The Great Rock Discography

Fifth Edition

Martin C. Strong

To Millar
From
Russ
AND
IT,
AINT
EVEN
YER
BIRTHDAY
X

MOJO
BOOKS

Fifth edition first published in the UK in 2000
by MOJO Books, an imprint of Canongate Books,
14 High Street, Edinburgh EH1 ITE, Scotland

Published simultaneously in the
United States of America and Canada
in 2001 by MOJO Books

10 9 8 7 6 5 4 3 2

British Library Cataloguing-in-Publication Data
A catalogue record for this book is available upon
request from the British Library.

ISBN 1 84195 017 3

Typeset by TexturAL, Edinburgh
Printed and bound in Finland by WS Bookwell.

Acknowledgements

I'd like to thank the following "GREAT" people who've helped me with this book (i.e. contributors):- MARY GLEN (the new woman in my life!), BRENDON GRIFFIN, ADAM STAFFORD, GYLLA-FIONA SIMPSON, KEITH MUNRO, STEFAN LEWANDOWSKI, ALAN LAWSON and a big thank-you to contributors from afar BOB PARR, PAUL & NAN McCARTHY, VAN JOHANN, GARY FERGUSON and JAMES TERRIS. Also "Great" friends ALLAN and ELAINE BREWSTER, VIC ZDZIEBLO, SANDY and CAROLINE McCRAE, PETER McGUCKIN, DOUGIE NIVEN, MIKEY KINNAIRD, BRIAN and MARGARET HUNTER, EILEEN SCOTT-MONCRIEFF (+ family), TAM MORRISON, MICHAEL FLETCHER + SHONA, KATE + GAV, JANET + TOM, CALLUM + MARY, KATY + BEAST, JENNI, everyone at Alex SMITH's bar/lounge including the manager ALLAN MANN, pint-pullers ANDY SHERIFF, GEORDIE CUNNINGHAM, COLIN ARMSTRONG, CARRIE DRUMMOND (now formerly), SARAH, STACY, CHRISTINE, regulars (at times!) PAUL KLEMM, JOHN HILL, BILL FISHER, IAN 'HARRY' HARRISON, BRIAN HAY + drummer TOMMY, BRIAN McLAUGHLIN, ANDREW RISK, IAIN ROBERTSON, STUART ROBERTSON, HAGGIS MacKENZIE, JOHN McARDLE, artist HAMISH, BILLY and ANN ROSS, GRANT BAILEY, TONY HUGHES, PAUL HUGHES, JOE SIMPSON, ELLA CRAWFORD, TONY WEIR, MARTIN 'No.2' McDERMOTT, IAIN McLEAN, DAVIE WALKER, ALEC GRAY, WATTY MORRISON, BARRY MOORE, Wee PYE and ARCHIE PARKER. Also FORREST DUNCAN, HAMISH McLEOD PRENTICE, BRIAN VAUSE, RUSSELL MAYES, ROY JACK, ANDREW MORLEY, MARK ROBERTSON, MURRAY ROWAN, TOM McINTYRE, DEREK ANDERSON, LAURIE DOOLAN, SHUG MACKIE, STEVIE CANAVAN, IAIN SUTHERLAND, GEORGE MAIN, RAY NOTLEY, DEREK IRVINE, DAVIE BLAIR, LES O'CONNOR (deceased), CHRIS REID (deceased), GEORDIE YOUNG (deceased), BUFF + SUSAN, TED MOCHAR, DAVIE SEATH, LINDA TONER, ERIC WEST, my accountant GRAHAM MINTO, DAVID BLUE, ALAN LIDDELL, GOGZ, BARRY LIDDELL, HUNTER WATT, MICK and WENDY (from Malta holiday), MALCOLM STEWART (of Jimpress fanzine), the Hebrides pub guys DAVIE BISSETT, MALCOLM YORK, ANDY SUTHERLAND and JOHN BISSETT, EWAN (of Europa Records, Friar Street, Stirling; a brilliant shop for every type of music buff), PIERCING THOUGHT / FLASHPOINT of the High Street, Falkirk (body piercing & tattoos done professionally), everyone at CANONGATE Books (they know who they are), DEREK KILLAH and all the staff who helped me at the Falkirk Library, plus RECORD COLLECTOR (and PETER DOGGETT) for finally reviewing this book (as if!). Other music journos I read are the NME, LASERLOG/R.E.D., MUSIC WEEK, BILLBOARD, KERRANG!, MOJO, SELECT and Q. A special thanks to Scots crime writer IAN RANKIN who credited me as one of his favourite authors (hope you enjoy this one too!). A note to all names mentioned above that I'm running out of space so don't be offended if I "un"-credit you in future editions (if I get 'round to doing any more that is!?). I'm gonna have to limit the names to about twelve close friends who I see on a regular basis and then it's "you know who are" type of thing. You ALL contributed to this book by listening, spreading the word and generally for having a laugh with me... thanks again.

A special mention to my daughters SUZANNE (aged 18) and SHIRLEY (aged 20), my grandson IVOR (aged 2), my granny ZENA MACKAY (who sadly passed away on the 15th of April, 2000), my auntie JOYCE (+ MICHAEL), my cousins PAUL, STEPHEN (+ NINA), BRIAN (+ JEANETTE), KEVIN (+ KAREN) and MAUREEN McELROY, AVRIL and JACKIE, uncle FRANK in Australia, RONNIE and MAISIE, ISOBEL and DANNY BUCHANNAN, JENNIFER and KEITH plus DANIEL. A message to a certain person:- Get on with your life and let "others" get on with theirs, The more you talk someone down the more people see how twisted you really are.

I'm "great"-ful to everyone who wrote to me over the last year or so:- JAN KUEHNEMUND (of the US girl band VIXEN; wow! makes you wanna visit the States!), Golden Earring fan(atic) TAEKE OOSTERWOUD, STEFFEN SCHMITT, HOLGER RINGEISEN, PAUL SIMMONDS (ex-Men They Couldn't Hang; sorry about omission!), KIP HANNAN, SEPPA KAUYYISER, ALBRECHT KOENIG, KLAUS HENSEL, NICK WOODHEAD, CHRIS RIGBY, MORTEN TANGAA, CLAUS HUTHMANN, BOB GOLDSBOROUGH, DAVID KAY, NICK WOODHEAD, CHRISTINE YOUNG, STEVE ELLIS, DARREL J BEVAN, LIAM RIGY, DEKE RIVERS, MATTHIAS GUDERJAN, ANDREW BASQUIL, NEIL CRUMP, AL HOLLYWOOD, ULI SCHMIDT, STEVE GORDON, KEVIN McCLURE, Black Metal fan DAVE SUMNER (KORN and BLACK SABBATH, so there!), SIMON DENHAM (no Tremeloes again, sorry!), MARC SIDDALL, GEORGE RAINEY, plus DAVID JOHNS, BJ PURDIE, IAN STEWART, JURGEN SCHAFER, PAUL WHITTINGHAM, CHRISTOPH CASSEL, MIKE ALEXANDER, WOLFGANG SCHMIDT, RITA GIACOMELLI, NEIL SANDERS, JAN SCHAEFER, MARTIN NISBET, RICHARD-MICHAEL KUJAS, ALEXANDER KAROTSCH, NICK MORONEY, RICHARD HENNESSEY, GRAEME LARMOUR, TERRY POULTON, JOEL A. STEIN, TONY McGROGAN, JOHN SIEWERT, RICHARD JONES, GUILLAUME BARREAU-DECHERF, MICHAEL YEATES, BERTHOLD NUCHTER, DOUGLAS A. BROWN, C. BLAIR, STEWART WILLIAMSON, MARK CHAMBERLIN, DAVID CLOUTER, ANDREAS DUDA, STUART MAZDON, SAM VANDIVER, STEVE ALLEN, WOLFGANG NUCHTER, ALEXEI ROUDITCHEV, STEFAN WEBER, STUART CAMERON, CHRIS CLARK, WIM VAN DER MARK, MARK O SULLIVAN, BERNARD PIERRE (Ambassador of Belgium in Prague!), JOHN MACKIE, NIGEL COUZINS, TONY FARNBOROUGH, CHRIS OWEN, JOHN STEEL, GEOFF WHITE, JONATHAN and PAUL COOK, HORST LUEDTKE, FRANZ ZEIDLER, OLIVER SEIDL, JOHN GREAVES, J. BENNINK, ANDREAS SCHOLLIG, SCOTT MURPHY (The Filth And The Fury fanzine), ALAN SPICER, BERNARD PIERRE (Ambassador of Belgium in Prague), PETER J. SMITH, AIDAN P. DOWNEY, JORG FOTH, SILVIO HELLEMANN, AXEL DREYER, ALAN OFFICER, DAVE NASH, JAMES MICHAEL CURLAND, ANDY CARR and NICK WALL.

* * * * *

Foreword

When I first received my hardback copy of The Great Rock Discography and being familiar with what I'm afraid you might feel compelled to style the obsessive attention to detail of Martin C. Strong, I turned to the Bob Seger section in the faint hope that I might read something like, "In the seventies and eighties an unknown middle-aged woman was often spotted in London's bustling Notting Hill Gate area wearing an ill-fitting Bob Seger Band tour jacket". That would have been my mother but, alas, Martin has chosen – recklessly in my view – not to include her in his book. So far, that is about the only notable omission I have spotted.

There is, inevitably, a lot of stuff here you're not going to need. Not for a while anyway. I mean Rhyl's The Alarm apparently started out as The Toilets. And Robert Palmer was in Mandrake Paddle Steamer. I've got two copies of their single, if you're interested.

But there are things here about people I thought I knew. I have always believed that The Fall – and I hope you'll excuse what may seem unpleasantly like bragging – had released their debut single by the time they came to record their first session for Radio 1. Not so, it seems. And I never knew that Captain Beefheart, as a child – and what can he have been like as a child? – made clay figurines for a local television programme. What a guy! And what's this? Did you know that Bill Oddie, the bird-watching former Goodie, sang on two Rick Wakeman albums? Armed with that fact alone, you could bring conversation to an awe-struck silence in most pubs in Britain.

I don't know, of course, what you're going to use this extraordinary work of scholarship for, but I suggest you use it for something. If nothing else, you'll know the answer the next time someone stops you on the street and asks, "Whatever happened to Fred Neil?"

I'm going to keep my copy by the bed, and plan to learn a fact a day. You have been warned.

John Peel
August 2000

Introduction

Doesn't two years just fly in when you're having fun. Yes it's been two short ones since the 4th Edition and now its time to sit/lie back and enjoy (hopefully) No.5 in the series.

This is my ninth published book in total:– 5 editions of The Great Rock Discography (1994, 1995, 1996, 1998 and 2000); The Great Psychedelic Discography (1997); The Great Metal Discography (1998); The Great Alternative & Indie Discography (1999); and not forgetting (although a lot of people did!) The Wee Rock Discography (1996).

Different again in content and comprehensiveness, the 5th Edition has over 1100 crammed pages of biographies (with updates), revised discographies, etc, of around 1000 top Rock artists (plus 1000 sub-entries) that graced our turntables, CD-players and whatever throughout the 20th Century (the cut-off date for releases being the 31st of December, 1999).

Exclusive to this edition are 250 brand new entries not included in 1998s 900-page tome. For instance, you'll see Italy's master composer Ennio Morricone, Belgium's Jacques Brel, France's finest Serge Gainsbourg, Germany's avant-rockers Neu!, Sweden's Roxette, America's Blues legends Robert Johnson and Leadbelly, Canada's Godspeed You Black Emperor! and Shania Twain, Australia's Natalie Imbruglia, England's Gomez and pop icons The Spice Girls, Wales' ageless pop star Tom Jones, Ireland's Saw Doctors and not forgetting Scotland's very own The Beta Band and Belle & Sebastian; all varying types of music from around nearly every part of the globe.

Also a new feature: an extended 'Album Rating' section which assesses (out of 10*) every long-player the artist recorded – although some of the more pop/singles-orientated artists have a 'Best CD compilation rating' (it would've also taken up too much space, thus excluding somebody else's favourite act!).

To make room for all of the above, things had to be axed: Harry Horse's illustrated pages sadly had to go, although it gave me around 50 more pages to play with. Also, you'll find a few hundred 'dig outs' of lesser-known groups that appeared either in one of the three off-shoot books (Psychedelic, Metal, Alt/Indie) or in the 4th Edition. I wanted a lot of them included in this extended tome, but most of you will realise you can't get everything – although there'll be one or two (again) complaining of a certain omission.

I have at my disposal all information of over 6000 acts, and if you're desperate to obtain any individual biog/discog just send a large SAE to Martin Strong, c/o Canongate, and enclose a cheque for £1.50 ($2.50 America/overseas) to cover my costs, and allow 28 days delivery. Anybody else who just simply wants to help me or anything, please do so as I'm always grateful for correspondence (although it's not always possible to write back or meet you in person, as I'm basically always writing books).

Talking about letters, I've received some weird ones in the last year or so, especially from some guy who wanted paragraphs in the 4th Edition biographies (it's not a bleedin novel, pal!). Just take a deep (very deep and long...) breath and, eh, carry on with the next sentence. One Canadian punk into DOA was slightly perturbed as I hadn't mentioned an early member of the said band. He went on to say he would not read the rest of the Alternative & Indie book (700 other pages!) as it would probably be crap; does this guy treat records like this?... I hope not. I was anticipating this would be a one-off and was getting along quite merrily until another letter popped its ugly head through my letter-box. Guess where it came from. Yes, Canada! This Maple-Leaf-wearing punter accused me (yes me!) of virtually ignoring Canadian artists. I, of course, looked into this and found I had included over 10% of Canadian acts in my 4th Edition and was about to give them a bigger percentage in this one (surely fair indeed). If you want a Canadian-only discography book, why not write it yourself, since you seem to think it's quite easy to compile, and good luck pal!

What makes up for these small gripes is when you get recognition for your work and in June of this year (awarded during their annual conference in Chapel Hill, North Carolina, USA) I was very proud to receive (by post) the ARSC (Association for Recorded Sound Collections) Certificate of Merit in Historical Recorded Sound Research for 'The Great Alternative & Indie Discography'; phew! Thank you to whoever voted for me. A year earlier, I was also on a high when monthly music journal MOJO considered my 'Great Rock Discography' Fourth Edition worthy of 10 out of 10. (Others didn't even review it, *Record Collector* again one of them; when oh when will it be, and should I really care?)

What's next on Martin C. Strong's agenda you may ask – apart from possibly some newspaper (music or otherwise) giving me a part-time or full-time job!, and meeting legendary DJ and good egg all round, John Peel (thanks for the Foreword). Having all this music biogs/discogs, etc, at my disposal, I'd like to get The Great Rock Discographies onto the Internet. The negotiations are still at an early stage with Canongate (www.canongate.net) and others, but maybe I'll just learn fast, plunder some money from somewhere, and do it on my own with a few friends 'in the know'. We'll see.

In the meantime, I wish to thank all the readers who have supported this quest for the best.

From Me To You, M C STRONG
Falkirk, August 2000

How To Read The Book

If you're struggling in any way how to comprehend some of the more complex parts of each discography, here are some examples to make it easier. Read below for around 10 minutes, taking a step at a time. The final lines/examples you see will give you a good guide before you proceed with the actual chronological discographies. However, I think that once you've read your own favourites you'll have a good idea.

GROUP / ARTIST

Formed/Born: Where/When ... biography including style/analysis, songwriters, cover versions, trivia, etc.
Album rating: i.e. rating between 1-10 amalgamated between music press reviews, your letters and my own personal opinion.

SINGER (born; b. day/month/year, town/city, country) – vocals, whatever (ex-GROUP; if any) / **MUSICIAN** (b. BIRTH NAME, 8 Sep'60, Musselburgh, Scotland) – instruments / **OTHER MUSICIANS** – other instruments, vocals, etc.

UKdate. (single, ep or album) *(UK cat.no.)* <*US cat.no.*> **THE TITLE**   [UK Label] [US Label] US date
    note:- UK label – might be another country's label if not released in UK.
    also:- Labels only appear when the group signs to a new one.
    note:- UK date – might be foreign, <even American at times>, if not initially issued in Britain.
    note:- *(UK catalogue number; in curved brackets)* <*US cat.no.; in angle brackets*>
    note:- chart positions, UK + US, are in the boxes below labels.
    also:- the boxes in the above example have been left blank, thus they did not hit either UK or US charts.
    note:- US date after the boxes indicates a variation from its UK counterpart.
    also:- Any other info on the right of the boxes (e.g. German) indicates it was not issued in the US.
UKdate. (7") *(UK cat.no.)* **A-SIDE. / B-SIDE**
US date. (7") <*US cat.no.*> **A-SIDE. / DIFFERENT B-SIDE**
    note:- The two examples above show that the UK + US release did not have an identical A-side & B-side, thus the chart boxes are marked with a – to indicate it was not released in either the UK or the US.
UKdate. (7"/c-s) *(CATNO 1/+C)* **A-SIDE. / B-SIDE**
    note:- above had two formats with the same tracks (i.e. 7"/c-s). However, catalogue numbers will always vary among different formats – often only slightly (e.g. CATNO 1/+C). Each cat.no. would read thus:- (7")=*(CATNO 1)* and (c-s)=*(CATNO 1C)*. To save space the (/) slash comes into effect. The (/) means "or" and in this case it is prefixed with a + sign for the equivalent cassette (c-s).
UKdate. (7"/c-s) *(example same as above)* **SEE ABOVE**
    (12"+=/cd-s+=) *(CATNO 1-12/1-CD)* – Extra tracks.
    note:- If there are more formats with extra or different tracks, a new line would be used. Obviously there would also be alternative catalogue numbers utilising the "(/)" as before. Extra tracks would therefore mean the addition of the sign "(+=)" to each format.

UKdate. (lp/c/cd) *(CATNO 200/+MC/CD)* <*US catno 4509*> **ALBUM TITLE**
    – Track listing / Track 2 / And so on. *(re-issued = re-iss. A later date, and other 'Label' mentioned, if different from original; new cat.no.) (could be re-iss. many times and if "(+=)" sign occurs there will be extra tracks from the original) <could also apply to the US release if in pointed brackets>*
    note:- Album above released in 3 formats, thus 3 catalogue numbers are neccessary. The "long-player" lp *(CATNO 200)* is obvious. The "cassette" c = +MC *(CATNO 200MC)* or "compact disc" CD *(CATNO 200CD)*. The US <*cat.no.*> will normally be just one set of numbers (or see further below for other details).
UKdate. (cd/c/lp) *(CD/TC+/CATNO+200)* <*UScatno 4509*> **ALBUM TITLE**   [ ] [ ]US date
    note:- This time a prefix is used instead of a suffix, hence the difference before the standard lp catalogue number. For instance, the cd would read as *(CDCATNO 200)*.
Jun 97. (cd/c/lp) <*(5557 49860-2/-4/-1)*> **ALBUM TITLE**   [1] [1]May97
    note:- Some catalogue numbers don't include any letters, but instead consist of a number sequence followed by one digit which universally corresponds with the format (i.e. 2 = cd / 4 = c / 1 = lp).
    also:- If the US numbers are identical, there would be no need to list them separately, i.e. <*the numbers*>
    note:- I've also marked down an actual date of release and its variant in the US (you'll find this fictitious album also hit No.1 in both charts "and ah've no even heard it yet, man!")

──── **NEW MUSICIAN/SINGER** (b.whenever, etc.) – instruments (ex-GROUP(s) replaced = repl. DEPARTING MUSICIAN/SINGER, who joined whatever
    note:- Above denotes a line-up change.

GROUP or ARTIST with major change of name

note:- above would always be in grey.
                                                       UK Label US Label
Jun 97. (cd/c/lp; GROUP or ARTIST with minor change of name)
    <*(5557 49860)*> **ALBUM TITLE**   [1] [1]May97

– compilations, etc. –

UKdate. (cd) *compilation Label only; (cat.no.)* **ALBUM TITLE**   [100] [ ]
    – Track listing would be selective, only included if the release was deemed essential.

RECORD-LABEL ABBREVIATIONS

Nearly all the record-labels have been shown in full, but the following abbreviations have been used:

Amphetam. Reptile – Amphetamine Reptile	N'bourhood – Neighborhood
Better Youth Org'n. – Better Youth Organization	Pye Inter – Pye International
Castle Comms – Castle Communications	Transatla. – Transatlantic
Crepescule – Les Disques du Crepescule	Road Goes – Road Goes on Forever
Dead Good Dolly Platt. – Dead Good Dolly Platters	Rough Trade Sing. Club – Rough Trade Singles Club
Deconstr. – DeConstruction	Sympathy F – Sympathy For The Record Industry
EMI Internat. – EMI International	U.A. – United Artists
Fundam. – Fundamental	Warners – Warner Brothers
Guy from Paraguay – The Guy from Paraguay	92 Happy C. – 92 Happy Customers
New Europ. Records – New European Records	not iss. – not issued

Formats & Abbreviations

VINYL (black coloured unless stated)

(lp)	=	The (LONG PLAYER) record ... circular 12" plays at 33¹/³ r.p.m., and has photo or artwork sleeve. Approximate playing time ... 30–50 minutes with average 10 tracks. Introduced in the mid-50's on mono until stereo took over in the mid-60's. Quadrophonic had a spell in the 70's, but only on mainly best-selling lp's, that had been previously released. Because of higher costs to the manufacturer and buyer, the quad sunk around 1978. Also note that around the mid-50's, some albums were released on 10 inch. Note:– average cost to the customer as of now = £9.00 (new). Collectors can pay anything from £1 to over £500, depending on the quality of the recording. Very scratched records can be worthless, but unplayed-mint deletions are worth a small fortune to the right person. Auctions and record fairs can be the place to find that long lost recording that's eluded you. This applies to all other vinyl below.
(d-1p)	=	The (DOUBLE-LONG PLAYER) record ... as before. Playing time 50–90 minutes on 4 sides, with average 17 tracks. Introduced to rock/pop world in the late 60's, to complement compilations, concept & concert (aka live) albums.[1]
		Compilations:– are a selection of greatest hits or rare tracks, demos, etc.
		Concepts:– are near-uninterrupted pieces of music, based around a theme.
		Note that normal lp's could also be compilations, live or concept. Some record companies through the wishes of their artists, released double lp's at the price of one lp. If not, price new would be around £15.
(t-1p)	=	The (TRIPLE-LONG PLAYER) record ... as before. Playing time over 100 minutes with normally over 20 tracks. Because of the cost to the consumer, most artists steered clear of this format. Depending on the artwork on the sleeve, these cost over £17.50. (See its replacement, the CD.)
(4-1p-box)	=	The (BOXED-LONG PLAYER) record (could be between 4 and 10 in each boxed-set). As the triple album would deal with live, concept or compilation side, the boxed-set would be mostly re-issues of all the artist's album material, with probably a bonus lp thrown in, to make it collectable. Could be very pricey, due to lavish outlay in packaging. They cost over £25 new.
(m-lp)	=	The (MINI-LONG PLAYER) record ... playing time between 20 and 30 minutes and containing on average 7 tracks. Introduced for early 80's independent market, and cost around £5.
	=	Note:– This could be confused at times with the extended-play 12" single.
(pic-1p)	=	The (PICTURE DISC-LONG PLAYER) record... as before but with album artwork/ design on the vinyl-grooves. Mainly for the collector because of the slightly inferior sound quality. If unplayed, these can fetch between £10 and £250.
(coloured lp)	=	The (COLOURED-LONG PLAYER) record; can be in a variety of colours including ... white / blue / red / clear / purple / green / pink / gold / silver.
(red-1p)	=	The (RED VINYL-LONG PLAYER) record would be an example of this.
(7")	=	The (7 INCH SINGLE). Arrived in the late 50's, and plays at 45 r.p.m. Before this its equivalent was the 10" on 78 r.p.m. Playing time now averages 4 minutes per side, but during the late 50's up to mid-60's, each side averaged 2¹/² minutes. Punk rock/new wave in 1977/78 resurrected this idea. In the 80's, some disco releases increased playing time. Another idea that was resurrected in 1977 was the picture sleeve. This had been introduced in the 60's, but mostly only in the States.
		Note:– cost in mid-98 was just under £2.50; second-hand rarities can cost between 25p and £200, depending again on their condition. These might also contain limited freebies/gifts (i.e. posters, patches, stickers, badges, etc). Due to the confusion this would cause, I have omitted this information, and kept to the vinyl aspect in this book. Another omission has been DJ promos, demos, acetates, magazine freebies, various artists' compilations, etc. Only official shop releases get a mention.
(7" m)	=	The (7 INCH MAXI-SINGLE). Named so because of the extra track, mostly on the B-side. Introduced widely during the early 70's; one being ROCKET MAN by ELTON JOHN.
(7" ep)	=	The (7 INCH EXTENDED PLAY SINGLE). Plays mostly at 33¹/³ r.p.m., with average playing time 10–15 minutes and 4 tracks. Introduced in the late 50's as compilations for people to sample their albums. These had a *title* and were also re-introduced from 1977 onwards, but this time for punk groups' new songs.
(d7")	=	The (DOUBLE 7 INCH SINGLE). Basically just two singles combined ... 4 tracks. Introduced in the late 70's for the "new wave/romantics", and would cost slightly more than normal equivalent.
(7" pic-d)	=	The (7 INCH PICTURE-DISC SINGLE). This was vinyl that had a picture on the grooves, which could be viewed through a see-through plastic cover.
(7" sha-pic-d)	=	The (7 INCH SHAPED-PICTURE-DISC SINGLE). Vinyl as above but with shape (i.e. gun, mask, group) around the edge of the groove. Awkward because it would not fit into the collector's singles box. Initially limited, and this can still be obtained at record fairs for over £3. Note:– However, in the book the type of shape has not been mentioned, to save space.
(7" coloured)	=	The (7 INCH COLOURED SINGLE). Vinyl that is not black (i.e. any other colour; red, yellow, etc). Note:– (7" multi) would be a combination of two or more colours (i.e. pink/purple).

1: **Note**:– Interview long players mainly released on 'Babatak' label, have not been included due to the fact this book only gives artists' music discography.

(7" flexi)	=	The (7 INCH FLEXIBLE SINGLE). One-sided freebies, mostly given away by magazines, at concerts or as mentioned here; free with single or lp. Worth keeping in mint condition and well protected.
(12")	=	The (12 INCH SINGLE). Plays at 45 r.p.m., and can have extended or extra tracks to its 7" counterpart (+=) or (++=). B-side's playing speed could be at 33 r.p.m. Playing time could be between 8 and 15 minutes. Introduced in 1977 with the advent of new wave and punk. They were again a must for collectors, for the new wave of British heavy metal scene.
(12"ep)	=	The (12 INCH EXTENDED PLAY SINGLE). Virtually same as above but *titled* like the 7" ep. Playing time over 12 minutes, and could have between 3 and 5 tracks.
(d12")	=	The (DOUBLE 12 INCH SINGLE). See double 7". Can become very collectable and would cost new as normal 12", £4.50.
(12" pic-d)	=	The (12 INCH PICTURE-DISC SINGLE). As with 7" equivalent ... see above.
(12" sha-pic-d)	=	The (12 INCH SHAPED-PICTURE-DISC SINGLE). See above 7" equivalent.
(12" colrd)	=	The (12 INCH COLOURED SINGLE). Not black vinyl ... see above 7" equivalent.
(10")	=	The (10 INCH SINGLE). Plays at 45 r.p.m. and, like the 12", can have extra tracks (+=). Very collectable, it surfaced in its newer form around the early 80's, and can be obtained in shops at £4.50. Note:– also (10" ep) / (d10") / (10" coloured) / (10" pic-d) / (10" sha-pic-d).

CASSETTES

(c)	=	The (CASSETTE) album ... size in case 4$^{1/2}$ inches high. Playing-time same as lp album, although after the mid-80's cd revolution, some were released with extra tracks. Introduced in the late 60's, to compete with the much bulkier lp. Until the 80's, most cassettes were lacking in group info, lyric sheets, and freebies. Note:– cost to the consumer as of now = £8 new. But for a few exceptions, most do not increase in price, and can be bought second-hand or budget-priced for around £5.
(d-c)	=	The (DOUBLE-CASSETTE) album ... as above, and would hold same tracks as d-lp or even t-1p. Price between £12 and £16.
(c-s)	=	The (CASSETTE-SINGLE). Now released mostly with same two tracks as 7" equivalent. The other side played the same 2 or 3 tracks. Introduced unsuccessfully in the US around the late 60's. Re-introduced there and in Britain in the mid-80's. In the States, it and its cd counterpart have replaced the charting 7" single for the 90's. Cost new is around £1.50–£2.50, and might well become quite collectable.
(c-ep)	=	The (CASSETTE-EXTENDED PLAY SINGLE). Same as above but *titled* as 12".

COMPACT DISCS

(cd)	=	The (COMPACT DISC) album. All 5" circular and mostly silver on its playing side. Perspex casing also includes lyrics & info, etc. Introduced late in 1982, and widely the following year (even earlier for classical music). Initially for top recording artists, but now in 2000 nearly every release is in cd format. Playing time normally over 50 minutes with some containing extra tracks or mixes. Possible playing time is just over 75 minutes. Marketed as unscratchable, although if they go uncleaned, they will stick just as vinyl. Average price now is £15, and will become collectable if, like most gloomy predictions, they do not deteriorate with time.
(d-cd)	=	The (DOUBLE-COMPACT DISC) album ... same as above although very pricey, between £20 and £25.
(cd-s)	=	The (COMPACT DISC-SINGLE). Mainly all 5" (but some 3" cd-s could only be played with a compatible gadget inside the normal cd player). Playing time over 15 minutes to average 25 minutes, containing 4 or 5 tracks. Introduced in 1986 to compete with the 12" ep or cassette. 99% contained extra tracks to normal formats. Cost new: over £4.50.
(pic-cd-s)	=	The (PICTURE-COMPACT DISC-SINGLE). Has picture on disc, which gives it its collectability. Also on (pic-cd-ep).
(vid-pic-s)	=	The (VIDEO-COMPACT DISC-SINGLE). A video cd, which can be played through stereo onto normal compatible TV screen. Very costly procedure, but still might be the format of the future. Promo videos can be seen on pub jukeboxes, which has made redundant the returning Wurlitzer style.

DIGITAL AUDIO TAPE

(dat)	=	The (DIGITAL AUDIO TAPE) album. Introduced in the mid-80's and, except for Japan and the rich yuppie, are not widely issued. It is a smaller version of the cassette, with the quality of the cd.

Another format (which I have not included) is the CARTRIDGE, which was available at the same time as the cassette. When the cassette finally won the battle in the early 80's, the cartridge became redundant. All car-owners of the world were happy when thieves made them replace the stolen cartridge player with the resurrected cassette. You can still buy these second-hand, but remember you'll have to obtain a second-hand 20-year-old player, with parts possibly not available.

Other abbreviations: repl. = replaced / comp. = compilation / re-iss. = re-issued / re-dist. = re-distributed

ABBA

Formed: Stockholm, Sweden . . . 1971 by songwriting buddies BJORN and BENNY with partners AGNETHA and ANNI-FRID, each individual member already established in their own right previous to this inevitable formation (see further solo). In 1973, they entered for The Eurovision Song Contest with 'RING RING'. It didn't win, but the following year's 'WATERLOO' did, soon topping the UK charts. The accompanying album of the same name didn't perform so well, struggling to make the Top 30, and it took more than a year for them to get back on track commercially. The plangent 'S.O.S.' achieved this in fine style, while 'MAMMA MIA' made No.1 at Christmas '75 and the ABBA phenomenon really kicked into gear. Simultaneously one of the most cherished groups ever to come out of the continent and one of the most readily identifiable icons of 70's cheesiness, ABBA were a one-off, plain and simple. With their gorgeous lovelorn melodies, glossy harmonies, kissing couples charm and occasionally pigeon English, ABBA captured the hearts of everyone from teenyboppers to grannies, hell, even John Peel! In their mid-late 70's heyday, the group scored an incredible amount of No.1's including 'FERNANDO', 'DANCING QUEEN', 'KNOWING ME, KNOWING YOU', 'THE NAME OF THE GAME' and 'TAKE A CHANCE ON ME'. There was something about the ABBA sound, something undefinable that made their records magical, timeless; there are songs which, for anyone who grew up in the 70's, can conjure up long forgotten memories more vividly than any photograph. The albums, 'ARRIVAL' (1977), 'THE ALBUM' (1978), 'VOULEZ VOUS' (1979) and 'SUPER TROOPER' (1980) all made the UK No.1, achieving massive sales all over the world. In fact, at their peak, ABBA were one of the country's top exports, listed on the national stock exchange. Like FLEETWOOD MAC, the stormy inter-band relationships in ABBA fuelled their most affecting, poignant work, and, as the decade wore on, the sad songs became even sadder; the dreamy Euro-pop of 'ANGELEYES' and the cod-disco of 'DOES YOUR MOTHER KNOW' belied a band in emotional turmoil. The heartbroken opening piano chords of 'WINNER TAKES IT ALL' spoke volumes, a song of lost love as powerful as any ever written; the track gave ABBA yet another No.1. After a final long-player, 'THE VISITORS' (1981), the band drifted apart to solo ventures. Unmentionable in the style-conscious 80's, the ABBA legend had become almost an industry in itself by the mid-90's. Part of an overall 70's revival, ABBA's elevation to gurus of "the decade that taste forgot" was fuelled by Australian parody outfit BJORN AGAIN as well as multi-million selling retrospective compilation 'ABBA GOLD' (1992).

Best CD compilation: ABBA – GOLD GREATEST HITS (*8)

AGNETHA FALTSKOG (-ULVAEUS) (b. 5 Apr'50, Jonkopping, Sweden) – vocals / **BJORN ULVAEUS** (b.25 Apr'45, Gothenburg, Sweden) – guitar, vocals / **BENNY ANDERSSON** (b.16 Dec'46, Stockholm, Sweden) – keyboards, synth, vocals (both ex-HEP STARS, ex-HOOTENANNY SINGERS) / **ANNI-FRID LYNGSTAD-FREDRIKSSON** (b.15 Nov'45, Norway) – vocals

In May 72, a single by **BJORN, BENNY, AGNETHA + FRIDA** hit Swedish No. 2

ABBA

(below debut single released in Sweden Feb '73, hit No.1)

		Epic	Atlantic	
Oct 73.	(7") (EPC 1793) **RING RING. / ROCK'N'ROLL BAND**		–	
Apr 74.	(7") (EPC 2040) <3035> **WATERLOO. / WATCH OUT** (re-iss. Feb78; EPC 5961) (re-iss. 1986; 650252-7)	1	6	May74
May 74.	(lp/c) (EPC/40 80179) <18101> **WATERLOO** – Waterloo / Watch out / King Kong song / Hasta manana / My mama said / Dance (while the music still goes on) / Honey, honey / What about Livingstone / Gonna sing you my love song / Suzy hang around / Ring ring. (re-iss. Mar81 lp/c; EPC/40 32009) (re-iss. Sep92 on 'Polydor' cd/c; 843643-2/-4) (re-iss. Jun93 on 'Spectrum' cd/c; 550034-2/-4)	28		Aug74
Jul 74.	(7") (EPC 2452) **RING RING. / ROCK'N'ROLL BAND**	32	–	
Sep 74.	(7") <3209> **HONEY, HONEY. / DANCE (WHILE THE MUSIC STILL GOES ON)**	–	27	

		Epic	Atlantic	
Nov 74.	(7") (EPC 2848) **SO LONG. / I'VE BEEN WAITING FOR YOU**	–	–	
Apr 75.	(7") (EPC 3229) **I DO I DO I DO I DO I DO. / ROCK ME**	38	–	
Jun 75.	(7") <3240> **RING RING. / HASTA MANANA**	–	–	
Aug 75.	(7") (EPC 3576) <3265> **S.O.S. / MAN IN THE MIDDLE**	6	15	
Dec 75.	(7") (EPC 3790) **MAMMA MIA. / INTERMEZZO No.1**	1	–	
Jun 75.	(lp/c) (EPC/40 80835) <18146> **ABBA** – Mamma mia / Hey, hey Helen / Tropical loveland / S.O.S. / Man in the middle / Bang-a-boomerang / I do, I do, I do, I do, I do / Rock me / Intermezzo No.1 / I've been waiting for you / So long. (re-iss. Nov81 lp/c; EPC/40 32052) (re-iss. Sep92 on 'Polydor' cd/c+=; 831596-2/-4) – Waterloo / Hasta manana / Honey honey / Ring ring / Nina, pretty ballerina. (lp re-iss. Aug99 on 'Simply Vinyl'; SVLP 103)	13		Nov75
Jan 76.	(7") <3310> **I DO I DO I DO I DO I DO. / BANG-A-BOOMERANG**	–	15	
Mar 76.	(7") <3315> **MAMMA MIA. / TROPICAL LOVELAND**	–	–	
Mar 76.	(7") (EPC 4036) <3346> **FERNANDO. / HEY HEY HELEN** (re-iss. Feb78; EPC 5962)	1	13	Aug76
Apr 76.	(lp/c) (EPC/40 69218) <18189> **GREATEST HITS** (compilation) – Fernando / S.O.S. / He is your brother / Hasta manana / Dance (while the music still goes on) / Another town, another train / Mamma mia / Waterloo / I do I do I do I do / Honey honey / People need love / Ring ring / Bang-a-boomerang / Nina, pretty ballerina / So long. (re-iss. Apr85 lp/c; EPC/40 32571)	1	48	Sep76
May 76.	(7") <3315> **MAMMA MIA./ TROPICAL LOVELAND**	–	32	
Aug 76.	(7") (EPC 4499) <3372> **DANCING QUEEN. / THAT'S ME**	1	1	Nov76
Nov 76.	(7") (EPC 4713) <3434> **MONEY MONEY MONEY. / CRAZY WORLD**	3	56	Oct77
Nov 76.	(lp/c) (EPC/40 86018) <18207> **ARRIVAL** – My love my life / When I kissed the teacher / Dancing queen / Dum dum diddle / Knowing me knowing you / Money, money, money / That's me / Why did it have to be me / Tiger / Arrival. (re-iss. Jul83 lp/c; EPC/40 32320) (cd-iss. 1986; CD 86018) (re-iss. Sep92 on 'Polydor' cd/c; 821319-2/-4)	1	20	Jan77
Feb 77.	(7") (EPC 4955) <3387> **KNOWING ME KNOWING YOU. / HAPPY HAWAII**	1	14	May77
Oct 77.	(7") (EPC 5750) <3449> **THE NAME OF THE GAME. / I WONDER (DEPARTURE)**	1	12	Dec77
Jan 78.	(7") (EPC 5950) <3457> **TAKE A CHANCE ON ME. / I'M A MARIONETTE** (re-iss. May82; EPC 8088)	1	3	Apr78
Jan 78.	(lp/c) (EPC/40 86052) <19164> **THE ALBUM** – Eagle / Take a chance on me / One man, one woman / The name of the game / Move on / Hole in your soul / The girl with the golden hair (three scenes from a mini musical): Thank you for the music – I wonder (departure) – I'm a marionette. (re-iss. Mar84 lp/c; EPC/40 32321) (cd-iss. 1986; CD86052) (cd re-iss. Jun89; CD 32321) (re-iss. Sep92 on 'Polydor' cd/c; 821217-2/-4)	1	14	Feb78
Sep 78.	(7") (EPC 6595) <3515> **SUMMER NIGHT CITY. / MEDLEY (PICK A PALE OF COTTON – OLD SMOKEY – MAKING IT SPECIAL)**	5		
Jan 79.	(7") (EPC 7030) <3629> **CHIQUITITA. / LOVELIGHT** (re-iss. May82; EPC 7030)	2	29	Nov79
Apr 79.	(7") (EPC 7316) <3574> **DOES YOUR MOTHER KNOW. / KISSES OF FIRE**	4	19	May79
May 79.	(lp/pic/pic-lp) (EPC/40/EPC11 86086) <16000> **VOULEZ VOUS** – As good as new / Voulez-vous / I have a dream / Angeleyes / The king has lost his crown / Does your mother know / If it wasn't for the night / Chiquitita / Lovers (like a little longer) / Kisses of fire. (re-iss. Jul86 lp/c; EPC/40 32322) (cd-iss. Nov86; CD 86086) (cd re-iss. Jun89; CD 32322) (re-iss. Sep92 on 'Polydor' cd/c; 821320-2/-4)	1	19	Jun79
Jul 79.	(7") (EPC 7499) <3609> **ANGELEYES. / VOULEZ-VOUS** (re-iss. Feb89 on 'Old Gold'; OG 9856)	3	64 / 80	
Oct 79.	(7") (EPC 7914) <3652> **GIMME GIMME GIMME (A MAN AFTER MIDNIGHT). / THE KING HAS LOST HIS CROWN**	3		
Nov 79.	(lp/c) (EPC/40 10017) <16009> **GREATEST HITS VOL.2** (compilation 1976-79) – Take a chance on me / Gimme gimme gimme (a man after midnight) / Money money money / Rock me / Eagle / Angeleyes / Dancing queen / Does your mother know / Chiquitita / Summer night city / I wonder / Name of the game / Thank you for the music / Knowing me knowing you. (cd-iss. 1984; CD 10017) (re-iss. May87 lp/c; 450915-1/-4)	1	46	Dec79
Dec 79.	(7") (EPC 8088) **I HAVE A DREAM. / TAKE A CHANCE ON ME (live)**	2	–	
Jul 80.	(7"/12") (EPC/+12 8835) <3776> **THE WINNER TAKES IT ALL. / ELAINE**	1	8	Nov80
Nov 80.	(7") (EPC 9089) <3806> **SUPER TROUPER. / THE PIPER**	1	45	Mar81
Nov 80.	(lp/c) (EPC/40 10022) <16023> **SUPER TROUPER** – Super trouper / The winner takes it all / On and on and on / Andante andante / Me and I / Happy New Year / Our last summer / The piper / Lay all your love on me / The way old friends do. (also box-lp; ABBOX 1) (cd-iss. May83; CD 10022) (re-iss. Sep92 on 'Polydor' cd/c; 800023-2/-4)	1	17	Dec80
Jun 81.	(7") (EPCA 1314) <3826> **LAY ALL YOUR LOVE ON ME. / ON AND ON AND ON**	7	90	B-side
Dec 81.	(7"/7"pic-d) (EPCA/+11 1740) <89881> **ONE OF US. / SHOULD I LAUGH OR CRY**	3		
Dec 81.	(lp/c) (EPC/40 10032) <19332> **THE VISITORS** – The visitors / Head over heels / When all is said and done / Soldiers / I let the music speak / One of us / Two for the price of one / Slipping through my fingers / Like an angel / Passing through my room / Eagle. (cd-iss. May83; CD 10032) (re-iss. Sep92 on 'Polydor' cd/c; 800011-2/-4)	1	29	Jan82
Jan 82.	(7") <3889> **WHEN ALL IS SAID AND DONE. / SHOULD I LAUGH OR CRY**	–	27	
Feb 82.	(7") (EPCA 2037) <4031> **HEAD OVER HEELS. / THE VISITORS**	25	63	B-side
Oct 82.	(7") (EPCA 2847) <89948> **THE DAY BEFORE YOU CAME. / CASSANDRA**	32		
Nov 82.	(d-lp/d-c) (ABBA/+40 10) <80036> **THE SINGLES – THE FIRST TEN YEARS** (compilation) – Ring ring / Waterloo / So long / I do I do I do I do I do / S.O.S. / Mamma mia / Fernando / Ancing queen / Money money money / Knowing me knowing you / The name of the game / Take a chance on me / Summer night city / Chiquitita / Does your mother know / Voulez-vous / Gimme gimme gimme (a man after midnight) / I have a dream / The winner takes it all / Super trouper / One of us / The day	1	62	

before you came / Under attack. (also iss.d-pic-lp; ABBOX 11-1/2) (cd-iss. Sep83; ABBACD 10)

Dec 82. (7"/7"pic-d) (EPCA/+11 2971) **UNDER ATTACK. / YOU OWE ME ONE** | 26 | - |

—— broke up late '82, FALTSKOG + FRIDA both had successful solo careers

– compilations, others, etc. –

on 'Epic' UK / 'Atlantic' unless mentioned otherwise

Aug 82. (7"ep/c-ep) (EPCA/40 2618) **GREATEST ORIGINAL HITS (EP)** | | |
– Super trooper / The winner takes it all / Lay all your love on me.

Nov 83. (7"/7"sha-pic-d) (A/WA 3894) **THANK YOU FOR THE MUSIC (live). / OUR LAST SUMMER (live)** | 33 | |

Nov 83. (lp/c) (EPC/40 10043) **THANK YOU FOR THE MUSIC – A COLLECTION OF LOVE SONGS (live)** | 17 | - |
– My love, my life / I wonder / Happy New Year / Slipping through my fingers / Fernando / One man, one woman / Eagle / I have a dream / Our last summer / The day before you came / Chiquitita / Should I laugh or cry / The old way friends do / Thank you for the music. (originally rel.Mar81 as 'GRACIAS POR LA MUSICA'; EPC 86123) (re-iss. Aug92 on 'Ariola Express' cd/c; 2/4 90928)

Apr 84. (26x7"box) (ABBA 26) **ANNIVERSARY BOX SET**
– (all 26 singles)

Aug 86. (lp/c)(cd) Polydor; (POLH/+C 29)(829 951-2) **ABBA LIVE (live)** | | - |
(re-iss. Sep92 cd/c; 829951-2/-4)

Sep 87. (lp/c) Hallmark; (SHM/HSC 3215) **THE HITS** | | - |
(cd-iss. Jan89 on 'Pickwick' PCD 866)

Nov 87. (7") Old Gold; (OG 9726) **DANCING QUEEN. / FERNANDO** | | - |

Nov 87. (7") Old Gold; (OG 9727) **TAKE A CHANCE ON ME. / CHIQUITITA** | | - |

Dec 87. (d-lp/c/cd) Castle; (CCS LP/MC/CD 176) **ABBA – THE COLLECTION** | | - |

Jan 88. (7") Old Gold; (OG 9741) **WATERLOO. / MAMMA MIA** | | - |

Feb 88. (lp/c) Hallmark; (SHM/HSC 3229) **THE HITS 2** | | - |
(cd-iss. Jan89 on 'Pickwick'; PWKS 500)

Sep 88. (lp/c) Hallmark; (SHM/HSC 3241) **THE HITS 3** | | - |
(cd-iss. Jan89 on 'Pickwick'; PWKS 15)

Nov 88. (d-lp/c/cd) Castle; (CCS LP/MC/CD 198) **ABBA – THE COLLECTION 2** | | - |

Nov 88. (lp/c/cd) Telstar; (STAR/STAC/TCD 2329) **ABSOLUTE ABBA** | 70 | - |

Feb 89. (7") Old Gold; (OG 9858) **KNOWING ME KNOWING YOU. / THE WINNER TAKES IT ALL** | | - |

Feb 89. (7") Old Gold; (OG 9860) **GIMME GIMME GIMME (A MAN AFTER MIDNIGHT). / DOES YOUR MOTHER KNOW** | | - |

Dec 89. (lp/c) Hallmark; (SHM/HSC 3297) **THE LOVE SONGS** | | - |
(cd-iss. on 'Pickwick'; PWKS 564)

Jan 90. (12") Old Gold; (OG 4151) **LAY ALL YOUR LOVE ON ME. / SUMMER NIGHT CITY** | | - |

Nov 91. (t-cd/t-c;box) Carlton; (BOX D/C 1) **THE HITS BOX** | | - |

Aug 92. (7"/c-s) Polydor; (PO/+CS 231) **DANCING QUEEN. / LAY YOUR LOVE ON ME** | 16 | |
(12"+=/cd-s+=) (PZ/+CD 231) – The day before you came / Eagle.

Sep 92. (cd/c/d-lp) Polydor; (<517007-2/-4/-1>) **ABBA – GOLD GREATEST HITS** | 1 | 63 |
– Dancing queen / Knowing me, knowing you / Take a chance on me / Mamma mia / Lay all your love on me / Super trouper / I have a dream / The winner takes it all / Money, money, money / S.O.S. / Chiquitita / Fernando / Voulez vous / Gimme, gimme, gimme (a man after midnight) / Does your mother know / One of us / The name of the game / Thank you for the music / Waterloo. (re-iss. Feb99; same)

Nov 92. (7"/c-s) Polydor; (PO/+CS) **THANK YOU FOR THE MUSIC. / HAPPY NEW YEAR** | | |
(cd-s+=) (PZCD) – The way old friends do.

Dec 92. (cd-s) Polydor; **VOULEZ VOUS /** | | |

May 93. (cd/c/lp) Polydor; (<519353-2/-4/-1>) **ABBA GOLD VOL.2 – MORE ABBA HITS** | 14 | |
(re-iss. Jul99; same) – hit No.13

Nov 94. (4xcd-box) Polydor; (<523472-2>) **THANK YOU FOR THE MUSIC** | | |
(re-iss. May99; same)

Nov 95. (3xcd-box) Polydor; **VOULEZ VOUS / SUPER TROUPER / ARRIVAL** | | |

Mar 96. (cd/c) Spectrum; (551109-2/-4) **AND THE MUSIC STILL GOES ON** | | - |

Oct 96. (d-cd) Polydor; (<533083-2>) **FOREVER GOLD** | | - |

Oct 98. (cd/c) Polydor; (<559221-2/-4>) **LOVE SONGS** | 51 | |

Nov 98. (cd/c) Spectrum; (551109-2/-4) **THE MUSIC STILL GOES ON** | | - |

Apr 99. (28xcd-box) Polydor; (563286-2) **THE SINGLES COLLECTION 1972-1982** | | - |

Nov 99. (27xcd-s-box) Polydor; (561252-2) **THE SINGLES COLLECTION 1972-1982** | | - |

—— BENNY & BJORN in 1984 collaborated with TIM RICE on 'CHESS' stage show. Released as d-lp,d-c,d-cd on 'RCA' Oct84; it hit UK No.10. It featured many singers, including MURRAY HEAD who scored UK No.12 / US No.3 hit with ONE NIGHT IN BANGKOK. To end the year '84, ELAINE PAIGE & BARBARA DICKSON hit UK No.1 duetting on I KNOW HIM SO WELL. ELAINE was to release more solo flops from the musical between late 1984-Spring 1986. In Oct85 'Telstar' issued lp,c,cd. 'CHESS PIECES – THE BEST OF CHESS' to attemt to cash in musicals' success. In 1986, both wrote and backed brother/sister duo GEMINI. An eponymous album was issued on 'Polydor', as were 2 singles 'JUST LIKE THAT' & 'ANOTHER YOU, ANOTHER ME'. The following year, another album GEMINISM was released on 'Polar' in Sweden only. Later in '87, BENNY released debut solo album 'KLINGA MINA KLOCKOR' on own label 'Mono Music' in Sweden. BENNY and BJORN went on to work with and produce most artists on that label.

ABC

Formed: Sheffield, England ... 1979 as VICE VERSA by STEPHEN SINGLETON and MARK WHITE. In late 1980, they found 'Modern Drugs' fanzine editor, MARTIN FRY, and became ABC, starting their own 'Neutron' label which was soon (early 1982) distributed by 'Phonogram'. Their first 45, 'TEARS ARE NOT ENOUGH', broke through into the UK Top 20 and they soon became leading contenders in the New Romantic attempt to dethrone DURAN DURAN and SPANDAU BALLET. ABC touted unashamed glamour-pop who'd become tired of tuneless grimacing. A follow-up single, 'POISON ARROW', narrowly missed the Top 5 in addition to cracking the US Top 30, the Americans rapidly developing a taste for all things New Romantic. A third single, 'THE LOOK OF LOVE', remains the defining ABC moment, a lavish lamé suit of a record. This Top 5 success saw the debut album, 'THE LEXICON OF LOVE', unsurprisingly clinch a No.1 spot. Produced by ubiquitous 80's guru, TREVOR HORN, the record remains one of the most popular albums of the early 80's, not only a lexicon of love, but a kaleidoscope of kitsch and a dictionary of debonair cool. It spawned one further single, 'ALL OF MY HEART', later that year, FRY and Co. touring extensively before entering the studio for a follow-up set, 'BEAUTY STAB'. A more rock-centric affair, the album met with frowning reviews, although it did make the Top 20. With DAVID YARRITH and EDEN replacing SINGLETON and bassist MARK LICKLEY respectively, a further effort, the kitschy 'HOW TO BE A ZILLIONAIRE', (1985) reclaimed at least some of the lost ground with a Top 10 US hit in 'BE NEAR ME'. Although FRY was subsequently diagnosed with Hodgkin's Disease (a form of cancer), the group bounced back with a Top 10 album, 'ALPHABET CITY' (1987), and a transatlantic smash with the SMOKEY ROBINSON tribute song, 'WHEN SMOKEY SINGS'. Though a further couple of low-key sets followed, the group were fairly inactive for most of the 90's, a comeback album 'SKYSCRAPER' in 1997 failing to register any commercial success.

Album rating: THE LEXICON OF LOVE (*9) / BEAUTY STAB (*5) / HOW TO BE A ... ZILLIONAIRE! (*6) / ALPHABET CITY (*5) / UP (*4) / ABSOLUTELY ABC (compilation) (*7) / ABRACADABRA (*4) / SKYSCRAPING (*5)

VICE VERSA

MARK WHITE (b. 1 Apr'61) – guitar, synthesizers / **STEPHEN SINGLETON** (b.17 Apr'59) – saxophone, synthesizers / **DAVE WYNDHAM** – vocals

	Neutron	not iss.
Jan 80. (7"ep) (NT 001) **MUSIC 4** – New girls / Neutrons / Science-fact / Riot squad / Camille.		-

—— added **MARTIN FRY** (b. 9 Mar'58, Manchester) – vocals

| Jun 81. (7") (NT 003) **STILYAGI. / EYES OF CHRIST** | - | - Dutch |

ABC

—— added **MARK LICKLEY** – bass / **DAVID ROBINSON** – drums

	Neutron	Mercury
Oct 81. (7") (NT 101) **TEARS ARE NOT ENOUGH. / ALPHABET SOUP** (12"+=) (NTX 101) – ('A'+'B'extended).	19	
Feb 82. (7") (NT 102) <810340> **POISON ARROW. / THEME FROM MANTRAP** (12"+=) (NTX 102) – Mantrap (The Lounge Sequence).	6	25 Jan83

—— **DAVID PALMER** (b.29 May'61, Chesterfield) – drums; repl. ROBINSON

| May 82. (7") (NT 103) <76168> **THE LOOK OF LOVE. / (part 2)**
(12"+=) (NTX 103) – (parts 3 & 4). (re-iss. Oct83; same) | 4 | 18 Aug82 |
| Jun 82. (lp/c) (NTRS/+C 1) <4059> **THE LEXICON OF LOVE** | 1 | 24 Sep82 |

– Show me / Poison arrow / Many happy returns / Tears are not enough / Valentine's day / The look of love / Date stamp / All of my heart / 4 ever 2 gether / The look of love. (cd-iss. Feb83; 810003-2) (remastered Mar96; 514942-2)

| Aug 82. (7") (NT 104) **ALL OF MY HEART. / OVERTURE** | 5 | |

—— guest session man **ANDY NEWMARK** – drums repl. PALMER

| Oct 83. (7"/12") (NT/+X 105) <814631> **THAT WAS THEN BUT THIS IS NOW. / VERTIGO** | 18 | 89 Jan84 |
| Nov 83. (lp/c)(cd) (NTRL/+C 2)(<814661>) **BEAUTY STAB** | 12 | 69 |

– That was then but this is now / Love's a dangerous language / If I ever thought you'd be lonely / The power of persuasion / Beauty stab / By default by design / Hey citizen / King money / Bite the hand / Unzip / S.O.S. / United kingdom.

| Jan 84. (7"/7"pic-d/12") (NT/+P/X 106) **S.O.S. / UNITED KINGDOM** | 39 | |

—— **FRY** and **WHITE** recruited new members (alongside other sessioners) **DAVID YARRITH** – keyboards repl. SINGLETON / **EDEN** (b.FIONA RUSSELL-POWELL) – keyboards repl. LICKLEY

Oct 84. (7") (NT 107) <884382> **HOW TO BE A MILLIONAIRE. / HOW TO BE A BILLIONAIRE** (ext.12"+=) (NTX 107) – ('A'-acappella version) / How to be a ... zillionaire (mix). (12") (NTXR 107) – ('A'acappella & Zillionaire mixes only).	49	20 Jan86
Mar 85. (7") (NT 108) <880626> **BE NEAR ME. / A TO Z** (d7"+=) (NTD 108) – Poison arrow / The look of love (US mix). (12") (NTX 108) – ('A'disco mix) / What's your destination.	26	9 Aug85
Jun 85. (7"/7"sha-pic-d) (NT/+P 109) <884714> **VANITY KILLS. / JUDY'S JEWELS** (d7"+=) (NTD 109) – S.O.S. / United Kingdom. (12"+=) (NTX 109) – You love you (instrumental). (12"+=) (NTXR 109) – Be near me (ecstacy mix).	70	91 May86
Oct 85. (lp/c)(cd) (NTRH/+C 3)(<824904>) **HOW TO BE A ... ZILLIONAIRE!**	28	30

– Tower of London / How to be a millionaire / Ocean blue / Fear of the world* / Vanity kills* / Be near me* / A to Z / So hip it hurts / Between you and me / 15 storey halo. (c+=/cd+=) – (diff.track mixes*)

Jan 86. (7") *(NT 110)* **OCEAN BLUE. / TOWER OF LONDON (instrumental)** `51`
    (d7"+=) *(NTD 110)* – All of my heart / The look of love.
    (12"+=) *(NTX 110)* – ('A'mix) / Be near me (mix).
    (12"+=) *(NTXR 110)* – ABC Megamix.

—— trimmed to **FRY + WHITE** duo plus sessioners (unknown)

May 87. (7") *(NT 111)* <888604> **WHEN SMOKEY SINGS. / CHICAGO (pt.1)** `11` `5`
    (12"+=) *(NTX 111)* – Chicago (pt.2).
    (cd-s+=) *(NTCD 111)* – All of my heart (live).

Aug 87. (7") *(NT 112)* **THE NIGHT YOU MURDERED LOVE. / MINNEAPOLIS** `31`
    (12"+=/c-s+=) *(NT X/C 112)* – ('A'version).

Oct 87. (lp/c)(cd) *(NTRH/+C 4)*<832391> **ALPHABET CITY** `7` `48` Aug87
    – Avenue A / When smokey sings / The night you murdered love / Think again / rage and then regret / Arkangel / King without a crown / Bad blood / Jealous lover / One day / Avenue Z. *(cd+=)* – (4 versions of last 2 singles 7")

Nov 87. (7") *(NT 113)* **KING WITHOUT A CROWN. / THE LOOK OF LOVE (live)** `44`
    (c-s+=/12"pic-d+=) *(NT MC/XR 113)* – Poison arrow (live).
    (12"++=/cd-s+=) *(NT X/CD 113)* – All of my heart (live).

May 89. (7") *(NT 114)* **ONE BETTER WORLD. / ('A'-percapella mix)** `32`
    (12"+=/cd-s+=) *(NT X/CD 114)* – ('A'club mix) / ('A'garage mix).
    (12"+=) *(NTXR 114)* – (above 3 extra mixes only; not 7" version)

Aug 89. (lp/c/cd) *(<838646-1/-4/-2>)* **UP** `58`
    – Never more than now / The real thing / One better world / Where is the Heaven? / The greatest love of all / I'm in love with you / Paper thin. *(re-iss. cd Aug94; same)*

Sep 89. (7") *(NT 115)* **THE REAL THING. / THE GREATEST LOVE OF ALL** `68`
    (c-s+=) *(NTMC 115)* – North.
    (cd-s+=) *(NTCD 115)* – The look of love (pt.5).
    (12"+/12"pic-d+=) *(NTX/+R 115)* – When Smokey sings / Be near me.

Mar 90. (7") *(NT 116)* **THE LOOK OF LOVE (1990 remix). / OCEAN BLUE** `68`
    (12"+=/cd-s+=) *(NT X/CD 116)* – Vanity kills.

Apr 90. (cd/c/lp) *(<842967-2/-4/-1>)* **ABSOLUTELY ABC** (compilation) `7`
    – Poison arrow / The look of love / All of my heart / Tears are not enough / That was then but this is now / S.O.S. / How to be a millionaire / Be near me / When Smokey sings / The night you murdered love / King without a crown / One better world. *(c+=/cd+=)* – Look of love (1990 remix) / When smokey sings (12"remix) / Be near me (12"remix) / One better world (12"remix) / Ocean blue.

                                   Parlophone M.C.A.

Jun 91. (c-s/7") *(TC+/R 6292)* **LOVE CONQUERS ALL. / WHAT'S GOOD ABOUT GOODBYE** `47`
    (cd-s+=) *(CDR 6292)* – ('A'extended) / ('A'percapella).

Aug 91. (cd/c/lp) *(CD/TC+/PCS 7355)* **ABRACADABRA** `50` Oct91
    – Love conquers all / Unhook the secrets of your heart / Answered prayer / Spellbound / Say it / Welcome to the real world / Satori / All that matters / This must be magic.

Aug 91. (c-s/7") *(TC+/R 6298)* <54040> **SAY IT (Black Box mix). / ('A'-Abracadabra mix)**
    (12"+=) *(12R 6298)* <54055> – Satori.
    (cd-s+=) *(CDR 6298)* – ('A'-piano mix / ('A'instrumental).
    (re-iss. Jan92, hit UK No.42; same)

—— re-formed in 1996

                                   Blatant-Arista Deconstr.

Mar 97. (c-s) *(74321 45363-4)* **STRANGER THINGS / THE WORLD SPINS ON** `57`
    (cd-s+=) *(74321 45363-2)* – All we need.

Apr 97. (cd/c) *(74321 45653-2/-4)* **SKYSCRAPING**
    – Stranger things / Ask a thousand times / Skyscraping / Who can I turn to / Rolling sevens / Only the best will do / Love is its own reward / Light years / Seven day weekend / Heaven knows / Faraway.

May 97. (c-s) *(74321 48525-4)* **SKYSCRAPING / STRANGER THINGS**
    (10"+=/cd-s+=) *(74321 48525-1/-2)* – Light years / Skydubbing.

Jul 97. (c-s) *(74321 49807-4)* **ROLLING SEVENS / ALL OF MY HEART**
    (cd-s+=) *(74321 49807-2)* – The look of love / Heaven knows.

– compilations, etc. –

Mar 93. (cd/c) *Connoisseur; (VSOP CD/MC 182)* **THE REMIX COLLECTION**

May 93. (cd/c) *Spectrum; (550000-2/-4)* **TEARS ARE NOT ENOUGH**

Aug 95. (d-cd) *Neutron; (528600-2)* **LEXICON OF LOVE / BEAUTY STAB**

Mar 96. (cd/c) *Spectrum; (551831-2/-4)* **THE COLLECTION**

Sep 99. (cd) *Blatant; (BLATCD 1)* **THE LEXICON OF LIVE (live)**

ACCEPT (dig out; Great Metal . . .)

AC/DC

Formed: Sydney, Australia . . . 1973, by ex-pat Scots brothers MALCOLM and ANGUS YOUNG. After an initial single, 'CAN I SIT NEXT TO YOU', the siblings headed for Melbourne where they recruited another Caledonian exile, wildman BON SCOTT. Stabilizing the line-up with MARK EVANS and PHIL RUDD, the band signed up with 'Albert' records, a company run by the eldest YOUNG brother, GEORGE, and HARRY VANDA (both ex-EASYBEATS). AC/DC's first two releases, 'HIGH VOLTAGE' (1975) and 'TNT' (1976) were Australia-only affairs, competent boogie-rock that established their name on the domestic scene and generated enough interest for 'Atlantic' UK to come sniffing with chequebook in hand. With major label

muscle behind them, the band relocated to London just as punk was rearing its snotty, vomit-encrusted head. With their particular brand of no-frills rock and ANGUS' school uniform stage gear, the band were initially loosely affiliated to the scene. But with ANGUS' bowel-quaking riffs and SCOTT's high-pitched bellow, their eventual status as one of the archetypal heavy metal acts was almost inevitable from the off. 'Atlantic' introduced the band to Britain with a compilation drawn from the group's first two Australian releases (confusingly also titled 'HIGH VOLTAGE') and AC/DC's first album proper was 1976's 'DIRTY DEEDS DONE DIRT CHEAP'. While its follow-up, 'LET THERE BE ROCK' gave the band their first taste of chart action, AC/DC were first and foremost a live band. The bare-legged cheek of ANGUS was eminently entertaining, his body contorting and jerking like a clockwork toy on speed (NEIL YOUNG's more frenetic noodlings bear a striking similarity, long lost brothers perhaps?!). After a corking live album, 'IF YOU WANT BLOOD, YOU'VE GOT IT' (featuring that classic paean to the larger woman, 'WHOLE LOTTA ROSIE', no anorexic waifs for this lot!), the band hit the big time with 'HIGHWAY TO HELL' (1979). Despite a more commercial sheen courtesy of producer Mutt Lange, the likes of 'TOUCH TOO MUCH' and the title track were unforgettable AC/DC moments, utilising the band's trademark steamrolling rhythm section and their inimitable way with a testosterone-saturated chorus. As ever, the group's lyrics were, for the most part, positively neolithic although their reliably unreconstructed, feminist-baiting songs were never without humour, something of a novelty in the metal scene of that era. Being Scottish/Australian, and a rock star to boot, BON SCOTT wasn't exactly a lager shandy man, the 'Uisge Beath' ('Water of life', or whisky to sassenach readers) rather taking away his life after he drank himself into an early grave the following February (1980). Yet incredibly, by July, the band were back with a No. 1 album, 'BACK IN BLACK', a record that saw the band finally break big in America. Ex-GEORDIE singer, BRIAN JOHNSON, had been recruited on vocal duties and his gravelly yelp carried on where SCOTT left off. The likes of 'HELL'S BELLS' and the irrepressible 'YOU SHOOK ME ALL NIGHT LONG' were staples of rock discos (remember them?) up and down the land and the band became a top-drawer draw in the age of stadium rock, headlining the legendary Castle Donington Festival in its heyday. Yet from here on in, AC/DC lost their spark somewhat. 'FLICK OF THE SWITCH' and 'FLY ON THE WALL' were metal by numbers although 'WHO MADE WHO' (1986) was an interesting hotch-potch of new and old. 'BLOW UP YOUR VIDEO' (1988) and 'THE RAZOR'S EDGE' (1990) saw a resurgence of sorts, the respective sets making Top 5. The band continued to tour for the metal faithful, 1992's 'LIVE' documenting the visceral thrill of the AC/DC concert experience. But while their formula was wearing a bit thin, nobody seemed to have informed the band, 1995's hilariously titled 'BALLBREAKER' crudely retreading over-familiar ground. Still, in the (supposedly) sophisticated PC world of the 90's, you've got to hand it to a band who could still get away with titles like 'COVER YOU IN OIL', 'HARD AS A ROCK' and 'LOVE BOMB'. Vive le rock! • **Songwriters:** Most by YOUNG brothers, some with SCOTT or JOHNSON. Covered; BABY PLEASE DON'T GO / BONNY (trad).

Album rating: HIGH VOLTAGE (UK *8) / DIRTY DEEDS DONE DIRT CHEAP (*6) / LET THERE BE ROCK (*8) / POWERAGE (*6) / IF YOU WANT BLOOD – YOU'VE GOT IT (*8) / HIGHWAY TO HELL (*8) / BACK IN BLACK (*8) / FOR THOSE ABOUT TO ROCK (WE SALUTE YOU) (*4) / FLICK OF THE SWITCH (*5) / FLY ON THE WALL (*5) / WHO MADE WHO (*5) / BLOW UP YOUR VIDEO (*7) / THE RAZOR'S EDGE (*5) / LIVE (*7) / BALLBREAKER (*6)

ANGUS YOUNG (b.31 Mar'59, Glasgow, Scotland) – guitar / **MALCOLM YOUNG** (b. 6 Jan'53, Glasgow) – guitar / **DAVE EVANS** – vocals / **ROB BAILEY** – bass / **PETER CLACK** – drums

                                   not iss. Albert

Jul 74. (7") **CAN I SIT NEXT TO YOU. / ROCKIN' IN THE PARLOUR**   -   - Aust.

—— When all but the brothers departed, they recruited (i.e.DAVE joined RABBIT) **BON SCOTT** (b.RONALD SCOTT, 9 Jul'46, Kirriemuir, Scotland) – vocals (ex-VALENTINES, ex-FRATERNITY, ex-SPECTORS, ex-MOUNT LOFTY RANGERS) / **MARK EVANS** – (b. 2 Mar'56, Melbourne) – bass (ex-BUSTER BROWN) / **PHIL RUDD** (b.19 May'54, Melbourne) – drums

Jan 75. (lp) <APLP 009> **HIGH VOLTAGE**   -   - Austra
    – Baby please don't go / She's got balls / Little lover / Stick around / Soul stripper / You ain't got a hold of me / Love song / Show business.

1975. (7") **DOG EAT DOG. / CARRY ME HOME**   -   - Austra

Dec 75. (lp) <APLP 016> **T.N.T.**   -   - Austra
    – It's a long way to the top (if you wanna rock'n'roll) / The ock'n'roll singer / The jack / Live wire / T.N.T. / Rocker / Can I sit next to you girl / High voltage / School days.

                                   Atlantic Atco

Apr 76. (7") *(K 10745)* **IT'S A LONG WAY TO THE TOP (IF YOU WANNA ROCK'N'ROLL). / CAN I SIT NEXT TO YOU GIRL**
    (re-iss. Jun80 on 'Heavy Metal-Atlantic'; HM 3) (hit UK 55)

May 76. (lp/c) *(K/K4 50257)* **HIGH VOLTAGE** (compilation from two above)
    – It's a long way to the top (if you wanna rock'n'roll) / The rock'n'roll singer / The jack / Live wire / T.N.T. / Can I sit next to you girl / Little lover / She's got balls / High voltage. *(re-iss. Oct87; K2 50257) (re-iss. Jul94 cd/c; 7567 92413-2/-4) (cd re-iss. May98 on 'E.M.I.'; 494671-2)* <US-iss.Apr81; 142>

Aug 76. (7") *(K 10805)* **JAILBREAK. / FLING THING**
    (re-iss. Mar80)

Oct 76. (7") *(K 10860)* **HIGH VOLTAGE. / LIVE WIRE**
    (re-iss. Jun80 on 'Heavy Metal-Atlantic'; HM 1) (hit UK 48)

Dec 76. (7") <7068> **HIGH VOLTAGE. / IT'S A LONG WAY TO THE TOP (IF YOU WANNA ROCK'N'ROLL)**   -   -

Dec 76. (lp/c) *(K/K4 50323)* **DIRTY DEEDS DONE DIRT CHEAP**

– Dirty deeds done dirt cheap / Love at first feel / Big balls / Rocker / Problem child / There's gonna be some rockin' / Ain't no fun (waiting round to be a millionaire) / Ride on / Squealer. <US-iss.Apr81; 16033> – <hit No.3> (cd-iss. Aug87; K2 50323) (re-iss. Jul94 cd/c; 7567 92448-2/-4) (cd re-iss. May98 on 'E.M.I.'; 494670-2)

Jan 77. (7"m) (K 10899) <7086> **DIRTY DEEDS DONE DIRT CHEAP. / BIG BALLS / THE JACK** [☐] [-]
(re-iss. Jun80 on 'Heavy Metal-Atlantic'; HM 2) (hit UK 47)

—— **CLIFF WILLIAMS** (b.14 Dec'49, Romford, England) – bass (ex-HOME, ex-BANDIT) repl. MARK

Sep 77. (7") (K 11018) <7086> **LET THERE BE ROCK. / PROBLEM CHILD**
(re-iss. Mar80)

Oct 77. (lp/c) (K/K4 50366) <151> **LET THERE BE ROCK** [17]
– Go down / Dog eat dog / Let there be rock / Bad boy boogie / Overdose / Crapsody in blue / Hell ain't a bad place to be / Whole lotta Rosie. (cd-iss. Jun89; K2 50366) (re-iss. Oct94 cd/c; 7567 92445-2/-4) (cd re-iss. Sep98 on 'E.M.I.'; 497316-2)

Atlantic / Atlantic

May 78. (lp/c) (K/K4 50483) <19180> **POWERAGE** [26]
– Gimme a bullet / Down payment blues / Gone shootin' / Riff raff / Sin city / Up to my neck in you / What's next to the moon / Cold hearted man / Kicked in the teeth. (cd-iss. Jun89; K 781 548-2) (re-iss. Oct94 cd/c; 7567 92446-2/-4) (cd re-iss. May98 on 'E.M.I.'; 494672-2)

May 78. (7"/12") (K 11142/+T) **ROCK'N'ROLL DAMNATION. / SIN CITY** [24] [-]
(re-iss. Mar80; same)

Jun 78. (7") <3499> **ROCK'N'ROLL DAMNATION. / KICKED IN THE TEETH** [-] [-]

Oct 78. (lp/c) (K/K4 50532) <19212> **IF YOU WANT BLOOD, YOU'VE GOT IT** (live) [13]
– Riff raff / Hell ain't a bad place to be / Bad boy boogie / The jack / Problem child / Whole lotta Rosie / Rock'n'roll damnation / High voltage / Let there be rock / Rocker. (re-iss. Mar80; same) (cd-iss. Jun89; K 781 553-2) (re-iss. Oct94; 7567 92447-2/-4) (cd re-iss. May98 on 'E.M.I.'; 494669-2)

Oct 78. (7"/12") (K 11207/+T) <3553> **WHOLE LOTTA ROSIE (live). / HELL AIN'T A BAD PLACE TO BE (live)**
(re-iss. Mar80; same) (re-iss. Jun80 on 'Heavy Metal-Atlantic'; HM 4) (hit UK 36)

Aug 79. (lp/c) (K/K4 50628) <19244> **HIGHWAY TO HELL** [8] [17]
– Highway to hell / Girls got rhythm / Walk all over you / Touch too much / Beating around the bush / Shot down in flames / Get it hot / If you want blood (you've got it) / Love hungry man / Night prowler. (cd-iss. Jul87; 250 628-2) (cd re-iss. 1989; K2 50628) (cd re-iss. on 'E.M.I.'; 477088-2)

Aug 79. (7") (K 11321) **HIGHWAY TO HELL. / IF YOU WANT BLOOD (YOU'VE GOT IT)** [56] [-]
(re-iss. Mar80; same)

Aug 79. (7") <3617> **HIGHWAY TO HELL. / NIGHT PROWLER** [-] [47]

Oct 79. (7") (K 11406) **GIRLS GOT RHYTHM. / GET IT HOT** [-] [-]
(7"ep) (K 11406E) – ('A'side) / If you want blood (you've got it) / Hell ain't a bad place to be (live) / Rock'n'roll damnation.

Jan 80. (7"m) (K 11435) **TOUCH TOO MUCH (live). / LIVE WIRE (live) / SHOT DOWN IN FLAMES (live)** [29] [-]

Feb 80. (7") <3644> **TOUCH TOO MUCH (live). / WALK ALL OVER YOU (live)** [-] [-]

—— **BRIAN JOHNSON** (b.5 Oct'47, Newcastle, England) – vocals (ex-GEORDIE) repl. BON SCOTT who died 20 Feb'80 after drunken binge.

Jul 80. (lp/c) (K/K4 50735) <16018> **BACK IN BLACK** [1] [4]
– Hells bells / Shoot to thrill / What do you do for money honey / Give the dog a bone / Let me put my love into you / Back in black / You shook me all night long / Have a drink on me / Shake a leg / Rock and roll ain't noise pollution. (cd-iss. Feb87; K2 50735) (re-iss. Aug94 cd/c; 7567 92418-2/-4) (cd re-iss. Jun98 on 'E.M.I.'; 495153-2)

Sep 80. (7") (K 11600) <3761> **YOU SHOOK ME ALL NIGHT LONG. / HAVE A DRINK ON ME** [38] [35]

Nov 80. (7"/12") (K 11630/+T) **ROCK'N'ROLL AIN'T NOISE POLLUTION. / HELL'S BELLS** [15] [☐]

Feb 81. (7") <3787> **BACK IN BLACK. / WHAT DO YOU DO FOR MONEY HONEY** [-] [37]

Nov 81. (lp/c) (K/K4 50851) <11111> **FOR THOSE ABOUT TO ROCK (WE SALUTE YOU)** [3] [1]
– For those about to rock (we salute you) / Put the finger on you / Let's get it up / Inject the venom / Snowballed / Evil walk / C.O.D. / Breaking the laws / Night of the long knives / Spellbound. (cd-iss. Jul87; K2 50851) (re-iss. Jul94 cd/c; 7567 92412-2/-4) (cd re-iss. Jan98 on 'E.M.I.'; 477090-2)

Jan 82. (7") (K 11706) **LET'S GET IT UP. / BACK IN BLACK (live)** [13] [-]
(12"+=) (K 11706T) – T.N.T. (live).

Jan 82. (7")(12") <3894> <3898> **LET'S GET IT UP. / SNOWBALLED** [-] [44]

Jun 82. (7") <4029> **FOR THOSE ABOUT TO ROCK (WE SALUTE YOU). / T.N.T.** [-] [☐]

Jun 82. (7"/ext.12") (K 11721/+T) **FOR THOSE ABOUT TO ROCK (WE SALUTE YOU). / LET THERE BE ROCK (live)** [15] [-]

Aug 83. (lp/c) (780 100-1/-4) <80100> **FLICK OF THE SWITCH** [4] [15]
– Rising power / This house is on fire / Flick of the switch / Nervous shakedown / Landslide / Guns for fire / Deep in the hole / Bedlam in Belgium / Badlands / Brain shake. (re-iss. Jul87 lp/cd/cd; K781 455-1/-4/-2) (re-iss. Oct94 cd/c; 7567 92448-2/-4) (cd re-iss. Jan98 on 'E.M.I.'; 477091-2)

Sep 83. (7"/7"sha-pic-d) (A 9774/+P) <89774> **GUNS FOR HIRE. / LANDSLIDE** [37] [84]

Mar 84. (7") <89772> **FLICK OF THE SWITCH. / BADLANDS** [-] [☐]

—— **SIMON WRIGHT** (b.19 Jun'63) – drums (ex-A II Z, ex-TYTAN) repl. RUDD

Jul 84. (7"/7"sha-pic-d) (A 9651/+P) **NERVOUS SHAKEDOWN. / ROCK'N'ROLL AIN'T NOISE POLLUTION (live)** [35] [☐]
(12"+=/c-s+=) (A 9651 T/C) – Sin city (live) / This house is on fire (live).

Jun 85. (7"/7"w-poster/7"sha-pic-d/12") (A 9532/+W/P/T) <89532> **DANGER. / BACK IN BUSINESS** [48] [☐]

Jul 85. (lp/c/cd) (781 263-1/-4/-2) <81263> **FLY ON THE WALL** [7] [32]
– Fly on the wall / Shake your foundations / First blood / Danger / Sink the pink / Playing with the girls / Stand up / Hell or high water / Back in business / Send for the man. (cd re-iss. Jan98 on 'E.M.I.'; 477092-2)

Nov 85. (7") **SHAKE YOUR FOUNDATIONS. / SEND FOR THE MAN** [-] [☐]

Jan 86. (7"/7"w-poster/7"sha-pic-d) (A 9474/+C/P) **SHAKE YOUR FOUNDATIONS. / STAND UP** [24] [☐]
(12"+=) (A 9474T) – Jailbreak.

May 86. (7"/7"sha-pic-d) (A 9425/+P) <89425> **WHO MADE WHO. / GUNS FOR HIRE (live)** [16] [☐]
(12"+=/12"w-poster) (A 9425T/+W) – ('A'-Collectors mix).

May 86. (lp/c) (WX 57/+C) <81650> **WHO MADE WHO (Soundtrack; Maximum Overdrive) (part compilation)** [11] [33]
– Who made who / You shook me all night long / DT / Sink the pink / Ride on / Hells bells / Shake your foundations / Chase the ace / For those about to rock (we salute you). (cd-iss. 1988; 781 650-2) (cd re-iss. Sep98 on 'E.M.I.'; 746299-2)

Aug 86. (7"/7"sha-pic-d) (A 9377/+P) <89377> **YOU SHOOK ME ALL NIGHT LONG (live). / SHE'S GOT BALLS (live)** [46] [☐]
(12"/12"sha-pic-d) (A 9377 T/TP) – ('B'extended) / ('A'live).

Jan 88. (7") (A 9136) <89136> **HEATSEEKER / GO ZONE** [12] [☐]
(12"+=/12"g-f+=/12"pic-d+=/3"cd-s+=) (A 9136 T/TW/TP/CD) – Snake high.

Feb 88. (lp/c/cd) (WX 144/+C/cd)(781 828-2) <81828> **BLOW UP YOUR VIDEO** [2] [12]
– Heatseeker / That's the way I wanna rock'n'roll / Meanstreak / Go zone / Kissin' dynamite / Nick of time / Some sin for nuthin' / Ruff stuff / Two's up / Some sin for nuthin' / This means war. (cd re-iss. Sep98 on 'E.M.I.'; 748977-2)

Mar 88. (7") (A 9098) <89098> **THAT'S THE WAY I WANNA ROCK'N'ROLL. / KISSIN' DYNAMITE** [22] [☐]
(12"+=/12"g-f+=/12"pic-d+=) (A 9098T/+W/P) – Borrowed time.
(3"cd-s+=) (A 9098CD) – Shoot to thrill (live) / Whole lotta Rosie (live).

—— (Apr88) cousin **STEVE YOUNG** – guitar briefly replaced MALCOLM on tour

—— (1989) (ANGUS, MALCOLM, BRIAN & CLIFF) bring in **CHRIS SLADE** (b.30 Oct'46) – drums (ex-GARY MOORE, ex-MANFRED MANN EARTHBAND, ex-FIRM) repl. WRIGHT who had joined DIO.

Atco / Atco

Sep 90. (7"/c-s/10"pic-d) (B 8907/+C/P) **THUNDERSTRUCK. / FIRE YOUR GUNS** [13] [☐]
(12"+=/cd-s+=) (B 8907 TCD) – DT / Chase the ace.

Oct 90. (cd)(lp/pic-lp/c) (<91413>)(WX 364/+P/+C) **THE RAZOR'S EDGE** [4] [2]
– Thunderstruck / Fire your guns / Moneytalks / The razor's edge / Mistress for Christmas / Rock your heart out / Are you ready / Got you by the balls / Shot of love / Let's make it / Goodbye & good riddance to bad luck / If you dare. (cd re-iss. Jun98 on 'E.M.I.'; 495144-2)

Nov 90. (7"/c-s) (B 8886/+C) **MONEYTALKS. / MISTRESS FOR CHRISTMAS** [36] [-]
(12"+=/12"sha-pic-d+=/cd-s+=) (B 8886 T/P/CD) – Borrowed time.

Nov 90. (c-s) <98881> **MONEYTALKS. / BORROWED TIME** [-] [23]

Apr 91. (7"/7"w-patch/7"s/c-s) (88830/+X/W/C) **ARE YOU READY. / GOT YOU BY THE BALLS** [34] [☐]
(12"+=/12"g-f+=/cd-s+=) (88830 T/TW/CD) – The razor's edge.

Oct 92. (7") (B 8479) **HIGHWAY TO HELL (live) / HELL'S BELLS (live)** [14] [☐]
(12"pic-d) (B 8479TP) – ('A'side) / High voltage (live).
(cd-s) (B 8479CD) – ('A'side) / High voltage (live) / Hell ain't a bad place to be (live).
(cd-s) (B 8479CDX) – ('A'side) / High voltage (live) / The jack (live).

Oct 92. (cd/c/d-lp) (<7567 92212-2/-4/-1>) **LIVE (live)** [5] [15]
– Thunderstruck / Shoot to thrill / Back in black / Sin city / Who made who / Fire your guns / Jailbreak / The jack / Dirty deeds done dirt cheap / Hells bells / Heatseeker / That's the way I wanna rock'n'roll / High voltage / You shook me all night long / Whole lotta Rosie / Let there be rock / Medley:- Bonny – Highway to Hell / T.N.T. / For those about to rock (we salute you). <in the US, a SPECIAL COLLECTOR'S EDITION hit No.26; 92215-2> (cd/d-cd re-iss. Jun98 on 'E.M.I.'; 49514 5/6-2)

Feb 93. (12"/cd-s) (B 6073 T/CD) **DIRTY DEEDS DONE DIRT CHEAP (live). / SHOOT TO THRILL (live) / DIRTY DEEDS DONE DIRT CHEAP** [68] [☐]

Jun 93. (7"/c-s) (88396/+C) <98406> **BIG GUN. / BACK IN BLACK (live)** [23] [65]
(12"+=) (88396T) – For those about to rock (live).
(cd-s) (88396CD) – ('A'side) / For those about to rock (live).

Sep 95. (7"yellow/cd-s/s-cd-s) (A 4368 X/CD/CDX) **HARD AS A ROCK. / CAUGHT WITH YOUR PANTS DOWN** [33] [☐]

Sep 95. (cd/c/lp) (<7559 61780-2/-4/-2>) **BALLBREAKER** [6] [4]
– Whisky on the rocks / The honey roll / The furor / Love bomb / Hard as a rock / Hail Caesar / Cover you in oil / Caught with your pants down / Burnin' alive / Boogie man / Ballbreaker. (cd re-iss. Jun98 on 'E.M.I.'; 495149-2)

Apr 96. (c-s) (A 6051C) **HAIL CAESAR / WHISKEY ON THE ROCKS** [56] [☐]
(cd-s+=) (A 6051CD) – Whole lotta Rosie (live).

Jul 96. (cd-s) (7559-64286-2) **COVER YOU IN OIL / LOVE BOMB / BALLBREAKER**

– compilations, others, etc. –

Aug 84. (m-lp) Atco; <80178> **JAILBREAK '74 (early demos..)** [-] [76]
(UK re-iss. cd Oct94; 7567 92449-2)

Sep 84. (7") Atlantic; <89616> **JAILBREAK. / SHOW BUSINESS** [-] [-]

1991. (3xcd-box) Atco; **BOX SET** [-] [-]
– HIGHWAY TO HELL / BACK IN BLACK / FOR THOSE ABOUT TO ROCK

Nov 97. (d-cd; BON SCOTT & THE FRATERNITY) Raven; (RVCD 56) **COMPLETE SESSIONS 1971-1972**

Dec 97. (5xcd-box) (493273-2) **BONFIRE** [90]

Jan 98. (cd-s; BON SCOTT) Head Office; (HOR 002) **ROUND AND ROUND AND ROUND.** [-] [-]

Sep 98. (cd; by BON SCOTT & THE FRATERNITY) Connoisseur; VSOPCD 261) **LIVESTOCK – BON SCOTT WITH FRATERNITY**

ACE

Formed: Sheffield, England ... late '72, having briefly played gigs as ACE FLASH & THE DYNAMOS. Former MIGHTY BABY members BAM KING and PHIL HARRIS were instigators of this tightly-knit, FM-friendly 5-piece, the other three, PAUL CARRACK, TEX COMER and STEVE WITHERINGTON, all stemming from another pub-rock outfit, WARM DUST. Before the band had entered the studio, one personnel change was in place, that of FRAN BYRNE for the departing WITHERINGTON. Signing to 'Anchor' records in 1974, they surprised even themselves when their laid-back, CARRACK-penned debut single, 'HOW LONG', cracked the Top 20. However, mediocre reviews of the accompanying album, 'FIVE-A-SIDE' (1974), prevented it doing the same. Early the following year, both the aforementioned 45 and LP entered the US Billboard charts and eventually rose to No.3 and No.11 respectively. The wanted follow-up set, 'TIME FOR ANOTHER' (1975), demonstrated too readily that audiences were extremely fickle, a lowly US chart position of No.153 resulting in the band coming home to lick their wounds. By the time a third LP, 'NO STRINGS', had hit the shops in '77, Punk/New Wave was in fashion and mainstream pop-rock was not; a split was the only inevitable outcome; most of the group (including PAUL) went on to work with FRANKIE MILLER, while frontman/keyboard-player PAUL CARRACK also teamed up with ROXY MUSIC (on session). The singer's solo career commenced around the same period, his debut album 'NIGHTBIRD' (1980) falling short of expectations. However, PAUL's career was on the up from then on, kickstarted surprisingly enough when SQUEEZE invited him in to replace JOOLS HOLLAND. One of his first duties was to sing 'TEMPTED' (from their album 'East Side Story'), a song that characterised his smooth vocal abilities to the max and one that became a deserved 1981 chart hit on both sides of the Atlantic. The following year and with the guidance of producer NICK LOWE, CARRACK had his first taste of solo success when 'I NEED YOU' (from the LP, 'SUBURBAN VOODOO') hit the US Top 40. In 1985, after regularly featuring in ERIC CLAPTON's band, PAUL joined GENESIS man MICHAEL RUTHERFORD in his new soft-pop venture, MIKE + THE MECHANICS; he would sing lead on many of their hits including 'SILENT RUNNING (ON DANGEROUS GROUND)' and 'ALL I NEED IS A MIRACLE'. Now signed to 'Chrysalis', CARRACK had his biggest solo hit to date, 'DON'T SHED A TEAR', a US Top 10'er it was taken from his third and best album, 'ONE GOOD REASON' (1987). 'GROOVE APPROVED' (1989) was his last long-player for some time, the man much in-demand all over the world. In 1996 and now on 'I.R.S.', PAUL delivered some fresh solo material in the shape of his fifth set, 'BLUE VIEWS'. This time around, Britain was the country to give him chart status, 'EYES OF BLUE' (twice!) and a re-make of 'HOW LONG' both denting the Top 40 – he would follow it up in 1998 with 'BEAUTIFUL WORLD'.

Album rating: FIVE-A-SIDE (*5) / TIME FOR ANOTHER (*4) / NO STRINGS (*3) / SIX-A-SIDE compilation (*6) / THE BEST OF ACE compilation (*5) / Paul Carrack: NIGHTBIRD (*5) / SUBURBAN VOODOO (*5) / ACE MECHANIC (or) CARRACKTER REFERENCE (*6) / ONE GOOD REASON (*7) / GROOVE APPROVED (*5) / TWENTY-ONE GOOD REASONS compilation (*6) / BLUE VIEWS (*7) / BEAUTIFUL WORLD (*5)

ALAN 'BAM' KING (b. Sep'46, Kentish Town, London, England) – guitar, vocals (ex-MIGHTY BABY, ex-ACTION) / **PHIL HARRIS** (b. Jul'48, Muswell Hill, London) – guitar, vocals (ex-MIGHTY BABY) / **PAUL CARRACK** (b.22 Apr'51) – vocals, keyboards (ex-WARM DUST) / **TERRY 'TEX' COMER** (b.23 Feb'49, Burnley, England) – bass, vocals (ex-WARM DUST) / **FRAN BYRNE** (b. Mar'48) – drums (ex-BEES MAKE HONEY) repl. STEVE WITHERINGTON (ex-WARM DUST)

		Anchor	Anchor	
Oct 74.	(7") (ANC 1002) <21000> **HOW LONG. / SNIFFIN' ABOUT**	20	3	Feb75
Nov 74.	(lp) (<ANC 2001>) **FIVE-A-SIDE**		11	Mar75

– Sniffin' about / Rock & roll runaway / How long / The real feeling / 24 hours / Why / Time ain't long / Know how it feels / Satellite / So sorry baby. (re-iss. Jun90 on 'Connoisseur' lp/c/cd; CSAP+C/CD 103)

Mar 75.	(7") (ANC 1014) **I AIN'T GONNA STAND FOR THIS. / ROCK & ROLL RUNAWAY**			
Jul 75.	(7") <21002> **ROCK & ROLL RUNAWAY. / KNOW HOW IT FEELS**	-		
Nov 75.	(7") (ANC 1024) **NO FUTURE IN YOUR EYES. / I'M A MAN**			
Nov 75.	(lp) (<ANC 2013>) **TIME FOR ANOTHER**			

– I think it's gonna last / I'm a man / Tongue tied / Does it hurt you / Message to you / No future in your eyes / This is what you find / You can't lose / Sail on my brother / Ain't gonna stand for this no more.

— **JON WOODHEAD** – guitar, vocals repl.HARRIS

Jan 77.	(7") (ANC 1036) **YOU'RE ALL THAT I NEED. / CRAZY WORLD**			
Jan 77.	(lp) (<ANC 2020>) **NO STRINGS**			

– Rock'n'roll singer / You're all that I need / Crazy world / I'm not takin' it out on you / Movin' / Gleaming in the gloom / Let's hang on / Why did you leave me / Found out the hard way / C'est la vie.

May 77.	(7") (ANC 1040) **FOUND OUT THE HARD WAY. / WHY DID YOU LEAVE ME**		

— disbanded summer 1977, FRAN, TEX and PAUL joined FRANKIE MILLER BAND. PAUL joined ROXY MUSIC then went solo

– compilations, etc. –

Feb 82.	(7") Polydor; (POSP 416) **HOW LONG. / I'M NOT TAKING IT OUT ON YOU**		-
Jun 82.	(lp)(c) Polydor; (2478 159)(3192 663) **SIX-A-SIDE**		-

– Sniffin' about / Why / How long / I'm a man / Tongue tied / Does it hurt you / Rock'n'roll singer / Sail on brother / You're all that I need /

Jun 84.	(7") Old Gold; (OG 9392) **HOW LONG. / (B-side by Stretch)**		-
Nov 87.	(7") Old Gold; (OG 9731) **HOW LONG. / YOU'RE ALL THAT I NEED**		-
Nov 87.	(lp/cd) See For Miles; (SEE/+CD 214) **THE BEST OF ACE**		-

– How long / I'm a man / Ain't gonna stand for this no more / Rock & roll runaway / The real feeling / Rock and roll singer / You're all that I need / 24 hours / Crazy world / No future in your eyes / Tongue tied / Time ain't long / Sail on my brother / I think it's gonna last. (cd re-iss. May93; same)

Aug 93.	(cd/c) Music Club; (MC CD/TC 123) **THE VERY BEST OF ACE**		

– (virtually the same track listing as above)

Aug 95.	(7") Old Gold; (OG 6304) **HOW LONG. / SNIFFIN' ABOUT**		-

PAUL CARRACK

— **PAUL CARRACK** – vocals, keyboards / with session people

		Vertigo	not iss.	
Apr 80.	(7") (PAUL 1) **BEAUTY IS ONLY SKIN DEEP. / BET YOU NEVER BEEN IN LOVE**		-	
Jul 80.	(lp/c) (6359/7150 016) **NIGHTBIRD**		-	

– Beauty is only skin deep / There's a good chance / In love with me / Love is all it takes / Where you going babe / Foregone conclusion / Bet you never been in love / Nightbird.

— CARRACK became a member of SQUEEZE

		Epic	Epic	
Oct 82.	(7") (EPC 2874) <03146> **I NEED YOU. / CALL ME TONIGHT**		37	Aug82
Dec 82.	(lp/c) (EPC/40 85992) <38161> **SUBURBAN VOODOO**		78	Aug82

– Lesson in love / Always better with you / I need you / I'm in love / Don't give my heart a break / A little unkind / Out of touch / What a way to go / So right, so wrong / From now on / Call me tonight / I found love.

Feb 83.	(7") (EPC 3159) **A LITTLE UNKIND. / DON'T GIVE MY HEART A BREAK**		

— the singer now turned up for MIKE + THE MECHANICS (MIKE RUTHERFORD of GENESIS' band) while continuing solo

		Chrysalis	Chrysalis	
Apr 87.	(7") (CHS 3109) **WHEN YOU WALK IN THE ROOM. / COLLRANE**	48		

(12"+=)(cd-s+=) (CHS12 3109)(CDE 3) – How long (album medley).

Oct 87.	(7") (CHS 3164) <43164> **DON'T SHED A TEAR. / MERILEE**		9	

(12"+=) (CHS12 3164) – All your love is in vain.
(above actually hit UK charts No.60 in Mar'89)

Oct 87.	(lp/c/cd) (<CDL /ZCDL /CCD 1578>) **ONE GOOD REASON**		67	

– One good reason / When you walk in the room / Button off my shirt / Give me a chance / Double it up / Don't shed a tear / Fire with fire / Here I am / Collrane / (Do I figure) In your life.

May 88.	(7") (CHS 3204) **ONE GOOD REASON. / ALL YOUR LOVE IS IN VAIN**		28	Mar88

(12"+=/cd-s+=) (CHS 12/CD 3204) –

Jun 88.	(7") <43252> **WHEN YOU WALK IN THE ROOM. / IF YOU SEE HER WALKIN'**	-	90	
Sep 88.	(7") <43288> **BUTTON OFF MY SHIRT. / DOUBLE IT UP**	-	91	
Oct 89.	(7") (CHS 3403) <23427> **I LIVE BY THE GROOVE. / TAILFINDER**		31	

(12"+=/cd-s+=) (CHS 12/CD 3403) – Don't shed a tear

Oct 89.	(lp/c/cd) (<CHR /ZCHR /CCD 1709>) **GROOVE APPROVED**			

– Only my heart can tell / I live by the groove / Battlefield / Love can break your heart / I'm on your tail / After the love is gone / Loveless / Tip of my tongue / Dedicated / Bad news (at the best of times).

Feb 90.	(7") (CHS 3494) **BATTLEFIELD. / SHE'S SOULFUL**		

(12"+=/cd-s+=) (CHS 12/CD 3494) – ('A'extended)

Jan 94.	(cd/c) (CD/TC 6067) **TWENTY-ONE GOOD REASONS** (compilation)		

– How long (w/ ACE) / The real feeling (w/ ACE) / No future in your eyes (w/ ACE) / You're all that I need (w/ ACE) / Tempted (w/ SQUEEZE) / Do me lover (w/ CARLENE CARTER) / Oh how happy (w/ CARLENE CARTER) / Rumour / I need you / Always better with you / A little unkind / One good reason / Don't shed a tear / Button off my shirt / When you walk in the room / I live by the groove / Only my heart can tell / Battlefield / Loveless / Silent running (w/ MIKE + THE MECHANICS) / Living years (w/ MIKE + THE MECHANICS).

		I.R.S.	I.R.S.	
Dec 95.	(c-s/cd-s) (TC/CD EIRS 192) **EYES OF BLUE / OVER MY SHOULDER / PEOPLE GET REAL**	40		

(cd-s) (CDEIRSS 192) – ('A'side) / Tempted / Warm and tender love / Burning love

Jan 96.	(cd/c) (EIRS CD/TC 1075) **BLUE VIEWS**		

– Eyes of blue / For once in our lives / No easy way out / Oh oh oh my my my / Only a breath away / Nothing more than a memory / Somewhere in your heart / Love will keep us alive / Always have always will / Don't walk over me / How long. (cd re-iss. May97 on 'ARK-EMI'; ARKK 10007)

Mar 96.	(c-s/cd-s) (TC/CD EIRS 193) **HOW LONG / LOVE ME AS HARD AS YOU HURT ME / INTO THE MYSTIC / DON'T DREAM IT'S OVER**	32	

(cd-s) (CDEIRSS 193) – Into the mystic / The living years

Aug 96.	(c-s/cd-s) (TC/CD EIRS 194) **EYES OF BLUE / TEMPTED / OVER MY SHOULDER / WHEN YOU WALK IN THE ROOM**	45	

(cd-s) (CDEIRSS 194) – ('A'side) / For once in our lives / Don't shed a tear.

		Ark – EMI	
May 98.	(cd) (ARKCD 001) **BEAUTIFUL WORLD**		

– The way I'm feeling tonight / Time to let go / Beautiful world / Perfect love / You give me something / Satisfied / Close to me / It goes without saying / If you'd ever needed someone / Some kinda love.

– compilations, etc. –

Dec 87.	(lp) Demon; (FIEND 83) **ACE MECHANIC** (his best work & for other groups)		-

– Silent running (on dangerous ground) / A little unkind / Why did you leave me? / Always better with you / C'est la vie / I need you / How long / Tempted / From now on / Sniffin' about / Lesson in love / I think it's gonna last / Do me lover / I found love. *(re-iss. Jul91 as 'CARRACKTER REFERENCE' cd+=/c+=; FIEND/+CASS 700)* – Give me a chance / After the love is gone. *<US-iss.May95 on 'Demon'; same as UK re-issue>*

A CERTAIN RATIO (dig out; Great Alt & Indie . . .)

ADAM & THE ANTS

Formed: London, England . . . April '77 by STUART GODDARD (aka ADAM ANT) along with LESTER SQUARE, ANDY WARREN and PAUL FLANAGAN. Initially a fairly rote punk act with attitude, what got the band noticed was their lurid stage show and penchant for S&M trappings. Derek Jarman was sufficiently enamoured to offer ADAM a part in his controversial punk flick, 'Jubilee' (released Feb '78), a revised ANTS line-up (featuring new members DAVE BARBE and MARK GAUMONT) recording two songs for the soundtrack, 'Plastic Surgery' and 'Deutcher Girls'. Later that year, the group released a one-off debut single for 'Decca', 'YOUNG PARISIANS', before releasing their rated debut album, 'DIRK WEARS WHITE SOX' in late '79. A morose slab of post-punk doom-mongering, the record stood in stark contrast to their later albums by a remodelled ADAM & THE ANTS. The shake-up came courtesy of none other than ex-SEX PISTOLS svengali, MALCOLM McLAREN, who, after dreaming up the flamboyant new image (a surprisingly effective if retrospectively ridiculous Native Indian cum swashbuckling pirates concept), whisked ADAM's band off to become BOW WOW WOW. Virtually written off by his critics, ADAM came swaggering back with a new line-up (MARCO PIRRONI, CHRIS HUGHES aka MERRICK, KEVIN MOONEY and TERRY LEE MIALL), a new sound and a new album (his first for 'C.B.S.'), 'KINGS OF THE WILD FRONTIER' (1980). Taking their cue from the Burundi drummers of Africa, the band had stumbled on a unique musical mutant which combined retro rock'n'roll with pseudo-tribal, dayglo pouting pop; teenyboppers loved it and a string of anthemic singles, 'DOG EAT DOG', 'ANT MUSIC' and the thundering title track all made the UK Top 5. The album itself rode to the top of the charts (even scaping into the US Top 50) and for a brief but warpainted period, Britain was gripped with "Antmania". The sight of the ever photogenic ADAM striding boldly through his video adventures like some dandy Indiana Jones was the stuff of girly fantasy and if you didn't have a white stripe across your nose, well, you could forget getting lucky at the school disco. ANT was clever enough to slightly tweak his image on the follow-up set, 'PRINCE CHARMING' (1981), this time going for a dashing highwayman cum 18th century courtier get-up. It was even more effective, the group scoring two No.1 singles in quick succession with 'STAND AND DELIVER' and the title track, while 'ANT RAP' made the Top 3. To be fair to the man, he had the good sense to disband ADAM & THE ANTS at the height of their fame, although by carrying on as ADAM ANT in a vaguely similar vein, he was bound to suffer a backlash sooner or later. Retaining sidekick, PIRRONI, ANT's solo career nevertheless got off to an auspicious start with No.1 single, 'GOODY TWO SHOES', while the accompanying album, 'FRIEND OR FOE' (1982) made the Top 5 (and bizarrely the US Top 20). The following three years brought only one major hit in 'PUSS 'N' BOOTS' and after the 'VIVE LE ROCK' (1985) set, ANT took four years off to develop his acting career while PIRRONI joined SPEAR OF DESTINY. By the turn of the decade, the pair were back with an underwhelming new single, 'ROOM AT THE TOP', and album, 'MANNERS & PHYSIQUE', both enjoying a brief stint in the charts but largely ignored as the nation's pop kids raved to acid house. • **Trivia:** He acted in stage production of 'Entertaining Mr. Sloane'. After retiring to the States in 1986 he took parts in 'Slam Dance' film, and 'Equalizer' TV serial.

Album rating: DIRK WEARS WHITE SOX (*7) / KINGS OF THE WILD FRONTIER (*7) / PRINCE CHARMING (*5) / FRIEND OR FOE (*5) / STRIP (*4) / VIVE LE ROCK (*4) / MANNERS AND PHYSIQUE (*4) / WONDERFUL (*5) / HITS (1980-1985) compilation (*7)

ADAM ANT (b. STUART GODDARD, 3 Nov'54) – vocals, guitar / **MATTHEW ASHMAN** (b.'62) – guitar, vocals (ex-KAMERAS) / **ANDY WARREN** (b.'61) – bass, vocals / **DAVE BARBE** (b.'61) – drums (ex-DESOLATION ANGELS)

	Decca	not iss.
Oct 78. (7") (F 13803) **YOUNG PARISIANS. / LADY**	☐	–
(re-act.Dec80; hit No.9)		

	Do-It	not iss.
Jun 79. (7") (DUN 8) **ZEROX. / WHIP IN MY VALISE**	☐	–

—— (some copies had B-side playing 'PHYSICAL (YOU'RE SO)')
(re-act.Jan81; hit No.45)

Nov 79. (lp/c) (RIDE 3/+M) **DIRK WEARS WHITE SOX** ☐ –
– Cartrouble (part 1 & 2) / Digital tenderness / Nine plan failed / Day I met God * / Tabletalk / Cleopatra / Catholic day / Never trust a man (with egg on his face) / Animals and men / Family of noise / The idea. *(re-act.Jan81; hit No.16) (remixed & re-iss. Apr83 on 'C.B.S.' lp/c; CBS/40 25361) (track * replaced by)* – Zerox / Kick! / Whip in my valise. *(cd-iss. Jul95 on 'Columbia'; 480521-2)*

—— **LEIGH GORMAN** – bass (on B-side) repl. WARREN who joined MONOCHROME SET

Feb 80. (7") (DUN 10) **CARTROUBLE. / KICK!** ☐ –
(re-act.Jan81; hit No.33)

—— (Jan80) until (Mar'80 when ADAM brought in entire new group) **MARCO PIRRONI** (b.27 Apr'59) – guitar, vocals (ex-MODELS) / **MERRICK** (b.CHRIS HUGHES, 3 Mar'54) – drums repl. BARBE / **KEVIN MOONEY** – bass, vocals repl. GORMAN (who with above 2 formed BOW WOW WOW) / added **TERRY LEE MIALL** (b. 8 Nov'58) – 2nd drummer (ex-MODELS)

	C.B.S.	Columbia
Jul 80. (7") (CBS 8877) **KINGS OF THE WILD FRONTIER. / PRESS DARLINGS**	48	–
(re-act.Feb81; hit No.2)		
Sep 80. (7") (CBS 9039) **DOG EAT DOG. / PHYSICAL (YOU'RE SO)**	4	–
Nov 80. (lp/c) (CBS/40 84549) <37033> **KINGS OF THE WILD FRONTIER**	1	44 Feb81

– Dog eat dog / Ant music / Feed me to the lions / Los Rancheros / Ants invasion / Killer in the home / Kings of the wild frontier / The magnificent five / Don't be square (be there) / Jolly Roger / Making history / The human beings. *(cd-iss. Oct93 & Dec98 on 'Sony Europe'; 477902-2)*

Nov 80. (7") (CBS 9352) **ANT MUSIC. / FALL IN**	2	–
Jan 81. (7")(12") <02042><01061> **ANT MUSIC. / DON'T BE SQUARE (BE THERE)**	–	–

—— **GARY TIBBS** (b.25 Jan'58)- bass (ex-ROXY MUSIC, ex-VIBRATORS) repl. MOONEY

May 81. (7")<US-12"> (A-1065) <02193> **STAND AND DELIVER. / BEAT MY GUEST**	1	–
Sep 81. (7") (A-1408) **PRINCE CHARMING. / CHRISTIAN D'OR**	1	–
Nov 81. (lp/c) (CBS/40 85268) <37615> **PRINCE CHARMING**	2	94

– Prince charming / The Scorpios / Picasso visita el Planeta de los Simios / 5 guns west / That voodoo / Stand and deliver / Mile high club / Ant rap / Mowhok / S.E.X. *(re-iss. cd Mar96 on 'Columbia'; 474606-2)*

Dec 81. (7"/7"pic-d) (A/+11 1738) **ANT RAP. / FRIENDS**	3	–

—— they broke up early '82

ADAM ANT

continued solo augmented by **PIRRONI** and sessioners

	C.B.S.	Epic
May 82. (7"/7"pic-d) (A/+11 2367) **GOODY TWO SHOES. / RED SCAB**	1	–
Sep 82. (7"/7"pic-d) (A/+11 2736) **FRIEND OR FOE. / JUANITO THE BANDITO**	9	–
Oct 82. (lp/c) (CBS/40 25040) <38370> **FRIEND OR FOE**	5	16

– Friend or foe / Something girls / Place in the country / Desperate but not serious / Here comes the grump / Hello I love you / Goody two shoes / Crackpot history and the right to lie / Made of money / Cajun twisters / Try this for sighs / A man called Marco. *(cd-iss. Jul96 on 'Columbia'; 484436-2)*

Oct 82. (7") <03367> **GOODY TWO SHOES. / CRACKPOT HISTORY**	–	12
Nov 82. (7"/7"pic-d) (A/+11 2892) **DESPERATE BUT NOT SERIOUS. / WHY DO GIRLS LOVE HORSES?**	33	–
Feb 83. (7") <03688> **DESPERATE BUT NOT SERIOUS. / PLACE IN THE COUNTRY**	–	66
Oct 83. (7"/7"pic-d/ext.12") (A/WA/TA 3614) <04461> **PUSS 'N' BOOTS. / KISS THE DRUMMER**	5	May84
Nov 83. (lp/c) (CBS/40 25705) <39108> **STRIP**	20	65

– Baby let me scream at you / Libertine / Spanish games / Vanity / Puss'n'boots / Playboy / Strip / Montreal / Navel to neck / Amazon. *(cd-iss. Jul84/ CD 25705)*

Dec 83. (7"/7"pic-d/ext.12") (A/WA/TA 3589) <04337> **STRIP. / YOURS, YOURS, YOURS**	41	42
Sep 84. (7"/'A'-Orbit mix-12") (A/TA 4719) **APOLLO 9. / B SIDE BABY**	13	

(12") (QTA 4719) – ('A'-Splashdown remix & accappella instrumental).

Jul 85. (7") (A 6367) <05574> **VIVE LE ROCK. / GRETA X**	50	

(12"+=) (TA 6367) – ('A'instrumental dub mix).

Sep 85. (lp/c) (CBS/40 26583) <40159> **VIVE LE ROCK**	42	

– Vive le rock / Miss Thing / Razor keen / Rip down / Scorpio rising / Apollo 9 / Hell's eight acres / Mohair lockeroom pin-up boys / No zap / P.O.E. (c+=) – Human bondage den. *(cd-iss. 1988+=; CD 26583)* – Apollo 9 (accappella). *(re-iss. cd Mar95 on 'Rewind'; 478504-2)*

—— ADAM retired for 4 years. MARCO joined SPEAR OF DESTINY

ADAM ANT

brought back MARCO to resurrect career.

	M.C.A.	M.C.A.
Feb 90. (7"/7"s/c-s) (MCA/+R/C 1387) <53679> **ROOM AT THE TOP. / BRUCE LEE**	13	17

(cd-s+=/12"+=) (D+/MCAT 1387) – ('A'house vocals).
(cd-s+=) (DMCAX 1387) – ('A'mixes).

Mar 90. (cd/lp)(c) (D+/MCG 6068)(MCGC 6068) <6315> **MANNERS & PHYSIQUE**	19	57

– Room at the top / If you keep on / Can't set rules about love / Bright lights black leather / Young dumb and full of it / Rough stuff / Manners & physique / U.S.S.A. / Piccadilly / Anger Inc.

Apr 90. (7"/c-s) (MCA/+C 1404) **CAN'T SET RULES ABOUT LOVE. / HOW TO STEAL THE WORLD**	47	

(cd-s+=/12"+=) (D+/MCAT 1404) – Brand new torso.
(cd-s+++=) (DMCAP 1404) – ('A'-lp version).

Jun 90. (7") <79042> **BRIGHT LIGHTS BLACK LEATHER. / ROUGH STUFF**	–	–

—— w/ **PIRRONI / BOZ BOORER** – guitars / **BRUCE WITKIN** – bass / **DAVE RUFFY** – drums

	E.M.I.	Capitol
Jan 95. (c-s/7") (TC+/EM 366) <58239> **WONDERFUL. / GOES AROUND**	32	39 Mar95

(cd-s+=) (CDEMS 366) – Norman / Woman love run through me.
(cd-s) (CDEM 366) – ('A'side) / If / Phoenix.

Mar 95. (c-s/7"; withdrawn) (TC+/EM) **BEAUTIFUL DREAM. / LET'S HAVE A FIGHT**		

(cd-s+=; w-drawn) (CDEMS) – Billy boy / Wonderful (acoustic).
(cd-s; w-drawn) (CDEM) – ('A'side) / Shake your hips / Ant music (acoustic) / ('A'-Lucas master mix).

Apr 95. (cd/c) (CD/TC EMC 3687) <30335> **WONDERFUL**	24	39

– Won't take that talk / Beautiful dream / Wonderful / 1969 again / Yin & Yang /

ADAM & THE ANTS (cont)   THE GREAT ROCK DISCOGRAPHY

Image of yourself / Alien / Gotta be a sin / Vampires / Angel / Very long ride. *(cd re-iss. Sep97; same)*
May 95. (c-s) *(TCEM 379)* **GOTTA BE A SIN / DOG EAT DOG (live)** `48` `☐`
(cd-s) *(CDEM 379)* – ('A'side) / Cleopatra (live) / Beat my guest (live) / Red scab (live).
(cd-s) *(CDEMS 379)* – ('A'side) / Desperate but not serious (live) / Car trouble (live) / Physical (you're so) (live).

– compilations, others, etc. –

Feb 82. (7") *E.G.; (EGO 5)* **DEUTCHER GIRLS. / PLASTIC SURGERY** `13` `-`
Mar 82. (7"ep/7"pic-ep) *Do-It; (DUN/+X 20)* **THE B-SIDES** `46` `-`
– Friends / Kick! / Physical (you're so).
(12"ep+=) *(DUNIT 20)* – Cartrouble (pts. 1 & 2).
1982. (7"; as MANEATERS) *E.G.; (EGO 8)* **NINE TO FIVE. / (SUZI PINNS: Jerusalem)** `☐` `-`
(above another from the film 'Jubilee' & featuring TOYAH)
Sep 86. (lp/c) *C.B.S.; (CBS/40 450074-1/-4)* **HITS** `☐` `-`
– Kings of the wild frontier / Dog eat dog / Ant music / Stand and deliver / Prince Charming / Ant rap / Goody two shoes / Friend or foe / Desperate but not serious / Puss 'n' boots / Strip / Apollo 9 / Vive le rock. *(re-iss. Jul90 & Jul98 on 'Columbia' cd/c; R 450074-2/-4)*
Jan 88. (7") *Old Gold; (OG 9739)* **ANT MUSIC. / STAND AND DELIVER** `☐` `-`
Oct 89. (12"white/12"pic-d) *Damaged Goods; (FNARR/+P 7)* **YOUNG PARISIANS / LADY. / (interview)** `☐` `-`
Nov 90. (7") *Old Gold; (OG 9953)* **PRINCE CHARMING. / GOODY TWO SHOES** `☐` `-`
Feb 91. (cd/c/lp) *Strange Fruit; (SFR CD/MC/LP 115)* **THE PEEL SESSIONS** (early 1979 material) `☐` `-`
Jun 91. (cd/c) *Columbia; (468762-2/-4)* **ANTICS IN THE FORBIDDEN ZONE** `☐` `-`
Aug 93. (cd/c) *Arcade; (ARC 31000 5-2/6-4)* **ANTMUSIC – THE VERY BEST OF ADAM ANT** `6` `-`
(re-iss. Mar94 d-cd+ 'LIVE'; ARC 310000-2); hit No.30)
Oct 94. (cd) *Columbia; (477513-2)* **THE BEST (ADAM ANT)** `☐` `-`
May 95. (cd) *Columbia; (480362-2)* **B SIDES BABIES** `☐` `-`
Mar 99. (cd) *Columbia; (494229-2)* **THE VERY BEST OF . . .** `56` `☐`

Bryan ADAMS

Born: 5 Nov'59, Vancouver, Canada. In 1977 he set up a writing partnership with JIM VALLANCE, drummer with techno-rock band, PRISM. Numerous groups, including LOVERBOY, KISS, BACHMAN-TURNER OVERDRIVE, etc. used their songs before ADAMS signed a contract with 'A&M' early in 1979. While VALLANCE recorded with ADAMS on the low-key debut single and eponymous album, he soon bowed out (the writing partnership continued) and ADAMS assembled a new band for the follow-up, 'YOU WANT IT YOU GOT IT' (1982). However, it wasn't until Spring 1983, with the release of 'STRAIGHT FROM THE HEART', that ADAMS made a significant impact on the US charts. His gravel-voiced, sub-SPRINGSTEEN rock was soon to enter into an ongoing love affair with coffee tables the world over, the follow-up album, 'CUTS LIKE A KNIFE' making the Top 10 album chart in America. ADAMS really hit his stride with 'RECKLESS' (1984), a sturdy, professional set of soft-rockers and ballads. While 'SUMMER OF '69' was an entertaining piece of anthemic pop/rock and the album possessed just enough rough-edged charm to offset the cheese factor, the likes of 'THE KIDS WANNA ROCK' was downright cringeworthy. ADAMS also beat ELTON to a Princess Di tribute with the B-side of the 'HEAVEN' single, entitled, funnily enough, 'DIANA'. The album made the man a household name while the follow-up effort, 'INTO THE FIRE' (1987) marked the end of his songwriting partnerhip with VALLANCE and saw ADAMS lyrics take on a more political bent (the following year saw ADAMS playing the Nelson Mandela benefit concert at Wembley Stadium). Still, any hopes of a radical new direction were dashed several years later upon the release of the unashamed slush-pop ballad, '(EVERYTHING I DO) I DO IT FOR YOU'. The record (featured on the soundtrack to the Kevin Costner film, 'Robin Hood, Prince Of Thieves') went to No. 1 on both sides of the Atlantic for what seemed like an eternity. After 16 weeks of radio overkill, one might have suspected that the populace had satiated their Adams appetite, so to speak, but no, the follow-up, 'CAN'T STOP THIS THING WE STARTED' (more uptempo but equally bland), almost breached the UK Top 10. The album, 'WAKING UP THE NEIGHBOURS' (1992) went to the top of the album charts, although it's safe to say that by now, ADAMS was probably appealing to a slightly different market and had lost any credibility (if, that is, he actually had any in the first place!) with a younger, more discerning audience. More nauseatingly saccharine ballads followed ('ALL FOR LOVE', 'HAVE YOU EVER REALLY LOVED A WOMAN', etc., you get the picture) into the singles charts while his most recent attempts at rock (in the loosest sense of the term, naturally) make HANSON sound dangerous. • **Covered:** WALKING AFTER MIDNIGHT (D. Hecht / A. Block) / I FOUGHT THE LAW (Sonny Curtis) / LITTLE RED ROOSTER (Willie Dixon).

Album rating: BRYAN ADAMS (*3) / YOU WANT IT YOU GOT IT (*5) / CUTS LIKE A KNIFE (*7) / RECKLESS (*7) / INTO THE FIRE (*5) / WAKING UP THE NEIGHBOURS (*5) / SO FAR SO GOOD compilation (*6) / LIVE! LIVE! LIVE! (*4) / 18 TIL I DIE (*4) / UNPLUGGED (*4) / ON A DAY LIKE TODAY (*4)

BRYAN ADAMS – vocals, guitar / with **JIM VALLANCE** – drums, keyboards, guitar, bass

	A&M	A&M
Jul 79. (7"/ext.12") *(AMS/+P 7460)* <2163> **LET ME TAKE YOU DANCIN'. / DON'T TURN ME AWAY**	`☐`	`☐`

Apr 80. (7") *(AMS 7520)* <2220> **HIDIN' FROM LOVE. / WAIT AND SEE** `☐` `☐`
Mar 81. (lp) *(AMLH 64800)* <4800> **BRYAN ADAMS** `☐` `Nov80`
– Hidin' from love / Win some, lose some / Wait and see / Give me your love / Wastin' time / Don't ya say it / Remember / State of mind / Try to see it my way. *(re-iss. cd Jun 3100) (re-iss. cd 1988; CD MID 100)*
Apr 81. (7") *(AMS 2249)* **GIVE ME YOUR LOVE. / WAIT AND SEE** `-` `☐`
—— now with **TOMMY HANDEL** – keyboards / **BRIAN STANLEY** – bass + **MICKEY CURRY** – drums repl. VALLANCE (he continued to co-write + play piano + percussion for ADAMS until '88.)
Mar 82. (7") *(AMS 8183)* <2359> **LONELY NIGHTS. / DON'T LOOK NOW** `☐` `☐`
Apr 82. (lp) *(AMLH 64864)* <4864> **YOU WANT IT, YOU GOT IT** `78` `84` `Jan82`
– Lonely nights / One good reason / Don't look now / Jealousy / Coming home / Fits ya good / Tonight / You want it, you got it / Last chance / No one makes it right. *(cd-iss. Aug85; CDA 3154) (re-iss. cd 1988; CD MID 100)*
Jul 82. (7") <2409> **COMING HOME. / FITS YA GOOD** `☐` `☐`
—— **DAVE TAYLOR** – bass repl. STANLEY
—— added **KEITH SCOTT** – guitar, vocals
Mar 83. (lp) *(SMLH 64919)* <4919> **CUTS LIKE A KNIFE** `8` `Feb83`
– The only one / Take me back / This time / Straight from the heart / Cuts like a knife / I'm ready / What's it gonna be / Don't leave me lonely / The best has yet to come. *(re-iss. Mar86; same); hit UK 21) (cd-iss. Mar86; CDA 4919) (cd re-iss. 1988; CDMID 102)*
Mar 83. (7") <2536> **STRAIGHT FROM THE HEART. / ONE GOOD REASON** `-` `10`
Apr 83. (7"/12") *(AM/+X 103)* **STRAIGHT FROM THE HEART. / LONELY NIGHTS** `-`
Jun 83. (7") *(2553)* **CUTS LIKE A KNIFE. / LONELY NIGHTS** `-` `15`
Jul 83. (7") *(AM 129)* **CUTS LIKE A KNIFE. / FITS YA GOOD** `-`
(12"+=) *(AMP 129)* – Hidin' from love.
Aug 83. (7") <2574> **THIS TIME. / FITS YA GOOD** `-` `24`
Nov 83. (7") <26??> **THE BEST HAS YET TO COME. / I'M READY** `-`
Dec 84. (7") *(AM 224)* <2686> **RUN TO YOU. / I'M READY** `11` `6` `Oct84`
(12"+=) *(AMD 224)* – Cuts like a knife.
(d7"++=) *(AMY 224)* – Lonely nights.
Feb 85. (lp/c/cd) <(AMA/AMC/CDA 5013)> **RECKLESS** `7` `1` `Nov84`
– One night love affair / She's only happy when she's dancin' / Run to you / Heaven / Somebody / Summer of '69 / It's only love / Kids wanna rock / Long gone / Ain't gonna cry. *(re-iss. Jul92 & Sep97; 395013-2)*
Feb 85. (7"/7"pic-d/12") *(AM/+P/Y 236)* <2701> **SOMEBODY. / LONG GONE** `35` `11` `Jan85`
Mar 85. (7") <2722> **DIANA. / ('A'live)** `-` `11`
Apr 85. (7") <2729> **HEAVEN. / ('A'live)** `-` `1`
May 85. (7") *(AM 256)* **HEAVEN.** `38` `-`
(12"+=) *(AMY 256)* – Fits ya good / ('A'version).
(d7"+=) *(AMD 256)* – Straight from the heart / You want it, you got it.
Jun 85. (7") <2739> **SUMMER OF '69. / THE BEST HAS YET TO COME** `-` `5`
Jul 85. (7") *(AM 267)* **SUMMER OF '69. / KIDS WANNA ROCK (live)** `42` `-`
(12"+=) *(AMY 267)* – The Bryan Adamix.
Sep 85. (7") <2770> **ONE NIGHT LOVE AFFAIR. / LONELY NIGHTS** `-` `13`
Oct 85. (7"/12"; by BRYAN ADAMS & TINA TURNER) *(AM/+Y 285)* **IT'S ONLY LOVE. / THE BEST HAS YET TO COME** `29` `-`
(d7"+=) *(AMD 285)* – Somebody. / Long gone.
Nov 85. (7"; by BRYAN ADAMS & TINA TURNER) <2791> **IT'S ONLY LOVE. / THE ONLY ONE** `-` `15`
Dec 85. (7"/12") *(AM/+Y 297)* **CHRISTMAS TIME. / REGGAE CHRISTMAS** `55` `-`
Feb 86. (7") *(AM 295)* **THIS TIME. / I'M READY** `41` `-`
(12"+=) *(AMY 295)* – Lonely nights.
Jul 86. (7") *(AM 322)* **STRAIGHT FROM THE HEART. / FITS YA GOOD** `51` `-`
(12"+=) *(AMY 322)* – ('A'live).
Mar 87. (7") *(ADAM 2)* <2921> **HEAT OF THE NIGHT. / ANOTHER DAY** `50` `6`
(12"+=) *(ADAM 2-12)* – ('A'extended remix).
Apr 87. (lp/c/cd) <(AMA/AMC/CDA 3907)> **INTO THE FIRE** `10` `7`
– Heat of the night / Into the fire / Victim of love / Another day / Native son / Only the strong survive / Remembrance day / Rebel rebel / Hearts on fire / Home again. *(re-iss. Mar93 cd/c;)*
May 87. (7") <2948> **HEARTS ON FIRE. / THE BEST HAS YET TO COME** `-` `26`
May 87. (7"/c-s) *(ADAM/+C 3)* **HEARTS ON FIRE. / RUN TO YOU** `57` `-`
(12"+=) *(ADAM 3-12)* – Native sun.
Aug 87. (7") <2964> **VICTIM OF LOVE. / INTO THE FIRE** `-` `32`
Oct 87. (7"/7"box/c-s) *(AM/+F/C 407)* **VICTIM OF LOVE. / HEAT OF THE NIGHT (live)** `68` `-`
(12"+=) *(AMY 407)* – ('A'live).
—— BRYAN now used session people?
Jun 91. (7"/c-s) *(AM/+MC 789)* <1567> **(EVERYTHING I DO) I DO IT FOR YOU. / SHE'S ONLY HAPPY WHEN SHE'S DANCING (live)** `1` `1`
(12"+=/cd-s+=) *(AM Y/CD 789)* – ('A'extended) / Cuts like a knife.
Aug 91. (7"/c-s) *(AM/+MC 812)* <1576> **CAN'T STOP THIS THING WE STARTED. / IT'S ONLY LOVE (live)** `12` `2`
(etched-12"+=/cd-s+=) *(AM Y/CD 812)* – Hearts on fire.
Sep 91. (cd/c/lp) *(397164-2/-4/-1)* <5367> **WAKING UP THE NEIGHBOURS** `1` `6`
– Is your mama gonna miss ya? / Hey honey – I'm rockin' you in! / Can't stop this thing we started / Thought I'd died and gone to Heaven / Not guilty / House arrest / Vanishing / Do I have to say the words? / There will never be another tonight / All I want is you / Depend on me / (Everything I do) I do it for you / If you wanna leave me (can I come too?) / Touch the hand / Don't drop that bomb on me.
Nov 91. (7"/c-s) *(AM/+C 838)* <1588> **THERE WILL NEVER BE ANOTHER TONIGHT. / INTO THE FIRE (live)** `32` `31`
(etched-12"+=/pic-cd-s+=) *(AM Y/CD 838)* – One night love affair (live).

Feb 92. (7"/c-s) (AM/+C 848) <1592> **I THOUGHT I'D DIED AND GONE TO HEAVEN. / SOMEBODY (live)** `8` `13`
(12"+=) (AMY 848) – (Everything I do) I do it for you.
(cd-s+=) (AMCD 848) – Heart of the night (live).

Jul 92. (7"/c-s) (AM/+C 879) **ALL I WANT IS YOU. / RUN TO YOU** `22` `-`
(12"+=/cd-s+=) (AM Y/CD 879) – Long gone.

Sep 92. (7"/c-s) (AM/+C 0068) <1611> **DO I HAVE TO SAY THE WORDS?. / SUMMER OF '69** `30` `11` Jul92
(12"+=/cd-s+=) – Kids wanna rock / Can't stop this thing we started.

Oct 93. (7"/c-s) (580423-7/-4) <0422> **PLEASE FORGIVE ME. / C'MON EVERYBODY** `2` `7`
(cd-s+=) (580423-2) – Can't stop this thing we started / There will never be another tonight.

Nov 93. (cd/c/lp) (540157-2/-4/-1) <0157> **SO FAR SO GOOD** (compilation) `2` `7`
– Summer of '69 / Straight from the heart / It's only love / Can't stop this thing we started / Do I have to say the words? / This time / Run to you / Heaven / Cuts like a knife / (Everything I do) I do it for you / Somebody / Kids wanna rock / Heat of the night / Please forgive me.

Jan 94. (7"/c-s; BRYAN ADAMS, ROD STEWART & STING) (580477-7/-4) <0476> **ALL FOR LOVE.** / ('A'instrumental) `2` `1` Nov93
(cd-s) (580477-2) – ('A'side) / Straight from the heart (live) (BRYAN ADAMS) / If only (ROD STEWART) / Love is stronger than justice (live) (STING).
(above hit from the film 'The Three Musketeers')

Jul 94. (cd/c) (397094-2/-4) **LIVE! LIVE! LIVE!** (rec.live Belgium 1988) `17` `-`
– She's only happy when she's dancin' / It's only love / Cuts like a knife / Kids wanna rock / Hearts on fire / Take me back / The best was yet to come / Heaven / Heat of the night / Run to you / One night love affair / Long gone / Summer of '69 / Somebody / Walking after midnight / I fought the law / Into the fire.

Apr 95. (7"/c-s/cd-s) (581028-7/-4/-2) <1028> **HAVE YOU EVER REALLY LOVED A WOMAN? / LOW LIFE** `4` `1`

May 96. (c-s/cd-s) (581579-4/-2) <1578> **THE ONLY THING THAT LOOKS GOOD ON ME IS YOU / HEY ELVIS / I WANT IT ALL** `6` `52`
(cd-s) (581639-2) – ('A'side) / Summer of '69 / Cuts like a knife / Thought I'd died and gone to Heaven.

Jun 96. (cd/c) (540675-2/-4) <0551> **18 TIL I DIE** `1` `31`
– The only thing that looks good on me is you / Do to you / Let's make a night to remember / 18 til I die / Star / (I wanna be) Your underwear / We're gonna win / I think about you / I'll always be right there / It ain't a party . . . if you can't come 'round / Black pearl / You're still beautiful to me / Have you ever really loved a woman?

Aug 96. (c-ep) (581865-4) **LET'S MAKE A NIGHT TO REMEMBER / ROCK STEADY / HEY LITTLE GIRL / IF YA WANNA BE BAD YA GOTTA BE GOOD** `10` `-`
(cd-ep) – (first 3 tracks) / ('A'version).
(cd-ep) – ('A'side) / ('A'version) / If ya wanna be bad ya gotta be good / Little red rooster.

Aug 96. (c-s,cd-s) <1862> **LET'S MAKE A NIGHT TO REMEMBER / STAR** `-` `24`

Nov 96. (cd-ep) (582027-2) **STAR / THE ONLY THING THAT LOOKS GOOD ON ME IS YOU / IT'S ONLY LOVE (with MELISSA ETHERIDGE) / RUN TO YOU** `13` `-`
(c-ep/cd-ep) (582025-4/-2) – ('A'side) / Let's make it a night to remember / All for love / (Everything I do) I do it for you.

Jan 97. (c-s; by BARBRA STREISAND & BRYAN ADAMS) (582083-4) <78480> **I FINALLY FOUND SOMEONE / 18 TIL I DIE** `10` `8` Nov96
(cd-s) (582083-2) – ('A'side) / Star / I think about you / Do to you.
(above issued on 'Columbia' US)

Apr 97. (c-s/cd-s) (582183-4/-2) **18 TIL I DIE / DO TO YOU** `22` `-`
(cd-s+=) (582183-5) – Can't stop this thing we started / Touch the hand.

Dec 97. (cd/c) <540831-2/-4> **UNPLUGGED (live)** `19` `88`
– Summer of '69 / Back to you / Cuts like a knife / I'm ready / Fits ya good / When you love someone / 18 til i die / I think about you / If ya wanna be bad ya gotta be good / Let's make a night to remember / The only thing that looks good on me is you / A little love / Heaven / I'll always be right there.

Dec 97. (c-s/cd-s) (582475-4/-2) **BACK TO YOU / HEY ELVIS / CAN'T STOP THIS THING WE STARTED – IT AIN'T A PARTY . . . IF YOU CAN'T COME 'ROUND (medley)** `18` `-`

Mar 98. (c-s/cd-s) (582535-4/-2) **I'M READY / (I WANNA BE YOUR) UNDERWEAR / BACK TO YOU (original demo) / I'LL ALWAYS BE RIGHT THERE** `20` `-`
(cd-s) (582537-2) –

Sep 98. (c-s) (MERMC 516) **ON A DAY LIKE TODAY / SHE BELIEVES IN ME** `13` `-`　　*Mercury　Mercury*
(cd-s+=) (MERCD 516) – ('A'-Pants down mix).
(cd-s) (MERDD 516) – ('A'side) / The only thing that looks good on me (is you) / Bin there, done that.

Oct 98. (cd/c) <541016-2/-4> **ON A DAY LIKE TODAY** `11` `-`
– How do ya feel tonight / C'mon c'mon c'mon / Getaway / On a day like today / Fearless / I'm a liar / Cloud number nine / When you're gone (with MELANIE C) / Inside out / If I had you / Before the night is over / I don't wanna live forever / Where angels fear to tread / Lie to me.

Nov 98. (c-s; by BRYAN ADAMS & MEL C) (582818-4) **WHEN YOU'RE GONE / HEY BABY** `3` `-`
(cd-s+=) (582819-2) – When you're gone (without Melanie C).
(cd-s) (582821-2) – ('A'side) / I love ya too much / What does it do to your heart.

Apr 99. (c-s) (582646-4) **CLOUD NUMBER 9 / Bryan Adams & Mel C: WHEN YOU'RE GONE (acoustic)** `6` `-`
(cd-s+=) (582849-2) – Let's talk about love.
(cd-s) (582847-2) – ('A'mixes; Chicane / Bascombe / medley).

Nov 99. (cd/c) (490522-2/-4) **THE BEST OF ME** (compilation) `12` `-`
– The best of me / Can't stop this thing we started / I'm ready (MTV unplugged) / Summer of '69 / Let's make it a night to remember / All for love (w/ ROD STEWART & STING) / Have you ever really loved a woman / Run to you / Cloud number nine (Chicane mix) / Everything I do (I do it for you) / Back to you (MTV

unplugged) / When you're gone (w/ MEL C) / Please forgive me / The only thing that looks good on me is you / Inside out. (special cd+=; 490559-2) – South Africa live:- Summer of '69 / Back to you / Can't stop this thing we started / Have you ever really loved a woman / Rock steady.

Nov 99. (c-s) (497023-4) **THE BEST OF ME / CLOUD NUMBER NINE** `47` `-`
(cd-s+=) (497196-2) – Fearless.
(cd-s) (497195-2) – ('A'side) / Inside out / How do ya feel tonight.

– compilations, others, etc. –

Jun 89. (c) A&M; (AMC 24101) **CUTS LIKE A KNIFE / RECKLESS** `-` `-`

—— on the 2nd lp below he had replaced NICK GILDER

Jan 92. (cd/lp; SWEENEY TODD featuring BRYAN ADAMS)
Receiver; (RR CD/LP 154) **IF WISHES WERE HORSES** `-` `-`
– Tantalize / If wishes were horses / Until I find you / Pushin' and shovin' / No.5243605 Smith / Song for a star / Shut up / All of a sudden / Wastin' time / Say hello wave goodbye.

Barry ADAMSON (dig out; Great Alt & Indie . . .)

ADD N TO (X)

Formed: South London, England . . . 1994 by former Radio Prague DJ, BARRY SMITH, alongside ANN SHENTON and STEVEN CLAYTON, taking their puzzling moniker from a mathematical formula. Moog and theremin dole-meisters of the Nth degree, ADD N TO (X) debuted early in 1996 with 'VERO ELECTRONICS', a strangely strange set of mind-blowing knob twiddling. The following year, after inking a deal with 'Satellite', the eardrum-bashing futurists had two NME Singles Of The Week, 'THE BLACK REGENT' and 'KING WASP'. Early in 1998, they established themselves with an innovative electro A-Bomb of sound in their second long-player, 'ON THE WIRES OF OUR NERVES'. Extreme and trail-blazing, like STEREOLAB/SUICIDE with a rocket shoved up their rectum, the album's lengthy, disorientated tracks were a prime feature of DJ Mary Ann Hobbs' Radio One "Breeze Block" show. After turning down the majors, ADD N TO (X) subsequently signed to semi-seminal indie, 'Mute', their first outing being the wonderful 'LITTLE BLACK ROCKS IN THE SUN'. In September that year, they were probably the first band ever to play underground at a nuclear shelter, the bunker in question being in the rural backwaters of north east Fife near Anstruther. ADD N TO (X) caused a little rumpus the following Spring with the single 'METAL FINGERS IN MY BODY', due to the accompanying animated porn clip. This track, alongside classic electro-gems such as 'ROBOT NEW YORK' and 'REVENGE OF THE BLACK REGENT', made their third set 'AVANT HARD' (1999), the most pioneering cyberpunk since DEVO donned their boiler-suits.

Album rating: VERO ELECTRONICS (*5) / ON THE WIRES OF OUR NERVES (*8) / AVANT HARD (*9)

BARRY SMITH – synthesizer / **ANN SHENTON** – programming/ **STEVEN CLAYTON** – synthesizer

　　　　　　　　　　　　　　　　　　　　　　　Blow Up　not iss.
Jan 96. (cd/lp) (BLOW UP 004 CD/LP) **VERO ELECTRONICS** `-`
– Inevitable fast access / A silhouette of a man and a wasp / Meetings in compact boxes / A very uncomfortable status (wet disco) / Inevitable fast access (sleeze) / A very uncomfortable status (mathematical) / Aphine repetition. (cd re-iss. Aug97 & Nov99; same)

　　　　　　　　　　　　　　　　　　　　　　　Satellite　Mute
Jun 97. (12") (STL 003) **THE BLACK REGENT. / MURMUR ONE** `-` `-`
Oct 97. (12") (STL 007) **KING WASP./ HIT ME** `-` `-`
Nov 97. (ltd-12") (PIAO 10) **DEMON SEED. / (track by FRIDGE)** `-` `-`
(above single issued on 'Piao!')

—— added **ROB HALLUM** (of the HIGH LLAMAS)
Feb 98. (cd/d-lp) (STL 010 CD/LP) <69053> **ON THE WIRES OF OUR NERVES** `-` May98
– We are Add N To X / Murmur one / Sound of accelerating concrete / Gentle Germans / The black regent / Planet Munich / Nevermind / King Wasp / Orgy of Bubastus / Grey body, green gun / On the wires of our nerves / Hit me / Sir Ape.

—— all above as **ADD N TO (X)**

　　　　　　　　　　　　　　　　　　　　　　　Mute　Mute
Jul 98. (10"ep/cd-ep) (10/CD MUTE 219) **LITTLE BLACK ROCKS IN THE SUN. / VOICES 1-3** `-` `-`
Mar 99. (12"/cd-s) (12CD MUTE 224) **METAL FINGERS IN MY BODY. / THIS IS THE FLEX (Hi-Fi & Lo-Fi mixes)** `-` `-`
Apr 99. (cd/d-lp) (CD+/STUMM 170) **AVANT HARD** `-` `-`
– Barry 7's contraption / Robot New York / Skills / Steve's going to teach himself who's boss / FYUZ / Buckminster fuller / Revenge of the black regent / Metal fingers in my body / Ann's eveready equestrian / Oh yeah, oh no / Machine is bored with love.

Aug 99. (7") (7MUTE 231) **REVENGE OF THE BLACK REGENT. / IRON MAN** `-` `-`
(12"+=) (12MUTE 213) – ('A'side) / Old lady Ealing does man experiments / Is that alright FYUZ / March of the pure mathematical genius that ends (and results in war).
(cd-ep+=) (CDMUTE 231) – Metal fingers in my body (CD-Rom).

Oct 99. (7") (SMALL 008) **LIVE 1940 (Rommel & Raisin mix).** / **Canter: VOTEL, ANDY** `-` `-`
(above issued on 'Slut Smalls')

ADVERTS / TV SMITH ...   (dig out; Great Alt & Indie ...)

AERIAL-M (see under ⇒ SLINT)

AEROSMITH

Formed: Sunapee, New Hampshire, USA ... summer 1970, by JOE PERRY and STEVEN TYLER, who, with others (BRAD WHITFORD, TOM HAMILTON and JOEY KRAMER) moved to Boston, Massachusetts. By 1972, through a Max's Kansas City gig, they were signed to 'Columbia' by Clive Davis for a six figure sum. The band released their eponymous debut album the following year and the ROLLING STONES comparisons were inevitable from the off. While The 'Stones had taken American music, translated it and shipped it back across the water, AEROSMITH took the 'Stones interpretation of the Blues and customized it for a younger generation. Comparisons with LED ZEPPELIN were somewhat off the mark, the PERRY/TYLER partnership closely mimicking that of JAGGER and RICHARDS and while the latter two proclaimed themselves the 'Glimmer Twins', so it came to pass that Perry and Tyler were duly christened the 'Toxic Twins' in recognition of their legendary mid-70's decadence. 'MAMA KIN' and the Rufus Thomas cover, 'WALKIN' THE DOG' were fine examples of AEROSMITH's early revved-up R&B strut while the ballad, 'DREAM ON', scraped the lower regions of the US singles chart. The follow-up album, 'GET YOUR WINGS' (1974), consolidated the band's rock'n'raunch but it wasn't until the release of 'TOYS IN THE ATTIC' the following year that the band staked their claim as one of America's biggest and sexiest rock acts. Featuring the swaggering 'SWEET EMOTION' and the supple funk-rock of 'WALK THIS WAY', the record made AEROSMITH a household name, Stateside at least, going on to sell millions. Quintessentially American, the band cut little ice in Britain where punk was the order of the day. While Britain was pogoing to the strains of 'Anarchy in the UK', American heavy metal kids were skinning up to Aerosmith's 'ROCKS' (1976), a seminal record that saw the band at the peak of their powers. Dirty, sinewy riffs gyrated provocatively against diamond melodies, TYLER's pout almost audible as he casually reeled off his lurid tales of life on the road. While the band continued to pack out stadiums across America, their fabled penchant for nose candy was beginning to take its toll on their creative output. 'DRAW THE LINE' (1978) and 'NIGHT IN THE RUTS' (1980) fell woefully short of the band's capabilities, tension between TYLER and PERRY eventually leading to the latter leaving and forming The JOE PERRY PROJECT. Despite a near-fatal road accident, TYLER soldiered on with a revamped line-up for the equally uninspired 'ROCK IN A HARD PLACE' (1982). The all-important chemistry was gone while the chemicals seemingly continued to take their toll. Just as it looked like the end for the band, PERRY and TYLER settled their differences and the original AEROSMITH line-up signed to 'Geffen', getting it together for the 'DONE WITH MIRRORS' (1985) album, their best effort since the 70's heyday. AEROSMITH always had the funk and it seemed fitting that their miraculous commercial and creative rebirth was kickstarted by black hip hop crew RUN DMC. Their reworking of 'WALK THIS WAY' was released at the height of the rock/rap crossover in 1986 on 'Def Jam' was a force to be reckoned with and VW badges were in short supply, duly exposing AEROSMITH to a generation of kids who had never even heard of the band. Bang on cue, the band released 'PERMANENT VACATION' (1987), a masterful return to form which spawned a classic slice of AEROSMITH sleaze in 'DUDE (LOOKS LIKE A LADY)'. Moreover, the band had almost singlehandedly inspired a whole scene; almost every band in the late 80's glam-metal movement modelled themselves on prime 70's AEROSMITH (i.e. GUNS N' ROSES, FASTER PUSSYCAT, JUNKYARD, L.A. GUNS etc.). While the majority of these bands quickly faded into obscurity, AEROSMITH left the young pretenders for dust, releasing the adventurous and critically acclaimed 'PUMP' (1989). The single 'LOVE IN AN ELEVATOR', TYLER's tongue planted, as ever, firmly in cheek (probably not his own though), gave the band their first Top 20 hit in the UK. With the album reaching No.3, it seemed Britain had cottoned on, albeit fifteen years later. If 1993's 'GET A GRIP' sounded somewhat formulaic, it was another massive hit nevertheless. After just more than three years away, they returned to 'Columbia', releasing the wittily titled Top 50 hit, 'FALLING IN LOVE (IS HARD ON THE KNEES)', previewing yet another massive selling opus, 'NINE LIVES' (1997). Having scored a modest hit with 'PINK' (an even bigger UK hit in '99), AEROSMITH unplugged their amps to power-ballad to the top of the Hot 100 with 'I DON'T WANT TO MISS A THING'. Almost as sentimental as the film it was lifted from ('Armageddon'), TYLER and his cohorts crooned through every filled-up wrinkle whilst leaving a few mascara stains on their female fans. While the ROLLING STONES continue to roll (bankroll, that is), there's no reason to suggest that AEROSMITH won't continue in a creakily similar fashion. • **Songwriters:** PERRY / TYLER (aka TOXIC TWINS) except; COME TOGETHER (Beatles) / REMEMBER WALKIN' IN THE SAND (Shangri-la's) / TRAIN KEPT A-ROLLIN' (Johnny Burnette Trio) / MILK COW BLUES (Kokomo Arnold) / CRY ME A RIVER (Julie London) / MY ADIDAS (Run DMC). THE JOE PERRY PROJECT:- GET IT ON (BANG A GONG) (T. Rex) / BIG TEN-INCH RECORD (F.Weismantel; blues artist?) / ALL YOUR LOVE (Otis Rush) / HELTER SKELTER (Beatles) / CHIP AWAY THE STONE (Richie Supa). • **Miscellaneous:** In 1978 the group appeared in the 'SGT. PEPPER' Beatles film.

Album rating: AEROSMITH (*8) / GET YOUR WINGS (*7) / TOYS IN THE ATTIC

(*9) / ROCKS (*8) / DRAW THE LINE (*7) / LIVE BOOTLEG (*7) / AEROSMITH'S GREATEST HITS compilation (*9) / NIGHT IN THE RUTS (*6) / ROCK IN A HARD PLACE (*6) / DONE WITH MIRRORS (*4) / CLASSICS LIVE collection (*6) / CLASSICS LIVE 2 collection (*5) / PERMANENT VACATION (*8) / GEMS collection (*6) / PUMP (*8) / PANDORA'S BOX compilation boxed-set (*9) / GET A GRIP (*6) / BIG ONES compilation (*8) / NINE LIVES (*6) / Joe Perry Project: LET THE MUSIC DO THE TALKING (*6)

STEVEN TYLER (b. STEVEN TALLARICO, 26 Mar'48, New York City) – vocals / **JOE PERRY** (b.10 Sep'50, Lawrence, Mass.) – guitar (ex-JAM BAND) / **BRAD WHITFORD** (b.23 Feb'52, Winchester, Mass.) – guitar repl. RAY TABANO / **TOM HAMILTON** (b.31 Dec'51, Colorado Springs) – bass (ex-JAM BAND) / **JOEY KRAMER** (b.21 Jun'50, New York City) – drums

		C.B.S.	Columbia	
Jun 73.	(lp) <32005> **AEROSMITH** – Make it / Somebody / Dream on / One way street / Mama kin / Write me a letter / Movin' out / Walkin' the dog. *(UK-iss.Sep74; CBS 65486) <US re-dist.Mar76 hit No.21> <US re-iss. Sep87/ cd-May88; PC/CK 32005> (cd-iss. Nov94; CK 64401) (cd re-iss. May97 on 'Columbia'; 474962-2)*	–		
Nov 73.	(7") *(CBS 1898)* <45894> **DREAM ON. / SOMEBODY** <*US ext.re-iss. Jan76; 10728*> ; hit No.6 *(re-iss. Apr76; CBS 4000)*		59	Oct73
Feb 74.	(7") <46029> **SAME OLD SONG AND DANCE. / PANDORA'S BOX**		–	
Apr 74.	(7") <10034> **SPACED. / TRAIN KEPT A-ROLLIN'**		–	
Jun 74.	(7") <10105> **S.O.S. (TOO BAD). / LORD OF THE THIGHS**		–	
Nov 74.	(lp/c) <80015> <32847> **GET YOUR WINGS** – Same old song and dance / Lord of the thighs / Spaced / Woman of the world / S.O.S. (too bad) / Train kept a-rollin' / Seasons of wither / Pandora's box. *<US re-iss. Sep87/ cd-May88; PC/CK 32847> (UK-cd Mar92 & Dec93 & May97 on 'Columbia'; 474963-2)*		74	Mar74
May 75.	(7") <10155> **SWEET EMOTION. / UNCLE SALTY**		36	
Jul 75.	(lp/c) <80773> <33479> **TOYS IN THE ATTIC** – Toys in the attic / Uncle Salty / Adam's apple / Walk this way / Big ten inch record / Sweet emotion / No more no more / Round and round / You see me crying. *(re-iss. Feb88 on 'Castle' lp/c/cd; CLA LPX/MCX/CDX 135) <US re-iss. Sep87/ cd-iss. May88; PC/CK 33479> (UK re-iss. Apr91 & Nov93 & Jul95 & May97 on 'Columbia'; 480414-2) (re-iss. Oct97 on 'Simply Vinyl'; SVLP 0001)*		11	Apr75
Sep 75.	(7") <10206> **WALK THIS WAY. / ROUND AND ROUND**		–	
Nov 75.	(7") <10253> **TOYS IN THE ATTIC. / YOU SEE ME CRYING**		–	
Jun 76.	(lp/c) *(CBS/40 81379)* <34165> **ROCKS** – Back in the saddle / Last child / Rats in the cellar / Combination / Sick as a dog / Nobody's fault / Get the lead out / Lick and a promise / Home tonight. *<US re-iss. Sep87/May88; PC/CK 34165> (cd-iss. Jul89; CD 32517) (re-iss. cd Dec93 & May97 on 'Columbia'; 474965-2) (lp re-iss. Feb99 on 'Simply Vinyl'; SVLP 65)*		3	May76
Aug 76.	(7") *(CBS 4452)* <10359> **LAST CHILD. / COMBINATION**	21	Jun76
Sep 76.	(7") <10407> **HOME TONIGHT. / PANDORA'S BOX**	–	71	
Feb 77.	(7") *(CBS 4878)* <10449> **WALK THIS WAY. / UNCLE SALTY**	10	Nov76
Apr 77.	(7") <10516> **BACK IN THE SADDLE. / NOBODY'S FAULT**	–	38	
Oct 77.	(7") <10637> **DRAW THE LINE. / BRIGHT LIGHT FRIGHT**	42	
Jan 78.	(lp/c) <82147> <34856> **DRAW THE LINE** – Draw the line / I wanna know why / Critical mass / Get it up / Bright light fright / Kings and queens / The hand that feeds / Sight for sore eyes / Milk cow blues. *<US re-iss. Sep87; PC 34856> (re-iss. cd Dec93 & May97 on 'Columbia'; 474966-2)*	11	Dec77
Mar 78.	(7") <10699> **KINGS AND QUEENS. / CRITICAL MASS**	–	70	
Jun 78.	(7") <10727> **GET IT UP. / MILK COW BLUES**	–		
Aug 78.	(7") <10802> **COME TOGETHER. / KINGS AND QUEENS**	23	
Jan 79.	(d-lp) *(CBS 88325)* <35564> **LIVE! BOOTLEG (live)** – Back in the saddle / Sweet emotion / Lord of the thighs / Toys in the attic / Last child / Come together / Walk this way / Sick as a dog / Dream on / Chip away the stone / Sight for sore eyes / Mama kin / S.O.S. / I ain't got you / Mother popcorn / Train kept a rollin'. *<US re-iss. Dec87; PC 35564> (re-iss. cd Aug93/Dec93/May97 on 'Columbia'; 469004-2/474967-2)*	13	Nov78
Jan 79.	(7") <10880> **CHIP AWAY THE STONE (live). / CHIP AWAY THE STONE (studio)**	–	77	
Jan 80.	(lp/c) *(CBS/40 83680)* <36050> **NIGHT IN THE RUTS** – No surprize / Chiquita / Remember (walkin' in the sand) / Cheesecake / Three mile smile / Reefer head woman / Bone to bone (Coney Island white fish boy) / Think about it / Mia. *<US re-iss. Sep87; PC 36050> (cd-iss. Mar92 & Dec93 & May97 on 'Columbia'; 474968-2)*	14	Nov79
Feb 80.	(7") *(CBS 8220)* <11181> **REMEMBER (WALKIN' IN THE SAND). / BONE TO BONE (CONEY ISLAND WHITE FISH BOY)**	67	Jan80
——	(Dec79) **JIMMY CREPSO** – guitar (ex-FLAME) repl. JOE PERRY who went solo			
——	(Feb80) **RICK DUFAY** – guitar repl. WHITFORD who teamed up with ST. HOLMES			
Oct 82.	(lp/c) *(CBS/40 85931)* <38061> **ROCK IN A HARD PLACE** – Jailbait / Lightning strikes / Bitch's brew / Bolivian ragamuffin / Cry me a river / Prelude to Joanie / Joanie's butterfly / Rock in a hard place (Cheshire cat) / Jig it up / Push comes to shove. *<US re-iss. Sep87; PC 38061> (cd-iss. Aug93/Dec93/May97 on 'Columbia'; 469006-2/474970-2)*	32	Sep82
——	(Mar84) original 1970's line-up reform (see above)			

		Geffen	Geffen	
Nov 85.	(7") <28814> **SHEILA. / GYPSY BOOTS**	–		
Dec 85.	(lp/c) *(GEF/40 26695)* <24091> **DONE WITH MIRRORS** – Let the music do the talking / My fist your face / Shame on you / The reason a dog / Shela / Gypsy boots / She's on fire / The hop / Darkness. *<US cd-iss. Oct87; 20491-2> (UK re-iss. Jun89 on 'W.E.A.'; 924 091-1/-4/-2) (re-iss. Apr92 & Jun94 & Feb98 cd/c; GFLD/GFLC 19052)*	36	Nov85
——	In Aug'86, AEROSMITH were credited on RUN DMC's hit version of 'WALK THIS WAY'.			
Aug 87.	(lp/c/cd) (WX 126/+C)(924 162-2) <24162> **PERMANENT VACATION** – Heart's done time / Magic touch / Rag doll / Simoriah / Dude (looks like a lady) / St. John / Hangman jury / Girl keep coming apart / Angel / Permanent vacation / I'm down / The movie. *(re-iss. Jun94 cd/c; ; GFLD/GFLC 19254) (lp re-iss. Jul98 on 'Simply Vinyl'; SVLP 35)*	37	11
Oct 87.	(7") *(GEF 29)* <28240> **DUDE (LOOKS LIKE A LADY). / SIMORIAH** (12"+=/12"pic-d+=) *(GEF 29T/+P)* – Once is enough.	45	14	Sep87

Apr 88. (7"/12"/12"pic-d) (GEF 34/+T/TP) <28249> **ANGEL. / GIRL KEEPS COMING APART** `69` `3` Jan88
(3"cd-s+=) (GEF 34CD) – Angel (A.O.R. remix) / Dude (looks like a lady).

Jun 88. (12") <27915> **RAG DOLL. / ST.JOHN** `-` `17`

Aug 89. (7"/7"s/c-s) (GEF 63/+X/C) <22845> **LOVE IN AN ELEVATOR. / YOUNG LUST** `13` `5`
(10"pic-d+=/12"+=/3"cd-s+=) (GEF 63 TP/T/CD) – Ain't enough.

Sep 89. (lp/c)(cd) (WX 304/+C)(924 254-2) <24254> **PUMP** `3` `5`
– Young lust / F.I.N.E. / Love in an elevator / Monkey on my back / Janie's got a gun / The other side / My girl / Don't get mad, get even / Voodoo medicine man / What it takes. (re-iss. Jun94 cd/c; GFLD/GFLC 19255) (lp re-iss. Nov98 on 'Simply Vinyl'; SVLP 45)

Nov 89. (7"/7"sha-pic-d/c-s) (GEF 68/+P/C) <22727> **JANIE'S GOT A GUN. / VOODOO MEDICINE MAN** `4`
(12"+=/3"cd-s+=) (GEF 68 T/CD) – Rag doll (live).

Feb 90. (7"/7"sha-pic-d) (GEF 72/+P) **DUDE (LOOKS LIKE A LADY) (remix). / MONKEY ON MY BACK** `20` `-`
(12"/cd-s+=) (GEF 72 T/CD) – ('A'extended) / Love in an elevator (live) / Walk this way (live).

Mar 90. (7"/c-s) <19944> **WHAT IT TAKES. / MONKEY ON MY BACK** `-` `9`

Apr 90. (7") (GEF 76) **RAG DOLL / SIMORIAH** `42` `-`
(12"/12"s) (GEF 76 T/TW) – ('A'side) / Mama kin (live) / Let it rain (live).
(cd-s) (GEF 76CD) – ('A'side) / Mama kin (live) / Dream on (live).

Aug 90. (7"/c-s) (GEF 79/+C) <19927> **THE OTHER SIDE. / MY GIRL** `46` `22` Jun90
(12"+=) (GEFT 79) – Theme from 'Wayne's World' / ('A'-honky tonk).
(12") (GEFTW 79) – ('A'side) / Love in an elevator / Dude (looks like a lady) / Walk this way.

Apr 93. (12"pic-d/cd-s) (GFST/+D 35) <19149> **LIVIN' ON THE EDGE. / DON'T STOP / FLESH** `19` `18`
(cd-s) (GFSTX 35) – ('A'side) / ('A'acoustic) / Can't stop messin'.

Apr 93. (cd/c/lp) (GED/GEC/GEF 24444) <24455> **GET A GRIP** `2` `1`
– Intro / Eat the rich / Get a grip / Livin' on the edge / Flesh / Walk on down / Shut up and dance / Cryin' / Gotta love it / Crazy / Line up / Can't stop messin' / Amazing / Boogie man.

Jun 93. (10"colrd) (GFST 46) **EAT THE RICH. / FEVER / HEAD FIRST** `34` `-`
(cd-s+=) (GFSTD 46) – Livin' on the edge (demo).

Oct 93. (c-s) (GFSC 56) <19256> **CRYIN' / WALK ON DOWN** `17` `12` Jul93
(12"white+=) (GFST 56) – I'm down.
(cd-s++=) (GFSTD 56) – My fist your face.
(cd-s++=) (GFSXD 56) – Love in an elevator / Janie's got a gun.

Nov 93. (c-s,cd-s) <19264> **AMAZING / FEVER** `-` `24`
Dec 93. (c-s) (GFSC 63) <19264> **AMAZING / GOTTA LOVE IT** `57` `-`
(12"colrd+=) (GFST 63) – ('A'acoustic).
(cd-s+=) (GFSTD 63) – ('A'orchestral).

May 94. (c-s,cd-s) <19267> **CRAZY / GOTTA LOVE IT** `-` `17`

Jun 94. (c-s) (GFSC 75) **SHUT UP AND DANCE. / DEUCES ARE WILD** `24` `-`
(7"+=) (GFS 75) – Crazy (orchestral).
(cd-s++=) (GFSTD 75) – Line up.

Oct 94. (c-s) (GFSC 80) **CRAZY / BLIND MAN** `23` `-`
(cd-s+=) (GFSTD 80) – Shut up and dance (live) / Blind man (mix).

Nov 94. (cd/c/d-lp) (GED/GEC/GEF 24546) <24716> **BIG ONES** (compilation) `7` `6`
– Walk on water / Love in an elevator / Rag doll / What it takes / Dude (looks like a lady) / Janie's got a gun / Cryin' / Amazing / Blind man / Deuces are wild / The other side / Crazy / Eat the rich / Angel / Livin' on the edge / Dude (looks like a lady) (live).

Dec 94. (c-s,cd-s) <19377> **BLIND MAN / HEAD FIRST** `-` `49`
                Columbia   Columbia

Mar 97. (7"/c-s) (664075-7/-4) **FALLING IN LOVE (IS HARD ON THE KNEES). / FALL TOGETHER** `22` `35` Feb97
(cd-s+=) (664075-2) – Sweet emotion / Seasons of wither.

Mar 97. (cd/c) (485020-2/-4) <67547> **NINE LIVES** `4` `1`
– Nine lives / Falling in love (is hard on the knees) / Hole in my soul / Taste of India / Full circle / Something's gotta give / Ain't that a bitch / Farm / Crash / Kiss your past good-bye / Pink / Falling off / Attitude adjustment / Fallen angels.

Jun 97. (7"pic-d) (664501-7) **HOLE IN MY SOUL. / NINE LIVES (live)** `29` `51` Aug97
(cd-s+=) (664501-2) – Falling in love (is hard on the knees) (Butcher mix) / Falling in love (is hard on the knees) (Moby flawed mix).
(cd-s) (664501-5) – ('A'side) / Falling in love (is hard on the knees) (Moby f**kee mix) / Falling in love (is hard on the knees) (live) / Walk this way (live).

Dec 97. (7"pink) (664872-7) <78830> **PINK. / PINK (Chulo mix)** `38` `27` Feb98
(cd-s+=) (664872-2) – ('A'side) / ('A'-South Beach mix) / ('A'live).

Sep 98. (7"/cd-s) (666408-7/-2) <78952> **I DON'T WANT TO MISS A THING. / TASTE OF INDIA (rock remix)** `4` `1` Aug98
(cd-s+=) (666408-5) – Pink (live) / Crash.

Jun 99. (c-s) (667534-4) **PINK / HOLE IN MY SOUL** `13` `-`
(cd-s) (667534-2) – I don't want to miss a thing.
(cd-s) (667534-5) –

– compilations, others, etc. –

on 'CBS' UK / 'Columbia' US + UK (90's) unless otherwise mentioned

Jan 81. (lp/c) (CBS/40 84704) <36865> **AEROSMITH'S GREATEST HITS** `53` Nov80
– Dream on / Same old song and dance / Sweet emotion / Walk this way / Remember (walking in the sand) / Back in the saddle / Draw the line / Kings and queens / Come together / Last child. <US re-iss. Sep87/ cd-Feb88; FC/FCT/CK 36865> (re-iss. Nov89 pic-lp/cd; 460703-8/-2) (re-iss. cd Dec93 on 'Columbia'; 474969-2)

Sep 86. (lp/c) (CBS/40 26901) <40329> **CLASSICS LIVE!** (live 1977-1983) `84` Apr86
– Train kept a-rollin' / Kings and queens / Sweet emotion / Dream on / Mama kin / Three mile smile / Reefer head woman / Lord of the thighs / Major Barbra. <US re-iss. Nov87 lp/c/cd; FC/FCT/CK 40329> (re-iss. cd Dec93 on 'Columbia'; 474971-2)

Aug 87. (lp/c) <FC/+T 40855> **CLASSICS LIVE II (live)** `-`

– Back in the saddle / Walk this way / Movin' out / Draw the line / Same old song and dance / Last child / Let the music do the talking / Toys in the attic. (UK cd-iss. Nov89; 460037-2) (cd re-iss. Dec92 on 'Columbia'; 474972-2)

Jun 88. (d-lp/c/cd) Raw Power; (RAW LP/TC/CD 037) **ANTHOLOGY** `-`

1988. (7") <08536> **CHIP AWAY THE STONE. / S.O.S (TOO BAD)** `-`

Aug 88. (3"cd-s) <38K 0795-2> **WALK THIS WAY / DREAM ON** `-`

Nov 89. (lp/c/cd) (463224-1/-4/-2) <44487> **GEMS** `Dec88`
– Rats in the cellar / Lick and a promise / Chip away the stone / No surprize / Mama kin / Adam's apple / Nobody's fault / Round and round / Critical mass / Lord of the thighs / Jailbait / Train kept a rollin'. (re-iss. Apr91 & Dec93 on 'Columbia'; 474973-2) (cd re-iss. May98; 491236-2)

Dec 91. (t-cd/t-c) (469293-2/-4) <46209> **PANDORA'S BOX** `45`
– When I needed you / Make it / Movin' out / One way street / On the road again / Mama kin / Same old song and dance / Train kept a-rollin' / Seasons of wither / Write me a letter / Dream on / Pandora's Box / Rattlesnake shake / Walkin' the dog / Lord of the thighs // Toys in the attic / Round and round / You see me crying / Sweet emotion / No More no more / Walk this way / I wanna know why / Big ten inch record / Rats in the cellar / Last child / All your love / Soul saver / Nobody's fault / Lick and a promise / Adam's apple / Draw the line / Critical mass // Kings and queens / Milk cow blues / I live in Connecticut / Three mile smile / Let it slide / Cheese cake / Bone to bone (Coney Island white fish boy) / No surprize / Come together / Downtown Charlie / Sharpshooter / Shit house shuffle / South station blues / Riff & roll / Jailbait / Major Barbara / Chip away the stone / Helter skelter / Back in the saddle / Circle jerk. (3xcd-iss. Nov98; 487480-2)

Jun 93. (cd) (474038-2) **TOYS IN THE ATTIC / CLASSICS LIVE** `-` `-`
Jul 93. (cd) (463224-2) **ROCKS / GEMS** `-` `-`
Jun 94. (cd/c) (476956-2/-4) **PANDORA'S TOYS (BEST)** (compilation of 'PANDORA'S BOX') `-` `-`
– Sweet emotion / Draw the line / Walk this way / Dream on / Train kept a rollin' / Mama kin / Nobody's fault / Seasons of wither / Big ten-inch record / All your love / Helter skelter / Chip away the stone.

Aug 94. (c-s) (660449-4) <74101> **SWEET EMOTION / SUBWAY** `74` Dec91
(cd-s+=) (660449-2) – Circle jerk.

Dec 94. (12xcd-box) (477803-2) **BOX OF FIRE** `-`
– (AEROSMITH / GET YOUR WINGS / TOYS IN THE ATTICS / ROCKS / DRAW THE LINE / LIVE BOOTLEG / NIGHT IN THE RUTS / GREATEST HITS / ROCK IN A HARD PLACE / CLASSICS LIVE / CLASSICS LIVE II / GEMS / bonus cd)

May 97. (13xcd-box) (477803-2) **BOX OF FIRE** `-`
Nov 97. (3xcd-box) (485312-2) **TOYS IN THE ATTIC / DRAW THE LINE / ROCKS** `-`
Aug 98. (cd) (487351-2) **CLASSICS LIVE VOL.1 & 2** `-`
Oct 98. (d-cd/d-c) Geffen; <(GED/GEC 25221)> **A LITTLE SOUTH OF SANITY (live)** `36` `12`
– Eat the rich / Love in an elevator / Falling in love (is hard on the knees) / Same old song and dance / Hole in my soul / Monkey on my back / Livin' on the edge / Cryin' / Rag doll / Angel / Janie's got a gun / Amazing // Back in the saddle / Last child / The other side / Walk on down / Dream on / Crazy / Mama kin / Walk this way / Dude (looks like a lady) / What it takes / Sweet emotion.

JOE PERRY PROJECT

(while not an AEROSMITH member) with **RALPH NORMAN** – vocals / **DAVID HULL** – bass / **RONNIE STEWART** – drums

           C.B.S.   Columbia

Mar 80. (lp) (CBS 84213) <36388> **LET THE MUSIC DO THE TALKING** `47`
– Let the music do the talking / Conflict of interest / Discount dogs / Shooting star / Break song / Rockin' train / The mist is rising / Ready on the firing line / Life at a glance. (cd-iss. Aug95 on 'Columbia'; 480967-2)

Aug 80. (7") (CBS 8889) <11250> **LET THE MUSIC DO THE TALKING. / BONE TO BONE**

--- **CHARLIE FARREN** – vocals repl. NORMAN

Jun 81. (lp) <37364> **I'VE GOT THE ROCK'N'ROLLS AGAIN** `-`
– East Coast, West Coast / No substitute for arrogance / I've got the rock'n'rolls again / Buzz buzz / Soldier of fortune / T.V. police / Listen to the rock / Dirty little things / Play the game / South station blues.

Jul 81. (7") <02497> **BUZZ BUZZ. / EAST COAST, WEST COAST** `-`

--- **PERRY** new line-up **MARK BELL** – vocals / **DANNY HARGROVE** – bass / **JOE PET** – drums

         M.C.A.   M.C.A.

Jan 84. (lp/c) (MCF/+C 3205) **ONCE A ROCKER, ALWAYS A ROCKER**
– Once a rocker, always a rocker / Black velvet pants / Woman in chains / Guns west / Crossfire / King of the kings / Never wanna stop / Adrianna / Get it on (bang-a-gong) / Walk with me Sally.

WHITFORD / ST.HOLMES

BRAD WHITFORD – guitar, vocals / **ST.HOLMES** – guitar (ex-TED NUGENT) also **DAVID HEWITT** – bass / **STEVE PACE** – drums

        not iss.   Columbia

Jul 81. (7") <02555> **SHY AWAY. / MYSTERY GIRL** `-`
Aug 81. (lp) **WHITFORD / ST. HOLMES** `-`
– I need love / Whiskey woman / Hold on / Sharp shooter / Every morning / Action / Shy away / Does it really matter / Spanish box / Mystery girl.

AFGHAN WHIGS

Formed: Denver, Colorado, USA … Autumn '86, by GREG DULLI and RICK McCOLLUM who met in a prison. The pair moved to Cincinatti, Ohio, after signing for Seattle based indie label 'Sub Pop' in 1989, their independently released debut set, 'BIG TOP HALLOWEEN' (1988), having caused something of a stir with its proto-grunge exhortations. Produced by Seattle maestro, Jack Endino, the album, 'UP IN IT', worked around the same formula, hinting at their wider country and soul influences. After a further set for 'Sub Pop', 'CONGREGATION' (1992), and an EP of soul covers, 'UPTOWN AVONDALE', the group were plucked from the mire of grunge cultdom by 'Elektra' in the major label stampede following NIRVANA's success. A former film student, DULLI cannily negotiated the right to creative control over the band's videos, his acting ambitions duly realised in 1994 when he scored the part of JOHN LENNON in Stuart Sutcliffe's story, 'Backbeat'. The 'WHIGS major label debut, 'GENTLEMEN', pushed all the right critical buttons, fleshing out their grungy noir-soul sound against a typically hard-bitten lyrical background. Although the record surprisingly failed to make the US charts, it scored a Top 60 placing in the UK. DULLI's rendition of Barry White's 'CAN'T GET ENOUGH OF YOUR LOVE', was an indication of where AFGHAN WHIGS were headed with 'BLACK LOVE'. An even more soul-centric offering, the album almost scraped into the British Top 40, the band now signed to 'Mute' (still on 'Elektra' US). 'Columbia' took up the reins for, er . . . 1998's '1965', a celebration of rock music's debt to the power of sex. Recorded in New Orleans, the record was hailed as their long promised masterpiece, a writhing, sweaty slab of post-grunge voodoo soul. DULLI matched this aggression later in the year, after a brawl with a steward earned him a few days in intensive care and a fractured skull . . . er, to boot. Subsequently the singer threatened action against the Texas nightclub even though it was alleged that he was the main instigator. • **Songwriters:** DULLI, some McCOLLUM except; covers by MY WORLD IS EMPTY WITHOUT YOU (Diana Ross & The Supremes) / (Al Green) / BAND OF GOLD (Freda Payne) / I KEEP COMING BACK (Austell-Graham) / IF I ONLY HAD A HEART (from 'Wizard Of Oz') / CREEP (Radiohead) / LITTLE GIRL BLUE (Hart-Rodgers) / MR. SUPERLOVE (Ass Ponys) / LOST IN THE SUPERMARKET (Clash).

Album rating: BIG TOP HALLOWEEN (*4) / UP IN IT (*6) / CONGREGATION (*7) / GENTLEMEN (*7) / BLACK LOVE (*6) / 1965 (*8)

GREG DULLI – vocals, guitar / **RICK McCOLLUM** – guitar / **JOHN CURLEY** – bass / **STEVE EARLE** – drums

		not iss.	Ultrasuede
Oct 88.	(lp) <001> **BIG TOP HALLOWEEN**	-	

– Here comes Jesus / In my town / Priscilla's wedding day / Push / Scream / But listen / Big top Halloween / Life in a day / Sammy / Doughball / Back o' the line / Greek is extra.

		Sub Pop	Sub Pop
Aug 89.	(7") <SP 32> **I AM THE STICKS. / WHITE TRASH PARTY**	-	
Apr 90.	(cd/c/lp/orange-lp) <SP 60> **UP IN IT**	-	

– Retarded / White trash party / Hated / Southpaw / Amphetamines and coffee / Now can we begin / You my flower / Son of the south / I know your secret. (cd/c+=) – I am the sticks. (UK-iss.Aug90 on 'Glitterhouse'; GR 0092) (cd re-iss. Sep98; SPCD 60)

Oct 90.	(7",7"red) <SP 84> **SISTER BROTHER. / HEY CUZ**	-	
Dec 90.	(12"ep) <(SP 4-115)> **THE RETARD EP**		

– Retarded / Sister brother / Hey cuz / Turning in two. (cd-ep May93; SPCD 4-115)

Jan 92.	(lp/cd) <(SP 183/+CD)> **CONGREGATION**		

– Her against me / I'm her slave / Turn on the water / Conjure me / Kiss the floor / Congregation / This is my confession / Dedicate it / The temple / Let me lie to you / Tonight. (cd re-iss. Sep98; same)

Jan 92.	(12"ep) <(SP 187)> **TURN ON THE WATER. / MILES IZ DEAD / DELTA KONG**		

(cd-ep+=) (SPCD 187) – Chalk outline.

May 92.	(7"white,7"lavender) <(SP 142)> **CONJURE ME. / MY WORLD IS EMPTY WITHOUT YOU**		

(12"+=)(cd-s+=) <(SP 42)> <(SP 203CD)> – My flower.

Oct 92.	(7"ep) <(SP 216)> **UPTOWN AVONDALE EP: BAND OF GOLD. / COME SEE ABOUT ME**		

(12"+=) <(SP 215)> – True love travels on a gravel road / Beware. (cd-s+=) <(SP 215CD)> – Rebirth of the cool. (above release could have been issued earlier in US, early 1990)

		Blast First	Elektra
Sep 93.	(7") (BFFP 89) **GENTLEMEN. / MR. SUPERLOVE**		
Oct 93.	(lp/cd) (BFFP 90/+CD) <7559 61501-2> **GENTLEMEN**		58

(12"+=/cd-s+=) (BFFP 89 T/CD) – The dark end of the street.
– If I were going / Gentlemen / Be sweet / Debonair / When we two parted / Fountain and fairfax / What jail is like / My curse / Now you know / I keep coming back / Brother Woodrow – Closing prayer. (lp w /free 7"ep) – ROT. / TONIGHT

—— guests on the album: **HAROLD CHICHESTER** – keyboards / **BARB HUNTER** – cello / **JODY STEPHENS** – vocals / **MARCY MAYS** – vocals

Feb 94.	(7"ep/12"ep/cd-ep) (BFFP 95/+T/CD) **BROKEN PROMISES EP**		

– Debonair / My curse / Little girl blue / Ready.
(cd-ep) (BFFP 95CDL) – ('A'side) / Rot / I keep coming back / Tonight.

—— In Mar'94, 'MR.SUPERLOVE' was issued on B-side of ASS PONY's single on 'Monocat'.

Aug 94.	(7"ep/10"ep/cd-ep) (BFFP 96/+T/CD) <61708> **WHAT JAIL IS LIKE EP** (some live)		

– What jail is like / Mr. Superlove / Dark end of the street / Little girl blue / Gentlemen / Now you know / My world is empty without you.

		Mute	Elektra
Feb 96.	(10"ep/cd-ep) (10/CD MUTE 128) **HONKY'S LADDER E.P.**		
Mar 96.	(cd/c/lp) (CD/C+/STUMM 143) <61896> **BLACK LOVE**	41	79

– Honky's ladder / Blame, etc. / If I only had a heart / Creep.
– Crime scene part one / My enemy / Double day / Blame, etc. / Step into the light / Going to town / Honky's ladder / Night by candlelight / Bulletproof / Summer's kiss / Faded.

Aug 96.	(cd-ep) (CDMUTE 199) **GOING TO TOWN / GOING TO TOWN – MODERN ROCK LIVE / YOU'VE CHANGED / I WANT TO GO TO SLEEP / MOON RIVER**		

		Columbia	Columbia
Oct 98.	(7") (666576-7) **SOMETHIN' HOT / MISS WORLD**		
Oct 98.	(cd/c) (491486-2/-4) <69450> **1965**		

(cd-s+=) (666576-2) – Papa was a rascal.
– Somethin' hot / Crazy / Uptown again / Sweet son of a bitch / 66 / City soleil / John the baptist / The slide song / Neglekted / Omerta / The vampire Lanois.

—— added **JOSH PAXTON** – keyboards / **SUSAN MARSHALL + DOUG FALSETTI** – backing vocals

A-HA

Formed: Manglerud, Oslo, Norway . . . 1982 by songwriters MAGNE FURUHOLMEN and PAL WAAKTAAR (both ex-BRIDGES and DOORS-inspired SPIDER EMPIRE), who invited singer MORTEN HARKET to make up the trio. Relocating to London early the following year, A-HA secured the services of manager, Terry Slater, and it was through him and a demo of 'LESSON ONE' that the band would sign to 'Warners'. Subsequently remixed by Tony Mansfield and renamed as 'TAKE ON ME', the song initially failed to impress the British buying public when issued in October 1984. The following summer, with Alan Tarney overseeing production, it bombed yet again and led to the lads returning for a summer solstice in Norway. However, things looked brighter in the States when the song received a Steve Barron-directed $100,000 animated video facelift. This resulted in some precious MTV airtime and a trip to L.A. which paved the way for a surprise US chart entry. Topping Billboard in October, it was immediately given a third release in Britain where it peaked at No.2, MORTEN, PAL and MAGNE becoming pin-up boys in the process. The album 'HUNTING HIGH AND LOW' was finally unleashed in the UK towards the end of 1985, its blend of electro-pop and HARKET's falsetto vox setting it up nicely for a Top 3 chart placing. In 1986, the Norwegians had no less than five British Top 10 hits, 'THE SUN ALWAYS SHINES ON TV' (their only UK No.1), 'TRAIN OF THOUGHT', 'HUNTING HIGH AND LOW', 'I'VE BEEN LOSING YOU' and 'CRY WOLF', the latter two lifted from that year's sophomore Top 3 set, 'SCOUNDREL DAYS'. Although fading fast in America, the trio were still one of the most popular acts in Britain and continued to have hits right up until their demise in 1994. One of these, 'THE LIVING DAYLIGHTS', was co-written by JOHN BARRY and used for the similarly-titled James Bond movie in 1987, while three years later they covered the Everly Brothers' classic 'CRYING IN THE RAIN'. In 1995 – while the other two moonlighted with TIMBERSOUND and SAVOY – HARKET delivered his only solo album to date, 'WILD SEED', which was unsurprisingly given the thumbs down by critics and public alike. A-HA re-formed for a one-off Nobel Peace Prize concert on the 11th of December 1998 and were threatening to go full-time again in 2000 (not a laughing matter me thinks!?).

Album rating: HUNTING HIGH AND LOW (*6) / SCOUNDREL DAYS (*5) / STAY ON THESE ROADS (*4) / EAST OF THE SUN, WEST OF THE MOON (*5) / HEADLINES & DEADLINES – THE HITS OF A-HA compilation (*6) / MEMORIAL BEACH (*3) / Morten Harket: WILD SEED (*3)

PAL WAAKTAAR (b. 6 Sep'61) – guitar, vocals / **MAGNE "MAGS" FURUHOLMEN** (b. 1 Nov'62) – keyboards / plus **VIGGO BONDI** – bass / **OYSTEIN JEVANORD** – drums

		Vakenatt	not iss.
Oct 80.	(lp; as BRIDGES) **FAKKELTOG** (means TORCHLIGHT PROCESSION)	-	- Norway

—— (1982) **PAL + MAGS** (let go OYSTEIN and VIGGO; former still on session) + introduced **MORTEN HARKET** (b.14 Sep'59, Konigsberg, Norway) – vocals

		Warners	Warners
Oct 84.	(7") (W 9146) **TAKE ON ME. / AND YOU TELL ME**		
May 85.	(7") (W 9006) <29011> **TAKE ON ME. / LOVE IS REASON**		1 Jun85

(12"+=) (W 9146T) – Stop and make your mind up.
(12"+=) (W 9006T) – ('A'extended).
(re-iss. Sep85 – hit UK No.2)

Nov 85.	(lp/c)(cd) (WX 30/+C)(925300-2) <25300> **HUNTING HIGH AND LOW**	2	15 Jun85

– Take on me / Train of thought / Hunting high and low / The blue sky / Living a boy's adventure tale / The sun always shines on TV / And you tell me / Love is reason / Dream myself alive / Here I stand and face the rain.

Dec 85.	(7"/7"sha-pic-d) (W 8846/+P) <28846> **THE SUN ALWAYS SHINES ON TV. / DRIFTWOOD**	1	20 Nov85

(12"+=) (W 8846T) – ('A'instrumental).

Mar 86.	(7"/7"sha-pic-d/12") (W 8736/+P/T) **TRAIN OF THOUGHT. / AND YOU TELL ME**	8	

May 86.	(7") (W 6663) **HUNTING HIGH AND LOW. / THE BLUE SKY (demo)**	5	

(12"+=/12"pic-d+=) (W 6663 T/P) – ('A'version).

Sep 86.	(7") (W 8594) **I'VE BEEN LOSING YOU. / THIS ALONE IS LOVE**	8	

(12"+=/12"pic-d+=) (W 8594 T/P) – ('A'dub version).

Oct 86.	(lp/c)(cd) (WX 62/+C)(925501-2) <25501> **SCOUNDREL DAYS**	2	74

– Scoundrel days / The swing of things / I've been losing you / October / Manhattan skyline / Cry wolf / Looking for the whales / The weight of the wind / Maybe maybe / Soft rains of April. (cd re-iss. Feb95; same)

Nov 86.	(7"/7"g-f) (W 8500/+V) <28500> **CRY WOLF. / MAYBE MAYBE**	7	50 Jan87

(12"+=/12"pic-d+=) (W 8500 T/P) – ('A'extended).

Feb 87.	(7") (W 8405) **MANHATTAN SKYLINE. / WE'RE LOOKING FOR THE WHALES (live)**	13	

(12"+=/12"pic-d+=) (W 8405 T/P) – ('A'extended remix).

Jul 87.	(7"/7"g-f) (W 8305/+V) **THE LIVING DAYLIGHTS. / ('A'instrumental)**	5	

(12"+=/12"pic-d+=) (W 8305 T/P) – ('A'extended).

		Columbia	Columbia

Jun 90. (cd-s) **EP**
– We die young / etc. [-] [ ]

Sep 91. (cd/c/lp) *(467201-2/-4/-1)* *<46075>* **FACELIFT** [ ] [42] Mar91
– We die young / Man in the box / Sea of sorrow / Bleed the freak / I can't remember /
Love, hate, love / It ain't like that / Sunshine / Put you down / Confusion / I know
somethin' ('bout you) / Real thing.

Oct 91. (cd-ep) *<73851>* **MAN IN THE BOX / SEA OF SORROW /
BLEED THE FREAK / SUNSHINE** [-] [ ]

Feb 92. (c-ep)(cd-ep) *<74182><74305>* **SAP** [-] [ ]
– Brother / Got me wrong / Right turn / Am I inside / Love song.

──── **MIKE INEZ** (b.14 May'66, San Fernando, California) – bass; repl. MIKE STARR.
He formed MY SISTER'S MACHINE, who released album in May'92 'DIVA' on
'Caroline'.

Oct 92. (cd/c/lp) *(472330-2/-4/-1)* *<52475>* **DIRT** [42] [6]
– Them bones / Dam that river / Rain when I die / Down in a hole / Sickman /
Rooster / Junkhead / Dirt / God smack / Hate to feel / Angry chair / Would?

Jan 93. (7") *(658888-7)* **WOULD?. / MAN IN THE BOX** [19] [ ]
(12"green+=/pic-cd-s+=) *(658888-6/-2)* – Brother / Right Turn.

Mar 93. (7") *(659090-7)* **THEM BONES. / WE DIE YOUNG** [26] [ ]
(cd-s+=) *(659090-2)* – Got me wrong / Am I inside.

May 93. (7") *(659365-7)* **ANGRY CHAIR. / I KNOW SOMETHIN'
('BOUT YOU)** [33] [ ]
(12"+=) *(659365-6)* – Bleed the freak / It ain't like that.
(cd-s+=) *(659365-2)* – It ain't like that / Hate to feel.

Oct 93. (7"pic-d) *(659751-7)* **DOWN IN A HOLE. / ROOSTER** [36] [ ]
(12"+=) *(659751-6)* – A little bitter / Love, hate, love.
(cd-s+=) *(659751-2)* – What the hell I have I / ('A'radio edit).

Dec 93. (cd-s; w-drawn) *(660047-2)* **ROTTEN APPLE /** [-] [-]

Jan 94. (cd/c/lp) *(475713-2/-4/-1)* *<57628>* **JAR OF FLIES / SAP** [4] [1]
– Rotten apple / Nutshell / I stay away / No excuses / Whale & wasp / Don't follow /
Swing on this. (US-version w /out 'SAP')

Oct 95. (7"/c-s) *(662623-7/-4)* **GRIND. / NUTSHELL** [23] [ ]
(cd-s+=) *(662823-2)* – So close / Love, hate, love.

Nov 95. (cd/c/d-lp) *(481114-2/-4/-1)* *<67248>* **ALICE IN CHAINS** [37] [1]
– Grind / Brush away / Sludge factory / Heaven beside you / Head creeps / Again /
Shame in you / God am / So close / Nothin' song / Frogs / Over now.

Jan 96. (7"white) *(662893-7)* **HEAVEN BESIDE YOU. / WOULD?
(live)** [35] [ ]
(cd-s+=) *(662893-2)* – Rooster (live) / Junkhead (live).
(cd-s) *(662893-5)* – ('A'side) / Angry chair (live) / Man in a box (live) / Love, hate,
love (live).

──── added for below only; **SCOTT OLSEN** – guitar
Jul 96. (cd/c/d-lp) *(484300-2/-4/-1)* *<67703>* **MTV UNPLUGGED
(live)** [20] [3]
– Nutshell / Brother / No excuses / Sludge factory / Down in a hole / Angry chair /
Rooster / Got me wrong / Heaven beside you / Would? / Frogs / Over now / Killer
is me.

Jul 99. (cd/c) *(494005-2/-4)* *<63649>* **NOTHING SAFE (compilation)** [ ] [20]
– Get born again / We die young / Man in the box / Them bones / Iron gland / Angry
chair / Down in a hole / Rooster / Got me wrong / No excuses / I stay away / What
the hell have I / Grind / Again / Would?

– compilations, etc. –

Oct 99. (4xcd-box) *Columbia; (CKX 69580)* **MUSIC BANK** [ ] [ ]

MAD SEASON

──── were originally called GACY BUNCH with **LAYNE STALEY** – vocals / **MIKE
McCREADY** – guitar (of PEARL JAM) / **BARRETT MARTIN** – drums (of
SCREAMING TREES)
Mar 95. (cd/c/lp) *(478507-2/-4/-1)* *<67057>* **ABOVE** [41] [24]
– Wake up / X-ray mind / I'm above / River of deceit / Lifeless dead / Artificial red /
Long gone day / I don't know anything / November hotel / All alone.

JERRY CANTRELL

with **SEAN KINNEY + MIKE INEZ** / plus bassists **REX BROWN** (PANTERA),
NORWOOD FISHER (FISHBONE) + **LES CLAYPOOL** (PRIMUS) / guest **ANGELO MOORE**
(FISHBONE) – sax
Apr 98. (cd/c/lp) *(488705-2/-4/-1)* *<68147>* **BOGGY DEPOT** [ ] [28]
– Dickeye / Cut you in / My song / Settling down / Breaks my back / Jesus hands /
Devil by his side / Keep the light on / Satisfy / Hurt a long time / Between / Cold
piece.

May 98. (cd-s) *<4704>* **CUT YOU IN** [-] [ ]

ALIEN SEX FIEND (dig out; Great Alt & Indie . . .)

ALL ABOUT EVE (dig out; 4th edition or Great Alt & Indie . . .)

Daevid ALLEN (see under ⇒ GONG)

ALLMAN BROTHERS BAND

Formed: Jacksonville, Florida, USA . . . 1967 by brothers DUANE and
GREGG. They became The HOURGLASS, after previously gigging under
the ALLMAN JOYS banner with others:- BOB KELLER (bass), BILLY
CANELL or MANARD PORTWOOD (drums). HOURGLASS released two
albums and nearly a third for 'Liberty' before disbanding in 1968. They then
returned to their homeland to augment BUTCH TRUCKS in his outfit, 31st
OF FEBRUARY, with DUANE also relying on session work for 'Atlantic'.
In 1969, all three formed The ALLMAN BROTHERS BAND and moved to

Macon, Georgia. The brothers had already signed to the 'Atlantic' distributed
label 'Capricorn', run by one-time OTIS REDDING manager, Phil Walden.
With a final line-up of GREGG, DUANE, BUTCH TRUCKS, BERRY
OAKLEY (bass) and a second percussionist, JAIMO JOHANSON, the band
cut their self-titled debut in 1969, following it up a year later with 'IDLEWILD
SOUTH'. All the elements that would make the ALLMANs a legend were
in place; the smooth fluidity of the guitar runs, bible-belt country and gospel
in abundance, jazz-influenced explorations and dyed-in-the-wool Southern-
soaked vocals. During this time, DUANE continued his session work for the
likes of LAURA NYRO and DELANEY & BONNIE, as well as lending an
unmistakable hand to ERIC CLAPTON on DEREK AND THE DOMINOES'
'LAYLA' project (yes, that most famous of English rock refrains was created
by the blonde maned all-American boy). Like their spiritual brothers The
GRATEFUL DEAD, it was in a live setting that The ALLMAN BROTHERS
BAND could really cook up a soulful gumbo stew and 'THE ALLMAN
BROTHERS BAND AT FILLMORE EAST' (1971) was possibly the band's
defining moment as well as one of rock's great live albums. A sprawling double
set, the free-flowing jams often tripped out on their own momentum and despite
being spaced out over a whole side of vinyl, 'WHIPPING POST ' (from the
debut) lost none of its hypnotic power. Less than three months later, the band
were dealt a potentially fatal blow when DUANE was killed in a motorbike
accident. Bloodied but unbowed, the band released the 'EAT A PEACH'
(1972) album, a mixture of live tracks left over from the Fillmore recordings
and new studio material. Another double set, three tracks had been recorded
prior to the accident, including DUANE's fragile 'LITTLE MARTHA'. The
indulgence of the side-long DONOVAN adaptation, 'MOUNTAIN JAM', was
balanced by the pastoral beauty of tracks like BETTS' 'BLUE SKY'. After
BERRY OAKLEY was killed later that year in a crash spookily reminiscent
of DUANE's, BETTS' influence was even more pronounced as the band
struggled bravely on with the triumphant 'BROTHERS AND SISTERS'
(1973) album. Replacing OAKLEY with LAMAR WILLIAMS and drafting in
pianist CHUCK LEAVELL, the rootsier sounding album gave THE ALLMAN
BROTHERS BAND their first and only No.1. BETTS' glorious country-
flavoured 'RAMBLIN' MAN' provided their biggest hit single to date and
'JESSICA' fuelled countless boy racer fantasies after it was used as the theme
for Britain's 'Top Gear' TV show. The band then returned to their natural
habitat, the tourbus, playing a landmark gig to a crowd of over half a million
people in Watkins Glen, New York, alongside The GRATEFUL DEAD and
The BAND. Patchy solo projects followed in the shape of GREG's 'LAID
BACK' (1973) and BETTS' 'HIGHWAY CALL' (1974), while the next
band effort 'WIN, LOSE OR DRAW' (1975) signalled that The ALLMANS'
infamous fast living was beginning to sap their creativity. GREG began a
brief, torrid marriage with CHER in 1975, releasing the 'TWO THE HARD
WAY' album in 1977 under the moniker of ALLMAN AND WOMAN (no,
seriously!). The turning point, however, came when GREG testified against
his road manager/pusher, SCOOTER HERRING, who was up on a serious
drugs rap. After HERRING was sentenced to 75 years(!) in prison, the rest of
the band turned their backs on GREG, the all-brothers-together bravado gone,
at least until the reunion. Splitting and reforming numerous times throughout
the 80's, their studio output trawled a creative nadir on their 'Arista' albums.
Nevertheless, they can still put bums on seats in the American heartlands and
their Southern-fried innovation was given official recognition in 1995 when
they were inducted into the Rock 'n' Roll Hall Of Fame. • **Songwriters:** The
ALLMANS and BETTS. In the 90's most were written by BETTS, HAYNES
and NEEL. Covered; STATESBORO BLUES (Blind Willie McTell) / ONE
WAY OUT (Elmore James) / I'M YOUR HOOCHIE COOCHIE MAN
(Muddy Waters) / SLIP AWAY (Clarence Carter). • **Trivia:** DUANE sessioned
for WILSON PICKETT, BOZ SCAGGS, ARETHA FRANKLIN, KING
CURTIS, etc, etc . . .

Album rating: THE ALLMAN BROTHERS BAND (*8) / IDLEWILD SOUTH (*7) /
AT FILLMORE EAST (*9) / EAT A PEACH (*9) / BROTHERS AND SISTERS (*8) /
WIN, LOSE OR DRAW (*4) / WIPE THE WINDOWS, CHECK THE OIL, DOLLAR
GAS (*5) / ENLIGHTENED ROGUES (*5) / REACH FOR THE SKY (*4) / BROTHERS
OF THE ROAD (*4) / DREAMS boxed-set (*7) / SEVEN TURNS (*6) / A DECADE
OF HITS 1969-1979 (*8) / 2nd SET: AN EVENING WITH THE ALLMAN BROTHERS
(*6) / WHERE IT ALL BEGINS (*5) / Gregg Allman: LAID BACK (*5) / GREGG
ALLMAN TOUR (*3) / PLAYIN' UP A STORM (*4) / TWO THE HARD WAY as
Allman & Woman (*3) / I'M NO ANGEL (*5) / JUST BEFORE THE BULLETS FLY
(*4) / SEARCHING FOR SIMPLICITY (*4)

HOURGLASS

GREGG ALLMAN (b. 8 Dec'48, Nashville, Tenn.) – vocals, keyboards, guitar / **DUANE
ALLMAN** (b.20 Nov'46, Nashville) – guitars / **PAUL HORNSBY** – keyboards, guitar, vocals
/ **MABRON McKINNEY** – bass / **JOHN SANDLIN** – drums

		Liberty	Liberty

Feb 68. (7") *<56002>* **HEARTBEAT. / NOTHING BUT TEARS** [-] [ ]

Aug 68. (lp; mono/stereo) *(LBL/LBS 83219E)* *<7536>* **THE HOUR
GLASS** [ ] [ ] Feb68
– Out of the night / Nothing but tears / Love makes the world 'round / Cast off all
my fears / I've been trying / No easy way down / Heartbeat / So much love / Got to
get away / Silently / Bells.

──── **JESSE WILLARD CARR** – bass, vocals repl. MABRON McKINNEY
Jul 68. (7") *<56029>* **POWER OF LOVE. / I STILL WANT YOUR
LOVE** [-] [-]

Aug 68. (lp) *<7555>* **POWER OF LOVE** [-] [ ]
– Power of love / Changing of the guard / To things before / I'm not afraid / I can
stand alone / Down in Texas / I still want your love / Home for the summer / I'm

hangin' up my heart for you / Going nowhere / Norwegian wood / Now is the time. (re-iss. the 1968 lp's; Mar74 on 'United Artists'; USD 303/4) <013G2>

Sep 68. (7") <56053> **CHANGING OF THE GUARD. / D-I-V-O-R-C-E**　　－　☐
Nov 68. (7") <56065> **GOING NOWHERE. / SHE'S MY WOMAN**　　☐
Dec 68. (7") <56072> **NOW IS THE TIME. / SHE'S MY WOMAN**　　☐
Feb 69. (7") <56091> **I'VE BEEN TRYING. / SILENTLY**　　☐

—　3rd album was withdrawn

31st FEBRUARY

DUANE and **GREGG** with **BUTCH TRUCKS** – drums / **SCOTT BOYER** – guitar, vocals / **DAVID BROWN** – bass

not iss.

Mar 69. (7") **IN THE MORNING WHEN I'M REAL. / PORCELAIN MIRRORS**　　－　☐

—　An album DUANE AND GREGG was released 1973 on 'Polydor UK'/'Bold' US cont. these demos.

The ALLMAN BROTHERS BAND

(**GREGG** and **DUANE**) plus **DICKEY BETTS** (b.RICHARD, 12 Dec'43, West Palm Beach, Florida) – guitar, vocals / **BERRY OAKLEY** (b. 4 Apr'48, Chicago, Illinois) – bass / **BUTCH TRUCKS** (b.Jacksonville, Florida) – drums, timpani / **JAIMOE JOHANSON** (b.JOHN LEE JOHNSON, 8 Jul'44, Ocean Springs, Miss.) – percussion

Atco　Atco

Nov 69. (lp) (228 033) <308> **THE ALLMAN BROTHERS BAND**
– Don't want you no more / It's my cross to bear / Black hearted woman / Trouble no more / Every hungry woman / Dreams / Whipping post. (cd-iss. 1994 on 'Polydor'; 823 653-2) (cd re-iss. Jun98; 531257-2)
Mar 70. (7") (226 013) <8803> **BLACK HEARTED WOMAN. / EVERY HUNGRY WOMAN**
Nov 70. (lp) (2400 032) <342> **IDLEWIND SOUTH**　　38
– Revival (love is everywhere) / Don't keep me wonderin' / Midnight rider / In memory of Elizabeth Reed / I'm your hoochie coochie man / Please call home / Leave my blues at home. (cd-iss. Mar89 on 'Polydor'; 833 334-2) (cd re-iss. Jun98; 531258-2)
Nov 70. (7") (2091 040) <8011> **REVIVAL (LOVE IS EVERYWHERE). / LEAVE MY BLUES AT HOME**　　92
Mar 71. (7") (2091 070) <8014> **MIDNIGHT RIDER. / WHIPPING POST**

Capricorn　Capricorn

Jul 71. (d-lp) (2659 005) <802> **AT FILLMORE EAST (live)**　　13
– Statesboro blues / Done somebody wrong / Stormy Monday / You don't love me / Hot 'Lanta / In memory of Elizabeth Reed / Whipping post. (re-iss. Nov74;) (d-cd-iss. 1986 on 'Polydor'; 823 273-2) (d-cd re-iss. Jun98; 531260-2)

—　On 29 Oct'71, DUANE was killed in a motorcycle accident in Macon. He had already contributed to 3 tracks on below album.

Feb 72. (d-lp) (67501) <0102> **EAT A PEACH**　　4
– Ain't wastin' time no more / Les brers in A minor / Melissa / Mountain jam / One way out / Trouble no more / Stand back / Blue sky / Little Martha / Mountain jam (reprise). (re-iss. Nov74;) (cd-iss. 1986 on 'Polydor'; 823 654-2) (cd re-iss. Jun98; 531261-2)
Apr 72. (7") <0003> **AIN'T WASTIN' TIME NO MORE. / MELISSA**　　－　77
Jul 72. (7") <0007> **MELISSA. / BLUE SKY**　　－　86
Nov 72. (7") <0014> **ONE WAY OUT. / STAND BACK**　　－　86

—　(Jan'73) **LAMAR WILLIAMS** (b.1947) – bass; repl. BERRY OAKLEY who also died in a motorcycle accident, again in Macon, 11 Nov'72.

Sep 73. (lp/c) (2429/3129 102) <0111> **BROTHERS AND SISTERS**　　42　1　Aug73
– Wasted words / Ramblin' / Come and go blues / Jelly jelly / Southbound / Jessica / Pony boy. (re-iss. Jun81; 2482 504) (cd-iss. 1986 on 'Polydor'; 825 092-2) (cd re-iss. Jun87 on 'Polydor'; 823 721-2) (cd re-iss. Jun98; 531262-2)
Oct 73. (7") (2089 005) <0027> **RAMBLIN' MAN. / PONY BOY**　　2　Aug73
Jan 74. (7") <0036> **JESSICA. / WASTED WORDS**　　－　65
Oct 74. (7") (2089 006) **JESSICA. / COME AND GO BLUES**　　－
Sep 75. (lp) (2476 116) <0156> **WIN, LOSE OR DRAW**　　5
– Can't lose what you never had / Just another love song / Nevertheless / Win, lose or draw / Louisiana Lou And Three Card Monty John / High falls / Sweet mama. (cd-iss. Aug87; 827586-2) (cd re-iss. Jun98; 531263-2)
Sep 75. (7") <0246> **NEVERTHELESS. / LOUISIANA LOU AND THREE CARD MONTY JOHN**　　－　67　78

—　Jul 76 when GREGG was ostracized by others for giving evidence against convicted drug trafficker and road manager Scooter Herring. GREGG formed his own band. BETTS formed GREAT SOUTHERN and others formed SEA LEVEL who hit US No. 31 Mar 78 with lp 'CATS ON THE COAST'. When rifts were settled The ALLMAN BROTHERS BAND re-united early '79. GREGG, DICKEY, BUTCH, JAIMO plus newcomers **DAN TOLER** – guitar / **DAVID GOLDFLIES** – bass (both ex-GREAT SOUTHERN)

Polydor　Capricorn

Mar 79. (lp) (2429 185) <0218> **ENLIGHTENED ROGUES**　　9
– Crazy love / Can't take it with you / Pegasus / Need your love so bad / Blind love / Try it one more time / Just ain't easy / Sail away. (cd-iss. 1987 on 'Polydor'; 831 589-2) (cd re-iss. Jun98; 531265-2)
Apr 79. (7") (2089 068) <0320> **CRAZY LOVE. / IT JUST AIN'T EASY**　　29　Mar79
Jun 79. (7") <0326> **CAN'T TAKE IT WITH YOU. / SAIL AWAY**　　－

Arista　Arista

Sep 80. (lp) (SPART 1146) <9535> **REACH FOR THE SKY**　　27　Aug80
– Hell & high water / Mystery woman / From the madness of the west / I got a right to be wrong / Angeline / Famous last words / Keep on keepin' on / So long. (cd-iss. Agg97 on 'Razor & Tie'; RE 2131)
Sep 80. (7") <0555> **ANGELINE. / SO LONG**　　－　58
Jan 81. (7") <0584> **MYSTERY WOMAN. / HELL OR HIGH WATER**　　－
Sep 81. (lp) <9564> **BROTHERS OF THE ROAD**　　44　Aug81
– Brothers of the road / Leavin' / Straight from the road / The heat is on / Maybe we can go back to yesterday / The judgement / Two rights / Never knew how much (I needed you) / Things you used to do / I beg of you. (cd-iss. Aug97 on 'Razor & Tie'; RE 2132)

Sep 81. (7") (ARIST 432) <0618> **STRAIGHT FROM THE HEART. / LEAVING**　　39　Aug81
Nov 81. (7") <0643> **TWO RIGHTS. / NEVER KNEW HOW MUCH**

—　**CHUCK LEAVELL** rejoined but they soon disbanded once again. Past member **LAMAR** died of cancer on 25 Jan'83.

GREGG ALLMAN BAND

went solo again in 1987 with **DAN TOLER** – guitar / **DAVID 'FRANKIE' TOLER** – drums / **TIM HEDING** – keyboards / **BRUCE WAIBEL** – bass, vocals / **CHAZ TRIPPY** – percussion

Epic　Epic

May 87. (lp/cd) <(450392-1/-4/-2)> **I'M NO ANGEL**　　30　Feb87
– I'm no angel / Anything goes / Evidence of love / Yours for the asking / Things that might have been / Can't keep running / Faces without names / Lead me on / Don't want you no more / It's not my cross to bear.
Jul 87. (7") (6507 517) <06998> **I'M NO ANGEL. / LEAD ME ON**　　49　Mar87
Jul 87. (7") <07215> **CAN'T KEEP RUNNING. / ANYTHING GOES**
Sep 87. (7") <07430> **EVIDENCE OF LOVE. / ANYTHING GOES**　　－
Apr 89. (lp/c/cd) (462 477-1/-4/-2) <44033> **JUST BEFORE THE BULLETS FLY**　　Aug88
– Demons / Before the bullets fly / Slip away / Thorn and a wild rose / Ocean awash the gunwale / Can't get over you / Island / Fear of falling / Night games / Every hungry woman.
Apr 89. (7") <08041> **SLIP AWAY. / EVERY HUNGRY WOMAN**　　－
Jan 98. (cd/c) (481691-2/-4) **SEARCHING FOR SIMPLICITY**
– Whippin' post / House of blues / Come back and help me / Silence ain't golden no more / Rendezvous with the blues / Wolf's a howlin' / Love the poison / Don't deny me / Dark end of the street / Neighbour neighbour / I've got news for you / Memphis in the meantime / Startin' over.

– other GREGG ALLMAN releases, etc. –

—　with **SCOTT BOYER** – guitar, vocals / **TOMMY TALTON** – slide guitar / **CHUCK LEAVELL** – keyboards / **DAVID BROWN** – bass / **BILL STEWART** – drums / etc.

Capricorn　Capricorn

Nov 73. (lp) (47508) <0116> **LAID BACK**　　13
– Will the circle be unbroken / Don't mess up a good thing / Multi-colored lady / Please call home / Queen of hearts / Midnight rider / Don't mess up a good thing / All my friends / These days. (cd-iss. Aug87 on 'Polydor';)
Jan 74. (7") (2089 002) <0035> **MIDNIGHT RIDER. / MULTI-COLORED LADY**　　19　Dec73

—　(above releases were issued approx.half a year later in UK).

Mar 74. (7") <0042> **PLEASE CALL HOME. / DON'T MESS UP A GOOD THING**　　－
Oct 74. (7") <0053> **DON'T MESS WITH A GOOD THING. / MIDNIGHT RIDER**　　－
Nov 74. (d-lp) (2659 038) <0141> **GREGG ALLMAN TOUR (live)**　　50
– Don't mess up a good thing / Queen of hearts / Feel so bad / Stand back / Time will take us / Where can you go / Double cross / Dreams / Are you lonely for me / Turn on your love light / Oncoming traffic / Will the circle be unbroken?. (cd-iss. Oct87 on 'Polydor'; 831 940-2)

—　retained **BILL STEWART** and brought in **STEVE BECKMEIER + JOHN HUG** – guitar / **RICKY HIRSCH** – slide guitar / **NEIL LARSEN** – piano / **WILLIE WEEKS** – bass

Jun 77. (lp) (2476 131) <0181> **PLAYIN' UP A STORM**　　42
– Come and go blues / Let this be a lesson to ya / The brightest smile in town / Bring it on back / Cryin' shame / Sweet feelin' / It ain't no use / Matthew's arrival / One more try.
Aug 77. (7") <0279> **CRYIN' SHAME. / ONE MORE TRY**　　－

ALLMAN AND WOMAN

the (Woman being GREGG's wife and singer CHER) (same line-up)

Warners　Warners

Nov 77. (lp) (K 56436) <3120> **TWO THE HARD WAY**
– Move me / I found you / Can you fool / You've really got a hold on me / We're gonna make it / Do what you gotta do / In for the night / Shadow dream song / Island / I love makin' love to you / Love me.
Dec 77. (7") (K 17057) <8504> **LOVE ME. / MOVE ME**

—　they subsequently split and were divorced on 16th of January '79

The ALLMAN BROTHERS BAND

—　re-formed 1989, **GREGG, DICKEY, JAIMO, BUTCH** and newcomers **ALLEN WOODY** – bass / **WARREN HAYES** – guitar / **JOHNNY NEEL** – keyboards

Epic　Epic

Jul 90. (7") <73504> **GOOD CLEAN FUN. / SEVEN TURNS**　　－
Jul 90. (cd/c/lp) (466850-2/-4/-1) <46144> **SEVEN TURNS**　　53
– Good clean fun / Let me ride / Low down dirty mean / Shine it on / Loaded dice / Seven turns / Gambler's roll / True gravity / It ain't over yet.
Sep 90. (7") <73583> **SEVEN TURNS. / LET ME RIDE**
Jul 91. (cd/c/lp) (468525-2/-4/-1) <47877> **SHADES OF TWO WORLDS**　　85
– End of the line / Bad rain / Nobody knows / Desert blues / Get on with your life / Midnight man / Kind of bird / Come on in my kitchen.
Jun 92. (cd/c) <48998-2/-4> **AN EVENING WITH THE ALLMAN BROTHERS BAND**
– Southbound / Nobody knows / Revival (love is everywhere) / Midnight blues / Get on with your life / Dreams / End of the line / Blue sky.

—　**MARC QUINONES** – congas, percussion; repl. NEEL

Jul 94. (cd/c/lp) (476884-2/-4) **WHERE IT ALL BEGINS**
– All night train / Sailin' 'cross the Devil's sea / Back where it all begins / Soulshine / No one to run with / Change my way of living / Mean woman blues / Everybody's got a mountain to climb / What's done is done / Temptation is a gun.
May 95. (cd,c) <66795> **2ND SET – AN EVENING WITH THE ALLMAN BROTHERS BAND**　　－　88
– Sailin' 'cross the Devil's sea / You don't love me / Soul shine / Back where it all

begins / In memory of Elizabeth Reed / Same thing / No one to run with / Jessica. *(UK-iss.Apr99; 480606-2)*

– DUANE & GREGG ALLMAN compilations, etc. –

1972.	(7") *Bold*; **MORNING DEW. / (pt. 2)**		-	
1973.	(lp) *Polydor; (2310 235) / Bold; <33-301>* **DUANE & GREGG ALLMAN** (rec.'68)			

– Morning dew / God rest his soul / Nobody knows when you're down and out / Come down and get me / Melissa / I'll change for you / Back down home with you / Well I know too well / In the morning when I'm real.

– ALLMAN BROTHERS compilations, etc. –

Oct 73.	(lp; as ALLMAN JOYS) *Mercury; (6398 005) / Dial; <6005>* **EARLY ALLMANS**			
Nov 74.	(d-lp) *Capricorn; (60046) / Atco; <805>* **BEGINNINGS**		25	Mar73

– (first 2 ALLMAN BROTHERS BAND lp's) *(cd-iss. Oct87 on 'Polydor'; 827 588-2) (cd re-iss. Jun98; 531259-2)*

1974.	(7") *Capricorn; <0050>* **AIN'T WASTIN' TIME NO MORE. / BLUE SKY**		-	
1974.	(7") *Capricorn; <0051>* **MELISSA. / RAMBLIN' MAN**		-	
Feb 76.	(d-lp) *Capricorn; (2637 101) <0164>* **THE ROAD GOES ON FOREVER**	54	43	Dec75

– Black hearted woman / Dreams / Whipping post / Midnight rider / Statesboro blues / Stormy Monday / Hoochie coochie man / Stand back / One way out / Blue sky / Hot 'Lanta / Ain't wastin' time no more / Melissa / Wasted words / Jessica / Ramblin' man / Little Martha.

Dec 76.	(d-lp) *Capricorn; (2637 103) <0177>* **WIPE THE WINDOWS, CHECK THE OIL, DOLLAR GAS** (demos, rarities recorded live)		75	

– (introduction) / Wasted words / Southbound / Ramblin' man / In memory of Elizabeth Reed / Ain't wastin' time no more / Come and go blues / Can't lose what you never had / Don't want you no more / It's not my cross to bear / Jessica. *(cd-iss. Jun98; 531264-2)*

Aug 80.	(lp) *Capricorn; <6339>* **THE BEST OF THE ALLMAN BROTHERS BAND**			Nov81
Jun 81.	(d-lp) *Capricorn; (2637 105)* **THE STORY OF THE ALLMAN BROTHERS BAND**			
Sep 83.	(12"ep) *Polydor; (POSP 607)* **JESSICA / SOUTHBOUND. / WHIPPIN' POST / RAMBLIN' MAN**			
Jul 84.	(7") *Old Gold; (OG 9437)* **JESSICA. / RAMBLIN' MAN**		-	
Sep 85.	(lp; as HOURGLASS) *C5; (C5-524)* **THE SOUL OF TIME**		-	
Feb 88.	(7") *Old Gold; (OG 4046)* **JESSICA. / (b-side by; Derek & The Dominoes')**		-	
Jul 88.	(lp/c) *Knight; (KNLP/KNMC 10004)* **NIGHTRIDING** *(cd-iss. Sep89; KNCD 10004)*		-	
Apr 89.	(6xlp/4xc/4xcd) *Polydor; <(839417-1/-4/-2)>* **DREAMS**			Jul89
Jul 90.	(d-cd) *Polydor; 843260-2)* **LIVE AT LUDLOW GARAGE 1970** (live)		-	
May 92.	(cd/c) *Polydor; (511156-2/-4)* **A DECADE OF HITS 1969-1979**			Nov91

– Statesboro blues / Ramblin' man / Midnight rider / Southbound / Melissa / Jessica / Ain't wastin' time no more / Little Martha / Crazy love / Revival / Wasted words / Blue sky / One way out / In memory of Elizabeth Reed / Dreams / Whipping post.

May 92.	(cd/c) *Castle; (CCS CD/MC 327)* **THE COLLECTION**		-	
Sep 94.	(cd) *R.C.A.; (0782 218724-2)* **HELL & HIGH WATER (The Best Of the Arista Years)**			
Mar 93.	(d-cd) *Polydor; (517 294-2)* **THE FILLMORE CONCERTS** (live)			
Mar 98.	(cd) *Camden; (74321 5696124)* **MADNESS OF THE WEST**			
Jun 98.	(cd/c) *Epic; (489087-2/-4)* **MYCOLOGY**			
Sep 98.	(cd) *Spectrum; (551824-2)* **THE BEST OF THE ALLMAN BROTHERS BAND LIVE** (live)		-	

DUANE ALLMAN

exploitation compilations featuring all his guitar/sessions

Oct 74.	(d-lp) *Capricorn; <2CP 0108>* **AN ANTHOLOGY**		28	Dec72

– B.B. King medley / Hey Jude / The road of love / Goin' down slow / The weight / Games people play / Shake for me / Loan me a dime / Rollin' stone / Livin' on the open road / Down along the cove / lease be with me / Mean old world / Layla / Statesboro blues / Don't keep me wondering / Stand back / Dreams / Little Martha. *(d-cd.iss.Oct87 on 'Polydor'; 831 444-2)*

Jan 75.	(d-lp) *Capricorn; <CPN2-0139>* **AN ANTHOLOGY VOL.2**		49	Jul74

– Happily married man / It ain't fair / The weight / You reap what you sow / Matchbox / Born to be wild / No money down / Been gone too long / Stuff you gotta watch / Push push / Walk on gilded splinters / Waiting for a train / Don't tell me your troubles / Goin' upstairs / Come on in my kitchen / Dimples / Goin' up the country / Done somebody wrong / Leave my blues at home / Midnight rider. *(d-cd.iss.Oct87 on 'Polydor'; 831 445-2)*

Sep 79.	(lp) *Capricorn; (242 919-8)* **THE BEST OF DUANE ALLMAN**		-	

ALMIGHTY (dig out; 4th edition or Great Metal . . .)

Marc ALMOND

Born: PETER MARC ALMOND, 9 Jul'59, Southport, England. Having met DAVE BALL at Leeds Polytechnic, the pair formed SOFT CELL and with the help of visual technician, STEVEN GRIFFITHS, they embarked on studio and live work in 1980 with the 'MUTANT MOMENTS' EP. After appearing on the infamous 'Some Bizzare Album', with cut, 'The Girl With The Patent Leather Face', they secured a bonafide deal with the 'Some Bizzare' label. The following year, after a debut single, 'MEMORABILIA' failed to make an impression, a darkly compelling, electro-fuelled cover of 'TAINTED LOVE' (once the dancefloor domain of disco diva, GLORIA JONES) slipped in to the UK chart, peaking at No.1 for two weeks. To end the year, SOFT CELL cracked the Top 5 with both 'BEDSITTER' and their debut album, 'NON-STOP EROTIC CABARET', an early 80's classic which trawled the depths

of ALMOND's black-leather, neon-lit fantasies to a sleazy musical backdrop of low-rent alternative disco. Apart from the aforementioned singles, tracks such as 'YOUTH', 'SEX DWARF', 'SEEDY FILMS', 'CHIPS ON MY SHOULDER' and the forthcoming hit, 'SAY HELLO, WAVE GOODBYE', even found a rampant audience in the gay disco community of New York. The extroverted ALMOND was a figurehead for young homosexuals, although the media were scathing in their criticism of what they saw as the singer's effeminate posturing. Nevertheless, SOFT CELL continued to chalk up the hits, 'TORCH' (an exquisite duet featuring CINDY ECSTACY) narrowly missing No.1, while a revamped dance model of the debut, 'NON-STOP ECSTATIC DANCING', marked time as BALL and ALMOND worked on a follow-up. Early in '83, their second set proper, 'THE ART OF FALLING APART', hit the shops and subsequently the Top 5, the record coming with a free 12" single that saw ALMOND bravely attempting a HENDRIX medley. As the pair increasingly concentrated on separate projects, MARC & THE MAMBAS and DAVE BALL solo, a split seemed imminent; by the release of 'THIS LAST NIGHT . . . IN SODOM' in January '84, SOFT CELL was no more. After many threats of impending retirement, ALMOND was back in his beloved spotlight with the 'VERMIN IN ERMINE' (1984) album, cut with new backing band, The WILLING SINNERS. Developing further as an interpretive balladeer/torch singer with each successive release, ALMOND's mid-late 80's output found him marginalised to cult appeal despite an impressive array of cover material from such luminaries as JACQUES BREL, SCOTT WALKER and JOHNNIE RAY. This approach finally resulted in a massive comeback hit duet with GENE PITNEY, the melodramatic 'SOMETHING'S GOTTEN HOLD OF MY HEART', originally a Top 5 hit in 1967 for the singing/songwriting hearthrob. In the early 90's, SOFT CELL enjoyed a bit of a renaissance, remixed versions of 'SAY HELLO, WAVE GOODBYE' and 'TAINTED LOVE' making the charts, while ALMOND scored a surprise Top 20 hit with a dancefloor reworking of Jacques Brel's 'JACKY'. Taken from the album, 'TENEMENT SYMPHONY' (1991), this return to form also numbered future hits, 'MY HAND OVER MY HEART' and 'THE DAYS OF PEARLY SPENCER', the latter another blast from the 60's past and originally a hit for DAVID McWILLIAMS. ALMOND continued to work on various idoisyncratic projects, including a set of old French songs and poems, 'ABSINTHE' (1993). Having delivered what was to be a one-off album ('FANTASTIC STAR') for 'Mercury' in early '96, the long-suffering tainted soul that was MARC ALMOND made his re-appearance with the single 'BLACK KISS' in late '98. Having set up his own record label, 'Blue Star', the wee man unleashed his most advanced work since the early days in the shape of 'OPEN ALL NIGHT' (1999). With rave reviews (for once!), ALMOND set about publishing two works, the first a lyrics/poems collection entitled 'A Beautiful Twisted Night', the second an autobiography 'Tainted Life'. • **Covered:** WHERE DID OUR LOVE GO (Supremes). MARC & THE MAMBAS covered IF YOU GO AWAY + THE BULLS (Jacques Brel) / CAROLINE SAYS (Lou Reed) / TERRAPIN (Syd Barrett) / CATCH A FALLEN STAR (Perry Como). MARC ALMOND solo:- A WOMAN'S STORY (Cher) / A SALTY DOG (Procol Harum) / THE LITTLE WHITE CLOUD THAT CRIED (Johnnie Ray) / THE PLAGUE (Scott Walker). • **Trivia:** In 1983, DAVE BALL scored the music for Tennessee Williams' play 'Suddenly Last Summer'. In mid 1987, ALMOND guested and wrote on SALLY TIMMS' single 'This House Is A House Of Tears'.

Album rating: Soft Cell: NON-STOP EROTIC CABARET (*8) / NON-STOP ECSTATIC DANCING remix collection (*4) / THE ART OF FALLING APART (*6) / THIS LAST NIGHT . . . IN SODOM (*5) / MEMORABILIA – THE SINGLES compilation (*8) / Marc And The Mambas: UNTITLED (*8) / TORMENT AND TOREROS (*5) / Marc Almond: VERMIN IN ERMINE (*5) / STORIES OF JOHNNY (*5) / MOTHER FIST AND HER FIVE DAUGHTERS (*4) / THE STARS WE ARE (*5) / JACQUES (*5) / ENCHANTMENT (*5) / TENEMENT SYMPHONY (*4) / TWELVE YEARS OF TEARS (*5) / ABSINTHE (*5) / FANTASTIC STAR (*5) / THE SINGLES (1984-1987) compilation (*7) / THE BEST OF MARC ALMOND compilation (*6) / OPEN ALL NIGHT (*7)

SOFT CELL

MARC ALMOND – vocals / **DAVE BALL** – keyboards, synthesizer, drum programming

		Big Frock	not iss.
1980.	(7"ep) *(ABF 1)* **MUTANT MOMENTS**		-

– Potential / L.O.V.E. feelings / Metro MRX / Frustration.

		Some Bizzare	Sire
Mar 81.	(7") *(HARD 1)* **MEMORABILIA. / A MAN CAN GET LOST** (12") *(HARD 12)* – ('A'extended) / Persuasion (extended).		-
Jul 81.	(7") *(BZS 2) <49855>* **TAINTED LOVE. / WHERE DID OUR LOVE GO** (12"+=) *(BZS 2-12)* – Tainted dub / Memorabilia. *(re-iss. Jul82; hit 50, re-iss. Jan85; hit 43)*	1	8 Dec81
Nov 81.	(7"/ext-12") *(BZS 6/+12)* **BEDSITTER. / FACILITY GIRLS**	4	

—— guests **CINDY ECSTACY** – dual vox / **DAVE TOFANI** – sax / **JOHN GATHELL** – trumpet

Dec 81.	(lp/c) *(BZ LP/MC 2) <3647>* **NON-STOP EROTIC CABARET**	5	22 Jan82

– Frustration / Tainted love / Seedy films / Youth / Sex dwarf / Entertain me / Chips on my shoulder / Bedsitter / Secret life / Say hello, wave goodbye. *(re-iss. May90 on 'Vertigo' cd/c/lp; 800 061-2/-4/-1)*

Jan 82.	(7"/ext-12") *(BZS 7/+12)* **SAY HELLO, WAVE GOODBYE. / FUN CITY**	3	
May 82.	(7"/ext-12") *(BZS 9/+12)* **TORCH. / INSECURE ME**	2	

—— duo carried on without CINDY, who later formed SIX SEE RED

Jun 82.	(m-lp/m-c) *(BZ X/M 1012) <23694>* **NON-STOP ECSTATIC DANCING** (remixes)	6	57 Jul82

– Memorabilia / Where did our love go / What! / A man could get lost / Chips on my shoulder * / Sex dwarf. *<US version repl.* with =)* –

Insecure . . . me? *(re-iss. Mar92 on 'Mercury' cd/c; 510 295-2/-4)* – (extra tracks).

Aug 82. (7"/ext-12") *(BZS 11/+12)* **WHAT! / . . . SO (remix)** | 3 |

Nov 82. (7"/ext-12") *(BZS 16/+12)* **WHERE THE HEART IS. / IT'S A MUG GAME** | 21 |

Feb 83. (lp/c/+C 3) *<23769>* **THE ART OF FALLING APART** | 5 | 84
– Forever the same / Where the heart is / Numbers / Heat / Kitchen sink drama / Baby doll / Loving you, hating me / The art of falling apart. *(12"ep with above +=)* – MARTIN. / HENDRIX MEDLEY: HEY JOE – PURPLE HAZE – VOODOO CHILE *(re-iss. Nov87; SOD 2) (re-iss. Mar92 on 'Mercury' cd/c; 510 296-2/-4)* – (extra tracks).

Feb 83. (7"/ext-12") *(BZS 16/+12)* **NUMBERS. / BARRIERS** | 25 |

Apr 83. (7") **HEAT. / IT'S A MUGS GAME** | – |

Sep 83. (7") *(BZS 20)* **SOUL INSIDE. / YOU ONLY LIVE TWICE** | 16 |
(12"+=) *(BZS 20-12)* – Loving you, hating me / 007 theme.
(d7"+=) *(BZS 20-20)* – Loving you, hating me / Her imagination.

Feb 84. (7") *(BZS 22)* **DOWN IN THE SUBWAY. / DISEASE AND DESIRE** | 24 |
(ext-12"+=/12"remix+=) *(BZS/+R 22-12)* – Born to lose.

Mar 84. (lp/c) *(BIZL /+C 6)* **THIS LAST NIGHT . . . IN SODOM** | 12 |
– Mr. Self destruct / Slave to this / Little rough rhinestone / Meet murder my angel / The best way to kill / L'Esqualita / Down in the subway / Surrender (to a stranger) / Soul inside / Where was your heart (when you needed it most). *(cd-iss. Aug84; 818 436-2)*

—— waved goodbye just prior to the above album

– compilations, others, etc. –

1982. (6x12"box) *Some Bizzare; (CELBX 1)* **THE 12" SINGLES** | | – |

Dec 86. (lp/c/cd) *Some Cell; (BZ LP/MC 3)(830 708-2)* **SOFT CELL – THE SINGLES** | 58 | – |

Mar 91. (7"/-c-s) *Mercury; (SOF T/MC 1)* **SAY HELLO, WAVE GOODBYE '91. / MEMORABILIA (Grid remix)** | 38 | – |
(12"+=)(cd-s+=) *(SOFT 1-12)(SOFCD 1)* – ('A'-Mendelsohn extended remix).
(cd-s) *(SOFCP 1)* – ('A'side) / Numbers / Torch (12"version).

May 91. (7"/c-s)(12") *Mercury; (SOF T/MC 2)(SOFT 2-12)* **TAINTED LOVE ('91 remix). / ('A'-Original)** | 5 | – |
(cd-s+=) *(SOFCP 2)* – Where did our love go?
(cd-s) *(SOFCD 2)* – Tainted love / Where is our love / Loving you – hating me / Where the heart is.

May 91. (cd/c/lp) *Mercury; (848 512-2/-4/-1)* **MEMORABILIA – THE SINGLES** | 8 | |
– Memorabilia '91 / Tainted love / Bedsitter / Torch / What was the matter with Rachmaninov? / Say hello wave goodbye '91 / Where the heart is / I feel love / Tears run rings / A lover spurned / Something's gotten hold of my heart. *(cd+=)* – (Soul inside / Say hello wave goodbye (12"mix) / Waifs and strays (Grid twilight mix).

Mar 94. (cd/c) *Spectrum; (550 189-2/-4)* **DOWN IN THE SUBWAY** | | |

Mar 96. (cd) *Some Bizzare; (552 086-2)* **SAY HELLO TO SOFT CELL** | | |

Feb 99. (12"; as SOFT CELL vs CLUB 69) *Twisted; (TWD 55530)* **TAINTED LOVE** | | |

MARC AND THE MAMBAS

with **ANNIE HOGAN** – piano / **TIM TAYLOR** – bass / **DAVE BALL** – multi instruments

Mar 82. (12"; mail order) *(BZS 5-12)* **FUN CITY. / SLEAZE (TAKE IT, SHAKE IT) / TAKING IT SHAKING IT** | – | – |

—— guests on next 2 albums were **GENESIS P. ORRIDGE + MATT JOHNSON**

Oct 82. (lp/c) *(BZA/BZC 13)* **UNTITLED** | 42 | – |
– Untitled / Empty eyes / Angels / Big Louise / Caroline says / Margaret / If you go away. *(free-12"ep with above +=)* – Terrapin / Twilights and lowlifes (street walking soundtrack) / Twilights and lowlifes. *(re-iss. Mar92 on 'Mercury' cd/c; 510 298-2/-4)*

Nov 82. (7"; w-drawn) *(BZS 15)* **BIG LOUISE. / EMPTY EYES** | – | – |
(12"; w-drawn+=) *(BZS 15-12)* – The dirt behind the neon.

Jun 83. (7") *(BZS 19)* **BLACK HEART. / YOUR AURA** | 49 | |
(12"+=) *(BZS 19-12)* – Mamba.

Aug 83. (d-lp/c) *(BIZL /+C 4)* **TORMENT AND TOREROS** | 28 | |
– The animal in you / Narcissus / Gloomy Sunday / Vision / Your love is a lesson / The untouchable one / My little book of sorrows / In my room / First time / The bulls / Boss cat / Intro / Catch a fallen star / Beat out dat rhythm on a drum / A million manias / Torment / Black heart. *(re-iss. Mar92 on 'Mercury' cd/c; 812 872-2/-4) (cd re-iss. Oct97; SBZCD 028CD)*

Nov 83. (12"ep) *(BZS 21-12)* **TORMENT / FIRST TIME. / YOU'LL NEVER SEE ME ON A SUNDAY / MAGAMILLIONMANIA-MULTIMANIAMIX** | | – |

MARC ALMOND

—— went solo augmented by The **WILLING SINNERS: ANNIE HOGAN** – piano / **BILLY McGEE** – bass / **RICHARD RILEY** – guitar / **STEPHEN HUMPHRIES** – drums / **MARTIN McCARRICK** – cello

May 84. (7") *(BZS 23)* **THE BOY WHO CAME BACK. / JOEY DEMENTO** | 52 | |
(10"/12") *(BZS 23 10/12)* – ('A'-Loud cut) / ('B'extended).

Sep 84. (7") *(BZS 24)* **YOU HAVE. / SPLIT UP** | 57 | |
(ext-10"+=) *(BZS 24-10)* – Black mountain blues.
(ext-12"+=) *(BZS 24-12)* – Joey Demento.

Oct 84. (lp/c)(cd) *(BIZL /+C 8) (<822 832-2>)* **VERMINE IN ERMINE** | 36 | |
– Shining sinners / Hell was a city / You have / Crime sublime / Gutter hearts / Ugly head / The boy who came back / Solo adultos / Tenderness is a weakness. *(c+=/cd+=)* – Pink shack blues / Split lip / Joey Demento.

Nov 84. (7") *(BZS 25)* **TENDERNESS IS A WEAKNESS. / LOVE FOR SALE** | | |
(10"+=) *(BZS 25-10)* – Pink shack blues (live) / The heel (live).

—— In April '85, he teamed up with BRONSKI BEAT on Top 3 version of 'I FEEL LOVE'. Two months later, he featured anonymously on 12" 'SKIN' as The BURMOE BROTHERS.

Aug 85. (7") *(BONK 1)* **STORIES OF JOHNNY. / STORIES OF JOHNNY (with The Westminster City School Choir)** | 23 | – |

(12"+=) *(BONK 1-12)* – Take my heart.
(d7"++=/10"++=) *(BONK 1/+10)* – Blond boy.

Sep 85. (lp/c/cd) *(FAITH/TFTH/CDFTH 1)* **STORIES OF JOHNNY** | 22 |
– Traumas, traumas, traumas / Stories of Johnny / The house is haunted (by the echoes of your last goodbye) / Love letter / The flesh is willing / Always / Contempt / I who never / My candle burns / Love and little white lies. *(c+=/cd+=)* – Take my heart / Blond boy / Stories of Johnny (with The Westminster City School Choir).

Oct 85. (7") *(BONKP 2)* **LOVE LETTER. / LOVE LETTER (with The Westminster City School Choir)** | 68 | – |
(10"/12") *(BONK 2 10/12)* – ('A'-Special mix) / ('B'side).

Jan 86. (d7") *(GLOW D1)* **THE HOUSE IS HAUNTED (BY THE ECHO OF YOUR LAST GOODBYE). / BROKEN BARRICADES // CARA A CARA (FACE TO FACE). / MEDLEY: (UNCHAIN MY HEART – BLACK HEART – TAKE MY HEART)** | 55 | – |
('A'-Ectoplasm mix-12"+=) *(GLOW 1-12)* – Burning boats.

May 86. (7") *(GLOW2)* **A WOMAN'S STORY. / FOR ONE MOMENT** | 41 | |
(c-ep+=)(10"pic-d-ep+=)(12"ep+=) **SOME SONGS TO TAKE TO THE TOMB EP** *(TGLOW 2-12)(GLOWY 2-10)(GLOW 2-12)* – The heel / A salty dog / The plague / The little white cloud that cried / Just good friends.

Oct 86. (7") *(GLOW 3)* **RUBY RED. / I'M SICK OF YOU TASTING OF SOMEONE ELSE** | 47 | – |
('A'-Arnacoma mix-12"+=) *(GLOW 3-12)* – Broken hearted and beautiful / Jackal jackal (Mustapha Tomb Stone Teeth).
('A'ext.dance mix-12") *(GLOW 3-13)* – ('A'instrumental).

Jan 87. (7") *(GLOW 4)* **MELANCHOLY ROSE. / GYP THE BLOOD** | 71 | |
(12"+=) *(GLOW 4-12)* – A world full of people / Black lullaby.
(d7+=) *(GLOWD 4)* – Surabaya Johnny / Pirate Jenny.

Mar 87. (lp/c/cd) *(FAITH/TFTH/CDFTH 2)* **MOTHER FIST AND HER FIVE DAUGHTERS** | 40 |
– Mother Fist / There is a bed / Saint Judy / The room below / Angel in her kiss / The hustler / Melancholy rose / Mr. Sad / The sea says / Champ / Ruby red / The river.

Mar 87. (7") *(GLOW 5)* **MOTHER FIST. / TWO SAILORS ON THE BEACH** | | – |
(12"+=) *(GLOW 5-12)* – The hustler.

Nov 87. (lp/c/cd) *(FAITH/TFTH/CDFTH 3)* **THE SINGLES 1984-1987** (compilation)
– The boy who came back / You have / Tenderness is a weakness / Stories of Johnny / Love letters / The house is haunted / A woman's story / Ruby red / Melancholy rose / Mother Fist.

—— He was now backed by LA MAGIA. (aka HOGAN, HUMPHRIES + McGEE)

			Parlophone	Capitol

Aug 88. (7"/7"box) *(R/RX 6186) <44240>* **TEARS RUN RINGS. / EVERYTHING I WANTED LOVE TO BE** | 26 | 67 Jan89
(12"+=/cd-s+=) *(12R/CDR 6186)* – ('A'extended).
('A'-Justin Strauss mix-12"+=) *(12RX 6186)* – ('A'-La Magia dance mix).

Sep 88. (cd/c/lp) *(CD/TC/+/PCS 7324) <91042>* **THE STARS WE ARE** | 41 | Jan89
– The stars we are / These my dreams are true / Bitter sweet / Only the moment / Your kisses burn / Tears run rings / Something's gotten hold of my heart / The sensualist / She took my soul in Istanbul. *(c+=/cd+=)* – The frost comes tomorrow / Kept boy.

Oct 88. (7"/7"g-f/7"clear) *(R/RG/RC 6194)* **BITTER SWEET. / KING OF THE FOOLS** | 40 | – |
(12"+=/12"g-f+=/12"etched+=/'A'-Big Beat mix-12"+=/cd-s+=) *(12R/12RG/12RS/12RX/CDR 6194)* – Tears run rings (Justin Strauss remix).

Jan 89. (7"/7"box; by MARC ALMOND & GENE PITNEY) *(R/RX 6201)* **SOMETHING'S GOTTEN HOLD OF MY HEART. / ('A'-solo version)** | 1 | |
(12"+=/12"etched+=) *(12R/12RS/CDR 6201)* – The frost comes tomorrow.

Mar 89. (7"/7"clear) *(R 6210)* **ONLY THE MOMENT. / REAL EVIL** | 47 | – |
(cd-s+=) *(CDR 6210)* – She took my soul in Istanbul (The Blue Mosque mix).
(12"/12"etched) *(12R/+S 6210)* – ('A'-All The Time In The World mix) / She took my soul in Istanbul (The Blue Mosque mix).

Feb 90. (7"/ext-7"square-pic-d/ext-c-s) *(R/RPD/TCR 6229)* **A LOVER SPURNED. / EXOTICA ROSE** | 29 | – |
(12"+=/cd-s+=) *(12R/CDR 6229)* – ('A'version).

May 90. (c-s/7") *(TC+/R 6252)* **THE DESPERATE HOURS. / THE GAMBLER** | 45 | – |
(12"+=/12"clear-pic-d+=/cd-s+=) *(12R/12RPD/CDR 6252)* – ('A'extended Flamenco mix).

Jun 90. (cd/c/lp) *(CD/TC/+/PCS 7344) <94404>* **ENCHANTED** | 52 | |
– Madame de la luna / Waifs and strays / The desperate hours / Toreador in the rain / Widow weeds / A lover spurned / Death's diary / Sea still sings / Carnival of life / Orpheus in red velvet.

Oct 90. (c-s/7") *(TC+/R 6263)* **WAIFS AND STRAYS. / OLD JACK'S CHARM** | | |
(12") *(12R 6263)* – (2 'A'-Grid mixes).
(cd-s+=) *(CDR 6263)* – City of nights.

—— Wrote w/ **DAVE BALL + NORRIS** (The GRID)

			W.E.A.	Sire

Sep 91. (7"/c-s) *(YZ 610/+C)* **JACKY. / DEEP NIGHT** | 17 | |
(12"+=) *(YZ 610T)* – ('A'-Alpine dub).
(cd-s+=) *(YZ 610CD)* – A love outgrown.

Oct 91. (cd/c/lp) *(9031 75518-2/-4/-1) <26764>* **TENEMENT SYMPHONY** | 39 | |
– Meet me in my dream / Beautiful brutal thing / I've never seen your face / Vaudeville and burlesque / Champagne / Tenement symphony (i) Prelude, (ii) Jacky, (iii) What is love?, (iv) Trois Chansons de Bilitis – extract, (v) The days of Pearly Spencer, (vi) My hand over my heart. *(re-iss. cd Feb95; same)*

Dec 91. (7"/c-s) *(YZ 633/+C)* **MY HAND OVER MY HEART. / DEADLY SERENADE** | 33 | – |
(12"pic-d) *(YZ 633TP)* – ('A'-Grit & Glitter mix) / Money for love (2 versions).
(cd-s) *(YZ 633CD)* – (above 3 tracks) / Night and no morning.

Apr 92. (7"/c-s) *(YZ 638/+C)* **THE DAYS OF PEARLY SPENCER. / BRUISES** | 4 | – |
(cd-s+=) *(YZ 638CD)* – Dancing in a golden cage / Extract from 'Trois Chanson De Bilitis'.

—— with **DAVE CLAYTON** – keyboards, musical director / **MARTIN WATKINS** – piano /

ANDY HAMILTON – saxophone / **MICHELE DREES** – drums, perc. / **CRIS BONACCI** – guitars / **SHIRLEY LEWIS, ANNA ROSS & AILEEN McLAUGHLIN** – b.vox / **TENEMENT SYMPHONY ORCH.**

Mar 93. (7"/c-s) *(YZ 720/+C)* **WHAT MAKES A MAN A MAN (live).** / **TORCH (live)** | 60 | – |
(cd-s+=) *(YZ 720CD)* – The stars we are (live).
(cd-s) *(YZ 720CDX)* – ('A'side) / Tainted love (live) / Vision (live) / Only the moment (live).

Apr 93. (cd/c/lp) *(4509 92033-2/-4/-1) <45247>* **12 YEARS OF TEARS – LIVE AT THE ROYAL ALBERT HALL (live)** | | May93 |
– Tears run rings / Champagne / Bedsitter / Mr. Sad / There is a bed / Youth / If you go away / Jacky / Desperate hours / Waifs and strays / Something's gotten hold of my heart / What makes a man a man / Tainted love / Say hello wave goodbye.

| | Some Bizzare | not iss. |

Sep 93. (cd/c/lp) *(SBZ CD/MC/LP 10)* **ABSINTHE: THE FRENCH ALBUM** | | – |
– Undress me / Abel and Cain / Lost Paradise / Secret child / Rue Des Blancs Manteaux / The slave / Remorse of the dead / Incestuous love / A man / My little lovers / In your bed / Yesterday when I was young. *<US cd-iss. 1996 on 'Thirsty Ear'; 57026>*

| | Mercury | Mercury |

Apr 95. (c-s) *(MERMC 431)* **ADORED AND EXPLORED** / **('A'-original)** | 25 | – |
(cd-s) *(MERCD 431)* – ('A'side) / The user / Loveless world / ('A'-Andy Meecham's Slow Fat dub).
(cd-s) *(MERDD 431)* – ('A'side) / ('A'-Beatmasters 12 take 1) / ('A'-Andy Meecham club mix) / ('A'-X-Press 2 extre,me excess mix).

Jul 95. (c-s) *(MERMC 437)* **THE IDOL** / **('A'-Tin Tin Out mix)** | 44 | – |
(cd-s+=) *(MERDD 437)* – ('A'-Idolized mix) / ('A'-Teenage dream mix).
(cd-s) *(MERCD 437)* – ('A'-part 1) / Law of the night / Adored and explored (live) / Bedsitter (live).

Nov 95. (c-s) *(MERMC 450)* **CHILD STAR** / **EDGE OF HEARTBREAK** | 41 | – |
(cd-ep+=) **CHILD STAR EP** *(MERCD 450)* – Christmas in Vegas / My guardian angel.
(cd-ep) **CHILD STAR EP** *(MERDD 450)* – ('A'side) / We need jealousy (live) / The idol (live) / Out there (live).

Feb 96. (c-s) *(MERMC 444)* **OUT THERE** / **BRILLIANT CREATURES** | | – |
(cd-s+=) *(MERCD 444)* – Lie (Beatmasters mix) / Lie.
(12") *(MERX 444)* – ('A'mixes:- Tony De Vite parts 1 & 2 / Non Eric / House Of Usher / Valerie Singleton).

Feb 96. (cd/c) *(528 659-2/-4)* **FANTASTIC STAR** | 54 | – |
– Caged / Out there / We need jealousy / Idol (parts 1 & 2) / All gods fall / Baby night eyes / Adored and explored / Child star / Looking for love (in all the wrong places) / Addicted / Edge of heartbreak / Love to die for / Betrayed / On the prowl / Come in sweet assassin / Brilliant creatures / Shining brightly. *(cd re-iss. Sep97; same)*

—— In Dec'96, MARC was credited on PJ PROBY minor hit single 'YESTERDAY HAS GONE' on 'EMI Premier' *(PRESTC/CDPRES/CDPRESX 13)*.

| | Echo | Instinct |

Nov 98. (7"pic-d) *(ECS 58)* **BLACK KISS.** / **('A'-DJ mix)** | | – |
(cd-s) *(ECSCD 58)* – ('A'side) / Satan's child / ('A'live).

| | Blue Star | Incense |

Mar 99. (cd-s) *(BSRS 001)* **TRAGEDY (TAKE A LOOK AND SEE)** / **BEAUTIFUL LOSERS** / **BLACK KISS (hard vocal mix)** | | – |

Apr 99. (cd) *(BSRCD 01) <INS 435-2>* **OPEN ALL NIGHT** | | Aug99 |
– Night & dark / Bedroom shine / Tragedy (take a look and see) / Black kiss / Almost diamonds / Scarlet bedroom / My love / Heart in velvet / Open all night / Threat of love / Bad people kiss / Sleepwalker / Midnight soul. *<US+=> – Satan's child / Lonely go-go dancer / Beautiful losers.*

Nov 99. (cd-s) *(BRSCD 002)* **MY LOVE** / **THREAT OF LOVE** / **ONE BIG SOUL** | | |

– compilations, etc. –

Dec 89. (lp/c/cd) *Some Bizzare; (BREL/+C/CD 001)* **JACQUES** (most rec.1986) | | – |
– The Devil (okay) / If you need / The lockman / We must look / Alone / I'm coming / Litany for a return / If you go away / The town fell asleep / The bulls / (Never to be) Next / My death.
(above a tribute to Belgian singer, JACQUES BREL)

Sep 92. (cd/c) *Virgin; (CD/TC VM 9010)* **A VIRGIN'S TALE VOL.1 (1985-1988)** | | – |

Sep 92. (cd/c) *Virgin; (CD/TC VM 9011)* **A VIRGIN'S TALE VOL.2 (1988-1991)** | | – |
(re-iss. both above Nov92 as d-cd; DCDVM 901 0/1) (both re-iss. Nov97; SBZ 032/033 CD)

Aug 95. (d-cd) *E.M.I.; (CDMATBOX 1)* **TREASURE BOX** | | – |

Sep 97. (cd; MARC ALMOND & FOETUS) *Some Bizzare; (SBZ 022CD)* **VIOLENT SILENCE** | | – |

Nov 97. (cd; MARC ALMOND & FOETUS) *Some Bizzare; (SBZ 034CD)* **FLESH VOLCANO / SLUT** | | – |

Nov 98. (cd-enhanced) *Some Bizzare; (SBZ 037)* **LIVE IN CONCERT AT THE ASTORIA (with LA MAGIA)** | | – |

ALONE AGAIN OR (see under ⇒ SHAMEN)

ALT (see under ⇒ CROWDED HOUSE)

ALTERED IMAGES   (dig out; Great Alt & Indie . . .)

ALTERNATIVE TV / Mark PERRY / etc
(dig out; Great Alt & Indie . . .)

AMBOY DUKES (see under ⇒ NUGENT, Ted)

AMBROSE SLADE (see under ⇒ SLADE)

AMERICA

Formed: By sons of American servicemen DAN PEEK, GERRY BECKLEY and DEWEY BUNNELL based in London, England . . . 1969. Signing to 'Warner Brothers', their debut release, 'A HORSE WITH NO NAME', became a massive hit on both sides of the Atlantic. Very much in the mould of CROSBY, STILLS & NASH, they delivered vocal harmonies reminiscent of NEIL YOUNG's more folk-orientated meanderings. The singles success precipitated a chart-topping album and a string of Top 10 singles and worldwide concert sell-outs. Subsequent albums, 'HOMECOMING' (1972), 'HOLIDAY' (1974), 'HEARTS' (1975) and a compilation all made the US Top 10; only the more experimental 'HAT TRICK' in '73 failed to make the commercial grade. They also scored another US No.1 in summer '75 with the GEORGE MARTIN-produced 'SISTER GOLDEN HAIR' single. Never the greatest market for country-rock, Britain was ironically one of the few European territories where AMERICA failed to make an impact, at least after the initial success of their first two albums. The latter half of the 70's saw their dominance diminishing, the 'HARBOR' (1977) set just missing the US Top 20, while PEEK's departure (for born-again Christian-type activities) saw the duo of BECKLEY and BUNNELL taking a more commercial direction after signing to 'Capitol'. They persevered through a largely barren early 80's period, managing only one significant US hit with the RUSS BALLARD-penned 'YOU CAN DO MAGIC' in '82. Although a split finally came in 1985, the original trio reunited in 1993 to support The BEACH BOYS, subsequently recording a comeback album, 'HOURGLASS', in '94.

Album rating: AMERICA (*6) / HOMECOMING (*5) / HAT TRICK (*4) / HOLIDAY (*5) / HEARTS (*5) / HISTORY: GREATEST HITS compilation (*6) / HIDEAWAY (*5) / HARBOR (*4) / AMERICA – LIVE (*2) / SILENT LETTER (*3) / ALIBI (*3) / VIEW FROM THE GROUND (*3) / YOUR MOVE (*3) / PERSPECTIVE (*3) / IN CONCERT (*3) / THE LAST UNICORN (*1) / HOURGLASS (*3) / THE BEST OF AMERICA – The Centenary Collection (*5)

DAN PEEK (b. 1 Nov'50, Panama City, Florida) – vocals, guitar / **GERRY BECKLEY** (b.12 Sep'52, Fort Worth, Texas) – vocals, guitar / **DEWEY BUNNELL** (b.19 Jan'52, Yorkshire, England) – vocals, guitar with guest drummer and bassmen.

	Warners	Warners

Nov 71. (7") *(K 16128) <7555>* **A HORSE WITH NO NAME.** / **EVERYONE: MEET IS FROM CALIFORNIA** | 3 | 1 Jan72 |

Jan 72. (lp/c) *(K/K4 46093) <2576>* **AMERICA – HORSE WITH NO NAME** | 14 | 1 |
– A horse with no name / Here / Riverside / Sandman / Three roses / Children / I need you / Rainy day / Never found the time / Clarice / Donkey jaw / Pigeon song. *(cd-iss. Jan93 on 'WEA'; 7599 27257-2)*

Aug 72. (7") *(K 16178) <7580>* **I NEED YOU.** / **RIVERSIDE** | | 9 May72 |

Nov 72. (7") *(K 16219) <7641>* **VENTURA HIGHWAY.** / **SATURN NIGHTS** | 43 | 8 Oct72 |

Dec 72. (lp/c) *(K/K4 46180) <2655>* **HOMECOMING** | 21 | 9 Nov72 |
– Ventura highway / To each his own / Don't cross the river / Moon song / Only in your heart / Till the sun comes up again / Cornwall blank / Head & heart / California revisited / Saturn nights. *(cd-iss. Mar95;)*

Jan 73. (7") *<7670>* **DON'T CROSS THE RIVER.** / **TO EACH HIS OWN** | – | 35 |

Apr 73. (7") *(K 16259)* **DON'T CROSS THE RIVER.** / **TILL THE SUN COMES UP AGAIN** | | – |

Apr 73. (7") *<7694>* **ONLY IN YOUR HEART.** / **MOON SONG** | – | 62 |

Aug 73. (7") *(K 16302) <7725>* **MUSKRAT LOVE.** / **CORNWALL BLANK** | | 67 |

Nov 73. (lp/c) *(K/K4 56016) <2728>* **HAT TRICK** | 41 | 28 |
– Muskrat love / Wind wave / She's gonna let you down / Rainbow song / Submarine ladies / It's life / Hat trick / Molten love / Green monkey / Willow tree lullaby / Goodbye.

Nov 73. (7") *<7760>* **RAINBOW SONG.** / **WILLOW TREE LULLABY** | – | |

Jan 74. (7") *<7785>* **GREEN MONKEY.** / **SHE'S GONNA LET YOU DOWN** | – | |

Feb 74. (7") *(K 16348)* **GREEN MONKEY.** / **RAINBOW SONG** | | – |

Jul 74. (lp/c) *(K/K4 56045) <2808>* **HOLIDAY** | | 3 |
– Miniature / Tin man / Another try / Lonely people / Glad to see you / Mad dog / Hollywood / Baby it's up to you / You / Old man Took / What does it matter / In the country.

Apr 74. (7") *(K 16419)* **TIN MAN.** / **MAD DOG** | | – |

Aug 74. (7") *<7839>* **TIN MAN.** / **IN THE COUNTRY** | – | 4 |

Dec 74. (7") *<8048>* **LONELY PEOPLE.** / **MAD DOG** | – | 5 |

Apr 75. (7") *(K 16539)* **LONELY PEOPLE.** / **IN THE COUNTRY** | | 4 |

Apr 75. (lp/c) *(K/K4 56115) <2852>* **HEARTS** | | 4 |
– Daisy Jane / Half a man / Midnight / Bell tree / Old Virginia / People in the valley / Company / Woman tonight / Story of a teenager / Sister golden hair / Tomorrow / Seasons. *(cd-iss. Mar95 on 'WEA'; 9362 45986-2)*

Jun 75. (7") *(K 16547) <8086>* **SISTER GOLDEN HAIR.** / **MIDNIGHT** | | 1 Mar75 |

Jul 75. (7") *<8118>* **DAISY JANE.** / **TOMORROW** | – | 20 |

Aug 75. (7") *(K 16597)* **DAISY JANE.** / **WOMAN TONIGHT** | | |

Nov 75. (7") *<8157>* **WOMAN TONIGHT.** / **BELL TREE** | – | 44 |

Jan 76. (lp/c) *(K/K4 56169) <2894>* **HISTORY – AMERICA'S GREATEST HITS** (compilation) | 60 | 3 Nov75 |
– A horse with no name / I need you / Sandman / Ventura highway / Don't cross the river / Only in your heart / Muskrat love / Tin man / Lonely people / Sister golden hair / Daisy Jane / Woman tonight. *(cd-iss. Jan87; 256 169)*

Apr 76. (lp/c) *(K/K4 56230) <2932>* **HIDEAWAY** | | 11 |
– Lovely night / Amber cascades / Don't let it get you down / Watership Down / She's beside you / Hideaway (part 1) / She's a liar / Letter / Today's the day / Jet boy blue / Who loves you / Hideaway (part 2).

May 76. (7") <8212> **TODAY'S THE DAY. / HIDEAWAY (part 2)**	–	23
Aug 76. (7") <8238> **AMBER CASCADES. / WHO LOVES YOU**	–	75
Aug 76. (7") (K 16774) **TODAY'S THE DAY. / AMBER CASCADES**	–	–
Nov 76. (7") <8285> **SHE'S A LIAR. / SHE'S BESIDE YOU**	–	–
Feb 77. (7") <8373> **DOWN TO THE WATER. / GOD OF THE SUN**	–	–
Mar 77. (lp/c) (K/K4 56351) <3017> **HARBOR**		21

– God of the Sun / Sergeant Darkness / Sarah / These brown eyes / Don't you cry / Are you there / Monster / Down to the water / Hurricane / She's gone / Slow down / Political poachers.

Apr 77. (7") (K 16931) **SLOW DOWN. / SARAH**	–	
Jun 77. (7") <8397> **DON'T CRY BABY. / MONSTER**	–	
Jan 78. (lp/c) (K/K4 56434) <3136> **AMERICA/LIVE** (live at Greek Theater, LA)		Dec77

– Tin man / Muskrat love / I need you / Old man Took / Daisy Jane / Company / Hollywood / Sergeant Darkness / Amber cascades / To each his own / Another try / Ventura highway / Sister golden hair / A horse with no name. (cd-iss. Jan96 on 'WEA'; 7599 26690-2)

—— Now a duo when DAN PEEK went solo (released an album and a handful of 45's) and also a became Christian.

	not iss.	American Int.
1978. (7") <5001> **DON'T FORGET ABOUT ME. / DON'T MAKE ME OVER**	–	
Mar 79. (7") <700> **CALIFORNIA DREAMIN'. / SEE IT MY WAY (BY FAR)**	–	56

	Capitol	Capitol
Jul 79. (lp/c) <(EST/TC-EST 11950)> **THE SILENT LETTER**		

– Tall treasures / No fortune / 1960 / All night / Only game in town / Foolin' / And forever / One morning / All around / All my life / High in the city. (re-iss. Nov83 on 'Fame' lp/c; FA/TC-FA 413078-1/-4) (cd-iss. Nov98 on 'One Way'; 72438 19358-28) (cd re-iss. Jun99 on 'Magic'; 520116-2)

Aug 79. (7") (CL 16094) <4752> **ONLY GAME IN TOWN. / HIGH IN THE CITY**		
Oct 79. (7") (CL 16109) <4777> **ALL MY LIFE. / ONE MORNING**		
Dec 79. (7") <4915> **CATCH THAT TRAIN. / HE COULD HAVE BEEN THE ONE**	–	
Nov 80. (7") <4950> **ONE IN A MILLION. / HANGOVER**	–	
Nov 80. (lp/c) <(EST/TC-EST 12098)> **ALIBI**		Sep80

– Survival / Might be your love / Catch that train / You could've been the one / I don't believe in miracles / I do believe in you / Right back to me / Coast-line / Valentine / One in a million. (cd-iss. Mar98 on 'Magic'; 17657-2) (cd re-iss. Jun99 on 'Magic'; 520119-2)

Oct 82. (7") (CL 264) <5142> **YOU CAN DO MAGIC. / EVEN THE SCORE**	59	8 Jul82
Nov 82. (lp/c) <(EST/TC-EST 12209)> **VIEW FROM THE GROUND**		41 Aug82

– You can do magic / Never be lonely / Your girl / Inspector Mills / Love on the vine / Desperate love / Right before your eyes / Jody / Sometimes lovers / Even the score. (cd-iss. Apr95 on 'Connoisseur'; NSPCD 509) (cd re-iss. Jun99 on 'Magic'; 520115-2)

Nov 82. (7") <5177> **RIGHT BEFORE YOUR EYES. / INSPECTOR MILLS**	–	45
Jan 83. (7") (CL 274) **JODY. / INSPECTOR MILLS**	–	–

—— guest **RUSS BALLARD** – keyboards, etc. (ex-ARGENT, solo artist)

Jul 83. (7") (CL 301) <5236> **THE BORDER. / SOMETIMES LOVERS**		33 Jun83
Jul 83. (lp/c) <(EST/TC-EST 12277)> **YOUR MOVE**		81

– My kinda woman / She's a runaway / Cast the spirit / Love's worn out again / The border / Your move / Honey / My dear / Tonight is for dreamers / Don't let me be lonely / Someday woman. (cd-iss. Mar98 on 'Magic'; 17658-2) (cd re-iss. Jun99 on 'Magic'; 520114-2)

Oct 83. (7") <5275> **CAST THE SPIRIT. / MY DEAR**	–	
Nov 84. (lp) (240216-1) <12370> **PERSPECTIVE**		

– We got all night / See how the love goes / (Can't fall asleep to a) Lullaby / Special girl / 5th Avenue / (It's like you) Never left at all / Stereo / Lady with a bluebird / Cinderela / Unconditional love / Fallin' off the world. (cd-iss. Oct97 on 'Magic'; 17659-2) (cd re-iss. Jun99 on 'Magic'; 520118-2)

Nov 84. (7") <5398> **SPECIAL GIRL. / UNCONDITIONAL LOVE**	–	
Feb 85. (7") <5430> **(CAN'T FALL ASLEEP TO A) LULLABY. / FALLIN' OFF THE WORLD**	–	

—— with **LEACOX / MICHAEL WOODS** – guitar, vocals / **BRAD PALMER** – bass, vocals

1985. (lp) (064-240385-1) **AMERICA IN CONCERT** (live)	–	– German

– Tin man / I need you / The border / Sister golden hair / Company / You can do magic / Ventura highway / Daisy Jane / A horse with no name / Survival. (UK cd-iss. Oct96 on 'EMI Gold'; CDGOLD 1072)

—— split later in 1985 and then in '88, although the original trio re-formed in 1993 to support The BEACH BOYS

	Virgin	not iss.
1988. (cd) (610 388 222) **THE LAST UNICORN**	–	– German

	American Gramaphon	American Gramaphone
Jun 94. (c/cd) <(AGC/+D 494)> **HOURGLASS**		

– Young moon / Hope / Sleeper train / Mirror to mirror / Garden of peace / Call of the world / Whole wide world / Close to the wind / Greenhouse / Ports-of-call / Everyone I meet is from California / You can do magic.

	In Akustik	In Akustik
Nov 98. (cd) (90004-2) **HUMAN NATURE**		

– From a moving train / Wednesday morning / Town and country / Moment to moment / Hidden talent / The wheels are turning / World alone / Overwhelming world suite: Overwhelming world – Come back – Barstow / Pages / Hot town / Whispering / Oloololo.

– compilations, others, etc. –

1974. (7"ep) Warners; (K 16408) **A HORSE WITH NO NAME / SANDMAN. / VENTURA HIGHWAY / RIVERSIDE**	–	–
Jul 81. (7") Warners; (K 17814) **A HORSE WITH NO NAME. / VENTURA HIGHWAY**	–	–

(re-iss. Sep85 on 'Old Gold'; OG 9525)

Sep 91. (cd/c/lp) Rhino; **ENCORE: MORE GREATEST HITS**	–	–
Mar 96. (cd) Disky; (DC 86435-2) **YOU CAN DO MAGIC**	–	–

Feb 97. (cd) E.M.I.; (CTMCD 307) **THE BEST OF AMERICA (The Centenary Collection)**		–

– You can do magic / The border / The last unicorn / All my life / Survival / Tall treasures / One morning / Honey / My dear / One in a million / Right before your eyes / We got all night / Lady with a bluebird / Only game in town / Ventura highway / Daisy Jane / I need you / Tin man / Sister golden hair / A horse with no name.

Jul 98. (cd) King Biscuit; (KBFHCD 012) **KING BISCUIT PRESENTS . . .**		

AMERICAN MUSIC CLUB

Formed: Burbank, California, USA . . . 1983 by MARK EITZEL, who had set up home in San Francisco after his Columbus, Ohio band The NAKED SKINNIES broke up in '82; they released one US-only single, 'ALL MY LIFE' / 'THIS IS THE BEAUTIFUL NIGHT' for 'Naked House'; (103457). With a line-up of MARK 'VUDI' PANKLER, DAN PEARSON, BRAD JOHNSON and MATT NORELLI, the AMERICAN MUSIC CLUB cut a debut album, 'RESTLESS STRANGER', for the small 'Grifter' label in 1985, before signing to 'Zippo' for the 'THE ENGINE' (1987). Regularly cited as one of the most criminally undervalued songwriters in the US, EITZEL has captured many a critics hear with his neon-lit meditations on the tragic futility of human existence and the fleeting consolation of romantic love. Apart from a cult fanbase, however, AMC's appeal never translated to a wider audience, even after the band were picked up by 'Virgin' in the early 90's. By this point, the group had a clutch of austere, country-tinged classics under their belt, namely 'CALIFORNIA', 'UNITED KINGDOM' (1989) and 'EVERCLEAR' (1991), the latter set especially haunting in spite of its more accessible approach. EITZEL's wracked outpourings were often shot through with a kind of outraged desperation, the 'RISE' single, a poignant tribute to a friend who died of AIDS. Also featuring suck bleakly beautiful material as 'SICK OF FOOD', the album saw EITZEL named as Rolling Stone magazine's songwriter of the year in 1991. The acclaim didn't sit particularly well with the AMC frontman. EITZEL, perhaps in response, accentuated the self-mocking tone of his work on the major label debut, 'MERCURY' (1993). Critically acclaimed once again, the album failed to sell, although it did almost scrape into the UK Top 40. It was the same story with 'SAN FRANCISCO' (1994). Parting company with 'Virgin', the band also saw fit to part company with each other; at least they'd given it their best shot. EITZEL remained with the label for a further solo album, '60 WATT SILVER LINING' (1996), another critical success seemingly doomed to obscurity. • Covered: CALIFORNIA DREAMIN' (Mamas & The Papas). EITZEL covered THERE IS NO EASY WAY DOWN (Carole King). • Trivia: EITZEL also moonlighted with The TOILING MIDGETS (a 5-piece also featuring early 90's AMC newcomer TIM MOONEY; he had always been part of the early 80's combo). They released an album, 'SON' (1993), before signing to 'Reprise' the same year.

Album rating: THE RESTLESS STRANGER (*5) / ENGINE (*6) / CALIFORNIA (*7) / UNITED KINGDOM (*7) / EVERCLEAR (*8) / MERCURY (*7) / SAN FRANCISCO (*6) / Mark Eitzel: SONGS OF LOVE: LIVE AT THE BORDERLINE – 1/19/91 (6) / 60 WATT SILVER LINING (*6)

MARK EITZEL (b.30 Jan'59, Walnut Creek, Calif.) – vocals, guitar, keyboards / **MARK "VUDI" PANKLER** (b.22 Sep'52, Chicago, Illinois) – guitar, accordion, bass / **DAN PEARSON** (b.31 May'59, Walnut Creek) – bass, guitar, dulcimer, vocals, etc. / **BRAD JOHNSON** – keyboards / **MATT NORELLI** – drums

	not iss.	Grifter
Jan 86. (lp) **THE RESTLESS STRANGER**	–	

– $1,000,000 song / Away down my street / Yvonne gets dumped / Ms. Lucky / Point of desire / Goodbye reprise #54 / Tell yourself / When your love is gone / Heavenly smile / Broken glass / Hold on to your love.

—— **TOM MALLON** – guitar, drums, vocals / **DAVE SCHEFF** – drums repl. JOHNSON + NORELLI

	Zippo	Zippo
Oct 87. (lp/cd) (ZONG/+CD 020) **ENGINE**		

– Big night / Outside this bar / At my mercy / Gary's song / Nightwatchman / Lloyd / Electric light / Mom's TV / Art of love / Asleep / This year.

—— now without SCHEFF

	Demon	Zippo
Oct 88. (lp/cd) (FIEND/+CD 134) **CALIFORNIA**		

– Firefly / Somewhere / Laughing stock / Lonely / Pale skinny girl / Blue and grey shirt / Bad liquor / Now you're defeated / Jenny / Western sky / Highway 5 / Last harbor. (cd re-iss. Apr93; FMCD 1)

—— **MIKE SIMMS** – drums; repl. MALLON

Oct 89. (lp/cd) (FIEND/+CD 151) **UNITED KINGDOM**		

– Here they roll down / Dreamers of the dream / Never mind / United kingdom / Dream is gone / Heaven of your hands / Kathleen / The hula maiden / Animal pen. (cd+=) – California (album). (cd re-iss. Apr93; FMCD 2)

—— added **BRUCE KAPHAN** (b. 7 Jan'55, San Francisco) – pedal steel guitar, keyboards, bass, producer (now full-time)

	Alias	Alias
Oct 91. (lp/c/cd) <(A 015/+C/D)> **EVERCLEAR**		

– Why won't you stay / Rise / Miracle on 8th Street / Ex-girlfriend / Crabwalk / The confidential agent / Sick of food / The dead part of you / Royal cafe / What the pillar of salt held up / Jesus' hands.

Nov 91. (cd-s) (A 014D) **RISE /**		

—— **TIM MOONEY** (b. 6 Oct'58, Las Vegas, Nevada) – drums (of TOILING MIDGETS) repl. SIMMS

	Virgin	Reprise
Mar 93. (cd/c/lp) (CD/TC+/V 2708) **MERCURY**	41	

– Gratitude walks / If I had a hammer / Challenger / I've been a mess / Hollywood 4-5-92 / What Godzilla said to God when his name wasn't found in the book of life /

Keep me around / Dallas, airports, bodybags / Apology for an accident / Over and done / Johnny Mathis' feet / The hopes and dreams of Heaven's 10,000 whores / More hopes and dreams / Will you find me?

Apr 93. (c-s) *(VSC 1445)* **JOHNNY MATHIS' FEET / WILL YOU FIND ME / THE HOPES AND DREAMS OF HEAVEN'S 10,000** `58` ☐
(cd-s+=) *(VSCDX 1445)* – The amylnitrate dream of Pat Robertson.
(cd-s) *(VSCDT 1445)* – ('A'side) / What Godzilla said to God when his name wasn't found in the book of life / Dallas, airports, bodybags (demo).

Jun 93. (c-ep) *(VSC 1464)* **KEEP ME AROUND / CHALLENGER / IN MY ROLE AS THE MOST HATED SINGER IN THE LOCAL UNDERGROUND MUSIC SCENE / MEMO FROM AQUATIC PARK** ☐ ☐
(cd-ep+=) *(VSCDG 1464)* – (no 2nd track) / Walking tune.

Aug 94. (7"/c-s) *(VS/+C 1512)* **WISH THE WORLD AWAY. / I JUST TOOK TWO SLEEPING PILLS AND NOW I'M LIKE A BRIDEGROOM** `46` ☐
(cd-s+=) *(VSCDT 1512)* – The revolving door (demo).
(cd-s) *(VSCDX 1512)* – ('A'side) / The President's test for physical fitness / Cape Canaveral.

Sep 94. (cd/c/lp) *(CD/TC+/V 2752)* **SAN FRANCISCO** `72` ☐
– Fearless / It's your birthday / Can you help me / Love doesn't belong to anyone * / Wish the world away / How many six packs to screw in a light? / Cape Canaverai * / Hello Amsterdam / The revolving door / In the shadow of the valley * / What holds the world together / I broke my promise / The thorn in my side is gone / I'll be gone / Fearless (reprise) * / I just took my two sleeping pills and now I'm like a bridegroom. *(cd+=/c+= *)*

Feb 95. (7"/c-s) *(VS/+C 1523)* **CAN YOU HELP ME. / THE THORN IN MY SIDE IS GONE** ☐ ☐
(cd-s+=) *(VSCDT 1523)* – California dreamin' (alt.version).

MARK EITZEL

		Demon	Matador

Apr 91. (lp/cd) *(FIEND/+CD 213)* **SONGS OF LOVE: LIVE AT THE BORDERLINE 1/19/91 (live)** ☐ –
– Firefly / Chanel No.5 / Western sky / Blue and grey shirt / Gary's song / Outside this bar / Room above the club / Last harbour / Kathleen / Crabwalk / Jenny / Take courage / Nothing can bring me down. *(cd re-iss. Nov97 on 'Diablo'; DIAB 838) (lp re-iss. Aug98 on 'Fruit Tree'; FRUITTREE 801)*

Jul 92. (7") *<OLE 016>* **TAKE COURAGE. /** – –

		Virgin	Warners

Mar 96. (cd/c/lp) *(CD/TC+/V 2798)* **60 WATT SILVER LINING** ☐ ☐
– There is no way down / Sacred heart / Always turn away / Saved / Cleopatra Jones / When my plane finally goes down / Mission rock / Wild sea / Aspirin / Some bartenders have the gift of pardon / Southend on sea / Everything is beautiful.

		Warners	Warners

Jun 97. (cd) *<(9362 46602-2)>* **WEST** ☐ May96
– If you have to ask / Free of harm / Helium / Stunned and frozen / Then it really happens / In your life / Lower Eastside tourist / Three inches of wall / Move myself ahead / Old photographs / Fresh screwdriver / Live or die.

		Matador	Matador

Feb 98. (cd/lp) *<(OLE 179-2/-1)>* **CAUGHT IN A TRAP AND I CAN'T BACK OUT** ☐ Jan98
– Are you the trash / Xmas lights spin / Auctioneer's song / White rosary / If I had a gun / Goodbye / Queen of no one / Cold light of day / Go away / Atico 18 / Sun smog seahorse.

TOILING MIDGETS

TIM MOONEY – drums / **RICKY WILLIAMS** – vocals (ex-SLEEPERS) / **CRAIG GRAY** – guitar (ex-NEGATIVE TREND) /
PAUL HOOD – guitar / with **JONATHAN HENDRICKSON** – bass

		not iss.	Rough Trade

Apr 82. (lp) *<ROUGHUS 11>* **SEA OF UNREST** – ☐
– Destiny / Trauma girl / Late show / Microage / Wishful thinking / All the girls cry / DJMC / Shooting gallery / Again / Big surprise / Sea of unrest. *<cd-iss. Sep94 on 'Fist Puppet'; 16>*

—— **KARL J GOLDRING** – bass; repl. HENDRICKSON

—— **MARK EITZEL** – guitar; repl. WILLIAMS

		Hut	Matador

Oct 91. (7") *<OLE 037>* **MR. FOSTER. /** – ☐
Jan 93. (12"ep/cd-ep) *(HUT 25 T/CD)* **FAUX PONY. / GOLDEN FROG / MR. FOSTER'S SHOES** ☐ ☐

—— **LISA DAVIS** – bass; repl. KARL

Jan 93. (cd/lp) *(CDHUT/HUTLP 6) <OLE 030>* **SON** ☐ Jul92
– Faux pony / Fabric / Slaughter on Sumner St. / Mr. Foster's shoes / Process words / Clinging fire – Clams / Third chair / Listen / Chains.

—— signed to 'Reprise', although commitments elsewhere led to break-up

AMON DUUL   (dig out; Great Psychedelic . . .)

AMON DUUL II

Formed: Munich, Germany . . . Autumn 1968 from the original AMON DUUL commune. While the aforesaid outfit remained as a separate musical entity, CHRIS KARRER set-up AMON DUUL II with JOHANNES WEINZIERL, FALK-ULRICH ROGNER, RENATE KNAUP, CHRISTIAN 'SHRAT' THIERFELD an DIETER SERFAS. Securing a deal with 'Liberty', they released their first album in 1969, 'PHALLUS DEI' (God's Penis), which introduced a further two members, PETER LEOPOLD (from AMON DUUL I) and Englishman DAVE ANDERSON. Avant-garde space-rock in the mould of PINK FLOYD and GRATEFUL DEAD, the album brought home-produced, psychedelic improvisation to the German market. 'YETI', the follow-up in

1970, was a much more structured double-set featuring some excellent acid-rock numbers including the weird but wonderful single 'ARCHANGEL'S THUNDERBIRD'. Their next effort, 'DANCE OF THE LEMMINGS' (1971), concentrated more on lengthy, segued collages, including the outrageously brilliant, 'SYNTELMAN'S MARCH OF THE ROARING SEVENTIES'. With members coming and going at their leisure, it was difficult for the band to maintain any degree of consistency and records like 'CARNIVAL IN BABYLON' (1972), 'WOLF CITY' (1972), etc, sounded uninspired in comparison to their earlier work. Even a deal with 'Atlantic' in 1974 failed to result in a return to form. The band still exist today, WEINZIERL having brought back past members KARRER, ROGNER, RENATE, LEOPOLD and MEID for Christmas concerts in 1992. • **Trivia:** AMON DUUL II members guested on releases by POPOL VUH and EMBRYO.

Album rating: PHALLUS DEI (*6) / YETI (*8) / DANCE OF THE LEMMINGS (*6) / WOLF CITY (*6) / CARNIVAL IN BABYLON (*5) / LIVE IN LONDON (*6) / VIVE LA TRANCE (*4) / HIJACK (*4) / MADE IN GERMANY (*4) / PYRAGONY X (*4) / ALMOST ALIVE (*4) / ONLY HUMAN (*4) / VORTEX (*4) / HAWK MEETS PENGUIN (*4) / NADA MOONSHINE (*4) / ANTHOLOGY compilation (*7)

JOHN WEINZIERL – lead guitar, vocals / **RENATE KNAUP-KROTENSCHWANZ** – vocals / **CHRIS KARRER** – violin, guitar, vocals / **FALK-U ROGNER** – keyboards, synthesizers / **DAVE ANDERSON** – bass / **SCHRAT** (b. CHRISTIAN THIELE) – bongos, vocals / **PETER LEOPOLD** – drums / **DIETER SERFAS** – drums and guests / **HOLGER TRULZSCH** – percussion / **CHRISTIAN BUCHARD** – vibes

		Liberty	Liberty

1969. (lp) *(LSB 83279)* **PHALLUS DEI** ☐ –
– Kanaan / Dem guten' Schonen, wahren / Luzifers ghilom / Henriette Kroten schwantz / Phallus dei. *(re-iss. Feb72 on 'Sunset'; SLS 50257) (cd-iss. Nov92 on 'Repertoire' Germany; REP 4274-WY) (cd re-iss. Apr97 & Jun98 on 'Mantra'; MANTRA 012) (cd re-iss. Jan99 on 'Repertoire'; REP 4747)*

—— now without SERFAS, but with new guests **ULRICH LEOPOLD** – bass / **RAINER BAUER** – guitar, vocals (both of other AMON DUUL)

1970. (7") *(15355)* **SOAP SHOP ROCK. / ARCHANGEL'S THUNDERBIRD** – German

1970. (7") *(15417)* **RATTLESNAKE PLUMCAKE. / BETWEEN THE EYES** – German

1971. (7") *(15468)* **LIGHT. / LEMMINGMANIA** – German

Sep 70. (7") *(LBF 15355)* **ARCANGEL'S THUNDERBIRD / BURNING SISTER** ☐ ☐

Nov 70. (d-lp) *(LSP 101)* **YETI** ☐ ☐
– Soda shop rock; (a) Burning sister / (b) Halluzination guillotine / (c) Gulp a sonata / (d) Flesh-coloured anti-aircraft alarm / She came through the chimney / Archangel's thunderbird / Cerberus / The return of Ruebezahl / Eye-shaking king / Pale gallery / Yeti (improvisation) / Yeti talks to Yogi (improvisation) / Sandoz in the rain (improvisation). *(cd-iss. Nov92 on 'Repertoire' Germany; REP 4275) (cd re-iss. Aug97 & Jun98 on 'Mantra'; MANTRA 010) (cd re-iss. Jan99 on 'Repertoire'; RR 4748)*

—— **LOTHAR MEID** – bass, vocals; repl. ANDERSON who joined HAWKWIND

—— **KARL-HEINZ HAUSMANN** – keyboards; repl. SCHRAT who formed SAMETI / added guests : **JIMMY JACKSON** – mellotron / **AL GROMER** – sitar / **HENRIETTE KROTENSCHWANZ** – vocals / **ROLF ZACHER** – vocals

		U.A.	U.A.

Jun 71. (d-lp) *(UAD 60003-4)* **DANCE OF THE LEMMINGS** (German title 'TANZ DER LEMMING') ☐ –
– Syntelman's march of the roaring seventies: (a) In the glass garden – (b) Pull down your mask – (c) Prayer to the silence – (d) Telephonecomplex / (a) Restless skylight – transistor child – (b) Dehypnotized toothpaste – (c) A short stop to the Transylvanian brain surgery / Race from here to your ears: (a) Little tornados – (b) Overheated tiara – (c) The flyweighted five – (d) Riding on a cloud – (e) Paralized Paradise – (f) H.G. Well's take off / Chamsin soundtrack; The Marilyn Monroe memorial church / Chewing gum telegram / Stumbling over melted moonlight / Toxicological whispering. *(cd-iss. Nov92 on 'Repertoire' Germany; REP 4276-WY) (cd re-iss. Sep98 on 'Mantra'; MANTRA 014) (cd re-iss. Jan99 as 'TANZ DER LEMMINGE' on 'Repertoire' REP 4749)*

—— added **D. SECUNDUS FICHELSCHER** – drums, congas

Apr 72. (lp) *(UAG 29327)* **CARNIVAL IN BABYLON** ☐ ☐
– C.I.D. in Urik / All the years round / Shimmering sands / Kronwinkl 12 / Tables are turned / Hawknose harlequin. *(cd-iss. Jun98 on 'Mantra'; MANTRA 063) (cd re-iss. Mar99 on 'Repertoire'; REP 4581)*

1972. (7") *(UA 35338)* **ALL THE YEARS ROUND. / TABLES ARE TURNED** – German

—— now w/ out HAUSMANN

Nov 72. (lp) *(UAG 29406)* **WOLF CITY** ☐ ☐
– Surrounded by the stars / Jail-house frog / Green-bubble-raincoated man / Wolf city / Wie der wind am ende einer strasse / Deutsch Nepal / Sleepwalker's timeless bridge. *(cd-iss. Apr97 & Jun98 on 'Mantra'; MANTRA 013) (cd re-iss. Feb99 on 'Repertoire'; RR 4750)*

1973. (lp) *(USP 102)* **LIVE IN LONDON (live)** ☐ ☐
– Archangels thunderbird / Eye shaking king / Soap shop rock / Improvisation / Syntelman's march of the roaring seventies: (a) Pull down your mask – (b) Prayer to the silence – (c) Telephonecomplex) / (a) Restless skylight – Transistor child – Landing in a ditch – (b) Dehypnotized toothpaste – (c) A short stop at the Transylvanian brain surgery / Race from here to your ears: (a) Little tornadoes – (b) Riding on a cloud (c) Paralized paradise. *(cd-iss. Nov98 on 'Mystic'; MYSCD 128)*

—— **ROBBY HEIBL** – bass repl. MEID (although he later returned)

1974. (lp) *(UAS 29504)* **VIVE LA TRANCE** ☐ ☐
– A morning excuse / Fly united / Jalousie / Im krater bluhn weider die baume / Mozambique (dedicated to Monika Ertt) / Apocalyptic bore / Dr. Trap / Pigman / Manana / Ladies mimikry. *(cd-iss. Jun98 on 'Mantra'; MANTRA 062) (cd re-iss. Jan99 on 'Repertoire'; RR 4752)*

1974. (7") *(UA 35466) <419>* **PIGMAN. / MOZAMBIQUE** – German

—— **ROBBY HEIBL** returned to replace MEID, KRAMPER and SECUNDUS

—— (signed to 'Nova' in Germany)

		Atlantic	Atco

1975. (lp) *(K 50136)* **HIJACK**
— I can't wait (parts 1 & 2) / Mirror / Traveller / You're not alone / Explode like a star / Da Guadeloop / Lonely woman / Liquid whisper / Archy the robot.

		-	-

1975. (7") *(6.11579)* **MIRROR. / LIQUID WHISPER**   `-`   `-` German
1975. (d-lp) *(K 50182)* **MADE IN GERMANY**   `-`   `-` German
— Dreams / Ludwig / The king's chocolate waltz / Blue grotto / 5.5.55 / Emigrant song / La krautoma / Metropolis / Loosey girls / Gala gnome / Top of the mud / Mr.Kraut's jinx.

—— **KARRER, WEINZIERL** and **LEOPOLD** were joined by **KLAUS EBART** – bass who repl. ROGNER and **STEFAN ZAUNER** – keyboards repl. KNAUP and BALDERSON

1976. (lp) *(622 890)* **PYRAGONY X**   `-`   `-` German
— Flower of the Orient / Merlin / Crystal hexagram / Lost in space / Sally the seducer / Telly vision / The only thing / Capuccino.

1977. (lp) *(623 305)* **ALMOST ALIVE**   `-`   `-` German
— One blue morning / Goodbye my love / Ain't today tomorrow's yesterday / Hallelujah / Feeling uneasy / Live in Jericho.

—— now w/out WEINZIERL

—— (signed to 'Strand' in Germany)

		Vinyl	not iss.

Jan 79. (lp) *(LV 1004)* **ONLY HUMAN**   `-`   `-`
— Another morning / Don't turn to stone / Kirk Morgan / Spaniards & spacemen / Kismet / Pharaoh / Ruby lane.

1979. (7") *(6.12459)* **DON'T TURN TO STONE. / SPANIARDS & SPACEMEN**   `-`   `-` German

—— line-up **CHRIS KARRER** / **RENATE ASCHAUER KNAUP** / **JOERG EVERS** – bass, guitar, synthesizers / **DANIEL FICHELSCHER** – drums, percussion / **FALK ROGNER** – synth / plus **JOHN WEINZIERI** – guitar / **LOTHAR MEID** – bass / **STEFAN ZAUNER** – piano, synth

		Telefunken	not iss.

1981. (lp) *(624 852)* **VORTEX**   `-`   `-` German
— Vortex / Holy west / Die 7 fetten Jahr / Wings of the wind / Mona / We are machines / Das gestern ist das heute von Morgen / Vibes in the air.

—— Broke-up but reformed in the 80's with line-up below **JOHN WEINZIERL, DAVE ANDERSON, JULIE WAREING** – vocals / **ROBERT CALVERT** – vocals / **GUY EVANS** – drums (ex-VAN DER GRAAF GENERATOR)

		Illuminated	not iss.

Jan 83. (lp) *(JAMS 024)* **HAWK MEETS PENGUIN**   `-`   `-`
— One moment of anger is two pints of blood / Meditative music from the third o before the producers pt.1 & 2. *(re-iss. as 'HAWK MEETS PENGUIN VOL.1' Dec85 on 'Demi-Monde'; DM 04)* *(cd-iss. 1992 on 'Thunderbolt'; CDTB 102)* *(cd re-iss. Apr97 on 'Spalax'; 14848)*

Jan 85. (lp) *(JAMS 27)* **MEETING WITH MEN MACHINES**   `-`   `-`
— Pioneer / Old one / Marcus lied / Song / Things aren't always what they seem / Burundi drummer's nightmare. *(re-iss. 1985 on 'Demi-Monde'; DM 006)* *(cd-iss. Mar93 on 'Thunderbolt'; CDTB 107)* *(cd re-iss. Jun97 on 'Spalax'; 14820)*

		Demi-Monde	not iss.

Jan 89. (lp) *(DMLP 1013)* **FOOL MOON**   `-`   `-`
— Fool moon / Tribe / Tik tok song / Haupmotor / Hymn for the hardcore. *(cd-iss. Nov89 on 'The CD Label'; CDTL 011)* *(cd re-iss. Jun97 on 'Spalax'; 14516)*

—— disbanded again, but re-formed for gigs late 1992 with **KARRER, WEINZIERL, ROGNER, RENATE, LEOPOLD & MEID**

		Mantra	not iss.

Jun 93. (cd) **SURROUNDED BY THE STARS / BARS**   `-`   `-`

		Mystic	not iss.

Aug 96. (cd) *(MYS 106CD)* **NADA MOONSHINE**   `-`   `-`
Aug 97. (cd) *(MYS 113CD)* **FLAWLESS**   `-`   `-`
— Nada Cairo / Surrounded by the stars / Castaneda dream / Wie der wind am ende einer strasse / Kiss ma eee / Cerberus / Speed inside my shoes / La paloma / Nada moonshine union / Dancing on fire / Jam '71 / What you gonna do / Jim hai jam UK '96.

– compilations, others –

May 75. (lp) *United Artists; (UAS 29723)* **LEMMINGMANIA**   `-`
Mar 87. (d-lp) *Raw Power; (RAWLP 032)* **ANTHOLOGY**   `-`
— Soup shock rock / Burning sister / Halluzination guillotine / Gulp a sonata / Flesh-coloured anti-aircraft alarm / Kanaan / Trap / Phallus dei / Yet (improvisation) / Wolf city / C.I.D. in Uruk / Morning excuse / Apocalyptic bone / Jailhouse frog.

Nov 92. (cd) *Windsong; (WINCD 026)* **LIVE IN CONCERT (live BBC '73)**   `-`
Jan 99. (cd) *Repertoire; (REP 4753)* **LIVE IN TOKYO (live)**   `-`

UTOPIA

WEINZIERI, MEID, KROTEN SCHWANTZ, FICHELSCHER, OLAF KUSLER (producer) / **ROGNER, KARRER**

		U.A.	U.A.

1973. (lp) *(UAG 29438)* **UTOPIA**   `-`   `-`
— What you gonna do / The Wolf-man Jack show / Alice / Las Vegas / Deutsch Nepal / Utopiat No. 1 / Nasi Goreng / Jazz kiste.

Tori AMOS

Born: MYRA ELLEN AMOS, 22 Aug '63, Newton, North Carolina, USA. Daughter of a preacher father and part-Cherokee Indian mother, she incredibly scored a scholarship to the 'Peabody Conservatory' in Baltimore at five years old (youngest ever admitee!), studying classical piano. Parting company with this illustrious establishment at the age of eleven, AMOS embarked upon her rebellious phase, playing bars and subsequently relocating to L.A. where she was discovered by early 80's sophisto-disco star, NARADA MICHAEL WALDEN. Despite recording some professional demos and releasing a one-off independently released 45, 'BALTIMORE' (1981), it would be a few

years down the line before AMOS's career really began. Reinventing herself as TORI, AMOS formed a gaudy glitz-metal band, Y KANT TORI READ, eventually signing to 'Atlantic' and releasing a dodgy eponymous album in 1988. Almost universally lambasted by the critics, TORI underwent a considerably more horrific ordeal when she was raped at gunpoint by a would-be fan after offering him a lift home (this experience was later detailed in the song, 'ME AND A GUN'). Making the transition from leather-clad frontwoman to soul searching singer-songwriter, TORI AMOS "moved along the corridor" to the 'East West' stable and released her solo debut, 'LITTLE EARTHQUAKES' (1991). Breaking initially in Britain, the album's deep subject matter and orchestrated, piano-led atmospherics were the backdrop for AMOS's eye-of-the-hurricane emotional turmoil; from heavy-lidded lullaby to howling, KATE BUSH-esque melodrama, the singer exorcised her demons in compelling fashion. Tracks such as 'SILENT ALL THESE YEARS', 'CHINA', 'WINTER' and 'CRUCIFY' (all UK hit singles in their own right) saw the album eventually scale the American charts; it has since become regarded as one of the all-time classic rock/pop records. AMOS's career trajectory was given a turbo boost in the first days of '94 with the strangely-titled 'CORNFLAKE GIRL', a Top 5 UK hit which helped propel her accompanying album, 'UNDER THE PINK' to the top of the British charts (Top 20 in America). A more probing exploration of the female psyche, the album attempted to reconcile AMOS's religious upbringing and developing identity with songs such as 'PAST THE MISSION', 'GOD' and 'PRETTY GOOD YEAR' (her second Top 10 hit in Britain). In early '96, AMOS released her most commercially successful album to date, 'BOYS FOR PELE' narrowly missing the top slot in both Britain and America despite its overtly experimental nature. Once again it was littered with classy hit singles (albeit with oblique lyrics), 'CAUGHT A LITE SNEEZE', 'TALULA' and double A-side 'HEY JUPITER' / 'PROFESSIONAL WIDOW'. The latter track (allegedly written about the death of KURT COBAIN and its controversial aftermath) was subsequently deconstructed in stunning style from its more subdued album counterpart, dance guru ARMAND VAN HELDEN possibly inspired by BT's (BRIAN TRANSEAU) impressive use/sample of TORI's voice on his Top 30 hit, 'Blue Skies'. The remix scaled the British charts in early '97, exposing AMOS's uniquely challenging work to a whole new E-poppin' audience. On the 22nd of February, 1998, she married Mark Hawley, the engineer on her last two albums, her new husband also working on a mooted fourth set, tentatively titled 'FROM THE CHOIRGIRL HOTEL'. When released that Spring, the record shifted enough units to hit the Top 10 on both sides of the Atlantic, subsequently bringing further well-deserved acclaim to this eclectic lady; Jools Holland and his TV programme 'Later With . . .' intensified her complex image with a ubiquitous piano-playing performance that would put even RICK WAKEMAN to shame. Just over a year later, she followed this with a double-set helping, 'TO VENUS AND BACK', which fused live gems with new studio work. • **Covers:** SMELLS LIKE TEEN SPIRIT (Nirvana) / RING MY BELL (Anita Ward) / ANGIE (Rolling Stones) / THANK YOU (Led Zeppelin) / LITTLE DRUMMER BOY (UK-hit 1959) / HOME ON THE RANGE + HAVE YOURSELF A MERRY LITTLE CHRISTMAS (trad.) / IF SIX WAS NINE (Jimi Hendrix Experience) / STRANGE FRUIT (Billie Holliday) / FAMOUS BLUE RAINCOAT (Leonard Cohen). • **Trivia:** TORI sang backing for AL STEWART on 'Last Days of the Century' album, plus STAN RIDGWAY's 'Mosquitos'.

Album rating: LITTLE EARTHQUAKES (*9) / UNDER THE PINK (*7) / BOYS FOR PELE (*7) / FROM THE CHOIRGIRL MOTEL (*7) / TO VENUS AND BACK (*5)

ELLEN AMOS

		not iss.	MEA

Dec 80. (7") *<MEA 5290>* **BALTIMORE. / WALKING WITH YOU**   `-`

Y KANT TORI READ

TORI AMOS – vocals, piano with group: **STEVE FARRIS** – guitar (ex-MR. MISTER) / **MATT SORUM** – drums

		not iss.	Atlantic

Jun 88. (7") *<7-89086>* **THE BIG PICTURE. / YOU GO TO MY HEAD**   `-`   `-`
Jul 88. (cd,c,lp) *<81845>* **Y KANT TORI READ**   `-`   `-`
— The big picture / God on your island / Fayth / Fire on the side / Pirates / Floating city / Heart attack at 23 / On the boundary / You go to my head / Etienne trilogy
Aug 88. (7") *<7-89021>* **COOL ON YOUR ISLAND. / HEART ATTACK AT 23**   `-`   `-`

TORI AMOS

—— with **STEVE CATON** – guitar / **WILL McGREGOR** – bass / **ERIC ROSSE** – keyboards, co-producer / **JEFF SCOTT** – bass, guitar / **PAULINHO DaCOSTA** – percussion

		East West	Atlantic

Nov 91. (7") *(YZ 618/+C)* **SILENT ALL THESE YEARS. / ME AND A GUN**   **51**   `-`
(12"ep+=)(cd-ep+=) *(YZ 618 T/CD)* – Upside down / Thoughts.
Jan 92. (cd/c/lp) *<(7567 82358-2/-4/-1)>* **LITTLE EARTHQUAKES**   **14**   **54** Dec91
— Crucify / Girl / Silent all these years / Precious things / Winter / Happy phantom / China / Leather / Mother / Tear in your hand / Me and a gun / Little earthquakes. *(lp re-iss. Jun99; same)*
Jan 92. (7"/c-s) *(A 7531/+C)* **CHINA. / SUGAR**   **51**   `-`
(12"+=/cd-s+=) *(A 7531 T/CD)* – Flying Dutchman / Humpty Dumpty.
Mar 92. (7"/c-s) *(A 7504/+C)* **WINTER. / THE POOL**   **25**   `-`
(cd-s+=) *(A 7504CD)* – Take to the sky / Sweet dreams.
(cd-s) *(A 7504CDX)* – ('A'side) / Angie / Smells like teen spirit / Thank you.

May 92. (cd-ep) <82399-2> **CRUCIFY (remix) / WINTER / ANGIE / SMELL LIKE TEEN SPIRIT / THANK YOU** | - | □
Jun 92. (7"/c-s) (A 7479/+C) **CRUCIFY (remix). / HERE, IN MY HEAD** | 15 | -
(cd-s+=) (A 7479CD) – Mary / Crucify (version).
(cd-s) (A 7479CDX) – CRUCIFY LIVE EP – Crucify / Little earthquakes / Precious things / Mother.
Aug 92. (7"/c-s) (A 7433/+C) **SILENT ALL THESE YEARS. / SMELLS LIKE TEEN SPIRIT** | 26 | -
(cd-s) (A 7433CD) – ('A'side) / Upside down / Me and a gun / Thoughts.
(cd-s) (A 7433CDX) – ('A'side) / Ode to the banana king (part 1) / Song for Eric / Happy phantom (live).
Nov 92. (cd-ep) <85799-2> **WINTER / THE POOL / TAKE TO THE SKY / SWEET DREAMS / UPSIDE DOWN** | - | □
—— now w/ **GEORGE PORTER JR.** – bass / **CARLO NUCCIO** – drums / **ERIC ROSSE** – programming / **STEVE CATON** – guitar / **PAULINHO DaCOSTA** – percussion
Jan 94. (7"/c-s) (A 7281/+C) **CORNFLAKE GIRL. / SISTER JANET** | 4 | -
(cd-s+=) (A 7281CD) – Piano suite: All the girls hate her – Over it.
(cd-s) (A 7282CDX) – ('A'side) / A case of you / If 6 was 9 / Strange fruit.
Feb 94. (c-s) <87250> **GOD / SISTER JANET** | 72
(cd-s) <PRCD 5408> – ('A'side) / Home on the range (Cherokee edition) / Hand suite: All the girls hate her – Over it.
Feb 94. (cd/c/lp) <(7567 82567-2/-4/-1)> **UNDER THE PINK** | 1 | 12
– Pretty good year / God / Bells for her / Past the mission / Baker baker / The wrong band / The waitress / Cornflake girl / Icicle / Cloud on my tongue / Space dog / Yes, Anastasia.
Mar 94. (7"/c-s) (A 7263/+C) **PRETTY GOOD YEAR. / HONEY** | 7 | -
(cd-s+=) (A 7263CD) – The black swan.
(cd-s) (A 7263CDX) – ('A'side) / Daisy dead petals / Home on the range (Cherokee version).
Apr 94. (cd-ep) <85655-2> **CORNFLAKE GIRL / SISTER JANET / DAISY DEAD PETALS / HONEY** | - | □
—— TRENT REZNOR of NINE INCH NAILS guested vox on 'Past The Mission'.
May 94. (7"/c-s) (A 7257/+C) **PAST THE MISSION. / ('A'live)** | 31 | -
(cd-s) (A 7257CD) – Winter (live) / The waitress (live) / Here in my head (live).
(cd-s) (A 7257CDX) – ('A'live) / Upside down (live) / Icicle (live) / Flying Dutchman (live).
Oct 94. (7"pic-d/c-s) (A 7251/+C) **GOD. / ('A'-Acapella vocal & rain mix)** | 44 | -
(12"+=/cd-s+=) (A 7251 T/CD) – ('A'remixes from;- The Joy / Carl Craig / CJ Bolland).

Atlantic   Atlantic

Jan 96. (c-s) (A 5524C) **CAUGHT A LITE SNEEZE / GRAVEYARD / TOODLES MR JIM** | 20 | -
(cd-s) (A 5524CD1) – ('A'side) / London girls / That's what I like Mick (sandwich song) / Samurai.
(cd-s) (A 5524CD2) – ('A'side) / Toodles Mr. Jim / Hungarian wedding song / This old man.
Jan 96. (cd-ep) <85519> **CAUGHT A LITE SNEEZE. / SILLY SONGS (medley:- THIS OLD MAN – THAT'S WHAT I LIKE MICK – GRAVEYARD – TOODLES MR. JIM)** | - | 60
Jan 96. (cd/c) <(7567 82862-2/-4)> **BOYS FOR PELE** | 2 | 2
– Beauty queen – Horses / Blood roses / Father Lucifer / Professional widow / Mr Zebra / Marianne / Caught a lite sneeze / Muhammed my friend / Hey Jupiter / Way down / Little Amsterdam / Talula / Not the Red Baron / Agent Orange / Doughnut song / In the spring of his voodoo / Putting the damage on / Twinkle.
Mar 96. (c-s) (A 8512C) **TALULA / SISTER NAMED DESIRE** | 22 | -
(cd-s+=) (A 8512CD2) – Frog on my toe / Alamo.
(cd-s) (A 8512CD1) – ('A'-Tornado mix) / ('A'-Synethasia mix) / Til the chicken / Amazing Grace.
May 96. (cd-ep) <85504> **TALULA (Tornado version) / SAMURAI / FROG ON MY TOE / LONDON GIRLS / TATULA (BT's synethasia mix)** | - | □
Jul 96. (c-s/12") (A 5494 C/T) **HEY JUPITER. / TALULA** | 20 | 94 Aug96
(cd-s) (A 5494CD) <82955-2> – ('A'-Dakota version) / Professional widow / Sugar (live) / Honey (live). <US ep+=, hit album chart> – Somewhere over the rainbow.
Sep 96. (cd-s) <2-85475> **IN THE SPRINGTIME OF HIS VOODOO (mixes)** | - | □
—— Nov'96, she featured on BT single 'BLUE SKIES', which hit UK 26.
Dec 96. (c-s/12"/cd-s) (A 5450 C/T/CD) <2-85499> **PROFESSIONAL WIDOW (IT'S GOT TO BE BIG). / (remixes by Armand Van Helden & Mr. Roy)** | 1 | Jul96
Mar 97. (cd-s) <2-83001> **SILENT ALL THESE YEARS (live) / ('A'-album version)** | - | 65
—— now with **MATT CHAMBERLAIN** – drums / **JUSTIN MELDAL-JOHNSEN + GEORGE PORTER JR.** – bass / **STEVE CATON** – guitars / **ANDY GRAY** – programming / etc
Apr 98. (c-s) (AT 0031C) <84104> **SPARK / PURPLE PEOPLE** | 16 | 49 Jun98
(cd-s+=) (AT 0031CD1) – Have yourself a merry little Christmas / Bachelorette.
(cd-s) (AT 0031CD2) – ('A'side) / Do it again / Cooling.
May 98. (cd/c/lp) <(7567 83095-2/-4/-1)> **FROM THE CHOIRGIRL HOTEL** | 6 | 5
– Spark / Cruel / Black-dove (January) / Raspberry swirl / Jackie's strength / iieee / Liquid diamonds / She's your cocaine / Northern lad / Hotel / Playboy mommy / Pandora's aquarium.
Aug 98. (cd-s) <2-84163> **JACKIE'S STRENGTH / NEVER SEEN BLUE / BEULAH LAND** | - | 54
Aug 98. (cd-ep) (AT 0041CD) **JACKIE'S STRENGTH (Wedding Cake mixes) / FATHER LUCIFER (Silkscreen mixes)** | - | -
Aug 98. (c-s; w-drawn) (AT 0045C) **RASPBERRY SWIRL (Lip Gloss version) / ('A'extended)** | - | □
(12"+=/cd-s+=; w-drawn) (AT 0045 T/CD) – ('A'-Scarlet Spectrum Feels mix).
Apr 99. (cd-ep) <2-84412> **CRUEL (Shady Feline mix) / RASPBERRY SWIRL (Lip Gloss version) / AMBIENT RASPBERRY SWIRL (Scarlet Spectrum Feels) / MAINLINE CHERRY – AMBIENT SPARK** | - | □
Aug 99. (c-s/cd-s) <84532> **BLISS** | - | 91

Sep 99. (d-cd/d-c) (7567 83242-2) <83230> **TO VENUS AND BACK** | 22 | 12
– Bliss / Juarez / Concertina / Glory of the 80's / Lust / Suede / Riot proof / Datura / Spring haze / 1000 oceans / Precious things / Cornflake girl / Bells for her / Girl / Cooling / Mr. Zebra / Cloud on my tongue / Sugar / Little earthquakes / Space dog / Waitress / Purple people.
Nov 99. (c-s) (AT 0077 C/CD2) **GLORY OF THE 80'S / BAKER BAKER (live) / WINTER (live)** | 46
(cd-s) (AT 0077CD) – ('A'side) / Blue raincoat (live) / Twinkle (live).

– compilations, etc. –

Sep 98. (cd+book) Point; (8089) **STAR PROFILE** | □ | -

AMPS (see under ⇒ BREEDERS)

Eric ANDERSEN

Born: 14 Feb'43, Pittsburg, Pennsylvania, USA. One of the many beatnik folk troubadours to check out the burgeoning Greenwich Village circle, the young singer/guitarist soon established himself as part of that aforementioned NY culture. Inking a deal with 'Vanguard' (home of JOAN BAEZ, BUFFY SAINTE-MARIE, etc), the good-looking ANDERSEN soon delivered his debut LP, 'TODAY IS THE HIGHWAY', in 1965. Around a year later, his masterful follow-up set, 'BOUT CHANGES 'N' THINGS' (1966), should have given him his first sweet taste of success; how or why it failed was anybody's guess. Among other tracks, the aforementioned long-player featured such gems as 'THIRSTY BOOTS' (inspired by civil rights chief, Gil Turner and subsequently covered by JUDY COLLINS), 'VIOLETS OF DAWN' (the BLUES PROJECT interpreted this) and 'THE HUSTLER' (virtually an ode to DYLAN!). With the backing of an electric band – which his peer DYLAN was to pioneer! – ANDERSEN chose to re-record the album, 'BOUT CHANGES 'N' THINGS, TAKE 2' (1967) suffering a little backlash in the process. It was rumoured at the time that before he died, BEATLES manager BRIAN EPSTEIN was about to sign ANDERSEN, although it was unclear how far negotiations had gone Prolific if not outstanding on his subsequent (end of 60's) albums, 'MORE HITS FROM TIN CAN ALLEY', 'A COUNTRY DREAM' and 'AVALANCHE' (the latter his first for 'Warners'), ERIC was becoming somewhat too anti-commercial for most record buyers. An eponymous set in 1970 also literally went ignored. However, a comeback of sorts was just around the corner after his new label, 'Columbia', delivered a Top 200 album(!) and ANDERSEN's finest hour, 'BLUE RIVER' (1972). Just when his fortunes seemed to be on an upturn, his label suffered some major personnel changes, resulting in master tapes of his follow-up album, 'STAGE' (along with the sleeve work) getting mislaid. The president and former man in charge, Clive Davis, swiftly set about getting his own imprint together, 'Arista' finally delivering some of the "re-recorded" tracks under the new title of 'BE TRUE TO YOU', in 1975. For ERIC's next LP, 'SWEET SURPRISE' (1976), he wrote a handful of fresh tracks to sit alongside some cleverly crafted cover versions but this and his 'Arista' swansong compilation, 'THE BEST SONGS' (1977), accomplished little. Disillusioned by the music world, ANDERSEN retired for over a decade, only to resurface with a tidy comeback set for 'Goldcastle', 'GHOSTS UPON THE ROAD' (1989). The 90's saw ERIC achieve more than the cult status awarded to him by his peers and critics; in fact things had looked positively brighter, when in late October 1989, a number of boxes containing the tapes of 'STAGES – THE LOST ALBUM' was found; the album would finally hit the shops in '91. Collaborations with RICK DANKO and Norwegian JONAS FJELD also materialised, although his solo comeback was deservedly in full swing after 1998's 'MEMORY OF THE FUTURE'. Sounding like the "saved" DYLAN at times (although looking as serious as a wild DAVID BYRNE!), the set was a watershed of all his relationship preoccupations put into one great hour. • Covered: OL' 55 (Tom Waits) / etc.

Album rating: TODAY IS THE HIGHWAY (*5) / 'BOUT CHANGES 'N' THINGS (*6) / 'BOUT CHANGES 'N' THINGS, TAKE 2 (*5) / MORE HITS FROM TIN CAN ALLEY (*6) / A COUNTRY DREAM (*4) / AVALANCHE (*4) / ERIC ANDERSEN (*5) / THE BEST OF ERIC ANDERSEN compilation (*6) / BLUE RIVER (*8) / BE TRUE TO YOU (*5) / SWEET SURPRISE (*5) / THE BEST SONGS compilation (*6) / GHOSTS UPON THE ROAD (*5) / STAGES – THE LOST ALBUM (*6) / MEMORY OF THE FUTURE (*7)

ERIC ANDERSEN – vocals, guitar, harmonica

Fontana   Vanguard

1965. (lp) (TFL 6061) <VSD 79157> **TODAY IS THE HIGHWAY** | □ | □
– Today is the highway / Dusty box car wall / Time for my returning / Plains of Nebraska-O / Looking glass / Never coming home / Come to my bedside / Baby please don't go / Bay of Mexico / Everything ain't been said / Song to J.C.B. / Bumblebee.
—— added **PAUL HARRIS** – keyboards / **HARVEY BROOKS** – bass / **HERBIE LOVELLE** – drums
1966. (lp) (STFL 6068) <VSD 79206> **'BOUT CHANGES 'N' THINGS** | □ | □
– Violets of dawn / The girl I love / That's alright mama / Thirsty boots / The hustler / Cross your mind / I shall go unbounded / You been cheatin' / Champion at keepin' them rollin' / Blind fiddler / Close the door lightly when you go / My land is a good land.
—— added **DEBBIE GREEN** – guitar
1967. (lp) (STFL 6086) <VSD 79236> **'BOUT CHANGES 'N' THINGS TAKE 2** | □ | □
– Close the door lightly when you go / That's all right mama / Blind fiddler / The hustler / Thirsty boots / My land is a good land / Hey babe, have you been cheatin' / Cross your mind / Champion at keeping them rolling / I shall go unbounded / Violets of dawn / The girl I love.

—— **NORMAN PUTNAM** – bass, producer + many session people repl. BROOKS

			Vanguard	Vanguard

1968. (lp) *(SVRL 19003)* <VSD 79271> **MORE HITS FROM TIN CAN ALLEY**
– Tin can alley (part 1) / 16 year grudge / Miss lonely are you blue / Mary Sunshine / Honey / Just a little something / Rollin' home (it's a far cry from Heaven . . . .) / On the edge of you / Broken hearted mama / Hello sun / Woman is a prism / Tin can alley (part 2).

1969. (lp) <VSD 6540> **A COUNTRY DREAM**
– (Sitting on) The dock of the bay / All I remember is you / Deborah, I love you / Devon, you look like Heaven / Eyes gently rolling / Just a country dream / Lovesick blues / Smashville jam / Waves of freedom.

—— now w/ **BRUCE LANGHORN** – guitar, bass / **ERIC GALE, ANDY JOHNSON + JAY DEE MANESS** – guitar / **LEE CRABTREE** – piano / **STEVE ANANDER + CHUCK RAINEY** – bass

			Warners	Warners

1969. (lp) <WS 1748> **AVALANCHE**
– It's comin' and it won't be long / An old song / Louise / Think about it / So hard to fall / Good to be with you / We were foolish like the flowers / Avalanche / For what was gained. *(cd-iss. Jan96 on 'WEA'; 7599 26779-2)*

1970. (lp) <WS 1806> **ERIC ANDERSEN**
(cd-iss. Jan96 on 'WEA'; 7599 26778-2)

—— now with numerous session people

			C.B.S.	Columbia

Feb 73. (lp) *(CBS 65571)* <31062> **BLUE RIVER**   Jul72
– Is it really love at all / Pearl's goodtime blues / Wind and sand / Faithful / Blue river / Florentine / Sheila / More often than not / Round the bend.

—— ANDERSEN recorded the "lost" album, 'STAGE' in 1973

			Arista	Arista

Apr 75. (lp) *(ARTY 114)* <4033> **BE TRUE TO YOU**
– Moonchild river song / Be true to you / Wild crow blues / Ol' 55 / Time run like a freight train / Liza, light the candle / Woman, she was gentle / Can't get you out of my life / Blues keep fallin' like the rain / Love is just a game.

1976. (lp) <4075> **SWEET SURPRISE**
– Lost in a song / How it goes / Dreams of Mexico / San Diego serenade / Sweet surprise / Down at the cantina / Crazy river / Love will meet again.

1977. (lp) <4128> **THE BEST SONGS** (compilation of re-recorded tracks)
– Is if really love at all / I shall go unbounded / Violets of dawn / Be true to you / Hey babe, have you been cheatin' / Thirsty boots / Moonchild river song / Blue river / Close the door lightly / Time run like a freight train.

—— retired from music biz until . . .

			Gold Castle	Gold Castle

May 90. (cd/c/lp) *(CD/TC+/VGC 14)* **GHOSTS UPON THE ROAD**   Nov89
– Belgian bar / Spanish steps / It starts with a lie / Listen to the rain / Ghosts upon the road / Too many times (I will try) / Carry me away / Six senses of darkness / Irish lace. <cd re-iss. Apr96 on 'Plump'; PLUCD 003)>

—— In 1991, ANDERSEN teamed up with RICK DANKO (ex-BAND) and JONAS FJELD on the album, 'DANKO/FJELD/ANDERSEN' (Rykodisc; RCD 10270) – another with the same trio, 'RIDIN' ON THE BLINDS' surfaced in '95.

—— In Jun'95, ANDERSEN collaborated with ROBERT MAZUREK on the album, 'BADLANDS' (Hep; HEPCD 2065)

			Appleseed	Appleseed

Feb 99. (cd) <(1028)> **MEMORY OF THE FUTURE**   Nov98
– Sudden love / Foghorn / Rain falls down in Amsterdam / Blue heart / Goin' gone / Memory of the future / Sex with you / Chinatown / No mans land / When I'm gone / Hills of Tuscany.

– compilations, etc. –

1971. (d-lp) *Vanguard;* <(VSD 7/8)> **THE BEST OF ERIC ANDERSEN**
– My land is a good land / Hey babe, have you been cheatin' / Thirsty boots / The hustler / Close the door lightly / Song to J.C.B. / Dusty box car wall / Looking glass / Bumblebee / Violets of dawn / Eyes gently rolling / Just a country dream / All I remember is you / Rollin' home / Miss lonely are you blue / Broken hearted mama / A woman is a prism / Hello sun. *(re-iss. May89 on 'Start' lp/c/cd; VNP 5/6/7 316)*

Apr 91. (cd) *Columbia-Legacy;* **STAGES – THE LOST ALBUM**
– Baby, I'm lonesome / Moonchild river song / Can't get you out of my life / Woman, she was gentle / Time run like a freight train / It's been a long time / Wild crow blues / Be true to you / I love to sing my ballad, mama (but they . . . .) / Dream to Rimbaud / Make it last (angel in the wind) / Lie with me / Soul of my song.

Sep 97. (cd) *Archive;* **THE ERIC ANDERSEN COLLECTION**
Jul 99. (cd) *Vanguard;* <79539> **VIOLETS OF DAWN**
– (track listing nearly same as 'BEST OF . . .')

Ian ANDERSON (see under ⇒ JETHRO TULL)

Jon ANDERSON (see under ⇒ YES)

Laurie ANDERSON

Born: 5 Jun'47, Chicago, Illinois, USA. Graduating from Columbia University in the early 70's, she soon became the Mother Superior of the New York art-rock cognoscenti, after moving there to sculpt in the mid 70's. In 1977, a debut 45, 'IT'S NOT THE BULLET THAT KILLS YOU', saw her turn her talents to music although the single did nothing. She gave up history tuition to concentrate more on performance art and fashion, utilising her weird violin playing to great effect. It wasn't until 1981 that her recording career took off, when a surprise 8-minute nauseating UK hit, 'O SUPERMAN', paved the way for debut 'Warners' album 'BIG SCIENCE'. This highlighted her speech-based, hypnotic minimalism, rounding on such topics as technology, culture and alienation with a wry, insightful ease. The follow-up, 'MR

HEARTBREAK', was a slightly more mainstream effort, due in part to BILL LASWELL's production on a couple of tracks. Two live albums were released during the mid-80's; the later of them, 'HOME OF THE BRAVE', with its accompanying concert film, was a flop despite garnering critical plaudits at Cannes. 'STRANGE ANGELS' (1989) saw ANDERSON move towards "real" singing and a more melodic approach while 1994's 'BRIGHT RED', co-produced by BRIAN ENO was characterised by a more claustrophobic feel. Another live album and tour cemented her reputation as a witty and succinct cultural commentator, although her recorded output, while often being innovative, sometimes veered too close to theatre to warrant repeated listening.
• **Trivia:** Her audio-visual concerts, complete with orchestra, lasted for around 7 hours. Guests on her '84 lp, were PETER GABRIEL, NILE RODGERS and WILLIAM S. BURROUGHS. She was romantically involved with LOU REED in the early 90's. • **Bibliography:** THE PACKAGE: A MYSTERY (1971) / TRANSPORTATION (1974) / NOTEBOOK (1977) / WORDS IN REVERSE (1979) / HOME OF THE BRAVE (1979) / EMPTY PLACES (1991) / STORIES FROM THE NERVE BIBLE (1994).

Album rating: BIG SCIENCE (*6) / UNITED STATES LIVE (*5) / MISTER HEARTBREAK (*7) / HOME OF THE BRAVE (*6) / STRANGE ANGELS (*7) / BRIGHT RED (*6) / THE UGLY ONE WITH THE JEWELS AND OTHER STORIES (*7)

LAURIE ANDERSON – vocals, multi-instrumentalist (violin / synthesizers)

—— with many on session incl. **DAVID VAN TIEGHEM** – percussion, drums / **ROMA BARAN** – accordian / **BILL OBRECHE** – sax, flute / **CHICK FISHER** – sax, clarinet / **PETER GORDON** – clarinet, sax / etc

			not iss.	Holly Solomon Gallery

1977. (7"ltd) <004> **IT'S NOT THE BULLET THAT KILLS YOU – IT'S THE HOLE**   -

			not iss.	One-Ten

Sep 81. (7") <OT 005> **O SUPERMAN. / WALK THE DOG**

			Warners	Warners

Oct 81. (7") <K 17870> <49876> **O SUPERMAN. / WALK THE DOG**   2
Jan 82. (7") <K 17941> **BIG SCIENCE. / EXAMPLE 22**   -
Apr 82. (lp/c) *(K/K4 57002)* <3674> **BIG SCIENCE**   29
– From the air / Big science / Sweaters / Walking and falling / Born, never asked / O Superman (for Massenet) / Example #22 / Let x = x / It tango. *(cd-iss. Apr84; K2 57002)*
Jul 82. (7") *(K 17956)* **LET X = X. / IT TANGO**   -
(12"+=) *(K 17956)* – Sweaters.
Feb 84. (lp/c) *(925077-1/-4)* <25077> **MISTER HEARTBREAK**   93   60
– Sharkey's day / Language d'amour / Gravity's angel / Kokoku / Excellent birds / Blue lagoon / Sharkey's night. *(cd-iss. Jul84; 925077-2)*
Jan 85. (5-lp-box) *(925192-1)* <25192> **UNITED STATES LIVE (live)**
– Say hello / Walk the dog / Violin solo / Closed circuits / For a large and changing rooms / Pictures of it / The language of the future / Cartoon song / Small voice / Three walking songs / The healing horn / New Jersey turnpike / So happy birthday / English / Dance of electricity / Three songs for paper, film and video / Sax solo / Sax duet / Born, never asked / From the air / Beginning French / O Superman (for Massenet) / Talkshow / Frames for the pictures / Democratic why / Looking for you walking and falling / Private property / Neon duet / Let x = x / The Mailman's nightmare / Difficult listening hour / Language is a virus from Outer Space – (William S. Burroughs) / Reverb / If you can't talk about it, point to it / Violin walk / City song / Finnish farmers / Red map / Hey ah / Bagpipe solo / Steven Weed / Time and a half / Voices on paper / Example #22 / Strike / False documents / New York social life / A curious phenomenon / Yankee see / I dreamed I had to take a test . . . / Running dogs / Four, three, two, one / The big top / It was up in the mountains / Odd objects / Dr. Miller / Big science / Big science (reprise) / Cello solo / It tango / Blue lagoon / Hothead (la langue d'amour) / Stiff neck / Telephone song / Sweaters / We've got four big clocks (and they're all ticking) / Song for two Jims / Over the river / Mach 20 / Rising sun / The visitors / The stranger / Classified / Going somewhere / Fireworks / Dog show / Lighting out for the territories.
Apr 86. (lp/c/cd) *(925400-1/-4/-2)* <25400> **HOME OF THE BRAVE**
– Smoke rings / White lily / Late show / Talk normal / Radar / Language is a virus from outer space / Sharkey's night / Credit racket.
May 86. (7"/12") *(W 8701/+T)* **LANGUAGE IS A VIRUS FROM OUTER SPACE (edit). / WHITE LILY**   -
Nov 89. (lp/c/cd) *(WX 258/+C)(K 925900-2)* <25900> **STRANGE ANGELS**
– Strange angels / Monkey's paw / Coolsville / Ramon / Babydoll / Beautiful red dress / The day the Devil / The dream before / My eyes / Hiawatha.
Oct 94. (cd/c) <(9362 45534-2/-4)> **BRIGHT RED**
– Speechless / Bright red / The puppet motel / Speak my language / World without end / Freefall / Muddy river / Beautiful pea green boat / Love among the sailors / Poison / In our sleep / Night in Baghdad / Tightrope / Same time tomorrow.
Mar 95. (cd/c) <(9362 45347-2/-4)> **THE UGLY ONE WITH THE JEWELS & OTHER STORIES FROM THE NERVE BIBLE**
– The end of the world / The salesman / The night flight from Houston / Word of mouth / The soul is a bird / The ouija board / The ugly one with the jewels / The geographic North Pole / John Lilly / The rotowhirl / On the way to Jerusalem / The Hollywood strangler / Maria Teresa Teresa Maria / Someone else's dream / White lily / The mysterious "J" / The cultural ambassador / Same time tomorrow.

ANGELIC UPSTARTS   (dig out; Great Alt & Indie . . .)

ANIMALS

Formed: Newcastle, England . . . 1960, as The ALAN PRICE COMBO. BURDON's arrival in 1962 led to tension in the ranks, no doubt a major contributing factor to the band's increasingly manic stage show. After supporting the likes of legendary bluesmen SONNY BOY WILLIAMSON and JOHN LEE HOOKER, they moved to London early in '64 and were promptly signed to EMI's 'Columbia' label by then virtually unknown producer MICKIE MOST. Re-christened The ANIMALS by the fans, the band adopted the name with glee and hit paydirt in summer '64 with the blues standard, 'HOUSE OF THE RISING SUN'. A massive hit on both sides of the Atlantic, with BURDON's ominous vocal phrasing and PRICE's wailing organ, the record remains the band's defining moment. Rarely, if ever, has the United Kingdom produced a white guy who could sing the blues like ERIC BURDON. The whisky-soaked menace of his voice sounded at times like Old Nick incarnate and was a key component in The ANIMALS' feisty challenge to The ROLLING STONES' throne at the height of the 60's R&B boom. Much like The BYRDS, The ANIMALS had an uncanny knack of covering material which, on paper, seemed less than obvious, but worked a treat on vinyl. 'DON'T LET ME BE MISUNDERSTOOD' and 'WE GOTTA GET OUT OF THIS PLACE' both went Top 5 in the UK, ensuring respectable sales of their second album, 'ANIMAL TRACKS'. PRICE left in 1965, beginning a dispute (incredibly still ongoing after more than 30 years) with BURDON over the publishing rights to 'HOUSE OF THE RISING SUN'. With DAVE ROWBERRY as PRICE's replacement, the band cut a few more albums including the semi-classic 'ANIMALIZATION', which contained such powerful tracks as 'INSIDE – LOOKING OUT' and 'GIN HOUSE BLUES'. The original ANIMALS fell apart towards the end of '66, CHAS CHANDLER going on to manage JIMI HENDRIX. BURDON moved to San Francisco, where he immersed himself in the nascent psychedelic scene, consuming liberal quantities of LSD. Under the new and improved moniker ERIC BURDON & THE ANIMALS, he released in 1967 his paean to the emerging hippy culture, 'WINDS OF CHANGE'. Other highlights of this period include BURDON's tribute to the narcotic delights of the Swiss pharmaceutical industry, 'A GIRL NAMED SANDOZ', and 'MONTEREY', his reverential recollection of the legendary pop festival. BURDON kept his third eye in check enough to release a handful of introspective albums before this particular version of The ANIMALS split at the end of '68. He tasted major success for the last time with soul/funk band WAR, their debut single 'SPILL THE WINE', climbing into the Top 3 in the States mid-1970. The collaboration was short-lived, however, and BURDON went solo with weak support from the public. The original ANIMALS line-up (minus PRICE, of course) re-formed in 1977 and again in '83, although the new material was met with a lukewarm response in the UK. CHAS CHANDLER, who also went onto work with SLADE and others, died of a heart attack on the 17th July '96. • **Songwriters:** BURDON lyrics / PRICE arrangements songs, with covers BOOM BOOM + DIMPLES + I'M MAD AGAIN (John Lee Hooker) / I'M IN LOVE AGAIN (Fats Domino) / TALKIN' ABOUT YOU (Ray Charles) / GONNA SEND YOU BACK TO GEORGIA (Timmy Shaw) / DON'T LET ME BE MISUNDERSTOOD (Nina Simone) / PRETTY THING (Bo Diddley) / BABY LET ME TAKE YOU HOME (Russell-Farrell) / BRING IT ON HOME TO ME (Sam Cooke) / WE'VE GOTTA GET OUT OF THIS PLACE (Mann-Weil) / DON'T BRING ME DOWN (Goffin-King) / RIVER DEEP MOUNTAIN HIGH (Phil Spector) / PAINT IT BLACK (Rolling Stones) / etc.

Best CD compilation: THE COMPLETE ANIMALS (*9)

ERIC BURDON (b.11 May'41, Walker, nr.Newcastle, England) – vocals / **ALAN PRICE** (b.19 Apr'41, Fairfield, Durham, England) – keyboards, vocals / **HILTON VALENTINE** (b.21 May'43, North Shields, England) – guitar / **CHAS CHANDLER** (b.18 Dec'38, Heaton, nr.Newcastle, England) – bass / **JOHN STEEL** (b. 4 Feb'41, Gateshead, England) – drums

		Columbia	M.G.M.	
Apr 64.	(7") (DB 7247) <K 13242> **BABY LET ME TAKE YOU HOME. / GONNA SEND YOU BACK TO WALKER** (US 'A'side)	21	57	Sep64
Jun 64.	(7") (DB 7301) <K 13264> **THE HOUSE OF THE RISING SUN. / TALKIN' 'BOUT YOU**	1	1	Jul64
Sep 64.	(7") (DB 7354) <K 13274> **I'M CRYING. / TAKE IT EASY**	8	19	Oct64
Oct 64.	(lp; mono/stereo) (33SX 1669) <E/SE 4264> **THE ANIMALS**	6	7	Sep64

– Story of Bo Diddley / Bury my body / Dimples / I've been around / I'm in love again / The girl can't help it / She said yeah / The right time / Memphis / Boom boom / Around and around. (US diff. tracks +=> – The house of the rising sun. (re-iss.Oct69 on 'Regal Starline'; SRS 5006) (cd-iss. Oct97 on 'E.M.I.'; DORIG 125)

		Columbia	M.G.M.	
Nov 64.	(7") <K 13298> **BOOM BOOM. / BLUE FEELING**	-	43	
Jan 65.	(7") (DB 7445) <K 13311> **DON'T LET ME BE MISUNDERSTOOD. / CLUB A-GO-GO**	3	15	Feb65
Mar 65.	(lp; mono/stereo) <E/SE 4281> **THE ANIMALS ON TOUR (live)**	-	99	

– Boom boom / How you've changed / I believe to my soul / Mess around bright lights / Big city / Worried life blues / Let the good times roll / Crying dimples / She said yeah.

Apr 65.	(7") (DB 7539) <K 13339> **BRING IT ON HOME TO ME. / FOR MISS CAULKER**	7	32	May 65
May 65.	(lp; mono/stereo) (33SX 1708) <E/SE 4305> **ANIMAL TRACKS**	6	57	Sep65

– Mess around / How you've changed / Hallelujah / I believe to my soul / Worried life blues / Roberta / I ain't got you / Bright lights, big city / Let the good times roll / For Miss Caulker / Roadrunner. (re-iss. Sep84 on 'Fame' lp/c; FA/TCFA 413110) (cd-iss. Jan99 on 'E.M.I.'; 498936-2)

Jul 65.	(7") (DB 7639) <K 13382> **WE'VE GOTTA GET OUT OF THIS PLACE. / I CAN'T BELIEVE IT**	2	13	Aug65
Oct 65.	(7") (DB 7741) <K 13414> **IT'S MY LIFE. / I'M GONNA CHANGE THE WORLD**	7	23	Nov65

— **DAVE ROWBERRY** (b.27 Dec'43, Newcastle, England) – keyboards (ex-MIKE COTTON SOUND) repl. PRICE who went solo

		Decca	M.G.M.	
Feb 66.	(7") (F 2332) **INSIDE – LOOKING OUT. / OUTCAST**	12	-	
Mar 66.	(7") <K 13468> **INSIDE – LOOKING OUT. / YOU'RE ON MY MIND**	-	34	

— **BARRY JENKINS** (b.22 Dec'44, Leicester, England) – drums (ex-NASHVILLE TEENS) repl. STEEL

May 66.	(7") (F 12407) <K 13514> **DON'T BRING ME DOWN. / CHEATING**	6	12	
May 66.	(lp) (LK 4797) **ANIMALISMS**	4		

– One monkey don't stop no show / Maudie / Outcast / Sweet little sixteen / You're on my mind / Clapping / Gin house blues / Squeeze her – Tease her / What am I living for / I put a spell on you / That's all I am to you / She'll return it. (cd-iss. Sep99 on 'Repetoire'; RR 4772)

Aug 66.	(lp; mono/stereo) <E/SE 4384> **ANIMALIZATION**		20	

– Don't bring me down / One monkey don't stop no show / You're on my mind / She'll return it / Cheating / Inside – looking out / See see rider / Gin house blues / Maudie / Sweet little sixteen / I put a spell on you.

Sep 66.	(7") <K 13582> **SEE SEE RIDER. / SHE'LL RETURN IT**	-	10	
Nov 66.	(lp; mono/stereo) <E/SE 4414> **ANIMALISM**	-	33	

– All night long / Shake / Other side of this life / Rock me baby / Lucille / Smokestack lightning / Hey Gyp / Hit the road Jack / Outcast / Louisiana blues / That's all I am to you / Going down slow.

ERIC BURDON & THE ANIMALS

— ERIC with session musicians incl. BENNY GOULSON

Oct 66.	(7") (F 12502) **HELP ME GIRL. / SEE SEE RIDER**	14	-	
Dec 66.	(7") <K 13636> **HELP ME GIRL. / THAT AIN'T WHERE IT'S AT**	-	29	
Mar 67.	(lp; mono/stereo) <E/SE 4433> **ERIC IS HERE**	-		

– Help me girl / In the night / Mama told me not to come / I think it's gonna rain today / This side of goodbye / That ain't where it's at / Wait till next year / Losin' control / It's not easy / Biggest bundle of them all / It's been a long time coming / True love.

— ERIC who had earlier moved to California brought back **BARRY JENKINS** in Jan '67

— recruited **VIC BRIGGS** (b.14 Feb'45, London) – guitar (ex-STEAMPACKET) to finally repl ROWBERRY / **JOHN WIEDER** (b.21 Apr'47, London) – guitar, violin repl. VALENTINE who went solo / **DANNY McCULLOCH** (b.18 Jul'45, London) – bass repl. CHANDLER who became producer

		M.G.M.	M.G.M.	
May 67.	(7") (MGM 1340) <K 13721> **WHEN I WAS YOUNG. / A GIRL NAMED SANDOZ**	45	15	Apr67
Aug 67.	(7") (MGM 1344) **GOOD TIMES. / AIN'T THAT SO**	20	-	
Aug 67.	(7") <K 13769> **SAN FRANCISCAN NIGHTS. / GOOD TIMES**	-	9	
Oct 67.	(lp; mono/stereo) (C/CS 8052) <E/SE 4454> **WINDS OF CHANGE**		42	Sep67

– San Franciscan nights / Good times / Winds of change / Poem by the sea / Paint it black / Black plague / Yes I am experienced / Man-woman / Hotel hell / Anything / It's all meat. (re-iss.Apr71; 2354 001) (cd-iss. Oct85 on 'Polydor'; 825 717-2)

Oct 67.	(7") (MGM 1359) **SAN FRANCISCAN NIGHTS. / GRATEFULLY DEAD**	7	-	
Nov 67.	(7") <K 13868> **MONTEREY. / AIN'T IT SO**	-	15	
Feb 68.	(7") (MGM 1373) <K 13939> **SKY PILOT (pt.1). / SKY PILOT (pt.2)**	40	14	Jun68
Mar 68.	(7") <K 13917> **ANYTHING. / IT'S ALL MEAT**	-	80	
May 68.	(7") (MGM 1412) **MONTEREY. / ANYTHING**			
May 68.	(lp; mono/stereo) (C/CS 8075) <E/SE 4537> **THE TWAIN SHALL MEET**		79	Mar68

– Just the thought / Closer to the truth / No self pity / Orange and red beans / Sky pilot / We love you Lil / All is one.

— **ZOOT MONEY** – keyboards (ex-BIG ROLL BAND, ex-DANTALIAN'S CHARIOT) / **ANDY SOMERS** (aka SUMMERS) – guitar, bass (ex-BIG ROLL BAND, ex-DANTALIAN'S CHARIOT) repl. BRIGGS and McCULLOCH

Aug 68.	(lp; mono/stereo) <E/SE 4553> **EVERY ONE OF US**			

– Uppers and downers / Serenade to a sweet lady / The immigrant lad / Year of the guru / St.James infirmary / New York 1963 – America 1968 / White houses.

Nov 68.	(7") <K 14013> **WHITE HOUSES. / RIVER DEEP MOUNTAIN HIGH**	-	67	
Jan 69.	(7") (MGM 1461) **RING OF FIRE. / I'M AN ANIMAL**	25	-	
Dec 68.	(d-lp; mono/stereo) (C/CS 8105) <SE 4591-2> **LOVE IS**			

– River deep, mountain high / I'm the animal / I'm dying, or am I / Gemini / The madman / Ring of fire / Coloured rain / To love somebody / As tears go passing by. (UK re-iss. Apr71; 2354 006-007) (re-iss. 1973; 2619 002) (cd re-iss/Sep94 on 'One Way'; OW 30338)

May 69.	(7") (MGM 1481) **RIVER DEEP, MOUNTAIN HIGH. / HELP ME GIRL**		-	

— Split Feb69. WIEDER joined FAMILY, ZOOT went solo, JENKINS joined HEAVY JELLY, SOMERS became SUMMERS and joined KEVIN AYERS then KEVIN COYNE. He later helped form The POLICE

ERIC BURDON & WAR

ERIC BURDON – vocals, and WAR: **LONNIE (LEROY) JORDAN** – keyboards, vocals / **HOWARD SCOTT** – guitar, vocals / **CHARLES MILLER** – saxophone, clarinet / **HAROLD BROWN** – drums, percussion / **B.B. DICKERSON** – bass / **THOMAS 'PAPA DEE' ALLEN** – keyboards / **LEE OSKAR** – harmonica

		Polydor	M.G.M.	
Sep 70.	(lp) (2310 041) <SE 4663> **ERIC BURDON DECLARES WAR**	50	18	May70

– Dedication / Roll on Kirk / Tobacco road / I have a dream / Spill the wine / Blues for Memphis Slim / Birth / Mother Earth / Mr.Charlie / Danish pastry / You're no stranger. (re-iss. Oct79 on 'MCA'; MCF 3026) <cd-iss. Oct95 on 'Avenue'; 74321 30526-2)

Jul 70.	(7") (2001 072) <K 14118> **SPILL THE WINE. / MAGIC MOUNTAIN**		3	
		Liberty	M.G.M.	
Dec 70.	(7") (LBF 15434) <K 14196> **THEY CAN'T TAKE AWAY OUR MUSIC. / HOME COOKIN'**		50	
Feb 71.	(d-lp) (LDS 84003-4) <SE 4710-2> **BLACK MAN'S BURDON**		82	Dec70

– Black on black in black / Paint it black / Laurel and Hardy / P.C. 3 / Black bird / Paint it black / Spirit / Beautiful new born child / Nights in white satin / Bird and the squirrel / Nuts seed and life / Out of nowhere / Sun – Moon / Pretty colours / Gun /

Jimbo / Bare back ride / Home cookin' / They can't take away our music. *(re-iss. Oct79 on 'MCA'; MCSP 306) <US-cd 1993 on 'Avenue'; R2 71193>*

		U.A.	M.G.M.
Jun 71.	(7") *(UP 35217)* **PAINT IT BLACK. / SPIRIT**	☐	–

ERIC BURDON & JIMMY WITHERSPOON

JIMMY WITHERSPOON – blues guitarist + WAR backing.

		U.A.	M.G.M.
Aug 71.	(7") *(UP 35287) <K 14296>* **SOLEDAD. / HEADIN' FOR HOME**	☐	☐
Dec 71.	(lp) *(UAG 29251) <SE 4791>* **GUILTY!**	☐	☐

– I've been drinking / Once upon a time / Steam roller / The laws must change / Have mercy judge / Goin' down slow / Soledad / Home dream / Wicked wicked man / Headin' for home / The time has come. *<US re-iss. 1976 as 'BLACK AND WHITE BLUES' on 'LA'; GG 58001> (re-iss. Oct79 as 'BLACK AND WHITE BLUES' on 'M.C.A.'; MCF 3024)*

ERIC BURDON BAND

performed at Reading festival (Aug73), backed by **AARON BUTLER** – guitar / **RANDY RICE** – bass / **ALVIN TAYLOR** – drums. This line-up also featured on his next long awaited album

		Capitol	Capitol
Dec 74.	(7") *<3997>* **THE REAL ME. / LETTER FROM THE COUNTY FARM**	–	☐
Feb 75.	(lp) *(<E-ST 11359>)* **SUN SECRETS**		51 Dec74

– It's my life / Ring of fire / Medley: When I was young – Warchild – The real me / Don't let me be misunderstood – Nina's school / Letter from the county farm / Sun secrets.

Feb 75.	(7") *<4007>* **RING OF FIRE. / THE REAL ME**	–	☐

── added **JOHN STERLING** – guitar / **TERRY RYAN** – keyboards / **MOSES WHEELOCK** – percussion / **GEORGE SURANOVICH** – drums / and **KIM KESTERSON** – bass (repl. AARON BUTLER)

Aug 75.	(lp/<lp>) *(E-ST/<SMAS 11426>)* **STOP**	☐	☐

– City boy / Gotta get it on / The man / I'm lookin' up / Rainbow / All I do / Funky fever / By mine / The way it should be / Stop.

ORIGINAL ANIMALS

reformed to record below **BURDON, PRICE, VALENTINE, CHANDLER + STEEL**

		Barn	U.A.
Aug 77.	(7") *(2014 109)* **PLEASE SEND ME SOMEONE TO LOVE. / RIVERSIDE COUNTY**	☐	–
Aug 77.	(lp/c) *(2314 104) <790>* **BEFORE WE WERE SO RUDELY INTERRUPTED**		70

– Brother Bill (the last clean shirt) / Many rivers to cross / Lonely avenue / Please send me someone to love / Riverside county / It's all over now, baby blue / Fire on the sun / As the crow flies / Just a little bit / The fool.

Oct 77.	(7") *(2014 115)* **MANY RIVERS TO CROSS. / BROTHER BILL (THE LAST CLEAN SHIRT)**	☐	–
Nov 77.	(7") *<1070>* **FIRE ON THE SUN. / RIVERSIDE COUNTY**	☐	☐

── PRICE returned to solo work.

ERIC BURDON

── solo with many session people.

		Polydor	not iss.
Mar 78.	(lp) *(2302 078)* **SURVIVOR**	☐	–

– Rocky / Woman of the rings / The kid / Tomb of the unknown singer / Famous flames / Hollywood woman / Hook of Holland / I was born to live the blues / Highway dealer / P.O. box 500.

1980.	(lp) *(2344 147)* **DARKNESS – DARKNESS**		–

– Darkness darkness / On the horizon / Rat race / Gospel singer / Ride on / Baby what's wrong / Cry to me / So much love / Ecstasy / Too late.

		Ariola	not iss.
1981.	(lp; as ERIC BURDON'S FIRE DEPT.) *(S 202 800-320)* **THE LAST DRIVE**	–	– German

– The last drive / Power company / Bird on the beach / The rubbing out of long hair / Atom-most-fear / Dry / Female terrorist / The last poet.

ANIMALS

reformed again in 1983.

		I.R.S.	I.R.S.
Sep 83.	(7") *(PFP 1019) <9920>* **THE NIGHT. / NO JOHN NO**	☐	48
	(12"+=) *(PFXS 1019)* – Melt down.		
Sep 83.	(lp) *(<SP 70037>)* **ARK**	☐	66

– Loose change / Love is for all time / My favourite enemy / Prisoner of the light / Being there / Hard times / The night / Trying to get to you / Just can't get enough / Melt down / Gotta get back to you / Crystal nights. *(cd-iss. Nov96 on 'Castle'; CLACD 412)*

Nov 83.	(7"/12") *(PFP/+X 1030) <9923>* **LOVE IS FOR ALL TIME. / JUST CAN'T GET ENOUGH**		
Sep 84.	(lp) *(<IRSA 70043>)* **RIP IT TO SHREDS – THE GREATEST HITS LIVE (live 1983)**		

– It's too late / House of the rising Sun / It's my life / Don't bring me down / Don't let me be misunderstood / I'm cryin' / Bring it on home to me / O lucky man / Boom boom / We've gotta get out of this place.

── (split though they did reunion gigs)

ERIC BURDON BAND

with **JOHN STERLING + SNUFFY WALDEN** – guitar / **STEVE GOLDSTEIN + LUIS CABAZA + RONNIE BARRON** – keyboards / **BILL McCUBBIN + TERRY WILSON** – bass / **TONY BRUANAGLE** – drums

		Blackline	not iss.
1983.	(lp) *(BL 712)* **COMEBACK**	☐	–

– No more Elmore / The road / Crawling King Snake / Take it easy / Dey won't / Wall of silence / Streetwalker / It hurts me too / Lights out / Bird on the beach. *(UK-iss.Jun84 as 'THE ROAD' on 'Thunderbolt'; THBL 1017) (cd-iss. Sep94 on 'Line'; LICD 900058)*

		Bullfrog	Carrere
Mar 84.	(lp) *(BDL 4006) <267.003>* **POWER COMPANY**	☐	Dec83

– Power company / Devil's daughter / You can't kill my spirit / Do you feel it (today) / Wicked man / Heart attack / Who gives a f*** / Sweet blood call / House of the rising Sun / Comeback. *<US-iss.1988 as 'WICKED MAN on 'GNP Crescendo' lp/c/cd; GNP S/C/D 2194>*

		Striped Horse	not iss.
Aug 88.	(12") *(SH12 615)* **RUN FOR YOUR LIFE (extended). / RUN FOR YOUR LIFE / RUN FOR YOUR LIFE (instrumental)**	☐	☐
	(cd-s+=) *(SHCD 615)* – Run for your life (Animal remix).		
Aug 88.	(cd) *<SHD 5006>* **I USED TO BE AN ANIMAL**	–	☐

(UK-iss.Jul94 on 'Success' cd/c;)

		Rhino	Rhino
1990.	(c-s) *(4JM 74425)* **SIXTEEN TONS / ('A'instrumental)**	–	☐

– compilations, etc. –

on 'Columbia' UK / 'MGM' US, unless stated otherwise

Nov 64.	(7"ep) *(SEG 8374)* **THE ANIMALS IS HERE**	☐	–

– The house of the rising sun / I'm crying / Gonna send you back to Walker / Baby let me take you down.

Mar 65.	(7"ep) *(SEG 8400)* **THE ANIMALS**	☐	–

– Boom boom / Around and around / Dimples / I've been around.

Jul 65.	(7"ep) *(SEG 8439)* **THE ANIMALS NO.2**	☐	–

– I'm in love again / Bury my body / I'm mad again / She said yeah.

Oct 65.	(7"ep) *(SEG 8452)* **THE ANIMALS ARE BACK**	☐	–
Jan 66.	(7"ep) *Decca; (DFE 8643)* **IN THE BEGINNING THERE WAS EARLY ANIMALS**		–

– Boom boom / Pretty thing / I just wanna make love to you.

Feb 66.	(lp; mono/stereo) *<E/SE 4324>* **THE BEST OF THE ANIMALS**	–	6

– It's my life / Gonna send you back to Walker / Bring it on home to me / I'm mad again / The house of the rising sun / We've gotta get out of this place / Boom boom / I'm in love again / I'm crying / Don't let me be misunderstood. *(UK iss.Mar89 on 'Crusader')*

Apr 66.	(lp) *(SX 6035)* **MOST OF THE ANIMALS**	4	☐

– The house of the rising sun / We've gotta get out of this place / Roadrunner / Let the good times roll / Hallelujah I love her so / It's going to change the world / Bring it on home to me / Worried life blues / Baby let me take you home / For Miss Caulker / I believe to my soul / How you've changed. *(re-iss. Sep71 on 'Music For Pleasure'; MFP 5218, hit no.18) (re-iss. Feb92; CDMFP 5218)*

Sep 66.	(7"ep) *(SEG 8499)* **ANIMAL TRACKS**	☐	–
Jun 67.	(lp; mono/stereo) *<E/SE 4454>* **THE BEST OF ERIC BURDON & THE ANIMALS VOL.2**	–	71
Mar 69.	(lp) *<SE 4602>* **THE GREATEST HITS OF ERIC BURDON & THE ANIMALS**	–	
1971.	(d-lp) *M.G.M.;* **POP HISTORY**	–	
1971.	(d-lp) *M.G.M.;* **STAR PORTRAIT**	–	

– Good times / Sky pilot / We love you Lil / Hey Gyp, dig the slowness / San Franciscan nights / Paint it black / When I was young / See see rider / Ring of fire / River deep, mountain high / True love (comes only once in a lifetime) / Inside – looking out / I'm an animal / Monterey / To love somebody / Anything / I'm dying, or am I?. *(cd-iss. Jul88)*

Mar 71.	(7") *(2006 028)* **GOOD TIMES. / SAN FRANCISCAN NIGHTS**	☐	–

(re-iss. Nov82 flipped over on 'Polydor'; POSP 534)

Sep 72.	(7"m) *R.A.K.; (RR 1)* **THE HOUSE OF THE RISING SUN. / DON'T LET ME BE MISUNDERSTOOD / I'M CRYING**	25	–

(re-iss. Sep82 7",7"pic-d; RR/+P 1, hit UK No.11)

Oct 75.	(lp) *Polydor; (2356 142)* **ERIC BURDON & THE ANIMALS**	☐	☐
Apr 76.	(lp) *Polydor; (2368 106)* **ERIC BURDON AND THE ANIMALS**	☐	☐
Apr 76.	(lp) *D.J.M.; (DJSL 069)* **IN CONCERT FROM NEWCASTLE (live '63)**	☐	☐

(re-iss. Dec 76 as 'LIVE IN NEWCASTLE'; DJB 26069) (re-iss. Jan 77 as 'NEWCASTLE '63 on 'Charly'; CR 30016) (re-iss. Feb81; CR 30197) (re-iss. Nov88 as 'LIVE AT THE CLUB A GO GO, NEWCASTLE' on 'Decal'; LIK 88) (cd-iss. Feb93 on 'Charly'; CDCD 1037) (cd iss. Jun97 on 'Spalax'; 14550) (re-iss. Oct97 on 'Hallmark' cd/c; 30814-2/-4)

Nov 76.	(lp; by ERIC BURDON & WAR) *A.B.C.; (ABCL 5207) <ABCD 988>* **LOVE IS ALL AROUND** (out-takes)	☐	☐

<US-cd-iss 1993 on 'Avenue'; R2 71218>

Jan 77.	(7"; by ERIC BURDON & WAR) *A.B.C.; <(12244)>* **MAGIC MOUNTAIN / HOME DREAM**	☐	☐
Jan 77.	(lp) *Charly; (CR 30018)* **SONNY BOY WILLIAMSON AND THE ANIMALS (live '63)**	☐	–

(re-iss. Dec81 as 'THE ANIMALS WITH SONNY BOY WILLIAMSON'; CR 30199) (re-iss. Nov88 on 'Decal'; LIK 45) (cd-iss. Jul90; CDCHARLY 215)

Sep 83.	(lp) *Polydor; (SPELP 40)* **ERIC BURDON AND THE ANIMALS**	☐	☐

(cd-iss. Nov90; 847 046-2)

Oct 87.	(lp/c) *E.M.I.; (746605-1/-4)* **THE SINGLES**	☐	☐

– (first 10 singles 'A' & 'B') *(cd-iss. Aug88; CZ 10)*

Apr 88.	(lp/c) *Platinum; (PLAT/PLAC 006)* **GREATEST HITS : ERIC BURDON – THE ANIMALS**	☐	☐
Dec 85.	(cd) *In-Akustik; (INAK 854CD)* **THAT'S LIVE (live by "ERIC BURDON & BAND")**	☐	☐
1988.	(cd) *Pair; <PCD 2-4791>* **ERIC BURDON SINGS THE ANIMALS' GREATEST**	–	☐

<re-iss. Oct95 on 'Avenue'; R2 71708>

Dec 88.	(lp/c/cd) *See For Miles; (SEE/+K/CD 244)* **THE EP COLLECTION**	☐	–

(cd re-iss. Mar99; same)

Jun 90.	(cd) *Nightriding; (KNCD 10013)* **GOLDEN DECADE**	☐	–
Jul 90.	(d-cd/d-c/d-lp) *E.M.I.; (CD/TC+/EM 1367)* **THE COMPLETE ANIMALS**	☐	–
Oct 90.	(7"/c-s) *E.M.I.; (EM/TCEM 154)* **WE'VE GOTTA GET OUT OF THIS PLACE. / THE HOUSE OF THE RISING SUN**	☐	–

(12"+=) *(12EM 154)* – Baby let me follow you down.		
(cd-s++=) *(CDEM 154)* – Blue feeling.		
Dec 90. (cd/c/lp) *Decal; (CD/C+/LIK 72)* **TRACKIN' THE HITS**	☐	-
Mar 91. (cd/d-lp) *Sequel; (NEXCD/NEDLP 153)* **INSIDE LOOKING OUT (THE 1965-1966 SESSIONS)**(cd+= extra tracks)	☐	-
1992. (cd) *Blue Wax; <117>* **THE UNRELEASED**	☐	
1992. (7") *Old Gold; (OG 8000)* **HOUSE OF THE RISING SUN. / WE'VE GOTTA GET OUT OF THIS PLACE**	☐	
Sep 92. (cd/c) *Prestige; (PRC DSP/ASSP 500)* **RARITIES**	☐	-
Oct 92. (cd) *Raven; (RVCD 11)* **ROADRUNNERS (1966-1968) (live)**	☐	-
Oct 92. (cd; ERIC BURDON) *Thunderbolt; (CDTB 017)* **CRAWLING KING SNAKE**	☐	-
Sep 93. (cd/c) *Spectrum; (550119-2/-4)* **INSIDE OUT**	☐	-
1993. (cd; ERIC BURDON) *Avenue; <R2 71219>* **SUN SECRETS / STOP**	☐	-
Jul 93. (cd; ERIC BURDON) *Polydor; (511778-2)* **GOOD TIMES**	-	☐
May 94. (cd; ANIMALS AND SONNY BOY WILLIAMSON) *Sixteen; (CD 9011)* **16 GREAT HITS**	☐	-
Apr 95. (cd; ERIC BURDON) *Jet; (JETCD 1011)* **LOST WITHIN THE HALLS OF TIME**	☐	-
Jul 95. (cd) *Laserlight; (16137)* **THE ANIMALS**	☐	-
Oct 95. (cd; ERIC BURDON) *Aim; (AIM 1054)* **MISUNDERSTOOD**	☐	-
Jul 96. (cd; ERIC BURDON) *Receiver; (RRCD 220)* **ERIC BURDON LIVE (live)**	☐	-
Aug 96. (cd; ERIC BURDON) *S.P.V.; (SPV 0858999-2)* **RARE MASTERS VOL.1**	☐	-
Aug 96. (cd; ERIC BURDON) *S.P.V.; (SPV 0854423-2)* **RARE MASTERS VOL.2**	☐	-
Nov 96. (cd) *Castle; (CLACD 424)* **GREATEST HITS LIVE**	☐	-
Feb 97. (cd; ERIC BURDON) *Thunderbolt; (CDTB 180)* **SOLDIER OF FORTUNE**	☐	-
Apr 97. (cd; ERIC BURDON) *B.R. Music; (RM 1542)* **GREATEST HITS**	☐	
Feb 98. (cd) *Hallmark; (392402)* **THE ANIMALS**	☐	
Sep 99. (d-cd) *B.R. Music; (BS 81122)* **THE STORY OF THE ANIMALS**	☐	
Sep 99. (cd) *Akarma; (AK 074)* **GUNSIGHT**	☐	

ANIMALS THAT SWIM (dig out; Great Alt & Indie . . .)

ANOTHER PRETTY FACE (see under ⇒ WATERBOYS)

Adam ANT (see under ⇒ ADAM AND THE ANTS)

ANTHRAX

Formed: Queens, New York, USA . . . mid'81, by NEIL TURBIN and DAN LILKER. SCOTT 'NOT' IAN, CHARLIE BENANTE and the diminutive DAN SPITZ completed the line-up, the band consequently spotted and signed to the 'Megaforce' label (licensed to 'Music For Nations' in Europe) by the legendary JOHNNY Z. The 1984 debut, 'FISTFUL OF METAL' (if you think the title's cheesy, wait till you see the cover!) hardly set the rock world alight, although 'METAL THRASHING MAD' was good for a laugh and the ALICE COOPER cover, 'I'M EIGHTEEN' was passable. By the release of the mini-album, 'ARMED AND DANGEROUS', the following year, the more traditional metal tonsils of JOEY BELLADONNA were being employed, a canny move that lent the band a modicum of style and sophistication. This was evident on ANTHRAX's first outing for 'Island', 'SPREADING THE DISEASE', a classy thrash metal affair that frequently rose above the narrow confines of the genre. By turns humorous, impassioned, and bloody loud, the likes of 'MADHOUSE' (a must-see video), 'AFTERSHOCK', 'ARMED AND DANGEROUS' and 'MEDUSA' made this one of the key metal releases of the 80's. 'AMONG THE LIVING' (1987) was almost as good and for many aging metallers, 'I AM THE LAW' is the definitive ANTHRAX track, a tribute to the meanest cop in Mega City One, Judge Dredd. 'INDIANS', meanwhile, was a more serious affair, dealing with the plight of their Native American brethren. Yet accomplished as the music was, it was almost overshadowed by the band's image. A case of bullet belts (!) out, skateboards and surf shorts in, for a brief, heady time in the late 80's, ANTHRAX almost made metal (whisper it now) trendy. Proving there was always a hip-hop element to their hardcore, the band released 'I'M THE MAN', a rap/metal pastiche that quite probably pissed off SAXON fans everywhere. At this point, the band were up there with METALLICA as the great white hopes of thrash and fans waited with bated breath for their next album, 'STATE OF EUPHORIA' (1988). Inevitably, perhaps, the record was a letdown; on first listen it sounded dense, promising; on repeated listening it became obvious the songs just weren't there. Equally inevitably, the band's dayglo image prompted a backlash. They retaliated with a considerably darker, more introspective opus, 'PERSISTENCE OF TIME' (1990). While the JOE JACKSON cover, 'GOT THE TIME', was engaging, the songwriting still wasn't up to scratch. A 1991 collaboration with CHUCK D on a storming cover of PUBLIC ENEMY's 'BRING THE NOISE' was the band's most effective effort for years and showed what they were obviously still capable of. The single was included on 'ATTACK OF THE KILLER B's', a compilation of B-sides and rare tracks, while ANTHRAX went on to tour with PUBLIC ENEMY on a genre-busting double bill. Signing a new contract with 'Elektra', the band promptly ditched BELLADONNA in favour of ex-ARMOURED SAINT man, JOHN BUSH. These were tough times for ANTHRAX, as every metal band on the planet purchased a distortion pedal, grew a goatee, and insisted they weren't actually metal after all, no, they were GRUNGE!! (of course). All credit to ANTHRAX then, for sticking to

their metal guns and releasing 'THE SOUND OF WHITE NOISE' (1993), a barrage of furious riffing that almost topped the work of their mid-80's golden period. 'STOMP 442' (1995) was equally ferocious, and while ANTHRAX mightn't sell as many records as they used to, they remain one of metal's best-loved bands. • **Songwriters:** SCOTT IAN except; I'M EIGHTEEN (Alice Cooper) / SABBATH BLOODY SABBATH (Black Sabbath) / GOD SAVE THE QUEEN and FRIGGIN' IN THE RIGGIN' (Sex Pistols) / GOT THE TIME (Joe Jackson) / BRING THE NOISE (Public Enemy) / PROTEST AND SURVIVE (Discharge) / LOOKING DOWN THE BARREL OF A GUN (Beastie Boys) / SHE (Kiss) / THE BENDS (Radiohead). • **Trivia:** DAN SPITZ's older brother DAVID played bass in the mid'80's with BLACK SABBATH. ANTHRAX an acting/ singing appearance on a 1992 showing of US TV sit-com 'Married With Children'. • **Note:** Not to be confused with UK "oi" band of the same name.

Album rating: FISTFUL OF METAL (*4) / SPREADING THE DISEASE (*8) / AMONG THE LIVING (*8) / STATE OF EUPHORIA (*5) / PERSISTENCE OF TIME (*7) / SOUND OF WHITE NOISE (*6) / STOMP 442 (*6) / S.O.D.: SPEAK ENGLISH OR DIE (*8) / LIVE FROM BUDOKAN (*7)

NEIL TURBIN – vocals / **DAN SPITZ** (b.28 Jan'63) – lead guitar / **SCOTT 'Not' IAN** (b.31 Dec'63) – rhythm guitar / **DAN LILKER** (b.18 Oct'64) – bass / **CHARLIE BENANTE** (b.27 Nov'62, The Bronx) – drums

		Music For Nations	Megaforce
Nov 83. (7") **SOLDIERS OF DEATH. / HOWLING FURIES**		-	
Jan 84. (lp) *(MFN 14) <MRS 469>* **FISTFUL OF METAL**		☐	

– Deathrider / Metal thrashing mad / I'm eighteen / Panic / Subjagator / Death from above / Across the river / Anthrax. *(re-iss. Apr87 lp/pic-lp; MFN 14DM/P) (c+=/cd+=; CD/T MFN 14)* – Soldiers of metal / Howling furies. *<US-cd-iss. 1987 on 'Caroline'; CAROLCD 1383> (re-iss. cd Sep95 on 'Bulletproof'; CDMVEST 56)*
(Mid'84) **MATT FALLON** – vocals repl. TURBIN

——— **FRANK BELLO** (b. 7 Sep'65) – bass (ex-roadie) repl. LILKER

——— (Aug'84) **MATT** was replaced by **JOEY BELLADONNA** (b.30 Oct'60, Oswego, NY) – vocals (ex-BIBLE BLACK)

		Music For Nations	Megaforce
Feb 85. (m-lp/pic-m-lp) *<MRS 05/+P>* **ARMED AND DANGEROUS**		-	☐

– Armed and dangerous / Raise Hell / God save the Queen / Metal thrashing mad / Panic. *(UK-iss.Aug87 on 'Music For Nations' lp/c; MFN/CMFN 123) (cd-iss. Nov91; CDMFN 123) (cd re-iss. Sep95 on 'Bulletproof'; CDMVEST 55)*

		Music For Nations	Megaforce-Island
Feb 86. (lp/c) *(MFN/TMFN 62) <90460>* **SPREADING THE DISEASE**		☐	Dec85

– A.I.R. / Lone justice / Madhouse / S.S.C – Stand or fall / The enemy / Aftershock / Armed and dangerous / Medusa / Gung ho. *(cd-iss. May86 on 'Island'; CID 9806) (pic-lp Sep87; MFNP 62) (re-iss. Aug91 on 'Island' cd)(c; IMCD 136)(ICM 9806)*

		Island	Island
May 86. (12"/12"s/12"pic-d) *(12IS/+B/P 285)* **MADHOUSE. / A.I.R. / GOD SAVE THE QUEEN**		☐	☐
Feb 87. (7"pic-d)(12") *(LAWP 1)(12IS 316)* **I AM THE LAW. / BUD E. LUVBOMB AND SATAN'S LOUNGE BAND**		32	

('A'live-7"red+=) *(ISX 316)* – Madhouse (live).

Apr 87. (lp/pic-lp/c/cd) *(ILPS/PILPS/ICT/CID 9865) <90584>* **AMONG THE LIVING**		18	62

– Among the living / Caught in the mosh / I am the law / Efilnikufesin (N.F.L.) / A skeleton in the closet / One world / A.D.I.- horror of it all / Imitation of life. *(cd re-iss. Mar94; IMCD 186)*

Jun 87. (7"orange/7"pic-d) *(IS/+P 325)* **INDIANS. / SABBATH BLOODY SABBATH**		44	

(12"+=/12"pic-d+=) *(12IS/+P 325)* – Taint.

Nov 87. (7"/7"sha-pic-d) *(IS/+P 338)* **I'M THE MAN. / CAUGHT IN THE MOSH**		20	-

(12"+=) *(12IS 338)* – I am the law (live).

Dec 87. (m-lp,c,cd) *<90685>* **I'M THE MAN**		-	53

– I'm the man (censored version) / I'm the man (Def uncensored version) / Sabbath bloody sabbath / I'm the man (live & extremely Def II uncensored version) / Caught in a mosh (live) / I am the law (live).

Sep 88. (7"yellow) *(IS 379)* **MAKE ME LAUGH. / ANTI SOCIAL (live)**		26	

(12"+=/cd-s+=) *(12IS/CIDP 379)* – Friggin' in the riggin'.

Sep 88. (lp/c/cd) *(ILPS/ICT/CID 9916) <91004>* **STATE OF EUPHORIA**		12	30

– Be all, end all / Out of sight, out of mind / Make me laugh / Anti-social / Who cares wins / Now it's dark / Schism / Misery loves company / 13 / (finale). *(re-iss. cd Apr94; IMCD 187)*

Mar 89. (7"/7"amber/7"blue/7"red) *(IS/+A/B/R 409)* **ANTI-SOCIAL. / PARASITE**		44	

(12"+=/12"amber+=/12"blue+=/12"red+=)(3"cd-s+=) *(12IS/+A/B/R 409)(CIDX 409)* – Le sects.

		Island	Megaforce
Aug 90. (7") *(IS 470)* **IN MY WORLD. / KEEP IT IN THE FAMILY**		29	☐

(10"+=/12"+=/cd-s+=) *(10IS/12IS/CID 470)* – ('A'&'B'extended).

Aug 90. (cd/c/lp) *(CID/ICT/ILPS 9967) <846480>* **PERSISTENCE OF TIME**		13	24

– Time / Blood / Keep it in the family / In my world / Gridlock / Intro to reality / Belly of the beast / Got the time / H8 red / One man stands / Discharge. *(pic-lp Jan91; ILPSP 9967) (re-iss. Apr94 cd)(c; IMCD 178)(ICM 9967)*

Nov 90. (c-s/10"/7") *(C/10+/CIS 476)* **GOT THE TIME. / WHO PUT THIS TOGETHER**		16	☐

(12"+=/cd-s+=) *(12IS/CID 476)* – I'm the man (live).

Jun 91. (c-s/7"; ANTHRAX featuring CHUCK D) *(C+/IS 490)* **BRING THE NOISE. / I AM THE LAW '91**		14	☐

(10"+=/12"+=/cd-s+=)(10"pic-d+=/12"pic-d+=) *(10IS/12IS/CID 490)(10/12 ISP 490)* – Keep it in the family (live).

——— CHUCK D. (of-PUBLIC ENEMY)

Jun 91. (cd/c/lp) *(CID/ICT/ILPS 9980) <848804>* **ATTACK OF THE KILLER B's** (rare studio)		13	27

– Milk (ode to Billy) / Bring the noise / Keep it in the family (live) / Startin' up a posse / Protest and survive / Chromatic death / I'm the man '91 / Parasite / Pipeline /

Sects / Belly of the beast (live) / N.F.B. (dallabnikufesin). *(re-iss. Apr94 cd)(c; IMCD 179)(ICM 9980)*

—— (May92) **JOHN BUSH** (b.24 Aug'63, L.A.) – vocals (ex-ARMOURED SAINT) repl. MARK OSEGUEDA who had replaced BELLADONNA

	Elektra	Elektra
Apr 93. (7"/c-s) *(EKR 166/+C)* **ONLY. / ONLY (mix)**	36	

(cd-s+=) *(EKR 166CD1)* – Cowboy song / Sodium pentaghol.
(cd-s) *(EKR 166CD2)* – ('A'side) / Auf wiedersehen / Noisegate.

May 93. (cd/c/lp) <*7559 61430-2/-4/-1*)> **SOUND OF WHITE NOISE**	14	7

– Potter's field / Only / Room for one more / Packaged rebellion / Hy pro glo / Invisible / 1000 points of hate / C11 H17 N2 O2 SNA / Burst / This is not an exit. *(cd+=)* – Black lodge. *(cd re-iss. Jap version Apr98 on 'Victor'; VICP 80320)*

Sep 93. (7"/c-s) *(EKR 171/+W)* **BLACK LODGE. / ('A'-Black strings mix)**	53	

(10"+=/12"pic-d+=/cd-s+=) *(EKR 171 TE/TP/CD)* – Pottersfield / Love her all I can.

Nov 93. (7"/c-s) *(EKR 178/+C)* **HY PRO GLO. / LONDON**
(12"+=/cd-s+=) *(EKR 178 T/CD)* – Room for one more (live).

Oct 95. (cd/c) <*7559 61856-2/-4*)> **STOMP 442**		47

– Fueled / Nothing / Bare / Random acts of senseless violence / Tester / Drop the ball / American Pompeii / In a zone / Perpetual motion / Riding shotgun / King size.

Jan 96. (c-s) *(EKR 216C)* **NOTHING / FUELLED (remix)**
(cd-s+=) *(EKR 216CD1)* – Remember tomorrow / Grunt and click.
(cd-s) *(EKR 216CD2)* – ('A'side) / Dethroned emperor / No time this time.

	Ignition – Tommy Boy	Ignition – Tommy Boy
Jul 98. (cd/c) <*IGN7 4034-3/-4*)> **VOLUME 8 – THE THREAT IS REAL!**	73	

– Crush / Catharsis / Inside out / Piss n vinegar / 604 / Toast to the extras / Born again idiot / Killing box / Harms way / Hog tied / Big fat / Cupajoe / Alpha male / Stealing from a thief.

Oct 98. (7") *(IGN 740516)* **INSIDE OUT. / GIVING THE HORNS**
(cd-s+=) *(IGN 740513)* – The bends.

– compilations, others, etc. –

Nov 92. (d-cd) *Island; (ITSCD 6)* **AMONG THE LIVING / PERSISTENCE OF TIME**
Apr 94. (cd/c/lp) *Island; (CID/ICT/ILPS 8027)* **ANTHRAX LIVE – THE ISLAND YEARS (live)**
Mar 98. (cd) *Connoisseur; (VSOPCD 252)* **MOSHERS 1986-1991**
Feb 99. (cd) *S.P.V.; (SPV 0761818-2)* **FISTFUL OF METAL / ARMED AND DANGEROUS**
Nov 99. (cd) *Beyond; (6398 578067-2)* **RETURN OF THE KILLER A's**

S.O.D.

(STORMTROOPERS OF DEATH)(off-shoot band of **SCOTT IAN + DAN LILKER** with **BILLY MILANO** – vocals (ex-PSYCHOS)

	Roadrunner	not iss.
Dec 85. (lp) *(RR 9725)* **SPEAK ENGLISH OR DIE**		–

– March of the S.O.D. / Sergeant "D" & the S.O.D. / Kill yourself / Milano mosh / Speak English or die / United forces / Chromatic death / Pi Alpha Nu / Anti-procrastination song / What's the noise / Freddy Kruger / Milk / Pre-menstrual princess blues / Pussy whipped / Fist banging mania. *(re-iss. Oct89 c/cd; RR/+34 9725-4)*

Sep 92. (cd/c/lp) *Music For Nations; (CD/T+/MFN 144)* **LIVE AT BUDOKAN (live)**
Mar 98. (cd) *Connoisseur; (VSOPCD 252)* **MOSHERS 1986-1991**

ANTI-NOWHERE LEAGUE   (dig out; Great Alt & Indie . . .)

APHEX TWIN

Born: RICHARD JAMES, 18 Aug'71, Limerick, Ireland. Isolated in the wilds of the South West of Cornwall, James began his precocious electronic tinkering at an early age. In true bedroom boffin style, he made his first recordings using customised analog synths at a cherubic 14 years old. Credited to AFX, his first release was 'ANALOGUE BUBBLEBATH VOL.1' (1991), released on the small dance indie label, 'Rabbit City'. The record created something of a buzz but it was 'DIDGERIDOO', included on 'ANALOGUE BUBBLEBATH VOL.2' (1991), which had legendary dance label 'R&S' chasing JAMES' signature. A sinister, didgeridoo-driven bpm marathon, it still sounds unique today. 'XYLEM TUBE' (1992) wasn't quite so scary while 'SELECTED AMBIENT WORKS '85-'92' (1992) was a largely beatless compilation containing some of his earliest creations. Signing to 'Warp', he recorded 'SURFING ON SINE WAVES' (1992) under the pseudonym POLYGON WINDOW. The album spawned the punishing rhythmical workout of the 'QUOTH' (1993) single, its dark intensity recalling 'DIGERIDOO'. By this point, APHEX TWIN was something of a cause celebre among the press, the indie papers surprisingly vocal in their support. With previous single releases, JAMES had missed the top 40 by a small margin but 'ON' (1993) gave him his first chart hit, reaching No.32. The second volume of 'SELECTED AMBIENT WORKS' was released the following year, the record concentrating on darker, more avant-garde material. This went down none too well with the critics and a backlash started to form. Silencing at least some of his detractors with 1995's 'I CARE BECAUSE YOU DO', the record featured equally dark but more consumer-friendly fare reflecting the (then) current penchant for trip hop. With 1996's 'RICHARD D. JAMES' album, the boy wonder explored drum 'n' bass textures replete with lush strings and the requisite exotic electronica. Having already caused a little controversy with his weirdo 'COME TO DADDY' video/single in '97, the APHEX TWIN laid low until 1999's Chris Cunningham-directed 'WINDOWLICKER'. This time the video/promo shoots

saw his face superimposed on the bodies of bikini-clad models, although this first new track for three years hit the Top 20. He remains one of electronic music's most enduring enigmas and anyone who drives a tank around their back garden sporting a 3-week old chin growth should definitely get our vote. • **Songwriters:** Ideas JAMES; sampled various and covered; FILM ME (Luxuria) / ONE DAY (Bjork). • **Trivia:** Was credited on SEEFEEL's 12" 'Time To Find Me (remixes)'.

Album rating: SELECTED AMBIENT WORKS '85-'92 (*8) / ANALOGUE BUBBLEBATH III (*6) / SELECTED AMBIENT WORKS, VOL.2 (*6) / CLASSICS compilation (*6) / . . . I CARE BECAUSE YOU DO (*7) / RICHARD D. JAMES (*6)

RICHARD D. JAMES (aka The APHEX TWIN) – keyboards, synthesizer

	Rabbit City	not iss.
Dec 91. (12"ep; as AFX) *(CUT 001)* **ANALOGUE BUBBLEBATH VOL.1**		–
Dec 91. (12"promo) *(009)* **ANALOGUE BUBBLEBATH VOL.2 (DIDGERIDOO 'Aboriginal' mix)** *(re-iss. 1993 as 12"ep; CUT 002)*	–	–

	Outer Rhythm – R&S	Rephlex
Apr 92. (12"ep) *(RSUK 12)* **ANALOGUE BUBBLEBATH VOL.2**	55	–

– Didgeridoo / Flaphead / Isoprolex.
(12"ep+=) *(RSUK 12CD)* – Analogue bubblebath 1.

Jul 92. (12"ep/cd-ep) **XYLEM TUBE EP**

Nov 92. (cd/c/d-lp) *(AMB 3922 CD/MC/LP)* **SELECTED AMBIENT WORKS '85-'92**		

– Xtal / Tha / Pulsewidth / Ageispolis / I won't let the Sun go down on me / Greencalx / Heliosphan / We are the music makers / Schotkey / Hedphelym / Delphium / Actium / Ptolemy. *(re-iss. Feb98 cd/d-lp; same)*

	Warp	Sire
Dec 92. (cd/c/clear-lp; as POLYGON WINDOW) *(WARP CD/MC/LP 7)* **SURFING ON SINE WAVES**		–

– Polygon window / Audax powder / Quoth / If it really is me / Supremacy II / UT 1 – Dot / (0.07) / Quixote / Quino – Phec. *(cd re-iss. Apr96; same)*

Mar 93. (12"ep/cd-ep; as POLYGON WINDOW) **QUOTH / IKEATA. / QUOTH (wooden thump mix) / QUOTH (bike pump meets bucket)**	49	–

—— In Jul'93, he teamed up with SEEFEEL on 'PURE / IMPURE' EP for 'Too Pure' 12"/cd-s; *PURE/+CD 025*)

Dec 93. (12"ep/cd+ep) **ON. / 73 YIPS. / D-SCAPE / XEPHA**	32	

(12"ep/cd-ep) *(WAP 39 R/CDR)* – ('A'-D-Scape mix) / ('A'-Reload mix) / ('A'-M-21Q) / ('A'-28 mix).

Mar 94. (d-cd/d-c/2xd-lp) *(WARP CD/MC/LP 21)* **SELECTED AMBIENT WORKS VOLUME II**	11	

– (12 + 13 of mostly untitled tracks; 1 of them 'Blue Calx')

	Warp	Sire
Mar 95. (12"ep/cd-ep) *(WAP 60/+CD)* **VENTOLIN / ('A'-Salbutanol mix) / ('A'-Marazanovose mix) / ('A'-Plain-an-guarry mix) / ('A'-The Coppice mix) / ('A'-Crowsnegods mix)**	49	

(12"ep/cd-ep; remixes) *(WAP 60 R/CDR)* – ('A'-Wheeze mix) / ('A'-Carnarack mix) / ('A'-Cyclob mix) / ('A'-Deep gong mix) / ('A'-Asthma beats mix).

Apr 95. (cd/c/d-lp) *(WARP CD/MC/LP 30)* **. . .I CARE BECAUSE YOU DO**	24	

– Acrid avid Jan Shred / The waxen path / Wax the nip / Icct Hedral / Ventolin / Come on you slags / Start as you mean to go one / Wet tip hen ax / Mookid / Alberto Balsan / Cow cud is a twin / Next heap with.

Aug 95. (12"ep/cd-ep) *(WAP 63/+CD)* **DONKEY RHUBARB EP**
– Icct Hedral (credited with PHILIP GLASS) / Pancake lizard / Mass observation (the crackdown) / Film me and finish off / One day (Sabres of Paradise mix) / Vaz deferenz.

—— In Jul'96, he collaborated with The MIKE FLOWERS POPS on a a 'Lo Recordings' 12"/cd-s release, 'FREEBASE'.

	Warp	Elektra
Oct 96. (12"/cd-s) *(WAP 78/+CD)* **GIRL/BOY EP**	64	–

– Girl/boy (NLS mix) / Milk man / Inkey $ / Girl/boy (#18 snare rush mix) / Beatles under my carpet / Girl/boy (redruth mix).

Nov 96. (cd/c/lp) *(WARP CD/MC/LP 43)* **RICHARD D. JAMES ALBUM**	62	

– 4 / Cornish acid / Peek 824545201 / Fingerbob / Corn mouth / To cure a weakling child / Goon gumpos / Yellow calx – Girl/boy song / Logic fock witch.

Oct 97. (12"/cd-s) *(WAP 094/+CD)* **COME TO DADDY (Pappy & Little Lord Faulteroy mixes). / FILM / BUCEPHALUS BOUNCING BALL**	36	

(cd-s) *(WAP 094CDR)* – ('A'side) / To cure a weakling child (contour regard) / Funny little man / IZ-US.

Mar 99. (12"/cd-s) *(WAP 105/+CD)* **WINDOWLICKER. / (FORMULA) / NANNOU**	16	

(cd-s+=) *(WAP 105CDR)* – ('A'-CD-Rom video).

– compilations, others, etc. –

(all on 'Rephlex' unless mentioned otherwise)

1992. (d-12"ep; as Q-CHASTIC) *(002EP)* **Q-CHASTIC EP**		–
1994. (12"; as KOSMIC KOMMANDO) *(CAT 007)* **THE KOSMIC KOMMANDO** *(also issued 1994 same label; MC 202)*		–
1994. (12"ep/cd-ep; as AFX) *(CAT 008/+CD)* **ANALOGUE BUBBLEBATH VOL.3** – (track numbers) *(re-iss. Nov97; same)*		–
1994. (12"; as CAUSTIC WINDOW) *(CAT 009)* **JOYREX 1. / JOYREX 2**		–
Aug 94. (12"ep/cd-ep; as AFX) *(CAT 019/+CD)* **ANALOGUE BUBBLEBATH VOL.4** – I / II / III / IV. *(re-iss. Apr98; same)*		–
Jan 95. (blue-d-lp/c/cd) *R&S; (RS 95035/+MC/CD)* **CLASSICS**	24	

– Digeridoo / Flaphead / Phloam / Isoprolex / Polynomial-C / Tamphex / Phlange phace / Dodeccaheedron / Analogue bubblebath / En trance to exit / AFX 2 / Metapharstic / Digeridoo (live). *(re-iss. Feb98; same)*

APHRODITE'S CHILD (see under ⇒ VANGELIS)

APOLLO 440

Formed: Liverpool, England . . . 1990 by GRAY brothers TREVOR & HOWARD, plus NOKO. Initially, they set up their own label, 'Stealth Sonic', to release early singles 'BLACKOUT', 'DESTINY' & 'LOLITA'. Their rock sampling sound was a hit with many established bands and they were soon to become remixers of some repute for the likes of U2, POP WILL EAT ITSELF, EMF, etc. Early in 1994, they had the first of many chart entries with 'ASTRAL AMERICA', sampling THE NICE's controversial version of BERNSTEIN & SONDHEIM's 'America'. Frontier mix 'n' match, techno 'n' roll, heavily influenced by French philosopher, Jean Baudrillard, 'MILLENNIUM FEVER' was eventually released early in '95. After the following year's novelty jazz cut-up, 'KRUPA', the techno terrorists took a heavier turn with early 1997's Top 10 hit, 'AIN'T TALKIN BOUT DUB', the single deriving the greater part of its not inconsiderable genius from a looped EDDIE VAN HALEN guitar riff. The 'ELECTRO GLIDE IN BLUE' album followed soon after, taking its name a la PRIMAL SCREAM's 'Vanishing Point', from a cult 70's movie. One track, 'PAIN IN ANY LANGUAGE', featured a vocal by the late, great BILLY MACKENZIE who admired them so much he requested their production skills for his next album prior to his untimely death. In August 1999, APOLLO FOUR FORTY once again rocketed up the charts, this time utilizing a sample of Status Quo's 'CAROLINE' on their Top 10 smash, 'STOP THE ROCK'. This previewed their third and best set to date, 'GETTIN' HIGH ON YOUR OWN SUPPLY', which resulted in their first major album chart appearance.

Album rating: MILLENNIUM FEVER (*6) / ELECTRO GLIDE IN BLUE (*6) / GETTIN' HIGH ON YOUR OWN SUPPLY (*7)

TREVOR GRAY – keyboards, vocals / **HOWARD GRAY** – backing vocals / **NOKO** – vocals, guitar, keyboards (ex-LUXURIA)

		Reverb	not iss.
1991.	(12") *(RVBT 001)* **LOLITA.** / ('A'-ambient)	☐	-
1991.	(12") *(RVBT 002)* **DESTINY (definitive hardcore mix).** / **DESTINY (theta wave immorality mix)**	☐	-
1991.	(12") *(RVBT 006)* **LOLITA (original hardcore mix).** / **DESTINY (definitive digital hardcore mix)**	☐	-
	(cd-s+=) *(RVBCDS 006)* – Lolita (USA '92) / Destiny (USA '92).		
	(12"/cd-s) *(RVB T/CDS 006R)* – Lolita (USA '92) / Lolita (USA instrumental '92) / Destiny (USA '92).		
Nov 91.	(12") *(RVBT 009)* **BLACK OUT.** / ('A'mix)	☐	-

		Stealth Sonic-Epic	Epic
1993.	(12"/cd-s) *(SSX T/CD 1)* **RUMBLE / HYDRAGLIDE.** / **LIQUID COOL (tune for cryonic suspension) (remix)**	☐	-
Jan 94.	(c-s) *(SSXM 2)* **ASTRAL AMERICA** / ('A'-Spirit Of America mix)	36	
	(12"+=/cd-s+=) *(SSX T/CD 2)* – ('A'-Orgone accumulator mix) / ('A'-Acid America mix).		
Oct 94.	(12"ep) *(SSXT 3)* **LIQUID COOL (Deep Forest Ice Cold @ The Equator mix)** / ('A'-Future Sound Of London remix) / ('A'-theme from Cryonic suspension) / ('A'-Jah Wobble remix)	☐	
	(cd-s+=) *(SSXCDX 3)* – ('A'-Re-animation mix).		
	(cd-s+=) *(SSXCD 3)* – ('A'-Deep Forest trans Afrique life extension express) / ('A'-Space colonization) / ('A'-Ollie J's live dubs) / ('A'-Space – 320 degrees F biostatic ambient mix).		
Feb 95.	(d-lp/c/cd) *(SSX/+C/CD 440)* **MILLENNIUM FEVER**	☐	
	– Rumble – Spirit of America / Liquid cool / Film me and finish me off / I need something stronger / Pain is a close up / Omega point / (Don't fear) The reaper / Astral America / Millennium fever / Stelth requiem. *(cd re-iss. Aug98; same)*		
Mar 95.	(c-s) *(SSXM 4)* **(DON'T FEAR) THE REAPER / HOLD ON (2 WOT U GOT)**	35	
	(cd-s+=) *(SSXCD 4)* – ('A'-@ 440 Reaper remix) / Reaper Hoodlum Priest remix.		
	(12") *(SSXT 4)* – (3 versions above; but not c-s 2nd track).		

APOLLO FOUR FORTY

Jul 96.	(c-s) *(SSXM 5)* **KRUPA (edit) / KRUPA (original)**	23	
	(cd-s+=) *(SSXCD 5)* – ('A'-Serotina) / ('A'-Alcatraz within the joint mix) / ('A'-Narcotic trust remix).		
	(12") *(SSXT 5)* – (no edit version).		
	(re-entered chart at No.24 in Sep'96)		
Feb 97.	(c-s) *(SSXM 6)* **AIN'T TALKIN' 'BOUT DUB / GLAM (Rock'n'roll part III)**	7	
	(cd-s+=) *(SSXCD 6)* – ('A'-Matrix remix) / ('A'-Nok-hop remix). above vocals, supplied by MARY MARY (ex-GAYE BIKERS ON ACID)		
Mar 97.	(cd/c/lp) *(SSX 2440 CD/C/LP)* **ELECTRO GLIDE IN BLUE**	62	
	– Stealth overture / Ain't talkin' 'bout dub / Altamont super-highway revisited / Electro glide in blue / Vanishing point / Tears of the gods / Krupa / White man's throat / Pain in any language / Stealth mass in F/m.		
Jun 97.	(c-s) *(SSXM 7)* **RAW POWER** / (instrumental)	32	
	(12"+=/cd-s+=) *(SSX T/CD 7)* – ('A'-Urban takeover mix) / ('A'-Matthew Roberts bass in your face mix) / ('A'-Aquanauts black ark mix).		
Nov 97.	(12"/d-cd-s) *(SSX 8 T/CDX)* **CARRERA RAPIDA (mixes).** / **(excerpts:- STEALTH OVERTURE - AIN'T TALKIN' 'BOUT DUB - VANISHING POINT - TEARS OF GODS) / (excerpts: WHITE MAN'S THROAT - PAIN IN ANY LANGUAGE - STEALTH MASS IN FM - RAW POWER)**	☐	-

—— In June '98, the group were credited alongside JEAN-MICHEL JARRE's on his new UK Top 20 version of 'RENDEZVOUS'.

Jul 98.	(c-s) *(SSX 9C)* **LOST IN SPACE** / ('A'-Jason Nevins Lunar Landing mix) / ('A'-Will & Penny's theme)	4	
	(cd-s) *(SSX 9CD)* – (first & third tracks) / Alpha point.		
	(cd-s) *(SSX 9CDX)* – (First & second tracks) / Imaginary forces.		
Aug 99.	(c-s) *(SSX 10CA)* **STOP THE ROCK / RAW POWER**	10	
	(cd-s+=) *(SSX 10CD)* – ('A'mixes).		
	(cd-s+=) *(SSX 10CDX)* – ('A'mixes).		
Sep 99.	(cd/c) *<62238>* **GETTIN' HIGH ON YOUR OWN SUPPLY**	20	
	– "Are we a rock band or what . . .?" / Stop the rock / Crazee horse / Cold cold the mic / Lost in space / For forty days / Heart go boom / The machine in the ghost / Blackbeat / Stadium parking lot / Yo! future / High on your own supply / Perfect crime.		
Nov 99.	(c-s) *(SSX 11CA)* **HEART GO BOOM / THE MACHINE IN THE GHOST (live) / HEART GO BOOM (Olav Basoski mix)**	57	
	(cd-s) *(SSX 11CD)* – ('A'side) / Anatomy (live) / The machine in the ghost (live).		
	(cd-s) *(SSX 11CDX)* – ('A'side) / ('A'-Lionrock mix) / ('A'Bad Company recordings mix) / ('A'-Harry K mix).		
	(12") *(SSX 11T)* – ('A'mixes).		

Fiona APPLE

Born: FIONA APPLE MAGGART, 13 Sep'77, New York City, New York, USA; her unmarried parents were separated when she was four. Raised most of her childhood by her jazz-loving mother and her BEATLES-obsessed step-father, FIONA found her solace in the poetry of Maya Angelou. However, more trauma was just around the corner when at the age of only twelve, she was raped outside her mother's apartment. Taking up singing as a way of channeling her emotions, FIONA was discovered by music publicist, Kathy Schenker (her babysitter at the time!), who sent her bedroom-cut demo on to 'Clean Slate' records boss, Andy Slater ('Sony'/'Work' would subsequently give it backing). In July '96 and after over eighteen months in the making, FIONA's debut album 'TIDAL' made the shops. Described as ALANIS MORISSETTE or TANITA TIKARAM with further angst to boot, the impressive album subsequently caught the attention of the American buying public and finally crawled all the way up to No.15 in the charts. One of it's highlights, 'CRIMINAL', took the Best Female Rock Performance Award at the 1998 Grammies, while another 'SLEEP TO DREAM' was released as a UK single. At the turn of the century, FIONA was already setting new boundaries by releasing her follow-up set, 'WHEN THE PAWN . . .', the longest album title ever! (the full title taken from a poem).

Album rating: TIDAL (*7) / WHEN THE PAWN . . . (*8)

FIONA APPLE – vocals, piano / with session people

		Columbia	Sony
Sep 96.	(cd/c) *(483750-2/-4) <67439>* **TIDAL**	15	Jul96
	– Sleep to dream / Sullen girl / Shadowboxer / Criminal / Slow like honey / The first taste / Never is a promise / The child is gone / Pale September / Carrion.		
Apr 97.	(c-s) *(664428-4)* **SLEEP TO DREAM / PALE SEPTEMBER**		-
	(10"+=/cd-s+=) *(664428-0/-2)* – Never is a promise / Sullen girl.		
Sep 97.	(c-s/cd-s) *<78595>* **CRIMINAL**	-	21
Jun 98.	(cd-s) *(6834)* **CRIMINAL / SLEEP TO DREAM (live)**	-	-
Jul 98.	(c-s/cd-s) *<110509>* **SHADOWBOXER / SHADOWBOXER / NEVER IS A PROMISE / CARRION (live)**	-	
Nov 99.	(cd-s) *<4630>* **FAST AS YOU CAN / NEVER IS A PROMISE / ACROSS THE UNIVERSE**	-	
Nov 99.	(cd/c) *<69195>* **WHEN THE PAWN . . .**	-	13
	– On the bound / To your love / Limp / Love ridden / Paper bag / Mistake / Fast as you can / The way things are / Get gone / I know.		

APPLES (IN STEREO)   (dig out; Great Alt & Indie . . .)

APRIL WINE   (dig out; Great Metal . . .)

ARAB STRAP

Formed: Falkirk, Scotland . . . 1995 by AIDAN MOFFAT and MALCOLM MIDDLETON. The former had already given up his day job at the local Sleeves record shop to team up with songwriter, JASON "JT" TAYLOR, in his outfit, BAY. This low-key band with drummer! AIDAN (augmented on their second release by RONNIE YOUNG, WILL HEGGIE – ex-COCTEAU TWINS – and ROSS BALLANY), released a couple of RED HOUSE PAINTERS-esque cd's, namely 'HAPPY BEING DIFFERENT' (1994) and 'ALISON RAE' (1995), the latter including a Lo-Fi cover of Roxy Music's 'IN EVERY DREAM HOME A HEARTACHE' and also coming free with an acoustic cd featuring a version of Nick Drake's 'WHICH WILL'. AIDAN, meanwhile, was plotting his own breakaway group, ARAB STRAP (named after a device used for horse-breeding and better known for something bought from a sex shop), re-establishing a friendship with MALCOLM while writing songs together in the latter's bedroom. A debut ARAB STRAP single, 'THE FIRST BIG WEEKEND', was warmly received by the music press in September '96, critics describing it as "trainspotting for the music world". AIDAN's drug/drink-fuelled life was portrayed in painful detail in a couple of the narrative songs from debut album, 'THE WEEK NEVER STARTS ROUND HERE' (incidentally the rhythm section was completed by GARY MILLER and DAVID GOW). His bittersweet, off-the-cuff, Scots-accented demo-esque sagas of broken romance were squeezed between Lo-Fi mumblings of occasional pure genius. MALCOLM's guitar-plucking, meanwhile, came from the laid-back school of cool, often played while literally lying on his back. The album was heralded by many (including John Peel) as the next big thing in exotic sound. It included seminal classics, 'THE CLEARING', 'COMING DOWN', 'I WORK IN A SALOON', 'WASTING' and 'DEEPER'. Their live set (including an early afternoon spot at Scotland's 'T In The Park' that added a host of singalong friends), was a mixture of apathy-in-concrete attitude with most people shouting for their favourite, 'THE FIRST BIG WEEKEND'; the track was subsequently used as the backing (with a new coherent talker!) on the Guinness ad (yes, that one that says about 38 per cent of all strippers were educated in a convent!). A year on, with word-of-mouth cult status ensured, ARAB STRAP finally achieved minor chart glory when 'THE GIRLS OF SUMMER' EP dented the Top 75. Following on from a double header tour with drinking buddies, MOGWAI, the now bearded AIDAN and Co delivered a surprise Top 50 hit, 'HERE WE GO' (a double A-side with 'TRIPPY'), one of the many low-rent, X-rated classics on their Top 40 Spring 1998 follow-up, 'PHILOPHOBIA'. Having signed up with 'Go Beat' early in '99, ARAB STRAP proceeded to deliver a disappointing stop-gap limited-edition live set, 'MAD FOR SADNESS'. Four months later, the 'CHERUBS' EP made amends and was one of the highlights of their rush-released third studio album, 'ELEPHANT SHOE'.

Album rating: THE WEEK NEVER STARTS ROUND HERE (*8) / PHILOPHOBIA (*8) / MAD FOR SADNESS (*6) / ELEPHANT SHOE (*7)

AIDAN MOFFAT – vocals, keyboards / **MALCOLM MIDDLETON** – guitar / with mainly **GARY MILLER** – bass / **DAVID GOW** – drums

		Chemikal Underground	Chemikal Underground
Sep 96.	(7") (CHEM 007) **THE FIRST BIG WEEKEND. / GILDED**		-
Nov 96.	(lp/cd) (<CHEM 010/+CD>) **THE WEEK NEVER STARTS ROUND HERE**		1997

– Coming down / The clearing / Driving / Gourmet / I work in a saloon / Wasting / General plea to a girlfriend / The first big weekend / Kate Moss / Little girls / Phone me tonight / Blood / Deeper.

| Mar 97. | (12"/cd-s) (CHEM 013/+CD) **THE CLEARING (guest starring Isobel Campbell & Chris Geddes). / (remixed by Hungry Lions) / (remixed by Iain Hanlon & Jonathan Hilditch)** | | - |
| Sep 97. | (12"ep/cd-ep) (CHEM 017/+CD) **THE GIRLS OF SUMMER E.P.** | 74 | - |

– Hey! fever / Girls of summer / The beautiful barmaids of Dundee / One day, after school.

| Nov 97. | (7"m) (LISS 22) **THE SMELL OF OUTDOOR COOKING. / THEME TUNE / BLACKSTAR** | | |

(above issued on 'Lissy's', below on 'Too Many Cooks')

| 1998. | (7") (BROTH 001) **LIVE: PACKS OF THREE. / BLOOD** | | - |

		Chemikal Underground	Matador
Mar 98.	(10"/cd-s) (CHEM 20 T/CD) **HERE WE GO. / TRIPPY**	48	-
Apr 98.	(cd) (CHEM 21CD) <OLE 315> **PHILOPHOBIA**	37	May98

– Packs of three / Soaps / Here we go / New birds / One day, after school / Islands / The night before the funeral / Not quite a yes / Piglet / Afterwards / My favourite muse / I would've liked me a lot last night / The first time you're unfaithful.

| Sep 98. | (7") (CHEM 27) **(AFTERNOON) SOAPS. / PHONE ME TOMORROW** | 74 | - |

(12"+=/cd-s+=) (CHEM 27 T/CD) – ('A'side) / Toy fights / Forest hills.

		Go Beat	Universal
May 99.	(cd/lp) (547387-2/-1) **MAD FOR SADNESS (live)**		-

– Intro / My favourite muse / Packs of three / New birds / Toy fights / Here we go / Phone me tomorrow / Girls of summer / Piglet / Blood / Afterwards.

| Aug 99. | (12"ep/cd-ep) (GOB X/CD 21 – 561263-1/-2) **CHERUBS E.P.** | | - |

– Cherubs / Motown answers / An eventful day / Pulled.

—— next with guests, CORA BISSETT, BARRY BURNS + ALAN WYLIE

| Sep 99. | (cd/lp) (547805-2/-1) **ELEPHANT SHOE** | ?? | |

– Cherubs / One four seven one / Pyjamas / Autumnal / Lay the day free / Direction of strong man / Tanned / Aries the ram / The drinking eye / Pro-(your) life / Hello daylight.

BAY

JASON "JR" TAYLOR – vocals, guitar, bass / with **AIDAN MOFFAT** – drums!

		Noise Annoys	Cargo
Nov 94.	(m-cd) (ANANCD 2) **HAPPY BEING DIFFERENT**		-

– Four miles / Spleen / Embossed and embellished / A shock in store for Piggsy / Kate / Your day out.

—— JR now with **AIDAN** / + **WILL HEGGIE** – bass (of LOWLIFE, ex-COCTEAU TWINS) / **ROSS BALLANY** – drums / **RONNIE YOUNG** – guitar

| Oct 95. | (cd) (ANANCD 6) **ALISON RAE** | | - |

– Washington / Pure / Home / Dutch / Siamese / In every dream home a heartache / In Lisa's living room / Ruptured / Are you alone? / A great red shark / Surely someone somewhere. (w/ free cd) **ACOUSTIC** – Washington / Pure / Surely someone somewhere / Concrete lions / Spleen / Obligatory / Kate / Four years / Spaniard / Which will.

ARCADIA (see under ⇒ DURAN DURAN)

ARGENT (dig out; 4th edition or Great Psychedelic . . .)

Joan ARMATRADING

Born: 9 Dec'50, Basseterre, St. Kitts, West Indies, although she and her family moved to Birmingham, England in '58. In 1969, she befriended PAM NESTOR (b. 28 Apr'48, Berbice, Guyana) with whom she initiated songwriting and stage partnership. They severed this arrangement when ARMATRADING alone was credited on a debut album in '73 for 'Cube'. Two years later she signed to 'A&M', releasing a belated follow-up set, 'BACK TO THE NIGHT', in 1975. However, it was with her third set, 'JOAN ARMATRADING' (1976), that the black singer/songwriter/guitarist fully realised her distinctive blend of folk, rock, pop and soul. While JONI MITCHELL was an obvious reference point, ARMATRADING had patented her own, richly resonant style which latter-day singers such as TRACY CHAPMAN would subsequently draw on for inspiration. Buoyed by the British Top 10 success of the classic 'LOVE AND AFFECTION' single, the album made the UK Top 20. Further success followed with 'SHOW SOME EMOTION' (1977) and 'TO THE LIMIT' (1978), veteran producer GLYNN JOHNS at the helm for the bulk of this developmental late 70's period. Despite a harder-edged direction, 1980's 'ME, MYSELF, I' became her most successful album to date, making the UK Top 5. Other early 80's sets such as 'WALK UNDER LADDERS' (1981) and 'THE KEY' (1983) were also well received, while the latter represented ARMATRADING's sole sojourn into the American Top 40. While never maintaining a particularly high profile, ARMATRADING has continued to record and release albums at regular intervals throughout the 80's and the 90's. Though she doesn't enjoy the commercial success of her earlier period, a loyal core of fans ensure that she usually makes the British Top 40. • **Songwriters:** She writes all material, except when PAM NESTOR wrote lyrics until '75. Covered: MOONDANCE (Van Morrison). • **Trivia:** MARK KNOPFLER (Dire Straits) and MARK BRZEZICKI (Big Country) guested on her 1988 album 'THE SHOUTING STAGE'.

Album rating: WHATEVER'S FOR US (*4) / BACK TO THE NIGHT (*5) / JOAN ARMATRADING (*7) / SHOW SOME EMOTION (*5) / TO THE LIMIT (*5) / STEPPIN' OUT (*5) / ME, MYSELF, I (*6) / WALK UNDER LADDERS (*5) / THE KEY (*6) / TRACK RECORD compilation (*7) / SECRET SECRETS (*5) / SLEIGHT OF HAND (*4) / THE SHOUTING STAGE (*4) / HEARTS AND FLOWERS (*4) / THE VERY BEST OF JOAN ARMATRADING compilation (*7) / SQUARE THE CIRCLE (*5) / WHAT'S INSIDE (*4) / LOVE AND AFFECTION compilation (*7)

JOAN ARMATRADING – vocals, acoustic guitar with various session people

		Cube	A&M
Nov 72.	(lp/c) (HIFLY/ZCFLY 12) <4382> **WHATEVER'S FOR US**		

– My family / City girl / Spend a little time / Whatever's for us / Child star / Mean old man / Visionary mountains / It could have been better / Head of the table / Mister remember me / Give it a try / Alice / Conversation / Mean old man / All the King's garden. (re-iss. Oct81 lp/c; same) (re-iss. Apr89 on 'Castle' lp/c/cd; CLA LP/MC/CD 143)

| Jul 73. | (7") (BUG 31) **LONELY LADY. / TOGETHER IN WORDS AND MUSIC** | | - |

		A&M	A&M
Apr 75.	(lp/c) (AMLH/CAM 68305) <4525> **BACK TO THE NIGHT**		

– No love for free / Travelled so far / Steppin' out / Dry land / Cool blue / Stole my heart / Get in touch with Jesus / Body to dust / Back to the night / So good / Let's go dancing / Come when you need me. (re-iss. Mar82; AMID 112) (re-iss. Sep84 on 'Hallmark' lp/c; SHM/HSC 3153)

Jun 75.	(7") (AMS 7181) **BACK TO THE NIGHT. / SO GOOD**		-
Nov 75.	(7") (AMS 7205) **DRY LAND. / BODY INTO DUST**		
Aug 76.	(lp/c) (AMLH/CAM 64588) <4588> **JOAN ARMATRADING**	12	67

– Down to zero / Help yourself / Water with the vine / Love and affection / Save me / Join the boys / People / Somebody who loves you / Like fire / Tall in the saddle. (cd-iss. 1988; CDA 3228) (re-iss. Aug91 cd/c; CD/C MID 104)

| Aug 76. | (7") (AMS 7249) <1865> **LOVE AND AFFECTION. / HELP YOURSELF** | 10 | |

(re-iss. 1988)

Jan 77.	(7") (AMS 7270) <1898> **DOWN TO ZERO. / LIKE FIRE**		
Apr 77.	(7") <1914> **WATER WITH THE WINE. / PEOPLE**		-
Sep 77.	(lp/c) (AMLH/CAM 68433) <4663> **SHOW SOME EMOTION**	6	52

– Woncha come on home / Show some emotion / Warm love / Never is too late / Peace in mind / Opportunity / Mama mercy / Get in the sun / Willow / Kissin' and a huggin'. (cd-iss. 1988; CDA 4663) (cd re-iss. Aug89; 394 663-2) (re-iss. Oct92 cd/c; CD/C MID 105)

Oct 77.	(7") (AMS 7316) **WILLOW. / NO WAY OUT**		-
Jan 78.	(7") (AMS 7331) **SHOW SOME EMOTION. / PEACE IN MIND**		-
Feb 78.	(7") <1994> **SHOW SOME EMOTION. / NO WAY OUT**	-	
Mar 78.	(7") (AMS 7346) **WARM LOVE. / GET IN THE SUN**		-
May 78.	(7") <2018> **WARM LOVE. / NO WAY OUT**	-	
Jun 78.	(7") (AMS 7365) **FLIGHT OF THE WILD GEESE. / NO WAY OUT**		
Sep 78.	(lp/c) (AMLH/CAM 64732) <4732> **TO THE LIMIT**	13	

– Barefoot and pregnant / Your letter / Am I blue for you / You rope you tie me / Baby I / Bottom to the top / Taking my baby up town / What do you want / Wishing / Let it last. (cd-iss. 1988; CDA 4732)

Oct 78.	(7") (AMS 7393) <2102> **BOTTOM TO THE TOP. / YOUR LETTER**		
Jan 79.	(7") <2113> **BAREFOOT AND PREGNANT. / YOUR LETTER**	-	-
Aug 79.	(lp/c) (AMLH/CAM 64789) **STEPPING OUT (live)**		

– Mama mercy / Cool blue / Stole my heart / How cruel / Kissin' and a huggin' / Love song / Love and affection / Stepin' out / You rope you tie me / Kissin' and a huggin' / Tall in the saddle. (re-iss. Sep85 on 'Hallmark' lp/c; SHM/HSC 3176)

| Dec 79. | (m-lp) <3302> **HOW CRUEL** | - | - |

– How cruel / He wants her / I really must be going / Rosie.

Jan 80.	(7") (AMS 7506) <2210> **ROSIE. / HOW CRUEL**	49	
Apr 80.	(7") <2224> **HE WANTS HER. / SHOW SOME EMOTION**	-	
May 80.	(lp/c) (AMLH/CAM 64809) <4809> **ME MYSELF, I**	5	28

– Me myself, I / Ma-me-o-beach / Friends / Is it tomorrow yet / Turn out the light / When you kisses me / All the way from America / Feeling in my heart (for you) / Simon / I need you. (cd-iss. Sep86; CDA 4809) (re-iss. May93 on 'Spectrum' cd/c; 550058-2/-4)

Jun 80.	(7") (AMS 7527) **ME MYSELF, I. / WHEN YOU KISS ME**	21	-
Jun 80.	(7") <2240> **ME MYSELF, I. / FRIENDS**	-	
Aug 80.	(7") (AMS 7552) **ALL THE WAY FROM AMERICA. / IS IT TOMORROW YET**	54	-
Sep 80.	(7") <2262> **IS IT TOMORROW YET. / MA-ME-O-BEACH**	-	
Oct 80.	(7") (AMS 7571) **SIMON. / HE WANTS HER**	-	
Aug 81.	(7") (AMS 8163) **I'M LUCKY. / SHINE**	46	-
Sep 81.	(lp/c) (AMLH/CAM 64876) <4876> **WALK UNDER LADDERS**	6	88

– I'm lucky / When I get it right / Romancers / I wanna hold you / The weakness in me / No love / At the hop / I can't lie to myself / Eating the bear / Only one. (cd-iss. Nov88; 394 876-2)

Oct 81.	(7") (AMS 8180) **WHEN I GET IT RIGHT. / CRYING**	-	
Jan 82.	(7") (AMS 8179) **NO LOVE. / DOLLARS**	50	-
Jan 82.	(7") <2381> **THE WEAKNESS IN ME. / CRYING**	-	
Apr 82.	(7") <2400> **I WANNA HOLD YOU. / CRYING**	-	
Feb 83.	(7") (AMS 8306) <2538> **DROP THE PILOT. / BUSINESS IS BUSINESS**	11	78 May83
Mar 83.	(lp/c) (AMLX/CXM 64912) <4912> **THE KEY**	10	32

– (I love it when you) Call me names / Foolish pride / Drop the pilot / The key / Everybody gotta know / Tell tale / What do boys dream / The game of love / The dealer / Bad habit / I love my baby. (cd-iss. Jun86; CDA 64912)

May 83.	(7") (AM 116) **(I LOVE IT WHEN YOU) CALL ME NAMES. / FOR THE BEST**	-	
Nov 83.	(7") <2622> **HEAVEN. / FRUSTRATION**	-	
Nov 83.	(7") (AM 162) **HEAVEN. / BACK TO THE NIGHT**	14	-
Nov 83.	(lp/c) (JA/+C 2001) **TRACK RECORD** (compilation)	18	-

– Drop the pilot / (I love it when you) Call me names / Frustration / When I get it right / I'm lucky / Me myself I / The weakness in me / Heaven / Down to zero / Love and affection / Show some emotion / Willow / Rosie. (cd-iss. Oct84; CDA 63725)

Feb 85.	(lp/c/cd) (<AMA/AMC/CDA 5040>) **SECRET SECRETS**	14	73

– Persona grata / Temptation / Moves / Talking to the wall / Love by you / Thinking man / Friends not lovers / One night / Secret secrets / Strange.

Feb 85.	(7") (AM 238) <2712> **TEMPTATION. / TALKING TO THE WALL**	65	

(12"+=) (AMY 238) – Spanking brand new.

May 85.	(7") (AM AM 250) <2751> **THINKING MAN. / LOVE GROWS**		
Aug 85.	(7"/12") (AM/+Y 269) **LOVE BY YOU. / READ IT WRITE**	-	
Apr 86.	(7"/12") (AM/+Y 315) <2837> **KIND WORDS (AND A REAL GOOD HEART). / FIGURE OF SPEECH**		
May 86.	(lp/c/cd) (<AMA/AMC/CDA 5130>) **SLEIGHT OF HAND**	34	68

– Kind words (and a real good heart) / Reach out / Killing time / Angel man / Laurel and the rose / One more chance / Russian roulette / Jesse / Figure of speech / Don Juan.

Jun 86.	(7") <2868> **ANGEL MAN. / RIVERS OF FIRE**	-	
Jul 86.	(7") (AM 338) **REACH OUT. / RIVERS ON FIRE**	-	
Sep 86.	(7") (AM 350) **JESSE. / DON JUAN**	-	

(d7"+=/12"+=) (AM S/Y 350) – Love and affection / Willow.

Jul 88.	(7") (AM 460) **LIVING FOR YOU. / INNOCENT REQUEST**		-

(12"+=/cd-s+=) (AM Y/CD 460) – Cool Blue stole my heart.

Jul 88.	(lp/c/cd) (<AMA/AMC/CDA 5211>) **THE SHOUTING STAGE**	28	100

– The Devil I know / Living for you / Did I make you up / Stronger love / The shouting stage / Words / Straight talk / Watch you step / All a woman needs / Dark truths. (cd+=) – Innocent request.

Jul 88.	(7") <1235> **LIVING FOR YOU. / I REALLY MUST BE GOING**	-	
Sep 88.	(7") (AM 449) <1259> **THE SHOUTING STAGE. / I REALLY MUST BE GOING**		

(12"+=/cd-s+=) (AM Y/CD 449) – He wants her.

Nov 88.	(7") (AM 482) **STRONGER LOVE. / THE DEVIL I KNOW**	-	
May 90.	(7"/c-s) (AM/+C 561) **MORE THAN ONE KIND OF LOVE. / GOOD TIMES**	75	

(12"+=/cd-s+=) (AM Y/CD 561) – Love and affection.

Jun 90.	(cd/c/lp) (395298-2/-4/-1) <5298> **HEARTS AND FLOWERS**	29	

– More than one kind of love / Hearts and flowers / Promise land / Someone's in the background / Can't let go / Free / Something in the air tonight / Always / Good times / The power of dreams.

Jun 90.	(7"/c-s) (AM/+C 567) **PROMISE LAND. / DOWN TO ZERO (live)**		

(12"+=/cd-s+=) (AM Y/CD 567) – Dark truths (live).

Aug 90.	(7") (AM 595) **FREE. / THE SHOUTING STAGE (live)**		

(cd-s+=) (AMCD 595) – Always.

May 92.	(7") (AM 877) **WRAPPED AROUND HER. / PROMISE LAND (live at the BBC)**	56	-

(cd-s) (AMCD 877) – ('A'side) / All the way from America / I'm lucky / Can't lie to myself (all live at the BBC).

Jun 92.	(cd/c/lp) (395888-2/-4/-1) **SQUARE THE CIRCLE**	34	

– True love / Crazy / Wrapped around her / Sometimes I don't wanna go home / Square the circle / Weak woman / Can I get next to you / Can't get over (how I broke your heart) / If women ruled the world / Cradled in your love.

Jul 92.	(7") (AM 881) **TRUE LOVE. / MORE THAN ONE KIND OF LOVE (live)**	-	

(12"+=/cd-s+=) (AM Y/CD 881) – Love and affection (live) / Something in the air (live).

		R.C.A.	**R.C.A.**
May 95.	(cd/c) (<74321 27269-2/-4>) **WHAT'S INSIDE**	48	

– In your eyes / Everyday boy / Merchant of love / Shapes and sizes / Back on the road / Lost the love / Songs / Would you like to dance / Recommend my love / Beyond the blue / Can't stop loving you / Shape of a pony / Trouble.

Feb 96.	(c-s) 74321 34112-4) **EVERYDAY BOY /**	-	

(cd-s+=) (74321 34112-2) –

– compilations, others –

Dec 76.	(7") Cube; (BUG 74) **ALICE. / ALL THE KING'S GARDEN**	-	
Jun 82.	(7") Cube; (BUG 93) **LONELY LADY. / VISIONARY MOUNTAINS**	-	

May 81.	(d-c) A&M; (CAMCR 2) **JOAN ARMATRADING / TO THE LIMIT**		-
Feb 85.	(lp/c) Sierra; (FEDB/CFEDB 5005) **REPLAY OF JOAN ARMATRADING**		-
Apr 88.	(cd-ep) A&M; (AMCD 903) **COMPACT HITS**		-

– Love and affection / All the way from America / Willow / Flight of the wild geese.

Jun 89.	(c) A&M; (AMC 24107) **ME MYSELF I / TRACK RECORD**		
Jun 90.	(cd/c) Knight; **THE GOLDEN HOUR OF JOAN ARMATRADING**		
Feb 91.	(7") A&M; **LOVE AND AFFECTION (remix). / ALL THE WAY FROM AMERICA**		

(12"+=/cd-s+=) – Promise land.

Mar 91.	(cd/c/lp) A&M; (397122-2/-4/-1) **THE VERY BEST OF JOAN ARMATRADING**	9	

– Love and affection / Down to zero / Drop the pilot / Show some emotion / The shouting stage / Willow / Rosie / I'm lucky / Me, myself, I / (I love it when you) Call me names / Bottom to the top / More than one kind of love / The weakness in me / All the way from America.

Oct 93.	(cd) A&M; **ME MYSELF I / WALK UNDER LADDERS**		-
Sep 95.	(d-cd) A&M; (540 405-2) **LOVE AND AFFECTION (A JOAN ARMATRADING ANTHOLOGY)**		-

(re-iss. Jan97; same)

Nov 99.	(cd) Spectrum; (554423-2) **THE COLLECTION**		-

ARMS AND LEGS (see under ⇒ JACKSON, Joe)

ARRESTED DEVELOPMENT

Formed: Atlanta, Georgia, USA ... late 1988 by head honcho SPEECH, formerly known as PEECH, due to his pale skin. They subsequently hooked up with DJ HEADLINER to form DISCIPLES OF LYRICAL REBELLION, changing the name to SECRET SOCIETY before finally deciding on ARRESTED DEVELOPMENT, at which point they began to hone their SLY STONE-influenced sound. The band signed to Chrysalis off-shoot, 'Cooltempo' early in 1991, and unleashed, a year later, their appropriately titled debut album '3 YEARS, 5 MONTHS AND 2 DAYS IN THE LIFE OF'. Dubbed "The Acceptable Face Of Rap", it showed a distinctive eco-conscious, Earth Mother blend of hip hop, jazz, soul and reggae. Their self-proclaimed "Life Music" breathed fresh air into the stagnant cesspool of "Gangsta Rap", although their hippy sentiments sometimes verged on idealistic naivety. The long-player received almost universal acclaim, and gained them a Top 10 placing on both sides of the Atlantic and over 4 million sales due to hit singles 'TENNESSEE', 'PEOPLE EVERYDAY' and 'MR WENDAL'. Their sound and lyrical content carried the Afrocentric torch on from The NATIVE TONGUES era, adding a rural charm which was at odds with the urban outlook of traditional hip hop. They also communicated their ideas on race issues, feminism and the environment to a wider cross section of the record-buying industry. In 1993, at the peak of their success, the band proved they were no armchair philosophers by visiting black community centres in Manchester and Birmingham. That year also saw the group win two Grammy awards and release a fine live album, 'UNPLUGGED'. Their second studio album 'ZINGALAMADUNI' (Swahili for "Beehive For Culture"), released in '94, didn't match the heavyweight commercial success of its predecessor although it was a magical cornucopia of black musical delights. While not as overtly psychedelic as say DE LA SOUL or PM DAWN, ARRESTED DEVELOPMENT appear to have a considered interest in moving minds as well as feet, and SPEECH (solo) remains one of hip hop's brightest hopes.

Album rating: 3 YEARS, 5 MONTHS AND 2 DAYS IN THE LIFE OF ... (*8) / UNPLUGGED (*4) / ZINGALAMADUNI (*5) / THE BEST OF ARRESTED DEVELOPMENT compilation (*6) / Speech: SPEECH (*4)

SPEECH (b. TODD THOMAS, 25 Oct'68, Milwaukee, Wis.) – vocals, producer, co-music director / **HEADLINER** (b. TIM BARNWELL, 26 Jul'67, N.J.) – turntable / **AERLE TAREE** (b. TAREE JONES, 10 Jan'73, Wisconsin) – vocals, dancer, stylist / **MONTSHO ESHE** (b. TEMELCA GARTHER, 23 Dec'74, Georgia) – dancer, vocals / **RASA DON** (b. DONALD JONES, 22 Nov'68) – drums / **BABA OJE** (b. 15 May'32, Laurie, Miss.) – spiritual advisor / plus extended family **DIONNE FARRIS + SISTER PAULETTE** – vocals / **CINQUE** (TERRANCE MASON) / **BROTHER LARRY** – guitar (1) / **LARRY JACKSON** – saxophone (1)

		Cooltempo	Chrysalis
Apr 92.	(c-s/7") (TC+/COOL 253) <23829> **TENNESSEE. / NATURAL**	46	6 Mar92

(12"+=/cd-s+=) (12/CD COOL 253) – ('A'mix).

Oct 92.	(c-s/7") (TC+/COOL 265) <50397> **PEOPLE EVERYDAY. / ('A'mix)**	2	8 Jul92

(12"+=/cd-s+=) (12/CD COOL 265) – Tennessee.

Oct 92.	(cd/c/lp) (CCD/CMC/CLP 1929) <21929> **3 YEARS, 5 MONTHS AND 2 DAYS IN THE LIFE OF ...**	3	7 May92

– Man's final frontier / Mama's always on stage / People everyday / Blues happy / Mr. Wendal / Children play with earth / Raining revolution / Fishin' 4 religion / Give a man a fish / U / Eve of reality / Dawn of the dreads / Tennessee / Washed away. (re-iss. cd.Mar94; same)

Dec 92.	(c-s/7") (TC+/COOL 268) <2481-0/-2> **MR. WENDAL. / REVOLUTION**	4	6 / 90

(12"+=/cd-s+=) (12/CD COOL 268) – ('A'-Perfecto mix, or It ain't no baseline mix') / ('A'-full mix).

Mar 93.	(c-s/7") (TC+/COOL 270) **TENNESSEE. / FISHIN' 4 RELIGION**	18	-

(cd-s+=) (CDCOOL 270) – ('A' remix) / Mama's always on the stage.

— added **NADIRAH ALI** – vocals plus new extended family **KUNDALINI MARK BATSON** – co-music director, piano / **JU JU HOUSE** – drums / **FREDERICK CASH JR.** – bass / **BRANDON ROSS** – guitar / **ATIBA WILSON** – percussion, flute / **DAVID**

PLEASANT – handmade percussion / **TERRANCE** (retained), **KELLI SAE, ARNAE, KEVIN CARNES & FULANI HART**

Apr 93. (cd/c/lp) *(CT CD/MC/LP 33)* <21994> **UNPLUGGED** | 40 | | 60 | Mar93
– Time / Give a man a fish / The gettin' / Natural / Searchin' for one soul / Raining revolution / Fishin' 4 religion / Mama's always on stage / U / Mr. Wendal / People everyday / *(next 7 all instrumental-)* Give a man a fish / The gettin' / Natural / Searchin' for one soul / Raining revolution / Mama's always on stage / Mr. Wendal.

—— TAREE was repl. by **AJILE** – vocals, dancer / **KWESI** – DJ, vocals

May 94. (c-s/7") *(TC+/COOL 293)* <58158> **EASE MY MIND. / SHELL** | 33 | | 45 |
(12"+=/cd-s+=) *(12/cd COOL 293)* – (2 'A'versions).

Jun 94. (cd/c/lp) *(CT CD/MC/LP 42)* <29274> **ZINGALAMADUNI** | 16 | | 55 |
– WMFW (We Must Fight & Win) Fm / United minds / Ache'n for acres / United front / Africa's inside me / Pride / Shell / Mister Landlord / Warm sentiments / The drum / In the sunshine / Kneelin' at my altar / Fountain of youth / Ease my mind / Praisin' U.

– compilations, etc. –

May 98. (cd) *E.M.I.; (494745-2)* **THE BEST OF ARRESTED DEVELOPMENT**
– People everyday (metamorposis radio edit) / Mr. Wendal / Raining revolution / Tennessee / Africa's inside me (Zingalamaduni mix) / Revolution / Give a man a fish / Ease my mind / Fishing 4 religion / Natural / Pride / Shell / Mama's always on stage / Ease my mind (another perspective mix) / Mr. Wendel (Perfecto mix) / People everyday (live).

SPEECH

—— with **PAPPA JON** – vocals / **FOLEY** – bass / **D.J. BROOKS** – drums / **DAVE COOLEY** – organ / **RICHARD STEWART** – guitar, bass / **JASON "TAKE TWO" THOMPSON** – vocals / **B.J. THOMAS** – chants / **AVERY JOHNSON** – bass / **LAURNEA WILKERSON** – vocals / **C.C.** – vibes, kalimba / **D.J. NABS** – turntables / **ALVIN SPEIGHTS** – bass / **STONEY BROOKS** – harmonica / **FREDDY "LULK" LUSTER** – acoustic guitar / **KWESI "D.J. KEMIT" ASUD** – vocals / **RICK "BIG GARBAGE DRUMS" MORRIS** – drums / **DARIAN EMORY** – sax / **KELLY O'NEAL** – sax / **MELVIN MILLER** – trumpet
Cooltempo Cooltempo

Feb 96. (c-s/12"/cd-s) *(MC/12/CD COOL 314)* **LIKE MARVIN GAYE SAID (WHAT'S GOING ON) / Arrested Development: MR. WENDAL (Perfecto mix)** | 35 | | |

Mar 96. (cd/c/lp) *(CT CD/MC/LP 52)* **SPEECH**
– Can you hear me? / Ask somebody who ain't (if you think the system's workin' . . .) / Filled with real / Why u gotta be feelin like dat / If u was me / Impregnated tid bits of dope hits / Let's be hippies / Freestyle #8 from Speech's vault / Like Marvin Gaye said, (what's going on) / Hopelessly / Insomnia song / Poor little music boy / Ghetto sex / Tell me something (let me know) / Runnin' wild / Another day at the podium.

ART OF NOISE

Formed: London, England . . . mid'83 by ANNE DUDLEY and J.J. JECZALIK, who soon added GARY LANGAN. Signed to TREVOR HORN and PAUL MORLEY's new label 'Z.T.T.' through 'Island' (late in 1984), they secured their first UK Top 10 hit 'CLOSE TO THE EDIT'. Following on from their sonic innovations with the mutant hip-hop cut-up of 'BEATBOX', the single's eccentric appeal built on a pioneering collage of sound which combined sampled noises, snatches of vocals and a body-popping rhythm track. The accompanying album, '(WHO'S AFRAID OF?)' made the UK Top 30, although follow-up single, the sublime 'MOMENTS IN LOVE', stalled outside the Top 40. Subsequently breaking from mentor, HORN, the trio signed to 'China' records and secured the services of DUANE EDDY for an electro-enhanced revamp of the twang-tastic 'PETER GUNN', complete with filmic musical support. The single made the Top 10, while a follow-up, 'PARANOIMIA' (featuring the erm, "talents" of 80's icon, MAX HEADROOM) was almost as successful, both tracks taken from the Top 20 album, 'IN VISIBLE SILENCE' (1986). Although LANGAN later became a part-time member, The ART OF NOISE scored another sizeable hit with their ingenious remakes of PRINCE's 'KISS' in conjunction with Welsh warbler, TOM JONES. A further collaboration, this time with South African singers, MAHLATHIM & THE MAHOTELLA QUEENS, for the 'YEBO' single, failed to chart and as the three members increasingly concentrated on individual projects, the band disintegrated. As well as various film scores (see below:- trivia), ANNE went on to work with KILLING JOKE's JAZ COLEMAN on the exotic 'SONG FROM VICTORIOUS CITY' (1990) and later recorded an electronically enhanced classical set, 'ANCIENT AND MODERN', in 1995, before going on to work with trip-hop outfit, MOLOKO. DUDLEY, HORN and MORLEY came out of the proverbial wilderness in '99 with their tribute to 20th century classical composer, CLAUDE DEBUSSY. The album 'THE SEDUCTION OF . . .' – featuring actor John Hurt as narrator – started off in fine transcendental form although it turned out to be inconsistent and dance-orientated towards the latter half. • **Trivia:** ANNE was a pianist on children's BBC-TV programme 'Playschool' until she became part of CINDY & THE SAFFRONS with actress JOANNE WHALLEY-(KILMER). Their single 'PAST PRESENT & FUTURE' hit No.56 early 1983. She now writes / arranges / sessions for PHIL COLLINS ('Buster') / BOY GEORGE / A-HA / MOODY BLUES / PAUL McCARTNEY / LLOYD COLE / etc. Her film scores include; Disorderlines (1987), Hiding Out (1987), Dragnet (1987), Buster (1988), Silence Like Glass (1989), The Mighty Quinn (1989), Say Anything (1989), Wilt (1990), The Miracle (1991), The Pope Must Die (1991), The Crying Game (1992; nominated for an oscar) & Knight Moves (1993). JEKZALIK has produced PET SHOP BOYS / GODLEY & CREME /

PAUL McCARTNEY / etc. LANGAN too has produced ABC / BILLY IDOL / SPANDAU BALLET / PUBLIC IMAGE LTD. / etc. (PAUL MORLEY as JJ quoted 'Made tea and gave titles to songs'). ART OF NOISE have been heard on TV ads and programmes such as 'The Krypton Factor' and 'The Return Of Sherlock Holmes'.

Album rating: (WHO'S AFRAID OF?) THE ART OF NOISE (*7) / IN VISIBLE SILENCE (*4) / IN NO SENSE? NONSENSE (*4) / THE BEST OF THE ART OF NOISE compilation (*7) / BELOW THE WASTE (*5) / THE SEDUCTION OF CLAUDE DEBUSSY (*4) / Anne Dudley: SONGS FROM THE VICTORIOUS CITY with Jaz Coleman (*5) / ANCIENT & MODERN (*5)

ANNE DUDLEY (b. 7 May'56) – keyboards (ex-CINDY & THE SAFFRONS) / **J.J. JECZALIK** (b.11 May'55) – keyboards, programmer / **GARY LANGAN** – multi, synthesizers / with **TREVOR HORN** – keyboards, producer (ex-YES, ex-BUGGLES)

		Z.T.T.- Island	Island
Aug 83.	(12"ep/c-ep) *(Z/C TIS 100)* **INTO BATTLE WITH THE ART OF NOISE**		-

– Battle / The army now / Donna / Bright noise / Flesh in armour / Come and goes / Moments in love.

Mar 84. (12") *(ZTIS 108)* **BEATBOX (DIVERSIONS 1). / BEATBOX (DIVERSIONS 2)** | | | - |

Oct 84. (7"pic-d/7") *(P+/ZTPS 01)* **CLOSE (TO THE EDIT). / A TIME TO HEAR (WHO'S LISTENING)** | 8 | | |
(12") *(12ZTPS 01)* – CLOSE UP. / CLOSE UP (HOP)
(12") *(12ZTPS 01)* – (above 2 plus 'A'side).
(12"pic-d) *(12ZTPS 01)* – EDITED. / A TIME TO CLEAR (IT UP)
(12") *(12ZTPS 01)* – CLOSELY CLOSELY (ENOUGH'S ENOUGH). / (7"B-side)
(+=) – Close Up (Hop)// or / / Moments In Love.
(c-s) *(CTIS 106)* – ('A'side)/ (various mixes of 'A').

Oct 84. (lp/c) *(ZT/C TIQ 2)* <90179> **(WHO'S AFRAID OF?)** | 27 | | 85 |
– A time for fear (who's afraid?) / Beat box (diversion one) / Snapshot / Close (to the edit) / Who's afraid (of the Art Of Noise) / Moments in love / Momento / How to kill / Realisation. *(cd-iss. Dec85; ZCTIQ 2) (re-iss. May94 cd/c; 4509 94746-2/-4) (cd re-iss. Nov98; ZTT 111CD)*

Mar 85. (7"sha-pic-d/7") *(P+/ZTPS 02)* **MOMENTS IN LOVE. / BEATBOX** | 51 | | |
(12") *(12ZTPS 02)* – ('A'side) / Beaten / Beatbox diversion 10 / Love beat.
(c-s) *(CTIS 109)* – ('A'side) / (various mixes).
(re-iss. Jun87- 7"/12"; WEEP/+S 1)

—— added guest **GEOFF DUGMORE** – drums (ex-EUROPEANS) / HORN also departed

		China	Chrysalis
Oct 85.	(7") *(WOK 5)* **LEGS. / HOOPS AND MALLETS**	69	

(12"+=) *(WOKR 5)* – Legs (Inside leg mix).

Mar 86. (7"/7"sha-pic-d; by ART OF NOISE with DUANE EDDY) *(WOK/+P 6)* <42986> **PETER GUNN. / SOMETHING ALWAYS HAPPENS** | 8 | | 50 |
(12"+=) *(WOKR 6)* – ('A'-Twang mix).

Apr 86. (lp/c/cd) *(WOL/ZWOL 2)(835806-2)* <41528> **IN VISIBLE SILENCE** | 18 | | 53 |
– Opus 4 / Paranoimia / Eye of a needle / Legs / Peter Gunn / Slip of the tongue / Beatback / Instruments of darkness / Camilla / Chameleon's dish / Legs. *(cd+=)* – Peter Gunn (extended). *(re-iss. Jul91 cd/c; WOL CD/MC 1016)*

May 86. (7"/7"sha-pic-d; by ART OF NOISE & MAX HEADROOM) *(WOK/+P 9)* <43002> **PARANOIMIA. / WHY ME?** | 12 | | 34 |
(12"+=) *(WOKR 9)* – A nation rejects / ('A'version).

—— trimmed to duo when LANGAN was now only part-time

Oct 86. (7") *(WOK 11)* **LEGACY. / OPUS III** | | | |
(12"+=) *(WOKX 11)* – Legs / ('A'version).

Jul 87. (7") *(WOK 14)* **DRAGNET (ART OF NOISE '88). / ACTION ART** | 60 | | |
(12"+/c-s+=) *(WOK X/MC 14)* – Dragnet (Arthur Baker mix).

Aug 87. (lp/c/cd) *(WOO/ZWOO 4)(835807-2)* <41570> **IN NO SENSE? NONSENSE!** | 55 | | |
– Galleons of stone / Dragnet / Fin du temps / How rapid? / Opus for four / Debut / E.F.L. / Ode to Don Jose / A day at the races / Counterpoint / Roundabout 727 / Random on the sand / Roller 1 / Nothing was going to stop them anyway / Crusoe / One Earth. *(re-iss. Jul91 cd/c; WOL CD/MC 1011) (cd re-iss. Jul99; 450995913-2)*

Feb 88. (7") *(CHINA 4)* **DRAGNET. / DRAGNET (A-O-N mix)** | | | |
(12"+=) *(CHINAX 4)* – ('A' Arthur Baker mix).

Nov 88. (7"; by ART OF NOISE featuring TOM JONES) *(CHINA 11)* <871038> **KISS. / E.F.L.** | 5 | | 31 |
(cd-s+=) *(CHICD 11)* – Kiss (the battery mix).
(12") *(CHINX 11)* – ('A'version) / Ode to Don Jose.

Mar 89. (7"pic-d) *(CHIXP 14)* **PARANOIMIA '89. / LOCUS CASSICUS** | | | |
(12"+=/cd-s+=) *(CHINX/CHICD 14)* – One Earth / Rounding of the sand / Debut / Adananda.

Jul 89. (7"; as ART OF NOISE featuring MAHLATHINI AND THE MAHOTELLA QUEENS) *(CHINA 18)* **YEBO. / DAN DARE** | 63 | | |
(12"pic-d+=) *(CHIXP 18)* – ('A'remix).
(12"+=/cd-s+=) *(CHINX/CHICD 18)* – Add to the confusion / Yebo (mbaguana mix).

Sep 89. (lp/c/cd) *(839 404-1/-4/-2)* **BELOW THE WASTE** | | | |
– Yebo / Promenade 1 / Island / Chain gang / Back to back / Spit / Catwalk / Dilemma / Dan Dare / Promenade 2 / Flashback / Finale. *(re-iss. Apr91 lp/c/cd; WOL/+MC/CD 1011)*

Jun 90. (7") *(CHINA 23)* **ART OF LOVE. / HEART OF LOVE** | 67 | | |
(12"+=/cd-s+=) *(CHINX/CHICD 23)* – Ambience of love.

—— split until around the end of the 90's, **DUDLEY, HORN + MORLEY** were credited as the new line-up

		Z.T.T.	
Jun 99.	(12"/cd-s) *(ZTT 129 T/CD)* **METAFORCE (mixes; original / Rhythm masters / Roni Size)**	53	

(cd-s) *(ZTT 129CD2)* – ('A'mixes; intromix / Ollie J / Shark tank).

Jun 99. (cd/c) *(ZTT 130 C/CD)* **THE SEDUCTION OF CLAUDE DEBUSSY**
– Il pleure (at the turn of the century) / Born on a Sunday / Dreaming in colour / On being blue / Continued in colour / Rapt: in the evening air / Metaforce / The holy egoism of genius / La flute de pan / Metaphor on the floor / Approximate mood swing No:2 / Pause / Out of this world (version 138).

– compilations, others, etc. –

on 'China' unless mentioned otherwise
Dec 88. (lp/c/cd) *(837 367-1/-4/-2) <837367>* **THE BEST OF ART OF NOISE** `55` `83`
– Beatbox / Moments in love / Close (to the edit) / Peter Gunn / Paranoimia / Legacy / Dragnet '88 / Kiss / Something always happens / Opus 4. (cd+=) – (several extended remixes). *(re-iss.Jul91 lp/c/cd; WOL/+MC/CD 1010) (re-iss.Aug92 cd/c; WOL CD/MC 1027) (cd re-iss.Jul99; 450996102-2)*
Jul 90. (cd/c/lp) *(843403-2/-4/-1)* **THE AMBIENT COLLECTION (THE SOUND OF ONE MAN CLAPPING)**
(re-iss.Apr91 lp/c/cd; WOL/+MC/CD 1012) (cd re-iss.Jul99; 450996098-2)
Dec 91. (7"/c-s) *(WOK/+C 2012)* **INSTRUMENTS OF DARKNESS (ALL OF US ARE ONE PEOPLE) (The Prodigy mix). / L.E.F. (Mark Brydon mix)** `45`
(12"+=/cd-s+=) *(WOK X/CD 2012)* – ('A'&'B'-Prodigy remixes).
Jan 92. (lp/c/cd) *(WOL/+MC/CD 1023)* **THE FON REMIXES** `-`
(re-iss.Jul99; 450996101-2)
Feb 92. (7"/c-s) *(WOK/+C 2014)* **SHADES OF PARANOIMIA (Carl Cox mix). / ROLLER 20 (rhythmatic mix)** `53`
(12"+=/cd-s+=) *(WOK X/CD 2014)* – Kiss / Peter Gunn / Paranoimia.
May 94. (cd/c) *Z.T.T.; (4509 94747-2/-4)* **DAFT** `-`
(cd re-iss.Nov98; ZTT 112CD)
Mar 95. (12") *(WOKT 2052)* **YEBO (the trust mix). / YEBO (the arkarna dub)** `-`
Oct 96. (d-lp/cd) *(WOL/+CD 1072)* **THE DRUM & BASS COLLECTION** `-` `-`
(cd re-iss.Jul99; 0630 16463-2)
Aug 97. (t-cd) *(WOLCD 1075)* **STATE OF THE ART** `-`

ANNE DUDLEY & JAZ COLEMAN

(JAZ – vocals, keyboards, (of KILLING JOKE)

	China	China

Sep 90. (7"/c-s) **MINARETS AND MEMORIES. / THE AWAKENING**
(12"+=/cd-s+=) – ('A'dance mix).
Oct 90. (cd/c/lp) *(847098-2/-4/-1)* **SONGS FROM THE VICTORIOUS CITY**
– The awakening / Endless festival / Minarets and memories / Force and fire / Mabebe / Ziggaretts of cinnamon / Hannah / The conquerer / A survivor's tale / In a timeless place. *(re-iss.Apr91 lp/c/cd; WOL/+MC/CD 1009)*
Dec 90. (7") **MABEBE. / THE CONQUERER**
(12"+=/cd-s+=) – In a timeless place.

ANNE DUDLEY

	Echo	not iss.

Feb 95. (cd/c) *(ECH CD/MC 3)* **ANCIENT & MODERN**
– Canticles of the Sun and the Moon / Veni sancte spiritus / Communion / Veni Emmanuel / Tallis Canon / The holly and the ivy / Coventry carol / Prelude / 3 chorals in common time.
Nov 95. (c-s) *(ECSMC 15)* **VENI EMMANUEL / THE HOLLY AND THE IVY** `-`
(cd-s+=) *(ECSCD 15)* – The sunset carol / The testimony of John.

——— ANNE DUDLEY augmented MOLOKO (with ROISON MURPHY on vocals). Released album 'DO YOU LIKE MY TIGHT SWEATER?' March '96. The single 'FUN FOR ME' hit UK Top 40.

ART OF SILENCE

——— with JJ JECZALIK

	Permanent	not iss.

Aug 96. (12"/cd-s) *(AX 12X/CDX 001)* **WEST 4. / ('A'mixes)**
(12") *(AX12X 002)* – ('A'remixes).
Sep 96. (cd/d-lp) *(PERM CD/LP 032)* **ARTOFSILENCE.CO.UK** `-`
– West 4 / 4.34 / Who are you / Some other dream / No malice / Fear / Giant without / Giant within / Messenger of Heaven. *(cd re-iss.Sep98; PERMCDX 32)*

ASH

Formed: N.Ireland ... 1989 by TIM WHEELER (then 12 years of age) and MARK HAMILTON, relocating to Downpatrick, County Down a few years later where they officially formed the trio with RICK McMURRAY. ASH's precocious talents were quickly spotted by American record moguls eager for more punk-centric guitar music which would also cross over to the pop market. Though they eventually opted to sign with 'Reprise', the trio had already released their debut set, 'TRAILER' on 'Infectious'. Their starry-eyed, bushy-tailed but ultimately derivative blend of indie punk finally became a part of the pop vocabulary when the catchy 'GIRL FROM MARS' sky-rocketed into the UK Top 20 in summer '95. This was pursued by another Top 20 hit later that year in 'ANGEL INTERCEPTOR'. With the hype machine going into overload, the group hit the UK Top 5 in Spring of the following year with 'GOLDFINGER', the single trailing a No.1 album, '1977' (1996). Apparently a reference to the year 'Star Wars' was released rather than any reference to safety-pins and saliva, the record included all their hit singles to date and confirmed their increasingly melodic approach. Keeping their profile high with festival appearances, the band later added another guitarist, CHARLOTTE

HATHERLEY, in summer '97. She made her debut on ASH's theme for the much lauded Ewan McGregor/Cameron Diaz film, 'A LIFE LESS ORDINARY', another Top 10 in late '97. While the indie scene continues to cry out for something innovative, it remains difficult to envisage any figureheads less ordinary than ASH (songs!). Surprisingly 'Kerrang!-friendly, the quartet lost a little of their indie cred with the release of their third album proper, 'NU-CLEAR SOUNDS' (1998), a record that quickly vacated the Top 10 with the accompanying single, 'JESUS SAYS', only managing to make a Top 20 placing. With sex (group, that is), drugs (abuse) and rock'n'roll (Tim Wheeler in the buff!) all the ingredients were in the latest promo instalment for ASH's single 'NUMBSKULL'. Unfortunately the viewing public, and for that matter the buying public, didn't get much of a look-in, as the EP (like many others at the turn of the century) was ineligible for the charts via a new ruling by those pesky compilers. • **Songwriters:** WHEELER or w/ HAMILTON except covers; PUNKBOY (Helen Love) / GET READY (Temptations) / DOES YOUR MOTHER KNOW (Abba) / LOSE CONTROL (Backwater) / BLEW (Nirvana) / WHO YOU DRIVIN' NOW? (Mudhoney). • **Trivia:** The cover sleeve of their single, 'KUNG FU', had a photo of French former Man U star footballer, ERIC CANTONA, giving his famous throat and neck tackle on an abusive Crystal Palace supporter in 1995.
Album rating: TRAILER mini (*7) / 1977 (*9) / LIVE AT THE WIRELESS live official bootleg (*5) / NU-CLEAR SOUNDS (*7)

TIM WHEELER – vocals, guitar / **MARK HAMILTON** – bass / **RICK McMURRAY** – drums

	La La Land	not iss.

Feb 94. (7") *(LA LA 001)* **JACK NAMES THE PLANETS. / DON'T KNOW** `-`

	Infectious	Reprise

Aug 94. (7"ep) *(INFECT 13S)* **PETROL. / THE LITTLE POND / A MESSAGE FROM OSCAR WILDE AND PATRICK THE BREWER** `-`
(cd-s+=) *(INFEVT 13CD)* – Things. *(re-iss.Nov96; same)*
Oct 94. (cd/c/lp) *(INFECT 14CD/MC/LP) <45985>* **TRAILER** Oct95
– Season / Message from Oscar Wilde and Patrick the brewer / Jack names the planets / Intense thing / Uncle Pat / Message from Mr. Waterman / Get out / Petrol / Obscure thing. (lp w/ free 7"yellow) *(INFECT 14S)* SILVER SURFER. / JAZZ '59 *<diff.tracks US>*
Oct 94. (7") *(INFECT 16S)* **UNCLE PAT. / DIFFERENT TODAY**
(cd-s+=) *(INFECT 16CD)* – Hulk Hogan bubble bath. *(re-iss.Nov96; same)*
Mar 95. (7") *(INFECT 21J) <17706>* **KUNG FU. / DAY OF THE TRIFFIDS** `57` Nov95
(cd-s+=) *(INFECT 21CD)* – Luther Ingo's star cruiser. *(re-iss.Nov96; same)*
Jul 95. (7"/c-s) *(INFECT 24S/24MC)* **GIRL FROM MARS. / CANTINA BAND** `11`
(cd-s+=) *(INFECT 24CD)* – Astral conversations with Toulouse Lautrec. *(re-iss. Nov96; same)*
Sep 95. (7"colrd-various) *<G26>* **PETROL. / PUNKBOY** `-`
Oct 95. (7"/c-s/cd-s) *(INFECT 27S/27MC/27CD)* **ANGEL INTERCEPTOR. / 5 A.M. ETERNAL / GIVE ME SOME TRUTH** `14` `-`
(re-iss. cd-s Nov96; same)
Dec 95. (7"red) *(FP 004)* **GET READY. / ZERO ZERO ZERO**
(above 45 issued on 'Fantastic Plastic')
Apr 96. (7"/c-s) *(INFECT 39 S/MC)* **GOLDFINGER. / I NEED SOMEBODY / SNEAKER** `5` `-`
(cd-s+=) *(INFECT 39CD)* – Get ready. *(re-iss. Nov96; same)*
May 96. (cd/c/lp) *(INFECT 40 CD/MC/LP) <46191>* **1977** `1`
– Lose control / Goldfinger / Girl from Mars / I'd give you anything / Gone the dream / Kung Fu / Oh yeah / Let it flow / Innocent smile / Angel interceptor / Lost in you / Darkside lightside. (cd+=hidden track) – Sick of vomiting.
Jun 96. (7"yellow/c-s) *(INFECT 41 S/MC)* **OH YEAH / T. REX / EVERYWHERE IS ALL AROUND / OH YEAH (quartet version)** `6` `-`
(cd-s) *(INFECT 41CD)* – (first 3 tracks) / Does your mother know. *(re-iss. Nov96; same)*

——— added **CHARLOTTE HATHERLEY** – guitar (ex-NIGHTNURSE)

	Infectious	Imprint

Oct 97. (7"blue/c-s) *(INFECT 50 S/MC)* **A LIFE LESS ORDINARY. / WHERE IS LOVE GOING / WHAT DEANER WAS TALKING ABOUT** `10`
(cd-s+=) *(INFECT 50CD)* – Halloween.
Sep 98. (7") *(INFECT 059S)* **JESUS SAYS. / TAKEN OUT** `15`
(c-s+=/cd-s+=) *(INFECT 059 MCS/CDS)* – Heroin, vodka, white noise.
(cd-s) *(INFECT 059CDSX)* – ('A'side) / Radiation / Dancing on the Moon.
Oct 98. (cd/c/lp) *(INFECT 060 CD/MC/LP) <112507>* **NU-CLEAR SOUNDS** `7`
– Projects / Low ebb / Jesus says / Wild surf / Death trip 21 / Folk song / Numbskull / Burn out / Aphrodite / Fortune teller / I'm gonna fall.
Nov 98. (7") *(INFECT 061S)* **WILD SURF. / STORMY WATERS** `31`
(c-s+=/cd-s+=) *(INFECT 061 MCS/CDS)* – When I'm tired.
(cd-s) *(INFECT 061CDSX)* – ('A'side) / Lose control / Gonna do it soon.

——— added on tour **DJ DICK KURTAINE** – turntables
Apr 99. (d7"red-ep) *(INFECT 62)* **NUMBSKULL EP** `-` `-`
– Numbskull / Blew / Who you drivin' now? / Jesus says (live).
(cd-ep+=) *(INFECT 62EP)* – Girl from Mars (live) / Fortune teller (live).

– compilations, etc. –

Feb 97. (cd) *Death Star; (DEATH 3)* **LIVE AT THE WIRELESS (live)** `-`

Daniel ASH (see under ⇒ BAUHAUS)

ASIA

Formed: London, England . . . early 1981 by seasoned pomp-rockers, JOHN WETTON, STEVE HOWE, CARL PALMER and GEOFREY DOWNES. These supergroup stadium fillers had no trouble finding a record contract with 'Geffen', their eponymous debut soon climbing to No.1 in the States, supplanting them as top dogs over similar challengers, YES. Their smooth FM-friendly AOR blend fared particularly well in the US, 'HEAT OF THE MOMENT', 'ONLY TIME WILL TELL' and 'DON'T CRY', all becoming Top 20 hits in 1982. The follow-up, 'ALPHA', didn't live up to the high expectations afforded it, although it still reached the Top 10 on both sides of the Atlantic. For a brief two year period, GREG LAKE filled in for the absent WETTON, the singer returning to record a third album, 'ASTRA' in '85. HOWE was also missing, having returned to YES, his replacement being MANDY MEYER. All this disruption clearly had a knock-on effect on album sales, the record stiffing in the lower regions of the chart. With another experienced campaigner, PAT THRALL, drafted in, the group recorded 'THEN & NOW', a 1990 set of re-worked favourites and a handful of new tracks. In 1992, with only DOWNES and PALMER remaining from the original line-up, they left 'Geffen' and recorded a fifth album, 'AQUA', which was followed by some more unremarkable cd outings, DOWNES having taken on full control when PALMER returned to ELP. • **Trivia:** Their "Asia In Asia" concert at Budokan, Tokyo 6 Dec'83, went live to over 20 million people in US through MTV station.

Album rating: ASIA (*6) / ALPHA (*4) / ASTRA (*3) / THEN & NOW (*5) / AQUA (*3) / ARIA (*3)

JOHN WETTON (b.12 Jul'49, Derby, England) – vocals, bass (ex-URIAH HEEP, ex-ROXY MUSIC, ex-BRYAN FERRY, ex-KING CRIMSON, ex-FAMILY, ex-U.K.) / **STEVE HOWE** (b. 8 Apr'47) – guitar, vocals (ex-YES, ex-BODAST, ex-TOMORROW) / **GEOFFREY DOWNES** – keyboards, vocals (ex-YES, ex-BUGGLES, ex-ISOTOPE) / **CARL PALMER** (b.20 Mar'47, Birmingham, England) – drums, percussion (ex-EMERSON, LAKE & PALMER, ex-P.M.)

		Geffen	Geffen
Apr 82.	(lp/pic-lp/c) *(GEF/+11/40 85577)* <2008> **ASIA** – Heat of the moment / Only time will tell / Sole survivor / One step closer / Time again / Wildest dream / Without you / Cutting it fine / Here comes the feeling. *(cd-iss. Apr83; CDGEF 85577) (re-iss. Sep86 lp/c; 902008-1/-4) (cd-iss. Feb87; 902008-2) (re-iss. Apr91 cd/c; GEFD/GEFC 02008) (re-iss. cd Apr92; GFLD 19054)*	**11**	**1**
Jun 82.	(7") *(A 2494)* <50040> **HEAT OF THE MOMENT. / TIME AGAIN**	46	4 Apr82
Aug 82.	(7"/7"pic-d) *(A/+11 2228)* <29970> **ONLY TIME WILL TELL. / RIDE EASY**	54	17 Jul82
Oct 82.	(7") *(A 2884)* **SOLE SURVIVOR. / HERE COMES THE FEELING**		
Aug 83.	(7"/7"sha-pic-d) *(A/WA 3580)* <29571> **DON'T CRY. / DAYLIGHT** (12"+=) *(TA 3580)* – True Colours.	33	10 Jul83
Aug 83.	(lp/c) *(GEF/GEC 25508)* <4008> **ALPHA** – Don't cry / The smile has left your eyes / Never in a million years / My own time (I'll do what I want) / The heat goes on / Eye to eye / The last to know / True colours / Midnight Sun / Open your eyes. *(c+=)* – Daylight. *(re-iss. Sep86 lp/c; 940008-1/-4) (cd-iss. Jun89; 94008-2) (re-iss. Apr91 & Aug99 cd/c; GEFD/GEFC 04008)*	5	6
Oct 83.	(7") *(A 3836)* <29475> **THE SMILE HAS LEFT YOUR EYES. / LYING TO YOURSELF** (12"+=,12"red+=) *(TA 3836)* – Midnight Sun.		34
——	(Oct83) **GREG LAKE** (b.10 Nov'48, Bournemouth, England) – vocals, bass (ex-EMERSON, LAKE & PALMER, ex-Solo Artist, ex-KING CRIMSON) repl. WETTON		
——	(Mar84). **ARMAND 'Mandy' MEYER** – guitar (ex-KROKUS) repl. HOWE who returned to YES and formed G.T.R.		
——	**JOHN WETTON** returned to replace LAKE (re-joined E.L.P.)		
Nov 85.	(7") *(A 6737)* <28872> **GO. / AFTER THE WAR** (A-remix-12"+=) *(TA 6737)* – ('A'instrumental).		46
Dec 85.	(lp/c/cd) *(GEF/40GEF/CDGEF 26413)* <24072> **ASTRA** – Go / Voice of America / Hard on me / Wishing / Rock and roll dream / Countdown to zero / Love now till eternity / Too late / Suspicion / After the war.	68	67
Jan 86.	(7") **WISHING. / TOO LATE**	-	-
——	(early 1986, disbanded) **WETTON** teamed up with **PHIL MANZANERA**		
——	In Sep87, **GEOFFREY DOWNES** released solo lp/cd 'THE LIGHT PROGRAMME' on 'Geffen'; *K 924156-1/-2)*		
——	re-formed late 1989 (WETTON, DOWNES, PALMER plus **PAT THRALL** – guitar (ex-AUTOMATIC MAN). He was replaced by session men **STEVE LUKATHER, RON KOMIE, MANDY MEYER** and **SCOTT GORHAM**		
Aug 90.	(cd/c/lp) *(CD/40+/GEF 24298)* **THEN & NOW** (hits compilation & new songs) – (THEN) Only time will tell / Wildest dreams / The smile has left your eyes / Heat of the moment / Don't cry / (NOW) – Days like these / Prayin' 4 a miracle / Am I in love? / Voice of America / Summer (can't last too long). *(re-iss. Aug91 cd/c; GEF D/C 24298)*		
Sep 90.	(c-s/cd-s) <19677> **DAYS LIKE THESE. / VOICE OF AMERICA**	-	64
——	**JOHN PAYNE** – vocals, bass; repl. WETTON		
——	**AL PITRELLI** – guitar (ex-DANGER DANGER) repl. THRALL		
——	**STEVE HOWE** also made guest appearance		

		FM Coast To Coast	JRS
Jun 92.	(cd/c/lp) *(WKFM XD/XC/LP 180)* **AQUA** – Aqua (part one) / Who will stop the rain / Back in town / Love under fire / Someday / Little rich boy / The voice of reason / Lay down your arms / Crime of		Mar92

the heart / A far cry / Don't call me / Heaven on Earth / Aqua (part two). *(cd re-iss. Feb98 on 'Snapper'; SMMCD 521)*

		Musidisc	Sony
Aug 92.	(7") *(10952-7)* **WHO WILL STOP THE RAIN. / AQUA (part 1)** (10"pic-d+=/12"+=) *(10952-1/-6)* – Heart of gold. (cd-s++=) *(10952-2)* – Obsessing.		
——	**MICHAEL STURGIS** – drums; repl. PALMER		

		Bulletproof	M.F.N.
May 94.	(cd-ep) *(CDVEST 1001)* **ANYTIME / REALITY / ANYTIME (extended) / FEELS LIKE LOVE**		
May 94.	(cd/c/lp) *(CD/C+/VEST 8)* **ARIA** – Anytime / Are you big enough? / Desire / Summer / Sad situation / Don't cut the wire (brother) / Feels like love / Remembrance day / Enough's enough / Military man / Aria. *(cd re-iss. Feb98 on 'Snapper'; SMMCD 523)*		
——	**VINNIE BURNS + TREVOR THORNTON** repl. PITRELLI plus injured HOWE		

– compilations, etc. –

Jun 92.	(cd) *Essential; (ESSCD 174)* / Rhino; <R2 70377> **ASIA LIVE MOCKBA 09-XI-90** (live)		Nov90
Nov 97.	(d-cd) *Blueprint; (BP 255CD)* **LIVE IN PHILADELPHIA** (live)		-
Feb 98.	(cd) *Snapper; (SMMCD 522)* **ARENA**		
Mar 98.	(cd) *Eagle; (EAMCD 037)* **LIVE IN MOSCOW** (live)		
Jun 98.	(cd) *Resurgence; (LV 104CD)* **ARCHIVA VOL.1** *(re-iss. Sep99 on 'Snapper'; SMMCD 596)*		
Jun 98.	(cd) *Resurgence; (LV 105CD)* **ARCHIVA VOL.2** *(re-iss. Sep99 on 'Snapper'; SMMCD 597)*		
Feb 99.	(d-cd) *Recall; (SMDCD 217)* **AXIOMS** – Bella nova / Who will stop the rain / Heaven on Earth / Words / Turn it around / Summer / Heaven / Far cry / Love under fire / Tell me why / Anytime / Aqua part two / Into the arena / Military man / Hunter / Desire / Sad situation / The day before the war / Feels like love / Different worlds / Remembrance day / U bring me down / Aria.		-
Oct 99.	(cd) *Resurgence; (LV 107CD)* **LIVE AT THE TOWN & COUNTRY** (live)		
Nov 99.	(cd) *Resurgence; (LV 108CD)* **LIVE ACOUSTIC** (live)		

ASIAN DUB FOUNDATION

Formed: Farringdon, London, England . . . 1993 by DR. DAS, PANDIT G and MASTER D, a tutor, an assistant and a student respectively at an inner-city community music programme designed for young aspiring Asian musicians/DJ's/MC's/etc. Initially trading as a sound system, ADF began making their own records the following year. Signed to 'Nation' (home of TRANSGLOBAL UNDERGROUND), the trio issued the 'CONSCIOUS' EP prior to adding unorthodox sitar-influenced guitarist, CHANDRASONIC, synth man SUN-J and stage dancer, BUBBLE-E. Taking up the agit-prop, slash'n'burn politico-musical baton from the ailing SENSER, ADF fought off the neo-Nazis with an inflammatory combination of Bengali folk, drum'n'bass and punk that strangely and uniquely recalled the spirit of ALTERNATIVE TV's MARK PERRY. In 1995, this radical troupe unleashed their debut long player, 'FACTS AND FICTIONS', a surprising cohesive set given the amount of disparate musical strands running through each track. Amassing a cult following drawn from both the indie and dance communities (much in the same way that The PRODIGY had risen to such giddy heights a few years earlier), ADF soon found themselves under the wing of 'London' offshoot, 'FFRR' in 1997. Gaining more column inches and higher chart placings with each successive release via the incendiary singles, 'NAXALITE', 'BUZZIN', 'FREE SATPAL RAM' and 'BLACK WHITE', the long awaited follow-up set, 'RAFI'S REVENGE' (1998) blazed a trail into the UK Top 20. Nominated for a 'Mercury Award', the album didn't win but received some free televised publicity/criticism courtesy of Fantasy Football thingy/ 3 Lions/"comedian", David Baddiel, who obviously prefers the fluffier sounds of the LIGHTNING SEEDS. While working on their follow-up set (scheduled for 2000), ADF were trying to convince the Home Office to "Free SATPAL RAM", the Asian man still in prison after 13 years.

Album rating: FACTS AND FICTIONS (*7) / RAFI'S REVENGE (*9)

MASTER D (DEEDER ZAMAN) – rapping / **PANDIT G (JOHN PANDIT)** – turntables, voice / **DR. DAS (ANIRUDDHA DAS)** – bass, programming, voice

		Nation	not iss.
Aug 94.	(12"ep/cd-ep) *(NR 42 T/CD)* **CONSCIOUS EP.** – Debris / Tu meri / Jericho / Witness.		
——	added **CHANDRASONIC (STEVE CHANDRA SAVALE)** – guitar, programming, vocals (ex-HEADSPACE, ex-The HIGHER INTELLIGENCE AGENCY)		
——	added **SUN-J (TAILOR)** – synths / + dancer **BUBBLE-E**		
Apr 95.	(12"ep/cd-ep) *(NR 51 T/CD)* **REBEL WARRIOR. / STRONG CULTURE**		-
Oct 95.	(cd/lp) *(NAT CD/LP 58)* **FACTS AND FICTIONS** – Witness / Pknb / Jericho / Rebel warrior / Journey / Strong culture / Th9 / Tu meri / Debris / Box / Thacid 9 (dub) / Return to Jericho – dub. *(cd re-iss. Aug98; NATCDM 058)*		-
May 96.	(12"/cd-s) *(NR 61 T/CD)* **CHANGE A GONNA COME. / OPERATION EAGLE LIE / C.A.G.C. (VIA PIRATE SATELLITE) / JERICHO**		-

		Damaged Goods	not iss.
Jul 97.	(7"; split with ATARI TEENAGE RIOT) *(DAMGOOD 132)* **split**		-

	Sub Rosa	not iss.
Jul 97. (12"; split with EUPHONIC) *(QUANTUM 605)* **TRIBUTE: . . . SOUND SYSTEM / WAY OF THE EXPLODING FIST**	☐	-

— now as ASIANDUBFOUNDATION

	FFRR	Polygram
Oct 97. (7") *(F 320)* **NAXALITE. / CHARGE** (12"+=/cd-s+=) *(FX/FCD 320)* – ('A'+'B'mixes).	☐	-
Feb 98. (7") *(F 326)* **FREE SATPAL RAM. / TRIBUTE TO JOHN STEPHENS** (12"+=/cd-s+=) *(FX/FCD 326)* –	56	☐
Apr 98. (12"ep/cd-ep) *(FX/FCD 335)* **BUZZIN' (mixes) / DIGITAL UNDERCLASS** (cd-ep) *(FCDP 335)* – ('A'side) / Free Satpal Ram / Charge / Naxalite.	31	☐
May 98. (cd/c/d-lp) *(556 006-2/-4/-1) <556 053>* **RAFI'S REVENGE**	20	☐

– Naxalite / Buzzin' / Black white / Assassin / Hypocrite / Charge / Free Satpal Ram / Dub mentality / Culture move / Operation eagle lie / Change / Tribute to John Stevens.

| Jun 98. (12"/cd-s) *(FX/FCDP 337)* **BLACK WHITE / BLACK WHITE (maximum roach mix). / NAXALITE (Underdog mix) / NAXALITE (Underdog instrumental)** (cd-s) *(FCD 337)* – ('A'side) / Rafi / Assassin (live) / Buzzin' (live). | 52 | - |
| Sep 98. (12"ep/cd-ep) *(FX/FCD 348) <570289>* **NAXALITE / CULTURE MOVE EP** | ☐ | Nov98 |

– Naxalite (main mix) / Culture move (pusher sound mix) / Free Satpal Ram (Russell Simmons mix) / Culture move (urban decay mix) / Culture move (silver haze mix).

ASPHALT RIBBONS (see under ⇒ TINDERSTICKS)

ASSEMBLY (see under ⇒ YAZOO)

ASSOCIATES

Formed: Dundee, Scotland ... 1979 by BILLY MacKENZIE and ALAN RANKINE, who had worked as a duo in 1976, The ABSORBIC ONES. After a debut single on their own 'Double-Hip' label, they signed to Chris Parry's 'Fiction', a subsidiary of 'Polydor' records. Their glorious debut set, 'THE AFFECTIONATE PUNCH', was followed by a series of highly rated 45's for the independent 'Situation 2' label. In 1982, they enjoyed their first taste of success with stylish 'PARTY FEARS TWO' and 'CLUB COUNTRY' both hit the UK Top 20. Energetic alternative dance rock, featuring the high, passionate vocals of MacKENZIE, The ASSOCIATES inimitable, unclassifiable sound enjoyed only a very brief liaison with the pop charts. Now signed to 'Warners', the group's more accessible 'SULK' (1982) album made the UK Top 10, its lavish arrangements, white funk and stirring vocal histrionics going down well amid the craze for all things "New Romantic". Despite this belated recognition, the pair subsequently went their separate ways, losing their commercial momentum in the process. When they finally got back together in 1984 (with a line-up of STEVE GOULDING, IAN McINTOSH, ROBERT SUAVE and L. HOWARD JONES), MacKENZIE and RANKINE recorded only one further single together, 'THOSE FIRST IMPRESSIONS', before the latter finally bowed out. The remaining members recorded the 'PERHAPS' (1985) album, a relative flop which saw a further set, 'THE GLAMOUR CHASE', shelved and MacKENZIE returned in 1990 with an album on the 'Circa' label, 'WILD AND LONELY', to little reaction. The ASSOCIATES name had seemingly been laid to rest when, a couple of years later, the singer released a solo set, 'OUTERNATIONAL'. The next five years were quiet as MacKENZIE attended to his beloved greyhounds in his native Dundee. The music world was shocked, when, on the 22nd January '97, it was announced that the Scotsman had taken his own life; he'd reportedly been depressed after the death of his mother a little earlier. Ironically, MacKENZIE had signed to the hip 'Nude' label (home of SUEDE), and had been working on new material at the time of his death. This material was posthumously released as 'BEYOND THE SUN', pundits and public alike mourning the death at 39 of one of music's forgotten geniuses. • **Songwriters:** Lyrics / music by duo (until RANKINE's departure), except BOYS KEEP SWINGING (David Bowie) / LOVE HANGOVER (Diana Ross) / GOD BLESS THE CHILD (Billie Holiday) / HEART OF GLASS (Blondie) / KITES (Simon Dupree & The Big Sound) / GROOVIN' WITH MR. BLOE (Mr. Bloe) / GREEN TAMBOURINE (Lemon Pipers) / I'M GONNA RUN AWAY FROM YOU (Tammi Lynn). • **Trivia:** MacKENZIE featured on B.E.F.'s (HEAVEN 17) single 'IT'S OVER' circa '82.

Album rating: THE AFFECTIONATE PUNCH (*6) / FOURTH DRAWER DOWN singles compilation (*8) / SULK (*7) / PERHAPS (*5) / WILD AND LONELY (*4) / POPERA: THE SINGLES COLLECTION compilation (*8) / Billy MacKenzie: OUTERNATIONAL (*5) / BEYOND THE SUN (*8)

BILLY MacKENZIE (b.27 Mar'57) – vocals / **ALAN RANKINE** – keyboards, guitar, etc

	Double Hip	not iss.
Oct 79. (7") *(DHR 1)* **BOYS KEEP SWINGING. / MONA PROPERTY GIRL** (re-iss. Dec79 on 'M.C.A.'; MCA 537)	☐	-

— added **NIGEL GLOCKER** – drums / guest **ROBERT SMITH** – guitar (of-CURE) who replaced unknown guitarist

	Fiction	not iss.
Aug 80. (7") *(FICS 11)* **THE AFFECTIONATE PUNCH. / YOU WERE YOUNG**	☐	-
Aug 80. (lp/c) *(FIX/+C 5)* **THE AFFECTIONATE PUNCH**	☐	-

– The affectionate punch / Amused as always / Logan time / Paper house / Transport to Central / A matter of gender / Even dogs in the wild / Would I . . . bounce

back / Deeply concerned / A. *(remixed & re-iss. Nov82; FIXD 5) (re-iss. Aug83 on 'Polydor' lp/c; SPE LP/MC 33)*

— **JOHN MURPHY** (b. Australia) – drums repl. GLOCKER (to TOYAH)

	Situation 2	not iss.
Apr 81. (7"/12") *(SIT 1/+12)* **TELL ME EASTER'S ON FRIDAY. / STRAW TOWELS** (re-iss. but w-drawn Nov82 on 'Beggars Banquet'; BEG 86)	☐	-
Jun 81. (7") *(SIT 4)* **Q: QUARTERS. / KISSED** (12"+=) *(SIT 4T)* – Q: Quarters (original).	☐	-
Aug 81. (7"/12") *(SIT 7/+T)* **KITCHEN PERSON. / AN EVEN WHITER CAR**	☐	-
Oct 81. (7"/12") *(SIT 10/+T)* **MESSAGE OBLIQUE SPEECH. / BLUE SOAP**	☐	-
Nov 81. (7"/12") *(SIT 11/+T)* **WHITE CAR IN GERMANY. / THE ASSOCIATE**	☐	-
Jan 82. (lp/c) *(SITU 2/+C)* **FOURTH DRAWER DOWN**	☐	-

– White car in Germany / A girl named Property / Kitchen person / Q; quarters / Tell me Easter's on Friday / The associate / Message oblique speech / An even whiter car. *(re-iss. Nov82 on 'Beggars Banquet' lp/c; BEGA/BEGC 43)*

	R.S.O.	not iss.
1981. (7"/12"; as 39, LYON STREET) *(RSO/+X 78)* **KITES. / A GIRL NAMED POVERTY**	☐	-

— added **MICHAEL DEMPSEY** – bass (of CURE) / **MARTHA LADLY** – backing vocals (ex-MARTHA & THE MUFFINS)

	Associates	WEA
Mar 82. (7"/12") *(ASC 1/+T)* **PARTY FEARS TWO. / IT'S BETTER THIS WAY**	9	☐
May 82. (7") *(ASC 2)* **CLUB COUNTRY. / IT'S YOU AGAIN** (12"+=) *(ASC 2T)* – Ulcragyceptemol.	13	☐
Jun 82. (lp/c) *(ASCL/ASCC 1)* **SULK**	10	☐

– It's better this way / Party fears two / Club country / Love hangover / 18 carat love affair / Arrogance gave him up / No / Skipping / Nothing in something particular / Arrogance gave him up / White car in Germany / Gloomy Sunday / The associate. *(re-iss. Oct82 on 'WEA' lp/c; 240 005-1/-4) (cd-iss. Jul88 on 'WEA'; K 240005-2)*

| Jul 82. (7") *(ASC 3)* **18 CARAT LOVE AFFAIR. / LOVE HANGOVER** (12"+=) *(ASC 3T)* – Voluntary wishes, swapit production. | 21 | ☐ |

— split & reformed 1984 by **MacKENZIE + RANKINE** recruiting **STEVE GOULDING** – drums / **IAN McINTOSH** – rhythm guitar / **ROBERT SUAVE** – bass / **L. HOWARD JONES** – keyboards

	WEA	WEA
May 84. (7"/ext.12") *(YZ 6/+T)* **THOSE FIRST IMPRESSIONS. / THIRTEEN FEELINGS**	43	☐

— **STEPHEN REID** – guitar; repl. RANKINE who joined PAUL HAIG. He also had a solo career between 1986-87, releasing two albums, 'THE WORLD BEGINS TO LOOK HER AGE' for 'Crepescule' and 'SHE LOVES ME NOT' for 'Virgin'

Aug 84. (7"/ext.12") *(YZ 16/+T)* **WAITING FOR THE LOVE BOAT. / SCHAMP OUT**	53	☐
Jan 85. (7"/7"pic-d) *(YZ 28/+P)* **BREAKFAST. / BREAKFAST ALONE** (12"+=) *(YZ 28T)* – Kites.	49	☐
Feb 85. (lp/c) *(WX 9/+C)* **PERHAPS**	23	☐

– Those first impressions / Waiting for the love boat / Perhaps / Schampout / Helicopter helicopter / Breakfast / Thirteen feelings / The stranger in your voice / The best of you / Don't give me that I told you so look.

| Oct 85. (7") *(YZ 47)* **TAKE ME TO THE GIRL. / PERHAPS** (ext.12"+=) *(YZ 47T)* – The girl that took me / ('A'instrumental). (10"+=) *(YZ 47TE)* – God bless the child (live) / Even dogs in the wild (live) / The boy that Santa Claus forgot (live). | ☐ | - |

— The above 'A'side was later (in Mar88) covered by group/artist JIH.

— (early 1986) HUGHES and SUAVE joined PETE MURPHY. MacKENZIE now used different session people under The ASSOCIATES

Sep 88. (7") *(YZ 310)* **HEART OF GLASS. / HER ONLY WISH** (3"cd-s+=) *(YZ 310CD)* – Breakfast / Those first impressions. ('A'-Auchterhouse mix-12"+=) *(YZ 310T)* – ('A'-Auchterhouse instrumental). (12"+=) *(YZ 310TX)* – ('A'-Temperamental mix) / Heavens blue.	56	☐
Nov 88. (w-drawn lp/c)(cd) *(WX 222/+C)(244619-2)* **THE GLAMOUR CHASE**	-	-
Jan 89. (w-drawn 7") *(YZ 329)* **COUNTRY BOY. / JUST CAN'T SAY GOODBYE** (w-drawn 12"+=) *(YZ 329T)* – Heart of glass (dub mix). (w-drawn 3"cd-s+=) *(YZ 329CD)* – Take me to the girl.	-	-

	Circa	Charisma
Mar 90. (c/cd/lp) *(CIRC/+D/A 11)* **WILD AND LONELY**	71	☐

– Fire to ice / Fever / People we meet / Just can't say goodbye / Calling all around the world / The glamour chase / Where there's love / Something's got to give / Strasbourg Square / Ever since that day / Wild and lonely / Fever in the shadows.

Apr 90. (7"/c-s) *(YR/+C 46)* **FEVER. / FEVER IN THE SHADOWS** (12"+=/s12"+=/3"cd-s+=/cd-s+=) *(YR T/TB/CD/CDT 46)* – Groovin' with Mr.Bloe.	☐	-
Aug 90. (7"/c-s) *(YR/+C 49)* **FIRE TO ICE. / GREEN TAMBOURINE** (ext.12"+=) *(YRT 49)* – The glamour chase. (10"++=/ext.cd-s++=) *(YR TX/CD 49)* – Groovin' with Mr.Bloe.	☐	-
Sep 90. (12"ep) *<096448>* **FIRE TO ICE (mixes) / GREEN TAMBOURINE**	-	☐
Jan 91. (7"/c-s) *(YR/+C 56)* **JUST CAN'T SAY GOODBYE. / ONE TWO THREE** (12") *(YRT 56)* – ('A'-Time Unlimited mix) / ('A'-Time Unlimited instrumental) / ('A'-US mix). (12") *(YRTX 56)* – ('A'-Time Unlimited mix) / ('A'-Time Unlimited instrumental) / ('A'-Karma mix). (cd-s) *(YRCD 56)* – ('A'side) / ('A'-Time Unlimited piano mix) / ('A'-US version) / I'm gonna run away from you.	☐	-

BILLY MacKENZIE

Jun 92. (7") (YR 86) **BABY. / SACRIFICE AND BE SACRIFICED (CH 8032 mix)**
(cd-s+=) (YRCD 86) – Grooveature (D 1000 mix) / Colours will come (US 60659 mix).
(12") (YRT 86) – ('A'side) / Colours will come (Larry Heard remix) / Opal krush / Colours will come (Raw Stylus remix).

Aug 92. (7") (YR 91) **COLOURS WILL COME. / OPAL KRUSH**
(12"+=/cd-s+=) (YRT/YRCD 91) – Look what you've done / Feels like the richtergroove.

Sep 92. (c/cd) (CIRC/+D 22) **OUTERNATIONAL**
– Outernational / Feels like the richtergroove / Opal krusch / Colours wil come / Pastime paradise / Groovecture / Sacrifice and be sacrificed / Baby / What made me turn on the lights / Windows cell.

—— In Jul'96, BILLY was featured on a single by LOOM, 'ANACOSTIA BAY'.

—— Tragically on the 22nd January 1997, BILLY committed suicide in his father's garden shed; he had recently signed to 'Nude' records.

	Nude	not iss.
Oct 97. (cd) (NUDE 8CD) **BEYOND THE SUN** | 64 | - |
– Give me time / Winter academy / Blue it is / 14 mirrors / At the edge of the world / Beyond the sun / And this she knows / Sour jewel / 3 gypsies in a restaurant / Nocturne VII.

– (ASSOCIATES) compilations, others, etc. –

Sep 81. (7"/12") Fiction; (FICS/+X 13) **A. / WOULD I . . . BOUNCE BACK**

Nov 82. (7"/12") Fiction; (FIXS/+X 16) **A MATTER OF GENDER. / EVEN DOGS IN THE WILD**

Oct 89. (12"ep/cd-ep) Strange Fruit; (SFPS/+CD 075)) **THE PEEL SESSIONS** ('82)
– It's better this way / Nude spoons / Me myself and the tragic story / Natural gender / Ulcragyceptemol.

Jan 91. (cd)(lp/c) East West; (9031 72414-2)(WX 363/+C) **POPERA**
– Party fears two / Club country / 18 Carat love affair / Love hangover / Those first impressions / Waiting for the loveboat / Breakfast / Take me to the girl / Heart of glass / Country boy / The rhythm divine / Waiting for the loveboat (slight return) / Tell me Easter's on Friday / Q; quarters / Kitchen person / Message oblique speech / White car in Germany.

Jan 91. (7"/c-s) East West; (YZ 534/+C) **POPERETTA EP: WAITING FOR THE LOVEBOAT (Slight Return). / CLUB COUNTRY CLUB**
(12"+=/cd-s+=) (YZ 534 T/CD) – Waiting for the loveboat (extended voyage) / Club country club (Time Unlimited).

Sep 94. (cd) Nighttracks; (CDNT 006) **THE RADIO ONE SESSION**

ASYLUM CHOIR   (dig out; Great Psychedelic . . .)

ATARI TEENAGE RIOT

Formed: West Berlin, Germany . . . 1992 by anti-Nazi cyberpunks ALEC EMPIRE, Syrian-born punk goddess HANIN ELIAS and Swiss-born CARL CRACK. With his 'Digital Hardcore' label as the main weapon of attack, EMPIRE has waged war on what he sees as an increasingly corporate, decadently comatose German dance scene. His self proclaimed 'lo-fi' techno owes more to the headfuck onslaught of radical hardcore punk (like X-RAY SPEX or CRASS) than any regular notion of "dance" music and ATARI TEENAGE RIOT's staunch anti-nazi, anti-Ecstasy stance has made EMPIRE a spokesman of sorts for the disillusioned Berlin underground scene. After a trio of fearsome albums, 'DELETE YOURSELF' (1995), 'THE FUTURE OF WAR' and the well-received 'BURN, BERLIN, BURN!' (both 1997), they secured support slots with big guns RAGE AGAINST THE MACHINE and WU-TANG CLAN. More recently, the 'RIOT released the 'DESTROY 2,000 YEARS OF CULTURE EP', though presumably EMPIRE'll make an exception for dodgy 70's punk, having already covered the old SHAM 69 chestnut, 'IF THE KIDS ARE UNITED'. In 1998, with a number of solo releases behind him, EMPIRE worked on the JON SPENCER BLUES EXPLOSION while planning ATR's comeback complete with a second female, the German/Japanese, face-painted, NIC ENDO. She also delivered a solo EP in '98, 'WHITE HEAT', a searing, uncompromising, computerised set of five hardcore sounds that became NME's Single Of The Week!

Album rating: DELETE YOURSELF (*7) / THE FUTURE OF WAR (*4) / BURN, BERLIN, BURN (*7) / Alec Empire: LTD EDITIONS 90-94 compilation (*7) / GENERATION STAR WARS (*7) / HYPERMODERN JAZZ 2000.5 (*8) / THE DESTROYER (*7) / SQUEEZE THE TRIGGER (*6) / MISS BLACK AMERICA (*7) / Carl Crack: BLACK ARK (*6)

HANIN ELIAS – vocals / **ALEC EMPIRE** (b. 2 May'72) – programming, shouts / **CARL CRACK** (b. CARL BOHM) – MC

	Force Inc	not iss.	
Nov 92. (12") **HUNTING FOR NAZIS. /** | - | - | German

	Raver Bassline	not iss.
Aug 94. (7") (RB 4) **RAVER BASHING. /** | - | - |

	Digital Hardcore	not iss.
Apr 95. (cd/lp) (DHR CD/LP 001) **DELETE YOURSELF** | | |
– Start the riot / Into the death / Raver bashing / Speed / Sex / Midi junkies / Delete yourself you got no chance to wine / Hetzjagd auf nazis / Cyberpunks are dead / Atari teenage riot / The kids are united / Riot 1995.

1996. (cd/lp) **THE DESTROYER** | - | - | German
Nov 96. (7") (DHRUS 71) **DEUTSCHLAND HAS GOTTA DIE. / RIOT 1996** | | - |

Jan 97. (12"ep/cd-ep) (DHR/+MCD 012) **SICK TO DEATH EP**
– Sick to death / We got the fucking power / Waves of disaster.

Mar 97. (cd/d-lp) (DHR CD/LP 006) **THE FUTURE OF WAR**
– Get up while you can / Fuck all / Sick to death / P.R.E.S.S. / Deutschland (has gotta die) / Destroy 2000 years of culture / Not your business / You can't hold us back / The heatwave / Redefine the enemy / Deathstar / The future of war.

	Grand Royal	Grand Royal
Jun 97. (12") (GR 039) **NOT YOUR BUSINESS. /** | | |
(re-iss. Dec99; same)

Jul 97. (7"; split with ASIAN DUB FOUNDATION) (DAMGOOD 132) **split** | | - |
(above single on 'Damaged Goods')

Aug 97. (cd) (<GR 042>) **BURN, BERLIN, BURN!** | | |
– Start the riot / Fuck all! / Sick to death / Press / Deutschland (has gotta die!) / Destroy 2000 years of culture / Not your business / Heatwave / Atari teenage riot / Delete yourself / Into the death / Death star / Speed / Future of war. (re-iss. Jan98 lp/cd; same)

—— added **NIC ENDO** – programmer

	Digital Hardcore	unknown
Dec 97. (ltd;12"ep/cd-ep) (DHR/+MCD 015) **DESTROY 2000 YEARS OF CULTURE EP** | | - |
– Destroy 2000 years of culture / Paranoid / Destroy 2000 years of culture remix / You can't hold us back.

Apr 99. (12"ep/cd-ep) (DHR/+MCD 024) **REVOLUTION ACTION!!!!!!!!!! EP** | | - |
– Revolution action / No success (Digital Hardcore remix) / your uniform (does not impress me) (Digital Hardcore remix) / Hunt down the Nazis! (live in Washington DC).

Oct 99. (12"ep/cd-ep) (DHR/+MCD 026) **TOO DEAD FOR ME / REVOLUTION ACTION (live) / ANARCHY 999 (real mix) / DEATH OF A PRESIDENT DIY (acapella) / NO REMORSE (live)** | | - |

ALEC EMPIRE

	Mille Plateau	Grand Royal
May 94. (cd/lp) (EFA 00652-2/-6) **LTD EDITIONS** | | |
Oct 94. (12"ep) (DHR 4) **DEATH EP** | | - |
(above issued on 'Digital Hardcore') (below on 'Force Inc.')
Dec 94. (12"ep) (FIM 71) **JAGUAR EP** | | - |
Mar 95. (12"; by ALEC EMPIRE & IAN POOLEY) (MP 3) **PULSE CODE EP** | | - |
Mar 95. (cd/lp) (<EFA 00661-2/-6>) **GENERATION STAR WARS** | | |
– Lash the 90 ties / Stahl & Blausaure / 13465 / Maschinenvolk / Sonyprotitutes / Blutrote nacht uber Berlin / Pussy heroin / New acid / Smack / Konsumfreiheit / N.Y. summer II / Microchipkinder / Sieg uber die mayday – HJ.
Oct 95. (cd/lp) (<EFA 00688-2/-6>) **LOW ON ICE** | | |
Apr 96. (cd/lp) (<EFA 00673-2/-6>) **HYPERMODERN JAZZ 2000.5** | | |
– Walk the apocalypse / God told me how to kiss / Get some / I'm gonna die if I fall asleep again / The unknown stepdancer / Chilling through the lives / Many bars and no money / My funk is useless / Slowly falling in love / Dreaming is a form of astrotravel.

	Digital Hardcore	Grand Royal
Jun 96. (cd/d-lp) (DHR CD/LP 004) **THE DESTROYER** | | |
– Hard like it's a pose / What are you talking about / Down with the shit / We all die! / Suicide / Bang your head! / Heartbeat that isn't there / Nobody gets out alive! / Fire bombing / Bonus beats / I don't care what happens / My face would crack / Pleasure is our business (live).

Aug 99. (cd) **MISS BLACK AMERICA** | | |

ATOMIC ROOSTER   (dig out; 4th edition or Great Metal . . .)

ATTILA (see under ⇒ JOEL, Billy)

AUDIENCE   (dig out; Great Psychedelic . . .)

Brian AUGER   (dig out; 4th edition)

AU PAIRS   (dig out; Great Alt & Indie . . .)

AUTEURS

Formed: Southgate, London, England . . . early 1992 by LUKE HAINES (ex-SERVANTS) and girlfriend ALICE READMAN. They quickly signed to 'Fire', soon moving to Virgin off-shoot label, 'Hut', and indie chart surfing with their debut single, 'SOWGIRL', later in the year. Glossy garage indie/punk merchants, fronted by the flamboyant but cynical HAINES, The AUTEURS sound was characterised by the singer's brooding lyrical complexities. The addition of cellist, JAMES BANBURY produced an extra dimension to their standard guitar, bass, drums approach and the debut album's encouragingly critical reception was matched by a UK Top 40 placing for 'NEW WAVE' (1993) and a nomination for the Mercury Music Award. Their third single, 'LENNY VALENTINO', almost scraped into the UK Top 40, the track relating to the debut album sleeve, which depicted Lenny Bruce dressed as Rudolph Valentino, both preoccupations of HAINES. Another favoured subject of the controversial frontman was the British Class System, 'THE UPPER CLASS' appearing on the follow-up set, 'NOW I'M A COWBOY' (1994). The record secured a Top 30 placing, although the group's critical acclaim continued to outweigh their commercial appeal. A remix set, 'THE AUTEURS VS U-ZIQ' appeared, although it wasn't until 1996 that a long-awaited third album materialised. Produced by STEVE ALBINI, this atmospheric offering combined HAINES' downbeat tales of intrigue with grinding organs, discordant guitars and mournful strings to often hypnotic effect. Despite garnering further plaudits, the record sold poorly and after a clutch of final gigs, HAINES wound the band up, subsequently releasing an album under the moniker of BAADER-MEINHOF (first mentioned on the bleak 'TOMBSTONE' track). In 1998, HAINES teamed up with two former members of BALLOON, JOHN MOORE (ex-EXPRESSWAY) and singer, SARAH NIXEY, in the more melodic, BLACK BOX RECORDER. Signing a major deal with 'Chrysalis', it didn't look likely that either their singles, 'CHILD PSYCHOLOGY' and 'ENGLAND MADE ME' or the latterly-titled accompanying album, would return the moody HAINES to earlier heights. 1999 saw the man discarding previous projects to reincarnate The AUTEURS. Comeback set, 'HOW I LEARNED TO LOVE THE BOOTBOYS', included their nostalgic look back to 70's glam-rock in the shape of minor hit single, 'THE RUBETTES'.

Album rating: NEW WAVE (*7) / NOW I'M A COWBOY (*8) / AFTER MURDER PARK (*7) / HOW I LEARNED TO LOVE THE BOOT BOYS (*7) / Baader-Meinhof: BAADER-MEINHOF (*5) / Black Box Recorder: ENGLAND MADE ME (*6)

LUKE HAINES (b. 7 Oct'67, Walton-On-Thames, Surrey, England) – vocals, guitar (ex-SERVANTS) / **ALICE READMAN** (b. 1967, Harrow, England) – bass (ex-SERVANTS) / **GLENN COLLINS** (b. 8 Feb'68, Cheltenham, England) – drums (ex-DOG UNIT, ex-VORT PYLON)

	Hut	Caroline
Dec 92. (12"ep/cd-ep) (*HUT T/CD*) **SHOWGIRL. / GLAD TO BE GONE / STAYING POWER**	☐	-

—— added **JAMES BANBURY** – cello

	Hut	
Mar 93. (cd/c/lp) (*CDHUT/HUTMC/HUTLP 7*) <1735> **NEW WAVE**	35	☐

– Showgirl / Bailed out / American guitars / Junk shop clothes / Don't trust the stars / Starstruck / How could I be wrong / Housebreaker / Valet parking / Idiot brother / Early years / Home again. (*free 7"w/lp on cd+c+=*) – Untitled.

May 93. (10"ep/12"ep/cd-ep) (*HUT EN/T/CD 28*) **HOW COULD I BE WRONG. / HIGH DIVING HORSES / WEDDING DAY**	☐	☐

—— **BARNEY CROCKFORD** – drums; repl. COLLINS

	Hut	Vernon Yard
Nov 93. (7") (*HUT 36*) **LENNY VALENTINO. / DISNEY WORLD**	41	☐

(12"/cd-s) (*HUT T/CD 36*) – ('A'side) / Car crazy / Vacant lot / ('A'original mix).

Apr 94. (7") (*HUTG 41*) **CHINESE BAKERY. / ('A'acoustic)**	42	☐

(7"/cd-s) (*HUT/+CD 41*) – ('A'side) / Government bookstore / Everything you say will destroy you.
(12") (*HUTDX 41*) – ('A'side) / ('A'acoustic) / Modern history.

May 94. (cd/c/lp) (*CDHUT/HUTMC/HUTLP 16*) <39597> **NOW I'M A COWBOY**	27	☐

– Lenny Valentino / Brainchild / I'm a rich man's toy / New French girlfriend / The upper classes / Chinese bakery / A sister like you / Underground movies / Life classes – Life model / Modern history / Daughter of a child. (*lp w /free 1-sided 7"*) (*HUTLPX 16*) – MODERN HISTORY (acoustic).

Nov 94. (m-cd/m-lp) (*DGHUTM/HUTMLP 20*) **THE AUTEURS VS U-ZIQ** (remixes)	☐	-

– Lenny Valentino No.3 / Daughter of a child / Chinese bakery / Lenny Valentino No.1 / Lenny Valentino No.2 / Underground movies.

	Hut	Hut
Dec 95. (7"ep/c-ep/cd-ep) (*HUT/+C/CD 65*) **BACK WITH THE KILLER E.P.**	45	-

– Unsolved child murder / Back with the killer again / Former fan / Kenneth Anger's bad dream.

Feb 96. (10"ep/cd-ep) (*<HUT EN/CD 66>*) **LIGHT AIRCRAFT ON FIRE / BUDDHA (demo). / CAR CRASH / X – BOOGIE MAN**	58	☐

Mar 96. (cd/c/lp) (*<DGHUT/HUTMC/HUTLP 33>*) **AFTER MURDER PARK**	53	☐

– Light aircraft on fire / The child brides / Land lovers / New brat in town / Everything you say will destroy you / Unsolved child murder / Married to a lazy lover / Buddha / Tombstone / Fear of flying / Dead Sea navagators / After Murder Park.

May 96. (10"ep/cd-ep) (*<HUT EN/CD 68>*) **"KID'S ISSUE" EP**	☐	☐

– Buddha / A new life a new family / After murder park.

BAADER-MEINHOF

—— HAINES with others **JAMES BANBURY + ANDY NICE** – cello / **JUSTIN ARMITAGE** – violin / **GARY STRASBOURG** – drums / **KULJIT BHAMRA** – percussion, tabla

	Hi-Rise	not iss.
Nov 95. (7") (*FLAT 24*) **BAADER MEINHOFF. / MEET ME AT THE AIRPORT**	☐	-

	Hut	Hut
Oct 96. (cd/lp) (*<CDHUT/HUTLP 36>*) **BAADER-MEINHOF**	☐	☐ Feb97

– Baader Meinhof / Meet me at the airport / There's gonna be an accident / Mogadishu / Theme from Burn Warehouse Burn / GSG-29 / …It's a moral issue / Back on the farm / Kill Ramirez / Baader Meinhof.

BLACK BOX RECORDER

—— HAINES with **JOHN MOORE** – guitar (ex-JESUS & MARY CHAIN, ex-EXPRESSWAY, ex-REVOLUTION 9, ex-BALLOON) / **SARAH NIXEY** – vocals (ex-BALLOON)

	Chrysalis	Chrysalis
May 98. (7") (*CHS 5082*) **CHILD PSYCHOLOGY. / GIRL SINGING IN THE WRECKAGE**	☐	☐

(cd-s+=) (*CDCHS 5082*) – Seasons in the sun.

Jul 98. (7") (*CHS 5091*) **ENGLAND MADE ME. / LORD LUCAN IS MISSING**	☐	☐

(cd-s) (*CDCHS 5091*) – ('A'side) / Factory radio / Child psychology (audio) / Child psychology (video).

Jul 98. (cd/d-lp) (*493907-2/-1*) **ENGLAND MADE ME**	☐	☐

– Girl singing in the wreckage / England made me / New baby boom / It's only the end of the world / Ideal home / Child psychology / I C one female / Uptown top ranking / Swinging / Kidnapping an heiress / Hated Sunday.

—— JOHN MOORE would soon form ABSINTHE EXPORTER

AUTEURS

—— HAINES with old line-up

	Hut	
May 99. (cd/c) (*HUT CD/MC 53*) **HOW I LEARNED TO LOVE THE BOOTBOYS**	☐	☐

– The Rubettes / 1967 / How I learned to love the bootboys / Your gang our gang / Some changes / School / The south will rise again / Asti Spumante / Sick of Hare Krishna / Lights out / Future generation.

Jun 99. (7"/c-s) (*HUT/+MC 113*) **THE RUBETTES. / GET WRECKED AT HOME**	66	☐

(cd-s+=) (*HUTCD 113*) – Breaking up.

AVERAGE WHITE BAND

Formed: Dundee/Glasgow, Scotland . . . early 1972 by ALAN GORRIE and other noted session men, HAMISH STUART, ONNIE McINTYRE, ROBBIE McINTOSH, ROGER BALL and MALCOLM 'MOLLY' DUNCAN. After supporting ERIC CLAPTON at his comeback Rainbow concert in '73, they gained enough attention to attract 'M.C.A.'. After one album, 'SHOW YOUR HAND', they moved to Los Angeles and signed to 'Atlantic', where the US audiences related more easily to their sound. Early in 1975, they scored a US No.1 with chant-orientated 'PICK UP THE PIECES', which was lifted from their self-titled top selling album. One of the few bands from Scotland (never mind Dundee!) to make it big in the States, what was even more ironic was that they didn't fit the usual Celtic musical stereotypes (i.e. folky, anthemic etc.), instead opting for a white funk/soul sound with top flight harmonies inspired by black artists of the 60's, e.g. The ISLEY BROTHERS, MARVIN GAYE etc. The lock-tight rhythmic shuffle and classy horn stabs of the aforementioned 'PICK UP THE PIECES' assured the track a place in funk history, the record still being played out on dancefloors today. Although celebrations were cut short with the shock heroin overdose of McINTOSH later that summer, AWB eventually found a replacement in STEVE FERRONE and began work on a follow-up set, 'CUT THE CAKE' (1975). Another sizeable Stateside success, the record's largely instrumental workouts weren't so enthusiastically embraced by a British audience. As the UK musical climate changed during the ensuing few years, AWB concentrated on America, their laidback, sun-kissed soul continuing to soundtrack the Californian idyll. The creamy-rich 'QUEEN OF MY SOUL' was the group's last kiln in Britain for almost five years, the band eventually storming back into the UK Top 20 in 1979 with the strong 'FEEL NO FRET' album, the evocative 'ATLANTIC AVENUE' another defining AWB moment. After 'PICK UP THE PIECES', however, their most enduring track remains the yearning disco classic, 'LET'S GO ROUND AGAIN', only their second UK Top 20 hit. The accompanying album, 'SHINE' (1980), also went Top 20, although it marked a last stand of sorts, a subsequent effort, 'CUPID'S IN FASHION' (1982) seeing them floundering in tepid waters. Inevitably, they split the following year, while equally inevitably, perhaps, reforming at the end of the decade. A line-up of GORRIE, McINTYRE and BALL recruited ALEX LIGERTWOOD and a couple of session players, cutting a sole flop album, 'AFTERSHOCK' (1989). Though they've since turned their backs on the studio, AWB continue to draw in the crowds every year with regular tours of the UK including a residency at London's Jazz Cafe.
• **Songwriters:** GORRIE and STUART, except I HEARD IT THROUGH THE GRAPEVINE (Marvin Gaye) / IMAGINE (John Lennon) / WALK ON BY (Burt Bacharach) / etc. • **Trivia:** McINTYRE and McINTOSH sessioned on CHUCK BERRY's 'My Ding-A-Ling'.

Album rating: SHOW YOUR HAND (*5) / AVERAGE WHITE BAND (*7) / CUT THE CAKE (*5) / SOUL SEARCHING (*6) / PERSON TO PERSON (*5) / BENNY AND US with Ben E. King (*5) / WARMER COMMUNICATIONS (*4) / FEEL NO FRET (*7) / SHINE (*4) / THE BEST OF THE AVERAGE WHITE BAND compilation (*7) / CUPID'S IN FASHION (*4) / AFTER SHOCK (*5) / THE BEST OF THE AVERAGE WHITE BAND – LET'S GO ROUND AGAIN compilation (*7) / SOUL TATTOO (*4)

HAMISH STUART (b. 8 Oct'49, Glasgow, Scotland) – vocals, guitar / **ALAN GORRIE** (b.19 Jul'46, Perth, Scotland) – vocals, bass / **ONNIE McINTYRE** (b.25 Sep'45, Lennoxtown, Scotland) – lead guitar / **ROBBIE McINTOSH** (b. 1950, Scotland) – drums / **ROGER BALL** (b. 4 Jun'44, Dundee, Scotland) – saxophone / **MALCOLM 'MOLLY' DUNCAN** (b.24 Aug'44, Montrose, Scotland) – tenor/soprano sax

	M.C.A.	M.C.A.
Jan 73. (lp) (*MCF 2514*) <345> **SHOW YOUR HAND**	☐	☐

– The jugglers / This world has music / Twilight zone / Put it where you want it / Show your hand / How can you go home / Back in '67 / Reach out / T.L.C. <*US re-iss. Apr75 as 'PUT IT WHERE YOU WANT IT'; 475>* – hit No.39 (*UK re-iss. Feb82 under US title; MCL 1650*) (*re-iss. May83 on 'Fame' lp/c; FA/TC-FA 3062*)

Feb 73. (7") (*MU 1187*) **PUT IT WHERE YOU WANT IT. / REACH OUT**	☐	-
1973. (7") <40168> **THE JUGGLERS. / THIS WORLD HAS MUSIC**	-	-
Jan 74. (7") (*MCA 86*) **HOW CAN YOU GO HOME. / TWILIGHT ZONE**	☐	-

(*re-iss. Apr75; MCA 102*)

	Atlantic	Atlantic
Jul 74. (lp/c) (*K/K4 50058*) <7308> **AVERAGE WHITE BAND**	6	1 Sep74

– You got it / Got the love / Pick up the pieces / Person to person / Work to do /

Nothing you can do / Just wanna love you tonight / Keepin' it to myself / I just can't give you up / There's always someone waiting. (re-iss. Oct80 on 'RCA Int.'; INTS 5049) (re-iss. Jun86 on 'Fame' lp/c; FA/TC-FA 3157) (cd-iss. 1987; 781515-2) (cd re-iss. Oct96 as 'THE WHITE ALBUM' on 'Essential'; ESMCD 439)

Jul 74. (7") (K 10489) **PICK UP THE PIECES. / YOU GOT IT** (re-dist.Feb75, hit UK No.6)			–
Oct 74. (7") (K 10498) <3044> **NOTHING YOU CAN DO. / I JUST CAN'T GIVE YOU UP**			
Nov 74. (7") <3229> **PICK UP THE PIECES. / WORK TO DO**		–	1

—— STEVE FERRONE (b.25 Apr'50, Brighton, England) – drums (ex-BRIAN AUGER) repl. ROBBIE who died of a heroin overdose 23rd Sep'74

Apr 75. (7") (K 10605) <3261> **CUT THE CAKE. / PERSON TO PERSON**		31	10
Jun 75. (lp/c) (K/K4 50146) <18140> **CUT THE CAKE**		28	4

– Cut the cake / School boy crush / It's a mystery / Groovin' the night away / If I ever lose this Heaven / Why? / High flyin' woman / Cloudy / How sweet can you get / When they bring down the curtain. (cd-iss. Sep97 on 'Snapper'; SMMCD 508)

Aug 75. (7") (K 10655) <3285> **IF I EVER LOSE THIS HEAVEN. / HIGH FLYIN' WOMAN**			39
Nov 75. (7") (K 10701) <3304> **SCHOOL BOY CRUSH. / GROOVIN' THE NIGHT AWAY**			33
May 76. (7") (K 10778) **EVERYBODY'S DARLING. / WHY?**			
Jul 76. (lp/c) (K/K4 50272) <18179> **SOUL SEARCHING**		60	8

– Overture / Love your life / I'm the one / A love of your own / Queen of my soul / Soul searching / Goin' home / Everybody's darling / Would you say / Sunny days (make me think of you) / Digging deeper. (re-iss. Nov80 on 'RCA Int.' lp/c; INTS/INTK 5058)

Aug 76. (7") (K 10825) <3354> **QUEEN OF MY SOUL. / WOULD YOU STAY**		23	40
Dec 76. (7") (K 10880) **A LOVE OF YOUR OWN. / SOUL SEARCHIN'**			–
Jan 77. (d-lp/d-c) (K/K4 60127) <1002> **PERSON TO PERSON (live)**			28

– Person to person / Cut the cake / If I ever lose this Heaven / Cloudy / T.L.C. / I'm the one / Pick up the pieces / Love your life / School boy crush / I heard it through the grapevine.

Mar 77. (7") (K 10912) **GOIN' HOME (live). / I'M THE ONE (live)**			
Mar 77. (7") <3388> **CLOUDY (live). / LOVE YOUR LIFE (live)**		–	

AVERAGE WHITE BAND / BEN E. KING

Jun 77. (7") <3402> **KEEPIN' IT TO MYSELF. / GET IT UP FOR LOVE**		–	
Jul 77. (lp/c) (K/K4 50384) <19162> **BENNY AND US**			33

– Get it up for love / Fool for you anyway / A star in the ghetto / The message / What is soul / Someday we'll all be free / Imagine / Keepin' it to myself.

Jul 77. (7") (K 10977) **A STAR IN THE GHETTO. / KEEPIN' IT TO MYSELF**		–	
Aug 77. (7") <3427> **A STAR IN A GHETTO. / WHAT IS SOUL**		–	
Dec 77. (7") <3444> **FOOL FOR YOU ANYWAY. / THE MESSAGE**		–	

AVERAGE WHITE BAND

	R.C.A.	Atlantic
Jun 78. (lp/c) (XL/XC 13053) <19162> **WARMER COMMUNICATIONS**		28 Mar78

– Your love is a miracle / Same feeling, different song / Daddy's all gone / Big city lights / She's a dream / Sweet and sour / One look over my shoulder (is this really goodbye?).

Jun 78. (7") <3481> **ONE LOOK OVER MY SHOULDER. / LOVE IS A MIRACLE**	–	
Jun 78. (7"/7"colrd) (XB/XC 9270) **ONE LOOK OVER MY SHOULDER (IS THIS REALLY GOODBYE?). / BIG CITY LIGHTS**		
Aug 78. (7") <3500> **SHE'S A DREAM. / BIG CITY LIGHTS**		
Feb 79. (7") (XB 1061) **ATLANTIC AVENUE. / SHE'S A DREAM**		
Feb 79. (lp/c) (XL/ZX 13063) <19207> **FEEL NO FRET**	15	32

– When will you be mine / Please don't fall in love / Walk on by / Feel no fret / Stop the rain / Atlantic avenue / Ace of hearts / Too late to cry / Fire burning. (re-iss. Sep81 lp/c; INTS/INTK 5140)

Apr 79. (7"/7"colrd) (XB/XC 1087) <3563> **WALK ON BY. / TOO LATE TO CRY**	46	92
May 79. (7") <3581> **FEEL NO FRET. / FIRE BURNING**	–	
Jul 79. (7"/7"colrd) (XB/XC 1096) **WHEN WILL YOU BE MINE. / ACE OF HEARTS**	49	

	R.C.A.	Arista
Apr 80. (7"/12") (AWB/+12 1) **LET'S GO 'ROUND AGAIN. / (art 2)**	12	–
May 80. (lp/c) (XL/XC 13123) <9523> **SHINE**	14	

– Catch me / Let's go 'round again / Whatcha gonna do for me / Help is on the way / Shine / For you, for love / Into the night / Our time has come / If love only lasts for one night.

Jun 80. (7") <0515> **LET'S GO 'ROUND AGAIN. / SHINE**	–	53
Jul 80. (7"/12") (AWB/+12 2) **FOR YOU, FOR LOVE. / HELP IS ON THE WAY**	46	–
Jul 80. (7") <0553> **FOR YOU, FOR LOVE. / WHATCHA GONNA DO FOR ME**		–
Jul 80. (7") <0580> **INTO THE NIGHT. /**		

—— added guest RITCHIE STOTTS – guitar (ex-PLASMATICS)

Jul 82. (7"/12") (RCA/+T 250) **YOU'RE MY NUMBER ONE. / THEATRE OF EXCESS**		–
Sep 82. (lp/c) (RCA LP/K 6052) **CUPID'S IN FASHON**		–

– You're my number one / Easier said than done / You wanna belong / Cupid's in fashion / Theatre of excess / I believe / Is it love that you're running from? / Reach out I'll be there / Isn't it strange / Love's a heartache.

Sep 82. (7"/12") (RCA/+T 274) **I BELIEVE. / REACH OUT I'LL BE THERE**		–

—— split 1983 but reformed in 1989 with GORRIE, McINTYRE, BALL recruited ALEX LIGERTWOOD – guitar, vocals (ex-SANTANA, ex-BRIAN AUGER'S OBLIVION EXPRESS) / + on session ELIOT LEWIS – keyboards / TIGER McNEIL – drums

	Polydor	TRK
Aug 89. (lp/c/cd) (839 466-1/-4/-2) **AFTERSHOCK**		

– The spirit of love / Aftershock / I'll get over you / Let's go all the way / Sticky situation / Love at first sight / Later we'll be greater / We're in too deep.

Oct 89. (7") (PO 56) **THE SPIRIT OF LOVE. / ('A'beat mix)**		–
(12"/cd-s) (PZ/+CD 56) – ('A'dance) / ('A'-long beat) / ('A'-New York mix).		

—— HAMISH joined ERIC CLAPTON's band in 1990

—— In 1985, ALAN GORRIE released album **SLEEPLESS NIGHTS** for 'A&M-US', plus single; 'AGE OF STEAM / I CAN TAKE IT (after) / DIARY OF A FOOL / IN THE JUNGLE

—— re-formed Spring 1994 after the success of their compilation album

	Hit Label	not iss.
Mar 94. (cd/c) (AHL CD/MC 15) **THE BEST OF THE AVERAGE WHITE BAND – LET'S GO ROUND AGAIN** (cd re-iss. Oct96 on 'Music Club'; MCCD 274)	38	–
Mar 94. (7"/c-s) (HL/+C 5) **LET'S GO ROUND AGAIN (the CCN mix). / ('A'mix)** (cd-s+=) (HLCD 5) – ('A'mixes)	56	–

—— ALAN GORRIE, ONNIE McINTYRE, ROGER BALL plus ELIOT LEWIS – vocals, keyboards, bass, guitar / PETE ABBOTT – drums, percussion

	Artful	Foundation
Feb 97. (cd) (ARTFULCD 7) <1601> **SOUL TATTOO**		

– Soul mine / Back to basics / Livin' on borrowed time / Every beat of my heart / Oh Maceo / Do ya really / I wanna be loved / No easy way to say goodbye / Love is the bottom line / Welcome to the real world / Window to your soul.

– compilations etc. –

Jul 81. (7") RCA-Gold; (GOLD 514) **PICK UP THE PIECES. / CUT THE CAKE**		
Sep 80. (lp) Atlantic; <19266> **VOLUME VIII**		
Sep 81. (lp) R.C.A.; (RCA 5139) **THE BEST OF THE AVERAGE WHITE BAND**		–

– Pick up the pieces / Cut the cake / Queen of my soul / A love of your own / Person to person / I heard it through the grapevine / Walk on by / You got it / Cloudy / Work to do / Atlantic avenue / When will you be mine. (re-iss. Aug84 lp/c; NL/NK 89091) (re-iss. May94 on 'Repertoire'.)

Aug 94. (cd) Windsong; (WHISCD 005) **LIVE ON THE TEST (live)**		–
Oct 96. (cd) Castle; (CCSCD 438) **ABOVE AVERAGE**		–
Feb 97. (cd) Laserlight; (12891) **THE VERY BEST OF THE AVERAGE WHITE BAND**		–
May 97. (d-cd) Snapper; (SMDCD 173) **AVERAGE WHITE BAND**		–
Aug 97. (cd-ep) Club Classics; (CLCL 001) **PICK UP THE PIECES / LET'S GO 'ROUND AGAIN / QUEEN OF MY SOUL**		–

AXIOM FUNK (see under ⇒ LASWELL, Bill)

Hoyt AXTON

Born: 25 Mar'38, Duncan, Oklahoma, USA, the son of MAE AXTON whose claim to fame was being the co-writer of 'Heartbreak Hotel' (ELVIS' first No.1 hit in '56). Having performed live at the turn of the decade (he also served his time in the navy), HOYT's road to semi-stardom came early in 1963 when The KINGSTON TRIO took his 'GREENBACK DOLLAR' into the US Top 30. Taken from his debut album, 'THE BALLADEER' (1962) – subsequently re-issued as 'GREENBACK DOLLAR' – the song should have made him some big cash, instead he was "shafted" by a crooked publisher (on reflection he described it as "I was just a kid"). His label, 'Horizon' (which basically catered for jazz artists), also released his follow-up, 'THUNDER 'N' LIGHTNIN'' (1963), however, it would be 'Vee-Jay' who issued two further sets, 'HOYT AXTON EXPLODES' (1963) and 'SATURDAY'S CHILD' (1964); around the same time, covers LP 'HOYT AXTON SINGS BESSIE SMITH' was turned out by 'Exodus'. The singer's subsequent output dried up for around half a decade while AXTON's cocaine addiction kicked in. However from these barren times, one song did surface when STEPPENWOLF covered his infamous anti-drug opus, 'THE PUSHER' (the film 'Easy Rider' gave it cult status). In 1969, with his name revered once again, AXTON signed a new deal with 'Columbia' and finally delivered his "comeback" set, 'MY GRIFFIN IS GONE'. Having previously opened for covers specialists, THREE DOG NIGHT, 1971 saw AXTON provide the group with two major US hits, 'JOY TO THE WORLD' (a No.1 and the title of his own album for 'Capitol') and 'NEVER BEEN TO SPAIN' (a Top 5). Two years later and now on the roster of 'A&M', the clear-voiced country/folk artist was back at his very best with 'LESS THAN THE SONG' (1973). In fact, all his star-studded 'A&M' albums from the mid-70's, 'LIFE MACHINE' (1974), 'SOUTHBOUND' (1975) and 'FEARLESS' (1976), were of top quality, the latter two giving him US chart entries. Around the same time, other major artists were delivering their own AXTON interpretations, notably JOAN BAEZ, GLEN CAMPBELL, RINGO STARR, JOHN DENVER, WAYLON JENNINGS, TANYA TUCKER, COMMANDER CODY and STEPPENWOLF again. HOYT moved to 'M.C.A.' for 1977's 'SNOWBLIND FRIEND' and the following year's 'FREE SAILIN', although it was clear that his artistic peak had come and gone. Having rid himself of his drug addiction, the cherub-faced singer/guitarist founded his own imprint, 'Jeremiah' (a reference from his 'JOY TO THE WORLD' song), where he issued three low-key LP's, the first of which 'A RUSTY OLE HALO' (1979) produced a surprise UK Top 50 hit in 1980, 'DELLA AND THE DEALER'. HOYT was also fast becoming an established actor having worked on TV and films such as 'The Black Stallion' (his subsequent movie appearances were in 'Gremlins', 'E.T.' and 'Season

Of Change'). However, the rest of the 80's saw the man take a well-earned break from his recording schedule. In 1991, AXTON made a comeback album, 'SPIN OF THE WHEEL', an acclaimed set which was sadly his swansong due to heart problems. Sadly, after a few years confined to a wheelchair due to a series of heart attacks, HOYT was to meet his maker on the 26th of October, 1999. • Covers: DAYS ARE SHORT (Arlo Guthrie) / MAYBELLINE (Chuck Berry) / THAT'S ALL RIGHT (Arthur 'Big Boy' Crudup) / GERONIMO'S CADILLAC (Michael Martin Murphey) / BLIND FIDDLER (trad.) / ROLL YOUR OWN (Mel McDaniel) / GREENSLEEVES (trad) / LAY, LADY, LAY (Bob Dylan).

Album rating: THE BALLADEER – GREENBACK DOLLAR (*5) / THUNDER 'N' LIGHTNIN' (*5) / SATURDAY'S CHILD (*4) / HOYT AXTON EXPLODES (*5) / HOYT AXTON SINGS BESSIE SMITH (*6) / THE BEST OF HOYT AXTON compilation (*6) / MY GRIFFIN IS GONE (*5) / JOY TO THE WORLD (*5) / COUNTRY ANTHEM (*3) / LESS THAN A SONG (*7) / LIFE MACHINE (*7) / SOUTHBOUND (*7) / FEARLESS (*6) / SNOWBLIND FRIEND (*5) / FREE SAILIN' (*5) / ROAD SONGS (*7) / A RUSTY OLE HALO (*4) / WHERE DID THE MONEY GO (*3) / LIVE (*4) / EVERYBODY'S GOING ON THE ROAD (*4) / PISTOL PACKIN' MAMA (*4) / NEVER BEEN TO SPAIN compilation (*4) / SPIN OF THE WHEEL (*6) / AMERICAN ORIGINALS compilation (*5) / LONESOME ROAD collection (*4)

HOYT AXTON – vocals, guitar

		Saga	Horizon
1963.	(7") <1> GRIZZLY BEAR. / GYPSY WOMAN	-	
1963.	(7") <6> HAPPY SONG. / WE'LL SING IN THE SUNSHINE	-	
1964.	(7") (SS 503) <351> GREENBACK DOLLAR. / THE CRAWDAD SONG		

		Stateside	Horizon
			1963
1963.	(7") <360> GRIZZLY BEAR. / GYPSY WOMAN		
1963.	(7") <361> THIS LITTLE NIGHT. / THUNDER 'N' LIGHTNIN'		
1963.	(7") <362> ONE MORE ROUND. / GREENBACK DOLLAR	-	
1964.	(lp) (SL 10082) <1601> GREENBACK DOLLAR (known as 'THE BALLADEER' until this issue)		1962

– Greenback dollar / Ashville Junction / Brisbane ladies / Five hundred miles / The balladeer / Ox driver's song / Peggy-o / Walkin' to Georgia / Vandy / John Henry.

—— next album + 3 singles with the CHAMBERS BROTHERS

1964.	(lp) (SL 10096) <1613> THUNDER 'N' LIGHTNIN'		1963

– Thunder 'n' lightnin' / Blue prelude / Woman at the well / Grizzly bear / I never knew my father / Midnight special / This little light / Gypsy woman / Water boy / Daddy walked in darkness / Cocaine / House of the rising sun.

		not iss.	Vee-Jay
1964.	(lp) <1098> HOYT AXTON EXPLODES		

– Never gonna work / Wild about my loving / There's a tiger in my closet / Red white and blue / L.A. town / Heartbreak hotel / Big red / Lonesome road / I'll be there / Double double dare / ABC song / Young man. (UK-iss.1968 on 'Joy'; JOYS 1098)

1964.	(lp) <1127> SATURDAY'S CHILD	-	

– Willie Jean / Make me a pallet / Hoochie coochie man / St. James infirmary / Saturday's child / etc.

		not iss.	Exodus
1964.	(lp) <301> HOYT AXTON SINGS BESSIE SMITH	-	

—— next with the SHERWOOD SINGERS

		London	not iss.
May 66.	(lp) (SAF 8276) THE BEST OF HOYT AXTON (compilation)		

– Greenback dollar / Thunder 'n' lightnin' / This little night / Trombone cholly / Ox driving song / Gambler's blues / We'll sing in the sunshine / 500 miles / I'm gonna tell you a story / Hoochie coochie man / They've been on their jobs too long / Voodoo blues.

		not iss.	Colgems
1966.	(7") <1005> SAN FERNANDO. / TEN THOUSAND SUNSETS		

		C.B.S.	Columbia
1969.	(lp) (63588) <33103> MY GRIFFIN HAS GONE		

– On the natural / Chase down the Sun / Gypsy will / Seven come / Childhood's end / Kingswood Manor / To some cool ice blue shore / It's alright now / I know the answer / Beelzebub's laughter / Sunrise. <cd-iss. Apr98 on 'Edsel'; EDCD 553)>

Jun 69.	(7") (4316) IT'S ALRIGHT NOW. / WAY BEFORE THE TIME OF TOWNS		

		not iss.	Capitol
1971.	(lp) <EST 788> JOY TO THE WORLD		

– Joy to the world / Alice in Wonderland / Never been to Spain / The pusher / Ease your pain / Have a nice day / Indian song / California women / Lightnin' bar blues / Farther along – Old time religion.

1972.	(lp) <EST 850> COUNTRY ANTHEM	-	

below as above + now with numerous session people

		A&M	A&M
May 73.	(lp) (AMLH 64376) <4376> LESS THAN THE SONG		

– Sweet misery / Less than the song / Sweet fantasy / Days are short / Mary makes magic / Peacemaker / Nothin' to lose / Oklahoma song / Mexico City hangover / Hungry man / Somebody turned on the light / Blue prelude.

Jun 73.	(7") (AMS 7071) LESS THAN A SONG. / PEACEMAKER		
Feb 74.	(lp) (AMLH 63604) <3604> LIFE MACHINE		

– Maybelline / Life machine / That's all right / Geronimo's Cadillac / When the morning comes / Good lookin' child / I dream of highways / Pet parade / Telephone booth / Boney fingers / Billy's theme.

May 74.	(7") <1497> WHEN THE MORNING COMES. / BILLY'S THEME		
May 74.	(7") (AMS 7110) MAYBELLINE. / LIFE MACHINE	-	54
Apr 75.	(lp) (AMLH 64510) <4510> SOUTHBOUND		

– I love to sing / Southbound / Lion in the winter / Blind fiddler / Pride of man / Greensleeves / No no song / Nashville / Speed trap (out of state cars) / Roll your own / Whiskey / In a young girl's mind / Sometimes it's easy.

May 75.	(7") (AMS 7169) LION IN WINTER. / SPEED TRAP		
Apr 76.	(lp) (AMLH 64571) <4571> FEARLESS		

– Idol of the band / Evangelina / Flash of fire / Lay, lady, lay / Jealous man / Paid

in advance / An old greyhound / A stone and a feather / Gypsy moth / Beyond these walls / Penny whistle song / The Devil.

Jun 76.	(7") (AMS 7236) FLASH OF FIRE. / PAID IN ADVANCE		
Mar 77.	(7") (AMS 7338) BONEY FINGERS. / FLASH OF FIRE		

		M.C.A.	M.C.A.
Jul 77.	(lp) (MCF 2803) <2263> SNOWBLIND FRIEND		

– You're the hangnail in my life / Little white moon / Water for the horses / Funeral of the king / I light this candle / Never been to Spain / You taught me how to cry / Snowblind friend / Poncho and Lefty / Seven come / I don't know why I love you. (re-iss.Mar86; IMCA 647) (cd-iss. May95 on 'Edsel'; EDCD 426)

Sep 77.	(7") (MCA 321) I LIGHT THIS CANDLE. / YOU TAUGHT ME HOW TO CRY		
May 78.	(lp) (MCF 2831) <2319> FREE SAILIN'		

– Bluebird / Honky tonk music / The way of the world / The heart you break (may be your own) / Jive man / Free sailin' / Them downers / Left my gal in the mountains / Darrell and Judy / Endless road. (cd-iss. Apr96 on 'Edsel'; EDCD 471)

Youngblood Jeremiah

Jan 80.	(7") <1000> DELLA AND THE DEALER. / A YOUNG GIRL'S MIND	-	
Apr 80.	(7") (YB 82) DELLA AND THE DEALER. / GOTTA KEEP GOING	48	-
Jul 80.	(lp) (VBLP 800) <5000> A RUSTY OLE HALO		Nov79

– A rusty ole halo / Della and the dealer / The Hotel Ritz / So hard to give it all up / Evangelina / Torpedo / Viva Pancho Villa / Wild bull rider / In a young girl's mind / Gotta keep rollin'. (re-iss. Aug81 on 'M.f.P.' lp/c; MFP/TCMFP 50520)

Jul 80.	(7") <1001> A RUSTY OLD HALO. / KEEP ROLLIN'		
Jul 80.	(7") (YB 92) HOTEL RITZ. / EVANGELINA		
Oct 80.	(7") (YB 101) <1003> WILD BULL RIDER. / TORPEDO		
Oct 80.	(lp) <5001> WHERE DID THE MONEY GO		

– Everybody's goin' on the road / Betty La Rue / Boozers and losers / Politicians / You do not tango / Smile as you go by / Where did the money go / Some people ride / Midnight in Memphis / Ease your pain / The battle of New Orleans / The house song.

1981.	(7") <1005> EVANGELINA. / SO HARD TO GIVE IT ALL UP		
1981.	(7") <1006> BOOZERS ARE LOSERS (WHEN THE BENDERS DON'T END). / POLITICIANS		
1981.	(d-lp) <5002> LIVE (live)		

– Roanoke / Wild bull rider / Flash of fire / Boney fingers / Della and the dealer / When the morning comes / Evangelina / No no song / Mel Tillis / Roger Miller story / Lion in winter / Jealous man / The Devil / A rusty ole halo / Bus story / An old greyhound / Orange blossom special / Will the circle be unbroken / Maybelline / Never been to Spain / Joy to the world. <cd-iss. Oct98 on 'Edsel'; EDCD 575)>

1981.	(7") <1008> SMILE AS YOU GO BY. / WHERE DID THE MONEY GO		
1981.	(7") <1011> THE DEVIL. / JEALOUS MAN	-	
Jan 82.	(lp) (YBLP 120) EVERYBODY'S GOIN' ON THE ROAD		

– Where did the money go / Some people ride / Midnight in Memphis / Ease your pain / Battle of New Orleans / House song / Everybody's goin' on the road / Betty La Rue / Boozers and losers (when the benders don't end) / (When you dance) You do not tango / Politicians / Smile as you go by.

1982.	(7") <1012> EASE YOUR PAIN. / WIN THIS ONE		
1982.	(lp) <1013> PISTOL PACKIN' MAMA		

– She's too lazy to be crazy / Pistol packin' mama / I walk the line / Don't fence me in / There stands the glass / Warm storms and wild flowers / He played real good for me / James Dean and the junkman / Indian song / Fearless the wonder dog.

1982.	(7") <1014> SHE'S TOO LAZY TO BE CRAZY. / (WHEN YOU DANCE) YOU DO NOT TANGO	-	
1983.	(7") <1015> THERE STANDS THE GLASS. / JAMES DEAN AND THE JUNKMAN	-	
1983.	(7") <1016> PISTOL PACKIN' MAMA. / FEARLESS THE WONDERDOG		
1983.	(7") <1017> WARM STORMS AND WILD FLOWERS. / DON'T FENCE ME IN		
1984.	(7") <1018> IF YOU'RE A COWBOY. / I COLLECT HEARTS		

—— HOYT semi-retired from the music business and went into film acting

		not iss.	D.P.I.
1991.	(cd) SPIN OF THE WHEEL	-	

—— after suffering several strokes in the mid-90's, HOYT was to die on the 26th of October, 1999

– compilations, etc. –

Jan 78.	(lp) A&M; (AMLH 64669) <4669> ROADSONGS (live)		Dec77

– No no song / Honey fingers / In a young girl's mind / Lay, lady, lay / Telephone booth / Paid in advance / Lion in winter / Less than a song / I love to sing / hen the morning comes / Sweet misery / Flash of fire.

1985.	(7"ep) Youngblood; (YBEP 92) EVANGELINA. / HOTEL RITZ		-
1980's.	(7") Briar; <100> DRINKING GOURD. / GEORGIA HOSS SOLDIER	-	-
1986.	(lp/c) M.C.A.; <MCA/+C 20342> NEVER BEEN TO SPAIN	-	-

– Never been to Spain / You're the hangnail in my life / Snowblind friend / Poncho and Lefty / Water for my horses / Free sailing / Way of the world / You taught me how to cry.

Jan 93.	(cd/c) Capitol; <C2/C4 99920> AMERICAN ORIGINALS	-	-
Jul 95.	(lp) Chicago Music; <118> LONESOME ROAD (rec. 1964)		

– Poor man's blues / Me and my gin / Lonesome road / Young man / Big red / Send me to the electric chair / After you've gone / Nobody knows you when you're down and out / Red, white and blue / Bring me some lovin'.

Jul 98.	(d-cd) A&M; <(540957-2)> THE A&M YEARS		

– (LESS THAN THE SONG / LIFE MACHINE / SOUTHBOUND / FEARLESS). (re-iss. May99; same)

Sep 98.	(cd) Edsel; <(EDCD 574)> A RUSTY OLE HALO / WHERE DID THE MONEY GO		
Sep 98.	(cd) Edsel; <(EDCD 576)> PISTOL PACKIN' MAMA / SPIN OF THE WHEEL		
Jun 99.	(cd) Raven; (RVCD 91) GOTTA KEEP ROLLIN' (THE JEREMIAH YEARS 1979-1981)		-

Kevin AYERS

Born: 16 Aug'45, Herne Bay, Kent, England; raised in Malaysia. Left school and moved to Canterbury, where he and ROBERT WYATT helped form SOFT MACHINE in 1966. Burned out after a gruelling American tour supporting JIMI HENDRIX, the singer/songwriter decamped in 1968 to Ibiza to write material for the fledgling 'Harvest' label, the fruits of his labour being the following year's 'JOY OF A TOY' (title taken from an ORNETTE COLEMAN track). The album's idiosyncratic flair was indicative of the direction AYERS would take in his later work and contained some of his most enduring songs. In 1970, he hooked up with a young MIKE OLDFIELD to form KEVIN AYERS AND THE WHOLE WIDE WORLD. The unit, including saxophonist LOL COXHILL and keyboardist DAVID BEDFORD, released the experimental classic, 'SHOOTING FOR THE MOON', setting the standard for the emergent progressive rock of the 70's. Critics complained that his monotone vox lay too close to SYD BARRETT, NICK DRAKE or even NICO, although he did manage to retain a distinctive character on such songs as 'CLARENCE IN WONDERLAND' and 'COLORES PARA DOLORES'. While 'WHATEVERSHEBRINGSWESING' (1972) and 'BANANAMOUR' (1973) contained moments of inspired exprimentation, AYERS began to move towards more straightforward writing. He appeared on the 'Island' live recording 'JUNE 1, 1974' alongside JOHN CALE, ENO and NICO, but he increasingly shied away from from publicity. The quality of his recorded output became inconsistent and directionless throughout the rest of the 70's and 80's, although he retained a diehard cult following. On the 1976 album 'YES WE HAVE NO MANANAS', he unwisely chose to record an appalling version of 'FALLING IN LOVE AGAIN' (made famous in the 30's by MARLENE DIETRICH). • **Trivia:** In 1987, he contributed vocals to a MIKE OLDFIELD song, 'FLYING START', from the album 'ISLANDS'. AYERS had also largely contributed to an album (LINGUISTIC LEPROSY) in 1974 by friend and Deia neighbour LADY JUNE.

Album rating: JOY OF A TOY (*7) / SHOOTING AT THE MOON (*7) / WHATEVERSHEBRINGSWESING (*6) / BANANAMOUR (*5) / THE CONFESSIONS OF DR. DREAM (*5) / SWEET DECEIVER (*5) / ODD DITTIES collection (*5) / YES WE HAVE NO MANANAS (*5) / RAINBOW TAKEAWAY (*4) / THAT'S WHAT YOU GET BABE (*3) / DIAMOND JACK AND THE QUEEN OF PAIN (*3) / AS CLOSE AS YOU THINK (*4) / FALLING UP (*5) / STILL LIFE WITH GUITAR (*5) / BANANA PRODUCTIONS – BEST OF KEVIN AYERS compilation (*8)

KEVIN AYERS – vocals, guitar (ex-SOFT MACHINE, ex-WILDE FLOWERS) / with **DAVID BEDFORD** – keyboards / **MIKE RATLEDGE** – keys / **HUGH HOPPER** – bass / **ROB TAIT** and **ROBERT WYATT** – drums / etc.

		Harvest	not iss.
Nov 69.	(lp) (SHVL 763) **JOY OF A TOY**	☐	-

– Joy of a toy . . . / Town feeling / Clarietta rag / Girl on a swing / Song for insane times / Stop this train again doing it / Eleanor's cake which ate her / Lady Rachel / Oleh olah bandu bandong / All this crazy gift of time. (re-iss. Jun89 on 'Beat Goes On' lp/cd; BGO LP/CD 78)

Feb 70.	(7") (HAR 5011) **SINGING A SONG IN THE MORNING. / ELEANOR'S CAKE WHICH ATE HER**	☐	-

—— After being augmented on last single by CARAVAN members, he formed backing group The WHOLE WIDE WORLD, which included **DAVID BEDFORD** – keyboards / **MIKE OLDFIELD** – bass / **LOL COXHILL** – saxophone / **MICK FINCHER** – drums

Oct 70.	(lp; as KEVIN AYERS & THE WHOLE WORLD) (SHSP 4005) **SHOOTING AT THE MOON**	☐	-

– May I / Rheinhardt and Geraldine / Colores para Dolores / Lunatics lament / Pisser dans un violin / The oyster and the flying fish / Underwater / Clarence in wonderland / Red, green and you, blue / Shooting at the Moon. (re-iss. Jun89 on 'Beat Goes On' lp/cd; BGO LP/CD 13)

Oct 70.	(7") (HAR 5027) **BUTTERFLY DANCE. / PUIS-JE?**	☐	-
Aug 71.	(7") (HAR 5042) **STRANGER IN BLUE SUEDE SHOES. / STARS**	☐	-

—— The WHOLE WIDE WORLD were augmented by GONG members **DIDIER MALHERBE** – sax / **STEVE HILLAGE** – guitar / also session drummers **WYATT, DUFORT & TONY CARR**

Jan 72.	(lp) (SHVL 800) **WHATEVERSHEBRINGSWESING**	☐	-

– There is loving – Among us – There is loving / Margaret / Oh my / Song from the bottom of a well / Whatevershebringswesing / Stranger in blue suede shoes / Champagne cowboy blues / Lullaby. (re-iss. Jun89 on 'Beat Goes On' lp/cd; BGO LP/CD 11)

—— **ARCHIE LEGGAT** – bass (ex-WONDERWHEEL) repl. OLDFIELD who went solo / **EDDIE SPARROW** – drums / etc.

		Harvest	Sire
Nov 72.	(7") (HAR 5064) **OH! WOT A DREAM. / CONNIE ON A RUBBER BAND**	☐	-
Apr 73.	(7") (HAR 5071) **CARIBBEAN MOON. / TAKE ME TO TAHITI** (re-iss. Jul75; HAR 5100) (re-iss. May76; HAR 5109)	☐	
May 73.	(lp) (SHVL 807) <SAS 7406> **BANANAMOUR**	☐	☐

– Don't let it get you down / Shouting in a bucket-blues / When your parents go to sleep / Interview / International anthem / Decadence / Oh! wot a dream / Hymn / Beware of the dog. <US-iss.+=> – CARIBBEAN MOON (lp). (re-iss. May86 on 'E.M.I.'; EMS 1124) (cd-iss. Oct92 on 'Beat Goes On'; BGOCD 142)

—— His touring '747' band incl. **HENRY CRALLAN** – keyboards / **FREDDIE SMITH** – drums / **CAL BATCHELOR** – guitar. In the studio he now used many session people.

		Island	not iss.
Apr 74.	(7") (WIP 6194) **THE UP SONG. / EVERYBODY'S SOMETIMES AND SOME PEOPLE'S ALL THE TIME BLUES**	☐	-
May 74.	(lp) (ILPS 9263) **THE CONFESSIONS OF DR.DREAM AND OTHER STORIES**	☐	-

– Day by day / See you later / Didn't feel lonely till I thought of you / Everybody's sometimes and some people's all the time blues / It begins with a blessing, but it ends with a curse / Once I awsheared / Ball bearing blues / The confessions of Dr.Dream (a) Irreversible neural damage, (b) Invitation, (c) The one chance dance, (d) Doctor Dream theme, (e) Two into 4 goes. (re-iss. Nov90 on 'Beat Goes On' cd/lp; BGO CD/LP 86)

Jul 74.	(7") (WIP 6201) **AFTER THE SHOW. / THANK YOU VERY MUCH**	☐	-

—— He was credited alongside ENO, NICO and JOHN CALE on 'Island' Various Artists album 'JUNE 1st, 1974'; ILPS 9291, released that month. (cd-iss. Feb90; IMCD 92)

—— He formed backing group, which included **ZOOT MONEY** – keyboards / **RICK WILLS** – bass / **TONY NEWMAN** – drums / **OLLIE HALSALL** – guitar

Mar 75.	(lp) (ILPS 9322) **SWEET DECEIVER**	☐	-

– Observations / Guru banana / City waltz / Toujours la voyage / Sweet deceiver / Diminished but not finished / Once upon an ocean / Farewell again / Another dawn. (cd-iss. Oct92 on 'Beat Goes On'; BGOCD 98)

Feb 76.	(7") (WIP 6271) **FALLING IN LOVE AGAIN. / EVERYONE KNOWS THE SONG**	☐	-

—— Retained ZOOT, calling in **ANDY SOMERS** – guitar / **CHARLIE McCRACKEN** – bass / **ROB TOWNSEND** – drums

		Harvest	A.B.C.
Feb 76.	(7") (HAR 5107) **STRANGER IN BLUE SUEDE SHOES. / FAKE MEXICAN TOURIST BLUES**	☐	☐
Jun 76.	(lp) (SHSP 4057) **YES WE HAVE NO MANANAS**	☐	☐

– Star / Mr. Cool / The owl / Love's gonna turn you 'round / Falling in love again (ich bin von kopf bis fuss duf liebe eingestellt) / Help me / Ballad of Mr. Snake / Everyone knows the song / Yes I do / Blue. (cd-iss. Apr93 on 'Beat Goes On'; BGOCD 143)

1976.	(7") <12303> **MR. COOL. /**	-	☐
Apr 77.	(7") (HAR 5124) **STAR. / THE OWL**	☐	-

—— **BILL LIVESY** – keyboards repl. ZOOT, etc.

Apr 78.	(lp/c) (SHSP/TC-SHSP 4085) **RAINBOW TAKEAWAY**	☐	-

– Blaming it all on love / Ballad of a salesman who sold himself / A view from a mountain / Rainbow takeaway / Waltz for you / Beware of the dog 2 / Strange song / Goodnight goodnight / Hat song. (cd-iss. May93 on 'Beat Goes On';)

Feb 80.	(lp/c) (SHSP/TC-SHSP 4106) **THAT'S WHAT YOU GET, BABE**	☐	-

– That's what you get, babe / Where do I go from here / You never outrun your heart / Given and taken / Idiots / Super salesman / Money, money, money / Miss Hanagal / I'm so tired / Where do the stars end. (cd-iss. Jun93 on 'Beat Goes On'; BGOCD 190)

Feb 80.	(7") (HAR 5198) **MONEY, MONEY, MONEY. / STRANGER IN BLUE SUEDE SHOES**	☐	-

—— Retired to Majorca in Spain. Still retained **FOLLIE** + employed new Spanish musicians.

		not iss.	Columbia
1982.	(7") (MO 2113) **ANIMALS. / DON'T FALL IN LOVE WITH ME**	-	- Spain
		Charly	not iss.
Jun 83.	(lp) (CR 30224) **DIAMOND JACK AND THE QUEEN OF PAIN**		-

– Madame Butterfly / Lay lady lay / Who's still crazy / You keep me hangin' on / You are a big girl / Steppin' out / My speeding heart / Howling man / Give a little bit / Champagne and valium.

Jul 83.	(7") (CYZ 7107) **MY SPEEDING HEART. / CHAMPAGNE AND VALIUM**		-
		Blau	not iss.
1984.	(lp) (A-014) **DEIA VU**		- Spain
		Illuminated	not iss.
May 86.	(7"promo) (LEV 71) **STEPPING OUT. / ONLY HEAVEN KNOWS**	☐	
Jun 86.	(lp) (AMA 25) **AS CLOSE AS YOU THINK**	☐	

– Heaven only knows / Wish I could fall / etc.

		Virgin	not iss.
Feb 88.	(lp/c/cd) (V/TCV/CDV 2510) **FALLING UP**	☐	-

– Saturday night (in Deya) / Flying start / The best we have / Another rolling stone / Do you believe? / That's what we did / Night fighters / Am I really Marcel?.

		Permanent	not iss.
Feb 92.	(cd/c/lp) (PERM CD/MC/LP 5) **STILL LIFE WITH GUITAR** (cd re-iss. Mar98 on 'Indelible'; INDELCD 2)	☐	-
		Voiceprint	not iss.
Jun 98.	(m-cd) (VP 180CD) **THE GARDEN OF LOVE**	☐	-

– compilations, etc. –

on 'Harvest' unless mentioned otherwise

Jun 75.	(d-lp) (SHDW 407) **JOY OF A TOY / SHOOTING AT THE MOON**	☐	-
Feb 76.	(lp) (SHSM 2005) **ODD DITTIES**	☐	-
Jul 83.	(lp) See For Miles; (CM 117) **THE KEVIN AYERS COLLECTION** (re-iss. Jun86; same) (re-iss. Jul90 & Jun97 lp/cd; same/SEECD 117)	☐	-
Jun 89.	(d-lp/c)(cd) (EM/TC-EM 2032)(CZ 176) **BANANA PRODUCTIONS – THE BEST OF KEVIN AYERS**	☐	-

– Butterfly dance / Girl on a swing / Soon soon soon / Sweet deceiver / Caribbean moon / Decadence [not on cd] / Irreversible neural damage / Gemini child / The lady Rachel / Toujours le voyage [not on cd] / Stranger in blue suede shoes / There is loving – Among us – There is loving / The Clarietta rag / Reinhardt & Geraldine – Colores para Dolores / Stars / Don't let it get you down / Hat song / Singing a song in the morning / Ballad of a salesman who sold himself / Clarence in Wonderland / Diminished but not finished / Blue [not on cd] / Song from the bottom of a well.

Jul 92.	(cd) Windsong; (WINCD 018) **THE BBC RADIO LIVE IN CONCERT** (live)	☐	-
Oct 92.	(cd) Connoisseur; (CSAPCD 110) **DOCUMENT SERIES PRESENTS (CLASSIC ALBUM & SINGLE TRACKS 1969-1980)**	☐	☐
Sep 96.	(cd) Band Of Joy; (BOJCD 019) **SINGING THE BRUISE**	☐	☐
Nov 96.	(cd) Band Of Joy; (BOJCD 020) **1ST SHOW IN THE APPEARANCE BUSINESS**	☐	☐
Jul 98.	(d-cd) Hux; (HUX 006) **TOO OLD TO DIE YOUNG**	☐	☐

Jul 98.　(cd) *Hux; (HUX 007)* **BANANA FOLLIES**　　□　－
Nov 99.　(d-lp) *Turning Point; (TPM 99203)* **RADIO SESSIONS**　□　－

AZTEC CAMERA

Formed: East Kilbride, Scotland ... early 1980 by 15 year-old, RODDY FRAME, who released two independent 45's on ALAN HORNE's now semi-famous 'Postcard' label, before moving on to 'Rough Trade' in 1982. The following year, RODDY and Co. hit the top of the indie charts (reached Top 30 nationally) with debut album, 'HIGH LAND, HARD RAIN', a largely acoustic-based affair combining folkish flights of fancy, Latin/jazz rhythms and an incisive lyrical flair with stunning results. The record's breezy lead track, 'OBLIVIOUS', was re-issued by new label 'Warners' later that year on the back of the album's success, one of the few AZTEC CAMERA singles to break the Top 20. FRAME brought in a new cast of musicians for 1984's MARK KNOPFLER-produced 'KNIFE' set, including seasoned Scots players CRAIG GANNON and MALCOLM ROSS. A more commercial offering, the record almost made a UK hit with 'ALL I NEED IS EVERYTHING'. After a world tour, FRAME laid low for more than two years, penning material for 'LOVE' (1987), the most successful album of his career. Initially something of a non-starter, this over-produced yet affecting album eventually made the Top 10 almost a year after its release following the massive Top 5 success of the plaintive 'SOMEWHERE IN MY HEART' single. Despite courting the pop mainstream, FRAME's subsequent effort, 'STRAY' (1990), veered into more eclectic territory, the Top 20 hit, 'GOOD MORNING BRITAIN', featuring MICK JONES of BIG AUDIO DYNAMITE / CLASH fame. The 90's, meanwhile, witnessed FRAME developing his earlier style, especially on the 1995 set, 'FRESTONIA'. Come 1998, the Scots veteran had signed to 'Independiente', releasing a minor hit, 'REASON FOR LIVING' which accompanied the relatively low-key pop-rock album, 'THE NORTH STAR'.
• **Covered:** JUMP (Van Halen) / DO I LOVE YOU (Cole Porter) / I THREW IT ALL AWAY (Bob Dylan) / BAD EDUCATION (Blue Orchids) / IF PARADISE WAS HALF AS NICE (Amen Corner). • **Trivia:** In Autumn '83, while in the States supporting ELVIS COSTELLO, he lied about his age (19) to get into the country.
Album rating: HIGH LAND, HARD RAIN (*8) / KNIFE (*6) / LOVE (*5) / STRAY (*6) / DREAMLAND (*6) / FRESTONIA (*5) / THE BEST OF AZTEC CAMERA compilation (*7) / Roddy Frame: THE NORTH STAR

RODDY FRAME (b.29 Jan'64) – vocals, acoustic guitar / **DAVE MULHOLLAND** – bass / **CAMPBELL OWENS** – drums (He replaced ALAN WELSH)

		Postcard	not iss.
Mar 81.	(7") *(81-3)* **JUST LIKE GOLD. / WE COULD SEND LETTERS**	□	－
Jul 81.	(7") *(81-8)* **MATTRESS OF WIRE. / LOOK OUTSIDE THE TUNNEL**	□	－

──　(mid-'82) added temp. member **BERNIE CLARK** – keyboards / **DAVE RUFFY** – drums (ex-RUTS) repl. MULHOLLAND

		Rough Trade	Sire
Aug 82.	(7"/7"pic-d) *(RT 112/+P)* **PILLAR TO POST. / QUEEN'S TATTOO**	□	－
Jan 83.	(7") *(RT 122)* **OBLIVIOUS. / ORCHARD GIRL** (12"+=) *(RT 122T)* – Haywire.	47	－
Apr 83.	(lp) *(ROUGH 47) <23899>* **HIGH LAND, HARD RAIN**	22	Aug83

– Oblivious / The boy wonders / Walk out to winter / The bugle sounds again / We could send letters / Pillar to post / Release / Lost outside the tunnel / Back on board / Down the dip. *(cd-iss. Feb87 +=; ROUGHCD 47)* – Haywire / Queen's tattoo / Orchard girl. *(re-iss. Sep93 on 'WEA' cd/c; 4509 92849-2/-4)*

| May 83. | (7"/12") *(RT/+T 132)* **WALK OUT TO WINTER. / SET THE KILLING FREE** | 64 | □ |

		WEA	Sire
Oct 83.	(d7") *(AZTEC 1)* **OBLIVIOUS. / ORCHARD GIRL // WE COULD SEND LETTERS (live). / BACK ON BOARD (live)**	18	□

──　**RODDY FRAME** retained **DUFFY** and brought into line-up. **CRAIG GANNON** – bass (ex-BLUEBELLS) repl. OWENS / added **MALCOLM ROSS** – guitar (ex-ORANGE JUICE, ex-JOSEF K) / guest **GUY FLETCHER** – keyboards

| Aug 84. | (7") *(AC 1)* **ALL I NEED IS EVERYTHING. / JUMP** (12") *(AC 1T)* – 'A'-Latin mix) / Jump (Loaded version). | 34 | □ |
| Sep 84. | (lp/c)(cd) *(WX 8/+C)(240 483-2) <25183>* **KNIFE** | 14 | □ |

– Still on fire / Just like the U.S.A. / Head is happy (heart's insane) / The back door to Heaven / All I need is everything / Backwards and forwards / Birth of the true / Knife. *(cd-iss. Sep93; same)*

| Nov 84. | (7"/7"sha-pic-d) *(AC 2/+P)* **STILL ON FIRE. / WALK OUT TO WINTER** | | □ |

(12"+=) *(AC 2T)* – Mattress of wire (live) / The boy wonders (live) / The bugle sounds again (live).

| Apr 85. | (10"m-lp) *<25285>* **AZTEC CAMERA (live)** | － | □ |

– Birth of the true / Mattress of wire / Jump / The bugle sounds again / Backwards and forwards.

──　**FRAME & DUFFY** plus alongside other session musicians **MARCUS MILLER** – bass / **DAVID FRANK** – keyboards (ex-SYSTEM) / **STEVE JORDAN** – guitar

| Sep 87. | (7"/ext-12") *(YZ 154/+T)* **DEEP AND WIDE AND TALL. / BAD EDUCATION** | | □ |
| Oct 87. | (lp/c)(cd) *(WX 128/+C)(242 202-2) <25646>* **LOVE** | 10 | □ |

– Deep and wide and tall / How men are / Everybody is a number one / More than a law / Somewhere in my heart / Working in a goldmine / One and one / Paradise / Killermont Street. *(cd-iss. Sep93; same)*

| Jan 88. | (7") *(YZ 168)* **HOW MEN ARE. / THE RED FLAG** | 25 | □ |

(12"+=) *(YZ 168T)* – Killermont Street (live) / Pillar to post (live).
(cd-s+=) *(248 028-2)* – Oblivious / All I need is everything.

| Apr 88. | (7") *(YZ 181)* **SOMEWHERE IN MY HEART. / EVERYBODY IS A NUMBER ONE '86** | 3 | □ |

(12"+=) *(YZ 181T)* – Down the dip / Jump.
(cd-s+=) *(YZ 181CD)* – Walk out to winter / Still on fire.

| Jul 88. | (7") *(YZ 199)* **WORKING IN A GOLDMINE. / I THREW IT ALL AWAY** | 31 | □ |

(12"+=/12"s+=) *(YZ 199 T/W)* – ('A'version).
(cd-s++=) *(YZ 199CD)* – How men are.

| Sep 88. | (7") *(YZ 154)* **DEEP AND WIDE AND TALL. / BAD EDUCATION** | 55 | □ |

(12"+=/cd-s+=) *(YZ 154 T/CD)* – More than a law.

──　(live band '88: augmenting **FRAME + DUFFY**) **EDDIE KULAK** – keyboards / **GARY SANFORD** – guitar / **PAUL POWELL** – bass

──　(by 1990, **FRAME** had lost **DUFFY**) retained **POWELL** / and new **GARY SANCTUARY** – keyboards / **FRANK TONTOH** – drums / guests **PAUL CARRACK**, **EDWYN COLLINS**, **MICKEY GALLAGHER** & **STEVE SI DELYNK**.

| Jun 90. | (cd)(lp/c) *(<9031 71694-2>)(WX 350/+C)* **STRAY** | 22 | □ |

– Stray / The crying scene / Get outta London / Over my head / How it is / Good morning Britain (featuring MICK JONES) / The gentle kind / Notting Hill blues / Song for a friend. *(re-iss. cd+c Sep93)*

| Jun 90. | (7") *(YZ 492)* **THE CRYING SCENE. / TRUE COLOURS** | 70 | □ |

(12"+=/cd-s+=) *(YZ 492 T/CD)* – Salvation.
(12"+=) *(YZ 492X)* – I threw it all away (live).

| Sep 90. | (7"/c-s; AZTEC CAMERA and MICK JONES) *(YZ 521/+C)* **GOOD MORNING BRITAIN. / ('A'live version)** | 19 | □ |

(12"+=) *(YZ 521T)* – ('A'remix).
(cd-s+=) *(YZ 521CD)* – Consolation prize. (with EDWYN COLLINS)

| Jul 92. | (7"/c-s) *(YZ 688/+C)* **SPANISH HORSES. / JUST LIKE THE U.S.A. (live)** | 52 | □ |

(cd-s) *(YZ 688CD1)* – ('A'side) / Killermont street (live) / The birth of the true (live) / Song for a friend (live).
(cd-s) *(YZ 688CD2)* – ('A'live version) / Stray (live) / The bugle sounds again (live) / Dolphins (live).

| Apr 93. | (7"/c-s) *(YZ 740/+C)* **DREAM SWEET DREAMS. / GOOD MORNING BRITAIN (live)** | 67 | □ |

(cd-s+=) *(YZ 740CD1)* – Sister Anne (live) / How men are (live).
(cd-s) *(YZ 740CD2)* – ('A'side) / Mattress of wire (live) / Let your love decide (live) / Orchid girl (live).

| May 93. | (cd/c/lp) *(<4509 92492/-2/-4/-1>)* **DREAMLAND** | 21 | □ |

– Birds / Safe in sorrow / Black Lucia / Let your love decide / Spanish horses / Dream sweet dreams / Piano's clocks / Sister Ann / Vertigo / Valium Summer / Belle of the ball.

| Jun 93. | (7"/c-s) *(YZ 754/+C)* **BIRDS. / DEEP AND WIDE AND TALL** | | □ |

(cd-s) *(YZ 754CD1)* – ('A'side) / Working in a goldmine / Knife.
(cd-s) *(YZ 754CD2)* – ('A'side) / Somewhere in my heart / Oblivious / Good morning Britain.

		WEA	Reprise
Oct 95.	(c-s) *(WEA 007C)* **SUN / SUNSET**	□	

(cd-s+=) *(WEA 007CD)* – The crying scene (live).
(cd-s) *(WEA 007CDX)* – ('A'side) / We could send letters (live) / Black Lucia (live) / The rainy season (live).

| Nov 95. | (cd/c) *(<0630 11929-2/-4>)* **FRESTONIA** | | □ |

– The rainy season / Sun / Crazy / On the avenue / Imperfectly / Debutante / Beautiful girl / Phenomenal world / Method of love / Sunset.

– compilations, etc. –

| Sep 90. | (7") *Old Gold; (OG 9945)* **SOMEWHERE IN MY HEART. / OBLIVIOUS** | | － |

──　In Nov'90, 'DO I LOVE YOU?' appeared as the extra track on the 12" & cd-s of a Cole Porter tribute by The POGUES and KIRSTY MacCOLL

| Oct 94. | (cd) *Windsong; (WHISCD 006)* **LIVE ON THE TEST (live)** | | － |
| Jul 99. | (cd/c) *WEA; (3984 28984-2/-4)* **THE BEST OF AZREC CAMERA** | 36 | － |

– Oblivious / Good morning Britain / Somewhere in my heart / Working in a goldmine / How men are / Birth of the true / Walk out to winter / Jump / All I need is everything / Deep & wide & tall / The crying scene / Killermont street / Spanish horses / Reason for living.

RODDY FRAME

		Independiente	Sony
Sep 98.	(c-s) *(ISOM 18CS)* **REASON FOR LIVING / WINTER HAVEN HIGH**	45	Nov98

(cd-s) *(ISOM 18MS) <66231A>* – Rainy greys and blues.
(cd-s) *(ISOM 18SMS) <66231B>* – ('A'side) / Biba nova / The sea is wide.

| Sep 98. | (cd) *(ISOM 7CD) <120123>* **THE NORTH STAR** | 55 | Nov98 |

– Back to the one / The north star / Here comes the ocean / River of brightness / Strings / Bigger brighter better / Autumn flower / Reason for living / Sister shadow / Hymn to grace.

| Mar 99. | (cd-s) **SISTER SHADOW** | □ | － |

Eric B. & RAKIM

Formed: Long Island, New York, USA ... 1985 by DJ ERIC BARRIER and rapper WILLIAM 'RAKIM' GRIFFIN. The pair met while BARRIER was working at New York radio station, WBLS, the dextrous turntable manipulator finally finding the MC skills he was looking for in the subtle but deadly RAKIM. Their debut effort, 'ERIC B. FOR PRESIDENT', stripped hip hop to its bare bones with merciless intensity, RAKIM's understated but effective vocal delivery heightening the impact. Initially released on the obscure 'Zakia' label, the track caught the attention of '4th and Broadway', who released the landmark 'PAID IN FULL' in 1987. A low-slung, sample happy classic propelled by a hypnotically funky rhythm track and focused on RAKIM's mantra like lyrical flow, the cut remains one of the genre's defining moments. A transatlantic singles chart success, the track inspired a brace of remixes as the emerging house culture cross pollinated with rap and hip hop; the most famous of these, the COLDCUT "Seven Minutes Of Madness" epic, embellished the original with the ubiquitous sample of Arabic singer OFRA HAZA, ERIC B. & RAKIM's cool reception of the makeover well documented. The accompanying album of the same name was released to just as much controversy, JAMES BROWN and BOBBY BYRD's legal team none too happy at the splicing of their early 70's funk classic in 'I KNOW YOU GOT SOUL' (another brilliantly conceived sample fest that also borrowed from The JACKSON 5 and KOOL & THE GANG amongst others). Yet the result was a literal exhumation of 'The Godfather's work for "reappraisal" by rap artists, just one of the seismic effects felt by hip hop in the wake of this pivotal album. A second set, 'FOLLOW THE LEADER' (1988) changed tack without losing the effect, its denser collages and harder hitting rhymes seeing the duo stay ahead of the game, almost; a US Top 30 hit, the record was nevertheless overshadowed by the unstoppable momentum of PUBLIC ENEMY. Despite a brave attempt at getting back to basics on the sinewy funk of 'LET THE RHYTHM HIT 'EM' (1990), ERIC B. & RAKIM were inevitably being overtaken by the emerging gangsta rappers, the pair finally splitting after a final album, 'DON'T SWEAT THE TECHNIQUE' (1992). By this point, RAKIM had matured into a lyricist of biting depth, the rapper embarking on a low-key solo career before criminally fading into obscurity; his comeback album 'THE 18th LETTER' in 1997 gave him his first trip into US Top 5 territory. ERIC B. & RAKIM are up there with GRANDMASTER FLASH, AFRIKA BAMBAATAA, CHUCK D, pioneers in an era of hip hop creativity unrivalled since.

Album rating: PAID IN FULL (*8) / FOLLOW THE LEADER (*7) / LET THE RHYTHM HIT 'EM (*5) / DON'T SWEAT THE TECHNIQUE (*6) / Rakim: THE 18th LETTER (*6) / THE MASTER (*6)

ERIC B. (b. ERIC BARRIER, 8 Nov.64) – turntables / **RAKIM** (b. WILLIAM GRIFFIN Jr., 28 Jan'68) – vocals

			Cooltempo	Cooltempo
Aug 86.	(12") (COOLX 129) **ERIC B. FOR PRESIDENT. / ('A'instrumental)**			
Nov 86.	(7") **MY MELODY. / ('A'instrumental)**		-	
Jun 87.	(7"/12") (COOL/+X 146) **I KNOW YOU GOT SOUL. / ('A'instrumental)**			
	(remixed versions Feb88 hit UK No.13, 7"/12"; COOLR/+X 146)			

			4th & Broad	4th & Broad
Aug 87.	(lp/c/cd) (BR LP/CA/CD 514) <4005> **PAID IN FULL**		85	58
	– I ain't no joke / Eric B. is on the cut / My melody / I know you got soul / Move the crowd / As the rhyme goes on / Chinese arithmetic / Eric B. for president / Extended beat / Paid in full. (cd re-iss. Jun89; IMCD 9)			
Oct 87.	(7") (BRW 78) **PAID IN FULL. / ERIC B IS ON THE CUT**		15	
	(12"+=) – (12BRW 78) – ('A'extended).			
Feb 88.	(7") (BRW 88) **MOVE THE CROWD. / ('A'mix)**		53	
	(ext-12"+=) – (12BRW 88) – ('A'-Wild Bunch mix).			
May 88.	(7") (BRW 106) **AS THE RHYME GOES ON. / CHINESE ARITHMETIC**			
	(12"+=) – (12BRW 106) – ('A'mixes).			

			M.C.A.	Uni
Jun 88.	(7") (MCA 1256) **FOLLOW THE LEADER. / ('A'dub)**		21	
	(12"+=) (MCAT 1256) – ('A'extended).			
	(cd-s++=) (DMCA 1256) – ('A'-Accapella mix).			
Aug 88.	(lp/c/cd) (MCG/MCGC/DMCG 6031) <UNI 3> **FOLLOW THE LEADER**		25	22
	– Follow the leader / Microphone fiend / Lyrics of fury / Eric B. never scared / Just a beat / Put your hands together / To the listeners / No competition / The R / Musical massacre / Beats for the listeners.			
Nov 88.	(7") (MCA 1300) **MICROPHONE FIEND. / ('A'mix)**		74	
	(12"+=/cd-s+=) (MCAT/DMCA 1300) – ('A'mixes).			
Jan 89.	(7") (MCA 1303) **THE R. / ('A'mix)**			
	(12"+=/cd-s+=) (MCAT/DMCA 1303) – ('A'mixes).			

—— In Aug'89, ERIC B. & RAKIM were credited on JODY WATLEY's hit single, 'FRIENDS' (MCA 1352)<53669>

			M.C.A.	M.C.A.
May 90.	(12") <MCA 24026> **LET THE RHYTHM HIT 'EM (mixes)**		-	
Jun 90.	(cd/c/lp) (DMCG/MCGC/MCG 6097) <6416> **LET THE RHYTHM HIT 'EM**		58	32
	– Let the rhythm hit 'em / No omega / In the ghetto / Step back / Eric B. made my day / Run for cover / Untouchables / Mahogany / Keep 'em eager to listen / Set 'em straight. (cd+=) – Let the rhythm hit 'em (12" remix).			
Feb 92.	(cd-s) <54333> **JUICE (KNOW THE LEDGE) / ('A'instrumental)**		-	96
	(above from the film, 'Juice')			
Jun 92.	(lp/c/cd) <(MCA/+C/D 10594)> **DON'T SWEAT THE TECHNIQUE**		73	22
	– What's on your mind / Teach the children / Pass the hand grenade / Casualties of war / Rest assured / The punisher / Relax with Pep / Keep the beat / What's going on / Know the ledge / Don't sweat the technique / Kick along.			

RAKIM

			Universal	Universal
Nov 97.	(d-cd/d-c) <(UD2/UC2 53111)> **THE 18th LETTER / THE BOOK OF LIFE**		72	4
	– Intro / The 18th letter (always and forever) / Skit / It's been a long time / Remember that / The saga begins / Skit 2 / Guess who's back / Stay a while / New York (ya' out there) / Show me love / etc.			
Dec 97.	(c-s) (UNC 56151) **GUESS WHO'S BACK / IT'S BEEN A LONG TIME**		32	
	(12"+=/cd-s+=) (UNT/UND 56151) – ('A'mixes).			
Aug 98.	(c-s/12"/cd-s) (UNC/UNT/UND 56203) **STAY A LITTLE WHILE. / THE SAGA BEGINS (Desert Island Discs mix) / NEW YORK (ya out there mix)**		53	
Nov 99.	(cd/c) <(542082-2/-4)> **THE MASTER**			72
	– Intro / Flow forever / When I B on tha mic / Finest ones / All night long / State of hip ho interlude / Uplift / I know / It's the R / I'll be there / It's a must / Real shit / How I get down / L.I. interlude / Strong island / Waiting for the world to end / We'll never stop.			

BAADER-MEINHOF (see under ⇒ AUTEURS)

BABES IN TOYLAND

Formed: Minneapolis, Minnesota, USA ... 1987 by KAT BJELLAND, MICHELLE LEON and LORI BARBELO. Signing to influential local label, 'Twintone', the all-girl group released an early proto-grunge classic in the Jack Endino-produced 'SPANKING MACHINE' (1990). Featuring such white hot blasts of feminine subversiveness as 'HE'S MY THING' and 'PAIN IN MY HEART', the album opened the floodgates for a slew of similar angry young women (i.e. L7 and HOLE, whose JENNIFER FINCH and COURTNEY LOVE respectively, LYDIA LUNCH soundalike BJELLAND had previously played with in SUGAR BABY DOLL). Over the course of the next year, they released a mini-album, 'TO MOTHER', replaced MICHELLE with MAUREEN HERMAN and signed to 'Warner Brothers', releasing a second album proper, 'FONTANELLE' in the Spring of '92. Produced by LEE RANALDO of SONIC YOUTH, the record breached the UK Top 30 on the back of rave reviews from both the inkies and the metal press. Following a stop-gap part live set, 'PAINKILLERS', the BABES took a sabbatical, BJELLAND turning up in STUART GRAY (her new husband)'s outfit, LUBRICATED GOAT, while moonlighting with CRUNT. BABES IN TOYLAND returned in 1995 with 'NEMESISTERS', which disappointed many of their more hardcore following by including covers of 'WE ARE FAMILY' (Sister Sledge), 'DEEP SONG' (Billie Holiday) and 'ALL BY MYSELF' (Eric Carmen). • Other covers: WATCHING GIRL (Shonen Knife) / THE GIRL CAN'T HELP IT (Little Richard).

Album rating: SPANKING MACHINE (*7) / TO MOTHER (*7) / FONTANELLE (*8) / PAINKILLERS (*5) / NEMESISTERS (*6)

KAT BJELLAND (b. KATHERINE, 9 Dec'63, Woodburn, Oregon) – vocals, guitar / **MICHELLE LEON** – bass / **LORI BARBERO** (b.27 Nov'60) – drums, vocals

			not iss.	Treehouse
Jul 89.	(7",7"green) <TR 017> **DUST CAKE BOY. / SPIT TO SEE THE SHINE**		-	

			not iss.	Sub Pop
Apr 90.	(7",7"gold) <SP 66> **HOUSE. / ARRIBA**		-	

			Twin Tone	Twin Tone
Jul 90.	(cd/lp/mauve-lp) <TTR 89183-2/-4/-1> **SPANKING MACHINE**		-	
	– Swamp pussy / He's my thing / Vomit heart / Never / Boto (w)rap / Dogg / Pain in my heart / Lashes / You're right / Dust cake boy / Fork down throat. (re-iss. +c Dec91 on purple-lp)			

Jun 91. (m-cd/m-c/m-lp) <(TTR 89208-2/-4/-1)> **TO MOTHER** ☐ ☐
– Catatonic / Mad pilot / Primus / Laugh my head off / Spit to see the shine / Pipe / The quiet room.

—— (Mar'92) **MAUREEN HERMAN** (b.25 Jul'66, Philadelphia, Pensylvania) – bass (ex-M+M STIGMATA drummer) repl. MICHELLE whose roadie boyfriend John Cole was killed by a burglar

	Strange Fruit	not iss.
Mar 92. (cd/10"m-lp) (SFPMCD/SFPMA 211) **THE PEEL SESSIONS** (live on John Peel show)	☐	☐

– Catatonic / Ripe / Primus / Spit to see the shine / Pearl / Dogg / Laugh my head off / Mad pilot.

	Southern	Warners
Aug 92. (cd/c/red-lp) (18501-2/-4/-1) <2-/4-26998> **FONTANELLE**	24	☐

– Bruise violet / Right now / Blue bell / Handsome & Gretel / Blood / Magick flute / Won't tell / The quiet room / Spun / Short song / Jungle train / Pearl / Real eyes / Mother / Gone.

Nov 92. (7"purple) (18503-7) **BRUISE VIOLET. / GONE** ☐ ☐
(12"+=/cd-s+=) (18503-6/-2) – Magick flute.

Jun 93. (cd/c/lp) (18512-2/-4/-1) <45339> **PAINKILLERS (part live)** 53 ☐
– He's my thing / Laredo / Istigkeit / Ragweed / Angel hair / Fontanellette (live at CBGB's): Bruise violet – Bluebell – Angel hair – Pearl – Blood – Magick flute – Won't tell – Real eyes – Spun – Mother – Handsome & Gretel.

—— KAT married STUART GRAY and sidelined with bands, CRUNT and KATSTU

CRUNT

—— **KAT BJELLAND / STUART GRAY** (of LUBRICATED GOAT) + **RUSSELL SIMINIS** (of JON SPENCER BLUES EXPLOSION)

	Insipid	Insipid
1993. (7") (IV-31) **SWINE. / SEXY**	☐	☐

	Trance Syndicate	Trance Syndicate
Mar 94. (lp,blue-lp/cd) <(TR 19/+CD)> **CRUNT**	☐	☐ Feb94

– Theme from Crunt / Swine / Black heart / Unglued / Changing my mind / Snap out of it / Sexy / Punishment / Spam / Elephant.

BABES IN TOYLAND

—— re-formed (see last line-up)

	Reprise	Reprise
Apr 95. (cd/c/lp) <(9362 45868-2/-4/-1)> **NEMESISTERS**	☐	☐

– Hello / Oh yeah! / Drivin' / Sweet '69 / Surd / 22 / Ariel / Kiler on the road / Middle man / Memory / S.F.W. / All by myself / Deep song / We are family.

May 95. (12"ep/c-ep/cd-ep) (W 0291 TEX/C/CD) **SWEET '69 / S.F.W. (live) / SWAMP PUSSY (live)** ☐ ☐

Sep 95. (c-s/cd-s) (W 0313 C/CD) **WE ARE FAMILY (Arthur Baker remix) / ('A'-Ben Grosse remix)** ☐ ☐
(12"+=) (W 0313T) – (2 other Baker & Grosse mixes).

—— In 1998, KAT's alternative/metal supergroup rock opera, Songs Of The Witchblade: A Soundtrack To The Comic Books', was released on CD (Dreamworks; DRMD 50102) featuring her alongside PETER STEELE (Type O Negative), BUZZ OSBORNE (Melvins), JIM THIRLWELL (Foetus), among others.

BABYBIRD

Formed: Sheffield, England ... 1988 by Telford born singer STEPHEN JONES. He had been a prolific writer in his bedroom, composing over 400 songs, some of which appeared on five well-received albums between mid-'95 and mid-'96. Each album came with a voting section on which the buyer was asked to write in with their "best of" lists. The top 12 appeared on BABYBIRD's "GREATEST HITS" later in '96, JONES finally coming to prominence that summer as he signed to 'Echo', roped in a full band (JOHN PEDDER, ROBERT GREGORY, LUKE SCOTT and HUW CHADBOURN) and had his first bonafide Top 30 hit with the 'GOODNIGHT' single. BABYBIRD only really took flight with 'YOU'RE GORGEOUS', however, a massive Top 3 hit and a masterstroke of pop genius which managed to weld JONES' wonderfully subversive lyrics to a twinkling, soaring melody and chorus. A simultaneous album, 'UGLY BEAUTIFUL' (1996) made the Top 10, although critics who'd praised his more endearing amateurish early recordings were unsure about this leap into semi-accessible chartbound territory. Nevertheless, a growing army of fans who'd never even heard the other albums (mainly because they were so rare it was impossible to get hold of them!) put a third single, 'CANDY GIRL' into the Top 10. A series of much talked about live appearances emphasized JONES performance-arty background, the singer drawing comparisons with PULP's JARVIS COCKER. Of late, STEPHEN and Co have been back in the public eye, 1998 seeing them hovering around the fringes of the UK Top 30 with a couple of singles and an album, 'THERE'S SOMETHING GOING ON'.

Album rating: I WAS BORN A MAN (*8) / BAD SHAVE (*7) / FATHERHOOD (*6) / THE HAPPIEST MAN ALIVE (*8) / UGLY BEAUTIFUL (*6) / THERE'S SOMETHING GOING ON (*7)

STEPHEN JONES (b.16 Sep'62) – vocals, guitar – with band; **LUKE SCOTT** (b.25 Aug'69) – guitar / **HUW CHADBOURN** (b. 7 Dec'63) – keyboards / **JOHN PEDDER** (b.29 May'62) – bass / **ROBERT GREGORY** (b. 2 Jan'67) – drums

	Baby Bird	not iss.
Jul 95. (cd) (BABYBIRD 001) **I WAS BORN A MAN**	☐	☐

– Blow it to the Moon / Man's tight vest / Lemonade baby / C.F.C. / Cornershop / Kiss your country / Hong Kong blues / Dead bird sings / Baby bird / Farmer / Invisible tune / Alison / Love love love.

Oct 95. (cd/d-lp) (BABYBIRD CD/LP 002) **BAD SHAVE** ☐ ☐

– KW Jesus TV roof appeal / Bad jazz / Too handsome to be homeless / Steam train / Bad shave / Oh my God, you're a king / The restaurant is guilty / Valerie / Shop girl / W.B.T. / Hate song / 45 & fat / Sha na na / Bug in a breeze / It's okay / Happy bus / Swinging from tree to tree.

Dec 95. (cd/d-lp) (BABYBIRD CD/LP 003) **FATHERHOOD** ☐ -
– No children / Cooling towers / Cool and crazy things to do / Bad blood / Neil Armstrong / I was never here / Saturday / Goodnight / I don't want to wake up with you / Iceberg / Aluminium beach / Goddamn it, you're a kid / Daisies / Failed old singer / Fatherhood / Dustbin liner / Not about a girl / Good weather / But love / May me.

Apr 96. (cd/lp) (BABYBIRD CD/LP 004) **THE HAPPIEST MAN ALIVE** ☐ -
– Razorblade shower / Sundial in a tunnel / Little white man / Halfway up the hill / Horsesugar / Please don't be famous / Louse / Copper feel / Seagullably / Dead in love / Candy girl / Gunfingers / Married / In the country / Planecrash Xmas / This beautiful disease / You'll get a slap / In the morning.

	Echo	Atlantic
Jul 96. (7") (ECS 024) **GOODNIGHT. / JULY**	28	☐

(cd-s+=) (ECSCD 024) – Harry and Ida swop teeth.
(cd-s) (ECSCX 024) – ('A'side) / Shellfish / Girl with money.

Oct 96. (c-s) (ECSMC 026) **YOU'RE GORGEOUS / BEBE LIMONADE** 3 ☐
(cd-s+=) (ECSCX 026) – Ooh yeah / Car crash.
(cd-s) (ECSCX 026) – ('A'side) / You're gorgeous too / Honk Kong blues / KW Jesus TV roof appeal.

Oct 96. (cd/c/d-lp) (ECH CD/MC/LP 011) <83049> **UGLY BEAUTIFUL** 9 ☐ 1997
– Goodnight / Candy girl / Jesus is my girlfriend / I didn't want to wake you up / Dead bird sings / Atomic soda / You're gorgeous / Bad shave 2 / Cornershop / King Bing / You & me / 45 & fat / Too handsome to be homeless / July / Baby bird. (cd re-iss. Mar99; same)

Jan 97. (c-s) (ECSMC 031) **CANDY GIRL / FARMER** 14 ☐
(cd-s+=) (ECSCD 031) – You're gorgeous (BBC session) / Oh what a beautiful day.
(cd-s) (ECSCX 031) – ('A'side) / Bad shave (BBC session) / Cooling towers (BBC session) / Amtrack.

Apr 97. (ltd-7"pic-d) (ECSPD 033) **CORNERSHOP. / ALUMINIUM** ☐ -
May 97. (c-s) (ECSMC 033) **CORNERSHOP / HAPPIEST MAN ALIVE** 37 ☐
(cd-s) (ECSCD 033) – ('A'side) / Death of the neighbourhood II / Shop girl / You're gorgeous (original demo – 1991).
(cd-s) (ECSCX 033) – ('A'side) / Death of the neighbourhood I / Pretty little graves / Cornershop (original demo – 1987).

—— now without HUW who left left early in '98

	Echo	Imprint
Apr 98. (7"pic-d) (ECS 060) **BAD OLD MAN. / FUCKLOVE**	31	☐

(cd-s+=) (ECSCD 060) – Hospital bed.
(cd-s) (ECSCX 060) – ('A'side) / All I know / Comeback scumbag.

Aug 98. (7"pic-d) (ECS 065) **IF YOU'LL BE MINE. / POOLSIDE** 28 ☐
(c-s+=/cd-s+=) (ECS MC/CD 065) – Worn.
(cd-s) (ECSCX 065) – ('A'side) / Memorise / I want nothing.

Aug 98. (cd/c/lp) (ECH CD/MC/LP 024) <111059> **THERE'S SOMETHING GOING ON** 28 ☐
– Bad old man / If you'll be mine / Back together / I was never here / First man on the sun / You will always love me / The life / All men are evil / Take me back / It's not funny anymore / There's something going on.

Feb 99. (7"clear) (ECS 073) **BACK TOGETHER. / IF YOU'LL BE MINE (acoustic)** 22 -
(cd-s) (ECSCD 073) – ('A'side) / Like before / C.F.C.
(cd-s) (ECSCX 073) – ('A'side) / Sunshine / Hate song.

Jul 99. (7") (MUSE 006) **DRUNK CAR. / East River Pipe: CYBERCAR** ☐ -
(above issued on 'Easy Tiger')

– compilations, etc. –

Aug 97. (cd) Baby Bird; <60804> **GREATEST HITS** ☐ ☐
– Goddamn it, you're a kid / Man's tight vest / KW Jesus TV roof appeal / Bad blood / Kiss your country / Hong Kong blues / Razor blade shower / Sha na na / Aluminium beach / Alison / Grandma begs to be 18 again / I was never here / Petrol cigarette / Losing my hair / Saturday / Invisible tune / Failed old singer / Swinging from tree to tree / Anot about a girl / In the morning.

BABYS / BAD ENGLISH (dig out; 4th edition or Great Metal . . .)

BACHMAN-TURNER OVERDRIVE

Formed: Winnipeg, Canada ... 1972 by the BACHMAN brothers, RANDY, ROBBIE and TIM. The former had been part of late 60's rock outfit, GUESS WHO, before releasing a 1970 solo album, 'AXE'. He also formed a short-lived country-rock band, BRAVE BELT, who issued two albums for 'RCA' in the early 70's. Together with FRED TURNER, BACHMAN-TURNER OVERDRIVE signed to 'Mercury' in 1973, making steady inroads onto the US airwaves. By late '74, they had a No.1 US hit with the stuttering hard-rock anthem, 'YOU AIN'T SEEN NOTHING YET'. (In the 90's, its intro featured on Harry Enfield's UK TV show DJ creations, Chas Smash and Nicey Nice). The single formed the centrepiece of the album, 'NOT FRAGILE', which also topped the chart. Being of the Mormon persuasion, the BACHMAN's unfortunately couldn't live the rock'n'roll lifestyle to the hilt, their faith forbidding alcohol, drugs, tea or coffee. Nevertheless, they were adopted by the "blue collar" brigade (actually a title of one of their songs), enjoying a brief run of successful albums in the mid 70's. In 1978, without the departed RANDY, the BACHMAN's abbrieviated their moniker to BTO, releasing a few more albums while the former formed the similar sounding IRON HORSE. BACHMAN-TURNER OVERDRIVE were re-united in the mid 80's, with RANDY back at the helm.

Album rating: Brave Belt: BRAVE BELT (*3) / BRAVE BELT II (*3) / Bachman-

Turner Overdrive: BACHMAN-TURNER OVERDRIVE (*4) / BACHMAN-TURNER OVERDRIVE II (*5) / NOT FRAGILE (*6) / FOUR WHEEL DRIVE (*6) / THE BEST OF BTO (SO FAR) (*6) / HEAD ON (*4) / THE BEST OF B.T.O. compilation (*6) / FREEWAYS (*3) / STREET ACTION (*2) / ROCK'N'ROLL NIGHTS (*2) / GREATEST HITS compilation (*5)

RANDY BACHMAN

with **DAN TROIANO** – guitar / **GARRY PETERSON** – drums / **WES DAKUS** – steel guitar

		not iss.	R.C.A.
1970.	(lp) **AXE**	-	

– Zarahemia / Not to return / Pookie's shuffle / Tally's tune / Take the long way home / La Jolla / Tin Lizzie / Suite theam / Noah.

BRAVE BELT

RANDY BACHMAN (b.27 Sep'43) – vocals, guitar (ex-GUESS WHO) / **CHAD ALLAN** – keyboards, vocals (ex-GUESS WHO) / **C.F. (FRED) TURNER** (b.16 Oct'43) – bass, vocals / **ROBBIE BACHMAN** (b.18 Feb'53) – drums, percussion

		not iss.	Reprise
1971.	(7") **ROCK AND ROLL BAND. / ANY DAY MEANS TOMORROW**	-	
1971.	(lp) <6447> **BRAVE BELT**	-	

– Crazy arms, crazy eyes / Lifetime / Waitin' there for me / I am the man / French kin / It's over / Rock and roll band / Wandering fantasy girl / I wouldn't give up my guitar for a woman / Holy train / Anyday means tomorrow / Scarecrow.

1971.	(7") <1039> **CRAZY ARMS, CRAZY EYES. / HOLY TRAIN**	-	
1972.	(7") <1061> **NEVER COMIN' HOME. / CAN YOU FEEL IT**	-	
1972.	(lp) <2057> **BRAVE BELT II**		

– Too far away / Dunrobin's gone / Can you feel it / Put it in a song / Summer soldier / Never comin' home / Be a good man / Long way round / Another way out / Waterloo country.

1972.	(7") <1083> **ANOTHER WAY OUT. / DUNROBIN'S GONE**	-	

BACHMAN-TURNER OVERDRIVE

TIM BACHMAN – guitar repl. CHAD

		Mercury	Mercury
Aug 73.	(7") <73383> **GIMME YOUR MONEY PLEASE. / LITTLE GAWDY DANCER**	-	
Aug 73.	(lp) (6499 509) <SRMI 673> **BACHMAN-TURNER OVERDRIVE**		70

– Gimme your money please / Hold back the water / Blue collar / Little gandy dancer / Stayed awake all night / Down and out man / Don't get yourself in trouble / Thank you for the feelin'. (cd-iss. Jan93;)

Sep 73.	(7") <73417> **STAYED AWAKE ALL NIGHT. / DOWN AND OUT MAN**		-
Nov 73.	(7") <73417> **BLUE COLLAR. / HOLD BACK THE WATER**	-	68
Feb 74.	(7") <73457> **LET IT RIDE. / TRAMP**	-	23
Mar 74.	(7") (6052 605) **LET IT RIDE. / BLUE COLLAR**	-	-
Mar 74.	(lp) (6338 482) <SRMI 693> **BACHMAN-TURNER OVERDRIVE II**		4 Jan74

– Blown / Welcome home / Stonegates / Let it ride / Give it time / Tramp / I don't have to / Takin' care of business.

Aug 74.	(7") (6052 627) <73487> **TAKIN' CARE OF BUSINESS. / STONEGATES**		12 May74

—— **BLAIR THORNTON** (b.23 Jul'50, Vancouver) – guitar repl. TIM who became producer

Oct 74.	(7") (6167 025) <73622> **YOU AIN'T SEEN NOTHING YET. / FREE WHEELIN'**	2	1 Sep74
Oct 74.	(lp/c) (9100 007) <SRMI 1004> **NOT FRAGILE**	12	1 Aug74

– Not fragile / Rock is my life, and this is my song / Roll on down the highway / You ain't seen nothing yet / Free wheelin' / Sledgehammer / Blue moanin' / Second hand / Givin' it all away. (cd-iss. Mar91; 830178-2)

Jan 75.	(7") (6167 071) <73656> **ROLL ON DOWN THE HIGHWAY. / SLEDGEHAMMER**	22	14
May 75.	(7") (6167 173) <73683> **HEY YOU. / FLAT BROKE LOVE**		21
Jun 75.	(lp/c) (9100 012) <SRMI 1027> **FOUR WHEEL DRIVE**		5 May75

– Four wheel drive / She's a devil / Hey you / Flat broke love / She's keepin' time / Quick change artist / Lowland blues / Don't let the blues get you down.

Nov 75.	(7") <73724> **DOWN TO THE LINE. / SHE'S A DEVIL**		43
Jan 76.	(7") (6167 320) **AWAY FROM HOME. / DOWN TO THE LINE**		-
Feb 76.	(lp/c) (9100 020) <SRMI 1067> **HEAD ON**		23 Jan76

– Find out about love / It's over / Average man / Woncha take me for a while / Wild spirit / Take it like a man / Lookin' out for #1 / Away from home / Stay alive.

Feb 76.	(7") <73766> **TAKE IT LIKE A MAN. / WONCHA TAKE ME FOR A WHILE**	-	33
Apr 76.	(7") <73784> **LOOKING OUT FOR #1. / FIND OUT ABOUT LOVE**		65
May 77.	(7") <73903> **MY WHEELS WON'T TURN. / FREE WAYS**	-	
May 77.	(7") (6167 520) **MY WHEELS WON'T TURN. / LIFE STILL GOES ON**		
May 77.	(lp/c) (9100 035) <SRMI 3700> **FREEWAYS**		70 Mar77

– Can we all come together / Life still goes on (I'm lonely) / Shotgun rider / Just for you / My wheels won't turn / Down, down / Easy groove / Freeways.

Sep 77.	(7") <73926> **SHOTGUN RIDER. / DOWN, DOWN**	-	
Sep 77.	(7") (6167 567) **SHOTGUN RIDER. / JUST FOR YOU**	-	
Dec 77.	(7") <73951> **LIFE STILL GOES ON. / JUST FOR YOU**		

B.T.O.

—— **JIM CLENCH** – bass, vocals (ex-APRIL WINE) repl. RANDY who went solo

Mar 78.	(lp/c) (9100 051) <SRMI 3713> **STREET ACTION**		

– I'm in love / Down the road / Takes a lot of people / A long time for a little while / Street action / For love / Madison Avenue / You're gonna miss me / The world is waiting for a love song.

Mar 78.	(7") <73987> **DOWN THE ROAD. / A LONG TIME FOR A LITTLE WHILE**	-	

Mar 79.	(7") <74046> **HEARTACHES. / HEAVEN TONIGHT**	-	60
Mar 79.	(7") (6167 759) **HEARTACHES. / ROCK'N'ROLL NIGHTS**		
Apr 79.	(lp/c) <SRMI 3748> **ROCK'N'ROLL NIGHTS (live)**		

– Jamaica / Heartaches / Heaven tonight / Rock and roll nights / Wastin' time / Here she comes again / End of the line / Rock and roll hell / Amelia Earhart.

Jun 79.	(7") <74062> **END OF THE LINE (live). / JAMAICA (live)**	-	-

—— Broke-up in 1979

BACHMAN-TURNER OVERDRIVE

Re-united mid-84 with below line-up 1984. **RANDY, TIM, FRED TURNER** and newcomer **GARRY PETERSON** – drums

		Compleat	Compleat
Sep 84.	(7") (CLT 6) <127> **FOR THE WEEKEND. / JUST LOOK AT ME NOW**		
Nov 84.	(lp/c) (CLTLP/ZCCLT 353) <1010> **BACHMAN-TURNER OVERDRIVE**		Sep84

– For the weekend / Just look at me now / My sugaree / City's still growin' / Another fool / Lost in a fantasy / Toledo / Service with a smile.

		M.C.A.	Curb
Jan 85.	(7") <133> **SERVICE WITH A SMILE. / MY SUGAREE**	-	
Mar 85.	(7") <137> **MY SUGAREE. / (part 2)**	-	
Aug 86.	(lp/c) (IMCA/+C 5760) **LIVE!-LIVE!-LIVE! (live)**		

– Hey you / Mississippi queen / Sledgehammer / Fragile man / Bad news travels fast / You ain't seen nothin' yet / Roll on down the highway / Takin' care of business.

—— **RANDY** later joined with (ex-TROOPER), FRANK LUDWIG, in UNION. He also became a songwriter for BEACH BOYS, etc.

– compilations, others, etc. –

Mar 75.	(lp) Warners; (K 54036) <MS 2210> **BACHMAN-TURNER OVERDRIVE AS BRAVE BELT**		
Sep 76.	(7") Mercury; <73843> **GIMME YOUR MONEY PLEASE. / FOUR WHEEL DRIVE**	-	70
Sep 76.	(7") Mercury; (6167 425) **TAKIN' CARE OF BUSINESS. / WON'T CHA TAKE ME FOR A WHILE**		-
Nov 76.	(lp) Mercury; (9100 026) <SRMI 1101> **THE BEST OF B.T.O. (SO FAR)**		19 Aug76

(cd-iss. Aug98; 558234-2)

1977.	(lp) Mercury; **JAPAN TOUR (live)**	-	
Aug 81.	(lp)(c) Mercury; (6430 151)(7420 043) **GREATEST HITS**	-	

– Lookin' out for #1 / Hey you / Takin' care of business / You ain't seen nothin' yet / Flat broke love / Rock'n'roll nights / Roll on down the highway / Freeways / Down, down / Let it ride / Can we all come together / Jamaica. (cd-iss. Jan86; 830039-2)

Oct 83.	(lp/c) Mercury; (PRICE/PRIMC 46) **YOU AIN'T SEEN NOTHIN' YET**	-	
Oct 84.	(7") Mercury; (CUT 109) **YOU AIN'T SEEN NOTHIN' YET. / ROLL ON DOWN THE HIGHWAY**	-	
Mar 88.	(7") Old Gold; (OG 9764) **YOU AIN'T SEEN NOTHIN' YET. / (other track by – Thin Lizzy)**		
Jul 88.	(lp/c) Knight; (KNLP/KNMC 10008) **NIGHTRIDING**		
Aug 93.	(d-cd) Polygram; (514902-2) **ANTHOLOGY**		
Aug 94.	(cd/c) Spectrum; (550421-2/-4) **ROLL ON DOWN THE HIGHWAY**		
Jun 97.	(cd) Go On Deluxe; (1031-2) **THE VERY BEST OF BACHMAN-TURNER OVERDRIVE**		
Aug 98.	(cd) King Biscuit; (KBFHCD 013) **KING BISCUIT PRESENTS . . .**		-

RANDY BACHMAN

solo with **BURTON CUMMINGS** – keyboards / **IAN GARDINER** – bass / **JEFF PORCARO** – drums / **TOM SCOTT** – saxophone

		Polydor	Polydor
Jun 78.	(7") (2066 954) **JUST A KID. / SURVIVOR**		
Jul 78.	(lp/c) (2490 146) <PDI 6141> **SURVIVOR**		

– Just a kid / One hand clappin' / Lost in the shuffle / Is the night too cold for dancin' / You moved me / I am a star / Maybe again / Survivor.

IRONHORSE

was formed by **RANDY** with **TOM SPARKS** – guitar / **JOHN PIERCE** – bass / **MIKE BAIRD** – drums / **BARRY ALLEN** – vocals

		Warners	Scotti Bros
Mar 79.	(7") (K 11271) <406> **SWEET LUI-LOUISE. / WATCH ME FLY**	60	36
May 79.	(lp/c) (K 50598) <7103> **IRONHORSE**		

– One and only / Sweet Lui-Louise / Jump back in the light / You gotta let go / Tumbleweed / Stateline blues / Watch me fly / Old fashioned / Dedicated to Slowhand / She's got it / There ain't no clue.

Jul 79.	(7") (K 11319) <408> **ONE AND ONLY. / SHE'S GOT IT**		

—— **FRANK LUDWIG** – vocals, keyboards repl. BARRY / **RON FOOS** – bass / **CHRIS LEIGHTON** – drums repl. JOHN + MIKE

Nov 80.	(7") (K 11497) <512> **WHAT'S YOUR HURRY DARLIN'. / TRY A LITTLE HARDER**		89 Apr80
Nov 80.	(lp/c) (K 50730) <7108> **EVERYTHING IS GREY**		

– Everything is grey / What's your hurry darlin' / Symphony / Only way to fly / Try a little harder / I'm hurting inside / Playin' that same old song / Railroad love / Somewhere sometime / Keep your motor running.

BAD BRAINS

Formed: Washington DC, USA ... 1978 by Afro-Americans, H.R., his brother EARL, DR. KNOW and DARRYL JENNIFER. Prior to the advent of the punk rock movement in 1976/77, they had all played together in a jazz fusion outfit, carrying over the jazz dynamic to their frenetic, dub-

wise hardcore. Subsequently relocating to New York, the late 70's saw the release of two classic 45's, 'PAY TO CUM' and 'BIG TAKEOVER'. These virtually went unnoticed, the band's UK profile remaining low after being refused work permits to support The DAMNED on a British tour. In 1983, they finally delivered their debut album, 'ROCK FOR LIGHT' (produced by RIC OCASEK of The CARS), a set that featured one side of hardcore and the other reggae. For three years, H.R. went solo, returning to the fold for 1986's 'I AGAINST I', a more metallic affair which anticipated the funk-rock explosion of the late 80's. H.R. (with EARL) subsequently departed to realise his more reggae orientated ambitions, releasing several albums for 'S.S.T.'. The remainder of BAD BRAINS parted company with this label, eventually reactivating the band for touring purposes with the addition of CHUCK MOSELEY (ex-FAITH NO MORE). H.R. and EARL returned to the fold for the 'QUICKNESS' album in 1989, remaining for the live set, 'THE YOUTH ARE GETTING RESTLESS'. Once again, H.R. and EARL decided to take off, their replacements being ISRAEL JOSEPH-I and the returning MACKIE. This line-up was in place for their major label debut for 'Epic', 'RISE' (1993), although incredibly yet again H.R. and EARL were invited back as BAD BRAINS were offered a place on MADONNA's 'Maverick' label. The resulting 1995 album, 'GOD OF LOVE' (again produced by OCASEK) focused more on dub reggae stylings, proving that the band were as open to experimentation as ever. However, during the accompanying tour, the athletic H.R. left the band for good in controversial circumstances, fighting with his fellow musicians and eventually being pulled up on a drugs charge (BAD BRAINS right enough!). • **Songwriters:** H.R. / DR. KNOW / group, except DAY TRIPPER (Beatles) / SHE'S A RAINBOW (Rolling Stones).

Album rating: BAD BRAINS (*7) / ROCK FOR LIGHT (*8) / I AGAINST I (*8) / LIVE (*5) / QUICKNESS (*4) / RISE (*4) / GOD OF LOVE (*6)

H.R. (b. PAUL HUDSON, 11 Feb'56, London, England) – vocals / **DR. KNOW** (b. GARY WAYNE MILLER, 15 Sep'58, Washington) – guitar, keyboards / **DARRYL AARON JENIFER** (b.22 Oct'60, Washington) – bass, vocals / **EARL HUDSON** (b.17 Dec'57, Alabama) – drums, percussion

	not iss.	Bad Brains
Jun 80. (7") <BB 001> **PAY TO CUM. / STAY CLOSE TO ME**	-	

	Alternative Tentacles	Alternative Tentacles
Jun 82. (12"ep) (VIRUS 13) **THE BAD BRAINS EP**		

– I luv jah / Sailin' on / Big takeover.

	R.O.I.R.	R.O.I.R.
Dec 82. (c) (A 106) **BAD BRAINS**		

– Sailin' on / Don't need it / Attitude / The regulator / Banned in D.C. / Jah calling / Supertouch / FVK / Big take over / Pay to cum / Right brigade / I luv jah / Intro / Leaving Babylon. (cd-iss. Dec89 as 'ATTITUDE – THE ROIR SESSIONS' on 'We Bite' lp/cd; WB 056/+CD) <US re-iss. Nov89 on 'In-Effect'> (re-iss. cd/c/lp 1991 on 'Dutch East Wax' / re-iss. lp Mar93) (re-iss. cd Apr96; RUDCD 8223) (lp re-iss. Jul98 & Nov99; RUSLP 8223R)

	Food For Thought	Important
Mar 83. (12"ep) (YUMT 101) **I AND I SURVIVE / DESTROY BABYLON EP**		

	Abstract	P.V.C.
Mar 83. (lp) (ABT 007) <PVC 8933> **ROCK FOR LIGHT**		

– Coptic times / Attitude / We will not / Sailin' on / Rally around jah throne / Right brigade / F.V.K. (Fearless Vampire Killers) / Riot squad / The meek shall inherit the Earth / Joshua's song / Banned in D.C. / How low can a punk get / Big takeover / I and I survive / Destroy Babylon / Rock for light / At the movies. (re-mixed re-iss. Feb91 on 'Caroline' cd/c/lp; CAR CD/MC/LP 4) (re-iss. cd Sep91; same) (cd re-iss. Jun97; CAROLCD 1375)

	S.S.T.	S.S.T.
Feb 87. (lp/c) <(SST 065/+C)> **I AGAINST I**		Nov86

– Intro / I against I / House of suffering / Re-ignition / Secret '77 / Let me help / She's calling you / Sacred love / Hired gun / Return to Heaven. (cd-iss. Feb88 & May93; SST 065CD)

—— **CHUCK MOSELEY** – vocals (ex-FAITH NO MORE) repl. H.R.

—— **MACKIE JAYSON** (b.27 May'63, New York City) – drums repl. EARL

	S.S.T.	S.S.T.
Nov 88. (lp/c/cd) <(SST 160 LP/C/CD)> **LIVE** (live)		

– I cried / At the movies / The regulator / Right brigade / I against I / I and I survive / House of suffering / Re-ignition / Sacred love / She's calling you / Coptic times / F.V.K. (Fearless Vampire Killers) / Secret 77 / Day tripper. (re-iss. May93; same)

—— both **H.R. + EARL** returned

	Caroline	Caroline
Jul 89. (lp/c/cd) <(CAR LP/C/CD 4)> **QUICKNESS**		

– Soul craft / Voyage into infinity / The messengers / With the quickness / Gene machine / Don't bother me / Don't blow bubbles / Sheba / Yout' juice / No conditions / Silent tears / The prophet's eye / Endtro. (re-iss. cd Sep91; same) (cd re-iss. Jun97; CAROLCD 1375)

	S.S.T.	S.S.T.
Oct 89. (10"m-lp/m-c/m-cd) <SST 228> **SPIRIT ELECTRICITY**	-	

– Return to Heaven / Let me help / Day tripper / She's a rainbow / Banned in D.C. / Attitude / Youth are getting restless.

—— **ISRAEL JOSEPH-I** (b. DEXTER PINTO, 6 Feb'71, Trinidad) – vocals repl. H.R. / **MACKIE** returned EARL

	Epic	Epic
Sep 93. (cd/c/lp) <(474265-2/-4/-1)> **RISE**		

– Rise / Miss Freedom / Unidentified / Love is the answer / Free / Hair / Coming in numbers / Yes jah / Take your time / Peace of mind / Without you / Outro.

—— **H.R. + EARL** returned to repl. JOSEPH-I + JAYSON

	Maverick	Maverick
May 95. (cd/c) <(9362 45882-2/-4)> **GOD OF LOVE**		

– Cool mountaineer / Justic keepers / Long time / Rights of a child / God of love / Over the water / Tongue tee tie / Darling I need you / To the heavens / Thank jah / Big fun / How I love thee.

– compilations, etc. –

May 90. (cd/lp) Caroline; (CARCD/LP 8) **THE YOUTH ARE GETTING RESTLESS (1987 live)**		

– I / Rock for light / Right brigade / House of suffering / Day tripper – She's a rainbow / Coptic times / Sacred love / Re-ignition / Let me help / The youth are getting restless / Banned in D.C. / Sailin' on / Fearless vampire killer / At the movies / Revolution / Pay to cum / Big takeover. (cd re-iss. Jun97; CAROLCD 1617)

May 92. (d-cd) Line; (LICD 921176) **ROCK FOR LIGHT**	-	- German
Oct 96. (cd/lp) Caroline; (PCAROL 005CD/LP) **BLACK DOTS** (rec.1979)		

– Don't need it / At the Atlantis / Pay to cum / Supertouch – Shitfit / Regulator / You're a migraine / Don't bother me / Banned in D.C. / Why'd you have to go / Man won't annoy ya / Redbone in the city / Black dots / How low can a punk get / Just another damn song / Attitude / Send you no flowers.

Nov 97. (10"ep/cd-ep) Victory; (VR 064/+CD) **THE OMEGA SESSIONS**		

– I against you / Stay close to me / I love jah / At the movies / Attitude.

BAD COMPANY

Formed: In late Summer 1973, by the English seasoned-pro foursome of PAUL RODGERS and SIMON KIRKE (both ex-FREE), plus MICK RALPHS and BOZ BURRELL. They got together to form this power-rock supergroup, taking their name from a 1972 Western film starring Jeff Bridges. LED ZEPPELIN manager, PETER GRANT, signed the band to his new 'Swan Song' label in 1974 and they hit the big time almost immediately. No.1 in America, No.3 in the UK, their eponymous debut album set the blueprint; driving music par excellence with RODGERS' heavy, soulful vocals set against a rock solid musical backdrop. These were songs that were built to last, and indeed they have, it's just a pity the cock-rock lyrics haven't aged quite so well. Then again, with such timeless melodic fare as 'CAN'T GET ENOUGH OF YOUR LOVE' and 'BAD COMPANY', maybe the lyrics are besides the point (it was the 70's after all). 'STRAIGHT SHOOTER' (1975) was a bit tougher, yet ultimately more of the same. No bad thing, with the classic 'FEEL LIKE MAKIN' LOVE' on a par with FREE's best efforts. Within such a limited framework, however, there was never much room for experimentation and it was probably inevitable that BAD COMPANY would begin to tread water as they waded through the murky tail end of the 70's. Nevertheless, they continued to sell bucketloads of records and put bums on seats right up until their 1983 parting shot, 'ROUGH DIAMONDS'. While RODGERS went on to solo work, BAD CO. reformed three years later with ex-TED NUGENT frontman, BRIAN HOWE, taking RODGERS' place. Their subsequent releases were lukewarm AOR fodder without the saving grace of the latter's voice, although they sold moderately. Come the 90's, RALPHS was the only remaining member from the original line-up, 'COMPANY OF STRANGERS' in '95 being their last effort to date. • **Songwriters:** RALPHS penned most. In the 90's RALPHS and HOWE individually co-wrote with THOMAS. • **Note:** watch out! a dance act going by the name of BAD COMPANY exists.

Album rating: BAD CO. (*7) / STRAIGHT SHOOTER (*8) / RUN WITH THE PACK (*4) / BURNIN' SKY (*4) / DESOLATION ANGELS (*5) / ROUGH DIAMONDS (*4) / 10 FROM 6 compilation (*7) / FAME AND FORTUNE (*3) / DANGEROUS AGE (*3) / HOLY WATER (*4) / HERE COMES TROUBLE (*3) / THE BEST OF BAD COMPANY LIVE ... WHAT YOU HEAR IS WHAT YOU GET collection (*5) / COMPANY OF STRANGERS (*4) / STORIES TOLD AND UNTOLD (*4)

PAUL RODGERS (b.12 Dec'49) – vocals, piano (ex-FREE) / **MICK RALPHS** (b.31 Mar'48) – guitar, piano (ex-MOTT THE HOOPLE) / **BOZ BURRELL** (b.RAYMOND, 1946) – bass, vocals (ex-KING CRIMSON, ex-SNAFU) / **SIMON KIRKE** (b.28 Jul'49) – drums (ex-FREE)

	Island	Swan Song
May 74. (7") (WIP 6191) <70015> **CAN'T GET ENOUGH. / LITTLE MISS FORTUNE**	15	5
Jun 74. (lp/c) (ILPS/ICT 9279) <8410> **BAD CO.**	3	1

– Can't get enough / Rock steady / Ready for love / Don't let me down / Bad company / The way I choose / Movin' on / Seagull. (cd-iss. Oct94 on 'Atlantic'; 7567 92441-2)

Jan 75. (7") <70101> **MOVIN' ON. / EASY ON MY SOUL**	-	19
Mar 75. (7") (WIP 6223) <70103> **GOOD LOVIN' GONE BAD. / WHISKEY BOTTLE**	31	36
Apr 75. (lp/c) (ILPS/ICT 9304) <8413> **STRAIGHT SHOOTER**	3	3

– Good lovin' gone bad / Feel like makin' love / Weep no more / Shooting star / Deal with the preacher / Wild fire woman / Anna / Call on me. (cd-iss. Oct88 on 'Swan Song'; SS 8502-2) (cd re-iss. Jul94 on 'Atlantic'; 7567 82637-2)

Aug 75. (7") (WIP 6242) <70106> **FEEL LIKE MAKIN' LOVE. / WILD FIRE WOMEN**	20	10 Jul75
Feb 76. (lp/c) (ILPS/ICT 9346) <8415> **RUN WITH THE PACK**	4	5

– Live for the music / Simple man / Honey child / Love me somebody / Run with the pack / Silver, blue & gold / Young blood / Do right by your woman / Sweet lil' sister / Fade away. (cd-iss. Oct88 on 'Swan Song'; SS 8503-2) (cd re-iss. Jul94 on 'Atlantic'; 7567 92435-2)

Mar 76. (7") (WIP 6263) **RUN WITH THE PACK. / DO RIGHT BY YOUR WOMAN**		-
Mar 76. (7") <70108> **YOUNG BLOOD. / DO RIGHT BY YOUR WOMAN**	-	20
Jul 76. (7") <70109> **HONEY CHILD. / FADE AWAY**	-	59
Feb 77. (7") (WIP 6381) **EVERYTHING I NEED. / TOO BAD**		
Mar 77. (lp/c) (ILPS/ICT 9441) <8500> **BURNIN' SKY**	17	15

– Burnin' sky / Morning Sun / Leaving you / Like water / Everything I need / Heartbeat / Peace of mind / Passing time / Too bad / Man needs a woman / Master of ceremony. (cd-iss. Oct94 on 'Atlantic'; 7567 92450-2)

May 77. (7") <70112> **BURNIN' SKY. / EVERYTHING I NEED**	-	78

Mar 79. (7") (K 19416) <70119> **ROCK'N'ROLL FANTASY. / CRAZY CIRCLES** | | 13 |

Mar 79. (lp/c) (SS K/4 59408) <8506> **DESOLATION ANGELS** | 10 | 3 |
– Rock'n'roll fantasy / Crazy circles / Gone, gone, gone / Evil wind / Early in the morning / Lonely for your love / Oh, Atlanta / Take the time / Rhythm machine / She brings me love. (cd-iss. Sep94 on 'Atlantic'; 7567 92451-2)

Jul 79. (7") <71000> **GONE, GONE, GONE. / TAKE THE TIME** | - | 56 |

Aug 82. (lp/c) (SS K/4 59419) <90001> **ROUGH DIAMONDS** | 15 | 26 |
– Electricland / Untie the knot / Nuthin' on T.V. / Painted face / Kickdown / Ballad of the band / Cross country boy / Old Mexico / Downhill ryder / Racetrack. (cd-iss. Oct94 on 'Atlantic'; 7567 92452-2)

Sep 82. (7") <99966> **ELECTRICLAND. / UNTIE THE KNOT** | - | 74 |

—— (mid'83) Disbanded. RODGERS went solo before joining The FIRM. KIRKE played with WILDFIRE. BURRELL sessioned for ROGER CHAPMAN.

—— **BAD COMPANY** reformed 1986. **RALPHS, KIRKE, BURRELL** and the incoming **BRIAN HOWE** – vocals (ex-TED NUGENT)

Atlantic   Atlantic

Jan 86. (lp/c)(cd) (WX 31/+C)(781625-2) <81625> **10 FROM 6** (compilation)
– Can't get enough / Feel like makin' love / Run with the pack / Shooting star / Movin' on / Bad company / Rock'n'roll fantasy / Electricland / Ready for love / Live for the music.

Oct 86. (lp/c)(cd) (WX 69/+C)(781684-2) <81684> **FAME AND FORTUNE**
– Burning up / This love / Fame and fortune / That girl / Tell it like it is / Long walk / Hold on my heart / Valerie / When we made love / If I'm sleeping.

Nov 86. (7") (A 9355) <89355> **THIS LOVE. / TELL IT LIKE IT IS** | 85 | Oct86 |
(12"+=) (TA 9355) – Burning up / Fame & fortune.

Feb 87. (7") (A 9296) **FAME AND FORTUNE. / WHEN WE MADE LOVE** | - | - |

Feb 87. (7") <89299> **THAT GIRL. / IF I'M SLEEPING** | - | - |

Aug 88. (7") <89035> **NO SMOKE WITHOUT FIRE. / LOVE ATTACK** | - | - |

Aug 88. (lp/c/cd) (K 781884-1/-4/-2) <81884> **DANGEROUS AGE** | 58 |
– One night / Shake it up / No smoke without fire / Bad man / Dangerous age / Dirty boy / Rock of America / Something about you / The way it goes / Love attack. (cd+=) – Excited.

Apr 89. (7") <88939> **SHAKE IT UP. / DANGEROUS AGE** | - | 82 |

Mar 90. (7"/c-s) (A 7954/+MC) **CAN'T GET ENOUGH. / BAD COMPANY**
(12"+=/cd-s+=) (A 7954 T/CD) – No smoke without fire / Shake it up.

—— **GEOFF WHITEHORN** – guitar (ex-BACK STREET CRAWLER) repl. RALPHS / **PAUL CULLEN** – bass repl. BURRELL / added **DAVE COLWELL** – keyboards (ex-ASAP)

Atco   Atco

Jul 90. (cd/c/lp) (<7567 91371-2/-4/-1>) **HOLY WATER** | 35 | Jun90 |
– Holy water / Walk through fire / Stranger stranger / If you needed somebody / Fearless / Lay your love on me / Boys cry tough / With you in a heartbeat / I don't care / Never too late / Dead of the night / I can't live without you / 100 miles.

Jul 90. (7") <98944> **HOLY WATER. / I CAN'T LIVE WITHOUT YOU** | - | 89 |
(12"+=/cd-s+=) – Love attack.

Apr 91. (7") <98914> **IF YOU NEEDED SOMEBODY. / DEAD OF THE NIGHT** | 16 | Nov90 |
(12"+=/cd-s+=) – Love attack.

Jul 91. (c-s,cd-s) <98748> **WALK THROUGH FIRE / LAY YOUR LOVE ON ME** | - | 28 |

—— (May'91) **STEVE WALSH** – vocals (ex-KANSAS) repl. HOWE / **MICK RALPHS** also returned

Sep 92. (c-s,cd-s) <98509> **HOW ABOUT THAT / BROKENHEARTED** | - | 38 |

Sep 92. (7"/c-s) **HOW ABOUT THAT. / HERE COMES TROUBLE** | - | - |
(12") – No smoke without a fire (remix) / Stranger stranger.
(cd-s+=) – No smoke without a fire (remix) / If you needed somebody.

Sep 92. (cd/c/lp) (<7567 91759-2/-4/-1>) **HERE COMES TROUBLE** | 40 |
-- How about that / Stranger than fiction / Here comes trouble / This could be the one / Both feet in the water / Take this town / What about you / Little angel / Hold on to my heart / Brokenhearted / My only one.

Nov 92. (c-s,cd-s) <98463> **THIS COULD BE THE ONE / BOTH FEET IN THE WATER** | - | 87 |

—— **RICK WILLS** – bass (ex-ROXY MUSIC, ex-FOREIGNER, ex-PETER FRAMPTON) repl. WALSH

Dec 93. (cd/c) (<7567 92307-2/-4>) **WHAT YOU HEAR IS WHAT YOU GET (The Best Of Bad Company - live)**
– How about that / Holy water / Rock'n'roll fantasy / If you needed somebody / Here comes trouble / Ready for love / Shooting star / No smoke without a fire / Feel like makin' love / Take this town / Movin' on / Good lovin' gone bad / Fist full of blisters / Can't get enough / Bad company.

—— **RALPHS, KIRKE, COLWELL + WILLS** recruited **ROBERT HART** – vox

Jul 95. (cd/c) (<7559-61808-2/-4>) **COMPANY OF STRANGERS**
– Company of strangers / Clearwater highway / Judas my brother / Little Martha / Gimme gimme / Where I belong / Down down down / Abandoned and alone / Down and dirty / Pretty woman / You're the only reason / Dance with the Devil / Loving you out loud.

Nov 96. (cd) (7559 61976-2) **STORIES TOLD & UNTOLD** (new & old) | - | German |
– One on one / Oh Atlanta / You're never alone / I still believe in you / Ready for love / Waiting on love / Can't get enough / Is that all there is to love / Love so strong / Silver, blue and gold / Downpour in Cairo / Shooting star / Simple man / Weep no more.

Mar 99. (d-cd) (<7559 62391-2>) **THE ORIGINAL BAD COMPANY ANTHOLOGY** (compilation)
– Can't get enough / Rock steady / Bad company / Seagull / Superstar woman / Little Miss Fortune / Good lovin' gone bad / Shooting star / Deal with the preacher / Wildfire woman / Easy on my soul / Whiskey bottles / Honey child / Run with the pack / Silver, blue and gold / Do right by your woman / Burnin' sky / Heartbeat / Too bad / Smoking / Rock'n'roll fantasy / Evil wind / Oh Atlanta / Rhythm machine / Untie the knot / Downhill rider / Track down a runaway / Ain't it good / Hammer of love / Hey hey.

BADFINGER

Formed: Liverpool, England . . . 1967 as The IVEYS, by PETE HAM and MIKE GIBBONS. They were a melodic pop group in the vein of The HOLLIES, who had the dubious novelty value of being Welsh. By the time they'd signed to The BEATLES' fledgling 'Apple' label in 1968, Liverpudlian TOM EVANS had joined the group, replacing DAVID JENKINS. After one minor hit 'MAYBE TOMORROW', they ditched the IVEY's moniker in favour of the more 70's sounding BADFINGER. They scored their first major hit in the first month of the new decade with the PAUL McCARTNEY-penned 'COME AND GET IT'. JOEY MOLLAND then replaced other original RON GRIFFITHS during its chart run, while HAM switched to bass. The BEATLES comparisons were unavoidable and their next 45, 'NO MATTER WHAT', was as close an approximation of The Fab Four's mid-60's amphetamine kick as you're likely to hear. The BEATLES' connection continued with contributions to the soundtrack for the movie, 'MAGIC CHRISTIAN MUSIC' and guest appearances on GEORGE HARRISON's 'ALL THINGS MUST PASS' and JOHN LENNON's 'IMAGINE'. HARRISON returned the favour by producing 'DAY AFTER DAY', an American Top 5 hit from the 'STRAIGHT UP' album late in '71. The songwriting skills of the HAM / EVANS team were finally recognised in 1972, when NILSSON transformed their 'WITHOUT YOU' into his own tortured No.1 classic. Ironically, the band failed to capitalise on this and their subsequent material was fairly lacklustre. A reputed deal with 'Warner Brothers' for a $3 million advance was struck prior to their last album for 'Apple', 1973's 'ASS'. However, their 'WISH YOU WERE HERE' album in '74 was shifting plenty of units in the States when money in their account went mysteriously missing, the record removed from retail sale soon after. Frustrated by his band's lack of success and MOLLAND's departure, and troubled by personal worries, PETE HAM hanged himself on the 23rd April '75 in his London home. Reeling from this tragedy, the band split, only to be re-formed by EVANS and part-time pipefitter, MOLLAND, in 1978. They even secured a deal with 'Elektra' but again failed to achieve any real success. Incredibly, history repeated itself when, on 23rd November '83, TOM EVANS also hanged himself amid fits of depression and financial troubles. Business problems were sorted out around a year and a half later, too late, of course, to bring back these lost songwriters of the 70's.

Album rating: MAGIC CHRISTIAN MUSIC (*5) / NO DICE (*7) / STRAIGHT UP (*7) / ASS (*5) / BADFINGER (*3) / WISH YOU WERE HERE (*5) / AIRWAVES (*4) / SAY NO MORE (*3) / COME AND GET IT – THE BEST OF BADFINGER (*7) / Pete Ham: 7 PARK AVENUE (*7)

The IVEYS

PETE HAM (b.27 Apr'47, Swansea, Wales) – guitar, vocals / **TOM EVANS** (b. 5 Jun'47, Liverpool, England) – guitar repl. DAVID JENKINS / **RON GRIFFITHS** – bass, vocals / **MIKE GIBBONS** (b.12 Mar'49, Swansea) – drums

Apple   Apple

Nov 68. (7") (APPLE 5) <1803> **MAYBE TOMORROW. / AND HER DADDY'S A MILLIONAIRE** | - | 67 | Jan69 |

Jul 69. (lp) (SAPCOR 8) **MAYBE TOMORROW** (UK-iss.Jun92; same) (with free 12"; SAPCOR 82) | - | - | Europe |

Jul 69. (7") (APPLE 14) **DEAR ANGIE. / NO ESCAPING YOUR LOVE** | - | - | Europe |

—— Also appeared on Various Artists 'Apple' records comp. EP for Walls ice cream, singing 'STORM IN A TEACUP'.

BADFINGER

supplied 3 tracks (*) for THE MAGIC CHRISTIAN film soundtrack released Apr'70.

Dec 69. (7") (APPLE 20) <1815> **COME AND GET IT. / ROCK OF ALL AGES** | 4 | 7 | Jan70 |

—— **JOEY MOLLAND** (b.21 Jun'47, Liverpool) – lead guitar (ex-MERSEYS, etc) repl. GRIFFITHS. (EVANS switched to bass guitar)

Jan 70. (lp) (SAPCOR 12) <3364> **MAGIC CHRISTIAN MUSIC** | - | 55 | Mar70 |
– Come and get it / Crimson ship / Dear Angie / Fisherman / Midnight sun / Beautiful and blue / Rock of all ages / Carry on till tomorrow / Fisherman / I'm in love / Walk out in the rain / Knocking down our home / Give it a try / Maybe tomorrow. (re-iss. Oct91 cd+=/c/d-lp; same) – Storm in a teacup / Arthur.

Oct 70. (7") <1822> **NO MATTER WHAT. / CARRY ON UNTIL TOMORROW** | - | 8 |

Dec 70. (7") (APPLE 31) **NO MATTER WHAT. / BETTER DAYS** | 5 | - |

Dec 70. (lp) (SAPCOR 16) <3367> **NO DICE** | 28 | Nov70 |
– I can't take it / I don't mind / Love me do / Midnight caller / No matter what / Without you / Blodwyn / Better days / It had to be / Watford John / Believe me / We're for the dark. (cd-iss. Jun92+=;) – Get down / Friends are hard to find / Mean mean Jemima / Loving you / I'll be the one.

Nov 71. (7") <1841> **DAY AFTER DAY. / MONEY** | - | 4 |

Dec 71. (lp) (SAPCOR 19) <3387> **STRAIGHT UP** | - | 31 |
– Money / Flying / Suitcase / Sweet Tuesday morning / Perfection / I'd die babe / Take it all / Baby blue / Name of the game / Day after day / Sometimes / It's over. (cd-iss. Mar93 cd/c/lp; same) – (original sessions of songs).

Jan 72. (7") (APPLE 40) **DAY AFTER DAY. / SWEET TUESDAY MORNING** | 10 | - |

Apr 72. (7"; w-drawn UK) (APPLE 42) <1844> **BABY BLUE. / FLYING** | - | 14 | Mar72 |

Mar 74. (7") (APPLE 49) **APPLE OF MY EYE. / BLIND OWL** | | |

Mar 74. (lp) (SAPCOR 27) <3411> **ASS** | | Dec73 |
– Apple of my eye / Get away icicles / The winner / Blind owl / Constitution / When I say / Cowboy / Timeless / I can love you. (cd-iss. Feb97; CDSAPCOR 27)

Warners   Warners

Jun 74. (lp) (K 56023) <2762> **BADFINGER** | | Mar74 |
– I miss you / Shine on / Love is easy / Song for a lost friend / Why don't we talk /

Island / Matted spam / Where do we go from here? / My heart goes out / Lonely you / Give it up / Andy Norris.

Jul 74. (7") **I MISS YOU. / SHINE ON**

Oct 74. (7") *(K 16323)* **LOVE IS EASY. / MY HEART GOES OUT**

Oct 74. (lp) *(K 56076) <2827>* **WISH YOU WERE HERE**
– Just a chance / You're so fine / Got to get out of here / Know one knows / Dennis / In the meantime / Love time / Some other time / King of the load (T) / Meanwhile, back at the ranch – Should I smoke.

—— added **BOB JACKSON** – keyboards (MOLLAND also left to join NATURAL GAS) They split just after PETE HAM commited suicide on 23rd April. EVANS joined DODGERS. Re-formed '76 by **MOLLAND** and **EVANS** who recruited new members / **KENNY HARCK** – drums / **JOE TANZIN** – guitar / session man **ANDY NEWMARK** – drums repl. HARCK on half of album

	Elektra	Elektra
Apr 79. (7") *(K 12345)* **LOST INSIDE YOUR LOVE. / COME DOWN HARD**

Apr 79. (lp) *(K 52129) <6E 175>* **AIRWAVES**
– Airwaves / Look out California / Lost inside your love / Love is gonna come at last / Sympathy / The winner / The dreamer / Come down hard / Sail away. *(cd-iss. Mar99 on 'Permanent Press'; 70267 52712-2)*

Jun 79. (7") *(K 12369) <46025>* **LOVE IS GONNA COME AT LAST. / SAIL AWAY** — 69 Mar79

—— MOLLAND and EVANS brought in **TONY KAYE** – keyboards (ex-YES, ex-BADGER) / **GLENN SHERBA** – guitar / **RICHARD BRYANS** – drums

	not iss.	Radio-Atlantic
Feb 81. (7") *<3793>* **HOLD ON. / PASSIN' TIME** | - | 56 |
Mar 81. (lp) *<16030>* **SAY NO MORE**
– Hold on / I got you / Come on / Because I love you / Rock'n'roll contract / Passin' time / Three time loser / Too hung up on you / Crocadillo / No more.

May 81. (7") *<3815>* **I GOT YOU. / ROCK'N'ROLL CONTRACT**

Jul 81. (7") *<3833>* **BECAUSE I LOVE YOU. / TOO HUNG UP ON YOU**

—— They split again in '83. JOEY MOLLAND released solo album AFTER THE PEARL. He later (1992) released cd 'THE PILGRIM' for 'Rykodisc'. TOM EVANS also tragically killed himself 23 Nov'83. MOLLAND and MIKE GIBBONS still tour as BADFINGER in US 60's tour.

—— They reformed with **MOLLAND, GIBBONS** plus **RANDY ANDERSON** – guitar / **A.J. NICHOLAS** – bass

	not iss.	Independent
1988. (lp) **TIMELESS** | - | |

– compilations, others, etc. –

Apr 89. (lp/cd) *Edsel; (ED/+CD 302)* **SHINE ON**

Nov 90. (cd/c/lp) *Essential; (ESS CD/MC/LP 135)* **DAY AFTER DAY (live)**
– Sometimes / I don't mind / Blind owl / Give it up / Constitution / Baby blue / Name of the game / Day after day / Timeless / I can't take it.

Jul 92. (cd) *Raven;* **APPLE DAZE** (TOM EVANS interview)

Sep 93. (cd/c) *Gipsy;* **THE FINAL TRACKS**

Apr 95. (cd/lp) *Apple; (CD+/SAPCOR 28)* **COME AND GET IT – THE BEST OF BADFINGER**
– Come and get it / Maybe tomorrow / Rock of all ages / Dear Angie / Carry on till tomorrow / No matter what / Believe me / Midnight caller / Better days / Without you / Take it all / Money / Flying / The name of the game / Suitcase / Day after day / Baby blue / When I say / Icicles / I can love you / Apple of my eye.

Jun 97. (cd) *Strange Fruit; (SFRSCD 031)* **BBC LIVE IN CONCERT (live)**
(d-lp re-iss. Dec99 on 'Turning Point'; TPM 99201)

PETE HAM

—— posthumous solo release

	Rykodisc	Rykodisc
Apr 97. (cd) *<(RCD 10349)>* **7 PARK AVENUE**
– Catherine cares / Coppertone blues / It really doesn't matter / Live love all of your days / Would you deny / Dear father / Matted spam / No matter what / Leaving on a midnight train / Weep baby / Hand in hand / Sille veb / I know that you should / Island / Just look inside the cover / Just how lucky we are / No more / Ringside.

BADLANDS (dig out; Great Metal . . .)

BAD RELIGION

Formed: Los Angeles, California, USA . . . 1980 by teenagers, GREG GRAFFIN, BRETT GUREWITZ, JAY BENTLEY and JAY LISHROUT. To combat lack of interest from major labels, the group initiated their own label, 'Epitaph', which has since become a proverbial pillar of the US hardcore/punk fraternity (i.e. OFFSPRING, etc). After one self-titled EP in '81, they unleashed their cheerily-titled debut, 'HOW COULD HELL BE ANY WORSE'. After they withdrew their next album, 'INTO THE UNKNOWN' from sale, BAD RELIGION disappeared for a long spell in the mid 80's. GRAFFIN returned with a new line-up in '87, numbering GREG HETSON, PETE FINESTONE and TIM GALLEGOS. An album, 'SUFFER' was a triumphant comeback effort, defining the new BAD RELIGION sound, a hybrid of melodic punk and machine-gun metal. In 1989, the band consolidated their newfound cult popularity with the follow-up, 'NO CONTROL', although their early 90's output suffered a slight decline. After 'Epitaph' experienced problems with distribution in '93, they signed to 'Columbia', with the result that they cracked the US Top 100 with their umpteenth album, 'STRANGER THAN FICTION'. Two years later, GUREWITZ having earlier bailed out,

they released 'THE GRAY RACE' (produced by RIC OCASEK, ex-CARS), re-establishing them at the forefront of the burgeoning hardcore/metal scene.

Album rating: HOW COULD HELL BE ANY WORSE (*5) / INTO THE UNKNOWN (*7) / BACK TO THE KNOWN (*4) / SUFFER (*7) / NO CONTROL (*8) / AGAINST THE GRAIN (*7) / GENERATOR (*6) / RECIPE FOR HATE (*6) / STRANGER THAN FICTION (*7) / THE GRAY RACE (*6) / ALL AGES compilation (*8)

GREG GRAFFIN – vocals / **BRETT GUREWITZ** – guitar / **JAY BENTLEY** – bass / **JAY LISHROUT** – drums

	Epitaph	Epitaph
Sep 81. (m-lp) *<EP1 BRLP 1>* **HOW COULD HELL BE ANY WORSE** | - | |
– Bad religion / Along the way / New leaf / Bad religion / Slaves / Drastic actions.

—— **PETE FINESTONE** – drums repl. LISHROUT

—— **PAUL DEDONA** – bass + **DAVY GOLDMAN** – drums repl. JAY + PETE

Dec 83. (lp) *<BR 1>* **INTO THE UNKNOWN** | - | |

—— **GRAFFIN** the sole survivor recruited **GREG HETSON** – guitar / **TIM GALLEGOS** – bass / **PETE FINESTONE** – drums (returned) / GUREWITZ joined CIRCLE JERKS

1987. (7"ep) *<BREP 2>* **BACK TO THE KNOWN** | - | |

—— **GUREWITZ + BENTLEY** rejoined to repl. GALLEGOS

1988. (lp) *<6404-1>* **SUFFER** | - | |
– You are (the government) / 1000 more fools / How much is enough / When? / Give you nothing / Land of competition / Forbidden beat / Best for you / Suffer / Delirium of disorder / Part II (the numbers game) / What can you do? / Do what you want / Part IV (the index fossil) / Pessimistic lines. *(UK-iss.cd/lp Mar91 & Jun93; same)*

1989. (lp) *<6406-1>* **NO CONTROL** | - | |
– Change of ideas / Big bang / No control / Sometimes it feels like *?%+! / Automatic man / I want to conquer the world / Sanity / Henchman / It must look pretty appealing / You / Progress / I want something more / Anxiety / Billy / The world won't stop without you. *(UK-iss.cd/lp Mar91 & Jun93; same)*

Jan 91. (cd/c/lp) *<(6409-2/-4/-1)>* **AGAINST THE GRAIN** | | |
– Modern man / Turn on the light / Get off / Blenderhead / Positive aspect of negative thinking / Anesthesia / Flat Earth Society / Faith alone / Entropy / Against the grain / Operation rescue / God song / 21st century digital boy / Misery and famine / Unacceptable / Quality or quantity / Walk away.

Mar 92. (cd/c/lp) *<(6416-2/-4/-1)>* **GENERATOR** | | |
– Generator / Too much to ask / No direction / Tomorrow / Two babies in the dark / Heaven is falling / Atomic garden / Answer / Fertile crescent / Chimaera / Only entertainment.

Jun 93. (cd/c/lp) *<(6420-2/-4/-1)>* **RECIPE FOR HATE** | | |
– Recipe for hate / Kerosene / American Jesus / Portrait of authority / Man with a mission / All good soldiers / Watch it die / Struck a nerve / My poor friend me / Lookin' in / Don't pray on me / Modern day catastrophists / Skyscraper / Sheath.

—— GUREWITZ retired to spend time with his record label 'Epitaph'.

—— line-up:- GRAFFIN / HETSON / BENTLEY / + **BRIAN BAKER** – guitar (ex-MINOR THREAT, ex-DAG NASTY) / **BOBBY SCHAYER** – drums

	Plastic Head	Plastic Head
1993. (7") *(MRR 006)* **NOAM. /**		
	Sympathy F	Sympathy F
Aug 94. (7") *(SFTRI 158)* **ATOMIC. /**		
Aug 94. (7") *(SFTRI 232)* **AMERICAN JESUS. /**		
Aug 94. (7") *(SFTRI 326)* **STRANGER THAN FICTION. /**		
	Columbia	Atlantic
Sep 94. (cd/c/lp) *(477343-2/-4/-1) <82658>* **STRANGER THAN FICTION** | | 87 |
– Incomplete / Leave mine to me / Stranger than fiction / Tiny voices / The handshake / Better off dead / Infected / Television / Individual / Hooray for me / Slumber / Marked / Inner logic. *(cd re-iss. Jan99; same)*

Jan 95. (10"pic-d-ep) *(661143-0)* **21st CENTURY (DIGITAL BOY) / AMERICAN JESUS (live). / NO CONTROL (live) / WE'RE ONLY GONNA DIE (live)** | 41 | |
(c-ep/cd-ep) *(661143-8/-2)* – ('A'side) / Leaders and followers (live) / Mediocrity (live) / American Jesus (live).

Mar 96. (cd/c)(grey-lp) *(493524-2/-4/483652-0)* **THE GRAY RACE** | | |
– The gray race / Them and us / Walk / Parallel / Punk rock songs / Empty causes / Nobody listens / Pity the dead / Spirit shine / Streets of America / Ten in 2010 / Victory / Drunk sincerely come to / Cease / Punk rock song (German version).

Jun 96. (7") *(6628677-7)* **PUNK ROCK SONG. / CEASE** | | |
(cd-s+=) *(6628677-5)* – Leave mine to me (live) / Change of ideas (live).
(cd-s) *(6628677-2)* – ('A'-German version) / The universal cynic / The dodo.
(above was shelved when they decided to do some more German gigs)

Apr 97. (cd/lp) *(486986-2/-1) <82870-2/-1>* **TESTED (live)** | | 56 |
– Operation rescue / Punk rock song / Tomorrow / A walk / God song / Pity the dead / One thousand more fool / Drunk sincerity / Generator / Change of ideas / Portrait of authority / What it is / Dream of unity / Sanity / American Jesus / Do what you want / Part III / 10 in 2010 / No direction / Along the way / Recipe for hate / Fuck armageddon / It's reciprocal / Struck a nerve / Leave mine to me / Tested / No control.

May 98. (cd/c) *(489570-2/-4) <83094>* **NO SUBSTANCE** | | 78 |
– Hear it / Shades of truth / All fantastic images / Biggest killer in American history / No substance / Raise your voice / Sowing the seeds of Utopia / Hippy killers / State of the end of the millenium / Vocacious march of godlines / Mediocre / Victims of the revolution / Strange denial / At the mercy of imbeciles / Same person / In so many ways.

– compilations, etc. –

Nov 91. (cd/c) *Epitaph; <(86407-2X/4X)>* **(1980-1985)** | | |
– We're all gonna die / Latch key kids / Part III / Faith in God / F*** armageddon . . . this is Hell / Pitty / Into the night / Damned to be free / White trash (2nd generation) / American dream / Eat your dog / Voice of God is government / Oligarchy / Doing time / Politics / Sensory overload / Slaves / Drastic actions / World War III / Yesterday / Frogger. *(w/ free cd)* – HOW COULD HELL BE ANY WORSE

Nov 95. (cd/c/lp) *Epitaph; <(86443-2/-4/-1)>* **ALL AGES** (1988-1992) **+ 2 from '94** | | |
– I want to conquer the world / Do what you want / You are (the government) / Modern man / We're only gonna die / Answer / Flat Earth society / Against the grain /

Generator / Anesthesia / Suffer / Faith alone / No control / 21st century digital boy / Atomic garden / No direction / Automatic man / Change of ideas / Sanity / Walk away / Best for you / Fuck armageddon . . . this is Hell.

Joan BAEZ

Born: 9 Jan'41, Staten Island, New York, USA. After a successful 1959 Newport festival appearance, she signed to the 'Vanguard' label in the States. An innovator of protest folk music, that leant on early PETE SEEGER, BAEZ was an inspiration to the likes of DYLAN etc. Her defiant protest anthems made her the darling of the intellectual beatnik scene developing in America at the time. Although her early material concentrated on traditional folk fare delivered in a crystal pure vocal style, BAEZ became a figurehead for the protest movement in the mid-60's with her anthemic 'WE SHALL OVERCOME'. On 'JOAN BAEZ 5' (1965), she showcased her move towards interpreting more contemporary artists, covering Phil Och's 'THERE BUT FOR FORTUNE' and Bob Dylan's 'IT AIN'T ME BABE'. As well as becoming a celebrated interpreter of the latter's work, BAEZ and DYLAN became lovers, the King and Queen of folk, the couple were dubbed (their relationship was well documented in the film, 'Don't Look Back'). The aforementioned album went Top 5 in the UK as did her sixth set 'FAREWELL ANGELINA' (1965), a record featuring a further two DYLAN covers in 'IT'S ALL OVER NOW, BABY BLUE' and 'A HARD RAIN'S A-GONNA FALL'. The same year, BAEZ founded the Institute For The Study Of Nonviolence in California, her increasingly political activism directed mainly against US involvement in the Vietnam war. In 1968, the singer married fellow protest leader DAVID HARRIS, although he was subsequently jailed for resisting the draft. '68 also saw BAEZ's most ambitious album to date, 'BAPTISM – A JOURNEY THROUGH OUR TIME' (1968), wherein she turned her head to spoken word poems etc. The early 70's found the folk veteran covering material by more mainstream artists such as The BEATLES and The BAND, her reading of the latter's 'THE NIGHT THEY DROVE OLD DIXIE DOWN', making the US Top 3. Her commitment to humanitarian protest remained steadfast and indeed, throughout the first half of the 70's, the singer's political activities (she was a high profile opponent of the military coup in Chile) overshadowed her recorded output. With 'DIAMONDS AND RUST' (1975), however, BAEZ emerged as an important figure in the American singer/songwriter movement, the album making the US Top 20 and becoming one of her best loved works. The mid-70's also saw a belated reunion with DYLAN, the pair hooking up in the Rolling Thunder Revue. Autobiographical efforts such as 'GULF WINDS' (1976) and 'BLOWIN' AWAY' (1977) marked the end of BAEZ's career for almost a decade as she found herself without a record label. She nevertheless continued to perform throughout the 80's, playing benefit concerts for Amnesty International and, of course, appearing at Live Aid in 1985. Perhaps inspired by the new wave of young female troubadours (SUZANNE VEGA, TRACY CHAPMAN etc.), BAEZ returned to the recording front in the late 80's/early 90's, the 'PLAY ME BACKWARDS' (1993) set seeing her court an adult MOR audience, while a live set, 'RING THEM BELLS' (1995) featured duets with JANIS IAN, MARY CHAPIN-CARPENTER and MARY BLACK amongst others. • **Songwriters:** She writes her own work interspersed with covers:- (Her debut album contained some Scottish traditional ballads). She recorded a whole lp of DYLAN material, 'ANY DAY NOW', and 'PACK UP YOUR SORROWS' (Richard Farina, her brother-in-law, who was killed in a motorcycle accident, summer '66) / IN THE QUIET MORNING (Mimi Farina, her sister) / LET IT BE (Beatles) / AMSTERDAM (Janis Ian) / STONES IN THE ROAD (Mary-Chapin Carpenter) / STRANGE RIVERS (John Stewart) / STEAL ACROSS THE BORDER (Ron Davies) / THROUGH YOUR HANDS (John Hiatt) / lots more . . .

Album rating: JOAN BAEZ (*8) / JOAN BAEZ 2 (*5) / JOAN BAEZ IN CONCERT (*7) / JOAN BAEZ IN CONCERT PART 2 (*5) / JOAN BAEZ 5 (*6) / FAREWELL ANGELINA (*6) / PORTRAIT (*5) / NOEL (*4) / JOAN (*5) / BAPTISM (*5) / ANY DAY NOW (*5) / DAVID'S ALBUM (*4) / ONE DAY AT A TIME (*5) / BLESSED ARE (*5) / CARRY IT ON (*5) / COME FROM THE SHADOWS (*5) / WHERE ARE YOU NOW, MY SON? (*4) / GRACIAS A LA VIDA (*4) / DIAMONDS AND RUST (*7) / FROM EVERY STAGE (*4) / GULF WINDS (*4) / BLOWING AWAY (*5) / HONEST LULLABY (*4) / LIVE EUROPE 83 (*5) / RECENTLY (*6) / DIAMONDS AND RUST IN THE BULLRING (*3) / SPEAKING OF DREAMS (*5) / PLAY ME BACKWARDS (*5) / RING THEM BELLS (*4) / GONE FROM DANGER (*5) / GREATEST HITS compilation (*7)

JOAN BAEZ – vocals, acoustic guitar

		Fontana	Vanguard
Nov 60. (lp) (STFL 6002) <VSD 2077> **JOAN BAEZ**		☐	☐

– Silver dagger / East Virginia / Ten thousand miles / House of the rising sun / All my trials / Wildwood flower / Donna Donna / John Riley / Rake and rambling boy / Little Moses / Mary Hamilton / Henry Martin / El preso numero nueve (the ninth prisoner). <re-dist.US Apr62 hit No.15> (re-iss. UK Jun65 hit No.9) (re-iss. 1973 on 'Vanguard'; VSD 79073) (re-iss. Oct88 on 'Start'; VFCD 7101) (cd-iss. Jan94 & Oct95 on 'Vanguard'; VMD 2077)

Oct 61. (lp) (STFL 6025) <VSD 2097> **JOAN BAEZ 2**		☐	13

– Wagoner's lad / The trees they do grow high / The lily of the west / Silkie / Engine 143 / Once I knew a pretty girl / Lonesome road / Banks of the Ohio / Pal of mine / Barbara Allen / The cherry tree carol / Old blue / Railroad boy / Plaisir d'amour. (re-iss. 1973 on 'Vanguard'; VSD 79094) (re-iss. Oct88 on 'Start'; VFCD 7102) (cd-iss. Jan94 & Oct95 on 'Vanguard'; VMD 2097)

Oct 61. (7") <35012> **BANKS OF THE OHIO. / OLD BLUE**		-	-
Feb 62. (7") <35013> **LONESOME ROAD. / PAL OF MINE**		-	-
Oct 62. (lp) (STFL 6035) <VSD 2122> **JOAN BAEZ IN CONCERT (live)**		☐	10

– Babe, I'm gonna leave you / Geordie / Copper kettle / Kumbaya / What have they done to the rain / Black is the colour of my true love's hair / Danger waters / Gospel

ship / The house carpenter / Pretty Boy Floyd / Lady Mary / Ate Amanha / Matty Groves. (re-iss. 1973 on 'Vanguard'; VSD 79112) (cd-iss. Jan96 on 'Vanguard'; VMD 2122)

Nov 62. (7") <35018> **WHAT HAVE THEY DONE TO THE RAIN. / DANGER WATERS**		-	☐
Oct 63. (7") <35023> **WE SHALL OVERCOME (live). / WHAT HAVE THEY DONE TO THE RAIN (live)**		-	90
May 64. (lp) (STFL 6033) <VSD 2123> **JOAN BAEZ IN CONCERT, PART 2 (live)**		8	7 Dec63

– Once I had a sweetheart / Jackaroe / Don't think twice it's alright / We shall overcome / Portland town / Queen of hearts / Manha de carnaval / Te ador / Long black veil / Fennario / 'Nu Bello Cardillo / With God on our side / Three fishers / Hush little baby / Battle hymn of the republic. (re-iss. 1973 on 'Vanguard'; VSD 79113) (cd-iss. Jan96 on 'Vanguard'; VMD 2123)

Jun 64. (7") <35026> **WITH GOD ON OUR SIDE. / RAILROAD BILL – DADDY YOU BEEN ON MY MIND (MEDLEY)**		-	☐
Nov 64. (7") (TF 561) **IT AIN'T ME BABE. / GO 'WAY FROM MY WINDOW**		☐	-
Apr 65. (lp) (STFL 6043) <VSD 79160> **JOAN BAEZ 5**		3	12 Nov64

– There but for fortune / Stewball / It ain't me babe / The death of Queen Jane / Villa lobos: Bachianas Brasileias No.5 – aria / Go 'way from my window / I still miss someone / When you hear them cuckoos hollerin / Birmingham Sunday / So we'll go no more a-rovin' / O'cangaceiro / The unquiet grave. (re-iss. 1973 on 'Vanguard'; VSD 79160) (cd-iss. Apr97 on 'Vanguard'; VMD 79160)

Mar 65. (7") (TF 564) **WE SHALL OVERCOME. / DON'T THINK TWICE**		26	-
Jun 65. (7") <35031> **THERE BUT FOR FORTUNE. / DADDY YOU BEEN ON MY MIND**		-	50
Jul 65. (7") (TF 587) **THERE BUT FOR FORTUNE. / PLAISIR D'AMOUR**		8	-
Aug 65. (7") (TF 604) **IT'S ALL OVER NOW, BABY BLUE. / DADDY YOU'VE BEEN ON MY MIND**		22	-
Nov 65. (lp) (STFL 6058) <VSD 79200> **FAREWELL ANGELINA**		5	10 Oct65

– Farewell angelina / Daddy, you been on my mind / It's all over now, baby blue / The ranger's command / Colours / A satisfied mind / The river in the pines / Pauvre Rutebeouf / Sagt mir wo die blumen sind / A hard rain's a-gonna fall. (re-iss. 1973 on 'Vanguard'; VSD 79200) (re-iss. Oct88 on 'Start' lp/c/cd; VFLP5/VFTC6/VFCD7 105) (cd-iss. Jan94 & Oct95 on 'Vanguard'; VMD 79200)

Dec 65. (7") (TF 639) **FAREWELL ANGELINA. / QUEEN OF HEARTS**		35	-
Jun 66. (7") (TF 727) <35040> **PACK UP YOUR SORROWS. / SWALLOW SONG**		50	-
Aug 66. (lp) (STFL 6082) <VSD 79240> **JOAN**		☐	38

– Be not too hard / Eleanor Rigby / Turquoise / La colombe – the dove / Dangling conversation / The lady came from Baltimore / North / Children of darkness / The greenwood side / If you were a carpenter / Annabel Lee / Saigon bride. (re-iss. 1973 on 'Vanguard'; VSD 23011) (cd-iss. Apr97 on 'Vanguard'; VMD 79240)

Nov 66. (7") <35046> **CANTIQUE DE NOEL. / LITTLE DRUMMER BOY**		-	-
Nov 66. (lp) (STFL 6082) <VSD 79240> **NOEL** (festive album)		☐	☐

– O come, o come Emmanuel / Coventry carol / Good King Wecelas / Little drummer boy / Wonder as I wander, bring a torch Jeanette, Isabella / Down in yon forest / Carol of the birds / Angels we have heard on high / Ave Maria / Mary's wandering / Away in a manger / Cantique de nord / What child is this / Silent night. (re-iss. 1973 on 'Vanguard'; VSD 23018) (re-iss. Oct88 on 'Start' lp/c/cd; VFLP5/VFTC6/VFCD7 107) (cd re-iss. Oct96 on 'Vanguard'; VMD 79230)

Jun 67. (7") (TF 865) <35055> **BE NOT TOO HARD. / NORTH**		☐	☐
		Vanguard	Vanguard
Aug 68. (lp) (SVRL 19000) <VSD 79275> **BAPTISM – A JOURNEY THROUGH OUR TIME**		☐	84

– Old Welsh song / I saw the vision of armies / Minister of war / Casida of the lament / Of the dark past / London / In Guernica / Who murdered the minutes / Oh, little child / No man is an island / From portrait of the artist as a young man / All the pretty little horses / Childhood III / The magic wood / Poems from the Japanese / Colours / All in green went my love riding / Gacela of the dark death / The parable of the old man and the young / Evil / Epitaph for a poet / Old Welsh song (reprise). (re-iss. Aug89 on 'Start' lp/c/cd; VFLP5/VFTC6/VFCD7 103)

—— added many session people **NORMAN PUTTNAM** – bass / **KEN BUTTREY** – drums / **DAVID BRIGGS** – keyboards / **GRADY MARTIN** – dobro / **PETE WADE** – guitar / etc.

Jan 69. (d-lp) (55-66) <VSD 79306-7> **ANY DAY NOW**		☐	30

– Love minus zero – No limit / North country blues / You ain't goin' nowhere / Drifter's escape / I pity the poor immigrant / Tears of rage / Sad eyed lady of the Lowlands / Love is just a four-letter word / I dreamed I saw St. Augustine / The walls of Redwing / Dear landlord / One too many mornings / I shall be released / Boots of Spanish leather / Walkin' down the line / Restless farewell. (re-iss. Sep89 on 'Start' d-lp/d-c/cd; VSD/CVSD/VCD 79306-7)

Apr 69. (7") (VA 2) <35088> **LOVE IS JUST A FOUR-LETTER WORD. / LOVE MINUS ZERO – NO LIMIT**		-	86
Jun 69. (7") <35092> **IF I KNEW. / ROCK, SALT AND NAILS**		-	☐
Jun 69. (lp) (SVRL 19050) <VSD 79308> **DAVID'S ALBUM**		☐	36

– If I knew / Rock / Salt and nails / Glad bluebird of happiness / Green, green grass of home / Will the circle be unbroken / Tramp on the street / I'm a poor wayfaring stranger / Just a closer walk with thee / Hickory wind / My home's across the blue ridge mountains. (cd-iss. Jan94 & Oct98; VMD 79308)

Aug 69. (7") <35098> **HICKORY WIND. / FOUR DAYS GONE**		-	-
Mar 70. (7") <35103> **NO EXPECTATIONS. / ONE DAY AT A TIME**		-	-
Apr 70. (lp) (VSD 23010) <VSD 79310> **ONE DAY AT A TIME**		☐	80 Mar70

– Seven bridges road / David's song / Sweet Sir Galahad / Long black veil / Ghetto / Carry it on / Jolie blonde / Joe Hill / No expectations / Take me back to the sweet sunny south / One day at a time. (cd-iss. Oct96; VMD 79310)

Jun 70. (7") <35106> **SWEET SIR GALAHAD. / GHETTO**		-	-
Jan 71. (7") <35114> **CARRY IT ON. / ROCK SALT & NAILS**		-	-
Sep 71. (7") <(VRS 35138)> **THE NIGHT THEY DROVE OLD DIXIE DOWN. / WHEN TIME IS STOLEN**		6	3 Aug71
Sep 71. (d-lp) <(VSD 6570-1)> **BLESSED ARE**		11	

– Blessed are / The night they drove Dixie down / The salt of the Earth / Three horses / Brand new Tennessee waltz / Lost lonely and wretched / Lincoln freed me today / Outside the Nashville limits / San Francisco Mabel Joy / When time is stolen / Heaven help us all / Angeline / Help me make it through the night / Let it be / Put your hand in the hand / Gabriel and me / Milanese waltz / Marie Flore / The hitch-hiker's song / The 23rd of August / Fifteen months. (d-cd-iss. Jan97; VCD2 6570)

Nov 71. (7") <35145> **LET IT BE. / POOR WAYFARING STRANGER**　　- | 49
Nov 71. (7") (VAN 1002) **LET IT BE. / GABRIEL AND ME**　　- | -
Dec 71. (lp) (VSD 519042) <VSD 79313> **CARRY IT ON** (Soundtrack compilation)
– Oh, happy day / Carry it on / In forty days / Hickory wind / Last thing on my mind / Life is sacred / Joe Hill / I shall be released / Do right woman, do right man / Love is just another four-letter word / Suzanne / Idols and heroes / We shall overcome. *(cd-iss. Sep99; VCD 79313)*
Jan 72. (7") <35148> **WILL THE CIRCLE BE UNBROKEN. / JUST A CLOSER WALK WITH THEE**
Apr 72. (7") <35158> **BLESSED ARE. / THE BRAND NEW TENNESSEE WALTZ**　　-

—— she also issued 2 film s-tracks 'Sacco & Vanzetti' & 'Silent Running'

	A&M	A&M

Apr 72. (7") <1334> **PRISON TRILOGY (BILLY ROSE). / SONG OF BANGLADESH**　　- |
May 72. (lp/c) (AMLH/CAM 64339) <4339> **COME FROM THE SHADOWS**　　| 48
– Prison trilogy (Billy Rose) / Rainbow road / Love song to a stranger / Myths / In the quiet morning / Weary mothers / To Bobby / Song of Bangladesh / A stranger in my place / Tumbleweed / The partisan / Imagine.
Jul 72. (7") (AMS 7011) **IN THE QUIET MORNING. / SONG OF BANGLADESH**　　| -
Jul 72. (7") <1362> **IN THE QUIET MORNING. / TO BOBBY**　　- | 69
Sep 72. (7") <1393> **LOVE SONG TO A STRANGER. / TUMBLEWEED**　　-
Mar 73. (7") <1454> **BEST OF FRIENDS. / MARY CALL**　　-
Apr 73. (lp/c) (AMLH/CAM 64390) <4390> **WHERE ARE YOU NOW, MY SON?**
– Only Heaven knows / Less than the song / A young gypsy / Mary call / Rider pass by / Best of friends / Windrose / Where are you now, my son? / (one side was devoted to Vietnam bombing noises).

—— now with complete new set of session people.

Jun 73. (7") <1472> **LESS THAN A SONG. / WINDROSE**　　-
Jun 73. (7") (AMS 7072) **LESS THAN A SONG. / MARY CALL**　　-
May 74. (lp/c) (AMLH 63614) **GRACIAS A LA VIDA (HERE'S TO LIFE)**
– Gracias a la vida / Ilego contres heridas (Come with three wounds) / La llorona (The weeping woman) / El preso numero (Prisoner number nine) / Guantanamera / Te recuerdo Amanda (I remember Amanda) / Dida / Cucurrucucu Paloma / Paso Rio (I pass a river) / El rossinyol (The nightingale) / De colores (In colours) / Las madras cansades (All the weary mothers of the Earth) / No nos moveran (We shall not be moved) / Esquinazo del guerrillo (The guerilla's serenade).
Jun 74. (7") <1516> **GUANTANAMERA. / FOREVER YOUNG**　　-
May 75. (lp/c) (AMLH 64527) <4527> **DIAMONDS & RUST**　　| 11
– Diamonds and rust / Fountain of sorrow / Never dreamed you'd leave me in summer / Children and all that jazz / Simple twist of fate / Blue sky / Hello in there / Jesse / Winds of the old days / Dida / I dream of Jeannie / Danny boy.
Jun 75. (7") <1703> **BLUE SKY. / DIDA**　　- | 57
Jul 75. (7") **NEVER DREAMED YOU'D LEAVE ME IN SUMMER. / LAST SUMMER**　　-
Oct 75. (7") (AMS 7200) <1737> **DIAMONDS AND RUST. / WINDS OF THE OLD DAYS**　　| 35 Sep75
Jan 76. (7") **CHILDREN AND ALL THAT JAZZ. / NEVER DREAMED YOU'D LEAVE ME IN SUMMER**
Mar 76. (d-lp) (AMLH 64704) <3704> **FROM EVERY STAGE** (live)　　| 34 Jan76
– (Ain't gonna let nobody) Turn me around / Blessed are . . . / Suzanne / Love song to a stranger / I shall be released / Blowin' in the wind / Stewball / Natalia / The ballad of Sacco & Vanzetti / Joe Hill / Love is just a four-letter word / Forever young / Diamonds and rust / Boulder to Birmingham / Swing low sweet chariot / Oh, happy day / Please come to Boston / Lily, Rosemary and the jack of hearts / The night they drove old Dixie down / Amazing Grace.
Apr 76. (7") (AMS 7226) <1802> **PLEASE COME TO BOSTON. / LOVE SONG TO A STRANGER**
Nov 76. (lp/c) (AMLH/CAM 64603) <4603> **GULF WINDS**　　| 62
– Sweeter for me / Seabirds / Caruso / Still waters at night / Kingdom of childhood / O brother! / Time is passing us by / Stephanie's room / Gulf winds.
Nov 76. (7") <1884> **CARUSO. / TIME IS PASSING US BY**　　-
Feb 77. (7") <1906> **O BROTHER!. / STILL WATERS AT NIGHT**　　-

	Portrait	Portrait

Jul 77. (lp/c) (PRT/40 82011) <34697> **BLOWIN' AWAY**　　| 54 Jun77
– Sailing / Many a mile to freedom / Miracles / Yellow coat / Time rag / A heartfelt line or two / I'm blowin' away / Luba the baroness / Alter boy and the thief / Cry me a river.
Jul 77. (7") <70006> **I'M BLOWIN' AWAY. / ALTAR BOY AND THE THIEF**　　-
Jul 77. (7") (PRT 5442) **I'M BLOWIN' AWAY. / LUBA THE BARONESS**
Nov 77. (7") (PRT 5759) <70009> **TIME RAG. / MIRACLES**　　| -
Jul 79. (lp/c) (PRT/40 83474) <35766> **HONEST LULLABY**
– Let your love flow / No woman, no cry / Light a light / The song at the end of the movie / Before the deluge / Honest lullaby / Michael / For Sasha / For all we know / Free at last. *(cd-iss. Feb97 on 'Columbia'; 473695-2)*
Feb 81. (lp/c) (PRT/40 84790) **EUROPEAN TOUR** (live)　　| -
– The boxer / Don't cry for me Argentina / Gracias a la vida / The rose / For Sasha / Diamonds and rust / Soyuz druzyei / Cambodia / Kinder (sind so kleine hande) / Here's to you / Blowin' in the wind.

—— retired for several years, although she toured Europe again in '83.

	Virgin – Goldcastle	Cypress

May 88. (cd/c/lp) (CD/TC+/VGC 1) **RECENTLY**　　| 1987
– Brothers in arms / Recently / Asimbonanga / The Moon is a harsh mistress / James and the gang / Let us break bread together (freedom) / MLK / Do right man / Biko. *(re-iss. Aug91 on 'Virgin' lp/c; OVED/+C 354)*
Apr 89. (cd/c/lp) (CD/TC+/VGC 9) **DIAMONDS AND RUST IN THE BULLRING** (live)
– Diamonds and rust / (Ain't gotta let nobody) Turn me around / No woman, no cry / Famous blue raincoat / Swing low sweet chariot / Let it be / El preso numero nueve / Ilego contres Heridas / Txoria Txoria / Ellas danzan solas (cueca sola) /

Gracias a la vida / No nos moveran. *(re-iss. Aug91 on 'Virgin' lp/c; OVED/+C 370)*
Nov 89. (cd/c/lp) (CD/TC+/VGC 12) **SPEAKING OF DREAMS**
– China / Warriors of the sun / Carrickfergus / Hand to mouth / Speaking of dreams / El Salvador / Rambler gambler – Whispering bells / Fairfax country / A mi manera. *(re-iss. Aug91 on 'Virgin' lp/c; OVED/+C 371)*

—— now co-wrote with producers **WALLY WILSON** – (also) synthesizers / **KENNY GREENBERG** (also) guitars Other co-writers **KAREN O'CONNOR** or **PAT BUNCH**. Musicians:- **CHAD CROMWELL** – drums / **JERRY DOUGLAS** – various / **MARCOS SUZANO** – percussion / **EDGAR MEYER** – upright bass

	Virgin	Virgin

Jan 93. (cd/c) (CD/TC 2705) **PLAY ME BACKWARDS**　　| Nov92
– Play me backwards / Amsterdam / Isaac & Abraham / Stones in the road / Steal across the border / I'm with you / I'm with you (reprise) / Strange rivers / Through your hands / The dream song / Edge of glory. *(cd re-iss. Oct96 on 'Virgin-VIP'; CDVIP 164) (cd re-iss. Nov96 on 'Disky'; VI 87484-2)*

—— next feat. duets w/ JANIS IAN, MARY CHAPIN-CARPENTER, MARY BLACK . . .

	Grapevine	Asylum

Sep 95. (cd/c) (GRA CD/MC 208) **RING THEM BELLS** (live)
– Lily of the west / Sweet Sir Galahad / The band played Waltzing Matilda / Willie Moore / Swallow song / Don't make promises / Jesse / Ring the bells / Welcome me / Suzanne / You're ageing well / Pajarillo Barranqueno / Don't think twice it's all right / Diamonds and rust / The night they drove old Dixie down. *(re-iss. May99; same)*
May 99. (cd) (GRACD 223) **GONE FROM DANGER**
– No mermaid / Reunion hill / Crack in the mirror / February / Fishing / If I wrote you / Lily / Who do you think I am / Mercy bound / Money for floods.
Sep 99. (cd-s) (CDGPS 269) **NO MERMAID / FUSHING / DIAMONDS AND RUST (with Mary-Chapin Carpenter)**

– compilations, others, etc. –

on 'Vanguard' unless mentioned otherwise

Nov 63. (lp) Squire; <33001> **THE BEST OF JOAN BAEZ** (early '59 live Newport)　　- | 45
1963.. (7"ep) Fontana; (TE 18012) **WITH GOD ON OUR SIDE**　　- | -
1968. (lp) Saga; (EROS 8075) **THE BEST OF JOAN BAEZ**
1969. (7") (VA 4) **JUST A CLOSER WALK WITH THEE. / GREEN GREEN GRASS OF HOME**
Jun 69. (lp) (SVXL 100) **JOAN BAEZ ON VANGUARD**　　| 15
Dec 70. (d-lp) <(VSD 6560-1)> **THE FIRST 10 YEARS**　　| 41 | 73 Nov70
Nov 72. (d-lp) <(VSD 41-42)> **THE JOAN BAEZ BALLAD BOOK**
(re-iss. Aug89 on 'Start' lp/c/cd; VFLP5/VFTC6/VFCD7 108)
Jun 73. (7") (VAN 1007) **THERE BUT FOR FORTUNE. / LOVE IS JUST A FOUR-LETTER WORD**
Jun 73. (lp) <(VSD 79332)> **HITS GREATEST & OTHERS** *(cd-iss. May91)*
Nov 74. (d-lp) <(VSD 49-50)> **CONTEMPORARY BALLAD BOOK**
Mar 76. (lp) Golden Hour; (GH 843) **THE GOLDEN HOUR PRESENTS . . .**
Oct 76. (d-lp/c) (VSD/ZC-VSD 79) **THE JOAN BAEZ LOVE SONG ALBUM**
Apr 77. (lp) Golden Hour; (GH 863) **THE GOLDEN HOUR PRESENTS Vol.2**
Dec 77. (lp) A&M; (AMLH 64668) <4668> **THE BEST OF JOAN C. BAEZ**
(re-iss. Mar82 lp/c; AMID/CMID 114) (re-iss. Aug85 on 'Hallmark' lp/c; SHM/HSC 3173) (cd-iss. Nov89 on 'Pickwick'; PWKS 544)
Apr 79. (lp) Flyover-A&M; (GMX 9002) **SUPER DISC OF JOAN BAEZ**
Oct 79. (d-lp) (VSD 105) **THE COUNTRY MUSIC ALBUM**
(cd-iss. Jul91 & Oct98; VCD 105)
Oct 80. (lp/c) P.R.T.; (SPOT/ZCSPT 1008) **SPOTLIGHT ON . . .**
Jun 82. (c) P.R.T.; (ZCTON 106) **100 MINUTES OF JOAN BAEZ**
Jan 83. (7") Flashback; (FBS 12) **THE NIGHT THEY DROVE OLD DIXIE DOWN. / THERE BUT FOR FORTUNE**
Jan 83. (d-lp/d-c) <(VSD/ZCVSD 79436)> **VERY EARLY JOAN** (live 1961-63)
(cd-iss. Jan94)
Dec 88. (lp/c)(cd) Ariola; (206/205 742)(610 586) **LIVE EUROPE '83** (live)
Aug 89. (lp/c/cd) Start; (VFLP5/VFTC6/VFCD7 104) **THE NIGHT THEY DROVE OLD DIXIE DOWN**　　| -
Jan 90. (7") Old Gold; (OG 9931) **THE NIGHT THEY DROVE OLD DIXIE DOWN. / WE SHALL OVERCOME**
Jan 90. (7") Old Gold; (OG 9933) **THERE BUT FOR FORTUNE. / IT'S ALL OVER NOW, BABY BLUE**
Jun 92. (cd/c) Laserlight; (15/79 450) **NO WOMAN NO CRY**
Nov 92. (cd/c) Music Of The World; (CD/MC 12507) **WE SHALL OVERCOME**
Mar 93. (cd) A&M; (CDMID 180) **IMAGINE**
Jun 93. (cd/c) Ce De International; (CD/MC 62107) **QUEEN OF HEARTS**
Jun 93. (cd/c) Ce De International; (CD/MC 62120) **IT AIN'T ME BABE**
Sep 93. (d-cd) Duchesse; (CD 333505) **WHERE HAVE ALL THE FLOWERS GONE**
Oct 93. (cd/c) Spectrum; (550129-2/-4) **THE ESSENTIAL FROM THE HEART – LIVE** (live)
Dec 93. (3xcd-box) Virgin; (TPAK 30) **THE COMPACT COLLECTION**
– (RECENTLY / DIAMONDS AND RUST / SPEAKING OF DREAMS)
Apr 94. (3xcd-box) (VCD 3125) **RARE, LIVE AND CLASSIC 1958-1989**
Apr 94. (cd) That's Country; (TC 021) **JOE HILL & MORE COUNTRY SONGS**
Apr 96. (d-cd) A&M; (540 500-2) **DIAMONDS (A JOAN BAEZ ANTHOLOGY)**
Sep 98. (cd) (VCD 79512) **BAEZ SINGS DYLAN**

Ginger BAKER

Born: PETER BAKER, 19 Aug'39, Lewisham, London, playing the trumpet as his first instrument. Gaining drumming experience in the late 50's with jazz bands such as ACKER BILK, "GINGER" chose a new style when he joined BLUES INCORPORATED in 1962. Early the following year, he moved on to GRAHAM BOND ORGANISATION, although he subsequently left them mid-'66 to form CREAM with ERIC CLAPTON and JACK BRUCE. The thundering anchor holding down the band's psychedelic blues rock, the self-taught BAKER was also a pioneer of the dreaded drum solo. After their demise late '68, GINGER and ERIC formed BLIND FAITH (with STEVE WINWOOD and RIC GRECH), however, the supergroup split after releasing only one solitary album. Late in 1969, BAKER formed the AIRFORCE ensemble, releasing an eponymous set soon after which hit the UK Top 40 early in 1970. A second solo album followed later that year before he moved to Lagos, Nigeria, to buy land and build a 16-track studio. An album, 'STRATOVARIOUS' appeared in 1972, as well as a live set recorded with African star, FELA RANSOME KUTI. Taking time off to run his studio, he eventually hooked up with the GURVITZ brothers (PAUL and ADRIAN) to form the BAKER GURVITZ ARMY. This outfit released three jazz-rock efforts, one of which, the eponymous 1974 debut, almost made the UK Top 20. Not content with laying the groundwork for the world music boom of the 80's, the ever adventurous BAKER subsequently travelled to Italy where he ran a drum school in a mountain village! The mid-80's saw him tempted back into the musical slipstream, playing on PIL's 'ALBUM' in 1985 and working with leftfield guru, BILL LASWELL on a number of projects. More recently, this veritable grandmaster of rock drummers lent his inspired talents to the criminally underrated retro-rockers, MASTERS OF REALITY, most memorably and amusingly on the track 'T.U.S.A.'. The 90's have also seen BAKER continue to indulge his love of percussive based music, releasing a string of albums under the GINGER BAKER + AFRICAN FORCE moniker. He even found himself back in the Top 10 in the mid-90's, alongside JACK BRUCE and GARY MOORE. Going by the name of BBM, the trio scored with the 'Virgin' album, 'AROUND THE NEXT DREAM'. • Covered: SWEET WINE (Staple Singers) / TWELVE GATES OF THE CITY (Graham Bond) / STRAIGHT NO CHASER (Thelonius Monk) etc. • Trivia: He married in the mid-90's and took the surname of his wife, becoming GINGER LOUCKS-BAKER in the process.

Album rating: GINGER BAKER'S AIRFORCE (*5) / AIRFORCE II (*4) / STRATAVARIOUS (*4) / FELA RANSOME KUTI AND THE AFRICA '70 WITH GINGER BAKER (*5) / GINGER BAKER AT HIS BEST compilation (*6) / BAKER GURVITZ ARMY (*5) / ELYSIAN ENCOUNTER (*4) / HEARTS ON FIRE (*4) / 11 SIDES OF BAKER (*4) / FROM HUMBLE ORANGES (*4) / HORSES AND TREES (*5) / THE ALBUM (*4) / AFRICAN FORCE (*4) / PALANQUIN'S POLE (*4) / UNSEEN RAIN (*3) / GOING BACK HOME (*5) / FALLING OFF THE ROOF (*5)

GINGER BAKER'S AIRFORCE

with **GRAHAM BOND** – keyboards / **DENNY LAINE** – guitar / **RICK GRECH** – bass / **HAROLD McNAIR** – saxophone / **REMI KABAKA** – percussion / plus guests **STEVE WINWOOD, CHRIS WOOD, PHIL SEAMAN & BUD BEADLE**

			Polydor	Atco	
Feb 70.	(d-lp) (2662 001) <703> **GINGER BAKER'S AIRFORCE (live)**		37	33	May70

– Da da man / Early in the morning / Don't care / Toad / Aiko biaye / Man of constant sorrow / Do what you like / Doin' it.

Mar 70.	(7") (56380) <6750> **MAN OF CONSTANT SORROW. / DOIN' IT**			85	May70

—— guests now were mainly African percussionists, vocalists and keyboard players.

Sep 70. (lp) (2383 029) **AIRFORCE II**
– Let me ride / Sweet wine / Do u no hu yor phrenz r? / We free kings / I don't want to go on without you / Toady / Twelve gates of the city.

May 71. (7"; GINGER BAKER'S DRUM CHOIR) (2058 107) **ATUNDE (WE ARE HERE). / (part 2)**

1972. (lp) (2383 133) <7015> **STRATAVARIOUS**
– Ariwo / Something nice / Ju Ju / Blood brothers / 69 coda.

—— In 1971, he had moved to Akeja, Nigeria to buy land to build studio. He was augmented by FELA RANSOME KUTI and African musicians SALT.

			Regal Zonophone	Signpost	
1972.	(lp) (SLRZ 1023) **FELA RANSOME KUTI AND THE AFRICA '70 WITH GINGER BAKER LIVE!** (live)				

– Let's start / Black man's cry / Ye ye de smell / Egbe mi o.

—— He retired for a while early 1973, but returned to form

BAKER GURVITZ ARMY

with **ADRIAN GURVITZ** – guitar / **PAUL GURVITZ** – bass (both ex-GUN)

			Vertigo	Janus	
Dec 74.	(lp) (9103 201) <7015> **BAKER GURVITZ ARMY**		22		

– Help me / Love is / Memory Lane / Inside of me / I wanna live again / Mad Jack / 4 Phil / Since beginning. (re-iss.May77 on 'Mountain';)

Mar 75. (7") (6078 211) **HELP ME. / I WANNA LIVE AGAIN**

—— added **SNIPS** – vocals (ex-SHARKS) / **PETER LEMER** – keyboards (ex-SEVENTH WAVE)

			Mountain	Atco	
Aug 75.	(7") (TOP 2) **SPACE MACHINE. / THE DREAMER**				
Sep 75.	(lp) (TOPS 101) <123> **ELYSIAN ENCOUNTER**				

– People / The key / Time / The gambler / The dreamer / Remember / The artist / The hustler. (cd-iss.Sep93 on 'Repertoire';)

Oct 75. (7") (TOP 4) **THE GAMBLER. / TIME**

Nov 75. (7") **NIGHT PEOPLE. / ?**

—— Trimmed slightly when PETER LEMER departed.

Apr 76. (7") (TOP 10) **TRACKS OF MY LIFE. / THE ARTIST**

May 76. (lp) (TOPS 111) <36137> **HEARTS ON FIRE**
– Hearts on fire / Neon lights / Smiling / Tracks of my life / Flying in and out of stardom / Dancing the night away / My mind is healing / Thirsty for the blues / Night people / Mystery.

Jun 76. (7") (TOP 15) **DANCING THE NIGHT AWAY. / NIGHT PEOPLE**

GINGER BAKER & FRIENDS

with loads of session people.

			Mountain	Sire	
Jan 77.	(lp) (TOPC 5005) <7532> **ELEVEN SIDES OF BAKER**				

– Ginger man / Candlestick maker / High life / Don Dorango / Little bird / N'kon kin' n'kon n'kon / Howlin' wolf / Ice cream dragon / Winner / Pampero / Don't stop the carnival.

Jan 77. (7") (TOP 23) **DON DORANGO. / CANDLESTICK MAKER**

—— Retired again to breed ponies, but formed **ENERGY** in 1980 with **JOHN MIZAROLLI** – guitar / **MIKE DAVIS** – guitar / **HENRY THOMAS** – bass. In the early 80's, he joined ATOMIC ROOSTER briefly and HAWKWIND with his 2nd wife where she ran a drama school. In 1982, he emigrated to Italy where she ran a drama school.

GINGER BAKER & BAND

recorded 1982. **DOUG BROCKIE** – vocals, guitar / **KARL HILL** – bass, vocals

			C.D.G.	not iss.	
Jun 83.	(c/lp) (30+/INT 20303) **FROM HUMBLE ORANGES**		–	–	Italy

– The eleventh hour / Too many apples / It / Under the Sun / On the road to granma's house / The land of Morder / This planet / Sore head in the morning blues / Wasting time / Lament.

—— In 1985, he joined PUBLIC IMAGE LTD, recording 'ALBUM' with them. In 1986 with RAVI SHANKER and BILL LASWELL issued 'HORSES AND TREES' on 'Celluloid' lp/c/cd; CELL/+C/CD 6126)

			Onsala Int	not iss.	
Apr 87.	(lp) (ONS 2) **GINGER BAKER IN CONCERT (live 1982)**			–	

– Chemical blues / Perfect nation / Everything I say / Wheelchair dance festival / Lost in space / Where are you?

GINGER BAKER & AFRICAN FORCE

with **AMPOFO** – percussion, vocals / **ANSOU MANA BANGOURA** – perc., vocals / **FRANCIS MENSAH** – percussion / **JC COMMODORE** – percussion, vocals / **KAZDA** – co writers

			I.T.M.	not iss.	
1989.	(lp/cd) (ITM 0017/1417) **AFRICAN FORCE** (rec'86)			–	

– Brain damage / Sokoto / Ansoumania / Aboa / African force. (cd re-iss. Oct91; same)

Apr 90. (cd/lp) (ITM 1433/0033) **PALANQUIN'S POLE**
– Go do / Brain damage / Ansoumania / Palaquin's pole / Abyssinia-1.2.7. / Ginger's solo / Want come? go!.

Oct 91. (cd; GINGER BAKER, SONNY SHARROCK & PETER BROTZMANN) (ITM 1435) **NO MATERIAL**

May 92. (cd; GINGER BAKER with COURTNEY PINE) (ITM 1469) **THE ALBUM**
– Sunshine of your love / Dream battle / Black audience / Nice – jam / Brain damage.

—— now with **BILL LASWELL, JAH WOBBLE + NICK SKOPELTIS**

			Axiom	not iss.	
Feb 92.	(cd) (AXCD 3001) **MIDDLE PASSAGE**			–	German

– Mektoub / Under black skies / Time be time / Altamont / Basil / South to the dust.

—— next with **MIKE DAVIS** – guitar, vocals / **JOHN MIZAROLLI** – guitar / **HENRY THOMAS** – bass / **DAVID LENNOX** – keyboards

			Traditional Line	not iss.	
Jun 92.	(cd) (TL 1320) **GINGER BAKER'S ENERGY**			–	

– Just like you / Lost your love my love / Don't be so serious / Countain on you / Help yourself / Natural thing / Waisting time / Menopause / Feel so blue / Motown / Natural thing.

—— Having backed old friend JACK BRUCE on early 1994 live album 'CITIES', he became part of their trio BBM, alongside GARY MOORE. Their album 'AROUND THE NEXT DREAM' on 'Virgin' hit UK Top 10.

GINGER BAKER TRIO

—— with **CHARLIE HAYDEN** – bass (of ORNETTE COLEMAN band) / **BILL FRISELL** – guitars (of NAKED CITY + POWER TOOLS)

			Atlantic	Atlantic	
Dec 94.	(cd/c) (<7567 82652-2/-4>) **GOING BACK HOME**				

– Ramblin' / Straight no chaser / Ginger blues / When we go / East Timor / Spiritual / In the moment / etc.

Dec 95. (cd) <7567 82900-2> **FALLING OFF THE ROOF**
– Falling off the roof / Amarillo, Barbados / Bemsha swing / Sunday at the hillcrest / Au Privave / Our Spanish love song / C.B.C. mimps / Skeleton / Vino vecchio / The day the sun come out / Taney County.

Apr 99. (cd; as GINGER BAKER and the DJQ2O with special guest JAMES CARTER) (<7567 83168-2>) **COWARD OF THE COUNTY**
– Cyril Davies / Ginger Spice / Dangle the carrot / Megan showers / Jesus loves me / Coward of the county / Daylight / Jesus, I just want to go to sleep.

– compilations, etc. –

1973. (d-lp) Polydor; (2659 023) / Atco; <3504> **GINGER BAKER AT HIS BEST**
(re-iss. Feb76; same)

Jan 93. (cd; by BAKER GURVITZ ARMY) *Traditional Line; (TL 1311)* **LIVE IN LONDON 1975 (live)** □ -

Dec 99. (cd; as GINGER BAKER & FELA KUTI) *Masterplan; (MP 42003)* **AFRICA** □ -

Afrika BAMBAATAA

Born: KEVIN DONOVAN, 10 Apr'60, South Bronx, New York, USA. A former Black Spades gang member also known as KHAYAN AASIN, BAMBAATAA combined his street knowledge with a forward looking musical vision to create the Zulu Nation at the height of hip hop's 70's gestation period. A fraternal organisation designed to nurture the talents of young black rappers, DJ's and MC's, this collective promoted peace and racial harmony in an attempt to progress from the violence that characterised NY's gang life. BAMBAATAA was well qualified to head up such an ambitious project, his consummate DJ'ing skills and knowledge of popular music unsurpassed in his native city. Alongside contemporaries like GRANDMASTER FLASH, GRAND WIZARD THEODORE and KOOL HERC, the resourceful turntable maestro cut and pasted beats from a famously diverse array of source material including English punk groups like The CLASH and The SEX PISTOLS. Given this pivotal influence, then, the man's debut vinyl release arrived relatively late in the day, a 1980 double whammy of 'JAZZY SENSATION' and 'ZULU NATION THROWDOWN', two 12"ers cut by The JAZZY 5 and SOUL SONIC FORCE respectively, both crews under the aegis of the Zulu Nation and with BAMBAATAA as their driving creative force. It wasn't until the release of 1982's 'PLANET ROCK', however, that the name of AFRIKA BAMBAATAA became internationally synonymous with the cutting edge. In line with the developing hip hop trend, live backing musicians were dropped; in their place was a jaw-dropping synthesis of drum machine beats and pulsing electronica courtesy of KRAFTWERK's 'Trans Europe Express'. The record, only a minor hit at the time, remains one of the most pivotal releases of the last 20 years, providing a blueprint for the electro movement and the subsequent explosion of acid house, techno etc., through the pioneering work of producers Arthur Baker and John Robie. Inevitably perhaps, BAMBAATAA never really recovered from its seismic impact, coming close but never bettering it with a string of fine singles including the blistering follow-up SOUL SONIC FORCE single, 'LOOKING FOR THE PERFECT BEAT', and a couple of classic 1985 singles recorded under the TIME ZONE moniker, 'THE WILDSTYLE' and 'WORLD DESTRUCTION'. While the former utilised squelching synths, clipped depth-charge beats and samples of film dialogue to impressive effect, the latter was a link-up with ex-SEX PISTOL, JOHN LYDON in a cultural collision echoed years later with the LEFTFIELD/LYDON classic, 'Open Up'. Another collaboration, this time with fellow heavyweight, JAMES BROWN, failed to deliver, musically at least, on its promise of 'UNITY' in 1984. Album wise, BAMBAATAA released 'BEWARE (THE FUNK IS EVERYWHERE)' in 1986, as well as working with MATERIAL mainman, BILL LASWELL (who also contributed to the TIME ZONE releases) on the SHANGO project, a more straightforward soul/funk affair. With the emergence of sharp shooting young guns like PUBLIC ENEMY and LL COOL J, BAMBAATAA's profile dipped in the late 80's/early 90's and arguably, cheesy, Italian-produced house was hardly the best medium to win back lost street cred. Nevertheless, the big man from the Bronx remains a towering influence on underground dance and hip hop, his occasional DJ'ing appearances received as something akin to the holy grail among the faithful. A mark of the man's respect among the dance cognoscenti was the 1992 release of 'DON'T STOP', a 'PLANET ROCK' remix project undertaken by the collective effort of electronic dons such as LFO, 808 STATE and ex-KRAFTWERK man, KARL BARTOS. BAMBAATAA's 90's reformation of the TIME ZONE wasn't quite so well received, a handful of singles and an album, 'WARLOCKS AND WITCHES, COMPUTER CHIPS, MICROCHIPS' (1996) released to relatively minimal interest.

Album rating: BEWARE (THE FUNK IS EVERYWHERE) (*6) / the PLANET ROCK various artists (*7) / THE LIGHT (*5) / THE DECADE OF DARKNESS 1990-2000 (*5) / WARLOCKS AND WITCHES, COMPUTER CHIPS, MICROCHIPS AND YOU (*4)

AFRIKA BAMBAATAA and the SOUL SONIC FORCE

AFRIKA BAMBAATAA – DJ / with rappers, M.C. G.L.O.B.E. (JOHN B. MILLER), MR. BIGGS (ELLIS WILLIAMS) and POW WOW (ROBERT ALLEN) with D.J. JAZZY JAY

	Polydor	Tommy Boy
Aug 82. (12") *(POSPX 497) <823>* **PLANET ROCK. / ('A'instrumental)**	53	48 Jun82

(re-iss. Aug98 on 'Afrowax' 12"/cd-s; 12AWX/CDSAWX 1)+ remix. (re-iss. Feb99 on 'Tommy Boy'; TBV 341) (re-iss. Oct99 on 'Hot Classics'; HCL 2293)

Feb 83. (7") *(POSP 561)* **LOOKING FOR THE PERFECT BEAT. / BONUS BEATS**	□	□

(12"+=) *(POSPX 561)* – Bonus beats II / ('A'instrumental).

	Tommy Boy	Tommy Boy
Feb 84. (7") *(AFR 1)* **RENEGADES OF FUNK. / ('A'mix)**	30	□
Aug 84. (7"/ext-12"; AFRIKA BAMBAATAA & JAMES BROWN) *(AFR/+X 2)* **UNITY (PART 1 - THE THIRD COMING). / BECAUSE IT'S COMING**	49	□
Oct 84. (12") *(AFRX 3)* **FRANTIC SITUATION. / ('A'mix)**	□	□

—— in Jan'85, BAMBAATAA and JOHN LYDON (of PiL) featured on a second TIME ZONE (aka NICKY SKOPELITES and BILL LASWELL) single, 'WORLD DESTRUCTION', which hit the UK Top 50.

AFRIKA BAMBAATAA

	WEA	WEA
Aug 86. (12") *(U 8663T)* **BAMBAATAA'S THEME (ASSAULT ON PRECINCT 13). / TENSION**	□	□
Oct 86. (lp/c) *(253092-1/-4)* **BEWARE (THE FUNK IS EVERYWHERE)**	□	□

– Funk jam party / Funk you / Bionic kats / What time is it? / Beware (the funk is everywhere) / Bambaataa's theme / Tension / Rock America / Kick out the jams.

AFRIKA BAMBAATAA & THE FAMILY

	E.M.I.	Capitol
Feb 88. (7") *(EM 41)* **RECKLESS. / MIND BODY AND SOUL**	17	□

(12"+=) *(12EM 41)* – ('A'-vocal Wildstyle mix).
(cd-s+=) *(CDEM 41)* – Recklessly (Soca chant zouk mix).
(12"+=) *(12EMXS 41)* – ('A'-Fon Force remix).
(above single featured UB40)

Mar 88. (cd/c/lp) *(CD/TC+/EMC 3545)* **THE LIGHT**	□	□

– The light / Reckless / Radical music, revolutionary dance / Something he can feel / Clean up your act / Zouk your body / World racial war / Shout it out / Sho nuff funky / All I want.

May 88. (7") *(EM 57)* **SHO NUFF FUNKY. / TELL ME WHEN YOU NEED IT AGAIN (vocal mix 1)**	□	□

(12"+=) *(12EM 57)* – Tell me when you need it again (mix 2).
(12"+=) *(12EMX 57)* – Tell me when you need it again (mix 3).
(12"+=) *(12EMXS 57)* – ('A'-Funkin' all night mix).

	Manhattan	Manhattan
Oct 91. (7") *(MT 100)* **JUST GET UP AND DANCE. / ('A'mix)**	45	□
Oct 91. (cd/c) *(CD/TC MTL 1062) <9777>* **THE DECADE OF DARKNESS (1990-2000)**	□	□

AFRIKA BAMBAATAA PRESENTS TIME ZONE

	Profile	Profile
Apr 93. (12"/cd-s) *(PROF T/CD 389)* **TIME ZONE. / ('A'mixes)**	□	□
Mar 94. (12"ep/cd-ep) *(PROF 409/+CD)* **WHAT'S THE NAME E.P.**	□	□

– What's the name of this nation? Zulu! / Hold on, I'm coming / Ghost.

Nov 95. (12"/cd-s) *(PROF T/CD 442)* **THROW YOUR FUNKY HANDS UP. / ('A'mixes)**	□	□
Feb 96. (cd)(c/d-lp) *(FILECD 464)(PRO 1464-4/-1)* **WARLOCKS AND WITCHES, COMPUTER CHIPS, MICROCHIPS AND YOU**	□	□

	ZYX	ZYX
Aug 97. (cd-s) *(ZYX 86948)* **MIND CONTROL (mixes)**	□	□

	Hudson Vandam	Celluloid
Dec 97. (cd) *(HVD 5103)* **ZULU GROOVE**	□	□ Nov97

– World destruction / Shango message / Wild style / Zulu groove / Than you / Let's party down / Soca fever / World destruction.
(above was originally issued for 'Celluloid')

—— In Jun'99, AFRIKA BAMBAATAA was credited on the WESTBAM single for 'Mute', AGHARTA – THE CITY OF SHAMBALLA.

	Dust It!	Dust It!
Aug 99. (12"/cd-s) *(SPEC 130/+CD)* **ELECTRO FUNK EXPRESS (mixes)**	□	□

	Areeba	Areeba
Sep 99. (12"; as AFRIKA BAMBAATAA & THE SOUL SONIC FORCE) *(ARET 004)* **WHO'S IN THE HOUSE (mixes; Doppelganger vocal / Scope Funktastic vocal / Doppelganger dub)**	□	□

	ZYX	ZYX
Oct 99. (12") *(ZYX 91038)* **YOU ASK FOR THE MOON (mixes)**	□	-

(above with KHAYAN & THe NEW WORLD POWER)

	Jungle Sky	Jungle Sky
Nov 99. (2x12"ep; Vs DJ SOULSLINGER) *(JSK 160)* **FIRE (remixes)**	□	□

– compilations, etc. –

Jul 87. (lp/c) *Blatant; (BLAT LP/MC 2)* **DEATH MIX THROWDOWN**		-
Mar 88. (12") *E.M.I.; (12BAM 1)* **SHOUT IT OUT. / SHO NUFF FUNKY**		-
Jul 91. (lp/cd) *Music Of Life; (SPOCK 3/+CD)* **HIP HOP FUNK DANCE CLASSICS VOL.1**		□
Sep 92. (lp/cd; AFRIKA BAMBAATAA & THE UNIVERSAL ZULU NATION) *Music Of Life; (SPOCK 4/+CD)* **HIP HOP FUNK DANCE CLASSICS VOL.2**		□
Jun 93. (cd/lp) *Music Of Life; (MOL CD/LP 30)* **HIP HOP FUNK DANCE CLASSICS VOL.3**		□
Mar 99. (cd) *Tommy Boy; (TBCD 1052)* **DON'T STOP . . . PLANET ROCK**		□

BAND

Formed: 1967, by expatriate Canadians ROBBIE ROBERTSON, RICK DANKO, RICHARD MANUEL, LEVON HELM and GARTH HUDSON. Having previously backed up rockabilly singer RONNIE HAWKINS, the group recorded under the name The CANADIAN SQUIRES and later LEVON AND THE HAWKS. As The HAWKS, the group also backed BOB DYLAN on his 1965-66 world tour, HELM having fallen out with DYLAN at an earlier gig, the infamous Forest Hills concert where the folk messiah had "gone electric" much to the chagrin of his more purist fans. Following DYLAN's 1966 motorcycle accident and subsequent seclusion at Woodstock, the group also relocated to the area, HELM rejoining them. They then began work on a series of laid back, informal sessions with DYLAN which would later see the light of day as 'THE BASEMENT TAPES', released by DYLAN's label, 'Columbia', in 1975. A seminal set of experimental proto-country rock, the legendary recording sessions from which the album resulted saw The BAND developing their distinctive instrumental, vocal and songwriting dexterity which would mark out 'MUSIC FROM BIG PINK' (1968) as one of the pivotal debut releases of the decade. Named after the group's communal Woodstock home, it stood alongside 'Sweetheart Of The Rodeo' and 'John Wesley Harding' as a quietly confident display of back to basics musical integrity and an antidote to the psychedelic excesses of the previous year. The record highlighted the vocal diversity of HELM, DANKO and MANUEL both individually and collectively whether covering DYLAN material ('TEARS OF RAGE', 'I SHALL BE RELEASED') or tackling the compelling ROBERTSON / MANUEL penned originals. From the former's prudent guitar playing to the eclecticism of HUDSON's organ runs, the musicianship was flawless and while songs like 'THE WEIGHT' were deceptively simple, they possessed an air of strange grace. If this album introduced The BAND as major contenders, then their eponymous follow-up assured them of a place in rock history. A veritable distillation of classic American musical tradition, 'THE BAND' (1969) put rock into a bit of much needed perspective, its rich beauty a reminder of why people set words to song in the first place. Vivid narratives like 'THE NIGHT THEY DROVE OLD DIXIE DOWN' and 'KING HARVEST (HAS SURELY COME)' resonated as deeply as any Steinbeck novel yet no one could accuse ROBERTSON of misty eyed nostalgia; the characters and their attendant burdens that inhabit these songs were genuine, holding up a mirror to the struggles of modern society. By 'STAGE FRIGHT' (1970), ROBERTSON's songwriting prowess was becoming a little blunted. Much of the material centered around his on-the-road experiences and while the likes of 'THE SHAPE I'M IN' and the title track were enjoyable enough, there was nothing to match the depths of its predecessor. 'CAHOOTS' (1971) was even more bereft of fresh ideas, a VAN MORRISON collaboration, '4% PANTOMINE', one of the record's few saving graces. 'ROCK OF AGES' (1972) was a competent, if pointless, double live effort, embellished with horns courtesy of the ubiquitous ALLEN TOUSSAINT while 'MOONDOG MATINEE' (1973) was an even more inessential collection of rock'n'roll covers. 'NORTHERN LIGHTS – SOUTHERN CROSS' (1975) saw the verve (small V!) returning to ROBERTSON's songwriting while HUDSON's keyboard work came into its own. By the following year, however, they'd decided enough was enough, playing their farewell concert at San Francisco's Winterland ballroom on Thanksgiving Day. The event was recorded for posterity as 'THE LAST WALTZ', a triple album set that also served as a soundtrack for the rockumentary of the same name. With an all-star cast including the likes of NEIL YOUNG and JONI MITCHELL, the record was a spirited, poignant farewell to a group that had helped define an era. After a final album to fulfil contractual obligations, the rank 'ISLANDS' (1977), the various members went off to do their own thing and that should've been the end of it. Inevitably it wasn't, and while an initial comeback album attempt was dealt a severe blow when RICHARD MANUEL took his own life in 1986, The BAND did reform the following decade (minus ROBERTSON who knocked back an invitation to join). Without two of their mainstays, the group were always going to find it difficult and indeed, both their albums, 'JERICHO' (1994) and 'HIGH ON THE HOG' (1996) consisted largely of well below par cover material. A solo artist for many years, RICK DANKO was found dead in his New York home on the 10th of December, 1999. • **Covered:** WHEN I PAINT MY MASTERPIECE + FOREVER YOUNG + I MUST LOVE YOU TOO MUCH (Bob Dylan) / DON'T DO IT (Holland-Dozier-Holland) / LONG BLACK VEIL (Wilkin-Dill) / MYSTERY TRAIN (Elvis Presley) / THE GREAT PRETENDER (Platters) / SHE KNOWS (Procol Harum) / CRAZY MAMA (JJ Cale) / FREE YOUR MIND (D.Foster / T.McElroy) / WHERE SHOULD I ALWAYS BE (Bill Chaplin) / BACK TO MEMPHIS / STAND UP (B.Channel / R.Rector) / etc.

Album rating: MUSIC FROM BIG PINK (*8) / THE BAND (*10) / STAGE FRIGHT (*7) / CAHOOTS (*5) / ROCK OF AGES (*7) / MOONDOG MATINEE (*5) / NORTHERN LIGHTS – SOUTHERN CROSS (*6) / ISLANDS (*4) / THE LAST WALTZ with various artists (*7) / THE BEST OF THE BAND – ANTHOLOGY compilation (*7) / TO KINGDOM COME – THE DEFINITIVE COLLECTION compilation (*7) / JERICHO (*5) / LIVE AT WATKINS' GLEN live '73 (*6) / HIGH ON THE HOG (*2) / ACROSS THE GREAT DIVIDE boxed-set (*6)

ROBBIE ROBERTSON (b. 4 Jul'44, Toronto, Canada) – guitar, vocals / **RICHARD MANUEL** (b. 3 Apr'45, Stratford, Canada) – piano, vocals, drums, sax / **RICK DANKO** (b. 9 Dec'43, Simcoe, Canada) – vocals, bass, violin, trombone / **GARTH HUDSON** (b. 2 Aug'37, London, Canada) – organ, saxophone, accordion / **LEVON HELM** (b.26 May'42, Marvel, AR) – drums, vocvals, mandolin, guitar

		not iss.	Apex
1964.	(7"; as CANADIAN SQUIRES) **UH-UH-UH. / LEAVE ME ALONE** <re-iss. 1965 on 'Ware'; >	–	

		Atlantic	Atco
Nov 65.	(7"; as LEVON AND THE HAWKS) (4054) <6383> **THE STONES I THROW. / HE DON'T LOVE YOU AND HE'LL BREAK YOUR HEART**		Mar65
1968.	(7"; as LEVON AND THE HAWKS) <6625> **GO GO LISA JANE. / HE DON'T LOVE YOU AND HE'LL BREAK YOUR HEART**		

		Capitol	Capitol
Aug 68.	(lp; stereo/mono) (S+/ST <2955>) **MUSIC FROM BIG PINK** – Tears of rage / To kingdom come / In a station / Caledonian mission / The weight / We can talk / Long black veil / Chest fever / Lonesome Suzie / This wheel's on		30

fire / I shall be released. (re-iss. Jun81 on 'Greenlight' lp/c; GO/TC-GO 2001) (cd-iss. May87; CDP 746 069-2) (lp re-iss. Apr99 on 'E.M.I.'; 499465-2)

Sep 68.	(7") (CL 15559) <2269> **THE WEIGHT. / I SHALL BE RELEASED**	21	63 Aug68
Jan 70.	(lp) <(EST 132)> **THE BAND**	25	9 Sep69

– Across the great divide / Rag mama rag / The night they drove old Dixie down / When you awake / Up on Cripple Creek / Whispering pines / Jemima surrender / Rockin' chair / Look out Cleveland / Jawbone / The unfaithful servant / King harvest (has surely come). (re-iss. Aug86 lp/c; EMS/TCEMS 1192) (cd-iss. Aug88 on 'E.M.I.'; CZ 70) (cd re-iss. Aug97 on 'E.M.I.' hit UK No.41; CDP 746493-2)

Oct 69.	(7") (CL 15613) <2635> **UP ON CRIPPLE CREEK. / THE NIGHT THEY DROVE OLD DIXIE DOWN**		25
Feb 70.	(7") (CL 15629) <2705> **RAG MAMA RAG. / THE UNFAITHFUL SERVANT**	16	57
Oct 70.	(lp) <(EASW 425)> **STAGE FRIGHT**	15	5 Sep70

– Strawberry wine / Sleeping / Time to kill / Just another whistle stop / All la glory / The shape I'm in / The W.S. Walcott medicine show / Daniel and the sacred harp / Stage fright / The rumor. (re-iss. Jun81 on 'Greenlight' lp/c; GO/TC-GO 2003) (cd-iss. Mar91; CZ 405)

Oct 70.	(7") <2870> **TIME TO KILL. / THE SHAPE I'M IN**	–	77
Oct 70.	(7") (CL 15659) **TIME TO KILL. / SLEEPING**	–	
Mar 71.	(7") (CL 15675) **THE SHAPE I'M IN. / THE RUMOR**	–	
Oct 71.	(lp) <(EAST 651)> **CAHOOTS**	41	21

– Life is a carnival / When I paint my masterpiece / Last of the blacksmiths / Where do we go from here? / 4% pantomime / Shoot out in Chinatown / The Moon struck one / Thinkin' out loud / Smoke signal / Volcano / The river hymn. (re-iss. Jun81 on 'Greenlight' lp/c; GO/TC-GO 2015) (cd-iss. May89; CZ 138)

Oct 71.	(7") (CL 15700) <3199> **LIFE IS A CARNIVAL. / THE MOON STRUCK ONE**		72
Dec 71.	(7") <3249> **WHEN I PAINT MY MASTERPIECE. / WHERE DO WE GO FROM HERE?**	–	
Aug 72.	(d-lp) <(SABB 11045)> **ROCK OF AGES** (live)		6

– Don't do it / King harvest (has surely come) / Caledonia mission / Get up Jake / The W.S. Walcott medicine show / Stage fright / The night they drove all Dixie down / Across the great divide / This wheel's on fire / Rag mama rag / The weight / The shape I'm in / The unfaithful servant / Life is a carnival / Chest fever / (I don't want to) Hang up my rock and roll shoes. (re-iss. Jul83 on 'E.M.I.';) (re-iss. Apr87 – =*; CDP 746 617-2) <d-cd-iss. 1990 += *>

Nov 72.	(7") (CL 15737) <3433> **DON'T DO IT** (live). **/ RAG MAMA RAG** (live)		34 Sep72
Feb 73.	(7") <3500> **CALEDONIA MISSION. / (I DON'T WANT TO) HANG UP MY ROCK AND ROLL SHOES**	–	
Nov 73.	(7") (CL 15767) <3758> **AIN'T GOT NO HOME. / GET UP JAKE**		73
Dec 73.	(lp) <(ESW 11214)> **MOONDOG MATINEE**		28 Nov73

– Ain't got no home / Holy cow / Share your love / Mystery train / The Third Man theme / The promised land / The great pretender / I'm ready / Saved / A change is gonna come. (cd-iss. Mar91;)

—— Late '73, they renewed association with BOB DYLAN, helping out on album 'PLANET WAVES' and more so 'BEFORE THE FLOOD' a live album credited to BOB DYLAN / THE BAND. In '75 The BAND returned with brand new material.

Feb 74.	(7") <3828> **THE THIRD MAN THEME. / THE W.S. WALCOTT MEDICINE SHOW**	–	
Dec 75.	(lp) **NORTHERN LIGHTS – SOUTHERN CROSS**		26

– Forbidden fruit / Hobo jungle / Ophelia / Acadian driftwood / Ring your bell / It makes no difference / Jupiter hollow / Rags and bones. (cd-iss. Mar91; CZ 404)

Feb 76.	(7") <4230> **OPHELIA. / HOBO JUNGLE**	–	62
Mar 76.	(7") (CL 15861) **RING YOUR BELL. / FORBIDDEN FRUIT**	–	
Nov 76.	(7") <4316> **TWILIGHT. / ACADIAN DRIFTWOOD**	–	
Apr 77.	(lp) <(EST 11602)> **ISLANDS**	64	Mar77

– Right as rain / Street walker / Let the night fall / Ain't that a lot of love / Christmas must be tonight / Islands / The saga of Pepote Rouge / Georgia on my mind / Knockin' lost John / Livin' in a dream. (cd-iss. Mar91; CZ 406)

Apr 77.	(7") <4361> **GEORGIA ON MY MIND. / THE NIGHT THEY DROVE OLD DIXIE DOWN**	–	–
Apr 77.	(7") (CL 15921) **RIGHT AS RAIN. / KNOCKIN' LOST JOHN**	–	–

—— Joined by guests BOB DYLAN, NEIL YOUNG, RONNIE HAWKINS, JONI MITCHELL, ERIC CLAPTON, VAN MORRISON, NEIL DIAMOND, MUDDY WATERS, PAUL BUTTERFIELD, BOBBY CHARLES and DR. JOHN etc. Jams were from STEPHEN STILLS, RINGO STARR and RONNIE WOOD

		Warners	Warners
Apr 78.	(t-lp) (K 66076) <3WS 3146> **THE LAST WALTZ** (live 25th Nov'76 – film soundtrack)	39	16

– Theme from the last waltz / Up on cripple creek / Who do you love / Helpless / Stage fright / Coyote / Dry your eyes / Such a night / It makes no difference / Mystery train / The shape I'm in / The night they drove old Dixie down / Mannish boy / Further on up the road / The shape I'm in / Down south in New Orleans / Ophelia / Tura lura lural (that's an Irish lullaby) / Caravan / Life is a carnival / Baby let me follow you down / I don't believe you (she acts like we never have met) / Forever young / I shall be released / The well / Evangeline / Out of the blue / The weight / The last waltz refrain / Theme from the last waltz (with orchestra). (cd-iss. Jul88; K 266076)

Jun 78.	(7") (K 17187) **THEME FROM THE LAST WALTZ** (live). **/ OUT OF THE BLUE** (live)	–	–
Nov 78.	(7") <8592> **OUT OF THE BLUE** (live). **/ THE WELL** (live)	–	–

—— After their official split in 1978, HUDSON and MANUEL went into sessions. MANUEL hung himself 6 Mar'86, after a fit of depression. RICK DANKO and LEVON HELM went solo. In 1980, ROBBIE wrote score for film CARNY, before finally getting around to recording solo album in 1987.

—— Re-formed (now studio / earlier live) with **DANKO, HELM, HUDSON + JIM WEIDER** – bass / **RICHARD BELL** – piano / **RANDY CIARLANTE** – drums

		Essential	Pyramid
Feb 94.	(cd/c) (ESS CD/MC 199) **JERICHO**		Nov93

– Remedy / Blind Willie McTell / The caves of Jericho / Atlantic City / Too soon gone / Country boy / Move to Japan / Amazon (river of dreams) / Stuff you gotta watch / Same thing / Shine a light / Blues stay away from me.

Apr 96. (cd/c) (TRA CD/MC 228) **HIGH ON THE HOG**
   – Stand up / Back to Memphis / Where I should always be / Free your mind / Forever young / The high price of love / Crazy mama / I must love you too much / She knows / Ramble jungle.

	Transatla.	Pyramid

– compilations, etc. –

on 'Capitol' unless stated otherwise

Sep 76. (d-lp) (ST 3927) <ST 11553> **THE BEST OF THE BAND** — | | 51 |
   (re-iss. Jun82 on 'Fame' lp/c; FA/TC-FA 3016) (cd-iss. May87; CDP 746 070-2)
Oct 76. (7") (CL 115887) **TWILIGHT. / THE WEIGHT** — | – |
Jan 79. (d-lp) (ESTSP 19) <SKBO 11856> **ANTHOLOGY** — | – |
   (cd-iss. May89; CZ 63)
Jul 84. (7") EMI Gold; (G45 28) **RAG MAMA RAG. / THE WEIGHT** — | – |
Oct 89. (t-lp/d-c)(d-cd) (EN/TCEN 5010)(CDS 792 169-2) **TO KINGDOM COME – THE DEFINITIVE COLLECTION** — | – |
May 92. (cd) Castle; (CCS CD/MC 333) **THE COLLECTION** — | – |
   – Back to Memphis / Tears of rage / To kingdom come / Long black veil / Chest fever / The weight / I shall be released / Up on Cripple Creek / Loving you is sweeter than ever / Rag mama rag / The night they drove old Dixie down / Unfaithful servant / King Harvest (has surely come) / The shape I'm in / The W.S.Walcott medicine show / Daniel and the sacred harp / Stage fright / Don't do it (baby don't do it) / Life is a carnival / When I paint my masterpiece / 4% pantomine / The river hymn / Mystery train / Endless highway / Get up Jake / It makes no difference / Ophelia / Arcadian driftwood / Christmas must be tonight / The saga of Peopote rouge / Knockin' lost John.
Nov 94. (3xcd-box) (CDBAND 1) **ACROSS THE GREAT DIVIDE** — | – |
Apr 95. (cd) (CDP 831742-2) **LIVE AT WATKINS GLEN** (live) — | – |
   – Back to Memphis / Endless highway / I shall be released / Loving you is sweeter than ever / Too wet to work / Don't ya tell Henry / The rumour / Time to kill / Jam / Up on Cripple Creek.
Aug 98. (cd) E.M.I.; (495051-2) **THE SHAPE I'M IN (THE VERY BEST OF THE BAND)** — | – |

BAND AID (see under ⇒ BOOMTOWN RATS / Bob Geldof)

Thomas BANGALTER (see under ⇒ DAFT PUNK)

BANGLES

Formed: Los Angeles, California, USA … 1981 as The BANGS by sisters VICKI and DEBBI PETERSON alongside SUSANNA HOFFS, getting together after the siblings replied to an ad placed by the latter. After a one-off US indie 45, they became The BANGLES, added a bass player, ANNETTE ZILINSKAS and signed to Miles Copeland's 'IRS/Faulty' records in mid '82. An eponymous mini-set showed them to be a feisty garage-pop band whose sound was characterised by the harmonies of the PETERSON sisters and influenced by the likes of LOVE, GRASS ROOTS, The BYRDS, The BEATLES and The GO-GO's, an all-female quartet in the male dominated Paisley Underground. Replacing ZILINSKAS (who subsequently joined BLOOD ON THE SADDLE) with MICKI STEELE, the band secured a major label deal with 'CBS/Columbia' and breached the lower fringes of both the UK and US charts with debut album proper, 'ALL OVER THE PLACE' (1985). Although the rough edges had been smoothed out for public consumption, no hit singles were forthcoming and it would take the masterful pen of PRINCE to furnish the girls with a breakthrough track; 'MANIC MONDAY' was released in early '86, a MAMAS & PAPAS-esque tale of 9 to 5 frustration that quickly captured the popular imagination and climbed into the Top 3 on both sides of the Atlantic. 1986 proved to be The BANGLES' year, a follow-up album, 'DIFFERENT LIGHT', again achieving transatlantic Top 3 status and spawning a further minor hit in the melancholy reading of Jules Shear's 'IF SHE KNEW WHAT SHE WANTS' and a monster US No.1 in 'WALK LIKE AN EGYPTIAN'. To end the year, they were back in the Top 20 with a remix of 'WALKING DOWN YOUR STREET'. While only a solitary flop single, 'FOLLOW', appeared in '87, The BANGLES kickstarted their career in early '88 with a storming cover of Simon & Garfunkel's 'HAZY SHADE OF WINTER', cut for the soundtrack to cult 80's bratpack movie, 'Less Than Zero'. With seemingly no end to their pop ascendancy, the BANGLES again hired outside writers for the slick 'EVERYTHING' (1988), another massive Stateside success which spawned US Top 5, 'IN YOUR ROOM', as well as the band's syrupy calling card, 'ETERNAL FLAME', a transatlantic chart topper in early '89. With sex symbol HOFFS (who sang the latter unaccompanied) increasingly regarded as the band's focal point, tensions eventually split the band in 1990 as their run of hits stuttered to a halt. While HOFFS went on to a marginally successful solo career, the PETERSONS continued to work on the alternative/pop underground. • **Songwriters:** Mostly HOFFS collaborations, except GOING DOWN TO LIVERPOOL (Kimberley Rew – SOFT BOYS) / WALK LIKE AN EGYPTIAN (Liam Sternberg) / SEPTEMBER GURLS (Alex Chilton). HOFFS solo; BOYS KEEP SWINGING (David Bowie) + UNCONDITIONAL LOVE (Cyndi Lauper). • **Trivia:** SUSANNA HOFFS made film acting debut in 'The Allnighter' released 1987.

Album rating: ALL OVER THE PLACE (*6) / DIFFERENT LIGHT (*5) / EVERYTHING (*4) / BANGLES' GREATEST HITS compilation (*7)

The BANGS

SUSANNA HOFFS (b.17 Jan'57, Newport Beach, Calif.) – vocals, rhythm guitar / **VICKI PETERSON** (b.11 Jan'58) – lead guitar, vocals (ex-The FANS) / **DEBBI PETERSON** (b.22 Aug'61) – drums, vocals (ex-The FANS)

	not iss.	Down Kitty

Dec 81. (7") <BANG 1> **GETTING OUT OF HAND. / CALL ON ME** — | – | ☐ |

The BANGLES

—— added **ANNETTE ZILINSKAS** – bass

	not iss.	Faulty-IRS

Jun 82. (m-lp) **THE BANGLES**
   – How is the air up there? / Mary Street / The real world / Want you / I'm in line.

—— **MICKI STEELE** (b.MICHAEL, 2 Jun'54) – bass, vocals (ex-RUNAWAYS, ex-SLOW CHILDREN) repl. ANNETTE who joined BLOOD ON THE SADDLE

	C.B.S.	Columbia.

Sep 84. (7") (A 4527) **HERO TAKES A FALL. / WHERE WERE YOU WHEN I NEEDED YOU** — | | |
Mar 85. (lp/c) (CBS/40 26015) <39220> **ALL OVER THE PLACE** | 86 | 80 | Jul84
   – Hero takes a fall / Live / James / All about you / Dover beach / Tell me / Restless / Going down to Liverpool / He's got a secret / Silent treatment / More than meets the eye. (re-iss. Oct86 lp/c/cd; 450091-1/-4/-2) (re-iss. Apr93 on 'Columbia' cd/c;)
Mar 85. (7") (A 4914) **GOING DOWN TO LIVERPOOL. / DOVER BEACH** | 56 | |
   (12"+=) – (TX 4914) – The real world / I'm in line / How is the air up there?
   (d7"+=) (DA 4914) – Hero takes a fall / Where were you when I needed you?
Jan 86. (7"/7"w-poster) (A/QA 6796) <05757> **MANIC MONDAY. / IN A DIFFERENT LIGHT** | 2 | 2 |
   (12"+=) (TX 6796) – Going down to Liverpool / Dover beach.
Mar 86. (lp/c/cd) (CBS/40/CD 26659) <40039> **DIFFERENT LIGHT** | 3 | 2 | Jan86
   – Manic Monday / In a different light / Walking down your street / Walk like an Egyptian / Standing in the hallway / Return post / If she knew what she wants / Let it go / September gurls / Angels don't fall in love / September girls / Following / Not like you. (re-iss. Mar90 cd/c/lp; 46558-2/-4/-1)
Apr 86. (7"/7"sha-pic-d) (A/WA 7062) <05886> **IF SHE KNEW WHAT SHE WANTS. / ANGELS DON'T FALL IN LOVE** | 31 | 29 |
   (12"+=) (TA 7062) – Manic Monday (extended).
   (d7"+=) (DA 7062) – Hero takes a fall (remix) / James.
Jul 86. (7") (A 7255) **GOING DOWN TO LIVERPOOL. / LET IT GO** | | |
   (12"+=) (TA 7255) – Walking down your street – James (live medley).
Sep 86. (7"/7"w-poster) (650071-7/-0) <06257> **WALK LIKE AN EGYPTIAN. / NOT LIKE YOU** | 3 | 1 |
   (12"+=) (650071-6) – ('A'dub version) / ('A'acappella).
   (d7"+=) (650071-8) – Manic Monday / In a different light.
Dec 86. (7"/7"g-f/ext.12") (BANGS/+G/T 1) <06674> **WALKING DOWN YOUR STREET (remix). / RETURN POST** | 16 | 11 |
   (d7"+=) (BANGS D1) – Walk like an Egyptian / Not like you.
Apr 87. (7"/7"w-poster) (BANGS/+Q 2) **FOLLOWING. / DOVER BEACH** | 55 | |
   (12"+=)(d7"+=) (BANGS T/D 2) – Bangles hit mix medley (Manic Monday – If she knew what she wants – Walking down your street – Going down to Liverpool – Walk like an Egyptian).

—— next 45 was a one-off for movie 'Less Than Zero' on 'Def Jam-CBS' label

Jan 88. (7"/7"pic-d) (BANGS/+Q 3) <07630> **HAZY SHADE OF WINTER. / (b-side by "Joan Jett & the Blackhearts")** | 11 | 2 |
   (12") (BANGS T3) – ('A'-Purple haze mix) / ('A'dub) / ('A'-Shady haze mix).
   (cd-s+=) (BANGS C3) – (the 4 tracks) / Walk like an Egyptian.
Oct 88. (7"/7"w-poster) (BANGS/+Q 4) <08090> **IN YOUR ROOM. / BELL JAR** | 35 | 5 |
   (12"+=/12"pic-d+=/cd-s+=) (BANGS T/P/C 4) – Hazy shade of winter (remix).
Nov 88. (lp/c/cd) (462597-1/-4/-2) <44056> **EVERYTHING** | 5 | 15 |
   – In your room / Complicated girl / Bell jar / Something to believe in / Eternal flame / Be with you / Glitter years / I'll set you free / Watching the sky / Some dreams come true / Make a play for her now / Waiting for you / Crash and burn. (re-iss. Apr93 on 'Columbia' cd/c;)
Jan 89. (7") (BANGS R5) <68533> **ETERNAL FLAME. / WHAT I MEANT TO SAY** | 1 | 1 |
   (12"+=/cd-s+=) (BANGS T/C 5) – Walk like an Egyptian (dance mix).
   (12") (BANGS Q5) – ('A'side) / Bangles hitmix.
   (c-s) (BANGS M5) – ('A'side) / Going down to Liverpool / Hero takes a fall / James.
May 89. (7"/7"sha-pic-d/c-s) (BANGS/+P/M 6) <68744> **BE WITH YOU. / LET IT GO** | 23 | 30 |
   (12"+=/cd-s+=) (BANGS T/C 6) – In your room (extended).
   (pic-cd-s+=) (BANGS D6) – Manic Monday (extended California mix).
Oct 89. (7") (BANGS 7) **I'LL SET YOU FREE. / WATCHING THE SKY** | 74 | |
   (12"+=/cd-s+=) (BANGS T/C 7) – Walking down your street (extended).
May 90. (cd/c/lp) (466769-2/-4/-1) <46125> **BANGLES' GREATEST HITS** (compilation) | 4 | 97 |
   – Hero takes a fall / Going down to Liverpool / Manic Monday / If she knew what she wants / Walk like an Egyptian / Walking down your street / Following / Hazy shade of winter / In your room / Eternal flame / Be with you / I'll set you free / Everything I wanted / Where were you when I needed you. (re-iss. May95 + Dec95 on 'Columbia' cd/c;)
May 90. (7") (BANGS 8) **WALK LIKE AN EGYPTIAN (remix). / ('A'-Ozymandias remix)** | 73 | |
   (c-s+=/12"+=/cd-s+=) (BANGS M/T/C 8) – ('A'extended dance) / ('A'dub) / ('A'acappella).

—— In the autumn of 1990 they disbanded; HOFFS went solo releasing two albums, 'WHEN YOU'RE A BOY' (1991) and 'SUSANNA HOFFS' (1996)

– compilations, etc. –

Apr 99. (cd) Columbia; (494469-2) **THE BEST OF THE BANGLES** — | | |

Tony BANKS / BANKSTATEMENT
(see under ⇒ GENESIS)

BARCLAY JAMES HARVEST

Formed: Oldham, Lancashire, England ... Autumn 1966 by art school students JOHN LEES and STUART WOLSTENHOLME. After their initial 45 on 'Parlophone', EMI subsequently found a new home for them on their aptly named 'Harvest' label. In 1970, their eponymous debut album was recorded with a full orchestra conducted by ROBERT GODFREY, their typically prog-rock sound proving a hit with the student fraternity. However their heavy use of mellotron proved none too popular with the critics of the day, who at times lambasted them for their neo-classical pretensions. In fact they were unfairly described by the music press as "the poor man's MOODY BLUES". Their 1971 follow-up 'ONCE AGAIN', featured what was to become their finest song, 'MOCKINGBIRD', a combination of both tender harmonies and quality instrumentation. They carried on in the same vein with two other albums 'BJH AND OTHER SHORT STORIES' & 'BABY JAMES HARVEST', leading to a contract with 'Polydor' in 1974. Finally gaining wide-scale recognition upon the releases of their 4th album 'EVERYONE IS EVERYBODY ELSE', it remains a mystery to most why it didn't chart. By this stage their live appeal was such that 'Polydor' subsequently released a double live set, a piece of work that encompassed everything they'd been working towards during their career. Although Britain and the States had somehow ignored them, they won many converts in Europe, especially Germany, who were always interested in anything prog-rock or symphonic. With the onset of the "new wave" explosion, they were forced into the margins, although they retained a loyal family of fans.
• **Trivia:** A CONCERT FOR THE PEOPLE was recorded near the Berlin Wall and was transmitted live on German TV and radio.

Album rating: BARCLAY JAMES HARVEST (*6) / ONCE AGAIN (*7) / BJH AND OTHER SHORT STORIES (*6) / BABY JAMES HARVEST (*6) / EVERYONE IS EVERYBODY ELSE (*8) / BARCLAY JAMES HARVEST LIVE (*8) / TIME HONOURED GHOSTS (*5) / OCTOBERON (*5) / GONE TO EARTH (*7) / LIVE TAPES (*4) / EYES OF THE UNIVERSE (*4) / TURN OF THE TIDE (*5) / A CONCERT FOR THE PEOPLE (BERLIN) (*4) / RING OF CHANGES (*5) / VICTIM OF CIRCUMSTANCE (*5) / FACE TO FACE (*5) / THE COMPACT BARCLAY JAMES HARVEST compilation (*8) / GLASNOST (*4) / WELCOME TO THE SHOW (*5) / CAUGHT IN THE LIGHT (*5) / RIVER OF DREAMS (*3)

STUART 'WOOLY' WOLSTENHOLME (b.15 Apr'47) – keyboards, vocals / **JOHN LEES** (b.13 Jan'48) – guitar, vocals, wind / **LES HOLROYD** (b.12 Mar'48, Bolton, England) – bass, vocals / **MELVIN PRITCHARD** (b.20 Jan'48) – drums

		Parlophone	Sire
Apr 68.	(7") (R 5693) <4105> **EARLY MORNING. / MR. SUNSHINE**	-	-

		Harvest	Sire
Jun 69.	(7") (HAR 5003) <4112> **BROTHER THRUSH. / POOR WAGES**	-	-
Jun 70.	(lp) (SHVL 770) <SES 97026> **BARCLAY JAMES HARVEST**		
	– Taking some time on / Mother dear / The sun will never shine / When the world was waken / Good love child / The iron maiden / Dark now my sky.		
Aug 70.	(7") (HAR 5025) **TAKING SOME TIME ON. / THE IRON MAIDEN**		-
Feb 71.	(lp) (SHVL 788) <4904> **ONCE AGAIN**		
	– She said / Happy old world / Song for dying / Galadriel / Mockingbird / Vanessa Simmons / Ball and chain / Lady loves. (quad-lp Jul73; Q4SHVL 788) (re-iss. Jul83 on 'Fame' lp/c; FA/TCFA 3073) (cd-iss. Mar99 on 'Brimstone'; BRIM 002)		
Feb 71.	(7") (HAR 5034) **MOCKINGBIRD. / VANESSA SIMMONS**		-
Nov 71.	(lp) (SHVL 794) <5904> **BJH AND OTHER SHORT STORIES**		
	– Ow / Harry's song / Ursula / Little lapwing / Song with no meaning / Blue John's blues / The poet / After the day.		
Apr 72.	(7") (HAR 5051) **I'M OVER YOU. / CHILD OF MAN**		-
Sep 72.	(7"; as BOMBADIL) (HAR 5056) **BREATHLESS. / WHEN THE CITY SLEEPS**		-
	(re-iss. Mar75; HAR 5095)		

		Harvest	Harvest
Oct 72.	(7") (HAR 5058) **THANK YOU. / MEDICINE MAN**		
Oct 72.	(lp) (SHSP 4023) <11145> **BABY JAMES HARVEST**		Feb73
	– Crazy (over you) / Delph town morn / Summer soldier / Thank you / One hundred thousand smiles out / Moonwater. (re-iss. May85 on 'E.M.I.' lp/c; ATAK/TC-ATAK 8) (re-iss. Mar87 on 'Fame' lp/c; FA/TC-FA 3172)		
May 73.	(7") (HAR 5060) **ROCK AND ROLL WOMAN. / THE JOKER**		

		Polydor	Capitol
May 74.	(7") (2058 474) **POOR BOY BLUES. / CRAZY CITY**		-
Jun 74.	(lp)(c) (2383 286)(3170 186) <PD 6508> **EVERYONE IS EVERYBODY ELSE**		
	– Child of the universe / Negative Earth / Paper wings / The great 1974 mining disaster / Crazy city / See me see you / Poor boy blues / Mill boys / For no one. (re-iss. Aug83 lp/c; SPE LP/MC 11) (cd-iss. Nov87 & Feb92; 833 448-2)		
Jul 74.	(7") <15104> **CHILD OF THE UNIVERSE. / CRAZY CITY**		
Nov 74.	(d-lp) (2683 052) **BARCLAY JAMES HARVEST – LIVE (live)**	40	-
	– Summer soldier / Medicine man / Crazy city / After the day / The great 1974 mining disaster / Galadriel / Negative Earth / She said / Paper wings / For no one / Mockingbird. (cd-iss. Jul91 on 'Connoisseur'; VSOPCD 164)		
Oct 75.	(lp) (2383 361) <6617> **TIME HONOURED GHOSTS**	32	
	– In my life / Sweet Jesus / Titles / Jonathan / Beyond the grave / Song for you / Hymn for the children / Moon girl / One night. (re-iss. Aug83 lp/c; SPE LP/MC 12) (cd-iss. Apr87 & Feb92; 831 543-2)		
Nov 75.	(7") (2058 660) <15118> **TITLES. / SONG FOR YOU**		

		Polydor	M.C.A.
Oct 76.	(lp) (2442 144) <2234> **OCTOBERON**	19	
	– Polk street rag / Suicide? / May day / Ra / Believe in me / The world goes on / Rock'n'roll star. (re-iss. Aug83 lp/c; SPE LP/MC 13) (cd-iss. Jun84 & Feb92; 821 930-2)		

Nov 76.	(7") <40690> **POLK STREET RAG. / ROCK'N'ROLL STAR**	-	
Mar 77.	(7"ep) (2229 198) **LIVE EP (live)**	49	-
	– Rock'n'roll star / Medicine man (part 1 & 2).		
Jul 77.	(7") (2058 904) <40795> **HYMN. / OUR KID'S KID**		
Sep 77.	(lp)(c) (2442 148)(3170 460) <2302> **GONE TO EARTH**	30	
	– Hymn / Love is like a violin / Friend of mine / Poor man's Moody Blues / Hard hearted woman / Sea of tranquility / Spirit on the water / Leper's song / Taking me higher. (cd-iss. Mar83; 800 092-2)		
Mar 78.	(7") (2059 002) **FRIEND OF MINE. / SUICIDE**		
Apr 78.	(d-lp/d-c) (PODV/+C 2001) **LIVE TAPES (live)**		-
	– Child of the universe / Rock'n'roll star / Poor man's Moody Blues / Mockingbird / Hard hearted woman / One night / Take me higher / Suicide? / Crazy city / Jonathan / For no one / Polk street rag / Hymn. (d-cd iss.Feb85 & Sep99; 821 523-2)		

		Polydor	Polydor
Sep 78.	(lp/c) (POLD/+C 5006) <6173> **XII**	31	
	– Fantasy: Loving is easy / Berlin / Classics: A tale of two sixties / Turning in circles / Fact: The closed shop / In search of England / Sip of wine / Harbour / Science fiction: Nova Lepidoptera / Giving it up / Fiction: The streets of San Francisco. (cd-iss. Jan85; 821 941-2)		
Nov 78.	(7",7"blue) (POSP 012) **LOVING IS EASY. / POLK STREET RAG**		
Jan 79.	(7") **LOVING IS EASY. / TURNING IN CIRCLES**	-	

—— Trimmed to a trio plus session men when WOLSTENHOLME went solo / **KEVIN McALEA** – keyboards (ex-BEES MAKE HONEY, ex-KATE BUSH)

Nov 79.	(lp/c) (POLD/+C 5029) <6267> **EYES OF THE UNIVERSE**		
	– Love on the line / Alright get down boogie (Mu ala rusic) / The song they love to sing / Skin flicks / Sperratus / Capricorn / Play to the world. (cd-iss. Jun84; 821 591-2)		
Dec 79.	(7") (POSP 97) **LOVE ON THE LINE. / ALRIGHT GET DOWN BOOGIE (MU ALA RUSIC)**	63	
Feb 80.	(7") (POSP 140) **CAPRICORN. / BERLIN**		
Nov 80.	(7") (POSP 195) **LIFE IS FOR LIVING. / SHADES OF B. HILL**	61	
May 81.	(lp/c) (POLD/+C 5040) **TURN OF THE TIDE**	55	
	– Waiting on the borderline / How do you feel now / Back to the wall / Highway for fools / Echoes and shadows / Death of the city / I'm like a train / Doctor doctor / Life is for living / In memory of the martyrs. (cd-iss. Mar83 & Feb92; 800 013-2)		
Jun 82.	(lp/c) (POLD/+C 5052) **A CONCERT FOR THE PEOPLE (BERLIN)**	15	-
	– Berlin / Loving is easy / Mockingbird / Sip of wine / Nova Lepidoptera / In memory of the martyrs / Life is for living / Child of the universe / Hymn. (cd-iss. Mar83 & Feb92; 800 026-2)		
May 83.	(lp/c)(cd) (POLH/+C 3)(811 638-2) **RING OF CHANGES**	36	-
	– Fifties child / Looking from the outside / Teenage heart / High wire / Midnight drug / Waiting for the right time / Just a day away / Paradiso dos cavalos / Ring of changes. (cd-iss. Feb92 cd/c; 811 638-2/-4)		
May 83.	(7") (POSP 585) **JUST A DAY AWAY. / ROCK'N'ROLL LADY (live)**	68	
	(7"sha-pic-d) (POPPX 585) – ('A'side) / Looking from the outside.		
Oct 83.	(7") (POSP 640) **WAITING FOR THE RIGHT TIME. / BLOW ME DOWN**		
	(12"+=) (POSPX 640) – ('A'extended).		
Mar 84.	(7"/7"sha-pic-d) (POSP/+P 674) **VICTIMS OF CIRCUMSTANCE. / ('A'instrumental)**		
	(ext.12"+=) (POSPX 674) – Love on the line (live).		
Apr 84.	(lp/c)(cd) (POLD/+C 5135)(817 950-2) **VICTIMS OF CIRCUMSTANCE**	33	-
	– Sideshow / Hold on / Rebel woman / Say you'll stay / For your love / Victim of circumstance / Inside my nightmare / Watching you / I've got a feeling.		
Sep 84.	(7") (POSP 705) **I'VE GOT A FEELING. / REBEL WOMAN**		
Nov 86.	(7") (POSP 834) **HE SAID LOVE. / ON THE WINGS OF LOVE**		
	(12"+=) (POSPX 834) – Hymn (live).		
Feb 87.	(lp/c)(cd) (POLD/+C 5209)(831 483-2) **FACE TO FACE**	65	
	– Prisoner of your love / He said love / Alone in the night / Turn the key / Guitar blues / African / Following me / All my life / Panic / Kiev. (cd+=) – On the wings of love.		
Apr 88.	(lp/c)(cd) (POLD/+C 5219)(835 590-2) **GLASNOST (live)**		
	– Berlin / Alone in the night / Hold on / African / On the wings of love / Poor man's Moody Blues / Love on the line / Medicine man / Kiev / Hymn / Turn the key / He said love.		
Feb 90.	(7"; as BJH) (PO 67) **CHEAP THE BULLET. / SHADOWS ON THE SKY**		-
	(12"+=) (PZ 67) – Berlin (live).		
	(cd-s+=) (PZCD 67) – Alone in the night (live) / Hold on (live).		
Mar 90.	(cd/c/lp; as BJH) (841 751-2/-4/-1) **WELCOME TO THE SHOW**		
	– The life you lead / Lady Macbeth / Cheap the bullet / Welcome to the show / John Lennon's guitar / African nights / Psychedelic child / Where do we go / If love is king / Halfway to freedom.		
May 92.	(7"/c-s) (PO/+CS 208) **STAND UP. / LIFE IS FOR LIVING (live)**		-
	(cd-s+=) (PZCDB 208) – Alone in the night / Poor man's Moody Blues (live).		
	(cd-s) (PZCD 208) – ('A'side) / John Lennon's guitar (live) / Play to the world (live) / ('A'extended).		
Jun 93.	(cd/c) (519 303-2/-4) **CAUGHT IN THE LIGHT**		
	– Who do we think we are? / Knoydart / Copii Romania / Back to Earth / Cold war / Forever yesterday / The great unknown / Spud-u-like / Silver wings / Once more / A matter of time / Ballad of Denshaw Mill.		

		Eagle	not iss.
1997.	(cd) (535576-2) **RIVER OF DREAMS**	-	German
Feb 99.	(cd/c) (EAB CD/MC 52) **NEXUS**		-

– compilations, etc. –

on 'Harvest' unless otherwise mentioned

Sep 72.	(lp) EMI Starline; (SRS 5126) **EARLY MORNING ONWARDS**		-
	– Early morning / Poor wages / Brother thrush / Mr. Sunshine / Taking some time		

on / Mother dear / Mockingbird / Song with no meaning / I'm over you / Child of man / After the day. *(cd-iss. Mar99 on 'Brimstone'; BRIM 001)*

Mar 75.	(7") *(HAR 5094)* **MOCKINGBIRD. / GALADRIEL**	☐	-
Jan 77.	(lp) *(SHSM 2013)* **THE BEST OF BARCLAY JAMES HARVEST** *(re-iss. Aug86 on 'E.M.I.' lp/c; ATAK/TC-ATAK 95)*	☐	-
Sep 79.	(lp) *(SHSM 2023)* **THE BEST OF BARCLAY JAMES HARVEST VOL.2**	☐	-
Feb 81.	(lp) *(SHSM 2033)* **THE BEST OF BARCLAY JAMES HARVEST VOL.3**	☐	-
Nov 85.	(cd) *Polydor; (825 895-2)* **THE COMPACT STORY OF BARCLAY JAMES HARVEST**	☐	-
Oct 87.	(cd) *E.M.I.; (CDP 746 709-2)* **ANOTHER ARABLE PARABLE**	☐	-
Dec 90.	(cd/c) *Connoisseur; (VSOP CD/MC 140)* **ALONE WE FLY** – Crazy city / For no one / Mockingbird / Hymn / Our kid's kid / Berlin / Loving is easy / Love on the line / Rock'n'roll lady / Shades of B Hill / Fifties child / Waiting for the right time / Blow me down / Sideshow / He said love / Guitar blues.	☐	-
Mar 91.	(d-cd/d-c/d-lp) *Harvest; (CD/TC+/EN 5014)* **THE HARVEST YEARS**	☐	-
Jun 92.	(cd) *Polydor; (513 587-2)* **THE BEST OF BARCLAY JAMES HARVEST**	☐	-
Dec 92.	(cd) *Beat Goes On; (BGOCD 152)* **BARCLAY JAMES HARVEST / ONCE AGAIN** *(re-iss. Oct95 on 'One Way';)*	☐	-
Dec 92.	(cd) *Beat Goes On; (BGOCD 160)* **BJH & OTHER SHORT STORIES / BABY JAMES HARVEST** *(re-iss. Oct95 on 'One Way';)*	☐	-
May 93.	(cd/c) *Spectrum; (550029-2/-4)* **SORCERERS & KEEPERS**	☐	-
Feb 96.	(4xcd-box) *EMI-Barclay; (CDBARCLAY 1)* **FOUR ORIGINALS** – (first 4 albums)	☐	-
Aug 96.	(cd) *Connoisseur; VSOPCD 228* **ENDLESS DREAM**	☐	-
Mar 97.	(cd) *Disky; (DC 86721-2)* **MOCKINGBIRD**	☐	-

BARENAKED LADIES

Formed: Scarborough, Toronto, Canada ... 1988 by songwriting college students ED ROBERTSON and STEVEN PAGE, both having cut their teeth in a RUSH covers band; JIM CREEGGAN, his brother ANDREW and TYLER STEWART later forming the complete line-up. This kooky and incredibly strange North American combo didn't reach the level of international success until 1998, and before then had never cultivated their talents outside their native Canada. The band began playing in colleges and dingy venues in the heart of Toronto's cosmopolitan scene, when, after a solid year of performing, they respectively discovered that they had created a huge local following. BARENAKED LADIES decided to take their sublime blend of pop/rock/rap/folk to eager crowds in Europe and the remainder of Canada before releasing the now cult debut EP 'THE YELLOW TAPE' (featuring 'BE MY YOKO ONO'). It climbed the charts on their home soil, becoming the first independent Canadian release to go gold! Following this minor ego boost, the group subsequently signed a contract with 'Reprise' records a year later, issuing the first album proper 'GORDON' (1992), which would see the BNLs earning a No.1 spot in the official Canadian charts. 'GORDON' fused structured melodies and graceful pop with 'Sgt. Pepper'-esque dizziness and a little touch of BRIAN WILSON psychedelic rock; it went on to stay a further 8 weeks at the top of the charts (bubbled under the US Top 100). Sophomore set, 'MAYBE YOU SHOULD DRIVE', wasn't released until 1994 and included top singles 'JANE' and the side splitting attempt at a love song, 'MY ALTERNATIVE GIRLFRIEND', both now standard BARENAKED LADIES traits. Having steadily climbed into the US Top 60, the group went on to score with their first Stateside hit 'THE OLD APARTMENT' in the Spring of '97 (taken from their patchy long-player of '96 'BORN ON A PIRATE SHIP'). Appearances on various talk shows, including 'Showbiz Today' and the 'David Letterman Show', helped the band receive international acclaim (with a televised New Year's party apparently reaching a drunken riotous plateau). By the release of their third studio album, 'ROCK SPECTACLE' (1997), the band were now reaching the mainstream by selling out dates across America and Europe. After a well deserved break, the BARENAKED LADIES embarked on what was to become their breakthrough instalment, 'STUNT' (1998), which was released to great critical and audience acclaim – of course its success arrived after smash hit single 'ONE WEEK'. The platter displayed an old-fashioned formula while using rimshot drums with nifty rap and a melodic break where lead singer CREEGGAN described life's little mishaps and misfortunes after a one-night stand. All in all, an entertaining single and equally good album where The BARENAKED LADIES had proved themselves to MOR audiences whilst suffering a post ironic chump-change. The group subsequently devoted a track to the 'Ed TV' soundtrack, and although their song was popular, it didn't help the film's chances at the box office.

Album rating: GORDON (*7) / MAYBE YOU SHOULD DRIVE (*6) / BORN ON A PIRATE SHIP (*7) / ROCK SPECTACLE (*6) / STUNT (*5)

ED ROBERTSON (b.25 Oct'70) – vocals, guitar / **STEVEN PAGE** (b.22 Jun'70) – guitar, vocals

		not iss.	own
1989.	(c-ep) **BUCK NAKED**	-	-
—	added **JIM CREEGGAN** (b.12 Feb'70) – bass, keyboards / **ANDREW CREEGGAN** (b. 4 Jul'71) – congas		
1990.	(c-ep) **BARENAKED LUNCH**	☐	
—	added **TYLER STEWART** (b.21 Sep'67) – drums		
1991.	(c-ep) **THE YELLOW TAPE**	☐	☐

		Reprise	Sire
Aug 92.	(cd/c) *<(7599 26956-2/-4)>* **GORDON** – Hello city / Enid / Grade 9 / Brian Wilson / Be my Yoko Ono / Wrap your arms around me / What a good boy / King of bedside manor / Box set / I love you / New kid on the block / Blame it on me / The flag / If I had $1,000,000 / Crazy.	☐	☐
Jul 93.	(7"/c-s) **IF I HAD $1,000,000. / GRADE 9** (12"+=/cd-s+=) *(W 0186 T/CD)* – Crazy.	☐	☐
Aug 94.	(cd/c) *<(9362 45709-2/-4)>* **MAYBE YOU SHOULD DRIVE** – A / Life, in a nutshell / Great provider / You will be waiting / Jane / Intermittently / These apples / Everything old is new again / Alternative girlfriend / Am I the only one? / Little tiny song / The wrong man was convicted.	57	☐
Aug 94.	(7"/c-s) *(W 0262/+C)* **JANE. / WHAT A GOOD BOY** (cd-s+=) *(W 0262CD)* – Great provider (demo).	☐	☐
—	ANDREW departed and PAGE moved to lead vocals (**KEVIN HEARN** – keyboards; was to join on a part-time basis at first)		
Jul 96.	(c-s) *(W 0342C)* **IF I HAD $1,000,000 / TRUST ME** (cd-s+=) *(W 0342CD)* – Shoe box.	☐	☐
Jul 96.	(cd/c) *<(9362 46128-2/-4)>* **BORN ON A PIRATE SHIP** – Break your heart / The old apartment / Spider in my room / Stomach vs. heart / This is where it ends / When I fall / In the drink / Call me calmly / I live with it every day / I know / Just a toy / I live it every day / The same thing / Shoe box / Straw hat and old dirty Hank.	☐	☐
Apr 97.	(cd-s) **THE OLD APARTMENT /**	-	88
Oct 97.	(cd-s) *<17290>* **BRIAN WILSON / BREAK YOUR HEART / BACK**	-	68
Oct 97.	(cd/c) *<46393>* **ROCK SPECTACLE** – Brian Wilson / Straw hat and old dirt Hank / Break your heart / Jane / When I fall / Hello city / What a good boy / The old apartment / Life, in a nutshell / These apples / If I had a $1,000,000.	-	86
Feb 99.	(c-s/cd-s) *(W 468 C/CD)* *<17174>* **ONE WEEK / WHEN YOU DREAM (demo) / SHOEBOX (live)**	5	2 Sep98
Feb 99.	(cd/c) *<(9362 46963-2/-4)>* **STUNT** – One week / It's all been done / Light up my room / I'll be that girl / Leave / Alcohol / Call and answer / In the car / Never is enough / Who needs sleep? / Told you so / Some fantastic (ivory and ivory) / When you dream. *(special d-cd Nov99 +=; 9362 47507-2)* – Brian Wilson (2000) / Old apartment (live) / Jane (live) / When I fall (live) / If I had $1,000,000 (live) / Straw hat and old dirty Hank (live) / Brian Wilson.	24	3 Jul98
May 99.	(c-s/cd-s) *(W 476 C/CD)* *<44602>* **IT'S ALL BEEN DONE / BRIAN WILSON (live) / THE OLD APARTMENT (live)**	28	44 Dec98
Jul 99.	(c-s/cd-s) *(W 498 C/CD2)* *<44710>* **CALL AND ANSWER / IF I HAD $1,000,000 / JANE (live)** (cd-s) *(W 498CD1)* – ('A'side) / One week (Big Beat mix) / One week (Paul's mix).	52	☐ Jun99
Nov 99.	(c-s/cd-s) *(W 511 C/CD1)* **BRIAN WILSON (mixes; 2000 / album version / live from Rock Spectacle / instrumental)**	73	-

Lou BARLOW (see under ⇒ DINOSAUR JR.)

Syd BARRETT

Born: ROGER KEITH BARRETT, 6 Jan'46, Cambridge, England. Earned the nickname SID (which he later changed to SYD), after regulars at the local Riverside Jazz Club found out his surname and christened him after an old drummer from the area, SID BARRET. SYD was talented enough to secure a place at the prestigious Camberwell Art School in 1963 and once in London, he teamed up with his old friend ROGER WATERS, who had asked him to join his band The SCREAMING ABDABS. At SYD's suggestion, the band renamed themselves PINK FLOYD after two Georgia bluesmen featured on an old record he owned. Turned onto LSD by a friend, he became fascinated with the mysteries of the Universe, even carrying around a Times Astronomical Atlas. This obsession would later inspire such FLOYD classics as 'ASTRONOMY DOMINE' and 'INTERSTELLAR OVERDRIVE'. The latter's main riff was famously derived from a chord pattern SYD worked out after hearing manager PETER JENNER attempting to hum LOVE's version of BURT BACHARACH's 'My Little Red Book'. The 1967 album 'THE PIPER AT THE GATES OF DAWN' on which these two tracks appeared, made the group and especially BARRETT, major league pop stars. This was something that did SYD's increasingly erratic mental health no good whatsoever. By the time of the album's release, he had moved into the infamous Cromwell Road flat in London, living on a daily diet of hallucinogenics and was beginning to develop a piercing stare, which would scare even the most hardened person in his company. At EMI's request, BARRETT recorded two further tracks, 'SCREAM THY LAST SCREAM' and 'VEGETABLE MAN', which were unsurprisingly rejected, EMI staff producer NORMAN SMITH dubbing them "lunatic ravings". His penultimate offering for FLOYD, 'APPLES AND ORANGES', flopped, and SYD's mental condition deteriorated further. After missing some shows and performances, WATERS eventually made it clear he was surplus to requirements. His last effort with PINK FLOYD, 'JUGBAND BLUES', appeared after his departure, on the second FLOYD album 'A SAUCERFUL OF SECRETS' (mid-68). It was his last poignant statement for FLOYD, a self-diagnosis of his encroaching schizophrenia. EMI (actually 'Harvest') still had enough confidence in SYD to offer him a solo deal, as he set about recording his debut, 'THE MADCAP LAUGHS'. Released early in 1970 after a laborious year in the studio, it featured drummer NICK MASON and other FLOYD-ians, thus its brief entry into the UK Top 40. Despite SYD being high on the tranquiliser Mandrax, the album had its moments, with the likes of 'OCTOPUS', 'DARK GLOBE', 'TERRAPIN', 'NO GOOD TRYIN' and 'LONG GONE', making up for the other lost-in-the-ether tracks. The hastily recorded 'BARRETT', released later the same year, used a band featuring DAVE GILMOUR (the friend who replaced him in PINK FLOYD), RICK

WRIGHT and JERRY SHIRLEY, giving him some cohesion, and although it was more assured in depth, it lacked the fragility of its predecessor. The album was poorly received and SYD retreated to the cellar of his mother's home in Cambridge. He resurfaced in 1972 as part of the doomed STARS project (with TWINK & JACK MONK), before finally giving up music altogether. He never fully recovered from his debilitating mental illness and tragically, at the time of writing, he's become almost blind due to diabetes related problems. Whether the drugs actually caused his decline or merely assisted it is something that will no doubt continue to be debated long into the future, although you can be sure SYD won't care to listen. A flawed genius whose legend and influence grows stronger with each passing year, SYD BARRETT was the whimsical child-like star, burning brightly in a kaleidoscope of technicolour sound, before dropping out into a haze of drug-induced psychosis. He has since been tributed and stylised by many, including TELEVISION PERSONALITIES, ROBYN HITCHCOCK and The LEGENDARY PINK DOTS. • Trivia: PINK FLOYD paid homage to SYD on their album SHINE ON YOU CRAZY DIAMOND track from album 'WISH YOU WERE HERE'. SYD attended these sessions but didn't contribute.

Album rating: THE MADCAP LAUGHS (*8) / BARRETT (*6) / OPEL collection (*6)

SYD BARRETT – vocals, guitar; augmented by **DAVID GILMOUR + ROGER WATERS** with **MIKE RATLEDGE** – keyboards / **HUGH HOPPER** – bass / **ROBERT WYATT** – drums (all of SOFT MACHINE) plus **JOHN 'WILLIE' WATSON + JERRY SHIRLEY** – rhythm (latter of HUMBLE PIE)

	Harvest	Harvest
Oct 69. (7") (HAR 5009) **OCTOPUS. / GOLDEN HAIR**		
Jan 70. (lp) (SHVL 765) <SABB 11314> **THE MADCAP LAUGHS**	40	

– Terrapin / No good trying / Love you / No man's land / Dark globe / Here I go / Octopus / Golden Hair / Long gone / She took a long cold look / Feel / If it's in you / Late night. (cd-iss. Oct87; CDP 746 607-2) (re-iss. cd Jun94; CDGO 2053) (re-iss. Feb97 on 'E.M.I.'; LPCENT 1)

—— SYD retained GILMOUR, SHIRLEY + WILSON adding **RICK WRIGHT** – keyboards (of PINK FLOYD) and guest on one **VIC SAYWELL** – tuba

Nov 70. (lp) (SHSP 4007) **BARRETT**		-

– Baby lemonade / Love song / Dominoes / It is obvious / Rats / Maisie / Gigolo aunt / Waving my arms in the air / Wined and dined / Wolfpack / Effervescing elephant / I never lied to you. (cd-iss. May87; CDP 746 606-2) (re-iss. cd Jun94; CDGO 2054)

—— His solo career ended and he formed short-lived STARS early in '72, with **TWINK** – drums (ex-PINK FAIRIES) + **JACK MONK** – bass (they made no recordings)

—— In 1982, he was living with his mother having hung up guitar.

– compilations, others, etc. –

Sep 74. (d-lp) Harvest; (SHDW 404) **SYD BARRETT**		-

– (THE MADCAP LAUGHS & BARRETT).

Jan 88. (12"ep) Strange Fruit; (SFPS/+CD 043) **THE PEEL SESSIONS** (24.2.70)		-

– Terrapin / Gigolo aunt / Baby lemonade / Two of a kind / Effervescing elephant. (cd re-iss. Sep95; same)

Oct 88. (cd)(c)(lp) Harvest; (CDP 791 206-2)(TC+/SHSP 4126) **OPEL** (recorded 68-70)		

– Opel / Clowns and daggers (Octopus) / Rats / Golden hair (vocal) / Dollyrocker / Word song / Wined and dined / Swan Lee (Silas Lang) / Birdie hop / Let's split / Lanky (part 1) / Wouldn't you miss me / Golden hair (instrumental). (re-iss. cd Jun94; CDGO 2055) (lp re-iss. Dec99 on 'Simply Vinyl'; SVLP 153)

Apr 93. (3xcd-box) E.M.I.; (SYDBOX 1) **CRAZY DIAMOND – THE COMPLETE SYD BARRETT**		

– (all 3 albums above)

Apr 94. (cd) Cleopatra; (CLEO 5771-2) **OCTOPUS**		-

BASEMENT JAXX

Formed: South London, England ... 1993 by producer & DJ duo SIMON RATCLIFFE and FELIX BUXTON. The pair met at a Thames party organised by the latter on a riverboat. After conversation, sparks flew between the two DJs and they promptly set up 'Atlantic Jaxx' records in the summer of 1994. The pair were astounded when their idol and key influence TONY HUMPHRIES played 'DA UNDERGROUND' (a song from their first EP with the same title) to near annihilation on his 'Mix-show' in 1995. Later the same year the group also released 'SAMBA MAGIC' on single and conscripted vocalist CORRINA JOSEPHS into the outfit. 1996 was spent doing remixes for The PET SHOP BOYS, 'LIL' MO YIN' and various other artists. The collective also released an eponymous EP, which saw the track 'FLY LIFE' reach the British Top 20 and go on to become a massive house anthem. Relentlessly being pursued by major labels, RATCLIFFE and BUXTON settled for imprint 'X.L.' (home of The PRODIGY), where the band went on to issue their first major album 'REMEDY' (1999). The obvious highlight was the rare 12" single, 'SAME OLD SHOW', a sampletastic "rude girl!" beatbox of a song that incorporated The Selector's 1980 hit 'On My Radio'. Two singles, 'RED ALERT' and the bass-breaking 'RENDEZ-VU', both became massive Ibiza and London house tracks, mixing styles as far apart as Chicago (drum'n'bass) to eclectic Latin disco-funk, the scope was undeniably wide.

Album rating: ATLANTIC JAXX – A COMPILATION (*6) / REMEDY (*9)

SIMON RATCLIFFE + FELIX BUXTON

	Atlantic Jaxx	unknown
Mar 96. (12"; by CORRINA JOSEPH) (JAXX 005) **I WANNA GET DOWN (WHEN U GET DOWN). /**		-
Jun 96. (12"ep) (JAXX 001) **BASEMENT JAXX E.P. 1**		
Jul 96. (12"ep) (JAXX 002) **BASEMENT JAXX E.P. 2**		

– Be free / Deep jackin' / I'm thru with you / Dusk till dawn.

Jul 96. (12"ep) (JAXX 003) **SUMMER DAZE E.P.**		

– Paradise / Phase 2 hi / Aprino jam / Samba magic.

| Jul 96. (12"ep; by RATCLIFFE) (JAXX 004) **RATCLIFFE E.P.** | | |
| Jul 96. (12"ep) (JAXX 006) **BASEMENT JAXX E.P. 3** | | |

– Daluma / Jus becuz / Fly life / Slide slide.

Nov 96. (12"; by HEARTISTS) (JAXX 009) **BELO HORIZONTI. /**		-

(re-iss. Jul97 c-s/12"/cd-s; VCR C/T/D 23)

Feb 97. (12"ep) (JAXX 008) **SLEAZYCHEEKS E.P.**		

– Ennao / Moradi / Get down, get horny / Jump / Stanley.

Mar 97. (12"ep) (JAXX 010) **URBAN HAZE E.P.**		

– City people / Urban haze / Set yo' body free / Raw shit.

	Multiply	unknown
May 97. (c-s/12"/cd-s) (CA/12/CD MULTY 21) **FLY LIFE (mixes)**	19	
(12") (12MULTY 21X) – ('A'mixes).		

	Banana Krew	not iss.
Aug 98. (12") (001) **SAME OLD SHOW. / AUTOMATIC**		-
	X.L.	Astralwerks
Nov 98. (12") (JAXL 001) **RED ALERT. / YO-YO**		-
Apr 99. (12")(cd-s) (XLT 100)(XLS 100CD2) <6273> **RED ALERT (mixes; Jaxx club / Eric Morillo & Harry Choo Choo Romero dub / Steve Gurley)**	5	Jul99
(cd-s) (XLS 100CD) <6274> – ('A'side) / Razocaine / ('A'-Jaxx nite dub).		
May 99. (cd/c/d-lp) (XL CD/MC/LP 129) <6270> **REMEDY**	4	Aug99

– Rendez-vu / Yo-yo / Jump n' shout / U can't stop me / Jaxxalude / Red alert / Jazzalude / Always be there / Sneakalude / Same old show / Bingo bango / Gemilude / Stop 4 love / Don't give up / Being with U.

Jul 99. (c-s) (XLC 110) <6281> **RENDEZ-VU / MUSIC KEEPS ON PLAYIN' (Miracles mix of Red Alert)**	4	Oct99
(12") (XLT 110) – All U crazies.		
(cd-s) (XLS 110CD) – (some of above),		
Oct 99. (c-s)(cd-s) (XLC 116)(XLS 116CD) **JUMP N' SHOUT / LA PHOTO / I BEG YOU**	12	
(12") (XLT 116) – ('A'side) / I Beg U / Boo slings dub.		

– compilations, others, etc. –

Oct 97. (cd/d-lp) Atlantic Jaxx; (JAXX CD/LP 001) **ATLANTIC JAXX – A COMPILATION**		

– Intro / Be free / Smaba magic / CORRINA JOSEPH: Live your life / Fly life / Ennao / HEARTISTS: Belo horizonti / CORRINA JOSEPH: Lonely / Set yo' body free / CORRINA JOSEPH: Daluma / RATCLIFFE: Grapesoda / RONNIE RICHARDS: Missing you / Undaground.

Aug 99. (12") Altlantic Jaxx; (JAXX 013) **BETTA DAZE**		

BASH & POP (see under ⇒ REPLACEMENTS)

BASTRO (see under ⇒ SQUIRREL BAIT)

BAUHAUS

Formed: Northampton, England ... late 1978, by PETE MURPHY, DANIEL ASH, DAVID J and KEVIN HASKINS, initially calling themselves BAUHAUS 1919. Obtaining a one-off deal with indie label 'Small Wonder', releasing an 8-minute epic 'BELA LUGOSI'S DEAD', backed with the infamous 'DARK ENTRIES', the latter track subsequently issued as a follow-up 45. A gender-bending but hard-edged collage of glam and punk influences shrouded in gothic horror posturing, BAUHAUS carved out their own inimitable niche in the early 80's post-new wave wasteland. After an album, 'IN THE FLAT FIELD' (1981) and a couple of singles (one a cover of T.Rex's 'TELEGRAM SAM') on '4 a.d.', the band signed to 'Beggars Banquet', scoring a Top 30 hit with debut set, 'MASK' (1981). Featuring the minor hit singles, 'KICK IN THE EYE' and 'THE PASSION OF LOVERS', the album remains their most consistent set. Still, the underground cred was called into question after MURPHY appeared in a TV ad for Maxell tapes later that year. More appropriate, perhaps, was the band's performance of 'BELA LUGOSI'S DEAD' for 1982 vampire film, 'The Hunger' starring the band's boyhood hero, DAVID BOWIE. In fact, it was one of BOWIE's classics, 'ZIGGY STARDUST', that gave BAUHAUS their commercial breakthrough, the single's Top 20 success seeing the accompanying album, 'THE SKY'S GONE OUT' make the UK Top 5. The droning affectations of 'SHE'S IN PARTIES' remains one of the band's most recognisable tracks while the swan song album, 'BURNING FROM THE INSIDE' (1983), saw BAUHAUS signing off on an unsettling, if creatively high point. MURPHY soon reappeared with MICK KARN of JAPAN in a new outfit, DALI'S CAR, although only one album, 'THE WAKING HOUR', surfaced in '84. The singer went on to release a string of albums, surprising many in Britain when he had a US Top 50 placing with 'DEEP', which contained the 1990 hit, 'CUTS YOU UP'. Meanwhile, the rest were enjoying success as LOVE AND ROCKETS (from earlier incarnation of TONES ON TAILS and DAVID J solo) and this trio also took America by storm having had a Top 3 smash, 'SO ALIVE' in '89. With current offshoots failing to sparkle during the rest of the 90's, BAUHAUS decided to officially re-form in mid 1998 for two concerts, which enabled their record label to cash-in on an accompanying best-of collection, 'CRACKLE'. • Covered: THIRD UNCLE (Eno) / WAITING FOR THE MAN (Velvet Underground). PETER MURPHY solo, wrote with STREATHAM and covered; FINAL SOLUTION (Pere Ubu) / THE LIGHT POURS OUT OF ME (Magazine) / FUNTIME (Iggy Pop). LOVE AND ROCKETS covered BALL OF CONFUSION (Temptations) / BODY AND SOUL (trad). DAVID J covered 4 HOURS (ClockDva) / SHIP OF FOOLS (John Cale).

Album rating: IN THE FLAT FIELD (*5) / MASK (*6) / THE SKY'S GONE OUT (*6) / BURNING FROM THE INSIDE (*5) / BAUHAUS 1979-1983 compilation (*9) / CRACKLE collection (*6) / Dali's Car: THE WAKING HOUR (*5) / Pete Murphy: SHOULD THE WORLD FAIL TO FALL APART (*5) / LOVE HYSTERIA (*5) / DEEP (*6) / CASCADE (*4) / Tones On Tails: NIGHT MUSIC compilation (*6) / Love And Rockets: LOVE AND ROCKETS (*5)

PETER MURPHY (b.11 Jul'57) – vocals / **DANIEL ASH** (b.31 Jul'57) – guitar, vocals / **DAVID J** (b. HASKINS, 24 Apr'57) – bass, vocals / **KEVIN HASKINS** (b.19 Jul'60) – drums, percussion

	Small Wonder	not iss.
Aug 79. (12",12"white) (TEENY 2) **BELA LUGOSI'S DEAD. / BOYS / DARK ENTRIES** (re-dist.Mar81 & Mar82; same) (re-iss. Sep86 in various colours; same) (12"pic-d.1987; TEENY 2P) (re-iss. May88 & Jun98, c-s/cd-s; TEENY 2 C/CD)		–

	Axis	not iss.
Jan 80. (7") (AXIS 3) **DARK ENTRIES. / UNTITLED** (re-iss. Feb80 on '4.a.d.'; AD 3) (some mispressed on 'Beggars Banquet'; BEG 37)		–

	4.a.d.	not iss.
Jun 80. (7") (AD 7) **TERROR COUPLE KILL COLONEL. / SCOPES / TERROR COUPLE KILL COLONEL II**		–
Oct 80. (lp) (CAD 13) **IN THE FLAT FIELD** – Double dare / In the flat field / A god in an alcove / Dive / Spy in the cab / Small talk stinks / St. Vitus dance / Stigmata martyr / Nerves. (cd-iss. Apr88 +=; CAD 13CD) – Untitled.	72	
Oct 80. (7") (AD 17) **TELEGRAM SAM. / CROWDS** (12"+=) (AD 17T) – Rosegarden funeral of sores.		–

	Beggars Banquet	A&M
Mar 81. (7"/12") (BEG 54/+T) **KICK IN THE EYE. / SATORI**	59	–
Jun 81. (7") (BEG 59) **THE PASSION OF LOVERS. / 1: 2: 3: 4:**	56	–
Oct 81. (lp/c) (BEGA/BEGC 29) **MASK** – Hair of the dog / The passion of lovers / Of lillies and remains / Dancing / Hollow hills / Kick in the eye / Muscle in plastic / In fear of fear / Man with x-ray eyes / Mask. (re-iss. Feb88 & Jul91 on 'Beggars Banquet-Lowdown' lp/c; BBL/+C 29) (cd-iss. Oct88 & Jul91 +=; BBL 29CD) – Satori / Harry / Earwax / In fear of dub / Kick in the eye.	30	–
Feb 82. (7"ep) (BEG 74) **SEARCHING FOR SATORI** – Kick in the eye / Harry / Earwax. (12"ep+=) (BEG 74T) – In fear of dub.	45	–
Jun 82. (7"/7"pic-d) (BEG 79/+P) **SPIRIT. / TERROR COUPLE KILL COLONEL (live)**	42	–
Sep 82. (7") (BEG 83) **ZIGGY STARDUST. / THIRD UNCLE (live)** (12"+=) (BEG 83T) – Party of the first part / Waiting for the man.	15	–
Oct 82. (d-lp/d-c) (BEGA/BEGC 42) / (BEGA/BEGC 38) <SP 4918> **THE SKY'S GONE OUT / PRESS THE EJECT BUTTON AND GIVE ME THE TAPE (live)** – Third uncle / Silent hedges / In the night / Swing the heartache / Spirit / The three shadows (parts 1, 2, 3) / Silent hedges / All we ever wanted was everything / Exquisite corpse. (re-iss. Feb88 & Jul91 on 'Beggars Banquet-Lowdown' lp/c; BBL/+C 42) (cd-iss. Oct88 & Jul91 +=; BBL 42CD) – Ziggy Stardust / Watch that grandad go / Party of the first part / Spirit (extended). **PRESS THE EJECT BUTTON AND GIVE ME THE TAPE** – In the flat field / Rosegarden funeral of sores / Dancing / Man with the x-ray eyes / Bela Lugosi's dead / Spy in the cab / Kick in the eye / In fear of fear / Hollow hills / Stigmata martyr / Dark entries. (re-iss. Feb88 & Jul91 on 'Beggars Banquet-Lowdown'; BBL/+C 38) (cd-iss. Oct88 & Jul91 +=; BBL 38CD) – Terror couple kill colonel / Double dare / Waiting for the man / Hair of the dog / Of lillies and remains. (free 7"ep with above; BH 1) – SATORI IN PARIS (live)	4	
Jan 83. (7") (BEG 88) **LAGARTIJA NICK. / PARANOIA! PARANOIA!** (12"+=) (BEG 88T) – Watch that grandad go / In the flat field (live).	44	–
Mar 83. (7") <2524> **LAGARTIJA NICK. / ZIGGY STARDUST**	–	
Apr 83. (7"/7"pic-d) (BEG 91/+P) **SHE'S IN PARTIES. / DEPARTURE** (12"+=) (BEG 91T) – Here's the dub.	26	
Jul 83. (lp/c) (BEGA/BEGC 45) **BURNING FROM THE INSIDE** – She's in parties / Antonin Artaud / King Volcano / Who killed Mr. Moonlight? / Slice of life / Honeymoon croon / Kingdom's coming / Burning from the inside / Hope. (re-iss. Feb88 & Jul91 on 'Beggars Banquet-Lowdown' lp/c; BBL/+C 45) (cd-iss. Oct88 & Jul91 +=; BBL 45CD) – Lagartija Nick / Departure / Here's the dub / The sanity assassin.	13	

—— disbanded mid 1983. DAVID J. continued splinter solo venture before forming LOVE AND ROCKETS with DANIEL and KEVIN who had come from own outfit, TONES ON TAIL. MURPHY went solo (see below).

– compilations, others, etc. –

on 'Beggars Banquet' unless mentioned otherwise

Sep 83. (12"ep) 4 a.d. (BAD 312) **THE 4.A.D. SINGLES** – Dark entries / Terror couple kill colonel / Telegram Sam / Rosegarden full of sores / Crowds.		–
Oct 83. (12"ep) (BEG 100E) **THE SINGLES 1981-83** – The passion of lovers / Kick in the eye / Spirit / Ziggy Stardust / Lagartija Nick / She's in parties. (re-iss. Dec88 as 3"pic-cd; BBP 4CD)	52	–
Nov 85. (d-lp/c) (BEGA/BEGC 64) **BAUHAUS 1979-1983** (d-cd-iss. Feb88; BEG 64CD) (re-iss. d-cd Sep95)	36	
Jul 89. (d-lp/c)(d-cd) (BEGA/BEGC 103)(BEGA 103CD) <9804> **SWING THE HEARTACHE** (the BBC sessions) (re-iss. 2xcd Sep95; BBL 64 CD1/CD2)		
Aug 98. (cd) (BEGL 2018CD) **CRACKLE (live)** – Double dare / In the flat field / Passion of lovers / Bela Lugosi's dead / Sanity assassin / She's in parties / Silent hedges / Hollow hills / Mask / Kick in the eye / Ziggy stardust / Dark entries / Terror couple kill colonel / Spirit / Burning from the inside / Crowds.		
Nov 99. (d-lp/d-cd) KK; (KK 200/+CD) **GOTHAM (live)**		

DALI'S CAR

were formed by **PETE MURPHY** – vocals / **MICK KARN** – bass, multi (ex-JAPAN) / **PAUL VINCENT LAWFORD** – rhythms

	Paradox	Beggars Banquet
Oct 84. (7"/7"pic-d) (DOX/+Y 1) **THE JUDGEMENT IS THE MIRROR. / HIGH PLACES** (12"+=) (DOX 1-12) – Lifelong moment.	66	–
Nov 84. (lp/c/cd) (DOX LP/C/CD 1) **THE WAKING HOUR** – Dali's car / His box / Cornwall stone / Artemis / Create and melt / Moonlife / The judgement is the mirror. (re-iss. Jan89 on 'Beggars Banquet-Lowdown'; lp/c)(cd; BBL/+C 52)(BBL 52CD)	84	

PETER MURPHY

went solo, augmented by **JOHN McGEOGH** – guitar / **HOWARD HUGHES** – keyboards / **ROBERT SUAVE** – bass / **STEVE YOUNG** – rhythm prog. / **PLUG** – harmonica

	Beggars Banquet	Beggars Banquet
Nov 85. (7") (BEG 143) **THE FINAL SOLUTION. / THE ANSWER'S CLEAR** (12"+=) (BEG 143T) – ('A'full version). (12"pic-d+=) (BEG 143TP) – ('A'club mix).		
Jun 86. (7"/12") (BEG 162/+T) **BLUE HEART. / CANVAS BEAUTY**		
Jul 86. (lp/c) (BEGA/BEGC 69) **SHOULD THE WORLD FAIL TO FALL APART** – Canvas beauty / The light pours out of me / Confessions / Should the world fail to fall apart / Never man / God . . . sends / Blue heart / The answer is clear / The final solution / Jemal. (re-iss. Jul88 on 'Beggars Banquet-Lowdown' lp/c)(cd; BBL/+C 69)(BBL 69CD)	82	
Oct 86. (7") (BEG 174) **TALE OF THE TONGUE. / SHOULD THE WORLD FAIL TO FALL APART** (12"+=) (BEG 174T) – ('A'-2nd version).		

—— MURPHY brought in **PAUL STATHAM** – co-composer, keyboards (ex-B-MOVIE) / **EDDIE BRACH** – bass / **PETER BONAS** – guitar / **TERL BRYANT** – drums

Feb 88. (7") (BEG 207) **ALL NIGHT LONG. / I'VE GOT A SECRET CAMERA** (12"+=) (BEG 207T) – Funtime (in cabaret).		–
Mar 88. (lp/c)(cd) (BEGA/BEGC 92)(BEGA 92CD) <7634> **LOVE HYSTERIA** – All night long / His circle and hers meet / Dragnet drag / Socrates the python / Indigo eyes / Time has got nothing to do with it / Blind sublime / My last two weeks / Funtime. (cd+=) – I've got a miniature secret camera / Funtime (cabaret mix).		
Mar 88. (7") <8670> **ALL NIGHT LONG. / FUNTIME (Cabaret mix)**	–	
Apr 88. (7"/7"box) (BEG/+B 210) **INDIGO EYES. / GOD SENDS (live)** (12"+=) (BEG 210T) – Confessions (live).		
Jun 88. (7") <8707> **INDIGO EYES. / MY LAST TWO WEEKS**		
Mar 90. (7") (BEG 237) <9140> **CUTS YOU UP. / STRANGE KIND OF LOVE** (12"+=/cd-s+=) (BEG 237 T/CD) – Roll call (reprise).		55
May 90. (cd)(c/lp) (BEGA 107CD)(BEGC/BEGA 107) <9877> **DEEP** – Deep ocean vast sea / Crystal waters / Marlene Dietrich's favourite poem / Seven veils / The line between the Devil's teeth (and that which cannot be repeated) / Cuts you up / A strange kind of love / Roll call. (cd+=) – Strange kind of love (alt.version).		44
Apr 92. (7") (BBQ) **YOU'RE SO CLOSE. / THE SWEETEST DROP** (12"+=/cd-s+=) (BBQ) – Cuts you up (live) / All night long (live).		
Apr 92. (cd)(c/lp) (BEGA 123CD)(BEGC/BEGA 123) <66007> **HOLY SMOKE** – Keep me from harm / Kill the hate / You're so close / The sweetest drop / Low room / Let me love you / Our secret garden / Dream gone by / Hit song.		
Jul 92. (7") (BBQ) **HIT SONG. / SEVEN VEILS** (12"+=/cd-s+=) (BBQ) – The line between the Devil's teeth (and that which cannot be repeated).		
Apr 95. (cd-ep) (BBQ 52CD) **THE SCARLET THING IN YOU / CRYSTAL WRISTS / WISH / DRAGNET DRAG (live)**		
Apr 95. (cd/c) (BBQ CD/MC 175) **CASCADE** – Mirror to my woman's mind / Subway / Gliding like a whale / Disappearing / Mercy rain / I'll fall with your knife / Scarlet thing in you / Sails wave goodbye / Wild birds flock to me / Huuvola / Cascade.		

TONES ON TAILS

GLEN CAMPLING – vocals, bass, keyboards (roadie of BAUHAUS) / **DANIEL ASH** – guitar, vocals / **KEVIN HASKINS** – drums

	4.a.d.	not iss.
Apr 82. (12"ep) (BAD 203) **A BIGGER SPLASH / COPPER. / MEANS OF ESCAPE / INSTRUMENTAL**		–

	Beggars Banquet	not iss.
Sep 82. (12") (BEG 85T) **THERE'S ONLY ONE. / NOW WE LUSTRE**		–

	Situation 2	not iss.
May 83. (7") (SIT 21) **BURNING SKIES. / OK, THIS IS THE POPS** (12"+=) (SIT 21T) – When you're smiling / You, the night and the music.		–

—— In 1983, they broke from BAUHAUS. ASH and HASKINS joined The JAZZ BUTCHER. TONES ON TAILS soon re-actified their line-up.

	Beggars Banquet	not iss.
Mar 84. (7") (BEG 106) **PERFORMANCE. / SHAKES** (12"+=) (BEG 106T) – ('A'dub version).		
Apr 84. (lp/c) (BEGA/BEGC 51) **POP** – Performance / War / Lions / Happiness / The never never / Real life / Slender fungus / Movement of fear / Rain. (re-iss. Oct88 & Jul91 on 'Beggars Banquet-Lowdown' lp/c)(cd; BBL/+C 51)(BBL 51CD) (cd-iss. Oct88 as 'NIGHT MUSIC' +=; BEGA 51CD) – (rest of material).		
May 84. (7") (BEG 109) **LIONS. / GO! (LET'S GO TO YA YA'S NOW)**		–

	Situation 2	not iss.

(12",12"red) (BEG 109T) – ('A'side) / Go! (club mix).

Nov 84. (7"/12"blue) (BEG 121/+T) **CHRISTIAN SAYS. / TWIST**

—— split from this name

Feb 85. (lp/c) Situation 2; (SITU/SITC 12) **TONES ON TAILS** (the singles compilation)
(re-iss. Oct88 & Jul91 on 'Situation 2-Lowdown' lp/c; SITL/+C 12)

LOVE AND ROCKETS

ASH + HASKINS were joined by DAVID J. – vocals, bass, keyboards (also ex-BAUHAUS + a solo artist)

	Beggars Banquet	Beggars Banquet

May 85. (7"/12") (BEG 132/+T) **BALL OF CONFUSION. / INSIDE THE OUTSIDE**

Sep 85. (7"/12") (BEG 146/+T) **IF THERE'S A HEAVEN ABOVE. / GOD AND MR. SMITH**

Oct 85. (lp/c) (BEGA/BEGC 66) <85071> **7th DREAM OF TEENAGE HEAVEN**
– If there's a Heaven above / A private future / 7th dream of teenage Heaven / Saudade / Haunted when the minutes drag / The dog-end of a day gone by / The game. (cd-iss. May86; BEGA 66CD) (re-iss. Jan89 & Jul91 on 'Beggars Banquet-Lowdown' lp/c)(cd+=; BBL/+C 66)(BBL 66CD) – Ball of confusion (USA mix) / God and Mr. Smith (Mars mix) / If there's a Heaven above (Canadian mix).

	Beggars Banquet	Big Time

Jun 86. (12"m) (BEG 163T) **KUNDALINI EXPRESS. / LUCIFER SAM / HOLIDAY ON THE MOON**

Sep 86. (7"/12") (BEG 166/+T) **YIN AND YANG (THE FLOWERPOT MEN). / ANGELS AND DEVILS**

Sep 86. (lp/c) (BEGA/BEGC 74) <6011> **EXPRESS** | | 72 |
– Kundalini express / It could be sunshine / Love me / All in my mind / Life in Laralay / Yin and Yang (the flowerpot men) / An American dream / All in my mind (acoustic version). (cd-iss. Jan88; BEGA 74CD) (re-iss. Jan89 & Jul91 on 'Beggars Banquet-Lowdown' lp/c)(cd; BBL/+C 74)(BEGA 74CD)

Sep 87. (lp/c)(cd) (BEGA/BEGC 84)(BEGA 84CD) <6011> **EARTH, SUN, MOON** | | 64 |
– The light / Mirror people / Welcome tomorrow / Here on Earth / Lazy / Waiting for the flood / Rainbird / Telephone is empty / Everybody wants to go to Heaven / The sun / Youth. (re-iss. Jan89 & Jul91 on 'Beggars Banquet' lp/c)(cd+=; BBL/+C 84)(BBL 84CD) – Mirror people (slow version).

Oct 87. (7"/12") (BEG 186/+T) **THE LIGHT. / MIRROR PEOPLE (slow version)**

Mar 88. (7") (BEG 209) **NO NEW TALE TO TELL. / EARTH, SUN, MOON**
(12"+=) (BEG 209T) – 7th dream of teenage Heaven.

May 88. (7") (BEG 213) **MIRROR PEOPLE. / DAVID LANFAIR**
(12"+=) (BEG 213T) – ('A'live version).

Aug 88. (7") (BEG 217) **LAZY. / THE DOG-END OF A DAY GONE BY**
(12"+=) (BEG 217T) – The purest blue.

	Beggars Banquet	R.C.A.

Jan 89. (12"ep) (BEG 224T) **MOTORCYCLE / I FEEL SPEED. / BIKE / BIKEDANCE**

Jul 89. (7"/c-s/12") (BEG 229/+C/T) <8956> **SO ALIVE. / DREAMTIME** | | 3 May89 |
(cd-s+=) (BEG 229CD) – Motorcycle / Bike. (re-dist.Jan90)

Sep 89. (lp/c)(cd) (BEGA/BEGC 99)(BEGA 99CD) <9715> **LOVE AND ROCKETS** | | 14 |
– **** (Jungle law) / No big deal / The purest blue / Motorcycle / I feel speed / Bound for Hell / The teardrop collector / So alive / Rock and roll Babylon / No words no more.

Oct 89. (7") (BEG 234) <9045> **NO BIG DEAL. / NO WORDS NO MORE** | | 82 Sep89 |
(12"+=) (BEG 234T) - 100 watts of your love.

	Beggars Banquet	Beggars Banquet

Jul 94. (12"/cd-s) (BBQ 36 T/CD) **THIS HEAVEN / THIS HEAVEN (Secret Knowledge mix). / THIS HEAVEN (Lost In It) / THIS HEAVEN (Torched mix)**

Sep 94. (12"/cd-s) (BBQ 42 T/CD) **BODY AND SOUL (Secret Knowledge out of body mix) / BODY AND SOUL (Delta Lady Rebel Trouser mix)**
above featured **NATACHA ATLAS** – vocals (of TRANS-GLOBAL UNDERGROUND)

Sep 94. (cd/c/d-lp) (BBQ CD/MC/LP 145) **HOT TRIP TO HEAVEN**
– Body and soul (parts 1 & 2) / Ugly / Trip and glide / This Heaven / No worries / Hot trip to Heaven / Eclipse / Voodoo baby / Be the revolution / Set me free. (re-iss. cd Sep95; BBL 145CD)

Mar 96. (cd-ep; unreleased) (BBQ 67CD) **SWEET F.A. / THE GLITTERING DARKNESS / TRIP AND GLIDE / RITUAL RADIO / BAD MONKEY**

DANIEL ASH

	Beggars Banquet	Beggars Banquet

Jun 91. (cd)(c/lp) (BEGA 114CD)(BEGA/BEGC 114) <3014> **COMING DOWN**
– Blue moon / Coming down fast / Walk this way / Closer to you / Day tripper / This love / Blue angel / Me and my shadow / Candy darling / Sweet little liar / Not so fast / Coming down.
—— Above features covers DAY TRIPPER (Beatles) / BLUE MOON (Rodgers / Hart) / ME AND MY SHADOW (Al Jolson/+).

Jun 91. (7") **WALK THIS WAY. / HEAVEN IS WAITING**
(12") – ('A'side) / ('A'groovy vox) / ('A'groovy guitar).
(cd-s) – (all 4 tracks).

Apr 93. (12"ep/cd-ep) (BBQ 9 T/CD) **GET OUT OF CONTROL. / THE HEDONIST / GET OUT OF CONTROL (farewell mixes)**

May 93. (cd/c/lp) (BBQ CD/MC/LP 129) **FOOLISH THING DESIRE**
– Here she comes / Foolish thing desire / Bluebird / Dream machine / Get out of control / The void / Roll on / Here she comes again / The hedonist / Higher than this.

BAY (see under ⇒ ARAB STRAP)

BAY CITY ROLLERS

Formed: Edinburgh, Scotland . . . 1967 by the LONGMUIR brothers, DEREK and ALAN, the pair finding NOBBY CLARKE and JOHN DEVINE after lengthy auditions. After a spell as SAXON they changed their moniker to The BAY CITY ROLLERS, found at random after pointing at Bay City, Michigan, on a map of the States. Managed by Tam Paton, the group were signed to 'Bell' records in 1971, hitting the UK Top 10 soon after with a Jonathan King-produced cover of The Gentry's 'KEEP ON DANCING'. It proved a one-off, however, and it'd be 1974 before they graced the charts again. By the time 'REMEMBER (SHA-LA-LA)' had become a Top 10 hit, CLARKE and DEVINE had been replaced by frontman LES McKEOWN, STUART WOOD and ERIC FAULKNER, the line-up which would effect mid-70's chart domination and make tartan trendy into the bargain. With the help of songwriters Phil Coulter and Bill Martin, the Edinburgh lads couldn't put a foot wrong throughout that year, kicking up a teen storm with bubblegum pop anthems 'SHANG-A-LANG', 'SUMMERLOVE SENSATION' and 'ALL OF ME LOVES ALL OF YOU'. Having started out as a BEATLES covers outfit, the BAY CITY ROLLERS at their height ironically provoked a level of knicker-wetting teen hysteria not witnessed since the Fab Four's heyday. Gracing Top Of The Pops with their trademark tartan flares, scarves and platform shoes, McKEOWN & Co. topped the UK charts twice in a row in 1975, first with a cover of The Four Seasons' 'BYE BYE BABY' followed by 'GIVE A LITTLE LOVE'. It was only a matter of time before the States couldn't resist something so squeaky clean and identifiably Scottish at the same time, the boys hitting the US Top spot with 'SATURDAY NIGHT' (originally a UK flop two years previously!) towards the end of the year. Following the Top 5 success of 1976's 'LOVE ME LIKE I LOVE YOU', ALAN LONGMUIR departed for a short-lived solo career although he returned in 1978. By then, the press knives were out for Rollermania and it wasn't long before the band's less than wholesome pedigree was exposed with revelations of drug use. On top of that, Paton was charged with indecency involving underage kids. Nevertheless, the ROLLERS kept rolling around the golden oldie circuit in various incarnations over the forthcoming decades while, for better or worse, they remain the biggest pop export Scotland has ever produced. Amid the band's high-profile slot at Edinburgh's Hogmanay 2000 celebrations, yet more controversy reared its ugly and all too familiar head as former member DEREK LONGMUIR (now working as a hospital auxiliary!) was charged with possessing child porn.

Best CD compilation: ABSOLUTE ROLLERS: THE VERY BEST OF . . . (*6)

GORDON 'NOBBY' CLARKE – vocals / **JOHN DEVINE** – guitar / **ALAN LONGMUIR** (b.20 Jun'53) – bass, accordion / **DEREK LONGMUIR** (b.19 Mar'52) – drums, percussion

	Bell	Bell

Jun 71. (7") (BLL 1164) <45169> **KEEP ON DANCING. / ALRIGHT** | 9 | |

Mar 72. (7") (BLL 1220) **WE CAN MAKE MUSIC. / JENNY** | | – |

—— (Jun'72) **ERIC FAULKNER** (b.21 Oct'54) – guitar; repl. DEVINE

Sep 72. (7") (BLL 1262) <45274> **MANANA. / BECAUSE I LOVE YOU**

—— (Jan'73) **LES McKEOWN** (b.12 Nov'55) – vocals + **STUART WOOD** (b.25 Feb'57) – guitar, mandolin; repl. CLARKE

Jun 73. (7") (BLL 1319) **SATURDAY NIGHT. / HEY C.B.** | | – |

Jan 74. (7") (BLL 1338) **REMEMBER (SHA-LA-LA). / BYE BYE BARBARA** | 6 | – |

Apr 74. (7") (BLL 1355) <45481> **SHANG-A-LANG. / ARE YOU READY FOR THAT ROCK'N'ROLL** | 2 | |

Jul 74. (7") (BLL 1369) <45607> **SUMMERLOVE SENSATION. / BRINGING BACK THE GOOD TIMES** | 3 | |

Oct 74. (7") (BLL 1382) <45618> **ALL OF ME LOVES ALL OF YOU. / THE BUMP** | 4 | |
          | 1 | – |

Oct 74. (lp) (BELLS 244) **ROLLIN'**
– Shang-a-lang / Give it to me now / Angel angel / Be my baby / Just a little love / Remember (sha-la-la) / Saturday night / Ain't it strange / Please stay / Jenny gotta dance / There goes my baby / Summerlove sensation.

	Bell	Arista

Mar 75. (7") (BLL 1409) <0120> **BYE BYE BABY. / IT'S FOR YOU** | 1 | – |

May 75. (lp) (SYBEL 8001) **ONCE UPON A STAR** | 1 | – |
– Bye bye baby / The disco kid / La belle Jeane / When will you be mine / Angel baby / Keep on dancing / Once upon a star / Let's go / Marlina / My teenage heart / Rock and roll honeymoon / Hey! beautiful dreamer.

Jul 75. (7") (BLL 1409) **GIVE A LITTLE LOVE. / SHE'LL BE CRYING OVER YOU** | 1 | – |

Sep 75. (7") <0149> **SATURDAY NIGHT. / MARLINA** | – | 1 |

Sep 75. (lp) <4049> **BAY CITY ROLLERS** | – | 20 |
– Bye bye baby / Give a little love / Be my baby / Summerlove sensation / Keep on dancing / Marlina / Shang-a-lang / Let's go (a huggin' and a kissin' in the moonlight) / My teenage heart / Remember (sha la la) / Saturday night.

Nov 75. (7") (BLL 1461) <0170> **MONEY HONEY. / MARYANNE** | 3 | 9 Jan76 |

Dec 75. (lp) (SYBEL 8002) **WOULDN'T YOU LIKE IT** | 3 | |
– I only wanna dance with you / Don't stop the music / Shanghai'd in love / Love is . . . / Maybe I'm a fool to rock'n'roll / Give a little love / Wouldn't you like it / Here comes that feeling again / Lovely to see you again / Eagles fly / Derek's end piece.

Mar 76. (lp) <4071> **ROCK N' ROLL LOVE LETTER** | – | 31 |

– Money honey / La belle Jeane / Rock n' roll love letter / Maybe I'm a fool to love you / Wouldn't you like it / I only wanna dance with you / Shanghai'd in love / Don't stop the music / The disco kid / Eagles fly / Too young to rock & roll.

Apr 76.	(7") (BLL 1477) **LOVE ME LIKE I LOVE YOU. / MAMA LI**	4	-
Apr 76.	(7") <0185> **ROCK AND ROLL LOVE LETTER. / SHANGHAI'D IN LOVE**	-	28
Jun 76.	(7") <0193> **DON'T STOP THE MUSIC. / DON'T STOP THE MUSIC (long)**	-	

—— **IAN MITCHELL** (b.,22 Aug'58, Downpatrick, County Down, N. Ireland) – guitar; repl. ALAN LONGMUIR who tries a brief solo career

Aug 76.	(7") <0205> **I ONLY WANT TO BE WITH YOU. / WRITE A LETTER**	-	12
Sep 76.	(7") (BLL 1493) **I ONLY WANNA BE WITH YOU. / ROCK N' ROLLER**	4	-
Sep 76.	(lp) (SYBEL 8005) <4093> **DEDICATION**	4	26

– Let's pretend / You're a woman / Rock 'n roller / Don't worry baby / Yesterday's hero / My Lisa / Money honey / Rock n' roll love letter / Write a letter / Dedication.

Nov 76.	(7") <0216> **YESTERDAY'S HERO. / MY LISA**	-	54
Feb 77.	(7") <0233> **DEDICATION. / ROCK N' ROLLER**	-	60
		Arista	Arista
May 77.	(7") (ARIST 108) **IT'S A GAME. / DANCE DANCE DANCE**	16	-
May 77.	(7") <0256> **YOU MADE ME BELIEVE IN MAGIC. / DANCE DANCE DANCE**	-	10
Jul 77.	(7") (ARIST 127) **YOU MADE ME BELIEVE IN MAGIC. / ARE YOU CUCKOO / DEDICATION**	34	-
Aug 77.	(lp) (SPARTY 1009) <7004> **IT'S A GAME**	18	23 Jul77

– It's a game / You made me believe in magic / Don't let the music die / Love power / The way I feel tonight / Love fever / Sweet Virginia / Inside a broken dream / Dance dance dance / Rebel rebel.

Oct 77.	(7") (ARIST 144) <0272> **THE WAY I FEEL TONIGHT. / LOVE POWER**	-	24
Nov 77.	(lp) <4158> **GREATEST HITS** (compilation)	-	77

– I only wanna be with you / Money honey / Rock and roll love letter / The way I feel tonight / Yesterday's hero / Dedication / Maybe I'm a fool to love you / You made me believe in magic / Don't stop the music / Saturday night.

—— **PAT McGLYNN** (b.31 Mar'58) – guitar; repl. MITCHELL who formed ROSETTA STONE before formed his own named outfit who became LA ROX

—— **ALAN LONGMUIR** returned to repl. McGLYNN

Oct 78.	(7") (ARIST 212) **ALL OF THE WORLD IS FALLING IN LOVE. / IF YOU WERE MY WOMAN**		-
Oct 78.	(7") <0363> **WHERE WILL I BE NOW. / IF YOU WERE MY WOMAN**		
Oct 78.	(lp) (SPART 1075) <4194> **STRANGERS IN THE WIND**		

– Another rainy day in New York City / All of the world is falling in love / Where will I be now / Back on the street / Strangers in the wind / Love brought me such a magical thing / If you were my woman / Every tear I cry / Shoorah shoorah for Hollywood / When I say I love you (the pie).

ROLLERS

—— **DUNCAN FAURE** – vocals, keyboards (ex-RABBIT) repl. McKEOWN who went solo (released 'ALL WASHED UP' in 1979 on the 'Egotrip' label)

May 79.	(7") (ARIST 259) **TURN ON THE RADIO. / WASHINGTON'S BIRTHDAY**		-
Jun 79.	(lp) (064-63136) **ELEVATOR**	-	- German

– Stoned houses #1 / Elevator / Playing in a rock and roll band / Hello and welcome home / I was eleven / Stoned houses #2 / Turn on the radio / Instant relay / Tomorrow's just a day away / Who'll be my keeper / Back on the road again / Washington's birthday.

Jun 80.	(lp) (202204) **VOXX**	-	- German

– God save rock & roll / Working for the people / Soho / The hero / '85 / Honey don't leave L.A. / New York / The jig / Only the young die old / Rebel rebel.

		Epic	not iss.
May 81.	(7") (EPC 1225) **LIFE ON THE ROAD. / RICOCHET**		-
Jul 81.	(7") (EPC 1402) **NO DOUBT ABOUT IT. / SET THE FASHION**		-
Aug 81.	(lp/c) (EPC/40 85004) **RICOCHET**		-

– Doors, bars, metal / Life on the radio / No doubt about it / Roxy lady / Ricochet / Won't you come home with me / Ride / Lay your love on the line / That's where the boys are / Set the fashion / This is your life.

—— after they split, various BCR's play in versions of the band

– compilations, etc. –

Jun 92.	(c/cd) I.M.D.; (MC+/JHD 025) **GREATEST HITS**		-
Sep 92.	(cd/c) R.C.A.; (26/41 3001) **COLLECTION**		-
Dec 92.	(cd/c) Ariola Express; (2/4 95588) **BAY CITY ROLLERS**		-
Aug 95.	(cd) Arista; (<74321 26575-2>) **ABSOLUTE ROLLERS**		-

– Saturday night / Shang-a-lang / Bye bye baby / I only want to be with you / All of me loves all of you / Give a little love / Summer love sensation / Rebel rebel / Money honey / Keep on dancing / Love me like I love you / Once upon a star / Be my baby / You made me believe in magic / The way I feel tonight / Another rainy day in New York City / It's a game / There goes my baby / Rock n' roll love letter / Bay City Rollers megamix.

May 96.	(cd-s) Old Gold; (126236367-2) **BYE BYE BABY / GIVE A LITTLE LOVE**		-
Nov 96.	(cd) Tring; (<QED 106>) **BYE BYE BABY**		-
Apr 97.	(cd) BR Music; (BM 1551) **GREATEST HITS**		-
May 97.	(cd/c) A-Play Collection; (10060-2/-4) **THE VERY BEST OF THE BAY CITY ROLLERS**		-
Mar 98.	(cd/c) RCA-Camden; (<74321 5696025>) **SHANG-A-LANG**		Dec99
Jul 98.	(cd/c) Hallmark; (<30906-2/-4>) **THE VERY BEST OF THE BAY CITY ROLLERS**		Dec99
Apr 99.	(cd-box) BMG Int.; <37045> **THE COMPLETE ANTHOLOGY 1971-1980**		-

---

BBM (see under ⇒ BRUCE, Jack)

BEACH BOYS

Formed: Hawthorne, Los Angeles, California, USA . . . 1961 by WILSON brothers BRIAN, DENNIS and CARL, who were soon joined by their cousin MIKE LOVE and neighbour AL JARDINE. They went through a series of cringe-inducing names before being individually christened The BEACH BOYS by a local DIY studio, who had released their first single 'SURFIN' on their small 'Candix' label. As sales of the record mushroomed, the band decided to keep the name. MURRAY WILSON, the brothers' tyrannical father, seized the opportunity to become their manager, producer and song publisher; not exactly a healthy combination and one which the band would come to regret when financial troubles dogged them throughout the next decade and beyond. For the moment however, on the surface at least, everything was hunky dory, the band riding the commercial crest of their surfing wave as they signed to 'Capitol' in 1962 and became the very essence of the sun-tanned, Californian dream. The hits came thick and fast with the prodigiously talented BRIAN writing most of the material. Songs like 'SURFIN SAFARI' and 'SURFIN U.S.A.' were effervescent feelgood anthems, their jaw-dropping vocal harmonies framing images of surf, sea and beautiful girls. Early glimpses of BRIAN's penchant for introspection are evident on tracks like the poignant 'IN MY ROOM', co-written with GARY USHER, the first of many songwriters BRIAN would collaborate with during the course of his career. The execrable sentiments of songs like 'BE TRUE TO YOUR SCHOOL', were a result of a period of collaboration with lyricist ROGER CHRISTIAN, although this partnership also created livelier gems like 'LITTLE DEUCE COUPE' and 'I GET AROUND'. The latter song was probably the highlight of 'ALL SUMMER LONG', the 1964 album which saw the band make the leap from being primarily a singles act to creating consistent long players. By Christmas of that year, however, the strain of their horrendous recording/touring treadmill was too much for BRIAN and he suffered a series of nervous breakdowns. Producing and arranging 6 albums in just over 2 years as well as writing over 60 songs in the same period would've been too much for the hardiest of souls, let alone the painfully shy and sensitive BRIAN. This episode signalled the end of BRIAN's live commitment to the band, allowing him to concentrate solely on composing and recording. 'BEACH BOYS – TODAY' and 'SUMMER DAYS (AND SUMMER NIGHTS)' represented a career high with breathtaking material highlighting BRIAN's preoccupation with achieving the perfect sound. He had become obsessed with outdoing The BEATLES who he saw as a threat, a paranoia that grew stronger after his first forays into the world of LSD. He first took the drug in the summer of '65 and it changed his approach to music, to his whole life in fact, with BRIAN later stating that his mind was opened and it scared the shit out of him. BRIAN then enlisted the unlikely help of erstwhile ad sloganeer TONY ASHER to express the lyrical mood of these new pieces, and the result was 'PET SOUNDS'. Released in May '66, it still holds the coveted "best album of all-time" position among many critics, with fragile highlights being 'GOD ONLY KNOWS', 'WOULDN'T IT BE NICE' and 'CAROLINE NO', which perfectly evoked BRIAN's turbulent emotional state. Reportedly devastated at the album's lack of success in his home country (yes, it did hit Top 10) and feeling outdone by The BEATLES' 'Revolver' and DYLAN's 'Blonde On Blonde', he upped his drug use and vowed to go one better, dreaming of the ultimate studio masterpiece. Initially pencilled in for inclusion on 'PET SOUNDS' in its earliest incarnation, 'GOOD VIBRATIONS' was released in October that year and soon became their biggest-ever selling single. With its pioneering use of the theramin and complex vocal arrangements, its success vindicated BRIAN's vision of grand sonic tapestries over the formulaic pop that other members (most notably MIKE LOVE and his father) wanted to churn out. Around this time, BRIAN began working on his masterpiece (with self-styled L.A. boho scenester/songwriter VAN DYKE PARKS), which had a working title of 'DUMB ANGEL', later changing to 'SMILE'. The sessions that resulted are the stuff of legend, with BRIAN's mental condition deteriorating rapidly under the weight of his own expectation. Among BRIAN's more whimsical foibles were having a box filled with sand so he could play piano barefoot "like on the beach, man" (Surf's Up, indeed). More worrying was the pathological superstition which saw him attempt to destroy tapes of the abandoned 'SMILE' album, although these did surface later on albums 'SMILEY SMILE', 'HEROES AND VILLAINS' and 'SURF'S UP'. From this point on, BRIAN retreated even further from the world at large and spent much of the following decade in bed. A string of average, occasionally good albums followed with DENNIS emerging as a fairly talented songwriter. Recorded after the band's acrimonious split with 'Capitol', 1971's 'SURF'S UP' was the highlight of this period with its 'SMILE'-era title track and spirited contributions from other band members. DENNIS WILSON's association with the infamous CHARLES MANSON, albeit before he went on his killing spree in 1969, probably brought more attention than any music the band released at this time. With the exception of one outstanding BRIAN-penned song 'SAIL ON SAILOR' from the disappointing 'HOLLAND' set, much of the 70's material was creatively bland to say the least. On the 4th June 1973, their father died and eventually MIKE LOVE's brothers STAN and STEVE were removed from management after STEVE was found guilty of embezzling around $1 million. 1977's 'BEACH BOYS LOVE YOU' album saw BRIAN return to take the reins again for the first time in 10 years, and included some fine material. From here on in, The BEACH BOYS became nothing more than a nostalgic novelty act, living on past glories while producing stagnant albums for the over 40's. On the 28th December '83, tragedy struck when DENNIS drowned during a diving trip in Marina Del Ray. The band struggled on minus BRIAN who'd been sacked a year earlier. The band scored a surprise US No.1 hit in 1988 with the soppy 'KOKOMO', which was co-written with former MAMAS & THE PAPAS singer JOHN PHILLIPS. Meanwhile, BRIAN released a competent, not to mention long-awaited solo album under the guidance of his controversial therapist EUGENE LANDY. He even recorded a second album, which was strangely turned down by his new label 'Sire', despite garnering rave reviews from critics who'd heard the pre-release tapes. 1995 saw the release of BRIAN's 'I JUST WASN'T MADE FOR THESE TIMES', an album project combining re-working of older and rare material. A year later The BEACH BOYS scraped the barrel of banality when they did a nauseating run through of their 60's hit 'FUN, FUN, FUN' with STATUS QUO. This was surely the end of the sandy road for the once inspirational outfit; tragedy struck with the lung cancer death (on the 6th of February) of CARL. Remaining brother BRIAN carried on, his 'IMAGINATION' (1998) set receiving rave reviews from the "old fogey" brigade while reaching the Top 100 (Top 30 in Britain); he subsequently teamed up with BRIAN SETZER (ex-STRAY CATS) to record 'LITTLE DEUCE COUPE' for a V/A "save our beaches" benefit album, 'Music For Our Mother Ocean'. • Covered: THE TIMES THEY ARE A-CHANGIN' (Bob Dylan) / PAPA OOM MOW MOW (Rivingtons) / I CAN HEAR MUSIC (Ronettes) / BARBARA ANN (Regents) / LOUIE LOUIE (Kingsmen) / WHY DO FOOLS FALL IN LOVE? (Frankie Lymon & the Teenagers) / MONSTER MASH (Bobby Pickett) / JOHNNY B. GOODE (Chuck Berry) / DO YOU WANNA DANCE (Bobby Freeman) / YOU'VE GOT TO HIDE YOUR LOVE AWAY + I SHOULD HAVE KNOWN BETTER (Beatles) / ALLEY OOP (Hollywood Argyles) / BLUEBIRDS OVER THE MOUNTAIN (Ersel Hickey) / THEN I KISSED HER (Crystals) / COME GO WITH ME (Del-Vikings) / CALIFORNIA DREAMIN' (Mamas & The Papas) / THE WANDERER (Dion) / ROCK AND ROLL MUSIC (Chuck Berry) / BLUEBERRY HILL (Fats Domino) / MONA (Bo Diddley) / PEGGY SUE (Buddy Holly) / THE AIR THAT I BREATHE (Hollies) / HOT FUN IN THE SUMMERTIME (Sly & The Family Stone) / WALKING IN THE SAND (Shangri-la's) / UNDER THE BOARDWALK (Drifters) / etc.

Album rating: SURFIN' SAFARI (*4) / SURFIN' U.S.A. (*7) / SURFER GIRL (*5) / LITTLE DEUCE COUPE (*4) / SHUT DOWN VOL.2 (*6) / ALL SUMMER LONG (*7) / THE BEACH BOYS CONCERT (*4) / THE BEACH BOYS – TODAY! (*7) / SUMMER DAYS (AND SUMMER NIGHTS!!) (*7) / THE BEACH BOYS PARTY~ (*4) / PET SOUNDS (*10) / SMILEY SMILE (*7) / WILD HONEY (*6) / FRIENDS (*5) / SUNFLOWER (*7) / SURF'S UP (*7) / CARL AND THE PASSIONS: SO TOUGH (*4) / HOLLAND (*6) / THE BEACH BOYS IN CONCERT (*5) / ENDLESS SUMMER compilation (*8) / 15 BIG ONES (*5) / THE BEACH BOYS LOVE YOU (*5) / M.I.U. ALBUM (*5) / L.A. (LIGHT ALBUM) (*5) / KEEPIN' THE SUMMER ALIVE (*4) / THE BEACH BOYS (*4) / STILL CRUISIN' collection (*3) / SUMMER IN PARADISE (*2) / THE VERY BEST OF THE BEACH BOYS compilation (*9) / Brian Wilson: BRIAN WILSON (*6) / I JUST WASN'T MADE FOR THOSE TIMES (*6) / IMAGINATION (*7)

BRIAN WILSON (b.20 Jun'42, Inglewood, California) – vocals, percussion / **CARL WILSON** (b.21 Dec'46) – guitar, vocals / **DENNIS WILSON** (b. 4 Dec'44) – vocals, drums / **MIKE LOVE** (b.15 Mar'44, Baldwin Hills, California) – vocals / **AL JARDINE** (b. 3 Sep'42, Lima, Ohio) – vocals, guitar

		not iss.	Candix
Dec 61.	(7") <301> **SURFIN'. / LUAU**	-	-
Feb 62.	(7") <331> **SURFIN'. / LUAU**	-	75

—— **DAVID MARKS** – vocals repl. JARDINE who became a dentist

		Capitol	Capitol
Aug 62.	(7") (CL 15273) <4777> **SURFIN' SAFARI. / 409**		14 / 76
Nov 62.	(lp) <T 1808> **SURFIN' SAFARI**	-	32

– Surfin' safari / County fair / Ten little indians / Chug-a-lug / Little girl (you're my Miss America) / 409 / Surfin' * / Heads you win – tails I lose / Summertime blues / Cuckoo clock * / Moon dawg / The shift. (UK-iss.Apr63; SY 4572) (re-iss. Jun81 on Greenlight; GO 2014) – omitted *.

Jan 63.	(7") (CL 15285) <4880> **TEN LITTLE INDIANS. / COUNTY FAIR**		49 Nov62

(re-iss. Jun79; CL 16041)

Mar 63.	(7") (CL 15305) <4932> **SURFIN' U.S.A.. / SHUT DOWN**	34	3 / 23

(re-iss. Jun79; CL 16042)

Apr 63.	(lp; stereo/mono) <S+/T 1890> **SURFIN' U.S.A.**	-	2

– Surfin' U.S.A. / Farmer's daughter / Misirlou / Stoked / Lonely sea / Shut down / Noble surfer / Honky tonk / Lana / Surf jam / Let's go trippin' / Finders keepers. (UK-iss.Aug65; same); hit No.17)

—— **AL JARDINE** – vocals returned to repl. MARKS

Jul 63.	(7") <5009> **SURFER GIRL. / LITTLE DEUCE COUPE**	-	7 / 15
Sep 63.	(lp; stereo/mono) <S+/T 1981> **SURFER GIRL**	-	7

– Surfer girl / Catch a wave / Surfer Moon / South bay surfer / Rocking surfer / Little deuce Coupe / In my room / Hawaii / Surfer's rule / Our car club / Your summer dream / Boogie woogie. (UK-iss.Mar67; same); hit No.13) (re-iss. Aug86 lp/c; EMS/TC-EMS 1175)

Oct 63.	(lp; stereo/mono) <S+/T 1998> **LITTLE DEUCE COUPE**		4

– Little deuce Coupe / Ballad of ole' Betsy / Be true to your school / Car crazy cutie * / Cherry, cherry Coupe / 409 / Shut down / Spirit of America / Our car club * / No-go showboat / A young man is gone / Custom machine. (re-iss. Jun81 on 'Greenlight'; GO 2025) – omitted * (re-iss. Aug86 lp/c; EMS/TC-EMS 1174)

Nov 63.	(7") <5069> **BE TRUE TO YOUR SCHOOL. / IN MY ROOM**	-	6 / 23
Dec 63.	(7") <5096> **LITTLE SAINT NICK. / THE LORD'S PRAYER**	-	

Jan 64.	(7"; as SURVIVORS) <5102> **PAMELA JEAN. / AFTER THE GAME**	-	
Mar 64.	(7") (CL 15339) <5118> **FUN, FUN, FUN. / WHY DO FOOLS FALL IN LOVE**		5 Feb64

(re-iss. Jun79; CL 16043)

Jul 64.	(lp; stereo/mono) <S+/T 2027> **SHUT DOWN, VOLUME 2**		13 Apr64

– Fun, fun, fun / Don't worry baby / In the parkin' lot / "Cassius" Love vs "Sonny" Wilson / The warmth of the sun / This car of mine / Why do fools fall in love / Pom-pom play girl / Keep an eye on summer / Shut down (pt.II) / Louie louie / Denny's drum. (re-iss. May89 on 'C5'; C5-535)

—— Note:- 'SHUT DOWN' was a various artists surf US-lp issued Jul63 reaching No.7. It contained two BEACH BOYS tracks; 409 / Shut down.

Jun 64.	(7") (CL 15350) <5174> **I GET AROUND. / DON'T WORRY BABY**	7	1 May64

(re-iss. Jun79; CL 16044)

Jul 64.	(lp; stereo/mono) <S+/T 2110> **ALL SUMMER LONG**	-	4

– I get around / All summer long / Hushabye / Little Honda / We'll run away / Carl's big chance / Wendy / Do you remember? / Girls on the beach / Drive-in / Our favourite recording session / Don't back down. (UK-iss.Jun65; same) (re-iss. Jul73 on 'Music For Pleasure'; MfP 50065) (re-iss. Aug86 lp/c; EMS/TC-EMS 1176)

Oct 64.	(7") (CL 15361) <5245> **WHEN I GROW UP (TO BE A MAN). / SHE KNOWS ME TOO WELL**	27	9 Aug64

(re-iss. Jun79; CL 16045)

Oct 64.	(7"ep) <R-5267> **LITTLE HONDA / DON'T BACK DOWN. / WENDY / HUSHABYE**	-	65 / 44
Dec 64.	(7") <5312> **THE MAN WITH ALL THE TOYS. / BLUE CHRISTMAS**	-	
Jan 65.	(7") (CL 15370) <5306> **DANCE, DANCE, DANCE. / THE WARMTH OF THE SUN**	24	8 Oct64

(re-iss. Jun79; CL 16046)

Feb 65.	(lp; stereo/mono) <S+/T 2198> **BEACH BOYS CONCERT (live)**		1 Nov64

– Fun, fun, fun / The little old lady from Pasadena / Little deuce Coupe / Long tall Texan / In my room / Monster mash / Let's go trippin' / Papa-oom-mow-mow / The wanderer / Hawaii / Graduation day / I get around / Johnny B. Goode. (re-iss. Jun81 on 'Greenlight' lp/c; GO/TCGO 2005)

—— **GLEN CAMPBELL** – vocals (on tour) repl. BRIAN who suffered breakdown. However BRIAN did stay as writer/producer (6th member)

Feb 65.	(7") <5372> **DO YOU WANNA DANCE?. / PLEASE LET ME WONDER**	-	12 / 52
Mar 65.	(7") (CL 15384) **ALL SUMMER LONG. / DO YOU WANNA DANCE?**		-

(re-iss. Jun79; CL 16047)

Mar 65.	(lp; stereo/mono) <S+/T 2269> **THE BEACH BOYS TODAY!**	-	4

– Do you wanna dance? / Good to my baby / Don't hurt my little sister / When I grow up (to be a man) / Help me, Rhonda / Dance, dance, dance / Please let me wonder / I'm so young / Kiss me baby / She knows me too well / In the back of my mind / She knew me too well. (UK-iss.Apr66; same); hit No.6) (re-iss. Jan72 as 'DO YOU WANNA DANCE' on 'Music For Pleasure'; MFP 5235)

—— **BRUCE JOHNSTON** – vocals (ex-his combo) repl. GLEN CAMPBELL who went solo

May 65.	(7") (CL 15392) <5395> **HELP ME, RHONDA. / KISS ME BABY**	27	1 Apr65

(re-iss. Jun79; CL 16048)

Jul 65.	(lp; stereo/mono) <S+/T 2354> **SUMMER DAYS (AND SUMMER NIGHTS!!)**	-	2

– The girl from New York City / Amusements parks U.S.A. / Then I kissed her / Salt Lake City / Girl don't tell me / Help me Rhonda / Let him run wild / You're so good to me / Summer means new love / I'm bugged at my ol' man / And your dream comes true. (UK-iss.Jul66; same); hit No.4) (re-iss. Jun78; CAPS 1023) (re-iss. Aug86 lp/c; EMS/TC-EMS 1178)

Aug 65.	(7") (CL 15409) <5464> **CALIFORNIA GIRLS. / LET HIM RUN WILD**	26	3 Jul65

(re-iss. Jun79; CL 16049)

Dec 65.	(7") (CL 15425) <5540> **THE LITTLE GIRL I ONCE KNEW. / THERE'S NO OTHER (LIKE MY BABY)**		20 Nov65

(re-iss. Jun79; CL 16050)

Feb 66.	(7") (CL 15432) <5561> **BARBARA ANN. / GIRL DON'T TELL ME**	3	2 Dec65

(re-iss. Jun79; CL 16051)

Feb 66.	(lp; stereo/mono) <S+/T 2398> **BEACH BOYS' PARTY!**	3	6 Nov65

– Hully gully / I should have known better / Tell me why / Papa-oom-mow-mow / Mountain of love / You've got to hide your love away / Devoted to you / Alley oop / There's no other (like my baby) / I get around – Little deuce Coupe / The times they are a-changin' / Barbara Ann. (re-iss. Aug86 lp/c; EMS/TC-EMS 1177)

Apr 66.	(7"; by BRIAN WILSON (CL 15438) <5610> **CAROLINE, NO. / SUMMER MEANS NEW LOVE**		32 Mar66
Apr 66.	(7") (CL 15441) <5602> **SLOOP JOHN B. / YOU'RE SO GOOD TO ME**	2	3 Mar66

(re-iss. Jun79; CL 16052)

May 66.	(lp; stereo/mono) <S+/T 2458> **PET SOUNDS**	2	10

– Wouldn't it be nice / You still believe in me / That's not me / Don't talk (put your head on my shoulder) / I'm waiting for the day / Let's go away for awhile / Sloop John B. / God only knows / I know there's no answer / Here today / I just wasn't made for these times / Pet sounds / Caroline, no. (re-iss. Jun81 on 'Greenlight'; GO 2002) (re-iss. May82 on 'Fame'; FA 3018) (re-iss. Aug86 lp/c; EMS/TC-EMS 1179) <(cd-iss. Jun90; 7-48421)> – Hang on to your ego / Trombone Dixie. (re-iss. Nov93 on 'Fame' cd/c; CD/TC FA 3298) (lp re-iss. Dec99 on 'Simply Vinyl'; SVLP 149)

Jul 66.	(7") (CL 15459) <5706> **GOD ONLY KNOWS. / WOULDN'T IT BE NICE**	2	39 / 8

(re-iss. Jun79; CL 16053)

Oct 66.	(7") <5676> **GOOD VIBRATIONS. / LET'S GO AWAY FOR AWHILE**	-	1
Oct 66.	(7") (CL 15475) **GOOD VIBRATIONS. / WENDY**	1	-

(re-iss. Jun79; CL 16054)

Apr 67. (7") (*CL 15502*) **THEN I KISSED HER. / MOUNTAIN OF LOVE** | 4 | - |
(re-iss. Jun79; CL 16055)

	Capitol	Brother

Aug 67. (7") (*CL 15510*) <*1001*> **HEROES AND VILLAINS. / YOU'RE WELCOME** | 8 | 12 Jul67 |
(re-iss. Jun79; CL 16056)

Sep 67. (7"; BRIAN WILSON & MIKE LOVE) (*CL 15513*) <*1002*> **GETTIN' HUNGRY. / DEVOTED TO YOU**

Nov 67. (lp; stereo/mono) <(*S 9001*)> **SMILEY SMILE** | 9 | 41 Sep67 |
– Heroes and villains / Vegetables / Fall breaks and back to winter / She's goin' bald / Little pad / Good vibrations / With me tonight / Wind chimes / Gettin' hungry / Wonderful / Whistle in. (cd-iss. Nov98 on 'Magic'; 497576-2)

	Capitol	Capitol

Nov 67. (7") (*CL 15521*) <*2028*> **WILD HONEY. / WIND CHIMES** | 29 | 31 |
(re-iss. Jun79; CL 16057)

Dec 67. (7") <*2068*> **DARLIN'. / HERE TODAY** | - | 19 |

Jan 68. (7") (*CL 15527*) **DARLIN'. / COUNTRY AIR** | 11 | - |
(re-iss. Jun79; CL 16058)

Mar 68. (lp; stereo/mono) <(*S+/T 2859*)> **WILD HONEY** | 7 | 24 Dec67 |
– Wild honey / Aren't you glad / I was made to love her / Country air / A thing or two / Darlin' / I'd love just once to see you / Here comes the night / Let the wind blow / How she boogalooed it / Mama says.

May 68. (7") (*CL 15545*) <*2160*> **FRIENDS. / LITTLE BIRD** | 25 | 47 |
(re-iss. Jun79; CL 16059)

Jul 68. (7") (*CL 15554*) <*2239*> **DO IT AGAIN. / WAKE THE WORLD** | 1 | 20 |
(re-iss. Jun79; CL 16060)

Sep 68. (lp; stereo/mono) <(*S+/T 2895*)> **FRIENDS** | 13 | Jun68 |
– Meant for you / Friends / Wake the world / Be here in the mornin' / When a man needs a woman / Passing by / Anna Lee, the healer / Little bird / Be still / Busy doing nothin' / Diamond head / Transcendental meditation.

Dec 68. (7") (*CL 15572*) <*2360*> **BLUEBIRDS OVER THE MOUNTAIN. / NEVER LEARN NOT TO LOVE** | 33 | 61 |
(re-iss. Jun79; CL 16061)

Feb 69. (7") (*CL 15584*) <*2432*> **I CAN HEAR MUSIC. / ALL I WANT TO DO** | 10 | 24 |
(re-iss. Jun79; CL 16062)

Feb 69. (lp) <(*EST 133*)> **20/20** | 3 | 68 |
– Do it again / I can hear music / Bluebirds over the mountain / Be with me / All I want to do / The nearest faraway place / Cottonfields / I went to sleep / Time to get alone / Never learn not to love / Our prayer / Cabinessence.

Jun 69. (7") (*CL 15598*) <*2530*> **BREAK AWAY. / CELEBRATE THE NEWS** | 6 | 63 |
(re-iss. Jun79; CL 16063)

	Stateside	Reprise

Feb 70. (7") <*0894*> **ADD SOME MUSIC TO YOUR DAY. / SUSIE CINCINNATTI** | - | 64 |

Sep 70. (7") <*0929*> **SLIP ON THROUGH. / THIS WHOLE WORLD** | - | - |

Nov 70. (7") (*SS 2181*) <*0957*> **TEARS IN THE MORNING. / IT'S ABOUT ME** | - | - |

Nov 70. (lp) (*SSL 8251*) <*6382*> **SUNFLOWER** | 29 | Sep70 |
– Slip on through / This whole world / Add some music to your day / Got to know the woman / Deirdre / It's about time / Tears in the morning / All I wanna do / Forever / Our sweet love / At my window / Cool, cool water. *(re-iss. Nov80 on 'Caribou'; 31773)* – Cottonfields. *(re-iss. Jul91 on 'Epic' cd/c; 467836-2/-4)*

Dec 70. (7"; by DENNIS WILSON & RUMBO) (*SS 2184*) **SOUND OF FREE. / LADY** | - | - |

Feb 71. (7") <*0998*> **COOL, COOL WATER. / FOREVER** | - | - |

Jun 71. (7") (*SS 2190*) <*1015*> **LONG PROMISED ROAD. / DEIRDRE** | - | - |

Oct 71. (7") <*1047*> **LONG PROMISED ROAD. / TILL I DIE** | - | 89 |

Nov 71. (7") (*SS 2194*) **DON'T GO NEAR THE WATER. / STUDENT DEMONSTRATION TIME** | - | - |

Nov 71. (lp) (*SSL 10313*) <*6453*> **SURF'S UP** | 15 | 29 Aug71 |
– Don't go near the water / Long promised road / Take a load off your feet / Disney girls (1957) / Student demonstration time / Feel flows / Lookin' at tomorrow / A day in the life of a tree / 'Til I die / Surf's up. <re-iss. Nov80 on 'Caribou'; 31774> *(re-iss. Jul91 on 'Epic' cd/c; 467835-2/-4)*

Nov 71. (7") <*1058*> **SURF'S UP. / DON'T GO NEAR THE WATER** | - | - |

—— **BLONDIE CHAPLIN** – guitar repl. JOHNSTON who later went solo

—— added **RICKY FATAAR** – drums (DENNIS now just vocals)

	Reprise	Reprise

May 72. (7") (*K 14173*) <*1091*> **YOU NEED A MESS OF HELP TO STAND ALONE. / CUDDLE UP** | - | - |

Jun 72. (d-lp) (*K 44184*) <*2083*> **CARL AND THE PASSIONS – SO TOUGH** | 25 | 50 May72 |
– You need a mess of help to stand alone / Here she comes / He come down / Marcella / Hold on dear brother / Make it good / All this is that / Cuddle up. *(w/ 'PET SOUNDS')* *(re-iss. Jul91 on 'Epic' cd/c; 468349-2/-4)*

Aug 72. (7") <*1101*> **MARCELLA. / HOLD ON DEAD BROTHER** | - | - |

Jan 73. (lp) (*K 54008*) <*2118*> **HOLLAND** | 20 | 36 |
– Sail on sailor / Steamboat / California saga (on my way to sunny Californ-i-a (medley):- Big surf – Beaks of eagles – California / The trader / Leaving this town / Only with you / Funky pretty. *(7"ep free-w/a)* <*2118*> **MOUNT VERNON AND FAIRWAY (A FAIRY TALE)** – Better get back in bed / Magic transistor radio / Mount Vernon and Fairway / I'm the pied piper / Radio King Dom. *(re-iss. Jul91 on 'Epic' cd/c; 467837-2/-4)*

Feb 73. (7") <*1138*> **SAIL ON SAILOR. / ONLY WITH YOU** | - | 79 |

Feb 73. (7") (*K 14232*) **CALIFORNIA SAGA: CALIFORNIA. / SAIL ON SAILOR** | 37 | - |

May 73. (7") <*1156*> **CALIFORNIA SAGA (ON MY WAY TO SUNNY CALIFORN-I-A). / FUNKY PRETTY** | - | 84 |

Nov 73. (d-lp) (*K 84001*) <*6484*> **THE BEACH BOYS IN CONCERT (live)** | - | 25 |
– Sail on sailor / Sloop John B. / The trader / You still believe me / California girls / Darlin' / Marcella / Caroline, no / Leaving this town / Heroes and villains / We got love / Don't worry baby / Surfin' U.S.A. / Good vibrations / Fun, fun, fun / Funky pretty / Let the wind blow / Help me Rhonda / Surfer girl / Wouldn't it be nice. *(re-iss. Jun91 on 'Epic' cd/c; 468345-2/-4)*

Jul 74. (7") <*1310*> **I CAN HEAR MUSIC (live). / LET THE WIND BLOW (live)** | - | - |

Aug 74. (7"ep) (*K 14346*) **CALIFORNIA SAGA: CALIFORNIA / SAIL ON SAILOR. / MARCELLA / I'M THE PIED PIPER** | - | - |

—— **JAMES GUERICO** – bass (on tour) repl. BLONDIE and RICKY / **DENNIS** returned to his drums

Jun 75. (7") (*K 14394*) <*1325*> **SAIL ON SAILOR. / ONLY WITH YOU** | - | 49 |

Dec 75. (7"-w/drawn) (*K 14411*) <*1321*> **CHILD OF WINTER. / SUSIE CINCINNATI** | - | Dec74 |

—— **BRIAN** returned to live work

—— After this point, The BEACH BOYS abandoned even the slightest attempts to push their own musical boundaries, Instead relying upon tired retreads of their earlier sound. For details of their recordings from 1976 onwards, seek out The GREAT ROCK DISCOGRAPHY.

Jul 76. (7") (*K 14440*) <*1354*> **ROCK AND ROLL MUSIC. / THE T.M. SONG** | 36 | 5 May76 |

Jul 76. (lp/c) (*K/K4 54079*) <*MSK 2251*> **15 BIG ONES** | 31 | 8 |
– Rock and roll music / It's O.K. / Had to phone ya / Chapel of love / Everyone's in love with you / Talk to me / That same song / The T.M. song / Palisades park / Susie Cincinatti / A casual look / Blueberry Hill / Back home / In the still of the night / Just once in my life. *(re-iss. Jul91 on 'Epic' cd/c; 468346-2/-4)*

Aug 76. (7") (*K 14448*) <*1368*> **IT'S O.K. / HAD TO PHONE YA** | - | 29 |

Nov 76. (7") <*1375*> **SUSIE CINCINNATI. / EVERYONE'S IN LOVE WITH YOU** | - | - |

Apr 77. (7") <*1389*> **HONKIN' DOWN THE HIGHWAY. / SOLAR SYSTEM** | - | - |

Apr 77. (lp/c) (*K/K4 54079*) <*MSK 2258*> **THE BEACH BOYS LOVE YOU** | 26 | 53 |
– Roller skating child / I'll bet he's nice / Airplane / Love is a woman / Johnny Carson / Let us go on this way / I wanna pick you up / Let's put our hearts together / Solar system / The night was so young / Ding dang / Mona / Honkin' down the highway / Good time. *(re-iss. Jun91 on 'Epic' cd/c; 468347-2/-4)*

Aug 77. (7"ep) (*K 14481*) **MONA / ROCK AND ROLL MUSIC. / SAIL ON SAILOR / MARCELLA** | - | - |

Sep 78. (lp/c) (*K/K4 54102*) <*MSK 2268*> **M.I.U. ALBUM** | - | - |
– She's got rhythm / Come go with me / Hey little tomboy / Kona coast / Peggy Sue / Wontcha come out tonight / Sweet Sunday kinda love / Belles of Paris / Pitter patter / My Diane / Match point of your love / Winds of change. *(re-iss. Jul91 on 'Epic' cd/c; 468348-2/-4)*

Oct 78. (7") (*K 14489*) <*1394*> **PEGGY SUE. / HEY LITTLE TOMBOY** | - | 59 Aug78 |

Dec 78. (7") (*K 14494*) **KONA COAST. / SWEET SUNDAY KINDA LOVE** | - | - |

—— **BRUCE JOHNSTON** – vocals, returned to add to DENNIS, CARL, AL, MIKE + BRIAN

	Caribou	Caribou

Mar 79. (7") (*CRB 7204*) <*9026*> **HERE COMES THE NIGHT. / BABY BLUE** | 37 | 44 |
(12"blue+=) (*CRB 12-7204*) – ('A'-disco version).

Apr 79. (lp/c/pic-lp) (*CRB/40/11 86081*) <*35752*> **L.A. (LIGHT ALBUM)** | 32 | 100 |
– Angel come home / Baby blue / Love surrounds me / Good timin' / Goin' south / Shortenin' bread / Lady Lynda / Sumahama / Full sail / Sumahama / Here comes the night. *(re-iss. Aug86; 4032806)* (cd-iss. Jul89 on 'Pickwick'; 902127-2)

May 79. (7") <*9029*> **GOOD TIMIN'. / LOVE SURROUNDS ME** | - | 40 |

Jun 79. (7") (*CRB 7427*) <*9030*> **LADY LYNDA. / FULL SAIL** | 6 | - |

Aug 79. (7") (*CRB 7846*) **SUMAHAMA. / ANGEL COME HOME** | 6 | - |

Sep 79. (7") <*9031*> **SUMAHAMA. / IT'S A BEAUTIFUL DAY** | - | - |

Nov 79. (7") (*CRB 8055*) **GOOD TIMIN'. / GOIN' SOUTH** | - | - |

Mar 80. (7") <*9032*> **GOIN' ON. / ENDLESS HARMONY** | - | 83 |

Mar 80. (7") (*CRB 8367*) **OH DARLING. / ENDLESS HARMONY** | - | - |

Mar 80. (lp) (*CRB 86109*) <*36283*> **KEEPIN' THE SUMMER ALIVE** | 54 | 75 |
– Endless harmony / When girls get together / School day (ring! ring! goes the bell) / Sunshine / Santa Ana winds / Goin' on / Some of your love / Oh darlin' / Livin' with a heartache / Keepin' the summer alive. *(re-iss. Jun91 on 'Epic' cd/c; 468350-2/-4)*

Jun 80. (7") (*CRB 8663*) **KEEPIN' THE SUMMER ALIVE. / WHEN GIRLS GET TOGETHER** | - | - |

Jul 80. (7") <*9033*> **LIVING WITH A HEARTACHE. / SANTA ANA WINDS** | - | - |

Jul 80. (7") (*CRB 8633*) **SANTA ANA WINDS. / SUNSHINE** | - | - |

—— **ADRIAN BAKER** – vocals (ex-solo) repl. CARL and BRUCE

—— **CARL WILSON** returned after short solo career

Feb 82. (7") (*CRBA 2015*) <*02633*> **COME GO WITH ME. / DON'T GO NEAR THE WATER** | - | 18 Nov81 |

—— Tragically on 28th Dec83, DENNIS drowned (see above). The other original 4 (BRIAN, CARL, AL and MIKE) carried on. Mar'85, ere credited on JULIO IGLESIAS single 'THE AIR THAT I BREATHE' *(CBS A 5009)*

May 85. (7") (*A 6324*) <*04913*> **GETCHA BACK. / MALE EGO** | - | 26 |
(12"+=) (*TA 6324*) – Here comes the night / Lady Lynda.

Jun 85. (lp/c/cd) (*CRB/40/CD 26378*) <*39946*> **THE BEACH BOYS** | 60 | 52 |
– Getcha back / It's gettin' late / Crack at your love / Maybe I don't know / She believes in love again / California calling / Passing friend / I'm so lonely / Where I belong / I do love you / It's just a matter of time. *(cd+=)* – Male ego. *(re-iss. Ovt90 on 'C.B.S.' cd/c/lp; 467363-2/-4/-1)*

Jul 85. (7") <*05433*> **IT'S GETTIN' LATE. / IT'S O.K.** | - | 82 |

Aug 85. (7") (*A 6471*) **PASSING FRIEND. / IT'S O.K.** | - | - |

Nov 85. (7") <*05624*> **SHE BELIEVES IN LOVE AGAIN. / IT'S JUST A MATTER OF TIME** | - | - |

	Capitol	Capitol

Jun 86. (7") <*5595*> **ROCK'N'ROLL TO THE RESCUE. / GOOD VIBRATIONS (live)** | - | 68 |

Sep 86. (7") (*CL 425*) <*5630*> **CALIFORNIA DREAMIN'. / LADY LIBERTY** | - | 57 |
(12"+=) (*12CL 425*) – (Ballads medley).

—— **BRIAN** now departed to go solo, the rest did one-off (Jul'87) with The FAT BOYS on their UK No.2 hit single 'WIPE OUT' *(Urban; URB 5)* Also hit No.12 in the US on 'Tin Pan'; <*885960*>

Nov 88. (7"/12") (EKR 85/+T) <69385> **KOKOMO. / TUTTI FRUTTI
(by 'Little Richard')** | 25 | 1 Aug88
above single was from the film 'Cocktail' on 'Elektra' label.

Aug 89. (7") (CL 549) <44445> **STILL CRUISIN'. / KOKOMO** | | 93
(cd-s+=) (CDCL 549) – Rock'n'roll to the rescue (mix) / Lady Liberty.
(12"+=) (12CL 549) – Beach Boys Medley.

Jul 90. (c-s/cd-s) <44475> **SOMEWHERE NEAR JAPAN /
KOKOMO** | – |

── **MIKE LOVE, CARL WILSON, AL JARDINE, BRUCE JOHNSTON** (now keyboards),
MELCHER (keyboards + co-writer w/**LOVE**), **ADRIAN BAKER** (backing vocals),
KEITH WECHSLER (keyboards / some drums), **CRAIG FALL** – guitar, keyboards / **ROD
CLARK** – bass / **SAMMY MERENDINO** – drums / **VAN DYKE PARKS** – accordion,
keyboards / **DANNY KORTCHMAR** – guitars / **JOEL PESKIN** – saxophone / **JOHN
WESTON** – pedal steel

| | E.M.I. | Brother |

Jun 93. (cd/c) (CD/TC EMD 1046) **SUMMER IN PARADISE**
– Hot fun in the summertime / Surfin' / Slow summer dancin' (one summer night) /
Strange things happen / Remember walking in the sand / Lahaina aloha / Under the
boardwalk / Summer in Paradise forever. (re-iss. cd May95 on 'Fame'; CDFA 3321)

── guested on STATUS QUO's hit version of their 'FUN FUN FUN'.

| | Sub Pop | Sub Pop |

Jun 96. (7") **I JUST WASN'T MADE FOR THESE TIMES. /
WOULDN'T IT BE NICE / HERE TODAY**

– compilations, etc. –

on 'Capitol' unless stated otherwise

1963. (7"ep) (EAP 1-20540) **SURFIN' U.S.A.** | | –
1964. (7"ep) (EAP 1-20603) **FUN, FUN, FUN** | | –
1964. (7"ep) (EAP 5267) **FOUR BY THE BEACH BOYS** | | –
1964. (7"ep) (EAP 4-2198) **BEACH BOYS CONCERT** | | –
1964. (7"ep) (EAP 1-20781) **THE BEACH BOYS HITS** | | –
Nov 64. (lp; stereo/mono) (S+/T 2164) **BEACH BOYS CHRISTMAS
ALBUM**
(re-iss. Oct94 on 'Music For Pleasure' cd/c; CD/TC MFP 6150)
Oct 66. (lp; stereo/mono) (S+/T 20856) <2545> **THE BEST OF THE
BEACH BOYS** | 2 | 8
1967. (7"ep) (EAP 6-2458) **GOD ONLY KNOWS** | | –
Oct 67. (lp; stereo/mono) (S+/T 20956) <2706> **THE BEST OF THE
BEACH BOYS VOL.2** | 3 | 50 Aug67
Nov 68. (lp; stereo/mono) (S+/T 21142) <2905> **THE BEST OF THE
BEACH BOYS VOL.3** | 3 | Sep68
Aug 69. (d-lp) <253> **CLOSE UP** | – |
– (SURFIN' U.S.A. / ALL SUMMER LONG)
Mar 70. (lp) Regal Starline; (SRS 5014) **BUG-IN** | | –
May 70. (7") (CL 15640) <2765> **COTTONFIELDS. / THE NEAREST
FARAWAY PLACE** | 5 |
Sep 70. (lp) (T 21628) **GREATEST HITS** | 5 |
Jul 71. (lp) Regal Starline; (SRS 5074) **THE BEACH BOYS** | – |
Aug 72. (7"m) (CMS 1) **WOULDN'T IT BE NICE. / FUN FUN FUN /
CALIFORNIA GIRLS**
Aug 72. (lp) (ST 21715) <11584> **LIVE IN LONDON** (live 1969) | | 75 Dec76
(re-iss. Sep77 on 'Music For Pleasure'; 50345)
Nov 72. (7"m) (CMS 2) **BARBARA ANN. / DANCE DANCE DANCE /
YOU'RE SO GOOD TO ME**
Nov 73. (7") (CL 15772) **LITTLE SAINT NICK. / THE LORD'S PRAYER**
May 74. (7") (CL 15781) **ALL SUMMER LONG. / SURFIN' SAFARI**
Jul 74. (d-lp) <2166> **WILD HONEY / 20-20** | – | 50
Aug 74. (7") <3924> **SURFIN' U.S.A. / THE WARMTH OF THE
SUN** | – | 36
Nov 74. (d-lp) <(EA-ST 11307)> **ENDLESS SUMMER** | | 1 Jul74
(re-iss. Sep81 on 'Music For Pleasure'; MfP 50528) (cd-iss. Feb87 on 'E.M.I.';
CDP 746 467-2) (cd re-iss. May99; CDMFP 50528)
Oct 74. (d-lp) <2167> **FRIENDS / SMILEY SMILE** | – |
Apr 75. (d-lp) (VMP 1007) <SVBB 11384> **SPIRIT OF AMERICA** | | 8
(cd-iss. Jun87; CDP7 746 618-2)
May 75. (d-lp) (ESTSP 14) **WILD HONEY / FRIENDS** | – |
Jun 75. (7") (CL 15822) **BREAK AWAY. / CELEBRATE THE NEWS** | – |
Oct 75. (lp) Music For Pleasure; (MFP 50234) / Brother; <2223> **GOOD
VIBRATIONS – THE BEST OF BEACH BOYS** | | 25 Jul75
Jun 76. (7") (CL 15875) **GOOD VIBRATIONS. / WOULDN'T IT BE
NICE** | 18 | –
Jul 76. (lp/c) E.M.I.; (EMTV/TC-EMTV 1) **20 GOLDEN GREATS** | 1 |
(cd-iss. Nov87; CDEMTV 1) (re-iss. 1979 blue-lp; same) (re-iss. cd+c Sep94)
Dec 76. (lp) (EST 24009) **STACK O' TRACKS** | |
Nov 77. (7") (CL 15954) **LITTLE SAINT NICK. / SANTA CLAUSE IS
COMING TO TOWN / ('A'instrumental)** | | –
May 78. (7") (CL 15969) **LITTLE DEUCE COUPE. / (B-side by
SUNRAYS and SUPERSTOCKS)** | |
Jun 78. (7") (CL 15991) **CALIFORNIA GIRLS. / YOU'RE SO GOOD
TO ME / DO IT AGAIN** | |
Jun 79. (26x7"box) (BBP 26) **SINGLES COLLECTION**
(7"free-w/a) – (as "The SURVIVORS" – Pamela Jean / After the game.
Jun 80. (7"m) (CL 16148) **GOD ONLY KNOWS. / GIRLS ON THE
BEACH / IN MY ROOM** | |
Jun 80. (lp/c) (CAPS/TC-CAPS 1037) **GIRLS ON THE BEACH** | |
Dec 80. (7"m) Creole; (CR 214) **SURFIN' SAFARI. / SURFIN' /
SURFER GIRL** | |
Jan 81. (7xlp-box) World Records; (WRC SM 651-657) **THE CAPITOL
YEARS** | |
Jan 81. (7xlp-box) WRC; (SM 651/657) **THE CAPITOL YEARS** | |
Aug 81. (7") (CL 213) <5030> **BEACH BOYS MEDLEY. / GOD ONLY
KNOWS** | 47 | 12
Jun 82. (lp) <12220> **SUNSHINE DREAM** | – |
Jul 83. (d-lp) (BBTV 1867193) **THE VERY BEST OF THE BEACH
BOYS** | 1 |
– Surfin' safari / Surfin' U.S.A. / Shut down / Little deuce Coupe / In my room / Fun,
fun, fun / I get around / Don't worry baby / When I grow up (to be a man) / Wendy /

Little Honda / Dance dance dance / All summer long / Do you wanna dance / Help
me Rhonda / California girls / Little girl I once knew / Barbara Ann / You're so good
to me / Then I kissed her / Sloop John B. / God only knows / Wouldn't it be nice /
Here today / Good vibrations / Heroes and villains / Wild honey / Darlin' / Country
air / Here comes the night / Friends / Do it again / Bluebirds over the mountain / I
can hear music / Break away / Cottonfields.

1983. (d-c) Cambra; (CRT 009) **BEACH BOYS** | |
Oct 83. (lp/c) (EST/TC-EST 7122931) **THE BEACH BOYS' RARITIES** | |
(re-iss. 1985 lp/c; ATAK/TC-ATAK 6)
Mar 84. (7") EMI Gold; (G45 10) **BARBARA ANN. / GOD ONLY
KNOWS** | |
Oct 84. (c) Audio Fidelity; (ZCGAS 720) **BEACH BOYS** | |
Nov 84. (lp/c) Topline; (TOP/KTOP 109) **SURFER GIRL** (different) | |
Dec 84. (d-lp/d-c) C.B.S.; (22178) / Caribou; <37445> **TEN YEARS
OF HARMONY (1970-1980)** | | Dec81
Aug 86. (cd/c/d-lp) (CD/TC+/EN 5005) <12396> **MADE IN THE U.S.A.** | 96 | Jul86
Oct 86. (lp) Meteor; (MTM 022) **WIPE OUT** | |
Oct 86. (lp/c) Music For Pleasure; (MFP/TC-MFP 5763) **DO IT AGAIN** | |
Jul 87. (cd; with JAN & DEAN) Bescol; (CD 34) **15 GREATEST
HITS** | | –
Nov 87. (cd; with JAN & DEAN) Timeless Treasures; (MC 1635) **16
ORIGINAL HITS** | |
May 88. (cd-s) Rhino; (R 373001) **LIL' BIT OF GOLD: THE BEACH
BOYS**
– California girls / Help me Rhonda / Wouldn't it be nice / Good vibrations.
Jun 90. (7") (CL 579) **WOULDN'T IT BE NICE. / I GET AROUND** | 58 |
(12"+=/cd-s+=) (12/CD CL 579) – Medley of hits.
Jun 90. (cd)(c/d-lp) (CDP7 94620-2)(TC+/EMTVD 51) **SUMMER
DREAMS** | 2 |
Jun 90. (cd) (CDP7 93691-2) **SURFIN' SAFARI / SURFIN' U.S.A.**
(contains extra tracks) (c-iss.Jul91; C 493691)
Jun 90. (cd) (CDP7 93692-2) **SURFER GIRL / SHUT DOWN,
VOLUME 2**
(contains extra tracks) (c-iss.Jul91; C 493692)
Jul 90. (cd) (CDP7 93693-2) **LITTLE DEUCE COUPE / ALL SUMMER
LONG**
(contains extra tracks) (c-iss.Aug91; C 493693)
Aug 90. (cd) (CDP7 93694-2) **TODAY / SUMMER DAYS (AND
SUMMER NIGHTS!!)**
(contains extra tracks) (c-iss.Aug91; C 493694)
Aug 90. (cd) (CDP7 93695-2) **BEACH BOYS' CONCERT / LIVE IN
LONDON**
(contains extra tracks) (c-iss.Aug91; C 493695)
Aug 90. (cd) (CDP7 93696-2) **WILD HONEY / SMILEY SMILE**
(contains extra tracks) (c-iss.Aug91; C 493696)
Aug 90. (cd) (CDP7 93697-2) **FRIENDS / 20-20**
(contains extra tracks) (c-iss.Aug91; C 493697)
Aug 90. (cd) (CDP7 93698-2) **BEACH BOYS' PARTY / STACK
O-TRACKS**
(contains extra tracks) (c-iss.Aug91; C 493698)
Jun 91. (7"/c-s) E.M.I.; (EM/+C 1) **DO IT AGAIN. / GOOD
VIBRATIONS** | 61 |
(cd-s+=) (EMCT 1) – Wouldn't it be nice.
Jun 93. (cd/c) Fame; (CD/TC FA 3294) **CRUISIN'** | |
Jun 93. (cd/c) Music For Pleasure; (CD/TC MFP 5988) **I LOVE YOU** | | –
Jul 93. (5xcd-box) (CDS 789936-2) **GOOD VIBRATIONS – 30
YEARS OF THE BEACH BOYS** | |
Jul 94. (cd/c; with JAN & DEAN) Success; **BEACH PARTY** | |
Oct 94. (cd/c) Music For Pleasure; (CD/TC MFP 6150) **THE CHRISTMAS
ALBUM** | |
Feb 95. (cd) B.A.M.; **PEARLS OF THE PAST** | |
Jun 95. (d-cd/d-c) E.M.I.; (CD/TC ESTVD 3) **THE BEST OF THE BEACH
BOYS** | 26 |
Apr 96. (cd) <29418> **20 GOOD VIBRATIONS – THE GREATEST
HITS** | – |
Aug 96. (cd) River North; <1205> **STARS AND STRIPES VOL.1** (new
recordings of old songs – country style with various stars) | – |
Mar 97. (cd) Disky; (DC 878682) **ALL SUMMER LONG** (diff.) | – |
Mar 97. (3xcd-box) E.M.I.; (CDOMB 018) **TODAY / SUMMER DAYS
AND SUMMER NIGHTS / SMILEY SMILE** | |
Oct 97. (4xcd-box) (CDS 837662-2) **THE PET SOUNDS SESSIONS** | |
Feb 98. (cd) Disky; <(LS 86307-2) **20 GREAT LOVE SONGS** | |
Jun 98. (cd) E.M.I.; (495696-2/-4) **GREATEST HITS** | 28 |
Sep 98. (cd) E.M.I.; (496391-2) **ENDLESS HARMONY SOUNDTRACK** | 56 |
Nov 98. (cd) E.M.I.; (495734-2) **THE ULTIMATE CHRISTMAS** | |

BRIAN WILSON

| | Sire | Sire |

May 87. (7") <28350> **LET'S GO TO HEAVEN IN MY CAR. / TOO
MUCH SUGAR** | – | 54
Jul 88. (lp/c)(cd) (WX 157/+C)(925669-2) <25669> **BRIAN WILSON**
– Love and mercy / Walkin' the line / Melt away / Baby let your hair grow long /
Little children / One of the boys / There's so many / Night time / Let it shine / Rio
Grande / Meet me in my dreams tonight. (re-iss. cd Dec95; 7599 25669-2)
Aug 88. (7") (W 7814) <27814> **LOVE AND MERCY. / HE COULDN'T
GET HIS POOR OLD BODY TO MOVE** | | –
(12"+=/3"cd-s+=) (W 7814 T/CD) – One for the boys.
Nov 88. (7") (W 7787) **NIGHT TIME. / ONE FOR THE BOYS** | | –
(12"+=/3"cd-s+=) (W 7787 T/CD) – Being with the one you love.
Feb 89. (7") <27694> **MELT AWAY. / BEING WITH THE ONE YOU
LOVE** | – |

── with musicians **JIM KELTNER** – drums / **JAMES HUTCHINSON** – bass / **BENMONT
TENCH** – keyboards / **MARK GOLDENBERG + WADDY WACHTEL** – guitar / **DAVID
McMURRAY** – sax, flute

| | M.C.A. | M.C.A. |

Sep 95. (cd) (MCD 11270) **I JUST WASN'T MADE FOR THOSE
TIMES** | 59 |

– Meant for you / This whole world / Caroline, no / Let the wind blow / Love and mercy / Do it again / The warmth of the sun / Wonderful / Still I dream of it / Melt away / 'Til I die.

—— A few months later, BRIAN teamed up with VAN DYKE PARKS (the main writer) on an album, 'ORANGE CRATE ART' for 'Warners' 9362 45427-2/-4.

	R.C.A.	Paladin-Giant
Jun 98. (cd) *(74321 57303-2)* <24703> **IMAGINATION**	30	88

– Your imagination / She says that she loves me / South American / Where has love been / Keep an eye on summer / Dream angel / Cry / Lay down burden / Let him run wild / Sunshine / Happy days.

BEASTIE BOYS

Formed: Greenwich Village, New York, USA . . . 1981 by ADAM YAUCH and MIKE DIAMOND. They recruited ADAM HOROWITZ to replace two others (KATE SCHELLENBACH and JOHN BERRY), and after two US indie releases they signed to 'Def Jam', the label run by The BEASTIE's friend and sometime DJ, RICK RUBIN. RUBIN paired with the BEASTIE BOYS was a match made in Heaven (or Hell, if you were unfortunate enough to own a Volkswagen) and the debut album 'LICENSED TO ILL' (1986) was the first real attempt to create a white, rock-centric take on Afro-American Hip Hop. At turns hilarious and exhilarating, RUBIN and the BEASTIE's shared taste in classic metal was evident with samples from the likes of AC/DC and LED ZEPPELIN along with the theme tune from American TV show 'Mr. Ed'. With snotty rapping and riff-heavy rhymes, tracks like 'FIGHT FOR YOUR RIGHT (TO PARTY)' and 'NO SLEEP TILL BROOKLYN' stormed the charts on both sides of the Atlantic, 'LICENSED TO ILL' becoming the fastest selling debut in Columbia's history. The record turned the band into a phenomenon and in 1987 they undertook a riotous headlining tour. Courting controversy wherever they played, the band were savaged by the press, a dispute with 'Def Jam' not helping matters any. Despite all the upheaval, by the release of 'PAUL'S BOUTIQUE' in 1989, the group's profile was negligible and the album was more or less passed over. A tragedy, as it remains one of hip hop's lost gems, a widescreen sampladelic collage produced by the ultra-hip DUST BROTHERS (US). Bypassing the obvious guitar riffs for samples of The BEATLES, CURTIS MAYFIELD and PINK FLOYD along with a kaleidoscopic array of cultural debris and hip references, the album was a funky tour de force. After another extended sabbatical during which the group relocated to California, the BEASTIE BOYS returned in 1992 with 'CHECK YOUR HEAD'. Hipness and attitude were still there in abundance but by now, the group were using live instrumentation. Despite veering from all out thrash to supple funk, the record was a success and only the BEASTIE BOYS could get away with a TED NUGENT collaboration ('THE BIZ VS THE NUGE'). 'ILL COMMUNICATION' (1994) developed this strategy to stunning effect. From the irresistable funk of 'SURE SHOT' and 'ROOT DOWN' to the laid back swing of 'GET IT TOGETHER' and 'FLUTE LOOP', this was the group's most mature and accomplished work to date. The hardcore was still there, 'TOUGH GUY' and 'HEART ATTACK MAN' but it was offset by the sombre strings of 'EUGENE'S LAMENT' and the mellow 'RICKY'S THEME'. A double A-side 'GET IT TOGETHER' and the screechingly brilliant 'SABOTAGE' (complete with entertaining cop-pastiche video) quite rightly returning them into the UK Top 20. From the artwork to the meditative feel of the music (well o.k., maybe not the punk numbers) it was no surprise that YAUCH had become a buddhist and the band subsequently played a high profile benefit for the oppressed nation of Tibet. Ever industrious, the group also started their own label and fanzine 'Grand Royal', signing the likes of LUSCIOUS JACKSON and the now "Big In Japan" BIS. Between development on their magnum-opus comeback (see below), The BEASTIE BOYS dabbled in more electronic/hardcore/instrumental tomfoolery via three mini-albums/EP's, 'ROOT DOWN' (1995), 'AGLIO E OLIO' (1995) and 'THE IN SOUND FROM WAY OUT!' (1996). 1998's 'INTERGALACTIC' single (along with bizarre Power-Rangers-esque video) led the way for the release of the eagerly-awaited 5th set proper, 'HELLO NASTY', an uncompromising, no-holds barred 23-track blinder. With reviews getting near perfect results it was inevitable that The BEASTIEs would have their first transatlantic chart-topper. The band had not lost their tongue-in-cheek attitude despite their recent shifts to a more harmonic religion. Such examples of this would be UK hit singles, 'BODY MOVIN' and 'REMOTE CONTROL', which would also turn up on double-CD anthology 'THE SOUNDS OF SCIENCE' (1999). • **Songwriters:** Although they released few cover versions, they sampled many songs (see above). In 1992, they covered JIMMY JAMES (Jimi Hendrix) + TIME FOR LIVIN' (Stewart Frontline), also collaborating with NISHITA. • **Trivia:** ADAM HOROWITZ is the son of playwright ISRAEL. HOROWITZ played a cameo role in TV serial 'The Equalizer' (circa '88).

Album rating: LICENSED TO 'ILL (*8) / PAUL'S BOUTIQUE (*7) / CHECK YOUR HEAD (*7) / ILL: COMMUNICATION (*9) / HELLO NASTY (*9) / THE SOUNDS OF SCIENCE compilation (*8)

'MCA' ADAM YAUCH (b. 5 Aug'65, Brooklyn, New York) – vocals / **'MIKE D' MIKE DIAMOND** (b.20 Nov'66, New York) – vocals / **KATE SCHELLENBACH** (b. 5 Jan'66, New York City) – drums / **JOHN BERRY** – guitar

	Ratcage	Ratcage
Nov 82. (7"ep) <*(MOTR 21)*> **POLLY WOG STEW EP**		

– B.E.A.S.T.I.E. boys / Transit cop / Jimi / Holy snappers / Riot fight / Ode to . . . / Michelle's farm / Egg raid on mojo. *(UK-iss.Apr88 12"/c-s; same) (re-iss. 12"ep/c-ep/cd-ep Feb93; same)*

—— **KIND AD-ROCK – ADAM HOROWITZ** (b.31 Oct'67, New York City) – vocals,

guitar (ex-The YOUNG & THE USELESS) repl.BERRY + SCHELLENBACH (she later joined LUSCIOUS JACKSON)

Aug 83. (7") <*MOTR 26*> **COOKY PUSS. / BEASTIE REVOLUTION**	-	

(UK-iss.Jan85 + Jul87; MOTR 26 C/CD) (cd-ep-iss.Dec87; same) (re-issues +=) – Bonus batter / Cooky puss (censored version). *(re-iss. 12"ep/c-ep/cd-ep Feb93; same)*

—— added guest RICK RUBIN – scratcher, DJ

	Def Jam	Def Jam
Dec 85. (12"ep; w-drawn) <002> **ROCK HARD / BEASTIE GROOVE. / THE PARTY'S GETTING ROUGH / BEASTIE GROOVE (instrumental)**	-	-
Jan 86. (7"/12") *(A/TA 6686)* <05683> **SHE'S ON IT. / SLOW AND LOW**	-	-
May 86. (7"/12") *(A/TA 7055)* <05864> **HOLD IT NOW, HIT IT. / ACAPULCO (Hold it now, hit it acapella)**	-	-
Sep 86. (7") *(650 114-7)* **SHE'S ON IT. / SLOW AND LOW** (12"+=) *(650 114-6)* – Hold it now, hit it.	-	-
Nov 86. (7") *(650 169-7)* <06341> **IT'S THE NEW STYLE. / PAUL REVERE**	-	-

(12"+=) *(650 169-6)* – ('A'&'B' instrumentals). (d12"++=) *(650 169-8)* – Hold it now, hit it / Hold it now, hit it (Acapulco version) / Hold it now, hit it (instrumental).

Nov 86. (7"/c/cd) *(450 062-1/-4/-2)* <40238> **LICENSED TO 'ILL**	7	1

– Rhymin and stealin' / The new style / She's crafty / Posse in effect / Slow ride / Girls / (You gotta) Fight for your right (to party) / No sleep till Brooklyn / Paul Revere / Hold it now, hit it / Brass monkey / Slow and low / Time to get ill. *(re-iss. Nov89 on 'Capitol'; 460 949-1) (re-iss. Jun94 cd/c; 460 949-2/-4) (cd re-iss. Jul95 & Nov99; 527351-2)*

Dec 86. (7") <06595> **(YOU GOTTA) FIGHT FOR YOUR RIGHT (TO PARTY). / PAUL REVERE**	-	7
Feb 87. (7") *(650 418-7)* **(YOU GOTTA) FIGHT FOR YOUR RIGHT (TO PARTY). / TIME TO GET ILL**	11	-

(12"+=) *(650 418-6)* – No sleep till Brooklyn.

Apr 87. (7") <06675> **NO SLEEP TILL BROOKLYN. / SHE'S CRAFTY**	-	-
May 87. (7"/7"sha-pic-d) *(BEAST/+P 1)* **NO SLEEP TILL BROOKLYN. / POSSE IN EFFECT**	14	-

(12"+=) *(BEASTT 1)* – Hold it now, hit it / Brass monkey.

Jul 87. (7"/7"s/7"s) *(BEAST/+B/D 2)* **SHE'S ON IT. / SLOW AND LOW**	10	-

(12"+=) *(BEASTT 2)* – Hold it now, hit it.

Sep 87. (7"/7"s/7"s/10"sha-pic-d) *(BEAST/+P/S/Q/W 3)* **GIRLS. / SHE'S CRAFTY**	34	-

(12"+=/12"s+=) *(BEASTT/+Q 3)* – Rock hard.

Mar 88. (7") <07020> **BRASS MONKEY. / POSSE IN EFFECT**	-	48

—— no more RICK RUBIN as DJ

	Capitol	Capitol
Jul 89. (7") *(CL 540)* <44454> **HEY LADIES. / SHAKE YOUR RUMP**		36

(12"ep+=/cd-ep+=) *(12/CD CL 540)* **LOVE AMERICAN STYLE** – 33% God / Dis yourself in '89 (just do it). *(re-iss. Jul98 on 'Grand Royal'; GR 064)*

Jul 89. (cd/c/lp) *(DE/TC+/EST 2102)* <91743> **PAUL'S BOUTIQUE**	44	14

– To all the girls / Shake your rump / Johnny Ryall / Egg man / High plains drifter / The sound of science / 3-minute rule / Hey ladies / 5-piece chicken dinner / Looking down the barrel of a gun / Car thief / What comes around / Shadrach / Ask for Janice / B-boy bouillabaisse:- (a) 59 Chrystie Street, (b) Get on the mic, (c) Stop that train, (d) A year and a day, (e) Hello Brooklyn, (f) Dropping names, (g) Lay it on me, (h) Mike on the mic, (i) A.W.O.L.

Aug 89. (12"ep) <Y 15523> **AN EXCITING EVENING AT HOME WITH SHADRACH, MESHACH AND ABEDNEGO EP**	-	

– Shadrach / Caught in the middle of a 3-way mix / And what you give is what you get / Car thief / Some dumb cop gave me two tickets already / Your sister's def.

—— Trio now also on instruments; **MCA** – bass / **AD ROCK** – keyboards / **MIKE D** – drums

Apr 92. (c-s/7") *(TC+/CL 653)* **PASS THE MIC. / PROFESSOR BOOTY**	47	

(etched-12"+=/c-s+=) *(12CL/TCCLX 653)* – Time for livin' / Drunken Praying Mantis style. (cd-s) *(CDCL 653)* – ('A'side) / Netty's girl / Something's got to give / ('A'-pt.2 – The skills to pay the bills).

May 92. (cd/c/d-lp) *(CD/TC+/EST 2171)* <98938> **CHECK YOUR HEAD**		10

– Jimmy James / Funky boss / Pass the mic / Gratitude / Lighten up / Finger lickin' good / So what 'cha want / The biz .vs. the Nuge (with TED NUGENT) / Time for livin' / Something's got to give / The blue nun / Stand together / Pow / The maestro / Groove Holmes / Live at P.J.'s / Mark on the bus / Professor Booty / In 3's / Namaste. *(re-iss. Sep94; CDP 798938-2) (d-lp re-iss. Nov98; GR 066)*

May 92. (12"ep/c-ep/cd-ep) <Y/4Y/C2 15836> **JIMMY JAMES / THE MAESTRO / JIMMY JAMES (album version) / BOOMIN' GRANNY / JIMMY JAMES (original) / DRINKIN' WINE**	-	-
Jun 92. (12"ep/12"white-ep/c-ep) *(12CL 665)* **FROZEN METAL HEAD EP**	55	-

– Jimmy James / So what'cha want (All the way live freestyle version) / Jimmy James (original) / Drinkin' wine. (cd-ep) *(CDCL 665)* – The blue nun *[repl. original]*

Jun 92. (cd-ep) <15847> **SO WHAT'CHA WANT (3 versions; including pt.2 – The Skills to pay the bills) / GROOVE HOLMES (2 versions)**	-	93
Dec 92. (12"ep/cd-ep) <Y/C2 07777> **GRATITUDE EP**	-	

– Gratitude / Stand together (live) / Finger lickin' good (remix) / Gratitude (live) / Honkey rink.

	Capitol	Grand Royal
May 94. (cd/c/d-lp) *(CD/TC+/EST 2229)* <28599> **ILL: COMMUNICATION**	10	1

– Sure shot / Tough guy / Freak freak / Bobo on the corner / Root down / Sabotage / Get it together / Sabrosa / The update / Futterman's rule / Alright hear this / Eugene's lament / Flute loop / Do it / Rick's theme / Heart attack man / The scoop / Shambala / Bodhisattva vow / Transitions. *(lp re-iss. Apr97 on 'Grand Royal'; GR 006LP)*

Jul 94. (c-s/7"green) *(TC+/CL 716)* **GET IT TOGETHER. / SABOTAGE / DOPE LITTLE SONG**	19	

(10") *(10CL 716)* – (first 2 tracks) / ('A'-Buck Wild remix) / ('A'instrumental).

Nov 94. (7"maroon) (CL 726) **SURE SHOT. / MULLET HEAD / SURE SHOT (Mario mix)**　`27`
(10"+=) (10CL 726) – The vibes.
(cd-s+=) (CDCLS 726) – Son of neck bone.
(cd-s) (CDCL 726) – ('A'mixes:- Pruins – European B-Boy / Nardone / Large Professor / instrumental).

Jun 95. (m-cd/m-c/m-lp) (CD/TC+/EST 2262) <33603> **ROOT DOWN EP** (some live)　`23`　`50`
– Root down (free zone mix) / Root down / Root down (PP balloon mix) / Time to get ill / Heart attack man / The maestro / Sabrosa / Flute loop / Time for livin' / Something's got to give / So what'cha want. (m-lp-iss.Apr97 on 'Grand Royal'; GR 018)

Dec 95. (12"ep/cd-ep) <GR 026/+CD> **AGLIO E OLIO** (11 minutes of hardcore)　`-`
– Brand new / Deal with me / Believe me / Nervous assistant / Square wave in unison / You catch a bad one / I can't think straight / I want some. (UK-iss.Mar98; same)

—— added guest co-writers **(MONEY) MARK RAMOS NISHITA** – claviers / **ERIC BOBO** – percussion / **EUGENE GORE** – violin

Mar 96. (cd/c) (CD/TC EST 2281) <7243 8 33590-2/-4> **THE IN SOUND FROM WAY OUT!** (instrumental)　`45`　`45`
– Groove Holmes / Sabrosa / Namaste / Pow / Son of neckbone / In 3's / Eugene's lament / Bobo on the corner / Shambala / Lighten up / Ricky's theme / Transitions / Drinkin' wine. (lp re-iss. Jan99 on 'Grand Royal'; GRA 80013)

Jun 98. (c-s) (TCCL 803) <58705> **INTERGALACTIC / HAIL SAGAN (Special K)**　`5`　`28` Jul98
(cd-s+=) (CDCL 803) – ('A'-Prisoners Of Technology TMSI remix).
(10") (10CL 803) – ('A'side) / ('A'-Prisoners Of . . . remix).

Jul 98. (cd/c/d-lp) (495723-2/-4/-1) <37716> **HELLO NASTY**　`1`　`1`
– Super disco breakin' / The move / Remote control / Song for the man / Just a test / Body movin' / Intergalactic / Sneakin' out of hospital / Putting shame in your game / Flowin' prose / And me / Three MC's and one DJ / Can't, won't, don't stop / Song for Junior / I don't know / The negotiation Limerick file / Electrify / Picture this / Unite / Dedication / Dr. Lee PhD / Instant death.

Oct 98. (cd-s) (CDCLS 809) **BODY MOVIN' / (Mickey Finn mix) / DR. LEE phD (dub mix)**　`15`
(cd-s) (CDCL 809) – ('A'side) / (Fatboy Slim remix) / (Peanut butter and jelly mix).
(12") (12CL 809) – ('A'side) / (Kut Masta Kurt remix) / (Erick Sermon remix) / (instrumental).
(re-iss. /re-mixed May99 on GR 069/063)

May 99. (12"/cd-s) (12CL/CDCLS 812) **REMOTE CONTROL / THREE MC'S AND ONE DJ / THE NEGOTIATION LIMERICK FILE (Ganja Kru – or – the 41 Small Star remix)**　`21`
(cd-s) (CDCL 812) – ('A'side) / Three MC's and one DJ (live video version) / Putting shame in your game (mix) / Three MC's and one DJ (enhanced video).

Aug 99. (12"ep) <(GR 071)> **SCIENTIST OF SOUND**
– Negotiation Limerick file (mixes) / Intergalactic / Three MC's and one DJ / Body movin' (mixes) / Putting shame in your game.

Nov 99. (d-cd/d-c) (522940-2/-4) <22940> **THE SOUNDS OF SCIENCE** (compilation)　`36`　`19`
– Beastie Boys / Slow and low / Shake your rump / Gratitude / Skills to pay the bills / Root down / Believe me / Sure shot / Body movin' / Boomin' granny / (You gotta) Fight for your right (to party) / Country Mike's theme / Pass the mic / Something's got to give / Bodhisattva vow / Sabrosa / Song for the man / Soba violence / Alive / Jimmy James / Three MC's and one DJ / Biz vs. the Nuge / Sabotage / Shadrach / Brass monkey / Time for livin' / Dub the mic / Benny and the jets / Negotion limerick file / I want some / She's on it / Son of neckbone / Get it together / Twenty questions / Remote control / Railroad blues / Live wire / So what'cha want / Netty's girl / Egg raid on mojo / Hey ladies / Intergalactic.

Dec 99. (10") (10CL 818) **ALIVE / START! / ALIVE (B.R.A. remix)**　`28`
(cd-s+=) (CDCLS 818) – Start! (video).
(cd-s) (CDCL 818) – ('A'side) / You and me together / Big shot (live) / ('A'-video).

– compilations, etc. –

Feb 94. (cd/c) Honey World; (CD/TC EST 2225) / Grand Royal; <89843> **SOME OLD BULLSHIT**　`46`
– (compilation of 1st 2 EP's) (re-iss. Jan99; same)

BEAT

Formed: Birmingham, England . . . Autumn 1978 by DAVE WAKELING, ANDY COX, DAVID STEELE and EVERETT MORTON. Following a number of low-key gigs, the quartet expanded their musical horizons with the addition of rapper/toaster RANKING ROGER and veteran saxophonist, SAXA, the latter having previously played with the legendary PRINCE BUSTER (whose 'ROUGH RIDER' the BEAT later covered). Signed to the ultra-hip creative centre of the ska revival, '2-Tone', the BEAT hit the UK Top 10 straight-off in late '79 with a high-octane blue-beat cover of Smokey Robinson's 'TEARS OF A CLOWN' (backed by the equally frenetic 'RANKING FULL STOP'). Spurred on by their success, the band negotiated their own label, 'Go Feet', under the sponsorship of 'Arista', stipulating that they required full creative control. Thankfully they got it and 1980 proved their golden year; 'HANDS OFF . . . SHE'S MINE' made the Top 10 while the compulsive claustrophobia of 'MIRROR IN THE BATHROOM' went Top 5. Both a landmark album in the ska movement and a classic pop record in its own right, 'I JUST CAN'T STOP IT' (1980) was a nigh on perfect combination of black and white music styles laced with humour, caustic lyrical wit and biting politicism. 'STAND DOWN MARGARET' was a self explanatory message to Thatcher and her cronies with the band pledging their support to a number of left wing causes including CND. Yet as the 2-Tone movement lost its momentum with main players MADNESS and The SPECIALS pursuing new musical avenues, The BEAT chose to emphasise the reggae element to limited success on Top 3 follow-up set, 'WHA'PPEN' (1981). Although the

'DROWNING' single narrowly missed the Top 20, from this point on hits became thin on the ground and the band made a concerted effort to break the lucrative American market (where they were billed as The ENGLISH BEAT to avoid confusion with the US outfit of the same name). Although third album, 'SPECIAL BEAT SERVICE' (1982) scraped into the US Top 40 (UK Top 30), it failed to produce any hits with even the infectious 'JEANETTE' lingering outside the 40. This marked the end of the line for the ageing SAXA who retired due to ill health. His replacement was WESLEY MAGOOGAN, the band also augmenting their final recordings with keyboard player, DAVID 'Blockhead' WRIGHT. Paradoxically, The BEAT had a final piece of chart action when a remixed version of 'CAN'T GET USED TO LOSING YOU' (an ANDY WILLIAMS hit that originally appeared on the first album) went Top 3 in Spring '83. It was too little too late though and following the release of a retrospective, 'WHAT IS BEAT? (THE BEST OF THE BEAT)' later that year they finally threw in the towel. WAKELING and ROGER subsequently became GENERAL PUBLIC while COX and STEELE became pop stars all over again with The FINE YOUNG CANNIBALS.

Album rating: I JUST CAN'T STOP IT (*7) / WHA'PPEN? (*5) / SPECIAL BEAT SERVICE (*4) / WHAT IS BEAT? (THE BEST OF THE BEAT) compilation (*7) / BPM – THE VERY BEST OF THE BEAT compilation (*7)

DAVE WAKELING (b.19 Feb'56) – vocals, guitar / **ANDY COX** (b.25 Jan'56) – guitar / **DAVID STEELE** (b. 8 Sep'60, Isle Of Wight) – bass / **EVERETT MORTON** (b. 5 Apr'51, West Indies) – drums (ex-JOAN ARMATRADING BAND) / **RANKING ROGER** (b.ROGER CHARLEY, 21 Feb'61) – toaster/vocals (ex-DUM DUM BOYS) / **SAXA** (b.'31, Jamaica) – saxophone (ex-PRINCE BUSTER) (temp.then permanent)

	2-Tone-Chrysalis	not iss.
Dec 79. (7") (CHSTT 6) **TEARS OF A CLOWN. / RANKING FULL STOP**	6	-

	Go Feet-Arista	Sire
Feb 80. (7") (FEET 1) **HANDS OFF . . . SHE'S MINE. / TWIST AND CRAWL**	9	
Apr 80. (7") (FEET 2) **MIRROR IN THE BATHROOM. / JACKPOT**	4	
May 80. (lp/c) (BEAT/TCBT 1) <6091> **I JUST CAN'T STOP IT**	3	Jul80

– Mirror in the bathroom / Hands off . . . she's mine / Two swords / Twist and crawl / Rough rider / Click click / Big shot / Whine and grine – Ranking full stop / Stand down Margaret / Noise in this world / Can't get used to losing you / Best friend / Jackpot. (re-iss. Mar84 on 'Fame' lp/c; FA/TC-FA 413091-1/-4) (cd-iss. Oct99 on 'London'; BTCD 1)

	Go Feet-Arista	Sire
Aug 80. (7") (FEET 3) **BEST FRIEND. / STAND DOWN MARGARET**	22	
Nov 80. (7"/12") (FEET/+12 4) **TOO NICE TO TALK TO. / PSYCHEDELIC ROCKERS**	7	
Apr 81. (7") (FEET 6) **DROWNING. / ALL OUT TO GET YOU**	22	
May 81. (lp/c) (BEAT/TCBT 3) <3567> **WHA'PPEN?**	3	Jun81

– Doors of your heart / All out to get you / Monkey murders / I am your flag / French toast / Drowning / Dreamhouse in N.Z. / Walk away / Over and over / Cheated / Get a job / The limits we set. (cd-iss. Oct99 on 'London'; BTCD 3)

Jun 81. (7") (FEET 9) **DOORS OF YOUR HEART. / GET A JOB**	33	
(12") (FEET12 9) – ('A'side) / Drowning.		
Nov 81. (7"/12") (FEET/+12 11) **HIT IT. / WHICH SIDE OF THE BED**	70	

	Go Feet-Arista	I.R.S.
Apr 82. (7"/12") (FEET/+12 333) **SAVE IT FOR LATER. / WHAT'S YOUR BEST THING**	47	-
Sep 82. (7"/12") (FEET/+12 15) **JEANETTE. / MARCH OF THE SWIVELHEADS**	45	-
Sep 82. (lp/c) (BEAT/TCBT 5) <70032> **SPECIAL BEAT SERVICE**	21	39 Nov82

– I confess / Jeanette / Sorry / Sole salvation / Spar with me / Rotating head / Save it for later / She's going / Pato and Roger a go talk / Sugar and stress / End of the party / Ackee 1-2-3. (cd-iss. 1988 on 'Illegal-IRS'; CD 70032) (cd re-iss. Oct99 on 'London'; BTCD 5)

Nov 82. (7") **JEANETTE. / SAVE IT FOR LATER**	-	

—— **WESLEY MAGOOGAN** – sax (ex-HAZEL O'CONNOR) repl. SAXA due to ill health / (on tour) **DAVID 'Blockhead' WRIGHT** – keyboards

Nov 82. (7") (FEET 16) **I CONFESS. / SOLE SALVATION**	54	
(12") (FEET12 16) – ('A'&'B' remixed versions).		
(d7"+=) – Spar with me (live) / Doors of your heart (live) / Mirror in the bathroom (live).		
Jan 83. (7") **I CONFESS. / MARCH OF THE SWIVELHEADS**	-	
Apr 83. (7"/12") (FEET/+12 17) **CAN'T GET USED TO LOSING YOU (remix). / SPAR WITH ME**	3	
May 83. (lp/c) (BEAT/TCBT 6) <70040> **WHAT IS BEAT? (THE BEST OF THE BEAT)**	10	87 Dec83

– Tears of a clown / Hands off . . . she's mine / Mirror in the bathroom / Stand down Margaret / Twist and crawl / Doors of your heart / Save it for later / Too nice to talk to / I confess / Best friend / Drowning / Ackee 1-2-3 / Can't get used to losing you / Ranking full stop. (lp w/free cd of remixes incl. on US cd version)

Jun 83. (7") (FEET 18) **ACKEE 1-2-3. / MONKEY MURDERS**	54	-
(12") (FEET12 18) – ('A'side) / I confess (US remix).		

—— split in Jul'83 when WAKELING and ROGER formed GENERAL PUBLIC. COX and STEELE formed FINE YOUNG CANNIBALS in the mid-80's. In the early 90's, The BEAT teamed up with The SPECIALS (as The SPECIAL BEAT) and issued a couple of live albums, 'SPECIAL BEAT LIVE' and 'LIVE IN JAPAN'

– compilations, etc. –

Aug 83. (d-c) Go Feet-Arista; (XTWO 23) **I JUST CAN'T STOP IT / WHA'PPEN?**	-	
Jan 96. (7"/c-s/cd-s) Go Feet-Arista; (74321 23206-7/-4/-2) **MIRROR IN THE BATHROOM**	44	-
(cd-s) (74321 31923-2) – ('A'mixes).		
Feb 96. (cd/c) Go Feet-Arista; (74321 23195-2/-4) **B.P.M. – THE VERY BEST OF THE BEAT**	13	-

– Mirror in the bathroom / Hands off . . . she's mine / Twist and crawl / Jackpot / Tears of a clown / Ranking fullstop / Rough rider / Best friend / Stand down Margaret / Too nice to talk to / All out to get you / Door of

your heart / Drowning / Can't get used to losing you / I confess / Save it for later.
(below stuff was actually fresh recordings as the INTERNATIONAL BEAT)

Jan 99. (3xcd-box; shared with SKALETTE O'HARA & JUDGE DREAD) *Dressed To Kill; (DTKBOX 89)* **SKA HITS VOL.1** ☐ -

Aug 99. (cd) *Dressed To Kill; (DRESS 605)* **THEIR MOST EXPLOSIVE HITS** ☐ ☐

Sep 99. (cd; shared with SELECTER) *Proper; (ABCD 118)* **THE ULTIMATE TWO-TONE SKA ALBUM** ☐ -

BEATLES

Formed: Liverpool, England ... by JOHN LENNON and PAUL McCARTNEY as schoolboy band The QUARRYMEN in 1957. GEORGE HARRISON joined up the following year, although they split late '59. They reformed in the Spring of 1960 as The SILVER BEATLES, adding PETE BEST and STU SUTCLIFFE. Dropping the SILVER part of their name, they employed manager Alan Williams, who secured them local gigs. Later that year, they toured Hamburg, West Germany, although they had to return when HARRISON was deported for being under eighteen. On the 21st of March '61, they debuted at Liverpool's 'Cavern Club', preceding another 3-month stint in Hamburg. While there, they recorded for 'Polydor' records, backing cabaret-type pop singer TONY SHERIDAN. (These recordings were later released, when the band were at the peak of their popularity). Around mid-'61, STU stayed in Hamburg to get married and study art. There, he was to tragically die of a brain haemorrhage on the 10th April of 1962. With PAUL now on bass and BRIAN EPSTEIN as their new manager, they laid down a demo for 'Decca', which was subsequently disregarded by DICK ROWE. Instead he signed BRIAN POOLE & THE TREMELOES (!), although he soon found consolation when he contracted future rivals-to-be The ROLLING STONES. Summer '62 brought sunshine when George Martin introduced them to EMI's 'Parlophone' label. During rehearsals BEST was fired and replaced by the more experienced drummer RINGO STARR. By the end of 1962 their debut single 'LOVE ME DO' was in the UK Top 20. The follow-up 'PLEASE PLEASE ME' (1963) reached No.2 and The BEATLES had arrived, their breezy, fresh-faced pop striking a chord in a music scene that was crying out for a band with the effortless charisma of the cheeky Scousers. More, their mop-topped, sharp-suited image (courtesy of BRIAN EPSTEIN) remains one of the most enduring impressions in the history of pop culture. And thus did that dog-eared cliche of a phenomenon, 'BEATLEMANIA' tighten its grip as the band toured above ROY ORBISON later that year to unprecedented scenes of teenage delirium. They also found time to knock out a debut album, 'PLEASE PLEASE ME' (1963), produced by their mentor George Martin and featuring a heady cocktail of live wig-outs ('I SAW HER STANDING THERE', 'TWIST AND SHOUT' etc.) and LENNON/McCARTNEY originals. This precocious songwriting partnership was entering its golden period as the band notched up an incredible string of No.1 singles in quick succession, 'FROM ME TO YOU' (1963), 'SHE LOVES YOU' (1963), 'I WANT TO HOLD YOUR HAND' (1963) and 'CAN'T BUY ME LOVE' (1964). The BEATLES finished 1963 in fine style; a No.1 follow-up album, 'WITH THE BEATLES', the biggest selling single in British history, 'SHE LOVES YOU' and a performance before the Queen Mother at the Royal Command Variety Performance. With British domination well under way, the band flew to America in February 1964, droves of hysterical fans greeting them upon their landing at New York's Kennedy Airport. They made a legendary appearance on the 'Ed Sullivan Show' and by April The BEATLES held the top five positions in the American Billboard singles charts (i.e. No.1:- CAN'T BUY ME LOVE, 2:- TWIST AND SHOUT, 3:- SHE LOVES YOU, 4:- I WANT TO HOLD YOUR HAND, 5:- PLEASE PLEASE ME). Flying high, that summer saw the release of The BEATLES' first movie and accompanying soundtrack, 'A HARD DAY'S NIGHT'. The band proved themselves as compelling on screen as on stage, and the film's revolutionary shooting technique created the blueprint for decades of rockumentaries to come. The same year also saw the release of the band's third album, 'BEATLES FOR SALE', a record which included some of the last genuine LENNON/McCARTNEY collaborations. Each was developing his own particular style and although all their songs continued to be credited as joint efforts, by the following year the pair seldom wrote together. 'HELP' (1965), a filmic follow-up to 'A HARD DAY'S NIGHT', featured some of LENNON and McCARTNEY's most focused songwriting to date (notably the title track and 'YESTERDAY') and was filmed at various locations around the globe. The BEATLES performed before a record number of fans at New York's Shea Stadium in August, the same month as 'HELP' was opened in the U.S. By this point The BEATLES were undoubtedly the biggest pop/rock band in the world, unique in their ability to produce music that seemingly crossed all boundaries of age, race, class and gender. Even so, it was a shock to the rock world when the Queen announced in the summer of '65 that the band were each to receive an M.B.E.. It was almost unthinkable that bad boy rivals The ROLLING STONES would be given such a (dubious) honour, and while the two bands were poles apart musically, LSD and the burgeoning psychedelic culture brought them together briefly. 'RUBBER SOUL' (1965), written and recorded in just over a month, was the sound of The BEATLES in flux, shedding their clean cut image and interpreting the influence of BOB DYLAN's pioneering folk-rock experiments. Despite the transformation taking place, the sound was more fluid and assured, the songwriting more mature. LENNON's 'IN MY LIFE' was beautifully bittersweet while McCARTNEY almost equalled 'YESTERDAY' with 'MICHELLE', and the

lilting 'NORWEGIAN WOOD' saw HARRISON's first forays into sitar work. The album was sandwiched between pioneering double A-sided singles 'DAY TRIPPER' / 'WE CAN WORK IT OUT' (1965) and 'PAPERBACK WRITER' / 'RAIN' (1966). 'RAIN' was the first overtly psychedelic BEATLES record, innovative in its use of rhythm and featuring an undulating LENNON vocal (a style much mimicked by many of today's crop of young bands). Its potential was fully realised on 'REVOLVER' (1966), oft cited as The BEATLES' pinnacle achievement and as one of the best albums ever made. McCARTNEY excelled himself with the string-cloaked melancholy of 'ELEANOR RIGBY', while HARRISON's biting 'TAXMAN' kicked off the album in strident style. But it was the psychedelic numbers which made most impact. 'SHE SAID SHE SAID' was a swirling piece of trip-pop, while 'TOMORROW NEVER KNOWS' remains one of the most bizarre and enigmatic songs in The BEATLES' canon. With a working title of 'THE VOID', the song was based on one of LENNON's first profound acid trips and was partly inspired by the ancient religious text beloved of hippies at the time, 'The Tibetan Book Of The Dead'. With a hypnotic drum sound that many have since tried and failed to recreate, backwards guitar that sounded like a flock of screeching pterodactyls and LENNON's mantra-like vocals, the record set a precedent in psychedelic rock. At this stage The BEATLES were already preoccupied with the possibilities of the recording studio and significantly, the band played their last gig in San Francisco's Candlestick Park the same month 'REVOLVER' was released. Ensconced in Abbey Road Studios, the band came up with the double A-side, 'PENNY LANE' / 'STRAWBERRY FIELDS FOREVER'. Released in February '67, the single's effects-laden innovation was a taster for The BEATLES' much heralded psychedelic concept album 'SGT. PEPPER'S LONELY HEARTS CLUB BAND'. Its release coinciding perfectly with the fabled 1967 'Summer Of Love', the record was a landmark in new studio technique. Utilising the (then) pioneering four-track recording process, the band painstakingly pieced together ornate pieces of sonic intricacy that set new standards. It contained many classics such as 'LUCY IN THE SKY WITH DIAMONDS' (wrongly thought by many to be about L.S.D.), 'SHE'S LEAVING HOME' and the never-ending 'A DAY IN THE LIFE', complete with prolonged intentionally stuck-in-the-groove outro. Fans and critics alike made it "their greatest album of all time", although many others thought it too overblown as well as over-produced. A month later, the anthemic 'ALL YOU NEED IS LOVE' gave them another No.1, helped no doubt by its simultaneous worldwide TV broadcast. The death of BRIAN EPSTEIN cast a shadow over the celebrations but the band moved on, filming/recording 'MAGICAL MYSTERY TOUR' (1967). A trippy film and soundtrack inspired by KEN KESEY and his bunch of technicolour minstrels, it contained the infamous LENNON-penned surrealism of 'I AM THE WALRUS'. Screened on British TV on Boxing Day 1967, the film was almost universally panned. Unbowed, The BEATLES decamped to India for spiritual retreat with the Maharishi Mahesh Yogi, during which time they accumulated much of the material that would form the 'WHITE ALBUM'. Upon their return to English shores, they set about forming the 'Apple Corporation', which would handle all the business dealings of the band as well as functioning as a label for The BEATLES and likeminded talent. The first release was 'HEY JUDE' / 'REVOLUTION' (1968), the former a rousing torch song, the latter a stinging attack by LENNON on would-be radicals. Eventually released in November '68, 'THE BEATLES (White Album)' was a sprawling double set recorded in an environment of tension and breakdown of inter-band communications. Yet it contained some of The BEATLES finest songs, HARRISON's solemn 'WHILE MY GUITAR GENTLY WEEPS', LENNON's gorgeous 'DEAR PRUDENCE' and 'JULIA', a moving tribute to his mother. The album also included the cryptic genius of LENNON's 'HAPPINESS IS A WARM GUN' while 'REVOLUTION No.9' was The BEATLES at their most defiantly experimental. Nevertheless, the recording had strained relationships within the band to breaking point and the subsequent back to basics sessions in 1969 (eventually emerging as the 'LET IT BE' album) broke down in disarray. Incredibly, the band got it together one last time for 'ABBEY ROAD' (1969), a breathtaking sweep through the diverse styles of each of the songwriters. GEORGE HARRISON contributed two of his best tracks, 'SOMETHING' and the pastoral beauty of 'HERE COMES THE SUN'. McCARTNEY penned most of the medley which formed a sizeable chunk of the album and which included one of his most heartbreakingly lovely songs, 'GOLDEN SLUMBERS'. 'LET IT BE', eventually released in 1970 was hardly a fitting epitaph for The BEATLES, PHIL SPECTOR's production coming in for some flak. It did, however, contain such definitive BEATLES moments as the deeply reflective title track, the sleepy 'ACROSS THE UNIVERSE' and the beguiling 'THE LONG AND WINDING ROAD'. The BEATLES had officially split a couple of months before the album's release in April 1970, estranged amid personal rows and more serious business disagreements. LENNON, McCARTNEY and HARRISON all went on to resepectable solo careers, although none of the subsequent recordings had quite the same impact as The BEATLES' material. The band remain one of the greatest cultural icons of the 20th Century with a back catalogue that even OASIS will never be able to match. • **Covered:** TWIST AND SHOUT (Isley Brothers) / A TASTE OF HONEY (Bobby Scott) / THERE'S A PLACE / MONEY (Barrett Strong) / ROLL OVER BEETHOVEN + ROCK AND ROLL MUSIC (Chuck Berry) / YOU REALLY GOT A HOLD ON ME (Miracles) / PLEASE MR. POSTMAN (Marvelettes) / KANSAS CITY (Wilbert Harrison) / WORDS OF LOVE (Diamonds) / CHAINS (Cookies) / BABY IT'S YOU (Shirelles) / etc.

Album rating: PLEASE PLEASE ME (*8) / WITH THE BEATLES (*8) / A HARD DAY'S NIGHT (*8) / BEATLES FOR SALE (*7) / HELP! (*8) / RUBBER SOUL

(*9) / REVOLVER (*9) / SGT. PEPPER'S LONELY HEARTS CLUB BAND (*10) / MAGICAL MYSTERY TOUR (*8) / THE BEATLES 'White Album' (*10) / YELLOW SUBMARINE (*5) / ABBEY ROAD (*9) / LET IT BE (*7) / THE BEATLES 1967-70 compilation (*10) / THE BEATLES 1962-66 compilation (*10) / LIVE AT THE BBC collection (*8)

JOHN LENNON (b. JOHN WINSTON LENNON, 9 Oct'40) – vocals, rhythm guitar / **PAUL McCARTNEY** (b. JAMES PAUL McCARTNEY, 18 Jun'42) – vocals, guitar / **GEORGE HARRISON** (b.25 Feb'43) – vocals, lead guitar/ **STU SUTCLIFFE** (b. STUART, 23 Jun'40, Edinburgh, Scotland) – bass/ **PETE BEST** (b.1941) – drums

                                 Polydor   Decca

Jan 62. (7"; as TONY SHERIDAN & THE BEATLES) (NH 66-833) <31382> **MY BONNIE. / THE SAINTS**   [ ]   [ ] Apr62
(re-iss. May63 hit UK No.48; same) (re-iss. Feb64; same) <US re-iss. Jan64 on 'M.G.M.'; K 13213>; hit No. 26) (above A-side was released Aug61 in Germany as TONY SHERIDAN & The BEAT BROTHERS)

——— Were a quartet at the time, STU stayed in Germany, died 10 Apr'62 of brain haemorrhage. McCARTNEY now on bass and vocals.

——— (Aug62) **RINGO STARR** (b.RICHARD STARKEY, 7 Jul'40) – drums (ex-RORY STORM & THE HURRICANES)repl. BEST

                              Parlophone   not iss.

Oct 62. (7") (R 4949) **LOVE ME DO. / P.S. I LOVE YOU**   [17]   [-]
(re-iss. Feb63; same) <US-iss.Apr64 on 'Tollie'; 9008>; hit Nos. 1+10> <US re-iss. Aug64 on 'Oldies'; 45 OL 151> <US re-iss.Oct65 on 'Capitol Starline'; 6062> (re-iss. Oct82; same); hit No.4) (re-iss. cd-s.1989) (re-iss. Oct92; same); hit No.53)

                              Parlophone   Vee Jay

Jan 63. (7") (R 4983) <VJ 498> **PLEASE PLEASE ME. / ASK ME WHY**   [2]   [ ]
(re-iss. Feb63; same) (re-iss. Jan83; same); hit 29) (re-iss. cd-s.1989)

Mar 63. (lp; mono)(lp; stereo) (PMC 1202)(PCS 3042) **PLEASE PLEASE ME**   [1]   [-]
– I saw her standing there / Misery / Anna (go to him) / Chains / Boys / Ask me why / Please please me / Love me do / P.S. I love you / Baby, it's you / Do you want to know a secret / A taste of honey / There's a place / Twist and shout. (c-iss.1970's) (cd-iss. Feb87; CDP 746435-2; hit 32) (re-iss. Nov88 lp/c; PMC/TC-PMC 1202)

Apr 63. (7") (R 5015) <VJ 522> **FROM ME TO YOU. / THANK YOU GIRL**   [1]   [ ]
(re-iss. Apr83; same); hit No.40) (re-iss. cd-s.1989)

Jul 63. (lp) <1062> **INTRODUCING . . . THE BEATLES**   [-]   [2] Feb64
-(tracks nearly same as UK debut)

Aug 63. (7") (R 5055) <Swan; S-4152> **SHE LOVES YOU. / I'LL GET YOU**   [1]   [1] Sep63
(re-iss. Aug83; same); hit No.45) (re-iss. cd-s.1989)

Nov 63. (lp; mono)(lp; stereo) (PMC 1206)(PCS 3042) **WITH THE BEATLES**   [1]   [-]
– It won't be long / All I've got to do / All my loving / Don't bother me / Little child / Till there was you / Please Mr. Postman / Roll over Beethoven / Hold me tight / I really got a hold on me / I wanna be your man / Roll over Beethoven / Devil in her heart / Not a second time / Money. (cd-iss. Feb87; CDP 746436-2; hit No.40) (re-iss. Nov88 lp/c; PMC/TC-PMC 1206)

Nov 63. (7") (R 5084) **I WANT TO HOLD YOUR HAND. / THIS BOY**   [1]   [-]
(re-iss. Nov83; same); hit No.62) (re-iss. cd-s.1989)

Jan 64. (7") <VJ 581> **PLEASE PLEASE ME. / FROM ME TO YOU**   [-]   [3]
<US re-iss. Aug64 on 'Oldies'; 45 OL 150> <US re-iss. Oct65 on 'Capitol Starline'; 6063>

                              Parlophone   Capitol

Jan 64. (7") <5112> **I WANT TO HOLD YOUR HAND. / I SAW HER STANDING THERE**   [-]   [1] [14]

Jan 64. (lp) <2047> **MEET THE BEATLES!**   [-]   [1]
– I want to hold your hand / I saw her standing there / This boy / It won't be long / All I've got to do / All my loving / Don't bother me / Little child / Till there was you / Hold me tight / I wanna be your man / Not a second time.

Mar 64. (7") (R 5114) <5150> **CAN'T BUY ME LOVE. / YOU CAN'T DO THAT**   [1]   [1]
(re-iss. Mar84; same); hit No.53) (re-iss. cd-s.1989)

Apr 64. (lp) <2080> **THE BEATLES' SECOND ALBUM**   [-]   [1]
– Roll over Beethoven / Thank you girl / You really got a hold on me / Devil in her heart / Money / You can't do that / Long tall Sally / I call your name / Please Mr. Postman / I'll get you / She loves you.

Jul 64. (7") (R 5160) **A HARD DAY'S NIGHT. / THINGS WE SAID TODAY**   [1]   [-]
(re-iss. Jul84; same); hit No.52) (re-iss. cd-s.1989)

Jul 64. (7") <5222> **A HARD DAY'S NIGHT. / I SHOULD HAVE KNOWN BETTER**   [-]   [1] [53]

Jul 64. (lp; mono)(lp; stereo) (PMC 1230)(PCS 3058) <6366> **A HARD DAY'S NIGHT (Soundtrack)**   [1]   [1]
– A hard day's night / I should have known better / If I fell / I'm happy just to dance with you / And I love her / Tell me why / Can't buy me love / Anytime at all / I'll cry instead / Things we said today / When I get home / You can't do that / I'll be back. (re-iss. Jan71; same); hit 39) (cd-iss. Feb87; CDP 746437-2; hit No.30) (re-iss. Nov88 lp/c; PMC/TC-PMC 1230)

Aug 64. (7") <5234> **I'LL CRY INSTEAD. / I'M HAPPY JUST TO DANCE WITH YOU**   [-]   [25] [95]

Aug 64. (7") <5235> **AND I LOVE HER. / IF I FELL**   [-]   [12] [53]

Sep 64. (7") <5255> **MATCHBOX. / SLOW DOWN**   [-]   [17] [25]

Nov 64. (7") (R 5200) <5327> **I FEEL FINE. / SHE'S A WOMAN**   [1]   [1] [4]
(re-iss. Nov84; same); hit No.65) (re-iss. cd-s.1989)

Dec 64. (lp; mono)(lp; stereo) (PMC 1240)(PCS 3062) **BEATLES FOR SALE**   [1]   [-]
– No reply / I'm a loser / Baby's in black / Rock and roll music / I'll follow the sun / Mr. Moonlight / Medley: Kansas City – Hey hey hey hey / Eight days a week /

Words of love / Honey don't / Every little thing / I don't want to spoil the party / What you're doing / Everybody's trying to be my baby. (c-iss.1970's) (cd-iss. Feb87; CDP 746438-2); hit No.45) (re-iss. Nov88 lp/c; PMC/TC-PMC 1240)

Jan 65. (lp) <2228> **BEATLES '65**   [-]   [1]
– (track listing near as above)

Feb 65. (7") (5371) **EIGHT DAYS A WEEK. / I DON'T WANT TO SPOIL THE PARTY**   [-]   [1] [39]

Apr 65. (7") (R 5265) <5407> **TICKET TO RIDE. / YES IT IS**   [1]   [1]
(re-iss. Apr85; hit No.70) (re-iss. cd-s.1989)

Jul 65. (lp) <2358> **BEATLES VI**   [-]   [1]
– Kansas City / Eight days a week / You like me too much / Bad boy / I don't want to spoil the party / Words of love / What you're doing / Yes it is / Dizzy Miss Lizzy / Tell me what you see / Every little thing.

Jul 65. (7") (R 5305) <5476> **HELP!. / I'M DOWN**   [1]   [1]
(re-iss. Jul85; same); hit No.37) (re-iss. cd-s.1989)

Jul 65. (lp; mono)(lp; stereo) (PMC 1255)(PCS PCS 3071) <2386> **HELP! (Soundtrack)**   [1]   [1] Aug65
– Help! / The night before / You've got to hide your love away / I need you / Another girl / You're going to lose that girl / Ticket to ride / Act naturally / It's only love / You like me too much / Tell me what you see / I've just seen a face / Yesterday / Dizzy Miss Lizzy. (re-iss. Jul71 lp/c; same); hit No.33) (cd-iss. Apr87; CDP 746439-2); hit No.61) (re-iss. Nov88 lp/c; PMC/TC-PMC 1255)

Sep 65. (7") <5498> **YESTERDAY. / ACT NATURALLY**   [-]   [1]

Dec 65. (7") (R 5389) <5555> **DAY TRIPPER. / WE CAN WORK IT OUT**   [1]   [5] [1]
(re-iss. Dec85; same) (re-iss. cd-s.1989)

Dec 65. (lp; mono)(lp; stereo) (PMC 1267)(PCS 3075) <2442> **RUBBER SOUL**   [1]   [1]
– Drive my car / Norwegian wood (this bird has flown) / You won't see me / Nowhere man / Think for yourself / The word / Michelle / What goes on? / Girl / I'm looking through you / In my life / Wait / If I needed someone / Run for your life. (c-iss.1970's) (cd-iss. Apr87; CDP 746440-2); hit UK No.60) (re-iss. Nov88 lp/c; PMC/TC-PMC 1267)

Feb 66. (7") <5587> **NOWHERE MAN. / WHAT GOES ON**   [-]   [3] [81]

Jun 66. (7") (R 5452) <5651> **PAPERBACK WRITER. / RAIN**   [1]   [1] [23]
(re-iss. Mar76; same); hit No.23) (re-iss. Jun86; same) (re-iss. cd-s.1989)

Aug 66. (7") (R 5493) <5715> **YELLOW SUBMARINE. / ELEANOR RIGBY**   [1]   [2] [11]
(re-iss. Aug86; same); hit No.63) (re-iss. cd-s.1989)

Aug 66. (lp; mono/stereo) (PMC/PCS 7009) <2576> **REVOLVER**   [1]   [1]
– Taxman / Love you to / I want to tell you / Eleanor Rigby / Here, there and everywhere / Good day sunshine / For no one / Got to get you into my life / I'm only sleeping / She said she said / And your bird can sing / Doctor Robert / Tomorrow never knows / Yellow submarine. (c-iss.1970's) (cd-iss. Apr87; CDP 746441-2); hit UK No.55) (re-iss. Nov88 lp/c; PMC/TC-PMC 7009)

Feb 67. (7") (R 5570) <5810> **PENNY LANE. / STRAWBERRY FIELDS FOREVER**   [2]   [1] [8]
(re-iss. Mar76; same); hit No.32) (re-iss. Feb87; same); hit No.65) (re-iss. cd-s.1989)

Jun 67. (lp; mono/stereo) (PMC/PCS 7027) <2653> **SGT. PEPPER'S LONELY HEARTS CLUB BAND**   [1]   [1]
– Sgt.Pepper's lonely hearts club band / With a little help from my friends / Lucy in the sky with diamonds / Getting better / Fixing a hole / She's leaving home / Being for the benefit of Mr.Kite / Within you without you / When I'm sixty-four / Lovely Rita / Good morning, good morning / Sgt. Pepper's lonely hearts club band (reprise) / A day in the life. (c-iss.1970's) (cd-iss. Jun87; CDP 746442-2); hit UK No.3) (re-iss. Nov88 lp/c; PMC/TC-PMC 7027) (re-iss. Jun92; same); hit UK No.6)

Jul 67. (7") (R 5620) <5964> **ALL YOU NEED IS LOVE. / BABY YOU'RE A RICH MAN**   [1]   [1] [34]
(re-iss. Jul87; same); hit No.47) (re-iss. cd-s.1989)

Nov 67. (7") (R 5655) <2056> **HELLO GOODBYE. / I AM THE WALRUS**   [1]   [1] [56]
(re-iss. Nov87; same); hit No.63) (re-iss. cd-s.1989)

Dec 67. (d7"ep; stereo/mono) (S+/MMT 1) **MAGICAL MYSTERY TOUR**   [2]   [-]
– Magical mystery tour / Your mother should know / Flying / Fool on the hill / Blue Jay way / I am the walrus.

Dec 67. (lp) (imported) <2835> **MAGICAL MYSTERY TOUR (Soundtrack)**   [31]   [1]
– (above UK-ep, plus 1967 singles) (UK-iss.Oct76, cd-iss. Sep87; CDP 748 062-2); hit UK 52)

Mar 68. (7") (R 5675) <2138> **LADY MADONNA. / THE INNER LIGHT**   [1]   [4] [96]
(re-iss. Mar88; same); hit No.67) (re-iss. cd-s.1989)

                              Apple   Apple

Aug 68. (7") (R 5722) <2276> **HEY JUDE. / REVOLUTION**   [1]   [1] [12]
(re-iss. Mar76; same); hit No.12) (re-iss. Aug88; same); hit No.52) (re-iss. cd-s.1989)

Nov 68. (d-lp; mono/stereo) (PMC/PCS 7067-8) <101> **THE BEATLES (White Album)**   [1]   [1]
– Back in the U.S.S.R / Dear Prudence / Glass onion / Ob-la-di-ob-la-da / Wild honey pie / The continuing story of Bungalow Bill / While my guitar gently weeps / Happiness is a warm gun / Martha my dear / I'm so tired / Blackbird / Piggies / Rocky raccoon / Don't pass me by / Why don't we do it in the road / I will / Julia / Yer blues / Mother nature's son / Everybody's got something to hide except me and my monkey / Sexy Sadie / Helter skelter / Long long long / Revolution 1 / Honey pie / Savoy truffle / Cry baby cry / Revolution 9 / Good night. (re-iss. Sep78 white-lp; same) (cd-iss. Aug87; CDP CDS 746443-2); hit UK No.18) (re-iss. Nov88 lp/c; PCS/TCPCS 7067) (d-cd re-iss. Nov98; 496895-2)

Jan 69. (lp; mono/stereo) *(PMC/PCS 7070) <153>* **YELLOW SUBMARINE (Soundtrack)** `[4]` `[2]`
– Yellow submarine / Only a northern song / All together now / Hey bulldog / It's all too much / All you need is love / Pepperland / Sea of time / Sea of holes / Sea of monsters / March of the Meanies / Pepperland laid waste / Yellow submarine in Pepperland. (with GEORGE MARTIN ORCHESTRA) *(re-iss. Aug87; CDP 746445-2); hit UK 60) (re-iss. Nov88 lp/c; PCS/TC-PCS 7070)*

Apr 69. (7"; by BEATLES with BILLY PRESTON) *(R 5777) <2490>* **GET BACK. / DON'T LET ME DOWN** `[1]` `[1]` `[35]`
(re-iss. Mar76; same); hit No.28) (re-iss. Apr89; same); hit 74) (re-iss. cd-s.1989)

May 69. (7") *(R 5786) <2531>* **THE BALLAD OF JOHN AND YOKO. / OLD BROWN SHOE** `[1]` `[8]`
(UK re-iss. May89) (re-iss. cd-s.1989)

Sep 69. (lp/c) *(PCS/TC-PCS 7088) <383>* **ABBEY ROAD** `[1]` `[1]`
– Come together / Maxwell's silver hammer / Something / Oh darling / Octopus's garden / I want you (she's so heavy) / Here comes the sun / Because / You never give me your money / Sun king / Mean Mr. Mustard / Polythene Pam / She came in through the bathroom window / Golden slumbers / Carry that weight / The end / Her majesty. *(UK re-iss. Oct87; CDP 746 446-2); hit No.30) (re-iss. Nov88 lp/c; PCS/TC-PCS 7088)*

Oct 69. (7") *(R 5814) <2654>* **SOMETHING. / COME TOGETHER** `[4]` `[3]` `[1]`
(UK re-iss. Oct89) (re-iss. cd-s.1989)

Mar 70. (7") *(R 5833) <2764>* **LET IT BE. / YOU KNOW MY NAME (LOOK UP THE NUMBER)** `[2]` `[1]`
(re-iss. Mar90) (re-iss. cd-s.1989)

May 70. (lp/c) *(PCS/TC-PCS 7096) <34001>* **LET IT BE** `[1]` `[1]`
– Two of us / Dig a pony / Across the universe / I me mine / Dig it / Let it be / Maggie Mae / I've got a feeling / The one after 909 / The long and winding road / For you blue / Get back. *(cd-iss. Oct87; CDP 746 447-2); hit No.50) (re-iss. Nov88 lp/c; PCS/TC-PCS 7096)*

May 70. (7") *<2832>* **THE LONG AND WINDING ROAD. / FOR YOU BLUE** `[-]` `[1]`

—— Officially disbanded April 1970. All 4 had released, or were due to release, own albums. See **Paul McCARTNEY** ⇒ , **John LENNON** ⇒ , **George HARRISON** ⇒ , **Ringo STARR** ⇒ .

– compilations, others, etc. –

on 'Parlophone' UK / 'Capitol' US unless otherwise mentioned

Jul 63. (7"ep) *(GEP 8880)* **TWIST AND SHOUT** `[2]` `[-]`
– Twist and shout / A taste of honey / Do you want to know a secret / There's a place.

Sep 63. (7"ep) *(GEP 8882)* **THE BEATLES HITS** `[14]` `[-]`
– From me to you / Thank you girl / Please please me / Love me do.

Nov 63. (7"ep) *(GEP 8883)* **THE BEATLES (No.1)** `[19]` `[-]`
– I saw her standing there / Misery / Chains / Anna (go to him).

Jan 64. (7"; by TONY SHERIDAN & THE BEATLES) *Polydor; (NH 52-906)* **SWEET GEORGIA BROWN. / NOBODY'S CHILD** `[-]`

Feb 64. (7"ep) *(GEP GEP 8891)* **ALL MY LOVING** `[12]` `[-]`
– All my loving / Ask me why / Money / P.S. I love you.

Mar 64. (7"; by TONY SHERIDAN & THE BEATLES) *M.G.M.; <K 13227>* **WHY. / CRY FOR A SHADOW** `[-]` `[88]`

Mar 64. (7") *Tollie; <9001>* **TWIST AND SHOUT / THERE'S A PLACE** `[-]` `[2]` `[74]`

Apr 64. (7") *Vee Jay; <VJ 587>* **DO YOU WANT TO KNOW A SECRET. / THANK YOU GIRL** `[-]` `[2]` `[35]`

May 64. (7") *Swan; <S-4182>* **SIE LIEBT DICH. / I'LL GET YOU** `[-]` `[97]`

May 64. (7"; by TONY SHERIDAN & THE BEATLES) *Polydor; (NH 52-317)* **AIN'T SHE SWEET. / IF YOU LOVE ME BABY** `[29]` `[-]`

Jun 64. (lp; by TONY SHERIDAN & THE BEATLES) *Polydor Special; (236 201)* **THE BEATLES' FIRST** `[-]`
(re-iss. Jun71 as THE EARLY YEARS on 'Contour') (re-iss. as 'THE FIRST ALBUM' cd+c May93 on 'Spectrum', credited to TONY SHERIDAN & THE BEATLES)

Jun 64. (7"; by TONY SHERIDAN & THE BEATLES) *Atco; <6302>* **SWEET GEORGIA BROWN. / TAKE OUT SOME INSURANCE ON ME BABY** `[-]` `[-]`

Jun 64. (7"ep) *(GEP 8913)* **LONG TALL SALLY** `[14]` `[-]`
– Long tall sally / I call your name / Slow down / Matchbox.

Jun 64. (7"ep) *<EAP 2121>* **FOUR BY THE BEATLES** `[92]`
– All my loving / This boy / Roll over Beethoven / Please Mr.Postman.

Jul 64. (7"; by TONY SHERIDAN & THE BEATLES) *Atco; <6308>* **AIN'T SHE SWEET. / NOBODY'S CHILD** `[-]` `[19]`

Aug 64. (lp) *<2108>* **SOMETHING NEW** `[-]` `[2]`

Aug 64. (7") *Oldies; <45 OL 149>* **DO YOU WANT TO KNOW A SECRET. / THANK YOU GIRL** `[-]`
<US re-iss. Oct65 on 'Capitol Starline'; 6064>

Aug 64. (7") *Oldies; <45 OL 152>* **TWIST AND SHOUT. / THERE'S A PLACE** `[-]`
<US re-iss. Oct65 on 'Capitol Starline'; 6061>

Nov 64. (7"ep) *(GEP 8920)* **EXTRACTS FROM THE FILM 'A HARD DAY'S NIGHT'** `[34]` `[-]`
– I should have known better / If I fell / Tell me why / And I love her.

Dec 64. (7"ep) *(GEP 8924)* **EXTRACTS FROM THE ALBUM 'A HARD DAY'S NIGHT' 2** `[-]`
– Anytime at all / I'll cry instead / Things we said today / When I get home.

Dec 64. (lp) *<2222>* **THE BEATLES' STORY (narrative)** `[-]` `[7]`

Feb 65. (7"ep) *<R 5365>* **4-BY THE BEATLES** `[-]`
– Honey don't / I'm a loser / Mr.Moonlight / Everybody's trying to be my baby.

Apr 65. (7"ep) *(GEP 8931)* **BEATLES FOR SALE** `[-]`
– No reply / I'm a loser / Rock and roll music / Eight days a week.

Jun 65. (7"ep) *(GEP 8938)* **BEATLES FOR SALE (NO.2)** `[-]`
– I'll follow the sun / Baby's in black / Words of love / I don't want to spoil the party.

Oct 65. (7") *Capitol Starline; <6065>* **ROLL OVER BEETHOVEN. / MISERY** `[-]` `[-]`

Oct 65. (7") *Capitol Starline; <6066>* **BOYS. / KANSAS CITY** `[-]` `[-]`

Dec 65. (7"ep) *(GEP 8946)* **THE BEATLES' MILLION SELLERS** `[-]` `[-]`

– She loves you / Can't buy me love / I feel fine / I want to hold your hand.

Mar 66. (7"ep) *(GEP 8948)* **YESTERDAY** `[-]`
– Yesterday / Act naturally / You like me too much / It's only love.

Jul 66. (lp) *<2553>* **YESTERDAY . . . AND TODAY** `[-]` `[1]`

Jul 66. (7"ep) *(GEP 8952)* **NOWHERE MAN** `[-]`
– Nowhere man / Drive my car / Michelle / You won't see me.

Dec 66. (lp) *(PMC/PCS 7016)* **A COLLECTION OF BEATLES OLDIES** `[7]` `[-]`
– She loves you / From me to you / We can work it out / Help! / Michelle / Yesterday / I feel fine / Yellow submarine / Can't buy me love / Bad boy / Day tripper / A hard day's night / Ticket to ride / Paperback writer / Eleanor Rigby / I want to hold your hand. *(re-iss. Oct83 on 'Parlophone' lp/c; FA/TC-FA 3081)*

Mar 70. (lp) *Apple; <385>* **HEY JUDE** `[-]` `[2]`
(UK-iss.May79 on 'Parlophone' lp/c; PCS/TC-PCS 7184)

Apr 73. (d-lp/d-c) *Apple; (PCSP/TC2-PCSP 717) <3403>* **THE BEATLES 1962-1966** `[3]` `[3]`
– Love me do / Please please me / She loves you / From me to you / She loves you / I want to hold your hand / All my loving / Can't buy me love / A hard day's night / And I love her / Eight days a week / I feel fine / Ticket to ride / Yesterday / Help! / You've got to hide your love away / We can work it out / Day tripper / Drive my car / Norwegian wood (this bird has flown) / Nowhere man / Michelle / In my life / Girl / Paperback writer / Eleanor Rigby / Yellow submarine. *(re-iss. Sep78 & Feb94 red-lp) (d-cd-iss. Jul91;) (re-iss. d-cd Sep93 on 'Apple-Parlophone', hit UK No.3)*

Apr 73. (d-lp/d-c) *Apple; (PCSP/TC2-PCSP 718) <3404>* **THE BEATLES 1967-1970** `[2]` `[1]`
– Strawberry fields forever / Penny lane / Sgt. Pepper's lonely hearts club band / With a little help from my friends / Lucy in the sky with diamonds / A day in the life / All you need is love / I am the Walrus / Hello, goodbye / The fool on the hill / Magical mystery tour / Lady Madonna / Hey Jude / Revolution / Back in the U.S.S.R / While my guitar gently weeps / Ob-la-di, ob-la-da / Get back / Don't let me down / The ballad of John and Yoko / Old brown shoe / Here comes the sun / Come together / Something / Octopus's Garden / Let it be / Across the universe / The long and winding road. *(re-iss. Sep78 & Feb94 blue-lp;) (d-cd-iss. Jul91;) (re-iss. d-cd Sep93 on 'Apple-Parlophone', hit UK No.4)*

Mar 76. (7") *(R 6013)* **YESTERDAY. / I SHOULD HAVE KNOWN BETTER** `[8]` `[-]`

Jun 76. (lp/c) *(PCSP/TC-PCSP 719) <11537>* **ROCK'N'ROLL MUSIC** `[11]` `[2]`
(re-iss. Nov80 as . . . VOL.1 / . . . VOL.2 both on 'MfP')

Jun 76. (7") *<4274>* **GOT TO GET YOU INTO MY LIFE. / HELTER SKELTER** `[-]` `[7]`

Jul 76. (7") *(R 6016)* **BACK IN THE U.S.S.R. / TWIST AND SHOUT** `[19]` `[-]`

Aug 76. (d-lp) *Polydor; (2683 068)* **THE BEATLES TAPES (interviews)** `[45]` `[-]`

Nov 76. (7") *<4347>* **OB-LA-DI, OB-LA-DA. / JULIA** `[-]` `[49]`

Apr 77. (d-lp/d-c) *Lingasong; <7001>* **LIVE AT THE STAR CLUB, HAMBURG, GERMANY 1962** `[ ]`

May 77. (lp/c) *(EMTV/TC-EMTV 4) <11638>* **THE BEATLES AT THE HOLLYWOOD BOWL (live)** `[1]` `[2]`
(UK re-iss. Sep84 on 'MfP')

Dec 77. (d-lp/d-c) *(PCSP/TC-PCSP 721) <11711>* **LOVE SONGS** `[7]` `[24]`

Sep 78. (7") *(R 6022) <4612>* **SGT. PEPPER'S LONELY HEARTS CLUB BAND – WITH A LITTLE HELP FROM MY FRIENDS. / A DAY IN THE LIFE** `[63]` `[71]`

Nov 78. (14xlp-box) **THE BEATLES COLLECTION** `[ ]`
– (all original albums boxed)

Oct 79. (lp/c) *(PCM/TC-PCM 1001) <12060>* **RARITIES** `[71]` `[21]` Apr80

Nov 80. (lp/c) *(PCS/TC-PCS 7214)* **BEATLES BALLADS** `[17]`

Dec 81. (14x7"ep's) **THE BEATLES EP COLLECTION** `[ ]`
– (all ep's above plus new SHE'S A WOMAN)
– She's a woman / Baby you're a rich man / This boy / The inner light.

Apr 82. (lp/c) *( ) <12199>* **REEL MUSIC** `[ ]` `[19]`

May 82. (7") *(R 6055) <5107>* **BEATLES MOVIE MEDLEY. / I'M HAPPY JUST TO DANCE WITH YOU** `[10]` `[12]` Mar82
– ('A'medley) Magical Mystery Tour – All You Need Is Love – You've Got To Hide Your Love Away – I Should Have Known Better – A Hard Day's Night – Ticket To Ride – Get Back.

Oct 82. (d-lp/d-c) *(PCTC/TC-PCTC 260) <12245>* **20 GREATEST HITS** `[10]` `[50]`

Jul 81. (lp) *Phoenix; (PHX 1004)* **EARLY MUSIC VOL.1** `[ ]`

Jul 81. (lp) *Phoenix; (PHX 1005)* **EARLY MUSIC VOL.2** `[ ]`

Feb 82. (lp) *Phoenix; (PHX 1011)* **RARE BEATLES** `[ ]`

Aug 81. (d-lp)(c) *Audio Fidelity;* **HISTORIC BEATLES** `[ ]`

Sep 82. (lp/c) *Audio Fidelity;(AFELP/ZCALP 1047)* **THE COMPLETE SILVER BEATLES** `[ ]`

Jul 82. (10"lp) *Charly; (CFM 701)* **THE SAVAGE YOUNG BEATLES** `[ ]`
(re-iss. as THE BEATLES FEATURING TONY SHERIDAN, HAMBURG on 'Topline', cd-iss. Feb93 on 'Charly')

Sep 83. (lp) *Audio Fidelity;* **COMETS** `[ ]`

Nov 83. (lp) *Berkeley;* **AUDITION TAPES** `[ ]`

Dec 83. (lp) *Breakaway;* **HAMBURG TAPES VOL.1** `[ ]`

Dec 83. (lp) *Breakaway;* **HAMBURG TAPES VOL.2** `[ ]`

Dec 83. (lp) *Breakaway;* **HAMBURG TAPES VOL.3** `[ ]`

Apr 86. (lp/c) *Showcase; (SHLP/SHTC 130)* **LIVE BEATLES VOL.1 (live)** `[ ]`

Apr 86. (lp/c) *Showcase; (SHLP/SHTC 131)* **LIVE BEATLES VOL.2 (live)** `[ ]`

Oct 87. (lp/c)(cd) *Topline; (TOP/KTOP 181)(TOPCD 523)* **THE DECCA SESSIONS (1/1/62)** `[ ]`

Feb 88. (cd/c/d-lp) *E.M.I.; (CD/TC+/BPM 1)* **PAST MASTERS VOL.1** `[49]`

Feb 88. (cd/c/d-lp) *E.M.I.; (CD/TC+/BPM 2)* **PAST MASTERS VOL.2** `[46]`

Oct 88. (box-lp/box-c/box-cd) **THE ULTIMATE BOX SET** `[ ]`

Aug 91. (c-s x all) *E.M.I.;* **THE SINGLES** `[ ]`
– (all 7"singles boxed)

Jun 92. (cd-ep x14-box) **COMPACT DISC EP'S** `[ ]`

Jun 92. (cd/c) *Columbia; (468950-2/-4)* **ROCKIN' AT THE STAR-CLUB (live)** `[ ]`

Dec 94. (cd/d-c/d-lp) *Apple; (CD/TC+/PCSP 726)* **LIVE AT THE BBC (live)** `[1]` `[3]`
– Beatle greetings / From us to you / Riding on a bus / I got a woman / Too much monkey business / Keep your hands off my baby / I'll be on my way / Young blood / A shot of rhythm and blues / Sure to fall (in love with you) / Some other guy / Thank you girl / Sha la la la la! / Baby it's you / That's all right (mama) / Carol / Soldier

of love / A little rhyme / Clarabella / I'm gonna sit right down and cry (over you) / Crying, waiting, hoping / Dear Wack! / You really got a hold on me / To know her is to love her / A taste of honey / Long tall Sally / I saw her standing there / The honeymoon song / Johnny B Goode / Memphis, Tennessee / Lucille / Can't buy me love / From Fluff to you / Till there was you / Crinsk Dee night / A hard day's night / Have a banana! / I wanna be your man / Just a rumour / Roll over Beethoven / All my loving / Things we said today / She's a woman / Sweet little sixteen / 1882! / Lonesome tears in my eyes / Nothin' shakin' / The hippy hippy shake / Glad all over / I just don't understand / So how come (no one loves me) / I feel fine / I'm a loser / Everybody's trying to be my baby / Rock and roll music / Ticket to ride / Dizzy Miss Lizzy / Medley: – Kansas City – Hey! hey! hey! / Set fire to that lot! / Matchbox / I forgot to remember to forget / Love these Goon shows! / I got to find my baby / Ooh! my soul / Ooh! my arms / Don't ever change / Slow down / Honey don't / Love me do.

Mar 95. (c-s/7") *Apple; (TC+/R 6406) <58348>* **BABY IT'S YOU / I'LL FOLLOW THE SUN** [7] [67]
(cd-s+=) *(CDR 6406)* – Devil in her heart / Boys.

Nov 95. (d-cd/d-c/t-lp) *Apple; (CD/TC+/PCSP 727)* **ANTHOLOGY 1** [2] [1]
– Free as a bird / Speech (by JOHN LENNON) / That'll be the day / In spite of all the danger / Sometimes I'd borrow (speech by PAUL McCARTNEY) / Hallelujah I love her so / You'll be mine / Cayenne / First of all (speech by PAUL) / My Bonnie (w/ TONY SHERIDAN) / Ain't she sweet / Cry for a shadow / Brian was a beautiful guy (speech by JOHN) / Secured them an audition (speech by BRIAN EPSTEIN) / Searchin' / Three cool cats / The Sheik of Araby / Like dreamers do / Hello little girl / Well, the recording test (speech by BRIAN) / Besame mucho / Love me do / How do you do it? / Please please me / One after 909 (sequence) / One after 909 (complete) / Lend me your comb / I'll get you / We were performers (speech by JOHN) / I saw her standing there / From me to you / Money (that's what I want) / You really got a hold on me / Roll over Beethoven / She loves you / Till there was you (music man) / Twist and shout / This boy / I want to hold your hand / Boys, what I was thinking (speech by The BEATLES and MORECAMBE & WISE) / Moonlightbay (w/ MORECAMBE & WISE) / Can't buy me love / All my loving / You can't do that / And I love her / A hard day's night / I wanna be your man / Long tall Sally / Boys / Shout / I'll be back (take 2) / I'll be back (take 3) / You know what to do / No reply (demo) / Mr.Moonlight / Leave my kitten alone / No reply / Eight days a week (sequence) / Eight days a week (complete) / Kansas City – hey, hey, hey.
(below single was recently re-recorded from JOHN LENNON's 1977 cut)

Dec 95. (c-s/7") *Apple; (TC+/R 6422) <58497>* **FREE AS A BIRD / CHRISTMAS TIME (IS HERE AGAIN)** [2] [6]
(cd-s+=) *(CDR 6422)* – I saw her standing there (take 9) / This boy (take 13).

Mar 96. (c-s/7") *Apple; (TC+/R 6425) <58544>* **REAL LOVE / BABY'S IN BLACK** [4] [11]
(cd-s+=) *(CDR 6425)* – Yellow submarine / Here, there and everywhere.

Mar 96. (d-cd/d-c/t-lp) *(CD/TC+/PCSP 728)* **ANTHOLOGY 2** (compilation) [1] [2]

Oct 96. (d-cd/d-c/t-lp) *(CD/TC+/PCSP 729)* **ANTHOLOGY 3** [4] [1]

Feb 97. (7"red/cd-s; BEATLES featuring TONY SHERIDAN) *Gecko; (GECK 06/+CD)* **CRY FOR A SHADOW. / LET'S DANCE** [ ] [-]

Feb 97. (7"blue/cd-s; BEATLES featuring TONY SHERIDAN) *Gecko; (GECK 07/+CD)* **IF YOU LOVE ME BABY. / WHAT'D I SAY** [ ] [-]

Feb 97. (7"green/cd-s; BEATLES featuring TONY SHERIDAN) *Gecko; (GECK 08/+CD)* **SWEET GEORGIA BROWN. / RUBY RUBY** [ ] [-]

Feb 97. (7"yellow/cd-s; BEATLES featuring TONY SHERIDAN) *Gecko; (GECK 09/+CD)* **YA YA. / WHY / (George Martin on the making of the Beatles)** [ ] [-]

Apr 97. (cd/c) *Presstige 2; (SYB 1 CD/MC)* **CRY FOR A SHADOW – THE SAVAGE YOUNG BEATLES** [ ] [-]

May 97. (d-cd) *Metro; (OTR 1100026)* **THE LOST FAB FOUR TAPES**

Nov 98. (cd; as TONY SHERIDAN & THE BEATLES) *Spectrum; (550037-2)* **THE EARLY TAPES OF THE BEATLES**

Sep 99. (cd/c/lp) *Parlophone; (<521481-2/-4/-1>)* **YELLOW SUBMARINE SONGTRACK** [8] [15]

BEATS INTERNATIONAL
(see under ⇒ COOK, Norman)

BEATNIGS (see under ⇒ DISPOSABLE HEROES OF HIPHOPRISY)

BEAU BRUMMELS (dig out; Great Psychedelic . . .)

BEAUTIFUL SOUTH

Formed: Hull, England . . . early 1989 by PAUL HEATON, DAVE HEMMINGWAY and DAVID ROTHERAY, who added SEAN WELCH and ex-HOUSEMARTINS roadie, DAVID STEED. They stuck with their 'Go! Discs' contract, the former two having been the integral part of STEED's employers. A debut single, 'SONG FOR WHOEVER' climbed to UK No.2, its parody of love song overload belying a bittersweet appeal which no amount of clever, ironic lyrics could detract from over the course of their career. With the addition of BRIANNA CORRIGAN, the bulk of the group's subsequent work would be characterised by the vocal trade-offs between her and HEATON, some of them priceless. Melody was everything with The BEAUTIFUL SOUTH and an irrepressible follow-up track, 'YOU KEEP IT ALL IN', made the UK Top 10. Both cuts were featured on their debut set, 'WELCOME TO THE BEAUTIFUL SOUTH' (1989), an impressive start which included the enduringly charming 'FROM UNDER THE COVERS' and a spine-tingling cover of 'I'LL SAIL THIS SHIP ALONE', HEATON's little-boy-lost vocals working miracles. Shrugging off the controversy of the cover art (a woman with a gun in her mouth), the band topped the charts

the following year with the STEED / CORRIGAN duet, 'A LITTLE TIME', a classy follow-up album, 'CHOKE' (1990) also selling in bucketloads. The record marked out The BEAUTIFUL SOUTH as undisputed champions of chronicling everyday relationship breakdowns, although the set undoubtedly sold on the strength of their tunes rather than their lyrics. Previewed by the semi-tragic 'OLD RED EYES IS BACK', the occasionally brilliant '0898' (1992) album was a more bitterly realistic affair, the poignant small-time tragedy of 'BELL BOTTOMED TEAR' remaining one of their most emotionally jarring compositions to date. The record went Top 5, consolidating their position as mainstream pop mavericks. A fourth set, 'MIAOW' (1994), saw HEATON work with new recruit, JACQUELINE ABBOTT, a replacement for the solo bound CORRIGAN. The partnership worked equally well, HEATON developing as a songwriter, while also putting in a swooning cover of Fred Neil's 'EVERYBODY'S TALKIN'. The latter track was the record's biggest hit, although the band's popularity was confirmed as a greatest hits set, 'CARRY ON UP THE CHARTS' (1994), became one of the fastest selling albums in British history. They returned in suitably barbed style with 'BLUE IS THE COLOUR' (1996), another No.1 album which drew controversy with its Top 10 hit, 'DON'T MARRY HER', a slightly altered version provided for radio play. HEATON and ABBOTT teamed up exquisitely once again after yet another two-year spell, this time No.2 single 'PERFECT 10' from the chart-topping parent album, 'QUENCH' (1998), displayed the usual BEAUTIFUL SOUTH repartee. While critics continued to queue up in the hope of writing off HEATON and Co, the band's comfy nook in the adult pop pantheon looked increasingly secure. • **Songwriters:** HEATON and ROTHERAY, except LOVE WARS (Womack & Womack).

Album rating: WELCOME TO THE BEAUTIFUL SOUTH (*7) / CHOKE (*6) / 0898 (*6) / MIAOW (*6) / CARRY ON UP THE CHARTS compilation (*8) / BLUE IS THE COLOUR (*7) / QUENCH (*6)

PAUL HEATON (b. 9 May'62, Bromborough, England) – guitar, vocals / **DAVE HEMMINGWAY** – keyboards (both ex-HOUSEMARTINS) / **DAVID ROTHERAY** (b. 9 Feb'??) – vocals, guitar / **SEAN WELCH** (b.12 Apr'??, Enfield, England) – bass / **DAVID STEED** (b.15 Oct'??, Huddersfield, England) – drums

		Go! Discs	Elektra
May 89.	(7"/7"s/c-s) *(GOD/+P/MC 32)* **SONG FOR WHOEVER. / STRAIGHT IN AT 37**	2	
	(12"+=/cd-s+=) *(GODX/GOCD 32)* – You and your big ideas.		

—— added **BRIANNA CORRIGAN** (b.County Antrim, Ireland) – vocals (ex-ANTHILL RUNAWAYS). She was to join full-time in 1990.

Sep 89.	(7"/7"s/c-s) *(GOD/+P/MC 35)* **YOU KEEP IT ALL IN. / I LOVE YOU (BUT YOU'RE BORING)**	8	
	(12"+=/cd-s+=) *(GODX/GOCD 35)* – You can't just smile it away / ('A'version).		
Oct 89.	(lp/c/cd) *(AGO LP/MC/CD 16)* **WELCOME TO THE BEAUTIFUL SOUTH**	2	

– Song for whoever / Have you ever been away? / From under the covers / I'll sail this ship alone / Girlfriend / You keep it all in / Woman in the wall / Oh Blackpool / Love is . . . / I love you (but you're boring). *(cd+=)* – Straight in at 37. *(cd re-iss. Aug98; 84208026)*

Nov 89.	(7"/7"s/c-s) *(GOD/+P/MC 38)* **I'LL SAIL THIS SHIP ALONE. / BUT TILL THEN**	31	
	(12"+=/cd-s+=) *(GOD X/CD 38)* – ('A'orchestral version).		
	(7"white++=) *(GODT 38)* – ('A'white version).		
Sep 90.	(7"/7"s/c-s) *(GOD/+P/MC 47)* **A LITTLE TIME. / IN OTHER WORDS I HATE YOU**	1	
	(12"+=/cd-s+=) *(GOD X/CD 47)* – What you see is what you get.		
Oct 90.	(cd/c/lp) *(828 233-2/-4/-1)* **CHOKE**	2	

– Tonight I fancy myself / My book / Let love speak up itself / Should've kept my eyes shut / I've come for my award / Lips / I think the answer's yes / A little time / Mother's pride / I hate you (but you're interesting) / The rising of Grafton Street. *(cd+=)* – What you see is what you get. *(re-iss. cd Apr93 & Aug98; same)*

Nov 90.	(7"/7"s/c-s) *(GOD/+P/MC 48)* **MY BOOK. / BIG BEAUTIFUL SOUTH**	8	
	(12"+=/cd-s+=) *(GOD X/CD 48)* – Bigger doesn't mean better / Speak to me.		
Mar 91.	(7"/7"s/c-s) *(GOD/+MC 53)* **LET LOVE SPEAK UP ITSELF. / LOVE WARS**	51	
	(12"+=/cd-s+=) *(GOD X/CD 53)* – Danielle Steele / Headbutting husband.		

		Go! Discs	Chameleon
Jan 92.	(7"/c-s) *(GOD/+MC 66)* **OLD RED EYES IS BACK. / FLEET STREET B.C.**	22	
	(12"+=/cd-s+=) *(GOD X/CD 66)* – Diamonds.		
Mar 92.	(7"/c-s) *(GOD/+MC 71)* **WE ARE EACH OTHER. / HIS TIME RAN OUT**	30	
	(12"+=/cd-s+=) *(GOD X/CD 71)* – I started a joke.		
Apr 92.	(cd/c/lp) *(828 310-2/-4/-1)* **0898**	4	

– Old red eyes is back / We are each other / The rocking chair / We'll deal with you later / Domino man / 36D / Here it is again / Something that you said / I'm your No.1 fan / Bell bottomed tear / You play glockenspiel / I'll play drums / When I'm 84.

Jun 92.	(7"/c-s) *(GOD/+MC 78)* **BELL BOTTOMED TEAR. / A THOUSAND LIES / THEY USED TO WEAR BLACK**	16	
	(cd-s+=) *(GODCD 78)* – You should be dancing (live) / Woman in the wall (live).		
Sep 92.	(7"/c-s) *(GOD/+MC 88)* **36D. / THROWING HIS SONG AWAY / TREVOR YOU'RE BIZARRE**	46	
	(cd-s+=) *(GODCD 88)*		
	(cd-s) *(GOLCD 88)* – ('A'live) / From under the covers (live) / You keep it all in (live).		

—— **JACQUELINE ABBOTT** (b.1974) – vocals repl. CORRIGAN who went solo

Feb 94.	(7"/c-s) *(GOD/+MC 110)* **GOOD AS GOLD. / LOVE ADJOURNED**	23	
	(cd-s+=) *(GODCD 110)* – Mini-correct.		
	(cd-s) *(GOLCD 110)* – ('A'side) / Frank and Delores / One man's rubbish.		
Mar 94.	(cd/c/lp) *(828 332-2/-4/-1)* **MIAOW**	6	

– Hold on to what / Good as gold (stupid as muck) / Especially for you / Everybody's talkin' / Prettiest eyes / Worthless lie / Hooligans don't fall in love / Hidden jukebox / Hole me close (underground) / Tattoo / Mini correct / Poppy.

May 94. (7"/c-s/cd-s) *(GOD/+MC/CD 113)* **EVERYBODY'S TALKIN'. / A WAY WITH THE BLUES / LET LOVE SPEAK UP ITSELF** `12`
(cd-s) *(GOLCD 113)* – ('A'side) / Nearer to God / A piece of sky.

Aug 94. (7"/c-s/cd-s) *(GOD/+MC/CD 119)* **PRETTIEST EYES. / THE BEST WE CAN / SIZE** `37`
(cd-s) *(GOLCD 19)* – ('A'side) / Why can't I / Missing her now.

Oct 94. (7"/c-s/cd-s) *(GOD/+MC/CD 122)* **ONE LAST LOVE SONG. / RIGHT MAN FOR THE JOB / JAVA** `14`
(cd-s) *(GOLCD 122)* – ('A'side) / Mr. Obsession / You're only jealous.

Nov 94. (cd/c/lp) *(828 572-2/-4/-1)* **CARRY ON UP THE CHARTS – THE BEST OF THE BEAUTIFUL SOUTH** (compilation) `1`
– Song for whoever / You keep it all in / I'll sail this ship alone / A little time / My book / Let love speak up itself / Old red eyes is back / We are each other / Bell bottomed tear / 36D / Good as gold (stupid as mud) / Everybody's talkin' / Prettiest eyes / One last love song.

Nov 95. (c-s/cd-s) *(GOD MC/CD 134)* **PRETENDERS TO THE THRONE. / VIRGIN / A LONG DAY IN THE FIELD** `18`

Oct 96. (7"/c-s) *(GOD/+MC 155)* **ROTTERDAM. / A MINUTE'S SILENCE** `5`
(cd-s+=) *(GODCD 155)* – Pollard.

Oct 96. (cd/c/lp) *(828 845-2/-4/-1)* **BLUE IS THE COLOUR** `1`
– Don't marry her / Little blue / Mirror / Blackbird on the wire / The sound of North America / Have fun / Liar's bar / Rotterdam / Foundations / Artificial flowers / One God / Alone.

Dec 96. (c-s) *(GODMC 158)* **DON'T MARRY HER / DREAM A LITTLE DREAM / GOD BLESS THE CHILD** `8`
(cd-s) *(GODCD 158)* – ('A'side) / God bless the child / Without her.
(cd-s) *(GOLCD 158)* – ('A'side) / Dream a little dream / Les yeux ouverts.

Mar 97. (7"/c-s) *(582124-7/-4)* **BLACKBIRD ON THE WIRE. / LEAN ON ME** `23`
(cd-s+=) *(582125-2)* – You just can't smile it away (live).
(cd-s) *(582197-2)* – ('A'live) / I'll sail this ship alone (live) / The sound of North America (live)

Jun 97. (c-s) *(582238-4)* **LIAR'S BAR / THE OPENING OF A NEW BOOK / YOU'VE DONE NOTHING WRONG (live)** `43`
(cd-s) *(582239-2)* – ('A'side) / Dumb / You've done nothing wrong (live).
(cd-s) *(582241-2)* – ('A'side) / The opening of a new book / Hold on to what? (live).

Sep 98. (c-s) *(566480-4)* **PERFECT 10 / IF** `2`
(cd-s+=) *(566481-2)* – I'll sail this ship alone.
(cd-s) *(566483-2)* – ('A'side) / Loving arms (live) / One last love song.

Oct 98. (cd/c/lp) *(538166-2/-4/-1)* **QUENCH** `1`
– How long's a tear take to dry? / The lure of the sea / Big coin / Dumb / Perfect 10 / The slide / Look what I found in my beer / The table / Window shopping for blinds / Pockets / I may be ugly / Losing things / Your father and I.

Dec 98. (c-s) *(556752-4)* **DUMB / SUCK HARDER** `16`
(cd-s+=) *(566753-2)* – Especially for you.
(cd-s) *(556755-2)* – ('A'side) / I sold my heart to the junkman / Blackbird on the wire.

Mar 99. (c-s) *(870820-4)* **HOW LONG'S A TEAR TAKE TO DRY? / ('A'remix)** `12` `-`
(cd-s+=) *(870821-2)* – Perfect 10 (acoustic).
(cd-s) *(870823-2)* – ('A'side) / Big coin (acoustic) / Rotterdam (acoustic).

Jun 99. (c-s) *(562165-4)* **THE TABLE / YOUR FATHER AND I (live)** `47` `-`
(cd-s+=) *(562165-2)* – Old red eyes is back (live).
(cd-s) *(562165-5)* – ('A'side) / Don't marry her (live) / Look what I found in my beer (live).

BEAVER & KRAUSE (dig out; Great Psychedelic . . .)

BE-BOP DELUXE (see under ⇒ NELSON, Bill)

BECK

Born: BECK HANSEN, 8 Jul'70, Los Angeles, California, USA. After absorbing the strains of primitive country blues artists like LEADBELLY and MISSISSIPPI JOHN HURT, along with the aural terrorism of hardcore noise, the 17-year old BECK relocated to New York in 1989 to try his hand on the post-punk East Village folk scene. Broke, he retired to L.A., setting himself up in the (now) trendy Silverlake district, playing low key gigs in local coffeehouses. Spotted by 'Bongload' owner TOM ROTHROCK, he was offered some studio time and the resulting sessions produced the 'LOSER' (1993) single. Caned by L.A.'s alternative radio stations, its popularity led to BECK signing with 'Geffen'. 'LOSER' (1994) in its re-issued, major label form went top 20 in both Britain and America, its slow burning hip hop blues turning the rosy-cheeked BECK into an overnight slacker anti-hero. The 'MELLOW GOLD' (1994) album went some way towards crystallising BECK's skewed vision of a modern folk music that encapsulated roots blues, hip hop, country, noise-core and psychedelia. While the record went on to sell half a million copies, BECK's unique contract allowed him the option of recording for other labels. 'STEREOPATHIC SOUL MANURE' (1994) was a U.S.-only release of rough early material on the small 'Flipside' label, while 'ONE FOOT IN THE GRAVE' (1995) was a mainly acoustic set released on CALVIN JOHNSON's 'K' records, its stark harmonica-driven title track remaining a highlight of the BECK live experience. Any dubious whispers of one-hit wonder were cast aside with the release of 1996's 'ODELAY', a record that topped many end of year polls and turned BECK into the music world's coolest hep cat. Garnering gushing praise from the dance, rock and hip hop communities alike, the album's effortless fusion of disparate styles was breathtaking. The cut'n'paste surrealism of the lyrics flourished imagery of a lucidness to match BOB DYLAN's 60's work and indeed, the gorgeously

bittersweet 'JACKASS' used Dylan's 'IT'S ALL OVER NOW BABY BLUE' as a shimmering harmonic backdrop. The album segued smoothly from distortion and dissonance into downhome steel guitar hoedown, all the while retaining an irresistably funky backbeat. For now, this pop auteur/wunderkid can do no wrong, his live experience is a dayglo potted history of American music and any readers who were lucky enough to catch his glorious set at the Chelmsford V97 festival, will know that BECK doesn't take too kindly to bottle throwing eunuchs! Towards the end of 1998, BECK found himself in the midst of another legal wrangle with label 'Geffen' when a dispute over who was to release his new 14-day recorded 'MUTATIONS' resulted in the label taking full control. The latter was subsequently released to critical acclaim due to Nigel Godrich's production of BECK's live direction. With less label fuss but with more media frenzy, the Lo-Fi loner issued his 4th 'Geffen' set, 'MIDNITE VULTURES' (1999), which proved to be a dark contrast between that and the aforementioned 'MUTATIONS'. • **Songwriters:** BECK writes most of his material, some with KARL STEPHENSON. 'LOSER' used a sample of DR.JOHN's 'I Walk On Gilded Splinters'. Covered: I'M SO GREEN (Can) / HALO OF GOLD (Moby Grape). • **Trivia:** The 'Geffen Rarities Vol.1' album of various artists, featured the BECK track, 'Bogusflow'.

Album rating: A WESTERN HARVEST FIELD BY MOONLIGHT (*4) / GOLDEN FEELINGS mini (*3) / MELLOW GOLD (*7) / STEREOPATHIC SOULMANURE (*4) / ONE FOOT IN THE GRAVE (*6) / ODELAY (*9) / MUTATIONS (*7) / MIDNITE VULTURES (*8)

BECK (HANSEN) – vocals, acoustic guitar with guests **RACHEL HADEN** – drums, vocals / **ANNA WARONKER** – bass, vocals / **PETRA HADEN** – violin, vocals / **MIKE BOITO** – organ / **DAVID HARTE** – drums / **ROB ZABRECKY** – bass

			not iss.	Flipside
1992.	(ltd-7"blue-ep) *<FLIP 46>* **TO SEE THAT WOMAN OF MINE / MTV MAKES ME WANNA SMOKE CRACK. / (other side 2 tracks by BEAN)**		`-`	

			not iss.	Sonic Enemy
Jan 93.	(c-ep) *<none>* **GOLDEN FEELINGS**		`-`	

			not iss.	Bongload
1993.	(ltd-12") *<BL 5>* **LOSER. / STEAL MY BODY HOME**		`-`	
1994.	(ltd-7") *<BL 11>* **STEVE THREW UP. / MUTHERFUCKER / (CUPCAKE)** *(both above UK-iss.Jan95; same) (cd-s iss.Dec97; BL 11CDS)*		`-`	

			not iss.	Fingerpaint
1994.	(10"ep) *<FP 02>* **A WESTERN HARVEST FIELD BY MOONLIGHT** *<re-iss. Sep95; same> (UK cd-iss. Oct97; same)*		`-`	

			Geffen	D.G.C.
Mar 94.	(7"/c-s) *<DGC S7-19/CS-12 270>* **LOSER. / ALCOHOL** (cd-s+=) *<DGCDM-21930>* – Corvette bumper / Soul suckin' jerk (reject) / Fume.			`10`
Mar 94.	(7"/c-s) *(GFS/+C 67)* **LOSER. / ALCOHOL / FUME** (cd-s) *(GFSTD 67)* – ('A'side) / Totally confused / Corvette bumper / MTV makes me want to smoke crack.		`15`	`-`
Mar 94.	(cd/c/lp) *(GED/GEC/GEF 24634) <DGCD/DGC 24634>* **MELLOW GOLD** – Loser / Pay no mind (snoozer) / Fuckin with my head (mountain dew rock) / Whiskeyclone, Hotel City 1997 / Soul suckin jerk / Truckdrivin neighbors downstairs (yellow sweat) / Sweet sunshine / Beercan / Steal my body home / Nitemare hippy girl / Motherfuker / Blackhole. *<lp-iss. on 'Bongload'(hidden track cd+=)* – Analog odyssey. *(lp re-iss. Apr97 & Sep99 on 'Bongload'; BL 12> (lp re-iss. Nov98 on 'Simply Vinyl'; SVLP 44)*		`41`	`13`
May 94.	(cd-ep) *<DM-22000>* **BEERCAN / GOT NO MIND / ASSKIZZ POWERGRUDGE (PAYBACK '94) / TOTALLY CONFUSED / SPANKING ROOM / BONUS NOISE**		`-`	
May 94.	(7"/c-s; w-drawn) *(GFS/+C 73)* **PAY NO MIND (SNOOZER). / SPECIAL PEOPLE** (12"+=/cd-s+=)*<US cd-ep>* *(GFST/+D 73)<GED 21911>* – Trouble all my days / Supergolden (sunchild).		`-`	`-`

— BECK featured on Various Artists 'Mammoth' EP 'JABBERJAW: GOOD TO THE LAST DROP'. In the same year, with CHRIS BALLEW of The PRESIDENTS . . . and under the moniker of CASPAR AND MOLLUSK, they issued the single, 'TWIG'. He was also featured on below alongside CALVIN JOHNSON – vocals (ex-BEAT HAPPENING), SCOTT PLOUFF – drums / JAMES BERTRAM – bass / +2

			not iss.	K
Aug 94.	(cd/c) *<(KLP 28 CD/C)>* **ONE FOOT IN THE GRAVE** – He's a mighty good leader / Sleeping bag / I get lonesome / Burnt orange peel / Cyanide breath mint / See water / Ziplock bag / Hollow log / Forcefield / Fourteen rivers fourteen floods / Asshole / I've seen the land beyond / Outcome / Girl dreams / Painted eyelids / Atmospheric conditions. *(UK-iss.Nov95; lp-iss.Jun97; KLP 28) (re-iss. Oct98; same)*		`-`	

			D.G.C.	D.G.C.
Nov 94.	(7",7"brown) *<iPU 45>* **IT'S ALL IN YOUR MIND. / FEATHER IN YOUR CAP / WHISKEY CAN CAN**		`-`	`-`
Jun 96.	(c-s) *(GFSC 22156)* **WHERE IT'S AT / WHERE IT'S AT (Mario C & Mickey P remix)** (cd-s+=)*<US cd-ep>* *(GFSTD 22156)<DGC CD-22214>* – Bonus beats. (12"++=)*<US 12">* *(GFST 22156)<DGC 12-22214>* – ('A'-U.N.K.L.E. remix).		`35`	`61`
Jun 96.	(cd/c; as BECK!) *(GED/GEC 24908) <DGCD/DGC 24823>* **ODELAY** – Devils haircut / Hotwax / Lord only knows / The new pollution / Derelict / Novacane / Jack-ass / Where it's at / Minus / Sissyneck / Readymade / High 5 (rock the catskills) / Ramshackle / Diskobox. *<lp-iss.Apr97 & Sep99 on 'Bongload'; BL 030LP> (lp-iss.Nov98 on 'Simply Vinyl'; SVLP 51)*		`18`	`16`
Nov 96.	(7") *(GFSC 22183)* **DEVILS HAIRCUT. / LLOYD PRICE EXPRESS** (cd-s)*<US cd-ep>* *(GFSTD 22183)<GED 22175>* – ('A'side) / Dark and lovely (Dust Brothers remix) / American wasteland (Mickey P remix).		`22`	`94`

<US 12"ep++=> <*DGC 12-22222*> – Lloyd Price express / Clock.

(cd-s) (*GFSXD 22183*) – ('A'side) / ('A'-Noel Gallagher remix) / Groovy Sunday (Mike Simpson remix) / Trouble all my days.

Mar 97. (7") (*GFS 22205*) **THE NEW POLLUTION. / ELECTRIC MUSIC AND SUMMER PEOPLE** | 14 | 78 |

(c-s) (*GFSC 22205*) – ('A'side) / Richard's hairpiece (Aphex Twin remix).

(cd-s)<US cd-ep> (*GFSTD 22205*) <*GED 22204*> – (all 3 tracks).

(cd-s)<US 12"ep> (*GFSTXD 22205*) <*DGC12 22300*> – ('A'side) / ('A'-Mario C & Mickey P remix) / Lemonade.

(*rel.Europe 12" May97 on 'Play It Again Sam'; 22300*)

May 97. (7") (*GFS 22253*) **SISSYNECK. / FEATHER IN YOUR CAP** | 30 |

(c-s) (*GFSC 22253*) – ('A'side) / The new pollution (remix by Mickey P).

(cd-s) (*GFSTD 22253*) – (all 3 tracks).

Aug 97. (d7"/cd-ep) (*GFS/+TD 22276*) <*22303*> **JACK-ASS (Butch Vig mix). / STRANGE INVITATION (orchestral version) / DEVIL GOT MY WOMAN // JACK-ASS (Lowrider mix). / BURRO / BROTHER** | | – |

Aug 97. (12"ep) <*DGC12 22303*> **JACK-ASS / BURRO. / STRANGE INVITATION / BROTHER** | – | 97 |

Oct 97. (7"/c-s) (*GFS/+C 22293*) **DEADWEIGHT / ERASE THE SUN** | 23 |

(cd-s+=) (*GFSTD 22293*) – SA-5.

—— BECK with **SMOKEY HORMEL** – guitar / **ROGER MANNING** – keyboards, percussion / **JUSTIN MELDAL JOHNSON** – bass / **JOEY WARONKER** – drums

Nov 98. (cd/c) (*GED/GEC 25184*) <*25309*> **MUTATIONS** | 24 | 13 |

– Cold brains / Nobody's fault but my own / Lazy flies / Cancelled check / We live again / Tropicalia / Dead melodies / Bottle of blues / O Maria / Sing it again / Static / Diamond bollocks / Runners dial zero. (*lp-iss. on 'Bongload'; BL 39*)

Dec 98. (7"/c-s) (*GFS/+C 22365*) **TROPICALIA. / HALO OF GOLD** | 39 |

(cd-s+=) (*GFSTD 22365*) – Black balloon.

Oct 99. (7"pic-d/c-s) (*497181-7/-4*) **SEXX LAWS. / SALT IN THE WOUND** | 27 |

(cd-s+=) (*497181-2*) – ('A'-Wizeguyz mix).

(cd-s) (*497182-2*) – ('A'side) / This is my crew / ('A'-Malibu mix).

Nov 99. (cd/c) (*490485-2/-4*) **MIDNITE VULTURES** | 19 | 34 |

– Sexx laws / Nicotine & gravy / Mixed bizness / Get real paid / Hollywood freaks / Peaches & cream / Broken train / Milk & honey / Beautiful way / Pressure zone / Debra.

– compilations, etc. –

Apr 94. (cd) *Flipside*; <*FLIP 60*> **STEREOPATHETIC SOULMANURE** | | – | (home recordings '88–'93) (*UK-iss.Dec95 & Nov97; same*)

Jeff BECK

Born: 24 Jun '44, Surrey, England. His solo career began in earnest at the start of '67, BECK having successfully filled the shoes of ERIC CLAPTON in The YARDBIRDS over the preceding two years. Under the wing of pop maestro MICKIE MOST, he scored an immediate UK hit with the anthemic 'HI HO SILVER LINING'. Two further commercial pop-rock numbers, 'TALLYMAN' and 'LOVE IS BLUE' signalled the end of BECK's brief chart liaison, also terminating his period with MOST. With blues-rock back in vogue, the axeman steered a course back into heavier territory, forming The JEFF BECK GROUP alongside old cohorts, ROD STEWART (vocals), RON WOOD (guitar), NICKY HOPKINS (piano) and MICKEY WALLER (drums). The resulting two albums, 'TRUTH' (1968) and 'BECK-OLA' (1969), established BECK and co. as a major UK export across the Atlantic, both sets making the US Top 20. With ROD STEWART striking out his own, BECK turned to the unlikely source of hippy-dippy popster DONOVAN, who combined with the group on the summer '69 single, 'GOO GOO BARABAJAGAL'. In the early 70's, The JEFF BECK GROUP was re-modelled around newcomers COZY POWELL (drums) and BOBBY TENCH (vocals), the resulting two albums both making US Top 50 placings. With the country's top guitarist, ERIC CLAPTON, now partially sidelined, BECK took the opportunity to form his own supergroup, BECK, BOGART & APPICE. However, after only one album with the former VANILLA FUDGE heavyweights, BECK resumed a solo career. In the mid 70's he returned to form with the highly successful 'BLOW BY BLOW' opus, regarded by many as his finest hour. Along with many in the rock fraternity, BECK subsequently veered towards jazz-fusion, collaborating with JAN HAMMER on two albums, 'WIRED' (1976) and 'LIVE' (1977). After going to ground for a few years, BECK was 'THERE AND BACK' in the early 80's, although he spent the same amount of time recording his follow-up set, 'FLASH' (1985). This featured a belated reunion with old mucker, ROD STEWART, on the collaborative hit 45, 'PEOPLE GET READY'. After working with MICK JAGGER on his 1987 album, 'Primitive Cool', BECK returned in '89 with his 'GUITAR SHOP' project/album. In the early 90's, he collaborated (yet again!), this time with blues legend, BUDDY GUY, on a superb interpretation of the standard soul/blues classic, 'MUSTANG SALLY'. JEFF showcased yet another dimension to his talent when he recorded a 1993 GENE VINCENT tribute album, 'CRAZY LEGS', with his BIG TOWN PLAYBOYS. A six-year long wait resulted in 1999's 'WHO ELSE!', minor chart positions on both sides of the Atlantic reminding us that in some quarters the man has not been forgotten. • **Songwriters:** BECK with covers being; HI HO SILVER LINING (Scott English & Larry Weiss) / TALLYMAN (Graham Gouldman) / ALL SHOOK UP + JAILHOUSE ROCK (Leiber – Stoller) / I'VE BEEN DRINKIN' (D.Tauber & J.Mercer) / I AIN'T SUPERSTITIOUS (Willie Dixon) / MORNING DEW (Tim Rose) / SUPERSTITIOUS + CAUSE WE'VE ENDED AS LOVERS (Stevie Wonder) / GREENSLEEVES (trad.) / OL' MAN RIVER ('Showboat' musical) / GOODBYE PORK PIE HAT (Charlie

Mingus) / SHE'S A WOMAN (Beatles) / STAR CYCLE (Jan Hammer) / WILD THING (Troggs) / etc. • **Trivia:** His song 'STAR CYCLE' (written by band members Hymas & Philips), became theme tune for 'The Tube' in 1983.

Album rating: TRUTH (*6) / BECK-OLA (*6) / ROUGH AND READY (*7) / BLOW BY BLOW (*6) / WIRED (*5) / JEFF BECK WITH THE JAN HAMMER GROUP LIVE (*4) / THERE AND BACK (*5) / FLASH (*4) / JEFF BECK'S GUITAR SHOP (*6) / THE BEST OF BECKOLOGY compilation (*7) / CRAZY LEGS (*4) / UP (*4) / WHO ELSE! (*5)

JEFF BECK (solo) – vocals, lead guitar (ex-YARDBIRDS) with **JET HARRIS** – bass (ex-SHADOWS) / **VIV PRINCE** – drums (ex-PRETTY THINGS)

		Columbia	Epic
Mar 67.	(7") (*DB 8151*) <*10157*> **HI-HO SILVER LINING. / BECK'S BOLERO**	14	
——	**RAY COOK** – drums repl. PRINCE		
Jul 67.	(7") (*DB 8227*) **TALLYMAN. / ROCK MY PLIMSOUL**	30	–
Feb 68.	(7") (*DB 8359*) **LOVE IS BLUE. / I'VE BEEN DRINKING**	23	–

JEFF BECK GROUP

—— with **ROD STEWART** – vocals (also a solo artist, who sang on BECK's last 'B'side) / **RON WOOD** – bass (ex BIRDS) / **MICKY WALLER** (b. 6 Sep'44) – drums / **NICKY HOPKINS** – keyboards

Jul 68. (lp; stereo/mono) (*S+/CX 6293*) <*26413*> **TRUTH** | | 15 |

– Shapes of things / Let me love you / Morning dew / You shook me / Ol' man river / Greensleeves / Rock my plimsoul / Beck's bolero / Blues de luxe / I ain't superstitious. (*re-iss. 1985 lp/c; ATAK/TC-ATAK 42*) (*re-iss. Jun86 on 'Fame' lp/c; FA/TC-FA 3155*)

—— **TONY NEWMAN** – drums repl. WALLER

(mid'69) The JEFF BECK GROUP teamed up with ⇒ DONOVAN, on their joint hit GOO GOO BARABAJAGAL (LOVE IS HOT). (see ⇒ DONOVAN)

Jul 69. (lp) (*SCX 6351*) <*26478*> **BECK-OLA** | 39 | 15 |

– All shook up / Spanish boots / Girl from Mill Valley / Jailhouse rock / Plynth (water down the drain) / The hangman's knee / Rice pudding. (*re-iss. Jul85 on 'Capitol' lp/c; ED 260600-1/-4*)

Sep 69. (7"; w-drawn) (*DB 8590*) **PLYNTH (WATER DOWN THE DRAIN). / HANGMAN'S KNEE** | – | – |

—— split (Sep'69) when ROD STEWART and RON WOOD joined The FACES.

JEFF BECK GROUP reformed (Apr'71) with **JEFF BECK** – guitar (only) plus **BOBBY TENCH** – vocals / **MAX MIDDLETON** – keyboards / **CLIVE CHAPMAN** – bass / **COZY POWELL** – drums (ex-BIG BERTHA, ex-ACE KEFFORD STAND, ex-SORCERORS)

		Epic	Epic
Oct 71.	(lp/c) (*EPC/40 64619*) <*30973*> **ROUGH AND READY**		46

– Got the feeling / Situation / Short business / Max's tune / I've been used / New ways – Train train / Jody. (*re-iss. Aug84 lp/c; EPC/40 32037*) (*quad-lp 1974; Q 64619*) (*cd-iss. 1990; 471047-2*)

Jan 72. (7") (*EPC 7720*) <*10814*> **GOT THE FEELING. / SITUATION** | | |

Jul 72. (lp/c) (*EPC/40 64899*) <*31331*> **JEFF BECK GROUP** | | 19 | May72 |

– Ice cream cakes / Glad all over / Tonight I'll be staying here with you / Sugar cane / I can't give back the love I feel for you / Going down / I got to have a song / Highways / Definitely maybe. (*quad-lp 1974 on 'C.B.S.'; Q 31331*) (*cd-iss. 1990; 471047-2*)

Aug 72. (7") <*10938*> **DEFINITELY MAYBE. / HI HO SILVER LINING** | – | – |

—— Broke-up when COZY POWELL went solo & joined BEDLAM. Later to RAINBOW, etc. TENCH joined STREETWALKERS then VAN MORRISON. **JEFF** formed supergroup

BECK, BOGERT, APPICE

—— with **TIM BOGERT** – bass, vocals / **CARMINE APPICE** – drums (both ex-VANILLA FUDGE, etc.) plus **DUANE HITCHINS** – keyboards / **JIMMY GREENSPOON** – piano / **DANNY HUTTON** – vox

Mar 73.	(7") (*EPC 1251*) **BLACK CAT MOAN. / LIVIN' ALONE**		–
Apr 73.	(7") <*11027*> **LADY. / OH TO LOVE YOU**		
Jul 73.	(7") <*10998*> **I'M SO PROUD. / OH TO LOVE YOU**		
Apr 73.	(lp/c) (*EPC/40 65455*) <*32140*> **BECK, BOGERT, APPICE**	28	12

– Black cat moan / Lady / Oh to love you / Superstition / Sweet sweet surrender / Why should I care / Love myself with you / Livin' alone / I'm so proud. (*re-iss. Sep84 lp/c; EPC/40 32491*) (*re-iss. Nov89 on 'Essential' lp/c/cd; ESS LP/MC/CD 011*) (*quad-lp 1975 on 'C.B.S.'; Q 65455*)

—— This trio, also released widely available (JAP-import Nov74 d-lp) LIVE IN JAPAN

JEFF BECK

—— group reformed as instrumental line-up, **BECK + MIDDLETON / PHILIP CHEN** – bass / **RICHARD BAILEY** – drums

Mar 75. (lp/c) (*EPC/40 69117*) <*33409*> **BLOW BY BLOW** | | 4 |

– It doesn't really matter / You know what I mean / She's a woman / Constipated duck / Air blower / Scatterbrain / Cause we've ended as lovers / Thelonius / Freeway jam / Diamond dust. (*re-iss. Sep83 lp/c; EPC/40 32367*) (*re-iss. May94 & Nov95 & Sep99 cd/c; 469012-2/-4*)

May 75. (7") (*EPC 3334*) **SHE'S A WOMAN. / IT DOESN'T REALLY MATTER** | | |

Jun 75. (7") <*50112*> **CONSTIPATED DUCK. / YOU KNOW WHAT I MEAN** | – | – |

—— **JAN HAMMER** (b.1950, Prague, Czechoslavakia) – drums, synthesizer / **MICHAEL NARADA WALDEN** – keyboards, drums (both ex-MAHAVISHNU ORCHESTRA) / **WILBUR BASCOMBE** – bass (all 3 replaced CHEN)

Jul 76. (lp/c) (*EPC/40 86012*) <*33849*> **WIRED** | 38 | 16 | Jun76 |

– Led boots / Come dancing / Goodbye pork pie hat / Head for backstage pass / Blue wind / Sophie / Play with me / Love is green. (*re-iss. Mar82 lp/c; EPC/40 32067*) (*cd-iss. 1988; CD 86012*)

Aug 76. (7") <*50276*> **COME DANCING. / HEAD FOR BACKSTAGE PASS** | – | – |

—— (BECK, HAMMER) plus **TONY SMITH** – drums / **FERNANDO SAUNDERS** – bass / **STEVE KINDLER** – violin, synth.

Mar 77. (lp/c) (EPC/40 86025) <34433> **LIVE . . . WITH THE JAN HAMMER GROUP (live)** ☐ | 23
– Freeway jam / Earth (still our only home) / She's a woman / Full Moon boogie / Darkness – Earth in search of a sun / Scatterbrain / Blue wind. (re-iss. Jun85 lp/c; EPC/40 32297)

—— with **TONY HYMAS** – keyboards / **MO FOSTER** – bass / **SIMON PHILLIPS** – drums

Jul 80. (lp/c) (EPC/40 83288) <35684> **THERE AND BACK** | 38 | 21
– Star cycle / Too much to lose / You never know / The pump / The golden road / Space boogie / The final peace. (re-iss. Aug84 lp/c; EPC/40 32197) (cd-iss. Jan89; CD 83288)
Jul 80. (7") (EPC 8806) **THE FINAL PEACE. / SPACE BOOGIE** ☐ | ☐
Aug 80. (7") <50914> **THE FINAL PEACE. / TOO MUCH TO LOSE** | - | ☐
Feb 81. (12"ep) (EPCA 1009) **THE FINAL PEACE / SCATTERBRAIN. / TOO MUCH TO LOSE / LED BOOTS** ☐ | ☐

—— retired from the studio for half a decade, before returning 1985 with **HAMMER**, **APPICE, HYMAS** and **JIMMY HALL** – vocals

Jun 85. (7") (EPCA 6387) <05416> **PEOPLE GET READY. / BACK ON THE STREET** ☐ | 48
(12"+=) (TA 6387) – You know, we know.
(above single featured **ROD STEWART** on vox)
Jul 85. (lp/c) (EPC/40 26112) <39483> **FLASH** | 83 | 39
– Ambitious / Gets us all in the end / Escape / People get ready / Stop, look and listen / Get workin' / Ecstasy / Night after night / You know, we know. (re-iss. Mar94 on 'Pickwick'; 982838-2/-4)
Sep 85. (7") <05595> **GETS US ALL IN THE END. / YOU KNOW, WE KNOW** - | ☐
Sep 85. (7") (EPCA 6587) **STOP, LOOK AND LISTEN. / YOU KNOW, WE KNOW** ☐ | ☐
(12"+=) (TA 6587) – ('A'remix).
Mar 86. (7"/12") (EPCA/TA 6981) **AMBITIOUS. / ESCAPE** ☐ | ☐
Jul 86. (7") (EPCA 7271) **WILD THING. / GETS US ALL IN THE END** ☐ | ☐
(12"+=) (TA 7271) – Nighthawks.

—— In 1987, BECK went to session with **MICK JAGGER** on his 2nd album.

Oct 89. (lp/c/cd; JEFF BECK with TERRY BOZZIO & TONY HYMAS) (463472-1/-4/-2) <44313> **JEFF BECK'S GUITAR SHOP** ☐ | 49
– Guitar shop / Savoy / Behind the veil / Big block / Where were you / Stand on it / Day in the house / Two rivers / Sling shot.
Oct 89. (7") (BECK 1) **DAY IN THE HOUSE. / PEOPLE GET READY** ☐ | ☐
(cd-s+=) (BECK 1CD) – Cause we've ended as lovers / Blue wind.
(12") (BECK 1T) – ('A'side) / Guitar shop (guitar mix) / Cause we've ended as lovers.

—— In 1990, sessioned for **JON BON JOVI** on his BLAZE OF GLORY album.

—— In Sep'91 JEFF collaborated with **BUDDY GUY** on a single 'MUSTANG SALLY' on 'Silvertone'.

—— now with **MIKE SANCHEZ** – vocals, piano – / **IAN JENNINGS** – bass, vocals / **ADRIAN UTLEY** – rhythm guitar / **CLIVE DENVER** – drums, vocals / **LEO GREEN** – tenor sax / **NICK HUNT** – baritone sax

Jun 93. (cd/c/lp; as JEFF BECK & THE BIG TOWN PLAYBOYS) (473597-2/-4/-1) **CRAZY LEGS** ☐ | ☐
– Race with the devil / Cruisin' / Crazy legs / Double talkin' baby / Woman love / Lotta lovin' / Catman / Pink thunderbird / Baby blue / You better believe / Who slapped John? / Say mama / Red blue jeans and a pony tail / Five feet of lovin' / B-i-bickey-bi-bo-bo-go / Blues stay away from me / Pretty, pretty baby / Hold me, hug me, rock me.
(above was a tribute to GENE VINCENT & HIS BLUE CAPS)

—— 1999 with **TONY HYMAS** – keyboards, co-producer / **JENNIFER BATTEN** – guitars / **RANDY HOPE-TAYLOR** – bass / **STEVE ALEXANDER** – drums

	Columbia	Epic
Mar 99. (cd/c) (493041-2/-4) <67987> **WHO ELSE!** | 74 | 99
– What mama said / Psycho Sam / Brush with the blues / Blast from the east / Space for the papa / Angel (footsteps) / THX138 / Hip-notica / Even odds / Declan / Another place.

– compilations, others, etc. –

1969. (lp) Music For Pleasure; (MFP 5219) **THE MOST OF JEFF BECK** ☐ | -
Oct 72. (7"m) RAK; (RR 3) **HI HO SILVER LINING. / BECK'S BOLERO / ROCK MY PLIMSOUL** | 14 | -
(re-iss. Oct82 7"pic-d/12"; RRP/12RR 3) ; hit No.62.
Apr 73. (7"m; JEFF BECK AND ROD STEWART) RAK; (RR 4) **I'VE BEEN DRINKING. / MORNING DEW / GREENSLEEVES** ☐ | -
Nov 77. (lp) Embassy-CBS; (31546) **GOT THE FEELING** ☐ | -
Feb 83. (d-c) Epic; **BLOW BY BLOW / WIRED** ☐ | -
May 85. (lp/c) Fame; (FA 413125-1/-4) **THE BEST OF JEFF BECK featuring ROD STEWART** ☐ | -
(re-iss. Dec95 on 'Music For Pleasure' cd/c; CD/TC MFP 6202)
1985. (d-lp) Epic; (EPC 461009-1) **WIRED / FLASH** ☐ | -
Sep 88. (cd) E.M.I.; (CDP 746710-2) **LATE 60's WITH ROD STEWART** ☐ | -
May 89. (d-lp/d-c/d-cd) That's Original; (TFO LP/MC/CD 19) **JEFF BECK GROUP / ROUGH & READY** ☐ | -
Feb 91. (cd)(c) E.M.I.; (CZ 374)(TCEMS 1379) **TRUTH / BECK-OLA** ☐ | -
Feb 92. (7"/c-s; by JEFF BECK & ROD STEWART) Epic; (657756-7/-4) **PEOPLE GET READY. / TRAIN KEPT A ROLLIN'** | 49 | -
(cd-s) (657756-2) – ('A'side) / Cause we've ended as lovers / Where were you.
(cd-s) (657756-5) – ('A'side) / Train train / New ways.
Feb 92. (3xcd/3xc;box) Epic; (469262-2/-4) **BECKOLOGY** ☐ | ☐
(re-iss. May94; same)
Mar 92. (cd/c/lp) Epic; (471348-2/-4/-1) **THE BEST OF BECKOLOGY** ☐ | ☐
– Heart full of soul (YARDBIRDS) / Shapes of things (YARDBIRDS) / Over under sideways down (YARDBIRDS) / Hi ho silver lining / Tallyman / Jailhouse rock / I've been drinking / I ain't superstitious / Superstition (BECK, BOGART & APPICE) / Cause we've ended as lovers / The pump / Star cycle (theme from 'The Tube') /

People get ready (with ROD STEWART) / Wild thing / Where were you (w/ TERRY BOZZIO & TONY HYMAS) / Trouble in mind (TRIDENTS).
Mar 93. (3xcd-box) Epic; (468802-2) **FLASH / BLOW BY BLOW / THERE & BACK** ☐ | -
Jul 94. (cd) Wisepack; (LECD 080) **LEGENDS IN MUSIC** ☐ | -
—— ('Wisepack' also issued another collection Aug95, with some tracks by ERIC CLAPTON; LECDD 639)
Oct 94. (cd) Charly; (CDCD 1186) **SHAPES OF THINGS** ☐ | -
Aug 99. (cd) Dressed To Kill; (RECD 130) **JEFF BECK** ☐ | -

BEEFEATERS (See under ⇒ BYRDS)

BEE GEES

Formed: By the GIBB brothers in Brisbane, Australia (where they had emigrated from Manchester, England) in 1958. The boys' inaugural performance had taken place three years previous at their dad's Manchester 'Blue Cats' residency where they played skiffle covers (yes, LONNIE DONEGAN had a lot to answer for!). The brothers continued to cut their teeth (quite, er, literally!?) in the parochial talent contests/amateur shows in their new hometown of Brisbane, going under the name of the BROTHERS GIBB before abbreviating it to The BEE GEES. Interest in the talented schoolboy group was not long in coming and in 1959, DJ Bill Gates (no, not THE Bill Gates!) offered to manage the trio, promising them more lucrative gigs and air space. Becoming ever more adept at songwriting, the lads were subsequently signed to local label 'Leedon' where they released numerous 45's to moderate success. Realising that they were potentially big fish in the small Aussie music biz pond, they packed their bags and headed back to England in 1966. Ironically, as they made their plans to travel to the mother country, the title track from their album, 'SPICKS AND SPECKS', reached No.1 down under. However, their collective minds were made up and they settled in London, virtually unknown but totally confident of their ability to storm the world-leading UK charts. Recruiting a drummer (COLIN PETERSON), bass player (VINCE MELOUNEY) and manager (the notorious ROBERT STIGWOOD), they secured a deal with 'Polydor' and released their debut British single, 'NEW YORK MINING DISASTER 1941' (suffixed in the USA with the chorus, "Have You Seen My Wife, Mr. Jones"). Their distinctive combination of good looks, vocal harmony and astute lyrics slotted in seamlessly with other contemporary Brit beat groups and the single soon went Top 20. Hot on its heels came further classic singles, 'TO LOVE SOMEBODY', 'MASSACHUSETTS' (a UK No.1), 'WORDS' and 'I'VE GOT TO GET A MESSAGE TO YOU'. On the album front, the lads also scored a number of successes culminating in Spring '69 with an obligatory pseudo-psychedelic (double!) album, 'ODESSA'. Around the same time, MAURICE tied the knot with diminutive Glasgow popster LULU while the latter album's release marked the departure of solo bound ROBIN. He made it in his own right later that year with the massive selling single, 'SAVED BY THE BELL' as the remaining MAURICE and BARRY retaliated chart-wise with 'DON'T FORGET TO REMEMBER ME'. As the decade drew to a close, it seemed that the once mighty BEE GEES were falling apart; not for the first time the brothers had surfed the big pop wave only to wipeout! Even after ROBIN's return in 1970, their moment seemed to have passed in the UK at least. However, their Stateside momentum continued, hits such as 'LONELY DAYS' and the No.1 'HOW CAN YOU MEND A BROKEN HEART' keeping their name in the spotlight. The first years of the new decade found them quite possibly at their lowest creative ebb as the albums 'TRAFALGAR' (1972) and 'TO WHOM IT MAY CONCERN'(1973) sank without trace. Subsequently signing to Stigwood's new 'R.S.O.' label (also home of ERIC CLAPTON), The BEE GEES released 'LIFE IN A TIN CAN' (1973) to little response. Something different was needed to re-ignite the ol' Antipodean magic and the 1974 arrival of producer Arif Mardin for their 'MR. NATURAL' album marked a watershed in the brothers' career. Adopting a new dance-based sound, the icing on their funky rhythm-rich cake came in the form of the (then rare) falsetto harmonies, destined to become their trademark. Again guided by Mardin, they were onto a winner with 1975's 'MAIN COURSE'. Comeback single, 'JIVE TALKIN' deftly captured the essence of mid-70's funk and became a huge Stateside chart topper (Top 5 in Britain). 'NIGHTS ON BROADWAY' and er, 'FANNY (BE TENDER WITH MY LOVE)' repeated the formula as did the 'CHILDREN OF THE WORLD' album and its famous No.1 single, 'YOU SHOULD BE DANCING'. Yet again on the crest of a popular wave, their songs were much in demand by the disco/soul artists of the day including TAVARES and YVONNE ELLIMAN. They also ensured the success of a 1977 mid-budget movie entitled 'Saturday Night Fever' (which attempted to cash-in on the disco phenomenon) and an unknown young actor called John Travolta by penning a ditty or two for inclusion in its screenplay. One of the biggest grossing soundtracks of all-time, 'SATURDAY NIGHT FEVER', included THE "medallion man" anthem, 'STAYIN' ALIVE'. Never one to miss an opportunity, Stigwood lifted another two huge No.1 singles from the soundtrack, 'HOW DEEP IS YOUR LOVE' and 'NIGHT FEVER'. A rather bad career move in the form of the Stigwood-conceived musical version of the BEATLES' 'Sgt. Pepper' occupied them for much of the following year. In 1979, the album 'SPIRITS HAVING FLOWN' spawned three further US No.1's, 'TOO MUCH HEAVEN', 'TRAGEDY' and 'LOVE YOU INSIDE OUT', The BEE GEES continuing to flash their hairy chests as if Punk had never happened. Yet 1981's effort, 'LIVING EYES' surprisingly sank like a lead balloon, failing to break into either US or UK Top 40's. There were contributions to follow-up film 'STAYIN' ALIVE' but the disco medium was truly dead and the Brothers GIBB strategically withdrew to count their millions, do a bit of outside songwriting (for the likes of BARBRA STREISAND, DIONNE WARWICK, etc.) and ponder the next big thing. It was 1987 when they re-emerged on 'Warners' with 'ESP' and its hit single, 'YOU WIN AGAIN' although the storm clouds were gathering once again. Young brother, ANDY GIBB (who had a few hits in the latter half of '77) was found dead from a cocaine overdose. During the next four years, they released three fairly successful albums, 'ONE' (1989), 'HIGH CIVILIZATION' (1991) and 'SIZE ISN'T EVERYTHING' (1993). In 1997 the brothers became immortalised after their induction into the Rock'n'Roll Hall of Fame, releasing 'STILL WATERS' at the same time. In conclusion, there have been few more resilient bands through the last four decades. Just when they're considered dead and buried they reappear in a new and more commercial guise, always in command of melody, harmony and rhythm, with fingers and ears shrewdly on the pulse of musical fashion. The Ultimate Survivors! Now into their fifth decade of performing (wow!), the brothers GIBB continue to ride the changes in the music business.

Album rating: BEE GEES' FIRST (*6) / HORIZONTAL (*6) / IDEA (*4) / ODESSA (*7) / THE BEST OF THE BEE GEES VOL.1 compilation (*8) / CUCUMBER CASTLE (*3) / TWO YEARS ON (*5) / TRAFALGAR (*4) / TO WHOM IT MAY CONCERN (*4) / LIFE IN A TIN CAN (*4) / THE BEST OF THE BEE GEES VOL.2 compilation (*7) / MR. NATURAL (*3) / MAIN COURSE (*7) / CHILDREN OF THE WORLD (*5) / BEE GEES GOLD VOL.1 compilation (*7) / HERE AT LAST... BEE GEES LIVE (*5) / SATURDAY NIGHT FEVER with Various Artists soundtrack (*8) / SPIRITS HAVING FLOWN (*6) / GREATEST compilation (*7) / LIVING EYES (*4) / STAYIN' ALIVE soundtrack (*4) / E.S.P. (*4) / ONE (*5) / HIGH CIVILIZATION (*3) / SIZE ISN'T EVERYTHING (*4) / STILL WATERS (*5)

BARRY GIBB (b. 1 Sep'47, Manchester, England) – vocals, guitar / **MAURICE GIBB** (b.22 Dec'49, Isle Of Man) – vocals, bass / **ROBIN GIBB** (b.22 Dec'49, Isle Of Man) – vocals

		Leedon	not iss.
Mar 63. (7") (LK 346) **THE BATTLE OF THE BLUE AND GREY. / THE THREE KISSES OF LOVE**	–	–	Austra
Jun 63. (7") (LK 412) **TIMBER! / TAKE HOLD OF THAT STAR**	–	–	Austra
Feb 64. (7") (LK 534) **DON'T SAY GOODBYE. / PEACE OF MIND**	–	–	Austra

— in Jun'64, they backed JOHNNY DEVLIN on 'Festival' label single, 'BLUE SUEDE SHOES' / 'WHOLE LOTTA SHAKIN' GOIN' ON'

Aug 64. (7") (LK 696) **CLAUSTROPHOBIA. / COULD IT BE**	–	Aussie
Oct 64. (7") (LK 745) **TURN AROUND LOOK AT ME. / THEME FROM THE TRAVELS OF JAMIE McPHEETERS**	–	Aussie
Dec 64. (7"; with TREVOR GORDON) (LK 829) **HOUSE WITHOUT WINDOWS. / I'LL BE HAPPY**	–	Austra
Apr 65. (7") (LK 920) **EVERY DAY I HAVE TO CRY. / YOU WOULDN'T KNOW IT**	–	Austra
May 65. (7"; with TREVOR GORDON) (LK 924) **LITTLE MISS RHYTHM AND BLUES. / HERE I AM**	–	Austra
Aug 65. (7") (LK 1070) **WINE AND WOMEN. / FOLLOW THE WIND**	–	Austra
Nov 65. (7") (LK 1150) **I WAS A LOVER, A LEADER OF MEN. / AND THE CHILDREN LAUGHING**	–	Austra
Nov 65. (lp) (LL 31801) **BARRY GIBB AND THE BEE GEES SING AND PLAY 14 BARRY GIBB SONGS**	–	Austra

(re-iss.1968 as 'BARRY GIBB AND THE BEE GEES' on 'Calendar', R 66241)

		Spin	not iss.
Mar 66. (7") (LK 1282) **CHERRY RED. / I WANT HOME**	–	–	Austra
Jun 66. (7") (EK 1384) **MONDAY'S RAIN. / ALL OF MY LIFE**	–	–	Austra
Sep 66. (7") (EK 1474) **SPICKS AND SPECKS. / I AM THE WORLD**	–	–	Austra
Nov 66. (lp) (EL 32031) **SPICKS AND SPECKS**	–	–	Austra

(UK-iss.Sep93 on 'Remember' cd/c; RMB 7/4 5068)

| Jan 67. (7") (EK 1634) **BORN A MAN. / BIG CHANCE** | – | – |

(also iss.AUST. ep's THE BEE GEES (1964) / **WINE AND WOMEN** (1966) / **SPICKS AND SPECKS** (1967).

— added **VINCE MELOUNEY** (b. Australia) – guitar / **COLIN PETERSON** (b. Australia) – drums

		Polydor	Atco	
Feb 67. (7") (56727) **SPICKS AND SPECKS. / I AM THE WORLD**			–	
Apr 67. (7") (56161) <6487> **NEW YORK MINING DISASTER 1941. / I CAN'T SEE NOBODY**		12	14	May67

— <above 'A'side was prefixed with 'HAVE YOU SEEN MY WIFE, MR. JONES'>

| Jun 67. (7") (56178) <6503> **TO LOVE SOMEBODY. / CLOSE ANOTHER DOOR** | 41 | 17 | Jul67 |
| Jul 67. (lp; mono/stereo) (582/583 012) <223> **BEE GEES' FIRST** | 8 | 7 | Aug67 |

– Close another door / Craise Finton Kirk Royal Academy of Arts / Cucumber castle / Every Christian lion-hearted man will show you / Holiday / I can't see nobody / I close my eyes / In my own time / New York mining disaster 1941 / One minute woman / Please read me / Red chair, Fade away / To love somebody / Turn of the century. (re-iss.Nov83 lp/c; SPE LP/MC 56) (cd-iss. 1985; 825220-2)

Sep 67. (7") (56192) **MASSACHUSETTS. / BARKER OF THE F.O.**	1	–
Sep 67. (7") (6521) **HOLIDAY. / EVERY CHRISTIAN LION HEARTED MAN WILL SHOW YOU**	–	16
Nov 67. (7") (6532) **(THE LIGHTS WENT OUT IN) MASSACHUSETTS. / SIR GEOFFREY SAVED THE WORLD**	–	11
Nov 67. (7") (56220) **WORLD. / SIR GEOFFREY SAVED THE WORLD**	9	–
Jan 68. (7") (56229) <6548> **WORDS. / SINKING SHIPS**	8	15
Feb 68. (lp; mono/stereo) (582/583 020) <233> **HORIZONTAL**	16	12

– World / And the sun will shine / Lemons never forget / Really and sincerely / Birdie told me / With the sun in my eyes / Massachusetts / Harry Braff / Day time girl / The earnest of being George / Change is made / Horizontal. (cd-iss. Feb90; 833659-2)

Mar 68. (7") (56242) <6570> **JUMBO. / THE SINGER SANG HIS SONG**	25	57
Aug 68. (7") (56273) <6603> **I'VE GOTTA GET A MESSAGE TO YOU. / KITTY CAN**	1	8
Sep 68. (lp; mono/stereo) (582/583 036) <253> **IDEA**	4	17	Aug68

– Let there be love / In the summer of his years / Down to earth / I've gotta get a message to you / When the swallows fly / I started a joke / Swan song / Kitty can / Indian gin and whisky dry / Such a shame / Let there be love / I dea / I have decided to join the airforce / Kilburn Towers. (cd-iss. Nov89; 833660-2)

Dec 68. (7") <6639> **I STARTED A JOKE. / KILBURN TOWERS**	–	6
Feb 69. (7") (56304) <6657> **FIRST OF MAY. / LAMPLIGHT**	6	37	Mar69
Mar 69. (d-lp) (582 049-050) <702> **ODESSA**	10	20	Feb69

– Odessa (city on the Black Sea) / You'll never see my face again / Black diamond / Marley Purt drive / Edison / Melody fair / Give your best / Seven sea symphony with all nations (international anthem) * / Laugh in your face / Never say never again / First of May / The British opera. (cd-iss. May85 – * track; 825451-2)

— **BARRY + MAURICE** continue as a duo when ROBIN GIBB went solo (VINCE + COLIN also departed)

May 69. (7") (56331) <6682> **TOMORROW TOMORROW. / SUN IN THE MORNING**	23	54
Aug 69. (7") (56343) <6702> **DON'T FORGET TO REMEMBER. / THE LORD**	2	73	Sep69
Mar 70. (7") <6741> **IF ONLY I HAD MY MIND ON SOMETHING ELSE. / SWEETHEART**	–	91
Mar 70. (7") (56377) **I.O.I.O. / SWEETHEART**	49	–
May 70. (7") <6752> **I.O.I.O. / THEN YOU LEFT ME**	–	94
May 70. (lp) (2383 010) <327> **CUCUMBER CASTLE** (TV film soundtrack)	57	94

– If only I had my mind on something else / Then you left me / I was the child / Sweetheart / My thing / Turning tide / I.O.I.O. / I lay down and die / Bury me down the river / The chance of love / Don't forget to remember. (cd-iss. Nov89; 833783-2)

— **ROBIN** returned to make up the trio once again

| Nov 70. (7") (2001 104) 6795> **LONELY DAYS. / MAN FOR ALL SEASONS** | 33 | 3 |
| Dec 70. (lp) (2310 069) <353> **TWO YEARS ON** | | 32 | Jan71 |

– Two years on / Portrait of Louise / Man for all seasons / Sincere relation / Back home / The first mistake I made / Lonely days / Alone again / Tell me why / Lay it on me / Every second, every minute / I'm weeping. (cd-iss. Mar90; 833785-2)

| Jun 71. (7") (2058 115) <6824> **HOW CAN YOU MEND A BROKEN HEART. / COUNTRY WOMAN** | | 1 |

— added **GEOFF BRIDGEFORD** – drums / **ALAN KENDALL** – lead guitar

| Oct 71. (7") <6847> **DON'T WANNA LIVE INSIDE MYSELF. / WALKING BACK TO WATERLOO** | – | 53 |
| Nov 71. (lp) (2383 052) <7003> **TRAFALGAR** | 34 | Sep71 |

– How can you mend a broken heart / Israel / The greatest man in the world / It's just the day / Remembering / Somebody stop the music / Trafalgar / Don't wanna live inside myself / When do I / Dearest / Lion in winter / Walking back to Waterloo. (cd-iss. Mar90; 833786-2)

Jan 72. (7") (2058 185) <6871> **MY WORLD. / ON TIME**	16	16
Jul 72. (7") (2058 255) <6896> **RUN TO ME. / ROAD TO ALASKA**	9	16
Oct 72. (lp) (2383 139) <7012> **TO WHOM IT MAY CONCERN**	35	

– Run to me / We lost the road / Never been alone / Paper mache, cabbages & kings / I can bring love / I held a party / Please don't turn out the lights / Sea of smiling faces / Bad bad dreams / You know it's for you / Alive / Road to Alaska / Sweet song of summer. (cd-iss. Apr93; 833787-2)

		R.S.O.	R.S.O.
Nov 72. (7") (2058 304) <6909> **ALIVE. / PAPER MACHE, CABBAGES AND KINGS**		34
Mar 73. (7") (2090 105) <401> **SAW A NEW MORNING. / MY LIFE HAS BEEN A SONG**		94

— now with **RIC GRECH** – bass / **SNEAKY PETE** – pedal steel / **JIM KELTNER** – drums / **JEROME RICHARDSON** – flute / **TOMMY MORGAN** – harmonica

| Mar 73. (lp; w-drawn) <870> **LIFE IN A TIN CAN** | – | 69 | Jan73 |

– Saw a new morning / I don't wanna be the one / South Dakota morning / Living in Chicago / While I play / My life has been a song / Come home Johnny Bridie / Method to my madness. (cd-iss. Apr93; 833788-2)

Jun 73. (7") (2090 111) <404> **WOULDN'T I BE SOMEONE. / ELISA**		
Mar 74. (7") (2090 128) <408> **MR. NATURAL. / IT DOESN'T MATTER MUCH TO ME**		93
Jun 74. (7") <410> **THROW A PENNY. / I CAN'T LET YOU GO**	–	–
Jul 74. (lp) (2394 132) <4800> **MR. NATURAL**			Jun74

– Charade / Throw a penny / Down the road / Voices / Give a hand take a hand / Dogs / Mr. Natural / Lost in your love / I can't let you go / Heavy breathing / Had a lot of love last night. (cd-iss. Apr93; 833789-2)

| Aug 74. (7") (2090 136) <501> **CHARADE. / HEAVY BREATHING** | | |

— back-up now from **ALAN KENDALL** – guitar / **BLUE WEAVER** – keyboards / **DENNIS BYRON** – drums

| May 75. (7") (2090 160) <510> **JIVE TALKIN'. / WIND OF CHANGE** | 5 | 1 |
| Jun 75. (lp)(c) (2394 150)(3216 050) <4807> **MAIN COURSE** | | 14 |

– Nights on Broadway / Jive talkin' / Winds of change / Songbird / Fanny (be tender with my love) / All this making love / Country lanes / Come on over / Edge of the universe / Baby as you turn away. (re-iss.Aug84 lp/c; SPE Lp/MC 111) (cd-iss. May88; 833790-2)

Sep 75. (7") (2090 171) <515> **NIGHTS ON BROADWAY. / EDGE OF THE UNIVERSE**		7
Jan 76. (7") (2090 179) <519> **FANNY (BE TENDER WITH MY LOVE). / COUNTRY LANES**		12	Dec75
Jul 76. (7") (2090 195) <853> **YOU SHOULD BE DANCING. / SUBWAY**	5	1
Sep 76. (7") (2090 207) <859> **LOVE SO RIGHT. / YOU STEPPED INTO MY LIFE**	41	3
Oct 76. (lp) (2394 169) <3003> **CHILDREN OF THE WORLD**		8	Sep76

– You should be dancing / You stepped into my life / Love so right / Lovers / Can't keep a good man down / Boogie child / Love me / Subway / The way it was / Children of the world. (cd-iss. Nov89; 623658-2)

Jan 77. (7") <867> **BOOGIE CHILD. / LOVERS**	–	12
Feb 77. (7") (2090 224) **CHILDREN OF THE WORLD. / BOOGIE CHILD**	–	–
Jun 77. (d-lp)(d-c) (2658 120)(3517 013) <3901> **HERE AT LAST... BEE GEES ... LIVE** (live)		8	May77

– I've gotta get a message to you / Love so right / Edge of the universe / Come on over / Can't keep a good man down / New York mining disaster 1941 / Run to me / World / Holiday / I can't see nobody / I started a joke / Massachusetts / How can you mend a broken heart / To love somebody / You should be dancing / Boogie child /

Down the road / Words / Winds of change / Nights on Broadway / Jive talkin' / Lonely days. *(re-iss. Oct84; 3517013)*

Jul 77. (7") <880> **EDGE OF THE UNIVERSE (live). / WORDS (live)** | – | 26

Oct 77. (7") *(2090 259)* <882> **HOW DEEP IS YOUR LOVE. / CAN'T KEEP A GOOD MAN DOWN** | 3 | 1 Sep77

Jan 78. (7") *(2090 267)* <885> **STAYIN' ALIVE. / Yvonne Elliman: IF I CAN'T HAVE YOU** | 4 | 1 Dec77

Mar 78. (d-lp)(d-c) *(2658 123)(3517 014)* <4001> **SATURDAY NIGHT FEVER (soundtrack w/ Various Artists)** | 1 | 1 Nov77
– Stayin' alive / How deep is your love / Night fever / More than a woman / Jive talkin' / You should be dancing / More than a woman (TAVARES) / Calypso breakdown (RALPH DONALDSON) / If I can't have you (YVONNE ELLIMAN) / A fifth of Beethoven (WALTER MURPHY) / Open sesame (KOOL & THE GANG) / Boogie shoes (K.C. & THE SUNSHINE BAND) / M.F.S.B. (K.C. & THE SUNSHINE BAND) / K. Jee (K.C. & THE SUNSHINE BAND) / Disco inferno (TRAMMPS) / Manhattan skyline (TRAMMPS) / Night on disco mountain (TRAMMPS) / Salsation (TRAMMPS). *(d-cd-iss. Nov83; 800068-2) (d-lp re-iss. Jan84; SPDLP 5) (d-cd re-iss. Oct95; 825389-2)*

Apr 78. (7") *(2090 272)* <889> **NIGHT FEVER. / DOWN THE ROAD (live)** | 1 | 1 Jan78

Nov 78. (7") *(RSO 25)* <913> **TOO MUCH HEAVEN. / REST YOUR LOVE IN ME** | 3 | 1

Feb 79. (7") *(RSO 27)* <918> **TRAGEDY. / UNTIL** | 1 | 1

Feb 79. (lp/c) *(RSBG/TRSBG 1)* <3041> **SPIRITS HAVING FLOWN** | 1 | 1
– Tragedy / Too much Heaven / Love you inside out / Reaching out / Search find stop (think again) / Spirits (having flown) / Living together / I'm satisfied / Until. *(re-iss. Sep83 lp/c; SPE LP/MC 48) (also iss.on US pic-lp) (cd-iss. Nov89; 827335-2)*

Apr 79. (7") *(RSO 31)* <925> **LOVE YOU INSIDE OUT. / I'M SATISFIED** | 13 | 1

Nov 79. (d-lp/d-c) *(RSDX/+C 001)* <4200> **BEE GEES GREATEST (compilation)** | 6 | 1
– Children of the world / Don't throw it all away / Fanny (be tender with my love) / How deep is your love / If I can't have you / Jive talkin' / Love me / Love so right / Love you inside out / More than a woman / Night fever / Nights on Broadway / Rest of your love on me / Spirits (having flown) / Stayin' alive / Too much Heaven / Tragedy / Wind of change / You should be dancing / You stepped into my life. *(cd-iss. 1983; 800071-2)*

Dec 79. (7") *(RSO 52)* **SPIRITS (HAVING FLOWN). / WINDS OF CHANGE** | 16 | –

—— the trio were now augmented by many session people

Sep 81. (7") *(RSO 81)* <1066> **HE'S A LIAR. / (instrumental)** | – | 30

Nov 81. (lp/c) *(RSBG/TRSBG 2)* <3098> **LIVING EYES** | 73 | 41
– Living eyes / He's a liar / Paradise / Don't fall in love with me / Soldiers / I still love you / Wild flower / Nothing could be good / Cryin' every day / Be who you are. *(re-iss. Aug83 lp/c; SPE LP/MC 22) (cd-iss. Aug84; 813642-2)*

Nov 81. (7") *(RSO 85)* <1067> **LIVING EYES. / I STILL LOVE YOU** | – | 45

Jul 83. (7") *(RSO 94)* <813 713-7> **THE WOMAN IN YOU. / STAYIN' ALIVE** | – | 24 May83
(12") *(RSOX 94)* – ('A'side) / Saturday night segue.

Jul 83. (lp/c) *(RSBG/TRSBG 3)* <813269> **STAYING ALIVE (soundtrack with Various Artists)** | 14 | 6
– The woman in you / Love you too much / Breakout / Someone belonging to someone / Life goes on / Stayin' alive / Far from over (FRANK STALLONE) / Look out for number one (TOMMY FARAGHER) / Finding out the hard way (CYNTHIA RHODES) / Moody girl (FRANK STALLONE) / (We dance) So close to the fire (TOMMY FARAGHER) / I'm never gonna give you up (FRANK STALLONE & CYNTHIA RHODES).

Sep 83. (7") *(RSO 96)* <815 235-7> **SOMEONE BELONGING TO SOMEONE. / I LOVE YOU TOO MUCH** | 49 | 49 Aug83
(12") *(RSOX 96)* – ('A'side) / Saturday night fever medley.

| | Warners | Warners |

Sep 87. (7")/c-s/12"/12"pic-d *(W 8351/+C/T/TP)* <28351> **YOU WIN AGAIN. / BACKTAFUNK** | 1 | 75

Sep 87. (lp/c)(cd) *(WX 83/+C)(925541-2)* <25541> **E.S.P.** | 5 | 96 Oct87
– E.S.P. / You win again / Live or die / Giving up the ghost / The longest night / This is your life / Angela / Overnight / Crazy for your love / Backtafunk. *(re-iss. cd Feb95; same)*

Dec 87. (7") *(W 8139)* <28139> **E.S.P. / OVERNIGHT** | 51 | –
(ext-12"+=) *(W 8139T)* – ('A'-Extra house vocals mix).

Feb 88. (7") *(W 7966)* **CRAZY FOR YOUR LOVE. / YOU WIN AGAIN** | – | –
(12"+=) *(W 7966T)* – Giving up the ghost.

Mar 88. (7"/c-s) *(W 7523/+C)* **ORDINARY LIVES. / WING AND A PRAYER** | 54 | –
(12"+=/cd-s+=) *(W 7523 T/CD)* – ('A'extended).

Apr 89. (lp/c)(cd) *(WX 252/+C)(925887-2)* <25887> **ONE** | 29 | 68 Aug89
– Ordinary lives / Bodyguard / Flesh and blood / House of shame / One / It's my neighbourhood / Tokyo nights / Wish you were here / Will you ever let him. *(re-iss. cd Feb95; same)*

Jun 89. (7"/c-s) *(W 2916/+C)* **ONE. / FLESH AND BLOOD** | 71 | –
(12"+=/cd-s+=) *(W 2916 T/CD)* – ('A'dance mix).

Jul 89. (7") <22899> **ONE. / WING AND A PRAYER** | – | 7

Nov 89. (7") <22733> **YOU WIN AGAIN. / WILL YOU EVER LET ME** | – | –

Feb 91. (7"/c-s) *(W 0014/+C)* **SECRET LOVE. / TRUE CONFESSIONS** | 5 | –
(12"+=/cd-s+=) *(W 0014 T/CD)* – Human sacrifice.

Mar 91. (cd)(lp/c) *(<7599 26530-2>)(WX 417/+C)* **HIGH CIVILIZATION** | 24 | –
– High civilization / Secret love / When he's gone / Happy ever after / Party with no name / Ghost train / Dimensions / The only one / Human sacrifice / Evolution. *(re-iss. cd Feb95; same)*

May 91. (7"/c-s) **WHEN HE'S GONE. / MASSACHUSETTS (live)** | – | –
(12"+=/cd-s+=) – You win again (live).

—— now with **ALAN KENDALL + TIM CANSFIELD** – guitars / **GEORGE PERRY** – bass / **TIM MOORE** – keyboards / **TREVOR MURRELL** – drums / **LUIS JARDIM** – percussion / **ED CALLE** – sax / **GUSTAVO LEZCANO** – harmonica

| | Polydor | Polydor |

Aug 93. (7") *(PO 284)* <859164> **PAYING THE PRICE OF LOVE. / MY DESTINY** | 23 | 74 Oct93

(cd-s+=) *(PZCD 284)* – (2-'A'mixes)

Sep 93. (cd/c) *(519945-2/-4)* <521055> **SIZE ISN'T EVERYTHING** | 28 | – Oct93
– Paying the price of love / Kiss of life / How to fall in love, pt.1 / Omega man / Haunted house / Heart like mine / Anything for you / Blue island / Above and beyond / For whom the bell tolls / Fallen angel / Decadence.

Nov 93. (cd-s) *(PZCD 299)* **FOR WHOM THE BELL TOLLS. / DECADENCE (YOU SHOULD BE DANCING)** | 4 |
(12"/c-s) – ('A'side) / Staying alive / Too much Heaven / Massachusetts.

Apr 94. (7"/c-s) *(PO/+CS 311)* **HOW TO FALL IN LOVE PART 1. / 855 7019** | 30 |
(cd-s+=) *(PZCD 311)* – Fallen angel.
(cd-s) *(PZDD 311)* – ('A'side) / I've gotta get a message to you / Tragedy / New York mining disaster 1941.

Feb 97. (c-s/cd-s) *(573527-4/-2)* **ALONE / CLOSER THAN CLOSE / RINGS AROUND THE MOON** | 5 | 28 May97
(cd-s) *(573529-2)* – ('A'side) / How deep is your love / Words / I've gotta get a message to you

Mar 97. (cd/c) *(537302-2/-4)* **STILL WATERS** | 2 | 11 May97
– Alone / I surrender / I could not love you more / Still waters (run deep) / My lover's prayer / With my eyes closed / Irresistible force / Closer than close / I will / Obsessions / Miracles happen / Smoke and mirrors.

Jun 97. (c-s) *(571220-4)* **I COULD NOT LOVE YOU MORE / (Brits medley)** | 14 |
(cd-s) *(571299-2)* – ('A'side) / Stayin' alive / Jive talkin'.
(cd-s) *(571223-2)* – ('A'side) / To love somebody / Love never dies.

Oct 97. (c-s/cd-s) *(571628-4/-2)* <569218> **STILL WATERS (RUN DEEP) / OBSESSIONS** | 18 | 57
(cd-s) *(571885-2)* – ('A'side) / Night fever / More than a woman / You should be dancing.

Sep 98. (cd/c) *(<559220-2/-4>)* **LIVE ONE NIGHT ONLY (live)** | 4 | 72 Nov98
– Intro – You should be dancing / Alone / Massachusetts / To love somebody / Words / Closer than close / Islands in the stream / Our love (don't throw it all away) / Night fever / More than a woman / Lonely days / New York mining disaster 1941 / I can't see nobody / And the sun will shine / Nights on Broadway / How can you mend a broken heart / Heartbreaker / Guilty / Immortality (BEE GEES & CELINE DION) / Tragedy / I started a joke / Grease / Jive talkin' / How deep is your love / Stayin' alive / You should be dancing. *(re-iss. Nov99; same)*

– compilations, etc. –

Note; all below on 'Polydor' UK / 'Atco' US until stated otherwise

Nov 68. (lp) *(236 221)* <264> **RARE, PRECIOUS & BEAUTIFUL** | | 99

Oct 69. (lp) <292> **BEST OF THE BEE GEES** | 7 | 9 Jul69
– Holiday / I've got to get a message to you / I can't see nobody / Words / I started a joke / Spicks and specks / First of May / World / Massachusetts / To love somebody / Every Christian lion hearted man will show you / New York mining disaster 1941. *(cd-iss. Mar87 on 'R.S.O.'; 831594-2)*

Mar 70. (lp) *(236 513)* <321> **RARE, PRECIOUS & BEAUTIFUL VOL.2** | | 100

Apr 70. (lp) *(236 556)* **RARE, PRECIOUS & BEAUTIFUL VOL.3** | – | –

Jun 71. (lp) *(2447 012)* **MARLEY PURT DRIVE (TV Film Soundtrack)** | – | –
– Odessa (city on the black sea) / You'll never see my face again / Black diamond / Marley purt drive / Edison / Melody fair / Suddenly / Whisper whisper.

Jun 73. (lp) *(234 106)* / R.S.O.; <875> **THE BEST OF THE BEE GEES, VOL.2** | | 98 Jul73
(re-iss. Nov85; SPELP 90) (cd-iss. 1988 on 'R.S.O.'; 831960-2)

Jun 76. (lp/c) *Contour; (CN/+4 2002)* **MASSACHUSETTS** | | –

Nov 76. (lp) *R.S.O.; <3006>* **BEE GEES GOLD, VOLUME ONE** | – | 50

Nov 77. (lp/c) *Contour; (CN/+4 2028)* **I'VE GOTTA GET A MESSAGE TO YOU** | | –

Aug 78. (d-lp) *Pickwick; (PDA 048)* **BEE GEES BONANZA – THE EARLY DAYS** | | –

Jun 79. (lp) *Hallmark; (SHM 971)* **THE EARLY DAYS VOL.1** | | –

Jun 79. (lp) *Hallmark; (SHM 973)* **THE EARLY DAYS VOL.2** | | –

Jun 79. (lp) *Hallmark; (SHM 982)* **THE EARLY DAYS VOL.3** | | –

Mar 86. (7") *Old Gold; (OG 9581)* **MASSACHUSETTS. / NEW YORK MINING DISASTER 1941** | |

Mar 86. (7") *Old Gold; (OG 9583)* **DON'T FORGET TO REMEMBER. / FIRST OF MAY** | |

Mar 86. (7") *Old Gold; (OG 9585)* **I'VE GOTTA GET A MESSAGE TO YOU. / TO LOVE SOMEBODY** | |

Mar 86. (7") *Old Gold; (OG 9587)* **JIVE TALKIN'. / YOU SHOULD BE DANCING** | |

Feb 88. (7") *Old Gold; (OG 9773)* **SAVED BY THE BELL (Robin Gibb) / WORDS** | |

Oct 88. (lp/c) *BR Music; (BRLP/BRMC 45)* **THEIR MOST BEAUTIFUL SONGS** | |

Nov 90. (cd/c/lp) *Polydor; (847339-2/-4/-1)* **THE VERY BEST OF THE BEE GEES** | 8 |
– You win again / How deep is your love / Night fever / Tragedy / Massachusetts / I've gotta get a message to you / You should be dancing / New York mining disaster 1941 / World / First of May / Don't forget to remember / Saved by the bell (ROBIN GIBB) / Run to me / Jive talkin' / More than a woman / Stayin' alive / Too much Heaven / Ordinary lives / – To love somebody / Nights on Broadway. *(re-iss. Mar97; same)* – hit UK No.6

Nov 90. (7"/c-s) *Polydor;* **HOW DEEP IS YOUR LOVE (1990 remix). / YOU SHOULD BE DANCING (1990 remix)** | |
(12"+=/cd-s+=) – Too much Heaven / To love somebody.

Dec 90. (4xcd-box/4xc-box) *Polydor; (843911-2/-4)* **TALES FROM THE BROTHERS GIBB: A HISTORY IN SONG 1967-1990** | |
(re-iss. Nov99; same)

Jan 92. (cd) *Thunderbolt; (CDTB 132)* **EVER INCREASING CIRCLES (early)** | |
(re-iss. Mar98 on 'MagMid'; MM 001)

Apr 92. (cd) *Thunderbolt; (CDTB 135)* **TOMORROW THE WORLD (1964 material onwards)** | |
(re-iss. Mar99 on 'MagMid'; MM 027)

Jun 92. (c/cd) *Tring; (MC+/JHD 006)* **YOU WOULDN'T KNOW** | – | –

Jun 93. (cd-s) *Old Gold;* **NIGHT FEVER / STAYIN' ALIVE / HOW DEEP IS YOUR LOVE** | |

Jun 93. (cd-s) *Old Gold;* **TRAGEDY / TOO MUCH HEAVEN / LOVE YOU INSIDE OUT** ☐ -
Nov 93. (cd) *Koch; (322691)* **FOREVER YOUNG** ☐ -
Feb 94. (cd/c) *Javelin; (HAD CD/MC 105)* **SPOTLIGHT ON THE BEE GEES** ☐ -
Dec 95. (cd) *Thunderbolt; (CDTB 170)* **TO BE OR NOT TO BE** ☐ -
Jul 97. (cd/c) *Hallmark; (30766-2/-4)* **THE LEGEND BEGINS** ☐ -
Oct 97. (cd) *Prestige; (CDSGP 0307)* **CLAUSTROPHOBIA** ☐ -
Mar 99. (cd) *Hallmark; (31122-2)* **THE BEE GEES (THE EARLY YEARS)** ☐ -
Sep 99. (cd) *A.B.M.; (ABMMCD 1083)* **BIG CHANCE** ☐ -

B.E.F. (see under ⇒ HEAVEN 17)

Chris BELL (dig out; Great Alt & Indie . . .)

BELLE AND SEBASTIAN

Formed: Glasgow, Scotland . . . early '96 by ex-choirboy/boxer!, STUART MURDOCH (the main songwriter) and ISOBEL CAMPBELL, who met and recruited additional members STUART DAVID, RICHARD COLBURN, STEVIE JACKSON and CHRIS GEDDES in a local cafe. They borrowed the group name from a popular 70's children's TV series (from France) about a young boy and his Pyrenees mountain dog. Two months into their career, the expanded outfit released a very limited (1000 copies) college financed album, 'TIGERMILK', which gained sufficient airplay on national radio to ensure encroaching cult status. By the end of the year (and now with 7th member, SARAH MARTIN) they had unleashed their debut proper, 'IF YOU'RE FEELING SINISTER', which went on to sell in excess of 15,000 copies and gained much respect from end of the year critic polls. Since then, BELLE AND SEBASTIAN have hit the singles chart three times with a series of highly desirable EP's, culminating with their critically acclaimed Top 40 entry, '3.. 6.. 9 SECONDS OF LIGHT'. The fact that they've scaled such giddy heights of indie stardom with only a minimum of promotion and a handful of gigs speaks volumes for the quality of their vintage twee C-86-esque sound. By late summer '98, expectations for a new album had reached fever pitch, critics unanimously hailing 'THE BOY WITH THE ARAB STRAP' as one of the year's finest (sadly, too late for esteemed Mercury Prize) and helped ease it into the Top 20. They by now trademark combination of fey vocals, killer hooklines and avant-pop experimentalism resulted in some of B&S's most infectious tracks to date. With the spirit of NICK DRAKE ghosting in and out of focus (especially on 'SLEEP THE CLOCK AROUND' and 'A SUMMER WASTING'), this troupe of Glaswegian revivalists succeeded in putting the 60's and 70's through an 80's filter, incredibly coming up with something quintessentially 90's! The uninitiated should head straight for the holy trinity of tracks opening side two wherein BELLE & SEBASTIAN do an "ARAB STRAP" so to speak, the "Bairn"-like narrative of 'A SPACE BOY DREAM' complementing the BOLAN-esque stomp of the title track and sandwiching the brassy, BOO RADLEYS (but don't let that put you off!) style 'DIRTY DREAM NUMBER TWO'. Fans eager to get a glimpse of these elusive Scots shysters in the flesh should keep their eyes peeled, actual gigs are woefully few and far between. Extra-curricular activities, meanwhile, included a US 'Sub Pop' 7" from STUART DAVID's spoken word/electro outfit, LOOPER (with also his wife, Wee KARN and his brother, RONNIE BLACK). They would continue as a unit early in 1999, releasing a debut album for 'Jeepster', while ISOBEL's side project, The GENTLE WAVES, also released a long-player on the same label. In July that year and due to demand from everybody bar possibly PETE WATERMAN and his STEPS (who were somewhat peeved about losing the recent Brit Newcomers award due to internet voting), BELLE & SEBASTIAN re-distributed their semi-quasi debut 'TIGERMILK'. With the CD version riding high in the UK Top 20, it was thought the best time for CHRIS GEDDES and his V-TWIN crew to deliver their STUART MURDOCH-produced solo single effort, 'THANK YOU BABY'.

Album rating: TIGERMILK (*8) / IF YOU'RE FEELING SINISTER (*8) / THE BOY WITH THE ARAB STRAP (*9) / Looper: UP A TREE (*5) / Gentle Waves: THE GREEN FIELDS OF FOREVERLAND (*6)

STUART MURDOCH (b.1967) – vocals, acoustic guitar / **ISOBEL CAMPBELL** – violin / **STEVIE JACKSON** – guitars, vocals / **STUART DAVID** – bass / **RICHARD COLBURN** – drums / **CHRIS GEDDES** – piano

	Electric Honey	not iss.
Jun 96. (lp) *(EHRLP 5)* **TIGERMILK**	☐	-

– The state I am in / Expectations / She's losing it / You're just a baby / Electronic renaissance / I could be dreaming / We rule the school / My wandering days are over / I don't love anyone / Mary Jo. *(re-iss. Jul99 on 'Jeepster' cd/c/lp; JPR CD/MC/LP 007)* – hit No.13

—— added **SARAH MARTIN** – violin, saxophone / and also extra member **MICK COOKE** – trumpet

	Jeepster	Enclave-Capitol
Nov 96. (cd/c/lp) *(JPR CD/MC/LP 001)* <56713> **IF YOU'RE FEELING SINISTER**	☐	☐ Feb97

– Stars of track and field / Seeing other people / Me and the Major / Like Dylan in the movies / The fox in the snow / Get me away from here, I'm dying / If you're feeling sinister / Mayfly / The boy done wrong again / Judy and the dream of horses.

May 97. (7") *(JPR7 001)* **DOG ON WHEELS. / THE STATE I AM IN (demo)** 59 -
(12"+=/cd-s+=) *(JPR 12/CDS 001)* – String bean Jean / Belle & Sebastian.

—— guest on below, **MONICA QUEEN** – vocals (of THRUM)

Aug 97. (7") *(JPR7 002)* **LAZY LINE PAINTER JANE. / YOU MADE ME FORGET MY DREAMS** 41 -
(12"+=/cd-s+=) *(JPR 12/CDS 002)* – Photo Jenny / A century of Elvis.
Oct 97. (7"ep) *(JPR7 003)* **3.. 6.. 9 SECONDS OF LIGHT EP** 32 -
– A century of fakers / Le pastie de la bourgeoisie.
(12"ep+=/cd-ep+=) *(JPR 12/CDS 003)* – Beautiful / Put the book back on the shelf / *(hidden track-)* Songs for children.

—— added guest **NEIL ROBERTSON** – bass

	Jeepster	Matador
Sep 98. (cd/c) *(JPR CD/MC 003)* <311> **THE BOY WITH THE ARAB STRAP**	12	☐

– It could have been a brilliant career / Sleep the clock around / Is it wicked not to care? / Ease your feet in the sea / A summer wasting / Seymour Stein / A space boy dream / Dirty dream number two / The boy with the arab strap / Chickfactor / Simple things / The rollercoaster ride.
Dec 98. (12"ep/cd-ep) *(JPR 12/CDS 009)* **THIS IS JUST A MODERN ROCK SONG / I KNOW WHERE THE SUMMER GOES. / THE GATE / SLOW GRAFFITI** - --chart

LOOPER

STUART DAVID – voice / with **WEE KARN** + **RONNIE BLACK**

	Jeepster	Sub Pop
Jul 98. (7") <SP 446> **IMPOSSIBLE THINGS. / SPACEBOY DREAM No.3**	-	☐

Feb 99. (10"ep/cd-ep) *(JPR 10/CDS 010)* **BALLAD OF RAY SUZUKI. / RAY'S GOLDEN FIST (bananahand mix) / SUZUKI'S BIG RIP-OFF (twintub remix)** ☐ ☐
Mar 99. (cd/lp) *(JPR CD/LP 005)* <SP 453> **UP A TREE** ☐ ☐
– Treehouse / Impossible things / Burning flies / Festival '95 / Ballad of Ray Suzuki / Dave the Moon man / Quiet and small / Colombo's car / Up a tree again / Back to the treehouse.
Oct 99. (10"/cd-s) *(JPR 10/CDS 015)* **UP A TREE AGAIN. / WHO'S AFRAID OF Y2K?** ☐

GENTLE WAVES

ISOBEL CAMPBELL with **RICHARD COLBURN, STUART MURDOCH, CHRIS GEDDES + STEVIE JACKSON**

	Jeepster	Jeepster
Mar 99. (7") *(JPR7 011)* **WEATHERSHOW. / EVENSONG**	☐	☐

Apr 99. (cd/lp) *(JPR CD/LP 006)* <4026> **THE GREEN FIELDS OF FOREVERLAND . . .** ☐ ☐
– Hangman in the shadow / Evensong / Renew & restore / Emmanuelle, skating on thin ice / Rose I love you / Enchanted place / Tree lullaby / Dirty snow for the broken ground / Weathershow / Chapter in the life of Matthew / To salt a scar.

V-TWIN

—— **CHRIS GEDDES** plus **STUART**, etc

	Domino	Drag City
Aug 99. (7") *(RUG 95)* **THANK YOU BABY. / DERAILED**	☐	☐

(cd-s+=) *(RUG 95CD)* – Lunan.

BELLY

Formed: Providence, Rhode Island, USA . . . late '91 by ex-THROWING MUSES and BREEDERS co-leader TANYA DONELLY. Recruiting brothers, THOMAS and CHRIS GORMAN along with FRED ABONG, DONELLY set her pet project in motion with the 'SLOWDUST' EP in summer '92, BELLY remaining with '4 a.d.' (the label that had been home to both DONELLY's previous outfits). Produced by The PIXIES maestro, Gil Norton, the record introduced BELLY's hypnotic blend of provocative musings and strident, infectious indie-rock, a style which flowered on the follow-up EP, 'GEPETTO' (featuring a cover of The Flying Burrito Brothers' classic 'HOT BURRITO #2') and the hit single 'FEED THE TREE'. The debut album, 'STAR' narrowly missed the UK No.1 spot, DONELLY's little-girl-lost sweetness occasionally transforming into a fearsome howl. Similarly, DONELLY's lyrics were by turns twisted and twee, this delicate balance undoubtedly part of the band's appeal. Despite this incredible start, a second set, the Glyn Johns-produced, 'KING', took off in a rockier direction, losing some of the BELLY mystique in the process. Though the record made the UK Top 10, its relative critical and commercial failure eventually led to DONELLY splitting the group up and heading for a solo career. In 1997, her debut, 'LOVESONGS FOR UNDERDOGS', was released to minimal impact, although it did contain two minor hits, 'PRETTY DEEP' and 'THE BRIGHT LIGHT'. • Covered: TRUST IN ME (Sherman – Sherman; for 'Jungle Book') / ARE YOU EXPERIENCED (Jimi Hendrix).

Album rating: STAR (*8) / KING (*7) / Tanya Donelly: LOVESONGS FOR UNDERDOGS (*5)

TANYA DONELLY (b.16 Jul'66, Newport, Rhode Island) – vocals, guitar / **THOMAS GORMAN** (b.20 May '66, Buffalo, N.Y.) – guitar **FRED ABONG** – bass / **CHRIS GORMAN** (b.29 Jul'67, Buffalo) – drums

	4 a.d.	Sire
Jun 92. (12"ep/cd-ep) *(BAD 2009/+CD)* **SLOWDUST**	☐	☐

– Dusted / Slow dog / Dancing gold / Low red moon.

—— **GAIL GREENWOOD** (b.10 Mar'60) – bass repl. FRED

Nov 92. (7") *(AD 2018)* **GEPETTO. / SEXY S** ☐ ☐
(12"+=/cd-s+=) *(BAD 2018/+CD)* – Hot burrito #1 / Sweet ride.
Jan 93. (7"/c-s) *(AD/+C 3001)* **FEED THE TREE. / DREAM ON ME** 32 -

Jan 93. (cd)(lp/c) (CAD 3002CD)(CAD/+C 3002) <45187> **STAR**   `2` `59`
– Someone to die for / Angel / Dusted / Every word / Gepetto / Witch / Slow dog / Low red moon / Feed the tree / Full Moon, empty heart / White belly / Untogether / Star / Sad dress / Stay.

Mar 93. (c-ep)(cd-ep) (BADC 2018)(BADD 2018CD) **GEPETTO (remix) / IT'S NOT UNUSUAL / STAR (demo)**   `49` ☐
(12"ep)(cd-ep) (BADR 2018) (BAD 2018CD) – ('A'side) / Hot burrito #1 / Sexy S / Sweet ride.

Feb 93. (cd-ep) <941 547-2> **LOW RED MOON / ARE YOU EXPERIENCED? / IT'S NOT UNUSUAL (3 mixes) / FULL MOON, EMPTY HEART (3 mixes)**   `-` `-`

Apr 93. (c-s) <18570> **FEED THE TREE / STAR**   `-` `95`

Jan 95. (7"/c-s) (AD/+ 5003) **NOW THEY'LL SLEEP. / THIEF**   `28` ☐
(12"+=/cd-s+=) (BAD 5003/+CD) – Baby's arm John Dark.

Feb 95. (cd)(lp/c) (CAD 5004CD)(CAD/+C 5004) <45833> **KING**   `6` `57`
– Puberty / Seal my fate / Red / Silverfish / Super-connected / The bees / King / Now they'll sleep / Untitled and unsung / Lil' Ennio / Judas my heart.

Jul 95. (7"clear) (AD 5007) **SEAL MY FATE. / BROKEN / JUDAS MY HEART (live)**   `35` ☐
(cd-s) (BAD 5007CD) – ('A'-U.S. radio mix) / Spaceman / Diamond rib cage / Think about your troubles.
(cd-s) (BADD 5007CD) – ('A'live) / White belly (live) / Untitled and unsung (live) / The bees (live).

—— disbanded in July '96

TANYA DONELLY

—— with **DEAN FISHER + WALLY GAGEL** – bass / **RICH GILBERT** – guitars / **STACY JONES** – guitar / + others

	4 a.d.	Warners
Nov 96. (d7"ep)(cd-ep) (ADD 6018)(BAD 6018CD) **SLIDING & DRIVING**		
– Bum / Restless / Human / Swoon.		
Aug 97. (7") (AD 7007) **PRETTY DEEP. / VANILLA (Wally's mix)**	`55`	☐
(cd-s) (BAD 7007CD) – ('A'side) / Spaghetti / Morna.		
(cd-s) (BADD 7007CD) – ('A'side) / These days / Influenza.		
Sep 97. (cd)(lp/c) (CAD 7008CD)(CAD/+C 7008) <46495>		
LOVESONGS FOR UNDERDOGS		
– Pretty deep / The bright light / Landspeed song / Mysteries of the unexplained / Lantern / Acrobat / Breathe around you / Bum / Clipped / Goat girl / Manna / Swoon.		
Nov 97. (7") (AD 7012) **THE BRIGHT LIGHT. / THE BRIGHT LIGHT (live)**	`64`	☐
(cd-s) (BAD 7012) – ('A'side) / Bury my heart / How can you sleep.		
(cd-s) (BADD 7012) – ('A'side) / Life on Sirius / Moon over Boston.		

BELOVED (dig out; Great Alt & Indie . . .)

Pat BENATAR

Born: PATRICIA ANDRZEJEWSKI, 10 Jan '53, Brooklyn, New York, USA. In her late teens she married long-time boyfriend DENNIS BENATAR and moved to Richmond, Virginia. Returning to New York in the mid-70's, BENATAR turned her hand at the cabaret circuit, adopting a harder edged approach after meeting manager/mentor, RICK NEWMAN. In keeping with her new rock-chick image, PAT retained the (frankly, more rock'n'roll) BENATAR name after divorcing DENNIS in the early 80's. Signing a deal with 'Chrysalis', BENATAR had the soft metal/AOR thing down pat (ouch!) from the off, her debut album, 'IN THE HEAT OF THE NIGHT', eventually going platinum. Her undeniable vocal prowess almost made up for the weakness of the original material, BENATAR only really coming into her own singing other people's songs. She transformed SMOKIE's 'IF YOU THINK YOU KNOW HOW TO LOVE ME', into a sultry mood piece while JOHN MELLENCAMP's 'I NEED A LOVER' benefited from her scuffed velvet tones. Boasting the likes of 'HIT ME WITH YOUR BEST SHOT' and 'TREAT ME RIGHT', the 'CRIMES OF PASSION' (1980) album was a million seller, establishing BENATAR as a major contender in the American market. Subsequent albums, 'PRECIOUS TIME' (1981) and 'GET NERVOUS' (1982), continued to sell in abundance despite a dearth of decent songs. Things picked up with 'LOVE IS A BATTLEFIELD', a brooding, catchy pop-rock number which gave BENATAR her biggest US hit single to date, the record reaching Top 5 in late '83. A year later, the singer released what was probably her finest moment in 'WE BELONG', a seductively melodic single which secured BENATAR her first substantial UK success. After moderate sales of the 'TROPICO' (1984) and 'SEVEN THE HARD WAY' (1985) albums, BENATAR took an extended break to look after her daughter. During this time, 'Chrysalis' released 'BEST SHOTS' (1987), a compilation that did surprisingly well in Britain (No.6) and saw BENATAR's subsequent 1988 album, 'WIDE AWAKE IN DREAMLAND', make the UK Top 20. That's not to say the record was any good, and it was clear her career was in decline. Subsequent efforts have sold poorly, BENATAR even chancing her arm with an ill-advised album of blues tracks, 'TRUE LOVE' (1991).
• **Songwriters:** She collaborated with others, including CHINN / CHAPMAN plus her husband/producer (from 20th Feb'82) NEIL GERALDO. She also covered YOU BETTER RUN (Young Rascals) / PAYIN' THE COST TO BE THE BOSS (B.B. King) / HELTER SKELTER (Beatles) / IF YOU THINK YOU KNOW HOW TO LOVE ME (Smokie) / INVINCIBLE (Simon Climie).
• **Trivia:** Her first 7" in US 1976 as "PAT BENATAR" was DAY GIG. / LAST SATURDAY on the 'Trace' label.

Album rating: IN THE HEAT OF THE NIGHT (*6) / CRIMES OF PASSION (*6) /

PRECIOUS TIME (*4) / GET NERVOUS (*4) / LIVE FROM EARTH (*3) / TROPICO (*4) / SEVEN THE HARD WAY (*6) / WIDE AWAKE IN DREAMLAND (*4) / BEST SHOTS compilation (*7) / TRUE LOVE (*3) / GRAVITY'S RAINBOW (*3) / ALL FIRED UP: THE VERY BEST OF . . . compilation (*6) / INNAMORATA (*4)

PAT BENATAR – vocals / **NEIL GERALDO** – keyboards (ex-DERRINGER) / **SCOTT ST. CLAIR SHEETS** – guitar / **ROGER CAPPS** – bass / **GLEN ALEXANDER HAMILTON** – drums

	Chrysalis	Chrysalis
Oct 79. (7") (CHS 2373) **IF YOU THINK YOU KNOW HOW TO LOVE ME. / SO SINCERE**	☐	☐
Dec 79. (lp/c) <(CHR/ZCHR 1236)> **IN THE HEAT OF THE NIGHT**	☐	`12` Oct79
– Heartbreaker / I need a lover / If you think you know how to love me / In the heat of the night / My clone sleeps alone / We live for love / Rated X / Don't let it show / No you don't / So sincere. (re-iss. Jun85 lp/c/cd; same/same/ACCD 1236) – hit UK No.98 (re-iss. Dec92 on 'Fame' cd/c; CD/TC FA 3286) (cd re-iss. Apr99 on 'DCC'; GZS 1056)		
Jan 80. (7") <(CHS 2395)> **HEARTBREAKER. / MY CLONE SLEEPS ALONE**	☐	`23` Dec79
Mar 80. (7") <2419> **WE LIVE FOR LOVE. / SO SINCERE**	☐	`27`
Apr 80. (7") (CHS 2403) **WE LIVE FOR LOVE. / I NEED A LOVER**	☐	☐
(12"+=) (CHS12 2403) – If you think you know how to love me.		
—— **MYRON GROOMBACHER** – drums; repl. HAMILTON		
Jul 80. (7") <2450> **YOU BETTER RUN. / OUT-A-TOUCH**	☐	`42`
Aug 80. (lp/c) <(CHR/ZCHR 1275)> **CRIMES OF PASSION**	☐	`2`
– Treat me right / You better run / Never wanna leave you / Hit me with your best shot / Hell is for children / Little paradise / I'm gonna follow you / Wuthering heights / Prisoner of love / Out-a-touch. (cd-iss. Jun85; ACCD 1275)		
Sep 80. (7") <2464> **HIT ME WITH YOUR BEST SHOT. / PRISONER OF LOVE**	☐	`9`
Nov 80. (7") (CHS 2452) **HIT ME WITH YOUR BEST SHOT. / YOU BETTER RUN**	☐	`-`
(7"red-ep+=) (CHS 2474) – Heartbreaker / We live for love.		
Jan 81. (7") <2487> **TREAT ME RIGHT. / NEVER WANNA LEAVE YOU**	`-`	`18`
Jan 81. (7",7"clear) (CHS 2511) **TREAT ME RIGHT. / HELL IS FOR CHILDREN**	☐	`-`
Jul 81. (lp/c) <(CHR/ZCHR 1346)> **PRECIOUS TIME**	`30`	`1`
– Promises in the dark / Fire and ice / Just like me / Precious time / It's a tuff life / Take it anyway you want it / Evil genius / Hard to believe / Helter skelter. (cd-iss. Jun85; ACCD 1346)		
Jul 81. (7"clear/7"pic-d) <(CHS/+P 2529)> **FIRE AND ICE. / HARD TO BELIEVE**	☐	`17`
Sep 81. (7") <2555> **PROMISES IN THE DARK. / EVIL GENIUS**	`-`	`38`
—— (Feb'82) **NEIL GERALDO** now on guitar / co-production.		
Oct 82. (7",7"sha-pic-d/12"blue) (CHS/+12 2662) <2647><03541> **SHADOWS OF THE NIGHT. / THE VICTIM**	☐	`13`
(7"ep) (CHS 2662) – ('A'side) / Treat me right / Heartbreaker / Anxiety (get nervous).		
Nov 82. (lp/pic-lp/c) (CHR/PCHR/ZCHR 1386) <1396> **GET NERVOUS**	`73`	`4`
– Shadows of the night / Looking for a stranger / Anxiety (get nervous) / Fight it out / The victim / Little too late / I'll do it / I want out / Tell it to her / Silent partner. (cd-iss. Jun85; ACCD 1386)		
—— (Nov'82) **CHARLIE GIORDANO** – keyboards; repl. SHEETS		
Jan 83. (7") <03536> **LITTLE TOO LATE. / FIGHT IT OUT**	`-`	`20`
Apr 83. (7") <42688> **LOOKING FOR A STRANGER. / I'LL DO IT**	`-`	`39`
Oct 83. (7"/7"pic-d/12") (CHS/+P/12 2747) <42732> **LOVE IS A BATTLEFIELD. / HELL IS FOR CHILDREN (live)**	`49`	`5` Sep83
Oct 83. (lp/pic-lp/c) (CHR/CHRP/ZCHR 1451) <41444> **LIVE FROM EARTH (live)**	`60`	`13`
– Fire and ice / Lookin' for a stranger / I want out / We live for love / Hell is for children / Hit me with your best shot / Promises in the dark / Heartbreaker / Love is a battlefield * / Lipstick lies. (* studio track) (cd-iss. Jun85; ACCD 1451)		
Oct 84. (7",7"pic-d) (CHR 2821) <42826> **WE BELONG. / SUBURBAN KING**	`22`	`5`
(12"+=) (CHR12 2821) – We live for love '85.		
Nov 84. (lp/c) (CHR/ZCHR 1471) <41471> **TROPICO**	`34`	`14`
– Diamond field / We belong / Painted desert / Temporary heroes / Love in the ice age / Ooh ooh song / Outlaw blues / Suburban king / A crazy world like this / Takin' it back. (cd-iss. Apr86; ACCD 1471)		
Jan 85. (7") <42843> **OOH OOH SONG. / LA CANCION OOH OOH**	`-`	`36`
Mar 85. (7"/12") (PAT/+X 1) **LOVE IS A BATTLEFIELD. / HERE'S MY HEART**	`17`	`-`
Jun 85. (7"/7"sha-pic-d) (PAT/+P 2) **SHADOWS OF THE NIGHT. / HIT ME WITH YOUR BEST SHOT**	`50`	`-`
(12"+=) (PATX 2) – Fire and ice.		
—— **DONNIE NOSSOV** – bass repl. CAPPS		
(below is the theme from the film 'The Legend Of Billie Jean')		
Oct 85. (7") (PAT 3) <42877> **INVINCIBLE. / ('A'instrumental)**	`53`	`10` Jun85
(12"+=) (PATX 3) – Promises in the dark / Heartbreaker.		
Dec 85. (7"/12") (PAT/+X 4) <42927> **SEX AS A WEAPON. / RED VISION**	`67`	`28` Nov85
Dec 85. (lp/c) (CHR/ZCHR 1507) <41507> **SEVEN THE HARD WAY**	`69`	`26`
– Sex as a weapon / Le bel age / Walking in the underground / Big life / Red vision / 7 rooms of gloom / Run between the raindrops / Invincible (theme from The Legend Of Billie Jean) / The art of letting go. (cd-iss. Apr86; ACCD 1507)		
Feb 86. (7") <42968> **LE BEL AGE. / WALKING IN THE UNDERGROUND**	`-`	`54`
—— **FERNANDO SAUNDERS + FRANK LINX** – bass repl. NOSSOV		
Jul 88. (7") (PAT 5) <43268> **ALL FIRED UP. / COOL ZERO**	`19`	`19`
(12"+=) (PATX 5) – Hit me with your best shot / Fire and ice / Just like me / Promises in the dark / Precious time.		
(12"+=/cd-s+=) (PAT XD/CD 5) – ('A'-US version).		
Jul 88. (lp/c/cd) (CDL/ZCDL/CCD 1628) <41628> **WIDE AWAKE IN DREAMLAND**	`11`	`28`
– All fired up / One love / Let's stay together / Don't walk away / Too long a soldier / Cool zero / Cerebral man / Lift 'em on up / Suffer the little children / Wide awake in Dreamland. (re-iss. cd Mar94; CD23CR 19)		

Sep 88. (7") *(PAT 6)* **DON'T WALK AWAY. / LIFT 'EM ON UP** `42` ☐
(12"+=/cd-s+=) *(PAT X/CD 6)* – Hell is for children (live) / We live for love (special mix).

Dec 88. (7") *(PAT 7)* **ONE LOVE. / WIDE AWAKE IN DREAMLAND** `59` ☐
(12"+=/12"pic-d+=) *(PATX/+P 7)* – Sex as a weapon.
(cd-s+=) *(PATCD 7)* – Love is a battlefield.

Apr 91. (cd/c/lp) *(CCD/ZCHR/CHR 1805) <21805>* **TRUE LOVE** `40` `37`
– Bloodshot eyes / Payin' the cost to be the boss / So long / I've got papers on you / I feel lucky / True love / The good life / Evening / I get evil / Don't happen no more. *(re-iss. Mar94 cd/c; same)*

Jun 91. (c-s/7") **PAYIN' THE COST TO BE THE BOSS. / TRUE LOVE** ☐ ☐
(12"+=/cd-s+=) – Evening.

Sep 93. (c-s) *(TCCHS 5001)* **SOMEBODY'S BABY. / ('A'- A-C mix)** `48` ☐
(cd-s+=) *(CDCHS 5001)* – Temptation / Promises in the dark (live).

Nov 93. (cd/c) *(CHR 6054) <21982>* **GRAVITY'S RAINBOW** ☐ `85` Jun93
– Pictures of a gone world / Everybody lay down / Somebody's baby / Ties that bind / You and I / Disconnected / Crazy / Everytime I fall back / Sanctuary / Rise (part 2) / Kingdom key / Tradin' down.

                                                                      C.M.C. C.M.C.
Sep 97. (cd) *<(06076 86216-2)>* **INNAMORATA** ☐ Jun97
– (guitar intro) / Only love / River of love / I don't want to be your friend / Strawberry wine / Purgatory / At this time / Dirty little secrets / Angry / In these times / Innamorata / Gina's song. *(d-cd-iss. Oct98 as 'INNAMORATA 8/1/80' on 'SPV'; SPV 0852917-2)*

– compilations, others, etc. –

──── on 'Chrysalis' unless mentioned othewise
Dec 82. (d-c) *(ZCDP 108)* **IN THE HEAT OF THE NIGHT / CRIMES OF PASSION**

Nov 87. (cd)(c/lp) *(CCD 1538)(Z+/PATV 1) <21715>* **BEST SHOTS** `6` `67` Nov89
– Hit me with your best shot / Love is a battlefield / We belong / We live for love / Sex as a weapon / Invincible / Shadows of the night / Heartbreaker / Fire and ice / Treat me right / If you think you know how to love me / You better run. *(cd re-iss. Sep97; same)*

Apr 94. (cd/c) *(CD/TC CHR 6070)* **THE VERY BEST OF PAT BENATAR** ☐ ☐
– Heartbreaker / We live for love / Promises in the dark / Fire and ice / Ooh ooh song / Hit me with your best shot / Shadows of the night / Anxiety (get nervous) / I want out / Lipstick lies / Love is a battlefield / We belong / All fired up / Hell is for children / Invincible / Somebody's baby / We live for love / True love.

Jan 95. (d-cd) *Chrysalis; <31094>* **ALL FIRED UP: THE VERY BEST OF PAT BENATAR** `-` ☐

Jul 98. (cd) *Ranch Life; <(CRANCH 6)>* **CONCERT CLASSICS** `-` ☐

Sep 98. (cd) *Beat Goes On; (BGOCD 418)* **IN THE HEAT OF THE NIGHT / CRIMES OF PASSION** ☐ `-`

Nov 98. (cd) *Beat Goes On; (BGOCD 427)* **PRECIOUS TIME / GET NERVOUS** ☐ `-`

Mar 99. (cd) *Beat Goes On; (BGOCD 433)* **TROPICO / SEVEN THE HARD WAY** ☐ `-`

Mar 99. (cd) *E.M.I.; (CDP 852256-2)* **HEARTBREAKER** ☐ `-`

BENTLEY RHYTHM ACE

Formed: Birmingham, England . . . 1997 by former POP WILL EAT ITSELF man, RICH MARSH plus ex-tarmac layer, MIKE STOKES. Described as the Black Country's answer to The CHEMICAL BROTHERS, the band were the ACE in the pack of Big Beat connoisseurs, 'Skint', their debut single, 'MIDLANDER' becoming a cult classic upon its Spring '97 release. A self-titled debut album followed soon after, BRA motoring their way to the front of the breakbeat pack with a larger than life collection of dayglo dancefloor stompers. Putting the fun back into moody clubland, the band's customised live shows soon became the stuff of legend, the ubiquitous dance tent at summer festivals struggling to contain the group's ever growing fanbase of frugging nutters. With the buzz surrounding the duo almost drowning out the turbo thrum of the BENTLEY roadmaster, it wasn't long before the majors attempted to hitch a ride, 'Parlophone' finally managing to flag them down and tune up sales of the debut with some financial muscle. Late summer also saw the release of 'BENTLEY'S GONNA SORT YOU OUT!', possibly their finest moment to date, a Top 20 hit guaranteed to sort out the real ravers from the posing fakers. With Japanese and American success imminent, it seems only a foolhardy case of road rage can hold back these Brummie chancers from the brink of pop stardom.

Album rating: BENTLEY RHYTHM ACE (*8)

RICH MARSH – keyboards, samples (ex-POP WILL EAT ITSELF) / **MIKE STOKES** – samples, etc / **FUZZ TOWNSHEND** – drums

                                                                      Skint AstralWerks
Sep 96. (12") *(SKINT 13)* **LATE TRAIN 2 BENTLEY ON C. (mixes)** ☐ `-`

Apr 97. (12"/cd-s) *(SKINT 23/+CD)* **MIDLANDER (THERE CAN ONLY BE ONE . . .) / SOMETHING TO KEEP YOUR SANDWICHES IN / MAN WITH THE GOLDEN TOAST / ('A' edit)** ☐ `-`

May 97. (cd/d-lp) *(BRASSIC 5 CD/LP) <ASW 6223>* **BENTLEY RHYTHM ACE** `40` Oct97
– Let there be flutes / Midlander (there can only be one . . .) / Why is a frog too..? / Mind that gap / Run on the spot / Bentley's gonna sort you out! / Ragtopskodacarchase / Whoosh / Who put the bom in the bom bom diddleye bom / Spacehopper / Return of the hardcore jumble carbootechnodisco roadshow. *(re-iss. Oct97 on 'Parlophone' cd/c/d-lp; DC/TC+/PCS 7391)*

                                                                      Parlophone AstralWerks
Aug 97. (12"ep) *(12R 6476)* **BENTLEY'S GONNA SORT YOU OUT! / RUN ON THE SPOT / ON HER MAJESTY'S SECRET WHISTLE / RAGTOPSKODACARCHASE** `17` ☐

───────────────────────────────────

(cd-ep) *(CDR 6476)* – (first 3 tracks) / The spy who loved moose.
(cd-ep) *(CDRS 6476)* – (tracks 1,2 & 4) / Two turntables a powercut and the DJ's gone off.

──── In Oct98, BRA issued a V/A remix d-cd/t-lp-set 'FSUK3 (THE FUTURE SOUND OF THE UNITED KINGDOM)' on 'FSUK' *(FSUK CD/LP 3)*

Chuck BERRY

Born: CHARLES EDWARD ANDERSON BERRY, 18 Oct'26, St. Louis, Missouri, USA. Having learned the guitar while at school, BERRY had his first run-in with the law in his late teens, when he was sent to reform school for a 3-year stretch after being convicted of armed attempted robbery. Upon his release, he worked blue collar jobs by day, perfecting his playing and songwriting by night; BERRY's first professional combo (with pianist JOHNNIE JOHNSON and drummer EBBY HARDY) became a regular local attraction during the early to mid-50's with their upbeat blend of R&B/C&W. During a trip to Chicago ("home of the blues"), BERRY enjoyed an opportunistic encounter with the legendary MUDDY WATERS, who in turn, put him in touch with 'Chess' records. By the summer of '55, his first recording, 'MAYBELLENE' (an adaptation of an old country standard), was riding high in the US singles chart; this rock'n'roll template would be successfully utilised by BERRY right through to the end of the decade on such definitive R&B gems as 'TOO MUCH MONKEY BUSINESS', 'ROLL OVER BEETHOVEN', 'ROCK AND ROLL MUSIC', 'SWEET LITTLE SIXTEEN' and 'JOHNNY B. GOODE'. As well as inventing his inimitable stage party piece, the "duck-walk", BERRY injected a quintessentially Afro-American element of humour, wit and innuendo into the concept of pop music as teen rebellion, reclaiming the rock'n'roll crown from white pretenders such as BILL HALEY and ELVIS PRESLEY. However, the position of a famous black, anti-establishment star was a precarious one and BERRY fell foul of the authorities after employing a 14-year old Apache Indian as a hat-check girl in his nightclub. Unbeknown to BERRY, the girl had allegedly worked as a prostitute, and he was subsequently found guilty of contravening the 'Mann act' by bringing an under-age child across the Texas-Missouri border. In October '61, he was sentenced to jail for five years, although due to the judge's racist remarks, he was given a retrial. He was later successfully tried and sentenced to three years, although with good behaviour, he was out early in '64. While in jail, BERRY's work was being successfully reappraised with many British-invasion artists, including The BEATLES and The ROLLING STONES, covering his early material as a sizeable part of their repertoire. Inspired, "Crazy Legs" (as he was nicknamed) returned to the studio to record a new song, 'NADINE', the single becoming a Top 30 hit on both sides of the Atlantic. BERRY also set foot in Britain for the first time, wowing audiences with a further brace of recent hits including 'NO PARTICULAR PLACE TO GO' and 'YOU NEVER CAN TELL'. In June 1966, with flower-power just over the horizon, he signed to 'Mercury', although this ill-advised partnership proved commercially fruitless. In 1972, following a return to the 'Chess' label three years previous, he scored a UK No.1 novelty hit with the embarrassing 'MY DING-A-LING'. Its double entendre lyrical content sufficiently enraged morality pest, Mary Whitehouse, for her to press for a media ban. In June 1979, BERRY was again imprisoned (100 days this time) for tax evasion, although during this period he signed a deal with 'Atlantic'. Throughout the 80's, he continued to work sporadically, a docu-film 'HAIL! HAIL! ROCK'N'ROLL' being released early in '88, featuring footage from his 60th birthday concert (KEITH RICHARDS – his biggest fan – along with other star names formed his backing band at the time). BERRY subsequently retired from recording, choosing to live in his own amusement park in Wentzville, Missouri. He did, however, play live again in a November '89 revival concert alongside BO DIDDLEY, The COASTERS etc. The following month, more controversy surrounded him when it was claimed he had been videoing a ladies rest-room for immoral purposes! In June 1990, his house was raided by the drugs squad, who seized marijuana, guns and homemade pornography. He was later charged with possession of drugs and child abuse, although he was cleared of the latter and handed a fine and a 6-month suspended prison sentence for the drugs misdemeanour. Hail! hail!, rock'n'roll! right enough!

Best CD compilation: THE BEST OF CHUCK BERRY (*9)

CHUCK BERRY – vocals, guitar with **JOHNNIE JOHNSON** – piano / **JASPER THOMAS** – drums / **WILLIE DIXON** – bass / etc.

			London	Chess
Jul 55.	(7") *<1604>* **MAYBELLENE. / WEE WEE HOURS**		`-`	`5`
Oct 55.	(7") *<1610>* **THIRTY DAYS. / TOGETHER WE WILL ALWAYS BE**		`-`	☐
May 56.	(7",78) *(HLU 8275) <1615>* **NO MONEY DOWN. / THE DOWNBOUND TRAIN**		☐	Feb56
May 56.	(7") *<1626>* **ROLL OVER BEETHOVEN. / DRIFTING HEART** (UK-iss.May57 – 7",78; HLU 8428)		`-`	`29`
Aug 56.	(7") *<1635>* **TOO MUCH MONKEY BUSINESS. / BROWN EYED HANDSOME MAN**		`-`	☐
Feb 57.	(7",78) *(HLN 8375) <1645>* **YOU CAN'T CATCH ME. / HAVANA MOON**		☐	`29` Nov56
Jun 57.	(7",78) *(DB 3951) <1653>* **SCHOOL DAY (RING! RING! GOES THE BELL). / DEEP FEELING** (above was issued in UK on 'Columbia')		`24`	`3` Mar57

──── He retained **DIXON** and enlisted on most of 50's **FRED BELOW** – drums / **LAFAYETTE LEAKE** – piano

| Jun 57. | (7") *<1664>* **OH BABY DOLL / LA JAUNDA** | | `-` | `57` |

Dec 57. (7",78) *(HLM 8531)* <1671> **ROCK AND ROLL MUSIC. / BLUE FEELING** — [8] Sep57

1958. (lp) <1426> **AFTER SCHOOL SESSIONS** [-]
 – School day / Deep feeling / Too much monkey business / Wee wee hours / Roly poly / No money down / Brown-eyed handsome man / Berry pickin' / Together we will always be / Havana Moon / Downbound train / Drifting heart.

Mar 58. (7",78) *(HLM 8585)* <1683> **SWEET LITTLE SIXTEEN. / REELIN' AND ROCKIN'** [16] [2] Jan58

May 58. (7",78) *(HLM 8629)* <1691> **JOHNNY B. GOODE. / AROUND AND AROUND** [8] Apr58

Aug 58. (7",78) *(HL 8677)* <1697> **BEAUTIFUL DELILAH. / VACATION TIME** [81] Jun58

Oct 58. (7",78) *(HL 8712)* <1700> **CAROL. / HEY PEDRO** [18] Aug58

Nov 58. (lp; stereo/mono) *(HA/+M 2132)* <1432> **ONE DOZEN BERRYS**
 – Sweet little sixteen / Blue feeling / La juanda / Rockin' at the Philharmonic / Oh baby doll / Reelin' & rockin' / In-go / Rock and roll music / How you've changed / Low feeling / It don't take but a few minutes.

Dec 58. (7",78) *(HLM 8767)* <1709> **SWEET LITTLE ROCK AND ROLLER. / JOE JOE GUN** [47] [83] Oct58

Dec 58. (7") <1714> **RUN RUDOLPH RUN. / MERRY CHRISTMAS BABY** [-] [69] 71

Jan 59. (7") <1716> **ANTHONY BOY. / THAT'S MY DESIRE** [-] [60]

Apr 59. (7",78) *(HLM 8853)* <1722> **ALMOST GROWN. / LITTLE QUEENIE** [32] [80] Mar59

Jul 59. (7",78) *(HLM 8921)* <1729> **BACK IN THE U.S.A. / MEMPHIS, TENNESSEE** [37] Jun59

1959. (lp) <1435> **CHUCK BERRY IS ON TOP**
 – Almost grown / Carol / Maybellene / Sweet little rock and roller / Anthony boy / Johnny B. Goode / Little Queenie / Jo Jo Gunne / Roll over Beethoven / Around and around / Hey Pedro / Blues for Hawaiians. (UK-iss.Oct87;) (re-iss.Oct94 cd/c;)

Oct 59. (7") <1737> **CHILDHOOD SWEETHEART. / BROKEN ARROW** [-]

Mar 60. (7") *(HLM 9069)* <1747> **LET IT ROCK. / TOO POOPED TO POP** [64] [42] Jan60

Apr 60. (7") <1754> **BYE BYE JOHNNY. / WORRIED LIFE BLUES** [-]

Jun 60. (7") *(HLM 9159)* **BYE BYE JOHNNY. / MAD LAD** [-]

Jun 60. (7") <1763> **MAD LAD. / I GOT TO FIND MY BABY** [-]

1960. (lp) <1448> **ROCKIN' AT THE HOPS**
 – Bye bye Johnny / Worried life blues / Down the road apiece / Confessin' the blues / Too pooped to pop ("Casey") / Mad lad / I got to find my baby / Betty Jean / Childhood sweetheart / Broken arrow / Driftin' blues / Let it rock. (re-iss. +c.Aug87)

Sep 60. (7") <1767> **JAGUAR AND THUNDERBIRD. / OUR LITTLE RENDEZVOUS** [-] [-] (Pye Int. / Chess)

Sep 61. (7") *(7N 25100)* <1779> **I'M TALKIN' 'BOUT YOU. / LITTLE STAR** [-] Feb61

—— BERRY was convicted of an earlier crime of transporting a minor (14 year-old) across the border. He served two years in prison.

– early recordings, compilations, etc, while in prison –

Jun 62. (lp) *(NPL 28019)* <1456> **NEW JUKE BOX HITS** [-] Nov61
 – I'm talking about you / Diploma for two / Thirteen question method / Away from you / Don't you lie to me / The way it was before / Little star / Route 66 / Sweet sixteen / Run around / Stop and listen / Rip it up.

May 63. (lp) *(NPL 28024)* <1465> **CHUCK BERRY** (compilation) <US-title 'CHUCK BERRY TWIST' different tracks> [12] 1962
 – Come back / Maybellene / Down the road apiece / Mad lad / School day (ring ring goes the bell) / Sweet little sixteen / Confessin' the blues / Back in the U.S.A. / Johnny B. Goode / Oh, baby doll / Come on / I got to find my baby / Betty Jean / Round and round / Almost grown. (re-iss. US Dec63 as 'MORE CHUCK BERRY')(re-iss. 1984 on 'Audio Fidelity')(re-iss. Dec85 on 'Astan')

Jul 63. (7") *(7N 25209)* <1799> **GO GO GO. / COME ON** [38] Jun61

Aug 63. (7") <1853> **I'M TALKIN' 'BOUT YOU. / DIPLOMA FOR TWO** [-]

Oct 63. (lp) *(NPL 28027)* <1480> **CHUCK BERRY ON STAGE (fake live)** [6] [29] Aug63
 – Go go go / Memphis, Tennessee / Maybellene / Surfin' steel (blues for Hawaiians) / Rockin' on the railroad (let it rock) / Brown eyed handsome man (new version) / I still got the blues / Surfin' USA (sweet little sixteen) / Jaguar and thunderbird / I just want to make love to you / All aboard / Trick or treat / Man and the donkey / How high the moon.

Oct 63. (7") <1866> **MEMPHIS, TENNESSEE. / SWEET LITTLE SIXTEEN** [-]

Oct 63. (7") *(7N 25218)* **MEMPHIS, TENNESSEE. / LET IT ROCK** [6]

Dec 63. (7") *(7N 25228)* **RUN RUDOLPH RUN. / JOHNNY B. GOODE** [36] [-]

—— Released from prison early '64. New recordings ...

Feb 64. (7") *(7N 25236)* <1883> **NADINE (IS IT YOU?). / O RANGUTANG** [27] [23]

Apr 64. (7") *(7N 25242)* **NO PARTICULAR PLACE TO GO. / LIVERPOOL DRIVE** [3] [-]

May 64. (7") <1898> **NO PARTICULAR PLACE TO GO. / YOU TWO** [-] [10]

May 64. (lp) *(NPL 28031)* **THE LATEST AND THE GREATEST** [8] [-]
 – Nadine / Fraulein / Guitar boogie / Things I used to do / Don't you lie to me / Driftin' blues / Liverpool drive / No particular place to go / Lonely all the time (crazy arms) / Jaguar and Thunderbird / O rangutang / You two / Deep feeling / Bye bye Johnny.

Aug 64. (7") *(7N 25257)* <1906> **YOU NEVER CAN TELL. / BRENDA LEE** [23] [14] Jul64

Sep 64. (lp) *(NPL 28039)* **YOU NEVER CAN TELL** [18]
 – You never can tell / Diploma for two / The little girl from Central / The way it was before / Around and around / Big Ben / Promised land / Back in the USA / Run around / Brenda Lee / Reeling and rockin' / Come on. (re-iss. Dec67 on 'Marble Arch';)

Oct 64. (7") *(7N 25271)* <1912> **LITTLE MARIE. / GO BOBBY SOXER** [-] [54] Sep64

—— Late in '64, he paired up with BO DIDDLEY to record single CHUCK'S BEAT. / BO'S BEAT; <1089> and album TWO GREAT GUITARS. They had already appeared together on 1963 EP's 'CHUCK AND BO' Volumes 1,2 & 3.

Dec 64. (lp) <1488> **ST. LOUIS TO LIVERPOOL (live)**
 – Little Marie / Our little rendezvous / No particular place to go / You two / Promised land / You never can tell / Night beat / Liverpool drive / Merry Christmas baby / Brenda Lee. (re-iss.Aug86)

Jan 65. (7") *(7N 25285)* <1916> **THE PROMISED LAND. / THINGS I USED TO DO** [26] (Chess / Chess)

Mar 65. (7") *(CRS 8006)* **LONELY SCHOOL DAYS. / I GOT A BOOKING** [-]

Mar 65. (lp) *(CRL 4005)* <1495> **CHUCK BERRY IN LONDON (live)**
 – My little love light / She once was mine / After it's over / I got a booking / Night beat / His daughter Caroline / You came a long way from St. Louis / St. Louis blues / Jamaica farewell / Dead dad / Butterscotch / The song of my love / Why should we end this way / I want to be your driver.

May 65. (7") *(CRS 8012)* <1926> **DEAR DAD. / MY LITTLE LOVELIGHT** [95] Mar65

Oct 65. (7") <1943> **IT WASN'T ME. / WELCOME BACK PRETTY BABY** [-]

Oct 65. (7") *(CRS 8022)* **IT WASN'T ME. / IT'S MY OWN BUSINESS** [-]

Nov 65. (lp) *(CRL 4506)* <1498> **FRESH BERRYS**
 – It wasn't me / Run Joe / Everyday we rock and roll / One for my baby / Sad day long night * / It's my own business / Right off Rampart Street / Vaya con dios / Merrily we rock and roll / My Mustang Ford / Ain't that just like a woman / Wee hours blues. <US version omitted * for 'Welcome back pretty baby'>

Jul 66. (7") *(CRS 8037)* <1963> **RAMONA SAY YES. / LONELY SCHOOL DAYS** [-] Jun66 (Mercury / Mercury)

Dec 66. (7") *(MF 958)* <72643> **CLUB NITTY GRITTY. / LAUGH AND CRY** [-] Nov66

Jul 67. (7") *(MF 994)* <72680> **BACK TO MEMPHIS. / I DO REALLY LOVE YOU** [-] Jun67

Nov 67. (7") <72748> **FEELIN' IT. / IT HURTS ME TOO** [-]

Dec 67. (lp) *(SMCL 20110)* **IN MEMPHIS** [-]
 – Back to Memphis / I do really love you / My heart will always belong to you / Ramblin' Rose / Sweet little rock and roller / Oh baby doll / Check me out / It hurts me too / Bring another drink / So long / Goodnight, well it's time to go.

Apr 68. (lp) *(MCL 20112)* <SR 61138> **LIVE AT THE FILLMORE AUDITORIUM (live)**
 – Medley: Rockin' at the Fillmore – Everyday I have the blues / C.C. rider / Driftin' blues / Feelin' it / Flying home / Hoochie coochie man / It hurts me too / Fillmore blues / Wee baby James / Johnny B. Goode.

Oct 68. (7") *(MF 1057)* <7840> **ST. LOUIS TO FRISCO. / MA DEAR** [-] Aug68

Nov 68. (lp) <6463 015> **FROM ST. LOUIS TO FRISCO**
 – St. Louis to Frisco / Ma dear / The love I lost / I love her, I love her / Little fox / Rock cradle rock / Soul rockin' / I can't believe / Misery / My tambourine / Oh captain / Mum's the word.

Aug 69. (7") <72963> **GOOD LOOKING WOMAN. / IT'S TOO DARK IN THERE** [-]

Nov 69. (lp) <SMCL 20162> **CONCERTO IN B. GOODE**
 – Good looking woman / My woman / It's too dark in there / Put her down / Concerto in 'B Goode'. (Chess / Chess)

Aug 70. (7") <2090> **TULANE. / HAVE MERCY JUDGE** [-]

Jan 71. (lp) *(6310 13)* <1550> **BACK HOME** [-] 1970
 – Tulane / Have mercy judge / Instrumental / Christmas / Gun / I'm a rocker / Flyin' home / Fish and chips / Some people.

1971. (lp) *(6310 115)* **SAN FRANCISCO DUES** [-]
 – Oh Louisiana / Let's do our thing together / Your lick / Festival / Bound to lose / Bordeaux in my pirough / San Francisco dues / Viva rock and roll / My dream / Lonely school days (version 2).

Jun 72. (lp) *(6310 122)* **THE LONDON SESSIONS** [8] [-]
 – Let's boogie / Mean old world / I will not let you go / London Berry blues / I love you / Reeling and rockin'(live) / My ding-a-ling (live) / Johnny B. Goode (live).

Aug 72. (7") *(6145 012)* **DOWN THE ROAD APIECE. / JOHNNY B. GOODE** [-]

Aug 72. (7") <2131> **MY DING-A-LING. / JOHNNY B. GOODE** [-] [1]

Oct 72. (7") *(6145 019)* **MY DING-A-LING. / LET'S BOOGIE** [1] [-]

Dec 72. (7") <2136> **REELIN' AND ROCKIN' (live). / LET'S BOOGIE** [-] [27]

Jan 73. (7") *(6145 020)* **REELIN' AND ROCKIN' (live). / I WILL NOT LET YOU GO** [18] [-]

Sep 73. (7") <2140> **BIO. / ROLL 'EM PETE** [-]

Oct 73. (lp) *(6499 650)* **BIO**
 – Bio / Hello little girl, goodbye / Woodpecker / Rain eyes / Aimlessly driftin' / Got it and gone / Talkin' about my buddy. (re-iss.May88)

Nov 73. (7") *(6145 027)* **SOUTH OF THE BORDER. / BIO** [-]

—— duets with daughter INGRID GIBSON on some tracks in 1975

Feb 75. (7") <2169> **SHAKE, RATTLE AND ROLL. / BABY WHAT YOU WANT ME TO DO** [-]

Mar 75. (7") *(6145 038)* **SHAKE, RATTLE AND ROLL. / I'M JUST A NAME** [-]

Apr 75. (lp) *(9109 101)* **CHUCK BERRY '75**
 – Swanee river / I'm just a name / I just want to make love to you / Too late / South of the border / Hi-heel sneakers / You are my sunshine / My babe / Baby what you want me to do / A deuce / Shake, rattle and roll / Sue answer / Don't you to me.

—— on the 10th July '79, he was sentenced to four months in jail

Aug 79. (7") *(K 11354)* <7203> **OH WHAT A THRILL. / CALIFORNIA** (Atlantic / Atlantic)

Oct 79. (lp) *(50648)* <SD 38118> **ROCKIT** [-] Aug79
 – Move it / Oh what a thrill / I need you baby / If I were / House lights / I never thought / Havana moon / Pass away. (re-iss. +cd.Nov88 on 'Magnum Force')

—— Virtually retired from the studio

– compilations, others, etc. –

on 'Chess' unless mentioned otherwise

May 56. (7"ep) *London; (REU 1053)* **RHYTHM AND BLUES WITH CHUCK BERRY** [-] [-]

– (first 2 singles)

1957. (7"ep) <5118> **AFTER SCHOOL SESSION**
 – School day / Deep feeling / Brown eyed handsome man / Too much monkey business.

1957. (7"ep) <5119> **ROCK AND ROLL MUSIC**
 – Rock and roll music / Oh baby doll / La juanda / Blue feeling.

1958. (7"ep) <5121> **SWEET LITTLE SIXTEEN**
 – Sweet little sixteen / Reelin' and rockin' / Rock at the philharmonic / Guitar boogie.

Mar 59. (7"ep) *London;* (REM 1188) **REELIN' AND ROCKIN'**
 – (nearly as above).

1959. (7"ep) <5124> **PICKIN' BERRIES**
 – Beautiful Delilah / Vacation time / Carol / Hey Pedro.

1959. (7"ep) <5126> **SWEET LITTLE ROCK AND ROLLERS**
 – Johnny B. Goode / Around and around / Sweet little rock and roller / Jo Jo Gunne.

May 64. (lp) <1485> **GREATEST HITS** — **34**

Oct 63. (7"ep) *Pye International;* (NEP 44011) **CHUCK BERRY**
 – Johnny B. Goode / Oh baby doll / School day / Back in the U.S.A.

Dec 63. (7"ep) *Pye International;* (NEP 44013) **THIS IS CHUCK BERRY**
 – Bye bye Johnny / Rock and roll music / Childhood sweetheart / Broken arrow.

Apr 64. (7"ep) *Pye International;* (NEP 44018) **THE BEST OF CHUCK BERRY**
 – Memphis, Tennessee / Roll over Beethoven / I'm talking 'bout you / Sweet little sixteen.

Oct 64. (7"ep) *Pye International;* (NEP 44028) **CHUCK BERRY HITS**
 – Johnny B. Goode / Nadine / No particular place to go / Memphis Tennessee.

Dec 64. (7"ep) *Pye International;* (NEP 44033) **BLUE MOOD**
 – Driftin' blues / Lonely all the time / Things I used to do / Fraulein.

Mar 65. (7"ep) (CRE 6002) **THE PROMISED LAND**
 – You never can tell / Brenda Lee / The promised land / Things I used to do.

Oct 65. (7"ep) (CRE 6005) **COME ON**
 – Reelin' and rockin' / Don't you lie to me / Around and around / Come on.

Feb 66. (7"ep) (CRE 6012) **I GOT A BOOKING**
 – I want to be your driver / St.Louis blues / Dear dad / I got a booking.

Feb 66. (lp) *Golden Guinea;* (GGL 0352) **CHUCK BERRY**
 (re-iss. Sep66 on 'Marble Arch'; MAL 611)

May 66. (7"ep) (CRE 6016) **YOU CAME A LONG WAY FROM ST. LOUIS**
 – You came a long way from St. Louis / His daughter Caroline / My little love-light / Jamaica farewell.

Feb 67. (lp) *Marble Arch;* (MAL 660) **CHUCK BERRY'S GREATEST HITS**

May 68. (7") (CRS 8075) **JOHNNY B.GOODE. / SWEET LITTLE SIXTEEN**

Apr 69. (7") (CRS 8089) **NO PARTICULAR PLACE TO GO. / IT WASN'T ME**

Mar 72. (7"m) (6145 007) **ROCK AND ROLL MUSIC. / JOHNNY B. GOODE / SCHOOL DAY**

May 72. (d-lp) (6641 177) <LPS 1514D> **GOLDEN DECADE VOL.1** — **72**

1973. (d-lp) <2CH 60023> **GOLDEN DECADE VOLUME 2**

1973. (lp) *Philips;* (6336 216) **BACK IN THE U.S.A.**
 <US-iss.pic-lp Dec85 on 'Astan'; PD 5009>

1974. (d-lp) <2CH 60028> **GOLDEN DECADE VOLUME 3**

Nov 74. (lp) (6310 130) <ACB 00208> **ALL-TIME GREATEST ROCK AND ROLL PARTY HITS**

May 75. (lp) *Contour;* (6870 638) **I'M A ROCKER**

May 76. (7"m) (6190 080) **SWEET LITTLE ROCK AND ROLLER. / BACK IN THE U.S.A. / NO PARTICULAR PLACE TO GO**

Jan 77. (lp) (9288 690) **MOTORVATIN'** (Greatest live) **7**
 (re-iss. Dec87 on 'Starblend'; SMT 009)

May 77. (7") (6078 707) **SWEET LITTLE SIXTEEN. / GUITAR BOOGIE**

Jul 78. (lp) *Sonic;* **SWEET LITTLE SIXTEEN**

Sep 79. (7"ep) *Hammer;* **ROLL OVER BEETHOVEN**
 – Roll over Beethoven / Johnny B.Goode / Sweet little sixteen / Maybellene / Carol / Memphis, Tennessee.

Sep 79. (7"ep) *Hammer;* **SCHOOL DAY**
 – School day / Rock and roll music / Sweet little rock and roller / Reelin' and rockin' / Back in the U.S.A. / Thirty days.

Oct 79. (lp) *Hammer;* (HMR 9003) **20 GREATEST HITS**

Feb 80. (lp) *Mercury;* (6336 635) **MODS AND ROCKERS**

Oct 80. (lp/c) *Spotlight;* (SPOT/ZCSPT 1003) **SPOTLIGHT ON . . .**

1981. (lp/c) *Mercury;* (9279/7259 140) **ROCKIN' WITH CHUCK BERRY**

Jan 83. (7") *Flashback-Pye;* (FBS 18) **NO PARTICULAR PLACE TO GO. / SWEET LITTLE SIXTEEN**

Mar 83. (lp) (CXMP 2011) **CHUCK BERRY**

Mar 83. (lp) (CMMD 4016) **CHESS MASTERS**

May 83. (lp) *Stack-O-Hits;* **ALIVE AND ROCKIN'** (live)

1983. (lp) *Spot;* (1957) **THE GREATEST HITS – LIVE** (live)

Jun 83. (7") *Old Gold;* (OG 9296) **MEMPHIS, TENNESSEE. / NO PARTICULAR PLACE TO GO**

Jul 83. (10"lp/c) *P.R.T.;* (DOW/(ZADOW 14) **DUCK WALKING**
 (re-iss. Jul88 on 'Entertainers' lp/c; ENT LP/MC 13046)

Nov 83. (lp) *Bulldog;* (BDL 1051) **REELING, ROLLING & ROCKING**

Jun 84. (7") *S.M.P.;* (SKM 04) **MY DING-A-LING. / MAYBELLENE / REELIN' AND ROCKIN'**

Jun 84. (7") *S.M.P.;* (SKM 05) **SWEET LITTLE SIXTEEN. / NADINE / JOHNNY B. GOODE**

Dec 85. (lp/c) *P.R.T.;* (6/4 24372) **20 SUPER HITS**

1986. (cd) *Vogue;* (VG 600 085) **TWO DOZEN BERRY'S**

Apr 86. (lp/c) *Castle;* (SHLP/SHTC 136) **GREATEST HITS**

Jul 86. (lp/c) (GCH/+K7 8008) **NEW JUKE BOX HITS**

Jul 86. (lp/c) *Deja Vu;* (DVLP/DVMC 2068) **THE COLLECTION – 20 ROCK'N'ROLL GREATS**
 (cd-iss. Sep87; DVCD 2068)

Dec 86. (cd) *Vogue;* (VG 600 033) **BEST OF CHUCK BERRY**

May 87. (cd) *Bescoli;* (CD 30) **21 GREATEST HITS**
 (re-iss. Jan90 on 'Zeta'; ZET 520)

Aug 87. (cd) *The Collection;* (OR 016) **REELING AND ROCKING**

Nov 87. (lp) *Checkmate;* (CHECKMATE 1955) **LET IT ROCK**

Jan 88. (lp) *Joker;* <SM 3983> **ROLL OVER BEETHOVEN VOL.1**

Feb 88. (lp/c/cd) *M.C.A.* (MCF/MCFC/DMCF 3411) **HAIL, HAIL, ROCK'N'ROLL (Soundtrack)**
 (re-iss. cd.Nov93 on 'Charly')

Mar 88. (lp/c/cd) *Stylus;* (SMR/SMC/SMD 848) **CHESS MASTERS**

Apr 88. (lp/c/cd) *Platinum;* (PLAT/+C/CD 24) **DECADE 55-65**

Jun 88. (d-lp/c/cd) *Castle;* (CCS LP/MC/CD 194) **THE COLLECTION**
 – Sweet little sixteen / Johnny B.Goode / Back in the U.S.A. / Maybellene / Too much monkey business / Rock and roll music / Reelin' and rockin' / No particular place to go / Roll over Beethoven / You never can tell / Nadine / Carol / School days / My ding-a-ling / Let it rock / Little Queenie / Promised land / Memphis Tennessee / Sweet little rock'n'roller / Thirty days / Brown-eyed handsome man / Run Rudolph run / Merry Christmas baby.

Jun 88. (7"ep/12"ep) (GCH N/X 101) **MY DING A LING / SCHOOL DAY. / NO PARTICULAR PLACE TO GO / JOHNNY B. GOODE**

Jul 88. (lp) *Driving Wheel;* (C 7788) **CHUCK BERRY'S ROCK'N'ROLL PARTY**

Oct 88. (d-lp) *Vogue;* (427008) **CHICAGO GOLDEN YEARS (GOLDEN DECADE VOL.1)**

Oct 88. (d-lp) *Vogue;* (427009) **CHICAGO GOLDEN YEARS (GOLDEN DECADE VOL.2)**

Oct 88. (d-lp) *Vogue;* (427010) **CHICAGO GOLDEN YEARS (GOLDEN DECADE VOL.3)**

Dec 88. (c) *Fun;* (FUN 9012) **20 GREATEST HITS**

Jan 89. (7") *Old Gold;* (OG 9843) **NO PARTICULAR PLACE TO GO. / MEMPHIS TENNESSEE**

Jan 89. (7") *Old Gold;* (OG 9845) **MY DING-A-LING. / REELIN' AND ROCKIN'**

Jan 89. (7") *Old Gold;* (OG 9849) **SWEET LITTLE SIXTEEN. / ROCK AND ROLL MUSIC**

Jan 89. (7") *Old Gold;* (OG 9847) **ROLL OVER BEETHOVEN. / JOHNNY B. GOODE**

May 89. (cd-ep) *Old Gold;* (OG 6143) **ROLL OVER BEETHOVEN / JOHNNY B. GOODE / ROCK AND ROLL MUSIC**

Jun 89. (lp/c/cd) *Ocean;* (OCN 2033 WL/WK/WD) **ROLL OVER BEETHOVEN**

Jul 89. (cd/c/lp) *Instant;* (CD/TC+/INS 5002) **ROCK & ROLL MUSIC**
 (re-iss. cd Feb93 on 'Charly')

Sep 89. (3xlp-box/3xc-box/3xcd-box) *M.C.A.,;* (CH6/CHC4/CD 8001 **CHESS BOX**

Nov 89. (3xcd-box/3xc-box/3xlp-box) *Charly;* (CD/TC+/BOX 256) **CHUCK BERRY BOX SET**

Feb 90. (cd) *M.C.A.;* (CHD 92521) **ROCK'N'ROLL RARITIES**

Mar 90. (cd) *Roots;* (RTS 33006) **ROCK & ROLL MUSIC**

Apr 91. (cd/c) *Vogue;* (670/771 100) **THE BEST OF CHUCK BERRY VOL.1 1955-57**

Apr 91. (cd/c) *Vogue;* (670/771 101) **THE BEST OF CHUCK BERRY VOL.2 1959-60**

Apr 91. (cd/c) *Vogue;* (670/771 102) **THE BEST OF CHUCK BERRY VOL.3 1960-65**

May 91. (cd) *Magnum Force;* (CDMF 076) **THE CHESS MASTERS**

Jun 91. (lp/c/cd) *See For Miles;* (SEE/+K/CD 320) **THE EP COLLECTION**
 (cd re-iss. Jan99; same)

Aug 91. (cd) *Roots;* (RTS 3303-2) **SWEET LITTLE SIXTEEN VOL.2**

Dec 91. (cd) *Magnum Force;* (CDMF 080) **THE CHESS MASTERS VOL.2: 1958-65**

Apr 92. (cd/c) *Music For Pleasure;* (CD/TC MFP 5936) **20 GREAT TRACKS**

Apr 93. (cd/c) *Laserlight;* (509075) **MR. ROCK'N'ROLL**

Sep 93. (cd) *Ace-Charly;* (CDCH 397) **ON THE BLUES SIDE**

May 94. (cd; shared with BO DIDDLEY) *Charly;* (CDTT 2) **TWO ON ONE**

Oct 94. (cd) (CDCD 1192) **LET IT ROCK**

Nov 94. (cd) **OH YEAH**

Jan 95. (cd) *Wisepack;* (LECD 037) **LEGENDS IN MUSIC**

Apr 95. (4xcd-box+book) (CDDIG 1) **THE POET OF ROCK'N'ROLL**

Jun 95. (cd) *Collection;* (COL 002) **THE COLLECTION**

Nov 96. (cd/c) *M.C.A.;* <(MCD/MCC 11560)> **THE BEST OF CHUCK BERRY**
 – Roll over Beethoven / Sweet little sixteen / Johnny B Goode / You never can tell / You can't catch me / Downbound train / Too much monkey business / Havana moon / School days / Oh baby doll / Beautiful Delilah / Sweet little rock'n'roller / Anthony boy / Little Queenie / Almost grown / Let it rock / Back in the USA / Reelin' and rockin' / Around and around / Brown eyed handsome man / Maybelline / No particular place to go / Rock'n'roll / Run Rudolph run / Jo Jo Gunne / Carol / Confessin' the blues / Jaguar and Thunderbird / Down the road apiece / Thirty days / Merry Christmas baby / My ding-a-ling / I'm talking about you / Too pooped to pop / Bye bye Johnny / Promised land / Tulane / Come on / Nadine (is it you) / Memphis, Tennessee.

Dec 98. (cd) *Beat Goes On;* (BGOCD 428) **YOU NEVER CAN TELL / THE LATEST AND GREATEST**

Aug 99. (cd) *Beat Goes On;* (BGOCD 458) **ONE DOZEN BERRYS / JUKE BOX HITS**

BETA BAND

Formed: London, England ... 1994 by ex-patriate Scotsman, STEVE MASON, the St. Andrews-born singer meeting up with Edinburgh University students, decksman JOHN MacLEAN and drummer ROBIN JONES on a train down to London. There they worked at various day jobs while sharing a flat in Shepherd's Bush; Portsmouth-born RICHARD GREENTREE, formerly bassist of SINISTER FOOTWEAR would become part of the zany quartet in early '97 after being introduced through mutual friends, PUSHERMAN. Discovered and subsequently produced by THE VERVE's NICK McCABE, he saw some potential in their psychedelic transcendental dub malarky. A pot-pourri of sound right enough (STONE ROSES or The MOONFLOWERS – remember them? – on a mantric mission!), the lads issued three EP's in the space of a year, 'CHAMPION VERSIONS', 'THE PATTY PATTY SOUND' and the excellent 'LOS AMIGOS DEL BETA BANDIDOS'. By popular demand (the vinyl was changing hands for upwards of £40 a time!) these were soon collected together on one shiny cd/album, simply titled 'THE THREE EP'S'. Lauded by the more discerning factions of the music press (the NME for one!), the bumbling art-rockers (by-passing the fashion stakes completely; safari suits, judo gear and horror of horrors, STEVE's "smart-arse" shell-suit being the disorder of the day) found themselves in the Top 40 by autumn '98 with a long player that hung together surprisingly well. The sound of "baggy" ten years on, filtered through a kingsized bong, BETA standards such as 'DRY THE RAIN ("It Will Be Alright"), 'INNER MEET ME', 'SHE'S THE ONE', 'DR. BAKER' and 'NEEDLES IN MY EYES' will surely come to be regarded as underground classics. To end the year, MASON moonlighted as KING BISCUIT TIME, releasing (to coincide with the latest edition of the band's zany in-house comic!) a bizarre EP of spaced-out drum'n'bass, '"SINGS" NELLY FOGGIT'S BLUES IN "ME AND THE PHARAOHS"'. With expectation and hype rife about the recording schedules and rumoured double-disc set of their debut set proper, the band were finally ready to promote 'THE BETA BAND' long-player in June '99. However, delays due to an objection from JIM STEINMAN (for the sample/use of his BONNIE TYLER – 'Total Eclipse Of The Heart' collaboration) and the band's post-release qualms that it was "fucking awful" contributed to complete bewilderment within the press and its readers. At the end of June, the album shot into the Top 20 despite poor reviews stating over-production as its downfall (or was it just plain arsing about?). Opening with the self-explanatory 'THE BETA BAND RAP' (which might've been handled better by the BONZO's in the 60's!) and finishing with the baffling 'THE COW'S WRONG', the album shocked fans who thought the quartet were perhaps a tad over-indulgent. On reflection though, The BETA BAND's original stage interpretations of the tracks could not be faulted. It's just a pity that critical cohorts like the MANICS have been proved right; so far . . . • Trivia: They guested on SPIRITUALIZED's 'Abbey Road' EP early '98.

Album rating: THE THREE E.P.'S (*9) / THE BETA BAND (*6)

STEVE MASON – vocals, percussion, drums, etc / **JOHN MacLEAN** – turntable, sampling / **RICHARD GREENTREE** – bass (ex-SINISTER FOOTWEAR) / **ROBIN JONES** – drums, percussion

	Regal	not iss.
Jul 97. (12"ep) (REG 16) **CHAMPION VERSIONS**	☐	-
– Dry the rain / I know / B + A / Dogs got a bone.		
Mar 98. (2x12"ep/cd-ep) (REG 18/+CD) **THE PATTY PATTY SOUND**	☐	-
– Inner meet me / The house song / The monolith / She's the one.		
Jul 98. (cd-ep) (REG 20CD) **LOS AMIGOS DEL BETA BANDIDOS**	☐	-
– Push it out / It's over / Dr. Baker / Needles in my eyes.		
Sep 98. (cd) (7243 4 97385 2 2) **THE THREE E.P.'S** (compilation)	35	-
Jun 99. (cd/d-lp) (REG 30 CD/LP) **THE BETA BAND**	18	-

– The Beta Band rap / It's not too beautiful / Simple boy / Round the bend / Dance o'er the border / Brokenupadingdong / Number 15 / Smiling / The hard one / The cow's wrong.

KING BISCUIT TIME

aka **STEVE MASON** – vocals, etc
Dec 98. (12"ep/cd-ep) (REG 025/+CD) **"SINGS" NELLY FOGGIT'S BLUES IN "ME AND THE PHARAOHS"**   ☐   -
– Fatheriver / Niggling discrepancy / Little white / Eye o' the dug.

BETTER DAYS (see under ⇒ Paul BUTTERFIELD)

BETTER THAN EZRA

Formed: New Orleans, Louisiana, USA . . . 1988 by university pals, KEVIN GRIFFIN (their main songwriter), TOM DRUMMOND and CARY BONNECAZE. Debuting their rather derivative DINOSAUR JR guitar-based sound on a privately distributed cassette at the turn of the decade, the band spent the first half of the 90's rehearsing and touring extensively in their southern domain. In 1993/4, BETTER THAN EZRA self-financed their debut release, 'DELUXE' (on 'Swell'), the album shifting enough copies to attract major label interest. Eventually signing to 'Elektra', the band went back into the studio with producer, Dan Rothchild, the man helping them polish up their aforementioned debut for re-release in '95. Catchy grunge by numbers with a MICHAEL STIPE-esque vocal inflection, the record gradually ascended the US charts helped by the Top 30 success of single, 'GOOD'. The following year, after CARY was replaced by TRAVIS AARON McNABB, the trio returned with a second collection, 'FRICTION BABY', a record that barely reached the shallows of the US chart as the grunge wave subsided. Obviously WEA/Elektra had given up any hope of marketing the band in Britain and like its predecessor, 'HOW DOES YOUR GARDEN GROW?' (1998), was a US-only release.

Album rating: DELUXE (*6) / FRICTION BABY (*5) / HOW DOES YOUR GARDEN GROW? (*6)

KEVIN GRIFFIN – vocals, guitar / **TOM DRUMMOND** – bass / **CARY BONNECAZE** – drums

	WEA Int.	Elektra
May 95. (cd/c) <(7559 61784-2/-4)> **DELUXE**	☐	35

– In the blood / Good / Southern girl / The killer inside / Rosealia / Cry in the sun / Teenager / Untitled / Summerhouse / Porcelain / Heaven / This time of year / Coyote.

Jun 95. (c-s) <64428> **GOOD / CIRCLE OF FRIENDS** (live)	-	30
Jun 95. (c-s) (EKR 204C) **GOOD / SUMMERHOUSE**	-	30
(cd-s+=) (EKR 204CD) – Know you better (live) / Circle of friends (live).		
Nov 95. (c-s,cd-s) <64352> **ROSEALIA / IN THE BLOOD** (live)	-	71

— **TRAVIS AARON McNABB** – drums; repl. BONNECAZE

Aug 96. (cd/c) <61944-2/-4> **FRICTION BABY**	-	64

– King of New orleans / Rewind / Long lost / Normal town / Scared are you? / Return of the post moderns / Hung the Moon / Desperately wanting / Still life with Cooley / WWOZ / Happy endings / Speeding up to slow down / At CH, Degaulle, etc.

Dec 96. (c-s,cd-s) <64228> **DESPERATELY WANTING / PALACE HOTEL**	-	48
Sep 98. (cd/c) <62247-2> **HOW DOES YOUR GARDEN GROW?**	-	

– Je ne m'en souviens pas / One more murder / At the stars / Like it like that / Allison Foley / Under you / Live again / Happy day mama / Pull / Particle / Beautiful mistake / Everything in 2's / New kind of low: a) Low – b) Coma / Waxing or waning?

Mar 99. (-) <radio cut> **AT THE STARS**	-	78

BETTIE SERVEERT (dig out; Great Alt & Indie . . .)

BEVIS FROND (dig out; Great Alt & Indie . . .)

B-52's

Formed: Athens, Georgia, USA . . . late '76, by KATE PIERSON, FRED SCHNEIDER, KEITH STRICKLAND, RICKY WILSON and his sister CINDY. After one self-financed 45 sold out its limited 2,000 copies, they drew the attention of Island's Chris Blackwell, who signed them after they played residency at Max's Kansas City late in 1978. They subsequently re-issued their 'ROCK LOBSTER' debut, the single making UK Top 40 lists the following year. Combining a kitsch image and sound which took in everything from rock'n'roll and 60's beat to new wave REZILLOS-style dual harmonies, The B-52's brightened up the increasingly dour late 70's/early 80's punk/pop scene. The marine madness of the classic 'ROCK LOBSTER' eventually made its way into the US charts in early 1980, by which time the eponymous '79 debut album had made the US Top 30. Even JOHN LENNON was a fan, the former BEATLES man surprisingly admitting that The B-52's were one of the groups who inspired him to start writing again. A strong follow-up set, 'WILD PLANET' (1980), made the Top 20 in both Britain and America, although critics weren't quite so enamoured with the more mannered 'MESOPOTAMIA' set (1982), produced by DAVID BYRNE of TALKING HEADS. The mid-80's were a bleak time for the band as RICKY finally died from AIDS on the 12th October, 1985, and the group struggled to capture the inspired creativity of their earlier period (fans were content in making 'ROCK LOBSTER' an even bigger UK hit than before). Signing a new deal with 'Reprise', The B-52's reunited their roots on 'BOUNCING OFF SATELLITES', an album which should have spawned a hit single, 'WIG'. DON WAS / NILE RODGERS-produced 'COSMIC THING' (1989), was a remarkable comeback that showcased their alternative dancefloor smash, 'LOVE SHACK', the album becoming their most successful release to date, making the US Top 5. Trimmed to a trio of PIERSON, SCHNEIDER and STRICKLAND following the departure of CINDY in 1992, the group recorded another album in the classic B-52's style, 'GOOD STUFF', before setting to work on the soundtrack for the revamped 'Flintstones' movie. Something of a canny pairing, SCHNEIDER's nasal-voiced nonsense was a perfect backdrop for Fred and family's stone age adventures. • Songwriters: All mainly STRICKLAND or group compositions. PLANET CLAIRE (w/ Henry Mancini) • Trivia: In 1981, during lay-off, STRICKLAND, PIERSON and CINDY WILSON did one-off Japan venture as "MELON" with group The PLASTICS and ADRIAN BELEW. Late 1990, PIERSON contributed on singles by IGGY POP (Candy) and R.E.M. (Shiny Happy People).

Album rating: THE B-52's (*8) / WILD PLANET (*6) / PARTY MIX! remixes (*3) / MESOPOTAMIA mini (*4) / WHAMMY! (*5) / BOUNCING OFF THE SATELLITES (*4) / COSMIC THING (*7) / DANCE THIS MESS AROUND – THE BEST OF THE B-52's compilation (*9) / GOOD STUFF (*5) / Fred Schneider: FRED SCHNEIDER AND THE SNAKE SOCIETY (*5) / JUST . . . FRED (*5)

KATE PIERSON (b.27 Apr'48, Weehawken, N.J.) – vocals, organ, bass / **CINDY WILSON** (b.28 Feb'57) – vocals, percussion, guitar / **RICKY WILSON** (b.19 Mar'53) – guitar / **FRED SCHNEIDER** (III) (b. 1 Jul'56, Newark, N.J.) – vocals, keyboards / **KEITH 'Julian' STRICKLAND** (b.26 Oct'53) – drums

	not iss.	Boo-Fant
Nov 78. (7") <DB-52> **ROCK LOBSTER. / 52 GIRLS**	-	-
	Island	Warners
Jul 79. (7") (WIP 6506) **ROCK LOBSTER. / RUNNING AROUND**	37	-
Jul 79. (lp/c) (WIP/ICT 9580) <3355> **THE B-52's**	22	59

– Planet Claire / 52 girls / Dance this mess around / Rock lobster / Lava / There's a Moon in the sky (called the Moon) / Hero worship / 6060-842 / Downtown. (lp w/ free 7") (PSR 438) – ROCK LOBSTER. / 52 GIRLS (re-iss. May86; same) (cd-iss. Jan87; CID 9580) (re-iss. Jan94 + May94;.

Sep 79. (7") (WIP 6527) **6060-842. / HERO WORSHIP**	☐	☐
Nov 79. (7"pic-d/7") (P+/WIP 6551) <WBS 49212> **PLANET CLAIRE. / THERE'S A MOON IN THE SKY (CALLED THE MOON)**	☐	May80
Jan 80. (7") <WBS 49173> **ROCK LOBSTER. / 6060-842**	-	56
Jul 80. (7") (WIP 6579) **GIVE ME BACK MY MAN. / STROBE LIGHT**	61	-
Sep 80. (lp/c) (ILPS/ICT 9622) <BSK 3471> **WILD PLANET**	18	18

– Party out of bounds / Dirty back road / Runnin' around / Give me back my man / Private Idaho / Devil in my car / Quiche Lorraine / Strobe light / 53 miles west of Venus. (cd-iss. May90; 842436-2)

Oct 80. (7") <WBS 49537> **PRIVATE IDAHO. / PARTY OUT OF BOUNDS** — | **74**

Nov 80. (7") *(WIP 6685)* **DIRTY BACK ROAD. / STROBE LIGHT** — | —

Jan 81. (7") <WBS 49717> **QUICHE LORRAINE. / LAVA** — | —

Jul 81. (m-lp/c) *(IPM/ICT 1001)* <MINI 3596> **THE PARTY MIX ALBUM** (remixes) **36** | **55**
– Party out of bounds / Private Idaho / Give me back my man / Lava / Dance this mess around / 52 girls. *(cd-iss. May90; 846044-2)*

Aug 81. (7") *(WIP 6727)* **GIVE ME BACK MY MAN (Party mix). / PARTY OUT OF BOUNDS** (version) — | —

Feb 82. (m-lp/c) *(ISSP/ICT 4006)* <3641> **MESOPOTAMIA** **18** | **35**
– Loveland / Deep sleep / Mesopotamia / Cake / Throw that beat in the garbage can / Nip it in the bud. *(cd-iss. May90; 846239-2)*

Mar 82. (7") <50064> **DEEP SLEEP. / NIP IT IN THE BUD** — | —

Jun 82. (7") <29971> **MESOPOTAMIA. / THROW THAT BEAT IN THE GARBAGE CAN** — | —

Apr 83. (7") *(IS 107)* **SONG FOR A FUTURE GENERATION. / ('A'instrumental)** **63** | —
(12"+=) *(12IS 107)* – Planet Claire.
(d7"++=) *(ISD 107)* – There's a moon in the sky (called the moon).

May 83. (lp/c) *(ILPS 9759)* <23819> **WHAMMY!** **33** | **29**
– Legal tender / Whammy kiss / Song for a future generation / Butterbean / Trism / Queen of Las Vegas / Don't worry / Big bird / Work that skirt. *(cd-iss. May90; 842445-2)*

Jul 83. (7") <29579> **LEGAL TENDER. / MOON 83** — | **81**

Oct 83. (7") <29561> **SONG FOR A FUTURE GENERATION. / TREASON** — | —

—— **RICKY** suffering from full blown AIDS, died 12 Oct'85.

May 86. (7"/7"sha-pic-d; rock/planet/lobster) *(BFT+/G/P/L 1)* **ROCK LOBSTER (new version). / PLANET CLAIRE** **12** | —
(d7"+=) *(BFTD 1)* – Song for a future generation / 52 girls.
(12"+=) *(12BFT 1)* – Song for a future generation / Give me back my man.

—— They carry on, augmented by session man **RALPH CARNEY** – guitar

Jun 87. (7"/7"pic-d) *(BFT/+P 2)* **WIG. / SUMMER OF LOVE** — | —
(c-s+=/12+=) *(BFTD/12BFT 2)* – Song for a future generation.

Jul 87. (lp/c/cd) *(ILPS/ICT/CID 9871)* <25504> **BOUNCING OFF THE SATELLITES** **74** | **85** Sep86
– Summer of love / Girl from Ipanema goes to Greenland / Housework / Detour thru your mind / Wig / Theme for a nude beach / Ain't it a shame / Juicy jungle / Communicate / She brakes for rainbows. *(cd-iss. May90; 842480-2)*

Sep 87. (7") **SUMMER OF LOVE. / HOUSEWORK** — | —

	Reprise	Reprise

Jul 89. (lp/c)(cd) *(WX 283/+C)*(925854-2) <25854> **COSMIC THING** **8** | **4**
– Cosmic thing / Dry country / Deadbeat club / Love shack / Junebug / Roam / Bushfire / Channel Z / Topaz / Follow your blues.

Aug 89. (7") <22817> **LOVE SHACK. / CHANNEL Z** — | **3**

Sep 89. (7") *(W 2831)* **CHANNEL Z (remix). / JUNEBUG** **61** | —
(12")(cd-s) *(W 2831 T/CD)* – ('A'-Rock mix) / ('A'side) / ('A'dub mix). *(re-iss. Aug90)*

Dec 89. (7") <22667> **ROAM. / BUSHFIRE** — | **3**

Feb 90. (7"/7"g-f/7"pic-d/c-s/cd-s) *(W 9917/+X/P/C/CD)* **LOVE SHACK. / PLANET CLAIRE (live) / ROCK LOBSTER (live)** **2** | —
(12") *(W 9917T)* – ('A'-Dany Rampling remix) / ('A'-Ben Grosse mix) / ('A'side)

Apr 90. (7") <19938> **DEADBEAT CLUB. / PLANET CLAIRE** — | **30**

May 90. (7"/c-s/cd-s) *(W 9827/+C/CD)* **ROAM. / WHAMMY KISS (live) / DANCE THIS MESS AROUND (live)** **17** | —
(12"/12"w-poster) *(W 9827T/+W)* – ('A'-Radio mix) / ('A'remix) / ('A'extended remix).

Sep 90. (7"/c-s) **DEADBEAT CLUB. / LOVE SHACK** — | —
(12"+=/cd-s+=) – B-52's megamix.

—— now trimmed to basic trio of **PIERSON, SCHNEIDER** – vox / + **STRICKLAND** – guitar with guest musicians **IRWIN / ALFORD / LEE** / plus **JEFF PORCARO + STERLING CAMPBELL** – drums / **DAVID McMURRAY** – sax / **JAMIE MULHOBERAC + RICHARD HILTON** – keyboards / **LENNY CASTRO** – percussion / **TRACY WORMWORTH** – bass

Jun 92. (7"/c-s) *(W 0109/+C)* <18895> **GOOD STUFF. / BAD INFLUENCE** **21** | **28**
(12"+=/cd-s+=) *(W 0109 T/CD)* – Return to Dreamland.
(12") *(W 0109TX)* – (4-'A'mixes).

Jul 92. (cd/c/lp) <(7599 26943-2/-4/-1)> **GOOD STUFF** **8** | **16**
– Tell it like it t-i-is / Hot pants explosion / Good stuff / Revolution Earth / Dreamland / Is that you Mo-Dean? / The world's green laughter / Vision of a kiss / Breezin'/ Bad influence. *(re-iss. Feb95 cd/c;)*

Sep 92. (7"/c-s) *(W 0130/+C)* **TELL IT LIKE IT T-I-IS. / THE WORLD'S GREEN LAUGHTER** **61** | —
(12"/cd-s) *(W 0130 T/CD)* – ('A'-4 other mixes).

Nov 92. (7"/c-s) **IS THAT YOU MO-DEAN?. / ('A'-Moby mix)** — | —
(12"+=/cd-s+=) – ('A'-2 other mixes) / Tell it like it t-i-is.

Feb 93. (7"/c-s) **HOT PANTS EXPLOSION. / LOVE SHACK** — | —
(cd-s+=) – Channel Z / Roam.

—— **SCHNEIDER, PIERSON + STRICKLAND**

	M.C.A.	M.C.A.

Jun 94. (7"/c-s; BC-52's) *(MCS/+CS 1986)* <54839> **(MEET) THE FLINTSTONES. / ('A'-Barney's mix)** **3** | **33** May94
(cd-s+=) *(MCSTD 1986)* – (2-'A'mixes).
(above from that year's movie, 'The Flintstones')

– compilations, others, etc. –

Jun 90. (cd/c/lp) *Island; (ILPS/ICT/CID 9959)* **DANCE THIS MESS AROUND THE BEST OF THE B-52's** **36** | —
– Party out of bounds / Devil in my car / Dirty back road / 6060-842 / Wig / Dance this mess around / Private Idaho / Rock lobster / Strobe light / Give me back my man / Song for a future generation / Planet Claire / 52 girls. *(cd+=)* – (2 extra mixes).

Feb 91. (cd) *Reprise; <26401>* **PARTY MIX! / MESOPOTAMIA** — | —

Nov 92. (d-cd) *Island; (ITSCD 1)* **THE B-52'S / WILD PLANET** — | —

Sep 95. (cd) *Spectrum; (551210-2)* **PLANET CLAIRE** — | —

Jul 98. (cd/c) *Reprise; (9362 46995-2/-4)* <46920> **TIME CAPSULE – SONGS FOR A FUTURE GENERATION** **93** Jun98
– Planet Claire / Rock lobster / Private Idaho / Quiche Lorraine / Mesopotamia / Summer of love / Channel Z / Deadbeat club / Love shack / Roam / Good stuff / Is that you Mo-Dean? / Meet the Flintstones / Debbie / Hallucinating Pluto.

Jan 99. (c-s) *Reprise; (W 0461C)* **LOVE SHACK '99 (mix)** **66** | —
(cd-s+=) *(W 0461CD)* –

FRED SCHNEIDER

solo, recorded 1984 and written with COTE

—— with various session people

	Reprise	Reprise

May 91. (cd/c/lp) <(7559 26592-2/-4/-1)> **FRED SCHNEIDER & THE SHAKE SOCIETY** — | —
– Monster / Out the concrete / Summer in Hell / Orbit / I'm gonna haunt you / It's time to kiss / This planet's a mess / Wave / Boonga (the New Jersey caveman).

Jun 91. (cd-s) <19262> **MONSTER /** — | **85**

—— next with **STEVE ALBINI** – producing backing from **DEADLY CUPCAKE, SHADOWY MEN ON A SHADOWY PLANET + SIX FINGER SATELLITE**

	WEA	WEA

Jun 96. (cd) <(9362 46215-2)> **JUST . . . FRED** — | —
– Whip / Helicopter / Sugar in my hog / Bulldozer / Coconut / Center of the universe / Radioactive lady eyeball / Lick / Bad dream / Secret sharer / Stroke of genius.

Jello BIAFRA (see under ⇒ DEAD KENNEDYS)

BIG AUDIO DYNAMITE

Formed: London, England . . . 1984 by ex-CLASH guitarist/singer, MICK JONES, who was still under contract with 'C.B.S.' records. Amongst others, namely DAN DONOVAN, LEO WILLIAMS and GREG ROBERTS, he recruited film-maker/friend and non-musician DON LETTS. Although their 1985 debut 45, 'THE BOTTOM LINE', soon became a favourite, it narrowly missed out on a chart placing. However, the follow-up 'E=MC2', gave them a close brush with the Top 10 early the following year, resurrecting sales of the critically acclaimed but commercially disastrous album, 'THIS IS . . .'. Mick's unique punk-ish vocals with the band's sound was not unlike a danceable CLASH. Indeed, the band were attempting to fashion a gleaming new hip-hop/electro/alternative rock hybrid, using the latter day CLASH sound as a springboard. The debut set was at least partially successful in this endeavour, standout cuts being the aforementioned 'E=MC2' and its follow-up Top 30 hit, 'MEDICINE SHOW'. A second set, 'NO.10 UPPING STREET' (1986) was even more ambitious, featuring contributions from JONES's former mucker, JOE STRUMMER. The following two years saw the band struggle as JONES survived a near fatal bout of pneumonia, the albums 'TIGHTEN UP VOL.88' (1988) and 'MEGATOP PHOENIX' (1989) brave attempts at further pushing back the boundaries between different genres, mixing up reggae, hip-hop and even country. However, by the end of the decade, the B.A.D. blueprint was being more successfully and inventively interpreted by a new wave of white kids armed with samples, drum machines and an attitude, enter EMF, JESUS JONES etc. The original line-up split at the turn of the decade although JONES recruited new players for BIG AUDIO DYNAMITE II, namely NICK HAWKINS, GARY STONEAGE and CHRIS KAVANAGH. The revamped B.A.D. recorded a further couple of critically and commercially underwhelming albums, 'KOOL-AID' (1990) and 'THE GLOBE' (1991), DJ ZONKA adding his turntable skills to the latter. Though JONES continued working under the B.A.D. name into the 90's, his output is largely confined to a cult following. • **Songwriters:** Mainly JONES and LETTS, with other members contributing. Covers: DUELLING BANJOS (Arthur Smith's theme from 'Deliverance' Soundtrack) / BATTLE OF NEW ORLEANS (trad). • **Trivia:** In 1991, JONES was credited on AZTEC CAMERA's Top 20 UK hit, 'GOOD MORNING BRITAIN'.

Album rating: THIS IS BIG AUDIO DYNAMITE (*7) / No.10 UPPING STREET (*6) / TIGHTEN UP, VOL.'88 (*4) / MEWGATOP PHOENIX (*5) / THE GLOBE (*6) / HIGHER POWER (*4) / F-PUNK (*4) / GREATEST HITS compilation (*8)

MICK JONES (b.26 Jun'55) – vocals, guitar (ex-CLASH) / **DON LETTS** – effects, keyboards, vocals / **DAN DONOVAN** – keyboards / **LEO WILLIAMS** – bass / **GREG ROBERTS** – drums

	C.B.S.	Columbia

Sep 85. (7"/12") *(A/TA 6591)* **THE BOTTOM LINE. / B.A.D.** — | —

Nov 85. (lp/c) *(CBS/40 26714)* <40220> **THIS IS BIG AUDIO DYNAMITE** **27** | —
– Medicine show / Sony / E=MC2 / The bottom line / Sudden impact / Stone Thames / B.A.D. / A party. *(cd-iss. Jun86; CD 26714)* (re-iss. Nov88 lp/c/cd; 462 999-1/-4/-2)

Mar 86. (7"/12") *(A/TA 6963)* **E=MC2. / THIS IS BIG AUDIO DYNAMITE** **11** | —
(d12"+=) *(QTA 6963)* – The bottom line (US remix) / B.A.D.

May 86. (7") *(A 7181)* **MEDICINE SHOW. / A PARTY** **29** | —
(12") *(TA 7181)* – ('A'extended) / ('B'dub).
(d12"+=) *(DTA 7181)* – E=MC2 (remix) / Albert Einstein meets the human beatbox.

Oct 86. (7") *(650147-7)* **C'MON EVERY BEATBOX. / BEDROCK CITY** **51** | —
(12"+=) *(650147-8)* – Beatbox's at dawn.
(with free one-sided-12"++=) *(XPR 1320)* – The bottom line (Rick Rubin remix).

Oct 86. (lp/c/cd) *(450137-1/-4/-2)* <40445> **No.10 UPPING STREET** **11** | —

– C'mon every beatbox / Beyond the pale / Limbo the law / Sambadrome / V thirteen / Ticket / Hollywood boulevard / Dial a hitman / Sightsee M.C! *(c+=/cd+=)* – Ice cool killer (dial a hitman-instrumental) / The big V (V thirteen – instrumental). *(re-iss. Oct89 lp/c; 463398-1/-4)*

Feb 87. (7") *(BAD 2)* **V THIRTEEN. / HOLLYWOOD BOULEVARD** `49`
(12"+=) *(BADT 2)* – ('B'club).

Jul 87. (12"m) *(BAADT 3)* **SIGHTSEE MC! (radio cut) / ANOTHER ONE RIDES THE BUS / SIGHTSEE MC! / SIGHTSEE – WEST LONDON** `-`

May 88. (7"/ext-12") *(BAAD/+T 4)* **JUST PLAY MUSIC. / MUCH WORSE** `51`
(12"+=/cd-s++) *(BAADQTA/CDBAAD 4)* – ('A'remix).

Jun 88. (lp/c/cd) *(461199-1/-4/-2) <44074>* **TIGHTEN UP VOL.'88** `33`
– Rock non stop (all night long) / Other 99 / Funny names / Applecart / Esquerita / Champagne / Mr. Walker said / The battle of All Saints Road, incorporating:- Battle of New Orleans – Duelling banjos / Hip neck and thigh / 2000 shoes / Tighten up vol.88 / Just play music. *(re-iss. Oct94 on 'Columbia' cd/c; 461199-2/-4)*

Jul 88. (7"/7"box) *(BAAD/+B 5)* **OTHER 99. / WHAT HAPPENED TO EDDIE?** `-`
(12"/cd-s) *(BAADT/CDBAAD 5)* – ('A'extended) / Just play music (club mix).

Sep 89. (lp/c/cd) *(465790-1/-4/-2) <45212>* **MEGATOP PHOENIX** `26` `85`
– Start / Rewind / All mink and no manners / Union, Jack / Contact / Dragon town / Baby don't apologise / Is yours working yet? / Around the girls in 80 ways / James Brown / Everybody needs a holiday / Mick's a hippie burning / House arrest / The green lady / London Bridge / Stalag 123 / End.

Oct 89. (7") *(BAAD 6)* **CONTACT. / IN FULL EFFECT**
(12"+=/cd-s+=) *(BAADT/CDBAAD 6)* – Who beats / If I were John Carpenter.

BIG AUDIO DYNAMITE II

—— were formed by **JONES + DONOVAN** (latter left mid'90) **NICK HAWKINS** (b. 3 Feb'65, Luton, England) – guitar / **GARY STONAGE** (b.24 Nov'62, Southampton, England) – bass / **CHRIS KAVANAGH** (b. 4 Jun'64, Woolwich, England) – drums (ex-SIGUE SIGUE SPUTNIK) all repl. others who formed SCREAMING TARGET in 1991

Oct 90. (cd/c/lp) *(467466-2/-4/-1)* **KOOL-AID** `55`
– Change of atmosphere / Can't wait / Kickin' in / Innocent child / On one / Kool-aid / In my dreams / When the time comes.

—— added **DJ ZONKA** (b. MICHAEL CUSTANCE, 4 Jul'62) – DJ

Columbia   Columbia

Jul 91. (cd/c/lp) *(467706-2/-4/-1) <46147>* **THE GLOBE** `63` `72`
– Rush / Can't wait (live) / I don't know / The globe / Innocent child / Green grass / Kool-aid / In my dreams / When the time comes / The tea party.

Jul 91. (7") *(657588-7) <74149>* **THE GLOBE (remix). / CITY LIGHTS** `76` Jan92
('A'-Danny Rampling remix-12"+=) *(657588-6)* – ('A'dub mix) / ('A'instrumental) / ('A'-Orb ambient mix).
(cd-s+=) *(657588-2)* – ('A'-Danny Rampling dub).

Nov 91. (7"/c-s) *(657640-7/-4) <73987>* **RUSH. / (A3 version)** `32` Sep91
(cd-s+=) *(657640-2)* – City lights (full version).
(12") *(657640-6)* – ('A'side) / ('A'-3 other mixes).
(above A-side was issued Feb'91 on other side of the CLASH single, 'Should I Stay Or Should I Go')

BIG AUDIO

—— added **ANDRE SHAPPS** – keyboards

Nov 94. (c-s) *(661018-4)* **LOOKING FOR A SONG / MODERN STONEAGE BLUES** `68`
(12"+=/cd-s+=) *(661018-6/-2)* – ('A'-Zonka-Shapps early mix) / ('A'-Zonka-Shapps remix).
(cd-s) *(661018-5)* – ('A'extended) / ('A'-Zonka-Shapps Adventures In Space mix) / Medicine show (live) / Rush (live).

Nov 94. (cd/c/d-lp) *(477239-2/-4/-1)* **HIGHER POWER**
– Got to wake up / Harrow Road / Looking for a song / Some people / Slender Loris / Modern stoneage blues / Melancholy maybe / Over the rise / Why is it? / Moon / Lucan / Light up my life / Hope.

BIG AUDIO DYNAMITE

Radioactive   Radioactive

Jun 95. (c-s) *(RAXC 15)* **I TURNED OUT A PUNK / WHAT ABOUT LOVE**
(cd-s+=) *(RAXTD 15)* – ('A'-Live fast, live fast mix).
(12") *(RAXT 15)* – ('A'side) / (A'-Live fast mix) / ('A'-Live fast instrumental) / ('A'-Feelin' lucky mix).

Jun 95. (cd/c) *(RAD/RAC 11280)* **F-PUNK**
– I turned out a punk / Vitamin C / Psycho wing / Push those blues away / Gonna try / It's a jungle out there / Got to set her free / Get it all from my TV / Singapore / I can't go on like this / What about love?

– compilations, etc. –

Nov 88. (d-cd) *C.B.S.; (CDBAD 241)* **THIS IS BIG AUDIO DYNAMITE / No.10 UPPING STREET** `-`

Sep 95. (cd/c) *Columbia; (481133-2/-4)* **PLANET B.A.D.** `-`
– The bottom line / E=MC2 / Medicine show / C'mon every beatbox / V thirteen / Sightsee MC! / Just play music / Other 99 / Contact / Free / Rush / The globe / Looking for a song / Harrow road (ska mix) / I turned out a punk.

BIG BLACK

Formed: Evanston, Illinois, USA ... 1982 by mainman STEVE ALBINI (vocals/guitar). The first official release, 'LUNGS' appeared later that year on local independent label, 'Ruthless', a six-track drum-machine driven EP that announced ALBINI's intent to take punk/hardcore into uncharted territory.

Now with an expanded line-up numbering SANTIAGO DURANGO on guitar and JEFF PEZZATI on bass, the BIG BLACK trio unleashed two more 12"ep's/mini-lp's in the mid 80's, 'BULLDOZER' (1983) and 'RACER X' (1985), prior to the seminal 'IL DUCE' single in '86. Replacing PEZZATI with DAVE RILEY (aka LOVERING), they created a minor hardcore classic in 'ATOMIZER' (1986), its bleak examinations of small-town American despair a theme which would be echoed countless times by their grunge/industrial successors. With DURANGO off to study law, MERVIN BELLI came in for the inflammatorily-titled, 'SONGS ABOUT *!?KING', BIG BLACK giving their all on an album which they knew would be their last. However, they did bow out in uncharacteristic style with a double A-sided 45 covering Cheap Trick's 'HE'S A WHORE' and Kraftwerk's 'THE MODEL'. Taking his twisted vision to its warped conclusion, ALBINI formed the controversially named RAPEMAN with two former SCRATCH ACID players, DAVID WM. SIMS and REY WASHAM. It wasn't just the name that provoked outrage, tracks such as 'HATED CHINEE', 'SUPERPUSSY' and 'KIM GORDON'S PANTIES' causing a fuss which possibly contributed to ALBINI abandoning the operation early in '89. Having already turned in classic productions for the likes of The PIXIES ('Surfer Rosa'), ALBINI, along with BUTCH VIG became one of the highest profile and most respected/hard working figures of the grunge era (credits include NIRVANA, TAD, PJ HARVEY, etc). ALBINI also sorted out another side project, SHELLAC, who released two spaced-out, metallic albums, 'AT ACTION PARK' (1994) and 'TERRAFORM' (1998).
• **Songwriters:** ALBINI and group compositions except; HEARTBEAT (Wire) / REMA REMA (Rema Rema) / Rapeman: JUST GOT PAID (ZZ Top).

Album rating: ATOMIZER (*7) / SONGS ABOUT *!?KING (*8) / PIGPILE live compilation (*7) / Shellac: AT ACTION PARK (*6) / TERRAFORM (*7)

STEVE ALBINI – vocals, guitar

not iss.   Ruthless

1982. (c) *<none>* **BIG BLACK LIVE (live)** `-`
(UK-iss.Oct89 on 'Blast First' lp/c/cd; BFFP 49/+C/CD)

Nov 82. (12"ep) *<RRBB 02>* **LUNGS** `-`
– Steelworker / Live in a hole / Dead Billy / I can be killed / Crack / R.I.P.
(UK-iss.Nov92 on 'Touch & Go'; TG 89)

—— added **SANTIAGO DURANGO** – guitar (ex-NAKED RAYGUN, ex-SILVER ABUSE) / **JEFF PEZZATI** – bass (ex-NAKED RAYGUN) / + on session 4th member **PAT BYRNE** – drums

Nov 83. (12"ep) *<RRBB 07>* **BULLDOZER** `-`
– Cables / Pigeon kill / I'm a mess / Texas / Seth / Jump the climb. (UK-iss.Nov92 on 'Touch & Go'; TG 90)

Homestead   Homestead

Apr 85. (m-lp) *<HMS 007>* **RACER-X** `1984`
– Racer-x / Shotgun / The ugly American / Deep six / Sleep! / Big payback. (re-iss. Nov92 on 'Touch & Go'; TG 91)

Sep 86. (7") *(HMS 042)* **IL DUCE. / BIG MONEY** `1985`
(re-iss. Nov92 on 'Touch & Go'; TG 96)

—— **DAVE RILEY** (aka LOVERING) – bass (ex-SAVAGE BELIEFS) repl. PEZZATI / drum machine replaced BYRNE

Sep 86. (lp) *<(HMS 43)>* **ATOMIZER**
– Jordan, Minnesota / Passing complexion / Big money / Kerosene / Bad houses / Kerosene / Fists of love / Stinking drunk / Bazooka Joe / Strange things. (re-iss. Nov86 on 'Blast First'; BFFP 11) (re-iss. Nov92 on 'Touch & Go' lp/cd; TG 93/+CD)

Blast First   Touch&Go

Jun 87. (12"ep/c-ep) *(BFFP 14/+C) <TG 20>* **HEADACHE** `1986`
– My disco / Grinder / Ready men / Pete, king of all detectives.
(free 7"w.a./tracks on c-ep) *(TG 21)* – **HEARTBEAT. / THINGS TO DO TODAY / I CAN'T BELIEVE** (UK re-iss. Nov92 on 'Touch & Go'; TG 20)

—— **MELVYN BELLI** – guitar; repl. DURANGO

Jul 87. (lp/c/cd) *(BFFP 19/+C/CD) <TG 24/+C/CD>* **SONGS ABOUT *!?KING**
– The power of independent trucking / The model / Bad penny / El doper / Precious thing / Columbian neck-tie / Kitty empire / Ergot / Kashmir S. Pulasiday / Fish fry / Pavement saw / Tiny, the king of the Jews / Bombastic intro. (re-iss. Nov90 on 'Touch & Go' lp/cd +=; TG 24/+CD) – He's A Whore.

Aug 87. (7") *(BFFP 24) <TG 23>* **HE'S A WHORE. / THE MODEL**
(re-iss. Nov92 on 'Touch & Go'; TG 23)

—— Disbanded in 1988.

– compilations, etc. –

Mar 87. (lp) *Homestead; (HMS 044)* **THE HAMMER PARTY** `-`
– (LUNGS + BULLDOZER) (re-iss. Nov92 on 'Touch & Go' lp/cd +=; TG 92/+CD) – RACER-X

Jun 87. (lp) *Not 2; (BUT 1)* **SOUND OF IMPACT (live bootleg)** `-`
(re-iss. 1990)

Jan 88. (cd) *Blast First; (BFFP 23)* **RICH MAN'S EIGHT TRACK TAPE** `-`
– (ATOMIZER + HEADACHE + HEARTBEAT) (re-iss. Nov92 on 'Touch & Go'; TG 94CD)

Oct 92. (lp/cd) *Touch & Go; <(TG 81/+CD)>* **PIGPILE (live)**

RAPEMAN

—— were formed by **ALBINI** with **DAVID WM. SIMS** – bass / **REY WASHAM** – drums (both ex-SCRATCH ACID, latter ex-BIG BOYS)

not iss.   Fierce

1988. (7") *<none>* **HATED CHINEE. / MARMOSET** `-`
Blast First   Touch & Go

Nov 88. (12"ep) *(BFFP 27) <TG 34>* **BUDD (live) / SUPERPUSSY (live). / LOG BASS (live) / DUTCH COURAGE**

Dec 88. (lp/c/cd) *(BFFP 33/+C/CD) <TG 36/+C/CD>* **TWO NUNS AND BLACK MULE**

– Steak and black onions / Monobrow / Up beat / Cotition ignition mission / Kim Gordon's panties / Hated Chinee / Radar love wizard / Marmoset / Just got paid / Trouser minnow. *(cd+=)* – Budd / Superpussy / Log brass / Dutch courage.

Aug 89. (7",7"clear) <*(SP 40)*> **INKI'S BUTT CRACK. / SONG NUMBER ONE**   [Sub Pop] [Sub Pop]

—— Had to split in Feb'89 due to the backlash against group name. SIMS returned to Austin, where he re-united with ex-SCRATCH ACID members to form JESUS LIZARD. They were produced by ALBINI who continued as a producer, notably for others The PIXIES, The BREEDERS, NIRVANA, WEDDING PRESENT. ALBINI formed below in '93.

SHELLAC

STEVE ALBINI – guitar, vocals / **BOB WESTON** – bass (ex-VOLCANO SONS) / **TODD TRAINER** – drums (ex-RIFLE SPORT, etc)

       Touch & Go / Touch & Go

1994. (7") **URANUS. /**
1994. (7") **THE ADMIRAL. /**
Sep 94. (7") <*TG 123*> **THE RUDE GESTURE: A PICTORIAL HISTORY. /**
Oct 94. (lp/c/cd) <*TG 141/+C/CD*> **AT ACTION PARK**
– My black ass / Pull the cup / Admiral / Crow / Song of the minerals / Minute / Idea of north / Dog and pony show / Boche's dick / Il porno star.
Feb 98. (lp/cd) <*TG 200/+CD*> **TERRAFORM**
– Didn't we deserve a look at you the way you really are / This is a picture / Disgrace / Mothpiece / Canada / Rush job / House full of garbage / Copper.

BIG BROTHER & THE HOLDING CO.

Formed: San Francisco, California, USA ... late '65 by SAM ANDREW, PETER ALBIN, DAVE ESKERSON and CHUCK JONES. Shortly after, the latter two were replaced by JAMES GURLEY and DAVID GETZ respectively. Through promoter CHET HELMS, they enlisted Texan JANIS JOPLIN, who had just turned down an opportunity to join The 13th FLOOR ELEVATORS. Signing to 'Mainstream' records in 1967, they turned in an excellent Monterey festival performance just prior to releasing their eponymous debut album. However, their blistering set caught the attention of 'Columbia', who subsequently released the 'CHEAP THRILLS' album, which hit No.1 in the States for 7 weeks in the fall of '68. This roughshod and at times ramshackle affair nevertheless captured the tremendous vocal talent of JOPLIN on soul-wrenching numbers such as 'PIECE OF MY HEART' (a Top 20 hit) and 'BALL AND CHAIN' (blues rock for acid heads). Her star rating outstripped her backing band at a rate of knots, and it was inevitable that she would take off for a solo career (see own entry). This all but killed any further success for BIG BROTHER, although they continued, releasing two further lacklustre albums in the early 70's. In 1987 however, GETZ, ANDREW, GURLEY and ALBIN recruited new singer MICHELLE BASTIAN for a series of low-key gigs. • **Note:** Nothing whatsoever to do with 80's outfit BIG BROTHER, who released 12" 'Adventures In Success'.

Album rating: BIG BROTHER AND THE HOLDING CO. (*5) / CHEAP THRILLS (*8) / BE A BROTHER (*3) / HOW HARD IT IS (*3) / CHEAPER THRILLS posthumous live (*4)

SAM ANDREW (b.18 Dec'41, Taft, California) – guitar, vocals / **PETE ALBIN** (b. 6 Jun'44) – bass, vocals / **JAMES GURLEY** (b.22 Dec'39, Detroit, Mich.) – guitar repl. DAVE ESKERSON (left Nov65) / **DAVID GETZ** (b.24 Jan'40, Brooklyn, N.Y.) – drums repl. CHUCK JONES (left Feb66) also on occasion / **ED BOGAS** – violin (left before Summer'66, to NEW RIDERS OF THE PURPLE SAGE)

—— (Jun'66) added **JANIS JOPLIN** (b.19 Jan'43, Port Arthur, Texas) – vocals

       Fontana / Mainstream

Jul 67. (7") <*657*> **BLIND MAN. / ALL IS LONELINESS**
Sep 67. (7") <*662*> **DOWN ON ME. / CALL ON ME**
<*hit US No.43 in Aug'68*> (*UK-iss.Sep68 on 'London'; HLT 10226*)
Nov 67. (lp; stereo/mono) (S+/TL 5457) <*6099*> **BIG BROTHER & THE HOLDING COMPANY**   [60] Aug67
– Bye bye baby / Easy rider / Intruder / Light is faster than sound / Call on me / Women is losers / Blind man / Down on me / Caterpillar / All is loneliness. *(re-iss. 1969 on 'London' mono/stereo; HA-T/SH-T 8377)* <*US re-iss. May71 on 'Columbia'; 30631*> – Coo Coo / The last mile. *(cd-iss.Apr93 as 'FIRST ALBUM' on 'Sony Europe';)*
Nov 67. (7") <*666*> **BYE BYE BABY. / INTRUDER**
Dec 67. (7") (TF 881) **BYE BYE BABY. / ALL IS LONELINESS**
Feb 68. (7") <*675*> **WOMEN IS LOSERS. / LIGHT IS FASTER THAN SOUND**

       C.B.S. / Columbia

Aug 68. (7") (CBS 3683) <*44626*> **PIECE OF MY HEART. / TURTLE BLUES**   [12]
Sep 68. (lp) (CBS 63392) <*PC 9700*> **CHEAP THRILLS**   [1] Aug68
– Combination of the two / I need a man to love / Summertime / Piece of my heart / Turtle blues / O sweet Mary / Ball and chain. <*US re-iss. Mar81;*> *(cd-iss. Jan91 & Jun92 on 'Columbia'; CD 32004)*

—— Folded late 1968. JANIS JOPLIN went solo, taking SAM ANDREW. In Aug69 GETZ and ALBIN re-formed BIG BROTHER & THE HOLDING COMPANY with **NICK GRAVENITES** – vocals / **MIKE PRENDERGAST** – guitar / **TED ASHBURTON** – piano

—— soon split again, GETZ was also in NU BUGALOO EXPRESS.

—— **GETZ, GURLEY, ALBIN, SAM ANDREW + NICK GRAVENITES** – vocals re-grouped

BIG BROTHER & THE HOLDING COMPANY with **KATHI McDONALD** – vocals / **MIKE FINNEGAN** – keyboards / **DAVID SCHALLOCK** – guitar (both ex-NU BUGALOO EXPRESS)

Jan 71. (lp) (CBS 64118) <*PC 30222*> **BE A BROTHER**   Nov70
– Keep on / Joseph's coat / Home on the strange / Someday / Heartache people / Sunshine baby / Mr. Natural / Funkie Jim / I'll change your flat tire Merle / Be a brother.
Jan 71. (7") <*45284*> **KEEP ON. / HOME ON THE STRANGE**
Aug 71. (lp) <*KC 30738*> **HOW HARD IT IS**
– How hard it is / You've been talkin' 'bout me, baby / House on fire / Black widow spider / Last band on side one / Nu Boogaloo jam / Maui / Shine on / Buried alive in the blues / Promise her anything but give her Arpeggio.
Sep 71. (7") <*45502*> **NU BOOGALOO JAM. / BLACK WIDOW SPIDER**

—— Split Feb'72. ALBIN rejoined COUNTRY JOE (McDonald) & THE FISH. He and GETZ were part of them in 1969. FINNEGAN played live with STEPHEN STILLS etc. GRAVENITES tried to revitalise ELECTRIC FLAG.

– compilations, etc. –

Nov 68. (7") *Mainstream*; <*678*> **COO COO. / THE LAST MILE**   [84]
Jan 84. (lp) *Edsel*; (ED 135) **CHEAPER THRILLS** (live 26th July '66) *(cd-iss. Sep90; EDCD 135)*
Apr 86. (lp) *Edsel*; (ED 170) **JOSEPH'S COAT** (best of 71's two albums)

BIG COUNTRY

Formed: Dunfermline, Scotland ... Autumn 1981 by STUART ADAMSON and BRUCE WATSON, following the former's departure from The SKIDS. They recruited brothers PETER (keyboards) and ALAN WISHART (bass) plus CLIVE PARKER (drums, ex-SPIZZ ...) although by early 1982, the latter three had been replaced by the lynchpin rhythm section of MARK BRZEZICKI and TONY BUTLER. After they turned down a contract with 'Ensign', the band signed to 'Mercury-Phonogram' in Spring '82, soon moving to London where they began work on a debut set, 'THE CROSSING' (1983). Previewed by the classic singles, 'FIELDS OF FIRE' & 'IN A BIG COUNTRY', the album traversed the charts in both Britain and America, introducing the famous (and, in certain quarters, much maligned) 'bagpipe' twin-guitar sound. Very much in the Celtic, stir-the-blood tradition, 'THE CROSSING' was a call to arms in a posturing, terminally pretentious early 80's music scene, its expansive, soaring sound transporting even the most smog-bound city dweller to the Scottish highlands. ADAMSON somehow managed to sing from the heart without sounding earnest, the chiming lament, 'CHANCE', displaying the raw emotive power this band once harnessed. Despite their straightforward approach, BIG COUNTRY were initially lauded by the press, even making something of a fashion statement with their trademark check shirts. With follow-up set, 'STEELTOWN' (1984), ADAMSON's voice of conscience examined Scottish industrial and economic decay; despite the subject matter, tracks such as the rousing 'FLAME OF THE WEST' burned with hope and optimism. Though the record entered the British chart at No.1, its less immediate appeal failed to translate into further Stateside success. This is where BIG COUNTRY began to lose their vision; although subsequent releases like 'THE SEER' (1986) and 'PEACE IN OUR TIME' (1988) continued to chart high and feature some inspired moments, creatively the band were merely treading water. The fact that the track 'ONE GREAT THING' was used on a Tennent's lager advert only seemed to underline its more pedestrian qualities. Despite periods where the band came perilously close to splitting, BIG COUNTRY survived into the 90's, their albums never breaking the mould but eagerly received by the band's fiercely partisan fans. ADAMSON has always addressed social/political issues in a challenging and often sympathetic fashion, the band releasing a 1995 EP, 'NON!', in protest at France's nuclear testing programme. Currently signed to 'Transatlantic', however, the poor commercial showing of the band's last two albums, 'WHY THE LONG FACE?' (1995) and 'ECLECTIC' (1996), suggests that their appeal may finally be waning. • **Songwriters:** Mostly ADAMSON / WATSON, except TRACKS OF MY TEARS (Smokey Robinson & The Miracles) / HONKY TONK WOMAN + RUBY TUESDAY (Rolling Stones) / AULD LANG SYNE (trad.) / ROCKIN' IN THE FREE WORLD (Neil Young) / FLY LIKE AN EAGLE (Steve Miller) / BLACK SKINNED BLUE EYED BOYS (Equals / Eddy Grant) / OH WELL (Fleetwood Mac) / (DON'T FEAR) THE REAPER (Blue Oyster Cult) / WOODSTOCK + BIG YELLOW TAXI (Joni Mitchell) / CRACKED ACTOR (David Bowie) / PARANOID (Black Sabbath) / SUMMERTIME (Gershwin / Du Bose Heyward) / ELEANOR RIGBY (Beatles) / SLING IT (Steve Harley) / I'M ON FIRE (Bruce Springsteen).

Album rating: THE CROSSING (*8) / STEELTOWN (*7) / THE SEER (*6) / PEACE IN OUR TIME (*4) / NO PLACE LIKE HOME (*5) / THE BUFFALO SKINNERS (*4) / WHY THE LONG FACE? (*4) / THROUGH A BIG COUNTRY – GREATEST HITS compilation (*8) / ECLECTIC (*4) / DRIVING TO DAMASCUS (*4)

STUART ADAMSON (b.11 Apr'58, Manchester, England) – vocals, lead guitar, synthesizer (ex-SKIDS) / **BRUCE WATSON** (b.11 Mar'61, Timmins, Ontario, Canada) – guitar (ex-DELINX) / **TONY BUTLER** (b. 3 Feb'57, London, England) – bass (ex-ON THE AIR) / **MARK BRZEZICKI** (b.21 Jun'57, Slough, England) – drums (ex-ON THE AIR)

       Mercury / Mercury

Sep 82. (7") (COUNT 1) **HARVEST HOME. / BALCONY**
(12"+=)(12"clear+=) (COUNT 12)(COUNX 1) – Flag of nations (swimming).
Feb 83. (7") (COUNT 2) <*811450*> **FIELDS OF FIRE. / ANGLE PARK**   [10] [52] Jan84
(12"+=/12"clear+=) (COUN T/X 2-12) – ('A'-alternative mix).

(7"sha-pic-d+=) (COUP 2) – Harvest home.

May 83. (7") (COUNT 3) <814467> **IN A BIG COUNTRY. / ALL OF US** | 17 | 17 Sep83
(12"+=) (COUNT 3-12) – ('A'-pure mix).
(12"++=) (COUNT 313) – Heart and soul.

Jun 83. (lp/c) (MERH/+C 27) <812870> **THE CROSSING** | 3 | 18 Jul83
– In a big country / Inwards / Chance / 1,000 stars / The storm / Harvest home / Lost patrol / Close action / Fields of fire / Porrohman. (c+=) – (4 remixes).
(re-dist.Mar84 lp/c; MERS/+C 27) (cd-iss. 1986; 812 870-2)

Aug 83. (7") (COUNT 4) **CHANCE. / TRACKS OF MY TEARS** (live) | 9 |
(ext.12"pic-d+=) (COUNT 4-12) – The crossing.

Jan 84. (7") (COUNT 5) <818834> **WONDERLAND. / GIANT** | 8 | 86
(12"+=) (COUNT 5-12) – ('A'extended).
(12"clear+=) (COUNX 5) – Lost patrol (live).
(d7"+=) (COUNT 5-5) – Lost patrol (live – parts one & two).

Apr 84. (m-lp) <818835> **WONDERLAND** | - | 65
– Wonderland / Angle park / The crossing / All fall together.

Sep 84. (7"/7"w-poster) (MER/+P 175) **EAST OF EDEN. / PRAIRIE ROSE.** | 17 |
(12"+=/12"w-poster+=) (MERX/+P 175) – ('A'extended).

Oct 84. (lp/c) (MERH/+C 49) <822831> **STEELTOWN** | 1 | 70
– Flame of the west / East of Eden / Steeltown / Where the rose is sown / Come back to me / Tall ships go / Girl with grey eyes / Rain dance / The great divide / Just a shadow. (cd-iss. 1986; 822 831-2) (re-iss. May93 on 'Spectrum' cd/c;)

Nov 84. (7") (MER 185) **WHERE THE ROSE IS SOWN. / BELIEF IN THE SMALL MAN** | 29 |
(12"+=) (MERX 185) – ('A'extended remix) / Bass dance.
(d7"+=) (MERD 185) – Wonderland (live) / In a big country (live) / Auld Lang Syne (live).

Jan 85. (7") (BCO 8) **JUST A SHADOW. / WINTER SKY** | 26 |
(12"+=) (BCO 8-12) – ('A'extended remix).

Apr 86. (7"/7"sha-pic-d) (BIGC/+P 1) **LOOK AWAY. / RESTLESS NATIVES** | 7 |
(d7"+=) (BIGCD 1) – Margo's theme / Highland scenery.
(ext.12"+=) (BIGCX 1-1) – ('A'-Outlaw mix).
(12") (BIG CX 1) – ('A'extended) / Restless natives (soundtrack part one).

Jun 86. (7") (BIGC 2) **THE TEACHER. / HOME CAME THE ANGELS** | 28 |
(12") (BIGCX 2) – ('A'-Mystery mix) / Restless natives (soundtrack part two).

Jul 86. (lp/c/cd) (MERH/+C 87)(826 844-2) <826 844> **THE SEER** | 2 | 59
– Look away / The seer / The teacher / I walk the hill / Eiledon / One great thing / Hold the heart / Remembrance day / The red fox / The sailor. (re-iss. cd Aug94 on 'Vertigo';)

Sep 86. (7"/s7")('A'-Boston mix-12") (BIGC/+G 3)(BIGCX 3-3) **ONE GREAT THING. / SONG OF THE SOUTH** | 19 |
(d7"+=) (BIGCD 3) – Porrohman (live) / Chance (live).
(d7"+=) (BIGCE 3) – Wonderland (live) / Inwards (live).
('A'-Big Baad Country mix.c-s+=) (BIGCM 3) – In a big country (pure mix) / Fields of fire (live).
('A'-Big Baad Country mix.12"+=) (BIGCR 3) – Look away (outlaw mix).

Nov 86. (7"/remix-12") (BIGC/+X 4) **HOLD THE HEART. / HONKY TONK WOMAN** (live) | 55 |
(d12"+=) (BIGCX 4-4) – (interview parts one & two).

—— added on tour **JOSS PHILIP-GORSE** – keyboards

| | Mercury | Reprise |
Aug 88. (7") (BIGC 5) **KING OF EMOTION. / THE TRAVELLERS** | 16 |
(12"+=) (BIGC 5-12) – Starred and Crossed.
(cd-s++=) (BIGCD 5) – Not waving but drowning.
(c-s+=) (BIGMC 5) – Starred and crossed / On the shore.

Sep 88. (7") (BIGC 5) **KING OF EMOTION. / IN A BIG COUNTRY** | - |

Sep 88. (lp/c)(cd) (MERH/+C 130)(836 325-2) <25787> **PEACE IN OUR TIME** | 9 |
– King of emotion / Broken heart (thirteen valleys) / Thousand yard stare / From here to eternity / Everything I need / Peace in our time / Time for leaving / River of hope / In this place / I could be happy here. (cd+=) – The travellers.

Oct 88. (7") (BIGC 6) **BROKEN HEART (THIRTEEN VALLEYS). / SOAPY SOUTAR STRIKES BACK** | 47 |
(12"+=/12"red+=) (BIGC/+R 6-12) – When a drum beats / On the shore.
(cd-s+=) (BIGCD 6) – Wonderland (12"mix).
(cd-s+=) (BIGCDR 6) – Made in Heaven / When a drum beats.

Jan 89. (7"/s7") (BIGC/+P 7) **PEACE IN OUR TIME. / PROMISED LAND** | 39 |
(12"+=) (BIGC 7-12) – Over the border / The longest day.
(12"+=) (BIGCR 7-12) – In a big country (live) / Chance (live).
(cd-s+=) (BIGCD 7) – Chance / The longest day.

—— (Feb'90) **PAT AHERN** – drums (ex-DAVE HOWARD SINGERS) repl. BRZEZICKI who joined PRETENDERS

Apr 90. (7"/c-s) (BIG C/MC 8) **SAVE ME. / PASS ME BY** | 41 |
(12"+=) (BIGC 8-12) – Dead on arrival.
(cd-s+=) (BIGCD 8) – World on fire.
(cd-s+=) (BIGCD 8-12) – Wonderland (live) / Thousand yard stare (live).

May 90. (cd/c/lp) (846 022-2/-4/-1) **THROUGH A BIG COUNTRY – GREATEST HITS** (compilation) | 2 |
– Save me / In a big country / Fields of fire / Chance / Wonderland / Where the rose is sown / Just a shadow / Look away / King of emotion / East of Eden / One great thing / The teacher / Broken heart (thirteen valleys) / Peace in our time. (c+=/cd+=) – Eiledon / The seer / Harvest home. (re-iss. Feb90 cd/c;)

Jul 90. (7"/c-s) (BIG C/MC 9) **HEART OF THE WORLD. / BLACK SKINNED BLUE EYED BOYS** | 50 |
(12"+=) (BIGC 9-12) – Broken heart (thirteen valleys) (acoustic) / Peace in our time (acoustic).
(cd-s+=) (BIGCD 9) – Restless Natives.

| | Vertigo | not iss. |
Aug 91. (7") (BIC 1) **REPUBLICAN PARTY REPTILE / COMES A TIME / YOU, ME AND THE TRUTH** | 37 | - |
(10"ep+=/12"ep+=) (BIC T/X 1) – Comes a time.
(cd-ep) (BIGCD 1) – ('A'side) / Freedom song / Kiss the girl goodbye / I'm only waiting.

Sep 91. (cd/c/lp) (510230-2/-4/-1) **NO PLACE LIKE HOME** | 28 | - |

– We're not in Kansas / Republican party reptile / Dynamic lady / Keep on dreaming / Beautiful people / The hostage speaks / Beat the Devil / Heap of faith / Ships / Into the fire. (cd+=) – You, me and the truth / Comes a time. (re-iss. Aug94; same)

Oct 91. (7"/c-s) (BIC/+C 2) **BEAUTIFUL PEOPLE. / RETURN OF THE TWO HEADED KING** | 72 | - |
(12"pic-d+=) (BICX 2) – Fly like an eagle.
(cd-s+=) (BICCD 2) – Rockin' in the free world (live).

—— **ADAMSON, BUTLER + WATSON** were joined by session men **SIMON PHILLIPS** – drums / **COLIN BERWICK** – keyboards

| | Compulsion Fox-RCA |
Mar 93. (c-s/7") (TC+/PULSS 4) **ALONE. / NEVER TAKE YOUR PLACE** | 24 | |
(12"pic-d+=) (12PULSS 4) – Winter sky / Look away.
(cd-s) (CDPULSS 4) – ('A'side) / Chance / Rockin' in the free world / Eastworld.

Mar 93. (cd/c/lp) (CD/TC+/NOIS 2) **THE BUFFALO SKINNERS** | 25 |
– Alone / Seven waves / What are you working for / The one I love / Long way home / The selling of America / We're not in Kansas / Ships / All go together / Winding wind / Pink marshmallow moon / Chester's farm. (re-iss. Sep94; same)

Apr 93. (c-s/7") (TC+/PULSS 6) **SHIPS (WHERE WERE YOU). / OH WELL** | 29 |
(12"+=/cd-s+=) (12/CD PULSS 6) – (Don't fear) The reaper / Woodstock.
(cd-s+=) (CDXPULSS 6) – The buffalo skinners / Cracked actor / Paranoid.

Jun 94. (cd/c/lp) (CD/TC+/NOIS 5) **WITHOUT THE AID OF A SAFETY NET** (live) | 35 |
– Harvest home / Peace in our time / Just a shadow / Broken heart (thirteen valleys) / The storm / Chance / Look away / Steeltown / Ships / Wonderland / What are you working for / Long way home / In a big country / Lost patrol.

| | Transatla. | not iss. |
May 95. (c-ep/cd-ep) (TRAM/TRAX 1009) **I'M NOT ASHAMED / ONE IN A MILLION (1st visit) / MONDAY TUESDAY GIRL / ('A'edit)** | 69 | - |
(cd-ep) (TRAX 1010) – ('A'side) / Crazytimes / In a big country / Blue on a green planet.

Jun 95. (cd/c) (TRA CD/MC/LP 109) **WHY THE LONG FACE?** | 48 |
– You dreamer / Message of love / I'm not ashamed / ail into nothing / Thunder & lightning / Send you / One in a million / God's great mistake / Wild land in my heart / Thank you to the Moon / Far from me to you / Charlotte / Post nuclear talking blues / Blue on a green planet.

Aug 95. (12"ep/cd-ep) (TRAT/TRAD 1012) **YOU DREAMER. / ICE CREAM SMILE / MAGIC IN YOUR ICE / BIANCA** | - |
(cd-ep) (TRAX 1012) – ('A'side) / I'm eighteen / Melons / I'm on the road again

Nov 95. (cd-ep) (TRAD) **NON!** | - |
– Post nuclear talking blues / Blue on a green planet / God's great mistake / All go together.
above was an action awareness record for Greenpeace.
below featured guests **BOBBY VALENTINO** – violin / **AARON EMERSON** – keyboards / **HOSSAM RAMZY + MOHAMMED TOUFIQ** – percussion / **CAROL LAULA + STEVE HARLEY + KYM MAZELLE** – vocals

Aug 96. (cd/c) (TRA CD/MC 234) **ECLECTIC** | 41 |
– River of hope / King of emotion / Big yellow taxi / The buffalo skinners / Summertime / The night they drove old Dixie down / Eleanor Rigby / Winter sky / Sling it / I'm on fire / Where the rose is sown / Come back to me / Ruby Tuesday.

| | Track Record | not iss. |
Aug 99. (10"; BIG COUNTRY featuring EDDI READER) (TRACK 0004C) **FRAGILE THING. / I GET HURT / LOSERVILLE** | 69 | - |
(cd-s) (TRACK 0004A) – (first & third tracks) / Dust on the road.
(cd-s) (TRACK 0004B) – (first two tracks) / John Wayne's dream.

Sep 99. (cd/c) (TRK 1000 CD/CAS) **DRIVING TO DAMASCUS** | - |
– Driving to Damascus / Dive in to me / See you / Perfect world / Somebody else / Fragile thing / The president slipped and fell / Devil in the eye / Trouble the waters / Bella / Your spirit to me / Grace. (special cd+=; TRK 1000CDSP) – Shattered cross / Too many ghosts.

Nov 99. (c-s) (TRACK 0005C) **SEE YOU /** | - |
(cd-s) (TRACK 0005A) –
(cd-s) (TRACK 0005B) – ('A'side) / Perfect world / Camp Smedley's theme.

—— **STUART ADAMSON** retired from the music business late in '99

– compilations, etc. –

Aug 94. (cd) *Nighttracks; (CDNT 007)* **RADIO 1 SESSIONS** | | - |
Aug 94. (cd) *Legends In Music; (LECD 043)* **BIG COUNTRY** | | - |
Aug 95. (cd) *Spectrum; (550 879-2)* **IN A BIG COUNTRY** | | - |
Oct 95. (cd) *Windsong; (WINCD 075)* **BBC LIVE IN CONCERT** (live) | | - |

BIG HEAD TODD & THE MONSTERS

Formed: Boulder, Colorado, USA . . . 1986 by songwriter/namesake TODD PARK MOHR, along with ROB SQUIRES and BRIAN NEVIN. Two albums appeared around the turn of the decade, namely 'ANOTHER MAYBERRY' (1989) and 'MIDNIGHT RADIO' (1990), the latter featuring artwork by fan CHRIS MARS (of the REPLACEMENTS). Moving from their own label to 'Warners', TODD and Co delivered their debut for the imprint, 'SISTER SWEETLY' (1993). The latter was subsequently re-issued on RCA/Arista outlet, 'Giant', a label that led them into the US Top 30 with their 1994 follow-up set, 'STRATEGEM'. Progressing further into earthy blues territory, TODD and his MOR monsters released 'BEAUTIFUL WORLD' (1997), a Top 60 success which featured a contribution from JOHN LEE HOOKER on their cover of 'BOOM BOOM'. • Covered: POOR MISS (John Lee Hooker) / TANGERINE (Led Zeppelin).

Album rating: ANOTHER MAYBERRY (*5) / MIDNIGHT RADIO (*6) / SISTER SWEETLY (*7) / STRATEGEM (*4) / BEAUTIFUL WORLD (*6)

TODD PARK MOHR – vocals, guitar, keyboards / **ROB SQUIRES** – vocals, bass / **BRIAN NEVIN** – vocals, drums

		not iss.	Big

1989. (lp) <0001> **ANOTHER MAYBERRY**
– Flander's fields / Another Mayberry / Salvation / I will carry / Blues of Annie / Blue water / Geography of a horse dreamer / It all comes down / American boy / Waiting in America / Hymn. <cd-iss. 1994 on 'Warners'; 24589>

1991. (lp) <0002> **MIDNIGHT RADIO**
– Vincent of Jersey / Leaving song / Dinner with Ivan / Bittersweet / Moose song / Cold blooded / Soul children / Love Betsy / Midnight radio / City on fire / Monument in green / Ann Arbor grandfather / Elvis. <cd-iss. 1994 on 'Warners'; 24590>

		Warners	Warners

Apr 93. (cd) <(7599 24486-2)> **SISTER SWEETLY**   Feb93
– Broken hearted savior / Sister sweetly / Turn the light out / Tomorrow never comes / It's alright / Groove thing / Soul for every cowboy / Ellis Island / Bittersweet / Circle / Brother John. (re-iss. Jun94 on 'Giant-RCA' cd/c; 74321 14799-2/-4)

Feb 94. (cd-s) <18381> **BITTERSWEET / CIRCLE / EVERYDAY PEOPLE**

		Giant	Giant

Oct 94. (cd/c) <(74321 22904-2/-4)> **STRATEGEM**   **30**
– Kensington line / Strategem / Wearing only flowers / Neckbreaker / Magdelina / Angel leads me on / In the morning / Candle 99 / Greyhound / Poor Miss / Shadowlands.

		Revolution	Warners

May 97. (cd) <(74321 44109-2)> **BEAUTIFUL WORLD**   **54** Feb97
– Resignation superman / Caroline / Crazy Mary / Helpless / Please don't tell her / Beautiful world / True lady / Heart of wilderness / If you can't slow down / Boom boom (with JOHN LEE HOOKER) / These days without you.

Nov 98. (cd) <24714> **LIVE MONSTERS** (live)
– Bittersweet / Turn the light out / Broken hearted savior / Resignation Superman / Sister sweetly / Please don't tell here / Tangerine / Circle / Kensington line / It's alright / Poor Miss / Vincent of Jersey / Leaving song / Tower / If you can't slow down / Boom boom.

BIG STAR (see under ⇒ BOX TOPS)

BIKINI KILL (dig out; Great Alt & Indie . . .)

BIOHAZARD (dig out; Great Metal . . .)

BIOSPHERE (dig out; Great Psychedelic . . .)

BIRDLAND (dig out; Great Alt & Indie . . .)

BIRTHDAY PARTY (see under ⇒ CAVE, Nick)

BIS (dig out; Great Alt & Indie . . .)

BJORK

Born: BJORK GUDMUNDSDOTTIR, 21 Oct'65, Reykjavik, Iceland. Growing up in a creative communal family and something of a child prodigy, the strikingly unique BJORK enjoyed her first taste of the music business at the age of 11 when she impressed her teachers with her rendition of TINA CHARLES' No.1 'I LOVE TO LOVE', who in turn convinced a local radio station to play it. This led to her recording a self-titled album with many of Iceland's top musicians. It also included other covers; YOUR KISS IS SWEET (hit; Syreeta) / ALFUR UT UR HOL (FOOL ON THE HILL; Beatles) / CHRISTOPHER ROBIN (Melanie) / ALTA MIRA (Edgar Winter). BJORK graduated to her first band EXODUS, and in 1981 aged 14, she instigated another; TAPPI TIKARRASS, which meant 'Cork The Bitch's Arse'. In the next two years, the X-RAY SPEX-type outfit completed two albums 'BITID FAST I VITID' and 'MIRANDA'. She subsequently worked with KILLING JOKE theorists, JAZ COLEMAN and YOUTH, who had both fled to the frozen north in fear of a supposed impending apocalypse. In the interim, she guested for free-form jazz-rock duo STIFGRIM, who comprised comedian/vocalist KRISTINN JON GUDMUNDSSON and guitarist STEINN SKAPTASON. They went down in the record books as one of over a hundred bands who took part in the longest ever continuous live performances (seven weeks!). She then spent two summer seasons playing synthesizer in a covers band named CACTUS. In 1984, she teamed up with friends EINAR ORN BENEDIKTSSON (he of the legendary, erm, rapping 'talent') and SIGTRYGGUR 'SIGGI' BALDERSSON to form KUKL ('Sorcery'), this FALL/BANSHEES influenced lot finding their way into Britain's earlobes (via the 'Crass' label) with two albums 'THE EYE' and 'HOLIDAYS IN EUROPE'. During this mid 80's period, she was also part of ROKHA ROKHA DRUM (as a drummer! and voice). They included lead vocalist JOHNNY TRIUMPH (b. SJON), who collaborated with BJORK's most famous and productive outfit The SUGARCUBES. Hooking up with BRAGI OLAFSSON, THOR ELDON (the father of BJORK's son, Sindri) and EINAR MELLAX, BJORK and Co. formed Iceland's first (and so far only) internationally renowned band. Signed to Derek Birkett's 'One Little Indian', the group had the critics frothing with their debut single, the sublime 'BIRTHDAY'. Like pop music from another planet, the song's reverberating bassline, celestial brass and ethereal production conspired to make this the aural equivalent of a particularly sensual massage. The track also introduced BJORK's inimitable vocals, a perversely melodic combination of wide-eyed child and Icelandic banshee. A further two slices of avant-garde strangeness, 'COLD SWEAT'

and 'DEUS' followed into the UK Top 75 before a debut album, 'LIFE'S TOO GOOD', crashed into the Top 20 in Spring '88. An intoxicating blend of jazz instrumentation, indie stylings and wilful weirdness, the album's success allowed the band to set up their own multi-media enterprise, 'Bad Taste Ltd.' back in Iceland. Though a follow-up, 'HERE TODAY, TOMORROW, NEXT WEEK' (1989) again made the UK Top 20, the critical reception was poor, particular vitriol reserved for EINER's (ORN) jarring vocal exhortations. After extensive touring the band headed back to Iceland to work on various outside jazz-styled projects, BJORK keeping her name in the music press via collaborative work with 808 STATE on their 'Ex:El' album. Then, in late '91, The SUGARCUBES bounced back with the celebratory avant-funk of 'HIT', the band putting in an unforgettable performance on Channel 4's 'The Word'. The accompanying album, 'STICK AROUND FOR JOY' (1992) saw the group back in critical favour, a brassy pot-pourri of spiked melody and faultless instrumental dexterity. To consolidate the new dancefloor-friendly direction, a set of remixes, 'IT'S IT', was released in late '92, coinciding with the voluntary demise of The SUGARCUBES. It had been a short strange trip, but not as strange as BJORK's forthcoming rise to international pop superstardom. While she undoubtedly had a distinctive, beguiling charm, few would've predicted the massive critical and commercial achievements of her solo debut, entitled, er . . . 'DEBUT' actually. Released in summer '93, co-written with ex-SOUL II SOUL/MASSIVE ATTACK guru, NELLEE HOOPER and featuring such underrated talents as TALVIN SINGH and JHELISA ANDERSON, proceedings were dominated by pulsing, house-orientated material, although there was a fair smattering of off-the-wall BJORK oddities. Lauded by the indie and dance press alike, the album's kudos was further boosted by the success of the 'PLAY DEAD' single, a collaboration with soundtrack man, DAVID ARNOLD recorded for the movie, 'Young Americans'. A UK Top 3 success and a Mercury Music Prize nominee, 'DEBUT' turned BJORK into a household name, remixers clamouring to get to grips with her work. A true celebrity hobnobber, BJORK co-wrote the title track to MADONNA's 'Bedtime Stories' set, while 1995's follow-up album, 'POST', saw her working with everyone from TRICKY and SKUNK ANANSIE to The BRODSKY QUARTET and EVELYN GLENNIE! The latter two featured on the experimental/schizophrenic (delete according to taste) Top 5 hit, 'IT'S OH SO QUIET', an, ahem, 'adaptation' of Betty Hutton's 40's big band number which saw BJORK veer wildly from hushed reverence to shouting the rafters down in fine style. The song was characteristic of the album's more fragmented nature, a challenging listen but proof positive that the elfen firebrand wasn't content to rest on her laurels. The following year saw BJORK take up residence in the gossip columns rather than the charts, what with her highly publicised relationship with GOLDIE and her unfortunate fracas with a reporter at Bangkok airport (19th February '96). In September, an obsessed fan from Florida blew his brains out and sent a letter bomb to BJORK. Luckily neighbours contacted police after smelling his decomposed body and the bomb was averted, although unsurprisingly it caused her much distress. The stresses and strains of stardom formed the lyrical backbone for her acclaimed 1997 set, 'HOMOGENIC', a return to more electronic waters that was nevertheless more downbeat than dancefloor. One of the music world's more unpredictable stars, her maverick genius is sorely needed in a chart choked with indie loser clones. With a plethora of mixes behind her, BJORK looked set to be a film star, her part in the film, 'Dancer In The Dark' (alongside Catherine Deneuve) won her praise at Cannes 2000; she also wrote the score. • **Songwriters:** SUGARCUBES – all written by BJORK and EINAR, except TOP OF THE WORLD (Carpenters) / MOTORCYCLE MAMA (Sailcat). • **Trivia:** BJORK was married to THOR, although after they had a child, he soon married new SUGARCUBE, MAGGI. SIGGI and BRAGI were former brother-in-laws who were married to twin sisters. In 1989, they divorced and moved to Denmark to get married to each other!. The first openly gay marriage in rock/pop history.

Album rating: Tappi Tikarrass: MIRANDA (*4) / Kukl: THE EYE mini (*4) / HOLIDAYS IN EUROPE mini (*4) / Sugarcubes: LIFE'S BEEN GOOD (*9) / STICK AROUND FOR JOY (*8) / HERE TODAY, TOMORROW, NEXT WEEK (*8) / Bjork: DEBUT (*9) / POST (*8) / TELEGRAM remixes (*7) / HOMOGENIC (*7)

BJORK GUDMUNDSDOTTIR

		Falkinn	not iss.
Dec 77. (lp/c) (FA 006/+C) **BJORK**		-	- Icelan

TAPPI TiKARRASS

BJORK – vocals, keyboards, etc / **JAKOB MAGNUSSON** – bass (ex-EXODUS) / etc.

		Spor	not iss.
Sep 81. (m-lp) (SPOR 4) **BITID FAST I VITID**		-	- Icelan
		Gramm	not iss.
Aug 83. (lp) (GRAMM 16) **MIRANDA**		-	- Icelan

KUKL

BJORK – vocals, keyboards / **EINAR ORN BENEDIKTSSON** (b.29 Oct'62, Copenhagen, Denmark) – trumpet, vocals / **SIGTRYGGUR 'Siggi' BALDURSSON** (b. 2 Oct'62, Stavanger, Norway) – drums, percussion / **EINAR MELLAX** – keyboards

		Gramm	not iss.
Sep 83. (7") (GRAMM 17) **SONGULL. / POKN FYRIR BYRJENDUR**		-	- Icelan
		Crass	not iss.
Nov 84. (m-lp) (1984-1) **THE EYE**			-

– Dismembered / Assassin / Anna. (cd-iss. Mar97; 1984 2CD)

Mar 86. (m-lp) (Cat.No.4) **HOLIDAYS IN EUROPE (THE NAUGHTY NOUGHT)**			-

SUGARCUBES

BJORK, EINAR, EINAR + SIGGI recruited **THOR ELDON JONSON** (b. 2 Jun'62, Reykjavik) – guitar / **BRAGI OLAFSSON** (b.11 Aug'62, Reykjavik) – bass

		One Little Indian	Elektra
Sep 87.	(7") *(7TP 7)* **BIRTHDAY. / BIRTHDAY** (Icelandic)	65	-
	(12"+=) *(12TP 7)* – Cat (Icelandic).		
	(cd-s;Dec87;++=) *(7TP 7CD)* – Motorcrash.		
Feb 88.	(7") *(7TP 9)* **COLD SWEAT. / DRAGON** (Icelandic)	56	-
	(12"+=) *(12TP 9)* – Traitor (Icelandic).		
	(12"++=) *(L12TP 9)* – Birthday (demo).		
	(cd-s+=) *(7TP 9CD)* – Traitor (Icelandic) / Revolution.		
Apr 88.	(7") *(7TP 10)* **DEUS. / LUFTGITAR** (Icelandic) (with **JOHNNY TRIUMPH**)	51	-
	(10"+=/12"+=) *(10TP/12TP 10)* – Organic prankster.		
	(cd-s+=) *(7TP 10CD)* – Night of steel (Icelandic).		
Apr 88.	(lp/c/cd/dat) *(TPLP/TPC/TPCD/DTPLP 5)* **LIFE'S TOO GOOD**	14	54 Jun 88
	– Mama / Delicious demon / Birthday / Traitor / Blue eyed pop / Petrol / F***ing in rhythm and sorrow / Cold sweat / Deus / Sick for toys. *(cd+=)* – I want.		
May 88.	(12"ep)(cd-ep) **COLD SWEAT / COLD SWEAT (meat mix). / BIRTHDAY** (Icelandic) **/ DELICIOUS DEMON / COLD SWEAT** (instrumental)	-	

── **MARGRET 'Magga' ORNOLFSDOTTIR** (b.21 Nov'67, Reykjavik) – keyboards repl. MELLAX

Sep 88.	(7") *(7TP 11)* **BIRTHDAY. / CHRISTMAS** (with Jesus & Mary Chain)	65	-
	(12")(cd-s) *(12TP 11)(7TP 11CD)* – ('A'side) / Fucking in rhythm and sorrow (live) / Cowboy (live) / Cold sweat (live).		
	(12") *(12TP 11L)(7TP 11CDL)* – BIRTHDAY CHRISTMAS MIX: – Christmas eve / Christmas day / Christmas present / Petrol (live).		
	(US-green-ep title 'DELICIOUS DEMONS')		
Dec 88.	(c-s) **MOTORCRASH** (live) / **POLO**	-	
	(12"+=)(3"cd-s+=) – Blue eyed pop.		
Aug 89.	(7"/c-s) *(26 TP7/+C)* **REGINA. / HOT MEAT**	55	
	(7"ep+=) *(26 TP7L)* – Hey / Propeller vs jet.		
	(12"+=) *(26 TP12)* – Regina (Icelandic).		
	(cd-s+=) *(26 TP7CD)* – Hey / Regina (Icelandic).		
	(12") *(26 TP12L)* – ('A'-Propeller mix) / ('A'-Jet mix).		
Oct 89.	(lp/silver-lp/c)(cd) *(TPLP 15/+SP/C)(TPCD 15)* **HERE TODAY, TOMORROW, NEXT WEEK**	15	70
	– Tidal wave / Regina / Speed is the key / Dream T.V. / Nail / Pump / Eat the menu / Bee / Dear plastic / Shoot him / Water / Day called Zero / Planet. *(cd+=)* – Hey / Dark disco! / Hot meat.		
Feb 90.	(7") *(32 TP7)* **PLANET. / PLANET** (somersault version)	-	
	(12"+=/cd-s+=) *(32 TP 12/7CD)* – Planet (Icelandic) / Cindy.		
Dec 91.	(7") *(62 TP7)* **HIT. / HIT** (instrumental)	17	
	(12"+=) *(62 TP12)* – Theft.		
	(cd-s++=) *(62 TP7CD)* – Chihuahua (instrumental).		
	(12"+=) *(62 TP12L)* – Leash called love.		
Feb 92.	(lp/c/cd) *(TPLP 30/+C/CD)* **STICK AROUND FOR JOY**	16	95
	– Gold / Hit / Leash called love / Lucky night / Happy nurse / I'm hungry / Walkabout / Hetero scum / Vitamin / Chihuahua.		
Mar 92.	(7"/c-s) *(72 TP7/+C)* **WALKABOUT** (remix). / **STONE DRILL (IN THE ROCK)**	-	
	(12"+=) *(72 TP12)* – Top of the world (live).		
	(cd-s++=) *(72 TP7CD)* – Bravo pop.		
Aug 92.	(12"ep) *(102 TP12)* **VITAMIN REMIXES**	-	
	– ('A'-Babylon's Burnin mix) / ('A'-Earth dub) / ('A'-Laser dub in Hell mix) / ('A'-Decline of Rome part II & III) / ('A'-Meditation mix).		
	(cd-ep+=) *(102 TP7CD)* – ('A'-E mix).		
Sep 92.	(c-ep/12"ep/cd-ep) *(104 TP 7C/12/7CD)* **BIRTHDAY REMIX EP**	64	
	– ('A'-Justin Robertson remix) / ('A'-Tommy D. dub mix) / ('A'-Jim & William Reid Christmas Eve mix) / ('A'original) / ('A'-Tommy D. 12" or dub mix) / ('A'-Justin Robertson dub) / ('A'-Jim & William Reid Christmas Day mix) / ('A'demo).		
	(cd-ep) *(104 TP7CDL)* – Birthday (Justin Robertson edit) / Birthday (Tommy D. edit) / Hit (Tony Humphries mix) / Mama (Mark Saunders mix).		
Oct 92.	(lp/c/cd/d-cd) *(TPLP 40/+C/CD/CDL)* **IT'S IT** (remixes)	47	
	(cd w/ bonus cd)		

── officially disbanded late 1992

– compilations, others, etc. –

all on 'One Little Indian'.

Apr 90.	(11x12"box) *(TP BOX 1)* **12.11** (box set)	-	
Apr 90.	(8x7"box) *(TP BOX 2)* **7.8** (box set)	-	
Apr 90.	(6xcd-s-box) *(TP BOX 3)* **CD.6**	-	
Jul 98.	(cd/c/lp) *(TPLP 333 CD/MC/LP)* **THE GREAT CROSSOVER POTENTIAL**	-	
	– Birthday / Cold sweat / Mama / Motor crash / Deus / Regina / Pump / Planet / Water / Hit / Vitamin / Walkabout / Gold / Chihuahua.		

BJORK GUDMUNDSDOTTIR & TRIO GUDMUNDAR INGOLFSSONAR

		Smekkleysa	not iss.
Oct 90.	(lp/c/cd) *(SM 27/+C/CD)* **GLING-GLO**	-	- Icelan

BJORK

── solo, with **MARIUS DE VRIES, PAUL WALLER, MARTIN VIRGO + GARRY HUGHES** – keyboards / **NELLEE HOOPER** (co-writer of some), **LUIS JARDIM** (also bass) + **BRUCE SMITH** – drums, percussion / **JON MALLISON** – guitar / **TALVIN SINGH** – tabla / **CORKI HALE** – harp / **JHELISA ANDERSON** – backing vocals / **OLIVER LAKE, GARY BARNACLE, MIKE MOWER** – brass

		One Little Indian	Elektra
Jun 93.	(c-s) *(112 TP7C)* **HUMAN BEHAVIOUR / ATLANTIC**	36	

	(12") *(112 TP12)* – ('A'-Underworld mix) / ('A'-Close to human mix) / ('A'-Dom T. mix).		
	(cd-s) *(112 TP7CD)* – ('A'side) / (above extras) / ('A'-Bassheads edit).		
Jul 93.	(cd/c/lp) *(TPLP 31 CD/C/L)* **DEBUT**	3	61
	– Human behaviour / Crying / Venus as a boy / There's more to life than this recorded live at the Milk Bar toilets / Like someone in love / Big time sensuality / One day / Aeroplane / Come to me / Violently happy / The anchor song. *(re-iss. Nov93 cd/c; TPLP 31 CDX/CX)(+=)* – Play dead.		
Aug 93.	(7"/c-s) *(122 TP7/+C)* **VENUS AS A BOY. / ('A'-Dream mix)**	29	
	(cd-s) *(122 TP7CD)* – ('A'side) / ('A'-Mykaell Riley mix) / There's more to life than this (non toilet mix) / Violently happy.		
	(cd-s) *(122 TP7CDL)* – ('A'side) / Stigdu mig / Anchor song (Black Dog mix) / I remember you.		
	(below single credited with **DAVID ARNOLD** and from the movie 'Young Americans', released on 'Island' records)		
Oct 93.	(7"/c-s) *(IS/CIS 573)* **PLAY DEAD. / ('A'-Tim Simenon remix)**	12	
	(12"+=/cd-s+=) *(12IS/CID 573)* – ('A'-Tim Simenon mixes; Orchestral / 12" / Instrumental) / ('A'-Original film mix).		
Nov 93.	(c-s) *(132 TP7C)* **BIG TIME SENSUALITY / SiDASTA EG**	17	
	(cd-s+=) *(132 TP7CD)* – Gloria / Come to me (Black Dog Productions).		
	(12"/cd-s) *(132 TP 12/7CDL)* – ('A'-Dave Morales def radio mix) / ('A'-Fluke mixes) / ('A'-Justin Robertson – Lionrock Wigout & Prankster's Joyride mix) / ('A'-Dom T. mix).		
Jan 94.	(c-s) *<64561>* **BIG TIME SENSUALITY / THERE'S MORE TO LIFE THAN THIS**	-	88

── In Mar'94, BJORK was accused by SIMON FISHER (LOVEJOY) of not crediting him on 4 of her songs on her 'DEBUT' album.

Mar 94.	(c-s) *(142 TP7C)* **VIOLENTLY HAPPY. / ('A'-Fluke mix)**	13	
	(cd-s) *(142 TP7CD)* – ('A'side) / Anchor song (acoustic) / Come to me (acoustic) / Human behavior (acoustic).		
	(d-cd-s) *(142 TP7CDL)* – ('B'side) / ('A'-5 other mixes).		
Sep 94.	(cd/c) *(MUM CD/SC 59)* **BEST MIXES FROM THE ALBUM DEBUT (For All The People Who Don't Buy White Labels)**	-	
	(above rel. on 'Mother')		
Apr 95.	(c-s) *(162 TP7C)* **ARMY OF ME / ('A'-ABA All-Stars mix)**	10	
	(cd-s+=) *(162 TP7CD)* – You've been flirting again / Sweet intuition.		
	(cd-s+=) *(162 TP7CDL)* – ('A'-Massey mix) / ('A'-featuring SKUNK ANANSIE) / ('A'-ABA All-Stars instrumental).		
	(cd-s) *(162 TP7)* – ('A'side) / Cover me.		
Jun 95.	(cd/c/lp) *(TPLP 51 CD/C/L)* *<612740>* **POST**	2	32
	– Army of me / Hyper-ballad / The modern things / It's oh so quiet / Enjoy / You've been flirting again / Isobel / Possibly maybe / I miss you / Cover me / Headphones. *(cd re-iss. Oct99; TPLP 51CD)*		
Aug 95.	(c-s/cd-s) *(172 TP7 C/CD)* **ISOBEL / CHARLENE (Black Dog mix) / I GO HUMBLE / VENUS AS A BOY (harpsicord version)**	23	
	(cd-s) *(172 TP7CDL)* – ('A'side) / ('A'-Goldie mix) / ('A'-Eumir Deodato mix) / ('A'-Siggi mix).		
Nov 95.	(c-s) *(182 TP7C)* **IT'S OH SO QUIET / YOU'VE BEEN FLIRTING AGAIN (flat is a promise mix)**	4	
	(cd-s+=) *(182 TP7CD)* – Hyper-ballad (Over the edge mix) / Sweet sweet intuition.		
	(cd-s) *(182 TP7CDL)* – ('A'side) / Hyper-ballad (Girl's blouse mix) / Hyper-ballad (with The Brodsky Quartet) / My spine (featuring Evelyn Glennie).		
Feb 96.	(c-s) *(192 TP7C)* **HYPER-BALLAD / HYPER-BALLAD (Robin Hood riding through the glen mix)**	8	
	(cd-s+=) *(192 TP7CD)* – ('A'-The stomp remix) / ('A'-Fluke mix) / ('A'-Subtle abuse mix) / ('A'-Tee's freeze mix).		
	(cd-s) *(192 TP7CDL)* – ('A'side) / Isobel (the Carcass remix) / Cover me (Plaid mix) / ('A'-Towa Tei remix).		
Oct 96.	(cd-s) *(193 TP7CD)* **POSSIBLY MAYBE (mixes; Lucy / Calcutta Cyber Cafe / Dalas Austin)**	13	
	(cd-s) *(193 TP7CDT)* – ('A'-Calcutta Cyber Cafe dub) / Cover me (Dillinja mix) / One day (Trevor Morais mix) / I miss you (Photek mix).		
	(cd-s) *(193 TP7CDL)* – ('A'live mix) / Big time sensuality (Plaid remix) / Visur vatnsenda-rosu / Hyper-ballad (live).		
Nov 96.	(cd/c/lp) *(TPLP 51 CDT/CT/T)* **TELEGRAM** (remixes)	-	66 Jan97
	(cd re-iss. Aug99; TPLP 51CDT)		
Feb 97.	(c-s) *(194 TP7C)* **I MISS YOU / I MISS YOU (Photek mix)**	36	
	(cd-s) *(194 TP7CD)* – ('A'side) / ('A'-Dobie part 2) / ('A'Darren Emerson mix) / Karvel (Graham Massey mix).		
	(cd-s) *(194 TP7CDL)* – ('A'-Dobie part 1) / Hyperballad (LFO) Violently happy (live) / Headphones (Miko Vainio remix).		
Sep 97.	(cd-s) *(202 TP7CD)* **JOGA (mixes; album / Alec Empire / Alec Empire Digital Hardcore 1 & 2)**	-	
	(cd-s) *(202 TP7CDL)* – ('A'album mix) / Sod off / Immature (Bjork's version) / So broken.		
	(cd-s) *(202 TP7CDX)* – (mixes; Howie B. main / String & Vocal / Buzzwater) / All is full of love (original).		
Sep 97.	(lp/c/cd) *(TPLP 71/+C/CD)* **HOMOGENIC**	4	28
	– Hunter / Joga / Unravel / Bachelorette / All neon like / 5 years / Immature / Alarm call / Pluto / All is full of love.		
Dec 97.	(c-s) *(212 TP7C)* **BACHELORETTE / ('A'-Howie "Spread" mix)**	21	
	(cd-s+=) *(212 TP7CD)* – My snare / Scary.		
	(12") *(212 TP12P1)* – ('A'-Alec Empire remix) / ('B'side).		
	(12") *(212 TP12P2)* – ('A'-Mark Bell "Optimism" remix) / ('A'-Mark Bell "Zip" remix).		
	(cd-s) *(212 TP7CDL)* – (mixes; above + RZA / Grooverider / etc.).		

── In Aug'98. BJORK collaborated with FUNKSTORUNG on a single, 'ALL IS FULL OF LOVE', released on 'Fat Cat' cd-s; *CDFAT 022)*

Oct 98.	(cd/c) *(222 TP7CD)* **HUNTER / ALL IS FULL OF LOVE (In Love With Funkstorung remix) / ('A'-U-Ziq remix)**	44	
	(cd-s) *(222 TP7CDL)* – ('A'side) / ('A'-State Of Bengal mix) / ('A'-Skothus mix).		
	(cd-s) *(222 TP7CDX)* – ('A'-Moodswing mix) / So broken (DK Krust remix) / ('A'live).		

Nov 98. (cd-s) *(232TP7CD)* **ALARM CALL (mixes; radio / Rhythmic Phonetics / Bjeck)**   `33`   ☐
(cd-s) *(232 TP7CDL)* – (mixes; Potage du jour / French edit / French dub).
(cd-s) *(232 TP7CDX)* – (mixes; Phunk you / Gangsta / Locked).
(12") *(232 TP12P1)* – (mixes; Bjeck [Beck] / Rhythmic Phonetics [Matmos] / Speech therapy [Matmos]).
(12") *(232 TP12P2)* – (mixes; Enough is enough [Mark Bell] / Rise & shine [Mark Bell]) / All is full of love (Mark Bell mix).
(12") *(232 TP12P3)* – (mix; Repression [DJ Krust] / So broken (DJ Krush mix).
(12") *(232 TP12P4)* – (mixes; Alan Braxe & Ben Diamond [Stardust] / Teesmade dub [Swag] / Alan Braxe & Ben Diamond).
(12") *(232 TP12P5)* – (mixes; Andy Bradford & Mark Bell / album / Snooze button [Dom T] / (Moodswing [Mark Bell]).
Jun 99. (cd-s) *(242 TP7CD)* **ALL IS FULL OF LOVE (mixes; original / Funkstorung exclusive / strings)**   `24`   ☐
(cd-s) *(242 TP7CDL)* – ('A'mixes; Howie B / Plaid / Guy Sigsworth).
(12") *(242 TP12)* – ('A'mixes; Mark Stent / Funkstorung exclusive / Mark Stent radio strings).
(12") *(242 TP12L)* – ('A'mixes; U-Ziq 7 minute / U-Ziq 1 minute / Funkstorung exclusive).

– others, etc. –

Aug 96. (12"ltd) *(193 TP12TD)* **POSSIBLY MAYBE (Talvin Singh mix). / I MISS YOU (Dobie mix)**   ☐   -
Sep 96. (12"ltd) *(193 TP12DM)* **POSSIBLY MAYBE (LFO mix). / ENJOY (Dom T mix)**   ☐   -
Oct 96. (12"ltd) *(193 TP12PT)* **BIG TIME SENSUALITY (Plaid mix). / ONE DAY (Trevor Morais mix)**   ☐   -
Jun 97. (12"ltd) *(193 TP12PT)* **BIG TIME SENSUALITY. / ONE DAY**   ☐   -
Jun 97. (12"ltd) *(193 TP12PD)* **I MISS YOU (Photek mix). / COVER ME (Dillinja mix)**   ☐   -
Jun 97. (12"ltd) *(193 TP12GH)* **ISOBEL'S LONELY HEART (Goldie remix). / HYPERBALLAD (Robin Hood Riding Through The Glen mix)**   ☐   -
Jun 97. (12"ltd) *(193 TP12MO)* **POSSIBLY MAYBE (Lucy mix – Mark Bell). / ENJOY (Further Over The Edge mix – Outkast)**   ☐   -
Jun 97. (12"ltd) *(193 TP12TT)* **HYPERBALLAD (Towa Tei remix). / ENJOY (The Beats mix – Dom T)**   ☐   -
Aug 98. (12"/cd-s; BJORK & FUNKSTORUNG) Fat Cat; *(12/CD FAT 022)* **ALL IS FULL OF LOVE (mixes)**   ☐   -

---

BLACK (dig out; Great Alt & Indie . . .)

Frank BLACK (see under ⇒ **PIXIES**)

BLACK BOX RECORDER (see under ⇒ **AUTEURS**)

BLACK CROWES

Formed: Atlanta, Georgia, USA . . . 1984 under the name MR CROWE'S GARDEN by the ROBINSON brothers, CHRIS and RICH (sons of STAN ROBINSON, who had a minor US hit in 1959 with 'Boom A Dip Dip'). By 1988, they'd adopted the BLACK CROWES moniker and assembled the line-up that would remain more or less stable throughout their career. Picked up by the ever eclectic RICK RUBIN, for his fledgling 'Def American' label, the band released their debut album in 1990 to almost universal acclaim. Taking its title ('SHAKE YOUR MONEY MAKER') from an old ELMORE JAMES song, the record was steeped in classic American musical tradition; a seamless mesh of hard-rock, blues, soul, country and R&B that drew inevitable comparisons with The FACES and The ROLLING STONES. Yet the BLACK CROWES were unmistakably American, Southern American in the tradition of The ALLMAN BROTHERS and LYNYRD SKYNYRD. The songwriting was simple but effective, while CHRIS ROBINSON's voice was a revelation, if a little wearing after prolonged exposure. This was feelgood music, genuine rough'n'ready soul music as opposed to the slick, neutered wallpaper that passes for much modern black soul. 'TWICE AS HARD', 'JEALOUS AGAIN', 'COULD'VE BEEN SO BLIND' and a rough hewn cover of OTIS REDDING's 'HARD TO HANDLE' sounded effortless, while ROBINSON put in a spine-tingling vocal performance on the emotive ballad, 'SHE TALKS TO ANGELS'. Live, the BLACK CROWES were naturally in their element and following the album's release, the band embarked on a punishing touring schedule, playing with everyone from DOGS D'AMOUR to ZZ TOP (in a well documented incident, the band were dropped from the ZZ TOP tour following CHRIS ROBINSON's criticisms of corporate sponsorship). With the permanent addition of keyboardist EDDIE HAWRYSCH to flesh out the sound, and replacing guitarist JEFF CEASE with MARC FORD (ex-BURNING TREE), the band cut 'THE SOUTHERN HARMONY AND MUSICAL COMPANION'. Released May 1992 (incredibly, recorded in just over a week), the album built on the solid blueprint of the debut. The band had amassed a sizeable following through their ceaseless live work and the album deservedly hit the top spot in America, No.2 in the UK. With the songwriting more assured and the arrangements more ambitious, The 'CROWES succeeded in carving out a musical identity distinct from their weighty musical influences. The addition of female backing singers added a richness to the sound and the record segued smoothly from the raucous R&B of opener 'STING ME' to the stoned melancholy of 'THORN IN MY PRIDE' and on to the darker, 'Midnight Rambler'-esque 'BLACK MOON CREEPING'. Just to make sure people knew where he was coming from (man), ROBINSON closed the set with a mellow, acoustic reading of BOB MARLEY's 'TIME WILL TELL'. Soon after

the album's release, the band hit the road once more, a headlining spot at the 1994 Glastonbury Festival illustrating just how high the 'CROWES had flown. Released later that year amid a storm of controversy over the cover shot (Uncle Sam[antha] in a compromising position, you could say), 'AMORICA' was something of a disappointment. Perhaps the relentless touring was beginning to take its toll, as the record sounded claustrophobic and turgid, the pace rarely rising above a monotonous plod. The songs were also lacking in cohesion and focus, although moments of genius were still evident on the likes of 'A CONSPIRACY' and the single, 'WISER TIME'. The band continued to cut it live, getting further out both musically and image wise. While The 'CROWES had always been defiantly 70's in their choice of apparel, CHRIS ROBINSON, in particular, had graduated from a vaguely glam look to a latter day CHARLES MANSON-alike. This was the revenge of the 70's; oriental rugs, ragged denim flares, bare feet, hell, even a GRATEFUL DEAD t-shirt! Rambling organ solos were also de rigeur of course, but fans lucky enough to catch the band at their low-key London gigs at the tail end of '96/early '97, were treated to a stripped down, largely acoustic set. While completely clueless, mullet-headed rock bores voiced their disapproval, the Christ-like ROBINSON mesmerised the more discerning 'CROWES fans with sterling covers of BOB DYLAN, BYRDS and LITTLE FEAT material. The 1996 album, 'THREE SNAKES AND ONE CHARM' was also a return to form, encompassing a greater diversity of styles and adding a bit of SLY STONE-style funkiness to their ragged retro patchwork. Where the band go from here is anybody's guess although a drum'n'bass remix is unlikely. With bassist JOHNNY COLT and guitarist FORD both leaving within a few months of each other, things didn't look too good. However, all was well again by early '99 with the release of their fifth set, 'BY YOUR SIDE', a typical FACES-meets-'STONES effort that highlighted their best track for some time, 'KICKIN' MY HEART AROUND' (a minor hit from late the previous year). • **Songwriters:** All written by ROBINSON brothers, except HARD TO HANDLE (Otis Redding) / RAINY DAY WOMAN NOS.12 & 35 + WHEN THE NIGHT COMES FALLING FROM THE SKY (Bob Dylan) / TIME WILL TELL (Bob Marley) / DREAMS (Allman Brothers). • **Trivia:** CHRIS and RICH's father STAN ROBINSON had a minor US hit in 59 with 'BOOM-A-DIP-DIP'. Chuck Leavell (ex-ALLMANS) produced and guested on the 1992 lp.
Album rating: SHAKE YOUR MONEY MAKER (*9) / THE SOUTHERN HARMONY AND MUSICAL COMPANION (*9) / AMORICA (*7) / THREE SNAKES AND ONE CHARM (*7) / BY YOUR SIDE (*7)

CHRIS ROBINSON (b.20 Dec'66) – vocals / **'Young' RICH ROBINSON** (b. RICHARD, 24 May'69) – guitar / **JEFF CEASE** (b.24 Jun'67, Nashville, USA) – guitar / **JOHNNY COLT** (b. 1 May'68, Cherry Point, New Connecticut) – bass (repl. 2 earlier) / **STEVE GORMAN** (b.17 Aug'65, Hopkinsville, Kentucky) – drums (repl. 5 earlier)

		Def American	Def American	
Mar 90.	(cd/c/lp) *(842515-2/-4/-1)* <24278> **SHAKE YOUR MONEY MAKER**	☐	`4`	Oct89
	– Twice as hard / Jealous again / Sister luck / Could I've been so blind / Hard to handle / Seeing things / Thick'n'thin / She talks to angels / Struttin' blues / Stare it cold. *(finally hit UK No.36 Aug91 – re-dist.Sep92)* (re-iss. Dec94 on 'American-BMG' cd/c; 74321 24839-2/-4) (cd re-iss. Feb99 on 'Columbia'; 491790-2)			
May 90.	(7") *(DEFA 4)* <19697> **JEALOUS AGAIN. / THICK'N'THIN**	☐	`75`	Apr90
	(12"+=/12"pic-d+=)(cd-s+=) *(DEFA/+P 4-12)(DEFAC 4)* – Waitin' guilty.			
Aug 90.	(7"/c-s) *(DEFA/+M 6)* <19668> **HARD TO HANDLE. / JEALOUS AGAIN (acoustic)**	`45`	`45`	Oct90
	(12"+=/12"sha-pic-d+=) *(DEFA/+P 6-12)* – Twice as hard / Stare it cold (both live).			
	(cd-s+=) *(DEFAC 6)* – Twice as hard (remix).			
Jan 91.	(7"/c-s) *(DEFA/+M 7)* **TWICE AS HARD. / JEALOUS AGAIN (live)**	`47`	-	
	(12"+=) *(DEFA 7-12)(DEFAC 7)* – Jealous guy (live).			
	(12"pic-d+=) *(DEFAP 7-12)* – Could I've been so blind (live).			
Mar 91.	(c-s/7") <19403> **SHE TALKS TO ANGELS. / ('A'live video version)**	-	`30`	
Jun 91.	(7") *(DEFA 8)* **JEALOUS AGAIN. / SHE TALKS TO ANGELS**	`70`	-	
	(12"+=) *(DEFA 8-12)* – She talks to angels (live).			
	(cd-s+=) *(DEFAC 8)* – Could I've been so blind (live).			
	(12"pic-d) *(DEFAP 8-12)* – ('A'acoustic) / ('B'acoustic) / Waitin' guilty / Struttin' blues.			
Jun 91.	(7") <19245> **HARD TO HANDLE. / WAITIN' GUILTY**	-	`26`	
Aug 91.	(7") *(DEFA 10)* **HARD TO HANDLE. / SISTER LUCK (live)**	`39`	-	
	(cd-s+=) *(DEFCD 10)* – Sister Luck (live).			
	(7"sha-pic-d) *(DEFAP 10)* – Hard to handle / Stare it cold (live).			
	(12"+=) *(DEFA 10-12)* – Dreams (live).			
Oct 91.	(7") *(DEFA 13)* **SEEING THINGS. / COULD I'VE BEEN SO BLIND (live)**	`72`	-	
	(12"+=) *(DEFAG 13-12)* – She talks to angels (live) / Sister luck (live).			
	(cd-s) *(DEFAC 13)* – ('A'side) / Hard to handle / Jealous again / Twice as hard.			

—— **MARK FORD** (b.13 Apr'66, Los Angeles, Calif.) – guitar (ex-BURNING TREE) repl. CEASE / added **EDDIE HAWRYSCH** – keyboards

Apr 92.	(etched-7") *(DEFA 16)* <18877> **REMEDY / DARLING OF THE UNDERGROUND PRESS**	`24`	`48`	Jun92
	(12"+=)(cd-s+=) *(DEFA 16-12)(DEFCD 16)* – Time will tell.			
May 92.	(cd/c/lp) *(512263-2/-4/-1)* <26916> **THE SOUTHERN HARMONY AND MUSICAL COMPANION**	`2`	`1`	
	– Sting me / Remedy / Thorn in my pride / Bad luck blue eyes goodbye / Sometime salvation / Hotel illness / Black moon creeping / No speak, no slave / My morning song / Time will tell. *(re-iss. Dec94 on 'American-BMG' cd/c; 74321 24840-2/-4)* (cd re-iss. Feb99 on 'Columbia'; 491791-2)			
Aug 92.	(c-s,cd-s) <18803> **THORN IN MY PRIDE. / STING ME**	-	`80`	
Sep 92.	(7") *(DEFA 21)* **STING ME. / RAINY DAY WOMEN NOS.12 & 35**	`42`	-	
	(cd-s) *(DEFCD 21)* – ('A'side) / She talks to angels / Thorn in my pride / Darling of the underground press.			

Nov 92. (7") *(DEFA 23)* **HOTEL ILLNESS. / NO SPEAK, NO SLAVE**   `47`
(12"clear) *(DEFX 23)* – ('A'side) / Words you throw away / Rainy day women
Nos.12 & 35.
(cd-s) *(DEFCD 23)* – ('A'side) / Rainy day / (Chris interview).
(cd-s) *(DEFCB 23)* – ('A'side) / Words you throw away / (Rich interview).

Jun 93. (7"/cd-s) *(862202-7/-2)* **REMEDY. / HARD TO HANDLE**   `-`
(12"++/cd-s++) *(862203-1/-2)* – Hotel illness / Jealous again.

—— added **EDDIE HARSCH** (b.27 May'57, Toronto, Ontario) – keyboards

	American-BMG	American-BMG
Nov 94. (cd/c/lp) *(74321 23682-2/-4/-1)* <43000> **AMORICA**   `8` `11`
– Gone / A conspiracy / High head blues / Cursed diamond / Non-fiction / She gave
good sunflower / P.25 London / Ballad in urgency / Wiser time / Downtown money
waster / Descending. *(cd+=/c+=)* – Tied up and swallowed. *(cd re-iss. Feb99 on
'Columbia'; 491792-2)*

Jan 95. (7"blue) *(74321 25849-7)* **HIGH HEAD BLUES. / A**
CONSPIRACY / REMEDY (live)   `25`
(ext'B'live; 12"+=) *(74321 25849-6)* – Thick'n'thin (live).
(cd-s++=) *(74321 25849-2)* – ('A'extended).
('B'live-cd-s+=) *(74321 25849-5)* – P25 London (live).

Jul 95. (7") *(74321 27267-7)* **WISER TIME. / CHEVROLET**   `34`
('A'-Rock mix; cd-s+=) *(74321 27267-2)* – She talks to angels (acoustic).
(cd-s) *(74321 29827-2)* – ('A'acoustic) / Jealous again (acoustic) / Non fiction
(acoustic) / Thorn in my pride (acoustic).

Jul 96. (10"pic-d/cd-s) *(74321 39857-1/-2)* **ONE MIRROR TOO**
MANY. / PIMPERS PARADISE / SOMEBODY'S ON YOUR
CASE   `51`

Jul 96. (cd/c) *(74321 38484-2/-4)* <43082> **THREE SNAKES AND**
ONE CHARM   `17` `15`
– Under a mountain / Good Friday / Nebakanezer / One mirror too many /
Blackberry / Girl from a pawnshop / (Only) Halfway to everywhere / Bring on, bring
on / How much for your wings? / Let me share the ride / Better when you're not
alone / Evil eye. *(cd re-iss. Feb99 on 'Columbia'; 491793-2)*

—— COLT + FORD left; repl. by **SVEN PIPPEN** – bass (ex-MARY MY HOPE)

—— added touring guitarist **AUDLEY FREED** (ex-CRY OF LOVE)

	Columbia	Columbia
Oct 98. (c-s) *(666666-4)* **KICKIN' MY HEART AROUND / IT MUST**
BE OVER   `55`
(cd-s+=) *(666666-2)* – You don't have to go.
(cd-s+=) *(666666-5)* – Diamond ring (version).

Jan 99. (cd/c) *(491669-2/-4)* <69361> **BY YOUR SIDE**   `34` `26`
– Go faster / Kickin' my heart around / By your side / Horsehead / Only a fool /
Heavy / Welcome to the goodtimes / Go tell the congregation / Diamond ring / Then
she said my name / Virtue and vice.

Jul 99. (7"/cd-s) **ONLY A FOOL. / WHEN THE NIGHT COMES**
FALLING FROM THE SKY   `-`

– compilations, etc. –

Aug 98. (5xcd-box) *Columbia; (C5K 65741)* **SHO 'NUFF**

BLACK FLAG

Formed: Hermosa Beach, California, USA . . . 1976 by GREG GINN and
CHUCK DUKOWSKI. In 1977, their demo reached local indie label 'Bomp',
who, after over half a year decided not to release BLACK FLAG's debut
45, 'NERVOUS BREAKDOWN'. Instead, GREG and CHUCK, with sound
men MUGGER and SPOT, formed their own label, 'S.S.T.' (Solid State
Tuners), issuing the aforesaid single in 1978. By the time BLACK FLAG's
debut lp, 'DAMAGED', was released in 1981, the group had suffered label
difficulties with 'MCA-Unicorn', who didn't like the outrageous content of the
tracks. Numerous personnel changes had also occurred, mainly the substitution
of KEITH MORRIS with the harder looking and now legendary HENRY
ROLLINS. SST took the major label to court and although the pivotal hardcore
group won, they had to pay out a 6-figure sum. The influential label went on to
help kickstart the careers of many hardcore/alternative acts such as HUSKER
DU, MINUTEMEN, DINOSAUR JR, MEAT PUPPETS, etc. Meanwhile,
BLACK FLAG (with GINN and ROLLINS at the helm), completed a series
of near brilliant albums, ROLLINS even contributing a spoken word side on
the half instrumental album, 'FAMILY MAN' (1984), a thing that he would
do more when he took off on a successful solo venture that year. GINN and
some new cohorts completed two more mid 80's sets, 'IN MY HEAD' and
'WHO'S GOT THE 10 1/2', before he too pursued a solo sojourn, although
at first with instrumental punk-jazz fusion, GONE. BLACK FLAG were one
of the first US acts to take DIY punk into hardcore, a hybrid sound that would
later be revered by metal fans who had picked up on 90's US hardcore/punk
groups like BAD RELIGION and OFFSPRING.

Album rating: DAMAGED (*8) / EVERYTHING WENT BLACK (*5) / THE FIRST
FOUR YEARS (*7) compilation / MY WAR (*6) / FAMILY MAN (*4) / SLIP IT IN (*5) /
LOOSE NUT (*5) / IN MY HEAD (*6) / WHO'S GOT THE 10 1/2 (*6) / WASTED . . .
AGAIN (*7)

KEITH MORRIS – vocals / **GREG GINN** (b. 8 Jun'54) – guitar / **CHUCK DUKOWSKI** –
bass / **BRIAN MIGDOL** – drums

	not iss.	S.S.T.
Oct 78. (7"ep) <SST 001> **NERVOUS BREAKDOWN. / FIX ME /**
I'VE HAD IT / WASTED   `-`
<US 10"colrd-ep/12"ep/cd-ep iss.1990; same>

—— **CHAVO PEDERAST** (aka RON REYES) – vocals (ex-RED CROSS) repl. KEITH
who formed CIRCLE JERKS. **ROBO** – drums repl. MIGDOL
Mar 80. (12"ep) <SST 003> **JEALOUS AGAIN / REVENGE. /**
WHITE MINORITY / NO VALUES / YOU BET WE'VE GOT
SOMETHING PERSONAL AGAINST YOU!   `-`

<US-iss.Mar83; same> <US 10"colrd-ep/12"ep/cd-ep iss.1990; same>

—— **DEZ CADENA** – vocals, guitar (ex-RED CROSS) repl. REYES
Jan 81. (7"ep) <SST 005> **SIX PACK. / I'VE HEARD IT ALL BEFORE /**
AMERICAN WASTE   `-`
(UK-iss.Dec81 on 'Alternative Tentacles'; VIRUS 9) <US 10"colrd-ep/12"/ep/cd-
ep iss.1990; same>

—— **HENRY ROLLINS** (b. HENRY GARFIELD, 13 Feb '61, Washington, D.C.) – vocals
(ex-SOA) repl. CHUCK who formed WURM (with ED DANKY and SIMON
SMALLWOOD (vocalist of DEAD HIPPIE) – one lp surfaced in '85, 'FEAST'
<SST 041>. CHUCK later formed SWA and was part of OCTOBERFACTION

—— group now **ROLLINS, GINN, CADENA** (now rhythm guitar only) + **ROBO**

	S.S.T.	S.S.T.
Nov 81. (lp) <(SST 007)> **DAMAGED**
– Rise above / Spray paint / Six pack / What I see / TV party / Thirsty and miserable /
Police story / Gimmie gimmie gimmie / Depression / Room 13 / Damaged II / No
more / Padded cell / Life of pain / Damaged I.

—— In the US, 'Posh Boy' issued '79 recording LOUIE LOUIE. / DAMAGED 1 *(PBS 13)*
(This was finally issued 10"coloured 1988 on 'SST' US) (re-iss. cd/c/lp Oct95; same) LOUIE
LOUIE was a KINGSMEN original.

—— **BILL STEVENSON** + guest **EMIL** – drums repl. ROBO
1982. (7"ep) <SST 012> **TV PARTY. / I'VE GOT TO RUN / MY**
RULES   `-`
<US 12"+cd-ep iss.1990; same>

—— guest on half **DALE NIXON** – bass (actually GREG under pseudonym) repl.
CADENA who formed DC3
Mar 84. (lp) <(SST 023)> **MY WAR**
– My war / Can't decide / Beat my head against the wall / I love you / The swinging
man / Forever time / Nothing left inside / Three nights / Scream. *(cd-iss. 1990; SST
023CD) (re-iss. cd/c/lp Oct95; same)*

—— added **KIRA ROESSLER** – bass
Sep 84. (lp) <(SST 026)> **FAMILY MAN**
– Family man / Salt on a slug / The pups are doggin' it / Let your fingers do the
walking / Long lost dog of it / I won't stick any of you unless and until I can stick all
of you / Hollywood diary / Armageddon man / Account for what? / Shred reading
(rattus norvegicus) / No deposit, no return. *(cd-iss. 1990; SST 026CD) (re-iss. cd/c/lp
Oct95; same)*

Oct 84. (12") <(SST1 2001)> **FAMILY MAN. / I WON'T STICK ANY**
OF YOU UNLESS AND UNTIL I CAN STICK ALL OF YOU

Dec 84. (lp) <(SST 029)> **SLIP IT IN**
– Slip it in / Black coffee / Wound up / Rat's eyes / Obliteration / The bars / My
ghetto / You're not evil. *(cd-iss. 1990; SST 029CD) (re-iss. cd/c/lp Oct95; same)*

Jan 85. (c) <(SST 030)> **LIVE '84 (live)**
– The process of weeding out / My ghetto / Jealous again / I love you / Swinging
man / Three nights / Nothing left inside / Black coffee. *(cd-iss. 1990; SST 030CD)
(re-iss. cd/c/lp Oct95; same)*

Jun 85. (lp) <(SST 035)> **LOOSE NUT**
– Loose nut / Bastard in love / Annihilate this week / Best one yet / Modern man /
This is good / I'm the one / Sinking / Now she's black. *(cd-iss. 1990; SST 035CD)
(re-iss. cd/c/lp Oct95; same)*

—— trimmed to **GINN, KIRA + STEVENSON** when ROLLINS went solo
Sep 85. (m-lp) <(SST 037)> **THE PROCESS OF WEEDING OUT**
– Your last affront / Screw the law / The process of weeding out / Southern rise. *(US
10"colrd/m-cd iss.1990)*

Nov 85. (lp) <(SST 045)> **IN MY HEAD**
– Paralyzed / The crazy girl / Black love / Retired at 21 / Drinking and driving /
White hot / In my head / Society's tease / It's all up to you / You let me down. *(cd-
iss. 1990 +=; SST 045CD)* – Out of this world / I can see you. *(cd re-iss. Oct95;
same)*

—— **ANTHONY MARTINEZ** – drums; repl. STEVENSON who had already joined
OCTOBERFACTION
May 86. (lp) <(SST 060)> **WHO'S GOT THE 10 1/2 (live in Portland**
23/8/85)
– I'm the one / Loose nut / Bastard in love / Slip it in / This is good / Gimmie gimmie
gimmie / Drinking and driving / Modern man / My war. *(cd-iss. 1990; re-iss. cd/c/lp
Oct95; same) (cd+=)* – Annihilate / Wasted / Sinking / Jam / Louie Louie / Best
one yet.

—— had already split earlier in '86. KIRA continued with DOS, alongside MIKE WATT
of The MINUTEMEN. After playing bass on a one-off trio project/eponymous
album in 1985 with TOM TROCCOLI'S DOG <SST 047> – solo artist GINN had
also been part of TOM's own quintet, OCTOBERFACTION – he also teamed up
with ANDREW WEISS to form instrumental group, GONE.

– compilations, others, etc. –
on 'S.S.T.' unless mentioned otherwise
Mar 83. (d-lp) <(SST 015)> **EVERYTHING WENT BLACK** (rare 78-81)
(re-iss. Oct95 lp/c/cd; SST 015/+C/CD)

1984. (lp) <SST 021> **THE FIRST FOUR YEARS**   `-`
(UK-iss.Oct95 & Oct99 lp/c/cd; SST 021/+C/CD)

Dec 87. (lp/c/cd) <(SST 166/+C/CD)> **WASTED . . . AGAIN**
– Wasted / TV party / Six pack / I don't care / I've had it / Jealous again / Slip it
in / Annihilate this week / Loose nut / Gimmie gimmie / Louie Louie / Drinking and
driving. *(re-iss. Oct95; same)*

Jun 93. (12"/c-s/cd-s) <(SST 226/+C/CD)> **I CAN SEE YOU**

BLACKFOOT (dig out; Great Metal . . .)

BLACK GRAPE (see under ⇒ HAPPY MONDAYS)

BLACKMORE'S RAINBOW (see under ⇒ RAINBOW)

BLACK OAK ARKANSAS (dig out; Great Metal . . .)

BLACK ROSE (see under ⇒ CHER)

BLACK SABBATH

Formed: Aston, Birmingham, England ... early 1969 by TONY IOMMI, OZZY OSBOURNE, TERRY 'GEEZER' BUTLER and BILL WARD, out of the jazz fusion combo, EARTH (IOMMI had also filled in as JETHRO TULL guitarist for a few weeks). Taking the name, BLACK SABBATH from a horror film adapted from a Dennis Wheatley novel of the same name, they signed to 'Fontana' in late '69. After a flop single, 'EVIL WOMAN (DON'T PLAY YOUR GAMES WITH ME)', they were shunted to the more progressive 'Vertigo' label in early 1970. The inimitable SABBATH sound was stunningly defined on the opening title cut from the self-titled debut album, the record storming into the UK Top 10. Occult influenced, BLACK SABBATH fused IOMMI's deceptively basic, doom-laden guitar riffs with OZZY's (much-mimicked since) banshee shriek. Lyrically morbid, with futuristic/medieval themes, tracks like 'THE WIZARD' highlighting their tongue-in-cheek protest against God! The band then branded their name on the nation's musical consciousness with a Top 5 hit single!!! 'PARANOID', a skullcrushing but strangely melodic track which remains one of the most (in)famous metal songs of all time. Not surprisingly, the album of the same name (also in 1970!) bludgeoned its way straight to No.1, a metal classic rammed full of blinding tracks, not least the stop-start dynamics of 'WAR PIGS', the spiralling melancholy of 'IRON MAN' and the doom-driven 'FAIRIES WEAR BOOTS' ("and you gotta believe me!"). Their third set, 'MASTER OF REALITY' (1971), was another dark jewel in the SABBATH legend, softer tracks like 'EMBRYO' and 'ORCHID' sledgehammered into oblivion by mogadon monsters, 'CHILDREN OF THE GRAVE' and 'SWEET LEAF'. The last two years had witnessed SABBATH taking America by the throat, 'VOL. 4' in '72 loosening the grip somewhat, although it did boast a classic rock ballad, 'CHANGES'. Returning to more pseudo-satanic territory, 'SABBATH BLOODY SABBATH' was another milestone, its demonic credibility nevertheless diminished somewhat by the fact that the instrumental, 'FLUFF', was subsequently adopted by namesake Radio One DJ ALAN FREEMAN on his Saturday afternoon prog-rock show! Returning from a year-long sabbatical, the release of the largely disappointing sixth album, 'SABOTAGE', was indicative of the cracks appearing in the IOMMI/OSBOURNE relationship. However, the album did contain two brilliant opening salvos, 'HOLE IN THE SKY' and 'SYMPTOM OF THE UNIVERSE'. The beginning of the end came with the ill-advised experimentation of 'TECHNICAL ECSTASY' (1976), an album which led to OZZY's brief departure (his supernatural consumption of the demon drink was also a factor). However, a newly rehabilitated OSBOURNE was back at the helm for 1978's 'NEVER SAY DIE', sales of which were boosted by a near UK Top 20 title shot. In 1979, OZZY took off on a solo career, leaving behind IOMMI, BUTLER and WARD to pick up the pieces in LA (where the band had relocated). With a new manager, Don Arden, in tow, they finally recruited American, RONNIE JAMES DIO (from RAINBOW), after auditioning many would-be OZZY clones. This proved to be SABBATH's blackest period, pitch in fact, with the release of two mediocre albums in the early 80's, 'HEAVEN AND HELL' and 'MOB RULES'. Things went from bad to ridiculous in 1983, when DIO was substituted by another hard-rock frontman celebrity, IAN GILLAN, taken straight from the proverbial heart of DEEP PURPLE. The resulting, ironically-titled album, 'BORN AGAIN', was an exercise in heavy-metal cliche, although it still managed to hit the UK Top 5. The original SABBATH reunited on the 13th of July '85 for a rather disappointing one-off performance at the 'Live Aid' concert in Philadelphia. In 1986, IOMMI was in full control once more, even giving his name co-billing on the appalling, 'SEVENTH STAR' set. Astonishingly, SABBATH were given another chance by Miles Copeland's 'I.R.S.' records, IOMMI having found a new vocalist, TONY MARTIN, also securing the services of veteran drummer, COZY POWELL (ex-everyband) to boost the sales of their comeback album, 'HEADLESS CROSS' (1989). The 1990's saw IOMMI and group trying to relive past glories, the 1995 album 'FORBIDDEN' even including a vocal piece from US rapper, ICE-T. At the turn of 1997/8, IOMMI and OZZY had finally settled their differences, coming together in a much heralded SABBATH reunion, which will apparently result in a comeback album, 20 years too late for some! • **Footnote:** Not a band for the easily-led and weak-minded, as the blame for teenage suicide attempts was always laid at their darkended door. Nevertheless, their influence on the worldwide metal scene is inestimable; as well as playing grunge before it was even invented, the likes of METALLICA et al, owe SABBATH a massive debt. • **Songwriters:** Mainly group compositions. Covered EVIL WOMAN (DON'T PLAY YOUR GAMES WITH ME) (Crow) / WARNING (Aynsley Dunbar).

Album rating: BLACK SABBATH (*8) / PARANOID (*9) / MASTER OF REALITY (*9) / VOLUME 4 (*8) / SABBATH BLOODY SABBATH (*8) / SABOTAGE (*7) / WE SOLD OUR SOULS FOR ROCK'N'ROLL compilation (*8) / TECHNICAL ECSTASY (*5) / NEVER SAY DIE (*5) / HEAVEN AND HELL (*7) / LIVE AT LAST (*4) / MOB RULES (*6) / LIVE EVIL (*7) / BORN AGAIN (*5) / SEVENTH STAR (*4) / THE ETERNAL IDOL (*4) / HEADLESS CROSS (*5) / BLACKEST SABBATH compilation (*7) / TYR (*5) / DEHUMANIZER (*5) / CROSS PURPOSES (*5) / FORBIDDEN (*5)

OZZY OSBOURNE (b. JOHN, 3 Dec'48) – vocals / **TONY IOMMI** (b.19 Feb'48) – guitars / **TERRY 'GEEZER' BUTLER** (b.17 Jul'49) – bass / **BILL WARD** (b. 5 May'48) – drums

			Fontana	Warners
Jan 70.	(7") *(TF 1067)* **EVIL WOMAN, DON'T PLAY YOUR GAMES WITH ME. / WICKED WORLD**			-

			Vertigo	Warners
Feb 70.	(lp) *(VO 6)* <1871> **BLACK SABBATH**		8	23 Jul 70

– Black Sabbath / The wizard / Behind the wall of sleep / N.I.B. / Evil woman, don't play your games with me / Sleeping village / Warning. *(re-iss. Jan74 on 'W.W.A.'; WWA 006) (re-iss. Jun80 + Nov85 on 'NEMS'; NEL 6002) (cd-iss. Dec86+=; NELCD 6002)* – Wicked world.

Mar 70.	(7") *(V2)* **EVIL WOMAN (DON'T PLAY YOUR GAMES WITH ME). / WICKED WORLD**			
Aug 70.	(7") *(6059 010)* <7437> **PARANOID. / THE WIZARD**		4	61 Nov70
Sep 70.	(lp) *(6360 011)* <1887> **PARANOID**		1	12 Feb71

– War pigs / Paranoid / Planet Caravan / Iron man / Electric funeral / Hand of doom / Rat salad / Fairies wear boots. *(re-iss. Jan74 on 'W.W.A.'; WWA 007) (re-iss. Jun80 on 'NEMS'; NEL 6003; hit UK 54. (re-iss. Nov85 on 'NEMS' lp/pic-lp/c/cd; NEL/NEP/NELMC/NELCD 6003) (re-iss. Jun89 on 'Vertigo' lp/c/cd+=; 832701-1/-4/-2)* – Tomorrow's world (live). *(re-iss. cd Feb96 on 'Essential'; ESMCD 302)*

Aug 71.	(lp) *(6360 050)* <2562> **MASTER OF REALITY**		5	8

– Sweet leaf / After forever / Embryo / Children of the grave / Orchid / Lord of this world / Solitude / Into the void. *(re-iss. Jan74 on 'W.W.A.'; WWA 008) (re-iss. Nov80 on 'NEMS'; NEL 6004) (re-iss. Nov85 on 'NEMS' lp/c/cd; NEL/+MC/CD 6004) (re-iss. cd Jun89 on 'Vertigo' lp/c/cd+=; 832707-1/-4/-2)* – Killing yourself to live (live). *(re-iss. cd Feb96 on 'Essential'; ESMCD 303)*

Jan 72.	(7") *<7530>* **IRON MAN. / ELECTRIC FUNERAL**	-	52

<re-iss. 1974; 7802>

Sep 72.	(7") *(6059 061)* <7625> **TOMORROW'S DREAM. / LAGUNA SUNRISE**			
Sep 72.	(lp) *(6360 071)* <2602> **BLACK SABBATH VOL.4**		8	13 Oct72

– Wheels of confusion / Tomorrow's dream / Changes / FX / Supernaut / Snowblind / Cornucopia / Laguna sunrise / St. Vitus' dance / Under the sun. *(re-iss. Jan74 on 'W.W.A.'; WWA 009) (re-iss. Jun80 on 'NEMS'; NEL 6005) (cd/cd-iss. 1988+=; NEL MC/CD 6005)* – Children of the grave (live). *(re-iss. cd Feb96 on 'Essential'; ESMCD 304)*

			W.W.A.	Warners
Oct 73.	(7") *(WWS 002)* <7764> **SABBATH BLOODY SABBATH. / CHANGES**			
Dec 73.	(lp) *(WWA 005)* <2695> **SABBATH BLOODY SABBATH**		4	11 Jan74

– Sabbath bloody sabbath / A national acrobat / Fluff / Sabbra cadabra / Killing yourself to live / Who are you? / Looking for today / Spiral architect. *(w-drawn copies were on 'Vertigo'; 6360 115) (re-iss. Jun80 on 'NEMS'; NEL 6017) (re-iss. Nov85 c/cd; NEL MC/CD 6017) (re-iss. Jun89 on 'Vertigo' lp/c/cd+=; 832700-1/-4/-2)* – Cornucopia (live). *(re-iss. cd Feb96 on 'Essential'; ESMCD 305)*

			N.E.M.S.	Warners
Sep 75.	(lp) *(9119 001)* <2822> **SABOTAGE**		7	28

– Hole in the sky / Don't start (too late) / Symptom of the universe / Megalomania / Thrill of it all / Supertzar / Am I going insane (radio) / The writ. *(re-iss. Nov80 on 'NEMS'; NEL 6018) (re-iss. Nov85 c/cd; NEL MC/CD 6018) (re-iss. Jun89 on 'Vertigo' lp/c/cd+=; 832706-1/-4/-2)* – Sweat leaf (live). *(re-iss. cd Feb96 on 'Essential'; ESMCD 306)*

Feb 76.	(d-lp) *(6641 335)* <2923> **WE SOLD OUR SOULS FOR ROCK'N'ROLL** (compilation)		35	48

– Black sabbath / The wizard / Warning / Paranoid / Wicked world / Tomorrow's dream / Fairies wear boots / Changes / Sweet leaf / Children of the grave / Sabbath bloody sabbath / Am I going insane (radio) / Laguna sunrise / Snowblind / N.I.B. *(re-iss. Nov80; NELD 101) (re-iss. Apr86 on 'Raw Power' d-lp/c/cd; RAW LP/TC/CD 017) (re-iss. Dec90 on 'Castle' cd/c/d-lp; CCS CD/MC/LP 249)*

Feb 76.	(7") *(6165 300)* **AM I GOING INSANE (RADIO). / HOLE IN THE SKY**			

			Vertigo	Warners
Oct 76.	(lp) *(9102 750)* <2969> **TECHNICAL ECSTASY**		13	51

– Back street kids / You won't change me / It's alright / Gypsy / All moving parts (stand still) / Rock'n'roll doctor / She's gone / Dirty women. *(re-iss. Aug83 lp/c; PRICE/PRIMC 40) (cd-iss. Jun89; 838224-2) (re-iss. cd Jan96 on 'Essential'; ESMCD 328)*

Nov 76.	(7") *<8315>* **IT'S ALRIGHT. / ROCK'N'ROLL DOCTOR**	-	

—— Late '77 OZZY leaves and is briefly repl. by **DAVE WALKER** (ex-SAVOY BROWN) Early 1978 **OZZY** returned.

May 78.	(7") *(SAB 001)* **NEVER SAY DIE. / SHE'S GONE**	21	-
Sep 78.	(7",7"purple) *(SAB 002)* **HARD ROAD. / SYMPTOM OF THE UNIVERSE**	33	-
Oct 78.	(lp) *(9102 751)* <3186> **NEVER SAY DIE!**	12	69

– Never say die / Johnny Blade / Juniors eyes / Hard road / Shock wave / Air dance / Over to you / Breakout / Swinging the chain. *(re-iss. May83 lp/c; PRICE/PRIMC 9) (re-iss. Sep93 on 'Spectrum' cd/c;) (re-iss. cd Jan96 on 'Essential'; ESMCD 329)*

—— **RONNIE JAMES DIO** (b.1950, Cortland, N.J.) – vocals (ex-(RITCHIE BLACKMORE'S) RAINBOW, ex-ELF etc.) repl.OZZY who went solo.

Apr 80.	(lp)(c) *(9102 752)(7231 402)* <3372> **HEAVEN AND HELL**	9	28 Jun80

– Neon knights / Children of the sea / Lady evil / Heaven and Hell / Wishing well / Die young / Walk away / Lonely is the word. *(re-iss. May83 lp/c; PRICE/PRIMC 10) (cd-iss. 1987; 830171-2) (re-iss. May93 on 'Spectrum' cd/c;) (re-iss. cd Jan96 on 'Essential'; ESMCD 330)*

Jun 80.	(7") *(SAB 3)* **NEON KNIGHTS. / CHILDREN OF THE SEA**	22	-
Jul 80.	(7") *<49549>* **LADY EVIL. / CHILDREN OF THE SEA**	-	-
Nov 80.	(7"/ext.12") *(SAB 4/+12)* **DIE YOUNG. / HEAVEN AND HELL (live)**	41	-

—— **VINNIE APPICE** (b.Staten Island, N.Y.) – drums, percussion repl. WARD

Oct 81.	(7"/12") *(SAB 5/+12)* **MOB RULES. / DIE YOUNG**	46	-
Nov 81.	(lp/c) *(6302/7144 119)* <3605> **MOB RULES**	12	29

– Turn up the night / Voodoo / The sign of the southern cross / E5150 / The mob rules / Country girl / Slippin' away / Falling off the edge of the world / Over and over. *(re-iss. Jan85 lp/c; PRICE/PRIMC 77) (re-iss. cd Jan96 on 'Essential'; ESMCD 332)*

Feb 82.	(7")(12"/12"pic-d) *(SAB 6)(SABP 6/+12)* **TURN UP THE NIGHT. / LONELY IS THE WORD**	37	-
Jan 83.	(d-lp/d-c) *(SAB/+M 10)* <23742> **LIVE EVIL (live)**	13	37

– E5150 / Neon knights / N.I.B. / Children of the sea / Voodoo / Black sabbath / War pigs / Iron man / Mob rules / Heaven and Hell / The sign of the southern cross / Heaven and Hell (continued) / Paranoid / Children of the grave / Fluff. *(re-iss. Apr86 lp/c; PRID/+C 11) (cd-iss. Apr96 on 'Essential'; ESMCD 333)*

—— **IAN GILLAN** (b.19 Aug'45, Hounslow, England) – vocals (ex-DEEP PURPLE, ex-

GILLAN) repl. RONNIE who formed DIO. **BILL WARD** – drums returned replacing VINNIE who also joined DIO. **BEV BEVAN** – drums (ex-ELECTRIC LIGHT ORCHESTRA) repl BILL, only originals in band were IOMMI and BUTLER

Sep 83. (lp/c) (VERL/+C 8) <23978> **BORN AGAIN**   `4` `39`
– Trashed / Stonehenge / Disturbing the priest / The dark / Zero the hero / Digital bitch / Born again / Hot line / Keep it warm. (cd-iss. Apr96 on 'Essential'; ESMCD 334)

Oct 83. (7") <29434> **STONEHENGE. / THRASHED**   `-` `☐`

—— **DAVE DONATO** – vocals repl. GILLAN who rejoined DEEP PURPLE

—— **TONY IOMMI** recruited **GLENN HUGHES** – vocals (ex-DEEP PURPLE, etc.) repl. DONATO / **DAVE SPITZ** (b. New York City) – bass repl. BUTLER / **ERIC SINGER** (b.Cleveland, Ohio) – drums repl. BEVAN / added **GEOFF NICHOLLS** (b.Birmingham) – keyboards (ex-QUARTZ) had toured '79.

Feb 86. (lp/c/cd; as BLACK SABBATH featuring TONY IOMMI) (VERH/+C 29)(826704-2) <25337> **SEVENTH STAR**   `27` `78`
– In for the kill / No stranger to love / Turn to stone / Sphinx (the guardian) / Seventh star / Danger zone / Heart like a wheel / Angry heart / In memory. (re-iss. cd Apr96 on 'Essential'; ESMCD 335)

     TONY IOMMI again added **BOB DAISLEY** – bass / **BEV BEVAN** – percussion / **TONY MARTIN** – vocals repl. HUGHES

Nov 87. (lp/c)(cd) (VERH/+C 51)(832708-2) <25548> **THE ETERNAL IDOL**   `66`
– The shining / Ancient warrior / Hard life to love / Glory ride / Born to lose / Scarlet Pimpernel / Lost forever / The eternal idol. (cd+=) – Nightmare. (re-iss. cd Apr96 on 'Essential'; ESMCD 336)

—— **IOMMI + MARTIN** recruited **COZY POWELL** – drums (ex-RAINBOW, ex-ELP) **LAURENCE COTTLE** – bass (on session)

                                       I.R.S.   **I.R.S.**

Apr 89. (7"/7"s) (EIRS/+CB 107) **HEADLESS CROSS. / CLOAK AND DAGGER**   `62`
(12"+=/12"w-poster+=) (EIRST/+PB 107) – ('A'extended).

Apr 89. (lp/pic-lp/c/cd) (EIRSA/+PD/C/CD 1002) <82002> **HEADLESS CROSS**   `31`
– The gates of Hell / Headless cross / Devil & daughter / When death calls / Kill in the spirit world / Call of the wild / Black moon / Nightwing. (pic-lp+=) – Cloak and dagger. (re-iss. cd Apr94) (cd re-iss. Aug99 on 'E.M.I.'; 521299-2)

Jun 89. (one-sided; 7"/7"s/7"pic-d) (EIRS/+B/PD 115) **DEVIL AND DAUGHTER**
(12"+=) (EIRST 115) – (15 minute interview).

—— **NEIL MURRAY** – bass (ex-VOW WOW, etc.) joined mid'89 repl.COTTLE

Aug 90. (lp/pic-lp/c/cd) (EIRSA/+PD/C/CD 1038) <X2-13049> **TYR**   `24`
– Anno Mundi / The law maker / Jerusalem / The sabbath stones / The battle of Tyr / Odin's court / Valhalla / Feels good to me / Heaven in black. (pic-lp+=) – Paranoid (live) / Heaven and Hell (live). (re-iss. cd Apr94) i(cd re-iss. Aug99 on 'E.M.I.'; 521298-2)

Sep 90. (7"/c-s) (EIRS/C 148) **FEELS GOOD TO ME. / PARANOID (live)**
(12"+=/cd-s+=) (EIRS T/CD 148) – Heaven and Hell (live).

—— The 1981-83 line-up reformed Oct91, **IOMMI, GEEZER, VINNIE** and **R.JAMES DIO.**

                                       I.R.S.   **Reprise**

Jun 92. (lp/c/cd) (EIRS A/C/CD 1064) <26965> **DEHUMANIZER**   `28` `44`
– Computer god / After all (the dead) / TV crimes / Letters from Earth / Masters of insanity / Time machine / Sins of the father / Too late / I / Buried alive. (re-iss. cd Apr94)

Jun 92. (7"pic-d) (EIRSP 178) **TV CRIMES. / LETTERS FROM EARTH**   `33` `-`
(12"pic-d+=) (12EIRSPD 178) – Mob rules (live).
(cd-s+=) (CDEIRS 178) – Paranoid (live).
(cd-s+=) (CDEIRSS 178) – Heaven and Hell (live).

—— **TONY MARTIN** returned on vocals to repl. DIO

—— **BOBBY RONDINELLI** – drums (ex-RAINBOW) repl. APPICE

Feb 94. (cd/c/lp) (EIRS CD/TC/LP 1067) <13222> **CROSS PURPOSES**   `41`
– I witness / Cross of thorns / Psychophobia / Virtual death / Immaculate deception / Dying for love / Back to Eden / The hand that rocks the cradle / Cardinal sin / Evil eye.

—— The 1990 line-up was once again in force although COZY departed once again after below to be repl. by the returning RONDINELLI

Jun 95. (cd/c) (EIRS CD/TC 1072) **FORBIDDEN**   `71`
– The illusion of power / Get a grip / Can't get close enough / Shaking off the chains / I won't cry for you / Guilty as hell / Sick and tired / Rusty angels / Forbidden / Kiss of death.

—— the original BLACK SABBATH reformed for live gigs

                                       Epic   **Epic**

Oct 98. (cd/c) (491954-2/-4) <69115> **REUNION (live late '97)**   `41` `11`
– War pigs / Beyond the wall of sleep / N.I.B. / Fairies wear boots / Electric funeral / Sweet leaf / Spiral architect / Into the void / Snowblind / Sabbath bloody sabbath / Iron man / Children of the grave / Paranoid / Psycho man (studio) / Selling my soul (studio). (also d-cd; 491954-9)

                                       N.M.C.   **not iss.**

Dec 99. (cd-ep) (PILOT 49) **BLACK MASS**
– Paranoid / Black sabbath / Iron man / Blue suded shoes.

– compilations etc. –

on 'NEMS' / 'Warners' unless otherwise stated

Dec 77. (lp) (NEL 6009) **BLACK SABBATH'S GREATEST HITS**
(re-iss. Nov90 on 'Castle' lp/c/cd+=; CLA LP/MC/CD 200)

Aug 78. (7") (NES 121) **PARANOID. / SNOWBLIND**   `-`

Jun 80. (lp) (BS 001) **LIVE AT LAST (live)**   `5`
– Tomorrows dream / Sweet leaf / Killing yourself to live / Cornucopia / Snowblind / Children of the grave / War pigs / Wicked world / Paranoid. (cd-iss. Aug96 on 'Essential'; ESMCD 331)

Aug 80. (7") (BSS 101) **PARANOID. / SABBATH BLOODY SABBATH**   `14` `-`

Aug 82. (7"pic-d) (NEP 1) **PARANOID. / IRON MAN**
(12"+=) (12NEX 01) – Fairies wear boots / War pigs.

Aug 85. (d-lp/c) Castle; (CCS LP/MC 109) **THE COLLECTION**
(cd-iss. 1986; CCSCD 109)

Dec 85. (7xlp-box) Castle; (BSBOX 01) **BOXED SET**

—— (all albums with OZZY)

Jun 86. (12"ep) That's Original; (TOF 101) **CLASSIC CUTS FROM THE VAULTS**
– Paranoid / War pigs / Iron man / Black sabbath.

Jun 88. (d-lp/d-c/d-cd) That's Original; (TFO LP/MC/CD 10) **SABBATH BLOODY SABBATH / BLACK SABBATH**

Nov 88. (3"cd-ep) Castle; (CD 3-5) **BLACK SABBATH LIMITED EDITION**
– Paranoid / Iron man / War pigs.

Dec 88. (6xcd-box) Castle; (BSBCD 001) **THE BLACK SABBATH CD COLLECTION**

Mar 89. (cd-ep) Old Gold; (OG 6129) **PARANOID / ELECTRIC FUNERAL / SABBATH BLOODY SABBATH**

Nov 89. (d-lp/c/cd) Vertigo; (838 818-1/-4/-2) **BLACKEST SABBATH**

Dec 89. (d-lp/d-c/cd) Masterpiece; (TRK LP/MC/CD 103) **BACKTRACKIN' (20th ANNIVERSARY EDITION)**

Mar 90. (7") Old Gold; (OG 9467) **PARANOID. / IRON MAN**

Oct 90. (cd/c/lp) Castle; (CCS CD/MC/LP 199) **THE BLACK SABBATH COLLECTION VOL.II**

May 91. (3xcd/5xlp-box) Essential; (ESB CD/LP 142) **THE OZZY OSBOURNE YEARS**
– (features first 6 albums)

Sep 94. (cd/c) Spectrum; (550720-2/-4) **IRON MAN**

1995. (cd-box with video) P.M.I.; (7243-8-30069-2) **CROSS PURPOSES LIVE (live 1994)**

Sep 95. (cd/c) Raw Power; (RAW CD/MC 104) **BETWEEN HEAVEN AND HELL (THE BEST OF BLACK SABBATH)**

Nov 95. (3xcd-box) E.M.I.; (CDOMB 014) **THE ORIGINALS**
– (HEADLESS CROSS / TYR / DEHUMANISER)

Apr 96. (cd/c) Essential; (EIRS CD/TC 1076) **THE SABBATH STONES**

Nov 96. (4xcd-box) Essential; (ESFCD 419) **UNDER THE WHEELS OF CONFUSION**

Oct 98. (3xcd-box) Essential; (ESMBX 300) **BLACK SABBATH / PARANOID / MASTER OF REALITY**

Oct 98. (3xcd-box) Essential; (ESMBX 301) **TECHNICAL ECSTASY / NEVER SAY DIE / HEAVEN AND HELL**

BLACK UHURU   (dig out; 4th edition)

BLACK WIDOW   (dig out; Great Metal . . .)

BLASTERS   (dig out; Great Alt & Indie . . .)

BLIND FAITH

Formed: London, England . . . May '69 . . . as supergroup of musicians ERIC CLAPTON, GINGER BAKER, STEVE WINWOOD and RIC GRECH. They introduced their accomplished style of roots blues at the BRIAN JONES memorial concert in Hyde Park, supporting The ROLLING STONES. Their first and only album, recorded virtually live in the studio, was a massive seller on both sides of the Atlantic and included some stellar moments ('CAN'T FIND MY WAY HOME', 'PRESENCE OF THE LORD'). They subsequently undertook a promotional tour of the States that Autumn, although to the disappointment of many fans, the project was abruptly aborted. • **Songwriters:** CLAPTON and WINWOOD, with cover WELL ALL RIGHT (Buddy Holly). • **Trivia:** GINGER BAKER's 11 year-old daughter was controversially used posing topless on UK album sleeve. This was subsequently banned in the States.

Album rating: BLIND FAITH (*7)

STEVE WINWOOD (b.12 May'48, Birmingham, England) – vocals, keyboards (ex-TRAFFIC, ex-SPENCER DAVIS GROUP) / **ERIC CLAPTON** (b.30 Mar'45, Ripley, England) – guitar, vocals (ex-CREAM, ex-JOHN MAYALL . . . , ex-YARDBIRDS, etc) / **RIC GRECH** (b. 1 Nov'46, Bordeaux, France) – bass (ex-FAMILY) / **GINGER BAKER** (b.19 Aug'39, Lewisham, England) – drums (ex-CREAM, ex-GRAHAM BOND ORGANISATION, ex-BLUES INC.)

                                       Polydor   **R.S.O.**

Aug 69. (lp) (583-059) <304> **BLIND FAITH**   `1` `1` Jul69
– Had to cry today / Can't find my way home / Well all right / Presence of the Lord / Sea of joy / Do what you like. <US re-iss. Feb77 on 'R.S.O.'; 3016> (re-iss. Nov77 on 'R.S.O.'; 2394 142) (re-iss. Aug83 on 'R.S.O.'; SPELP 14) (cd-iss. Apr86+=; 825 094-2) (cd re-iss. Sep95) – Exchange and mart / Spending all my days. (lp re-iss. Aug99 on 'Simply Vinyl'; SVLP 104)

—— Disbanded later 1969. GINGER BAKER formed AIRFORCE with STEVE WINWOOD. The latter returned to TRAFFIC before carving out a solo career. RIC GRECH went solo. As did ERIC CLAPTON who also formed DEREK & THE DOMINOES in 1970.

– compilations, others, etc. –

1977. (7") R.S.O.; <873> **CAN'T FIND MY WAY HOME. / PRESENCE OF THE LORD**   `-`
Obviously no albums were released, although some BLIND FAITH tracks did surface on ERIC CLAPTON compilations, 'CROSSROADS' and 'THE HISTORY OF ERIC CLAPTON' (see ⇒)

BLIND MELON

Formed: Newport Beach, Los Angeles, California, USA . . . 1989 by West Point, Mississippi born BRAD SMITH and ROGER STEVENS. In the early 90's, they were joined by SHANNON HOON, CHRISTOPHER THORN and a little later, GLEN GRAHAM. After recording a widely circulated demo, the band were eventually picked up by 'Capitol'. While awaiting release of their self-titled debut, SHANNON (cousin of AXL ROSE) guested on the GUNS N' ROSES set, 'Use Your Illusion'. With MTV heralding their excellent 'NO RAIN' track, their debut album finally shot into the US Top 3 in 1993. A laid back 70's/GRATEFUL DEAD influenced affair, alternately jangly and funky, HOON's vocals weren't too dissimilar to AXL's. Following a disappointing second set, 'SOUP' (1995), HOON died of a drug overdose on the 21st October '95. Three years on and the sad death now behind them, THORN and SMITH re-united in the outfit LUMA; frontman CHRIS SIHN and veteran drummer DAVE KRUSEN were also part of the set-up on an internet-only EP in '99.

Album rating: BLIND MELON (*6) / SOUP (*5) / NICO posthumous (*4)

SHANNON HOON (b. RICHARD SHANNON HOON, 26 Sep'67, Lafayette, Indiana) – vocals / **ROGER STEVENS** (b.31 Oct'70, West Point, Mis.) – guitar / **CHRISTOPHER THORN** (b.16 Dec'68, Dover, Pensylvania) – guitar / **BRAD SMITH** (b.29 Sep'68, West Point) – bass / **GLEN GRAHAM** (b. 5 Dec'68, Columbus, Miss.) – drums

		Capitol	Capitol
Jun 93.	(12"pic-d-ep/12"ep/cd-ep) (12P/12/CD CL 687) **TONES OF HOME / NO RAIN** (live). / **DRIVE** (live) / **SOAK THE SIN** (live)	62	-
Aug 93.	(cd/c) (CD/TC EST 2188) <96585> **BLIND MELON**	53	3
	– Soak the sin / Tones of home / I wonder / Paper scratcher / Dear ol' dad / Change / No rain / Deserted / Sleepy house / Holyman / Seed to a tree / Drive / Time. (re-dist.Jul94 w/ free cd, hit UK 53)		
Aug 93.	(c-s) <44939> **NO RAIN / NO RAIN (live) / SOAK THE SIN**	-	20
Dec 93.	(c-s/7"yellow) (TC+/CL 699) **NO RAIN. / NO BIDNESS (live)**	17	-
	(12"+=/cd-s+=) (12/CD CL 699) – I wonder.		
	(12"pic-d/pic-cd-s) (12P/CDP CL 699) – ('A'live) / Soak the sin / Paper scratcher / Deserted.		
Jun 94.	(c-s/7"green) (TC+/CL 717) **CHANGE. / PAPER SCRATCHER (acoustic)**	35	
	(12"pic-d/pic-cd-s) (12/CDS CL 717) – ('A'side) / No rain (live) / Candy says (live) / Time.		
Jul 95.	(cd-s) (CDCL 755) **GALAXIE / WILT / CAR SEAT (GOD'S PRESENTS)**	37	
	(12"+=) (12CL 755) – 2 x 4.		
	(cd-s) (CDCLS 755) – (first 2 tracks) / 2 x 4 / Change.		
Aug 95.	(cd/c) (CD/TC EST 2261) <28732> **SOUP**	48	28
	– Galaxie / 2 x 4 / Vernie / Skinned / Toes across the floor / Walk / Dumptruck / Car seat (God's presents) / Wilt / The duke / St.Andrew's fall / New life / Mouthful of cavities / Lemonade.		

—— On October 21st, '95, frontman SHANNON HOON died of drug overdose.

– compilations, etc. –

Feb 97.	(cd) Capitol; (CDEST 2291) **NICO**		
	– Pusher / Hell / Soup / No rain / Soul one / John Sinclair / All that I need / Glitch / Life ain't so shitty / Swallowed / Oull / St. Andrew's hall / Letters from a porcupine.		

BLINK-182

Formed: Poway, nr. San Diego, California, USA ... 1992 by TOM DELONGE, MARK HOPPUS and TRAVIS 'MAD DOG' BARKER. This post new cartoon punk outfit began when DELONGE and BARKER met in college. Soon, they were distributing their collection of demos (all of which would later appear on 'BUDDHA') to A&R upstarts. Unfortunately their quest did not succeed, forcing our mangled, spiky-haired heroes to issue their debut, self-financed set 'CHESHIRE CAT' (1995), whilst still under the name of BLINK. However, with pressures from an Irish group of the same name, the band re-emerged as BLINK-182 – the 182 in question, being the number of times Al Pacino said "fuck" in the movie, 'Scarface' – and issued the more successful 'DUDE RANCH' (1997). The album boasted college anthem 'DICK LIPS' which sent the boys quite literally on the road to semi-stardom via a little help from supportive peers GREEN DAY and NOFX. Major labels began to show interest, BLINK-182 finally signing on the dotted line with 'M.C.A.' at the beginning of 1999. 'ENEMA OF THE STATE' (which featured porn actress Janine scantily clad in a nurse's uniform) surfaced in that summer and went on to achieve double platinum sales throughout America and Europe. Memorable single, 'WHAT'S MY AGE AGAIN?' (a catchy two minute punk/pop rant), saw the trio run naked through L.A. (in the video at least!) and earned them a cameo performance in "ironic" teen sex movie, 'American Pie'. No underlying message, it seemed that BLINK 182 were just out to drink, party and get nekid!

Album rating: CHESHIRE CAT (*5) / DUDE RANCH (*7) / BUDDHA (*5) / ENEMA OF THE STATE (*6)

TOM DELONGE – vocals, guitar / **MARK HOPPUS** – bass / **SCOTT RAYNOR** – drums

		not iss.	unknown
1993.	(7"ep; as BLINK) **FLY SWATTER EP**	-	
		not iss.	Rapido
Jun 96.	(cd-ep) <RAP 14> **WASTING TIME EP** (UK-iss.Apr98; RAP 30)	-	
		Grilled Cheese	Grilled Cheese
Nov 96.	(cd) (GRL 001) **CHESHIRE CAT**		May95
	– Carousel / M+M's / Fentoozler / Touchdown boy / Strings / Peggy Sue / Sometimes / Does my breath smell? / Cacophony / T.V. / Toast and bananas / Wasting time / Romeo and Rebecca / Ben wah balls / Just about done / Depends.		
Nov 96.	(cd-s) (GRL 701) **THEY CAME TO CONQUER. /**		-

May 97.	(cd-ep) <(CSGRL 004)> **DICK LIPS / APPLE SHAMPOO / WRECKED HIM / ZULU**		
Jul 97.	(cd/lp) <(CRGD/LPGRL 4)> **DUDE RANCH**		67
	– Pathetic / Voyeur / Dammit / Boring / Dick lips / Waggy / Enthused / Untitled / Apple shampoo / Emo / Josie / New hope / Degenerate / Lemmings / I'm sorry. <(cd re-iss. Nov97 on 'M.C.A.'; MCD 11624)>		
Oct 97.	(cd/lp) <78765-2/-1> **BUDDHA** (demos)		
	– Carousel / T.V. / Strings / Fentoozler / Time / Romeo & Rebecca / 21 days / Sometimes / Point of view / My pet Sally / Reebok commercial / Toast and bananas / The girl next door / Don't. (re-iss. Jan99 & Jul99; same)		
	(above issued on 'Kung Fu')		
Nov 98.	(cd-s) <55513> **JOSIE / WASTING TIME / CAROUSER / I WON'T BE HOME FOR CHRISTMAS**	-	-
		M.C.A.	M.C.A.
Sep 99.	(c-s) (MCSC 40219) <radio cut> **WHAT'S MY AGE AGAIN?** / **PATHETIC (live)**	38	59 Jul99
	(cd-s+=) <(MCSTD 40219)> – Untitled (live).		
	(cd-s) <(MCSXD 40219)> – ('A'side) / Josie (live) / Aliens exist (live).		
Oct 99.	(cd) (MCD 11950) <111950> **ENEMA OF THE STATE**		9 Jun99
	– Dumpweed / Don't leave me / Aliens exist / Going away to college / What's my age again? / Dysentry Gary / Adam's song / All the small things / Party song / Mutt / Wendy clear / Anthem.		
	(above will hit UK Top10 in the year 2000) (below repeated the feat)		
Nov 99.	(-) <album cut> **ALL THE SMALL THINGS**	-	52

BLODWYN PIG (dig out; Great Psychedelic ...)

BLONDIE

Formed: New York City, New York, USA ... August 1974 by former Playboy bunny girl, DEBBIE HARRY and boyfriend CHRIS STEIN. Other original members (excluding female backing singers) were sticksman, BILLY O'CONNOR (soon replaced by CLEM BURKE), bassist FRED SMITH (later of TELEVISION) and guitarist IVAN KRAL (later of PATTI SMITH GROUP). After line-up changes which saw the latter two replaced by GARY VALENTINE and JIMMY DESTRI respectively, the group soon found themselves supporting the likes of punk legend, IGGY POP. Subsequently hooking up with veteran producer, Richard Gottehrer, the group released their debut single, 'X-OFFENDER', on his 'Private Stock' label in late '76. This was followed with a second track, 'IN THE FLESH', while the eponymous debut hit the shelves later that Spring. Trawling tacky 60's girly pop and sprucing it up with a healthy dose of punk muscle and attitude, BLONDIE laid the foundations for their swoonsomely infectious late 70's/early 80's hits. With HARRY as the peroxide Marilyn Monroe of new wave, BLONDIE almost immediately caught the eye of the UK scene, where a follow-up album, 'PLASTIC LETTERS', made the Top 10 in Spring '78. By this point BLONDIE had signed to 'Chrysalis' (who had reputedly bought the contract out for $500,000 in August of the previous year) and had replaced VALENTINE with FRANK INFANTE. A cover of Randy & The Rainbows 60's nugget, 'DENISE' (aka 'DENIS') almost topped the British charts, while another single pulled from the album, '(I'M ALWAYS TOUCHED BY YOUR) PRESENCE DEAR', made the Top 10. With the subsequent recruitment of bassist NIGEL HARRISON, INFANTE switched to rhythm guitar, the music taking on a whole new dimension with the seminal 'PARALLEL LINES' (1978). Produced by legendary pop picker, MIKE CHAPMAN, the album spawned a UK Top 5 in 'HANGING ON THE TELEPHONE', plus two No.1's with 'SUNDAY GIRL' and 'HEART OF GLASS'. The latter track's throbbing disco feel was further developed on fourth album, 'EAT TO THE BEAT', a set which featured yet another UK chart topper in the moody dancefloor classic, 'ATOMIC' (later famous for providing the aural backdrop to the disco scene in 'Trainspotting'). BLONDIE even teamed up with electro disco guru, GEORGIO MORODER, for 'CALL ME' (recorded for the soundtrack to 'American Gigolo'), the band's second transatlantic No.1. They repeated this feat with 'THE TIDE IS HIGH', a wonderfully dreamy cover of a track originally cut by reggae outfit, The PARAGONS, while also having a bash at hip hop with 'RAPTURE', their fourth US No.1. Both tracks were included on 1980's 'AUTOAMERICAN', an album which suggested BLONDIE were beginning to lose their musical curls. Although 'THE HUNTER' (1982) spawned a further British No.1 in 'ISLAND OF LOST SOULS', the album met with a less than rapturous reception, likewise their final tour. The band finally split in summer '82, STEIN forming his own 'Chrysalis'-backed label, 'Animal', before falling ill the following year. This put HARRY's solo career (begun rather non-eventfully with 1981's BERNARD EDWARDS / NILE RODGERS collaborative set, 'KOO KOO') temporarily on the back burner, the singer re-emerging in late '86 with the UK Top 10, 'FRENCH KISSIN' IN THE U.S.A.'. The accompanying album, 'ROCKBIRD' made the Top 40 although 1989's 'DEF, DUMB AND BLONDE' was more successful, its shiny, poppy single 'I WANT THAT MAN' making the UK Top 20. If nothing else, she proved herself an adaptable stylist although much more interesting was a tongue in cheek duet with IGGY POP in 1990, 'WELL, DID YOU EVAH!'. Throughout her career, HARRY had also made the occasional venture into celluloid (see below). At the tender age of 53, but still looking every inch (or two) the ideal peroxide sex symbol, DEBBIE and her slightly younger crew of CHRIS, JIMMY and CLEM, re-formed BLONDIE for round the world tours. By early 1999, the band were topping the UK charts with the catchy 'MARIA', a song lifted from their aptly-titled Top 5 (US Top 40) parent album, 'NO EXIT'. • **Songwriters:** Most written by STEIN-HARRY except; HANGING ON THE TELEPHONE (Jack Lee; Nerves) / RING OF

FIRE (Johnny Cash) / HEROES (David Bowie). • **Trivia:** DEBBIE HARRY filmography:- UNION CITY (1979) / ROADIE (1980) / VIDEODROME (1982) / HAIRSPRAY (1982) / Broadway play 'TEANECK TANZI: THE VENUS FLYTRAP' (1983), which bombed after one night. She also appeared on 'The Muppet Show' circa 1980.

Album rating: BLONDIE (*6) / PLASTIC LETTERS (*7) / PARALLEL LINES (*8) / EAT TO THE BEAT (*6) / AUTOAMERICAN (*5) / THE BEST OF BLONDIE compilation (*9) / THE HUNTER (*4) / THE COMPLETE PICTURE – THE VERY BEST OF DEBORAH HARRY & BLONDIE compilation (*9) / BLONDE AND BEYOND compilation (*5) / NO EXIT (*6) / Debbie Harry: KOOKOO (*5) / ROCKBIRD (*6) / DEF, DUMB & BLONDE (*5) / DEBRAVATION (*4)

DEBBIE HARRY (b. 1 Jul'45, Miami, Florida) – vocals (ex-WIND IN THE WILLOWS) / **CHRIS STEIN** (b. 5 Jan'50, Brooklyn, New York) – guitar / **JIMMY STEIN** (b.13 Apr'54) – keyboards (ex-KNICKERS) / **GARY VALENTINE** – bass / **CLEM BURKE** (b.CLEMENT, 24 Nov'55) – drums (ex-SWEET REVENGE)

		Private Stock	Private Stock
Dec 76.	(7") <PVT 90> **X OFFENDER. / IN THE SUN**	-	-
Dec 76.	(lp) <PS 2023> **BLONDIE**	-	-

– X offender / Little girl lies / In the flesh / Look good in blue / In the sun / A shark in jet's clothing / Man overboard / Rip her to shreds / Rifle range / Kung Fu girls / The attack of the giant ants. <re-iss. Feb77; PVLP 1017> (UK-iss.Dec77 on 'Chrysalis'; CHR 1165) – (hit UK No.75 in Mar79) (re-iss. Oct82 on 'Hallmark' lp/c; SHM/HSC 3119) (re-iss. Apr85 on 'M.F.P.' lp/c; MFP 41-5696-1/-4) (cd-iss. Sep94 on 'Chrysalis'; CDCHR 6081)

Feb 77.	(7") <PVT 105> **IN THE FLESH. / MAN OVERBOARD**	-	-
May 77.	(7") (PVT 105) **IN THE FLESH. / X OFFENDER**	-	-

		Chrysalis	Chrysalis
Nov 77.	(7"m/12"m) <CHS 2180/+12> **RIP HER TO SHREDS. / IN THE FLESH / X OFFENDER**	-	-

(re-iss. 12"m Dec81; same)

—— (Oct'77) **FRANK INFANTE** – bass (ex-WORLD WAR III) repl. VALENTINE

Feb 78.	(7"m/12") <CHS 2180/+12> **DENIS. / CONTACT IN RED SQUARE / KUNG FU GIRLS**	2	

(re-iss. 12"white Dec81; same)

Feb 78.	(lp/c) <CHR/ZCHR 1166> **PLASTIC LETTERS**	10	72 Feb78

– Fan mail / Denis / Bermuda Triangle blues (Flight 45) / Youth nabbed as sniper / Contact in Red Square / (I'm always touched by your) Presence, dear / I'm on E / I didn't have the nerve to say no / Love at the pier / No imagination / Kidnapper / Detroit 442 / Cautious lip. (cd-iss. Sep94; CDCHR 6085)

Apr 78.	(7"m/12") <CHS/+12 2217> **(I'M ALWAYS TOUCHED BY YOUR) PRESENCE, DEAR. / POET'S PROBLEM / DETROIT 442**	10	

(re-iss. Dec81; same)

—— (Nov77 on recording of 2nd lp) added **NIGEL HARRISON** – bass (b.24 Apr'51, Stockport, England) now sextet with **INFANTE** – now on rhythm guitar

Aug 78.	(7"yellow) <CHS 2204> **PICTURE THIS. / FADE AWAY (AND RADIATE)**	12	
Sep 78.	(7") <2251> **I'M GONNA LOVE YOU TOO. / JUST GO AWAY**	-	-
Sep 78.	(lp/c) <CHR/ZCHR 1192> **PARALLEL LINES**	1	6

– Fade away (and radiate) / Hanging on the telephone / One way or another / Picture this / Pretty baby / I know but I don't know / 11:59 / Will anything happen / Sunday girl / Heart of glass / I'm gonna love you too / Just go away. (re-iss. Nov83 on 'Fame' lp/c; FA/TCFA 3089-1/-4) (re-iss. Jul88 lp/c/cd; CDL/ZCDL/CCD 1192) (re-iss. Dec92 on 'Fame' cd/c; CD/TC FA 3282) (re-iss. Jul94 cd/c; CCD/ZCDL 1192)

Nov 78.	(7") (CHS 2266) **HANGING ON THE TELEPHONE. / WILL ANYTHING HAPPEN**	5	-
Nov 78.	(7") <CHS 2266> **HANGING ON THE TELEPHONE. / FADE AWAY AND RADIATE**	-	-
Jan 79.	(7") (CHS 2275) **HEART OF GLASS. / RIFLE RANGE** (12"+=) – ('A'instrumental). (re-iss. 12" Dec81; same)	1	-
Feb 79.	(7") <CHS 2275> **HEART OF GLASS. / 11:59**	-	1
May 79.	(7") (CHS 2320) **SUNDAY GIRL. / I KNOW BUT I DON'T KNOW** (12"+=) – ('A' French version). (re-iss. 12"clear Dec81; same)	1	-
May 79.	(7") (CHS 2336) **ONE WAY OR ANOTHER. / JUST GO AWAY**	-	24
Sep 79.	(7") (CHS 2350) **DREAMING. / SOUND ASLEEP**	2	-
Sep 79.	(7") <CHS 2379> **DREAMING. / LIVING IN THE REAL WORLD**	-	27
Oct 79.	(lp/c) <CHR/ZCHR 1225> **EAT TO THE BEAT**	1	17

– Dreaming / The hardest part / Union city blue / Shayla / Eat to the beat / Accidents never happen / Die young stay pretty Slow motion / Atomic / Sound-a-sleep / Victor / Living in the real world. (cd-iss. Jun87; CPCD 1225) (cd-iss. Nov92; CDCHR 1225)

Nov 79.	(7") (CHS 2400) **UNION CITY BLUE. / LIVING IN THE REAL WORLD**	13	
Jan 80.	(7") <CHS 2408> **THE HARDEST PART. / SOUND-A-SLEEP**	-	84
Feb 80.	(7") (CHS 2410) **ATOMIC. / DIE YOUNG STAY PRETTY** (12"+=) (CHS12 2410) – Heroes. (re-iss. 12" Dec81; same)	1	39 May80
Apr 80.	(7") <(CHS 2414)> **CALL ME. / ('A'instrumental)** (12"+=) (CHS12 2414) – ('A'-Spanish version).	1	1 Feb80
Oct 80.	(7") <CHS 2465> **THE TIDE IS HIGH. / SUZIE AND JEFFREY**	1	1 Nov80
Nov 80.	(lp/c) <(CDL/ZCDL 1290)> **AUTOAMERICAN**	3	7

– Europa / Live it up / Here's looking at you / The tide is high / Angels on the balcony / Go through it / Do the dark / Rapture / Faces / Do the dark / T-Birds / Walk like me / Follow me. (cd-iss. Sep94; CDCHR 6084)

Jan 81.	(7") <CHS 2485> **RAPTURE. / WALK LIKE ME** (12") (CHS12 2485) – ('A'side / Live it up.	5	1
Oct 81.	(lp/c) (CDLTV/ZCLTV 1) <1371> **THE BEST OF BLONDIE** (compilation)	4	30

– Denis / The tide is high / In the flesh / Sunday girl / (I'm always touched by your) Presence dear / Dreaming / Hanging on the telephone / Rapture / Picture this / Union

city blue / Call me / Atomic / Rip her to shreds / Heart of glass. (cd-iss. Jan88; CCD 1371)

Apr 82.	(7"/7"pic-d) <(CHS/+P 2608)> **ISLAND OF LOST SOULS. / DRAGONFLY**	1	37 May82
May 82.	(lp/c/pic-lp) <(CDL/ZCDL/PCDL 1384)> **THE HUNTER**	9	33

– Orchid club / Island of lost souls / Dragonfly / For your eyes only / The beast / War child / Little Caesar / Danceaway / (Can I) Find the right words (to say) / English boys / The hunter gets captured by the game. (cd-iss. Sep94; CDCHR 6083)

Jul 82.	(7"/7"pic-d/12") <(CHS/+P/12 2624)> **WAR CHILD. / LITTLE CAESAR**	39	

—— (Aug'82) STEIN formed own 'Animal' label through 'Chrysalis'. CLEM BURKE joins EURYTHMICS and later RAMONES. He also teams up with HARRISON to form CHEQUERED PAST. A solo album, 'HEART ON THE WALL', was released by JIMMY DESTRI in 1982 and featured most of BLONDIE.

DEBBIE HARRY

solo, with **NILE RODGERS** and **BERNARD EDWARDS** on production, etc.

		Chrysalis	Chrysalis
Jul 81.	(7"/12") <(CHS/+12 2526)> **BACKFIRED. / MILITARY RAP**	32	43
Aug 81.	(lp/c) <(CHR/ZCCHR 1347)> **KOO KOO**	6	23

– Jump jump / The jam was moving / Chrome / Under arrest / Inner city spillover / Surrender / Backfired / Now I know you / Military rap / Oasis. (cd-iss. Sep94; CDCHR 6082)

Sep 81.	(7") <CHS 2554> **THE JAM WAS MOVING. / CHROME** (12"+=) (CHS12 2554) – Inner city spillover.	82	

—— now worked with various session musicians.

		Chrysalis	Geffen
Jan 84.	(7") **RUSH RUSH. / DANCE DANCE DANCE**	-	
Jan 84.	(7"/12") (CHS/12CHS 2752) **RUSH RUSH. / RUSH RUSH (dub)**		-
Nov 86.	(7") (CHS 3066) **FRENCH KISSIN' IN THE U.S.A. / ROCKBIRD** ('A'dance; 12"+=/12"pic-d+=) (CHS12 3066/+B) – ('A'dub version).	8	-
Nov 86.	(7") <28546> **FRENCH KISSIN' IN THE U.S.A. / BUCKLE UP**	-	57
Nov 86.	(lp/c/cd) (CHR/ZCHR/CCD 1540) <24123> **ROCKBIRD**	31	97

– I want you / French kissin' in the U.S.A. / Buckle up / In love with love / You got me in trouble / Free to fall / Rockbird / Secret life / Beyond the limit. (cd re-iss. Sep94; CCD 1540)

Feb 87.	(7") <CHS 3093> **FREE TO FALL. / FEEL THE SPIN** (12"+=/12"pic-d+=) (CHS12 3093/+B) – Secret life. (d7"+=) (CHSD 3093) – French kissin' in the U.S.A. / Rockbird.	46	
Apr 87.	(7") (CHS 3128) **IN LOVE WITH LOVE. / FEEL THE SPIN** (12"+=/12"pic-d+=) (CHS/+P 12-3128) – French kissin' in the U.S.A. (French version).	45	-
Jun 87.	(7") <28476> **IN LOVE WITH LOVE. / SECRET LIFE**	-	70

DEBORAH HARRY

—— with **CHRIS STEIN** – guitar / **LEIGH FOXX** – bass / **TERRY BOZZIO** – drums / **TOMMY PRICE** – drums / **PHIL ASHLEY** – synthesizers / **STEVE GOLDSTEIN** – keyboards, etc.

		Chrysalis	Sire
Sep 89.	(7"/c-s) (CHS/+MC 3369) **I WANT THAT MAN. / BIKE BOY** (12"pic-d+=/cd-s+=) (CHS 12P/CD 3369) – ('A'remix) / ('A'instrumental).	13	
Oct 89.	(lp/c/cd) (CHR/ZCHR/CCD 1650) <25938> **DEF, DUMB & BLONDE**	12	

– I want that man / Lovelight / KIss it better / Bike boy * / Get your way / Maybe for sure / I'll never fall in love / Calmarie / Sweet and low / He is so / Bugeye / Comic books / Brite side / End of the run *. (cd+=*) (cd re-iss. Sep94; CCD 1650)

Nov 89.	(7"/7"s) (CHS/+PB 3452) **BRITE SIDE. / BUGEYE** (12"+=/cd-s+=) (CHS 12/CD 3452) – In love with love. ('A'remix-cd-s++=) (CHSCCD 3452) – French kissin' in the U.S.A.	59	

—— Her touring group at time included **STEIN** and **FOXX** plus **SUZY DAVIS** – keyboards / **CARLA OLLA** – rhythm guitar / **JIMMY CLARK** – drums

Mar 90.	(7"/7"s) (CHS/+PB 3491) **SWEET AND LOW. / LOVELIGHT** (12"/12"pic-d/cd-s) (CHS 12/P12/CD 3491) – (3-'A'mixes).	57	
May 90.	(7") (CHS 3537) **MAYBE FOR SURE. / GET YOUR WAY** (12"+=/cd-s+=) (12/CD CHS 3537) – ('A'extended). below featured on a Cole Porter tribute album, 'Red Hot & Blue'.		
Dec 90.	(7"/12"; by DEBORAH HARRY & IGGY POP) (CHS/+12 3646) **WELL DID YOU EVAH! / (b-side by The Thompson Twins)** (cd-s+=) (CHSCD 3646) – (track by 'Aztec Camera').	42	
Jun 93.	(c-s/7") (TC+/CHS 4900) **I CAN SEE CLEARLY. / STANDING IN MY WAY** (12"+=/cd-s+=) (12/CD CHS 4900) – Atomic / Heart of glass. (cd-s+=) (CDCHSS 4900) – Call me / In love with love.	23	
Jul 93.	(cd/c/lp) (CD/TC+/CHR 6033) **DEBRAVATION**	24	

– I can see clearly / Stability / Strike me pink / Rain / Communion / Lip service / Mood ring / Dancing down the moon / Standing in my way / The fugitive / Dog star girl.

Sep 93.	(c-s) (TCCHS 5000) **STRIKE ME PINK / 8 AND A HALF RHUMBA** (cd-s) (CDCHS 5000) – Dreaming. (12"pic-d/cd-s) (12CHSPD/CDCHSS 5000) – ('A'side) / Sweet and low / On a breath.	46	

BLONDIE

—— re-formed in 1998 with **DEBBIE, CHRIS, CLEM + JIMMY**

		Beyond-RCA	Logic
Feb 99.	(c-s) (74321 64563-4) <78040> **MARIA / MARIA (Soul Soultion mix)** (cd-s+=) (74321 64563-2) – Maria (Talvin Singh remix). (cd-s) (74321 63737-2) – ('A'side) / In the flesh (live) / Screaming skin (live).	1	82 Mar99
Feb 99.	(cd/c) (74321 64114-2/-4) <78003> **NO EXIT**	3	18

– Screaming skin / Forgive & forget / Maria / No exit / Double take / Nothing is real but the girl / Boom boom in the zoom zoom room / Night wind sent / Under the gun / Out in the streets / Happy dog (for Caggy) / The dream's lost on me / Divine / Dig up the Congo.

Jun 99. (c-s) (74321 66948-4) **NOTHING IS REAL BUT THE GIRL (Boilerhouse mix) / RIP HER TO SHREDS (live)** | 26 | |
(cd-s) (74321 66380-2) – ('A'side) / ('A'-Danny Tenaglia mix) / ('A'-Danny Tenaglia instradub).
(cd-s) (74321 66947-2) – ('A'-US radio mix) / Hanging on the telephone (live) / Shayla (live).

Nov 99. (cd-ep) (74321 71653-2) **NO EXIT / MARIA (J&B mix) / MARIA (Talvin Singh rhythmic mix) / NOTHING IS REAL BUT THE GIRL (Danny Tenaglia mix & his trance version)** | | |

– compilations, others, etc. –

on 'Chrysalis' unless mentioned otherwise

Dec 82. (d-c) (2CDP 101) **EAT TO THE BEAT / AUTOAMERICAN** | | - |
Feb 87. (7") Old Gold; (OG 9672) **DENIS. / PICTURE THIS** | | - |
Feb 87. (7") Old Gold; (OG 9674) **SUNDAY GIRL. / HANGING ON THE TELEPHONE** | | - |
Feb 87. (7") Old Gold; (OG 9676) **CALL ME. / UNION CITY BLUE** | | - |
Feb 87. (7") Old Gold; (OG 9678) **HEART OF GLASS / THE TIDE IS HIGH** | | - |
Feb 87. (7") Old Gold; (OG 9680) **DREAMING. / ATOMIC** | | - |
Nov 88. (7") (CHS 3328) **DENIS (remix). / RAPTURE (Teddy Riley remix)** | 50 | - |
(12"+=/12"pic-d+=/cd-s+=) (CHS/12/12P/CD 3328) – Heart of glass (remix) / Atomic (remix).
Dec 88. (lp/c/cd) (CJB/ZCJB/CDJB 2) **ONCE MORE INTO THE BLEACH (GREATEST HITS)** | 50 | - |
– Denis / Heart of glass / Call me / Rapture / Rapture (bonus beats) / The tide is high / The jam was moving (DEBBIE HARRY) / In love with love (DEBBIE HARRY) / Rush rush (DEBBIE HARRY) / French kissin' in the U.S.A. (DEBBIE HARRY) / Feel the spin (DEBBIE HARRY) / Backfired (DEBBIE HARRY) / Sunday girl (French version).
Dec 88. (lp/c/cd) Star; (84026-1/-4) **BLONDIE HIT COLLECTION** | | - |
Feb 89. (7") (CHS 3342) **CALL ME. / CALL ME (version)** | 61 | - |
(12"+=/cd-s+=) (CHS 12/CD 3342) – Backfired (DEBBIE HARRY).
Mar 91. (cd/c/d-lp) (CCD/ZCHR/CHR 1817) **THE COMPLETE PICTURE – THE VERY BEST OF DEBORAH HARRY & BLONDIE** | 3 | |
– Heart of glass / I want that man / Call me / Sunday girl / French kissin' in the USA / Denis / Rapture / Brite side / (I'm always touched by your) Presence dear / Well, did you evah! / The tide is high / In love with love / Hanging on the telephone / Island of lost souls / Picture this / Dreaming / Sweet and low / Union city blue / Atomic / Rip her to shreds.
Jan 94. (cd/c) (CD/TC CHR 6063) **BLONDIE AND BEYOND – RARITIES AND ODDITIES** | | - |
Aug 94. (c-s/12"/cd-s) (12/ZC/CD CHS 5013) **ATOMIC (re-mix). / ('A'mixes by Diddy & Alan Thompson)** | 19 | - |
(cd-s) (CDCHS 5013) – ('A'side) / Sunday girl (re-mix) / Union City blues (re-mix).
Nov 94. (d-cd) (CDCHR 6089) **THE PLATINUM COLLECTION** | | |
Jun 95. (12") (12CHS 5023) HEART OF GLASS (re-mix). / CALL ME (re-mix) | 15 | |
(c-s) (CDCHS 5023) – ('A'side) / Rapture / Atomic (re-mix).
(cd-s+=) (CDCHSS 5023) – ('A'mixes).
Jul 95. (cd/c/d-lp) (CD/TC+/CHR 6105) **BEAUTIFUL – THE REMIX ALBUM** | 25 | - |
Oct 95. (12"blue/cd-s) (12/CD CHS 5027) **UNION CITY BLUE (re-mix) / I FEEL LOVE (live)** | 31 | - |
(cd-s) (CDCHSS 5027) – (other mixes by:- Diddy / The Burger Queens / OPM / Vinny Vero & Jammin' Hot).
Jul 98. (cd/c) E.M.I.; (494996-2/-4) **ATOMIC – THE VERY BEST OF . . .** | 12 | |
(d-cd-iss.Feb99 +=; 499288-2) – ATOMIX
Jul 98. (c-s) E.M.I.; (TCATOM 150) **ATOMIC (1998 remix)** | | |
(12"+=/cd-s+=) (12/CD ATOM 150) – ('A'mixes).
Mar 99. (cd) EMI Gold; (499421-2) **THE ESSENTIAL COLLECTION** | | - |
Jun 99. (cd) E.M.I.; (521233-2) **LIVE (live Philadelphia 1978 / Dallas 1980)** | | |

BLOODHOUND GANG

Formed: King Of Prussia, Pennsylvania, USA . . . 1994 by JIMMY ALI POP and LUPUS. Not much can be said for these cheeky US punks who have so obviously ripped off quality comedic acts such as JERKY BOYS and BEASTIE BOYS (latter strictly 80's period only!). The BLOODHOUND GANG quite literally stamped on their peers', attempting to crush their credibility with sexual innuendos within nasty, juvenile rock. A topsy turvy blend of hip hop, metal, rap, quirky funk and a galaxy of fart jokes, the, er . . . BG's signed to 'Columbia' after the minor success of the 'DINGLEBERRY HAZE' EP. The group issued the seminal classic 'USE YOUR FINGERS' (1995) and were subsequently dropped due to an abundance of irate listeners who even disliked their manic version of 'KIDS IN AMERICA'. However, once these pesky youths were knocked down, they rose to their feet once more, rebelling with the 'ONE FIERCE BEER COASTER' album (which was originally delivered through the small 'Republic' label). In 1996, David Geffen and his associates found some relative humour within the group, signing them and re-releasing the aforementioned set. The US hit album was heavily promoted with tongue-in-cheek single, 'KISS ME WHERE IT SMELLS FUNNY'; its video apparently featured a bowler-hatted guy sprinting off to somewhere with a fish(!). This single sent giggling American teens ballistic in campuses everywhere and became the most alternative party tune since '(Y~ou've Gotta) Fight For Your Right (To Party)'. Echoes of KING

MISSILE's frank and subtle-as-a-sledgehammer humour could be heard within the realms of the group's madness, although vaguely comparing such acts who were so diverse would be in itself insane. Later (in 1999), the band respectfully (not!) celebrated the female form with another long-player, 'HOORAY FOR BOOBIES', ahhem. To much critical lauding, it went on to win five Grammys and a whole host of international music awards, the best track being the hit single, 'THE BAD TOUCH'.
Album rating: USE YOUR FINGERS (*4) / ONE FIERCE BEER COASTER (*3) / HOORAY FOR BOOBIES (*8)

JIMMY POP ALI (b. JAMES BOWE) – vocals / **LUPUS** (b. FRANKS) – guitar

	not iss.	Cheese Factory
Oct 94. (cd-ep) <9401> **DINGLEBERRY HAZE EP**	-	

– Go down / Cheese tidbit / Legend in my spare time / Neighbour invasion / Mama say / Hang dang / Earlamayer the butt pirate / One way / Record offer / Co costs choo / Live at the Apollo
<re-iss. 1999 on 'Interscope'; 90455>

	not iss.	TVT-Sony
May 95. (c-s/cd-s) <7792-9/-8> **MAMA SAY /**	-	
Jun 95. (cd/c) <67225> **USE YOUR FINGERS**	-	

– Rip Taylor is God / We are the knuckleheads / Legend in my spare time / B.H.G.P.S.A. / Mama say / Kids in America / You're pretty when I'm drunk / The evils of placenta hustling / One way / Shitty record offer / Go down / Earlamayer the butt pirate / No rest for the wicked / She ain't got no legs / We like meat / Coo coo ca choo / Rang dang / Nightmare at the Apollo – K.I.D.S . . . . (UK-iss.Feb98 on 'TVT-Sony'; same as US)

—— added **EVIL JARED** – bass / **SPANKY G** – drums / **Q-BALL** – DJ

	not iss.	Republic
Dec 96. (lp) <REP 26903-1> **ONE FIERCE BEER COASTER**	-	57

– Kiss me where it smells funny / Lift your head up high (and blow your . . . .) / Fire water burn / I wish I was queer so I could get . . . . / Why's everybody always pickin' on me? / It's tricky / Asleep at the wheel / Shut up / Your only friends are make believe / Boom / Going nowhere slow / Reflections of Remoh. <cd-iss. Sep97 on 'Geffen'; GED 25124> (UK lp-iss.Oct97 on 'Republic'; same as US)

	Geffen	Geffen
Aug 97. (c-s) (GFSC 22252) **WHY'S EVERYBODY ALWAYS PICKIN' ON ME? (Xankus Maximus mix) / 'A' Hemlock mix**		

(12"+=/cd-s+=) (GFS V/TD 22252) – ('A' - Greek salad mix)
Nov 97. (12") <(REP 9603-1)> **FIRE WATER BURN (Rudimental Jammy Jam). / FIRE WATER BURN (Jim Makin' Jamaican mix)** | | |
(above on 'Republic', below on 'Bloodhound Gang')
Dec 97. (7") <(BHG 002)> **ONE CENSORED BEER COASTER** | | |
Oct 99. (cd) <(90455)> **HOORAY FOR BOOBIES** | | Sep99 |
– I hope you die / The inevitable return of the great white dope / Mama's boy / Three point one four / Mope / Yummy down on this / The ballad of Chasey Lain / R.S.V.P. / Magna cum nada / The bad touch / That cough came with a prize / Take the long way home / Hell yeah / Right turn Klyde / This is stupid / A lap dance is so much better when the stripper is crying / 10 coolest things about New Jersey / Along comes Mary.

BLOOD, SWEAT & TEARS

Formed: New York, USA . . . late 1967 by BLUES PROJECT defectors, AL KOOPER and STEVE KATZ, together with rhythm section BOBBY COLOMBY and JIM FIELDER; FRED LIPSIUS subsequently joined on sax while original members were supplemented by a brass section of DICK HALLIGAN, RANDY BRECKER and JERRY WEISS. The first album (for 'Columbia') 'CHILD IS FATHER TO THE MAN' was released in early '68 to critical acclaim but only moderate commercial success. Internal strife caused KOOPER to leave soon after the record's release, his place taken by DAVID CLAYTON-THOMAS. BRECKER and WEISS also left, CHUCK WINFIELD and Brooklyn buddies JERRY HYMAN and LEW SOLOFF subsequently bolstering their ranks. Produced by JAMES GUERCIO, the eponymous second album was issued at the dawn of '69, a much more popular effort which hit the commercial bullseye, going triple platinum and winning a Grammy award; three hit singles, 'YOU'VE MADE ME SO VERY HAPPY', 'SPINNING WHEEL' plus 'AND WHEN I DIE', helped make it Album Of The Year. Although his powerful, soulful larynx perfectly complemented the brass-heavy jazz-pop sound, GUERCIO found CLAYTON-THOMAS' ego in the studio too much to take; the producer decided to quit while he was ahead, taking his skills to the more commercial (and less volatile) CHICAGO. With BST's lead vocalist beginning to dominate the outfit more and more, further friction was inevitable. However, the band began to court the media and became the critics' darlings for a short time (even appearing at Woodstock – much to the bemusement of the love children). The third album, 'BLOOD, SWEAT & TEARS 3' (1970) and 'B,S & T; 4' (1971), saw the band reconciled with KOOPER, although he returned in a production capacity. The winning formula continued, notably with the valedictory CLAYTON-THOMAS-penned 'GO DOWN GAMBLIN'. While DAVID's vocals helped win chart success, there were continual arguments over the band's musical direction (most of the members were classically-trained) which resulted in a huge bust-up in 1972. Exit one DAVID CLAYTON-THOMAS. He was almost immediately replaced on vocals by BOB DOYLE then JERRY FISHER, the subsequent domino effect seeing chaos reign supreme; different factions within the band had been pulling in different directions. Time for a Greatest Hits compilation perhaps?, 'BLOOD, SWEAT & TEARS GREATEST HITS' was issued in Spring '72 and went gold, peaking at 19 in the charts. Yet more musical chairs ensued when HENDERSON and HALLIGAN departed, the pair superseded by LOU MARINI JR and LARRY WILLIS respectively for subsequent albums, 'NEW BLOOD' (1972) and 'NO SWEAT' (1973). They were now, however, losing their reputation as a crowd-pulling band, and even with CLAYTON-THOMAS' return, the writing was on the wall. Their ninth and final album for 'Columbia', 'MORE THAN EVER' (1976) was actually less than ever in terms of the quality control; it was time for a parting of the ways. 'BRAND NEW DAY' (1977) – their first for 'A.B.C.' – continued the creative slump and failed (for the first time!) to break into the US Top 200. In truth, the once great BS&T was in its death throes, breathing its last as a backing section for CLAYTON-THOMAS' similarly expiring career. • Songwriters: Most by KOOPER until CLAYTON-THOMAS took over. Covered AND WHEN I DIE (Laura Nyro) / YOU'VE MADE ME SO VERY HAPPY (Brenda Holloway) / MORNING GLORY (Tim Buckley) / HI-DE-HO (Goffin-King) / GOT TO GET YOU INTO MY LIFE (Beatles) / etc.

Album rating: CHILD IS FATHER TO THE MAN (*7) / BLOOD, SWEAT & TEARS (*7) / BLOOD, SWEAT & TEARS 3 (*5) / B, S & T; 4 (*4) / BLOOD, SWEAT & TEARS GREATEST HITS compilation (*7) / NEW BLOOD (*3) / NO SWEAT (*3) / MIRROR IMAGE (*3) / NEW CITY (*3) / MORE THAN EVER (*3) / BRAND NEW DAY (*3) / NUCLEAR BLUES (*3) / CLASSIC . . . compilation (*6) / SMILING PHASES compilation (*5) / WHAT GOES UP: BEST OF . . . compilation (*7)

AL KOOPER (b. 5 Feb'44, Brooklyn, NY) – vocals, keyboards (ex-BLUES PROJECT, ex-BOB DYLAN Band) / **STEVE KATZ** (b. 9 May'45, New York City) – vocals, guitar (ex-BLUES PROJECT) / **RANDY BRECKER** (b.27 Nov'44, Philadelphia) – trumpet, flugelhorn / **JERRY WEISS** (b. 1 May'46, New York City) – trumpet, flugelhorn / **FRED LIPSIUS** (b.19 Nov'43, New York City) – alto sax, piano / **DICK HALLIGAN** (b.29 Aug'43, Troy, New York) – trombone, flute, keyboards / **JIM FIELDER** (b. 4 Oct'47, Dallas, Texas) – bass (ex-BUFFALO SPRINGFIELD) / **BOBBY COLOMBY** (b.20 Dec'44, New York City) – drums

			C.B.S.	Columbia
Jun 68.	(lp) (CBS 63296) <9619> **CHILD IS FATHER TO THE MAN**		40	47 Apr68

– Overture / I love you more than you'll ever know / Morning glory / My days are numbered / Without her / Just one smile / Meagan's gypsy eyes / House in the country / I can't quit her / Somethin' goin' on / The modern adventures of Plato, Diogenes and Freud / So much love / Underture. *(re-iss. Jul77 as 'THE FIRST ALBUM' on 'Embassy-CBS'; CBS 31942) (cd-iss. 1988; 30DP 303) (cd re-iss. Nov95; CK 64214) (cd re-iss. Apr99 on 'Mobile Fidelity'; UDCD 742)*

Jun 68.	(7") (CBS 3563) <44559> **I CAN'T QUIT HER. / HOUSE IN THE COUNTRY**			

—— (Mar'69) **DAVID CLAYTON-THOMAS** (b.DAVID THOMSETT, 13 Sep'41, Surrey, England, raised Canada) – vocals; repl. KOOPER who went solo

—— **CHUCK WINFIELD** (b.5 Feb'43, Monessen, Pennsylvania) – trumpet, flugelhorn repl. BRECKER who later formed BRECKER BROTHERS. **LEW SOLOFF** (b.20 Feb'44, Brooklyn, New York) – trumpet, flugelhorn and **JERRY HYMAN** (b.19 May'47, New York) – trombone repl. WEISS

Apr 69.	(lp) (CBS 63504) <9720> **BLOOD, SWEAT & TEARS**		15	1 Jan69

– Variations on a theme by Eric Satie (1st & 2nd movements) / Smiling phases / Sometimes in winter / More and more / And when I die / God bless the child / Spinning wheel / You've made me so very happy / Blues (part 2) / Variations on a theme by Eric Satie (reprise). *(re-iss. Dec88 on 'Beat Goes On'lp/cd; BGO LP/CD 28)*

Apr 69.	(7") (CBS 4116) <44776> **YOU'VE MADE ME SO VERY HAPPY. / THE BLUES (part 2)**		35	2 Feb69
Jun 69.	(7") (CBS 4220) <44871> **SPINNING WHEEL. / MORE AND MORE**			2 May69
Dec 69.	(7") (CBS 4613) <45008> **AND WHEN I DIE. / SOMETIMES IN WINTER**			2 Oct69
Aug 70.	(lp) (CBS 64024) <30090> **BLOOD, SWEAT & TEARS 3**		14	1 Jul70

– Hi-de-ho / The battle / Lucretia Mac Evil / Lucretia's reprise / Fire and rain / Lonesome Suzie / Symphony for the Devil / Sympathy for the Devil: Emergence – Evil's game; (a) Labyrinth, (b) Satan's dance, (c) The demand – Submergence / Contemplation – Return / He's a miner / Somethin' comin' on / 40,000 headman.

Aug 70.	(7") (CBS 5137) <45204> **HI-DE-HO. / THE BATTLE**			14 Jul70
Oct 70.	(7") (CBS 5220) <45235> **LUCRETIA MAC EVIL. / LUCRETIA'S REPRISE**			29

—— **DAVID BARGERON** (b. 6 Sep'42, Massachusetts) – horns; repl. HYMAN

Jul 71.	(lp) (CBS 64355) <30590> **B, S & T; 4**			10

– Go down gamblin' / Cowboys and Indians / John The Baptist (holy John) / Redemption / Lisa, listen to me / Look to my heart / High on a mountain / Valentine's day / Take me in your arms (rock me a little while) / For my lady / Mama gets high / Look to my heart. *(cd-iss. Mar96 on 'Columbia'; CK 66422)*

Jul 71.	(7") (CBS 7417) <45427> **GO DOWN GAMBLIN'. / VALENTINE'S DAY**			32
Dec 71.	(7") (CBS 7578) <45477> **LISA, LISTEN TO ME. / COWBOYS AND INDIANS**			73 Oct71
Mar 72.	(lp/c) (CBS/40 64803) <31170> **GREATEST HITS** (compilation)			19

– You've made me so very happy / I can't quit her / Go down gamblin' / Hi-de-ho / Sometimes in winter / And when I die / Spinning wheel / Lisa, listen to me / I love you more than you'll ever know / Lucretia Mac Evil / God bless the child. *(re-iss. Jul83; CBS 32159) (cd-iss. Nov87; CD 64803) (quad-lp 1973; Q 64803) <US-quad; CQ 31170>*

—— **JERRY FISHER** (b. 1943, Texas) – vocals; repl. BOBBY DOYLE who had repl. solo bound CLAYTON-THOMAS / **LOU MARINI Jr.** – saxophone; repl. LIPSIUS / **LARRY WILLIS** – keyboards; repl. HALLIGAN

Jul 72.	(7") (CBS 8267) <45...> **SO LONG DIXIE. / KRAKBERGARNINGEN (CROWS FUNERAL)**			
Sep 72.	(7") <45661> **SO LONG DIXIE. / ALONE**		-	44
Oct 72.	(lp) (CBS 65252) <31780> **NEW BLOOD**			32

– Down in the flood / Touch me / Alone / Velvet / I can't move no mountains / Over the hill / So long Dixie / Snow queen / Maiden voyage.

Nov 72.	(7") (CBS 1051) **TOUCH ME. / VELVET**			
Dec 72.	(7") <45755> **I CAN'T MOVE NO MOUNTAINS. / VELVET**		-	-
May 73.	(7") (CBS 1519) **BACK UP AGAINST THE WALL. / OVER THE HILL**		-	-
Aug 73.	(7") <45937> **ROLLER COASTER. / INNER CRISIS**		-	-
Aug 73.	(lp) (CBS 65275) <32180> **NO SWEAT**			72

– Roller coaster / Save our ship / Django / Rosemary / Song for John / Almost sorry /

Back up against the wall / Hip pickles / My old lady / Empty pages / Mary Miles / Inner crisis.

Oct 73.	(7") <45965> **SAVE OUR SHIP. / SONG FOR JOHN**		-	-
Nov 73.	(7") (CBS 1845) **SAVE OUR SHIP. / INNER CRISIS**		-	-

—— **DAVID CLAYTON-THOMAS** returned to repl. JERRY LaCROIX who had briefly replaced KATZ (he was later to join AMERICAN FLYER)

—— **TOM MALONE** – horns; repl. WINFIELD

Jun 74.	(7") (CBS 2462) **TELL ME THAT I'M WRONG. / ROCK REPRISE**			-
Sep 74.	(lp) (CBS 80153) <32929> **MIRROR IMAGE**			83

– Tell me that I'm wrong / Look up to the sky / Love looks good on you (you're candy sweet) / Hold on to me / Thinking of you / Are you satisfied / Rock reprise / She's coming home.

Oct 74.	(7") (CBS 2594) **LOVE LOOKS GOOD ON YOU. / ARE YOU SATISFIED**			-

—— **RON McCLURE** – bass; repl. FIELDER

—— **BILL TILLMAN** – saxophone; repl. SOLOFF

Jun 75.	(lp) (CBS 80784) <33484> **NEW CITY**			47 May75

– Ride captain ride / Life / No show / I was a witness to a war / One room country shack / Applause / Yesterday's music / Naked man / Got to get you into my life / Takin' it home.

Jun 75.	(7") <10151> **GOT TO GET YOU INTO MY LIFE. / NAKED MAN**		-	-
Sep 75.	(7") <10189> **YESTERDAY'S MUSIC. / NO SHOW**			62

—— **CLAYTON-THOMAS, COLOMBY, BARGERON, WILLIS, TILLMAN + McCLURE** brought in guests **PATTI AUSTIN / CHAKA KHAN** – vocals plus newcomers **MIKE STERN** – guitar / **DON ALIAS** – percussion / **STEVE KHAN** – guitar / **F.BUCHTELL** – trumpet

Aug 76.	(lp) (CBS 81465) <34233> **MORE THAN EVER**			Jul76

– They / I love you more than ever / Kathy Bell / Sweet Sadie the savior / Hollywood / You're the one / Heavy blue / Saved by the grace of your love.

Jan 77.	(7") <10400> **YOU'RE THE ONE. / HEAVY BLUE**		-	-

—— **DANNY TRIFAN** – bass repl. McCLURE / added **ROY McCURDY** – drums / **RANDY BERNSEN** – guitar repl. KHAN / **TONY KLATKA** – trumpet repl. ALIAS

			A.B.C.	A.B.C.
Nov 77.	(lp) (ABCL 5234) <1015> **BRAND NEW DAY**			

– Somebody I trusted / Dreaming as one / Same old blues / Lady put out the light / Womanizer / Blue street / Gimme that wine / Rock & roll queen / Don't explain.

Nov 77.	(7") (ABC 4202) **BLUE STREET. / PUT ON THE LIGHT**		-	-
Jan 78.	(7") <12310> **BLUE STREET. / SOMEBODY I TRUSTED**		-	-

—— added **CHRIS ALBERT** – trumpet / **GREG HERBERT** – sax / **NEIL STUBENHAUS** – bass

—— (1979) **CLAYTON-THOMAS** brought in new members **ROBERT PILTCH** – guitar / **RICHARD MARTINEZ** – keyboards / **BRUCE CASSIDY** – trumpet / **BOBBY ECONOMOU** – drums / **DAVID PILTCH** – bass / **EARL SEYMOUR** – sax, flute / **VERNON DORGE** – sax, flute

			A.B.C.	M.C.A.
Feb 80.	(7") <41198> **NUCLEAR BLUES. / AGITATO**		-	
Feb 80.	(7"/12") (MCA/+T 569) **NUCLEAR BLUES. / I'LL DROWN IN MY OWN TEARS**			-
Mar 80.	(lp/c) (MCF/+C 3061) **NUCLEAR BLUES**			-

– Agitato / Nuclear blues / Manic depression / I'll drown in my own tears / Fantasy stage / Spanish wine suite: La cantina – Spanish wine – The challenge – The duel – Amor – Spanish wine (reprise). *(re-iss. Sep89 on 'Big Time' lp/c; 221/211 5235)*

—— BS&T broke-up in 1980, CLAYTON-THOMAS and COLOMBY did some reunion concerts and even re-formed with varied line-up in 1988

– compilations, etc. –

on 'CBS' UK 'Columbia' US unless mentioned otherwise

Mar 73.	(7") (CBS 1142) **SPINNING WHEEL. / AND WHEN I DIE**			
1975.	(7") (13-33194) **AND WHEN I DIE. / LUCRETIA MAC EVIL**			
Feb 76.	(7") (CBS 3947) **YOU MADE ME SO VERY HAPPY. / SPINNING WHEEL**			

(re-iss. Jul84; A 4576)

Jul 78.	(lp) Hallmark; (SHM 963) **BLOOD, SWEAT & TEARS**			
May 80.	(lp/c) (CBS/40 31824) **CLASSIC BLOOD, SWEAT & TEARS**			
Nov 84.	(lp/c) Astan; (2/4 0140) **THE CHALLENGE**			
Oct 85.	(lp/c) Platinum; (PLP/PMC 25) **LATIN FIRE**			
May 91.	(cd/c) Elite; (ELITE 005 CD/MC) **SMILING PHASES**			

– Smiling phases / More and more / Fire and rain / Lonesome Suzie / Somethin' comin' on / Cowboys and Indians / High on a mountain / Take me in your arms (rock me a little while) / Down in the flood / Touch me / Alone / Morning glory / Without her / Just one smile / Roller coaster / Rosemary / Back up against the wall / Velvet. *(re-iss. cd Sep93; same)*

Sep 93.	(cd/c) Castle; (CCS CD/MC 379) **THE COLLECTION**			-
Jan 96.	(d-cd) Columbia (481019-2) / Sony; **WHAT GOES UP (THE BEST OF BLOOD, SWEAT & TEARS)**			Nov95

– I can't quit her / House in the country / I love you more than you'll ever know / You've made me so very happy / More and more / And when I die / Sometimes in winter / Smiling phases / Spinning wheel / God bless the child / Children of the wind / Hi-de-ho / Lucretia Mac Evil / He's a runner / Somethin' comin' on / 40,000 headman / Go down gamblin' / Mama gets high / Lisa, listen to me / Valentine's day / John the Baptist (Holy John) / So long Dixie / Snow queen / Maiden voyage / I can't move to the mountains / Time remembered / Roller coaster / Tell me that I'm wrong / Got to get you into my life / You're the one / Mean ole world (live).

Sep 99.	(cd) Mastertone; (MM 5104) **HIP PICKLES**			

Mike BLOOMFIELD (see under ⇒ELECTRIC FLAG)

Kurtis BLOW

Born: KURT WALKER, 9 Aug'59, New York City, New York, USA. A communications student at Harlem's City College Of NY, BLOW earned his first break at a party promoted by his friend and fellow student, RUSSELL 'RUSH' SIMMONS, wowing the crowd with his rapping abilities and making sure that RUSH's 'Force' events soon became a place to be seen at. BLOW subsequently found himself working alongside such future stars as GRANDMASTER FLASH and JOEY 'RUN' SIMMONS (RUSSELL's kid brother and soon to be the RUN in RUN DMC), RUSSELL Snr. duly procuring the services of Billboard journos Robert 'Rocky' Ford and J.B. Moore who wrote and financed BLOW's debut single, 'CHRISTMAS RAPPIN'. While not exactly a key moment in the evolution of the genre or even the first rap record per se (pipped at the post by The SUGARHILL GANG's seminal 'Rapper's Delight'), the track did become the first rap single to be distributed by a major label. The label in question was 'Mercury' and BLOW was promptly signed to a long term contract. Things got off to a promising start with 1980's 'THE BREAKS', a rap classic that presaged the lyrical pessimism of FLASH's 'The Message' by a couple of years and sold over half a million copies into the bargain. As many critics have pointed out, however, BLOW was essentially a singles artist and while subsequent albums such as 'PARTY TIME' (1983) and 'AMERICA' (1985) had their moments, the rapper struggled to develop his art as the young bucks began to overtake him. Roping in veterans GEORGE CLINTON and BOB DYLAN (!) for 'KINGDOM BLOW' (1986) didn't improve matters and BLOW's recording career (bar a German-only set, 'BACK BY POPULAR DEMAND') stuttered to a halt soon after. Following a brief spell in production work (for RENE AND ANGELA), BLOW fell in with the 90's mania for revival and began promoting and performing at old school spectaculars featuring the cream of the genre's pioneers.

Album rating: KURTIS BLOW (*7) / DEUCE (*6) / TOUGH mini (*5) / THE BEST RAPPER ON THE SCENE (*5) / EGO TRIP (*5) / AMERICA (*4) / KINGDOM BLOW (*4) / BACK BY POPULAR DEMAND (*3) / BEST OF KURTIS BLOW compilation (*8)

KURTIS BLOW – vocals / with mainly **JIMMY BRALOWER** – drums, percussion / **ROBBIE KONDOR** – keyboards / **RICHARD PASCUAL + TOMMY WOUK** – bass / **JOHN TROPEA** – guitar / **ONAJE ALLAN GUMBS** – piano / **JB MOORE** – guitar, keyboards / **JAMIE DELGADO** – bongos / etc

	Mercury	Mercury
Dec 79. (7"/12") (BLOW 7/+12) **CHRISTMAS RAPPIN'. / DO IT YOURSELF RAPPIN'**	30	
Sep 80. (7"/12") (BLOW 8/+12) <76075> **THE BREAKS. / (instrumental)**	47	87 Aug80
Nov 80. (lp) (6337 137) <3854> **KURTIS BLOW**		71 Oct80
– Rappin' Blow (part 2) / The breaks / Way out west / Throughout your years / Hard times / All I want in this world (is to find that girl) / Takin' care of business.		
Dec 80. (7"/12") (BLOW 9/+12) **THROUGHOUT YOUR YEARS (part 1). / CHRISTMAS RAPPIN'**		
── **SETH GLASSMAN** – bass; repl. WOUK + PASCUAL		
Jul 81. (lp) <4020> **DEUCE**	-	
– The deuce / It's gettin' hot / Getaway / Starlife / Take it to the bridge / Do the do / Rockin'.		
Oct 82. (7"/12") (BLOW 10/+12) **TOUGH. / (instrumental)**		
Oct 82. (m-lp/m-c) (MX/M4X 1505) <505> **TOUGH**		
– Tough / Juice / Daydreamin' / Boogie blues / Baby, you've got to go.		
1983. (7"/12") (BLOW 11/+12) **PARTY TIME. / THE BREAKS**		-
Nov 83. (7") (BLOW 13) **CHRISTMAS RAPPIN'. / NERVOUS**		-
Oct 84. (lp/c) (822283-1/-4) **THE BEST RAPPER IN TOWN**		
– Party time / Do the do / Boogie blues / The breaks / One two five / Throughout your years.		
Nov 84. (lp/c) <(822420-1/-4)> **EGO TRIP**		83 Oct84
– 8 million stories / AJ scratch / Basketball / Under fire / I can't take it no more / Ego trip / Fallin' back in love again.		

	Club – Mercury	Mercury
Feb 85. (7") (JAB 12) **PARTY TIME (the Go-Go edit). / THE BREAKS** (12"+=) (JABX 12) – ('A'instrumental).	67	
Apr 85. (7") <881529> **BASKETBALL. / Ralph McDonald: (IT'S) THE GAME**	-	71
Jun 85. (7"/12"; by RENE AND ANGELA featuring KURTIS BLOW) (JAB/+X 14) **SAVE YOUR LOVE (FOR NUMBER ONE). / (instrumental)**	66	
Dec 85. (7") (JAB 26) **IF I RULED THE WORLD. / (dub)** (12"+=) (JABX 26) – (instrumental).	24	
Dec 85. (lp/c) <(826141-1/-4)> **AMERICA**		Oct85
– America / America (dub) / Super sperm / AJ meets Davy DMX / Hello baby / If I ruled the world / Respect to the king / Summertime groove / MC lullaby / Don't cha like making love.		
── next featured **TROUBLE FUNK, GEORGE CLINTON + BOB DYLAN!**		
Oct 86. (7"/12") (JAB/+X 42) **I'M CHILLIN'. / DON'T CHA FEEL LIKE MAKIN' LOVE**	64	
Nov 86. (lp/c)(cd) (JABH/+C 22) <(830215-2)> **KINGDOM BLOW**		
– Street rock / The Bronx / Unity party jam / Sunshine / Magilla gorilla / I'm chillin' / Kingdom Blow / Reasons for wanting you.		
1988. (lp/cd) (834692-1/-2) **BACK BY POPULAR DEMAND**	-	- German
– Back by popular demand / Only the strong survive / I'm true to this / Get on up / Suckers in the place / Love don't love nobody / Still on the scene / Blue iguana / Express yourself / I'm feeling good.		
── **KURTIS** retired from solo work		

– compilations, etc. –

	Mercury	
Jun 94. (cd) Mercury; <(522456-2)> **THE BEST OF KURTIS BLOW**		
Jun 99. (12") Eukahouse; (EUHO 016) **THE REMIXED EP**		-

BLUE ANGEL (see under ⇒ LAUPER, Cyndi)

BLUE CHEER (dig out; Great Metal . . .)

BLUE NILE

Formed: Glasgow, Scotland . . . 1981 by songwriter PAUL BUCHANAN, PAUL JOSEPH MOORE and ROBERT BELL. After a debut 45 on 'R.S.O.' (just prior to the label going belly up!), they were offered an unusual record contract by Scottish (East Lothian) label, 'Linn', the hi-fi manufacturer using their tape as a demo and subsequently being sufficiently impressed to sign the band up for their recently formed music business venture. After an initial single, 'STAY', in Spring '84, the label issued the languorous debut album, 'A WALK ACROSS THE ROOFTOPS'. Garnering gushing reviews, this classic set of understated pop elegance created enough of a buzz for 'Virgin' to take over distribution. Its relatively lowly final chart position of No.80 belied the record's influence and impact, although it would be another five years before a follow-up as the trio locked themselves in the studio and diligently attempted to create another masterpiece. After a few false starts, they finally emerged in 1989 with 'HATS', a record which arguably topped the debut in the late night sophistication stakes, its moody atmospherics delicately caressed by PAUL BUCHANAN's silky croon (a singer who undoubtedly has the potential of being the next SINATRA). A UK Top 20 hit, the record's success saw The BLUE NILE leave their studio cocoon in the early 90's for a tour of America where they ended up working with such luminaries as ROBBIE ROBERTSON and RICKIE LEE JONES amongst others. Now signed to 'Warners', it looked as if The BLUE NILE were finally destined to leave cultdom behind with a third set, 'PEACE AT LAST' (1996). Another classy effort, again the trio enjoyed critical plaudits and modest chart success while simultaneously failing to corner the wider pop market.

Album rating: A WALK ACROSS THE ROOFTOPS (*8) / HATS (*9) / PEACE AT LAST (*6)

PAUL BUCHANAN – vocals, guitar, synthesizer / **PAUL JOSEPH MOORE** – keyboards, synthesizer, etc. / **ROBERT BELL** – bass, synthesizer, etc.

	R.S.O.	not iss.
Oct 81. (7") (RSO 84) **I LOVE THIS LIFE. / SECOND ACT**		-
── added guests **CALUM MALCOLM** – keyboards, vocals (ex-BADGER, ex-HEADBOYS) / **NIGEL THOMAS** – drums		

	Linn-Virgin	A&M
Apr 84. (7"/12") (LKS 1/+12) **STAY. / SADDLE THE HORSES** (re-iss. Jan89 remixed 7"/12"/d7"+=; same/same/LKSD 1) – Tinseltown in the rain / Heatwave (instrumental).		1985
Apr 84. (lp/c) (LKH/+C 1) **A WALK ACROSS THE ROOFTOPS**	80	1985
– A walk across the rooftops / Tinseltown in the rain / From rags to riches / Stay / Easter parade / Heatwave / Automobile noise. (cd-iss. Jan89; LKHCD 1)		
Jul 84. (7") (LKS 2) **TINSELTOWN IN THE RAIN. / HEATWAVE (instrumental)** ('A'ext-12") (LKS 2-12) – Regret.		-
── now a basic trio plus session musicians.		
Sep 89. (7") (LKS 3) **THE DOWNTOWN LIGHTS. / THE WIRES ARE DOWN** (12"+=/3"cd-s+=) (LKS 3-12/CD3) – Halfway to Paradise (TV theme).	67	
Oct 89. (lp/c/cd) (LKH/+C/CD 2) <5284> **HATS**	12	
– Over the hillside / The downtown lights / Let's go out tonight / Headlights on the parade / From a late night train / Seven a.m. / Saturday night. (re-iss. Apr92 on 'Virgin' cd/c; OVED CD/C 391)		
Sep 90. (7"/c-s) (LKS/+C 4) **HEADLIGHTS ON THE PARADE (Bob Clearmount mix). / ('A'-lp version)** (12"+=/cd-s+=) (LKS 4-12/CD4) – Easter parade (with RICKIE LEE JONES).	72	
Jan 91. (7"/c-s) (LKS/+C 5) **SATURDAY NIGHT. / ('A'version)** (12"+=/cd-s+=) (LKS 5-12/CD5) – Seven a.m. (live in the U.S.) / or / Our lives.	50	

	Warners	Warners
Jun 96. (cd/c/lp) (<9362 45848-2/-4/-1>) **PEACE AT LAST**	13	
– Happiness / Tomorrow morning / Sentimental man / Love came down / Body and soul / Holy love / Family life / War is love / God bless you kid / Soon.		
Sep 96. (c-ep/cd-ep) (W 0373 C/CD2) **HAPPINESS / NEW YORK MAN / WISH ME WELL** (cd-ep) (W 0373CD1) – ('A'side) / War is love / O Lolita.		

BLUE OYSTER CULT

Formed: Long Island, New York, USA . . . 1970 as SOFT WHITE UNDERBELLY by BUCK DHARMA, ALLEN LANIER and AL BOUCHARD. They became STALK-FORREST GROUP and signed to 'Elektra', where they released one 45, 'WHAT IS QUICKSAND' / 'ARTHUR COMICS' <45693> but had an album rejected. In late 1971 they renamed themselves The BLUE OYSTER CULT, their manager/guru SANDY PEARLMAN securing them a recording contract with 'Columbia'. The first two albums, 'BLUE OYSTER CULT' (1972) and 'TYRANNY AND MEDITATION' (1973 and containing lyrics by producer Richard Meltzer), were sophisticated proto-metal classics, infusing the crunching guitar and rhythm with a keen sense of melody and keeping tight enough a rein on proceedings to avoid the hoary bombast that characterised other bands of their ilk. Lyrically the band peddled fairly cliched, if more intelligent than average, dark musings and with 1974's 'SECRET TREATIES', the music began to sound similarly predictable. Throughout the remainder of the 70's, the band gravitated to a cleaner cut hard rock sound, although the darkly shimmering 'DON'T FEAR THE REAPER' was a one-off return to their 60's psychedelic roots. The song gave the band a surprise Top 20 UK hit, and while they continued to enjoy minor chart successes with their subsequent releases, the quality of their output struggled to rise above stale cliche. • Songwriters: Group compositions, except CAREER OF EVIL (written by LANIER's one-time girlfriend PATTI SMITH) / BLACK BLADE (co-written with Michael Moorcock; ex-Hawkwind) / KICK OUT THE JAMS (MC5) / WE GOTTA GET OUT OF THIS PLACE (Animals) / BORN TO BE WILD (Steppenwolf). • Trivia: AL BOUCHARD claimed he was the inspiration for the 1988 album, 'IMAGINOS'.

Album rating: BLUE OYSTER CULT (*6) / TYRANNY & MUTATION (*5) / SECRET TREATIES (*8) / ON YOUR FEET ON YOUR KNEES (*7) / AGENTS OF FORTUNE (*8) / SPECTRES (*5) / SOME ENCHANTED EVENING (*8) / MIRRORS (*5) / CULTOSAURUS ERECTUS (*4) / FIRE OF UNKNOWN ORIGIN (*6) / EXTRATERRESTRIAL LIVE (*3) / THE REVOLUTION BY NIGHT (*5) / CLUB NINJA (*4) / IMAGINOS (*6) / WORKSHOP OF THE TELESCOPES compilation (*7) / CULT CLASSICS (*3) / HEAVEN FORBID (*4)

ERIC BLOOM – vocals, "stun" guitar / **BUCK DHARMA** (b.DONALD ROSIER) – lead guitar, vocals / **ALLEN LANIER** – rhythm guitar, keyboards / **JOE BOUCHARD** (b. 9 Nov'48, Watertown, N.Y.) – bass, vocals / **ALBERT BOUCHARD** (b.24 May'47, Watertown) – drums, vocals

			not iss.	Reichstag
1972.	(7"ep) <1106> **LIVE BOOTLEG (live)** – In my mouth or on the ground / etc.		-	

			C.B.S.	Columbia
1973.	(lp) (64904) <31063> **BLUE OYSTER CULT** – Transmaniacon MC / I'm on the lamb but I ain't no sheep / Then came the last days of May / Stairway to the stars / Before the kiss, a redcap / Screams / She's as beautiful as a foot / Cities on flame with rock and roll / Workshop of the telescopes / Redeemed. (re-iss. Mar81; 32025)			May72
1973.	(7") <45598> **CITIES ON FLAME WITH ROCK AND ROLL. / BEFORE THE KISS, A REDCAP**		-	
1973.	(7") <45879> **SCREAMING DIZ-BUSTERS. / HOT RAILS TO HELL**		-	
1974.	(lp) (65331) <32107> **TYRANNY AND MUTATION** – The red & the black / O.D.'d on life itself / Hot rails to Hell / 7 screaming diz-busters / Baby ice dog / Wings wetted down / Teen archer / Mistress of the salmon salt (quicklime girl). (re-iss. 1981; 32056)			Mar74
1974.	(7") <10046> **CAREER OF EVIL. / DOMINANCE AND SUBMISSION**		-	
Sep 74.	(lp) (80103) <32858> **SECRET TREATIES** – Career of evil / Subhuman / Dominance and submission / ME 262 / Cagey cretins / Harvester of eyes / Flaming telepaths / Astronomy. (re-iss. Mar82; 32055)		53	Apr74
Nov 75.	(d-lp) (88116) <33317> **ON YOUR FEET OR ON YOUR KNEES (live)** – Subhuman / Harvester of eyes / Hot rails to Hell / The red and the black / 7 screaming diz-busters / Buck's boogie / Then came the last days of May / Cities on flame / ME 262 / Before the kiss (a redcap) / I ain't got you / Born to be wild. (re-iss. Sep87 lp/c; 460113-1/-4)		22	Mar75
Nov 75.	(7") <10169> **BORN TO BE WILD (live). / (part 2)**			
Jun 76.	(lp/c) (CBS/40 81835) <34164> **AGENTS OF FORTUNE** – This ain't the summer of love / True confessions / (Don't fear) The reaper / E.T.I. (Extra Terrestrial Intelligence) / The revenge of Vera Gemini / Sinful love / Tattoo vampire / Morning final / Tenderloin / Debbie Denise. (re-iss. Jul89; CDCBS 32221) (cd-iss. Jun94 on 'Sony'; 982732-2) (cd-iss. May95 on 'Columbia'; 468019-2)	26	29	
Jul 76.	(7") <10384> **(DON'T FEAR) THE REAPER. / TATTOO VAMPIRE**		-	12
Jul 76.	(7") (4483) **(DON'T FEAR) THE REAPER. / R.U. READY 2 ROCK**		-	
Jan 77.	(7") <10560> **DEBBIE DENISE. / THIS AIN'T THE SUMMER OF LOVE**		-	
Dec 77.	(lp/c) (CBS/40 86050) <35019> **SPECTRES** – Godzilla / Golden age of leather / Death valley nights / Searchin' for Celine / Fireworks / R.U. ready 2 rock / Celestial the queen / Goin' through the motions / I love the night / Nosferatu. (re-iss. Feb86 lp/c; CBS/40 32715) (cd-iss. Dec88; CDCBS 82371)	60	43	Nov77
Dec 77.	(7") (5689) <10659> **GOING THROUGH THE MOTIONS. / SEARCHIN' FOR CELINE**			
Feb 78.	(7") <10697> **GODZILLA. / NOSFERATU**			
May 78.	(7"/12") (7/12 6333) **(DON'T FEAR) THE REAPER. / R U READY 2 ROCK** (re-iss. Jun84 on 'Old Gold'; OG 9398)	16	-	
Jun 78.	(7") <10725> **GODZILLA. / GODZILLA (live)**		-	
Aug 78.	(7") (6514) **I LOVE THE NIGHT. / NOSFERATU**		-	
Sep 78.	(lp) (CBS/40 86074) <35563> **SOME ENCHANTED EVENING (live)** – R.U. ready 2 rock / E.T.I. (Extra Terrestrial Intelligence) / Astronomy / Kick out the jams / Godzilla / (Don't fear) The reaper / We gotta get out of this place.	18	44	
Oct 78.	(7") <10841> **WE GOTTA GET OUT OF THIS PLACE. / E.T.I. (EXTRA TERRESTRIAL INTELLIGENCE)**			
Nov 78.	(7") (6909) **WE GOTTA GET OUT OF THIS PLACE (live). / STAIRWAY TO THE STARS**		-	
Aug 79.	(lp/c) (CBS/40 86087) <36009> **MIRRORS** – Dr. Music / The great sun jester / In thee / Mirrors / Moon crazy / The vigil / I am the storm / You're not the one (I was looking for) / Lonely teardrops.	46	44	Jul79
Aug 79.	(7"clear) (7763) **MIRRORS. / LONELY TEARDROPS**		-	
Sep 79.	(7") <11055> **IN THEE. / LONELY TEARDROPS**		-	74
Oct 79.	(7") (8003) **IN THEE. / THE VIGIL**		-	
Feb 80.	(7") <11145> **YOU'RE NOT THE ONE (I WAS LOOKING FOR). / MOON CRAZY**		-	-
Jul 80.	(lp) (86120) <36550> **CULTOSAURUS ERECTUS**	12	34	

– Black blade / Monsters / Divine wind / Deadline / Here's Johnny / The Marshall plan / Hungry boys / Fallen angel / Lips in the hills / Unknown tongue.

Jul 80.	(7") <11401> **HERE'S JOHNNY (THE MARSHALL PLAN). / DIVINE WIND**	-	
Jul 80.	(7") (8790) **FALLEN ANGEL. / LIPS IN THE HILLS**	-	
Oct 80.	(7") (8986) **DEADLINES. / MONSTERS**	-	
Jul 81.	(lp) (CBS 85137) <37389> **FIRE OF UNKNOWN ORIGIN** – Fire of unknown origin / Burnin' for you / Veteran of the psychic wars / Sole survivor / Heaven metal: the black and silver / Vengeance (the pact) / After dark / Joan Crawford / Don't turn your back. <cd-iss. 1987; CK 85137>	29	24
Aug 81.	(7") <02415> **BURNIN' FOR YOU. / VENGEANCE (THE PACT)**	-	40
Sep 81.	(7"+=) (A 1453) **BURNIN' FOR YOU. / HEAVY METAL** (12"+=) (A13 1453) – The black & silver.	-	-
May 82.	(d-lp) (CBS 22203) <KF 37946> **EXTRATERRESTRIAL LIVE (live)** – Dominance and submission / Cities on flame / Dr. Music / The red and the black / Joan Crawford / Burnin' for you / Roadhouse blues / Black blade / Hot rails to Hell / Godzilla / Veteran of the psychic wars / E.T.I. (Extra Terrestrial Intelligence) / (Don't fear) the reaper.	39	29
Jun 82.	(7") <03137> **BURNIN' FOR YOU (live). / (DON'T FEAR) THE REAPER (live)**	-	

	(late 1981) **RICK DOWNEY** – drums repl. ALBERT		
Nov 83.	(lp/c) (CBS/40 25686) <38947> **THE REVOLUTION BY NIGHT** – Take me away / Eyes on fire / Shooting shark / Veins / Shadows of California / Feel the thunder / Let go / Dragon lady / Light years of love. <cd-iss. Dec88; CK 38947>	95	93
Nov 83.	(7") (A 3937) **TAKE ME AWAY. / FEEL THE THUNDER** (12"+=) (TA 3937) – Burnin' for you / Dr. Music.		
Feb 84.	(7"/12") (A/TA 4117) <04298> **SHOOTING SHARK. / DRAGON LADY**		83
May 84.	(7") <04436> **TAKE ME AWAY. / LET GO**	-	

—— **TONY ZVONCHEK** – keyboards (ex-ALDO NOVA) repl. LANIER

—— **TOMMY PRICE** – drums repl. DOWNEY.

Oct 85.	(7") <05845> **DANCIN' IN THE RUINS. / SHADOW WARRIOR**	-	-
Dec 85.	(lp/c/cd) (CBS/40/CD 26775) <39979> **CLUB NINJA** – White flags / Dancin' in the ruins / Rock not war / Perfect water / Spy in the house of the night / Beat 'em up / When the war comes / Shadow warrior / Madness to the method. (cd-iss. Jun97 on 'Koch Int.'; 37943-2)		63
Dec 85.	(7") (A 6779) **WHITE FLAGS. / ROCK NOT WAR** (12"+=) (TA 6779) – Shooting shark.	-	-
Feb 86.	(7") <06199> **PERFECT WATER. / SPY IN THE HOUSE OF NIGHT**	-	

—— added **ALBERT BOUCHARD** – guitar, percussion, vocals

ALLEN LANIER – keyboards, returned to repl. TONY

Sep 88.	(lp/c/cd) (460036-1/-4/-2) <40618> **IMAGINOS** – I am the one you warned me of / Les invisibles / In the presence of another world / Del Rio's song / The siege and investiture of Baron Von Frankenstein's castle at Weisseria / Astronomy (new version) / Magna of illusion. (pic-lp Mar89; 460036-0)		Aug88
Oct 88.	(7") (652 985) **ASTRONOMY. / MAGNA OF ILLUSION** (12"+=) (652 985-8) – ('A'-wild mix). (12"+=/cd-s+=) (652 985-6/-2) – (Don't fear) The reaper.	-	

—— (early '89 tour) **JON ROGERS** – bass repl. JOE BOUCHARD / **CHUCK BURGI** – drums repl. RON RIDDLE who repl. RICK DOWNEY

		Fragile	Herald
Jun 94.	(cd/c) (CD/C FRL 003) <HER 008> **CULT CLASSICS (re-recorded best of)** – (Don't fear) The reaper / E.T.I. (Extra Terrestrial Intelligence) / Me 262 / This ain't the summer of love / Burnin' for you / O.D.'d on life itself / Flaming telepaths / Godzilla / Astronomy / Cities on fire with rock and roll / Harvester of eyes / Buck's boogie / (Don't fear) The reaper / Godzilla.		
Jul 94.	(c-s/7") (TC+/FRS 1001) **(DON'T FEAR) THE REAPER. / BURNIN' FOR YOU** (cd-s+=) (CDFRS 1001) – ('A'extended). above were re-recordings of best known material.		-

—— reformed in '97 with **BLOOM, DHARMA + LANIER**

		C.M.C.	C.M.C.
Mar 98.	(cd) <(6076 86241-2)> **HEAVEN FORBID** – See you in black / Harvest moon / Power underneath despair / X-ray eyes / Hammer back / Damaged / Cold gay light of dawn / Real world / Live for me / Still burnin' / In thee.		

		Angel Air	Angel Air
Nov 99.	(cd) <(SJPCD 046)> **BAD CHANNELS (original soundtrack)** – Demon kiss / Horsemen arrive / Joker: That's how it is – Jane Jane (the hurricane) / Fair game: Somewhere in the night – Blind faith / Synkotik sinfoney: Manic depresso – Mr. Cool / DMT: Myth of freedom – Touching myself again / Little old lady polka / Ukelaliens / Bad channels overture / Power station / Shadow / VU / Cosmos rules but lump controls / Battering ram / This dude is fucked / Pick up her feed / Spray that scumbag / Out of station / Tree full of owls / Cookie in bottle / Corky gets it / Eulogy for Corky / Spore bomb / Remodelling / Ginger snaps / The moon gets in.		

– compilations, others, etc. –

Below on 'CBS' / 'Columbia' unless otherwise mentioned.

1984.	(7") (A 4584) **(DON'T FEAR) THE REAPER. / I LOVE THE NIGHT**		-
Apr 90.	(cd/c/lp) (465929-2/-4/-1) **CAREER OF EVIL: THE METAL YEARS** – Cities on flame / The red and the black / Hot rails to Hell / Dominance and submission / Seven screaming Diz-busters / M.E. 262 / E.T.I. (Extra Terrestrial Intelligence) / Beat 'em up / Black blade / The harvester of eyes / Flaming telepaths / Godzilla / (Don't fear) The reaper.		
Jan 92.	(cd/c) Castle; (CLA CD/MC 269) **LIVE 1976 (live)**		-
Jan 96.	(d-cd) Columbia; (480949-2) **WORKSHOP OF THE TELESCOPES** – Cities in flames with rock'n'roll / Transmaniacon MC / Before the kiss / Redcap /		-

Stairway to the stairs / Buck's boogie / Workshop of the telescopes / Red and the black / 7 screaming dizbusters / Career of evil / Flaming telepaths / Astronomy / Subhuman / Harvester of eyes / M.E. 262 / Born to be wild / (Don't fear) The reaper / This ain't the summer of love / E.T.I. (Extra Terrestrial Intelligence) / Godzilla / Goin' through the motions / Golden age of leather / Kick out the jams / We gotta get out of this place / In thee / Marshall plane / Veteran of the psychic wars / Burnin' for you / Dominnance and submission / Take me away / Shooting shark / Dancin' in the ruins / Perfect water.

BLUESBREAKERS (see under ⇒ MAYALL, John)

BLUES MAGOOS　(dig out; Great Psychedelic . . .)

BLUESOLOGY (see under ⇒ Elton John)

BLUES PROJECT

Formed: New York City, USA . . . mid-65 by DANNY KALB and ROY BLUMENFELD, the former enlisting TOMMY FLANDERS and STEVE KATZ (who replaced short-lived member ARTIE TRAUM) while the latter found ANDY KULBERG. Up and coming session hustler, AL KOOPER (straight from recording with DYLAN on his 'Highway 61 . . .' set) rounded off a line-up which signed to 'Verve Folkways' and made their live debut at the Cafe Au Go Go; the set was duly recorded and released as their inaugural album in May '66, although by the time of its release, FLANDERS had already broken ranks. More representative of the band's talent was sophomore studio set, 'PROJECTIONS' (1966), an ambitious album drawing its aural inspiration from country-blues, jazz and folk. Featuring the dual vocals of KATZ and KOOPER, the record stayed in the album charts (peaking at No.52) for around nine months by which time third set, ' . . .LIVE AT TOWN HALL' had taken its place. This was an underwhelming effort marred by overdubbed applause, an indication that the band's musical eclecticism was taking them in opposing directions rather than galvanising their sound. The inevitable split came in 1968 after KOOPER jumped ship to form his new baby, BLOOD, SWEAT & TEARS, almost immediately recruiting KATZ who had gone AWOL during The BLUES PROJECT's final days. Dead but not quite buried, the band was resurrected in the early 70's by founding members KALB and BLUMENFELD who released 'LAZARUS' as their comeback set for 'Capitol' in 1971. FLANDERS was then invited back to take the helm for the following year's dismal eponymous effort, precipitating a second split. Incredibly, the band thought it was worth one more effort and even hooked up with KOOPER once more to bring us the 'REUNION AT CENTRAL PARK' set in '73. • **Songwriters:** AL KOOPER or KATZ until former's departure. Covered VIOLETS OF DAWN (Eric Andersen) / CATCH THE WIND (Donovan) / I WANT TO BE YOUR DRIVER (Chuck Berry) / SPOONFUL (Willie Dixon) / TWO TRAINS RUNNING (Muddy Waters) / etc.

Album rating: LIVE AT THE CAFE AU GO GO (*5) / PROJECTIONS (*6) / THE BLUES PROJECT LIVE AT TOWN HALL (*5) / PLANNED OBSOLESCENCE (*4) / THE BEST OF THE BLUES PROJECT compilation (*7) / LAZARUS (*4) / BLUES PROJECT (*4) / ORIGINAL BLUES PROJECT REUNION IN CENTRAL PARK (*5) / ANTHOLOGY compilation (*6)

TOMMY FLANDERS – vocals / **STEVE KATZ** (b. 9 May'45, Brooklyn, N.Y.) – guitar, vocals / **DANNY KALB** (b.19 Sep'42, Brooklyn) – guitar / **AL KOOPER** (b. 5 Feb'44, Brooklyn) – organ, vocals / **ANDY KULBERG** (b.1944, Buffalo, N.Y.) – bass, flute / **ROY BLUMENFELD** – drums

		Verve	Verve Folkways
1965.	(7") <5004> **BACK DOOR MAN. / VIOLETS OF DAWN**	-	
May 66.	(lp; mono/stereo) <FT/+S 3000> **LIVE AT THE CAFE AU-GO-GO** (live)	-	77

– Goin' down Louisiana / You go, and I'll go with you / Catch the wind / I want to be your driver / Alberta / The way my baby walks / Violets of dawn / Back door man / Jelly jelly blues / Spoonful / Who do you love.

1966.	(7") <5013> **I WANT TO BE YOUR DRIVER. / CATCH THE WIND**	-	

—— KATZ and KOOPER now share vocal duties when FLANDERS leaves (later solo)

Oct 66.	(lp; mono/stereo) (VLP/SVLP 6004) <FT/+S 3008> **PROJECTIONS**		52

– I can't keep from crying / Steve's song / You can't catch me / Two trains running / Wake me, shake me / Cheryl's going home / Flute thing / Caress me baby / Fly away.

Nov 66.	(7") <5019> **WHERE THERE'S SMOKE THERE'S FIRE. / GOIN' DOWN LOUISIANA**	-	
Jan 67.	(7") (VS 1505) <5032> **I CAN'T KEEP FROM CRYING. / THE WAY MY BABY WALKS**	-	
Mar 67.	(7") <5040> **NO TIME LIKE THE RIGHT TIME. / STEVE'S SONG**	-	96
Sep 67.	(lp; mono/stereo) <FT/FTS 3025> **THE BLUES PROJECT LIVE AT TOWN HALL**	-	71

– (introduction) / Electric flute thing / I can't keep from crying / Mean old Southern / No time like the right time / Love will endure / Where there's smoke, there's fire / Wake me, shake me. (cd-iss. Jul94 on 'One Way'; OW 30010)

—— KOOPER went solo and then formed BLOOD, SWEAT AND TEARS; KATZ also joined. The remaining members with KALB on a few tracks, brought in **JOHN GREGORY** – guitar / **RICHARD GREENE** – violin

1968.	(7") <5063> **GENTLE DREAMS. / LOST IN THE SHUFFLE**		
1968.	(lp; mono/stereo) <FT/+S 3046> **PLANNED OBSOLESCENCE**	-	

– If you gotta make a fool of somebody / Calypso / The endless sleep / Nairt aes hornpipe / Turtledove / Mojo Hanna / Frank and Curt incensed / She raised her hand / Dakota recollection.

—— the rhythm section (KOLBERG & BLUMENFELD) became SEA TRAIN

Aug 69.	(lp) <3077> **THE BEST OF THE BLUES PROJECT** (compilation)	-	

<re-iss. 1989 on 'Rhino' lp/cd+; R1/R2 70165>(cd+=) – Flute thing.

—— in 1971, BLUES PROJECT re-formed with BLUMENFELD and KALB; they recruited **DON KRETMAR** – bass, saxophone

		Capitol	Capitol
1971.	(lp) <ST 872> **LAZARUS**	-	-

– It's alright / Personal mercy / Black night / Visions of flowers / Yellow cab / Lazarus / Brown eyed handsome man / Reachings / Midnight rain / So far, so hear.

—— added **DAVID COHEN** (b.1942, Brooklyn) – piano / **TOMMY FLANDERS** – vox / **BILL LUSSENDEN** – guitar

1972.	(lp) <EST 11017> **THE BLUES PROJECT**	-	

– Back door man / Danville dame / Railroad boy / Rainbow / Easy lady / Plain & fancy / Little rain / Crazy girl / I'm ready.

1972.	(7") **CRAZY GIRL. / EASY LADY**	-	

—— disbanded again 1972, but originals minus FLANDERS re-united mid'73

		M.C.A.	M.C.A.
Jul 73.	(d-lp) <MCA 8003> **ORIGINAL BLUES PROJECT REUNION IN CENTRAL PARK** (live 24 Jun'73)	-	-

– Louisiana blues / Steve's song / I can't keep from crying / You can't catch me / Fly away / Caress me baby / Catch the wind / Wake me, shake me / Two trains running / (closing audience).

—— same line-up rekindle group for gig in New York 17 Mar'81. KATZ had joined AMERICAN FLYER earlier in the 70's

– compilations, etc. –

1986.	(lp/c) Polydor; (SPE LP/MC 104) **BLUES PROJECT**		-
Jun 97.	(d-cd) Polydor; <(529785-2)> **ANTHOLOGY**		-

– I'm troubled / Back door man / Violets of dawn / Goin' down Louisiana / Hoochie coochie man / Parchman farm / You go and I'll go with you / Catch the wind / I want to be your driver / Alberta / Have you ever had the blues / The way my baby walks / Bright lights big city / Jelly roll blues / Spoonful / Who do you love / Love will endure / I can't keep from crying sometimes / Steve's song / You can't catch me / Two trains running / Wake me shake me / Cheryl's going home / Flute thing / Caress me baby / Fly away / No time like the right time / Mean old southern / Gentle dreams / Lost in the shuffle / Black night / Visions of flowers / Little rain.

—— please note a 1964 album 'BLUES PROJECT' on 'Elektra' only featured KALB augmenting with DYLAN (aka BOB LANDY), JOHN SEBASTIAN, GEOFF MULDAUR, etc.

BLUES TRAVELER

Formed: New York City, New York, USA . . . mid 80's by JOHN POPPER. While at school in Connecticut, he became friends with BLUES BROTHERS keyboard player PAUL SHAFFER, who, at the time, was arranger for the David Letterman show. They soon appeared on his show (many times) as The BLUES BAND, but after moving from Princeton, New Jersey to New York, they opted for the more appropriate BLUES TRAVELER moniker. By the late 80's, their distribution of demo tapes enabled the legendary BILL GRAHAM to set up prestigious support slots to the likes of SANTANA and The ALLMAN BROTHERS, subsequently leading to a contract with 'A&M'. Further appearances on the Letterman show boosted sales of their eponymous 1990 debut, a set of organic blues inspired by the 'Blues Brothers' film (and especially the late, great JOHN BELUSHI). In the Autumn of '92, POPPER was seriously hurt in a motorcycle accident, although he returned just over half a year later, taking the stage in a wheelchair!. Their biggest highlight came when celebrating the 25th anniversary of the Woodstock Festival in August '94, while the following year (the band now signed to 'Polydor') saw them go Top 10 with the 'FOUR' album and 'RUN-AROUND' single. 'LIVE FROM THE FALL' (1996) and 'STRAIGHT ON TILL MORNING' (1997) were also major sellers but only in America; it seemed Britain was still unimpressed. The BLUES TRAVELERS suffered the ultimate loss when bassist BOBBY SHEEHAN died, compounded soon after when POPPER himself underwent a major heart operation. However, JP was to resurface as a solo artist in 1999, the album 'ZYGOTE' keeping up the good tradition of alternative blues. • **Covered:** IMAGINE (John Lennon) / LOW RIDER (War). • **Trivia:** GREGG ALLMAN (Allman Brothers) and close friend CHRIS BARRON (Spin Doctors) guested on their 2nd album.

Album rating: BLUES TRAVELER (*7) / TRAVELERS & THIEVES (*6) / SAVE HIS SOUL (*6) / FOUR (*7) / LIVE FROM THE FALL (*7) / STRAIGHT ON TILL MORNING (*6) / John Popper: ZYGOTE (*5)

JOHN POPPER (b.1967, Cleveland, Ohio) – vocals, harmonica, guitar / **CHAN KINCHLA** – guitar / **BOBBY SHEEHAN** – bass / **BRENDAN HILL** – drums, percussion

		not iss.	A&M
Nov 90.	(cd/c/lp) <75021 5308-2/-4/-1> **BLUES TRAVELER**	-	

– But anyway / Gina / Mulling it over / 100 years / Dropping some NYC / Slow change / Warmer days / Gotta get mean / Alone / Sweet talking hippie. (cd+=) – Crystal flame.

Sep 91.	(cd/c/lp) <75021 5373-2/-4/-1> **TRAVELERS & THIEVES**	-	

– The tiding / Onslaught / Ivory tusk / What's for breakfast / I have my moments / Optimistic thoughts / The best part / Sweet pain / All in the groove / Support your local emperor / Bagheera / Mountain cry. (w/ free cd) – ON TOUR FOREVER (live)

Apr 93.	(cd,c) <0080> **SAVE HIS SOUL**	-	72

– Trina magna / Love and greed / Letter from a friend / Believe me / Go outside and drive / Defense and desire / Whoops / Manhattan Bridge / Love of my life / My prophesie / Save his soul / Bullshitter's lament / Conquer me / Fledgling.

		Polydor	Polydor
Nov 94.	(cd/c) (540265-2/-4) <0265> **FOUR**		9　Sep94

– Run-around / Stand / Look around / Fallible / The mountains win again / Freedom / Crash burn / Price to pay / Hook / The good the bad and the ugly / Just wait / Brother John.

			Superior	Polydor
Mar 95.	(c-s,cd-s) <0982> **RUN-AROUND / TRUST IN TRUST**		–	8
Nov 95.	(c-s) (POCS 339) **RUN-AROUND / SAVE HIS SOUL**		–	–
	(cd-s+=) (PZCD 339) – Escaping.			
Sep 95.	(c-s,cd-s) <1176> **HOOK / LOVE & GREED**		–	23
Jul 96.	(d-cd/d-c) <540515-2/-4> **LIVE FROM THE FALL (live)**		–	46

– Love and greed / Mulling it over / Closing down the park / Regarding Steven / New York prophesie / 100 years / Crash burn / Gina / But anyway / Mountain cry / Alone / Freedom / Mountains win / Breakfast / Go / Low / Go / Run / Hippie / Imagine.

Jun 97.	(cd/c) <(540750-2/-4)> **STRAIGHT ON TILL MORNING**			11

– Carolina blues / Felicia / Justify the thrill / Canadian rose / Business as usual / Yours / Psycho Joe / Great big world / Battle of someone / Most precarious / Gunfighter / Last night I dreamed / Make my way.

—— now without, SHEEHAN who died in 1998

JOHN POPPER

—— with **ROB CLORES** – keyboards / **DAVE ARES** – bass / **CRUGIE** – rhythm guitar / **CARTER BEAUFORD** – drums, percussion

			not iss.	A&M
Sep 99.	(cd/c) <490408> **ZYGOTE**		–	–

– Miserable bastard / Once you wake up / Growing in dirt / Tip the domino / His own ideas / Home / Love for free / How about now / Evil in my chair / Lunatic / Open letter / Fledgling.

BLUETONES

Formed: Hounslow, London, England ... 1994 by brothers MARK and SCOTT MORRISS, along with ADAM DEVLIN and ED CHESTERS. An indie band in the classic sense of the term, The BLUETONES stood somewhat apart and aloof from the Brit-pop class of '95. The previous year, they'd contributed the track, 'No.11', (later retitled 'BLUETONIC') to a 'Fierce Panda' compilation EP, 'Return To Splendour', before attracting attention from A&M's 'Superior Quality' label early in 1995. A strutingly assured live proposition, the initial buzz surrounding the band was almost tangible. It came as little surprise when a debut single, 'ARE YOU BLUE OR ARE YOU BLIND?', crashed into the charts at No.31, followed later in the long, hot summer of '95 by Top 20 hit, 'BLUETONIC'. A further series of gigs followed before the band narrowly missed the UK No.1 spot in early '96 with the 'SLIGHT RETURN' single. A classic slice of jangle-pop following the time-honoured lineage of The BYRDS, The SMITHS, The LA's and The STONE ROSES, MORRIS even donned a duffel coat(!) for the video, his nimble footed shuffle and boyish good looks generating talk of another IAN BROWN in the ascendant. The long awaited album, 'EXPECTING TO FLY' was released almost simultaneously, reaching the UK No.1 spot and eventually going platinum. Listeners expecting a series of breezy strumalong's were disappointed; the album's dense, evershifting sound rewarded repeated listening, classic rock references slipping in and out of focus but never revealing themselves fully. The catchy 'CUT SOME RUG' was the next single, making the Top 10 ahead of a new track, 'MARBLEHEAD JOHNSON' later that year.

Album rating: EXPECTING TO FLY (*9) / RETURN TO THE LAST CHANCE SALOON (*6)

MARK MORRISS – vocals / **ADAM DEVLIN** – guitars / **SCOTT MORRISS** – bass, vocals / **ED CHESTERS** – drums, percussion

			Superior	Polydor
Feb 95.	(7"blue; mail-o) (TONE 001) **SLIGHT RETURN. / FOUNTAINHEAD**		–	–
Jun 95.	(7") (BLUE 001X) **ARE YOU BLUE OR ARE YOU BLIND?. / STRING ALONG**		31	
	(12"+=/cd-s+=) (BLUE 001 T/CD) – Driftwood.			
Oct 95.	(7"/c-s) (BLUE 002 X/MC) **BLUETONIC. / GLAD TO SEE Y'BACK AGAIN?**		19	
	(12"+=/cd-s+=) (BLUE 002 T/CD) – Colorado beetle.			
Dec 95.	(cd-ep) <1142> **BLUETONES COMPANION**		–	

– Are you blue or are you blind? / String along / Driftwood / Bluetonic / Colorado beetle / Glad to see y' back again.

			Superior	A&M
Jan 96.	(7"/c-s) (BLUE 003 X/MC) **SLIGHT RETURN. / DON'T STAND ME DOWN**		2	
	(cd-s+=) (BLUE 003CD) – Nae hair on't.			
Feb 96.	(cd/c/lp/s-lp) (BLUECD/BLUEMC/BLUELP/BLUELPX 004) <540475> **EXPECTING TO FLY**		1	

– Talking to Clarry / Bluetonic / Cut some rug / Things change / he fountainhead / Carnt be trusted / Slight return / Putting out fires / Vampire / A parting gesture / Time & again.

Apr 96.	(7"/c-s) (BLUE 005 X/MC) **CUT SOME RUG. / CASTLE ROCK**		7	
	(cd-s+=) (BLUE 005CD) – The devil behind my smile.			
Sep 96.	(7"/c-s) (BLUE 006 X/MC) **MARBLEHEAD JOHNSON. / THE SIMPLE THINGS / NIFKIN'S BRIDGE**		7	
	(cd-s+=) (BLUE 006CD) – Are you blue or are you blind?			
Feb 98.	(7"/c-s) (BLUE X/M 007) **SOLOMON BITES THE WORM. / I WAS A TEENAGE JESUS**		10	
	(cd-s+=) (BLUED 007) – I walked all night.			
Mar 98.	(cd/c/lp) (BLUE D/M/V 008) <LC 0485> **RETURN TO THE LAST CHANCE SALOON**		10	

– Tone blooze / Unpainted Arizona / Solomon bites the worm / U.T.A. / 4-day weekend / Sleazy bed track / If . . . / The jub-jub bird / Sky will fall / Ames / Down

at the reservoir / Heard you were dead / Broken starr. (hidden track on cd+=) – Woman done gone left me.

Apr 98.	(7"/c-s) (BLUE X/M 009) **IF . . . / BLUE SHADOWS**		13	
	(cd-s+=) (BLUED 009) – The watchman.			
Jul 98.	(7"/c-s) (BLUE X/M 010) **SLEAZY BED TRACK. / THE BALLAD OF MULDOON**		35	
	(cd-s+=) (BLUED 010) – Blue.			

BLUE VELVETS (see under ⇒ CREEDENCE CLEARWATER REVIVAL)

BLUR

Formed: Colchester, Essex, England ... 1989 by DAMON ALBARN, GRAHAM COXON, ALEX JAMES and DAVE ROWNTREE. Initially they went under the moniker of SEYMOUR before opting for The GREAT WHITE HOPES. Finally settling with BLUR, they were on the books of David Balfe's 'Food' label, a subsidiary of Parlophone. There, they secured their first UK Top 50 entry with 'SHE'S SO HIGH', an early PINK FLOYD-influenced single, that rode the coat-tails of the baggy brigade. With the ghost of SYD BARRETT even more pronounced, they created one of the more psychedelic singles of the era in 'THERE'S NO OTHER WAY', the record hitting Top 10 in '91. Another single, 'BANG', preceded their debut album, 'LEISURE', a record that received mixed reviews at the time. Still mainly a singles-orientated outfit, they progressed dramatically with the much-improved, 'MODERN LIFE IS RUBBISH' (1993) album, which featured some classy tracks including the hits, 'FOR TOMORROW', 'CHEMICAL WORLD' and 'SUNDAY SUNDAY'. Although they had come on leaps and bounds creatively, this wasn't translated into sales. With the release of 'GIRLS AND BOYS', however, they embarked upon a commercial renaissance that saw the record become their biggest hit to date. It was the opening track on the critically approved 'PARKLIFE' album, which also spawned further hits, 'TO THE END' and the title track (co-sung with actor PHIL DANIELS). By this point they had evolved into a mod-ish indie-pop combo, ALBARN supplying the cockney barrow-boy delivery over a musical backdrop that drew from the rich English pop heritage, once the domain of such luminaries as The SMALL FACES and The KINKS. The following year, 1995, saw them win the battle for the coveted No.1 spot with 'COUNTRY HOUSE', beating rivals OASIS who were sharpening their tongues for an onslaught of media slagging. However, BLUR lost ground in the credibility stakes, when their 'GREAT ESCAPE' album failed to impress the critics. OASIS, on the other hand, were scaling new heights with their 2nd album. 1997 marked a slight return to favour, both the single, 'BEETLEBUM', and their eponymous 5th album hitting pole position. With BLUR taking a slight sabbatical from the recording studio, GRAHAM COXON took the opportunity to release a respectable solo effort, 'THE SKY IS TOO HIGH', the BLUR factor and a few good reviews nearly carrying it into the Top 30. Having involved themselves with various remixers (including WILLIAM ORBIT, MOBY, THURSTON MOORE, ADRIAN SHERWOOD and JOHN McENTIRE on the once Japanese-only 'BUSTIN' & DRONIN') over the course of the last year or so, BLUR were seeing clearly once again. In March '99, the gospel-led 'TENDER' went straight to No.2 while the accompanying album, '13' (DAMON had recently split with ELASTICA's JUSTINE FRISCHMANN) topped the chart. Further singles, 'COFFEE & TV' (with COXON taking the lead) and 'NO DISTANCE LEFT TO RUN', only managed to reach the Top 20; it would seem BLUR (like possibly OASIS to come) were beginning to falter slightly. • **Covered:** MAGGIE MAY (Rod Stewart) / LAZY SUNDAY (Small Faces). • **Trivia:** DAMON's father, KEITH ALBARN, used to be the manager of 60's rock outfit, The SOFT MACHINE.

Album rating: LEISURE (*6) / MODERN LIFE IS RUBBISH (*8) / PARKLIFE (*9) / THE GREAT ESCAPE (*7) / BLUR (*8) / 13 (*6) / Graham Coxon: THE SKY IS TOO HIGH (*6)

DAMON ALBARN (b.23 Mar'68, Whitechapel, London) – vocals / **GRAHAM COXON** (b.12 Mar'69, Germany) – guitars / **ALEX JAMES** (b.21 Nov'68, Dorset, England) – bass, vocals / **DAVE ROWNTREE** (b. 8 Apr'63) – drums

			Food-EMI	S.B.K.
Oct 90.	(c-s/7") (TC+/FOOD 26) **SHE'S SO HIGH. / I KNOW**		48	–
	(12") (12FOOD 26) – ('A'-Definitive) / Sing / I know (extended).			
	(cd-s) (CDFOOD 26) – ('A'side) / I know (extended) / Down.			
Apr 91.	(c-s/7") (TC+/FOOD 29) **THERE'S NO OTHER WAY. / INERTIA**		8	–
	(ext.12"+=/cd-s+=) (12/CD FOOD 29) – Mr.Briggs / I'm all over.			
	(12") (12FOODX 20) – ('A'remix) / Won't do it / Day upon day (live).			
Jul 91.	(c-s/7") (TC+/FOOD 31) **BANG. / LUMINOUS**		24	
	(ext.12"+=) (12FOOD 31) – Explain / Uncle Love.			
	(cd-s+=) (CDFOOD 31) – Explain / Beserk.			
Aug 91.	(cd/c/lp) (FOOD CD/TC/LP 6) <97880> **LEISURE**		7	

– She's so high / Bang / Slow down / Repetition / Bad day / Sing / There's no other way / Fool / Come together / High cool / Birthday / Wear me down.

Dec 91.	(c-s,cd-s) <07374> **THERE'S NO OTHER WAY / EXPLAIN**		–	82
Mar 92.	(c-s/7") (TC+/FOOD 37) **POPSCENE. / MACE**		32	
	(12"+=) (12FOOD 37) – I'm fine / Garden central.			
	(cd-s+=) (CDFOOD 37) – Badgeman Brown.			
Apr 93.	(c-s) (TCFOOD 40) **FOR TOMORROW. / INTO ANOTHER / HANGING OVER**		28	
	(12"+=) (12FOOD 40) – Peach.			
	(cd-s) (CDFOOD 40) – ('A'extended) / Peach / Bone bag.			
	(cd-s) (CDSFOOD 40) – ('A'side) / When the cows come home / Beachcoma / For tomorrow (acoustic).			

May 93. (cd/c/lp) *(FOOD CD/TC/LP 9)* <89442> **MODERN LIFE IS RUBBISH** ☐15☐ ☐
– For tomorrow / Advert / Colin Zeal / Pressure on Julian / Star shaped / Blue jeans / Chemical world / Sunday Sunday / Oily water / Miss America / Villa Rosie / Coping / Turn it up / Resigned.

Jun 93. (7"red) *(FOODS 45)* **CHEMICAL WORLD. / MAGGIE MAY** ☐28☐ ☐
(12"/cd-s) *(12/CD FOOD 45)* – ('A'side) / Es Schmecht / Young and lovely / My ark.
(cd-s) *(CDFOODS 45)* – ('A'side) / Never clever (live) / Pressure on Julian (live) / Come together (live).

Oct 93. (7"yellow) *(FOODS 46)* **SUNDAY SUNDAY. / TELL ME, TELL ME** ☐26☐ ☐
(12") *(12FOODS 46)* – ('A'side) / Long legged / Mixed up.
(cd-s) *(CDFOODS 46)* – ('A'side) / Dizzy / Fried / Shimmer.
(cd-s) *(CDFOODX 46)* – ('A'side) / Daisy bell / Let's all go The Strand.

Mar 94. (7"/c-s) *(FOODS/TCFOOD 47)* **GIRLS AND BOYS. / MAGPIE / PEOPLE IN EUROPE** ☐5☐ ☐–☐
(cd) *(CDFOOD 47)* – ('A'side) / People in Europe / Peter Panic.
(cd-s) *(CDFOODS 47)* – ('A'side) / Magpie / Anniversary waltz.

Apr 94. (cd/c/lp) *(FOOD CD/TC/LP 10)* <29194> **PARKLIFE** ☐1☐ ☐Jun94☐
– Girls and boys / Tracy Jacks / End of a century / Park life / Bank holiday / Bad head / The debt collector / Far out / To the end / London loves / Trouble in the message centre / Clover over Dover / Magic America / Jubilee / This is a low / Lot 105.

May 94. (c-s) *(TCFOOD 50)* **TO THE END / GIRLS AND BOYS (Pet Shop Boys remix) / THREADNEEDLE STREET** ☐16☐ ☐
(12"/cd-s) *(12/CD FOOD 50)* – (1st 2 tracks; 2 versions of 2nd).
(cd-s) *(CDFOODS 50)* – ('A'side) / Threadneedle Street / Got yer.
(above featured LETITIA of STEREOLAB. Next with actor PHIL DANIELS.)

Jun 94. (c-s,cd-s) <58155> **GIRLS AND BOYS / GIRLS AND BOYS (Pet Shop Boys radio mix) / MAGGIE MAY** ☐–☐ ☐59☐

Aug 94. (c-s/cd-s) *(TC/CDS FOOD 53)* **PARKLIFE. / SUPA SHOPPA / THEME FROM AN IMAGINARY FILM** ☐10☐ ☐
(12") *(12FOOD 53)* – (1st 2 tracks) / To the end (French version).
(cd-s) *(CDFOOD 53)* – (1st track) / Beard / To the end (French version).

Nov 94. (c-s/7") *(TCFOOD/FOODS 56)* **END OF A CENTURY. / RED NECKS** ☐19☐ ☐
(cd-s+=) *(CDFOOD 56)* – Alex's song.

                                    Food   **Virgin**

Aug 95. (c-s/7") *(TC+/FOOD 63)* **COUNTRY HOUSE. / ONE BORN EVERY MINUTE** ☐1☐ ☐
(cd-s+=) *(CDFOOD 63)* – To the end (with FRANCOISE HARDY).
(cd-ep) *(CDFOODS 63)* – ('A'live) / Girls and boys (live) / Parklife (live) / For tomorrow (live).

Sep 95. (cd/c/lp) *(FOOD CD/MC/LP 14)* <40855> **THE GREAT ESCAPE** ☐1☐ ☐
– Stereotypes / Country house / Best days / Charmless man / Fade away / Top man / The universal / Mr. Robinson's quango / He thought of cars / It could be you / Ernold Same / Globe alone / Dan Abnormal / Entertain me / Yuko and Hiro.

Nov 95. (c-s) *(TCFOOD 69)* **THE UNIVERSAL / ENTERTAIN ME (the live it! remix)** ☐5☐ ☐
(cd-s+=) *(CDFOODS 69)* – Ultranol / No monsters in me.
(cd-ep) *(CDFOOD 69)* – ('A'live) / Mr. Robinson's quango (live) / It could be you (live) / Stereotypes (live).

Feb 96. (c-s/7") *(TC+/FOOD 73)* **STEREOTYPES. / THE MAN WHO LEFT HIMSELF / TAME** ☐7☐ ☐
(cd-s+=) *(CDFOOD 73)* – Ludwig.

Apr 96. (c-s/7") *(TC+/FOOD 77)* **CHARMLESS MAN. / THE HORRORS** ☐5☐ ☐
(cd-s+=) *(CDFOOD 77)* – A song / St. Louis.

—— BLUR were joint winners (with rivals OASIS; NOEL) of the Ivor Novello Award for songwriter of the year.

May 96. (d-cd; ltd on 'EMI Japan') *(TOCP 8400)* **LIVE AT THE BUDOKAN (live)** ☐–☐ ☐–☐

—— ALEX JAMES helped to form one-off indie supergroup ME ME ME alongside JUSTIN WELCH (Elastica –), STEPHEN DUFFY and CHARLIE BLOOR. Had a UK Top 20 hit in Aug'96 with 'HANGING AROUND'.

                                    Food   **Virgin**

Jan 97. (7"red) *(FOOD 89)* **BEETLEBUM. / WOODPIGEON SONG** ☐1☐ ☐
(cd-s+=) *(CDFOODS 89)* – ('A'-Mario Caldato Jr mix) / Dancehall.
(cd-s) *(CDFOOD 89)* – ('A'side) / All your life / A spell for money.

Feb 97. (cd/c/lp) *(FOOD CD/TC/LP 19)* **BLUR** ☐1☐ ☐61☐
– Beetlebum / Song 2 / Country sad ballad man / M.O.R. / On your own / Theme from retro / You're so great / Death of a party / Chinese bombs / I'm just a killer for your love / Look inside America / Strange news from another star / Movin' on / Essex dogs.

Apr 97. (7"purple) *(FOOD 93)* **SONG 2 / GET OUT OF THE CITIES** ☐2☐ ☐
(cd-s+=) *(CDFOODS 93)* – Polished stone.
(cd-s) *(CDFOOD 93)* – ('A'side) / Bustin' & dronin' / Country sad ballad man (live acoustic).

Jun 97. (7"white) *(FOOD 98)* **ON YOUR OWN. / POP SCENE (live) / SONG 2 (live)** ☐5☐ ☐
(cd-s+=) *(CDFOODS 98)* – On your own (live).
(cd-s) *(CDFOODS 98)* – ('A'side) / Chinese bombs (live) / Moving on (live) / M.O.R. (live).

Sep 97. (c-s/7"orange) *(TC+/FOOD 107)* **M.O.R. (Alan Moulder road version). / SWALLOWS IN THE HEATWAVE** ☐15☐ ☐–☐
(cd-s+=) *(CDFOOD 107)* – Movin' on (William Orbit mix) / Beetlebum (Moby's minimal house mix).

Mar 98. (d-cd) *(TOCP 504445)* **BUSTIN' AND DRONIN'** ☐☐ ☐–☐

Mar 99. (c-s/7"blue) *(TC+/FOOD 117)* **TENDER. / ALL WE WANT** ☐2☐ ☐
(cd-s+=) *(CDFOOD 117)* – Mellow jam (short version).
(cd-s) *(CDFOODS 117)* – ('A'side) / French song (full version) / Song 2 (video).

Mar 99. (cd/c/d-lp) *(FOOD CD/MC/LP 29)* <99129> **13** ☐1☐ ☐80☐
– Tender / Bugman / Coffee & TV / Swamp song / 1992 / B.L.U.R.E.M.I. / Battle / Mellow song / Trailerpark / Caramel / No distance left to run / Trimm trabb / Optigan 1.

Jun 99. (c-s) *(TCFOOD 122)* **COFFEE & TV / X-OFFENDER (Damon – Controls freaks bugman remix)** ☐11☐ ☐–☐

(cd-s+=) *(CDFOOD 122)* – Coyote (Dave's bugman remix).
(12"++=) *(12FOOD 122)* – Trade stylee (Alex's bugman remix) / Metal hip slop (Graham's bugman remix).
(cd-s) *(CDFOODS 122)* – ('A'side) / (above 2).

Nov 99. (c-s) *(TCFOOD 123)* **NO DISTANCE LEFT TO RUN / BEAGLE 2 / SO YOU** ☐14☐ ☐–☐
(cd-s) *(CDFOODS 123)* – ('A'side) / Battle (U.N.K.L.E. remix).
(cd-s) *(CDFOOD 123)* – ('A'side) / Tender (Cornelius mix).

– compilations, etc. –

Sep 99. (cd-ep-box) *Food; (BLURBOX 10)* **10th ANNIVERSARY BOX SET** ☐☐ ☐–☐
– (all 22 hit singles)

GRAHAM COXON

                                    Transcopic Caroline

Aug 98. (cd/c) <7560> **THE SKY IS TOO HIGH** ☐31☐ ☐
– That's all I wanna do / Where'd you go? / In a salty sea / Day is far too long / R U lonely? / I wish / Hard and slow / Me you, we two / Waiting / Who the fuck? / Morning blues.

BMX BANDITS (dig out; Great Alt & Indie . . .)

BODY COUNT (see under ⇒ ICE-T)

Marc BOLAN

Born: MARC FELD, 30 Sep'47, London, England. He began his performing career under the improbable moniker of TOBY TYLER, before ditching it and signing to 'Decca'. After 3 flop singles, he enjoyed a brief stint with JOHN'S CHILDREN ('Desdemona') before teaming up in 1968 with bongo player STEVE PEREGRINE TOOK to form TYRANNOSAURUS REX. Far from the hoary, chest-beating proto-metal that name might imply, the band's sound was a folky melange of acoustic guitar, manic bongos and pop melodies. Unfortunately the band were victims of their era and prone to lyrical flights of fancy that often broke down into hippy cliche; just check out the title of their debut mid-68 album 'MY PEOPLE WERE FAIR AND HAD SKY IN THEIR HAIR . . . BUT NOW THEY'RE CONTENT TO WEAR STARS ON THEIR BROWS'. A bit of a hippy himself at the time, Radio One DJ JOHN PEEL championed their first single, 'DEBORA', as well as material from their next 3 albums. They became a big draw on the underground circuit, helping the albums gain minor placings in the UK charts. MARC's ex-model features and effeminate charisma did no harm in making him an object of hippy chick lust, and it was about time the band had a sexier name to match. Just before the group became T.REX, TOOK was replaced by MICKEY FINN, as they gradually adopted an all-electric sound. The spanking new single, 'RIDE A WHITE SWAN', nearly nailed the No.1 spot in October 1970 and made BOLAN a fully fledged pop idol. A jaunty little number with a stabbing guitar-line, it heralded the band's strident new sound, although it retained the quasi-mystical lyrical schtick. STEVE CURRY and BILL LEGEND were drafted in and the band notched up 8 consecutive Top 3 hits, including 4 UK chart-toppers. The celebratory 'HOT LOVE' and the timeless 'GET IT ON' both hit the top spot as did the 'ELECTRIC WARRIOR' album, displaying a welcome move to raunchier (but often equally silly) lyrics. BOLAN then set up his own label through EMI after 'JEEPSTER' was re-issued without his consent. He almost single-handedly invented the "glam-rock" phenomenon, achieving the rare feat of being a rock idol and pop star at the same time. 'TELEGRAM SAM', 'METAL GURU' and the evergreen '20th CENTURY BOY' are still guaranteed to get you dusting down your 6" platforms a quarter of a century on. After the single 'THE GROOVER' was released in 1973 and after splitting with his wife JUNE CHILD, BOLAN brought in his new girlfriend GLORIA JONES to record 'TRUCK ON (TYKE)'. This was the first single by T.REX not to make the Top 10. His creativity was ebbing and he moved to America to record some lacklustre formulaic material in a variety of styles. Like early fan JOHN PEEL, BOLAN embraced the subsequent punk takeover and had a new deal with 'R.C.A.' before he met his untimely end on 16th September 1977. In yet another bizarre rock'n'roll death, his girlfriend crashed their car into a tree near Barnes Common, which soon became a shrine. Since his death, obsessive fans and curious observers alike have lapped up a stream of documentaries, greatest hits packages, tributes and re-issues (mostly on fan club label 'Marc On Wax'), which shows no sign of abating. • **Covers:** SUMMERTIME BLUES (Eddie Cochran) / DO YOU WANNA DANCE (Bobby Freeman) / DOCK OF THE BAY (Otis Redding) / TO KNOW HIM IS TO LOVE HIM (Teddy Bears) / RIP IT UP (Little Richard) / ENDLESS SLEEP (Joey Reynolds) / A TEENAGER IN LOVE (Dion).

Album rating: Tyrannosaurus Rex: MY PEOPLE WERE FAIR AND HAD SKY IN THE HAIR, BUT NOW THEY'RE CONTENT TO WEAR STARS ON THEIR BROWS (*6) / PROPHETS, SEERS AND SAGES, THE ANGEL OF THE AGES (*6) / UNICORN (*7) / A BEARD OF STARS (*6) / T.Rex: T.REX (*5) / ELECTRIC WARRIOR (*8) / THE SLIDER (*7) / TANX (*6) / ZINC ALLOY & THE HIDDEN RIDERS OF TOMORROW (*4) / BOLAN'S ZIP GUN (*4) / FUTURISTIC DRAGON (*5) / DANDY IN THE UNDERWORLD (*5) / THE ULTIMATE COLLECTION compilation (*9)

Marc BOLAN

—— solo using session men

			Decca	not iss.
Nov 65.	(7")	(F 12288) **THE WIZARD. / BEYOND THE RISING SUN**	☐	☐ -
Jun 66.	(7")	(F 12413) **THE THIRD DEGREE. / SAN FRANCISCO POET**	☐	☐ -

			Parlophone	not iss.
Dec 66.	(7")	(R 5539) **HIPPY GUMBO. / MISFIT**	☐	☐ -

—— BOLAN then joined JOHN'S CHILDREN before forming own band

TYRANNOSAURUS REX

MARC – vocals, guitars / **STEVE PEREGRINE TOOK** (b.28 Jul'49, London) – bongos, vocals

			Regal Zonophone	A&M
Apr 68.	(7")	(RZ 3008) **DEBORA. / CHILD STAR**	34	☐
Jun 68.	(lp; stereo/mono) (S+/LRZ 1003) **MY PEOPLE WERE FAIR AND HAD SKY IN THEIR HAIR . . . BUT NOW THEY'RE CONTENT TO WEAR STARS ON THEIR BROWS**		15	☐

– Red hot mama / Scenesof / Child star / Strange orchestras / Chateau in Virginia Waters / Dwarfish trumpet blues / Mustang Ford / Afghan woman / Knight / Graceful fat shake / Weilder of words / Frowning Atahuallpa. *(re-iss. May85 on 'Sierra' lp/c; FEDB/CFEDB 5013) (cd-iss. Oct98 on 'Polydor'; 541009-2)*

			Regal Zonophone	Blue Thumb
Aug 68.	(7")	(RZ 3011) **ONE INCH ROCK. / SALAMANDA PALAGANDA**	28	☐
Oct 68.	(lp; stereo/mono) (S+/LRZ 1005) **PROPHETS, SEERS AND SAGES, THE ANGELS OF THE AGES**		☐	☐

– Deboraarobed / Stacey grove / Wind quartets / Conesuala / Trelawny lawn / Aznagell the mage / Salamanda Palaganda / Our wonderful brownskin man / Oh Harley (the Saltimbanques) / Eastern spell / The travelling tragition / Juniper suction / Scenes of dynasty. *(re-iss. May85 on 'Sierra' lp/c; FEDB/CFEDB 5022) (cd-iss. Oct94 on 'Disky'; CUCD 10) (cd re-iss. Oct98 on 'Polydor'; 541010-2)*

Jan 69.	(7")	(RZ 3016) **PEWTER SUITOR. / WARLORD OF THE ROYAL CROCODILES**	☐	☐
May 69.	(lp; stereo/mono) (S+/LRZ 1007) **UNICORN**		12	☐

– Chariots of silk / 'Pon a hill / The seal of seasons / The throat of winter / Cat black (the wizard's hat) / Stones of Avalon / She was born to be my unicorn / Like a white star, tangled and far, Tulip that's what you are / Warlord of the royal crocodiles / Evenings of Damask / The sea beasts / Iscariot / Nijinsky hind / The pilgrim's tale / The misty coast of Albany / Romany soup. *(re-iss. May85 on 'Sierra' lp/c; FEDB/CFEDB 5024) (cd-iss. Oct94 on 'Disky'; CUCD 11) (cd re-iss. Oct98 on 'Polydor'; 541012-2)*

Jul 69.	(7")	(RZ 3022) **KING OF THE RUMBLING SPIRES. / DO YOU REMEMBER?**	44	☐

—— **MICKEY FINN** (b. 3 Jan'47) – bongos, vocals repl. TOOK who joined PINK FAIRIES (He died Nov80)

Jan 70.	(7")	(RZ 3025) **BY THE LIGHT OF THE MAGICAL MOON. / FIND A LITTLE WOOD**	☐	☐
Mar 70.	(lp) (SLRZ 1013) **A BEARD OF STARS**		21	☐

– Prelude / A day laye / The woodland bop / First heart mighty dawn dart / Pavillions of sun / Organ blues / By the light of the magical Moon / Wind cheetah / A beard of stars / Dragon's ear / Lofty skies / Dove / Elemental child. <US-import had free 7"; BLUE THING> *(re-iss. May85 on 'Sierra' lp/c; FEDB/CFEDB 5035) (cd-iss. Oct98 on 'Polydor'; 541003-2)*

T.REX

			Fly	Blue Thumb
Oct 70.	(7"m) (BUG 1) <121> **RIDE A WHITE SWAN. / IS IT LOVE / SUMMERTIME BLUES**		2	76 Jan71

—— added **STEVE CURRY** (b.21 May'47, Grimsby, England) – bass / **BILL LEGEND** (b. 8 May'44, Essex, England) – drums

			Fly	Reprise
Dec 70.	(lp/c) (HIFLY/ZCFLY 2) <6440> **T.REX**		13	☐ Apr71

– The children of Rarn / Jewel / The visit / Childe / The time of love is now / Diamond meadows / Root of star / Beltane walk / Is it love / One inch rock / Summer deep / Seagull woman / Sun eye / The wizard / The children of Rarn (reprise). *(re-iss. Mar78 + Oct81; same) (re-iss. May85 on 'Sierra' lp/c; FEDB/CFEDB 5010) (cd-iss. May92 on 'Castle';) (cd re-iss. Oct98 on 'Polydor'; 541011-2)*

Feb 71.	(7"m) (BUG 6) **HOT LOVE. / WOODLAND ROCK / KING OF THE MOUNTAIN COMETH**		1	☐
Apr 71.	(7"m) <1006> **HOT LOVE. / ONE INCH ROCK / SEAGULL WOMAN**		-	72
Jul 71.	(7"m) (BUG 10) **GET IT ON (BANG A GONG). / THERE WAS A TIME / RAW RAMP**		1	-
Sep 71.	(lp/c) (HIFLY/ZCFLY 6) <6466> **ELECTRIC WARRIOR**		1	32 Oct71

– Mambo sun / Cosmic dancer / Jeepster / Monolith / Lean woman blues / Get it on (bang a gong) / Planet queen / Girl / The motivator / Life's a gas / Rip off. *(re-iss. Mar78 + Oct81; same) (cd-iss. May87 on 'Sierra; CDTR 2) (re-iss. Apr90 on 'Castle' c/cd+=; CLA MC/CD 180) – Hot love / Deborah. (cd re-iss. Oct98 on 'Polydor'; 541007-2) (lp re-iss. Sep99 on 'Simply Vinyl'; SVLP 117)*

Nov 71.	(7") (BUG 16) **JEEPSTER. / LIFE'S A GAS**		2	-
Nov 71.	(7") <1056> **JEEPSTER. / RIP OFF**		-	-
Dec 71.	(7") <1032> **BANG A GONG (GET IT ON). /**		-	10

			E.M.I.	Reprise
Jan 72.	(7"m) (T REX 1) <1078> **TELEGRAM SAM. / CADILLAC / BABY STRANGE**		1	67 Apr72

(re-iss. Mar82; same); hit No.69)

May 72.	(lp/c) (HIFLY/ZCFLY 8) **BOLAN BOOGIE** (compilation)		1	

– Get it on (bang a gong) / The king of the mountain cometh / She was born to be my unicorn / Dove / Woodland bop / Ride a white swan / Raw ramp / Jeepster / First heart mighty dawn dart / By the light of the magical Moon / Summertime blues / Hot love. *(re-iss. Mar78 & Oct81; same) (re-iss. Apr89 on 'Castle' lp/c/cd; CLA LP/MC/CD 145) (cd re-iss. Oct98 on 'Polydor'; 541006-2)*

May 72.	(7"m) (MARC 1) <1095> **METAL GURU. / LADY / THUNDERWING**		1	
Jul 72.	(lp/c) (BLN/ 5001) <2095> **THE SLIDER**		4	17 Aug72

– Metal guru / Mystic lady / Rock on / The slider / Baby boomerang / Spaceball ricochet / Buick MacKane / Telegram Sam / Rabbit fighter / Baby strange / Ballrooms of Mars / Chariot choogle / Main man. *(re-iss. Nov89 on 'Marc On Wax' lp/c/cd; MARC L/K/D 503) (cd re-iss. Jul94 on 'Edsel'; EDCD 390)*

Jul 72.	(7") <1122> **THE SLIDER. / ROCK ON**		-	-
Sep 72.	(7"m) (MARC 2) **CHILDREN OF THE REVOLUTION. / JITTERBUG LOVE / SUNKEN RAGS**		2	
Dec 72.	(7") (MARC 3) **SOLID GOLD EASY ACTION. / BORN TO BOOGIE**		2	
Mar 73.	(7") (MARC 4) **20th CENTURY BOY. / FREE ANGEL**		3	
Mar 73.	(lp/c) (BLN/ 5002) <2132> **TANX**		4	

– Tenement lady / Rapids / Mister mister / Broken hearted blues / Shock rock / Country honey / Electric Slim and the factory man / Mad Donna / Born to boogie / Life is strange / The street and the babe shadow / Highway knees / Left hand Luke and the beggar boys. *(re-iss. Oct87 on 'Marc On Wax' lp/pic-lp/c/cd; RAP/+D/C/CD 504) (re-iss. Nov89 lp/c/cd; MARC L/K/D 504) (cd re-iss. Jul94 on 'Edsel'; EDCD 391)*

Jun 73.	(7") (MARC 5) **THE GROOVER. / MIDNIGHT**		4	-
Jun 73.	(7") **THE GROOVER. / BORN TO BOOGIE**		-	

—— added **JACK GREEN** – guitar (plus 3 female backing singers incl. **GLORIA JONES**)

Nov 73.	(7") (MARC 6) **TRUCK ON (TYKE). / SITTING HERE**		12	-

—— (T.REX = FINN, CURRIE, GREEN, JONES – keyboards, vocals) / **DAVY LUTTON** – drums (ex-HEAVY JELLY), repl. LEGEND (2 more female singers)

Feb 74.	(7"; as MARC BOLAN & T.REX) (MARC 7) **TEENAGE DREAM. / SATISFACTION PONY**		13	
Mar 74.	(lp/c; as MARC BOLAN & T.REX) (BNLA 7751) **ZINC ALLOY AND THE EASY RIDERS OF TOMORROW**		12	

– Venus loon / Sound pit / Explosive mouth / Galaxy / Orange / Nameless wildness / Teenage dream / Liquid gang / Carsmile Smith & the old one / You've got to jive to stay alive – Spanish midnight / Interstellar soul / Painless persuasion and the meathawk / Interstellar / The avengers (superbad) / The leopards (featuring Gardinia and The Mighty Slug). *(re-iss. Oct87 on 'Marc On Wax' lp/pic-lp/c/cd; RAP/+D/C/CD 505) (re-iss. Nov89 lp/c/cd; MARC L/K/D 505) (cd re-iss. Jul94 on 'Edsel'; EDCD 392)*

Jul 74.	(7") (MARC 8) **LIGHT OF LOVE. / EXPLOSIVE MOUTH**		22	-

—— added **DINO DINES** – keyboards

Nov 74.	(7") (MARC 9) **ZIP GUN BOOGIE. / SPACE BOSS**		41	
Feb 75.	(lp/c) (BNLA 7752) **BOLAN'S ZIP GUN**			

– Light of love / Solid baby / Precious star / Zip gun boogie / Token of my love / Think zine / 'Till dawn / Girl in the thunderbolt suit / I really love you baby / Golden belt. *(re-iss. Jul87 on 'Marc On Wax' lp/pic-lp/c/cd; RAP/+D/C/CD 506) (cd re-iss. Jul94 on 'Edsel'; EDCD 393)*

—— members FINN and GREEN departed. The latter to PRETTY THINGS. Now 5-piece comprising BOLAN, JONES, CURRIE, LUTTON + DINES

Jul 75.	(7") (MARC 10) **NEW YORK CITY. / CHROME SITAR**		15	

—— next with **BILLY PRESTON** – keyboards

Oct 75.	(7"m; as T.REX DISCO PARTY) (MARC 11) **DREAMY LADY. / DO YOU WANNA DANCE / DOCK OF THE BAY**		30	
Feb 76.	(lp/c) (BLNA/ 5004) **FUTURISTIC DRAGON**		50	

– Futuristic dragon / Jupiter lion / All alone / Chrome sitar / New York City / My little baby / Calling all destroyers / Theme for a dragon / Sensation boulevard / Ride my wheels / Dreamy lady / Dawn storm / Casual agent. *(re-iss. Oct87 on 'Marc On Wax' lp/pic-lp/c/cd; RAP/+D/C/CD 507) (re-iss. Nov89 lp/c/cd; MARC L/K/D 507) (cd re-iss. Jul94 on 'Edsel'; EDCD 394)*

Feb 76.	(7") (MARC 13) **LONDON BOYS. / SOLID BABY**		40	-
Jun 76.	(7") (MARC 14) **I LOVE TO BOOGIE. / BABY BOOMERANG**		13	-
Sep 76.	(7") (MARC 15) **LASER LOVE. / LIFE'S AN ELEVATOR**		41	-
Jan 77.	(7"; by MARC BOLAN & GLORIA JONES) (EMI 2572) **TO KNOW HIM IS TO LOVE HIM. / CITY PORT**		☐	☐

—— now comprised BOLAN and DINES who brought in **MILLER ANDERSON** – guitar (ex-SAVOY BROWN) repl. GLORIA JONES who went solo / **HERBIE FLOWERS** – bass repl. CURRIE who went into sessions **TONY BRENNAN** – drums repl. LUTTON who joined WRECKLESS ERIC

Mar 77.	(7") (MARC 16) **THE SOUL OF MY SUIT. / ALL ALONE**		42	
Mar 77.	(lp/c) (BLNA 5005) **DANDY IN THE UNDERWORLD**		26	

– Dandy in the underworld / Crimson moon / Universe / I'm a fool for you / I love to boogie / Visions of Domino / Jason B. Sad / Groove a little / Hang-ups / The soul of my suit / Pain and love / Teen riot structure. *(re-iss. Oct87 on 'Marc On Wax'; lp/pic-lp/c/cd; RAP/+D/C/CD 508) (re-iss. Nov89 lp/c/cd; MARC L/K/D 508) (cd re-iss. Jul94 on 'Edsel'; EDCD 395)*

May 77.	(7") (MARC 17) **DANDY IN THE UNDERWORLD. / GROOVE A LITTLE**		☐	☐
Aug 77.	(7") (MARC 18) **CELEBRATE SUMMER. / RIDE MY WHEELS**		☐	☐

—— On 16th Sep'77 MARC BOLAN died when his car driven by GLORIA hit a tree. ANDERSON joined SOUTHSIDE JOHNNY and FLOWERS formed SKY.

Apr 78.	(7") (MARC 19) **CRIMSON MOON. / JASON B. SAD**		☐	☐

– compilations, etc. –

On 'Fly' UK / 'Reprise' US unless mentioned otherwise.

Aug 71.	(lp/c) (TON/CTON 2) **THE BEST OF T.REX**		21	
Mar 72.	(d-lp/d-c) (TOOFA/ZCTOF 3-4) / A&M / <3514> **PROPHETS, SEERS AND SAGES, THE ANGELS OF THE AGES / MY PEOPLE WERE FAIR . . .** <US-title 'TYRANNOSAURUS REX – A BEGINNING'>		1	

(re-iss. Oct81; same)

Mar 72.	(7"ep) Magni Fly; (ECHO 102) **DEBORA / ONE INCH ROCK. / WOODLAND BOP / SEAL OF SEASONS**		7	
1973.	(7") <1149> **BANG A GONG. / TELEGRAM SAM**		-	-
1973.	(7") <1151> **METAL GURU. / JEEPSTER**		-	-
1973.	(7") **HOT LOVE. / RIP OFF**		-	-
Oct 72.	(lp/c) Music For Pleasure; **RIDE A WHITE SWAN**		-	
Dec 72.	(d-lp/d-c) Cube; (TOOFA/ZCTOF 9-10) **A BEARD OF STARS / UNICORN**		44	☐

(re-iss. Mar78 + Oct81; same) (re-iss. Sep88 on 'That's Original' d-lp/c/cd;) (re-iss. cd Oct94 on 'Disky';)

Sep 73. (7"; as BIG CARROT) E.M.I.; (EMI 2047) **BLACKJACK. / SQUINT EYE MANGLE** | | - |

Nov 73. (lp/c) E.M.I.; (BLN/ 5003) **GREAT HITS** | 32 | - |

Jun 74. (lp; by MARC BOLAN) Track; (2410 201) **THE BEGINNING OF DOVES** | | - |
(re-iss. Aug89 on 'Media Motion' lp/c/cd; MEDIA/+C/CD 2) (cd-iss. Oct91 on 'Receiver';)

Jun 74. (7"m; by MARC BOLAN) Track; (2094 013) **JASPER C. DEBUSSY. / HIPPY GUMBO / THE PERFUMED GARDEN OF GULLIVER SMITH** | | - |

Nov 74. (lp) Sounds Superb; (90059) **GET IT ON** | | - |
(re-iss. Jun86 on 'Fame'; FA/TC-FA 3154)

Apr 76. (7") Cube; (BUG 66) **HOT LOVE. / GET IT ON** | | - |

Sep 77. (7"ep) Cube; (ANT 1) **BOLAN'S BEST PLUS ONE** | | - |
– Ride a white swan / Motivator / Jeepster / Demon queen.

Mar 78. (7"m) Cube; (ANT 2) **HOT LOVE. / RAW RAMP / LEAN WOMAN BLUES** | | - |

Apr 78. (d-lp) Cube; (HIFLD 1) **MARC, THE WORDS AND MUSIC OF MARC BOLAN** | | - |
(with free interview disc; BINT 1)

Apr 78. (d-lp) Pickwick; (PDA 044) **THE T.REX COLLECTION / GREATEST HITS** | | - |
(d-c-iss.Feb80; PDC 044)

Jun 78. (lp/c) Hallmark; (SHM/+C 953) **GREATEST HITS VOL.1** | | - |
(re-iss. Jan87 as 'THE VERY BEST OF VOLUME 1' lp/c; SMH/HSC 3204)

Jun 79. (lp/c) E.M.I.; (NUT 5) **SOLID GOLD T.REX** | 51 | - |
(re-iss. May82 on 'Fame' lp/c; FA/TC-FA 3005) (cd-iss. Feb99 on 'Repertoire'; RR 4800)

Jul 79. (12"ep) Cube; (ANTS 001) **LIFE'S A GAS / FIND A LITTLE WOOD. / ONCE UPON THE SEAS OF ABYSSINIA / BLESSED WILD APPLE GIRL** | | - |
(re-iss. Jul82 on 'Rarn'; MBFS RAP 1)

Sep 80. (lp/c) E.M.I.; (NUT/TC-NUT 28) **THE UNOBTAINABLE T.REX** | | - |

Mar 81. (12"pic-ep/12"clear-ep) Rarn; (MBFS 001 C/P) **THE RETURN OF THE ELECTRIC WARRIOR** | 50 | - |
– Sing me a song / Endless sleep (extended) / The lilac hand of Menthol Dan. (re-iss. 7"pic-d.Jul82;)

Aug 81. (pic-lp; 2 diff) Marc; (ABOLAN 1P) **T.REX IN CONCERT (live)** | 35 | - |

Sep 81. (7"/7"pic-d; by MARC BOLAN) Cherry Red; (CHERRY/+P 29) **YOU SCARE ME TO DEATH. / THE PERFUMED GARDEN OF GULLIVER SMITH** | 51 | - |

Oct 81. (pic-lp/lp; by MARC BOLAN) Cherry Red; (P+/ERED 20) **YOU SCARE ME TO DEATH** | 88 | - |
(re-iss. Nov94 on 'Emporio' cd/c; EMPR CD/MC 545)

Oct 81. (7"; by MARC BOLAN) Cherry Red; (CHERRY 32) **CAT BLACK. / JASPER C. DEBUSSY** | | - |

Nov 81. (d-lp/c) Countdown; (PLAT/ZCPLAT 1002) **THE PLATINUM COLLECTION OF T.REX** | | - |

Jan 82. (lp/pic-lp; as MARC BOLAN & T.REX) Cube; (ICS/+X 1004) **ACROSS THE AIRWAVES** | | - |
(cd-iss. Oct98 on 'Polydor'; 541004-2)

Jan 82. (7"blue) Marc; (SBOLAN 13) **MELLOW LOVE. / FOXY BOX / LUNACY'S BACK** | | - |
(12"+=) (SBOLAN 13) – Rock me.

May 82. (7"m; by MARC BOLAN) Cherry Red; (CHERRY 39) **THE WIZARD. / BEYOND THE RISING SUN / RINGS OF FORTUNE** | | - |

Jun 82. (10"ep) Marc On Wax; (ABOLAN 2) **CHILDREN OF RARN SUITE** | | - |
(free one-side 7"w-above) – MISTER MOTION

Jul 82. (12"blue) Rarn; (MBFS RAP 2) **DEEP SUMMER. / OH BABY / ONE INCH ROCK** | | - |

Jul 82. (7") Old Gold; (OG 9230) **GET IT ON. / JEEPSTER** | | - |

Jul 82. (7"ep) E.M.I.; (MARC 20) **CHILDREN OF THE REVOLUTION / I LOVE TO BOOGIE. / LONDON BOYS / SOLID GOLD EASY ACTION** | | - |

Aug 82. (7") Dakota; (BAK 3) **HOT LOVE. / JEEPSTER** | | - |

Aug 82. (7") Dakota; (BAK 4) **GET IT ON. / DEBORA** | | - |

Aug 82. (7") Dakota; (BAK 5) **RIDE A WHITE SWAN. / ONE INCH ROCK** | | - |

Aug 82. (7") Old Gold; (OG 9229) **HOT LOVE. / RIDE A WHITE SWAN** | | - |

Aug 82. (7") Old Gold; (OG 9230) **GET IT ON. / JEEPSTER** | | - |

Aug 82. (7") Old Gold; (OG 9234) **DEBORA. / ONE INCH ROCK** | | - |

Sep 82. (7"ep) E.M.I.; (MARC 22) **TRUCK ON (TYKE) / ZIP GUN BOOGIE. / TEENAGE DREAM / LIGHT OF LOVE** | | - |

Sep 82. (7"ep) E.M.I.; (MARC 23) **TELEGRAM SAM / THE SOUL OF MY SUIT. / METAL GURU / LASER LOVE** | | - |

Oct 82. (lp/c) Countdown; (COUNT/ZCCNT 11) **T.REX** | | - |

Dec 82. (7"ep) Marc; (SBOLAN 1) **CHRISTMAS BOP. / SHY BOY / RIDE A WHITE SWAN** | | - |
(12"ep+=/12"pic-d-ep+=) (SBOLAN 12/+EP) – King of the rumbling spires / Savage Beethoven.

Jun 83. (7"pic-d) Marc; (SBOLAN 14PD) **THINK ZINC. / MAGICAL MOON / TILL DAWN** | | - |
(12") – ('A'side) / Rip it up / A teenager in love.

Aug 83. (7") Cube; (BUG 90) **JEEPSTER. / GET IT ON** | | - |

Sep 83. (lp/c; by MARC BOLAN) Marc On Wax; (MARC L/K 501) **DANCE IN THE MIDNIGHT** | 83 | - |
(re-iss. Apr85; same)

Apr 84. (d-lp/d-c; by MARC BOLAN) Cambra; (CR/+T 115) **BEYOND THE RISING SUN** | | - |

Jun 84. (7"promo' by MARC BOLAN) Cube; (BUG 99) **SAILOR OF THE HIGHWAY. / DO YOU REMEMBER** | | - |
(12"+=) **RARE MAGIC EP** (HBUG 99) – Demon queen / Pewtor suitor / The wizard.

Aug 84. (red-lp/c) Marc On Wax; (MARC L/K 500) **BILLY SUPER DUPER** | | - |
(re-iss. Apr85 lp/c; same)

Aug 84. (lp) Marc On Wax; (ABOLAN 5) **T.REXTASY** | | - |
(free 12"w-above) (ABOLAN 5F) JAM (live). / ELEMENTAL CHILD (live)

Nov 84. (lp/c) Sierra; (FEDD/CFEDD 1000) **OFF THE RECORD WITH T.REX** | | - |

Jan 85. (7") Old Gold; (OG 9505) **METAL GURU. / CHILDREN OF THE REVOLUTION** | | - |

Jan 85. (7") Old Gold; (OG 9506) **TELEGRAM SAM. / I LOVE TO BOOGIE** | | - |

Jan 85. (7") Old Gold; (OG 9507) **SOLID GOLD EASY ACTION. / THE GROOVER** | | - |

Mar 85. (d-lp/d-c) Cambra; (CR/+T 5161) **THE MAIN MAN** | | - |
(7"pic-d. w/above) – TEENAGE DREAM. / SOLID GOLD SEGUE

Apr 85. (d-lp/d-c; as MARC BOLAN & T.REX) K-Tel; (NE/CE 1297) **THE BEST OF THE 20th CENTURY BOY** | 5 | - |
(cd-iss. Oct87; NCD 3325)

May 85. (12"ep) Sierra; (FED 12) **GET IT ON / THERE WAS A TIME. / RAW RAMP / ELECTRIC BOOGIE** | | - |

May 85. (7"ep) Marc On Wax; (TANX 1) **MEGAREX 1 (medley). / CHARIOT CHOOGLE / LIFE'S AN ELEVATOR** | 72 | - |
(12TANX 1) – Solid baby.

May 85. (7"pic-ep) Marc On Wax; (PTANX 1) **MEGAREX 2 (medley). / TAME MY TIGER / CHROME SITAR / SOLID BABY** | | - |
(MEGAREX 3: was a 12"sha-pic-ep; STANX 1)

Jul 85. (7"m) Marc On Wax; (TANX 2) **SUNKEN RAGS. / JITTERBUG LOVE / DOWN HOME LADY** | | - |
(12"+=) (12TANX 2) – Funky London / Childhood.

Jul 85. (lp/c; as MARC BOLAN & T.REX) Dojo; (DOJO LP/TC 12) **A CROWN OF JEWELS** | | - |

Nov 85. (lp/c/cd) Marc On Wax; (MARC L/K/D 509) **TILL DAWN** | | - |
(cd-iss. Oct91 on 'Castle'; CLACD 247)

Jun 86. (12"ep) Archive 4; (TOF 102) **CLASSIC CUTS** | | - |
– Jeepster / Ride a white swan / Get it on / Hot love.

Feb 87. (7") Marc On Wax; (MARC 9) **CHILDREN OF THE REVOLUTION (remix). / THE SLIDER (remix) / TEAR FOR THE HIGH STAR** (by 'Dave Ashby') | | - |
(12"+=) – Free angel (TV remix).

Mar 87. (d-lp/d-c/d-cd) Marc On Wax; (MARC L/K/CD 510) **THE SINGLES COLLECTION** | | - |

May 87. (7"; as MARC BOLAN & T.REX) Marc On Wax; (MARC 10) **GET IT ON. / JEEPSTER** | 54 | - |
(12"+=/c-s+=/cd-s+=) (MARC B/C/CD 10) – Cadillac.

May 87. (cd; as T.REX & MARC BOLAN) Sierra; (CDTR 1) **GREATEST HITS** | | - |

Aug 87. (12"ep) Strange Fruit; (SFPS 031) **THE PEEL SESSIONS** (27.10.70) | | - |
– Jewel / Ride a white swan / Elemental child / Sun eye. (cd-ep-iss.Dec94; SFPSCD 031)

1987. (lp/c/cd; as MARC BOLAN & T.REX) Connoisseur; (VSOP LP/MC/CD 100) **STAND BY ME** | | - |

Sep 87. (7"m; as MARC BOLAN & T.REX) Marc On Wax; (MARC 11) **I LOVE TO BOOGIE. / RIDE A WHITE SWAN / HOT LOVE** | | - |
(12"+=/cd-s+=) (12MARC/MARCD 11) – Hot George.

Oct 87. (lp/c; as MARC BOLAN & T.REX) Hallmark; (SHM/HSC 3217) **TEENAGE DREAM** | | - |
(cd-iss. Oct87 on 'Pickwick'; PWK 040)

Jan 88. (3"cd-ep) Special Edition; (CD3-13) **HOT LOVE / GET IT ON / TELEGRAM SAM / METAL GURU** | | - |

1988. (lp) Fun; (FUN 9029) **18 GREATEST HITS** | | - |

Jul 88. (lp/c/cd) Knight; (KN LP/MC/CD 10003) **NIGHTRIDING** | | - |

Mar 89. (cd-s) Old Gold; (OG 6130) **TELEGRAM SAM / METAL GURU / CHILDREN OF THE REVOLUTION** | | - |

May 89. (cd-s) Old Gold; (OG 6134) **SOLID GOLD EASY ACTION / 20th CENTURY BOY / THE GROOVER** | | - |

Aug 89. (lp/c/cd) Marc On Wax; (MARC L/K/D 513) **THE MARC SHOWS** (Granada TV shows) | | - |

1990. (4xlp-box) Rhino; **WHERE THERE'S CHAMPAGNE** | - | - |

Apr 91. S.P.S.; (lp)(cd) **RARITIES VOLUME ONE** | | |

Jun 91. (cd/c) Music Club; (MC CD/TC 030) **THE VERY BEST OF MARC BOLAN & T.REX** | | - |
(gold-cd-iss. Mar96; MCCDSE 030)

Aug 91. (7"/c-s; as MARC BOLAN & T.REX) Marc On Wax; (MARC/+ 501) **20th CENTURY BOY. / MIDNIGHT / THE GROOVER** | 13 | - |
(12"+=)(cd-s+=) – Telegram Sam.

Sep 91. (cd/c/lp; MARC BOLAN & T.REX) Telstar; (TCD/STAC/STAR 2539) **THE ULTIMATE COLLECTION** | 4 | - |
– 20th century boy / Metal guru / I love to boogie / Debora / New York City / Telegram Sam / Hot love / Dreamy lady / One inch rock / The soul of my suit / London boys / Ride a white swan / Get it on / Light of love / Children of the revolution / Jeepster / Laser love / Zip gun boogie / The groover / King of the rumbling spires / Plateau skull / Truck on (Tyke) / Solid gold easy action / Teenage dream. (cd has 4 extra above)

Oct 91. Marc On Wax; (7"/c-s; as MARC BOLAN & T.REX) **METAL GURU. / THUNDERWIND / BOLAN'S ZIP GUN** | | - |
(12"+=/cd-s+=) – Solid baby (remix).

Nov 91. (cd; by MARC BOLAN) Cherry Red; (CBRED 70) **LOVE AND DEATH** | | - |
(re-iss. Aug98; same)

Nov 91. (7") Marc On Wax; **SLEEPY MAURICE. / (1968 interview)** | | - |

Dec 91. (cd/c/d-lp) Marc On Wax; (MARC CD/MC/LP 514) **BORN TO BOOGIE** (live & poetry) | | - |

Dec 91. (cd) Dojo; **THE EARLY YEARS** | | - |
(re-iss. +lp+c)

Dec 91. (3xcd-box; as MARC BOLAN & T.REX) Essential; (ESBCD 965) **ANTHOLOGY** | | - |

– (THE EARLY YEARS / THE SINGLES A'S & B'S / GLAM ROCK TO FAST PUNK 1972-1977)

Feb 92. (cd; *Castle; (CLABX 909)* **3 ORIGINALS** – (T.REX / BOLAN BOOGIE / ELECTRIC WARRIOR)	□	-
Jun 92. (cd/c) *Action Replay; (CDAR/ARLC 1031)* **THE BEST OF THE REST OF MARC BOLAN**	□	-
Apr 93. (cd; TYRANNOSAURUS REX) *Windsong; (WINCD 032)* **BBC RADIO 1 LIVE IN CONCERT (live)**	□	-
Apr 93. (cd-ep) *Deram;* **THE WIZARD / BEYOND THE RISIN' SUN / THE THIRD DEGREE / SAN FRANCISCO POET**	□	-
Jun 93. (cd) *Deram;* **THE WIZARD**	□	-
Jun 93. (cd-ep) *Zinc Alloy;* **BLOWIN' IN THE WIND / THE ROAD I'M ON (GLORIA) / BLOWIN' IN THE WIND (session version)**	□	-
Sep 93. (cd) *Sequel; (NEXCD 250)* **THE DEFINITIVE TYRANNOSAURUS REX**	□	-
Nov 93. (cd) *Soundwind; (ACD 105106)* **16 GREATEST HITS**	□	-
Apr 94. (cd) *Remember;* **20th CENTURY BOY**	□	-
Oct 94. (cd) *Edsel; (EDCD 401)* **GREAT HITS (1972-1977): THE A SIDES)**	□	-
Oct 94. (cd) *Edsel; (EDCD 402)* **GREAT HITS (1972-1977): THE B SIDES)**	□	-
Oct 94. (cd) *Edsel; (EDCD 403)* **RABBIT FIGHTER (THE ALTERNATIVE SLIDER)**	□	-
Oct 94. (cd) *Edsel; (EDCD 404)* **MESSING WITH THE MYSTIC**	□	-
May 95. (cd) *Edsel; (EDCD 410)* **LEFT HAND LUKE (THE ALTERNATIVE TANX)**	□	-
May 95. (cd) *Edsel; (EDCD 413)* **LIGHT OF LOVE**	□	-
Jun 95. (cd; MARC BOLAN & T.REX) *Edsel; (EDCD 411)* **UNCHAINED: VOLUME 1 (UNRELEASED RECORDINGS 1972)**	□	-
Jun 95. (cd; MARC BOLAN & T.REX) *Edsel; (EDCD 412)* **UNCHAINED: VOLUME 2 (UNRELEASED RECORDINGS 1972)**	□	-
Aug 95. (cd-s) *Old Gold;* **TELEGRAM SAM / 20th CENTURY BOY**	□	-
Sep 95. (cd/c; as MARC BOLAN & T.REX) *Polygram TV; (525 961-2/-4)* **THE ESSENTIAL COLLECTION**	24	-
Sep 95. (cd/c) *Emporio; (EMPR CD/MC 589)* **PREHISTORIC**	□	-
Oct 95. (cd; MARC BOLAN & T.REX) *Edsel;* **UNCHAINED: VOLUME 3 (UNRELEASED RECORDINGS 1973 PART 1)**	□	-
Oct 95. (cd; MARC BOLAN & T.REX) *Edsel;* **UNCHAINED: VOLUME 4 (UNRELEASED RECORDINGS 1973 PART 2)**	□	-
Oct 95. (cd; as MARC BOLAN & T.REX) *Edsel; (EDCD 440)* **CHANGE (THE ALTERNATIVE ZINC ALLOY)**	□	-
Jun 96. (cd) *Edsel; (EDCD 443)* **PRECIOUS STAR (THE ALTERNATIVE BOLAN'S ZIP GUN)**	□	-
Jun 96. (cd; MARC BOLAN & T.REX) *Edsel; (EDCD 444)* **UNCHAINED: VOLUME 5 (UNRELEASED RECORDINGS 1974)**	□	-
Jun 96. (cd; MARC BOLAN & T.REX) *Edsel; (EDCD 445)* **UNCHAINED: VOLUME 6 (UNRELEASED RECORDINGS 1975)**	□	-
Jun 96. (cd) *Band Of Joy; (BOJCD 016)* **LIVE AT THE BBC**	□	-
Sep 96. (cd/c) *Telstar; (TCD/STAC 2858)* **ACOUSTIC WARRIOR** (*cd re-iss. Nov99 on 'Camden'; 74321 71001-2*)	□	-
Jan 97. (cd; as MARC BOLAN & T.REX) *Burning Airlines; (PILOT 4)* **ELECTRIC WARRIOR SESSIONS** (*lp-iss.Mar97 on 'Get Back'; GET 502*)	□	-
May 97. (cd-s) *BMG; (MASSCD 1000)* **GET IT ON**	□	-
May 97. (cd/c) *BMG; (MASQ CD/MC 1010)* **GET IT ON**	□	-
Jun 97. (cd) *Edsel; (EDCD 522)* **DAZZLING RAIMENT (THE ALTERNATIVE FUTURISTIC DRAGON)**	□	-
Jun 97. (cd) *Edsel; (EDCD 524)* **UNCHAINED: UNRELEASED RECORDINGS VOL.7**	□	-
Jun 97. (d-cd) *Edsel; (EDCD 530)* **LIVE**	□	-
Nov 97. (d-cd) *Burning Airlines; (PILOT 021)* **SPACEBALL (US TOURS 1971-1972)**	□	-
Aug 98. (d-cd) *Burning Airlines; (PILOT 028)* **MIDNIGHT COURT AT THE LYCEUM (live)**	□	-
Sep 98. (cd) *Edsel; (MEDCD 573)* **THE VERY BEST OF MARC BOLAN & T.REX VOL.2**	□	-
Oct 98. (cd) *Polydor; (541008-2)* **MARC – WORDS AND MUSIC OF MARC BOLAN 1947-1977**	□	-
Jan 99. (4xcd-box) *Edsel; (MARCBOX 99)* **T.REX BOXED**	□	-
Feb 99. (cd) *Masquerade; (MASQ CD/MC 1010)* **GET IT ON**	□	-
Mar 99. (cd) *Music Club; (MCCD 030)* **THE VERY BEST OF T.REX VOL.1**	□	-
Mar 99. (cd) *Music Club; (MCCD 374)* **THE VERY BEST OF T.REX VOL.2**	□	-
Apr 99. (4xcd-box) *Burning Airlines; (XPILOT 017)* **THE WARRIOR BOX SET** – (ELECTRIC WARRIOR SESSIONS / ELECTRIC BOOGIE / SPACEBALL / T.REX)		-
Sep 99. (d-cd) *Cleopatra; (CLP 577)* **T.REX CLASSICS**	□	-

Tommy BOLIN (dig out; Great Metal . . .)

Graham BOND

Born: 28 Oct'37, Romford, Essex, England. Adopted as a child from a Dr. Bernardo's home, BOND cut his teeth in the late 50's as an alto sax player with The DON RENDELL QUINTET. In 1962, he replaced CYRIL DAVIES in BLUES INCORPORATED, an influential London-based R&B combo headed by ALEXIS KORNER; like many artists who'd pass through the band's ranks, BOND was a pioneer in his own right. Eager to implement his innovative use of the electric organ as a Blues tool, he formed his own outfit in 1963, The GRAHAM BOND ORGANISATION, taking JACK BRUCE and GINGER BAKER with him; future jazz guitar virtuoso JOHN McLAUGHLIN was also a short-lived early member. With the latter being quickly replaced by another time-served BLUES INCORPORATED man, DICK HECKSTALL-SMITH, the ORGANISATION cut a one-off 45 for 'Decca', 'LONG TALL SHORTY', before new manager, Robert Stigwood, helped them sign a deal with 'Columbia'. Early in 1965, the quartet showcased their hard-edged jazz-inspired R&B on their debut album, 'THE SOUND OF '65'. A second set, 'THERE'S A BOND BETWEEN US', appeared later the same year, again serving up a mixed platter of BOND originals and Blues standards with GRAHAM pioneering the soon-to-be ubiquitous mellotron. By '67, BOND's lack of commercial success had been compounded with the loss of both BRUCE and BAKER who'd soon make their mark as two-thirds of power trio supergroup, CREAM. A short stay in the USA – during which he issued the LP, 'LOVE IS THE LAW' – found him working with HARVEY MANDEL. Meanwhile, back in Britain, GB was finally hitting the Top 40, albeit with a set of early recordings 'SOLID BOND' (1970). After a brief call-up for GINGER BAKER's AIRFORCE, the restless wildman formed MAGICK with new like-minded wife DIANE STEWART; having initially dabbled in Eastern mystical influences in 1967, BOND became increasingly entrenched in the occult and even maintained he was the bastard son of the infamous Aleister Crowley. GRAHAM's latest incarnation delivered two 1971 albums, 'HOLY MAGICK' and 'WE PUT OUR MAGICK ON YOU', before his marriage and in turn the band fell apart. The following year, he collaborated with former CREAM lyricist PETE BROWN on a one-off album, 'TWO HEADS ARE BETTER THAN ONE'. BOND's final music venture came in the shape of MAGUS, a project put together with folkie CAROL ANNE PEGG. Again this ended in disarray and amid mounting financial difficulties, drug addiction and mental health problems, BOND was found dead under a London train on the 8th of May, 1974; mystery surrounds this as to whether it was suicide or a "cult" murder. It was a messy end for a man who has sometimes been referred to as The Godfather Of British R&B. • **Songwriters:** Self/group penned, except GOT MY MOJO WORKING (Muddy Waters) / WHAT'D I SAY (Ray Charles) / etc. • **Trivia:** BOND appeared on B-side of WHO single, 'Substitute' under the billing of The WHO ORCHESTRA (the track, 'Waltz For A Pig').

Album rating: THE SOUND OF '65 (*7) / THERE'S A BOND BETWEEN US (*6) / LOVE IS THE LAW (*4) / SOLID BOND compilation (*6) / Magick: HOLY MAGICK (*5) / WE PUT OUR MAGICK ON YOU (*5) / TWO HEADS ARE BETTER THAN ONE with Pete Brown (*5) / LIVE AT KLOOK'S KLEEK live collection (*5)

GRAHAM BOND ORGANISATION

GRAHAM BOND – vocals, organ (ex-BLUES INCORPORATED, ex-DUFFY POWER) / **DICK HECKSTALL-SMITH** – saxophone repl. guitarist JOHN McLAUGHLIN / **JACK BRUCE** – bass, vocals / **PETER 'GINGER' BAKER** – drums

	Decca	not iss.
Jun 64. (7") *(F 11909)* **LONG TALL SHORTY. / LONG LEGGED BABY**	□	-
	Columbia	**Ascot**
Jan 65. (7") *(DB 7471)* **WADE IN THE WATER. / TAMMY**	□	-
Mar 65. (lp) *(SX 1711)* **THE SOUND OF '65** – Hoochie coochie / Baby make love to me / Neighbour, neighbour / Early in the morning / Spanish blues / Oh baby / Little girl / I want you / Wade in the water / Got my mojo working / Train time / Baby, be good to me / Half a man / Tammy.	□	-
Mar 65. (7") *(DB 7528)* **TELL ME (I'M GONNA LOVE AGAIN). / LOVE COMES SHINING THROUGH**	□	-
Jul 65. (7") *(DB 7647)* **LEASE ON LOVE. / MY HEART'S IN LITTLE PIECES**	□	-
Nov 65. (lp) *(SX 1750)* **THERE'S A BOND BETWEEN US** – Who's afraid of Virgina Woolf / Hear me calling your name / The night time is the right time / Walkin' in the park / Last night / Baby it can't be true / What'd I say / Dick's instrumental / Don't let go / Keep-a-drivin' / Have you ever loved a woman / Camels and elephants.	□	-

—— (Oct65) **NEIL HUBBARD** – guitar repl. BRUCE (to JOHN MAYALL and solo, then CREAM)

| Feb 66. (7") *(DB 7838)* **ST. JAMES INFIRMARY. / SOUL TANGO** | □ | - |
| Apr 66. (7") *<2211>* **ST. JAMES INFIRMARY. / WADE IN THE WATER** | - | - |

—— BOND retained HECKSTALL-SMITH and HUBBARD plus **JON HISEMAN** – drums repl. BAKER who (with BRUCE) formed CREAM

	Page One	not iss.
Feb 67. (7") *(POF 014)* **YOU'VE GOT TO HAVE LOVE BABE. / I LOVE YOU**	□	-

—— Split Sep67, HECKSTALL-SMITH and HISEMAN joined JOHN MAYALL then COLOSSEUM. HUBBARD joined GREASE BAND then JUICY LUCY

GRAHAM BOND

—— moved to the States & went solo, with **HARVEY MANDEL** – guitar / **HARVEY BROOKS** – bass / **EDDIE HOH** – drums

	not iss.	Pulsar
1968. (lp) *<AR 10604>* **LOVE IS THE LAW** – Water, water / Oh shining on / Pictures in the fire / Baroque / Sisters and brothers / Stiffnecked chicken / Freaky beak / Walk onto me / Magic mojo / Brothers and sisters.	-	□

—— (Dec69) returned to UK. He joined GINGER BAKER in AIRFORCE

	Warners	Warners
Jan 70. (d-lp) *(WS 3001) <2555>* **SOLID BOND** (compilation 63-66) – Green onions / Springtime in the city / Can't stand it / The grass is greener / Doxy /	40	

Only sixteen / Last night / Long legged baby / Walkin' in the park / It's not goodbye / Neighbour nightbour / Ho ho country kicking blues.

Feb 70. (7") *(WB 8004) <7391>* **WALKING IN THE PARK. / SPRINGTIME IN THE CITY**

MAGICK

— were formed by **GRAHAM BOND** plus **DIANE STEWART** – vocals / **HENRY WILLIAMS** – guitar / **TERRY POOLE** – guitar / **STEVE GREGORY** – saxophone / **JOHN WEATHERS** – drums / **GASPER WILLIAMS** – percussion

	Vertigo	Mercury

Feb 71. (lp) *(6360 021) <61327>* **HOLY MAGICK**
– Holy magick suite:- Meditation aumgn / The Qabalistic cross / The word of the Aeon / Invocation to the light / The pentagram ritual / The Qabablistic cross / Hymn of praise / Twelve gates to the city / The holy words Iao Saluco (these are the words) / Aquarius mantra (in Egyptian) / Enochian (Atlantean) call / Abrahadabra the word of the Aeon / Praise "city of light" / The Qabalistic cross aumgn / Return of Arthur / The magician / The judgement / An archangel Mikael. *(cd-iss. Aug91 on 'Repertoire'; REP 4106WP)*

Apr 71. (7") *(6059 042)* **WATER WATER. / TWELVE GATES TO THE CITY**

Dec 71. (lp) *(6360 042)* **WE PUT OUR MAGICK ON YOU**
– Forbidden fruit (part 1) / Moving towards the light / Ajama / Druid / I put my magick on you / Time to die / Hail Ra Haraknite / Forbidden fruit (part 2). *(re-iss. '74 on 'Philips'; SRM1 0612) (re-iss. Nov88 on 'Beat Goes On'; BGOLP 73) (cd-iss. Aug91 on 'Repertoire'; REP 4107WP)*

GRAHAM BOND & PETE BROWN

	Chapter One	not iss.

Nov 72. (lp) *(CHSR 813)* **TWO HEADS ARE BETTER THAN ONE**
– Lost tribe / Ig the pig / Oobati / Amazing grass / Scunthorpe crabmeat train sideways boogie shuffle stomp / C.F.D.T. (Colonel Fright's dancing terrapins) / Mass debate / Looking for time.
(cd-iss.Jul92 on 'See For Miles'+=; SEECD 345) – Milk is turning sour in my shoes / Macumbe / The beginning / Aeroplane drinking man (Gladiator song) / Italian song / Spend my nights in armour / Fury of war / Magpie man / Drum roll / Swing song / Sailor's song / The ending.

	Greenwich	not iss.

1972. (7"m) *(GSS 104)* **LOST TRIBE. / MACUMBE / MILK IS TURNING SOUR IN MY SHOES**

— They also both recorded for soundtrack 'MALTAMOUR'. In 1973, BOND formed MAGUS with folk singer, CAROL ANNE PEGG. They split, and on the 8th of May '74 – after a bout of depression due to heroin addiction – he was found dead under a tube train in Finsbury.

– compilations etc. –

1964. (7"ep) *Decca;* **THE GRAHAM BOND ORGANISATION**
– Hoochie coochie man / High healed sneakers / Little girl / Long legged baby / Strut around.

1971. (d-lp) *Philips; (6499 200-1)* **BOND IN AMERICA**

1972. (lp) *Philips; (6382 010)* **THIS IS GRAHAM BOND**

Jan 77. (lp; by GRAHAM BOND ORGANISATION) *Charly; (CR 30198)* **THE BEGINNING OF JAZZ ROCK** (live 1964)

Mar 88. (d-lp) *Edsel; (DED 254)* **THE SOUND OF '65 / THERE'S A BOND BETWEEN US**
(cd-iss. Oct99 on 'Beat Goes On'; BGOCD 500)

Oct 88. (lp) *Decal; (LIK 47)* **LIVE AT KLOOKS KLEEK** (live)
– Wade in the water / Big boss man / Early in the morning / Person to person blues / Spanish blues / Introduction by Dick Jordan / First time I met the blues / Stormy Monday / Train time / What'd I say. *(cd-iss. Dec97 on 'Charly'; CDGR 195)*

Aug 98. (cd; shared with the ANIMALS) *Spalax; (14553)* **ROCK GENERATION**

Nov 99. (cd) *Beat Goes On; (BGOCD 483)* **HOLY MAGICK / WE PUT OUR MAGICK ON YOU**

BONGWATER　(dig out; Great Alt & Indie . . .)

BON JOVI

Formed: Sayreville, New Jersey, USA . . . Spring '83, by JON BON JOVI and DAVID BRYAN, who duly recruited RICHIE SAMBORA, ALEC SUCH and TICO TORRES. Gaining a toehold on the music business ladder by helping out at his cousin's recording studio, JON found time to cut a rough demo of 'RUNAWAY', which subsequently gained radio play after being featured on a local various artists compilation. A line-up that would remain stable throughout BON JOVI's career was soon established and by the summer of 1983, the band had signed to a worldwide deal with 'Polygram'. The first two albums, 'BON JOVI' (1984) and '7800 DEGREES FAHRENHEIT' (1985), were generally derided by critics for their formulaic, glossy pop-metal content, yet the latter sold respectably, 'Polygram's marketing muscle and JON's pretty boy looks certainly not doing the band any harm. At this point, BON JOVI were just another name in an endless sea of wet-permed 'hair' bands on the hard-rock circuit and no one was quite expecting the splash that 'SLIPPERY WHEN WET' would make upon its release in 1986. Preceded by the squalling riff and anthemic chorus of 'YOU GIVE LOVE A BAD NAME', the album was heavy metal (in the broadest possible sense) for people who didn't like heavy metal (housewives, junior schoolgirls, construction workers, etc.). The next single taken from it was 'LIVIN' ON A PRAYER', a hard-bitten tale of love on the breadline (rather ironic considering the moolah rolling into BON JOVI's coffers) that featured what must rank as one of the most bombastic choruses in the history of rock. Elsewhere on the record, the

production loomed equally large and the songs were relentlessly hook-laden, with just enough edge to convince "real" rock fans that the band hadn't sold out. 'WANTED DEAD OR ALIVE' marked the beginning of JON's cowboy fantasies while 'I'D DIE FOR YOU' and 'NEVER SAY GOODBYE' were the obligatory 'sensitive' numbers. The album's success was partly down to the band hiring soft rock songsmith extrordinaire, DESMOND CHILD, whose unerringly catchy way with a tune saw the album going on to sell millions. BON JOVI were at the top of their career already, headlining the Monsters Of Rock shows in Britain and Europe. No doubt feeling more confident about his songwriting abilities, JON BON JOVI followed a more SPRINGSTEEN-esque direction on 'NEW JERSEY' (1988); more rock, less metal, while still retaining the spotless production and impeccable hooks. 'LIVING IN SIN', 'BLOOD ON BLOOD' (title taken from SPRINGSTEEN's 'HIGHWAY PATROLMAN', perchance?) and 'WILD IS THE WIND' were all reassuringly strident, the album again selling in mindboggling quantities. In many ways, JON BON JOVI is BON JOVI, so when JON-boy released his 'BLAZE OF GLORY' solo effort (a result of his acting role in 'Young Guns II'), it was a case of more of the same. When the band re-emerged in 1992 with 'KEEP THE FAITH', there was no question of the album failing to scale the heights of its predecessors. The songs were intact although the likes of 'I'LL SLEEP WHEN I'M DEAD' were verging on self-parody. Needless to say, a compilation, 'CROSSROADS', sold phenomenally with the subsequent studio album, 'THESE DAYS' also hitting No.1 in Britain. While the band continued to win the hearts of coffee table browsers the world over, most metal fans probably lost interest years ago. Something of a celeb these days with his short(er) hair, pseudo-trendy image and acting career, JON recently completed his own short film and accompanying soundtrack (he'd previously made his acting debut proper, in the 1996 film, 'Moonlight And Valentino'). • **Covered:** IT'S ONLY ROCK'N'ROLL (Rolling Stones) / WITH A LITTLE HELP FROM MY FRIENDS + HELTER SKELTER (Beatles) / I DON'T LIKE MONDAYS (Boomtown Rats) / ROCKIN' IN THE FREE WORLD (Neil Young) / HOUSE OF THE RISING SUN (trad). • **Miscellaneous:** April 1988 saw their manager DOC McGEE convicted for drug offences. He was sentenced to five years suspended, although he ended up doing community work. JON married his childhood sweetheart Dorothea Hurley on the 29th April '89. SAMBORA is married to actress Heather Locklear, while TORRES tied the knot with supermodel Eva Herzigova on the 7th of September '96 (but now split).

Album rating: BON JOVI (*6) / 7800° FAHRENHEIT (*5) / SLIPPERY WHEN WET (*9) / NEW JERSEY (*7) / BLAZE OF GLORY solo (*5) / STRANGER IN THIS TOWN; Sambora solo (*6) / KEEP THE FAITH (*8) / CROSS ROAD – THE BEST OF BON JOVI compilation (*8) / (THESE DAYS) (*6) / DESTINATION ANYWHERE solo (*6)

JON BON JOVI (b. JOHN BONGIOVI, 2 Mar'62) – vocals, guitar / **RICHIE SAMBORA** (b.11 Jul'59, Woodbridge, N.J.) – lead guitar / **DAVID BRYAN** (b. DAVID BRYAN RASHBAUM, 7 Feb'62, New York City) – keyboards / **ALEC JOHN SUCH** (b.14 Nov'56, Yonkers, N.Y.) – bass (ex-PHANTON'S OPERA) / **TICO 'Tar Monster' TORRES** (b. HECTOR TORRES, 7 Oct'53, New York City) – drums (ex-FRANKIE & THE KNOCKOUTS)

	Vertigo	Mercury
Apr 84. (lp/c) *(VERL/+C 14) <814982>* **BON JOVI**	71	43 Feb84

– Runaway / Roulette / She don't know me / Shot through the heart / Love lies / Breakout / Burning for love / Come back / Get ready. *(cd-iss. Jul86; 814 982-2) (cd-enhanced.Oct98 on 'Jambco'; 538025-2)*

May 84. (7"/12") *(VER/+X 11) <818958>* **SHE DON'T KNOW ME. / BREAKOUT**		48
Oct 84. (7") *(VER 14) <818309>* **RUNAWAY. / BREAKOUT** (live)		39 Feb84

(12"+=) *(VERX 14)* – Runaway (live).

Apr 85. (7") *<880736>* **ONLY LONELY. /**	-	54
May 85. (lp/c) *(VERL/+H 24) <824509>* **7800° FAHRENHEIT**	28	37

– In and out of love / The price of love / Only lonely / King of the mountain / Silent night / Tokyo road / The hardest part is the night / Always run to you / To the fire / Secret dreams. *(cd-iss. Jul86; 824 509-2) (cd-enhanced; Oct98 on 'Jambco'; 538026-2)*

May 85. (7"/7"pic-d) *(VER/+P 19) <880951>* **IN AND OUT OF LOVE. / ROULETTE** (live)		69 Jul85

(12"+=) *(VERX 19)* – Shot through the heart (live).

Jul 85. (7") *(VER 22)* **THE HARDEST PART IS THE NIGHT. / ALWAYS RUN TO YOU**	68	-

(12"+=) *(VERX 22)* – Tokyo Road (live).
(d7"++=) *(VERDP 22)* – Shot through the heart (live).
(12"red) *(VERXR 22)* – ('A'side) / Tokyo Road (live) / In and out of love (live).

Aug 86. (7"/10"sha-pic-d) *(VER/+P 26) <884953>* **YOU GIVE LOVE A BAD NAME / LET IT ROCK**	14	1

(12"+=) *(VERX 26)* – Borderline.
(12"blue+=) *(VERXR 26)* – The hardest part is the night (live) / Burning for love (live).

Sep 86. (lp/c)(cd) *(VERH/+C 38)(<830 264-2>)* **SLIPPERY WHEN WET**	6	1

– Let it rock / You give love a bad name / Livin' on a prayer / Social disease / Wanted dead or alive / Raise your hands / Without love / I'd die for you / Never say goodbye / Wild in the streets. *(re-iss.Aug88; VERHP 38) (re-iss. Dec90; same); hit 46) (re-charted.Jun91 No.42, Sep92 re-issue) (cd-enhanced.Oct98 on 'Jambco'; 538025-2) (lp re-iss. Jun99 on 'Simply Vinyl'; SVLP 93)*

Oct 86. (7"/7"s) *<888184>* **LIVIN' ON A PRAYER. / WILD IN THE STREETS**	4	1 Dec86

(12"+=/12"green+=) *(VERX/+P 28)* – Edge of a broken heart.
(d12"+=) *(VERXG 28)* – Only lonely (live) / Runaway (live).

Mar 87. (7"/7"s) *(JOV/+S 1) <888467>* **WANTED DEAD OR ALIVE. / SHOT THROUGH THE HEART**	13	7

(12"+=) *(JOV 1-12)* – Social disease.
(12"silver++=) – *(JOVR 1-12)* – Get ready (live).

Aug 87. (7") *(JOV 2)* **NEVER SAY GOODBYE. / RAISE YOUR HANDS** — `21` `-`
(c-s+=) *(JOVC 2)* – ('A'acoustic).
(12"+=/12"yellow+=) *(JOV/+R 2-12)* – Wanted dead or alive (acoustic).
Sep 88. (7") *(JOV 3)* **BAD MEDICINE. / 99 IN THE SHADE** `17` `1`
(12"+=/cd-s+=) *(JOV 3-12/CD3)* – Lay your hands on me.
(12") *(JOVR 3-12)* – ('A'side) / You give love a bad name / Livin' on a prayer (live).
Sep 88. (lp/c)(cd) *(VERH/+C 62)(<836 345-2>)* **NEW JERSEY** `1` `1`
– Lay your hands on me / Bad medicine / Born to be my baby / Living in sin / Blood on blood / Stick to your guns / Homebound train / I'll be there for you / 99 in the shade / Love for sale / Wild is the wind / Ride cowboy ride. *(re-iss. Mar93 cd/c;) (cd-enhanced.Oct98 on 'Jambco'; 538024-2)*
Nov 88. (7"/7"s) *(JOV/+S 4)* <872156> **BORN TO MY BABY. / LOVE FOR SALE** `22` `3`
(12"+=/12"g-f+=/12"pic-d+=) *(JOV/+R/P 4-12)* – Wanted dead or alive.
(cd-s+=) *(JOVCD 4)* – Runaway / Livin' on a prayer.
Apr 89. (7"/7"w-poster) *(JOV/+PB 5)* <872564> **I'LL BE THERE FOR YOU. / HOMEBOUND TRAIN** `18` `1` Feb89
(12"+=) *(JOV 5-12)* – Wild in the streets (live).
(cd-s+=) *(JOVCD 5)* – Borderline / Edge of a broken heart.
May 89. (7") <874452> **LAY YOUR HANDS ON ME. / RUNAWAY (live)** `-` `7`
Aug 89. (7"/-c-s)(7"red/7"white/7"blue) *(JOV/+MC 6)(JOVS 6 61/62/63)* **LAY YOUR HANDS ON ME. / BAD MEDICINE** `18` `-`
(10"pic-d+=) *(JOV 6-10)* – Blood on blood.
(12") *(JOVG 6-12)* – ('A'side) / Blood on blood (live) / Born to be my baby (acoustic).
(cd-s) *(JOVCD 6)* – ('A'side) / You give love a bad name / Let it rock.
Nov 89. (7"/-c-s) *(JOV/+MC 7)* <876070> **LIVING IN SIN. / LOVE IS WAR** `35` `9` Oct89
(12"+=/box-cd-s+=) *(JOV 7-12/CD7)* – Ride cowboy ride / Stick to your guns.
(12"white+=) *(JOVR 7-12)* **The boys are back in town.**

JON BON JOVI

Jul 90. (7") *(JBJ 1)* <875896> **BLAZE OF GLORY. / YOU REALLY GOT ME NOW (with LITTLE RICHARD)** `13` `1`
(12"+=/cd-s+=) *(JBJ T/CD 1)* – Blood money.
Aug 90. (cd/c/lp) <(846473-2/-4/-1)> **BLAZE OF GLORY – YOUNG GUNS II** `2` `3`
– Billy get your guns / Miracle / Blaze of glory / Blood money / Santa Fe / Justice in the barrel / Never say die / You really got me now / Bang a drum / Dyin' ain't much of a livin' / Guano City. *(re-iss. Apr95 cd/c;)*
Oct 90. (c-s) <878392> **MIRACLE / BLOOD MONEY** `-` `12`
Nov 90. (7"/-c-s) *(JBJ/+C 2)* **MIRACLE. / BANG A DRUM** `29` `-`
(12"+=/cd-s+=) *(JBJ T/CD 2)* – Dyin' ain't much of a livin' / (interview).

BON JOVI

	Jambco	Jambco
Oct 92. (7"/-c-s) *(JOV/+MC 8)* <864432> **KEEP THE FAITH. / I WISH EVERYDAY COULD BE CHRISTMAS** `5` `29`
(cd-s+=) *(JOVCB 8)* – Living in sin.
(cd-s+=) *(JOVCA 8)* – Little bit of soul.
Nov 92. (cd/c/lp) *(514197-2/-4/-1)* <514045> **KEEP THE FAITH** `1` `5`
– I believe / Keep the faith / I'll sleep when I'm dead / In these arms / Bed of roses / If I was your mother / Dry country / Woman in love / Fear / I want you / Blame it on the love of rock'n'roll / Little bit of soul. *(d-cd-iss. Aug93; 518 019-2)* – (live versions). *(cd-enhanced.Oct98)*
Jan 93. (c-s) <864852> **BED OF ROSES / LAY YOUR HANDS ON ME (live)** `-` `10`
Jan 93. (7"/-c-s) *(JOV/+MC 9)* **BED OF ROSES. / STARTING ALL OVER AGAIN** `13` `-`
(12"+=) *(JOVT 9)* – Lay your hands on me (live).
(cd-s) *(JOVCD 9)* – ('A'side) / Lay your hands on me (live) / I'll be there for you (live) / Tokyo road (live).
May 93. (cd-s) <862088> **IN THESE ARMS / SAVE A PRAYER / IN THESE ARMS (live)** `-` `27`
May 93. (7") *(JOV 10)* **IN THESE ARMS. / BED OF ROSES (acoustic)** `9` `-`
(cd-s) *(JOVCD 10)* – ('A'side) / Keep the faith (live) / In these arms (live).
(c-s) *(JOVMC 10)* – ('A'side) / Blaze of glory (acoustic).
Jul 93. (7"/-c-s) *(JOV/+MC 11)* <862428> **I'LL SLEEP WHEN I'M DEAD. / NEVER SAY GOODBYE (live acoustic)** `17` `97`
(cd-s) *(JOVCD 11)* – ('A'side) / Blaze of glory / Wild in the streets (both live).
(cd-ep) **HITS LIVE EP** *(JOVD 11)* – ('A'side) / Blaze of glory / You give love a bad name / Bad medicine.
Sep 93. (7"/-c-s) *(JOV/+MC 12)* **I BELIEVE (Clearmountain mix). / ('A'live)** `11` `-`
(cd-s) *(JOVCD 12)* – ('A'side) / Runaway (live) / Livin' on the prayer (live) / Wanted dead or alive ('HITS LIVE PART 2 EP').
(cd-s) *(JOVCB 12)* – ('A'side) / You give love a bad name (live) / Born to be my baby (live) / I'll sleep when I'm dead (live).
Mar 94. (7"/-c-s) *(JOV/+MC 13)* **DRY COUNTY. / STRANGER IN THIS TOWN (live)** `9` `-`
(gold-cd-s+=) *(JOVBX 13)* – Blood money (live).
(cd-s) *(JOVCD 13)* – ('A'side) / It's only rock'n'roll (live) / Waltzing Matilda (live).
Sep 94. (c-s) *(JOVMC 14)* **ALWAYS. / THE BOYS ARE BACK IN TOWN** `2` `-`
(12"colrd) *(JOVT 14)* – ('A'side) / Prayer '94.
(cd-s) *(JOVCD)* – ('A'side) / ('A'mix) / Edge of a broken heart.
Sep 94. (cd-s) <856227> **ALWAYS / NEVER SAY GOODBYE / EDGE OF A BROKEN HEART** `-` `4`
Oct 94. (cd/c/lp) *(522 936-2/-4/-1)* <526013> **CROSS ROAD – THE BEST OF BON JOVI (compilation)** `1` `8`
– Livin' on a prayer / Keep the faith / Someday I'll be Saturday night / Always / Wanted dead or alive / Lay your hands on me / You give love a bad name / Bed of roses / Blaze of glory / In these arms / Bad medicine / I'll be there for you / In and out of love / Runaway / Never say goodbye. *(cd-enhanced.Oct98; same)*

Dec 94. (7"pic-d/c-s) *(JOV P/MC 16)* **PLEASE COME HOME FOR CHRISTMAS / BACK DOOR SANTA** `7` `-`
(cd-s+=) *(JOVCD 16)* – I wish every day could be like Christmas.
Feb 95. (7"pic-d/c-s) *(JOV P/MC 15)* **SOMEDAY I'LL BE SATURDAY NIGHT. / GOOD GUYS DON'T ALWAYS WEAR WHITE (live)** `7` `-`
(cd-s+=) *(JOVCD 15)* – With a little help from my friends (live).
(cd-s+=) *(JOVDD 15)* – Always (live).
May 95. (cd-s) *(JOVMC 17)* **THIS AIN'T A LOVE SONG. / LONELY AT THE TOP** `6` `-`
(cd-s+=) *(JOVCX 17)* – The end.
(cd-s) *(JOVCD 17)* – ('A'side) / When she comes / Wedding day / Prostitute.
May 95. (c-s) <856227> **THIS AIN'T A LOVE SONG / ALWAYS (live) / PROSTITUTE** `-` `14`
Jun 95. (cd/c/d-lp) *(528 248-2/-4/-1)* <528181> **(THESE DAYS)** `1` `9`
– Hey God / Something for the pain / This ain't a love song / These days / Lie to me / Damned / My guitar lies bleeding in my arms / (It's hard) Letting you go / Hearts breaking even / Something to believe in / If that's what it takes / Diamond ring / All I want is everything / Bitter wine. *(re-iss. w/ free cd+=)* – (8 tracks). *(iss.w/ tour pack Jun96; 532 644-2) (cd-enhanced.Oct98; 538036-2)*
Sep 95. (c-s) *(JOVMC 18)* **SOMETHING FOR THE PAIN / THIS AIN'T A LOVE SONG** `8` `-`
(cd-s+=) *(JOVCX 18)* – I don't like Mondays.
(cd-s) *(JOVCD 18)* – ('A'side) / Living on a prayer / You give love a bad name / Wild in the streets.
Nov 95. (c-s) *(JOVMC 19)* <852296> **LIE TO ME / SOMETHING FOR THE PAIN (live)** `10` `88` `76`
(cd-s+=) *(JOVCX 19)* – Always (live) / Keep the faith (live).
(cd-s) *(JOVCD 19)* – ('A'side) / Something for the pain / Hey God (live) / I'll sleep when I'm dead (live).
Feb 96. (c-s) *(JOVMC 20)* **THESE DAYS / 634-5789** `7` `-`
(cd-s+=) *(JOVCX 20)* – Rockin' in the free world (live) / (It's hard) Letting you go (live).
(cd-s) *(JOVCD 20)* – ('A'side) / Someday I'll be Saturday night / These days (live) / Helter skelter (live).
Jun 96. (c-s) *(JOVMC 21)* **HEY GOD / LIE TO ME (remix)** `13` `-`
(cd-s+=) *(JOVCX 21)* – House of the rising sun / Livin' on a prayer.
(cd-s) *(JOVCD 21)* – ('A'side) / The end / When she comes / ('A'live).

JON BON JOVI

— with **DAVID BRYAN** – keyboards / **KENNY ARONOFF** – drums / **ERIC BAZILIAN + DAVE STEWART**

	Mercury	Mercury
Jun 97. (c-s) *(MERMC 488)* **MIDNIGHT IN CHELSEA / MIDNIGHT IN CHELSEA (album version)** `4` ` `
(cd-s+=) *(MERCD 488)* – Sad song tonight / August 7th (acoustic).
(cd-s+=) *(MERCX 488)* – Drive / Every word was a piece of my heart.
Jun 97. (cd/c) *(536 011-2/-4)* **DESTINATION ANYWHERE** `2` `31`
– Queen of New Orleans / Janie, don't take your love to town / Midnight in Chelsea / Ugly / Staring at your window with a suitcase in my hand / Every word was a piece of my heart / It's just me / Destination anywhere / Learning how to fall / Naked / Little city / August 4, 4:15 / Cold hard heart. *(cd re-iss. Dec97 with bonus cd of live tracks; 536 758-2)* – Queen of New Orleans / Midnight in Chelsea / Destination anywhere / Ugly / It's just me / August 7, 4:15 / Jailbreak / Not fade away / Janie, don't take your love to town.
Aug 97. (c-s) *(MERMC 493)* **QUEEN OF NEW ORLEANS / MIDNIGHT IN CHELSEA (live)** `10` `-`
(cd-s+=) *(MERCD 493)* – ('A'album version) / Destination anywhere (live).
(cd-s) *(MERCX 493)* – ('A'side) / ('A'album version) / Every piece of my heart (acoustic) / Jailbreak (live).
Nov 97. (c-s) *(574986-4)* **JANIE, DON'T TAKE YOUR LOVE TO TOWN / TALK TO JESUS (demo)** `13` `-`
(cd-s+=) *(574987-2)* – Billy get your guns (live).
(cd-s) *(574989-2)* – ('A'album version) / Destination anywhere (MTV acoustic) / It's just me (MTV acoustic) / ('A'-MTV acoustic).

BON JOVI

	Warners	Reprise
Mar 99. (c-s) *(W 479C)* **REAL LIFE / KEEP THE FAITH (live)** `21` ` `
(cd-s+=) *(W 479CD)* – Real life (instrumental).

– (JOHN BONGIOVI) compilations, etc. –

Jul 97. (cd/c) *Masquerade; (MASQ CD/MC 1011)* **THE POWER STATION YEARS** *(rec.1980-1983; remixed 1997)* `  ` `  `
(re-iss. Feb99; same)
Aug 97. (cd-ep) *Masquerade; (MASSCD 1001)* **MORE THAN WE BARGAINED FOR** `  ` `  `
Nov 99. (cd) *Laserlight; (21490)* **JOHN BONGIOVI** `  ` `-`

RICHIE SAMBORA

(solo with **BRYAN + TORRES + TONY LEVIN** – bass)

	Mercury	Mercury
Aug 91. (7") *(MER 350)* <868790> **BALLAD OF YOUTH. / REST IN PEACE** `59` `63`
(12"+=/cd-s+=) *(MER X/CD 350)* – The wind cries Mary.
Sep 91. (cd/c/lp) <(848895-2/-4/-1>) **STRANGER IN THIS TOWN** `20` `36`
– Rest in peace / Church of desire / Stranger in this town / Ballad of youth / One light burning / Mr.Bluesman / Rosie / River of love / Father time / The answer. *(re-iss. Apr95 cd/c;)*

— DAVID BRYAN also had solo album 'NETHERWORLD' (1992) for 'Moonstone'.

Feb 98. (cd-s) *(568503-2)* **HARD TIMES COME EASY / MIDNIGHT RIDER – WANTED DEAD OR ALIVE (live) / WE ALL SLEEP ALONE (live) / BAD MEDICINE (live)** `37` `-`

(cd-s) *(568503-5)* – ('A'side) / Little help from my friends (live) / Stranger in this town (live) / I'll be there for you (live).

Mar 98. (cd/c) <*(536972-2/-4)*> **UNDISCOVERED SOUL**   `24`   □
– Made in America / Hard times come easy / Fallen from Graceland / If God was a woman / All that really matters / You're not alone / In it for love / Chained / Harlem rain / Who am I / Downside of love / Undiscovered soul.

Jul 98. (cd-s) *(566063-2)* **IN IT FOR LOVE / MADE IN AMERICA (German acoustic) / IN IT FOR LOVE (German acoustic)**   `58`   □
(cd-s) *(568825-2)* – ('A'side) / Livin' on a prayer (live at Ronnie Scott's) / I'll be there for you (live '91).

BONNIE 'PRINCE' BILLY (see under ⇒ OLDHAM, Will)

BONZO DOG BAND

Formed: London, England . . . 1965 by art students RODNEY SLATER and ROGER 'RUSKIN' SPEAR, who soon enlisted fellow eccentrics VIV STANSHALL, NEIL INNES and 'LEGS' LARRY SMITH. Their flexible line-up also numbered VERNON DUDLEY BOHAY-NOWELL, SAM SPOONS and BOB KERR. They took elements of The NEW VAUDEVILLE BAND and The TEMPERANCE SEVEN to a more modern conclusion, much in evidence on two early 'Parlophone' 45's in 1966. A year later, they released their debut album, 'GORILLA', on 'Liberty' and performed on The BEATLES' film 'MAGICAL MYSTERY TOUR'. The album skillfully parodied 20's Englishness on comic tracks like 'JOLLITY FARM', 'THE INTRO AND THE OUTRO' and 'DEATH CAB FOR CUTIE', STANSHALL and INNES being the main protagonists behind the surreal humour. Early in 1968 they secured a weekly slot on the satirical London Weekend TV show, 'Do Not Adjust Your Set'. By the end of the year, they were at No.5 with the surprise novelty hit, 'I'M THE URBAN SPACEMAN', which was produced by PAUL McCARTNEY under the pseudonym of APOLLO C. VERMOUTH. They released a further clutch of albums over the course of the next few years, some incorporating a more rock-based format, more convincingly executed by US counterparts, The MOTHERS OF INVENTION. After their final split in 1972, INNES and STANSHALL went onto greater things. INNES wrote for his GRIMMS project with a plethora of artists such as The SCAFFOLD. After a TV comedy, 'RUTLAND WEEKEND TELEVISION' (1976), with ERIC IDLE (of MONTY PYTHON), he later worked on children's television programmes such as 'The Raggy Dolls'. Meanwhile, STANSHALL released his first solo album, 'MEN OPENING UMBRELLAS AHEAD' (1974), and set to work on his finest hour, 'SIR HENRY AT RAWLINSON END' (1978), an excellent production of comic genius that was played to death each night on the John Peel show before being made into a film. Sadly, VIVIAN STANSHALL died in a fire at his home on the 3rd of March 1995. Two days later early member VERNON also died. • **Covered:** ALLEY OOP (Hollywood Argyles) / Monster Mash (Bobby Pickett) / etc. STANSHALL solo:- SUSPICION (Elvis Presley) / YOUNG ONES (Cliff Richard).

Album rating: GORILLA (*5) / THE DOUGHNUT IN GRANNY'S GREENHOUSE (*6) / TADPOLES (*5) / KEYNSHAM (*4) / LET'S MAKE UP AND BE FRIENDLY (*3) / THE HISTORY OF THE BONZOS compilation (*7) / THE BESTILALTY OF THE BONZO DOG BAND compilation (*7) / Vivian Stanshall: SIR HENRY AT RAWLINSON'S END (*9)

BONZO DOG DOO-DAH BAND

VIVIAN STANSHALL (b.21 Mar'43, Shillingford, England) – vocals, trumpet / **NEIL INNES** (b. 9 Dec'44, Essex, England) – piano, vocals, guitar / **'LEGS' LARRY SMITH** (b.18 Jan'44, Oxford, England) – drums / **RODNEY SLATER** (b. 8 Nov'44, Lincolnshire, England) – horns / **ROGER RUSKIN SPEAR** (b.29 Jun'43, London) – tenor sax, kazoo, objects / **VERNON DUDLEY BOHAY-NOWELL** (b.29 Jul'32, Plymouth, England) – bass, banjo, guitar / **SAM SPOONS** (b. MARTIN STAFFORD ASH, 8 Feb'42, Bridgewater, England) – percussion

	Stateside	not iss.
Apr 66. (7") *(R 5430)* **MY BROTHER MAKES THE NOISES FOR THE TALKIES. / I'M GONNA BRING A WATERMELON TO MY GAL TONIGHT**	□	–
Sep 66. (7") *(R 5499)* **ALLEY OOP. / BUTTON UP YOUR OVERCOAT**	□	–

	Liberty	Imperial
Oct 67. (lp; mono/stereo) *(LBL/LBS 83056)* <*12370*> **GORILLA**	□	□

– Cool Britannia / Equestrian statue / Jollity farm / I left my heart in San Francisco / Look out, there's a monster coming / Jazz, delicious hot, disgusting cold / Death cab for Cutie / Narcissus / The intro and the outro / Mickey's son and daughter / Big shot / Music for head ballet / Piggy bank love / I'm bored / The sound of music. *(re-iss. Nov70 on 'Sunset'; SLS 50160) (re-iss. Aug80; LBR 1019) (cd-iss. Jul95 on 'Beat Goes On';)*

Nov 67. (7") *(LBF 15040)* **EQUESTRIAN STATUE. / THE INTRO AND THE OUTRO**   □ □

—— **DENNIS COWAN** (b. 6 May'47, London) – bass repl. BOHAY-NOWELL. Also SPOONS departed. For a short while BOB KERR "the nearly unknown" played sax.

Oct 68. (7") *(LBF 15144)* <*66345*> **I'M THE URBAN SPACEMAN. / THE CANYONS OF YOUR MIND**   `5`   □
<US re-iss. 1972 on 'United Artists'; 50809>

BONZO DOG BAND

Nov 68. (lp; mono/stereo) *(LBL/LBS 83158E)* **THE DOUGHNUT IN GRANNY'S GREENHOUSE**   `40`   □
– We are normal / Postcard / Beautiful Zelda / Can blue men sing the whites / Hello Mabel / Kama Sutra / Humanoid boogie / The trouser press / My pink half of the drainpipe / Rockaliser baby / Rhinocratic oaths / Eleven mustachioed daughters. *(re-iss. Mar71 on 'Sunset'; SLS 50210) (re-iss. Mar87 on 'Edsel'; XED 209)*

Jul 69. (7") *(LBF 15201)* <*66373*> **MR. APOLLO. / READY MADES**   □ □

Aug 69. (lp) *(LBS 83257)* <*12445*> **TADPOLES**   `36` □
– Hunting tigers out in 'Indiah' / Shirt / Tubas in the moonlight / Dr. Jazz / Monster mash / I'm the urban spaceman / Ali Baba's camel / Laughing blues / By a waterfall / Mr. Apollo / Canyons of your mind. *(re-iss. Sep73 as 'URBAN SPACEMAN' on 'Sunset'; SLS 50350) (re-iss. May86 on 'Edsel'; ED 186)*

Nov 69. (7") *(LBF 15273)* **I WANT TO BE WITH YOU. / WE WERE WRONG**   □ –

Nov 69. (lp) *(LBS 83290)* <*12457*> **KEYNSHAM**   □ □
– You done my brain in / Keynsham / Quiet talks and summer walks / Tent / We were wrong / Joke shop man / The bride stripped bare by "The Bachelors" / Look at me, I'm wonderful / What do you do? / Mr. Slater's parrot / Sport (the odd boy) / I want to be with you / Noises for the leg / "Busted". *(re-iss. Nov75 on 'Sunset'; SLS 50375) (re-iss. Dec80; LBR 1041) (re-iss. Sep87 on 'Edsel'; XED 235)*

Feb 70. (7") *(LBF 15314)* **YOU DONE MY BRAIN IN. / MR. SLATER'S PARROT**   □ –

—— Split early 1970 with each member doing own disastrous projects. STANSHALL, INNES, SMITH, RUSKIN-SPEAR and COWAN re-formed late '71. Also using session people **HUGHIE FLINT** – drums / **BUBS WHITE** – guitar / **ANDY ROBERTS** – guitar / **DAVE RICHARDS** – bass / **DICK PARRY** – woodwind

	U.A.	U.A.
Mar 72. (lp) *(UAS 29288)* **LET'S MAKE UP AND BE FRIENDLY**		

– The strain / Turkeys / King of scurf / Waiting for the wardrobe / Straight from my heart / Rusty / Rawlinson End / Don't get me wrong / Fresh wound / Slush / Bad blood. *(re-iss. May78 on 'Sunset'; SLS 50418) (re-iss. Apr87 on 'Awareness' lp/c; AWL/AWT 1004)*

May 72. (7") *<50943>* **SLUSH. /**   – □

—— NEIL INNES joined GRIMMS before going solo. He then augmented the MONTY PYTHON team (part-time) before actually appearing in their films. He also created the Beatles spoof The RUTLES. He went on to host an under-5 children's TV show. LARRY SMITH went on tour with ELTON JOHN and ERIC CLAPTON. RUSKIN-SPEAR formed his KINETIC WARDROBE. SLATER became a government officer. STANSHALL narrating on MIKE OLDFIELD's "Tubular Bells" album, while also going solo. In 1978, he released the side-splitting 'SIR HENRY AT RAWLINSON END'.

– compilations, others, etc. –

on 'United Artists' unless mentioned otherwise

Aug 70. (lp) *Liberty;* *(LBS 83332)* <*5517*> **THE BEAST OF THE BONZOS**   □ □

Oct 73. (7") *(UP 35602)* **THE INTRO AND THE OUTRO. / HELLO MABEL**   □ –
(re-iss. 1975; UP 36002)

Mar 74. (7") *(UP 35662)* **MR. SLATER'S PARROT. / NOISES FOR THE LEG**   □ –

Apr 74. (d-lp) *(UAD 60071-2)* <*LA 321*> **THE HISTORY OF THE BONZOS**   `42` □

May 78. (7"m) *(UP 36397)* **I'M THE URBAN SPACEMAN. / THE INTRO AND THE OUTRO / STRAIN**   □ □

Jul 84. (7") *EMI Golden 45's;* *(G 4533)* **I'M THE URBAN SPACEMAN. / THE INTRO AND THE OUTRO**   □ □

Oct 84. (lp/c) *M.F.P.;* *(MFP/TCMFP 5680)* **THE VERY BEST OF THE BONZO DOG DOO-DAH BAND**   □ □

Jul 88. (12"ep) *Strange Fruit;* *(SFPS 051)* **THE PEEL SESSIONS (29.7.69)**   □ □
– We're going to bring it on home / Sofa Head / Tent / Monster mash.

Apr 90. (cd)(c/lp) *E.M.I.;* *(CDP 792675-2)(TC+/EMS 1335)* **THE BESTIALITY OF THE BONZO DOG BAND**   □ □
– The intro and the outro / Canyons of your mind / Trouser press / Postcard / Mickey's son and daughter / Sport (the odd boy) / Tent / I'm the urban spaceman / Mr. Apollo / Shirt / Bad blood / Ready mades / Rhinocratic oaths / Can blue men sing the whites / Mr.Slater's parrot / The strain / We are normal / My pink half of the drainpipe / Jazz, delicious hot, disgusting cold / Big shot / Jollity farm / Humanoid boogie.

Jul 91. (cd) *Rhino;* **THE BEST OF THE BONZOS**   □

Apr 92. (cd-ep) *China;* *(WOKCD 2021)* **NO MATTER WHO YOU VOTE FOR, THE GOVERNMENT ALWAYS GETS IN / URBAN SPACEMAN / THE INTRO /** Neil Innes: **THEM**   □ –

Jul 92. (cd) *E.M.I.;* *(CDP 799596-2)* **THE INTRO**   □ –

Jul 92. (cd) *E.M.I.;* *(CDP 799597-2)* **THE OUTRO**   □ –
(cd re-iss. Mar97 on 'Music For Pleasure'; CDMFP 6311)

Jul 92. (cd) *E.M.I.;* *(CDP 799598-2)* **DOG-ENDS**   □ –

Aug 92. (3xcd-box) *E.M.I.;* *(CDDOG 1)* **CORNOLOGY**   □ –
– (THE INTRO / THE OUTRO / DOG-ENDS)

Jun 95. (cd) *Strange Fruit;* *(SFRCD 134)* **UNPEELED**   □ –

Feb 96. (4xcd-box) *E.M.I.;* *(CDBONZO 1)* **FOUR BONZO ORIGINALS**   □ –

Mar 99. (cd) *D.J.C.;* *(DJC 008)* **ANTHROPOLOGY**   □ –

VIVIAN STANSHALL

solo using session people

	Liberty	not iss.
Feb 70. (7"; with SEAN HEAD SHOW BAND featuring ERIC CLAPTON) *(15309)* **LABIO-DENTAL FRICATIVE. / PAPER ROUND**	□	–

	Fly	not iss.
Dec 70. (7") *(BUG 4)* **SUSPICION (with Gargantuan Chums). / BLIND DATE (with biG GRunt)**	□	–

	Warners	not iss.
Jul 74. (7") *(K 16424)* **LAKONGA. / BABA TUNDE**	□	–
Aug 74. (lp) *(K 56052)* **MEN OPENING UMBRELLAS AHEAD**	□	–

– Afoju ti ole rirtan / Truck-track / Yelp, below, rasp et cetera / Prong / Redeye / How the zebra got his spots / Dwarf succulents / Bout of sobriety / Prong and Toots go steady / Strange tongues.

	Harvest	not iss.
Nov 76. (7"m) *(HAR 5114)* **THE YOUNG ONES. / ARE YOU HAVIN' ANY FUN / THE QUESTION**	□	–

1978. (lp) *(CAS 1139)* **SIR HENRY AT RAWLINSON END**

– Aunt Florrie's waltz / Interlewd / Wheelbarrow / Nice'n'tidy / Socks / The rub / Pigs 'ere purse / 6/8 hoodoo / Smeeton / Fool and bladder / Endroar / Jungle bunny / The beasht inshide / Rawlinsons & Maynards / Papadumb. *(cd-iss. Jul91 & May95 on 'Virgin'; CASCD 1139)*

—— (This comic concept was later made into feature film in which VIV appeared alongside TREVOR HOWARD as Sir Henry)

Sep 80. (7") *(CB 373)* **TERRY KEEPS HIS CLIPS ON. / KING KRIPPLE**

Jun 81. (7") *(CB 382)* **CALYPSO TO COLAPSO. / SMOKE SIGNALS AT NIGHT**

Jun 81. (lp) *(CAS 1153)* **TEDDY BOYS DON'T KNIT**
– King Kripple / Slave Valse / Calypso to colapso / The tube / Biwilderbeeste / Ginger geezer / The cracks are showing / Flung a dummy / Possibly an armchair (and embodying) / Gums / Fresh faced boys / Terry keeps his clips on / Bass Macaw and broken bottles / Nose hymn / Everyday I have the blows / Smoke signals at night / Nouveau riffe. *(cd-iss. Jul91 on 'Virgin'; CASCD 1153)*

—— next with **SEAN OLIVER** – bass / **BRUCE SMITH** – drums (both ex-POP GROUP, etc)

Sep 84. (lp) *(VERB 1)* **SIR HENRY AT NDIDI'S KRAAL** (spoken word)
– (further adventures of Sir Henry, this time in deepest Africa). *(cd-iss. May92; VERB CD1)*

—— VIVIAN died in a fire in his London home on the 3rd of March '95. Two days later, another original, VERNON DUDLEY BOHAY-NOWELL ,also died.

BOOGIE DOWN PRODUCTIONS (see under ⇒ KRS-ONE)

BOOKER T. & THE M.G.'S

Formed: Memphis, Tennessee, USA ... 1962 when 'Stax' in-house musicians, BOOKER T. JONES, STEVE CROPPER, LEWIS STEINBERG (subsequently replaced with DONALD 'DUCK' DUNN) and AL JACKSON Jr. recorded a couple of instrumental tracks for label owner Jim Stewart. He duly released a single with 'BEHAVE YOURSELF' as the lead track; it was the B-side, however, 'GREEN ONIONS' which became a massive Top 3 US hit and a subsequent mod floor filler. This classic slice of lean, stinging R&B was a stunning showcase for the M.G.'s (Memphis Group) unique chemistry, JONES' organ stabbing and churning away over the taut rhythm section, while CROPPER snaked in with his wiry guitar playing. While continuing to work as part of the MAR-KEYS backing band in the early 60's, The M.G.'s also backed up a gamut of 'Stax' stars, not least the legendary OTIS REDDING, who himself had started out as a session player at the label. As the 60's progressed, the band's lock-tight R&B dance sound not only played a pivotal part in the emerging British mod culture but regularly saw them hit the American charts, especially towards the end of the decade when they scored with classics 'HIP HUG-HER', 'GROOVIN' and the Caribbean-flavoured barnstormer, 'SOUL LIMBO'. The latter track hit the US Top 20 in late '68, while the album of the same name spawned another American Top 10 in 'HANG 'EM HIGH'. Like most of their albums, the record featured a fair smattering of finger-poppin' contemporary cover versions alongside the funky originals. The following year, they ventured into soundtrack work with 'UPTIGHT', a set which provided a rare UK Top 5 in 'TIME IS TIGHT'. As 'Stax' foundered in the early 70's, so The M.G.'s signed off after the 'McLEMORE AVENUE' (1970) set of 'Abbey Road' covers and the 'MELTING POT' (1971) album. While JONES married Priscilla Coolidge (sister of Rita) and recorded a number of albums with her, DUNN and JACKSON carried on as The M.G.'s for one further eponymous album in 1972. Like JONES, CROPPER had already co-written a string of soul classics and he subsequently went into production work. Tragically, JACKSON was not part of the intermittent BOOKER T. & THE M.G.'s reunions, having been shot dead by a burglar on 1st of October '75. The most recent incarnation of the group hooked up with NEIL YOUNG for a 1994 tour. • **Songwriters:** BOOKER T, except GROOVIN' (Young Rascals) / FOXY LADY (Jimi Hendrix) / THE HORSE (Jesse James) / LOVE CHILD (Richards-Sawyer-Taylor-Wilson) / SING A SIMPLE SONG (Pepper-Watt) / LADY MADONNA & MICHELLE (Beatles) / MRS.ROBINSON (Simon & Garfunkel) / THIS GUY'S IN LOVE WITH YOU (Bacharach-David) / LIGHT MY FIRE (Doors) / YOU'RE ALL I NEED TO GET BY (Ashford-Simpson) / IT'S YOUR THING (Isley Brothers) / and loads more. • **Trivia:** SOUL LIMBO was/is used for theme tune to BBC TV's cricket coverage.

Album rating: GREEN ONIONS (*9) / MO' ONIONS (*7) / SOUL DRESSING (*7) / AND NOW! (*5) / IN THE CHRISTMAS SPIRIT (*3) / HIP HUG-HER (*5) / DOIN' OUR THING (*5) / SOUL LIMBO (*5) / UPTIGHT (*4) / THE BOOKER T. SET (*4) / McLEMORE AVENUE (*4) / MELTING POT (*4) / MEMPHIS SOUND (*4) / UNION EXTENDED (*4) / UNIVERSAL LANGUAGE (*4) / THE VERY BEST OF BOOKER T. & THE MG'S compilation (*7) / THAT'S THE WAY IT SHOULD BE (*3)

BOOKER T.JONES (b.12 Nov'44) – keyboards, multi (ex-MAR-KEYS) / **STEVE CROPPER** (b.21 Oct'41, Willow Springs, Missouri) – guitar (ex-MAR-KEYS) / **LEWIS STEINBERG** (b.13 Sep'33) – bass / **AL JACKSON Jr.** (b.27 Nov'35) – drums (ex-ROY MILTON BAND)

May 62. (7") *<102>* **BEHAVE YOURSELF. / GREEN ONIONS**

Sep 62. (7") *(HLK 9595) <STAX 127>* **GREEN ONIONS. / BEHAVE YOURSELF** | | 3 Jul62

Nov 62. (lp) *<STAX 701>* **GREEN ONIONS** | | 33
– Green onions / Rinky-dink / I got a woman / Mo' onions / Twist and shout / Behave yourself / Stranger on the shore / Lonely avenue / One who really loves you / You can't sit down / A woman, a lover, a friend / Comin' home baby. *(UK-iss.Jul64; HA-*

K 8182) – (hit No.11) *(re-iss. 1966 on 'Atlantic' mono/stereo; 587/588 033) (re-iss. Feb80 on 'Atlantic'; K 40072) (cd-iss. Jul91 & Dec94 on 'Atco'; 7567 82255-2)*

Feb 63. (7") *(HLK 9670) <STAX 131>* **JELLY BREAD. / AW' MERCY** | | 82 Dec62

May 63. (7") *<STAX 134>* **HOME GROWN / BIG TRAIN**

Oct 63. (7") *(HLK 9784) <STAX 137>* **CHINESE CHECKERS. / PLUM NELLIE** | | 78 Jul63
(re-iss. Jan68 on 'Stax'; 601 026)

Feb 64. (7") *<STAX 142>* **MO' ONIONS. / TIC-TAC-TOE** | - | 97

—— **DONALD 'DUCK' DUNN** (b.24 Nov'41) – bass (ex-MAR-KEYS) repl. LEWIS

Jul 64. (7") *<STAX 153>* **SOUL DRESSING. / M.G. PARTY** | - | 95

Aug 64. (lp) *<STAX 705>* **SOUL DRESSING**
– Soul dressing / Tic-tac-toe / Big train / Jelly bread / Aw' mercy / Outrage / Night owl walk / Chinese checkers / Home grown / Mercy, mercy / Plum Nellie / Can't be still. *(UK-iss.1965 on 'Atlantic', ATL 5027) (re-iss. 1967 on 'Atlantic'; 587 047) (cd-iss. May93 & Feb95 on 'Rhino-Atlantic'; 7567 82337-2)*

Sep 64. (7") *<STAX 161>* **CAN'T BE STILL. / TERRIBLE THING** | - | -

May 65. (7") *(AT 4033) <STAX 169>* **BOOT-LEG. / OUTRAGE** | | 58

Jan 66. (7") *(AT 4063) <STAX 182>* **BE MY LADY. / RED BEANS & RICE** | - | -

Jun 66. (lp) *<STAX 711>* **AND NOW!**
– My sweet potato / Jericho / No matter what shape / One mint julep / In the midnight hour / Summertime / Working in the coal mine / Don't mess up a good thing / Think / Taboo / Soul jam / Sentimental journey. *(UK-iss.1967; 589 002) (cd-iss. Aug93 on 'Rhino-Atlantic'; 8122 70297-2)*

Oct 66. (7") *(584 044) <1STAX 96>* **MY SWEET POTATO. / BOOKER LOO** | | 85 Aug66

Dec 66. (7") *(584 060) <STAX 203>* **JINGLE BELLS. / WINTER WONDERLAND** | | -

Dec 66. (lp) *<STAX 715>* **IN THE CHRISTMAS SPIRIT** (festive) | - | -
(UK-iss.Nov68 as 'SOUL CHRISTMAS'; 589 013) (cd-iss. Aug93 & Dec95 on 'Rhino-Atlantic'; 7567 82338-2)

Mar 67. (7") *(584 088)* **GREEN ONIONS. / BOOT-LEG** | | -
(re-iss. Jun72; K 10109) – hit No.7 in Dec79 *(re-iss. 12" Apr80; K 10109T)*

Apr 67. (7") *(601 009) <STAX 211>* **HIP HUG-HER. / SUMMERTIME** | - | 37

Jun 67. (lp) *<STAX 717>* **HIP HUG-HER** | - | 35
– Hip hug-her / Soul sanction / Get ready / More / Double or nothing / Carnaby St. / Slim Jenkins' joint / Pigmy / Groovin' / Booker's motive / Sunny. *(re-iss. Aug93 on 'Rhino-Atlantic'; 8122 71013-2)*

Aug 67. (lp; by MAR-KEYS & BOOKET T & THE MG'S) *<STAX 720>* **BACK TO BACK** (live) | - | 98

Sep 67. (7") *(601 018) <STAX 224>* **SLIM JENKINS' PLACE. / GROOVIN'** | | 70

May 68. (lp) *<STAX 724>* **DOIN' OUR THING** | 21 Jul67 | -
– I can dig it / Expressway (to your heart) / Doin' our thing / You don't love me / Never my love / The exodus song / The beat goes on / Ode to Billy Joe / Blue on green / You keep me hanging on / Let's go get stoned. *(UK-iss.1969 mono/stereo; 230/231 002) (cd-iss. Aug93 on 'Rhino-Atlantic'; 8122 70142-2)*

Oct 68. (7") *(STAX 102) <STAX 0001>* **SOUL LIMBO. / HEADS OR TAILS** | 30 | 17 Jul68

Oct 68. (lp; stereo/mono) *(S+/XATS 1001) <STAX 2001>* **SOUL LIMBO**
– Be young, be foolish, be happy / La la means I love you / Hang 'em high / Willow weep for me / Over easy / Soul limbo / Eleanor Rigby / Heads or tails / (Sweet, sweet baby) Since you've been gone / Born under a bad sign / Foxy lady. *(re-iss. Feb88; SXE 009) (cd-iss. Apr90; CDSXE 009)*

Nov 68. (7") *<STAX 0013>* **HANG 'EM HIGH. / OVER EASY** | - | 9
(re-iss. Sep87; STAX 813)

Mar 69. (7") *<STAX 0028>* **TIME IS TIGHT. / JOHNNY I LOVE YOU** | - | 6

Apr 69. (7") *(STAX 119)* **TIME IS TIGHT. / HANG 'EM HIGH** | 4 | -

Apr 69. (lp; stereo/mono) *(S+/XATS 1005) <2006>* **UPTIGHT (Soundtrack)** | | 98 Feb69
– Johnny, I love you / Cleveland now / Children, don't get weary / Tank's lament / Blues in the gutter / We've got Johnny Wells / Down at Ralph's joint / Deadwood Dick / Run tank run / Time is tight. *(re-iss. +cd.Jan90)*

Jul 69. (7") *(STAX 127) <STAX 0037>* **MRS. ROBINSON. / SOUL CLAP '69** | 35 | 37 May69

Jul 69. (lp; stereo/mono) *(S+/XATS 1015) <STAX 2009>* **THE BOOKER T. SET** | | 53 Jun69
– The horse / Love child / Sing a simple song / Lady Madonna / Mrs.Robinson / This guy's in love with you / Light my fire / Michelle / You're all I need to get by / I've never found a girl (to love me like you do) / It's your thing. *(re-iss. 1971; 2362 012) <re-iss. Dec86 on 'Mobile Fidelity Sound' lp/c; MFS/+5 8531> (re-iss. May90 cd/lp; CD+/SXE 026)*

Aug 69. (7") *<0049>* **SLUM BABY. / MEDITATION** | - | 88

Nov 69. (7") *(STAX 136)* **THE HORSE. / SLUM BABY** | - | -

May 70. (lp) *(SXATS 1031) <2027>* **McLEMORE AVENUE** | 70 | Apr70
– Golden slumbers – Carry that weight – The end – Here comes the sun – Come together / Something / Because – You never give me your money / Sun king – Mean Mr. Mustard – Polythene Pam / She came in through the bathroom window – I want you – She's so heavy. *(re-iss. 1971; 2362 016) (re-iss. Dec88; SXE 016) (cd-iss. 1988 on 'Mobile Fidelity Sound'; MFCD 835)*

Jul 70. (7") *<0073>* **SOMETHING. / SUNDAY SERMON** | - | 76

Sep 70. (7") *(STAX 152)* **SOMETHING. / DOWN AT RALPH'S JOINT** | | -

Mar 71. (lp) *(2325 030) <2035>* **MELTING POT** | | 43 Feb71
– Melting pot / Back home / Chicken pox / Fuquawi / Kinda easy like / Hi ride / L.A. jazz song / Sunny Monday. *(re-iss. Jun76; STAX 1054) (cd-iss. Dec92 on 'Ace-Stax')*

Jun 71. (7") *(2025 026) <0082>* **MELTING POT. / KINDA EASY LIKE** | | 45 Mar71

Sep 71. (7") *<0108>* **FUQUAWI. / JAMAICA THIS MORNING** | - | -

—— May'71 they disbanded. JONES went solo and married singer PRISCILLA COOLIDGE (sister of RITA). He issued 3 albums with her 'BOOKER T. & PRISCILLA' / 'HOME GROWN' + 'CHRONICLES' (for 'A&M'), plus 'EVERGREEN' (for 'Epic' Feb75). CROPPER became workaholic session man and producer. DUNN and JACKSON continued as The MG's with newcomers **BOBBY MANUEL** – guitar / **CARSON WHITSETT** – keyboards. They issued a self-titled album and a few singles for 'Stax' in 1972.

—— On the 1st October 1975, AL JACKSON was shot dead by a burglar.

—— BOOKER T. & THE MG'S re-united (**BOOKER T., CROPPER and DUNN**) brought in **WILLIE HALL** (b. 8 Aug'50) – drums

	Asylum	Asylum
Mar 77. (lp) (K 53057) <7E 1093> **UNIVERSAL LANGUAGE**	☐	☐

– Sticky stuff / Grab bag / Space nuts / Love wheels / Motor cross / Last tango in Memphis / MG's salsa / Tie stick / Reincarnation.

Mar 77. (7") <45392> **STICKY STUFF. / TIE STICK**	☐	-
Jun 77. (7") <45424> **GRAB BAG. / REINCARNATION**	☐	-

—— Broke-up again. CROPPER and DUNN were in backing band that featured in the film 'The BLUES BROTHERS' in 1980. They continued to work on session/production.

—— BOOKER T went solo, releasing 3 albums for 'A&M'; 'TRY AND LOVE AGAIN' (Nov'78),'THE BEST OF YOU' (Feb'80) and 'I WANT YOU' (1981). Also issued a single, 'LET'S GO DANCING' in '79.

—— The BOOKER T TRIO released a cd-album, 'GO TELL IT TO THE MOUNTAIN' for 'Silkheart' (SHCD 114) Oct'92.

—— JONES, CROPPER + DUNN recruited in 1992; **STEVE JORDAN** – drums who was replaced in 1994 by **STEVE POTTS** (b.12 Nov'53 – nephew of the late AL JACKSON).

	Columbia	Columbia
Jun 94. (cd/c) (474470-2/-4) **THAT'S THE WAY IT SHOULD BE**	☐	☐

– Slip slidin' / Mo' greens / Gotta serve somebody / Let's wait awhile / That's the way it should be / Just my imagination (running away with me) / Camel ride / Have a heart / Cruisin' / I can't stand the rain / Sarasota sunset / I still haven't found what I'm looking for.

– compilations, others, etc. –

on 'Stax' unless mentioned otherwise

1963. (7"ep) London; (REK 1367) **R&B WITH BOOKER T**	☐	-
1964. (7"ep) Atlantic; (AET 6002) **R&B WITH BOOKER T VOL.2**	☐	-
Nov 68. (lp) Atco; (228 015) / Atlantic; <8202> **THE BEST OF BOOKER T. & THE MG'S**	☐	☐

– Green onions / Slim Jenkins' place / Hip hug-her / Soul dressing / Summertime / Bootleg / Jellybread / Tic-tac-toe / Can't be still / Groovin' / Mo' onions / Red beans and rice. (re-iss.Jul84 on 'Atlantic' lp/c; K/K4 40072) (cd-iss.Apr87 on 'London'; FCE 60004) (cd re-iss. Jan93 on 'Atlantic'; 7567 81218-2)

Dec 68. (7") <STAX 236> **SILVER BELLS. / WINTER SNOW**	☐	-
Nov 70. (lp) (2362 002) <2033> **GREATEST HITS**	☐	-

(re-iss. Aug74; STX 1037)

1973. (d-lp) Warners; (K 30042) **STAR COLLECTION**	☐	-
Nov 74. (7"m) (2025 207) **TIME IS TIGHT. / BRING IT HOME TO ME / MY BABY SPECIALISES**	☐	-
Nov 75. (lp) (STX 1037) **MEMPHIS SOUND**	☐	-
Jan 76. (lp) (STX 1045) **UNION EXTENDED** (rare tracks)	☐	-
Jul 76. (7") (STXS 2041) **SOUL LIMBO. / MRS. ROBINSON**	☐	-
Nov 77. (7") (STAX 1011) **SOUL LIMBO. / SOUL CLAP '69**	☐	-
Nov 77. (7") (STAX 2001) **TIME IS TIGHT. / SOUL LIMBO**	☐	-

(re-iss. Sep85 on 'Old Gold'; OG 9530)

Dec 77. (7"ep) Buddah-Pye; (BD 109) **TIME IS TIGHT. / (3 other artists)**	☐	-
May 80. (lp; with The MARKEYS) (STX 3007) **TIME IS TIGHT**	☐	-
Mar 80. (7") Atlantic; (K 11454) **HIP HUG HER. / SLIM JENKINS' PLACE**	☐	-
Jun 80. (lp) Hallmark; (SHM 3031) **BOOKER T. & THE MG'S**	☐	-
Jan 85. (7") Old Gold; (OG 9499) **GREEN ONIONS. / CHINESE CHECKERS**	☐	-
Jun 87. (7") (STAX 803) **TIME IS TIGHT. / JOHNNY I LOVE YOU**	☐	-
Aug 87. (7"/7"pic-d/12") (STA X/P/T 808) **SOUL LIMBO. / HEADS OR TAILS**	☐	-
Apr 93. (cd) (CDSX 46) **THE BEST OF BOOKER T. & THE MG'S** (different)	☐	-
Apr 95. (cd) (CDSXD 065) **PLAY THE FLIP HITS**	☐	-
Nov 97. (12"; BOOKER T) Junior Boys Own; (JBO 43) **GROOVE ME** (mixes; vocal mix / Bookstone dub / Swag's feeling alive / Swags 2x dub)	☐	-

(12" (JBO 43) – (mixes; Farley & Heller's summer flava / original vocal – Benji's edit).

Nov 97. (12"; BOOKER T & TUFF JAM) Fatt Boy; (FBOY 1) **SWING LOW** (mixes)	☐	-
Oct 98. (3xcd-box) Stax; (3SCD 4424) **TIME IS TIGHT**	☐	-
Oct 98. (cd) Stax; (CDSXK 123) **THE BEST OF BOOKER T. & THE MG'S**	☐	☐

BOOMTOWN RATS

Formed: Dun Laoghaire (near Dublin), Ireland ... 1975 by former NME journalist BOB GELDOF, JOHNNIE FINGERS, GERRY COTT, PETE BRIQUETTE, GERRY ROBERTS and SIMON CROWE. Moving to London in late 1976, they signed to the newly formed 'Ensign' records. Though their music was rooted in R&B and they were more of a New Wave outfit than anything, The BOOMTOWN RATS were loosely affiliated with the burgeoning punk scene, at least initially. In the long, hot summer of '77, their debut single, 'LOOKIN' AFTER No.1' made the UK Top 20. This was closely followed by a similarly successful eponymous debut album and a second Top 20 hit, 'MARY OF THE 4th FORM'. With a lean sound lying somewhere between EDDIE & THE HOT RODS and The ROLLING STONES, The BOOMTOWN RATS were also a compelling live proposition, GELDOF's moody charisma helping to give the band a distinct identity. Major success came with 'A TONIC FOR THE TROOPS' (1978), this album spawning a number of hits including their first No.1 in the insistent 'RAT TRAP'. They scored a second number one and a massive worldwide hit with 'I DON'T LIKE MONDAYS', a stunningly effective, piano-driven

belter inspired (if that's the appropriate word) by schoolgirl Brenda Spencer, who snipered/shot dead several of her school colleagues. The accompanying album, 'THE ART OF SURFACING' (1979) showed the 'RATS at the peak of their power, although subsequent albums increasingly followed a more mundane pop/rock direction and the band slowly faded from view, finally splitting in 1984. GELDOF's profile remained high, however, the Irishman helping to mastermind the mammoth undertaking that was LIVE AID. He and ULTRAVOX's MIDGE URE, assembled together all the major stars of the time to sing 'DO THEY KNOW IT'S CHRISTMAS', the resulting 45 making millions of pounds/dollars/etc for famine relief in Ethiopia. Not content with this, BOB and MIDGE reunited most of them again for the LIVE AID concert at Wembley Stadium on the 13th of July '85 (this was simultaneously broadcast over the Atlantic at JFK Stadium, Philadelphia). At the time, it amassed well over £10m, the money also being spread around other needy charities as well as Ethiopia (the total at the end of 1991 was over £100m). In June 1986, BOB was now Sir BOB GELDOF, after being knighted by the Queen and two months later he married long-time fiancee, PAULA YATES (TV presenter/writer/etc). She gave birth to FIFI TRIXIBELLE and in 1989, their second daughter, PEACHES, was born. During the latter half of a very busy decade for GELDOF, he managed to maintain a solo career, a hit single, 'THIS IS THE WORLD CALLING', was appropriate enough to become a Top 30 hit in 1986, while 1990's 'THE GREAT SONG OF INDIFFERENCE' went one step better. His backing band at the time, The VEGETARIANS OF LOVE, provided the title of the single's folky/cajun parent album, which also sold reasonably well. His last solo album, 'THE HAPPY CLUB' (1992), was something of a disappointment and Sir BOB virtually retired from the studio side of things to run his own Planet 24 company and The Big Breakfast on Channel 4. PAULA was also part of the latter, although by 1995, she had opted to bed MICHAEL HUTCHENCE of INXS, citing BOB as the adulterer. BOB and PAULA were subsequently divorced as the new couple became the media focal point (tragically, this was cut short when MICHAEL took his own life on the 22nd November, 1997 – see INXS). • **Songwriters:** Most written by GELDOF except; BAREFOOTIN' (Robert Parker). GELDOF solo covered SUNNY AFTERNOON (Kinks). • **Trivia:** GELDOF starred in the feature films, 'The Wall' (1982) and 'Number One' (1984).

Album rating: THE BOOMTOWN RATS (*6) / A TONIC FOR THE TROOPS (*5) / THE FINE ART OF SURFACING (*5) / MONDO BONGO (*4) / V DEEP (*4) / IN THE LONG GRASS (*5) / Bob Geldof: DEEP IN THE HEART OF NOWHERE (*5) / THE VEGETARIANS OF LOVE (*5) / THE HAPPY CLUB (*4) / LOUDMOUTH – THE BEST OF THE BOOMTOWN RATS AND BOB GELDOF compilation (*8)

BOB GELDOF (b. 5 Oct'54, Dublin, Ireland) – vocals / **JOHNNIE FINGERS** (b. JOHNNY MOYLETT) – keyboards, vocals / **GERRY COTT** – guitar / **PETE BRIQUETTE** (b. PATRICK CUSACK) – bass / **GERRY ROBERTS** – guitar, vocals / **SIMON CROWE** – drums, vocals

	Ensign	Mercury
Aug 77. (12"m) (ENY 4) **LOOKIN' AFTER No.1. / BORN TO BURN (live) / BAREFOOTIN'** (live)	11	-
Sep 77. (lp/c) (ENVY/ENCAS 1) <SRM 1188> **THE BOOMTOWN RATS**	18	☐

– Lookin' after No.1 / Neon heart / Joey's on the street again / Never bite the hand that feeds / Mary of the 4th form / (She gonna) Do you in / Close as you'll ever be / I can make it if you can / Kicks. (re-iss.Dec83 on 'Mercury' lp/c; PRICE/PRIMC 57)

	Ensign	Columbia
Nov 77. (7") (ENY 9) **MARY OF THE 4th FORM. / DO THE RAT**	15	-
Mar 78. (7") (ENY 13) **SHE'S SO MODERN. / LYING AGAIN**	12	☐
Jun 78. (7") (ENY 14) **LIKE CLOCKWORK. / HOW DO YOU DO?**	6	☐
Jul 78. (lp/c) (ENVY/ENCAS 3) <35750> **A TONIC FOR THE TROOPS**	8	☐

– Like clockwork / Blind date / (I never loved) Eva Braun / Living in an island / Don't believe what you read / She's so modern / Me and Howard Hughes / Can't stop * / (Watch out for) The normal people / Rat trap. <US version repl.* with – Joey> (re-iss. Dec83 on 'Mercury' lp/c; PRICE/PRIMC 58)

Oct 78. (7") (ENY 16) **RAT TRAP. / SO STRANGE**	1	-
Nov 78. (7") **RAT TRAP. / DO THE RAT**	-	
Jul 79. (7") (ENY 30) <11117> **I DON'T LIKE MONDAYS. / IT'S ALL THE RAGE**	1	73 Jan80
Oct 79. (lp/c) (ENROX/ENCAS 11) <36248> **THE FINE ART OF SURFACING**	7	☐

– Someone's looking at you / Diamond smiles / Wind chill factor (minus zero) / Having my picture taken / Sleep (Fingers' lullaby) / I don't like Mondays / Nothing happened today / Keep it up / Nice 'n' neat / When the night comes. (re-iss. Nov84 on 'Mercury' lp/c; PRICE/PRIMC 73)

Nov 79. (7") (ENY 33) **DIAMOND SMILES. / LATE LAST NIGHT**	13	-
Jan 80. (7",12") (ENY 34) **SOMEONE'S LOOKING AT YOU. / WHEN THE NIGHT COMES**	4	-
May 80. (7") <11248> **SOMEONE'S LOOKING AT YOU. / I DON'T LIKE MONDAYS** (live)	-	-

	Mercury	Columbia
Nov 80. (7") (BONGO 1) **BANANA REPUBLIC. / MAN AT THE TOP**	3	-
Dec 80. (lp/c) (6359/7150 042) <37062> **MONDO BONGO**	6	☐

– Please don't go / The elephant's graveyard (guilty) / Banana republic / Fall down / Hurt hurts / Whitehall 1212 * / Mood mambo / Straight up / This is my room / Another piece of red / Under their thumb ... is under my thumb / Go man go. <US version repl. * with – Don't talk to me>

Jan 81. (7") (BONGO 2) **THE ELEPHANT'S GRAVEYARD (GUILTY). / REAL DIFFERENT**	26	-

—— (Mar'81) trimmed to a quintet when GERRY COTT left to go solo

Nov 81. (7") <60512> **UP ALL NIGHT. / ANOTHER PIECE OF RED**	-	☐
Nov 81. (7") (MER 87) **NEVER IN A MILLION YEARS. / DON'T TALK TO ME**	62	-
Mar 82. (7"/12") (MER/+X 91) **HOUSE ON FIRE. / EUROPE LOOKED UGLY**	24	
Mar 82. (lp/c) (6359/7150 082) **V DEEP**	64	

– Never in a million years / The bitter end / Talking in code / He watches it all /

Storm breaks / Charmed lives / House on fire / Up all night / Skin on skin / Little death.

Jun 82. (7") *(MER 106)* **CHARMED LIVES. / NO HIDING PLACE** ☐ ☐–
(d7"+=) *(MER 106-2)* – Nothing happened today (live) / Storm breaks (instrumental).
(12") *(MERX 106)* – ('A'side) / A storm breaks.

Aug 82. (7") *<03386>* **CHARMED LIVES. / NEVER IN A MILLION YEARS** ☐– ☐

Jan 84. (7") *(MER 154)* **TONIGHT. / PRECIOUS TIME** 73 ☐
(12"+=) *(MERX 154)* – Walking downtown.

May 84. (7") *(MER 163)* **DRAG ME DOWN. / AN ICICLE IN THE SUN** 50
(12"+=) *(MERX 163)* – Rat trap / She's so modern.

Nov 84. (7"pic-d) *(MER 179)* **DAVE. / HARD TIMES** ☐ ☐–
(d7"+=) *(MER 179-2)* – I don't like Mondays / It's all the rage.
(12"+=) *(MERX 179)* – Banana republic (live) / Close as you'll ever be (live).

Dec 84. (lp/c) *(MERL/+C 38)* *<39335>* **IN THE LONG GRASS** ☐ ☐
– A hold of me / Drag me down / Dave / Over again / Another sad story / Tonight / Hard times / Lucky / Icicle in the Sun / Up or down.

Feb 85. (7") *(MER 184)* **A HOLD OF ME. / NEVER IN A MILLION YEARS** ☐ ☐–
(12"+=) *(MERX 184)* – Say hi to Mick.

Mar 85. (7") *<04892>* **ICICLE IN THE SUN. / RAIN** ☐– ☐

Jun 85. (7") *<05590>* **DRAG ME DOWN. / HARD TIMES** ☐– ☐

—— had already split late '84. FINGERS and CROWE formed GUNG HO. BOB GELDOF pieced together BAND/LIVE AID before going solo.

– compilations, others, etc. –

Dec 83. (6x7"box) *Mercury; (none)* **RAT PACK** (6 best of singles pack) ☐ ☐–

Jan 88. (7") *Old Gold; (OG 9790)* **I DON'T LIKE MONDAYS. / RAT TRAP** ☐ ☐–

BOB GELDOF

—— solo, with guests **DAVE STEWART, ERIC CLAPTON**, etc.

		Mercury	Atlantic
Oct 86.	(7"/12") *(BOB/+X 101)* *<89341>* **THIS IS THE WORLD CALLING. / TALK ME UP**	25	82

Nov 86. (lp/c)(cd) *(BOB LP/MC 1)(830 607-2)* *<812687>* **DEEP IN THE HEART OF NOWHERE** 79
– Love you like a rocket / In the pouring rain / This heartless night / Words from Heaven / Deep in the heart of nowhere / Night turns to day / The beat of the night / When I was young / This is the world calling / August was a heavy month.
(cd+=) – Pulled apart by horses / Good boys in the wrong / Truly true blue.

Jan 87. (7") *(BOB 102)* **LOVE YOU LIKE A ROCKET. / THIS IS THE WORLD CALLING** 61 ☐
(12"+=) *(BOBX 102)* – ('A'extended).
(cd-s+=) *(BOBCD 102)* – Pulled apart by horses / Truly true blue.

Mar 87. (7") *<89309>* **LOVE YOU LIKE A ROCKET. / PULLED APART BY HORSES** ☐– ☐

Jun 87. (7") *<89261>* **THE HEARTLESS NIGHT. / PULLED APART BY HORSES** ☐– ☐

Jun 87. (7") *(BOB 103)* **I CRY TOO. / LET'S GO** ☐– ☐
(12"+=) *(BOBX 103)* – Night turns to day / Deep in the heart of nowhere.

—— He was now augmented by his **VEGETARIANS OF LOVE** backing band **GEOFF RICHARDSON** – viola, clarinet, etc. / **BOB LOVEDAY** – violin, bass, penny whistle / **PETE BRIQUETTE** – bass, keyboards / **PHIL PALMER** – guitars / **STEVE FLETCHER** – keyboard ALUN DUNN – accordion, organ / **RUPERT HINE** – keyboards, percussion, producer,

Jun 90. (7") *(BOB 104)* **THE GREAT SONG OF INDIFFERENCE. / HOTEL 75** 15
(12"+=/cd-s+=) *(BOB X/CD 104)* – In the pouring rain.

Jul 90. (cd/c/lp) *(846 250-2/-4/-1)* **THE VEGETARIANS OF LOVE** 21
– A gospel song / Love or something / Thinking Voyager 2 type things / The great song of indifference / Crucified me / Big romance stuff / The chains of pain / A rose at night / Let it go / No small wonder / Walking back to happiness / The end of the world.

Aug 90. (7"/c-s) **LOVE OR SOMETHING. / OUT OF ORDER** ☐ ☐
(12"+=) – The great song of indifference (mix) / Friends for life / One of these girls.

Nov 90. (7"/c-s) **A GOSPEL SONG. / VEGETARIANS OF LOVE** ☐ ☐
(12"+=/cd-s+=) – The warmest fire.

—— now with The HAPPY CLUBSTERS (same as last)

		Vertigo	Mercury
Jun 92.	(7"/c-s) **ROOM 19 (SHA LA LA LEE). / HUGE BIRDLESS SILENCE**	☐	☐

(cd-s+=) – The great song of indifference / Sweat for you (BRIQUETTE & SHARKEY CO.).

Sep 92. (7"/c-s) **MY HIPPY ANGEL. / MAYBE HEAVEN** ☐ ☐
(cd-s+=) – Love or something / ('A'extended).

Oct 92. (cd/c/lp) *(512 896-2/-4/-1)* **THE HAPPY CLUB** ☐ ☐
– Room 19 (sha la la la lee) / Attitude chicken / The soft soil / A hole to fill / The song of the emergent nationalist / My hippy angel / The happy club / Like down on me / Too late God / Roads of Germany (after BD) / A sex thing / The house at the top of the world.

Apr 94. (7"/c-s) *(MER/+MC 85)* **CRAZY. / THE HAPPY CLUB** 65 ☐
(cd-s) *(MERCX 85)* – ('A'side) / Room 19 (sha la la lee) (live) / The beat of the night (live) / Rat trap (live).
Note; below single by BOOMTOWN RATS (also compilation tracks *)

Jun 94. (7"colrd/c-s) *(VER/+MC 87)* **I DON'T LIKE MONDAYS. / BORN TO BURN / DO THE RAT** 38
(cd-s) *(MERCD 87)* – ('A'side) / Looking after No.1 / Mary of the 4th form / She's so modern.
(cd-s) *(MERCX 87)* – ('A'side) / Rat trap / Someone's looking at you / Banana republic.

Jul 94. (cd/c) *(522 283-2/-4)* **LOUDMOUTH – THE BEST OF THE BOOMTOWN RATS & BOB GELDOF** (compilation) 10 ☐

– I don't like Mondays * / This is the world calling / Rat trap * / The great song of indifference / Love or something / Banana republic * / Crazy / The elephant's graveyard (guilty) * / Someone's looking at you * / She's so modern * / House on fire * / The beat of the night / Diamond smiles * / Like clockwork * / Room 19 (sha la la la lee) / Mary of the 4th form * / Looking after No.1 *. (* tracks by The BOOMTOWN RATS)

Clint BOON EXPERIENCE! (see under ⇒ INSPIRAL CARPETS)

BOO RADLEYS

Formed: Liverpool, England . . . 1988, by schoolmates SICE and MARTIN CARR. Another friend, TIM BROWN, was invited to join after teaching MARTIN how to play guitar. They took the group name from a weird character in the film, 'To Kill A Mockingbird'. The quartet was complete when they found drummer STEVE HEWITT. They worked hard on the Mersey gig circuit but no major deal was forthcoming. Come 1990, they finally found a home with small indie label, 'Action', who released their debut lp 'ICHABOD AND I'. On its merit, they were invited by the illustrious DJ John Peel to session for Radio 1. This led to a signing for 'Rough Trade', who issued 3 popular EP's between late 1990 & 91. They then moved to 'Creation', their psychedelic, BYRDS-influenced jangle-pop soon making them favourites of the music press (Singles Of The Week, etc). The release of 1992's 'EVERYTHING'S ALRIGHT FOREVER' and the following year's masterful 'GIANT STEPS' album infused their sugary pop with screeching guitars and jagged brass accompaniment. The latter secured them their first Top 20 placing, the tracks 'I HANG SUSPENDED', 'BARNEY (. . . AND ME)' and 'LAZARUS' being effervescent highlights. Early to rise in '95, they scored their first Top 10 hit with 'WAKE UP BOO!', taken from their similarly titled No.1 album. The single was subsequently spoiled after it was played to death as the theme tune for ITV's Breakfast TV. In 1996, SICE (aka EGGMAN) delivered a solo album, while The BOO's returned with another slice (or SICE!) of nostalgic pop, 'C'MON KIDS'. After the album 'KINGSIZE' was released to some mixed reviews (towards the end of '98), the unhappy BOO's were quite literally treading water(beds) until their demise early the following year. • **Songwriters:** CARR lyrics / group music, except TRUE FAITH (New Order) / ALONE AGAIN OR (Love) / ONE OF US MUST KNOW (Bob Dylan) / THE QUEEN IS DEAD (Smiths). • **Trivia:** MERIEL BARHAM of The PALE SAINTS provided vocals on 2 tracks for GIANT STEPS album. ED BALL (ex-TV PERSONALITIES) often made guest appearances.

Album rating: ICHABOD AND I (*5) / EVERYTHING'S ALRIGHT FOREVER (*7) / GIANT STEPS (*9) / WAKE UP! (*8) / C'MON KIDS (*6) / KINGSIZE (*6) / Eggman: FIRST FRUITS (*5)

SICE (b. SIMON ROWBOTTOM, 18 Jun'69, Wallasey, England) – vocals, guitar / **MARTIN CARR** (b.29 Nov'68, Thurso, Scotland) – guitar / **TIM BROWN** (b.26 Feb'69, Wallasey) – bass / **STEVE DREWITT** (b. Northwich, England) – drums

		Action	not iss.
Jul 90.	(lp) *(TAKE 4)* **ICHABOD AND I**	☐	☐–

– Eleanor everything / Bodenheim Jr. / Catweazle / Sweet salad birth / Hip clown rag / Walking 5th carnival / Kaleidoscope / Happens to us all.

—— **ROB CIEKA** (b. 4 Aug'68, Birmingham, England) – drums repl. DREWITT to BREED

		Rough Trade	not iss.
Oct 90.	(12"ep/cd-ep) *(RTT 241/+CD)* **KALEIDOSCOPE EP**	☐	☐–

– Kaleidoscope / How I feel / Aldous / Swansong.

Apr 91. (12"ep/cd-ep) *(R 201127-10/-13)* **EVERY HEAVEN EP** ☐ ☐–
– The finest kiss / Tortoiseshell / Bluebird / Naomi.

Sep 91. (12"ep/cd-ep) *(R 275-0/-3)* **BOO UP! EP (Peel sessions)** ☐ ☐–
– Everybird / Sometime soon she said / Foster's van / Song for up!

Dec 91. (cd) *(R 3012)* **LEARNING TO WALK** (compilation of above 3 EP's) ☐ ☐–

		Creation	Columbia
Feb 92.	(12"ep)(cd-ep) *(CRE 128T)CRESCD 124)* **ADRENALIN EP**	☐	☐

– Lazy day / Vegas / Feels like tomorrow / Whiplashed.

Mar 92. (cd/c/lp) *(CRE CD/MC/LP 120)* *<52912>* **EVERYTHING'S ALRIGHT FOREVER** 55 ☐ Aug92
– Spaniard / Towards the light / Losing it (song for Abigail) / Memory babe / Skyscraper / I feel nothing / Room at the top / Does this hurt / Sparrow / Smile fades fast / Firesky / Song for the morning to sing / Lazy day / Paradise.

Jun 92. (7") *(CRE 128)* **BOO! FOREVER. / DOES THIS HURT** 67 ☐
(12"+=)(cd-s+=) *(CRE 128T)(CRESCD 128)* – Buffalo Bill / Sunfly II: Walking with the kings.

Nov 92. (7") *(CRE 137)* **LAZARUS. / LET ME BE YOUR FAITH** 76 ☐
(12"+=)(cd-s+=) *(CRE 137T)(CRESCD 137)* – At the sound of speed / Petroleum.

—— added **STEVE KITCHEN** – trumpet, flugel horn / **JACKIE ROY** – clarinet / **LINDSAY JOHNSTON** – cello

Jul 93. (7") *(CRE 147)* **I HANG SUSPENDED. / RODNEY KING (St. Etienne mix)** 77 ☐–
(12"+=)(cd-s+=) *(CRE 147T)(CRESCD 147)* – As bound a stomorrow / I will always ask where you have been though I know the answer.

Jul 93. (cd/c-d-lp) *(CRE CD/MC/LP 149)* *<53794>* **GIANT STEPS** 17 ☐ Aug93
– I hang suspended / Upon 9th and Fairchild / Wish I was skinny / Leaves and sand / Butterfly McQueen / Rodney King (song for Lenny Bruce) / Thinking of ways / Barney (. . . and me) / Spun around / If you want it, take it / Best lose the fear / Take the time around / Lazarus / One is for / Run my way runway / I've lost the reason / The white noise revisited. (cd re-iss. Aug98; same)

Oct 93. (7"/c-s) *(CRE/+CD 169)* **WISH I WAS SKINNY. / PEACHY KEEN** 75 ☐–
(12"+=)(cd-s+=) *(CRE 169T)(CRESCD 169)* – Furthur / Crow eye.

Feb 94. (7"/c-s) *(CRE/+CS 178)* **BARNEY (. . .AND ME). / ZOOM** | 48 | - |
(12"+=)(cd-s+=) *(CRE 178T)(CRESCD 178)* – Tortoiseshell / Cracked lips, homesick.

May 94. (7") *(CRE 187)* **LAZARUS. / (I WANNA BE) TOUCHDOWN JESUS** | 50 | - |
(12"+=) *(CRE 187T)* – ('A'-Secret Knowledge mix) / ('A'-Ultramarine radio mix).
(cd-s+=) *(CRESCD 187)* – ('A'acoustic) / ('A'-St. Etienne mix).
(cd-s) *(CRESCD 187X)* – ('A'-Secret Knowledge mix) / ('A'-Ultramarine mix) / ('A'-Augustus Pablo mix) / ('A'-12"mix).

Feb 95. (c-s) *(CRECS 191)* **WAKE UP BOO! / JANUS** | 9 | - |
(cd-s+=) *(CRESCD 191)* – Blues for George Michael / Friendship song.
(12") *(CRE 191T)* – Wake up Boo!: Music for astronauts / Janus / Blues for George Michael.
(cd-s) *(CRESCD 191X)* – Wake up Boo!: Music for astronauts / . . .And tomorrow the world / The history of Creation parts 17 & 36.

Mar 95. (cd/c/lp) *(CRE CD/MC/LP 179)* <67249> **WAKE UP!** | 1 | - |
– Wake up Boo! / Fairfax scene / It's Lulu / Joel / Find the answer within / Reaching out from here / Martin, Doom! it's 7 o'clock / Stuck on amber / Charles Bukowski is dead / 4am conversation / Twinside / Wilder. *(cd re-iss. Aug98; same)*

May 95. (c-s) *(CRECS 202)* **FIND THE ANSWER WITHIN / DON'T TAKE YOUR GUN TO TOWN** | 37 | - |
(cd-s+=) *(CRESCD 202)* – Wallpaper.
(12"++=) *(CRE 202T)* – The only word I can find / Very together.
(cd-s) *(CRESCD 202X)* – ('A'-High Llamas mix) / The only word I can find / Very together.

Jul 95. (c-s) *(CRECS 211)* **IT'S LULU / THIS IS NOT ABOUT ME** | 25 | - |
(cd-s+=) *(CRESCD 211)* – Reaching out from here (the High Llamas mix / Martin, doom! it's seven o'clock (Stereolab mix).
(cd-s) *(CRESCD 211X)* – ('A'side) / Joel (Justin Warfield mix) / Tambo / Donkey.

Sep 95. (c-s/7") *(C+/CRE 214)* **FROM THE BENCH AT BELVIDERE. / HI FALUTIN'** | 24 | - |
(cd-s+=) *(CRESCD 214)* – Crushed / Nearly almost time.

<table>
<tr><td></td><td>Creation</td><td>Mercury</td></tr>
</table>

Aug 96. (7") *(CRE 220)* **WHAT'S IN THE BOX? (SEE WHATCHA GOT). / BLOKE IN A DRESS** | 25 | - |
(cd-s+=) *(CRESCD CRESCD 220)* – Flakes / ('A'-Kris Needs mix).
(cd-s) *(CRESCD 220X)* – ('A'side) / Atlantic / The absent boy / Annie and Marnie.

Sep 96. (cd/c)(d-lp) *(CRECD/CCRE 194)(CRELP 194L)* <534256> **C'MON KIDS** | 20 | - |
– C'mon kids / Meltin's worm / Melodies for the deaf / Get on the bus / Everything is sorrow / Bullfrog green / What's in the box? (see whatcha got) / Four saints / New Brighton promenade / Fortunate sons / Shelter / Ride the tiger / One last hurrah. *(lp w/ free 7")* SKYWALKER. / FRENCH CANADIAN BEAN SOUP

Oct 96. (7") *(CRE 236)* **C'MON KIDS. / SPION COP** | 18 | - |
(cd-s+=) *(CRESCD 236)* – Too beautiful / Bullfrog green (ultra living mix).
• (cd-s) *(CRESCD 236X)* – ('A'side) / Nothing to do but scare myself / From the bench at Belvidere (Ultramarine mix) / Fortunate sons (Greg Hunter remix).

Jan 97. (7") *(CRE 248)* **RIDE THE TIGER. / VOTE YOU** | 38 | - |
(cd-s) *(CRESCD 248)* – A part I know so well / Everything is sorrow
(cd-s) *(CRESCD 248X)* – ('A' side / Roadie / Safe at home /

<table>
<tr><td></td><td>Creation</td><td>Creation</td></tr>
</table>

Oct 98. (10") *(CRE 299X)* **FREE HUEY. / ('A' mix)** | 54 | - |
(cd-s) *(CRESCD 299)* – Everything falls away / In a galaxy far, far away
(cd-s) *(CRESCD 299X)* –

Oct 98. (cd/d-lp)(c) *(CRE CD/LP 228)(CCRE 228)* **KINGSIZE** | 62 | - |
– Blueroom in archway / The old newsstand at Hamilton Square / Free Huey / Monuments for a dead century / Heaven's at the bottom of this glass / Kingsize / High as monkeys / Eurostar / Adieu clo clo / Jimmy Webb is God / She is everywhere / Comb your hair / Song for the blueroom / The future is now.

──　the band split early '99; CARR formed BRAVE CAPTAIN

EGGMAN

──　i.e. SICE with **ROB CIEKA** – drums / **ED BALL** – bass / **SEAN JACKSON** – lead guitar / **TIM BROWN** – piano, etc / others

<table>
<tr><td></td><td>Creation</td><td>Tristar</td></tr>
</table>

May 96. (7"/c-s) *(CRE/+CS 225)* **NOT BAD ENOUGH. / IDENTIKIT** | | - |
(cd-s+=) *(CRESCD 225)* – We won the war.

May 96. (cd/lp)(c) *(CRE CD/LP 201)(CCRE 201)* <36910> **FIRST FRUITS** | | |
– Purple patches / Tomas / That's that then (for now) / Not bad enough / The funeral song / Replace all your lies with truth / Out of my window / Look up / I'll watch your back / First fruits fall.

BOOTH AND THE BAD ANGEL
(see under ⇒ JAMES)

BOOTSY'S RUBBER BAND

Formed: mid-70's by Cincinatti-born bass player WILLIAM 'BOOTSY' COLLINS. After JAMES BROWN fell out with his backing band in 1969, he recruited BOOTSY's band The PACEMAKERS to play on the single 'GET UP (I FEEL LIKE BEING A SEX MACHINE)'. The distinctive polyrhythmic fluidity of his playing, not only helped lay the foundations for funk, but, along with SLY & THE FAMILY STONE bassist LARRY GRAHAM, changed the way the instrument was played. After a series of groundbreaking singles, BOOTSY and "The Godfather Of Funk" went their separate ways with COLLINS forming his own short-lived band before hooking up with that dayglo Grand Wizard of funk, GEORGE CLINTON, in the early 70's. BOOTSY became a part of the ever-evolving freak show that was FUNKADELIC & PARLIAMENT. This was alongside other refugees from the JAMES BROWN camp, including his brother PHELPS 'CATFISH' COLLINS, MACEO PARKER, FRED WESLEY and BERNIE WORRELL.

In keeping with the spirit of things, COLLINS became CASPAR THE FRIENDLY GHOST complete with a star-shaped guitar to match his glasses and a larger-than-life persona. In 1976, CLINTON inspired COLLINS to form BOOTSY'S RUBBER BAND, a solo spin-off featuring the aforementioned musicians amongst others, notably soul singer GARY 'MUDBONE' COOPER. The first two albums 'STRETCHIN OUT . . .' and 'AHH . . . THE NAME IS BOOTSY, BABY', released in '76 & '77 respectively, fell somewhere between both sides of the P-FUNK. The group nailed its fun-loving cartoon, politico-sexual manifests with deft rhythmic aplomb. CASPAR was abandoned in favour of BOOTZILLA on the 1978 album 'BOOTSY? PLAYER OF THE YEAR', a record which at times experimented successfully with jazz fusion and topped the R&B charts. Come the 80's, the ever adatable COLLINS altered his bass style to fit with the prevailing mood and the spare, mechanical sound was evident on the one-off single 'BODY SLAM' from 1982. He kept a fairly low profile for much of the 80's, popping up on various projects such as MALCOLM McLAREN's 'Waltz Darling' and SLY & ROBBIE's 'Rhythm Killers' as well as releasing 1988 comeback album, 'WHAT'S BOOTSY DOIN?'. 1995 saw The RUBBER BAND touring once more, preaching the funky gospel to a generation of hip hop kids who'd been blessed with the word through the prolification of old P-FUNK samples.

Album rating: STRETCHIN' OUT IN BOOTSY'S RUBBER BAND (*6) / AHH . . . THE NAME IS BOOTSY, BABY! (*7) / BOOTSY? PLAYER OF THE YEAR (*6) / THIS BOOT IS MADE FOR FONK-N (*5) / ULTRA WAVE (*5) / THE ONE GIVETH, THE COUNT TAKETH AWAY (*5) / WHAT'S BOOTSY DOIN? (*6) / JUNGLE BASS (*5) / BLASTERS OF THE UNIVERSE (*5) / BACK IN THE DAY – THE BEST OF BOOTSY compilation (*7) / FRESH OUTTA "P" UNIVERSITY (*5)

WILLIAM "BOOTSY" COLLINS (b.26 Oct'51) – guitar, bass, vocals / **PHELPS "CATFISH" COLLINS** – bass, guitar / **GARY SHIDER + MIKE HAMPTON** – guitar / **GARY "MUD-BONE" COOPER + FRANKIE "KASH" WADDY + BOOGIE** – drums / **FRED WESLEY** – trombone / **MACEO PARKER + RANDY BRECKER** – sax / **MICHAEL BRECKER + RICK GARDNER** – trumpet / **CASPER** – bass, drums, guitar / **BERNIE WORRELL + FREDERICK ALLEN + SONNY TALBERT** – keyboards / **ROBERT "P-NUT" JOHNSON + LESLYN BAILEY** – vox

<table>
<tr><td></td><td>Warners</td><td>Warners</td></tr>
</table>

Aug 76. (lp) *(K 56200)* <BS 2920> **STRETCHIN' OUT IN BOOTSY'S RUBBER BAND** | | 59 Apr76 |
– Stretchin' out (in a rubber band) / Psychoticbumpschool / Another point of view / I'd rather be with you / Love vibes / Physical love / Vanish in our sleep. *(cd-iss. Jan96; 7599 26334-2)*

──　**GLENN GOINS** – guitar / **JEROME BAILEY** – drums / **JOEL "RAZOR-SHARP" JOHNSON** – keyboards / **RICHARD GRIFFITH** – horns repl. BOOGIE, ALLEN, TARBERT + BAILEY

Jan 77. (lp) *(K 56302)* <BS 2972> **AHH . . .THE NAME IS BOOTSY, BABY** | | 16 |
– Ahh . . .the name is Bootsy, baby / The Pinocchio theory / Rubber duckie / Preview side too / What's a telephone bill? / Munchies for your love / Can't stay away / Reprise: We want Bootsy. *(cd-iss. Jan96; 7599 22972-2)*

Jul 77. (7") *(K 16964)* **THE PINOCCHIO THEORY. / PSYCHOTICBUMPSCHOOL** | | - |
(12"+=) *(K 16964T)* – What's a telephone bill?

──　now without HAMPTON, BAILEY, GOINS + BRECKER BROTHERS

Feb 78. (lp) *(K 56424)* <BS 3093> **BOOTSY? PLAYER OF THE YEAR** | | 16 |
– As in (I love you) / Bootsy (what's the name of this town?) / Bootzilla / Hollywood squares – Funk attack / May the force be with you / Roto-rooter / Very yes "Player of the year". *(cd-iss. an96; 7599 26335-2)*

Jun 78. (7"/12") *(K 17196/+T)* **BOOTZILLA./ HOLLYWOOD SQUARES** | 43 | |

──　added **STARR-MON** – percussion, drums / **LARRY FRATANGELO** – percussion

Aug 79. (lp) *(K 56615)* <BS 3295> **THIS BOOT IS MADE FOR FONK-N** | | 52 Jul79 |
– Under the influence of a groove / Bootsy get live / Oh boy gorl / Jam fan (hot) / Chug-a-lug (the bun patrol) / Shejam (almost Bootsy show). *(cd-iss. Jan96; 7599 23295-2)*

──　with **CATFISH / RAZOR-SHARP / MACEO / FRED / KUSH GRIFFIN + SHIDER + JOHNSON**

Dec 80. (lp; as BOOTSY) *()* <BS 3433> **ULTRA WAVE** | | 70 |
– Mug push / F-Encounter / Is that my song? / It's a musical / Fat cat / Scared flower / Sound crack. *(cd-iss. Jan96; 7599 26336-2)*

──　with usual array of friends incl. guest spot from GEORGE CLINTON

May 82. (lp; as WILLIAM "BOOTSY" COLLINS) *(K 56998)* <BS 3667> **THE ONE GIVETH, THE COUNT TAKETH AWAY** | | |
– Shine-o-myte (rag popping) / Landshark (just when you thought it was safe) / Countracula (this one's for you) / #1 funkateer / Excon (of love) / So nice you name him twice / What's W-R-O-N-G radio / Music to smile by / Play on playboy / Take a lickin' and keep on kickin' / The funky funktioneer. *(cd-iss. Jan96; 7599 23667-2)*

BOOTSY COLLINS

<table>
<tr><td></td><td>Bluebird</td><td>Bluebird</td></tr>
<tr><td></td><td>C.B.S.</td><td>Columbia</td></tr>
</table>

Aug 86. (12") *(9299190)* **BODY SLAM. /** | | |

Sep 88. (7") *(653003-7)* **PARTY ON PLASTIC. /** | | |
(12"+=) *(653003-6)* –

Nov 88. (lp/c/cd) *(462 918-1/-4/-2)* <FC 44107> **WHAT'S BOOTSY DOIN'?** | | Oct88 |
– Party on plastic (what's Bootsy doin'?) / Subliminal seduction (funk-me dirty) / Leakin' / Electro-cutie (shock-it-to-me) / 1st 1 2 the egg wins (the human race) / Love song / (I wannabe) Kissin' the "luv gun" / Yo-mama-loves ya / Save what's mine for me. *(cd re-iss. Mar99 on 'Columbia'; 494187-2)*

──　BOOTSY and his BOOTZILLA ORCHESTRA were credited on MALCOLM McLAREN's 1989 album 'Waltz Darling'. The RUBBER BAND were touring again in the early 90's and BOOTSY could be heard backing dance group DEEE-LITE.

Jul 90. (m-cd; as BOOTSY'S RUBBER BAND) (*BRECD 550*) **JUNGLE BASS**
– Jungle bass / Disciples of funk / Interzone / Jungle bass (mix).

	4th & Broad	Zillatron
	□	□

ZILLATRON

COLLINS, WORRELL / + BUCKETHEAD – guitar

	Rykodisc	Rykodisc

Jul 94. (cd) <(*RCD 10301*)> **LORD OF THE HARVEST**   □   □
– Bigg light / Fuzz face / Exterminate / Smell the secrets / Count zero / Bootsy and the beast / No fly zone the Devil's playground / The passion continues.

BOOTSY COLLINS & BOOTSY'S NEW RUBBER BAND

featured BERNIE WORRELL

	Rykodisc	Rykodisc

Aug 94. (d-cd/d-c) <(*RCD/RAC 90307-8*)> **BLASTER OF THE UNIVERSE**   □   □
– Blasters of the universe / J.R. (just right) / Funk express card / Bad girls / Back n the day / Where r the children / Female troubles (the national anthem) / Wide track / Funk me dirty / Blasters of the universe 2 (the sequel) / Good night Eddie / A sacred place / Half pass midnight / It's a silly serious world / J.R. (just right) / Funk express card / Back n the day / Bad girls / Good night Eddie / Where r the children / Funk me dirty / It's a silly serious world / A sacred place.

Aug 95. (d-cd) <(*RCD 90323-4*)> **KEEPIN' DAH FUNK ALIVE 4 – 1995**   □   □
– Intro / Ahh . . . the name is Bootsy, baby / Bootsy? (what's the name of this town) / Psychoticbumpschool (live) / The Pinocchio theory / Hollywood squares / Bernie solo / One nation under a groove / P. Funk (wants to get funked up) / Cosmic slop / Flash light / Bootzilla / Roto-rooter / I'd rather be with you / A sacred place (R.I.P.) / Stretchin' out – Touch somebody / Night of the Thumpasaurus peoples / Keepin' da funk alive 1994-95.

BOOTSY COLLINS

	WEA	Warners

Aug 98. (c-s/12"/cd-s) (*WEA 170 C/T/CD*) **DO THE FREAK**   □   □
Feb 99. (12"/cd-s) (*WEA 200 T/CD*) **PARTY LICK-A-BLE'S** (mixes; Norman Cook original & club / Headrush house)   □   □

– compilations, etc. –

Aug 94. (cd) *Warners*; <(*7599 26581-2*)> **BACK IN THE DAY: THE BEST OF BOOTSY**
– Ahh . . . the name is Bootsy, baby / Stretchin' out (in a rubber band) / The Pinocchio theory / Hollywood squares / I'd rather be with you / Bootzilla / What so never the dance / Can't stay away / Jam fan (hot) / Mug push / Body slam / Scenery / Vanish in our sleep / Psychoticbumpschool (live).

BOSTON

Formed: 1975 by technical whizz and sometime musical genius, TOM SCHOLZ, who had set up his own basement studio in Boston, Massachusetts, USA. Signed to 'Epic' on the strength of some home-crafted demos, SCHOLZ assembled a crew of musician friends (BRAD DELP, BARRY GOUDREAU, FRAN SHEEHAN and JIM MASDEA) and set about creating his first opus. Quintessentially 70's yet one of the most enduring AOR tracks ever recorded, BOSTON's debut single, 'MORE THAN A FEELING', gave the band instant UK and US success upon its release in Christmas 1976. With its powerful twin lead guitar attack, softened with flawless harmonies, the song set a blueprint for the eponymous debut album. While the record contained nothing else quite as affecting, it was all well written stuff and highly listenable if you ignored the cliched lyrics. Inevitably, the album sold in its millions and the pressure was on to record a follow-up. Notoriously perfectionist in the studio, SCHOLZ was unhappy with a mere two years to craft 'DON'T LOOK BACK' (1978). While the title track was top drawer car-stereo material, the formula was sounding tired and the bulk of the album didn't lend itself to repeated listening. While SCHOLZ complained that its relatively disappointing sales (still in the millions!) were down to the record being released prematurely, it was, after all, the height of the punk explosion, when sleeve designs of intergalactic guitars weren't particularly appreciated by the kids (in Britain, at least). It was to be another seven years before BOSTON returned with a follow-up and during this period, SCHOLZ signed with 'M.C.A.', a legal battle with 'C.B.S.' ensuing. The boffin-like SCHOLZ also found time to invent the 'Rockman', a device that amplified guitar sound at low volume for home recording. 'THIRD STAGE' (1986) boasted another airbrushed space fantasy cover and another set of reliable melodic rock songs, 'AMANDA' reaching No.1 in the US singles chart, the album itself achieving a similar feat. Yet again it quickly sold over a million but the BOSTON concept reeked of staleness and after another interminably long lay-off, SCHOLZ/BOSTON came up with 'WALK ON' in 1994. Unsurprisingly, the album only made it to No.51 in the US chart; SCHOLZ had clearly tested his fans' patience once too often.

Album rating: BOSTON (*7) / DON'T LOOK BACK (*5) / THIRD STAGE (*5) / WALK ON (*4) / GREATEST HITS compilation (*7)

BRAD DELP (b.12 Jun'51) – vocals, guitar / **TOM SCHOLZ** (b.10 Mar'47, Toledo, Ohio) – guitar, keyboards, vocals / **BARRY GOUDREAU** (b.29 Nov'51) – guitar / **FRAN SHEEHAN** (b.26 Mar'49) – bass / **SIB HASHIAN** (b.17 Aug'49) – drums repl. debut lp session drummer JIM MASDEA

	Epic	Epic

Jan 77. (7") (*EPC 4658*) <*50266*> **MORE THAN A FEELING. / SMOKIN'**   22   5 Sep76

Jan 77. (lp/c) (*EPC/40 81611*) <*34188*> **BOSTON**   11   3 Sep76
– More than a feeling / Peace of mind / Foreplay – Long time / Rock & roll band / Smokin' / Hitch a ride / Something about you / Let me take you home tonight. (re-iss. Mar81 lp/c; EPC/40 32038) – hit UK 58) (cd-iss. Mar87; CD 81611) (cd re-iss. Dec98; 4894129)

Mar 77. (7") (*EPC 5043*) <*50329*> **LONG TIME. / LET ME TAKE YOU HOME TONIGHT**   22 Jan77

Jun 77. (7") (*EPC 5288*) <*50381*> **PEACE OF MIND. / FOREPLAY**   38 May77

Sep 78. (lp/c)<US-pic-lp> (*EPC/40 86057*) <*35050*> **DON'T LOOK BACK**   9   1 Aug78
– Don't look back / The journey / It's easy / A man I'll never be / Feelin' satisfied / Party / Used to bad news / Don't be afraid. (re-iss. Jun81 lp/c; EPC/40 32048) (cd-iss. Mar87; CD 86057)

Oct 78. (7") (*EPC 6653*) <*50590*> **DON'T LOOK BACK. / THE JOURNEY**   43   4 Aug78

Jan 79. (7") (*EPC 6837*) <*50638*> **A MAN I'LL NEVER BE. / DON'T BE AFRAID**   31 Nov78

May 79. (7") (*EPC 7295*) <*50677*> **FEELIN' SATISFIED. / USED TO BAD NEWS**   46 Mar79

—— (broke up for a while, after 3rd album was shelved / not completed) BARRY GOUDREAU made solo album late '80 before in '82 forming ORION THE HUNTER. He was augmented by SCHOLZ and DELP. HASHIAN joined SAMMY HAGAR band.

BOSTON re-grouped around **SCHOLZ** and **DELP** plus **GARY PHIL** – guitar and the returning of **JIM MASDEA** – drums

	M.C.A.	M.C.A.

Oct 86. (7"/12") (*MCA/+S 1091*) <*52756*> **AMANDA. / MY DESTINATION**   1 Sep86

Oct 86. (lp/c/cd) (*MCG/MCGC/DMCG 6017*) <*6188*> **THIRD STAGE**   37   1
– Amanda / We're ready / The launch: Countdown – Ignition – Third stage separation / Cool the engines / My Destination / A new world / To be a man / I think I like it / Can'tcha say (you believe in me) / Still in love / Hollyann. (cd re-iss. Jun92; MCLD 19066)

Nov 86. (7") <*52985*> **WE'RE READY. / THE LAUNCH: COUNTDOWN – IGNITION – THIRD STAGE SEPARATION**   –   9

Apr 87. (7") (*MCA 1150*) <*53029*> **CAN'TCHA SAY (YOU BELIEVE IN ME). / STILL IN LOVE**   20 Mar87
(12"+=) (*MCAT 1150*) – Cool the engines.
(cd-s+=) (*DMCA 1150*) – The launch: Countdown – Ignition – Third stage separation.

—— Early in '90 SCHOLZ (aka BOSTON) won $million lawsuit against CBS.

RTZ

—— (RETURN TO ZERO) were formed by **BRAD + BARRY** with **BRIAN MAES** – keyboards / **TIM ARCHIBALD** – bass / **DAVID STEFANELLI** – drums

	Giant	Giant

Aug 91. (c-s,cd-s) <*19273*> **FACE THE MUSIC / RETURN TO ZERO**   –   49

Apr 92. (7") (*543918955-7*) <*19051*> **UNTIL YOUR LOVE COMES BACK AROUND. / EVERY DOOR IS OPEN**   26 Jan92
(c-s+=)(12"+=/cd-s+=) (*543918955-4*)(*93624040-30/-42*) – Return to zero / ('A'extended).

Apr 92. (cd/c) <(*7599 24422-2/-4*)> **RETURN TO ZERO**   Feb92
– Face the music / There's another side / All you've got / This is my life / Rain down on me / Every door is open / Devil to pay / Until your love comes back around / Livin' for the rock'n'roll / Hard time (in the big house) / Return to zero.

May 92. (c-s,cd-s) <*19112*> **ALL YOU'VE GOT / LIVIN' FOR THE ROCK'N'ROLL**   –   56

BOSTON

—— another comeback album with; **TOM SHOLTZ** – guitar, keyboards, bass, drums / **GARY 'PIHL'** – keyboards / **DAVID SIKES** – vocals, bass / **DOUG HOFFMAN** – drums / **FRAN COSMO + TOMMY FUNDERBURK** – vocals

	M.C.A.	M.C.A.

Jun 94. (cd/c) <(*MCD/MCC 10973*)> **WALK ON**   56   7
– I need your love / Surrender to me / Livin' for your love / Walkin' at night / Walk on / Get organ-ized / Get reorgan-ized / Walk on (some more) / What's your name / Magdalene / We can make it.

Jul 94. (c-s) (*MCSC 1983*) <*54803*> **I NEED YOUR LOVE / WE CAN MAKE IT**   51 Jun94
(cd-s+=) (*MCSTD 1983*) – The launch: The countdown – Ignition – Third stage separation.

– compilations etc. –

Sep 79. (7"m) *Epic*; (*EPC 7888*) **DON'T LOOK BACK. / MORE THAN A FEELING / SMOKIN'**   □   –

Apr 83. (7") *Old Gold*; (*OG 9299*) **MORE THAN A FEELING. / DON'T LOOK BACK**   □   –

Aug 83. (d-c) *C.B.S.*; (*4022155*) **BOSTON / DON'T LOOK BACK**   □   □

Aug 88. (3"cd-ep) *Epic*; <*34K 02355*> **MORE THAN A FEELING / FOREPLAY / LONG TIME**   –   □

Jun 97. (cd/c) <(*484333-2/-4*)> **GREATEST HITS**   47
– Tell me / Higher power / More than a feeling / Peace of mind / Don't look back / Cool the engines / Livin' for you / Feelin' satisfied / Party / Foreplay / Long time / Amanda / Rock'n'roll band / Smokin' / A man I'll never be / Star spangled banner / 4th of July reprise / Higher power.

David BOWIE

Born: DAVID ROBERT JONES, 8 Jan'47, Brixton, London. In 1964 he formed The KING BEES with schoolmate GEORGE UNDERWOOD but after one single they split when BOWIE joined The MANNISH BOYS. They also lasted half a year, DAVID going solo with backing from The LOWER THIRD. In early 1966, he became DAVID BOWIE and signed to 'Pye' although commercial success continued to elude him. After three years of trying, he finally charted with 'SPACE ODDITY', a classic that introduced his "MAJOR TOM" character. That year (1969) his father died, but he was compensated by the introduction to ANGIE, his future wife. Although he was regarded as one of the top newcomers to the rock/pop scene, it took him until 1972 to finally establish himself as *the* rock star. He formed his now famous backing band, The SPIDERS, and announced his bisexuality to the music press. The single, 'STARMAN', and parent album, 'ZIGGY STARDUST' (an archetype alter-ego), were to hit the UK top 10. By this stage he'd come a long way from being a 60's ANTHONY NEWLEY copyist, innovating a risque, glam rock style and pioneering the 'feathercut', make-up for men and stage-mime (the latter being learnt from LINDSEY KEMP). Signed to R.C.A., the company duly re-issued his past three albums which all broke into the U.K. charts and 'ALADDIN SANE' (1973) was the first of his many No.1 albums. 'DIAMOND DOGS' (1974) represented the finale of his futuristic concept work and bore the hit single, 'REBEL, REBEL', while the follow-up concert album, 'DAVID LIVE' (1974), documented the mammoth tour that followed. With 'YOUNG AMERICANS' in 1975, his music took a dramatic and not entirely well-received turn towards Philadelphia soul/disco. Nevertheless, the album hit No.2 in the UK and a collaborative single with JOHN LENNON, 'FAME', gave him a US No.1. BOWIE then made yet another about-face; dallying briefly with themes of fascism and dictatorship, he recorded the stark 'STATION TO STATION' (1976) album, before relocating to Berlin with BRIAN ENO and continuing his move towards experimental/avant-garde rock. The resulting albums, 'LOW' and 'HEROES', both released in 1977, were fairly successful in the UK despite containing some of BOWIE's most uncommercial work to date. After a final album with ENO, BOWIE returned to more conventional rock, gaining another No.1 hit with his resurrection of Major Tom on 'ASHES TO ASHES' (1980). After a two and a half year hiatus, he returned with the NILE RODGERS-produced 'LET'S DANCE' album. A typically polished, 80's-sounding record, it featured the single 'CHINA GIRL', complete with controversial video (in 1977, BOWIE had originally collaborated on the track with IGGY POP for the wild man's 'The Idiot' album). The rest of BOWIE's 80's output was hardly essential and at the turn of the decade he set up the embarrassing TIN MACHINE project, a misguided attempt at a return to spontaneous rock'n'roll. Ignoring the critical barbs, he carried on with this set-up until 1991 but couldn't substantiate any major hits. The release of 'OUTSIDE' (1995), (a collaboration with his old mucker ENO) saw BOWIE back in critical favour, while more recently 'EART HL ING' (1997) was an admirable attempt to incorporate cutting-edge dance styles into his music, collaborating with drum 'n' bass don, A GUY CALLED GERALD. More recently and trying desperately to get his new material noticed by an ailing public (he was still excellent live), BOWIE delivered his final set towards the end of the 90's, 'HOURS . . .' – it had in fact been "years . . ." since his last great album. • **Songwriters:** He wrote all his own material even managing some for others (e.g. ALL THE YOUNG DUDES for (Mott The Hoople) / OH YOU PRETTY THINGS (Peter Noone) / THE MAN WHO SOLD THE WORLD / (Lulu) / PINK ROSE (Adrian Belew) / etc. He produced 'RCA' acts LOU REED (Transformer) / MICK RONSON (Slaughter on Tenth Avenue) / etc. BOWIE's cover album PIN-UPS featured SORROW (Merseys) / ROSALYN (Pretty Things) / HERE COMES THE NIGHT (Them) / SHAPES OF THINGS (Yardbirds) / FRIDAY ON MY MIND (Easybeats) / ANYWAY ANYHOW ANYWHERE + I CAN'T EXPLAIN (Who) / SEE EMILY PLAY (Pink Floyd) / WHERE HAVE ALL THE GOOD TIMES GONE (Kinks) / DON'T BRING ME DOWN + I WISH YOU WOULD (Pretty Things) / EVERYTHING'S ALRIGHT (Mojos) /. Other covers:- LET'S SPEND THE NIGHT TOGETHER (Rolling Stones) / KNOCK ON WOOD (Eddie Floyd) / ALABAMA SONG (Brecht-Weill) / DANCING IN THE STREET (Martha & The Vandellas). I FEEL FREE (Cream) / NITE FLIGHT (Scott Walker) / I KNOW IT'S GONNA HAPPEN SOMEDAY (Morrissey) / DON'T LET ME DOWN & DOWN (Tacha-Valmont) / THE SEEKER (Who). – TIN MACHINE :- He co-wrote with GABRELS except MAGGIE'S FARM (Bob Dylan) / WORKING CLASS HERO (John Lennon, who also co-wrote FAME for BOWIE in 1975) / IF THERE IS SOMETHING (Roxy Music). • **Trivia:** BOWIE'S acting career started in 1976 with the film 'THE MAN WHO FELL TO EARTH' and 'JUST A GIGOLO' (1978). After starring in stage production of ELEPHANT MAN in 1980, he returned to films THE HUNGER (1982) / MERRY XMAS MR. LAWRENCE (1983) / LABYRINTH (1986) / ABSOLUTE BEGINNERS (1986) / THE LAST TEMPTATION OF CHRIST (1989). In 1985, he was one of the major stars of LIVE AID concert, and co-sang on 'DANCIN' IN THE STREET' with MICK JAGGER.

Album rating: DAVID BOWIE (*4) / MAN OF WORDS, MAN OF MUSIC aka SPACE ODDITY (*6) / THE MAN WHO SOLD THE WORLD (*8) / HUNKY DORY (*9) / THE RISE AND FALL OF ZIGGY STARDUST . . . (*10) / ALADDIN SANE (*8) / BOWIE PIN-UPS (*5) / DIAMOND DOGS (*6) / DAVID LIVE (*5) / YOUNG AMERICANS (*6) / STATION TO STATION (*8) / LOW (*10) / HEROES (*9) / STAGE (*5) / LODGER (*4) / SCARY MONSTERS (AND SUPER CREEPS) (*9) / CHANGESONEBOWIE compilation (*10) / LET'S DANCE (*6) / TONIGHT (*4) / NEVER LET ME DOWN (*4) / CHANGESBOWIE compilation (*9) / Tin Machine: TIN MACHINE (*4) / TIN MACHINE II (*3) / OY VEY BABY (*3) / David Bowie: BLACK TIE, WHITE NOISE (*5) / THE BUDDHA OF SUBURBIA soundtrack for TV (*5) / OUTSIDE (*6) / EART HL ING (*6) / HOURS . . . (*6)

DAVID BOWIE – vocals, acoustic guitar

		Vocalion	not iss.
Jun 64.	(7"; as DAVIE JONES with The KING BEES) *(Pop V 9221)* **LIZA JANE. / LOUIE LOUIE GO HOME** *(re-iss. Sep78 on 'Decca'; F 13807)*	☐	-

		Parlophone	not iss.
Mar 65.	(7"; as The MANNISH BOYS) *(R 5250)* **I PITY THE FOOL. / TAKE MY TIP**	☐	-
Aug 65.	(7"; as DAVY JONES) *(R 5315)* **YOU'VE GOT A HABIT OF LEAVING. / BABY LOVES THAT WAY**	☐	-

		Pye	Warners
Jan 66.	(7"; as DAVID BOWIE with The LOWER THIRD) *(7N 17020) <5814>* **CAN'T HELP THINKING ABOUT ME. / AND I SAID TO MYSELF**	☐	-
Apr 66.	(7") *(7N 17079)* **DO ANYTHING YOU SAY. / GOOD MORNING GIRL**	☐	-
Aug 66.	(7") *(7N 17157)* **I DIG EVERYTHING. / I'M NOT LOSING SLEEP**	☐	-

		Deram	Deram
Dec 66.	(7") *(DM 107)* **RUBBER BAND. / THE LONDON BOYS**	☐	-
Feb 67.	(7") *<85009>* **RUBBER BAND. / THERE IS A HAPY LAND**	-	☐
Apr 67.	(7") *(DM 123)* **THE LAUGHING GNOME. / THE GOSPEL ACCORDING TO TONY DAY** *(re-iss. Sep73; same); hit UK No.6 (re-iss. Jun82)*	☐	-
Jun 67.	(lp; mono/stereo) *(DML/SML 1007)* **DAVID BOWIE** – Uncle Arthur / Sell me a coat / Rubber band / Love you till Tuesday There is a happy land / We are hungry men / When I live my dream / Little bombadier / Silly boy blue / Come and buy me toys / Join the gang / She's got medals / Maids of Bond Street / Please Mr. Gravedigger. *(re-iss. Nov69 on 'Philips'; SBL 7912) (re-iss. Aug84 lp/c; DOA 1) (cd-iss. Oct88; 800 087-2)*	☐	-
Jul 67.	(7") *(DM 135) <85016>* **LOVE YOU TILL TUESDAY. / DID YOU EVER HAVE A DREAM**	☐	☐

—— (Jul68-Feb69) **BOWIE** formed FEATHERS with girlfriend **HERMOINE FARTHINGALE** + **JOHN HUTCHINSON** – bass. BOWIE went solo, recording solo album with session players **RICK WAKEMAN** – keyboards

		Philips	Mercury
Jul 69.	(7") *(BF 1801) <72949>* **SPACE ODDITY. / THE WILD EYED BOY FROM FREECLOUD**	5	☐
Nov 69.	(lp) *(SBL 7912)* **DAVID BOWIE – MAN OF WORDS MAN OF MUSIC** – Space oddity / Unwashed and somewhat slightly dazed / Letter to Hermione / Cygnet committee / Janine / An occasional dream / The wild eyed boy from Freecloud / God knows I'm good / Memory of a free festival. *(re-iss. Nov72 as 'SPACE ODDITY' on 'RCA' lp/c; LSP/PK 4813) (hit No.17 UK + No.16 US; <ST 61246>) (re-iss. Oct84 on 'RCA' lp/c/cd; PL/PK/PD 84813) (re-iss. Apr90 on 'EMI' cd/c/lp; CD/TC+/EMC 3571) (+=) – Conversation piece / Don't sit down. (hit UK No.64) (cd re-iss. Sep97 on 'Premier-EMI'; CDP 791835-2)*	☐	-

—— **BOWIE** formed backing band **HYPE** with **TONY VISCONTI** – bass / **MICK RONSON** – guitar / **JOHN CAMBRIDGE** – drums

		Mercury	Mercury
Mar 70.	(7") *(MF 1135)* **THE PRETTIEST STAR. / CONVERSATION PIECE**	☐	-

—— **MICK 'Woody' WOODMANSEY** – drums repl. CAMBRIDGE

Jun 70.	(7") *(6052 026) <73075>* **MEMORY OF A FREE FESTIVAL (part 1). / (part 2)**	☐	-
Jan 71.	(7") *(6052 049)* **HOLY HOLY. / BLACK COUNTRY ROCK**	☐	-
Apr 71.	(lp) *(6338 041) <61325>* **THE MAN WHO SOLD THE WORLD** – The width of a circle / All the madmen / Black country rock / After all / Running gun blues / Saviour machine / She took me cold / The man who sold the world / The supermen. *(re-iss. Nov72 on 'RCA' lp/c; LSP/PK 4816) (hit No.26 UK) (re-iss. Apr83 on 'RCA' lp/c; INTS/INTK 5237) (hit UK 64) (re-iss. Oct84 on 'RCA Int.' lp/c/cd; NL/NK/PD 84654) (re-iss. Apr90 on 'EMI' cd/c/lp; CD/TC+/EMC 3573) (+=) – Lightning frightening / Moonage daydream / Holy holy / Hang on to yourself. (hit UK No.66) (cd re-iss. Sep97 on 'Premier-EMI'; CDP 791837-2)*	☐	☐
Jun 71.	(7") *<73175>* **ALL THE MADMEN**	-	☐

—— Became **SPIDERS FROM MARS (BOWIE, RONSON, WOODMANSEY), TREVOR BOULDER** – bass repl. VISCONTI

		R.C.A.	R.C.A.
Dec 71.	(lp/c) *(SF/PK 8244) <AFL-1 4623>* **HUNKY DORY** – Changes / Oh! you pretty things / Eight line poem / Life on Mars? / Kooks / Quicksand / Fill your heart / Andy Warhol / Song for Bob Dylan / Queen bitch / The Bewlay Brothers. *(re-dist.Sep72 reached No.3 UK) (re-iss. Jan81 lp/c; INTS/INTK 5064) (hit No.32 UK) (pic-lp Apr84; BOPIC 2) (re-iss. Oct84 on 'RCA Int.' lp/c/cd; NL/NK/PD 83844) (re-iss. Apr90 on 'EMI' cd/c/lp; CD/TC+/EMC 3572) (+=) – Bombers / The supermen (alt.) / Quicksand (demo) / The Bewlay Brothers (alt.). (hit UK No.39) (cd re-iss. Sep97 on 'Premier-EMI'; LPCENT 21) (lp re-iss. Nov97 on 'E.M.I.'; CDP 791843-2)*	☐	93
Jan 72.	(7") *(RCA 2160) <74-0605>* **CHANGES. / ANDY WARHOL** *(re-iss. Dec74; same); reached No.41 UK*		66 Apr72
Apr 72.	(7") *(RCA 2199) <74-0719>* **STARMAN. / SUFFRAGETTE CITY**	10	65 Jun72
Jun 72.	(lp/c) *(SF/PK 8267) <AFL-1 4702>* **THE RISE AND FALL OF ZIGGY STARDUST AND THE SPIDERS FROM MARS** – Five years / Soul love / Moonage daydream / Starman / It ain't easy / Lady Stardust / Star / Hang on to yourself / Ziggy Stardust / Suffragette city / Rock'n'roll suicide. *(re-iss. Jan81 lp/c; INTS/INTK 5063) (hit No.33 UK) (pic-lp Apr84; BOPIC 3) (re-iss. Oct84 on 'RCA Int.' lp/c/cd; NL/NK/PD 83843) (re-iss. Apr90 on 'EMI' cd+=/c+=/lp; CD/TC+/EMC 3577) <re-iss. Jun90 on 'Rykodisc'+=; 10134>; hit No.93. – John, I'm only dancing (demo) / Velvet goldmine / Sweet head / Ziggy Stardust (demo) / Lady Stardust (demo). (hit UK No.25) (re-iss. Feb97 on 'E.M.I.'; LPCENT 4)*	5	75
Sep 72.	(7") *(RCA 2263)* **JOHN, I'M ONLY DANCING. / HANG ON TO YOURSELF**	12	-
Nov 72.	(7") *(RCA 2302)* **THE JEAN GENIE. / ZIGGY STARDUST**	2	-
Nov 72.	(7") *<74-0838>* **THE JEAN GENIE. / HANG ON TO YOURSELF**	-	71
Jan 73.	(7") *<74-0876>* **SPACE ODDITY. / THE MAN WHO SOLD THE WORLD**	-	15
Apr 73.	(7") *(RCA 2352)* **DRIVE-IN-SATURDAY. / ROUND AND ROUND**	3	-

—— with guests **MIKE GARSON** – piano / **KEN FORDHAM** and **BUX** – saxophone, flute

| Apr 73. | (lp/c) *(RS/PK 1001) <AFL-1 4852>* **ALADDIN SANE** | 1 | 17 May73 |

– Watch that man / Aladdin Sane (1913-1938-197?) / Drive-in Saturday / Panic in Detroit / Cracked actor / Time / The prettiest star / Let's spend the night together / The Jean genie / Lady grinning soul. *(re-iss. Feb81 on 'RCA Int.' lp/c; INTS/INTK 5067)* (hit No.49 UK Feb82) *(re-iss. Mar84 on 'RCA Int.' lp/c; NL/NK 83890) (pic-lp Apr84; BOPIC 1) (cd-iss. Jun85; PD 83890) (re-iss. Jul90 on 'EMI' cd/c/lp; CD/TC+/EMC 3579)(+=) – (other rare tracks). (hit UK No.43) (cd re-iss. Sep97 on 'Premier-EMI'; CDP 794768-2)*

Jun 73. (7") *<APBO 0001>* **TIME. / THE PRETTIEST STAR** | – | |

Jun 73. (7") *(RCA 2316)* **LIFE ON MARS. / THE MAN WHO SOLD THE WORLD** | 3 | – |

Aug 73. (7") *<APBO 0028>* **LET'S SPEND THE NIGHT TOGETHER. / LADY GRINNING SOUL**

——— **AYNSLEY DUNBAR** – drums repl. WOODY

Oct 73. (7") *(RCA 2424) <APBO 0160>* **SORROW. / AMSTERDAM** | 3 | 23 | Nov73

Oct 73. (lp/c) *(RS/PK 1003) <AFL-1 0291>* **PIN-UPS**
– Rosalyn / Here comes the night / I wish you would / See Emily play / Everything's alright / I can't explain / Friday on my mind / Sorrow / Don't bring me down / Shapes of things / Anyway anyhow anywhere / Where have all the good times gone!. *(re-iss. Sep81 lp/c; RCA LP/K 3004) (re-iss. Apr83 on 'RCA Int.' lp/c; INTS/INTK 5236) (hit UK 57) (pic-lp Apr84; BOPIC 4) (re-iss. Jul90 on 'EMI' cd/c/lp; CD/TC+/EMC 3580) (hit No.52)*

——— **DUNBAR** and **TONY NEWMAN** – drums / **HERBIE FLOWERS** – bass / **MIKE GARSON** – keyboards

Feb 74. (7") *(LPBO 5009)* **REBEL REBEL. / QUEEN BITCH** | 5 | – |

Apr 74. (7") *(RCA 5021)* **ROCK'N'ROLL SUICIDE. / QUICKSAND** | 22 | – |

May 74. (7") *<APBO 0287>* **REBEL REBEL. / LADY GRINNING SOUL** | – | 64 |

May 74. (lp/c; as BOWIE) *(<APL/APK 1-0576>)* **DIAMOND DOGS** | 1 | |
– Future legend / Diamond dogs / Sweet thing / Candidate / Sweet thing (reprise) / Rebel rebel / Rock'n'roll with me / We are the dead / 1984 / Big brother (including 'Chant of the ever circling skeletal family'). *(re-iss. Feb81 on 'RCA Int.' lp/c; INTS/INTK 5068) (hit UK 60 in May83) (re-iss. Mar84 on 'RCA Int.' lp/c/cd; NL/NK/PD 83889) (pic-lp Apr84; BOPIC 5) (re-iss. Jun90 on 'E.M.I.' cd/c/lp; CD/TC+/EMC 3584) (+=) – Dodo / Candidate. (hit UK No.67)*

Jun 74. (7") *<APBO 0293>* **DIAMOND DOGS. / HOLY HOLY** | 21 | |

——— added **EARL SLICK** – guitar / **DAVID SANBORN** – saxophone

Sep 74. (7") *(RCA 2466)* **KNOCK ON WOOD (live). / PANIC IN DETROIT (live)** | 10 | |

Oct 74. (7") *<10026>* **1984 (live). / QUEEN BITCH** | – | |

Nov 74. (d-lp/c) *(<APL/APK 2-0771>)* **DAVID LIVE (live at the Tower theatre Philadelphia '74)** | 2 | 8 |
– 1984 / Rebel rebel / Moonage daydream / Sweet thing / Changes / Suffragette city / Aladdin Sane (1913-1938-197?) / All the young dudes / Cracked actor / Rock'n'roll with me / Watch that man / Knock on wood / Diamond dogs/ Big brother / The width of a circle / The Jean genie / Rock'n'roll suicide. *(re-iss. May84 lp/c; PL/PK 80771) (re-iss. Jun90 on 'EMI' cd/c/d-lp+=; CD/TC+/DBLD 1) – (band intro) / Here today, gone tomorrow / Time. (re-iss. d-cd Jun95 on 'EMI'; same)*

Dec 74. (7") *<10105>* **ROCK'N'ROLL WITH ME (live). / PANIC IN DETROIT (live)** | – | |

——— **ANDY NEWMARK** – drums / **WILLIE WEEKS** – bass / **CARLOS ALOMAR** – guitar / **EARL SLICK** – guitar / guests **LUTHER VANDROSS** + **JOHN LENNON** – backing vocals

Feb 75. (7") *(RCA 2523)* **YOUNG AMERICANS. / SUFFRAGETTE CITY** | 18 | – |

Mar 75. (7") *<10152>* **YOUNG AMERICANS. / KNOCK ON WOOD (live)** | – | 28 |

Mar 75. (lp/c) *(APL/APK 1-1006) <0998>* **YOUNG AMERICANS** | 2 | 9 |
– Young americans / Win / Fascination / Right / Somebody up there like me / Across the universe / Can you hear me / Fame. *(re-iss. Sep81 lp/c; RCA LP/K 3009) (re-iss. Oct84 lp/c/cd; PL/PK/PD 80998) (re-iss. Apr91 on 'E.M.I.' cd+=/c+=/lp; CD/TC+/EMD 1021) – Who can I be now? / John, I'm only dancing (again) (1975) / It's gonna be me. (hit UK No.54)*

Jul 75. (7") *<10320>* **FAME. / RIGHT** | 17 | 1 | Jun75

Sep 75. (7"m) *(RCA 2593)* **SPACE ODDITY. / CHANGES / VELVET GOLDMINE** | 1 | – |

——— retained **SLICK** + **ALOMAR**

——— **GEORGE MURRAY** – bass + **DENNIS DAVIS** – drums repl. WEEKS + NEWMARK

Nov 75. (7") *(RCA 2640) <10441>* **GOLDEN YEARS. / CAN YOU HEAR ME** | 8 | 10 |

Jan 76. (lp/c) *(<APL/APK 1-1327>)* **STATION TO STATION** | 5 | 3 |
– Station to station / Golden years / Word on a wing / TVC 15 / Stay / Wild is the wind. *(re-iss. Sep81 lp/c; RCA LP/K 3013) (re-iss. Oct84 lp/c/cd; PL/PK/PD 81327) (re-iss. Apr91 on 'E.M.I.' cd/c/lp; CD/TC+/EMD 1020) (+=) – Word on the wing (live) / Stay (live). (hit UK No.54)*

May 76. (7") *(RCA 2682) <10664>* **TVC 15. / WE ARE THE DEAD** | 33 | 64 |

Jun 76. (lp/c) *(RS/PK 1055) <1732>* **CHANGESONEBOWIE** (compilation) | 2 | 10 |
– Space oddity / John, I'm only dancing / Changes / Ziggy Stardust / Suffragette city / The Jean genie / Diamond dogs / Rebel rebel / Young Americans / Fame / Golden years. *(re-iss. May84 lp/c/cd; PL/PK/PD 81732)*

Jul 76. (7") *(RCA 2726)* **SUFFRAGETTE CITY. / STAY** | | |

Aug 76. (7") *<10736>* **STAY. / WORD ON A WING** | – | |

——— now collaborated with **BRIAN ENO** – synthesizers

——— **RICKY GARDINER** – guitar repl. SLICK

Jan 77. (lp/c) *(PL/PK 12030) <2030>* **LOW** | 2 | 11 |
– Speed of life / Breaking glass / What in the world / Sound and vision / Always crashing in the same car / Be my wife / A new career in a new town / Warszawa / Art decade / Weeping wall / Subterraneans. *(re-iss. Dec80 on 'RCA Int.' lp/c; INTS/INTK 5065) ;hit UK 85 in Jun83) (re-iss. Mar84 on 'RCA Int.' lp/c/cd; NL/NK/PD 83856) (re-iss. Aug91 on 'E.M.I.' cd/c/lp; CD/TC+/EMD 1027) (+=) – (bonus tracks). (hit UK No.64)*

Feb 77. (7") *(PB 0905) <10905>* **SOUND AND VISION. / A NEW CAREER IN A NEW TOWN** | 3 | 69 |

Jun 77. (7") *(PB 1017) <11017>* **BE MY WIFE. / SPEED OF LIFE** | | |

——— next guest **ROBERT FRIPP** – guitar who repl. RICKY GARDINER.

Oct 77. (7") *(PB 1121) <11121>* **HEROES. / V2-SCHNEIDER** | 24 | |

Oct 77. (lp/c) *(PL/PK 12522) <2522>* **"HEROES"** | 3 | 35 |
– Beauty and the beast / Joe the lion / Heroes / Sons of the silent age / Blackout / V-2 Schneider / Sense of doubt / Moss garden / Neukoln / Black out / The secret

life of Arabia. *(re-iss. Dec80 lp/c; INTS/INTK 5066) (hit UK 75 in Jun83) (re-iss. Nov84 lp/c/cd; NL/NK/PD 83857) (re-iss. Apr91 on 'E.M.I.' cd/c/lp; CD/TC+/EMD 1025) (+=) – Joe the Lion (1991 remix) / Abolumajor.*

Jan 78. (7") *(PB 1190) <11190>* **THE BEAUTY AND THE BEAST. / SENSE OF DOUBT** | 39 | |

——— added **ADRIAN BELEW** – guitar / **SIMON HOUSE** – violin (ex-HIGH TIDE, ex-HAWKWIND) / **SEAN MAYES** – piano

Sep 78. (d-lp,yellow-d-lp/d-c) *(PL/PK 02913) <2913>* **STAGE (live)** | 5 | 44 |
– Hang on to yourself / Ziggy Stardust / Five years / Soul love / Star / Station to station / Fame / TVC 15 / Warszawa / Speed of life / Art decade / Breaking glass / Heroes / What in the world / Blackout / Beauty and the beast. *(re-iss. Jul84 d-lp/d-c; PL/PD 89002) (re-iss. Feb92 on 'EMI' d-cd/c; CD/TC EMD 1030) – (bonus tracks).*

Oct 78. (7"ep) *(BOW 1)* **BREAKING GLASS (live). / ZIGGY STARDUST (live) / ART DECADE (live)** | 54 | – |

Apr 79. (7") *(BOW 2) <11585>* **BOYS KEEP SWINGING. / FANTASTIC VOYAGE** | 7 | 20 |

May 79. (lp/c) *(BOW LP/K 1) <3254>* **LODGER** | 4 | 20 |
– Fantastic voyage / African night flight / Move on / Yassassin / Red sails / D.J. / Look back in anger / Boys keep swinging / Repetition / Red money. *(re-iss. May82 on 'RCA Int.' lp/c; INTS/INTK 5212) (re-iss. Mar84 on 'RCA Int.' lp/c/cd; NL/NK/PD 84234) (re-iss. Aug91 on 'E.M.I.' cd/c/lp; CD/TC+/EMD 1026) – (2 tracks).*

Jul 79. (7") *(BOW 3)* **D.J. / REPETITION** | 29 | – |

Aug 79. (7") *<11661>* **D.J. / FANTASTIC VOYAGE** | – | |

Oct 79. (7") *<11724>* **LOOK BACK IN ANGER. / REPITITION** | – | |

Dec 79. (7"/ext.12") *(BOW 4/12-4)* **JOHN, I'M ONLY DANCING (AGAIN) (1975). / JOHN, I'M ONLY DANCING (1972)** | 12 | – |

Jan 80. (7") *<11887>* **JOHN, I'M ONLY DANCING (1972). / JOE THE LION** | – | |

Feb 80. (7") *(BOW 5)* **ALABAMA SONG. / SPACE ODDITY** | 23 | |

——— guest **ROBERT FRIPP** – guitar repl. BRIAN ENO

Aug 80. (7") *(BOW 6)* **ASHES TO ASHES. / MOVE ON** | 1 | – |

Sep 80. (7") *<12078>* **ASHES TO ASHES. / IT'S NO GAME** | – | |

Sep 80. (lp/c) *(BOW LP/K 2) <3647>* **SCARY MONSTERS** | 1 | 12 |
– It's no game (No.1) / Up the hill backwards / Scary monsters (and super creeps) / Ashes to ashes / Fashion / Teenage wildlife / Scream like a baby / Kingdom come / Because you're young / It's no game (No.2). *(re-iss. Oct84 lp/c/cd; PL/PK/PD 83647) (re-iss. Jun92 on 'EMI' cd/c; CD/TC EMD 1029) (+=) – Space oddity / Panic in Detroit / Crystal Japan / Alabama song.*

Oct 80. (7"/12") *(BOW/+T 7) <12134>* **FASHION. / SCREAM LIKE A BABY** | 5 | 70 |

Jan 81. (7"/c-s) *(BOW/+C 8)* **SCARY MONSTERS (AND SUPER CREEPS). / BECAUSE YOU'RE YOUNG** | 20 | – |

Mar 81. (7"/c-s) *(BOW/+C 9)* **UP THE HILL BACKWARDS. / CRYSTAL JAPAN** | 32 | – |

——— (next single "UNDER PRESSURE" was a No.1 collaboration w/ "QUEEN")

Nov 81. (7"/12") *(BOW/+T 10)* **WILD IS THE WIND. / GOLDEN YEARS** | 24 | |

Nov 81. (lp/c) *(BOW LP/K 3) <4202>* **CHANGESTWOBOWIE** (compilation) | 24 | 68 |
– Aladdin Sane / Oh you pretty things / Starman / 1984 / Ashes to ashes / Sound and vision / Fashion / Wild is the wind / John, I'm only dancing (again) (1975) / D.J. *(re-iss. May84 lp/c/cd; PL/PK/PD 84202)*

Feb 82. (7"ep) *(BOW 11)* **BAAL'S HYMN** | 29 | |
– Baal's hymn / Remembering Marie / Ballad of the adventurers / The drowned girl / The dirty song.

Apr 82. (7"/ext.12") *(MCA/+T 770) <52024>* **CAT PEOPLE (PUTTING OUT FIRE). / PAUL'S THEME (by GIORGIO MORODER)** | 26 | 67 |

——— (above single taken from the feature film of the same name on 'MCA-UK' / 'Backstreet' US)

Nov 82. (7"/12"; by DAVID BOWIE & BING CROSBY) *(BOW/+T 12) <13400>* **PEACE ON EARTH – LITTLE DRUMMER BOY. / FANTASTIC VOYAGE** | 3 | |

——— now with **NILE RODGERS + STEVIE RAY VAUGHAN** – guitar / **BERNARD EDWARDS + CARMINE ROJAS** – bass / **OMAR HAKIM + TONY THOMPSON** – drums / **SAMMY FIGUEROA** – percussion

	EMI America	EMI America
Mar 83. (7"/12"/c-s) *(EA/12EA/45-TCEA 152) <8158>* **LET'S DANCE. / CAT PEOPLE (PUTTING OUT FIRE)**	1	1
Apr 83. (lp/pic-lp/c) *(AML/AMLP/TCAML 3029) <17093>* **LET'S DANCE**	1	4

– Modern love / China girl / Let's dance / China girl / Without you / Ricochet / Criminal world / Cat people (putting out fire) / Shake it. *(cd-iss. Jan84; CD 7460022) (re-iss. cd Nov95 on 'Virgin American'; CDVUS 96) (cd re-iss. Jan98 on 'E.M.I.'; 493094-2)*

Jun 83. (7"/7"pic-d/12") *(EA/EAP/12EA 157) <8165>* **CHINA GIRL. / SHAKE IT** | 2 | 10 |

Sep 83. (7"/12") *(EA/12EA 158) <8177>* **MODERN LOVE. / MODERN LOVE (live)** | 2 | 14 |

Feb 84. (7") *<8190>* **WITHOUT YOU. / CRIMINAL WORLD** | – | 73 |

——— retained **HAKIM, ROJAS, FIGUEROA** / brought back **ALOMAR** and recruited **DEREK BRAMBLE** – bass, synths, etc.

Sep 84. (7"/12") *(EA/12EA 181) <8231>* **BLUE JEAN. / DANCING WITH THE BIG BOYS** | 6 | 8 |

Sep 84. (lp/c/)(cd) *(DB/TCDB 1)(CDP 746052-2) <17138>* **TONIGHT** | 1 | 11 |
– Loving the alien / Don't look down / God only knows / Tonight / Neighbourhood threat / Blue Jean / Tumble and twirl / I keep forgetting / Dancing with the big boys. *(re-iss. cd Nov95 on 'Virgin American'; CDVUS 97) (cd re-iss. Jan 98 on 'E.M.I.'; 493102-2)*

Nov 84. (7") *(EA 187) <8246>* **TONIGHT. / TUMBLE AND TWIRL** | 53 | 53 |
(12") *(12EA 187)* – ('A'vocal dance mix) / ('B'extended dance mix) / ('A'dub mix).

——— (next single, from the film "Falcon And The Snowman")

Jan 85. (7"/12"; by DAVID BOWIE with The PAT METHENY GROUP) *(EA 190) <8251>* **THIS IS NOT AMERICA. / ('A'instrumental by The PAT METHENY GROUP)** | 14 | 32 |

May 85. (7"/7"pic-d) *(EA/+P 195) <8271>* **LOVING THE ALIEN. / DON'T LOOK DOWN** | 19 | |

(ext.12"+=/ext.12"sha-pic-d+=) *(12EA/+P 195)* – ('A'extended dub mix).

Sep 85. (7"; by DAVID BOWIE & MICK JAGGER) *(EA 204)* <8288> **DANCING IN THE STREET (Clearmountain mix). / ('A'instrumental)** — [1] [7]
(12") *(12EA 204)* – ('A'-Steve Thompson mix) / ('A'dub version) / ('A'edit.
(below single from 'Virgin' records film & album of the same name, cont. 3 BOWIE tracks, album reached No.19 UK)

Mar 86. (7"/7"sha-pic-d)(ext.12") *(VS/+S 838)(VS 838-12)* <8308> **ABSOLUTE BEGINNERS. / ('A'dub version)** — [2] [53]
(re-iss. 3"cd-s Nov88; CDT 20)

—— (below single from the feature film "Labyrinth" which cont. 5 BOWIE tracks, album reached No.38 UK)

—— now with **ALOMAR, ROJAS + ERDAL KIZILCAY** – keyboards / **PHILIPPE SAISSE** – keyboards, etc. / **PETER FRAMPTON** – guitar

Jun 86. (7"/7"sha-pic-d) *(EA/+P 216)* <8323> **UNDERGROUND. / ('A'instrumental)** — [21] [ ]
(ext.dance-12"+=) – ('A'dub).

—— (the next, was from animated film of the same name on 'Virgin')

Nov 86. (7"/7"sha-pic-d) *(VS/+S 906)* **WHEN THE WIND BLOWS. / ('A'instrumental)** — [44] [-]
(12"+=) *(VS 906-12)* – ('A'dub).

Mar 87. (7"/7"red) *(EA/+X 230)* <8380> **DAY-IN DAY-OUT. / JULIE** — [17] [21]
(ext.dance-12"+=/remix-12"+=)(ext.dance c-s+=) *(12EA/+X 230)(TCEA 230)* – ('A'extended dub).

Apr 87. (lp/c/cd) *(AMLS/TCAMLS/CDAMLS 3117)* <17267> **NEVER LET ME DOWN** — [6] [34]
– Day-in day-out / Time will crawl / Beat of your drum / Never let me down / Zeroes / Glass spider / Shining star (makin' my love) / New York's in love / '87 and cry / Bang bang / Too dizzy. (cd+=) – Time will crawl (extended dance) / Never let me down (version) / Day-in day-out (Groucho mix).*(re-iss. cd Nov95 on 'Virgin American'; CDVUS 98) (cd re-iss. Jan98 on 'E.M.I.'; 493097-2)*

Jun 87. (7"/7"w-poster) *(EA/+P 237)* <43020> **TIME WILL CRAWL. / GIRLS** — [33] [ ]
(12") *(12EA 237)* – ('A'extended dance mix) / ('A'version) / ('B'extended).
(12") *(12EAX 237)* – ('A'dance crew mix) / ('A'dub) / ('B'-Japanese version).

Aug 87. (7"/7"pic-d) *(EA/+P 239)* <43031> **NEVER LET ME DOWN. / '87 AND CRY** — [34] [27]
(c-s+=) *(TCEA 239)* – Time will crawl (extended dance mix) / Day-in day-out (Groucho mix).
(ext.dance-12"+=) *(12EA 239)* – ('A'dub) / ('A'acappella).

TIN MACHINE

was the name of **BOWIE's** next project/band. **DAVID BOWIE** – vocals, saxophone / **REEVES GABRELS** – lead guitar / **TONY SALES** – bass / **HUNT SALES** – drums (both ex-IGGY POP, ex-TODD RUNDGREN RUNT)plus p/t member **KEVIN ARMSTRONG** – guitar

Manhattan Manhattan

May 89. (cd/c/lp) *(CD/MC+/MTLS 1044)* <91990> **TIN MACHINE** — [3] [28]
– Heaven's in here / Tin machine / Prisoner of love / Crack city / I can't read / Under the god / Amazing / Working class hero / Bus stop / Pretty thing / Video crimes / Run * / Sacrifice yourself * / Baby can dance. *(cd+= *)* *(re-iss. cd Nov95 on 'Virgin American'; CDVUS 99)*

Jun 89. (7"/c-s) *(MT/TCMT 68)* **UNDER THE GOD. / SACRIFICE YOURSELF** — [51] [ ]
(10"+=/12"+=/cd-s+=) *(10/12/CD MT 68)* – (the interview).

Aug 89. (7"/7"s/7"sha-pic-d/c-s) *(MT/MTG/MTPD/TCMT 73)* **TIN MACHINE. / MAGGIE'S FARM (live)** — [48] [ ]
(12"+=) *(12MT 73)* – I can't read (live).
(cd-s+=) *(CDMT 73)* – Bus stop (live country version).

Oct 89. (7"/7"s/7"sha-pic-d/c-s) *(MT/MTS/MTPD/TCMT 76)* **PRISONER OF LOVE. / BABY CAN DANCE (live)** — [ ] [ ]
(12"+=) *(12MT 76)* – Crack city (live).
(cd-s++=) *(CDMT 76)* – ('A'version).

London Victory

Aug 91. (7"/12") *(LON/+X 305)* **YOU BELONG IN ROCK'N'ROLL. / AMLAPURA** — [33] [ ]
(pic-cd+=) *(LONCD 305)* – Stateside / Hammerhead.

Sep 91. (cd/c/lp) *(828 272-2/-4/-1)* <511216> **TIN MACHINE II** — [23] [ ]
– Baby universal / One shot / You belong in rock'n'roll / If there is something / Amlapura / Betty wrong / You can't talk / Stateside / Shopping for girls / Big hurt / I'm sorry / Goodbye Mr. Ed / Hammerhead.

Oct 91. (7"/c-s) *(LON/+CS 310)* **BABY UNIVERSAL. / YOU BELONG IN ROCK'N'ROLL** — [48] [ ]
(12") *(LONT 310)* – ('A'side) / A big hurt (live) / ('A'live).
(cd-s) *(LONCD 310)* – ('A'side) / Stateside (live) / If there is something (live) / Heaven's in here (live).

—— In Feb'92, BOWIE's song 'SOUND AND VISION (remix)' was re-done with himself and 808 STATE on label 'Tommy Boy'.

Jul 92. (cd/c/lp) *(828 328-2/-4/-1)* **TIN MACHINE LIVE – OY VEY, BABY (live)** — [ ] [ ]
– If there is something / Amazing / I can't read / Stateside / Under the god / Goodbye Mr. Ed / Heaven's in here / You belong in rock'n'roll.

DAVID BOWIE

(solo again) and starred in the film 'THE LINGUINI INCIDENT'.

Warners Warners

Aug 92. (7"/c-s) *(W 0127/+C)* **REAL COOL WORLD. / ('A'instrumental)** — [53] [ ]
(12") *(W 0127T)* – ('A'club) / ('A'dub thing 1 & 2) / ('A'dub overture).
(cd-s+=) *(W 0127CD)* – (2 more 'A'mixes).

—— with **NILE RODGERS** – guitar, co-producer / **DAVE RICHARDS + RICHARD HILTON + PHILIPPE SAISSE + RICHARD TEE** – keyboards / **BARRY CAMPBELL + JOHN REGAN** – bass / **PUGI BELL & STERLING CAMPBELL** – bass / **GERADO VELEZ** – percussion. Plus guests **MICK RONSON** – guitar / **LESTER BOWIE** – trumpet / **REEVES GABRELS** – guitar / **MIKE GARSON** – piano / **AL B.SURE!** – vocals / **WILD T.SPRINGER** – guitar

Savage- Savage-
BMG BMG

Mar 93. (c-s) *(74321 139424)* **JUMP THEY SAY. / PALLAS ATHENA (Don't Stop Praying mix)** — [9] [ ]
(cd-s+=) *(74321 139422)* – ('A'-Hard Hands mix) / ('A'-JAE-E remix).
(cd-s) *(74321 139432)* – ('A'-Brothers In Rhythm mix) / ('A'-Brothers In Rhythm instrumental) / ('A'-Leftfield vocal) / ('A'ext).
(12") *(74321 139424-1)* – ('A'-Hard Hands mix) / ('A'version) / ('A'-Leftfield 12" vocal) / ('A'-extended).

Apr 93. (cd/c/lp) *(<74321 13697-2/-4/-1>)* **BLACK TIE WHITE NOISE** — [1] [39]
– The wedding / You've been around / I feel free / Black tie white noise / Jump they say / Nite flight / Pallas Athena / Miracle tonight / Don't let me down & down / Looking for Lester / I know it's gonna happen someday / The wedding song / Jump they say (alternate mix) / Lucy can't dance.

Jun 93. (7"/c-s) *(74321 14868-7/-4)* **BLACK TIE WHITE NOISE. / YOU'VE BEEN AROUND (Jack Dangers remix)** — [36] [ ]
(cd-s+=) *(74321 14868-2)* – ('A'-extended remix) / ('A'-Urban).
(12") *(74321 14868-1)* – ('A'extended) / ('A'trance mix) / ('A'version) / ('A'club mix with AL B.SURE!) / ('A'-extended urban mix).

Oct 93. (7"/c-s) *(74321 16226-7/-4)* **MIRACLE TONIGHT. / LOOKING FOR LESTER** — [40] [ ]
(cd-s+=) *(74321 16226-2)* – ('A'-Philly mix) / ('A'-Masereti mix).
(12") *(74321 16226-1)* – ('A'-Blunted mix) / ('A'-Make believe mix) / ('A'-Philly mix) / ('A'dance dub).

Nov 93. (7"/c-s) *(74321 17705-7/-4)* **BUDDHA OF SUBURBIA. / DEAD AGAINST IT** — [35] [ ]
(cd-s+=) *(74321 17705-2)* – South horizon / ('A'-Lenny Kravitz rock mix).

Nov 93. (cd/c) *(74321 17004-2/-4)* **BUDDHA OF SUBURBIA (TV soundtrack)** — [ ] [-]
– Buddah of suburbia / Sex and the church / South horizon / The mysteries / Bleed like a craze, dad / Strangers when we meet / Read against it / Untitled No.1 / Ian Fish / UK heir / Buddah of suburbia (featuring LENNY KRAVITZ).

—— now with **ENO** – synthesizers, co-writer (on most) / **REEVES GABRELS / ERDAL KIZILCAY / MIKE GARSON / STERLING CAMPBELL / CARLOS ALOMAR / JOEY BARON / YOSSI FINE**

R.C.A. Virgin

Sep 95. (c-s/cd-s) *(74321 30703-4/-2)* **THE HEARTS FILTHY LESSON / I AM WITH NAME** — [35] [-]
(cd-s+=) *(74321 30703-2)* – ('A'-Bowie mix) / ('A'-Tony Maserati remix).
(12"pic-d) *(74321 30703-2)* – (5-'A'mixes; Bowie / alt. / Rubber / Simple text / Filthy).

Sep 95. (cd/c/d-lp) *(<74321 30702-2/-4/-1>)* **OUTSIDE** — [8] [21]
– THE NATHAN ADLER DIARIES: A Hyper Cycle:- Leon takes us outside / Outside / The hearts filthy lesson / A small plot of land / segue – Baby Grace (a horrid cassette) / Hallo spaceboy / The motel / I have not been to Oxford Town / No control / segue – Algeria touchshriek / The voyeur of utter destruction (as beauty) / segue – Ramona A. Stone / I am with name / Wishful beginnings / We prick you / segue – Nathan Adler / Strangers when we meet.

Sep 95. (c-s) *<38518>* **THE HEARTS FILTHY LESSON / NOTHING TO BE DESIRED** — [-] [92]

Nov 95. (7"/c-s) *(74321 32940-7/-4)* **STRANGERS WHEN WE MEET. / THE MAN WHO SOLD THE WORLD (live)** — [39] [ ]
(cd-s+=) *(74321 32940-2)* – ('A'side again) / Get real.
(12") *(74321 32940-1)* – ('A'side) / The seeker / Hang ten high.

Feb 96. (7"pink/c-s) *(74321 35384-7/-4)* **HALLO SPACEBOY. / THE HEARTS FILTHY LESSON** — [12] [ ]
(cd-s+=) *(74321 35384/-2)* – Moonage daydream (live) / Under pressure (live).
below a collaboration with A GUY CALLED GERALD. His main band:- REEVES GABRELS, MIKE GARSON + ZACHARY ALFORD + GAIL ANN DORSEY – vocals

Nov 96. (12"/cd-s) *(74321 39741-1/-2)* **TELLING LIES (mixes; Paradox / Feelgood / Adam F)** — [ ] [-]

Jan 97. (12"/cd-s) *(74321 45207-1/-2)* **LITTLE WONDER. / TELLING LIES (Adam F mix)** — [14] [ ]
(cd-s) *(74321 45208-2)* – ('A'mixes by Junior Vasquez & Danny Saber) / Jump they say (Leftfield mix).

Feb 97. (cd/c) *(<74321 44944-2/-4>)* **EART HL ING** — [6] [39]
– Little wonder / Looking for satellites / Battle for Britain (the letter) / Seven years in Tibet / Dead man walking / Telling lies / Last thing you should do / I'm afraid of Americans / Law (earthlings on fire).

Apr 97. (12"/cd-s) *(74321 47584-1/-2)* **DEAD MAN WALKING. / TELLING LIES** — [32] [ ]
(cd-s) *(74321 47585-2)* – ('A'mixes) / I'm deranged / Heart's filthy lesson.

Aug 97. (12"clear/cd-s) *(74321 51254-7/-2)* **SEVEN YEARS IN TIBET (mixes; Mandarin). / PALLAS ATHENA** — [61] [ ]

Nov 97. (c-s,cd-s) *<38618>* **I'M AFRAID OF AMERICANS /** — [-] [56]
Velvel not iss.

Feb 98. (cd-ep) *(ZYX 87578)* **I CAN'T READ (short & long version) / THIS IS NOT AMERICA** — [73] [-]
Virgin Virgin

Sep 99. (c-s/cd-s) *(VSC/+DT 1753)* **THURSDAY'S CHILD / WE ALL GO THROUGH / NO ONE CALLS** — [16] [-]
(cd-s) *(VSCDTX 1753)* – ('A'-Rock mix) / We shall all go to town / 1917 / ('A'-CD-Rom video).

Oct 99. (cd/c) *(CDV/TCV 2900)* <48157> **HOURS ...** — [5] [47]
– Thursday's child / Something in the air / Survive / If I'm dreaming my life / Seven / What's really happening / Pretty things are going to hell / New angels of promise / Brilliant adventure / Dreamers.

– compilations, etc. –

Note; All below on 'RCA' unless otherwise mentioned

Mar 70. (lp; mono/stereo)(c) Decca; *(PA/SPA 58)(KCSP 58)* **THE WORLD OF DAVID BOWIE** — [ ] [-]
(re-iss. Feb73)

Oct 72. (7"ep) Pye; *(7N 8002)* **DO ANYTHING YOU SAY / CAN'T HELP THINKING ABOUT ME. / I DIG EVERYTHING / I'M NOT LOSING SLEEP** — [ ] [-]

May 75.	(d-lp) Decca; (DPA 3017-8) / London; <628-9> **IMAGES 66-67**		
May 75.	(7") Decca; (F 13579) **THE LONDON BOYS. / LOVE YOU TILL TUESDAY**		-
Mar 79.	(7"ep) E.M.I.; (EMI 2925) **I PITY THE FOOL / TAKE MY TIP. / YOU'VE GOT A HABIT OF LEAVING / BABY LOVES THAT WAY**		
	(re-iss. Nov82 on 'Charly'; CYM 1)		
Dec 80.	(lp/c) K-Tel; (NE/+C 1111) **THE BEST OF DAVID BOWIE**	3	-
Apr 81.	(lp/c) Decca; (TAB/KTAB 17) **ANOTHER FACE**		-
Apr 81.	(lp) (BL 43606) **CHRISTIANE F. – WIR KINDER VOM BAHNHOF ZOO (soundtrack)**	-	- Europe
Jun 81.	(10"m-lp/c) P.R.T.; (DOW/ZCDOW 1) **DON'T BE FOOLED BY THE NAME**		
Dec 82.	(10x7"pic-d-singles) (BOW 100) **FASHIONS** – SPACE ODDITY / LIFE ON MARS / THE JEAN GENIE / REBEL REBEL / SOUND & VISION / DRIVE-IN SATURDAY / SORROW / GOLDEN YEARS / BOYS KEEP SWINGING / ASHES TO ASHES		-
Jan 83.	(lp/c) (PL/PK 45406) **RARE**	34	-
Aug 83.	(lp/c) (BOW LP/K 004) <4792> **GOLDEN YEARS (live recent)**	33	99
Aug 83.	(lp) Decca Rock Echoes; (TAB 71) **A SECOND FACE**		
Oct 83.	(d-lp/d-c) (PL/PK 84862) <4862> **ZIGGY STARDUST – THE MOTION PICTURE (live '73 film)**	17	89
	(cd-iss. Sep92 on 'EMI'; CDP 780411-2)		
Oct 83.	(7") (RCA 372) <13660> **WHITE LIGHT WHITE HEAT (live). / CRACKED ACTOR (live)**	46	
Jan 84.	(7") <13769> **1984. / TVC 15**	-	
Apr 84.	(lp/c/cd) (PL/PK/PD 84919) <4919> **FAME AND FASHION (ALL TIME GREATEST HITS)**	40	
May 84.	(lp/c) Deram; (BOWIE/BOWMC 1) **LOVE YOU TILL TUESDAY (soundtrack)**	53	-
May 85.	(12"ep; by ARNOLD CORNS & THE SPIDERS FROM MARS) Krazy Kat; (PAST 2) **HANG ON TO YOURSELF. / LOOKING FOR A FRIEND / MAN IN THE MIDDLE**		-
Nov 85.	(d-lp/c) Castle; (CCS LP/MC 118) **THE COLLECTION**		-
	(cd-iss. Aug92; CCSCD 118)		
Apr 86.	(lp/c) Showcase; (SHLP/SHTC 137) **RARE TRACKS**		-
Aug 86.	(12"ep) Archive 4; (TOF 105) **ARCHIVE 4** – London boys / Love you till Tuesday / Laughing gnome / Maid of Bond Street.		-
Oct 87.	(m-lp/c/cd) P.R.T.; (PYL/PYM/PYC 6001) **1966: DAVID BOWIE**		-
	(pic-m-lp Jun88; PYX 6001) (re-iss. Dec89 on 'Castle' lp/c/cd; CLA LP/MC/CD 154)		
Jan 89.	(cd) Deram; (820 570-2) **CHAMELEON**		-
Sep 89.	(cd) Rykodisc; <0120> **SOUND + VISION**	-	97
Mar 90.	(c-s/7") EMI-USA; (TC+/FAME 90) **FAME 90 (Gass mix). / ('A'-Queen Latifah's version)**	28	
	(cd-s+=) (CDFAME 90) – ('A'house mix) / ('A'hip mix).		
	(12") (12FAME 90) – ('A'side) / ('A'house) / ('A'hip hop).		
	(7"pic-d) (FAMEPD 90) – ('A'side) / ('A'-bonus beats mix).		
Apr 90.	(cd/c/d-lp) E.M.I.; (CD/TC+/DBTV 1) / Rykodisc; <20171> **CHANGESBOWIE** – Space oddity / John, I'm only dancing / Changes / Ziggy stardust / Suffragette city / The Jean genie / Diamond dogs / Rebel rebel / Young Americans / Fame ('90 remix) / Golden years / Heroes / Ashes to ashes / Fashion / Let's dance / China girl / Modern love / Blue Jean.	1	39
Apr 91.	(cd/c) Rhino; **EARLY ON (1964-66)**	-	
May 93.	(cd/c) Spectrum; (550021-2/-4) **THE GOSPEL ACCORDING TO DAVID BOWIE**		-
Nov 93.	(d-cd/d-c/t-lp) E.M.I.; (7243 828099-2/-4/-1) **THE SINGLES COLLECTION**	9	
	(re-iss. Nov95 d-cd/d-c/t-lp; CD/TC+/EM 1512)		
May 94.	(cd/c/d-lp) Trident; (GY/+MC/LP 002) **SANTA MONICA '72 (live)**	74	-
Jul 95.	(cd) Trident; (GY 014) **RARESTONEBOWIE**		-
Mar 96.	(cd/c) Spectrum; (551706-2/-4) **LONDON BOY**		-
Jun 97.	(cd) O.T.R.; (OTR 1100048) **EARTH CALLING ZIGGY**		-
Aug 97.	(cd) Deram; (844784-2) **THE DERAM ANTHOLOGY 1966-1968**		-
Oct 97.	(cd/c) E.M.I.; (821849-2/-4) **THE BEST OF DAVID BOWIE 1969-1974**	13	
Apr 98.	(cd/c) E.M.I.; (494300-2/-4) **THE BEST OF DAVID BOWIE 1974-1979**	39	-
Nov 98.	(cd) Spectrum; (551706-2) **LONDON BOY**		-
Apr 99.	(cd) Essential; (ESMCD 712) **1966**		-

BOW WOW WOW (dig out; Great Alt & Indie . . .)

BOX TOPS

Formed: Memphis, Tennessee, USA . . . 1967 originally as RONNIE & THE DeVILLES. They signed to 'Bell' label offshoot 'Mala', and with the legendary DANN PENN producing, the band soon topped the US chart with their debut 45, 'THE LETTER', which subsequently became a well covered standard for many artists. Throughout the 60's, they had a large number of hits, with CHILTON virtually taking over the reins just prior to their 1969 demise. CHILTON headed back to Memphis, where he hooked up with his old schoolfriend CHRIS BELL to form the hugely influential but desperately unlucky BIG STAR. The first two albums sounded like a rougher take on the pop sensibilities of The BEATLES and The BEACH BOYS, with the 1972 debut 'NO.1 RECORD', especially, having great commercial potential. Guitarist BELL acted as a foil for CHILTON's inspired outpourings and the album contained such acoustic gems as 'BALLAD OF EL GOODOO'. Despite garnering rave reviews, the album failed to sell, due almost wholly to the distribution problems of their label 'Ardent' (a 'Stax' offshoot). BELL left at the end of '72, after a fallout with CHILTON over live work, the upshot

being that BIG STAR became CHILTON's "power-pop" baby. Generally thought to be his artistic peak, early '74's 'RADIO CITY' had a gloriously raw spontaneity, with 'SEPTEMBER GURLS' proving the pained highlight. Distribution problems continued to dog 'Ardent' and as the record stiffed, BIG STAR gradually broke-up. Although released under the BIG STAR moniker, 'BIG STAR'S THE THIRD ALBUM', later re-released as 'SISTER LOVERS', was more or less the work of CHILTON. A difficult album, although nonetheless rewarding, it showcased a vulnerable man exorcising his demons in haunting and deeply introspective songs. CHRIS BELL's similarly downbeat 'I AM THE COSMOS' was recorded around the time of his death in a car accident in 1978, and was posthumously released by 'Rykodisc' in the early 90's. In 1979, CHILTON re-surfaced after a quiet period in New York, where his makeshift band toured with the likes of TELEVISION and The CRAMPS, whom he went on to produce. That same year saw him record the folk-punk 'BANGKOK' single and 'FLIES ON SHERBET', a cult classic which featured a hotch-potch of inspired covers and CHILTON originals. In the 80's, he worked with TAV FALCO under the name The PANTHER BURNS before releasing a solo album 'HIGH PRIEST' in 1987, a fairly enjoyable romp through a patchwork of ragged styles. The praise lavished upon BIG STAR by the likes of PRIMAL SCREAM and TEENAGE FANCLUB, brought about a renaissance of sorts, and CHILTON re-formed the band in 1993. He also released a further solo album in 1995, 'A MAN CALLED DESTRUCTION'.

Best CD compilation: THE BEST OF THE BOX TOPS (*6)

Other Ratings: #1 RECORD (*7; Big Star) / RADIO CITY (*7; Big Star) / SISTER LOVERS – THIRD ALBUM (*8; Big Star) / LIKE FLIES ON SHERBET (*3; Alex Chilton) / BLACK LIST (*4; Alex Chilton) / 19 YEARS: A COLLECTION compilation (*7; Alex Chilton) / COLUMBIA: LIVE AT MISSOURI UNIVERSITY (*4; Big Star) / CLICHES (*5; Alex Chilton) / A MAN CALLED DESTRUCTION (*3; Alex Chilton)

ALEX CHILTON (b.28 Dec'50) – vocals, guitar / **JOHN EVANS** – organ / **GARY TALLEY** (b.17 Aug'47) – guitar / **BILL CUNNINGHAM** (b.23 Jan'50) – bass, piano / **DANNY SMYTHE** – drums

		Stateside	Mala-Bell	
Sep 67.	(7") (SS 2044) <565> **THE LETTER. / HAPPY TIMES**	5	1	Jul67
Nov 67.	(7") (SS 2070) <580> **NEON RAINBOW. / SHE KNOWS HOW**		24	
Jan 68.	(lp; stereo/mono) (S+/SL 10218) <6011> **THE LETTER – NEON RAINBOW** – The letter / She knows how / Trains & boats & planes / Break my mind / A whiter shade of pale / Everything I am / Neon rainbow / People make the world / I'm your puppet / Happy times / Gonna find somebody / I pray for rain.	87	Nov67	

		Bell	Mala	
Mar 68.	(7") (BLL 1001) <593> **CRY LIKE A BABY. / THE DOOR YOU CLOSED ON ME**	15	2	
Apr 68.	(lp; mono/stereo) (M/S BLL 105) <6017> **CRY LIKE A BABY** – Cry like a baby / Deep in Kentucky / I'm the one for you / Weeping Analeah / Every time / Fields of clover / Trouble with Sam / Lost / Good morning dear / 727 / You keep me hanging on / The door you closed to me.	59		
May 68.	(7") (BLL 1017) <12005> **CHOO CHOO TRAIN. / FIELDS OF CLOVER**		26	

—— **RICK ALLEN** (b.28 Jan'46, Little Rock, Arkansas) – organ, drums repl. EVANS **TOM BOGGS** (b.16 Jul'47, Wynn, Arkansas) – drums repl. SMYTHE (both return to college)

Sep 68.	(7") (BLL 1035) <12017> **I MET HER IN CHURCH. / PEOPLE GONNA TALK**		37	
Oct 68.	(lp; mono/stereo) (M/S BLL 108) <6023> **NON-STOP** – Choo choo train / I'm movin' on / Sandman / She shot a hole in my soul / People gonna talk / I met her in church / Rock me baby / Rollin' in my sleep / I can dig it / Yesterday / Where's my mind / If I had let you in.			
Dec 68.	(lp) <6025> **SUPER HITS** (compilation) – The letter / Trains & boats & planes / Break my mind / A whiter shade of pale / She sot a hole in my soul / Neon rainbow / Cry like a baby / I'm your puppet / I met her in church / You keep me hanging on / Choo choo train. (UK-iss.1970 mono/stereo; M/S BLL 129)	-	45	
Jan 69.	(7") (BLL 1045) <12035> **SWEET CREAM LADIES, FORWARD MARCH. / SANDMAN**		28	Dec68
Mar 69.	(7") (BLL 1063) <12038> **I SHALL BE RELEASED. / I MUST BE THE DEVIL**		67	

—— **JERRY RILEY** – guitar repl. TALLEY

Jul 69.	(7") (BLL 1068) <12040> **SOUL DEEP. / HAPPY SONG**	22	18	
Oct 69.	(7") (BLL 1084) <12042> **TURN ON A DREAM. / TOGETHER**		58	
Oct 69.	(lp) (SBLL 120) <6032> **DIMENSIONS** – Soul deep / I shall be released / Midnight angel / Together / I'll hold out my hand / I must be the Devil / Sweet cream ladies, forward march / The happy song / Ain't no way / Rock me baby.		77	Sep69
Jul 70.	(7") (BLL 1097) <865> **YOU KEEP TIGHTENING UP ON ME. / COME ON HONEY**		92	Mar70

—— CHILTON (now the only original member), ALLEN, BOGGS and RILEY brought in **SWAIN SCHAEFER** – piano / **HAROLD CLOUD** – bass (both) repl. CUNNINGHAM

Sep 71.	(lp) (BELLS 149) **BOX TOPS** – The letter / Cry like a baby / Soul deep / I'm movin' on / Lost / A whiter shade of pale / Together / The happy song / Fields of clover / Weeping Analeah / I'll hold out my hand / I pray for rain.		-

– UK compilations etc. –

Jan 73.	(7") London; (HLU 10402) **SUGAR CREEK WOMAN. / IT'S ALL OVER**		
Jun 74.	(lp) Sound Superb; (SPR 90051) **THE BEST OF THE BOX TOPS**		
May 78.	(7") Stiff; (BUY 28) **CRY LIKE A BABY. / THE LETTER**		
Mar 82.	(7") J.B.; (JB 04) **THE LETTER. / CRY LIKE A BABY**		
Jul 82.	(7") Old Gold; (OG 9116) **THE LETTER. / CRY LIKE A BABY**		
Aug 82.	(7"m) Creole; (CR 178) **THE LETTER. / (2 tracks by other artists)**		

Aug 82. (7"m) *Creole; (CR 179)* **CRY LIKE A BABY. / (2 tracks by other artists)** □ -

1988. (cd) *Warner Super Savers; (WSP 27611)* **THE ULTIMATE BOX TOPS** □ -

Nov 88. (lp) *Decal; (LIK 41)* **THE BEST OF THE BOX TOPS featuring ALEX CHILTON** □ -
– The letter / Neon rainbow / I pray for rain / The door you closed to me / Cry like a baby / Deep in Kentucky / Fields of clover / You keep me hangin' on / Choo choo train / I can dig it / Yesterday where's my mind / Soul deep / I shall be released / Together / I must be the Devil / Sweet cream ladies, forward march / Happy song.

Jun 89. (cd-ep) *Arista; (162071)* **THE LETTER / HAPPY TIMES / CRY LIKE A BABY / THE DOOR YOU CLOSED ON ME** □ -

Jun 99. (cd) *Camden-RCA; (74321 67452-2)* **SOUL DEEP (THE BEST OF THE BOX TOPS)** □ -

BIG STAR

were formed in 1971 by singer/ songwriter/ guitarist **CHRIS BELL** (b.12 Jan'51, Memphis) plus **ALEX CHILTON / ANDY HUMMEL** (b.26 Jan'51) – bass / **JODY STEPHENS** (b. 4 Oct'52) – drums

		not iss.	Ardent
Apr 72.	(lp) *<ADS 1501>* **#1 RECORD**	-	□

– Feel / The ballad of El Goodo / In the street / Don't lie to me / Thirteen / The India song / When my baby's beside me / My life is right / Give me another chance / Try again / Watch the sunrise / St 100-6. *(re-iss. Nov86 & Jan90 on 'Big Beat' lp/c; WIK/+C 53)*

Apr 72. (7") *<2902>* **IN THE STREET. / WHEN MY BABY'S BESIDE ME** - □

Jul 72. (7") *<2904>* **DON'T LIE TO ME. / WATCH THE SUNRISE** - □

—— now trio when BELL left to go solo, He's killed in car crash 27th Dec'78.

Feb 74. (lp) *<ADS 2803>* **RADIO CITY** □ □
– O, my soul / Life is white / Way out west / What's going on / You got what you deserve / Mod Lang / Back of a car / Daisy glaze / She's a mover / September gurls / Morpha too – I'm in love with a girl. *(re-iss. Nov86 & Mar95 on 'Big Beat' lp/c; WIK/+C 54)*

Feb 74. (7") *<2909>* **O, MY SOUL / MORPHATOO – I'M IN LOVE WITH A GIRL** - □

May 74. (7") *<2912>* **SEPTEMBER GURLS. / MOD LANG** - □
(UK-iss.Sep78 on 'Stax'; STAX 504)

1974. (7"; as BOX TOPS) *<0199>* **WILLOBEE AND DALE. / I'M GONNA BE ALRIGHT** - □

—— ALEX CHILTON now sole BIG STAR with session people, incl. STEPHENS + STEVE CROPPER. In 1975, after recording below album, they disbanded. It was finally released.

		Aura	P.V.C.
Jul 78.	(lp) *(AUL 703) <7903>* **BIG STAR'S THE THIRD ALBUM**	□	□

– Stroke it Noel / For you / Kizza me / You can't have me / Nightime / Blue moon / Take care / Jesus Christ / Femme fatale / O Dana / Big black car / Holocaust / Kangaroo / Thank you friends. *(re-iss. 1987 on 'Dojo' lp/cd; DOJO LP/CD 55) <US re-iss. Nov87 lp/c/cd; PVC/+CD 8917> (UK cd-iss. Mar92 & Apr97 on 'Rykodisc'; RCD 10220) (cd re-iss. Oct94 on 'Line'; LICD 900492)*

Jul 78. (7") *(AUS 103)* **KIZZA ME. / DREAM LOVER** □ □

Dec 78. (7") *(AUS 107)* **JESUS CHRIST. / BIG BLACK CAR** □ □

– (BIG STAR) compilations etc. –

Jul 78. (d-lp) *Stax; (SXSP 302)* **#1 RECORD / RADIO CITY** □ □
(cd-iss. Jun87 & Jan90 on 'Big Beat'; CDWIK 910) – (omits; In the street / St 100-6.

1988. (lp) *Line; (LILP 400509)* **BIG STAR'S BIGGEST** - German
– The ballad of El Goodo / In the street / Don't lie to me / When my baby's beside me / Try again / Watch the sunrise / Life is white / What's goin' ahn / Back of a car / She's a mover / Way out west / September gurls / Jesus Christ / O'Dana / Holocaust / Kangaroo / Big black car / Thank you friends. *(UK cd-iss. Oct94; LICD 900509)*

Mar 92. (cd) *Rykodisc; (RCD 10221)* **LIVE** □ □
(re-iss. Apr97; same)

Dec 99. (cd) *Big Beat; (CDWIKK 197)* **THE BEST OF BIG STAR** □ -

ALEX CHILTON

went solo in 1977, with **RICHARD ROSEBROUGH** – drums / etc.

		not iss.	Ork
1977.	(lp) *<81978>* **ONE DAY IN NEW YORK**	-	□
1977.	(12"ep) **SINGER NOT THE SONG**	-	□

		Aura	Peabody
Feb 80.	(lp) *(AUL 710)* **LIKE FLIES ON SHERBET**	□	□

– Boogie shoes / My rival / Hey! little child / Hook or crook / I've had it / Rock hard / Girl after girl / Waltz across Texas / Alligator man / Like flies on sherbet. *(cd-iss. Sep92 on 'Great Expectations' +=;)* – No more the Moon shines on Lorena. *(cd re-iss. Oct94 on 'Line'; LICD 900486) (cd re-iss. Jan96 on 'Cooking Vinyl'; COOKCD 095)*

Jun 80. (7") *(AUS 117)* **HEY! LITTLE CHILD. / NO MORE THE MOON SHINES ON LORENA** □ □

—— with **KNOX** – guitar / **MATTHEW SELIGMAN** – bass + **MORRIS WINDSOR** – drums

		Line	not iss.
1981.	Line; (lp) *<OLLP 5081>* **BACH'S BOTTOM** (rec.1975)	□	- German

– Take me home / Make me like it / Everytime I close my eyes / All of the time / Oh baby I'm free / I'm so tired / Alligator man / Jesus Christ / Free again / The singer not the song / Summertime blues / Take me home again. *(cd-iss. Nov87; LICD 900091) (cd re-iss. Mar97 on 'Razor & Tie'; RE 2010)*

Jan 83. (lp) *(OLLP 5264)* **LIVE IN LONDON (live)** □ □
– Bangkok / Tramp / In the street / Hey little child / Nightime / Rock hard / Alligator man / The letter / Train kept a rollin' / Kanga roo / My rival / Stranded on a dateless night / September gurls / No more the Moon shines on Lorena. *(cd-iss. May93 on 'Rev-Ola'; CREV 015CD)*

		New Rose	Big Time
Jul 85.	(lp) *(ROSE 68)* **FEUDALIST TARTS**	□	- France

(cd-iss. 1986 as 'STUFF'; ROSE 68CD) – (with 10 extra tracks).

May 86. (7") *(NEW 068)* **NO SEX. / UNDERCRASS** - - France
(12"+=) *(NEW12 068)* – Wild kingdom.
(d7"+=) *(NEW 69)* – September gurls / I'm gonna make you mine (live Paris'85).

Nov 87. (7") *(NEW 96)* **MAKE A LITTLE MOVE. / LONELY WEEKENDS** - - France

Nov 87. (lp/c/cd) *(ROSE 130/+C/CD)* **HIGH PRIEST** - - France
– Take it off / Let me get close to you / Dalai Lama * / Volare / Thing for you / Forbidden love / Make a little love / Trouble don't last / Don't be a drag / Nobody's fool / Come by here / Raunchy / Junkyard * / Lonely weekends / Margie * / Rubber room *. *(cd+= *)*

Feb 88. (d7"-ltd) *(NEW 102)* **DALAI LAMA. / MARGIE // JUNKYARD. / RUBBER ROOM** - - France

Jan 90. (m-lp/cd) *(ROSE 194/+CD)* **BLACKLIST** - - France
– Little GTO / Guantanamerika / Jailbait / Baby baby baby / Nice and easy does it / I will turn your money green.
(above cont.some covers). In 1992 CHILTON resurrected BIG STAR (see below).

		New Rose	Ardent
Feb 94.	(cd) **CLICHES**	□	□

		Ruf	Ardent
Jun 95.	(cd) *(RRCD 90131-2)* **A MAN CALLED DESTRUCTION**	□	□

		Shoeshine	not iss.
Oct 96.	(7") *(SHOE 005)* **MARGIE. /**	□	□

– (ALEX CHILTON) compilations etc. –

Sep 85. (lp/cd) *Aura;* **DOCUMENT** □
– Kizza me / Downs / Holocaust / Big black car / Kangaroo / Dream lover / My rival / Hey little child / Hook or crook / Like flies on sherbet / Bangkok / September gurls / In the street.

Mar 86. (d-lp) *Fan Club; (FC 015)* **LOST DECADE (1969-77)** - - France

May 91. (cd) *Rhino;* **19 YEARS (1969-87)** □ -

Feb 92. (cd) *New Rose;* **ALEX CHILTON** □ -

Mar 96. (cd) *Rev-ola; (CREV 044CD)* **1970** □ -

Mar 97. (cd) *Razor & Tie; (RE 2032)* **FEUDALISTIC TARTS / NO SEX** □ -

Mar 97. (cd) *Razor & Tie; (RE 2033)* **HIGH PRIEST / BLACKLIST** □ -

May 97. (d-cd) *Arcade; (302108-2)* **TOP 30** □ -

BIG STAR

—— re-formation with **CHILTON / JONATHAN BAUER** – guitar, vocals / **KEN STRINGFELLOW** – guitar, bass (ex-POSIES)

		Zoo	Zoo
Sep 93.	(cd/c) **LIVE AT MISSOURI UNIVERSITY (4.25.93) (live)**	□	□

– In the street / Don't lie to me / When my baby's beside me / I am the cosmos / The ballad of El Goodo / Back of a car / Way out west / Daisy glaze / Baby strange / For you / Fool / September gurls / Thank you friends / Slut / Jeepster.

—— CHILTON teamed up with VEGA (from SUICIDE) and BEN VAUGHN on album 'CUBIST BLUES' for 'Last Call'; (7422466)

BOY GEORGE

Born: GEORGE O'DOWD, 14 Jun'61, Eltham, Kent, England. Ironically the son of a boxing club manager, GEORGE became a familiar face on London's turn of the decade New Romantic scene, MALCOLM McLAREN even picking him out for a brief tenure in BOW WOW WOW (as LIEUTENANT LUSH) before the cross-dressing gender-bender formed his own outfit, IN PRAISE OF LEMMINGS alongside MIKEY CRAIG and JOHN SUEDE. Wisely, they soon opted for the moniker CULTURE CLUB instead as ex-DAMNED drummer JON MOSS was brought into the fold and ROY HAY replaced SUEDE. After having their demos turned down by 'E.M.I.', the group secured a contract with 'Virgin' in 1982 and proceeded to fire a couple of chart blanks in the shape of 'WHITE BOY' and 'I'M AFRAID OF ME'. Much more potent was 'DO YOU REALLY WANT TO HURT ME', a winning combinaiton of white cod-reggae and candy-coated soul-pop that topped the UK chart and sold millions around the world. Decked out in flowing tunics and striking make-up, the dread-locked BOY GEORGE became an overnight sensation on the still fairly conservative MTV, beguiling fans by sheer force of his charisma and a lilting, sensual vocal style that transformed the often fairly average songs/arrangements. In retrospect, it's still surprising how big America was on CULTURE CLUB, almost putting second single, 'TIME (CLOCK OF THE HEART)' atop the chart at the tail end of '82 and affording a US issue of 'DO YOU REALLY..' the same treatment. The accompanying album, 'KISSING TO BE CLEVER' (1982), went Top 5 in the UK, Top 20 in America, and CULTURE CLUB were ready to take on the world. The following year saw a slew of hits breach the Top 10 on both sides of the Atlantic, 'CHURCH OF THE POISON MIND', 'I'LL TUMBLE 4 YA' and the evergreen 'KARMA CHAMELEON', a transatlantic No.1. All three were lifted from sophomore effort, 'COLOUR BY NUMBERS' (1983), female backing vocalist HELEN TERRY adding an extra dimension to the established sound. After hitting such stratospheric peaks, however, the only way was down; as a sweetener for third album, 'WAKING UP WITH THE HOUSE ON FIRE' (1984), 'WAR SONG' left a sour taste in the mouth, at least for critics, who derided the sanctimonious inanity of its anti-war "message". Although both single and album made the No.2 position in the UK (they were already beginning to flag across the pond), a second single, 'THE MEDAL SONG', didn't even make the Top 30. The band's final two years were characterised by BOY GEORGE's worsening drug addiction and inter-band tension, their final album, 'FROM LUXURY TO HEARTACHE' (1986), drawing enthusiasm from only the most ardent of fans. The shit really hit the fan(s) later that summer when GEORGE's heroin problem had the tabloids sharpening their claws. He was easy prey, especially after being arrested for possession of cannabis. If that wasn't bad enough, keyboard player, MIKE RUDETSKI was found dead from a drugs overdose in GEORGE's house only days later. Amid the scandal, CULTURE CLUB officially split in Spring '87 with GEORGE pursuing a solo career. Although his first effort – a tame cover of 'EVERYTHING I OWN' – topped the chart, successive singles met with diminishing returns and the album, 'SOLD' (1987), barely scraped the Top 30. 'Virgin' kept the faith though, furnishing the man with his own label, 'More Protein'. This functioned as a platform for his new project, JESUS LOVES YOU, (re)born of GEORGE's newfound interest in the Hare Krishna religion. Surprisingly, perhaps, some of his most interesting compositions surfaced during this period, not least the acid-house influenced 'GENERATIONS OF LOVE' and the joyous 'BOW DOWN MISTER', which gave him a rare Top 30 hit in Spring '91. Having finally come to terms with his drug problem, GEORGE became increasingly focused on DJ'ing, making a name for himself on the burgeoning UK club scene. Save for a genius one-off cover of Dave Berry's 'THE CRYING GAME' (featured on the brilliant UK film of the same name) in 1992, it would be the mid-90's before the veteran star released another solo album, 'Virgin' once again home for the largely ignored 'CHEAPNESS AND BEAUTY' (1995). Over the course of the next few years, GEORGE concentrated on DJ'ing and made his name as a top draw for many of the "superclubs", signing a lucrative deal with 'Ministry Of Sound' in Spring '96. A year on, his long drawn-out court battle with former "mate" KIRK BRANDON (ex-SPEAR OF DESTINY) came to an end when the judge dismissed BRANDON's objections to GEORGE's published comments regarding their former relationship. It was inevitable that GEORGE and his former CULTURE CLUB bandmates would make up, the lure of the lucre tempting the band to re-form in summer 1998 for massive sell-out concerts in Monte Carlo and America. A new single, 'I JUST WANNA BE LOVED', subsequently hit the UK Top 5 which prompted 'Virgin' to re-package their greatest hits in lieu of a flop new album, 'DON'T MIND IF I DO' (1999). • Songwriters: All written by GEORGE and HAY except STARMAN (David Bowie). GEORGE solo covered EVERYTHING I OWN (Bread; hit. Ken Boothe) / WHAT BECOMES OF THE BROKEN HEARTED (Jimmy Ruffin) / THE CRYING GAME (Dave Berry) / MY SWEET LORD (George Harrison) / FUNTIME (Iggy Pop) and co-wrote with DUST & THEWLIS. • Trivia: In 1988, BOY GEORGE protested about the 'CLAUSE 28' law which the government used to ban homosexual literature. In 1989, he duetted with CONNIE FRANCIS on a version of Frank & Nancy Sinatra's 'Something Stupid'.

Album rating: Culture Club: KISSING TO BE CLEVER (*7) / COLOUR BY NUMBERS (*6) / WAKING UP WITH THE HOUSE ON FIRE (*5) / FROM LUXURY TO HEARTACHE (*4) / THIS TIME: THE FIRST 4 YEARS compilation (*7) / THE BEST OF CULTURE CLUB compilation (*6) / GREATEST MOMENTS compilation (*6) / DON'T MIND IF I DO (*5) / Boy George: SOLD (*4) / HIGH HAT (*3) / THE DEVIL IN SISTER GEORGE mini (*4) / CHEAPNESS AND BEAUTY (*3) / AT WORST . . . THE BEST OF BOY GEORGE & CULTURE CLUB compilation (*6) / Jesus Loves You: THE MARTYR MANTRAS (*4)

CULTURE CLUB

BOY GEORGE – vocals / **ROY HAY** (b.12 Aug'61) – guitar, keyboards (ex-RUSSIAN BOUQUET) repl. JOHN SUEDE / **MIKEY CRAIG** (b.15 Feb'60) – bass / **JON MOSS** (b.11 Sep'57) – drums, percussion (ex-EDGE, ex-DAMNED)

		Virgin	Epic
May 82.	(7"/12") (VS 496/+12) **WHITE BOY. / LOVE TWIST**		
Jun 82.	(7"/12") (VS 509/+12) **I'M AFRAID OF ME. / MURDER RAP TRAP**		
Sep 82.	(7"/7"pic-d) (VS/+Y 518) **DO YOU REALLY WANT TO HURT ME. / (dub version)**	1	-
	(12"+=) (VS 518-12) – Love is cold (you were never so good).		
Oct 82.	(lp/c) (V/TCV 2232) <38398> **KISSING TO BE CLEVER**	5	14 Dec82
	– White boy / You know I'm not crazy / I'll tumble 4 ya / Take control / Love twist / Boy boy (I'm the boy) / I'm afraid of me (remix) / White boys can't control it / Do you really want to hurt me. (re-iss. 1987 lp/c; OVED/+C 209) (cd-iss. Jul87; CDV 2232) (cd re-iss. Oct96 on 'Virgin-VIP'; CDVIP 158)		
Nov 82.	(7"/7"pic-d) (VS/+Y 558) **TIME (CLOCK OF THE HEART). / WHITE BOYS CAN'T CONTROL IT**	3	-
	(12"+=) (VS 558-12) – Romance beyond the alphabet.		
Nov 82.	(7") <03368> **DO YOU REALLY WANT TO HURT ME. / YOU KNOW I'M NOT CRAZY**	-	2
	(12") – ('A'side) / Love is cold (you were never so good.)		
Apr 83.	(7") <03796> **TIME (CLOCK OF THE HEART). / ROMANCE BEYOND THE ALPHABET**	-	2
–––	added guest vocalist HELEN TERRY in '83		
Apr 83.	(7"/7"pic-d) (VS/+Y 571) **CHURCH OF THE POISON MIND. / MAN SHAKE**	2	-
	(12"+=) (VS 571-12) – Mystery boy.		
Jun 83.	(7") <03912> **I'LL TUMBLE 4 YA. / MYSTERY BOY**	-	9
	(12"+=) - Man shake.		
Sep 83.	(7"/7"pic-d) (VS/+Y 612) <04221> **KARMA CHAMELEON. / THAT'S THE WAY**	1	1 Nov83
	(12") – ('A'side) / I'll tumble 4 ya.		
Oct 83.	(7") <04144> **CHURCH OF THE POISONED MIND. / MYSTERY BOY**	-	10
Oct 83.	(lp/c/cd/pic-lp) (V/TCV/CDV/VP 2285) <39107> **COLOUR BY NUMBERS**	1	2
	– Karma chameleon / It's a miracle / Black money / Changing every day / That's the way (I'm only trying to help you) / Church of the poison mind / Miss me blind / Mister man / Stormkeeper* / Victims. (c+=*/cd+=*) (re-iss. 1989 lp/c; OVED/+C 238) (cd re-iss. Feb92; CDV 2285) (cd re-iss. Dec98 on 'Virgin-VIP'; CDVIP 230)		
Nov 83.	(7"/7"pic-d) (VS/+Y 641) **VICTIMS. / COLOUR BY NUMBERS**	3	-
	(12"+=) (VS 641-12) – Romance revisited.		

		Virgin	Epic
Feb 84.	(7") <04388> **MISS ME BLIND. / COLOUR BY NUMBERS**	-	5
Mar 84.	(7"/7"pic-d) (VS/+Y 662) <04457> **IT'S A MIRACLE. / LOVE TWIST (live)**	4	13 May84
	(12"+=) (VS 662-12) – Miss me blind.		
Sep 84.	(7",7"red) (VS 694) <04638> **THE WAR SONG. / LA CANCION DE GUERRA**	2	17
	(12"+=) (VS 694-12) – ('A'-Shriek mix).		
Oct 84.	(lp/c/cd/pic-lp) (V/TCV/CDV/VP 2330) <39881> **WAKING UP WITH THE HOUSE ON FIRE**	2	26 Nov84
	– Dangerous man / The war song / Unfortunate thing / Crime time / Mistake No.3 / The dive / The medal song / Don't talk about it / Mannequin / Hello goodbye. (re-iss. Jun88 lp/c; OVED/+C 184) (cd re-iss. Aug98 on 'Virgin-VIP'; CDVIP 205)		
Nov 84.	(7"/7"pic-d)(ext.12") (VS/+Y 730)(VS 730-12) **THE MEDAL SONG. / DON'T GO DOWN THAT STREET**	32	-
Nov 84.	(7") <04727> **MISTAKE NO.3. / DON'T GO DOWN THAT STREET**	-	33
Mar 86.	(7"/5"pic-d) (VS/+X 845) <05847> **MOVE AWAY. / SEXUALITY**	7	12
	(12"+=) (VS 845-12) – ('A'-Tango dub remix).		
Apr 86.	(lp/c/cd) (V/TC/CDV 2380) <40345> **FROM LUXURY TO HEARTACHE**	10	32
	– Move away / I pray / Work on me baby / Gusto blusto / Heaven's children / Thank God you woman / Reasons / Too bad / Come clean / Sexuality. (c+=) – Move away (remix) / Thank God you woman (remix). (cd++=) – Sexuality (remix). (re-iss. 1989 lp/c; OVED/+C 251)		
May 86.	(7"/7"pic-d)(12") (VS/+Y 861)(VS 861-12) **THANK GOD YOU WOMAN. / FROM LUXURY TO HEARTACHE**	31	
–––	split in the Autumn of '86. MOSS formed HEARTBEAT UK while BOY GEORGE went solo		

BOY GEORGE

––– solo although backed by WELL RED

		Virgin	Virgin
Feb 87.	(7") (BOY 100) **EVERYTHING I OWN. / USE ME**	1	
	('A'-P.W. Botha mix; 12"+=) (BOY 100-12) – ('A'dub).		
May 87.	(7") (BOY 101) **KEEP ME IN MIND. / STATE OF LOVE**	29	
	(ext; 12") (BOY 101-12) – I pray.		
	(c-s+=/12"pic-d=) (BOY C/Z 101-12) – Everything I own.		
Jun 87.	(cd/c/lp) (CD/TC+/V 2430) <90617> **SOLD**	29	Jul87
	– Sold / I asked for love / Keep me in mind / Everything I own / Freedom / Just ain't enough / Where are you now? / Little ghost / Next time / We've got the right / To be reborn. (cd re-iss. Aug98 on 'Virgin-VIP'; CDVIP 204)		
Jul 87.	(7") (BOY 102) **SOLD. / ARE YOU TOO AFRAID**	24	
	(12"+=/c-s+=) (BOY/+C 102-12) – Everything I own (go-go mix).		
Nov 87.	(7") (BOY 103) **TO BE REBORN. / WHERE ARE YOU NOW?**	13	
	(12"+=) (BOY 103-12) –		
Feb 88.	(7") (BOY 105) <99390> **LIVE MY LIFE. / ('A'-Soul remix)**	62	40 Dec87
	(12"+=) (BOY 105-12) – ('A'-Klub mix).		
	(12"+=) (BOY 105-13) – ('A'-Business mix) / ('A'-12"club).		
Jun 88.	(7") (BOY 106) **NO CLAUSE 28. / ('A'mix)**	57	
	(ext; 12"+=/cd-s+=) (BOY 106-12/CD 106) – ('A'-beats mix).		
	(12"+=) (BOY 106-13) – ('A'-Emilio Pasquez space mix).		
Sep 88.	(7") (BOY 107) **DON'T CRY. / LEAVE IN LOVE**		
	(12"+=) (BOY 107-12) – ('A'&'B' versions).		
	(cd-s+=) (BOYCD 107) – ('A'&'B' versions) / A boy called Alice.		
Feb 89.	(7") (BOY 108) **DON'T TAKE MY MIND ON A TRIP. / GIRLFRIEND**	68	
	(12"+=)(3"cd-s+=) (BOY 108-12)(BOYCD 108) – I go where I go.		
Mar 89.	(cd/c/lp) (CD/TC+/V 2555) <91022> **HIGH HAT**		
	– Don't cry / You are my heroin / I go where I go / Girl, with combination skin / Whisper / Something strange called love / I love you / Mama never knew / What becomes of the broken hearted. (c+=/cd+=) – American boys / Happy family. (above was the withdrawn 'TENSE NERVOUS HEADACHE' set from last Oct)		
–––	BOY GEORGE formed		

JESUS LOVES YOU

		More Protein	not iss.
Nov 89.	(7") (PROT 2) **AFTER THE LOVE. / ('A'version)**	68	-
	(12"+=)(cd-s+=) (PROT 2-12)(PROCD 2) – ('A'version).		
Jun 90.	(7"/c-s) (PRO T/C 5) **GENERATIONS OF LOVE. / ('A'dub version)**		
	(12"+=)(cd-s+=) (PROT 5-12)(PROCD 5) – ('A'-Sisters Of Mercy mix).		
Nov 90.	(7"/c-s) (PRO T/C 7) **ONE ON ONE. / ('A'-Massive mix)**		-
	(12"+=) (PROT 7-12) – Generations of love (90's mix).		
	(cd-s++=) (PROCD 7) – After the love.		
Feb 91.	(7"/c-s) (PRO T/C 8) **BOW DOWN MISTER. / LOVE HURTS**	27	-
	(12"+=) (PROT 8-12) – ('A'-different mix).		
	(cd-s+=) (PROCD 8) – ('A'-different mix).		
Apr 91.	(cd/c/lp) (CUM CD/TC/LP 1) **THE MARTYR MANTRAS**	60	-
	– Generations of love / One on one / Love's gonna let you down / After the love / I specialize in loneliness / No clause 28 / Love hurts / Siempre te amare / Too much love / Bow down mister. (cd+=) – Generations of love (90's mix).		
May 91.	(7") (PROT 10) **GENERATIONS OF LOVE. / ('A'mix)**	35	-
	(12"+=) (PROT 10-12) – ('A'-Love dub mix).		
	(cd-s++=) (PROCD 10) – ('A'-different mixes).		
	(re-iss. 12" Aug96; PROT 115)		
Sep 91.	(7") (PROT 10) **AFTER THE LOVE '91. / ('A'version)**		
	(cd-s+=) – ('A'diff edit) / ('A'-10 glorious years mix).		

BOY GEORGE

		Spaghetti	S.B.K.
Sep 92.	(7"/c-s) (CIOA 6/+C) **THE CRYING GAME. / I SPECIALIZE IN LONELINESS**	22	
	(12"+=/cd-s+=) – ('A'extended dance mix).		

		Virgin	Virgin
Feb 93.	(c-s/cd-s) <50437> **THE CRYING GAME.** / (the original Dave Berry version)	-	15

		Virgin	Virgin
Nov 92.	(7"/c-s; by JESUS LOVES YOU) (VS/+C 1449) **SWEET TOXIC THING. / AM I LOSING CONTROL**	65	

(12"+=/cd-s+=) (VST/VSCDX 1449) – ('B'-Dizzy tequila mix) / Oh Lord.

—— In Jun'93, GEORGE was credited on the UK hit single, 'More Than Likely' with PM DAWN

Mar 95.	(7"/c-s) (VS/+C 1538) **FUNTIME. / GENOCIDE PEROXIDE**	45	-

(12"+=/cd-s+=) (VST/VSCDG 1538) – ('A'mixes).

May 95.	(cd/c/lp) (CD/V+/V 2780) **CHEAPNESS AND BEAUTY**	44	

– Funtime / Satans butterfly ball / Sad / God don't hold a grudge / Genocide peroxide / If I could fly / Same thing in reverse / Cheapness and beauty / Evil is so civilised / Blind man / Your love is what I am / Unfinished business / Il adore. (cd re-iss. Aug98 on 'Virgin-VIP'; CDVIP 203)

Jun 95.	(c-s) (VSC 1543) **IL ADORE / THESE BOOTS ARE MADE FOR WALKING**	50	

(cd-s+=) (VSCDX 1543) – Sad / ('A'mixes).
(cd-s) (VSCDD 1543) – ('A'side) / Cheapness and beauty.

Sep 95.	(c-s) (VSC 1561) **SAME THING IN REVERSE / ('A'-Evolution radio screamer mix)**	56	

(cd-s+=) (VSCDT 1561) – ('A'-Evolution brick in my hand mix) / ('A'-Clubzone).
(12") (VST 1561) – (2 'A'-Clubzone mixes) / (2 'A'-Evolution mixes).

		More Protein	not iss.
Apr 96.	(c-s) (PROC 112) **SAD / SATAN'S BUTTERFLY BALL**		-

(cd-s+=/12"+=) (PRO CD/T 112) – ('A'+'B'mixes).

CULTURE CLUB

—— re-formed original line-up for apparently one new song

		Virgin	Virgin
Oct 98.	(c-s/cd-s) (VSC/+DT 1710) **I JUST WANNA BE LOVED / DO YOU REALLY WANT TO HURT ME (mixes)**	4	
Nov 98.	(cd/c) (CDVX/TCV 2865) **GREATEST MOMENTS** (compilation)	21	

– Do you really want to hurt me / Time (clock of the heart) / Church of the poisoned mind / Karma chameleon / Victims / I'll tumble 4 ya / It's a miracle / Miss me blind / Move away / Love is love / Everything I own / The crying game / I just wanna be loved / Generations of love (the Timewriter bootleg mix).

Jul 99.	(c-s/cd-s) (VSC/+DT 1736) **YOUR KISSES ARE CHARITY / ('A'mixes)**	25	

(cd-s) (VSCDX 1736) – ('A'side) / Do you really want to hurt me (Kinky Disco mix) / Time (clock of the heart) (Quivver's Amityville mix).

Nov 99.	(c-s) (VSC 1758) **COLD SHOULDER / STARMAN**	43	

(cd-s+=) (VSCDT 1758) – Your kisses are charity.

Nov 99.	(cd/c) (CDV/TCV 2887) **DON'T MIND IF I DO**	64	

– I just wanna be loved / Cold shoulder / Maybe I'm a fool / Sign language / Mirror / Black comedy / Your kisses are charity / Weep for the child / See thru / Strange voodoo / Truth behind the smile / Fat cat / Confidence trick / Starman / Less than perfect.

– compilations, etc. –

Apr 87.	(lp/c/cd) Virgin; (VTV/VTVC/CDVTV 1) **THIS TIME: THE FIRST FOUR YEARS**	8	-

– Do you really want to hurt me / Move away / I'll tumble 4 ya / Love is love / Victims / Karma chameleon / Church of the poison mind / Miss me blind / Time (clock of the heart) / It's a miracle / Black money / The war song. (cd+=) – I'll tumble 4 ya (US 12"remix) / Miss me blind (US 12"remix). (c re-iss. Apr92; OVEDC 435)

Nov 88.	(7") Old Gold; (OG 9816) **DO YOU REALLY WANT TO HURT ME. / I'LL TUMBLE 4 YA**		

(Feb89; 12"+=) OG 4101) – Time (clock of the heart).

Nov 88.	(7") Old Gold; (OG 9822) **KARMA CHAMELEON. / IT'S A MIRACLE**		

(Mar89; 12"+=) (OG 4107) – Miss me blind.

Nov 88.	(7") Old Gold; (OG 9832) **CHURCH OF THE POISON MIND. / VICTIMS**	-	-

Sep 89.	(lp/c/cd) VIP-Virgin; (VVIP/+C/D 102) **THE BEST OF CULTURE CLUB**	-	-

(re-iss. Oct94 cd/c; CD/TC VIP 102)

Sep 93.	(cd/c/lp) Virgin; (VT CD/TC/LP 19) / S.B.K.; <39014> **AT WORST... THE BEST OF BOY GEORGE & CULTURE CLUB**	26	Nov93

– CULTURE CLUB: Do you really want to hurt me / Time (clock of the heart) / Church of the poisoned mind / Karma chameleon / Victims / I'll tumble 4 ya / It's a miracle / Miss me blind / Move away / BOY GEORGE or JESUS LOVES YOU: Love is love / Love hurts / Everything I own / Don't cry / After the love / More likely / The crying game / Generations of love (La la gone gaga mix) / Bow down mister (a small portion 28 polite mix) / Sweet toxic love (Deliverance mix).

Mar 94.	(m-cd/m-lp) Virgin; (VSCDG/VST 1490) **THE DEVIL IN SISTER GEORGE EP**	26	-

– Miss me blind / Generations of love / Am I losing control / Love hurts / Everything I own.

May 94.	(cd/c) VIP-Virgin; (CD/TC VIP 116) **COLLECT 12" MIXES PLUS**		-
Jul 99.	(d-cd) Disky; (HR 85774-2) **ORIGINAL GOLD**		-
Sep 99.	(cd; by BOY GEORGE) Back Door; (BDCD 01) **UNRECOUPABLE ONE MAN BANDIT 1996-1998**		-

BOYS NEXT DOOR (see under ⇒ CAVE, Nick)

Billy BRAGG

Born: STEVEN WILLIAM BRAGG, 20 Dec'57, Barking, Essex, England. Inspired by The CLASH, he formed Peterborough-based R&B/punk band, RIFF RAFF, in 1977. After releasing a string of indie 7" singles, (including the wonderfully titled 'I WANNA BE A COSMONAUT'), the band split in 1981,

BILLY incredibly going off to join the army. Thankfully, a career in the military wasn't to be though, and he bought himself out after only 90 days. Complete with amplifier and guitar, he busked around Britain, finally furnished with some studio time in 1983 courtesy of 'Charisma' indie subsidiary, 'Utility'. The result was 'LIFE'S A RIOT WITH SPY VS SPY', and with the help and distribution of new label 'Go! Discs', the record finally hit the UK Top 30 in early '84. BRAGG's stark musical backdrop (for the most part, a roughly strummed electric guitar) and even starker vocals, belied a keen sense of melody and passionate, deeply humane lyrics. 'THE MILKMAN OF HUMAN KINDNESS' was a love song of the most compassionate variety which illustrated that BRAGG approached politics from a humanist perspective rather than a soapbox. After seeing firsthand how Thatcher had decimated mining communities, BRAGG's songs became more overtly political. 'BREWING UP WITH BILLY BRAGG' (1984) opened with the fierce 'IT SAYS HERE', but again the most affecting moments were to be found on heartfelt love songs like the wistful 'ST. SWITHIN'S DAY'. It would be another two years before he released a new album, in the interim taking time to make his Top Of The Pops debut and play a lead role in the 'Red Wedge' campaign. A well intentioned but ultimately hopeless initiative to persuade people to vote Labour, BRAGG toured alongside The STYLE COUNCIL, MADNESS, The COMMUNARDS and MORRISSEY. As the Conservatives romped home to another sickening victory, BRAGG licked his wounds and bounced back with a third album, 'TALKING WITH THE TAXMAN ABOUT POETRY' (1986). His most successful and accomplished release to date, the record spawned the classic single, 'LEVI STUBBS' TEARS' as well as the JOHNNY MARR collaboration, 'GREETINGS TO THE NEW BRUNETTE'. And of course, who could argue with the sentiments of 'HELP SAVE THE YOUTH OF AMERICA'?! Not content with saving our transatlantic cousins, BRAGG also did his bit for kids back in Blighty. Recording a cover of 'SHE'S LEAVING HOME' with CARA TIVEY, BRAGG found himself at No.1 when the song was released as the B-side to WET WET WET's cover of 'WITH A LITTLE HELP FROM MY FRIENDS', the not inconsiderable proceeds going to the Childline charity. BRAGG's next album, 'WORKER'S PLAYTIME' (1988), saw a move away from the sparse accompaniment of old, while lyrically the record focused more on matters of the heart than the ballot box. 'THE INTERNATIONALE' (1990), meanwhile, was BRAGG's most political work to date, with the likes of 'NICARAGUITA' and 'THE RED FLAG'. On 'DON'T TRY THIS AT HOME' (1991), BRAGG enlisted a cast of musicians to flesh out the sound, a tactic that elicited mixed results. His stance with CND and anti-apartheid, anti-poll tax, etc, has often seen him on wrong side of the law. In 1998, BILLY and the alt-country group WILCO decided to do a tribute album dedicated to their dustbowl hero, WOODY GUTHRIE. 'MERMAID AVENUE' (a street in Coney Island where WOODY lived with his family in the late 40's and early 50's) was the title, the lyrics seemingly found in an attic while messers BRAGG and WILCO set them to tunes. Also noted was the track, 'CALIFORNIA STARS', which featured guest vocals via NATALIE MERCHANT.

• **Covered:** WALK AWAY RENEE (Four Tops) / SHE'S LEAVING HOME + REVOLUTION (Beatles) / JEANE (Smiths) / SEVEN AND SEVEN IS (Love) / THERE IS POWER IN A UNION (trad.new words) / THINK AGAIN (Dick Gaughan) / CHILE YOUR WATERS RUN RED THROUGH SOWETO (B.Johnson Reagan) / TRAIN TRAIN (Z.Delfeur) / DOLPHINS (Fred Neil) / EVERYWHERE (Sid Griffin-Greg Trooper) / JERUSALEM (William Blake) / WHEN WILL I SEE YOU AGAIN (Three Degrees) / NEVER HAD NO ONE EVER (Smiths).

Album rating: LIFE'S A RIOT WITH SPY VS. SPY mini (*7) / BREWING UP WITH BILLY BRAGG (*8) / TALKING WITH THE TAXMAN ABOUT POETRY (*8) / BACK TO BASICS compilation (*7) / WORKERS PLAYTIME (*7) / THE INTERNATIONALE (*5) / DON'T TRY THIS AT HOME (*8) / WILLIAM BLOKE (*7) / BLOKE ON BLOKE (*6) / MERMAID AVENUE (*8; with Wilco) / REACHING TO THE CONVERTED (MINDING THE GAPS) collection (*7)

RIFF RAFF

(BILLY BRAGG – vocals, guitar) and other members

		Chiswick	not iss.
May 78.	(7"ep) (SW 34) **I WANNA BE A COSMONAUT**		-

– Cosmonaut / Romford girls / What's the latest? / Sweet as pie.

		Geezer	not iss.
Oct 80.	(7") (GZ 1) **EVERY GIRL AN ENGLISH ROSE. / U SHAPED HOUSE**		-
Oct 80.	(7") (GZ 2) **KITTEN. / FANTOCIDE**		-
Oct 80.	(7") (GZ 3) **LITTLE GIRLS KNOW. / SHE DON'T MATTER**		-
Oct 80.	(7") (GZ 4) **NEW HOME TOWN. / RICHARD**		-

BILLY BRAGG

went solo

		Utility	not iss.
Jun 83.	(m-lp) (UTIL 1) **LIFE'S A RIOT WITH SPY VS. SPY**	30	-

– The milkman of human kindness / To have and have not / A new England / The man in the iron mask / The busy girl buys beauty / Lover's town revisited / Richard. (re-iss. Jan84 on 'Go! Discs' lp/c; UTIL/+C 1) (cd-iss. Sep96 on 'Cooking Vinyl'; COOKCD 106)

—— added for back-up **KENNY CRADDOCK** – organ / **DAVE WOODHEAD** – trumpet

		Go! Discs	Elektra
Oct 84.	(lp/c) (A/Z GOLP 4) **BREWING UP WITH BILLY BRAGG**	16	

– It says here / Love gets dangerous / The myth of trust / From a Vauxhall Velox / The Saturday boy / Island of no return / St. Swithin's Day / Like soldiers do / This guitar says sorry / Strange things happen / A lover sings. (cd-iss. Sep96 on 'Cooking Vinyl'; COOKCD 107)

Feb 85. (7") **ST. SWITHIN'S DAY. / A NEW ENGLAND**   `-`   `-` Euro
Mar 85. (7"ep) *(AGOEP 1)* **BETWEEN THE WARS**   `15`   `-`
– Between the wars / Which side are you on? / World turned upside down / It says here.
Dec 85. (7"m) *(GOD 8)* **DAYS LIKE THESE. / I DON'T NEED THIS PRESSURE RON / SCHOLARSHIP IS THE ENEMY OF ROMANCE**   `43`   `-`

—— + guests **JOHNNY MARR** – guitar / **KIRSTY MacCOLL** – b.vocals / **KENNY JONES** – drums, co-producer / **JOHN PORTER** – bass, co-producer / **SIMON MORTEON** – percussion / **BOBBY VALENTINO** – violin

Jun 86. (7"m) *(GOD 12)* **LEVI STUBBS' TEARS. / THINK AGAIN / WALK AWAY RENEE**   `29`   `-`
(12"+=) *(GODX 12)* – Between the wars (live).
Sep 86. (lp/c) *(A/Z GOLP 6)* **TALKING WITH THE TAXMAN ABOUT POETRY**   `8`   `☐`
– Greetings to the new brunette / Train train / The marriage / Ideology / Levi Stubbs' tears / Honey, I'm a big boy now / There is power in a union / Help save the youth of America / Wishing the days away / The passion / The warmest room / The home front. *(cd-iss. May87; AGOCD 6)* *(cd re-iss/Sep96 on 'Cooking Vinyl'; COOKCD 108)*
Nov 86. (7"m) *(GOD 15)* **GREETINGS TO THE NEW BRUNETTE. / DEPORTEES / THE TATLER**   `58`   `-`
(12"+=) *(GODX 15)* – Jeane / There is power in a union (instrumental).

—— Oct'87, BRAGG is credited with OYSTER BAND backing **LEON ROSSELSON** on his single **BALLAD OF A SPYCATCHER** (Upside Down records).

—— May'88, he's credited with **CARA TIVEY** on 45 **SHE'S LEAVING HOME** the B-side of **WET WET WET** – With A little Help From My Friends. This UK No.1 single issued on 'Childline' gave all proceeds to children's charity, with backing including his usual friends.

Go! Discs   Elektra
May 88. (12"ep/cd-ep) *(A/ZA GOLP 1)* <960-787-2> **HELP SAVE THE YOUTH OF AMERICA (LIVE AND DUBIOUS)**   `☐`   `☐`
– Help save the youth of America / Think again / Chile your waters run red through Soweto / Days like these (DC mix) / To have and have not / There is power in a union (with The PATTERSONS).
Aug 88. (7"m) *(GOD 23)* **WAITING FOR THE GREAT LEAP FORWARD. / WISHING THE DAYS AWAY / SIN CITY**   `52`   `☐`
Sep 88. (lp/c/cd) *(AGOLP/ZGOLP/AGOCD 15)* <60824> **WORKER'S PLAYTIME**   `17`   `☐`
– She's got a brand new spell / Must I paint you a picture / The price I pay / Little timb-bomb / Rotting on demand / Valentine's day is over / Life with the lions / The only one / The short answer / Waiting for the great leap forward. *(cd re-iss. Sep96 on 'Cooking Vinyl'; COOKCD 109)*
Nov 88. (7") *(GOD 24)* **SHE'S GOT A BRAND NEW SPELL. / MUST I PAINT YOU A PICTURE**   `☐`   `-`

—— In Jul'89, BRAGG was credited on a NORMAN COOK Top 30 single 'Won't Talk About it'.
May 90. (m-lp/m-c/m-cd; on 'Utility') *(UTIL/+C/CD 011)* **THE INTERNATIONALE**   `34`   `☐`
– The internationale / I dreamed I saw Phil Ochs last night / The marching song of the convent battalions / Jerusalem / Nicaraguita / The red flag / My youngest son came home today.

—— still holding on to **MARR, MacCOLL, TIVEY** (keyboards) and WOODHEAD plus **WIGGY** – guitar, bass / **J.F.T. HOOD** – drums / **AMANDA VINCENT** – keyboards / etc.
Jun 91. (7") *(GOD 56)* **SEXUALITY. / BAD PENNY**   `27`   `☐`
(12"+=/cd-s+=) *(GOD X/CD 56)* – (2 'A'mixes).
Aug 91. (7") *(GOD 60)* **YOU WOKE UP MY NEIGHBOURHOOD. / ONTARIO, QUEBEC AND ME**   `54`   `☐`
(12"+=/cd-s+=) *(GOD X/CD 60)* – Bread and circuses / Heart like a wheel.
(above single 'A'featured **MICHAEL STIPE and PETER BUCK (R.E.M.)** with first 12"extra track with **NATALIE MERCHANT** (10,000 MANIACS) – also backing vocals
Sep 91. (cd/c/d-lp)(8x7"box) *(828279-2/-4/-1)* **DON'T TRY THIS AT HOME**   `8`   `☐`
– Accident waiting to happen / Moving the goalposts / Everywhere / Cindy of a thousand lives / You woke up my neighbourhood / Trust / God's footballer / The few / Sexuality / Mother of the bride / Tank park salute / Dolphins / North sea bubble / Rumours of war / Wish you were here / Body of water. *(re-iss. Nov93 & Apr98 on 'Cooking Vinyl' lp/c/cd; COOK/+C/CD 062)* *(cd re-iss. Sep96; COOKCD 110)*
Feb 92. (7"ep) *(GOD 67)* **ACCIDENT WAITING TO HAPPEN (Red Star version) / SULK. / THE WARMEST ROOM (live) / REVOLUTION**   `33`   `-`
(12"+=/cd-s+=) *(GOD X/CD 67)* – ('A'live version) / Levi Stubbs' tears / Valentine's day is over / North Sea bubble.

Cooking Vinyl   Elektra
Aug 96. (7"/c-s) *(FRY/+C 051)* **UPFIELD / THATCHERITES**   `46`   `☐`
(cd-s+=) *(FRYCD 051)* – Rule nor reason.
Sep 96. (lp/c/cd) *(COOK/+C/CD 100)* **WILLIAM BLOKE**   `16`   `☐`
– From red to blue / Upfield / Everybody loves you babe / Sugardaddy / A Pict song / Brickbat / The space race is over / Northern industrial town / The fourteenth of February / King James version / Goalhanger.
May 97. (7") *(FRY 064)* **THE BOY DONE GOOD. / SUGARDADDY**   `55`   `☐`
(cd-s+=) *(FRYCD 064)* – Just one victory / Qualifications.
(cd-s+=) *(FRYCDX 064)* – Never had no one ever / Run out of reasons.
Jun 97. (cd) *(COOKCD 127)* **BLOKE ON BLOKE**   `72`   `☐`
– The boy done good / Just one victory / Qualifications / Sugar daddy / Never had no one ever / Run out of seasons / Rule nor reason / Thatcherites.

Elektra   Elektra
Jun 98. (cd/c; BILLY BRAGG & WILCO) <7559 62204-2/-4> **MERMAID AVENUE**   `34`   `90`
– Walt Whitman's niece / California stars / Way over yonder in the minor key / Birds and ships / Hoodoo voodoo / She came along to me / At my window sad and lonely / Ingrid Bergman / Christ for President / I guess I planted / One by one / Eisler on the go / Hesitating beauty / Another man's done gone / The unwelcome guest.

Nov 98. (7"/c-s; BILLY BRAGG & WILCO) *(E 3798/+C)* **WAY OVER YONDER IN THE MINOR KEY. / MY THIRTY THOUSAND**   `☐`   `-`
(cd-s+=) *(E 3798CD)* – Bug-eyed Jim.

– compilations, others, etc. –

May 87. (12"ep) *Strange Fruit; (SFPS 027)* **THE PEEL SESSIONS**   `☐`   `-`
– A new England / Strange things happen / This guitar says sorry / Love gets dangerous / A13 trunk road to the sea / Fear . . . *(cd-iss. 1988; SFPSCD 027)*
Jun 87. (d-lp/d-c/cd) *Go! Discs; (AGOLP/ZGOLP/AGOCD 8)* **BACK TO BASICS** (best 83-85 material)   `37`   `☐`
(re-iss. Apr98 on 'Cooking Vinyl' d-lp/c/cd; COOK/+C/CD 060)
Feb 92. (cd/c/lp) *Strange Fruit; (SFR CD/MC/LP 117)* **THE PEEL SESSIONS ALBUM**   `☐`   `-`
(cd with extra tracks)
Nov 93. (d-lp/c/cd) *Cooking Vinyl; (COOK/+C/CD 061)* **VICTIM OF GEOGRAPHY**   `☐`   `-`
– Greetings to the new brunette / Train train / Marriage / Idealogy / Levi Stubbs' tears / Honey, I'm a big boy now / There is a power in a union / Help save the youth of America / Wishing the days away / Passion / The warmest room / Home front / She's got a new spell / Must I paint you a picture / Tender comrade / The price I pay / Little timb bomb / Rotting on demand / Valentine's day is over / Life with the lions / The only one / Short answer / Waiting for the great leap forward. *(re-iss. Apr98 cd/c; same)*
Aug 99. (cd/c/lp) *Cooking Vinyl; (COOK CD/MC/LP 186)* **REACHING TO THE CONVERTED (MINDING THE GAPS)** (collection)   `41`   `☐`
– Shirley / Sulk / Accident waiting to happen / Boy done good / Heart like a wheel / Bad penny / Ontario Quebec and me / Walk away Renee / Rule nor reason / Days like these / Think again / Scholarship is the enemy of romance / Wishing the days away (ballad version) / Tatler / Jeane / She's leaving home.

BRAINBOX (see under ⇒ FOCUS)

BRAND NEW HEAVIES

Formed: Ealing, London, England . . . 1985 by ANDREW LEVY, SIMON BARTHOLOMEW and JAN KINCAID. Fascinated by the prime 70's funk of JAMES BROWN, The METERS, The JB's, etc., this teenage trio began cutting instrumental demos which they aired on the capital's thriving rare groove club scene. Subsequent live gigs amassed a loyal following and together with singer LINDA MURIEL, the fledgling BRAND NEW HEAVIES released 'GOT TO GIVE' as their debut single for 'Cooltempo' in 1987. After a protracted dispute with the label's parent company, 'Chrysalis', the band moved on to Eddie Pilar's independent 'Acid Jazz' imprint. One of the hubs of London's acid-jazz scene (alongside 'Talkin' Loud') – which had evolved from rare groove and mutated through the house revolution – as well as the springboard for JAMIROQUAI's career, the label was home for The BRAND NEW HEAVIES' eponymous 1990 debut album. Recorded on a miniscule budget with vocalist JAYE ELLA RUTH, the record was a breath of funky fresh air for a UK dance scene in thrall to bpm madness and countless novelty rave records. It was also enough to impress 'Delicious Vinyl', an American-based indie who already had sultry Southern-born soulstress N'DEA DAVENPORT on their books. The label suggested the band re-record a handful of tracks – with DAVENPORT on vocals – for a US debut album, the results appearing in 1992. One of the revamped tracks, 'DREAM COME TRUE', became their first UK Top 30 hit and soon the group were snapped up by 'ffrr/London' for a long-term major label deal. Back in America, meanwhile, the 'HEAVIES had hit the R&B charts with 'NEVER STOP', while a New York gig alongside A TRIBE CALLED QUEST mainman, Q-TIP, planted the seeds of 'HEAVY RHYME EXPERIENCE VOL.1' (1992). This was an inspired set of collaborations with the cream of the era's funkier hip hop crews (MAIN SOURCE, GANG STARR etc.), the record proving if nothing else that good old guitar/bass/drums and rap weren't mutually exclusive. If 'HEAVY RHYME . . .' had taken hip hop back to its 70's roots, 'BROTHER SISTER' (1994) polished up those self-same 70's roots with a 90's production sheen; again featuring N'DEA (now in a full-time capacity), BNH's third set occasionally sounded too slick for its own good. Nevertheless, gorgeous singing by the outrageously sexy DAVENPORT helped furnish the band with some of their biggest hits to date i.e 'DREAM ON DREAMER', a cover of Maria Muldaur's 'MIDNIGHT AT THE OASIS' etc. After a hugely successful tour, The BRAND NEW HEAVIES went to ground as N'DEA subsequently departed for a solo career. It was the end of a beautiful partnership but the band eventually re-emerged in 1997 with a new vocalist, SIEDAH GARRETT and album, 'SHELTER'. Somehow, the essential funk ingredient of old had become replaced by a more commercial R&B sound and the record arguably represented a substantial pop compromise even by the standards of its predecessor. Carrying on the band's tradition of unlikely cover versions, a reading of Carole King's 'YOU'VE GOT A FRIEND' became the album's biggest hit single (Top 10) and was featured alongside the cream of BNH's career on the 1999 retrospective 'TRUNK FUNK – THE BEST OF THE BRAND NEW HEAVIES'. (Note: The discography below does not include full details of the different mixes which were employed for their releases.)

Album rating: THE BRAND NEW HEAVIES (*7) / HEAVY RHYME EXPERIENCE: VOL.1 (*6) / BROTHER SISTER (*7) / ORIGINAL FLAVA (*4) / SHELTER (*4) / TRUNK FUNK – THE BEST OF THE BRAND NEW HEAVIES compilation (*7)

SIMON BARTHOLOMEW (b. 16 Oct'65) – guitar / **ANDREW LEVY** (b.20 Jul'66) – keyboards / **JAN KINCAID** (b.17 May'66) – drums, keyboards / **CERI EVANS** – keyboards / **LINDA MURIEL** – vocals / also **MIKE SMITH** – saxophone / **PAUL DIAS** – trumpet

			Cooltempo	not iss.
May 88. (7"/12") (COOL/+X 167) **GOT TO GIVE (part 1)**. / **GOT TO GIVE (part 2)**			☐	–

—— **JAY ELLA RUTH** – vocals; repl. MURIEL

		Acid Jazz	Delicious
Nov 89. (12") (JAZID 17T) **PEOPLE GET READY**. / ('A'mix)		☐	–
Apr 90. (lp/c/cd) (JAZID LP/MC/CD 023) **THE BRAND NEW HEAVIES**		☐	–

– BNH / Gimme one of these / Dream come true / Put the funk back in it / People get ready / Ride in the sky / Sphynx / Stay this way / Shake down. (re-iss. Feb95 & Aug99 cd/c/lp; same)

Sep 90. (cd-s) (JAZIDCD 025) **DREAM COME TRUE** /   ☐   –

—— added **LASCELLES GORDON** – percussion, guitar / **JIM WELLMAN** – saxophone, keyboards

Sep 91. (7") (F 165) <868552> **NEVER STOP**. / ('A'remix)   43   54
(12"+=/cd-s+=) (FX 165) – ('A'mixes)

—— now without EVANS who went solo as SUNSHIP and also produce GALLIANO and ALISON LIMERICK

Feb 92. (7") (F 180) **DREAM COME TRUE**. / ('A'mix)   24
(12"+=/cd-s+=) (FX 180) – ('A'mixes)

Mar 92. (cd/c/lp) (828 333-2/-4/-1) **THE BRAND NEW HEAVIES** (SECOND VERSION)   25
– Dream come true / Stay this way / People get ready / Never stop / Put the funk back in it / Ride in the sky / Brand new heavies / Gimme one of these / Got to give / Sphynx / Dream come true (reality mix) / Don't let it go to your head.

Apr 92. (7"ep/12"ep/cd-ep) (F 185) **ULTIMATE TRUNK FUNK – THE EP**   19
– Never stop / Stay this way / Mr. Tanaka / Never stop (remix).

Jul 92. (7") (BNH 1) **DON'T LET IT GO TO YOUR HEAD**. / ('A'mix)   24
(12"+=/cd-s+=) (BNH X/CD 1) – ('A'mixes).

—— now with guest vocalists **BLACK SHEEP / GANG STARR / GRAND PUBA / MAIN SOURCE / KOOL G. RAP / ED O.G. / MASTA ACE / JAMALSKI / TIGER / THE PHARCYDE**

Aug 92. (cd/c/lp) (828 355-2/-4/-1) <92178> **HEAVY RHYME EXPERIENCE: VOL.1**   38
– Bonafied funk / It's gettin' hectic / Who makes the loot? / Wake me when I'm dead / Jump n' move / Death threat / State of yo / Do whatta I gotta do / Whatgabouthat / Soul flower.

Dec 92. (7"/c-s) (BNH 2) **STAY THIS WAY (club mix)**. / ('A'-Lunar Dub version)   40
(12"+=/cd-s+=) (BNH X/CD 2) – Bang / O-Fa-Fu.

—— now with **N'DEA DAVENPORT** (b. Atlanta, Georgia, USA) – vocals (now full-time; had guested from 1991) but without JIM + LASCELLES

Mar 94. (12") (BNHX 3) <98321> **DREAM ON DREAMER**. / (3-'A'mixes)   15   51
(c-s+=/cd-s+=) (BNH MC/CD 3) – ('A'mix).
(12") (BNHXR 3) – ('A'mixes).

Apr 94. (cd/c/d-lp) (828 557-2/-4/-1) <92319> **BROTHER SISTER**   4   95
– Back to love / Ten ton take / Mind trips / Spend some time / Keep together / Snake hips / Fake / People giving love / World keeps spinning / Forever / Daybreak / Midnight at the oasis / Dream on dreamer / Have a good time / Brother sister. (re-iss. Aug99; same)

Jun 94. (c-s/cd-s) (BNH MC/CD 4) **BACK TO LOVE** / ('A'mixes)   28
(12"+=) (BNHX 4) – ('A'mix).
(cd-s) (BNHCDP 4) – ('A'side).

Aug 94. (c-s/cd-s) (BNH MC/CD 5) **MIDNIGHT AT THE OASIS** / ('A'mixes)   13
(12"+=) (BNHX 5) – ('A'mix).
(cd-s) (BNHCDP 5) – ('A'mix) / Back to love / Fake / Mind trips.

Oct 94. (c-s) (BNHMC 6) **SPEND SOME TIME** / ('A'mix)   26
(12"+=/cd-s+=) (BNH X/CD 6) – ('A'mixes).

Mar 95. (c-s) (BNHMC 7) **CLOSE TO YOU** / ('A'mix)   38
(cd-s+=) (BNHCD 7) – ('A'mixes).

—— **SIEDAH GARRETT** – vocals; repl. DAVENPORT

Apr 97. (c-s) (BNHMC 8) **SOMETIMES** / ('A'mix)   11   88
(cd-s) (BNHCD 8) – ('A'mix).
(cds) (BNCDP 8) – ('A'mixes).

Apr 97. (cd/c/lp) (828887-2/-4/-1) **SHELTER**   5
– I like it / Sometimes / Shelter / You are the universe / Crying water / Day by day / Feels like right / The highest high / Stay gone / You've got a friend / Once is twice enough / After forever / Last to know. (version II – iss.Oct97 & Sep99; 828975-2/-4)

Jun 97. (12"/cd-s) (BNH X/CDP 9) **YOU ARE THE UNIVERSE**. / ('A'mix)   21
(12"/cd-s) (BNH XX/CDP 9) – ('A'mixes).

Oct 97. (c-s) (BNHMC 10) **YOU'VE GOT A FRIEND** / ('A'mix)   9
(12"/cd-s) (BNH X/CD 10) – ('A'mixes).
(cd-s) (BNCDP 10) – ('A'mixes).

Dec 97. (12"/cd-s) (BNH X/CD 11) **SHELTER**. / ('A'-Dan's groove pt.2)   31
(cd-s) (BNCDP 11) – ('A'mixes; Jan's big funk / Brand New Harvey's / Doble's The Way It Should Be).

Aug 99. (c-s) (BNHMC 12) **SATURDAY NITE** / ('A'mix)   35
(cd-s) (BNHCD 12) – ('A'mixes).
(cd-s) (BNCDP 12) – ('A'mixes).
(12") (BNHX 12) – ('A'mixes).

Sep 99. (cd/c) (3984 2916-42/-54) **TRUNK FUNK – THE BEST OF THE BRAND NEW HEAVIES** (compilation)   13
– Dream come true / Stay this way / Never stop / Dream on dreamer / Back to love / Midnight at the oasis / Spend some time / Close to you / You are the universe / Forever / You've got a friend / Shelter / Sometimes / BNH / Gimme one of those / Apparantly nothin' / Saturday nite / Try my love.

– compilations, others, etc. –

Nov 94. (cd/c/lp) Acid Jazz; (JAZID CD/MC/LP 114) **ORIGINAL FLAVA**   64
– Rest of me / Put yourself in my shoes / Reality / Country funkin' / Got to give / Mother's tongue / Dream come true / Never stop / Headhunters (live) / Day at the seaside.

BRAN VAN 3000

Formed: New York, USA . . . early 1997 by DJ and former video director "BRAN MAN" (JAMES DI SALVIO), who, after a video shoot which earned him big bucks, phoned "ELECTRONIC-PIERRE" BERGEN in Montreal. He arrived in the Big Apple with around twenty Canadian musicians, rappers, et al and set about helping to arrange a unique blend of lo-fi country and hip hop! (take the BEASTIES, BECK, ZZ TOP and HANK WILLIAMS and you get the drift). Eventually they cut the ensemble down to a neat 9-piece and toured promoting their 'GLEE' album for 'Capitol' (it had been released on 'Audiogram' records in '97). By the time of its release in June '98, they had already notched up a Top 40 hit via 'DRINKING IN L.A.'. • **Covered:** CUM ON FEEL THE NOIZE (Slade). 'GIMME SHELDON' sampled DE LA SOUL, RIMSKY KORSAKOV, YOUNG MC, PEANUT BUTTER WOLF and JEEP BEAT COLLECTIVE. 'UNE CHANSON' contained elements of 'Perfect' MATT JOHNSON/THE THE. • **Trivia:** Was DI SALVIO in bands called SHINE LIKE STARS and GREENDOORNYO?

Album rating: GLEE (*6)

"BRAN MAN" (JAMES DI SALVIO) – vocals / "ELECTRONIC-PIERRE" BERGEN – / STEPHANE MORAILLE – vocals / SARA JOHNSTON, JAYNE HILL, STEVE "LIQUID" HAWLEY, GARY McKENZIE, ROB JOANISSE, NICK HYNES plus others NERVOUS DUANE LARSON, ADAM CHAKI, HAIG VARTZBEDIAN, SIDAFFA "DODGE" BAKEL, LENA FANKHAUSER, MARTHA WAINWRIGHT, MONICA HYNES, LUCIE LAURIER, RICK RIGBY, BOB EAGLESHAM, JEAN LELOUP, DANIELE LINDY, TOM WALSH, EVAL MANIGATT, DOROTHY CLARKE, LEANNA WHITE, J.F. LEMIEUX, DAVE HODGE, RICK D'ANJOU, JOHN KASTNER, JIMMY, R-KADE + guest GRYM REAPER

		Capitol	Capitol
May 98. (c-s/7") (TC+/CL 802) **DRINKING IN L.A.** / **THE PROBLEM WITH SHELDON** / **DRINKING IN L.A. (Fink mix)**		34	☐

(cd-s+=) (CDCL 802) – Thinking in L.A. (Zoobone mix).

Jun 98. (cd/c) <(8 23604-2/-4)> **GLEE**
– Gimme sheldon / Couch surfer / Drinking in L.A. / Problems / Highway to heck / Forest / Rainshine / Carry on / Afrodiziak / Lucknow / Cum on feel the noize / Exactly like me / Everywhere / Une chanson / Old school / Willard / Supermodel / Oblonging / Mama don't smoke.

Aug 99. (c-s) (TCCL 811) **DRINKING IN L.A.** / **THE PROBLEM WITH SHELDON** / **DRINKING IN L.A. (Fink mix)**   3
(cd-s+=) (CDCL 811) – ('A'mixes; intro / Fink / Zoobone).

BREAD

Formed: Los Angeles, California, USA . . . late 1968 by DAVID GATES, JAMES GRIFFIN and ROB ROYER. GATES grew up in a musical family in Tulsa, Oklahoma learning piano, bass and guitar to a high standard by the time he reached high school. His composition, 'JO BABY', written about his girlfriend (and future wife) Jo Rita, was turned into a minor hit in '57 by CHUCK BERRY (who had visited Tulsa around that time). GATES was only sixteen at this point; by the time he was twenty he had recorded with LEON RUSSELL, moved to L.A. and established himself as a studio musician and producer. In this capacity he worked with a number of legends including ELVIS PRESLEY, MERLE HAGGARD and CAPTAIN BEEFHEART. Another band he produced were PLEASURE FAIRE whose members included ROB ROYER and JAMES GRIFFIN, who had already released his own solo record, 'SUMMER HOLIDAY'. He subsequently asked GATES to join the band and the trio signed to 'Elektra', changing their name to BREAD in the process. The first LP, 'BREAD' (1969) introduced their unique sound of melody-driven soft-rock ballads with a hint of American folk, one of the highlights being the gorgeous 'IT DON'T MATTER TO ME'. Enriched with strings, it became the only the track from their debut to hit the charts, making the US Top 10 the following year. Its belated success came on the back of 'MAKE IT WITH YOU', their chart-topping masterpiece and signature song taken from 'ON THE WATERS' (1970). This album was an instant success and left them deeply embedded in the mainstream, the subsequent tour seeing new drummer MIKE BOTTS brought into the fold. The quartet went back to the studio to produce 'MANNA' (1971) and although its sales did not scale the dizzy heights of the previous effort, it did spawn their most recorded song (TELLY SAVALAS took it to No.1 in Britain), the slow ballad, 'IF'. A further single, 'MOTHER FREEDOM', barely dipped its toe into the charts, a poor attempt by the group to diversify into the rock territory stalked by bands like FREE. BREAD were back on form with two other Top 5 hits 'BABY I'M-A WANT YOU' (from the album of the same name) and 'EVERYTHING I OWN' (a two-times UK No.1, first for reggae star KEN BOOTHE and latterly for gay icon BOY GEORGE). The same year, the 'GUITAR MAN' album provided a further three Top 20 singles before the band split in 1973; internal difficulties between GATES and GRIFFIN over the former's songwriting domination of the group's hits caused the dissolution. However they did reunite in '76 for one more album, 'LOST WITHOUT YOUR LOVE' (1977), but even with the success of the Top 10 title track, the pair just couldn't bury the hatchet. Both went back to the pursuit of solo careers and unsurprisingly GATES had by far the more success of the two. He released two albums in between the BREAD years providing two hits with 'NEVER LET HER GO' and 'GOODBYE GIRL'. His only other hit, 'TOOK THE LAST TRAIN' came in '78 and although he continued to record into the '90s, he never managed to match the success he enjoyed with BREAD. • **Trivia:** GRIFFIN and ROYER (under pseudonyms) wrote 'FOR ALL WE KNOW', used in the film, 'Lovers And Other Strangers'; it subsequently became a hit for The CARPENTERS in 1971.

Best CD compilation: DAVID GATES & BREAD: ESSENTIALS (*7)

DAVID GATES (b.11 Dec'40, Tulsa, Oklahoma, USA) - vocals, keyboards / **JAMES GRIFFIN** (b. Memphis) – guitar, keyboards, vocals / **ROB ROYER** – bass, vocals (ex-PLEASURE FAIRE) **JIM GORDON + RON EDGAR** – session drummers

Elektra / Elektra

Oct 69. (7") <(EKSN 45071)> **DISMAL DAY. / LONDON BRIDGE**
Nov 69. (lp) <(EKS 74044)> **BREAD** — Oct69
– Dismal day / London Bridge / Could I / Look at me / Last time / Anyway you want me / Move over / Don't shut me down / You can't measure the cost / Family doctor / It don't matter to me / Friends & lovers. (re-iss. Nov71; K 42029) (cd-iss. Jan96; 0349 73502-2)
Feb 70. (7") <(EKSN 45083)> **MOVE OVER. / YOU CAN'T MEASURE THE COST**
—— **MIKE BOTTS** (b. Sacramento) – drums (ex-WES MONTGOMERY) repl. session people
Jul 70. (7") (2101 010) <45686> **MAKE IT WITH YOU. / WHY DO YOU KEEP ME WAITING** — 5 / 1 Jun70
Aug 70. (lp) (2469 005) <EKS 74076> **ON THE WATERS** — 34 / 12 Jul70
– Why do you keep me waiting / Make it with you / Blue satin pillow / Look what you've done / I am what I am / Been too long on the road / I want you with me / Coming apart / Easy love / In the afterglow / Call on me / The other side of love. (re-iss. Nov71; K 42050) (cd-iss. Jan96; 0349 73503-2)
Oct 70. (7") (2101 015) <EKSN 45701> **IT DON'T MATTER TO ME. / CALL ON ME** — 10 Sep70
Feb 71. (7") <(K 45711)> **LET YOUR LOVE GO. / TOO MUCH LOVE** — 28
May 71. (7") (K 12014) <45720> **IF. / TAKE COMFORT** — 4 Mar71
Jul 71. (lp) <(EKS 74086)> **MANNA** — 21 Mar71
– Let your love go / Take comfort / Too much love / If / Be kind to me / He's a good lad / She was my lady / Live in your love / What a change / I say again / Come again / Truckin'. (re-iss. 1972; K 52001) (cd-iss. Jan96; 0349 73504-2)
—— **LARRY KNECHTEL** (b. Bell, California) – guitar, multi (ex-DUANE EDDY) (also played piano on 'Bridge Over Troubled Water') repl. ROYER
Jul 71. (7") <K 45740> **MOTHER FREEDOM. / LIVE IN YOUR LOVE** — - / 37
Nov 71. (7") (K 12033) <45751> **BABY I'M A-WANT YOU. / TRUCKIN'** — 14 / 3 Oct71
Mar 72. (7") (K 12041) <45765> **EVERYTHING I OWN. / I DON'T LIKE YOU** — 32 / 5 Jan72
Mar 72. (lp/c) (K/K4 42100) <75015> **BABY I'M A-WANT YOU** — 9 / 3 Jan72
– Baby I'm-a want you / Everything I own / Diary / Mother Freedom / Down on my knees / Nobody like you / Dream lady / Games of magic / This isn't what the government / Just like yesterday / I don't love you. (re-iss. Nov76; same)
Apr 72. (7") <45784> **DIARY. / DOWN ON MY KNEES** — - / 15
Sep 72. (7") (K 12066) <45803> **THE GUITAR MAN. / JUST LIKE YESTERDAY** — 16 / 11 Jul72
Nov 72. (lp/c) (K/K4 52004) <75047> **GUITAR MAN** — 18
– The guitar man / Sweet surrender / Aubrey / Welcome to the music / Make it by yourself / Fancy dancer / Tecotote / Let me go / Yours for life / Picture in your mind / Don't tell me no / Didn't even know her name. (re-iss. Nov76; same)
Jan 73. (7") (K 12075) <45818> **SWEET SURRENDER. / MAKE IT BY YOURSELF** — 15 Nov72
Feb 73. (7") <45832> **AUBREY. / DIDN'T EVEN KNOW HER NAME** — - / 11
—— BREAD broke-up in May '73, BOTTS joined the LINDA RONSTADT band and KNECHTEL returned to sessions. GRIFFIN went solo (2 lp's 1974 & 1975)

DAVID GATES

—— solo, although not including his pre-BREAD stuff
Aug 73. (7") (K 12114) **CLOUDS. / I USE THE SOAP** — 47 Jul73
Oct 73. (lp/c) (K/K4 42150) <75066> **DAVID GATES – FIRST**
– Sail around the world / Sunday rider / I use the soap / Suite: Clouds – Rain / Help is on the way / Ann / Do you believe he's coming / Sight and sound / Lorilee. (re-iss. Nov76; same) (cd-iss. Jan96; 7559 60610-2)
Nov 73. (7") (K 12126) <45868> **SAIL AROUND THE WORLD. / HELP IS ON THE WAY**
May 74. (7") (K 12162) **SUITE: CLOUDS – RAIN. / (part 2)** — 50 Oct73
Jan 75. (7") (K 12165) <45223> **NEVER LET HER GO. / WATCH OUT**
May 75. (lp/c) (K/K4 52012) 1028> **NEVER LET HER GO** — 32 / 29 Feb75
– Never let her go / Angel / Playin' on my guitar / Watch out / Part time love / Chain me / Light of my life / Someday / Greener days / Strangers. (re-iss. Nov76; same)
Jun 75. (7") (K 12179) **PART TIME LOVE. / SUNDAY RIDER**

BREAD

—— re-formed (see last line-up)
Dec 76. (7") (K 12241) <45365> **LOST WITHOUT YOUR LOVE. / CHANGE OF HEART** — 27 / 9 Nov76
Jan 77. (lp/c) (K/K4 52044) 1094> **LOST WITHOUT YOUR LOVE** — 17 / 26
– Hooked on you / She's the only one / Lost without your love / Change of heart / Belonging / Fly away / Lay your money down / The chosen one / Today the first day / Hold tight / Our lady of sorrow.
Mar 77. (7") (K 12250) **HOOKED ON YOU. / FLY AWAY**
Apr 77. (7") <45389> **HOOKED ON YOU. / OUR LADY OF SORROW** — - / 60
—— split:- GRIFFIN soon teamed up with TERRY SYLVESTER (ex-The HOLLIES)

– compilations, etc. –

on 'Elektra' unless mentioned otherwise
Oct 72. (lp/c) (K/K4 42115) <75056> **THE BEST OF BREAD** — 7 / 2 Mar73
– Make it with you / Everything I own / Diary / Baby I'm a-want you / It don't matter to me / Mother freedom / Down on my knees / Too much love / Let your love go / Look what you've done / Truckin'. (re-iss. Nov76; same)
May 73. (7"m) **IF. / IT DON'T MATTER TO ME / LET YOUR LOVE GO**

Jun 74. (lp/c) (K/K4 42161) <1005> **THE BEST OF BREAD VOL.2** — 48 / 32 May74
– Sweet surrender / Fancy dancer / The guitar man / Been too long on the coast / Friends and lovers / Aubrey / Daughter / Dream lady / Yours for life / Just like yesterday / He's a good lad / London Bridge. (re-iss. Nov76; same)
Aug 74. (7") (K 12155) **SWEET SURRENDER. / BEEN TOO LONG ON THE COAST**
Jun 76. (7") (K 12210) **GUITAR MAN. / BABY I'M A-WANT YOU**
Jun 76. (7") (K 12221) **MAKE IT WITH YOU. / EVERYTHING I OWN** (re-iss. Sep85 on 'Old Gold'; OG 9512)
Jun 76. (7") (K 12222) **IF. / SWEET SURRENDER**
Oct 77. (lp/c) (K/K4 52062) **THE SOUND OF BREAD** — 1
– Make it with you / Dismal day / London Bridge / Anyway you want me / Look what you've done / It don't matter to me / The last time / Let your love go / Truckin' / If / Baby I'm a-want you / Everything I own / Down on my knees / Aubrey / Diary / Sweet surrender / The guitar man / Fancy dancer / She's the only one / Lost without your love. (cd-iss. Jan87 +=; K2 52062) – Just like yesterday. (lp re-iss. Oct97 on 'Simply Vinyl'; SVLP 5)
Nov 83. (d-c) (960 284-2) **THE BEST OF BREAD VOL.1 & 2**
Sep 85. (7") Old Gold; (OG 9513) **BABY I'M A-WANT YOU. / IF**
Nov 87. (lp/c/cd) Telstar; (STAR/STAC/TCD 2303) **THE BREAD COLLECTION**
Oct 88. (lp/c) Hallmark; (SHM/HSC 3244) **THE VERY BEST OF BREAD** (cd-is.Oct89 on 'Pickwick'+=) – (3 DAVID GATES tracks).
Aug 92. (cd) Remember; (RMB 75063) **LET YOUR LOVE GO**
Sep 96. (cd/c; DAVID GATES & BREAD) <(7559 61961-2/-4)> **ESSENTIALS**
– Dismal day / Any way you want me / It don't matter to me / Make it with you / Look what you've done / I want you with me / Let your love go / Too much love / If / He's a good lad / Mother freedom / Baby I'm-a want you / Down on my knees / Everything I own / Diary / The guitar man / Aubrey / Sweet surrender / She's the only one / Lost without your love / Soap (I use the) / Ann / Never let her go / Goodbye girl. (re-iss. Jun97; 9548 35408-2/-4) – hit UK No.11

DAVID GATES

—— was solo again in 1978
Jan 78. (7") (K 12276) <45450> **GOODBYE GIRL. / SUNDAY RIDER** — 15
Jul 78. (7") (K 12307) <45500> **TOOK THE LAST TRAIN. / ANN** — 50 / 30
Jul 78. (lp/c) (K/K4 52091) <148> **GOODBYE GIRL** — 28
– Goodbye girl / Took the last train / Overnight sensation / California lady / Ann / Drifter / He don't know how to love you / Sunday rider. (cd-iss. Jan96; 7559 61172-2)
Sep 78. (7") (K 12318) **NEVER LET HER GO. / LORILEE**
Jan 80. (7") (K 52206) <251> **FALLING IN LOVE AGAIN**
– Can I call you / Where does the lovin' go / 20th century man / She was so young / Silky / Falling in love again / Starship ride / Chingo / Sweet desire.
Jan 80. (7") <46588> **WHERE DOES THE LOVIN' GO. / STARSHIP RIDE** — 46
Feb 80. (7") (K 12423) **FALLING IN LOVE AGAIN. / STARSHIP RIDE**
Apr 80. (7") (K 12439) **WHERE DOES THE LOVIN' GO. / CHINGO**

Arista / Arista

Sep 81. (7") <0615> **TAKE ME NOW. / IT'S WHAT YOU SAY** — 62
Nov 81. (7") (ARIST 446) **COME HOME FOR CHRISTMAS. / IT'S WHAT YOU SAY**
Jan 82. (lp) (SPART 1175) <9563> **TAKE ME NOW** — Nov81
– It's you / Take me now / She's a heartbreaker / This could be forever / Come home for Christmas / Still in love / Vanity / Nineteen on the Richter scale / Lady Valentine / It's what you say.
—— GATES went quiet for a long spell

Discovery / Discovery

May 95. (cd) <(1046 77012-2)> **LOVE IS ALWAYS SEVENTEEN**
– Avenue of love / Love is always seventeen / Ordinary man / I will wait for you / Save this dance for me / No secrets in a small town / Heart, it's all over / I don't want to share your love / I can't find the words to say goodbye / Dear world / Thankin' you sweet baby James.

– (DAVID GATES) compilations, etc. –

1976. (7") (K 12229) **SUITE: CLOUDS – RAIN. / PART TIME LOVE**
1976. (7") (K 12230) **AIL AROUND THE WORLD. / NEVER LET HER GO**
1977. (lp) <6002> **DAVID GATES SONGBOOK** (early material)

BREAKBEAT ERA (see under ⇒ SIZE, Roni)

BREEDERS

Formed: Boston, Massachusetts, USA … 1989 by TANYA DONELLY (of THROWING MUSES) and KIM DEAL (of The PIXIES) as a side project to their respective musical careers, an opportunity to exercise their frustrated songwriting talent. Recruiting JOSEPHINE WIGGS (of PERFECT DISASTER) on bass and SHANNON DOUGHTY (of the late, great SLINT) on drums, the BREEDERS cut their debut outing, 'POD', in a matter of weeks. Released in May 1990, the album rapidly achieved cult status, even enjoying a hearty endorsement from one KURT COBAIN. Inevitably, the record was compared with The PIXIES by critics although in reality there was little in common between the two bands. Where The PIXIES were enigmatic and frenetic, The BREEDERS were deliberate, dark and intense. While the pace picked up with 'HELLBOUND', tracks like the opener, 'GLORIOUS', and 'IRIS' were more representative of the record as a whole, and if their cover of LENNON's 'HAPPINESS IS A WARM GUN' didn't add much to the original, it sounded so BREEDERS-like within the context of the album that they could've conceivably penned it themselves. The group recorded a further

EP, 'SAFARI' (1992), with the original line-up before DONELLY went off to work full-time with her own outfit, BELLY. Following The PIXIES' demise later that year, DEAL devoted all her energies to a BREEDERS follow-up album. Enlisting her sister KELLEY in place of the departed DONELLY, the band released the 'CANNONBALL' single in Autumn '93. With its undulating guitar riff and pneumatic rhythm section, the track became an alternative classic, tearing up indie dancefloors across the country. The subsequent album, 'LAST SPLASH', powered into the UK Top 5 upon its release the following month. While much of the set sounded less focused than the debut, it nevertheless contained another stellar guitar pop moment in 'DIVINE HAMMER', also released as a single. Although the album's sales topped the million mark, things have been quiet on The BREEDERS front of late, save for a lone 10" EP in 1994. The following year, (KIM) DEAL did surface in the guise of The AMPS, releasing an album, 'PACER', on '4 a.d.'. • **Songwriters:** KIM DEAL wrote bulk from 1992 onwards. • **Covered:** HAPPINESS IS A WARM GUN (Beatles / George Harrison) / LORD OF THE THIGHS (Aerosmith) / SO SAD ABOUT US (Who). The AMPS covered JUST LIKE A BRIAR (Tasties).

Album rating: POD (*7) / LAST SPLASH (*9) / Amps: PACER (*6)

TANYA DONELLY (b.14 Jul'66, Newport, Rhode Island) – rhythm guitar, vocals (of THROWING MUSES) / **KIM DEAL** (b.10 Jun'61, Dayton, Ohio, USA) – guitar, vocals (of The PIXIES) / **JOSEPHINE WIGGS** (b.26 Feb'65, Letchworth, England) – bass, cello, vocals (of PERFECT DISASTER) / **SHANNON DOUGHTY** (aka MIKE HUNT) (b. BRITT WALFORD, Louisville, Kentucky) – drums (of SLINT) repl. NARCIZO and another from HUMAN SEXUAL RESPONSE

		4 a.d.	Elektra
May 90.	(cd)(lp/c) *(CAD 0006CD)(CAD/+C 0006)* **POD**	22	

– Glorious / Doe / Happiness is a warm gun / Oh! / Hellbound / When I was a painter / Fortunately gone / Iris / Opened / Only in 3's / Limehouse / Metal man.

—— **DONELLY, KIM DEAL, JO WIGGS + JON MATLOCK** (of SPIRITUALIZED)

Apr 92.	(12"cd/cd-ep) *(BAD 2003/+CD)* **SAFARI**	69	

– Safari / So sad about us / Do you love me now? / Don't call home.

—— now **KIM** her sister **KELLEY DEAL** (b.10 Jun'61, Dayton) – guitar, vocals / **JO WIGGS** – bass, vox / **JIM MacPHERSON** (b.23 Jun'66, Dayton) – drums, vocals (ex-RAGING MANTRAS) / (DONELLY formed BELLY)

Aug 93.	(12"cd/cd-ep) *(BAD 3011/+CD) <64566>* **CANNONBALL. / CRO-ALOHA / LORD OF THE THIGHS / 900**	40	44 Nov93
Sep 93.	(cd)(lp/c) *(CAD 3014CD)(CAD/+C 3014) <61508>* **LAST SPLASH**	5	33

– New Year / Cannonball / Invisible man / No aloha / Roi / Do you love me now? / Flipside / I just wanna get along / Mad Lucas / Divine hammer / S.O.S. / Hag / Saints / Drivin' on 9 / Roi (reprise).

Oct 93.	(7"clear/c-s) *(AD/+C 3017)* **DIVINE HAMMER. / HOVERIN'**	59	

(10"ep+=)(cd-ep+=) *(BADD 3017)(BAD 3017CD)* – I can't help it (if I'm still in love with you) / Do you love me now Jr (J. Mascis remix).

Jul 94.	(10"ep) *(BADD 4012)* **HEAD TO TOE. / SHOCKER IN GLOOMTOWN / FREED PIG**	68	

(cd-ep+=) – *(BAD 4014CD)* – Saints.

—— new 1997 line-up, includes **KIM DEAL + JIM MacPHERSON** plus **MICHAEL O'DEAN** – guitar / **NATE FARLEY** – guitar / **LOUIS NERMA** – bass / **CARRIE BRADLEY** – violin

AMPS

KIM DEAL / JIM MacPHERSON / NATHAN FARLEY + LUIS LERMA

		4 a.d.	4 a.d.
Oct 95.	(12"ep/cd-ep) *(BAD 5015/+CD)* **TIPP CITY / JUST LIKE A BRIAR. / EMPTY GLASSES (Kim's basement 4 track version)**	61	
Oct 95.	(cd)(lp/c) *(CAD 5016CD)(CAD/+C 5016)* **PACER**	60	

– Pacer / Tipp city / I am decided / Mom's drunk / Bragging party / Hoverin' / First revival / Full on idle / Breaking the split screen barrier / Empty glasses / She's a girl / Dedicated.

Jacques BREL

Born: 8 Apr'29, Brussels, Belgium. Reared in a conservative middle-class environment, BREL went on to study law before entering the family business. He soon tired of a conventional lifestyle and instead relocated to Paris where he thought he'd try his hand at songwriting. Despite an awkward gait and buck-teeth, he soon graduated to performing his own compositions, appearing regularly at the Theatre Des Trois Baudets. BREL enthralled fans with a magnetic stage presence and a gift for dramaticism that helped define his vision of the doomed romantic, translating this to the wider record-buying public with his first French hit, 'QUAND ON N'A QUE L'AMOUR'. Signed to 'Barclay' in France, BREL proceeded to release a string of singles which documented the dark underbelly of modern society in shrewdly observed style. A one-off album for 'C.B.S.', the self explanatory 'AMERICAN DEBUT' (1957), introduced BREL's literate genius to a whole new English-speaking audience and influenced a host of future stars; while the likes of LEONARD COHEN would incorporate the spirit of BREL into his dark balladry, The KINGSTON TRIO interpreted him more literally, transforming 'LE MORIBUND' into the sentimental 'Seasons In The Sun' (later a UK hit for TERRY JACKS). British artists influenced by his work include SCOTT WALKER, DAVID BOWIE, RAY DAVIES, MARC ALMOND and The SENSATIONAL ALEX HARVEY BAND who covered 'NEXT' (a track centering on an army base brothel) as the title track to a 1973 album (mainman ALEX HARVEY had heard the track in a cult continental film, 'Jacques Brel Is Alive And Well And Living In Paris'). A hugely popular and hard working live performer, BREL had sold out

both New York's Carnegie Hall and London's Royal Albert before giving up performing for good in the late 60's; he'd already stated his intention to boycott the USA after it became involved in the Vietnam war. He subsequently retired to French Polynesia from where he'd make sporadic recording trips back to Paris. Diagnosed with cancer in the mid-70's, BREL succumbed to the disease on the 10th of October 1978. Despite his dearth of either British or American chart success, he remains one of the last century's most influential songwriters.

Best CD compilation: QUINZE ANS D'AMOUR (*8)

JACQUES BREL – vocals / with orchestra/session people

		Barclay	Columbia	
1956.	(7") **QUAND ON N'A QUE L'AMOUR. /**	–	–	French
1957.	(lp) *<AWS 324>* **AMERICAN DEBUT**		–	French
1959.	(lp) **LA VALSE A MILLE TEMPS**	–		French
1962.	(lp) **LES BOURGEOIS** (live)	–		French
——	still signed to 'Barclay' in France			

		Fontana	unknown	
1962.	(lp) *(SFJL 967)* **A L'OLYMPIA** (cd-iss. 1988 on 'Philips'; 814372-2)		–	
1963.	(lp) *(817004)* **LE PLAT PAYS**	–	–	French

– Les bourgeois / Les paumes du petit matin / Le plat pays / Zangra / Une ile / Madeleine / Bruxelles / Chanson sans parole / Les biches / Caporal / Casse-pompom / La statue / Rosa. *(UK-iss.1970's on 'Barclay Logo-RCA'; 90015) (cd-iss. 1988 on 'Philips'; 817004-2)*

1964.	(lp) **CES GENS-LA**	–	–	French

– Ces gens-la / Jef / Jacky / Les bergers / Tango funebre / Fernand / Mathilde / L'age idiot / Frand'mere / Les desperes. *(UK-iss.1978 on 'Barclay Logo-RCA'; 90021) <US cd-iss. 1998 on 'Polydor'; 821594>*

1965.	(lp) *(TL 5330)* **JACQUES BREL** (UK-iss.of 'LE PLAT PAYS')			
1965.	(lp) *(TL 5391)* **JACQUES BREL, VOL.2**			
1966.	(lp) **LES BONBONS**		–	French
1967.	(lp) *(STL 5429)* **JACQUES BREL '67**			
1968.	(lp) **J'ARRIVE**	–	–	French

(<US cd-iss. 1998 on 'Polydor'; 821595>

		Barclay	not iss.	
1972.	(lp) *(90022)* **NE ME QUITTE PAS**	–		

– Ne me quitte pas / Marieke / On n'oublie rien / Les flamandes / Les prenoms de Paris / Quand on n'a que l'amour / Les biches / Le prochain amour / Le moribund / La valse a mille temps / Je ne sais pas pourquoi. *(cd-iss. 1980's on 'Phonogram'; 813009-2) (cd re-iss. Jul90 on 'E.C.M.'; 813009-2)*

1977.	(lp) *(96010)* **BREL: LES MARQUISES**	–	–	French

– Jaures / La ville s'endormait / Viellir / Le bon dieu / Les f . . . / Orly / Les remparts de varsovie / Voie un ami pleurer / Knokke-le-soute tango / Jojo / Le lion / Les marquises. *(cd-iss. 1984 on 'Phonogram'; 810537-2)*

—— JACQUES died of cancer on the 10th of October, 1978

– others, compilations, etc. –

Nov 79.	(lp) *Barclay; (920492)* **LA CHANSON FRANCAISE**	–	–	French

– J'aimais / Vasoul / Ces gens la / Amsterdam / Chanson des vieux amants / Les flamandes / Le plat pays / Quand on n' a que l'amour / Les paumes du petit matin / Jef.

1980's.	(lp) *Barclay Logo-RCA; (90016)* **LA CHANSON DES VIEUX AMANTS**		–	French

– Mon enfance / Le cheval / Mon pere disait / La la la / Les coeurs tendres, du film "un idiot a Paris" / Files de . . . / Les bonbons 67 / La chanson des vieuz amants / A jeun / Le gaz.

1980's.	(lp) *Barclay Logo-RCA; (90017)* **AMSTERDAM**	–	–	French

– Amsterdam / Les timies / Le dernier repas / Les jardins du casino / Les vieux / Les bonbons / Au suivant / La fanette / Les bigotes / Les filles et les chiens / Les fenetres.

1980's.	(lp) *Barclay Logo-RCA; (90018)* **VESOUL**	–	–	French

– J'arrive / Vesoul / L'ostendaise / Je suis un soir d'ete / Regarde bien petit Comment tuer l'amant / de sa femme quand on a ete eleve comme moi dans la tradition / L'eclusier / Un enfant / La biere.

1980's.	(lp) *Barclay Logo-RCA; (90019)* **LA FANETTE**	–	–	French

– Mathilde / La fanette / Jef / Titine / Rosa / Jacky / Fernand / Zangra / Madeleine.

1980's.	(lp) *Barclay Logo-RCA; (90020)* **LES VIEUX**	–	–	French

– Les bonbons / Les vieux / La parlote / Le dernier repas / Titine / Au suivant / Les toros / La fanette / J'aimais / Les filles et les chiens / Les bigotes / Les fenetres. *(cd-iss. 1988 on 'Barclay'; 815989-2)*

Apr 83.	(lp/c) *Philips; (6395/7206 216)* **MUSIC FOR THE MILLIONS**	–	–	French
Aug 86.	(d-lp) *Vanguard; (VS2LP 2779)* **BREL ALIVE IN PARIS**			
Sep 86.	(c) *Philips; (818359-4)* **JACQUES BREL**	–	–	French

– Les prenoms de Paris / Clara / On n'oubile rien / Les singes / Madeleine / Les biches / Les paumes du petit matin / Zangra / La statue / Les bourgeois / Marieke / Ne me quitte pas / Le prochain amour / Le moribund / Au printemps / Le colombe / Les flamandes / L'Ivrogne / La valse a mille temps / Mivre debout.

Feb 88.	(cd/c) *Philips; (816458-2/-4)* **JACQUES BREL: MASTER SERIES**	–	–	French

– Jaures / Ne me quitte pas / Les vieux / La quete / On n'oublie rien / Le plat pays / Mathilde / Les remparts de varsovie / Amsterdam / J'arive / Ces gens la / Jef / Vesoul / Au suivant / Madeleine / Les bourgeois.

Jan 89.	(d-lp/c)(cd; Various Artists) *Silva Screen; (SD/CD 1000)(CGK 40817)* **JACQUES BREL IS ALIVE AND WELL AND LIVING IN PARIS**			
1988.	(cd) *Barclay; (810537-2)* **JAURES**	–	–	French
1990's.	(cd) *Vanguard; <79265>* **LE FORMIDABLE JACQUES BREL**	–	–	
Jun 92.	(d-cd) *Verve; <816458-2>* **MASTER SERIE: JACQUES BREL**	–	–	
Nov 92.	(cd) *Musicrama; <1668>* **QUINZE ANS D'AMOUR**	–	–	

– Grand Jacques (c'est trop facile) / Quand on n'a que l'amour / Valse a mille temps / Ne me quitte pas / Les flamandes / Le plat pays / Les bourgeois / Quete / Les vieux / Les bonbons / Jef / Mathilde / Au suivant / Chanson de Jacky / Ces gens-la / Mon enfance / Chanson des vieux amants / J'arrive / Amsterdam.

Nov 92.	(cd) *Alex; <3063>* **ORLY**	–	–	French
Jul 93.	(cd) *Duchesse; (CD3/MC2 52111)* **GREATEST HITS**	–	–	
Mar 96.	(cd) *Isba; (5009)* **L'UNIVERS SYMPHONIQUE**	–	–	French
1996.	(d-cd) *Polygram; (531707)* **QUAND ON N'A QUE L'AMOUR**	–	–	French
Oct 97.	(cd) *Musicrama; <4015>* **AMSTERDAM**	–	–	
Jan 98.	(cd) *Polygram; <521237-2>* **KNOKKE LIVE 1963 (live)**			

Jan 98. (cd) *Polydor; <839586-2>* **L'HOMME DE LA MANCHA (with JOAN DIENER)**

Jan 98. (d-cd) *Polydor; <515753>* **MASTER SERIE**

Jan 98. (cd) *Polydor; <845001>* **AMSTERDAM: THE BEST OF JACQUES BREL**

Jan 98. (10xcd-box) *Polydor; <816719-2>* **GRAND JACQUES**
– (GRAND JACQUES / LA VALSE A MILLE TEMPS / LES FLAMANDES / LE PLAT PAYS / JEF / J'ARRIVE / ORLY / BREL EN PUBLIC OLYMPIA 1961 / BREL EN PUBLIC 1964 / NE ME QUITTE PAS).

Jan 98. (cd) *<816720-2>* **JACQUES BREL 1: GRAND JACQUES** (rec.1955)
– Haine / Grand Jacques (c'est trop facile) / Il pleut (les carreaux) / Diable (ca va) / Il nous faut regarder / C'est comme ca / Il peut pleuvoir / Fou du roi / Sur la place / S'll te faut / Bastille / Priere paienne / L'air de la betise / Qu'avons-nous fait, bonnes gens / Pardons / Saint Pierre / Pieds dans le ruisseau / Quand on n'a que l'amour / J'en appelle / Bourree du celibataire / Heureux / Bles / Demain l'on se Marie (la chanson des vieux amants).

Jan 98. (cd) *<816721-2>* **JACQUES BREL 2: LA VALSE A MILLE TEMPS** (rec.1958)
– Au printemps / Je ne sais pas / Dors ma mie bonsoir / Dites, si c'tait vrai (poeme) / Colonel / L'homme dans la cite / Lumiere jaillira / Voici / Litanies pour un retour / Seul / Dame patronnesse / La mort / La valse a mille temps / Je t'aime / Ne me quitte pas / Isabelle / Tendresse / Colombe.

Jan 98. (cd) *<816722-2>* **JACQUES BREL 3: LES FLAMANDES** (rec.1961)
– Les flamandes / L'ivrogne / Marieke / Prochain amour / Vivre debout / Prenoms de Paris / Clara / On n'oublie rien / Singes / Voir / L'adventure / Moutons / Amants de coeur (the lovers) / Il neige sur Liege / Pourquoi faut-il que les hommes / Coeurs tendres / L'enfance / Chanson de Van Horst / Il y a / Foire.

Jan 98. (cd) *<816723-2>* **JACQUES BREL 4: LE PLAT PAYS** (rec.1963)
– Le plat pays / Zangra / Caporal casse-pompon / La statue / Rosa / Les bourgeois / Madeleine / Les paumes du petit matin / Bruxelles / Chanson sans parole / Une ile / Le bigotes / Le vieux / Fenetres / Toros / Parlote / Filles et les chiens / La fanette / J'aimais / Bergers / Bonbons.

Jan 98. (cd) *<816724-2>* **JACQUES BREL 5: JEF** (rec.1964)
– Jef / Tango funebre / Desespreres / L'age idiot / Mathilde / Au suivant / Titine / Quand maman reviendra / Dernier repas / Grand-mere / Fernand / Chanson de Jacky / Ces gens-la / La, la / Cheval / Mon enfance / Bonbons 67.

Jan 98. (cd) *<816725-2>* **JACQUES BREL 6: J'ARRIVE** (rec.1968)
– Chanson des vieux amants / Jeun / Fils de / Mon pere disait / Gaz / L'ostendaise / Je suis un soir d'ete / Enfant / Comment tuer l'amant de sa femme quand o a / Vesoul / J'arrive / Biere / L'eclusier / Regarde bien petit / Quete / Mijn vlakke land (le plat pays) / De burgerij / Rosa / De nuttelozen de nacht.

Jan 98. (cd) *<816726-2>* **JACQUES BREL 7: ORLY** (rec.1977)
– Jaures / Ville s'endormait / Viellir / Bon dieu / Les f . . . / Orly / Remparts de varsovie / Voir un ami pleurer / Knokke-le-soute tango / JoJo / Le lion / Les marquises.

Jan 98. (cd) *<816727-2>* **JACQUES BREL 8: BREL EN PUBLIC OLYMPIA 1961** (live)
– Prenoms de Paris / Les bourgeois / Paumes du petit matin / Les Flamandes / La statue / Zangra / Marieke / Le biches / Madeleine / Singes / L'ivrogne / La valse a mille temps / Ne me quitte pas / Le moribund / Quand on n'a que l'amour.

Jan 98. (cd) *<816729-2>* **JACQUES BREL 9: BREL UN PUBLIC OLYMPIA 1964** (live)
– Amsterdam / Le timides / Dernier repas / Jardins du casino / Le vieux / Toros / Tango funebre / Le pat pays / Le bonbons / Mathilde / Les bigotes / Les bourgeois / Jef / Au suivant / Madeleine.

Jan 98. (cd) *<616729-2>* **JACQUES BREL 10: NE ME QUITTE PAS** (rec.1972)
– Ne me quitte pas / Marieke / On n'oublie rien / Les Flamandes / Renoms de Paris / Quand on n'a que l'amour / Les biches / Prochain amour / Le moribund / Le valse a mille temps / Je ne sais pas pourquoi.

Apr 99. (cd) *Polygram; <559231-2>* **EN SCENES (ENREGISTREMENT INEDITS) (live)**

Edie BRICKELL

Born: 10 Mar '66, Oak Cliff, Texas, USA. She joined Dallas group The NEW BOHEMIANS in 1985 after she drank enough to pluck up enough courage to venture on stage to front the band. As a group (alongside KENNY WITHROW, BRAD HOUSER, WES BURT-MARTIN, MATT CHAMBERLAIN and JOHN BUSH), they signed to 'Geffen' records, recording a debut album, 'SHOOTING RUBBERBANDS AT THE STARS', with producer Pat Moran in Wales. This went platinum in the States, reaching Top 5, after the release of the single, 'WHAT I AM'. A soft-rock campus crooner, her voice/range was similar to that of RICKIE LEE JONES, JONI MITCHELL or even MELANIE. Though a follow-up 45, 'CIRCLE', failed to consolidate this success, the band were praised for their live work, touring with BOB DYLAN and generally becoming critical favourites. They further refined their loose, folky jazz/muso sound on 'GHOST OF A DOG' (1990), yet despite favourable reviews, the album's sales were disappointing. BRICKELL subsequently embarked upon a relationship with PAUL SIMON, marrying him in summer '92 and giving birth to his son later that year. By this point, the band had already split and BRICKELL worked on 'PICTURE PERFECT MORNING', a pared-down solo set. Despite a few more star collaborations (including ART NEVILLE, DR. JOHN and BARRY WHITE!), the album was given a cool critical reception upon its 1994 release. • **Songwriters:** EDIE wrote most of material, except some with WITHROW (and also BUSH). Covered; A HARD RAIN'S A-GONNA FALL (Bob Dylan) / WALK ON THE WILD SIDE (Lou Reed) / THE EARLY DAY (John Williams). • **Trivia:** In Dec'89, EDIE and Co. collaborated on vinyl with SOUL II SOUL, recording their own composition 'CIRCLE'.

Album rating: SHOOTING RUBBERBANDS AT THE STARS (*6) / GHOST OF A DOG (*5) / PICTURE PERFECT MORNING (*4)

EDIE BRICKELL & THE NEW BOHEMIANS

EDIE BRICKELL – vocals, acoustic guitar / **KENNY WITHROW** (b.13 Apr'65) – guitar / **BRAD HOUSER** (b. 7 Sep'60) – bass / **WES BURT-MARTIN** (b.28 May'64) – guitar / **MATT CHAMBERLAIN** (b.17 Apr'67) – drums / **JOHN BUSH** – percussion / guests **WIX** – keyboards / (some by **BRENDAN ALY**)

		Geffen	Geffen	
Sep 88. (lp/c)(cd) *(WX 215/+C)(924192-2) <24192>* **SHOOTING RUBBERBANDS AT THE STARS**		25	4	
– What I am / Little Miss S. / Air of December / Love like we do / The wheel / Circle / Beat the time / She / Nothing / Now / Keep coming back. *(cd+=) – I do. (re-iss. Jan91 lp/c/cd; GEF/+C/D 24192) (cd re-iss. Mar95; GFLD 19268)*				
Jan 89. (7"/7"box) *(GEF 49/+B)* **WHAT I AM. / I DO**		31	7	Nov88
(12"+=/cd-s+=) (GEF 49 T/CD) – Walk on the wild side.				
Apr 89. (7") *(GEF 51) <27580>* **CIRCLE. / NOW**		74	48	Mar89
(12"+=/cd-s+=) (GEF 51 T/CD) – Plain Jane.				
Nov 89. (7") *(GEF 61)* **LOVE LIKE WE DO. /**			-	

— Next 45, was from the film 'Born On The 4th Of July' on 'M.C.A.'

Mar 90. (7") *(MCA 1397)* **A HARD RAIN'S A-GONNA FALL. / THE EARLY DAY, MASSAPEQUA 1957**				
(12"+=/cd-s+=) (MCAT/DMCA 1397) – ('A'version).				
Nov 90. (cd)(lp/c) *<(7599 24304-2)>(WX 386/+C)* **GHOST OF A DOG**		63	32	
– Mama help me / Black and blue / Carmelito / He said / Times like this / Ghost of a dog / 10,000 angels / Strings of love / Woyaha / Oak cliff bra / Stwisted / This eye. *(re-iss. May91 lp/c/cd; GEF/+C/D 24304) (cd re-iss. Mar95; GFLD 19269)*				
Jan 91. (7"/c-s) *(GEF)* **MAMA HELP ME. / OAK CLIFF BRA**				
(12"+=/cd-s+=) (GEF T/CD) – What I am / Beat the time (live).				

EDIE BRICKELL

— with **BILL DILLON, KENNY WITHROW, JOHN LEVENTHAL + BRIAN SOLTZ** – guitar / **TONY HALL, BAKIITHI KUMALO + BRAD HOUSER** – bass / **SHAWN PELTON or WILLIE GREEN** – drums / + guests hubby **PAUL SIMON + ART NEVILLE**

Aug 94. (cd/c) *<(GED/GEC 24715)>* **PICTURE PERFECT MORNING**		59	68	
– Tomorrow comes / Green / When the lights go down / Good times / Another woman's dream / Stay awhile / Hard times / Olivia / In the bath / Picture perfect morning / Lost in the moment. *(cd re-iss. Sep96; GFLD 19332)*				
Sep 94. (c-s) *(GEFC 78) <19273>* **GOOD TIMES / PICTURE PERFECT MORNING**		40	60	
(cd-s+=) (GEFTD 78) – Look out for me.				

above featured BARRY WHITE on dual vocals! HOUSER and CHAMBERLAIN formed their own eclectic funky jazz outfit, CRITTERS BUGGIN

BRIDGES (see under ⇒ A-HA)

BRINSLEY SCHWARZ

Formed: Turnbridge Wells, England . . . 1965 as the beat/psychedelic combo KIPPINGTON LODGE by SCHWARZ and NICK LOWE. After 5 flop singles between '67 & '69 (the first, 'SHY BOY', should have been a hit), they renamed themselves in Autumn '69. They came under the wing of DAVID ROBINSON, former tour manager for JIMI HENDRIX, who now headed the Famepushers Agency. On 3rd April '70, he chartered a plane to fly 150 music journalists to New York to see them support VAN MORRISON at the Fillmore East. This proved to be a six-figure sum disaster, due to an admittedly dodgy performance. Predictably, the press ignored their debut album for 'United Artists' and not surprisingly it bombed. Unbowed, they went off to take stock and write new material, resurfacing late in the year with follow-up 'DESPITE IT ALL'. The preceding single 'COUNTRY GIRL' was reminiscent of 'SWEETHEART OF THE RODEO'-era BYRDS and was as fine an example of country-rock as anything coming out of America at the time. Pioneers of the genre in the UK, the band went on to experiment with many other areas of American roots music, evidenced on their 1972 album, 'NERVOUS ON THE ROAD'. Their interest in the "down home" sound had deepened upon seeing American bar band EGGS OVER EASY playing at the Tally Ho club in London. The venue had become a focus for the burgeoning "pub rock" scene of which The BRINSLEY's would soon be such an integral part, along with acts such as BEES MAKE HONEY and DUCKS DELUXE. As well as digging the band's R&B boogie, BRINSLEY SCHWARZ were heavily influenced by EGGS OVER EASY's freewheeling attitude which didn't give a fig for the banks of Marshall stacks and sprawling concept albums which were de rigeur in the early 70's. The same back to basics spirit that inspired the BRINSLEY's to scale down the length of their songs and cut their hair, laid the foundations for the punk explosion later in the decade as well as breaking such important figures as ELVIS COSTELLO and JOE STRUMMER (101'ERS). For the moment though, the band had found a comfortable niche and the track 'HAPPY DOING WHAT WE'RE DOING', from the 'NERVOUS ON THE ROAD' set seemed to confirm this. Another two excellent albums followed, showcasing LOWE's comprehensive songwriting talent on such classic tracks as '(WHAT'S SO FUNNY 'BOUT) PEACE, LOVE AND UNDERSTANDING'. Ironically, no commercial breakthrough came and the band split amicably in 1975, with NICK LOWE going on to a successful solo career, while BRINSLEY and keyboard player BOB ANDREWS helped to form The RUMOUR (GRAHAM PARKER's backing band). • **Covered:** (The Beatles') I SHOULD HAVE KNOWN BETTER. / TELL ME WHY as 'The LIMELIGHT' in '75. • **Trivia:** In 1974, they were featured as The ELECTRICIANS (with DAVE EDMUNDS; their sometimes producer) in the film 'Stardust'.

Album rating: BRINSLEY SCHWARZ (*5) / DESPITE IT ALL (*5) / SILVER PISTOL

(*7) / NERVOUS ON THE ROAD (*6) / PLEASE DON'T EVER CHANGE (*6) / THE NEW FAVOURITES OF BRINSLEY SCHWARZ (*7) / SURRENDER TO THE RHYTHM (THE BEST OF BRINSLEY SCHWARZ) compilation (*7)

KIPPINGTON LODGE

BRINSLEY SCHWARZ – guitar, sax / **NICK LOWE** (b.25 Mar'49, Woodbridge, England) – vocals, bass / **BARRY LANDERMAN** – organ / **PETE WHALE** – drums

		Parlophone	Capitol
Oct 67.	(7") (R 5645) **SHY BOY. / LADY ON A BICYCLE**		-
Mar 68.	(7") (R 5677) <2236> **RUMOURS. / AND SHE CRIED** (above 4 tracks re-iss. Nov78.7"ep on 'EMI')		

—— **BOB ANDREWS** (b.20 Jun'49) – organ, vox repl. BARRY to VANITY FARE

Aug 68.	(7") (R 5717) **TELL ME A STORY. / UNDERSTAND A WOMAN**		-
Dec 68.	(7") (R 5750) **TOMORROW TODAY. / TURN OUT THE LIGHT**		-
May 69.	(7") (R 5776) **IN MY LIFE. / I CAN SEE HER FACE**		-

BRINSLEY SCHWARZ

—— (**BRINSLEY, NICK + BOB**) recruited **BILLY RANKIN** – drums; to repl. PETE

		U.A.	Capitol
Apr 70.	(lp) (UAS 29111) <SWBC 11869> **BRINSLEY SCHWARZ** – Hymn to me / Shining brightly / Rock & roll women / Lady constant / What do you suggest / Mayfly / Ballad of a has-been beauty queen. (cd-iss. Feb94 on 'Repertoire'; REP 4421WY)		
May 70.	(7") (UP 35118) **SHINING BRIGHTLY. / WHAT DO YOU SUGGEST**		
Jun 70.	(7") <3004> **HYMN TO ME. / ROCK & ROLL WOMAN**	-	

		Liberty	not iss.
Nov 70.	(7") (LBY 15419) **COUNTRY GIRL. / FUNK ANGEL** (re-iss. 1972 on 'United Artists'; UP 35312)	-	
Dec 70.	(lp) (LBG 83427) **DESPITE IT ALL** – Country girl / The slow one / Funk angel / Piece of home / Love song / Starship / Ebury down / Old Jarrow.		

—— added **IAN GOMM** (b.17 Mar'47) – guitar, vocals

		U.A.	U.A.
Oct 71.	(lp) (UAS 29217) <5566> **SILVER PISTOL** – Dry land / Merry go round / One more day / Nightingale / Silver pistol / The last time I was fooled / Unknown number / Range war / Egypt / Niki Hoeke speedway / Ju ju man / Rockin' chair. (re-iss. Apr86 on 'Edsel'; ED 190) (cd-iss. Sep90; EDCD 190)		
Jan 72.	(7") <50915> **SILVER PISTOL. / NIGHTINGALE**	-	

—— Contributed 5 tracks to 'GREASY TRUCKERS' live lp, Apr72.

Sep 72.	(lp) (UAS 29374) <5647> **NERVOUS ON THE ROAD** – It's been so long / Happy doing what we're doing / Surrender to the rhythm / Don't lose your grip on love / Nervous on the road (but can't stay at home) / Feel a little funky / I like it like that / Brand new you, brand new me / Home in my hand / Why, why, why, why, why. (re-iss. Dec80 on 'Liberty'; LBR 1040) (cd-iss. Oct95 on 'Beat Goes On'; BGOCD 289)		
Oct 72.	(7") <50976> **NERVOUS ON THE ROAD. / HARRY DOING WHAT WE'RE DOING**	-	
May 73.	(7"; as The HITTERS) (UP 35530) **THE HYPOCRITE. / THE VERSION**		-
Aug 73.	(7") (UP 35588) **SPEEDO. / I WORRY**		-
Oct 73.	(lp) (UAS 29489) **PLEASE DON'T EVER CHANGE** – Hooked on love / Why do we hurt the one we love? / I worry ('bout you baby) / Don't ever change / Home in my hand / Play that fast thing (one more time) / I won't make it without you / Down in Mexico / Speedo / Hypocrite (the version). (re-iss. Jan88 on 'Edsel'; ED 237) (cd-iss. Sep90; EDCD 237)		
Mar 74.	(7") (UP 35642) **I'VE CRIED MY LAST TEAR. / (IT'S GONNA BE A) BRINGDOWN**		-
May 74.	(7") (UP 35700) **(WHAT'S SO FUNNY 'BOUT) PEACE, LOVE AND UNDERSTANDING. / EVER SINCE YOU'RE GONE**		-
Jul 74.	(lp) (UAS 29641) **THE NEW FAVOURITES OF BRINSLEY SCHWARZ** – Peace, love and understanding / Ever since you're gone / Ugly things / I got the real thing / Look what's in your eye tonight / Now's the time / Small town, big city / Trying to live my life without you / I like you I don't love you / Down in the dive. (re-iss. Aug80 on 'Liberty'; LBR 1033)		
Jan 75.	(7") (UP 35768) **I LIKE YOU, I DON'T LOVE YOU. / EVERYBODY**		-
Jan 75.	(7"; as LIMELIGHT) (UP 35779) **I SHOULD HAVE KNOWN BETTER. / TELL ME WHY**		-
Mar 75.	(7") (UP 35812) **THERE'S A CLOUD IN MY HEART. / I GOT THE REAL THING**		-

—— Disbanded Mar75. SCHWARZ and RANKIN joined DUCKS DELUXE, The former later joining with ANDREWS in GRAHAM PARKER & THE RUMOUR. IAN GOMM later went solo, as did NICK LOWE.

– compilations, others, etc. –

on 'United Artists' unless mentioned otherwise

Mar 74.	(lp) (USP 101) **ORIGINAL GOLDEN GREATS**		-
Jun 76.	(7"m) (UP 36409) **COUNTRY GIRL. / HOOKED ON LOVE / SURRENDER TO THE RHYTHM**		-
Jul 78.	(lp) (UAK 30177) **FIFTEEN THOUGHTS OF BRINSLEY SCHWARZ**		-
Sep 78.	(7") (UP 36466) **PEACE, LOVE AND UNDERSTANDING. / I'VE CRIED MY LAST TEAR**		-
1978.	(7"ep; by KIPPINGTON LODGE) E.M.I.; (NUT 2894) **KIPPINGTON LODGE**		
May 88.	(lp/c/cd on 'Charly') Decal; (LIK/TCLIK 22/CDCHARLY 22) **IT'S ALL OVER NOW**		
Jul 91.	(cd/c/lp) E.M.I.; (CD/TC+/EMS 1407) **SURRENDER TO THE RHYTHM (THE BEST OF BRINSLEY SCHWARZ)**		-

—— Country girl / Surrender to the rhythm / Ugly things / Happy what we're doing / The look what's in your eyes / Last time I was fooled / Silver pistol / Nightingale / Hypocrite / Trying to live my life without you / I like it like that / Nervous on the road / Down in Mexico / I worry ('bout you baby) / Play that fast thing (one more time) / Don't lose your grip on love / Ju Ju man / Down in the dive / Home in my hand.

| Jul 94. | (cd) Beat Goes On; (BGOCD 239) **BRINSLEY SCHWARZ / DESPITE IT ALL** | | - |
| Dec 95. | (cd) Beat Goes On; (BGOCD 289) **NERVOUS ON THE ROAD / THE NEW FAVOURITES OF . . .** | | - |

BRITISH LIONS (see under ⇒ MOTT THE HOOPLE)

Meredith BROOKS

Born: 1966, Oregon, USA. Learning to play guitar at the age of 10, BROOKS began writing songs soon after. In the mid-80's, she helped form The GRACES, an all-female trio headed by ex-GO-GO's guitarist, CHARLOTTE CAFFEY, although they split after one album, 'PERFECT VIEW' (1989), a minor hit 45, 'LAY DOWN YOUR ARMS', and record company failures. She subsequently relocated to L.A. and secured a deal with 'Capitol', finally releasing a debut single, 'BITCH' in Spring '97. Believed to be about PMT, the track obviously struck a chord with moodswing-happy females who'd bought the last ALANIS MORISSETTE album. A massive transatlantic Top 10 hit, the track's success was repeated by her debut album, 'BLURRING THE EDGES'. The raven-haired angst-ridden singer looks set for big things as the female singer/songwriter lobby continues to gather strength.

Album rating: BLURRING THE EDGES (*6)

GRACES

MEREDITH BROOKS – vocals, guitar / **CHARLOTTE CAFFEY** – vocals, guitar (ex-GO-GO's) / **GIA CIAMBOTTI** – guitar / + a plethora of session people

		A&M	A&M	
Sep 89.	(7"/12") (AM/+Y 526) <1440> **LAY DOWN YOUR ARMS. / OUT IN THE FIELDS** (cd-s+=) (CDEE 526) – Should I let you in.		56	Aug89
Oct 89.	(lp/c/cd) <(AMA/AMC/CDA 5265)> **PERFECT VIEW** – Lay down your arms / When the sun goes down / Perfect view / Fear no love / Time waits for no one / 50,000 candles burning / Should I let you in / We never met / Tomorrow / Out in the fields.			
Jan 90.	(7") (AM 538) <1453> **PERFECT VIEW. / OUT IN THE FIELDS** (12"+=/cd-s+=) (AMY/CDQ 538) – We never meet.			

—— split some time in 1990, CAFFEY continued to write songs

MEREDITH BROOKS

		Capitol	Capitol	
Jul 97.	(c-s/7") (TC+/CL 790) <58634> **BITCH. / BITCH (Madgroove mix)** (cd-s+=) (CDCL 790) – ('A'-Transistor mix) / ('A'-E Team funky radio edit).	6	2	Apr97
Aug 97.	(cd/c) (CD/TC EST 2298) <36919> **BLURRING THE EDGES** – I need / Bitch / Watched you fall / Pollyanne / Shatter / My little town / What would happen / It don't get better / Birthday / Stop / Wash my hands.	5	22	May97
Nov 97.	(c-s) (TCCL 794) **I NEED / EVERYTIME SHE WALKS AWAY** (cd-s+=) (CDCL 794) – Down by the river / ('A'original). (cd-s) (CDCLS 794) – ('A'side) / ('A'-Crusty mix) / Bitch (Todd Terry mix) / Bitch (united mix).	28		
Feb 98.	(c-s/cd-s) (TCCL/CDCL 798) <58681> **WHAT WOULD HAPPEN / COME UNDONE / STOP / BITCH**	49	46	

Edgar BROUGHTON BAND

(dig out; Great Psychedelic . . .)

Arthur BROWN

(dig out; 4th edition & Great Psychedelic . . .)

Ian BROWN (see under ⇒ STONE ROSES)

James BROWN

Born: 3 May'33 in Barnwell, South Carolina. At the age of five, BROWN moved to his Aunt's brothel in Augusta, Georgia, during which time he learned to play piano, drums and guitar. By the time he was nineteen, after a brief spell as a semi-pro boxer and a brief spell in jail, he had settled in Georgia and was a member of BOBBY BYRD's quartet, The GOSPEL STARLIGHTERS. A raw Southern gospel group, they subsequently evolved into a R&B outfit, in the process changing their name to The AVONS, then The FLAMES. The band performed R&B covers, among them an ORIOLES song, 'BABY PLEASE DON'T GO'. After some fine tuning, BROWN brought the "please" to the forefront, crafting the showstopping 'PLEASE, PLEASE, PLEASE'. On hearing the tune, LITTLE RICHARD, at the time Georgia's most celebrated black musician, told Brown to move to Macon, where the song was cut at a local radio station under the band name the FAMOUS FLAMES, the prefix added courtesy of Richard's manager, Clint Brantly. Although the song was refused by a number of labels, when Ralph Bass of 'King' Records heard the tune, he immediately signed the group and the track was re-recorded at King's Ohio studio. The session proved to be more troublesome than expected, as the musical director and owner of the label couldn't come to grips with BROWN's unusual and now heavily influential writing style of hitting on the downbeat instead of the upbeat. Nevertheless, the track was eventually released on King's 'Federal' label in March '56, making #5 on the Billboard R&B chart. It would be another three years before their next hit, the infectious 'TRY ME' reached #1 on the R&B chart and crucially created enough money for BROWN to hire a backing band, the first quintet led by the tenor sax of J.C. DAVIS. It was during the end of the 50's, with the components all in place, that the band set about touring to sharpen their sound and BROWN's routines of knee-drops, flying splits and cochlea-piercing screams. Whilst BROWN continued to supply hits for 'King', he still hadn't hit the big time, subsequently trying to persuade the label to front the money for a live recorded performance. With 'King' not convinced that such a record would sell, BROWN decided to put up his own cash, coming up with one of the most successful live LP's of all time, the '63 killer 'LIVE AT THE APOLLO'. The record not only made it to #2 on the Billboard album charts, it also had the knock-on effect of mammoth audience attendances, and in turn increased sales figures and the high profile that BROWN craved. This mushroomed to an even greater height when, in '65, he released the definitive funk single, 'PAPA'S GOT A BRAND NEW BAG', featuring a larger band led by the trumpet of LEWIS HAMLIN, in the process modifying his style from the gospel and blues structure to a more straight-ahead approach. His singing was also reaching new heights of primordial intensity, fusing with a tight and oh-so-funky backing band. The middle to late 60's proved a purple patch for BROWN, with one classic single following another, 'IT'S A MAN'S WORLD' in '66, 'COLD SWEAT' in '67, 'SAY IT LOUD – I'M BLACK AND PROUD' in '68 and 'GET UP / I FEEL LIKE BEING A SEX MACHINE' in '70, his backing band including the likes of the PARKER brothers (MACEO and MELVIN) and older stalwarts like JIMMY NOLAN and ALPHONSO KELLUM on guitars. The early 70's saw the line-up constantly changing, PEE WEE ELLIS, BOOTSY COLLINS and PHELPS COLLINS the leading lights in the backing band dubbed first The PACEMAKERS, then latterly the now familiar J.B.'s, FRED WESLEY joining soon after to form the backbone of the band alongside MACEO. BROWN's '72 single, 'KING HEROIN' is often cited as the first rap record (although the waters are cloudy on this one), and he even made it to Zaire for the "Rumble In The Jungle", solidifying his status as Soul Brother Number One. He continued to tour the world throughout the '70s, simultaneously influencing popular music styles wherever he went, although the quality of his recordings became ever more infrequent set next to the standards he had already set, a prime example being the '79 offering 'TAKE A LOOK AT THOSE CAKES'. However, his spectacular cameo as the rocking reverend in the 80's cult classic film, 'The Blues Brothers', opened the gates to a whole new generation of fans, and as the Stars & Stripes clad special guest in 'Rocky IV', he stole the show whilst achieving yet another Top 10 hit with the cheesy 'LIVING IN AMERICA'. BROWN has had his problems with the law along the way, the most publicised event occuring in September '88, when he walked into an insurance seminar with a shotgun in an attempt to find out who had used his private toilet, the tale ending in a two-state police chase and two years in jail. Having amassed 98 entries on Billboard's Top 40 R&B singles chart over his career, earning the nickname 'the hardest working man in showbusiness', as well as being sampled by other musicians an estimated 4000 times, his journey from juvenile delinquent to the Godfather Of Soul bears all the hallmarks of greatness.

Album rating (selective): PLEASE, PLEASE, PLEASE (*6) / TRY ME! (*6) / LIVE AT THE APOLLO (*9) / PURE DYNAMITE! LIVE AT THE ROYAL (*6) / LIVE AT THE APOLLO, VOL.II (*7) / REVOLUTION OF THE MIND – LIVE AT THE APOLLO, VOL. III (*8) / THE PAYBACK (*7) / HELL (*7) / THERE IT IS (*7) / FUNKY PRESIDENT (*7) / THE BEST OF JAMES BROWN (THE GODFATHER OF SOUL) compilation (*9) / STAR TIME boxed set (*9)

JAMES BROWN & THE FAMOUS FLAMES

JAMES BROWN – vocals, multi / **BOBBY BYRD** – organ / **JOHNNY TERRY** / **SYLVESTER KEELS** / **NAFLOYD SCOTT** – guitar / etc.

		not iss.	Federal
Feb 56.	(7") <12258> **PLEASE, PLEASE, PLEASE. / WHY DO YOU DO ME**	-	☐
May 56.	(7") <12264> **I DON'T KNOW. / I FEEL THAT OLD FEELING COMING ON**	-	☐
Aug 56.	(7") <12277> **NO, NO, NO, NO. / HOLD MY BABY'S HAND**	-	☐
Dec 56.	(7") <12289> **JUST WON'T DO ME RIGHT. / LET'S MAKE IT**	-	☐
Jan 57.	(7") <12290> **CHONNIE-ON-CHON. / I WON'T PLEAD NO MORE**	-	☐
Feb 57.	(lp) <610> **PLEASE, PLEASE, PLEASE**	-	☐

– Please, please, please / Chonnie-on-chon / Hold my baby's hand / I feel that same old feeling coming on / Just won't do right / Baby cries over the ocean / I don't know / Tell me what I did wrong / Try me / That dood it / Begging, begging / I walked alone / No, no, no, no / That's when I lost my heart / Let's make it / Love or a game.

Mar 57.	(7") <12292> **CAN'T BE THE SAME. / GONNA TRY**	-	☐
Jul 57.	(7") <12295> **LOVE OR A GAME. / MESSING WITH THE BLUES**	-	☐
Nov 57.	(7") <12300> **YOU'RE MINE, YOU'RE MINE. / I WALKED ALONE**	-	☐
Mar 58.	(7") <12311> **THAT DOOD IT. / BABY CRIES OVER THE OCEAN**	-	☐
May 58.	(7") <12316> **BEGGING, BEGGING. / THAT'S WHEN I LOST MY HEART**	-	☐

Nov 58.	(7") <12337> **TRY ME. / TELL ME WHAT I DID WRONG**	-	48
Apr 59.	(7") <12348> **I WANT YOU SO BAD. / THERE MUST BE THE REASON**	-	☐
Jun 59.	(7") <12352> **I'VE GOT TO CHANGE. / IT HURTS TO TELL YOU**	-	☐
Jul 59.	(lp) <635> **TRY ME**	-	☐

– Try me / There must be a reason / Strange things happen / Messing with the blues / Why do you do me / I've got to cry / Fine old foxy self / I want you so bad / It was you / I've got to change / Can't be the same / It hurts to tell you / I won't plead no more / You're mine, you're mine / Gonna try / Don't let it happen to me.

| Oct 59. | (7") <12361> **GOOD GOOD LOVIN'. / DON'T LET IT HAPPEN TO ME** | - | ☐ |
| Dec 59. | (7") <12364> **IT WAS YOU. / GOT TO CRY** | - | ☐ |

—— Released MASHED POTATOES on 'Dade' label, as NAT KENDRICK & THE SWANS.

| Feb 60. | (7") <683> **THINK** | - | ☐ |

– Think / Good good lovin' / Wonder when you're coming home / I'll go crazy / This old heart / I know it's true / Bewildered / I'll never never let you go / You've got the power / If you want me / Baby, you're right / So long.

| Mar 60. | (7") <12369> **I'LL GO CRAZY. / I KNOW IT'S TRUE** | - | ☐ |

		Parlophone	Federal
Jun 60.	(7") (R 4667) <12370> **THINK. / YOU'VE GOT THE POWER**	33	86 Apr60
Nov 60.	(7") (H 273) <12378> **THIS OLD HEART. / WONDER WHEN YOU'RE GOING HOME** (above issued on 'Fontana' UK)	-	79 Jul60

		Parlophone	King
Nov 60.	(7") <5423> **THE BELLS. / AND I DO JUST WHAT I WANT**	-	68
Jan 61.	(7") <5438> **HOLD IT (instrumental). / THE SCRATCH (instrumental)**	-	☐
Feb 61.	(7") <5442> **BEWILDERED. / IF YOU WANT ME**	-	40
Apr 61.	(7") <5466> **I DON'T MIND. / LOVE DON'T LOVE NOBODY**	-	47
Jun 61.	(7") <5485> **SUDS (instrumental). / STICKY (instrumental)**	-	☐
Aug 61.	(7") <5519> **CROSSFIRING (instrumental). / NIGHT FLYING (instrumental)**	-	☐
Sep 61.	(7") <5524> **BABY, YOU'RE RIGHT. / I'LL NEVER NEVER LET YOU GO**	-	47
1961.	(lp) <743> **THE AMAZING JAMES BROWN**	-	☐

– I love you, yes I do / Lost someone / You don't have to go / Dancin' little thing / The bells / Tell me what you're gonna do / So long / Just you and me / And I do just what I want / Come over here / I don't mind / Love don't love nobody.

Nov 61.	(7") <5547> **I LOVE YOU, YES I DO. / JUST YOU AND ME DARLING**	-	☐
Jan 62.	(7") <5573> **LOST SOMEONE. / CROSS FIRING (instrumental)**	-	48
Jul 62.	(7") (R 4922) <5614> **NIGHT TRAIN (instrumental). / WHY DOES EVERYTHING HAPPEN TO ME** (re-iss. Dec64 on 'Sue'; WI 360)	-	35 Apr62
Aug 62.	(7") (R 4952) <5657> **SHOUT AND SHIMMY. / COME OVER HERE**	-	61
Sep 62.	(7") <5672> **MASHED POTATOES U.S.A. / YOU DON'T HAVE TO GO**	-	82
Nov 62.	(7") <5698> **(CAN YOU) FEEL IT. / (part 2)**	-	☐
Dec 62.	(7") <5701> **THREE HEARTS IN A TANGLE. / I'VE GOT MONEY**	-	93

		London	King
Dec 62.	(lp) <826> **LIVE AT THE APOLLO (live)**	-	2

– I'll go crazy / Try me / Think / I don't mind / Lost someone / I found someone / Why do you do me like you do / I want you so bad / I love you yes I do / Why does everything happen to me / Bewildered / Please don't go / Night train. (UK-iss.Sep64; HA 8184) (re-iss. Aug75 on 'Polydor') <re-iss. Nov80 as 'LIVE AND LOWDOWN AT THE APOLLO, VOL.1' on 'Solid Smoke'; 8006> (re-iss. Sep73 on 'Polydor' lp/c; SPE LP/MC 46) (cd-iss. Jul90; 843479-2)

Jan 63.	(7") <5710> **EVERY BEAT OF MY HEART (instrumental). / LIKE A BABY**	-	99
Apr 63.	(7") (HL 9730) <5739> **PRISONER OF LOVE. / CHOO CHOO (LOCOMOTION)**	-	18
Jun 63.	(7") (HL 9775) <5767> **THESE FOOLISH THINGS. / (CAN YOU) FEEL IT**	55	73
Sep 63.	(lp) <851> **PRISONER OF LOVE**	-	73

– Prisoner of love / Waiting in vain / Again / Lost someone / Bewildered / So long / Signed, sealed & delivered / Try me / (Can you) Feel it (pt.1) / How long darling / The thing in 'G'. (re-iss.Nov83 on 'Polydor'; 8134 911)

Oct 63.	(7") <5803> **SIGNED, SEALED AND DELIVERED. / WAITING IN VAIN**	-	77
Jan 64.	(7") <5829> **I'VE GOT TO CHANGE. / THE BELLS**	-	☐
Feb 64.	(7") <5842> **OH BABY DON'T YOU WEEP. / (part 2)**	-	23
Mar 64.	(7") <5853> **PLEASE, PLEASE, PLEASE. / IN THE WEE WEE HOURS**	-	95

—— He signed to 'Smash' records in the US and was also retained by 'King'. In the UK, 'King' was licensed by 'London' until late '65. The releases on 'Smash' US were on 'Philips' UK, and marked *.

May 64.	(7") *<1898> **CALEDONIA. / EVIL**	-	95
Jun 64.	(7") <5876> **AGAIN. / HOW LONG DARLING**	-	☐
Jul 64.	(lp) (HA 8177) <883> **PURE DYNAMITE! LIVE AT THE ROYAL (live)**	10 Feb64	

– Shout and shimmy / These foolish things / Signed, sealed and delivered / Like a baby / I'll never let you go / Please, please, please / Oh, baby, don't you weep / Good, good lovin'.

Jul 64.	(7") <5899> **SO LONG. / DANCIN' LITTLE THING**	-	☐
Aug 64.	(7") *<1908> **THE THINGS I USED TO DO. / OUT OF THE BLUE**	-	99
Sep 64.	(7") (BF 1368)*<1919> **OUT OF SIGHT. / MAYBE THE LAST TIME**	24 Aug64	
Jun 64.	(7") <5922> **TELL ME WHAT YOU'RE GONNA DO. / I DON'T CARE**	-	☐

Sep 64. (lp) (BL 7630)*<67054> **SHOWTIME (live)** — 61 May64

Sep 64. (lp) Ember; (EMB 3357) **TELL ME WHAT YOU'RE GONNA DO** — -
– Just you and me darling / I love, yes I do / I don't mind / Come over here / The bells / Love don't love nobody / Dancin' little thing / Lost someone / And I do just what I want / So long / You don't have to go / Tell me what you're gonna do. (cd-iss. Mar95 on 'Charly'; CPCD 8053)

Oct 64. (7") <5952> **THINK. / TRY ME** - -

Oct 64. (7") <5956> **FINE OLD FOXY SELF. / MEDLEY** - -

Dec 64. (7") (HL 9945) <5968> **HAVE MERCY BABY. / JUST WON'T DO RIGHT** - 92

Mar 65. (7") *<1975> **DEVIL'S HIDEAWAY (instrumental). / WHO'S AFRAID OF VIRGINIA WOOLF (instrumental)** - -

Apr 65. (lp) (BL 7664)*<67057> **GRITS AND SOUL (instrumental)** -
– Grits / Tempted / There / After you're through / Devil's den / Who's afraid of Virginia Woolf / Infatuation / Wee wee / Mister hip / Headache.

Apr 65. (7") <5995> **THIS OLD HEART. / IT WAS YOU** - -

Jul 65. (lp) (HA 8231) <909> **PLEASE, PLEASE, PLEASE** -
– Try me / Please, please, please / I feel that old feeling coming on / That's when I lost my heart / Chonnie on chon / Hold my baby's hand / Tell me what I did wrong / Baby cries over the ocean / Begging, begging / No, no, no, no / That dood it / I don't know / I walked alone / Love or a game / Let's make it / Just won't do right. (re-iss. Nov83; 2489 194)

—— His UK touring band 1965 **BOBBY BYRD, BOBBY BENNETT, JAMES CRAWFORD + LLOYD STALLWORTH**

Aug 65. (7") (HL 9990) <5999> **PAPA'S GOT A BRAND NEW BAG. / (part 2)** 25 8 Jul65

Sep 65. (lp) <938> **PAPA'S GOT A BRAND NEW BAG** - 26
– Papa's got a brand new bag / Mashed potatoes U.S.A. / This old heart / Cross firing / Doin' the limbo / Baby, you're right / Love don't love nobody / Have mercy baby / And I do just what I want / I stay in the chapel every night / You don't have to go. (UK-iss.Mar66; HA 8262) (re-iss. May67 on 'Pye International'; NPL 28099) (re-iss. Nov83 on 'Polydor'; 2489 195)

Oct 65. (lp) (HA 8240) **JAMES BROWN AND HIS FAMOUS FLAMES TOUR THE U.S.A. (live)** - -

Dec 65. (7") (BF 1458)*<2008> **TRY ME (instrumental) / PAPA'S GOT A BRAND NEW BAG (instrumental)** 63

Dec 65. (lp) (BL 7697)*<67072> **JAMES BROWN PLAYS JAMES BROWN TODAY AND YESTERDAY** 42 Nov65
– Papa's got a brand new bag / Oh baby don't you weep / Every beat of my heart / Out of sight / Sidewinder / Maybe the last time / Hold it / Song for my father.

	Pye Int.	King	

Feb 66. (7") (7N 25350) <6015> **I GOT YOU (I FEEL GOOD). / I CAN'T HELP IT** 29 3 Nov65

Mar 66. (7") <6020> **LOST SOMEONE. / I'LL GO CRAZY** - 94 Jan66 / 73

Apr 66. (lp) (NPL 28072) <946> **I GOT YOU (I FEEL GOOD)** 36 Jan66
– I got you (I feel good) / Good good lovin' / Lost someone / I can't help it / You've got the power / Night train / I've got money / Dancin' little thing / Three hearts in a tangle / Suds / Love don't love nobody.

Apr 66. (7") (7N 25367) <6025> **AIN'T THAT A GROOVE. / (part 2)** 42 Feb66

Apr 66. (7") <6029> **PRISONER OF LOVE. / I'VE GOT TO CHANGE** -

May 66. (7") <6032> **COME OVER HERE. / TELL ME WHAT YOU'RE GONNA DO** -

Apr 66. (7") (BF 1481)*<2028> **NEW BREED (instrumental) / (part 2)** -

May 66. (lp) (BL 7718)*<67090> **JAMES BROWN PLAYS NEW BREED** Apr66
– New breed / Slow walk / Fat bag / Vanshelia / Jabo / Lost in the mood of changes / All about my girl / Hooks / Something else.

Jun 66. (7") (7N 25371) <6035> **IT'S A MAN'S MAN'S MAN'S WORLD. / IS IT YES OR IS IT NO?** 13 8 Apr66

Jun 66. (7") <6037> **JUST WON'T DO RIGHT. / I'VE GOT MONEY** -

Jun 66. (7") *<2042> **JAMES BROWN'S BOO-GA-LOO (instrumental) / LOST IN A MOOD OF CHANGES (instrumental)** -

Jul 66. (lp) (NPL 28079) <985> **IT'S A MAN'S, MAN'S, MAN'S WORLD** 90
– It's a man's, man's man's world / Is it yes or is it no? / Ain't that a groove (pt.1 & 2) / The scratch / Bewildered / The bells in the wee wee hours / Come over here / I don't mind / Just you and me / I love you, yes I do. (re-iss. Nov83 on 'Polydor'; 2489 197)

Jul 66. (7") <6040> **IT WAS YOU. / I DON'T CARE** - -

Aug 66. (7") <6044> **THIS OLD HEART. / HOW LONG DARLING** - -

Sep 66. (7") (7N 25379) <6048> **MONEY WON'T CHANGE YOU. / (pt.2)** 53 Jul66

Nov 66. (7") <6056> **DON'T BE A DROP-OUT. / TELL ME THAT YOU LOVE ME** - 50

Dec 66. (7") <6064> **THE CHRISTMAS SONG. / (pt.2)** - -

Dec 66. (7") <6065> **SWEET LITTLE BABY BOY. / (pt.2)** - -

Dec 66. (lp) (NPL 28097) **THE JAMES BROWN CHRISTMAS ALBUM** (festive songs)

Dec 66. (7") (7N 25411) <6071> **BRING IT UP. / NOBODY KNOWS** 29

Dec 66. (7") <6072> **LET'S MAKE CHRISTMAS MEAN SOMETHING THIS YEAR. / (pt.2)** - -

Feb 67. (lp) (NPL 28093) **MIGHTY INSTRUMENTALS** -
– Papa's got a brand new bag (part 1) / Feel it / Hold it / Sticky / Scratch / James Brown's house party / Night train / Every beat of my heart / Cross firing / Suds / Doin' the limbo / Choo choo.

Mar 67. (7") *<2064> **LET'S GO GET STONED (instrumental) / OUR DAY WILL COME (instrumental)** -

Mar 67. (lp; stereo/mono) (S+BL 7761)*<67064> **HANDFUL OF SOUL** Nov66
– Our day will come / Get loose / Oh Henry / Let's go get stoned / Hot mix / Hold on, I'm coming / King / When a man loves a woman / Message to Michael / 6345-789.

Apr 67. (7") (7N 25418) <6086> **KANSAS CITY / STONE FOX (instrumental)** 55

May 67. (lp) (NPL 28103) <1016> **SINGS RAW SOUL** 88 Apr67
– Bring it up / Don't be a drop out / Till then / Tell me that you love me / Yours and mine / Money won't change you (part 1 & 2) / Only you / Let yourself go / The

nearness of you / Nobody knows / Stone fox.

—— In May '67, he issued 7" 'THINK' a collaboration with VICKI ANDERSON hit No.100 in the US.

Nov 67. (lp) (NPL 28104) <1018> **LIVE AT THE GARDEN (live)** 41 Jun67
– Out of sight / Bring it up / Try me / Let yourself go / Hip bag '67 / Prisoner of love / It may be the last time / I got you / Ain't that a groove (parts 1 & 2) / Please, please, please / Bring it up.

Jul 67. (7") (7N 25423) <6100> **LET YOURSELF GO. / GOOD ROCKIN' TONIGHT** 46

Jul 67. (lp) (NPL 28100) **MR. EXCITEMENT** (recordings from 1962) (re-iss. Nov83 on 'Polydor')

Jul 67. (7") *<2075> **JIMMY MACK (instrumental) / WHAT DO YOU LIKE (instrumental)** -

—— In mid'67, he released 'I LOVE YOU PORGY'. / 'YOURS AND MINE' on 'Bethlehem' <3089>.

—— **ALFRED 'Pee-Wee' ELLIS** – brass; repl. JONES new **JIMMY NOLEN** – guitar / **CLYDE STUBBLEFIELD** – drums / **MACEO PARKER** – tenor sax / **ST. CLAIR PINCKNEY** – tenor sax / etc.

Sep 67. (7") (7N 25430) <6110> **COLD SWEAT. / (pt.2)** 7 Jul67

Oct 67. (lp) (658 043) <1020> **COLD SWEAT** 35 Sep67
– Cold sweat (pt.1 & 2) / Nature boy / Come rain or come shine / I love you Porgy / Back stabbin' / Fever / Mona Lisa / I want to be around / Good rockin' tonight / Stagger Lee / Kansas City. (re-iss. Nov83 on 'Polydor')

Oct 67. (7") <6112> **AMERICA IS MY HOME. / (part 2)** -
<hit US No.52 in May68>

Nov 67. (lp) (582 703) **THE JAMES BROWN SHOW (live)** -
– I'll go crazy / Try me / Think / I don't mind / Lost someone / Please, please, please / You've got the power / I found someone / Why do you do me / I want you so bad / I love you yes I do / Why does everything happen to me / Bewildered / Please don't go / Night train.

Nov 67. (7") (7N 25441) <6122> **GET IT TOGETHER. / (pt.2)** 40 Oct67

Nov 67. (7") <6133> **FUNKY SOUL No.1 (instrumental) / THE SOUL OF J.B. (instrumental)** -

Nov 67. (7") <6141> **I GUESS I'LL HAVE TO CRY, CRY, CRY. / JUST PLAIN FUNK (instrumental)** -
<hit No.US 55 in Jul68>

		Polydor	King

Dec 67. (7") (56740) <6144> **I CAN'T STAND MYSELF (WHEN YOU TOUCH ME). / THERE WAS A TIME** 28 / 36

Mar 68. (lp) (184 136) <1030> **I CAN'T STAND MYSELF (WHEN YOU TOUCH ME)** 17
– I can't stand myself (when you touch me) (part 1) / There was a time / Get it together (part 1) / Baby, baby, baby / Time after time / The soul of J.B. (instrumental) / I can't stand myself (when you touch me) (part 2) / Get it together (part 2) / Why did you take your love away from me / Need your love so bad / You've got to change your mind / Fat Eddie [US] / Funky soul #1 [UK].

Mar 68. (7"; with BOBBY BYRD) <6151> **YOU'VE GOT TO CHANGE YOUR MIND. / I'LL LOSE MY MIND** -

Mar 68. (7"; with VICKI ANDERSON) <6152> **YOU'VE GOT THE POWER. / WHAT THE WORLD NEEDS NOW IS LOVE** -

May 68. (7") (56743) <6155> **I GOT THE FEELIN'. / IF I RULED THE WORLD** 6 Mar68 / -

Apr 68. (lp) (623 032) **MR. DYNAMITE** -
– Money won't change you (part 1 & 2) / I don't mind / Doin' the limbo / I stay in the chapel every night / Scratch / Night train / I can't help it / Is it yes or is it no / Come over here / In the wee wee hours / Choo choo.

Apr 68. (7") <6159> **MAYBE GOOD, MAYBE BAD (instrumental). / (pt.2)** -

May 68. (7") <6164> **SHHHHHHHH (FOR A LITTLE WHILE) (instrumental). / HERE I GO (instrumental)** -

May 68. (lp) <1031> **I GOT THE FEELIN'** -
– I got the feelin' / Maybe I'll understand – part 1 / You've got the power / Maybe good, maybe bad – part 1 / Shhhhhhh (for a little while) / Just plain funk / If I ruled the world / Maybe I'll understand – part 2 / Stone fox / It won't be me / Maybe good, maybe bad – part 2 / Here I go.

Jun 68. (7") (56744) <6166> **LICKING STICK, LICKING STICK. / (pt.2)** 14 May68

JAMES BROWN

—— solo, but still with The FAMOUS FLAMES

Sep 68. (7") (56752) <6187> **SAY IT LOUD – I'M BLACK AND I'M PROUD. / (pt.2)** - 10

Sep 68. (d-lp) <1022> **LIVE AT THE APOLLO VOLUME 2 (live)** - 32
– Introduction / Think / I want to be around / Thanks / That's life / Kansas City / Let yourself go / There was a time / I feel all right / Cold sweat / It may be the last time / I feel good / Prisoner of love / Out of sight / Try me / Bring it up / It's a man's man's world / Lost someone / Please, please, please. (UK-iss.Jun69; 583 729/30) (re-iss. Jun70; 2612 005) (cd-iss. Dec88 on 'Polydor') (cd-iss. Jan 93)

Nov 68. (7") <6198> **GOODBYE MY LOVE. / SHADES OF BROWN (instrumental)** - 31

Nov 68. (7") (BM 56540) **THAT'S LIFE. / PLEASE, PLEASE, PLEASE** - -

Dec 68. (7") <6203> **SANTA CLAUS GOES STRAIGHT TO THE GHETTO. / YOU KNOW IT (instrumental)** - -

Dec 68. (7") <6204> **TIT FOR TAT (AIN'T NO TAKING BACK). / BELIEVERS SHALL ENJOY** - 86

Dec 68. (7") <6205> **LET'S UNITE THE WHOLE WORLD AT CHRISTMAS. / IN THE MIDDLE (pt.1)** - -

Jan 69. (7") <6213> **GIVE IT UP OR TURNIT A LOOSE. / I'LL LOSE MY MIND** - 15

Jan 69. (lp) (580 701) **TURN IT LOOSE** -
– Give it up or turnit a loose / I'll lose my mind / I don't want nobody to give me tonight (open up the door, I'll get it myself) (parts 1 & 2).

Mar 69. (7") <6216> **ATTACK WITH THE NEWS. / SHADES OF BROWN** - -

Mar 69. (7"; with MARVA WHITNEY) <6218> **YOU'VE GOT TO HAVE A JOB. / I'M TIRED, I'M TIRED, I'M TIRED** - -

Mar 69. (7") <6222> **SOUL PROUD.** / (pt.2) | - |

Mar 69. (7") <6223> **YOU'VE GOT TO HAVE A MOTHER FOR ME.** / (part 2) | - |

Apr 69. (7") <6224> **I DON'T WANT NOBODY TO GIVE ME NOTHIN'** (OPEN UP THE DOOR, I'LL GET IT MYSELF). / (pt.2) | - | 20

Apr 69. (lp) <1047> **SAY IT LOUD – I'M BLACK AND I'M PROUD** | - | 53
  – Say it loud I'm black and proud (parts 1 & 2) / I guess I'll have to cry, cry, cry / Goodbye my love (parts 1 & 2) / Shades of brown / Licking stick / I love you / Then you can tell me goodbye / Let them talk / Maybe I'll understand / I'll lose my mind. (UK-iss.Sep69; 583 741)

May 69. (7") <6235> **THE LITTLE GROOVE MAKER ME.** / **I'M SHOOK** | - |

May 69. (lp) <1051> **GETTIN' DOWN TO IT** | - | 99
  – Sunny / That's life / Strangers in the night / Willow weep for me / Cold sweat / There was a time / Chicago / For sentimental reasons / Time after time / All the way / It had to be you / Uncle. (UK-iss.Jan70; 583 742)

Jun 69. (7") <6240> **THE POPCORN** (instrumental) / **THE CHICKEN** (instrumental) | - | 30

Jul 69. (7") (56776) <6245> **MOTHER POPCORN** (YOU GOT TO HAVE A MOTHER FOR ME). / (pt.2) | 11 | Jun69

Aug 69. (7") <6250> **LOWDOWN POPCORN** (instrumental) / **TOP OF THE STACK** (instrumental) | - | 41

Aug 69. (lp) <1055> **JAMES BROWN PLAYS AND DIRECTS THE POPCORN** | - | 40
  – The popcorn / Why am I treated so bad / In the middle / Soul pride / A new shift / Sudsy / The chicken / The chase. (UK-iss.Mar70 as 'THE POPCORN'; 184 319)

Sep 69. (7") <6255> **LET A MAN COME IN AND DO THE POPCORN PART ONE.** / **SOMETIME** | | 21

Sep 69. (7") (56780) <6258> **THE WORLD.** / (pt.2) | | 37

Oct 69. (lp) (583 768) <1063> **IT'S A MOTHER** | 26 | Sep69
  – Mother popcorn (you got to have a mother for me) (parts 1 & 2) / Mashed potato popcorn (parts 1 & 2) / I'm shook / Popcorn with a feeling / Little groove maker me (parts 1 & 2) / Any day now (my wild beautiful bird) / If I ruled the world / You're still out of sight / Top of the stack.

Nov 69. (7") <6273> **I'M NOT DEMANDING.** / (part 2) | - |

Dec 69. (7") <6275> **PART TWO** (LET A MAN COME IN AND DO THE POPCORN). / **GETTIN' A LITTLE HIPPER** (pt.1) | - | 40

Dec 69. (7") <6277> **IT'S CHRISTMAS TIME.** / (pt.2) | - |

Jan 70. (7") (56787) **THERE WAS A TIME.** / **I CAN'T STAND MYSELF** (WHEN YOU TOUCH ME) | - | -

Jan 70. (7") <6285> **BROTHER RAPP.** / (part 2) | - |

Feb 70. (7") <6290> **FUNKY DRUMMER** (instrumental) / (pt.2) | - | 51

Feb 70. (7") <6292> **IT'S A NEW DAY.** / (pt.2) | - | 32

Feb 70. (lp) <1092> **AIN'T IT FUNKY** | - | 43
  – Ain't it funky now (parts 1 & 2) / Fat wood (parts 1 & 2) / Cold sweat / Give it up or turnit a loose / Nose job / Use your mother / After you done it. (UK-iss.Aug70; 2343 010)

Mar 70. (7") (56793) <6280> **AIN'T IT FUNKY NOW** (instrumental). / (pt.2) | 24 | Nov69

Mar 70. (7") <6300> **TALKIN" LOUD AND SAYIN' NOTHIN'.** / (part 2) | - |

Apr 70. (7") <6310> **BROTHER RAPP** (pt.1). / **BEWILDERED** | - | 32

Jul 70. (7") (2001 018) **IT'S A NEW DAY.** / **GEORGIA ON MY MIND** | - |

Jul 70. (lp) (2310 029) <1095> **IT'S A NEW DAY SO LET A MAN COME IN** | | -
  – It's a new day so let a man come in / Do the popcorn / World / Georgia on my mind / It's a man's man's world / Give it up or turn it a loose / If I ruled the world / The man in the glass / I'm not demanding.

——— (Also released lp SOUL ON TOP with The LOUIE BELLSON ORCHESTRA (Jul70) Released another duet 7" with VICKI ANDERSON – Let It Be Me.

——— He breaks up The FAMOUS FLAMES to introduce his new band The JB's. They included **BOOTSY COLLINS, FRED WESLEY, BOBBY BYRD, JIMMY PARKER**, etc.

Sep 70. (7") (2001 071) <6318> **GET UP, I FEEL LIKE BEING A SEX MACHINE.** / (pt.2) | 32 | 15 Jul70

——— (released gospel 45, A MAN HAS TO GO BACK TO THE CROSSROADS on 'Bethlehem')

Sep 70. (7") <6322> **I'M NOT DEMANDING.** / (part 2) | - |

Nov 70. (7") (2001 097) <6329> **CALL ME SUPER BAD.** / (pt.2) | - | 13 Sep70

Nov 70. (7") <6339> **HEY AMERICA** (vocal). / (instrumental) | - |

Dec 70. (7") (2625 004) <1115> **SEX MACHINE** (live) | | 29 Sep70
  – Get up I feel like being a sex machine / Brother Rapp (parts 1 & 2) / Bewildered / I got the feelin' / Give it up or turn it a loose / I don't want nobody / To give me nothing / Licking stick / Lowdown / Popcorn / Spinning wheel / If I ruled the world / There was a time / It's a man's man's world / Please, please, please / I can't stand myself / Mother popcorn. (cd-iss.Sep98; 517984-2)

Dec 70. (7") <6340> **SANTA CLAUS IS DEFINITELY HERE TO STAY.** / (instrumental) | - |

Jan 71. (7") <6347> **GET UP, GET INTO IT, GET INVOLVED.** / (pt.2) | - | 34

Feb 71. (7") <6359> **TALKING LOUD AND SAYING NOTHING.** / (pt.2) | - |

Feb 71. (7") <6366> **SPINNING WHEEL** (instrumental) / (part 2) | - | 90

Mar 71. (7") (2001 163) <6368> **SOUL POWER.** / (pt.2) | - | 29 Feb71

May 71. (7") (2001 190) <6363> **I CRIED.** / **GET UP, GET INTO IT, GET INVOLVED** | 50 | 61 Jan71

May 71. (lp) (2310 089) <1127> **SUPER BAD** | 61 | Jan71
  – Superbad (parts 1 & 2) / Let it be me / Sometime a man has to go back to the crossroads / Giving out my juice / By the time I get to Phoenix.

——— Most of his band except WESLEY, joined PARLIAMENT/FUNKADELIC.

                              Polydor   People

Jun 71. (7") <2500> **ESCAPE-ISM.** / (part 2) | - | 35

Jul 71. (7") (2001 213) <2501> **HOT PANTS** (SHE GOT TO USE WHAT SHE GOT, TO GET WHAT SHE WANTS). / (pt.2) | - | 15
                              Polydor   Polydor

Sep 71. (lp) (2425 086) <4054> **HOT PANTS** | | 22 Aug71
  – Blues and pants / Can't stand it / Escape-ism (part 1) / Escape-ism (Part 2) / Hot pants (she got to use what she got to get what she wants) / Escape-ism. (re-iss. Sep98 lp/cd; 517985-1/-2)

Sep 71. (7") (2001 223) <14088> **MAKE IT FUNKY.** / (pt.2) | | 22

Oct 71. (7") <14098> **MY PART: MAKE IT FUNKY PART 3.** / (other version) | - | 68

Nov 71. (7") (2066 153) <14100> **I'M A GREEDY MAN.** / (part 2) | - | 35

Feb 72. (d-lp) (2659 011) <3003> **REVOLUTION OF THE MIND – LIVE AT THE APOLLO, VOLUME III** (live) | | 39 Dec71
  – It's a new day so let a man come in and do the popcorn / Bewildered / Sex machine / Escape-ism / Make it funky / Try me / Fast medley: I can't stand myself – Mother popcorn – I got the feelin' / Give it up or turn it a loose / Call me Superbad / Get up, get into it, get involved (parts 1 & 2) / Soul power / Hot pants (she got to use what she got to get what she wants).

Feb 72. (7") (2066 185) <14116> **KING HEROIN.** / **THEME FROM KING HEROIN** | | 40

Apr 72. (7") (2066 210) <14126> **THERE IT IS.** / (part 2) | | 43

Jun 72. (7") (2066 216) <14129> **HONKY TONK.** / (part 2) | | 44

Aug 72. (7") (2066 231) <14139> **GET ON THE GOOD FOOT.** / (part 2) | | 18

Nov 72. (lp) (2391 033) <5028> **THERE IT IS** | | Jun72
  – There it is (parts 1 & 2) / King heroin / I'm a greedy man (parts 1 & 2) / Who am I / Talkin' loud and sayin' nothing / Public enemy #1 (part 1) / Public enemy #1 (part 2) / I need help (I can't do it alone) / Never can say goodbye. (re-iss. Sep98 lp/cd; 517986-1/-2)

Nov 72. (7") (2066 283) <14157> **WHAT MY BABY NEEDS NOW IS A LITTLE MORE LOVIN'.** / **THIS GUY'S IN LOVE WITH YOU** (with LYN COLLINS) | | 56 Dec72

Dec 72. (7") (2066 285) <14153> **I GOT A BAG OF MY OWN.** / **I KNOW IT'S TIME** | | 44 Nov72

Dec 72. (7") <14161> **SANTA CLAUS GOES STRAIGHT TO THE GHETTO.** / **SWEET LITTLE BABY BOY** | - |

Jan 73. (7") <14162> **I GOT ANTS IN MY PANTS** (AND I WANT TO DANCE). / (part 2) | | 27

Jan 73. (d-lp) (2659 018) <3004> **GET ON THE GOOD FOOT** | | 68 Dec72
  – Get on the good foot (parts 1 & 2) / The whole world needs liberation / Your love was good for me / Cold sweat / Recitation by Hank Ballard / I got a bag of my own / Nothing beats a try but a fail / Lost someone / Funky side of town / Please, please, please / Ain't it a groove / My part – Make it funky (parts 3 & 4) / Dirty Harry / I know it's true. (cd-iss. Mar99 on 'IMS-Universal'; E 523982-2)

Mar 73. (7") <14168> **DOWN AND OUT IN NEW YORK CITY.** / **MAMA'S DEAD** | - | 50

Mar 73. (7") <14169> **LIKE IT IS, LIKE IT WAS.** / **THE BASS** | - |

May 73. (lp) (2490 117) <6014> **BLACK CAESAR** (Soundtrack) | | 31 Feb73
  – Down and out in New York city / Blind man can see it / Sportin' life / Dirty Harri / The boss / Make it good to yourself / Mama Feelgood / Mama's dead / White lightning (I mean moonshine) / Chase / Like it is, like it was. (re-iss. Sep98 lp/cd; 517735-1/-2)

May 73. (7") (2066 329) <14177> **THINK.** / **SOMETHING** | | 77
(above and below 2 different versions)

Jun 73. (7") <14185> **THINK.** / **SOMETHING** | | 80

Jul 73. (7") <14193> **WOMAN.** / (part 2) | - |

Aug 73. (lp) (2391 084) <6015> **SLAUGHTER'S BIG RIP-OFF** (Soundtrack) | | 92 Jul73
  – Slaughter theme / Tryin' to get over / Transmographication / Happy for the poor / Brother Rapp / Big strong / Really, really, really / Sexy, sexy, sexy / To my brother / How long can I keep it up / People get up and drive your funky soul / King Slaughter / Straight ahead. (cd-iss. Aug96; 3145 17136-2) (cd re-iss. Sep98; 517136-2)

Aug 73. (7") <14194> **SEXY, SEXY, SEXY.** / **SLAUGHTER THEME** | - | 50

Sep 73. (7"; JAMES BROWN with LYN COLLINS) <14199> **LET IT BE ME.** / **IT'S ALL RIGHT** | - |

Oct 73. (7") <14206> **I'VE GOT A GOOD THING.** / (part 2) | - |

Nov 73. (7") <14210> **STONED(D) TO THE BONE.** / (part 2) | - | 58

Jan 74. (7") (2066 411) **STONE(D) TO THE BONE.** / **SEXY, SEXY, SEXY** | | -

Mar 74. (7") <14223> **THE PAYBACK.** / (part 2) | - | 26

Apr 74. (d-lp) (2659 030) <3007> **THE PAYBACK** | | 34 Jan74
  – The payback / Doing the best I can / Take some – leave some / Shoot your shot / Forever suffering / Time is running out fast / Stoned to the bone / Mind power. (cd-iss. Sep98; 517137-2)

Jun 74. (7") (2066 485) **MY THANG.** / **THE PAYBACK** | - |

Jul 74. (7") <14244> **MY THANG.** / **PUBLIC ENEMY #1** | - | 29

Sep 74. (7") <14255> **PAPA DON'T TAKE NO MESS.** / (part 2) | - | 31

Sep 74. (d-lp) (2659 036) <9001> **IT'S HELL** <US-title 'HELL'> | | 35 Jul74
  – Coldblooded / Hell / My thang / Savin' it and doin' it / Please, please, please / When the saints go marching in / These foolish things / Storming Monday / A man has to go back to the cross road before he finds himself / Sometime / I can't stand it / Lost someone / Don't tell a lie about me and I won't tell the truth about you / Papa don't take no mess. (re-iss. Jul88)

Jan 75. (7") (2066 520) <14258> **FUNKY PRESIDENT** (PEOPLE IT'S BAD). / **COLD BLOODED** | | 44 Nov74

Feb 75. (7") <14268> **REALITY.** / **TWIST** | - | 80

Mar 75. (lp) (2391 164) <6039> **REALITY** | | 56 Jan75
  – Reality / Funky President (people it's bad) / Further on up the road / Check your body / Don't fence me in / All for one / I'm broken hearted / The twist / Who can I turn to.

Apr 75. (7") <14270> **SEX MACHINE** (remix). / (part 2) | - |

May 75. (lp) (2391 175) <6042> **SEX MACHINE TODAY** | | -
  – Sex machine (pt.1 & 2) / I feel good / Problems / Dead on it / Get up off of me / Deep in it.

Jun 75. (7") <14279> **DEAD ON IT.** / (part 2) | - |

Jul 75. (7") <14281> **HUSTLE!!!** (DEAD ON IT). / (part 2) | - |

Nov 75. (7") <14295> **SUPERBAD, SUPERSLICK.** / (part 2) | - |

Dec 75. (lp) (2391 197) <6054> **EVERYBODY'S DOIN' THE HUSTLE AND DEAD ON THE DOUBLE BUMP** | | Oct75
  – Hustle!!! (dead on it) / Papa's got a brand new bag / Your love / Turn on the heat and build some fire / Superbad, superslick / Calm & cool / Kansas City.

Jan 76. (7") (2066 642) <14301> **HOT** (I NEED TO BE LOVED, LOVED, LOVED). / **SUPERBAD, SUPERSLICK** (part 1) | |

Feb 76. (7") <14303> **DOOLEY'S JUNKYARD DOGS.** / (part 2) | - |

Feb 76. (7") <14304> **(I LOVE YOU) FOR SENTIMENTAL REASONS. / GOODNIGHT MY LOVE** — | -

Mar 76. (lp) (2391 214) **HOT**
— Hot (I need to be loved, loved, loved) / so long / For sentimental reasons / Try me / The future shock of the world / woman / Most of all / Goodnight my love / Please, please, please. (re-iss. Jul88; PD 6059)

Jul 76. (7") (2066 687) <14326> **GET UP OFFA THAT THING. / RELEASE THE PRESSURE** — 22 | 45

Sep 76. (lp) (2391 228) <6071> **GET UP OFFA THAT THING** — | Aug76
— Get up offa that thing / Release the pressure / You took my heart / I refuse to lose / Can't take it with you / Home again / This feeling.

Nov 76. (7") <14354> **I REFUSE TO LOSE. / HOME AGAIN** — | -

Jan 77. (7") (2066 763) <14360> **BODYHEAT. / (part 2)** — 36 | 88

Feb 77. (lp) (2391 258) <6093> **BODYHEAT** — | Jan77
— Bodyheat / Woman / Kiss in '77 / I'm satisfied / What the world needs now is love / Wake up and give yourself a chance / Don't feel it. (re-iss. Oct82 on 'Phoenix'; PHX 1025) (re-iss. Jul88; PD 6093)

Jun 77. (7") <14388> **KISS IN '77. / WOMAN** — | -

Jul 77. (7") (2066 834) **HONKY TONK. / BROTHER RAPP**

Sep 77. (7") <14409> **GIVE ME SOME SKIN. / PEOPLE WAKE UP AND LIVE**

Sep 77. (lp) (2391 300) <6111> **MUTHA'S NATURE**
— Give me some skin / People who criticize / Have a happy day / Bessie / If you don't give a doggone about it / Summertime / People wake up and live / Take me higher and groove me.

Nov 77. (7") <14433> **TAKE ME HIGHER AND GROOVE ME. / SUMMERTIME** (Martha & James) — | -

Jan 78. (7") <14438> **IF YOU DON'T GIVE A DOGGONE ABOUT IT. / PEOPLE WHO CRITICIZE** — | -

—— His backing group, left for a while, but soon returned. JIMMY NOLAN was to die of a heart attack 18 Dec'83.

May 78. (7") <14460> **LOVE ME TENDER. / HAVE A HAPPY DAY** — | -

May 78. (lp) (2391 342) <6140> **JAM / 1980's**
— Jam / The spank / Nature / Eyesight / I never never never will forget.

Jun 78. (7") (2066 915) <14465> **EYESIGHT. / NEVER, NEVER, NEVER WILL FORGET**

Aug 78. (7") <14487> **LOVE ME TENDER. / THE SPANK** — | -

Oct 78. (7") (2066 984) <14512> **NATURE. / (part 2)**

Dec 78. (7") <14522> **FOR GOODNESS SAKES, LOOK AT THOSE CAKES. / (part 2)** — | -

Jan 79. (7") (POSP 24) **FOR GOODNESS SAKES, LOOK AT THOSE CAKES. / GET UP, I FEEL LIKE BEING A SEX MACHINE**

Jan 79. (lp) (2391 384) <6181> **TAKE A LOOK AT THOSE CAKES**
— For goodness sakes, take a look at those cakes / A man understands / As long as I love you / Someone to talk about / Spring.

Apr 79. (7") <14540> **SOMEONE TO TALK ABOUT. / (part 2)** — | -

Jul 79. (7") (POSP 68) <14557> **IT'S TOO FUNKY IN HERE. / ARE WE REALLY DANCING**

Aug 79. (lp) (2391 412) <6212> **THE ORIGINAL DISCO MAN**
— It's too funky in here / Let the boogie do the rest / Still / The original disco man / Star generation / Women are something else.

Aug 79. (7") <2005> **STAR GENERATION. / WOMEN ARE SOMETHING ELSE** — | -

Sep 79. (7"/12") (STEP/+X 2) **STAR GENERATION. / LET THE BOOGIE DO THE REST**

Nov 79. (7") <2034> **THE ORIGINAL DISCO MAN. / LET THE BOOGIE DO THE REST**

Feb 80. (7") (POSP 121) <2054> **REGRETS. / STONE COLD DRAG**

Apr 80. (lp) (2391 446) <6258> **PEOPLE**
— Regrets / Don't stop the funk / That's sweet music / Let the funk flow / Stone cold drag / Are we really dancing / Sometimes that's all there is. (re-iss. Jul88; PD 16258)

May 80. (7") <2078> **LET THE FUNK FLOW. / SOMETIMES THAT'S ALL THERE IS** — | -

Aug 80. (7") <2129> **IT'S TOO FUNKY FOR ME IN HERE. / GET UP OFFA THAT THING** — | -

Oct 80. (d-lp) (2683 085) <6290> **JAMES BROWN . . . LIVE – HOT ON THE ONE** (live) — | Aug80
— It's too funky in here / Gonna have a funky good time / Get up offa that thing / Bodyheat / I got the feelin' / Try me / Sex machine / It's a man's man's man's world / Get on the good foot / Papa's got a brand new bag / Please, please, please / Jam. (cd-iss. Apr91; 847856-2)

Oct 80. (7") <2167> **GIVE THE BASS PLAYER SOME. / (part 2)** — | -

R.C.A. | T.K.

Dec 80. (7"/12") (RCA/+T 28) <1039> **RAPP PAYBACK (WHERE IZ MOSES?). / (pt.2)** — 39

Dec 80. (lp) (RCALP 5006) <5334> **SOUL SYNDROME**
— Rapp payback / Mashed potatoes / Smokin' and drinkin' / Stay with me / Honky tonk. (re-iss. Sep81 lp/c; RCA LP/K 3048)

Feb 81. (7") (RCA 44) <1042> **STAY WITH ME. / SMOKIN' AND DRINKIN'**

May 81. (7") (RCA 65) **FUNKY MAN. / (part 2)**
(12"+=) (RCAT 65) – Mashed potatoes.

Polydor | not iss.

Apr 81. (lp) (POLS 1029) **THE THIRD COMING**
— Popcorn 80's / Give that bass player some / You're my only love / World cycle inc. / Superball / Superbad 80's / I go crazy.

Jun 81. (7") (POSP 290) **I GO CRAZY. / WORLD CYCLE INC.** — | -

Sonet | not iss.

Jun 83. (7"/12") (SON/+L 2258) **BRING IT ON . . . BRING IT ON. / NIGHT TIME IS THE RIGHT TIME** — 45 | -

Sep 83. (lp) (SNTF 906) **BRING IT ON** — | -
— Bring it on . . . bring it on / Today / You can't keep a good man down / Nighttime is the right time / Tennessee waltz / For your precious love.

—— In Aug'84, he teamed up with **AFRIKA BAMBAATAA** for one-off 7+12" **UNITY** (THE THIRD COMING) on 'Tommy Boy' (US No.49).

Scotti Bros | Scotti Bros

Jan 86. (7") (A 6701) <05682> **LIVING IN AMERICA. / Vince Di Cola: FAREWELL** — 5 | 4 Dec85
(12"+=) (TA 6701) – ('B'extended).

—— (above from the film 'Rocky IV', and written by DAN HARTMAN)

Oct 86. (7") (650059-7) <06275> **GRAVITY. / GRAVITY (dub)** — 65 | 93
(12") (650059-6) – ('A'side) / The big G (dig this myth).

Oct 86. (lp/c) (SCT/40 57108) <40380> **GRAVITY** — 85
— How do you stop / Turn me loose, I'm Dr.Feelgood / Living in America / Goliath / Repeat the beat (faith) / Return to me / Gravity. (cd-iss. Mar87; CD 57108) (re-iss. Jul88; FZ 40380)

Mar 87. (7") <06568> **HOW DO YOU STOP. / HOUSE OF ROCK** — | -

Apr 87. (7") (JAMES 1) **HOW DO YOU STOP. / REPEAT THE BEAT (FAITH)**
(12"+=) (JAMEST 1) – Living in America.
(12"+=) (JAMESQ 1) – ('A'-House mix).

Jun 87. (7") <07090> **LET'S GET PERSONAL. / REPEAT THE BEAT** — | -

Urban-Polydor | Scotti Bros

May 88. (7") <07783> **I'M REAL. / TRIBUTE** — | -

May 88. (7") (JSB 1) **I'M REAL. / KEEP KEEPING** — 31
(12"+=) (JSBX 1) – Tribute.
(cd-s+=) (JSBCD 1) – ('A'-Hype mix).

Jun 88. (lp/c)(cd) (POLD/+C 5230)(834755-2) <44241> **I'M REAL** — 27 | 96
— Tribute / I'm real / Static / Time to get busy / She looks types a good / Keep keeping / Can't git enuf / It's your money / Godfather runnin' the joint.

Aug 88. (7") (JSB 1) <07975> **STATIC. / GODFATHER RUNNIN' THE JOINT**
(12"+=) (JSBX 2) – I'm real (US remix).
(cd-s+=) (JSBCD 2) – ('A'-Full Force mix).

Nov 88. (7") <08088> **TIME TO GET BUSY. / BUSY J.B.** — | -

Feb 89. (7") <68559> **IT'S YOUR MONEY. / YOU AND ME** — | -

—— He guested on ARETHA FRANKLIN single Nov88, 'GIMME YOUR LOVE'.

—— In Apr-May'88, JAMES and his wife ADRIANNE were arrested for possession of substances and guns. She also filed for divorce and pleaded not guilty. Later that year, after resisting arrest in a car chase, etc., he was sentenced to 6 years. He was released on parole on 27th Feb'91, but had to return until late 1993 to serve full sentence. In 1992, he was awarded a special grammy award, for his contribution to music. He appeared there with his wife, to sing finale.

Polydor | Polydor

Jul 91. (cd/c/lp) (510079-2/-4/-1) **LOVE OVERDUE**
— (So tired of standing still we got to) Move on / Show me – dance, dance, dance / To the funk / Teardrops on your letter / Standing on higher ground / Later for dancing / You are my everything / It's time for love (put a little love).

Jul 91. (7") **(SO TIRED OF STANDING STILL WE GOT TO) MOVE ON / YOU ARE MY EVERYTHING** — | -
(12"+=) – ('A' extended).

Mar 93. (cd/c) (514329-2/-4) **UNIVERSAL JAMES**
— Can't get any harder / Just do it / Mine all mine / Watch me / Georgia-Lina / Show me your friends / Everybody's got a thang / How long / Make it funky 2000 / Moments.

Apr 93. (7"/c-s) (PO/+CS 262) **CAN'T GET ANY HARDER. / ('A'-O.B.C. mix)** — 59
(12"+=/cd-s+=) (PZ/+CD 262) – ('A'mixes).

Eagle | Crash

Nov 98. (cd) (EAGCD 054) <417081> **I'M BACK**
— Can't stand it / Funk on ah roll / Kare / What it takes / Papa's got a brand new bag / Break away / Funk on ah roll / Lucky old sun / I don't hear no music / Every part of my heart / Eden / Peace in the world / Funk on ah roll / James on the loose.

Apr 99. (12"/cd-s) (EAG 12/XS 073) **FUNK ON AH ROLL / ('A'mix)** — 40
(cd-s) (EAGXA 073) – ('A'mixes).

– compilations, others, etc. –

on Polydor UK / King + Polydor (+'75) US, unless mentioned otherwise

Apr 65. (lp) *London; (HA 8203) / King; <919>* **16 UNBEATABLE HITS**

Oct 65. (7"ep) *Ember; (EMBEP 4549)* **I DO JUST WHAT I WANT**
— I do just what I want / So long / Bells / I love you, yes I do.

May 66. (7"ep) *Pye International; (NEP 44059)* **I GOT YOU**
— I got you / Good good loving / I can't help it.

Aug 66. (7"ep) *Pye International; (NEP 44068)* **I'LL GO CRAZY**
— I'll go crazy / I've got money / Love don't love nobody / You've got the power.

Oct 66. (7"ep) *Pye International; (NEP 44076)* **HOW LONG DARLING**
— How long darling / This old heart / Three hearts in a tangle / Lost someone.

May 67. (7"ep) *Pye International; (NEP 44088)* **BRING IT UP**
— Bring it up / Tell me that you love me / Don't be a drop out / Nobody knows.

Apr 68. (lp) (623 017) **JAMES BROWN'S GREATEST HITS**

Jan 69. (lp) (184 148) **SOUL FIRE**

Mar 69. (lp) (184 159) **KING OF SOUL**

Nov 69. (lp) (583 765) **THE BEST OF JAMES BROWN** (re-iss. Jul82)

Jan 70. (7"ep) (580 701) **TURN IT LOOSE**
— Give it up or turnit a loose / I'll lose my mind / I don't want nobody . . . / I'll get it myself.

May 71. (lp) (2343 036) **SOUL BROTHER NUMBER 1** (re-iss. +cd.May88 on 'Arcade')

Aug 72. (lp) (2391 057) <5401> **JAMES BROWN SOUL CLASSICS** — | 83

Feb 73. (7"m) (2141 008) **PAPA'S GOT A BRAND NEW BAG. / OUT OF SIGHT / IT'S A MAN'S MAN'S MAN'S WORLD**

Mar 73. (lp) (2391 116) **SOUL CLASSICS VOL.2**

May 75. (7") <14270> **SEX MACHINE (part 1). / (part 2)** — | 61

May 75. (lp) (2391 166) **SOUL CLASSICS VOLUME 3**

May 77. (lp) (2679 044) **SOLID GOLD**

Jun 82. (lp) (248 253-0) **JAMES BROWN LIVE AND LOWDOWN AT THE APOLLO VOL.1**

Jul 82. (lp)(c) (239 152-9)(317 752-9) **THE BEST OF JAMES BROWN**

Jul 82. (12"ep) (POSPX 605) **PAPA'S GOT A BRAND NEW BAG / GET UP OFFA THAT THING / GET UP I FEEL LIKE BEING A SEX MACHINE / GET ON THE GOOD FOOT**

(re-iss. May87 on 'Perfect'; PER12 8607)

Nov 83. (lp) *(2489 194)* **PLEASE PLEASE PLEASE**
(re-iss. 1988 on 'Sing' lp/c/cd; SING/+4/8 610)

Jan 84. (d-lp) *(REVO 1)* **ROOTS OF A REVOLUTION**
(d-cd.iss.Nov89; 817 304-2)

Sep 85. (cd) *(825 714-2)* **THE COMPACT DISC OF JAMES BROWN**

Mar 86. (lp/c) *(827 439-1/-4)* **DEAD ON THE HEAVY FUNK 74-76**

May 86. (lp/c) *(POLD/+C 5192)* **THE LP OF J.B. (SEX MACHINE & OTHER SOUL CLASSICS)**

Jan 88. (lp/cd) *(834 085-1/-4/-2)* **JAMES BROWN & FRIENDS (live)**

Jul 88. (lp) *(PD 6318)* **NON STOP**

Feb 90. (cd/c/lp) *(841516-2/-4/-1)* **DUETS**
(cd-iss. Jan93)

Jan 91. (d-cd) *(847258-2)* **MESSIN' WITH THE BLUES** (rare R&B/Blues)

May 91. (4xcd-box/4xc-box) *(849 108-2/-4)* **STAR TIME**

Nov 91. (cd/c/lp) *(845 828-2/-4/-1)* **SEX MACHINE – THE VERY BEST OF JAMES BROWN** | **19** |
– (see K-Tel album except replacement of tracks marked * by:-) Night train / Out of sight / I'm a greedy man (pt.1) / Get up offa that thing / I'm real / It's too funky in here / Soul power (live).

Nov 91. (7") **GET UP (I FEEL LIKE BEING A) SEX MACHINE (1991 EQ'd Version) / GET UP (I FEEL LIKE BEING A) SEX MACHINE**
(12"+=/cd-s+=) – Think / I got you (I feel good).

Feb 93. (cd/c) **MASTER SERIES**

Apr 93. (d-cd) *(517 845-2)* **CHRONICLES – SOUL PRIDE**

Jul 93. (cd/c/d-lp) *(519 854-2/-4/-1)* **FUNKY PRESIDENT – THE VERY BEAT OF JAMES BROWN VOL.2**

– more compilations, etc. –

Apr 85. (7") *Boiling Point; (FROG 1)* **FROGGY MIX. / (pt.2)** | **50** |
(12"+=) *(FROGX 1)* – (extra mixes).

Jun 85. (7") *(POSP 751)* **GET UP, I FEEL LIKE BEING A SEX MACHINE (pt.2). / PAPA'S GOT A BRAND NEW BAG** | **47** |
(12"+=) *(POSPX 751)* – Get up offa that thing (release the pressure) / Get on the good foot. *(re-iss. Feb86 hit UK-No.46)*

Apr 86. (7") *(POSP 783)* **SOUL POWER (pt.1). / IT'S A MAN'S, MAN'S, MAN'S WORLD**
(12"+=) *(POSPX 783)* – King Heroin / Don't tell it.

May 86. (d-lp) *Urban; (URB LP/DC 11)* **IN THE JUNGLE GROOVE**
(cd-iss. May88 on 'Polydor'; 829624-2)

Jan 88. (7") *Urban; (URB 13)* **SHE'S THE ONE. / FUNKY PRESIDENT (PEOPLE IT'S BAD)** | **45** |
(12"+=) *(URBX 13)* – Funky drummer (edit) / Funky drummer (boms beat reprise).

Apr 88. (7") *Urban; (URB 17)* **THE PAYBACK MIX (pt.1). / GIVE IT UP OR TURNIT A LOOSE**
(12") *(URBX 17)* – ('A'side) / Keep on doing what you're doing but keep it funky / Stoned to the bone / Cold sweat.

– more compilations, etc. –

Feb 68. (lp) *Philips; (SBL 7823)* **JAMES BROWN PLAYS THE REAL THING**

Feb 72. (lp) *Philips; (6336 201)* **THIS IS JAMES BROWN**

1969. (7") *Federal;* **SOUL PRESIDENT. / POPCORN WITH A FEELING**

Dec 81. (lp) *Audio Fidelity; (AFESD 1030)* **LIVE IN NEW YORK (live)**

Sep 81. (lp) *R.C.A.; (RCA LP/K 3048)* **SOUL SYNDROME**
(re-iss. Oct91 on 'Roulette' cd/c/d-lp; CD/TC+/ROUS 1043)

Oct 82. (lp) *Phoenix; (PHX 1016)* **MEAN ON THE SCENE**

Jul 84. (7") *Old Gold; (OG 9438)* **GET UP I FEEL LIKE BEING A SEX MACHINE. / GET UP OFFA THAT THING**

Jan 90. (7") *Old Gold; (OG 9930)* **IT'S A MAN'S, MAN'S, MAN'S WORLD. / PAPA'S GOT A BRAND NEW BAG**

May 86. (12") *Konnexion; (PER 128601)* **IT'S A MAN'S, MAN'S, MAN'S WORLD. / SEX MACHINE**

Aug 86. (lp/c; Various Artists) *People; (829 417-1/-4)* **JAMES BROWN'S FUNKY PEOPLE**
– (side 2 was by his JB's) *(re-iss. +cd.on 'Urban')* (cd-iss Jan93)

Jul 88. (lp/c; Various Artists) *Urban; (URB LP/MC 14)* **JAMES BROWN'S FUNKY PEOPLE VOL.2**

—— **JAMES BROWN'S FUNKY PEOPLE 2** (cd-iss. Jan93)

Apr 87. (lp) *Perfect; (PER 33 8605)* **COLD SWEAT (live)**

Sep 87. (lp/c/cd) *K-Tel; (NE1/CE2/NCD3 376)* **THE BEST OF JAMES BROWN (THE GODFATHER OF SOUL)** | **17** |
– Living in America /* Body heat / Hey America / Please, please, please / Hot pants (pt.1) / Think / I got you (I feel good) / Say it loud, I'm black and proud (pt.1) / Get up (I feel like being a) sex machine / Make it funky (pt.1) / Papa's got a brand new bag (pt.1) / Get on the good foot / * Gonna have a funky good time / Cold sweat / * Honky tonk / It's a man's man's man's world / * Gravity.

—— May'88 'A&M' released I GOT YOU (I FEEL GOOD) hit UK 52, from the film 'Good Morning Vietnam', B-side by Martha Reeves & The Vandellas.

Aug 88. (cd/c/lp) *Jambalaya; (CD/TC+/JAM 1984)* **JAMES BROWN & THE SOUL G's – LIVE AT CHASTAIN PARK (live)**

Oct 88. (12") *Lucky; (12LSD 101)* **LET'S GET SERIOUS. /**

Feb 89. (cd) *Mainline; (266202-2)* **20 GREATEST HITS**

Jul 84. (lp) *Solid Smoke; (SS 8023)* **FEDERAL YEARS VOL.1**

Jul 84. (lp) *Solid Smoke; (SS 8024)* **FEDERAL YEARS VOL.2**

Apr 90. (cd/lp) *Blue Moon; (CDBM/BMLP 081)* **SOUL JUBILEE**

Jul 91. (cd/c) *Entelekeg; (UCD1/UMK9 9018)* **LIVE IN NEW YORK (live)**

Oct 92. (7"; JAMES BROWN VS DAKEYNE) *F.B.I.; (FBI 9)* **I GOT YOU (I FEEL GOOD) (remix). / PROCESSED B'S** | **72** |
(cd-s+=) *(FBICD 9)* – B-Funked.

Jul 93. (cd/c) *Laserlight;* **LIVE (live)**

Sep 93. (cd/c) *Yesterday's Gold; (YDG 7613/45704)* **GREATEST HITS**

Nov 93. (cd/c) *Spectrum; (550 040-2/-4)* **GODFATHER OF SOUL**

Mar 94. (cd) *Charly;* **AT STUDIO 54**

Jul 94. (cd) *Charly; (CDCD 1151)* **LIVE AT CHASTAIN PARK – 25th ANNIVERSARY CONCERT**

Jun 94. (cd/c) *Javelin; (HAD CD/MC 164)* **COLD SWEAT**

Sep 94. (cd/c) *Spectrum; (550 199-2/-4)* **THE GODFATHER RETURNS**

Jan 95. (cd) *Success;* **SEX MACHINE – LIVE IN CONCERT**

Feb 95. (cd) *B.A.M.; (KLMCD 018)* **PEARLS FROM THE PAST**

Mar 95. (cd) *Collection; (COL 003)* **THE COLLECTION**

Mar 95. (cd/c) *Muskateer; (MUCD/MUCA 9009)* **THE GODFATHER OF SOUL & FUNK**

Apr 95. (d-cd) *Wisepack; (LECD 623)* **THE ESSENTIAL COLLECTION**

Nov 95. (3xcd-box) *(523943-2)* **LIVE AT THE APOLLO 1 / & 2 / HOT ON THE ONE**

Mar 96. (cd) *Prism; (PLATCD 153)* **FUNKY GOODTIME (live in Atlanta)**

May 96. (cd) *Double Gold; (DBG 53045)* **EARLY STUDIO HITS**

Sep 98. (d-cd) *Polydor; (535888-2)* **THE 40th ANNIVERSARY COLLECTION**

Sep 98. (cd) *Polydor; (531165-2)* **THE FOUNDATIONS OF FUNK 1964-1969**

Sep 98. (cd) *Members Edition; (UAE 3011-2)* **JAMES BROWN**

Oct 98. (d-cd) *Polydor; (537901-2)* **DREAD ON HEAVY FUNK 1975-1983**

Nov 98. (cd) *MagMid; (MM 016)* **SOUL JUBILEE**

Nov 98. (cd) *Spectrum; (554756-2)* **JAMES BROWN'S FUNKY CHRISTMAS**

Dec 98. (cd) *Dressed To Kill; (DRESS 608)* **THE GODFATHER LIVE IN NYC (live)**

Mar 99. (d-cd) *IMS-Universal; (E 531684-2)* **FUNK POWER 1970**

Mar 99. (d-cd) *IMS-Universal; (E 533052-2)* **MAKE IT FUNKY 1971-1975**

Jun 99. (cd) *Proper; (EMCD 14)* **THE ESSENTIAL MASTERS**

Jackson BROWNE

Born: 9 Oct'48, Heidelberg, Germany. BROWNE's parents were actually American (father was in the Army) and the family subsequently moved back to Orange County, California. During the 60's, the budding singer/songwriter worked with the likes of TIM BUCKLEY, NITTY GRITTY DIRT BAND and even NICO, BROWNE later providing material for such luminaries as The BYRDS and LINDA RONSTADT. He duly signed a solo deal with 'Elektra', initially as a house writer, before being picked up by David Geffen's new 'Asylum' label in 1971. With the help of a number of high-profile cover versions, 'DOCTOR MY EYES' (Jackson 5) / 'SHADOW DREAM SONG' (Tom Paxton), BROWNE's eponymous debut album hit the US Top 60. Featuring such ubiquitous L.A. session men as LELAND SKLAR and RUSS KUNKEL alongside such esteemed company as DAVID CROSBY, CLARENCE WHITE and SNEAKY PETE KLEINOW, the album established BROWNE at the forefront of the navel-gazing Californian singer/songwriter scene. His fragile melodies and bookish, confessional lyrics saw him adopted as a kind of genre figurehead, BROWNE garnering further kudos after co-penning the classic EAGLES track, 'TAKE IT EASY'. But while The EAGLES took that song's philosophy to its ultimate conclusion, BROWNE continued to analyse himself and his relationships on classic sets, 'FOR EVERYMAN' (1973) and 'LATE FOR THE SKY' (1974). Tragedy struck on 25th March 1976, when his wife, PHYLLIS, committed suicide, something that undoubtedly contributed to the bleak feel of 'THE PRETENDER' (1976), BROWNE's first album to make the US Top 10. The singer forged on nevertheless, releasing a further set, 'RUNNING ON EMPTY' (1978), which featured previously unreleased material and songs recorded on the road, notably a smash hit version of Maurice Williams & the Zodiacs' 'STAY'. His popularity had been steadily increasing as the decade wore on and BROWNE finally topped the American charts in summer 1980 with the 'HOLD OUT' album. The new decade saw BROWNE becoming increasingly politically active and outspoken on such controversial issues as nuclear power and US foreign policy. Inevitably, this was reflected in BROWNE's writing, the 'LAWYERS IN LOVE' set marking a move away from the personal towards the socially conscious. Subsequent politicised sets, 'LIVES IN THE BALANCE' (1986) and 'WORLD IN MOTION' (1989), were relative commercial failures, some sections of BROWNE's fanbase perhaps not impressed with his liberal convictions. With a star cast including DAVID CROSBY, JENNIFER WARNES, DON HENLEY and longtime collaborator, DAVID LINDLEY, BROWNE returned to more personal fare on 1993's 'I'M ALIVE'. While he might not enjoy the critical and commercial plaudits of his 70's heyday, the singer retains a loyal following, even in Britain, where he made a rare appearance, headlining the 1997 Cambridge Folk Festival. • **Trivia:** He found new love in the 80's with actress girlfriend DARRYL HANNAH.

Album rating: JACKSON BROWNE (*8) / FOR EVERYMAN (*7) / LATE FOR THE SKY (*8) / THE PRETENDER (*6) / RUNNING ON EMPTY (*6) / HOLD OUT (*4) / LAWYERS IN LOVE (*5) / LIVES IN THE BALANCE (*6) / WORLD IN MOTION (*4) / I'M ALIVE (*6) / LOOKING EAST (*5) / THE NEXT VOICE YOU HEAR – THE BEST OF JACKSON BROWNE compilation (*8)

JACKSON BROWNE – vocals, guitar, piano / with **CRAIG DOERGE** – keyboards / **LELAND SKLAR** – bass / **RUSS KUNKEL** – drums / **CLARENCE WHITE** – guitar / **DAVID CROSBY** – b.vocals

				Asylum	Asylum

Mar 72. (7") (K 13043) <11004> **DOCTOR MY EYES. / I'M LOOKING INTO YOU** — | 8 | Feb72

Apr 72. (lp) (SYL 9002) <5051> **JACKSON BROWNE** | 53 | Mar72
– Jamaica say you will / A child in these hills / Song for Adam / Doctor my eyes / From Silver Lake / Something fine / Under the falling sky / Looking into you / Rock me on the water / My opening farewell. (re-iss. Jun76 lp/c; K/K4 53022) (cd-iss. Jan87; K2 53022)

Aug 72. (7") (AYM 506) <11006> **ROCK ME ON THE WATER. / SOMETHING FINE** | 48 | Jul72

—— added **DAVID LINDLEY** – guitar, violin, etc. (ex-KALEIDOSCOPE)

Nov 73. (7") (AYM 522) <11023> **REDNECK FRIEND. / THE TIMES YOU'VE COME** | 85 | Sep73

Dec 73. (lp/c) (K/K4 43003) <5067> **FOR EVERYMAN** | 43 | Nov73
– Take it easy / Our lady of the well / Colors of the sun / I thought I was a child / These days / Redneck friend / The times you've come / Ready or not / Sing my songs to me / For everyman. (cd-iss. Jan87; K2 43003)

Apr 74. (7") (AYM 526) <11030> **TAKE IT EASY. / READY OR NOT**

—— retained **LINDLEY** and brought in **JAI WINDING** – keyboards / **DOUG HAYWOOD** – bass, vocals / **LARRY ZACK** – drums

Oct 74. (7") <45227> **WALKING SLOW. / BEFORE THE DELUGE** | - | -

Nov 74. (7") (AYM 535) **WALKING SLOW. / THE LATE SHOW**

Dec 74. (lp/c) (SYL 9018) <EQ 1017> **LATE FOR THE SKY** | 14 | Oct74
– Late for the sky / Fountain of sorrow / Farther on / The late show / The road and the sky / For a dancer / Walking slow / Before the deluge. (re-iss. Jun76 lp/c; K/K4 43007) (cd-iss. Jan87; K2 43007)

Mar 75. (7") (K 13022) <45242> **FOUNTAIN OF SORROW. / THE LATE SHOW**

—— now with **KUNKEL, SKLAR, DOERGE and LINDLEY** plus **JEFF PORCARO** – drums / **JIM GORDON** – drums / **BOB GLAUB and CHUCK RAINEY** – bass / **ROY BITTAN and BILL PAYNE** – organ / **LUIS F.DAMIAN** – guitar / etc.

Nov 76. (lp/c) (K/K4 53048) <7E 1079> **THE PRETENDER** | 26 | 5
– The fuse / Your bright baby blues / Linda Paloma / Here come those tears again / Daddy's tune / The only child / Daddy's tune / Sleep's dark and silent gate / The pretender. (cd-iss. Jan87)

Feb 77. (7") (K 13073) <45379> **HERE COME THOSE TEARS AGAIN. / LINDA PALOMA** | 23

Jul 77. (7") (K 13086) <45399> **THE PRETENDER. / DADDY'S TUNE** | 58 | May77

Jan 78. (7") (K 13105) **YOU LOVE THE THUNDER. / COCAINE**

Jan 78. (lp/c) (K/K4 53070) <6E 113> **RUNNING ON EMPTY** | 28 | 3
– Running on empty / The road / Rosie / You love the thunder / Cocaine / Shaky town / Love needs a heart / Nothing but time / The load-out / Stay. (cd-iss. Jan87; K2 53070)

Mar 78. (7") (K 13118) <45460> **RUNNING ON EMPTY. / NOTHING BUT TIME** | 11 | Feb78

Jun 78. (7") (K 13128) **STAY. / ROSIE** | 12 | -

Sep 78. (7") <45485> **STAY. / THE LOAD-OUT** | - | 20

Nov 78. (7") <45543> **THE ROAD. / YOU LOVE THE THUNDER** | -

Jul 80. (7") (K 12466) <47003> **BOULEVARD. / CALL IT A LOAN** | 19

Jul 80. (lp/c) (K/K4 52226) <5E 511> **HOLD OUT** | 44 | 1
– Disco apocalypse / Hold out / That girl could sing / Boulevard / Of missing persons / Call it a loan / Hold on hold out. (cd-iss. Jan87; K2 52226)

Oct 80. (7") (K 12479) **DISCO APOCALYPSE. / BOULEVARD** | -

Oct 80. (7") <47036> **THAT GIRL COULD SING. / OF MISSING PERSONS** | - | 22

—— next single was from "Fast Times at Ridgemont High" Soundtrack featuring GRAHAM NASH + DAVID LINDLEY

Aug 82. (7") (K 13185) <69982> **SOMEBODY'S BABY. / THE CROW ON THE CRADLE** | 7 | Jul82

—— **BROWNE** retained **KUNKEL, DOERGE, HAYWOOD, GLAUB / + RICK VITO** – guitar repl. LINDLEY

				Elektra	Asylum

Jul 83. (7") (E 9826) <69826> **LAWYERS IN LOVE. / SAY IT ISN'T TRUE** | 13
(with free 7") – TENDER IS THE NIGHT. / ON THE DAY

Aug 83. (lp/c) <(960 268-1/-4)> **LAWYERS IN LOVE** | 37 | 8
– Lawyers in love / On the day / Cut it away / Downtown / Tender is the night / Knock on any door / For a rocker. (cd-iss. Jul87; 960 268-2)

Oct 83. (7") (E 9791) <69791> **TENDER IS THE NIGHT. / ON THE DAY** | 25 | Sep83

Jan 84. (7") <69764> **FOR A ROCKER. / DOWNTOWN** | - | 45

—— Late '85 / early in '86, JACKSON was credited on US Top 20 single 'You're A Friend Of Mine', with CLARENCE CLEMONS (ex-BRUCE SPRINGSTEEN). His girlfriend DARRYL HANNAH guested, backing vocals.

Feb 86. (lp/c)(cd) (EKT 31/+C)<(960 457-2)> **LIVES IN THE BALANCE** | 36 | 23
– For America / Soldier of plenty / In the shape of a heart / Candy / Lawless avenues / Lives in the balance / Till I go down / Black and white.

Feb 86. (7"/7"sha-pic-d) (EKR 35/+P) <69566> **FOR AMERICA. / TILL I GO DOWN** | 30

Oct 86. (7"/7"sha-pic-d) (EKR 42/+P) <69543> **IN THE SHAPE OF A HEART. / VOICE OF AMERICA** | 66 | 70 | Jun86
(d7"+=) (EKR 42) – Running on empty / The pretender.

Jan 87. (7"/12") (W 8698/+T) **EGO MANIAC. / LOVE'S GONNA GET YOU** | -
(above single on 'Warners')

Jun 89. (lp/c)(cd) (EKT 50/+C)<(960 832-2)> **WORLD IN MOTION** | 39 | 45
– World in motion / Enough of the night / Chasing you into the light / How long / Anything can happen / When the stone begins to turn / The worst justice / My personal revenge / I am a patriot / Lights and virtues. (cd re-iss. Feb95; same)

Jun 89. (7") <69292> **WORLD IN MOTION. / PERSONAL REVENGE** | - | -

Oct 89. (7") <69284> **ANYTHING CAN HAPPEN. / LIGHTS AND VIRTUES**

Jan 90. (7") <69262> **CHASING YOU INTO THE NIGHT. / HOW LONG**

—— now with **DAVID LINDLEY, MARK GOLDENBERG, SCOTT THURSTON, MIKE CAMPBELL, WALLY WACHTEL** – guitars / **KEVIN McCORMICK** – bass / **BENMONT TENCH** – organ / **MAURICIO LEWAK** – drums / **LUIS CONTE + LENNY CASTRO** –

percussion / plus guests **DAVID CROSBY / DON HENLEY / JENNIFER WARNES / SWEET PEA ATKINSON + SIR HARRY BOWENS**

Oct 93. (cd/c) (7559 61524-2/-4)> **I'M ALIVE** | 35 | 40
– I'm alive / My problem is you / Everywhere I go / I'll do anything / Miles away / Too many angels / Take this rain / Two of me, two of you / Sky blue and black / All good things.

Nov 93. (7"/c-s) (EKR 176/+C) **I'M ALIVE / TOO MANY ANGELS**
(cd-s) (EKR 176CD) – ('A'side) / Late for the sky / Running on empty / The pretender.

Jun 94. (7"/c-s) (EKR 184/+C) **EVERYWHERE I GO. / I'M ALIVE (live)** | 67
(cd-s+=) (EKR 184CD2) – The pretender (live) / Running on empty (live).
(cd-s) (EKR 184CD1) – ('A'side) / Take it easy / Doctor my eyes / In the shape of a heart.

Nov 94. (7"/c-s) (EKR 193/+C) **SKY BLUE AND BLACK. / TENDER IS THE NIGHT** | | |
(12"+=/cd-s+=) (EKR 193 T/CD) – Everywhere I go.

—— guests on below; BONNIE RAITT / RY COODER / DAVID CROSBY / DAVID LINDLEY / etc.

Feb 96. (cd/c) <(7559 61867-2/-4)> **LOOKING EAST** | 47 | 36
– Looking east / The barricades of Heaven / Some bridges / Information wars / I'm the cat / Culver moon / Baby how long / Nino / Alive in the world / It is one.

Jul 96. (c-s/cd-s) (EKR 221 C/CD) **I'M THE CAT / BEFORE THE DELUGE** | |

Nov 97. (cd/c) <(7559 62111-2/-4)> **THE NEXT VOICE YOU HEAR – THE BEST OF JACKSON BROWNE** (compilation) | 47 | Oct97
– Doctor my eyes / These days / Late for the sky / Fountain of sorrow / The pretender / Running on empty / Call it a loan / Somebody's baby / Tender is the night / Lives in the balance / In the shape of a heart / Sky blue and black / Barricades of Heaven / The rebel Jesus / The next voice you hear.

– compilations, etc. –

on 'Asylum' unless mentioned otherwise

Sep 76. (7") (K 13043) **DOCTOR MY EYES. / TAKE IT EASY** | | -

Oct 82. (d-c) (K4 62041) **THE PRETENDER / LATE FOR THE SKY** | | -

Nov 83. (d-c) (960 277-4) **JACKSON BROWNE / RUNNING ON EMPTY** | | -

Jack BRUCE

Born: JOHN SYMON ASHER BRUCE, 14 May'43, Bishopbriggs, Lanarkshire, Scotland. At 17 he won a scholarship to R.S.A. of music although the prodigiously talented teenager joined local band JIM McHARG'S SCOTSVILLE JAZZBAND, before moving to London and playing in BLUES INCORPORATED with ALEXIS KORNER. In 1963 he became a member of GRAHAM BOND ORGANISATION, joining JOHN MAYALL'S BLUESBREAKERS a couple of years later. He also released a one-off debut solo 45 around the same time and after a six month spell with MANFRED MANN, he made his greatest ever career move, co-forming legendary power trio, CREAM, alongside ERIC CLAPTON and GINGER BAKER. One of the greatest bass players of all time, his hard-hitting style and booming vocals were an integral part of the CREAM sound, his technique mimicked by countless heavy rock bands in the years that followed. After the band's demise in late 1968, he went solo, remaining with 'Polydor'. Recorded with a backing band including DICK HECKSTALL-SMITH and CHRIS SPEDDING, his debut album, 'SONGS FOR A TAILOR' (1969), hit the UK Top 10 despite its ambitious, idiosyncratic blend of jazz-fusion (the track 'THEME FOR AN IMAGINARY WESTERN' subsequently becoming a hit for MOUNTAIN). This was his only commercial success though, and subsequent albums such as 'HARMONY ROW' (1971) and 'OUT OF THE STORM' (1974) failed to chart. Featuring MICK TAYLOR on guitar, the latter set was a more straightforward hard rock effort, while the 1977 set, 'HOW'S TRICKS', was recorded under the JACK BRUCE BAND moniker. 1980 saw him team up with DAVID SANCIOUS, DAVE CLEMPSON and BILLY COBHAM as JACK BRUCE & FRIENDS, releasing an album for 'Epic'. He then teamed up with another veteran guitarist, ROBIN TROWER, for an album on 'Chrysalis', although throughout much of the ensuing decade he focused on his drug and alcohol problems. The 90's saw BRUCE reunited with old mucker GINGER BAKER for the ethnic flavoured 'A QUESTION OF TIME', the pair subsequently forming BBM along with GARY MOORE and enjoying Top 10 success with 'AROUND THE NEXT DREAM'. • **Trivia:** During 1970, he was also part of US jazz-rock outfit TONY WILLIAMS' LIFETIME, releasing album of same name.

Album rating: SONGS FOR A TAILOR (*8) / THINGS WE LIKE (*5) / HARMONY ROW (*6) / AT HIS BEST compilation (*6) / OUT OF THE STORM (*5) / HOW'S TRICKS (*5) / GREATEST HITS compilation (*6) / I'VE ALWAYS WANTED TO DO THIS (*5) / AUTOMATIC (*4) / A QUESTION OF TIME (*5) / SOMETHIN ELS (*5) / CITIES OF THE HEART (*5) / AROUND THE NEXT DREAM with BBM (*6) / MONKJACK (*4)

JACK BRUCE – vocals, bass (ex-BLUES INCORPORATED, ex-GRAHAM BOND ORGANISATION) with session people

				Polydor	Atco

Dec 65. (7") (BM 56036) **I'M GETTIN' TIRED (OF DRINKING AND GAMBLING). / ROOTIN' TOOTIN'** | | -

—— (see above for details between 1966 and 1968.) He brought in friends **JON HISEMAN** – drums / **DICK HECKSTALL-SMITH** – sax / **CHRIS SPEDDING** – guitar / etc.

Sep 69. (lp) (583 058) <33306> **SONGS FOR A TAILOR** | 6 | 55
– Never tell your mother she's out of tune / Theme for an imaginary western / Tickets to water falls / Weird of Hermiston / Rope ladder to the Moon / The ministry of bag /

He the Richmond / Boston ball game, 1967 / To Isengard / The clearout. (re-iss. May84; 2459 360) (cd-iss. May88 & Apr97; 835 242-2)

— **JOHN McLAUGHLIN** – guitar (solo artist), repl. SPEDDING
Jan 71. (lp) (2343 033) <33349> **THINGS WE LIKE**
   – Over the cliff / Statues / Sam enchanted Dick (medley:- Sam's back / Rill's thrills) / Born to be blue / Hchhh blues / Ballad of Arthur / Things we like. (re-iss. Apr71; 2310 070)

— retained some past musicians, bringing in **LARRY COYRELL** – guitar / **MIKE MANDEL** – keyboards / **MITCH MITCHELL** – drums
Sep 71. (lp) (2310 107) <33365> **HARMONY ROW**
   – Can you follow? / Escape to the Royal wood (on ice) / You burned the tables on me / There's a forest / Morning story / Folk song / Smiles and grins / Post war / Letter of thanks / Victoria sage / The consul at sunset. (cd-iss. 1980's;)
Oct 71. (7") (2058 153) **THE CONSUL AT SUNSET. / LETTER OF THANKS**

— In 1972/73, he became part of WEST, BRUCE & LAING (see; MOUNTAIN) He also collaborated on lp ESCALATOR OVER THE HILL with PAUL HAINES and CARLA.

— now with **MICK TAYLOR** – guitar / **CARLA BLEY** – piano / **RONNIE LEAHY** – keyboards / **BRUCE GARY** – drums

R.S.O.   R.S.O.
Oct 74. (7") (2090 141) **KEEP IT DOWN. / GOLDEN DAYS**
Nov 74. (lp) (2394 143) <4805> **OUT OF THE STORM**
   – Pieces of mind / Golden days / Running through our hands / Keep on wondering / Keep it down / Into the storm / One / Timeslip. (cd-iss.)

— now with **SIMON PHILIPS** – drums / **HUGH BURNS** – guitar / **TONY HYMAS** – keyboards
Mar 77. (lp; as JACK BRUCE BAND) (2394 180) <1-3021> **HOW'S TRICKS**
   – Without a word / Johnny B '77 / Times / Baby Jane / Lost inside a song / How's tricks / Madhouse / Waiting for the call / Outsiders / Something to live for.

— Friends: **DAVID SANCIOUS** – guitar, keyboards / **DAVE CLEMPSON** – guitar / **BILLY COBHAM** – drums

Epic   Epic
Dec 80. (lp; as JACK BRUCE & FRIENDS) (84672) <JE 36827> **I'VE ALWAYS WANTED TO DO THIS**
   – Hit and run / Running back / Facelift 318 / In this way / Mickey the fiddler / Dancing on air / Livin' without ja / Wind and the sea / Out to lunch / Bird alone.

— In 1981 he teamed up with BILL LORDAN and ROBIN TROWER to release lp 'B.L.T.' Early the following year he and ROBIN TROWER (see ⇒ released 'TRUCE' album on 'Chrysalis'; CHR/ZCHR 1352). He returned to solo work after below 45 was featured on TV car advert.

Virgin   Virgin
Jun 86. (7"/12") (VS 875/+12) **I FEEL FREE. / MAKE LOVE**

President Intercord
Jan 87. (lp/c) (PTLS/PTLC 1082) **AUTOMATIC**
   – A boogie / Uptown breakdown / Travelling child / New world / Make love (part 2) / Green and blue / The swarm / Encore / Automatic pilot.

— next with **ANTON FIER** – drums (ex-PERE UBU) / **KENJI SUZUKI** – guitar

Epic   Epic
Jan 88. (lp/c/cd; JACK BRUCE, ANTON FIER & KENJI SUZUKI) **INAZUMA SUPER SESSION – ABSOLUTELY LIVE (live)**
   – Generation breakdown / White room / Out into the field / Working harder / Sittin' on top of the world / Sunshine of your love / Crossroads / Spoonful – Beat of rock.

— now with **VERNON REID, NICKY HOPKINS, ALLAN HOLDSWORTH, GINGER BAKER**
Jan 90. (cd/c/lp) (465 692-2/-4/-1) **A QUESTION OF TIME**
   – Life on Earth / Make love / No surrender! / Flying / Hey now princess / Blues you can't lose / Obsession / Kwela / Let me be / Only playing games / A question of time. (re-iss. Feb91;)

— with **PETE BROWN** still lyricist / plus **ERIC CLAPTON** – lead guitar / **STUART ELLIOT** – drums / **PETER WIEHE** – rhythm guitar / **MAGGIE REILLY** – b.vocals / **CLEM CLEMPSON** – rhythm guitar, etc / **TRILOK GURTU** – percussion / and guests on 1 each **DICK HECKSTALL-SMITH + DAVID LIEBMAN** – saxophones

C.M.P.   C.M.P.
Mar 93. (cd/c/lp) **SOMETHIN ELS**
   – Waiting on a word / Willpower / Ships in the night / Peace of the East / Close enough for love / G.B. dawn blues / Criminality / Childsong / F.M.

— with **GARY MOORE** – guitar, vocals / **MAGGIE REILLY** – vocals / **GARY 'Mudbone' COOPER** – vocals, percussion / **CLEM CLEMPSON** – guitars / **DICK HECKSTALL-SMITH** – saxophone / **BERNIE WORRELL** – keyboards / **PETE BROWN** – vocals, percussion / **GINGER BAKER & SIMON PHILLIPS + GARY HUSBAND** – drums / **FRANCOIS GARNY** – bass / **MALCOLM BRUCE** – acoustic guitar, keyboards / **JONAS BRUCE** – keyboards / **ART THEMEN** – saxophone / **HENRY LOWTHER** – trumpet / **JOHN MUMFORD** – trombone / + **KIP HANRAHAN**
Mar 94. (d-cd/d-c) (CMP CD/MC 1005) **CITIES OF THE HEART (live)**
   – Can you follow? / Running thro' our hands / Over the cliff / Statues / First time I met the blues / Smiles & grins / Over the cliff / Neighbor, neighbor / Born under a bad sign / Ships in the night / Never tell your mother she's out of tune / Theme for an imaginary western / Golden days / Life on Earth / NSU / Sitting on top of the world / Politician / Spoonful / Sunshine of your love. (cd re-iss. Aug94 + Nov94 + Mar96; CMPCD 1005)
Sep 95. (cd) (CMPCD 1010) **MONKJACK**
   – Third degree / The boy / Shouldn't we / David's harp / Know one blues / Time repairs / Laughing on music / Street / Folksong / Weird of Hermiston / Tightrope / The food / Immoral ninth.

BBM

(aka GINGER BAKER, JACK BRUCE & GARY MOORE) A near reformation of CREAM with MOORE taking the place of CLAPTON.

Virgin   Virgin
Jun 94. (cd/c/lp) (CD/TC+/V 2745) **AROUND THE NEXT DREAM** | 9 |

   – Waiting in the wings / City of gold / Where in the world / Can't fool the blues / High cost of living / Glory days / Why does love (have to go wrong) / Naked flame / I wonder (why are you so mean to me?) / Wrong side of town.
Jul 94. (7"/c-s) (VS/+C 1495) **WHERE IN THE WORLD. / DANGER ZONE** | 57 |
   (cd-s+=) (VSCDG 1495) – The world keeps on turnin'.
   (cd-s) (VSCDX 1495) – ('A'side) / Sittin' on top of the world / I wonder (why are you so mean to me?).

– compilations, others, etc. –

on 'Polydor' UK unless mentioned otherwise
1974. (d-lp) (2659 024) / R.S.O.; <PD 3505> **AT HIS BEST** | | 1972
Nov 80. (d-lp)(d-c) (2658 137)(3524 218) **GREATEST HITS**
Jul 89. (d-lp/c/cd) (837 806-1/-4/-2) **WILLPOWER**
   (cd re-iss. Apr95; same)
May 92. (cd/c) Castle; (CCS CD/MC 326) **THE COLLECTION**
Nov 92. (cd; JACK BRUCE & FRIENDS) Traditional Line; (TL 1324) **LIVE AT THE BOTTOM LINE (live)**
May 94. (cd; by DICK HECKSTALL-SMITH, JACK BRUCE & JOHN STEVENS) Atonal; (EFA 11956-2) **THIS THAT**
Sep 95. (cd) Windsong; (WINCD 076) **BBC LIVE IN CONCERT**
Aug 96. (cd) C.M.P.; (CMPCD 1013) **THE COLLECTORS EDITION**
Nov 99. (cd) Ranch Life; (CRANCH 15) **CONCERT CLASSICS**

B.T.O. (see under ⇒ BACHMAN-TURNER OVERDRIVE)

Tim BUCKLEY

Born: 14 Feb'47, Washington DC, USA. Signed to 'Elektra' in 1966 by FRANK ZAPPA manager HERB COHEN, who'd discovered him playing folk clubs around L.A. He recorded an eponymous debut with ZAPPA's musicians backing him up, before moving to New York where he was influenced by Greenwich Village troubadour FRED NEIL (whose 'DOLPHINS' he would later cover on his 1974 album 'SEFRONIA'). 1967's 'GOODBYE AND HELLO' wore its influences on its sleeve but won critical plaudits for its cascading vocal versatility and meandering grace. Released a couple of years later, 'HAPPY / SAD's introspective intimations abandoned conventional song structures for abstract folk-jazz workouts. Desite their more experimental nature, the songs retained a tangible warmth of feeling, especially the lovely 'BUZZIN' FLY'. A frenetic period of creativity followed in 1970, with BUCKLEY releasing three albums in the space of a year. 'BLUE AFTERNOON' carried on in much the same vein while he took a further sidestep into improvisation with 'LORCA', culminating in the uncompromising 'STARSAILOR'. In true BUCKLEY fashion, he veered wildly into new territory with the sexually explicit 1972 album 'GREETINGS FROM L.A.', which exhibited an interest in black music. The doomed singer recorded two final rather patchy and self-indulgent albums before he died of an accidental drug overdose on 29th June '75. His poetic awareness and uncompromising efforts to push musical boundaries, had taken him down a solitary path that bypassed commercial success and eventually led to disillusionment and death, although he left behind a musical legacy of shimmering beauty. In 1990, 'DREAM LETTER', an album of live material from 1968, was unearthed to critical acclaim and along with various other re-issues, has only served to feed the myth of one of rock's greatest enigmas.
• **Covered:** SALLY GO ROUND THE ROSES (Jaynettes). • **Trivia:** His songs were later recorded by THIS MORTAL COIL (Song To The Siren + I Must Have Been Blind) and BLOOD, SWEAT & TEARS (Morning Glory).

Album rating: TIM BUCKLEY (*7) / GOODBYE & HELLO (*7) / HAPPY SAD (*7) / BLUE AFTERNOON (*7) / LORCA (*5) / STARSAILOR (*7) / GREETINGS FROM L.A. (*7) / SEFRONIA (*4) / LOOK AT THE FOOL (*4) / BEST OF TIM BUCKLEY – 1983 US-import lp (*8) / DREAM LETTER – LIVE IN LONDON (*7) / LIVE AT THE TROUBADOUR 1969 (*5) / HONEYMAN (*5)

TIM BUCKLEY – vocals, guitar with **LEE UNDERWOOD** – guitar, keyboards / **BILLY MUNDI** – drums / **JIM FIELDER** – bass / **VAN DYKE PARKS** – piano / **JACK NITZSCHE** – string arrangements

Elektra   Elektra
Nov 66. (7") <45606> **GRIEF IN MY SOUL. / WINGS**
Dec 66. (lp; mono/stereo) (EKL/EKS 4004) <74004> **TIM BUCKLEY** | | Oct66
   – I can't see you / Wings / Song of the magician / Strange street affair under blue / Valentine melody / Aren't you the girl / Song slowly sung / It happens every time / Song for Jainie / Grief in my soul / She is / Understand your man. <re-iss. Jul71 & Mar75; same>
Jan 67. (7") (EKSN 45008) <45612> **AREN'T YOU THE GIRL. / STRANGE STREET AFFAIR UNDER BLUE**

— BUCKLEY retained UNDERWOOD, recruiting **CARTER C. COLLINS** – congas
Aug 67. (7") <45618> **LADY GIVE ME YOUR HEART. / ONCE UPON A TIME**
Oct 67. (7") <45623> **MORNING GLORY. / ONCE I WAS**
Nov 67. (7") (EKSN 45018) **MORNING GLORY. / KNIGHT-ERRANT**
Dec 67. (lp; mono/stereo) (EKL/EKS 318) <7318> **GOODBYE AND HELLO** | | Oct67
   – No man can find the war / Carnival song / Pleasant street / Hallucinations / I never asked to be your mountain / Once I was / Phantasmagoria in two / Knight-Errant / Goodbye and hello / Morning glory. (re-iss. Jul71; K 42070) (re-iss. Mar93 & Sep95 on 'Warners' cd/c; 7559 60896-2/-4)
Jan 68. (7") (EKSN 45023) **ONCE I WAS. / PHANTASMAGORIA IN TWO**
Mar 68. (7") (EKSN 45031) **WINGS. / I CAN'T SEE YOU**

— added **JOHN MILLER** – acoustic & electric bass / **DAVID FREEDMAN** – vibes, percussion

Oct 68. (7") *(EKSN 45041)* **PLEASANT STREET. / CARNIVAL SONG** ☐ ☐

Jul 69. (lp) *<(EKS 74045)>* **HAPPY – SAD** ☐ | 81 |
— Strange feeling / Buzzin' fly / Love from room 109 at the Islander (on Pacific Coast Highway) / Dream letter / Gypsy woman / Sing a song for you. *(re-iss. Jul71; K 42072)* *(cd-iss. Feb93; 7559 74045-2)*

—— added **JIMMY MADISON** – drums

                                   Straight   Straight

Feb 70. (7") *(S 4799)* **HAPPY TIME. / SO LONELY** ☐ ☐

Feb 70. (lp) *<(STS 1060)>* **BLUE AFTERNOON** ☐ ☐
— Happy time / Chase the blues away / I must have been blind / The river / So lonely / Cafe / Blue melody / Train. *<US re-iss. Jul71 on 'Warners'; WS 1842>*

—— BUCKLEY retained only UNDERWOOD and COLLINS, recruiting **JOHN BLAKIN** – bass

                                   Elektra   Elektra

Oct 70. (lp) *(2410 005)* *<EKS 74074>* **LORCA** ☐ ☐
— Lorca / Anonymous proposition / I had a talk with a woman / Driftin' / Nobody walkin'. *<US re-iss. Jul71; K 42053>* *(re-iss. Mar75; same)*

—— BUCKLEY retained only UNDERWOOD and BALKIN, recruiting co-write **LARRY BECKETT / MAURI BAKET** – timpani / **BUZZ GARDNER and BUNK GARDNER** on wind and horns

                                   Straight   Straight

Jan 71. (lp) *<(STS 1064)>* **STARSAILOR** ☐ ☐
— Come here woman / I woke up / Monterey / Moulin Rouge / Song to the siren / Jungle fire / Starsailor / The healing festival / Down by the borderline. *<US re-iss. Jul71 on 'Warners'; WS 1881>*

—— from now on BUCKLEY used loads of session people plus past friends.

                                   Warners   Warners

Oct 72. (7") *<7623>* **MOVE WITH ME. / NIGHTHAWKIN'** - ☐

Oct 72. (lp) *(K 46176)* *<BS 2631>* **GREETINGS FROM L.A.** - ☐
— Move with me / Get on top / Sweet surrender / Nighthawkin' / Devil eyes / Hong Kong bar / Make it right. *<cd-iss. Jul89 on 'Disc Int.'; EN 73506>* *(cd-iss. Feb96; 7599 27261-2)*

                               Discreet- Discreet-
                               Warners Warners

May 74. (lp) *(K 49201)* *<MS 2157>* **SEFRONIA** ☐ ☐
— Dolphins / Honeyman / Because of you / Peanut man / Martha / Quicksand / I know I'd recognise your face / Stone in love / Sefronia – After Asklepiades, after Kafka / Sefronia – The King's chain / Sally go 'round the roses. *(re-iss. Oct89 on 'Edsel' lp/cd; ED/+CD 277)* *(cd re-iss. Feb97 on 'Manifesto'; PT 340701)*

May 74. (7") *<1187>* **STONE IN LOVE. / QUICKSAND** - ☐

Jul 74. (7") *<1189>* **HONEYMAN. / DOLPHINS** - ☐

Nov 74. (lp) *(K 59204)* *<DS 2201>* **LOOK AT THE FOOL** - ☐
— Look at the fool / Bring it on up / Helpless / Freeway blues / Tijuana moon / Ain't it peculiar / Who could deny you? / Mexicali voodoo / Down in the street / Wanda Lu. *(re-iss. Oct89 on 'Edsel' lp/cd; ED/+CD 294)* *(cd re-iss. Feb97 on 'Manifesto'; PT 340702)*

Nov 74. (7") *<1311>* **WANDA LU. / WHO COULD DENY YOU** - ☐

—— TIM died on the 29th of June '75 (see biog.)

– compilations, etc. –

Sep 76. (7") *Elektra; (K 12223)* **MORNING GLORY. / ONCE I WAS** ☐ ☐

Jun 90. (d-lp/d-cd) *Demon; (DFIEND/+CD 200)* **DREAM LETTER – LIVE IN LONDON 1968 (live)** ☐ -
(cd re-iss. Feb97 on 'Manifesto'; PT 340703)

Aug 91. (cd-ep) *Strange Fruit; (SFPSCD 082)* **THE PEEL SESSIONS** -
— Morning glory / Coming home to you / Sing a song for you / Hallucinations / Troubadour / Once I was.

Mar 94. (cd) *Demon; (EDCD 400)* **LIVE AT TROUBADOUR 1969 (live)** ☐ ☐
(re-iss. May97 on 'Manifesto'; PT 340705)

Aug 94. (cd) *Band Of Joy; (BOJCD 009)* **MORNING GLORY** ☐ ☐

Sep 95. (cd) *Edsel; (EDCD 450)* **HONEYMAN** (live 27th Nov'73) ☐ ☐

Jeff BUCKLEY

Born: 17 Nov'66, Orange County, California, USA. The offspring of the late, great TIM BUCKLEY, JEFF's chosen career as a musician, singer and songwriter was always destined to bear the heavy burden of his father's unique legacy (note: in this instance JEFF appears out of alphabetical sequence). To his credit, BUCKLEY Jnr. persevered at carving out a distinctive niche in the musical landscape of the early 90's, plugging away on the once legendary Greenwich Village scene of New York. Torch rather than tortured, JEFF utilised his inherited multi-octave vocal chords in ever more impressive and innovative fashion, both in tackling an eclectic variety of cover material (see below) and lavishly dramatic originals. Given his first British break in 1994, via 'LIVE AT THE SIN-E' EP (1992 in America) on the 'Big Cat' label, BUCKLEY was a surprise success at the grunge overload of Reading 1994. Coinciding with his appearance was the release of his major label ('Columbia') debut, 'GRACE', an emotionally raw and occasionally claustrophobic listen that gained almost unanimous praise from UK critics and enjoyed a brief residence in the Top 50. Tracks such as 'SO REAL', 'LAST GOODBYE' and 'DREAM LOVER', suggested a mercurial talent in the ascendant, although the lad had possibly listened to too much LED ZEPPELIN as a youth. Eventually resuming his recording career early in 1997 with TOM VERLAINE (ex-TELEVISION) at the controls, JEFF looked like making a severe dent in the rock mainstream with a follow-up to 'GRACE', although subsequent sessions proved problematic. Fate was to deal a cruel hand when, on the 29th of May '98, JEFF, like his father before him, was cut down in his prime; hardly a typical rock'n'roll death, the young singer was swept away by a powerful current while swimming in Memphis harbor. Exactly a year later, the half-finished project BUCKLEY had been working on at the time of his death was posthumously

released as 'SKETCHES FOR MY SWEETHEART THE DRUNK'. A double CD partly curated by his mother, the UK Top 10 set gave an indication as to where JEFF was headed as well as serving as a convincing last word on the career of a man many considered a genius. • **Covers:** JE N'EN CONNAIS PAS LA FIN (Edith Piaf) / THE WAY YOUNG LOVERS DO (Van Morrison) / LILAC WINE (Elkie Brooks) / HALLELUJAH (Leonard Cohen) / KANGA ROO (Big Star) / KICK OUT THE JAMS (MC5) / YARD OF BLONDE GIRLS (Audrey Clark) / BACK IN N.Y.C. (Genesis) / SATISFIED MIND (J.Hayes & J.Rhodes).

Album rating: LIVE AT SIN-E mini (*6) / GRACE (*8) / SKETCHES FOR MY SWEETHEART THE DRUNK (*7)

JEFF BUCKLEY – vocals, guitars, harmonium, organ, dulcimer / with **MICK GRONDAHL** – bass / **MATT JOHNSON** – drums, percussion / plus MICHAEL TIGHE – guitar / **GARLY LUCAS** – magicalguitarness

                                   Big Cat   Big Cat

Apr 94. (m-lp/m-cd) *(ABB 61/+CD)* **LIVE AT SIN-E** (live) ☐ ☐
— Mojo pin / Eternal life / Je n'en connais pas la fin / The way young lovers do.

                                 Columbia Columbia

Aug 94. (cd/c/lp) *(475928-2/-4/-1)* *<57528>* **GRACE** | 50 | ☐
— Mojo pin / Grace / Last goodbye / Lilac wine / So real / Hallelujah / Lover, you should've come over / Corpus christi Carol / Eternal life / Dream brother.

May 95. (10"ep/cd-ep) *(662042-0/-2)* **LAST GOODBYE. / LOVER, YOU SHOULD'VE COME OVER / TONGUE** (live) | 54 | ☐
(cd-ep) *(662042-5)* – ('A'side) / Dream brother (live) / So real (live).

1996. (m-cd) **LIVE FROM YHE BATACLAN** (live) - ☐

—— Sadly, JEFF was to die in a drowning accident on the 29th of May '97 (see biography)

May 98. (d-cd/d-c/d-lp) *(488661-2/-4/-1)* *<67228>* **SKETCHES FOR MY SWEETHEART THE DRUNK** | 7 | 64 |
— The sky is a landfill / Everybody here wants you / Opened once / Nightmares by the sea / Yard of blonde girls / Witches' rave / Morning theft / Vancouver / You & I // Nightmares by the sea / New Year's prayer / Haven't you heard / I know we could be so happy baby (if we wanted to be) / Murder suicide meteor slave / Back in N.Y.C. / Gunshot glitter *[cd-only]* / Demon John / Your flesh is so nice / Jewel box / Satisfied mind.

May 98. (cd-ep) *(665791-2)* **EVERYBODY HERE WANTS YOU / THOUSAND FOLD / ETERNAL LIFE / HALLELUJAH** | 43 | ☐
(cd-ep) *(665791-5)* – ('A'side) / Lover, you should've come over / Tongue.

BUDGIE (dig out; Great Metal . . .)

BUFFALO SPRINGFIELD

Formed: Los Angeles, California, USA . . . March '66. In a well-documented incident, STEPHEN STILLS and guitarist RICHIE FUREY were caught in a traffic jam on Sunset Strip, when by pure chance, STILLS recognised the driver of a black hearse, NEIL YOUNG. Along with bass player and fellow Canadian BRUCE PALMER, YOUNG had travelled down to Hollywood to try his luck in the fabled City of Angels. This fateful get-together also led to another member being recruited, drummer DEWEY MARTIN. STILLS and YOUNG clashed right from the off, but it was essentially this tension that fuelled the band's creative spark in a JAGGERS/RICHARDS kind of fashion. Taking their name from a type of steamroller, and with the help of the SONNY & CHER management team of CHARLIE GREENE and BRIAN STONE, the band were signed to Atlantic offshoot 'Atco' in a matter of months. With the combined talent of STILLS and YOUNG's soaring harmonies and driving rhythm, the band often came on like a country-fied BEATLES, although their albums were notable for their striking stylistic diversity. The ambitiously eccentric, YOUNG-penned debut single, 'NOWADAYS CLANCY CAN'T EVEN SING', did nothing, while 'BURNED', the 2-minute pop thrill of a follow-up, fared equally badly. But then STILLS struck gold with the famous protest anthem, 'FOR WHAT IT'S WORTH', released in the same month as the band's fine eponymous debut album. The song concerned itself with the previous summer's riots whereby a coterie of businessmen had threatened Sunset Strip's nightlife by proposing the building of a business district. Of course the students were none too happy, especially when 300 protesters were arrested. The song was duly adopted by rebels everywhere as a general mascot for fighting the good fight, and its vaguely psychedelic, menacing tone perfectly evoked the feelings of persecution felt by the emerging flower children. Throughout 1967, the band was rocked by internal squabbling with various members coming and going. An album, 'STAMPEDE', was recorded but never quite completed. It later surfaced as a bootleg and one track from it, 'DOWN TO THE WIRE', featuring an impassioned YOUNG vocal, was included on his 'DECADE' (1976) compilation. YOUNG also missed the band's slot at the Monterey Pop Festival, DAVID CROSBY taking his place. Despite all this, the band completed a follow-up, 'BUFFALO SPRINGFIELD AGAIN', which was issued in late '67. Opinions on the album are mixed with some critics deeming it a classic of its time, others criticising its watered-down production. The best moments are YOUNG's JACK NITZSCHE-arranged numbers, 'BROKEN ARROW' and 'EXPECTING TO FLY', the latter possessed a haunting, lysergic quality. STILL's compositions, 'BLUEBIRD' and 'ROCK AND ROLL WOMAN', lack the sophistication of YOUNG's surreal epics but are enjoyable nonetheless. The tension between YOUNG and STILLS eventually finished the band (DAVID CROSBY once commenting that they used their guitars as weapons, on stage and off!) with a final album, 'LAST TIME AROUND', released after the split. YOUNG contributed the fragile 'I AM A CHILD' and one other song before leaving the band early on during the sessions. YOUNG went on to an erratic, often mercurial career, while STILLS went off to help form CROSBY, STILLS and NASH (re-united with YOUNG in 1970). FURAY, meanwhile, went off to join country rockers POCO. Along with The BYRDS and LOVE, BUFFALO SPRINGFIELD were one of the most influential, if somewhat short-lived bands to come out of L.A.

Album rating: BUFFALO SPRINGFIELD (*7) / BUFFALO SPRINGFIELD AGAIN (*9) / LAST TIME AROUND (*6) / THE BEST OF BUFFALO SPRINGFIELD ... RETROSPECTIVE compilation (*8) / EXPECTING TO FLY compilation (*7)

STEPHEN STILLS (b. 3 Jan'45, Dallas, Texas) – lead guitar, vocals / NEIL YOUNG (b.12 Nov'45, Toronto, Canada) – lead guitar, vocals / RICHIE FURAY (b. 9 May'44, Dayton, Ohio) – vocals, guitar / BRUCE PALMER (b. 1944, Liverpool, Canada) – bass; repl. KEN KOBLUN / DEWEY MARTIN (b.30 Sep'42, Chesterville, Canada) – drums (ex-DILLARDS)

		Atlantic	Atco
Oct 66.	(7") <6428> NOWADAYS CLANCY CAN'T EVEN SING. / GO AND SAY GOODBYE	-	
Dec 66.	(7"w-drawn) <6452> BURNED. / EVERYBODY'S WRONG	-	
Jan 67.	(lp; stereo/mono) (588/587 070) <SD+/33-200> BUFFALO SPRINGFIELD		Dec66

– Don't scold me (*) / Go and say goodbye / Sit down I think I love you / Nowadays Clancy can't even sing / Everybody's wrong / Hot dusty roads / Flying on the ground / Burned / Do I have to come right out and say it? / Leave / Pay the price / Out of my mind. *re-iss. Feb67 stereo/mono; SD+/33-200-A) – For what it's worth (repl.track (*) ; hit US No.80> (re-iss. 1971; K 30028) (cd-iss. Feb93; 7567 90389-2)

| Jan 67. | (7") (584 077) <6459> FOR WHAT IT'S WORTH. / DO I HAVE TO COME RIGHT OUT AND SAY IT? | | 7 |

—— on stage KEN KOBLUN and JIM FIELDER, latter of The MOTHERS, repl. PALMER, although PALMER did return occasionally. / DOUG HASTINGS – guitar repl. YOUNG (also DAVID CROSBY guested at Monterey)

—— BOB WEST – bass & CHARLIE CHIN – banjo deputise for above reshuffles

| Jul 67. | (7") <6499> BLUEBIRD. / MR. SOUL | - | 58 |

STILLS, FURAY, MARTIN and the returning YOUNG recruit JIM MESSINA (b. 5 Dec'47, Maywood, Calif.) – bass repl. FIELDER who joined BLOOD SWEAT & TEARS

| Oct 67. | (7") (584 145) <6519> ROCK'N'ROLL WOMAN. / A CHILD'S CLAIM TO FAME | | 44 Sep67 |
| Jan 68. | (lp; stereo/mono) (588/587 091) <SD+/33-226> BUFFALO SPRINGFIELD AGAIN | | 44 Nov67 |

– Mr. Soul / A child's claim to fame / Everydays / Expecting to fly / Bluebird / Hung upside down / Sad memory / Good time boy / Rock'n'roll woman / Broken arrow. (re-iss. 1971; K 40014) (cd-iss. Jul88; 790 417-2)

Feb 68.	(7") (584 165) <6545> EXPECTING TO FLY. / EVERYDAYS		98 Jan68
Jun 68.	(7") (584 189) <6572> UNO MUNDO. / MERRY-GO-ROUND		
Aug 68.	(7") <6602> KIND WOMAN. / SPECIAL CARE	-	

—— with original line-up they recorded another album, but they had split by May'68. MESSINA who had always been their sound recordist posthumously assembled line-up

| Oct 68. | (7") <6615> ON THE WAY HOME. / FOUR DAYS GONE | - | 82 |
| Dec 68. | (lp) (228 024) <SD33-256> LAST TIME AROUND | | 42 Aug68 |

– On the way home / It's so hard to wait / Pretty girl why / Four days gone / Carefree country day / Special care / The hour of not quite rain / Questions / I am a child / Merry-go-round / Uno mundo / Kind woman. (re-iss. 1971; K 40077) (cd-iss. Mar94 on 'Atco'; 7567 90393-2)

—— After their split, NEIL YOUNG went solo and joined STEPHEN STILLS in CROSBY, STILLS NASH & YOUNG. FURAY formed POCO adding later MESSINA. DEWEY MARTIN tried in vain to use BUFFALO SPRINGFIELD name.

– compilations, etc. –

on 'Atlantic' UK / 'Atco' US; unless otherwise mentioned

| Mar 69. | (lp) (228 012) <SD33-283> RETROSPECTIVE – THE BEST OF BUFFALO SPRINGFIELD | | 42 Feb69 |

– For what it's worth / Mr. Soul / Sit down I think I love you / Kind woman / Bluebird / On the way home / Nowadays Clancy can't even sing / Broken arrow / Rock'n'roll woman / I am a child / Go and say goodbye / Expecting to fly. (re-iss. 1971; K 40071) (cd-iss. Jul88; 790 417-2)

Oct 69.	(7") Atco; (226 006) PRETTY GIRL WHY / QUESTIONS	-	-
Oct 70.	(lp) (K 2462 012) EXPECTING TO FLY		-
Oct 72.	(7"ep) (K 10237) BLUEBIRD / MR. SOUL. / ROCK'N'ROLL WOMAN / EXPECTING TO FLY		
Dec 73.	(d-lp) (K 70001) <SD2 806> BUFFALO SPRINGFIELD		

—— some BUFFALO SPRINGFIELD live tracks appeared on NEIL YOUNG's compilation lp 'JOURNEY THROUGH THE PAST', and two on his 'DECADE' triple in '77.

BUFFALO TOM

Formed: Boston, Massachusetts, USA ... 1986 by BILL JANOVITZ, CHRIS COLBOURN and TOM MAGINNIS. Signed to 'S.S.T.', the band debuted in summer '89 with an eponymous album of high octane melodic hardcore. Though drawing countless comparisons with DINOSAUR JR. (J. MASCIS produced them), the group ploughed on, developing their own unique sound and garnering critical praise for the impressive writing talents of JANOVITZ and COLBOURN. Somewhat akin to a grunge hybrid of HUSKER DU and VAN MORRISON, these soulful indie rockers signed to 'Beggars Banquet' subsidiary, 'Situation 2', for their follow-up set, 'BIRD BRAIN'. However, it was with the acclaimed 'LET ME COME OVER' (1992), that BUFFALO TOM's bruised beauty really began to resonate, the classic 'TAILLIGHTS FADE' warranting gushing but deserved praise from the music press. By taking their collective foot off the noise accelerator, the group had given the

songs time to catch their breath and enjoy the scenery. This didn't translate into major sales, however, the record stalling just inside the UK Top 50. 'BIG RED LETTER DAY' (1993) went for a slicker sound, this approach paying off as the album became the first BUFFALO TOM record to make the Top 20. Released just prior to the band's 1995 Reading Festival appearance, 'SLEEPY EYED' proved that JANOVITZ and co. have the talent and ability to last the course, their sound noticeably more confident and mature. In fact, JANOVITZ was sufficiently sure of his talents to attempt a solo set in 1996, the rootsy 'LONESOME BILLY'. • **Songwriters:** As said, except SHE BELONGS TO ME (Bob Dylan) / HEAVEN (Psychedelic Furs) / THE SPIDER AND THE FLY (Rolling Stones).

Album rating: BUFFALO TOM (*5) / BIRDBRAIN (*5) / LET ME COME OVER (*7) / (BIG RED LETTER DAY) (*7) / SLEEPY EYED (*6) / SMITTEN (*5) / Bill Janovitz: LONESOME BILLY (*5)

BILL JANOVITZ – vocals, guitar / CHRIS COLBOURN – bass / TOM MAGINNIS – drums

		S.S.T.	S.S.T.
Oct 89.	(lp/c/cd) <(SST/+C/CD 250)> BUFFALO TOM		Jul89

– Sunflower suit / The plank / Impossible / 500,000 warnings / The bus / Racine / In the attic / Flushing stars / Walk away / Reason why. (cd-iss. Oct92 on 'Beggars Banquet'; MDC 7896) (re-iss. Oct92 on 'Beggars Banquet' lp/c/cd+=; BBQ LP/MC/CD 126) – Blue / Deep in the ground.

		Caff	not iss.
Feb 90.	(7"ltd) (CAFF 6) ENEMY. / DEEP IN THE GROUND		-
		Megadisc	Megadisc
Jun 90.	(12"/cd-s) <(MD/+C 125276)> CRAWL. / THE BUS		
		Situation 2	Beggars Banquet
Oct 90.	(12"ep/cd-ep) BIRDBRAIN. / REASON WHY (live acoustic) / HEAVEN (live acoustic)		
Oct 90.	(cd/c/lp) (SITU 31CD)(SIT C/U 31) <2434-2/-4> BIRDBRAIN		

– Birdbrain / Skeleton key / Caress / Guy who is me / Enemy / Crawl / Fortune teller / Baby / Directive / Bleeding heart. (cd+=) – Heaven / Reason why (acoustic). (cd re-iss. Sep95 & Nov97 on 'Beggars Banquet'; BBL 31CD)

May 91.	(12"/cd-s) FORTUNE TELLER. / WAH WAH		-
Feb 92.	(12"ep/cd-ep) VELVET ROOF / SHE BELONGS TO ME. / CRUTCH / SALLY BROWN		
Mar 92.	(cd)(c/lp) (SITU 36CD)(SIT C/U 36) <61105> LET ME COME OVER	49	

– Staples / Taillights fade / Mountains of your head / Mineral / Darry / Larry / Velvet roof / I'm not there / Stymied / Porch light / Frozen lake / Saving grace. (cd+=) – Crutch. (cd re-iss. Nov97 on 'Beggars Banquet'; BBL 36CD)

May 92.	(10"ep/12"ep/cd-ep) (SIT 96 TT/TCD) TAILLIGHTS FADE / BIRDBRAIN (live). / LARRY (live) / SKELETON KEY (live)		
		Beggars Banquet	Beggars Banquet
Oct 92.	(7"/7"green) MINERAL. / SUNFLOWER SUIT		

(cd-s+=) – Crawl / The bus.

| Sep 93. | (cd/c/lp) (BBQ CD/MC/LP 142) <92292> (BIG RED LETTER DAY) | 17 | |

– Sodajerk / I'm allowed / Tree house / Would not be denied / Latest monkey / My responsibility / Dry land / Torch singer / Late at night / Suppose / Anything that way. (cd re-iss. Nov97; BBL 142CD)

| Sep 93. | (12"ep/cd-ep) (BBQ 20 T/CD) SODA JERK / WOULD NOT BE DENIED. / WITCHES / THE WAY BACK | | |
| Nov 93. | (7") (BBQ 25) TREE HOUSE. / ANYTHING THAT WAY (acoustic) | | |

(12"+=/cd-s+=) – Late at night (acoustic).

		Beggars Banquet	Atlantic
Apr 94.	(12"ep/cd-ep) (BBQ 30 T/CD) <95942> I'M ALLOWED. / FOR ALL TO SEE / BUTTERSCOTCH		
		Beggars Banquet	East West
Jun 95.	(10"ep/cd-ep) (BBQ 49 TT/CD) SUMMER. / CLOUDS / DOES THIS MEAN YOU'RE NOT MY FRIEND?		-
Jul 95.	(cd/c/lp) (BBQ CD/MC/LP 177) <61782> SLEEPY EYED	31	-

– Tangerine / Summer / Kitchen door / Rules / It's you / When you discover / Sunday night / Your stripes / Sparklers / Clobbered / Sundress / Twenty-points (the ballad of sexual dependency) / Souvenir / Crueler. (cd re-iss. Nov97; BBL 177CD)

| Nov 95. | (7") (BBQ 64) TANGERINE. / BREATH | | - |

(cd-s+=) (BBQ 64CD) – The spider and the fly.

		Beggars Banquet	Polydor
Sep 98.	(7") (BBQ 329) WISER. / CUPID COME		

(cd-s+=) (BBQ 329CD) – Hawaiian baby.

| Sep 98. | (cd/lp) (BBQ CD/LP 205) <557867> SMITTEN | | |

– Rachael / Postcard / Knot it in / Bible / Scottish windows / White paint morning / Wiser / See to me / Register side / Do you in / Under milkwood / Walking wounded.

		Ignition	not iss.
Oct 99.	(7"/c-s/cd-s) (IGN/+SMC/SCD 16) GOING UNDERGROUND. / Liam Gallagher & Steve Craddock: CARNATION	6	-

BILL JANOVITZ

—— with JOEY BURNS – upright bass, vocals / JOHN CONVERTINO – drums / and guests CRAIG SCHUMACHER, HOWE GELB + NEIL HARRY

| Dec 96. | (cd/lp) (BBQ CD/LP 186) LONESOME BILLY | | |

– Girl's club / Think of all / Shoulder / Gaslight / Ghost in my piano / Strangers / My funny valentine / Peninsula / Talking to the Queen / Red balloon.

The BUNCH (see under ⇒ FAIRPORT CONVENTION)

Eric BURDON (see under ⇒ ANIMALS)

BURNING SPEAR

Formed: 1969, St. Anns, Jamaica. Mainman, WINSTON RODNEY, traced the path of 'the master of music' after a brief conversation with BOB MARLEY outside his nearby farm. Following MARLEY's advice to check out 'Studio One', the late 60's saw him record two classic LPs for the label, 'BURNING SPEAR', the superb eponymous debut, and 'ROCKING TIME', a true 'SPEAR classic, produced by Coxsone Dodd and featuring gritty keyboard sounds mixed with thumping bass lines and RODNEY's soaring vocals on extraordinary tracks such as 'SWELL HEADED', 'FOGGY ROAD' and the hypnotic title tune. BURNING SPEAR took his name from Jomo Kenyatta, Kenya's first head of state and an African freedom fighter; black history became synonymous with 'SPEAR after the release of his third album, 'MARCUS GARVEY', the first of eleven for 'Island/Mango'. He subsequently devoted a large part of his life and recordings to promoting the teachings of GARVEY – also born in St Anns – a prominent spokesman for self-determination and self-reliance for all of African descent; the leader became prominent for a time in America at the turn of the century before his message was distilled and to a large extent forgotten. The album dripped with quality, as did the next two offerings released between '75 and '76, 'GARVEY'S GHOST', a dub version of 'MARCUS GARVEY', and 'MAN IN THE HILLS'. 'SOCIAL LIVING', released in '78, continued this run of form with head-nodding aplenty and after some well received albums on the 'Heartbeat' label in the early and mid-'80s, 88's 'LIVE IN PARIS' set proved SPEAR's status as a true Reggae great. His concerts were always more of an event than just a live version of the album and this two disc recording became the quintessential SPEAR album, the recording featuring such outstanding tracks as 'MISTRESS MUSIC' and 'PEOPLE OF THE WORLD' as well as some early gems. 'MEK WE DWEET', the follow up to 'LIVE IN PARIS', recorded at the Tuff Gong studio in Kingston, continued SPEAR's lyrical message of social justice but missed the groove of his earlier work. This was underlined in 1990 when 'MARCUS GARVEY' and 'GARVEY'S GHOST' were issued side by side on one CD in celebration of the 100th anniversary of GARVEY's birth. A recent return to form with 'AN APPOINTMENT WITH HIS MAJESTY' included a tribute to JERRY GARCIA, 'PLAY JERRY', and featured SPEAR's BURNING BAND in top form. Fusing his roots philosophy with dub and reggae over the past three decades, WINSTON RODNEY continues to educate through his positive music and inspirational lyrics.

Album rating (selective): MARCUS GARVEY (*8) / MAN IN THE HELLS (*7) / GARVEY'S GHOST (*6) / DRY AND HEAVY (*7) / SOCIAL LIVING (*7) / RESISTANCE (*7) / CHANT DOWN BABYLON: THE ISLAND ANTHOLOGY compilation (*8)

WINSTON RODNEY (b. 1 Mar'45, St.Ann's) – vocals / **RUPERT WILLINGTON** – vocals
    released 2 unknown singles

——— added **DELROY HINES** – vocals

		Fab	not iss.
1970's.	(7") **MARCUS GARVEY. /**	-	-
1970's.	(7") **SLAVERY DAYS. /**	-	-
1970's.	(7") **SWELL HEADED. /**	-	-
1970's.	(lp) **BURNING SPEAR**	-	-
1970's.	(7") (FAB 240) **FOGGY ROAD. / VERSION**	-	-
1970's.	(7") **ETHIOPIANS LIVE IT OUT. /**	-	-
1970's.	(lp) **ROCKING TIME**	-	-

(UK-iss.Sep84 on 'Studio Worx'; SOL 1123)
above were imported into Britain having been recorded 1969-1971

——— trio now with **EARL SMITH + TONY CHIN** – guitar / **ASTON BARRETT + ROBBIE SHAKESPEARE** – bass / **TYRONE DOWNIE + BERNARD HARVEY** – keyboards / **LEROY WALLACE** – drums / **HERMAN MARQUIS + RICHARD HALL** – saxes / **CARLTON SAMUELS** – flute / **VINCENT GORDON** – trombone

		Island	not iss.
Dec 75.	(lp) (ILPS 9377) **MARCUS GARVEY**	□	-

– Marcus Garvey / Slavery days / The invasion (a.k.a. Black wa-da-da) / Live good / Give me / Old Marcus Garvey / Tradition / Jordan river / Red, gold and green / Resting place. (cd-iss. Aug87; CID 9377) (re-iss. Jan89 on 'Rita Marley Music'; RMM 1654)

Jan 76.	(7") (WIP 6264) **OLD MARCUS GARVEY. / TRADITION**	□	-
Mar 76.	(7") (WIP 6294) **I & I SURVIVE. / BLACK WA-DA-DA**	□	-
Apr 76.	(lp/c) (ILPS/ZCI 9382) **GARVEY'S GHOST** (dub versions)	□	-

– The ghost / I & I survive / Black wa-dad-da / John Burns Shank / Brain food / Father – East of Jack / 2000 years / Dread river / Workshop / Reggaelation.

——— **WINSTON RODNEY** now took BURNING SPEAR name (RUPERT + DELROY now not part of set-up)

Aug 76.	(lp/c) (ILPS/ZCI 9412) **MAN IN THE HILLS**	□	-

– Man in the hills / It's good / No more war / Black soul / The lion / People get ready / Children / Mother / Door peep / Groovy. (cd-iss. Sep90 on 'Reggae Refreshers' RRCD 15)

Oct 76.	(7") (WIP 6346) **THE LION. / DOOR PEEP**	□	-

——— **WIRE LINDO** – keyboards repl. DOWNIE

Jul 77.	(m-lp) (MLPS 9431) **DRY & HEAVY**	□	-

– Any river / The sun / It's a long way around / I.W.I.N. / Throw down your arms / Dry & heavy / Wailing / Black disciples / Shout it out. (cd-iss. Jul92 on 'Reggae Refreshers'; RRCD 40)

——— now with new line-ups from now on

Dec 77.	(lp/c) (ILPS/ZCI 9513) **LIVE (live)**	□	-

– Marcus Garvey / Slavery days / Black soul / The lion / Old Marcus Garvey / Man in the hills / Throw down your arms.

		Stop	not iss.
Aug 78.	(lp) (1001) **SOCIAL LIVING**	□	-

– Marcus children suffer / Social living / Nyah Keith / Institution / Marcus Senior / Civilize reggae / Mister Garvey come / Marcus say jah no dead. (re-iss. Jul80 on 'Island'; ILPS 9556) (re-iss. Oct94 on 'Blood & Fire' lp/cd; BAF LP/CD 4)

		Radic	not iss.
Apr 80.	(lp/c) (RDC/TC-RDC 2003) **HAIL H.I.M.**	□	-

– Hail H.I.M. / Columbus / Road foggy / Follow Marcus Garvey / Jah see and now / African teacher / African postman / Cry blood Africa / Jah a God raid. (re-iss. Dec88; DSR 4422) (re-iss. Jun94 on 'Heartbeat' cd/c; HB CD/MC 145)

May 82.	(lp/c) (RDC/TC-RDC 2004) **FAROVER**	□	-

– Farover / Greetings / Image / Rock / Education / She's mine / Message / O jah / Jah is my driver. (re-iss. 1988 on 'Heartbeat' lp/c/cd; HB/+C/CD 11)

Jun 82.	(7") (RIC 113) **SHE'S MINE. / EDUCATION**	□	-
Sep 82.	(12"ep) (12RIC 114) **JAH IS MY DRIVER / DRIVER / DISTANCE / FAROVER DUB**	□	-
Sep 83.	(lp) (RDC 1077681) **THE FITTEST OF THE FITTEST**	□	-

– 2000 years / For you / In Africa / Vision / Fire man / Bad to worse / Repatriation / The fittest of the fittest / Old boy Garvey. (re-iss. 1988 on 'Heartbeat' lp/c/cd; HB/+C/CD 22)

		Heartbeat	Rounder
Sep 85.	(cd) (HB 33) **RESISTANCE**	□	-

– Resistance / Mek we Yadd / Holy foundation / Queen of the mountain / The force / Jah say / We been there / Jah feeling / Love to you. (re-iss. 1988 c/cd; HBC/+D 33)

		Greensleeves	Slash
Oct 86.	(lp/cd) (GREL/+CD 100) <2606439> **PEOPLE OF THE WORLD**	□	□

– We are going / This experience / Seville land / Who's the winner / Distant drum / People of the world / I'm not the worst / Built this city / No worry you'self / Little love song.

——— BURNING SPEAR with **ANTHONY BRADSHAW** – guitar, vocals / **DEVON BRADSHAW** – vass / **NELSON MILLER** – drums / **LENFORD RICHARDS** – guitar / **ALVIN HAUGHTON** – percussion / **JENNIFER HILL** – saxophone / **NILDA RICHARDS** – trombone / **PAMELA FLEMING** – trumpet

Jun 88.	(lp/cd) (GREL/+CD 116) **MISTRESS MUSIC**	□	□

– Tell the children / Leader / Woman I love you / One way / Negril / Mistress music / Love Garvey / Tell me tell me / Say you are in love / Fly me to the Moon.

		Blue Moon	WEA
Sep 88.	(7") (BMS 608) **TELL THE CHILDREN. /**	□	-
Dec 88.	(d-lp/c/cd) (BM/+C/CD 120) <925842-1/-4/-2> **LIVE IN PARIS: ZENITH (live)**	□	□

– Spear burning / We are going / The youth / New experience / African postman / Hapy day / Woman I love you / Queen of the mountain / Creation rebel / Mistress music / Built this city / The wilderness / Driver.

		Mango	Mango
Jun 90.	(cd/c/cd) (DIDM/MCT/MLPS 1045) **MEK WE DWEET**	□	□

– Mek we dweet / Garvey / Civilization / Elephants / My roots / Great man / African woman / Take a look / One people / Mek we dweet in dub.

Aug 91.	(cd/c/lp) (CIDM/MCT/MLPS 1089) **JAH KINGDOM**	□	□

– Jah kingdom / Praise him / Come, come / World power / Tumble down / Call on Jah / Should I / When jah call / Thank you / Land of my birth / Estimated prophet.

		Heartbeat	
Feb 93.	(lp/c/cd) (HB/+C/CD 119) **THE WORLD SHOULD KNOW**	□	□

(cd re-iss. May96 on 'Declic'; 841212-2)

		Tribesman	not iss.
1994.	(lp; BURNING SPEAR & FRED LOCKS) (TMLP 1) **12 THE HARD WAY**	□	-
Apr 94.	(12") (TM 20) **FREE THE WHOLE WIDE WORLD. / JAH NO DEAD**	□	-

		Declic	Declic
Sep 94.	(cd/c/lp) (50358-2/-4/-1) **LIVE 1993 (live)**	□	□

		Heartbeat	not iss.
Nov 95.	(cd/c) (40604-2/-4) **RASTA BUSINESS**	□	-
Nov 99.	(lp) (HBLP 211) **AN APPOINTMENT WITH HIS MAJESTY**	□	□

– An appointment with his majesty / Play Jerry / Reggae physician / Music / African Jamaican / Loving you / My island / Don't sell out / Commercial develpment / Glory be to Jah / Clean it up / Come in peace.

– compilations, etc. –

Aug 79.	(lp/c) Island; (ILPS/ZCI 9567) **HARDER THAN THE REST**	□	-

– Marcus Garvey / Dry & heavy / Throw down your arms / Social living / The invasion / Black wa-dad-da / Slavery days / Old Marcus Garvey / Man in the hills / The sun / Civilize reggae.

Jul 85.	(lp) Island; (885083) **REGGAE GREATS**	□	-

(cd-iss. 1988 on 'Mango'; CIDRG 5) (cd re-iss. Jul89; IMCD 5)

Aug 87.	(12") Island; (12IS 332) **MARCUS GARVEY. / TRADITION**	□	-
Oct 87.	(cd) E.M.I.; (CDP 748 271-2) **SELECTION**	□	-

– The fittest of the fittest / Bad to worse / Road foggy / African teacher / She's mine / Fire man / Cry blood Africa / Jah a go raid / Message / Farover / Distance – Farover dub.

Jul 88.	(lp) World Records; (WRLP 102) **MARCUS CHILDREN**	□	-
Jan 89.	(lp) Rita Marley Music; (RMM 118) **LIVING DUB VOL.1**	□	-

(cd-iss. Jul93 on 'Heartbeat'; HBCD 131)

Jan 89.	(lp) Rita Marley Music; (RMM 1209) **LIVING DUB VOL.2**	□	-

(cd-iss. Sep93 on 'Heartbeat'; HBCD 132)

1989.	(cd) Island; (CIDD 9377) **KEEP THE SPEAR BURNING**	□	-
Nov 90.	(cd/c) Reggae Refreshers; (RR CD/CT 20) **MARCUS GARVEY / GARVEY'S GHOST**	□	-
Apr 92.	(cd) Sonic Sounds; (SONCD 0023) **THE ORIGINAL BURNING SPEAR**	□	-
Jan 95.	(cd) Heartbeat; (CDHB 175) **LOVE AND PEACE (live)**	□	-
Jul 96.	(d-cd) Island; (524190-2) **CHANT DOWN BABYLON: THE ISLAND ANTHOLOGY**	□	-
Nov 96.	(cd) Declic; (842 539-2) **LIVING DUB VOL.3**	□	-

Apr 99. (cd) *Declic; (B 1101-2)* **THE BEST OF BURNING SPEAR**
Jun 99. (cd) *Musidisc; (12306-2)* **LIVING DUB VOL.4**

JAKE BURNS & THE WHEEL (see under ⇒
STIFF LITTLE FINGERS)

BURRITO BROTHERS (see under ⇒
FLYING BURRITO BROTHERS)

BUSH

Formed: Kilburn, London, England . . . 1992, as FUTURE PRIMITIVE, by the seasoned Brit team of singer and lyricist GAVIN ROSSDALE, guitarist NIGEL PULSFORD, bassist DAVE PARSONS (from TRANSVISION VAMP!) and drummer ROBIN GOODRIDGE. Virtually ignored outright in the capital, BUSH's luck changed after American label 'Trauma' got hold of a demo, their signature obviously worth its weight in gold to US A&R men looking for the British answer to the recently defunct grungesters, NIRVANA. They relocated to the States early '95, a highlight at this point playing New York's CBGB's. The following year, they issued their debut, 'SIXTEEN STONE', an album that garnered critical acclaim from more rockcentric quarters and massive US sales from all quarters. Finally hitting the Top 5, the set contained a handful of impressive NIRVANA-esque numbers, among them 'EVERYTHING ZEN', 'COMEDOWN' and 'TESTOSTERONE', tracks that were to break the band in the UK a year later. By the end of 1996, BUSH were burning a proverbial trail with their chart-topping follow-up, 'RAZORBLADE SUITCASE', an album that made the UK Top 5 early the next year. A string of British hit singles completed their rise to transatlantic fame, the Top 10 'SWALLOWED' being one of their more memorable efforts. • **Covers:** REVOLUTION BLUES (Neil Young).

Album rating: SIXTEEN STONE (*7) / RAZORBLADE SUITCASE (*6) / THE SCIENCE OF THINGS (*6)

GAVIN ROSSDALE (b.30 Oct'67, London) – vocals, guitar (ex-MIDNIGHT) / **NIGEL PULSFORD** (b.11 Apr'65, Newport, Wales) – guitar (ex-KING BLANK) / **DAVE PARSONS** (b. 2 Jul'66, Uxbridge, England) – bass (ex-TRANSVISION VAMP) / **ROBIN GOODRIDGE** (b.10 Sep'66, Crawley, England) – drums (ex-BEAUTIFUL PEOPLE)

	Atlantic	Trauma
Apr 95. (c-s) *(A 8196C)* **EVERYTHING ZEN / BUD**		-
(12"+=/cd-s+=) *(A 8196 T/CD)* – Monkey.		
May 95. (cd/c/lp) *(<6544-92531-2/-4/-1>)* **SIXTEEN STONE**		4

 – Everything zen / Swim / Bomb / Little things / Comedown / Body / Machinehead / Testosterone / Monkey / Glycerine / Alien / X-girlfriend. *(re-iss. Jun96 on 'Interscope' cd/c; IND/INC 92531) – w/ bonus cd; hit UK 42)*

Jul 95. (5"ltd/c-s) *(A 8160/+C)* **LITTLE THINGS. / X-GIRLFRIEND**		-
(cd-s+=) *(A 8160CD)* – Swim.		
Aug 95. (c-s) *<98134>* **COMEDOWN / TESTOSTERONE**	-	30
Dec 95. (c-s) *(A 8152C)* **COMEDOWN / REVOLUTION BLUES**	-	-
(cd-s+=) *(A 8152CD)* – Testosterone.		
Jan 96. (c-s) *<98088>* **GLYCERINE / SOLOMON'S BONES**	-	28

	Interscope	Trauma
Apr 96. (c-s) *<98079>* **MACHINEHEAD / ALIEN (live)**	-	43
May 96. (10"ep) *(INV 95505)* **MACHINEHEAD. / COMEDOWN /**		
SOLOMON'S BONES	48	-
(cd-s) *(IND 95505)* – (first & third track) / Bud.		
(cd-s) *(INDX 95505)* – (first & second track) / X-girlfriend.		
Jan 97. (cd/c) *(<IND/INC 90091>)* **RAZORBLADE SUITCASE**	4	1 Nov96

 – Personal Holloway / Greedy fly / Swallowed / Insect kin / Cold contagious / Tendency to start fires / Mouth / Straight no chaser / History / Synapse / Communicator / Bonedriven / Distant voices. *(d-lp-iss.Sep99 on 'Simply Vinyl'; SVLP 120)*

Feb 97. (c-ep/cd-ep) *(INC/IND 95528)* **SWALLOWED / BROKEN**		
TV. / GLYCERINE / IN A LONELY PLACE	7	-

 (cd-ep) *(INDX 95528)* – ('A'side) / ('A'-Toasted both sides) / Insect kin (live) / Cold contagious (16oz demo).

May 97. (c-s) *(INC 95536)* **GREEDY FLY / GREEDY FLY (album**		
version)	22	-

 (cd-s+=) *(IND 95536)* – ('A'-16 oz demo).
 (cd-s) *(INDX 95536)* – ('A'side) / Old / Insect kin (live) / Personal Holloway (live).

Nov 97. (c-s) *(INC 95553)* **BONEDRIVEN / SYNAPSE (Philip Steir**		
remix)	49	-

 (cd-s+=) *(IND 95553)* – Personal Holloway (Soundclash Republic remix) / Straight no chaser.
 (cd-s) *(INDX 95553)* – ('A'version) / ('A'-Beat Me Clever mix) / Everything zen (Derek DeLarge mix) / ('A'-Video cd-rom).

Nov 97. (cd) *(<IND 90161>)* **DECONSTRUCTED**		36

 – Everything zen (The lhasa free mix) / Mouth (the stingray mix) / Swallowed (toasted both sides please – Goldie remix) / Synapse (my ghost in the bush of life remix) / History (Dub Pistols mix) / etc

Oct 99. (cd/c/lp) *<(490483-2/-4/-1)>* **THE SCIENCE OF THINGS**	28	11

 – Warm machine / Jesus online / The chemicals between us / English fire / Spacetravel / 40 miles from the sun / Prizefighter / Disease of the dancing cat / Altered states / Dead meat / Letting the cables sleep / Mindchanger.

Nov 99. (7"clear) *(497222-7)* *<album cut>* **THE CHEMICALS BETWEEN**		
US. / HOMEBODY	46	67 Sep99

 (cd-s+=) *(497223-2)* – Letting the cables sleep (original demo).
 (cd-s) *(497222-2)* – ('A'side) / ('A'-Supercollider remix) / ('A'-video).

Kate BUSH

Born: CATHERINE BUSH, 30 Jul'58. Bexleyheath, Kent, England. In 1974, this child prodigy formed her own K.T.BUSH band with brother PADDY and future boyfriend DEL PALMER, having already stockpiled a sizeable number of songs. By summer '76, with help from DAVE GILMOUR (Pink Floyd), she had secured a development contract with EMI, subsequently setting to work on the songs which would make up her debut set. Things couldn't have got off to a better start in early '78 when the classic 'WUTHERING HEIGHTS' warbled its way to the top of the charts. The single announced the arrival of a distinctively original talent, a swooping, soaring epic of a track which fully exhibited BUSH's stunning four-octave vocal range. The debut album, 'THE KICK INSIDE', followed into the Top 3 shortly after, the singer's ambitious, idiosyncratic brand of art-rock set to probing, intelligent and often fantastical lyrics. A second track, 'THE MAN WITH THE CHILD IN HIS EYES', also made the Top 10, while a hastily recorded follow-up album, 'LIONHEART', was released later that year. BUSH subsequently undertook her first and only tour, the experience proving so trying that she'd later keep her promotional work to a minimum. This freed her up to concentrate on lavish videos, characterised by her inspired eccentricity and imaginative choreography. Fuelled by the Top 5 success of the sassy 'BABOOSHKA', a third set, 'NEVER FOR EVER' (1980), became her first No.1 album, the record spawning further hits in 'ARMY DREAMERS' and the bizarre 'BREATHING'. The latter track's overtly experimental nature was carried over into her next album, 'THE DREAMING' (1982). Her first self-produced effort, the record's intricate inaccessiblity and conceptual weirdness tested even her most devoted fans. Although it made the UK Top 3, the record sold relatively poorly and BUSH retreated to her newly built, hi-tech home studio to create as near as she could get to a perfect album. She eventually emerged in summer '85 with the hypnotic grace of 'RUNNING UP THAT HILL', its foghorn-like synth refrain and mature, sensual vocals taking BUSH back into the Top 5 for the first time in five years and even giving her a rare US hit. The accompanying album, 'HOUNDS OF LOVE' (1985), was raved over by a wide cross section of critics, BUSH at her creative peak on a record which saw the singer rein in her more wayward tendencies and achieve a perfect balance of melody, drama and mystery. The album spawned a further two Top 20 hits in 'CLOUDBUSTING' and the title track while late in '86, she teamed up with hero PETER GABRIEL on the Top 10 hit, 'DON'T GIVE UP'. After this critical and commercial rebirth, BUSH returned in 1989 with 'THE SENSUAL WORLD', a markedly more reflective affair, its title track inspired by the Molly Bloom character in James Joyce's classic novel, 'Ulysses'. The record narrowly missed the No.1 spot and consolidated BUSH's position as the elder stateswoman of fiercely original femme-pop. Though her most recent album, 'THE RED SHOES' received a mixed critical reception, the singer remains a towering influence on todays more, erm, wayward songstresses; step forward TORI AMOS. • **Covered:** ROCKET MAN + CANDLE IN THE WIND (Elton John) / I'M STILL WAITING (Diana Ross) / WHEN YOU WISH UPON A STAR (Walt Disney soundtrack). • **Trivia:** Her first major tour came in April'79, and although it was mildly successful, she only once appeared live again at 'The Secret Policeman's Third Ball' in 1987. Actor Donald Sutherland appeared in her video for 'CLOUDBUSTING' 45.

Album rating: THE KICK INSIDE (*7) / LIONHEART (*5) / NEVER FOR EVER (*6) / THE DREAMING (*6) / HOUNDS OF LOVE (*7) / THE WHOLE STORY compilation (*9) / THE SENSUAL WORLD (*7) / THE RED SHOES (*5)

KATE BUSH – vocals, keyboards with **PADDY BUSH** – mandolin, etc. / **DEL PALMER** – bass / **IAN BAIRNSON** – guitar / **DUNCAN MACKAY** – keyboards / **ANDREW POWELL** – keyboards / **STUART ELLIOTT** – drums / **DAVID PATON** – bass / **MORRIS PERT** – percussion / **BRIAN BATH** – guitar / + others (her backing musicians changed from time to time, see 2nd edition)

	E.M.I.	EMI America
Jan 78. (7") *(EMI 2719)* *<8003>* **WUTHERING HEIGHTS. / KITE**	1	
Feb 78. (lp/c) *(EMC/TC-EMC 3223)* *<11761>* **THE KICK INSIDE**	3	

 – Moving / The saxophone song / Strange phenomena / Kite / The man with the child in his eyes / Wuthering heights / James and the cold gun / Feel it / Oh to be in love / L'amour looks something like you / Them heavy people / Room for the life / The kick inside. *(pic-lp 1979; EMPC 3223) (cd-iss. Jan84; CDP 746012-2) (re-iss. Oct88 on 'Fame' lp/c/cd; FA/TCFA/CDFA 3207) (re-iss. Sep94 cd/c; CD/TC EMS 1522)*

May 78. (7") *(EMI 2806)* *<8006>* **THE MAN WITH THE CHILD IN**		
HIS EYES. / MOVING	6	85 Feb79
Nov 78. (7") *(EMI 2887)* **HAMMER HORROR. / COFFEE**		
HOMEGROUND	44	-
Nov 78. (lp/c) *(EMA/TC-EMA 787)* *<1978>* **LIONHEART**	6	-

 – Symphony in blue / In search of Peter Pan (incl. When you wish upon a star) / Wow / Don't push your foot on the heartbrake / Oh England my lionheart / Fullhouse / In the warm room / Hammer horror / Kashka from Baghdad / Coffee homeground / Hammer horror. *(re-iss. Apr84 on 'Fame' lp/c; FA 41-3094-1/-4) (re-iss. Oct88 on 'Fame' lp/c/cd; FA/TCFA/CDFA 3094) (re-iss. Sep94 cd/c; CD/TC EMS 1523)*

Mar 79. (7") *(EMI 2911)* **WOW. / FULLHOUSE**	14	-
Sep 79. (d7"ep) *(MIEP 2991)* **KATE BUSH ON STAGE (live)**	10	-

 – Them heavy people / Don't put you foot on the heartbrake / James and the cold gun / L'amour looks something like you.

Apr 80. (7") *(EMI 5058)* **BREATHING. / THE EMPTY BULLRING**	16	-
Jun 80. (7") *(EMI 5085)* **BABOOSHKA. / RAN TAN WALTZ**	5	-
Sep 80. (lp/c) *(EMA/TC-EMA 794)* **NEVER FOR EVER**	1	

 – Babooshka / Delius / Blow away / All we ever look for / Egypt / The wedding list / Violin / The infant kiss / Night scented stock / Army dreamers / Breathing. *(re-iss. Sep82 lp/c; ATAK/TCATAK 91) (cd-iss. Mar87; CDP 746360-2) (cd-iss. Oct90; CDP 746360-2)*

Sep 80. (7"m) *(EMI 5106)* **ARMY DREAMERS. / DELIUS / PASSING THROUGH THE AIR** `16` `-`

Nov 80. (7") *(EMI 5121)* **DECEMBER WILL BE MAGIC AGAIN. / WARM AND SOOTHING** `29` `-`

Jul 81. (7") *(EMI 5201)* **SAT IN YOUR LAP. / LORD OF THE REEDY RIVER** `11` `-`

Jul 82. (7") *(EMI 5296)* **THE DREAMING. / DREAMTIME (instrumental)** `48` `-`

Sep 82. (lp/c) *(EMC/TC-EMC 3419)* <17084> **THE DREAMING** `3`
– Sat in your lap / There goes a tenner / Pull out the pin / Suspended in Gaffa / Leave it open / The dreaming / Night of the swallow Houdini / Get out of my house / All the love. *(cd-iss. Jan87; CDP 746361-2)* (re-iss. Mar91 lp/c; ATAK/TCATAK 45) *(cd-iss. Mar91; CDP 746361-2)*

Nov 82. (7") *(EMI 5350)* **THERE GOES A TENNER. / NE T'ENFUIS PAS** `☐` `☐`

Aug 85. (7") *(KB 1)* <8285> **RUNNING UP THAT HILL. / UNDER THE IVY** `3` `30`
(ext.12"+=) *(12KB 1)* – ('A'instrumental).

Sep 85. (lp/c)(cd) *(KAB/TC 1)(CDP 746164-2)* <17171> **HOUNDS OF LOVE** `1` `30`
– Running up that hill / Hounds of love / The big sky / Mother stands for comfort / Cloudbusting / And dream of sheep / Under ice / Waking the witch / Watching you without me / Jig of life / Hello Earth / The morning fog. *(cd+=)* – Cloudbusting (extended). (re-iss. Oct90 lp/c; ATAK/TCATAK 157) *(cd-iss. Sep90; CDP 746164-2)*

Oct 85. (7") *(KB 2)* **CLOUDBUSTING. / BURNING BRIDGES** `20` `-`
('A'-Organon mix-12"+=) *(12KB 2)* – My Lagan Love.

Feb 86. (7") *(KB 3)* **HOUNDS OF LOVE. / HANDSOME CABIN BOY** `18` `-`
(12"+=) *(12KB 3)* – The alternative hounds of love / Jig of life.

May 86. (7"/7"pic-d) *(KB/+P 4)* **THE BIG SKY. / NOT THIS TIME** `37` `-`
(12"+=) *(12KB 4)* – The morning fog.

—— In Oct 86, she did a duet **DON'T GIVE UP** with **PETER GABRIEL** which hit for 'Geffen' UK No.9 / US No.72.

Nov 86. (7") *(KB 5)* **EXPERIMENT IV. / WUTHERING HEIGHTS (vocal)** `23` `-`
(12"+=) *(12KB 5)* – December will be magic again.

Nov 86. (lp/c)(cd) *(KBTV/TCKBTV 1)(CDP 746414-2)* <17242> **THE WHOLE STORY** (compilation) `1` `76`
– Wuthering heights / Cloudbusting / The man with the child in his eyes / Breathing / Wow / Hounds of love / Running up that hill / Army dreamers / Sat in your lap / Experiment IV / The dreaming / Babooshka.

	E.M.I.	Columbia
Sep 89. (7"/c-s) *(EM/TCEM 102)* **THE SENSUAL WORLD. / WALK STRAIGHT DOWN THE MIDDLE** (ext.12"+=/ext.cd-s+=) *(12/CD EM 102)* – ('A'instrumental).	`12`	`-`

Oct 89. (lp/c)(cd) *(EMD/TCEMD/CDEMD 1010)* <44164> **THE SENSUAL WORLD** `2` `43`
– The sensual world / Love and anger / The fog / Reaching out / Heads we're dancing / Deeper understanding / Between a man and a woman / Never be mine / Rocket's tail / This woman's work. *(cd+=)* – Walk straight down the middle.

Nov 89. (7"/7"pic-d) *(EM/TCEM 119)* **THIS WOMAN'S WORK. / BE KIND TO MY MISTAKES** `25` `-`
(12"+=/cd-s+=) *(12/CD EM 119)* – ('A'version) / I'm still waiting.

Mar 90. (7"/c-s) *(EM/TCEM 134)* **LOVE AND ANGER. / KEN** `38` `-`
(12"+=/cd-s+=) *(12/CD EM 134)* – The confrontation / Just one last look around the house before we go.

Apr 90. (7") <73092> **LOVE AND ANGER. / WALK STRAIGHT DOWN THE MIDDLE** `-` `☐`
(c-s+=) <73098> – This woman's work.

Nov 91. (7"/c-s) *(TRIBO/+C 2)* **ROCKET MAN (I THINK IT'S GOING TO BE A LONG LONG TIME). / CANDLE IN THE WIND** `12` `☐`
(12"+=/cd-s+=) *(TRIBOT 2)* – ('B'instrumental). (above single on 'Mercury')

—— with **STUART ELLIOTT** – drums / **JOHN GIBLIN** – bass / **DANNY McINTOSH** – guitar / **GARY BROOKER** – hammond organ / **PADDY BUSH + COLIN LLOYD TUCKER** – vocals / **PAUL SPONG + STEVE SLOWER** – trumpet / **NEIL SIDWELL** – trombone / **NIGEL HITCHCOCK** – sax / **NIGEL KENNEDY** – violin / + guests **PRINCE + ERIC CLAPTON**

Sep 93. (7"/c-s) *(EM/TCEM 280)* **RUBBERBAND GIRL. / BIG STRIPEY LIE** `12` `-`
(12"pic-d+=/cd-s+=) *(12/CD EM 280)* – ('A'extended remix).

Nov 93. (cd/c/lp) *(CD/TC+/EMD 1047)* **THE RED SHOES** `2` `28`
– Rubberband girl / And so is love / Eat the music / Moments of pleasure / The song of Solomon / Lily / The red shoes / Top of the city / Constellation of the heart / Big stripey lie / Why should I love you? / You're the one.

Nov 93. (7"/c-s) *(EM/TCEM 297)* **MOMENTS OF PLEASURE. / SHOW A LITTLE DEVOTION** `26` `☐`
(12") *(12EM 297)* – ('A'side) / ('A'instrumental) / Home for Christmas.
(cd-s) *(CDEM 297)* – ('A'side) / December will be magic again / Experiment IV.

Dec 93. (c-s) <77280> **RUBBERBAND GIRL / THIS WOMAN'S WORK** `-` `88`

Apr 94. (7"/c-s) *(EMS/TCEM 316)* **THE RED SHOES. / YOU WANT ALCHEMY** `21` `☐`
(cd-s+=) *(CDEM 316)* – Cloudbusting (video mix) / This woman's work.
(cd-s) *(CDEMX 316)* – ('A'shoedance mix) / The big sky / Running up that hill.

—— In Jul 94, KATE partnered **LARRY ADLER** on 'Mercury' single 'THE MAN I LOVE'; *(MER/+C/CD 408)*. It hit UK No.27, and was from his tribute album 'The Glory Of Gershwin'.

Nov 94. (7"pic-d/c-s) *(EMS/TCEMS 355)* **AND SO IS LOVE. / RUBBERBAND GIRL (U.S.mix)** `26` `☐`
(cd-s+=) *(CDEM 355)* – Eat the music (U.S. mix).

– compilations, others, etc. –

Jun 83. (m-lp) *EMI America; <19004>* **KATE BUSH** `-` `☐`

Oct 83. (7") *Old Gold; (OG 9380)* **WUTHERING HEIGHTS. / THE MAN WITH THE CHILD IN HIS EYES** `☐` `☐`

Jan 84. (7"x13) *E.M.I.; (KBS 1)* **THE SINGLES FILE** `☐` `-`

– (all previous singles +) NE T'ENFUIS PAS. / UN BAISER D'ENFANT

Oct 90. (9xcd-box/8xc-box/8xlp-box) *(KBBX/+CD/C 1)* **THIS WOMAN'S WORK – ANTHOLOGY 1978-1990** `☐` `☐`

Oct 92. (12"-box+cd) *(KB 2)* **NEVER FOREVER** `☐` `☐`
(above issued w / free booklet & T-shirt)

Aug 94. E.M.I.; (cd-vid) *(SAV 4913063)* **LIVE AT HAMMERSMITH ODEON** (live) `☐` `☐`
– (a complete history of all her songs, re-issuing albums)

BUSTA RHYMES

Born: 1972, Brooklyn, New York, USA. Growing up as a teenager in Long Island, NY (or Strong Island as it was known among the hip hop fraternity, subsequently immortalised in song by JVC FORCE), the young BUSTA RHYMES hooked up with MC's CUT MONITOR MILO, DINCO D and CHARLIE BROWN to form LEADERS OF THE NEW SCHOOL. A well established hotbed of talent, Long Island had already spawned the likes of PUBLIC ENEMY, RAKIM and EPMD. LEADERS OF THE NEW SCHOOL were next in line, 'Elektra' picking up BUSTA & Co when the frontman was barely out of school. Touting a distinctive rapping style influenced by his Jamaican background and the freestyle ethos of the genre's pioneers, RHYMES stamped his not inconsiderable personality firmly over the group's debut album, 'FUTURE WITHOUT A PAST' (1991). Although they only recorded one more long player before breaking up, 'T.I.M.E.' (1993), they left behind a couple of interesting collaborations, with funk godfather JAMES BROWN on 'CAN'T GET ANY HARDER' and A TRIBE CALLED QUEST on the freestyling classic, 'SCENARIO'. After working with various artists in the soul/R&B field including the delectable MARY J. BLIGE, BUSTA RHYMES launched his solo career with the wild 'WOO-HAH!! GOT YOU ALL IN CHECK', making the US Top 10 and boosting sales of debut album, 'THE COMING' (1996). The man's finest moment, however, arguably arrived with the gloriously funky 'PUT YOUR HANDS WHERE MY EYES CAN SEE' leaving the cliched world of gangsta rap for dead and proving that less is more with a minimalist, shuffling rhythm, spooked-out rapping and a riveting dayglo video. The accompanying album, 'WHEN DISASTER STRIKES' (1997) entered the US chart at No.3 and confirmed RHYMES' place among the new Hip Hop elite. The rapper wasted little time in consolidating his success, releasing a third set, 'EXTINCTION LEVEL EVENT – THE FINAL WORLD FRONT', a year later.

Album rating: THE COMING (*6) / WHEN DISASTER STRIKES (*7) / EXTINCTION LEVEL EVENT – THE FINAL WORLD FRONT (*7)

BUSTA RHYMES – vocals / with various personnel

	Elektra	Elektra
Mar 96. (cd/c/lp) <(7559 61742-2/-4/-1)> **THE COMING**	`☐`	`6`

– The coming / Do my thing / Abandon ship / Everything remains raw / Hot fudge – interlude / Flipmode squad meets the Def squad / Keep it movin' / End of the world / Finish line / Still shining / Ill vibe / It's a party / Woo-hah!! got you all in the check.

May 96. (c-s) *(EKR 220C)* <64335> **WOO-HAH!! GOT YOU ALL IN CHECK / EVERYTHING REMAINS RAW** `☐` `8` Feb96
(12"+=/cd-s+=) *(EKR 220 T/C)* – ('A'mix).

Jul 96. (c-s; BUSTA RHYMES featuring ZHANE) <64268> **IT'S A PARTY / ILL VIBE (with Q-TIP)** `-` `52`

Sep 96. (c-s; BUSTA RHYMES featuring ZHANE) <64268> **IT'S A PARTY / EVERYTHING REMAINS RAW** `23` `-`
(12"+=/cd-s+=) *(EKR 226 T/CD)* – ('A'mixes).

—— In Mar'97, BUSTA featured on B REAL UK Top 10 single, 'HIT EM HIGH (THE MONSTARS' ANTHEM)'.

Apr 97. (c-s) *(EKR 235C)* **DO MY THING / ('A'-LP version), ('A' instrumental)** `39` `☐`
(12"+=/cd-s+=) *(EKR 235 T/CD)* – ('A'- Fila Brazilia 1–3 mixes)

Jul 97. (cd) *(7559 63992-2)* **FLIPMODE REMIXES** `☐` `☐`
– Woo-hah!! got you all in check / It's a party / Do my thing / Abandon ship.

Sep 97. (cd/c) <(7559 62064-2/-4)> **WHEN DISASTER STRIKES** `34` `3`
– (intro) / Whole world lookin' at me / Survival hungry / When disaster strikes / So hardcore / Get high tonight / Turn it up / Put your hands where my eyes can see / It's all good / There's not a problem my squad can't fix / We can take it outside / Rhymes galore / Thing we be doin' for money (parts 1 & 2) / One / Dangerous / Body rock / Get off my block / (outro).

Oct 97. (c-s) *(E 3900C)* **PUT YOUR HANDS WHERE MY EYES CAN SEE / ('A'instrumental)** `16` `☐`
(12"+=/cd-s+=) *(E 3900 T/CD)* – Audio bio

Dec 97. (c-s) *(E 3877C)* <64131> **DANGEROUS / DANGEROUS (dirty)** `32` `9`
(12"+=/cd-s+=) *(E 3877 T/CD)* – ('A'mixes); Soul society / Natural born chillers

—— In Mar'98, the BUSTA man featured with The NOTORIOUS B.I.G. on PUFF DADDY & THE FAMILY's Top 20 (US) hit, 'Victory'.

Apr 98. (c-s) *(E 3847C)* <64104> **TURN IT UP / FIRE IT UP** `2` `10`
(12"+=/cd-s+=) *(E 3847 T/CD)* – ('A'&'B'mixes).

Jun 98. (c-s/cd-s; BUSTA RHYMES featuring ERYKAH BADU) *(E 3833 C/CD1)* **ONE / FIRE IT UP / WOO HAH** `23` `☐`
(12"+=/cd-s+=) *(E 3833 T/CD2)* – ('A'side) / Rhymes galore.

Dec 98. (cd/c/lp) <(7559 62211-2/-4/-1)> **EXTINCTION LEVEL EVENT – THE FINAL WORLD FRONT** `65` `12`
– There's only one year left / Everybody rise / Where we're about to take it / Extinction level event (the salvation song) / Tear da roof off / Against all odds (with FLIPMODE SQUAD) / Just don't give it to me raw (what U asking 4) / Do it to death / Gimme some more / Iz they wildin' wit' us or gettin' rowdy wit' us (with MYSTIKAL) / A party goin' on over here / Bus a bus / Take it off / What's it gonna be?! (with JANET JACKSON) / Hot shit makin' you bounce / What the fuck you want / This means war (with OZZY OSBOURNE) / Outro (the burial).

Jan 99. (c-s/12"/cd-s) *(E 3782 C/T/CD)* **GIMME SOME MORE. / DO IT LIKE NEVER BEFORE** `5` `☐`

Apr 99. (c-s/12"/cd-s; BUSTA RHYMES featuring JANET) *(E 3762 C/T/CD1) <64051>* **WHAT'S IT GONNA BE?! / TEAR DA ROOF OFF** | 6 | | 3 | Mar99
(cd-s) *(E 3762CD2)* – ('A' Micky Finn D&B mix).

Bernard BUTLER

Born: 1 May'70, Stamford Hill, London, England. Temporarily putting aside his violin and piano, BUTLER took up guitar as a young teenager, idolising JOHNNY MARR (of The SMITHS) in the mid-80's. In 1989, after an unsuccessful year at London's Queen Mary College, he answered an ad in the NME; it was to join SUEDE. His creative and imaginative songwriting helped the band and their chief wordsmith, BRETT ANDERSON, reach the heady heights in the first half of the 90's, although a personality clash with the SUEDE mainman BUTLER led to him seeking out pastures new in the summer of '94. After a brief spell working with ALL ABOUT EVE singer JULIANNE REGAN, he began putting pen to paper once more in his new London abode (which he shares with wife, Elisa). He provided the song, 'YES', for the up-and-coming, flashily extravagant soul singer, DAVID McALMONT, the partnership McALMONT & BUTLER duly signing to Virgin offshoot, 'Hut'. A terrific follow-up single, 'YOU DO', gave the pair another UK Top 20 hit, while the accompanying album, 'THE SOUND OF . . .' became their swansong in late 1995; unfortunately they just couldn't stop backstabbing each other in the press. BERNARD subsequently worked with BRYAN FERRY, AIMEE MANN, EDWYN COLLINS, EDDI READER, and NENEH CHERRY, and made a substantial contribution to the BOOTH & THE BAD ANGEL project (aka TIM BOOTH of JAMES and ANGELO "Twin Peaks" BADALAMENTI). The following year (1997), BUTLER signed to 'Creation' and worked on his debut solo album, 'PEOPLE MOVE ON'. Released in the Spring of '98 and containing two Top 30 hits, 'STAY' and 'NOT ALONE', it knocked on the door of the Top 10 after receiving rave reviews. A largely acoustic affair, the record saw BUTLER re-invent himself as a tortured balladeer, although the OTT production and ghosts of his more elaborate recent past seemed to haunt him. The esteemed guitarist went on to play the festival circuit, his axework outshining even the great MARR, especially his electric set at 'T In The Park'.

Album rating: PEOPLE MOVE ON (*6) / FRIENDS AND LOVERS (*5)

BERNARD BUTLER – vocals, guitar (ex-SUEDE, ex-McALMONT & BUTLER) / with **MAKOTO SAKAMOTO** – drums / and guests DENISE JOHNSON – backing vocals / NICK WOLLAGE – sax / EDWYN COLLINS – vocals / GEORGE SHILLING – cello / RICHARD BISSILL – French horn / & The Brilliant Strings conducted by BILLY McGEE: GINI BALL, JACKIE NORRIE, MARGARET ROSEBERRY, ANNE WOOD, ANNA HEMERY, SALLY HERBERT + ANNE STEPHENSON – violins / CHRIS PITISILLIDES + ELLEN BLAIR – viola / DINAH BEAMISH + SIAN BELL – cello

	Creation	Columbia
Jan 98. (7"/c-s) *(CRE/+CS 281)* **STAY. / HOTEL SPLENDIDE** (cd-s+=) *(CRESCD 281)* – Sea.	12	–
Mar 98. (7"/c-s) *(CRE/+CS 289)* **NOT ALONE. / BYE BYE** (cd-s+=) *(CRESCD 289)* – It's alright.	27	–
Apr 98. (cd/lp)(c) *(CRE CD/LP 221)(CCRE 221) <69332>* **PEOPLE MOVE ON** – Woman I know / You just know / People move on / A change of heart / Autograph / You light the fire / Not alone / When you grow / You've got what it takes / Stay / In vain / I'm tired.	11	
Jun 98. (7"/c-s) *(CRE/+CS 297)* **A CHANGE OF HEART. / MY DOMAIN** (cd-s+=) *(CRESCD 297)* – More than I thought.	45	
Oct 99. (7"/c-s) *(CRE/+CS 324)* **YOU MUST GO ON. /** (cd-s+=) *(CRESCD 324)*	44	
Oct 99. (cd/c/lp) *(CRECD/C-CRE/CRELP 248)* **FRIENDS AND LOVERS** – Friends and lovers / I'd do it again if I could / Cocoon / Smile / You must go on / No easy way out / Everyone I know is falling apart / What happened to me / Let's go away / Precious / Has your mind got away / You'll feel it when you're mine.	43	

Paul BUTTERFIELD BLUES BAND

Formed: Chicago, Illinois, USA . . . 1963 by PAUL (born 17th December 1942, Chicago, Illinois, USA). He was a catalyst for the development of blues music played by white musicians in almost the same way that JOHN MAYALL was in Britain, although BUTTERFIELD held an advantage over MAYALL, in that he was able to sit in and play with HOWLIN' WOLF, MUDDY WATERS and LITTLE WALTER (with the latter taking on the role of mentor for the talented young harmonica player). BUTTERFIELD didn't have the greatest voice in the world but he was a formidable harpist, strictly following in the footsteps of LITTLE WALTER, JAMES COTTON, BIG WALTER HORTON and SONNY BOY WILLIAMSON and he was arguably the first white man to play blues with the same passion as the great black players. His first band was a quartet consisting of ex-HOWLIN' WOLF rhythm section, SAM LAY on drums and bassist JEROME ARNOLD (brother of harpist BILLY BOY ARNOLD), BUTTERFIELD and guitarist ELVIN BISHOP, but by the time they signed to 'Elektra' in 1965 the band had swelled to a sextet with the notable inclusion of MIKE BLOOMFIELD on lead guitar, who was to become a first class guitar hero. The debut album, 'THE PAUL BUTTERFIELD BLUES BAND' was released in 1966 and from

the first bars of 'BORN IN CHICAGO' it was clear that the band knew exactly what they were doing. They heavily covered ELMORE JAMES and LITTLE WALTER on the record and when LAY sang on their version of MUDDY WATERS', 'GOT MY MOJO WORKING', people thought that it was actually the great bluesman himself. On the second album, 'EAST WEST', ARNOLD was replaced by BILLY DAVENPORT and they went beyond the strict realms of blues by using compositions by CANNONBALL ADDERLEY, ALLEN TOUSSAINT and MONKEE-to-be, MIKE NESMITH, although the highlight was ROBERT JOHNSON's 'WALKING BLUES'. BUTTERFIELD also contributed five tracks to an Elektra various artists album, 'What's Shakin', alongside LOVIN' SPOONFUL, ERIC CLAPTON, TOM RUSH and AL KOOPER. Supporting BOB DYLAN at the 1965 Newport Folk Festival, BUTTERFIELD and Co gained the infamous distinction of being the band who helped in DYLAN'S 'musical heresy' of going electric. BLOOMFIELD played on the first two albums which became high points for white blues in the sixties, although he quit in 1967 to form the psychedelic ELECTRIC FLAG. BUTTERFIELD, meanwhile, added a horn section and turned to soul, the band losing its direction with each successive album ('THE RESURRECTION OF PIGBOY CRABSHAW', 'IN MY OWN DREAMS', 'KEEP ON MOVING' and 'LIVE'). The low point came with the appalling 'LOVE MARCH' from the equally appalling 'KEEP ON MOVING', which he chose, for reasons only known to himself, to play at Woodstock in 1969. BUTTERFIELD started to play less and less harmonica and was turning more and more vocals over to other band members and it came as no surprise, and some relief, that he broke up the band in 1971 and moved to Woodstock. A retrospective 'BEST OF' was released in 1972 and specialist blues label 'Red Lightnin' produced 'AN OFFER YOU CAN'T REFUSE ', an album of early recordings, in the same year. In 1973, BUTTERFIELD formed BETTER DAYS and signed to 'Bearsville' Records for whom he recorded two poor albums before they split. Nothing was heard from BUTTERFIELD until 1976 when he made a guest appearance at The BAND'S farewell concert in San Francisco which was later documented in Martin Scorcese's film of the event, 'The Last Waltz'. (He duetted with LEVON HELM on 'Mystery Train', played harmonica for MUDDY WATERS on 'Mannish Boy' and was part of the all star cast on 'I Shall Be Released'). In 1981, BUTTERFIELD attempted a comeback recording 'NORTH SOUTH' for 'Bearsville', although he fell ill with peritonitis (caused by his powerful harmonica playing) during the sessions, the album being delayed while he underwent two operations. He returned to live work after the release of the album although this failed to sell and he never regained his past popularity. In 1986, after a further lengthy recording silence, 'THE LEGENDARY PAUL BUTTERFIELD RIDES AGAIN' was released in America by 'Amherst' Records. BUTTERFIELD was found dead on the 4th of May 1987 in his North Hollywood flat. He found to his cost that it was easier to get into the blues than it was to get out, but his legacy remains and much of his catalogue is still available. • **Songwriters:** BUTTERFIELD and BISHOP except some covers. Time w / BETTER DAYS covered TOO MANY DRIVERS (Big Bill Broonzy) / NOBODY'S FAULT BUT MINE (trad; Nina Simone) / BORN UNDER A BAD SIGN (Booker T.) / HIGHWAY 28 (Dan Hicks) / RULE THE ROAD (Von Schmidt) / BABY PLEASE DON'T GO (Big Joe Williams) / IF YOU LIVE (Mose Allison). • **Trivia:** In 1965 they did back-up on record for BOB DYLAN, on manager Albert Grossman's recommendation. Album 'PIGBOY CRABSHAW' was actually ELVIN BISHOP's nick-name. BUZZ FIETON (a member in 1969) was later to resurface in US chart toppers Mr. Mister.

Album rating: PAUL BUTTERFIELD BLUES BAND (*7) / EAST-WEST (*8) / THE RESURRECTION OF PIGBOY CRABSHAW (*6) / IN MY OWN DREAM (*5) / KEEP ON MOVIN' (*4) / LIVE (*4) / SOMETIMES I JUST FEEL LIKE SMILIN' (*4) / OFFER YOU CAN'T REFUSE old material (*5) / GOLDEN BUTTER – THE BEST OF THE PAUL BUTTERFIELD BLUES BAND compilation (*6) / IT ALL COMES BACK (*4; by Better Days) / BETTER DAYS (*4; by Better Days) / PUT IT IN YOUR EAR (*4) / NORTH SOUTH (*4) / THE LEGENDARY PAUL BUTTERFIELD RIDES AGAIN (*4) / THE ORIGINAL LOST ELEKTRA SESSIONS exploitation (*7) / STRAWBERRY JAM exploitation (*5) / EAST-WEST LIVE exploitation (*6)

PAUL BUTTERFIELD (b.17 Dec'42) – vocals, harmonica (ex-MUDDY WATERS) / **MIKE BLOOMFIELD** (b.24 Jul'44) – slide guitar, lead guitar (ex-BOB DYLAN) / **ELVIN BISHOP** (b.21 Oct'42, Tulsa, Oklahoma) – guitar / **JEROME ARNOLD** – bass (ex-HOWLIN' WOLF) / **SAMMY LAY** – drums (ex-HOWLIN' WOLF)

	London	Elektra
1966. (7") *(HLZ 10100) <45609>* **COME ON IN. / I GOT A MIND TO GIVE UP LIVING**		

	Elektra	Elektra
May 66. (lp; mono/stereo) *<(EKL/EKS 7294)>* **THE PAUL BUTTERFIELD BLUES BAND** – Born in Chicago / Shake your money-maker / Blues with a feeling / Thank you Mr. Poobah / I got my Mojo working / Mellow down easy / Screamin' / Our love is drifting / Mystery train / Last train / Look over yonders wall. *(re-iss. Feb71; K 42004) (re-iss. Mar85 on 'Edsel'; ED 150) (cd-iss. 1989 on 'WEA'; 960 647-2) (re-iss. Mar93 & Dec94 & Sep95 cd/c; 7559 60647-2/-4)*		Oct65
Oct 66. (7") *(EKSN 45007)* **ALL THESE BLUES. / NEVER SAY NO**		–

——— added **BARTY GOLDBERG** – guitar and **AL KOOPER** (b.5 Feb'44, Brooklyn, New York) – keyboards (ex-BOB DYLAN)

——— **MARK NAFTALIN** – organ (appears on debut 8-tracks) repl. GOLDBERG and KOOPER who went solo & etc.

Dec 66. (lp; mono/stereo) *<(EKL/EKS 7315)>* **EAST – WEST** – Walkin' blues / Get out of my life woman / I've got a mind to give up living / Work song / Never say no / Mary, Mary / Two trains running / All these blues / East west. *(re-iss. Feb71; K 22004) (re-iss. Feb87 on 'Edsel'; ED 212) (cd-iss. 1989 on 'WEA'; 960 751-2) (re-iss. Sep95 on 'Warners' cd/c; 7559 60751-2/-4)*		65 Aug66

―― Recorded EP with JOHN MAYALL BLUESBREAKERS see ⟹
1967. (7") *(EKSN 45007)* **ALL THESE BLUES. / NEVER SAY NO** 　[ ] -

―― **BILLY DAVENPORT** – drums repl. SAMMY LAY above now in 5-piece with **BUTTERFIELD, BISHOP, NAFTALIN** and **ARNOLD**

―― then added brass section **GENE DINWIDDIE, DAVE SANBORN and KEITH JOHNSON / PHIL WILSON** – drums, vocals repl. DAVENPORT / **BUGSY MAUGH** – bass, vocals repl. ARNOLD

Nov 67. (7") *(EKSN 45020) <45620>* **RUN OUT OF TIME. / ONE MORE HEARTACHE** 　[ ] [ ]

Feb 68. (lp; mono/stereo) *<EKL/EKS 74015>* **THE RESURRECTION OF PIGBOY CRABSHAW** 　[ ] [52] Jan68
– One more heartache / Driftin' and driftin' / Pity the fool / Born under a bad sign / Run out of time / Double trouble / Drivin' wheel / Droppin' out / Tollin' bells. *(re-iss. 1971; K 42017) (re-iss. Feb89 on 'Edsel'; ED 301)*

Apr 68. (7") *(EKSN 45047)* **GET YOURSELF TOGETHER. / MINE TO LOVE** 　[ ] -

―― guest **AL KOOPER** – organ note; NAFTALIN aka NAFFY MARHAM

Sep 68. (lp) *(EKL 4025) <74025>* **IN MY OWN DREAM** 　[ ] [79] Aug68
– Last hope's gone / Mine to love / Get yourself together / Just be with you / Morning blues / Drunk again / In my own dream. *(re-iss. 1971; K 42042)*

Nov 68. (7") *<45643>* **IN MY OWN DREAM. / GOT MY MOJO WORKING** 　- [ ]

―― **BUZZ FEITON** – guitar, organ, French horn, vocals repl. BISHOP who went solo

Sep 69. (7") *(EKSN 45069) <45658>* **WHERE DID MY BABY GO. / IN MY OWN DREAM** 　[ ] [ ]

Nov 69. (lp) *<(EKS 74053)>* **KEEP ON MOVING** 　[ ] Oct69
– Love march / No amount of loving / Morning sunrise / Losing hand / Walking by myself / Except you / Love disease / Where did my baby go / All in a day / So far so good / Buddy's advice / Keep on moving *(re-iss. 1971; K 42033)*

Feb 70. (7") *(2101 012) <45692>* **LOVE MARCH. / LOVE DISEASE** 　[ ] [ ]

―― **BUTTERFIELD** retained **HARRIS** and **DINWIDDIE** and brought in **RALPH WALSH** – guitar GEORGE DAVIDSON – drums TREVOR LAWRENCE – brass

Feb 71. (d-lp) *<(EKD 2001)>* **LIVE** (live) 　[ ] [72] Jan71
– Everything's going to be alright / Love disease / The boxer / No amount of loving / Driftin' and driftin' / Intro the musicians / Number nine / I want to be with you / Born under a bad sign / Get together again / So far, so good.

―― **DENNIS WHITTED** – drums repl. DAVIDSON augmented by guests **BOBBY HALL** – congos BIG BLACK – bongos with **CLYDIE KING, MERRY CLAYTON, VENETTA FIELDS & ONA DRAKE** – vocal harmonies

Sep 71. (lp) *(K 42095) <EKS 75013>* **SOMETIMES I JUST FEEL LIKE SMILIN'** 　[ ] [ ]
– Play on / 1000 ways / Pretty woman / Little piece of dying / Song for Lee / Trainman / Night child / Drowned in my own tears / Blind leading the blind.

―― Disbanded late '71

Jun 72. (d-lp) *(K 62001) <7E 2005>* **GOLDEN BUTTER – THE BEST OF THE PAUL BUTTERFIELD BLUES BAND** (compilation) 　[ ] [ ] May72
– Born in Chicago / Shake your moneymaker / Mellow down easy / Our love is drifting / Mystery train / Look over yonders wall / East West / Walkin' blues / Get out of my life / Woman / Mary, Mary / Spoonful / One more mile, one more heartache / Last hope's gone / In my own dreams / Love march / Driftin' and driftin' / Blind leading the blind.

BETTER DAYS

were formed by **PAUL BUTTERFIELD** who recruited **GEOFF MULDAUR** – vocals, guitar, vibes (ex-JIM KWESKIN BAND) / **RONNIE BARRON** – keyboard, vocals, co-composer (ex-DR. JOHN) / **AMOS GARRETT** – guitar, bass (ex-JESSIE WINCHESTER BAND etc.) / **BILLY RICH** – bass / **CHRISTOPHER PARKER** – drums guests were **MARIA MULDAUR** – occ. violin & b.vocals / **DAVID SANDBORN** – horns / **BOBBY CHARLES** – b.vocals, co-composer, as was **DAVID WHITTED**

	Bearsville	Bearsville
Feb 73. (lp) *(K 45515) <BR 2119>* **BETTER DAYS**	[ ]	[ ] Jan73

– New walkin' blues / Please send me home to love / Broke my baby's heart / Baby please don't go / Nobody's fault but mine / Done a lot of wrong things / Buried alive in the blues / Rule the road / Highway 28. *(cd-iss. Feb93 on 'Rhino'; 8122 70877-2)*

Jan 74. (lp) *(K 45517) <BR 2170>* **IT ALL COMES BACK** 　[ ] [ ] Oct73
– It all comes back / Take your pleasure where you find it / Louisiana flood / Poor boy / If you live / It's getting harder to survive / Small town talk / Win or lose / Too many drivers. *(cd-iss. Feb93 on 'Rhino'; 8122 70880-2)*

―― Split '74. GARRET joined MARIA MULDAUR and PARKER joined ARETHA FRANKLIN.

PAUL BUTTERFIELD

solo with sessioners
Feb 76. (lp) *(K 55509) <BR 6960>* **PUT IT IN YOUR EAR** 　[ ] [ ] Nov75
– You can run but you can't hide / (If I never sing) My song / The animal / Breadline / Ain't that a lot of love? / I don't wanna go / Day to day / Here I go again / The flame / Watch 'em tell a lie.

―― PAUL then toured with LEVON HELM's ALL-STARS, before teaming up with RICK DANKO. He realeased another solo effort (below) augmented by MICHAEL TOLES – multi

	not iss.	Warners
1981. (lp) *<6995>* **NORTH SOUTH**		[ ]

– I get excited / Get some fun in your life / Footprints on the windshield / Upside down / Entch a train / Bread & Butterfield / Living in Memphis / Glow down / I let it go / Baby blue. *(UK cd-iss. Feb93 on 'Rhino'; 8122 70880-2)*

1981. (7") **LIVING IN MEMPHIS. / FOOTPRINTS ON THE WINDSHIELD** 　- [ ]

―― went into session work in the 80's before making a come-back (below)

	not iss.	Bearsville
1986. (lp) **THE LEGENDARY PAUL BUTTERFIELD RIDES AGAIN**	-	[ ]

―― On 4th of May '87, BUTTERFIELD died of a long illness; peritonitis.

– compilations, etc. –

1972. (lp; PAUL BUTTERFIELD & WALTER HORTON) *Red Lightnin'; (R 008)* **AN OFFER YOU CAN'T REFUSE** (recorded 1963) 　[ ] -
– Easy / Have a good time / Mean mistreater / In the mood / West side blues / Louise / Tin pan alley / Walter's boogie / Everything's gonna be alright / Last night / Loaded / One room country shack. *(re-iss. 1982; same)*

Sep 98. (cd) *Winner; (WINNER 446)* **STRAWBERRY JAM** 　[ ] [ ]

BUTTHOLE SURFERS

Formed: San Antonio, Texas, USA … 1980 originally as The ASHTRAY BABY HEELS by ex-accountant GIBBY (son of US children's TV presenter "Mr. Peppermint") and PAUL LEARY, who met at Trinity College, San Antonio. By 1983, they had signed to JELLO BIAFRA's (Dead Kennedys) label, 'Alternative Tentacles'. Around the mid-80's, they gigged heavily in Britain due to lack of Stateside interest, and this, together with radio play from John Peel, helped them make it into the UK indie charts. Heavy psychedelia mixing noise, confusion and futuristic art-punk, the manic GIBBY, (complete with loudspeaker, etc), was always offensive and disturbing while their weird stage act included the nude dancer, KATHLEEN. She covered herself in green jello, while GIBBY simulated sex with her! GIBBY was well-known for other stage antics; pissing in plastic baseball bats ('piss wands') and annointing the audience at the front. There were other obscenities, too rude to print here (no need to mention President Carter's creamy briefcase). In 1987, they unleashed the brilliantly crazed 'LOCUST ABORTION TECHNICIAN', complete with a parody of BLACK SABBATH's 'SWEET LEAF', the humorously titled 'SWEAT LOAF'. Also deep inside its nightmarish musical grooves was their gem, 'TWENTY TWO GOING ON TWENTY THREE', a track that made John Peel's Festive 50. A longer sojourn in Britain culminated in some riotous, oversubscribed London gigs. The follow-up, 'HAIRWAY TO STEVEN' (another piss-take; this time of LED ZEPPELIN – Stairway To Heaven), deliberately left the tracks nameless (instead using obscene looking symbols) as a twisted tribute to ZEPPELIN's "untitled" symbols album. 1990 saw them shift to a more commercial sound with 'PIOUGHD' (which means "pissed-off" in Native American), which featured a re-working of DONOVAN's 'HURDY GURDY MAN'. Having signed to 'Capitol' in 1992, they were back to their abrasive sound of old with the JOHN PAUL JONES-produced album, 'INDEPENDENT WORM SALOON'. This, together with their previous effort, had given them their first taste of chart success in Britain, this being well surpassed in 1996 when 'ELECTRICLARRYLAND' hit the US Top 30. It was due, no doubt, to a surprise domestic hit with 'PEPPER', and probably their "fiery" guest appearance on American mock talk show, The Larry Sanders Show' in '97. • **Songwriters:** GIBBY and co., except AMERICAN WOMAN (Guess Who) / THE ONE I LOVE (R.E.M.). P covered DANCING QUEEN (Abba).

Album rating: BROWN REASONS TO LIVE mini (*6) / PSYCHIC … POWERLESS … ANOTHER MAN'S SAC (*7) / LOCUST ABORTION TECHNICIAN (*8) / HAIRWAY TO STEVEN (*7) / DOUBLE LIVE (*4) / PHIOGHD (*6) / INDEPENDENT WORM SALOON (*7) / ELECTRICLARRYLAND (*7)

GIBBY HAYNES (b. GIBSON JEROME HAYNES, 1957) – vocals / **PAUL LEARY** (b.1958) – guitar / **KING COFFEY** – drums repl. ? / **ALAN ?** – bass

	Alternative Tentacles	Alternative Tentacles
Apr 84. (m-lp) *(VIRUS 32)* **BUTTHOLE SURFERS** <'BROWN REASONS TO LIVE; US-title>	[ ]	[ ] 1983

– The Shah sleeps in Lee Harvey's grave / Hey / Something / Bar-b-que / Pope / Wichita cathedral / Suicide / The legend of Anus Presley. *(re-iss. Sep93 as 'BROWN REASONS TO LIVE' brown-lp; same)*

Jan 85. (12"ep) *(VIRUS 39)* **LIVE PCPPEP** (live)
– Cowboy Bob / Bar-b-q pope / Dance of the cobras / The Shah sleeps in Lee Harvey's grave / Wichita cathedral / Hey / Something.

―― **TERENCE** – bass repl. ALAN (?)

	Fundam.	Touch&Go
Apr 85. (7") **LADY SNIFF. /**	-	[ ]
Jul 85. (lp) *(SAVE 5)* **PSYCHIC … POWERLESS … ANOTHER MAN'S SAC**	[ ]	[ ]

– Concubine / Eye of the chicken / Dum dum / Woly boly / Negro observer / Butthole surfer / Lady sniff / Cherub / Mexican caravan / Cowboy Bob / Gary Floyd. *(cd-iss. Jan88+=)* – CREAM CORN FROM THE SOCKET OF DAVIS

―― **MARK KRAMER** – bass (of SHOCKABILLY) repl. TREVOR who had repl. TERENCE

Oct 85. (12"ep) *(PRAY 69)* **CREAM CORN FROM THE SOCKET OF DAVIS** 　[ ] [ ]
– Moving to Florida / Comb – Lou Reed (two parter) / Tornados.

	Red Rhino Europe	Touch&Go
Apr 86. (lp) *(RRELP 2) <TGLP 8>* **REMBRANDT PUSSYHORSE**	[ ]	[ ]

– Creep in the cellar / Sea ferring / American woman / Waiting for Jimmy to kick / Strangers die / Perry / Whirling hall of knives / Mark says alright / In the cellar. *(cd-iss. May88; RRECD 2)*

―― **JEFF 'TOOTER' PINKUS** – bass repl. KRAMER who formed BONGWATER

	Blast First	Blast First
Mar 87. (lp/c/cd) *(BFFP 15/+C/CD)* **LOCUST ABORTION TECHNICIAN**	[ ]	[ ]

– Sweat loaf / Graveyard 1 / Pittsburgh to Lebanon / Weber / Hay / Human cannonball / U.S.S.A. / Theoman / Kintz / Graveyard 2 / 22 going on 23 / The G-men.

―― added **THERESA NERVOSA (NAYLOR)** – 2nd drummer / **KATHLEEN** – naked dancer (above with GIBBY, PAUL, COFFEY and PINKUS)

Apr 88. (lp/cd) (BFFP 29/+CD) **HAIRWAY TO STEVEN** ☐ ☐
– Hairway part 1 / Hairway part 2 / Hairway part 3 / Hairway part 4 / Hairway part 5 / Hairway part 6 / Hairway part 7 / Hairway part 8 / Hairway part 9. (9 tracks marked rude symbols as titles)

Aug 89. (12"ep/10"ep/cd-ep) (BFFP 41/+T/CD) **WIDOWERMAKER** ☐ ☐
– Bong song / 1401 / Booze tobacco / Helicopter.

—— now without THERESA

Rough Trade   Rough Trade

Nov 90. (7") (RT 240) **THE HURDY GURDY MAN. / BARKING DOGS** ☐ ☐
(12"+=/cd-s+=) (RTT 240/+CD) – ('A'-Paul Leary remix).

Feb 91. (cd/c/lp) (R 2081260-2/-4/-1) <RTE R2601> **PIOUGHD** [68] ☐
– Revolution pt.1 & 2 / Lonesome bulldog pt.1 & 2 / The hurdy gurdy man / Golden showers / Lonesome bulldog pt.3 / Blindman / No, I'm iron man / Something / P.S.Y. / Lonesome bulldog pt.IV. (cd+=) – Barking dogs. (cd-iss. Dec 94 on 'Danceteria';)

—— In Apr'92, GIBBY guested for MINISTRY on single 'Jesus Built My Hotrod'. PAUL LEARY had earlier issued a solo set, while DRAIN (COFFEY's outfit) delivered a further two albums.

Capitol   Capitol

Mar 93. (cd/c/lp) (CD/TC+/EST 2192) <98798> **INDEPENDENT WORM SALOON** [73] ☐
– Who was in my room last night / The wooden song / Tongue / Chewin' George Lucas' chocolate / Goofy's concern / Alcohol / Dog inside your body / Strawberry / Some dispute over T-shirt sales / Dancing fool / You don't know me / The annoying song / Dust devil / Leave me alone / Edgar / The ballad of a naked man / Clean it up.

May 96. (cd/c/d-lp) (CD/TC+/EST 2285) <29842>
ELECTRICLARRYLAND [31]
– Birds / Cough syrup / Pepper / Thermador / Ulcer breakout / Jingle of a dog's collar / TV star / My brother's wife / Ah ha / The Lord is a monkey / Let's talk about cars / L.A. / Space.

Sep 96. (7") (CL 778) **PEPPER. / HYBRID** [59] ☐
(cd-s+=) (CDCL 778) – Pepper (Butcha' Bros remix) / The Lord is a monkey.

– compilations, others, etc. –

Jun 89. (d-lp/cd) Latino Bugger; (LBV ?) **DOUBLE LIVE** (live) ☐ –
Nov 94. (7"/7"pic-d) Trance Syndicate; (TR 30/+PD) **GOOD KING WENCENSLAUS. / THE LORD IS A MONKEY** ☐ –
Apr 95. (cd) Trance Syndicate; (TR 35CD) **THE HOLE TRUTH & NOTHING BUTT!** (early demos) ☐ –

JACKOFFICERS

off-shoot with **GIBBY, JEFF & KATHLEEN**

Naked Brain   Rough Trade

Dec 90. (lp/c/cd) (NBX 003/+C/CD) <ROUGHUS 100> **DIGITAL DUMP** ☐ ☐
– Love-o-maniac / Time machine pt.1 & 2 / L.A.name peanut butter / Do it / Swingers club / Ventricular retribution / 6 / Don't touch that / An Hawaiian Christmas song / Flush.

P

—— formed 1993 by **GIBBY + JOHNNY DEPP** – bass, guitar (yes! the actor & beau of supermodel Kate Moss) / **BILL CARTER** – bass / **SAL JENCO** – drums

Capitol   Capitol

Feb 96. (cd/c/lp) (CD/TC PCS 7379) <7243 8 32942-2/-4/-1> **P** ☐ ☐
– I save cigarette butts / Zing Splash / Michael Stipe / Oklahoma / Dancing queen / Jon Glenn (megamix) / Mr Officer / White man sings the blues / Die Anne / Scrapings from ring / The deal.

BUZZCOCKS

Formed: Manchester, England . . . April 1976 by HOWARD DEVOTO and PETE SHELLEY who met at the Bolton Institute Of Higher Education. Having recruited STEVE DIGGLE and JOHN MAHER, they played their first gig on the 20th of July '76 supporting the SEX PISTOLS. Early the following year, they released the first ever DIY punk "indie" 45 on 'New Hormones' in the form of the 'SPIRAL SCRATCH' EP. They then suffered a major bust up when frontman DEVOTO departed (to form MAGAZINE), although the rest carried on having signed to 'United Artists' on the strength of featuring on the now famous 'LIVE AT THE ROXY' various artists compilation (with tracks 'Breakdown' and 'Love Battery'). By this time, SHELLEY had taken over vocal duties, while DIGGLE switched to guitar, having found a new bassist, GARTH SMITH. Early in 1978, they stormed the charts with the brooding love gem, 'WHAT DO I GET', a two-minute rush of bittersweet pop/punk angst which saw SHELLEY emerging as a serious frontman in his own right. The previous year's masturbating classic, 'ORGASM ADDICT', was too frenetic to allow SHELLEY's effeminate romance'n'roll stylings a look-in, although he blossomed on subsequent releases. A debut album, 'ANOTHER MUSIC IN A DIFFERENT KITCHEN' (1978), made the UK Top 20, while another SHELLEY-penned classic, 'EVER FALLEN IN LOVE (WITH SOMEONE YOU SHOULDN'T'VE?)', almost made the Top 10 later that year. With fervent suport from Radio One DJ, John Peel, the band had squarely cornered the more accessible end of the punk market, although the 'LOVE BITES' album marked a move away from the short, sharp melodic shock which had become their trademark as songwriting duties were more democratically distributed. A final clutch of Top 30 hits, 'PROMISES' (their fifth hit in 1978), 'EVERYBODY'S HAPPY NOWADAYS' and 'HARMONY IN MY HEAD', saw the increasing influence of DIGGLE. 1979's 'A DIFFERENT KIND OF

TENSION' saw SHELLEY's influence begin to dissipate and the album's mixed reviews signalled the band were running out of creative steam. After 'Liberty' took over their contract in 1980 and a further three 45's flopped, the BUZZCOCKS split, DIGGLE forming FLAG OF CONVENIENCE with MAHER. SHELLEY, meanwhile, went solo, making his debut in 1981 with the 'HOMOSAPIEN' album. Although the album made little commercial headway in Britain, the title track, bizarrely enough, topped the Australian charts. He released another two sets, 'XL-1' (1983) and 'HEAVEN AND THE SEA' (1986) to mild interest; far more newsworthy was the band's reformation in 1990 with a line-up of SHELLEY, DIGGLE, STEVE GARVEY and ex-SMITHS drummer, MIKE JOYCE. A comeback album, 'TRADE TEST TRANSMISSION' (1993) was lapped up by old punks and new converts alike, while a slightly modified line-up undertook a heartily received tour. A live set culled from the dates, 'FRENCH', was released in 1995, while a follow-up album, 'ALL SET', appeared a year later. The band's classic late 70's output remains one of the most influential bodies of work from the punk era, second only to perhaps the SEX PISTOLS. • **Covered:** HERE COMES THE NICE (Small Faces). • **Trivia:** In 1978, SHELLEY produced fun group, ALBERTO Y LOST TRIOS PARANOIAS.

Album rating: ANOTHER MUSIC IN A DIFFERENT KITCHEN (*9) / LOVE BITES (*7) / DIFFERENT KIND OF TENSION (*6) / SINGLES – GOING STEADY compilation (*9) / TRADE TEST TRANSMISSION (*5) / FRENCH (*4) / ALL SET (*5) / Pete Shelley: SKY YEN (*4) / HOMOSAPIEN (*7) / XL-1 (*5) / HEAVEN AND THE SEA (*6)

HOWARD DEVOTO (b.HOWARD TRAFFORD) – vocals / **PETE SHELLEY** (b.PETER McNEISH, 17 Apr'55) – guitar, vocals / **STEVE DIGGLE** – bass, vocals / **JOHN MAHER** – drums

New Hormones   not iss.

Jan 77. (7"ep) (ORG 1) **SPIRAL SCRATCH** ☐ –
– Breakdown / Times up / Boredom / Friends of mine. (re-iss. Aug79 credited as "BUZZCOCKS with HOWARD DEVOTO"; same); hit No.31) (re-iss. 1994 on 'Document' 12"ep/cd-ep)

—— (Mar'77) **GARTH SMITH** – bass; repl. DEVOTO who formed MAGAZINE SHELLEY now lead vocals, guitar / **DIGGLE** switched to guitar, vocals

U.A.   not iss.

Oct 77. (7") (UP 36316) **ORGASM ADDICT. / WHATEVER HAPPENED TO . . . ?** ☐ –

—— **STEVE GARVEY** – bass repl. GARTH (on tour at first)

Jan 78. (7") (UP 36348) **WHAT DO I GET?. / OH SHIT** [37] –

U.A.   I.R.S.

Mar 78. (lp/c) (UAG/TCK 30159) **ANOTHER MUSIC IN A DIFFERENT KITCHEN** [15] ☐
– Fast cars / No reply / You tear me up / Get on our own / Love battery / 16 / I don't mind / Fiction romance / Autonomy / I need / Moving away from the pulsebeat. (re-iss. Aug85 on 'Liberty' lp/c; ATAK/TC-ATAK 51) (re-iss. Jun87 on 'Fan Club' blue-lp; FC 021) (re-iss. May88 on 'Fame' lp/c/cd; FA/TC-FA/CD-FA 3199) (re-iss. cd Jul88 on 'E.M.I.'; CDP 790299-2) (cd re-iss. Jul96; PRDFCD 3)

Apr 78. (7") (UP 36386) **I DON'T MIND. / AUTONOMY** [55] ☐
Jul 78. (7") (UP 36433) **LOVE YOU MORE. / NOISE ANNOYS** [34] ☐
Sep 78. (7") (UP 36455) **EVER FALLEN IN LOVE (WITH SOMEONE YOU SHOULDN'T'VE). / JUST LUST** [12] ☐
Sep 78. (lp/c) (UAG/TCK 30197) **LOVE BITES** [13] ☐
– Real world / Ever fallen in love with someone you shouldn't've / Operator's manuel / Nostalgia / Just lust / Sixteen again / Walking distance / Love is lies / Nothing left / E.S.P. / Late for the train. (re-iss. Mar87 on 'Fame' lp/c; FA/TC-FA 3174) (re-iss. Jun87 on 'Fan Club' blue-lp; FC 022) (cd-iss. Jul88 on 'Fame'; CD-FA 3174) (cd re-iss. Jul96; PRDFCD 4)

Nov 78. (7") (UP 36471) **PROMISES. / LIPSTICK** [20] ☐
Mar 79. (7") (UP 36499) **EVERYBODY'S HAPPY NOWADAYS. / WHY CAN'T I TOUCH IT** [29] ☐
Jul 79. (7") (UP 36541) **HARMONY IN MY HEAD. / SOMETHING'S GONE WRONG AGAIN** [32] –
Sep 79. (7") (BP 316) **YOU SAY YOU DON'T LOVE ME. / RAISON D'ETRE** ☐ ☐
Sep 79. (lp/c) (UAG/TCK 30260) <009> **A DIFFERENT KIND OF TENSION** [26] ☐
– Paradise / Sitting round at home / You say you don't love me / You know you can't help it / Mad mad Judy / Raison d'etre / I don't know what to do with my life / Money / Hollow inside / A different kind of tension / I believe / Radio Nine. (initial copies cont. previous 45) (re-iss. Jun87 on 'Fan Club' blue-lp; FC 023) (cd-iss. Jul88 on 'E.M.I.'; CZ 93)

Oct 79. (7") **I BELIEVE. / SOMETHING'S GONE WRONG AGAIN** – ☐
Nov 79. (lp/c) <010> **SINGLES – GOING STEADY** (compilation) – ☐
– Orgasm addict / What do I get / I don't mind / Love you more / Ever fallen in love with someone you shouldn't've / Promises / Everybody's happy nowadays / Harmony in my head / Whatever happened to . . . ? / Oh shit! / Autonomy / Noise annoys / Just luck / Lipstick / Why can't I touch it / Something's gone wrong again. (UK-iss.Nov81 on 'Liberty' lp/c; LBR/TC-LBR 1043) (re-iss. Aug85 lp/c; ATAK/TC-ATAK 52) (cd-iss. Jun87 + Jun88 on 'E.M.I.'; CDP 746449-2) (re-iss. Sep90 cd/c/lp; CD/TC+/FA 3241)

Liberty   I.R.S.

Aug 80. (7") (BP 365) **WHY SHE'S A GIRL FROM THE CHAINSTORE. / ARE EVERYTHING** [61] ☐
Oct 80. (7") (BP 371) **STRANGE THING. / AIRWAVES DREAM** ☐ ☐
Nov 80. (7") (BP 392) **RUNNING FREE. / WHAT DO YOU KNOW** ☐ ☐

—— (split Feb81) **DIGGLE** went solo and formed FLAG OF CONVENIENCE, with MAHER

PETE SHELLEY

solo, augmented by **STEVE GARVEY** – bass / **JIM RUSSELL** – drums.

	Genetic-Island	Arista
Aug 81. (7"/12") (WIP/12WIP 6720) **HOMOSAPIEN. / KEAT'S SONG**	☐	☐
Sep 81. (lp/c) (ILPS/ICT 9676) **HOMOSAPIEN**		Jun82

– Homosapien / Yesterday's here / I generate a feeling / Keat's song / Qu'est-ce que c'est que ca / I don't know what it is / Guess I must have been in love with myself / Pusher man / Just one of those affairs / It's hard enough knowing. (re-iss. cd Sep94 on 'Grapevine';)

Nov 81. (d7"/12") (U/12 WIP 6740) **I DON'T KNOW WHAT IT IS. / WITNESS THE CHANGE/ / IN LOVE WITH SOMEBODY ELSE. / MAXINE**	☐	☐
Apr 82. (7"/12") (WIP/12WIP 6720) **HOMOSAPIEN. / LOVE IN VAIN**	☐	☐

—— **BARRY ADAMSON** – bass (ex-MAGAZINE, ex-BIRTHDAY PARTY) repl. GARVEY / added **MARTIN RUSHENT** – keyboards, producer

	Island	Arista
Feb 83. (7"/12") (XX/+T 1) **TELEPHONE OPERATOR. / MANY A TIME**	**66**	☐
Apr 83. (lp) (XL 1) **XL-1**	**42**	Jul83

– Telephone operator / If you ask me (I won't say no) / What was Heaven? / You better than I know / Twilight / (Millions of people) No one like you / Many a time / I just wanna touch / You and I / XL-1 *. (c+= dub tracks) (track* = only playable on ZX Spectrum computer) (re-iss. cd Sep94 on 'Grapevine';)

	Immaculate	not iss.
Nov 84. (7") (IMMAC 1) **NEVER AGAIN. / ONE ONE ONE**	☐	-
(12"+=) (12IMMAC 1) – Give it to me.		

—— **SHELLEY** brought in new **JOHN DOYLE** – drums / **MARK SANDERSON** – bass / **NORMAN FISCHER-JONES** – guitar / **GERARD COOKSON** – keyboards / **JIM GARDNER** – synth.

	Mercury	Mercury
Mar 86. (7"/12") (MER/+X 215) **WAITING FOR LOVE. / DESIGNER LAMPS**	☐	☐
May 86. (7"/12") (MER/+X 221) **ON YOUR OWN. / PLEASE FORGIVE ME . . . BUT I CANNOT ENDURE IT ANY LONGER**	☐	☐
Jun 86. (lp/c)(cd) (MERH/+C 90)(830004-2) **HEAVEN AND THE SEA**	☐	☐

– Never again / My dreams / Blue eyes / You can't take that away / No Moon . . . / Waiting for love / On your own / They're coming for you / I surrender / Life without reason / Need a minit.

Aug 86. (7"/12") (MER/+X 225) **BLUE EYES. / NELSON'S RIDDLE**	☐	☐
Nov 86. (7"/12") (MER/+X 234) **I SURRENDER. / I NEED A MINUTE**	☐	☐

—— In 1988, **SHELLEY** formed **ZIP** with COOKSON and SANDERSON.

– his compilations, others, etc. –

Apr 80. (m-lp) Groovy; (STP 2) **SKY YEN** (rec.1974)	☐	-
Apr 89. (7"/12") Immaculate; (IMMAC/12IMMAC 11) **HOMOSAPIEN. PETE SHELLEY VS. POWER, WONDER AND LOVE / ('A'mix)**	☐	-
(3"cd-s+=) (IMMACD 11) – ('A'-Icon mix) / ('A'-shower mix).		

STEVE DIGGLE

	Liberty	not iss.
Feb 81. (7"m) (BP 389) **SHUT OUT THE LIGHTS. / 50 YEARS OF COMPARATIVE WEALTH / HERE COMES THE FIRE BRIGADE**	☐	-

FLAG OF CONVENIENCE

were formed by **DIGGLE, MAHER + DAVE FARROW** – bass / **D.P.** – keyboards

	Sire	not iss.
Sep 82. (7") (SIR 4057) **LIFE ON THE TELEPHONE. / THE OTHER MAN'S SIN**	☐	-

—— **DIGGLE, MAHER + GARY HAMER** – bass / **MARK** – keyboards

	Weird Systems	not iss.
Dec 84. (7") **CHANGE. / LONGEST LIFE**	☐	-

—— **JOHN CAINE** – drums repl. MAHER and MARK

	M.C.M.	not iss.
Apr 86. (7") (MCM 186) **NEW HOUSE. / KEEP ON PUSHING**	☐	-
	Flag of Convenience	not iss.
Apr 87. (12") (FOC 1) **LAST TRAIN TO SAFETY. / ?**	☐	-
	M.C.M.	not iss.
Oct 87. (12"ep; as F.O.C.) (MCM 001) **SHOULD I EVER GO DEAF / PICTURES IN MY MIND. / THE GREATEST SIN / DROWNED IN YOUR HEARTACHES**	☐	-
Aug 88. (12"ep; as F.O.C.) (MCM 002) **EXILES / I CAN'T STOP THE WORLD. / SHOT DOWN WITH YOUR GUN / TRAGEDY IN MARKET SQUARE**	☐	-

BUZZCOCKS F.O.C.

—— **DIGGLE, HAMMER + ANDY COUZENS** – guitar / **CHRIS GOODWIN** – drums

	Thin Line	not iss.
Jul 89. (12"/cd-s) (THIN 003/+CD) **TOMORROW'S SUNSET. / LIFE WITH THE LIONS** ('A'version)	☐	-

BUZZCOCKS

—— re-formed in 1990 **SHELLEY, DIGGLE, GARVEY** and **MIKE JOYCE** – drums (ex-SMITHS) repl. ANDY and CHRIS who formed The HIGH

	Planet Pacific	not iss.
Apr 91. (7"ep/12"ep/c-ep/cd-ep) **ALIVE TONIGHT**	☐	-

– Alive tonight / Successful street / Serious crime / Last to know.

—— **JOHN MAHER** – drums returned to repl. MIKE who joined PIL.

—— **TONY BARBER** – bass / **PHIL BARKER** – drums repl.GARVEY and MAHER

	Essential	Caroline
May 93. (7") (ESS 2025) **INNOCENT. /**	☐	-
(12"+=/cd-s+=) (ESS T/X 2025) –		
Jun 93. (cd/c/lp) (ESM CD/MC/LP 389) <1747> **TRADE TEST TRANSMISSION**	☐	☐

– Innocent / Smile / Palm of your hand / Last to know / Do it/ Who will help me to forget / Energy / Alive tonight / Inside / Isolation / Never gonna give it up / Crystal night / 369 / Chegga / It's unthinkable / Somewhere. (reiss.cd Jul96; same)

Aug 93. (12"/cd-s) **DO IT. / TRASH AWAY / ALL OVER YOU**	☐	-
Apr 94. (12"/cd-s) **LIBERTINE ANGEL. / ROLL IT OVER / EXCERPT FROM PRISON RIOT HOSTAGE**	☐	-

	Dojo	I.R.S.
Nov 95. (cd) (DOJOCD 237) <36761> **FRENCH (live in Paris 12th April 1995)**	☐	Jan96

– I don't mind / Who'll help me to forget / Get on our own / Unthinkable / Strange thing / Energy / Breakdown / Innocent / Roll it over / Why she's a girl from the chainstore / Last to know? / Running free / Libertine angel / Why can't I touch it / Noise annoys / Isolation / Boredom / Do it / Harmony in my head / I believe.

	I.R.S.	I.R.S.
Apr 96. (cd) (EIRSCD 1078) **ALL SET**	☐	☐

– Totally from the heart / Without you / Give it to me / Your love / Point of no return / Hold me close / Kiss & tell / What am I supposed to do? / Some kind of wonderful / (What you) Mean to me / Playing for time / Pariah / Back with you.

– compilations, others, etc. –

Apr 87. (lp/c) Weird Systems; (WS 021/+X1) **TOTAL POP**	☐	-
Jan 88. (12"ep) Strange Fruit; (SFPS 044) **THE PEEL SESSIONS** (7.9.77)	☐	-

– Fast cars / What do I get / Moving away from the pulsebeat.

Oct 88. (c) R.O.I.R.; (A 158) **LEST WE FORGET** (live) (cd-iss. 1990;)	☐	-
Sep 89. (lp/cd) Absolutely Free; (FREE LP/CD 002) **LIVE AT THE ROXY CLUB, 2 APRIL 1977** (live)	☐	-

– (cd= 1 extra track) (re-iss. Jul90 on 'Receiver'; RR CD/LC/LP 131)

Oct 89. (7"ep/12"ep/cd-ep) E.M.I.; (EM/12EM/CDEM 104) **THE FAB FOUR**	☐	-

– Ever fallen in love with someone you shouldn't've / Promises / Everybody's happy nowadays / Harmony in my head.

Nov 89. (4xlp/2xd-c/2xd-cd) E.M.I.; (LP/TC/CD PROD 1) **PRODUCT**	☐	-

– (cont. first 3 albums + 1 live and rare) (re-iss. May95 cd; PRODUCT 1)

Feb 90. (cd/lp) Strange Fruit; (SFR CD/LP 104) **THE PEEL SESSIONS ALBUM**	☐	-
Sep 91. (cd/c/d-lp) E.M.I.; (CD/TC+/EM 1421) **OPERATOR'S MANUEL**	☐	-
May 92. (cd) EMI Gold; (CDGOLD 1029) **ENTERTAINING FRIENDS LIVE** (live)	☐	-
Oct 92. (cd-s) Old Gold; (OG 6182) **EVER FALLEN IN LOVE WITH SOMEONE . . . / WHAT DO I GET / PROMISES**	☐	-
Feb 94. (cd; STEVE DIGGLE & THE FLAG OF CONVENIENCE) Anagram; (CDMGRAM 74) **THE BEST OF . . . THE SECRET PUBLIC YEARS 1981-1989**	☐	-
Apr 94. (cd) E.M.I.; (CDPRDT 12) **ANOTHER MUSIC IN A DIFFERENT KITCHEN / LOVE BITES**	☐	-
1995. (7") One Stop Music; (ONE 7001) **NOISE ANNOYS. / ISOLATION** (live)	☐	-
Jul 95. (cd) Dojo; (DLP 2) **TIME'S UP**	☐	-
Nov 95. (cd-s) Old Gold; (12623 6332-2) **EVER FALLEN IN LOVE WITH SOMEONE YOU SHOULDN'T HAVE FALLEN IN LOVE WITH / PROMISES**	☐	-
Oct 98. (cd) E.M.I.; (497771-2) **THE BBC SESSIONS**	☐	-
Jun 99. (cd) Almafame; (YEAAH 1) **PARIS ENCORE DU PAIN**	☐	-
Sep 99. (d-cd) E.M.I.; (521767-2) **MODERN / A DIFFERENT KIND** (lp-iss.Sep99 on 'Go Kart'; GK 058)	☐	-

STEVE DIGGLE & THE FLAG OF CONVENIENCE

	3:30	not iss.
Nov 93. (cd-ep) (330001) **HEATED AND RISING / OVER AND OUT / TERMINAL / WEDNESDAYS FLOWERS**	☐	-
	Ax-s	not iss.
Oct 95. (cd) (AXSO 2CD) **HERE'S ONE I MADE EARLIER**	☐	-

BYRDS

Formed: Los Angeles, California, USA . . . 1964 as The JETSET by JIM McGUINN, GENE CLARK and DAVID CROSBY. All three had come from folky backgrounds, McGUINN having toured with The CHAD MITCHELL TRIO as a teenager and CLARK already having proved an accomplished songwriter with The NEW CHRISTY MINSTRELS. CROSBY, meanwhile, was an ambitious singer/songwriter who'd performed with LES BAXTER'S BALLADEERS. The JETSET recorded a one-off flop single for 'Elektra', 'PLEASE LET ME LOVE YOU', under the pseudonym of The BEEFEATERS. Later the same year, they recruited expert bluegrass player CHRIS HILLMAN, previously of The HILLMEN, who'd incorporated his instrumental dexterity on the mandolin into his bass playing. Drummer MICHAEL CLARKE, with his chiselled, BRIAN JONES-esque looks, completed the line-up, initially playing on cardboard boxes when the band were too hard-up to afford a real drum-kit! Profoundly influenced by The BEATLES, they soon changed their name to The BYRDS (the mis-spelling a tribute to their heroes), and set about realising their vision of marrying the fab four's electric energy to the folk music which was their stock in trade. With the help of long-time manager JIM DICKSON and the unlikely recommendation of MILES DAVIS, the band signed to 'Columbia'. At the insistence of DICKSON and producer TERRY MELCHER, the reluctant BYRDS eventually agreed to re-work their earlier demo of 'MR. TAMBOURINE MAN' (this and other demos later surfaced on 'PREFLYTE'). It was a canny decision which did nothing less than change the course of pop/rock history. The resulting song's unforgettable euphoric rush charged DYLAN's lyrics with a youthful romanticism, encapsulating in 3 minutes what it was to be young and have the world at your feet. It soon hit No.1 on both sides of the Atlantic and it still sounds as fresh today as it did then, a timeless slice of hypnotic, bittersweet pop with McGUINN's delivery forging an affecting DYLAN / LENNON hybrid. Much has since been made of the fact that only one BYRD, McGUINN, actually played on the record, with MELCHER hiring session musicians like LEON RUSSELL, LARRY KNECHTAL and HAL BLAINE. However, any doubts about The BYRDS ability as a band were dispelled with the self-titled debut album, a folk-rock classic. It was a case of more of the same really, with the band turning in a dazzling string of DYLAN covers, making the songs distinctly their own. 'CHIMES OF FREEDOM' was a ringing, hippy call to arms, fuelled by a starry-eyed optimism, and they even managed to transform the Welsh mining disaster ballad, 'BELLS OF RHYMNEY', into an effervescent swirl. GENE CLARK was the band's chief songwriter at this stage, contributing the classic BEATLES-esque originals 'FEEL A WHOLE LOT BETTER', 'I KNEW I'D WANT YOU' and 'HERE WITHOUT YOU'. In the summer of '65, they played a residency at Ciro's nightclub on Sunset Strip, often cited as the origin of the L.A. hippy movement (described by The L.A. Times as being frequented by people who looked like they'd been dragged from Sherwood Forest!). They were back at No.1 by the end of 1965, when they managed to transform PETE SEEGER's Book Of Ecclesiastes-adaptation 'TURN! TURN! TURN!' into a classic pop record, a miracle of biblical proportions. Very early the next year, the second album boasted two more DYLAN covers, an uninspiring update of 'THE TIMES THEY ARE A-CHANGIN' and 'LAY DOWN YOUR WEARY TUNE', apparently the song that finally persuaded DYLAN that The BYRDS were doing something above and beyond mere imitation. McGUINN contributed two songs, one of which was his tribute to the assassinated JOHN F. KENNEDY, 'HE WAS A FRIEND OF MINE', while CLARK offered three originals, including the classic 'SET YOU FREE THIS TIME'. Recorded the previous January, 'EIGHT MILES HIGH' pioneered psychedelic rock, predating the efforts of The BEATLES, The BEACH BOYS and the San Franciscan bands. The JOHN COLTRANE-inspired track was promptly vetoed by radio stations on its spring '66 release, amid allegations that the song was an explicit account of an LSD trip. After the completion of the third album, 'FIFTH DIMENSION', CLARK departed, citing his paranoia-fuelled fear of flying and CROSBY's digs regarding his tambourine playing. The new album heralded a move away from sparkling pop to a more complex, ambitious and intelligent sound. Influenced heavily by Indian sitar player RAVI SHANKAR, and modal jazz, the record didn't fulfill the promise of the preceding single but still contained some memorable moments. McGUINN's 'MR SPACEMAN' hinted at the country sound the band would later embrace. Just prior to releasing the fourth album, 'YOUNGER THAN YESTERDAY', the band issued 'SO YOU WANT TO BE A ROCK'N'ROLL STAR', a sarcastic reaction to manufactured bands by a group that had fallen out of favour with the Hollywood set. The album was an assorted bag of styles, with HILLMAN emerging as a talented songwriter on the likes of 'TIME BETWEEN' and 'THOUGHTS AND WORDS', while CROSBY had his finest moment with the haunting 'EVERYBODY'S BEEN BURNED'. Despite the melange of styles, the album predated 'SGT PEPPER', once again proving that The BYRDS were ahead of their time. By the time of 'THE NOTORIOUS BYRD BROTHERS' in 1968, CROSBY's dictational manner had led to his ejection from the band, along with MICHAEL CLARKE. A contender for the The BYRDS' best album, the record was again stylistically diverse but included possibly the band's finest moment in the GOFFIN/KING number, 'GOIN' BACK' (later a hit for DUSTY SPRINGFIELD). Its wistful musings on the passage from childhood to maturity were set against a backdrop of heavenly harmonies and celestial pedal steel while 'WASN'T BORN TO FOLLOW' (another GERRY GOFFIN-CAROLE KING cover) was a triumphant clarion call of phased, psychedelic country. With the addition of GRAM PARSONS and HILLMAN's cousin KEVIN KELLEY, the band steered radically away from the studio-enhanced sound of 'NOTORIOUS' straight into the heart of country, once again staying one step ahead of their peers and foreshadowing the country-rock boom of the early 70's. 'SWEETHEART OF THE RODEO', with its purist sound, confounded the hippies and despite playing a show at the Grand Ole Opry, and even, God forbid, cutting their hair(!) for the occasion, the country crowd remained suspicious of their druggy image, thereby ensuring little commercial success. Released in '68, PARSONS was the driving force behind the album, contributing beautiful songs like 'HICKORY WIND' and 'ONE HUNDRED YEARS FROM NOW', which sat majestically alongside covers of LOUVIN BROTHERS and DYLAN material. The gypsy-like PARSONS soon left, taking HILLMAN with him to form The FLYING BURRITO BROTHERS. McGUINN (who'd now changed his name to ROGER, following his immersion in the Indonesian religion, Subud) recruited country guitar maestro CLARENCE WHITE along with a cast of other musicians. The albums that followed were inconsistent, although they contained a few BYRDS classics and highlighted WHITE's virtuoso guitar playing. 'DR BYRDS & MR HYDE' featured the ironic stab at the country establishment, 'DRUG STORE

TRUCK DRIVING MAN', while 'THE BALLAD OF EASY RIDER's gentle meandering title track was a minor classic. The half live/half studio set, 'UNTITLED', from 1970, included an impassioned performance from WHITE on 'LOVER OF THE BAYOU' and a lovely version of LOWELL GEORGE's 'TRUCK STOP GIRL'. Probably the strongest set of the latter-day BYRDS, it also included the single 'CHESTNUT MARE', and the evocative McGUINN and JACQUES LEVY song 'ALL THE THINGS'. Many of McGUINN's songs during this period came from the abandoned 'Gene Tryp' project which he had begun with New York psychologist LEVY to chart the history of American music. The last few albums weren't quite as ambitious in their scope, but 'BYRDMANIAX' and 'FARTHER ALONG' were enjoyable despite having the weight of such an illustrious career on their shoulders. McGUINN did the right thing and called it a day at last in mid-72, later joining up with the original BYRDS for an uninspired album a year later. Two of the BYRDS most talented members died in separate incidents in the early 70's, CLARENCE WHITE killed by a drunken driver, GRAM PARSONS from a heroin overdose. CROSBY survived a descent into free-base cocaine addiction and a liver transplant to record songs in Nashville with McGUINN and HILLMAN in 1990. A proposed tour never happened but the tracks are included on the wonderful 'Columbia' boxed set released the same year. More recently, McGUINN was sighted running through some old numbers on 'Later With Jools (Holland)' in true troubadour style. An endless list of artists and bands (TOM PETTY, R.E.M., LONG RYDERS, SMITHS, PRIMAL SCREAM, RIDE, etc), have kept alive the spirit of The BYRDS in their own particular style, while the band's own recordings remain timeless treasures.

Album rating: MR. TAMBOURINE MAN (*8) / TURN! TURN! TURN! (*8) / FIFTH DIMENSION (*6) / YOUNGER THAN YESTERDAY (*8) / THE BYRDS' GREATEST HITS compilation (*10) / THE NOTORIOUS BYRD BROTHERS (*9) / SWEETHEART OF THE RODEO (*8) / DR. BYRDS & MR. HYDE (*5) / THE BALLAD OF EASY RIDER (*5) / UNTITLED (*6) / BYRDMANIAX (*4) / GREATEST HITS VOL.2 compilation (*8) / FARTHER ALONG (*4) / THE BYRDS (*4) / THE VERY BEST OF THE BYRDS compilation (*8) / Roger McGuinn: ROGER McGUINN (*6) / PEACE ON YOU (*5) / ROGER McGuinn & HIS BAND (*5) / CARDIFF ROSE (*7) / THUNDERBYRD (*5) / McGUINN, CLARK & HILLMAN (*6) / CITY (*4) / MEAN STREETS with Chris Hillman (*3) / BACK FROM RIO (*6) / BORN TO ROCK'N'ROLL compilation (*7) / LIVE FROM MARS (*5)

GENE CLARK (b. HAROLD EUGENE CLARK, 17 Nov'41, Tipton, Missouri, USA) – vocals, tambourine / **JIM McGUINN** (b.JAMES JOSEPH McGUINN, 13 Jul'42, Chicago, Illinois, USA) – guitar, vocals / **DAVID CROSBY** (b.DAVID VAN CORTLAND, 14 Aug'41, L.A.) – guitar, vocals

		Pye Inter.	Elektra
Nov 64.	(7"; as BEEFEATERS) (7N 25277) <45013> **PLEASE LET ME LOVE YOU. / DON'T BE LONG**		Sep64

— added **CHRIS HILLMAN** (b. 4 Dec'42, L.A.) – bass, vocals (ex-HILLMEN) / **MICHAEL CLARKE** (b. 3 Jun'43, New York City) – drums

		C.B.S.	Columbia
Jun 65.	(7") (201765) <43271> **MR. TAMBOURINE MAN. / I KNEW I'D WANT TO**	1	1 May65
Aug 65.	(7") (201796) <43332> **ALL I REALLY WANT TO DO. / I'LL FEEL A WHOLE LOT BETTER**	4	40 Jul65
Aug 65.	(lp; stereo/mono) (S+/BPG 62571) <9172> **MR. TAMBOURINE MAN**	7	6 Jun65

– Mr. Tambourine man / I'll feel a whole lot better / Spanish Harlem incident / You won't have to cry / Here without you / The bells of Rhymney / All I really want to do / I knew I'd want you / It's no use / Don't doubt yourself, babe / Chimes of freedom / We'll meet again. (re-iss. Jul77; CBS/40 31503) (cd-iss. May96 on 'Columbia'; 483705-2) (lp re-iss. Jul98 on 'Simply Vinyl'; SVLP 32) (lp re-iss. Jun99 on 'Sundazed'; SUNLP 5057)

Oct 65.	(7") (202008) <43424> **TURN! TURN! TURN!. / SHE DON'T CARE ABOUT TIME**	26	1
Feb 66.	(7") (202037) <43501> **SET YOU FREE THIS TIME. / IT WON'T BE WRONG**		79 63
Mar 66.	(lp; stereo/mono) (S+/SPG 62652) <9254> **TURN! TURN! TURN!**	11	17 Dec65

– Turn! Turn! Turn! / It won't be wrong / Set you free this time / Lay down your weary tune / He was a friend of mine / The world turns all around her / Satisfied mind / If you're gone / The times they are a-changin' / Wait and see / Oh! Susannah. (re-iss. Jul77; CBS/40 31526) (cd-iss. May96 on 'Columbia'; 483706-2) (lp re-iss. Nov98 on 'Simply Vinyl'; SVLP 27) (lp re-iss. Jun99 on 'Sundazed'; SUNLP 5058)

— trimmed to a quartet when GENE CLARK went solo

Apr 66.	(7") (202067) <43578> **EIGHT MILES HIGH. / WHY?**	24	14
Jul 66.	(7") (202259) <43702> **5D (FIFTH DIMENSION). / CAPTAIN SOUL**		44
Sep 66.	(lp; stereo/mono) (S+/BPG 62783) <9349> **FIFTH DIMENSION**	27	24 Aug66

– 5D (Fifth Dimension) / Wild mountain thyme / Mr. Spaceman / I see you / What's happening?!?! / I come and stand at every door / Eight miles high / Hey Joe / John Riley / Captain Soul / 2-4-2 Foxtrot (the Lear jet song). (re-iss. Jul83 lp/c; CBS/40 32284) (cd-iss. May96 on 'Sony'; 483707-2) (lp re-iss. Nov98 on 'Simply Vinyl'; SVLP 47) (lp re-iss. Jun99 on 'Sundazed'; SUNLP 5059)

Oct 66.	(7") (202295) <43766> **MR. SPACEMAN. / WHAT'S HAPPENING?!?!**		36 Sep66
Feb 67.	(7") (202559) <43987> **SO YOU WANT TO BE A ROCK'N'ROLL STAR. / EVERYBODY'S BEEN BURNED**		29 Jan67
Apr 67.	(lp; stereo/mono) (S+/BPG 62988) <9442> **YOUNGER THAN YESTERDAY**	37	24 Mar67

– So you want to be a rock'n'roll star / Have you seen her face / C.T.A. - 102 / Renaissance fair / Time between / Everybody's been burned / Thoughts and words / Mind gardens / My back pages / The girl with no name / Why. (re-iss. Mar87 on 'Edsel' cd/c/lp; CD/C+/ED 227) (re-iss. Oct94 & May96 on 'Columbia' cd/c; 483708-2) (lp re-iss. Oct97 on 'Simply Vinyl'; SVLP 7) (lp re-iss. Jun99 on 'Sundazed'; SUNLP 5060)

May 67. (7") (2648) <44054> **MY BACK PAGES. / RENAISSANCE MAN** □ 30 Mar67

Jun 67. (7") <44157> **HAVE YOU SEEN HER FACE. / DON'T MAKE WAVES** - 74

Sep 67. (7") <44230> **LADY FRIEND. / OLD JOHN ROBERTSON** - 82

Sep 67. (7") (2924) **LADY FRIEND. / DON'T MAKE WAVES** - □

Oct 67. (lp; stereo/mono) (S+/BPG 63107) <9516> **THE BYRDS' GREATEST HITS** (compilation) □ 6 Aug67
– Mr. Tambourine man / I'll feel a whole lot better / Bells of rhymney / Turn! turn! turn! / All I really want to do / Chimes of freedom / Eight miles high / Mr.Spaceman / 5D (Fifth Dimension) / So you want to be a rock'n'roll star / My back pages. (re-iss. Jan84; CBS/40 32068) (cd-iss. Jun89; CD 32068) (REMASTERED cd.Feb91; 467843-2) (cd re-iss. May96 on 'Sony'; 483705-2)

— **GENE CLARK** – guitar, vocals returned to repl. DAVID who formed CROSBY, STILLS and NASH (JIM also changed name to ROGER McGUINN)

Dec 67. (7") (3093) <44362> **GOIN' BACK. / CHANGE IS NOW** □ 89 Nov67
(re-iss. Jun77; 5300)
Now a trio of McGUINN, HILLMAN and CLARKE (GENE continued solo career)

Apr 68. (lp; stereo/mono) (S+/BPG 63169) <9575> **THE NOTORIOUS BYRD BROTHERS** 12 47 Jan68
– Artificial energy / Goin' back / Natural harmony / Draft morning / Wasn't born to follow / Get to you / Change is now / Old John Robertson / Tribal gathering / Dolphin's smile / Space odyssey. (re-iss. Aug88 on 'Edsel' cd/lp; CD+/ED 262) (cd re-iss. Mar97 on 'Columbia'; 486751-2)

— **KEVIN KELLEY** (b.1945, California) – drums (ex-RISING SONS) repl. MICHAEL who joined DILLARD & CLARK. Also added **GRAM PARSONS** (b.INGRAM CECIL CONNOR III, 5 Nov'46, Winterhaven, Florida) – guitar, vocals, keyboards (ex-INTERNATIONAL SUBMARINE BAND) / guests on album – **SNEAKY PETE** – pedal steel guitar / **DOUG DILLARD** – banjo

May 68. (7") (3411) <44499> **YOU AIN'T GOING NOWHERE. / ARTIFICIAL ENERGY** 45 74

Sep 68. (lp) (63353) <9670> **SWEETHEART OF THE RODEO** 77 Aug68
– You ain't going nowhere / I am a pilgrim / The Christian life / You're still on my mind / Pretty Boy Floyd / You don't miss your water / Hickory wind / One hundred years from now / Blue Canadian Rockies / Life in prison / Nothing was delivered. (re-iss. Jun87 on 'Edsel' cd/lp; CD+/ED 234) (cd re-iss. Mar97 on 'Columbia'; 486752-2) (lp re-iss. Nov98 on 'Simply Vinyl'; SVLP 57) (cd re-iss. Oct99 on 'Columbia'; MILLEN 6)

Oct 68. (7") (3752) <44643> **PRETTY BOY FLOYD. / I AM A PILGRIM** □ □

— **CARLOS BERNAL** – guitar played on US tour replacing GRAM who joined FLYING BURRITO BROTHERS alongside HILLMAN and SNEAKY PETE. Soon McGUINN recruited entirely new members **CLARENCE WHITE** (b. 6 Jun'44, Lewiston, Maine, USA) – guitar, vocals (ex-NASHVILLE WEST) repl. BERNAL / **GENE PARSONS** (b. 9 Apr'44) – drums, vocals (ex-NASHVILLE WEST) repl. KELLEY / **JOHN YORK** – bass, vocals repl. HILLMAN

Mar 69. (7") (4055) <44746> **BAD NIGHT AT THE WHISKEY. / DRUG STORE TRUCK DRIVIN' MAN** 15 □ Mar69

Apr 69. (lp) (63545) <9755> **DR. BYRDS AND MR. HYDE** 15 □
– This wheel's on fire / Old blue / Your gentle way of loving me / Child of the universe / Nashville West / Drug store truck drivin' man / King Apathy III / Candy / Bad night at the Whiskey / My back pages / B.J.blues – Stanhope you want me to do. (cd-iss. Aug91 on 'Beat Goes On'; BGOCD 107) (cd re-iss. Mar97 on 'Columbia'; 486753-2) (lp re-iss. Feb99 on 'Simply Vinyl'; SVLP 70)

Jun 69. (7") (4284) <44868> **LAY LADY LAY. / OLD BLUE** □ □

Sep 69. (7") (4572) **WASN'T BORN TO FOLLOW. / CHILD OF THE UNIVERSE** □

Oct 69. (7") <44990> **THE BALLAD OF EASY RIDER. / WASN'T BORN TO FOLLOW** - 5

Jan 70. (lp) (63795) <9942> **THE BALLAD OF EASY RIDER** 41 36 Dec69
– The ballad of Easy rider / Fido / Oil in my lamp / Tulsa County / Jack Tarr the sailor / Jesus is just alright / It's all over now, baby blue / There must be someone / Gunga Din / Deportee (plane wreck at Los Gatos) / Armstrong, Aldrin and Collins. (cd-iss. Mar97 on 'Columbia'; 486751-2)

Feb 70. (7") (4753) <45071> **JESUS IS JUST ALRIGHT. / IT'S ALL OVER NOW, BABY BLUE** □ 97

— **SKIP BATTIN** (b. 2 Feb'34, Gallipolis, Ohio) – bass, repl. YORK

Nov 70. (d-lp) (66253) <30127> **UNTITLED** (1/2 live) 11 40 Oct70
– Lover of the bayou / Positively 4th Street / Nashville West / So you want to be a rock'n'roll star / Mr.Tambourine man / Mr.Spaceman / Eight miles high / Chestnut mare / Truck stop girl / All the things / Yesterday's train / Hungry planet / Just a season / Take a whiff (on me) / You all look alike / Well come back home.

Dec 70. (7") (5322) <45259> **CHESTNUT MARE. / JUST A SEASON** 19 □

May 71. (7") (7253) **I TRUST (EVERYTHING'S GONNA WORK OUT FINE). / THIS IS MY DESTINY** □ -

Aug 71. (lp) (64389) <30640> **BIRDMANIAX** 46 Jul71
– Glory, glory / Pale fire / I trust / Tunnel of love / Citizen Kane / I wanna grow up to be a politician / Absolute happiness / Green apple quick step / My destiny / Kathleen's song / Jamaica say you will. (cd-iss. Sep90 on 'Line'; CLCD 900930)

Oct 71. (7") (7501) <45440> **GLORY, GLORY. / CITIZEN KANE** □ □

Oct 71. (lp) (64650) <31795> **THE BYRDS' GREATEST HITS VOLUME 2** (compilation) <US title 'THE BEST OF THE BYRDS (GREATEST HITS, VOLUME II'> □ Dec72
– The ballad of Easy rider / Jesus is just alright / Chestnut mare / You ain't goin' nowhere / I am a pilgrim / Goin' back / I trust / Lay lady lay / Wasn't born to follow / The times are a-changin' / Drug store truck drivin' man / Get to you.

Jan 72. (lp) (64676) <31050> **FARTHER ALONG** □ Dec71
– Tiffany queen / Get down your line / B.B. class road / Bugler / America's great national pastime / Antique Sandy / Precious Kate / So fine / Lazy waters / Bristol steam convention blues / Farther along.

Jan 72. (7") (7712) <45514> **AMERICA'S GREAT NATIONAL PASTIME. / FARTHER ALONG** □

— They split mid '72, SKIP joined NEW RIDERS OF THE PURPLE SAGE. CLARENCE WHITE was killed in a road accident 14 Jul'73. / **JOHN GUERRIN** – drums (session men) took over briefly when reforming

— **McGUINN** then re-formed the original "BYRDS" Himself, CROSBY, CLARK, HILLMAN + CLARKE

	Asylum	Asylum
Apr 73. (lp) (SYLA 8754) <5058> **THE BYRDS**	31	20 Mar73

– Full circle / Sweet Mary / Changing heart / For free / Born to rock'n'roll / Things will be better / Cowgirl in the sand / Long live the King / Borrowing time / Laughing / (See the sky) about to rain. (cd-iss. Feb93 on 'Warners'; 7559 60955-2)

May 73. (7") (AYM 516) **THINGS WILL BE BETTER. / FOR FREE** □ -

Jun 73. (7") (AYM 517) <11016> **FULL CIRCLE. / LONG LIVE THE KING** □ -

Jul 73. (7") <11019> **COWGIRL IN THE SAND. / LONG LIVE THE KING** □ Apr73

— McGUINN, HILLMAN and CLARK all went solo, later teaming up together on album. CROSBY re-formed CROSBY, STILL and NASH. Sadly, MICHAEL CLARKE was to die of liver failure 19th December '93.

– (BYRDS) compilations, etc. –

On 'CBS' / 'Columbia' unless mentioned otherwise.

Feb 66. (7"ep) (EP 6069) **THE TIMES ARE A-CHANGING** 15 -

Oct 66. (7"ep) (EP 6077) **EIGHT MILES HIGH** 18 -

Aug 69. (lp) Together; <ST-T 1001> **PREFLYTE** (demo recordings of '64) - □
<re-iss. 1973 on 'Columbia'; C 32183> (UK-iss.Sep73 on 'Bumble'; GEXP 8001)

Dec 69. (lp) Together; <ST-T 1019> **EARLY L.A.** - □

May 73. (d-lp) (68242) **THE HISTORY OF THE BYRDS** 47 -
– Mr. Tambourine man / Turn! turn! turn! / She don't care about time / Wild mountain thyme / Eight miles high / Mr.Spaceman / 5D (Fifth Dimension) / So you want to be a rock'n'roll star / Time between / My back pages / Lady friend / Goin' back / Old John Robertson / Wasn't born to follow / You ain't goin' nowhere / Hickory wind / Nashville West / Drug store truck drivin' man / Gunga Din / Jesus is just alright / The ballad of Easy Rider / Chestnut mare / Yesterday's train / Just a season / Citizen Kane / Jamaica say you will / Tiffany queen / America's great national pastime. (re-iss. Sep87 d-lp/c; 460115-1/-4)

Jul 73. (7") (8210) **MR. TAMBOURINE MAN. / TURN! TURN! TURN!** □ -
(re-iss. Feb78; 5951)

Aug 75. (7") Asylum; (AYM 545) **FULL CIRCLE. / THINGS WILL BE BETTER** □ -

Feb 76. (7") (3952) **CHESTNUT MARE. / ALL I REALLY WANT TO DO** □ -

Jul 76. (7") (4411) **TURN! TURN! TURN!. / YOU AIN'T GOIN' NOWHERE** □ -

Jul 76. (d-lp) (22040) **SWEETHEART OF THE RODEO / THE NOTORIOUS BYRD BROTHERS** □ -

Feb 80. (lp/c) (CBS/40 31795) **THE BYRDS PLAY DYLAN** □ -
(cd-iss. Apr94 & Feb96 on 'Sony'; 476757-2)

Aug 80. (lp/c) (CBS/40 31851) **THE ORIGINAL SINGLES 1965-1967** □ -
(re-iss. Nov81 lp/c; CBS/40 32069)

Feb 82. (lp/c) (CBS/40 32103) **THE ORIGINAL SINGLES 1967-1969** □ -

Jul 82. (7") Old Gold; (OG 9182) **CHESTNUT MARE. / WASN'T BORN TO FOLLOW** □ -

Sep 83. (7"ep/c-ep) Scoop 33; (7SR/7SC 5016) **6-TRACK HITS** □ -
– Lay lady lay / Turn! turn! turn! / Goin' nowhere / So you want to be a rock'n'roll star / Chestnut mare / All I really want to do.

Jul 84. (7") Epic; (EPCA 4575) **MR. TAMBOURINE MAN. / WASN'T BORN TO FOLLOW** □ -

Sep 86. (d-lp/c) Castle; (CCS LP/MC 151) **THE BYRDS COLLECTION** □ -
(cd-iss. 1988; CCSCD 151) – (omits some tracks).

Jan 88. (7") Old Gold; (OG 9747) **MR. TAMBOURINE MAN. / TURN! TURN! TURN!** □ -

May 88. (lp) Murray Hill; <MH 70318> **NEVER BEFORE** -
<cd-iss. Aug89; D 22808>

1988. (lp/cd) Rhino; <R1/R2 70244> **IN THE BEGINNING** -

1989. (3"cd-ep) **MR. TAMBOURINE MAN / TURN! TURN! TURN!. / ALL I REALLY WANT TO DO / LAY LADY LAY** -

Nov 90. (4xcd-box) Columbia; (467611-2) <46773> **THE ULTIMATE BYRDS** -
– (above included 4 new songs)

1990. (7"ep) Columbia; **FOUR DIMENSIONS** -
– Eight miles high / Mr.Tambourine man / Turn! turn! turn! (to everything there is a season) / I feel a whole lot better

Feb 91. (cd/c) Raven; (RV CD/CA 10) **FULL FLYTE 1965-1970** -

Jul 91. (3xcd-box) Columbia; (468338-2) **MR. TAMBOURINE MAN / TURN! TURN! TURN! / YOUNGER THAN YESTERDAY** -

Mar 93. (cd/c) Columbia; (471665-2/-4) **20 ESSENTIAL TRACKS** -

Oct 94. (cd) Columbia; **THE BEST** -

Oct 94. (cd-ep) Columbia; **TURN! TURN! TURN!. / (other artists)** -

Jun 97. (d-cd) Columbia; (487995-2) **THE VERY BEST OF THE BYRDS** -
(above from the soundtrack of Oscar winning film 'Forrest Gump')

ROGER McGUINN

	C.B.S.	Columbia
Jun 73. (7") (45931) **DRAGGIN'. / TIME CUBE**	-	

Jun 73. (lp) (CBS 65274) <31946> **ROGER McGUINN** □
– I'm so restless / My new woman / Lost my drivin' wheel / Draggin' / Time cube / Bag full of money / Hanoi Hannah / Stone / Heave away / M'Linda / The water is wide. (re-iss. Jul88 on 'Edsel'; ED 281) (cd-iss. Feb91; EDCD 281)

Jul 74. (7") <10019> **SAME OLD SOUND. / GATE OF HORN** - -

Sep 74. (lp) (CBS 80171) <32956> **PEACE ON YOU** 92
– Peace on you / Without you / Going to the country / One more time / Same old sound / Do what you want / Together / Better change / Gate of horn / Lady.

Sep 74. (7") (2649) <10044> **PEACE ON YOU. / WITHOUT YOU** □

— his band; **GREG ATTAWAY / STEVE LOVE / DAVID LOVELACE**

Jul 75. (lp; as ROGER McGUINN & BAND) (CBS 80877) <33541> **ROGER McGUINN AND BAND** □ Jun75
– Somebody loves you / Knockin' on Heaven's door / Bull Dog / Painted lady / Lover of the bayou / Lisa / Circle song / So long / Easy does it / Born to rock and roll.

Jul 75. (7"; as ROGER McGUINN & BAND) <10181> **SOMEBODY LOVES YOU / EASY DOES IT** - □

Oct 75. (7"; as ROGER McGUINN & BAND) <10201> **LOVER OF THE BAYOU. / EASY DOES IT**

	-	

Jun 76. (7") <10385> **TAKE ME AWAY. / FRIEND**

	-	

Jun 76. (lp) (CBS 81369) **CARDIFF ROSE**
– Jolly Roger / Take me away / Rock and roll time / Partners in crime / Friend / Up to me / Round table / Prettly Polly / Dream land.

May 77. (lp) (CBS 81883) **THUNDERBYRD**
– All night long / It's gone / Dixie highway / American girl / We can do it all over again / Why, baby why / I'm not lonely anymore / Golden loom / Russian Hill.

May 77. (7") (5231) **AMERICAN GIRL. / RUSSIAN HILL**

	-	

May 77. (7") (10543) **AMERICAN GIRL. / I'M NOT LONELY ANYMORE**

	-	

McGUINN, CLARK & HILLMAN

—— (nearly a BYRDS reformation; ROGER, GENE & CHRIS)

	Capitol	Capitol
Feb 79. (7") (CL 16065) **SURRENDER TO ME. / BYE BYE BABY**		-
Feb 79. (lp/c) <(EST/TC-EST 11910)> **McGUINN, CLARK & HILLMAN**		39

– Long long time / Little mama / Don't you write her off / Sad boy / Surrender to me / Backstage pass / Stopping traffic / Feeling higher / Release me girl / Bye bye baby. (cd-iss. Feb99 on 'E.M.I.'; CDP 796355-2)

Apr 79. (7") (CL 16077) <4693> **DON'T YOU WRITE HER OFF. / SAD BOY**		33	Mar79
Jun 79. (7") <4739> **SURRENDER TO ME. / LITTLE MAMA**	-		
Sep 79. (7") <4763> **BYE BYE BABY. / BACKSTAGE PASS**	-		

Jan 80. (lp; by ROGER McGUINN and CHRIS HILLMAN featuring GENE CLARK) <(EST/TC-EST 12043)> **CITY**
– Who taught the night / One more chance / Won't let you down / Street talk / City / Skate date / Givin' herself away / Let me down easy / Deeper in / Painter fire.

Feb 80. (7") <4821> **STREET TALK. / ONE MORE CHANCE**	-	
Apr 80. (7") <4855> **CITY. / DEEPER IN**	-	

McGUINN / HILLMAN

Mar 81. (lp/c) <(EST/TC-EST 12108)> **McGUINN / HILLMAN – MEAN STREETS**
– Mean streets / Entertainment / Soul shoes / Between you and me / Angel / Ain't no money / Love me tonight / King for a night / A secret side of you / Turn your radio on. (cd-iss. Feb91;)

Mar 81. (7") (4952) **TURN YOUR RADIO ON. / MAKING MOVIES**	-	
May 81. (7") <4973> **LOVE ME TONIGHT. / KING FOR A NIGHT**	-	

	not iss.	Universal
1983. (7") <66006> **YOU AIN'T GOIN' NOWHERE. / DON'T YOU HEAR JERUSALEM MOAN**	-	

ROGER McGUINN

—— used session people **STAN LYNCH** – drums / **GEORGE HAWKINS** – bass / **DAVID COLE** – acoustic guitar / **JOHN JORGENSEN** – guitar / **BELMONT TENCH** – keyboards / **MICHAEL THOMPSON** – acoustic guitar

	Arista	Arista
Feb 91. (cd/c/lp) (261/411/211 348) <8648> **BACK FROM RIO**		44	Jan91

– Someone to love / Car phone / You bowed down / Suddenly blue / The trees are all gone / king of the hill / Without your love / The time has come / Your love is a gold mine / If we never meet again.

Feb 91. (7") **KING OF THE HILL. / YOUR LOVE IS A GOLD MINE**
(cd-s+=) – The time has come.

	Polydor	Hollywood
Jan 97. (cd) (162090-2) **LIVE FROM MARS** (live)			Nov96

– compilations, etc. –

Mar 92. (cd/c) Columbia; (471269-2/-4) **BORN TO ROCK AND ROLL**		
Dec 92. (cd; McGUINN / CLARK / HILLMAN) Edsel; (EDCD 358) **RETURN FLYTE**		-
Jun 93. (cd) Edsel; (EDCD 373) **RETURN FLIGHT VOL.2**		
Feb 97. (d-cd; McGUIIN, HILLMAN & CLARK) Strange Fruit (SFRCD 001) **3 BYRDS LAND IN LONDON**		-

David BYRNE (see under ⇒ TALKING HEADS)

BYSTANDERS (see under ⇒ MAN)

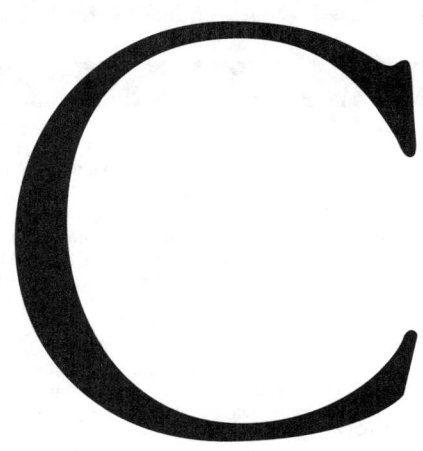

Melanie C (see under ⇒ SPICE GIRLS)

CABARET VOLTAIRE

Formed: Sheffield, England ... 1973 by STEPHEN MALLINDER, RICHARD H. KIRK and CHRIS WATSON, naming themselves after the experimental Parisian Dadaist performances of pre-20's France. A farcical 1975 debut gig saw them using a backing tape of a steamhammer while KIRK played clarinet; his jacket was also covered in fairy lights (!), the whole set-up not going down with a rioting audience who proceeded to beat him up! Inspired by the likes of CAN and BRIAN ENO, the CABS contributed two songs (one of them, 'BAADER MEINHOF', was nearly chosen as a debut 45!) to a 1978 various artists double EP, 'A FACTORY SAMPLER', before they signed to Geoff Travis's new independent operation, 'Rough Trade'. Later that year, the trio issued their debut release, 'EXTENDED PLAY', a four track EP that included their industrial mangling of The Velvet Underground's 'HERE SHE COMES NOW'. A classic follow-up, 'NAG NAG NAG', fused electronic sound with the yobbish rush of adrenaline-fuelled punk to devastating effect. 1979 also saw the release of their debut long-player, 'MIX-UP', a pivotal experimental affair which, although marking out new territory, was a challenging listen end to end. The early years of the following decade found CABARET VOLTAIRE ploughing their own idiosyncratic furrow over the course of three studio albums (two live events were also issued), namely 'THE VOICE OF AMERICA' (1980), 'RED MECCA' (1981) and '2 X 45' (1982), before WATSON's departure left MALLINDER and KIRK as a duo. In 1983, they were sought out by Virgin off-shoot, 'Some Bizzare', their avant-garde inaccessibility now taking on a more commercial hue with 'THE CRACKDOWN', an album which nearly took them into the UK Top 30. Incorporating elements of Eastern exotica, the record was also more dancefloor friendly than anything they had recorded to date; tracks such as 'JUST FASCINATION', '24-24', 'ANIMATION' and 'WHY KILL TIME (WHEN YOU CAN KILL YOURSELF)', were lent the rhythmic expertise of SOFT CELL's DAVE BALL (later of The GRID). Ironically, the more overtly pop approach of SOFT CELL and their ilk (DEPECHE MODE, HUMAN LEAGUE and OMD) led to the more adventurous CABS being squeezed out of the market. They did, however, maintain a loyal if not massive following who stuck by them through a series of lesser mid-80's albums, 'MICRO-PHONIES' (1984), 'THE COVENANT, THE SWORD AND THE ARM OF THE LORD' (1985) and 'CODE' (1987), the latter set their first for 'Parlophone'. Since 1983, both MALLINDER and KIRK had moonlighted in various side projects, the former releasing a solo album, 'POW-WOW', the latter far more prolific in his output with 'BLACK JESUS VOICE' (1986) the pick of the bunch. The late 80's house scene, meanwhile, saw CABARET VOLTAIRE cited as a prominent influence on many of the genre's prime movers; the result was a creative renaissance of sorts which led to a remix by PETE WATERMAN (!) for the 'KEEP ON' single, while house producer, MARSHALL JEFFERSON, took controls on the comeback set, 'GROOVY, LAID BACK AND NASTY' (1990). Despite this uncharacteristic dalliance with the mainstream, the CABS slipped back into semi-obscurity with their former Belgian label, 'Les Disques Du Crepuscule' releasing a handful of low profile sets, 'BODY AND SOUL' (1991), 'PERCUSSION FORCE' (1991), 'INTERNATIONAL LANGUAGE' (1993) and 'THE CONVERSATION' (1994).

Album rating: MIX-UP (*5) / THE VOICE OF AMERICA (*4) / RED MECCA (*7) / 2x45 (*7) / JOHNNY YES NO soundtrack (*3) / THE CRACKDOWN (*8) / MICRO-PHONIES (*6) / DRINKING GASOLINE (*6) / THE COVENANT, THE SWORD & THE ARM (*6) / CODE (*7) / GROOVY, LAIDBACK & NASTY (*6) / THE LIVING LEGENDS compilation (*9) / THE GOLDEN MOMENTS OF CABARET VOLTAIRE compilation (*7) / LISTEN UP WITH CABARET VOLTAIRE compilation (*7) / COLOURS (*5) / PLASTICITY (*5) / Stephen Mallinder: POW WOW (*5) / Richard H. Kirk: BLACK JESUS VOICE (*5)

STEPHEN MALLINDER – vocals, bass, electronics, percussion, trumpet, piano / **RICHARD H. KIRK** – guitar, vocals, synthesizer, bongos, piano / **CHRISTOPHER R. WATSON** – electronics, tapes
(issued cassette 25 copies LIMITED EDITION in 1976 on own label)

		Rough Trade	not iss.
Nov 78.	(7"ep) *(RT 003)* **EXTENDED PLAY** – Talkover / Here she comes now / Do the Mussolini – headkick / The set up.	□	–
Jun 79.	(7") *(RT 018)* **"NAG NAG NAG." / IS THAT ME (FINDING SOMEONE AT THE DOOR AGAIN)?**	□	–
Oct 79.	(lp) *(ROUGH 4)* **MIX-UP** – Kurlian photograph / No escape / 4th shot / Heaven and Hell / Eyeless sight (live) / Photophobia / On every other street / Expect nothing / Capsules. *(re-iss. Sep90 on 'Mute' lp/cd; CABS 8/+CD)*	□	–
Dec 79.	(7") *(RT 035)* **SILENT COMMAND. / The Soundtrack 'CHANCE VERSUS CAUSALITY'**	□	–
——	added guest **MARK TATTERSALL** – drums		
Jan 80.	(lp) *(ROUGH 7)* **LIVE AT THE Y.M.C.A. 27.10.79 (live)** – Untitled / On every other street / Nag nag nag / The set up / Havoc / Expect nothing / Here she comes now / No escape / Baader Meinhof. *(re-iss. Jun90 on 'Mute' lp/cd; CABS 4/+CD)*	□	–
——	now with guests **JOHN CLAYTON** – percussion / **JANE** – tapes		
Mar 80.	(12"ep) *(RT 038)* **THREE MANTRAS** – Eastern mantra / Western mantra. *(re-iss. Jun90 on 'Mute' m-lp/cd; CABS 7/+CD)*	□	–
——	with guest **HAYDN BOYES-WESTON** – drums (ex-2.3) (also on debut lp)		
Jul 80.	(lp) *(ROUGH 11)* **THE VOICE OF AMERICA** – The voice of America / Damage is done / Partially submerged / Kneel to the boss / Premonition / This is entertainment / If the shadows could march? / Stay out of it / Obsession / News from nowhere / Messages received. *(re-iss. Jun90 on 'Mute' lp/cd; CABS 2/+CD)*	□	–
Nov 80.	(7") *(RT 060)* **SECONDS TOO LATE. / CONTROL ADDICT**	□	–
Jul 81.	(12"ep) *(TWI 018)* **3 CREPUSCULE TRACKS** – Sluggin' fer Jesus (Pt.1) / Your agent man / Sluggin' fer Jesus (Pt.2). (above released on 'Crepuscule')	–	– Belg.
——	**NICK ALLDAY** – drums (ex-GRAPH) repl. HAYDN		
Aug 81.	(lp) *(ROUGH 27)* **RED MECCA** – Touch of evil / Sly doubt / Landslide / A thousand ways / Red mask / Split second feling / Black mask / Spread the virus / A touch of evil (reprise). *(re-iss. Jun90 on 'Mute' lp/cd; CABS 3/+CD)*	□	–
Sep 81.	(lp) *(COPY 002)* **LIVE AT THE LYCEUM (live)** – Taxi music / Seconds too late / Your agent man / Split second feeling / Sluggin' fer Jesus (Pt.1) / Kneel to the boss / Obsession / A thousand ways. *(re-iss. Sep90 on 'Mute' lp/cd; CABS 13/+CD)*		–
Nov 81.	(7") *(RT 095)* **JAZZ THE GLASS. / BURNT TO THE GROUND**	□	–
Dec 81.	(12") *(RT 096)* **EDDIE'S OUT. / WALLS OF JERICHO** *(limited copies contained last 7" free) (below on 'Solidarity')*	□	–
Mar 82.	(12"ep; by PRESSURE COMPANY) *(SOLID 1)* **LIVE IN SHEFFIELD 19th JANUARY 1982 (live)** – War of nerves / Wait & shuffle / Get out of my face / Vitrions China (paradox).	□	–
——	**ALAN FISH** – drums, percussion (of HULA) repl. ALLDAY / guest **ERIC RANDOM** – guitar (also a solo artist)		
Jun 82.	(2x12"lp) *(ROUGH 42)* **2 x 45** – Breathe deep / Yashar / Protection / War of nerves (T.E.S.) / Wait and shuffle / Get out of my face. *(re-iss. Sep90 on 'Mute' lp/cd; CABS 9/+CD)*	98	–
Nov 82.	(lp) *(RTD 1)* **HAI! (live)** – Walls of Kyoto / 3 days monk / Yashar (version) / Over and over / Diskono / Taxi music (version). *(re-iss. Sep90 on 'Mute' lp/cd; CABS 11/+CD)*	–	– German
——	trimmed to a duo (**MALLINDER + KIRK**) when WATSON departed. Retained **ALAN FISH** and brought in **DAVE BALL** – keyboards (of SOFT CELL)		
Feb 83.	(12") *(TWI 020)* **FOOLS GAME (SLUGGIN' FER JESUS Pt.3). / GUT LEVEL** (above released on 'Crepuscule')	–	– Belg.

		Some Bizzare – Virgin	Virgin
Jul 83.	(7") *(CVS 1)* **JUST FASCINATION. / EMPTY WALLS** (12") *(CVS 1-12)* – ('A'side) / The crackdown.	□	–
Aug 83.	(lp/c) *(CV/TCV 1)* **THE CRACKDOWN** – 24-24 / In the shadows / Talking time / Animation / Over and over / Just fascination / Why kill time (when you can kill yourself) / Haiti / Crackdown. *(free 12"w/ above + on c+cd)* – MOSCOW / BADGE OF EVIL. / DISKONO / DOUBLE VISION *(cd-iss. 1984; CDCV 1) (re-iss. Aug86 lp/c; OVED/+C 156)*	31	□
Nov 83.	(lp) *(DVR 1)* **JOHNNY YESNO** *(1982 video)* – Taxi music / Hallucination sequence / DT's / Cold turkey / The quarry (in the wilderness) / Title sequence / Taxi music dub. *(re-iss. Sep90 on 'Mute' lp/cd; CABS 10/+CD)* (above released on 'DoubleVision')		
Dec 83.	(7"/ext.12") *(CVS 2/+12)* **THE DREAM TICKET. / SAFETY ZONE**	□	□
Sep 84.	(7"/ext.12") *(CVS 3/+12)* **SENSORIA. / CUT THE DAMN CAMERA**	□	□
Nov 84.	(lp/c/cd) *(CV/TCV/CVCD 2)* **MICRO-PHONIES** – Do right / The operative / Digital rasta / Spies in the wires / Theme from Earthshaker / James Brown / Slammer / Blue heat / Sensoria. *(cd+=)* – Blue heat (extended) / Sensoria (extended). *(re-iss. Sep91 on 'Virgin'; cd/c; same)*	69	□
Jan 85.	(7"/12") *(CVS 4/+12)* **JAMES BROWN. / BAD SELF (part 1)**	□	□
Jun 85.	(2x12"/c) *(CVM/TCVM 1)* **DRINKING GASOLINE** – Kino / Sleepwalking / Big funk / Ghost talk. *(re-iss. Sep91 on 'Virgin'; same)*	71	□
Sep 85.	(7") *(CVS 5)* **I WANT YOU. / DRINK YOUR POISON** (12") *(CVS 5-12)* – ('A'side) / Drink your poison, C.O.M.A.	□	□
Oct 85.	(lp/c/cd) *(CV/TCV/CDCV 3)* **THE COVENANT, THE SWORD AND THE ARM OF THE LORD** – L21st / I want you / Hell's home / Kickback / The arm of the Lord / Warm / Golden halos / Motion rotation / Whip blow / The web. *(cd+=)* – Sleepwalking / Big funk *(re-iss. Sep91 on 'Virgin'; same)*	57	□
——	guest **DEE BOYLE** – drums (of CHAAK) repl. FISH		

		DoubleVision	not iss.
Jun 86.	(12"ep) *(DVR-DVRP 21)* **THE DRAIN TRAIN** – Shakedown (the whole thing) / Menace / Electro-motive.	–	–

(w/ free-12") – SHAKEDOWN (The Whole Thing). / SHAKEDOWN (dub).

Parlophone Capitol

Jul 87. (7") (R 6157) **DON'T ARGUE. / DON'T ARGUE (WHO'S ARGUING)** | 69 | - |
(12") (12R 6157) – ('A'extended) / ('A'-Hate & Destroy mix).
(12") (12RX 6157) – ('A'dance mix) / ('A'dub).

Sep 87. (7") (R 6166) **HERE TO GO. / HERE TO GO (dub)**
(12") (12R 6166) – ('A'extended mix) / ('A'-Space dub mix).
(12") (12RX 6166) – ('A'-Eleven Eleven mix).

Oct 87. (lp/c/cd) (PCS/TCPCS/CDPCS 7312) **CODE**
– Don't argue / Sex, money, freaks / Thank you America / Here to go / Trouble (won't stop) / White car / No one here / Life slips by / Code. (cd+=) – Here to go (little dub) / Hey hey.

Oct 89. (7") (RS 6227) **HYPNOTISED (Daniel Miller mix). /** ('A'-Gerald's vocal mix) | 66 |
(12") (12RS 6227) – ('A'-Fon Force mix) / ('A'-Fon Force dub) / ('A'-Daniel Miller dub mix) / ('A'-Robert Gordon mix).
(cd-s) (CDCDR 6227) – ('A'-Fon Force mix) / ('A'-Gerald's vocal mix).
(12") (12RX 6227) – (cd tracks) / ('A'-A Guy Called Gerald's music mix) / ('A'-Western Works mix).

Mar 90. (7") (R 6250) **KEEP ON. / KEEP ON (Les dub)** | 55 |
(12") (12R 6250) – ('A'-Sweet Exorcist mix) / ('A'-Sleazy Dog mix) / ('A'-Mayday mix).
(cd-s) – ('A'-western works mix) / ('A'club mix).

Jun 90. (cd/c/lp) (CD/TC+/PCS 7338) **GROOVY, LAIDBACK AND NASTY**
– Searchin' / Hypnotised / Minute by minute / Runaway / Keep on (I got this feeling) / Magic / Time beats / Easy life. (free 12"ep w/ above) **GROOVY, LAIDBACK AND NASTY** (remixes) – Runaway / Magic / Searchin' / Rescue me (city lights) * / Easy life. (cd+= *)

Jul 90. (7") (R 6261) **EASY LIFE. / ('A'-Robert Gordon mix)** | 61 |
(12") (12R 6261) – ('A'side) / Fluid / Positive I.D.
(cd-s) (CDR 6261) – ('A'side) / ('A'-Jive Turkey mix) / Fluid.
(12") (12RX 6261) – ('A'vocal) / ('A'-Strange mix) / ('A'-Very strange mixes by Robert Gordon and Fon Force).

Crepuscule not iss.

Feb 91. (12") (TWI 948) **WHAT IS REAL. / ('A'-Virtual reality mix)**
(cd-s+=) (TWI 948-2) – Legacy of a computer.

Mar 91. (lp/cd) (TWI 944/+2) **BODY AND SOUL**
– No resistance / Shout / Happy / Decoy / Bad chemistry / Vibration / What is real / Western land. (cd+=) – What is real (dreamtime mix).

Jul 91. (m-lp/cd) (TWI 951/+2) **PERCUSSION FORCE**
– Don't walk away / Keep on pushin' / Don't walk away (Robert Gordon mix) / Dynamic zone / Jazz the computer (part 1) / Keep on pushin' (version). (cd+=) – T.Phunk / Don't walk away (version) / Jazz the computer part 2.

Plastex Instinct

Oct 91. (m-lp) (EXL 001) <93> **COLOURS**

Oct 92. (d-lp/c/cd) (EXL/+C/CD 003) <255> **PLASTICITY**
– Low cool / Soul vine (70 billion people) / Resonator /Inside the electronic revolution / From another source / Deep time / Back to Brazilia / Neuron factory / Delmas 19 / Cooled out / Invisible generation / Soulenoid (scream at the right time).

Jun 93. (cd) <264> **INTERNATIONAL LANGUAGE**
– Everything is true / Radical chic / Taxi mutant / Let it come down / Afterglow / The rest / Millenium / Belly of the beast (back in Babylon) / Other world.

Apollo- R&S Instinct

Jul 94. (q-lp/d-cd) (AMB 4934/+CD) <273> **THE CONVERSATION**
– Exterminating angel (intro) / Brutal but clean / The message / Let's start / Night rider / Night rider / I think / The heat / Harmonic parallel / Project 80 (parts 1-4) / Exterminating angel (outro).

– compilations, others, etc. –

1981. (c) Industrial; (IRC 35) **74-76**
(cd-iss. Jun92 on 'Grey Area-Mute'; CABS 15CD)
Feb 88. (lp/cd) Crepuscule; (TWI 749/+2) **8 CREPUSCULE TRACKS** | - | - | Belgium
Jul 83. (12") Factory Benelux; (FBN 25) **YASHAR (5.00). / YASHAR (7.20)** | - | Belgium
Nov 87. (cd) Rough Trade; (RUFCD 6001) **THE GOLDEN MOMENTS OF CABARET VOLTAIRE**
– Do the Mussolini (Head Kick) / Nag nag nag / Photophobia / Expect nothing / Seconds Too late / This is entertainment / Obsession / Sluggin for Jesus / Landslide / Red mask / Get out of my face.
(below releases on 'Mute' unless otherwise mentioned)
May 90. (cd-ep) (CABS 1CD) **"NAG NAG NAG." / YASHAR / YASHAR (John Robie remixes)**
Jun 90. (lp/c/cd) (CABS 5/+C/CD) **LISTEN UP WITH CABARET VOLTAIRE** (rare demos)
Jun 90. (d-lp/c/cd) (CABS 6/+C/CD) **THE LIVING LEGENDS . . . CABARET VOLTAIRE** (the singles)
– Do the Mussolini (head kick) / Talk over / Here she comes now / The set up / Nag, nag, nag / Silent command / Jazz the glass / Walls of Jericho / Seconds too late / Eddie's out / Burnt to the ground / Extract from : Chance Verses Casuality / Control addict / Is that me (finding someone at the door again).
Jun 90. (c) (CABS 2C) **LIVE AT THE LYCEUM / THE VOICE OF AMERICA**
Jun 90. (c) (CABS 7C) **THE DRAIN TRAIN / THREE MANTRAS**
Jun 90. (c) (CABS 8C) **MIX-UP / LIVE AT THE Y.M.C.A.**
Jun 90. (c) (CABS 10C) **2 x 45 / JOHNNY YESNO**
Jun 90. (c) (CABS 11C) **HAI! / RED MECCA**
Apr 92. (12"/cd-s) Virgin; **I WANT YOU. / KINO**
– (Altern 8 remixes / Western re-works '92)
May 92. (d-lp/cd)(c) Virgin; (CV/+CD 4)(TCV 4) **TECHNOLOGY**
(remixes late 70's & early 80's)

CACTUS (see under ⇒ VANILLA FUDGE)

CAKE

Formed: Sacramento, California, USA . . . 1994 by JOHN McCREA, GREG BROWN, VICTOR DAMIANI, VINCENT DI FIORE and TODD ROPER. Along with fellow mavericks, 311, the success of CAKE has helped resurrect that long-forgotten bastion of southern rock, 'Capricorn' records (once home to the legendary ALLMAN BROTHERS BAND). Don't expect mutton chops and slide guitar though, as CAKE were raised on more eclectic influences, CRACKER and THEY MIGHT BE GIANTS among them. McCREA and BROWN's complex guitar numbers were matched with countrified covers:- MULTIPLY THE HEARTACHES (Kathy Dee) / I WILL SURVIVE (hit; Gloria Gaynor) / PERHAPS, PERHAPS, PERHAPS (Davis-Farres) / SAD SONGS AND WALTZES (Willie Nelson). After a US-only album, 'MOTORCADE OF GENEROSITY' failed to gain much attention in '94/'95, they returned two years later, playing with much fervour on the million seller, 'FASHION NUGGET'. Two semi-classics were subsequently lifted from the record, both 'THE DISTANCE' and 'IT'S COMING DOWN' distinguished from the alternative rock pack by the hazily melancholy trumpet flurries of VINCENT DI FIORE. 1998 saw them break the US Top 40 once again with a further slice of post-ironic US indie, 'PROLONGING THE MAGIC', although their attempts to woo the mainstream were hit and miss.

Album rating: MOTORCADE OF GENEROSITY (*4) / FASHION NUGGET (*6) / PROLONGING THE MAGIC (*6)

JOHN McCREA – vocals, acoustic guitar, organ / **GREG BROWN** – electric guitar, organ / **VICTOR DAMIANI** – bass / **VINCENT DI FIORE** – trumpet, percussion / **TODD ROPER** – drums, percussion

Capricorn Capricorn

Nov 94. (cd) <532 506-2> **MOTORCADE OF GENEROSITY** | - | - |
– Comanche / Up so close / Jolene / You part the waters / Jesus wrote a blank cheque / I bombed Korea / Ain't no good / Ruby sees all / Pentagram / Haze of love / Is this love / Rock'n'roll lifestyle / Mr. Mastodon farm. (UK-iss.Jul97; same)
Mar 97. (7"/c-s) (574 220-7/-4) **THE DISTANCE. /** | 22 |
(cd-s) (574 220-2) – ('A'side) / Multiply the heartaches / Jolene (live) / It's coming down.
Mar 97. (cd/c) <(532 857-2/-4)> **FASHION NUGGET** | 53 | 36 | Sep96
– Frank Sinatra / The distance / Friend is a four letter word / Open book / Daria / Race car ya-yas / I will survive / Stickshifts and safetybelts / Perhaps, perhaps, perhaps / It's coming down / Nugget / She'll come back to me / Italian leather sofa / Sad songs and waltzes. <clean version Sep97; 534228>
May 97. (7"/c-s) (574 470-7/-4) **I WILL SURVIVE. / RUBY SEES ALL** | 29 | - |
(cd-s+=) (574 470-2) – Rock'n'roll lifestyle.
Aug 97. (7") (574 716-7) **FRANK SINATRA. /** | - |
(cd-s+=) (574 717-2) –
(cd-s) (574 825-2) –
Oct 98. (cd) <(538092-2)> **PROLONGING THE MAGIC** | 33 |
– Satan is my motor / Mexico / Never there / Guitar out the window / You turn the screws / Walk on by / Sheep go to Heaven / When you sleep / Hem of your garment / Alpha beta parking lot / Let me go / Cool blue reason / Where would I be?
Apr 99. (c-s) (870810-7) <radio play> **NEVER THERE / I WILL SURVIVE** | 66 | 78 | Nov98
(cd-s) (870811-2) – ('A'side) / Cool blue reason / Is this love (live) / Never there (video).
(cd-s) (870813-2) – ('A'side) / The Distance / You part the waters (live) / The distance (video).

J.J. CALE

Born: JEAN-JACQUES CALE, 5 Dec'38, Oklahoma, U.S.A. After a childhood spent immersing himself in the blues and rockabilly, CALE's first foray into the music business was as a country player in Nashville. When this came to little, CALE followed the bright lights and Tulsa musical compadres RUSSELL BRIDGES (aka LEON RUSSELL), CARL RADLE (later of DEREK & THE DOMINOES) and JIMMY KARSTEIN to L.A. where he worked as an engineer for 'Liberty' records. Around this time he was also performing solo in L.A. clubs, releasing a one-off single for the label, 'OUTSIDE LOOKING IN' in summer 66. CALE's most sought-after artefact from this period, however, is his pseudo-psychedelic project, 'A TRIP DOWN SUNSET STRIP', recorded under the moniker of The LEATHERCOATED MINDS. One track left over from this session was eventually revamped and released as 'AFTER MIDNIGHT', a slow burning piano blues groove which was pivotal in getting CALE's career off the ground. Subsequently covered by ERIC CLAPTON (who had heard the track through DELANEY & BONNIE) in 1970, the single's success (and a little encouragement from producer Audie Ashworth) spurred on CALE (now eking out a living back in TULSA after another ill-fated period in Nashville) to write a whole album's worth of songs. The result was 'NATURALLY' (1972), a back porch blend of country, blues, rockabilly and R&B which would serve the singer well over more than 30 years as a recording artist. Released on LEON RUSSELL's 'Shelter' records, the set included a re-recorded 'AFTER MIDNIGHT' as well as such CALE staples as 'CALL ME THE BREEZE' (later covered by LYNYRD SKYNYRD), 'MAGNOLIA' (later covered by POCO and JOSE FELICIANO) and the languorous 'CRAZY MAMA' (CALE's US Top 30 hit). The record also introduced CALE's trademark vocal style, a tersely minimalist, often barely audible drawl which complemented the unadorned music perfectly; interestingly, CALE's insistence that his voice be mixed down was drawn from his conviction that this would draw the listener in. Maybe there was something in this, most of CALE's albums pulsing with a subtly hypnotic power that was hard to resist. A follow-up set, 'REALLY' (1973), was more upbeat, recorded in various studios including Muscle Shoals where CALE cut the moody, horn-embellished R&B of 'LIES'. 'OKIE' (1974) was a more organic affair, with several of the tracks recorded at CALE's house. The singer subseqently moved to Nashville where he and ASHWORTH set up a studio in the producer's house, recording most of the material which would make up the excellent 'TROUBADOUR' (1976) album. It became his first album to chart in the UK (Top 60) while the brassy swing of 'HEY BABY' enjoyed a brief tenure in the US Hot 100. The set also included the brooding road fever of 'TRAVELIN' LIGHT' (arguably one of CALE's finest moments, positively frenetic against the bulk of his work!) and his most famous track, 'COCAINE', covered, of course, to much success by ERIC CLAPTON. Yet again, CALE could've taken the bit between his teeth and made a shot at the big time on the back of the single's success; instead, he chose to spend the proceeds on building a studio in his Nashville home. '5' (1979) became CALE's highest charting album to date, making the UK Top 40, though you could hardly call this reticent studiophile a pop star. Shunning most publicity at any opportunity, it's just as well that it often took an interpretation by another artist for CALE's songs to gain radio airplay. Nevertheless, in the early 80's, he signed a major label deal with 'Phonogram International', releasing 'GRASSHOPPER' (1982) and '#8' (1983); though they both sold fairly well in Britain, CALE was apparently unhappy and asked to be released from his contract. He then retired from the music business for the bulk of the 80's and his hardly prolific recording rate slowed to nought. CALE eventually returned at the end of the decade with 'TRAVEL-LOG', courtesy of a new deal with 'Silvertone' (who'd also taken on JOHN LEE HOOKER). The mid-90's saw him again thrown in his lot with a major label, this time 'Virgin', who released 'CLOSER TO YOU' in summer '94. 'Phonogram', meanwhile, issued a long overdue overview of CALE's career in 1997; entitled 'ANYWAY THE WIND BLOWS', the record is worth picking up for the previously unissued tracks alone, especially the neon-lit desert psych-out (no, seriously!) of 'DURANGO' (no, seriously!) • Trivia: MARK KNOPFLER and RICHARD THOMPSON guested on his '#8' album in 1983.

Album rating: NATURALLY (*7) / REALLY (*5) / OKIE (*5) / TROUBADOUR (*7) / 5 (*4) / SHADES (*4) / GRASSHOPPER (*4) / #8 (*4) TRAVEL-LOG (*7) / NUMBER 10 (*6) / CLOSER TO YOU (*4) / GUITAR MAN (*5) / SPECIAL EDITION compilation (*7) / WHEN THE WIND BLOWS anthology (*7)

J.J. CALE – vocals, guitar, piano; with loads of session musicians (too numerous to mention)

			Liberty	Liberty
Jun 66.	(7")	<(LIB 55881)> **OUTSIDE LOOKIN' IN. / IN OUR TIME**		Apr66
Dec 66.	(7")	<LIB 55931> **AFTER MIDNIGHT. / SLOW MOTION**	-	

— In 1967, CALE and LEON RUSSELL formed The LEATHERCOATED MINDS who issued one lp, 'A TRIP DOWN SUNSET STRIP' for 'Fontana'; (STL 5412)

			A&M	Shelter
Oct 71.	(7")	<7306> **CRAZY MAMA. / MAGNOLIA**	-	
Jan 72.	(lp)	(AMLS 68105) <8098> **NATURALLY**		51

– Call me the breeze / Call the doctor / Don't go to strangers / Woman I love / Magnolia / Clyde / Crazy mama / Nowhere to run / After midnight / River runs deep / Bringing it back / Crying eyes. (re-iss.Apr76 on 'Island'; ISA 5003) (re-iss.Aug83 on 'Mercury' lp/c; PRICE/PRIMC 25) (cd-iss.Jan87 on 'Mercury'; 830 042-2) (lp re-iss/Dec98 on 'Vivante'; VPLP 002)

Jan 72.	(7")	<7314> **CRAZY MAMA. / DON'T GO TO STRANGERS**	-	22
Aug 72.	(7")	(AMS 7022) <7321> **AFTER MIDNIGHT. / CRAZY MAMA**		42 May72
Jan 73.	(7")	(AMS 7042) <7326> **LIES. / RIDING HOME**		42 Oct72
Jan 73.	(lp)	(AMLS 68157) <8912> **REALLY**		92 Dec72

– Lies / Everything will be alright / I'll kiss the world goodbye / Changes / Right down here / If you're ever in Oklahoma / Ridin' home / Going down / Soulin' / Playin' in the streets / Mo Jo / Louisiana women. (re-iss.Apr76 on 'Island'; ISA 5002) (re-iss.Aug83 on 'Mercury' lp/c; PRICE/PRIMC 26) (cd-iss.May90 on 'Mercury'; 810 314-2)

May 73.	(7")	<7332> **GOING DOWN. / LOISIANA WOMEN**	-	-
Jun 74.	(7")	(AMS 7018) **CAJUN MOON. / STARBOUND**	-	-
Jun 74.	(lp)	(AMLS 68261) <2107> **OKIE**	-	-

– Crying / I'll be there (if you ever want me) / Everlovin' woman / Cajun moon / I'd like to love you baby / Starbound / Rock and roll records / The old man and me / Everlovin' woman / Cajun moon / I'd like to love you baby / Anyway the wind blows / Precious memories / Okie / I got the same old blues. (re-iss.Apr76 on 'Island'; ISA 5004) (re-iss.Aug83 on 'Mercury' lp/c; PRICE/PRIMC 34) (cd-iss. May90 on 'Mercury'; 842 102-2)

Aug 74.	(7")	<40290> **I'LL BE THERE (IF YOU EVER WANT ME). / PRECIOUS MEMORIES**	-	-
Mar 75.	(7")	<40366> **I GOT THE SAME OLD BLUES. / ROCK AND ROLL RECORDS**	-	-

			Island	Shelter
Sep 76.	(lp)	(ISA 5011) <52002> **TROUBADOUR**	53	84

– Hey baby / Travelin' light / You got something / Ride me high / Hold on / Cocaine / I'm a gypsy man / The woman that got away / Super blue / Let me do it to you / Cherry / You got me on so bad. (re-iss.Aug83 on 'Mercury' lp/c; PRICE/PRIMC 35) (cd-iss.Oct83 on 'Mercury'; 800 001-2)

Oct 76.	(7")	(WIP 6339) **HEY BABY. / MAGNOLIA**	-	-
Dec 76.	(7")	<62002> **HEY BABY. / COCAINE**	-	96
Jan 77.	(7")	(WIP 6366) **TRAVELIN' LIGHT. / COCAINE**	-	-
Feb 78.	(7")	(WIP 6434) **I'M A GYPSY MAN. / CHERRY**	-	-

			Island	M.C.A.
Jun 79.	(7")	(WIP 6479) **KATY KOOL LADY. / JUAREZ BLUES**	-	
Jul 79.	(lp)	(ISA 5018) <3163> **5**	40	

– Thirteen days / Boilin' point / I'll make love to you anytime / Don't cry sister / Too much for me / A sensitive kind / Friday / Lou-Easy-Ann / Let's go to Tahiti / Katy kool lady / Fate of a fool / Mona. (with free 7"; JJ-1) – KATY

KOOL LADY. / JUAN AND MARIA JUAREZ BLUES (re-iss.May90; 810 313-2)

Aug 79.	(7")	(WIP 6521) **KATY KOOL LADY. / JUAN AND MARIA JUAREZ BLUES**		
Feb 81.	(lp)	(ISA 5021) <5158> **SHADES**	44	

– Carry on / Deep dark dungeon / Wish I had not said that / Pack my jack / If you leave her / Mama don't / Runaround / What do you expect / Love has been gone / Cloudy day. (cd-iss.Oct83 on 'Mercury'; 800 105-2) (re-iss.May84 on 'Mercury' lp/c; PRICE/PRIMC 65)

Feb 81.	(7")	<51095> **CARRY ON. / DEEP DARK DUNGEON**	-	-
Mar 81.	(7")	(WIP 6696) **CARRY ON. / CLOUDY DAY**	-	-
May 81.	(7")	(WIP 6697) **MAMA DON'T. / WHAT DO YOU EXPECT**	-	-

			Island	Mercury
Jan 82.	(7")	<76145> **DEVIL IN DISGUISE. / DRIFTER'S WIFE**	36	-
Mar 82.	(lp/c)	(ISA 5022) <SRM1 4038> **GRASSHOPPER**	36	

– City girls / Devil in disguise / One step ahead of the blues / You keep me hangin' on / Downtown L.A. / Can't live here / Grasshopper / Drifters wife / Don't wait / A thing going on / Nobody but you / Mississippi river / Does your mama like to reggae / Dr.Jive. (cd-iss. Oct83 on 'Mercury'; 800 038-2) (re-iss.Nov84 on 'Mercury' lp/c; PRICE/PRIMC 74)

			Mercury	Mercury
Mar 82.	(7")	(WIP 6775) **CITY GIRLS. / ONE STEP AHEAD OF THE BLUES**	-	-
Sep 83.	(lp/c)	(MERL/+C 22) <811 152> **#8**	47	

– Money talks / Losers / Hard times / Reality / Takin' care of business / People lie / Unemployment / Trouble in the city / Teardrops in my tequila / Livin' here too. (cd-iss. 1984; 811 152-2)

Sep 83.	(7")	(MER 146) **TEARDROPS IN MY TEQUILA. / AFTER MIDNIGHT**	-	-
	(12"+=)	(MERX 146) – Cocaine.		
Jun 84.	(lp/c)	(814 401-1/-4) **LA FEMME DE MON POTE**	-	- French

– Bringing it back / City girls / Mons (5) / Right down here / The woman that got away / Ride me high / Starbound (okie) / You keep me hangin' on / Super blue / Magnolia. (above album was Soundtrack to French film MY BEST FRIEND'S GIRL)

— CALE retired from music business, writing only score for German film 50/50 around mid-1986. Below album took 5 years to record using backing band TIM DRUMMOND + DOUG BELL – bass / JIM KARSTEIN – drums, percussion / JIM KELTNER – drums, percussion, organ / CHRISTINE LAKELAND – guitar, organ, vocals / SPOONER OLDHAM – keyboards / JAY MITTHAUER – drums guests on * HOYT AXTON + JAMES BURTON

			Silvertone	Silvertone
Oct 89.	(7")	(ORE 12) **SHANGHAID. / ARTIFICIAL PARADISE**	-	-
	(cd-s+=)	(ORE 12CD) – Hang ups.		
Oct 89.	(lp/c/cd)	(ORE LP/C/CD 507) <1306> **TRAVEL-LOG**	-	Mar90

– Shanghaid / Hold on baby / No time / Lady luck / Disadvantage / Lean on me / End of the line / New Orleans / Tijuana / That kind of thing / Who's talking / Change your mind / Humdinger / River boat song. (re-iss.Apr94 cd/c; same)

Aug 92.	(lp/c/cd)	(ORE/+C/CD 523) **NUMBER 10**	58	

– Lonesome train / Digital blues / Feeling in love / Artificial paradise / Passion / Take out some insurance / Jailer / Low rider / Traces / She's in love / Shady grove / Roll on mama. (re-iss.Apr95 cd/c; same))

Aug 92.	(7")	**LONESOME TRAIN. / LOW RIDER**		
	(cd-s+=)	– Passion.		

— During this period, he produced JOHN PAUL HAMMOND's albums 'Got Love If You Want It' and 'Trouble No More'.

			Virgin	Virgin
Jun 94.	(cd/c)	(CDV/TCV 2746) **CLOSER TO YOU**		

– Long way home / Sho-biz blues / Slower baby / Devil's nurse / Like you used to / Borrowed time / Rose in the garden / Brown dirt / Hard love / Ain't love funny / Closer to you / Steve's song.

Apr 96.	(cd)	(CDVIR 48) **GUITAR MAN**		

– Death in the wilderness / It's hard to tell / Days go by / Low down / This town / Guitar man / If I had a rocket / Perfect woman / Old Blue / The doctor told me / Miss of St. Louie / Nobody knows.

– compilations, etc. –

May 77.	(7")	Island; (WIP 6393) **AFTER MIDNIGHT. / BRINGING IT BACK**		-
Jun 84.	(lp/c)(cd)	Mercury; (MERL/+C 42)(818 633-2) **SPECIAL EDITION**		-

– Cocaine / Don't wait / Magnolia / Devil in disguise / A sensitive kind / Carry on / After midnight / Money talks / Call me the breeze / Lies / City girls / Cajun Moon / Don't cry sister / Crazy mama.

May 88.	(d-lp)	Mercury; (830 179-1) **NATURALLY / OKIE**		-
Jul 88.	(lp/c)	Knight; (KNLP/KNMC 10006) **NIGHTRIDING**		-
Jun 97.	(d-cd)	Mercury; (532901-2) **WHEN THE WIND BLOWS (THE ANTHOLOGY)**		

John CALE

Born: 9 Mar'42, Cwmamman, Garnant, Wales. He studied classical piano and later viola at London's Guildhall School Of Music. As an 8 year old schoolboy prodigy, he'd already composed music for the BBC. In 1963, he moved to New York on a scholarship, and under JOHN CAGE and LaMONTE YOUNG's tuition, he experimented with avant-garde music. In 1965, he met LOU REED, and formed the legendary VELVET UNDERGROUND, CALE's wailing viola and white noise experimentation meshing with REED's pop sensibilities and dark lyrics to create their distinctive sound. After being fired by the band in 1968, he went solo, releasing a couple of albums for 'Columbia'. His debut in 1970 'VINTAGE VIOLENCE', saw him exhibiting a more traditional side to his enigmatic persona, with gentle folky songs. A collaboration entitled 'CHURCH OF ANTHRAX', with minimalist composer TERRY RILEY, followed in 1971. CALE continued the trend towards his roots with 'ACADEMY OF PERIL', before returning once more to the songwriter format of his first album. With LITTLE FEAT members LOWELL GEORGE and RICHIE HAYWARD among his backing band, he cut the classic 'PARIS 1919', which infused his melancholic songwriting with a disturbing unease. This was the template for much of CALE's 70's output with 1974's 'FEAR' also introducing a more aggressive element. 'HELEN OF TROY' (1975), featured a version of 'HEARTBREAK HOTEL' guaranteed to send a shiver up anyone's spine, although the album was generally disappointing overall. In 1976, he cemented his reputation by producing the legendary PATTI SMITH album, 'HORSES', having previously worked on the classic blast of primal noise that was THE STOOGES first album. His career went into a bit of a slump in the latter half of the 70's, and after an infamous incident in which he allegedly beheaded a chicken onstage (!), he had a brief dalliance with the New York punk scene. He regained his footing with 1982's 'MUSIC FOR A NEW SOCIETY', an intelligent, minimalistic affair. The mid-80's saw him sign to British label 'Beggars Banquet', and release the more mainstream 'ARTIFICIAL INTELLIGENCE'. 'WORDS FOR THE DYING', released in 1989, was a return to the classical field which included a collaboration with BRIAN ENO. They also teamed up on the sparse 'WRONG WAY UP' from 1990. 'SONGS FOR DRELLA' (a tribute to mentor ANDY WARHOL), saw CALE hook up once more with his old sparring partner LOU REED, together producing an album that outshone CALE's more recent solo outings. He and REED re-united with the others in VELVET UNDERGROUND for live work which resulted in the comeback album 'LIVE MCMXCIII'. A year later, another collaboration, this time with BOB NEUWIRTH, was largely ignored by the public. Throughout his career, he also sessioned for others, including ENO, and produced MODERN LOVERS (JONATHAN RICHMAN), SQUEEZE, etc. • **Style:** Described initially as 'Baroque'n'roll', he drifted back into avant-garde. As an 'Island' artist, he shifted into more accessible rock forms, becoming one of the genre's most gifted and influential artists. His vocal monotone drew comparisons with stablemate like NICK DRAKE or even KEVIN AYERS.

Album rating: VINTAGE VIOLENCE (*5) / CHURCH OF ANTHRAX with Terry Riley (*5) / THE ACADEMY IN PERIL (*5) / PARIS 1919 (*8) / FEAR (*7) / SLOW DAZZLE (*6) / HELEN OF TROY (*5) / GUTS compilation (*7) / SABOTAGE – LIVE (*4) / HONI SOIT (*4) / MUSIC FOR A NEW SOCIETY (*6) / CARIBBEAN SUNSET (*4) / COMES ALIVE (*4) / ARTIFICIAL INTELLIGENCE (*5) / WORDS FOR THE DYING (*6) / SONGS FOR DRELLA with Lou Reed (*7) / WRONG WAY UP with Eno (*7) / EVEN COWGIRLS GET THE BLUES live compilation (*5) / FRAGMENTS OF A RAINY SEASON (*7) / LAST DAYS ON EARTH with Bob Neuwirth (*5) / SEDUCING DOWN THE DOOR a collection (*7) / PARIS S'EVEILLE . . . (*5) / 23 SOLO PIECES FOR LA NAISSANCE DE L'AMOUR (*5) / THE ISLAND YEARS compilation (*7) / WALKING ON LOCUSTS (*4) / EAT/KISS: MUSIC FOR THE FILMS OF ANDY WARHOL (*5)

JOHN CALE – vocals, viola, keyboards, bass, guitar (with session people)

			C.B.S.	Columbia
Nov 70.	(7") <45154> **FAIRWEATHER FRIEND. / CLEO**		-	
Dec 70.	(lp) (64256) <CS 1037> **VINTAGE VIOLENCE**			

– Hello there / Gideon's bible / Adelaide / Big white cloud / Cleo / Please / Charlemagne / Bring it on up / Amsterdam / Ghost story / Fairweather friend. *(re-iss. May87 on 'Edsel' lp/cd; ED/+CD 230) (cd-iss. Sep94 on 'Columbia'; 477356-2)*

| Jan 71. | (7") <45266> **GIDEON'S BIBLE. / BIG WHITE CLOUD** | | - | |
| Apr 71. | (lp; JOHN CALE & TERRY RILEY) (64259) <CS 30131> **CHURCH OF ANTHRAX** | | | |

– Church of anthrax / The hall of mirrors in the palace at Versailles / The soul of Patrick Lee / Ides of March / The protege. *(cd-iss. Oct93 on 'Sony Europe';) (cd re-iss. Mar96 on 'Columbia'; 476640-2)*

			Reprise	Reprise
Apr 72.	(lp) (K 44212) <MS 2079> **ACADEMY IN PERIL**			

– The philosopher / Brahms / Legs Larry at Television Centre / Academy in peril / Intro: days of steam / 3 orchestral pieces: (a) Faust, (b) The balance, (c) Capt. Morgan's lament / King Harry / John Milton. *(re-iss. Apr86 on 'Edsel'; XED 182) (cd-iss. Apr89; EDCD 182) (cd-iss. Oct93 on 'Warners'; 7599 26930-2)*

| May 72. | (7") <1108> **DAYS OF STEAM. / LEGS LARRY AT TELEVISION CENTER** | | | |
| Mar 73. | (lp) (K 44239) <MS 2131> **PARIS 1919** | | | |

– Child's Christmas in Wales / Hanky panky nohow / The endless plain of fortune / Andalucia / Macbeth / Paris 1919 / Graham Greene / Half past France / Antartica starts here. *(cd-iss. Oct93 on 'Warners'; 7599 25926-2)*

—   Around this time he contributed to album 'JUNE 1st, 1974' on 'Island' with others ENO, NICO, KEVIN AYERS. *(ILPS 9291)*

—   now with **ENO** – synth / **PHIL MANZANERA** – guitar / **ARCHIE LEGGAT** – bass / **FRED SMITH** – drums guest on below 'A'side **JUDY NYLON** – vocals

			Island	A&M
Jul 74.	(7") (WIP 6202) **THE MAN WHO COULDN'T AFFORD TO ORGY. / SYLVIA SAID**			-
Sep 74.	(lp) (ILPS 9301) **FEAR**			

– Fear is a man's best friend / Buffalo ballet / Barracuda / Emily / Ship of fools / Gun / The man who couldn't afford to orgy / You know more than I know / Momamma scuba. *(re-iss. Aug91 cd)(c; IMCD 140)(ICM 9301)*

—   with **CHRIS SPEDDING + PHIL MANZANERA** – guitar / **PAT DONALDSON** – bass / **TIMI DONALD + GERRY CONWAY** – drums / **ENO** – synthesizer / **CHRIS THOMAS** – violin, electric piano

| Apr 75. | (lp) (ILPS 9317) **SLOW DAZZLE** | | | |

– Mr. Wilson / Taking it all away / Dirty ass rock'n'roll / Darling I need you / Rollaroll / Heartbreak hotel / Ski patrol / I'm not the loving kind / Guts / The jeweller. *(re-iss. Jun88; CID 9317) (re-iss Aug94; IMCD 202)*

—   **PHIL COLLINS** – drums repl. CONWAY, MANZANERA + THOMAS.

| Nov 75. | (lp) (ILPS 9350) **HELEN OF TROY** | | | |

– My Maria / Helen of Troy / China sea / Engine / Save us / Cable Hogue / I keep a close watch / Pablo Picasso / Leaving it up to you * / Baby what you wanna do? / Sudden death. *(some copies repl.* by) – Coral Moon'. (cd-iss. Apr94; IMCD 177)*

| Feb 77. | (lp) (ILPS 9459) **GUTS** (compilation) | | | |

– Guts / Mary Lou / Helen of Troy / Pablo Picasso / Leaving it up to you / Fear is a man's best friend / Gun / Dirty ass rock 'n' roll / Heartbreak hotel. *(cd-iss. Aug94; IMCD 203)*

—   with **RITCHIE FLIEGLER** – lead guitar / **BRUCE BRODY** – mogg synthesizer / **JIMMY BAIN** – bass / **KEVIN CURRIE** – drums

			Illegal	not iss.
Sep 77.	(7"ep) (ILL 003) **ANIMAL JUSTICE**			

– Chicken shit / Memphis / Hedda Gabbler.

—   with **MARK AARON** – guitar / **JOE BIDWELL** – keyboards / **GEORGE SCOTT** – bass / **DOUG BROWN** – drums / **DEERFRANCE** – vocals

			not iss.	Spy
Dec 79.	(lp) <SP 004> **SABOTAGE (live)**		-	

– Mercenaries (ready for war) / Baby you know / Evidence / Dr.Mudd / Walkin' the dog / Captain Hook / Only time will tell / Sabotage / Chorale.

			not iss.	I.R.S.
1980.	(7") <9008> **MERCENARIES (READY FOR WAR). / ROSEGARDEN FUNERAL OF SORES**		-	

—   with **STURGIS NIKIDES** – guitar, vocals / **JIM GOODWIN** – keyboards, synth. / **PETER MUNY** – bass / **ROBERT MEDECI** – drums

			A&M	A&M
Mar 81.	(lp) (AMLH 64849) **HONI SOIT**			

– Dead or alive / Strange times in Casablanca / Fighter pilot / Wilson Joliet / Streets of Laredo / Honi soit (la premiere Lecon de Francaise) / Riverbank / Russian roulette / Magic & lies. *(cd-iss. Jul94; CDMID 1936)*

| Apr 81. | (7") (AMS 8130) **DEAD OR ALIVE. / HONI SOIT** | | | |

—   now w/ **ALAN LANIER** – keyboards / **D. J. YOUNG** – guitar / **DAVID LICHTENSTEIN** – drums / **JOHN WONDERLING / MIKE McCLINTOCK / ROBERT ELK**

			Ze-Island	Ze
Aug 82.	(lp/c) (ILPS/ICT 7019) **MUSIC FOR A NEW SOCIETY**			

– Taking your life in your hands / Thoughtless kind / Sanities / If you were still around / Close watch / Mama's song / Broken bird / Chinese envoy / Changes made / Damn life / Rise, Sam and Rimsky Korsakov. *(cd-iss. Mar94 on 'Yellow Moon'; YMCD 003)*

| Apr 83. | (7") (IS 113) **I KEEP A CLOSE WATCH. / CLOSE WATCH (instrumental)** | | | |

—   **ANDY HEERMANS** – bass, vocals repl. LANIER

| Jun 83. | (lp/c) (ILPS/ICT 7024) **CARIBBEAN SUNSET** | | | |

– Hungry for love / Experiment number 1 / Model Beirut recital / Caribbean sunset / Praetorian underground / Magazines / Where there's a will / The hunt / Villa Albani.

| Aug 84. | (7") (IS 197) **OOH LA LA. / MAGAZINES** | | | |
| Sep 84. | (lp/c) (ILPS/ICT 7026) **JOHN CALE COMES ALIVE (live)** | | | |

– Ooh la la / Evidence / Dead or alive / Chinese envoy / Leaving it up to you / Dr. Mudd / Waiting for the man / Heartbreak hotel / Fear / Never give up on you.

—   with **DAVID YOUNG** – guitar / **JAMES YOUNG** – keyboards / **GRAHAM DOWDALL** – percussion

			Beggars Banquet	Warners
Jul 85.	(7"/12") (BEG 145/+T) **DYING ON THE VINE. / EVERYTIME THE DOGS BARK**			-
Nov 85.	(lp/c) (BEG A/C 68) **ARTIFICIAL INTELLIGENCE**			

– Everytime the dogs bark / Dying on the vine / The sleeper / Vigilante lover / Chinese takeaway (Hong Kong 1997) (medley) / Song of the valley / Fade away tomorrow / Black rose / Satellite walk. *(re-iss. Jan89 on 'Lowdown-Beggars Banquet' lp/c; BBL/+C 68) (cd-iss. Mar96; BBL 68CD)*

| Nov 85. | (12"m) (BEG 153T) **SATELLITE WALK. / DYING ON THE VINE / CRASH COURSE IN HARMONICS** | | | |

—   now w/ **BRIAN ENO** – synthesizers, keyboards / **NEIL CATCHPOLE** – viola, violin / choir

			Land	Warners
Oct 89.	(lp/c/cd) (LAND/+C/CD 009) **WORDS FOR THE DYING**			

– The Falkland suite:- Introduction-There was a saviour – Interlude 1 / On a wedding anniversary – Interlude II – Lie still, sleep becalmed – Do not go gentle into that good night / Songs without words 1 & 2 / The soul of Carmen Miranda. *(re-iss. cd Oct95 & Aug99 on 'All Saints'; ASCD 009)*

—   Apr'90, CALE & Lou REED⇒, collaborated on Andy Warhol tribute album SONGS FOR DRELLA. On 'Warners' records lp/c//cdWX 345/+C //7599 26140-2. It was CALE's first excursion into the Top 30.

—   Oct'90, he teamed up with ENO (see –), on album 'WRONG WAY UP' on 'Land' and a single 'ONE WORD'.

			Delabel	not iss.
Nov 91.	(cd) **PARIS S'EVEILLE, SUIVI D'AUTRES COMPOSITIONS**		-	- France

– Paris s'eveille, suivi d'autres / Sanctus (four etudes for electronic orchestra) / Animals at night / The cowboy laughs at round-up / Primary motive 1) Factory speech, 2) Strategy session, 3) Closing titles / Antartica starts here / Booker T. (by VELVET UNDERGROUND) *(UK-iss.Mar93 on 'Crepuscule';) (re-iss. Nov95 on 'Yellow Moon'; YMCD 007)*

			Crepuscule	not iss.
Nov 93.	(cd) (TWI 9542) **23 SOLO PIECES FOR LA NAISSANCE DE L'AMOUR**			-

– La naissance de l'amour / If you love me no more / And if I love you still / Judith / Converging themes / Opposites attract / I will do it, I will keep it / Keep it to yourself / Walk towards the sea / Unquiet heart / Waking up to love / Mysterious relief / Never been so hapy / Beyond expectations / Conversations in the garden / La naissance de l'amour II / Secret dialogue / Roma / On the dark side / La naissance de l'amour III / Eye to eye / Maria's car crash and hotel rooms / La naissance de l'amour IV. *(re-iss. Nov95 on 'Yellow Moon'; YMCD 007)*

			M.C.A.	M.C.A.
May 94.	(cd; JOHN CALE / BOB NEUWIRTH) **LAST DAY ON EARTH (Soundtrack)**			

– Overture- a) A tourist, b) A contract, c) A prisoner / Cafe Shabu / Pastoral angst / Who's in charge? / Short of time / Angel of death / Paradise Nevada / Old China / Ocean life / Instrumental / Modern world / Streets come alive / Secrets / Maps of the world / Broken hearts / The high and the mighty road.

				Hannibal	Hannibal

Sep 96. (cd) (<HNCD 1395>) **WALKING ON LOCUSTS**
– Dancing undercover / Set me free / So what / Crazy Egypt / So much for love / Tell me why / Indistinct notion of cool / Secret corrida / Circus / Gatorville and points east / Some friends / Entre nous.

Jun 97. (cd) (<HNCD 1407>) **EAT / KISS – MUSIC FOR THE FILMS OF ANDY WARHOL**
– KISS:- Infinite guitar, quartet / Frozen warning, Jimmy, metal-violin solo – Daid Tiye (backing vocal) / B.J., quartet, Moe / Violin solo – Todd, Tiye, quartet / Harpsichord, infinite guitar / Quartet, Moe – Harpsichord, Tiye – percussion / Quartet, cello solo – Dawn, harpsichord / B.J., quartet, electric piano / B.J., quartet, electric piano / Quartet solo / Solo Tiye, strings // EAT:- B.J., 12-string guitar intro – David / Reading from 'Melanethon' (Swedenborg) / Todd solo, 12-string, Moe / Piano, B.J.

				Erato	Erato

Nov 98. (cd) (<3984 22122-2>) **NICO**
– intro / New York underground / Night club theme / Modelling / Out of China / Death camp / Ari sleepy / Iceberg / Jim / Iceberg / Espana / Nibelungen.

– compilations, etc. –

Jul 91. (c) Danceteria; (DANCD 113) **EVEN COWBOYS GET THE BLUES** (live 1978-79 at CBGB's)
(cd-iss. Jun97; same)

Oct 92. (cd) Hannibal; (HNCD 1372) **FRAGMENTS OF A RAINY SEASON** (live)

Oct 92. (cd) Traditional Line; (TL 001326) **BROKEN HEARTS LIVE 1984-1992** (live)

Jul 94. (d-cd) Rhino; **SEDUCING DOWN THE DOOR: A JOHN CALE COLLECTION**

Sep 96. (d-cd) Island; (524235-2) **THE ISLAND YEARS ANTHOLOGY**

Feb 99. (cd) Island; (IMCD 259) **CLOSE WATCH (AN INTRODUCTION TO JOHN CALE)**
– Paris 1919 / Mr. Wilson / Leaving it up to you / Dying on the vine / Guts / Heartbreak hotel / Ship of fools / Cable hogue / Gun / Riverbank / Child's Christmas in Wales / Fear is a man's best friend / If you were still around / Wilson Joilet / I keep a close watch.

Randy CALIFORNIA (see under ⇒ SPIRIT)

Terry CALLIER

Born: 24 May '45, Chicago, Illinois, USA. A vocalist of astonishing gifts, CALLIER initially emerged on the US troubadour scene of the mid-60's (although one 'Chess' single, 'LOOK AT ME NOW' appeared in '63) with the belated 1968 release of 'THE NEW FOLK SOUND OF TERRY CALLIER'. Over the years, the sound in question has been variously described as soul-folk, folk-jazz, soul-jazz, hell, even operatic-soul! While a lazy comparison could be made with fellow Afro-American songsmith, RICHIE HAVENS, CALLIER remains an oddity, until very recently a criminally overlooked oddity at that. While the man achieved a nominal amount of fame via the apocalyptic rumblings of his debut set, subsequent early 70's releases languished in obscurity despite moments of stellar inspiration. If CALLIER had a theme tune, it'd surely be 'ORDINARY JOE', ironically the most charismatic slice of sun-kissed, blue-eyed soul this side of STEVIE WONDER. A highlight of 1972's 'OCCASIONAL RAIN' album alongside the downcast beauty of 'GOLDEN CIRCLE', it remains a mystery as to why these songs failed to capture the imagination of the record buying public first time round. No doubt part of the problem was marketing, there really is no classification for the likes of 'YOU GOIN' MISS YOUR CANDYMAN' (from 1973's 'WHAT COLOR IS LOVE'), the kind of sparse, foreboding harangue in which CALLIER really comes into his own. After a further extended break, the ochre-voiced singer returned for another ill-fated crack at success, this time signed to 'Elektra'. The albums 'FIRE ON ICE' (1978) and 'TURN YOU TO LOVE' (1979) signalled the end of CALLIER's recording career, his small but loyal band of fans left with a relatively slim legacy as he turned his hand to computer programming (no kidding!) for most of the next 15 years. Perhaps this was a blessing in disguise, given the amount of musical abortions churned out in the 80's; whatever, CALLIER was eventually rehabilitated from being the sole preserve of chin-stroking jazz buffs/soul weekender types after a collaboration with nu-folk chanteuse BETH ORTON. Released in late '97, 'THE BEST BIT' EP featured goose-bump duets on a cover of Tim Buckley's 'DOLPHINS' and a revamped 'LEAN ON ME' (a track originally recorded for 'OCCASIONAL RAIN'), its success encouraging CALLIER to plough ahead with a whole new album of original material for the 'Talking Loud' label. The result was 'TIMEPEACE', one of '98's warmest, most stress-defying and altogether most satisfyingly contented albums, the sound of a man who quietly knew all along that his talent was too strong to be kept down indefinitely. CALLIER's rich, sage tones against BETH ORTON's girlish folkiness may not be everyone's cup of tea, but their double act was arguably one of the highlights of the man's long overdue '98 tour, an event that was almost akin to the second coming among his more enthusiastic fans.

Album rating (selective): THE NEW FOLK SOUND OF TERRY CALLIER (*7) / OCCASIONAL RAIN (*7) / ESSENTIAL (THE VERY BEST OF TERRY CALLIER) compilation (*8) / TIMEPEACE (*7)

TERRY CALLIER – vocals, guitar (with various session people)

				not iss.	Chess
1963.	(7") **LOOK AT ME NOW.** /			-	

				not iss.	Prestige

1968. (lp) <PR 7383> **THE NEW FOLK SOUND OF TERRY CALLIER**
– 900 miles / Oh dear, what can the matter be / Johnny be gay if you can / Cotton eyed Joe / It's about time / Promenade in green / Spin spin spin / I'm a drifter. (UK-iss.Nov95 & Mar98 on 'Beat Goes Public' cd/lp; CD+/BGPM 1101)

				not iss.	Cadet

1968. (7") <5623> **LOOK AT ME NOW. / YOU GOIN' MISS YOUR CANDY MAN**

1972. (lp) <CA 50007> **OCCASIONAL RAIN**
– Segue #1 – Go ahead on / Ordinary Joe / Golden circle / Segue #5 – Go head on / Trance on Sedgewick Street / Do you finally need a friend / Segue #4 – Go head on / Sweet Edie-D / Occasional rain / Segue #2 – Go head on / Blues for Marcus / Lean on me / Last segue – Go head on. <(cd-iss. Jun98 on 'Universal'; UMD 80512)> (cd re-iss. Oct99 on 'Universal'; 380512-2)

1972. (7") <5692> **ORDINARY JOE. / GOLDEN CIRCLE OF YOUR LOVE**

1973. (lp) <CA 50019> **WHAT COLOR IS LOVE**
– Dancing girl / What color is love / You goin' miss your candyman / Just as long as we're in love / Ho tsing mee (a song of the sun) / I'd rather be with you / You don't care. <(cd-iss. Jun98 on 'Universal'; UMD 80510)> (cd re-iss. Oct99 on 'Universal'; 380510-2)

1973. (7") <5697> **I JUST CAN'T HELP MYSELF (I DON'T WANT NOBODY ELSE). / GOTTA GET CLOSER TO YOU**

1973. (lp) <CA 50041> **I JUST CAN'T HELP MYSELF**
– (I just can't help myself) I don't want nobody else / Brown-eyed lady / Gotta get closer to you / Satin doll / Until tomorrow / Alley-wind song / Can't catch the trane / Bowlin' green. <(cd-iss. Jun98 on 'Universal'; UMD 80511)> (cd re-iss. Oct99 on 'Universal'; 380511-2)

				Elektra	Elektra

Aug 78. (lp) <K 52096> <6E-143> **FIRE ON ICE**
– Be a believer / Holdin' on to your love / Street fever / I been doin' alright / Butterfly / Disco in the sky / African violet / Love to love / Martin St. Martin.

Oct 78. (7") <45527> **STREET FEVER. / BUTTERFLY**

Jul 79. (7") <K 12372> <46054> **SIGN OF THE TIMES. / OCCASIONAL RAIN**

Nov 79. (lp) <K 52140> <6E-189> **TURN YOU TO LOVE**
– Sign of the times / Pyramids of love / Turn you to love / Do it again / Ordinary Joe / Occasional rain / Still water / You and me / Mother's love. (re-iss. May85; same)

				not iss.	Erect

1982. (12") <ERD 1214> **I DON'T WANT TO SEE MYSELF (WITHOUT YOU). / IF I COULD MAKE YOU (CHANGE YOUR MIND)**
(UK-iss.Jul90 on 'Acid Jazz'; JAZID 27T)

—— In 1997, TERRY was involved with two collaborations, 'Religion & Politics' with URBAN SPECIES and 'Best Bit' EP with BETH ORTON.

				Talkin' Loud	unknown

Feb 98. (cd/lp) (539 249-2/-1) **TIMEPEACE**
– Lazarus man / Keep your heart right / Java sparrow / People get ready / Brotherly love / Love theme from Spartacus / No more blues / Timepeace / Following your footprints / C'est la vie / Coyote moon / Aka New York Al / Traitor to the race. (cd re-iss. Oct99; same)

May 98. (cd-s) (TLCD 32) **LOVE THEME FROM SPARTACUS / KEEP YOUR HEART RIGHT / AFRICAN VIOLET (live) / WHAT COLOR IS LOVE? (live)** | 57 | |
(12"/cd-s) (TLX/TLDD 32) – ('A'side) / ('A'-Zero 7 mix) / ('A'-4 Hero mix) / Roy Stepper's delight / ('A'-Aqua mental mix).

Oct 99. (7") (LOUD 7) **HOLDIN' ON. / WHEN THE LADY DANCED**

Nov 99. (2x12"/cd-ep) (TL X/CD 52) **I DON'T WANT TO SEE MYSELF**

– compilations, etc. –

Apr 94. (cd/d-lp) Charly; (CD+/ARC 514) **THE VERY BEST OF TERRY CALLIER ON CADET**

1996. (cd) Premonition; <PREM 739-2> **T.C. IN D.C.** (live in 1982 with ERIC HOCHBERG & PENN McGEE)

Apr 98. (cd/d-lp) M.C.A.; <(MCD/MCA 11781)> **ESSENTIAL (THE VERY BEST OF TERRY CALLIER)**
– Ordinary Joe / Gotta get closer to you / Lover (where have you gone) / Just as lobg as we're in love / Baby take your time / Occasional rain / Dancing girl / Look at me now / You were just foolin' me / etc. (cd re-iss. Oct99; 11781-2)

Apr 98. (cd) Premonition; (7669 178740-2) **FIRST LIGHT**
– Ordinary Joe / If I could make you mine / Can't catch the train / Golden circle / Lean on me / Gravy waltz / Alley wind song / Naomi / Trick all your time away / Blues for Marcus / 900 miles / Occasional rain.

Robert CALVERT (see under ⇒ HAWKWIND)

CAMEL

Formed: London, England ... 1972 by R&B veteran PETE BARDENS, plus ex-backing band of PHILIP GOODHAND-TAIT; DOUG FERGUSON, ANDY WARD and ANDY LATIMER. Their first recording, 'GOD OF LIGHT REVISITED – PARTS ONE, TWO, THREE', featured on 1 side of a various double album, 'Greasy Truckers – Live At Dingwalls'. The following year, they issued their eponymous debut on 'M.C.A.', before moving to 'Deram' for the follow-up, 'MIRAGE' (1974). CAMEL really came into their own with their conceptual interpretation of Paul Gallico's 'THE SNOW GOOSE'. A Top 30 breakthrough, it was dominated by excellent instrumental pieces which perfectly translated Gallico's children story into a prog-rock framework. However, Gallico served a writ against the group for copyright infringement. Unbowed, CAMEL came up with yet another successful album, 'MOONMADNESS', this time utilising vocals which took them a stage further in their musical development. Another Top 20 album followed in 1977,

'RAIN DANCES', a softer, more conventional affair, as was the 1978 studio follow-up, 'BREATHLESS'. Although they retained a loyal fan-base within the college fraternity, the onset of more hip sounds (i.e. punk & new wave) effectively swept them under the carpet. They disbanded in '84, but re-formed seven years later. Their comeback album, 'DUST AND DREAMS' (1992), was inspired by John Steinbeck's book, 'The Grapes Of Wrath', while CAMEL's (virtually down to friends of LATIMER and COLIN BASS – a member since '79) 1996 effort, 'HARBOUR OF KINGS', was Irish folk inspired.

Album rating: CAMEL (*4) / MIRAGE (*5) / THE SNOW GOOSE (*8) / MOONMADNESS (*6) / RAIN DANCES (*6) / BREATHLESS (*5) / I CAN SEE YOUR HOUSE FROM HERE (*6) / NUDE (*6) / THE SINGLE FACTOR (*4) / STATIONARY TRAVELLER (*5) / PRESSURE POINTS – CAMEL LIVE (*4) / DUST AND DREAMS (*5) / NEVER LET GO (*4) / ECHOES – THE RETROSPECTIVE compilation (*7) / HARBOUR OF TEARS (*4) / COMING OF AGE (*4)

PETER BARDENS – keyboards, vocals (ex-THEM, ex-solo, ex-SHOTGUN EXPRESS) / **ANDY LATIMER** – vocals, guitar / **DOUG FERGUSON** – bass / **ANDY WARD** – drums, percussion

			M.C.A.	not iss.
Nov 72.	(7") *(MU 1177)* **NEVER LET GO. / CURIOSITY**		☐	-
Dec 73.	(lp) *(MUPS 477)* **CAMEL**		☐	-

– Slow yourself down / Mystic queen / Six ate / Separation / Never let go / Curiosity / Arubaluba. *(re-iss. 1974; MCF 2065) (re-iss. Aug81 lp/c; MCL/+C 1601) (re-iss. Nov82 on 'Fame' lp/c; FA/TCFA 3054) (cd-iss. Jul93 on 'Camel Prod.'; CP 002CD)*

			Deram	Janus
1974.	(lp) *(SML 1107) <7009>* **MIRAGE**		☐	☐

– Freefall / Supertwister / Nimrodel: – The procession – The white rider / Earthrise / Lady fantasy: – Encounter – Smiles for you – Lady fantasy. *(cd-iss. Jun89; 820 613-2)*

			Decca	Janus
May 75.	(lp/c) *(SKLR/KSKC 5207) <7016>* **THE SNOW GOOSE**		22	☐

– The great marsh – Rhayader – Rhayader goes to town – Sanctuary – Fritha – The snow goose – Friendship – Migration – Rhayader alone / Flight of the snow goose – Preparation – Dunkirk – Epitaph – Fritha alone – La princesse Perdue – The great marsh. *(re-iss. Nov76; same) (cd-iss. Jul88; 800 080-2)*

May 75.	(7") *(FR 13581)* **FLIGHT OF THE SNOW GOOSE. / RHAYADER**		☐	-
Sep 75.	(7") *(FR 13603)* **THE SNOW GOOSE. / FREEFALL**		☐	-
Apr 76.	(lp/c) *(TXSR/KTXCR 115) <7024>* **MOONMADNESS**		15	☐

– Aristillus / Song within a song / Chord change / Spirit of the water / Another night / Air born / Lunar sea. *(cd-iss. 1983 & Jul89; 810 879-2)*

Jun 76.	(7") *(FR 13656) <262>* **ANOTHER NIGHT. / LUNAR SEA**		☐	-

—— **RICHARD SINCLAIR** – bass (ex-CARAVAN) repl. FERGUSON

Sep 77.	(lp/c) *(TXSR/KTXCR 124) <7035>* **RAIN DANCES**		20	☐

– First light / Metrognome / Tell me / Highways of the sun / Unevensong / One of these days I'll get an early night / Elke / Skylines / Rain dances. *(cd-iss. Dec91 on 'London' += ; 820 725-2)* – Highways of the sun (single edit).

Sep 77.	(7") *(FR 13729)* **HIGHWAYS OF THE SUN. / TELL ME**		☐	-

—— added **MEL COLLINS** – saxophone (ex-KING CRIMSON etc.) / **DAVE SINCLAIR** – keyboards (ex-CARAVAN etc.)

Apr 78.	(d-lp/d-c) *(DBCR/KBC 7-8)* **A LIVE RECORD (live)**		☐	-

– Never let go / Song within a song / Lunar sea / Skylines / Lady fantasy: Encounter– Smiles for you – Lady fantasy / The great marsh – Rhayader – Rhayader goes to town – Sanctuary – Fritha – The snow goose – Friendship – Migration – Rhayader alone / Flight of the snow goose – Preparation – Dunkirk – Epitaph – Fritha alone – La princesse Perdue – The great marsh / Ligging at Louis'.*(re-iss. Jul93 cd/c;)*

			Decca	Arista
Sep 78.	(lp/c) *(TXSR/KTXSR 132) <4206>* **BREATHLESS**		26	☐

– Breathless / Echoes / Wing and a prayer / Down on the farm / Starlight ride / Summer lightning / You make me smile / The sleeper / Rainbow's end. *(re-iss. Aug92 on 'Deram' cd/c; 820 726-2/-4)*

—— **COLIN BASS** – bass, vocals repl. RICHARD who later rejoined CARAVAN / **KIT WATKINS** – keyboards, flute repl. PETER who went solo then LATIMER, WARD

Sep 79.	(lp/c) *(TXSR/KTXSR 137) <4254>* **I CAN SEE YOUR HOUSE FROM HERE**		45	☐

– Wait / Your love is no stronger than mine / Eye of the storm / Who are we / Survival / Hymn to her / Neon magic / Remote romance. *(cd-iss. Jan89 & Oct93 on 'London'; 820 614-2)*

Oct 79.	(7") *(FR 13871)* **YOUR LOVE IS NO STRONGER THAN MINE. / NEON MAGIC**		☐	-
Feb 80.	(7") *(FR 13879)* **REMOTE ROMANCE. / RAINBOW'S END / TELL ME**		☐	-

—— **DUNCAN MACKAY** – keyboards (ex-COCKNEY REBEL) repl. KIT

Jan 81.	(lp/c) *(SKL/KSKC 5323)* **NUDE**		36	-

– City life / Nude / Drafted / Docks / Beached / Landscapes / Changing places / Pomp and circumstance / Please come home / Reflections / Captures / The homecoming / Lies / The last farewell / The birthday cake / Nude's return. *(cd-iss. 1987; 810 880-2)*

—— **JAN SCHELHAAS** – keyboards (ex-CARAVAN) repl. MACKAY who joined BUDGIE

			Decca	Passport
May 82.	(lp/c) *(SKL/KSKC 5328) <PB 6013>* **THE SINGLE FACTOR**		57	☐

– No easy answer / You are the one / Heroes / Selva / Manic / Lullaby / Sasquatch / Camelogue / Today's goodbye / A heart's desire / End piece. *(cd-iss. 1983 & May94; 800 081-2)*

—— **PAUL BURGESS** – drums, percussion repl. WARD (who joined MARILLION)

Mar 84.	(lp/c/cd) *(SKL/KSKC 5334)(820 020-2)* **STATIONARY TRAVELLER**		57	-

– Pressure points / Refugee / Copos / Cloak and dagger man / Stationary traveller / West Berlin / Fingertips / Missing / Afterwords / Long goodbyes. *(cd re-iss. Jul89; same)*

Mar 84.	(7"/12") *(CAMEL/CAMEX 1)* **CLOAK AND DAGGER MAN. / PRESSURE POINTS**		☐	-

—— **LATIMER, BASS + BURGESS** with returning guests **MEL COLLINS & PETER BARDENS** brought in **TOM SCHERPENZEEL** – keyboards / **RICHIE CLOSE** – keyboards + **CHRIS RAINBOW** – vocals, keyboards

Nov 84.	(lp/c)(cd) *(SKL/KSKC 5338)(823 812-2)* **PRESSURE POINTS – CAMEL LIVE (live 11th May'84)**		☐	-

– West Berlin / Pressure points / Drafted / Captured / Lies / Rhayader goes to town / Sasquatch / Fingertips / Rhayader / Wait. *(cd re-iss. 1987 on 'London'; 820 166-2)*

—— CAMEL disbanded in '84 but re-formed again in 1991

			Camel	not iss.
Sep 92.	(cd/c) *(CP 001 CD/C)* **DUST AND DREAMS**		☐	-

– Dust bowl / Go west / Dusted out / Mother road / Needles / Rose of Sharon / End of the line / Storm clouds / Cotton camp / Broken ranks / Sheet rain / Whispers / Little rivers and little Rose / Hopeless anger / Whispers in the rain. *(cd re-iss. Jul93; same)*

Nov 93.	(d-cd) *(CP 004CD)* **NEVER LET GO (live '92)**		☐	-

LATIMER + BASS + MICKEY SIMMONDS – keyboards / **DAVID PATON** – bass, vocals / **MAE McKENNA** – a capella vocal / **JOHN XEPOLEAS** – drums / **NEIL PANTON** – oboe, soprano sax, harmonium / **JOHN BURTON** – french horn / **BARRY PHILLIPS** – cello / **KAREN BENTLEY** – violin / **ANITA STONEHAM** – violin

Jan 96.	(cd) *(CP-006CD)* **HARBOUR OF TEARS**		☐	-

– Irish air / Irish air (instrumental reprise) / Harbour of tears / Cobh / Send home the slates / Under the moon / Watching the bobbins / Generations / Eyes of Ireland / Running from paradise / End of the day / Coming of age / The hour candle (a song for my father).

—— **LATIMER + BASS** recruited **FOSS PATTERSON** – keyboards, vocals / **DAVE STEWART** – drums, percussion, octapad

Apr 98.	(d-cd) *(CP 008CD)* **COMING OF AGE**		☐	-

– Lunar sea / Hymn to her / Rhayader / Rhayader goes to town / Preparation / Dunkirk / Drafted / Docks / Beached / Spirit of the water / Ice / Sasquatch // Milk 'n honey / Mother road / Needles / Rose of Sharon / Irish air / Irish air (reprise) / Harbour of tears / Cobh / Send home the slates / Under the moon / Watching the Bobbins / Eyes of Ireland / Running from Paradise / End of the day / Coming of age / The hour candle.

– compilations etc. –

Sep 81.	(lp/c) *Decca; (SKL/KSKC 5325)* **CHAMELEON**		☐	-
Nov 85.	(d-lp/c/cd) *Castle; (CCS LP/MC/CD 116)* **THE COLLECTION**		☐	-

– Aristilus / Freefall / Supertwister / Spirit of the water / Lunar sea / The white rider / Earthrise / Song within a song / Rhayader – Rhayader goes to town – Migration – Rhayader alone – La princesse Perdue – The great marsh / Drafted / Captured / Sasquatch / Rain dances / Highways of the sun / First light.

May 91.	(cd/c) *Elite;* **LANDSCAPE**		☐	-
Jul 93.	(cd) *Camel Prod.; (CP 003CD)* **CAMEL ON THE ROAD 1972 (live)**		☐	-
Nov 94.	(cd) *Deram; (844 340-2)* **ECHOES**		☐	-
Jan 95.	(cd) *Camel Prod.; (CP 005CD)* **CAMEL ON THE ROAD 1982 (live)**		☐	-
Mar 97.	(cd) *Camel Prod.; (CP 007CD)* **CAMEL ON THE ROAD 1981 (live)**		☐	-

—— In July '94, PETE BARDENS released cd 'BIG SKY' for 'H.T.D.'.

CAMPAG VELOCET

Formed: London, England ... early '93 by Portsmouth-born schoolfriends ARGE (IAN CATER) and PETE VOSS, the latter deemed a misfit, who actually found out later in life that he had an indentation to the brain (apparently due to a boyhood accident in which he fell out of a loft). Having acquired a home at bassist BARNEY SLATER's Kentish Town (London) pad, the trio began marathon rehearsal sessions, only stopping for the occasional bag of mushrooms (magic they weren't!). Having gone through a plethora of drummers, CAMPAG VELOCET finally recruited LASCELLES' LASCELLE GORDON (ex-guitarist with the BRAND NEW HEAVIES, wow!) and supported other local lads, LO FIDELITY ALLSTARS. CV released a couple of singles at the turn of '97, a split affair with the REGULAR FRIES and a highly-rated EP, 'DRENCROM VELOCET SYNTHEMESC'. Akin to HAWKWIND, STEVE HILLAGE and CRISPY AMBULANCE, their hard musical soundscapes of repetitive "Laandaan beat" rhythms were on full course for the 'SAUNTRY SLY CHIC' single in April '98. A whole year later, the CAMPAG's were back in town (so to speak) with a new single, 'TO LOSE LA TREK', although it would be another six months before its parent album would appear. The S&M-obsessed 'BON CHIC BON GENRE' (1999), hit all the right buttons on nearly every track. From the short-sharp-shock of the opening title track to arguably the record's finest modern-day prog-punk piece, 'PIKE IN MY LIFE', the album was a seminal work worthy of the heaps of praise it received.

Album rating: BON CHIC BON GENRE (*8)

PETE VOSS – vocals, percussion / **IAN CATER (aka ARGE)** – guitars, keyboards, programming / **BARNEY SLATER** – bass / **LASCELLES LASCELLE (GORDON)** – drums, percussion, samples (ex-BRAND NEW HEAVIES)

			Fierce Panda	not iss.
Nov 97.	(12"; split with REGULAR FRIES) *(Ning 41)* **split**		☐	-

			Rabid Badger	not iss.
Nov 97.	(12"ep) *(Nang 1)* **DRENCROM VELOCET SYNTHEMESC EP**		☐	-
Apr 98.	(12"ep/cd-ep) *(Nang 3/+CD)* **SAUNTRY SLY CHIC / GAK STACKERS / TV EYE**		☐	-

			Play It Again Sam	not iss.
Mar 99.	(7") *(PIASX 001)* **TO LOSE LA TREK. / POSTPONED NATIVE PLEASURES (part 1)**		☐	-

(12"+=/cd-s+=) *(PIASX 001 T/CD)* – I forget.

Sep 99.	(cd/d-lp) *(PIAS CD/LP 003)* **BON CHIC BON GENRE**		☐	-

– Bon chic bon genre / Only answers delay our time / Cacophonous bubblegum / To lose la trek / Vito Satan / Sauntry sly chic / Drencrom velocet synthemesc / Skin so soft / Pike in my life – Schiaparelli cat / Caught unawares / Harsh shark.

Ali CAMPBELL (see under ⇒ UB40)

CAMPER VAN BEETHOVEN

Formed: Redlands / Santa Cruz, California, USA ... 1983 by DAVE LOWERY and DAVID McDANIELS, who had relocated to college in Santa Cruz. Touted as one of the first real "alternative" acts to come out of America, CAMPER VAN BEETHOVEN were a reaction to the rigid conformity of the all-pervasive Californian hardcore scene, taking it upon themselves to brew up an exotic concoction of avant-folk-pop/cow-punk taking in elements of stone country, reggae, ska and even oompa-jazz. By the release of debut album, 'TELEPHONE FREE LANDSLIDE VICTORY' (1985), the line-up had stabilised around LOWERY, CHRIS MOLLA, VICTOR KRUMMENACHER, GREG LISHER and JONATHAN SEGAL (CHRIS PEDERSON was recruited later), the SEGAL's strident violin flourishes adding the quintessential Eastern European flavour prevalent in much of the band's work. Ranging from the John Peel favourite, 'TAKE THE SKINHEADS BOWLING' to Cossack-style howdowns like 'BALALAIKA GAP' and 'VLADIVOSTOCK' and even an irreverent Black Flag cover, 'WASTED', the record's tongue-in-cheek humour and headlong eclecticism caused a major buzz on the US underground, even prompting R.E.M.'s MICHAEL STIPE to name it as one of his Top 10 albums of the year. A subsequent distribution deal with 'Rough Trade' saw the record gain a UK release, yet both British and US sales weren't as high as expected and the group formed their own 'Pitch-A-Tent' label for the release of follow-up double set, 'CAMPER VAN BEETHOVEN II/III' (1986). The latter included one of their most infamous creations, 'ZZ TOP GOES TO EGYPT' alongside another hardcore makeover, Sonic Youth's 'I LOVE HER ALL THE TIME'. An eponymous third album and further couple of EP's, 'GOOD GUYS, BAD GUYS' and 'VAMPIRE CAN MATING OVEN', kept the band's profile high and a subsequent major label bidding war ended in a move to 'Virgin' in 1988. With the luxuries of a decent sized studio budget behind them, CVB made the record they'd probably always wanted to make in 'OUR REVOLUTIONARY SWEETHEART' (1988). Polishing off the rough edges but retaining the spontaneity, this should've been the record to propel them into the indie mainstream. In the event, crossover success proved out of reach and SEGAL bailed out for a solo career. The cracks were beginning to show on what proved to be the band's swansong set, 'KEY LIME PIE' (1990), a final split occuring later that year as PEDERSON, LISHER and KRUMMENACHER resurrected their MONKS OF DOOM, releasing their third album, 'THE INSECT GOD'; LOWERY eventually formed CRACKER. • **Covers:** PHOTOGRAPH (Ringo Starr) / I'M NOT LIKE EVERYBODY ELSE (Kinks) / INTERSTELLAR OVERDRIVE (Pink Floyd) / PICTURES OF MATCHSTICK MEN (Status Quo). The MONKS OF DOOM covered; WHO ARE THE BRAIN POLICE? (Mothers Of Invention; Frank Zappa) / THE VIVIAN GIRLS (Snakefinger – Residents) / VOODOO VENGEANCE (Eugene Chadbourne).

Album rating: TELEPHONE FREE LANDSCAPE VICTORY (*7) / II & III (*6) / CAMPER VAN BEETHOVEN (*6) / VAMPIRE CAN MATING OVEN mini (*6) / OUR BELOVED REVOLUTIONARY SWEETHEART (*8) / KEY LIME PIE (*7) / CAMPER VANTIQUES compilation (*5) / Monks Of Doom: BREAKFAST ON THE BEACH OF DECEPTION (*7) / THE COSMODEMONIC TELEGRAPH COMPANY (*6) / MERIDIAN (*5) / FORGERY (*5) / Victor Krummenacher: OUT IN THE HEAT (*6) / SAINT JOHN'S MERCY (*5)

DAVID LOWERY (b.10 Sep'60, San Antonio, Texas) – vocals, guitar, drums / **JONATHAN SEGAL** (b. 3 Sep'63, Marseilles, France) – keyboards, violin, mandolin, vocals / **GREG LISHER** (b.29 Nov'63, Santa Cruz) – guitar / **VICTOR KRUMMENACHER** (b. 7 Apr'65, Riverside, Calif.) – bass, vocals / **CHRIS MOLLA** – guitar, vocals, drums

	Rough Trade	Independents
Apr 86. (lp) *(ROUGH 95)* *<IP 016>* **TELEPHONE FREE LANDSCAPE VICTORY**	☐	☐ Oct85

– Border ska / The day that Lassie went to the moon / Wasted / Yanqui go home / Oh no! / The day of disks / Payed vacation: Greece / Where the hell is Bill? / Vladivostock / Skinhead stomp / Tina / Take the skinheads bowling / Mao reminisces about his days / I don't see you / Balalaika gap / Opi rides again – Club Med sucks / Ambiguity song. *<re-iss. 1993 on 'I.R.S.'; X2 13208>*

	not iss.	Pitch A Tent
Jan 86. (d-lp) *<PITCH 1>* **CAMPER VAN BEETHOVEN II/III**	-	☐

– Abundance / Cowboys from Hollywood / Sad lovers waltz / Turtlehead / I love her all the time / No flies on us / Down and out / No krugerrands for David / (Don't you go to) Goleta / 4 year plan / (We're a) Bad trip / Circles / Dustpan / Sometimes / Chain of circumstances / ZZ Top goes to Egypt / Cattle (reversed) / From another stone / No more bullshit / Take the skinheads bowling / Epigram No.2 / Cowboys from Hollywood / At Kuda? / Epigram No.1 / Colonel Enrique Adolfo Bermudas. *(UK/German-iss.Nov87 on 'Full Blast'; FBLP 400320) <cd-iss. 1993 on 'I.R.S.'; 13209>*

——— added **CHRIS PEDERSEN** (b.16 Aug'60, San Diego, Calif.) – drums
below featured **EUGENE CHADBOURNE** – banjo (of SHOCKABILLY)

Dec 86. (lp) *(ROUGH 109)* *<PITCH 2>* **CAMPER VAN BEETHOVEN (THE THIRD LP)**	☐	☐ Aug86

– Good guys, bad guys / Jo Stalin's Cadillac / Five sticks / Lulu land / Une fois / We saw Jerry's daughter / Surprise truck / Stairway to Heaven / The history of Utah / Still wishing to course / We love you / Hoe yourself down / Peace & love / Folly / Interstellar overdrive / Shut us down. *<cd-iss. 1993 on 'I.R.S.'; 13210>*

Mar 87. (7"ep/12"ep) *(RT/+T 161)* **TAKE THE SKINHEADS BOWLING** ☐ ☐
Oct 87. (12"ep) *(RTT 205)* **GOOD GUYS, BAD GUYS EP** ☐ ☐

——— now without MOLLA

Nov 87. (m-lp) *<PITCH 05>* **VAMPIRE CAN MATING OVEN**	-	

– Opi rides again / Club Med sucks / Oh no / Where the hell is Bill? / etc.

——— In Feb 88, they teamed up with EUGENE CHADBOURNE on the lp, 'CAMPER VAN CHADBOURNE', on 'Fundamental' records.

	Virgin	Virgin
May 88. (cd/c/lp) *(CD/TC+/V 2516)* *<90918>* **OUR BELOVED REVOLUTIONARY SWEETHEART**	☐	☐

– Eye of Fatima (pt.1) / Turquoise jewelry / O death / She divines water / Devil song / One of these days / Waka / Change your mind / My path belated / Never go back / Eye of Fatima (pt.2) / Tania / Life is grand / The fool.

Sep 88. (7") *(VS 1122)* **LIFE IS GRAND. / LOVE IS A WEED** ☐ ☐
(12"+=/cd-s+=) *(VS T/CD 1122)* – Harmony in my head / Wade in the water.

——— **MORGAN FICHTER** – violin, vocals; repl. SEGAL who went solo

	Virgin America	Virgin
Jan 90. (cd/c/lp) *(VUS CD/CM/LP 8)* *<91289>* **KEY LIME PIE**	☐	☐ Oct89

– Opening theme / Jack Ruby / Sweethearts / When I win the lottery / (I was born in a) Laundromat / Borderline / The light from a cake / June / All her favourite fruit / Interlude / Flowers / The humid press of days / Pictures of matchstick men / Come on darkness.

Jan 90. (7") *(VUS 8)* **PICTURES OF MATCHSTICK MEN. / JACK RUBY** ☐ ☐
(12"+=) *(VUST 8)* – Closing theme / The humid press of days.

——— disbanded in Spring 1990; LOWERY formed CRACKER.

– compilations, etc. –

Mar 93. (cd,c) *I.R.S.; <13211>* **CAMPER VANTIQUES** (B-sides, rarities, etc) - ☐
Oct 99. (cd) *Knitting Factory; <(KFW 252)>* **USED RECORD PILE** - ☐

MONKS OF DOOM

PEDERSON, LISHER + KRUMMENACHER with also **DAVID IMMERGLUCK** – guitar, vocals, piano (drummer of OPHELIAS)

	not iss.	Pitch A Tent
Dec 87. (lp) *<PITCH 6>* **BREAKFAST ON THE BEACH OF DECEPTION (soundtrack)**	-	☐

– In anticipation of the pope / Blues on Sunday / Facts about spiders / Ukranian technological faith dance / Lappish tea song / B-music / Fall from grace / Save me from myself / Visions from the acid couch / Insana and her manchild / Jim Gore and the ghost of Missouri / The haunting of an eastern man's mind / Eldridge street. *<cd-iss. Mar93 on 'IRS-Capitol'; X2-13213>*

Sep 89. (lp/c/cd) *<PITCH 13/+C/CD>* **THE COSMODEMONIC TELEGRAPH COMPANY**	-	☐

– Vaporize your crystals / The Vivian girls / All in good time / Voodoo vengeance / Taste of tendon / Trapped / The evidence you hide / Unexplained murders / The beach of deception / Broadcast at midday. *<cd re-iss. Mar93 on 'IRS-Capitol'; X2-13214>*

	not iss.	Baited Breath
1991. (cd) *<4>* **MERIDIAN**	-	☐

– Cherry blossom baptism / Riverbed / Turn it on himself / Geode / Door to success / The traveler / Argentine dilemma / The better angels of our nature / Going south / Follow the queen / Hieroglyphic / The harbor incident / Miracle mile / Circassian beauty.

	not iss.	C/Z
Jun 92. (cd-ep) *<CZ 047>* **THE INSECT GOD**	-	☐

– Chang / Let's split / If it didn't kill me / Who are the brain police?

	not iss.	IRS-Capitol
Sep 92. (cd/c) *<X2/X4 13163>* **FORGERY**	-	☐

– Flint Jack / Flow / Tanguedia (for Astor Piazzolla) / Virtual lover / Queen of fortune / Dust / What does a man require? / A.O.A. / Cigarette man / Off on a comet / Tanguedia (reprise) / Chaos is not dead.

VICTOR KRUMMENACHER

——— with **CHRIS XEFOS, GREG LISHER, BRUCE KAPHAN, JOHN NELSON**, etc

	not iss.	Magnetic
1995. (cd; as VICTOR KRUMMENACHER'S GREAT LAUGH) *<0006>* **OUT IN THE HEAT**	☐	☐

– All right / Clean as filth and finesse / Evangelina will sleep No.1 / Water gone to mist / '48 or '47 / Out in the heat / New Mexico / Insomniac / Foot on the pedal (instrumental) / Resurrection plant / Not an inch / Sweet talking Bill / Sister & me / Antebellum / As real as your dreams.

1996. (7") *<007>* **PRINCE OF LIES. / ROBERT** ☐ ☐
1998. (cd) *<0009>* **SAINT JOHN'S MERCY** ☐ ☐

– Tear-stained road / Nothing outside / Now that you're gone / Dreams die hard / No sin to wandering / Tierra o' Muerte / Expanse / Thunderhead / Quest sunset / Raven / Saint John's mercy / Long way home.

CAN

Formed: Cologne, Germany ... 1968 initially as INNER SPACE by HOLGER CZUKAY and IRMIN SCHMIDT. MICHAEL KAROLI and JAKI LEIBEZEIT were soon recruited along with DAVID JOHNSON and black American vocalist MALCOLM MOONEY. Later that year, JOHNSON bailed out prior to their debut album, 'MONSTER MOVIE' (1970). Having studied under KARL-HEINZ STOCKHAUSEN, CZUKAY and SCHMIDT (who were also influenced by JOHN CAGE, TERRY RILEY and The VELVET UNDERGROUND) pioneered their own take on avant-garde minimalism, creating a hypnotic, free-form sound, relentless in its intensity. The album included a 20-minute piece, 'YOU DOO RIGHT', extracted from a marathon improv-session and highlighting the very real dementia of MOONEY's ravings. He suffered a nervous breakdown soon after and was subsequently replaced by the Japanese 'vocalist' DAMO SUZUKI prior to recording 'SOUNDTRACKS'. More improvised beauty was evidenced on their next set, the German Top 40 classic, 'TAGO MAGO' (1971), a sprawling double-set that featured two of their more hypnotic tracks, 'HALLELUWAH' and 'MUSHROOM'. On their next two releases, 'EGE BAMYASI' and 'FUTURE DAYS', CAN explored even more ritualistic textures alongside SUZUKI's partly-spoken tri-lingual ramblings. SUZUKI subsequently returned to Japan to become a Jehovah's Witness, after a final gig at the 1973 Edinburgh Festival. Vocal duties were now shared by KAROLI and SCHMIDT on the more percussive 'SOON OVER BABALUMA' album (1974). They signed to Richard Branson's innovative 'Virgin' label the following year, 'LANDED' being a prime example of British-influenced avant-garde rock. In 1976, they surprised many by having a Top 30 hit, 'I WANT MORE', penned by PINK FLOYD's DAVID GILMOUR. With the addition of ROSKO GEE and sessionman REEBOP KWAKU BAAH, they moved in a more African/reggae influenced direction, CZUKAY having already withdrawn from most of the proceedings. Their final efforts were of little significance, the 1979 album interesting only for its re-hash of Offenbach's 'CAN-CAN', which had previously been released as a single. KAROLI, SCHMIDT and CZUKAY all continued in the 80's as solo artists, the latter teaming up once again with LEIBEZEIT (and JAH WOBBLE) on the 1982 album 'FULL CIRCLE'. The original line-up reformed in 1986 for an album, 'RITE TIME', but the record lacked the inspiration and originality that characterised CAN's earlier work. The band remain highly regarded, cited as a major influence by artists as diverse as CARL CRAIG and PRIMAL SCREAM. Even The FALL payed homage to them by crediting a song as 'I AM DAMO SUZUKI'.

Album rating: MONSTER MOVIE (*7) / SOUNDTRACKS (*6) / TAGO MAGO (*8) / EGE BAMYASI (*7) / FUTURE DAYS (*7) / LIMITED EDITION collection (*6) / SOON OVER BABALUMA (*6) / LANDED (*5) / FLOW MOTION (*5) / UNLIMITED EDITION collection (*5) / SAW DELIGHT (*6) / CANNIBALISM compilation (*7) / OUT OF REACH (*3) / CAN (*4) / DELAY 1968 exploitation (*5) / RITE TIME (*5) / CANNIBALISM II compilation (*6) / CANNIBALISM III compilation (*5) / ANTHOLOGY 1968-1993 compilation (*8) / Holger Czukay: CANAXIS 5 with Rolf Dammers (*7) / MOVIES (*7) / ON THE WAY TO THE PEAK OF NORMAL (*5) / FULL CIRCLE (*5) / DER OSTEN IST ROT (*5) / ROME REMAINS ROME (*7) / RADIO WAVE SURFER (*4) / MOVING PICTURES (*5) / Michael Karoli with Polly Estes: DELUGE (*7) / Jaki Liebezeit: PHANTOM BAND (*5) / FREEDOM OF SPEECH (*5) / NOWHERE (*5) / Irmin Schmidt: FILM MUSIK (*5) / TOY PLANET (*5) / FILM MUSIK VOL.2 (*5) / FILM MUSIK VOL.3 & 4 (*5) / MUSIC AT DUSK (*5) / IMPOSSIBLE HOLIDAYS (*5)

IRMIN SCHMIDT (b.29 May'37, Berlin, Germany) – keyboards / **HOLGER CZUKAY** (b.24 Mar'38, Danzig, Germany) – bass, electronics / **DAVID JOHNSON** – flute / **MICHAEL KAROLI** (b.29 Apr'48, Straubing, Germany) – guitar, violin / **JAKI LEIBEZEIT** (b.26 May'38, nr.Dresden, Germany) – drums / **MALCOLM MOONEY** – vocals

			Music Factory	not iss.	
Nov 68.	(7"; by IRMIN SCHMIDT) **KAMA SUTRA. /**		☐	☐	German

—— Now a quintet when JOHNSON departed (below issued Germany Aug'69)

			U.A.	U.A.	
May 70.	(lp) (UAS 29094) **MONSTER MOVIE**		☐	☐	

– Father cannot yell / Mary, Mary so contrary / You doo right / Outside my door. (cd-iss. Jun89 on 'Spoon-Mute'; SPOONCD 004)

—— **KENJI 'DAMO' SUZUKI** (b.16 Jan'50, Japan) – vocals repl.MOONEY who suffered a nervous breakdown

Sep 70.	Liberty; (7") **SOUL DESERT. / SHE BRINGS THE RAIN**		☐	☐	German
Sep 71.	(lp) (UAS 29283) **SOUNDTRACKS**		☐	☐	

– Deadlock / Tango whiskeyman / Don't turn the light off / Leave me alone / Soul desert / Mother sky / She brings the rain. (cd-iss. Jun89 on 'Spoon-Mute'; SPOONCD 005)

1971.	(7") **TURTLES HAVE SHORT LEGS. / HALLELUWAH (edit)**		☐	☐	German
1971.	(7") **SPOON. / SHIKAKO MARU TEN**		☐	☐	German
Feb 72.	(d-lp) (UAD 60009-10) **TAGO MAGO**		☐	☐	

– Paperhouse / Mushroom / Oh yeah / Halleluwah / Aumgn / Peking O / Bring me coffee or tea. (cd-iss. Jul89 on 'Spoon-Mute'; SPOONCD 006-007)

Nov 72.	(lp) (UAS 29414) <063> **EGE BAMYASI**		☐	☐	

– Pinch / Sing swan song / One more night / Vitamin C / Soup / I'm so green / Spoon. (cd-iss. Jun89 on 'Spoon-Mute'; SPOONCD 008)

Feb 73.	(7") (UP 35506) **SPOON. / I'M SO GREEN**		☐	☐	
Jun 73.	(lp) (UAS 29505) <213> **FUTURE DAYS**		☐	☐	

– Future days / Spray / Moonshake / Bel Air. (cd-iss. Jun89 on 'Spoon-Mute'; SPOONCD 009)

Oct 73.	(7") (UP 35596) <446> **MOONSHAKE. / FUTURE DAYS (edit)**		☐	☐	

—— trimmed to a quartet when DAMO SUZUKI left to become a Jehovah's Witness. Now **SCHMIDT / KAROLI** (shared vocals) **CZUKAY + LEIBEZEIT**

Nov 74.	(lp) (UAG 29673) <343> **SOON OVER BABALUMA**		☐	☐	

– Dizzy dizzy / Come sta, la luna / Splash / Chain reaction / Quantum physics. (cd-iss. Jun89 on 'Spoon-Mute'; SPOONCD 010)

Dec 74.	(7") (UP 35749) **DIZZY DIZZY. / SPLASH**		☐	☐	

			Virgin	Polydor	
Sep 75.	(lp) (V 2041) **LANDED**		☐	☐	

– Full moon on the highway / Half past one / Hunters and collectors / Vernal equinox / Red hot Indians / Unfinished. (cd-iss. Jun87; CDV 2041) (re-iss. Aug88; OVED 194)

—— approx Mar76, tried two vocalists one a Malayan, the other **MICHAEL COUSINS** (English). added **DAVID JOHNSON** – guest/composer (3) b.vocals of PINK FLOYD

Jul 76.	(7") (VS 153) **I WANT MORE. / . . . AND MORE**		26		
Oct 76.	(lp) (V 2071) **FLOW MOTION**		☐	☐	

– I want more / Cascade waltz / Laugh till you cry . . . live till you die / . . .And more / Babylonian pearl / Smoke (E.F.S. No.59) / Flow motion. (cd-iss. Jun87; CDV 2071) (re-iss. Aug88; OVED 88)

Nov 76.	(7") (VS 166) **SILENT NIGHT. / CASCADE WALTZ**		☐	☐	

—— added **ROSKO GEE** – bass + **REEBOP KWAKU BAAH** (b. Konongo, Ghana) – percussion (both ex-TRAFFIC) (HOLGER now synths., samplers)

Mar 77.	(lp) (V 2079) **SAW DELIGHT**		☐	☐	

– Don't say no / Sunshine day and night / Call me / Animal waves / Fly by night. (cd-iss. Jun87; CDV 2079) (re-iss. Aug88; OVED 195)

Apr 77.	(7") (VS 172) **DON'T SAY NO. / RETURN**		☐	☐	

—— HOLGER went on a few holidays (& solo). The rest of the band below (**SCHMIDT, KAROLI, LIEBEZEIT, BAAH & GEE**) recorded album.

			Lightning	Peters Int.	
Jun 78.	(7") (LIG 545) **CAN-CAN. / CAN BE**		☐	☐	
Jul 78.	(lp) (LIP 4) <9024> **OUT OF REACH**		☐	☐	

– Serpentine / Pauper's daughter and I / November / Seven days awake / Give me no roses / Like Inobe God / One more day. (cd-iss. Nov88; CDTB 025) (cd re-iss. May99 on 'MagMid'; MM 030)

			Laser	not iss.	
Jul 79.	(lp) (LASL 2) **CAN**		☐	☐	

– All gates open / Safe / Sunday jam / Sodom / Aspectacle / E.F.S. No.99: "can can" / Ping pong / Can be. (re-iss. Feb85 as 'INNER SPACE' on 'Thunderbolt'; THBL 020) (cd-iss. Jun87; THBL 020)

—— had already split late '78. JAKI formed PHANTOM BAND and collaborated with HOLGER. IRMIN went solo and formed BRUNO SPOERRI. MICHAEL in '84 went solo. All their releases were mainly German only. **CAN** reformed 1969 line-up 20 years on.

			Mercury	not iss.	
Oct 89.	(lp/c/cd) (838 883-1/-4/-2) **RITE TIME**		☐	☐	

– On the beautiful side of a romance / The without law man / Below this level (patient's song) / Movin' right along / Like a new world / Hoolah hoolah / Give the drummer some / In the distance lies the future. (cd-iss. Oct94 on 'Spoon-Mute'; SPOONCD 029)

			White Label	not iss.	
Sep 90.	(cd)(c)(lp) **FISHERMAN'S FRIEND REMIXES**		☐	☐	

– compilations, others, etc. –

on 'United Artists' unless otherwise mentioned

Aug 74.	(lp) (USP 103) **LIMITED EDITION**		☐	☐	
May 76.	(d-lp) Caroline; (CAD 3001) **UNLIMITED EDITION**		☐	☐	
Nov 76.	(lp) Sunset; (SLS 50400) **OPENER** (71-74 material)		☐	☐	
Oct 78.	(d-lp) (UDM 105-6) **CANNIBALISM**		☐	☐	
May 81.	(7") Virgin; (VS 422) / Polydor; **I WANT MORE. / . . . AND MORE**		☐	☐	

(12"+=) (VS 422-12) – Silent night.

1981.	(lp) (SPOON 012) **DELAY 1968**		☐	☐	German

– Butterfly / Pnoom / 19th century man / Thief / Man named Joe / Uphill / Little star of Bethlehem. (cd-iss. Jun89 on 'Spoon-Mute'; SPOONCD 012)

Oct 81.	(lp) Virgin; (OVED 3) **INCANDESCENCE**		☐	☐	
1982.	(lp) Pure Freude; (PF 23) **ONLYOU**		☐	☐	German
Mar 83.	(12"ep) Cherry Red; (12CHERRY 57) **MOONSHAKE. / TURTLES HAVE SHORT LEGS / ONE MORE NIGHT**		☐	☐	
Jan 85.	(c) Tago Mago; (TM 4755) **PREHISTORIC FUTURE**		☐	☐	France
Jun 91.	(cd) Spoon-Mute; (SPOONCD 23-24) **UNLIMITED EDITION** (new collection)		☐	☐	
Nov 92.	(cd) Spoon-Mute; (SPOONCD 021) **CANNIBALISM II**		☐	☐	

– Uphill / Pnoom / Connection / Mother Upduff / Little star / T.V. spot / Doko E. / Turtles have short legs / Shikaku maru ten / Gomorrha / Blue bag / Red hot Indians / Half past one / Flow motion / Smoke / I want more . . .and more / Laugh till you cry / Aspectacle animal waves / Sunshine day and night / E.F.S. No.7 / Melting away.

Oct 94.	(cd) Spoon-Mute; (SPOONCD 3031) **ANTHOLOGY 1968-1993**		☐	☐	
Feb 95.	(cd) Spoon-Mute; (SPOONCD 022) **CANNIBALISM III**		☐	☐	

– (solo work 1979-1991 from CZUKAY, SCHMIDT, LIEBEZEIT & KAROLI)

Oct 95.	(cd) Strange Fruit; (SFRCD 135) **LIVE AT THE BBC (Peel sessions)**		☐	☐	
May 97.	(t-lp/d-cd) Grey Area; (SPOON/+CD 39-40) **SACRILEGE**		☐	☐	
Mar 99.	(d-cd+video+book) Spoon-Mute; (SPOON 041) **CAN BOX**		☐	☐	
Sep 99.	(d-cd) Spoon-Mute; (SPOON 042/043) **CAN LIVE** (live)		☐	☐	

HOLGER CZUKAY

			Music Factory	not iss.	
1968.	(lp; by HOLGER CZUKAY with ROLF DAMMERS) (SRS 002) **CANAXIS 5**		☐	☐	German

– Boat woman song / Canaxis. (re-iss. 1981 on 'Spoon'; SPOON 015) (cd-iss. Feb95 on 'Spoon-Mute'; SPOONCD 015)

—— CZUKAY with other CAN members augenting

			E.M.I.	not iss.	
Nov 79.	(7") (EMI 5005) **COOL IN THE POOL. / OH LORD GIVE US MORE MONEY**		☐	☐	

(re-iss. Jul83; same)

Jan 80.	(lp) (EMC 3319) **MOVIES**		☐	☐	

– Cool in the pool / Oh Lord give us some money / Persian love / Hollywood symphony.

—— 1980, CZUKAY released 12"ep 'LES VAMPYRETTES' in Germany with CONRAD PLANK & AXEL GROS on 'Electrola'; (F 667.226)

—— mid'81, CZUKAY teamed up with JAH WOBBLE and JAKI LIEBEZEIT to releases 12"ep 'HOW MUCH ARE THEY?' for 'Island'; (12WIP 6701)

—— most of the tracks appeared on below 'Virgin' German album.

Feb 82.	(lp/c) (EMC/TC-EMC 3394) **ON THE WAY TO THE PEAK OF NORMAL**		☐	☐	

– Ode to perfume / On the way to the peak of normal / Witches multiplication table / Two bass shuffle / Hiss'n'listen.

			Virgin	not iss.	
Mar 82.	(7") (EMI 5280) **ODE TO PERFUME. / PERSIAN LOVE**		☐	☐	

1982.	(lp; by HOLGER CZUKAY, JAH WOBBLE & JAKI LIEBEZEIT) (205 866-320) **FULL CIRCLE**		☐	☐	German

– How much are they? / Where's the money? / Full circle R.P.S. (No.7) / Mystery R.P.S. (No.8) / Trench warfare / Twilight world. (cd-iss. May92 on 'Virgin'; CDOVD 437)

—— In Oct'83, he teamed up with JAH WOBBLE (again) & The EDGE (U2), to release mini-album 'SNAKE CHARMER' for 'Island'; (IMA 1)

May 84. (lp/c) (V/TCV 2307) **DER OSTEN IST ROT** ☐ –
– The photo song / Bankel rap '82 / Michy / Rhonrad / Collage / Esperanto socialiste / Der osten ist rot / Das massenmedium / Schaue vertrauensvoll in die zukunft / Traum mal wieder. (re-iss. Apr86 lp/c; OVED/+C 161)

May 84. (7") (VS 671) **THE PHOTO SONG. / DAS MASSENMEDIUM** ☐ –
(12"+=) (VS 671-12) – Biomutanten.

Jan 87. (lp/c) (V/TCV 2408) **ROME REMAINS ROME** ☐ –
– Hey ba ba re bob / Blessed Easter / Sudentenland / Hit hit flop flop / Perfect world / Music in the air. (cd-iss. Jan88+=; CDV 2408) – DER OSTEN IST ROT (lp)

—— (Mar'88) collaborated next with DAVID SYLVIAN on album 'PLIGHT AND PREMONITION' for 'Venture' cd/c/lp; (CD/TC+/VE 11)

—— next with **SHELDON ANCEL** – vocals / **M.KAROLI** – guitar / **J.LIEBEZEIT** – drums

Jan 91. (cd/c/lp) (CD/TC+/V 2651) **RADIO WAVE SURFER** ☐ –
– Rhine water / It ain't no crime / I get weird dreams / Saturday night movie / Dr. Oblivion / We can fight all night / Get it sweet / Ride a radio wave / Atmosphere tuning / Voice of Bulgaria / Late night radio / Through the freezing snow / Encore.

Mute   not iss.

May 93. (cd) (CDSTUMM 125) **MOVING PICTURES** ☐ –
– Longing for daydreams / All night long / Radio in an hourglass / Dark moon / Floatspace / Rhythms of a secret life.

JAKI LEIBEZEIT

PHANTOM BAND
with others **DOMINIK VON SENGER** – guitar / **HELMUT ZERLETT** – keyboards / **OLEK GELBA** – percussion / **ROSKO GEE** – bass, vocals

Sky   not iss.

1980. (lp) (048) **PHANTOM BAND** – – German
– You inspired me / I'm the one / For M. / Phantom drums / Absolutely straight / Rolling / Without desire / No more fooling / Pulsar / Latest news. (UK cd-iss. Feb95 on 'Spoon-Mute'; SPOONCD 017)

—— **SHELDON ANCEL** – vocals repl. GEE

1981. (lp) (065) **FREEDOM OF SPEECH** – – German
– Freedom of speech / E.F.1 / Brain police / No question / Relax / Gravity / Trapped again.

—— In 1981 he and CZUKAY teamed up with PHEW on lp 'PHEW'

—— now without OLEK

Spoon   not iss.

1983. (lp) (SPOON 017) **NOWHERE** – – German
– Loading zone / Planned obsolescene / Mind probe / Morning alarm / Weird love / Neon man / Positive day / Nervous breakdown / The party / George the space monster / This is the rule / Cricket talk / Nowhere. (cd-iss. Feb95; SPOONCD 17)

—— SCHMIDT + KAROLI also issued several albums (not together)

CANDLEBOX

Formed: Beverly Hills, California, USA . . . 1992 by KEVIN MARTIN, PETER KLETT, BARDI MARTIN and SCOTT MERCADO. The band's career got off to a promising start, when MADONNA procured them for her eclectic, high-profile 'Maverick' label. Virtually guaranteed press coverage, then, the group delivered their eponymous debut album the following year to widespread critical acclaim. The record scaled the American charts slowly but surely over the course of a year, finally securing a Top 10 spot and selling a good few million in the process. Combining elements of melodic rock and post-grunge, the album spawned two hit singles, including the Top 20 hit, 'FAR BEHIND'. Unfortunately, this musical recipe for success had obviously been mislaid by the release of 'LUCY' (1995), an album which let down fans and critics alike despite its initial high chart placing. Further post-grunge misery was to beset the CANDLEBOX makers when MERCADO departed during the sessions of their third set. However, former PEARL JAM sticksman, DAVE KRUSEN, stepped in just in time to save the day, although the pundits and critics alike gave the LED ZEPPELIN-esque 'HAPPY PILLS' (1998) the proverbial thumbs down. • **Covered:** VOODOO CHILE (Jimi Hendrix).

Album rating: CANDLEBOX (*6) / LUCY (*4) / HAPPY PILLS (*4)

KEVIN MARTIN – vocals / **PETER KLETT** – guitar / **BARDI MARTIN** – bass / **SCOTT MERCADO** – drums

			Maverick-Sire	Maverick-Sire
Jul 93.	(cd/c) <(9362 45313-2/-4)> **CANDLEBOX**		☐	7

– Don't you / Change / You / No easy / Far behind / Blossom / Arrow / Rain / Mothers dream / Cover me / He calls home.

| Mar 94. | (c-s) <18304> **YOU / PULL AWAY** | – | 78 |
| Aug 94. | (7"/c-s) (W 0258/+C) <18118> **FAR BEHIND. / YOU (live)** | – | 18 |

(cd-s+=) (W 0258CD) – Live medley: Far behind – Voodoo chile (slight return).

| Oct 95. | (cd/c) <(9362 45962-2/-4)> **LUCY** | ☐ | 11 |

– Simple lessons / Drowned / Lucy / Best friend / Become (to tell) / Understanding / Crooked halo / Bothered / Butterfly / It's amazing / Vulgar before me / Butterfly (reprise).

—— **DAVE KRUSEN** – drums (ex-PEARL JAM) repl. MERCADO

| Jul 98. | (cd-s) **IT'S ALRIGHT /** | – | ☐ |
| Jul 98. | (cd/c) <46975> **HAPPY PILLS** | – | 65 |

– 10,000 horses / Happy pills / Blinders / It's alright / Stone's throw away / So real / Offerings / Sometimes / Step back / Belmore place / Breakaway / Look what you've done.

CANIBUS

Born: GERMAINE WILLIAMS, 1975, USA. Naming himself after a similarly-monikered weed, CANIBUS wafted onto the rap scene via guest spots for such luminaries as LL COOL J and the LOST BOYZ. The eclectic rapper (described by some as the ISAAC HAYES for the new 90's generation!) swaggered his way through streetwise hip-hop sketches as sharp and incisive as a surgeon's scalpel. 'SECOND ROUND K.O.' was (as most were) co-written with manager WYCLEF JEAN (FUGEES), a transatlantic hit featuring the bulky talents of boxer, MIKE TYSON. The self-titled/hyphenated samplemungus debut set, 'CAN-I-BUS' (1998), saw him join the million-selling rap aristocracy as the record barely missed the elusive US top slot. This was another release to carry the ubiquitous black and white parental advisory sticker due to its supposed explicit lyrical content; the Moral Majority winning or losing? Take your pick, just don't forget to consult mummy and daddy first.

Album rating: CAN-I-BUS (*8)

CAN-I-BUS – vocals / with **WYCLEF JEAN** – co-production, guitar, etc (of FUGEES)

			Universal	Universal
Jun 98.	(12"/cd-s) (UNT/UND 56198) <56175> **SECOND ROUND K.O. / (clean version) / (album version)**		35	28 Mar98
Sep 98.	(cd/c) <(UND/UNC 53222)> **CAN-I-BUS**		43	2

– Intro / Patriots / Get retarded / Niggonometry / Second round K.O. / What's going on / I honor U / Hype-nitis / How we roll / Channel zero / Let's ride / Buckingham Palace / Rip rock / How come.

| Sep 98. | (c-s/12"/cd-s; YOUSSOU N'DOUR & CANIBUS) (INC/INT/IND 95598) **HOW COME (mixes:- original / instrumental / acappella)** | | 52 | ☐ |

(above issued on 'Interscope')

CANNED HEAT

Formed: 1966, Los Angeles, California, USA by ALAN WILSON and BOB HITE. WILSON, nicknamed 'BLIND OWL' because of his thick-lensed glasses, was already a renowned harmonica player and had accompanied SON HOUSE on his album, 'FATHER OF FOLK BLUES'. He met HITE (known as 'THE BEAR' due to his massive 300 pound frame) in 1965 and they soon discovered a shared passion for blues archives (WILSON had studied music at Boston University and did a thesis on blues music while HITE had a collection of blues 78s that numbered in the thousands). They were joined by FRANK COOK on drums and HENRY 'SUNFLOWER' VESTINE, a former member of The MOTHERS OF INVENTION, on guitar. Taking their name from TOMMY JOHNSON, 'CANNED HEAT BLUES' they completed the line-up with the addition of LARRY 'THE MOLE' TAYLOR who was a session bass player with CHUCK BERRY, JERRY LEE LEWIS and The MONKEES. CANNED HEAT's eponymous debut album was released in 1967 and showed some promise, although it only offered copies of 12-bar standards such as, 'ROLLIN' AND TUMBLIN', 'DUST MY BROOM' and 'BULLFROG BLUES'. Later the same year they performed with distinction at the Monterey Festival, while things got even better with the arrival of new drummer ALFREDO FITO and the subsequent release of the second album, 'BOOGIE WITH CANNED HEAT' in 1968. This was an impressive selection which included, 'FRIED HOCKEY BOOGIE' (a song destined to become a concert favourite) and the hypnotic 'ON THE ROAD AGAIN' (originally recorded by The MEMPHIS JUG BAND in the early Twenties) which gave them a UK Top 10 and US Top 20 hit single. For the next album, 'LIVIN' THE BLUES', WILSON adapted a HENRY THOMAS song, 'BULLDOZE BLUES', by keeping the tune and rewriting the lyric, the result being 'GOIN' UP THE COUNTRY', which highlighted WILSON's trademark falsetto (seemingly taken from SKIP JAMES) and gave them a UK and US Top 20 hit as well as being one of the highlights of the Woodstock movie. Their new-found chart status allowed them to bully their record company, 'Liberty', into giving ALBERT COLLINS a deal with their subsidiary, 'Imperial'. CANNED HEAT recorded a further four albums between 1969-70 including a self-financed collaboration with JOHN LEE HOOKER (which gave HOOKER his first chart album). For 'HALLELUJAH', guitarist HARVEY MANDEL replaced HENRY VESTINE who could no longer work with LARRY TAYLOR. They enjoyed further UK hits with a cover of WILBERT HARRISON's, 'LET'S WORK TOGETHER', which reached number 2, and the cajun-like, 'SUGAR BEE' (originally by CLEVELAND CROCHET) but they were shocked by the suicide of ALAN WILSON, whose body was found in HITE'S backyard on the 3rd of September 1970. His death brought about a major reshuffle with TAYLOR and MANDEL going to JOHN MAYALL's BLUESBREAKERS, VESTINE returning and ANTONIO DE LA BARREDA becoming the new bassist. The new line-up completed one album, 'HISTORICAL FIGURES AND ANCIENT HEADS', before BOB HITE's brother RICHARD, replaced BARREDA for the 1973 release, 'THE NEW AGE'. Throughout the next decade, HITE tried to keep the band going although he was unable to get a permanent record deal. A new impetus came with 'HUMAN CONDITION' but the years of struggle took their toll on HITE, who collapsed and died after a gig on the 5th of April 1981. The band's name lived on with TAYLOR and DE LA PARRA recruiting new guitarists JAMES THORNBURY and JUNIOR WATSON and they still tour today although their line-up is constantly changing. • **Songwriters:** HITE and WILSON, except ROLLIN' AND TUMBLIN' (Muddy Waters) / WOOLY BULLY (Sam The Sham & The Pharoahs) / SUGAR BEE (Cleveland Crotchet) / BULLDOZE BLUES (Henry

Thomas). • **Trivia:** 'Blind Owl' WILSON was so-called due to his bespectacled eyes.

Album rating: CANNED HEAT (*6) / BOOGIE WITH CANNED HEAT (*6) / LIVIN' THE BLUES (*6) / HALLELUJAH (*7) / CANNED HEAT '70 CONCERT (*4) / CANNED HEAT COOKBOOK compilation (*9) / FUTURE BLUES (*5) / HOOKER 'N' HEAT with John Lee Hooker (*5) / HISTORICAL FIGURES AND ANCIENT HEADS (*5) / NEW AGE (*3) / ONE MORE RIVER TO CROSS (*3) / LIVE AT TOPANGA CORRAL (*3) / THE HUMAN CONDITION (*4) / KINGS OF THE BOOGIE (*4) / THE BOOGIE ASSAULT – LIVE IN AUSTRALIA (*3) / RE-HEATED (*3) / INTERNAL COMBUSTION (*4) / UNCANNED – THE BEST OF CANNED HEAT compilation (*8)

BOB 'THE BEAR' HITE (b.26 Feb'45, Torrance, California) – vocals, harmonica / **AL 'BLIND OWL' WILSON** (b. 4 Jul'43, Boston, Mass.) – vocals, guitar, harmonica / **HENRY VESTINE** (b.25 Dec'44, Washington, D.C.) – guitar (ex-MOTHERS OF../ZAPPA) / **LARRY TAYLOR** (b.SAMUEL TAYLOR, 26 Jun'42, Brooklyn, N.Y.) – bass repl. MARK ANDES who had repl. STUART BROTMAN (to KALEIDOSCOPE) / **FRANK COOK** – drums

			Liberty	Liberty
Aug 67.	(lp; mono/stereo) (LBL/LBS 83059) <7526> **CANNED HEAT**			76

– Rollin' and tumblin' / Bullfrog blues / Evil is going on / Goin' down slow / Catfish blues / Dust my broom / Help me / Big road blues / The story of my life / The road song / Rich woman. (re-iss. Feb73 as 'ROLLIN' & TUMBLIN' on 'Sunset'; SLS 50321) (re-iss. Jun89 on 'See for Miles'; SEE 268) (cd-iss. Aug90; SEECD 268)

| Jan 68. | (7") (LBF 150) <55979> **ROLLIN' AND TUMBLIN'. / BULLFROG BLUES** | | |

FITO 'ADOLPHO' DE LA PARRA (b. 3 Feb'46, Mexico City, Mexico) – drums (ex-BLUESBERRY JAM) repl. COOK

| Mar 68. | (7") <56005> **EVIL WOMAN. / THE WORLD IS A JUDGE** | | - | |
| May 68. | (7") (LBF 15090) **ON THE ROAD AGAIN. / THE WORLD IN A JUG** | | 8 | - |

(re-iss. Sep75 on 'United Artists'; UP 36001)

| Jun 68. | (lp; mono/stereo) (LBL/LBS 83103) <7541> **BOOGIE WITH CANNED HEAT** | | 5 | 16 Feb68 |

– Evil woman / My crime / On the road again / World in a jug / Turpentine music / Whiskey headed woman No.2 / Amphetamine Annie / An owl song / Marie Laveau / Fried hockey boogie. (re-iss. Feb86 on 'See for Miles'; SEE 62) (cd-iss. Feb90; SEECD 62)

Jul 68.	(7") <56038> **ON THE ROAD AGAIN. / BOOGIE MUSIC**		-	16
Nov 68.	(7") (LBF 15169) <56077> **GOING UP THE COUNTRY. / ONE KIND FAVOUR**		19	11
Dec 68.	(d-lp) (LDS 84001) <27200> **LIVING THE BLUES**			18

– Pony blues / My mistake / Sandy's blues / Going up the country / Walking by myself / Boogie music / One kind favour / Parthenogenesis:- Nebulosity – Rollin' and tumblin' – Five owls – Bear wires – Snooky flowers – Sunflower power – Ragi Kafi – Icebag – Childhood's / Refried the boogie (part 1 – live) / Refried the boogie (part 2 – live). (re-iss. Jul87 on 'See for Miles' lp; SEE 97) (cd-iss. Feb90; SEECD 97) (re-iss. May99 on 'Akarma' d-cd/d-lp; AK 051 CD/LP)

| Apr 69. | (7") (LBF 15200) <56097> **TIME WAS. / LOW DOWN** | | | 67 Mar69 |

HARVEY MANDEL (b.11 Mar'45, Detroit, Mich.) – guitar (+ solo artist) repl. VESTINE

| Aug 69. | (lp) (LBS 83239) <7618> **HALLELUJAH** | | | 37 |

– Same all over / Change my ways / Canned Heat / Sic 'em pigs / I'm her man / Time was / Do not enter / Big fat / Huautla / Get off my back / Down in the gutter, but free. (re-iss. Feb89 on 'See for Miles'; SEE 248) (cd-iss. Aug90; SEECD 248)

Sep 69.	(7") (LBF 15255) **POOR MAN. / SIC 'EM PIGS**		
Dec 69.	(7") <56140> **CHANGE MY WAYS. / GET OFF MY BACK**		-	
Jan 70.	(lp) (LBS 83303) <11000> **CANNED HEAT COOKBOOK** (compilation)		8	86 Nov69

– Bullfrog blues / Rollin' and tumblin' / Going up the country / Time was / Boogie music / On the road again / Same all over / Sic 'em pigs / Fried hockey boogie / I will wait for you. (re-iss. Nov75 on 'Sunset'; SLS 50377)

Jan 70.	(7") (LBF 15302) <56151> **LET'S WORK TOGETHER. / I'M HER MAN**		2	26 Sep70
Jun 70.	(7") (LBF 15350) **SUGAR BEE. / SHAKE IT AND BREAK IT**		49	-
Jun 70.	(lp) (LBS 83333) <5509> **CANNED HEAT '70 CONCERT (live in Europe)**		15	Jul71

– That's all right mama / Bring it on home / Pulling hair blues / Back out on the road – On the road again / London blues / Let's work together / Goodbye for now. (re-iss. Oct88 as '70: LIVE IN EUROPE' on 'Beat Goes On'; BGOLP 12) (cd-iss. Sep89; BGOCD 12)

ANTONIO DE LA BARREDA (aka TONY OLAV) – bass repl. LARRY TAYLOR

| Sep 70. | (7") (LBF 15395) **FUTURE BLUES. / SKAT** | | - | |
| Sep 70. | (lp) (LBS 83364) <11002> **FUTURE BLUES** | | 27 | 59 |

– Sugar bee / Shake it and break it / That's all right mama / My time ain't long / Scat / Let's work together / London blues / So sad (the world's in a tangle) / Future blues. (re-iss. Jul89 on 'Beat Goes On' lp/cd; BGO LP/CD 49)

On 3rd Sep70, AL WILSON suffering depression died of drug o/d. He appeared on the releases below until stated.

| Dec 70. | (7") (LBF 15429) **CHRISTMAS BLUES. / DO NOT ENTER** | | | - |
| Jan 71. | (7") (LBF 15439) **WOOLY BULLY. / MY TIME AIN'T LONG** | | |

HENRY VESTINE – guitar returned to repl. MANDEL who returned to JOHN MAYALL (next with veteran US blues legend)

| Mar 71. | (d-lp; by CANNED HEAT / JOHN LEE HOOKER) (LPS 103-4) <35002> **HOOKER'N'HEAT** | | | 73 Feb71 |

– Messin' with the Hook / The feelin' is gone / Send me your pillow / Sittin' here thinkin' / Meet me in the bottom / Altmonia blues / Drifter / You talk too much / Burning Hell / Bottle up and go / The world today / I got my eyes on you / Whiskey and wimmen' / Just you and me / Let's make it / Peavine / Boogie chillen No.2. (re-iss. Oct71 on 'United Artists'; 9955> (re-iss. Sep88 as lp 'THE BEST OF HOOKER'N'HEAT' on 'See for Miles'; SEE 234) (cd-iss. Aug89 as 'HOOKER'N'HEAT (THE BEST OF PLUS)'; SEECD 234)

JOEL SCOTT HILL – guitar, vocals finally repl. AL WILSON, now alongside HITE, BARREDA, PARRA and VESTINE

			U.A.	U.A.
Mar 71.	(7"; CANNED HEAT & JOHN LEE HOOKER) <50779> **LET'S MAKE IT. / WHISKEY AND WIMMEN**			-
Sep 71.	(7") (UP 35279) <50831> **LONG WAY FROM L.A.. / HILL'S STOMP**		-	

LITTLE RICHARD – piano, vocals guested on next album

| Mar 72. | (lp) (UAG 29304) <5557> **HISTORICAL FIGURES AND ANCIENT HEADS** | | 87 Feb72 |

– Sneakin' around / Hill's stomp / Rockin' with the king / I don't care what you tell me / Long way from L.A. / Cherokee dance / That's all right / Utah. (re-iss. Aug90 on 'Beat Goes On' cd/lp; BGO CD/LP 83)

| Apr 72. | (7") (UP 35348) <50892> **ROCKIN' WITH THE KING. / I DON'T CARE WHAT YOU TELL ME** | | 88 Mar72 |
| Jul 72. | (7") <50927> **CHEROKEE DANCE. / SNEAKIN' AROUND** | | |

RICHARD HITE – bass (BOB's brother) (ex-POPPA HOP) repl. BARREDA / added **JAMES SHANE** – guitar / **ED BEYER** – keyboards

| Jun 73. | (7") (UP 35562) **KEEP IT CLEAN. / YOU CAN RUN, BUT YOU SURE CAN'T HIDE** | | |
| Sep 73. | (lp) (UAS 29455) <049F> **NEW AGE** | | |

– Keep it clean / Harley Davidson blues / Don't deceive me / You can run, but you sure can't hide / Rock and roll music / Lookin' for my rainbow / Framed / Election blues / So long wrong. (cd-iss. May91 on 'Beat Goes On'; BGOCD 85)

| Sep 73. | (7") <167> **LOOKIN' FOR MY RAINBOW. / ROCK AND ROLL MUSIC** | | - |
| Nov 73. | (7") <243> **HARLEY DAVIDSON BLUES. /** | | - |

		Atlantic	Atlantic
Feb 74.	(7") (K 10420) <3010> **ONE MORE RIVER TO CROSS. / HIGHWAY 401**		
Mar 74.	(lp) (K 50026) <SD 7289> **ONE MORE RIVER TO CROSS**		

– L.A. town / I need someone / Bagful of boogie / I'm a hog for you baby / You am what I am / Shake rattle & roll / Bright times are comin' / Highway 401 / We remember Fats.

| Jan 75. | (7") <3236> **THE HARDER THEY COME. / ROCK 'N' ROLL SHOW** | | - |

RICHARD HITE + FITO DE LA PARRA took over control of band when BOB & HENRY got stoned. ED BAYER also departed. Recruited **CHRIS MORGAN** – guitar / **GENE TAYLOR** – keyboards (both ex-POPPA HOP)

		Sonet	Takoma
Dec 78.	(lp) (SNTF 783) <7066> **THE HUMAN CONDITION**		

– Strut my stuff / Hot money / House of blue lights / Just got to be there / You just got the rock / Human condition / She's lookin' good / Open up your backdoor / Wrapped up.

(later in 70's) BOB HITE returned (he was to die of heart attack 4th Apr81)

re-united + re-formed with FITO, VESTINE, and TAYLOR and others, **RAUL E. RODRIGUEZ + F.M. HALEY.**

		not iss.	Destiny
1981.	(lp) **KINGS OF THE BOOGIE**	-	

– Kings of the boogie / Stoned bad street fighting man / So fine / You just can't get close to me / Hell's just on down the road / I was wrong / Little crystal / Chicken shack. <re-iss. 1981 as 'DOG HOUSE BLUES' on 'Rhino'; > (re-iss. Oct85 on 'Platinum' lp/c; PLP/PMC 20)

		not iss.	A.L.A.
1984.	(12"ep) <1996> **THE HEAT BROS '84**		

JAMES THORNBERRY – slide guitar, vocals, harmonica repl. VESTINE.

		Bedrock	not iss.
Dec 87.	(blue-lp) (BEDLP 5) **THE BOOGIE ASSAULT (LIVE IN AUSTRALIA)**		

– Kings of the boogie / Stoned bad street fighting man / So fine / You just can't get close to me / Hell's just on down the road / I was wrong / Little crystal / Dog house blues / Sleepy hollow baby / Chicken shack. (cd-iss. Mar89; BEDLP 5CD)

		not iss.	Chameleon
1990.	(cd) <SPV 858805> **REHEATED**		

– Looking for the party / Driftin' / I'm watching you / Bullfrog blues / Hucklebuck / Mercury blues / Gunstreet girl / I love to rock and roll / So fine (Betty Jean) / Take me to the river / Red headed woman / Built for comfort. (UK-iss.Mar96 on 'SPV'; same)

new line-up: **VESTINE / DE LA PARRA / THORNBURY / + JUNIOR WATSON** – guitar, vocals / **RON SHUMAKE** – bass, vocals

		Aim	Topic
Sep 93.	(cd)(c) (AIM CD/C 1033) **BURNIN' (live in Australia 1990)**		

– Let's work together / Gamblin' woman / Hucklebuck / Sunnyland / Rollin' and tumblin' / Nitwit / Gunstreet girl / One way out / J.J. jump / Mercury blues.

TAYLOR + MANDEL returned

		Aim	River Road
Jul 95.	(cd) (AIM 1044) **INTERNAL COMBUSTION**		

(re-iss. Jan96 on 'Connoisseur'; FPCCD 01)

– compilations, etc. –

– On the road again / Let's work together / Going up the country.

(12"+=) (12EM 100) – Rollin' and tumblin'.
(cd-s+=) (CDEM 100) – Amphetamine Annie.

Sep 89. (lp/c)(cd) *E.M.I.; (GO/TC-GO 2026)(CDP 793114-2)* **LET'S WORK TOGETHER (THE BEST OF CANNED HEAT)**
– On the road again / Bullfrog blues / Rollin' and tumblin' / Amphetamine / Annie / Fried hockey boogie / Sic 'em pigs / Poor Moon / Let's work together / Going up the country / Boogie music / Same all over / Time was / Sugar bee / Rockin' with the king / That's alright mama / My time ain't long.

Apr 90. (d-lp)(cd) *Bear Family; (BTS 964410)(BTCD 9779 409)* **LIVE AT THE TURKU ROCK FESTIVAL (live in Finland)** — German

Feb 92. (cd) *Thunderbolt; (CDTB 130)* **STRAIGHT AHEAD** (re-iss. Apr97; same)

Oct 92. (cd) *Carlton; (SMS 053)* **ROCK LEGENDS VOL.1**

Nov 92. (3xcd-box) *Liberty; (CANNED 780275-2)* **THE BIG HEAT**

Jul 93. (cd) *Charly; (CCCD 1104)* **LIVE**

Aug 94. (d-cd) *E.M.I.; (CDEM 15431)* **UNCANNED (THE BEST OF CANNED HEAT)**

Feb 95. (cd) *In-Akustik; (INAK 8804)* **BOOGIE UP THE COUNTRY (live in West Germany 1987)**

Feb 95. (cd) *B.A.M.; (KLMCD 015)* **PEARLS OF THE PAST VOL.2 – CANNED HEAT**

Feb 96. (cd) *Prestige; (CSGSP 079)* **BIG ROAD BLUES**

Feb 97. (cd) *EMI Gold; (CDGOLD 1076)* **ON THE ROAD AGAIN**

May 97. (cd) *Disky; (DC 87865-2)* **THE BEST OF CANNED HEAT**

Mar 99. (cd) *Start; (SRH 806)* **ON THE ROAD AGAIN**

Jerry CANTRELL (see under ⇒ ALICE IN CHAINS)

CAPPADONNA (see under ⇒ WU-TANG CLAN)

CAPTAIN BEEFHEART AND HIS MAGIC BAND

Formed: Los Angeles, California, USA . . . 1964 by DON VAN VLIET, a child-prodigy sculptor who, between the ages of five and thirteen, had his clay animals featured on a weekly TV show hosted by Portuguese sculptor Augustino Rodriguez. An opportunity to develop his art skills were halted when his parents declined a scholarship on his behalf to study art in Europe, preferring instead to move to Lancaster in the Mojave desert. Here he met FRANK ZAPPA at the local high school, setting up a few local bands while ZAPPA started to write a script for a B-movie 'CAPTAIN BEEFHEART MEETS THE GRUNT PEOPLE'. When FRANK went to Los Angeles to form The MOTHERS OF INVENTION, he adopted the name CAPTAIN BEEFHEART and set about recruiting The MAGIC BAND. They signed to 'A&M' in 1964, releasing their version of BO DIDDLEY's 'DIDDY WAH DIDDY', which sold enough copies to encourage the label to buy studio time for an album. When completed, president Jerry Moss rejected the tapes, citing it too strange and anti-commercial. Undaunted, VAN VLIET and a new set of musicians, including RY COODER, re-recorded most of these masters, the album 'SAFE AS MILK' finally surfacing in 1967 on the 'Buddah' label. This was a masterpiece of its time, full of BEEFHEART on a HOWLIN' WOLF-style trip; the great tracks being 'ELECTRICITY', 'ABBA ZABA', 'AUTUMN CHILD' & 'ZIG ZAG WANDERER'. However, RY COODER departed for safer pastures when VAN VLIET/BEEFHEART left the stage halfway through their set at the 1967 Monterey Pop Festival, leaving the band to play to a bewildered but carefree hippy audience. BEEFHEART often showed signs of outlandish behaviour which split the band up as much as his personality. Late in 1968, they recorded another album, 'MIRROR MAN', although this was shelved until his popularity had grown in the early 70's. However, one album did appear that year, 'STRICTLY PERSONAL', which BEEFHEART slammed for its radical remix by producer BOB KRASNOW. This riled him so much that he signed a new contract with old friend ZAPPA who gave him complete artistic control on his new 'Straight' label. Having written about 30 songs in a day, BEEFHEART took his new bunch of weirdo musicians (ANTENNAE JIMMY SEMENS, DRUMBO, ART TRIPP III, ZOOT HORN ROLLO and THE MASCARA SNAKE) to rehearse in a house which was close-by an old friend JIMMY CARL BLACK (drummer for ZAPPA). They stayed there for a full eight months, only one of them at a time venturing out if the band was in need of food & drink, etc. This was VAN VLIET's tyrannical way of keeping the band tight, so as to establish virtuoso musicianship while he got on with the weird vocals. The resulting album (a double!) 'TROUT MASK REPLICA' was handed to ZAPPA, much to his surprise, after four and a half hours in the studio. When released at the turn of the decade, it was initially given the thumbs down by many critics and fans. Those hardy enough to give it a few tolerant spins, however, were convinced of its genius. The record surprisingly nearly made the UK Top 20, having been played to death on John Peel's Radio 1 night-time show. Its virtual insanity was literally not of this world, utilising the complex structures of jazz legend ORNETTE COLEMAN; the best tracks to break through – to the sane among us – were 'THE BLIMP', 'PENA', 'DALI'S CAR', 'ELLA GURU' & 'OLD FART AT PLAY'. It has since become regarded as a classic, although it should never be played to someone not of your generation. He returned a thank-you to ZAPPA, when he sang a track, 'WILLIE THE WIMP', on his 'Hot Rats' album, although their friendship was fraying with every meeting, two egos too big for one room. In 1970, he settled down to a more conventional avant-garde Delta-blues album 'LICK MY DECALS OFF, BABY' (compared that is, to their last). It was another excellent set; combing through the depths of his unearthly roots to find tracks such as 'DOCTOR DARK', 'I LOVE YOU, YOU BIG DUMMY' and the title track. 1972 saw another great album 'THE

SPOTLIGHT KID', featuring the delights of 'CLICK CLACK', 'I'M GONNA BOOGLARIZE YOU BABY' & 'WHEN IT GROWS IT STACKS'. Their next, 'CLEAR SPOT' covered new territory on softer tracks like 'TOO MUCH TIME' & 'MY HEAD IS MY ONLY HOUSE UNLESS IT RAINS', tempting the MAGIC BAND to bail out and form their own outfit, MALLARD. The album did, however, include another powerful BEEFHEART special in the shape of 'BIG EYED BEANS FROM VENUS'. In 1974, with a new line-up, he signed to UK's 'Virgin' label but his work at this point, especially on the albums 'UNCONDITIONALLY GUARANTEED' & 'BLUEJEANS AND MOONBEAMS', was just about average. He tried to escape yet another restrictive deal; it was said he would sign anything, and teamed up with his old pal FRANK ZAPPA and The MOTHERS. Their collaboration, 'BONGO FURY', set the ball rolling for a litigation battle between him and 'Virgin' UK, resulting in another deal!, this time with 'Warner Brothers' for the 1978 album 'SHINY BEAST (BAT CHAIN PULLER)', a marked return to form on some tracks. Virgin won the rights to this album, which gained a UK release in early 1980. Two other records surfaced in the next two years; 'DOC AT RADAR STATION' and the considerably better 'ICE CREAM FOR CROW', the latter containing the excellent title track, his final epitaph. He retired from the music business and set up home with his wife JAN at a trailer park in the Mojave desert. Still an avid sculptor and painter, with the help of fan Julian Schnabel, he began exhibiting his primitive canvases which made him more money than his records ever did. In the mid-80's, a host of young British indie acts including STUMP, McKENZIES, The SHRUBS, etc, took on the mantle of the BEEFHEART sound. Always asked if he would return, BEEFHEART has repeatedly refused to get back on the bandwagon (having fallen into ill-health, both physically and mentally), a return to the recording studio is unlikely to say the least). A remarkable figure of his time, DON VAN VLIET exemplified the glory of not worrying about the exploitation of the music industry, only happy with his own, and of course the MAGIC BAND's work. Let's just hope he's around for several more years to enjoy whatever he creates. • **Trivia:** He also covered Jack Nitzsche's 'HARD WORKIN' MAN' on the 1978 film 'Blue Collar', which starred Harvey Keitel.

Album rating: SAFE AS MILK (*9) / STRICTLY PERSONAL (*7) / TROUT MASK REPLICA (*10) / LICK MY DECALS OFF, BABY (*8) / MIRROR MAN earlier recording (*7) / THE SPOTLIGHT KID (*8) / CLEAR SPOT (*7) / UNCONDITIONALLY GUARANTEED (*6) / BLUEJEANS AND MOONBEAMS (*7) / BONGO FURY; with Frank Zappa (*5) / SHINY BEAST (BAT CHAIN PULLER (*6) / DOC AT RADAR STATION (*5) / ICE CREAM FOR CROW (*6) / THE LEGENDARY A&M SESSIONS mini of early stuff (*5) / I MAY BE HUNGRY BUT I SURE AIN'T WEIRD (*5) / GROW FINS boxed set (*8)

CAPTAIN BEEFHEART (b. DON VAN VLIET, 15 Jan'41, Glendale, California) – vocals, harmonica, occasional guitar, wind instruments / **ALEX ST. CLAIRE** – guitar / **DOUG MOON** – guitar / **JERRY HANDLEY** – bass / **PAUL BLAKELY** – drums

		A&M	A&M
1966.	(7") <794> **DIDDY WAH DIDDY. / WHO DO YOU THINK YOU'RE FOOLING**	-	
1966.	(7") <818> **MOONCHILD. / FRYING PAN**	-	
1968.	(7") (AMS 726) **MOONCHILD. / WHO DO YOU THINK YOU'RE FOOLING**		-

—— The CAPTAIN recruited an entire new band . . . **RY COODER** – slide guitar repl. MOON + ST.CLAIRE (they later joined DENNY KING) / **HERB BERMANN** – bass, co-composer repl. HANDLEY / **JOHN FRENCH (DRUMBO)** – drums repl. BLAKELY

		Pye Inter	Kama Sutra
Jan 68.	(7") (7N 25443) **YELLOW BRICK ROAD. / ABBA ZABA**		
Feb 68.	(lp) (NPL 28110) <BDS 5001> **SAFE AS MILK**		1967

– Sure 'nuff n yes I do / Zig zag wanderer / Call on me / Dropout boogie / I'm glad / Electricity / Yellow brick road / Abba zaba / Plastic factory / Where there's woman / Plastic factory / Grown so ugly / Autumn child. (re-iss. 1968 on 'Marble Arch' 2 tracks less; MAL 1117) (re-iss. 1970 on 'Buddah' stereo; 623 171) (re-iss. Jan82 on 'P.R.T.'; NCP 1004) (re-iss. Jul85 on 'Buddah' lp/c; 252260-1/-4) (cd-iss. May91 on 'Castle'; CLACD 234) (cd re-mast.Sep99 on 'Buddha-RCA'; 74321 89175-2) (lp re-iss. Sep99 on 'Simply Vinyl'; SVLP 122)

—— **JEFF COTTON** (ANTENNAE JIMMY SEMENS) – guitar; repl. COODER who went solo

		not iss.	Buddah
1968.	(lp) <BDS 5077> **MIRROR MAN** (rec.1965)	-	

– Tarot plane / Kandy korn / 25th century Quaker / Mirror man. (UK-iss.May71 on 'Buddah'; 2365 002); reached No.49) (re-iss. May82 on 'P.R.T.'; NCP 1006) (re-iss. Apr86 on 'Edsel'; ED 184) (cd-iss. May91 on 'Castle'; CLACD 235) (cd re-mast.Sep99 w/sessions on 'Buddha-RCA'; 74321 69174-2)

		Liberty	Blue Thumb
Dec 68.	(lp; mono/stereo) (LBL/LBS 83172) <BTS 1> **STRICTLY PERSONAL**		

– Ah feel like acid / Safe as milk / Trust us / Son of Mirror Man – Mere man / On tomorrow / Beatles bones 'n' smokin' stones / Gimme that harp boy / Kandy korn. (re-iss. Nov79 lp/c; LBR/TCR 1006) (cd-iss. Aug94 on 'E.M.I.'; CZ 529)

—— The **CAPTAIN** retained **DRUMBO** and **ANTANNAE** plus new members **ZOOT HORN ROLLO** (b.BILL HARKLEROAD) – brass, narrator, guitar, flute / **ROCKETTE NORTON** (b.MARK BOSTON) – bass, narrator repl. HERB / **THE MASCARA SNAKE** (b.VICTOR HAYDEN) – clarinet / guest **DOUG MOON** returned

		Straight	Straight
Nov 69.	(d-lp) (STS 1053) <RS 2027> **TROUT MASK REPLICA**	21	

– Frownland / The dust blows forward 'n dust blows back / Dachau blues / Ella guru / Hair pie: bake 1 / Moonlight on Vermont / Hair pie: bake 2 / Pena / Well / When big Joan sets up / Fallin' ditch / Sugar 'n spikes / Ant man bee / Pachuco cadaver / Bills corpse / Sweet sweet bulbs / Neon meate dream of an octafish / China pig / My human gets me blues / Dali's car / Orange claw hammer / Wild life / She's too much for my mirror / Hobo chang ba / The blimp (mousetrap replica) / Steal softly thru snow / Old fart at play / Veteran's day poppy. *(re-iss. May75 on 'Reprise'; K 64026) (re-iss. cd Sep94 on 'WEA'; K 927 196-2)*

—— **ED MARIMBA** (ART TRIPP) – marimba (ex-MOTHERS OF INVENTION) repl. THE MASCARA SNAKE

Jan 71. (lp) *(STS 1063)* <*RS 6240*> **LICK MY DECALS OFF, BABY**   20
 – Lick my decals off, baby / Doctor Dark / I love you, you big dummy / Peon / Bellerin' plain / Woe-is-uh-me-bop / Japan in a dishpan / I wanna find a woman that'll hold my big toe till I have a go / Petrified forest / One rose that I mean / The Buggy boogie woogie / The Smithsonian Institute blues (or the big dig) / Space-age couple / The clouds are full of wine (not whiskey or rye) / Flash Gordon's ape. *(re-iss. Jul73 on 'Reprise')*

—— **THE WINGED EEL FINGERLING** (r.n. ELLIOT INGBER) – guitar, etc. (ex-MOTHERS etc.) repl. SEMENS who had already formed MU

Reprise   Reprise

Jan 72. (7") <*1068*> **CLICK CLACK. / I'M GONNA BOOGLARIZE YOU BABY**   -

Feb 72. (lp; by CAPTAIN BEEFHEART) *(K 44162)* <*RS 2050*> **THE SPOTLIGHT KID**   44
 – I'm gonna booglarize you baby / White jam / Blabber 'n smoke / When it blows its stacks / Alice in Blunderland / The spotlight kid / Click clack / Grow fins / There ain't no Santa Claus on the evenin' stage / Glider.

—— **ROY 'OREJON' ESTRADA** – bass (ex-LITTLE FEAT, ex-MOTHERS OF INVENTION) repl. INGBER. ROCKETTE moved to guitar, and augmented by backing vocals The **BLACKBERRIES / RUSS TITELMAN** – guitar (guested, as he did on "Safe as Milk")

Nov 72. (lp) *(K 54007)* <*MS 2115*> **CLEAR SPOT**
 – Low yo yo stuff / Nowadays a woman's gotta hit a man / Too much time / Circumstances / My head is my only house unless it rains / Sun zoom sparks / Clear spot / Crazy little thing / Long neck bottles / Her eyes are a blue million miles / Big eyed beans from Venus / Golden birdies.

Mar 73. (7") *(K 14233)* <*1133*> **TOO MUCH TIME. / MY HEAD IS MY ONLY HOUSE UNLESS IT RAINS**

—— **ALEX ST.CLAIRE** – guitar returned to repl. ROY. Added **MARK MERCELLO** – keyboards

Virgin   Mercury

Apr 74. (lp) *(V 2015)* <*SRMI 709*> **UNCONDITIONALLY GUARANTEED**
 – Upon the my-oh-my / Sugar bowl / New electric ride / Magic be / Happy love song / Full Moon, hot Sun / This is the day / Lazy music / Peaches. *(re-iss. Aug82 + Aug85 on 'Fame' lp/c; FA/TCFA 3034) (cd-iss. Jun88; CDV 2015)*

Apr 74. (7") *(VS 110)* **UPON THE MY-OH-MY. / MAGIC BE**   -

Apr 74. (7") <*73494*> **UPON THE MY-OH-MY. / I GOT LOVE ON MY MIND**   -

—— **ELLIOT INGBER** – guitar returned to repl. ST.CLAIRE plus session men **MARK GIBBONS, MICHAEL SMOTHERMAN, JIMMY CARAVAN** – all keyboards repl. MARCELLO.

—— **DEAN SMITH** – guitar / **BOB WEST** – bass / **GENE PELLO** – drums / **TV GRIMES** – percussion

Nov 74. (lp) *(V 2123)* **BLUEJEANS AND MOONBEAMS**
 – Party of special things do / Same old blues / Observatory crest / Pompadour swamp / Captain's holiday / Rock'n'roll's evil doll / Further than we've gone / Twist ah luck / Bluejeans and moonbeams. *(re-iss. Mar84; OVED 19) (cd-iss. Jun88; CDV 2023)*

—— Late '75 **BEEFHEART** collaborated with **FRANK ZAPPA** on "BONGO FURY" album. This was a near live album with 2 studio tracks.

—— His new touring band featured past members **ELLIOT, INGBER** and **JOHN FRENCH** plus **DENNY WHALLEY** – slide guitar / **BRUCE FOWLER** – trombone (both on bongos)

—— His '76 band were **DRUMBO, WHALLEY, JEFF MORRIS TEPPER** – guitar, and **JOHN THOMAS** – piano. They recorded first sessions for the next album

—— **ERIC DREW FELDMAN** – keyboards, bass repl. THOMAS / **ROBERT WILLIAMS** – drums repl. DRUMBO / **RICHARD REDISS** – slide guitar repl. WHALLEY / **ART TRIPP** – marimba returned from MALLARD. **BRUCE FOWLER** also returned.

Virgin   Warners

Feb 80. (lp) *(V 2149)* <*BSK 3256*> **BAT CHAIN PULLER** (US-title 'SHINY BEAST')   1978
 – The floppy boot stomp / Tropical hot dog night / Ice rose / Harry Irene / You know you're a man / Bat chain puller / When I see mommy I feel like a mummy / Owed t'Alex / Candle mambo / Love lies / Suction prints / Apes-ma. *(re-iss. Aug88; OVED 67) (cd-iss. Jun87; CDV 2149)*

—— **GARY LUCAS** – guitar repl. REDISS

Virgin   Virgin

Aug 80. (lp) *(V 2172)* **DOC AT RADAR STATION**
 – Hot head / Ashtray heart / A carrot is as close as a rabbit gets to a diamond / Run paint run run / Sue Egypt / Brickbats / Dirty blue Gene / Best batch yet / Telephone / Flavour bud living / Sheriff of Hong Kong / Making love to a vampire with a monkey on my knee. *(re-iss. Aug88; OVED 68) (cd-iss. Jun88; CDV 2172)*

—— The CAPTAIN brought in **HATSIZE SNYDER, CLIFF MARTINEZ, WILLIAMS, LAMBOURNE FOWLER** and DRUMBO

Virgin   Epic

Aug 82. (12") *(VS 534-12)* <*03190*> **LIGHT REFLECTED OFF THE OCEANS OF THE MOON. / ICE CREAM FOR CROW**

Sep 82. (lp) *(V 2237)* **ICE CREAM FOR CROW**   90
 – Ice cream for crow / The host, the ghost, the most holy-o / Semi-multi-(coloured) caucasian / Hey Garland, I dig your tweed coat / Evening bell / Cardboard cut-out sundown / The past is sure tense / Ink mathematics / The witch doctor life / "81" poop hatch / The thousand and tenth day of the human totem pole / Skeleton makes good. *(re-iss. Aug88; OVED 121) (cd-iss. Apr88; CDV 2237)*

—— He retired from music business to concentrate on painting/sculpting in his recently bought Mojave desert home.

– compilations etc. –

Jul 70. (lp) *Buddah; (2349 002)* **DROPOUT BOOGIE**   -
 (a re-iss. of "SAFE AS MILK" 2 tracks less)

1975. (lp) *WRMB;* **WHAT'S ALL THIS BOOGA-BOOGA MUSIC (live)**

Aug 76. (d-lp) *Reprise; (K 84006)* **TWO ORIGINALS OF . . .**
 – LICK MY DECALS OFF, BABY / THE SPOTLIGHT KID.

Nov 77. (d-lp/d-c) *Pye; (FILD/ZCFILD 008)* **THE CAPTAIN BEEFHEART FILE** (first 2-lp's)

1978. (d-lp) *Impossible;* **EASY TEETH**

Jan 78. (7") *Buddah; (BDS 466)* **SURE 'NUFF 'N' YES I DO. / ELECTRICITY**

May 78. (7") *M.C.A.; (MCA 366)* **HARD WORKIN' MAN** (by Jack Nitzsche featuring Captain Beefheart). **/ Coke Machine (by Jack Nitzsche)**   -

—— Above also features RY COODER – on guitar

1978. (7"pic-ep) *Virgin; (SIXPACK 1)* **SIX-PACK / SIX TRACK**   -
 – Sugar bowl / Same old blues / Upon the My-Oh-My / Magic be / Rock'n'roll's evil doll / New electric ride.

Jul 83. (10"lp/c) *P.R.T.; (DOW/ZCDOW 15)* **MUSIC IN SEA MINOR**

Jul 84. (lp/pic-lp) *Design; (PIL/+P 4)* **TOP SECRET**

Oct 84. (m-lp) *A&M; (AMY 226)* **THE LEGENDARY SESSIONS**
 – Diddy wah diddy / Who do you think you're folling / Moonchild / Frying pan / Here I am, I always am. *(re-iss. Oct86 on 'Edsel'; BLIMP 902) (cd-iss. Mar92; BLIMPCD 902)*

Jun 88. (d-lp)(c)(d-cd) *That's Original; (TFO LP/MC/CD 11)* **SAFE AS MILK / MIRROR MAN**
 (re-iss. d-cd.May91 on 'Castle')

Feb 91. (d-cd) *Reprise; (7599 26249-2)* **THE SPOTLIGHT KID / CLEAR SPOT**

Jul 91. (cd) *The Collection; (ORO 146)* **ZIG ZAG WANDERER**
 (re-iss. Nov96 on 'Wooden Hill'; HILLCD 6)

Jun 92. (cd) *Sequel; (NEXCD 215)* **I MAY BE HUNGRY BUT I SURE AIN'T WEIRD – THE ALTERNATIVE CAPTAIN BEEFHEART**

Jun 93. (cd) *Virgin; (CDVM 9028)* **A CARROT IS AS CLOSE AS A RABBIT GETS TO A DIAMOND**

Nov 93. (cd) *Movieplay Gold; (MPG 74025)* **LONDON 1974 (live)**

Jan 98. (cd) *Camden-RCA; (74321 55846-2)* **ELECTRICITY**

May 99. (5xcd-box) *Revenant; (REV 210)* **GROW FINS** (rarities 1965-1982)

May 99. (d-lp) *Xeric; (XERLP 96)* **GROW FINS VOL.1 – JUST GOT BACK FROM THE CITY 1965-1967 / ELECTRICITY 1968**

Sep 99. (d-lp) *Xeric; (XERLP 97)* **GROW FINS VOL.2 – THE TROUT MASK REPLICA HOUSE SESSIONS 1969**

CAPTAIN SENSIBLE   (dig out; Great Alt & Indie . . .)

CARAVAN   (dig out; Great Psychedelic . . .)

CARDIACS   (dig out; Great Alt & Indie . . .)

CARDIGANS

Formed: Jonkoping, Sweden . . . October 1992 by songwriters PETER SVENSSON and MAGNUS SVENINGSSON, along with LARS-OLAF JOHANSSON, BENGT LAGERBERG and cutesy bombshell, NINA PERSSON. Despite the fact the band's founding members came from a heavy-metal background, The CARDIGANS' sound leaned more towards fragile, angelic indie-pop drawing on the melodic traditions of fellow Swedes, ABBA and UK pop ironists BEAUTIFUL SOUTH as well as French 60's pop (especially FRANCOISE HARDY's Burt Bacharach period). They initially released an album in Sweden before signing to 'Polydor' UK and in 1995/96, scored minor successes with 'CARNIVAL', 'SICK & TIRED' and 'RISE & SHINE', all stemming from their UK debut album, 'LIFE' (1995). In the late summer of '96, they peaked critically with the starry-eyed 'LOVEFOOL', a near Top 20 hit first time around and an even bigger success upon its re-issue in conjunction with the 'Romeo & Juliet' soundtrack in 1997. The song was a standout track on their acclaimed follow-up set, 'THE FIRST BAND ON THE MOON', although the band no doubt came to regard it as something of an albatross round their necks. Presumably a reaction to being filed under Scando-pop, the more deliberately experimental 'GRAN TURISMO' (1998) saw the band sacrifice some of their charm for instant "alternative" appeal.
• **Covered:** SABBATH BLOODY SABBATH + IRON MAN (Black Sabbath) / MR. CROWLEY (Ozzy Osbourne) / BOYS ARE BACK IN TOWN (Thin Lizzy).

Album rating: EMMERDALE (*6) / LIFE (*8) / FIRST BAND ON THE MOON (*7) / GRAN TURISMO (*6)

NINA PERSSON (b. Karlskoga, Sweden) – vocals / **PETER SVENSSON** – guitar / **MAGNUS SVENINGSSON** – bass / **LARS-OLAF JOHANSSON** – keyboards / **BENGT LAGERBERG** – drums, flute

Trampolene   not iss.

Feb 94. (cd) *(TRACD 1501)* **EMMERDALE**   -   Sweden
 – Sick & tired / Black letter day / In the afternoon / Over the water / After all . . . / Cloudy sky / Our space / Rise and shine / Celia inside / Sabbath bloody sabbath / Seems hard / The last song. *(UK-iss.Jan97 on 'Stockholm' cd/c; 523215-2/-4) (re-iss. May99; same)*

May 94. (cd-s) *(TRACDS 501)* **RISE & SHINE / AFTER ALL**   -   Sweden

Aug 94. (cd-s) *(TRACDS 502)* **BLACK LETTER DAY / I FIGURED OUT**   -   Sweden

Sep 94. (cd-s) *(TRACDS 503)* **SICK & TIRED / PLAIN PARADE / LAIKA / POOH SONG**   -   Sweden

		Stockholm–Polydor	Minty Fresh
Nov 94.	(7"/c-s) *(PO/+CS 336)* **SICK & TIRED. / PLAIN PARADE**		

(cd-s) *(PZCD 336)* – ('A'side) / Pooh song / The boys are back in town / Carnival (Puck version).

		Stockholm–Polydor	Minty Fresh
May 95.	(7"/c-s) *(PO/+CS 345)* **CARNIVAL. / MR. CROWLEY (live)**	72	-

(cd-s+=) *(PZCD 345)* – Emmerdale.
(re-iss. Nov95, hit No.35; same)

Jun 95.	(c-s) *(577311-4)* **SICK & TIRED / PLAIN PARADE**	58	

– Carnival / Gordon's garden party / Daddy's car / Sick & tired / Tomorrow / Rise & shine / Beautiful one / Travelling with Charley / Fine / Celia inside / Hey! get out of my way / After all. *(cd re-iss. May99; same) (lp re-iss. Sep99 on 'Simply Vinyl'; SVLP 114)*

Sep 95.	(c-s) *(577311-4)* **SICK & TIRED / PLAIN PARADE**	34	

(cd-s+=) *(577311-2)* – Laika / Pooh song.

Feb 96.	(7"/c-s) *(577824-7/-4)* **RISE & SHINE. / PIKE BUBBLES**	29	

(cd-s+=) *(577825-2)* – Cocktail party bloody cocktail party.

		Stockholm–Polydor	Mercury
Sep 96.	(7"white/c-s) *(575528-7/-4)* **LOVEFOOL. / NASTY SUNNY BEAM**	21	

(cd-s+=) *(575295-2)* – Iron man (first try).

Sep 96.	(cd/c/lp) *(<533117-2/-4/-1>)* **FIRST BAND ON THE MOON**	18	35

– Your new cuckoo / Been it / Heartbreaker / Happy meal II / Never recover / Step on me / Lovefool / Loser / Iron man / The great divide / Choke. *(cd re-iss. May99; same*

Nov 96.	(7"brown/c-s) *(575966-7/-4)* **BEEN IT. / BEEN IT (radio)**	56	

(cd-s+=) *(575966-2)* – Blah blah blah / Losers (first try).
below was featured on the film 'Romeo & Juliet'

Apr 97.	(c-s) *(571050-4)* **LOVEFOOL / ('A'-Todd Terry remix)**	2	

(cd-s+=) *(571050-2)* – ('A'-Todd Terry's frozen sun mix).
(cd-s) *(571051-2)* – ('A'side) / Sick & tired (live) / Carnival (live) / Rise & shine (live).

Aug 97.	(7"/c-s) *(571633-7/-4)* **YOUR NEW CUCKOO. / LOVEFOOL (radio)**	35	

(cd-s+=) *(571633-2)* – I figured out (demo '93) / After all (demo '93).
(cd-s) *(571661-2)* – ('A'radio) / ('A'-Hyper disco mix) / ('A'-Super stereo mix).

Oct 98.	(c-s) *(567988-4)* **MY FAVOURITE GAME / LOVEFOOL (live)**	14	-

(cd-s+=) *(567991-2)* – ('A'-Wubbledub mix).
(cd-s) *(567989-2)* – ('A'side) / War / Sick and tired (live).

Oct 98.	(cd/c) *(<559081-2/-4>)* **GRAN TURISMO**	8	

– Paralyzed / Erase – Rewind / Explode / Starter / Hanging around / Higher / Marvel hill / My favourite game / Do you believe / Junk of the hearts / Nil.

Feb 99.	(c-s) *(563535-4)* **ERASE – REWIND / MY FAVOURITE GAME**	7	-

(cd-s+=) *(563533-2)* – Explode (remixed) / ('B'-CD-Rom).
(cd-s) *(563535-2)* – ('A'side) / ('A'mixes; Cut La Roc vocal mix & Naid remix).

Jul 99.	(c-s) *(561268-4)* **HANGING AROUND / MY FAVOURITE GAME (acoustic radio session)**	17	-

(cd-s) *(561268-2)* – ('A'side) / Erase – Rewind (CD-Rom video; banned directors cut).
(cd-s) *(561269-2)* – ('A'side) / My favourite game (Rollo from Faithless remix) / ('A'-CD-ROM video).

—— The CARDIGANS backed TOM JONES on a collaborative single, 'Burning Down The House'.

– compilations, etc. –

May 97.	(10xcd-ep-box) *Border; (CARDSIN 1)* **THE COMPLETE SINGLES COLLECTION**		

—— there is also a Various Artists tribute album *(TR 012CD)*

Belinda CARLISLE (see under ⇒ GO-GO'S)

CARPENTERS

Formed: Downey, California, USA . . . early 1969 by the brother and sister team of RICHARD and KAREN CARPENTER. Eldest child RICHARD grew up in a musical household, initially learning the accordion and transferring his skills to the piano at the age of nine. He eventually ended up at Yale studying classical music at the tender age of sixteen. As a student he filled in for local jazz combos in his spare time and this put him in good stead for his later years as did his spell as local choir arranger. Meanwhile, sister KAREN, following in his footsteps four years later, decided that her talents lay in drumming(!). When, in their latter teens, they decided to form the short-lived jazz group, The CARPENTER TRIO, they enlisted the help of a tuba and bass playing friend, WES JACOBS. The combo survived just long enough to secure a recording contract with 'R.C.A.' after winning a Hollywood talent show in 1965. Although they had moved to California and were surrounded by bands like The BYRDS and The GRATEFUL DEAD, the trio had decided that romantic schmaltz was their thing and, with typical Mormon thoroughness, proceeded to increase and multiply into a six-piece outfit called SPECTRUM (other members being DANNY WOODHAM and JOHN BETTIS). The new look combo unsurprisingly flopped in the era of acid and free love. Brother and sister duly took up various odd jobs while continuing to hone their talents; the pair also signed up for some singing lessons and even performed as a twosome at Disneyland. Subsequently discovering their talent for close harmony, they proceeded to cut a few demos which eventually reached the ears of HERB ALPERT at 'A&M' records. Sensing the gap in a market overrun with heavy rock bands, he signed them immediately. Their debut album, 'TICKET TO RIDE' (1969), which obviously featured their easy-listening (minor hit) rendition of the BEATLES classic, showed at least some promise although it was subsequently decided that their brand of vocals needed a professionally crafted tune to best showcase their talents. This

was achieved with a BURT BACHARACH number, '(THEY LONG TO BE) CLOSE TO YOU', which sold over a million copies and topped the US charts (Top 10 in the UK) in the summer of 1970; middle American could sleep safe in their beds again, the hippy dominance of the charts was finally over! From then on, The CARPENTERS' flawless MOR formula saw them conquering the charts on both sides of the Atlantic. Massive hits came thick and fast, starting with 'WE'VE ONLY JUST BEGUN' and running through 'FOR ALL WE KNOW', 'RAINY DAYS AND MONDAYS', 'SUPERSTAR', 'HURTING EACH OTHER', 'GOODBYE TO LOVE', 'SING', 'YESTERDAY ONCE MORE' and 'TOP OF THE WORLD'. By the end of '73, the duo certainly were on top of the world as a singles compilation went multi-platinum and cemented their reputation as everyone's favourite purveyors of clean-cut all-American ballad-pop. An old HANK WILLIAMS favourite, 'JAMBALAYA (ON THE BAYOU)', provided them with yet another smash hit, although only in Britain. After two further classy Top 10 hits ('PLEASE MR. POSTMAN' and 'ONLY YESTERDAY') in late '74/early '75, the duo's cutesy appeal began to wane. Perhaps as a result, they cut the uncharacteristically spaced-out 'CALLING OCCUPANTS OF INTERPLANETARY CRAFT'. The track was a UK Top 10 hit in 1977 although America wasn't quite so appreciative and it lingered outside the Billboard Top 30. They continued recording and touring sporadically prior to KAREN's death from heart failure on February the 4th, 1983. This was a direct result of the anorexia nervosa problem which had dogged her in her final years and which she tried in vain to keep secret from her adoring fans. • **Songwriters:** RICHARD co-wrote most with JOHN BETTIS, except covers WE'VE ONLY JUST BEGUN + I WON'T LAST A DAY WITHOUT YOU (Paul Williams-Roger Nichols) / HURTING EACH OTHER + OUR DAY WILL COME (Ruby & The Romantics) / FUN, FUN, FUN (Beach Boys) / THE END OF THE WORLD (Skeeter Davis) / DA DOO RON RON (Crystals) / DEADMAN'S CURVE (Jan & Dean) / JOHNNY ANGEL (Shelley Fabares) / THE NIGHT HAS A THOUSAND EYES (Bobby Vee) / ONE FINE DAY (Chiffons) / PLEASE MR.POSTMAN + BEECHWOOD 4-5789 (Marvelettes) / THERE'S A KIND OF HUSH (Herman's Hermits) / GOOFUS (Wayne King) / BREAKING UP IS HARD TO DO (Neil Sedaka) / DON'T CRY FOR ME ARGENTINA (Julie Covington; hit) / MAN SMART, WOMAN SMARTER (Robert Palmer) / DESPERADO (Eagles).

Best CD compilation: ONLY YESTERDAY (*8)

KAREN CARPENTER (b. 2 Mar'50, New Haven, Connecticut, USA) – vocals, drums / **RICHARD CARPENTER** (15 Oct'46, New Haven) – keyboards, vocals

		A&M	A&M
Nov 69.	(lp) *<4205>* **TICKET TO RIDE**	-	

– Invocation / Your wonderful parade / Someday / Get together / All of my life / Turn away / Ticket to ride / Don't be afraid / What's the use / All I can do / Eve / Nowadays Clancy can't even sing / Benediction. *<re-dist.Feb71> (UK-iss.Apr72; AMLS 64342)* – hit No.20 *(re-iss. Jun75 on 'Hamlet-A&M'; AMLP 8001)* – hit No.35 *(re-iss. Jul79 on 'Music For Pleasure' lp/c; MFP/TC-MFP 50431) (cd-iss. Jul87; CDA 4205) (re-iss. Oct92 cd/c; CD/C MID 137) (cd re-iss. Nov98; 394205-2)*

Feb 70.	(7") *(1142)* **TICKET TO RIDE. / YOUR WONDERFUL PARADE**	-	54
Aug 70.	(7") *(AMS 800) <1183>* **(THEY LONG TO BE) CLOSE TO YOU. / I KEPT ON LOVING YOU**	6	1 Jun70
Dec 70.	(7") *(AMS 813) <1217>* **WE'VE ONLY JUST BEGUN. / ALL OF MY LIFE**	28	2 Sep70
Dec 70.	(7") *<1236>* **MERRY CHRISTMAS DARLING. / MR. GUDER**	-	
Jan 71.	(lp/c) *(AMLS/CAM 998) <4271>* **CLOSE TO YOU**	23	2 Sep70

– We've only just begun / Love is surrender / Maybe it's you / Reason to believe / Help / (They long to be) Close to you / Baby it's you / I'll never fall in love again / Crescent moon / Mr. Guder / I kept on loving you / Another song. *(cd-iss. 1988; CDA 3184) (re-iss. Oct92 cd/c; CD/C MID 136) (cd re-iss. Nov98; 393184-2)*

Jan 71.	(7") *<1243>* **FOR ALL WE KNOW. / DON'T BE AFRAID**	-	3
May 71.	(7") *<1260>* **RAINY DAYS AND MONDAYS. / SATURDAY**	-	2
Aug 71.	(7") *<1289>* **SUPERSTAR. / BLESS THE BEASTS AND CHILDREN**	-	2
			67
Sep 71.	(7") *(AMS 864)* **SUPERSTAR. / FOR ALL WE KNOW**	18	-
Oct 71.	(lp/c) *(AMLH/CAM 63502) <3502>* **THE CARPENTERS**	12	2 May71

– Rainy days and Mondays / Saturday / Let me be the one / (A place to) Hideaway / For all we know / Superstar / Druscilla Penny / One love / Bacharach-David medley:- Knowing when to leave – Make it easy on yourself – (There's) Always something there to remind me – I'll never fall in love again – Walk on by – Do you know the way to San Jose / Sometimes. *(cd-iss. Jul87; CD 3502) (re-iss. Oct92 cd/c; CD/C MID 145) (re-iss. May93 on 'Spectrum' cd/c; 550063-2/-4) (cd re-iss. Nov98; 393502-2)*

Dec 71.	(7"m) *(AME 601)* **MERRY CHRISTMAS DARLING. / TICKET TO RIDE / SATURDAY**	45	-
Jan 72.	(7") *<1322>* **HURTING EACH OTHER. / MAYBE IT'S YOU**	-	2
Jun 72.	(7") *(AMS 7006) <1351>* **IT'S GONNA TAKE SOME TIME. / FLAT BAROQUE**	-	12 Apr72
Jul 72.	(7") *<1367>* **GOODBYE TO LOVE. / CRYSTAL LULLABY**	-	7
Aug 72.	(7") *(AMS 7023)* **GOODBYE TO LOVE. / I WON'T LAST A DAY WITHOUT YOU**	9	-
Sep 72.	(lp/c) *(AMLS/CAM 63511) <3511>* **A SONG FOR YOU**	13	4 Jul72

– A song for you / Top of the world / Hurting each other / It's going to take some time / Goodbye to love / Intermission / Bless the beasts and children / Flat baroque / Piano picker / I won't last a day without you / Crystal lullaby / Road ode / A song for you – reprise. *(cd-iss. 1988; CDA 3511) (re-iss. Oct92 cd/c; CD/C MID 139) (cd re-iss. Nov98; 393511-2)*

Mar 73.	(7") *(AMS 7059) <1413>* **SING. / DRUSCILLA PENNY**		3 Feb73
Jun 73.	(7") *(AMS 7073) <1446>* **YESTERDAY ONCE MORE. / ROAD ODE**	2	2 May73
Jul 73.	(lp/c) *(AMLH/CAM 63519) <3519>* **NOW AND THEN**	2	2 May72

– Sing / This masquerade / Heather / Jambalaya (on the bayou) / I can't make music / Yesterday once more / Fun, fun, fun – The end of the world – Da doo ron ron – Deadman's curve – Johnny Angel – The night has a thousand eyes – Our day will come – One fine day / Yesterday once more (reprise). *(cd-iss. Nov88; CDA 3519) (re-iss. Oct92 cd/c; CD/C MID 140) (re-iss. Nov98; 393519-2)*

Sep 73. (7") *<1468>* **TOP OF THE WORLD. / HEATHER** | - | 1 |

Oct 73. (7") *(AMS 7086)* **TOP OF THE WORLD. / YOUR WONDERFUL PARADE** | 5 | - |

Jan 74. (lp/c) *(AMLH/CAM 63601) <3601>* **THE SINGLES 1969-1973 (compilation)** | 1 | 1 | Nov73
– We've only just begun / Top of the world / Ticket to ride / Superstar / Rainy days and Mondays / Goodbye to love / Yesterday once more / It's going to take some time / Sing / For all we know / Hurting each other / Close to you. *(cd-iss. Jun84; CDA 63601)*

Feb 74. (7") *(AMS 7098)* **JAMBALAYA (ON THE BAYOU). / MR. GUDER** | 12 | - |

May 74. (7") *(AMS 7111) <1521>* **I WON'T LAST A DAY WITHOUT YOU. / ONE LOVE** | 32 | 11 | Apr74

Dec 74. (7") *(AMS 7141) <1646>* **PLEASE MR. POSTMAN. / THIS MASQUERADE** | 2 | 1 | Nov74

Dec 74. (7") *(AMS 7144) <1648>* **SANTA CLAUS IS COMING TO TOWN. / MERRY CHRISTMAS DARLING**
(re-iss. Dec75 – hit UK No.37) (re-iss. Dec78)

Apr 75. (7") *(AMS 7159) <1677>* **ONLY YESTERDAY. / HAPPY** | 7 | 4 | Mar75

Jun 75. (lp/c) *(AMLK/CAM 64530) <4530>* **HORIZON** | 1 | 13 |
– Aurora / Only yesterday / Desperado / Please Mr. Postman / I can dream can't I / Solitaire / Happy / (I'm caught between) Goodbye and I love you / Love me for what I am / Eventide. *(re-iss. 1988 cd/c; 394530-2/-4) (re-iss. Oct92 cd/c; CD/C MID 141) (cd re-iss. Nov98; 394530-2)*

Aug 75. (7") *(AMS 7187) <1721>* **SOLITAIRE. / LOVE ME FOR WHAT I AM** | 32 | 17 | Jul75

Mar 76. (7") *(AMS 7219) <1800>* **THERE'S A KIND OF HUSH (ALL OVER THE WORLD). / (I'M CAUGHT BETWEEN) GOODBYE AND I LOVE YOU** | 22 | 12 | Feb76

Jun 76. (lp/c) *(AMLK 64581) <4581>* **A KIND OF HUSH** | 3 | 33 | Jul76
– There's a kind of hush (all over the world) / You / Sandy / Goofus / Can't smile without you / I need to be in love / One more time / Boat to sail / I have you / Breaking up is hard to do. *(re-iss. Mar82 lp/c; AMID/CMID 117) (cd-iss. 1987; 393197-2) (re-iss. Oct92 cd/c; CD/C MID 142) (cd re-iss. Nov98; 393197-2)*

Jun 76. (7") *(AMS 7238) <1828>* **I NEED TO BE IN LOVE. / SANDY** | 36 | 25 |

Aug 76. (7") *<1859>* **GOOFUS. / BOAT TO SAIL** | - | 56 |

Jan 77. (lp/c) *(AMLS/CAM 68403)* **LIVE AT THE PALLADIUM (live)** | 28 | - |
– Flat baroque / There's a kind of hush (all over the world) / Jambalaya (on the bayou) / Medley; Piano picker – Strike up the band – S'wonderful – Fascinating rhythm – Warsaw concerto – From this moment on / Medley; (They long to be) Close to you – For all we know – Top of the world – Ticket to ride / Only yesterday / I won't last a day without you / Hurting each other / Superstar / Rainy days and Mondays / Goodbye to love / We've only just begun. *(re-iss. May84 on 'Hallmark' lp/c; SHM/HSC 3142) (cd-iss. Mar90 on 'Pickwick'; PWKS 572)*

May 77. (7") *(AMS 7294) <1940>* **ALL YOU GET FROM LOVE IS A LOVE SONG. / I HAVE YOU** | | 35 |

Oct 77. (7") *(AMS 7318) <1978>* **CALLING OCCUPANTS OF INTERPLANETARY CRAFT. / CAN'T SMILE WITHOUT YOU** | 9 | 32 |

Oct 77. (lp/c) *(AMLK 64703) <4703>* **PASSAGE** | 12 | 49 |
– B'wanna she no home / All you get from love is a love song / I just fell in love again / On the balcony of the Casa Rosada – Don't cry for me Argentina / Sweet, sweet smile / Two sides / Man smart, woman smarter / Calling occupants of interplanetary craft. *(cd-iss. 1988; 393188-2) (re-iss. Oct92 cd/c; CD/C MID 143) (cd re-iss. Nov98; 394703-2)*

Jan 78. (7") *<2008>* **SWEET, SWEET SMILE. / I HAVE YOU** | | 44 |

Feb 78. (7") *(AMS 7327)* **SWEET, SWEET SMILE. / TWO SIDES** | 40 | - |

Nov 78. (lp/c) *(AMLT/CTM 19748)* **THE SINGLES 1974-1978 (compilation)** | 2 | - |
– Sweet, sweet smile / Jambalaya (on the bayou) / Can't smile without you / I won't last a day without you / All you get from love is a long song / Only yesterday / Solitaire / Please Mr. Postman / I need to be in love / Happy / There's a kind of hush (all over the world) / Calling occupants of interplanetary craft. *(cd-iss. 1988 & Nov98; CDA 19748)*

Dec 78. (7") *<2097>* **I BELIEVE YOU. / B'WANNA SHE NO HOME** | - | 68 |

—— in 1979, KAREN recorded an unfinished album with producer Phil Ramone

Jun 81. (7") *(AMS 8141) <2344>* **TOUCH ME WHEN WE'RE DANCING. / BECAUSE WE ARE IN LOVE (THE WEDDING SONG)** | | 16 |

Jun 81. (lp/c) *(AMLK 63723) <3723>* **MADE IN AMERICA** | 12 | |
– Those good old dreams / Strength of a woman / (Want you) Back in my life again / When you've got what it takes / Somebody's been lyin' / I believe you / Touch me when we're dancing / When it's gone / Beechwood 4-5789 / Because we are in love. *(cd-iss. 1987; 393723-2) (re-iss. Oct92 cd/c; CD/C MID 146) (cd re-iss. Nov98; 393723-2)*

Aug 81. (7") *(AMS 8153)* **BEECHWOOD 4-5789. / SOMEBODY'S BEEN LYIN'** | | - |

Sep 81. (7") *<2370>* **(WANT YOU) BACK IN MY LIFE AGAIN. / SOMEBODY'S BEEN LYIN'** | - | 72 |

Oct 81. (7") *(AMS 8181)* **THOSE GOOD OLD DREAMS. / (WANT YOU) BACK IN MY LIFE AGAIN**

Dec 81. (7") *<2386>* **THOSE GOOD OLD DREAMS. / WHEN IT'S GONE (IT'S JUST GONE)** | - | 63 |

Apr 82. (7") *<2405>* **BEECHWOOD 4-5789. / TWO SIDES** | - | 74 |

—— Sadly, on the 4th of February '83, KAREN died of heart failure. The duo had just recorded – what was to be – their final album.

Oct 83. (7") *(AM 147) <2585>* **MAKE BELIEVE IT'S YOUR FIRST TIME. / LOOK TO YOUR DREAMS** | 60 | |
(re-iss. Oct84 on 'E.M.I.'; EMI 5501)

Oct 83. (lp/c/cd) *(AMLX/CAM/CDA 64954) <4954>* **VOICE OF THE HEART** | 6 | 46 | Nov83
– Now / Sailing on the tide / Make believe it's your first time / Two lives / At the end of a song / Ordinary fool / Your baby doesn't love you anymore / Look to your dreams. *(re-iss. Oct92 cd/c; CD/C MID 144) (cd re-iss. Nov98; 394954-2)*

Dec 83. (7") *(AM 166)* **NOW. / LOOK TO YOUR DREAMS** | | - |

Jan 84. (7") *<2620>* **YOUR BABY DOESN'T LOVE YOU ANYMORE. / SAILING ON THE TIDE** | - | - |

– compilations, etc. –

on 'A&M' unless mentioned otherwise

Dec 75. (d-lp) *(CSW 301-02)* **LIVE IN JAPAN (live)** | | | Japan

Mar 76. (3xlp-box) *(CARP 1000)* **THE CARPENTERS COLLECTION** – (first 3 albums from 69/70/71)

Dec 78. (lp/c) *(AMLH/CAM 64726) <4726>* **CHRISTMAS PORTRAIT (festive songs)** | | |
(cd-iss. 1988; 395173-2) (re-iss. Oct92 cd/c; CD/C MID 147)

Apr 79. (d-lp) *(GXF 9001/2)* **SILVER DOUBLE DISC OF THE CARPENTERS** | | |

Dec 81. (4xlp-box) *World; (ALBUM 92)* **THE BEST OF THE CARPENTERS** | | | mail-o

Oct 84. (d-lp) *(SING 1) <6601>* **YESTERDAY ONCE MORE (THE CARPENTERS COLLECTION – THE VERY BEST OF . . .)** | 10 | | May85
(cd-iss. 1988 on 'E.M.I.'; CDP 260296-8) (d-cd re-iss. Nov98; 541000-2)

Dec 84. (lp/c) *<(AMA/AMC 3270)>* **AN OLD-FASHIONED CHRISTMAS (festive songs)** | | |

Dec 84. (7") *<2700>* **DO YOU HEAR WHAT I HEAR? / LITTLE ALTAR BOY** | - | |

Sep 85. (7") *Old Gold; (OG 9541)* **YESTERDAY ONCE MORE. / (THEY LONG TO BE) CLOSE TO YOU** | - | |

May 87. (cd) *(CDA 6750)* **CARPENTERS CLASSICS** | | |

Apr 88. (cd-ep) *(AMCD 901)* **COMPACT HITS** | | |
– (They long to be) Close to you / We've only just begun / I won't last a day without you / Goodbye to love.

Dec 88. (lp/c/cd) *Telstar; (1011-1/-4/-2)* **THE HIT COLLECTION** | | - |

Oct 89. (lp/c/cd) *(AMA/AMC/CDA 3931)* **LOVELINES (rare tracks & 4 KAREN CARPENTER solo)** | 73 | |
– Lovelines / Where do I go from here? / The uninvited guest / If we try / I just fall in love again / Kiss me the way you did last night / Remember when lovin' took all night / You're the one / Honolulu city lights / Slow dance / If I had you / Little girl blue. *(re-iss. Oct92 cd/c; CD/C MID 148) (cd re-iss. Nov98; 395282-2)*

Oct 89. (7") *<8667>* **HONOLULU CITY LIGHTS. / I JUST FALL IN LOVE AGAIN** | - | |

Nov 89. (12xcd-box) *(CARCD 20)* **THE COMPACT DISC COLLECTION** *(re-iss. Nov90 on 12xc-box; CARMC 12)* | | |

Feb 90. (7"; by KAREN CARPENTER) *<1471>* **THE UNINVITED GUEST. / IF I HAD YOU** | - | |

Mar 90. (cd/c/d-lp) *(CDA/AMC/AMA 1990)* **ONLY YESTERDAY: RICHARD AND KAREN CARPENTER'S GREATEST HITS (some remixed)** | 1 | - |
– Yesterday once more / Superstar / Rainy days and Mondays / Top of the world / Ticket to ride / Goodbye to love / This masquerade / Hurting each other / Solitaire / We've only just begun / Those good old dreams / Please Mr. Postman / I won't last a day without you / Touch me when we're dancing / Jambalaya (on the bayou) / For all we know / All you get from love is a love song / (They long to be) Close to you / Only yesterday / Calling occupants of interplanetary craft.

Nov 90. (7") *(AM 716)* **MERRY CHRISTMAS DARLING. / (THEY LONG TO BE) CLOSE TO YOU** | 25 | |

Oct 91. (4xcd-box) *(396875-2)* **FROM THE TOP** | | |

Feb 93. (7"c-s) *(AM/+C 0180)* **RAINY DAYS AND MONDAYS (radio remix). / GOODBYE TO LOVE** | 63 | |
(cd-s+=) (AMCD 0180) – Still crazy after all these years / Let me be the one.

May 93. (cd/c) *Royal Collection; (RC 83103)* **RADIO YEARS** | | |

Sep 94. (cd/c) *Pickwick; PWK S/MC 4089)* **TREASURES** | | |

Oct 94. (cd/c) *(540251-2/-4)* **INTERPRETATIONS (A 25th ANNIVERSARY CELEBRATION)** | 29 | |
(re-iss. Nov98; same)

Dec 94. (7"/c-s) *(580761-7/-4)* **TRYIN' TO GET THE FEELING AGAIN. /** | 44 | - |
(cd-s+=) (580761-2) –

Nov 95. (cd/c) *Spectrum; (551593-2/-4)* **REFLECTIONS** | | |
(re-iss. Nov98; same)

Nov 96. (cd/c; by KAREN CARPENTER) *<(540588-2/-4)>* **KAREN CARPENTER** | | |

Nov 96. (d-cd) *(540603-2)* **CHRISTMAS COLLECTION** | | |

Jun 97. (cd) *Harmony; (HM 004)* **THE CARPENTERS** | | |

Nov 97. (cd/c) *<(540838-2/-4)>* **LOVE SONGS** | 53 | |

RICHARD CARPENTER

Sep 87. (7"; with DUSTY SPRINGFIELD) *(AM 406) <2940>* **SOMETHING IN YOUR EYES. / TIME** | | |
(12"+=) (AMY 406) – Say yeah!

Sep 87. (lp/c/cd) *<(AMA/AMC/CDA 5117)>* **TIME** | | |
– Say yeah! / Who do you love? / When time was all we had / Time / Calling your name again / In love alone / Remind me to tell you / That's what I believe / I'm still not over you.

Oct 87. (7") *(AM 417)* **IN LOVE ALONE. / THAT'S WHAT I BELIEVE** | | - |

Nov 87. (7") *<2998>* **CALLING YOUR NAME AGAIN. / TIME** | - | |

Paul CARRACK (see under ⇒ ACE)

CARS

Formed: Boston, Massachusetts, USA ... 1976 by BENJAMIN ORR, GREG HAWKES and ELLIOT EASTON who started out touring as CAP 'N' SWING. Manager Fred Davis was successful in getting a demo of 'JUST WHAT I NEEDED' playlisted on US radio and they duly signed to 'Elektra', having added RIC OCASEK and DAVID ROBINSON. The track was released simultaneously with their eponymous 1978 debut album, an American new wave milestone which also caught the attention of UK hipsters eager for something a bit easier on the ear than British punk. Taking 70's Anglo art-rock as base material, The CARS combined synthesized cool with an American classic rock sensibility. This recipe was realised in irresistably infectious style with 'MY BEST FRIEND'S GIRL', a UK Top 3 hit later that year. On subsequent albums however, the band's predeliction for moody experimentation saw the singles dry up. Though 'CANDY-O' (1979), 'PANORAMA' (1980) and 'SHAKE IT UP' (1981), all reached the US Top 10, they spawned only a couple of major hits in the former's 'LET'S GO' and the latter's title track while further success in Britain had faltered completely. After a two year break, however (during which time, OCASEK released a solo set, 'BEATITUDE' – 1983), the band returned with the commercially revved-up 'HEARTBEAT CITY' (1984). Motoring squarely for the AOR market, the group scored a sizeable Top 5 transatlantic hit with the polished atmospherics of the ORR-penned 'DRIVE'. The song would later become forever linked with images of famine-plagued Ethiopia after it was used as part of a Live Aid documentary. The album itself made the Top 5 and provided a further two major Stateside hits in 'YOU MIGHT THINK' and 'MAGIC'. After a mid-80's break during which the various members pursued solo projects, The CARS spluttered to a halt with the poorly received 'DOOR TO DOOR' in 1987. OCASEK reappeared from time to time in the following years, mainly in connection with his production work. • Songwriters: All written by OCASEK, ORR and EASTON, except THINK IT OVER and MAYBE BABY (Buddy Holly).

Album rating: THE CARS (*7) / CANDY-O (*5) / PANORAMA (*4) / SHAKE IT UP (*5) / HEARTBEAT CITY (*7) / THE CARS' GREATEST HITS compilation (*7) / DOOR TO DOOR (*3) / JUST WHAT I NEEDED – ANTHOLOGY compilation (*7) / Ric Ocasek: BEATITUDE (*4) / THIS SIDE OF PARADISE (*4) / FIREBALL ZONE (*4) / QUICK CHANGE WORLD (*4) / TROUBLIZING (*3) / Elliott Easton: CHANGE NO CHANGE (*4) / Benjamin Orr: THE LACE (*4) / Greg Hawkes: NIAGARA FALLS (*3)

RIC OCASEK (b. RICHARD OTCASEK, 23 Mar'49, Baltimore, Maryland) – vocals, guitar / **BENJAMIN ORR** (b. ORZECHOWSKI, in Cleveland, Ohio) – vocals, bass / **ELLIOT EASTON** (b. ELLIOT STEINBERG, 18 Dec'53, Brooklyn, N.Y.) – guitar / **GREG HAWKES** – keyboards, saxophone (ex-MILKWOOD, with ORR and OCASEK) / **DAVID ROBINSON** – drums (ex-The POP, ex-DMZ, ex-MODERN LOVERS)

		Elektra	Elektra
Aug 78.	(7") <45491> **JUST WHAT I NEEDED. / I'M IN TOUCH WITH YOUR WORLD**	-	27
Aug 78.	(lp/c) (K/K4 52088) <135> **THE CARS**	29	18 Jun78
	– Good times roll / My best friend's girl / Just what I needed / I'm in touch with your world / Don't cha stop / You're all I've got tonight / Bye bye love / Moving in stereo / All mixed up. (cd-iss. Jan84; 252 088)		
Oct 78.	(7"pic-d) (K 12301) **MY BEST FRIEND'S GIRL. / MOVING IN STEREO**	3	-
Oct 78.	(7") <45537> **MY BEST FRIEND'S GIRL. / DON'T CHA STOP**	-	35
Jan 79.	(7"pic-d) (K 12312) **JUST WHAT I NEEDED. / I'M IN TOUCH WITH YOUR WORLD**	17	-
May 79.	(7") <46014> **GOOD TIMES ROLL. / ALL MIXED UP**	-	41 Mar79
Jun 79.	(lp/c) (K/K4 52088) <507> **CANDY-O**	30	3
	– Let's go / Since I held you / It's all can do / Double life / Shoo be doo / Candy-O / Nightspots / You can't hold on too long / Lust for kicks / Got a lot on my head / Dangerous type. (cd-iss. Jan84; 252 148)		
Jul 79.	(7"pic-d) (K 12371) <46063> **LET'S GO.** / THAT'S IT	51	14 Jun79
Sep 79.	(7"pic-d) (K 12385) **DOUBLE LIFE. / COME AROUND**	-	-
Oct 79.	(7") <46546> **IT'S ALL I CAN DO. / GOT A LOT ON MY HEAD**	-	41
Jan 80.	(7") <46580> **DOUBLE LIFE. / CANDY-O**	-	-
Jan 80.	(7") (K 12416) **IT'S ALL I CAN DO. / CANDY-O**	-	5
Sep 80.	(lp/c) (K/K4 52240) <514> **PANORAMA**		
	– Panorama / Touch and go / Gimme some slack / Don't tell me no / Getting through / Misfit kid / Down boys / You wear those eyes / Running to you / Up and down. (cd-iss. 1986; 252 240)		
Sep 80.	(7") <47039> **TOUCH AND GO. / DOWN BOYS**		37
Jan 81.	(7") <47080> **DON'T TELL ME NO. / DON'T GO TO PIECES**	-	
Mar 81.	(7") <47101> **GIMME SOME SLACK. / DON'T GO TO PIECES**	-	
Nov 81.	(lp/c) (K/K4 52330) <567> **SHAKE IT UP**		9
	– Since you're gone / Shake it up / I'm not the one / Victim of love / Cruiser / A dream away / This could be love / Think it over / Maybe baby. (cd-iss. 1986; 252 330)		
Nov 81.	7"pic-d) (K 12583) <47250> **SHAKE IT UP. / CRUISER**	-	4
Mar 82.	(7") (K 12433) **SINCE YOU'RE GONE. / THINK IT OVER**	-	41
May 82.	(7") (K 13177) **SINCE YOU'RE GONE. / MAYBE BABY**	37	-
Jun 82.	(7") <47479> **THIS COULD BE LOVE. / VICTIM OF LOVE**	-	
Aug 82.	(7") (K 13187) **THINK IT OVER. / I'M NOT THE ONE**	-	
Mar 84.	(7") <69744> **YOU MIGHT THINK. / HEARTBEAT CITY**	-	7
Mar 84.	(lp/c) (960 296-1/-4) <60296> **HEARTBEAT CITY**	25	3
	– Hello again / Magic / Stranger eyes / It's not the night / I refuse / Looking for love / Drive / You might think / Why can't I have you / Heartbeat city. <cd-iss. Jul84>		
Apr 84.	(7") <69741> **WHY CAN'T I HAVE YOU. / JACKIE**	-	
May 84.	(7") <69724> **MAGIC. / I REFUSE**	-	12
Sep 84.	(7"/12") (E 9706/+T) <69706> **DRIVE. / STRANGER EYES**	5	3 Jul84
	(re-iss. Jul85; hit UK No.4)		
Oct 84.	(7") <69681> **HELLO AGAIN. / ('A'dub)**	-	20
Nov 84.	(7") <69718> **YOU MIGHT THINK. / I REFUSE**	-	
	(12"+=) (E 9710T) – Let's go.		
Jan 85.	(7") <69657> **WHY CAN'T I HAVE YOU. / HEARTBEAT CITY**	-	33
	(12"+=) (E 9741T) – Hello again (remix) / Moving in stereo.		
Sep 85.	(7") (EKR 3) **HEARTBEAT CITY. / WHY CAN'T I HAVE YOU**		
	(12"+=) (EKR 3T) – Chemistry / Hello again.		
Oct 85.	(7") <69589> **TONIGHT SHE COMES. / JUST WHAT I NEEDED**	-	7
Nov 85.	(7"pic-d) (EKR 30) **TONIGHT SHE COMES. / BREAKAWAY**	-	

	(12"+=) (EKR 30T) – Just what I needed.		
Nov 85.	(lp/c)(cd) (EKT 25/+C)(960 464-2) <60464> **THE CARS' GREATEST HITS** (compilation)	27	12
	– Just what I needed / Since you're gone / You might think / Good times roll / Touch and go / Drive / Tonight she comes / My best friend's girl / Heartbeat city / Let's go / Magic / Shake it up. (c+=/cd+=) – I'm not the one.		
Jan 86.	(7") <69569> **I'M NOT THE ONE. / HEARTBEAT CITY**	-	32
Mar 86.	(7") (EKR 38) **I'M NOT THE ONE (remix). / SINCE YOU'RE GONE**	-	-
	(12"+=) (EKR 38T) – Shake it up.		
Sep 87.	(7") (EKR 63) <69446> **YOU ARE THE GIRL. / TA TA WAYO WAYO**	-	17 Aug87
	(12"+=/12"pic-d+=) (EKR 63T/+P) – Tonight she comes.		
Sep 87.	(lp/c)(cd) (EKT 42/+C)(960 747-2) <60747> **DOOR TO DOOR**	72	26
	– Leave or stay / You are the girl / Double trouble / Fine line / Everything you say / Ta ta wayo wayo / Strap me in / Coming up you / Wound up on you / Go away / Door to door.		
Nov 87.	(7") <69427> **STRAP ME IN. / DOOR TO DOOR**	-	85
Jan 88.	(7") <69432> **COMING UP YOU. / DOUBLE TROUBLE**	-	74

—— disbanded early 1988. OCASEK married Paulina Porizkova (23 Aug'89) while continuing his solo career; ORR and EASTON also released solo sets

– compilations, etc. –

Jan 96.	(d-cd) Elektra; (0349 73506-2) **JUST WHAT I NEEDED – ANTHOLOGY**		
May 99.	(d-cd) Rhino Deluxe; <(8122 75700-2)> **THE CARS**		

CARTER THE UNSTOPPABLE SEX MACHINE

Formed: Streatham, South London, England . . . 1988 by FRUITBAT (LES CARTER) and JIM BOB (JIM MORRISON). They had both been in early 80's outfit The BALLPOINTS, and after a lengthy period with real jobs, they formed the group JAMIE WEDNESDAY in 1984; signing to 'Rough Trade' subsidiary label 'Pink', they released two singles before disbanding in early '87. The following year they became CARTER THE UNSTOPPABLE SEX MACHINE, debuting that summer with 'SHELTERED LIFE', railing against shady landlords. It was the first in a memorable, if occasionally grating series of DIY agit-pop/punk singles which characterised an era of British indie music; "baggy" had died a lingering death and "grunge" was lumbering over the horizon, a time when all kinds of sub-standard ephemera made the cover of the NME. CARTER were at least entertaining, an undulatingly melodic follow-up single, 'SHERIFF FATMAN', unlucky not to chart (it later became their first Top 30 hit when re-released in the summer of '91). By this point, CARTER mania had firmly gripped the student nation and you couldn't go to any gig without seeing the ubiquitous '30 SOMETHING' baseball shirt. The 1991 album of the same name followed on from the sample-happy drum machine-driven crusty pop of the debut, '101 DAMNATIONS' (1990), and provided a further controversial hit in the anti-army brutality rant, 'BLOODSPORTS FOR ALL'. The chirpy cockney duo (now signed to 'Chrysalis') topped off their annus glorious with a riotous headlining slot at the Reading Festival. There was some grief, however, as the ever vigilant ROLLING STONES legal team made explicit their concern over 'AFTER THE WATERSHED's none too subtle lift from JAGGER and Co.'s 'RUBY TUESDAY'. Following a Christmas re-issue of 'RUBBISH' (featuring one of their inimitable cover versions on the b-side, The Pet Shop Boys' 'RENT' coming in for the CARTER treatment this time around), the group returned in Spring '92 with one of their finest singles, 'THE ONLY LIVING BOY IN NEW CROSS'. A third set, ironically titled '1992 – THE LOVE ALBUM' topped the UK chart, another round of witty punning and HALF MAN HALF BISCUIT style humour. With the advent of American underground domination however, CARTER sounded increasingly tame, subsequent albums 'POST HISTORIC MONSTERS' and 'WORRY BOMB' entering the Top 10 but not hanging around. After a mid-90's split, the band, now signed to indie label, 'Cooking Vinyl', returned in 1997 with the largely ignored 'A WORLD WITHOUT DAVE'. MORRISON has since resurfaced with his own JIM'S SUPER STEREOWORLD. • Covered: RANDY SCOUSE GIT (Monkees) / EVERYBODY'S HAPPY NOWADAYS (Buzzcocks) / BEDSITTER (Soft Cell) / THIS IS HOW IT FEELS (Inspiral Carpets) / PANIC (Smiths) / MANNEQUIN (Wire) / KING ROCKER (Generation X) / DOWN IN THE TUBE STATION AT MIDNIGHT (Jam) / ANOTHER BRICK IN THE WALL (Pink Floyd) / THE IMPOSSIBLE DREAM (Mitch Leigh – Joe Darion) / HIT (Sugarcubes) / SPEEED KING (These Animal Men) / SILVER DREAM MACHINE (David Essex). • Trivia: Surprisingly it was JONATHAN KING who gave them tabloid exposure in his 'Sun' column.

Album rating: 101 DAMNATIONS (*9) / 30 SOMETHING (*8) / 1992 – THE LOVE ALBUM (*7) / POST-HISTORIC MONSTERS (*8) / STARRY EYED AND BOLLOCK NAKED (A COLLECTION OF B-SIDES) (*6) / WORRY BOMB (*5) / STRAW DONKEYS – THE SINGLES compilation (*6) / A WORLD WITHOUT DAVE (*5) / I BLAME THE GOVERNMENT (*4)

JAMIE WEDNESDAY

JIM 'Jim Bob' MORRISON (b.22 Nov'60) – vocals, acoustic guitar / **LES 'Fruitbat' CARTER** (b.12 Feb'58) – bass / **LINDSEY HENRY** – trumpet / **SIMON LOWE** – brass / **DEAS LEGGETT** – drums

		Pink	not iss.
Nov 85.	(12"ep) *(PINKY 6)* **VOTE FOR LOVE / THE WALL. / WHITE HORSES / BUTTONS AND BOWS**	☐	-
May 86.	(12"ep) *(PINKY 10)* **WE THREE KINGS OF ORIENT AREN'T. / LAST NIGHT I HAD THE STRANGEST DREAM / I THINK I'LL THROW A PARTY FOR MYSELF**	☐	-

—— disbanded Feb'87

CARTER THE UNSTOPPABLE SEX MACHINE

—— was duo formed by **JIM BOB & FRUITBAT** who now both played guitar with back-up of tape machines & **JIM BOB** – vocals

		Big Cat	not iss.
Aug 88.	(12"m) *(BBA 03)* **SHELTERED LIFE. / IS THIS THE ONLY WAY THROUGH TO YOU? / GRANNY FARMING IN THE U.K.** *(re-iss. Jun94 on 'Southern' cd-ep; 18620-2)*	☐	-
Nov 89.	(12"ep) *(ABB 100T)* **SHERIFF FATMAN / R.S.P.C.E.. / TWIN-TUB WITH GUITAR / EVERYBODY'S HAPPY NOWADAYS**	☐	-
Jan 90.	(lp/c/cd) *(ABB/+C/CD 101)* **101 DAMNATIONS** – A perfect day to drop the bomb / Midnight on the murder mile / The road to Domestos / An all-American sport / 24 minutes to Tulsa Hill / Good grief / Charlie Brown / Everytime a churchbell rings / Good grief / Sheriff Fatman / G.I. blues. *(re-dist.Sep91; same); hit No.29)*	☐	-
May 90.	(12"/cd-s) *(ABB 102 T/CD)* **RUBBISH. / RENT / ALTERNATIVE ALF GARNET**	☐	-
Oct 90.	(export; m-lp/m-cd) *(ABB 103X/+CD)* **HANDBUILT FOR PERVERTS**	-	-

		Rough Trade	not iss.
Oct 90.	(7") *(RT 242)* **ANYTIME, ANYPLACE, ANYWHERE. / RE-EDUCATING RITA** *(12"+=/cd-s+=) (RTT 242/+CD)* – Alternative title / Randy sarf git.	☐	-
Jan 91.	(7"/c-s) *(R 2011 268-7/-6)* **BLOODSPORTS FOR ALL. / 2001: A CLOCKWORK ORANGE** *(12"+=/cd-s+=) (R 2011 268-0/-3)* – Bedsitter.	48	
Feb 91.	(cd/c/lp) *(RT 2011 270-2/-4/-1)* **30 SOMETHING** – Surfin' USM / My second to last will and testament / Anytime anyplace anywhere / Prince in a pauper's grave / Shopper's paradise / Billy's smart circus / Bloodsport for all / Sealed with a Glasgow kiss / Say it with flowers / Falling on a bruise / The final comedown. *<US-iss.Aug91 on 'Chrysalis'; > (re-iss. Jan92 on 'Chrysalis' cd/c/lp; CCD/ZCHR/CHR 1897); hit UK 21) (re-iss. Feb95;)*	8	

		Chrysalis	Chrysalis
Jun 91.	(7") *(USM 1)* **SHERIFF FATMAN. / R.S.P.C.E.** *(c-s+=/12"+=/cd-s+=) (USM X/XMS/CD 1)* – Twin-tub with guitar / Everybody's happy nowadays.	23	
Oct 91.	(7"/c-s) *(USM/+XMC 2)* **AFTER THE WATERSHED. / THE 90's REVIVAL / A NATION OF SHOPLIFTERS** *(12"+=/cd-s+=) (USM X/CD 2)* – This is how it feels.	11	
Dec 91.	(7"/c-s) *(USM/+XMC 3)* **RUBBISH. / ALTERNATIVE ALF GARNET** *(12"+=/cd-s+=) (USM X/CD 3)* – Rent.	14	
Apr 92.	(7"/c-s/12"/cd-s) *(USM/+XMC/X/CD 4)* **THE ONLY LIVING BOY IN NEW CROSS. / WATCHING THE BIG APPLE TURN / PANIC**	7	
May 92.	(cd/c/lp) *(CCD/ZCHR/CHR 1946)* **1992 – THE LOVE ALBUM** – 1993 / Is wrestling fixed? / The only living boy in New Cross / Suppose you gave a funeral and nobody came / England / Do re mi, so far so good / Look mum, no hands / While you were out / Skywest and crooked / The impossible dream. *(re-iss. Mar94 & Feb95 cd/c;)*	1	
Jun 92.	(7"/c-s/12"/cd-s) *(USM/+XMC/X/CD 5)* **DO RE MI, SO FAR SO GOOD / MANNEQUIN / KING ROCKER / DOWN IN THE TUBE-STATION AT MIDNIGHT**	22	
Nov 92.	(7"/c-s/12"/cd-s) *(USM/+XMC/X/CD 6)* **THE IMPOSSIBLE DREAM / TURN ON, TUNE IN AND SWITCH OFF / WHEN THESAURUSES RULED THE WORLD / BRING ON THE GIRLS**	21	
Aug 93.	(7"/c-s) *(USM/+XMC 7)* **LEAN ON ME I WON'T FALL OVER. / HIT** *(12"+=/cd-s+=) (12/CD USM 7)* – Always the bridesmaid never the bride.	16	
Sep 93.	(cd/c/lp) *(CD/TC+/CHR 7090)* **POST HISTORIC MONSTERS** – 2 million years B.C. / The music that nobody likes / Mid day crisis / Cheer up, it might never happen / Stuff the jubilee! / A bachelor for Baden Powell / Spoilsports personality of the year / Suicide isn't painless / Being here / Evil / Sing fat lady sing / Travis / Lean on me I won't fall over / Lenny and Terence / Under the thumb and over the Moon. *(re-iss. Feb95;)*	5	
Oct 93.	(7"/c-s) *(USM/+XMC 8)* **LENNY AND TERENCE. / HER SONG** *(12"+=/cd-s+=) (12/CD USM 8)* – Commercial fucking suicide (part 1) / Stuff the jubilee (1977).	40	
Mar 94.	(c-s/7") *(TC+/USM 10)* **GLAM ROCK COPS. / LEAN ON ME (I WON'T FALL OVER) (by The FAMILY CAT)** *(12"+=/cd-s+=) (12/USM/CDUSM5 10)* – ('A'-GRID mixes). *(cd-s) (CDUSM 10)* – ('A'side) / Bloodsports for all (by SULTANS OF PING F.C.) / Lenny and Terence (by BLADE) / Falling on a bruise (by PUBLIC WORKS).	24	
Mar 94.	(cd/c/lp) *(CD/TC+/CHR 6069)* **STARRY EYED AND BOLLOCK NAKED (A COLLECTION OF B-SIDES)** (compilation) – Is this the only way to get through to you? / Granny farming in the UK / R.S.P.C.E. / Twin tub with guitar / Alternative Alf Garnett / Re educating Rita / 2001: A clockwork orange / The 90's revival / A nation of shoplifters / Watching the big apple turn over / Turn on, tune in and switch off / When Thesauruses ruled the Earth / Bring on the girls! / Always the bridesmaid never the bride / Her song / Commercial f**king suicide / Stuff the jubilee (1977) / Glam rock cops. *(re-iss. Feb95; same)*	22	

—— added **WEZ BOYNTON** – drums (ex-RESQUE)

| Nov 94. | (c-s/7") *(TC+/USM 11)* **LET'S GET TATTOOS. / ESPECIALLY 4 U** *(cd-s+=) (CDUSMS 11)* – Speed king / Silver dream machine. | 30 | |

Jan 95.	(cd-s) *(CDUSM 11)* – ('A'side) / Turbulence / King for a day.		
	(c-s/7"colrd) *(TC+/USM 12)* **THE YOUNG OFFENDER'S MUM. / TROUBLE** *(cd-s+=) (CDUSMS 12)* – This one's for me. *(cd-s) (CDUSM 12)* – ('A'side) / Rubbish (live) / Suicide isn't painless (live) / Falling on a bruise (live).	34	
Feb 95.	(cd/c/d-lp) *(CD/TC+/CHR 6096)* **WORRY BOMB** – Cheap'n'cheesy / Airplane food – airplane fest food / The young offender's mum / Gas (man) / The life and soul of the party dies / My defeatest attitude / Worry bomb / Senile delinquent / Me and Mr.Jones / Let's get tattoos / Going straight / God, Saint Peter and the guardian angel / The only looney left in town / Ceasefire. *(d-cd+=) (CDCHRX 6096)* **DOMA SPORTOVA . . . LIVE IN ZAGREB, 20/5/94** – Alternative Alf Garnett / Do re me so far so good / A bachelor pad for Baden Powell / Re-educating Rita / The only living boy in New Cross / Lean on me I won't fall over / Granny farming in the U.K. / Travis / Sing fat lady sing / Lenny and Terence / Commercial fucking suicide part 1.	9	
Sep 95.	(c-s/7"red) *(TC+/USM 13)* **BORN ON THE 5th OF NOVEMBER. / D.I.V.O.R.C.E.F.G.** *(cd-s) (CDUSM 13)* – ('A'side) / Tomorrow when you die / The aftertaste of Paradise / Airplane food.	35	
Oct 95.	(cd/c/lp) *(CD/TC+/CHR 6110)* **STRAW DONKEY . . . THE SINGLES** (compilation) – A sheltered life / Sheriff Fatman / Rubbish / Antime anyplace anywhere / Bloodsport for all / After the watershed (early learning the hard way) / The only living boy in New Cross / Do re mi, so far so good / The impossible dream / Lean on me (I won't fall over) / Lenny and Terence / Glam rock cops / Let's get tattoos / The young offender's mum / Born on the 5th of November.	37	

—— CARTER split for around a year after above

		Cooking Vinyl	Cooking Vinyl
Mar 97.	(lp/cd) *(<COOK/+CD 120>)* **A WORLD WITHOUT DAVE** – Broken down in broken town / A world without dave / Before the war / Nowhere fast / Johnny Cash / And God created Brixton / Stand up and be counted / Negative equity / Road rage.	73	Apr97

		True North	True North
Sep 98.	(cd) *(<163>)* **I BLAME THE GOVERNMENT** – Wrong place at the wrong time / 23:59 end of the world / Sunshine / The undertaker and the hippy protest / Sweetheart sugar baby / Growing old disgracefully / The man who bought the world / Winning the war / I blame the government / Citizen's band radio / Psycho Bill / Closedown / Girls can keep a secret.		

JIM'S SUPER STEREOWORLD

—— yes, JIM MORRISON (the – only – living one in New Cross!) all alone

		Fierce Panda	not iss.
Jul 99.	(7") *(NING 076)* **BONKERS IN THE NUT. / YOU'RE MY MATE (AND I LIKE YOU)** *(cd-s+=) (NING 076CD)* – Rock'n'roll relay race.	☐	-
Nov 99.	(7") *(NING 086)* **COULD U BE THE 1 I WAITED 4. / JIM'S SUPER STEREOWORLD SIGN TO FIERCE PANDA** *(cd-s) (NING 086CD)* – ('A'side) / Put your lips together and blow / World of disco.	☐	-

Johnny CASH

Born: 26 Feb'32, Kingsland, Arkansas, USA (where a statue of "The Man in Black" now stands). The third of seven children born to poor sharecropper parents, Ray and Annie Cash, JOHNNY attended Dyess High School in Arkansas and won his first talent contest at age seventeen. In 1950, he joined the Air Force and served overseas in Germany, being discharged in 1954 as a staff sergeant (his other pre-musical jobs included salesman, assembly line worker and margarine factory operative). Young CASH, however, was destined for greater things; the birth of Rock'n'Roll, or more correctly its rockabilly predecessor, was the perfect vehicle for his budding singing and songwriting talents. After initially playing in a combo called the TENNESSEE TWO (later the TENNESSEE THREE), he was subsequently spotted and signed by Sam Phillips for his influential 'Sun' record label in 1955 as a fellow stable-mate to rockers ROY ORBISON, JERRY LEE LEWIS, CARL PERKINS and a little-known truck driver named ELVIS PRESLEY (CASH, PERKINS, LEWIS and PRESLEY were to become known as "The Million Dollar Quartet"). While the others took the rock road, CASH churned out a string of country-influenced hit singles and albums ('BIG RIVER', 'I WALK THE LINE', 'RING OF FIRE', 'SAN QUENTIN' and 'FOLSOM PRISON' being typical of his slow western, macho, half-spoken/half-sung drawl) between 1955 and 1968, his rising fame running parallel with a notorious reputation offstage as a violent, hot-headed heavy boozer and pill-popper. As his career soared, so his personal life disintegrated, ending in divorce after a stormy marriage to first wife, Vivien Liberto. Along with the infamous Folsom Prison and San Quentin Prison live albums (Grammy award winners both), this image established his blue-collar following and consolidated his position as the champion of the underdog in America. He rapidly established himself as the hottest property in country music, selling over fifty million records and even outselling the Beatles in America for a time. He married June Carter in 1968, erstwhile member of the legendary all-singing CARTER FAMILY. Her calming influence on him was to prove a major factor in the style and quality of his later recordings. As the decade turned, he became involved in TV, hosting 'The Johnny Cash Show' and bringing many cult names, (BOB DYLAN, NEIL YOUNG, HANK WILLIAMS Jnr. et al.) to a wider audience. CASH, influenced by his new wife, turned to religion around this time, making a film 'Gospel Road', while various religious organisations and charities benefitted from the newly converted wild man of country. He continued to tour non-stop during the 70's and 80's, including shows for Vietnam draftees and tours behind the then Iron

Curtain. Two books were published, 'Man in Black' in 1975 and 'Man in White' in 1987. The 80's also saw him becoming a member of "outlaw" country band, The HIGHWAYMEN alongside KRIS KRISTOFFERSON, WAYLON JENNINGS and WILLIE NELSON, with whom he toured the world to sellout concerts and more recording success. The 90's, meanwhile, saw CASH resurrected as an alternative hero (via a guest track – 'THE WANDERER' – on U2's 1993 album, 'Zooropa') by Rick Rubin and his 'American' label, who released comeback set, 'AMERICAN RECORDINGS' (1994). He garnered even more critical kudos with 1996's 'UNCHAINED', wherein he even had a crack at Soundgarden's 'RUSTY CAGE' and Beck's 'ROWBOAT'. His compositions are still covered by today's up-and-coming artists while his frequent appearances on MTV have kept his popularity high, despite failing health and a less rigourous tour schedule. Now in his sixties, he is head of a family of five, the most famous of whom is ROSANNE CASH, a minor C&W star in her own right. He has been inducted into all of music's four Halls of Fame: Songwriters (1989), Rock'n'Roll (1992) and, of course, Country Music (1980) and Rockabilly (1994), a unique achievement among his peers as is his grand total of seven Grammys, three multi-platinum albums ('FOLSOM PRISON', 'SAN QUENTIN' and 'GREATEST HITS') and 130 (yes 130!) hits on the Billboard charts. On a more depressing note, CASH has had to contend with ongoing health problems over the last few years and has recently been diagnosed with Parkinson's disease, having to abandon a US show midway through. • **Songwriters:** CASH penned except; THE WAYS OF A WOMAN IN LOVE (Charlie Rich) / RING OF FIRE (Merle Haggard & June Carter) / IT AIN'T ME BABE + WANTED MAN (Bob Dylan) / A BOY NAMED SUE (Shel Silverstein) / IF I WERE A CARPENTER (Tim Hardin) / SUNDAY MORNING COMING DOWN (Kris Kristopherson) / JOHNNY 99 (Bruce Springsteen) / DADDY SANG BASS (Carl Perkins) / THE HIGHWAYMAN (Jimmy Webb) / BIRD ON A WIRE (Leonard Cohen) / THIRTEEN (Glen Danzig) / THE BEAST IN ME (Nick Lowe) / THE MAN WHO COULDN'T CRY (Loudon Wainwright III). The 1964 album BITTER TEARS was written by PETER LA FARGE. **Trivia:** In 1969, he guested on BOB DYLAN's 'Nashville Skyline' lp track, 'THE GIRL FROM NORTH COUNTRY'.

Album rating (selective): RIDE THIS TRAIN (*7) / I WALK THE LINE (*7) / AT FOLSOM PRISON (*8) / AT SAN QUENTIN (*7) / ONE PIECE AT A TIME (*6) / THE MAN IN BLACK – THE DEFINITIVE JOHNNY CASH compilation (*8) / THE MYSTERY OF LIFE (*6) / AMERICAN RECORDINGS (*7) / UNCHAINED (*7)

JOHNNY CASH – vocals, guitar / with various backers

				London	Sun		
Jun 55.	(7",78) <221> **CRY! CRY! CRY! / HEY PORTER** (UK-iss.Oct70 on 'Sun'; 6094 005)			-			
Jan 56.	(7",78) <232> **FOLSOM PRISON BLUES. / SO DOGGONE LONESOME**			-			
Jan 57.	(7",78) (HL 8358) <241> **I WALK THE LINE. / GET RHYTHM**				17 Aug56		
Jun 57.	(7",78) (HLS 8427) <258> **TRAIN OF THOUGHT. / THERE YOU GO**				Nov56		
Aug 57.	(7",78) (HLS 8461) <266> **NEXT IN LINE. / DON'T MAKE ME GO**				99 Jun57		

Oct 57. (lp) <SLP 1220> **JOHNNY CASH WITH HIS HOT & BLUE GUITAR**   [-]
– The rock island line / I heard that lonesome whistle blow / Country boy / If the good Lord's willing and the creeks don't rise / Cry cry cry / Remember me / I'm so doggone lonesome / I was there when it happened / I walk the line / The wreck of the old 97 / Folsom Prison blues / Doin' my time. *(UK-iss.Feb81 on 'Charly'; CRM 2013)*

Dec 57.	(7",78) (HLS 8514) <279> **HOME OF THE BLUES. / GIVE MY LOVE TO ROSE**	88 Sep57
Apr 58.	(7",78) (HLS 8586) <283> **BALLAD OF A TEENAGE QUEEN. / BIG RIVER**	14 Jan58
Jul 58.	(7",78) (HLS 8656) <295> **GUESS THINGS HAPPEN THAT WAY. / COME IN STRANGER**	11 / 66 May58
Oct 58.	(7",78) (HLS 8709) <302> **THE WAYS OF A WOMAN IN LOVE. / YOU'RE THE NEAREST THING TO HEAVEN**	24 Aug58

                             Philips   Columbia

Nov 58.	(7",78) (PB 874) <41251> **ALL OVER AGAIN. / WHAT DO I CARE**	38 / 52 Sep58

—— In Dec'58, 'Sun' and CASH had their first of a number of Top 100 successes with 'IT'S JUST ABOUT TIME'.

Jan 59.	(7",78) (PB 897) <41313> **DON'T TAKE YOUR GUNS TO TOWN. / I STILL MISS SOMEONE**	32

Jan 59. (lp) (BBL 7298) <1253> **THE FABULOUS JOHNNY CASH**   19
– Run softly, blue river / Frankie's man, Johnny / That's all over / The troubadour / One more ride / That's enough / I still miss someone / Don't take your guns to town / I'd rather die young / Pickin' time / Shepherd of my heart / Supper-time. *(UK re-iss. Jun62 on 'C.B.S.'; 62042)*

May 59.	(7",78) (PB 928) <41371> **FRANKIE'S MAN, JOHNNY. / YOU DREAMER YOU**	57 Apr59
Sep 59.	(7",78) (PB 953) <41427> **I GOT STRIPES. / FIVE FEET HIGH AND RISING**	43 / 76

—— recruited new drummer **W.S.HOLLAND** who stayed for next 30 years.

Dec 59.	(7",78) (PB 979) <41481> **THE LITTLE DRUMMER BOY. / I'LL REMEMBER YOU**	63

Jan 60. (lp) (BBL 7353) <CS 8148> **SONGS OF OUR SOIL**
– Drink to me / Five feet high and rising / Man on the hill / Hank and Joe and me / Clementine / Don't step on mother's roses / Great speckled bird / I want to go home / Caretaker / Old Apache squaw / My grandfather's clock / It could happen to you.

Apr 60. (7") (PB 1017) <41618> **SEASONS OF MY HEART. / SMILING BILL McCALL**

Jun 60.	(lp) (BBL 7373) <CS 8522> **HYMNS BY JOHNNY CASH**		
	– It was Jesus / I saw a man / Are all the children in / The old account / Lead me gently home / Swing low, sweet chariot / Snow in his hair / Lead me, father / I called him / These things shall pass / He'll be a friend / God will.		
Jul 60.	(7") <41707> **SECOND HONEYMOON. / HONKY-TONK GIRL**	-	
Oct 60.	(7") (PB 1075) <41804> **GOING TO MEMPHIS. / LOADING COAL**		
Oct 60.	(lp) (BBL 7358) <CS 8254> **NOW THERE WAS A SONG**		

   – Seasons of my heart / I couldn't keep from crying / I feel better all over / My shoes keep walking back to you / Time changes everything / I'd just be a fool enough (to fall) / Why do you punish me / Transfusion blues / I will miss you when you go / I'm so lonesome, I could cry / Just one more / Honky-tonk girl. *(re-iss. May62 on 'C.B.S.'; 62028) (cd-iss. Feb95;)*

Dec 60. (lp) (BBL 7417) <CS 8255> **RIDE THIS TRAIN**
– Loading coal / Slow rider / Lumberjack / Dorraine of Ponchartrain / Going to Memphis / When papa played the dobro / Boss Jack / Old Doc Brown. *(re-iss. May62 on 'C.B.S.'; 62575)*

Jan 61.	(7") <41920> **LOCOMOTIVE MAN. / GIRL IN SASKATOON**	-	
May 61.	(7") (PB 1148) <41995> **THE REBEL – JOHNNY YUMA. / FORTY SHADES OF GREEN**		
Nov 61.	(7") (PB 1200) <42147> **TENNESSEE FLAT-TOP BOX. / TALL MEN**		84 Sep61
Jan 62.	(7") <42301> **THE BIG BATTLE. / WHEN I'VE LEARNED**	-	
May 62.	(7") <42425> **IN THE JAILHOUSE NOW. / LITTLE AT A TIME**	-	
Aug 62.	(7") <42512> **BONANZA! / PICK A BALE O' COTTON**	-	94
Nov 62.	(7"; JOHNNY CASH with The CARTER FAMILY) <42615> **WERE YOU THERE (WHEN THEY CRUCIFIED MY LORD). / (THERE'LL BE) PEACE IN THE VALLEY (FOR ME)**	-	

                          C.B.S.   Columbia

Mar 63.	(7") <42665> **BUSTED. / SEND A PICTURE OF MOTHER**	-	
May 63.	(lp) (BPG 62119) <8730> **BLOOD, SWEAT AND TEARS**		80 Mar63

   – The legend of John Henry's hammer / Tell him I'm gone / Another man done gone / Busted / Casey Jones / Nine pound hammer / Chain gang / Waiting for a train / Roughneck. *(cd-iss. Feb95;)*

Jul 63.	(7") (AAG 159) <42788> **RING OF FIRE. / I'D STILL BE THERE**		17 May63
Oct 63.	(lp; stereo/mono) (S+/BPG 62171) <8853> **RING OF FIRE – THE BEST OF JOHNNY CASH** (compilation)		26 Jul63

   – Ring of fire / I'd still be there / What do I care / I still miss someone / Forty shades of green / Were you there (when they crucified my Lord) / The rebel – Johnny Yuma / Bonanza / The big battle / Remember the Alamo / Tennessee flat-top box / (There'll be) Peace in the valley (for me).

Nov 63.	(7") (AAG 173) <42880> **THE MATADOR. / STILL IN TOWN**		44 Oct63
Nov 63.	(lp; stereo/mono) (S+/BPG 62284) **THE CHRISTMAS SPIRIT** (festive)	-	
Feb 64.	(7") <42964> **UNDERSTAND YOUR MAN. / DARK AS A DUNGEON**	-	35
Sep 64.	(lp; stereo/mono) (S+/BPG 62371) <8990> **I WALK THE LINE** (new versions of old recordings)		53

   – I walk the line / Bad news / Folsom Prison blues / Give my love to Rose / Hey Porter / I still miss someone / Understand your man / Wreck of old '97 / Still in town / Goodbye, little darlin' / Big river / Troublesome waters.

Dec 64.	(7") <43058> **BAD NEWS. / THE BALLAD OF IRA HAYES**	-	
Jan 65.	(lp; stereo/mono) (S+/BPG 62463) <9048> **BITTER TEARS (BALLADS OF THE AMERICAN INDIAN)**		47

   – As long as the grass shall grow / Apache tears / Custer / The talking leaves / The ballad of Ira Hayes / Drums / White girl / The vanishing race. *(cd-iss. Feb95;)*

Mar 65.	(7") (201741) <43206> **ORANGE BLOSSOM SPECIAL. / ALL OF GOD'S CHILDREN AIN'T FREE**		80 Feb65
Apr 65.	(lp; stereo/mono) (S+/BPG 62501) <9109> **ORANGE BLOSSOM SPECIAL**		49 Mar65

   – Orange blossom special / The long black veil / It ain't me babe / The wall / Don't think twice, it's alright / You wild Colorado / Mama, you've been on my mind / When it's springtime in Alaska (it's forty below) / All of God's children ain't free / Danny boy / Wildwood flower / Amen.

May 65.	(7") (201760) <43145> **IT AIN'T ME BABE. / TIME AND TIME AGAIN**	28	58 Oct64
Jun 65.	(7") <43313> **STREETS OF LAREDO. / MISTER GARFIELD**	-	
Aug 65.	(7") (210809) **RING OF FIRE. / STREETS OF LAREDO**	-	
Sep 65.	(7") <43342> **THE SONS OF KATIE ELDER. / CERTAIN KINDA HURTIN'**	-	
Nov 65.	(7") <43420> **PICKIN' TIME. / HAPPY TO BE WITH YOU**	-	
Mar 66.	(7") (202046) <43496> **THE ONE ON THE RIGHT IS ON THE LEFT. / COTTON PICKIN' HANDS**		46 Feb66
Jul 66.	(7") (202256) <43673> **EVERYBODY LOVES A NUT. / AUSTIN PRISON**		96
Jul 66.	(lp; stereo/mono) (S+/BPG 62717) <9292> **EVERYBODY LOVES A NUT**	28	88

   – Everybody loves a nut / The one on the right is on the left / A cup of coffee / The bug that tried to crawl around the world / The singing star's queen / Austin Prison / Dirty old egg / Sucking dog / Take me home / Please don't play / Red river valley / Boa constrictor / Joe Bean.

Oct 66.	(7") <43763> **BOA CONSTRICTOR. / BOTTOM OF A MOUNTAIN**	-	
Nov 66.	(lp; stereo/mono) (S+/BPG 62760) **HAPPINESS IS YOU**	-	

   – Happiness is you / Guess things happen that way / Ancient history / You comb her hair / She came from the mountains / For lovin' me / No one will ever know / Is this my destiny / A wound time can't erase / Happy to be with you / Wabash cannonball.

Jan 67.	(7") (202546) <43921> **YOU BEAT ALL I EVER SAW. / PUT THE SUGAR TO BED**		
Mar 67.	(lp; stereo/mono) (S+/BPG 62972) **FROM SEA TO SHINING SEA**	-	

   – From sea to shining sea / Whirl anmd the suck / Call daddy from the mine / The frozen four-hundred-pound fair-to-middlin' cotton picker / The walls of a prison / The masterpiece / You and Tennessee / Another song to sing / The flint arrowhead / Cisco Clifton's fillin' station / Shrimpin' sailin' / From sea to shining sea (reprise). *(hit No.40 in May68)*

Jul 67. (7"; with JUNE CARTER) <44011> **JACKSON. / PACK UP YOUR SORROWS** `-` `☐`

Sep 67. (lp; stereo/mono) (S+/BPG 63062) <9478> **JOHNNY CASH'S GREATEST HITS, VOLUME 1** (compilation) `82` Jul67
– Jackson (with JUNE CARTER) / I walk the line / Understand your man / Orange blossom special / The one on the right is on the left / Ring of fire / It ain't me babe / The balad of Ira Hayes / The rebel – Johnny Yuma / Five feet high and rising / Don't take your guns to town. *(UK hit No.23 Dec69) (cd+c.iss.Nov93 on 'Sony Europe')*

Sep 67. (7"; with JUNE CARTER) <44158> **YOU'LL BE ALRIGHT. / LONG-LEGGED GUITAR-PICKIN' MAN** `☐`

Nov 67. (lp; stereo/mono) (S+/BPG 63105) <9528> **CARRYIN' ON WITH JOHNNY CASH & JUNE CARTER** Sep67
– Long-legged guitar pickin' man / Shantytown / It ain't me babe / Fast boat to Sydney / Pack up your sorrows / I got a woman / Jackson / Oh, what a good thing we had / You'll be all right / No, no, no / What'd I say.

Nov 67. (7") <44288> **RED VELVET. / THE WIND CHANGES** `☐`

Jan 68. (7") <44373> **ROSANNA'S GOING WILD. / ROLL CALL** `-` `91`

Feb 68. (CBS 3268) **ROSANNA'S GOING WILD. / LONG-LEGGED GUITAR-PICKIN' MAN (with JUNE CARTER)** `-`

Apr 68. (7") (CBS 3433) **A CERTAIN KIND OF HURTIN'. / ANOTHER SONG TO SING** `☐`

Jun 68. (7") (CBS 3549) **FOLSOM PRISON BLUES (live). / THE FOLK SINGER** `32` May68

Jun 68. (lp) (CBS 63308) <9639> **JOHNNY CASH AT FOLSOM PRISON (live prison gig)** `13`
– Folsom prison blues / Dark as a dungeon / I still miss someone / Cocaine blues / 25 minutes to go / Orange blossom special / The long black veil / Send a picture of mother / The wall / Dirty old egg sucking dog / Flushed from the bathroom of your heart / Jackson (with JUNE CARTER) / Give my love to Rose / I got stripes / Green green grass of home / Greystone chapel. *(cd/c-iss.Jan95 on 'Success';)*

Jan 69. (7") (CBS 3878) <44689> **DADDY SANG BASS. / HE TURNED THE WATER INTO WINE** `42` Dec68

May 69. (lp) (CBS 63428) <KC 9726> **THE HOLY LAND** `54` Feb69
– Prologue / Land of Israel / A mother's love / This is Nazareth / Nazareth town of Canaan / He turned the water into wine / My wife June at the sea of Galilee / Beautiful words / Our guide Jacob at Mount Tabor / The ten commandments / Daddy sang bass / At the wailing wall / Come to the wailing wall / In Bethlehem / In garden of Gethsemane / The fourth man / On the Via Dolorosa / Church of the holy / Sepulchre / At Calvary / God is not dead.

—— CASH guested on BOB DYLAN's country 1969 album 'Nashville Skyline'.

—— In Jun'69, he also began own self-titled TV show, with The CARTER FAMILY, CARL PERKINS, etc.

—— BOB WOTTON – guitar repl. LUTHER who died in a house fire.

Aug 69. (lp) (CBS 63629) <CS 9827> **JOHNNY CASH AT SAN QUENTIN (live prison gig)** `2` `1` Jun69
– Wanted man / Wreck of the old 97 / I walk the line / Darling companion / Starkville city jail / San Quentin / A boy named Sue / Peace in the valley / Folsom prison blues. *(cd-iss.Mar94 on 'Sony Collectors')*

Aug 69. (7") (CBS 4460) <44944> **A BOY NAMED SUE. / SAN QUENTIN** `4` `2` Jul69

Dec 69. (7") (CBS 4638) <45020> **BLISTERED. / SEE RUBY FALL** `50` `75` Nov69

Feb 70. (7"; with JUNE CARTER) <45064> **IF I WERE A CARPENTER. / 'CAUSE I LOVE YOU** `-` `36`

Feb 70. (lp) (CBS 63796) <9943> **HELLO, I'M JOHNNY CASH** `6` `6`
– Southwind / The Devil to pay / Cause I love you / See Ruby fall / If I were a carpenter / To beat the Devil / Blistered / Wrinkled, crinkled, wadded dollar bill / I've got a thing about trains / Jesus was a carpenter.

May 70. (7") (CBS 4934) <45134> **WHAT IS TRUTH. / SING A TRAVELLING SONG** `21` `19` Apr70

Aug 70. (d-lp) (CBS 66237) <29> **THE WORLD OF JOHNNY CASH** (compilation) `5` `54` May70
– I still miss someone / Pickin' time / My shoes keep walking back to you / I want to go home / I feel better all over / I'm so lonesome I could cry / Supper-time / In them old cotton fields back home / Delia's gone / One more ride / Accidentally on purpose / In the jailhouse now / I gorgot more than you'll ever know / Casey Jones / Frankie's man, Johnny / The legend of John Henry's hammer / When papa played the dobro / Busted / Sing it pretty, Sue / Waiting for a train.

Aug 70. (7") <45211> **SUNDAY MORNING COMING DOWN. / I'M GONNA TRY TO BE THAT WAY** `-` `46`

Oct 70. (7") (CBS 5252) **25 MINUTES TO GO. / I'M GONNA TRY TO BE THAT WAY** `-` `☐`

Dec 70. (lp) (CBS 64089) <30100> **THE JOHNNY CASH SHOW (live)** `18` `44` Nov70
– Sunday morning coming down / Come along and ride this train (medley): Six days on the road – There ain't no easy run – The sailor on a concrete sea / These hands / I'm gonna try to be that way / Come along and ride this train (medley): Mississippi Delta land – Detroit City – Uncloudy day – No setting sun – Mississippi Delta land / Here was a man (dialogue).

Jan 71. (7") (CBS 5364) <45269> **FLESH AND BLOOD. / THIS SIDE OF THE LAW** `54` Dec70

Mar 71. (lp) (CBS 70087) **LITTLE FAUSS AND BIG HALSY (soundtrack)** `-`
– Rollin' free / The ballad of Little Fauss and Big Halsy / The ballad of Little Fauss and Big Halsy (instrumental) / 7:06 union / The little man / The little man (instrumental) / Wanted man / Rollin' free (instrumental) / True love is greater than friendship / Movin'.

Apr 71. (7") (CBS 7122) <45339> **MAN IN BLACK. / LITTLE BIT OF YESTERDAY** `58` Mar71

Jun 71. (7"ep) (CBSEP 9155) **THE BALLAD OF LITTLE FAUSS & BIG HALSY** `-`

Jun 71. (7") (CBS 7300) <45393> **SINGING IN VIETNAM TALKING BLUES. / YOU'VE GOT A NEW LIGHT SHINING** `☐`

Sep 71. (lp) (CBS 64331) <30550> **THE MAN IN BLACK** `18` `56` Jun71
– The preacher said Jesus said / Orphan of the road / You've got a new light shining in your eyes / If not for love / The man in black / Singin' in Vietnam talkin' blues / Ned Kelly / Look for me / Dear Mrs. / I talk to Jesus every day. *(included a duet with evangelist BILLY GRAHAM)*

Sep 71. (7"; with JUNE CARTER) <45431> **I'LL BE LOVING YOU. / NO NEED TO WORRY** `-` `☐`

Oct 71. (lp) <30887> **THE JOHNNY CASH COLLECTION (HIS GREATEST HITS, VOLUME II)** (compilation) `-` `94`

Nov 71. (7") <45460> **I PROMISE YOU. / PAPA WAS A GOOD MAN** `-`

—— early '72, he appeared in the film, 'A Gunfight' and TV's 'Colombo'

Mar 72. (7") (CBS 7797) <45534> **A THING CALLED LOVE. / DADDY** `4`

May 72. (lp) (CBS 64898) <31332> **A THING CALLED LOVE** `8`
– Kate / Melva's wine / A thing called love / I promise you / Papa was a good man / Tear stained letter / Mississippi sand / Daddy / Arkansas lovin' man / The miracle man. *(re-iss.Dec85;)*

Jun 72. (7") (CBS 8036) <45590> **KATE. / THE MIRACLE MAN** `75` May72

Aug 72. (7"; with JUNE CARTER) <45631> **IF I HAD A HAMMER. / I GOTTA BOY** `-` `☐`

Oct 72. (7") <45660> **COUNTRY TRASH. / ONEY** `☐`

Nov 72. (lp) (CBS 65163) <31465> **JOHNNY CASH: AMERICA (A 200-YEAR SALUTE IN STORY AND SONG)**
– (Opening dialogue) / Paul Revere / Begin West movement / The road to Kaintuck / To the shining mountains / Southwestward / Remember the Alamo / Opening the west / Lorena / The Gettysburg address / The west / Big foot / Like a young colt / Mister Garfield / A proud land / The big battle / On wheels and wings / Come take a trip in my airship / Reaching for the stars / These are my people.

Dec 72. (7"; with others) <45679> **THE WORLD NEEDS A MELODY. / A BIRD WITH BROKEN WINGS CAN'T FLY** `-` `☐`

Mar 73. (7") (CBS 1115) <45740> **ANY OLD WIND THAT BLOWS. / KENTUCKY STRAIGHT** `Feb73`

Apr 73. (lp) (CBS 65431) <32091> **ANY OLD WIND THAT BLOWS** `Feb73`
– Any old wind that blows / Kentucky Straight / The loving gift / The good Earth / Best friend / Oney / The ballad of Annie Palmer / Too little, too late / If I had a hammer / Country trash / Welcome back Jesus.

Jun 73. (7"; with JUNE CARTER) <45758> **HELP ME MAKE IT THROUGH THE NIGHT. / A LOVING GIFT** `-` `☐`

Jun 73. (d-lp) (CBS 68243) **THE GOSPEL ROAD** (religious & narrations)

Aug 73. (7") (CBS 1490) <45786> **CHILDREN. / LAST SUPPER** `☐`

Oct 73. (7"; with The CARTER FAMILY) <45890> **BALLAD OF BARBARA. / PRAISE THE LORD AND PASS THE SOUP** `☐`

Oct 73. (lp) (CBS 65689) <32443> **JOHNNY CASH AND HIS WOMAN**
– The color of love / Saturday night in Hickman County / Allegheny / Life has it's ups and downs / Matthew 24 (is knocking at the door) / The city of New Orleans / Tony / The pine tree / We're for love / Godshine.

Oct 73. (7"; with JUNE CARTER CASH) <45929> **ALLEGHENY. / WE'RE FOR LOVE** `-` `☐`

Nov 73. (7"; with MOTHER MAYBELLE CARTER) <45938> **DIAMONDS IN THE ROUGH. / PICK THE WILDWOOD FLOWERS** `☐`

Dec 73. (7"; with JUNE CARTER CASH) (CBS 1994) **JACKSON. / WE'RE FOR LOVE** `☐`

Dec 73. (7") <45979> **CHRISTMAS AS I KNEW IT. / THAT CHRISTMAS FEELING (with TOMMY CASH)** `-` `☐`

Feb 74. (7") <45997> **JACOB GREEN. / ORLEANS PARISH PRISON** `-` `☐`

Apr 74. (7") <46028> **RAGGED OLD FLAG. / DON'T GO NEAR THE WATER** `-` `☐`

May 74. (lp) (CBS 80113) <32917> **RAGGED OLD FLAG**
– Ragged old flag / Don't go near the water / All I do is drive / Southern comfort / King of the hill / Pie in the sky / Lonesome to the bone / While I've got it on my mind / Good morning friend / I'm a worried man / Please don't let me out / What on Earth (will you do for Heaven's sake).

Jun 74. (7") (CBS 2396) **SOUTHERN COMFORT. / DON'T GO NEAR THE WATER** `☐`

Aug 74. (7") <10011> **CRYSTAL CHANDELIERS & BURGANDY. / THE JUNKIE AND THE JUICEHEAD (MINUS ME)** `-` `☐`

Oct 74. (7"; with ROSIE NIX) <10048> **FATHER AND DAUGHTER. / DON'T TAKE YOUR GUNS TO TOWN** `☐`

Oct 74. (lp) (CBS 80348) <33086> **THE JUNKIE AND THE JUICEHEAD MINUS ME**
– The junkie and the juicehead (minus me) / Don't take your guns to town / Broken freedom song / I do believe / Ole slewfoot / Keep on the sunny side / Father and daughter (father and son) / Crystal chandeliers and burgandy / Friendly gates / Billy & Rex & Oral & Bob / Jesus / Lay back with my woman.

Jan 75. (7") (CBS 2900) <10066> **THE LADY CAME FROM BALTIMORE. / LONESOME TO THE BONE** `☐`

May 75. (7") <10116> **MY OLD KENTUCKY HOME. / HARD TIMES COMIN'** `-` `☐`

May 75. (lp) (CBS 80634) <33370> **JOHN R. CASH**
– My old Kentucky home (turpentine and dandelion wine) / Hard times comin' / The lady came from Baltimore / Lonesome to the bone / The night they drove old Dixie down / Clean your own tables / Jesus was our saviour (cotton was our king) / Reason to believe / Cocaine Carolina / Smokey factory blues.

Aug 75. (7") (CBS 3499) **SMOKEY FACTORY BLUES. / CLEAN YOUR OWN TABLES** `☐` `☐`

Nov 75. (lp) (CBS 81012) <34193> **LOOK AT THEM BEANS**
– Texas 1947 / What have you got / Planned tonight, Diana / Look at them beans / No charge / I hardly ever sing / Beer drinking songs / Down the road I go / I never met a man like you before / All round cowboy / Gone / Down at Drippin' Springs.

Nov 75. (7") <10177> **LOOK AT THEM BEANS. / ALL AROUND COWBOY** `-` `☐`

Jan 76. (7") <10237> **TEXAS 1947. / I HARDLY EVER SING BEER DRINKING SONGS** `☐`

Mar 76. (7") (CBS 4096) <10279> **STRAWBERRY CAKE. / I GOT STRIPES** `☐` `☐`

Mar 76. (lp) (CBS 81211) <34088> **STRAWBERRY CAKE (live)**
– Big river / Doin' my time / I still miss / Someone / I got stripes / Medley: Church in the wildwood – Lonesone valley / Strawberry cake / Rock Island Line / Navajo / Destination / Victoria Station / The fourth man.

May 76. (7"; with The TENNESSEE THREE) (CBS 4287) <10321> **ONE PIECE AT A TIME. / GO ON BLUES** `32` `29` Apr76

Jun 76. (lp; with The TENNESSEE THREE) *(CBS 81416)* <34193>
ONE PIECE AT A TIME | 49 |
– Let there be country / One piece at a time / In a young girl's mind / Mountain lady / Michigan city howdy do / Sold out of flagpoles / Committed to Parkview / Daughter of a railroad man / Love has lost again / Go on blues. *(re-iss. Mar81 lp/c; CBS/40 32016)*

Jul 76. (7") <10381> **MOUNTAIN LADY. / SOLD OUT OF FLAGPOLES** | - |

Sep 76. (7") <10424> **RIDIN' ON THE COTTON BELT. / IT'S ALL OVER** | - |

Nov 76. (7"; with JUNE CARTER CASH) <10436> **FAR SIDE BANKS OF JORDAN / OLD TIME FEELING** | - |

Feb 77. (lp) *(CBS 81566)* <34314> **THE LAST GUNFIGHTER BALLAD**
– I will dance with you / The last gunfighter ballad / Far side banks of Jordan (with JUNE CARTER CASH) / Ridin' on the cotton belt / Give it away / You're so close to me / City jail / Cindy / I love you / Ballad of Barbara / That silver haired daddy of mine.

Apr 77. (7") *(CBS 5107)* <10483> **THE LAST GUNFIGHTER BALLAD. / CITY JAIL** | | |

Aug 77. (lp) *(CBS 82156)* <34833> **THE RAMBLER**
– Hit the road and go / If it wasn't for the Wabash River / Lady / After the ball / No earthly good / A Wednesday car / My cowboy's last ride / Calilou.

Sep 77. (7") *(CBS 5564)* <10587> **LADY. / HIT THE ROAD AND GO** | | |

Dec 77. (7") <10623> **CALILOU. / AFTER THE BALL** | - |

Apr 78. (7") <10681> **I WOULD LIKE TO SEE YOU AGAIN. / LATELY** | - |

Apr 78. (lp) *(CBS 82676)* <35313> **I WOULD LIKE TO SEE YOU AGAIN**
– I would like to see you again / Lately / I wish I was crazy again / Who's Gene Autrey / Hurt so bad / I don't think I could take you back again / Abner Brown / After taxes / There ain't no good / Chain gang / That's the way it is / I'm alright now.

Jun 78. (7"; by JOHNNY CASH & WAYLON JENNINGS) *(CBS 6401)* <10742> **THERE AIN'T NO GOOD CHAIN GANG. / I WISH I WAS CRAZY AGAIN** | | |

Sep 78. (7") <10817> **GONE GIRL. / I'M ALRIGHT NOW** | - |

Jan 79. (7") <10855> **IT'LL BE HER. / IT COMES AND GOES** | - |

Mar 79. (7") *(CBS 7153)* <10888> **I WILL ROCK AND ROLL WITH YOU. / A SONG FOR THE LIFE** | | |

Apr 79. (lp/c) *(CBS/40 83323)* <35646> **GONE GIRL**
– Gone girl / I will rock and roll with you / Diplomat / No expectations / It comes and goes / It'll be her / Gambler / Cajun born / You and me / A song for the life.

Sep 79. (lp/c) *(CBS/40 83757)* <36086> **SILVER**
– The L&N don't stop here anymore / Lonesome to the bone / Bull rider / I'll say it's true (with GEORGE JONES) / Ghost riders in the sky / Cocaine blues / Muddy waters / West Canterbury / Subdivision blues / Lately I been leanin' towards the blues / I'm gonna sit on the porch and pick my old guitar.

Oct 79. (7") <10961> **GHOST RIDERS IN THE SKY. / I'M GONNA SIT ON THE PORCH AND PICK MY OLD GUITAR** | - |

Dec 79. (7") <11103> **I'LL SAY IT'S TRUE. / COCAINE BLUES** | - |

Mar 80. (7") <11237> **BULL RIDER. / LONESOME TO THE BONE** | - |

Mar 80. (lp/c) *(CBS/40 84132)* **A BELIEVER SINGS THE TRUTH**
– Wings in the morning / Gospel boogie (a wonderful time up there) / Over the next hill / He's alive / I've got Jesus in my soul / When he comes / I was there when it happened (so I guess I ought to know) / I'm a new born man / There are strange things happening every day / Children go where I send thee / I'm just an old chunk of coal (but I'll be a diamond someday) / Lay me down in Dixie / Don't take everybody for your friend / You'll get yours, I'll get mine / O come angel band / This train is bound for glory / I'm gonna try to be that way / What on earth (will you do for Heaven's sake) / That's enough / The greatest cowboy of them all.

Oct 80. (7"; with MARTY ROBBINS) <11283> **SONG OF THE PATRIOT. / SHE'S A GO-ER** | - |

Dec 80. (lp/c) *(CBS/40 84607)* <36779> **ROCKABILLY BLUES**
– Cold lonesome morning / Without love / W.O.M.A.N. / The cowboy who started the fight / The 20th century is almost over / Rockabilly blues (Texas 1955) / The last time / She's a go-er / It ain't nothin' new babe / One way rider.

Dec 80. (7") <11340> **COLD LONESOME MORNING. / THE COWBOY WHO STARTED TO FIGHT** | - |

Feb 81. (7") <11399> **THE LAST TIME. / ROCKABILLY BLUES (TEXAS 1965)** | - |

Apr 81. (7") <11424> **WITHOUT LOVE. / IT AIN'T NOTHIN' NEW BABE** | - |

Jun 81. (lp/c) *(CBS/40 84990)* <37179> **THE BARON**
– The baron / Mobile boy / Magnolia blossoms / I learned the hard way / A ceiling, four walls and a floor / Hey hey train / The reverend Mr.Black / The blues keep gettin' bluer / Chattanooga city limit sign / Thanks to you / The greatest love affair.

Oct 81. (7") *(A 1155)* <60516> **THE BARON. / I WILL DANCE WITH YOU** | - |

Jan 82. (7") <02189> **MOBILE BOY. / THE HARD WAY** | - |

Mar 82. (7") <02669> **THE REVEREND MR. BLACK. / CHATTANOOGA CITY LIMIT SIGN** | - |

May 82. (lp/c; by JOHNNY CASH, JERRY LEE LEWIS & CARL PERKINS) *(CBS/40 85609)* **THE SURVIVORS** | | Mar82 |
– Get rhythm / I forgot to remember to forget / Goin' down the road feeling bad / That silver haired daddy of mine / Matchbox / I'll fly away / Whole lotta shakin' goin' on / Rockin' my life away / Blue suede shoes / There will be peace in the valley for me / Will the circle be unbroken / I saw the light. *(re-iss. Sep85 on 'Hallmark')*

Nov 82. (7") <03058> **I'VE BEEN TO GEORGIA ON A FAST TRAIN. / SING A SONG** | - |

Nov 82. (lp/c) *(CBS/40 85881)* <38094> **THE ADVENTURES OF JOHNNY CASH**
– I've been to Georgia on a fast train / John's fair weather friends / Paradise / we must believe in magic / Only love / Good old American guest / I'll cross over Jordan some day / Sing a song / Ain't gonna hobo no more.

Jan 83. (7") <03317> **AIN'T GONNA HOBO NO MORE. / JOHN'S FAIR WEATHER FRIENDS** | - |

Apr 83. (7") <03524> **I'LL CROSS OVER JORDAN SOME DAY. / WE MUST BELIEVE IN MAGIC** | - |

Oct 83. (7"; with JUNE CARTER) <04060> **BRAND NEW DANCE. / I'M RAGGED BUT I'M RIGHT** | - |

Oct 83. (7"; with JUNE CARTER) *(A 3804)* **JOHNNY 99. / BRAND NEW DANCE** | - | - |

Nov 83. (lp/c) *(CBS/40 25471)* **JOHNNY 99**
– Highway patrolman / That's the truth / God bless Robert E.Lee / New cut road / Johnny 99 / Ballad of the ark / Joshua gone to Barbados / Girl from the canyon / Brand new dance / I'm ragged but I'm right.

Jan 84. (7") <04227> **JOHNNY 99. / NEW CUT ROAD** | - | - |

Apr 84. (7") <04428> **THAT'S THE TRUTH. / JOSHUA GONE TO BARBADOS** | - |

Oct 84. (7") *(A 4722)* <04513> **CHICKEN IN BLACK. / BATTLE OF NASHVILLE** | | |

The HIGHWAYMAN

—— were formed by country stars **JOHNNY CASH, WAYLON JENNINGS, WILLIE NELSON & KRIS KRISTOFFERSON** (same label)

Aug 85. (7") <04881> **THE HIGHWAYMAN. / THE HUMAN CONDITION** | - |

Sep 85. (lp/c) *(CBS/40 26466)* <40056> **THE HIGHWAYMAN** | 92 | May85
– The highwayman / The last cowboy song / Jim, I wore a tie today / Big river / Committed to Parkview / Desperados waiting for the train / Deportees (plane wreck at Los Gatos) / Welfare line / Against the wind / The twentieth century is almost over. *(cd-iss. 1987; CD 26466) (cd re-iss. Apr90; 902296-2)*

Apr 90. (cd/c/lp; as WILLIE NELSON, JOHNNY CASH, WAYLON JENNINGS & KRIS KRISTOFFERSON) *(466652-2/-4/-1)* <45240> **THE HIGHWAYMAN 2** | | 79 | Mar90
– Silver stallion / Born and raised in black and white / Two stories wide / We're all in the corner / American remains / Anthem '84 / Angels love bad men / Songs that made a difference / Living legend / Texas. *(d-cd-iss. Oct93 on 'Sony Europe' incl. 1985 lp)*

Apr 90. (7") <73233> **SILVER STALLION. / AMERICAN DREAMS** | - |

Jun 90. (7") <73381> **BORN AND RAISED IN BLACK AND WHITE. / TEXAS** | - |
(above singles were credited as the second album)

JOHNNY CASH

—— had continued with solo career

Oct 85. (7") <05594> **DESPERADOES WAITING FOR A TRAIN. / THE TWENTIETH CENTURY IS ALMOST OVER** | - |

Dec 85. (7") <05672> **I'M LEAVING NOW. / EASY STREET** | - |

Dec 85. (lp/c) *(CBS/40 26689)* **RAINBOW**
– I'm leaving now / Here comes that rainbow again / They're all the same to me / Easy street / Have you ever seen the rain / You beat all I ever saw / Unwed fathers / Love me like you used to / Casey's last ride / Borderline (a musical whodunit).

Jun 86. (lp/c; JOHNNY CASH & WAYLON JENNINGS) *(CBS/40 26922)* **HEROES**
– Folks out on the road / I'm never gonna roam again / American by birth / Field of diamonds / Heroes / Even cowgirls get the blues / Love is the way / The ballad of forty dollars / I'll always love you in my own crazy way / One too many mornings. *(cd-iss. Nov93 on 'Sony';)*

Jun 86. (7"; by JOHNNY CASH & WAYLON JENNINGS) <05896> **AMERICAN BY BIRTH. / EVEN COWGIRLS GET THE BLUES** | - |

Sep 86. (7"; by JOHNNY CASH & WAYLON JENNINGS) <06287> **THE BALLAD OF FORTY DOLLARS. / FIELD OF DIAMONDS** | - |

May 87. (lp/c)(cd) *(MERH/+C 108)* <(832031-2)> **JOHNNY CASH IS COMING TO TOWN**   Mercury   Mercury
– The big light / The ballad of Barbra / I'd rather have you / Let him roll / The night Hank Williams came to town / Sixteen tons / Letters from home / W.Lee O'Daniel and the light crust dough boys / Heavy metal (don't mean rock'n'roll to me) / My ship will sail.

Aug 87. (7"; JOHNNY CASH & WAYLON JENNINGS) *(MER 225)* <888459-7> **THE NIGHT HANK WILLIAMS CAME TO TOWN. / I'D RATHER HAVE YOU** | | |

Jan 88. (7") <888719-7> **THE BALLAD OF BARBRA. / SIXTEEN TONS** | - | - |

May 88. (7") *(MER 263)* **THE BIG LIGHT. / SIXTEEN TONS** | | |

—— next feat. daughter and son **ROSANNE + JOHN** plus other guests **HANK WILLIAMS JR., PAUL McCARTNEY, EMMYLOU HARRIS, WAYLON JENNINGS and The EVERLYS**

Oct 88. (lp/c/cd) <(834778-1/-4/-2)> **WATER FROM THE WELLS OF HOME** | | |
– As long as I live / Ballad of a teenage queen / Last of the drifters / Where did we go right / Call me the breeze / That ole wheel / Sweeter than the flowers / Ballad of Robb MacDunn / New moon over Jamaica.

Nov 88. (7") <874562-7> **THAT OLE WHEEL. / THE LAST OF THE DRIFTERS** | | Jan89

Feb 89. (7") <872420-7> **BALLAD OF A TEENAGE QUEEN. / GET RHYTHM** | | Oct88

Feb 90. (cd/c/lp) <842155-2/-4/-1)> **BOOM CHICKABOOM**
– A backstage pass / Farmer's almanac / Family bible / I love you, I love you / Monteagle mountain / Cat's in the cradle / Don't go near the water / Harley / Hidden shame / That's one you owe me.

Feb 90. (7") <875626-7> **CAT'S IN THE CRADLE. / I LOVE YOU, I LOVE YOU** | - |

Mar 91. (cd/c/lp) <(848051-2/-4/-1)> **THE MYSTERY OF LIFE**
– The greatest cowboy of them all / I'm an easy rider / The mystery of life / Hey porter / Beans for breakfast / Goin' by the book / Wanted man / I'll go somewhere and sing my songs again / The hobo song / The angel and the badman.

Apr 91. (7") **THE MYSTERY OF LIFE. / I'M AN EASY RIDER**
(cd-s+=) – Veterans' day.

Oct 93. (cd/c) **IT AIN'T ME BABE**   Spirit Of America   Spirit Of America / American   American

Oct 94. (cd/c) *(74321 23685-2/-4)* <45520> **AMERICAN RECORDINGS** | | May94
– Delia's gone / Let the train blow the whistle / The beast in me / Drive on / Why

me / Thirteen / Oh bury me nought / Bird on a wire / Tennessee stud / Down there by the train / Like a soldier / The man who couldn't cry.

Nov 96. (cd/c) *(74321 39742-2)* **UNCHAINED**
– Rowboat / Sea of heartbreak / Rusty cage / One rose / Country boy / Memories are made of this / Spiritual / Kneeling drunkard's plea / Southern accents / Mean eyed cat / Meet me in Heaven / I never picked cotton / Unchained / I've been elsewhere.

– compilations, etc. –

			UK	US
Nov 58.	(7"ep) *London; (RES 1120)* **JOHNNY CASH**			–
Jan 59.	(7",78) *London; (HLS 8789) / Sun; <309>* **IT'S JUST ABOUT TIME. / I JUST THOUGHT YOU'D LIKE TO KNOW**			47
				85 Dec58
Mar 59.	(7"ep) *London; (RES 1193)* **JOHNNY CASH SINGS HANK WILLIAMS**			
Apr 59.	(lp) *London; (HA-S 2157) / Sun; N1235>* **SINGS THE SONGS THAT MADE HIM FAMOUS**			
May 59.	(7",78) *London; (HLS 8847) / Sun; <316>* **LUTHER PLAYED THE BOOGIE. / THANKS A LOT**			Mar59
Jun 59.	(7"ep) *London; (RES 1212)* **COUNTRY BOY**			
Jun 59.	(7"ep) *London; (RES 1230)* **JOHNNY CASH NO.2**			
Jul 59.	(lp) *London; (HA-S 2179)* **THE ROCK ISLAND LINE**			
Aug 59.	(7",78) *London; (HLS 8928) / Sun; <321>* **KATY TOO. / I FORGOT TO REMEMBER TO FORGET**			66 Jul59
Nov 59.	(7",78) *London; (HLS 8978) / Sun; <331>* **YOU TELL ME. / GOODBYE, LITTLE DARLIN', GOODBYE**			Sep59
Mar 60.	(7") *London; (HLS 9070) / Sun; <334>* **STRAIGHT A'S IN LOVE. / I LOVE YOU BECAUSE**			84
Jun 60.	(7"ep) *Philips; (BBE 12377)* **THE TROUBADOUR**			
Sep 60.	(7") *London; (HLS 9182) / Sun; <343>* **DOWN THE STREET TO 301. / THE STORY OF A BROKEN HEART**			85 Jul60
Nov 60.	(7") *Sun; <347>* **MEAN EYES CAT. / PORT OF LONELY HEARTS**			–
Nov 60.	(7"ep) *Philips; (BBE 12395)* **SONGS OF OUR SOIL**			–
Mar 61.	(7") *London; (HLS 9314) / Sun; <355>* **OH LONESOME ME. / LIFE GOES ON**			93 Dec60
Dec 61.	(7"ep) *Philips; (BBE 12494)* **STRICTLY CASH**			–
Apr 62.	(lp; stereo/mono) *C.B.S.; (S+/BPG 62015)* **HYMNS FROM THE HEART**			–
Jul 62.	(lp; stereo/mono) *C.B.S.; (S+/BPG 62073)* **THE SOUND OF JOHNNY CASH**			–
1962.	(7") *Sun; <363>* **SUGARTIME. / MY TREASURER**			–
1963.	(7") *Sun; <376>* **BLUE TRAIN. / BORN TO LOSE**			–
Sep 64.	(7"ep) *C.B.S.; (AGG 20050)* **FORTY SHADES OF GREEN**			–
1965.	(7") *Sun; <392>* **WIDE OPEN ROAD. / BELSHAZAH**			–
1965.	(c-ep) *Fontana; (FJS 301)* **JOHNNY CASH'S COUNTRY ROUND-UP**			
May 65.	(lp) *London; (HA-S 8220) / Sun; <SLP 1275>* **THE ORIGINAL SUN SOUND OF JOHNNY CASH**			1964
Sep 65.	(7"ep) *C.B.S.; (EP 6061)* **IT AIN'T ME BABE**			–
Nov 65.	(lp; stereo/mono) *C.B.S.; (S+/BPG 62538)* **BALLADS OF THE TRUE WEST VOL.1**			–
Nov 65.	(lp; stereo/mono) *C.B.S.; (S+/BPG 62591)* **BALLADS OF THE TRUE WEST VOL.2**			–
Jan 66.	(lp; stereo/mono) *C.B.S.; (S+/BPG 62575)* **RIDE THIS TRAIN**			–
Jul 66.	(7"ep; with STATLER BROTHERS & CARTER FAMILY) *C.B.S.; (EP 6073)* **MEAN AS HELL! – BALLADS FROM THE TRUE WEST**			–
Jan 66.	(lp) *London; (HA-S 8253)* **LONESOME ME**			–
Jun 68.	(lp) *C.B.S.; (CBS 63316)* **OLD GOLDEN THROAT** (re-iss. Sep82 on 'Bear Family'; BF 15072)		37	–
Jul 69.	(lp) *C.B.S.; (CBS 63521)* **MORE OF OLD GOLDEN THROAT** (re-iss. Sep82 on 'Bear Family'; BFX 15073)			–
Oct 69.	(lp; stereo/mono) *C.B.S.; (S+/BPG 52705) / Harmony; <11342>* **JOHNNY CASH**			
Nov 69.	(7") *Sun; <1103>* **GET RHYTHM. / HEY PORTER**		–	60
Feb 70.	(7") *Sun; <1111>* **ROCK ISLAND LINE. / NEXT IN LINE**		–	93
May 70.	(7") *Sun; <1121>* **BIG RIVER. / COME IN STRANGER**			–
Dec 70.	(lp) *Hallmark; (SHM 696)* **THE GREAT JOHNNY CASH**			
Dec 70.	(lp) *Sun; (6467 001) <100>* **ORIGINAL GOLDEN HITS, VOLUME 1**			
Dec 70.	(lp) *Sun; (6467 007) <101>* **ORIGINAL GOLDEN HITS, VOLUME 2**			95 Sep69
Mar 71.	(lp) *Sun; (6467 012) <104>* **STORY SONGS OF THE TRAINS AND RIVERS**			98 Sep69
Jul 71.	(lp) *Sun; (6467 014) <105>* **GET RHYTHM** (cd-iss. Feb93 on 'Charly';)			Nov69
Jul 71.	(lp) *Sun; (6467 016) <106>* **SHOWTIME**			Nov69
Sep 71.	(7"m) *Sun; (6094 008)* **I WALK THE LINE. / FOLSOM PRISON BLUES / WRECK OF THE OL' 97**			Nov69
Oct 71.	(lp; shared with JERRY LEE LEWIS) *Sun; (BI 1572)* **. . . SING HANK WILLIAMS**			–
Nov 71.	(d-lp) *Sun; (6641 008) <126>* **THE MAN, HIS WORLD, HIS MUSIC**			
Nov 71.	(lp) *Hallmark; (SHM 739)* **JOHNNY CASH**		43	
Dec 71.	(lp) *C.B.S.; (64516)* **A JOHNNY CASH PORTRAIT**			–
Aug 72.	(lp) *Sun; (6467 022) <127>* **ORIGINAL GOLDEN HITS, VOLUME 3**			
Sep 72.	(7"m) *Sun; (6094 009)* **SUGARTIME / OH LONESOME ME. / HEY GOOD LOOKIN' / I FORGOT TO REMEMBER TO FORGET**			
Sep 72.	(d-lp) *C.B.S.; (67201)* **STAR PORTRAIT**		16	
Nov 72.	(lp; shared with JERRY LEE LEWIS) *Sun; (6467 024) <119>* **SUNDAY DOWN SOUTH**			
Nov 72.	(lp) *Hallmark; (SHM 777)* **THE MAGNIFICENT JOHNNY CASH**			–

			UK	US
Mar 73.	(lp) *Hallmark; (SHM 804)* **THE MIGHTY JOHNNY CASH**			–
May 73.	(7") *C.B.S.; (1152)* **A BOY NAMED SUE. / FOLSOM PRISON BLUES**			–
Feb 74.	(d-lp) *Sun; (6641 161)* **THE GIANT OF COUNTRY AND WESTERN MUSIC**			–
Mar 74.	(lp) *Sun; <122>* **THE ROUGH-CUT KING OF COUNTRY AND WESTERN**		–	
Mar 74.	(lp) *Embassy-CBS; (70083)* **I WALK THE LINE**			–
Jun 74.	(lp) *Sun; (SHM 822)* **FOLSOM PRISON BLUES**			–
Nov 74.	(lp) *Embassy-CBS;* **THE SOUND OF JOHNNY CASH**			–
Jun 75.	(lp) *Hallmark; (SHM 862)* **BALLAD OF A TEENAGE QUEEN**			–
Aug 75.	(d-lp) *C.B.S.; (88153)* **RIDING THE RAILS**			–
Oct 75.	(lp) *Charly; (CR 30005)* **OLD GOLDEN THROAT**			–
Nov 75.	(lp) *Hallmark; (SHM 884)* **I FORGOT TO REMEMBER TO FORGET**			–
Feb 76.	(7") *C.B.S.; (3944)* **I WALK THE LINE. / RING OF FIRE**			–
Mar 76.	(lp) *Pickwick; (PDA 005)* **THE JOHNNY CASH COLLECTION**			–
Oct 76.	(lp) *C.B.S.; (10000)* **THE BEST OF JOHNNY CASH**		48	
Oct 76.	(lp) *Charly; (CR 30113)* **THE ORIGINAL JOHNNY CASH**			–
Nov 76.	(lp) *Hallmark; (SHM 897)* **THE STORY OF A BROKEN HEART**			–
Dec 76.	(7"ep) *Charly; (CEP 108)* **BALLAD OF A TEENAGE QUEEN**			–
Jul 77.	(lp) *Embassy-CBS;* **BALLADS OF THE TRUE WEST**			–
Jul 77.	(lp) *Embassy-CBS;* **JOHNNY CASH**			–
Jul 77.	(lp) *Charly; (CR 30153)* **SUN SOUNDS SPECIAL**			–
Jun 78.	(lp/c) *C.B.S.; (CBS/40 10009)* **ITCHY FEET – 20 FOOT TAPPIN' GREATS**		36	–
	– Folsom prison blues / I walk the line / Ring of fire / Forty shades of green / I still miss someone / There ain't no good chain gang / Busted / Twenty five minutes to go / Orange blossom special / It ain't me babe / A boy named Sue / San Quentin / Don't take your guns to town / The one on the right is on the left / Jackson / Hey porter / Daddy sang bass / I got stripes / A thing called love / One piece at a time. *(cd-iss. Oct94 on 'Columbia'; 477504-2) (re-iss. Apr95 on 'Columbia'; 468116-2/-4)*			
Aug 78.	(d-lp/d-c) *Pickwick; (PDA/PDC 033)* **THE JOHNNY CASH COLLECTION**			–
Apr 79.	(lp) *Hallmark; (SHM 998)* **RING OF FIRE**			–
Jun 79.	(7") *Charly; (CYS 1052)* **MEAN EYED CAT. / GET RHYTHM**			–
Jul 79.	(lp) *Pickwick; (PDC 005)* **THE JOHNNY CASH COLLECTION VOL.3**			–
Jul 79.	(lp) *Hammer; (HMB 7001)* **JOHNNY CASH**			–
Sep 79.	(7") *Hammer; (HB 606)* **I WALK THE LINE. / ROCK ISLAND LINE**			–
1979.	(lp; with JUNE CARTER) *Bear Family; (BFX 15030)* **JOHNNY & JUNE**			–
Feb 80.	(lp) *Hallmark; (SHM 3027)* **I'M SO LONESOME I COULD CRY**			–
May 80.	(lp/c) *C.B.S.; (CBS/40 31827)* **A BOY NAMED SUE**			–
Mar 82.	(d-lp/d-c; shared with MARTY ROBBINS) *Ronco; (RTL/4CRTL 2070)* **THE COWBOYS**			–
Jul 82.	(7") *Old Gold; (OG 9177)* **A THING CALLED LOVE. / ONE PIECE AT A TIME**			–
Jul 82.	(7") *Old Gold; (OG 9180)* **A BOY NAMED SUE. / SAN QUENTIN**			–
Oct 82.	(lp) *Bear Family; (BFX 15092)* **INSIDE A SWEDISH PRISON**			–
Mar 83.	(lp/c) *C.B.S.; (CBS/40 32304)* **BIGGEST HITS**			–
Aug 83.	(7"; JULIE ANDREWS & JOHNNY CASH) *Peach River; (BBPR 5)* **LOVE ME TENDER. / (other by her)**			–
Oct 83.	(7"ep/c-ep) *Scoop; (7SR/7SC 5015)* **6 TRACK HITS**			–
	– A boy named Sue / I walk the line / Ring of fire / If I were a carpenter / Folsom Prison blues / What is truth?			
Apr 84.	(5xlp-box) *Charly; (SUNBOX 103)* **THE SUN YEARS**			–
Apr 84.	(lp/c) *Allegience; (ALEB/ZCALB)* **THE FIRST YEARS**			–
Jul 84.	(lp) *Bear Family; (BFX 15127)* **BITTER TEARS**			–
Sep 84.	(lp) *Bear Family; (BFX 15016)* **THE UNISSUED JOHNNY CASH**			–
Sep 84.	(lp) *Bear Family; (BFX 15021)* **DESTINATION VICTORIA STATION**			–
Sep 84.	(lp) *Bear Family; (BFX 15033)* **TALL MAN**			–
Nov 84.	(lp/c) *Astan; (2/4 0086)* **GREAT SONGS OF JOHNNY CASH** (pic-lp Dec85; PD 50004)			–
Dec 84.	(lp) *Premier; (CRB 1015)* **18 LEGENDARY PERFORMANCES**			–
Feb 85.	(lp/c) *C.B.S.; (CBS/40 32565)* **GREATEST HITS VOL.1**			–
May 85.	(lp/c) *Word; (WST/WC 9629)* **A DIAMOND IN THE ROUGH**			–
May 85.	(lp/c) *Word; (WRD/TCWR 3008)* **WELCOME FRIEND**			–
Dec 85.	(lp/c) *Country Store; (CST/+K 11)* **AT THE COUNTRY STORE** (cd-iss. 1988; CDCST 11)			–
Mar 86.	(lp/c) *C.B.S.; (CBS/40 32766)* **GREATEST HITS VOL.2**			–
Apr 86.	(cd) *Charly; (CDCHARLY 18)* **COUNTRY BOY**			–
Apr 86.	(cd) *Pickwick; (PCD 813)* **JOHNNY CASH – I LOVE COUNTRY**			–
Sep 86.	(lp/c) *Word; (WST R/C 9678)* **BELIEVE IN HIM** (re-iss. Sep88 on 'Music For Pleasure' lp/c; MFP/TC-MFP 5840)			–
Nov 86.	(cd) *Bear Family; (BCD 15247)* **UP THROUGH THE YEARS 1955-57**			–
Dec 86.	(lp/c/cd) *Castle; (CCS LP/MC/CD 146)* **THE COLLECTION**			–
Feb 87.	(lp/c) *Premier; (PMP/+K 1004)* **LADY**			–
Apr 87.	(lp/c/cd) *C.B.S.; (450466-1/-4/-2)* **1958-1986 THE CBS YEARS**			–
May 87.	(cd) *Topline; (TOPCD 521)* **HOME OF THE BLUES**			–
May 88.	(cd-ep) *Rhino; (R 37300-2)* **LIL BIT O' GOLD**			–
	– I walk the line / Folsom Prison blues / Guess things happen that way / Ballad of a teenage queen.			
May 88.	(lp/c/cd) *Big Country; (22/21/24 30712)* **ORIGINAL HITS**			–
Jul 88.	(lp/c) *Connoisseur; (VSOP LP/MC 121)* **COUNTRY BOOGIE** (cd-iss. Apr90; VSOPCD 121)			–
Jul 88.	(lp/c) *Exel; (XEL LP/MC 111)* **BALLAD OF A TEENAGE QUEEN**			–
1988.	(cd) *Starr; (29013 001)* **20 GREATEST HITS**			–
Nov 88.	(lp/c) *Sierra; (FED B/C 5015)* **REPLAY ON . . .**			–
Dec 88.	(cd) *Spectrum; (SPEC 85008)* **18 GOLDEN HITS**			–
Mar 89.	(lp/c/cd) *C.B.S.; (834526-1/-4/-2)* **CLASSIC CASH**			Dec88
Jul 89.	(lp/c/cd) *Instant; (INS/TCINS/CDINS 5007)* **BORN TO LOSE**			–

Sep 90. (5xcd-box) *Bear Family; (BCD 15517)* **THE MAN IN BLACK VOL.1**

May 91. (4xcd-box) *Bear Family; (BCD 15563)* **COME ALONG AND RIDE THIS TRAIN**

Aug 91. (5xcd-box) *Bear Family; (BCD 15562)* **THE MAN IN BLACK VOL.2 – 1959-1962**

Aug 92. (cd/c) *Woodford; (WMCD5/WMMC4 661)* **GREATEST HITS** | | -

Sep 92. (cd) *Music Club; (MCCD 082)* **THE BEST OF THE SUN YEARS 1955-1961** | | -

Oct 93. (7") *Columbia; (659785-7)* **RING OF FIRE. / A THING CALLED LOVE**
(cd-s+=) *(659785-2)* – A boy named Sue.

Aug 94. (cd/c) *Columbia; (MOOD CD/C 35)* **THE MAN IN BLACK – THE DEFINITIVE COLLECTION** | 15 |
– Ring of fire / I walk the line / Get rhythm (live) / It ain't me babe / I still miss someone / (Ghost) Riders in the sky / The baron / Sunday morning coming down / Daddy sang bass / Jackson (with JUNE CARTER) / One piece at a time / Orange blossom special / Folsom prison blues (live) / San Quentin (live) / A boy named Sue (live) / A thing called love / Don't take your guns to town / Wanted man / Big river / Without love / No expectations / Highway patrolman / Singin' in Vietnam talkin' blues / Man in black.

Mar 94. (cd) *Charly; (CDCD 1154)* **GUESS THINGS HAPPEN THAT WAY** | | -

Sep 94. (cd) *Sixteen; (CD 1100-2)* **16 GREATEST HITS** | | -

Jan 95. (cd) *Collection; (COL 004)* **THE COLLECTION** | | -

Mar 95. (cd/c) *Spectrum; (550932-2/-4)* **RING OF FIRE** | | -

Jun 95. (cd/c) *Marble Arch; (MAT CD/MC 331)* **THE BEST OF JOHNNY CASH** | | -

Jun 95. (cd/c) *Truetrax;* **IN CONCERT** | | -

Jul 95. (cd) *Charly; (CDCD 1253)* **RING OF FIRE – HIS GREATEST HITS LIVE** | | -

Jul 95. (cd) *Charly; (CPCD 8101)* **FOLSOM PRISON BLUES (THE ORIGINAL SUN HITS)** | | -

Sep 95. (cd/c) *Hallmark; (30003-2)* **JOHNNY CASH LIVE (HIS GREATEST HITS OLD AND NEW)** | | -

Nov 95. (6xcd-box) *Bear Family; (BRCD 15588)* **THE MAN IN BLACK VOL.3 – 1963-1969**

Nov 95. (3xcd-box) *Charly; (CDSUNBOX 5)* **THE SUN YEARS**

Nov 95. (cd/c) *Columbia; (CK/CT 64154)* **PERSONAL CHRISTMAS COLLECTION**

Feb 96. (cd) *Columbia; (483725-2)* **THE BEST OF JOHNNY CASH**

Apr 96. (cd/c) *Pulse; (PLS CD/MC 132)* **THE BEST OF JOHNNY CASH** | | -

Aug 96. (cd/c) *Autograph; (MAC CD/MC 145)* **THE BEST OF JOHNNY CASH** | | -

Oct 96. (d-cd) *Charly; (CPCD 8241-2)* **THE VERY BEST OF JOHNNY CASH**

Nov 96. (cd) *Summit; (SUMCD 4020)* **LIVE IN THE RING OF FIRE**

Nov 97. (cd) *Eagle; (EABCD 058)* **SINGS THE COUNTRY CLASSICS**

Nov 97. (cd) *Eagle; (EABCD 059)* **THE MASTERS**

Jun 98. (cd/c; shared with WILLIE NELSON) *(491531-2/-4)* **VH1 STORYTELLERS**

Feb 99. (cd) *Koch Int.; (379802)* **JOHNNY 99**

Mar 99. (3xcd-box) *REDX; (RXBOX 31056)* **THE GREAT**

Apr 99. (cd) *Repertoire; (RR 4824)* **THE BEST OF THE SUN YEARS**

May 99. (cd) *Essential; (RX 1040)* **THE ESSENTIAL**

Jul 99. (3xcd-box) *Goldies; (GLD 25345)* **RING OF FIRE**

Jul 99. (cd) *Columbia; (494896-2)* **THE FABULOUS / THE SONGS OF OUR SOUL**

Aug 99. (cd) *Galaxy; (HIB 10023-2)* **HITS** | | -

Aug 99. (cd) *Koch; (37979-2)* **ROCKABILLY BLUES** | | -

Aug 99. (d-cd) *Snapper; (SMDCD 213)* **THE ESSENTIAL SUN COLLECTION** | | -

CAST

Formed: Liverpool, England . . . 1994 by ex-LA'S guitarist JOHN POWER, alongside KEITH O'NEIL, LIAM TYSON and PETER WILKINSON. Bassist POWER had become increasingly disillusioned with The LA'S interminable absence from the music scene, taking his future into his own hands and developing his 60's influenced songwriting within a more solid framework. Fortuitously, POWERS' strident, melodic sound was perfectly in tune with the emerging retro fixated Brit-pop sound and, with the influential backing of OASIS, CAST crashed into the Top 20 in the summer of '95 with 'FINETIME'. Surfing on a wave of frothy powerchords and an irrepressibly buoyant melody, 'ALRIGHT' followed soon after, the track becoming something of a theme tune and a definitive highlight of their debut set, 'ALL CHANGE'. Released later that Autumn, the album divided the critics, some raving over its immaculate melodic appeal, some deriding its workmanlike adherence to "classic songwriting". Whatever, there was no doubting POWER's ear for a tune, and the sublime 'SANDSTORM' gave the band a further Top 10 hit in early '96. CAST's solid style inevitably translated well to the live arena and they built up a rabid following of beany-topped fans, the same constituency of check-shirted "lads" who frequented OASIS and OCEAN COLOUR SCENE gigs. In Autumn '96, the group scored their first Top 5 with 'FLYING', a lilting new track which further showcased their mastery of BEATLES-esque pop dynamics. However, the critics were just dying to sink their claws into this resolutely untrendy outfit, with the fine 'MOTHER NATURE CALLS' (1997) unfairly receiving mixed reviews. Detractors rounded on POWER's spiritually-enhanced muse and mystical leanings but there was no arguing with the life-affirming power inherent in songs like 'GLIDING STAR', another Top 10 smash in summer '97. Influenced by the WHO on a 'Magic Bus'-type thing (with production from GIL NORTON and string accompaniment courtesy of

DAVID ARNOLD) POWER and Co retro-fied their way back into the charts with 'BEAT MAMA'. A hook-line festival-friendly tune, it previewed their third Top 10 album, 'MAGIC HOUR' (1999), yet another to gain the support from both the Indie and Modern Rock factions.

Album rating: ALL CHANGE (*7) / MOTHER NATURE CALLS (*6) / MAGIC HOUR (*5)

JOHN POWER (b.14 Sep'67) – vocals, guitar (ex-LA'S) / **LIAM TYSON** (b. 7 Feb'69) – guitar / **PETER WILKINSON** (b. 9 May'69) – bass (ex-SHACK) / **KEITH O'NEIL** (b.18 Feb'69) – drums

		Polydor	Polydor
Jul 95.	(7"green/c-s/cd-s) *(579 506-7/-4/-2)* **FINETIME. / BETTER MAN / SATELLITES**	17	-
Sep 95.	(7"blue/c-s/cd-s) *(579 926-7/-4/-2)* **ALRIGHT. / FOLLOW ME DOWN / MEET ME**	13	-
Oct 95.	(cd/c/d-lp) *(529 312-2/-4/-2)* **ALL CHANGE**	7	

– Alright / Promised land / Sandstorm / Mankind / Tell it like it is / Four walls / Finetime / Back of my mind / Walkaway / Reflections / History / Two of a kind.

Jan 96.	(7"orange/c-s) *(577 872-7/-4)* **SANDSTORM. / HOURGLASS / BACK OF MY MIND (live)**	8	-

(cd-s+=/tin-cd-s+=) *(577 873/903-2)* – Alright (live).

Mar 96.	(7"clear/c-s) *(576 284-7/-4)* **WALKAWAY. / FULFILL / FINETIME (acoustic)**	9	-

(cd-s) *(576 285-2)* – (first 2 tracks) / Mother.

Oct 96.	(7"/c-s) *(575 476-7/-4)* **FLYING. / BETWEEN THE EYES / FOR SO LONG**	4	-

(pic-cd-s+=) *(575 477-2)* – Walkaway.

Mar 97.	(7"/c-s) *(573 648-7/-4)* **FREE ME. / COME ON EVERYBODY / CANTER**	7	-

(cd-s+=) *(573 649-2)* – ('A'acoustic).
(cd-s) *(573 651-2)* – ('A'side) / Release my soul / Dancing on the flames.

Apr 97.	(cd/c/lp) *(537 567-2/-4/-1)* **MOTHER NATURE CALLS**	3	

– Free me / On the run / Live the dream / Soul tied / She sun shines / I'm so lonely / The mad hatter / Mirror me / Guiding star / Never gonna tell you what to do (revolution) / Dance of the stars. *(special edition d-cd Nov97; 539681-2)*

Jun 97.	(7") *(571 172-7)* **GUIDING STAR. / OUT OF THE BLUE**		

(c-s+=) *(571 172-4)* – Keep it alive.
(cd-s+=) *(571 173-2)* – Free me (live) / Mirror me (live).
(cd-s) *(571 295-2)* – ('A'side) / Keep it alive / Redemption song (live) / ('A'acoustic).

Sep 97.	(c-s) *(571 500-4)* <6025> **LIVE THE DREAM / HOLD ON / FLOW**	7	Apr98

(cd-s) *(571 501-2)* – (first 2 tracks) / Effectomatic who / ('A'acoustic).
(cd-s) *(571 685-2)* – (first & third tracks) / On the run.

Nov 97.	(c-s) *(569 256-4)* **I'M SO LONELY / THINGS YOU MAKE ME DO / THEME FROM**	14	-

(cd-s) *(569 057-2)* – (first 2 tracks) / Never gonna tell you / History.
(cd-s) *(569 059-2)* – (tracks 1 & 3) / History.

Apr 99.	(c-s) *(563592-4)* **BEAT MAMA / GET ON YOU / HOEDOWN**	9	-

(cd-s) *(563593-2)* – (first 2 tracks) / 3 nines are 28.
(cd-s) *(563595-2)* – (first & third tracks) / Whiskey song.

May 99.	(cd/c/d-lp) *(547176-2/-4/-1)* **MAGIC HOUR**	6	

– Beat mama / Compared to you / She falls / Dreamer / Magic hour / Company man / Alien / Higher / Chasing the day / The feeling remains / Burn the light / Hideaway.

Jul 99.	(c-s) *(561227-4)* **MAGIC HOUR / ALLBRIGHT**	28	

(cd-s) *(561227-2)* – ('A'side) / Gypsy song / I never wanna lose you.
(cd-s) *(561228-2)* – ('A'side) / Beat mama / What you gonna do.

CATATONIA

Formed: Cardiff, Wales . . . 1991 by songwriters MARK ROBERTS and PAUL JONES, who had both been part of 'Ankst' label outfit, Y CRYFF (The BODY). Having found OWEN POWELL from The CRUMB BLOWERS and sultry blonde singer, CERYS MATTHEWS, they set about taking their style of Welsh accented hooks to the alternative indie scene. However, things did not get off to a flying start, when the group offended the label's strict Welsh-only language policy and were moved on to another leek-biased label, 'Crai', where they released two singles in 1993/94. In the summer of '94, Geoff Travis's 'Rough Trade Singles Club' label issued 'WHALE', Travis subsequently grabbing them for his 'Blanco Y Negro'. 1996 became a shining year for them with four hit singles and a well-received album, the Stephen Street-produced 'WAY BEYOND BLUE' denting the Top 40. Much was anticipated for a glorious 1998 after they hit the Top 40 in late '97 with 'I AM THE MOB'. All predictions came true as CERYS and Co stormed the Top 3 as early as January that year with the X-Files inspired 'MULDER AND SCULLY'. This was only one of the many successes (others being 'ROAD RAGE', 'STRANGE GLUE' and 'GAME ON') taken from their acclaimed chart-topping album, 'INTERNATIONAL VELVET', although indie sex symbol CERYS would also team up with SPACE for the tongue-in-cheek romantic duet, 'The Ballad Of Tom Jones'. Never far away from the limelight and with the help of producer TOMMY D., CATATONIA returned in Spring '99 via Top 10 smash, 'DEAD FROM THE WAIST DOWN'. The highest of three hits (the other two being 'LONDINIUM' and 'KARAOKE QUEEN') taken from their follow-up No.1 album, 'EQUALLY CURSED AND BLESSED', the 5-piece indie-pop outfit were going into the 21st Century on a high note.

Album rating: THE SUBLIME MAGIC OF CATATONIA European compilation or THE CRAI EP'S (*7) / WAY BEYOND BLUE (*7) / INTERNATIONAL VELVET (*8) / EQUALLY CURSED AND BLESSED (*6)

CERYS MATTHEWS (b.11 Apr'69) – vocals / **MARK ROBERTS** (b. 3 Nov'69, Colwyn Bay, Wales) – guitar / **OWEN POWELL** (b. 9 Jul'67, Cambridge, England) – guitar (ex-CRUMB

BLOWERS) / **PAUL JONES** (b. 5 Apr'60, Colwyn Bay) – bass / **ALED RICHARDS** (b. 5 Jul'69, Carmathen, Wales) – drums

		Crai	not iss.
Sep 93.	(c-ep)(cd-ep) *(C 039L)(CD 039B)* **FOR TINKERBELL EP**		-

– For Tinkerbell / New mercurial heights / Dimbran / Sweet Catatonia / Gyda Gwen – New mercurial heights (Welsh mix).

| Jun 94. | (c-s)(cd-s) *(C 042L)(CD 042B)* **HOOKED. / FALL BESIDE HER / DIFRYCHEULYD (SNAIL AMBITION)** | | - |

(above 2 re-iss. together Dec98; CRAI 064)

		Rough Trade Sing. Club	not iss.
Aug 94.	(7") *(45rev 33)* **WHALE. / YOU CAN**		-

		Nursery	not iss.
Feb 95.	(7"red) *(NYS 12L)* **BLEED. / THIS BOY CAN'T SWIM**		-
	(cd-s+=) *(NYSCD 12)* – Painful.		
Nov 95.	(cd) *(NYSCD 12X)* **THE SUBLIME MAGIC OF CATATONIA** (compilation)	-	Europe

– Bleed / This boy can't swim / Painful / Dream on / Whale / You can / Hooked / Fall beside her / Difrycheulyd (Snail ambition). *(hidden track +=)* – Cariadon ffol.

		Blanco Y Negro	Blanco Y Negro
Dec 95.	(7"white; mail-o) *(SAM 1746)* **BLOW THE MILLENNIUM BLOW. / BEAUTIFUL SAILOR**	-	-
Jan 96.	(7"/c-s) *(NEG 85/+C)* **SWEET CATATONIA. / TOURIST**	61	-
	(cd-s) *(NEG 85CD)* – ('A'side) / Acapulco gold / Cut you inside (demo).		
Apr 96.	(7"yellow) *(NEGAT 88X)* **LOST CAT. / TO AND FRO**	41	-
	(c-s/cd-s) *(NEGAT 88 CAS/CD1)* – ('A'side) / All girls are fly / Indigo blind.		
	(cd-s) *(NEG 88CD2)* – ('A'side) / Sweet Catatonia (live – Mark Radcliffe 1FM session) / Whale (live – Mark Radcliffe 1FM session).		
Sep 96.	(7") *(NEG 93)* **YOU'VE GOT A LOT TO ANSWER FOR. / DO YOU BELIEVE IN ME?**	35	-
	(cd-s+=) *(NEG 93CD1)* – Dimbran.		
	(cd-s) *(NEG 93CD2)* – ('A'side) / You can / All girls are fly.		
	(c-s) *(NEG 93CAS)* – ('A'side) / Blow the millennium blow (Splott remix).		
Sep 96.	(cd/c/lp) *(0630 16305-2/-4/-1)* **WAY BEYOND BLUE**	40	-

– Lost cat / Sweet Catatonia / Some half baked / Ideal called wonderful / You've got a lot to answer for / Infantile / Dream on. *(lp w/free 7"/cd w/hidden track)* – Gyda Gwen. *(lp re-iss. Jun99; same)*

Nov 96.	(7"red) *(NEG 97)* **BLEED. / DO YOU BELIEVE IN ME? (live – Reading Festival 1FM)**	46	-
	(cd-s+=) *(NEG 97CD2)* – Bleed (live evening session 1FM).		
	(cd-s) *(NEG 97CD1)* – ('A'side) / Way beyond blue (live – Mark Radcliffe 1FM session) / Painful (live – Reading Festival 1FM).		
	(c-s) *(NEG 97CASS)* – ('A'side) / Way beyond blue (live – Mark Radckiffe 1FM session) / Bleed (live – evening session 1FM).		
Oct 97.	(7"orange/c-s) *(NEG 107/+CASS)* **I AM THE MOB. / JUMP OR BE SANE**	40	-
	(cd-s+=) *(NEG 107CD)* – My selfish Gene / ('A'-Luca Brasi mix).		
Jan 98.	(7"blue/c-s) *(NEG 109/+CASS)* **MULDER AND SCULLY. / NO STONE UNTURNED**	3	-
	(cd-s+=) *(NEG 109CD)* – Mantra for the lost / ('A'-The Ex-files).		
Feb 98.	(cd/c/lp) *(<3984 20834-2/-4/-1>)* **INTERNATIONAL VELVET**	1	

– Mulder and Scully / Game on / I am the mob / Road rage / Johnny come lately / Goldfish and paracetamol / International velvet / Why I can't stand one night stands / Part of the furniture / Don't need the sunshine / Strange glue / My selfish gene. *(lp w/ free 12"radio sessions)* – International velvet / No stione unturned / Murder & Scully / Strange glue.

—— Feb'98:- CERYS featured on a SPACE hit, 'The Ballad Of Tom Jones'

| Apr 98. | (7"yellow/c-s) *(NEG 112/+CASS)* **ROAD RAGE. / I'M CURED** | 5 | - |
| | (cd-s+=) *(NEG 112CD)* – Blow the millennium (pt.2) / ('A'-Ghia). | | |

		Blanco Y Negro	Imprint
Jul 98.	(7"red/c-s) *(NEG 113/+CASS)* **STRANGE GLUE. / THAT'S ALL FOLKS**	11	
	(cd-s+=) *(NEG 113CD)* – Road rage (live).		
Oct 98.	(7"green/c-s) *(NEG 114/+CASS)* **GAME ON. / STRANGE GLUE (live acoustic)**	33	-
	(cd-s+=) *(NEG 114CD)* – Mulder and Scully (live in Newport).		
Mar 99.	(7"orange/c-s) *(NEG 115/+C)* **DEAD FROM THE WAIST DOWN. / BRANDING A MOUNTAIN**	7	
	(cd-s+=) *(NEG 115CD)* – Bad bad boy.		
Apr 99.	(cd/lp) *(3984 27094-2/-4/-1)* **EQUALLY CURSED & BLESSED**	1	

– Dead from the waist down / Londinium / She's a millionaire / Storm the palace / Karaoke queen / Bulimic beats / Shoot the messenger / Postscript / Valarian unwanted / Nothing hurts / Dazed beautiful and bruised.

Jul 99.	(7"/c-s) *(NEG 117/+C)* **LONDINIUM. / INTERCONTINENTAL**	20	
	(cd-s+=) *(NEG 117CD)* – Apathy revolution.		
Nov 99.	(7"/c-s) *(NEG 119/+C)* **KARAOKE QUEEN. / DON'T WANNA TALK ABOUT IT**	36	
	(cd-s+=) *(NEG 119CD)* – All girls are fly (da-be).		

CATCH (see under ⇒ EURYTHMICS)

CATHERINE WHEEL (dig out; Great Alt & Indie . . .)

Nick CAVE

Born: NICHOLAS EDWARD CAVE, 22 Sep'57, Warracknabeal, Australia. He was the main man behind punk/power-pop outfit, The BOYS NEXT DOOR, completing the band with neighbours MICK HARVEY, TRACY PEW and PHIL CALVERT. Formed in Caulfield, Melbourne in late '77, they issued a one-off version of Nancy Sinatra's 'THESE BOOTS WERE MADE FOR WALKING', before they added a fifth member, ROWLAND S. HOWARD. After an album, 'DOOR, DOOR', was released on 'Mushroom' records in 1979, they came to England as The BIRTHDAY PARTY, taking their name

from a Harold Pinter play. The band were subsequently snapped up by IVO on the (then) new indie label '4 a.d.', after a recent 'HEE-HAW' EP was given some night time airing by John Peel. About as extreme as any music ever released by the label, The BIRTHDAY PARTY were more a wake than a celebration, albeit one with more than its fair share of black humour. Their first UK album, 'PRAYERS ON FIRE' (1981), featured such enduringly sharp material as 'ZOO MUSIC GIRL', 'CRY', 'CAPERS' and 'NICK THE STRIPPER', although for many obsessive fans and critics alike, 'RELEASE THE BATS' remains the definitive track. Issued in summer '81, the single was a gothic slice of avant-garde that took over the territory once belonging to the likes of PERE UBU and The POP GROUP. Later that year, TRACY PEW was jailed for drunk driving, a revolving cast of BARRY ADAMSON, CHRIS WALSH and HARRY HOWARD deputising for him on tour. Live, The BIRTHDAY PARTY were even more unhinged than on vinyl, their demented stage show setting them apart from the masses of up and coming goth-rock acts around at the time. While TRACY was behind bars, NICK, ROWLAND and MICK teamed up as The TUFF MONKS with fellow Australians, The GO-BETWEENS on a one-off 45, 'AFTER THE FIREWORKS'. A further album, 'JUNKYARD' (which hit UK Top 75 in 1982), assured The BIRTHDAY PARTY's position as cult favourites among those who favoured black as a fashion statement. Later that year, ROWLAND hooked up with mistress of soft-porn new wave, LYDIA LUNCH, for a cover of Lee Hazlewood & Nancy Sinatra's 'SOME VELVET MORNING', while The BIRTHDAY PARTY were trimmed to a quartet for 'THE BAD SEED' EP. Released in early '83, the set included the incendiary 'SONNY'S BURNING', arguably the group's finest track. Having moved to Berlin to escape the pressures of critical adulation, the party was finally over after the appropriately titled 'MUTINY' EP. CAVE, who at the time also lived in London, played a few low-key gigs in '83 backed by The CAVEMEN who subsequently became The BAD SEEDS. Including a couple of his cronies from the BIRTHDAY PARTY days, MICK HARVEY and BLIXA BARGELD (also a member of cheery industrial types, EINSTURZENDE NEUBAUTEN), the initial line-up also boasted ex-MAGAZINE man, BARRY ADAMSON, who stayed with the band for the first four albums. Released on 'Mute' (whom CAVE was still contracted to), the debut long player, 'FROM HER TO ETERNITY' (1984), introduced CAVE's preoccupation with the ELVIS myth on a cover of 'IN THE GHETTO', an obsession indulged in greater depth on 'THE FIRSTBORN IS DEAD' (1985). The spit and thrash of the BIRTHDAY PARTY had now been replaced with a skeletal, funereal musical backing to accompany CAVE's ominous crooning. Part hellfire preacher, part damned sinner, CAVE's tales of murder most foul and general debauchery were almost always set in a context (real or implied) of Old Testament morality. Yep, this crazy cat's got that old-time religion, his songs steeped in the shadowy blues of the Mississippi Delta and the lure of his namesake, Old Nick himself. While 'KICKING AGAINST THE PRICKS' (1986), an album of covers, saw the likes of 'BLACK BETTY' and 'BY THE TIME I GET TO PHOENIX', falling under CAVE's dark spell like lambs to the slaughter, the singer came into his own on 'YOUR FUNERAL . . . MY TRIAL' later that year. Rich in dark, dense imagery, the compelling narratives of crime and punishment were further developed on 'TENDER PREY' (1988). In the couple of years preceding the next BAD SEEDS release, CAVE published his first novel, 'AND THE ASS SAW THE ANGEL', and appeared in the film, 'GHOSTS OF THE CIVIL DEAD', as well as scoring the soundtrack (along with HARVEY and BARGELD). Largely acoustic, 'THE GOOD SON' (1990) saw CAVE and his BAD SEEDS return in moodily intense style, grandiose string arrangements complementing CAVE's sombre intonations. 'HENRY'S DREAM' (1992) was somewhat more menacing with the chilling 'JACK THE RIPPER', although 'STRAIGHT TO YOU' found CAVE applying his vocal intensity in lovelorn ballad mode with impressive results. Further musings on the nature of love pervaded 'LET LOVE IN' (1994), although the apocalyptic antipode was back on familiar blood stained ground with 'MURDER BALLADS' a couple of years later. Against a minimal musical backdrop, CAVE recounted tales of a lyrical savagery that made his earlier work read like nursery rhymes. As well as a duet with POLLY HARVEY, the record saw an unlikely, but interesting pairing with KYLIE MINOGUE (!) on 'WHERE THE WILD ROSES GROW'. In comparison, 'THE BOATMAN'S CALL' (1997) was almost evangelical, an opus that seemed to find NICK as at peace with himself and the world as he's ever been. That's not to say this was a happy record, far from it, as CAVE reflected on the redemptive power of love, and the pain of love lost. Mooted by many critics as his best work to date, it was certainly his most accessible and possessed an atmosphere of meditative grace that sets it apart from much of his previous output. In a music world of MTV mediocrity, CAVE's dark, defiantly individual stance is somehow comforting, though you wouldn't necessarily want to meet the man down a dark alley late at night. Later in 1997, CAVE was rumoured to be working on a blues covers album with TIM ROSE, while he was also set to star alongside Ewan Bremner in the film, 'Rhinoceros Hunting In Budapest'. A second volume of 'King Ink' hit the book shops in March '98 although more publicity was generated via the release of a long-overdue NICK CAVE & THE BAD SEEDS best of compilation. • **Covered:** RUNNING SCARED (Roy Orbison) / BLACK BETTY (Ram Jam) / BY THE TIME I GET TO PHOENIX (Jim Webb) / MUDDY WATER (Johnny Rivers) / HEY JOE (Jimi Hendrix) / ALL TOMORROW'S PARTIES (Velvet Underground) / THE CARNIVAL IS OVER (Seekers) / SOMETHING'S GOTTEN HOLD OF MY HEART (Gene Pitney) / HELPLESS (Neil Young) / WHAT A WONDERFUL WORLD (Ray Charles) / etc. mainly from his covers album KICKING AGAINST THE PRICKS.

Album rating: Boys Next Door: DOOR DOOR (*6) / Birthday Party: PRAYERS ON FIRE (*8) / DRUNK ON THE POPE'S BLOOD (*6) / JUNKYARD (*6) / HITS compilation (*8) / LIVE 1981-1982 collection (*7) / Nick Cave & The Bad Seeds: FROM HER TO ETERNITY (*7) / THE FIRSTBORN IS DEAD (*8) / KICKING AGAINST THE PRICKS (*6) / YOUR FUNERAL . . . MY TRIAL (*6) / TENDER PREY (*6) / THE GHOST OF THE CIVIL DEAD soundtrack (*5) / THE GOOD SON (*8) / HENRY'S DREAM (*8) / LIVE SEEDS (*6) / LET LOVE IN (*8) / MURDER BALLADS (*7) / THE BOATMAN'S CALL (*9) / THE BEST OF NICK CAVE & THE BAD SEEDS compilation (*9)

BOYS NEXT DOOR

NICK CAVE – vocals / **MICK HARVEY** (b.29 Sep'58, Rochester, Australia) – guitar / **TRACY PEW** – bass / **PHIL CALVERT** – drums

		Suicide	not iss.
May 78.	(7") (103140) **THESE BOOTS ARE MADE FOR WALKING. / BOY HERO**	-	- Austra

— (Dec'78) added **ROWLAND S. HOWARD** (b.24 Oct'59, Melbourne) – guitar (ex-YOUNG CHARLATANS)

		Mushroom	not iss.
May 79.	(7") (K 7492) **SHIVERS. / DIVE POSITION**	-	- Austra
May 79.	(lp) (L 36931) **DOOR, DOOR**	-	- Austra

– The nightwatchman / Brave exhibitions / Friends of my world / The voice / Roman Roman / Somebody's watching / After a fashion / Dive position / I mistake myself / Shivers. (Australian cd-iss. 1987; D 19227) (cd-iss. Mar93 on 'Grey Area-Mute';)

		Missing Link	not iss.
Dec 79.	(12"ep) (MLEP-3) **HEE-HAW**	-	- Austra

– Catholic skin / The red clock / Faint heart / The hair shirt / Death by drowning. (Australia re-iss. Dec83; credited as BIRTHDAY PARTY; ING 008)

Feb 80.	(7"gig freebie) (MLS 16) **HAPPY BIRTHDAY. / THE RIDDLE HOUSE**	-	- Austra

BIRTHDAY PARTY

— (same line-up & label)

Jul 80.	(7") (MLS 18) **MR. CLARINET. / HAPPY BIRTHDAY**	-	- Austra
Nov 80.	(lp) (LINK 7) **THE FIRST ALBUM** (originally credited to BOYS NEXT DOOR)	-	- Austra

– The friend catcher / Waving my arms / Catman / The red clock / (below Australian releases only are with different label mentioned)

		4.a.d.	not iss.
Oct 80.	(7"m) (AD 12) **THE FRIEND CATCHER. / WAVING MY ARMS / CATMAN**	-	-
Apr 81.	(lp) (CAD 104) **PRAYERS ON FIRE**	-	-

– Zoo music girl / Cry / Capers / Nick the stripper / Ho-ho / Figure of fun / King Ink / A dead song / Yard / Dull day / Just you and me. (cd-iss. Apr88+=; CAD 104CD) – Blundertown / Kathy's kisses.

Jun 81.	Missing Link; (12"m) (MSD 479) **NICK THE STRIPPER. / BLUNDER TOWN / KATHY'S KISSES**	-	- Austra
Aug 81.	(7") (AD 111) **RELEASE THE BATS. / BLAST OFF**	-	-
Oct 81.	(7") (AD 114) **MR. CLARINET. / HAPPY BIRTHDAY**	-	-
Feb 82.	(m-lp) (JAD 202) **DRUNK ON THE POPE'S BLOOD (live)**	-	-

– (Sometimes) Pleasure heads must burn / King Ink / Zoo music girl / Loose / LYDIA LUNCH:- The Agony Is The Ecstasy.

— (Dec81) while **TRACY PEW** was in jail for drunk driving he was replaced on tour only by either BARRY ADAMSON, CHRIS WALSH or **HARRY HOWARD**

May 82.	(lp) (CAD 207) **JUNKYARD**	73	-

– She's hit / Dead Joe / Dim locator / Hamlet (pow-pow-pow) / Several sins / Big-Jesus-trash-can / Kiss me back / 6" gold blade / Kewpie doll / Junkyard. (cd-iss. Apr88+=; CAD 207CD) – Dead Joe (version) / Release the bats / Blast off.

— In Sep'82, ROLAND S. HOWARD did duet with LYDIA LUNCH on 12" 'Some Velvet Morning. / I Fell In Love With A Ghost'; BAD 210)

Nov 82.	Missing Link; (7") (MLS 32) **NICK THE STRIPPER. / BLUNDERTOWN**	-	- Austra

— Now quartet when **CALVERT** joined **PSYCHEDELIC FURS**. (HARVEY now drums)

Feb 83.	(12"ep) (BAD 301) **THE BAD SEED**	-	-

– Sonny's burning / Wild world / Fears of gun / Deep in the woods.

— **JEFFREY WEGENER** – drums (ex-LAUGHING CLOWNS) repl. HARVEY Also **BLIXA BARGELD** – guitar (of EINSTURZENDE NEUBAUTEN) repl. absent HOWARD

		Mute	not iss.
Nov 83.	(12"ep) (12MUTE 29) **MUTINY!**	-	-

– Jennifer's veil / Mutiny in Heaven / Swampland / Say a spell.

— Disbanded Autumn 1983. TRACY joined The SAINTS. (He was later to die late '86 of epileptic fit aged 28). ROWLAND HOWARD formed CRIME & THE CITY SOLUTION. NICK CAVE went solo, forming his BAD SEEDS taking with him MICK HARVEY.

– compilations, etc. – (all mostly UK)

on '4 a.d.' unless otherwise stated

Jun 83.	(12"ep) (BAD 307) **THE BIRTHDAY PARTY EP**	-	-

– Release the bats / Blast off / The friend catcher / Mr. Clarinet / Happy birthday.

Apr 84.	(d-lp) Missing Link; (ING 009) **IT'S STILL LIVING (live)**	-	- Austra
Dec 85.	(lp) Missing Link; (LINK 22) **A COLLECTION – BEST AND RAREST**	-	- Austra
Feb 87.	(12"ep) Strange Fruit; (SFPS 020) **THE PEEL SESSION** (21.4.81)	-	-

– Release the bats / Rowland around in that stuff / (Sometimes) Pleasure heads must burn / Loose. (re-iss. Aug88 cd-ep; SFPSCD 020)

Oct 88.	(12"ep/cd-ep) Strange Fruit; (SFPS/+CD 058) **THE PEEL SESSIONS** (2.12.81)	-	-

– Big-Jesus-trash-can / She's hit / Bully bones / 6" gold blade.

Aug 89.	(cd) (CAD 301CD) **MUTINY / THE BAD SEED**	-	-
Aug 89.	(cd) (CAD 307CD) **HEE-HAW**	-	-

– (contains tracks from THE BIRTHDAY PARTY lp)

Oct 92.	(d-lp/cd)(c) (DAD 2016/+CD)(DADC 2016) **HITS**	-	-

– The friend catcher / Happy birthday / Mr Clarinet / Nick the stripper / Zoo music girl / King Ink / Release the bats / Blast off / She's hit / 6" Gold blade / Hamlet (pow, pow, pow) / Dead Joe / Junkyard / Big-Jesus-Trash-Can / Wild world / Sonny's burning / Deep in the woods / Swampland / Jennifer's veil / Mutiny in Heaven.

Jul 99.	(cd) (CAD 9005CD) **LIVE 1981-1982 (live)**	-	-

NICK CAVE & THE BAD SEEDS

NICK CAVE – vocals / **MICK HARVEY** – guitar, keyboards / **BLIXA BARGELD** (b.12 Jan'59, Berlin, Germany) – guitar (of EINSTURZENDE NEUBAUTEN) / **BARRY ADAMSON** (b. 1 Jun'58, Manchester, England) – bass, guitar (ex-MAGAZINE, ex-PETE SHELLEY) / **HUGO RACE** – drums

		Mute	Restless
Jun 84.	(7") (MUTE 32) **IN THE GHETTO. / THE MOON IS IN THE GUTTER**	-	-

— added **ANITA LANE** – synthesizers (ex-solo artist)

Jun 84.	(lp) (STUMM 17) <71435> **FROM HER TO ETERNITY**	40	-

– Avalanche / Cabin fever / Well of misery / From her to eternity / Wings of flies / Saint Huck / A box for black Paul. (cd-iss. 1987+=; CDSTUMM 17) – In the ghetto / The Moon is in the gutter / From her to eternity (1987).

— **THOMAS WYDLER** (b. 9 Oct'59, Zurich, Switzerland) – drums (ex-DIE HAUT) repl. HUGO + ANITA

		Mute	Homestead
Jun 85.	(lp/c) (STUMM/CSTUMM 21) <HMS 026> **THE FIRSTBORN IS DEAD**	53	-

– Tupelo / Say goodbye to the little girl tree / Train long suffering / Black crow king / Knockin' on Joe / Wanted man / Blind Lemon Jefferson. (cd-iss. Apr88; CDSTUMM 21)

Jul 85.	(7") (7MUTE 38) **TUPELO. / THE SIX STRINGS THAT DREW BLOOD**	-	-
Jun 86.	(7") (7MUTE 47) **THE SINGER. / RUNNING SCARED**	-	-

(12"+=) (12MUTE 47) – Black Betty.

Aug 86.	(cd/c/lp) (CD/C+/STUMM 28) <HMS 065> **KICKING AGAINST THE PRICKS**	89	-

– Muddy water / I'm gonna kill that woman / Sleeping Annaleah / Long black veil / Hey Joe / The singer / Black Betty * / Running scared * / All tomorrow's parties / By the time I get to Phoenix / The hammer song / Something's gotten hold of my heart / Jesus met the woman at the well / The carnival is over. (cd+= *)

Nov 86.	(cd/c/lp) (CD/C+/STUMM 34) <HMS 073> **YOUR FUNERAL . . . MY TRIAL**	-	-

– Sad waters / The Carny / Your funeral . . . my trial / Stranger than kindness / Jack's shadow / Hard on for love / She fell away / Long time man. (cd+=) – Scum.

— **CAVE** retained **HARVEY, BARGELD** and **WYDLER**, bringing in **ROLAND WOLF** – bass / **KID CONGO POWERS** (b. BRIAN TRISTAN, 27 Mar'61, La Puente, Calif.) – guitar (ex-CRAMPS, ex-GUN CLUB)

		Mute	Mute-Elektra
May 88.	(7") (MUTE 52) **THE MERCY SEAT. / NEW DAY**	-	-

(12"+=) (12MUTE 52) – ('A'video mix).
(cd-s+=) (CDMUTE 52) – From her to eternity (film version) / Tupelo (version).

Sep 88.	(cd/c/lp) (CD/C+STUMM 52) <75401> **TENDER PREY**	67	-

– The mercy seat / Up jumped the Devil / Deanna / Watching Alice / Mercy / City of refuge / Slowly goes the night / Sunday's slave / Sugar, sugar, sugar / New morning. (cd+=) – The mercy seat (video mix). (free-12"ep.w/above) **AND THE ASS SAW THE ANGEL** (narration/book) – One Autumn / Animal static / Mah sanctum / Lamentation.

Sep 88.	(12") (12MUTE 86) **DEANNA. / THE GIRL AT THE BOTTOM OF MY GLASS**	-	-
Mar 89.	(cd/c/lp; NICK CAVE – MICK HARVEY – BLIXA BARGELD) (<CD/C+/IONIC 3>) **GHOSTS . . . OF THE CIVIL DEAD** (Soundtrack w/ dialogue)	-	-

– The news / Introduction / A prison in the desert / David Hale – I've been a prison guard since I was 18 years old / Glover – I was 16 when they put me in prison / David Hale – you're danglin' us like a bunch of meat on a hook / Pop mix / Glover – we were united once / David Hale – the day of the murders / Lilly's theme ("A touch of warmth") / Maynard mix / David Hale – what I'm tellin' is the truth / Outro – The free world / Glover – one man released so they can imprison the rest of the world.

— (now a 5-piece, without WOLF)

Mar 90.	(12"/cd-s/7") (12/CD+/MUTE 108) **THE SHIP SONG. / THE TRAIN SONG**	-	-
Apr 90.	(cd/c/lp) (CD/C+/STUMM 76) <60988> **THE GOOD SON**	47	Oct90

– Foi na cruz / The good son / Sorrow's child / The weeping song / The ship song / The hammer song / Lament / The witness song / Lucy. (w/-7"/cd-s) **THE MERCY SEAT / CITY OF REFUGE / DEANNA (all acoustic)**

Sep 90.	(12"/7") (12+/MUTE 118) **THE WEEPING SONG. / COCKS 'N' ASSES**	-	-

(cd-s+=) (12/CD MUTE 118) – Helpless / (some with hidden track).

— **CONWAY SAVAGE** (b.27 Jul'60, Foster, Australia) – keyboards + **MARTYN P. CASEY** – 10 Jul'60, Chesterfield, England) – bass (ex-TRIFFIDS) repl. KID CONGO

Mar 92.	(7") (MUTE 140) **STRAIGHT TO YOU. / JACK THE RIPPER (acoustic)**	68	-

(12"+=/cd-s+=) (12/CD MUTE 140) – Blue bird.

Apr 92.	(cd/c/lp) (CD/C+/STUMM 92) <61323> **HENRY'S DREAM**	29	May92

– Papa won't leave you Henry / I had a dream, Joe / Straight to you / Brother, my cup is empty / Christina the astonishing / When I first came to town / John Finn's wife / Loom of the land / Jack the ripper.

Aug 92.	(7") (LMUTE 147) **I HAD A DREAM, JOE. / THE GOOD SON (live)**	-	-

(12"+=/cd-s+=) (12/CD MUTE 147) – ('A'side) / The Carny (live) / The mercy seat (live) / The ship song (live).

Nov 92.	(c-s/7"; by NICK CAVE & SHANE MacGOWAN) (C+/MUTE 151) **WHAT A WONDERFUL WORLD. / A RAINY NIGHT IN SOHO**	72	-

(7") (MUTE 151D) – ('A'side / Lucy (by SHANE MacGOWAN).
(12"/cd-s) (12/CD MUTE 151) – (all 3 tracks).

Sep 93. (cd) *(CDMUTE 122) <61554>* **LIVE SEEDS (live)** — **67** — [ ]
— Mercy seat / Deanna / The ship song / Papa won't leave you Henry / Plain gold ring / John Finn's wife / Tupelo / Brother my cup is empty / The weeping song / Jack the ripper / The good son / From her to eternity. *(re-iss. Sep96; LCDSTUMM 122)*

Mar 94. (12"/cd-s/7"silver) *(12/CD/MUTE 160)* **DO YOU LOVE ME? / CASSIEL'S SONG / SAIL AWAY** — **68** — [ ]

Apr 94. (cd/c/lp) *(CD/C+/STUMM 123) <61645>* **LET LOVE IN** — **12** [ ]
— Do you love me? / Nobody's baby now / Loverman / Jangling Jack / Red right hand / I let love in / Thirsty dog / Ain't gonna rain anymore / Lay me low / Do you love me? (part 2).

—— **JAMES JOHNSON** – guitar (of GALLON DRUNK) repl. on tour only BLIXA

Jul 94. (7"pic-d) *(MUTE 169)* **LOVERMAN. / (I'LL LOVE YOU) TILL THE END OF THE WORLD** — [ ] [ ]
(12"/cd-s) *(12/CD MUTE 169)* – ('A'side) / B side.

Oct 94. (7"red) *(MUTE 172)* **RED RIGHT HAND. / THAT'S WHAT JAZZ IS TO ME** — [ ] [ ]
(cd-s+=) *(CDMUTE 172)* – Where the action is.

Oct 95. (c-s/7"; NICK CAVE & THE BAD SEEDS featuring KYLIE MINOGUE) *(C+/MUTE 185)* **WHERE THE WILD ROSES GROW. / THE BALLAD OF ROBERT MOORE & BETTY COLTRANE** — **11** [ ]
(cd-s+=) *(CDMUTE 185)* – The willow garden.

Feb 96. (cd/c/lp) *(CD/C+/STUMM 138) <46195>* **MURDER BALLADS** — **8** [ ]
— Song of joy / Stagger Lee / Henry Lee / Lovely creature / Where the wild roses grow (featuring KYLIE MINOGUE) / The curse of Millhaven / The kindness of strangers / Crow Jane / O'Malley's bar / Death is not the end.

Feb 96. (7"; by NICK CAVE & PJ HARVEY) *(MUTE 189)* **HENRY LEE. / KING KONG KITCHEE KITCHEE KI-MI-O** — **36** [ ]
(c-s+=/cd-s+=) *(C/CD MUTE 189)* – Knoxville girl.

<most UK singles were given a US release in 1996>

—— JOHNSON was repl. by **JIM SCLAVUNOS + WARREN ELLIS**

Feb 97. (7") *(MUTE 192)* **INTO MY ARMS. / LITTLE EMPTY BOAT** — **53** [ ]
(cd-s+=) *(CDMUTE 192)* – Right now I'm a-roaming.

Mar 97. (cd/c) *(CD/C+/STUMM 142) <46530>* **THE BOATMAN'S CALL** — **22** [ ]
— Into my arms / Lime tree harbour / People ain't no good / Brompton oratory / There is a kingdom / (Are you) The one that I've been waiting for? / Where do we go now but nowhere? / West country girl / Black hair / Idiot prayer / Far from me / Green eyes.

May 97. (7") *(MUTE 206)* **(ARE YOU) THE ONE THAT I'VE BEEN WAITING FOR? / COME INTO MY SLEEP** — **67** [ ]
(cd-s+=) *(CDMUTE 206)* – Black hair (band version) / Babe, I got you bad.

May 98. (cd/c/d-lp) *(CD/C+/MUTEL 004) <46960>* **THE BEST OF NICK CAVE & THE BAD SEEDS** (compilation) — **11** [ ]
— Deanna / Red right hand / Straight to you / Tupelo / Nobody's baby now / Stranger than kindness / Into my arms / (Are you) The one that I've been waiting for? / The weeping song / The ship song / Where the wild roses grow (feat. KYLIE MINOGUE) / For her to eternity. *(special d-cd; LCDMUTEL 004)* **LIVE AT THE ROYAL ALBERT HALL** – Stranger than kindness / The ship song / Let love in / Brompton oratory / Red right hand / Lime tree arbour / The weeping song / Henry Lee / Where the wild roses grow / Deanna / Straight to you / Tupelo / Nobody's baby now / Into my arms / (Are you) The one that I've been waiting for? / The Carny / Do you love me? / The mercy seat / From her to eternity.

Exene CERVENKA (see under ⇒ X)

Guy CHADWICK (see under ⇒ HOUSE OF LOVE)

CHAMBERS BROTHERS (dig out; Great Psychedelic . . .)

CHAMELEONS (dig out; Great Alt & Indie . . .)

James CHANCE (dig out; Great Alt & Indie . . .)

Harry CHAPIN

Born: 7 Dec'42, Greenwich Village, New York City, USA. Son of a big band drummer, he played in Brooklyn Heights Boys' Choir before forming a trio with his brothers, TOM and STEPHEN. Becoming a documentary film maker in the 60's, he directed the Oscar-nominated 'Legendary Champions' in 1968 before forming his own backing group and signing for 'Elektra' in 1971. His narrative folk-rock style served him well over the early-mid 70's period, CHAPIN's debut set, 'HEADS AND TALES' (1972) enjoying an extended residency in the American charts following the Top 30 success of the 'TAXI' single. CHAPIN later became something of a mini-star when radio staple, 'W-O-L-D' (about a morning DJ) hit the Top 40 on both sides of the Atlantic in 1974. In the space of a few months he released a fourth set, 'VERITIES & BALDERDASH', his most commercially successful to date. The album's appeal was considerably sweetened with the inclusion of 'CAT'S IN THE CRADLE', a treatise on injustice which became CHAPIN's only No.1 single (and a big hit for snotty metallers, UGLY KID JOE). The following year, CHAPIN concentrated on his anti-hunger initiatives, becoming a tireless social activist whose lobbying drew more recognition than his subsequent musical output. He continued to play more than his fair share of benefit concerts, although tragically he was killed in a car crash (on the 16th July 1981), travelling to just such a gig. Ironically, CHAPIN had made a brief return from commercial oblivion the previous year with the 'SEQUEL' single (billed, funnily enough, as a sequel to 'TAXI'), which almost made the American Top

20. • **Trivia:** His younger TOM CHAPIN released an album in 1988 for 'Flying Fish'; 'LET ME BACK INTO YOUR LIFE'.

Album rating: HEAD & TALES (*6) / SNIPER AND OTHER LOVE SONGS (*4) / SHORT STORIES (*5) / VERITIES & BALDERDASH (*7) / PORTRAIT GALLERY (*5) / GREATEST STORIES – LIVE (*4) / ON THE ROAD TO KINGDOM COME (*4) / DANCE BAND ON THE TITANIC (*5) / LIVING ROOM SUITE (*4) / LEGENDS OF THE LOST AND FOUND – NEW GREATEST STORIES LIVE (*4) / SEQUEL (*5) / ANTHOLOGY compilation (*7) / THE LAST PROTEST SINGER posthumous (*4)

HARRY CHAPIN – vocals, guitar, with **RON PALMER** – guitar / **TIM SCOTT** – cello / **JOHN WALLACE** – bass / **STEVE CHAPIN** – keyboards / **RUSS KUNKEL** – drums, percussion

	Elektra	Elektra
Feb 72. (7") <45-770> **TAXI. / EMPTY**	-	**24**
Mar 72. (lp) *(K 42107) <75023>* **HEADS & TALES**		**60**

— Could you put your light on, please / Greyhound / Everybody's lonely / Sometime, somewhere wife / Empty / Taxi / Any old kind of day / Dogtown / Same sad singer.

Jul 72. (7") *(K 12060) <45-792>* **COULD YOU PUT YOUR LIGHT ON, PLEASE. / ANY OLD KIND OF DAY** — [ ] [ ]

Oct 72. (7") *(K 42125) <45-811>* **SUNDAY MORNING SUNSHINE. / BURNING HERSELF** — - **75**

Oct 72. (lp) *(K 42125) <75042>* **SNIPER AND OTHER LOVE SONGS** — [ ] [ ]
— Sunday morning sunshine / Sniper / And the baby never cries / Burning herself / Barefoot boy / Better place to be (parts 1 & 2) / Circle / Woman child / Winter song.

Jan 73. (7") *<45-828>* **BETTER PLACE TO BE. / WINTER SONG** — - [ ]

—— **MICHAEL MASTERS** – cello / **PAUL LEKA** – keyboards / **JIM CHAPIN** – drums, repl. SCOTT, brother STEVE CHAPIN + KUNKEL

Apr 74. (lp) *(K 42155) <75065>* **SHORT STORIES** — **61** Dec73
— Short stories / W-O-L-D / Song for myself / Changes / They call her easy / Mr. Tanner / Mail order Annie / There's a lot of lonely people tonight / Old College Avenue.

Apr 74. (7") *(K 12133) <45-874>* **W-O-L-D. / SHORT STORIES** — **34** **36** Dec73

May 74. (7") *(K 12133) <45-893>* **OLD COLLEGE AVENUE. / WHAT MADE AMERICA FAMOUS** — - [ ]

—— **STEVE CHAPIN** returned and added **ALLAN SCHWARTZBERG** – drums

Sep 74. (7") *<45-203>* **CAT'S IN THE CRADLE. / VACANCY** — - **1**

Sep 74. (lp) *(K 52007) <1012>* **VERITIES & BALDERDASH** — **4**
— Cat's in the cradle / I wanna learn a love song / Shooting star / 30,000 pounds of bananas / She sings songs without words / What made America famous / Vacancy / Halfway to Heaven / Six-string orchestra.

Oct 74. (7") *(K 12157)* **CAT'S IN THE CRADLE. / SHOOTING STAR** — [ ] -

Mar 75. (7") *(K 12173) <45-236>* **I WANNA LEARN A LOVE SONG. / SHE SINGS SONGS WITHOUT WORDS** — **44** Feb75

Jul 75. (7") *(K 12184) <45-264>* **DREAMS GO BY. / SANDY** — [ ]

Nov 75. (lp) *(K 52023) <1041>* **PORTRAIT GALLERY** — **53** Sep75
— Dreams go by / Tangled up puppet / Star tripper / Babysitter / Someone keeps calling my name / The rock / Sandy / Dirt gets under the fingernails / Bummer / Stop singing those sad songs.

Jan 76. (7") *(K 12194) <45-285>* **TANGLED UP PUPPET. / DIRT GETS UNDER THE FINGERNAILS** — [ ] [ ]

Mar 76. (7") *<45-304>* **THE ROCK. / STAR TRIPPER** — - [ ]

—— **HOWIE FIELDS** – drums + **DOUG WALKER** – guitar were added

Apr 76. (d-lp) *(K 62017) <2009>* **GREATEST STORIES – LIVE (live)** — **48**
— Dreams go by / W.O.L.D. / Saturday morning / I wanna learn a love song / Mr.Tanner / Better place to be / Let time go lightly / Cat's in the cradle / Taxi / Circle / 30,000 pounds of bananas / She is always seventeen / Love is just another word / The shortest story. *(cd-iss. 1989; 960 630-2)*

Jun 76. (7") *<45-327>* **BETTER PLACE TO BE. / (part 2) (live)** — - **86**

Aug 76. (7") *(K 12211)* **BETTER PLACE TO BE (live). / TAXI (live)** — - [ ]

—— now w/ **WALKER, WALLACE, FIELDS, S. CHAPIN + RON EVANUIK**

Oct 76. (lp/c) *(K/K4 52040) <1082>* **ON THE ROAD TO KINGDOM COME** — **87**
— On the road to kingdom come / The parade's still passing by / The mayor of Candor lied / Laugh man / Corey's coming / If my Mary was here / Fall in love with him / Caroline / Roll down the river.

Jan 77. (7") *<45-368>* **IF MY MARY WAS HERE. / COREY'S COMING** — - [ ]

—— **KIM SCHOLES** – cello, repl. EVANUIK

Sep 77. (7") *<45-426>* **DANCE BAND ON THE TITANIC. / I WONDER WHAT HAPPENED TO HIM** — - [ ]

Sep 77. (d-lp) *(K 62021) <301>* **DANCE BAND ON THE TITANIC** — **58**
— Dance band on the Titanic / Why people should stay the same / My old lady / We grew up a little bit / Bluesman / Country dreams / I do it for you, Jane / I wonder what happened to him / Paint a picture of yourself (Michael) / Mismatch / Merceneries / Manhood / One light in a dark valley (an imitation spiritual) / There was only one choice.

Oct 77. (7") *(K 12271)* **DANCE BAND ON THE TITANIC. / (part 2)** — [ ] -

May 78. (7") *<45-445>* **MY OLD LADY. / I'D DO IT FOR YOU, JANE** — - [ ]

Jun 78. (lp/c) *(K/K4 52089) <142>* **LIVING ROOM SUITE** — [ ]
— Dancin' boy / If you want to feel / Poor damned fool / I wonder what happened to this world / Jenny / It seems you only love me when it rains / Why do little girls / Flowers are red / Somebody said.

Aug 78. (7") *(K 12308) <45-497>* **IF YOU WANT TO FEEL. / I WONDER WHAT WOULD HAPPEN TO THE WORLD** — [ ] -

May 79. (7") *(K 12361)* **FLOWERS ARE RED. / WHY DO LITTLE GIRLS** — [ ] -

—— w/ **WALLACE, WALKER, FIELDS, S. CHAPIN + SCHOLES**

Nov 79. (d-lp) *(K 62026) <703>* **LEGENDS OF THE LOST AND FOUND – NEW GREATEST STORIES LIVE (live)** — [ ] Oct79
— Stranger with the melodies / Copper / The day they closed the factory down / Pretzel man / Old folkie / Get on with it / We were three / Odd job man / Legends of the lost and found / You are the only song / Mail order Annie / Tangled up puppet / Poor damned fool / Corey's coming / If my Mary were here / Flowers are red.

Nov 79. (7") *<45-524>* **FLOWERS ARE RED. / JENNY** — - [ ]

—— **YVONNE CABLE** – cello repl. SCHOLES

			Boardwalk	Boardwalk
Oct 80.	(7") *(FWS 1)* <5700> **SEQUEL. / I FINALLY FOUND IT SANDY**			23
			Epic	Boardwalk
Apr 81.	(7") *(EPCA 1168)* <5705> **REMEMBER WHEN THE MUSIC. / NORTH WEST 222**			
May 81.	(lp) *(EPC 84996)* **SEQUEL**			58 Oct80

– Sequel / I miss America / Story of a life / Remember when the music / Up on the shelf / Salt and pepper / God babe, you've been good for me / Northwest 222 / I finally found it Sandy / Remember when the music (reprise).

Aug 81.	(7") <119> **STORY OF A LIFE. / SALT AND PEPPER**	-	-

—— HARRY was killed in a motor crash on 16th July 1981

– compilations, etc. –

on 'Elektra' unless mentioned otherwise

Jun 76.	(7") *(K 12224)* **W.O.L.D. / CAT'S IN THE CRADLE**	-	-
Nov 85.	(lp/c) *(EKT 16/+C)* **ANTHOLOGY**	-	-

– W.O.L.D. / Any old kind of day / Cat's in the cradle / 30,000 pounds of bananas / Taxi / She is always seventeen / Sunday morning sunshine / I wanna learn a love song / Better place to be / Song man.

1989.	(7") *Old Gold; (OG 9907)* **CAT'S IN THE CRADLE. / W.O.L.D.**	-	-
1989.	(lp/c/cd) *Sequel; (NEX LP/MC/CD 101)* **THE LAST PROTEST SINGER**	-	-

– Last of the protest singers / November rains / Basic protest song / Last stand / Sounds like America to me / Word wizard / Anthem / A quiet little love affair / I don't want to be president / Silly little girl / You only own the light.

Roger CHAPMAN (see under ⇒ FAMILY)

Tracy CHAPMAN

Born: 20 Mar'64, Cleveland, Ohio, USA. A budding singer/songwriter from childhood, CHAPMAN's break came while attending Medford University (Tufts) where she met Brian Koppelman, son of industry bigwig, Charles. Through this valuable contact, CHAPMAN secured a manager in Elliot Roberts and a deal with 'Elektra', an eponymous debut album following in Spring '88. Critically acclaimed upon release, its sparse, grainy yet soulful and cathartic nu-folk sketched vivid portraits of everyday suffering shot through with the desire for individual freedom and the redemptive power of love. Although the record's initial release was fairly low-key, CHAPMAN landed a support slot with 10,000 MANIACS and the rave reviews continued, so far, so good; what really kicked off her career, however, was a show stopping performance at the Nelson Mandela 70th birthday concert in London, an event beamed around the globe via satellite. Sales of her debut went into overdrive, the album eventually topping both the UK and US charts, while 'FAST CAR' raced up the singles chart. A cliche perhaps, but CHAPMAN had literally become an international superstar almost overnight, her success especially surprising bearing in mind she was a young black woman singing about issues many people would rather ignore. She subsequently undertook a high profile Amnesty International tour, a strong follow-up set, 'CROSSROADS' (1989) giving her another UK No.1. Some felt the album had been a bit hastily recorded, the record inevitably failing to scale the commercial heights of its predecessor; while CHAPMAN was an articulate, observant voice for the dispossessed, she was also a singer who shied away from the showbiz limelight. It would be another three years before 'MATTERS OF THE HEART' (1992), a competent effort which nevertheless brought criticisms of water treading. Although CHAPMAN's profile had diminished considerably by the mid-90's, a fourth set, 'NEW BEGINNING' made the US Top 5, while 'GIVE ME ONE REASON' became her highest charting single to date. • **Covered:** traditional song HOUSE OF THE RISING SUN (Glenn Yarborough).

Album rating: TRACY CHAPMAN (*8) / CROSSROADS (*5) / MATTERS OF THE HEART (*4) / NEW BEGINNING (*5)

TRACY CHAPMAN – vocals, acoustic guitar / with **JACK HOLDER** – guitar, organ / **LARRY KLEIN** – bass / **DENNY FONGHEISER** – drums

Apr 88.	(lp/c)(cd) *(EKT 44/+C)*<*(K 960774-2)*> **TRACY CHAPMAN**	1	1

– Talkin' bout a revolution / Fast car / Across the lines / Behind the wall / Baby can I hold you / Mountains o' things / She's got her ticket / Why? / For my lover / If not now . . . / For you.

May 88.	(7") *(EKR 73)* <69412> **FAST CAR. / FOR YOU**	5	6
	(12"+=) *(EKR 73T)* – Behind the wall.		
Aug 88.	(7"/12") *(EKR 78/+T)* **TALKIN' BOUT A REVOLUTION. / IF NOT NOW . . .**		-
	(cd-s+=) *(EKR 78CD)* – She's got her ticket.		
Sep 88.	(7") <69383> **TALKIN' BOUT A REVOLUTION. / BEHIND THE WALL**	-	75
Oct 88.	(7") <69356> **BABY CAN I HOLD YOU. / IF NOT NOW . . .**	-	48
Nov 88.	(7") *(EKR 82)* **BABY CAN I HOLD YOU. / ACROOS THE LINES**		-
	(12"+=/cd-s+=) *(EKR 82 T/CD)* – Mountain o' things.		
Sep 89.	(7"/c-s) *(EKR 95/+C)* <69273> **CROSSROADS. / BORN TO FIGHT**	61	90
	(12"+=) *(EKR 95T)* – Fast car.		
	(cd-s+=) *(EKR 95CD)* – Mountain o' things (live).		
Oct 89.	(lp/c)(cd) *(EKT 61/+C)*<*(K 960888-2)*> **CROSSROADS**	1	9

– Crossroads / Bridges / Freedom now / Material world / Be careful of my heart / Subcity / Born to fight / A hundred years / This time / All that you have is your soul.

Feb 90.	(7") *(EKR 107)* **ALL THAT YOU HAVE IS YOUR SOUL. / SUBCITY**		-
	(12"+=) *(EKR 107T)* – Freedom now.		
Feb 90.	(7") **ALL THAT YOU HAVE IS YOUR SOUL. / MATERIAL WORLD**	-	-

---

Apr 92.	(7"/c-s) **BANG BANG BANG. / WOMAN'S WORK**		
	(12"+=/cd-s+=) – House of the rising Sun.		
May 92.	(cd)(lp/c) <*(7559 61215-2)*>*(EKT 98/+C)* **MATTERS OF THE HEART**		19

– Bang bang bang / So / I used to be a sailor / The love that you had / Woman's work / These are the things / Short supply / Dreaming on a world / Open arms / Matters of the heart. *(re-iss. cd+c Nov93)*

Jul 92.	(7"/c-s) **DREAMING ON A WORLD. / WOMAN'S WORK**		
	(cd-s+=) – ('A'extended) / House of the rising Sun.		
Nov 95.	(cd/c) <*(7559 61850-2/-4)*> **NEW BEGINNING**		4

– Heaven's here on Earth / New beginning / Smoke and ashes / Cold feet / At this point in my life / the promise / The rape of the world / Tell it like it is / Give me one reason / Remember the tin man / I'm ready.

Mar 96.	(c-s) <64346> **GIVE ME ONE REASON. / THE RAPE OF THE WORLD**	-	3
May 96.	(cd-s) *(EKR 222CD)* **GIVE ME ONE REASON / THE RAPE OF THE WORLD / HOUSE OF THE RISING SUN**	-	-
Mar 97.	(c-s) *(E 3969C)* **GIVE ME ONE REASON / FAST CAR**		
	(cd-s+=) *(E 3969CD)* – Talking 'bout a revolution.		

CHAPTERHOUSE   (dig out; Great Alt & Indie . . .)

CHARLATANS (US)   (dig out; Great Psychedelic . . .)

CHARLATANS (UK)

Formed: Northwich, Cheshire, England . . . late 1989 by MARTIN BLUNT, ROB COLLINS, JON BROOKES and JON BAKER. They soon found a frontman in singer TIM BURGESS and after a few attempts at getting a record deal, they set up their own 'Dead Dead Good' label. Early in 1990, they scored a massive indie hit with the 'INDIAN ROPE' single. Following the explosion of the "Madchester" scene, the label was taken over by the Beggars Banquet subsidiary, 'Situation 2', for whom they recorded their first Top 10 hit, 'THE ONLY ONE I KNOW'. Another hammond-driven classic, 'THEN', preceded a late summer chart topping debut album, 'SOME FRIENDLY'. A relatively quiet year followed, during which MARTIN BLUNT nearly retired due to severe depression. However, it was actually BAKER who departed after playing at London's Royal Albert Hall. Come 1992, MARK COLLINS was drafted in and things look brighter when the single, 'WEIRDO', gave them another Top 20 hit. Their second album, however, ('BETWEEN 10TH AND 11TH'), was given the thumbs down by the music press, hence its failure to secure a respectable chart placing. This was not the only setback that year, as ROB COLLINS was charged with aiding and abetting an armed robbery. A year later, although maintaining his innocence, he was sentenced to several months in jail, later being released in early 1994 on good behaviour. 'CAN'T GET OUT OF BED', saw them return in fine style, and was lifted from the Top 10 album 'UP TO OUR HIPS'. TIM then moonlighted on singles by SAINT ETIENNE and The CHEMICAL BROTHERS, before the group were back to their best on the eponymous 1995 album. From its retro cover art, to the 'Sympathy For The Devil'-style single, 'JUST WHEN YOU'RE THINKIN' THINGS OVER', the album was an obvious homage to The ROLLING STONES. Tragically, on 23rd of July '96, ROB COLLINS was killed when his car spun off a road in Wales. The coroner's report concluded that he was the driver and also that he had twice the legal amount of alcohol in his blood. They had just recorded their fifth album, 'TELLIN' STORIES', preceded by their biggest hit singles to date, 'ONE TO ANOTHER' and 'NORTH COUNTRY BOY'. With The CHARLATANS' momentum seemingly unstoppable while every other 'baggy' band fell by the wayside, BURGESS and Co celebrated their longevity with a career retrospective, 'MELTING POT' (1998). With newboy TONY ROGERS finally getting his chance to perform in the place of COLLINS and with the group signing a major deal via 'M.C.A.', The CHARLATANS were ready to take their place back in indie-rock – albeit minus a few hundred thousand admittedly stolen by their accountant, Trevor Williams. Their sixth album, 'US AND US ONLY' (1999), was a test of sorts, its subsequent No.2 peak position in the UK charts an indication that they were still wanted by their ageing fanbase; the STONE ROSES, THE VERVE and OASIS, where were they now? • **Songwriters:** Group compositions except; I FEEL MUCH BETTER ROLLING OVER (Small Faces). On their eponymous 1995 album, the track 'HERE COMES A SOUL SAVER' featured a guitar riff remarkably similar to that of PINK FLOYD's 'Fearless' (from 'Meddle' 1971).

Album rating: SOME FRIENDLY (*8) / BETWEEN 10th & 11th (*5) / UP TO OUR HIPS (*7) / THE CHARLATANS (*8) / TELLIN' STORIES (*8) / MELTING POT compilation (*8) / US AND US ONLY (*7)

TIM BURGESS (b.30 May'68) – vocals (ex-ELECTRIC CRAYONS) repl. BAZ KETTLEY / **ROB COLLINS** (b.23 Feb'63) – organ / **JON BAKER** (b.1969) – guitar / **JON BROOKS** (b.1969) – drums / **MARTIN BLUNT** (b.1965) – bass (ex-MAKIN' TIME, ex-TOO MUCH TEXAS w / TIM)

			Dead Dead Good	not iss.
Feb 90.	(7") *(GOOD ONE SEVEN)* **INDIAN ROPE. / WHO WANTS TO KNOW**		89	-

(12"+=) *(GOOD ONE TWELVE)* – You can talk to me. *(re-iss. Jul91 12"/cd-s; GOOD 1 T/CD, hit No.57) (re-iss. cd-s Oct96)*

			Situation 2	Beggars Banquet
May 90.	(7") *(SIT 70)* **THE ONLY ONE I KNOW. / EVERYTHING CHANGED**		9	

(12"+=) *(SIT 70T)* – Imperial 109.

(cd-s++=) *(SIT 70CD)* – You can talk to me.

Sep 90. (7"/c-s) *(SIT 74/+C)* **THEN. / TAURUS MOANER** 　12
(12"+=/cd-s+=) *(SIT 74 T/CD)* – ('A'-alternate take) / ('B'instrumental).

Oct 90. (lp/c/cd/s-lp) *(SITU 30/+MC/CD/R)* <2411> **SOME FRIENDLY** 　1　　73
– You're not very well / White shirt / Opportunity / Then / 109 pt.2 / Polar bear /
Believe you me / Flower / Sonic / Sproston Green. *(cd+=)* – The only one I know.
(cd re-iss. Sep95 on 'Beggars Banquet'; BBL 30CD)

Feb 91. (7"/c-s) *(SIT 76/+CS)* **OVER RISING. / WAY UP THERE** 　15
(12"+=/cd-s+=) *(SIT 76 T/TC/CD)* – Happen to die / Opportunity Three
(re-work).

—— **MARK COLLINS** – guitar (ex-CANDLESTICK PARK) repl. BAKER

Oct 91. (7"/c-s) *(SIT 84/+C)* **ME IN TIME. / OCCUPATION H.
MONSTER** 　28
(12"+=/cd-s+=) *(SIT 84 T/CD)* – Subtitle.

Feb 92. (7"/c-s) *(SIT 88/+C)* **WEIRDO. / THEME FROM 'THE WISH'** 　19
(12"+=/cd-s+=) *(SIT 88 T/CD)* – Sproston Green (U.S. remix) / ('A'-alternate take).

Mar 92. (lp/c/cd) *(SITU 37/+MC/CD)* <61108> **BETWEEN 10th AND
11th** 　21
– I don't want to see the lights / Ignition / Page one / Tremelo song / The end of
everything etc / Subtitle / Can't even be bothered / Weirdo / Chewing gum weekend /
(No one) Not even the rain. *(re-iss. cd Sep95 on 'Beggars Banquet'; BBL 37CD)*

Jun 92. (c-s) *(SIT 97C)* **TREMELO SONG (alternate take) / THEN
(live) / CHEWING GUM WEEKEND (live) / TREMELO
SONG** 　44
(12") *(SIT 97T)* – Happen to die (unedited) repl. last version.
(cd-s) *(SIT 97CD1)* – ('A'side) / Happen to die (unedited) / Normality swing
(demo).
(cd-s) *(SIT 97CD2)* – ('A'live April '92) / Then (live) / Chewing gum weekend
(live).

—— ROB COLLINS was imprisoned in Sep'93 for taking part in a robbery. (see above)
He had already recorded below while awaiting trial, and was free just in time to
feature on Top Of The Pops.

	Beggars Banquet	Beggars Banquet

Jan 94. (7"/c-s) *(BBQ 27/+C)* **CAN'T GET OUT OF BED. /
WITHDRAWN** 　24　　-
(12"+=/cd-s+=) *(BBQ 27 T/CD)* – Out.

Mar 94. (cd-ep) *(BBQ 31CD)* **I NEVER WANT AN EASY LIFE IF ME
AND HE WERE EVER TO GET THERE / ONLY A BOHO /
SUBTERRAINEAN / CAN'T GET OUT OF BED (demo)** 　38　　-

Mar 94. (cd/c/lp) *(BBQ CD/MC/LP 147)* <92352> **UP TO OUR HIPS** 　8　　-
– Come in number 21 / I never want an easy life / If me and he were ever to get
there / Can't get out of bed / Feel flows / Autograph / Jesus hairdo / Up to our hips /
Patrol / Another rider up in flames / Inside – looking out. *(re-iss. cd Sep95; BBL
147CD)*

Jun 94. (c-s) *(BBQ 32C)* **JESUS HAIRDO / PATROL (Dust Brothers
mix)** 　48
(12"+=) *(BBQ 32T)* – Feel flows (the carpet kiss mix).
(cd-s+=) *(BBQ 32CD1)* – Stir it up / Feel flows (Van Basten mix).
(cd-s) *(BBQ 32CD2)* – ('A'side) / I never want an easy life / Another rider up in
flames / Up to our hips (BBC Radio 1 live sessions).

Dec 94. (7"/c-s) *(BBQ 44/+C)* **CRASHIN' IN. / BACK ROOM
WINDOW** 　31　　-
(12"+=/cd-s+=) *(BBQ 44 T/CD)* – Green flashing eyes.

May 95. (7"/c-s) *(BBQ 55/+C)* **JUST LOOKIN'. / BULLET COMES** 　32　　-
(cd-s+=) *(BBQ 55CD)* – Floor nine.

Aug 95. (c-s) *(BBQ 60C)* **JUST WHEN YOU'RE THINKIN' THINGS
OVER / FRINCK / YOUR SKIES ARE MINE** 　12　　-
(cd-s+=) *(BBQ 60CD)* – Chemical risk (toothache remix).
(12") *(BBQ 60T)* – (first 2 tracks) / Chemical risk dub (toothache remix) / Nine
acre dust (Dust Brothers mix).

Aug 95. (cd/c/d-lp) *(BBQ CD/MC/LP 174)* <92602> **THE CHARLATANS** 　1　　-
– Nine acre court / Feeling holy / Just lookin' / Crashin' in / Bullet comes /
Here comes a soul saver / Just when you're thinkin' things over / Tell everyone /
Toothache / No fiction / See it through / Thank you. *(d-lp+=)* – Chemical risk
(toothache remix).

—— On 23rd July '96, ROB COLLINS was killed in a car crash (see above).

Aug 96. (7"/c-s/cd-s) *(BBQ 301/+C/CD)* **ONE TO ANOTHER. / TWO
OF US / REPUTATION** 　3　　-

—— **MARTIN DUFFY** – keyboards (of PRIMAL SCREAM) augmented

	Beggars Banquet	M.C.A.

Mar 97. (7"/c-s/cd-s) *(BBQ 309/+C/CD)* **NORTH COUNTRY BOY. /
AREA 51 / DON'T NEED A GUN** 　4　　-

Apr 97. (cd/c/lp) *(BBQ CD/MC/LP 190)* <11622> **TELLIN' STORIES** 　1　　-
– With no shoes / North country boy / Tellin' stories / One to another / You're a big
girl now / How can you leave us / Area 51 / How high / Only teethin' / Get on it /
Rob's theme / Two of us / Reputation.

Jun 97. (7"/c-s) *(BBQ 312/+C)* **HOW HIGH. / DOWN WITH THE
MOOK** 　6　　-
(cd-s+=) *(BBQ 312CD)* – Title fight.

Oct 97. (7") *(BBQ 318)* **TELLIN' STORIES. / KEEP IT TO YOURSELF** 　16　　-
(c-s+=) *(BBQ 318C)* – Thank you (live).
(cd-s++=) *(BBQ 318CD)* – Clean up kid.

	Beggars Banquet	Beggars Banquet

Feb 98. (cd/c/lp) *(BBQ CD/MC/LP 198)* <80198> **MELTING POT**
(compilation) 　4
– The only one I know / Then / Opportunity three / Over rising / Sproston Green
(U.S. version) / Weirdo / Theme from the wish / Patrol (The Chemical Brothers mix) /
Can't get out of bed / I never want an easy life if me & he were ever to get there /
Jesus hairdo / Crashin' in / Just lookin' / Here comes a soul saver / Just when you're
thinkin' things over / One to another / North country boy.

—— (1997) **TONY RODGERS** was now the replacement for ROB

	M.C.A.	M.C.A.

Oct 99. (7") *(MCS 40220)* **FOREVER. / WHEN YOUR SHIP
COMES IN** 　12
(c-s/cd-s+=) *(MCS C/TD 40220)* – Great place to leave.
(cd-s) *(MCSXD 40220)* – ('A'side) / Sleepy little sunshine boy / ('A'-CD enhanced).

Oct 99. (cd/c/lp) *(MCD/MCC/MCA 60069)* **US AND US ONLY** 　2
– Good witch bad witch / Impossible / Blonde waltz / House is not a home / Senses /
My beautiful friend / I don't care where you live / Blind stagger / Good witch bad
witch / Watching you.

Dec 99. (7") *(MCS 40225)* **MY BEAUTIFUL FRIEND. / SCORCHED** 　31
(c-s/cd-s+=) *(MCS C/TD 40225)* – Your precious love.
(cd-s) *(MCSXD 40225)* – ('A'mixes + CD-enhanced).

Ray CHARLES

Born: RAY CHARLES ROBINSON, 23 Sep'30, Albany, Georgia, USA.
While encouraged to take up the piano at an early age after his family moved
to Greenville, Florida, the young ROBINSON was afflicted by glaucoma (after
witnessing the death of his brother) at the age of seven and subsequently
went blind. Using Braille, he studied composition at the St. Augustine School
for the Deaf and the Blind as well as learning instruments such as organ and
saxophone. The troubles continued to pile up, however, as both his mother and
father died before he reached the age of sixteen. Leaving school, he survived
by playing in various dance bands around Florida before saving enough
money to move to Seattle. As R.C. ROBINSON he began playing with The
McSON TRIO (alongside guitarist GOSSADY McGHEE and bassist MILTON
GARRAD) before signing to Jack Lauderdale's 'Downbeat' label in 1949.
To avoid confusion with boxer Sugar Ray Robinson, he began recording as
RAY CHARLES (accompanied by The MAXIM TRIO) and released his debut
single, 'CONFESSION BLUES', the same year; a further two singles followed
before the label was taken over by 'Swingtime'. Subsequently working with
JOHNNY MOORE'S THREE BLAZERS, CHARLES continued cutting sides
in the 'sepia Sinatra' style of singers such as NAT 'KING' COLE and
CHARLES BROWN. 1951's 'BABY LET ME HOLD YOUR HAND' and
'KISS-A-ME BABY' marked his first couple of R&B Top 10 hits, during
which time he embarked on a national tour with blues man LOWELL
FULSON. Starting out as a sideman, CHARLES soon advanced to musical
director and the experience put him in good stead for a subsequent stint in New
Orleans with GUITAR SLIM. He both arranged and played piano on SLIM's
million-selling 1954 hit for 'Specialty', 'The Things That I Used To Do',
CHARLES duly incorporating a more organic, gospel-influenced style into his
own recordings. Adding alto sax and a quartet of horn players, the singer signed
to 'Atlantic' and perfected his thrilling marriage of earthy, hollering gospel and
raw R&B with 1955's 'I'VE GOT A WOMAN'. The track narrowly missed top
spot on the R&B chart and initiated a string of such hits wherein CHARLES
alchemised various black music styles in what amounted to a blueprint for
60's soul. His first brush with the pop chart came in summer '59 with the
classic 'WHAT'D I SAY', a raucous combination of gospel, jump-blues and
rock'n'roll that made him a national star overnight. A cover of Hank Snow's
'I'M MOVIN' ON' followed into the Top 40 while 'THE GENIUS OF RAY
CHARLES' (1960) album made the Top 20, its combination of sentimental
balladry and big-band ebullience setting the tone for many of his future
recordings. 1960 was also the year he moved to 'ABC Paramount', thrashing
out a deal whereby he was given far more creative control as well as full
ownership of the mastertapes (virtually unheard of in those days). Things got
off to a great start with a stunning US No.1 cover of pop standard, 'GEORGIA
ON MY MIND', while female backing singers, The RAELETTES, spiced up
CHARLES' rasp on 'HIT THE ROAD JACK' (another No.1) and a rollicking
'UNCHAIN MY HEART'. 1962 saw him recording a set of duets with BETTY
CARTER as well as making a shock move into country with the No.1 album,
'MODERN SOUNDS IN COUNTRY AND WESTERN MUSIC'. Having
already cut a number of straight jazz albums at 'Atlantic', CHARLES proved
there were few boundaries to his eclectic talent with unique interpretations
of country standards like Don Gibson's 'I CAN'T STOP LOVING YOU'
(a transatlantic No.1) and Hank Williams' 'HEY GOOD LOOKIN'. 1963's
brassy Top 5 remake of Harlan Howard's 'BUSTED' proved uncannily
prophetic as CHARLES was arrested for possession of heroin two years later;
though he took a year out to fight his addiction, he was back in court on
a second drugs rap in 1967, the judge refraining from handing out a prison
sentence but fining him heavily and putting him on four years probation. By
the time he'd formed his own label, 'Tangerine' (through which he released
material by other artists as well as his own), in the mid-late 60's, his sound
was increasingly catering to the MOR market though he could still come up
with funky little gems like the 1969 collaboration with JIMMY LEWIS, 'IF
IT WASN'T FOR BAD LUCK' and 1971's instrumental 'BOOTY BUTT'. He
also cut a couple of notable albums during the 70's, the black consciousness-
centred (CHARLES was a vocal supporter of the civil rights movement and
its leader, Martin Luther King) 'A MESSAGE FROM THE PEOPLE' (1972)
and 1975's 'RENAISSANCE'. 1976, meanwhile, found him recording a pop
interpretation of 'PORGY AND BESS' with CLEO LAINE, CHARLES going
on to cut unlikely recordings with everyone from CLINT EASTWOOD!
(a track from the film 'Any Which Way You Can') and BILLY JOEL to
INXS. An early 80's move to 'Columbia' saw him attempt a fully fledged
transformation into country on 'WISH YOU WERE HERE TONIGHT' (1983)
and 'FRIENDSHIP' (1984), the latter an album of collaborations with the likes
of JOHNNY CASH, MERLE HAGGARD and WILLIE NELSON. If critics
weren't too enamoured with these efforts, CHARLES certainly didn't redeem
himself with 1985's Xmas set, 'THE SPIRIT OF CHRISTMAS'. Nevertheless,
he won a Grammy for his 1990 duet with CHAKA KHAN, 'I'LL BE GOOD
TO YOU' (from QUINCY JONES' 'Back On The Block' album) while he
endeared himself to a whole new generation of American youth with a series

of ads for Diet Pepsi. While it undoubtedly seems his glory days are behind him, RAY CHARLES remains one of the true giants and founding fathers of modern music, his part in the development of soul especially, beyond question. His versatility and eclecticism remain unparalleled with his influence apparent in the vocal style of everyone from STEVIE WONDER to VAN MORRISON and JOE COCKER. • **Songwriters:** RAY wrote most of material, although at times lending from others, i.e.- LET THE GOOD TIMES ROLL (Shirley & Lee) / GEORGIA ON MY MIND (Hoagy Carmichael) / HIT THE ROAD JACK (Percy Mayfield) / YOU ARE MY SUNSHINE (Jimmie Davis) / YOUR CHEATIN' HEART + TAKE THESE CHAINS FROM MY HEART (Hank Williams) / THAT LUCKY OLD SUN (?) / MAKIN' WHOOPEE (?) / CRY (Johnny Ray) / I'M A FOOL TO CARE (Joe Barry) / TOGETHER AGAIN (Buck Owens) / ELEANOR RIGBY + YESTERDAY (Beatles) / WHAT AM I LIVING FOR? (Chuck Willis) / LOOK WHAT THEY'VE DONE TO MY SONG, MA? (Melanie) / LIVING FOR THE CITY (Stevie Wonder) / etc. • **Miscellaneous:** Many didn't know at the time, but RAY was married to gospel singer DELLA REESE for 22 years, until they divorced late 1977. Also note that The Ray Charles Singers, who had US hits in the 60's, were in fact conductor Charles Ray Offenberg.

Best CD compilation: RAY CHARLES – THE LIVING LEGEND (*8)

RAY CHARLES – vocals, piano / **GISADY McGHEE** – guitar / **MILTON GARRAD** – bass

		not iss.	Downbeat
1949.	(78; as the MAXIM TRIO) <171> **CONFESSION BLUES. / I LOVE YOU, I LOVE YOU**	-	
1949.	(78) <178> **BLUES BEFORE SUNRISE. / HOW LONG BLUES**	-	
1949.	(78) <179> **A SENTIMENTAL BLUES. / YOU'LL NEVER MISS THE WATER**	-	

		not iss.	Swingtime
1949.	(78; as the MAXIM TRIO) <211> **ALONE IN THIS CITY. / CAN ANYONE ASK FOR MORE**	-	
1949.	(78; as the MAXIM TRIO) <212> **LET'S HAVE A BALL. / ROCKIN' CHAIR BLUES**	-	
1949.	(78) <213> **IF I GIVE YOU MY LOVE. / unknown**	-	
1950.	(78) <215> **I'VE HAD MY FUN. / SITTIN' ON TOP OF THE WORLD**	-	
1950.	(78) <216> **AIN'T THAT FINE. / DON'T PUT YOUR DREAMS ALL IN ONE BASKET**	-	
1950.	(78) <217> **SEE SEE RIDER. / WHAT HAVE I DONE**	-	
1950.	(78) <218> **HONEY, HONEY. / SHE'S ON THE BALL**	-	
1950.	(78) <228> **LATE IN THE EVENING BLUES. / TH' EGO SONG**	-	
1950.	(78) <229> **I'LL DO ANYTHING BUT WORK. / SOMEDAY**	-	
1951.	(78) <249> **ALL TO MYSELF. / I WONDER WHO'S KISSING HER NOW**	-	
1951.	(7",78) <250> **BABY, LET ME HOLD YOUR HAND. / (I'M JUST A) LONELY BOY**	-	
1952.	(7",78) <274> **KISS-A-ME BABY (ALL NIGHT LONG). / I'M GLAD FOR YOUR SAKE**	-	
1952.	(7") <276> **CHANGEABLE WOMAN BLUES. / MOONRISE**	-	
1952.	(7",78) <297> **HEY, NOW. / BABY WON'T YOU PLEASE COME HOME**	-	
1952.	(7",78) <300> **GUITAR BLUES. / BABY LET ME HEAR YOU CALL MY NAME**	-	
	<re-iss. 1952 on 'Sittin-In-With'; 641>		

—— **RAY** added sax / + **4 other horn players** / + **DAVID NEWMAN** – saxophone

		not iss.	Atlantic
Jun 52.	(7") <976> **ROLL WITH MY BABY. / THE MIDNIGHT HOUR**	-	
1953.	(7") <984> **THE SUN'S GONNA SHINE AGAIN. / JUMPIN' IN THE MORNING**	-	
1953.	(7") <999> **MESS AROUND. / FUNNY (BUT I STILL LOVE YOU)**	-	
1953.	(7") <1008> **HEARTBREAKER. / FEELIN' SAD**	-	
1954.	(7") <1021> **IT SHOULD'VE BEEN ME. / SINNER'S PRAYER**	-	
1954.	(7") <1037> **DON'T YOU KNOW (BABY)?. / LOSING HAND**	-	
1954.	(7") <1050> **I'VE GOT A WOMAN. / COME BACK BABY**	-	
1955.	(7") <1063> **THIS LITTLE GIRL OF MINE. / A FOOL FOR YOU**	-	
1955.	(7") <1076> **BLACKJACK. / GREENBACKS**	-	
1956.	(7") <1085> **I'LL DROWN IN MY OWN TEARS. / MARY ANN**	-	
1956.	(7") <1096> **HALLELUJAH, I LOVE HER SO. / WHAT WOULD I DO WITHOUT YOU?**	-	
1956.	(7") <1108> **LONELY AVENUE. / LEAVE MY WOMAN ALONE**	-	
1957.	(7") <1124> **AIN'T THAT LOVE. / I WANT TO KNOW**	-	
1957.	(7") <1143> **IT'S ALL RIGHT. / GET ON THE RIGHT TRACK BABY**	-	
Jul 57.	(lp) <8006> **RAY CHARLES SINGS**	-	

– Ain't that love / I'll drown in my own tears / Come back baby / Sinner's prayer / Funny / Losing hand / A fool for you / Hallelujah I love her so / Mess around / This little girl of mine / Mary Ann / Greenbacks / Don't you know / I got a woman. <UK-iss.Mar67 as 'HALLELUJAH, I LOVE HER SO'; 587 056>

Oct 57.	(7") <1154> **SWANEE RIVER ROCK (TALKIN' 'BOUT THAT RIVER). / I WANT A LITTLE GIRL**	-	34
1957.	(lp) <1259> **THE GREAT RAY CHARLES**		

– The Ray / My melancholy baby / Black coffee / There's no you / Doodlin' / Sweet sixteen bars / I surrender dear / Undecided. (UK-iss.Nov58 on 'London-Jazz'; LTZK 15134)

1958.	(7") <1172> **TALKIN' 'BOUT YOU. / THAT'S ENOUGH**		
1958.	(lp) <1289> **RAY CHARLES AT NEWPORT (live)**		

– The right time / In a little Spanish town / I got a woman / Blues waltz / Hot rod / Talkin' 'bout you / Sherry / A fool for you. (UK-iss.Mar59 on 'London-Jazz'; LTZK 15149) (re-iss. Feb69 & Mar73 on 'Atlantic')

1958.	(lp) as RAY CHARLES & MILT JACKSON) <1279> **SOUL BROTHERS**	-	

– How long blues / Cosmic Ray / The genius after hours / Charlesville / Bags of blues / 'Deed I do / Blue funk / Soul brothers / Bags' guitar blues / Soul meeting / Hallelujah I love her so / Blue genius / X-Ray blues / Love on my mind. (UK-iss.Feb59 on 'London-Jazz'; LTZK 15146) <re-iss. 1961 as 'SOUL MEETING'; 1360> (UK-iss.Mar64 on 'London' mono/stereo; HAK/SHK 8045) (re-iss. 1973 & Jul76 on 'Atlantic') (d-cd-iss. May93)

1958.	(7") <1180> **YES INDEED. / I HAD A DREAM**	-	
1958.	(lp) <8025> **YES INDEED!**	-	

– What would I do without you / It's all right / I want to know / Yes indeed / Got on the right track baby / Talkin' 'bout you / Swanee River rock / Lonely Avenue / Blackjack / The sun's gonna shine again / I had a dream / I want a little girl / Heartbreaker / Leave my woman alone. (UK-iss.Mar59 on 'London'; HAE 2168) (re-iss. 1968 on 'Atlantic')

1958.	(7") <1196> **YOU BE MY BABY. / MY BONNIE**	-	

		London	Atlantic
Dec 58.	(7",78) (HLE 8768) <2006> **ROCKHOUSE (part 1). / ROCKHOUSE (part 2)**		79
Feb 59.	(7") <2010> **(THE NIGHT TIME IS) THE RIGHT TIME. / TELL ALL THE WORLD ABOUT YOU**	-	95
May 59.	(7") <2022> **THAT'S ENOUGH. / TELL ME, HOW YOU FEEL?**	-	
Jul 59.	(7",78) (HLE 8917) <2031> **WHAT'D I SAY (part 1). / WHAT'D I SAY (part 2)**		6 Jun59
Aug 59.	(lp) <8029> **WHAT'D I SAY**	-	

– What'd I say (part 1&2) / Jumping in the mornin' / You be my baby / Tell me how you feel / What kind of man are you / Rock house (part 1&2) / Roll with my baby / Tell all the world about you / My Bonnie / That's enough. (UK-iss.Mar60 on 'London'; HAE 2226) <US re-iss. Aug61, hit No.20> (re-iss. Oct69)

Dec 59.	(7",78) (HLE 9009) <2043> **I'M MOVIN' ON. / I BELIEVE TO MY SOUL**		40 Oct59
Feb 60.	(7") (HLE 9058) <2047> **LET THE GOOD TIMES ROLL. / DON'T LET THE SUN CATCH YOU CRYIN'**		78 / 95 Jan60
Feb 60.	(lp) <1312> **THE GENIUS OF RAY CHARLES**		17

– Let the good times roll / It had to be you / Alexander's ragtime band / Two years of torture / When your lover has gone / 'Deed I do / Just for a thrill / You won't let me go / Tell me you'll wait for me / Don't let the sun catch you cryin' / Am I blue? / Come rain or come shine. (UK-iss.May60 on 'London'Jazz'; LTZK 15190) (cd-iss. Aug93)

		H.M.V.	ABC Paramount
1960.	(7") <10081> **WHO YOU GONNA LOVE? / MY BABY (I LOVE HER, YES I DO)**	-	
Aug 60.	(7") (POP 774) <10118> **STICKS AND STONES. / WORRIED LIFE BLUES**		40 Jun60
Oct 60.	(lp) (CLP 1387) <335> **THE GENIUS HITS THE ROAD**		9 Sep60

– Alabama bound / Georgia on my mind / Basin Street blues / Mississippi mud / Moonlight in Vermont / New York's my home / California, here I come / Moon over Miami / Deep in the heart of Texas / Carry me back to Old Virginny / Blue Hawaii / Chattanooga choo choo.

Oct 60.	(7",78) (POP 792) <10135> **GEORGIA ON MY MIND. / CARRY ME BACK TO OLD VIRGINNY**	24	1 Sep60
Feb 61.	(7") (POP 825) <10164> **RUBY. / HARDHEARTED HANNAH**		28 / 55 Nov60
May 61.	(7") (POP 838) <10141> **THEM THAT GOT. / I WONDER**		58 Jan61

		H.M.V.	Impulse!
Jun 61.	(7") <202> **I'VE GOT NEWS FOR YOU. / I'M GONNA MOVE TO THE OUTSKIRTS OF TOWN**	-	66 / 84
Jul 61.	(7") (POP 862) <200> **ONE MINT JULEP. / LET'S GO**		8 Feb61
Sep 61.	(lp) (CLP 1449) <355> **DEDICATED TO YOU**		11 Feb61

– Hardhearted Hannah / Nancy / Margie / Ruby / Rosetta / Stella by starlight / Cherry / Josephine / Candy / Marie / Diane / Sweet Georgia Brown.

Nov 61.	(lp) (CLP 1475) <2> **GENIUS + SOUL = JAZZ**		4 Mar61

– From the heart / I've got news for you / Moanin' / Let's go / One mint julep / I'm gonna move to the outskirts of town / Stompi' room only / Mister C / Strike up the band / Birth of the blues. (re-iss. +c+cd.Sep89 on 'Essential') (re-iss. cd Jul95 on 'Actual Jazz')

		H.M.V.	ABC Paramount
Oct 61.	(7") (POP 935) <10244> **HIT THE ROAD JACK. / THE DANGER ZONE**	6	1 Sep61
Jan 62.	(7") (POP 969) <10244> **UNCHAIN MY HEART. / BUT ON THE OTHER HAND BABY**		9 / 72 Nov61
Feb 62.	(7"; by RAY CHARLES & BETTY CARTER) <10298> **BABY IT'S COLD OUTSIDE. / WE'LL BE TOGETHER AGAIN**	-	91
Mar 62.	(lp; by RAY CHARLES and BETTY CARTER) (CLP 1520) <385> **RAY CHARLES AND BETTY CARTER**		52 Sep61

– Everytime we say goodbye / You and I / Intro; Goodbye / We'll be together again / People will say we're in love / Cocktails for two / Side by side / Baby it's cold outside / Together / For all we know / It takes twoo to tango / Alone together. (re-iss. c+cd.Nov89 on 'Essential')

Apr 62.	(7") (POP 1017) <10314> **HIDE NOR HAIR. / AT THE CLUB**		20 / 44 Mar62
May 62.	(lp) (CLP 1580) <410> **MODERN SOUNDS IN COUNTRY AND WESTERN MUSIC**	6	1 Apr62

– Bye bye love / You don't know me / Half as much / I love you so much it hurts / Just a little lovin' / Born to lose / Worried mind / It makes no difference now / You win again / Careless love / I can't stop loving you / Hey, good lookin'.

May 62.	(7") (POP 1034) <10330> **I CAN'T STOP LOVING YOU. / BORN TO LOSE**	1	1 / 41 Apr62
Sep 62.	(7") (POP 1064) <10345> **YOU DON'T KNOW ME. / CARELESS LOVE**	9	2 / 60 Jul62

Nov 62. (7") (POP 1099) <10375> **YOUR CHEATING HEART. / YOU ARE MY SUNSHINE** `13` `29` `7`

Feb 63. (lp) (CLP 1613) <435> **MODERN SOUNDS IN COUNTRY AND WESTERN MUSIC VOL.2** `15` `2` Oct62
– You are my sunshine / No letter today / Someday (you'll want me to want you)/ Don't tell me your troubles / Midnight / Oh, lonesome me / Take these chains from my heart / Your cheating heart / I'll never stand in your way / Making believe / Teardrops in my heart / Hang your head in shame.

Mar 63. (7") (POP 1133) <10405> **DON'T SET ME FREE. / THE BRIGHTEST SMILE IN TOWN** `37` `20` `92` Feb63

Apr 63. (lp) (CLP 1626) <415> **RAY CHARLES' GREATEST HITS** (compilation of hits) `16` `5` Aug62

May 63. (7") (POP 1161) <10435> **TAKE THESE CHAINS FROM MY HEART. / NO LETTER TODAY** `5` `8` Apr63

Jul 63. (7") (POP 1202) <10453> **NO ONE. / WITHOUT LOVE (THERE IS NOTHING)** `35` `21` `29` Jun63

Oct 63. (7") (POP 1221) <10481> **BUSTED. / MAKE BELIEVE** `21` `4` Aug63

Oct 63. (lp) (CLP 1678) <465> **INGREDIENTS IN A RECIPE FOR SOUL** `9` Aug63
– Busted / Where can I go / Born to the blue / That lucky old sun / Ol' man river / In the evening / A stranger in town / Ol' man time / Over the rainbow / You'll never walk alone. (cd-iss. Jun95 on 'Personality') (re-iss. cd Jul95 on 'Actual Jazz')

Jan 64. (7") <10509> **THAT LUCKY OLD SUN. / OL' MAN TIME** `-` `20`

Jan 64. (7") (POP 1251) **THAT LUCKY OLD SUN. / MISSISSIPPI MUD** `-`

Mar 64. (7") (POP 1272) <10530> **BABY, DON'T YOU CRY. / MY HEART CRIES FOR YOU** `39` `38` Feb64

May 64. (lp) (CLP 1728) <480> **SWEET AND SOUR TEARS** `9` Mar64
– Cry / Guess I'll hang my tears out to dry / A tear fell / No one to cry to / You've got me crying again / After my laughter came tears / Teardrops from my eyes / Don't cry baby / Cry me a river / Baby, don't you cry / Willow weep for me / I cried for you.

Jun 64. (7") (POP 1315) <10557> **MY BABY DON'T DIG ME. / SOMETHING'S WRONG** `51` May64

Sep 64. (7") (POP 1333) <10571> **NO ONE TO CRY TO. / A TEAR FELL** `38` `50` `55` Jul64

Nov 64. (lp) (CLP 1728) <495> **HAVE A SMILE WITH ME** `36` Aug64
– Smack dab in the middle / Feudin' and fightin' / Two ton Tessie / I never see Maggie alone / Move it on over / Ma (she's making eyes at me) / The thing / The man with the weird beard / The naughty lady of Shady Lane / Who cares (for me).

Nov 64. (7") (POP 1350) <10588> **SMACK DAB IN THE MIDDLE. / I WAKE UP CRYING** `52` Sep64

Dec 64. (7") <10609> **MAKIN' WHOOPEE. / (instrumental)** `-` `46`

Jan 65. (7") (POP 1383) **MAKIN' WHOOPEE. / MOVE IT ON OVER** `42` `-`

Mar 65. (7") (POP 1392) <10615> **CRY. / TEARDROPS FROM MY EYES** `58`

Apr 65. (7") (POP 1414) **LIGHT OUT OF DARKNESS. / PLEASE FORGIVE & FORGET** `-`

Apr 65. (lp) (CLP 1872) <500> **RAY CHARLES LIVE IN CONCERT** (live) `80` Feb65
– Opening (introduction) / Swing a little taste / I gotta woman / Margie / You don't know me / Hide nor hair / Baby, don't you cry / Makin' whoopee / Hallelujah I love her so / Don't set me free / What'd I say / Finale. (cd-iss. Aug93)

Apr 65. (7") <10649> **I GOTTA WOMAN (part 1). / I GOTTA WOMAN (part 2)** `-` `79`

May 65. (7") <10663> **WITHOUT A SONG (part 1) / WITHOUT A SONG (part 2)** `-`

Jul 65. (7") (POP 1437) **I GOTTA WOMAN. / WITHOUT A SONG** `-`

Aug 65. (7") (POP 1457) <10700> **I'M A FOOL TO CARE. / LOVE'S GONNA LIVE HERE** `84` Jul65

Oct 65. (7") (POP 1484) <10720> **THE CINCINNATI KID. / THAT'S ALL I AM TO YOU**

Oct 65. (lp) (CLP 1914) <520> **COUNTRY AND WESTERN MEETS RHYTHM & BLUES** `Aug65`
– Together again / I like to hear it sometime / I've got a tiger by the tail / Please forgive and forget / I don't care / Next door to the blues / Blue moon of Kentucky / Light out of darkness / Maybe it's nothing at all / All night long / Don't let her know / Watch it baby.

Dec 65. (7") (POP 1502) <10739> **CRYING TIME. / WHEN MY DREAMBOAT COMES HOME** `6`

Apr 66. (7") (POP 1519) <10785> **TOGETHER AGAIN. / YOU'RE JUST ABOUT TO LOSE YOUR CLOWN** `48` `19` `91` Mar66

May 66. (lp; mono/stereo) (CLP/CSD 3533) <544> **CRYING TIME** `15` Mar66
– Crying time / No use crying / Let's go get stoned / Going down slow / Peace of mind / Tears / Drifting blues / We don't see eye to eye / You're in for a big surprise / You're just about to lose your crown / Don't you think I ought to know / You've got a problem.

H.M.V.   ABC-TRC

Jun 66. (7") (POP 1537) <10808> **LET'S GO GET STONED. / THE TRAIN** `31` May66

Sep 66. (7") (POP 1551) <10840> **I CHOSE TO SING THE BLUES. / HOPELESSLY** `32` Aug66 `52` Sep66

Nov 66. (lp; mono/stereo) (CLP/CSD 3574) <550> **RAY'S MOODS**
– What-cha doing in there (I wanna know) / Please say you're fooling / By the light of the silvery Moon / You don't understand / Maybe it's because of love / Chitlins with candied yams / Granny wasn't grinning that day / She's lonesome again / Sentimental journey / A born loser / It's a man's world / A girl I used to know.

Nov 66. (7") (POP 1556) <10865> **PLEASE SAY YOU'RE FOOLING. / I DON'T NEED NO DOCTOR** `64` `72`

––– some of the above singles were cred. to RAY CHARLES & HIS ORCHESTRA

Mar 67. (7") <10901> **I WANT TO TALK ABOUT YOU. / PLEASE SAY YOU'RE FOOLING** `-` `98`

Apr 67. (7") (POP 1589) **YOU WIN AGAIN. / BYE BYE BYE** `-`

Jun 67. (7") (POP 1595) <10938> **HERE WE GO AGAIN. / SOMEBODY OUGHT TO WRITE A BOOK ABOUT IT** `38` `15` May67

Sep 67. (lp; mono/stereo) (CLP/CSD 3630) <595> **RAY CHARLES INVITES YOU TO LISTEN** `76` Jul67
– She's funny that way (I got a woman crazy for me) / How deep is the ocean (how high is the sky) / You made me love you (I didn't wanna do it) / Yesterday / I'll be seeing you / Here we go again / All for you / Love walked in / Gee, baby ain't I good to you / People.

Sep 67. (7") (POP 1607) <10970> **IN THE HEAT OF THE NIGHT. / SOMETHING'S GOT TO CHANGE** `33` Aug67
Stateside   ABC-TRC

Dec 67. (7") (SS 2071) <11009> **YESTERDAY. / NEVER HAD ENOUGH OF NOTHING YET** `44` `25` Nov67

Mar 68. (7") (SS 2091) <11045> **THAT'S A LIE. / GO ON HOME** `64` Feb68

Jul 68. (7") (SS 2120) <11090> **ELEANOR RIGBY. / UNDERSTANDING** `36` `35` `46` May68

Nov 68. (7") (SS 2132) <11133> **SWEET YOUNG THING LIKE YOU. / LISTEN, THEY'RE PLAYING OUR SONG** `83` `92` Aug68

Jan 69. (7"; as RAY CHARLES & JIMMY LEWIS) <11170> **IF IT WASN'T FOR BAD LUCK. / WHEN I STOP DREAMING** `-` `77`

Feb 69. (lp; stereo/mono) (S+/SL 10269) <625> **A PORTRAIT OF RAY** `51` Apr68
– Eleanor Rigby / Am I blue / Never say naw / Sun died / Yesterday / When I stop dreaming / I won't leave / Sweet young thing like you / Bright lights and you girl / Understanding.

Mar 69. (7") <11193> **I'LL BE YOUR SERVANT. / I DIDN'T KNOW WHAT TIME IT WAS** `-`

May 69. (7") <11213> **LET ME LOVE YOU. / I'M SATISFIED** `-` `94`

Jul 69. (lp; stereo/mono) (S+/SL 10281) <675> **I'M ALL YOURS – BABY!** `Mar69`
– Yours / I didn't know what the time was / Love is here to stay / Memories of you / Till the end of time / I had the craziest dream / Someday / Indian love call / I dream of you (more than you dream I do) / Gloomy Sunday.

Sep 69. (7") (SS 2155) <11239> **WE CAN MAKE IT. / I CAN'T STOP LOVING YOU BABY** `-`

Nov 69. (7") <11251> **CLAUDIE MAE. / SOMEONE TO WATCH OVER ME** `-`

Feb 70. (lp; stereo/mono) (S+/SL 10293) <695> **DOING HIS THING** `Jul69`
– The same thing that can make you laugh (can make you cry) / Finders keepers, losers weepers / You ought to change your ways / Baby please / Come and get it / We can make it / I'm ready / That thing called love / If it wasn't for bad luck / I told you so.

Feb 70. (7") <11259> **LAUGHIN' AND CLOWNIN'. / THAT THING CALLED LOVE** `-` `98`
Tangerine   Tangerine

May 71. (7"; as RAY CHARLES ORCHESTRA) (6121 001) <1015> **BOOTY BUTT (instrumental). / ZIG ZAG (instrumental)** `36` Mar71

Jul 71. (lp) (6495 001) <1512> **MY KIND OF JAZZ** (instrumental) `Jul70`
– Golden boy / Booty butt / This here / I remember Clifford / Sidewinder / Bluesette / Pas-se-o-ne blues / Zig zag / Senior blues.

Probe   ABC-Tangerine

Oct 70. (7") (SS 2170) <11271> **TILL I CAN'T TAKE IT ANYMORE. / IF YOU WERE MINE** `41` Sep70

Nov 70. (lp) (SPB 1015) <707> **LOVE COUNTRY STYLE** `Aug70`
– f you were mine / Ring of fire / Your love is so doggone good / Don't change on me / Till I can't take it anymore / You've still got a place in my heart / I keep it hid / Sweet memories / Good morning dear / Show me the sunshine.

Mar 71. (7") (PRO 524) <11219> **DON'T CHANGE ON ME. / SWEET MEMORIES** `36`

Jul 71. (lp) (SPB 1039) <726> **VOLCANIC ACTION OF MY SOUL** `52` May71
– See you then / What am I living for / Feel so bad / The long and winding road / The three bells / All I ever need is you / Wichita lineman / Something / I may be wrong (but I think you're wonderful) / Down in the valley.

Aug 71. (7") <11308> **FEEL SO BAD. / YOUR LOVE IS SO DOGGONE GOOD** `68`

Oct 71. (7") (PRO 539) **THE LONG AND WINDING ROAD. / WICHITA LINEMAN** `-`

Dec 71. (7") <11317> **WHAT AM I LIVING FOR. / TIRED OF MY TEARS** `-` `54`

Jun 72. (7") (PRO 566) <11329> **LOOK WHAT THEY'VE DONE TO MY SONG, MA. / AMERICA THE BEAUTIFUL** `65`

Sep 72. (lp) (SPB 1060) <755> **A MESSAGE FROM THE PEOPLE** `52` Apr72
– Lift every voice and sing / Seems like I gotta do wrong / Heaven help us all / There'll be no peace without all men as one / Hey mister / What have they done to my song, ma / Abraham, Martin and John / Take me home, country roads / Every Saturday night / America the beautiful.

Aug 72. (7") <11337> **HEY MISTER. / THERE'LL BE NO PEACE WITHOUT ALL MEN AS ONE** `-`

Jan 73. (7") <11344> **EVERY SATURDAY NIGHT. / TAKE ME HOME, COUNTRY ROADS** `-`

Feb 73. (lp) (SPB 1066) <765> **THROUGH THE EYES OF LOVE** `Nov72`
– My first night alone without you / I can make it thru the days (but oh those lonely nights) / Someone to watch over me / A perfect love / If you wouldn't be my lady / You leave me breathless / Never ending song of love / Rainy night in Georgia.

May 73. (7") <11351> **I CAN MAKE IT THRU THE DAYS (BUT OH THOSE LONELY NIGHTS). / RING OF FIRE** `-` `81`
London   Crossover

Nov 73. (7") (HLU 10432) <973> **COME LIVE WITH ME. / EVERYBODY SING** `82`

Jan 74. (7") <974> **LOUISE. / SOMEBODY** `-`

Apr 74. (lp) (SHU 8467) <9000> **COME LIVE WITH ME** `Jan74`
– Till there was you / If you go away / It takes so little time / Somebody / Come live with me / Problems, problems / Louise / Where was he / Everybody sing.

Aug 75. (lp) (SHU 8485) <9005> **RENAISSANCE** [ ] [ ] Jun75
 – Living for the city / Then I'll be home / My God and I / We're gonna make it / For mama / Sunshine / Bein' green / Sail away.

Sep 75. (7") <981> **LIVING FOR THE CITY. / THEN I'LL BE HOME** [-] [**91**]

Sep 75. (7") (HLU 10505) **LIVING FOR THE CITY. / FOR MAMA** [-] [-]

Jan 76. (7") <985> **AMERICA THE BEAUTIFUL. / SUNSHINE** [-] [-]

London / **R.C.A.**

Oct 76. (7"; by RAY CHARLES & CLEO LAINE) (HLU 10541) <PB 10800> **OH LAWD, I'M ON MY WAY. / OH BESS, WHERE'S MY BESS?** [ ] [ ]

Dec 76. (d-lp; by RAY CHARLES & CLEO LAINE) (D 31-32) <1831> **PORGY AND BESS** [ ] [ ] Nov76
 – Summertime (instrumental) / Summertime / My man's gone now / A woman is a sometimes thing / They pass by singing / What you want wild Bess / I got plenty o' nothin' (instrumental) / I got plenty o' nothing / Buzzard song / Bess, you is a woman / Oh doctor Jesus / Crab man's call / Here come de honey man / Strawberry woman's call / It ain't necessarily so (instrumental) / It ain't necessarily so / There's a boat dat's leaving for New York (instrumental) / There's a boat dat's leaving for New York / Oh Bess, oh where's my Bess? / Oh lawd I'm on my way.

London / **Atlantic**

Jul 77. (7") (HLU 10554) **I CAN SEE CLEARLY NOW. / LET IT BE** [ ] [ ]

Nov 77. (7") <3443> **I CAN SEE CLEARLY NOW. / ANONYMOUS LOVE** [-] [ ]

Jan 78. (lp) (SHU 8509) <19142> **TRUE TO LIFE** [**78**] Nov77
 – I can see clearly now / The jealous kind / Oh what a beautiful morning / How long has this been goin' on / Be my love / Anonymous love / Heavenly music / Game number nine / Let it be.

1978. (7") <3473> **A PEACE THAT WE NEVER COULD ENJOY. / GAME NUMBER NINE** [ ] [ ]

1978. (7") <3527> **YOU FORGET YOUR MEMORY. / RIDING THUMB** [-] [ ]

Nov 78. (lp/c) (SHU/KSACU1 8519) <19199> **LOVE AND PEACE** [ ] [ ]
 – Take off that dress / She knows / You 20th century fox / Riding thumb / We had it all / A peace that we never could enjoy / No achievement showing / Is there anyone out there / Give the poor man a break.

Dec 78. (7") <3549> **CHRISTMAS TIME. / THERE'LL BE NO PEACE WITHOUT ALL MEN AS ONE** [-] [ ]

Aug 79. (7") <3611> **SOME ENCHANTED EVENING. / YOU 20TH CENTURY FOX** [ ] [ ]

Sep 79. (lp/c) (SHU/KSAC1 8537) <19251> **AIN'T IT SO** [ ] [ ]
 – Some enchanted evening / Blues in the night / Just because / What'll I do / One of these days / Love me or set me free / Drift away / Love me tonight.

Nov 79. (7") <3634> **LOVE ME OR SET ME FREE. / JUST BECAUSE** [-] [ ]

Oct 80. (7"; by RAY CHARLES & CLINT EASTWOOD) <49608> **BEERS TO YOU (w/CLINT EASTWOOD). / COTTON-EYED CLINT (by the TEXAS OPERA COMPANY)** [-] [ ]
 (above from the movie 'Any Which Way You Can' on 'Warners')

Dec 80. (7") (HL 10579) <3762> **COMPARED TO WHAT. / NOW THAT WE'VE FOUND EACH OTHER** [ ] [ ]

—— in Oct'80, he issued SHAKE YOUR TALL FEATHER. / MINNIE THE MOOCHER with "CAB CALLOWAY")

C.B.S. / **Columbia**

Mar 83. (7") <03429> **STRING BEAN. / BORN TO LOVE ME** [-] [ ]

Mar 83. (lp) (CBS 25065) <38293> **WISH YOU WERE HERE TONIGHT?** [ ] [ ]
 – 3/4 times / Ain't your memory got no pride at all / I don't want no stranger sleepin' in my bed / Born to love me / Let your love flow / Shakin' your head / String bean / I Wish you were here tonight? / You've got the longest leaving act / You feel good all over. (cd-iss. Apr90 on 'Pickwick')

May 83. (7") (CBS 3407) **I WISH YOU WERE HERE TONIGHT. / YOU FEEL GOOD ALL OVER** [ ] [ ]

1983. (7") <03810> **YOU FEEL GOOD ALL OVER. / 3/4 TIME** [ ] [ ]

1983. (7") <04083> **AIN'T YOUR MEMORY GOT NO PRIDE AT ALL. / I DON'T WANT NO STRANGERS SLEEPING IN MY BED** [ ] [ ]

1983. (7"; as RAY CHARLES with GEORGE JONES & CHET ATKINS) <04297> **I WISH YOU WERE HERE TONIGHT. / WE DIDN'T SEE A THING** [ ] [ ]

1984. (7") <04420> **DO I EVER CROSS YOUR MIND. / THEY CALL IT LOVE** [ ] [ ]

Jul 84. (lp/c) (CBS/40 25764) <38990> **DO I EVER CROSS YOUR MIND** [ ] [ ]
 – I had it all / Do I ever cross your mind / Woman sensuous woman / Then I'll be over you / Lay around and love on you / Love of my life / They call it love / If I were you / Workin' man's woman / I was on Georgia time.

1984. (7") <04500> **WOMAN, SENSUOUS WOMAN. / I WAS ON GEORGIA TIME** [ ] [ ]

Oct 84. (lp/c) (CBS/40 26060) <39415> **FRIENDSHIP** [ ] [**75**]
 – Two old cats like us / This old heart / We didn't see a thing / Who cares / Rock and roll shoes / Friendship / It ain't gonna worry my mind / Little hotel room / Crazy old soldier / Seven Spanish angels.

1984. (7"; by RAY CHARLES with B.J. THOMAS) <04531> **ROCK AND ROLL SHOES. / THEN I'LL BE OVER YOU** [ ] [ ]

Mar 85. (7"; by RAY CHARLES with WILLIE NELSON) (CBS 4991) <04715> **SEVEN SPANISH ANGELS. / WHO CARES (with JANE FRICKIE)** [ ] [ ]

1985. (7"; by RAY CHARLES with MICKEY GILLEY) <04860> **IT AIN'T GONNA WORRY MY MIND. / CRAZY OLD SOLDIER (with JOHNNY CASH)** [ ] [ ]

1985. (7"; by RAY CHARLES with HANK WILLIAMS JR.) <05575> **TWO OLD CATS LIKE US. / LITTLE HOTEL ROOM (with MERLE HAGGARD)** [ ] [ ]

Dec 85. (lp/c) (CBS/40 26562) <40125> **THE SPIRIT OF CHRISTMAS** [ ] [ ]
 – What child is this / Santa Claus is coming to town / This time of the year / Rudolph the red-nosed reindeer / That spirit of Christmas / All I want for Christmas / Christmas in my heart / Winter wonderland / Christmas time.

Aug 86. (7") <06172> **THE PAGES OF MY MIND. / SLIP AWAY** [ ] [ ]

Aug 86. (lp/c) (CBS/40 26856) <40338> **FROM THE PAGES OF MY MIND** [ ] [ ]
 – The pages of my mind / Slip away / Anybody wit the blues / Class reunion / Caught a touch of your love / A little bit of Heaven / Dixie Moon / Over and over (again) / Beaucoup love / Love is worth the pain.

Nov 86. (7") <06370> **DIXIE MOON. / A LITTLE BIT OF HEAVEN** [ ] [ ]

—— RAY was credited on BILLY JOEL's 'Baby Grand' 45 (Apr'87), then semi-retired from the music biz but continued acting mainly on 'Moonlighting' and 'St. Elsewhere'.

Sep 88. (lp/c/cd) (461183-1/-4/-2) <40703> **JUST BETWEEN US** [ ] [ ]
 – Nothing like a hundred miles / I wish I'd never loved you at all / Too hard to love you / Now I don't believe that anymore / Let's call the whole thing off / Stranger in my own hometown / Over the top / I'd walk a little more for you / If that's what cha want / Save the bones for Henry Jones.

—— In the early 90's, he featured on QUINCY JONES + CHAKA KHAN's hit, 'I'll Be Good To You'.

WEA / **Warners**

Oct 90. (cd/c/lp) <2/-4/-1-26343> **WOULD YOU BELIEVE?** [ ] [ ]
 – I'll take care of you / Your love keeps me satisfied / Ellie, my love / I can't get enough / Let's get back to where we left off / Child support, alimony / Fresh out of tears / Living without you / Where're the stairs? / Leave him!

Mar 93. (c-s) <18611> **A SONG FOR YOU / I CAN'T GET ENOUGH** [ ] [ ]

Mar 93. (cd/c) <7599 26735-2/-4> **MY WORLD** [ ] [ ]
 – My world / A song for you / None of us are free / So help me God / Let me take over / One drop of love / If I could / Love has a mind of its own / I'll be there / Still crazy after all these years.

—— BILLY PRESTON featured on keyboards

—— In Nov'93, RAY teamed up with INXS on their hit 'Please (You Got That . . .)'

Qwest / **Qwest**

Feb 96. (cd) <(9362 46107-2)> **STRONG LOVE AFFAIR** [ ] [ ] Jan96
 – All she wants to do is love me / Say no more / No time to waste time / Angelina / Tell me what you want me to do / Strong love affair / Everybody's handsome child / Out of my life / The fever / Separate ways / I need a good woman bad / If you give me your heart.

– compilations, others, etc. –

1952. (7") Sittin-In-With; <651> **I CAN'T DO MORE. / Rufus Beacham: ROLY POLY** [ ]

1952. (7") Rockin'; <504> **WALKIN' AND TALKIN' WITH MYSELF. / I'M WONDERIN' AND WONDERIN'** [ ]

1953. (7",78) Swingtime; <326> **MISERY IN MY HEART. / THE SNOW IS FALLING** [ ]

1950s. (7") Rockin'; **HARD TIMES. / (part 2)** [ ]

1956. (7"ep) Atlantic; <567> **RAY CHARLES** [ ]

1957. (7"ep) Atlantic; <587> **RAY CHARLES** [ ]

1957. (7"ep) Atlantic; <597> **THE GREAT RAY CHARLES** (UK-iss.Oct58 on 'London-Jazz'; EZK 19043) [ ]

1958. (7"ep) Atlantic; <607> **ROCK WITH RAY CHARLES** [ ]

1958. (7"ep; with MILT JACKSON) Atlantic; <614> **SOUL BROTHERS** (UK-iss.Apr59 on 'London-Jazz'; EZK 19048) [ ]

1959. (7"ep) Atlantic; <619> **THE GENIUS OF RAY CHARLES** [ ]

1960. (7") Rockin'; <5005> **DOODLIN. / (part 2)** [ ]

1960. (7") Atlantic; <2055> **JUST FOR A THRILL. / HEARTBREAKER** [ ]

1960. (7") Atlantic; <2068> **TELL THE TRUTH. / SWEET SIXTEEN BARS** [ ]

Sep 60. (7") London; (HLK 9181) **TELL THE TRUTH. / YOU BE MY BABY** [-]

Nov 60. (lp) London; (HAK 2284) / Atlantic; <8039> **RAY CHARLES IN PERSON** (live) [**13**] Jul60
 (re-iss. Apr69 on 'Atlantic')

1960. (7") Baronet; <7111> **SEE SEE RIDER. / I USED TO BE SO HAPPY** [ ]

1960. (7") Time; <1026> **I FOUND MY BABY. / GUITAR BLUES** [-]

Dec 60. (7") London; (HLK 9251) / Atlantic; <2084> **COME RAIN OR COME SHINE. / TELL ME YOU'LL WAIT FOR ME** [**83**]
 (re-iss. Jan68)

Jun 61. (7") London; (HLK 9364) / Atlantic; <2094> **EARLY IN THE MORNING. / A BIT OF SOUL** [ ] Apr61

1961. (7") Atlantic; <2106> **AM I BLUE? / IT SHOULD'VE BEEN ME** [-] [ ]

Oct 61. (7") London; (HLK 9435) / Atlantic; <2118> **HARD TIMES (NO ONE KNOWS BETTER THAN I). / I WONDER WHO (RAY'S BLUES)** [ ] [ ]

Oct 61. (7"ep) London; (REK 1306) **WHAT'D I SAY** [ ]

Nov 61. (7"ep) London; (REK 1317) **RAY CHARLES AT NEWPORT** [ ]

Nov 61. (lp) Atlantic; <8054> **DO THE TWIST!** [**11**] [-]

Feb 62. (7"ep) H.M.V.; (7EG 8729) **HIT THE ROAD JACK** [ ]

Mar 62. (lp) London-Jazz; (LTZK 15238) / Atlantic; <8052> **THE GENIUS SINGS THE BLUES** [**73**] Nov61

1962. (7") Time; <1054> **BACK HOME. / WHY DID YOU GO** [ ]

Aug 62. (d-lp) Atlantic; <900> **THE RAY CHARLES STORY** [**14**]

Nov 62. (lp) Atlantic; (HAB 8022) **THE ORIGINAL RAY CHARLES** [-]

Nov 62. (7"ep) H.M.V.; (7EG 8781) **I CAN'T STOP LOVING YOU** [-]

Jan 63. (lp) London; (HAK 8023) **THE RAY CHARLES STORY** [-]

Jan 63. (lp) London; (HAK 8024) **THE RAY CHARLES STORY VOL.2** [-]

Feb 63. (lp) London; (HAK 8035) / Atlantic; <1369> **THE GENIUS AFTER HOURS** [**49**] Aug61

Feb 63. (7"ep) H.M.V.; (7EG 8783) **THE BALLAD STYLE OF RAY CHARLES** [-]

Apr 63. (7"ep) H.M.V.; (7EG 8801) **THE SWINGING STYLE OF RAY CHARLES** [-]

May 63. (7"ep; with BETTY CARTER) H.M.V.; (7EG 8807) **BABY IT'S COLD OUTSIDE** [-]

1963. (7") Atlantic; <2174> **CARRYING THAT LOAD. / FEELIN' SAD** [-] [-]

1963. (lp) Saga; (RM 101) **RAY CHARLES IN R&B GREATS** [-] [-]

Sep 63. (7"ep) H.M.V.; (7EG 8812) **TAKE THESE CHAINS**	☐	-
Nov 63. (7"ep) London; (REB 1407) **THE ORIGINAL RAY CHARLES VOL.1**	☐	-
Nov 63. (7"ep) London; (REB 1408) **THE ORIGINAL RAY CHARLES VOL.2**	☐	-
Nov 63. (7"ep) London; (REB 1409) **THE ORIGINAL RAY CHARLES VOL.3**	☐	-
Jan 64. (7"ep) H.M.V.; (7EG 8841) **BUSTED**	☐	-
1964. (7") Atlantic; <2239> **TALKIN' 'BOUT YOU. / IN A LITTLE SPANISH TOWN**	-	
Jun 64. (7"ep) H.M.V.; (7EG 8861) **RAY CHARLES SINGS**	☐	-
Jun 64. (7"ep) Realm; (REP 4001) **THE YOUNG RAY CHARLES**	☐	-
1965. (lp) Concert Hall; (CJ 1250) **THE AUTHENTIC RAY CHARLES**	☐	-
1965. (lp) Society; (SOC 1007) **RAY CHARLES**	☐	-
Feb 66. (7"ep) H.M.V.; (7EG 8932) **LIVE IN CONCERT (live)**	☐	-
Jul 66. (7"ep) H.M.V.; (7EG 8951) **RAY CHARLES SINGS SONGS OF BUCK OWENS**	☐	-
Mar 67. (7") Atlantic; (584 093) **WHAT'D I SAY. / I GOT A WOMAN**	-	
Mar 67. (d-lp) ABC Paramount; <590> **A MAN AND HIS SOUL**	-	77
1968. (lp) Fidelity; (FID 2103) **RAY CHARLES**	☐	-
Sep 68. (lp; stereo/mono) Stateside; (S+/SL 10241) **GREATEST HITS VOL.2**	24	
1970. (lp) Crown; (CRS 2006) **THE INCOMPARABLE RAY CHARLES**	☐	-
1971. (lp) Transatlantic; (XTRA 1103) **RAY CHARLES**	☐	-
Dec 71. (d-lp) Atlantic; (2659 009) / A.B.C.; <731> **A 25th ANNIVERSARY IN SHOW BUSINESS SALUTE TO RAY CHARLES: HIS ALL-TIME GREAT PERFORMANCES**	☐	☐ Nov71
Nov 72. (7"m) Atlantic; (K 10329) **WHAT'D I SAY / YES INDEED. / I GOT A WOMAN / DON'T LET THE SUN CATCH YOU CRYING**	☐	-
Apr 73. (lp) Probe; (PBSB 108) **ALL-TIME GREAT C&W HITS**	☐	
Jun 73. (d-lp) Atlantic; (K 30032) **RAY CHARLES LIVE (Newport & Herndon)**	☐	
Aug 74. (lp) Decca; (SPA 361) **THE WORLD OF RAY CHARLES**	☐	
May 75. (lp) Decca; (SPA 422) **THE WORLD OF RAY CHARLES VOL.2**	☐	
Sep 75. (lp) London; (FOS 1/2) **FOCUS ON RAY CHARLES**	☐	
Jun 77. (lp) London; (ZGU 139) **WHAT HAVE I DONE TO THEIR SONGS**	☐	
1978. (lp) Ember; (CJS 854) **RAY CHARLES' BLUES**	☐	
Apr 79. (lp) Flyover; **SUPER DISC OF RAY CHARLES**	☐	
Sep 79. (lp) Bulldog; (BDL 2012) **20 GOLDEN PIECES OF RAY CHARLES**	☐	
May 80. (lp) Manhattan; (MAN 5019) **SIMPLY RAY**	☐	
Aug 80. (lp) Manhattan; (MAN 5020) **A RAY OF HOPE**	☐	
Aug 80. (lp) London; (RAYTV 1) **HEART TO HEART – 20 RAY CHARLES' HOTTEST HITS**	29	
Sep 80. (lp) Manhattan; (MAN 5029) **EVERYTHING**	☐	-
Sep 80. (lp) Pickwick; (SSP 3075) **I CAN'T STOP LOVING YOU**	☐	
Dec 80. (lp) London; (SH 8546) **BROTHER RAY**	☐	
Apr 81. (lp) Joker; <SM 3729> **RAY CHARLES VOL.2**		-
Sep 81. (c) Ampro; (AMP 011) **KING OF THE BLUES**	☐	
Oct 82. (lp) Phoenix; (PHX 1013) **GREAT HITS**	☐	
Mar 84. (lp/c) Charly; (CRB/TC-CRB 1071) **TELL THE TRUTH**	☐	
Jun 84. (lp) Meteor; (MTM 002) **GOING DOWN SLOW**	☐	
Nov 84. (lp/c) Astan; (2/4 0078) **JAMMIN' THE BLUES**	☐	
Mar 85. (d-lp) Musidisc; (ALB 103) **THE FANTASTIC RAY CHARLES**	☐	
Jun 85. (lp/c) Premier; (CBR/KCBR 1018) **SEE SEE RIDER**	☐	
Aug 85. (lp/c) Deja Vu; (DVLP/DVMC 2005) **COLLECTION (20 GOLDEN GREATS)** (cd-iss. Sep87; DVCD 2005)	☐	
Apr 86. (lp/c) Starjazz; <SJAZZ/+C 1> **THE COLLECTION**	-	-
Apr 86. (lp/c) Arcade; (ADAH/+C 447) **THE COUNTRY SIDE OF RAY CHARLES**	☐	
1986. (lp/c) Topline; (TOP/KTOP 126) **THIS LOVE OF MINE** (cd-iss. Apr87; TOPCD 512)	☐	
Feb 87. (12"/7") Charly; (CYZ/+7 119) **I WONDER WHO'S KISSING HER NOW. / SHE'S ON THE BALL / BABY WON'T YOU PLEASE COME HOME**	☐	
Jul 87. (lp/c/cd) Atlantic; (241119-1/-4/-2) **THE RIGHT TIME**	☐	
Sep 87. (c) Timeless; (MC 1631) **16 ORIGINAL HITS**	☐	
1988. (lp) Joker; <SM 3712> **RAY CHARLES**	☐	
1988. (lp) Joker; <SM 3871> **ROCKIN' WITH RAY**	-	
Mar 88. (lp/c/cd) Exel; (XEL LP/MC/CD 106) **THE GENIUS**	☐	
Mar 88. (lp/c) King; (K 5011) **14 ORIGINAL GREATEST HITS**	☐	
May 88. (lp/c/cd) Commander; (3/6/9 9009) **HITS OF A GENIUS**	☐	
May 88. (cd) Arcade; (ADEHCD 780) **THE LEGEND LIVES**	☐	
Jun 88. (lp/c/cd) Deja Vu; (DVLP/DVMC/DVCD 2123) **COLLECTION: RAY CHARLES (THE LOVE SONGS)**	☐	
Jun 88. (cd; shared with PERRY COMO) Spectrum; **CLASSIC DUO**	☐	
1988. (lp) Zeta; (ZET 707) **THE EARLY YEARS**	☐	
May 89. (lp) Object; (ONN 37) **BLUES IS MY MIDDLE NAME**	☐	
Jan 90. (cd/c) Mainline; (264823-2/-4) **16 GREATEST HITS**	☐	
Feb 90. (cd/c/lp) Sequel; (NEX CD/MC/LP 100) **GREATEST COUNTRY & WESTERN HITS** (re-iss. Jun95 on 'Personality';)	☐	-
Mar 90. (cd/c/lp) Arcade; (RCL D/C/P 101) **THE COLLECTION** – Your cheatin' heart / Hit the road Jack / Georgia on my mind / Unchain my heart / One mint julep / Take these chains from my heart / I can't stop loving you / You are my sunshine / Making whoopee / Let's go get stoned / My heart cries for you / Feel so bad / The lucky old Sun / Smack dab in the middle / Crying time / If it wasn't for bad luck / In the heat of the night / Eleanor Rigby / Born to lose / No one / Hard hearted / Hannah / Yesterday.	36	-
1990. (cd/c/d-lp) Castle; (CCS CD/MC/LP 241) **RAY CHARLES: THE COLLECTION**		-
Jun 91. (3xcd-set) Essential; (ESBCD 144) **THE CLASSIC YEARS**	☐	-
Jan 92. (cd) Audio Archive; (CD/MC AA 003) **RAY CHARLES**	☐	-
Jul 92. (cd/c) Castle; (CCS CD/MC 328) **THE RAY CHARLES COLLECTION VOLUME 2**	☐	-

Mar 93. (d-cd/d-c) Arcade; (ARC 9464-2/-4) **THE LIVING LEGEND**	48	-
Apr 93. (cd/c) Deja Vu; (D2 CD/MC 05) **THE GOLD COLLECTION** (re-iss. Jun95; same)	☐	-
May 93. (cd) Atlantic; <(7567 81368-2)> **THE BEST OF RAY CHARLES**	☐	-
Sep 93. (cd/c) Pickwick; (PWKS/+C 4169) **GEORGIA TIME**	☐	-
1993. (c/cd) Tring; (MC+/GRF 033) **BLUES IS MY MIDDLE NAME**	☐	-
May 94. (cd; with NAT KING COLE) Musidisc; (CDTT 8) **TWO IN ONE**	☐	-
Mar 94. (cd) Traditional Line; (TL 1332-2) **INGREDIENTS IN A RECIPE FOR SOUL**	☐	-
Mar 94. (d-cd) Rhino; <(8122 71607-2)> **THE BLUES & JAZZ ANTHOLOGY**	☐	-
Apr 94. (cd) Jazz Door; **LIVE (live)**	☐	-
Apr 94. (cd) Castle; (CLACD 340) **RAY CHARLES & BETTY CARTER**	☐	-
Jul 94. (cd/c) Prestige; (CD/CAS SGP 0121) **THE CLASSIC YEARS**	☐	-
Aug 94. (cd) Dynamite; (LECD 049) **RAY CHARLES**	☐	-
Apr 95. (d-cd) Wisepack; (LECD 607) **THE ESSENTIAL COLLECTION**	☐	-
Jun 96. (cd) Pablo; (PACD 5301) **BERLIN 1962 (JAZZ AT THE PHILHARMONIC)**	☐	-
Jul 96. (cd) Collection; (COL 005) **THE COLLECTION**	☐	-
Aug 96. (cd) Autograph; (MAC Cd/MC 227) **RAY CHARLES GOLD**	☐	-
Nov 96. (cd) Summit; (SUMCD 4044) **BLUES BEFORE SUNRISE**	☐	-
Nov 96. (cd) Tring; (QED 017) **THE GENIUS OF RAY CHARLES**	☐	-
Apr 97. (cd) King; (KCD 5011) **THE EARLY YEARS**	☐	-
May 97. (cd/c) K-Tel; (ECD3/EMC2 341) **BLUES IS MY MIDDLE NAME**	☐	-
May 97. (c) A-Play Collection; (101404) **HEY NOW**	☐	-
Jun 97. (cd/c) Koch; (3/2 99526) **RAY CHARLES**	☐	-
Sep 97. (cd/c) Music; (CDB6/MC7 101) **BLUES IS MY MIDDLE NAME**	☐	-
Sep 97. (d-cd) Charly; (CPCD 83162) **GREATEST HITS**	☐	-
Nov 97. (d-cd) Platinum; (PC 616) **THE PLATINUM COLLECTION** (re-iss. Mar99; same)	☐	-
Jan 98. (d-cd) UAE 3008-2) **RAY CHARLES**	☐	-
Apr 98. (d-cd) Deja Vu; (R2CD 4005) **RAY CHARLES**	☐	-
Apr 98. (cd/c) Hallmark; (30148-2/-4) **BLUES AND SOUL GREATS**	☐	-
Sep 98. (cd) Atlantic; (7567 80865-2) **AT NEWPORT (remastered)**	☐	-

CHEAP TRICK

Formed: Rockford, Illinois, USA . . . 1972 by main writer RICK NIELSEN and TOM PETERSSON, who were part of The GRIM REAPERS prior to becoming FUSE. This brief early period only produced one self-titled album, before they enlisted the help of THOM MOONEY and ROBERT 'STEWKEY' ANTONI, fresh from (TODD RUNDGREN's) NAZZ. In 1972, they changed their moniker yet again, this time to The SICK MAN OF EUROPE, recruiting BUN E. CARLOS in place of the departing MOONEY. This primitive incarnation of CHEAP TRICK also saw the inclusion new vocalist RANDY 'XENO' HOGAN, although after two years of steady touring he was replaced by ROBIN ZANDER. With the classic line-up now in place, the band secured a deal with 'Epic', releasing their eponymous debut album early in '77. Coming at a time of musical turbulence (new wave/punk had just arrived), the album failed to excite an interest of either critics or rock fans. More marketable was the band's highly original image, ZANDER and PETERSSEN the good-lookers, while CARLOS was the joker in the pack with his Tweedle-Dee/Dum attire (i.e. baseball cap, bow-tie and all-round eccentricity). Tours supporting KISS and QUEEN helped promote the band's off-the-wall appeal to a wider audience, the follow-up, 'IN COLOR' (also in '77) gaining healthy sales and a US Top 75 placing. The album featured the excellent 45, 'I WANT YOU TO WANT ME', a flop first time around, although a live equivalent subsequently made the US Top 10 in 1979. Following on from the success of their third studio album, 'HEAVEN TONIGHT' (1978), their harder-edged live set, 'AT BUDOKAN' turned their popularity in Japan into even greater commercial heights in America. The record struck platinum, hitting Top 5 in the process and making them virtual overnight international stars over the ensuing decade. Another Top 10'er, 'DREAM POLICE' (1979), consolidated their newfound fame, although this was nearly wrecked when The BEATLES-influenced CHEAP TRICK worked with the legendary GEORGE MARTIN on the album, 'ALL SHOOK UP'. PETERSSEN felt the strain and bailed out before their next album, 'ONE ON ONE' (1982), which had seen JON BRANDT come in as a replacement for the temporary PETE COMITA. In 1983, they employed the services of TODD RUNDGREN (who didn't!?) on their album of that year, 'NEXT POSITION PLEASE', which was a relative flop compared to the lofty chart heights of its predecessors. After a near return to form with the 1985 album, 'STANDING ON THE EDGE', they trawled a creative and commercial trough with 'THE DOCTOR'. Drastic measures were needed; PETERSSEN returned and the group drafted in outside writers to make 1988's 'LAP OF LUXURY' their most successful album of the decade. Of course, this was due in no small part to CHEAP TRICK achieving their first singles chart topper, 'THE FLAME'. Their AOR formula was utilised once more on their 1990 'BUSTED', although this was to be their last taste of major chart action for some time. The 1994 'Warner Brothers' set, 'WOKE UP WITH A MONSTER' saw the band attempting to recapture their heady 70's sound. Three years later, after a one-off for the seminal cult-indie label, 'Sub Pop', CHEAP TRICK released an eponymous set which dented the US Top 100. • **Covered:** AIN'T THAT A SHAME (Fats Domino) / DON'T BE CRUEL (Elvis Presley) / DANCING THE NIGHT AWAY (Motors) / SPEAK NOW (Terry Reid) / MONEY (Barrett Strong) / MAGICAL MYSTERY TOUR (Beatles).

Album rating: CHEAP TRICK (*7) / IN COLOR (*6) / HEAVEN TONIGHT (*7) / AT BUDOKAN (*7) / DREAM POLICE (*5) / ALL SHOOK UP (*4) / ONE ON ONE (*5) / NEXT POSITION PLEASE (*4) / STANDING ON THE EDGE (*5) / THE DOCTOR

(*3) / LAP OF LUXURY (*5) / BUSTED (*4) / THE GREATEST HITS compilation (*6) / BUDOKAN II early live (*5) / WOKE UP WITH A MONSTER (*4) / CHEAP TRICK on 'Red Ant' 1997 (*4)

FUSE

RICK NIELSEN (b.22 Dec'46, Rockford)– guitar / **JOE SUNBERG** – vocals / **CRAIG MYERS** – guitar / **TOM PETERSSON** (b. 9 May'50) – bass / **CHIP GREENMAN** – drums

			not iss.	Epic
Jul 68.	(7") <5-10514> **HOUND DOG. / CRUISIN' FOR BURGERS** <originally-iss.Jun68 as GRIM REAPERS on 'Smack'; >		-	
Jul 69.	(lp) **FUSE**		-	

—— split soon after above **NIELSEN** and **PETERSSON** teamed up invariably as NAZZ and FUSE with ex-NAZZ members **ROBERT 'STEWKEY' ANTONI** – vocals / **THOM MOONEY** – drums

—— In '72 they became **The SICK MAN OF EUROPE** and moved to Philadelphia / **BUN E. CARLOS** (b.BRAD CARLSON, 12 Jun'51) – drums (ex-PAGANS) repl. MOONEY / **XENO** (r.n. RANDY HOGAN) – vocals repl. STEWKEY / **RICK SZELUGA** – bass repl. PETERSSON for a short while, until they became in '73 ...

CHEAP TRICK

NIELSEN, PETERSSON, CARLOS and XENO)

—— Oct74 **ROBIN ZANDER** (b.23 Jan'53, Loves Park, Illinois) – vocals, guitar (ex-TOONS) repl. XENO who joined STRAIGHT UP

		Epic	Epic
Mar 77.	(7") <50375> **OH CANDY. / DADDY SHOULD HAVE STAYED IN HIGH SCHOOL**	-	
Mar 77.	(lp) (EPC 81917) <34400> **CHEAP TRICK** — Hot love / Speak now or forever hold your peace / He's a whore / Mandocello / The ballad of T.V. violence (I'm not the only boy) / Elo kiddies / Daddy should have stayed in high school / Taxman, Mr Thief / Cry cry / Oh Candy. (re-iss. Nov81 lp/c; EPC/40 32070) <cd-iss. Jun88 on 'Collector's Choice'; EK 34400> (cd re-iss. Jul97; 487933-2) (cd re-iss. Oct98 on 'Columbia'; 491229-2)		Jan77
Nov 77.	(7") (EPC 5701) <50435> **I WANT YOU TO WANT ME. / OH BOY** (instrumental) (re-iss. Mar78; same)		
Nov 77.	(lp/c) (EPC/40 82214) <34884> **IN COLOR** — Hello there / Big eyes / Downed / I want you to want me / You're all talk / Oh Caroline / Clock strikes ten / Southern girls / Come on, come on / So good to see you. <cd-iss. Jun88 on 'Collector's Choice'; EK 34884> (cd-iss. Oct93 on 'Sony Europe'; 982833-2) (cd re-iss. Oct98 on 'Columbia'; 491230-2)		73 Aug77
Nov 77.	(7") <50485> **SOUTHERN GIRLS. / YOU'RE ALL TALK**	-	
Mar 78.	(7") (EPC 6199) **SO GOOD TO SEE YOU. / YOU'RE ALL TALK**		-
May 78.	(7") (EPC 6394) <50570> **SURRENDER. / AUF WIEDERSEHEN**		62
May 78.	(lp/c) (EPC/40 82679) <35312> **HEAVEN TONIGHT** — Surrender / On top of the world / California man / High roller / Auf wiedersehen / Takin' me back / On the radio / Heaven tonight / Stiff competition / How are you / Oh Claire. (cd-iss. Sep93 on 'Sony Europe'; 982993-2) (cd re-iss. Oct98; 491231-2)		48
Jul 78.	(7") (EPC 6427) **CALIFORNIA MAN. / STIFF COMPETITION**		-
Aug 78.	(7") <50625> **CALIFORNIA MAN. / I WANT YOU TO WANT ME**	-	
Feb 79.	(lp,yellow-lp/c) (EPC/40 86083) <35795> **AT BUDOKAN** (live) — Hello there / Come on, come on / Look out / Big eyes / Need your love / Ain't that a shame / I want you to want me / Surrender / Goodnight now / Clock strikes ten. (re-iss. as d-lp.Nov81 EPC 32595) (cd-iss. Feb86; CDEPC 86083) (re-iss. Jul91 on 'Essential' cd/c; ESS CD/MC 949)	29	4
Feb 79.	(7"; w-drawn) (EPC 7144) <50814> **VOICES (live). / SURRENDER (live)**		32 Nov79
Mar 79.	(7",7"orange) (EPC 7258) <50680> **I WANT YOU TO WANT ME (live). / CLOCK STRIKES TEN (live)**	29	7
Jul 79.	(7") (EPC 7724) **SURRENDER (live). / AUF WIEDERSEHEN (live)**		-
Sep 79.	(7") (EPC 7839) <50743> **AIN'T THAT A SHAME (live). / ELO KIDDIES**		35 Jul79
Sep 79.	(lp/pic-lp/c) (EPC/11/40 83522) <35773> **DREAM POLICE** — Dream police / Way of the world / The house is rockin' (with domestic problems) / Gonna raise Hell / I'll be with you tonight / Voices / Writing on the wall / I know what I want / Need your love.	41	6
Oct 79.	(7") (EPC 7880) <50744> **DREAM POLICE. / HEAVEN TONIGHT**		26 Sep79
Jan 80.	(7") (EPC 8114) **WAY OF THE WORLD. / OH CANDY**	73	
Mar 80.	(7"ep) (EPC 8335) **I'LL BE WITH YOU TONIGHT. / HE'S A WHORE / SO GOOD TO SEE YOU**		-
Apr 80.	(7") <50887> **EVERYTHING WORKS IF YOU LET IT. / WAY OF THE WORLD**	-	44
Jul 80.	(7") (EPC 8755) **EVERYTHING WORKS IF YOU LET IT. / HEAVEN TONIGHT**		-
Oct 80.	(7") (EPC 9071) <50942> **STOP THIS GAME / WHO D'KING**	-	48
Oct 80.	(lp/c) (EPC/40 86124) <36498> **ALL SHOOK UP** — Stop this game / Just got back / Baby loves to rock / Can't stop it but I'm gonna try / World's greatest lover / High Priest of rhythmic noise / Love comes a-tumblin' down / I love you honey but I hate your friends / Go for the throat (use your own imagination) / Who d'king. <cd-iss. Jun88 on 'Collector's Choice'; EK 36498>		24
Jan 81.	(7") (EPC 9502) **WORLD'S GREATEST LOVER. / HIGH PRIEST OF RHYTHMIC NOISE**		

—— **PETE COMITA** (b. Italy) – bass repl. PETERSSON who formed own group with his wife

| Aug 81. | (7") <47187> **REACH OUT. / I MUST BE DREAMING** | - | |

—— (above single from the film 'Heavy Metal'. issued on 'Full Moon-Asylum') now alongside **NIELSEN** (some bass), **ZANDER + CARLOS**

—— (late '81) **JON BRANT** (b.20 Feb'54) – bass (on three songs) repl. COMITA

| May 82. | (7") (EPCA 2406) <02968> **IF YOU WANT MY LOVE. / FOUR LETTER WORD** | 57 | 45 |

May 82.	(lp,red-lp/pic-lp/c) (EPC/11/40 85740) <38021> **ONE ON ONE** — I want you / One on one / If you want my love / Oo la la la / Lookin' out for number one / She's tight / Time is runnin' / Saturday at midnight / Love's got a hold on me / I want be man / Four letter word. (re-iss. Jun85; EPC 32654)	95	39
Sep 82.	(7") <03233> **SHE'S TIGHT. / ALL I REALLY WANT TO DO**	-	65
Aug 83.	(7") <04078> **DANCING THE NIGHT AWAY. / DON'T MAKE OUR LOVE A CRIME**		
Sep 83.	(lp/c) (EPC/40 25490) <38794> **NEXT POSITION PLEASE** — I can't take it / Borderline / I don't love her anymore / Next position please / Younger girls / Dancing the night away / 3-D / You say jump / Y.O.Y.O.Y. / Won't take no for an answer / Heaven's falling / Invaders of the heart. <US c+=/cd+=> — You take too much / Don't make our love a crime.		61
Sep 83.	(12"ep) (EPCTA 3743) **DANCING THE NIGHT AWAY / AIN'T THAT A SHAME / I WANT YOU TO WANT ME / SURRENDER**		
Nov 83.	(7") <04216> **I CAN'T TAKE IT. / YOU TALK TOO MUCH**	-	-
Feb 84.	(7") <29723> **SPRING BREAK. / GET READY** (above from the film 'Spring Break', issued on 'Warner Bros') (below issued on 'Pasha' US)		
1984.	(7") <04392> **UP THE CREEK. / (other artist)**	-	
Sep 85.	(7") (A 6390) <05431> **TONIGHT IT'S YOU. / WILD WILD WOMEN** (12"+=) (EPCTX 6390) – I want you to want me / If you want my love.		44 Jul85
Oct 85.	(lp/c) (EPC/40 26374) <39592> **STANDING ON THE EDGE** — Little sister / Tonight it's you / She's got motion / Love comes / How about you / Standing on the edge / This time around / Rock all night / Cover girl / Wild wild women.		35 Aug85
Jun 86.	(7") <06137> **MIGHTY WINGS. / (other artist)**	-	
Nov 86.	(lp/c) (EPC/40 40405> **THE DOCTOR** — It's up to you / Rearview mirror romance / The doctor / Are you lonely tonight / Name of the game / Kiss me red / Take me to the top / Good girls go to heaven (bad girls go everywhere) / Man-u-lip-u-later / It's only love. (cd-iss. May87; CDEPC 57087)		Oct86
Nov 86.	(7") <06540> **IT'S ONLY LOVE. / NAME OF THE GAME**	-	-

—— **TOM PETERSSON** – bass, vocals returned to repl. BRANT

May 88.	(7"/7"sha-pic-d) (651466-7/-0) <07745> **THE FLAME. / THROUGH THE NIGHT** (12"+=/cd-s+=) (EPC 651466-6/-2) – I want you to want me / If you want my love. <re-iss. Dec88; EPC 73792>		1 Apr88
May 88.	(lp/c/cd) (460782-1/-4/-2) <40922> **LAP OF LUXURY** — Let go / No mercy / The flame / Space / Never had a lot to lose / Don't be cruel / Wrong side of love / All we need is a dream / Ghost town / All wound up. (re-iss. cd Oct93 on 'Sony Europe'; 982839-2)		18
Aug 88.	(7"/7"sha-pic-d) (652896-7/-0) <07965> **DON'T BE CRUEL. / I KNOW WHAT I WANT** (12"+=/cd-s+=) (652896-6/-2) – California man / Ain't that a shame. (3"cd-s+=) (653005-3) – Dream police / Way of the world.		4 Jul88
Oct 88.	(7"/c-s) <08097> **GHOST TOWN. / WRONG SIDE OF LOVE**	-	33
Jan 89.	(7"/c-s) <68563> **NEVER HAD A LOT TO LOSE. / ALL WE NEED IS A DREAM**	-	75

—— In Feb89, ZANDER dueted with Heart's ANN WILSON on US Top 10 single 'SURRENDER TO ME'

Aug 90.	(7"/c-s) (656148-7/-4) <73444> **CAN'T STOP FALLIN' INTO LOVE. / YOU DRIVE, I'LL STEER** (12"+=/cd-s+=) (656148-6/-2) – The flame.		12 Jul90
Sep 90.	(cd/c/lp) (466876-2/-4/-1) <46013> **BUSTED** — Back 'n blue / I can't understand it / Wherever would I be / If you need me / Can't stop falling into love / Busted / Walk away / You drive, I'll steer / When you need someone / Had to make you mine / Rock'n'roll tonight.		48 Jul90
Sep 90.	(7"/c-s; w-drawn) <73566> **IF YOU NEED ME. / BIG BANG**	-	-
Oct 90.	(7"/c-s) <73580> **WHEREVER WOULD I BE. / BUSTED**	-	50
Oct 91.	(cd/c) (469086-2/-4) <48681> **THE GREATEST HITS** (compilation) — Magical mystery tour / Dream police / Don't be cruel / Tonight it's you / She's tight / I want you to want me (live) / If you want my love / Ain't that a shame / Surrender / The flame / I can't take it / Can't stop fallin' into love / Voices (re-iss. May94; same)		

—— ROBIN ZANDER issued an eponymous solo set in '93

		Warners	Warners
Mar 94.	(cd/c) <(9362 45425-2/-4)> **WOKE UP WITH A MONSTER** — My gang / Woke up with a monster / You're all I wanna do / Never run out of love / Didn't know I had it / Ride the pony / Girlfriends / Let her go / Tell me everything / Cry baby / Love me for a minute.		

		Sub Pop	Sub Pop
Mar 97.	(7") <(SP 393)> **BABY TALK. / BRONTOSAURUS**		

		Red Ant	Red Ant
Jun 97.	(cd-ep) (RAAX 1001) **SAY GOODBYE / YEAH YEAH / VOICES (live) / SURRENDER (live)**		99
Jun 97.	(cd) (RAACD 002) **CHEAP TRICK** — Anytime / Hard to tell / Carnival game / Shelter / You let a lotta people down / Baby no more / Yeah yeah / Say goodbye / Wrong all along / Eight miles low / It all comes back to you.		

– compilations etc. –

Apr 80.	(10"m-lp) Epic; <36453> **FOUND ALL THE PARTS (rare '76-'79)** — Day tripper (live) / Can't hold on / Such a good girl / Take me I'm yours.	-	39
Oct 91.	(cd/c) Castle; (CCS CD/MC 309) **THE COLLECTION**	-	-
Feb 94.	(cd) Epic; <EK 53308> **BUDOKAN II (live)**	-	
Aug 96.	(cd-box) Elektra; (E4K 649384) **SEX, AMERICA, CHEAP TRICK**		

CHEMICAL BROTHERS

Formed: North London, England . . . 1989 by DJ's ED SIMONS and TOM ROWLANDS (the latter had been part of 'Deconstruction' act, ARIEL, who released one single, 'ROLLERCOASTER'). The pair had met at Manchester University, and, discovering a shared love of techno and classic hip hop, they set about creating their own club night, 'NAKED UNDER LEATHER'. The logical next step was to cut their own record and with 'SONG TO THE SIREN', they successfully blended their myriad influences into an abrasive chunk of freak-beat techno. Wildly impressed, 'Junior Boys Own' maestro ANDY WEATHERALL released the single in early 1993, the more discerning underground D.J.'s of the time caning the track at club nights across the country. The record was credited to The DUST BROTHERS, the name SIMONS and ROWLANDS assumed for their DJ work. Later the same year, they released the 'Fourteenth Century Sky' EP which included the definitive 'CHEMICAL BEATS'. 'MY MERCURY MOUTH' from the 1994 EP of the same name was equally impressive and by this point the DUST BROTHERS had become one of the hippest name-drops among the dance cognoscenti. Their seminal reworking of SAINT ETIENNE's 'Like A Motorway', together with a DJ spot on PRIMAL SCREAM's 1994 tour further increased their profile and it wasn't long before the major record labels came sniffing round. Signing to 'Virgin', they released 'LEAVE HOME' in 1995, following it up with the top ten debut album, 'EXIT PLANET DUST'. The duo were now trading under the moniker of The CHEMICAL BROTHERS following objections from The DUST BROTHERS (U.S), a highly rated hip hop production team (Responsible for the BEASTIE BOYS' classic, 'Paul's Boutique'). For the most part, the debut was an unrelenting, exhilarating, rollercoaster ride of breakbeat techno, only letting up on 'ALIVE: ALONE' (featuring a BETH ORTON vocal) and the TIM BURGESS (of CHARLATANS fame) collaboration, 'LIFE IS SWEET'. The 'LOOPS OF FURY EP' was as uncompromising as the title suggests while the 'SETTING SUN' (featuring NOEL GALLAGHER on vocals) single gave the CHEMICALS their first No.1 later that year. The track featured a 'TOMMORROW NEVER KNOWS'-style rhythm pattern, the follow-up album, 'DIG YOUR OWN HOLE' (1997), similarly psychedelic in its reach. Using samples from 60's theramin pioneers LOTHAR AND THE HAND PEOPLE, and featuring a guest spot from MERCURY REV's JONATHAN DONOHUE, the album was more thrillingly diverse than the debut. With a mindbending live show, universal critical acclaim and even a burgeoning Stateside career, The CHEMICAL BROTHERS could do no wrong. After initiating their own record label, 'Freestyle Dust' (which released DJ-styled set, 'BROTHER'S GONNA WORK IT OUT'), ROWLANDS and SIMONS were back with a third album, 'SURRENDER' (1999). Featuring guest vocals by NOEL GALLAGHER (on Top 10 hit, 'LET FOREVER BE'), BERNARD SUMNER (on 'OUT OF CONTROL'), BOBBY GILLESPIE (on 'UNDER THE INFLUENCE'), HOPE SANDOVAL (on 'ASLEEP FROM DAY') and JONATHAN DONAHUE (on 'DREAM ON'), the album crashed into the charts at No.1 and even cracked America by making the Top 40. • **Songwriters:** ROWLANDS-SIMONS except samples of Blake Baxters 'Brothers Gonna Work It Out' on 'LEAVE HOME'. Borrowed SWALLOW's; 'Peekaboo' & 'Follow Me Down'.

Album rating: EXIT PLANET DUST (*9) / DIG YOUR OWN HOLE (*9) / SURRENDER (*8)

DUST BROTHERS

TOM ROWLANDS (b.11 Jan'71, Kingston upon Thames, Surrey, England) – keyboards / **ED SIMONS** (b. 9 Jun'70, Oxford, England) – synthesizers, etc

		Junior Boys Own	not iss.
1993.	(12") *(JBO 10)* **SONG TO THE SIREN. / SONG TO THE SIREN (Sabres Of Paradise mixes)**		–
1993.	(12"ep) *(COLLECT 004)* **FOURTEENTH CENTURY SKY EP** – Chemical beats / One too many mornings / Dope coil / Her jazz. (above issued on 'Boys Own')		–
May 94.	(12"ep) *(JBO 20)* **MY MERCURY MOUTH EP** – My mercury mouth / If you kling to me I'll klong to you / Dust-up beats.		–

CHEMICAL BROTHERS

TOM ROWLANDS + ED SIMONS with voices by **TIM BURGESS** (CHARLATANS) + **BETH ORTON** (solo artist)

		Virgin	AstralWerks
Jun 95.	(12") *(CHEMST 1)* <6167> **LEAVE HOME (Sabres Of Paradise mix). / LET ME IN MATE** (12") *(CHEMSTX 1)* – ('A'-Underworld mixes). (cd-s) *(CHEMSD 1)* – (all above except 'Let Me In Mate')	17	Sep95
Jun 95.	(cd/c/d-lp) *(XDUST CD/MC/LP 1)* <6157> **EXIT PLANET DUST** – Leave home / In dust we trust / Song to he siren / Three little birdies down beats / Fuck up beats / Chemical beats / Chico's groove / One too many mornings / Life is sweet / Playground for a wedgeless firm / Alive alone.	9	Aug95
Aug 95.	(12") *(CHEMSD 2)* **LIFE IS SWEET. / ('A'-Daft Punk remix) / ('A'-remix 1) / ('A'-remix 2)** (cd-s) *(CHEMSD 2)* – ('A'-remix 1, repl.by) Leave home (terror drums). (cd-s) *(CHEMSDX 2)* – ('A'remix 1) / If you kling to me I'll klong to you / Chico's groove (mix 2).	25	–
Jan 96.	(12"ep/cd-ep) *(CHEMS T/D 3)* <6174> **LOOPS OF FURY EP** – Chemical beats (Dave Clarke remix) / Loops of fury / (The best part of) Breaking up / Get up on it like this.	13	

Oct 96.	(c-s/12"/cd-s) *(CHEMS C/T/D 4)* <6187> **SETTING SUN. / ('A'extended & instrumental mixes) / BUZZ TRACKS** above featured NOEL GALLAGHER (Oasis) on vocals/ co-writer	1	80 Jan97
Mar 97.	(12"/cd-s) *(CHEMS T/D 5)* <6195> **BLOCK ROCKIN' BEATS. / PRESCRIPTION BEATS / MORNING LEMON** (cd-s) *(CHEMSDX 5)* – ('A'mixes).	1	
Apr 97.	(cd/c/d-lp) *(XDUST CD/MC/LP 2)* <6180> **DIG YOUR OWN HOLE** – Block rockin' beats / Dig your own hole / Elektrobank / Piku / Setting sun / It doesn't matter / Don't stop the rock / Get up on it like this / Lost in the k-hole / Where do I begin / The private psychedelic reel.	1	14
Sep 97.	(12") *(CHEMST 6)* <6204> **ELEKTROBANK. / NOT ANOTHER DRUGSTORE / ('A'-Dust Brothers remix)** (cd-s+=) *(CHEMSD 6)* – Don't stop the rock (electronic version). (cd-s+=) *(CHEMSDX 6)* – These seats are made for breakin'.	17	
Dec 97.	(ltd;12"/cd-s) *(CHEMS T/DX 7)* **THE PRIVATE PSYCHEDELIC REEL. / SETTING SON (live)**		–
Sep 98.	(cd/c) *(XDUST CDX 101)* <6243> **BROTHER'S GONNA WORK IT OUT: A DJ REMIX ALBUM**	7	95
May 99.	(c-s/12"/cd-s) *(CHEMS C/D/T 8)* **HEY BOY HEY GIRL. / FLASHBACK / SCALE**	3	
Jun 99.	(cd/c/lp) *(XDUST CD/MC/LP 4)* <47610> **SURRENDER** – Music: response / Under the influence / Out of control / Orange wedge / Let forever be / The sunshine underground / Asleep from day / Got glint? / Hey boy hey girl / Surrender / Dream on.	1	32
Aug 99.	(7"/c-s) *(CHEMS LH/C 9)* **LET FOREVER BE. / ('A'-album version)** (12"/cd-s) *(CHEMS T/D 9)* – ('A'side) / Diamond sky / Studio K.	9	
Oct 99.	(c-s/cd-s) *(CHEMS C/D 10)* **OUT OF CONTROL / POWER MOVE** (12") *(CHEMST 10)* – ('A'mixes).	21	

CHER

Born: CHERILYN SARKASIAN LA PIER, 20 May'46, El Centro, California, USA. Relocating to L.A. in her late teens, the would-be actress fell in with SONNY BONO and had her first taste of the music business singing backup on PHIL SPECTOR sessions, the production maestro subsequently issuing her BEATLES tribute, 'RINGO I LOVE YOU' on his own 'Annette' label in 1964. She married BONO the same year and the pair proceeded to cut a handful of unsuccessful duets as CAESAR & CLEO for the small 'Vault' imprint. Playing alongside British invasion acts like The DAVE CLARK FIVE and HERMAN'S HERMITS, the duo were eventually picked up by 'Reprise' for a couple of singles, 'JUST YOU' and 'BABY DON'T GO'. These flopped upon initial release and the couple (renamed SONNY and CHER) moved on to 'Atco' where they hit paydirt in summer '65 with 'I GOT YOU BABE', a transatlantic No.1 marrying the cutesy pop appeal of the SPECTOR era to the new folk-rock sensibility of hip Hollywood. Decked out in garish hippie garb, the incongruous couple became the love generation darlings of Sunset Strip and 'Imperial' signed up CHER for a solo deal. Although her debut (as CHERILYN), 'DREAM BABY' had stiffed earlier in the year, her cover of Bob Dylan's 'ALL I REALLY WANT TO DO' competed with The BYRDS' version of the same song that summer while her Top 20 (Top 10 UK) album of the same name featured yet more DYLAN material. Meanwhile, the SONNY & CHER album, 'LOOK AT US' (1965) narrowly missed the US No.1 spot and over the course of the ensuing decade or so, CHER attempted (not always successfully) to maintain a solo career in tandem with her SONNY partnership. Her predeliction for cringeing puns was revealed with 'THE SONNY SIDE OF CHER' (1966), an album that spawned one of her biggest solo hits (transatlantic No.3), 'BANG BANG (MY BABY SHOT ME DOWN)'. 1966-67 proved rockier but CHER was back in the Top 10 in 1968 with 'YOU BETTER SIT DOWN KIDS'. This signalled the end of her tenure with 'Imperial' and she moved on to 'Atco' for a commercially bleak couple of years before her early-mid 70's revival. Her success with SONNY followed the same pattern and after 1967's 'THE BEAT GOES ON', it'd be a further four years before the duo racked up another Top 10 hit with 'ALL I EVER NEED IS YOU'. By this point both had signed to 'Kapp' ('M.C.A.' in Britain), churning out rubbish like 'A COWBOY'S WORK IS NEVER DONE'. The latter proved to be their last Top 10 hit and after a final couple of singles on 'Warners', the couple ended both their creative and marital partnership, divorcing on the 26th of June 1974. CHER's solo career, meanwhile, had been rekindled with a 1971 US No.1 hit, 'GYPSYS, TRAMPS & THIEVES', her charismatic half-Cherokee identity melodramatically stamped over further No.1's, 'HALF-BREED' and 'DARK LADY'. A matter of days after her divorce from BONO she married GREG ALLMAN with whom she recorded the execrable 'ALLMAN AND WOMAN: TWO THE HARD WAY' (1977). Her critical stock was hardly improved with her opportunistic disco effort, 'TAKE ME HOME' (1979) although it did put her back in the US Top 10. Newly signed to decadent disco/KISS stronghold, 'Casablanca', CHER followed up with an attempt at heavy rock/metal the following year with the 'BLACK ROSE' album (also billed as BLACK ROSE). By this point she'd divorced ALLMAN and was dating ex-STEVE MILLER BAND guitarist, LES DUDEK, who both played on and produced the latter set. Unsurprisingly it sank without trace and CHER moved on once more to 'Columbia' where she cut one album, 'I PARALYZE'(!), before turning her attention to film work. Although she was a veteran of the TV chat show (having hosted both a SONNY & CHER and solo version in the 60's/70's), a Broadway appearance in Robert Altman's 'Come Back To The Five And Dime, Jimmy Dean, Jimmy Dean' led to roles in 80's movies like 'Silkwood', 'Mask', 'Witches Of Eastwick', 'Moonstruck' (for which she netted an Oscar) and 'Suspect'. With her profile sufficiently raised, the mainstream late 80's resurgence of soft rock/AOR/metal was a perfect vehicle for CHER's commercial comeback; newly signed to 'Geffen', she hit the Top 10 in 1987 with "power-ballad", 'I FOUND SOMEONE'. A US Top 10 duet with PETER CETERA, 'AFTER ALL', spurred on the success of 1989's 'HEART OF STONE' album and its US Top 3 hit, 'IF I COULD TURN BACK TIME'. More tortuous Top 10 torch balladry followed with 'JUST LIKE JESSE JAMES' although CHER saved her most cloying material 'til last; taken from the film, 'Mermaids' (in which she starred), 'THE SHOOP SHOOP SONG (IT'S IN HIS KISS)' gave CHER her first solo UK No.1 in 1991. Tacked onto the 'LOVE HURTS' (1991) album, the song's massive popularity even pushed the album itself to No.1 and CHER enjoyed a British popularity previously unwitnessed. A 1992 greatest hits set gave her another UK No.1 while a reworking of 'I GOT YOU BABE' with the inimitable BEAVIS & BUTT-HEAD proved she at least had a sense of humour under all the histrionics. She was back at No.1 again in 1995 alongside CHRISSIE HYNDE, NENEH CHERRY and ERIC CLAPTON with the Comic Relief charity song, 'LOVE CAN BUILD A BRIDGE'. A year later, her comeback set, 'IT'S A MAN'S WORLD', stalled at No.10 and faired even worse in the States. Tragedy was to strike early in '98 (January 5th) when her ex-husband and recently elected politician SONNY BONO died instantly after hitting a tree during a skiing trip. Later that year, CHER was to gain some consolation when she scored a massive best-selling UK No.1 with 'BELIEVE' (later to do the same in America). • Covered: BLOWIN' IN THE WIND + LIKE A ROLLING STONE (Bob Dylan) / ALFIE (hit: Cilla Black) / SONNY (Bobby Hebb) / DARK LADY (Johnny Durill) / GYPSYS, TRAMPS AND THIEVES (Robert Stone) / HALF-BREED (Mary Dean & Al Capps) / NEEDLES AND PINS (Searchers) / IT'S NOT UNUSUAL (hit; Tom Jones) / TWELFTH OF NEVER (Johnny Mathis) / ELUSIVE BUTTERFLY (Bob Lind) / UNTIL IT'S TIME FOR YOU TO GO (Elvis Presley) / CATCH THE WIND (Donovan) / PIED PIPER (Crispan St. Peters) / YOU DON'T HAVE TO SAY YO LOVE ME (Dusty Springfield) / GIRL FROM IPANEMA (Stan Getz) / OUR DAY WILL COME (Ruby & The Romantics) / OLD MAN RIVER (Paul Robeson) / I WALK ON GILDED SPLINTERS (Dr.John) / FOR WHAT IT'S IT'S WORTH (Buffalo Springfield) / BABY I LOVE YOU (Ronettes) / LOVE HURTS (Everly Brothers) / I FOUND SOMEONE (Michael Bolton-Mark Mangold) / WE ALL SLEEP ALONE (Bon Jovi-Child) / OH NO NOT MY BABY (Goffin-King) / THE SHOOP SHOOP SONG (IT'S IN HIS KISS) (Rudy Clark) / Around this time in the 90's, DESMOND CHILD & DIANE WARREN wrote her material. HEART OF STONE (was originally written for BUCKS FIZZ!) • Trivia: In 1981, CHER dueted with MEAT LOAF on his 'Dead Ringer For Love' single. She appeared with SONNY on many TV specials in the 60's/70's.

Best CD compilation: GREATEST HITS 1965-1992 (*7)

CHER – vocals (with session people; no band at this time)

	Liberty	Imperial
Mar 65. (7"; as CHERILYN) <66081> **DREAM BABY. / STAN QUETZEL**	-	
Jun 65. (7") <(LIB 66114)> **ALL I REALLY WANT TO DO. / I'M GONNA SHOW YOU**	9	15
Sep 65. (lp; stereo/mono) (S+/LBY 3058) <12292> **ALL I REALLY WANT TO DO**	7	16

– All I really want to do / I go to sleep / Needles and pins / Don't turn twice / She thinks I still care / Dream baby / The bells of Rhymney / Girl don't come / See see rider / Come and stay with me / Cry myself to sleep / Blowin' in the wind.

	Liberty	Imperial
Oct 65. (7") <(LIB 66136)> **WHERE DO YOU GO. / SEE SEE RIDER**		25
Mar 66. (7") <(LIB 66160)> **BANG BANG (MY BABY SHOT ME DOWN). / OUR DAY WILL COME**	3	2
May 66. (lp; stereo/mono) (S+/LBY 3072) <12301> **THE SONNY SIDE OF CHER**	11	26 Apr66

– Bang bang (my baby shot me down) / Elusive butterfly / Where do you go / Our day will come / The girl from Ipanema / It's not unusual / Like a rolling stone / Time / Come to your window / Old man river / Milord / A young girl (une enfante).

	Liberty	Imperial
Jul 66. (7") <LIB 66192> **ALFIE. / SHE'S NO BETTER THAN ME**	-	32
Aug 66. (7") (LIB 12034) **I FEEL SOMETHING IN THE AIR. / COME TO YOUR WINDOW**	43	-
Sep 66. (7") (LIB 12038) **SUNNY. / SHE'S NO BETTER THAN ME**	32	-
Oct 66. (lp; stereo/mono) (S+/LBY 3081) <12320> **CHER**		59 Sep66

– Sunny / Twelfth of never / You don't have to say you love me / I feel something in the air (magic in the air) / Will you love me tomorrow / Until it's time for you to go / Cruel war / Catch the wind / Pied piper / Homeward bound / I want you / Alfie.

	Liberty	Imperial
Nov 66. (7") (LIB 12038) **MAMA (WHEN MY DOLLIES HAVE BABIES). / BEHIND THE DOOR**		-
Nov 66. (7") <66217> **BEHIND THE DOOR. / MAGIC IN THE AIR**	-	97
Feb 67. (7") <66223> **DREAM BABY. / MAMA (WHEN MY DOLLIES HAVE BABIES)**	-	
Aug 67. (7") <66252> **HEY JOE. / OUR DAY WILL COME**	-	94
Oct 67. (7") <66261> **YOU BETTER SIT DOWN KIDS. / MAMA (WHEN MY DOLLIES HAVE BABIES)**	-	9
Dec 67. (lp; stereo/mono) (LBS/LBL 83051) <12358> **WITH LOVE – CHER**	47	Nov67

– You better sit down, kids / But I can't love you more / Hey Joe / Mama (when my dollies have babies) / Behind the door / Sing for your supper / Look at me / There but for fortune / I will wait for you / The times they are a-changin'.

	Liberty	Imperial
Feb 68. (7") (LBF 15038) **YOU BETTER SIT DOWN KIDS. / ELUSIVE BUTTERFLY**		9-
Jun 68. (7") <66282> **THE CLICK SONG NUMBER ONE. / BUT I CAN'T LOVE YOU MORE**	-	
Jul 68. (lp; stereo/mono) (LBS/LBL 83156) <12373> **BACKSTAGE**		

– Go now / Carnival (manha de carnaval) (cancion de orfeo) / It all adds up now / Reason to believe / Masters of war / Do you believe in magic / I wasn't ready / A house is not a home / Take me for a little while / The impossible dream (the quest) / The click song number one / Song called children.

	Atlantic	Atco
Sep 68. (7") <6307> **TAKE ME FOR A LITTLE WHILE. / SONG CALLED CHILDREN**	-	
Feb 69. (7") <6658> **YOURS UNTIL TOMORROW. / THOUGHT OF LOVING YOU**	-	
Apr 69. (7") <6684> **CHASTITY'S SONG. / WALK ON GILDED SPLINTERS**	-	
Jun 69. (7") (584 278) **WALK ON GILDED SPLINTERS. / TONIGHT I'LL BE STAYING HERE WITH YOU**	-	
Jul 69. (lp; mono/stereo) (226/228 036) <SD33 298> **3614 JACKSON HIGHWAY**	-	

– For what it's worth / (Just enough to keep me) Hangin' on / (Sittin' on) The dock of the bay / Tonight I'll be staying here with you / I threw it all away / Walk on guilded splinters / Lay baby lay / Please don't tell me / Cry like a baby / Do right woman, do right man / Save the children.

	Atco	Atco
Sep 69. (7") (226 003) <6704> **FOR WHAT IT'S WORTH. / (JUST ENOUGH TO KEEP ME) HANGIN' ON**		
Nov 69. (7") <6713> **YOU MADE ME SO VERY HAPPY. / FIRST TIME**	-	
Jun 70. (7") <6793> **SUPERSTAR. / FIRST TIME**	-	
Feb 71. (7") <6868> **LAY LADY LAY. / (JUST ENOUGH TO KEEP ME) HANGIN' ON**	-	

	M.C.A.	Kapp
May 71. (7") (MU 1137) <2134> **CLASSIFIED 1A. / DON'T PUT IT ON ME**		
Sep 71. (7") (MU 1142) <2146> **GYPSYS, TRAMPS AND THIEVES. / HE'LL NEVER KNOW**	4	1
Nov 71. (lp) (MUPS 438) <3649> **CHER <US-title 'GYPSYS, TRAMPS & THIEVES'>**		16

– The way of love / Gypsys, tramps and thieves / He'll never know / Fire and rain / When you find out where you're goin' let me know / He ain't heavy, he's my brother / I hate to sleep alone / I'm in the middle / Touch and go / One honest man. (re-iss. Aug81 on 'Music For Pleasure';)

	M.C.A.	Kapp
Jan 72. (7") <2158> **THE WAY OF LOVE. / DON'T PUT IT ON ME**	-	7
Feb 72. (7") (MU 1148) **THE WAY OF LOVE. / FIRE AND RAIN**	-	
Jun 72. (7") (MU 1158) <2171> **LIVING IN A HOUSE DIVIDED. / ONE HONEST MAN**		22 May72
Aug 72. (lp) (MUPS 459) <5514> **FOXY LADY**		43 Jul72

– Living in a house divided / It might as well stay Monday (from now on) / Song for you / Down, down, down / Don't try to close a rose / The first time / Let me down easy / If I knew then / Don't hide your love / Never been to Spain.

	M.C.A.	Kapp
Nov 72. (7") (MU 1168) <2184> **DON'T HIDE YOUR LOVE. / THE FIRST TIME**		46 Sep72

	M.C.A.	M.C.A.
May 73. (lp) (MUPS 484) <2101> **BITTERSWEET WHITE LIGHT**		Apr73

– By myself / I got it bad and that ain't good / Am I blue / How long has this been going on / The man I love / Jolson medley: Sonny boy – My mammy – Rock-a-bye your baby with a Dixie melody / More than you know / Why was I born / The man that got away.

	M.C.A.	M.C.A.
Jun 73. (7") (MU 1196) <40039> **AM I BLUE. / HOW LONG WAS THIS BEEN GOING ON**		May73
Aug 73. (7") (MU 1215) <40102> **HALF-BREED. / MELODY**		1 Jul73
Oct 73. (lp) (MCF 2501) <2104> **HALF-BREED**		28 Sep73

– My love / Two people clinging to a thread / Half-breed / The greatest song I ever heard / How can you mend a broken heart / Carousel man / David's song / Melody / The long and winding road / This God-forsaken day / Ruby Jean & Billie Lee. <US = last track repl. by> – Chastity sun.

	M.C.A.	M.C.A.
Jan 74. (7") (MCA 101) <40161> **DARK LADY. / TWO PEOPLE CLINGING TO A THREAD**	36	1
May 74. (7") (MCA 140) <40245> **TRAIN OF THOUGHT. / DIXIE GIRL**		27
Jun 74. (lp) (MCF 2559) <2113> **DARK LADY**		69 May74

– Train of thought / I saw a man and he danced with his wife / Make the man love me / Just what I've been lookin' for / Dark lady / Miss Subway of 1952 / Dixie girl / Rescue me / What'll I do (from The Great Gatsby) / Apples don't fall from the tree.

	M.C.A.	M.C.A.
Aug 74. (7") (MCA 152) <40273> **I SAW A MAN AND HE DANCED WITH HIS WIFE. / I HATE TO SLEEP ALONE**		42
Apr 75. (7") (MCA 188) **RESCUE ME. / DIXIE GIRL**		-

	Warners	Warners
May 75. (lp) (K 56111) <2850> **STARS**		

– Love enough / Bell bottom blues / These days / Mr. Soul / Just this one time / Geronimo's Cadillac / The bigger they come the harder they fall / Love hurts / Rock and roll doctor / Stars.

	Warners	Warners
Jun 75. (7") <8096> **GERONIMO'S CADILLAC. / THESE DAYS**	-	

	Phil Spector Int.	Warner Spector
Jul 75. (7"; CHER & NILSSON) (2010 006) <402> **A LOVE LIKE YOURS (DON'T COME KNOCKING EVERY DAY). / (JUST ENOUGH TO KEEP ME) HANGIN' ON**		Apr75
Mar 76. (7") (2010 013) <400> **A WOMAN'S STORY. / BABY I LOVE YOU**		Feb75
Oct 76. (7") <8263> **LONG DISTANCE LOVE AFFAIR. / BORROWED TIME**		
Oct 76. (lp) (K 56292) <BS 2898> **I'D RATHER BELIEVE IN YOU**		

– Long distance love affair / I'd rather believe in you / I know (you don't love me) / Silver wings and golden rings / Flashback / It's a cryin' shame / Early morning strangers / Knock on wood / Spring / Borrowed time.

Jan 77. (7") <8311> **PIRATE. / SEND THE MAN OVER**	-	93
Apr 77. (lp) (K 56401) <3046> **CHERISHED**		

– Pirate / He was beautiful / War paint and soft feathers / Love the devil out of ya / She loves to hear the music / L.A. plane / Again / Dixie / Send the man over / Thunderstorm.

May 77. (7") <8366> **WAR PAINT AND SOFT FEATHERS. / SEND THE MAN OVER**	-	

—— CHER collaborated with husband GREGG ALLMAN late '77 on lp, 'TWO THE HARD WAY' and the single, 'LOVE ME' / 'MOVE ME'.

Casablanca Casablanca

Mar 79. (7") *(CAN 147)* <965> **TAKE ME HOME. / MY SONG (TOO FAR GONE)** | 8 | Feb79

Apr 79. (lp/c) *(CAL/ACCAN 2047)* <7133> **TAKE ME HOME** | 25 | Feb79
– Take me home / Wasn't it good / Say the word / Happy was the day we met / Git down (guitar groupie) / Pain in my heart / Let this be a lesson to you / It's too late to love me now / My song (too far gone).

Jul 79. (7") *(CAN 156)* <987> **WASN'T IT GOOD. / IT'S TOO LATE TO LOVE ME NOW** | 49 | May79
(12") *(CANL 156)* – ('A'side) / Take me home.

Oct 79. (7"/12") *(CAN/+L 164)* <2208> **HELL ON WHEELS. / GIT DOWN (GUITAR GROUPIE)** | 59 | Sep79

Mar 80. (lp) <*(NBLP 7184)*> **PRISONER** | | Oct79
– Prisoner / Holdin' out for love / Shoppin' / Boys and girls / Mirror image / Hell on wheels / Holy smoke / Outrageous.

Mar 80. (7") *(CAN 185)* **IT'S TOO LATE TO LEAVE ME NOW. / SHOPPIN'** | | -

Mar 80. (7") <2228> **HOLDING OUT FOR LOVE. / BOYS AND GIRLS** | - | -

Mar 82. (7") *(CAN 1009)* **HOLDIN' OUT FOR LOVE. / OUTRAGEOUS** | - | -

BLACK ROSE

—— **CHER** with boyfriend at the time **LES DUDEK** – guitar (ex-STEVE MILLER BAND) / **MIKE FINNEGAN** – keyboards, vocals / **GARY FURGASON** – drums / **TREY THOMPSON** – bass / **RON RITCHOTTE** – guitar

Casablanca Casablanca

Nov 80. (7") <2296> **YOUNG AND PRETTY. / TAKE IT FROM THE BOYS** | - | -

Nov 80. (lp) <*(NBLP 7234)*> **BLACK ROSE** | |
– Never should've started / Julie / Take it from the boys / We all fly home / 88 degrees / You know it / Young and pretty / Fast company.

Feb 81. (7") <2312> **NEVER SHOULD'VE STARTED. / YOUNG AND PRETTY** | - |

—— lack of success led the group to part

CHER

—— went solo again (with various session people)

C.B.S. Columbia

Mar 82. (7") *(CBS 2227)* <02850> **RUDY. / DO I EVER CROSS YOUR MIND** | |

Aug 82. (7") *(CBS 2609)* <03150> **I PARALYZE. / WALK WITH ME** | |

Nov 82. (lp/c) *(CBS/40 85850)* **I PARALYZE** | |
– Rudy / Games / I paralyze / When the love is gone / Say what's on your mind / Back on the street again / Walks with me / The book of love / Do I ever cross your mind. (cd-iss. Jun99 on 'Varese Sarabande'; VSD 6039)

—— CHER turned to acting (full-time) and subsequently appeared in many films (see above Filmography); she was back in the charts in '87

Geffen Geffen

Oct 87. (7"/7"pic-d) *(GEF 31/+P)* <28191> **I FOUND SOMEONE. / DANGEROUS TIMES** | 5 | 10
(12"+=/12"pic-d+=) *(GEF 31T/+P)* – ('A'version).

Dec 87. (lp/c)(cd) *(WX 132/+C)(924164-2)* <24164> **CHER** | 26 | 32 | Nov87
– I found someone / We all sleep alone / Bang bang (my baby shot me down) / Main man / Give our love a fightin' chance / Perfection / Dangerous times / Skin deep / Working girl / Hard enough getting over you. (re-iss.Jan91 lp/c/cd; GEF/+C/D 24164) (re-iss. Mar93 cd/c; GEF/+C/D 24164) (cd re-iss. Nov96; GED 24164)

Apr 88. (7") *(GEF 35)* <27986> **WE ALL SLEEP ALONE (remix). / WORKING GIRL** | 47 | 14
(12"+=/12"pic-d+=/3"cd-s+=) *(GEF 35 T/TP/CD)* – I found someone.

Sep 88. (7") *(GEF 44)* <27894> **SKIN DEEP. / PERFECTION** | | 79 | Jul88
(ext-12"+=/cd-s+=) *(GEF 44 T/CD)* – ('A'dub version).

Dec 88. (7") <27742> **MAIN MAN. / HARD ENOUGH GETTING OVER YOU** | - |

May 89. (7"/c-s; by CHER & PETER CETERA) *(GEF 52/+C)* **AFTER ALL. / DANGEROUS TIMES** | | 6 | Mar89
(12"+=/cd-s+=) *(GEF 52 T/CD)* – I found someone / Main man.

Jul 89. (lp/c)(cd) *(WX 262/+C)(924239-2)* <24239> **HEART OF STONE** | 7 | 10
– If I could turn back time / Just like Jesse James / You wouldn't know love / Heart of stone / Still in love with you / Love on a rooftop / Emotional fire / All because of you / Does anybody really fall in love anymore? / Starting over / Kiss to kiss / After all. (re-iss.Jan91 lp/c/cd; GEF/+C/D 24239)

Jul 89. (7"/c-s) *(GEF 59/+C)* <22886> **IF I COULD TURN BACK TIME. / SOME GUYS** | 6 | 3
(12"+=) *(GEF 59T)* – Kiss to kiss.
(cd-s+=) *(GEF 59CD)* – ('A'remix) / ('A'rock guitar mix) / I found someone.

Jan 90. (7"/c-s) *(GEF 69/+C)* <22844> **JUST LIKE JESSE JAMES. / STARTING OVER** | 11 | 8 | Oct89
(12"+=/cd-s+=) *(GEF 69 T/CD)* – I found someone.

Mar 90. (7"/c-s) *(GEF 75/+C)* <19953> **HEART OF STONE. / ALL BECAUSE OF YOU** | 43 | 20 | Feb90
(12"+=/cd-s+=) *(GEF 75 T/CD)* – Working girl.

Jul 90. (7"/c-s) *(GEF 77/+C)* **YOU WOULDN'T KNOW LOVE. / KISS TO KISS** | 55 | -
(12"+=) *(GEF 77T)* – Bang bang / Heart of stone.
(7"ep/cd-ep) *(GEF 77 D/CD)* – ('A'side) / If I could turn back time / I found someone / We all sleep alone (remix).

Oct 90. (7"/c-s) **BABY I'M YOURS. / (IT'S BEEN) HARD ENOUGH GETTING OVER YOU** | | -
(12"+=/cd-s+=) – Just like Jesse James.

Nov 90. (7") <19659> **THE SHOOP SHOOP SONG (IT'S IN HIS KISS). / LOVE ON A ROOFTOP** | - | 33

Apr 91. (7"/c-s) *(656673-7/-4)* **THE SHOOP SHOOP SONG (IT'S IN HIS KISS). / BABY I'M YOURS** | 1 | -
(12"+=/cd-s+=) *(656673-6/-2)* – We all sleep alone.
(above single from the film 'Mermaids' and released on 'Epic')

Jun 91. (lp/c/cd) <*(GEF/+C/CD 24427)*> **LOVE HURTS** | 1 | 48
– Save up all your tears / Love hurts / Love and understanding / Fires of Eden / I'll never stop loving you / The shoop shoop song (it's in his kiss) / One small step / A world without heroes / Could've been you / When love calls your name / When lovers become strangers / Who you gonna believe. (cd re-iss. Mar95; GFLD 19266)

Jul 91. (7"/c-s) *(GFS 5/+C)* <19023> **LOVE AND UNDERSTANDING. / TRAIL OF BROKEN HEARTS** | 10 | 17 | Jun91
(12"+=/cd-s+=) *(GFS 5 T/CD)* – If I could turn back time.

Sep 91. (7"/c-s) *(GFS 11/+C)* <19105> **SAVE UP ALL YOUR TEARS. / A WORLD WITHOUT HEROES** | 37 | 37
(12"+=/cd-s+=) *(GFS 11 T/CD)* – Love and understanding.

Nov 91. (7"/c-s) *(GFS 16/+C)* **LOVE HURTS. / ONE SMALL STEP** | 43 |
(12"+=/cd-s+=) *(GFS 16 T/CD)* – Just like Jesse James.

Mar 92. (7"/7"pic-d/c-s) *(GFS 19/+P/C)* **COULD'VE BEEN YOU. / LOVE AND UNDERSTANDING** | 31 |
(12"sha-pic-d+=/cd-s+=) *(GFS 19 T/CD)* – Save up all your tears.

Nov 92. (cd/c/d-lp) <*(GED/GEC/GEF 24439)*> **GREATEST HITS 1965-92** (compilation) | 1 |
– Oh no no baby / Whenever you're near / Many rivers to cross (live) / Love and understanding / Save up all your tears / The shoop shoop song (it's in his kiss) / If I could turn back time / Just like Jesse James / Heart of stone / We all sleep alone / Bang bang (my baby shot me down) (with SONNY) / Dead ringer for love (with MEAT LOAF) / Dark lady / Gypsys, tramps and thieves / I got you babe (with SONNY).

Nov 92. (7"/c-s) *(GFS 29/+C)* **OH NO NOT MY BABY. / LOVE HURTS** | 33 |
(cd-s+=) *(GFS 29TD)* – Love on a rooftop / Main man.

Jan 93. (7"/c-s) *(GFS 31/+C)* **MANY RIVERS TO CROSS. / WHO YOU GONNA BELIEVE** | 37 |
(cd-s+=) *(GFS 31TD)* –

Feb 93. (7"/c-s) *(GFS 32/+C)* **WHENEVER YOU'RE NEAR. / COULD'VE BEEN YOU** | 72 |
(12"pic-d+=/cd-s+=) *(GFS 32 TP/TD)* – You wouldn't know love / I'll never stop loving you.

Jan 94. (c-s/cd-s; by CHER with BEAVIS & BUTT-HEAD) *(GFS C/TD 64)* **I GOT YOU BABE / Sonny & Cher: I GOT YOU BABE** | 35 |

—— BEAVIS & BUTT-HEAD; cult TV cartoon characters who have already carved up a lot of parental hysteria by their use of foul language and violence. In March '95 – alongside CHRISSIE HYNDE, NENEH CHERRY and ERIC CLAPTON – she hit UK No.1 with charity Comic Relief song 'LOVE CAN BUILD A BRIDGE'.

WEA Reprise

Oct 95. (c-s) *(WEA 021C)* **WALKING IN MEMPHIS / THE FALL** | 11 |
(cd-s+=) *(WEA 021CD1)* – Angels running.
(cd-s) *(WEA 021CD2)* – ('A'-Shut up and dance instrumental) / ('A'mixes).

Nov 95. (cd/c) *(0630 12670-2/-4)* <46179> **IT'S A MAN'S WORLD** | 28 | 64
– Walking in Memphis / Not enough love in the world / One by one / I wouldn't treat a dog (the way you treated me) / Angels running / Paradise is here / I'm blowin' away / Don't come around tonite / What about the moonlight / The same mistake / The gunman / The sun ain't gonna shine anymore / Shape of things to come / It's a man's, man's, man's world.

Jan 96. (c-s) *(WEA 032C)* **ONE BY ONE / WALKING IN MEMPHIS (mix)** | 7 | -
(12"+=/cd-s+=) *(WEA 032 T/CD)* – It's a man's world.

Apr 96. (c-s) *(WEA 032C)* **NOT ENOUGH LOVE IN THE WORLD / ONE BY ONE (Sam Ward mix)** | 31 |
(cd-s+=) *(WEA 032CD)* – ('A'side) / One by one (Jr. Vasquez mixes).

Jun 96. (c-s) <17695> **ONE BY ONE / I WOULDN'T TREAT A DOG (THE WAY YOU TREATED ME)** | - | 52

Jul 96. (c-s) *(WEA 071C)* **THE SUN AIN'T GONNA SHINE ANYMORE / PARADISE IS HERE** | 26 |
(cd-s) *(WEA 071CD)* – Not enough love in the world (mix).

WEA Warners

Oct 98. (c-s/cd-s) *(WEA 175 C/CD)* <44576> **BELIEVE / ('A'mixes; Phat 'n' phunky / Club 69 phunk club / Almighty definitive)** | 1 | 1
(12"+=/cd-s+=) *(WEA 175 T/CD2)* – ('A'mixes; Xenomania Mad Tim.. Club 69 future anthem / Grips heartbroken / + 3 dub).

Oct 98. (cd/c) *(3984 25319-2/-4)* <47121> **BELIEVE** | 8 | 4
– Believe / The power / Runaway / All or nothing / Strong enough / Dov'e l'amore / Takin' back my heart / Taxi taxi / Love is the groove / We all sleep alone.

Feb 99. (c-s) *(WEA 201C)* <44644> **STRONG ENOUGH / ('A'mix)** | 5 | 57 | May99
(cd-s) *(WEA 201CD1)* – ('A'mixes; Club 69 / Pumpin' Dolls vocal epic / male / Club 69 phunk).
(cd-s) *(WEA 201CD2)* – ('A'mixes; Marc Andrews / Pumpin' Dolls cashmere / D-Bop melt / Club 69 phuture / Pumpin' Dolls radio).
(12") *(WEA 201T)* – ('A'mixes; some of above).

Jun 99. (c-s) *(WEA 212C)* **ALL OR NOTHING / STRONG ENOUGH (club)** | 12 | -
(cd-s+=) *(WEA 212CD1)* – ('A'-almighty mixes).
(cd-s) *(WEA 212CD2)* – ('A'-K-Klass mixes).

Oct 99. (c-s) *(WEA 230C)* **DOV'E L'AMORE / ('A'mix)** | 21 | -
(cd-s) *(WEA 230CD1)* – ('A'mixes).
(cd-s) *(WEA 230CD2)* – ('A'mixes).
(12") *(WEA 230T)* – ('A'mixes).

Nov 99. (cd/c) *(8573 80420-2/-4)* <24509> **GREATEST HITS** <US-title 'IF I COULD TURN BACK TIME – CHER'S GREATEST HITS'> (compilation) | 7 | 57 | Aug99
– Believe / The shoop shoop song (it's in his kiss) / If I could turn back time / Heart of stone / Love and understanding / Love hurts / Just like Jesse James / I found someone / One by one / Strong enough / All or nothing / Walking in Memphis / Love can build a bridge / All I really want to do / Bang bang / Gypsys, tramps and thieves / The beat goes on / I got you babe / Dov'e l'amore.

– compilations, others, etc. –

1966. (7"ep) *Liberty; (LEP 4047)* **THE HITS OF CHER** | | -

Nov 68. (lp) *Liberty; (LBS 83105) / Imperial; <12406>* **CHER'S GOLDEN GREATS** | |

Date	Release	UK	US
Jan 72.	(d-lp) *United Artists;* <88> **CHER SUPERPAK**	-	92
Nov 75.	(lp) *Sunset;* (SLS 50378) **GOLDEN HITS**	-	-
Oct 72.	(d-lp) *United Artists;* <94> **CHER SUPERPAK, VOL.II**	-	95
1972.	(lp) *United Artists;* (UAS 29317) **HITS OF CHER**	-	-
1970's.	(lp) *Imperial;* <5276> **THIS IS CHER**	-	-
1970's.	(lp) *Springboard;* <4028> **GREATEST HITS**	-	
1970's.	(lp) *Springboard;* <4029> **SINGS THE HITS**	-	
Jul 80.	(7") *M.C.A.;* (MCA 710) **GYPSYS, TRAMPS & THIEVES. / DARK LADY**		
Jul 82.	(7") *Old Gold;* (OG 9167) **GYPSYS, TRAMPS & THIEVES. / HALF-BREED**		
Jul 84.	(7") *EMI Gold;* (G45 32) **BANG BANG (MY BABY SHOT ME DOWN). / ALL I REALLY WANT TO DO**		
Sep 85.	(lp/c) *Liberty;* (EG 260723-1/-4) **THE BEST OF CHER**		
Oct 85.	(lp/c) *M.C.A.;* (MCM/+C 5019) **GOLDEN GREATS** *(cd/c re-iss. Apr92; MCL D/C 19003)*		
May 89.	(cd-s) *Old Gold;* (OG 6146) **GYPSYS, TRAMPS AND THIEVES / HALF-BREED / ALL I REALLY WANT TO DO** *(re-iss. Mar96; 126236349-2)*		
Mar 91.	(cd/c/lp) *E.M.I.;* (CD/TC+/EMS 1382) **BANG BANG (MY BABY SHOT ME DOWN) – THE BEST OF CHER**		
Jun 91.	(cd) *Thunderbolt;* (CDTB 131) **OUTRAGEOUS** *(re-iss. Sep99 on 'BR Music'; RM 1556)*		
Jun 92.	(cd) *Tring;* (JHD 021) **HOLDIN' OUT FOR LOVE**		
May 93.	(cd/c) *Spectrum;* (550038-2/-4) **TAKE ME HOME / PRISONER**		
Apr 93.	(cd) *Movieplay Gold;* (MPG 74017) **GYPSYS, TRAMPS & THIEVES**		
Jul 93.	(cd/c) *M.C.A.;* (MCL D/C 19208) **CHER / FOXY LADY**		
Jul 93.	(cd/c) *M.C.A.;* (MCL D/C 19209) **HALF BREED / DARK LADY**		
Nov 95.	(3xcd-box) CDOMB 005) **ALL I REALLY WANT TO DO / SONNY SIDE OF CHER / CHER**		
Sep 96.	(cd) *E.M.I.;* (CDP 792773-2) **BANG BANG (MY BABY SHOT ME DOWN)**		
Nov 98.	(cd) *Spectrum;* (550038-2) **TAKE ME HOME / PRISONER**		
Feb 99.	(cd) *Magic;* (497941-2) **SUNNY**		
Apr 99.	(cd) *E.M.I.;* (499900-2) **THE BEST OF CHER**		

SONNY & CHER

Date	Release	not iss.	Vault
1963.	(7"; as CAESAR & CLEO) <909> **THE LETTER. / SPRING FEVER**	-	

<re-iss. Oct65 as SONNY & CHER; 916> – hit No.75 (UK-iss.Oct65 on 'Vocalion'; VL 9247)

Date	Release	Reprise	Reprise
1964.	(7"; as CAESAR & CLEO) <0308> **LOVE IS STRANGE. / DO YOU WANT TO DANCE**	-	
1964.	(7") <0309> **BABY DON'T GO. / LOVE IS STRANGE**	-	
Feb 65.	(7") (R 20309) **BABY DON'T GO. / WALKING THE QUETZEL**	-	-

Date	Release	Atlantic	Atco
Oct 64.	(7") <6345> **JUST YOU. / SING C'EST LA VIE**	-	

<re-iss. Aug65> – hit No.20

Date	Release		
Jul 65.	(7") (AT 4035) <6359> **I GOT YOU BABE. / IT'S GONNA RAIN**	1	1

—— In Aug'65, SONNY had his first solo hit with 'LAUGH AT ME' which hit US No.10 and UK No.9 – the re-issue of 'BABY DON'T GO' also hit US No.8 at the same time. A month later, CHER contributed vocals to BONNIE + THE TREASURES 7", 'Home Of The Brave'

Date	Release		
Oct 65.	(7") (AT 4047) <6381> **BUT YOU'RE MINE. / HELLO**	17	15
Oct 65.	(lp; mono/stereo) (ATL/STL 5036) <177> **LOOK AT US**	7	2 Aug65

– I got you babe / Unchained melody / Then he kissed me / Sing c'est la vie / It's gonna rain / 500 miles / Just you / The letter / Let it be me / You don't love me / You've really got a hold on me / Why don't they let us fall in love. *(cd-iss. Jul98 on 'Sundazed'; SC 6139)*

Date	Release		
Feb 66.	(7") (AT 4069) <6395> **WHAT NOW MY LOVE. / I LOOK FOR YOU**	13	16 Jan66
Jun 66.	(7") (584 018) <6420> **HAVE I STAYED TOO LONG. / LEAVE ME BE**	42	49
May 66.	(lp; mono/stereo) (587/588 006) <183> **THE WONDROUS WORLD OF SONNY & CHER**	15	34 Apr66

– Summertime / Tell him / I'm leaving it all up to you / But you're mine / Bring it on home to me baby / Set me free / What now my love / Leave me be / I look for you / Laugh at me / Turn around / So fine. *(cd-iss. Jul98 on 'Sundazed'; SC 6140)*

Date	Release		
Sep 66.	(7") (584 040) <6440> **LITTLE MAN. / MONDAY**	4	21
Nov 66.	(7") <6449> **LIVING FOR YOU. / LOVE DON'T COME**	-	87
Nov 66.	(7") (584 057) **LIVING FOR YOU. / TURN AROUND**	44	-
Jan 67.	(7") (584 078) <6461> **THE BEAT GOES ON. / LOVE DON'T COME**	29	6
Apr 67.	(lp; mono/stereo) (587/588 052) <203> **IN CASE YOU'RE IN LOVE**		45 Mar66

– The beat goes on / Groovy kind of love / You baby / Monday / Love don't come / Podunk / Little man / We'll sing in the sunshine / Misty roses / Stand by me / Living for you / Cheryl's goin' home. *(cd-iss. Jul98 on 'Sundazed'; SC 6141)*

Date	Release		
May 67.	(7") (584 110) <6480> **A BEAUTIFUL STORY. / PODUNK**		53 Apr67
May 67.	(lp) <214> **GOOD TIMES (soundtrack)**	-	73

– I got you babe / It's the little things / Good times / Trust me / Don't talk to strangers / I'm gonna love you / Just a name / I got you babe.

Date	Release		
Aug 67.	(7") (584 129) <6486> **PLASTIC MAN. / IT'S THE LITTLE THINGS**		74 Jun67
Sep 67.	(7") <6507> **IT'S THE LITTLE THINGS. / DON'T TALK TO STRANGERS**	-	50
Dec 67.	(7") (584 162) <6541> **GOOD COMBINATION. / YOU AND ME**		56
Feb 68.	(7") (584 168) <6555> **CIRCUS. / Sonny Bono: I WOULD MARRY YOU TODAY**		
Sep 68.	(7") (584 215) <6605> **YOU GOTTA HAVE A THING OF YOUR OWN. / I GOT YOU BABE**		

Date	Release		
1969.	(7") <6683> **YOU'RE A FRIEND OF MINE. / I WOULD MARRY YOU TODAY**	- (Atco)	- (Atco)
Jul 70.	(7") (2091 021) <6758> **GET IT TOGETHER. / HOLD YOU TIGHTER**	(M.C.A.)	(Kapp)
Jun 71.	(7") (MU 1139) <2141> **REAL PEOPLE. / SOMEBODY**		
Oct 71.	(lp) (MUPS 435) <3654> **SONNY AND CHER LIVE (live)**		35 Sep71

– What now my love / The beat goes on / Once in a lifetime / More today than yesterday / Gotta get you into my life / Someday (you'll want me to want you) / Danny boy / Laugh at me / Something / Hey Jude / I got you babe.

Date	Release		
Nov 71.	(7") (MU 1145) <2151> **ALL I EVER NEED IS YOU. / I GOT YOU BABE (live)**	8	7 Oct71
Jun 72.	(lp) (MUPS 452) <3660> **ALL I EVER NEED IS YOU**		14 Feb72

– All I ever need is you / Here comes that rainy day feeling / More today than yesterday / Crystal clear / Muddy waters / United we stand / A cowboy's work is never done / I love what you did with the love I gave you / You better sit down kids / We'll watch the sun coming up / Somebody.

Date	Release		
Apr 72.	(7") (MU 1154) <2163> **A COWBOY'S WORK IS NEVER DONE. / SOMEBODY**		8 Feb72
Aug 72.	(7") (MU 1164) <2176> **WHEN YOU SAY LOVE. / CRYSTAL CLEAR – MUDDY WATERS**	(M.C.A.)	32 Jul72 (M.C.A.)
Feb 73.	(lp) (MCF 3672) <2101> **MAMA WAS A ROCK AND ROLL SINGER, PAPA USED TO WRITE ALL HER SONGS**		Jun73

– It never rains in Southern California / I believe in you / I can see clearly now / Rhythm of your heartbeat / Mama was a rock and roll singer, papa used to write all her songs (parts 1 & 2) / By love I mean / Brother Love's travelling salvation show / You know darn well / The greatest show on Earth / Listen to the music.

Date	Release		
Apr 73.	(7") (MU 1194) <40026> **MAMA WAS A ROCK AND ROLL SINGER, PAPA USED TO WRITE ALL HER SONGS. / (part 2)**		77 Mar73
Jul 73.	(7") (MUS 1211) <40083> **THE GREATEST SHOW ON EARTH. / YOU KNOW DARN WELL I DO**		
May 74.	(d-lp) (MCSP 257) <8004> **LIVE IN LAS VEGAS VOL.2 (live)**		Dec73

– All I ever need is you / I can see clearly now / You've got a friend / Where you lead / You'd better sit down kids / A cowboy's work is never done / I got you babe / Gypsies, tramps and thieves / Brother Love's travelling salvation show / You and I / Superstar / Bang bang (my baby shot me down).

—— they decided to end partnership as they separated and divorced on 26th June 1974 (see biography above). Professionally they did re-unite in 1976-77 on US TV 'SONNY & CHER SHOW' again

Date	Release	not iss.	Warners
1977.	(7") <8341> **YOU'RE NOT RIGHT FOR ME. / WRONG NUMBER**	-	

– compilations, others, etc. –

On 'Atlantic' UK, 'Atco' US unless mentioned otherwise

Date	Release		
Aug 65.	(7") *Reprise;* <0392> **BABY DON'T GO. / WALKIN' THE QUETZAL (or) LOVE IS STRANGE**	-	8
Oct 65.	(lp; with Various Artists) *Reprise;* <6177> **BABY DON'T GO**	-	69
Dec 65.	(7") *Reprise;* (R 30056) **CAESAR AND CLEO**	-	-
1966.	(7"; as CAESAR & CLEO) *Reprise;* <419> **LOVE IS STRANGE. / LET THE GOOD TIMES ROLL**	-	-
Mar 67.	(7") (584 095) **I GOT YOU BABE. / BUT YOU'RE MINE**	-	-
Oct 67.	(lp) (588 083) <33219> **THE BEST OF SONNY & CHER**		23 Aug67

– The beat goes on / What now my love / I got you babe / Little man / Just you / Let it be me / A beautiful story / It's the little things / But you're mine / Sing c'est la vie / Laugh at me / Living for you. *(re-iss. Aug72 lp/c; K/K4 40012)*

Date	Release		
Jun 72.	(7"m) (K 10186) **I GOT YOU BABE. / THE BEAT GOES ON / LITTLE MAN**		
Aug 72.	(7") (K 10200) **I GOT YOU BABE. / THE BEAT GOES ON**		
Sep 72.	(d-lp) **THE TWO OF US (LOOK AT US + IN CASE YOU'RE IN LOVE)**		
1974.	(7"m) (K 10388) **I GOT YOU BABE. / WHAT NOW MY LOVE / THE BEAT GOES ON**		
1975.	(lp) <11000> **THE BEAT GOES ON – THE BEST OF SONNY & CHER**	-	

(cd-iss. Jun93 on 'Atco'; 7567 91796-2)

Date	Release		
Jan 75.	(lp) *M.C.A.;* (K 20026) <2117> **GREATEST HITS**		Sep74

(cd-iss. Aug98; MCD 11745)

Date	Release		
Jun 81.	(lp/c) *Hallmark;* (SHM/HSC 3063) **THE VERY BEST OF SONNY & CHER**		
Sep 85.	(7") *Old Gold;* (OG 9523) **I GOT YOU BABE. / WHAT NOW MY LOVE**		
Dec 90.	(cd/c/lp) *W.E.A.;* (9548 30152-2/-4/-1) **THE SONNY & CHER COLLECTION**		
May 93.	(7"/c-s) *Epic;* (659240-7/-4) **I GOT YOU BABE. / (cd-s+=) –**	66	-

Eagle-Eye CHERRY

Born: 1970, Skane, Sweden (he was apparently given his real Christian name after opening one eye at birth under the inspection of his father). Evolving from a family of successful musicians (son of famous jazz trumpeter DON CHERRY and half brother to experimental hip-hop/soul singer NENEH CHERRY), EAGLE-EYE grew up in Brooklyn, New York. He spent most of his time on the road with his father and through experience learned to quickly become a skilled drummer and multi-instrumentalist. Bent on becoming an actor, he gravitated towards theatre and subsequently decided to enrol in Manhattan's School Of Performing Arts. It would be 1994 before he became involved in a band, balancing group commitments while studying for a degree. Two years on,

CHERRY was signed to Sony's 'Work' records, his first appearance being on MARVIN GAYE tribute, 'Inner City Blues: The Music Of Marv', while around the same time he concentrated on writing his own material. In 1998, following on from the huge success of UK hit singles 'STAY TONIGHT' and 'FALLING IN LOVE AGAIN', he released his debut set, 'DESIRELESS'. His renaissance of 70's funk styles, 80's drum programming techniques, DYLAN-esque guitars and Motown vocals drew press attention due to obvious similarities with LENNY KRAVITZ and even FINLAY QUAYE. It was not surprising that he was invited to provide the soundtrack to the "Generation X" movies, 'Best Laid Plans' and 'Go'.

Album rating: DESIRELESS (*6)

EAGLE-EYE CHERRY – vocals, guitar, keyboards, programming / with session people

		Super Studio	not iss.
Mar 98.	(cd-s) *(BLAD 5CD)* **WHEN MERMAIDS CRY / ('A'– Naid remix)**		–

		Polydor	Atlantic
Jun 98.	(c-s) *(569594-4)* <*radio cut*> **SAVE TONIGHT / CONVERSATION**	6	5 Nov98
	(cd-s+=) *(569595-2)* – ('A'mixes; Bacon & Quarmby / radio).		
Jul 98.	(cd/c) *(537226-2/-4)* <*69434*> **DESIRELESS**	3	45 Nov98

– Save tonight / Indecision / Comatose (in the arms of slumber) / Worried eyes / Rainbow wings / Falling in love again / Conversation / When mermaids cry / Shooting up in vain / Permanent tears / Death defied by Will / Desireless.

Nov 98.	(c-s) *(563024-4)* **FALLING IN LOVE AGAIN / SAVE TONIGHT**	8	
	(cd-s+=) *(563025-2)* – ('A'mix).		
	(cd-s) *(563027-2)* – ('A'side) / Miss fortune / Shooting in vain (live).		
Mar 99.	(c-s) *(563672-4)* **PERMANENT TEARS / MAMA SAID KNOCK YOU OUT**	43	
	(cd-s+=) *(563675-2)* – ('A'mix).		
	(cd-s) *(563677-2)* – ('A'mixes) / Desireless.		

Neneh CHERRY

Born: NENEH MARIANN KARLSSON, 10 March '64, Stockholm, Sweden. Raised and educated by her Swedish mother and stepfather DON CHERRY (the famous jazz trumpeter) in Manhattan, New York; her early influences were inevitably jazz luminaries such as ORNETTE COLEMAN. In 1981, she moved to London, augmenting The SLITS before joining Bristolian avant-garde indie-jazz collective, RIP, RIG & PANIC. They made three albums, 'GOD' (1981), 'I AM COLD' (1982) and 'ATTITUDE' (1983), before she left to form FLOAT UP CP. In 1986, CHERRY guested on THE THE's 'Slow Train To Dawn' (from the 'Infected' album). The same year, she met CAMERON McVEY (aka BOOGA BEAR) and together they started a writing partnership, launching her solo career in 1988, with McVEY as producer/musician. A revamped version of an old MORGAN-McVEY (mid-80's outfit of whom CAMERON formed one half alongside JAMIE MORGAN) track, 'BUFFALO STANCE' took CHERRY into the charts for the first time, the British and American Top 5 no less. A fresh 'n' funky lesson in street suss hip-hop, punctuated by CHERRY's cockney wide girl interludes, the record was a taster (along with the evocative 'MANCHILD', another Top 5 smash) for her acclaimed debut set, 'RAW LIKE SUSHI' (1989). Drawing on her avant-rock background and love of jazz, soul, pop and R&B, CHERRY had created an intelligent, sensual and uniquely feminine take on a male-dominated genre. CHERRY was already a mother of two and on tracks like 'INNER CITY MAMA', she displayed a lyrical maturity missing in much modern soul/R&B. Her feminist credibility was already rock solid, CHERRY having appeared on Top Of The Pops in a lycra bodysuit while heavily pregnant. In 1990, she covered Cole Porter's 'I'VE GOT YOU UNDER MY SKIN', for the 'Red, Hot + Blue' charity album, subsequently moving back to Sweden with new husband, McVEY and beginning work on a follow-up set. 'HOMEBREW' eventually appeared in 1992, a less immediate record which struggled to make the Top 30. Nevertheless, CHERRY was back in the UK Top 3 with the spine-tingling YOUSSOU N'DOUR collaboration, '7 SECONDS', possibly her most powerful vocal performance to date. Another piece of teamwork, this time with CHER, CHRISSIE HYNDE and ERIC CLAPTON on Comic Relief charity single, 'LOVE CAN BUILD A BRIDGE' saw her top the British singles chart. The following year, CHERRY signed to the hip 'Virgin' subsidiary, 'Hut', scoring her first solo Top 10 in years with 'WOMAN'. An accompanying album, 'MAN' (1996) made the Top 20, expanding her established lyrical themes and proving that she could still cut the proverbial mustard. • **Covered:** TROUBLE MAN (Marvin Gaye) / GOLDEN RING (S.Douglas-J.Skeete). Sampled BORN TO BE WILD (Steppenwolf) / FOR THE LOVE OF MONEY (O'Jays) / SUGAR FREE (Juicy).

Album rating: RAW LIKE SUSHI (*6) / HOMEBREW (*5) / MAN (*5)

NENEH CHERRY – vocals / **CAMERON McVEY** – keyboards / etc

		Circa	Virgin
Nov 88.	(7") *(YR 21)* <*99231*> **BUFFALO STANCE. / ('A'-Electro ski mix)**	3	3 Mar89
	(12"+=) *(YRTX 21)* – ('A'-Scratchappela mix).		
	(3"cd-s++=) *(YRCD 21)* – ('A'-Give me a muthaf**kin' break beat).		
	(12") *(YRT 21)* – ('A'instrumental).		
May 89.	(7"/c-s) *(YR/+C 30)* **MANCHILD. / ('A'version)**	5	–
	(12"+=/3"cd-s+=) *(YR T/CD 30)* – ('A'versions).		
	(12"+=) *(YRTX 30)* – Buffalo stance.		
Jun 89.	(c/lp/cd) *(CIRC/+A/D 8)* <*91252*> **RAW LIKE SUSHI**	2	40

– Buffalo stance * / Manchild * / Kisses on the wind / Inna city mama / The next generation / Love ghetto / Heart * / Phoney ladies / Outre risque

locomotive / So here I come. *(cd+=)* – My bitch / (tracks marked * = extra remixes).

Aug 89.	(7"/c-s) *(YR/+C 33)* <*99183*> **KISSES ON THE WIND. / BUFFALO BLUES**	20	8 Jul89	
	(12"+=/3"cd-s+=) *(TR T/CD 33)* – ('A'extended).			
	(12") *(TRTX 33)* – ('A'mixes).			
Nov 89.	(c-s) <*99153*> **HEART / PHONY LADIES**	–	73	
Dec 89.	(7"/c-s) *(YR/+C 42)* **INNA CITY MAMA. / THE NEXT GENERATION**	34	–	
	(12"+=) *(YRT 42)* – Kisses on the wind.			
	(cd-s++=) *(YRCD 42)* – So here I come.			
	(12") *(YRTX 42)* – ('A'mixes).			
Sep 90.	(7"/c-s) *(YR/+C 53)* **I'VE GOT YOU UNDER MY SKIN. / ('A'version)**	25	–	
	(12"+=/cd-s+=) *(YR T/CD 53)* – ('A'-long version).			
	(12") *(YRTX 53)* – ('A'-different mix).			
Sep 92.	(7"/c-s) *(YR/+C 83)* **MONEY LOVE. / TWISTED**	23		
	(ext;12"+=) *(YR T/CD 83)* – ('A'-Paul Oakenfield) / ('A'-Perfecto mix).			

—— Below album featured guests GURU from GANGSTARR / J$ / MICHAEL STIPE

Oct 92.	(c/cd/lp) *(CIRC/+A/D 25)* **HOMEBREW**	27	

– Sassy / Money love / Move with me / I ain't gone under yet / Twisted / Buddy X / Somedays / Trout / Peace in mind / Red paint. *(re-iss. Jul93; same)*

Mar 93.	(c-s) <*12648*> **BUDDY X / MOVE WITH ME**	–	43
Jun 93.	(7"/c-s) *(YR/+C 98)* <*12648*> **BUDDY X (What's Up Mix) / BUDDY X (Falcon & Fabian Remix)**	35	–
	(12"+=/cd-s+=) *(YR T/CD 98)* – (4 other 'A' mixes).		

—— In May '94, she was credited on UK Top 3 single '7 SECONDS' with YOUSSOU N'DOUR (Columbia; 660508-2/-4). In Mar '95, alongside CHER, CHRISSIE HYNDE and ERIC CLAPTON, she hit No.1 UK with Comic Relief charity song 'LOVE CAN BUILD A BRIDGE'.

		Hut	Virgin
Jul 96.	(c-s) *(HUTC 70)* **WOMAN / HAD YOU IN ME**	9	
	(cd-s+=) *(HUTCD 70)* – Heart throbs / Telephone pole.		
	(cd-s) *(HUTDX 70)* – ('A'mixes).		
Sep 96.	(cd/c) *(CDHUT/HUTMC 38)* **MAN**	16	
	– Woman / Feel it / Hornbeam / Trouble man / Golden ring / 7 seconds / Kootchi / Beastiality / Carry me / Together now / Everything.		
Dec 96.	(c-s) *(HUTC 75)* **KOOTCHI / CRACK BABY**	38	
	(cd-s+=) *(HUTCD 75)* – ('A'mix) / Somedays.		
	(cd-s) *(HUTDG 75)* – ('A'mixes).		
Feb 97.	(c-s) *(HUTC 79)* **FEEL IT / I WANNA KNOW**	68	
	(cd-s+=) *(HUTCD 79)* – Trout / Devotion.		
	(cd-s) *(HUTDX 79)* – ('A'mixes).		

—— In Nov'99, 'BUDDY X' was given ('99) duet treatment by DREEM TEAM VS. NENEH CHERRY, hitting UK No.15

CHERRY POPPIN' DADDIES

Formed: Eugene, Oregon, USA ... 1989 out of the JAZZ GREATS and The HUCKS by main frontman/songwriter STEVE 'Large Drink' PERRY and bassist DAN SCHMID. Adding TIM DONAHUE, JASON MOSS, DUSTIN LANKNER, DANA HEITMAN, SEAN FLANNERY and IAN EARLY, this swingin' ska-core 8-piece delivered their independently-released debut set, 'FEROCIOUSLY STONED', in 1990. By the time of their retrospective fourth album, 'ZOOT SUIT RIOT' (1997), the combo were high in the Top 20 and rivaling fellow "swing-rock" contemporaries the SQUIRREL NUT ZIPPERS.

Album rating: FEROCIOUSLY STONED (*4) / RAPID CITY MUSCLE CAR (*6) / KIDS ON THE STREET (*5) / ZOOT SUIT RIOT compilation (*6)

STEVE 'Large Drink' PERRY – vocals, guitar / **JASON MOSS** – guitar / **DAN SCHMID** – bass / **TIM DONAHUE** – drums / **DUSTIN LANKNER** – keyboards / **DANA HEITMAN** – trumpet / **SEAN FLANNERY** – saxophone / **IAN EARLY** – saxophone

		not iss.	Space Age Bachelor
1990.	(cd) <*SAB 224CD*> **FEROCIOUSLY STONED**	–	

– Drunk daddy / Teenage brainsurgeon / Answering machine / Midas in reverse / Lifeboat mutiny / Master and slave / Dirty mutha fuzz / You better move / Suicide kings / Flovilla thatch vs. the virile garbageman / Shake your lovemaker / Dr. Bones / Diabolic tastemaker / Up from the gutter / Cherry Poppin' Daddy strut. *(UK-iss.Oct98; same as US)*

1994.	(cd) <*SAB 225CD*> **RAPID CITY MUSCLE CAR**	–	

– Search / Sockable face club / Chrysalis / Ding-dong daddy of the D-car line / Equus / Mister white keys / Skyline drive / Pink elephant / Hazel, South Dakota / Lovers understand / Johanna of the spirits / Inertia rhapsody / Bobby Kennedy / Come back to me / Impossible dream. *(UK-iss.Oct98; same as US)*

		Nail	Space Age Bachelor
May 96.	(cd) *(PD 4228)* <*SAB 228CD*> **KIDS ON THE STREET**		

– Kids on the street / Say it to my face / We'll always have Paris / Trapped inside the planey of the roller . . . / Millionaire / Dave's pie shoppe / Cosa nostra / Irish whiskey / Flower fight with Morrissey / Modsquadrophenia / Silver-tongued devil / Here comes the snake / Enemy within / Luther Lane / Don Quixote. *(UK re-iss. Oct98; same as US)*

		Universal	Universal
Oct 98.	(7"/c-s/cd-s) *(UNS/UNC/UND 56211)* **ZOOT SUIT RIOT. / 2.29 / NO MERCY FOR SWINE**		–
Nov 98.	(cd/c) <*(UND/UNC 53081)*> **ZOOT SUIT RIOT** (compilation)		17 Jul97

– Zoot suit riot / Ding-dong daddy of the D-car line / When I change your mind / Here comes the snake / Mister white keys / Come back to me / Brown derby jump / Dr. Bones / Pink elephant / Master and slave / Drunk daddy / No mercy for swine / Cherry Poppin' Daddy strut / Shake your lovemaker.

Vic CHESNUTT (dig out; Great Alt & Indie . . .)

CHIC

Formed: New York City, New York, USA . . . 1972 as The BIG APPLE BAND by NILE RODGERS, BERNARD EDWARDS and TONY THOMPSON. They worked together sessioning for disco acts (i.e. NEW YORK CITY's hit 'I'm Doin' Fine' and CAROL DOUGLAS) before forming CHIC in 1976. They added singer NORMA JEAN WRIGHT who had previously cut a solo album with CHIC at the controls. CHIC were finally signed by 'Atlantic', after the company president at the time got an earful of their demo. Late in 1977, 'DANCE DANCE DANCE (YOWSAH YOWSAH YOWSAH)' hit the charts, eventually peaking at No.6 on both sides of the Atlantic. With a change of vocalists (LUCI MARTIN replacing NORMA) the following year, they issued 'LE FREAK', which gave them their first US No.1. It also introduced their instantly recognisable funky bass/guitar interplay which would go on to influence not only the disco scene but many British pop acts of the 80's. In 1979, RODGERS and EDWARDS produced another disco act, SISTER SLEDGE, presiding over their two classic dancefloor hits, 'He's The Greatest Dancer' and 'We Are Family'. Later in the year, CHIC had their second No.1 with 'GOOD TIMES', its insistent bassline "borrowed" by The SUGARHILL GANG for 1980's 'Rapper's Delight'; the group were subsequently collared for plagiarism and ordered to pay the due royalties. Meanwhile, offers poured in for production work from the likes of DIANA ROSS ('Diana'), DEBBIE HARRY ('Koo Koo') and DAVID BOWIE ('Let's Dance'), the growing demand for the seemingly invincible RODGERS-EDWARDS team contributing to the break-up of the band (RODGERS joined The HONEYDRIPPERS with former LED ZEPPELIN legends, PLANT and PAGE).

Best CD compilation: DANCE DANCE DANCE – THE BEST OF CHIC (*8)

NILE RODGERS (b.19 Sep'52, New York) – guitar / **BERNARD EDWARDS** (b.31 Oct'52, Greenville, New Connecticut) – bass / **TONY THOMPSON** – drums / **ALFA ANDERSON** (b. 7 Sep'46) + **NORMA JEAN WRIGHT** – vocals

		Atlantic	Atlantic	
Nov 77.	(7") (K 11038) <3435> **DANCE DANCE DANCE (YOWSAH YOWSAH YOWSAH). / SAO PAULO**	6	6	Oct77
Feb 78.	(lp/c) (K/K4 50441) <19153> **CHIC**		27	Nov77
	– Dance dance dance (yowsah yowsah yowsah) / Sao paulo / You can get by / Everybody dance / Est ce que c'est Chic / Falling in love with you / Strike up the band. (cd-iss. Nov93; 7567 80407-2)			
Mar 78.	(7") (K 11097) <3469> **EVERYBODY DANCE. / YOU CAN GET BY**	9	38	

LUCI MARTIN (b.10 Jan'55) – vocals repl. NORMA JEAN WRIGHT

Nov 78.	(7") (K 11209) <3519> **LE FREAK. / SAVOIR FAIRE**	7	1	Oct78
	(12"+=) (K 11209) – Chic (everybody say).			
Dec 78.	(lp/c) (K/K4 50565) <19209> **C'EST CHIC**	2	4	Nov78
	– Chic cheer / Le freak / I want your love / Happy man / Dance dance dance / Savoir faire / At last I am free / Sometimes you win / Funny bone / Everybody dance. (cd-iss. Nov93; 7567 81552-2)			
Feb 79.	(7") (K 11245) <3557> **I WANT YOUR LOVE. / FUNNY BONE**	4	7	
	(12") (K 11245T) – ('A'side) / Chic cheer / Le freak.			
Jun 79.	(7") (K 11310) <3584> **GOOD TIMES. / A WARM SUMMER NIGHT**	5	1	
Aug 79.	(lp/c) (K/K4 50634) <16003> **RISQUE**	29	5	
	– Good times / A warm summer night / My feet keep dancing / My forbidden lover / Can't stand to love you / Will you cry when you hear this song / What about me. (cd-iss. Nov93; 7567 80406-2)			
Sep 79.	(7") **MY FORBIDDEN LOVER. / WHAT ABOUT ME**	15	43	
Nov 79.	(7") (K 11415) <3638> **MY FEET KEEP DANCING. / WILL YOU CRY WHEN YOU HEAR THIS SONG**	21		
Dec 79.	(lp/c) (K/K4 50686) <16011> **(LES PLUS GRANDS SUCCES DE CHIC –) GREATEST HITS** (compilation)	30	88	
	– Le freak / I want your love / Dance dance dance (yowsah yowsah yowsah) / Everybody dance / My forbidden lover / Good times / My feet keep dancing.			
Jul 80.	(7") (K 11539) <3665> **REBELS ARE WE. / OPEN UP**		61	
Jul 80.	(lp/c) (K/K4 50711) <16016> **REAL PEOPLE**		30	
	– Real people / Rebels are we / You can't do it alone / Chip off the old block / I got protection / Open up / 26. (cd-iss. Jan96; 7567 80420-2)			
Sep 80.	(7") (K 11617) <3768> **26. / CHIP OFF THE OLD BLOCK**		–	
Nov 80.	(7") <3768> **REAL PEOPLE. / CHIP OFF THE OLD BLOCK**	–	79	
Nov 81.	(lp/c) (K/K4 50845) <19323> **TAKE IT OFF**			
	– Flashback / Take it off / Just out of reach / Telling lies / Stage fright / So fine / Baby doll / Your love is cancelled / Burn hard / Would you be my baby. (cd-iss. Jan96; 7567 80421-2)			
Jun 82.	(7") <4032> **SOUP FOR ONE. / BURN HARD**	–	80	
	(above was the title track from the film for which NILE & RODGERS wrote soundtrack released 'Mirage')			
Nov 82.	(lp) (780 031-1) <80031> **TONGUE IN CHIC**			
	– Hangin' / I feel your love comin' on / When you love someone / Chic (everybody say) / Hey fool / Sharing love / City lights. (cd-iss. Jan96; 7567 80031-2)			
Jan 83.	(7"/12") (A 9898/+T) **HANGIN'. / CITY LIGHTS**	64	–	
Jan 83.	(7") <89954> **HANGIN'. / CHIC (EVERYBODY SAY)**	–		
Dec 83.	(lp) (780 107-1) <80107> **BELIEVER**			
	– Believer / You are beautiful / Take a closer look / Give me the lovin' / Show me your light / You got some love for me / In love with music / Party everybody. (cd-iss. Jan96; 7567 80107-2)			
Dec 83.	(7") <89725> **YOU GOT SOME LOVE FOR ME. / GIVE ME THE LOVIN'**	–		

Early in 1983, they had already split. EDWARDS and THOMPSON later joined The POWER STATION with ROBERT PALMER and members of DURAN DURAN.

NILE RODGERS

went solo, also augmented by EDWARDS and THOMPSON

		Mirage-WEA	Mirage-WEA
Feb 83.	(lp/c) (B 0073) **ADVENTURES IN THE LAND OF THE GOOD GROOVE**		
	– The land of the good groove / Yum yum / Beat / Get her crazy / It's all in your hands / Rock bottom / My love song for you / Most down.		
Mar 83.	(7") (U 9911) **THE LAND OF GOOD GROOVE. / MY LOVE SONG FOR YOU**		
May 83.	(7") (U 9918) **YUM YUM. / GET HER CRAZY**		

After spell with The HONEYDRIPPERS (see LED ZEPPELIN), he continued solo.

		Warners	Warners
Jun 85.	(lp/c) (925290-1/-4) **B-MOVIE MATINEE**		
	– Groove master / Let's go out tonight / Same wavelength / Plan number 9 / State your mind / Face in the window / Doll squad.		
Jun 85.	(7"/12") (W/WT 9049) **LET'S GO OUT TONIGHT. / DOLL SQUAD**		
Jan 86.	(12") (WT 8921) **STATE OF MIND. / STAY OUT OF THE LIGHT**		

In 1986, RODGERS formed The OUTLOUD with PHILLIPE SAISSE + FELICIA COLLINS. Made one eponymous album that year.

CHIC

reformed 1991; **STERLING CAMPBELL** – drums repl. THOMPSON / + new vocalists **SYLVER LOGAN SHARP + JENN THOMAS**

		W.E.A.	W.E.A.
Jan 92.	(7"/c-s) (W 0083/+C) **CHIC MYSTIQUE. / ('A'-Lovely without rap mix)**	48	
	(12"+=) (W 0083T) – ('A'-4 a.m. mix) / ('A'-Lovely mix).		
	(cd-s++=) (W 0083CD) – ('A'extended) / ('A'acappella mix).		
Mar 92.	(cd)(lp/c) <(7599 26394-2)>(WX 463/+C) **CHIC-ISM**		
	– Chic mystique / Your love / Jusagroove / Something you can feel / One and only one / Doin' that thing to me / Chicism / In it to win it / My love's for real / Take my love / High / M.M.F.T.C.F. (cd re-iss. Feb95; same)		
May 92.	(7") (W) **YOUR LOVE. / ('A'mix)**		
	(12"+=/cd-s+=) (W) – ('A'extended).		

On the 18 April '96, BERNARD EDWARDS died of unknown causes.

– compilations, others, etc. –

on 'Atlantic' unless mentioned otherwise

Nov 84.	(7") (A 9604) **CHIC CHEERS. / SAVOIR FAIRE**		
	(12"+=) (TA 9604) – Dance, dance, dance (yowsah, yowsah, yowsah).		
Sep 87.	(7"/12") (A/AT 9198) **JACK LE FREAK. / SAVOIR FAIRE**	19	
Nov 87.	(lp/c/cd; shared with SISTER SLEDGE) Telstar; (STAR/STAC/TCD 2319) **FREAK OUT**	72	–
Jul 90.	(7"/c-s) East West; (A 7949) **MEGACHIC (Chic Medley). / LE FREAK**	58	–
	(12"+=/cd-s+=) (A 7949 T/CD) – ('A'edit).		
Aug 90.	(cd/c/lp) East West; (2292 41750-2/-4/-1) **MEGACHIC (THE BEST OF CHIC VOL.1)**		
Jul 91.	(cd/c/d-lp; shared with ROSE ROYCE) Dino; (DIN CD/MC/TV 23) **THEIR GREATEST HITS – SIDE BY SIDE**	–	–
Nov 91.	(cd) **DANCE DANCE DANCE – THE BEST OF CHIC**	–	
Jun 93.	(cd) <(8122 71086-2)> **THE BEST OF CHIC – VOL.2**		Nov92

CHICAGO

Formed: Chicago, Illinois, USA . . . 1966 by WALTER PARAZAIDER, LEE LOUGHNANE, TERRY KATH, DANNY SERAPHINE, JAMES PANKOW and ROBERT LAMM. Originally named CHICAGO TRANSIT AUTHORITY by manager and producer JAMES WILLIAM GUERCIO, the group were the first US pop-rock band to include a horn section and were the most successful American act of all time (running pretty close behind THE BEACH BOYS of course). After the recruitment of bassist, vocalist and organ player PETER CETERA, the group redirected themselves to Hollywood where they signed a permanent contract with 'Columbia' records, albeit shortening their name to CHICAGO. The band issued their debut album, 'CHICAGO TRANSIT AUTHORITY' (1969), stunning critics with their fusion of jazz, rock'n'roll and good-old spirited R&B and selling an awesome two million copies in the process. Like the proverbial domino effect, this marked the beginning of a string of unforgettable albums which all bore the CHICAGO logo and were simply titled in the numerical sense as they were released in (i.e. 'CHICAGO 2' 'CHICAGO 3', need I go on!?). The band churned out a number of hit singles during the 70's, culminating with the smoochiest and bed-cert 'IF YOU LEAVE ME NOW' (1976) being the most prominent of the bunch. Penned by bassist CETERA himself, the song displayed all of the romantic codes, with slow vocals and a memorable horn section, which, in itself, proved CHICAGO's talent to drive a song into new heights. The track became a best-selling hit, earning a top spot in the American Billboard charts and going double gold; even more success which was added to the band's ever growing CV. Afterwards, the troupe became familiar with swooping ballads, which the majority of their audience seemed to like, although one would argue that they had peaked with their prolific earlier works. CHICAGO had now run into their teens ('CHICAGO 13', 'CHICAGO 14', aarrgghh!) in the late '70's/early 80's after the release of the disappointing 'HOT STREETS' (1978) – er, working title '12'. It was around about this point when the band slowly began to deteriorate: they left the side of their long-term manager GUERICO just before the accidental and tragic death of guitarist/vocalist TERRY KATH. However, things weren't that bad, the 'CHICAGO 16' (1982) set selling over a million copies and the single 'HARD TO SAY I'M SORRY' entering the Top 5 on both sides of the Atlantic. The band continued to flaunt their dizzy orchestrations and trademark jazzy textures with 'CHICAGO 17' and 'CHIGAGO 18', although a few live albums were a bit beyond the pale. The group subsequently retired in the early '90's, although they issued a Big Band-style CD-disc in 1995 (what!). • **Songwriters:** LAMM wrote lyrics, KATH and group the music. Covered I'M A MAN (Spencer Davis Group). • **Trivia:** 80's newcomer JASON SCHEFF was son of Elvis Presley's bassman JERRY.

Album rating: CHICAGO TRANSIT AUTHORITY (*7) / CHICAGO II (*6) / CHICAGO III (*5) / CHICAGO AT CARNEGIE HALL (*3) / CHICAGO V (*5) / CHICAGO VI (*5) / CHICAGO VII (*5) / CHICAGO VIII (*5) / CHICAGO IX – CHICAGO'S GREATEST HITS compilation (*6) / CHICAGO X (*4) / CHICAGO XI (*4) / HOT STREETS (*4) / CHICAGO 13 (*3) / CHICAGO XIV (*3) / CHICAGO – GREATEST HITS VOLUME II compilation (*5) / CHICAGO 16 (*4) / CHICAGO 17 (*4) / CHICAGO 18 (*4) / CHICAGO 19 (*4) / GREATEST HITS 1982-1989 compilation (*5) / TWENTY 1 (*4) / NIGHT AND DAY (*2) / HEART OF CHICAGO 1967-97 compilation (*7)

ROBERT LAMM (b.13 Oct'44, Brooklyn, N.Y.) – vocals, keyboards / **TERRY KATH** (b.31 Jan'46) – vocals, guitar / **PETER CETERA** (b.13 Sep'44) – vocals, bass / **DAN SERAPHINE** (b.28 Aug'48) – drums / **LEE LOUGHNANE** (b.21 Oct'46) – trumpet, vocals / **JAMES PANKOW** (b.20 Aug'47) – trombone / **WALTER PARAZAIDER** (b.14 Mar'48) – reeds

C.B.S.   Columbia

Sep 69. (d-lp; as CHICAGO TRANSIT AUTHORITY) (CBS 66221) <8> **CHICAGO TRANSIT AUTHORITY** — `9` | `17` May69
– (introduction) / Does anybody really know what time it is? / Beginnings / Questions 67 and 68 / Listen / Poem 58 / Free form guitar / South California purples / I'm a man / (prologue, August 29, 1968) / Someday / Liberation. (re-iss. Sep87) (cd-iss. Oct93 on 'Sony Europe') (re-iss. cd+c Jun94 on 'Columbia')

Jul 69. (7") (CBS 4381) <44909> **QUESTIONS 67 AND 68. / LISTEN** `71`

Nov 69. (7") <45011> **BEGINNINGS. / POEM 58** `-`

Dec 69. (7") (CBS 4715) **I'M A MAN. / DOES ANYBODY REALLY KNOW WHAT THE TIME IS?** `8` | `-`

Mar 70. (d-lp) (CBS 66233) <24> **CHICAGO II** `6` | `4` Feb70
– Movin' in / The road / Poem for the people / In the country / Wake up sunshine (ballet for a girl in Buchannon) / Make me smile / So much to say, so much to give / Anxiety's moment / West Virginia fantasies / Colour my world / To be free / Now more than ever / Fancy colours / 25 or 6 to 4 / (prelude) / A.M. mourning / P.M. mourning / Memories of love / It better end soon (movements 1-5) / Where do we go from here. (cd-iss. Oct93 on 'Sony Europe')

Apr 70. (7") (CBS 4919) <45127> **MAKE ME SMILE. / COLOUR MY WORLD** `9`

Jul 70. (7") (CBS 5076) <45194> **25 OR 6 TO 4. / WHERE DO WE GO FROM HERE** `7` | `4`

Nov 70. (7") <45264> **DOES ANYBODY REALLY KNOW WHAT THE TIME IS? / LISTEN** `-` | `7`

Mar 71. (7") (CBS 7061) <45331> **FREE. / FREE COUNTRY** `20` Feb71

Mar 71. (d-lp) (CBS 66260) <30110> **CHICAGO III** `31` | `2` Jan71
– Sing a mean tune kid / Loneliness is just a word / What else can I say / I don't want your money / Flight 602 / Motorboat to Mars / Free / Free country / At the sunrise / Happy 'cause I'm going home / Mother / Lowdown / A hard risin' morning without breakfast / Off to work / Fallin' out / Morning blues again / When all the laughter dies in sorrow / Canon / Once upon a time / Progress? / The approaching storm / Man vs. man / The end. (cd-iss. Oct93 on 'Sony Europe')

May 71. (7") (CBS 7218) <45370> **LOWDOWN. / LONELINESS IS JUST A WORD** `35`

Jul 71. (7") (CBS 7348) <45417> **BEGINNINGS. / COLOUR MY WORLD** `7` Jun71

Nov 71. (q-lp) (CBS 66405) <30865> **LIVE AT CARNEGIE HALL – IV** (live 5-10 April '71) `3`
– In the country / Fancy colours / Does anybody really know what time it is? / Free form guitar / South California purples / Questions 67 and 68 / Sing a mean tune kid / Beginnings / It better end soon (5 movements) / (introduction) / Mother / Lowdown / Flight 602 / Motorboat to Mars / Where do we go from here / I don't want your money / Happy 'cause I'm going home / Wake up sunshine (ballet for a girl in Buchannon) / Make me smile / So much to say, so much to give / Anxiety's moment / West Virginia fantasies / Colour my world / To be free / Free / Now more than ever / A song for Richard and his friends / 25 or 6 to 4 / I'm a man. (cd-iss. Apr89; CD 66405)

Jan 72. (7") <45467> **QUESTIONS 67 AND 68 (live). / I'M A MAN (live)** `-`

Aug 72. (7") (CBS 8331) <45657> **SATURDAY IN THE PARK. / ALMA MATER** `3`

Sep 72. (lp) (CBS 69018) <31102> **CHICAGO V** `24` | `1` Jul72
– Saturday in the park / A hit by Varese / All is well / Now that you've gone / Dialogue (part 1 & 2) / While the city sleeps / State of the union / Alma mater / Goodbye. (cd-iss. May88; CD 69018) (re-iss. Nov93 on 'Pickwick'; 983301-2)

Nov 72. (7") (CBS 847?) <45717> **DIALOGUE (part I & II). / NOW THAT YOU'VE GONE** `24` Oct72

Aug 73. (7") (CBS 1653) <45880> **FEELIN' STRONGER EVERY DAY. / JENNY** `10` Jun73

Aug 73. (lp) (CBS 69041) <32400> **CHICAGO VI** `1` Jul73
– Critic's choice / Just you 'n' me / Darlin' dear / Jenny / What's this world comin' to / Something in this city changes people / Hollywood / Jenny / In terms of two / Rediscovery / Feelin' stronger every day. (cd-iss. May88; 69041)

Sep 73. (7") <45933> **JUST YOU 'N' ME. / CRITIC'S CHOICE** `-` | `4`

Oct 73. (7") (CBS 1819) **JUST YOU 'N' ME. / FEELIN' STRONGER EVERY DAY** `-`

Apr 74. (7") (CBS 2245) <46020> **(I'VE BEEN) SEARCHIN' SO LONG. / BYBLOS** `9` Mar74

May 74. (d-lp/c) (CBS/40 88015) <32810> **CHICAGO VII** `1` Mar74
– (prelude to Aire) / Aire / Devil's sweet / Halian from New York / Hanky panky / Life saver / Happy man / (I've been) Searchin' so long / Mongonucleosis / Song of the evergreens / Byblos / Wishing you were here / Call on me / Woman don't want to love me / Skinny boy. (cd-iss. May88; CK 32810)

Jun 74. (7") <46062> **CALL ON ME. / PRELUDE TO AIRE** `-` | `6`

Oct 74. (7") (CBS 2468) **CALL ON ME. / AIRE** `-` | `-`

Oct 74. (7") <10049> **WISHING YOU WERE HERE. / LIFE SAVER** `-` | `11`

Dec 74. (7") (CBS 2510) **WISHING YOU WERE HERE. / SONG OF THE EVERGREENS** `-`

Apr 75. (7") (CBS 3103) <10092> **HARRY TRUMAN. / TILL WE MEET AGAIN** `13` Feb75

Apr 75. (lp/c) (CBS/40 80348) <33100> **CHICAGO VIII** `1`
– Anyway you want / Brand new love affair (part I & II) / Never been in love before / Hideaway / Till we meet again / Harry Truman / Oh, thank you great spirit / Long time no see / Ain't it blue / Old days.

Jun 75. (7") (CBS 3335) <10131> **OLD DAYS. / HIDEAWAY** `5` Apr75

Oct 75. (7") (CBS 3745) <10185> **NEVER BEEN IN LOVE BEFORE. / (part 2)** `Aug75`

Oct 75. (7") <10200> **BRAND NEW LOVE AFFAIR. / HIDEAWAY** `-` | `61`

Nov 75. (lp/c) (CBS/40 69187) <33900> **CHICAGO IX – CHICAGO'S GREATEST HITS** (compilation) `1`
– 25 or 6 to 4 / Does anybody really know what time it is? / Colour my world / Just you 'n' me / Saturday in the park / Feelin' stronger every day / Make me smile / Wishing you were here / Call on me / (I've been) Searchin' so long / Beginnings. (re-iss. Nov84 lp/c; CBS/40 32535) (cd-iss. Jul87; CD 69187) (re-iss. Mar91 cd/c; CD/40 32535)

Jul 76. (7") (CBS 4458) <10360> **ANOTHER RAINY DAY IN NEW YORK. / HOPE FOR LOVE** `32` Jun76

Jul 76. (lp/c) (CBS/40 86010) <34200> **CHICAGO X** `21` | `3` Jun76
– Once or twice / You are on my mind / Skin tight / If you leave me now / Together again / Another rainy day in New York City / Mama mama / Scrapbook / Gently I'll wake you / You get it up / Hope for love. (cd-iss. May88; CD 86010)

Sep 76. (7") (CBS 4603) <10390> **IF YOU LEAVE ME NOW. / TOGETHER AGAIN** `1` | `1` Aug76

Feb 77. (7") <10523> **YOU ARE ON MY MIND. / GENTLY I'LL WAKE YOU** `-` | `49`

Sep 77. (lp/c) (CBS/40 86031) <34860> **CHICAGO XI** `6`
– Mississippi Delta queen blues / Baby, what a big surprise / Policeman / Till the end of time / Take me back to Chicago / Vote for me / Takin' it on uptown / This time / The inner struggles of a man / (prelude) / Little one. (cd-iss. May88; CD 86031)

Oct 77. (7") (CBS 5672) <10620> **BABY, WHAT A BIG SURPRISE. / TAKIN' IT ON UPTOWN** `41` | `4` Sep77

Jan 78. (7") (CBS 5924) <10737> **TAKE ME BACK TO CHICAGO. / POLICEMAN** `63` May78

Mar 78. (7") (CBS 6174) <10683> **LITTLE ONE. / TILL THE END OF TIME** `44` Feb78

—— On the 23rd of January '78, TERRY KATH died after accidentally shooting himself in the head. Later in year, he was repl. by **DONNIE DACUS** – guitar (ex-STEPHEN STILLS)

Sep 78. (lp/c) (CBS/40 86069) <35512> **HOT STREETS** `12`
– Alive again / The greatest love on earth / Little Miss Lovin' / Hot streets / Take a chance / Gone long gone / Ain't it time / Love was new / No tell lover / Show me the way. (re-iss. Mar94 on 'Pickwick'; 982942-2)

Oct 78. (7") (CBS 6787) <10845> **ALIVE AGAIN. / LOVE WAS NEW** `14`

Mar 79. (7") (CBS 7050) <10879> **NO TELL LOVER. / TAKE A CHANCE** `14` Dec78

Apr 79. (7") <10935> **GONE LONG GONE. / THE GREATEST LOVE ON EARTH** `-` | `73`

Aug 79. (7") (CBS 7822) <11061> **MUST HAVE BEEN CRAZY. / CLOSER TO YOU** `83`

Sep 79. (lp/c) (CBS/40 86093) <36105> **CHICAGO 13 – STREET PLAYER** `21` Aug79
– Street player / Mama take / Must have been crazy / Window dreamin' / Paradise alley / Aloha mama / Reruns / Loser with a broken heart / Life is what it is / Run away.

Oct 79. (7") (CBS 7991) **MAMA TAKE. / WINDOW DREAMIN'** `-`

Apr 80. (7") (CBS 8040) <11138> **STREET PLAYER. / WINDOW DREAMIN'**

—— **CHRIS PINNICK** – guitar; repl. DACUS

Aug 80. (7") (CBS 8921) <11341> **SONG FOR YOU. / I'D RATHER BE RICH** `Jul80`

Aug 80. (7") <11345> **THUNDER AND LIGHTNING. / I'D RATHER BE RICH** `-` | `56`

Sep 80. (lp/c) (CBS/40 86118) <36517> **CHICAGO XIV** `71` Aug80
– Manipulation / Upon arrival / Song for you / Where did the lovin' go / Birthday boy / Hold on / Overnight cafe / Thunder and lightning / I'd rather be rich / The American dream. (re-iss. Dec92 cd/c on 'Sony Collectors'; 982834-2/-4)

Dec 81. (lp/c) (CBS/40 85444) <37682> **CHICAGO – GREATEST HITS, VOLUME II** (compilation)
– Baby, what a big surprise / Dialogue (part 1 & 2) / No tell lover / Alive again / Old days / If you leave me now / Questions 67 and 68 / Happy man / Gone long gone / Take me back to Chicago.

—— added **BILL CHAMPLIN** – vocals, bass, guitar (ex-SONS OF CHAMPLIN)

Full Moon   Full Moon

Jun 82. (lp/c) (K/K4 99235) <23689> **CHICAGO 16** `44` | `9`
– What you're missing / Waiting for you to decide / Bad advice / Chains / Hard to say I'm sorry / Get away / Follow me / Sonny think twice / Rescue you / What can I say / Love me tomorrow. (cd-iss. 1983; 299235)

Aug 82. (7") (K 79301) <29979> **HARD TO SAY I'M SORRY. / SONNY THINK TWICE** `4` | `1` Jun82

Nov 82. (7") (K 79338) <29911> **LOVE TOMORROW. / BAD ADVICE** `22` Sep82

Jan 83. (7") <29798> **WHAT YOU'RE MISSING. / RESCUE YOU** `-` | `81`

Full Moon –   Full Moon –
Warners   Warners

Jun 84. (7") (W 9306) <29306> **STAY THE NIGHT. / ONLY YOU** `16` Apr84

Jun 84. (lp/c/cd) (925060-1/-4/-2) <25060> **CHICAGO 17** `4` May84
– Stay the night / We can stop the hurtin' / Hard habit to break / Only you / Remember the feeling / Along comes a woman / You're the inspiration / Please hold on / Prima Donna / Once in a lifetime. (hit No.24 in Dec84)

Oct 84. (7"/12") (W 9214/+T) <29214> **HARD HABIT TO BREAK. / REMEMBER THE FEELING** `8` | `3` Aug84

Nov 84. (7") <29126> **YOU'RE THE INSPIRATION. / ONCE IN A LIFETIME** `-` | `3`

Jan 85. (7") *(W 9126)* **YOU'RE THE INSPIRATION. / LOVE ME TOMORROW** | 14 | - |
(12"+=) *(W 9126T)* – Once in a lifetime.

Apr 85. (7"/12") *(W 9082/+T) <29082>* **ALONG COMES A WOMAN. / WE CAN STOP THE HURTIN'** | | 14 | Feb85

—— **JERRY SCHEFF** – bass; repl. CETERA who went solo

Oct 86. (7") *(W 8628) <28628>* **25 OR 6 TO 4 (remix). / ONE MORE DAY** | | 48 | Aug86
(12"+=) *(W 8628T)* – Hard habit to break.

Oct 86. (lp/c)(cd) *(WX 61/+C)(925714-2) <25714>* **CHICAGO 18** | | 35 |
– Niagara Falls / Forever / If she would have been faithful . . . / 25 or 6 to 4 / Will you still love me? / Over and over / It's alright / Nothin' gonna stop us now / I believe / One more day. *(cd re-iss. Feb93; same)*

Nov 86. (7") *<28512>* **WILL YOU STILL LOVE ME? / 25 OR 6 TO 4** | - | 3 |
Feb 87. (7") *(W 8439)* **WILL YOU STILL LOVE ME? / FOREVER** | - | - |
(12"+=) *(W 8439T)* – Hard habit to break.

Jul 87. (7") *<28283>* **NIAGARA FALLS. / I BELIEVE** | - | 91 |
Oct 87. (7") *(W 8424) <28424>* **IF SHE WOULD HAVE BEEN FAITHFUL . . . / FOREVER** | - | 17 | Mar87
(12"+=) *(W 8424T)* – 25 or 6 to 4.

		Warners	Reprise

Jun 88. (lp/c)(cd) *(WX 161/+C)(925714-2) <25714>* **CHICAGO 19** | | 43 |
– Heart in pieces / I don't want to live without your love / I stand up / We can last forever / Come in from the night / Look away / What kind of man would I be? / Runaround / You're not alone / Victorious.

Aug 88. (7"/c-s) *(W 7855/+C) <27855>* **I DON'T WANNA LIVE WITHOUT YOUR LOVE. / I STAND UP** | | 3 | May88
(12"+=) *(W 7855T)* – 25 or 6 to 4.
(cd-s+=) *(W 7855CD)* – Will you still love me?

Sep 88. (7"/c-s) *(W 7766/+C) <27766>* **LOOK AWAY. / COME IN FROM THE NIGHT** | | 1 |
(12"+=/cd-s+=) *(W 7766 T/CD)* – 25 or 6 to 4.

Jan 89. (7") *<27757>* **YOU'RE NOT ALONE. / IT'S ALRIGHT** | - | 10 |
May 89. (7") *<22985>* **WE CAN LAST FOREVER. / ONE MORE DAY** | - | 55 |

Oct 89. (cd)(lp/c) *(K 926107-2)(WX 328/+C) <26080>* **THE HEART OF CHICAGO** <US title 'GREATEST HITS 1982-1989'> (compilation) | 9 | 37 | Nov89
– If you leave me now / Baby, what a big surprise / Where did the lovin go / Take me back to Chicago / Hard to say I'm sorry / Love me tomorrow / Hard habit to break / Only you / You're the inspiration / Along comes a woman / Remember the feeling / If she would have been faithful . . . *(c+=/cd+=)* – Will you still love me? / What kind of man would I be? / Look away. *(re-iss. Feb94; same)* – hit UK No.6

Feb 90. (7") *(W 2741) <22741>* **WHAT KIND OF MAN WOULD I BE? / 25 OR 6 TO 4** | | 5 | Nov89
(12"+=/cd-s+=) *(W 2741 T/CD)* – You're the inspiration / Hard to say I'm sorry.

Jul 90. (7") *<19679>* **HEARTS IN TROUBLE. / (B-side by Hans Zimmer)** | | 75 |
(12"+=/cd-s+=) – (track by other artist). *(above on 'D.G.C.' in the US)*

—— trimmed when SERAPHINE departed Aug'90

Jan 91. (c-s) *<19466>* **CHASIN' THE WIND / ONLY TIME CAN HEAL THE WOUNDED** | - | 39 |
Feb 91. (cd/c/lp) *<(7599 26391-2/-4/-1)>* **TWENTY 1** | | 66 |
– Explain to my heart / If it were you / You come to my senses / Somebody somewhere / What does it take / One from the heart / Chasin' the wind / God save the Queen / Man to woman / Only time can heal the wounded / Who do you love / Holdin' on.

		Giant-RCA	Giant-RCA

Jun 95. (cd) *(74321 26767-2) <24615>* **NIGHT AND DAY** | | 90 |
– Moonlight serenade / Night and day / Chicago (from 'The Joker Is Wild') / Sing, sing, sing / Dream a little dream / Goody goody / Sophisticated lady / Don't get around much anymore / String of pearls / Take the 'A' train / Caravan / In the mood / Blues in the night. *(re-iss. Sep97; same)*

		not iss.	Chicago

Nov 98. (cd,c) *<3035>* **CHICAGO 25 – THE CHRISTMAS ALBUM** (festive) | - | 47 |
– Little drummer boy / God rest ye merry gentlemen / Have yourself a merry little Christmas / The Christmas song / O come all ye faithful / Child's prayer / Felix Navidad / Santa Claus is coming to town / Christmas time is here / Let it snow! let it snow! let it snow! / What child is this / White Christmas / Silent night / One little candle.

– compilations, etc. –

on 'C.B.S.' / 'Columbia' unless stated otherwise

Apr 73. (7") *(CBS 1167)* **25 OR 6 TO 4. / MAKE ME SMILE** | | - |
(re-iss. 1975; 13-33193) (re-iss. Mar76; 3961)
1975. (7") *(13-33197)* **DOES ANYBODY REALLY KNOW WHAT THE TIME IS? / FREE** | | - |
1975. (7") *(13-33201)* **BEGINNINGS. / QUESTIONS 67 AND 68** | | - |
1975. (7") *(13-33210)* **COLOUR MY WORLD. / I'M A MAN** | | - |
1975. (7") *(13-33241)* **SATURDAY IN THE PARK. / DIALOGUE** | | - |
Aug 75. (7") *(CBS 2815)* **WISHING YOU WERE HERE. / LIFE SAVER** | | - |
Jan 77. (7") *(CBS 4940)* **WISHING YOU WERE HERE. / GENTLY I'LL WAKE YOU** | | - |
Mar 79. (7") *(CBS 7079)* **I'M A MAN. / 25 OR 6 TO 4** | | - |
Nov 82. (lp/c) *TV; (TVA/TVC 6)* **LOVE SONGS** | 42 | - |
Nov 82. (7") *(A 2939)* **IF YOU LEAVE ME NOW. / 25 OR 6 TO 4** | | - |
Nov 82. (lp/c) *(CBS/40 25133)* **IF YOU LEAVE ME NOW** | | - |
(re-iss. Dec89; CD 32391) (cd-iss. Dec89; CD 32391)
Jan 83. (c-ep) *(40 3064)* **GREATEST ORIGINAL HITS** | | - |
– If you leave me now / 25 or 6 to 4 / Baby, what a big surprise / Wishing you were here.
Dec 83. (lp) *Meteor; (MTLP 1003)* **BEGINNINGS** | | - |
(re-iss. Jan85 on 'Topline' lp/c; TOP/KTOP 116) (cd-iss. Feb93 on 'Charly'; CDCD 1034)
Jul 84. (pic-lp) *Design; (PIXLP 2)* **TORONTO ROCK'N'ROLL REVIVAL (live)** | | - |

(cd-iss. Jul91 as 'LIVE IN TORONTO' on 'Thunderbolt'; CDTB 103) (cd re-iss. Mar99 as 'LIVE IN TORONTO' on 'MagMid'; MM 021)
Apr 86. (lp/c) *Showcase; (SHLP/SHTC 121)* **CHICAGO LIVE (live)** | | - |
(cd-iss. Dec88 on 'Spectrum'; SPEC 85019)
Aug 88. (3"cd-s) *<38K 33193>* **25 OR 6 TO 4. / MAKE ME SMILE** | - | - |
Feb 89. (lp) *Crusader; (RMB 5649)* **THE BEST OF CHICAGO** | | - |
May 89. (lp/c/cd) *That's Original; (TFO LP/MC/CD 18)* **THE COLLECTION** | | - |
– (CHIGAGO XIII / STREET PLAYER)
Jul 91. (3xcd-box) *(468332-2)* **IF YOU LEAVE ME NOW / CHICAGO V / CHICAGO X** | | - |
Apr 93. (cd) *Pulsar;* **I'M A MAN & OTHER GREAT HITS LIVE (live)** | | - |
(re-iss. Jul97 on 'Hallmark' cd/c; 30565-2/-4)
May 94. (4xcd-box/4xc-box) *Columbia-Legacy; (469209-2/-4)* **GROUP PORTRAIT** | | - |
Jun 94. (cd) *Javelin; (HADCD 172)* **IN CONCERT (live)** | | - |
Aug 94. (cd) *Wisepack; (LECD 075)* **LEGENDS IN MUSIC – CHICAGO** | | - |
Sep 94. (cd/c) *Prestige; (CDS/CASS GP 0126)* **25 OR 6 TO 4** | | - |
Sep 96. (cd) *Experience; (EXP 006)* **CHICAGO** | | - |
Mar 98. (cd) *Eagle; (EABCD 088)* **THE MASTERS** | | - |
Feb 99. (cd/c) *Warner ESP; <(9362 46554-2/-4)>* **THE HEART OF CHICAGO 1967-1997** | 21 | 55 | May97
– You're the inspiration / If you leave me now / Make me smile / Hard habit to break / Saturday in the park / Wishing you were here / The only one / Colour my world / Look away / Here in my heart / Just you 'n' me / Does anyone really know what time it is / Will you still love me / Beginnings / Hard to say I'm sorry / Get away.
May 99. (d-cd) *Collection; (KBOX 234)* **CHICAGO** | | - |

CHICKEN SHACK (dig out 4th edition)

CHILLS (dig out; Great Alt & Indie . . .)

Alex CHILTON (see under ⇒ BOX TOPS)

CHINA CRISIS (dig out; Great Alt & Indie . . .)

CHUMBAWAMBA

Formed: Burnley / Barnsley, Yorkshire, England . . . 1980 by vegan sextet, ALICE NUTTER, BOFF, LOU, MAVIS, HARRY and DANBERT NOBACON, who shacked up in a Leeds commune. In 1982, they appeared as SKIN DISEASE on a single 'BACK ON THE STREETS', and toured as CHUMBAWAMBA a year later with CRASS, while releasing three cassettes independently. In 1985/86, they caused a little controversy by issuing records arguing the merits of the BAND/LIVE AID charity causes. Needless to say, these were banned from radio airplay. More publicity surrounded them around this time, when they poured red paint over The CLASH, after the one-time punks arrived in Leeds for their 'Busking Britain Tour'. 1987's 'NEVER MIND THE BALLOTS: HERE'S THE REST OF YOUR LIFE', meanwhile, berated all parties in the forthcoming general election although obviously the Tories came in for the main disdain ('MR HESELTINE MEETS HIS PUBLIC'. The same year, CHUMBAWAMBA railed against tabloid hypocrisy when they released 'LET IT BE' under the moniker of SCAB AID. Perhaps as a reaction to yet another Conservative victory, the band released an album of traditional folk protest songs, 'ENGLISH REBEL SONGS 1381-1914' (1988), their MADDY PRIOR (Steeleye Span) meets CRASS sound rising with ease to the challenge. Discovering the subversive possibilities in the emerging rave culture, the band turned in the dancefloor-friendly 'SLAP!' in summer 1990, although it took a pair-up with agit-hip hoppers CREDIT TO THE NATION for CHUMBAWAMBA to finally get their message across to a wider audience. Now signed to 'One Little Indian', the track in question, 'ENOUGH IS ENOUGH', gave the band a minor UK chart hit. Its call to challenge the rise of right-wing activism was echoed in a similarly successful follow-up, 'TIMEBOMB'. The attendant album, 'ANARCHY', made the British Top 30. Unimaginable ten years earlier, the once crustie band signed to conglomorate, 'E.M.I.' in the mid-90's, obviously deciding to subvert the pop world from within (a likely story!). Not only did they come pretty damn close with the annoyingly infectious 'TUBTHUMPING' (a No.2 UK hit!), but they broke the normally impenetrable American market. The accompanying album, 'TUBTHUMPER' (1997) made the US Top 5 (having earlier made UK Top 20), proving that patience is a virtue, even for those committed to radical social change. Love them or loathe them (and there's never usually any waverers!), CHUMBAWAMBA are now something of an institution, their newfound pop/MTV-friendly sound ushering in a new era of chart topping protest, possibly . . . • **Songwriters:** Group, except some traditional Hungarian folk tunes. Also sampled JOHN LENNON (Imagine), ELVIS, ALTERNATIVE TV, GANG OF FOUR, CRASS, FALL, X-RAY SPEX, STIFF LITTLE FINGERS, DAGMAR KRAUSE and GERSHWIN!. The lp tracks on 'ENGLISH REBEL SONGS' were all traditional. Covered on 'JESUS H CHRIST'; ALRIGHT NOW (Free) / MONEY, MONEY, MONEY (Abba) / SOLID GOLD EASY ACTION (T.Rex) / HEY YOU GET OFF MY CLOUD (Rolling Stones) / STAIRWAY TO HEAVEN (Led Zeppelin) / BIGMOUTH STRIKES AGAIN (Smiths) / I SHOULD BE SO LUCKY (Kylie Minogue) / MANNEQUIN (Wire) / HUNCHBACK OF NOTRE DAME (Frantic Elevators; Mick Hucknall). • **Trivia:** In 1982, track 'THREE YEARS LATER' appeared on 'Crass' label album 'BULLSHIT DETECTOR 2'. ALICE NUTTER was named after a 17th century witch. DANBERT NOBACON released a single before he joined them, which featured a picture of his utensil on the cover!.

'NEVER SAY DI' single (proceeds to charity) was surprisingly in support of Princess Diana, as they were anti-royalists. 'BEHAVE!' was a tribute ha!, about 'The Hit Man And Her' (aka PETE WATERMAN & MICHAELA).

Album rating: PICTURES OF STARVING CHILDREN SELL RECORDS (*7) / NEVER MIND THE BALLOTS: HERE'S THE REST OF YOUR LIFE (*7) / ENGLISH REBEL SONGS 1381-1914 mini (*5) / SLAP! (*6) / SHHH (*8) / ANARCHY (*9) / SHOWBUSINESS! CHUMBAWAMBA LIVE (*5) / SWINGIN' WITH RAYMOND (*5) / TUBTHUMPER (*5) / UNEASY LISTENING compilation (*7)

ALICE NUTTER – vocals / **BOFF** (b. BILLY McCOID) – guitar, vocals, clarinet / **LOU** (b. LOUISE MARY WATTS) – vocals, guitar / **MAVIS DILLAN** – bass, trumpet, French horn / **HARRY** (b. DARREN HAMMER) drums / **DANBERT NOBACON** (b. ALAN WHALEY) – vocals / with **SIMON COMMONKNOWLEDGE** – keyboards, accordion, piano

—— (released 3 cassettes before the mid-80's)

Sep 85. (7"ep) *(AGIT 001)* **REVOLUTION**
Apr 86. (7") *(AGIT 002)* **WE ARE THE WORLD. / A STATE OF MIND**
In '86, they issued DESTROY FASCISM as The ANTIDOTE; alongside The EX
Oct 86. (lp) *(PROP 001)* **PICTURES OF STARVING CHILDREN SELL RECORDS**
– (prologue) / How to get your band on television / British colonialism and the BBC – Flickering pictures hypnotise / Commercial break / Unilever / More whitewashing / . . . An interlude. Beginning to take it back / Dutiful servants and political masters / Coca- colanisation / . . . And in a nutshell "food aid is our most powerful weapon" / Invasion.
Jul 87. (lp) *(PROP 002)* **NEVER MIND THE BALLOTS: HERE'S THE REST OF YOUR LIFE**
– Always tell the voter what the voter wants to hear / Come on baby (let's do the revolution) / The wasteland / Today's sermon / Ah-men / Mr. Heseltine meets his public / The candidates find common ground / Here's the rest of your life.
—— Under the name SCAB AID, they issued 'Let It Be' on the 'Scum' label.
Jul 88. (7") *(AGIT 003)* **FIGHT THE ALTON BILL. / SMASH CLAUSE 28**
Oct 88. (10"m-lp) *(PROP 003)* **ENGLISH REBEL SONGS 1381-1914**
– The Cutty wren / The diggers song / Colliers march / The triumph of General Ludd / Chartist anthem / Song of the times / Smashing of the van / World turned upside down / Poverty knock / Idris strike song / Hanging on the old barbed wire / The Cutty wren (reprise). *(re-iss. Feb93 lp/cd; PROP 3/+CD) on 'One Little Indian' lp/c/cd; TPLP 64/+C/CD) <US cd-iss. Jun98 on 'Imprint'; 8769>*
—— In Dec'89; they appeared on 'Agit Prop' Various Artists (SPORTCHESTRA) lp '101 SONGS ABOUT SPORT' *PROP 004*. Another Various 'THIS SPORTING LIFE' was iss.Aug'90.
—— added **DUNST** (b. DUNSTON BRUCE) – vocals, percussion, soprano sax / **COBIE** – live sound / + others
Jul 90. (cd/lp) *(CD+/PROP 7)* **SLAP!**
– Ulrike / Tiananmen Square / Cartrouble / Chase PC's flee attack by own dog / Rubens has been shot! / I never gave up: Rappoport's testament / Slap! / That's how grateful we are / Meinhof. *(re-iss. Feb95 & Jan99 on 'One Little Indian' lp/c/cd; TPLP 65/+C/CD)*
—— In Mar'91, CHUMBAWAMBA AND OTHER SUBVERSIVES released 7"; GREATEST HITS for 'Peasant Revolt'. At the same time ALICE and LOUISE (I think?) as The PASSION KILLERS released mail-order EP 'FOUR WAR IS SHIT SONGS' featuring tracks 'Shipbuilding', 'Reuters' + 2 for 'Rugger Bugger' records.
—— added **MATTY** (MC FUSION) – vocals (of CREDIT TO THE NATION) / **NEIL FERGUSON** – guitar, keyboards / **GEOFF SLAPHEAD** – fiddle / **HOWARD STOREY** – vocals
Jan 92. (7") **I NEVER GAVE UP: RAPPOPORT'S TESTAMENT. / LAUGHING**
(12") – ('A'-Rondo mix) / ('A'-Cass mix).
(cd-s) – (all 4 tracks). *(re-iss. Jul94 on 'Southern' 12"/cd-s; 18521-1/-2)*
Jun 92. (cd/c/lp) *(CD/TC+/PROP 11)* **SHHH**
– Shhh / Big mouth strikes again / Nothing that's new / Behave! / Snip snip snip / Look! no strings! / Happiness is just a chant away / Pop star kidnap / Sometimes plunder / You can't trust anyone nowadays / Stitch that. *(re-iss. Nov94 & Sep97 on 'Southern' cd/c/lp; 18515-2/-4/-1)*
Jul 92. (7") **NEVER SAY DI. / FOR THE LOVE OF A PRINCESS**
Nov 92. (12"/cd-s) *(AGIT 666/+CD)* **SOMEONE'S ALWAYS TELLING YOU HOW TO BEHAVE!** / (2-'A'mixes by PAPA BRITTLE)
Dec 92. (cd/c/lp) **JESUS H CHRIST**
– Alright now / Money, money, money / Solid gold easy action / Silly love songs / Hey you get off my cloud / Stairway to Heaven / Bigmouth strikes again / I should be so lucky.

Sep 93. (12"ep/c-ep/cd-ep; CHUMBAWAMBA & CREDIT TO THE NATION) *(79 TP 7C/12/7CD)* **ENOUGH IS ENOUGH. / HEAR NO BULLSHIT (on fire mix) / THE DAY THE NAZI DIED (1993 mix)**
Nov 93. (12"ep/c-ep/cd-ep) *(89 TP 12/7C/7CD)* **TIMEBOMB. / TECHNO THE BOMB / THE WORLD TURNED UPSIDE DOWN**
May 94. (lp/c/cd) *(TPLP 46/+C/CD) <40903>* **ANARCHY**
– Give the anarchist a cigarette / Timebomb / Homophobia / On being pushed / Heaven – Hell / Love me / Georgina / Doh! / Blackpool rock / This year's thing / Mouthful of shit / Never do what you are told / Bad dog / Enough is enough / Rage.
May 94. (12"ep-c-ep/cd-ep) *(119 TP 12/7C/7CD)* **HOMOPHOBIA (with The SISTERS OF PERPETUAL INDULGENCE). / MORALITY PLAY IN THREE ACTS / ('A'acappella mix) / SONG FOR DEREK JARMEN**
(cd-ep) *(119 TP7CDL)* – ('A'side) / Enough is enough (w / CREDIT TO THE NATION) / The day the Nazi died (w / CREDIT TO THE NATION) / Morality play in three acts.
Mar 95. (lp/c/cd) *(TPLP 56/+C/CD)* **SHOWBUSINESS! CHUMBAWAMBA LIVE (live)**
– Never do what you are told / I never gave up / Give the anarchist a cigarette / Heaven-Hell / That's how grateful we are / Homophobia / Morality play in three

acts / Bad dog / Stitch that / Mouthful of shit / The day the Nazi died / Time bomb (Jimmy Echo vocal) / Slag aid.
Oct 95. (7"/c-s) *(139 TP7/+C)* **UGH! YOUR UGLY HOUSES! / THIS GIRL**
(cd-s+=) *(139 TPCD)* – Mannequin / Hunchback of Notre Dame.
Oct 95. (d-lp/c/d-cd) *(TPLP 66/+C/CD)* **SWINGIN' WITH RAYMOND**
– This girl / Never let go / Just look at me now / Not the girl I used to be / The morning after (the night before) / Love can knock you over / All mixed up / This dress kills / Salome (let's twist again) / Oxymoron / Waiting, shouting / Hey you! outside now! / Ugh! your ugly houses.

E.M.I.   Republic

Aug 97. (c-s) *(TCEM 486) <56146>* **TUBTHUMPING / (Buttthumping mix) / (Danny Boy mix)**
(cd-s+=) *(CDEM 486)* – ('A'-Mawr mix: Pablo & Lawrie) / ('A'-Timeshard mix) / ('A'-Gunshot mix).
(7"red) *(EM 486)* – ('A'side) / Farewell to the Crown (featuring The OYSTER BAND) / Football song ("Shit ground, no fans").
Sep 97. (cd/c) *(CD/TC EMC 3773) <53099>* **TUBTHUMPER**
– Tubthumping / Amnesia / Drip drip drip / Big issue / Good ship lifestyle / One by one / Outsider / Creepy crawling / Mary Mary / Small town / I want more / Scapegoat. *(re-iss. Jun98 cd+=/c+=; 495238-2/-4)* – Top of the world (ole, ole, ole).
Jan 98. (c-s) *(TCEM 498)* **AMNESIA / AMNESIA (Zion Train 359 Amherst Road mix) / TUBTHUMPING (Escape From New York mix)**
(cd-s) *(CDEM 498)* – (first 2 tracks) / ('A'-Done Lying Down mix) / ('A'-Jimmy Echo version) / ('A'-Decontrol mix).
(cd-s) *(CDEMS 498)* – (first & third tracks) / Tubthumping (original) / Tubthumping (Tin Tin Out mix).
May 98. (c-s) *(TCEM 511)* **TOP OF THE WORLD (OLE, OLE, OLE) / I'M A WINNER BABY / STRIKE! (Barnsley 3, Man Utd 2 mix)**
(cd-s) *(CDEM 511)* – (first 2 tracks) / The best is yet to come (acoustic) / The best is yet to come.
Feb 99. (cd) *(499231-2)* **UNEASY LISTENING** (compilation)
– And in a nutshell / Mouthful of shit / Behave / Timebomb / Morality play in three acts / Enough is enough / On being pushed / Hanging on the old barb wire / Ugh! your ugly houses! / Look no strings! / Bigmouth strikes again / This girl / Smash clause 28 / Waiting, shouting / Song of the mother in debt / On the day the Nazi died / Give the anarchist a cigarette / Nothing knocks me over / We don't go to God's house anymore.

Seeland   Seeland

Apr 99. (cd-s; with NEGATIVLAND) *<(SEELAND 020CD)>* **ABC'S OF ANARCHISM**

– compilations, others, etc. –

Feb 92. (lp/cd) Agit Prop; *(PROP 4)* **FIRST 2**
– (as said 1st 2 albums, originally Aug89 as '100 SONGS ABOUT SPORT'; *PROP 004) (re-iss. Feb95 on 'One Little Indian' d-lp/c/cd; TPLP 63/+C/CD)*
Apr 96. (cd+book) One Little Indian; *(EYE 1)* **PORTRAITS OF ANARCHISTS**
—— DANBERT released a CD, 'THE UNFAIRYTALE' in Mar'98
Jan 99. (cd) One Little Indian; *(TPLP 65CD)* **LOVE / HATE**

CHURCH (dig out; Great Alt & Indie . . .)

CINDERELLA (dig out; Great Metal . . .)

CINERAMA (see under ⇒ **WEDDING PRESENT**)

CITY (see under ⇒ **KING, Carole**)

CLANNAD (dig out; 4th edition)

Eric CLAPTON

Born: ERIC PATRICK CLAPP, March 30th 1945, Ripley, Surrey, England. Brought up by his grandparents, CLAPTON later attended Kingston Art College where he studied stained glass design. Heavily influenced by ROBERT JOHNSON, B.B. KING and BUDDY GUY, CLAPTON was a self taught musician (he had been given a £14 guitar by his grandparents on his 14th birthday) and began playing with TOM McGUINNESS in his first band, The ROOSTERS, in January 1963. Eight months later, they left The ROOSTERS and joined CASEY JONES AND THE ENGINEERS, although this didn't last long and CLAPTON's first big break came in October 1963 when he was asked to replace TOP TOPHAM in The YARDBIRDS. The latter act had just taken over from The ROLLING STONES as the resident band at the Crawdaddy Club in Richmond; CLAPTON, nicknamed "Slowhand" by the band's manager, GIORGIO GOMELSKY, quickly outshone the singer, KEITH RELF, and became the principal focal point of the group, although he left them on the eve of their chart success in 1965, complaining that their music had become too commercial. CLAPTON had recorded only one album with The YARDBIRDS but his potential shone out on 'FIVE LONG YEARS' and 'SMOKESTACK LIGHTNING'. The highlight of the album, entitled, 'FIVE LIVE YARDBIRDS', was a rendition of Chuck Berry's 'TOO MUCH MONKEY BUSINESS'. He then joined JOHN MAYALL's BLUESBREAKERS in April 1965 and around this time the famous, although unsubstantiated phrase, 'CLAPTON IS GOD' was coined. Again, he only recorded one album although it was to be the spark for the blues boom of the sixties. That album was 'BLUESBREAKERS WITH ERIC CLAPTON', recorded over one weekend with no track laid down in more than one take. He left THE BLUESBREAKERS in 1966 and immediately formed CREAM with GINGER BAKER and JACK BRUCE. CREAM broke up in November 1968 and CLAPTON played on the GEORGE HARRISON-penned BEATLES track, 'While My Guitar Gently Weeps' (under the name, L'ANGELO MYSTERIOSO), and also contributed to HARRISON's solo album, 'WONDERWALL MUSIC'. CLAPTON subsequently formed BLIND FAITH with BAKER, STEVE WINWOOD and RIC GRECH, and although they topped the charts on both sides of the Atlantic with their eponymous debut set, they could not cope with the high pressure expected of a "supergroup", and broke up in 1970. He was still only 24 but fame had taken its toll and he retreated into the ranks of DELANEY & BONNIE AND FRIENDS from which he formed his own, equally laid back DEREK AND THE DOMINOES. By this time CLAPTON was actively trying to shun publicity and even refused to have his name on the cover of the classic album, 'LAYLA AND OTHER ASSORTED LOVE SONGS'. Meanwhile, his debut solo lp was recorded in Los Angeles in 1970; issued shortly after, it reached the UK and US Top 20. The following year, the second DEREK AND THE DOMINOES album was scrapped due to the band's worsening drugs problem and they decided to call it a day. CLAPTON went into seclusion, only coming out for the occasional charity performance (including the Concert For Bangladesh). Ironically, 'LAYLA' (a song written about GEORGE HARRISON's wife PATTI), gave the now defunct DEREK AND THE DOMINOES a belated Top 10 hit in the UK in 1972. PETE TOWNSHEND, concerned for his friend's health, persuaded CLAPTON to take part in an all-star comeback concert in 1973 at London's Rainbow Theatre with RON WOOD, STEVE WINWOOD, JIM CAPALDI and many others. The performance was recorded and the resulting album, 'ERIC CLAPTON'S RAINBOW CONCERT' reached a respectable Top 20 slot on both sides of the Atlantic. The success of the project and the album did not, however, convince CLAPTON to step back into the limelight and he retreated once more. The guitarist underwent a course of electronically adapted acupuncture in 1974, eventually got rid of the habit and told record boss, Robert Stigwood, that he was ready to come back. TOM DOWD was brought in as producer although CLAPTON had only two songs in mind, 'PLEASE BE WITH ME' by Charles Scott Boyer and his own, 'GIVE ME STRENGTH'. A new band was assembled with CARL RADLE, JAMIE OLDAKER, DICK SIMS, GEORGE TERRY and YVONNE ELLIMAN and MARCY LEVY (LEVY would later resurface as MARCELLA DETROIT in SHAKESPEAR'S SISTER). In August 1974, the first single from the comeback sessions, a brilliant version of Bob Marley's 'I SHOT THE SHERIFF', was released and reached an unexpected UK number 9; many observers speculated that he was ill-advised in trying to cross over music boundaries. Later the same month, the accompanying album, '461 OCEAN BOULEVARD' (named after the address of the recording studio), was released to UK Top 3 success. His long guitar solos had now been trimmed down in line with his more basic approach to songwriting, apparent on subsequent hit album, 'THERE'S ONE IN EVERY CROWD' (1975); his version of 'SWING LOW SWEET CHARIOT' reached UK Top 20. In August of the same year, he hit the charts with yet another cover, Bob Dylan's 'KNOCKIN'ON HEAVEN'S DOOR', while the live album, 'E.C. WAS HERE', kept his profile high. During this period, GEORGE TERRY was taking on most of the lead guitar work as CLAPTON was still reluctant to be in the forefront. In September 1976, 'NO REASON TO CRY' reached UK Top 10, its credibility factor enhanced by the talents of BOB DYLAN & THE BAND. CLAPTON reciprocated by performing 'FURTHER ON UP THE ROAD' (with new band member, SERGIO PASTORA, on percussion) at THE BAND's 'LAST WALTZ' farewell concert. 'SLOWHAND' released in 1977, was only kept off the US top spot by 'Saturday Night Fever', while the painfully sentimental single, 'WONDERFUL TONIGHT' (the second song written for PATTI) reached Top 20; other highlights were JJ Cale's 'COCAINE' and John Martyn's 'MAY YOU NEVER'. The following year's 'BACKLESS' followed in much the same head-nodding vein, CLAPTON obviously remaining oblivious to the energy and attitude of the burgeoning punk scene. In March 1979, he decided to embark on a world tour with an all new UK band consisting of ALBERT LEE, CHRIS STAINTON, DAVE MARKEE and HENRY SPINETTI. The veteran troupe recorded live tracks at the Budokan in Japan (the resulting album, 'JUST ONE NIGHT' was a transatlantic Top 5 success the following year), and during the tour, CLAPTON finally married his long time love, PATTI. The 70's had not been an easy time for CLAPTON and his disciples, his heroin addiction subsequently replaced by a copious intake of cognac. In May 1980, ex-PROCOL HARUM stalwart, GARY BROOKER, replaced STAINTON for a British tour, although later in the month, CLAPTON was saddened to hear that his former bass player, CARL RADLE, had died of chronic kidney disease. CLAPTON wasn't in the best of health himself, the guitarist admitted to hospital in Minnesota during his 1980 tour of America with doctors estimating that he would have had under an hour to live had his ulcer burst. With his health restored, and with the revitalisation of the adult rock market (beginning with the early 80's introduction of the Compact Disc), CLAPTON re-emerged as a revered elder statesman of rock, although he had a further setback when he was hospitalised in April 1981 after a car accident. He recovered from this and went on to contribute to PHIL COLLINS' debut album (beginning a long standing friendship/working relationship) and also returned to live work by performing with JEFF BECK at 'The Secret Policeman's Other Ball'. CLAPTON's last album for 'R.S.O.', 'ANOTHER TICKET', reached the UK Top 20, although success was limited in the States; later that year he decided to form his own 'Duck' Records. The following year he released 'MONEY AND CIGARETTES', the album (featuring RY COODER

and ALBERT LEE amongst others) seeing him back in the Top 20 on both sides of the Atlantic. In between numerous charity concerts, "God" managed to record his next album, 'BEHIND THE SUN' (1985), the Top 10 (US Top 40) set being produced by PHIL COLLINS, TED TEMPLEMAN and RUSS TITELMAN. Later that year, CLAPTON ventured into TV soundtrack work, co-writing the Ivor Novello award winning 'EDGE OF DARKNESS' theme with MICHAEL KAMEN. By this point, CLAPTON was in his slick, Armani suit-wearing period, his polished follow-up, 'AUGUST' (again produced by COLLINS), contained the semi-classic tracks, 'BEHIND THE MASK' and the TINA TURNER duet 'TEARING US APART'. In 1987 he began his first series of concerts at the Royal Albert Hall, London (they would become an annual event and by 1990, he had built up to 18 consecutive nights). Towards the end of the decade, CLAPTON completed the score for the Mickey Rourke-starring film, 'Homeboy', while his next album proper, 'JOURNEYMAN' (1989; Top 5), found CLAPTON rediscovering his guitar. Tragedy was to rear its ugly head again in 1990, when, on August the 27th, three members of his entourage died along with STEVIE RAY VAUGHAN in a helicopter crash following a concert in East Troy, Wisconsin. In 1991, at his annual Albert Hall residency (now up to a staggering 24 shows; the performances would subsequently be released as concert set, '24 NIGHTS'), he decided to split each show into five segments – a four piece band, a second four piece band with different percussion, a nine piece band, a blues band with guitarists ALBERT COLLINS, ROBERT CRAY, BUDDY GUY and JIMMIE VAUGHAN, and a nine piece band with orchestra conducted by MICHAEL KAMEN. Incredibly, CLAPTON underwent further emotional trauma, when in March that year, his 4-year old son, CONOR, died after falling out of a skyscraper window. Not surprisingly, CLAPTON shunned the world for some time, only reappearing in September on BUDDY GUY's first album for over a decade, 'Damn Right I've Got The Blues'. A live version of 'WONDERFUL TONIGHT' (from the '24 NIGHTS' set) reached the UK Top 30 and rounded off a year of highs and lows to match any that he'd faced previously. 1992 began with a recording of an 'MTV UNPLUGGED' show, and, backed by NATHAN EAST, ANDY FAIRWEATHER LOW, RAY COOPER and CHUCK LEAVELL, he performed new material, 'THE CIRCUS LEFT TOWN' and 'TEARS IN HEAVEN' along with standards including a drastically pared down version of 'LAYLA'. The resulting album went on to be the most successful of his career (UK No.2 and US No.1), although he allegedly didn't even want it released! It also showed CLAPTON's return to his blues roots with Big Bill Broozny's 'HEY HEY', a stunning version of Robert Johnson's 'MALTED MILK' and Muddy Waters' 'ROLLIN AND TUMBLIN'. However, it was the aforementioned heart rendering tribute to his son, 'TEARS IN HEAVEN' (lyrics by Will Jennings) that stole the show, CLAPTON's voice wracked with the pain of his bereavement (the song subsequently won him another Ivor Novello award). Following on from more film soundtrack work (i.e. 'LETHAL WEAPON 3' and 'RUSH'), his 1994 album, 'FROM THE CRADLE', saw him completely back to his blues roots with standards like Willie Dixon's 'GROANIN THE BLUES' and Lowell Fulson's 'RECONSIDER BABY'. Although the brilliant 'MOTHERLESS CHILD' lingered in the lower regions of the charts, he finally scored his first No.1 single backing CHRISSIE HYNDE, CHER and NENEH CHERRY on the 1995 Childline single, 'LOVE CAN BUILD A BRIDGE'. CLAPTON continues to tour, play charity gigs and has even taken to giving interviews (something he wasn't exactly noted for in the past). • **Covered:** AFTER MIDNIGHT + I'LL MAKE LOVE TO YOU ANYTIME (J.J. Cale) / SWING LOW SWEET CHARIOT (spiritual/gospel trad.) / WILLIE AND THE HAND JIVE + CRAZY COUNTRY HOP (Johnny Otis) / HAVE YOU EVER LOVED A WOMAN (Billy Myles) / NOBODY KNOWS YOU WHEN YOU'RE DOWN AND OUT (Jimmy Cox) / KEY TO THE HIGHWAY (Sager/Broozny) / KNOCK ON WOOD (Eddie Floyd) / BEHIND THE MASK (Michael Jackson co-wrote w/others; covered by Yellow Magic Orchestra) / WATCH YOURSELF (Buddy Guy) / WORRIED LIFE BLUES (Mecio Merryweather) / HOODOO MAN (Sonny Boy Williamson) / HOUND DOG (hit; Elvis Presley) / DOUBLE TROUBLE (Otis Rush) / SIGN LANGUAGE (Bob Dylan) / FLOATING BRIDGE and EVERYBODY OUGHTA (Sleepy John Estes) / LEAD ME ON (Womack/Womack) / BEFORE YOU ACCUSE ME (Bo Diddley) / RUNNING ON FAITH + PRETENDING (. . . Williams) / RUN SO FAR (Wilbert Harrison) / DON'T KNOW WHICH WAY TO GO (Willie Dixon) / etc. • **Trivia:** In 1966 (with JACK BRUCE, PAUL JONES, STEVE WINWOOD and PETE YORK), CLAPTON briefly formed The POWERHOUSE, who recorded three songs for 'Elektra' compilation, 'WHAT'S SHAKIN'.

Album rating: ERIC CLAPTON (*7) / LAYLA AND OTHER ASSORTED LOVE SONGS; Derek & The Dominoes (*9) / THE RAINBOW CONCERT (*5) / IN CONCERT; Derek & The Dominoes (*5) / 461 OCEAN BOULEVARD (*8) / THERE'S ONE IN EVERY CROWD (*5) / E.C. WAS HERE (*5) / NO REASON TO CRY (*6) / SLOWHAND (*7) / BACKLESS (*6) / JUST ONE NIGHT (*3) / ANOTHER TICKET (*6) / TIME PIECES: BEST OF ERIC CLAPTON compilation (*7) / MONEY AND CIGARETTES (*6) / TIME PIECES II: LIVE IN THE 70'S collection (*6) / BEHIND THE SUN (*5) / AUGUST (*6) / CROSSROADS compilation (*9) / JOURNEYMAN (*7) / 24 NIGHTS (*4) / UNPLUGGED (*7) / FROM THE CRADLE (*6) / THE CREAM OF ERIC CLAPTON collection (*7) / CROSSROADS 2: LIVE IN THE 70's collection (*6) / PILGRIM (*5)

ERIC CLAPTON – vocals, guitar (ex-DELANEY & BONNIE, ex-BLIND FAITH ex-CREAM, ex-JOHN MAYALL'S BLUESBREAKERS, ex-YARDBIRDS, etc) featured his **DOMINOES** musicians plus **STEPHEN STILLS** – guitar

		Polydor	Atco	
Aug 70. (lp) (2383 021) <329> **ERIC CLAPTON**		17	13	Jul70

– Slunky / Bad boy / Lonesome and a long way from home / After midnight / Easy now / Blues power / Bottle of red wine / Lovin' you lovin' me / I've told you for the last time / I don't know why / Let it rain. *(re-iss. Nov82 & Feb83)*

—— In Oct 70, CLAPTON guested on KING CURTIS single 'TEASIN'. / 'SOULIN'

Nov 70. (7") *(2001 096)* <6784> **AFTER MIDNIGHT. / EASY NOW** ☐ 18 Oct70

DEREK AND THE DOMINOES

ERIC CLAPTON – vox, guitar with **BOBBY WHITLOCK** – keyboards, vocals / **CARL RADLE** – bass / **JIM GORDON** – drums / **and guest DUANE ALLMAN** – guitar

Sep 70. (7"w-drawn) *(2058 057)* **TELL THE TRUTH. / ROLL IT OVER** ☐ –
Dec 70. (7") *(2058 130)* <6809> **LAYLA. / BELL BOTTOM BLUES** ☐ –
Jan 71. (d-lp) *(2625 005)* <SD2 704> **LAYLA & OTHER ASSORTED**
LOVE SONGS 16 Nov70
– I looked away / Bell bottom blues / Keep on growing / Nobody knows you when you're down and out / I am yours / Anyday / Key to the highway / Tell the truth / Why does love got to be so sad? / Have you ever loved a woman / Little wing / It's too late / Layla / Thorn tree in the garden. *(re-iss. Aug74 & Nov77; 2671 110) (re-iss. Jan84; SPDLP 1) (cd-iss. Mar91; 823277-2) (LAYLA REMASTERED – 20th ANNIVERSARY EDITION d-cd/d-c; 847083-2/4)*
Feb 71. (7") <6803> **BELL BOTTOM BLUES. / KEEP ON GROWING** – 91
Mar 71. (7") <6809> **LAYLA. / I AM YOURS** – 51
     <re-iss. Apr72; 15040> – hit No.10
Jul 72. (7") *(2058 130)* **LAYLA. / I AM YOURS** 7 –

—— split Spring '71 but left behind posthumous album below, etc

			R.S.O.	Polydor
Sep 72. (7") *<15049>* **LET IT RAIN. / EASY NOW** – 48
Mar 73. (d-lp) *(2659 020)* <28800> **DEREK AND THE DOMINOES –**
IN CONCERT (live) 36 20 Jan73
– Why does love got to be so sad? / Got to get better in a little while / Let it rain / Presence of the Lord / Tell the truth / Bottle of red wine / Roll it over / Blues power / Have you ever loved a woman. *(d-cd-iss. Jan94)*
Apr 73. (7") *(2090 104)* **WHY DOES LOVE GOT TO BE SO SAD?**
(live). / PRESENCE OF THE LORD (live) ☐ –
Jun 73. (7") *<15056>* **BELL BOTTOM BLUES. / LITTLE WING** – 78 Feb73

—— In '71 ERIC had virtually retired into session work. He appeared in GEORGE HARRISON's Bangla Desh concert, 1st Aug'71.

ERIC CLAPTON

returned for a one-off concert at the Rainbow, 13Jan73 with **PETE TOWNSHEND** – guitar / **RON WOOD** – guitar / **STEVE WINWOOD** – keyboards / **JIMMY KARSTEIN & JIM CAPALDI** – drums / **REE BOP** – percussion / **RIC GRECH** – bass

			Polydor	R.S.O.
Sep 73. (lp) *(2479 116)* <877> **THE RAINBOW CONCERT** 19 18
– Badge / Roll it over / Presence of the Lord / Pearly queen / After midnight / Little wing. *(re-iss. Aug83 on 'R.S.O.' lp/c; SPE LP/MC 23) (cd-iss. 1988; 831 320-2) (re-iss. 1993; 527472-2/-4)*
Oct 73. (7") *<400>* **PRESENCE OF THE LORD (live). / WHY DOES**
LOVE GOT TO BE SO BAD? – ☐

—— **ERIC CLAPTON** went solo again with **GEORGE TERRY** – guitar (ex-sessions) / **CARL RADLE** – bass (ex-DEREK AND THE DOMINOES, ex-DELANEY & BONNIE) / **DICK SIMS** – keyboards (ex-BOB SEGER) / **JAMIE OLDAKER** – drums (ex-BOB SEGER) / **MARCY LEVY** – b.vocals (ex-BOB SEGER) / **YVONNE ELLIMAN**

			R.S.O.	R.S.O.
Jul 74. (7") *(2090 132)* <409> **I SHOT THE SHERRIF. / GIVE ME**
STRENGTH 9 1
Aug 74. (lp/c) *(2479/ 116)* <4801> **461 OCEAN BOULEVARD** 3 1 Jul74
– Motherless children / Give me strength / Willie and the hand jive / Get ready / I shot the sheriff / I can't hold out / Please be with me / Steady rollin' man / Mainline Florida. *(re-iss. Aug83 lp/c; SPE LP/TC 24) (cd-iss. Nov89; 839 874-2)*
Oct 74. (7") *(2090 139)* <503> **WILLIE AND THE HAND JIVE. /**
MAINLINE FLORIDA ☐ 26

—— added **MARCY LEVY** – vocals, tambourine
Apr 75. (7") *(2058 560)* <509> **SWING LOW SWEET CHARIOT. /**
PRETTY BLUE EYES 19 ☐
Apr 75. (lp/c) *(2479/ 132)* <4806> **THERE'S ONE IN EVERY CROWD** 15 21
– We've been told (Jesus soon coming) / Swing low sweet chariot / Little Rachel / Don't blame me / The sky is crying / Singing the blues / Better make it through today / Pretty blue eyes / High / Opposites. *(re-iss. Mar85 lp/c; SPE LP/MC 92) (cd-iss. Nov86; 829 649-2)*
Aug 75. (7") *(2090 166)* <513> **KNOCKIN' ON HEAVEN'S DOOR. /**
SOMEONE LIKE YOU 38 ☐
Sep 75. (lp/c) *(2479 179)* <4809> **E.C. WAS HERE (live)** 14 20
– Have you ever loved a woman / Presence of the Lord / Drifting blues / Can't find my way home / Ramblin' on my mind / Further on up the road. *(re-iss. Aug83 lp/c; SPE LP/MC 21) (cd-iss. Jul92; 831519-2)*

—— added **SERGIO PASTORA** – percussion (ex-BOB SEGER)
Aug 76. (lp/c) *(2479 179)* <3801> **NO REASON TO CRY** 8 15 Sep76
– Beautiful thing / Carnival / Sign language / County jail blues / All our past times / Hello old friend / Double trouble / Innocent times / Hungry / Black summer rain. *(re-iss. Aug83 lp/c; SPE LP/MC 2) (cd-iss. Dec86; 813 582-2)*
Oct 76. (7") *(2090 208)* <861> **HELLO OLD FRIEND. / ALL OUT**
PAST TIMES ☐ 24
Feb 77. (7") *(2090 284)* <868> **CARNIVAL. / HUNGRY** ☐ ☐

—— augmented by five piece when ELLIMAN then PASTORA both went solo
Nov 77. (7") *(2090 294)* <886> **LAY DOWN SALLY. / COCAINE** 39 3
Nov 77. (lp/c) *(2479 201)* <3030> **SLOWHAND** 23 2
– Cocaine / Wonderful tonight / Lay down sally / Next time you see her / We're all the way / The core / May you never / Mean old Frisco / Peaches and diesel. *(re-iss. Aug83 lp/c)(cd; SPE LP/MC)(823 276-2)*
Mar 78. (7") *(2090 275)* <895> **WONDERFUL TONIGHT. / PEACHES**
AND DIESEL ☐ 16 May78

ERIC CLAPTON & HIS BAND
ERIC now backed up only by **SIMS, OLDAKER** and **RADLE** when MARCY LEVY went solo and GEORGE TERRY went into sessions.
Sep 78. (7") *(RSO 21)* <910> **PROMISES. / WATCH OUT FOR LUCY** 37 9
     40

Nov 78. (lp/c) *(RSD/TRSD 5001)* <3039> **BACKLESS** 18 8
– Walk out in the rain / Watch for Lucy / I'll make love to you anytime / Roll it / Tell me that you love me / If I don't be there by morning / Early in the morning / Promises / Golden ring / Tulsa time. *(re-iss. Aug83 lp/c; SPE LP/MC 1) (cd-iss. Jan89; 813 581-2)*
Mar 79. (7") *<928>* **TULSA TIME. / COCAINE** –
Mar 79. (7") *(RSO 24)* **IF I DON'T GET THERE BY MORNING. /**
TULSA TIME –

—— added **ALBERT LEE** – guitar (ex-solo artist, etc.) to complete new band, **DAVE MARKEE** – bass repl.CARL / **HENRY SPINETTI** drums repl. JAMIE
May 80. (d-lp/d-c) *(RSDX/+C 2)* <4202> **JUST ONE NIGHT (live at**
Budokhan) 3 2
– Tulsa time / Early in the morning / Lay down Sally / Wonderful tonight / If I don't be there by morning / Worried life blues / All our past times / After midnight / Double trouble / Setting me up / Blues power / Ramblin' on my mind / Cocaine / Farther on up the road. *(d-cd-iss. Nov88; 800 093-2)*
Jul 80. (7") *<1039>* **TULSA TIME (live). / COCAINE (live)** 30 Jun80
Oct 80. (7") *<1051>* **BLUES POWER (live). / EARLY IN THE**
MORNING (live) – 76

—— **GARY BROOKER & CHRIS STAINTON** – keyboards repl. DICK
Feb 81. (7") *(RSO 74)* <1060> **I CAN'T STAND IT. / BLACK ROSE** 10
Feb 81. (lp/c) *(RSD/TRSD 5008)* <3095> **ANOTHER TICKET** 18 7 Mar81
– Something special / Black rose / Blow wind blow / Another ticket / I can't stand it / Hold me Lord / Floating bridge / Catch me if you can / Rita Mae. *(re-iss. Apr84 lp/c; SPE LP/MC 67) (cd-iss. Feb87; 827 579-2)*
Apr 81. (7") *(RSO 75)* <1064> **ANOTHER TICKET. / RITA MAE** 78

—— **ERIC CLAPTON** retained **LEE** and recruited **RY COODER, ROGER HAWKINS, DONALD 'DUCK' DUNN** plus backing vocalists **JOHN SAMBATAO** and **CHUCK KIRKPATRICK**

			Duck-Warners	Duck-Warners
Feb 83. (7") *(W 9780)* <29780> **I'VE GOT A ROCK'N'ROLL HEART. /**
MAN OVERBOARD 18 Jan83
     (12"+=) *(W 9780T)* – Everybody oughta make a change.
Feb 83. (lp/c) *(W 3773/+4)* <23773> **MONEY AND CIGARETTES** 13 16
– Everybody outta make a change / The shape you're in / Ain't going down / I've got a rock'n'roll heart / Man overboard / Pretty girl / Man in love / Crosscut saw / Slow down Linda / Crazy country hop. *(cd-iss. 1984; 923 773-2) (cd re-iss. Feb95;)*
Apr 83. (7"/7"pic-d) *(W 9701/+P)* **THE SHAPE YOU'RE IN. /**
CROSSCUT SAW 75
     (12"+=) *(W 9701T)* – Pretty girl.
May 83. (7") *(W 9651)* **SLOW DOWN LINDA. / CRAZY COUNTRY**
HOP ☐
     (12"+=) *(W 9651T)* – The shape you're in.

—— **CLAPTON** put together a new band. **TIM RENWICK** – guitar (ex-SUTHERLAND BROTHERS & QUIVER) / **CHRIS STAINTON** – keyboards (ex-solo, ex-JOE COCKER) / **DONALD 'DUCK' DUNN** – bass (ex-BOOKER T. AND THE M.G.'s) / **JAMIE OLDAKER** – drums (returned) **MARCY LEVY** (returned) **& SHAUN MURPHY** – backing vocals
Mar 85. (7") *(W 9069)* <29081> **FOREVER MAN. / TOO BAD** 51 26
     (12"+=) *(W 9069T)* – Something's happening.
Mar 85. (lp/c/cd) *(925166-1/-4/-2)* <25166> **BEHIND THE SUN** 8 34
– She's waiting / See what love can do / Same old blues / Knock on wood / Something's happening / Forever man / It all depends / Tangled in love / Never make you cry / Just like a prisoner / Behind the sun. *(re-iss. cd Feb95;)*
May 85. (7") *<28986>* **SEE WHAT LOVE CAN DO. / SHE'S WAITING** 89
Jul 85. (7") *(W 8954)* **SHE'S WAITING. / JAILBAIT** –
Dec 85. (7") by ERIC CLAPTON & MICHAEL KAMEN *(RESL 178)* **EDGE OF DARKNESS. / SHOOT OUT** 65 –
     (c-s)(12") *(Z/12 RSL 178)* – ('A'side) / Escape from North Moor. *(re-iss. cd-ep.Feb89; CDRSL 178)*
     (above from TV series 'Edge Of Darkness' on 'BBC' records)
Nov 86. (lp/c)(cd) *(WX 71/+C)(925476-2)* <25476> **AUGUST** 3 37 Dec86
– It's in the way that you use it / Run / Tearing us apart / Bad influence / Hung up on your love / Take a chance / Hold on / Miss you / Holy mother / Behind the mask. *(cd+=)* – Grand illusion. *(re-iss. cd Feb95;)*
Jan 87. (7") *(W 8461)* **BEHIND THE MASK. / GRAND ILLUSION** 15
     (12"+=) *(W 8461T)* – Wanna make love to you.
     (d7"+=) *(W 8461F)* – White room (live) / Crossroads (live).
Mar 87. (7") *(W 8397)* **IT'S IN THE WAY THAT YOU USE IT. / BAD**
INFLUENCE ☐
     (d7+=/12"+=) *(W 8397 8397 F/T)* – Old ways / Pretty girl.

—— **GREG PHILLINGANES** also joined
Jun 87. (7") by ERIC CLAPTON & TINA TURNER *(W 8299)*
TEARING US APART. / HOLD ON 56
     (12"+=) *(W 8299T)* – Run.
Nov 87. (7") *(W 8141)* **HOLY MOTHER. / TANGLED IN LOVE** ☐
     (12"+=) *(W 8141T)* – Behind the mask / Forever man.

—— now backed in concert by **BUCKWHEAT ZYDECO**
Feb 89. (cd/c/lp) *(CD/TC+/V 2741)* **HOMEBOY (Soundtrack w/**
others on 'Virgin' records UK) ☐
– Travelling east / Johnny / Call me if you need me (MAGIC SAM) / Bridge / Pretty baby (J.B. HUTTO & THE NEW HAWKS) / Dixie / Ruby's loft / I want to love you baby (PEGGY SCOTT / JO JO BENSON) / Bike ride / Ruby / Living in the real world (The BRAKES) / Final flight / Dixie / Homeboy. *(cd+=)* – Country bikin' / Party / Training / Chase.

—— now with **ALAN CLARKE, ROBERT CRAY, GEORGE HARRISON, PHIL COLLINS,** etc
Nov 89. (7") *<22732>* **PRETENDING. / BEFORE YOU ACCUSE ME** – 55
Nov 89. (lp)(c/cd) *(WX 322)(926074-4/-2)* <26074> **JOURNEYMAN** 3 16
– Pretending / Anything for your love / Bad love / Running on faith / Hard times / Hound dog / No alibis / Run so far / Old love / Breaking point / Lead me on / Before you accuse me.
Jan 90. (7") *(W 2644)* **BAD LOVE. / BEFORE YOU ACCUSE ME** – –
     (c-s/12"/cd-s) *(W 2644 C/T/CD)* – ('A'side) / Badge (live) / Let it rain (live).
Mar 90. (7") *<19980>* **BAD LOVE. / HARD TIMES** – 88
Mar 90. (7"/7"box/c-s) *(W 9981/+B/C)* **NO ALIBIS. / RUNNING**
ON FAITH 53 ☐

(12"+=) (W 9981T) – Behind the mask (live) / Cocaine (live).
(cd-s+=) (W 9981CD) – No alibis (live) / Cocaine (live).
Jun 90. (7") (W 9970) **PRETENDING. / HARD TIMES**
(12"+=) (W 9970T) – Knock on wood.
(cd-s++=) (W 9970CD) – Behind the sun.
—— with **ALAN CLARKE** – keyboards / **NATHAN EAST** – bass / **STEVE FERRONE** – drums / **PHIL PALMER** – guitar / **RAY COOPER** – guitar / **RICHARD TEE** – piano / **CRAIG PHILLINGAMES** – keyboards, synths. and The NATIONAL PHILHARMONIC ORCHESTRA.
Oct 91. (d-cd)(d-lp/d-c) (7599 <26420-2>)(WX 373/+C) **24 NIGHTS (live)** `17` `38`
– Badge / Running on faith / White room / Sunshine of your love / Watch yourself / Have you ever loved a woman / Worried life blues / Hoodoo man / Pretending / Bad love / Old love / Wonderful tonight / Bell bottom blues / Hard times / Edge of darkness.
Nov 91. (7") (W 0069) **WONDERFUL TONIGHT (live). / EDGE OF DARKNESS (live)** `30` `-`
(c-s/12"/cd-s) (W 0069 C/T/CD) – ('A'side) / Layla (band version) / Cocaine.
Jan 92. (cd) (7599 <26794-2>) **RUSH (Soundtrack)** `24`
– Tears in Heaven / Will Gaines / Tracks and lines / Realization / New recruit / Preludia fugue / Kristen and Jim / Help me up / Cold turkey / Don't know which way to go. (re-iss. cd Feb95;)
—— **CHUCK LEAVELL** – keyboards (ex-ALLMANS) repl. CRAIG and RICHARD / **ANDY FAIRWEATHER-LOW** – guitar (ex-AMEN CORNER, ex-solo) repl. PHIL / backing singers **KATIE KISSOON + TESSA NILES**
Jan 92. (7"/c-s) (W 0081/+C) **TEARS IN HEAVEN / WHITE ROOM (live)** `5` `-`
(12"+=/cd-s+=) (W 0081 T/CD) – Tracks & lines / Bad love (live).
Jan 92. (c-s) <19038> **TEARS IN HEAVEN / TRACKS AND LINES** `-` `2`
—— In Jul'92, ERIC teamed up with ELTON JOHN on single 'RUNAWAY TRAIN'. A month later, STING was his co-collaborator on another hit 'IT'S PROBABLY ME'.
Sep 92. (7"/c-s) (W 0134/+C) **LAYLA (live acoustic). / TEARS IN HEAVEN (live acoustic)** `45` `-`
(cd-s+=) (W 0134CD) – (MTV unplugged interview).
Sep 92. (c-s) <18787> **LAYLA (live acoustic) / SIGNE (live acoustic)** `-` `12`
Sep 92. (cd)(lp/c) (9362 <45024-2>)(WX 480/+C) **UNPLUGGED (live acoustic)** `2` `1`
– Signe / Before you accuse me / Hey hey / Tears in Heaven / Lonely stranger / Nobody knows when you're down & out / Layla / Running on faith / Walkin' blues / Alberta / San Francisco Bay blues / Malted milk / Old love / Rollin' & tumblin'.
Sep 94. (cd/c/lp) (9362 <45737-2/-4/-1>) **FROM THE CRADLE** `1` `1`
– Third degree / Hoochie coochie man / Standin' round cryin' / Groanin' the blues / Blues before sunrise / Reconsider baby / Five long years / I'm tore down / How long blues / Goin' away baby / Blues leave me alone / Sinner's prayer / Motherless child / It hurts me too / Someday after a while.
Oct 94. (c-s) (W 0271C) **MOTHERLESS CHILD. / DRIFTIN'** `63`
(12"+=/cd-s+=) (W 0271CD) – County jail blues / 32-20 blues.
—— In Mar'95, alongside CHER, CHRISSIE HYNDE and NENEH CHERRY, he hit UK No.1 with charity Comic Relief single 'LOVE CAN BUILD A BRIDGE'.
Jul 96. (c-s) (W 0358C) <17621> **CHANGE THE WORLD / DANNY BOY** `18` `5`
(cd-s+=) (W 0358CD) – ('A'instrumental).
Mar 98. (cd/c) (<9362 46577-2/-4>) **PILGRIM** `6` `4`
– My father's eyes / River of tears / Pilgrim / Broken hearted / One chance / Circus / Going down slow / Fall like rain / Born in time / Sick and tired / Needs his woman / She's gone / You were there / Inside of me.
Mar 98. (c-s) (W 0443C) **MY FATHER'S EYES / THEME FROM A MOVIE THAT NEVER HAPPENED** `33`
(cd-s+=) (W 0443CD) – Inside of me.
Jun 98. (c-s) (W 0447C) **CIRCUS / TEARS IN HEAVEN** `39`
(cd-s+=) (W 0447CDX) – Wonderful tonight / Edge of darkness.
(cd-s) (W 0447CD) – ('A'side) / Behind the mask / Bad love / Tearing us apart.
Nov 98. (c-s) (W 456C) **PILGRIM / NEED HIS WOMAN**
(cd-s+=) (W 456CD) – ('A'mix).
Oct 99. (c-s/cd-s) (W 508 C/CD) **BLUE EYES BLUE / CIRCUS / OLD LOVE**
(cd-s+=) (W 508CDX) – Tearing us apart.
Oct 99. (cd/c) (9362 47564-2/-4) <47553> **CLAPTON CHRONICLES – THE BEST OF ERIC CLAPTON (compilation)** `6` `20`
– Blue eyes blue / Change the world / My father's eyes / Tears in Heaven / Layla / Pretending / Bad love / Before you accuse me / It's in the way that you use it / Forever man / Running on faith / She's waiting / River of tears / I get lost / Wonderful tonight.

– compilations, etc. –

issued 'Polydor' UK / 'Atco' US, unless mentioned otherwise.
Aug 72. (lp) (2659 012) <803> **THE HISTORY OF ERIC CLAPTON** `20` `6` Apr72
Feb 73. (lp) (5526) **CLAPTON** `-` `67`
Apr 73. (lp) (2659 025) <3503> **AT HIS BEST** `87` Oct72
1970. (7"; by ERIC CLAPTON & KING CURTIS) **TEASIN'. / SOULIN'** `-` `-`
now 'R.S.O.' UK+US until mentioned
Jun 81. (lp) Decca; (TAB/KTAB 81) **STEPPIN' OUT (live)**
Jan 82. (7"/12") (RSO/+X 87) **LAYLA (Derek & The Dominoes). / WONDERFUL TONIGHT** `4`
Mar 82. (7") (RSO 88) **I SHOT THE SHERIFF. / COCAINE** `64`
(12"+=) (RSOX 88) – Knockin' on heaven's door (live).
Apr 82. (lp/c) (RSD/TRSD 5010) <3099> **TIME PIECES – THE BEST OF ERIC CLAPTON** `20`
(cd-iss. 1984; 800 014-2) (re-iss. Nov88 & Apr95; same)
Aug 82. (d-c) (3524 229) **SLOWHAND / BACKLESS**
Nov 82. (t-lp-set) (BOX 3) **461 OCEAN BOULEVARD / BACKLESS / SLOWHAND**
May 83. (lp/c) (RSD/TRSD 502) **TIME PIECES VOL.II – 'LIVE' IN THE SEVENTIES**
(cd-iss. 1985; 811 835-2)
Jun 83. (d-c) (TWOMC 6) **461 OCEAN BOULEVARD / ANOTHER TICKET** `-`

Apr 84. (7") (RSO 98) **WONDERFUL TONIGHT. / COCAINE**
May 84. (d-lp/d-c) Starblend; (ERIC/ERIK 1) **BACK TRACKIN'** `29` `-`
– I shot the sheriff / Knockin' on heaven's door / Lay down Sally / Promises / Swing low sweet chariot / Wonderful tonight / Sunshine of your love (CREAM) / Tales of brave Ulysses (CREAM) / Badge (CREAM) / Little wing (DEREK & THE DOMINOES) / Layla (DEREK & THE DOMINOES) / Cocaine / Strange brew (CREAM) / Spoonful (CREAM) / Let it rain / Have you ever loved a woman? (DEREK & THE DOMINOES) / Presence of the Lord (BLIND FAITH) / Crossroads (CREAM) / Roll it over (DEREK & THE DOMINOES live) / Can't find my way home (live) / Blues power (live) / Further on up the road (live). (re-iss. Feb85 on 'Polydor' d-cd; 821 937-2) (re-iss. cd Feb91;)
Jul 84. (7") Old Gold; (OG 9422) **LAYLA (Derek & the Dominoes) / ONLY YOU KNOW AND I KNOW**
Nov 84. (lp/c) Astan; <2/4 0118> **TOO MUCH MONKEY BUSINESS** `-` `-`
Mar 86. (lp/c) Thunderbolt; (THB L/C 013) **SURVIVOR**
(cd-iss. Mar88; CDTB 013)
Mar 86. (7") Old Gold; (OG 9586) **I SHOT THE SHERIFF. / KNOCKIN' ON HEAVEN'S DOOR** `-` `-`
Apr 86. (lp/c) Arcade; (ADAH/+C 428) **GREATEST HITS** `-` `-`
Aug 87. (7") Polydor; (POSP 881) **WONDERFUL TONIGHT. / I SHOT THE SHERIFF**
(12"+=) (POSPX 881) – Layla (full version).
(cd-s+=) (POCD 881) – Swing low sweet chariot.
Sep 87. (d-lp/c)(cd) Polydor; (ECTV/+C 1)(833 519-2) **THE CREAM OF ERIC CLAPTON** `9` `-`
(re-charted Sep92, hit UK No.49) (re-iss. Mar94 cd/c; 521881-2/-4) <US re-iss. Mar95; >; hit No.80)
Apr 88. (d-lp/c/cd) Castle; (CCS LP/MC/CD 162) **THE EARLY CLAPTON COLLECTION**
Apr 88. (6xlp/4xc/4xcd) (<835 261-1/-4/-2>) **CROSSROADS** `34`
(above features all his work of past 25 years) (YARDBIRDS to solo)
May 88. (lp/c) Big Time; (22/21 15515) **FIVE LONG YEARS** `-`
Jul 88. (7") Polydor; (PO 8) **AFTER MIDNIGHT. / I CAN'T STAND IT**
(12"+=) (PZ 8) – What you doing today.
(cd-s++=) (PZCD 8) – Sunshine of your love (CREAM).
Feb 89. (c) Venus; (VENUMC 4) **THE MAGIC OF ERIC CLAPTON**
(re-iss. Jun93 on 'Royal Collection' cd/c; RC 83/82 107)
Oct 90. (cd/c) O.N.N.; (ONN 73 CD/MC) **THE FIRST TIME I MET THE BLUES**
Nov 90. (4xcd/3xc; DEREK & THE DOMINOES) Polydor; (847 083-2/-4) **THE LAYLA SESSIONS (Derek & The Dominoes)**
Jul 91. (7") Polydor; **LAYLA. (Edit) / BELL BOTTOM BLUES**
Nov 91. (cd/c/d-lp) Polydor; **THE BEST OF ERIC CLAPTON (with CREAM)**
(re-iss. Jul93 cd/c;)
Jul 92. (cd) Koch Int.; (TL 1322) **BLUES YOU CAN'T LOOSE**
Apr 93. (cd) Pulsar; (PULS 201) **MISTER SLOWHAND**
Dec 93. (cd) Immediate; (CSL 6040) **THE EARLY YEARS**
Mar 94. (d-cd; DEREK & THE DOMINOES) Polydor; (521 682-2) **LIVE AT FILLMORE (live)**
(re-iss. Sep95; same)
Aug 94. (cd) Charly; (CDCD 1174) **BEGINNINGS**
Nov 95. (3xcd-box) Polydor; **SLOWHAND / 461 OCEAN BOULEVARD / THERE'S ONE IN EVERY CROWD**
Mar 96. (4xcd-box) Polydor; (529 305-2) **CROSSROADS 2 (LIVE IN THE SEVENTIES)** `-`
Apr 96. (cd/c) Hallmark; (30300-2/-4) **BLUES POWER** `-`
(re-iss. Apr98; same)
Oct 98. (10"lp/cd) Get Back; (GET 540/+CD) **FROM YARDBIRDS TO BLUESBREAKERS** `-` `-`
May 99. (d-cd) Collection; (KBOX 235) **ERIC CLAPTON**
May 99. (3xcd-box) Dressed To Kill; (REDTK 124) **CLAPTON, PAGE & BECK** `-` `-`
Jun 99. (d-cd/d-c) (<547178-2/-4>) **BLUES** `52` `52`
(also see under CREAM)

Gene CLARK

Born: HAROLD EUGENE CLARK, 17 Nov'41, Tipton, Missouri, USA. Born into a large farming family, GENE grew up listening to country, bluegrass and rockabilly before taking up the guitar and learning to write songs as he entered his teens. Plucked from obscurity in Kansas by The NEW CHRISTY MINSTRELS' RANDY SPARKS, CLARK left college to sing with the folk outfit that also unleashed KENNY ROGERS and JOHN DENVER on an unsuspecting world. In the event, he only appeared on two albums before his concept of music was turned upside down upon hearing The BEATLES. Deciding that this was the future of music, he quit the MINSTRELS and headed to L.A. where he figured he'd meet some musicians who felt the same way. He figured correct and was soon bringing the house down at Ciro's nightclub alongside JIM (later ROGER) McGUINN, DAVID CROSBY and MICHAEL CLARKE. Calling themselves The BYRDS, they represented an American folk-rock teen sensation equivalent to The BEATLES. What's more, CLARK had penned one of the best songs on their debut album, namely 'I'LL FEEL A WHOLE LOT BETTER'. While the band rapidly became one of the biggest in the world, CLARK's innate fear of flying quickly became a major problem. That, coupled with a dispute over publishing royalties and GENE's increasing alienation from the endless round of touring and interviews led to his eventual departure in February 1966 – this despite being the band's most prolific, versatile and accomplished songwriter (he'd also co-written the groundbreaking 'EIGHT MILES HIGH') as well as their most imposing stage presence. A debut solo single, the orchestrated 'ECHOES', emerged in December while CLARK wasted little time in assembling a formidable team of session players for his impressive proto-country rock album, 'GENE

CLARK WITH THE GODSIN BROTHERS' (1967). Alongside bluegrass singers, VERN and REX GODSIN, the album boasted the talents of GLEN CAMPBELL, CLARENCE WHITE, DOUG DILLARD and LEON RUSSELL as well as BYRDS, CHRIS HILLMAN and MICHAEL CLARKE yet its release date clashed with The BYRDS' 'Younger Than Yesterday' and it sank without trace; both were issued on 'C.B.S.'. The harpsichord orchestration of mooted follow-up single, 'THE FRENCH GIRL', wasn't heard until 1991 when it was belatedly included on a repackaged version of CLARK's debut album, confusingly titled 'ECHOES'. GENE duly decided he was unhappy with this musical direction and a follow-up album was abandoned. Instead, the singer signed a solo deal with 'A&M' and a further round of sessions came to nothing. Present at those sessions, however, was DOUG DILLARD and by Autumn '67, the pair's musical partnership had resulted in 'THE FANTASTIC EXPEDITION OF DILLARD & CLARK'. A pioneering fusion of bluegrass and harmony-rich country-rock, the album featuring guitarist BERNIE LEADON, who'd go on to work within a similar musical format with The EAGLES. 'THROUGH THE MORNING, THROUGH THE NIGHT' (1969) continued in a similar vein albeit with a profusion of covers. Restless due to his lack of commercial success, CLARK enlisted the original BYRDS line-up to back him up on a one-off 1970 single, 'ONE IN A HUNDRED'. This was followed by a brief period with the FLYING BURRITO BROTHERS before he began work on a new solo set with guitarist JESSE ED DAVIS. The result was the eponymous 'GENE CLARK' (1971; usually referred to as 'WHITE LIGHT'), a sparser, more affecting DYLAN-influenced affair that drew rave reviews in both the States and Europe; GENE's vocals, especially, were more immediate and intimate. After contributing material to the soundtrack for a Dennis Hopper movie, 'The American Dreamer', CLARK began work on the 'ROADMASTER' album; yet again the sessions were abandoned before completion although a version surfaced in Holland (where, bizarrely enough, CLARK has a huge fanbase) on the 'Ariola' label. Following an ill-fated BYRDS reunion, CLARK cut 'NO OTHER' (1974) for 'Asylum'. Certainly his most talked about album – if only for its back cover shot of a fully made-up GENE in glam-rock image shock – it marked the most daringly experimental work of his career, combining state of the art studio techniques, trippy sound effects and female backing vocals with his trademark country-rock. Again, with national touring out of the question due to GENE's fear of flying, the record was destined for cult classic status. Following a further solo album on 'R.S.O.', 'TWO SIDES TO EVERY STORY' (1977), he again hooked up with ex-BYRDS McGUINN and HILLMAN for a couple of unremarkable albums on 'Capitol'. The 80's, meanwhile, found him working with the likes of The LONG RYDERS and TEXTONES singer, CARLA OLSON, with whom he cut a fine album of duets, 'SO REBELLIOUS A LOVER' (1987). By the release of 'SILHOUETTED IN LIGHT' (1992), a CLARK/OLSON live set, GENE had already passed away, dying of natural causes on the 24th of May '91. Held back by personal fears and natural modesty, CLARK never reaped the commercial rewards he deserved yet his rich, emotive songs attract ever more devotees with each passing year while his spirit lives on in the work of many young alt-country bands.

Album rating: GENE CLARK WITH THE GODSIN BROTHERS (*6) / THE FANTASTIC EXPEDITION OF DILLARD & CLARK or ECHOES (*7) / THROUGH THE MORNING, THROUGH THE NIGHT by Dillard & Clark (*5) / GENE CLARK (WHITE LIGHT) (*7) / ROADMASTER (*7) / NO OTHER (*7) / TWO SIDES TO EVERY STORY (*4) / FIREBYRD (*4) / SO REBELLIOUS A LOVER with Carla Olson (*5) / SILHOUETTED IN LIGHT (*5) / AMERICAN DREAMER compilation (*7) / FLYING HIGH compilation (*8)

GENE CLARK – vocals, guitar / with The **GODSIN BROTHERS (REX + VERN** – both guitars + vocals)

	C.B.S.	Columbia
Apr 67. (lp) *(CBS 62934)* **GENE CLARK WITH THE GODSIN BROTHERS** – Echoes / Think I'm gonna feel better / Tried so hard / Is yours mine / Keep on pushing / I found you / So you say you lost your baby / Elevator operator * / The same one / Couldn't believe her / Needing someone. *<US remixed & re-iss. 1972 as 'EARLY L.A. SESSIONS' extra track *>* (re-iss. May88 on 'Edsel'; ED 263) (re-iss. 1991 original) (CBS-Epic re-issued in 1991+= & Sep97+=; 488224-2) – (6 extra BYRDS tracks). (cd-iss. Jun97 on 'Edsel'; EDCD 529)*		
1967. (7") *(202523) <43903>* **ECHOES. / I FOUND YOU**		
1967. (7") **SO YOU SAY YOU LOST YOUR BABY. / IS YOURS MINE**	-	

— CLARK briefly re-joined The BYRDS in October '67

— In Aug68, **GENE CLARK** and occasional ex-BYRD; **DOUG DILLARD** – banjo formed . . .

DILLARD & CLARK

— with also **MICHAEL CLARKE** – drums (ex-BYRDS) / **DON BECK** – pedal steel / **BERNIE LEADON** – guitar, vocals / **DAVID JACKSON** – bass (both ex-HEARTS & FLOWERS)

	A&M	A&M
Oct 68. (lp) *(AMLS 939) <SP 4158>* **THE FANTASTIC EXPEDITION OF DILLARD & CLARK** – Out on the side / She darkened the sun / Don't come rollin' / Train leaves here this mornin' / With care from somewhere / The radio song / Git it on brother (git in line brother) / In the plan / Something's wrong / Why not your baby / Lyin' down the middle / Don't be cruel. *(cd-iss. Jun90 on 'Demon'; FIENDCD 62)*		
Nov 68. (7") **OUT ON THE SIDE. / TRAIN LEAVES HERE THIS MORNIN'**		
Feb 69. (7") **LYIN' DOWN THE MIDDLE. / DON'T BE CRUEL**	-	
May 69. (7") **WHY NOT YOUR BABY. / THE RADIO SONG**	-	

— (Jan69) **JON CORNEAL** – drums (ex-FLYING BURRITO BROTHERS) repl. MICHAEL CLARKE who joined FLYING BURITTO BROTHERS / **DONNA WASHBURN** – guitar, vocals repl. BECK

— (May69) **BYRON BERLINE** – fiddle repl. LEADON to FLYING BURRITO BROTHERS

Sep 69. (lp) *(AML 966) <SP 4203>* **THROUGH THE MORNING, THROUGH THE NIGHT** – No longer a sweetheart of mine / Through the morning, through the night / Rocky top / So sad / Corner street bar / I bowed my head and cried holy / Kansas city southern / Four walls / Polly / Roll in my sweet baby's arms / Don't let me down. *(cd-iss. Jan91 on 'Edsel'; EDCD 195)*		
Nov 69. (7") **ROCKY TOP. / DON'T LET ME DOWN**	-	

— DOUG DILLARD continued with other solo albums & The DILLARDS

GENE CLARK

— after a rest period he continued solo

	A&M	A&M
1971. (lp) *(64297) <SP 4292>* **GENE CLARK (WHITE LIGHT)** – The virgin / With tomorrow / White light / Because of you / One in a hundred / Spanish guitar / Where my love lies asleep / Tears of rage / 1975. *<US cd-iss. 1990's; D32Y 3530>*		

	Ariola	not iss.
Dec 72. (lp) *(27897)* **ROADMASTER** – She's the kind of girl / One in a hundred / Here tonight / Full circle song / In a misty morning / Rough and rocky / Roadmaster / I really don't want to know / I remember the railroad / She don't care about time / Shooting star. *(UK-iss.1988 on 'Edsel'; ED 198) (cd-iss. Jun90; EDCD 198)*	-	Dutch

	Asylum	Asylum
Oct 74. (lp) *(SYL 9020) <1016>* **NO OTHER** – Life's greatest fool / Silver raven / No other / Strength of strings / From a silver phial / Some misunderstanding / The true one / Lady of the north. *(re-iss. 1988 on 'Edsel'; ED 299) (cd-iss. Sep94 on 'Line'; LECD 9008890)*		
Jan 75. (7") *(AYM 536)* **NO OTHER. / THE TRUE ONE**		
Mar 75. (7") *(AYM 540) <45222>* **LIFE'S GREATEST FOOL. / FROM A SILVER PHIAL**		

	Polydor	R.S.O.
Mar 77. (lp) *(2394 176)* **TWO SIDES TO EVERY STORY** – Home run King / Lonely Saturday / In the pines / Kansas city southern / Silent crusade / Give my love to Maria / Sister moon / Mary Lou / Hear the wind / Past address.		
1977. (7") *<876>* **HOME RUN KING. / LONELY SATURDAY**	-	

	Spindrift	Takoma
1984. (lp) *(SPIN 122) <TAK 7112>* **FIREBYRD** – Mr. Tambourine man / Something about you / Rain song / Rodeo rider / Vanessa / If you could read my mind / Feel a whole lot better / Made for love / Blue raven. *(cd-iss. Jul95 as 'THIS BIRD HAS FLOWN' on 'Edsel'+=; EDCD 436)* – C'est la Bonne Rue / Dixie flyer / All I want. *(cd-iss. Dec97 on 'Spindrift'; SPINCD 122) (cd re-iss. Mar98 on 'Movieplay Gold'; MPG 74053)*		

— other solo (import) releases below **CARLA** – vocals of TEXTONES)

	Demon	Razor&Tie
Apr 87. (lp; by GENE CLARK & CARLA OLSON) *(FIEND 89)* **SO REBELLIOUS A LOVER** – The drifter / Gypsy rider / Every angel in heaven / Del gato / Deportee / Fair and tender ladies / Almost Saturday night / I'm your toy / Are we still making love / Why did you leave me today / Don't it make you want to go home. *(cd-iss. Aug87+=; FIENDCD 89)* – Lover's turnaround.		

— GENE CLARK died of natural causes on 24th May '91

Mar 92. (cd/c) *(FIEND CD/CASS 710)* **SILHOUETTED IN LIGHT (live in concert with CARLA OLSON)** – Your fire burning / Number one is to survive / Love wins again / Fair and tender ladies / Photograph / Set you free this time / Last thing on my mind / Gypsy rider / Train leaves here this morning / Almost Saturday night / Delgato / Feel a whole lot better / She don't care about time / Speed of the sound of loneliness / Will the circle be unbroken.		

– posthumous releases, etc. –

Mar 93. (cd) *Raven; (RVCD 21)* **AMERICAN DREAMER 1964-1974** – I feel a whole lot better / Set you free this time / She don't care about time / Echoes / So you say you lost your baby / Radio song / With care from someone / Out on the side / The train leaves here this morning / Something's wrong / Through the morning, through the night / She's the kind of girl / One in a hundred / Here tonight / Virgin / With tomorrow / White light / Spanish guitar / American dreamer / Outlaw song / Full circle / From a silver phial / Silver raven.		
Sep 98. (d-cd) *Polydor; (540725-2)* **FLYING HIGH** – You showed me / Feel a whole lot better / Set you free this time / She don't care about time / Tried so hard / So you say you lost your baby / French girl / Los Angeles / I pity the poor immigrant / That's alright for me / The train leaves here this morning / Why not your baby / Radio song / Git it on brother / Something's wrong / Stone must be the wall / No longer a sweetheart of mine / Through the morning through the night / Kansas City southern / Polly / Dark hollow / One in a hundred / She's the kind of girl.		

Guy CLARK

Born: 6 Nov'41, Rockport, Texas, USA. Raised in Monahans, Texas, by his grandparents, CLARK first picked up a guitar at the age of sixteen before moving to Houston. There, he worked the coffee-shop folk circuit alongside the likes of TOWNES VAN ZANDT (to whom he became a lifelong friend and occasional musical partner) and KAY OSLIN (KT OSLIN). Briefly relocating to San Francisco at the tail end of the hippy boom, CLARK met his soon-to-be-wife, SUSANNA, a painter/songwriter with whom he subsequently set up home in L.A. Scraping a living in a musical instrument factory as well as writing for publishers (Sunbury Music), CLARK had soon had enough of life

in the metropolis and the pair headed to Nashville. The experience provided the inspiration for his most enduring and well known song, the classic 'L.A. FREEWAY'. One of his Nashville compadres, JERRY JEFF WALKER, took the track into the Billboard Top 100 in 1973, while CLARK's own version was one of the highlights of his 'R.C.A.' debut album, 'OLD No.1' (1975). Heading a coterie of Texan singer/songwriters (including VAN ZANDT) based in music city, CLARK helped define the outlaw stance and his reputation among his contemporaries was second to none. Lending a hand on the debut were the likes of DAVID BRIGGS (whose previous credits included NEIL YOUNG), a young STEVE EARLE, RODNEY CROWELL and EMMYLOU HARRIS, whose unmistakable harmonies can be heard to spine-tingling effect on 'THAT OLD TIME FEELING'. While the album was hailed as a landmark by critics, commerical radio programmers weren't too keen on CLARK's grits'n'gravy Texas drawl and the songwriter seemed destined for cult status. Not that he was too bothered, preferring to let the music do the talking and cutting another classic album in 'TEXAS COOKIN' (1976). Added to the roll-call this time around were veterans like CHIPS MOMAN (whose studio the album was recorded in), WAYLON JENNINGS and NICOLETTE LARSON, CLARK at his best on wine-stained tributes to booze and doomed love, 'BROKEN HEARTED PEOPLE' and 'BLACK HAIRED BOY' (co-written with SUSANNA) while the joyous country hoedown of 'ME I'M FEELING THE SAME' surely had hit written all over it. JOHNNY CASH even used closer, 'THE LAST GUNFIGHTER BALLAD' as the title track of a 1977 album. Yet again, CLARK's critical stock was high while his sales remained modest. 1978 saw him sign to 'Warners' where he released an eponymous album the same year, providing yet more material for other artists. Fellow Texan RODNEY CROWELL produced his early 80's sets, 'GULF COAST OF TEXAS' (1981) and 'BETTER DAYS' (1983), subsequently taking the former's 'SHE'S CRAZY FOR LEAVING' (which he also co-wrote with CLARK) to the top of the country charts; other country stars to benefit from CLARK's pen include VINCE GILL, BOBBY BARE and RICKY SKAGGS. CLARK himself finally returned in 1989 with the 'OLD FRIENDS' album on US indie label, 'Sugar Hill'. As the title might suggest, CLARK roped in another cast of pals for a fine set that included a cover of Van Zandt's 'TO LIVE IS TO FLY' and a humorous swipe at America's other obsession with 'HEAVY METAL (DON'T MEAN ROCK & ROLL TO ME)'. More recently, CLARK recorded 'BOATS TO BUILD' (1992) for 'Elektra'. Fairly prolific during the 90's, CLARK released three more sets, 'DUBLIN BLUES' (1995), the live 'KEEPERS' (1997) and 'COLD DOG SOUP' (1999). One of country music's great unsung heroes, he remains an inspiration for seasoned campaigners and young bucks alike. • Covers: ONE PAPER KID (. . . Cowart) / IN THE JAILHOUSE NOW (. . . Rodgers) / DON'T YOU TAKE IT TOO BAD + TO LIVE IS TO FLY (Townes Van Zandt) / THE INDIAN COWBOY (Joe Ely) / FORT WORTH BLUES (Steve Earle) / FOREVER, FOR ALWAYS, FOR CERTAIN (. . . Dobson) / BE GONE FOREVER (McGarrigle – Sykes) / etc.
Album rating: OLD No.1 (*8) / TEXAS COOKIN' (*7) / GUY CLARK (*5) / THE SOUTH COAST OF TEXAS (*6) / BETTER DAYS (*6) / OLD FRIENDS (*5) / BOATS TO BUILD (*5) / DUBLIN BLUES (*5) / KEEPERS (*5) / THE ESSENTIAL GUY CLARK compilation (*8) / COLD DOG SOUP (*6)

GUY CLARK – vocals, acoustic guitar / with session people

	R.C.A.	R.C.A.

1975. (lp) <APL1 1303> **OLD NO.1**
– Rita Ballou / L.A. freeway / She ain't goin' nowhere / Nickel for the fiddler / That old time feeling / Texas, 1947 / Desperados waiting for the train / Like a coat from the cold / Instant coffee blues / Let him roll. (UK-iss.Aug76; same as US) (re-iss. May88 on 'Edsel'; ED 285) (cd-iss. Apr96; EDCD 285) <(cd/c-iss.Jan97 on 'Sugar Hill'; SH MC/CD 1030)>

1976. (lp) <RS 1097> <1994> **TEXAS COOKIN'**
– Texas cookin' / Anyhow, I love you / Virginia's real / It's about time / Good to love you lady / Broken hearted people (take me to a barroom) / Black haired boy / Me I'm feeling the same / Ballad of Laverne and Captain Flint / Last gunfighter ballad. (re-iss. Jun88 on 'Edsel'; ED 287) (cd-iss. Apr96; EDCD 287) <(cd/c-iss.Jan97 on 'Sugar Hill'; SH MC/CD 1031)>

	Warners	Warners

May 78. (lp) <K 56565> <3241> **GUY CLARK**
– Fool on the roof / Fools for each other / Shade of all greens / Viola, an American dream / One paper kid / In the jailhouse now / Comfort and crazy / Don't you take it too bad / Houston kid / Fool on the roof blues. <cd/c-iss.Jan97 on 'Sugar Hill'; SH MC/CD 1025>

Feb 81. (lp) <K 56902> <BSK 3381> **THE SOUTH COAST OF TEXAS**
– Who do you think you are / Crystelle / New cut road / Rita Ballou / South coast of Texas / Heartbroke / The partner nobody chose / She's crazy for leavin' / Calf-rope / Lone star hotel. (UK-iss.Aug90; same as US)

1983. (lp) <923880-1> **BETTER DAYS**
– Blowin' like a bandit / Better days / Homegrown tomatoes / Supply & demand / The Randall knife / The carpenter / Uncertain Texas / No deal / Tears / Fool in the mirror. (UK-iss.Aug90; 23880-1)

	Mother	Sugar Hill

Mar 89. (lp/c/cd) (MUM/+CD 893) <SH/+C/CD 1026> **OLD FRIENDS** / Jan89
– Old friends / Hands / I'm all through throwin' good love after bad / Immigrant eyes / Heavy metal / Come from the heart / The Indian cowboy / To live is to fly / Watermelon dream / Doctor good doctor. (cd re-iss. Aug95 on 'Sugar Hill'; same as US)

May 89. (7") (MUM 11) **GOOD LOVE AFTER BAD. / OLD FRIENDS**
(cd-s+=) (MUMCD 11) – Watermelon dream.

	Nonesuch Elektra	–Nonesuch Elektra

Jul 93. (cd/c) <(7559 61442-2/-4)> **BOATS TO BUILD** / Nov92
– Baton rouge / Picasso's mandolin / How'd you get this number / Boats to build / Too much / Ramblin' Jack and Mahan / I don't love you much do I / Jack of all trades / Madonna w/ child c.1969 / Must be my baby.

Apr 95. (cd/c) <(7559 61723-2/-4)> **DUBLIN BLUES**

– Dublin blues / Black diamond strings / Shut up and talk to me / Stuff that works / Hank Williams said it best / The Cape / Baby took a limo to Memphis / Tryin' to try / Hangin' your life on the wall / The Randall knife.

	Sugar Hill	Sugar Hill

Apr 97. (cd/c) <(SH CD/MC 1055)> **KEEPERS (a live recording)**
– L.A. freeway / Texas, 1947 / Like a coat from the cold / Heartbroke / Last gunfighter ballad / Better days / Homegrown tomatoes / She ain't goin' nowhere / The south coast of Texas / That old time feeling / A little of both / Out in the parking lot / Let him roll / Texas cookin' / Desperados waiting for a train.

Nov 99. (cd) <(SHCD 1063)> **COLD DOG SOUP** / Oct99
– Cold dog soup / Fort Worth blues / Sis Draper / Ain't no trouble to me / Water under the bridge / Forever, for always, for certain / Men will be boys / Indian head penny / Bunkhouse blues / Red river / Die tryin' / Be gone forever.

– compilations, etc. –

May 82. (lp/c) RCA Inter.; (INT S/K 5196) **THE BEST OF GUY CLARK** / -

Jun 95. (d-cd/c) Philo; <(CD/C PH 118485)> **CRAFTSMAN**
– (GUY CLARK / THE SOUTH COAST OF TEXAS / BETTER DAYS).

May 97. (cd) R.C.A.; <(7863 67404-2)> **THE ESSENTIAL GUY CLARK** / Jan97
– Texas / Desperados waiting for the train / Like a coat from the cold / Instant coffee blues / Let him roll / Rita Ballou / L.A. freeway / She ain't goin' nowhere / Nickel for the fiddler / That old time feeling / Texas cookin' / Anyhow, I love you / Virginia's real / Broken hearted people / Black haired boy / Me I'm feelin' the same / Ballad of Laverne and Captain Flint / Don't let the sunshine fool you / Last gunfighter ballad / Fools for each other.

Jun 98. (cd) RCA Camden; (74321 58813-2) **OLD NO.1 / TEXAS COOKIN'** / -

John Cooper CLARKE (dig out; Great Alt & Indie . . .)

Vince CLARKE & PAUL QUINN (see under ⇒ YAZOO)

Dave CLARK FIVE

Formed: Tottenham, London, England . . . 1958 by singing drummer DAVE CLARK and original bass player, CHRIS WALSH. After a series of personnel changes, CLARK finally settled on a line-up of MIKE SMITH, LENNY DAVIDSON, RICK HUXLEY and DENNY PAYTON. Following a couple of early instrumental efforts for the 'Piccadilly' label, the band signed to 'Columbia' in 1963 and debuted that Spring with 'THE MULBERRY BUSH'. The raucous 'DO YOU LOVE ME' followed later that year and became their first UK success with third single, 'GLAD ALL OVER', knocked The BEATLES off the No.1 spot and saw the DC5 briefly touted as a serious challenge to the Fab Four. While that prediction may have been a bit wild, the band's booming, big-production sound and stomping R&B beat provided ample ammunition for a sustained chart assault during the British Invasion of the US charts; 'BITS AND PIECES' was a transatlantic Top 5 in early '64 while 'CAN'T YOU SEE THAT SHE'S MINE' and 'BECAUSE' both made the American Top 5 later that summer. Their US profile was so successful they appeared on the Ed Sullivan show more times than any other English band and even released a US live set, 'AMERICAN TOUR' (1964). What distinguished them from many of their peers was their self-determination; most of the songs were self-penned while CLARK handled both the production and management. As a unit, then, they sounded more cohesive and this perhaps explains their relative longevity with regards to the short-lived beat-pop era. Summer '65 saw another US/UK Top 5 with 'CATCH US IF YOU CAN', lifted from the soundtrack of the obligatory group film; they'd already made their acting debut the previous year with 'Get Yourself A College Girl'. Later that year they scored their first (and only) US No.1 with a cover of Bobby Day's 'OVER AND OVER'. While the hits increasingly became thinner on the ground (and dried up completely in the States by 1968) during the psychedelic revolution of the late 60's, the DC5 scored the occasional UK Top 10 right up until 1970 when they hit with a cover of The Youngbloods' 'EVERYBODY GET TOGETHER'. By the release of a final single in summer '71, 'WON'T YOU BE MY LADY', the group had already disbanded. CLARK and SMITH continued to record for 'Columbia' as DAVE CLARK & FRIENDS although even this was abandoned in 1973. CLARK subsequently undertook session work etc. although he was back in the spotlight in 1986 having written and produced the hit musical, 'Time' (featuring a host of superstars including CLIFF RICHARD, FREDDIE MERCURY, DIONNE WARWICK, LEO SAYER and STEVIE WONDER). The man was back again in 1990 with a 50's revival set, 'IT'S ONLY ROCK'N'ROLL'. • **Songwriters:** CLARK and vocalist MIKE SMITH. Covered (singles only); THE MULBURY BUSH (nursery rhyme) / DO YOU LOVE ME (Contours) / I LIKE IT LIKE THAT (Chris Kenner) / OVER AND OVER (Bobby Day) / YOU GOT WHAT IT TAKES (Marv Johnson) / YOU MUST HAVE BEEN A BEAUTIFUL BABY (Bobby Darin) / EVERYBODY KNOWS (Les Reed & Barry Mason) / RED BALLOON (Raymond Froggatt) / PUT A LITTLE LOVE IN YOUR HEART (Jackie DeShannon) / BRING IT ON HOME TO ME (Sam Cooke) / PARADISE (Amen Corner) / GOOD OLD ROCK'N'ROLL (Cat Mother & The All-Night Newsboys) / DRAGGIN' THE LINE (Tommy James) / SWEET CITY WOMAN (Stampeders) / SOUTHERN MAN (Neil Young) / etc.

Best CD compilation: 25 THUMPING HITS (*7)

DAVE CLARK (b.15 Dec'42, Tottenham, London, England) – drums, vocals / **MIKE SMITH** (b.12 Dec'43, Edmunton, London) – vocals, keyboards / **LENNY DAVIDSON** (b.30 May'44, Enfield, London) – guitar, vocals / **RICK HUXLEY** (b. 5 Aug'42, Dartford, Kent, England) – bass, vocals / **DENNY PAYTON** (b. 8 Aug'43, Walthamstow, London) – saxophone, etc.

	Ember	not iss.
Aug 62. (7") *(EMBS 156)* **CHAQUITA. / IN YOUR HEART** <*US re-iss. May64 on 'Jubilee'; 5476>*	□	–

	Piccadilly	Laurie
Jun 62. (7") *(7N 35088)* <*3188*> **FIRST LOVE. / I WALK THE LINE** <*US re-iss. & flipped over; Mar64 on 'Rust'; 5078>*	□	□ Jul63
Dec 62. (7") *(7N 35500)* **I KNEW IT ALL THE TIME. / THAT'S WHAT I SAID** <*US re-iss. May64 on 'Congress'; 212>; hit No.53*		–

	Columbia	Epic
Mar 63. (7") *(DB 7011)* **THE MULBERRY BUSH. / CHAQUITA**		
Sep 63. (7") *(DB 7112)* **DO YOU LOVE ME. / DOO-DAH**	30	
Nov 63. (7") *(DB 7154)* <*9656*> **GLAD ALL OVER. / I KNOW YOU**	1	6 Jan64
Feb 64. (7") *(DB 7210)* <*9671*> **BITS AND PIECES. / ALL OF THE TIME**	2	4 Mar64
Apr 64. (7") <*9678*> **DO YOU LOVE ME. / CHAQUITA**	–	11
Apr 64. (lp) *<BN 26093>* **GLAD ALL OVER** – Glad all over / All of the time / Stay / Chaquita / Do you love me / Bits and pieces / I know you / No time to lose / Doo dah / Time / She's all mine.	–	3
Apr 64. (lp) *(33SX 1598)* **A SESSION WITH THE DAVE CLARK FIVE** – Can't you see that she's mine / I need you, I love you / I love you no more / Rumble / Funny / On Broadway / Zip-a-dee-doo-dah / Can I trust you / Forever and a day / Theme without a name / She's all mine / Time. *(re-iss. '68 on 'Music For Pleasure';)*	3	
May 64. (7") *(DB 7291)* **CAN'T YOU SEE THAT SHE'S MINE. / BECAUSE**	10	
Jun 64. (7") <*9692*> **CAN'T YOU SEE THAT SHE'S MINE. / NO TIME TO LOSE**	–	4
Jun 64. (lp) *<BN 26104>* **THE DAVE CLARK FIVE RETURN!** – Can't you see that she's mine / I need you, I love you / I love you, no more / Rumble / Funny / Zip-a-dee-doo-dah / Can I trust you / Forever and a day / Theme without a name / On Broadway.	–	5
Jul 64. (7") <*9704*> **BECAUSE. / THEME WITHOUT A NAME**	–	3
Aug 64. (7") *(DB 7335)* **THINKING OF YOU BABY. / WHENEVER YOU'RE AROUND**	26	–
Aug 64. (lp) *<BN 26117>* **AMERICAN TOUR (live)** – Because / Who does he thinks he is / Move on / Whenever you're around / I want you still / Long ago / Come on over / Blue Monday / Sometimes / Any time you want love / I cried over you / Ol' soul.		11
Sep 64. (7") <*9722*> **EVERYBODY KNOWS (I STILL LOVE YOU). / OL' SOL**	–	15
Oct 64. (7") *(DB 7377)* <*9739*> **ANYWAY YOU WANT IT. / CRYING OVER YOU**	25	14 Nov64
Dec 64. (lp) *<BN 26128>* **COAST TO COAST** – Any way you want it / Give me love / I can't stand it / I'm left without you / Say you want me / Everybody knows (I still love you) / Crying over you / Say you want me / When / Don't you want me / It's not true.		6
Jan 65. (7") *(DB 7453)* **EVERYBODY KNOWS. / SAY YOU WANT ME**	37	–
Jan 65. (7") <*9763*> **COME HOME. / YOUR TURN TO CRY**	–	14
Mar 65. (7") *(DB 7503)* **REELIN' AND ROCKIN'. / LITTLE BITTY PRETTY ONE**	24	
Apr 65. (7") <*9786*> **REELIN' AND ROCKIN'. / I'M THINKING**	–	23
May 65. (7") *(DB 7580)* **COME HOME. / MIGHTY GOOD LOVING**	16	
Apr 65. (lp) *<BN 26139>* **WEEKEND IN LONDON** – Come home / We'll be running / Blue suede shoes / Hurting inside / I'll never know / 'Til the right one comes along / I'm thinking / Your turn to cry / Little bitty pretty one / Remember, it's me / Mighty good loving.	–	24
Jun 65. (7") <*9811*> **I LIKE IT LIKE THAT. / HURTING INSIDE**	–	7
Jul 65. (7") *(DB 7625)* <*9833*> **CATCH US IF YOU CAN. / ON THE MOVE**	5	4 Aug65
Aug 65. (lp) *(SX 1756)* *<BN 26162>* **CATCH US IF YOU CAN (Soundtrack)** <*US-title 'HAVING A WILD WEEKEND'*> – Catch us if you can / On the move / If you come back / Long ago / Any time you want love / I can't stand it / Your turn to cry / Hurtin' inside / Don't be taken in / Don't you realize / I cried over you / Sweet memories.	8	15
Nov 65. (7") *(DB 7744)* <*9863*> **OVER AND OVER. / I'LL BE YOURS**	45	1
Nov 65. (lp) *<BN 26178>* **I LIKE IT LIKE THAT** – I like it like that / Pumping / I need love / Maybe it's you / That's how long our love will last / A little bit of love / I'll be yours my love / Please love me / Goodbye my friends / I am on my own / She's loving girl / You know you're lying.		32
Jan 66. (7") <*9882*> **AT THE SCENE. / I MISS YOU**	–	18
Mar 66. (7") *(DB 7863)* <*10004*> **TRY TOO HARD. / ALL NIGHT LONG**		12
May 66. (7" <*US flipped over*>) *(DB 7909)* <*10031*> **LOOK BEFORE YOU LEAP. / PLEASE TELL ME WHY**	50	28 Jun66
Jun 66. (lp) *<BN 26198>* **TRY TOO HARD** – Try too hard / Today / I never will / Looking in / Ever since you've been away / Somebody find a new love / I really love you / It don't feel good / Scared of falling in love / I know.	–	77
Aug 66. (7") <*10053*> **SATISFIED WITH YOU. / DON'T LET ME DOWN**	–	50
Sep 66. (lp) *<BN 26212>* **SATISFIED WITH YOU** – Satisfied with you / Go on / Do you still love me / I meant you / Look before you leap / Please tell me why / You never listen / I still need you / It'll only hurt for a little while / Good lovin'.	–	
Oct 66. (7") *(DB 8028)* **NINETEEN DAYS. / I NEED LOVE**	□	–
Oct 66. (7") <*10076*> **NINETEEN DAYS. / SITTING HERE BABY**	–	48
Jan 67. (7") <*10114*> **I'VE GOT TO HAVE A REASON. / GOOD TIME WOMAN**	–	44
Mar 67. (7") *(DB 8152)* **YOU GOT WHAT IT TAKES. / SITTING HERE BABY**	28	–
Mar 67. (7") <*10144*> **YOU GOT WHAT IT TAKES. / DOCTOR RHYTHM**	–	7
Apr 67. (lp) *<BN 26236>* **5 BY 5 = GO!** – Just a little bit now / Maze of love / Return my love / Best day's work / Who do you think you're talking to / Got love if you want it / Red balloon / Please stay / Devoted to me / 3406 / Away from the noises / When I am alone / I still need you / No one can break a heart like you.	–	

	Columbia	Epic
May 67. (7") *(DB 8194)* **TABATHA TWITCHIT. / MAN IN A PIN-STRIPED SUIT**		–
Jun 67. (7") <*10179*> **YOU MUST HAVE BEEN A BEAUTIFUL BABY. / THE MAN IN THE PIN-STRIPED SUIT**	–	35
Aug 67. (7") <*10209*> **A LITTLE BIT NOW. / YOU DON'T PLAY ME AROUND**	–	67
Aug 67. (lp) *<BN 26312>* **YOU GOT WHAT IT TAKES** – You've got what it takes / I've got to have a reason / You won't play me around / Thinkin' of you baby / Lovin' so good / Doctor Rhythm / Play with me / Let me be / Blueberry Hill / Tabatha twitchit.	–	
Oct 67. (7") <*10244*> **RED AND BLUE. / CONCENTRATION BABY**		89
Nov 67. (7") *(DB 8286)* **EVERYBODY KNOWS. / CONCENTRATION BABY**	2	–
Dec 67. (7") <*10265*> **EVERYBODY KNOWS. / INSIDE AND OUT**		43
Feb 68. (7") *(SX 6207)* *<BN 26354>* **EVERYBODY KNOWS** – Everybody knows / Little bit now / At the place / Inside and out / Red and blue / You must have been a beautiful baby / Good love is hard to find / Lost in his dreams / Hold on tight / I'll do the best I can / Concentration baby.		
Feb 68. (7") *(DB 8342)* **NO ONE CAN BREAK A HEART LIKE YOU. / YOU DON'T WANT MY LOVIN'**	28	–
May 68. (7") <*10325*> **PLEASE STAY. / FORGET**	–	–
Sep 68. (7") *(DB 8465)* <*10375*> **THE RED BALLOON. / MAZE OF LOVE**	7	
Nov 68. (7") *(DB 8505)* **LIVE IN THE SKY. / CHILDREN**	38	
Feb 69. (7") *(DB 8545)* **THE MULBERRY TREE. / SMALL TALK**		
Mar 69. (lp) *(SX 6309)* **5 BY 5 1964-69: 14 TITLES BY DAVE CLARK FIVE** (compilation)		
May 69. (7") <*10474*> **(IF) PARADISE (WAS HALF AS NICE). / 34-06**	–	
Jul 69. (7") <*10509*> **IF SOMEBODY LOVES YOU. / BEST DAY'S WORK**	–	
Oct 69. (7") *(DB 8624)* **PUT A LITTLE LOVE IN YOUR HEART. / 34-06**	31	–
Dec 69. (7") <*10547*> **BRING IT ON HOME TO ME. / DARLING I LOVE YOU**	–	
Dec 69. (7") *(DB 8638)* **GOOD OLD ROCK'N'ROLL MEDLEY: Good Old Rock'n'roll – Sweet Little Sixteen – Long Tall Sally – / Whole Lotta Shakin' Goin' On. / GOOD OLD ROCK'N'ROLL MEDLEY part 2: Blue Suede Shoes – Lucille – Reelin' And Rockin' – Memphis Tennessee**	7	
Feb 70. (7") *(DB 8660)* **EVERYBODY GET TOGETHER / DARLING I LOVE YOU**	8	
Apr 70. (7") *(DB 8681)* **JULIA. / FIVE BY FIVE**		
Jun 70. (7") *(DB 8689)* **HERE COMES SUMMER. / BREAK DOWN AND CRY** *(re-iss. Jun75 on 'EMI')*	44	–
Sep 70. (7") <*10635*> **HERE COMES SUMMER. / FIVE BY FIVE**	–	
Oct 70. (7") *(DB 8724)* <*10684*> **MORE GOOD OLD ROCK'N'ROLL MEDLEY:- Rock And Roll Music – Blueberry Hill – Good Golly Miss Molly – My Blue Heaven. / MORE GOOD OLD ROCK'N'ROLL MEDLEY part 2:- Keep A Knockin' – Loving You – One Night – Lawdy Miss Clawdy**	34	
Dec 70. (7") *(DB 8749)* <*10704*> **SOUTHERN MAN. / IF YOU WANNA SEE ME CRY**		
Dec 70. (lp) *(SCX 6437)* **IF SOMEBODY LOVES YOU** – If somebody loves you / It ain't what you do / Live in the sky / Five by five / Here comes summer / How do you get to Heaven / Everybody get together / Julia / Break down and cry / I'm on my own / Red and blue / If you wanna see me cry / Worried time / Darling I love you.		–
Jun 71. (7") *(DB 8791)* <*10768*> **WON'T YOU BE MY LADY. / INTO YOUR LIFE**	□	□

— They had already officially disbanded.

DAVE CLARK & FRIENDS

DAVE CLARK & MIKE SMITH

	Columbia	Epic
Oct 71. (7") *(DB 8834)* **ONE EYED, BLUES SUITED, GUN TOTIN' MAN. / DRAGGIN' THE LINE**	□	□
Feb 72. (7") *(DB 8862)* **THINK OF ME. / RIGHT OR WRONG**	□	□
Jun 72. (7") *(8907)* <*10894*> **RUB IT IN. / I'M SORRY BABY** *(re-iss. Aug74 on 'E.M.I.'; EMI 2205)*	□	□
Sep 72. (lp) *(SCX 6494)* **DAVE CLARK & FRIENDS** – Southern man / Bring it on home to me / Signs / Won't you be my lady / The time has come / If you got a little love to give / Officer McKirk / (If) Paradise (is half as nice) / Draggin' the line / Think of me / One-eyed, blue-suited, gun-totin' man / Right or wrong / I don't know / Put a little love in your heart.		

	E.M.I.	not iss.
Mar 73. (7") *(EMI 2013)* **SWEET CITY WOMAN. / LOVE COMES BUT ONCE**	□	□
Oct 73. (7") *(EMI 2082)* **SHA-NA-NA. / I DON'T KNOW**	□	□

— CLARK ended musical career, and concentrated on his business. In 1986 he co-wrote musical TIME, which featured many superstars including CLIFF RICHARD, FREDDIE MERCURY, DIONNE WARWICK, LEO SAYER, STEVIE WONDER, etc. DAVID CASSIDY replaced CLIFF in the lead role.

May 86. (d-lp/d-c) **DAVE CLARK'S TIME – THE ALBUM** – (various artists album)	21	–

	Mooncrest	not iss.
Nov 90. (cd/c/lp; DAVE CLARK) **IT'S ONLY ROCK'N'ROLL**	□	□

– compilations, others, etc. –

on 'Columbia' UK 'Epic' US unless otherwise stated

Jan 64. (7"ep) *(SEG 8289)* **THE DAVE CLARK FIVE** – I know you / Poison Ivy / Twist and shout / No time to lose.	28	
1964. Ember; (lp) *(FA 2003)* **THE DAVE CLARK FIVE AND THE WASHINGTON DC's**		
Mar 65. (7"ep) *(SEG 8381)* **THE HITS OF THE DAVE CLARK FIVE**	□	□

Sep 65.	(7"ep) (SEG 8447) **WILD WEEKEND**		-
Mar 66.	(lp) (BN 26185) **DAVE CLARK FIVE'S GREATEST HITS**	-	9
	– Over and over / Everybody knows (I still love you) / Can't you see that she's mine / Bits and pieces / I like it like that / Catch us if you can / Because / Any way you want it / Do you love me / Glad all over.		
Dec 66.	(lp) <BN 26221> **DAVE CLARK FIVE'S: MORE GREATEST HITS**	-	-
Mar 67.	(lp) (SX 6105) **GREATEST HITS**	-	-
	– Over and over / Glad all over / Catch us if you can / Bits and pieces / I like it like that / Can't you see that she's mine / Everybody knows (I still love you) / Because / Any way you want it / Do you love me.		
1970.	(lp) Regal Starline; (SRS 5037) **THE BEST OF THE DAVE CLARK FIVE**	-	-
Mar 71.	(d-lp) <EG 30434> **THE DAVE CLARK FIVE**	-	-
1971.	(lp) Regal Starline; (SRS 5090) **PLAYS GOOD OLD ROCK'N'ROLL**	-	-
	(re-iss. Oct75 on 'Music For Pleasure';)		
Dec 72.	(7") (DB 8963) **ALL TIME GREATS MEDLEY. / WILD WEEKEND**	-	-
Mar 75.	(d-lp) (33459) **GLAD ALL OVER AGAIN: THE DAVE CLARK FIVE'S GREATEST HITS**	-	-
1975.	(7") Epic; **BECAUSE. / DO YOU LOVE ME**	-	-
1975.	(7") Epic; **CATCH US IF YOU CAN. / OVER AND OVER**	-	-
1975.	(7") Epic; **GLAD ALL OVER. / BITS AND PIECES**	-	-
1975.	(7") Epic; **YOU GOT WHAT IT TAKES. / COME HOME**	-	-
Feb 77.	(d-lp) Polydor; (POLTV 7) **25 THUMPING GREAT HITS**	7	-
	– Glad all over / Do you love me? / Bits and pieces / Can't you see / Catch us if you can / Because / Over and over / Reelin' and rockin' / You got what it takes / Everybody knows / Good old rock'n'roll / Sweet little sixteen / Long tall Sally / Chantilly lace / Whole lotta shakin' goin' on / Blue suede shoes / Wild weekend / Here comes summer / Live in the sky / Red balloon / Come home / Sweet city woman / Sha-na-na / Put a little love in your heart / Everybody get together.		
Nov 77.	(7") Polydor; (2058 953) **EVERYBODY KNOWS. / ALWAYS ME**		-
Apr 93.	(cd/c/d-lp) E.M.I.; (CD/TC+/EMTV 75) / Hollywood; **GLAD ALL OVER AGAIN** <US title 'THE HISTORY OF . . .'>	28	
Apr 93.	(12"ep/c-ep/cd-ep) E.M.I.; (12/TC/CD EMCT 8) **GLAD ALL OVER EP**	37	-

CLASH

Formed: London, England … early '76, by MICK JONES, PAUL SIMONON, JOE STRUMMER (ex-101'ers) and TERRY CHIMES (future PIL member, KEITH LEVENE, also had a brief spell). After a riotous tour supporting the SEX PISTOLS, their manager, BERNIE RHODES, attained a deal with major label big boys 'C.B.S.' in early '77 and subsequently unleashed the two minute classic, 'WHITE RIOT'. A driving chantalong stomp, the record smashed into the UK Top 40 and announced the arrival of a band whose influence and impact was second only to the 'PISTOLS. In contrast to LYDON and Co., The CLASH manipulated the energy of punk as a means of political protest and musical experimentation. 'THE CLASH' (1977) was a blinding statement of intent, a finely balanced masterwork of infectious hooklines and raging conviction. 'I'M SO BORED WITH THE U.S.A.' and 'CAREER OPPORTUNITIES' railed against inertia, while a cover of Junior Murvin's 'POLICE AND THIEVES' was the first of many sporadic forays into dub reggae. The album went Top 20, lauded by many critics as the definitive punk set, while a further two classic singles (not on the album), 'CLASH CITY ROCKERS' and 'WHITE MAN IN HAMMERSMITH PALAIS' made the Top 40 (the latter addressing the issue of racism, a subject never far from the band's agenda). CBS (and no doubt the band themselves) were keen to break America, subsequently enlisting the production services of BLUE OYSTER CULT guru, SANDY PERLMAN for follow-up set, 'GIVE 'EM ENOUGH ROPE' (1978). The album's more rockest, less frenetic approach met with some criticism and despite the label's best efforts, the record just failed to crack the American Top 100. It had, however, made No.2 in Britain and spawned the band's first Top 20 hit in 'TOMMY GUN'. The CLASH subsequently set out to tour the States, while British fans lapped up 'THE COST OF LIVING' EP and its incendiary cover of Sonny Curtis's 'I FOUGHT THE LAW'. Finally, in late '79, The CLASH delivered their marathon masterwork, 'LONDON CALLING'. Overseen by seasoned producer, Guy Stevens, the double set showed The CLASH at an assured creative peak, from the anthemic echo of the title track to the brooding 'GUNS OF BRIXTON'. A UK Top 10'er, it finally cracked the States (Top 30), its universal acclaim spurred them on to ever more ambitious endeavours. After the plangent dub of the 'BANKROBBER' and 'THE CALL-UP' singles, the band unleashed the sprawling, triple vinyl set, 'SANDINISTA!' in December 1980. The record's wildly experimental material met with critical pasting, the bulk of the album's tracks failing to withstand repeated listening. Its relatively poor sales (still at single vinyl price) forced a back to basics rethink for 'COMBAT ROCK' (1982). Although the record was a healthy seller, it sounded laboured; ironically, it became The CLASH's biggest selling album in America, where the 'ROCK THE CASBAH' single made the Top 10. Drummer TOPPER HEADON was already long gone by this point and was replaced by CHIMES, who had left after the 1977 debut; JONES too, was kicked out the following year. The band stumbled on for a further album, 'CUT THE CRAP' in 1985, before finally disbanding the following month. While JONES enjoyed mid-80's success with BIG AUDIO DYNAMITE, STRUMMER embarked on a low-key solo career before working with his pal SHANE MacGOWAN in The POGUES. The CLASH fever gripped the nation again in 1991 when 'SHOULD I STAY OR SHOULD I GO' (a Top 20 hit in 1983), hit the top of the charts after being

used in a Levi jeans advert (what else!?). A best of double set, 'THE STORY OF THE CLASH VOL.1', flew off the shelves and rumours were rife of a CLASH reunion (unceremoniously quashed by STRUMMER). • **Songwriters:** Either STRUMMER / – JONES until 1980 group penned, except PRESSURE DROP (Maytals) / POLICE ON MY BACK (Equals) / ARMAGIDEON TIME (Willie Williams) / JUNCO PARTNER + ENGLISH CIVIL WAR (unknown trad) / EVERY LITTLE BIT HURTS (Ed Cobb) / BRAND NEW CADILLAC (Vince Taylor). • **Trivia:** Early in 1980, the band featured live in the docu-film 'Rude Boy' about a fictionalised CLASH roadie. JOE STRUMMER went into acting 1986 (Straight To Hell) / 1989 (Lost In Space).

Album rating: THE CLASH (*10) / GIVE 'EM ENOUGH ROPE (*8) / LONDON CALLING (*9) / SANDINISTA! (*7) / COMBAT ROCK (*6) / CUT THE CRAP (*4) / THE STORY OF THE CLASH, VOL.1 compilation (*9) / CLASH ON BROADWAY (*7) / SUPER BLACK MARKET CLASH (*7) / FROM HERE TO ETERNITY live collection (*8) / Joe Strummer: EARTHQUAKE WEATHER (*5) / ROCK ART AND THE X-RAY STYLE (*5)

JOE STRUMMER (b. JOHN GRAHAM MELLOR, 21 Aug'52, Ankara, Turkey / raised London) – vocals, guitar (ex-101'ers) / **PAUL SIMONON** (b.15 Dec'55, Brixton, England) – bass, vocals / **MICK JONES** (b. MICHAEL JONES, 26 Jun'55) – guitar, vocals / **TORY CRIMES** (b. TERRY CHIMES, 25 Jan'55) – drums

		C.B.S.	Epic
Mar 77.	(7") (S-CBS 5058) **WHITE RIOT. / 1977**	38	-
Apr 77.	(lp/c) (CBS/40 82000) **THE CLASH**	12	-
	– Janie Jones / Remote control / I'm so bored with the U.S.A. / White riot / Hate and war / What's my name / Deny / London's burning / Career opportunities / Cheat / Protex blue / Police and thieves / 48 hours / Garage land. <US-iss.Aug79 on 'Epic'; 36060> (tracks differed & contained free 7") – GROOVY TIMES. / GATES OF THE WEST (this lp version UK-iss.Jan91 on cd) (re-iss. Nov82 lp/c; CBS/40 32232) (cd-iss. Apr89 on 'Columbia'; CD 32232) (cd re-iss. Aug91 on 'Columbia'; 468783-2)		
—	(Jan'77) (NICKY) **TOPPER HEADON** (b.30 May'55, Bromley, Kent, England) – drums; repl. CHIMES who later joined COWBOYS INTERNATIONAL and GENERATION X		
May 77.	(7") (S-CBS 5293) **REMOTE CONTROL. / LONDON'S BURNING (live)**		-
Sep 77.	(7") (S-CBS 5664) **COMPLETE CONTROL. / THE CITY OF THE DEAD**	28	-
Feb 78.	(7") (S-CBS 5834) **CLASH CITY ROCKERS. / JAIL GUITAR DOORS**	35	-
Jun 78.	(7") (S-CBS 6383) **(WHITE MAN) IN HAMMERSMITH PALAIS. / THE PRISONER**	32	-
Nov 78.	(lp/c) (CBS/40 82431) <35543> **GIVE 'EM ENOUGH ROPE**	2	Feb79
	– Safe European home / English civil war / Tommy gun / Julie's been working for the drug squad / Guns on the roof / Drug-stabbing time / Stay free / Cheapstakes / All the young punks (new boots and contracts). (re-iss. 1984 lp/c; CBS/40 32444) (cd-iss. Jan91; CD 32444)		
Nov 78.	(7") (S-CBS 6788) **TOMMY GUN. / 1, 2, CRUSH ON YOU**	19	-
Feb 79.	(7") (S-CBS 7082) **ENGLISH CIVIL WAR. / PRESSURE DROP**	25	-
May 79.	(7"ep) (S-CBS 7324) **THE COST OF LIVING**	22	-
	– I fought the law / Groovy times / Gates of the west / Capital radio.		
Jul 79.	(7") <50738> **I FOUGHT THE LAW. / (WHITE MAN) IN HAMMERSMITH PALAIS**	-	-
—	added on tour MICKEY GALLAGHER – keyboards (ex-IAN DURY)		
Dec 79.	(7") (S-CBS 8087) **LONDON CALLING. / ARMAGIDEON TIME**	11	-
	(12"+=) (CBS12 8087) – Justice tonight (version) / Kick it over (version).		
Dec 79.	(d-lp/c) (CLASH/+C 3) <36328> **LONDON CALLING**	9	27 Jan80
	– London calling / Brand new cadillac / Jimmy Jazz / Hateful / Rudie can't fail / Wrong 'em boyo / Death or glory / Koka Kola / The card cheat / Spanish bombs / The right profile / Lost in the supermarket / The guns of Brixton / Lover's rock / Four horsemen / I'm not down / Revolution rock / Train in vain. (re-iss. Feb88 on 'Columbia' d-lp/c; 460114-1/-4) (cd-iss. Apr89 on 'Columbia'; 460114-2)		
Mar 80.	(7") <50851> **TRAIN IN VAIN (STAND BY ME). / LONDON CALLING**	-	27
Aug 80.	(7") (S-CBS 8323) **BANKROBBER. / Mickey Dread: ROCKERS GALORE . . . UK TOUR**	12	-
Nov 80.	(7") (S-CBS 9339) **THE CALL-UP. / STOP THE WORLD**	40	-
Nov 80.	(10"m-lp) <36846> **BLACK MARKET CLASH**	-	74
	– Time is tight / Capital radio / Bankrobber / Pressure drop / The prisoner / City of the dead / Justice tonight – kick it over (version). (UK-iss.Sep91 on 'Columbia' cd/c; 468763-2/-4)		
Dec 80.	(t-lp/d-c) (CBS/40 FSLN 1) <37037> **SANDINISTA!**	19	24
	– The magnificent seven / Hitsville U.K. / Junco partner / Ivan meets G.I. Joe / The leader / Something about England / Rebel waltz / Look here / The crooked beat / Somebody got murdered / One more time / One more dub / Lightning strikes (not once but twice) / Up in Heaven (not only here) / Corner soul / Let's go crazy / If music could talk / The sound of the sinners / Police on my back / Midnight log / The equaliser / The call up / Washington bullets / Broadway / Lose this skin / Charlie don't surf / Mensforth Hill / Junkie slip / Kingston advice / The street parade / Version city / Living in fame / Silicone on sapphire / Version pardner / Career opportunites (version) / Shepherds delight. (d-cd-iss. Apr89 on 'Columbia'; 463364-2)		
Jan 81.	(7") (S-CBS 9480) **HITSVILLE U.K. / RADIO ONE**	56	-
Feb 81.	(7") <51013> **HITSVILLE U.K. / POLICE ON MY BACK**	-	-
Apr 81.	(12"ep) <02036> **THE CALL-UP / THE COOL-OUT. / THE MAGNIFICENT SEVEN / THE MAGNIFICENT DANCE**	-	-
Apr 81.	(7"/12") (A/+12 1133) **THE MAGNIFICENT SEVEN. / THE MAGNIFICENT DANCE**	34	-
Nov 81.	(7") (A 1797) **THIS IS RADIO CLASH. / RADIO CLASH**	47	-
	(12"+=) (A12 1797) – Outside broadcast / Radio 5.		
—	**TERRY CHIMES** returned to repl. HEADON who later went solo (signed to 'Mercury', released a couple of singles – 'DRUMMIN' MAN', 'LEAVE IT TO LUCK' and 'I'LL GIVE YOU EVERYTHING' – all from the 1986 album, 'WAKING UP', which featured 60's soul singer, JIMMY HELMS)		
Apr 82.	(7") (A 2309) **KNOW YOUR RIGHTS. / FIRST NIGHT BACK IN LONDON**	43	-

May 82. (lp/c) *(CBS/40 FMLN 2)* <37689> **COMBAT ROCK** | 2 | 7 |
– Know your rights / Car jamming / Should I stay or should I go / Rock the Casbah / Red angel dragnet / Straight to Hell / Overpowered by funk / Atom tan / Sean Flynn / Ghetto defendant / Inoculated city / Death is a star. *(re-iss. Nov86 lp/c; CBS/40 32787)* *(cd-iss. on 'Columbia'; CD 32787)*

May 82. (7") <03006> **SHOULD I STAY OR SHOULD I GO. / INNOCULATED CITY** | - | |

Jun 82. (7"/7"pic-d) *(A/+11 2479)* <03245> **ROCK THE CASBAH. / LONG TIME JERK** | 30 | 8 Sep82 |
(12") *(A12 2479)* – ('A'side) / Mustapha dance.

Jul 82. (7") <03061> **SHOULD I STAY OR SHOULD I GO. / FIRST NIGHT BACK IN LONDON** | - | 45 |

Sep 82. (7"/7"pic-d/12") *(A/+11/12 2646)* **SHOULD I STAY OR SHOULD I GO. / STRAIGHT TO HELL** | 17 | - |

Feb 83. (7") <03547> **SHOULD I STAY OR SHOULD I GO? / COOL CONFUSION** | - | 50 |

—— (Feb83-Jan84) STRUMMER & SIMONON brought in new musicians PETE HOWARD – drums (ex-COLD FISH),repl. CHIMES who later joined HANOI ROCKS / NICK SHEPHERD – guitar (ex-CORTINAS) + VINCE WHITE – guitar; repl. JONES who formed BIG AUDIO DYNAMITE

Sep 85. (7") *(A 6122)* **THIS IS ENGLAND. / DO IT NOW** | 24 | - |
(12"+=) *(A12 6122)* – Sex mad roar.

Nov 85. (lp/c) *(CBS/40 26601)* <40017> **CUT THE CRAP** | 16 | 88 |
– Dictator / Dirty punk / We are The Clash / Are you red.. Y / Cool under heat / Movers and shakers / This is England / Three card trick / Play to win / Fingerpoppin' / North and south / Life is wild. *(cd-iss. Apr89 on 'Columbia'; CD 465110-2)* *(cd-iss. Dec92 on 'Columbia';)*

—— disbanded Dec'85 and STRUMMER went solo (see below). SHEPHERD formed HEAD. In the early 90's, SIMONON formed HAVANA 3 A.M. who comprised NIGEL DIXON (ex-WHIRLWIND), GARY MYRICK and TRAVIS WILLIAMS. Signing to 'I.R.S.', they released only one 50's style eponymous rock album in 1991 before splitting their quiffs.

– compilations, others, etc. –

on 'C.B.S.' unless mentioned otherwise

Nov 82. (c-ep) *(A40 2907)* **COMPLETE CONTROL / LONDON CALLING / BANKROBBER / CLASH CITY ROCKERS** | | |

Sep 86. (c-ep) *(450 123-4)* **THE 12" TAPE** | | |
– London calling / The magnificent dance / This is Radio Clash / Rock the Casbah / This is England. *(cd-iss. Nov92 on 'Columbia'; 450123-2)*

Mar 88. (7") *(CLASH 1)* **I FOUGHT THE LAW. / THE CITY OF THE DEAD / 1977** | 29 | - |
(12"+=) *(CLASH T/C 1)* – Police on my back / 48 hours.

Mar 88. (d-lp/c/cd) *(460244-1/-4/-2)* <44035> **THE STORY OF THE CLASH** | 7 | |
– The magnificent seven / Rock the Casbah / This is Radio Clash / Should I stay or should I go / Straight to Hell / Armagideon time / Clampdown / Train in vain / Guns of Brixton / I fought the law / Somebody got murdered / Lost in the supermarket / Bank robber / White man in Hammersmith Palais / London's burning / Janie Jones / Tommy gun / Complete control / Capital radio / White riot / Career opportunities / Clash city rockers / Safe European home / Stay free / London calling / Spanish bombs / English civil war / Police and thieves. *(re-iss. Mar91 as THE STORY OF THE CLASH VOL.1, on 'Columbia'; same)* – (hit UK 13) *(re-iss. Oct95 on 'Columbia'; same)*

Apr 88. (7"/7"box) *(CLASH/+B 2)* **LONDON CALLING. / BRAND NEW CADILLAC** | 46 | |
(12"+=) *(CLASHT 2)* – Rudie can't fail.
(cd-s+=) *(CLASHC 2)* – The street parade.

Jul 90. (7"/c-s) *(656072-7/-4)* **RETURN TO BRIXTON (remix). / ('A'-SW2 mix)** | 57 | |
(12"+=/cd-s+=) *(656072-6/-2)* – The guns of Brixton.

Feb 91. (7"/c-s) Columbia; *(656667-7/-4)* **SHOULD I STAY OR SHOULD I GO. / B.A.D. II: Rush** | 1 | |
(12"+=/cd-s+=) *(656667-6/-2)* – ('B'dance mix) / Protex blue.
(cd-s) *(656667-5)* – ('A'side) / London calling / Train in vain / I fought the law.

Apr 91. (7"/c-s) Columbia; *(656814-7/-4)* **ROCK THE CASBAH. / MUSTAPHA DANCE** | 15 | |
(12"+=/cd-s+=) *(656814-6/-2)* – The magnificent dance / This is Radio Clash.
(cd-s) *(656814-5)* – ('A'side) / Tommy gun / (White man) In Hammersmith Palais / Straight to Hell.

Jun 91. (7"/c-s) Columbia; *(656946-7/-4)* **LONDON CALLING. / BRAND NEW CADILLAC** | 64 | |
(12"+=) *(656946-6)* – Return to Brixton (remix).
(cd-s++=) *(656946-2)* – The call-up.

Oct 91. (7"/c-s) Columbia; *(656-7/-4)* **TRAIN IN VAIN (STAND BY ME). / THE RIGHT PROFILE** | | - |
(cd-s+=) *(656-2)* – Groovy times / Gates to the west.
(pic-cd-s+=) *(656-5)* – ('A'remix) / Death or glory.

Nov 91. (cd/c) Columbia; *(468946-2/-4)* **THE SINGLES COLLECTION** | 68 | |

Nov 93. (cd) Columbia; *(474546-2)* **SUPER BLACK MARKET CLASH** | | |

May 94. (3xcd-box/3xc-box) Columbia; *(469308-2/-4)* **ON BROADWAY** | | |

Oct 99. (cd-c/d-lp) Columbia; *(496183-2/-4/-1)* **FROM HERE TO ETERNITY (live)** | 13 | |
– Complete control / London's burning / What's my name / Clash city rockers / Career opportunities / White man in Hammersmith Palais / Capitol radio / City of the dead / I fought the law / London calling / Armagideon time / Train in vain / Guns of Brixton / The magnificent seven / Should I stay or should I go / Straight to Hell.

—— The CLASH also appeared under different guises for singles below

May 83. (12"; FUTURA 2000 with The Clash) Celluloid; *(CYZ 104)* **ESCAPADES OF FUTURA 2000** | | - |

Dec 83. (7"; JANIE JONES & THE LASH) Big Beat; *(NS 91)* **HOUSE OF THE JU-JU QUEEN. / SEX MACHINE** | - | |

—— They can also be heard on TYMON DOGG's 45; 'Lose This Skin' (May80)

JOE STRUMMER

| | C.B.S. | Epic |
Oct 86. (7"/12") *(A/TA 7244)* **LOVE KILLS. / DUM DUM CLUB** | 69 | - |
| | Virgin | Virgin |
Feb 88. (cd/c/lp) *(CD/TC/V 2497)* **WALKER (Soundtrack)** | | |
– Filibustero / Omotepe / Sandstorm / Machete / Viperland / Nica libre / Latin romance / The brooding side of madness / Tennessee rain / Smash everything / Tropic of no return / The unknown immortal / Musket waltz.

| | Epic | Epic |
Jun 88. (7"/7"s) *(TRASH/+P 1)* **TRASH CITY. / THEME FROM A PERMANENT RECORD** | | - |
(12"+=/pic-cd-s+=) *(TRASH T/C 1)* – Nerfititi rock.

—— STRUMMER was augmented by new band JACK IRONS – drums (of RED HOT CHILI PEPPERS) / ZANDON SCHLOSS – guitar (ex-CIRCLE JERKS) / RONNIE MARSHALL – bass (of TONE LOC).

Aug 89. (7"/c-s) *(STRUM/+M 1)* **GANGSTERVILLE. / JEWELLERS AND BUMS** | | - |
(7"ep+=) *(STRUME 1)* – Passport to Detroit / Punk rock blues.
(12"+=/cd-s+=) *(STRUM T/C 1)* – Don't tango with my django.

Sep 89. (lp/c/cd) *(465347-1/-4/-2)* **EARTHQUAKE WEATHER** | 58 | |
– Gangsterville / King of the bayou / Island hopping / Slant six / Dizzy's goatee / Shouting street / Boogie with your children / Leopardskin limousines / Sikorsky parts / Jewellers and bums / Highway on zero street / Ride your donkey / Passport to Detroit / Sleepwalk.

Oct 89. (7") *(STRUM 2)* **ISLAND HOPPING. / CHOLO VEST** | | |
(12"+=/cd-s+=/7"ep+=) *(STRUM T/C/E 2)* – Mango street / Baby o' boogie.

—— STRUMMER joined The POGUES on tour, deputising when SHANE McGOWAN was under the bottle. At the start of 1992, he had begun writing with them, so who knows? At least it will quell the dogged persistent rumours of a CLASH reformation.

JOE STRUMMER & THE MESCALEROS

—— STRUMMER with ... NORRIS / ... DYSON / ... GENN

| | Mercury | Mercury |
Aug 99. (12"/cd-s) *(MER/+CD 523)* **YALLA YALLA. / X-RAY STYLE / TIME AND THE TIDE** | | - |
Oct 99. (cd/c/lp) *(546654-2/-4/-1)* <80424> **ROCK ART & THE X-RAY STYLE** | 71 | |
– Tony Adams / Sandpaper blues / X-ray style / Techno D-day / Road to rock'n'roll / Diggin' the new / Nitcomb / Forbidden city / Yalla yalla / Willesden to Cricklewood.

Adam CLAYTON & Larry MULLEN (see under ⇒ U2)

Jimmy CLIFF

Born: JAMES CHAMBERS, 1 Apr'48, St. Catherine, Jamaica, his earliest musical influences stemmed from Trinidad, the birthplace of Calypso. However, by the time JIMMY left home for Kingston in '62, his real interest lay in the imported sounds of boogie and blues from the States. As the boogie sound blended with calypso, mento and Jamaican folk music, so "Ska" was born. CLIFF cut his first track at Federal studio (owned at the time by the dominant force in Jamaican recording, Ken Khouri) for Count Boysie's sound system, who, in turn, would air the track at dances. The single was never released, although after a few more attempts with various systems, 'HURRICANE HATTIE' delivered CLIFF's first hit, produced by Leslie Kong, who at the time had little knowledge of the music business, but plenty of money to hire the best musicians on the islands, and was to be involved in CLIFF's finest work. By '63, CLIFF had his second hit with 'MISS JAMAICA', going on to score with 'MY LUCKY DAY' and 'MISS UNIVERSE', although he was barely earning a decent living. A brief attempt to break "Ska" in the States led to CLIFF meeting Chris Blackwell (head of 'Island' records), who persuaded him to try his luck in England, CLIFF moving over in '65. The trip to America had opened the singer's eyes to soul music, this inflence subsequently coming to the fore in both his gigs and recordings of the mid-'60s. After a couple of near misses with 'Island', the album, 'HARD ROAD TO TRAVEL', was released in '67, amongst the tracks a poppy version of Procol Harum's 'WHITER SHADE OF PALE'. During this period, he built up a strong fanbase in Britain without the hits and cash to go with it; unsurprisingly, his spirits were low, made apparent in his classic track, 'MANY RIVERS TO CROSS', which he wrote in '68. A trip to Brazil the same year to attend an international song contest saw CLIFF pulling off a hit in the country with 'WATERFALL', as well as inspiring him to write 'WONDERFUL WORLD BEAUTIFUL PEOPLE'. On the way back from Brazil, CLIFF stopped off in Jamaica for the first time since '65, recording material for his subsequent debut LP for 'Trojan', 'JIMMY CLIFF', and catching up with the sounds of rock-steady and reggae, the new style coming to the fore on the LP. Released in England at a time when Trojan scored the majority of their hits, the LP proved the pinnacle of CLIFF's recording career, listing 'MANY RIVERS TO CROSS' and the sublime 'USE WHAT I GOT', as well as the melancholy sounds of a rare ballad, 'COME INTO MY LIFE'. After the international success of 'WONDERFUL WORLD, BEAUTIFUL PEOPLE', CLIFF recorded the inspired protest song, 'VIETNAM', although the major success he craved continued to evade him with the record being rejected for US release as it was considered "too upbeat". 'WILD WORLD', penned by CAT STEVENS, gave CLIFF a glimmer of success, in the meantime producing DESMOND DEKKER's 'You Can Get It If You Really Want' and The PIONEERS' hit 'Let Your Yeah Be Yeah', before launching his second set, the unforgettable 'ANOTHER CYCLE' in '71. Superstar status was eventually achieved through an unforseen medium; film. 'THE HARDER THEY COME' not only starred CLIFF but used four of his songs, including the title track, as well as the infectious 'YOU CAN GET IT IF YOU REALLY WANT'. Incredibly, when 'THE HARDER THEY COME' was released in '72, it failed to chart, CLIFF becoming disillusioned with 'Island' and moving to 'E.M.I.' in '73. From this point onwards, his output failed to match the high standards he had previously set for himself, his style shifting away from the reggae sound that had formed the basis of his fame. • **Trivia:** In 1985, he wrote 'TRAPPED' for BRUCE SPRINGSTEEN, who sang it on the charity album, 'USA FOR AFRICA'.

Album rating: JIMMY CLIFF (*6) / WONDERFUL WORLD, BEAUTIFUL PEOPLE (*7) / HARD ROAD TO TRAVEL (*5) / ANOTHER CYCLE (*6) / THE HARDER THEY COME (*9) / UNLIMITED (*5) / STRUGGLING MAN (*5) / THE BEST OF JIMMY CLIFF compilation (*7) / BRAVE WARRIOR (*5) / FOLLOW MY MIND (*4) / GIVE THANX (*4) / OH JAMAICA (*4) / I AM THE LIVING (*4) / GIVE THE PEOPLE WHAT THEY WANT (*4) / HOUSE OF EXILE (*4) / SPECIAL (*4) / THE POWER AND THE GLORY (*5) / CAN'T GET ENOUGH OF IT (*4) / CLIFF HANGER (*4) / SENSE OF DIRECTION (*5) / HANG FIRE (*5) / IMAGES (*5) / SAVE OUR PLANET EARTH (*4) / BREAKOUT (*5) / THE COOL RUNNER LIVE IN LONDON (*3)

JIMMY CLIFF – vocals / with various session people

		Blue Beat	not iss.
1962.	(7"; JIMMY CLIFF with CAVALIERS COMBO) (BB 78) **I'M SORRY.** / The BLUE BEATS with RED PRICE: Roarin'		-

		Island	not iss.
1962.	(7") (WI 012) **HURRICANE HATTY.** / **DEAREST BEVERLEY**		-
1962.	(7") (WI 016) **MISS JAMAICA.** / **GOLD DIGGER**		-
1962.	(7") (WI 025) **SINCE LATELY.** / **I'M FREE**		-
1963.	(7") (WI 062) **MY LUCKY DAY.** / **ONE EYED JACKS**		-
1963.	(7") (WI 070) **KING OF KINGS.** / Sir Percy: OH YEAH		-
1963.	(7") (WI 112) **MISS UNIVERSE.** / **THE PRODIGAL**		-

		Black Swan	not iss.
1963.	(7") (WI 403) **THE MAN.** / **YOU ARE NEVER TOO OLD**		-

		Stateside	not iss.
Sep 64.	(7") (SS 342) **ONE EYED JACKS.** / **KING OF KINGS**		-

		Fontana	not iss.
Jan 66.	(7") (TF 641) **CALL ON ME.** / **PRIDE AND PASSION**		-

		Island	not iss.
Feb 67.	(7") (WIP 6004) **AIM AND AMBITION.** / **GIVE AND TAKE**		-
May 67.	(7") (WIP 6011) **I GOT A FEELING.** / **HARD ROAD TO TRAVEL**		-
Oct 67.	(7") (WIP 6024) **THAT'S THE WAY LIFE GOES.** / **THANK YOU**		-
Jan 68.	(lp) (ILP 962) **HARD ROAD TO TRAVEL**		-

– Reward / Let's dance / Can't get enough of it / I've got a feeling / All I know about you / Give and take / Pride and passion / Searchin' for my baby / Hard road to travel / A whiter shade of pale / Call on me / Aim and ambition.

Jun 68.	(7"; JACKIE EDWARDS & JIMMY CLIFF) (WIP 6036) **SET ME FREE.** / **HERE I COME**		-
Jul 68.	(7") (WIP 6039) **WATERFALL.** / **REWARD**		-

		Trojan	A&M
Oct 69.	(7") (TR 690) **WONDERFUL WORLD, BEAUTIFUL PEOPLE.** / **HARD ROAD TO TRAVEL**	6	-
Nov 69.	(7") <1146> **WONDERFUL WORLD, BEAUTIFUL PEOPLE.** / **WATERFALL**	-	25
Dec 69.	(lp) (TRLS 16) <4251> **JIMMY CLIFF** <US-title 'WONDERFUL WORLD'>		

– Many rivers to cross / Vietnam / My ancestors / Hard road to travel / Hello sunshine / Wonderful world, beautiful people / Sufferin' in the land / Use what I got / That's the way it goes / Come into my life. (re-iss. 1983 lp/c; TRLS/ZCTRLS 16) (cd-iss. Mar94 on 'Trojan'; CDTRL 16)

Jan 70.	(7") (TR 7722) **VIETNAM.** / **SHE DOES IT RIGHT**	46	-
Feb 70.	(7") <1167> **COME INTO MY LIFE.** / **VIETNAM**	-	89
Mar 70.	(7") (TR 7745) **SUFFERING.** / **COME INTO MY LIFE**		-
May 70.	(7") (TR 7767) <1201> **YOU CAN GET IT IF YOU REALLY WANT.** / **BE AWARE**		

		Island	A&M
Jul 70.	(7") (WIP 6087) **WILD WORLD.** / **BE AWARE**	8	-
Nov 70.	(7") (WIP 6097) **SYNTHETIC WORLD.** / **I GO TO PIECES**		-
Feb 71.	(7") (WIP 6103) **GOODBYE YESTERDAY.** / **BREAKDOWN**		-
May 71.	(7") <1270> **GOODBYE YESTERDAY.** / **LET'S SEIZE THE TIME**	-	
Aug 71.	(7") (WIP 6110) **SITTING IN LIMBO.** / **THE BIGGER THEY COME**		-
Sep 71.	(lp) (ILPS 9159) **ANOTHER CYCLE**		-

– Take a look at yourself / Please tell me why / Rap / Opportunity only knocks once / My friend's wife / Another cycle / Sitting in limbo / Oh, how I miss you / Inside out, upside down / One thing is over.

—— In 1972, he appeared and contributed some tracks to 'THE HARDER THEY COME' film soundtrack on 'Island'. In US, it was released early 1975. (cd-iss. Sep86) (cd-re-iss. Oct90 on 'Mango')

Jul 72.	(7") (WIP 6132) **TRAPPED.** / **STRUGGLIN' MAN**		-
Oct 72.	(7") (WIP 6139) **THE HARDER THEY COME.** / **MANY RIVERS TO CROSS**		-

		E.M.I.	Reprise
May 73.	(7") <1177> **BORN TO WIN.** / **BLACK QUEEN**	-	
Jul 73.	(7") (EMI 2042) **OH MY LOVE.** / **OH JAMAICA**		
Aug 73.	(lp) (EMA 757) <2147> **UNLIMITED**		

– Under the Sun, Moon and stars / Fundamental reggay / World of peace / Black queen / Be true / Oh Jamaica / Commercialization / The price of peace / On my life / I see the light / Rip off / Poor slave / Born to win. (re-iss. Oct90 lp/c/cd; CDTRJ/ZCTRJ/TRJC 100)

Oct 73.	(7") (EMI 2065) **FUNDAMENTAL REGGAY.** / **THE MONEY VERSION**		-

May 74.	(7") (EMI 2160) **LOOK WHAT YOU DONE TO MY LIFE.** / **I'VE BEEN DEAD 400 YEARS**		-
Jun 74.	(lp) (ILPS 9235) **STRUGGLING MAN**		

– Struggling man / When you're young / Better days are coming / Sooner or later / Those good old days / Can't stop worrying, can't stop loving you / Let's seize the time / I can't live without you / Going back west / Come on people.

Jul 74.	(7") (EMI 2189) **MONEY WON'T SAVE YOU.** / **YOU CAN'T BE WRONG AND GET IT RIGHT**		-
Nov 74.	(7") (EMI 2244) **DON'T LET IT DIE.** / **ACTIONS SPEAK LOUDER THAN WORDS**		-
Dec 74.	(lp) (EMC 3035) <2188> **HOUSE OF EXILE** <US-title 'MUSIC MAKER'>		

– Brother / I want to know / House of exile / Foolish pride / No.1 rip-off man / Long time no see / Music maker / My love is solid as a rock / You can't be wrong and get it right / Look what you do to my life, devil woman / Money won't save you / I've been dead 400 years. (cd-iss. Dec95 on 'EMI Europe')

Dec 74.	(7") <1315> **MUSIC MAKER.** / **YOU CAN'T BE WRONG AND GET RIGHT**	-	-
1975.	(lp) (EMC 3078) **BRAVE WARRIOR**		

– My people / Bandwagon / Every tub / Don't let it die / Actions speak louder than words / A million teardrops / Brave warrior / Save a little loving / My people (reprise).

		Reprise	Reprise
Sep 75.	(7") (EMI 2346) **OH JAMAICA.** / **MILLION TEARDROPS**		
Nov 75.	(lp) (K 54061) <2218> **FOLLOW MY MIND**		

– Look at the mountains / The news / I'm gonna live, I'm gonna love / Going mad / Dear mother / Who feels it, knows it / Remake the world / No woman no cry / Wahjhaka man / Hypocrite / If I follow my mind / You're the only one. (cd-iss. Jan96; 26311-2)

Apr 76.	(7") K 14423) **LOOK AT MY MOUNTAINS.** / **NO WOMAN NO CRY**		-
1976.	(lp) (K 54086) <2256> **LIVE IN CONCERT** (live)		

– You can get it if you really want / Vietnam / Fountain of life / Many rivers to cross / Wonderful world, beautiful people / Under the Sun, Moon and stars / Wild world / Sitting in limbo / Struggling man / The harder they come. (cd-iss. Feb92 on 'WEA'; 759927232-2)

		Warners	Warners
1976.	(7") <1383> **HARDER THEY COME** (live). / **VIETNAM** (live)	-	
1978.	(lp) (K 56558) <3240> **GIVE THANX**		

– Bongo man / Stand up and fight back / She is a woman / You left me standing by the door / Footprints / Medley in Afrika / Wanted man / Lonely street / Love I need / Universal love (beyond the boundaries).

Jan 79.	(7") (K 17295) **STAND UP AND FIGHT BACK.** / **FOOTPRINTS**		
Jun 80.	(7") (K 79135) **ALL THE STRENGTH WE GOT.** / **LOVE AGAIN**		
Jul 80.	(lp) (K 99089) <5153> **I AM THE LIVING**		

– I am the living / Another summer / All the strength we got / It's the beginning of the end / Gone clear / Love again / Morning train / Satan's kingdom. (cd-iss. Jan96; 0630 12991-2)

Oct 80.	(7") (K 79182) **ANOTHER SUMMER.** / **SATAN'S KINGDOM**		-
Jan 81.	(7") (K 79182) **ANOTHER SUMMER.** / **IT'S THE BEGINNING OF THE END**	-	
Sep 81.	(lp) (K 99160) <5153> **GIVE THE PEOPLE WHAT THEY WANT**		

– Son of man / Give the people what they want / Experience / Shelter of your love / Majority rule / Let's turn the tables / Material world / World in trap / What are you doing with your life / My philosophy. (cd-iss. Jan96; 9031 74825-2)

Sep 81.	(7") **MY PHILOSOPHY.** / **SHELTER OF YOUR LOVE**	-	

—— 1982 with backing group ONENESS

		C.B.S.	Columbia
Jul 82.	(7") (A 2605) **ROOTS RADICAL.** / **RUB-A-DUB PARTNER**	-	
Jul 82.	(7") **PEACE OFFICER.** / **SPECIAL**	-	
Jul 82.	(lp/c) (CBS/40 85878) **SPECIAL**		

– Special / Love is all / Peace officer / Treat the youths right / Keep on dancing / Rub-a-dub partner / Roots radical / Love heights / Originator / Rock children / Where there is love.

Sep 82.	(7") (A 2825) **SPECIAL.** / **KEEP ON DANCING** (dub)		-
Jan 83.	(7") (A 3037) **LOVE IS ALL.** / **ORIGINATOR** / **ROOTS RADICAL**		
Oct 83.	(7") (A 3849) **REGGAE NIGHTS.** / **LOVE HEIGHTS** (12"+=) (TA 3849) – ('A'instrumental).		
Oct 83.	(lp/c) (CBS/40 25761) **THE POWER AND THE GLORY**		

– We all are one / Sunshine in the music / Reggae nights / Piece of the pie / American dream / Roots woman / Love solution / The power and the glory / Journey. (cd-iss. 1988; CD 25761)

Jan 84.	(7") <04335> **WE ALL ARE ONE.** / **ROOTS WOMAN**		
Jan 84.	(7") (A 4056) **WE ARE ALL ONE.** / **NO APOLOGY** (12"+=) (TA 4056) – Piece of the pie.		
Aug 84.	(7") (A 4636) **REGGAE MOVEMENT.** / **TREAT THE YOUTHS RIGHT** (12"+=) (TA 4636) – ('A'dub movement).		
Jul 85.	(7") (A 6370) <05396> **HOTSHOT.** / **MODERN WORLD** (12"+=) (TA 6370) – Reggae night / ('A'instrumental).		
Aug 85.	(lp/c/cd) (CBS/40/CD 26528) **CLIFF HANGER**		

– Hitting with music / American sweet / Arrival / Brown eyes / Reggae street / Hot shot / Sunrise / Dead and awake / Now and forever / Nuclear war. (cd re-iss. Feb97 on 'Columbia'; 471220-2)

Aug 85.	(7") <05716> **AMERICAN SWEET.** / **REGGAE MOVEMENT**		
1986.	(7"; with ELVIS COSTELLO & THE ATTRACTIONS) <06135> **7-DAY WEEKEND.** / **BRIGHTEST STAR**		
1986.	(7") <06235> **CLUB PARADISE.** / **THIRD WORLD PEOPLE**		

—— In 1986, JIMMY starred in the film 'Club Paradise' on soundtrack.

Mar 88.	(lp/c/cd) (460139-1/-4/-2) **HANGING FIRE**		

– Love me love me / Hanging fire / Girls and cars / She was so right for me / It's time / Reggae down Babylon / Hold tight (eye for an eye) / Soar like an angel.

Mar 88. (7") **LOVE ME LOVE ME. / SUNSHINE IN THE MUSIC**	-		Cliff
	not iss.		
Oct 89. (lp/cd) **IMAGES**	-		-
	Musidisc		not iss.
Oct 90. (cd/c/lp) *(10655-2/-4/-1)* **SAVE OUR PLANET EARTH**			

Oct 90. (cd/c/lp) *(10655-2/-4/-1)* **SAVE OUR PLANET EARTH**
– Turning point / Rebel in me / First love / Everliving love / Trapped / Pressure / Image of the beast / Save our Planet Earth / No justice / Johnny too bad.

		Columbia	Chaos
Mar 94. (7"/c-s) *(660 198-7/-4) <77207>* **I CAN SEE CLEARLY NOW. /**			
(track by Tony Rebel)		23	18 Oct93

(cd-s+=) *(660 198-2)* – (track by other artist).
(above from the film 'Cool Runnings')

– compilations, etc. –

Note; on 'Island' unless mentioned otherwise

Mar 76. (lp) *(ICD 6)* **THE BEST OF JIMMY CLIFF**			-

– Hard road to travel / Sooner or later / Sufferin' in the land / Keep your eye on the sparrow / Struggling man / Wild world / Vietnam / Another cycle / Wonderful world, beautiful people / The harder they come / Let your yeah be yeah / Synthetic world / I'm no immigrant / Give and take / Many rivers to cross / Going back west / Sitting in limbo / Come into my life / You can get it if you really want / Goodbye yesterday. *(cd-iss. 1988 on 'Mango'; CICD 6) (cd re-iss. Mar96 on 'Reggae Refreshers'; RRCD 50)*

May 77. (7") *(WIP 6397)* **YOU CAN GET IT IF YOU REALLY WANT. / MANY RIVERS TO CROSS**		-
Jun 78. (7") *(WIP 6447)* /A&M; *<1473>* **MANY RIVERS TO CROSS. / WONDERFUL WORLD, BEAUTIFUL PEOPLE**		-
Apr 83. (7") Old Gold; *(OG 9269)* **WONDERFUL WORLD, BEAUTIFUL PEOPLE. / (track by Dandy Livingstone)**		-
1983. (12") Trojan; *(TROT 9075)* **MANY RIVERS TO CROSS. /**		-
1985. (lp/c) *(IRG/+C 1)* **REGGAE GREATS**		-
(re-iss. Jan91 on 'Reggae Refreshers' cd/c; RR CD/CT 22)		
Feb 87. (lp) See For Miles; *(SEE 83)* **FUNDAMENTAL REGGAY**		-
(cd-iss. Jan91 +=; SEECD 83) – (extra tracks).		
May 88. (7") *(IS 377)* **WILD WORLD. / HARD ROAD TO TRAVEL**		-
Feb 89. (12") Greensleeves; *(GRED 235)* **PRESSURE (version). / (b-side by JOSEY WALES)**		-
Nov 92. (cd/c) Ammi-JMS; *(JRS CD/CA 1001)* **BREAKOUT**		-
May 94. (cd) Lagoon; *(LG 21085)* **JIMMY CLIFF LIVE**		-
Jun 94. (d-cd) Trojan; *(CDTRL 342)* **MANY RIVERS TO CROSS**		-
Aug 94. (cd) Success; *(16224CD)* **LIVE (live)**		-
Feb 95. (cd/c) More Music; *(MO CD/MC 3010)* **THE COOL RUNNER LIVE IN LONDON**		-
Dec 96. (cd/c) Hallmark; *(30285-2/-4)* **MANY RIVERS TO CROSS**		-
May 97. (cd) Experience; *(EXP 009)* **JIMMY CLIFF**		-
Jul 97. (cd) Milan; *(74321 49170-2)* **100% PURE REGGAE**		-
Nov 98. (cd) Jamaican Vibes; *(JMY 200376)* **LIVE AND IN THE STUDIO**		-

CLINTON (see under ⇒ CORNERSHOP)

George CLINTON

Born: 22 Jul'40, Kannapolis, North Carolina, USA. Raised in Newark, New Jersey, CLINTON's love of doo-wop inspired him to form The PARLIAMENTS. They released a couple of singles in 1955, before moving to Detroit and recording for 'Gordy (Tamla Motown)' in 1962. The band made little progress, although GEORGE wrote songs for Motown artists such as The JACKSON 5 and DIANA ROSS. In 1965, unsuccessful in their attempts to land a deal, they issued a one-off 45, 'THAT WAS MY GIRL', for 'Golden World'. In 1967, he created the earliest incarnations of his future psychedelic image and added new musicians such as EDDIE HAZEL and BERNIE WORRELL. Signing to 'Revilot' in the States, they then hit Top 20 with single '(I WANNA) TESTIFY'. After a series of flops, he was stopped temporarily by Motown writers HOLLAND-DOZIER-HOLLAND from using PARLIAMENT'S name. Meanwhile, CLINTON was being heavily influenced by The MC5, JIMI HENDRIX, SLY & THE FAMILY STONE, the primal throb of The STOOGES and radical politics, not to mention a hefty dose of LSD. By the late 60's, his group had evolved into FUNKADELIC and signed to 'Westbound'. The eponymous debut album of 1970 set the scene with its marriage of skintight rhythm, slow burning vocals and searing psychedelic guitar freakouts. Meanwhile, CLINTON had been given back the rights to The PARLIAMENTS moniker, changing it simply to PARLIAMENT, and signing to 'Invictus'. More or less the same line-up that'd recorded 'FUNKADELIC', worked on 'OSMIUM', PARLIAMENT's 1971 debut. While this album was more in keeping with the free range psychedelia of FUNKADELIC, PARLIAMENT became a vehicle for the more groove-orientated instalments in the P-FUNK saga. The 'PARLIAFUNKADELICAMENT THANG' effect was akin to a mind-bending 60's trip put through the blender of 70's excess with a soundtrack that combined soul, blues, gospel, psychedelic rock, sex and politics to create P-FUNK. Over the coming years the collective would grow into a large musical corporation that featured over 35 members, releasing such classic albums as FUNKADELIC's 'MAGGOT BRAIN' (1971) and 'COSMIC SLOP' (1973), while PARLIAMENT's first two dancefloor friendly albums, 'UP FOR THE DOWN STROKE' (1974) and 'CHOCOLATE CITY' (1975), set the scene for the landmark 'MOTHERSHIP CONNECTION', an interstellar concept piece from the inner galaxy of CLINTON's fevered mind. His re-definition of the black man's past and sci-fi vision of the future was underpinned by the precocious instrumental precision of former JB's trio BOOTSY COLLINS, BERNIE WORRELL and FRED WESLEY. CLINTON furthered his conceptual reach with 1977's 'FUNKENTELECHY VS THE

PLACEBO SYNDROME', in which he presented his ideas of the Man keeping the kids oppressed through material dependency. In the meantime, FUNKADELIC had signed to 'Warners' and 1978's anthemic celebration of P-Funk, 'ONE NATION UNDER A GROOVE,' saw them reach a commercial and artistic peak, having already hit the US Top 30 two years previously with 'TEAR THE ROOF OFF THE SUCKER'. By the turn of the decade, there were so many side projects taking up the creative energy of the P-FUNK posse (BOOTSY'S RUBBER BAND, PARLET, HORNY HORNS, etc), that both PARLIAMENT and FUNKADELIC fizzled out, the latter releasing the last decent effort in 1981's 'ELECTRIC SPANKING OF WAR BABIES'. CLINTON went on to a solo career, offering the excellent 'COMPUTER GAMES' album and accompanying canine madness of the 'ATOMIC DOG' single. In the 90's, the ageing, dayglo warrior guested on records by PRIMAL SCREAM and ICE CUBE, as well as playing to sold out shows worldwide with The P-FUNK ALLSTARS. CLINTON's unswerving belief in the power of the funk to set people free (in every sense) lends his music a delirious, hedonistic quality, which, together with his synthesis of disparate musical styles and technology, is an ever present influence on a diverse range of artists, not leaset the P-FUNK sampling hip-hop community. • **Songwriters:** He covered SUNSHINE OF YOUR LOVE (Cream). • **Trivia:** In 1985, he collaborated with THOMAS DOLBY on 'DOLBY'S CUBE' single 'May The Cube Be With You'. Note: – An entirely different George Clinton surprised us with 'ABC' release 'Please Don't Run From Me'.

Album rating: Parliament: OSMIUM (*5) / UP FOR THE DOWN STROKE (*6) / CHOCOLATE CITY (*6) / MOTHERSHIP CONNECTION (*8) / CLONES OF DR. FUNKENSTEIN (*7) / LIVE – P FUNK EARTH TOUR (*6) / FUNKENTELECHY VS. THE PLACEBO SYNDROME (*8) / MOTOR BOOTY AFFAIR (*7) / GLORYHALLASTOOPID (*6) / TROMBIPULATION (*5) / GREATEST HITS (THE BOMB) compilation (*7) / TEAR THE ROOF OFF compilation (*8) / DOPE DOGS (*6) / THE BEST OF PARLIAMENT: GIVE UP THE FUNK compilation (*9) / Funkadelic: FUNKADELIC (*7) / FREE YOUR MIND . . . AND YOUR ASS WILL FOLLOW (*6) / MAGGOT BRAIN (*8) / AMERICA EATS ITS YOUNG (*6) / COSMIC SLOP (*7) / STANDING ON THE EDGE OF GETTING IT ON (*6) / LET'S TAKE IT TO THE STAGE (*7) / FUNKADELIC'S GREATEST HITS compilation (*6) / TALES OF KIDD FUNKADELIC (*6) / HARDCORE JOLLIES (*6) / ONE NATION UNDER A GROOVE (*8) / UNCLE JAM WANTS YOU (*7) / THE ELECTRIC SPANKING OF WAR BABIES (*7) / MUSIC FOR YOUR MOTHER compilation (*8) / George Clinton: COMPUTER GAMES (*6) / YOU SHOULDN'T-NUF BIT FISH (*6) / SOME OF MY BEST FRIENDS ARE JOKES (*7) / R&B SKELETONS IN THE CLOSET (*7) / THE CINDERELLA THEORY (*6) / HEY MAN . . . SMELL MY FINGER (*6) / THE AWESOME POWER OF A FULLY OPERATIONAL MOTHERSHIP (*5) / GREATEST FUNKIN' HITS compilation (*6)

The PARLIAMENTS

GEORGE CLINTON – vox / **CHARLES BUTCH DAVIS** – vocals / **CALVIN SIMON** – vocals repl. GENE BOYKIN / **ROBERT LAMBERT** – vocals repl. HERBIE JENKINS / **GRADY THOMAS** – vocals repl. DANNY MITCHELL

		not iss.	Hull-/Apt
May 59. (7") *<25036>* **POOR WILLIE. / PARTY BOYS**		-	

—— **JOHNNY MURRAY** repl. LAMBERT

		not iss.	Flip
1959. (7") *<100>* **LONELY ISLAND. / (YOU MAKE ME WANNA) CRY**		-	
		not iss.	Symbol
1961. (7") *<917>* **I'LL GET YOU YET. / YOU'RE CUTE**		-	
		not iss.	U.S.A.
1961. (7") *<719>* **MY ONLY LOVE. / TO BE ALONE**		-	

—— Spent 4 years writing for Motown . . . then sign to (see below)

—— **CLARENCE 'Fuzzy' HASKINS** – vocals repl. JOHNNY MURRAY + CALVIN SIMON **RAYMOND DAVIS** – vocals repl. BUTCH DAVIS

		not iss.	Golden World
1966. (7") *<46>* **HEART TROUBLE. / THAT WAS MY GIRL**		-	

—— added **EDDIE HAZEL** – lead guitar / **TAWL ROSS** – rhythm guitar / **BILLY NELSON** – bass / **MICKEY ATKINS** – organ (on some) / **TIKI FULWOOD** – drums

		not iss.	Revilot
Jun 67. (7") *<207>* **(I WANNA) TESTIFY. / I CAN FEEL THE ICE MELTING**		-	20
Sep 67. (7") *<211>* **ALL YOUR GOODIES ARE GONE (THE LOSER'S SEAT). / DON'T BE SORE AT ME**		-	80
Nov 67. (7") *<214>* **THE GOOSE (THAT LAID THE GOLDEN EGG). / LITTLE MAN**		-	
Jan 68. (7") *<217>* **LOOK AT WHAT I ALMOST MISSED. / WHAT YOU BEEN GROWING**		-	
Nov 68. (7") *<228>* **A NEW DAY BEGINS. / I'LL WAIT**		-	

<re-iss. Jan69 on 'Atco'; 6675>; hit No.44>

—— 12 years later, this song was to give CLINTON rights to group name.

		not iss.	Funkedelic
1969. (7"; ROSE WILLIAMS with GEORGE CLINTON & FUNKADELICS) *<6709>* **WHATEVER MAKES MY BABY FEEL GOOD. / ('A'instrumental)**		-	

FUNKADELIC

—— **CLINTON + RAYMOND DAVIS** – vocals / **CLARENCE 'Fuzzy' HASKINS** – vocals / **EDDIE HAZEL** – lead guitar / **TAWL ROSS** – rhythm guitar / **TIKI FULTON** – drums / **MICKEY ATKINS** – some organ

BERNIE WORRELL – keyboards repl. ATKINS

			Pye Int.	Westbound	
1969.	(7") <148> **MUSIC FOR MY MOTHER.** / ('A'instrumental)		–		
Sep 69.	(7") <150> **I'LL BET YOU.** / QUALIFY AND SATISFY			63	
Apr 70.	(7") (7N 25519) <158> **I GOT A THING, YOU GOT A THING, EVERYBODY'S GOT A THING.** / FISH, CHIPS & SWEAT			80	Feb70
Sep 70.	(lp) (NSPL 28137) <2000> **FUNKADELIC**				Mar70

– Mommy, what's a Funkadelic? / I'll bet you / Music for my mother / I got a thing, you got a thing, everybody's got a thing / Good old music / Quality and satisfaction / What is soul?. (re-iss.Aug89 on 'Westbound' lp/c/cd; SEW/SEWC/CDSEW 010)

Dec 70.	(7") <167> **I WANNA KNOW IF IT'S GOOD TO YOU.** / ('A'instrumental)		–	81	
1971.	(lp) (NSPL 28137) <2001> **FREE YOUR MIND . . . AND YOUR ASS WILL FOLLOW**			92	Oct70

– Free your mind and your ass will follow / Friday night, August 14th / Funky dollar bill / I wanna know if it's good to you / Some more / Eulogy and light. (re-iss.Feb90 on 'Westbound' lp/c/cd; SEW/SEWC/CDSEW 012)

Apr 71.	(7") (7N 25548) <175> **YOU & YOUR FOLKS, ME & MINE.** / FUNKY DOLLAR BILL			91	Feb71

PARLIAMENT

(i.e. CLINTON & FUNKADELIC musicians) + R.DAVIS / G.THOMAS / F.HASKINS / C.SIMON

			Invictus	Invictus	
Dec 70.	(7") <9077> **I CALL MY BABY PUSSYCAT.** / LITTLE OLE COUNTRY BOY	(UK-iss.Dec84 on 'H.D.H.'; HDH 457)	–		
Feb 71.	(7") <9091> **RED HOT MAMA.** / LITTLE OLE COUNTRY BOY		–		
Jul 71.	(lp) (SVT 1004) <7302> **OSMIUM**		–		Dec70

– The breakdown / Call my baby Pussycat / Little ole country boy / Moonshine Heather / Oh Lord – why Lord – prayer / Red hot mama / My automobile / Nothing before me but thang / Funky woman / Come on in out of the rain / The silent boatman. (re-iss.Feb90 as 'RHENIUM' on 'H.D.H.' cd/c/lp; HDH CD/MC/LP 008) – (extra tracks) (cd-iss.Jul93;)

Jul 71.	(7") (INV 513) **LIVIN' THE LIFE.** / THE SILENT BOATMAN		–	–	
Jul 71.	(7") <9095> **THE BREAKDOWN.** / LITTLE OLE COUNTRY BOY		–		
Sep 71.	(7") <9123> **COME IN OUT OF THE RAIN.** / LITTLE OLE COUNTRY BOY		–		

FUNKADELIC

Now without NELSON + ROSS. Replaced by **GARY SHIDER** – guitar

			Westbound	Westbound	
Sep 71.	(7") <185> **CAN YOU GET TO THAT.** / BACK IN OUR MINDS		–	93	
Sep 71.	(lp) (6310 200) <2007> **MAGGOT BRAIN**				Aug71

– Maggot brain / Can you get to that / Hit it and quit it / You and your folks, me and mine / Super stupid / Back in our minds / Wars of armageddon. (re-iss.Aug89 lp/c/cd; SEW/SEWC/CDSEW 002)

added **WILLIAM BOOTSY COLLINS** – bass / **CATFISH COLLINS** – guitar / **FRANKIE 'Kash' WADDY** – drums (all of The J.B.'s, ex-JAMES BROWN)

Jul 72.	(d-lp) <2020> **AMERICA EATS IT'S YOUNG**		–		

– You hit the nail on the head / If you don't like the effects / Don't produce the cause / Everybody is going to make it this time / A joyful process / We hurt too / Loose booty / Philmore / I call my baby Pussycat / America eats its young / Biological speculation / That was my girl / Balance / Miss Lucifer's love / Wake up. (UK cd-iss.Jul90 cd/c/lp; CDSEWD/SEWC2/SEW2 029)

1972.	(7") <197> **I MISS MY BABY.** / BABY I OWE YOU SOMETHING GOOD		–		
1972.	(7") <198> **HIT AND QUIT IT.** / A WHOLE LOT OF BS		–		
1973.	(7") <205> **LOOSE BOOTY.** / A JOYFUL PROCESS		–		
Jul 73.	(lp) <2022> **COSMIC SLOP**		–		

– Happy dug out / You can't miss what you can't measure / March to the witches castle / Let's make it last / Cosmic slop / No compute (alias spit don't make no babies) / Broken heart / Trash a go-go / Can't stand the strain. (UK-iss.Feb91 cd/c/lp; CDSEW/SEWC/SEWA 035)

1973.	(7") <218> **COSMIC SLOP.** / YOU DON'T LIKE THE EFFECTS, DON'T PRODUCE THE CAUSE		–		

added **FRED WESLEY & MACEO PARKER** – horns (both of J.B.'s)

Nov 74.	(lp) <1001> **STANDING ON THE VERGE OF GETTING IT ON**		–		Sep74

– Red hot mama / Alice in my fantasies / I'll stay / Sexy ways / Standing on the verge of getting it on / Jimmy's got a little bit of bitch in him / Good thoughts, bad thoughts. (re-iss.Aug91 cd/c/lp; CDSEW/SEWC/SEWA 040)

Nov 74.	(7") <224> **(STANDING) ON THE VERGE OF GETTING IT ON.** / JIMMY'S GOT A LITTLE BIT OF BITCH IN HIM.		–		
1975.	(7") <5000> **RED HOT MAMA.** / VITAL JUICES		–		
1975.	(lp) <1004> **FUNKADELIC'S GREATEST HITS** (compilation)				Jul74

			20th Century	Westbound	
Jun 75.	(lp) (215) **LET'S TAKE IT TO THE STAGE**				

– Good to your earhole / Better by the pound / Be my beach / No head no backstage pass / Let's take it to the stage / Get off your ass and jam / Baby I owe you something good / Stuffs & things / The song is familiar / Atmosphere. (UK re-iss.Mar92 cd/c/lp; CDSEW/SEWC/SEWA 044)

Oct 75.	(7") <5014> **BETTER BY THE POUND.** / STUFFS AND THINGS		–	99	
Jan 76.	(7") <5026> **LET'S TAKE IT TO THE STAGE.** / BIOLOGICAL SPECULATION		–		

MIKE HAMPTON – guitar repl. EDDIE HAZEL who went solo

1976.	(lp) <227> **TALES OF KIDD FUNKADELIC**		–		

– Butt to butt resuscitation / Let's take it to the people / Undisco kid / Take your dead ass home / I'm never gonna tell it / Takes of Kidd Funkadelic / How do yeaw view you. (UK re-iss.Mar93 cd/lp; CDSEW/SEWA 054)

1976.	(7") <5029> **UNDISCO KIDD.** / HOW DO YEAW VIEW YOU		–		

After one more compilation 'THE BEST OF FUNKADELIC EARLY YEARS,

VOL.1' in 1977, COLLINS continued with BOOTSY'S RUBBER BAND. Also leaving were HASKINS, SIMON and DAVIS who were to form own FUNKADELIC in the early 80's. They and 'Lax' label issued album CONNECTIONS AND DISCONNECTIONS (without CLINTON).

Meanwhile in the mid-70's,

PARLIAMENT

(CLINTON, etc.) were signed to . . .

			Casablanca	Casablanca	
Dec 74.	(7") <0003> **THE GOOSE (pt.1).** / (pt.2)		–		
Dec 74.	(lp) (CAL 2011) <7002> **UP FOR THE DOWN STROKE**				Aug74

– Up for the down stroke / Testify / The goose / I can move you (if you let me) / I just got back / All your goodies are gone / Whatever makes baby feel good / Presence of a brain. (re-iss.May77 & Nov78; same)

Feb 75.	(7") (CBX 505) <0013> **UP FOR THE DOWN STROKE.** / PRESENCE OF A BRAIN			63	Aug74
Feb 75.	(7") <811> **TESTIFY.** / I CAN MOVE YOU (IF YOU LET ME)		–		
May 75.	(7") <831> **CHOCOLATE CITY.** / ('A'long version)			94	
Jun 75.	(lp) (CAL 2012) <7014> **CHOCOLATE CITY**			91	Apr75

– Chocolate city / Ride on / Together / Side effects / What comes funky / Let me be / If it don't fit (don't force it) / Misjudged you / Big footin'. (re-iss.May77; same)

Nov 75.	(7") <843> **RIDE ON.** / BIG FOOTIN'		–		
Jun 76.	(7") <852> **P. FUNK (WANTS TO GET FUNKED UP).** / NIGHT OF THE THUMPASORUS PEOPLES		–		
Jun 76.	(lp) (CAL 2013) <7022> **MOTHERSHIP CONNECTION**			13	Feb76

– P. Funk (wants to get funked up) / Mothership connection (star child) / Unfunky UFO / Supergroovalisticprosifunkstication (the thumps bump) / Handcuffs / Tear the roof off the sucker (give up the funk) / Night of the thumpasorus people. (re-iss.May77; same) (re-iss.Aug87; 824 502-1/-4)

Jun 76.	(7") (CBX 518) <856> **TEAR THE ROOF OFF THE SUCKER (GIVE UP THE FUNK).** / P. FUNK (WANTS TO GET FUNKED UP)			15	May76
1976.	(7") <864> **STAR CHILD.** / SUPERGROOVALISTICPROSIFUNKSTACATION (THE THUMPS BUMB)		–	–	
Oct 76.	(7",12") <871> **DO THAT STUFF.** / HANDCUFFS		–		
May 77.	(lp) (CAL 2001) <7034> **THE CLONES OF DR. FUNKENSTEIN**			20	Oct76

– Prelude / Gamin' on ya / Dr. Funkenstein / Children of productions / Gettin' to know you / Do that stuff / Everything is on the one / I've been watching you (move your sexy body) / Funkin' for fun. (re-iss.Feb91 cd/c/lp; 842620-2)

Jan 77.	(7") <875> **DR. FUNKENSTEIN.** / CHILDREN OF PRODUCTION		–		
May 77.	(7"m) (CAN 103) **TEAR THE ROOF OFF THE SUCKER (GIVE UP THE FUNK).** / DR. FUNKENSTEIN / P. FUNK (WANTS TO GET FUNKED UP)			–	
Jun 77.	(d-lp) (CALD 5002) <7053> **PARLIAMENT LIVE – P.FUNK EARTH TOUR** (live)			29	May77

– P. Funk (wants to get funked up) / Dr. Funkenstein's supergroovalisticprosi-funkstication / Medley: (a) Let's take it to the stage, (b) Take your dead ass home, (c) Say som'n nasty / Do that stuff / The landing (of the holy mothership) / The undisco Kidd (the girl is bad) / Children of production / Mothership connection (star child) / Swing down, sweet chariot / This is the way we funk with you (featuring Mike Hampton; lead snare) / Dr. Funkenstein / Gamin' on you / Tear the roof off the sucker medley:- (a) Give up the funk (tear the roof off the sucker) (b) Get off your ass and jam / Night of the thumpasorus people / Fantasy is reality.

1977.	(7") <892> **FANTASY IS REALITY.** / THE LANDING (OF THE HOLY MOTHERSHIP)		–		
Dec 77.	(lp) (CALN 2021) <7084> **FUNKENTELECHY VS. THE PLACEBO SYNDROME**			13	

– Bop gun (endangered species) / Sir Nose D'voidoffunk / Pay attention B-3M / Wizard of finance / Funkentelechy / Placebo syndrome / Flash light.

Jan 78.	(7") (CAN 115) <900> **BOP GUN (ENDANGERED SPECIES).** / I'VE BEEN WATCHING YOU (MOVE YOUR SEXY BODY)				Nov77

(12"+=) (CANL 115) – Do that stuff. <US-12" has 2 'A'mixes>

Apr 78.	(7") (CAN 123) <909> **FLASH LIGHT.** / SWING LOW, SWEET CHARIOT (live)			16	Feb78

(US-12") <same> – (2 'A'mixes).

1978.	(7") <921> **FUNKENTELECHY (part 1).** / (part 2)		–	–	

Early '78, other PARLIAMENT / FUNKADELIC off-shoots "PARLET" (vocalists MALLIA FRANKLIN, JEANETTE WASHINGTON and SHIRLEY HAYDEN) released album 'THE PLEASURE PRINCIPLE'. Another album 'INVASIONS OF THE BODY SNATCHERS' was further issued Jul 79. "The BRIDES OF FUNKENSTEIN" (vocalists LYNN MABRY and DAWN SILVA) released album 'FUNK OR WALK' on 'Atlantic' late 1978.

FUNKADELIC

meanwhile had reappeared signing to . . .

			Warners	Warners	
1977.	(7") <8309> **COMIN' ROUND THE MOUNTAIN.** / IF YOU GOT FUNK, YOU GOT STYLE		–		
Feb 78.	(lp) (K 56299) <2973> **HARDCORE JOLLIES**			96	Nov77

– Osmosis phase one / Comin' round the mountain / Smokey / If you got funk, you got style / Hardcore jollies / Territibus phase two / Sould mate / Cosmic slop / You scared the lovin' outta me / Adolescent funk. (re-iss.Jul93 on 'Charly' cd/lp; CDGR/LPGR 101)

Feb 78.	(7") <8367> **SMOKEY.** / SOUL MATE		–	–	

add **JEROME BRAILEY** – drums (who had joined PARLIAMENT mid '76) / **WALTER 'JUNIE' MORRISON** – keyboards (ex-OHIO PLAYERS)

Nov 78.	(7"/12") (K 17246/+T) <8618> **ONE NATION UNDER A GROOVE (part 1).** / (part 2)		9	28	Oct78
Dec 78.	(lp) (K 56539) <3209> **ONE NATION UNDER A GROOVE**		56	16	Sep78

– One nation under a groove / Groovallegience / Who says a funk band can't play rock / Promentalashitbackwashpsychosisenema squad / Into you / Cholly (funk getting ready to roll) / Lunchmeat and phobia / P.E.squad / Doodoo chasers / Maggot brain. (re-iss.Jul93 on 'Charly' cd/lp; CDGR/LPGR 100)

Apr 79. (7") (K 17321) <8735> **CHOLLY (FUNK GETTING READY TO ROLL). / INTO YOU**
(US-12") <same> – (2-'A'mixes).

—— drummer BRAILEY left to form own group MUTINY.

Oct 79. (lp) (K 56712) <3371> **UNCLE JAM WANTS YOU** ☐ **18**
– Freak of the week / (Not just) Knee deep / Uncle Jam / Field manoeuvres / Cholly wants to go to California / Foot soldiers. (re-iss. Jun93 on 'Charly' cd/lp; CDGR/LPGR 103)

Jan 80. (7") (K 17494) <49040> **(NOT JUST) KNEE DEEP. / (part 2)** **77** Oct79

1980. (7") <49117> **UNCLE JAM. / (part 2)** –

Aug 81. (7"/12") (K 17786/+T) <49667> **THE ELECTRIC SPANKING OF WAR BABIES. / THE ELECTRIC SPANKING (instrumental)**

Apr 81. (lp) (K 56874) <3482> **THE ELECTRIC SPANKING OF WAR BABIES**
– The electric spanking of war babies / Electrocuties / Funk gets stronger / Brettino's bounce / She loves you / Shockwaves / Oh, I / Laka-prick. (re-iss. Jun93 on 'Charly' cd/lp; CDGR/LPGR 102)

1981. (7") <49807> **SHOCKWAVES. / BRETTINO'S BOUNCE** –

—— (above featured CLINTON's long-time friend SLY STONE)

—— The FUNKADELIC project had now been abandoned, due to splinter band.

PARLIAMENT

were still around simultaneously with FUNKADELIC and continued throughout the 80's.
                    Casablanca Casablanca

Dec 78. (7") (CAN 136) <950> **AQUA BOOGIE (A PSYCHOALPHADISCOBETABIOQUADOLOOP). / (YOU'RE A FISH AND I'M A) WATER SIGN** **89**

Dec 78. (lp/pic-lp) (CAL N/H 2043) <7125> **MOTOR-BOOTY AFFAIR** **23**
– Mr. Wiggles / Rumpopsteelskin / (You're a fish and I'm a) Water sign / Aqua boogie (a psychoalphadiscobetabioquadoloop) / One of those funky things / Liquid sunshine / Motor-booty affair / Deep. (re-iss. Feb91 cd/c/lp; 842621-2)

1979. (7") <976> **RUMPOFSTEELSKIN. / LIQUID SUNSHINE**

Jul 79. (7"/12") (CAN/+L 154) **DEEP. / FLASH LIGHT** –

Dec 79. (lp) <(NBLP 7195)> **GLORYHALLASTOOPID – OR PIN THE TALE ON THE FUNKY** – **44**
– Party people / Big bang theory / Freeze (sizzaleenmean) / Colour me funky / Theme from the black hole / May we bang you / Gloryhallastoopid (or pin the tale on the funky).

Jan 80. (12") (CANL 188) **THEME FROM THE BLACK HOLE. / THE BIG BANG THEORY** –

Apr 80. (7") <(NR 2222)> **PARTY PEOPLE. / PARTY PEOPLE (reprise)** Dec79
(12") – ('A'side) / Tear the roof off the sucker (give up the funk) / Flash light.

1980. (7") <2235> **THEME FROM THE BLACK HOLE. / (YOU'RE A FISH AND I'M A) WATER SIGN** –

Apr 81. (7"/12") (CAN/+L 223) <2250> **AGONY OF DE FEET. / THE FREEZE (SIZZALEENMEAN)**

Apr 81. (lp) <(NBLP 7249)> **TROMBIPULATION** **61** Jan81
– Trombipulation / crush it / Long way round / Agony of de feet / Now doo review / Let's play house / Body language / Peck-a-groove. (cd-iss. Feb91; 842623-2)

—— PARLIAMENT were also defunkt, leaving behind a few exploitation releases

1981. (12") <NBD 20235> **CRUSH IT. / BODY LANGUAGE** –

GEORGE CLINTON

(solo) with numerous session people and **BOOTSY COLLINS / FRED WESLEY**

—— another GEORGE CLINTON issued 1979 single 'Please Don't Run From Me'
               Capitol   Capitol

Nov 82. (lp/c) <(EST/TCEST 12246)> **COMPUTER GAMES** **40**
– Get dressed / Man's best friend / Loopzilla / Pot sharing tots / Computer games / Atomic dog / Free alterations / One fun at a time. (re-iss. May95 on 'MCI' cd/c; MUS CD/MC 511) (cd-iss. Apr97 on 'E.M.I.'; REPLAYCD 45)

Nov 82. (7") <5160> **LOOPZILLA. / POT SHARING TOTS** **57**
(12"+=) (12CL 271) – ('A'-broadcast version).
(US-12") <8538> – (2-'A'versions).

Feb 83. (7")(12") (CL 280) <5201><8556> **ATOMIC DOG. / MAN'S BEST FRIEND**
(12"+=) (12CL 280) <8544> – ('A'instrumental).

1983. (7") <5222> **GET DRESSED. / FREE ALTERATIONS** –

Dec 83. (7"/12") (CL 319) <5296><8572> **NUBIAN NUT. / FREE ALTERATIONS** –
(12") <9039> – (2-'A'versions).

Jan 84. (lp/c) <(EST/TCEST 12308)> **YOU SHOULDN'T NUF BIT FISH** Dec83
– Nubian nut / Quickie / Last dance / Silly millameter / Stingy / You shouldn't – Nuf bit fish. (cd-iss. Sep91 on 'E.M.I.'; CZ 469)

1984. (7")(12") <5324><8580> **QUICKIE. / LAST DANCE** –

1984. (7")(ext-12") <5332><9065> **LAST DANCE. / LAST DANCE (version)** –

Jul 85. (7") (CL 365) <5473> **DOUBLE OH-OH. / BANGLADESH** –
(12") <8642> – (2-'A'versions).

Sep 85. (lp/c) (CLINT/TC-CLINT 1) <12417> **SOME OF MY BEST JOKES ARE FRIENDS** Aug85
– Some of my best jokes are friends / Double oh-oh / Bulletproof / Pleasures of exhaustion (do it till I drop) / Bodyguard / Bangladesh / Thrashin' / Some of my best jokes are friends – reprise.

Dec 85. (7")(12") <5504><8653> **BULLETPROOF. / SILLY MILLAMETER** –

Apr 86. (7") (CL 402) **DO FRIES GO WITH THAT SHAKE. / PLEASURES OF EXHAUSTION (DO IT TILL I DROP)** **57**
(UK-12"+=) (12CL 402) – Scratch medley.
(US-12") <15219> – (2-'A'versions).

—— Did he release IRON EAGLE (Soundtrack) album around this time?

May 86. (7") <5602> **HEY GOOD LOOKIN'. / ('A'mix)** –
(12"+=) <15263> – ('A'extended).

May 86. (lp) <12481> **R&B SKELETONS (IN THE CLOSET)** –

– Hey good looking / Do fries go with that shake / Mix master suite – Startin' from scratch – Counter irritant – Nothing left to burn – Electric Pygmies – Intense – Cool Joe – R&B Skeleton (in the closet). (UK cd-iss. Sep91 on 'E.M.I.'; CZ 470)

1986. (7") <5642> **R&B SKELETONS IN THE CLOSET. / NUBIAN NUT** –

1987. (lp) <12534> **THE BEST OF GEORGE CLINTON & THE MOTHERSHIP CONNECTION LIVE FROM HOUSTON (live)** –
– Atomic dog / R&B skeletons (in the closet) / Quickie / Do fries go with that shake / Hey good lookin' / Double oh-oh / Nubian nut / Last dance.
               Paisley   Paisley
               Park   Park

Jul 89. (7"/12") (W 7557/+T) <27557> **WHY SHOULD I DOG U OUT (part 1). / (part 2)**

Aug 89. (lp/c/cd) (K 925994-1/-4/-2) <25994> **THE CINDERELLA THEORY**
– Airbound / Tweakin' / The Cinderella theory / Why should I dog you out? / Serious slammin' / There I go again / (She's got it) Goin' on / The banana boat song / French kiss / Rita bewitched / Kredit-Kard / Airbound (reprise).

1989. (7") <22190> **TWEAKIN'. / FRENCH KISS** –
(12") <21337> – ('A'side) / Hysterical / ('A'remix).

Oct 93. (cd/c) (7599 25518-2/-4) **HEY MAN, SMELL MY FINGER**
– Martial law / Paint the White House black / Way up / Dis beat disrupts / Get satisfied / Hollywood / Rhythm and rhyme / The big pump / If true love / High in my hello / Maximumisness / Kickback / The flag was still there / Martial law (hey man . . . smell my finger) (single version). (re-iss. Mar95 on 'New Power Generation' cd/c; NPG 6053-2/-4)

—— CLINTON guested for PRIMAL SCREAM on their early 1994 album 'GIVE OUT BUT DON'T GIVE UP'. To start the second half of '94, he featured on ICE CUBE single 'BOP GUN (ONE NATION) ', a re-indition of his old FUNKADELIC number.
               Essential   Rykodisc

Feb 95. (cd) (ESSCD 280) **FIFTH OF FUNK**
– Flatman and Robin / Count Funkula (I didn't know that funk was loaded) / Thumparella (Oh Kay) / Eyes of a dreamer / I found you / Ice melting in your heart / Clone ranger / Who do you love / Up up up and away / Can't get over losing you / Rat kissed the cat / Too tight for light / Every little bit hurts. (re-iss. Apr97; ESMCD 490)

P-FUNK ALL STARS

—— another CLINTON aggregation
               not iss.   Hump

1982. (7") <1> **HYDRAULIC PUMP. / (part 2)** –

1982. (7") <3> **ONE OF THOSE SUMMERS. / IT'S TOO FUNKY IN HERE** –
               not iss.   CBS

1983. (7") <04032> **GENERATOR POP. / (part 2)** –
               not iss.   Uncle Jam

1983. (lp) <39168> **URBAN DANCEFLOOR GUERRILLAS** –
               Westbound Westbound

Oct 90. (d-cd/d-c/d-lp) (CDSEW2/SEWC2/SEW2 031) **P-FUNK ALL STARS LIVE (live at The Beverly Theater 1983)**

Jun 95. (cd/lp) (CD+/SEWD 097) **HYDRAULIC FUNK** (early material) –
– Pump up and down / Pumpin' it up / Copy cat / Throw your hand up in the air / Generator pop / Acupuncture / One of those summers / Catch a keeper / Pumpin' you is so easy / Generator pop (mix).

PARLIAMENT, FUNKADELIC & THE P-FUNK ALL STARS

               Hot Hands Hot Hands

Apr 95. (12"/cd-s) (12/CD HOTH 1) **FOLLOW THE LEADER. / ('A'-D&S radio mix) / ('A'-Kool az phuk mix)**

May 95. (cd/c) (HOTH CD/CD/MC/LP 1) **DOPE DOGS** Mar95
– Dog star (fly on) / U.S. custom coast guard dope dog / Some next shit / Just say ding (databoy) / Help Scottie, help I'm tweaking and I . . . .) / Pepe (the pill popper) / Back against the wall / Fifi / All songs of bitches / Sick 'em / I ain't the lady (he ain't the tramp) / Pack of wild dogs / Tales that wag the dog / My dog.

GEORGE CLINTON & THE P-FUNK ALLSTARS

               MJJ-Epic MJJ-Epic

May 96. (c-s) (663321-4) **IF ANYBODY'S GONNA GET FUNKED UP / ('A' instrumentals)**
(12"/cd-s) (663321-6/-2) – ('A'– Colin Wolfe remixes)

Jun 96. (cd/c/lp) (483833-2/-4/-1) **T.A.P.O.A.F.O.M.**
– If anybody gets funked up (it's gonna be you) / Summer swim / Funky kind (gonna knock it down) / Mathematics / Hard as steel / New spaceship / Underground angel / Let's get funky / Flatman and Bobbin / Sloppy seconds / Rock the party / Get your funk on / T.A.P.O.A.F.O.M. (fly away).

—— also P-FUNK singles on UK 'Frontline' in 1995; 'P-FUNK ERA' & 'RETURN OF THE GANGSTA'

– (GEORGE CLINTON compilations) –

Aug 92. (cd/c/lp; Various) Essential; (ESS CD/MC/LP 185) **GEORGE CLINTON FAMILY SERIES – VOL.1** –
(cd re-iss. Jul96; ESMCD 383)

Jan 93. (cd/c/lp; Various) Essential; (ESS CD/MC/LP 189) **GEORGE CLINTON FAMILY SERIES – VOL.2** –
(cd re-iss. Jul96; ESMCD 384)

Feb 93. (cd/lp) Music Of Life; (MOL CD/LP 026) **SAMPLE SOME OF DISC, SAMPLE SOME OF DAT** –
(re-iss. Nov94 cd/lp; MOL CD/LP 36)

Jun 93. (cd/c/lp; Various) Esantial; (ESS CD/MC/LP 190) **GEORGE CLINTON FAMILY SERIES PART 3 – P IS THE FUNK** –
(cd re-iss. Jul96; ESMCD 385)

Sep 93. (cd/c/lp; Various) Essential; (ESS CD/MC/LP 198) **GEORGE CLINTON FAMILY SERIES – VOL.4** –

Oct 93. (cd/lp) *Music For Life; (MOL CD/LP 33)* **SAMPLE SOME OF DISC, SAMPLE SOME OF DAT, VOL.II** ☐ ☐

Mar 97. (d-lp/cd) *EMI Premier; (PRMD/+CD 20)* **THE GREATEST FUNKIN' HITS** ☐ ☐

– (PARLIAMENT) compilations –

Sep 86. (lp/c) *Club; (JAB B/C 18)* **UNCUT FUNK – THE BOMB (THE BEST OF PARLIAMENT)** ☐ ☐

May 93. (d-cd) *Mercury; (514417-2)* **TEAR THE ROOF OFF: 1974-80** ☐ ☐
(re-iss. Sep95; same)

Oct 94. (cd; PARLIAMENTS) *Goldmine; (GSCD 052)* **I WANNA TESTIFY** ☐ ☐

Sep 95. (cd) *Mercury; (526995-2)* **GIVE UP THE FUNK** ☐ ☐

Jun 97. (cd) *Deepbeats; (DEEPMO 23)* **PARLIAMENT – THE EARLY YEARS** ☐ ☐

– (FUNKADELIC) compilations, etc –

1989. (12") *M.C.A.; <23953>* **BY THE WAY OF THE DRUM. / ('A'edit) / ('A'instrumental)** ☐ ☐

Aug 90. (4xpic-cd-box) *Westbound; (WBOXPD 1)* **FUNKADELIC PICTURE DISC BOX SET** ☐ ☐

Oct 92. (d-cd/d-c/d-lp) *Westbound; (CDSEW/SEWC/SEW 2055)* **MUSIC FOR YOUR MOTHER (the singles)** ☐ ☐

Mar 94. (4xpic-cd-box) *Westbound; (WBOXPD 5)* **PICTURE DISC BOXED SET VOLUME 2** ☐ ☐
– (COSMIC SLOP / TALES OF KIDD FUNKADELIC / LET'S TAKE IT TO THE STAGE / STANDING ON THE VERGE OF GETTING IT ON)

Mar 94. (cd/lp) *Charly; (CDGR/LPGR 104)* **THE BEST OF FUNKADELIC 1976-1981** ☐ ☐

Nov 94. (cd) *Charly; (CPCD 8064)* **HARDCORE FUNK JAM** ☐ ☐

Oct 94. (4xcd-box) *Sequal; (NEFCD 273)* **PARLIAMENT / FUNKADELIC LIVE (live)** ☐ ☐

Apr 96. (c-s/12"/cd-s) *Charly; (MC/12/CD NATION 1)* **ONE NATION UNDER A GROOVE** ☐ ☐

Apr 96. (cd) *Westbound; (CDSEWD 108)* **FUNKADELIC LIVE (live Rochester 1971)** ☐ ☐

May 97. (cd/c) *Southbound; (CD+/SEWD 115)* **FINEST** ☐ ☐

CLOCKDVA (dig out; Great Alt & Indie . . .)

COAL CHAMBER

Formed: Los Angeles, California, USA . . . mid 90's by vocalist DEZ FAFARA, guitarist MIGUEL "MEEGS" RASCON, bassist RAYNA FOSS and drummer MIKE "BUG" COX. Despite initially splitting soon after their inception, the facial-piercing group quickly re-formed and signed a deal with 'Roadrunner'. In 1996/97, they unleashed their eponymous debut set, a very KORN-like affair (the intro of 'LOCO' virtually a clone of 'Daddy') which saw them become the darlings of the metal press. Wielding a powerful, RATM-esque bass groove overlaid with FAFARA's tongue-twistingly distinctive death growl, COAL CHAMBER boasted one of the most exciting sound blueprints in the current metal scene. Around the middle of '97, they were rumoured to be working on a version of Peter Gabriel's 'SHOCK THE MONKEY'!!!, most people (even myself!) questioning this until its inclusion (and release as single) on their sophomore set, 'CHAMBER MUSIC' (1999). Harking back to the days of industrial-goth rock (ALIEN SEX FIEND their new mentors!?), the "spook-core" album lacked the bite of their debut although it nearly hit the Top 20 on both sides of the Atlantic. Now married to SEVENDUST's drummer MORGAN ROSE, pregnant RAYNA FOSS-ROSE (who had been temp'd by the stunning NADJA POROMBKA) was absent from tour and promotion duties.

Album rating: COAL CHAMBER (*7) / CHAMBER MUSIC (*5)

DEZ FAFARA – vocals / **MIGUEL "MEEGS" RASCON** – guitar, vocals / **RAYNA FOSS** – bass / **MIKE "BUG" COX** – drums

	Roadrunner	I.R.S.

Mar 97. (cd/c) *(RR 8863-2/-4) <983.063>* **COAL CHAMBER** ☐ ☐
– Loco / Bradley / Oddity / Unspoiled / Big truck / Sway / First / Maricon puto / I / Clock / My frustration / Amir of the desert / Dreamtime / Pig. *(cd re-iss. Dec97; RR 8863-5)*

Jun 98. (cd-ep) *(RR 2229-3)* **LOCO / BLISTERS / SWAY (remix) / LOCO (remastered)** ☐ ☐

— temp **NADJA POROMBKA** – bass; repl. RAYNA (see above)

	Roadrunner	Roadrunner

Sep 99. (cd) *<(RR 8659-2)>* **CHAMBER MUSIC** [21] [22]
– Tragedy / El cu cuy / Untrue / Tyler's song / What's in your mind / Not living / Shock the monkey / Burgundy / Anahstasia / Feed my dreams / My mercy / No home / Shari Vegas / Notion / Anything but you. *(special-cd+=; RR 8659-5)* – Apparation / Wishes.

Nov 99. (cd-s) *(RR 2134-3)* **SHOCK THE MONKEY / SHOCK THE MONKEY (Gorilla mix) / EL CU CUY (remix)** ☐ ☐

COAL PORTERS (see under ⇒ LONG RYDERS)

Eddie COCHRAN

Born: EDWARD RAY COCHRAN, 3 Oct'38, Oklahoma City, Oklahoma. Raised in Albert Lea, Minnesota, he later moved with his Irish parents to Bell Gardens, Los Angeles in 1951. Four years later, the young, self-taught guitarist EDDIE formed The COCHRANS with his hillbilly friend, HANK COCHRAN

(no relation), the pair soon securing a deal with 'Ekko'. Songwriter JERRY CAPEHEART joined the duo early in 1956 for a single 'WALKIN' STICK BOOGIE', although HANK subsequently moved to Nashville after CAPEHEART became EDDIE's new writing partner (and later manager). Although their first collaboration, 'SKINNY JIM', flopped, CAPEHEART negotiated a deal with 'Liberty', who, in turn, released his major label debut, 'SITTIN' IN THE BALCONY'. Boosted by a cameo role in the rock'n'roll movie, 'The Girl Can't Help It' (performing 'TWENTY FLIGHT ROCK'), the single became a Top 20 hit in the Spring of '57. After a couple of flops and minor hits during the next year, he finally recorded a commercial follow-up in 'SUMMERTIME BLUES', a lip-curling, deceptively simple, all-time classic, which introduced COCHRAN the leather-clad, rebellious rocker to hordes of screaming female fans. Rock'n'roll's answer to James Dean, he eventually followed up with two more attitude-stoked nuggets, 'C'MON EVERYBODY' and 'SOMETHIN' ELSE'; twenty years on, the SEX PISTOLS – with SID VICIOUS at the helm – resurrected these hits in appropriately snotty punk style. In the interim, COCHRAN took part in the Alan Freed / Hal Roach film, 'Go, Johnny Go!', although he had to withdraw from a winter tour alongside his famous friend, BUDDY HOLLY. The tour in question was the ill-fated jaunt that claimed the lives of not just HOLLY, but RICHIE VALENS and BIG BOPPER, all three dying when their plane crashed in February '59. Early the following year, on the strength of his UK success (he was now a bigger star in Britain than he was in the States!), COCHRAN toured around England with co-headliner, GENE VINCENT, for a few months. Having accepted an extension to stay for further shows, he invited girlfriend, SHARON SHEELEY, to come over for her birthday. However, on the 17th of April 1960, COCHRAN, SHEELEY and VINCENT were involved in a car crash, when their London cab skidded off the road. While SHEELEY and VINCENT suffered a few broken bones, EDDIE COCHRAN died after being propelled through the windscreen. A month later, the poignantly titled 'THREE STEPS TO HEAVEN' hit the top of the British charts while criminally ignored in his native America. A plethora of material was posthumously issued, most selling well enough to again hit the UK charts; nearly four decades on, his best songs still retain a primal power which successive generations of musicians have strived to capture. To think that EDDIE was only twenty-one when he died, one can only speculate as to what heights he might have scaled. • **Songwriters:** As said above plus covers: SITTIN' IN THE BALCONY (Johnny Dee) / SOMETHIN' ELSE + LONELY (c.Sharon Sheeley) / HALLELUJAH I LOVE HER SO (Ray Charles) / MY WAY (Paul Anka) / WEEKEND (Post-Post) / CUT ACROSS SHORTY (Wilkin-Walker) / NERVOUS BREAKDOWN (. . . Roccuzzo) / etc.

Best CD compilation: LEGENDARY MASTERS (*9)

COCHRAN BROTHERS

EDDIE – guitar, vocals / **HANK COCHRAN** (no relation) – vocals, guitar / with **CONNIE 'GUMBO' SMITH** – bass / **HAROLD HENSLEY** – fiddle

	not iss.	Ekko

Jul 55. (7",78) *<1003>* **MR. FIDDLE. / TWO BLUE SINGIN' STARS** [-] ☐

Nov 55. (7",78) *<1005>* **GUILTY CONSCIENCE. / YOUR TOMORROW MAY NEVER COME** [-] ☐

— (next 7", in Feb'56 **WALKIN' STICK BOOGIE. / ROLLIN'** was credited to **JERRY CAPEHEART** with The **COCHRAN BROTHERS** on 'Cash' records.

Jun 56. (7",78) *<3001>* **TIRED AND SLEEPY. / FOOL'S PARADISE** [-] ☐

EDDIE COCHRAN

	not iss.	Crest

Oct 56. (7",78) *<1026>* **SKINNY JIM. / HALF LOVED** [-] ☐

	London	Liberty

Apr 57. (7",78) *(HLU 8386)* **20 FLIGHT ROCK. / DARK LONELY STREET** ☐ [-]

Jul 57. (7",78) *(HLU 8433) <55056>* **SITTIN' IN THE BALCONY. / DARK LONELY STREET** ☐ [18] Mar57

Jun 57. (7",78) *<55070>* **MEAN WHILE I'M MAD. / ONE KISS** [-] ☐

Aug 57. (7",78) *<55087>* **DRIVE IN-SHOW. / AM I BLUE** [-] [82]

Nov 57. (7",78) *<55112>* **20 FLIGHT ROCK. / CRADLE BABY** [-] ☐

Jan 58. (7",78) *<55123>* **JEANIE, JEANIE, JEANIE. / POCKET FULL OF HEARTACHES** [-] [94]

Apr 58. (7",78) *<55138>* **PRETTY GIRL. / THERESA** [-] [-]

Aug 58. (lp) *(HA-U 2093)* **SINGIN' TO MY BABY** [-] [-]
– Sittin' in the balcony / Completely sweet / Undying love / I'm alone because I love you / Lovin' time / Proud of you / Am I blue / Twenty flight rock / Drive-in show / Mean when I'm mad / Stockin's 'n' shoes / Tell me why / Have I told you lately that I love you / Cradle baby / One kiss. *(re-dist.Jul60, hit UK No.19) (re-iss. Sep63 on 'Liberty'; LBY 1158)* – hit No.20 *(re-iss. Nov68 on 'Liberty' mono/stereo; LBL/LBS 83152)*

Sep 58. (7",78) *(HLU 8702) <55144>* **SUMMERTIME BLUES. / LOVE AGAIN** [18] [8] Aug58

Jan 59. (7",78) *(HLU 8792) <55166>* **C'MON EVERYBODY. / DON'T EVER LET ME GO** [6] [35] Dec58
(re-iss. Mar84 on 'United Artists'; UP 603)

— Augmented by The **KELLY FOUR: JIM STIVERS** – piano / **MIKE HENDERSON** – sax / **DAVE SCHREIBER** – bass / **GENE RIDGIO** – drums

Jun 59. (7",78) *(HLU 8880) <55177>* **TEENAGE HEAVEN. / I REMEMBER** ☐ [99] Jan59

Sep 59. (7",78) *(HLU 8944) <55203>* **SOMETHIN' ELSE. / BOLL WEEVIL SONG** [22] [58] Aug59
(re-iss. Sep79 on 'United Artists'; UP 36521)

Jan 60. (7",78) *(HLW 9022) <55217>* **HALLELUJAH I LOVE HER SO. / LITTLE ANGEL** [22] ☐ Dec59
Tragedy struck on the 17th of April 1960 when EDDIE was killed (see above). Below release was already recorded and due out.

May 60. (7",78) (HLG 9115) <55242> **THREE STEPS TO HEAVEN. / CUT ACROSS SHORTY** | **1** | -

– compilations, exploitation, etc. –
on 'Liberty' unless mentioned otherwise

May 59. (7"ep) London; (REU 1214) **C'MON EVERYBODY** | | -
(re-iss. Sep63 on 'Liberty'; LEP 2111)
Feb 60. (7"ep) London; (REU 1239) **SOMETHIN' ELSE** | | -
(re-iss. Nov63 on 'Liberty'; LEP 2122)
Sep 60. (lp) London; (HAG 2267) **THE EDDIE COCHRAN MEMORIAL ALBUM** | **9** | -
– C'mon everybody / Three steps to Heaven / Cut across Shorty / Jeannie, Jeannie, Jeannie / Pocketful of hearts / Hallelujah, I love her so / Don't ever let me go / Summertime blues / Teresa / Pretty girl / Teenage heaven / Boll Weevil song / I remember. *(re-iss. Apr63 on 'Liberty'; LBY 1127) – hit No.11 (re-iss. Apr68 on 'Liberty' mono/stereo; LBL/LBS 83009)*
Sep 60. (7") London; (HLG 9196) / Liberty; <55278> **SWEETIE PIE. / LONELY** | **38** |
(above was flipped over after 3 weeks and hit UK No.41)
Nov 60. (7"ep) London; (REG 1262) **EDDIE'S HITS** | |
(re-iss. Nov63 on 'Liberty'; LEP 2124)
Dec 60. (7") <55389> **WEEKEND. / LONELY** | | -
Jun 61. (7") London; (HLG 9362) **WEEKEND. / CHERISHED MEMORIES** | **15** |
Nov 61. (7") London; (HLG 9460) **JEANNIE, JEANNIE, JEANNIE. / POCKETFUL OF HEARTS** | **31** |
Nov 61. (7") London; (HLG 9464) **PRETTY GIRL. / TERESA** | |
Nov 61. (7"ep) London; (REG 1301) **CHERISHED MEMORIES OF EDDIE COCHRAN** | |
(re-iss. Nov63 on 'Liberty'; LEP 2123)
Dec 61. (7") London; (HLG 9467) **UNDYING LOVE. / STOCKIN'S 'N' SHOES** | |
Nov 62. (7") (LIB 10049) **NEVER. / THINK OF ME** | |
Nov 62. (7"ep) (LEP 2052) **NEVER TO BE FORGOTTEN** | |
Dec 62. (lp) (LBY 1109) **CHERISHED MEMORIES** | **15** |
– Cherished memories / I've waited so long / Never / Skinny Jim / Half loved / Weekend / Nervous breakdown / Let's go together / Rock and roll blues / Dark lonely street / Pink pegged slacks / That's my desire / Sweetie pie / Think of me. *(re-iss. Nov68 mono/stereo; LBL/LBS 83072E) (re-iss. Feb72 on 'Sunset'; SLS 50289) (re-iss. Sep83 lp/c; LBR/TC-LBR 182701-1/-4)*
Dec 62. (7"ep) (LEP 2090) **CHERISHED MEMORIES (VOL.1)** | | -
Apr 63. (7") (LIB 10088) **MY WAY. / ROCK AND ROLL BLUES** | **23** | -
Sep 63. (7") (LIB 10108) **DRIVE-IN SHOW. / I ALMOST LOST MY MIND** | | -
Jul 64. (7") (LIB 10151) **SKINNY JIM. / NERVOUS BREAKDOWN** | | -
Sep 64. (lp) (LBY 1205) **MY WAY** | |
(re-iss. Apr68; LBL 83104)
Nov 64. (7"ep) (LEP 2180) **STOCKIN'S AND SHOES** | |
Jun 65. (7"ep) (LEP 2165) **C'MON AGAIN** | |
Apr 66. (7") (LIB 10233) **C'MON EVERYBODY. / SUMMERTIME BLUES** | |
Sep 66. (7") (LIB 10249) **THREE STARS. / SOMETHIN' ELSE** | |
Feb 67. (7") (LIB 10276) **THREE STEPS TO HEAVEN. / EDDIE'S BLUES** | | -
Apr 68. (7") (LBF 15071) **SUMMERTIME BLUES. / LET'S GET TOGETHER** | | -
Aug 68. (7") (LBF 15109) **MILK COW BLUES. / SOMETHIN' ELSE** | **34** | -
Apr 70. (7") (LBS 83337) **THE VERY BEST OF EDDIE COCHRAN (10th ANNIVERSARY ALBUM)** | **34** | -
Aug 70. (7") (LBF 15366) **C'MON EVERYBODY. / MEAN WHEN I'M MAD** | | -
Nov 70. (lp) Sunset; (SLS 50155) **C'MON EVERYBODY** | |
(re-iss. Mar88 on 'Liberty' cd/c/lp with extra tracks; CD/TC+/ECR 1) – hit UK No.53
Jun 71. (lp) United Artists; (UAS 29163) **THE LEGENDARY EDDIE COCHRAN** | | -
Apr 72. (lp) United Artists; (UAD 60017) **LEGENDARY MASTERS** | | -
Jul 72. (7") United Artists; (UP 35408) **SUMMERTIME BLUES. / COTTON PICKER** | | -
Sep 72. (lp) United Artists; (UAS 29380) **ON THE AIR** | | -
Apr 75. (lp) United Artists; (UAG 29760) <LA 428E> **THE VERY BEST OF EDDIE COCHRAN (15th ANNIVERSARY ALBUM)** | |
(re-iss. May82 on 'Fame' lp/c; FA/TC-FA 3019) (cd-iss. May90; CDFA 3019)
Jun 76. (7") United Artists; (UP 603) **C'MON EVERYBODY. / MILK COW BLUES** | | -
1979. (lp) Charly; (CR 30168) / Union Pacific; <UP 001> **A LEGEND IN OUR TIME** | |
Aug 79. (lp/c) United Artists; (UAK/TCK 30244) **THE EDDIE COCHRAN SINGLES ALBUM** | **39** | -
Mar 80. (7") United Artists; (UP 618) **TWENTY FLIGHT ROCK. / TEENAGE CUTIE** | | -
May 79. (lp) Rockstar; (RSRLP 1001) **THE MANY SIDES OF EDDIE COCHRAN** | |
Sep 79. (7") Rockstar; (RSPSP 3001) **WHAT'D I SAY. / MILK COW BLUES** | |
1979. (7"ep; with BO DAVIS) Rockstar; (RSREP 2003) **LET'S COAST AWHILE** | |
1979. (7"ep) Rockstar; (RSREP 2004) **WALKIN' STICK BOOGIE** | |
1979. (7"ep) Rockstar; (RSREP 2005) **TIRED AND SLEEPY** | |
1979. (7"ep) Rockstar; (RSREP 2006) **COUNTRY STYLE** | |
Apr 80. (4xlp-box) United Artists; (UPECSP 20) **20th ANNIVERSARY ALBUM** | |
Apr 80. (7"ep) Rockstar; (RSREP 2007) **20th ANNIVERSARY SPECIAL** | |
Dec 80. (7"; as HOLLY TWINS & EDDIE COCHRAN) Rockstar; (RSRSP 3004) **I WANT ELVIS FOR CHRISTMAS. / THE TENDER AGE** | |
Jan 82. (lp) Rockstar; (RSRLP 1004) **ROCK'N'ROLL HEROES** | |
Sep 82. (lp) Rockstar; (RSRLP 1006) **THE YOUNG EDDIE COCHRAN** | | -

1984. (7"ep) Rockstar; (RSREP 2009) **PINK PEG SLACKS** | | -
May 84. (7") EMI Gold; (G45 19) **SUMMERTIME BLUES. / 20 FLIGHT ROCK** | | -
Mar 85. (lp) Rockstar; (RSRLP 1005) **WORDS AND MUSIC** | | -
Apr 85. (lp) Rockstar; (RSLP 1008) **PORTRAIT OF A LEGEND** | | -
1985. (7"ep) Rockstar; (RSREP 2010) **MORE SIDES OF EDDIE COCHRAN** | | -
Oct 85. (lp/c) (EG 260757-1/-4) **THE BEST OF EDDIE COCHRAN** | | -
(cd-iss. 1987 on 'E.M.I.'; CDP 746580-2) (re-iss. Sep96 on 'Music For Pleasure' cd/c; CD/TC MFP 6268)
Dec 85. (lp) Rockstar; (RSRLP 1009) **THE HOLLYWOOD SESSIONS** | | -
Dec 85. (lp/c) Conifer; (CFRC/MCFRC 505) **THE MANY STYLES OF EDDIE COCHRAN** | | -
Apr 86. (lp/c) Music For Pleasure; (MFP/TC-MFP 5748) **EDDIE COCHRAN** | | -
Jun 86. (cd) Card; (CD 86070-2) **A LEGEND LIVES ON** | | -
1986. (7"ep) Rockstar; (RSREP 2012) **RARE ITEMS** | | -
1986. (7"ep; shared with GENE VINCENT) Rockstar; (RSREP 2013) **ON TOUR** | | -
Apr 87. (cd) (RSRCD 001) **ROCK'N'ROLL LEGEND** | | -
Jul 87. (lp) Capeheart; (5003) **SOMETHIN' ELSE** | | -
Jan 88. (lp/c/cd) Charly-Ace; (CHA/CHC/CDCH 237) **THE EARLY YEARS** | | -
– (cd has 4 extra tracks). *(cd re-iss. Nov93; same)*
Jan 88. (7") (EDDIE 501) **C'MON EVERYBODY. / DON'T EVER LET ME GO** | **14** | -
(12"+=/cd-s+=) (12/CD EDDIE 501) – Skinny Jim / Jeannie, Jeannie, Jeannie.
Apr 88. (lp) Sunjay; (SJLP 571) **HOLLYWOOD ROCKER** | | -
May 88. (cd-ep) Rhino; (R 373005) **LIL' BIT OF GOLD** | | -
– Summertime blues / Somethin' else / C'mon everybody / Nervous breakdown.
Jul 88. (lp) Hydra; (BLK 7706) **RECORD DATE** | | -
Oct 88. (d-cd/d-c/d-lp) CD/TC+/ECB 1) **EDDIE COCHRAN BOX SET** | | -
Dec 88. (c) Capitol; (4XLL 9086) **SUMMERTIME BLUES AND OTHER HITS** | | -
Sep 89. (lp) Rockstar; (RSRLP 1019) **THINKIN' ABOUT YOU** | | -
Sep 89. (lp/c) See For Miles; (SEE/+K 271) **THE EP COLLECTION** | | -
(cd-iss. Mar91; SEECD 271)
Mar 90. (cd) EMI America; **LEGENDARY MASTERS** | - | -
Apr 90. (cd) Rockstar; (RSRLP 1021) **30TH ANNIVERSARY ALBUM** | | -
Aug 90. (lp) Rockstar; (RSRLP 1022) **EDDIE & HANK** | | -
Mar 91. (4xcd-box) (CDECB 1) **THE EDDIE COCHRAN BOX SET** | | -
May 92. (cd) Sunjay; (cd) **GUITAR PICKIN' RARITIES ("EDDIE COCHRAN & GARY LAMBERT")** | | -
Sep 92. (cd-s) Old Gold; (OG 6179) **THREE STEPS TO HEAVEN / SUMMERTIME BLUES / HALLELUJAH I LOVE HER SO** | | -
Oct 92. (cd-s) Old Gold; (OG 6183) **C'MON EVERYBODY / SOMETHIN' ELSE / WEEKEND** | | -
Apr 93. (cd) Remember; (RMB 75054) **SUMMERTIME BLUES** | | -
(re-iss. Sep96 on 'Laserlight'; 16151)
Apr 94. (cd; by COCHRAN BROTHERS) Rockstar; (RSRCD 001) **ROCK'N'ROLL LEGEND** | | -
Apr 94. (cd) Rockstar; (RSRCD 003) **L.A. SESSIONS** | | -
May 95. (cd) Rockstar; (RSRCD 006) **MIGHTY MEAN** | | -
Jan 96. (cd) Rockstar; (RSRCD 009) **CRUISIN' THE DRIVE IN** | | -
Oct 96. (cd) Rockstar; (RSRCD 010) **ONE MINUTE TO ONE** | | -
Mar 97. (3xcd-box; shared with GENE VINCENT / EDDIE COCHRAN) E.M.I.; CDOMB 006) **ROCK'N'ROLL** | | -
Sep 98. (cd; shared with GENE VINCENT) EMI Gold; (496847-2) **BACK 2 BACK** | | -
Oct 98. (cd) Rockstar; (RSRCD 014) **DON'T FORGET ME** | | -

Bruce COCKBURN

Born: 27 May'45, Pembroke, Ontario, Canada. After growing up in Ottowa, COCKBURN travelled around Europe in his late teens, ending up in Paris where he busked as a street musician. Able to make a living this way thanks to much musical encouragement from his family, COCKBURN was already proficient on piano, clarinet, trumpet and guitar as well as composition. He further enhanced these talents on return to the Americas where he studied at Boston's Berklee School of Music between '64 and '66. During this period, COCKBURN's work and spare time were intensely geared towards music having, on top of his studies, committed to several bands. One of these groups was the ESQUIRES with whom he released a single ('THE CHILDREN') in '65 on 'Capitol'. The band he joined upon his return to Ottawa in the summer of '66 subsequently achieved a bi-weekly regular live slot. Although he was simultaneously moonlighting in another band, HEAVENLY BLUE (a blues 3-piece where he played organ and harmonica), COCKBURN was looking to go it alone; he made his first solo performance at the Mariposa Folk Festival in '67. This led to Canadian band, THREE'S A CROWD recording a trio of his songs, COCKBURN joining the group on a TV performance the following year. With his increasingly high profile, the inevitable record company interest came courtesy of 'Columbia' records. The singer concentrated on songwriting during '69, resulting in his debut LP, 'BRUCE COCKBURN' (1970; 1971 in the US). A diverse album with folk at its core, it was probably the most enthusiastic COCKBURN ever sounded. Less innocent was 'HIGH WINDS WHITE SKY' (1971), another worthwhile folk-rock outing that won him the Juno Best Canadian Folk Singer in '72. This didn't help the sales of his next LP, 'SUNWHEEL DANCE' (1972), his most diverse work to date; while subtly flirting with jazz, the record drew influences from the burgeoning folk-rock boom in England. His next album, and indeed the next few showed him going from strength to strength artistically, often producing a gutsier sound in tracks such as 'YOU DON'T HAVE TO PLAY THE HORSES'. Commercially, as with many artists that choose to write about Christian themes, COCKBURN struggled to reach the mainstream. He made an exception to this rule following the release of 'DANCING IN THE DRAGON'S JAWS' (1979) which contained the single 'WONDERING WHERE THE LIONS ARE'. It narrowly missed the Top 20 in the US, becoming COCKBURN's one and only major US hit in the process. Like much of the album it was lifted from, the track drew influences from South American/African music and rhythms. COCKBURN dug deeper into his soul for the next album 'HUMANS' (1980) which was more of a political statement than any he'd written before. It saw COCKBURN's withdrawal from Christian ideology towards a knowledgeable socialist stance against capitalist manipulation and worldwide environmental plunder. This theme (obviously witnessed firsthand by the well travelled musician) continued throughout the '80s during which time he produced a few songwriting nuggets like 1983's 'WAITING FOR THE MOON' and 1984's harder-hitting 'IF I HAD A ROCKET LAUNCHER'. However, by the end of the decade, this concept was sounding a little tired; COCKBURN had few fresh ideas for the next decade either, reintroducing his Christian beliefs on the somewhat paltry 'NOTHING BUT A BURNING LIGHT' (1991). He even unashamedly released a Christmas album, before rediscovering the plot with 'CLARITY OF THE NIGHT' (1997) and 'BREAKFAST IN NEW ORLEANS DINNER IN TIMBUKTU', the latter enlisting the eerie but glorious voice of MARGO TIMMINS (of THE COWBOY JUNKIES) on the tracks 'MANGO' and 'BLUEBERRY HILL'. Although having seen little success outside his native Canada, this prolific singer/songwriter has amassed a considerable and consistently rewarding body of work, spanning three decades from '70 to the present day.

Album rating: BRUCE COCKBURN (*5) / HIGH WINDS WHITE SKY (*5) / SUNWHEEL DRIVE (*5) / NIGHT VISION (*5) / SALT, SUN AND TIME (*5) / JOY WILL FIND A WAY (*5) / IN THE FALLING DARK (*6) / CIRCLES IN THE STREAM (*5) / FURTHER ADVENTURES OF (*5) / DANCING IN THE DRAGON'S JAWS (*7) / HUMANS (*7) / RESUME compilation (*5) / MUMMY DUST compilation (*5) / INNER CITY FRONT (*5) / THE TROUBLE WITH NORMAL (*6) / STEALING FIRE (*5) / WORLD OF WONDERS (*5) / WAITING FOR A MIRACLE – THE SINGLES 1970-1987 compilation (*7) / BIG CIRCUMSTANCE (*5) / BRUCE COCKBURN LIVE (*5) / NOTHING BUT A BURNING LIGHT (*5) / CHRISTMAS (*4) / DART TO THE HEART (*5) / CLARITY OF THE NIGHT (*4) / BREAKFAST IN NEW ORLEANS DINNER IN TIMBUKTU (*5)

BRUCE COCKBURN – vocals, guitar, piano, etc / with various session people

not iss. True North

1970. (lp) <TN 1> **BRUCE COCKBURN**   -   - Canada
– Going to the country / Thoughts of a rainy afternoon / Together alone / The bicycle trip / The thirteenth mountain / Musical friends / Change your mind / Man of a thousand faces / Spring song / Keep it open. <US-iss.1971 on 'Epic'; 30812> <US/UK re-iss. Feb85 lp/c; TN/+T 1) > <cd-iss. 1995 on 'Sony'; 67102>

1971. (lp) <TN 3> **HIGH WINDS WHITE SKY**   -   - Canada
– Happy good morning blues / Let us go laughing / Love song / One day I walk / Golden serpent blues / High winds white sky / You point the sky / Life's mistress / Ting – The cauldron / Shining mountain.
<(UK/US-iss.Feb85 lp/c; TN/+T 3)> <cd-iss. 1990 on 'East Side Digital'; 80152> <US cd-iss. 1993 on 'Sony'; 48738>

1972. (lp) <TN 7> **SUNWHEEL DANCE**   -   - Canada
– My lady and my lord / Feet fall on the road / Fall / Sunwheel dance / Up on the hillside / Life will open / I'm going down slow / When the sun falls / He came from the mountain / Dialogue with the Devil / For the birds. <US-iss.1972 on 'Epic'; 31768> (UK-iss.1972 on 'Epic'; 65187) <(US/UK re-iss. Feb85 lp/c; TN/+T 7)> <cd-iss. 1993 on 'Sony'; 48740>

1973. (lp/c) <TN/+T 11> **NIGHT VISION**   -   - Canada
– Foxglove / You don't have to play the horses / Blues got the world . . . / Mama just wants to barrelhouse all night long / Island in a black sky / Clocks don't bring tomorrow – Knives . . . . / When the sun goes Nova / Deja vu / Lightstorm / God bless the children. <US/UK-iss. Feb85 lp/c; same as Canadian)> <cd-iss. 1990 on 'East Side Digital'; 80172> <cd-iss. 1993 on 'Sony'; 48741>

1974. (lp/c) <TN/+T 16> **SALT, SUN AND TIME**   -   - Canada
– All the diamonds in the world / Salt, sun and time / Don't have to tell you why / Stained glass / Rouler sa bosse / Never so free / Seeds on the wind / It won't be long / Christmas song. <(US/UK-iss.Feb85; same as Canadian)> <cd-iss. 1990 on 'East Side Digital'; 80162> <cd-iss. 1995 on 'Sony'; 67103>

1975. (lp/c) <TN/+T 23> **JOY WILL FIND A WAY**   -   - Canada
– Hand-dancing / January in the Halifax airport lounge / Starwheel / Lament for the last days / Joy will find a way / Burn / Skylarking / Long-time love song / Life story / Arrows of light. <(US/UK-iss.Feb85 lp/c; same as Canadian)> <cd-iss. 1990 on 'East Side Digital'; 80092> <cd-iss. 1995 on 'Sony'; 48744>

not iss. Island

1976. (lp) <ILTA 9463> **IN THE FALLING DARK**   -
– Lord of the starfields / Vagabondage / In the falling dark / Little seahorse / Water into wine / Silver wheels / Giftbearer / Gavin's woodpile / I'm gonna fly someday / Festival of friends. <(US/UK re-iss. Feb85 on 'True North' lp/c; TN/+T 26 = original Canadian cat.no.)> <cd-iss. 1990 on 'East Side Digital'; BRUCE 2> <cd re-iss. 1995 on 'Sony'; 48745>

1977. (d-lp) <ILTA 9475> **CIRCLES IN THE STREAM (live at Massey Hall, Toronto)**
– The pipes, the pipes / Starwheel / Never so free / Deer dancing round a broken mirror / Homme brulant / Free to be / Mama just wants to barrelhouse all night long / Cader Idris / Arrows of light / One day I walk / Love song / Red brother red sister / Lord of the starfields / All the diamonds in the world / Joy will find a way / God bless the children. (<UK/US-iss.Feb85 on 'True North'; TN 31 = original Canadian cat.no.)

1978. (lp) <ILTA 9528> **FURTHER ADVENTURES OF**   -
– Rainfall / Montreal song / Outside a broken phone booth with money in my hand / Prenons la mer / Red ships take off in the distance / Laughter / Bright sky / Feast of fools / an I go with you / Nanzen Fi. <(US/UK re-iss. Feb85 on 'True North'; TN 33 = original Canadian cat.no.)> <cd-iss. 1990 on 'East Side Digital'; 80182>

R.C.A. Millennium

May 80. (7") (PB 1786) <11786> **WONDERING WHERE THE LIONS ARE. / AFTER THE RAIN**   21 Mar80

Jul 80. (lp/c) (FL/FK 17747) <BXL1-7747> **DANCING IN THE DRAGON'S JAWS**   45 Feb80
– Creation dream / Hills of morning / Badlands flashback / Northern lights / After the rain / Wondering where the lions are / Incandescent blue / No footprints. (US/UK re-iss. Feb85 on 'True North'; TN 37 = original Canadian cat.no.)> (re-iss. 1988 on 'Myrrh' lp/c; MYR R/C 6840) (re-iss. Jul89 on 'FM-Revolver' lp/c/cd; REV LP/MC/XD 127) <cd-iss. 1990 on 'Capitol'; 71309> (cd re-iss. Apr95 on 'Columbia'; 480364-2)

Oct 80. (7") (PB 1795) **RUMOURS OF GLORY. / YOU GET BIGGER AS YOU GO**

Nov 80. (lp) (FL 17752) <BXL1-7752> **HUMANS**   81 Oct80
– Grim travellers / Rumours of glory / More not more / You get bigger as you go / What about the bond / How I spent my fall vacation / Guerilla betrayed / Tokyo / Fascist architecture / The rose above the sky. <(UK/US re-iss. Feb85 on 'True North' lp/c; TN/+T 42 = original Canadian cat.no.)> (re-iss. Jul89 on 'FM-Revolver' lp/c/cd; REV LP/MC/XD 124) <cd-iss. 1990 on 'East Side Digital'; 80072> <cd re-iss. 1995 on 'Sony'; 48748>

May 81. (lp) <BXL1-7757> **RESUME (compilation 1976-1981)**   -
– Silver wheels / The coldest night of the year / Can I go with you / Laughter / Mama just wants to barrelhouse all night long / Lord of the starfields / Outside a broken phone booth with money in my hand / Dialogue with the Devil.

Jun 81. (lp) <TN 45> **MUMMY DUST** (compilation 1969-1981)   -   - Canada
– Silver wheels / Loner / Joy will find a way / Thoughts on a rainy afternoon / It's going down slow / The coldest night of the year / Laughter / Red brother red sister / You don't have to play the horses / Dweller by a dark stream / All the diamonds in the world.

Dec 81. (lp) <BXL1-7761> **INNER CITY FRONT**   -
– You pay your money and you take your chance / The strong one / All' quiet on the inner city front / Radio shoes / Wanna go walking / And we dance / Justice / Broken wheel / Loner. <(UK/US re-iss. Feb85 on 'True North' lp/c; TN/+T 47 = original Canadian cat.no.)> <cd-iss. 1990 on 'East Side Digital'; BR 4> <cd re-iss. 1995 on 'Sony'; 48749>

not iss. True North

Feb 84. (lp/c) <TN/+T 53> **THE TROUBLE WITH NORMAL**   -   - Canada
– The trouble with normal / Candy man's gone / Hoop dancer / Waiting for the moon / Tropic moon / Going up against chaos / Put our hearts together / Civilization and it's discontents / Planet of the clowns. (US/UK-iss.Feb85; same as Canadian)> (re-iss. Jul89 on 'FM-Revolver' lp/c/cd; REV LP/MC/XD 126) <cd-iss. 1990 on 'Capitol'; 71308> <cd re-iss. 1995 on 'Sony'; 48750>

Spindrift Gold Mountain

Nov 84. (lp) (SPIN 112) <80012> **STEALING FIRE**   74 Aug84
– Lovers in a dangerous time / Maybe the poet / Sahara gold / Making contact / Peggy's kitchen wall / To raise the morning star / Nicaragua / If I had a rocket launcher / Dust and diesel. (re-iss. Jul89 on 'FM-Revolver' lp/c/cd; REV LP/MC/XD 125) <cd-iss. 1990 on 'Capitol'; 71310> <cd re-iss. 1995 on 'Sony'; 48735> (cd re-iss. Apr95 on 'Columbia'; 480365-2)

Jan 85. (7") <82013> **IF I HAD A ROCKET LAUNCHER. / NICARAGUA**   -   88

Jun 85. (7") (DRIFT 102) **IF I HAD A ROCKET LAUNCHER. / MAYBE THE POET**   -

FM-Revolver M.C.A.

Feb 87. (lp/c/cd) (REV LP/MC/XD 73) <MCA/+C/D 5772> **WORLD OF WONDERS**   Jul86
– Call it democracy / Lily of the midnight sky / World of wonders / Berlin tonight / People see through you / See how I miss you / Santiago dawn / Dancing in Paradise / Down here tonight. <cd re-iss. 1990 on 'Columbia'; 48751>

FM-Revolver Gold Castle

May 87. (d-lp/c/cd) (REV LP/MC/XD 90) <71305> **WAITING FOR A MIRACLE – THE SINGLES 1970-1987** (compilation)   Jan87
– Going to the country / One day I walk / It's going down slow / Mama wants to barrelhouse all night long / All the diamonds in the world / Burn / Silver wheels / Laughter / Wondering where the lions are / Tokyo / Fascist architecture / The trouble with normal / Rumours of glory / The coldest night of the year / You pay your money and you take your chance / Lovers in a dangerous time / If I had a rocket launcher / Peggy's kitchen wall / People see through you / Call it democracy / Stolen land / Waiting for a miracle. <cd re-iss. 1990 on 'Capitol'; 71305>

Jan 89. (7") (VHF 49) **IF A TREE FALLS.**

Jan 89. (lp/c/cd) (REV LP/MC/XD 122) <D1/D4/D2 71320> **BIG CIRCUMSTANCE**   Feb89
– If a tree falls / Shipwrecked at the stable door / Gospel of bondage / Don't feel your touch / Tibetan side of town / Understanding nothing / Where the death squad lives / Radium rain / Pangs of love / The gift / Anything can happen. <cd re-iss. 1995 on 'Sony'; 48737>

Feb 90. (7") (REV 53) **SHIPWRECKED AT THE STABLE DOOR. /**

Cooking Vinyl Gold Castle

Apr 90. (lp/c/cd) (COOK/+C/CD 034) <D1/D4/D2 71346> **BRUCE COCKBURN LIVE** (live)   Jun90
– Silver wheels / World of wonders / Rumours of glory / See how I miss you / After the rain / Call it democracy / Wondering where the lions are / Nicaragua / Broken wheel / Stolen land / Always look on the bright side of life. (cd+=/c+=) – Tibetan side of town / To raise the morning star / Maybe the poet.

Columbia Columbia

Feb 92. (cd/c/lp) (468898-2/-4/-1) <CK/CT 47983> **NOTHING BUT A BURNING LIGHT**   Nov91
– Dream like mine / Kit Carson / Mighty trucks of midnight / Soul of a man / Great big love / One of the best ones / Somebody touched me / Cry of a tiny babe / Actions speak louder / Indian wars / When it's gone, it's gone / Child of the wind.

Dec 93. (cd/c/lp) (474712-2/-4) <CK/CT 53026> **CHRISTMAS** (festive)
– Adeste fidelis / Early on one Christmas morn / O little town of Bethlehem / Riu riu chiu / I saw three ships / Down in yon forest / Anges dans nos campagnes / Go tell it to the mountain / Shepherds / Silent night / Jeus Ahatonnia / God rest ye merry gentlemen / It came upon a midnight clear / Mary had a baby / Joy to the world.

Jun 94. (cd/c) (475649-2/-4) <CK/CT 53831> **DART TO THE HEART**   Mar94
– Listen for the laugh / All the ways I want you / Bone in my ear / Burden of the angel – The beast / Scanning these crowds / Southland of the heart / Train in the rain / Someone I used to love / Sunrise on the Mississippi / Closer to the light / Tie me at the crossroads.

Apr 94. (cd-ep) <*CSK 5671*> **LISTEN FOR THE LAUGH / LISTEN FOR THE LAUGH / BURDEN OF THE ANGEL – THE BEAST / SOUTHLAND OF THE HEART / TIE ME AT THE CROSSROADS**

-	
Rykodisc	Rykodisc

Feb 97. (cd/c) <*(RCD/RAC 10366)*> **CLARITY OF THE NIGHT**
– Night train / Get up Jonah / Pacing the cage / Mistress of storms / Whole night sky / Coming rains / Birmingham shadows / Mines of Mozambique / Live on my mind / Clarity of night / Strange waters.

Jan 98. (m-cd) <*(RCD 10435)*> **YOU PAY YOUR MONEY AND YOU TAKE YOUR CHANCE** (live)
– Call it democracy / Stolen land / Strange waters / Fascist architecture / You pay your money and you take your chance / Birmingham shadows.

Sep 99. (cd) <*(RCD 10407)*> **BREAKFAST IN NEW ORLEANS DINNER IN TIMBUKTU**
– When you give it away / Mango / Last night of the world / Isn't that what friends are for / Down to the delta / Embers of Eden / Blueberry hill / Let the bad air out / Look how far / Deep lake / Use me while you can.

Joe COCKER

Born: JOHN ROBERT COCKER, 20 May'44, Sheffield, England. COCKER's first musical influence was RAY CHARLES, after hearing the track 'What'd I Say', also taking in the blues sounds of LIGHTNIN' HOPKINS, MUDDY WATERS and JOHN LEE HOOKER. Pipefitter by day and pub singer by night, his band, VANCE ARNOLD & THE AVENGERS were signed to 'Decca' in '65, cutting the BEATLES cover, 'I'LL CRY INSTEAD'. Although the single failed to achieve any real success, COCKER gave it a second bash in '67, making a demo tape for the influential Denny Cordell, the producer of Procol Harum's 'A WHITER SHADE OF PALE'. This proved a shrewd move, his subsequent single (cut by Cordell), 'MARJORINE', leading to a deal with A&M. '68 saw COCKER catapulted to fame with a cover of the Beatles 'WITH A LITTLE HELP FROM MY FRIENDS', featuring JIMMY PAGE on guitar. Reaching #1 in Britain, the song showcased COCKER's powerful, gravel-throated voice and his ability to make a song his own. With heavyweight fame looming large, COCKER hired manager Dee Anthony, who promptly booked him for gigs in America with his group, the GREASE BAND, and in '69, the Cordell produced album, 'WITH A LITTLE HELP FROM MY FRIENDS' was issued, featuring the talents of STEVE WINWOOD and MATTHEW FISHER, amongst others. The set received critical and commercial acclaim, featuring an inspired version of Dylan's 'I SHALL BE RELEASED' as well as the spell-binding rendition of Traffic's 'FEELIN ALRIGHT', the next single to be lifted from the album. With the festival scene buzzing, JOE and the GREASE BAND appeared in America on a series of five gigs, the last being the Woodstock Music and Arts Fair in Bethal, New York, where his full-on performance of 'WITH A LITTLE HELP . . .' summed up the mood of the weekend. His second long-player, 'JOE COCKER!', produced a Top 10 in the UK with a LEON RUSSELL-penned 'DELTA LADY', the album characterised by COCKER's primordial, blasting vocals. Dismantling the GREASE BAND in 1970 after a hectic two years on the road, his next outfit was assembled a matter of weeks later for a few gigs he had forgotten about. The MAD DOGS band, made up of LEON RUSSELL and a full horn section from the recently disbanded DELANEY & BONNIE & FRIENDS, almost immediately created a hit with 'THE LETTER', a cover of the Box Tops' 1967 pop hit. A live recording, 70's 'MAD DOGS AND ENGLISHMEN' (recorded at Fillmore during the tour of the same name), solidified COCKER's fame, the album rocketing to #2 on the Billboard chart and the tour being released as a film, premiering at Cannes in '71. Ironically, the tour left COCKER a wreck and led to his withdrawal from the music buisness. A half-hearted comeback in '72 saw the release of 'JOE COCKER' (without the exclamation mark, which is exactly what it was) while another comeback set in May '74, 'I CAN STAND A LITTLE RAIN' was equally disastrous. Although 'YOU ARE SO BEAUTIFUL' (taken from the current album) charted in March '75, the personal turmoil continued, painfully illustrated by John Belushi's hilarious impersonation of COCKER on Saturday Night Live. The rest of the 70's saw the release of a string of lacklustre albums and an end to his relationship with 'A&M'. COCKER subsequently signed to 'Elektra / Asylum' in '78, before moving to 'Island' in '82, his first release for the label, 'SHEFFIELD STEEL', borrowing the talents of SLY & ROBBIE to lukewarm effect. The comeback that had threatened to happen with the release of the album actually came a year later when 'UP WHERE WE BELONG', a duet sung with JENNIFER WARNES and the love theme to the movie, 'An Officer And A Gentleman', COCKER was on the move again in '84, signing to 'Capitol', where he released six albums, appealing largely to the AOR market, while the '90s saw JOE teaming up with BRYAN ADAMS before rehashing his two most celebrated recordings, 'WITH A LITTLE HELP . . .' and 'FEELIN' ALRIGHT' for the commercial re-run of Woodstock '94. Now with Sony's '550' label, he continues to tour the globe and confound the critics with his durability. • **Songwriters:** Pens some with band (GREASE BAND) member CHRIS STAINTON. Covers:- SHE CAME IN THROUGH THE BATHROOM WINDOW + YOU'VE GOT TO HIDE YOUR LOVE AWAY (Beatles) / YOU ARE SO BEAUTIFUL (Billy Preston-Jim Price) / JUST LIKE A WOMAN + I SHALL BE RELEASED + WATCHING THE RIVER FLOW (Bob Dylan) / DON'T LET ME BE MISUNDERSTOOD (Nina Simone) / DARLING BE HOME SOON (Lovin' Spoonful) / BIRD ON THE WIRE + I'M YOUR MAN (Leonard Cohen) / HONKY TONK WOMEN (Rolling Stones) / I'VE BEEN LOVING YOU TOO LONG (Otis Redding) / GIVE PEACE A CHANCE (John Lennon) / ST.JAMES INFIRMARY (Graham Bond) / LAWDY MISS CLAWDY (Little Richard) / MANY RIVERS TO CROSS (Jimmy Cliff) / I HEARD IT THROUGH THE GRAPEVINE (Barrett Strong) / TALKING BACK TO THE NIGHT (Steve Winwood) / INNER CITY BLUES (Marvin Gaye) / UNCHAIN MY HEART (Ray Charles) / UP WHERE WE BELONG (Buffy Sainte Marie-Will Jennings-Jack Nitzchse) / DON'T LET THE SUN GO DOWN ON ME (Elton John) / CAN'T FIND MY WAY HOME (Blind Faith) / THE MOON IS A HARSH MISTRESS (Jimmy Webb) / FIVE WOMEN (Prince) / TWO WRONGS DON'T MAKE A RIGHT (Bendith-Schwartz) / TEMPTED (Squeeze) / I STILL CAN'T BELIEVE IT'S TRUE (. . . Cadd) / LET THE HEALING BEGIN (Tony Joe White) / HAVE A LITTLE FAITH IN ME (John Hiatt) / THE SIMPLE THINGS (Shanks-Neigher-Roy) / SUMMER IN THE CITY (Lovin' Spoonful) / THE GREAT DIVIDE (J.D. Souther) / HIGHWAY HIGHWAY (Steven Allen Davis) / TOO COOL (G.Sutton-K.Fleming) / SOUL TIME (Will Jennings-Frankie Miller) / OUT OF THE BLUE (Robbie Robertson) / HELL AND HIGHWATER (John Miles) / STANDING KNEE DEEP IN A RIVER (Bob McDill-Dickey Lee-Bucky Jones) / TAKE ME HOME (Kipner-Capek-Jordan) / and many more.

Album rating: WITH A LITTLE HELP FROM MY FRIENDS (*7) / JOE COCKER! (*7) / MAD DOGS AND ENGLISHMEN (*7) / COCKER HAPPY early stuff (*5) / SOMETHING TO SAY (*4) / I CAN STAND A LITTLE RAIN (*5) / JAMAICA SAY YOU WILL (*3) / STINGRAY (*5) / LUXURY YOU CAN AFFORD (*5) / SHEFFIELD STEEL (*5) / A CIVILIZED MAN (*4) / COCKER (*4) / UNCHAIN MY HEART (*5) / ONE NIGHT OF SIN (*3) / JOE COCKER LIVE! (*4) / NIGHT CALLS (*4) / THE LEGEND: THE ESSENTIAL COLLECTION compilation (*7) / HAVE A FAITH (*5) / ORGANIC (*5) / ACROSS FROM MIDNIGHT (*5) / NO ORDINARY WORLD (*4)

JOE COCKER – vocals, (touring band JOE COCKER'S BIG BLUES) with **DAVE HOPPER** – guitar / **VERNON NASH** – piano / **DAVE GREEN** – bass / **DAVE MEMMOT** – drums Record company used session men instead incl. **BIG JIM SULLIVAN** – guitar

			Decca	not iss.
Oct 64.	(7")	(F 11974) **I'LL CRY INSTEAD. / PRECIOUS WORDS**	☐	-

—— He formed **The GREASE BAND** in '67 retaining **NASH** and **MEMMOTT** and recruited **CHRIS STAINTON** – bass, and **FRANK MYLES** – guitar. But once again opted for session musicians incl. **CLEM CATTINI** – drums / **J. PAGE & A. LEE** – guitar. Although STAINTON did appear. (JIMMY PAGE also appeared on next 45)

			Regal Zonophone	A&M
Sep 68.	(7")	(RZ 3006) <928> **MARJORINE. / THE NEW AGE OF LILY**	48	☐

JOE COCKER & THE GREASE BAND with **STAINTON** brought in new guys **TOMMY EYRE** – keyboards / **MICKEY GEE** – guitar / **TOMMY REILLY** – drums

Sep 68.	(7")	(RZ 3013) <991> **WITH A LITTLE HELP FROM MY FRIENDS. / SOMETHING'S COMING ON**	1	68 Nov68

—— **MENRY McCULLOCH** – guitar repl. MICKEY GEE (he later joined SHAKIN' STEVENS) **KENNY SLADE** – drums repl. REILLY Plus of course a huge selection of session people

May 69.	(lp)	(SLRZ 1006) <AM 4182> **WITH A LITTLE HELP FROM MY FRIENDS**	☐	35

– Feeling alright / Bye bye blackbird / Change in Louise / Marjorine / Just like a woman / Do I still figure in your life / Sandpaper Cadillac / Don't let me be misunderstood / With a little help from my friends / I shall be released. (cd-iss. 1988 on 'Cube'; TOOFA/ZCTOF 1) (cd-iss. 1988 on 'Cube'; 846316) (re-iss. Feb90 on 'Castle' cd/c; CLA CD/MC 172) (cd re-iss. Oct98 on 'Polydor'; 393106-2)

Jun 69.	(7")	<1063> **FEELING ALRIGHT. / SANDPAPER CADILLAC**	-	69

<re-iss. Dec71, hit No.33>

—— **JOE'S GREASE BAND** retained **STAINTON** – now keyboards and **McCULLOCH ALAN SPENNER** – bass repl. TOMMY EYRE who joines AYNSLEY DUNBAR, etc. **BRUCE ROWLANDS** – drums repl. KENNY SLADE who went into sessions

Sep 69.	(7")	(RZ 3024) <1112> **DELTA LADY. / SHE'S GOOD TO ME**	10	69
Nov 69.	(lp)	(SLRZ 1011) <AM 4224> **JOE COCKER!**	11	

– Dear landlord / Bird on the wire / Lawdy Miss Clawdy / She came in through the bathroom window / Hitchcock railway / That's your business now / Something / Delta lady / Hello little friend / Darling be home soon. (re-iss. May91 on 'Castle' cd/c; CLA CD/MC 238) (cd re-iss. Oct98 on 'Polydor'; 394224-2)

Dec 69.	(7")	<1147> **SHE CAME IN THROUGH THE BATHROOM WINDOW. / CHANGE IN LOUISE**		30
Jun 70.	(7")	(RZ 3027) <1174> **THE LETTER. / SPACE CAPTAIN**	39	7 Apr70

—— Early '70, he retained **STAINTON** and assembled his **MAD DOGS AND ENGLISHMEN** entourage which included **LEON RUSSELL & THE SHELTER PEOPLE** – guitar, piano / **DON PRESTON** – guitar CARL RADLE – bass / **BOBBY KEYS** – sax / **JIM PRICE** – trumpet / **JIM KELTNER** – drums plus even more session people, over 10, which was documented on film in '71.

			A&M	A&M
Sep 70.	(d-lp)	(<AMLD 6002>) **MAD DOGS & ENGLISHMEN** (live)	16	2

– (introduction) / Honky tonk women / Sticks and stones / Cry me a river / Bird on the wire / Feeling alright / Superstar / Let's go get stoned / Blue medley: I'll drown in my own tears – When something is wrong with my baby – I've been loving you too long / Girl from North Country / Give peace a chance / She came in through the bathroom window / Space captain / The letter / Delta lady. (re-iss. 1983 d-lp/d-c; AMLS/CDM 6002) (cd-iss. 1988; CDA 6002) <US d-cd-iss. Jan86 on 'Mobile Fidelity'; MFCD 2-824> (cd re-iss. Jan97; 396002-2) (cd re-iss. Oct98 on 'Polydor'; 540698-2) (cd re-iss. Dec98 on 'Mobile Fidelity'; UDCD 736)

			Fly	A&M
Oct 70.	(7")	(BUG 3) <1200> **CRY ME A RIVER** (live). / **GIVE PEACE A CHANCE** (live)		11
Apr 71.	(lp)	(HIFLY 3) **COCKER HAPPY** (older material)	-	-

– Hitchcock railway / She came in through the bathroom window / Marjorine / She's good to me / Hello little friend / With a little help from my friends / Delta lady / Darlin be home soon / Do I still figure in your life / Feeling alright / Something's coming on / The letter. (re-iss. May85 on 'Sierra' lp/c; FEDB/CFEDB 5011) (cd-iss. Oct94 on 'Disky'; CUCD 01)

—— JOE retained **STAINTON** and some of his past session men

May 71. (7") (BUG 9) <1258> **HIGH TIME WE WENT. / BLACK EYED BLUES** | | 22 |

—— now with the CHRIS STAINTON BAND" (a 12-piece) retaining **KEYS, PRICE** and **KELTNER.** (also had loads of session men)

Aug 72. (7") (BUG 25) <1370> **MIDNIGHT RIDER. / WOMAN TO WOMAN** | | 27 | | 56 |

Dec 72. (lp) (HIFLY 13) <AM 4368> **SOMETHING TO SAY** <US-title 'JOE COCKER'> | | 30 |
– Pardon me sir / High time we went / She don't mind / Black eyed blues / Something to say / Midnight rider / Do right woman / Woman to woman / St. James infirmary blues. (cd-iss. Oct98 on 'Polydor'; 394368-2)

Feb 73. (7") (BUG 28) **PARDON ME SIR. / SHE DON'T MIND** | | - |

Feb 73. (7") <1407> **PARDON ME SIR. / ST. JAMES INFIRMARY BLUES** | - | 51 |

—— now (complete new line-up) **STAINTON** joined **TUNDRA / HENRY McCULLOCH** – guitar / **MICK WEAVER** (aka **WYNDER K. FROG**) – keyboards / **BUFFALO GELBER** – bass / **JIMMY KARSTEIN** – drums

Jun 74. (7") (BUG 47) <1539> **PUT OUT THE LIGHT. / IF I LOVE YOU** | | 46 |

Aug 74. (lp/c) (HIFLY/ZCFLY 18) <AM 3633> **I CAN STAND A LITTLE RAIN** | | 11 |
– Put out the light / I can stand a little rain / I get mad / Sing me a song / The moon is a harsh mistress / Don't forget me / You are so beautiful / It's a sin when you love somebody / Performance / Guilty. (re-iss. Apr89 on 'Castle' lp/c/cd; CLA LP/MC/CD 144) (cd re-iss. Oct98 on 'Polydor'; 393175-2)

Dec 74. (7") (BUG 57) **YOU ARE SO BEAUTIFUL. / I GET MAD** | | - |

Dec 74. (7") <1641> **YOU ARE SO BEAUTIFUL. / IT'S A SIN WHEN YOU LOVE SOMEBODY** | - | 5 |

—— He then formed **JOE COCKER & The COCK'N'BULL BAND** with **WEAVER** plus **ALBERT LEE** – guitar / **PETER GAVIN** – drums / **ANDY DENNO** – bass
JOE COCKER retained **LEE, GAVIN** plus touring band **RICHARD TEE** – keyboards / **GORDON EDWARDS** – bass / **CORNELL DUPREE** – guitar / **KENNY SLADE** – percussion and three girl backing singers

Jul 75. (7") <1749> **I THINK IT'S GONNA RAIN TODAY. / OH MAMA** | | - |

Aug 75. (lp/c) (HIFLY/ZCFLY 20) <AM 4529> **JAMAICA SAY YOU WILL** | | 42 |
– (That's what I like) In my woman / Where am I now / I think it's going to rain today / Forgive me now / Oh mama / Lucinda / If I love you / Jamaica say you will / It's all over but the shoutin' / Jack-a-diamonds. (cd-iss. Oct98 on 'Polydor'; 394529-2)

Oct 75. (7") (BUG 61) **IT'S ALL OVER BUT THE SHOUTIN'. / SANDPAPER CADILLAC** | | - |

Oct 75. (7") <1758> **JAMAICA SAY YOU WILL. / IT'S ALL OVER BUT THE SHOUTIN'** | - | |

—— **JOE COCKER & STUFF** retained **TEE, EDWARDS** and **DUPREE** added **ERIC GALE** – guitar repl. LEE who went solo **STEVE GADD** drums repl. GAVIN

	A&M	A&M
Apr 76. (7") <1805> **THE MAN IN ME. / (part 2)** | - | |

Apr 76. (lp/c) (AMLH/CAM 64574) <AM 4574> **STINGRAY** | | 70 |
– The jealous kind / I broke down / You came along / Catfish / Moon dew / The man in me / She is my lady / Worrier / Born thru indifference with you / A song for you. (cd-iss. Oct98 on 'Polydor'; 394574-2)

Jul 76. (7") (AMS 7243) <1830> **THE JEALOUS KIND. / YOU CAME ALONG** | | |

Sep 76. (7") (AMS 7257) <1855> **I BROKE DOWN. / YOU CAME ALONG** | | |

—— JOE then joined **KOKOMO** for a month late '76 (no recordings). Took a long time off from studio & stage. Returned with a host of session people

	Asylum	Asylum
Sep 78. (7") <45540> **FUN TIME. / WATCHING THE RIVER FLOW** | - | |

Sep 78. (lp/c) (K/K4 53087) <6E 145> **LUXURY YOU CAN AFFORD** | | 76 |
– Fun time / Watching the river flow / Boogie baby / A white shade of pale / I can't say no / Southern lady / I know (you don't want me no more) / What you did to me last night / Lady put the light out / Wasted years / I heard it through the grapevine. (cd-iss. Jan96 on 'WEA'; 7559 60821-2)

Sep 78. (7") (K 13138) **FUN TIME. / I CAN'T SAY NO** | | - |

Jan 79. (7") (K 13148) **A WHITER SHADE OF PALE. / WATCHING THE RIVER FLOW** | | |

—— In Sep'81, JOE was credited on a single 'I'm So Glad I'm Standing Here Today' and guested on 'Standing Still' by the CRUSADERS.

JOE COCKER returned to solo work '82, (first w/ SLY DUNBAR + ROBBIE SHAKESPEARE)

	Island	Island
Jun 82. (7"/12") (WIP/12WIP 6708) **SWEET LITTLE WOMAN. / LOOK WHAT YOU'VE DONE** | | |

Jul 82. (lp/c) (ILPS/ICT 9700) <9750> **SHEFFIELD STEEL** | | |
– Look what you've done / Shocked / Sweet little woman / Seven days / Marie / Ruby Lee / Many rivers to cross / So good so right / Talking back to the night / Just like always. (cd-iss. Jul92; IMCD 149)

Aug 82. (7") (WIP 6802) **MANY RIVERS TO CROSS. / TALKING BACK TO THE NIGHT** | | |
below from the film 'An Officer and a Gentleman'

Jan 83. (7"; JOE COCKER & JENNIFER WARNES) (WIP 6830) <99996> **UP WHERE WE BELONG. / SWEET LITTLE WOMAN** | 7 | 1 Aug82 |

Jun 83. (7") (IS 115) **THROW IT AWAY. / EASY RIDER** | | |

	Capitol	Capitol
Jun 84. (7") (CL 333) <5338> **CIVILIZED MAN. / A GIRL LIKE YOU** | | |

Jun 84. (lp/c/cd) (EJ 240139-1/-4)(CDP 746038-2) <12335> **CIVILIZED MAN** | 100 | May84 |
– Civilized / There goes my baby / Come on in / Tempted / Long drag off a cigarette / I love the night / Crazy in love / A girl like you / Hold on (I feel our love is changing) / Even a fool would let go. (re-iss. Jul88 lp/c; ATAK/TC-ATAK 115) (cd re-iss. Apr92; EJ 240139-2)

Aug 84. (7") <5390> **CRAZY IN LOVE. / COME ON IN** | - | |

Nov 84. (7") (CL 347) <5412> **EDGE OF A DREAM (from the film 'Teachers'). / TEMPTED** | 69 Oct84 | |

Feb 86. (7") <5557> **SHELTER ME. / TELL ME THERE'S A WAY** | - | 91 |

Mar 86. (7") (CL 362) **SHELTER ME. / ONE MORE TIME** | | |
(12"+=) – If you have love, give me some.

Apr 86. (lp/c)(cd) (EST/TC-EST 2009)(CDP 746268-2) <12394> **COCKER** | 50 | |
– Shelter / A to Z / Don't you love me anymore / Living without your love / Don't drink the water / You can leave your hat on / Heart of the matter / Inner city blues / Love is on a fade / Heaven. (re-iss. Oct89 on 'Fame' cd/c/lp; CD/TC+/FA 3227) (re-iss. Jul94; CDEST 2009)

May 86. (7"/12") (CL/12CL 404) **DON'T YOU LOVE ME ANYMORE. / TELL ME THERE'S WAY** | | |

May 86. (7") <5626> **DON'T YOU LOVE ME ANYMORE. / DON'T DRINK THE WATER** | - | |

Jun 86. (7"/12") (CL/12CL 413) **YOU CAN LEAVE YOUR HAT ON. / LONG DRAG OFF THE CIGARETTE** | | |

Oct 87. (7") (CL 465) **UNCHAIN MY HEART. / THE ONE** | 46 | - |
(12") (12CL 465) – ('A'side) / ('A'-Rock mix) / The one.
(cd-s+=) (CDCL 465) – ('A'dance mix) / You can leave your hat on.

Oct 87. (7") <44072> **UNCHAIN MY HEART. / SATISFIED** | - | |

Oct 87. (cd/c/lp) (CD/TC+/EST 2045) <48285> **UNCHAIN MY HEART** | 89 | |
– Unchain my heart / Two wrongs (don't make a right) / I stand in wonder / The river's rising / Isolation / All our tomorrows / A woman loves a man / Trust in me / The one / Satisfied. (re-iss. Jun89; CDP 748285-2) (cd re-iss. Aug92; CDEST 2045)

Dec 87. (7") <44101> **TWO WRONGS (DON'T MAKE A RIGHT). / ISOLATION** | - | |

Dec 87. (7"/12") (MCA/+S 129) <53077> **LOVE LIVES ON. / ON MY WAY TO YOU** | - | |
(above from the movie, 'Bigfoot & The Hendersons' – US title 'Harry & The Hendersons', on 'M.C.A.')

May 88. (7") (CL 493) **DON'T YOU LOVE ME NO MORE. / ALL OUR TOMORROWS** | - | |
(12"+=) (12CL 493) – Tell me there's a way.
(cd-s++=) (CDCL 493) – With a little help from my friends.

Jul 89. (cd/c/lp) (CD/TC+/EST 2098) <92861> **ONE NIGHT OF SIN** | 52 | |
– When the night comes / I will live for you / I've got to use my imagination / Letting go / Just to keep from drowning / The unforgiven * / Another mind gone / Fever / You know it's gonna hurt / Bad bad sign / I'm your man / One night of sin. (cd+= *) (cd re-iss. Mar94; same)

Oct 89. (c-s,cd-s) <44437> **WHEN THE NIGHT COMES. / ONE NIGHT OF SIN** | - | 11 |

Nov 89. (7") (CL 535) **WHEN THE NIGHT COMES. / RUBY LEE** | 65 | - |
(12"+=/cd-s+=) (12/CD CL 535) – ('A'extended).

—— **JOE COCKER BAND** is **DERIC DYER** – sax, keys, perc. / **STEVE HOLLEY** – drums / **PHIL GRANDE** – lead guitar / **JEFF LEVINE** – keyboards / **KEITH MACK** – rhythm guitar / **CHRIS STAINTON** – keyboards / **T.M. STEVENS** – bass, vocals / **DOREEN CHANTER** – vocals / **MAXINE GREEN** – vocals / **CRYSTAL TALIEFERO** – vocals, percussion / The **MEMPHIS HORNS:- WAYNE JACKSON, ANDREW LOVE, GARY GAZAWAY**

Jun 90. (cd/c/d-lp) (CD/TC+/ESTSP 25) <93416> **JOE COCKER LIVE (live)** | 95 | |
– Feeling alright? / Shelter me / Hitchcock railway / Up where we belong / You can leave your hat on / Guilty / When the night comes / Unchain my heart / With a little help from my friends / You are so beautiful / The letter / She came in through the bathroom window / High time we went / What are you doing with a fool like me (studio) / Living in the promise land (studio).

May 90. (c-s,cd-s) <44543> **WHAT ARE YOU DOING WITH A FOOL LIKE ME? / ANOTHER MIND GONE** | - | 96 |
(studio:- KENNY RICHARDS – drums / EARL SLICK – guitar / BASHARI JOHNSON – percussion, b.vocals – TAWATHA AGEE, VANEESE THOMAS & FONZI THORNTON.)

Oct 91. (cd/c/lp) (CD/TC+/ESTU 2167) **NIGHT CALLS** | | |
– Love is alive / Little bit of love / Please no more / There's a storm coming / You've got to hide your love away / I can hear the river / Don't let the Sun go down on me / Night calls / Five women / Can't find my way home / Not too young to die of a broken heart / Out of the rain. (re-dist.Apr92, hit UK No.25)

Oct 91. (c-s/7") (TC+/CL) **NIGHT CALLS. / OUT OF THE RAIN** | | |
(12"+=/cd-s+=) (12/CD CL) – Not too young to die of a broken heart.

Mar 92. (c-s/7") (TC+/CL 645) **(ALL I KNOW) FEELS LIKE FOREVER. / WHEN THE NIGHT COMES** | 25 | |
(cd-s+=) (CDCL 645) – Up where we belong / With a little help from my friends.

May 92. (c-s/7") (TC+/CL 657) **NOW THAT THE MAGIC HAS GONE. / FIVE WOMEN** | 28 | |
(12"+=/cd-s+=) (12/CD CL 657) – Two wrongs don't make a right / The letter.

Jun 92. (c-s/7") (TC+/CL 664) **UNCHAIN MY HEART. / YOU CAN LEAVE YOUR HAT ON** | 17 | - |
(12"+=/cd-s+=) (12/CD CL 664) – The one / ('A'-Rock mix).

Nov 92. (c-s/7") (TC+/CL 674) **WHEN THE NIGHT COMES. / YOU'VE GOT TO HIDE YOUR LOVE AWAY** | 61 | |
(cd-s+=) (CDCL 674) – Tempted / I still can't believe it's true.
(cd-s) (CDCLS 674) – ('A'side) / The Moon is a harsh mistress / I'm your man / She came in through the bathroom window.

—— now w/ **JACK BRUNO** – drums / **BOB FEIT + TONY JOE WHITE + TIM PIERCE** – guitar / **CHRIS STAINTON** – keyboards / **LENNY CASTRO** – percussion / **C.J. VANSTON** – organ

Aug 94. (c-s) (TCCL 722) **THE SIMPLE THINGS / SUMMER IN THE CITY** | 17 | |
(cd-s+=) (CDCL 722) – With a little help from my friends (live).
(cd-s) (CDCLS 722) – ('A'side) / Angeline / My strongest weakness.

Sep 94. (cd/c/lp) (CD/TC+/EST 2233) **HAVE A LITTLE FAITH** | 9 | |
– Let the healing begin / Have a little faith in me / The simple things / Summer in the city / The great divide / Highway highway / Too cool / Soul time / Out of the blue / Angeline / Hell and highwater / Standing knee deep in a river / Take me home.

Oct 94. (c-s/cd-s) (TC/CD CL 729) **TAKE ME HOME. (featuring BEKKA BRAMBLETT) / TEMPTED / UNCHAIN MY HEART (90's version)** | 41 | |
(cd-s) (CDCLS 729) – ('A'side) / Up where we belong / You can leave your hat on.

Dec 94. (c-s/cd-s) *(TC/CD CL 727)* **LET THE HEALING BEGIN / SUMMER IN THE CITY (2-mixes)** `32`
(cd-s) *(CDCLS 727)* – ('A'side) / You are so beautiful (live) / The letter (live).

Sep 95. (c-s) *(TCCL 744)* **HAVE A LITTLE FAITH / THE SIMPLE THINGS (live) / LET THE HEALING BEGIN (live)** `67`
(cd-s) *(CDCLS 744)* – ('A'side) / Summer in the city (live) / Angeline (live).

Oct 96. (c-s) *(TCCL 779)* **DON'T LET ME BE MISUNDERSTOOD / SOMETHING / HIGH LONESOME BLUE** `53`
(cd-s) *(CDCLS 779)* – ('A'side) / Human touch / Anybody seen my girl.

Oct 96. (cd/c/lp) *(CD/TC+/ESTD 6)* **ORGANIC** `49`
– Into the mystic / Bye bye blackbird / Delta lady / Heartful of rain / Don't let me be misunderstood / Many rivers to cross / High lonesome blue / Sail away / You and I / Darlin' be home soon / Dignity / You can leave your hat on / You are so beautiful / Can't find my way home.

Aug 97. (c-s) *(TCCL 793)* **COULD YOU BE LOVED / THAT'S THE WAY HER LOVE IS**
(cd-s+=) *(CDCLS 793)* – ('A'-Catania mix) / Summer in the city.

Sep 97. (cd/c/lp) *(CD/TC+/EST 2301)* **ACROSS FROM MIDNIGHT**
– Tonight / Could you be loved / That's all I need to know / N'oubliez jamais / What do I tell my heart / Wayward soul / Loving you tonight / Across from midnight / What do you say / Last one to know / That's the way love is / Need your love so bad.

Parlophone   Capitol

Oct 99. (cd-s) *(CDR 6526)* **DIFFERENT ROADS / YOU CAN LEAVE YOUR HAT ON (live) / WHEN THE NIGHT COMES (live)**

Oct 99. (cd/c) *(523091-2/-4)* **NO ORDINARY WORLD** `63`
– First we take Manhattan / Different roads / My father's son / While you see a chance / She believes in me / No ordinary world / Where would I be now / Ain't gonna cry again / Soul rising / Naked without you / Love to lean on / On my way home.

– compilations etc. –

Apr 72. (d-lp) *Cube; (TOOFA 1-2)* **WITH A LITTLE HELP FROM MY FRIENDS / JOE COCKER!** `29` –

Dec 76. (lp) *Fly; (HIFLY 23)* **LIVE IN L.A. (live)**
(re-iss. May86 on 'Sierra'; lp/c; FEDB/CFEDB 5037)

1977. (7") *A&M;* **CRY ME A RIVER. / FEELING ALRIGHT** – –

May 78. (lp) *Hallmark; (SHM 954)* / *A&M; <AM 4670>* **GREATEST HITS Vol.I** Nov77

Oct 81. (d-lp/d-c) *Platinum; (PLAT/ZCPLT 1004)* **THE JOE COCKER PLATINUM COLLECTION** –

Dec 81. (7") *Cube; (BUG 91)* **LET IT BE. / MARJORINE** –

Apr 82. (lp/c) *ICS/ZCICS 1002)* **SPACE CAPTAIN (live)** –
(cd-iss. 1988; CD 853010)

Jul 82. (7") *Old Gold; (OG 9232)* **WITH A LITTLE HELP FROM MY FRIENDS. / DELTA LADY** –

Oct 82. (lp/c) *Countdown; (COUNT/ZCCNT 12)* **JOE COCKER** –

May 83. (7") *Cube; (BUG 97)* **YOU ARE SO BEAUTIFUL. / MARJORINE** –

Nov 84. (lp/c) *Sierra; (FEDD/CFEDD 1002)* **OFF THE RECORD WITH JOE COCKER** –

Apr 86. (d-lp/c/cd) *Castle; (CCS LP/MC/CD 126)* **THE COLLECTION** –

May 86. (lp/c/cd) *(STAR/STAC/TCD 2258)* **THE VERY BEST OF JOE COCKER** –

Sep 86. (12"ep) *Archive 4; (TOF 109)* **WITH A LITTLE HELP FROM MY FRIENDS / MARJORINE / THE LETTER / DELTA LADY (live)** –
(3"cd-iss. 1988 on 'Special Edition'; CD3-8)

Mar 88. (d-lp/c/d-cd) *That's Original; (TFO LP/MC/CD 4)* **JAMAICA SAY YOU WILL / COCKER HAPPY** –
(d-cd.iss-Sep91)

1988. (cd) *K-Tel; (ONCD 5121)* **THE BEST OF JOE COCKER** –

Jul 88. (lp/c/cd) *Knight; (KN LP/MC/CD 10001)* **NIGHTRIDING** –

1988. (lp) *Fun; (FUN 9015)* **16 GREATEST HITS** –

Jan 92. (cd) *Raven-Topic; (RVCD 01)* **CONNOISSEUR'S COCKER** –

Feb 92. (3xcd-box) *Castle; (CLABX 902)* **3 ORIGINALS** –
– (COCKER HAPPY / SOMETHING TO SAY / WITH A LITTLE HELP FROM MY FRIENDS)

Jun 92. (cd/c) *Polygram TV; (515411-2/-4)* **THE LEGEND** `4` –
– Up where we belong (with JENNIFER WARNES) / With a little help from my friends / Delta lady / The letter / She came in through the bathroom window / A whiter shade of pale / Love the one you're with (live) / You are so beautiful / Let it be / Just like a woman / Many rivers to cross / Talking back to the night / Fun time / I heard it through the grapevine / Please give peace a chance (live) / Don't let me be misunderstood / Honky tonk woman (live) / Cry me a river (live).

Jun 92. (c/cd) *Tring; (MC+/JHD 030)* **HITCHCOCK RAILWAY** –

Oct 93. (cd/c) *Spectrum; (550126-2/-4)* **THE FIRST TIME** –

Jul 94. (cd/c) *BR Music; (BRCD 104)* **THE VERY BEST OF JOE COCKER** –

Oct 94. (cd) *Rare; (RA 9502-2)* **FAVOURITE RARITIES** –

Aug 94. (cd,cd-vid) *E.M.I.; (SAV 4913123)* **THE BEST OF JOE COCKER – LIVE (live)** –

Oct 94. (cd) *Woodford; (WMCD 5701)* **MIDNIGHT RIDER** –

Oct 94. (cd) *Woodford; (WMCD 5705)* **SIMPLY THE BEST** –

Sep 95. (cd/c) *Spectrum; (551408-2/-4)* **THE ESSENTIAL JOE COCKER** –
(re-iss. Nov98; same)

Dec 95. (4xcd-box) *A&M; (540236-2)* **THE LONG VOYAGE HOME** –

Mar 97. (3xcd-box) *E.M.I.; (CDOMB 024)* **CIVILIZED MAN / COCKER / UNCHAIN MY HEART** –

Jul 97. (cd; JOE COCKER & THE GREASE BAND) *Strange Fruit; (SFRSCD 036)* **ON AIR** –

Feb 99. (cd/c) *Parlophone; (497719-2/-4)* **THE BEST OF JOE COCKER** `24`

COCKNEY REJECTS (dig out; Great Alt & Indie . . .)

COCTEAU TWINS

Formed: Grangemouth, Scotland . . . late 1981 when the (then) trio of ELIZABETH FRASER, ROBIN GUTHRIE and WILL HEGGIE visited London to hand DJ John Peel a demo tape. He booked them for sessions on his Radio One night time show and they subsequently signed to IVO WATT-RUSSELL's indie label, '4 a.d.'. The COCTEAUS' debut offering, 'GARLANDS', was hastily recorded, hitting the shops just over a week later and giving a hint of things to come with an interesting fusion of monochromatic rhythms, textured guitar distortion and sampling technology. Resisting many offers from the majors, they were back in the studio again for 1983's 'LULLABIES' EP and 'HEAD OVER HEELS' album. A mesmerising collage of irridescent guitar soundscapes and sheets of feedback perforated with FRASER's unintelligible but highly emotive warbling, the latter record was a blueprint for the best of The COCTEAU TWINS work. After a support slot to OMD, WILL HEGGIE departed, making the long trip back north to set up his own outfit, LOWLIFE. Around the same time ROBIN and LIZ hit No.1 in the indie charts when guesting for 'IVO/4 a.d.' ensemble, THIS MORTAL COIL on 'SONG TO THE SIREN'; it was mistakenly thought by many to be a COCTEAU TWINS off-shoot, rather than IVO's project. That idea was laid to rest after the album, 'IT'LL END IN TEARS', was issued in '84. Meanwhile, The COCTEAU TWINS were back with another blissed out masterpiece, 'TREASURE', introducing newcomer, SIMON RAYMONDE on bass and seeing LIZ explore hitherto uncharted vocal territory in a fascinating, enigmatic and occasionally unsettling language that communicated everything and nothing. It also marked their first taste of Top 30 success although they surpassed this with 1986's more inscrutably minimalist Top 10 effort, 'VICTORIALAND'. An abortive film project collaboration with HAROLD BUDD was issued at the end of the year as they headed towards an increasingly "New Age"-style sound. Two more classics, 'BLUE BELL KNOLL' and 'HEAVEN OR LAS VEGAS' were released over the next half decade, both finding a home in the US charts for 'Capitol' records. In 1992, they finally succumbed to signing for 'Fontana' in the UK, leading to a comeback album, 'FOUR CALENDAR CAFE' in '93. Many longtime fans were disappointed with what was surely the duo's most accessible, grounded album to date yet devoid of much of the mystery that made their earlier work so alluring. The following year saw LIZ guest on FUTURE SOUND OF LONDON's ambient venture, 'Lifeforms'; she would subsequently go on to perform on MASSIVE ATTACK's 'Teardrops' single in '98. After another 3-year hiatus, FRAZER and GUTHRIE returned with 'MILK & KISSES', a typically COCTEAU-esque affair that moved some critics to suggest the band were treading water. • **Trivia:** ROBIN has produced many '4.a.d.' outfits in addition to The GUN CLUB (1987). An item for some time, LIZ and ROBIN became parents in 1989. Early in 1991, LIZ was surprisingly but not undeservedly nominated for Best Female Vocalist at the 'Brit' awards.

Album rating: GARLANDS (*7) / HEAD OVER HEELS (*8) / TREASURE (*9) / VICTORIALAND (*8) / THE MOON AND THE MELODIES with Harold Budd (*5) / THE PINK OPAQUE compilation (*8) / BLUE BELL KNOLL (*7) / HEAVEN OR LAS VEGAS (*7) / FOUR CALENDAR CAFE (*6) / MILK & KISSES (*7) / THE BBC SESSIONS collection (*7)

ELIZABETH FRASER (b.29 Aug'63) – vocals / **ROBIN GUTHRIE** (b. 4 Jan'62) – guitar, drum programming, keyboards / **WILL HEGGIE** – bass

4 a.d.   not iss.

Jul 82. (lp) *(CAD 211)* **GARLANDS**
– Blood bitch / Wax and wane / But I'm not / Blind dumb deaf / Grail overfloweth / Shallow than halo / The hollow men / Garlands. *(c-iss.Apr84 +=; CADC 211)* – Dear heart / Blind dumb deaf / Hearsay please / Hazel. *(cd-iss. 1986 ++=; CAD 211CD)* – Speak no evil / Perhaps some other acorn. *<US cd-iss. 1991 on 'Alliance'; 96415>*

Sep 82. (12"ep) *(BAD 213)* **LULLABIES**
– It's all but an ark lark / Alas dies laughing / Feathers-Oar-Blades.

Mar 83. (7") *(AD 303)* **PEPPERMINT PIG. / LAUGH LINES**
(12"+=) (BAD 303) – Hazel.

—— Trimmed to a duo when HEGGIE left to form LOWLIFE

Oct 83. (lp) *(CAD 313)* **HEAD OVER HEELS** `51` –
– When mama was moth / Sugar hiccup / In our anglehood / Glass candle grenades / Multifoiled / In the gold dust rush / The tinderbox (of a heart) / My love paramour / Musette and drums / Five ten fiftyfold. *(c-iss.Apr84 +=; CADC 313)* *(cd-iss. 1986 +=; CAD 313CD)* – SUNBURST AND SNOWBLIND EP *<US cd-iss. 1991 on 'Alliance'; 96416>*

Oct 83. (12"ep) *(BAD 314)* **SUNBURST AND SNOWBLIND** –
– Sugar hiccup / From the flagstones / Because of whirl-Jack / Hitherto.

—— added **SIMON RAYMONDE** (b. 3 Apr'62, London, England) – bass, keyboards, guitar (ex-DROWNING CRAZE)

Apr 84. (7") *(AD 405)* **PEARLY DEWDROPS DROP. / PEPPER-TREE** `29` –
(12"+=) (BAD 405) – The spangle maker.

Nov 84. (lp/c) *(CAD/+C 412)* **TREASURE** `29` –
– Ivo / Lorelei / Beatrix / Persephone / Pandora – for Cindy / Amelia / Aloysius / Cicely / Otterley / Donimo. *(cd-iss. 1986; CAD 412CD)* *<US cd-iss. 1991 on 'Alliance'; 96418>*

Mar 85. (7") *(AD 501)* **AIKEA-GUINEA. / KOOKABURRA** `41` –
(12"+=) (BAD 501) – Rococo / Quiquose.

Nov 85. (12"ep) *(BAD 510)* **TINY DYNAMITE** `52` –
– Pink orange red / Ribbed and veined / Sultitan Itan / Plain tiger.

Nov 85. (12"ep) *(BAD 511)* **ECHOES IN A SHALLOW BAY** `65` –

– Great spangled fritillary / Melonella / Pale clouded white / Eggs and their shells *(cd-iss. Oct86 +=; BAD 510/511)* – TINY DYNAMITE

—— **RICHARD THOMAS** – saxophone, bass (of DIF JUZ) repl. SIMON who fell ill

Apr 86. (lp/c)(cd) *(CAD/+C 602)(CAD 602CD)* **VICTORIALAND**   **10**   ☐
– Lazy calm / Fluffy tufts / Throughout the dark months of April and May / Whales tales / Oomingmak / Little Spacey / Feet-like fins / How to bring a blush to the snow / The thinner the air. *<US cd-iss. 1991 on 'Alliance'; 96417>*

—— **SIMON RAYMONDE** returned repl.temp. RICHARD (back to DIF JUZ)

Oct 86. (7") *(AD 610)* **LOVE'S EASY TEARS. / THOSE EYES, THAT MOUTH**   **53**   -
(12"+=) *(BAD 610)* – Sigh's smell of farewell.

—— next was a one-off collaboration with label new signing **HAROLD BUDD** – piano

                  4 a.d. Relativity

Nov 86. (lp/c)(cd; by HAROLD BUDD, ELIZABETH FRASER, ROBIN GUTHRIE, SIMON RAYMONDE) *(CAD/+C 611)(CAD 611CD)* *<8143>* **THE MOON AND THE MELODIES** **46**   ☐
– Sea, swallow me / Memory gongs / Why do you love me? / Eyes are mosaics / She will destroy you / The ghost has no home / Bloody and blunt / Ooze out and away, one how.

                  4 a.d. Capitol

Sep 88. (lp/c/dat)(cd) *(CAD/+C/T 807)(CAD 807CD)* *<90892>* **BLUE BELL KNOLL**   **15**   ☐
– Blue bell knoll / Athol-brose / Carolyn's fingers / For Phoebe still a baby / The itchy glowbo blow / Cico buff / Suckling the mender / Spooning good singing gum / A kissed out red floatboat / Ella megablast burls forever.

Oct 88. (7") **CAROLYN'S FINGERS. / BLUE BELL KNOLL**   -   ☐

—— In Apr'90, LIZ was heard on Ian McCulloch's (ex-ECHO & THE BUNNYMEN) 'Candleland' single.

Aug 90. (7"/c-s) *(AD 0011/+C)* **ICEBLINK LUCK. / MIZAKE THE MIZAN**   **38**   -
(12"+=/cd-s+=) *(AD 0011 T/CD)* – Watchiar.

Sep 90. (cd)(lp/c) *(CAD 0012CD)(CAD/+C 0012)* *<C2/C1/C4 93669>* **HEAVEN OR LAS VEGAS**   **7**   **99**
– Cherry coloured funk / Pitch the baby / Iceblink luck / Fifty-fifty clown / Heaven or Las Vegas / I wear your ring / Fotzepolitic / Wolf in the breast / Road, river and rail / Frou-frou foxes in midsummer fires.

—— on U.S. tour, augmented by **MITSUO TATE + BEN BLAKEMAN** – guitars

                  Fontana Capitol

Sep 93. (7"/c-s) *(CT/+C 1)* **EVANGELINE. / MUD AND LARK**   **34**   -
(12"pic-d+=/cd-s+=) *(CT X/CD 1)* – Summer-blink.

Oct 93. (cd/c/lp) *(518259-2/-4/-1)* *<C2/C4/C1 99375>* **FOUR CALENDAR CAFE**   **13**   **78**
– Know who you are ate every age / Evangeline / Blue beard / Theft and wandering around lost / Oil of angels / Squeeze-wax / My truth / Essence / Summerhead / Pur.

Dec 93. (cd-s) *(COCCD 1)* **WINTER WONDERLAND. / FROSTY THE SNOWMAN**   **58**   -
(above festive tracks, deleted after a week in UK Top 60)

Feb 94. (7"/c-s) *(CT/+C 2)* **BLUEBEARD. / THREE SWEPT**   **33**   ☐
(12"+=) *(CTX 2)* – Ice-pulse.
(cd-s+++=) *(CTCD 2)* – ('A'acoustic).

Sep 95. (7"//7"/cd-ep) *(CCT//CTT/CTCD 3)* *<30548>* **TWINLIGHTS**   **59**   ☐ Dec95
– Rilkean heart / Golden-vein // Pink orange red / Half-gifts.

Oct 95. (12"ep/cd-ep) *(CT X/CD 4)* *<36240>* **OTHERNESS** (An Ambient EP)   **59**   ☐ Dec95
– Feet like fins / Seekers who are lovers / Violaine / Cherry coloured funk.

Mar 96. (cd-ep) *(CTCD 5)* **TISHBITE / PRIMITIVE HEART / FLOCK OF SOUL**   **34**   ☐
(12"ep/cd-ep) *(CT X/DDD 5)* – (title track) / Round / An Elan.

Apr 96. (cd/c/lp) *(514 501-2/4/-1)* *<37049-2/-4/-1>* **MILK & KISSES**   **17**   **99**
– Violaine / Serpent skirt / Tishbite / Half-gifts / Calfskin smack / Rilkean heart / Ups / Eperdu / Treasure hiding / Seekers who are lovers. *(also ltd.cd; 532 363-2)*

Jul 96. (12") *(CTX 6)* **VIOLAINE. / ALICE**   **56**   ☐
(cd-s+=) *(CTDD 6)* – Circling girl.
(cd-s) *(CTCD 6)* – ('A'side) / Tranquil eye / Smile.

– compilations, others, etc. –

Dec 85. (cd) *4 a.d.; (CAD 513CD)* / Relativity; *<ENC 8040>* **THE PINK OPAQUE**   ☐   ☐ Sep85
– The spangle maker / Millimillenary / Wax and wane / Hitherto / Pearly-dewdrops' drops (12" Version) / From the flagstones / Aikea-Guinea / Lorelei / Pepper-tree / Musette and drums.

Nov 91. (10xcd-ep-box) *Capitol; (CTBOX 1)* **THE SINGLES COLLECTION**   ☐   -
– (above featured previous 9 singles + new 1) (sold separately Mar92)

Sep 99. (d-cd) *Bella Union; (BELLACD 14)* **THE BBC SESSIONS**   ☐   ☐

Leonard COHEN

Born: 21 Sep'34, Montreal, Canada. Emerging from the tail end of the beatnik scene in the early 60's, COHEN was nearing his mid thirties and had already published several volumes of poetry as well as two novels when he came to record his debut album, 'SONGS OF LEONARD COHEN'. Released in 1968, the record is still regarded by many as his finest work and includes two of his best loved and well known songs in 'SUZANNE' and 'SISTERS OF MERCY'. Musically, the album was sparse, fragile acoustic guitar accompanying COHEN's highly distinctive, tortured sliver of a voice. All ravaged sophistication and doomed romance, COHEN was inevitably compared with the likes of JACQUES BREL, although the richness of the imagery he employed immediately set him apart. While the seemingly self-pitying, bedsit-friendly image saw him panned and parodied by critics, he found an appreciative audience among disillusioned hippies as the singer/songwriter movement began to gather strength. Always more popular

in Britain and Europe than America, his debut album reached No.13 in the UK charts. The follow-up, 'SONGS FROM A ROOM' (1969) was almost as good, another opus cloaked in a melancholic intensity and an aching sense of loss, boasting such timeless COHEN fare as 'BIRD ON A WIRE', 'THE PARTISAN' and 'LADY MIDNIGHT'. The record reached No.2 in Britain and COHEN set off for Europe on an extensive round of touring that included an appearance at the Isle Of Wight festival in 1970. Following the release of 'SONGS OF LOVE AND HATE' (1971), the singer embarked on another soujourn to foreign shores, even playing for Israeli soldiers at various military bases, an experience that informed a large part of the lyrical themes on 'NEW SKIN FOR THE OLD CEREMONY' (1974). It was to be another three years before the next studio release and in the interim, 'Columbia' issued a fairly representative best of package. Upon its release, 'DEATH OF A LADIES MAN' (1977) was met with puzzlement and derision, COHEN's subtle, quasi-mystical lyricism suffocated under a typically high powered PHIL SPECTOR production. Vocal in his embarrassment over the album, COHEN returned to more complementary arrangements and structures on 'RECENT SONGS' (1979). The early 80's saw COHEN concentrate on poetry and prose, even making a film, 'I Am A Hotel', in 1983. Returning to the music scene in 1985 with 'VARIOUS POSITIONS', COHEN still had a cult audience in Europe, one that mushroomed with the release of 'I'M YOUR MAN' in 1988. As a purveyor of effortlessly cool urban existentialism on the likes of 'FIRST WE TAKE MANHATTAN', COHEN attracted a new generation of disaffected music fans. It seems he was also held in high regard by the younger generation of fellow artists who showed their appreciation with a 1991 tribute album, 'I'M YOUR FAN'. Among those interpreting COHEN's finer moments (with mixed results) were NICK CAVE, R.E.M., IAN McCULLOCH and The PIXIES. 'THE FUTURE' (1992) saw COHEN achieve his biggest commercial success since the 70's; although never the most prolific of artists, the record has been his sole studio release of the 90's. At the time of writing, COHEN is currently residing in a monastary, so don't hold your breath for a new album (unless it's of the Gregorian chant variety!). • **Covered:** ALWAYS (Irving Berlin) / THE PARTISAN (A.Marly & H.Zaret-Bernard) / BE FOR REAL (Frederick Knight). • **Trivia:** His long-time dual backing singer and solo artist JENNIFER WARNES released album 'FAMOUS BLUE RAINCOAT' which contained all songs written by COHEN.

Album rating: THE SONGS OF LEONARD COHEN (*8) / SONGS FROM A ROOM (*6) / SONGS OF LOVE AND HATE (*6) / LIVE SONGS (*4) / NEW SKIN FOR THE OLD CEREMONY (*5) / GREATEST HITS compilation (*9) / DEATH OF A LADIES' MAN (*4) / RECENT SONGS (*5) / VARIOUS POSITIONS (*5) / I'M YOUR MAN (*7) / THE FUTURE (*7) / COHEN LIVE (*4)

LEONARD COHEN – vocals, guitar(with various session people)

                  C.B.S. Columbia

Feb 68. (lp) *(CBS 63241)* *<9533>* **SONGS OF LEONARD COHEN** **13**   **83**
– Suzanne / Master song / Winter lady / The stranger song / Sisters of mercy / So long, Marianne / Hey, that's no way to say goodbye / Stories of the street / Teachers / One of us cannot be wrong. *(re-iss. Nov91;)*

Apr 68. (7") *<44439>* **SUZANNE. / HEY, THAT'S NO WAY TO SAY GOODBYE**   -   -

May 68. (7") *(CBS 3337)* **SUZANNE. / SO LONG, MARIANNE**   -   ☐

Apr 69. (lp) *(CBS 63587)* *<9767>* **SONGS FROM A ROOM**   **2**   **63**
– Bird on the wire / Story of Isaac / Bunch of lonesome heroes / The partisan / Seems so long ago, Nancy / Old revolution / The butcher / You know who I am / Lady midnight / Tonight will be fine. *(re-iss. Nov81; CBS 32074) (cd-iss. Feb88; CDCBS 63587) (re-iss. cd Jun90; CD 32074)*

May 69. (7") *(CBS 4245)* *<44827>* **BIRD ON THE WIRE. / SEEMS SO LONG AGO, NANCY**   ☐   ☐

Mar 71. (lp) *(CBS 69004)* *<30103>* **SONGS OF LOVE AND HATE**   **4**   ☐
– Avalanche / Last year's man / Dress rehearsal rag / Diamonds in the mine / Love call you by your first name / Famous blue raincoat / Sing another song / Boys / Joan of Arc. *(re-iss. Sep82 lp/c; CBS/40 32219) (re-iss. Jun94 on 'Columbia' cd/c; 476799-2/-4)*

Jul 71. (7") *(CBS 7292)* **JOAN OF ARC. / DIAMONDS IN THE MINE**   ☐   -

Jul 72. (7"ep) *(CBS 9162)* **McCABE & MRS. MILLER**   ☐   ☐
– Sisters of mercy / Winter lady / The stranger song.

—— w / **RON CORNELIUS** – guitar / **BOB JOHNSTON** – organ, guitar, harmonica / **CHARLIE DANIELS** – bass, fiddle / **ELKIN FOWLER** – banjo, guitar / **JENNIFER WARNES** – vocals / **PETER MARSHALL** – bass / **DAVID O'CONNOR** – guitar

Apr 73. (lp) *(CBS 65224)* *<31724>* **LIVE SONGS** (live)   ☐   ☐
– (minute prologue) / Passing through / You know who I am / Bird on the wire / Nancy / Improvisation / Story of Isaac / Please don't pass me by (a disgrace) / Tonight will be fine / Queen Victoria. *(re-iss. Mar84 lp/c; CBS/40 32272) (cd-iss. May88; CDCBS 65224)*

Apr 73. (7") *<45852>* **NANCY (live). / PASSING THROUGH (live)**   -   ☐

Jul 74. (7") *(CBS 2494)* **BIRD ON THE WIRE (live). / TONIGHT WILL BE FINE (live)**   ☐   ☐

—— now w/ loads of sessioners

Aug 74. (lp) *(CBS 69087)* *<33167>* **NEW SKIN FOR THE OLD CEREMONY**   **24**   ☐
– Is this what you wanted / Chelsea hotel No.2 / Lover lover lover / Field Commander Cohen / Why don't you try / There is a war / A singer must die / I tried to leave you / Who by fire / Take this longing / Leaving Green sleeves. *(c-iss.Jun86; CBS40 32660) (cd-iss. Jun88; CDCBS 69087) (cd re-iss. Apr96; CD 32660)*

Nov 74. (7") *(CBS 2699)* **LOVER LOVER LOVER. / WHO BY FIRE**   ☐   ☐

Nov 75. (lp) *(CBS 69161)* *<34077>* **GREATEST HITS** (compilation)   ☐   ☐
– Suzanne / Sisters of mercy / So long, Marianne / Bird on the wire / Lady Midnight / The partisan / Hey, that's no way to say goodbye / Famous blue raincoat / Last year's man / Chelsea hotel No.2 / Who by fire / Take this longing. *(re-iss. Apr85 lp/c; CBS/40 32644) (cd-iss. Jun88; CDCBS 69161; hit UK No.99) (re-iss. cd Jun89; CDCBS 32644)*

Nov 77. (lp/c) *(CBS/40 86042)* *<3125>* **DEATH OF A LADIES MAN**   **35**   ☐

– True love leaves no traces / Iodine / Paper thin hotel / Memories / I left a woman waiting / Don't go home with your hard-on / Fingerprints / Death of a ladies man. (cd-iss. Jun88; CDCBS 86042) (re-iss. cd May95; CD 86042)

Dec 77. (7") (CBS 5882) **MEMORIES. / DON'T GO HOME WITH YOUR HARD-ON**

Mar 78. (7") (CBS 6095) **TRUE LOVE LEAVES NO TRACES. / I LEFT A WOMAN WAITING**

Sep 79. (lp/c) (CBS/40 86097) <36364> **RECENT SONGS**
– The guests / Humbled in love / Came so far for beauty / The lost Canadian (un Canadien errant) / The traitor / Our lady of solitude / The gypsy's wife / The smokey life / The ballad of absent mare. (cd-iss. Jun88; CDCBS 86097) <US cd-iss. May88; CK 36264> (re-iss. cd.Dec93 on 'Sony Europe';) (re-iss. May94 on 'Columbia' cd/c; 474750-2/-4)

—— took time out during the first half of the 80's

		C.B.S.	Passport
Feb 85. (lp/c) (CBS/40 26222) **VARIOUS POSITIONS**		52	

– Dance me to the end of love / Come back to you / The law / Night comes on / Hallelujah / The captain / Hunter's lullaby / Heart with no companion / If it be your will. (cd-iss. May87; CDCBS 26222) (re-iss. Oct89 cd/c; 465 569-1/-4)

Feb 85. (7") (A 6052) **DANCE ME TO THE END OF LOVE. / THE LAW**

Jan 88. (7") (651 352-7) **FIRST WE TAKE MANHATTAN. / SISTERS OF MERCY**
(12"+=/cd-s+=) (651 352-6/-2) – Bird on the wire / Suzanne.

Feb 88. (lp/c/cd) (460642-1/-4/-2) **I'M YOUR MAN** `48`
– First we take Manhattan / Ain't no cure for love / Everybody knows / I'm your man / Take this waltz / Jazz police / I can't forget / Tower of song. (re-iss. Jul90 lp/c; same) (re-iss. cd Dec95; 460642-9)

May 88. (7") (651 599-7) **AIN'T NO CURE FOR LOVE. / JAZZ POLICE**
(12"+=/cd-s+=) (651 599-6/-2) – Hey that's no way to say goodbye / So long, Marianne.

		Columbia	Columbia
Nov 92. (cd/c/lp) (472498-2/-4/-1) **THE FUTURE**		36	

– The future / Waiting for the miracle / Be for real / Closing time / Anthem / Democracy / Light as the breeze / Always / Tacoma trailer. (d-cd-iss. Feb93; 472498-2D) – SONGS OF LEONARD COHEN

May 93. (cd-ep) **CLOSING TIME / FIRST WE TAKE MANHATTAN / FAMOUS BLUE RAINCOAT / WINTER LADY**
(above ep might have been called 'THE FUTURE EP')

Jul 94. (cd) (477171-2) **COHEN LIVE (live)**
– Dance me to the end of love / Bird on the wire / Everybody knows / Joan Of Arc / There is a war / Sisters of mercy / Hallelujah / I'm your man / Who by fire / One of us cannot be wrong / If it be your will / Heart with no companion / Suzanne. (cd re-iss. Jan99; same)

– compilations, others, etc. –

on 'CBS' (later 'Columbia') UK / 'Columbia' US unless stated.

Mar 73. (7") (CBS 8353) **SUZANNE. / BIRD ON THE WIRE**

May 76. (7") (CBS 4306) **SUZANNE. / TAKE THIS LONGING**

Aug 83. (7"ep/c-ep) Pickwick; (7SR/7SC 5022) **SCOOP 33**
– Suzanne / Hey, that's no way to say goodbye / Joan of Arc / Bird on the wire / Paper thin hotel / Lady midnight.

May 88. (cd) <CK 34077> **THE BEST OF LEONARD COHEN**
(UK-iss.Oct94;)

Apr 90. (cd) Collectors Choice; (902 297-2) **SO LONG, MARIANNE**
(re-iss. Nov93; same) (re-iss. Dec95 on 'Columbia' cd/c; 460500-2/-4)

Sep 92. (cd) (461012-2) **NEW SKIN FOR THE OLD CEREMONY / SONGS FROM A ROOM**

Oct 92. (3xcd-box) (472268-2) **SONGS FROM A ROOM / VARIOUS POSITIONS / I'M YOUR MAN**

Oct 93. (3xcd-box) (474146-2) **SONGS OF LEONARD COHEN / SONGS OF LOVE & HATE / LIVE SONGS**

Feb 95. (d-cd) (478480-2) **SONGS FROM A ROOM / SONGS OF LOVE & HATE**

Lloyd COLE

Born: 31 Jan'61, Buxton, England. In summer of '83, COLE and BLAIR COWAN formed LLOYD COLE & THE COMMOTIONS after a meeting at Glasgow University. They subsequently recruited some fellow students, NEIL CLARK, LAWRENCE DONEGAN (son of LONNIE) and STEPHEN IRVINE, signing with 'Polydor' and scoring almost immediately with the classic 'PERFECT SKIN' single, a Top 30 hit in Spring '84. This was followed up by 'FOREST FIRE' and by the time the band's seminal debut set, 'RATTLESNAKES' was released later that Autumn, the critics were already fawning over the group's subtle, intelligent retro pop/rock. They scored extra points for the intellectual ruminations and name dropping in the lyrics, COLE's languorous croon a model of detached cool inevitably drawing comparisons with LOU REED. An auspicious start to their career, the album sold well enough to guarantee a Top 20 placing for the following year's 'BRAND NEW FRIEND' single. More readily endearing, the track's lilting pop melancholy was characteristic of the general mood on 'EASY PIECES' (1985), although the blackly humorous 'LOST WEEKEND' upped the tempo and provided the band with another Top 20 hit. By this point, COLE and his COMMOTIONS had graduated from being the darlings of the college circuit to achieve considerable crossover success and the future looked good. A third set, 'MAINSTREAM' (1987), sounded lacklustre in comparison, only 'SEAN PENN BLUES' partly recovering the sly wit of old. After a further flop EP and a relatively successful best of compilation, the band went their separate ways. COLE embarked on a solo career, taking COWAN and relocating to New York, where he recruited ex-LOU REED players, ROBERT QUINE and FRED MAHER. The resulting album, 'LLOYD COLE' (1990) achieved a respectable chart placing but a muted critical reception, despite some genuinely

evocative moments. Subsequent sets, the more buoyant 'DON'T GET WEIRD ON ME BABE' (1991) and 'BAD VIBES' (1993) rather unfairly met a similar fate. 1995's 'LOVE STORY', on the other hand, saw something of a belated critical comeback, the classy single, 'LIKE LOVERS DO', COLE's biggest hit in years, with the singer proving that a midnight shadow and artful lyrics still had a place in the pop jungle. • **Covered:** GLORY (Television) / MYSTERY TRAIN (Elvis Presley) / I DON'T BELIEVE YOU + IF YOU GOTTA GO, GO NOW (Bob Dylan) / CHILDREN OF THE REVOLUTION (T.Rex). • **Trivia:** 60's chanteuse/singer, SANDIE SHAW, had minor UK chart hit in 1986 with their 'ARE YOU READY TO BE HEARTBROKEN?'.

Album rating: RATTLESNAKES (*7) / EASY PIECES (*6) / MAINSTREAM (*5) / 1984-1989 compilation (*7) / LLOYD COLE (*5) / DON'T GET WEIRD ON ME, BABE (*5) / BAD VIBES (*4) / LOVE STORY (*5) / THE COLLECTION compilation (*7)

LLOYD COLE & THE COMMOTIONS

LLOYD COLE (b.31 Jan'61, Derbyshire, England) – vocals, guitar / **NEIL CLARK** (b. 3 Jul'55) – guitar / **BLAIR COWAN** – keyboards, vocals / **LAWRENCE DONEGAN** (b.13 Jul'61) – bass (ex-BLUEBELLS) / **STEPHEN IRVINE** (b.16 Dec'59) – drums

		Polydor	Geffen
Apr 84. (7") (COLE 1) **PERFECT SKIN. / THE SEA AND THE SAND**		26	

(12"+=) (COLEX 1) – You will never be so good.

Aug 84. (7"/7"g-f) (COLE/+G 2) **FOREST FIRE. / ANDY'S BABY** `41`
(12"+=) (COLEX 2) – Glory.

Oct 84. (lp/c)(cd) (LCLP/LCMC 1)(823 683-2) **RATTLESNAKES** `13`
– Perfect skin / Speedboat / Rattlesnakes / Down on Mission Street / Forest fire / Charlotte Street / 2CV / Four flights up / Patience / Are you ready to be heartbroken? (cd+=) – The sea and the sand / You will never be no good / Sweetness / Andy's babies. (cd re-iss. Jan92; same)

Oct 84. (7") (COLE 3) **RATTLESNAKES. / SWEETNESS** `65`
(12"+=) (COLEX 3) – Four flights up.

Aug 85. (7") (COLE 4) **BRAND NEW FRIEND. / HER LAST FLING** `19`
(12"+=) (COLEX 4) – Speedboat (live) / 2CV (live).

Oct 85. (7"/10") (COLE/+T 5) **LOST WEEKEND. / BIG WORLD** `17`
(12"+=) (COLEX 5) – Never ends.

Nov 85. (lp/c)(cd) (LCLP/LCMC 2)(827 670-2) **EASY PIECES** `5`
– Rich / Why I love country music / Pretty gone / Grace / Cut me down / Brand new friend / Lost weekend / James / Minor characters / Perfect blue. (c+=) – Her last fling / Big world. (cd++=) – Never ends. (cd re-iss. Jan92; same) (re-iss. May93 on 'Spectrum' cd/c; 550035-2/-4)

Jan 86. (7") (COLE 6) **CUT ME DOWN (remix). / ARE YOU READY TO BE HEARTBROKEN? (live)** `38`
(12"+=) (COLEX 6) – Forest fire (live).
(d7"++=) (COLEG 6) – Perfect blue (instrumental).

—— trimmed to a studio quartet when COWAN became part-time (gigs only)

		Polydor	Capitol
Sep 87. (7") (COLE 7) **MY BAG. / JESUS SAID**		46	-

('A'dance-12"+=/cd-s+=) (COL EX/CD 7) – Perfect skin.

Oct 87. (lp/c)(cd) (LCLP/LCMC 3)(833 691-2) **MAINSTREAM** `9`
– My bag / From the hip / 29 / Mainstream / Jennifer she said / Mister malcontent / Sean Penn blues / Big snake / Hey Rusty / These days.

Oct 87. (7") <44253> **MY BAG. / LOVE YOUR WIFE** `-`

Jan 88. (7"/7"g-f) (COLE/+G 8) **JENNIFER SHE SAID. / PERFECT BLUE** `31`
(12"+=) (COLEX 8) – Mystery train (live) / I don't believe you (live).
(cd-s+=) (COLCD 8) – My bag (mix).

Apr 88. (7"ep/ext-12"ep/cd-ep) (COL E/EX/CD 9) **FROM THE HIP** `59`
– From the hip / Please / Lonely mile / Love you wife.

Mar 89. (lp/c/cd) (837 736-1/-4/-2) **1984-1989** (compilation) `14`
– Perfect skin / Are you ready to be heartbroken? / Forest fire / You will never be so good / Rattlesnakes / Perfect blue / Brand new friend / Cut me down / Lost weekend / Her last fling / Mr. Malcontent / My bag / Jennifer she said / From the hip.

Apr 89. (7") (COLE 10) **FOREST FIRE ('89 remix). / PERFECT BLUE**
(12"+=/cd-s+=) – ('A'&'B'extended).

—— DONEGAN left and subsequently became a journalist. The group folded in the Spring of '89.

LLOYD COLE

—— solo with **BLAIR COWAN** – keyboards / **DARYLL SWEET** – bass / **ROBEDRT QUINE** – guitar / **FRED MAHER** – drums, etc / **NICKY HOLLAND + PARKER DU LANY** – backing vocals / (on tour; **DAN McCARROLL** repl. MAHER / **DAVID BALL** repl. SWEET)

		Polydor	Capitol
Jan 90. (7"/c-s) (COL E/CS 11) **NO BLUE SKIES. / SHELLY I DO**		42	

(10"+=/12"+=/cd-s+=) (COL ET/EX/CD 11) – Wild orphan.

Feb 90. (cd/c/lp) (841 907-2/-4/-1) **LLOYD COLE** `11`
– Don't look back / What do you know about love? / Loveless / No blue skies / Sweetheart / To the church / Downtown / A long way down / Ice cream girl / I hate to see you baby doing that shift / Undressed / Waterline / Mercy killing. (cd re-iss. Apr95;)

Mar 90. (7"/c-s) (COL E/CS 12) **DON'T LOOK BACK. / BLAME MARY JANE** `59`
(10"+=/12"+=/cd-s+=) (COL ET/EX/CD 12) – Witching hour.

Oct 90. (7"/c-s) (COL E/CS 13) **DOWNTOWN. / A LONG WAY DOWN (live)**
(12"+=/cd-s+=) (COL EX/CD 13) – Sweetheart (live).

—— **COLE** now with **COWAN + CLARK**

Aug 91. (7"/c-s) (COL E/CS 14) **SHE'S A GIRL AND I'M A MAN. / WEIRD ON ME** `55`
(12"+=/cd-s+=) (COL EX/CD 14) – Children of the revolution.

Sep 91. (cd/c/lp) (511093-2/-4/-1) **DON'T GET WEIRD ON ME BABE** `21`
-Butterfly / Theme for her / Margo's waltz / Half of everything / Man enough / What he doesn't know / Tell your sister / Weeping wine / To the lions / Pay for it / The one you never had / She's a girl and I'm a man.

Oct 91. (7"/c-s) *(COL E/CS 15)* **WEEPING WINE. / TELL YOUR SISTER**
(12"+=/cd-s+=) *(COL EX/CD 15)* – Somewhere out in the east.

Mar 92. (7"/c-s) *(COL E/CS 16)* **BUTTERFLY. / JENNIFER SHE SAID**
(12"+=/cd-s+=) *(COL EX/CD 16)* – ('A'-The Planet Anne Charlotte mix).

| | | Fontana | Rykodisc |

Sep 93. (7"/c-s) *(VIBE D1/C1)* **SO YOU'D LIKE TO SAVE THE WORLD. / VICIOUS** | 72 | - |
(cd-s+=) *(VIBE 1)* – Mystic lady.
(cd-s) *(VIBE 1)* – ('A'side) / For your pleasure for your company / 4 M.B.

Oct 93. (cd/c/lp) *(518318-2/-4/-1)* **BAD VIBES** | 38 | | Jan94
– Morning is broken / So you'd like to save the world / Holier than thou / Love you so what / Wild mushrooms / My way to you / Too much of a good thing / Fall together / Mister Wrong / Seen the future / Can't get arrested.

Nov 93. (7"/c-s) **MORNING IS BROKEN. / RADIO CITY MUSIC HALL** | | - |
(cd-s+=) – Radio City music hall / Eat your greens.
(cd-s+=) – The slider / Mannish girl.
above album w/ **ADAM PETERS, ANN CHARLOTTE VENGSGAARD, JOHN MICCO, JOHN CARRUTHERS, NEIL CLARK, MATTHEW SWEET, DAN McCARROLL, ANTON FIER, CURTIS WATTS, FRED MAHER, DANA VLCEK, Lightning BOB HOFFNAR + PETER MARK**

Sep 95. (cd-s) *(LCCD 1)* **LIKE LOVERS DO / TRAFFIC / FOREST FIRE** | 24 | |
(cd-s) *(LCDD 1)* – ('A'side) / I will not leave you alone / Rattlesnakes.
(cd-s) *(LCDC 1)* – ('A'side) / Brand new baby blues (demo) / Perfect skin.

Sep 95. (cd/c) *(528529-2/-4)* **LOVE STORY** | 27 | |
– Trigger happy / Sentimental fool / I didn't know that you cared / Love ruins everything / Baby / Be there / The June bride / Like lovers do / Happy for you / Traffic / Let's get lost / For crying out loud.

Nov 95. (c-s) *(LCMCC 2)* **SENTIMENTAL FOOL / BRAND NEW FRIEND** | 73 | |
(cd-s+=) *(LCCD 2)* – Lost weekend / Cut me down.
(cd-s) *(LCDD 2)* – ('A'side) / Most of the time / Millionaire / Sold.

Jan 96. (c-s/cd-s) *(LCCMC/LCCD 3)* **BABY / MY BAG / JENNIFER SHE SAID / FROM THE HIP**
(cd-s) *(LCDD 3)* – ('A'side) / The steady slowing down of the heart / Like lovers do.

| | | Mercury | not iss. |

Sep 98. (c-s) *(MERMC 511)* **THAT BOY / IF YOU GOTTA GO, GO NOW** | | - |
(cd-s+=) *(MERCD 511)* – Tie me down.
(cd-s) *(MERDD 511)* – ('A'side) / Rain on the parade / Missing.

– compilations, etc. –

Jan 91. (cd/c) *Polydor; (847733-2/-4)* **RATTLESNAKES / EASY PIECES** | | - |
Jan 99. (cd/c) *Universal TV; (538104-2/-4)* **THE COLLECTION** | 24 | - |

COLLECTIVE SOUL

Formed: Stockbridge, Georgia, USA . . .late 80's by ED ROLAND, who had studied at Boston's Berklee School Of Music. After numerous rejections from major record companies, he split the band in 1992. ED continued to try his hand at penning songs for other artists while making a songwriting demo for some radio stations in the process. Interest in the song, 'SHINE', saw 'Atlantic' taking note and they duly signed the group to their roster in 1993. The singer/guitarist brought in musicians, namely his brother DEAN, ROSS CHILDRESS, WILL TURPIN and original drummer SHANE EVANS. The aforementioned track became a near Top 10 smash in the States, as did their debut album 'HINTS, ALLEGATIONS AND THINGS LEFT UNSAID', helped no doubt by the band playing Woodstock's 25th Anniversary Festival in '94. They further developed their consummate, perfectly formed hard rock/pop sound with an eponymous follow-up set in summer '95. Previewed by the 'GEL' single (included on the soundtrack to cult US comedy, 'The Jerky Boys'), the album made the American Top 30. Another steady seller, the record spawned a further two Top 20 hits with 'DECEMBER' and 'THE WORLD I KNOW', COLLECTIVE SOUL's Stateside profile heightened with a prestigious support slot to VAN HALEN. While the band enjoyed further success with a third set, 'DISCIPLINED BREAKDOWN' in 1997, commercial headway in Britain continued to elude them.

Album rating: HINTS, ALLEGATIONS AND THINGS LEFT UNSAID (*6) / COLLECTIVE SOUL (*7) / DISCIPLINED BREAKDOWN (*7) / DOSAGE (*6)

ED ROLAND – vocals, guitar / **ROSS CHILDRESS** – lead guitar / **DEAN ROLAND** – guitar / **WILL TURPIN** – bass / **SHANE EVANS** – drums

| | | Atlantic | Atlantic |

Apr 94. (c-s) *<87237>* **SHINE / ('A'-remix)** | - | 11 |
May 94. (c-s) *(A 5647C)* **SHINE / LOVE LIFTED ME** | | - |
(12"+=/cd-s+=) *(A 5647 T/CD)* – Burning bridges / ('A'version).
Sep 94. (cd/c) *<(7567 82596-2/-4)>* **HINTS, ALLEGATIONS AND THINGS LEFT UNSAID** | | 15 | Mar94
– Shine / Goodnight, good guy / Wasting time / Sister don't cry / Love lifted me / In a moment / Heaven's already here / Pretty Donna / Reach / Breathe / Scream / Burning bridges / All.
Jun 95. (cd/c) *<(7567 82745-2/-4)>* **COLLECTIVE SOUL** | | 23 | Mar95
– Simple / Untitled / The world I know / Smashing young man / December / Where the river flows / Gel / She gathers rain / When the water falls / Collection of goods / Bleed / Reunion.
May 95. (c-s) *<87157>* **DECEMBER / WHERE THE RIVER FLOWS** | - | 20 |
Dec 95. (c-s) *<87088>* **THE WORLD I KNOW / WHEN THE WATER FALLS** | - | 19 |
Mar 97. (cd/c) *<(7559 82984-2/-4)>* **DISCIPLINED BREAKDOWN** | - | 16 |
– Precious declaration / Listen / Maybe / Full circle / Blame / Disciplined

breakdown / Forgiveness / Link / Giving / In between / Crowded head / Everything.

Mar 97. (cd-s) **PRECIOUS DECLARATION /** | - | 65 |
Jun 97. (cd-s) **LISTEN /** | - | 72 |
Feb 99. (–) *<radio cut>* **HEAVY** | - | 73 |
May 99. (cd) *<(7567 83162-2)>* **DOSAGE** | | 21 | Feb99
– Tremble for my beloved / Heavy / No more no less / Needs / Slow / Dandy life / Run / Generate / Compliment / Not the one / Crown.
Jun 99. (cd-s) *(AT 0066CD)* *<radio cut>* **RUN /** | | 76 | Mar99

Albert COLLINS   (dig out; 4th edition)

Allen COLLINS BAND (see under ⇒ LYNYRD SKYNYRD)

Bootsy COLLINS (see under ⇒ BOOTSY'S RUBBER BAND)

Edwyn COLLINS

Born: 23 Aug'59, Edinburgh, Scotland. COLLINS formed ORANGE JUICE in Glasgow, . . . 1977 initially as the NU-SONICS with JAMES KIRK, STEPHEN DALY and ALAN DUNCAN, who was subsequently replaced by DAVID McCLYMONT. In 1979, ORANGE JUICE signed to local indie label 'Postcard', the hub of the burgeoning Glasgow indie scene masterminded by ALAN HORNE. In contrast to the post-punk miserabilism coming out of England, ORANGE JUICE were purveyors of studiedly naive, wide-eyed indie pop as best sampled on the brace of early 45's, 'FALLING AND LAUGHING', 'BLUE BOY', 'SIMPLY THRILLED HONEY' and 'POOR OLD SOUL' (later collected on 1993's retrospective, 'THE HEATHER'S ON FIRE'). They subsequently signed to 'Polydor' in 1981, releasing a debut album, 'YOU CAN'T HIDE YOUR LOVE FOREVER', early the following year. Though some of their die-hard fans inevitably accused them of selling out, the set almost made the UK Top 20, its charming guitar pop auguring well for the future. The band suffered internal ruction soon after the album's release, however, MALCOLM ROSS and ZEKE MANYIKA replacing KIRK and DALY respectively. The Nigerian-born MANYIKA injected a newfound rhythmic thrust into the follow-up album, 'RIP IT UP' (1982), the clipped funk of the title track providing the band with their only Top 40 hit, albeit a sizeable one. Despite this belated success, further tensions reduced the band to a duo of COLLINS and MANYIKA who recorded an impressive mini-set, 'TEXAS FEVER' (1984) under the production auspices of reggae veteran, DENNIS BOVELL. Later that year, saw the release of swansong set, 'THE ORANGE JUICE – THE THIRD ALBUM', a far more introspective affair which found COLLINS at a low ebb. The singer had already released a cover of The Velvet Underground's 'PALE BLUE EYES', with PAUL QUINN and subsequently embarked on a solo career which remained low key for the ensuing decade. Initially signed to ALAN McGEE's "side" label, 'Elevation', his first two solo singles flopped and as the label went belly-up, COLLINS opted for 'Demon' records. He finally issued a long-awaited album, 'HOPE AND DESPAIR' in summer '89. An eclectic, rootsy affair borne of COLLINS' troubled wilderness years, the record was hailed by the same critics who so vehemently supported ORANGE JUICE. Yet despite the praise, it seemed COLLINS was destined for cult appeal; a second 'Demon' set, 'HELLBENT ON COMPROMISE' (1990) failed to lift his profile and COLLINS went to ground. Well, not completely, the singer honing his production skills for indie outfits such as A HOUSE and The ROCKINGBIRDS. The throaty-voxed singer finally re-emerged in 1994 with 'GORGEOUS GEORGE', the record he'd been threatening to make for years. Recorded on classic studio equipment, the record's organic feel coupled with COLLINS's mordant cynicism and razor sharp songwriting resulted in a massive worldwide hit, 'A GIRL LIKE YOU'. With its crunching, NEIL YOUNG-like riffing and infectious delivery, the record was initially in Europe and Australia before eventually hitting the Top 5 in the UK a year on. Though 1997's 'THE MAGIC PIPER' (from the album 'I'M NOT FOLLOWING YOU') didn't quite match this commercial feat, COLLINS remains one of Scotland's most accomplished songwriters with a reliable line in caustic wit. • **Songwriters:** ORANGE JUICE: most written by COLLINS, some with MANYIKA. Note that KIRK was the writer of FELICITY, and ROSS provided PUNCH DRUNK. They covered L.O.V.E. (Al Green), while COLLINS solo tried his hand at MY GIRL HAS GONE (Smokey Robinson) + TIME OF THE PREACHER (Willie Nelson) / WON'T TURN BACK (Vic Godard).

Album rating: Orange Juice: YOU CAN'T HIDE YOUR LOVE FOREVER (*7) / RIP IT UP (*6) / TEXAS FEVER mini (*5) / THE ORANGE JUICE (*5) / THE ESTEEMED ORANGE JUICE (THE VERY BEST OF ORANGE JUICE) compilation (*9) / Edwyn Collins: HOPE AND DESPAIR (*6) / HELLBENT ON COMPROMISE (*6) / GORGEOUS GEORGE (*8) / I'M NOT FOLLOWING YOU (*6)

ORANGE JUICE

EDWYN COLLINS – vocals, guitar, occasional violin / **JAMES KIRK** – guitar, vocals / **DAVID McCLYMONT** – bass, synths; repl. ALAN DUNCAN / **STEPHEN DALY** – drums

| | | Postcard | not iss. |

Feb 80. (7") *(80-1)* **FALLING AND LAUGHING. / MOSCOW** | | - |
(free 7"flexi) *(LYN 7609)* – FELICITY (live).
Aug 80. (7") *(80-2)* **BLUE BOY. / LOVE SICK** | | - |
Dec 80. (7") *(80-6)* **SIMPLY THRILLED HONEY. / BREAKFAST TIME** | | - |
Mar 81. (7") *(81-2)* **POOR OLD SOUL. / (part 2)** | | - |

	Polydor	Polydor

Oct 81. (7") *(POSP 357)* **L.O.V.E. LOVE. / INTUITION TOLD ME PT.2** — `65` `-`
(12"+=) *(POSPX 357)* – Moscow.

Jan 82. (7") *(POSP 386)* **FELICITY. / IN A NUTSHELL** — `63` `-`
(12"+=) *(POSPX 386)* – You old eccentric.

Feb 82. (lp/c) *(POLS/+C 1057)* **YOU CAN'T HIDE YOUR LOVE FOREVER** — `21`
– Falling and laughing / Untitled melody / Wan light / Tender object / Dying day / L.O.V.E. love / Intuition told me (part 1) / Upwards and onwards / Satellite city / Three cheers for our side / Consolation prize / Felicity / In a nutshell.

—— **MALCOLM ROSS** – guitar (ex-JOSEF K) + **ZEKE MANYIKA** (b. Nigeria) – percussion, vocals, synths; repl. KIRK DALY who subsequently formed MEMPHIS, releasing only one single for 'Swamplands', 'YOU SUPPLY THE ROSES', early 1985

Jul 82. (7"/10") *(POSP/+T 470)* **TWO HEARTS TOGETHER. / HOKOYO** — `60` `-`

Oct 82. (7") *(POSP 522)* **I CAN'T HELP MYSELF. / TONGUES BEGIN TO WAG** — `42`
(12"+=) *(POSPX 522)* – Barbeque.

Nov 82. (lp/c) *(POLS/+C 1076)* **RIP IT UP** — `39`
– Rip it up / Breakfast time / A million pleading faces / Mud in your eye / Turn away / I can't help myself / Flesh of my flesh / Louise Louise / Hokoyo / Tenter hook. *(cd-iss. Jul89; 839768-2)*

Feb 83. (7") *(POSP 547)* **RIP IT UP (remix). / SNAKE CHARMER** `8`
(some w/ live c-s+=) – The Felicity Flexi Session: The formative years – Simply thrilled honey / Botswana / Time to develop / Blue boy.
(d7"+=) *(POSPD 547)* – Sad lament / Lovesick.
(12") *(POSPX 547)* – ('A'side) / Sad lament / ('A'long version).

May 83. (7"/7"pic-d/ext.12") *(OJ/OJP/OJX 4)* **FLESH OF MY FLESH. / LORD JOHN WHITE AND THE BOTTLENECK TRAIN** — `41`

—— basically now a duo of **COLLINS + MANYIKA** with session people replacing ROSS (who joined AZTEC CAMERA) and McCLYMONT (to The MOODISTS)

Feb 84. (7") *(OJ 5)* **BRIDGE. / OUT FOR THE COUNT** — `67`
(free 7"flexi w/ above) *(JUICE 1)* – Poor old soul (live).
(12"+=) *(OJX 5)* – ('A'-Summer '83 mix).

Feb 84. (m-lp/c) *(OJM LP/MC 1)* **TEXAS FEVER** — `34`
– A sad lament / Craziest feeling / A place in my heart / The day I went down to Texas / Punch drunk / Bridge.

Apr 84. (7") *(OJ 6)* **WHAT PRESENCE?!. / A PLACE IN MY HEART (dub)** — `47`
(free c-s w/ above) *(OJC 6)* – In a nutshell (live) / Simply thrilled honey (live) / Dying day (live).
(12"+=) *(OJX 6)* – ('A'extended).

Oct 84. (7") *(OJ 7)* **LEAN PERIOD. / BURY MY HEAD IN MY HANDS** — `74`
(free 7"flexi w/ above) *(JUICE 3)* – Rip it up / What presence?!.
(12"+=) *(OJX 7)* – ('A'extended).

Nov 84. (lp/c) *(OJ LP/MC 1)* **THE ORANGE JUICE – THE THIRD ALBUM**
– Get while the goings good / Salmon fishing in New York / I guess I'm just a little sensitive / Burning desire / The artisan / Lean period / What presence?! / Out for the count / All that mattered / Seacharger. *(re-iss. Aug86 lp/c; SPE LP/MC 102)* *(c+=remixes)* – I can't help myself / Rip it up / Love struck / Flesh of my flesh / Out for the count / What presence?! / Lean period.

—— Disbanded after above album. MANYIKA went solo, as did EDWYN COLLINS. He had already in Aug'84 hit UK 72 with PAUL QUINN on 7"/12" 'PALE BLUES EYES' (a Velvet Underground cover) released on 'Swamplands'.

– compilations, etc. –

Jul 85. (lp/c) *Polydor; (OJ LP/MC 3)* **IN A NUTSHELL** — `-`
(w/free 7"flexi) – FELICITY.

Jan 91. (cd/c) *Polydor; (847 727-2/-4)* **THE ORANGE JUICE / YOU CAN'T HIDE YOUR LOVE FOREVER** — `-`

Jul 92. (cd) *Polydor; (513618)* **THE VERY BEST OF ORANGE JUICE (THE ESTEEMED ORANGE JUICE)** — Oct95
– Falling and laughing / Consolation prize (live) / Old encentric / L.O.V.E. love / Felicity / In a nutshell / Rip it up / I can't help myself / Flesh of my flesh / Tenterhook / Bridge / The day I went down to Texas / Punch drunk / A place in my heart / A sad lament / Lean period / I guess I'm just a little too sensitive / The artisans / Salmon fishing in New York / What presence?! / Out for the count. *(re-iss. cd Sep95; same)* – (extra track).

Jul 92. (lp/c/cd) *Postcard; (DUBH 922/+MC/CD)* **OSTRICH CHURCHYARD (live in Glasgow)** — `-`
(cd re-iss. Oct95; DUBH 954CD)

May 93. (7") *Postcard; (DUBH 934)* **BLUEBOY. / LOVESICK** — `-`
(cd-s+=) *(DUBH 934CD)* – Poor old soul (French version) / Poor old soul (instrumental).

Jul 93. (lp/cd) *Postcard; (DUBH 932/+CD)* **THE HEATHER'S ON FIRE** — `-`
– Falling and laughing / Moscow / Moscow Olympics / Blue boy / Love sick / Simply thrilled honey / Breakfast time / Poor old soul / Poor old soul pt.2 / Felicity / Upwards and onwards / Dying day / Holiday hymn. *(re-iss. cd Oct95; DUBH 955CD)*

EDWYN COLLINS

solo, with **DENNIS BOVELL, MALCOLM ROSS, ALEX GRAY + CHRIS TAYLOR**

	Elevation	not iss.

May 87. (7") *(ACID 4)* **DON'T SHILLY SHALLY. / IF EVER YOU'RE READY** — `-`
(12"+=) *(ACID 4T)* – Queer fish.

	Elevation	not iss.

Nov 87. (7") *(ACID 6)* **MY BELOVED GIRL. / CLOUDS (FOGGING UP MY MIND)** — `-`
(12"+=) *(ACID 6T)* – My (long time) beloved girl.
(7"box+=) *(ACID 6B)* – 50 shades of blue (acoustic) / What's the big idea.

—— now with **BERNARD CLARKE** – keyboards / **DENNIS BOVELL** – bass / **DAVE RUFFY** – drums

	Demon	not iss.

Jun 89. (lp/c/cd) *(FIEND/+C/CD 144)* **HOPE AND DESPAIR** — `-`
– Coffee table song / 50 shades of blue / You're better than you know / Pushing it to the back of my mind / The wheels of love / Darling, they want it all / The beginning of the end / The measure of the man / Testing time / Let me put my arms around you / The wide eyed child in me / Ghost of a chance. *(c+=/cd+=)* – If ever you're ready. *(re-iss. cd Sep95)*

Jul 89. (7") *(D 1064)* **THE COFFEE TABLE SONG. / JUDAS IN BLUE JEANS** — `-`
(12"+=) *(D 1064T)* – Out there.

Oct 89. (7") *(D 1065)* **50 SHADES OF BLUE (new mix). / IF EVER YOU'RE READY** — `-`
(12") *(D 1065T)* – ('A'extended) / Kindred spirit / Just call her name / Ain't that always the way.
(cd-s) *(D 1065CD)* – ('A'side) / Judas in blue jeans / Kindred spirit / Just call her name.

Oct 90. (lp/c/cd) *(FIEND/+C/CD 195)* **HELLBENT ON COMPROMISE** — `-`
– Means to an end / You poor deluded fool / It might as well be you / Take care of yourself / Graciously / Someone else besides / My girl has gone / Everything and more / What's the big idea / Hellbent medley:- Time of the preacher – Long time gone. *(re-iss. cd Oct95; same)*

—— now with **STEVEN SKINNER** – guitar / **PHIL THORNALLEY** – bass / **PAUL COOK** – drums

	Setanta	Bar None

Aug 94. (cd/c/lp) *(SET CD/MC/LP 014) <058>* **GEORGEOUS GEORGE** — Sep95
– The campaign for real rock / A girl like you / Low expectations / Out of this world / If you could love me / North of Heaven / Gorgeous George / It's right in front of you / Make me feel again / You got it all / Subsidence / Occupy your mind. *(re-iss. Jul95, hit UK No.8)*

Oct 94. (c-ep) *(ZOP 001C)* **EXPRESSLY EP** — `42` `-`
– A girl like you / A girl like you (Macrame remix by Youth).
(cd-ep+=) *(ZOP 001CD1)* – Out of this world (I hear a new world) (St.Etienne remix) / Occupy your mind.
(cd-ep) *(ZOP 001CD2)* – ('A'side) / Don't shilly shally (Spotters'86 demo) / Something's brewing / Bring it on back.

Mar 95. (12"ep) *(ZOP 002CD1)* **IF YOU COULD LOVE ME (radio edit). / IN A BROKEN DREAM / INSIDER DEALING / ('A'-MC Esher mix)** — `-`
(cd-ep) *(ZOP 002CD1)* – (first 3 tracks) / Hope and despair.
(cd-ep) *(ZOP 002CD2)* – ('A'side) / If ever you're ready / Come to your senses / A girl like you (the Victoria Spaceman mix).

Jun 95. (7") *(ZOP 0037)* **A GIRL LIKE YOU. / YOU'RE ON YOUR OWN** — `4` `-`
(c-s+=) *(ZOP 003C)* – If you could love me (acoustic version).
(cd-s++=) *(ZOP 003CD)* – Don't shilly shally (Spotters '86 demo).

Oct 95. (c-s) *<58-1234>* **A GIRL LIKE YOU / IF YOU COULD LOVE ME** — `-` `32`
(above used on the film 'Empire Records')

Feb 96. (c-s) *(ZOP 004C)* **KEEP ON BURNING / IF YOU COULD LOVE ME (IN TIME AND SPACE)** — `45` `-`
(cd-s+=) *(ZOP 004CD1)* – Lava lamp / The campaign for real rock.
(cd-s) *(ZOP 004CD2)* – Won't turn back / You've grown a beard / A girl like you (live) / White room.

	Setanta	Sony

Jul 97. (12") *(SET 041T)* **THE MAGIC PIPER. / A GIRL LIKE YOU (Makrame mix) / WELWYN GARDEN CITY** — `32` `-`
(cd-s) *(SETCDA 041)* – ('A'side) / More than you bargained for / Red menace / It takes a little time.
(cd-s) *(SETCDB 041)* – ('A'side) / Who is it? / Who is it? (halterbacked by the Victorian spaceman / Welwyn Garden City.

Sep 97. (cd/c/lp) *(SET CD/MC/LP 039) <68716>* **I'M NOT FOLLOWING YOU** — `55` Oct97
– It's a steal / The magic piper (of love) / Seventies night / No one waved goodbye / Downer / Keep on burning / Running away with myself / Country rock / For the rest of my life / Superficial cat / Adidas world / I'm not following you.

Oct 97. (7") *(SET 045)* **ADIDAS WORLD. / HIGH FASHION** — `71` `-`
(cd-s+=) *(SETCDA 045)* – Mr. Bojangles / Talking 'bout the times.
(cd-s) *(SETCDB 045)* – ('A'side) / Episode 3 / Episode 5 / Episode 10 (no, no, no Adidas – Adilated by . . .).

Nov 97. (d12") *(ZOPPR 005)* **I HEAR A NEW WORLD (mixes; Red Snapper / Deadly Avenger Supershine / Red Snapper vocal / DOWNER (James Lavelle mix) // THE MAGIC PIPER (the Wiseguys sniper mix) / ADIDAS WORLD (adilated by Sebastian Lawsely) / DOWNER (James Lavelle vocal)** — `-`

Judy COLLINS

Born: 1 May'39, Denver, Colorado, USA. Her father encouraged her to follow a musical career and by the age of ten, JUDY was studying piano with female composer Antonia Brica. A career as a concert pianist was well within her grasp (having performed Mozart upon her live debut at the age of thirteen) but the then revolutionary music of WOODY GUTHRIE began to turn her head and she soon deserted the piano for the more portable (and trendy) guitar. By the age of sixteen she was wowing them in the Colorado folk scene and had her sights set on Greenwich Village in New York City. Arriving there in 1961, she was immediately signed by 'Elektra's Jac Holzman who was impressed by her crystal-pure vocals and recognised her innate talent for sympathetic interpretation of trad folk material. Her relationship with the label was to endure over three decades while her recordings brought the raw material of such composers as BOB DYLAN, LEONARD COHEN, JONI MITCHELL, SANDY DENNY and many others to a professional polish. Like many 60's artists, she began to experiment with different types of music and her repertoire expanded to encompass material by cult European

composers like BRECHT, WEILL and JACQUES BREL. She also moved towards stage and film work which she adopted with the same enthusiasm as her music career. Having already released a string of critically acclaimed albums, her 1966 set, 'IN MY LIFE', highlighted her increasing diversity while 'WILDFLOWERS' marked her first foray into singer/songwriting and featured arrangements by classic ragtime producer, JOSHUA RIFKIN. The latter album also saw her break into the US Top 5 for the first time while spawning a rare hit single in the shape of Joni Mitchell's 'BOTH SIDES NOW'. Late 1970, meanwhile, saw COLLINS score the biggest hit single (US Top 5/UK Top 20) of her career with an unaccompanied version of 'AMAZING GRACE', the track lifted from 'WHALES AND NIGHTINGALES' (1971). The following year's retrospective, 'COLOURS OF THE DAY' made the US Top 40 and it's a mark of JUDY's popularity that this record still sells in considerable numbers; apparently it's President Bill Clinton's fave album and he even named his daughter after the Joni Mitchell cover, 'CHELSEA MORNING'. COLLINS extended her vocal reach even further in 1975 with a Top 10 reading of the Stephen Sondheim Broadway weepie, 'SEND IN THE CLOWNS'. The accompanying album, 'JUDITH', confirmed her increasing tendency toward contemporary ballads in the form of both cover material and her own compositions. Throughout the remainder of the 70's and on into the 80's she continued to record and sell albums to her loyal following in respectable amounts although the chart hits faded. At the dawn of the 90's she released 'FIRES OF EDEN' (1991) which relied more heavily on her own songs than many previous collections had done and included classic track, 'THE BLIZZARD'. COLLINS fulfilled a lifelong ambition by releasing an album of BOB DYLAN compositions the following year and in 1995 completed a project entitled 'SHAMELESS', also publishing a book of the same name later that year. As she moves into her sixties her appetite for work has hardly abated with punishing concert tours and TV/stage work still featuring prominently in her busy schedule. COLLINS' commitment to the underprivileged continues unswervingly, the singer undertaking anti-landmine tours as a UNICEF representative in the former Yugoslavia. Her autobiography, 'Singing Lessons' was released in 1999 to critical and popular acclaim while she continues to explore new avenues in music with the forthcoming 'BOTH SIDES NOW – CLASSIC BROADWAY', a Broadway hits album.
• **Songwriters:** Wrote songs/lyrics herself and many covers by BOB DYLAN, LEONARD COHEN, JONI MITCHELL, The BYRDS, etc. Others included; WHO KNOWS WHERE THE TIME GOES (Sandy Denny) / IN MY LIFE (Beatles) / CATS IN THE CRADLE (Harry Chapin) / FROM A DISTANCE (Julie Gold) / WIND BENEATH MY WINGS (Henley/Silbar) / I PITY THE POOR IMMIGRANT (Bob Dylan) / THE AIR THAT I BREATHE (Hollies).
• **Trivia:** Her 1969 boyfriend, STEPHEN STILLS, wrote a song inspired by her 'SUITE: JUDY BLUE EYES'. ROGER McGUINN played on her third album.

Album rating: MAID OF CONSTANT SORROW (6) / GOLDEN APPLES OF THE SUN (*6) / JUDY COLLINS #3 (*6) / THE JUDY COLLINS CONCERT (*4) / JUDY COLLINS' FIFTH ALBUM (*6) / IN MY LIFE (*7) / WILDFLOWERS (*7) / WHO KNOWS WHERE THE TIME GOES (*7) / RECOLLECTIONS compilation (*7) / WHALES & NIGHTINGALES (*6) / LIVING (*5) / COLORS OF THE DAY – THE BEST OF JUDY COLLINS compilation (*7) / TRUE STORIES AND OTHER DREAMS (*6) / JUDITH (*6) / BREAD & ROSES (*6) / SO EARLY IN THE SPRING, THE FIRST 15 YEARS compilation (*8) / HARD TIMES FOR LOVERS (*4) / RUNNING FOR LIFE (*4) / TIME OF OUR LIVES (*4) / HOME AGAIN (*4) / TRUST YOUR HEART (*4) / SANITY AND GRACE (*4) / FIRES OF EDEN (*5) / JUDY SINGS DYLAN . . . JUST LIKE A WOMAN (*4) / COME REJOICE . . . A JUDY COLLINS CHRISTMAS (*5) / SHAMELESS (*5)

JUDY COLLINS – vocals, acoustic guitar (with session people)

		not iss.	Elektra
Oct 61.	(lp) <EKS 7209> **MAID OF CONSTANT SORROW**	-	

– Maid of constant sorrow / The prickle bush / Wild mountain thyme / Tim Evans / Sailor's life / Bold Fenian men / Wars of Germany / O daddy be gay / I know where I'm going / John Riley / Pretty Savo / The rising of the moon. (UK-iss.1965 on 'Elektra'; EKL 209) (re-iss. 1975; K 52032)

| Jul 62. | (lp) <EKS 7222> **GOLDEN APPLES OF THE SUN** | - | |

– Golden apples of the sun / Bonnie ship the Diamond / Little brown dog / Twelve gates to the city / Christ child lullaby / Great Selchie of Shule Skerry / Tell me who I'll marry / Fannerio / Crow on the cradle / Lark in the morning / Sing hallelujah / Shule Aaron.

| Mar 64. | (lp) <EKS 7243> **#3** | - | |

– Anathea / Bullgine run / Farewell / Hey, Nelly, Nelly / Ten o'clock all is well / The dove / Masters of war / In the hills of Shiloh / The bells of Rhymney / Deportee / Come away Melinda / Turn turn turn.

| 1964. | (7") **TURN TURN TURN. / FAREWELL** | - | - |
| Oct 64. | (lp) <EKS 7280> **IN CONCERT – TOWN HALL** (live) | - | |

– Winter sky / That was the last thing on my mind / Tear down the walls / Bonnie boy is young / Me & my uncle / Wild ripping water / The lonesome death of Hattie Carroll / My ramblin' boy / Redwinged blackbird / Coal tattoo / Cruel mother / Bottle of wine / Medgar Evers lullaby / Hey, Nelly, Nelly.

		London	Elektra
Sep 65.	(lp) <EKS 7300> **JUDY COLLINS' FIFTH ALBUM**		69

– Pack up your sorrows / The coming of the roads / So early, early in the Spring / Tomorrow is a long time / Daddy you've been on my mind / Thirsty boots / Mr. Tambourine man / Lord Gregory / In the heat of the summer / Early morning rain / Carry it on / It isn't nice.

| Mar 66. | (7") (HLZ 10029) **I'LL KEEP IT WITH MINE. / THIRSTY BOOTS** | - | - |
| Dec 66. | (lp) <EKS 7320> **IN MY LIFE** | | 46 |

– Tom Thumb's blues / Hard lovin' loser / Pirate Jenny / Suzanne / La Colombe / Marat / Sade / I think it's going to rain today / Sunny Goodge Street / Liverpool lullaby / Dress rehearsal rag / In my life. (UK-iss.1971; K 42009)

| Jan 67. | (7") **HARD LOVIN' LOSER. / I THINK IT'S GOING TO RAIN TODAY** | - | - |
| Jan 67. | (7") (EKSN 45011) **HARD LOVIN' LOSER. / IN MY LIFE** | - | - |

		Elektra	Elektra
Jan 68.	(lp) <(EKS 74012)> **WILDFLOWERS**		5

– Both sides now / Michael from the mountains / Since you asked / Sisters of mercy / A ballata of Francesco Landini / Lasso di Donna / La chanson des vieux amants (the song of old lovers) / Sky fell / Albatross / Hey that's no way to say goodbye. (re-iss. May87 lp/cd; K/K2 42014)

| Oct 68. | (7") <45639> **BOTH SIDES NOW. / WHO KNOWS WHERE THE TIME GOES** | - | 8 |
| Nov 68. | (7") (EKSN 45043) **BOTH SIDES NOW. / HEY THAT'S NO WAY TO SAY GOODBYE** | - | - |

(re-prom.Jan70) – hit No.14 (re-iss. Oct73; K 12005) (re-iss. Sep76; K 12225)

| Dec 68. | (lp) <(EKS 74033)> **WHO KNOWS WHERE THE TIMES GOES** | | 29 |

– Hello, hurray / Story of Isaac / My father / Someday soon / Who knows where the time goes / I pity the poor immigrant / The first boy I loved / Bird on the wire / Pretty Polly. (cd-iss. Feb93 & Mar95)

Feb 69.	(7") (EKSN 45649) **SOMEDAY SOON. / MY FATHER**		55 Jan69
Oct 69.	(7") (EKSN 45073) <45657> **CHELSEA MORNING. / PRETTY POLLY**		78 Jul69
Nov 69.	(7") <45680> **TURN! TURN! TURN! – TO EVERYTHING THERE IS A SEASON. / PACK UP YOUR SORROWS**	-	69
Dec 69.	(7") (EKSN 45077) **TURN! TURN! TURN! / MR. TAMBOURINE MAN**	-	-
Jan 70.	(7") **PACK UP YOUR SORROWS. / TURN! TUR~N! TURN!**	-	-
Nov 70.	(7") (2101 020) **AMAZING GRACE. / I PITY THE POOR IMMIGRANT**	5	-
Nov 70.	(7") <45709> **AMAZING GRACE. / NIGHTINGALE**	-	15

—— back into UK Top 40 Sep71, In Apr72 dented UK Top 20, re-iss. Nov76)

| Jan 71. | (lp) (K 42059) <75010> **WHALES & NIGHTINGALES** | 37 | 17 Nov70 |

– Farewell to Tarwathie / Song for David / Sons of / The patriot game / Oh had I a golden thread / Prothalmum / Gene's song / Time passes slowly / Maricke / Nightingale I / Nightingale II / Simple gifts / Amazing Grace.

| Nov 71. | (7") (K 12035) <45755> **OPEN THE DOOR (SONG FOR JUDITH). / INNISFREE** | | 90 |
| Jan 72. | (lp) (K 42102) <75014> **LIVING** (part live) | | 64 Nov71 |

– Joan of Arc / Four strong winds / Vietnam love song / Innisfree / Open the door (song for Judith) / All things are quite silent / Easy times / Chelsea morning / Famous blue raincoat / Just like Tom Thumb's blues.

| Feb 73. | (7") (K 12089) <45831> **COOK WITH HONEY. / SO BEGINS THE TASK** | | 32 |
| Mar 73. | (lp) (K 42132) <75053> **TRUE STORIES & OTHER DREAMS** | | 27 Feb72 |

– Che / Song for Martin / Cook with honey / So begins the task / Fisherman song / Dealer (done and losin') / The secret gardens / Holly Ann / The hostage song.

| 1973. | (7") **THE SECRET GARDENS. / THE HOSTAGE** | - | - |
| May 75. | (7") (K 12177) <45253> **SEND IN THE CLOWNS. / HOUSES** | 6 | 36 Jun75 |

<US re-prom.Sep77> – hit No.19

| May 75. | (lp/c) (K/K4 52019) <1032> **JUDITH** | 7 | 17 Apr75 |

– Born to the breed / Send in the clowns / The Moon is a harsh mistress / Angel spread your wings / Houses / The loving of the game / Song for Duke / Salt of the earth / Brother can you spare a dime / City of New Orleans / I'll be seeing you / Pirate ships. (cd-iss. 1983; K2 52019)

Jul 75.	(7") (K 12181) **I'LL BE SEEING YOU. / BORN TO THE BREED**		-
Sep 75.	(7") (K 12189) **SALT OF THE EARTH. / SONG FOR DUKE**		-
Sep 76.	(lp/c) (K/K4 52039) <1076> **BREAD & ROSES**		25

– Bread and roses / Everything must change / Special delivery / Out of control / Plegaria del labrador / Come down in time / Spanish is the loving tongue / I didn't know about you / Take this longing / Love hurts / Marjorie / King David.

Oct 76.	(7") **BREAD AND ROSES. / OUT OF CONTROL**		-
Nov 76.	(7") (K 12239) **BREAD AND ROSES. / KING DAVID**		-
Feb 77.	(7") **SPECIAL DELIVERY. / EVERYTHING MUST CHANGE**		-
May 77.	(7") **BORN TO THE BREED. / SPECIAL DELIVERY**		-
Mar 79.	(7") **DOROTHY. / WHERE OR WHEN**		-
Mar 79.	(lp/c) (K/K4 52121) <6E 171> **HARD TIMES FOR LOVERS**		54

– Hard times for lovers / Marie / Happy end / Desperado / I remember sky / Theme from 'The Promise' (I'll never say goodbye) / Starmaker / Dorothy / Theme from 'The Ice Castle' (Through the eyes of love) / Where or when. (cd-iss. Oct94; 7599 60536-2)

| Mar 79. | (7") (K 12343) <46020> **HARD TIMES FOR LOVERS. / HAPPY END** | | 66 |
| May 80. | (lp/c) (K/K4 52205) <6E 253> **RUNNING FOR MY LIFE** | | |

– Running for my life / Bright morning star / Green Finch & Linnet bird / Marieke / Pretty woman / Almost free / I could really show you around / I've done enough dying for today / Anyone would love you / Rainbow connection / This is the day.

May 80.	(7") **BRIGHT MORNING STAR. / ALMOST FREE**		-
Jul 80.	(7") **THE RAINBOW CONNECTION. / RUNNING FOR MY LIFE**		-
Jan 82.	(7") **MEMORY. / THE LIFE YOU DREAM**		-
Mar 82.	(lp/c) (K/K4 52347) <E 60001> **THE TIME OF OUR LIVES**		-

– Great expectations / The rest of your life / Grandaddy / It's gonna be one of those nights / Memory / Sun son / Mama mama / Drink a round to Ireland / Don't say goodbye love.

May 82.	(7") (K 13180) **GREAT EXPECTATIONS. / MEMORY**		-
1982.	(7") **MAMA MAMA. / IT'S GONNA BE ONE OF THOSE NIGHTS**	-	-
Nov 84.	(7"; JUDY COLLINS with T.G. SHEPHERD) **HOME AGAIN. / DREAM ON**	-	Nov84
Jan 85.	(lp) <(9 60304-1)> **HOME AGAIN**		Nov84

– Only you / Sweetheart on parade / Everybody works in China / Yellow kimono (Tokyo time) / From where I stand / Home again / Shoot first / Don't say love / Dream on / The best is yet to come.

| Feb 85. | (7") **ONLY YOU. /** | - | - |

		Goldcastle	Goldcastle
Nov 88.	(cd/c/lp) <(CD/TC+/VGC 7)> **TRUST YOUR HEART**		Nov87

– Amazing Grace / Trust your heart / Jerusalem / Day by day / The life you dream / The rose / Moonfall / Morning has broken / When a child is born / When you wish upon a star. (re-iss. Aug91 on 'Virgin' lp/c; OVED/+C 372)

| Jun 89. | (cd/c/lp) <(CD/TC+/VGC 11)> **SANITY AND GRACE** (live) | | |

– History / Wind beneath my wings / Lovin' and leavin' / From a distance / Sanity and grace / daughters of time / Cats in the cradle / Pretty Polly / Born to the breed. *(re-iss. Aug91 on 'Virgin' lp/c; OVED/+C 373)*

	Columbia	Columbia
Feb 91. (cd/c/lp) *(467373-2/-4/-1)* **FIRES OF EDEN**	☐	☐

– The blizzard / Fortune of soldiers / Test of time / Fires of eden / Home before dark / The air that I breathe / City of cities / Dreaming / Queen of the night / From a distance / The blizzard – reprise.

—— next album covers by BOB DYLAN

	Geffen	Geffen
Mar 94. (cd) *<(GED 24612)>* **JUDY SINGS DYLAN . . . JUST LIKE A WOMAN**	☐	☐

– Like a rolling stone / It's all over now, baby blue / Simple twist of fate / Sweetheart like you / Gotta serve somebody / Dark eyes / Love minus zero – No limit / Just like a woman / I believe in you / With God on our side / Bob Dylan's dream.

– compilations, etc. –

on 'Elektra' unless mentioned otherwise

Nov 69. (lp) *(K 42035) <74055>* **RECOLLECTIONS (THE BEST OF JUDY COLLINS)**	☐	29 Sep69
1972. (7") **SUZANNE. / SOMEDAY SOON**	-	☐
1972. (7") **IN MY LIFE. / SUNNY GOODGE STREET**	-	☐
May 72. (lp) *<75030>* **COLORS OF THE DAY – THE BEST OF JUDY COLLINS**	-	37

– Somebody soon / Since you've asked / Both sides now / Sons of Susan / Farewell / Tarwathie / Who knows where the time goes / Sunny Goodge Street / My father always promised / Albatross / In my life. *(UK cd-iss. 1989; 960681-2)*

Jul 72. (lp/c) *(K/K4 42110)* **AMAZING GRACE – THE BEST OF JUDY COLLINS**	☐	-

(cd-iss. Jun85; K2 42110) (cd re-iss. Sep95;)

Aug 77. (d-lp) *(K 62019) <6002>* **SO EARLY IN THE SPRING: THE FIRST 15 YEARS**	☐	42 Jul77

– Pretty Polly / So early, early in the spring / Pretty Saro / Golden apples of the Sun / Bonnie ship the diamond / Farewell to Tarwathie / The hostage / La Colombe / Coal tattoo / Carry it on / Bread and roses / The Marat-Sade / Special delivery / The lovin' of the game / Both sides now / Marieke / Send in the clowns / Bird on the wire / Since you've asked / Born to the breed / My father / Holly Ann / Houses / Secret gardens.

1977. (lp/c) *(K 62006)* **MOST BEAUTIFUL SONGS OF . . .**	☐	☐
Aug 77. (7"ep) *(K 12270)* **AMAZING GRACE / SEND IN THE CLOWNS. / HOSTAGE / BOTH SIDES NOW**	☐	☐
Jul 81. (7") *(K 12534)* **AMAZING GRACE. / BOTH SIDES NOW**	☐	-
Oct 82. (lp/c) *Hallmark; (SHM/HSC 3061)* **BOTH SIDES NOW**	☐	-
Sep 85. (7") *Old Gold; (OG 9516)* **AMAZING GRACE. / SEND IN THE CLOWNS**	☐	-
Dec 85. (lp/c) *Telstar; (STAR/STAC/TCD 2265)* **AMAZING GRACE**	34	-

(re-iss. cd/c Mar93 on 'Pickwick'; 9548 31616-2/-4)

Jun 92. (c/cd) *Laserlight; (79/15 451)* **WIND BENEATH MY WINGS**	☐	☐
Oct 95. (cd) *Vanguard; <(VCD 77013)>* **LIVE AT NEWPORT 1959-1966 (live)**	☐	☐

Phil COLLINS

Born: 31 Jan'51, London, England. COLLINS began his career with FLAMING YOUTH before joining art-prog rockers, GENESIS, replacing JOHN MAYHEW on the drum stool for the 1970 album, 'Trespass'. His impeccable playing anchored the GENESIS sound over their early mid-70's, PETER GABRIEL-fronted peak on such classic sets as 'Nursery Cryme' (1971), 'Foxtrot' (1972) and 'Selling England By The Pound' (1973). With GABRIEL subsequently leaving after the epic 'Lamb Lies Down On Broadway' (1974), COLLINS was promoted from drummer to frontman in one fell swoop when auditions proved fruitless. Proving that he was more than capable of filling GABRIEL's hallowed shoes, COLLINS successfully steered the band through the rocky patch of late 70's punk and beyond. Mirroring his band's move into glossy MOR with the 'DUKE' (1980) album, COLLINS' solo career came ready made for the heart of the mainstream pop/rock crossover market. Trailed by overweight radio favourite 'IN THE AIR TONIGHT', 'FACE VALUE' (1981) was a transatlantic million seller and a British No.1 to boot. Here was a man who truly polarised opinion from the start, his ubiquitous smugness and increasingly sterile pop making him a favourite target for critics. Yet his breezy melodies, cheeky chappy demeanour and soul-lite hollering made him hugely popular as the cult of the 80's coffee-table star took hold. A second set, 'HELLO, I MUST BE GOING' (1982) was another massive seller, again blessed with an insidiously catchy No.1 single in the form of 'YOU CAN'T HURRY LOVE' (originally a 60's hit for The SUPREMES). A string of subsequent singles failed to make any commercial impression and for a while it looked like COLLINS' career was faltering. Any such doubts were cast aside with the hugely successful ballad, 'AGAINST ALL ODDS (TAKE A LOOK AT ME NOW)'. While many detractors would've preferred an empty space, COLLINS inhabited the American No.1 spot for a good few weeks with this soundtrack piece which subsequently won a Grammy. He was back again early the following year with the pop/funk of 'SUSSIDIO' and his biggest album to date in 'NO JACKET REQUIRED' (1985). This was the set that really broke America, the record selling faster than Michael Jackson's 'Thriller'; its success was boosted by a further two US No.1's, the American release of 'SUSSIDIO' and the slushy ballad, 'ONE MORE NIGHT'. Seemingly unable to get enough of the man, the Americans secured a LIVE AID performance and put him back astride the US charts with the STEPHEN BISHOP-penned 'SEPARATE LIVES', a collaborative ballad with MARILYN MARTIN (he had earlier struck big time with a duet with PHILIP BAILEY on 'EASY LOVER'). Having acted as a child, COLLINS procured the star part in the film 'Buster' (1988) as well as contributing several songs

to the soundtrack. One of these was a nauseous cover of The Mindbenders' 'GROOVY KIND OF LOVE', while the asinine 'TWO HEARTS' (co-written with LAMONT DOZIER) gave him another US peak position. A transatlantic No.1 (what else?!), COLLINS' fourth studio set, ' . . . BUT SERIOUSLY' (1989) was a lame attempt at addressing more serious issues . Many people found 'ANOTHER DAY IN PARADISE' downright offensive, COLLINS masquerading as a friend of the street dwellers, although the man did contribute a lot of his earnings to this and certain charities (was 'I WISH IT WOULD RAIN DOWN' Pink Floyd's 'Wish You Were Here' Part 2, or what?). He continued in inimitably goal-getting fashion throughout the 90's, eventually leaving GENESIS in the mid-90's. Having released 'BOTH SIDES' in '93, he returned in 1996 with, 'DANCE INTO THE LIGHT', his first album for the unfortunately named new label, 'Face Value'. The accompanying single, 'WEAR MY HAT', was another to trigger mass deja vu in the listening public, PAUL SIMON's 'You Can Call Me Al' strangely coming to mind this time around. Rock on though, PHIL, GENESIS are missing you badly. • **Also covered:** ALWAYS (Irving Berlin) / THE TIMES THEY ARE A-CHANGIN' (Bob Dylan).

Album rating: FACE VALUE (*7) / HELLO, I MUST BE GOING! (*6) / NO JACKET REQUIRED (*6) / . . . BUT SERIOUSLY (*5) / SERIOUS HITS . . . LIVE! (*4) / BOTH SIDES (*5) / DANCE INTO THE NIGHT (*4) / . . .HITS compilation (*7) / A HOT NIGHT IN PARIS (*4)

PHIL COLLINS – vocals, piano, drums, etc (with session people)

	Virgin	Atlantic
Jan 81. (7") *(VSK 102) <3824>* **IN THE AIR TONIGHT. / THE ROOF IS LEAKING**	2	19 May81

(re-iss. & remixed Jun88; same); hit UK No.4.

Feb 81. (lp/c) *(V/TCV 2185) <16029>* **FACE VALUE**	1	7

– In the air tonight / This must be love / Behind the lines / The roof is leaking / Droned / Hand in hand / I missed again / You know what I mean / I'm not moving / If leaving me is easy / Tomorrow never knows / Thunder and lightning. *(cd-iss. Jun88; CDV 2185)*

Mar 81. (7"/12") *(VS 402/+12) <3790>* **I MISSED AGAIN. / I'M NOT MOVING**	14	19
May 81. (7") *(VS 423)* **IF LEAVING ME IS EASY. / DRAWING BOARD: IN THE AIR TONIGHT – I MISSED AGAIN – IF LEAVING ME IS EASY (demo versions)**	17	-
Oct 82. (7"/7"pic-d) *(VS/+Y 524)* **THRU' THESE WALLS. / DO YOU KNOW, DO YOU CARE**	56	-
Nov 82. (lp/c) *(V/TCV 2252) <80035>* **HELLO, I MUST BE GOING!**	2	8

– I don't care anymore / I cannot believe it's true / Like China / Do you know, do you care? / You can't hurry love / It don't matter to me / Thru' these walls / Don't let him steal your love away / The west side / Why can't it wait 'til morning. *(cd-iss. Jun88; CDV 2252) (re-iss. Jun91;)*

Nov 82. (7"/7"pic-d) *(VS/+Y 531)* **YOU CAN'T HURRY LOVE. / I CANNOT BELIEVE IT'S TRUE**	1	-
(12"+=) *(VST 531)* – Oddball. *(cd-iss. 1988; CDT 1)*		
Nov 82. (7") *<89933>* **YOU CAN'T HURRY LOVE. / DO YOU KNOW, DO YOU CARE**	-	10
Mar 83. (7") *(VS 572)* **DON'T LET HIM STEAL YOUR HEART AWAY. / THUNDER AND LIGHTNING**	45	-
(12") *(VS 572-12)* – ('A'side) / And so to f . . . (live).		
Feb 83. (7") *<89877>* **I DON'T CARE ANYMORE. / THE WEST SIDE**	-	39
May 83. (7") *(VS 603)* **WHY CAN'T IT WAIT 'TIL MORNING. / LIKE CHINA**	☐	☐
May 83. (7") *<89864>* **I CANNOT BELIEVE IT'S TRUE. / THRU THESE WALLS**	-	79
Feb 84. (7") *<89700>* **AGAINST ALL ODDS (TAKE A LOK AT ME NOW). / (b-side by Larry Carlton)**	-	1
Mar 84. (7"/7"pic-d) *(VS/+Y 674)* **AGAINST ALL ODDS. / MAKING A BIG MISTAKE (by Mike Rutherford)**	2	-
(above from the film of the same name)		
May 84. (7") *<89668>* **WALK THROUGH THE FIRE. / MAKING A BIG MISTAKE (by Mike Rutherford)**	☐	☐
Jan 85. (7") *(VS 736)* **SUSSUDIO. / THE MAN WITH THE HORN**	12	☐
(12"+=/12"pic-d+=) *(VS/+Y 736-12)* – ('A'extended).		
Feb 85. (lp/c/cd) *(V/TCV/CDV 2345) <81240>* **NO JACKET REQUIRED**	1	1

– Sussudio / Only you know and I know / Long long way to go / Don't want to know / One more night / Don't lose my number / Who said I would / Doesn't anybody stay together anymore? / Inside out / Take me home. *(cd+=) – We said hello, goodbye.*

Feb 85. (7") *<89588>* **ONE MORE NIGHT. / THE MAN WITH THE HORN**	-	1

—— Mar'85 saw him duet with **PHIL BAILEY (ex-EARTH, WIND & FIRE)** on single **EASY LOVER** which hit UK No.1 & US No.2 (Nov84)

Apr 85. (7"/7"sha-pic-d) *(VS/+S 755)* **ONE MORE NIGHT. / I LIKE THE WAY**	4	-
(12"+=) *(VS 755-12)* – ('A'extended).		
Apr 85. (7") *<89560>* **SUSSUDIO. / I LIKE THE WAY**	-	1
Jul 85. (7") *(VS 777)* **TAKE ME HOME. / WE SAID HELLO, GOODBYE**	19	-
(w/ free 7"+=) *(VS 674)* – Against all odds / Making a big mistake. (12"+=) *(VS 777-12)* – ('A'extended).		
Jul 85. (7") *<89536>* **DON'T LOSE MY NUMBER. / WE SAID HELLO GOODBYE**	-	4
Sep 85. (7"; by PHIL COLLINS & MARILYN MARTIN) *<89498>* **SEPARATE LIVES. / I DON'T WANNA KNOW**	-	1
Nov 85. (7"/7"white/7";2-interlocking pic-discs; by PHIL COLLINS & MARILYN MARTIN) *(VS/+S/SD 818)* **SEPARATE LIVES. / ONLY YOU KNOW AND I KNOW**	4	-
Mar 86. (7") *<89472>* **TAKE ME HOME. / ONLY YOU KNOW AND I KNOW**	-	7
Aug 88. (7"/12"/12"g-f) *(VS/+T/TG 1117) <89017>* **GROOVY KIND OF LOVE. / BIG NOISE (instrumental)**	1	1

(cd-s+=) *(VSCD 1117)* – Will you still be waiting.

—— (above & below singles were from the film 'BUSTER', in which he starred and contributed some tracks to soundtrack released Sep88)

Nov 88. (7") *(VS 1141)* <88980> **TWO HEARTS. / THE ROBBERY (excerpt by Anne Dudley)** | 6 | 1
(12"/cd-s) *(VS T/CD 1141)* – ('A'side) / ('B'extended).

Nov 89. (7"/12") *(VS/+T 1234)* <88774> **ANOTHER DAY IN PARADISE. / HEAT ON THE STREET** | 2 | 1
(c-s/cd-s/3"cd-s+=) *(VSC/VSCD 1234)* – Saturday night and Sunday morning.

Nov 89. (lp/c/cd) *(V/TCV/CDV 2620)* <82050> **. . . BUT SERIOUSLY** | 1 | 1
– Hang in long enough / That's just the way it is / Do you remember? / Something happened on the way to Heaven / Colours / I wish it would rain down / Another day in Paradise / Heat on the street / All of my life / Saturday night and Sunday morning / Father to son / Find a way to my heart.

Jan 90. (7") *(VS 1240)* **I WISH IT WOULD RAIN DOWN. / HOMELESS (ANOTHER DAY IN PARADISE) (demo)** | 7 | -
(12"+=/12"s+=/3"cd-s+=) *(VS T/TX/CD 1240)* – You've been in love just (that little bit too long).

Jan 90. (7") <88738> **I WISH IT WOULD RAIN DOWN. / YOU'VE BEEN IN LOVE JUST (THAT LITTLE BIT TOO LONG)** | - | 3

Apr 90. (7") <87955> **DO YOU REMEMBER?. / I WISH IT WOULD RAIN DOWN** | - | 4

Apr 90. (7"/7"s/c-s) *(VS/+P/C 1251)* **SOMETHING HAPPENED ON THE WAY TO HEAVEN. / RAIN DOWN (demo)** | 15 | -
(12"+=/cd-s+=) *(VS T/CD 1251)* – ('A'remix).

Jul 90. (7"/c-s) *(VS/+C 1277)* **THAT'S JUST THE WAY IT IS. / BROADWAY CHORUS (SOMETHING HAPPENED ON THE WAY TO HEAVEN)** | 26 | -
(12"+=/cd-s+=) *(VS T/CD 1277)* – In the air tonight (extended).

Jul 90. (7") <87885> **SOMETHING HAPPENED ON THE WAY TO HEAVEN. / LIONEL (DO YOU REMEMBER? – DEMO)** | - | 4

Sep 90. (7"/c-s) *(VS/+C 1300)* **HANG IN LONG ENOUGH. / AROUND THE WORLD IN 80 PRESETS** | 34 | -
(cd-s+=) *(VSCD 1300)* – ('A'-12"mix).
(pic-cd-s) *(VSCDX 1300)* – ('A'side) / That's how I feel / ('A'dub).
(12") *(VST 1300)* – ('A'side) / ('A'dub) / ('A'-12"mix).

Nov 90. (c-s) <87800> **HANG IN LONG ENOUGH. / SEPARATE LIVES (live)** | - | 23

—— live with **LELAND SKLAR** – bass / **CHESTER THOMPSON** – drums / **DARYL STUERMER** – guitar / **BRAD COLE** – keyboards / **BRIDGETTE BRYANT, ARNOLD McCULLER and FRED WHITE** – backing vocals. plus **DON MYRICK** – alto sax / **LUI LUI** – trombone / **RAHMLEE MICHAEL DAVIS** – trumpet / **HARRY KIM** – trumpet.

Nov 90. (cd/c/lp) *(PC CD/TC/LP 1)* <82157> **SERIOUS HITS . . . LIVE! (live)** | 2 | 11
– Something happened on the way to Heaven / Against all odds (take a look at me now) / Who said I would / One more night / Don't lose my number / Another day in Paradise / Do you remember? / Separate lives / In the air tonight / You can't hurry love / Two hearts / Sussidio / Groovy kind of love / Easy lover / Take me home.

Nov 90. (7"/c-s) *(VS/+C 1305)* **DO YOU REMEMBER? (live). / AGAINST THE ODDS (live)** | 57 | -
(12"+=) *(VST 1305)* – Doesn't anyone stay together anymore (live).
(cd-s+++=) *(VSCDT 1305)* – The roof is leaking (live).
(cd-s) *(VSCDG 1305)* – ('A'side) / Doesn't anyone stay together anymore (live) / The roof is leaking (live).

Jan 91. (promo-cd-s) <PR-3758> **WHO SAID I WOULD (live)** | - | 73

—— In May 93, PHIL was credited on DAVID CROSBY'S Top 50 hit 'Hero'.

Oct 93. (7"/c-s) *(VS/+C 1500)* <87299> **BOTH SIDES OF THE STORY. / ALWAYS (live)** | 7 | 25
(cd-s+=) *(VSCDT 1500)* – Both sides of the demo.
(cd-s++=) *(VSCDG 1500)* – Rad Dudeski.

Nov 93. (cd/c/lp) *(CD/TC/+V 2800)* <82550> **BOTH SIDES** | 1 | 13
– Both sides of the story / Can't turn back the years / Everyday / I've forgotten everything / We're sons of our fathers / Can't find my way / Survivors / We fly so close / There's a place for us / We wait and wonder / Please come out tonight.

Jan 94. (7"/c-s) *(VS/+C 1505)* <87300> **EVERYDAY. / DON'T CALL ME ASHLEY** | 15 | 24
(cd-s+=) *(VSCDT 1505)* – ('A'demo).
(cd-s+=) *(VSCDG 1505)* – Doesn't anybody stay together anymore (live).

Apr 94. (7"/c-s) *(VS/+C 1510)* **WE WAIT AND WE WONDER. / HERO (with DAVID CROSBY)** | 45 | -
(cd-s+=) *(VSCDX 1510)* – For a friend.
(cd-s) *(VSCDG 1510)* – ('A'side) / Take me with you / Stevie's blues – There's a place for us (instrumental).

—— now not a GENESIS member, having announced departure early '96.

East West / Atlantic

Sep 96. (c-s) *(EW 066C)* **DANCE INTO THE LIGHT / TAKE ME DOWN** | 9 | 45
(cd-s+=) *(EW 066CD)* <87043> – It's over (demo).

Oct 96. (cd/c) *(0630 16000-2/-4)* **DANCE INTO THE LIGHT** | 4 | 23
– Dance into the light / That's what you said / Lorenzo / Just another story / Love police / Wear my hat / It's in your eyes / Oughta know by now / Take me down / The same moon / River so wide / No matter who / The times they are a-changin'.

Dec 96. (c-s) *(EW 076C)* **IT'S IN YOUR EYES / DON'T WANT TO GO** | 30 | 77 Feb97
(cd-s+=) *(EW 076CD1)* – Always (live).
(cd-s) *(EW 076CD2)* – ('A'side) / Easy lover (live) / Separate lives (live).

Jul 97. (c-s) *(EW 113C)* **WEAR MY HAT / ('A'-edited hat dance mix)** | 43 |
(cd-s+=) *(EW 113CD)* – ('A' hat dance mix) / ('A'- Wear my dub)

Oct 98. (cd/c) *(CDV/TCV 2870)* <83139> **. . . HITS (compilation)** | 1 | 18
– Easy lover / Dance into the light / True colours / One more night / In the air tonight / I wish it would rain down / Another day in Paradise / Something happened on the way to Heaven / You can't hurry love / Two hearts / Take me home / Both sides of the story / Groovy kind of love / Against all odds (take a look at me now) / Sussidio.

Oct 98. (c-s/cd-s) *(VSC/+DT 1715)* **TRUE COLOURS / IN THE AIR TONIGHT / I MISSED AGAIN** | 26 |
(cd-s) *(VSCDG 1715)* – ('A'side) / Don't lose my number / Take me home.

—— next with **GEORGE DUKE + BRAD COLE** – piano / **DARYL STUERMER** – guitar / **GERALD ALBRIGHT** – alto sax / **JAMES CARTER** – tenor sax

WEA / WEA

May 99. (cd/c; the PHIL COLLINS BIG BAND) *(3984 27221-2/-4)* <83198> **A HOT NIGHT IN PARIS** | | Jul99
– Sussidio / That's all / Invisible touch / Hold on my heart / Chips and salsa / I don't care anymore / Milestones / Against all odds / Pick up the pieces / Los endos suite.

Nov 99. (c-s/cd-s) *(010073 9/5 DNY)* <860025> **YOU'LL BE IN MY HEART / (version) / TRASHIN' THE CAMP** | 17 | 21 Jun99
(above from the animated movie, 'Tarzan' on 'Edel' UK 'Hollywood' US)

– compilations, others, etc. –

Jan 88. (cd)<US-lp/cd> *Virgin; (CDEP 4)* **12 INCHERS** | |
– (12" remixed extended versions of 6 hits)

COLOSSEUM (dig out; Great Psychedelic . . .)

COLOUR FIELD (see under ⇒ HALL, Terry)

COMSAT ANGELS (dig out; Great Alt & Indie . . .)

CONCRETE BLONDE (dig out; Great Alt & Indie . . .)

CONNELLS (dig out; Great Alt & Indie . . .)

Ry COODER

Born: RYLAND COODER, 15 Mar'47, Los Angeles, California, USA. He sessioned for the likes of JACKIE DE SHANNON and TAJ MAHAL, before moving on to CAPTAIN BEEFHEART in 1967. He nearly replaced BRIAN JONES in The ROLLING STONES, although he chose to only guest on their 'Let It Bleed' album, contributing searing bottleneck slide work to a number of songs, most effectively on the classic title track. By the time COODER was offered a solo deal by 'Reprise' in 1970, he was already one of the most adaptable, respected and gifted guitarists in the world, equally adept at playing other instruments such as the banjo and mandolin. Guesting on LITTLE FEAT's eponymous 1970 debut, COODER released his own self-titled solo set the following year. An impressive start, the record was largely made up of cover material, including an abrasive cover of Woody Guthrie's 'DO RE MI', a mandolin rendition of Sleepy John Este's 'GOIN' TO BROWNSVILLE' and a brilliantly drawling version of Randy Newman's biting 'OLD KENTUCKY HOME'. A follow-up long-player, 'INTO THE PURPLE VALLEY' (1972) was a more stripped down affair, highlighting his slide work, most notably on another Woody Guthrie number, 'VIGILANTE MAN'. Subsequent albums, 'BOOMER'S STORY' (1972) and PARADISE AND LUNCH' (1974), covered similar territory, jazz pianist EARL HINES guesting on the latter. It was 1978's 'CHICKEN SKIN MUSIC', that had the critics in rapture, however, its Hawaiian slack guitar and Tex-Mex stylings lent genuine authenticity by the contributions of star players GABBY PAHINUI and FLACO JIMENEZ together with the gospel vocals of BOBBY KING. These collaborations with respected players in the field of world music were a blueprint for much of COODER's subsequent output. In the meantime, he dabbled in ragtime and vaudeville with 'JAZZ' (1978), while 1979's 'BOP TILL YOU DROP' signalled a move away from traditional music to rock'n'roll and R&B. The latter album also saw COODER make a rare entry into the UK Top 40, something he only repeated with 1982's 'THE SLIDE AREA'. During the 80's, COODER moved sideways into soundtrack work, his atmospheric slide work fitting the bill for a number of Hollywood studios. Having already worked on 'Performance' in the late 60's, COODER proceeded to turn in impressive scores including 'THE LONG RIDERS' (1980), 'THE BORDER' (1982), 'JOHHNY HANDSOME' (1989) and most famously (and effectively) 'PARIS, TEXAS' (1985). The 90's saw the irrepressible guitarist team up with Indian musician, VISHANA MOHAN BHATT, for 'A MEETING BY THE RIVER' (1993), a magical, hypnotic fusion of Delta blues and Eastern classical/folk. Another groundbreaking set was released the following year in 'TALKING TIMBUKTU' (1994), a Grammy winning piece upon which COODER sparred with African guitarist ALI FARKA TOURE. The greatest critical praise, however, was probably reserved for the celebrated 'BUENA VISTA SOCIAL CLUB' (1997), a benchmark recording which saw COODER jam with some of Cuba's oldest (we're talking in their 80's and 90's here!) most accomplished musicians. • **Covered:** VIGILANTE MAN (Woody Guthrie) / GET RHYTHM (Johnny Cash) / HE'LL HAVE TO GO (hit; Jim Reeves) / LITTLE SISTER (Pomus-Shuman) / 13 QUESTION METHOD (Chuck Berry) / MONEY HONEY (hit; Drifters) / STAND BY ME (Ben E. King) / IT'S ALL OVER NOW (Bobby Womack) / GOODNIGHT IRENE (Leadbelly) / NEED A WOMAN (Bob Dylan) / BLUE SUEDE SHOES (Carl Perkins) / ALL SHOOK UP (Elvis Presley) / and loads more. The JAZZ album had early 1940's covers, etc. • **Trivia:** He also wrote score for 1980 film SOUTHERN COMFORT which sadly was not issued on soundtrack.

Album rating: RY COODER (*6) / INTO THE PURPLE VALLEY (*7) / BOOMER'S STORY (*7) / PARADISE AND LUNCH (*7) / CHICKEN SKIN MUSIC (*8) / SHOWTIME (*5) / JAZZ (*5) / BOP TILL YOU DROP (*5) / BORDERLINE (*3) / THE LONG RIDERS soundtrack (*4) / THE BORDER soundtrack (*5) / RY COODER LIVE (*5) / THE SLIDE AREA (*4) / PARIS, TEXAS soundtrack (*7) / ALAMO BAY soundtrack (*5) / WHY DON'T YOU TRY ME TONIGHT compilation (*7) /

BLUE CITY soundtrack (*4) / CROSSROADS soundtrack (*4) / GET RHYTHM (*5) / JOHNNY HANDSOME soundtrack (*5) / TRESPASS soundtrack (*5) / A MEETING BY THE RIVER with V.M. Bhatt (*5) / TALKING TIMBUKTU with Ali Farka Toure (*7) / GERONIMO soundtrack (*5) / MUSIC BY RY COODER compilation/soundtracks (*7) / THE BEST OF RY COODER compilation (*8) / BEUNA VISTA SOCIAL CLUB (*6)

RY COODER – vocals, guitar (ex-CAPTAIN BEEFHEART & HIS MAGIC BAND) plus session people too numerous to mention

		Reprise	Reprise
Oct 70.	(7") <0910> **GOIN' TO BROWNSVILLE. / AVAILABLE SPACE**	-	-
Dec 70.	(7") <0940> **ALIMONY. / PIGMEAT**	-	
Jan 71.	(lp) (K 44093) <RSLP 6402> **RY COODER**		Dec70

– Alimony / France chance / One meat ball / Do re mi / Old Kentucky home (turpentine & dandelion wine) / How can a poor man stand such times and live? / Available space / Pig meat / Police dog blues / Goin' to Brownsville / Dark is the night. (cd-iss. May95 on 'Warners'; 7599-27510-2)

May 71.	(7") (RS 23497) **HOW CAN A POOR MAN STAND SUCH TIMES AND LIVE. / GOIN' TO BROWNSVILLE**		-
Feb 72.	(7") <1009> **ON A MONDAY. / DARK IS THE NIGHT**	-	-
Feb 72.	(lp) (K 44142) <2052> **INTO THE PURPLE VALLEY**		-

– How can you keep on moving / Billy the kid / Money honey / F.D.R. in Trinidad / Teardrops will fall / Denomination blues / On a Monday / Hey porter / Great dreams from heaven / Taxes on the farmer feeds us all / Vigilante man. (cd-iss. 1988; K2 44142)

Feb 72.	(7") (K 14151) **MONEY HONEY. / ON A MONDAY**		-
Apr 72.	(7") <1071> **MONEY MONEY. / BILLY THE KID**		-
Oct 72.	(7") <1167> **BOOMER'S STORY. / BILLY THE KID**		-
Nov 72.	(lp) (K 44224) <2117> **BOOMER'S STORY**		-

– Boomer's story / Cherry ball blues / Crow black children / Axe sweet mama / Maria Elena / Dark end of the street / Rally 'round the flag / Comin' in on a wing and a prayer / President Kennedy / Good morning Mr. Railroad man. (cd-iss. Jan93 on 'WEA'; 7599 26398-2)

| May 74. | (lp) (K 44260) <2179> **PARADISE AND LUNCH** | | - |

– Tamp 'em up solid / Tattler / Married man's a fool / Jesus on the mainline / It's all over now / Fool about a cigarette – Feelin' good / If walls could talk / Mexican divorce / Ditty wa ditty. (cd-iss. 1988; K2 44260)

—— next with **FLACO JIMENEZ** – accordion / **GABBY PAHINUI** – steel guitar / **BOBBY KING** – gospel vocals

| Oct 76. | (lp/c) (K/K4 54083) <2254> **CHICKEN SKIN MUSIC** | | - |

– The bourgeois blues / I got mine / Always lift him up / He'll have to go / Smack dab in the middle / Stand by me / Yellow roses / Chloe / Goodnight Irene. (cd-iss. 1988; 254083)

| Mar 77. | (7") (K 14457) **HE'LL HAVE TO GO. / THE BOURGEOIS BLUES** | | - |

		Warners	Warners
Aug 77.	(lp/c) (K/K4 56386) <3059> **SHOW TIME (live)**		

– School is out / Alimony / Jesus on the mainline / ark end of the street / Viva sequin – Do re mi / Volver, volver / How can a poor man stand such times and live? / Smack dab in the middle. (cd-iss. Nov93; 7599 27319-2)

| Aug 77. | (7") <8384> **SCHOOL IS OUT (live). / JESUS ON THE MAINLINE (live)** | | - |
| Jun 78. | (lp/c) (K/K4 56488) <3197> **JAZZ** | | - |

– Face to face I shall meet him / Davenport blues / In a mist / Big bad Bill is sweet William now / Happy meeting in glory / We shall be happy / Nobody / Shine / Flashes / Dream / Pearls / Tia Juana. (cd-iss. 1988; K2 25688)

| Jun 79. | (7") <49055> **LITTLE SISTER. / DOWN IN HOLLYWOOD** | | - |
| Aug 79. | (lp/c) (K/K4 56691) <3358> **BOP TILL YOU DROP** | 36 | 62 |

– Little sister / Go home girl / The very thing that makes you rich (makes me poor) / I think it's gonna work out fine / Down in Hollywood / Look at granny run run / Trouble, you can't fool me / Don't mess up a good thing / I can't win. (cd-iss. 1983; K2 56691)

Aug 79.	(7") (K 17460) **LITTLE SISTER. / GO HOME GIRL**		-
Oct 79.	(7") <49081> **THE VERY THING THAT MAKES YOU RICH (MAKES ME POOR). / LITTLE SISTER**		-
Jun 80.	(lp) (K 56826) <3448> **THE LONG RIDERS (Soundtrack)**		-

– (main title) The long riders / I'm a good old rebel / Seneca square dance / Archie's funeral (hold to God's unchanging hand) / I always knew that you were the one / Rally 'round the flag / Wildwood boys / Better things to talkabout / My grandfather / Cole Younger polka / Escape from Northfield / Leaving Missouri / Jesse James.

| Oct 80. | (lp/c) (K/K4 56864) <3489> **BORDERLINE** | 35 | 43 | Jan81 |

– 634-5789 / Speedo / Why don't you try me / Down in the Boondocks / Johnny Porter / The way we make a broken heart / Crazy 'bout an automobile (every woman I know) / The girls from Texas / Borderline / Never make a move too soon. (cd-iss. 1988; 25686-2)

Oct 80.	(7") <49677> **BORDERLINE. / THE GIRLS FROM TEXAS**		-
Oct 80.	(7") (K 17713) **634-5789. / THE GIRLS FROM TEXAS**		-
Dec 80.	(7") **CRAZY 'BOUT AN AUTOMOBILE. / BORDERLINE**		-
Aug 81.	(7") (K 17844) **CRAZY 'BOUT AN AUTOMOBILE (EVERY WOMAN I KNOW) / THE VERY THING THAT MAKES YOU RICH (MAKES ME POOR)**		-

(12"+=) (K 17844T) – If walls could talk / Look at granny run run.

—— In March '82, he contributed tracks to 'THE BORDER' soundtrack, which was issued on 'M.C.A.' (MCF 3133) / 'Backstreet' US

| Apr 82. | (lp/c) (K/K4 56960) <3651> **THE SLIDE AREA** | 18 | |

– UFO has landed in the ghetto / I need a woman / Gypsy woman / Blue suede shoes / Mama, don't treat your daughter mean / I'm drinking again / Which came first / That's the way love turned out for me. (cd-iss. Jul88; K2 56976)

| May 82. | (d7") (K 17952) **GYSPY WOMAN / ALIMONY** | | - |

(with free 7") (SAM 149) – TEARDROPS WILL FALL / IT'S ALL OVER NOW

| Feb 85. | (lp) (925270-1) <25270> **PARIS, TEXAS (Soundtrack)** | | - |

– Paris, Texas / Brothers / Nothing out there / Cancion Mixteca / No safety zone / Houston in two seconds / She's leaving the bank / On the couch / I knew these people / Dark was the night.

| Aug 85. | (lp) **MUSIC FROM ALAMO BAY (Soundtrack)** | | - |

– Theme from Alamo Bay / Gooks on main street / Klan meeting / Too close / Sailfish evening / The last stand / Glory / Search and destroy / Quatro vicios.

(above issued on 'London' UK / 'Slash' US)

| Mar 86. | (lp/c)(cd) (WX 37/+C)(40864-2) **WHY DON'T YOU TRY ME TONIGHT (THE BEST OF RY COODER)** (compilation) | | - |

– How can a poor man stand such times and live? / Available space / Money honey / Tattler / He'll have to go / Smack dab in the middle / Dark end of the street / Down in Hollywood (every woman I know) / 634-5789 / Why don't you try me tonight.

| Jul 86. | (lp) (925386-1) <25386> **BLUE CITY (Soundtrack)** | | - |

– Blue city down / Elevation 13 foot / True believers – Marianne / Nice bike / Greenhouse / Billy and Annie / Pops and 'timer – Tell me something slick / Blue city / Don't take your guns to town / A leader of men / Not even Key West.

Jul 86.	(7") **BILLY AND ANNIE. / TELL ME SOMETHING SLICK**		-
Jul 86.	(7") <28723> **CROSSROADS. / FEEL IT (BAD BLUES)**		-
Jul 86.	(lp) (925399-1) <25399> **CROSSROADS**	85	May86

– Crossroads / Down in Mississippi / Cotton needs pickin' / Viola Lee blues / See you in Hell, blind boy / Walkin' away blues / Nitty gritty Mississippi / He made a woman out of me / Feelin' bad blues / Somebody's callin' my name / Willie Brown blues.

| Dec 87. | (lp/c)(cd) (WX 121/+C)(925639-2) <25639> **GET RHYTHM** | 75 | Nov87 |

– Get rhythm / Low-commotion / Going back to Okinawa / 13 question method / Women will rule the world / All shook up / I can tell by the way you smell / Across the borderline / Let's have a ball.

Jan 88.	(7") <> **GET RHYTHM. / GOING BACK TO OKINAWA**		-
Apr 88.	(7") <> **ALL SHOOK UP. / GET YOUR LIES STRAIGHT**		-
Apr 88.	(7"/10") (WB/WTE 8107) **GET RHYTHM. / GET YOUR LIES STRAIGHT**		-

(12"+=/3"cd-s+=) (WT/WCD 8107) – Down in Hollywood.

| Oct 89. | (lp/c/cd) () <> **JOHNNY HANDSOME (Soundtrack)** | | - |

– Main theme / I can't walk this time – The prestige / Angola / Clip joint rhumba / Sad story / Fountain walk / Cajun metal / First week at work / Greasy oysters / Smells like money / Sunny's tune / I like your eyes / Adios Donna / Cruising wife Rafe / How's my face / End theme. (re-iss. cd Feb95;)

—— In 1991, he recorded Soundtrack for Robin Williams film 'PECOS BILL'. He also teamed up with NICK LOWE, JOHN HIATT and JIM KELTNER in band LITTLE VILLAGE. In 1992, he and DAVID LINDLEY were part of The PAHINUI BROTHERS who released Aug'92 eponymous album for 'Private'.

		WEA	Sire
Jan 93.	(cd/c) <(6362 45220-2/-4)> **TRESPASS** (soundtrack w/ other artists)		82

– Video drive-by / Trespass / East St.Louis toodle-oo / Orgil Bros. / Goose and lucky / You think it's on now / Solid gold / Heroin / Totally boxed in / Give 'm cops / Lucy in the trunk / We're rich / King of the street / Party lights. (re-iss. Feb95;)

—— **RY** – bottle neck guitar; with **VISHWA MOHAN BHATT** – mohan vina / **JOACHIM COODER** (his 14 year old son) / **SUKHVINDER** – tabla

		Topic	Water Lily
Apr 93.	(cd; RY COODER & V.M. BHATT) (WLACS 029) **A MEETING BY THE RIVER**		

– A meeting by the river / Longing / Ganges Delta blues / Isa Lei. (re-iss. Aug98; same)

		World Circuit	Nonesuch
Mar 94.	(cd/c/lp; ALI FARKA TOURE & RY COODER) (WCD/WCC/WCB 040) **TALKING TIMBUKTU**	44	

– Blonde / Soukora / Gomni / Sega / Amandrai / Lasidan / Keito / Banga / Ai du / Diaraby.

—— now **COODER** with **ELIADES OCHOA / COMPAY SEGUNDO / IBRAHIM FERRER / RUBEN GONZALEZ** etc

| Jun 97. | (cd; as BUENA VISTA SOCIAL CLUB) (WCD 050) <79478> **BUENA VISTA SOCIAL CLUB** | 44 | |

– Chan chan / Camino por vereda / Veinte anos / Pueblo nuevo / Dos gardinerias / El carretero / Candela / Amor de loca juventud / Orgullecida / Murmullo / El cuarto de tula / Y tu que has hecho / Buena Vista social club / La bayamesa. (lp-iss.Dec98 on 'Rock The House'; RTH 79468)

– compilations, etc. –

| May 93. | (cd; by The RISING SONS featuring RY COODER & TAJ MAHAL) Columbia; (472865-2) **THE RISING SONS** | | |

Norman COOK

Born: QUENTIN COOK, 31 Jul'63, London, England. Following the demise of sunny agit-prop popsters, the HOUSEMARTINS, bassist COOK returned to his Brighton base and pursued his interest in the burgeoning dance culture. Already a budding DJ by the time HEATON & Co. split, the future man of many pseudonyms initially began recording club orientated music under his own name. Signed to 'Go! Beat', the dance arm of his previous band's now defunct label, 'Go! Discs', COOK enjoyed his debut hit via a collaboration with labelmate BILLY BRAGG on 'WON'T TALK ABOUT IT'. After a further minor solo hit, COOK initiated the BEATS INTERNATIONAL project with the classic 'DUB BE GOOD TO ME' single. Splicing the bassline from The CLASH's 'Guns Of Brixton' with the S.O.S BAND's 'Just Be Good To Me' proved a masterstroke, LINDY LAYTON (soon to be a solo star in her own right) teasing, girlish vocal the icing on a vinyl cake which furnished COOK with a massive-selling No.1 record in 1990. Also on board for the new venture were LESTER NOEL, keyboardist ANDY BOUCHER and percussionist LUKE CRESSWELL, the attendant Top 20 album 'LET THEM EAT BINGO' (1990) in addition finding COOK collaborating with a diverse cast of names including hip hop'ers DOUBLE TROUBLE and ex-DAMNED man, CAPTAIN SENSIBLE. A follow-up single revamping 'WON'T TALK..' with LAYTON on vocals made the Top 10 while the album's pot-pourri of rythmic styles provided a further minor single in the innovative 'BURUNDI BLUES'. 1991's follow-up album, 'EXCURSION ON THE VERSION' followed in a more dub-centric vein, evidenced by the 'ECHO CHAMBER' single. A willingness to experiment was nevertheless the record's enduring characteristic, with further attempts at COOK-style soul and hip-hop. Although he failed to repeat the success of the debut single, his kudos as a remixer and producer were now firmly established. By 1992, BEATS INTERNATIONAL had run its natural course and COOK secured a new outlet for his rapidly improving songwriting talents through FREAK POWER, a more conventional band comprising bonafide musicians and dealing in sounds of a decidedly acid-jazzy persuasion. Signed to 'Island' subsidiary, '4th & Broadway', the tongue-in-cheek, smokily laid-back grooves of the group's debut single, 'TURN ON, TUNE IN, COP OUT' furnished them with a minor Top 30 hit upon its initial release in 1993. A highlight of the fine album, 'DRIVE-THRU BOOTY' (1995) alongside rump-shaking follow-up single, 'RUSH', the track was subsequently used on a Levi's 501 commercial, becoming one of '95's biggest hits. Like many other acts given the Levi's treatment, however, it eventually proved to be the kiss of death for the outfit, a second album, 'MORE OF EVERYTHING FOR EVERYBODY' (1997) failing to chart and subsequent releases flopping amid drug-related touring problems. By this point, however, the industrious COOK had already notched up a series of massive club smashes under his PIZZAMAN alias, many of his anthemic house monsters crossing over into the pop charts with 'TRIPPIN' ON SUNSHINE' becoming a Top 20 hit second time around in Spring '96. Concurrent with the rise of The CHEMICAL BROTHERS, The Heavenly Social club and all things "Big Beat", the chameleon-like COOK then turned his hand to some block rockin' beats and came up with one of 1997's most critically acclaimed albums, 'BETTER LIVING THROUGH CHEMISTRY'. Released under the FATBOY SLIM moniker and preceded by a clutch of blistering breakbeat 12"ers including 'SANTA CRUZ' (featured on the seminal 'BRIT HOP AND AMYL HOUSE' compilation) and 'EVERYBODY LOVES A 303', the record proved to be COOK's most cohesive and thrilling dalliance with dance music to date. A year later, FATBOY SLIM's 'ROCKAFELLER SKANK' (a take-off from a FALL tune) was racing up the charts and even broke this unusual set-up into the American Hot 100. Incredibly, COOK almost made No.1 yet again with a follow-up FATBOY SLIM album, 'YOU'VE COME A LONG WAY, BABY', possibly his most contagious, outrageous release to date. However, it was 'PRAISE YOU' indeed, after the single of that name topped the UK chart early in 1999 and eventually gave him a US Top 40 entry later in the year. COOK subsequently married "hyper" TV presenter/radio DJ, Zoe Ball, ah! showbiz couples, aren't they just worth reading about every day in the tabloids. • **Songwriters:** COOK, and some with ASHLEY SLATER in FREAK POWER. Covered RUNNING AWAY (Sly & The Family Stone).

Album rating: Beats International: LET THEM EAT BINGO (*6) / EXCURSION OF THE VERSION (*4) / Freak Power: DRIVE THRU BOOTY (*5) / MORE OF EVERYTHING FOR EVERYBODY (*4) / Fatboy Slim: BETTER LIVING THROUGH CHEMISTRY (*8) / YOU'VE COME A LONG WAY, BABY (*8)

NORMAN COOK – multi (solo) with various people

		Go! Discs	Elektra
Jun 89.	(7"/c-s; NORMAN COOK featuring BILLY BRAGG. / NORMAN COOK featuring MC WILDSKI) (GOD/+MC 33) **WON'T TALK ABOUT IT. / BLAME IT ON THE BASSLINE**	29	

(12"+=/cd-s+=) (GOD X/CD 33) – Blame it on the bonus beats / Blame it on the acappella.
(12"+=) (GODXR 33) – Blame it on the bonus beats / ('B'dub).

| Oct 89. | (7"/c-s; NORMAN COOK featuring LESTER) (GOD/+MC 37) **FOR SPACIOUS LIES. / FOR SPACIOUS LIES (dance mix) / THE INVASION OF THE ESTATE AGENTS** | 48 | |

(12"+=/cd-s+=) (GOD X/CD 37) – For spacious ballad.

BEATS INTERNATIONAL

NORMAN COOK with **LINDY LAYTON & LESTER NOEL** – vocals / **ANDY BOUCHER** – keyboards / **LUKE CRESSWELL** – percussion

| Feb 90. | (7"/c-s; BEATS INTERNATIONAL featuring LINDY LAYTON) (GOD/+MC 39) <64970> **DUB BE GOOD TO ME. / THE INVASION OF THE ESTATE AGENTS** | 1 | 76 Mar90 |

(12"+=/cd-s+=) (GOD X/CD 39) – Just be good to me (acappella) / The invasion of the freestyle – Discuss.
(12") (GODXR 39) – ('A'-Smith & Mighty mix) / Before I go too dub / ('A'-Norman Cook's excursion on the version) / ('A'-Smith & Mighty mellow mix).

| Mar 90. | (cd/c/lp) (842 196-2/-4/-1) <60921> **LET THEM EAT BINGO** | 17 | |

– Burundi blues / Dub be good to me / Before I grow too old / The ragged trousered percussionists / For spacious lies / Blame it on the bassline / Won't talk about it / Dance to the drummer's beat / Babies makin' babies (stoop rap) / The whole world's down on me / Tribute to King Tubby. (some lp's cont. 12"ep) – BINGO BEATS (cd+=) – For spacious lies.

| May 90. | (7"/c-s) (GOD/+MC 43) <64948> **WON'T TALK ABOUT IT. / BEATS INTERNATIONAL THEME** | 9 | 76 Aug90 |

(12"+=/cd-s+=) (GOD X/CD 43) – ('A'extended).
(12") (GODXR 43) – ('A'-Frankie Foncett mix) / ('A'-Chad Jackson mix) / (bonus beats).

| Sep 90. | (7"/c-s) (GOD/+MC 45) **BURUNDI BLUES. / THEME FROM THE DEERSTALKER** | 51 | |

(12"+=/cd-s+=) (GOD X/CD 45) – Burundi dub.
(12") (GODXR 45) – ('A'-Boilerhouse mix) / ('A'-Boilerhouse guitar & vocal mix) / ('A'-Traditional version).

| Feb 91. | (7"/c-s) (GOD/+MC 51) **ECHO CHAMBER. / INCH BY INCH** | 60 | - |

(12"+=/cd-s+=) (GOD X/CD 51) – ('A'-version) / ('A- Daddy Freddy version)

| Sep 91. | (7"/c-s) (GOD/+MC 59) **THE SUN DOESN'T SHINE. /** | 66 | - |

(12"+=/cd-s+=) (GOD X/CD 59) –

| Oct 91. | (cd/c/lp) (828 290-2/-4/-1) **EXCURSION OF THE VERSION** | | |

– Brand new beat / Change your mind / Love is green / Echo chamber / The sun doesn't shine / Herman / Three foot skank / No more Mr. Nice guy / Eyes on the prize / Ten long years / In the ghetto. (cd+=/c+=) – Come home.

| Nov 91. | (7"/c-s) (GOD/+MC 64) **IN THE GHETTO. / OH THAT'S DEEP** | 44 | - |

(12"+=/cd-s+=) (GOD X/CD 64) – ('A'-version two & three)

FREAK POWER

NORMAN COOK – guitar, vox / **ASHLEY SLATER** – vocals, trombone / **CYRIL McCAMMON** – keyboards, vox / **DALE DAVIES** – bass / **PETE ECKFORD** – percussion / **JIM CARMICHAEL** – drums

		4th & Broadway	4th & Broadway
Oct 93.	(7"/c-s) (BRW/BRCA 284) **TURN ON, TUNE IN, COP OUT. / ('A'mix)**	29	
	(12"+=/cd-s+=) (12BRW/BRCD 284) – (2-'A'mixes).		
Feb 94.	(7"/c-s) (BRW/BRCA 291) **RUSH. / PARTY TILL WE PART**	62	
	(12"+=/cd-s+=) (12BRW/BRCD 291) – (2-'A'mixes).		
Oct 94.	(c-s) (BRCA 298) **GET IN TOUCH / CHEW THE BONE**		
	(12"+=/cd-s+=) (12BRW/BRCD 298) – (2-'A'mixes).		
Mar 95.	(7"/c-s) (BRW/BRCA 317) **TURN ON, TUNE IN, COP OUT. / GETTING OVER THE HUMP**	3	
	(12"+=) (12BRW 317) – (2-'A'mixes).		
	(cd-s+=) (BRCD 317) – ('A'mix).		
Apr 95.	(cd/lp) (BRCD/BRLP 606) **DRIVE-THRU BOOTY**	11	

– Moonbeam woman / Turn on, tune in, cop out / Get in touch / Freak power / Running away / Change my mind / What it is? / Waiting for the story to end / Rush / Big time / The whip. (re-iss. Oct95 d-cd+=/d-lp+=; BRCDX/BRLPX 606) – IN DUB

May 96.	(c-s) (BRCA 331) **NEW DIRECTION / ('A'mix)**	60	-
	(12"+=/cd-s+=) (12BRW/BRCD 331) – ('A'mixes).		
Jun 96.	(cd/c/lp) (BRCD/BRCA/BRLP 619) **MORE OF EVERYTHING FOR EVERYBODY**		
Aug 96.	(c-s) (BRCA 335) **CAN YOU FEEL IT / ('A'mix)**		
	(12"+=/cd-s+=) (12BRW/BRCD 335) – ('A'mixes).		

		Southern	unknown
Dec 97.	(12") (ECB 14) **NO WAY. ('A'mixes)**		

		DeConstruct	unknown
Apr 98.	(c-s) (74321 57857-4) **NO WAY / ('A'mix)**	29	
	(12"+=/cd-s+=) (74321 57857-1/-2) – ('A'mixes).		

PIZZAMAN

– aka **NORMAN COOK** with various members

		Loaded	unknown
Aug 94.	(7"/c-s) (LOAD/+MC 16) **TRIPPIN' ON SUNSHINE. / ('A'mix)**	33	
	(12"+=/cd-s+=) (LOAD 16 12/CD) – ('A'mixes).		
Jun 95.	(c-s) (CALOAD 24) **SEX ON THE STREETS / ('A'mix)**	24	
	(12"+=/cd-s+=) (12/CD LOAD 24) – ('A'mixes).		
	(re-entered the chart Jan96 and hit No.23)		
Nov 95.	(c-s) (CALOAD 29) **HAPPINESS / ('A'mix)**	19	
	(12"+=/cd-s+=) (12/CD LOAD 29) – ('A'mixes).		
May 96.	(c-s) (CALOAD 32) **TRIPPIN' ON SUNSHINE / ('A'mix)**	18	
	(12"+=/cd-s+=) (12/CD LOAD 32) – ('A'mixes).		
Sep 96.	(c-s) (CALOAD 39) **HELLO HONKY TONKS (ROCK YOUR BODY) / ('A'mix)**	41	
	(12"+=/cd-s+=) (12/CD LOAD 39) – ('A'mixes).		

FATBOY SLIM

– aka **NORMAN COOK**

		Skint	Astralwerks
Mar 96.	(12") (SKINT 1) **SANTA CRUZ. / THE WEEKEND STARTS HERE**		-
Mar 96.	(12"/cd-s) (SKINT 6/+CD) **EVERYBODY LOVES A 303. / ('A'mixes)**		-
Sep 96.	(12"/cd-s) (SKINT 12/+CD) **PUNK TO FUNK. / ('A'mixes)**		-
Apr 97.	(12"/cd-s) (SKINT 19/+CD) **GOING OUT OF MY HEAD. / MICHAEL JACKSON**	57	
Oct 97.	(12"/cd-s) (SKINT 31/+CD) **EVERYBODY NEEDS A 303. / ('A'mixes)**	34	

(cd-s) (SKINT 31XCD) – Everybody loves a carnival / Everybody loves a filter / Es paradis / Where you're at.

| Nov 97. | (cd/c/d-lp) (BRASSIC 2 CD/MC/LP) **BETTER LIVING THROUGH CHEMISTRY** | | |

– Song for Lindy / Santa Cruz / Going out of my head / The weekend starts here / Everybody needs a 303 / Give the po' man a break / 10th and Crenshaw / First down / Punk to funk / The sound of Milwaukee / Michael Jackson / Next to nothing.

| Jun 98. | (c-s) (SKINT 35MC) <6 6242> **THE ROCKAFELLER SKANK / THE ROCKAFELLER SKANK (long version)** | 6 | 77 Nov98 |

(12"+=/cd-s+=) (SKINT 35/+CD) – Always read the label / Tweakers delight.

Jul 98.	(cd/c; FATBOY SLIM mixes Various Artists) (BRASSIC 9 CD/MC) **ON THE FLOOR AT THE BIG BEAT BOUTIQUE**		
Oct 98.	(c-s) (SKINT 39MC) **GANGSTER TRIPPIN' (mixes)**	3	
	(12"+=/cd-s+=) (SKINT 39/+CD) – (mixes).		
Oct 98.	(cd/c/d-lp) (BRASSIC 11 CD/MC/LP) <ASW 66247> **YOU'VE COME A LONG WAY, BABY**	1	34

– Right here, right now / The Rockafeller skank / In Heaven / Gangster tripping / Build it up – Tear it down / Kalifornia / Soul surfing / You're not from Brighton / Praise you / Love island / Acid 8000.

| Jan 99. | (c-s) (SKINT 42MC) <66254> **PRAISE YOU / SHO NUFF** | 1 | 36 Feb99 |

(12"+=/cd-s+=) (SKINT 42/+CD) – Rockafeller skank (Urban takeover remix).

| Apr 99. | (c-s) (SKINT 46MC) **RIGHT HERE, RIGHT NOW / DON'T FORGET YOUR TEETH** | 2 | |

(12"+=/cd-s+=) (SKINT 46/+CD) – Praise you (original).

– FATBOY SLIM was also credited on FREDDY FRESH's hit, 'Badder Badder Schwing'

Sam COOKE

Born: SAMUEL COOK, 22 Jan'31, Clarksdale, Mississippi, USA. The son of a Baptist minister, SAM was steeped in gospel from his earliest days, singing in the church choir before graduating to bonafide gospel groups in his teens. In 1951 he became lead tenor with The SOUL STIRRERS, achieving widespread critical acclaim within the gospel community for his stunning interpretations of traditional hymns and self-penned material like 'TOUCH THE HEM OF HIS GARMENT'. The outfit signed to Art Rupe's L.A.-based 'Specialty' label (also home to JOE LIGGINS, PERCY MAYFIELD and most famously, LITTLE RICHARD) where they cut a string of singles throughout the early 50's. In 1956, SAM made a move into the pop market with a debut solo track, 'LOVEABLE', released under the alias DALE COOK so as not to offend his gospel fanbase. Following another handful of singles and an album, 'TWO SIDES OF SAM COOKE' (1957), the singer's ongoing wish to become a fully fledged secular star brought him to a final showdown with Rupe who was strongly opposed to any transformation. 'Specialty' producer Bumps Blackwell had backed COOKE all the way and in 1957, Rupe washed his hands of both of them. Armed with the freshly penned 'YOU SEND ME', the pair signed with Hollywood label, 'Keen' and duly took the track to the top of the US chart. While Rupe was quite possibly kicking himself, the yearning ballad made COOKE a star overnight; his clean-cut good looks, sophisticated phrasing and luminous delivery endearing him to a massive youth-orientated audience that held more than its fair share of teenage girls. A string of Top 20/Top 30 hits followed in an overtly pop vein, COOKE and Bumps adapting to the demise of straightahead R&B with airy romantic singles like 'WIN YOUR LOVE FOR ME', 'LOVE YOU MOST OF ALL' and the brilliant 'WONDERFUL WORLD', actually written as a joint effort between future biz moguls Lou Adler (under the pseudonym Barbara Campbell) and Herb Alpert. COOKE was also savvy enough to start his own label, 'SAR', publishing arm, 'Kags Music' and even film company, 'SAR Pictures'; together with his manager, JW Alexander, COOKE helped initiate the careers of future stars like BOBBY WOMACK and BILLY PRESTON. While SAR's output remained on the grittier side of R&B, COOKE's 1960 signing to 'R.C.A.' saw the singer veer towards a supper club, orchestrated easy listening style courtesy of in-house producers like Hugo Peretti and Luigi Creatore. Even so, COOKE still managed to get back to his roots on hits like 'TWISTIN' THE NIGHT AWAY' (a UK/US Top 10 in 1962), the sublime 'BRING IT ON HOME TO ME' (featuring a wonderful call-and-response section with former PILGRIM TRAVELLER, LOU RAWLS) and the 1963 Top 20 cover of Willie Dixon's 'LITTLE RED ROOSTER'. The latter track appeared on 'NIGHT BEAT' (1963), one of his better albums of the period featuring COOKE in hollering blues mode. 1963 was also the proposed year of release for 'LIVE AT THE HARLEM SQUARE CLUB', a gritty concert set recorded at a show on the infamous chitlin' circuit. The record never saw the light of day until the mid-80's with COOKE's paymasters eager to cater to his newfound white MOR audience instead. The record couldn't have been in starker contrast to 'AT THE COPA' (1965), a live set recorded the previous summer during SAM's residency at New York's swish 'Copacabana' nightclub. Tragically, COOKE wasn't around to see its release; on 11th December 1964, he was shot dead by motel manageress, Bertha Franklin, who maintained she acted in self defence after the singer had allegedly raped 22-year old Elisa Boyer. The controversial nature of the case has since fuelled countless rumours that COOKE's death was set up as a result of vested interests and rivalry in the music business. Whatever the truth, his shockingly premature demise was a body blow for soul music and the whole black community; 1965's posthumous Top 10 single, 'A CHANGE IS GONNA COME' was a poignant reminder of COOKE's commitment to ending racial segregation. One of the singer's closest friends and admirers, CASSIUS CLAY (aka MOHAMMED ALI), once described COOKE as "the world's greatest rock'n'roll singer . . .". Few would disagree. • **Songwriters:** COOKE wrote mostly all material, except SEND ME SOME LOVIN' (Little Richard) / LITTLE RED ROOSTER (Willie Dixon) / etc.

Best CD collection: THE MAN AND HIS MUSIC (*8)

SAM COOKE – vocals (with various session people)

		not iss.	Specialty
1956.	(7",78; as DALE COOK) <596> **LOVEABLE. / FOREVER**	-	
1956.	(7",78) <619> **I'LL COME RUNNING BACK TO YOU. / FOREVER**	-	
	<re-iss.Dec57> – hit No.18 B-side No.60		
1957.	(7",78) <627> **THAT'S ALL I NEED TO KNOW. / I DON'T WANT TO CRY**	-	
	(UK-iss.May58 on 'London'; HLU 8615)		
1957.	(7",78) <667> **I NEED YOU NOW. / HAPPY IN LOVE**	-	
1957.	(lp) <2116> **TWO SIDES OF SAM COOKE**	-	

– The last mile of the way / Touch the hem of his garment / Jesus gave me water / Were you there / Pilgrim of sorrow / He's my guide / I'll come running back to you / I don't want to cry / Loveable / That's all I need to know / Forever / Happy in love.

		London	Keen
1957.	(7",78) <3-4002> **(I LOVE YOU FOR) SENTIMENTAL REASONS. / DESIRE ME**	-	
	<re-iss.Dec57> – hit No.17 + B-side No.47		
1957.	(7",78) <3-4009> **LONELY ISLAND. / YOU WERE MADE FOR ME**	-	
	<re-iss.Mar58> – hit No.26 + B-side No.27		

—— next with the BUMPS BLACKWELL ORCHESTRA

Jan 58.	(7",78) (HLU 8506) <3-4013> **YOU SEND ME. / SUMMERTIME**	29	1 81 Oct57

Mar 58.	(lp) (CLP 1261) <A-2001> **SAM COOKE**		

H.M.V. Keen

– You send me / The lonesome road / Tammy / Ol' man river / Moonlight in Vermont / Canadian sunset / Summertime / Around the world / Ain't misbehavin' / The bells of St. Mary's / So long / Danny boy / That lucky old sun. (cd-iss. Dec93 on 'Entertainers')

May 58.	(7",78) <3-2005> **ALL OF MY LIFE. / STEALING KISSES**	□	□
Jul 58.	(7",78) <3-2006> **WIN YOUR LOVE FOR ME. / LOVE SONG FROM "HOUSEBOAT" (ALMOST IN YOUR ARMS)**	-	22
Nov 58.	(7",78) <3-2008> **LOVE YOU MOST OF ALL. / BLUE MOON**	-	26
Nov 58.	(lp) (CLP 1273) <A-2003> **ENCORE**		

– When I fall in love / I cover the waterfront / My foolish heart / Today I sing the blues / The gypsy / It's the talk of the town / Oh look at me now / Someday (You'll want me to want you) / Along the Navajo Trail / Running wild / Ac-cent-tchu-aet the positive / Mary, Mary Lou.

Feb 59.	(7",78) (POP 568) **LOVE YOU MOST OF ALL. / WIN YOUR LOVE FOR ME**	-	
May 59.	(7",78) (POP 610) <3-2018> **EVERYBODY LIKES TO CHA CHA CHA. / LITTLE THINGS YOU DO**		31 Mar59
Aug 59.	(7",78) (POP 642) <3-2022> **ONLY SIXTEEN. / LET'S GO STEADY AGAIN**	23	28 Jun59
Sep 59.	(7") <8-2101> **SUMMERTIME. / (part 2)**	-	
Nov 59.	(lp) <A-2004> **TRIBUTE TO THE LADY – BILLIE HOLIDAY**	-	
Dec 59.	(7") (POP 675) <8-2105> **THERE, I'VE SAID IT AGAIN. / ONE HOUR AHEAD OF THE POSSE**		81 Nov59
Feb 60.	(7") <8-2111> **'TAIN'T NOBODY'S BIZNESS (IF I DO). / NO ONE**	-	
Feb 60.	(lp) <8-6101> **HIT KIT**	-	

—— now orchestration by his new 'R.C.A.' producers HUGO & LUIGI

R.C.A. RCA Victor

—— some 45's/lp's were still being issued by 'Keen' ('H.M.V.' UK)

May 60.	(7") (RCA 1184) <47-7701> **TEENAGE SONATA. / IF YOU WERE THE ONLY GIRL**		50 Mar60
May 60.	(7") <47-7730> **YOU UNDERSTAND ME. / I BELONG TO YOUR HEART**	-	
Jun 60.	(7"; on 'Keen') (POP 754) <8-2112> **WONDERFUL WORLD. / ALONG THE NAVAJO TRAIL**	27	12 May60
Jun 60.	(7"; on 'Keen') <8-2117> **WITH YOU. / I THANK GOD**	-	
Jun 60.	(lp; on 'Keen') <8-6103> **I THANK GOD**	-	
Sep 60.	(7") (RCA 1202) <47-7783> **CHAIN GANG. / I FALL IN LOVE EVERY DAY**	9	2 Aug60
Oct 60.	(7"; on 'Keen') <8-2118> **STEAL AWAY. / SO GLAMOUROUS**	-	
Nov 60.	(lp; on 'Keen') <8-6106> **THE WONDERFUL WORLD OF SAM COOKE**	-	

– Wonderful world / Desire me / Summertime / Almost in your arms / That's heaven to me / No one / With you / Blue moon / Stealing kisses / You were made for me / There, I've said it again / I thank God. (UK-iss.1966 on 'Immediate'; IMLP 002)

Dec 60.	(7"; on 'Keen') <8-2122> **MARY, MARY LOU. / EEE-YI-EEE-YI-OH**	-	
Jan 61.	(7") (RCA 1221) <47-7816> **SAD MOOD. / LOVE ME**		29 Nov60
Feb 61.	(lp) (RD 27190) <LPM 2221> **COOKE'S TOUR**		Nov60

– Faraway places / Under Paris skies / South of the border / Bali Ha'l / The coffee song / Arrivederci Roma / London by night / Jamaica farewell / Galway bay / Sweet Leilani / The Japenese farewell song / The house I live in.

Apr 61.	(7") (RCA 1230) <47-7853> **THAT'S IT – I QUIT – I'M MOVIN' ON. / WHAT DO YOU SAY**		31 Feb61
Apr 61.	(lp) (RD 27215) <LPM 2236> **HITS OF THE 50's**		Jan61

– Hey there / Mona Lisa / Too young / The great pretender / You, you, you / Unchained melody / The wayward wind / Secret love / The song from Moulin Rouge / I'm walking behind you / Cry / Venus. (cd-iss. Jun95; 74321 26056-2)

Jul 61.	(7") (RCA 1242) <47-7883> **CUPID. / FAREWELL, MY DARLING**	7	17 May61
	(re-iss. 1969; RCA 1817)		
Sep 61.	(7") (RCA 1260) <47-7927> **FEEL IT. / IT'S ALL RIGHT**		56 93
Oct 61.	(lp) (RD 27222) <LPM 2293> **SWING LOW**		Aug61

– Swing low, sweet chariot / I'm just a country boy / They call the wind Maria / Twilight on the trail / If I had you / Chain gang / Grandfather's clock / I dream of Jeanie with the light brown hair / Long, long ago / Pray / You belong to me / Goin' home.

Feb 62.	(lp) (RD 27245) <LPM 2392> **MY KIND OF BLUES**		Dec61

– Don't get around much anymore / Little girl blue / Nobody knows you when you're down and out / Out in the cold again / But not for me / Exactly like you / I'm just a lucky so and so / Since I met you baby / Baby, won't you please come home / Trouble in mind / You're always on my mind / The song is ended.

Feb 62.	(7") (RCA 1277) <47-7983> **TWISTIN' THE NIGHT AWAY. / ONE MORE TIME**	6	9 Jan62 72
Jun 62.	(lp) (RD 27263) <LPM 2555> **TWISTIN' THE NIGHT AWAY**		

– Twistin' the night away / Sugar dumpling / Twistin' in the kitchen with Dinah / Somebody's gonna miss me / A whole lotta woman / The twist / Twistin' in the old town tonight / Movin' and a-groovin' / Camptown twist / Somebody have mercy / Soothe me / That's it – I quit – I'm movin' on.

Jul 62.	(7") (RCA 1296) <47-8036> **BRING IT ON HOME TO ME. / HAVING A PARTY**		13 17 May62
Oct 62.	(7") (RCA 1310) <47-8088> **NOTHING CAN CHANGE THIS LOVE. / SOMEBODY HAVE MERCY**		12 70 Sep62
Oct 62.	(lp) <lpm 2625> **THE BEST OF SAM COOKE** (compilation)	-	22

– You send me / Only sixteen / Everybody loves to cha cha cha / For sentimental reasons / Wonderful world / Summertime / Chain gang / Twistin' the night away / Sad mood / Having a party / Bring it on home to me.

Jan 63.	(7") (RCA 1327) <47-8129> **SEND ME SOME LOVIN'. / BABY, BABY, BABY**		13 60
Mar 63.	(lp; mono/stereo) (RD/SF 7539) <LPM/LSP 2673> **MR. SOUL**		94

– I wish you love / Willow weep for me / Chains of love / Smoke rings / All the way /

Send me some lovin' / Cry me a river / Driftin' blues / (I love you for) Sentimental reasons / Nothing can change this love / Little girl / These foolish things. *(re-iss. Jul80 on 'RCA Int.'; INTS/INTK 5024)*

May 63. (7") *(RCA 1341)* *<47-8164>* **ANOTHER SATURDAY NIGHT. / LOVE WILL FIND A WAY** | 23 | 10 | Apr63

Aug 63. (7") *(RCA 1361)* *<47-8215>* **FRANKIE AND JOHNNY. / COOL TRAIN** | 30 | 11 | Jul63

Sep 63. (lp; mono/stereo) *(RD/SF 7583)* *<LPM/LSP 2709>* **NIGHT BEAT** | 62
– Nobody knows the trouble I've seen / Lost and lookin' / Mean old world / Please don't drive me away / I lost everything / Get yourself another fool / Little red rooster / Laughin' and clownin' / Trouble blues / You gotta move / Fool's paradise / Shake, rattle and roll. *(cd-iss. Sep95 on 'London'; 528567-2)*

Oct 63. (7") *<47-8247>* **LITTLE RED ROOSTER. / YOU GOTTA MOVE** | - | 11

Nov 63. (7") *(RCA 1367)* **LITTLE RED ROOSTER. / SHAKE RATTLE AND ROLL** | - | -

Feb 64. (7") *(RCA 1386)* *<47-8299>* **GOOD NEWS. / BASIN STREET BLUES** | - | 11 | Jan64

May 64. (lp; mono/stereo) *(RD/SF 7635)* *<LPM/LSP 2899>* **AIN'T THAT GOOD NEWS** | 34 | Mar64
– Ain't that good news / Meet me at Mary's place / Good times / Rome wasn't built in a day / Another Saturday night / Tennessee waltz / change is gonna come / Falling in love / Home / Sittin' in the sun / No second time / The riddle song.

Jun 64. (7") *(RCA 1405)* *<47-8368>* **GOOD TIMES. / TENNESSEE WALTZ** | - | 11 / 35

Oct 64. (7") *<47-8426>* **COUSIN OF MINE. / THAT'S WHERE IT'S AT** | - | 31 / 93

Jan 65. (lp; mono/stereo) *(RD/SF 7674)* *<LPM/LSP 2970>* **SAM COOKE AT THE COPA (live)** | 29 | Oct64
– (opening introduction) / The best things in life are free / Bill Bailey / Nobody knows you when you're down and out / Frankie and Johnny / Medley: Try a little tenderness – (I love you) For sentimental reasons – You send me / If I had a hammer / When I fall in love / This little light of mine / Blowin' in the wind / Tennessee waltz.

—— on 11th of December '64, COOKE was shot dead (see biography)

– posthumous, exploitation, etc. –

Jan 65. (7") *(RCA 1436)* *<47-8486>* **SHAKE. / A CHANGE IS GONNA COME** | - | 7 / 31 / 44

Feb 65. (lp; mono/stereo) *(RD/SF 7730)* *<LPM/LSP 3367>* **SHAKE** | -
– Shake / Yeah man / Win your love for me / Love you most of all / Meet me at Mary's place / I've got the whole world shakin' / A change is gonna come / I'm in the mood for love / I'm just a country boy / You're nobody 'til somebody loves you / Comes love / Ease my troublin' mind.

Apr 65. (7") *(RCA 1452)* *<47-8539>* **IT'S GOT THE WHOLE WORLD SHAKIN'. / (SOMEBODY) EASE MY TROUBLIN' MIND** | - | 41 | Mar65

May 65. (7") *<47-8586>* **WHEN A BOY FALLS IN LOVE. / THE PIPER** | - | 52

Jul 65. (lp; mono/stereo) *<LMP/LSP 3373>* **THE BEST OF SAM COOKE VOLUME 2** (compilation) | -
– Frankie and Johnny / That's where it's at / Shake / Baby, baby, baby / Another Saturday night / Little red rooster / Good news / Cousin of mine / Tennessee waltz / A change is gonna come / Basin Street blues / Love will find a way.

Sep 65. (7") *(RCA 1476)* *<47-8631>* **SUGAR DUMPLING. / BRIDGE OF TEARS** | - | 32 | Jul65

Jan 66. (lp; mono/stereo) *(RD/SF 7764)* *<LPM/LSP 3435>* **TRY A LITTLE LOVE** | - | Oct65
– Try a little love / Don't cry on my shoulder / Bridge of tears / I fall in love every day / You're always on my mind / Almost in your arms / When a boy falls in love / To each his own / Tammy / The gypsy / The little things you do / You send me.

Feb 66. (7") *<47-8751>* **FEEL IT. / THAT'S ALL** | - | 95

Apr 66. (7") *<47-8803>* **LET'S GO STEADY AGAIN. / TROUBLE BLUES** | - | 97

Oct 66. (lp; mono/stereo) *<LPM/LSP 3517>* **THE UNFORGETTABLE SAM COOKE** | -
– I'm gonna forget about you / Sugar dumpling / I ain't gonna cheat on you no more / Soothe me / With you / One more time / Feel it / Wonderful world / It's all right / A whole lotta woman / No one / That's all.

Dec 66. (7") *<47-8934>* **MEET ME AT MARY'S PLACE. / IF I HAD A HAMMER** | - |

– compilations, others, etc. –

also on 'RCA (Victor)' unless stated otherwise

1957. (7"ep) *Keen; <2001>* **SAM COOKE VOL.1** | -
1957. (7"ep) *Keen; <2002>* **SAM COOKE VOL.2** | -
1957. (7"ep) *Keen; <2003>* **SAM COOKE VOL.3** | -
1958. (7"ep) *Keen; <2007>* **ENCORE VOL.1** | -
1958. (7"ep) *Keen; <2008>* **ENCORE VOL.2** | -
1958. (7"ep) *Keen; <2009>* **ENCORE VOL.3** | -
1959. (7"ep) *Keen; <2012>* **TRIBUTE TO THE LADY VOL.1** | -
1959. (7"ep) *Keen; <2013>* **TRIBUTE TO THE LADY VOL.2** | -
1959. (7"ep) *Keen; <2014>* **TRIBUTE TO THE LADY VOL.3** | -
1959. (lp) *Specialty; <SPS 2106>* **THE SOUL STIRRERS FEATURING SAM COOKE** | -
(UK-iss.1965 on 'London'; HA-U 8232)
1960. (7"; with The SOUL STIRRERS) *SAR; <105>* **NEARER TO THEE. / (part 2)** | -
1960. (7"; as L.C. COOKE) *SAR; <112>* **THE LOVER. / SUFFERIN'** | -
1961. (7"; as SAM COOK) *SAR; <122>* **JUST FOR YOU. / MADE FOR ME** | -
1961. (7"; as L.C. COOKE) *<148>* **TAKE ME FOR WHAT I AM. / PUT ME DOWN EASY** | -
1961. (7"ep) *<LPC 126>* **SAM COOKE SINGS** | -
1963. (7"ep) *<EPA 4375>* **ANOTHER SATURDAY NIGHT** | -
1963. (7"ep) *(RCX 7117)* **HEART AND SOUL** | -

1964. (7"ep) *(RCX 7128)* **SWING SWEETLY** | | -
1968. (lp) *<LSP 3991>* **THE MAN WHO INVENTED SOUL** | -
Jul 69. (lp) *RCA Int,; (INTS 1005) / Camden; <2264>* **THE ONE AND ONLY SAM COOKE** | | 1968
1969. (lp) *Camden; <CAS 2392>* **MY KIND OF SOUL** | -
1969. (lp) *Famous; <F-502>* **SAM'S SONGS** | -
1969. (lp) *Famous; <F-505>* **ONLY SIXTEEN** | -
1969. (lp) *Famous; <F-508>* **SO WONDERFUL** | -
1969. (lp) *Famous; <F-509>* **YOU SEND ME** | -
1969. (lp) *Famous; <F-512>* **CHA CHA CHA** | -
1969. (lp) *Specialty; <SPS 2113>* **TWO SIDES OF SAM COOKE** | -
1970. (lp) *Specialty; <SPS 2128>* **THE GOSPEL SOUL OF SAM COOKE VOL.2** | -
1970. (lp) *Camden; <2433>* **SAM COOKE** | -
1970. (lp) *RCA Int.; (INTS 1080)* **THE LATE GREAT SAM COOKE** | -
1970. (7"; with The SOUL STIRRERS) *Specialty; <921>* **MUST JESUS BEAR THE CROSS ALONE** | -
1971. (lp) *Cherie; <1001>* **RIGHT ON** | -
1971. (7") *Cherie; <4501>* **DARLING I NEED YOU NOW. / WIN YOUR LOVE FOR ME** | -
1971. (d-lp) *(DPS 2007)* **THIS IS ...** |
1972. (lp) *Sonet; (SNTF 5009) / Specialty; <SPS 2116>* **THE GOSPEL SOUL OF SAM COOKE VOL.1** | | 1969
1972. (lp) *Trip; <8030>* **GOLDEN SOUNDS** |
1972. (lp) *Up-Front; <UPF 148>* **SAM COOKE** |
1973. (lp) *Up-Front; <UPF 160>* **BILLIE HOLIDAY STORY** |
1973. (7"; with The SOUL STIRRERS) *Specialty; <928>* **CHRIST IS ALL. / JUST ANOTHER DAY** | -
1973. (7") *Specialty; <930>* **THAT'S HEAVEN TO ME. / LORD, REMEMBER ME** | -
1973. (lp) *Camden; <2610>* **UNFORGETTABLE** | -
1974. (lp) *Camden; <0445>* **YOU SEND ME** | -
Mar 76. (lp) *RCA-Starcall; (HY 1030) / <APL1 0899>* **INTERPRETES BILLIE HOLIDAY** | | Nov75
Oct 76. (lp) *(RS 1054)* **GOLDEN AGE OF SAM COOKE** |
1977. (lp) *<AYL1 3863>* **THE BEST OF SAM COOKE** |
Aug 79. (lp/c) *EMI-Nut; (NUTM/TC-NUTM 23)* **WHEN I FALL IN LOVE** |
(re-iss. Feb87 on 'Arena' lp/c; ARA/+C 1007)
Jun 80. (12") *(PE 9511)* **ANOTHER SATURDAY NIGHT. / SOOTHE ME** | | -
Oct 82. (lp/c) *Dakota; (COUNT/ZCCNT 2)* **SAM COOKE** | | -
1983. (d-lp/d-c) *Cambra; (CR/+T 050)* **THE FABULOUS SAM COOKE** |
Apr 84. (lp/c) *Cambra; (CR/+T 117)* **SOLITUDE** | | -
1984. (lp/c) *Premier; (CBR/KCBR 1012)* **TWISTIN' THE NIGHT AWAY** | | -
Feb 85. (7") *Golden Grooves; (G45 44)* **YOU SEND ME. / ONLY SIXTEEN** |
Jun 85. (cd) *(PCD 15181) <5181>* **LIVE AT THE HARLEM SQUARE CLUB, 1963 (live)** |
(cd/c re-iss. Feb90; ND/NK 90454)
Jul 85. (lp/c) *Topline; (TOP/KTOP 125)* **YOU SEND ME** | | -
(cd-iss. Aug87 on 'The Collection'; OR 0017) (re-iss. Jul93 on 'Charly' cd/c; CDCD/CDMC 1093)
1985. (7") *<PB 14146>* **BRING IT ON HOME TO ME. / NOTHING CAN CHANGE THIS LOVE** | -
Feb 86. (7") *(PB 49871)* **WONDERFUL WORLD. / CHAIN GANG** | 2
(12"+=) (PT 49872) – Cupid / A change is gonna come.
Apr 86. (d-lp/d-c/d-cd) *(PL/PK/PD 87127) <7127>* **THE MAN AND HIS MUSIC** | 8 | Mar86
– Meet me at Mary's place / Good times / Shake / Sad mood / Bring it on home to me / That's where it's at / That's heaven to me / Touch the hem of his garment / You send me / I'll come running back to you / Win your love for me / Wonderful world / Cupid / Just for you / Chain gang / Only sixteen / When a boy falls in love / Rome wasn't built in a day / Everybody loves to cha cha cha / Nothing can change this love / Love will find a way / Another Saturday night / Having a party / Twistin' the night away / Somebody have mercy / Good news / Soothe me / A change is gonna come.
Apr 86. (7") *(RCA 49849)* **ANOTHER SATURDAY NIGHT. / LITTLE RED ROOSTER** | 75 | -
(12"+=) (PT 49850) – Frankie and Johnny.
Apr 87. (cd) *Card; (CD 180001)* **WONDERFUL WORLD: BEST OF SAM COOKE** | | -
Apr 87. (lp/c) *Topline; (TOP/KTOP 171)* **SWING OUT BROTHER** | | -
Apr 87. (cd-ep) *Topline; (TOPCD 507)* **YOU SEND ME EP** | | -
May 87. (12"ep) *Perfect; (PER12 8605)* **YOU SEND ME EP** | | -
Sep 87. (cd) *Compact Collection; (9404-2)* **20 GREATEST HITS** | | -
Dec 87. (cd) *Deja Vu; (DVCD 2095)* **SAM COOKE COLLECTION** | | -
Apr 88. (cd) *(CD 90122)* **SAM COOKE – DIAMOND SERIES** | | -
Apr 88. (cd) *(ND 89903)* **WONDERFUL WORLD – THE BEST OF SAM COOKE** | | -
(re-iss. Aug95; same)
Apr 88. (cd/c/lp) *Fame; (CD/TC+/FA 3195)* **WONDERFUL WORLD** | | -
Jul 88. (lp/cd; with The SOUL STIRRERS) *(C5CD 523)* **HEAVEN IS MY HOME** | | -
Feb 89. (lp) *Crusader; (RMB 5615)* **YOU SEND ME** | | -
May 89. (lp/c) *Performance; (PFP/PFC 1008)* **WONDERFUL WORLD** | | -
Jun 89. (cd-ep) *(PD 49455)* **CHAIN GANG EP** | | -
Jul 89. (cd/c/lp) *Instant; (CD/TC+/INS 5001)* **THE WORLD OF SAM COOKE** | | -
Nov 89. (cd/lp; with The SOUL STIRRERS) *Charly-Ace; (CD+/CHD 280)* **IN THE BEGINNING** | | -
Aug 90. (cd) *Graffiti; (GRCD/GRMC 04)* **THE GRAFFITI COLLECTION** | | -
Jun 91. (cd) *Music Club; (MCCD/MCTC 021)* **THE MAGIC OF SAM COOKE** | | -
Nov 91. (cd; with The SOUL STIRRERS) *Charly-Ace; (CDCHD 359)* **SAM COOKE WITH THE SOUL STIRRERS** | | -

May 94. (cd; shared with JACKIE WILSON) *Charly*; *(CDTT 1)* **TWO ON ONE**

Oct 94. (cd/c) *Ariola Express*; *(2/4 95039)* **SAM COOKE**

Alice COOPER

Formed: Initially as a group by VINCENT FURNIER (son of a preacher), Phoenix, Arizona . . . 1965 as The EARWIGS. Together with his partners in musical crime, GLEN BUXTON, MICHAEL BRUCE, DENNIS DUNAWAY and NEAL SMITH, FURNIER relocated to L.A., becoming The SPIDERS and enjoying healthy airplay for their debut single, 'DON'T BLOW YOUR MIND', released on the local 'Santa Cruz' label. After another low key single and a brief name change to NAZZ, the band adopted the improbable moniker of ALICE COOPER (a 17th Century witch, apparently), signing to FRANK ZAPPA's 'Straight' records. Turgid, clumsy cod-psychedelia, the debut album, 'PRETTIES FOR YOU' (1969) didn't bode well, while 'EASY ACTION' (1970) fared little better. Moving to Detroit in 1970, the band were inspired by the Motor City madness of MC5 and The STOOGES, tightening up their sound and developing their theatrical shock tactics. FURNIER simultaneously used the band name for his ghoulish, androgynous alter-ego, infamously embellishing the band's stage show with all manner of sick trickery: simulated hangings, mangled baby dolls, a live snake, mmm . . . nice. Signing to 'Warners' and drafting in BOB EZRIN on production, the band actually started writing material to match the effectiveness of their live shows. This wasn't gloomy, horror soundtrack minimalism, however, it was freewheeling, revved-up rock'n'roll, often with more than a touch of tongue-in-cheek humour. While 'KILLER' probably stands as COOPER's peak achievement, with the hilarious 'UNDER MY WHEELS' and the classic 'BE MY LOVER', the band really hit big with 'SCHOOL'S OUT' (1972). The title track was an irrepressible blast of adolescent-style attitude that made the UK No.1 spot and propelled the album to the upper reaches of the charts on both sides of the Atlantic. The 'ELECTED' single was another hit and the accompanying 'BILLION DOLLAR BABIES' (1973) album made UK and US No.1. 'MUSCLE OF LOVE' (1974) didn't fare quite so well and cracks were beginning to show in the songwriting armoury. COOPER subsequently sacked the rest of the band in the Summer of '74, hiring a cast of musicians that had previously backed up LOU REED. 'WELCOME TO MY NIGHTMARE' (1975; complete with eerie narration by the legendary VINCENT PRICE) was the last great vintage COOPER effort, a macabre concept album that spawned the hit single, 'ONLY WOMEN BLEED'. In contrast to his superfreak, anti-hero stage character, offstage COOPER was becoming something of a celebrity, hobnobbing with the Hollywood elite and even hosting his own TV show, wherein the band shamelessly retreaded past glories. By the end of the decade, his musical output had degenerated into AOR mush and he spent time in rehab for alcohol addiction. His early 80's work was hardly inspiring and even after a new deal with 'M.C.A.', the subsequent albums, 'CONSTRICTOR' and 'RAISE YOUR FIST AND YELL' failed to resurrect the (unclean) spirit of old. The latter did contain the anthemic 'FREEDOM' and the records were an attempt at the heady rock'n'roll of yore, COOPER even resuming the schlock shock for the subsequent tour. However, it was only with the help of hair-rock writer, DESMOND CHILD, that ALICE once again became a major player on the metal scene, the 'POISON' single seeing COOPER return to the Top 10 for the first time since his 70's heyday. The accompanying album, 'TRASH', fared almost as well, although it sounded about as menacing as BON JOVI. 'HEY STOOPID' (1989) consolidated COOPER's newfound success, as did 'THE LAST TEMPTATION' (1994). Things have gone quiet on the recording front of late, although the pro-am golfing COOPER continues to pop up in places where you most expect him, 'Wayne's World' (1992 movie), US chat shows etc, zzzzz . . . . . • **Songwriters:** ALICE wrote / co-wrote with band most of material, also using producer BOB EZRIN. DICK WAGNER to BERNIE TAUPIN also contributed in the 70's. On 'CONSTRICTOR' album, ALICE co-wrote with ROBERTS, some with KELLY and WEGENER. Collaborated with DESMOND CHILD in '89 and JACK PONTI, VIC PEPE, BOB PFEIFER in 1991. Covered:- SUN ARISE (trad.; a Rolf Harris hit) / SEVEN AND SEVEN IS (Love) / FIRE (Jimi Hendrix). • **Trivia:** Film cameo appearances have been:- DIARY OF A HOUSEWIFE (1970) / SGT. PEPPER'S LONELY HEARTS CLUB BAND (1978) / ROADIE (1980) / PRINCE OF DARKNESS (1987) / FREDDIE'S DEAD: THE FINAL NIGHTMARE (1991) he also acted). In 1975 he sang 'I'M FLASH' on the Various Artists concept album 'FLASH FEARLESS VS.THE ZORG WOMEN Pts.5 & 6'.

Album rating: PRETTIES FOR YOU (*5) / EASY ACTION (*5) / LOVE IT TO DEATH (*8) / KILLER (*8) / SCHOOL'S OUT (*7) / BILLION DOLLAR BABIES (*8) / MUSCLE OF LOVE (*6) / WELCOME TO MY NIGHTMARE (*8) / ALICE COOPER GOES TO HELL (*6) / LACE AND WHISKEY (*5) / THE ALICE COOPER SHOW (*6) / FROM THE INSIDE (*6) / FLUSH THE FASHION (*6) / SPECIAL FORCES (*6) / ZIPPER CATCHES SKIN (*6) / DA DA (*6) / CONSTRICTOR (*5) / RAISE YOUR FIST AND YELL (*5) / TRASH (*5) / HEY STOOPID (*5) / BEAST OF ALICE COOPER compilation (*8) / THE LAST TEMPTATION (*5)

The SPIDERS

ALICE COOPER (b.VINCENT DAMON FURNIER, 4 Feb'48, Detroit) – vocals / **GLEN BUXTON** (b.17 Jun'47, Washington DC) – lead guitar / **MICHAEL BRUCE** (b.21 Nov'48, California) – rhythm guitar, keyboards / **DENNIS DUNAWAY** (b.15 Mar'46, California) – bass / **NEAL SMITH** (b.10 Jan'48, Washington DC) – drums

		not iss.	Santa Cruz
1967.	(7") *<SCR 10.003>* **DON'T BLOW YOUR MIND. / NO PRICE TAG**	-	-

		not iss.	Very
1967.	(7") *<001>* **WONDER WHO'S LOVING HER NOW. / LAY DOWN AND DIE, GOODBYE**		-

ALICE COOPER

		Straight	Straight
Dec 69.	(lp) *<(STS 1051)>* **PRETTIES FOR YOU**		Jun69
	– Titanic overture / 10 minutes before the worm / Sing low sweet cheerio / Today Mueller / Living / Fields of regret / No longer umpire / Levity ball / B.B. on Mars / Reflected / Apple bush / Earwigs to eternity / Changing, arranging.		
Jan 70.	(7") *<101>* **LIVING. / REFLECTED**		
Jun 70.	(lp) *<(STS 1061)>* **EASY ACTION**		
	– Mr. and Misdemeaner / Shoe salesman / Still no air / Below your means / Return of the spiders / Laughing at me / Refridgerator heaven / Beautiful flyaway / Lay down and die, goodbye.		
Jun 70.	(7") *<7141>* **CAUGHT IN A DREAM. / EIGHTEEN**	-	
Nov 70.	(7") *<7398>* **RETURN OF THE SPIDERS. / SHOE SALESMAN**	-	
		Straight	Warners
Apr 71.	(7") *(S 7209) <7499>* **EIGHTEEN. / IS IT MY BODY**	21	Feb71
Jun 71.	(lp) *(STS 1065) <1883>* **LOVE IT TO DEATH**	35	Mar71
	– Caught in a dream / Eighteen / Long way to go / Black Juju / Is it my body / Hallowed be my name / Second coming / Ballad of Dwight Fry / Sun arise. (re-iss. *Dec71 on 'Warners' lp/c; K/K4 46177*) – hit UK No.28 in Sep'72.		
		Warners	Warners
Jun 71.	(7") *(7490)* **CAUGHT IN A DREAM. / HALLOWED BE THY NAME**	-	94
Dec 71.	(7") *(K 16127) <7529>* **UNDER MY WHEELS. / DESPERADO** (re-iss. *Aug74; same*)	-	59
Dec 71.	(lp/c) *(K/K4 56005) <2567>* **KILLER**	27	21 Nov71
	– Under my wheels / Be my lover / Halo of flies / Desperado / You drive me nervous / Yeah yeah yeah / Dead babies / Killer. (cd-iss. *Sep89 on 'WEA'; 927255-2*)		
Jan 72.	(7") *<7568>* **BE MY LOVER. / YEAH YEAH YEAH**		49
Feb 72.	(7") *(K 16154)* **BE MY LOVER. / YOU DRIVE ME NERVOUS**	-	
Jul 72.	(7") *(K 16188) <7596>* **SCHOOL'S OUT. / GUTTER CAT**	1	7 May72
Jul 72.	(lp/c) *(K/K4 56007) <2623>* **SCHOOL'S OUT**	4	2 Jun72
	– School's out / Luney tune / Gutter cat vs. the jets / Street fight / Blue Turk / My stars / Public animal No.9 / Alma mater / Grande finale. (cd-iss. *Sep89 on 'WEA'; 927260-2*)		
Oct 72.	(7") *(K 16214) <7631>* **ELECTED. / LUNEY TUNE**	4	26
Feb 73.	(7") *(K 16248) <7673>* **HELLO HURRAY. / GENERATION LANDSLIDE**	6	35 Jan73
Mar 73.	(lp/c) *(K/K4 56013) <2685>* **BILLION DOLLAR BABIES**	1	1
	– Hello hurray / Raped and freezin' / Elected / Billion dollar babies / Unfinished sweet / No more Mr. Nice guy / Generation landslide / Sick things / Mary Ann / I love the dead.		
Apr 73.	(7") *(K 16262) <7691>* **NO MORE MR. NICE GUY. / RAPED AND FREEZIN'**	10	25
Jul 73.	(7") *<7724>* **BILLION DOLLAR BABIES. / MARY ANN**	-	57
Jan 74.	(lp/c) *(K/K4 56018) <2748>* **MUSCLE OF LOVE**	34	10 Dec73
	– Muscle of love / Woman machine / Hard hearted Alice / Man with the golden gun / Big apple dreamin' (hippo) / Never been sold before / Working up a sweat / Crazy little child / Teenage lament '74.		
Jan 74.	(7") *(K 16345) <7762>* **TEENAGE LAMENT '74. / HARD HEARTED ALICE**	12	48 Dec73
Mar 74.	(7") *(K 16345) <7783>* **MUSCLE OF LOVE. / CRAZY LITTLE CHILD**	-	
Jun 74.	(7") *<8023>* **MUSCLE OF LOVE. / I'M EIGHTEEN**	-	
Sep 74.	(lp/c) *(K/K4 56043) <2803>* **ALICE COOPER'S GREATEST HITS** (compilation)		8 Aug74
	– I'm eighteen / Is it my body / Desperado / Under my wheels / Be my lover / School's out / Hello hurray / Elected / No more Mr. Nice guy / Billion dollar babies / Teenage lament '74 / Muscle of love. (cd-iss. *Jun89; K2 56045*)		

---- ALICE sacked rest of band, who became BILLION DOLLAR BABIES. He brought in **DICK WAGNER** – guitar, vocals / **STEVE (DEACON) HUNTER** – guitars / **PRAKASH JOHN** – bass / **PENTII 'Whitey' GLAN** – drums / **JOSEF CHIROWSKI** – drums. (all ex-LOU REED band)

		Anchor	Atlantic
Feb 75.	(7") *(1012) <3280>* **DEPARTMENT OF YOUTH. / COLD ETHYL**		-
Mar 75.	(lp/c) *(ANC L/K 2011) <18130>* **WELCOME TO MY NIGHTMARE**	19	5
	– Welcome to my nightmare / Devil's food / The black widow / Some folks / Only women bleed / Department of youth / Cold Ethyl / Years ago / Steven / The awakening / Escape. *<cd-iss. Sep87 on 'Atlantic'; SD 19157>*		
Apr 75.	(7") *<3254>* **ONLY WOMEN BLEED. / COLD ETHYL**	-	12
Jun 75.	(7") *(1018)* **ONLY WOMEN BLEED. / DEVIL'S FOOD**	-	
Aug 75.	(7") *<3280>* **DEPARTMENT OF YOUTH. / SOME FOLKS**	-	67
Oct 75.	(7") *<3298>* **WELCOME TO MY NIGHTMARE. / COLD ETHYL**	-	45
Nov 75.	(7") *(1025)* **WELCOME TO MY NIGHTMARE. / BLACK WIDOW**	-	-
		Warners	Warners
Jun 76.	(lp/c) *(K/K4 56171) <2896>* **ALICE COOPER GOES TO HELL**	23	27
	– Go to Hell / You gotta dance / I'm the coolest / Didn't we meet / I never cry / Give the kid a break / Guilty / Wake me gently / Wish you were here / I'm always chasing rainbows / Going home.		
Jun 76.	(7") *(K 16792) <8228>* **I NEVER CRY. / GO TO HELL**	-	12
Apr 77.	(7") *<8349>* **YOU AND ME. / IT'S HOT TONIGHT**	-	9
Apr 77.	(7") *(K 16935)* **(NO MORE) LOVE AT YOUR CONVENIENCE. / IT'S HOT TONIGHT**	44	-
May 77.	(lp/c) *(K/K4 56365) <3027>* **LACE AND WHISKEY**	33	42
	– It's hot tonight / Lace and whiskey / Road rats / Damned if you do / You and me / King of the silver screen / Ubangi stomp / (No more) Love at your convenience / I never wrote those songs / My God.		
Jul 77.	(7") *(K 16984)* **YOU AND ME. / MY GOD**	-	-
Jul 77.	(7") *<8448>* **(NO MORE) LOVE AT YOUR CONVENIENCE. / I NEVER WROTE THOSE SONGS**	-	-

---- **FRED MANDEL** – keyboards repl. JOSEF

Dec 77. (lp/c) (K/K4 56439) <3138> **THE ALICE COOPER SHOW (live)**
– Under my wheels / I'm eighteen / Only women / Sick things / Is it my body / I never cry / Billion dollar babies / Devil's food – The black widow / You and me / a. I love the dead – b. Go to hell – c. Wish you were here / School's out.

—— **Alice COOPER** now basically a solo artist with session people, which retaining **MANDEL, DAVEY JOHNSTONE** – guitar (ex-ELTON JOHN) / **MARK VOLMAN + HOWARD KAYLAN** – backing vocals (ex-TURTLES)

Dec 78. (7") (K 17270) <8695> **HOW YOU GONNA SEE ME NOW. / NO TRICKS** `61` `12` Oct78

Dec 78. (lp/c) (K/K4 56577) <3263> **FROM THE INSIDE** `68` `60`
– From the inside / Wish I were born in Beverly Hills / The quiet room / Nurse Rozetta / Millie and Billie / Serious / How you gonna see me now / For Veronica's sake / Jacknife Johnny / Inmates (we're all crazy).

Jan 79. (7") <8760> **FROM THE INSIDE. / NURSE ROZETTA** `-`
above w / **JOHN Lo PRESTI** – bass / **DENNIS CONWAY** – drums

May 80. (lp/c) (K/K4 56805) <3436> **FLUSH THE FASHION** `56` `44`
– Talk talk / Clones (we're all) / Pain / Leather boots / Aspirin damage / Nuclear infected / Grim facts / Model citizen / Dance yourself to death / Headlines.

Jun 80. (7") (K 17598) <49204> **CLONES (WE'RE ALL). / MODEL CITIZEN** `40` May80

Sep 80. (7") <49526> **DANCE YOURSELF TO DEATH. / TALK TALK**

—— now w / **MIKE PINERA + DAVEY JOHNSTONE** – guitar / **DUANE HITCHINGS** – keyboards / **ERIC SCOTT** – bass / **CRAIG KRAMPF** – drums

Sep 81. (7") <49780> **WHO DO YOU THINK WE ARE. / YOU WANT IT, YOU GOT IT** `-`

Sep 81. (lp/c) (K/K4 56927) <3581> **SPECIAL FORCES** `96`
– Who do you think we are / Seven and seven is / Prettiest cop in the block / Don't talk old to me / Generation landslide '81 / Skeletons in the closet / You want it, you got it / You look good in rags / You're a movie / Vicious rumours.

Feb 82. (7") (K 17924) <49848> **SEVEN AND SEVEN IS (live). / GENERATION LANDSLIDE '81 (live)** `62`

May 82. (7"/7"pic-d) (K 17940/+M) **FOR BRITAIN ONLY. / UNDER MY WHEELS (live)** `66`
(12"+=) (K 17940T) – Who do you think we are (live) / Model citizen (live).

—— now w / **MIKE PINERA + DAVEY JOHNSTONE** – guitar / **DUANE HITCHINGS** – keyboards / **ERIC SCOTT** – bass / **CRAIG KRAMPF** – drums

Oct 82. (7") <29928> **I LIKE GIRLS. / ZORRO'S ASCENT** `-`

Oct 82. (lp/c) (K/K4 57021) <23719-1/-4> **ZIPPER CATCHES SKIN**
– Zorro's ascent / Make that money (Scrooge's song) / I am the future / No baloney homosapiens / Adaptable (anything for you) / I like girls / Remarkably insincere / Tag, you're it / I better be good / I'm alive (that was the day my dead pet returned to save my life).

—— **COOPER + WAGNER** re-united w / **EZRIN + PRAKASH** and recruited **GRAHAN SHAW** – synth / **JOHN ANDERSON + RICHARD KOLINGA** – drums

Mar 83. (7") (K 15004) **I AM THE FUTURE (remix). / ZORRO'S ASCENT**

Mar 83. (7") <29928> **I AM THE FUTURE (remix). / TAG, YOU'RE IT** `-`

Nov 83. (lp/c) (923969-1/-4) <23969-1/-4> **DA DA** `93`
– Da da / Enough's enough / Former Lee Warner / No man's land / Dyslexia / Scarlet and Sheba / I love America / Fresh blood / Pass the gun around.

Nov 83. (12"m) (ALICE 1T) **I LOVE AMERICA. / FRESH BLOOD / PASS THE GUN AROUND**

—— band now consisted of **KANE ROBERTS** (b.16 Jan'59) – guitar, vocals / **DAVID ROSENBERG** – drums / **PAUL DELPH** – keyboards, vocals / **DONNIE KISSELBACK** – bass, vocals / **KIP WINGER**

	M.C.A.	M.C.A.

Oct 86. (7") (MCA 1090) <52904> **HE'S BACK (THE MAN BEHIND THE MASK). / BILLION DOLLAR BABIES** `61`
(12"+=) (MCAT 1090) – I'm eighteen.

Oct 86. (lp/c) (MCF/+C 3341) <5761> **CONSTRICTOR** `41` `59`
– Teenage Frankenstein / Give it up / Thrill my gorilla / Life and death of the party / Simple disobedience / The world needs guts / Trick bag / Crawlin' / The great American success story / He's back (the man behind the mask).

Apr 87. (7") (MCA 1113) **TEENAGE FRANKENSTEIN / SCHOOL'S OUT (live)** `-`
(12"+=) (MCAT 1113) – Only women bleed.

—— **KEN K. MARY** – drums repl.ROSENBERG / **PAUL HOROWITZ** – keyboards, repl. DELPH + KISSELBACH.

Oct 87. (lp/pic-lp/c) (MCF/+P/C 3392) <42091> **RAISE YOUR FIST AND YELL** `48` `73`
– Freedom / Lock me up / Give the radio back / Step on you / Not that kind of love / Prince of darkness / Time to kill / Chop, chop, chop / Gail / Roses on white lace. (cd-iss. May88; DMCF 3392)

Mar 88. (7") (MCA 1241) <53212> **FREEDOM. / TIME TO KILL** `50`
(12"+=/12"s+=) (MCA T/X 1241) – School's out (live).

—— retained **KIP WINGER** bringing in guests **JON BON JOVI, RICHIE SAMBORA** plus **JOE PERRY, TOM HAMILTON, JOEY KRAMER** etc.

—— **COOPER + WAGNER** re-united w / **EZRIN + PRAKASH** and recruited **GRAHAN SHAW** – synth / **JOHN ANDERSON + RICHARD KOLINGA** – drums

	Epic	Epic

1988. (7") <08114> **I GOT A LINE ON YOU. / LIVIN' ON THE EDGE** `-`

Jul 89. (7") (655061-7) <68958> **POISON. / TRASH** `2` `7` Sep89
(12"+=) (655061-8) – The ballad of Dwight Fry.
(cd-s++=) (655061-2) – I got a line on you (live).
(12"+=) (655061-9) – Cold Ethyl (live).

Aug 89. (lp/c/cd) (465130-1/-4/-2) <45137> **TRASH** `2` `20`
– Poison / Spark in the dark / House of fire / Why trust you / Only my heart talkin' / Bed of nails / This maniac's in love with you / Trash / Hell is living without you / I'm your gun. (re-iss. Sep93 cd/c; same)

Sep 89. (7"/7"green/7"red/7"blue/c-s) (ALICE/+G/R/B/M 3) **BED OF NAILS. / I'M YOUR GUN** `38` `-`
(12"+=/12"w-poster/12"pic-d+=) (ALICE T/Q/P 3) – Go to Hell (live).
(cd-s++=) (ALICEC 3) – Only women bleed (live).

Dec 89. (7"/7"sha-pic-d/c-s) (ALICE/+P/M 4) **HOUSE OF FIRE. / THIS MANIAC'S IN LOVE WITH YOU** `65` `-`

(12"+=/cd-s+=) (ALICE T/C 4) – Billion dollar babies (live) / Under my wheels (live).
(7"sha-pic-d) (ALICEX 4) – ('A'side) / POISON (live).
(12"pic-d+=/12"w-poster+=) (ALICE S/Q 4) – Spark in the dark (live) / Under my wheels (live).

Jan 90. (c-s) <73085> **HOUSE OF FIRE / BALLAD OF DWIGHT FRY** `-` `56`

Apr 90. (cd-s) <73268> **ONLY MY HEART TALKIN'. / UNDER MY WHEELS (live)** `-` `89`

—— (Mar'90) touring band **PETE FRIEZZEN** – guitar / **AL PITRELLI** – guitar / **TOMMY CARADONNA** – bass / **DEREK SHERINIAN** – keyboards / **JONATHAN MOVER** – drums

—— (1991 sessions) **STEVE VAI, JOE SATRIANI, STEF BURNS** (on tour), **VINNIE MOORE, MICK MARS, SLASH** – guitars / **HUGH McDONALD, NIKKI SIXX** – bass / **MICKEY CURRY** – drums / **ROBERT SALLEY, JOHN WEBSTER** – keyboards / **STEVE CROES** – synclaiver

Jun 91. (7"/c-s) (656983-7/-4) **HEY STOOPID. / WIND-UP TOY** `21` `-`
(12"+=/12"pic-d+=/cd-s+=) (656983-6/-8/-9) – It rained all night.

Jun 91. (cd/c/lp) (468416-2/-4/-1) <46786> **HEY STOOPID** `4` `47`
– Hey stoopid / Love's a loaded gun / Snakebite / Burning our bed / Dangerous tonight / Might as well be on Mars / Feed me Frankenstein / Hurricane years / Little by little / Die for you / Dirty dreams / Wind-up toy.

Jul 91. (c-s) <73845> **HEY STOOPID. / IT RAINED ALL NIGHT** `-` `78`

Sep 91. (7"/c-s) (657438-7/-4) **LOVE'S A LOADED GUN. / FIRE** `38`
(12"+=/12"pic-d+=/sha-pic-d-s+=) (657438-6/-8/-9) – Eighteen (live '91).

Jun 92. (7"/c-s) (658092-7/-4) **FEED MY FRANKENSTEIN. / BURNING OUR BED** `27`
(12"pic-d+=/cd-s+=) (658092-6/-2) – Poison / Only my heart talkin'.
(cd-s+=) (658092-5) – Hey stoopid / Bed of nails.

—— w / **STEF BURNS** – guitar, vocals / **GREG SMITH** – bass, vocals / **DEREK SHERINIAN** – keyboards, vocals / **DAVID VOSIKKINEN** – drums

May 94. (c-s) (660347-4) **LOST IN AMERICA. / HEY STOOPID (live)** `22`
(12"pic-d+=/pic-cd-s+=) (660347-2) – Billion dollar babies (live) / No more Mr.Nice Guy (live).

Jun 94. (cd/c/lp) (476594-2/-4/-1) <52771> **THE LAST TEMPTATION** `6` `68`
(w /free comic)
– Sideshow / Nothing's free / Lost in America / Bad place alone / You're my temptation / Stolen prayer / Unholy war / Lullaby / It's me / Cleansed by fire.

Jul 94. (c-s) (660563-4) **IT'S ME. / BAD PLACE ALONE** `34`
(12"pic-d+=/pic-cd-s+=) (660563-2) – Poison / Sick things.

Oct 95. (cd/c) (480845-2/-4) **CLASSICKS** (compilation)
– Poison / Hey stoopid / Feed my Frankenstein / Love's a loaded gun / Stolen prayer / House of fire / Lost in America / It's me / Under my wheels (live) / Billion dollar babies (live) / I'm eighteen (live) / No more Mr. Nice guy (live) / Only women bleed (live) / School's out (live) / Fire.

—— now with **REB BEACH** – guitar / **RYAN ROXIE** – guitar / **PAUL TAYLOR** – keyboards / **TODD JENSEN** – bass / **JIMMT DeGRASSO** – drums / guests; SAMMY HAGAR, BOB ZOMBIE + SLASH

	E.M.I.	Capitol

Jun 97. (cd) (CTM CD/MC 331) **A FISTFUL OF ALICE (live)**
– School's out / Under my wheels / I'm eighteen / Desperado / Lost in America / Teenage lament '74 / I never cry / Poison / No more Mr. Nice guy / Welcome to my nightmare / Only women bleed / Feed my Frankenstein / Elected / Is anyone home? (studio).

– compilations, others, etc. –

on 'Warners' unless otherwise stated

Mar 73. (7") **BE MY LOVER. / UNDER MY WHEELS** `-` `-`

Jun 73. (d-lp) (K 66021) **SCHOOLDAYS** (1st-2 lp's)

Feb 75. (7"ep) (K 16409) **SCHOOL'S OUT / NO MORE MR.NICE GUY. / BILLION DOLLAR BABIES / ELECTED** `-`

Feb 76. (7") (K 16287) **SCHOOL'S OUT. / ELECTED** `-`
(re-iss. Dec80; same) (re-iss. Sep85 on 'Old Gold'; OG 9519)

Dec 77. (7"ep/12"ep) Anchor; (ANE 7/12 001) **DEPARTMENT OF YOUTH EP**
– Department of youth / Welcome to my nightmare / Black widow / Only women bleed.

1978. (7") **I'M EIGHTEEN. / SCHOOL'S OUT** `-` `-`

Apr 84. (pic-lp) Design; (PXLP 3) **ROCK'N'ROLL REVIVAL: TORONTO LIVE '69 (live)** `-`
(re-iss. Apr86 as 'FREAKOUT SONG' on 'Showcase'; SHLP 115)

Apr 87. (m-lp/c) Thunderbolt; (THBM/+C 005) **LADIES MAN (live'69)** `-`
(cd-iss. Aug88; CDTHBM 005) (re-iss cd.Jun91; same) (cd re-iss. Aug98 on 'MagMid'; MM 011)

Dec 89. (lp/c)(cd) W.E.A.; (WX 331/+C)(241781-2) **THE BEAST OF ALICE COOPER**
– School's out / Under my wheels / Billion dollar babies / Be my lover / Desperado / Is it my body? / Only women bleed / Elected / I'm eighteen / Hello hurray / No more Mr. Nice guy / Teenage lament '74 / Muscle of love / Department of youth.

Jul 90. (cd-box) Enigma; (773 362-2) **PRETTIES FOR YOU** `-`

Jul 90. (cd-box) Enigma; (773 391-2) **EASY ACTION** `-`

May 92. (lp/cd) Edsel; (NEST/+CD 903) **LIVE AT THE WHISKEY A GO GO, 1969 (live)** `-`

Oct 92. (cd) Pickwick; (SMA 054) **ROCK LEGENDS VOL.2** `-`

Apr 93. (cd) Pulsar; (PULS 010) **NOBODY LIKES ME** `-`

Sep 94. (cd) Wisepack; (LECD 085) **LEGENDS IN MUSIC** `-`

Apr 99. (4xcd-box) Rhino; <(8122 75680-2)> **THE LIFE AND CRIMES OF ALICE COOPER** `-`

Julian COPE

Born: 21 Oct'57, Bargeld, Wales although he was raised in Liverpool, England. His first foray into the music business was with CRUCIAL THREE, alongside IAN McCULLOCH and PETE WYLIE. In the Autumn of '78 he formed The TEARDROP EXPLODES, originally named A SHALLOW

MADNESS with MICK FINKLER and PAUL SIMPSON. In late '78 a deal was inked with local UK indie label, 'Zoo,' and after three critically acclaimed singles, they transferred to the major label, 'Mercury,' in July 1980. They scored their first hit with 'WHEN I DREAM', from the classic album, Top 30 'KILIMANJARO'. Early in 1981, they cashed-in when 'REWARD' delivered them a Top tenner. 'TREASON', the next 45, didn't emulate this feat, although it still managed a Top 20 placing. Their second album, 'WILDER' was another commercial success, although it lacked the bite of its predecessor. A few minor hits followed over the next year and a bit, but it was clear JULIAN was gearing up for a solo career. Remaining with 'Mercury' records, he released two albums in 1984, 'WORLD SHUT YOUR MOUTH' and 'FRIED', both receiving a lukewarm response from the music press. He then signed for 'Island' in 1985, leaving behind the unissued (until 1990) 'SKELLINGTON' lp. Around the same time he suffered a marriage break-up and drug problems, although he re-married in 1986. Re-emerging triumphantly in 1986, he scored with the Top 20 hit 45, 'WORLD SHUT YOUR MOUTH' (curiously enough, the song wasn't included on the 1984 album of the same name). The single was a taster for the following year's comeback album 'SAINT JULIAN', a record which almost gave him his first solo top ten hit. A disappointing pop album, 'MY NATION UNDERGROUND', lent his street cred a bitter blow and he retreated somewhat with two (meant for mail-order) 1990 albums 'SKELLINGTON' & 'DROOLIAN'. He returned in fine fashion a year later with the splendid double, 'PEGGY SUICIDE', a record that targeted pollution and even the dreadful Tory poll tax (something he protested against vehemently). In 1992, he brought back his old influences (CAN, FAUST, "Kraut-rock") with 'JEHOVAKILL'. Creatively, the album was an admirable effort although it bombed both commercially and critically. This was his last for 'Island', who dropped him unceremoniously after he recorded the 'RITE' cd-album for German release. In 1994, he signed with 'Echo' and returned with two mediocre and great albums respectively; 'AUTOGEDDON' & '20 MOTHERS' (1995). • **Style:** Keyboard-biased (TEARDROP EXPLODES) were mostly influenced by 60's pop psychedelia, sounding like a modern, post-new wave SCOTT WALKER. On-stage antics like cutting his stomach (IGGY POP-like), and singing perched on a high pole, saw him develop a weird new character. Often he perfomed through his alter-ego (SQWUBBSY a seven foot giant). • **Songwriters:** COPE penned except; READ IT IN BOOKS (co-with; Ian McCulloch). He wrote all material, except NON-ALIGNMENT PACT (Pere Ubu) / BOOKS (Teardrop Explodes). • **Trivia:** The album DROOLIAN, was released as part of a campaign to free from jail ROKY ERICKSON (ex-13th FLOOR ELEVATORS). In '90, COPE took part in the Anti-Poll tax march from Brixton to Trafalgar Square.

Album rating: Teardrop Explodes: KILIMANJARO (*9) / WILDER (*7) / EVERYBODY WANTS TO SHAG THE TEARDROP EXPLODES posthumous (*7) / PIANO early (*4) / Julian Cope: WORLD SHUT YOUR MOUTH (*7) / FRIED (*7) / SAINT JULIAN (*7) / MY NATION UNDERGROUND (*8) / SKELLINGTON (*7) / DROOLIAN (*7) / PEGGY SUICIDE (*8) / JEHOVAHKILL (*5) / AUTOGEDDON (*6) / 20 MOTHERS (*8) / FLOORED GENIUS: THE BEST OF JULIAN COPE & THE TEARDROP EXPLODES 1979-1991 compilation (*8) / FLOORED GENIUS, VOL.2 (1983-91) compilation (*7)

TEARDROP EXPLODES

JULIAN COPE (b.21 Oct'57, Bargoed, Wales) – vocals, bass / **PAUL SIMPSON** – keyboards / **MICK FINKLER** – guitar / **GARY DWYER** – drums

			Zoo	not iss.
Feb 79.	(7"m) (CAGE 003) **SLEEPING GAS. / CAMERA CAMERA / KIRBY WORKERS' DREAM FADES**		☐	-

— **GERARD QUINN** – keyboards repl. SIMPSON who formed The WILD SWANS

| May 79. | (7") (CAGE 005) **BOUNCING BABIES. / ALL I AM IS LOVING YOU** | | ☐ | |

— **DAVID BALFE** – keyboards (ex-LORI & THE CHAMELEONS, ex-BIG IN JAPAN, ex-THOSE NAUGHTY LUMPS) repl. QUINN who joined The WILD SWANS

| Mar 80. | (7") (CAGE 008) **TREASON (IT'S JUST A STORY). / READ IT IN BOOKS** | | ☐ | - |

— **ALAN GILL** – guitar (ex-DALEK I) repl. FINKLER now (COPE, DWYER, BALFE + GILL)

			Mercury	Mercury
Sep 80.	(7") (TEAR 1) **WHEN I DREAM. / KILIMANJARO**		47	☐
Oct 80.	(lp) (6359 035) <4016> **KILIMANJARO**		24	☐

– Ha, ha, I'm drowning / Sleeping gas / Treason (it's just a story) / Second head / Poppies in the field / Brave boys keep their promises / Bouncing babies / Books / Thief of Baghdad / When I dream. (re-iss. Mar81 lp/c +=; 6359/7150 035) – Reward. (re-iss. Jul84 lp/c; PRICE/PRIMC 59) (re-iss. May89 lp/c/cd; 836 897-1/-4/-2)
(below trumpet by RAY MARTINEZ)

Jan 81.	(7") (TEAR 2) **REWARD. / STRANGE HOUSE IN THE SNOW**		6	☐
Apr 81.	(7") (TEAR 3) **TREASON (IT'S JUST A STORY). / USE ME**		18	☐
	(12"+=) – Traison (c'est juste une histoire).			
Jun 81.	(7") (TEAR 4) **POPPIES IN THE FIELD. / HA HA I'M DROWNING**			☐
	(d7"+=) (TEAR 44) – Bouncing babies / Read it in books.			

— **TROY TATE** – guitar, vocals (ex-INDEX, ex-SHAKE) repl. GILL

| Sep 81. | (7") (TEAR 5) **PASSIONATE FRIEND. / CHRIST VS. WARHOL** | | 25 | ☐ |

— on session/gigs **ALFIE ALGIUS** (b.Malta) – bass / **JEFF HAMMER** – keyboards

| Nov 81. | (lp/c) (6359/7150 056) <4035> **WILDER** | | 29 | ☐ |

– Bent out of shape / Tiny children / The culture bunker / Falling down around me / Passionate friend / Colours fly away / Pure joy / Seven views of Jerusalem / The great dominions / Like Leila Khaled said / . . .And the fighting takes over. (re-iss. Jun87 lp/c; PRICE/PRIMC 112) (re-iss. May89 lp/c/cd; 836 896-1/-4/-2)

| Nov 81. | (7") (TEAR 6) **COLOURS FLY AWAY. / WINDOW SHOPPING FOR A NEW CROWN OF THORNS** | | 54 | ☐ |
| | (12"+=) (TEAR 6-12) – East of the equator. | | | |

— **DAVID BALFE** returned

— **RON FRANCOIS** – bass (ex-SINCEROS) repl. guests

| Jun 82. | (7"/7"g-f) (TEAR 7/+G) **TINY CHILDREN. / RACHEL BUILT A STEAMBOAT** | | 44 | ☐ |
| | (12"+=) (TEAR 7-12) – Sleeping gas (live). | | | |

— now trio of **COPE, DWYER + BALFE** plus session man **FRANCOIS**

— TROY TATE went solo and joined FASHION

| Mar 83. | (7") (TEAR 8) **YOU DISAPPEAR FROM VIEW. / SUFFOCATE** | | 41 | ☐ |
| | (d7"+=/12"+=) (TEAR 88/8-12) – Soft enough for you / Ouch monkey's / The in-psychlopedia. | | | |

— Disbanded early '83. BALFE went into producing films and music. JULIAN COPE went solo augmented by DWYER.

– compilations, others, etc. –

Jun 85.	(7") Mercury; (TEAR 9) **REWARD (remix). / TREASON (IT'S JUST A STORY)**		☐	-
	(12"+=) (TEAR 9-12) – Strange house in the snow / Use me.			
Jan 90.	(7") Fontana; (DROP 1) **SERIOUS DANGER. / SLEEPING GAS**		☐	-
	(12"+=)(c-s+=)/cd-s+=) (DROP 1-12)(DRO MC/CD 1) – Seven views of Jerusalem.			
Mar 90.	(cd/c/lp) Fontana; (842 439-2/-4/-1) **EVERYBODY WANTS TO SHAG THE TEARDROP EXPLODES** (long lost 3rd album)		72	-

– Ouch monkey's / Serious danger / Metranil Vavin / Count to ten and run forever / In-psychlopaedia / Soft enough for you / You disappear from view / The challenger / Not only my friend / Sex / Terrorist / Strange house in the snow.

Apr 90.	(7") Fontana; (DROP 2) **COUNT TO TEN AND RUN FOR COVER. / REWARD**		☐	-
	(12"+=)(cd-s+=) (DROP 2-12)(DROCD 2) – Poppies / Khaled said.			
Jan 91.	(cd/c/lp) Document; (DCD/DMC/DLP 004) **PIANO**		☐	-

– (early 'Zoo' material)

JULIAN COPE

with **GARY DWYER** / **STEVE CREASE + ANDREW EDGE** – drums / **STEPHEN LOWELL** – lead guitar / **RON FRANCOIS** – bass / **KATE ST. JOHN** – oboe

			Mercury	Mercury
Nov 83.	(7") (COPE 1) **SUNSHINE PLAYROOM. / HEY HIGH CLASS BUTCHER**		64	☐
	(12"+=) (COPE 1-12) – Wreck my car / Eat the poor.			
Feb 84.	(lp/c) (MERL/+C 37) **WORLD SHUT YOUR MOUTH**		40	☐

– Bandy's first jump / Metranil Vavin / Strasbourg / An elegant chaos / Quizmaster / Kolly Kibber's birthday / Sunshine playroom / Head hang low / Pussy face / The greatness and perfection of love / Lunatic and fire pistol. (cd-iss. 1986; 818 365-2)

Mar 84.	(7") (MER 155) **THE GREATNESS AND PERFECTION OF LOVE. / 24a VELOCITY CRESCENT**		52	☐
	(12"+=) (MERX 155) – Pussyface.			
Nov 84.	(lp/c) (MERL/+C 48) **FRIED**		87	☐

– Reynard the fox / Bill Drummond said / Laughing boy / Me singing / Sunspots / Me singing / Bloody Assizes / Search party / O king of chaos / Holy love / Torpedo. (cd-iss. 1986; 822 832-2)

| Feb 85. | (7") (MER 182) **SUNSPOTS. / I WENT ON A CHOURNEY** | | | ☐ |
| | (d7"+=) (MER 182-2) – Mik mak mok / Land of fear. | | | |

— **COPE** recruited Americans **DONALD ROSS SKINNER** – guitar / **JAMES ELLER** – bass / **DOUBLE DE HARRISON** – keyboards / **CHRIS WHITTEN** – drums

			Island	Island
Sep 86.	(7") (IS 290) <99479> **WORLD SHUT YOUR MOUTH. / UMPTEENTH UNNATURAL BLUES**		19	84 Feb87
	(d7"+=) (ISB 290) – ('A'-Trouble Funk remix) / Transportation.			
	(c-s+=) (CIS 290) – I've got levitation / Non-alignment pact.			
	(12"++=) (12IS 290) – (all extra above).			
Jan 87.	(7") (IS 305) **TRAMPOLENE. / DISASTER**		☐	
	(7"ep+=/12"ep+=) (ISW/12IS 305) – Mock Turtle / Warwick the kingmaker.			
Feb 87.	(m-lp) <90560> **JULIAN COPE**		-	☐

– World shut your mouth / Transportation / Umpteenth unnatural blues / Non-alignment pact / I've got levitation.

| Mar 87. | (lp/c/cd) (ILPS/ICT/CID 9861) <90571> **SAINT JULIAN** | | 11 | ☐ |

– Trampolene / Shot down / Eve's volcano (covered in sin) / Spacehopper / Planet ride / Trampolene / World shut your mouth / Saint Julian / Pulsar NX / Space hopper / Screaming secrets / A crack in the clouds. (re-iss. Aug91 cd)(c; IMCD 137)(ICM 2023)

Apr 87.	(7") (IS 318) **EVE'S VOLCANO (COVERED IN SIN). / ALMOST BEAUTIFUL CHILD**		☐	
	(12"+=) (12IS 318) – Pulsar NX (live) / Shot down (live).			
	(12"+=) (12ISX 318) – Spacehopper – Annexe) / ('B'side; pt.II).			
	(cd-s+=) (CID 318) – (all 3 extra above).			

— **DAVE PALMER** – drums (studio) / **MIKE JOYCE** – drums (tour) repl. WHITTEN / added **RON FAIR** – keyboards / **ROOSTER COSBY** – percussion, some drums

Sep 88.	(7") (IS 380) **CHARLOTTE ANNE. / CHRISTMAS MOURNING**		35	☐
	(12"+=/12"pic-d+=/pic-cd-s+=) (12IS/12ISP/CIDP 380) – Books / A question of temptation.			
Oct 88.	(lp/c/cd) (ILPS/ICT/CID 9918) <91025> **MY NATION UNDERGROUND**		42	☐

– 5 o'clock world / Vegetation / Charlotte Anne / My nation underground / China doll / Someone like me / Easter everywhere / I'm not losing sleep / The great white hoax. (re-iss. Aug91 cd)(c; IMCD 138)(ICM 9918)

Nov 88.	(7") (IS 399) **5 O'CLOCK WORLD. / S.P.Q.R.**		42	☐
	(10"+=/12"+=/pic-cd-s+=) (10IS/12IS/CIDP 399) – Reynard in Tokyo (extended live).			
Jun 89.	(7") (IS 406) **CHINA DOLL. / CRAZY FARM ANIMAL**		53	☐
	(10"+=/10"pic-d+=/12"+=) (10IS/10ISP/12IS 406) – Desi.			
	(cd-s++=) (CID 406) – Rail on.			

— **COPE** retained **SKINNER & COSBY** plus **J.D. HASSINGER** – drums / **TIM** – keyboards / **BRAN** – bass (both of Guernsey)

Jan 91. (7"/c-s) *(IS/CIS 483)* **BEAUTIFUL LOVE. / PORT OF SAINTS** `32`
(12"+=/cd-s+=) *(12IS/CID 483)* – Love L.U.V. / Unisex cathedral.
(12"pink+=) *(12ISX 483)* – Love L.U.V. / Dragonfly.

Mar 91. (cd/c/d-lp) *(CID/ICT/ILPSD 9977) <848338-2/-4>* **PEGGY SUICIDE** `23`
– Pristeen / Double vegetation / East easy rider / Promised land / Hanging out & hung up on the line / Safesurfer / If you loved me at all / Drive, she said / Soldier blue / You . . . / Not raving but drowning / Head / Leperskin / Beautiful love / Uptight / Western Front 1992 CE / Hung up & hanging out to dry / The American Lite / Las Vegas basement. *(cd re-iss. Aug94; IMCD 188)*

Apr 91. (7"/c-s) *(IS/CIS 492)* **EAST EASY RIDER. / BUTTERFLY E** `51`
(12"+=/cd-s+=) *(12IS/CID 492)* – Almost live / Little donkey.
(12"pic-d+=) *(12ISX 492)* – Easty Risin' / Ravebury stones.

Jul 91. (7"/c-s) *(IS/CIS 497)* **HEAD. / BAGGED – OUT KEN** `57`
(12"+=/cd-s+=) *(12IS/CID 497)* – Straw dogs / Animals at all.

Oct 92. (7"/c-s) *(IS/CIS 545)* **FEAR LOVES THE SPACE. / SIZEWELL B.** `42`
(12"pic-d+=) *(12ISX 545)* – I have always been here before / Gogmagog.

Oct 92. (cd/c/d-lp) *(<514052-2/-4/-1>)* **JEHOVAHKILL** `20` Dec92
– Soul desert / No harder shoulder to cry on / Akhenaten / The mystery trend / Upwards at 45° / Cut my friends down / Necropolis / Slow rider / Gimme back my flag / Poet is priest / Julian H Cope / The subtle energies commission / Fa-fa-fa-fine / Fear loves this place / Peggy Suicide is missing. *(cd re-iss. Aug94; IMCD 189)*

—— Next was last in the 90's album trilogy about pollution. Its theme this time was the car, (coincidentally he had just passed his driving test). It featured usual musicians.

	Echo	American

Jul 94. (cd/c/lp) *(ECH CD/MC/LP 001) <45705>* **AUTOGEDDON** `16` Aug94
– Autogeddon blues / Madmax / Don't call me Mark Chapman / I gotta walk / Ain't no gettin' round gettin' round / Paranormal in the West Country (medley): i) Paranormal pt.1, ii) Archdrude's roadtrip. iii) Kar-ma-kanik / Ain't but the one way / S.t.a.r.c.a.r. *(cd re-iss. Mar99; same)*

Aug 95. (7"yellow/c-s) *(ECS/+MC 11)* **TRY TRY TRY. / WESSEXY** `24` –
(cd-s+=) *(ECSCD 11)* – Baby, let's play vet / Don't jump me, mother.

Aug 95. (cd/c/d-lp) *(ECH CD/MC/LP 005)* **20 MOTHERS** `20` –
– Wheelbarrow man / I wandered lonely as a child / Try try try / Stone circles 'n' you / Queen – Mother / I'm your daddy / Highway to the sun / 1995 / By the light of the Silbury moon / Adam and Eve hit the road / Just like Pooh Bear / Girl-call / Greedhead detector / Don't take roots / Senile get / The lonely guy / Cryingbabiessleeplessnights / Leli B. / Road of dreams / When I walk through the land of fear.

	Echo	Cooking Vinyl

Jul 96. (7"white-ep/cd-ep) *(ECS/+CDX 022)* **I COME FROM ANOTHER PLANET, BABY. / HOW DO I UNDERSTAND MY MOTORMAN? / IF I COULD DO IT ALL OVER AGAIN, I'D DO IT OVER YOU** `34` –
(cd-s) *(ECSCD 022)* – Ambulance: Weesex post-ambient therapy.

Sep 96. (7"white) *(ECS 025)* **PLANETARY SIT-IN. / CUMMER IN SUMMERTIME / TORCH** `34` –
(cd-s) *(ECSCX 025)* – ('A'-Radio sit-in mixes).

Oct 96. (cd/c/lp) *(ECH CD/MC/LP 12) <9007>* **INTERPRETER** `39` Feb97
– I come from another planet, baby / I've got my TV and my pills / Planetary sit-in / Since I lost my head, it's awl-right / Cheap new age fix / Battle for the trees / Arthur / Spacerock with me / Re-directed male / Maid of constant sorrow / Loveboat / Dust.

– compilations, others, etc. –

Feb 85. (7"; as RABBI JOSEPH GORDON) *Bam Caruso; (NRICO 30)* **COMPETITION. / BELIEF IN HIM** –

May 90. (cd/lp) *Copeco-Zippo; (JUCD/JULP 89)* **SKELLINGTON** (1985 lost lp) –
– Doomed / Beaver / Me & Jimmy Jones / Robert Mitchum / Out of my mind on dope and speed / Don't crash here / Everything playing at once / Little donkey / Great white wonder / Incredibly ugly girl / No how, no why, no way, no where, no when / Comin' soon.

Jul 90. (cd/lp) *Mofo-Zippo; (MOFOCO CD/LP 90)* **DROOLIAN** –

Jul 92. (c-s/7") *Island; (C+/IS 534)* **WORLD SHUT YOUR MOUTH (remix). / DOOMED** `44`
(12"+=/cd-s+=) *(12/CD IS 534)* – Reynard the fox / The elevators / Levitation.

Aug 92. (cd/c/d-lp) *Island; (CID/ICT/ILPSD 8000)* **FLOORED GENIUS – THE BEST OF JULIAN COPE AND THE TEARDROP EXPLODES 1981-1991** `22`
– Reward / Treason / Sleeping gas / Bouncing babies / Passionate friend / The great dominions (; all TEARDROP EXPLODES) / The greatness & perfection of love / An elegant chaos / Sunspots / Reynard the fox / World shut your mouth / Trampolene / Spacehopper / Charlotte Anne / China doll / Out of my mind on dope & speed / Jellypop perky Jean / Beautiful love / East easy rider / Safesurfer.

Nov 92. (d-cd) *Island; (ITSCD 11)* **SAINT JULIAN / MY NATION UNDERGROUND** –

Nov 93. (cd/lp) *Night Tracks; (CD/LP NT 003)* **BEST OF THE BBC SESSIONS 1983-91 (FLOORED GENIUS VOL.2)** –

Jun 97. (cd) *Island; (IMCD 251)* **THE FOLLOWERS OF SAINT JULIAN**

Feb 99. (cd) *Island; (IMCD 260)* **LEPER SKIN (AN INTRODUCTION TO JULIAN COPE)**

Chris CORNELL (see under ⇒ SOUNDGARDEN)

CORNERSHOP

Formed: Preston, England . . . 1987, evolving from GENERAL HAVOC by Asian songwriting brothers, TJINDER and AVTAR SINGH. They first came to attention of the music press late in 1992, when they publicly derided MORRISSEY for his alleged racist leanings. Already signed to the up and coming 'Wiiija' label, they delivered their debut EP, 'IN THE DAYS OF FORD CORTINA', in a blaze of publicity. Described as JESUS & MARY CHAIN with sitars, the unconventional Sikh/white thrash fusion was entertaining if hardly professional. Inevitably the initial press hype soon backfired on them, although they struggled on through a clutch of patchy albums including 'HOLD

ON IT HURTS' (1994) and 'WOMAN'S GOTTA HAVE IT' (1995). Major alterations were subsequently carried out on the 'SHOP, after which TJINDER re-opened for business in 1997 with the sonic nirvana of 'WHEN I WAS BORN FOR THE 7th TIME'. A surprise Top 40 success, well worthy of merit with its consummate blend of hip hop, Indian folk, country and indie funk, the album spawned the classic 'BRIMFUL OF ASHA' (a ltd-edition original release, it went on to hit the top of the charts in early '98). The record also featured a suitably exotic version of the Beatles' 'NORWEGIAN WOOD (THIS BIRD HAS FLOWN)', while 'CANDYMAN' took elements from LARRY CORYELL's 'The Opening'. CORNERSHOP subsequently toured the States and Europe for almost a year after the album's release. Mentally and physically exhausted, the irate TJINDER SINGH and his equally worn associate BEN AYRES hibernated in a South London studio, preparing their off-shoot band, CLINTON's debut album (following a back-catalogue of three 12" singles over four years). Released on their own 'Meccico' imprint (through 'Hut'), 'DISCO AND THE HALFWAY TO DISCONTENT' (1999), didn't exactly sound like the kind of record that was made by two men who were on the verge of musical breakdown. Opening track, 'PEOPLE POWER IN THE DISCO HOUR', made the speakers pound like a nomadic tribesman beating from the inside. Other tracks dabbled in sitar techniques, that for once, didn't sound like some mystical KULA SHAKER thing! The theme of disco ran throughout the set, occasionally taking inspiration from their dub reggae peers, proving that CLINTON had, most definitely, danced those blues away!

Album rating: HOLD ON IT HURTS (*5) / WOMAN'S GOTTA HAVE IT (*5) / WHEN I WAS BORN FOR THE 7th TIME (*9) / Clinton: DISCO AND THE HALFWAY TO DISCONTENT (*8)

TJINDER SINGH (b. 8 Feb'68, New Cross, Wolverhampton, England) – guitar / **AVTAR SINGH** (b.11 May'65, Punjab, India) – bass, vocals / **DAVID CHAMBERS** (b.1969, Lincoln, England) – drums / **ANTHONY SAFFERY** – sitar / **NEIL MILNER** – tapes

	Chapati Heat	not iss.

Dec 91. (7"ep; as the GENERAL HAVOC) *(BIRD 1)* **FAST JASPAL EP** –
– Moonshine / Vacuum cleaner / Another cup of tea, Arch Deacon?

—— **BEN AYRES** (b. BENEDICT, 30 Apr'68, St John's, Canada) – guitar, vocals; repl. ANTHONY + NEIL

	Wiiija	Merge

Jan 93. (7"ep; some colrd) *(WIJ 019V)* **IN THE DAYS OF FORD CORTINA EP** –
– Waterlogged / Moonshine / Kawasaki (more heat than chapati) / Hanif Kureishi scene.

Apr 93. (10"ep) *(WIJ 22V)* **LOCK STOCK & DOUBLE-BARREL** –
– England's dreaming / Trip easy / Summer fun in a beat up Datsun / Breaking every rule language English.
(cd-ep+=) *(WIJ 22CD)* – (hidden track).

Jul 93. (m-cd) *(WAKEUP 001)* **ELVIS SEX-CHANGE** –
– (above 2 EP's)

Jan 94. (7"ep/cd-ep) *(WIJ 29 V/CD)* **READERS' WIVES EP** –
– Readers' wives / Inside Rani (short version) / Tandoori chicken.

Jan 94. (cd/c/lp) *(WIJ 030 CD/C/V) <74>* **HOLD ON IT HURTS** Jan95
– Jason Donovan / Tessa Sanderson / Kalluri's radio / Readers' wives / Change / Inside Rani (long version) / Born disco; died heavy metal / Counteraction / Where d'u get your information / Tera mera pyar / You always said my language would get me into trouble. *(lp w/ free 7")* – BORN DISCO; DIED HEAVY METAL (disco mix) / ENGLAND'S DREAMING

Mar 94. (7"ep/cd-ep) *(WIJ 033 V/CD)* **BORN DISCO; DIED HEAVY METAL. / THE SAFETY OF OBJECTS / REHOUSED** –

Apr 94. (7") *(XPI 24)* **SEETAR MAN. / (track by Blood Sausage)** –
(above issued on 'Clawfist')

—— CHAMBERS departed before below album

	Wiiija	Luaka Bop – Warners

Apr 95. (7"etched) *(LTD 004)* **6 A.M. JULLANDAR SHERE** –

May 95. (cd/lp) *(WIJ 045 CD/V) <46018>* **WOMAN'S GOTTA HAVE IT**
– 6 a.m. Jullandar shere / Hong Kong book of Kung Fu / Roof rack / My dancing days are done / Call all destroyer / Camp orange / Never leave yourself (vocal overload mix) / Jamsimran king / Wog / Looking for a way in / 7.20 a.m. Jullander shere.

Aug 95. (7") *(CIP 101)* **MY DANCING DAYS ARE DONE. / Prohibition: I AM NOT A FISH** – French
(above issued on French label, 'Bruit Distordu')

Feb 96. (12"ep/cd-ep) *(WIJ 048 V/CD)* **6 A.M. JULLANDAR SHERE: The Grid & Star Liner mixes** –
– (Jeh Jeh mix) / (All Fetters Loose mix) / (original).

—— AVTAR departed around 1995/96, leaving **TJINDER + BEN** to recruit **PETER BENGRY** – percussion / **ANTHONY SAFFREY** – sitar, harmonium, keyboards (returned) / **NICK SIMMS** – drums, tambourine

Jun 96. (12"ep) *(WIJ 049V)* **W.O.G. – THE U.S. WESTERN ORIENTAL MIXES** –
– (original) / (Freaky's) / (Witchman's Assimilation) / Freaky's Acid DJ) / (Witchman's extended beats).

Dec 96. (12"etched) *(ROOT 011)* **BUTTER THE SOUL** –
(above released on 'Art Bus')

Jun 97. (7") *(WIJ 70)* **GOOD SHIPS. / FUNKY DAYS ARE BACK AGAIN** –
(12"+=/cd-s+=) *(WIJ 70 T/CD)* – ('A'-Intro – instrumental / 'B'extended beats mix).

Aug 97. (7") *(WIJ 75)* **BRIMFUL OF ASHA. / EASY WINNERS (part 1)** `60`
(cd-s+=) *(WIJ 75CD)* – Rehoused / ('A'mix).
(cd-s) *(WIJ 75CDX)* – ('A'remixes; Sofa Surfers / Mucho Macho).

Sep 97. (cd/c/d-lp) *(WIJ CD/MC/LP 1065) <46576>* **WHEN I WAS BORN FOR THE 7th TIME** `17`
– Sleep on the left side / Brimful of Asha / Butter the soul / Chocolat / We're in yr corner / Funky days are back again / What is happening? / When the light appears

boy / Coming up / Good shit / Good to be on the road back home again / It's Indian tobacco my friend / Candyman / State troopers / Norwegian wood (this bird has flown).

Nov 97.	(12"etched) *(ROOT 014T)* **BRIMFUL OF ASHA (Norman Cook remix)**	☐	-
Feb 98.	(7"/c-s) *(WIJ 81/+MC)* **BRIMFUL OF ASHA. / ('A'-Norman Cook remix)**	1	☐
	(12"+=) *(ROOT 014T)* – ('A'-Norman Cook extended).		
	(cd-s++=) *(WIJ 81CD)* – U47S.		
May 98.	(c-s) *(WIJ 80C)* *<44524>* **SLEEP ON THE LEFT SIDE. / ('A'-Les Rhythms Digitales mix)**	23	☐
	(12"+=/cd-s+=) *(WIJ 80 T/CD)* – ('A'-Ashley Beadle mix) / ('A'-Ashley Beadle extended).		
Nov 98.	(12"ltd) *(WIJ 093T)* **CANDYMAN (mixes; Rob Swift vocal & instrumental / Schizoid Man / Uptight Vienna)**	☐	-

CLINTON

—— alter-ego of **TJINDER + BEN**

		Wiiija	not iss.
Dec 94.	(etched-12") *(JJAR 001)* **JAM JAR (Marv Johnson mix) / EVERYBODY KNOWS THAT THE MOST IMPORTANT PEOPLE SPEAK FIRST**	☐	-
Sep 95.	(etched-12") *(ROOT 010)* **SUPERLOOSE! (Bobby Austin mix) / FINANCIAL HEADACHE**	☐	-
Apr 97.	(12") *(ROOT 012)* **SUPERLOOSE! (Automator Hot Vox mix). / SUPERLOOSE! (Automator instrumental)**	☐	-
Mar 99.	(7") *(ROOT 013)* **DAVID D. CHAMBERS. / INSTRUMENTAL / VOCAL**	☐	-

		Hut	not iss.
Aug 99.	(12"/cd-s) *(HUT T/CD 116)* **BUTTONED DOWN DISCO. / ('A'-Scratch perverts boil in the bag mix) / ('A'-Fila Brazillia disco frisco mix)**	☐	-
Sep 99.	(cd/c/lp) *(CDHUT/HUTMC/HUTLP 56)* **DISCO AND THE HALFWAY TO DISCONTENT**	☐	-

– People power in the disco hour / Saturday night and dancing / Buttoned down disco / Hip hop bricks / Electric ice cream (Miami jammies) / GT road / Hot for May sound / Sing hosana / Mr. President / Giddian di rani / Before the fizz is gone / Welcome to Tokyo Otis Clay.

CORROSION OF CONFORMITY   (dig out; Great Metal . . .)

Elvis COSTELLO

Born: DECLAN McMANUS, 25 Aug'55, Liverpool, England. The son of a jazz bandleader, he grew up listening to the sounds of the day; the BEATLES (he was a member of their fanclub), the KINKS, the WHO and the sounds of Motown were all to instil in him a love of rock'n'roll and help shape his own musical style. Dividing his time between playing clubs at night and working as a computer operator during working hours (the strain on his eyes leading to the wearing of his now trademark glasses), he subsequently moved to London in 1974 to become frontman and songwriter for a country-rock group called Flip City. Flogging his demos far and wide, the newly formed 'Stiff' label duly took on his talent, McMANUS changing his name to ELVIS COSTELLO; 'Elvis', a challenge to the rock establishment, and 'Costello', his mother's maiden name. While at Stiff he met his long time collaborators NICK LOWE and Jake Rivera, who would in turn become producer and manager to COSTELLO. His first album was recorded in 24 hours, backed by CLOVER, a country and western bar band with a certain HUEY LEWIS at the helm (although he did not participate in the sessions). After little success with the first two singles, 'ALISON' and 'LESS THAN ZERO', the man resorted to playing outside a CBS Records international convention taking place at the Hilton in London. Although arrested, the stunt worked, and in '77 his first album, 'MY AIM IS TRUE' was released by 'Columbia' (US), stand out tracks including the aforementioned singles and 'WATCHING THE DETECTIVES'. Produced by LOWE, the record was hailed as one of the finest debuts in rock history, blending the Stiff sound of punk and new wave with COSTELLO's cynical observations on life. Voted Album of the Year in Rolling Stone's annual poll, COSTELLO toured the States with his newly assembled backing band, The ATTRACTIONS. America got its first taste of COSTELLO's independent stance when his appearance on Saturday Night Live turned into a scathing attack on the media. His next two albums, 'THIS YEARS MODEL' and 'ARMED FORCES' (originally titled Emotional Fascism) were to prove an artistic peak, as well as being commercially successful, the latter charting in the Top 10. Released in 1980, 'GET HAPPY' abandoned the new wave sound for a more 60's Motown approach. With 20 songs on the original LP (and 10 more on the CD reissue), it proved COSTELLO in prime songwriting mode, the record swiftly followed by his fifth set, 'TRUST' (1981), sounding as captivating and twisted as its predecessor was fast and loose. In between these two sets was the Nashville covers album, 'ALMOST BLUE' more a curiosity than a stand out success. 'IMPERIAL BEDROOM', released in '82, is often cited as COSTELLO's best album, and was produced by the Beatles engineer, Geoff Emerick (who would later go on to produce the '96 effort 'ALL THIS USELESS BEAUTY'). Not surprisingly then, it was compared to the masterpieces of the BEATLES and the BEACH BOYS, and included such fan favourites as 'MAN OUT OF TIME' and 'THE LONG HONEYMOON'. 'PUNCH THE CLOCK', released in '83, and featuring CHET BAKER on the track 'SHIPBUILDING', was less ambitious than the previous album, while 'GOODBYE CRUEL WORLD', released the following year, was his worst

record by some margin, starting out as an attempt at folk-rock, but ending up as an example of the '80s sound gone wrong. By this time, a split had developed between COSTELLO and the ATTRACTIONS, and 'KING OF AMERICA' was the penultimate album recorded with this combination until 'BRUTAL YOUTH' in '94. With backing from The CONFEDERATES and co-production by T-BONE BURNETT, it featured a mixture of country and folk with a fair splattering of rockabilly with varied success. 'BLOOD AND CHOCOLATE' (1986) was notable both for the return of NICK LOWE as producer and the man's split from the ATTRACTIONS. With LOWE at the helm, the record was far removed from his '84 effort, featuring a nastier, meatier version of 'THIS YEARS MODEL' plus 'POISONED ROSE', the latter track boasting the bass playing of the legendary jazz bassist RAY BROWN. Subsequently signing to 'Warner Brothers', his first release was the darkly comic and commercially successful 'SPIKE' (1989), its considerable sales due largely to the hit single, 'VERONICA', although it also featured songs of genuine outrage such as 'TRAMP THE DIRT DOWN' and 'LET HIM DANGLE'. The next few years saw COSTELLO become more adventurous in an attempt to break away from the past, symbolised by a change of image. 'MIGHTY LIKE A ROSE' remains arguably his most underrated album, while the follow up, 'THE JULIET LETTERS' (featuring The Brodsky Quartet), mixed pop with chamber music to commercial failure but critical praise. 'BRUTAL YOUTH' in '94 saw the reunion of COSTELLO and the ATTRACTIONS (dubbed the Distractions) and included one of the most beautiful recordings of his career in 'ROCKING HORSE ROAD', while the follow up, 'ALL THIS USELESS BEAUTY', was the ATTRACTIONS' swansong and inexplicably a commercial failure. Collaborations outside of his albums for 'Columbia' and 'Warners' are numerous, COSTELLO winning a BAFTA with RICHARD HARVEY for the soundtrack to 'G.B.H.' and also recently contributing the track, 'MY MOOD SWINGS' to the Coen Brothers latest film, 'The Big Lebowski'. Perhaps the most intriguing partnership never to see the light of day, save for three releases as obscure B-Sides, was his collaboration with country legend, GEORGE JONES, singing 'non-country' songs such as Hoagy Carmichael's 'MY RESISTANCE IS LOW' and Bruce Springsteen's 'BRILLIANT SURPRISE'. A collaboration was released at the back end of '98 featuring an album's worth of COSTELLO and BURT BACHARACH material, 'PAINTED FROM MEMORY', together again after the magnificent 'God Give Me Strength' (which was originally recorded on the 'Grace Of My Heart' soundtrack). Released recently, a tribute album of COSTELLO's songs by the likes of JOHNNY CASH, JUNE TABOR, NICK LOWE and ROBERT WYATT demonstrate both the man's musical versatility and the songwriting skills which have made him such an integral part of the last two decades of popular music. • **Songwriters:** All penned by COSTELLO, bar NEAT NEAT NEAT (Damned) / I CAN'T STAND UP FOR FALLING DOWN (Sam & Dave) / SWEET DREAMS (Patsy Cline) / A GOOD YEAR FOR THE ROSES (Jerry Chestnut) / DON'T LET ME BE MISUNDERSTOOD (Nina Simone) / I WANNA BE LOVED (Farnell Jenkins) / THE UGLY THINGS (Nick Lowe) / YOU'RE NO GOOD (Swinging Blue Jeans) / FULL FORCE GALE (Van Morrison) / YOU'VE GOT TO HIDE YOUR LOVE AWAY (Beatles) / STEP INSIDE LOVE (Cilla Black) / STICKS & STONES (Ray Charles) / FROM HEAD TO TOE (Smokey Robinson) / CONGRATULATIONS (Paul Simon) / STRANGE (Screaming Jay Hawkins) / HIDDEN CHARMS (Willie Dixon) / REMOVE THIS DOUBT (Supremes) / I THREW IT ALL AWAY (Bob Dylan) / LEAVE MY KITTEN ALONE (Little Willie John) / EVERYBODY'S CRYIN' MERCY (Mose Allison) / I'VE BEEN WRONG BEFORE (Randy Newman) / BAMA LAMA BAMA LOO (Little Richard) / MUST YOU THROW DIRT IN MY FACE (Louvin Bros.) / POURING WATER ON A DROWNING MAN (James Carr) / THE VERY THOUGHT OF YOU (Ray Noble) / PAYDAY (Jesse Winchester) / PLEASE STAY (Bacharach-David) / RUNNING OUT OF FOOLS (Jerry Ragavoy) / DAYS (Kinks) / SHE (hit; Charles Aznavour) / etc. • **Trivia:** He has also produced The SPECIALS (1979) / SQUEEZE (1981) / POGUES (1985) retaining a latter acquaintance in CAIT O'RIORDON, whom he married on 16 May'86.

Album rating: MY AIM IS TRUE (*9) / THIS YEAR'S MODEL (*9) / ARMED FORCES (*9) / GET HAPPY!! (*8) / TRUST (*8) / ALMOST BLUE (*5) / IMPERIAL BEDROOM (*8) / PUNCH THE CLOCK (*7) / GOODBYE CRUEL WORLD (*5) / KING OF AMERICA (*7) / BLOOD AND CHOCOLATE (*7) / OUT OF OUR IDIOT collection (*5) / SPIKE (*5) / MIGHTY LIKE A ROSE (*5) / THE JULIET LETTERS with Brodsky Quartet (*5) / BRUTAL YOUTH (*6) / KOJAK VARIETY (*4) / ALL THIS USELESS BEAUTY (*5) / PAINTED FROM MEMORY with Burt Bacharach (*5) / THE VERY BEST OF ELVIS COSTELLO & THE ATTRACTIONS compilation (*8)

ELVIS COSTELLO

(solo) – vocals, guitar with backing band The **SHAMROCKS**, (alias CLOVER) / **JOHN McFEE** – guitar / **ALEX CALL** – guitar, vocals / **SEAN HOPPER** – keyboards / **JOHN CIAMBOTTI** – bass / **MICHAEL SHINE** – drums

		Stiff	Columbia
Mar 77.	(7") *(BUY 11)* **LESS THAN ZERO. / RADIO SWEETHEART**	☐	-
May 77.	(7") *(BUY 14)* **ALISON. / WELCOME TO THE WORKING WEEK**	☐	☐
Jun 77.	(7") *<3-10641>* **ALISON. / MIRACLE MAN**	-	☐
Jul 77.	(7") *(BUY 15)* **(THE ANGELS WANNA WEAR MY) RED SHOES. / MYSTERY DANCE**	☐	☐
Jul 77.	(lp/c) *(SEEZ/ZSEEZ 3)* *<JC 35037>* **MY AIM IS TRUE**	14	32 Nov77

– Welcome to the working week / Miracle man / No dancing / Blame it on Cain / Alison / Sneaky feelings / (The angels wanna wear my) Red shoes / Less than zero / Mystery dance / Pay it back / I'm not angry / Waiting for the end of the world. *<re-iss. US Mar78 +=> (AL 35037)* – Watching the detectives. *(re-iss. Jul86 on*

'Imp' lp/c/cd; FIEND/+CASS/CD 13) (re-mast.Mar93 & Aug99 w/ extra tracks on 'Demon'; DPAM 1)

ELVIS COSTELLO & THE ATTRACTIONS

—— **STEVE NIEVE** (b.NASON)– keyboards repl. HOPPER to HUEY LEWIS & THE NEWS **BRUCE THOMAS** – bass, vocals (ex-QUIVER)repl. CIAMBOTTI, CALL + McFEE / **PETE THOMAS** (b.9 Aug'54, Sheffield, England)– drums (ex-CILLI WILLI, ex-WILKO JOHNSON)repl. SHINE

Oct 77.	(7"m) *(BUY 20)* **WATCHING THE DETECTIVES. / BLAME IT ON CAIN** (live) / **MYSTERY DANCE** (live)			15	–
Nov 77.	(7" *<3-10705>* **WATCHING THE DETECTIVES. / ALISON**			–	–

Radar   Columbia

Mar 78.	(7") *(ADA 3)* **(I DON'T WANT TO GO TO) CHELSEA. / YOU BELONG TO ME** — `16` `–`
Mar 78.	(lp/c) *(XX LP/C 11) <35331>* **THIS YEAR'S MODEL** — `4` `30`

– No action / This year's girl / The beat / Pump it up / Little Triggers / You belong to me / Hand in hand / (I don't want to go to) Chelsea * / Lip service / Living in Paradise / Lipstick vogue / Night rally *. (free-7"w/ above) (SAM 83) – STRANGER IN THE HOUSE. / NEAT NEAT NEAT <tracks * repl. by 'Radio Radio' on US version> (re-iss. May80 on 'F-Beat'; XXLP 4) (re-iss. Apr84 on 'Imp'; FIEND/+CASS 18) (cd-iss. Jan86; FIENDCD 18) (re-mast.Mar93 & Aug99 w/ extra tracks on 'Demon'; DPAM 2)

May 78.	(7") *(ADA 10)* **PUMP IT UP. / BIG TEARS** — `24` `–`
Jul 78.	(7") *<3-10762>* **THIS YEAR'S GIRL. / BIG TEARS** — `–` `–`
Oct 78.	(7") *(ADA 24)* **RADIO RADIO. / TINY STEPS** — `29` `–`
Jan 79.	(lp/c) *(RAD/RAC 14) <35709>* **ARMED FORCES** — `2` `10`

– Senior service / Oliver's army / Big boys / Green shirt / Party girl / Goon squad / Busy bodies / Sunday's best * / Moods for moderns / Chemistry class / Two little Hitlers / Accidents will happen. (free 7"w/ above) (SAM 90) <AE 71171> LIVE AT HOLLYWOOD HIGH EP:- Accidents Will Happen / Alison / Watching The Detectives. <track * repl. by '(What's So Funny 'Bout) Peace, Love And Understanding' on US version> (re-iss. May80 on 'F-Beat'; XXLP 5) (re-iss. Apr84 on 'Imp' lp/c; FIEND/+CASS 21) (cd-iss. Jan86; FIENDCD 21) (re-mast.Mar93 & Aug99 on 'Demon' w/ extra tracks; DPAM 3)

Feb 79.	(7") *(ADA 31)* **OLIVER'S ARMY. / MY FUNNY VALENTINE** — `2` `☐`
May 79.	(7"m) *(ADA 35)* **ACCIDENTS WILL HAPPEN. / TALKING IN THE DARK / WEDNESDAY WEEK** — `28` `☐`

ELVIS COSTELLO

solo, but still used ATTRACTIONS

F-Beat   Columbia

Feb 80.	(7") *(XX 1)* **I CAN'T STAND UP FOR FALLING DOWN. / GIRLS TALK** — `4` `☐`
Feb 80.	(lp/c) *(XX LP/C 1) <36347>* **GET HAPPY!!** — `2` `11`

– Love for tender / Opportunity / The imposter / Secondary modern / King Horse / Possession / Man called Uncle / Clowntime is over / New Amsterdam / High fidelity / I can't stand up for falling down / Black and white world / Five years in reverse / B movie / Motel matches / Human touch / Beaten to the punch / Temptation / I stand accused / Riot act. (re-iss. Apr84 on 'Imp' lp/c; FIEND/+CASS 24) (cd-iss. Jan86; FIENDCD 24) (re-mast.May94 & Aug99 on 'Demon' w/ extra tracks; DPAM 5)

Apr 80.	(7") *(XX 3)* **HIGH FIDELITY. / GETTING MIGHTY CROWDED** — `30` `☐`
	(12"+=) *(XX 3T)* – Clowntime is over (version 2).
Jun 80.	(7") *(XX5)* **NEW AMSTERDAM. / DR. LUTHER'S ASSISTANT** — `36` `☐`
	(7"ep+=) *(XX 5E)* – Ghost train / Just a memory.

ELVIS COSTELLO & THE ATTRACTIONS

(same line-up)

Dec 80.	(7"m) *(XX 12)* **CLUBLAND. / CLEAN MONEY / HOOVER FACTORY** — `60` `☐`
Jan 81.	(lp/c) *(XX LP/C 11) <37051>* **TRUST** — `9` `28`

– Clubland / Lovers walk / You'll never be a man / Pretty words / Strict time / Luxembourg / Watch your step / New lace sleeves / From a whisper to a scream / Different finger / White knuckles / Shot with his own gun / Fish 'n' chip paper / Big sister's clothes. (re-iss. Apr84 on 'Imp'; lp/c; FIEND/+CASS 30) (cd-iss. Jan86; FIENDCD 30) (re-mast.May94 & Aug99 on 'Demon' w/ extra tracks; DPAM 6)

Feb 81.	(7") *(XX 14)* **FROM A WHISPER TO A SCREAM. / LUXEMBOURG** — `☐` `☐`
Sep 81.	(7") *(XX 17)* **GOOD YEAR FOR THE ROSES. / YOUR ANGEL STEPS OUT OF HEAVEN** — `6` `☐`
Oct 81.	(lp/c) *(XX LP/C 13) <37562>* **ALMOST BLUE** — `7` `50`

– Why don't you love me (like you used to do) / Sweet dreams / Sucess / I'm your toy / Tonight the bottle let me down / Brown to blue / Good year for the roses / Sittin' and thinkin' / Colour of the blues / Too far gone / Honey hush / How much I lied. (re-iss. Apr84 on 'Imp' lp/c; FIEND/+CASS 33) (cd-iss. Jan86; FIENDCD 33) (re-mast.Oct94 & Aug99 on 'Demon' w/extra tracks; DPAM 7)

Dec 81.	(7") *(XX 19)* **SWEET DREAMS. / PSYCHO** (live) — `42` `☐`
Apr 82.	(7"m) *(XX 21)* **I'M YOUR TOY** (live). / **CRY CRY CRY / WONDERING** — `51` `☐`
	(12"ep) *(XX 21T)* – ('A'side) / My shoes keep walking back to you / Blues keep calling / Honky tonk girl. (w/ The ROYAL PHILHARMONIC)
Jun 82.	(7"m) *(XX 26)* **YOU LITTLE FOOL. / BIG SISTER / THE STAMPING GROUND** (The Emotional Toothpaste) — `52` `☐`
Jul 82.	(lp/c) *(XX LP/C 17) <38157>* **IMPERIAL BEDROOM** — `6` `30`

– Beyond belief / Tears before bedtime / Shabby doll / The long honeymoon / Man out of time / Almost blue / ... And in every home / The loved ones / Human hands / Kid about it / Little savage / Boy with a problem / Pidgin English / You little fool / Town cryer. (re-iss. Apr84 on 'Imp' lp/c; FIEND/+CASS 36) (cd-iss. Jan86; FIENDCD 36) (re-mast.Oct94 & Aug99 on 'Demon' w/ extra tracks; DPAM 8)

Jul 82.	(7") *(XX 28)* **MAN OUT OF TIME. / TOWN CRYER** (alt.take) — `58` `–`
Jul 82.	(7") *<CNR 03269>* **MAN OUT OF TIME. / (one-side)** — `–` `–`
	(12"+=) *(XX 28T)* – Imperial bedroom.
Sep 82.	(7") *(XX 30)* **FROM HEAD TO TOE. / THE WORLD OF BROKEN HEARTS** — `43` `☐`
	(below from the film 'Party Party' and released on 'A&M')
Nov 82.	(7") *(AMS 8267)* **PARTY PARTY. / IMPERIAL BEDROOM** — `48` `☐`
	(below ELVIS as "The IMPOSTER" and issued on 'Imp-Demon')

May 83.	(7") *(IMP 001)* **PILLS AND SOAP.** / **('A'extended)** — `16` `☐`
Jul 83.	(7") *(XX 32) <04045>* **EVERYDAY I WRITE THE BOOK. / HEATHEN TOWN** — `28` `36`
	(12"+=) *(XX 32T) <44-04115>* – Night time.
Jul 83.	(lp/c) *(XX LP/C 19) <38897>* **PUNCH THE CLOCK** — `3` `24`

– Let them all talk / Everyday I write the book / The greatest thing / The element within her / Love went mad / Shipbuilding / T.K.O. (boxing day) / Charm school / The invisible man / Mouth almighty / King of thieves / Pills and soap / The world and his wife. (re-iss. Sep84 lp/c/cd; ZL /ZK/ZD 70026) (re-iss. Jan88 on 'Demon' lp/c/cd; FIEND/+CASS/CD 72) (re-mast.Feb95 & Aug99 on 'Demon' w/ extra tracks; DPAM 9)

Sep 83.	(7"/ext.12") *(XX 33/+T) <04266>* **LET THEM ALL TALK. / KEEP IT CONFIDENTIAL** — `59` `☐`
	(below also as "The IMPOSTER" and issued on 'Imp')
Apr 84.	(7") *(TRUCE 1)* **PEACE IN OUR TIME. / WITHERED AND DEAD** — `48` `☐`
Jun 84.	(7") *(XX 35) <05625>* **I WANNA BE LOVED. / TURNING THE TOWN RED** — `25` `☐`
	(12"+=) *(XX 35T)* – ('A'extended smoochy'n'runny mix).
	(12"+=) *(XX 35Z)* – ('A'discotheque version).
Jun 84.	(lp/c/cd) *(XX LP/C 21) <39429>* **GOODBYE CRUEL WORLD** — `10` `35`

– The only flame in town / Room with no number / Inch by inch / Worthless thing / Love field / I wanna be loved / The comedians / Joe Porterhouse / Sour milk cow blues / The great unknown / The deportees club / Peace in our time. (cd-iss. Mar86; ZD 70317) (re-iss. Jan88 on 'Demon' lp/c/cd; FIEND/+CASS/CD 75) (cd re-mast.Feb95 & Aug99 on 'Demon' w/extra tracks; DPAM 10)

Aug 84.	(7"/'A'disco-12") *(XX 37/+T) <04502>* **THE ONLY FLAME IN TOWN. / THE COMEDIANS** — `71` `56` Jul84
	('A'disco-12"+=) *(XX 37Z) <44-05081>* – Pump it up (1984 dance mix).
——	(In May'85, guested on JOHN HIATT single 'Living A Little')
	(below as The COWARD BROTHERS (w/ T-BONE BURNETT) + issued on 'Imp')
Jul 85.	(7") *(IMP 006)* **THE PEOPLE'S LIMOUSINE. / THEY'LL NEVER TAKE THEIR LOVE FROM ME** — `☐` `☐`

The COSTELLO SHOW

featuring The ATTRACTIONS and The CONFEDERATES

—— added **JAMES BURTON** – guitar / **MITCHELL FROOM** – keyboards / **JERRY SCHEFF** – bass / **JIM KELTNER** – drums / **RON TUTT** – drums (i.e. The CONFEDERATES)

F-Beat   Columbia

Jan 86.	(7") *(ZB 40555) <05809>* **DON'T LET ME BE MISUNDERSTOOD. / BABY'S GOT A BRAND NEW HAIRDO** — `33` `☐`
	(12"+=) *(ZT 40556)* – Get yourself another fool.
Feb 86.	(lp/c/cd) *(ZL/ZK/ZD 70946) <40173>* **KING OF AMERICA** — `11` `39`

– Brilliant mistake / Loveable / Our little angel / Don't let me be misunderstood / Glitter gulch / Indoor fireworks / Little palaces / I'll wear it proudly / American without tears / Eisenhower blues / Poisoned rose / The big light / Jack of all parades / Suit of lights / Sleep of the just. (re-iss. Jan88 on 'Demon' lp/c/cd; FIEND/+CASS/CD 78) (re-mast.Jul95 & Aug99 on 'Demon' cd/d-lp; DPAM/LP 11) (cd w/ bonus cd of 'LIVE ON BROADWAY' EP)

ELVIS COSTELLO & THE ATTRACTIONS

(ELVIS, BRUCE, STEVE & PETE) plus guest **NICK LOWE** – guitar

Imp-Demon   Columbia

Aug 86.	(7") *(IMP 007) <06326>* **TOKYO STORM WARNING. / (part 2)** — `73` `☐`
	(12"+=) *(IMP 007T)* – Black sails in the sunset.
Sep 86.	(lp/c/cd) *(FIEND/+CASS/CD 80) <40518>* **BLOOD AND CHOCOLATE** — `16` `84`

– Uncomplicated / I hope you're happy now / Tokyo storm warning / Home is anywhere you hang your head / I want you / Honey are you straight or are you blind? / Blue chair / Battered old bird / Crimes of Paris / Poor Napoleon / Next time around. (cd re-mast.Sep95 & Aug99 on 'Demon'; DPAM 12) (cd w/ bonus interview disc)

Nov 86.	(7") *(IMP 008)* **I WANT YOU. / (part 2)** — `☐` `☐`
	(12"+=) *(IMP 008T)* – I hope you say you're happy.

Demon   Columbia

Jan 87.	(7") *(D 1047)* **BLUE CHAIR. / AMERICA WITHOUT TEARS NO.2 (Twilight version)** — `☐` `☐`
	(12"+=) *(D 1047T)* – Shoes without heels.
May 87.	(7"/12") *(D 1052/+T)* **A TOWN CALLED BIG NOTHING. / RETURN TO BIG NOTHING** — `☐` `–`
	(above as "McMANUS GANG" featuring SY RICHARDSON)

ELVIS COSTELLO

solo, with mostly **FROOM, KELTNER, PETE THOMAS** (2), **MICHAEL BLAIR** – percussion / **MARC RIBOT** – guitar / **JERRY MAROTTA** – drums / **PAUL McCARTNEY, ROGER McGUINN, CAIT O'RIORDAN, T-BONE BURNETT, CHRISSIE HYNDE** on 1 or 2, plus The DIRTY DOZEN BRASS BAND (GREGORY DAVIS, EFREM TOWNS, ROGER LEWIS, KEVIN HARRIS, KIRK JOSEPH, C. JOSEPH, plus loads more)

Warners   Warners

Feb 89.	(lp/c/)(cd) *(WX 238/+C)(925848-2) <25848>* **SPIKE** — `5` `32`

– ... This town ... / Let him dangle / Deep dark truthful mirror / Veronica / God's comic / Chewing gum / Tramp dirt town / Stalin Malone / Satellite / Pads, paws and claws / Baby plays around / Miss Macbeth / Any king's shilling / Coal train robbers * / Last boat leaving. (cd.+ = *) (re-iss. cd Nov93;) (w/ extra tracks).

Feb 89.	(7") *(W 7558) <22981>* **VERONICA. / YOU'RE NO GOOD** — `31` `19`
	(12"+=/12"poster+=/cd-s+=/pic-cd-s) *(W 7558 T/TW/CD/CDX)* – The room nobody lives in / Coal train robberies.
May 89.	(7"ep/10"ep) *(W 2949/+TE)* **BABY PLAYS AROUND / POISONED ROSE. / ALMOST BLUE / MY FUNNY VALENTINE** — `65` `☐`
	(c-ep/12"ep/cd-ep) *(W 2949 C/T/CD)* – (2nd track repl. by) Point of no return.

Apr 91. (7"/c-s) (W 0025/+C) **THE OTHER SIDE OF SUMMER. / COULDN'T CALL IT UNEXPECTED #4** `43`
(12"+=/cd-s+=) (W 0025 T/CD) – The ugly things.
May 91. (lp/c/cd) (WX 419/+C/CD) <26575> **MIGHTY LIKE A ROSE** `5` `55`
– The other side of summer / How to be dumb / All grown up / Invasion hit parade / Harpers bizarre / Hurry down doomsday (the bugs are taking over) / After the fall / Georgie and her rival / So like Candy / Interlude: Couldn't call it unexpected #2 / Playboy to a man / Sweet pear / Broken / Couldn't call it unexpected #4. (re-iss. cd Feb95; 7599 26675-2)
Oct 91. (7"/c-s) **SO LIKE CANDY. / VERONICA (demo)**
(12"+=/cd-s+=) – Couldn't call it unexpected (live) / Hurry down doomsday (the blues are taking over).

—— In 1992, he wrote material for WENDY JAMES (Transvision Vamp)

ELVIS COSTELLO / THE BRODSKY QUARTET

with **MICHAEL THOMAS + IAN BELTON** – violins / **PAUL CASSIDY** – viola / **JACQUELINE THOMAS** – violincello (all co-wrote music with him)
Jan 93. (cd/c) (<9362 45180-2/-4>) **THE JULIET LETTERS** `18`
– Deliver us / For other eyes / Swine / Expert rites / Dead letter / I almost had a weakness / Why? / Who do you think you are? / Taking my life in your hands / This offer is unrepeatable / Dear sweet filthy world / The letter home / Jacksons, Monk and Rowe / This sad burlesque / Romeo's seance / I thought I'd write to Juliet / Last post / The first to leave / Damnation's cellar / The birds will still be singing.
Feb 93. (c-s) (W 0159) **JACKSONS, MONK AND ROWE / THIS SAD BURLESQUE**
(cd-s+=) (W 0159CDX) – (interviews).

Elvis COSTELLO

Mar 94. (7"/c-s) (W 0234/+C) **SULKY GIRL. / A DRUNKEN MAN'S PRAISE OF SOBRIETY** `22`
(cd-s+=) (W 0234CD) – Idiophone / ('A'album version).
Mar 94. (cd/c) (<9362 45535-2/-4>) **BRUTAL YOUTH** `2` `34`
– Pony St. / Kinder murder / 13 steps lead down / This is Hell / Clown strike / You tripped at every step / Still too soon to know / 20% amnesia / Sulky girl / London's brilliant parade / My science fiction twin / Rocking horse road / Just about glad / All the rage / Favourite hour.
Apr 94. (7"/c-s) (W 0245/+C) **13 STEPS LEAD DOWN. / DO YOU KNOW WHAT I'M SAYING?** `59`
(cd-s+=) (W 0245CD) – ('A'side) / Puppet girl / Basement kiss / We despise you.
Jul 94. (7"/c-s) (W 0251/+C) **YOU TRIPPED AT EVERY STEP. / YOU'VE GOT TO HIDE YOUR LOVE AWAY**
(cd-s+=) (W 0251CD) – Step inside love / Sticks & stones.
Nov 94. (c-s) (W 0270C) **LONDON'S BRILLIANT PARADE / LONDON'S BRILLIANT** `48`
(12"+=) (W 0270T) – My resistance is low / Congratulations.
(cd-s) (W 270CD1) – ('A'side) / Sweet dreams / The loved ones / From head to toe.
(cd-s) (W 270CD2) – ('A'side) / New Amsterdam / Beyond belief / Shipbuilding.
May 95. (cd/c) (<9362 45903-2/-4>) **KOJAK VARIETY** `21`
– Strange / Hidden charms / Remove this doubt / I threw it all way / Leave my kitten alone / Everybody's cryin' mercy / I've been wrong before / Bama lama bama loo / Must you throw dirt in my face / Pouring water on a drowning man / The very thought of you / Payday / Please stay / Running out of fools / Days.

ELVIS COSTELLO & THE ATTRACTIONS

Apr 96. (c-s) (W 0348C) **IT'S TIME / LIFE SHRINKS** `58`
(cd-s+=) (W 0348CD) – Brilliant disguise.
May 96. (cd/c) (<9362 46198-2/-4>) **ALL THIS USELESS BEAUTY** `28` `53`
– The other end of the telescope / Little atoms / All this useless beauty / Complicated shadows / Why can't a man stand alone / Distorted angel / Shallow grave / Poor fractured atlas.
Jul 96. (cd-s) (W 0364CD) **LITTLE ATOMS / WHY CAN'T A MAN STAND ALONE / ALMOST IDEAL EYES / JUST ABOUT GLAD**
Jul 96. (cd-s) (W 0365CD) **THE OTHER END OF THE TELESCOPE / ALMOST IDEAL EYES / BASEMENT KISS (live) / COMPLICATED SHADOWS (demo)**
Jul 96. (cd-s) (W 0366CD) **DISTORTED ANGEL / ALMOST IDEAL EYES / LITTLE ATOMS (DJ Food mix) / Lush: ALL THIS USELESS BEAUTY**
Jul 96. (cd-s) (W 0367CD) **ALL THIS USELESS BEAUTY / ALMOST IDEAL EYES / Sleeper: THE OTHER END OF THE TELESCOPE / DISTORTED ANGEL (Tricky mix)**

ELVIS COSTELLO with BURT BACHARACH

	Mercury	Mercury
Sep 98. (cd/c) (<538002-2/-4>) **PAINTED FROM MEMORY** `32` `78`
– In the darkest place / Toledo / I still have that other girl / This house is empty now / Tears at the birthday party / Such unlikely lovers / My thief / Long division / Painted from memory / Sweetest punch / What's her name today? / God give me strength. (special iss.Apr99; 546165-2)
Apr 99. (cd-s) (870965-2) **TOLEDO / TEARS AT THE BIRTHDAY PARTY (live) / INCH BY INCH (live)** `72`
(cd-s) (870967-2) – ('A'side) / Such unlikely lovers (live) / Baby plays around (live).
Jul 99. (c-s) (MERMC 521) **SHE / THE HOUSE IS EMPTY NOW** `19`
(cd-s+=) (MERDD 521) – What's her name today.
(cd-s) (MERCD 521) – ('A'side) / Painted from memory / Sweetest punch.

– compilations, others, etc. –

Mar 80. (c) F-Beat; (XXC 6) **TEN BLOODY MARY'S & TEN HOW'S YOUR FATHERS**
(re-iss. Apr84 on 'Imp' lp/c; FIEND/+CASS 27) (cd-iss. Jan86; FIENDCD 27) (re-iss. cd Mar93; FIENDCD 27X)
Oct 80. (lp) Columbia; (JC 36839) **TAKING LIBERTIES** `-` `28`

Apr 85. (lp/c/cd) Telstar; (STAR/STAC/TCD 2247) **THE BEST OF ELVIS COSTELLO – THE MAN** `8` `-`
– Watching the detectives / Oliver's army / Alison / Accidents will happen / Pump it up / High fidelity / Pills and soap (THE IMPOSTER) / (I don't want to go to) Chelsea / New lace sleeves / A good year for the roses / I can't stand up for falling down / Clubland / Beyond belief / New Amsterdam / Green shirt / Everyday I write the book / I wanna be loved / Shipbuilding (THE IMPOSTER). (re-iss. May86 on 'Imp' lp/c/cd; FIEND/+CASS 52) (re-iss. cd Mar93 on 'Demon'; FIENDCD 52X)
Apr 85. (7",7"green) F-Beat; (ZB 40086) **GREEN SHIRT. / BEYOND BELIEF** `68` `-`
(12"+=,12"green+=) (ZT 40086) – ('A'extended).
(d7"+=) (ZB 40085-7) – Oliver's army / A good year for the roses.
(Nov85; d7"+=) (same) – The people's limousine / They'll never take her love away from me.
Nov 85. (12"ep) Stiff; (BUYIT 239) **WATCHING THE DETECTIVES / RADIO SWEETHEART. / LESS THAN ZERO / ALISON** `-`
Oct 87. (lp/c/cd; VARIOUS ARTISTS) Demon; (FIEND/+CASS/CD 67) **OUT OF OUR IDIOT**
(re-iss. cd Mar93; FIENDCD 67X)
Oct 89. (d-lp/c/cd/dat) Demon; (D-)FIEND CASS/CD/DAT 160) **GIRLS, GIRLS, GIRLS** `67` `-`
Nov 89. (c) Demon; (FIENDCASS 161) **GIRLS, GIRLS, GIRLS VOL. 2** `-`
Nov 93. (4xcd-box) Demon; (DPAM BOX1) **THE FIRST 2 1/2 YEARS** `-`
Nov 94. (cd/c/lp) Demon; (DMAM CD/MC/LP 13) Rykodisc; **THE VERY BEST OF ELVIS COSTELLO** `57`
Aug 99. (d-cd/d-c) Universal TV; (546490-2/-4) **THE VERY BEST OF ELVIS COSTELLO** `4`

—— The first 4 singles were also re-issued together around 1980 and could be found on 'Stiff' 10-pack Nos.11-20).
—— The ATTRACTIONS released two singles and an album (Aug80) 'MAD ABOUT THE WRONG BOY' on 'F-Beat'.

ELVIS COSTELLO & RICHARD HARVEY

	Demon	not iss.
Jul 91. (cd/lp) (DSCD/DSLP 4) **G.B.H. (TV Soundtrack)** | | `-` |

ELVIS COSTELLO & BILL FRISELL

	Warners	Nonesuch
Aug 95. (cd) (<9362 46073-2>) **DEEP DEAD BLUE** | | Nov95 |
– Weird nightmare / Love field / Shamed into love / Gigi / Poor Napoleon / Baby plays around / Deep dead blue.

John COUGAR
(see under ⇒ MELLENCAMP, John Cougar)

Cathal COUGHLAN / MICRODISNEY / FATIMA
MANSIONS (dig out; Great Alt & Indie . . .)

COUNT FIVE (dig out; Great Psychedelic . . .)

COUNTING CROWS

Formed: Bay Area, San Francisco, California, USA . . . August '91 out of early 90's outfit, SORDID HUMOR. CROWS vocalist/songwriter ADAM DURITZ and guitarist DAVID BRYSON had both been members of this folky outfit, releasing the album, 'LIGHT MUSIC FOR DYING PEOPLE', on 'Capricorn'. The record remained unreleased until COUNTING CROWS became massive in 1994. Their success was mainly due to 'MR JONES', a highly melodic slice of melancholic rock that was caned by both MTV and radio, resulting in the T-BONE BURNETT-produced album, 'AUGUST AND EVERYTHING AFTER' (1993), selling by the million. The record (which featured MARIA McKEE on backing vocals) was a professional, coffee table-friendly package of Roots rock that at times came across like a more polished JAYHAWKS. Two further singles, 'ROUND HERE' and 'RAIN KING' were issued, although they failed to dent the Top 40, by which time BEN MIZE had been drafted in to replace BOWMAN. Their long-awaited GIL NORTON-produced sophomore set, 'RECOVERING OF THE SATELLITES' (1996), disappointed no one and duly climbed to No.1 (UK Top 5), minor British hits such as 'ANGEL OF THE SILENCES', 'A LONG DECEMBER' and 'DAYLIGHT FADING', obvious highlights. A tad ambitious was their next album (a double live set!), 'ACROSS THE WIRE' (1998); all the best tunes were there of course although it was only a moderate seller peaking at No.19 in the US chart. That three year long wait for a studio album was up in November '99, 'THIS DESERT LIFE' finally making it to the shelves and returning the reclusive COUNTING CROWS to the Top 10. • Songwriters: DURITZ; some w /BRYSON, except THE GHOST IN YOU (Psychedelic Furs).

Album rating: AUGUST AND EVERYTHING AFTER (*8) / RECOVERING THE SATELLITES (*7) / ACROSS THE WIRE – ALIVE IN NEW YORK (*6) / THIS DESERT LIFE (*7)

ADAM DURITZ (b. 1 Aug'64, Baltimore, Maryland) – vocals, piano, harmonica / **DAVID BRYSON** (b. 5 Nov'61) – guitar, vocals / **DAN VICKREY** (b.26 Aug'66, Walnut Creek, Calif.) – guitar / **MATT MALLEY** (b. 4 Jul'63) – bass, vocals / **CHARLIE GILLINGHAM** (b.12 Jan'60, Torrance, Calif.) – piano, organ, accordion, chamberlain, vocals / **STEVE BOWMAN** (b.14 Jan'67) – drums, vocals

		Geffen	Geffen
Oct 93.	(cd/c) <(GED/GEC 24528)> **AUGUST AND EVERYTHING AFTER**	16	4

– Round here / Omaha / Mr. Jones / Perfect blue buildings / Anna begins / Time and time again / Rain king / Sullivan Street / Ghost train / Raining in Baltimore / A murder of one.

Apr 94.	(7"/c-s) (GFS/+C 69) **MR. JONES. / RAINING IN BALTIMORE**	28	-

(cd-s+=) (GFSTD 69) – Rain king / ('A'acoustic).

Jun 94.	(7"/c-s) (GFS/+C 74) **ROUND HERE. / GHOST TRAIN**	70	-

(cd-s+=) (GFSTD 74) – The ghost in you (live).

Oct 94.	(c-s) (GFSC 82) **RAIN KING / A MURDER OF ONE**	49	

(cd-s+=) (GFSTD 82) – Mr. Jones (acoustic live).

—— **BEN MIZE** (b. 2 Feb'71) – drums, vocals; repl. BOWMAN

Oct 96.	(c-s) (GFSC 22182) **ANGEL OF THE SILENCES / ROUND HERE (live)**	41	-

(cd-s+=) (GFSTD 22182) – Recovering the satellites.

Oct 96.	(cd/c) <(GED/GEC 24975)> **RECOVERING OF THE SATELLITES**	4	1

– Catapult / Angel of the silences / Daylight fading / Goodnight Elisabeth / Children in bloom / Have you seen me lately? / Miller's angels / Another horsedreamer's blues / Recovering the satellites / Monkey / Mercury / A long December / Walkaways.

Dec 96.	(c-s) (GFSC 22190) **A LONG DECEMBER. / GHOST TRAIN (live)**	62	-

(cd-s+=) (GFSTD 22190) – Sullivan Street (live).

May 97.	(c-s) (GFSC 22247) **DAYLIGHT FADING / DAYLIGHT FADING (live)**	54	-

(cd-s+=) (GFSTD 22247) – Rain king (live).
(cd-s) (GFSXD 22247) – ('A'side) / Time and time again (live) / Miller's angels (demo).

Dec 97.	(cd-s) (GFSTD 21910) **A LONG DECEMBER / GHOST TRAIN (live)**	68	-

(cd-s+=) (GFSXD 21910) – Sullivan Street (live).

Jul 98.	(d-cd) <(GED 25226)> **ACROSS THE WIRE – LIVE IN NEW YORK** (VH1 storytellers // MTV live from the 10 spot)	27	19

– Round here / Have you seen me lately? / Angels of the silences / Catapult / Mr. Jones / Rain king / Mercury / Ghost train / Anna begins // Recovering the satellites / Angels of the silences / Rain king / Sullivan Street / Children in bloom / Have you seen me lately? / Raining in Baltimore / Round here / I'm not sleeping / A murder of one / A long December / Walkaways.

—— disc 1 recorded live at Chelsea Studios, New York, August 12, 1997 // disc 2 recorded live at Hammersmith Ballroom, New York, November 6th, 1997

Oct 99.	(cd-s) (497188-2) <album cut> **HANGINAROUND / MERCURY / GOODNIGHT ELIZABETH**	46	33

(cd-s) (497184-2) – ('A'side) / Baby I'm a big star / Omaha.

Nov 99.	(cd/c) <(490415-2/-4)> **THIS DESERT LIFE**	19	8

– Hanginaround / Mrs. Potter's lullabye / Army hit the atmosphere / Four days / All my friends / High life / Colourblind / I wish I was a girl / Speedway / Saint Robinson and his Cadillac dream.

COUNTRY JOE AND THE FISH
(see under ⇒ McDONALD, Country Joe)

Wayne/Jayne COUNTY (dig out; Great Alt & Indie . . .)

COVERDALE PAGE (see under ⇒ WHITESNAKE)

COWBOY JUNKIES

Formed: Toronto, Canada . . . 1985 by MICHAEL TIMMINS, with younger brother PETER and sister MARGO; all inviting ALAN ANTON to the fold. In the late 70's and early 80's, MICHAEL had been in groups, HUNGER PROJECT and GERMINAL, before moving to New York and London in the process. In the mid-80's, The COWBOY JUNKIES recorded a debut lp, 'WHITES OFF EARTH NOW!!' in their garage, releasing it on their own Canadian indie label 'Latent'. By 1988, they were on the roster of 'R.C.A.', with 'Cooking Vinyl' licensing them in UK. That year's album, 'THE TRINITY SESSION' was famously cut in a Toronto Church with the most basic of recording equipment. Despite this, or more likely because of it, the album remains 'JUNKIES most enduring effort. Proving that at its heart, real country music really is a religious experience, the band drifted grace through perceptive covers and original material alike. Whether investing in Hank Williams' 'I'M SO LONESOME I COULD CRY' and Patsy Cline's 'WALKIN' AFTER MIDNIGHT' with latter day angst or re-inventing Lou Reed's 'SWEET JANE' with a languorous poignancy, The COWBOY JUNKIES' melancholic, minimalistic take on Americana was hypnotic and groundbreaking. Though they initially appealed to the college market, the group successfully crossed over with follow-up set, 'THE CAUTION HORSES' (1990). A slightly more robust album, it included one of the group's most affecting originals to date 'CAUSE CHEAP IS HOW I FEEL', while they even managed to transform NEIL YOUNG's classic 'POWDERFINGER', into a spectral lament. 'BLACK EYED MAN' (1992) was even better, JOHN PRINE and the late, lamented TOWNES VAN ZANDT guesting on an album which mined a rawer country seam. The record also marked the peak of their commercial success, the band playing a prestigious gig at London's Royal Albert Hall. Since then, the band have lost their momentum somewhat, despite a further couple of critically acclaimed albums, 'PALE SUN, CRESCENT MOON' (1993) and 'LAY IT DOWN' (1996). The latter marked their debut for 'Geffen', their tenure with 'R.C.A.' ending in the mid-90's. • **Songwriters:** MICHAEL wrote & produced most songs, except other covers BLUE MOON (hit; Elvis Presley) / SHINING MOON (Lightning Hopkins) / STATE TROOPER (Bruce Springsteen) / ME AND THE DEVIL + CROSSROADS (Robert Johnson) / DECORATION DAY + I'LL NEVER GET OUT OF THESE BLUES ALIVE + FORGIVE ME (John Lee Hooker) / BABY PLEASE DON'T GO (Bukka White) / COWBOY JUNKIES LAMENT + TO LIVE IS TO FLY (Townes Van Zandt) / IF YOU'VE GOTTA GO, GO NOW (Bob Dylan) / LOST MY DRIVING WHEEL (Wiffen) / THE POST (Dinosaur Jr).

Album rating: WHITES OFF EARTH NOW!! (*6) / THE TRINITY SESSION (*7) / THE CAUTION HORSES (*5) / BLACK EYED MAN (*6) / PALE SUN, CRESCENT MOON (*7) / 200 MORE MILES live 1985-1994 (*5) / LAY IT DOWN (*5) / MILES FROM OUR HOME (*5) / STUDIO compilation (*6)

MICHAEL TIMMINS (b.21 Apr'59, Montreal, Canada) – guitar / **MARGO TIMMINS** (b.27 Jun'61, Montreal) – vocals / **PETER TIMMINS** (b.29 Oct'65, Montreal) – drums / **ALAN ANTON** (b. ALAN ALIZOJVODIC, 22 Jun'59, Montreal) – bass

		not iss.	Latent
Nov 86.	(lp) **WHITES OFF EARTH NOW!!**	-	Canada

– Shining moon / State trooper / Me and the Devil / Decoration day / Baby please don't go / I'll never get out of these blues alive / Take me / Forgive me / Crossroads. (UK-iss.Feb91 on 'R.C.A.' cd/c/lp; PD/PK/PL 82380)

		Cooking Vinyl	R.C.A.
Mar 89.	(7") (FRY 008) **SWEET JANE. / 200 MORE MILES**		Nov88

(12"+=) (FRY 008T) – Postcard blues.

Mar 89.	(lp/c/cd) (COOK/+C/CD 011) <8568> **THE TRINITY SESSION**		26 Oct88

– Mining for gold / Misguided angel / Blue moon revisited (a song for Elvis) / I don't get in / I'm so lonesome I could cry / To love is to bury / 200 more miles / Dreaming my dreams with you / Working on a building / Sweet Jane / Postcard blues / Walking after midnight. (cd re-iss. Feb94; 74321 18356-2)

May 89.	(7") (FRY 011) **MISGUIDED ANGEL. / POSTCARD BLUES**	-	
Jul 89.	(7") (FRY 011) **BLUE MOON REVISITED (SONG FOR ELVIS). / TO LOVE IS TO BURY**		

(12"+=/cd-s+=) (FRY 011 T/CD) – ('A'live version).
(10") (FRY 011X) – ('A'side) / You won't be loved again / Shining moon / Walking after midnight.

		R.C.A.	R.C.A.
Feb 90.	(7") (PB 49301) **SUN COMES UP, IT'S TUESDAY MORNING. / WITCHES**		

(12"+=) (PT 49302) – Powderfinger.
(cd-s++=) (PD 49302) – Misguided angel.
(c-s+=) (PK 49302) – Dead flowers.

Mar 90.	(cd/c/lp) (PD/PK/PL 90450) <2058> **THE CAUTION HORSES**	33	47

– Sun comes up, it's Tuesday morning / 'Cause cheap is how I feel / Thirty summers / Mariner's song / Powderfinger / Where are you tonight / Witches / Rock and bird / Escape is so easy / You will be loved again. (cd re-iss. Feb94; 74321 18537-2)

Jun 90.	(7") **'CAUSE CHEAP IS HOW I FEEL / THIRTY SUMMERS**		

(12"+=/cd-s+=) – Declaration day / State trooper / Take me.

Sep 90.	(c-s) **ROCK AND BIRD /**	-	
Jan 92.	(cd-ep) **SOUTHERN RAIN / MURDER, TONIGHT, IN THE TRAILER PARK / LOST MY DRIVING WHEEL / IF YOU'VE GOTTA GO, GO NOW**		
Feb 92.	(cd/c/lp) (PD/PK/PL 90620) <61049> **BLACK EYED MAN**	21	76

– Southern rain / Oregon hill / This street, that man, this life / A horse in the country / If you were the woman and I was the man / Murder, tonight, in the trailer park / Black eyed man / Winter's song / The last spike / Cowboy Junkies lament / Townes' blues / To live is to fly. (w/ free cd-ep) – DEAD FLOWERS / CAPTAIN KIDD / TAKE ME / 'CAUSE CHEAP IS HOW I FEEL (cd re-iss. Jun96; 74321 36913-2)

Mar 92.	(7") **A HORSE IN THE COUNTRY. / OREGON HILL**		

(cd-s+=) – Five room love story.

Nov 93.	(cd/c) <(74321 16808-2/-4)> **PALE SUN, CRESCENT MOON**		

– Crescent moon / First recollection / Ring on the sill / Anniversary song / White sail / Seven years / Pale Sun / The post / Cold tea blues / Hard to explain / Hunted / Floorboard blues. (cd re-iss. Jun96; same)

Feb 96.	(d-cd) <(74321 29643-2)> **200 MORE MILES (live)**		

– Blue moon revisited (a song for Elvis) / 200 more miles / Me and the Devil / State trooper / Sun comes up, it's Tuesday morning / Oregon hill / Where are you tonight / 'Cause cheap is how I feel / Floorboard blues / Murder tonight in the trailer park / Sweet Jane / If you were the woman and I was the man / Pale sun / Hunted / Lost mny driving wheel / Forgive me / Misguided angel / I'm so lonesome I could cry / Walking after midnight.

		Geffen	Geffen
Mar 96.	(c-s) (GFSC 22117) **A COMMON DISASTER / COME CALLING (HER SONG)**		-

(cd-s+=) (GFSTD 22117) – In the long run.

May 96.	(cd/c) <(GED/GEC 24952)> **LAY IT DOWN**		55 Mar96

– Something more besides you / A common disaster / Lay it down / Hold on to me / Come calling (his song) / Just want to see / Lonely sinking feeling / Angel mine / Bea's song (river song trilogy: part II) / Musical key / Speaking confidentially / Come calling (her song) / Now I know.

Aug 96.	(cd-s) (GED 2216-2) **ANGEL MINE / NOW I KNOW / CARMELITA**		
Sep 98.	(cd/c) <(GED/GEC 25201)> **MILES FROM OUR HOME**		98 Jun98

– New dawn coming / Blue guitar / Miles from our home / Good Friday / Darkling days / Hollow as a bone / Someone out there / Summer of discontent / No birds today / Those final feet.

– compilations, etc. –

Feb 98.	(cd) R.C.A.; (07863 67412-2) **STUDIO** (selected studio recordings 1986-1995)		

– Shining moon / Misguided angel / Blue moon revisited (a song for Elvis) / Sweet Jane / Sun comes up, it's Tuesday morning / 'Cause cheap is how I feel / Powderfinger / Southern rain / A horse in the country / This street, that man, this life / Anniversary song / Ring on the sill / A common disaster / Lost my driving wheel.

Graham COXON (see under ⇒ BLUR)

Kevin COYNE

Born: 21 Jan '44, Derby, England. At 19, after attending a local art college, he worked as a social therapist at a mental hospital in Preston. COYNE moved to London in 1968, where he was initially employed as a social worker in Camden, while moonlighting on vocal duties for local act SIREN. Signing to John Peel's 'Dandelion' label, they released two competent albums between 1969 and 1971, the eponymous debut containing some fine numbers including, 'GET RIGHT CHURCH', 'AND I WONDER' and 'ASYLUM'. In 1972, COYNE left his job and the band to go solo full-time, releasing 'CASE HISTORY' the same year. A more acoustic set, his throaty, mannered vocal chords (described as a cross between ROGER CHAPMAN or JOE COCKER) went hand-in-hand with the record's heavy subject material (i.e. 'UGGY'S SONG', 'EVIL ISLAND' & 'MAD BOY'). In 1973, he was picked up by Richard Branson's new 'Virgin' label, where he released the seminal critically-acclaimed 'MARJORY RAZORBLADE', a disturbing double-set drawing on his past experiences dealing with mental patients. His subsequent work for 'Virgin' continued to make no concessions to commerciality and a final outing, 'SANITY STOMP' (1980), was backed by punk/dub outfit, The RUTS. Throughout the 80's and beyond, he released several albums, some only finding favour in Germany where he has resided for several years. • **Songwriters:** COYNE wrote all, except some with CLAGUE. In 1980, he wrote with PAUL WICKENS. Covered KNOCKIN' ON HEAVEN'S DOOR (Bob Dylan) / OL' MAN RIVER (Paul Robeson) / ONE FINE DAY (Chiffons).

Album rating: Siren: SIREN (*6) / STRANGE LOCOMOTION (*5) / Kevin Coyne: CASE HISTORY (*7) / MARJORY RAZORBLADE (*8) / BLAME IT ON THE NIGHT (*7) / MATCHING HEAD AND FEET (*6) / HEARTBURN (*5) / IN LIVING BLACK AND WHITE (*7) / DYNAMITE DAZE (*6) / MILLIONAIRES AND TEDDYBEARS (*5) / BEAUTIFUL EXTREMES (*5) / BABBLE with Dagmar Krause (*6) / THE DANDELION YEARS boxed-set collection (*8) / BURSTING BUBBLES (*5) / SANITY STOMP (*4) / POINTING THE FINGER (*5) / POLITCZ (*5) / LEGLESS IN MANILA (*4) / ROUGH – LIVE (*4) / STUMBLING ON TO PARADISE (*5) / EVERYBODY'S NAKED (*4) / WILD TIGER LOVE (*5) / TOUGH AND SWEET (*4) SIGN OF THE TIMES compilation (*7) / ELVIRA: SONGS FROM THE ARCHIVE collection (*5) / THE ADVENTURES OF CRAZY FRANK (*5)

SIREN

KEVIN COYNE – vocals, guitar / **DAVID CLAGUE** – bass, guitar, producer / **NICK CUDWORTH** – guitar, piano / **JOHN CHICHESTER** – lead guitar / **TAT MEAGER** – drums / with guests **COLIN WOOD** – keyboards, flute / **DAVID GIBBONS / ALISTAIR CAMPBELL**

		Dandelion	Elektra
1969.	(7"; as CLAGUE with KEVIN COYNE) (S 4493) **BOTTLE UP AND GO. / MANDY LEE**	☐	-
1969.	(lp) (63755) **SIREN**	☐	-

– Ze-ze-ze-ze / Get right church / Rock me baby / Wake up my children / Wasting my time / Sixteen women / First time I saw your face / Gardener man / And I wonder / The war is over / Asylum / Bertha Lee / I wonder where. (cd-iss. Aug91 on 'Repertoire'; REP 4202WP)

Sep 69.	(7"; as COYNE-CLAGUE) (S 4494) **THE STRIDE. / I WONDER WHERE**	☐	-
1970.	(7") <45714> **ZE-ZE-ZE-ZE. / AND I WONDER**	-	☐

— **MICK GRATTON** – guitar, repl. CHICHESTER.

Jan 71.	(lp) (DAN 8001) **STRANGE LOCOMOTION**	☐	-

– Relaxing with Bonnie Lou / Some dark day / Hot potato / Soon / Gigolo / I'm all aching / Strange locomotion / Fetch me my woman / Fat moaning Minnie / Squeeze me. (cd-iss. Aug91 on 'Repertoire'; REP 4083WP)

May 71.	(7") (DAN 7002) **STRANGE LOCOMOTION. / I'M ALL ACHING**	☐	-

KEVIN COYNE

solo, retaining **CLAGUE**, (+ with session people)

1972.	(lp) (2310 228) **CASE HISTORY**		

– God bless the bride / White horse / Uggy's song / Need somebody / Evil Island home / Araby / Mad boy / My message to the people / Sand all yellow. (cd-iss. Sep94 on 'See For Miles'+=; SEECD 410) – I'm all aching / A leopard never changes its spots.

		Polydor	not iss.
1972.	(7") (2001 357) **CHEAT ME. / FLOWERING CHERRY**	☐	-

		Virgin	Virgin
1973.	(d-lp) <lp> (VD 2501) **MARJORY RAZORBLADE**		

– Marjory Razorblade / Marlene / Talking to no one / Eastbourne ladies / Old soldiers / I want my crown / Nasty, lonesome valley / House on the hill / Cheat me / Jackie and Edna / Everybody says / Mummy / Heaven in my view / Karate king / Dog Latin / This is Spain / Chairman's ball / Good boy / Chicken wing. (cd-iss. Oct90+=; CDVM 2501) – Lovesick fool / Sea of love.

Aug 73.	(7") (VS 102) **MARLENE. / EVERYBODY SAYS**	☐	-
Nov 73.	(7") (VS 104) **LOVESICK FOOL. / SEA OF LOVE**	☐	-
1974.	(lp) (V 2012) **BLAME IT ON THE NIGHT**	☐	-

– River of sin / Sign of the times / I believe in love / Don't delude me / Wanting you is not easy / Take a train / Blame it on the night / Poor swine / Light up you little light / Choose / Witch / Right on her side. (cd-iss. Apr91; CDV 2012)

1974.	(7") (VS 107) **I BELIEVE IN LOVE. / QUEENIE QUEENIE CAROLINE**	☐	-

— His band were **GORDON SMITH** – slide guitar / **ANDY SUMMERS** – guitar / **TIM PENN** – keyboards / **PETER WOOLF** – drums / **ARCHIE LEGGAT** – bass

Apr 75.	(lp) (V 2033) **MATCHING HEAD AND FEET**	☐	-

– Saviour / Lucy / Lonely lover / Sunday morning sunrise / Rock'n'roll hymn / Mrs.

Hooley go home / It's not me / Turpentine / Tulip / One fine day. (cd-iss. Jun91; CDV 2033)

Apr 75.	(7") (VS 119) **ROCK'N'ROLL HYMN. / IT'S NOT ME**	☐	-

— **STEVE THOMPSON** – bass repl. LEGGAT who went solo. **ZOOT MONEY** – keyboards, vocals (ex-ERIC BURDON) repl. PENN and SMITH

Nov 75.	(7") (VS 126) **LORNA. / SHANGRI-LA**	☐	-
Feb 76.	(7") (VS 136) **DON'T MAKE WAVES. / MONA WHERE'S MY TROUSERS**	☐	-
Feb 76.	(lp) (V 2047) **HEARTBURN**	☐	-

– Strange locomotion / Don't make waves / Happy band / I love my mother / Shangri-la / America / Big white bird / Games games games / My mother's eyes / Daddy. (cd-iss. Apr91; CDV 2047)

May 76.	(7") (VS 148) **WALK ON BY. / SHANGRI-LA**	☐	-

— ZOOT & ANDY joined KEVIN AYERS. The latter formed The POLICE.

Oct 76.	(7") (VS 160) **FEVER. / DADDY**	☐	-
Jan 77.	(d-lp) (VD 2505) **IN LIVING BLACK AND WHITE (live)**	☐	-

– Case history No.2 / Fat girl / Talking to no-one / My mother's eyes / Ol' man river / Eastbourne ladies / Sunday morning sunrise / One fine day / Marjory Razorblade / Coconut Island / Turpentine / House on the hill / Knockin' on Heaven's door / Saviour / Mummy / Big white bird / America. (cd-iss. Feb91; CDVM 2505)

Apr 77.	(7") (VS 175) **MARLENE. / ENGLAND IS DYING**	☐	-
Jan 78.	(7") (VS 203) **AMSTERDAM. / I REALLY LOVE YOU**	☐	-
Feb 78.	(lp) (V 2095) **DYNAMITE DAZE**	☐	-

– Dynamite daze / Brothers of mine / Lunatic / Are we dreaming / (Take me back to) Dear old Blighty / I really live round here (fake friends) / I am / Amsterdam / I only want to see you smile / Juliet and Mark / Woman, woman, woman / Cry / Dance of the bourgeoisie. (cd-iss. Jun91; CDV 2096)

1978.	(lp) (V 2110) **MILLIONAIRES AND TEDDYBEARS**	☐	-

– People / Having a party / I'll go too / I'm just a man / Pretty park / Let me be with you / Marigold / Don't blame Mandy / Little Miss Portobello / Wendy's dream / The world is full of fools. (cd-iss. Apr91; CDV 2110)

Mar 79.	(7") (VS 255) **I'LL GO TOO. / HAVING A PARTY**	☐	-
Aug 79.	(lp; KEVIN COYNE & DAGMAR KRAUSE) (V 2128) **BABBLE**	☐	-

– Are you deceiving me? / Come down here / Dead, dying, gone / Stand up / Lonely man / I really love you / Sun shines down on me / I confess / Sweetheart / Shaking hands with the Sun / My mind's joined forces / It's my mind / Love together / Happy homes / It really doesn't matter / We know who we are. (cd-iss. Mar91; CDV 2128)

Feb 80.	(lp) (V 2151) **BURSTING BUBBLES**	☐	-

– The only one / Children's crusade / No melody / Learn to swim – learn to drown / Mad boy No.2 / Dark dance hall / Don't know what to do / A little piece of Heaven / Day to day / Golden days / The old fashioned love song. (cd-iss. Mar91; CDV 2151)

— next release had backing by punk group The **RUTS**.

1980.	(d-lp) (V 3504) **SANITY STOMP**	☐	-

– Fat man / The monkey man / How strange / When (see you again) / Taking on the world / No romance / Too dark (one for the hero) / Admit you're wrong / Formula eyes / New motorway / A lovin' hand / Fear of breathing / In silence / Take on the Bowers / Wonderful wilderness / My wife says / The world speaks / You can't kill us. (cd-iss. Apr91+=; CDV 3504) – Somewhere in my mind.

with **BRIAN GODDING** – guitar / **STEVE BULL** – synthesizers / **STEVE LAMB** – bass / **DAVE SHEEN** – drums, vocals

		Cherry Red	not iss.
Oct 81.	(lp) (RED 23) **POINTING THE FINGER**	☐	-

– There she goes / As I recall / Children of the deaf / One little moment / Let love reside / Sleeping – Waking / Pointing the finger / You can't do that / Song of the womb / Old lady. (cd-iss. Jan94 on 'Mau Mau'; MAUCD 640)

PETER KIRTLEY – guitar + **JIM WOODLAND** – vocals repl. GODDING / LAMB + SHEEN although the latter 2 returned in 1983

1982.	(lp) (BRED 30) **POLITICZ**		

– Your holiness / Liberation / Fun flesh / Flashing back / Tell the truth / Banzai / Poisoning you / Magnolia street / I've got the photographs.

		Rough Trade	not iss.
Nov 82.	(7") (CHERRY 49) **SO STRANGE. / FATHER DEAR FATHER**	☐	-
Feb 84.	(lp) (RTD 22) **LEGLESS IN MANILA**	☐	-

– Big money man / Gina's song / Money machine / Raindrop on the river / Nigel in Napoli / Zoo wars / Black clouds / Legless in Manila / Don't raise an argument / Cycling. (cd-iss. Nov94 on 'Golden Hind'; GH 7006-2)

PETER KIRTLEY – guitar, returned to repl. HOPE-EVANS

		On	not iss.
1985.	(lp) (12-1250) **ROUGH – LIVE (live)**	☐	- German

– The house on the hill / Singing the blues / Gina's song / Lucille / Pretty park / Dark dance hall / A loving hand / The monkey man / The old fashioned love song / I wander (poem).

with **HANS PUKKE** – guitar / **ROBERT STEINHART** – bass / **FALK STEFFEN** – drums

		Line	not iss.
1987.	(lp/cd; as KEVIN COYNE BAND) (LILP/842 438) **STUMBLING ON TO PARADISE**	☐	- German

– I'm still here / Pack of lies / How is your luck / Sunshine home / Tear me up / No revolution / Victoria smiles / Charming / Winter into summer / Love for five minutes / Back home boogie. (UK cd-iss. Nov94 on 'Golden Hind'; GH 7010-2)

		Future Earth	not iss.
Feb 90.	(cd/c; by KEVIN COYNE & THE PARADISE BAND) (IMC 5721 8023-2/-0) **EVERYBODY'S NAKED**	☐	-

– The millionaires song / I couldn't love you / Not the way / We don't talk too much / Here comes the morning / City crazy / Take me back in your arms / Last time blues / The slave / Old hippie / Radio / Everybody's naked. (cd re-iss. Nov94 on 'Zabo'; IMC 5721 8023CK)

		Golden Hind	Rockport
1991.	(cd; by KEVIN COYNE & THE PARADISE BAND) **WILD TIGER LOVE**	-	- Europe

– The bungalow song / Sensual / Cafe crazy / Looking in your eyes / Open up the gates / Go Sally go / American girls / Fish brain / Fooled again / Don't you look (that way) / Raindrops on the window / Passion's pleasure. (UK-iss.Nov94 on 'Golden Hind'; CD 3887001240)

Jun 94.	(cd) (GH 7009-2) **TOUGH AND SWEET**	☐	☐

– Little Miss Dynamite / Precious love / Burning head II / Really in love / Pony tail song / Elvis is dead / Totally naked II / Walls have ears / Baby blue / Talking money / Slow burner / All the loving / No lullabies / It's amazing II / Tell me Tony / Now's the time / Getting old / Some day / Love and money / Let's get romantic / Creeper.

Voiceprint   not iss.

Dec 94. (cd; KEVIN COYNE & THE PARADISE BAND) *(SPV 849260-2)* **ROMANCE – ROMANCE**
– Ready for love / Happy, happy / Chances / It's all over / The 17th floor / Theresa / No kindness, no pity / The Heaven song / Lovers and friends / Wild eyes / Best friend / Impossible child / Neighbourhood girl.

Rockport   Rockport

Oct 95. (cd) *(<CD 388701724-2>)* **THE ADVENTURES OF CRAZY FRANK**
– Born crazy / Drunk again / Moon madness / You're so wonderful / Crazy dream / Devil calling / Married / Deep the darkness / I stood up / Playing the fool / Heart of hearts / Perversion / Frankie's dream No.1 / Frankie's dream No.2 / Time for tears / Blast of glory / Never ending.

– compilations, others, etc. –

1978. (lp) *Virgin; (V 2527)* **BEAUTIFUL EXTREMES**
– Something gone wrong / Looking for the river / Roses in your room / Face in the mirror / All the battered babies / Right in hand / Love in your heart / Hello friends, hello everyone / Mona, where's my trousers / So strange / Rainbow curve / Fool fool fool. *(re-iss. Feb83 on 'Cherry Red'; MRED 43)*

Feb 82. (3xlp-box) *Butt; (BUTBOX 1)* **THE DANDELION YEARS**
– (SIREN / STRANGE LOCOMOTION / CASE HISTORY lp's)

Jun 90. (cd/lp) *Strange Fruit; (SFR CD/LP 112)* **THE PEEL SESSIONS (73-79)**
– Marlene / Cheat me / By up me duck / The miner's song / Evil island home / Araby / Dance of the bourgenoise / Do not shout at me father / Need somebody / Poor swine / Rivers of blood / Lunatic / I only want to see you smile / That's rock'n'roll / A leopard never changes its spots / I couldn't love you.

Feb 91. (d-cd) *Virgin;* **MARJORY RAZORBLADE / MILLIONAIRE AND TEDDY BEARS**

Aug 92. (cd) *Virgin; (CDVM 9029)* **SIGN OF THE TIMES**
– Marjory razorblade / Marlene / Eastbourne ladies / House on the hill / Dog Latin / Good boy / Karateking / Fat girl / Saviour / Brothers of mine / Dynamite daze / Having a party / I'm just a man / The only one / Children's crusade / Mona, where's my trousers / Sign of the times / Witch / Blame it on the night.

Aug 94. (cd) *Mau Mau; (MAUCD 640)* **POINTING THE FINGER / POLITCZ**

Oct 94. (cd; KEVIN COYNE & SIREN) *Voiceprint; (DJC 001)* **RABBITS**

Dec 94. (cd; by SIREN) *See For Miles; (SEECD 413)* **STRANGE LOCOMOTION / SIREN**

Mar 95. (cd) *Golden Hind; (GH 7012-2)* **ELVIRA: SONGS FROM THE ARCHIVES 1979-83**

Sep 95. (cd; by SIREN) *Blueprint; (DJC 002CD)* **LET'S DO IT**

May 96. (cd; by SIREN) *Blueprint; (DJC 003CD)* **CLUB RONDO**

CRACKER

Formed: Redlands, California, USA ... 1990 by DAVID LOWERY and DAVE LOVERING (former members of top cult US acts). While LOVERING had been a sidekick for FRANK BLACK in The PIXIES, LOWERY had been in CAMPER VAN BEETHOVEN, who were known for releasing a string of albums for 'Rough Trade' in the 80's and the classic track 'TAKE THE SKINHEADS BOWLING'. Alternately acoustic laid-back/hard rockin' grunge cowpunks fusing TOM PETTY or IAN HUNTER like songs with twanging country rock, CRACKER emerged in 1992 with the tongue in cheek, 'TEEN ANGST (WHAT THE WORLD NEEDS NOW)'. This was swiftly followed up with an impressive eponymous debut set. Though not a straight grunge act by any means, the band nevertheless appealed to a similar college crowd and a follow-up set, 'KEROSENE HAT' (1994) spawned a grunge mini-anthem in 'LOW'. The album itself sold close to a half million copies, a more experimental outing that saw them cover The Grateful Dead's 'LOSER'. A third set, 'THE GOLDEN AGE' (1996) meanwhile, saw LOVERING getting back to his roots in line with the burgeoning "No Depression" alternative country scene. Another US-only release, 'GENTLEMEN'S BLUES', was released in September '98 to a lukewarm critical reception. • **Covered:** WITHERING AWAY (Vic Chesnutt).

Album rating: CRACKER (*7) / KEROSENE HAT (*8) / THE GOLDEN AGE (*5) / GENTLEMEN'S BLUES (*5)

DAVID LOWERY (b.10 Sep'60, San Antonio, Texas) – vocals, guitars (ex-CAMPER VAN BEETHOVEN) / **JOHNNY HICKMAN** – guitar, vocals / **BOB RUPE** (b.16 Sep'56, Michigan) – bass (ex-SILOS) / **DAVE LOVERING** (b. 6 Dec'61, Boston, Mass.) – drums (ex-PIXIES)

Virgin America   Virgin

Mar 92. (7") **TEEN ANGST (WHAT THE WORLD NEEDS NOW). / CAN I TAKE MY GUN TO HEAVEN**
(12"+=) – China.
(cd-s+++=) – ('A'version).

Apr 92. (cd/c/lp) *(CDVUS/VUSMC/VUSLP 48) <91816-2/-4>* **CRACKER**
– Teen angst (what the world needs now) / Happy birthday to me / This is Cracker soul / I see the light / St. Cajetan / Mr. Wrong / Someday / Can I take my gun to Heaven / Satify you / Another song about the rain / Don't f*** me up (with peace and love) / Dr. Bernice.

`—` **DAVEY FARAGHER** – bass, vocals; repl. RUPE
`—` **MICHAEL URBANO** – drums; repl. LOVERING

Mar 94. (c-s) *<38427>* **LOW / NOSTALGIA**   – | 64

May 94. (7"/c-s) *(VUS/+C 80)* **LOW. / TEEN ANGST (WHAT THE WORLD NEEDS NOW)**   43 | –
(cd-s) *(VUSDG 80)* – ('A'side) / I ride my bike / Sunday train / Whole lotta trouble.

(10"colrd) *(VUSA 80)* – ('A'side) / River Euphrates / Euro-trash girl / Bad vibes everybody.
(re-iss. Nov94; same) – (hit UK No.54)

Jun 94. (cd/c) *(CDVUS/VUSMC 67) <39012>* **KEROSENE HAT**   44 | 59 Sep93
– Low / Movie star / Get off this / Kerosene hat / Take me down to the infirmary / Nostalgia / Sweet potato / Sick of goodbyes / I want everything / Lonesome Johnny blues / Let's go for a ride / Loser. *(cd+=)* – No songs: Eurotrash girl + I ride my bike / Hi-desert biker meth lab. *(c+=)* – No songs; Euro-trash girl + I ride my bike / Kerosene hat (acoustic).

Jul 94. (c-ep/cd-ep) *(VUSC/+D 83)* **GET OFF THIS / HAPPY BIRTHDAY TO ME / CHINA / DR. BERNICE**   41
(cd-ep) *(VUSDG 83)* – ('A'side) / Fucking up (live) / Blue Danube / Don't f*ck me up (with peace and love).
(10"ep) *(VUSA 83)* – ('A'side) / Steve's hornpipe / Mr. Wrong / I want everything (acoustic).

Apr 96. (cd/c) *<41498>* **THE GOLDEN AGE**   – | 83
– I hate my generation / I'm a little rocket ship / Big dipper / Nothing to believe in / The golden age / 1000 flower power maximum / Dixie Babylon / I can't forget you / Sweet thistle pie / Useless stuff / How can I live without you / Bicycle Spaniard.

Sep 98. (cd/c) *<46263>* **GENTLEMEN'S BLUES**
– Good life / Seven days / Star / James river / My life is totally boring without you / Been around the world / World is mine / Lullabye / Waiting for you girl / Trails and tribulations / Wild one / Gentlemen's blues / I want out of the circus / Wedding day / Hallelujah.

Sarah CRACKNELL (see under ⇒ SAINT ETIENNE)

CRADLE OF FILTH

Formed: Suffolk, England ... 1991 by gothic grave robbers fronted by former journalist, DANI DAVEY. Influenced by the Scandinavian black-metal scene, the group nevertheless carved out their own inimitably gothic-punk-orchestral English sound. Their 1994 debut, 'THE PRINCIPLE OF EVIL MADE FLESH' had distinct gothic overtones, although bludgeoning death-metal was their stock-in-trade. Another set, 'VEMPIRE' (1996), was quickly succeeded by their first for 'Music For Nations', 'DUSK ... AND HER EMBRACE', although CRADLE OF FILTH garnered more attention for their controversial promo-shoots and "masturbating-nun" T-shirts. 1998 satanism and sex always on the agenda, DANI was the focal point since his awakening from the grave in '96. A TV documentary was made for BBC2, the band a tad uncomfortable when a devoted fan's mum followed them around in her camper van. However, 'CRUELTY AND THE BEAST' (1998), saw them in the UK Top 50, Europe (especially Scandinavia) having already succumbed to their majesty. • **Covered:** DEATH COMES RIPPING (Misfits) / SLEEPLESS (Anathema).

Album rating: THE PRINCIPLE OF EVIL MADE FLESH (*5) / DUSK AND HER VEMPIRE – OR DARK FAIRYTALES IN PHALLUSTEIN (*5) / DUSK ... AND HER EMBRACE (*6) / CRUELTY AND THE BEAST (*6) / FROM THE CRADLE TO ENSLAVE mini (*4)

DANI DAVEY – vocals / **DAMIEN GREGORI** – keyboards / **STUART ANSTIS** – guitar / **GIAN PYRES** – guitar / **ROBIN EAGLESTONE** – bass / **NICHOLAS BARKER** – drums

Cacophonous not iss.

Mar 94. (cd/lp,blue-lp) *(NIHL 1 CD/LP)* **THE PRINCIPLE OF EVIL MADE FLESH**   – | –
– Darkness our bride (jugular wedding) / The principle of evil made flesh / The forest whispers my name / Iscariot / The black goddess rises / One final graven kiss / A crescendo of passion bleeding / To Eve the art of witchcraft / Of mist and midnight skies / In secret love we drown / A dream of wolves in the snow / Summer dying fast. *(re-iss. Jul98; same)*

Apr 96. (cd/lp) *(NIHL 8/+LP)* **VEMPIRE – OR DARK FAIRYTALES IN PHALLUSTEIN**   – | –
– Ebony dressed for sunset / Forest whispers my name / Queen of winter throned / Nocturnal supremacy / She mourns a lengthening shadow / Rape and ruin of angels (hosanas in extremis). *(re-iss. Jul98; same)*

Music For Nations   Music For Nations

Nov 96. (cd/c/lp) *(CD/T+/MFN 208)* **DUSK ... AND HER EMBRACE**   – | –
– Humana inspired to nightmare / Heaven from asunder / Funeral in Carpathia / Gothic romance / Malice through the looking glass / Duske and her embrace / Graveyard moonlight / Beauty sleeps in Sodom / Haunted shores. *(sha-cd-iss. Mar97 +=; CDMFNC 208)* – Hell awaits / Camilia's masque. *(other cd; CDMFNX 208)* – Nocturnal supremacy '96.

`—` **LES 'LECTOR' SMITH** – keyboards; repl. DAMIEN GREGORI who departed mid-97

May 98. (cd/c/lp) *(CD/T+/MFN 242)* **CRUELTY AND THE BEAST**   48
– Thirteen autumns and a widow / Cruelty beneath the orchids / Beneath the howling stars / Venus in fear / Desire in violent overture / Twisted nails of faith / Bathory aria / Portrait of the dead countess / Lustmord and wargasm (the lick of carnivorous winds). *(other cd+=; CDMFNX 242)* – (bonus tracks).

`—` **STUART SMITH** – guitar; repl. PYRES

Nov 99. (m-cd) *(CDMFN 254)* **FROM THE CRADLE TO ENSLAVE**   – | –
– From the cradle to enslave / Of dark blood and fucking / Death comes ripping / Sleepless / Perverts church (from the cradle to deprave) / Funeral in Carpathia (be quick or be dead version).

CRAMPS

Formed: New York City, New York, USA ... 1975 by LUX INTERIOR and POISON IVY, who recruited fellow weirdos BRYAN GREGORY and PAM 'BALAM' GREGORY (the latter was replaced by MIRIAM LINNA, who in turn was superseded by NICK KNOX). The trashiest, sleaziest 50's throwbacks to ever besmirch the good name of rock'n'roll, The CRAMPS took the genre's inherit debauchery to its thrilling (and often hilarious) conclusion. Crawling from the mire of CBGB's punk scene like the proverbial Swamp Thing in one of their beloved B-movies, The CRAMPS started as they meant to go on, initiating their vinyl career in 1978 with an obscure cover, 'THE WAY I WALK'. The single was backed with a riotous mangling of The Trashmen's 'SURFIN' BIRD', as close to a theme tune as the band came. A follow-up, 'HUMAN FLY', introduced LUX's impressive capacity for disturbingly accurate animal (and insect!) noises, its voodoo surf twang and creeping tempo scarier than the frontman's skintight leotard. Subsequently signed to Miles Copeland's 'I.R.S.' label, The CRAMPS set up shop in Sun Studios, Memphis (where else?!) with producer ALEX CHILTON at the production helm, working on the material for their acclaimed debut set, 'SONGS THE LORD TAUGHT US' (1980). Featuring such bad taste gems as 'GARBAGEMAN' (more animal noises!), 'I WAS A TEENAGE WEREWOLF' and 'STRYCHNINE', the record further boosted the band's cult following. The departure of GREGORY after the 'DRUG TRAIN' single was the first in a long series of line-up changes through which IVY (the sexiest thing in stockings!) and INTERIOR were the only constants. With KID CONGO POWERS as a replacement, the band cut the less convincing 'PSYCHEDELIC JUNGLE' (1981), their final release for Copeland who they later sued. A short spell with the French 'New Rose' label and then 'Big Beat' saw the release of the live mini 'SMELL OF FEMALE' (1983). This went at least some way to capturing the cheap thrills of a CRAMPS gig, though readers are advised to experience the real thing; if the primeval spirit of raw rock'n'roll doesn't move you, then the sight of a grown man in a leather thong and and high heels just might! INTERIOR had always modelled himself on a kind of ELVIS-from-the-crypt and in 1986, the CRAMPS met their maker, so to speak, on the classic 'A DATE WITH ELVIS'. The likes of 'THE HOT PEARL SNATCH', 'CAN YOUR PUSSY DO THE DOG?' and 'WHAT'S INSIDE A GIRL?', need no further explanation save that THE KING was no doubt turning in his grave. Though this marked a creative and commercial peak of sorts, The CRAMPS continued to think up the best song titles in the Western World over a string of late 80's/90's albums, including 'STAY SICK' (1990), 'LOOK MOM, NO HEAD' (1991; essential if only for the IGGY POP collaboration, 'MINISKIRT BLUES'), 'FLAME JOB' (1994) and 'BIG BEAT FROM BADSVILLE' (1997). Though they've hardly pushed back the boundaries of music, The CRAMPS are arguably even more essential now than in their heyday, if only to remind he current crop of indie dullards what it REALLY means to play "The Devil's Music". • Songwriters: Most written by LUX and IVY except SURFIN' BIRD (Trashmen) / FEVER (Little Willie John) / THE WAY I WALK (Robert Gordon) / GREEN DOOR (Jim Lowe) / JAILHOUSE ROCK (Elvis Presley) / MULESKINNER BLUES (Fendermen) / PSYCHOTIC REACTION (Count Five) / LONESOME TOWN (Ricky Nelson) / HARD WORKIN' MAN (Jack Nitzche) / HITSVILLE 29 B.C. (Turnbow) / WHEN I GET THE BLUES (Larry Mize) / HOW COME YOU DO ME? (. . .Joiner) / STRANGE LOVE (. . .West) / BLUES BLUES BLUES (. . .Thompson) / TRAPPED LOVE (Kohler-Fana) / SINNERS (. . .Aldrich) / ROUTE 66 (. . . Troup) / etc. • Trivia: Their fan club was surprisingly based in Grangemouth, Scotland (wee Marty fi the Nash ran it!)

Album rating: SONGS THE LORD TAUGHT US (*7) / PSYCHEDELIC JUNGLE (*7) / OFF THE BONE compilation (*8) / SMELL OF FEMALE (*6) / A DATE WITH ELVIS (*7) / STAY SICK (*6) / LOOK MOM, NO HEAD! (*5) / FLAMEJOB (*6) / BIG BEAT FROM BADSVILLE (*5)

LUX INTERIOR (b. ERICK LEE PURKHISER, 1948, Akron, Ohio) – vocals / **POISON IVY RORSCHACH** (b. KIRSTY MARLANA WALLACE, 1954, Sacramento, Calif.) – guitar / **BRYAN GREGORY** (b. Detroit, Mich.) – guitar / **NICK KNOX** (b. NICHOLAS STEPHANOFF) – drums repl. MIRIAM LINNA (later to The ZANTEES & The A-BONES) who had repl. PAM 'BALAM' GREGORY

			not iss.	Vengeance
Apr 78.	(7") <666> **THE WAY I WALK. / SURFIN' BIRD**		-	-
Nov 78.	(7") <668> **HUMAN FLY. / DOMINO**		-	-

			Illegal	I.R.S.
Jun 79.	(12"ep) (ILS 12-013) **GRAVEST HITS**			-

– Human fly / The way I walk / Domino / Surfin' bird / Lonesome town. (re-iss. Sep82 - 7"blue-ep / re-iss. Mar83- 7"red-ep; same)

Mar 80.	(7") (ILS 0017) **FEVER. / GARBAGEMAN**			-
Apr 80.	(lp) (ILP 005) <SP 007> **SONGS THE LORD TAUGHT US**			-

– TV set / Rock on the Moon / Garbageman / I was a teenage werewolf / Sunglasses after dark / The mad daddy / Mystery plane / Zombie dance / What's behind the mask / Strychnine / I'm cramped / Tear it up / Fever. (re-iss. Feb90;)

May 80.	(7") <IR 9014> **DRUG TRAIN. / GARAGEMAN**		-	
Jul 80.	(7"m) (ILS 021) **DRUG TRAIN. / LOVE ME I CAN HARDLY STAND IT**			-

KID CONGO POWERS (b. BRIAN TRISTAN, 27 Mar'61, La Puente, Calif.) – guitar; repl. JULIEN BOND, who had repl. GREGORY for two months mid 1980.

			I.R.S.	I.R.S.
May 81.	(7"yellow) (PFS 1003) <IR 9021> **GOO GOO MUCK. / SHE SAID**			Aug81
May 81.	(lp) <(SP 70016)> **PSYCHEDELIC JUNGLE**			Jul81

– Green fuzz / Goo goo muck / Rockin' bones / Voodoo idol / Primitive / Caveman / The crusher / Don't eat stuff off the sidewalk / Can't find my mind / Jungle hop / The natives are restless / Under the wires / Beautiful gardens / Green door. (cd-iss. Sep98 on 'E.M.I.'; 496504-2)

Oct 81.	(12"m) (PFSX 1008) **THE CRUSHER. / SAVE IT / NEW KIND OF KICK**			-

(LUX, IVY & NICK were joined by **IKE KNOX** (Nick's cousin) – guitar; repl. KID CONGO who returned to GUN CLUB (appeared on live tracks 83-84)

			Big Beat	not iss.
Nov 83.	(red-m-lp) (NED 6) **SMELL OF FEMALE (live)**		74	-

– Faster pussycat / I ain't nuthin' but a gorehound / Psychotic reaction / The most

---

exhalted potentate of love / You got good taste / Call of the wig hat. (pic-lp Jun84; NED6) (re-iss. Feb91 cd+=/c+=; CDWIKM/WIKMC 95) – Beautiful gardens / She said / Surfin' dead.

(signed to below label in France)

			New Rose	New Rose
Mar 84.	(7"/7"pic-d) (NEW 28/+P) **FASTER PUSSYCAT. / YOU GOT GOOD TASTE**		-	- French
Mar 84.	(7"colrd;various) (NEW 33) **I AIN'T NUTHIN' BUT A GOREHOUND. / WEEKEND ON MARS**		-	- French

CANDY FUR (DEL-MAR) – guitar; repl. IKE

			Big Beat	not iss.
Nov 85.	(7"orange) (NS 110) **CAN YOUR PUSSY DO THE DOG? / BLUE MOON BABY**		68	-
	(12"blue+=) (NST 110) – Georgia Lee Brown.			
Feb 86.	(blue-lp/c/cd) (WIKA/WIKC/DCWIK 46) **A DATE WITH ELVIS**		34	-

– How can too far go / The hot pearl snatch / People ain't too good / What's inside a girl / Can your pussy do the dog? / Kizmiaz / Cornfed dames / Chicken / (Hot pool of) Woman need / Aloha from Hell / It's just that song. <US-iss.1994 on 'Capitol'; 73579>

May 86.	(7") (NS 115) **WHAT'S INSIDE A GIRL? / GET OFF THE ROAD**			-

(12"+=) (NST 115) – Give me a woman.
(Mar87; cd-s++=) (CRAMP 1) – Scene / Heart of darkness.

			Enigma	Enigma
Jan 90.	(7"/7"sha-pic-d/c-s) (ENV/+PD/TC 17) **BIKINI GIRLS WITH MACHINE GUNS. / JACKYARD BACKOFF**		35	
	(12"+=/cd-s+=) (12ENV/ENVCD 17) – Her love rubbed off.			
Feb 90.	(cd/c/lp) (CDENV/TCENV/ENVLP 1001) <73543> **STAY SICK**		62	

– Bop pills / Goddam rock'n'roll / Bikini girls with machine guns / All women are bad / Creature from the black leather lagoon / Shortenini' bread / Daisy's up your butterfly / Everything goes / Journey to the centre of a girl / Mama oo pow pow / Saddle up a buzz buzz / Muleskinner blues. (cd+=) – Her love rubbed off. (pic-lp Nov90; ENVLPPD 101) (re-iss. Feb94 cd/lp; CD+/WIKD 126)

Apr 90.	(7"/c-s) (ENV/+TC 19) **ALL WOMEN ARE BAD. / TEENAGE RAGE (live)**			-

(12"+=/12"pic-d+=/cd-s+=) (12ENV/12ENVPD/ENVCD 19) – King of the drapes (live) / High school hellcats (live).

Aug 90.	(7") **CREATURES FROM THE BLACK LEATHER LAGOON. / JAILHOUSE ROCK**			-

(12"+=/cd-s+=) – Beat out my love.

LUX & IVY were joined by **SLIM CHANCE** – guitar (ex-PANTHER BURNS) / **JIM SCLAVUNOS** – drums

			Big Beat	Restless
Sep 91.	(7") (NST 135) **EYEBALL IN MY MARTINI. / WILDER WILDER FASTER FASTER**			
	(12"+=/cd-s+=) (12/CD NST 135) – Wilder wilder faster faster.			
Sep 91.	(cd/c/lp) (CDWIK/WIKDC/WIKAD 101) <72586> **LOOK MOM, NO HEAD!**			

– Dames, booze, chains and boots / Two headed sex change / Blow up your mind / Hard workin' man / Miniskirt blues / Alligator stomp / I wanna get in your pants Bend over / I'll drive / Don't get funny with me / Eyeball in my Martini / Hipsville 29 B.C. / When I get the blues (the strangeness in me). (also pic-lp/pic-cd; WIKDP/CDWIKD 101)

NICKY ALEXANDER – drums (ex-WEIRDOS); repl. JIM

Sep 92.	(cd-ep) (CDNST 136) **BLUES FIX EP**			-

– Hard workin' man / It's mighty crazy / Jelly roll rock / Shombalor.

HARRY DRUMDINI – drums; repl. NICKY

			Creation	Medicine – Warners
Oct 94.	(7") (CRE 180) **ULTRA TWIST! / CONFESSIONS OF A PSYCHO CAT**			
	(12"+=)(cd-s+=) (CRE 180T)(CRESCD 180) – No club love wolf.			
Oct 94.	(cd/c/lp) (CRECD/C-CRE/CRELP 170) <24592> **FLAMEJOB**			

– Mean machine / Ultra twist / Let's get f*cked up / Nest of the cuckoo bird / I'm customized / Sado country auto show / Naked girl falling down the stairs / How come you do me? / Inside out and upside down (with you) / Trapped love / Swing the big eyed rabbit / Strange love / Blues blues blues / Sinners / Route 66 (get your kicks on).

Feb 95.	(7") (CRE 196) **NAKED GIRL FALLING DOWN THE STAIRS. / LET'S GET F*CKED UP**			

(cd-s+=) (CRESCD 196) – Surfin' bird.

			Epitaph	Epitaph
Oct 97.	(cd/c/lp) <(6516-2/-4/-1)> **BIG BEAT FROM BADSVILLE**			

– Cramp stomp / God monster / It thing hard on / Like a bad girl should / Sheena's in a goth gang / Queen of pain / Monkey with your tail / Devil behind that bush / Super goo / Hypno sex ray / Burn she devil, burn / Wet nightmare / Badass bug / Haulass hyena.

Dec 97.	(7") (6527-7) **LIKE A BAD GIRL SHOULD. / WET NIGHTMARE**			

(cd-s+=) (6527-2) – I walked all night.

– compilations, others, etc. –

May 83.	(lp) Illegal; (ILP 012) / I.R.S.; <SP 70042> **OFF THE BONE** <US-title 'BAD MUSIC FOR BAD PEOPLE'>		44	Feb84

– Human fly / Domino / Surfin' bird / Lonesome town / Garbageman / Fever / Drug train / Love me / I can't hardly stand it / Goo goo muck / She said / The crusher / Save it / New kind of kick. (cd-iss. Jan87; ILPCD 012) (cd re-iss. 1992 on 'Castle'+=;) – Uranium Rock / Good taste (live)

1984.	(4x7"box) New Rose; **I AIN'T NUTHIN' BUT A GOREHOUND. / WEEKEND ON MARS // FASTER PUSSYCAT. / YOU GOT GOOD TASTE // CALL OF THE WIG HAT. / THE MOST EXHALTED POTENTATE OF LOVE // PSYCHOTIC REACTION. / (one sided)**		-	- French

(all 4 either blue/white/black/green)

May 86.	(7") New Rose; (NEW 71) **KIZMIAZ. / GET OFF THE ROAD**		-	-

(12"+=) (NEW 70) – Give me a woman.

Nov 87. (lp) *Vengeance*; **ROCKIN' AND REELIN' IN AUCKLAND, NEW ZEALAND (live)**   `-`   ☐
(*UK cd-iss. Sep94 on 'Big Beat'; CDWIKD 132*)

CRANBERRIES

Formed: Limerick, Ireland ... 1990 initially as covers band The CRANBERRY SAW US (corny, or what!) by brothers NOEL and MIKE HOGAN, plus FERGAL LAWLER. The inclusion of singer DOLORES O'RIORDAN, saw the release the following year of an independent single, 'UNCERTAIN'. The quartet returned to the studio late in '91, subsequently resurfacing on the 'Island' label with 'DREAMS', 'LINGER' and 'PUT ME DOWN'. These tracks were featured on 1993's glorious debut album, 'EVERYBODY ELSE IS DOING IT, SO WHY CAN'T WE', which went on to sell a million in America (a year later it went platinum in Britain). An indie style major outfit, initially described as The Irish SUNDAYS, The CRANBERRIES were distinguished by DOLORES' heavily accented vocals, endearing naive and girlish one minute, howling banshee-style the next. An acquired taste, definitely, but one which millions seemingly, erm, acquired, drawn in no doubt by their canny way with a romantic Celtic melody. After their slow beginnings, The CRANBERRIES were now hot property, the UK music press finally recognising their unique talent. Confusingly for newly acquainted fans, a follow-up album, 'NO NEED TO ARGUE' hit the shops the same year ('94), previewed by the grunge-like 'ZOMBIE', a "loud" single (in every sense of the word), it made the UK Top 20. Incredibly, the track became a massive international hit for rave outfit, AMY, who took it back into the UK Top 20 in 1995. A third set, 'TO THE FAITHFUL DEPARTED' (1996) saw the band enlisting gloss-rock producer, Bruce Fairbairn, in what was surely a move to further dominate the American market. Songs about Bosnia, John Lennon etc, didn't detract it from cleaning up commercially once more, although most critics were unimpressed. If the CRANBERRIES thought they were harshly treated by the press on this occasion, they hadn't dreamt of the stick they would endure for next record, 'BURY THE HATCHET' (1999). Although its initial sales were once again promising both in the UK and US, the album quickly tailed off into the proverbial oblivion (six feet under it would seem); surely babe DOLORES and her melancholic muckers can't get away with this sort of thing again. • **Songwriters:** DOLORES / N. HOGAN, except (THEY LONG TO BE) CLOSE TO YOU (Carpenters). • **Trivia:** They supported MOOSE in the summer of '91, DOLORES guesting on their 1992 album, 'XYZ'.

Album rating: EVERYBODY ELSE IS DOING IT, SO WHY CAN'T WE (*8) / NO NEED TO ARGUE (*7) / TO THE FAITHFUL DEPARTED (*4) / BURY THE HATCHET (*4)

DOLORES O'RIORDAN (b. 6 Sep'71) – vocals, acoustic guitar / **NOEL HOGAN** (b.25 Dec'71) – guitar / **MIKE HOGAN** (b.29 Apr'73) – bass / **FERGAL LAWLER** (b. 4 Mar'71) – drums

		Xerica	not iss.
Oct 91.	(12"ep) (*XER 14T*) **UNCERTAIN / NOTHING LEFT AT ALL. / PATHETIC SENSES / THEM**	☐	`-`

		Island	Island
Sep 92.	(7") (*IS 548*) **DREAMS. / WHAT YOU WERE** (12"+=/cd-s+=) (*12IS/CID 548*) – Liar.	☐	`-`
Feb 93.	(c-s/7") (*C+/IS 556*) **LINGER. / REASON** (12"/cd-s) (*12IS/CID 556*) – ('A'side) / How (radical mix).	74	`-`
Mar 93.	(cd/c/lp) (*CID/ICT/ILPS 8003*) <514156> **EVERYBODY ELSE IS DOING IT, SO WHY CAN'T WE?** – I still do / Dreams / Sunday / Pretty / Waltzing black / Not sorry / Linger / Wanted / Still can't . . . / I will always / How / Put me down. (*re-dist.Nov93; same*) (*re-iss. Mar94, hit UK No.1*)	64	18
Oct 93.	(c-s) <862800> **LINGER / HOW**	`-`	8
Jan 94.	(c-s/7") (*C+/IS 559*) **LINGER. / PRETTY (live)** (10"+=/cd-s+=) (*10IS/CID 559*) – Waltzing black (live) / I still do (live).	14	`-`
Apr 94.	(c-s/7") (*C+/IS 594*) <864436> **DREAMS. / WHAT YOU WERE** (cd-s+=) (*CID 594*) – Liar. (cd-s) (*CIDX 594*) – ('A'live) / Liar (live) / Not sorry (live) / Wanted (live).	27	42 Mar94

—— Jun'94; DOLORES featured on JAH WOBBLE's hit 'The Sun Does Rise'.

Sep 94.	(c-s/7") (*C+/IS 600*) **ZOMBIE. / AWAY** (cd-s+=) (*CID 600*) – I don't need. (cd-s) (*CIDX 600*) – ('A'extended) / Waltzing black (live) / Linger (live).	14	`-`
Oct 94.	(cd/c/lp) (*CIS/ICT/ILPS 8029*) <524050> **NO NEED TO ARGUE** – Ode to my family / I can't be with you / 21 / Zombie / Empty / Everything I said / The icicle melts / Disappointment / Ridiculous thoughts / Dreaming my dreams / Yeats' grave / Daffodil lament / No need to argue.	2	6
Nov 94.	(c-s/7") (*C+/IS 601*) **ODE TO MY FAMILY. / SO COLD IN IRELAND** (cd-s+=) (*CID 601*) – No need to argue / Dreaming my dreams. (cd-s) (*CIDX 601*) – ('A'live) / Dreams (live) / Ridiculous thoughts (live) / Zombie (live).	29	`-`
Feb 95.	(c-s/7") (*C+/IS 605*) **I CAN'T BE WITH YOU. / (THEY LONG TO BE) CLOSE TO YOU** (cd-s+=) (*CID 605*) – Empty (BBC session). (cd-s) (*CIDX 605*) – ('A'-BBC session) / Zombie (acoustic) / Daffodil lament (live).	23	`-`
Jul 95.	(c-s/7") (*C+/IS 616*) **RIDICULOUS THOUGHTS. / LINGER** (cd-s+=) (*CID 616*) – Twenty one (live) / Ridiculous thoughts (live).	20	`-`
Apr 96.	(c-s) (*CIS 633*) **SALVATION / I'M STILL REMEMBERING** (cd-s) (*CID 633*) – I just shot John Lennon.	13	`-`
May 96.	(cd/c/colrd-lp) (*CID/ICT/ILPS 8048*) <524234> **TO THE FAITHFUL DEPARTED** – Hollywood / Salvation / When you're gone / Free to decide / War child / Forever	2	4

yellow skies / The rebels / I just shot John Lennon / Electric blue / I'm still remembering / Will you remember? / Joe / Bosnia.

Jul 96.	(c-s) (*CIS 637*) **FREE TO DECIDE / CORDELL** (cd-s+=) (*CID 637*) – The picture I view. (cd-s) (*CIDX 637*) – ('A'side) / Salvation (live) / Bosnia.	33	`-`
Nov 96.	(c-s) <854802> **FREE TO DECIDE / WHEN YOU'RE GONE**	`-`	22
Apr 99.	(c-s) (*572568-4*) **PROMISES / SWEETEST THING** (cd-s+=) (*572591-2*) – Linger (live). (cd-s) (*572593-2*) – ('A'side) / Dreams (live) / Promises (live).	13	
Apr 99.	(cd/c/d-lp) (*524644-2/-4/-1*) <524611> **BURY THE HATCHET** – Animal instinct / Loud and clear / Promises / You and me / Just my imagination / Shattered / Desperate Andy / Saving grace / Copycat / What's on my mind / Fee fi fo / Dying in the sun.	7	13
Jul 99.	(c-s/cd-s) (*56219 1-4/7-2*) **ANIMAL INSTINCT / PAPARAZZI ON MOPEDS** (cd-s) (*562198-2*) – ('A'side) / Ode to my family (live) / Baby blues / Salvation (live).	54	
Oct 99.	(c-s) (*562412-4*) **JUST MY IMAGINATION / GOD TO BE WITH YOU** (cd-s+=) (*562414-2*) – Zombie (live). (cd-s) (*562415-2*) – ('A'side) / Such a shame / Promises (live).	☐	☐

– compilations, etc. –

Nov 95. (d-cd) **EVERYBODY ELSE IS DOING IT, SO WHY CAN'T WE? / NO NEED TO ARGUE**   ☐   ☐

CRANES (dig out; Great Alt & Indie . . .)

CRASH TEST DUMMIES

Formed: Winnipeg, Manitoba, Canada ... late 80's by songwriter BRAD ROBERTS and his younger brother, DAN. Initially a barroom-playing outfit, BRAD took a back seat on the singing front, thinking his voice was unsuitable for the cover versions the band played in their performance repertoire. However, on the advice of his singing tutor, who told him he was a competent bass-baritone, BRAD took up the front role once again. In the early 90's, with the recruitment of a more settled line-up (i.e. ELLEN REID, VINCE LAMBERT and BENJAMIN DARVILL), BRAD and the group signed to 'Arista'. Combining his work by day as a literature/philosophy student, BRAD developed into the complete wordsmith, his ability to compose strange storytelling now ready to be heard on record. Initially released in Canada only, the low-key, lo-fi album, 'THE GHOSTS THAT HAUNT ME' (boasting their US Hot 100 breakthrough single, 'SUPERMAN'S SONG'), finally cracked platinum sales and made inroads across the American border. The record impressed former TALKING HEADS man, JERRY HARRISON, who subsequently took over production on their follow-up set, 'GOD SHUFFLED HIS FEET' (1993/94) – MITCH DORGE was now in place of LAMBERT. Full of wit and deep insight into offbeat life, the long-player soon took off, helped no doubt by "alternative rock" favourite and Top 5 single, 'MMM MMM MMM MMM' (their only classic – so far!). Had the group peaked too soon? It was clear that the answer was, well, MMMM, yes, when their third album, 'A WORM'S LIFE' (1996), failed to win over any new fanbase. • **Covered:** ALL YOU PRETTY GIRLS + THE BALLAD OF PETER PUMPKINHEAD (Xtc).

Album rating: THE GHOSTS THAT HAUNT ME (*6) / GOD SHUFFLED HIS FEET (*6) / A WORM'S LIFE (*4) / GIVE YOURSELF A HAND (*4)

BRAD ROBERTS (b.10 Jan'64) – vocals, guitars / **ELLEN REID** (b.14 Jul'66, Selkirk, Manitoba) – keyboards, accordion / **BENJAMIN DARVILL** (b. 4 Jan'67) – mandolin, harmonicas / **DAN ROBERTS** (b.22 May'67) – bass / **VINCE LAMBERT** – drums

		Arista	Arista
Sep 91.	(c-s/cd-s) <12339> **SUPERMAN'S SONG / THE VOYAGE**	☐	56
Oct 91.	(cd/c) (*261/411 521*) <ARCD/AC 8677> **THE GHOSTS THAT HAUNT ME** – Winter song / Comin' back soon (the bereft man's song) / Superman's song / The country life / Here on Earth (I'll have my cake) / The ghosts that haunt me / Thick-necked man / Androgynous / The voyage / At my funeral. (*re-iss. Oct95 cd/c; 74321 20152-2/-4*)	☐	☐

—— **MITCH DORGE** (b.15 Sep'60) – drums, percussion; repl. LAMBERT

		R.C.A.	Arista
Jan 94.	(c-s) <12654> **MMM MMM MMM MMM. / SUPERMAN'S SONG**	`-`	4
Apr 94.	(7"/c-s/cd-s) (*74321 20151-7/-4/-2*) **MMM MMM MMM MMM. / HERE I STAND BEFORE ME (live)** (cd-s+=) (*74321 20676-2*) – Superman's song (live).	2	`-`
May 94.	(cd/c) (*74321 20152-2/-4*) <16531> **GOD SHUFFLED HIS FEET** – God shuffled his feet / Afternoons & coffeespoons / Mmm mmm mmm mmm / In the days of the caveman / Swimming in your ocean / Here I stand before me / I think I'll disappear now / How does a duck know? / When I go out with artists / The psychic / Two knights and maidens / Untitled.	2	9 Feb94
Jun 94.	(7"/c-s) (*74321 21962-7/-4*) **AFTERNOONS & COFFEESPOONS. / IN THE DAYS OF THE CAVEMAN (live)** (cd-s+=) (*74321 21962-2*) – The ghosts that haunt me / Androgynous (live). (cd-s) (*74321 21963-2*) – ('A'side) / Mmm mmm mmm mmm (live) / God shuffled his feet (live).	23	`-`
Jun 94.	(c-s) <12706> **AFTERNOONS & COFFEESPOONS / MMM MMM MMM MMM**	☐	66
Oct 94.	(7"/c-s/cd-s) (*74321 23808-7/-4/-2*) **GOD SHUFFLED HIS FEET. / AFTERNOONS & COFFEESPOONS (live)** (cd-s+=) (*74321 23809-2*) – Winter song / Mmm mmm mmm mmm.	☐	`-`

below featured vocals by ELLEN REID

Apr 95. (c-s) (74321 27676-4) <64262> **THE BALLAD OF PETER**
PUMPKINHEAD / GOD SHUFFLED HIS FEET | 30 | | | Jan95
(cd-s+=) (74321 27676-2) – Afternoons and coffeespoons (live) / Swimming in your
ocean.
(cd-s) (74321 27677-2) – ('A'side) / Afternoons and coffeespoons (live) / When I
go out with artists (live) / Swimming in your ocean (live).
Oct 96. (c-s) (74321 40200-4) **HE LIKED TO FEEL IT** / ('A'mix) | | | - |
(cd-s) (74321 40200-2) – ('A'side) / Afternoons and coffeespoons / Swimming in
your ocean.
Oct 96. (cd/c) (74321 40201-2/-4) <39779> **A WORM'S LIFE** | | | 78 |
– Overachievers / He liked to feel it / A worm's life / Our driver gestures / My
enemies / There are many dangers / I'm outlived by that thing / All of this ugly / An
old scab / My own sunrise / I'm a dog / Swatting flies.
Jun 99. (cd-s) (74321 64834-2) **KEEP A LID ON THINGS / FILTER**
QUEEN / HANDY CANDYMAN | | | |
Jun 99. (cd/c) (74321 64833-2/-4) **GIVE YOURSELF A HAND** | | | |
– Keep a lid on things / A cigarette is all you get / Just chillin' / I want to par-tay /
Give yourself a hand / Get you in the morning / Pissed with me / Just shoot me,
baby / A little something / I love your goo / Aching to squeeze / Playing dead.

CRASS (dig out; Great Alt & Indie . . .)

Robert CRAY

Born: 1 Aug'53, Columbus, Georgia, USA. A long time admirer of ALBERT
COLLINS, CRAY formed his first band ONE WAY STREET, in high
school (where, incidentally, COLLINS performed), graduating to support the
legendary bluesman on his future forays in the area. He subsequently met
bass player, RICHARD COUSINS, in 1973, both of them serving a two
year apprenticeship with COLLINS and later stepping out independently to
form what was to become The ROBERT CRAY BAND, featuring CRAY
(guitar and vocals), COUSINS (bass), PETER BOE (keyboards) and DAVID
OLSON (drums). Their debut album, 'WHO'S BEEN TALKIN' was cut
during constant touring throughout the US in 1978 and showed CRAY'S
clean cut style of blues and soul, owing much to ALBERT COLLINS and
PETER GREEN, (with the influence of JIMI HENDRIX showing on the
faster numbers). Although the record was initially shelved for two years, it
was eventually issued in the US by the short lived 'Tomato' label (whose
licence was picked up by 'Atlantic' and by 'Charly' Records in the UK). He
recorded 'BAD INFLUENCE' in 1983 (with ERIC CLAPTON – who held
CRAY in high regard – guesting) the record released on 'Hightone' in the US
and 'Demon' in Britain (it would take 4 years to chart!). The album showed
that his talent as a songwriter was flourishing and as a result there were
only two covers although, one of them, 'GOT TO MAKE A COMEBACK',
by EDDIE FLOYD, is one of the highlights. In 1984, The ROBERT CRAY
BAND completed their first European tour to critical acclaim and in 1985,
had their first chart entry with 'FALSE ACCUSATIONS', the set topping
the UK Independent chart and reaching number 68 in the national album
chart. In the US meanwhile, it won the 'Best Blues Album' award from the
National Association of Independent Record Distributors, although it only
reached number 141 in the charts. The album featured such enduring tracks
as, 'PLAYIN' IN THE DIRT', 'THE LAST TIME (I GET BURNED LIKE
THIS)', 'PAYIN' FOR IT NOW' and 'SONNY', a classic CRAY set. A
collaboration with ALBERT COLLINS and JOHNNY COPELAND followed
in the form of 'SHOWDOWN' and he subsequently signed to 'Mercury'
Records where he began work on his debut album, 'STRONG PERSUADER'.
During 1986 he played 170 gigs, including his seventh Euro tour since 1984,
building on his increasing reputation in the UK. In October, he joined KEITH
RICHARDS, ERIC CLAPTON and others on stage in St. Louis for CHUCK
BERRY's 60th birthday concert, later featured in the film 'HAIL HAIL ROCK
N ROLL'. One month later, he won a record six Handy awards at America's
7th National Blues ceremony. CRAY's first stadium tour started in May 1987
as support to HUEY LEWIS AND THE NEWS, just as 'BAD INFLUENCE',
originally released in 1983, charted in the US. April 1987 saw the outstanding
'STRONG PERSUADER' at 13 in the US charts, becoming the first blues
album to crack the Top 20 since 1972. Lyrically he was improving all the
time, his guitar was as crisp as ever and the album went on to sell over a
million copies. The single from the album, 'SMOKING GUN' (although there
were better tracks on the album), was to be his breakthrough, reaching 22
in the US and as his fame spread, he was invited to back ERIC CLAPTON
on a month-long tour of the States. His next single, 'RIGHT NEXT DOOR
(BECAUSE OF ME)', didn't fare so well at home, although it did give him
his first single hit in the UK, reaching number 50. He was back touring with
ERIC CLAPTON again in November (this time in Japan) and it was clear that
a great friendship was forming. The following year, 1988, he won the Grammy
for 'Best Contemporary Blues Recording' on 'STRONG PERSUADER', and
recorded his next album, 'DON'T BE AFRAID OF THE DARK', in Los
Angeles with DAVID SANBORN guesting on saxophone. The record was his
most successful to date (number 13 in the UK and number 32 in the US)
although the title track, released as a single, failed to make any significant
impact. He won his second Grammy for 'DON'T BE AFRAID OF THE
DARK' and went on to guest on ERIC CLAPTON'S 'JOURNEYMAN'
while being on the bill at CLAPTON's eighteen-show marathon at the Albert
Hall. His sixth album, 'MIDNIGHT STROLL', an altogether tougher album,
recorded with a new line-up, reached UK number 19 and US number 51. In
1991, he was selected to present HOWLIN' WOLF's induction trophy to the
WOLF's widow, Lilly Burnett, at the sixth annual Rock & Roll Hall of Fame
Awards. Later that year, he took part in the Newport Jazz Festival with B.B.

KING and JOHN LEE HOOKER, which led to him playing on HOOKER'S
album 'MR. LUCKY'. He took the stage in Seville, Spain as part of a
five-concert series, 'Guitar Legends' to celebrate Expo 92 and later joined
BOZ SCAGGS, JOHNNY RIVERS and The DOOBIE BROTHERS with
MICHAEL McDONALD to celebrate the 25th anniversary of The MEMPHIS
HORNS in Memphis. CRAY'S next two albums seemed to show a slide in
his chart status with the bland 'I WAS WARNED' reaching UK number 29
and US 103, while 'SHAME AND A SIN', although showing some signs of
the earlier spark, peaked at only 48 and 143 in the UK and US respectively.
His 1995 album, 'SOME RAINY MORNING' leaves you wondering whether
he is looking forwards or backwards, CRAY obviously suffering a lack of
direction. Although his chart success may be waning he will always have the
respect of the public and his fellow performers by virtue of the unassuming
way he goes about his business. • **Songwriters:** Mostly CRAY compositions
with group collaborations. 1992 producer DENNIS WALKER wrote most with
CRAY or PUGH. The same album saw CRAY co-write with BOZ SCAGGS
and STEVE CROPPER on 'A PICTURE OF A BROKEN HEART' & 'ON
THE ROAD DOWN' respectively. Covered; GOT TO MAKE A COMEBACK
(Eddie Floyd) / DON'T TOUCH ME (Johnny 'Guitar' Watson) / TOO MANY
COOKS (Willie Dixon) / YOU'RE GONNA NEED ME (Albert King) / SAVE
IT (Bordleaux Bryant) / TRICK OR TREAT (Otis Redding) / etc. • **Trivia:** In
1980 he and band appeared in the film 'Animal House' as OTIS DAY's house
group.

Album rating: WHO'S BEEN TALKIN' (*5) / BAD INFLUENCE (*7) / FALSE
ACCUSATIONS (*6) /STRONG PERSUADER (*6) / DON'T BE AFRAID OF THE
DARK (*7) / MIDNIGHT STROLL (*7) / I WAS WARNED (*5) / SHAME + A SIN
(*5) / SOME RAINY MORNING (*5) / SWEET POTATO PIE (*6)

ROBERT CRAY BAND

ROBERT CRAY – vocals, guitar / **RICHARD COUSINS** – bass / **DAVE OLSON** – drums / also
MIKE VANNICE – sax, keyboards / **WARREN RAND** – sax / **CURTIS SALADO** – (guest)
harmonica

			not iss.	Tomato
1980.	(lp) <7041> **WHO'S BEEN TALKIN'**		-	

– Too many cooks / The score / The welfare (turns its back on you) / That's what I'll
do / I'd rather be a wino / Who's been talkin' / Sleeping in the ground / I'm gonna
forget about you / Nice as a fool can be / If you're thinkin' what I'm thinkin'. (UK
cd-iss. Oct86 on 'Charly'; CDCHARLY 28) (re-iss. Oct87 on 'Charly-R&B' lp/c;
CRB/TC-CRB 1140) <US-re-iss. May88 lp/c/cd; 269 601-1/-4/-2> (re-iss. Oct88 on
'Charly' cd/c/lp; CD/TC+/CLM 101) (re-iss. Apr92 as 'THE SCORE' on 'Charly'
cd/c; CDBM/TCBM 16)

— retained **COUSINS, OLSON + SALADO**

			Demon	Hightone
Mar 84.	(lp) (FIEND 23) <H 8001> **BAD INFLUENCE**			Nov83

– Phone booth / The grinder / Got to make a comeback / So many women, so little
time / Where do I go from here / Waiting for a train / March on / Don't touch me / No
big deal. <cd-iss. Feb87; HCD 8001> (re-iss. Jul87 lp/c/cd+=; FIEND/+CASS/CD
23) – I got loaded / Share what you've got, Keep what you need. (cd re-iss. Apr96
on 'Hightone'; HCD 8001)

— **PETER BOE** – keyboards, vocals repl. SALADO, VANNICE + RAND

Oct 85.	(lp/c) (FIEND/+CASS 43) <H 8005> **FALSE ACCUSATIONS**	68		

– Porch light / Change of heart, change of mind (S.O.F.T.) / She's gone / Playin' in
the dirt / I've slipped her mind / False accusations / The last time (I get burned like
this) / Payin' for it now / Sonny. (cd-iss. 1986; FIENDCD 43) (cd re-iss. Apr96 on
'Hightone'; HCD 8005)

Nov 85.	(12"ep) (D 1038T) **CHANGE OF HEART, CHANGE OF** **MIND (soft) / I GOT LOADED. / PHONE BOOTH / BAD** **INFLUENCE**			

— In Nov'85, an album, 'SHOWDOWN!' with ALBERT COLLINS and JOHNNY
COPELAND was released by 'Sonet' (SNTF 954)

			Mercury	Mercury
Oct 86.	(7") (CRAY 1) **I GUESS I SHOWED HER. / DIVIDED HEART**			

(12"+=) (CRAY 1-12) – Got to be a comeback / Share what you've got, keep what
you need.

Nov 86.	(lp/c)(cd) (MERH/+C 97)<(830568-2)> **STRONG PERSUADER**	34		13

– Smoking gun / I guess I showed her / Right next door (because of me) / Nothin' but
a woman / Still around / More than I can stand / Foul play / I wonder / Fantasized /
New blood.

Feb 87.	(7") (CRAY 2) <888343> **SMOKING GUN. / FANTASIZED**			22

(12"+=) (CRAY 2-12) – Divided heart.

May 87.	(7") (CRAY 3) <888327> **RIGHT NEXT DOOR (BECAUSE** **OF ME). / NEW BLOOD**	50		80

(12"+=) (CRAY 3-12) – Share what you've got, keep what you need.
(10"+=) (CRAY 3-10) – I wonder / Smoking gun.

Aug 87.	(7") (CRAY 4) **NOTHIN' BUT A WOMAN / I WONDER**			

(12"+=) (CRAY 4-12) – Still around / New blood.
(10"+=) (CRAY 4-10) – Right next door (because of me).

Aug 88.	(7") (CRAY 5) <870569> **DON'T BE AFRAID OF THE DARK. /** **AT LAST**			74

(12"+=) (CRAY 5-12) – Without a trace.
(cd-s+=) (CRACD 5) – Smoking gun.

Aug 88.	(lp/c)(cd) (MERH/+C 129)<(834923-2)> **DON'T BE AFRAID** **OF THE DARK**	13		32

– Don't be afraid of the dark / Don't you even care? / Your secret's safe with me / I
can't go home / Night patrol / Acting this way / Gotta change the rules / Across the
line / At last / Laugh out loud.

Oct 88.	(7") (CRAY 6) **NIGHT PATROL. / MORE THAN I CAN** **STAND**			

(12"+=) (CRAY 6-12) – Divided heart.
(cd-s+=) (CRACD 6) – I wonder.

Jan 89.	(7") (CRAY 7) **ACTING THIS WAY. / LAUGH OUT LOUD**			

(12"+=) (CRAY 7-12) – ('A'-Guitar version).
(cd-s+=) (CRACD 7) – Smoking gun.

ROBERT CRAY

—— solo, retained only **COUSINS** plus **JIMMY PUGH** – keyboards / **KEVIN HAYES** – drums, percussion / **TIM KAIHATSU** – guitar / & The MEMPHIS HORNS: **WAYNE JACKSON** – trumpet, trombone / **ANDREW LOVE** – tenor saxophone (credited later as **ROBERT CRAY BAND with The MEMPHIS HORNS**)

Aug 90. (12"ep/cd-ep) **THE FORECAST (CALLS FOR PAIN) / HOLDIN' COURT. / LABOUR OF LOVE / MIDNIGHT STROLL**

Sep 90. (cd/c/lp) <(846652-2/-4/-1)> **MIDNIGHT STROLL** — [19] [51]
– The forecast (calls for pain) / These things / My problem / Labour of love / Bouncin' back / Consequences / The things you do to me / Wall around time / Move a mountain / Midnight stroll. (cd+=) – Holdin' court. (re-iss. Mar93 cd/c; same)

Jan 91. (7") **CONSEQUENCES. / SMOKING GUN**
(12"+=/cd-s+=) – Right next door (because of me).

—— **KARL SEVAREID** – bass; repl. COUSINS

Aug 92. (cd/c/lp) <(512721-2/-4/-1)> **I WAS WARNED** — [29]
– Just a loser / I'm a good man / I was warned / The price I pay / Won the battle / On the road down / A whole lotta pride / A picture of a broken heart / He don't live here anymore / Our last time. (cd re-iss. Apr95; same)

—— **EDWARD MANION** – saxophone + **MARK PENDER** – trumpet; repl. horn section

Oct 93. (cd/c) <(518517-2/-4)> **SHAME + A SIN** — [48]
– 1040 blues / Some pain, some shame / I shiver / You're gonna need me / Don't break this ring / Stay go / Leave well enough alone / Passing by / I'm just lucky that way / Well I lied / Up and down.

Nov 93. (7"/c-s) **I HATE TAXES. / SMOKING GUN**
(cd-s+=) – 1040 blues / Right next door.

—— with **PUGH / SEVAREID / HAYES**

May 95. (cd/c) <(526928-2/-4)> **SOME RAINY MORNING** — [63]
– Moan / I'll go on / Steppin' out / Never mattered much / Tell the landlord / Little boy big / Enough for me / Jealous love / Will you think of me / Holdin' on / Love well spent.

—— Apr'96, he returned to the UK chart (at 65) augmenting JOHN LEE HOOKER on his single 'BABY LEE'.

May 97. (cd/c) (534698-2/-4) **SWEET POTATO PIE**
– Nothing against you / Do that for me / Back home / Save it / The one in the middle / Little birds / Trick or treat / Simple things / Jealous minds / Not bad for love / I can't quit.

Feb 99. (cd) (IGOXCD 516) **IN CONCERT** (live) — *Indigo Indigo*
– Chicken (intro) / That will never do / I've gotta take a chance / One more kiss / I'm so satisfied / A Collins (intro) / Don't lose your cool / Angel of mercy / That ain't the way to do it / I don't want you cuttin' my hair / Don't want no woman / Watch me baby / Collins' instrumental jam / Albert's alley.

Apr 99. (cd/c) <(RCD/RAC 10479)> **TAKE YOUR SHOES OFF** — *Rykodisc Rykodisc*
– Love gone to waste / That wasn't me / All the way / There's nothing wrong / 24-7 man / Pardon / Let me know / It's all gone / Won't you give him one more chance / Living proof / What about me / Tollin' bells.

– compilations, others, etc. –

Jan 92. (cd/c/lp) *Tomato-Rhino; (269653-2/-4/-1)* **TOO MANY COOKS** (1978 session)

Jun 97. (cd/c) *Hallmark; (30664-2/-4)* **NEW BLUES**

CRAZY HORSE

Formed: California, USA ... 1962 as DANNY & THE MEMORIES by DANNY WHITTEN, BILLY TALBOT and RALPH MOLINA. After recording one 45 for 'Valiant', they finally settled for The ROCKETS moniker in 1967. Releasing an eponymous album early the following year, the group subsequently attracted the attention of NEIL YOUNG who procured them as a credited backing band on his early solo sets, 'Everybody Knows This Is Nowhere' (1969) and 'After The Goldrush' (1970). Signing to 'Reprise' in their own right, CRAZY HORSE delivered an eponymous solo album early in 1971. Featuring such West Coast luminaries as JACK NITZCHE, NILS LOFGREN, RY COODER and BARRY GUILBEAU and deservedly receiving rave reviews, the record alternated hard-bitten, country-ish rockers with desolate, lovelorn ballads; WHITTEN's tortured 'I DON'T WANT TO TALK ABOUT IT' was subsequently covered by everyone from ROD STEWART to EVERYTHING BUT THE GIRL, taking on an added poignancy following his untimely, fatal heroin overdose on the 18th November 1972. At the time of his death, WHITTEN had already been replaced as frontman by GREG LEROY, who had made his debut earlier that year on the album, 'LOOSE'; others new members numbered JOHN BLANTON and GEORGE WHITSELL, who deputised for producer, NITZSCHE. Nevertheless, the shock of WHITTEN's death eventually led to the group's break-up, although a final album, 'CRAZY HORSE AT CROOKED CREEK' appeared on 'Epic' records early in '73. YOUNG had also been affected by WHITTEN's death and the same year gathered together TALBOT and MOLINA (alongside new guitarist, FRANK SAMPEDRO) to record the compelling 'Tonight's The Night' album, a tribute of sorts to both WHITTEN and BRUCE BERRY (their roadie who had met a similar fate). Upon its belated 1975 release, the record was credited to NEIL YOUNG & CRAZY HORSE, the core of TALBOT, MOLINA and SAMPEDRO remaining at YOUNG's side from that point on (although the singer alternated with solo material) and working their gritty magic on such classic albums as 'Zuma' (1975), 'Rust Never Sleeps' (1979), 'Ragged Glory' (1990) and 'Weld' (1991). CRAZY HORSE themselves went back into the studio in the late 70's to record 'CRAZY MOON', a follow-up to the debut finally worth the name. With SAMPEDRO a worthy successor to WHITTEN,

the likes of 'GOING DOWN AGAIN' (on which SAMPEDRO, in retrospect, sounds uncannily like NOEL GALLAGHER! – apparently a CRAZY HORSE fan) as soulful as anything on the debut. In 1993/94, CRAZY HORSE hooked up with another one of their admirers, ex-ICICLE WORKS frontman, IAN McNABB, on his Mercury-nominated set, 'Head Like A Rock'.

Album rating: CRAZY HORSE (*8) / LOOSE (*5) / CRAZY HORSE AT CROOKED CREEK (*5) / CRAZY MOON (*6)

DANNY & THE MEMORIES

DANNY WHITTEN (b. Los Angeles) – vocals, guitar / **BILLY TALBOT** (b. New York) – bass / **RALPH MOLINA** (b. Puerto Rica) – drums

not iss.   Valiant

1964.   (7") <6049> **CAN'T HELP LOVIN' THAT GIRL OF MINE. / DON'T GO**
<re-iss. 1965; 705>

—— Later in 1965, they were backing band to EDDIE HODGES on single 'LOVE MINUS ZERO – NO LIMIT' on 'Stateside' UK / 'Aurora' US.

The ROCKETS

with guests **LEON WHITSELL** – guitar, vocals / **GEORGE WHITSELL** – guitar, vocals / **BOBBY NOTKOFF** – violin

not iss.   White Whale

Mar 68. (7") <270> **HOLE IN MY POCKET. / LET ME GO**
Mar 68. (lp) <WWS 7116> **THE ROCKETS**
– Hole in my pocket / Won't you say you'll stay / Mr. Chips / It's a mistake / Let me go / Try my patience / I won't always be around / Pill's blues / Stretch your skin / Eraser. (UK cd-iss. May97 on 'Edsel'; EDCD 520)

CRAZY HORSE

WHITTEN, TALBOT & MOLINA plus **JACK NITZSCHE** – keyboards, with **NILS LOFGREN** – guitar / **RY COODER** – steel guitar / **BOB GUILBEAU** – fiddle

Reprise   Reprise

Feb 71. (7"w/drawn) **DOWNTOWN. / CROW JANE LADY**
Apr 71. (lp) (<RSLP 6438>) **CRAZY HORSE** — [84] Feb71
– Gone dead train / Dance, dance, dance / Look at all the things / Beggars day / I don't want to talk about it / Downtown / Carolay / Dirty, dirty / Nobody / I'll get by / Crow Jane lady. (re-iss. Mar86 on 'Edsel') (cd-iss. Apr94)
Apr 71. (7") (RS 23503) **DANCE, DANCE, DANCE. / LOOK AT ALL THE THINGS**
1971.   (7") <1025> **DANCE, DANCE, DANCE. / CAROLAY**
1971.   (7") <1046> **DIRTY, DIRTY. / BEGGARS DAY**

—— **GREG LEROY** – guitar, vocals repl. WHITTEN (He later died, see above) **JOHN BLANTON** – keyboards / **GEORGE WHITSELL** – guitar repl. NITZSCHE (producer)

Apr 72. (lp) (K 44171) <MS 2059> **LOOSE** — [ ] Jan 72
– Hit and run / Try / One thing I love / Move / All alone now / All the little things / Fair weather friend / You won't miss me / Going home / I don't believe it / Kind of woman / One sided love / And she won't even blow smoke in my direction.
Apr 72. (7") (K 14159) <1075> **ALL ALONE NOW. / ONE THING I LOVE**

—— **RICK CURTIS** – guitar, vocals repl. WHITSELL. **MICHAEL CURTIS** – keyboards, guitar repl. BLANTON

Epic   Epic

Jan 73. (lp) (EPC 65223) <KE 31710> **CRAZY HORSE AT CROOKED CREEK**
– Rock and roll band / Love is gone / We ride / Outside lookin' in / Don't keep me burning / Vehicle / Your song / Lady soul / Don't look back / 85 El Paso's.
Feb 73. (7") <10925> **ROCK AND ROLL BAND. / OUTSIDE LOOKIN' IN**
Jun 73. (7") (EPC 1121) **WE RIDE. / OUTSIDE LOOKING IN**

—— CRAZY HORSE now concentrated on working with NEIL YOUNG

—— **FRANK SAMPEDRO** – guitar, vox had now been recruited by TALBOT and MOLINA. CRAZY HORSE re-united for another studio album.

R.C.A.   R.C.A.

Apr 79. (lp) (PL 13054) <AFL1-3054> **CRAZY MOON** — [ ] Nov 78
– She's hot / Going down again / Lost and lonely / Dancin' lady / End of the line / New Orleans / Love don't come easy / Downhill / Too late now / That day / Thunder & lightning. (cd-iss. Apr98 on 'Camden-BMG'; 74321 578212)

—— As a trio, they continued to augment NEIL YOUNG well into the 90's.

—— **SONNY MONE + MATT PUICCI** – guitars, vocals repl. MOLINA

World Service   Curb

1989.   (lp) (SERV 009) **LEFT FOR DEAD**

—— In 1993/94, the best known trio (TALBOT, MOLINA & SAMPEDRO), worked with IAN McNABB (ex-ICICLE WORKS)

CREAM

Formed: London, England ... mid '66 as the first ever supergroup, by ERIC CLAPTON, GINGER BAKER and JACK BRUCE, who'd all cut their teeth with top-flight R&B outfits earlier in the decade. This fine pedigree led to Robert Stigwood signing them to his newly-founded 'Reaction' label, after their lauded debut at The National Jazz & Blues Festival in Windsor on the 3rd of July '66. Their initial 45, 'WRAPPING PAPER', gave them the first of many Top 40 hits, a track that didn't inspire much critical praise. To end the year, they issued a debut album, 'FRESH CREAM', lifting from it, the breezy psychedelic single, 'I FEEL FREE', a number which united BRUCE and poet/lyricist PETE BROWN in a new songwriting partnership. It also gave

CREAM their biggest hit to date, reaching No.11 in the UK. Alongside original material, the album featured updated blues standards, 'SPOONFUL' (Willie Dixon), 'ROLLIN' & TUMBLIN' (Muddy Waters) and 'I'M SO GLAD' (Skip James). Over the course of the next six months, they became increasingly influenced by the pioneering psychedelic blues of JIMI HENDRIX. This was much in evidence on the next 45, 'STRANGE BREW', a slow-burning piece of sinister psych-blues. One of the highlights of their second album, 'DISRAELI GEARS', this record also featured such enduring CREAM classics as, 'SUNSHINE OF YOUR LOVE' (a US-only Top 5 hit), 'TALES OF BRAVE ULYSSES' & 'WORLD OF PAIN'. In fact every track was fantastic and the album remains an essential purchase for any self-respecting record collector. Their third set, 'WHEELS OF FIRE', recorded in San Francisco and New York, consisted of two records, one studio – one live. The former featured an ominous cover of BOOKER T's 'BORN UNDER A BAD SIGN', while the live disc included a definitive re-working of ROBERT JOHNSON's 'CROSSROADS'. However, the album (which was soon split into two single lp's) failed to garner the same critical praise as its predecessor, pandering too heavily to commerciality. They played their farewell tour in November '68, culminating in a legendary sell-out show on the 26th at The Royal Albert Hall. They were already in the US Top 10 with the GEORGE HARRISON and CLAPTON-penned 'WHITE ROOM', the song later becoming a fitting epitaph after it was given a UK release in early '69. All went on to high profile solo careers, the most obvious being ERIC 'God' CLAPTON.

Album rating: FRESH CREAM (*6) / DISRAELI GEARS (*9) / WHEELS OF FIRE (*8) / GOODBYE (*5) / THE BEST OF CREAM compilation (*7) / LIVE CREAM collection (*5) / LIVE CREAM VOL.2 collection (*5) / HEAVY CREAM compilation (*6) / STRANGE BREW – THE VERY BEST OF CREAM compilation (*9)

ERIC CLAPTON (b.ERIC PATRICK CLAPP, 30 May'45, Ripley, Surrey, England) – guitar, vocals (ex-YARDBIRDS, ex-JOHN MAYALL'S BLUESBREAKERS) / **JACK BRUCE** (b.JOHN BRUCE, 14 May'43, Glasgow, Scotland) – vocals, bass (ex-GRAHAM BOND, ex-JOHN MAYALL'S BLUESBREAKERS, ex-MANFRED MANN) / **GINGER BAKER** (b.PETER BAKER, 19 Aug'39, Lewisham, London, England) – drums (ex-GRAHAM BOND ORGANISATION, ex-ALEXIS KORNER'S BLUES INCORPORATED)

			Reaction	Atco
Oct 66.	(7") (591 007) **WRAPPING PAPER. / CAT'S SQUIRREL**		34	
Dec 66.	(lp; mono/stereo) (593/594 001) <33206> **FRESH CREAM** – N.S.U. / Sleepy time time / Dreaming / Sweet wine / Spoonful / Cat's squirrel / Four until late / Rollin' and tumblin' / I'm so glad / Toad. (re-iss.Feb69; stereo); reached No.7 UK. (re-iss.Oct70 as 'FULL CREAM'; 2447 010) (re-iss.Mar75 as 'CREAM' on 'Polydor'+=; 2384 067); 2 tracks) (cd-iss.Jan84+=; 827 576-2) – Wrapping paper / The coffee song.		6	39
Dec 66.	(7") (591 011) <6462> **I FEEL FREE. / N.S.U.**		11	
Jun 67.	(7") (591 015) <6488> **STRANGE BREW. / TALES OF BRAVE ULYSSES**		17	
Nov 67.	(7") <6522> **SPOONFUL. / (part 2)**		-	4
Nov 67.	(lp; mono/stereo) (593/594 003) <33232> **DISRAELI GEARS** – Strange brew / Sunshine of your love / World of pain / Dance the night away / Blue condition / Tales of brave Ulysses / S.W.L.A.B.R. / We're going wrong / Outside woman blues / Take it back / Mother's lament. <US re-iss.Nov77 on 'R.S.O.'; 3010> (re-iss.Nov77 on 'R.S.O.'; 239 412-2) (cd-iss.Jan84 on 'Track'; 823 636-2)		5	4
			Polydor	Atco
Jan 68.	(7") <6544> **SUNSHINE OF YOUR LOVE. / S.W.L.A.B.R.** (UK-iss.Sep68; 56286); hit No.25)		-	5
May 68.	(7") (56258) <6575> **ANYONE FOR TENNIS. / PRESSED RAT AND WARTHOG**		40	64
—	**FELIX PAPPALARDI** – producer, instruments guested as 4th p/t member			
Aug 68.	(d-lp; mono/stereo) (582/583 031-2) <2-700> **WHEELS OF FIRE** (re-iss.1972; 2612 001) <US re-iss.Feb77 on 'R.S.O.'; 3802> (re-iss.Jan84 on 'R.S.O.'; 3216 036) (cd-iss.Jan84; 8254 142) (cd re-iss.Feb89; 827 658-2)		3	1 Jul68
Aug 68.	(lp; mono/stereo) (582/583 033) **WHEELS OF FIRE – IN THE STUDIO** – White room / Sitting on top of the world / Passing the time / As you said / Pressed rat and warthog / Politician / Those were the days / Born under a bad sign / Deserted cities of the heart. (re-iss.Nov77 on 'R.S.O.'; 2394 136)		7	
Aug 68.	(lp; mono/stereo) (582/583 040) **WHEELS OF FIRE – LIVE AT THE FILLMORE (live)** – Crossroads / Spoonful / Traintime / Toad. (re-iss.Nov77 on 'R.S.O.'; 2394 137)		-	-
Jan 69.	(7") (65300) <6617> **WHITE ROOM. / THOSE WERE THE DAYS**		28	6 Sep68
—	They split around mid-'68. The rest of their releases were posthumous and CLAPTON went solo after forming BLIND FAITH with BAKER. He also went solo. JACK BRUCE went solo, etc.			

– compilations, others, etc. –

either 'Polydor' in UK and 'Atco' in the US.

Jan 69.	(7") <6646> **CROSSROADS. / PASSING THE TIME**	-	28
Mar 69.	(lp) (583 053) <7001> **GOODBYE** – I'm so glad (live) / Politician (live) / Sitting on top of the world (live) / Badge / Doing that scrapyard thing / What a bringdown. (re-iss.Nov77 & Aug84 on 'R.S.O.'; 2394 178) (cd-iss.Jan84.+=; 823 660-2) – Anyone for tennis.	1	2
Apr 69.	(7") (56315) <6315> **BADGE. / WHAT A BRINGDOWN** (re-iss.Oct72; 2058 285)	18	60 Mar69
Nov 69.	(lp) (583 060) <291> **BEST OF CREAM** (re-iss.Nov77 on 'R.S.O.'; 3216 031) (re-iss.Apr86 on 'Arcade'; ADAH 429)	6	3 Jul69
Jun 70.	(lp) (2383 016) <33-328> **LIVE CREAM (live)** – N.S.U. / Sleepy time time / Lawdy mama / Sweet wine / Rollin' and tumblin'. (re-iss.Nov77 & Mar85 on 'R.S.O.' lp/c; SPE LP/MC 93) (cd-iss.May88; 827 577-2)	4	15 Apr70
Jul 70.	(7") **LAWDY MAMA (live). / SWEET WINE (live)**	-	-
Jul 71.	(7") **I FEEL FREE. / WRAPPING PAPER** (re-iss.Jul84 on 'Old Gold'; OG 9423)	-	-
Jun 72.	(lp) (2383 119) <7005> **LIVE CREAM VOL.2** – Deserted cities of the heart / White room / Politician / Tales of brave Ulysses /	15	27 Mar72

	Sunshine of your love / Steppin' out. (re-iss.Nov77 on 'R.S.O.';) (cd-iss.May88; 823 661-2)		
Apr 73.	(d-lp) (2659 022) <3502> **HEAVY CREAM**		Oct72
1973.	(lp) Polydor; <PD 5529> **OFF THE TOP**	-	
Oct 80.	(6xlp-box) (2658 142) **CREAM BOX SET**	-	
Oct 83.	(lp)(c) (2479 212)(3215 038) **THE STORY OF CREAM VOL.1**	-	
Oct 83.	(lp)(c) (2479 213)(3215 039) **THE STORY OF CREAM VOL.2**		-
Apr 78.	(lp)(c) R.S.O.; (3228 005) **CREAM VOLUME TWO**		
Feb 83.	(lp/c) R.S.O.; (RSD/TRSD 5021) **STRANGE BREW – THE VERY BEST OF CREAM** – Badge / Sunshine of your love / Crossroads / White room / Born under a bad sign / Swlabr / Strange brew / Anyone for tennis / I feel free / Tales of brave Ulysses / Politician / Spoonful. (cd-iss.Nov87 on 'Polydor';)		
Aug 82.	(7") R.S.O.; (RSO 91) **BADGE. / TALES OF BRAVE ULYSSES** (12"+=) (RSOX 91) – White room.		
Jul 86.	(7") (POSP 812) **I FEEL FREE. / BADGE**		
Jul 84.	(7") Old Gold; (OG 9425) **WHITE ROOM. / BADGE**		
Jul 84.	(7") Old Gold; (OG 9426) **SUNSHINE OF YOUR LOVE. / ANYONE FOR TENNIS**		
Feb 89.	(cd) Koine; (K 880803) **LIVE 1968 (live)**		
Dec 91.	(cd; w/booklet) **U.F.O.; IN GEAR**		
Nov 92.	(cd) I.T.M.; (ITM 960002) **THE ALTERNATIVE ALBUM** (re-iss.Jan97 on 'Masterplan'; MP 42009)		
Dec 92.	(cd/c) Pickwick; (PWK S/MC 4127P) **DESERTED CITIES: THE CREAM COLLECTION**		
Feb 95.	(cd/c) (523 752-2/-4) **THE VERY BEST OF CREAM**		

CREATION (dig out; Great Psychedelic . . .)

CREATURES (see under ⇒ SIOUXSIE & THE BANSHEES)

CREED

Formed: Tallahassee, Florida, USA . . . 1994 by singer SCOTT STAPP and guitarist MARK TREMONTI, who hooked up with rhythm section BRIAN MARSHALL and SCOTT PHILLIPS. Another band to emerge from the post-Grunge scene, although EDDIE VEDDER and LAYNE STALEY have no fears here about their mantle being taken by these lads. A year or two into their career, CREED released a self-financed debut set, 'MY OWN PRISON', which sold its initial batch and made major labels take note. 'Epic' (through subsidiary 'Wind-Up') finally won the battle for their signatures early in '97 and with a new producer, Ron St. Germain, remixed and re-issued the album later in the year. "Grunge was not dead!" was the claim of their teen-metal followers, although CREED themselves dismissed they were part of that genre and just a basic rock'n'roll band – basic being the key word. 'MY OWN PRISON' started a steady rise up the American charts finally peaking at No.22 a year later, although Britain had to wait until early '99 to get its first taste of million-sellers CREED. By which point, Grunge had certainly been well and truly buried. Meanwhile, back in States, the glum-rockers were just about to serve up a second helping in the shape of 'HUMAN CLAY' (1999) – a difficult second album indeed that nevertheless topped the chart. • **Note:** not to be confused with mid-90's act who issued 12" singles on 'Rectory'.

Album rating: MY OWN PRISON (*6) / HUMAN CLAY (*5)

SCOTT STAPP – vocals / **MARK TREMONTI** – guitar, vocals / **BRIAN MARSHALL** – bass / **SCOTT PHILLIPS** – drums

			Wind Up-Epic	Wind Up-Epic
Oct 97.	(cd) <13049> **MY OWN PRISON** – Torn / Ode / My own prison / Pity for a dime / In America / Illusion / Unforgiven / Sister / What's this life for / One. <US originally iss.1997 on 'Blue Collar'; 5066> (UK-iss.Feb99 on 'Wind-Up – Epic'; 493072)		-	22
Feb 99.	(-) <radio cut> **ONE**			70
Aug 99.	(-) <radio cut> **HIGHER**			52
Sep 99.	(cd/c) (495027-2/-4) <13053> **HUMAN CLAY** – Are you ready / What if / Beautiful / Say I / Wrong way / Faceless man / Never die / With arms wide open / Higher / Wash away those years / Inside us all.			1

CREEDENCE CLEARWATER REVIVAL

Formed: El Cerrito, California, USA . . . late 1959 as school group The BLUE VELVETS by JOHN FOGERTY, STU COOK and DOUG CLIFFORD. JOHN soon invited other multi-instrumentalist and brother TOM. After one 45 on a local label, they became The GOLLIWOGS in 1964 and signed to label 'Fantasy' where TOM was working as a clerk. The 'BROWN EYED GIRL' single was a moderate success although subsequent releases stiffed. Following DOUG and JOHN's compulsory spell in the forces (no hippy draft dodging for these guys!) the group became CREEDENCE CLEARWATER REVIVAL, releasing their debut single, an inspired cover of 'SUZIE Q,' in September '68. A top 20 hit, it was closely followed by another cover, SCREAMIN' JAY HAWKINS', 'I PUT A SPELL ON YOU' (1968) and a self-titled debut album the following year. Despite hailing from Berkeley in California, CREEDENCE, or at least JOHN FOGERTY lived and breathed a Southern fantasy of "Backwood Bayous", "Cajun Queens" and "Hoodoos" (eh?!). This was swamp R&B of the rootsiest pedigree, utilising a simple but stunningly effective hybrid of raw rock'n'roll, country and blues. FOGERTY's voice was an instrument in its own right, a life-affirming bellow that equalled MARVIN

GAYE and OTIS REDDING for soulfulness and if his early classics fail to send a shiver up your spine, it'd be an idea to check your pulse. The man was also blessed with the ability to write insanely catchy songs which were nevertheless steeped in Southern authenticity. 'PROUD MARY' / 'BORN ON THE BAYOU' (1969) was the first in an avalanche of hits that saw CREEDENCE become one of the world's biggest selling bands during their heyday of '69-70. The classic 'GREEN RIVER' (1969) spawned perhaps their best known track, the apocalyptic swamp-pop of 'BAD MOON RISING' as well as the poignant country soul of 'LODI' and the blistering title track. 'DOWN ON THE CORNER' (1970) kept up the run of hit singles while 'WILLY AND THE POOR BOYS' (1970) remains the definitive CCR album. From the passionate politicism of 'FORTUNATE SON' to the desolate strangeness of 'EFFIGY', the album ran the gamut of the band's influences. There was no stopping the prolific FOGERTY at this point and a mere six months later the band released 'COSMO'S FACTORY' (1970). Coming within a whisker of its predecessor, the album produced the top ten hits 'TRAVELLIN' MAN' (1970), 'UP AROUND THE BEND' (1970) and 'LONG AS I CAN SEE THE LIGHT' (1970) as well as their driving cover of MARVIN GAYE's 'I HEARD IT THROUGH THE GRAPEVINE'. While 'PENDULUM' (1971) was slated as a disappointment, it nevertheless held nuggets like the gorgeous 'HAVE YOU EVER SEEN THE RAIN' and the rousing 'HEY TONIGHT'. By this point, however, internal disputes were rife and TOM left for a solo career a month after the album's release. Pared down to a trio, CCR cut a final studio album, 'MARDI GRAS' (1971) before splitting in 1973. JOHN released his first solo outing the same year, a collection of purist country under the BLUE RIDGE RANGERS moniker, following it up with JOHN FOGERTY' in 1975. While the album contained the FOGERTY classics, 'ROCKIN' ALL OVER THE WORLD' and 'ALMOST SATURDAY NIGHT', and his voice was still incredible, his earlier songwriting sharpness sounded blunted. Retreating to a farm for a life of rural bliss with his family, it was 10 years before FOGERTY returned with 'CENTERFIELD' (1985). Although it sold two million copies, the album was again slightly disappointing and led to FOGERTY gaining a place in the history books for being possibly the only artist ever to be sued (by 'Fantasy' owner SAUL ZAENTZ) for plagiarising his own material. 'EYE OF THE ZOMBIE' (1986) was average while 'BLUE SWAMP' (1996) was hardly worth waiting a decade for. Despite being the driving force behind a band that has influenced artists as diverse as SONIC YOUTH, HANOI ROCKS and STATUS QUO (!), it seems increasingly unlikely that FOGERTY is going to come up with something that does his legend justice. • Covered: SUZIE Q (Dale Hawkins) / OOBY DOOBY (Roy Orbison) / HELLO MARY LOU (Ricky Nelson) / etc. • Miscellaneous: TOM FOGERTY was to die of tuberculosis on the 6th September '90.

Album rating: CREEDENCE CLEARWATER REVIVAL (*5) / BAYOU COUNTRY (*6) / GREEN RIVER (*8) / WILLY AND THE POOR BOYS (*9) / COSMO'S FACTORY (*7) / PENDULUM (*8) / MARDI GRAS (*4) / CREEDENCE GOLD compilation (*8) / MORE CREEDENCE GOLD compilation (*7) / LIVE IN EUROPE (*4) / THE ROYAL ALBERT HALL CONCERT (*4) / THE COLLECTION double compilation (*9) / John Fogerty: THE BLUE RIDGE RANGERS (*5) / JOHN FOGERTY (*4) / CENTERFIELD (*7) / EYE OF THE ZOMBIE (*4) / BLUE MOON SWAMP (*7)

The BLUE VELVETS

JOHN FOGERTY (b.28 May'45, Berkeley, Calif.)– vocals, guitar / **TOM FOGERTY** (b. 9 Nov'41, Berkeley)– rhythm guitar, piano / **STU COOK** (b.25 Apr'45, Portland, Calif.)– bass / **DOUG 'COSMO' CLIFFORD** (b.24 Apr'45, Palo Alto, Calif.)- drums

		not iss.	Orkhestra
1962.	(7") <1010> **HAVE YOU EVER BEEN LONELY. / BONITA**	-	

The GOLLIWOGS

same line-up (TOM sang lead on first)

			not iss.	Fantasy
Nov 64.	(7") <590> **DON'T TELL ME NO LIES. / LITTLE GIRL**		-	
Jun 65.	(7") <597> **YOU CAME WALKING. / WHERE YOU BEEN**		-	
Aug 65.	(7") <599> **YOU CAN'T BE TRUE. / YOU GOT NOTHIN' ON ME**			
			Vocalion	Scorpio
Jan 66.	(7") (VF 9266) <404> **BROWN-EYED GIRL. / YOU BETTER BE CAREFUL**			
Mar 66.	(7") (VF 9283) <405> **FRAGILE CHILD. / FIGHT FIRE**			
Dec 66.	(7") <408> **WALKING ON THE WATER. / YOU BETTER GET IT**			
Nov 67.	(7") <412> **PORTERVILLE. / CALL IT PRETENDING**		-	

(above single was soon later credited to below group name) *(also, a compilation album of some singles above was released in '74 on 'Fantasy')*

CREEDENCE CLEARWATER REVIVAL

same line-up

		Liberty	Fantasy
Sep 68.	(7") <616> **SUZIE Q. (part 1). / SUZIE Q. (part 2)**	-	11
Nov 68.	(7") <617> **I PUT A SPELL ON YOU. / WALK ON THE WATER**		
Apr 69.	(lp) (LBS 83259) <8382> **CREEDENCE CLEARWATER REVIVAL**		52 Jul68

– I put a spell on you / Suzie Q. / The working man / Ninety-nine and a half (won't do) / Get down woman / Porterville / Gloomy / Walk on the water. *(re-iss. Mar73 on 'Fantasy'; FT 506) (re-iss. Jul84 on 'Fantasy' lp/c; FAS LP/K 5002) (re-iss. Aug87 on 'Fantasy' lp/c/cd; FACE/FACC/CDFE 501)*

May 69.	(7") (LBF 15223) <619> **PROUD MARY. / BORN ON THE BAYOU**	8	2 Jan69

Jun 69.	(lp) (LBS 83261) <8387> **BAYOU COUNTRY**		7 Feb69

– Born on the bayou / Bootleg / Graveyard train / Good golly Miss Molly / Penthouse pauper / Keep on chooglin' / Proud Mary. (hit UK No.62 in May'70) *(re-iss. Mar73 on 'Fantasy'; FT 507) (re-iss. Jul84 on 'Fantasy' lp/c; FAS LP/K 5003) (re-iss. Aug87 on 'Fantasy' lp/c/cd; FACE/FACC/CDFE 502)*

Aug 69.	(7") (LBF 15230) <622> **BAD MOON RISING. / LODI**	1	2	
			52 May69	
Nov 69.	(7") (LBF 15250) <625> **GREEN RIVER. / COMMOTION**	19	2	
			30 Jul69	
Dec 69.	(lp) (LBS 83273) <8393> **GREEN RIVER**	20	1 Sep69	

– Green river / Commotion / Tombstone shadow / Wrote a song for everyone / Bad moon rising / Lodi / Cross-tie walker / Sinister purpose / Lodi / Wrote a song for everyone / Night time is the right time. *(re-iss. Mar73 on 'Fantasy'; FT 504) (re-iss. Jul84 on 'Fantasy' lp/c; FAS LP/K 5004) (re-iss. Aug87 on 'Fantasy' lp/c/cd; FACE/FACC/CDFE 503)*

Feb 70.	(7") (LBF 15283) <634> **DOWN ON THE CORNER. / FORTUNATE SON**	31	3 Oct 69
			14
Mar 70.	(lp) (LBS 83338) <8397> **WILLY AND THE POOR BOYS**	10	3 Dec69

– Down on the corner / It came out of the sky / Cotton fields / Poor boy shuffle / Feelin' blue / Fortunate son / Don't look now (it ain't you or me) / The midnight special / Side of the road / Effigy. *(re-iss. Mar73 on 'Fantasy'; FT 503) (re-iss. Jul84 on 'Fantasy' lp/c; FAS LP/K 5005) (re-iss. Aug87 on 'Fantasy' lp/c/cd; FACE/FACC/CDFE 504)*

Mar 70.	(7") (LBF 15310) <637> **TRAVELIN' BAND. / WHO'LL STOP THE RAIN**	8	2 Jan70
Jun 70.	(7") (LBF 15354) <641> **UP AROUND THE BEND. / RUN THROUGH THE JUNGLE**	3	4 Apr70
Aug 70.	(7") (LBF 15384) <645> **LONG AS I CAN SEE THE LIGHT. / LOOKIN' OUT MY BACK DOOR**	20	2 B-side
Sep 70.	(lp) (LBS 83388) <8402> **COSMO'S FACTORY**	1	1 Jul70

– Ramble tamble / Before you accuse me / Travelin' band / Ooby dooby / Lookin' out my back door / Run through the jungle / Up around the bend / My baby left me / Who'll stop the rain / I heard it through the grapevine / Long as I can see the light. *(re-iss. Mar73 on 'Fantasy'; FT 502) (re-iss. Jul84 lp/c; FAS LP/K 506) (re-iss. Aug87 on 'Fantasy' lp/c/cd; FACE/FACC/CDFE 505)*

Jan 71.	(lp) (LBG 83400) <8410> **PENDULUM**	23	5 Dec70

– Pagan baby / Sailor's lament / Chameleon / Have you ever seen the rain / (Wish I could) Hideaway / Born to move / Hey tonight / It's just a thought / Molina / Rude awakening No.2. *(re-iss. Mar73 on 'Fantasy'; FT 508) (re-iss. Jul84 on 'Fantasy' lp/c; FAS LP/K 507) (re-iss. Nov89 on 'Fantasy' lp/c/cd; FACE/FACC/CDFE 512) (cd re-iss. Jan99 on 'Akarma'; 8410)*

Mar 71.	(7") (LBF 15440) <655> **HAVE YOU EVER SEEN THE RAIN. / HEY TONIGHT**	36	8 Jan71

(re-iss. Apr71 on 'United Artists'; UP 35210)

—— now a trio when TOM FOGERTY departed to go solo (Feb'71)

		U.A.	Fantasy
Jul 71.	(7") (UP 35261) <665> **SWEET HITCH-HIKER. / DOOR TO DOOR**		
		36	6
		Fantasy	Fantasy
Apr 72.	(7") <676> **SOMEDAY NEVER COMES. / TEARIN' UP THE COUNTRY**	-	25
Jul 72.	(lp) <(FAN 9404)> **MARDI GRAS**		12 Apr72

– Lookin' for a reason / Take it like a friend / Need someone to hold / Tearin' up the country / Hello Mary Lou / Someday never comes / What are you gonna do / Hello Mary Lou / Door to door / Sweet hitch-hiker. *(re-iss. Mar73; FT 505) (re-iss. Jul84 lp/c; FAS LP/K 5008) (re-iss. Nov89 lp/c/cd; FACE/FACC/CDFE 513)*

—— split Oct'72

– compilations etc. –

on 'Fantasy' unless mentioned otherwise

Dec 72.	(7") (FRC 101) **BORN ON THE BAYOU. / I PUT A SPELL ON YOU**		
Jan 73.	(lp) (501) <9418> **CREEDENCE GOLD**		15 Nov72

– Proud Mary / Down on the corner / Bad Moon rising / I heard it through the grapevine / Midnight special / Have you ever seen the rain / Born on the bayou / Suzie Q. *(cd-iss. Sep91; CDFE 515)*

Mar 73.	(7") (FRC 104) **IT CAME OUT OF THE SKY. / SIDE O' THE ROAD**		-
Sep 73.	(lp) (512) <9430> **MORE CREEDENCE GOLD**		61 Jul73

– Hey tonight / Run through the jungle / Fortunate son / Bootleg / Lookin' out my back door / Molina / Who'll stop the rain / Sweet hitch-hiker / Good golly Miss Molly / I put a spell on you / Don't look now / Lodi / Porterville / Up around the bend. *(cd-iss. Sep91; CDFE 516)*

May 74.	(d-lp) (520) <FCCR 1> **LIVE IN EUROPE (live 1971)**		Nov73

– Born on the bayou / Green river / It came out of the sky / Door to door / Travellin' band / Fortunate son / Porterville / Up around the bend / Suzie Q / Commotion / Lodi. *(re-iss. Feb90 lp/c/cd; FACE/FACC/CDFE 514)*

Mar 76.	(d-lp) (528) <FCCR 2> **CHRONICLE (THE 20 GREATEST HITS)**		100 Feb76

– Suzie Q. / I put a spell on you / Proud Mary / Bad Moon rising / Lodi / Green river / Commotion / Down on the corner / Fortunate son / Travellin' band / Who'll stop the rain / Up around the bend / Run through the jungle / Lookin' out my back door / Long as I can see the light / Have you ever seen the rain? / Hey tonight / Sweet hitch-hiker / Someday never comes. *(cd-iss. Jun87 on 'Polydor'+=; 821 742-2)* – I heard it through the grapevine.

Mar 76.	(7") (FTC 128) <759> **I HEARD IT THROUGH THE GRAPEVINE. / GOOD GOLLY MISS MOLLY**		43 Dec75
Jul 77.	(7"m) (FTC 142) **BAD MOON RISING. / PROUD MARY / GREEN RIVER**		-
Nov 78.	(7"m) (FTC 164) **WHO'LL STOP THE RAIN. / PROUD MARY / HEY TONIGHT**		-
Jun 79.	(lp) (FT 558) **GREATEST HITS (20 GOLDEN)**	35	
Jul 79.	(7") (FRC 178) **I HEARD IT THROUGH THE GRAPEVINE. / John Fogerty: ROCKIN' ALL OVER THE WORLD**		-

(12") (12FTC 178) – ('A'side) / Keep on chooglin' (extended).

1979.	(7") <908> **COMMOTION. / TOMBSTONE SHADOW**	-	-
1979.	(7") <917> **BAD MOON RISING. / MEDLEY U.S.A.**	-	-
1979.	(7") <920> **LODI. / COTTON FIELDS**	-	-

1979. (7") <957> **I HEARD IT THROUGH THE GRAPEVINE – UP AROUND THE BEND (medley). / PROUD MARY – LODI (medley)** | - | |

Feb 81. (lp/c) *Music For Pleasure-Fantasy;* <*(MPF/+5 4501)* **LIVE AT THE ROYAL ALBERT HALL** (live) <US-title 'THE CONCERT'> | | 62 Dec80
(re-iss. Jul89 as 'THE CONCERT' on 'Fantasy' lp/c/cd; FACE/FACC/CDFE 511)

Aug 81. (7") *Golden Grooves; (GOLD 521)* **PROUD MARY. / UP AROUND THE BEND**

Oct 81. (7") *Golden Grooves; (GOLD 530)* **BAD MOON RISING. / GOOD GOLLY MISS MOLLY**

Feb 82. (lp/c) *Music For Pleasure-Fantasy; (MPF/+5 4500)* **THE HITS ALBUM**

Sep 85. (7") *Old Gold; (OG 9569)* **BAD MOON RISING. / LONG AS I SEE THE LIGHT**

Sep 85. (7") *Old Gold; (OG 9570)* **PROUD MARY. / TRAVELLIN' BAND**

Oct 85. (d-lp/c) *Impression; (IMD P/K 3)* **THE CREEDENCE COLLECTION** | 68 |

Jun 87. (cd) <*(CDCCR 3)*> **CHRONICLE VOL.2**

May 88. (cd) *Arcade; (01279161)* **THE COMPLETE HITS ALBUM VOL.1**

May 88. (cd) *Arcade; (01279261)* **THE COMPLETE HITS ALBUM VOL.2**

Jun 88. (7") *Ace; (NS 124)* **BAD MOON RISING. / HAVE YOU EVER SEEN THE RAIN?**
(12"+=) *(NST 124)* – Keep on chooglin'.

Jun 88. (lp/c/cd) *(FACE/FACC/FAX 509)* **THE BEST OF – VOLUME 1**

Aug 88. (lp/c) *(FACE/FACC 510)* **THE BEST OF – VOLUME 2**

Dec 88. (cd) <*8029 852-2*> **CHOOGLIN'**
(UK-iss.Nov92; CDFE 517)

Apr 92. (7") *Epic; (658004-7)* **BAD MOON RISING. / AS LONG AS I CAN SEE THE LIGHT** | 71 |
(cd-s+=) *(658004-2)* –

Dec 92. (cd) *(CDFE 518)* **CREEDENCE COUNTRY**

Aug 95. (cd-s) *Old Gold; (OG 6306)* **TRAVELLIN' BAND. / WHO'LL STOP THE RAIN**

Sep 95. (cd-s) *Old Gold; (12623 6326-2)* **UP AROUND THE BEND / RUN THROUGH THE JUNGLE** | | -

BLUE RIDGE RANGERS

—— was JOHN FOGERTY's first total solo venture

	Fantasy	Fantasy

Dec 72. (7") <689> **JAMBALAYA (ON THE BAYOU). / WORKING ON A BUILDING** | - | 16

Apr 73. (lp) *(F 1511)* <9415> **BLUE RIDGE RANGERS** | | 47
– Blue ridge mountain blues / Somewhere listening (for my name) / You're the reason / Jambalaya (on the bayou) / She thinks I still care / California blues (blue yodel #4) / Workin' on a building / Please help me I'm falling / Have thine own way, Lord / I ain't never / Hearts of stone / Today I started loving you. <*re-iss. Aug86; 1061150*> *(re-iss. Sep87 lp/c/cd; FACE/FACC/CDFA 506)*

May 73. (7") *(FRC 105)* <700> **HEARTS OF STONE. / SOMEWHERE LISTENING (FOR MY NAME)** | | 37 Mar73

Oct 73. (7") *(FRC 110)* <710> **BACK IN THE HILLS. / YOU DON'T OWN ME** | | Jul73

JOHN FOGERTY

solo, plays / sings everything

	Fantasy	Fantasy

Mar 74. (7") *(FTC 111)* <717> **COMING DOWN THE ROAD. / RICOCHET**

	Fantasy	Asylum

Sep 75. (7") *(FTC 119)* <45274> **ROCKIN' ALL OVER THE WORLD. / THE WALL** | | 27

Oct 75. (lp) *(FT 526)* <1046> **JOHN FOGERTY** | | 78
– Rockin' all over the world / You rascal you / The wall / Travelin' high / Lonely teardrops / Almost Saturday night / Where the river flows / Sea cruise / Dream – Song / Flyin' away. *(re-iss. Sep87 lp/c/cd; FACE/FACC/CDFE 507)*

Dec 75. (7") <45291> **ALMOST SATURDAY NIGHT. / SEA CRUISE** | - | 78

May 76. (7") *(FTC 133)* <45309> **YOU GOT THE MAGIC. / EVIL THING** | | 87

—— JOHN FOGERTY returned after 9 years complete with new session people

	Warners	Warners

Feb 85. (7") *(W 9100)* <29100> **THE OLD MAN DOWN THE ROAD. / BIG TRAIN (FROM MEMPHIS)** | | 10 Dec84

Feb 85. (lp/c/cd) *(925203-1/-4/-2)* <25203> **CENTERFIELD** | 48 | 1 Jan85
– The old man down the road / Rock and roll girls / Big train (from Memphis) / I saw it on T.V. / Mr. Greed / Searchlight / Centerfield / I can't help myself / Zant Kant danz. *(cd re-iss. Nov93; same)*

Jun 85. (7") *(W 9053)* <29053> **ROCK AND ROLL GIRLS. / CENTERFIELD** | | 20
| | | 44 Mar85

—— now with **JOHN ROBINSON** – drums / **NEIL STUBENHAUS** – bass

Oct 86. (lp/c/cd) *(925449-1/-4/-2)* <25449> **EYE OF THE ZOMBIE** | 44 | 26
– Goin' back home / Eye of the zombie / Headlines / Knockin' on your door / Change in the weather / Violence is golden / Wasn't that a woman / Soda pop / Sail away.

Oct 86. (7") *(W 8657)* <28657> **EYE OF THE ZOMBIE. / I CONFESS** (with Bobby King) | | 81
(12"+=) *(W 8657T)* – I can't help myself.

Dec 86. (7") <28535> **CHANGE IN THE WEATHER. / MY TOOT TOOT** | - | -

—— returned after another 10 years in the proverbial wilderness

	Warners	Warners

Jun 97. (cd/c) <*(9362 45426-2/-4)*> **BLUE MOON SWAMP** | | 37 May97
– Southern streamline / Hot rod heart / Blueboy / Hundred and ten in the shade / Rattlesnake highway / Bring it down to Jelly Roll / Walking in a hurricane / Swamp river days / Rambunctions boy / Joy of my life / Blue moon nights / Bad bad boy.

—— his live band were basically **KENNY ARONOFF** – drums / **BOB GLAUB** – bass / **MIKE CANIPE** – guitar

Jun 98. (cd) <*(9362 46908-2)*> **PREMONITION** (live) | | 29
– Born on the bayou / Green river / Susie Q. / I put a spell on you / Who'll stop the rain / Premonition / Almost Saturday night / Rockin' all over the world / Joy of my life / Down on the corner / Centerfield / Swamp river days / Hot rod heart / The old man down the road / Bad moon rising / Fortunate son / Proud Mary / Travelin' band.

Marshall CRENSHAW (dig out; Great Alt & Indie . . .)

Michael CRETU (see under ⇒ ENIGMA)

CRIME & THE CITY SOLUTION
(dig out; Great Alt & Indie . . .)

CRISPY AMBULANCE (dig out; Great Alt & Indie . . .)

Peter CRISS (see under ⇒ KISS)

Jim CROCE

Born: 10 Jan'43, Philadelphia, Pennsylvania, USA, although he moved to New York in 1967 with his wife INGRID. He'd already started playing guitar by the early 60's, forced to adapt his guitar-picking technique after suffering a broken finger; this was sustained during one of his many jobs which also included broadcasting a university campus folk/blues radio show in 1963. Signing to 'Capitol, he and his spouse cut a one-off album, 'APPROACHING DAY' (1968), before returning to Pennsylvania. A soft-rock acoustic singer/songwriter/guitarist in the JAMES TAYLOR mould, CROCE (who was driving trucks in his spare time to make ends meet) would subsequently sign to 'A.B.C.' with the help of an old college mate turned record producer, Tommy West. His debut solo set, 'YOU DON'T MESS AROUND WITH JIM' (1972), began a steady ascent of the US chart, finally peaking at No.1 thanks to the success of its title track and 'OPERATOR (THAT'S NOT THE WAY IT FEELS)'. Concentrating on streetwise subject matter and accompanied by the distinctive lead acoustic guitar of MAURY MUELHLIESEN, CROCE's unique, laid back approach was further developed on the man's 1973 sophomore set, 'LIFE AND TIMES'. This was preceded by what was to become CROCE's signature tune, 'BAD, BAD LEROY BROWN', a surprise but worthy No.1 in America which sadly went unnoticed in Britain. CROCE was obviously on the brink of a huge career with a cover of the latter song soon-to-be recorded by no less a personage than Ol' Blue Eyes himself, FRANK SINATRA, the ultimate songwriting acclaim. This popularity was largely achieved on the back of a punishing touring schedule which was ultimately to cost him and his guitarist their lives as they flew all over the states promoting their work. On September the 20th, 1973, JIM and MAURY's charter plane crashed after take-off, killing them both along with four other passengers. He was survived by his wife and child, Adrian, whose baby pic appears on the inner cover of top-selling posthumous compilation album, 'PHOTOGRAPHS AND MEMORIES' (1974); Adrian is now a recording artist in his own right. One can only speculate as to whether JC's easy-going style would have survived the 70's. All the signs were that he would have probably broadened out into a mainstream lyric writer. • **Songwriters:** CROCE except, SALON SALOON (Maury Meuhleisen) / THURSDAY (S.Joseph) / I GOT A NAME (Fox-Gimbel) / CHAIN GANG (Sam Cooke) / HE DON'T LOVE YOU (Impressions) / SEARCHIN' (Coasters) / OLD MAN RIVER (Kern-Hammerstein) / etc.

Album rating: APPROACHING DAY (*4) / YOU DON'T MESS AROUND WITH JIM (*6) / LIFE AND TIMES (*6) / I GOT A NAME posthumous (*6) / PHOTOGRAPHS AND MEMORIES – HIS GREATEST HITS compilation (*6) / THE VERY BEST OF JIM CROCE compilation (*7)

INGRID & JIM CROCE

JIM CROCE – vocals, acoustic guitar / with **INGRID** (b.27 Apr'47) – vocals, acoustic guitar

	not iss.	Capitol

Jan 69. (lp) <*ST 315*> **APPROACHING DAY** | - |
– Age / Spin spin spin / I am who I am / What do people do / Another day, another town / Vespers / Big wheel / Just another day / The next man that I marry / What the hell / The man that is me. *(UK-iss.1977 as 'ANOTHER DAY' on 'Pickwick'; PWK 3332) (cd-iss. May96 as 'BOMBS OVER PUERTO RICO' on 'Bear Family'; BCD 15894)*

—— in 1970, JIM guested on MAURY MUEHLIESEN's debut album 'Gingerbread'

JIM CROCE

—— JIM now used session players

	Vertigo	A.B.C.

Apr 72. (lp) *(6360 700)* <356> **YOU DON'T MESS AROUND WITH JIM** | | 1
– You don't mess around with Jim / Tomorrow's gonna be a brighter day / New York's not my home / Hard time losin' man / A long time ago / Walkin' back to Georgia / Operator (that's not the way it feels) / Time in a bottle / Rapid Roy (the stock car boy) / Box 10 / Photographs and memories / Hey tomorrow.

Jul 72. (7") *(6000 069)* <11328> **YOU DON'T MESS AROUND WITH JIM. / PHOTOGRAPHS AND MEMORIES** | | 8 Jun72

Oct 72. (7") *(6073 251)* <11335> **OPERATOR (THAT'S NOT THE WAY IT FEELS). / RAPID ROY (THE STOCK CAR BOY)** | | 17

Jan 73. (7") <11346> **ONE LESS SET OF FOOTSTEPS. / IT DOESN'T HAVE TO BE THAT WAY** | - | 37

Apr 73. (7") <11359> **BAD, BAD LEROY BROWN. / A GOOD TIME MAN LIKE ME AIN'T GO NO BUSINESS (SINGIN' THE BLUES)** | - | 1

Jul 73. (lp) (6360 701) <769> **LIFE AND TIMES** | 7 | Feb73
– One less set of footsteps / Roller derby queen / Dreamin' again / Careful man / Alabama rain / A good time man like me ain't got no business (singin' the blues) / Next time, this time / Bad, bad Leroy Brown / These dreams / Speedball Tucker / 't doesn't have to be that way. (re-iss. Nov76; same)

May 73. (7") (6073 258) **BAD, BAD LEROY BROWN. / ROLLER DERBY QUEEN** | □ | -

Nov 73. (7") (6073 260) <11389> **I GOT A NAME. / ALABAMA RAIN** | □ | 10 | Sep73

—— JIM was killed on the 20th of September '73 when his chartered plane crashed on take-off. His guitarist MAURY MUEHLEISEN was also to die.

– compilations, others. etc. –

Nov 73. (7") A.B.C.; (11405) **TIME IN A BOTTLE. / HARD TIME LOSIN' MAN** | - | 1

Dec 73. (7") A.B.C.; (11413) **IT DOESN'T HAVE TO BE THAT WAY. / ROLLER DERBY QUEEN** | - | 64

Feb 74. (7") Vertigo; (6073 272) **TIME IN A BOTTLE. / HEY TOMORROW** | □ | -

Apr 74. (lp) Vertigo; (6360 703) / A.B.C.; <797> **I GOT A NAME** | - | 2 | Dec73
– I got a name / Lover's cross / Five short minutes / Ages / Workin' at the carwash blues / I'll have to say I love you in a song / Salon and saloon / Thursday / Top hat bar and grill / Recently / The hard way / Every time.

Mar 74. (7") A.B.C.; <11424> **I'LL HAVE TO SAY I LOVE YOU IN A SONG. / SALON AND SALOON** | - | 9

May 74. (7") A.B.C.; <11447> **WORKIN' AT THE CAR WASH BLUES. / THURSDAY** | - | 32
<re-iss. 1970's; 12015>

Sep 74. (lp) A.B.C.; <835> **PHOTOGRAPHS AND MEMORIES – HIS GREATEST HITS** | - | 2
– Bad, bad Leroy Brown / Operator (that's not the way it feels) / Photographs and memories / Rapid Roy (the stock car boy) / Time in a bottle / New York's not my home / Workin' at the car wash blues / I got a name / I'll have to say I love you in a song / Lover's cross / One less set of footsteps / These dreams. (UK-iss.Jul77 on 'Lifesong'; LSLP 5000) (re-iss. Jun88 on 'Castle' lp/c/cd; CLA LP/MC/CD 119) (cd re-iss. Apr99 on 'Essential'; ESMCD 699)

Apr 75. (7") Philips; (6072 278) **BAD, BAD LEROY BROWN. / I GOT A NAME** | □ | -

Jun 75. (7") Philips; (6073 280) **I'LL HAVE TO SAY I LOVE YOU IN A SONG. / WORKIN' AT THE CAR WASH BLUES** | □ | -

Sep 75. (7") Philips; (6073 281) **LOVER'S CROSS. / SPEEDBALL TUCKER** | □ | -

Oct 75. (d-lp) Lifesong; <LSDP 900> **THE FACES I'VE BEEN** (early recordings from 1961-1971) | - | 87
– This land is your land / Greenback dollar / Pig's song / Gunga Din / Sun come up / Big fat woman / Charlie Green play the slide trombone / Railroads and riverboats / Railroad song / The way we used to / Maybe tomorrow / Stone walls / I remember Mary / Country girl / Which way are you going / King's song / Mississippi lady / Chain gang medley: Chain gang – He don't love you – Searchin' / Old man river / Carmella / South Philly / Cars and dates / Chrome and clubs / The Chinese / Trucks and ups / The army. (UK-iss.Jul77; same as US)

Dec 75. (7") Lifesong; <45001> **CHAIN GANG MEDLEY: CHAIN GANG – HE DON'T LOVE YOU – SEARCHIN'. / STONE WALLS** | - | 63

1976. (7") Lifesong; <45005> **MISSISSIPPI LADY. / MAYBE TOMORROW** | □ | -

1970's. (7") Golddiggers; <1005> **YOU DON'T MESS AROUND WITH JIM. / LOVER'S CROSS** | - | □

Jan 77. (7") Lifesong; (ELS 3500) **I'LL HAVE TO SAY I LOVE YOU IN A SONG. / PHOTOGRAPHS AND MEMORIES** | □ | -

Feb 77. (lp) Lifesong; <6007> **TIME IN A BOTTLE: JIM CROCE'S GREATEST LOVE SONGS** | - | □
(re-iss. Sep86 on 'Castle' lp/c/cd; CLA LP/MC/CD 117) (cd re-iss. Apr99 on 'Essential'; ESMCD 697)

1979. (lp) Lifesong; <35571> **BAD, BAD LEROY BROWN: JIM CROCE'S GREATEST CHARACTER SONGS** | □ | -

Mar 80. (c) K-Tel; (CE 2059) **HIS GREATEST HITS** | □ | -

Sep 86. (lp/c/cd) Castle; (CLA LP/MC/CD 118) **DOWN THE HIGHWAY** | □ | -
(cd re-iss. Apr99 on 'Essential'; ESMCD 698)

Dec 86. (d-lp/c/cd) Castle; (CCS LP/MC/CD 154) **THE JIM CROCE COLLECTION** | □ | -
– Time in a bottle / Operator (that's not the way it feels) / Salon saloon / Alabama rain / Dreamin' again / It doesn't have to be that way / I'll have to say I love you in a song / Lover's cross / Thursday / These dreams / A long time ago / Photographs and memories / I got a name / Mississippi lady / New York's not my home / Chain gang medley:- Chain gang – He don't love you – Searchin' / You don't mess around with Jim / Old man river / Which way are you goin' / Bad, bad Leroy Brown / Walkin' back to Georgia / Box 10 / Speedball Tucker / Rapid Roy (the stock car boy).

May 88. (d-lp/d-c) Commander; (80044 1-2) **JIM CROCE SONGBOOK** | □ | -

May 88. (lp/c/cd) Commander; (3/6/9 9010) **GREATEST HITS** | □ | -

1988. (cd) Roadrunner; (RR34 9841) **THE LEGEND OF JIM CROCE** | □ | -

Feb 90. (cd/c/lp) Essential; (ESS CD/MC/LP 020) **THE FINAL TOUR (live)** | □ | -
(cd re-iss. May94 on 'Castle'; CLACD 341) (cd re-iss. Apr99 on 'Essential'; ESMCD 700)

Nov 92. (d-cd) Essential; (ESDCD 188) **50th ANNIVERSARY COLLECTION** | □ | -

Oct 94. (cd) Woodford Music; (WMCD 5703) **SIMPLY THE BEST** | □ | -

May 97. (cd) Music Club; (MCCD 295) **THE BEST OF JIM CROCE** | □ | -

May 97. (d-cd) Snapper; (SMDCD 102) **BAD, BAD LEROY BROWN – THE DEFINITIVE JIM CROCE** | □ | -

Mar 98. (cd/c) Castle Select; (SEL CD/MC 505) **THE VERY BEST OF JIM CROCE** | □ | -

Feb 99. (d-cd) Castle Select; (SELDD 558) **TIME IN A BOTTLE – THE DEFINITIVE COLLECTION** | □ | -

Oct 99. (cd) Castle Pie; (PIESCD 137) **THE COLLECTION** | □ | -

CROSBY, STILLS, NASH (& YOUNG)

Formed: Los Angeles, California, USA ... Summer 1968 as a superband trio (DAVID) CROSBY, (STEPHEN) STILLS and (GRAHAM) NASH. Their eponymous first offering was released in Summer '69 and soon broke into the US Top 10. Featuring the distinctive songwriting talent of each member respectively on 'GUINNEVERE', 'SUITE: JUDY BLUE EYES' and 'MARRAKESH EXPRESS', the album introduced the close harmonising that would come to characterise the band. Later that year the trio recruited NEIL YOUNG (ex-BUFFALO SPRINGFIELD) who'd played an electric set on their mid-'69 gigs and who'd already embarked on his successful solo career. The newly augmented line-up played Woodstock as well as supporting The ROLLING STONES at their ill-fated Altamont concert which, ironically, saw the dreams of the Woodstock generation shatter. Nevertheless the band were adopted as hippy flagbearers and after lifting the coveted 'Best Newcomers' award at The Grammys, they released their magnum opus, 'DEJA VU' (1970). With YOUNG contributing the achingly gorgeous 'HELPLESS' and the sublime 'COUNTRY GIRL' suite, his intensity, both vocal and instrumental was a towering influence although STILLS offered a powerful cover of JONI MITCHELL's 'WOODSTOCK'. NASH's 'TEACH YOUR CHILDREN' and 'OUR HOUSE' were slighter in comparison but rounded out the record perfectly. Blighted by ego problems with drug habits to match, the band split the same month as YOUNG's ominous 'OHIO' single was released, an inpired protest against the killing of four students by the National Guard during an anti-war demo at Kent State University. The patchy, posthumous live album 'FOUR-WAY STREET' (1971) was hardly a fitting epitaph although predictably it sold in bucketloads. While YOUNG continued with his mercurial solo career, STILLS released a follow-up to his well-received debut solo album and later recorded with the country-inflected MANASSAS. CROSBY and NASH, meanwhile, worked as a duo, releasing their eponymous debut in 1972. Minus STILLS and YOUNG, the record was pleasant if hardly essential, lacking the tension that had made CSN&Y so compelling. The inevitable reunion took place in 1974 and the biggest personality clash in rock toured the world to ecstatic audiences although the band couldn't keep it together long enough to record anything concrete in the studio (the fact that YOUNG travelled in his own tourbus didn't bode too well). STILLS and YOUNG recorded the 'LONG MAY YOU RUN' album in 1976 which boasted the wistful charm of the title track and the exquisite 'FONTAINEBLEU' but was otherwise fairly lacklustre. The following year CROSBY, STILLS and NASH reformed and recorded the million selling 'CSN', again another inoffensive collection which lacked the focus YOUNG had brought to the group in the past. Indeed, while CSN were touring their particular brand of polite folk-Pop, YOUNG was interpreting punk with his 'LIVE RUST' and 'RUST NEVER SLEEPS' albums, outstripping CSN creatively and commercially. 'DAYLIGHT AGAIN' (1982) spawned the American singles 'WASTED ON THE WAY' and 'SOUTHERN CROSS' while the band split later the same year as CROSBY was sentenced to five years for drugs and firearms offences. In the event, he was allowed to attend a rehabilitation program as an alternative which he later reneged on and did actually serve some time during the mid-80's. Out on bail, he appeared live with STILLS, NASH and YOUNG at Live Aid and the quartet made a long-awaited second album in 1988, 'AMERICAN DREAM'. Although it eclipsed most of the YOUNG-less CSN material, it was hardly the masterpiece people had waited almost two decades for. The standout track was CROSBY's 'COMPASS', a song borne of his drug-induced hardships. NEIL YOUNG subsequently refused to tour the record and that, more or less, was that. CSN continued unbowed, even after CROSBY underwent a liver transplant following the release of the 'AFTER THE STORM' (1994) album. With YOUNG now almost in the 30th year of a solo career which shows no sign of letting up (even if his recent output has been under par), it didn't appear likely that he would ever re-unite with his old sparring partners. However, the er, 'LOOKING FORWARD' (1999) set (was it?) heralded the one-off return of C, S, N & Y. • **Songwriters:** All 4 took a hand individually and later together in all songs. Also covered; WOODSTOCK (Joni Mitchell) / DEAR MR. FANTASY (Traffic) / and a few more.

Album rating: CROSBY, STILLS & NASH (*8) / DEJA VU (*9; & Young) / FOUR-WAY STREET (*7; & Young) / SO FAR compilation (*7; & Young) / CSN (*7) / REPLAY compilation (*7) / DAYLIGHT AGAIN (*6) / ALLIES (*5) / AMERICAN DREAM (*5; & Young) / LIVE IT UP (*4) / AFTER THE STORM (*4) / LOOKING FORWARD (*4; & Young) / David Crosby: IF I COULD ONLY REMEMBER MY NAME (*8) / GRAHAM NASH & DAVID CROSBY (*5; with Graham Nash) / WIND ON THE WATER (*5; with Graham Nash) / WHISTLING DOWN THE WIRE (*4; with Graham Nash) / CROSBY/NASH LIVE (*4; with Graham Nash) / THE BEST OF CROSBY/NASH compilation (*5; with Graham Nash) / OH YES I CAN (*5) / THOUSAND ROADS (*5) / IT'S ALL COMING BACK TO ME NOW (*4) / Stephen Stills: STEPHEN STILLS (*8) / STEPHEN STILLS 2 (*6) / MANASSAS (*6) / DOWN THE ROAD (*4; with Manassas) / STILLS (*5) / STEPHEN STILLS LIVE (*5) / ILLEGAL STILLS (*5) / LONG MAY YOU RUN (*5; as Stills-Young Band) / STILL STILLS – THE BEST OF STEPHEN STILLS compilation (*6) / THOROUGHFARE GAP (*3) / RIGHT BY YOU (*5) / STILLS ALONE (*5) / Graham Nash: SONGS FOR BEGINNERS (*7) / WILD TALES (*5) / EARTH AND SKY (*4) / INNOCENT EYES (*4)

CROSBY, STILLS & NASH

DAVID CROSBY (b. DAVID VAN CORTLAND, 14 Aug'41, Los Angeles, Calif.) – vocals, guitar (ex-BYRDS) / **STEPHEN STILLS** (b. 3 Jan'45, Dallas, Texas)– vocals, guitar, bass, keyboards (ex-BUFFALO SPRINGFIELD) / **GRAHAM NASH** (b. 2 Feb'42, Blackpool, England)– vocals, guitar (ex-HOLLIES) with **DALLAS TAYLOR** – drums

		Atlantic	Atlantic
Jun 69.	(lp) (588 189) <8229> **CROSBY, STILLS & NASH**	25	6

– Suite: Judy blue eyes / Marrakesh express / Guinnevere / You don't have to cry / Pre-road downs / Wooden ships / Lady of the island / Helplessly hoping / Long time gone / 49 bye-byes. (re-iss. 1972; K 40033) (cd-iss. Jul87; K2 40033)

Jul 69.	(7") (584 283) <2652> **MARRAKESH EXPRESS. / HELPLESSLY HOPING**	17	28
Oct 69.	(7") (584 304) <2676> **SUITE: JUDY BLUE EYES. / LONG TIME GONE**	☐	21 Sep69

CROSBY, STILLS, NASH & YOUNG

–––– added **NEIL YOUNG** (b.12 Nov'45, Toronto, Canada) – guitar, vocals (ex-BUFFALO SPRINGFIELD) also **GREG REEVES** – bass

Mar 70.	(lp) (2401 001) <7200> **DEJA VU**	5	1

– Carry on / Teach your children / Almost cut my hair / Helpless / Woodstock / Deja vu / Our house / 4 + 20 / Country girl: Whiskey boot hill – Down, down, down – Country girl / Everybody I love you. (re-iss. 1972 lp/c; K/K4 50001) (cd-iss. May87; K2 50001)

Apr 70.	(7") (2091 002) **TEACH YOUR CHILDREN. / COUNTRY GIRL**	☐	–
May 70.	(7") (2091 010) <2723> **WOODSTOCK. / HELPLESS**	☐	11 Mar70
May 70.	(7") <2735> **TEACH YOUR CHILDREN. / CARRY ON**	–	16
Aug 70.	(7") (2091 023) <2740> **OHIO. / FIND THE COST OF FREEDOM**	☐	14 Jun70
Nov 70.	(7") (2091 039) <2760> **OUR HOUSE. / DEJA VU**	☐	30 Sep70

–––– (May'70) **CALVIN 'FUZZY' SAMUELS** – bass repl. REEVES **JOHN BARBATA** – drums (ex-TURTLES) repl. TAYLOR

–––– (Aug'70) split before release of posthumous album below with last line-up

Apr 71.	(d-lp) (2657 007) <2-902> **FOUR-WAY STREET (live)**	5	1

– On the way home / Teach your children / Triad / The Lee shore / Chicago / Right between the eyes / Cowgirl in the sand / Don't let it bring you down / 49 bye-byes / Love the one you're with / Pre-road downs / Long time gone / Southern man / Ohio / Carry on / Find the cost of freedom. (re-iss. 1972 lp/c; K/K4 60003) (cd-iss. Jul87; K2 60003) (d-cd re-iss. Aug92)

–––– Their solo recordings, excluding NEIL YOUNG's, are below

STEPHEN STILLS

–––– - vocals, guitar with **STEPHEN FROMHOLTZ** – guitar / **PAUL HARRIS** – keyboards / **DALLAS TAYLOR** – drums / **CALVIN SAMUELS** – bass / plus **Memphis Horns**

		Atlantic	Atlantic
Nov 70.	(lp) (2401 004) <7202> **STEPHEN STILLS**	30	3

– Love the one you're with / Do for the others / Church (part of someone) / Old times, good times / Go back home / Sit yourself down / To a flame / Black queen / Cheroke / We are not helpless. (cd-iss. Oct95; 7567 82809-2)

Dec 70.	(7") (2091 046) <2778> **LOVE THE ONE YOU'RE WITH. / TO A FLAME**	37	14
May 71.	(7") (2091 069) <2790> **SIT YOURSELF DOWN. / WE ARE NOT HELPLESS**	☐	37 Mar71
Jul 71.	(lp) (2401 013) <7206> **STEPHEN STILLS II**	22	8

– Change partners / Nothin' to do but today / Fishes and scorpions / Sugar babe / Know you got to run / Open secret / Relaxing town / Singin' call / Ecology song / Word game / Marianne / Bluebird revisited. (re-iss. 1978;)

Jul 71.	(7") (2091 117) <2806> **CHANGE PARTNERS. / RELAXING TOWN**	☐	43 Jun71
Sep 71.	(7") (2091 141) <2820> **MARIANNE. / NOTHIN' TO DO BUT TODAY**	☐	42 Aug71

STEPHEN STILLS & MANASSAS

STILLS retained **SAMUELS, HARRIS** and **TAYLOR**, brought in **CHRIS HILLMAN** – guitar, vocals / **AL PERKINS** – steel guitar, guitar / **JOE LALA** – percussion / **KENNY PASSARELLI** – bass (ex-JOE WALSH) repl. SAMUELS

		Atlantic	Atlantic
May 72.	(d-lp/c) (K/K4 60021) <2-903> **MANASSAS**	30	4 Apr72

– Fallen eagle / Jesus gave love away for free / Colorado / So begins the task / Hide to the deep / Don't look at my shadow / It doesn't matter / Johnny's garden / Bound to fall / How far / Move around / The love gangster / Song of love / Rock'n'roll crazies – Cuban bluegrass / Jet set (sigh) / Anyway / Both of us (bound to lose) / What to do / Right now / The treasure (take one) / Blues man. (cd-iss. Feb93 & Oct95; 7567 82808-2)

May 72.	(7") <2876> **IT DOESN'T MATTER. / ROCK'N'ROLL CRAZIES – CUBAN BLUEGRASS**	–	61
Aug 72.	(7") (K 10147) **IT DOESN'T MATTER. / FALLEN ANGEL**	–	–
Nov 72.	(7") <2888> **ROCK'N'ROLL CRAZIES. / COLORADO**	33	92
May 73.	(lp/c) (K/K4 44040) <7250> **DOWN THE ROAD**	33	26

– Isn't it about time / Lies / Pensamiento / So many times / Business on the street / Do you remember the Americans / Down road / City junkies / Guaguanco de Vero / Rollin' my stone. (cd-iss. Nov93; 7567 81424-2)

May 73.	(7") (K 10306) <2959> **ISN'T IT ABOUT TIME. / SO MANY TIMES**	☐	56 Apr73
Jul 73.	(7") (K 10340) <2917> **GUAGUANCO DE VERO. / DOWN THE ROAD**	☐	Feb73

–––– (Sep73) **HARRIS, PERKINS** and **HILLMAN joined SOUTHERN HILLMAN FURAY BAND. STEPHEN STILLS** formed his own band, retaining **PASSARELLI** and **LALA** plus **DONNIE DACUS** – guitar / **JERRY AIELLO** – keyboards / **HUSS KUNKEL** – drums

CROSBY, STILLS NASH & YOUNG

–––– (May'74) re-formed, mainly for concerts. Augmented by **TIM DRUMMOND** – bass / **RUSS KUNKEL** – drums / **JOE LALA** – percussion

STEPHEN STILLS

–––– went solo again (Feb75) with new band **LALA, DACUS, AIELLO** plus **GEORGE PERRY** – bass / **RONNIE ZIEGLER** – drums

		C.B.S.	Columbia
Jun 75.	(lp/c) (69146) <33575> **STILLS**	31	19

– Turn back the pages / My favorite changes / My angel / In the way / Love story / To mama Christopher and the old man / First things first / New mama / As I come of age / Shuffle just as bad / Cold cold world / Myth of Sisyphus.

Jul 75.	(7") (3497) <10179> **TURN BACK THE PAGES. / SHUFFLE JUST AS BAD**	☐	84

–––– added **RICK ROBERTS** – guitar, vocals (of FIREFALL)

Apr 76.	(7") <10369> **BUYIN' TIME. / SOLDIER**	–	–
May 76.	(lp/c) (81330) <34148> **ILLEGAL STILLS**	54	30

– Buyin' time / Midnight in Paris / Different tongues / Closer to you / Soldier / The loner / Stateline blues / No me nieges / Ring of love / Circlin'.

Jul 76.	(7") (4416) **THE LONER. / STATELINE BLUES**	☐	–

STILLS-YOUNG BAND

STEPHEN STILLS – vocals, guitar / **NEIL YOUNG** – vocals, guitar with **AIELLO, PERRY, VITALE + LALA**

		Reprise	Reprise
Sep 76.	(7") (K 14446) <1365> **LONG MAY YOU RUN. / 12:8 BLUES**	☐	☐
Oct 76.	(lp/c) (K/K4 54081) <2253> **LONG MAY YOU RUN**	12	26

– Long may you run / Make love to you / Midnight on the bay / Black coral / Ocean girl / Let it shine / 12/8 blues (all the same) / Fontainebleau / Guardian angel. (cd-iss. Jul93; K2 54081)

Dec 76.	(7") <1370> **MIDNIGHT ON THE BAY. / BLACK CORAL**	–	–

–––– CROSBY, STILLS & NASH re-formed in '77 (see further on for more solo STILLS)

DAVID CROSBY

with loads of session people, too numerous to mention.

		Atlantic	Atlantic
Feb 71.	(lp) (2401 005) <SD 7203> **IF I COULD ONLY REMEMBER MY NAME**	12	12

– Music is love / Cowboy movie / Tamalpais High (at about 3) / Laughing / What are their names / Traction in the rain / Song with no name (tree with no leaves) / Orleans / I'd swear there was somebody here. (re-iss. 1972 lp/c; K/K4 40320) (cd-iss. Nov93; 56781415-2)

Apr 71.	(7") <2792> **MUSIC IS LOVE. / LAUGHING**	–	95
Jul 71.	(7") <2809> **ORLEANS. / TRACTION IN THE RAIN**	–	☐

GRAHAM NASH & DAVID CROSBY

duo (DAVID & GRAHAM with more sessioners and left over GRATEFUL DEAD members which were included on DAVID's debut solo album.

May 72.	(lp/c) (K/K4 50011) <7220> **GRAHAM NASH & DAVID CROSBY**	13	4 Apr72

– Southbound train / Whole cloth / Black notes / Strangers room / Where will I be / Page 43 / Frozen smiles / Games / Girl to be on my mind / The wall song / Immigration man.

May 72.	(7") <2873> **IMMIGRATION MAN. / WHOLE CLOTH**	–	36
May 72.	(7") <2877> **SOUTHBOUND TRAIN. / WHOLE CLOTH**	–	–
Jul 72.	(7") <2892> **SOUTHBOUND TRAIN. / THE WALL SONG**	–	99

–––– after CROSBY, STILLS, NASH & YOUNG reunion May74-Feb75

–––– resurrected partnership, with steady band members **CRAIG DOERGE** – keyboards / **LEE SKLAR + TIM DRUMMOND** – bass / **DANNY KOOTCH & RUSS KUNKEL** – drums / **DAVID LINDLEY** – guitar, violin.

		Polydor	A.B.C.
Jan 76.	(lp) (2310 428) <902> **WIND ON THE WATER**	☐	6 Oct75

– Carry me / Mama lion / Bittersweet / Take the money and run / Naked in the rain / Love work out / Low down payment / Cowboy of dreams / Homeward through the haze / Fieldworker / To the last whale. (cd re-iss. Nov91 on 'Thunderbolt'; CDTB 128) (cd re-iss. Mar97 on 'Nectar'; NTMCD 550)

Nov 75.	(7") (2001 615) <12140> **CARRY ME. / MAMA LION**	☐	52
Mar 76.	(7") <12165> **TAKE THE MONEY AND RUN. / BITTERSWEET**	–	–
May 76.	(7") (2001 660) <12185> **LOVE WORK OUT. / BITTERSWEET**	☐	26
Jul 76.	(lp) (2319 468) <956> **WHISTLING DOWN THE WIRE**	☐	26

– Spotlight / Broken bird / Time after time / Dancer / Mutiny / J.B.'s blues / Marguerita / Taken at all / Foolish man / Out of the darkness.

Aug 76.	(7") **OUT OF THE DARKNESS. / LOVE WORK OUT**	☐	–
Aug 76.	(7") <12199> **OUT OF THE DARKNESS. / BROKEN BIRD**	–	89
Oct 76.	(7") <12217> **SPOTLIGHT. / FOOLISH MAN**	–	☐

–––– CROSBY STILLS & NASH re-formed '77 (see further on)

GRAHAM NASH

solo using C,S & N past members plus GRATEFUL DEAD main men

		Atlantic	Atlantic
Jun 71.	(lp) (2401 011) <SD 7204> **SONGS FOR BEGINNERS**	13	15

– Military madness / Better days / Wounded bird / I used to be a king / Be yourself / Simple man / Man in the mirror / There's only one / Sleep song / Chicago / We can change the world. (cd-iss. Feb93; 7567 81416-2)

Jun 71.	(7") (2091 096) <2804> **CHICAGO. / SIMPLE MAN**	☐	35 May71
Aug 71.	(7") <2827> **MILITARY MADNESS. / SLEEP SONG**	–	73
Sep 71.	(7") (2091 135) **MILITARY MADNESS. / I USED TO BE A KING**	☐	–

Nov 71. (7") <2840> **I USED TO BE A KING. / WOUNDED BIRD**   – / ☐
Nov 73. (7") <2990> **PRISON SONG. / HEY YOU (LOOKING AT HTE MOON)**   – / ☐
Mar 74. (lp/c) (K/K4 50025) <SD 7288> **WILD TALES**   **34** Dec73
    – Wild tales / Hey you (looking at the Moon) / Prison song / You'll never be the same / And so it goes / Oh! Camil (the winter soldier) / I miss you / On the line / Another sleep song.
Mar 74. (7") (K 10425) **ON THE LINE. / I MISS YOU**   ☐ / –
Aug 74. (7") (K 10470) **GRAVE CONCERN. / ANOTHER SLEEP SONG**   ☐ / –

—— GRAHAM rejoined below and had more solo releases later.

CROSBY, STILLS & NASH

reformed in '77, with various session men.

	Atlantic	Atlantic
Jun 77. (lp/c) (K 50369) <19104> **CSN**	23	2

– Shadow captain / See the changes / Carried away / Fair game / Anything at all / Cathedral / Dark star / Just a song before I go / Cold rain / In my dreams / I give you give blind.

Jun 77. (7") (K 10947) <3401> **JUST A SONG BEFORE I GO. / DARK STAR**   ☐ / **7** May77
Oct 77. (7") (K 11024) <3432> **FAIR GAME. / ANYTHING AT ALL**   ☐ / **43** Sep77
Dec 77. (7") <3453> **CARRIED AWAY. / I GIVE YOU GIVE BLIND**   ☐ / –

STEPHEN STILLS

more solo releases with session people & his tour band **DALLAS TAYLOR** – drums / **GEORGE PERRY** – bass / **MIKE FINNEGAN** – keyboards / **JERRY TOLMAN & BONNIE BRAMLETT** – b.vocals

	C.B.S.	Columbia
Sep 78. (7") (6662) <10804> **CAN'T GET NO BOOTY. / LOWDOWN**	☐	☐
Oct 78. (lp) (82859) <35380> **THOROUGHFARE GAP**		83

– You can't dance alone / Thoroughfare gap / We will go / Beaucoup yumbo / What's the game / Midnight rider / Woman Lleva / Lowdown / Not fade away / Can't get no booty.

Nov 78. (7") <10872> **THOROUGHFARE GAP. / LOWDOWN**   – / ☐

GRAHAM NASH

solo, with usual and past session people + CROSBY, STILLS & YOUNG

	Capitol	Capitol
Jan 80. (7") <4812> **IN THE 80'S. / T.V. GUIDE**	☐	–
Mar 80. (7") <4849> **OUT ON THE ISLAND. / HELICOPTER SONG**	☐	–
Mar 80. (lp) (12014) **EARTH & SKY**	☐	☐

– Earth & sky / Love has come / Out on the island / Skychild / Helicopter song / Barrel of pain / T.V. guide / It's alright / Magical child / In the 80's.

May 80. (7") <4879> **EARTH & SKY. / MAGICAL CHILD**   – / ☐

CROSBY, STILLS & NASH

re-formed mid '82, with session men

	Atlantic	Atlantic
Jul 82. (lp/c) (K/K4 50896) <19360> **DAYLIGHT AGAIN**	☐	8

– Turn your back on love / Wasted on the way / Southern cross / Into the darkness / Delta / Since I met you / Too much love to hide / Song for Susan / You are alive / Might as well have a good time / Daylight again. (cd-iss. Oct94; 7567 82672-2)

Nov 82. (7") <4058> **WASTED ON THE WAY. / DELTA**   ☐ / **9** Jul82
Nov 82. (7") (K 11749) <89969> **SOUTHERN CROSS. / INTO THE DARKNESS**   ☐ / **18** Sep82
Jan 83. (7") <89888> **TOO MUCH LOVE TO HIDE. / SONG FOR SUSAN**   ☐ / **69**
Jun 83. (lp) (78-0075-1) <80075> **ALLIES (live)**   ☐ / **43**
– War games / Raise a voice / Turn your back on love / Barrel of pain / Shadow captain / Dark star / Blackbird / He played real good for free / Wasted on my way / For what it's worth. (cd-iss. 1984; 780 075-2)
Jul 83. (7") (A 9818) <89812> **WAR GAMES (live). / SHADOW CAPTAIN (live)**   ☐ / **45** Jun83
    (12") (A 9818T) – ('A'side) / Dark star (live) / Keep your . . .
Sep 83. (7") <89775> **RAISE A VOICE (live). / FOR WHAT IT'S WORTH (live)**   – / ☐

—— split Aug'82, when CROSBY was sentenced to 5 years for drugs. He got leniency, when he agreed to rehabilitate himself in a drug hospital Dec'84.

STEPHEN STILLS

solo again (2nd single featured WALTER FINNEGAN)

	W.E.A.	Atlantic
Aug 84. (7") <89633> **STRANGER. / NO HIDING PLACE**	–	61
Sep 84. (lp/c) (780 177-1) <80177> **RIGHT BY YOU**		75 Aug84

– 50/50 / Stranger / Flaming heart / Love again / No problem / Can't let go / Grey to green / Only love can break your heart / No hiding place / Right by you. (cd-iss. Nov93; 7567 80177-2)

Oct 84. (7") <89611> **CAN'T LET GO. / GREY TO GREEN**   – / **67**
    (above as STEPHEN STILLS featuring MICHAEL FINNIGAN)
Dec 84. (7") <89597> **ONLY LOVE CAN BREAK YOUR HEART. / LOVE AGAIN**   – / ☐

	not iss.	Goldhill
1990. (cd) **STILLS ALONE**	–	☐

– Isn't it so / Everybody's talkin' / Just isn't like you / In my life / Ballad of Hollis Brown / Singin call / The right girl / Blind fiddler medley / Amazonia / Treetop flyer.

GRAHAM NASH

solo, he had rejoined The HOLLIES between Sep81-Apr83.

	Atlantic	Atlantic
Apr 86. (7") (A 9434) <89434> **INNOCENT EYES. / I GOT A ROCK**	☐	84
Apr 86. (lp/c) (781-633-1/-4) <81633> **INNOCENT EYES**		

– See you in Prague / Keep away from me / Innocent eyes / Chippin' away / Over the wall / Don't listen to the rumours / Sad eyes / Newday / Glass and steel / I got a rock.

Jul 86. (7") <89396> **SAD EYES. / NEWDAY**   – / ☐
Oct 86. (7") <89373> **CHIPPIN' AWAY. / NEWDAY**   – / ☐

CROSBY, STILLS, NASH & YOUNG

re-formed yet again

	Atlantic	Atlantic
Nov 88. (7") <88966> **GOT IT MADE. / THIS OLD HOUSE**	–	69
Nov 88. (lp/c)(cd) (WX 233/+C)(781 886-2) <81888> **AMERICAN DREAM**		16

– American dream / Got it made / Name of love / Don't say goodbye / This old house / Nighttime for the generals / Shadowland / Drivin' thunder / Clear blue skies / That girl / Compass / Soldiers of peace / Feel your love / Night song.

Jan 89. (7") (A 9003) <88966> **AMERICAN DREAM. / COMPASS**   55 / ☐
    (12"+=) (A 9003T) – Soldiers of peace.
    (12"g-f++=) (A 9003TX) – Ohio.

DAVID CROSBY

solo again

	A&M	A&M
Feb 89. (lp/c/cd) <(AMA/AMC/CDA 5232)> **OH YES I CAN**	☐	☐

– Drive my car / Melody / Monkey and the underdog / In the wide ruin / Tracks in the dust / Drop down mama / Lady of the harbour / Distances / Flying man / Oh yes I can / My country 'tis of thee.

Feb 89. (7") (AM 500) **DRIVE MY CAR. / TRACKS IN THE DUST**   ☐ / ☐
    (12"+=) (AMY 500) – Flying men.
Apr 89. (7"/12") (AM/+Y 502) **LADY OF THE HARBOR. / DROP DOWN MAMA**   ☐ / ☐

—— with band **LELAND SKLAR** – bass / **RUSSELL KUNKEL + JEFF PORCARO** – drums / **CRAIG DOERGE** – keyboards / **ANDY FAIRWEATHER-LOWE** – guitar / **DEAN PARKS** – guitar, flute / **BERNIE LEADON** – acoustic guitar / **C.J. VANSTON** – keyboards / with many guests **JACKSON BROWNE + DON WAS** plus outside writers + on session **PHIL COLLINS, JONI MITCHELL, MARC COHN, JIMMY WEBB, PAUL BRADY, STEPHEN BISHOP, JOHN HIATT, BONNIE HAYES + NOEL BRAZIL.**

	Atlantic	Atlantic
May 93. (7"/c-s; by DAVID CROSBY featuring PHIL COLLINS) <87360> **HERO. / COVERAGE**	☐	44

    (cd-s+=) – Fare thee well.

Jun 93. (cd/c) <(7567 82484-2/-4)> **THOUSAND ROADS**   ☐ / ☐
– Hero / Too young to die / Old soldier / Through your hands / Yvette in English / Thousand roads / Columbus / Helpless heart / Coverage / Natalie.
Mar 95. (cd/c) <(7567 82620-2/-4)> **IT'S ALL COMING BACK TO ME NOW (live '93)**   ☐ / ☐
– In my dreams / Rusty and blue / Hero / Till it shines on you / 1000 roads / Cowboy movie / Almosy cut my hair / Deja vu / Long time gone / Wooden ships.

	Sams	Sams
Sep 98. (cd) (145) **CPR**	☐	☐

CROSBY, STILLS & NASH

with **JOE VITALE** – drums, organ, synth bass / **LELAND SKLAR** – bass / **CRAIG DOERGE** – keyboards / **MIKE LANDAU** – guitar / **MIKE FISHER** – percussion

	East West	Atlantic
Jun 90. (cd/c/lp) <(7567 82101-2/-4/-1)> **LIVE IT UP**	☐	57

– Live it up / If anybody had a heart / Tomboy / Haven't we lost enough / Yours and mine / (Got to keep) Open / Straight line / House of broken dreams / Arrows / After the dolphin.

Jul 90. (7") <87909> **LIVE IT UP. / CHUCK'S LAMENT**   – / ☐
Aug 94. (cd/c) <(7567 82654-2/-4)> **AFTER THE STORM**   ☐ / **98**
– Only waiting for you / Find a dream / Camera / Unequal love / Till it shines / It won't go away / These empty days / In my life / Street to lean on / Bad boyz / After the storm / Panama.

CROSBY, STILLS, NASH & YOUNG

Nov 99. (cd/c) <(9362 47436-2/-4)> **LOOKING FORWARD**	54	26

– Faith in me / Looking forward / Stand and be counted / Heartland / Seen enough / Slowpoke / Dream for him / No tears left / Out of control / Someday soon / Queen of them all / Sanibel.

– their compilations etc. –

on 'Atlantic' unless mentioned otherwise

Aug 74. (lp/c) (K/K4 50023) <18100> **SO FAR – THE BEST OF . . .**	25	1

– Woodstock / Marrakesh express / You don't have to cry / Teach your children / Love the one you're with / Almost cut my hair / Wooden ships / Dark star / Helpless / Chicago – We can change the world / Cathedral / 4 + 20 / Our house / Change partners / Just a song before I go / Ohio / Wasted on the way / Southern cross / Suite: Judy blue eyes / Carry on – Questions / Horses through a rainstorm / Johnny's garden / Guinnevere / Helplessly hoping / The Lee Shore / Taken it all / Shadow captain / As I come of age / Drive my car / Dear Mr. Fantasy / In my dreams / Yours and mine / Haven't we lost enough? / After the dolphin / Find the cost of freedom. (cd-iss. Jan87; K2 50023) (cd re-iss. Oct94; 7567 82648-2)

Oct 75. (d-lp) (K 60063) **TWO ORIGINALS OF STEPHEN STILLS (1st 2 lp's)**   ☐ / –
Dec 75. (lp) (K 50214) <18156> **STEPHEN STILLS – LIVE (live)**   ☐ / ☐
Jan 77. (lp) (K 50327) <18201> **STEPHEN STILLS – THE BEST OF STEPHEN STILLS**   ☐ / ☐
– Love the one you're with / It doesn't matter / We are not helpless / Marianne / Bound to fall / Isn't it about time / Change partners / Go back home / Johnny's garden / Rock and roll crazies – Cuban bluegrass / Sit yourself down.

Nov 77. (lp; CROSBY & NASH) *Polydor; (2310 565) / A.B.C.; <1042>*
LIVE (live) ▢ | 52
Jan 79. (lp; CROSBY & NASH) *Polydor; (2310 626) / A.B.C.; <1102>*
THE BEST OF CROSBY & NASH ▢ | Oct78
(re-iss. Nov80)
Nov 80. (lp/c) *Atlantic; (K/K4 50766) <16026>* **REPLAY** ▢ | Sep80
– Carry on / Marrakesh express / Just a song before I go / First things first / Shadow captain / To the last whale / Love the one you're with / Pre-road downs / Change partners / I give you give blind / Cathedral. *(cd-iss. Oct94; 7567 82648-2)*
Dec 91. (d-cd/d-c) *(7567 80487-2/-4)* **CARRY ON**
Dec 91. (4xcd-box/4xc-box) *East West; (7567 82319-2/-4)* **THE BEST OF CROSBY, STILLS & NASH** ▢ | –
Feb 92. (7"/c-s) *East West;* **OUR HOUSE. / MARRAKESH EXPRESS**
(12"+=/cd-s+=) – Carry on / Dear Mr. Fantasy (STEPHEN STILLS / GRAHAM NASH).
(above A-side was re-actified on a famous building society TV ad)

CROSS (see under ⇒ QUEEN)

Sheryl CROW

Born: 11 Feb'62, Kennett, Missouri, USA. She left university after studying classical music before subsequently relocating to St. Louis. In the mid-80's, SHERYL set off to L.A. and finally cut her teeth as SHIRLEY CROW on MICHAEL JACKSON's 1988 'Bad' tour. The singer/songwriter then earned her crust by singing back-up for ROD STEWART, DON HENLEY and JOE COCKER. With ambitions of becoming a solo singer, she handed a demo tape to producer, Hugh Padgham, who, with a recommendation from STING, got her signed to 'A&M' in '91. An album of unproductive songs was shelved but with the help of a second producer, Bill Bottrill, she emerged late in 1993 with debut set, 'TUESDAY NIGHT MUSIC CLUB'. Although it didn't sell immediately, it became a deserved smash a year later after a support slot to the re-formed EAGLES and a well-received appearance at WOODSTOCK II. Suddenly her album turned gold and a single, 'ALL I WANNA DO', almost hit No.1. Its easy-going swing was characteristic of the album as a whole and the singer's EDIE BRICKELL / ROSIE VELA-esque narratives translated into further hits with 'CAN'T CRY ANYMORE' and the evocative 'RUN BABY RUN'. Now as much of a female role model as ALANIS MORISSETTE, SHERYL scored a second UK Top 10 with 'IF IT MAKES YOU HAPPY'. Arguably her finest moment to date, the song had a gritty passion missing from her earlier work and the rootsier, harder hitting sound indicated the direction of the new album. Simply titled, 'SHERYL CROW' (1996), the record saw her paying homage to her musical heroes, primarily The ROLLING STONES but also BOB DYLAN. A second transatlantic success, the album spawned further hits in 'EVERYDAY IS A WINDING ROAD', 'HARD TO MAKE A STAND' and 'A CHANGE WOULD DO YOU GOOD'. Yet despite the promise of the first single, the bulk of the album sounded as though she was merely going through the motions, especially on the lacklustre 'A CHANGE ...'. A crowd-buoying performance at a mud-caked Glastonbury Festival proved she's made of sterner stuff than her glossy image might suggest. SHERYL undoubtably has the potential, it's just a shame she doesn't harness it more often. • **Songwriters:** Writes lyrics mainly / songs by BILL BOTTRELL or BAERWALD-GILBERT-McLEOD, etc. except I'M GONNA BE A WHEEL SOMEDAY (Fats Domino) / D'YER MAKER (Led Zeppelin) / MISSISSIPPI (Bob Dylan). • **Trivia:** The track, 'HUNDREDS OF TEARS', featured on 'Pointbreak' movie soundtrack. Another two, 'STRONG ENOUGH' and 'NO ONE SAID IT WOULD BE EASY', were heard in the 1994 film 'Kalifornia'.
Album rating: TUESDAY NIGHT MUSIC CLUB (*7) / SHERYL CROW (*8) / THE GLOBE SESSIONS (*6) / ... AND FRIENDS: LIVE AT CENTRAL PARK (*5)

SHERYL CROW – vocals + sessioners incl. **BILL BOTTRILL**

	A&M	A&M
Sep 93. (7"/c-s) *(580 380-7/-4)* **RUN, BABY, RUN. / ALL BY MYSELF**	▢	▢
(cd-s+=) *(580 381-2)* – The na-na song / Reach around jerk.		
Oct 93. (cd/c) *(540 126-2/-4) <0126>* **TUESDAY NIGHT MUSIC CLUB**	68	3

– Run, baby, run / Leaving Las Vegas / Strong enough / Can't cry anymore / Solidify / The na-na song / No one said it would be easy / What I can do for you / All I wanna do / We do what we can / I shall believe. *<re-dist.US Feb94> (re-dist.Sep94; hit UK No.22 + No.8 early '95) (re-iss. cd May95; 540 368-2) – (w/ free cd '6 TRACK LIVE MINI-ALBUM'; 540 126-18)*

Feb 94. (7"/c-s) *(580 462-7/-4)* **WHAT I CAN DO FOR YOU. / VOLVO COWGIRL 99**	▢	▢
(cd-s+=) *(580 463-2)* – ('A'version) / I shall believe.		
Apr 94. (7"/c-s) *(580 568-7/-4)* **RUN, BABY, RUN. / LEAVING VEGAS (acoustic)**	▢	▢
(cd-s+=) *(580 569-2)* – All by myself / Reach around jerk.		
Apr 94. (c-s) *<0582>* **LEAVING LAS VEGAS / THE NA-NA SONG**	–	60
Jun 94. (7"/c-s) *(580 644-7/-4)* **LEAVING LAS VEGAS. / LEAVING LAS VEGAS (live)**	66	–
(cd-s) *(580 645-2)* – ('A'side) / I shall believe (live) / What I can do for you (live).		
(cd-s) *(580 647-2)* – ('A'side) / No one said it would be easy (live) / The na-na song (live).		
Oct 94. (7"/c-s) *(580 842-7/-4) <0702>* **ALL I WANNA DO (remix). / SOLIDIFY**	5	2 Jul94
(cd-s+=) *(580 843-2)* – I'm gonna be a wheel someday.		
(cd-s) *(580 845-2)* – ('A'acoustic live) / Run, baby, run (acoustic live) / Leaving Las Vegas (acoustic live).		
Dec 94. (c-s) *<0798>* **STRONG ENOUGH / WHAT I CAN DO FOR YOU**	–	5
Jan 95. (7"/c-s) *(580 918-7/-4)* **STRONG ENOUGH. / NO ONE SAID IT WOULD BE EASY**	33	–

(cd-s+=) *(580 919-2)* – All I wanna do (live).
(cd-s) *(580 921-2)* – ('A'side) / All by myself / ('A'live) / Reach around jerk.
May 95. (c-s/cd-s) *(581 055-4/-2)* **CAN'T CRY ANYMORE / ALL I WANNA DO / STRONG ENOUGH (US version) / WE DO WHAT WE CAN** | 33 | –
(cd-ep) *(581 057-2)* – ('A'side) / What I can do for you (live) / No one said it would be easy (live) / I shall believe (live).
Jun 95. (c-s) *<0798>* **CAN'T CRY ANYMORE / WE DO WHAT WE CAN** | – | 36
Jul 95. (c-s) *(581 146-4)* **RUN, BABY, RUN / LEAVING LAS VEGAS** | 24 | –
(cd-s) *(581 147-2)* – ('A'side) / Can't cry anymore (live) / Reach around jerk (live) / I shall believe (live).
(cd-s) *(581 149-2)* – ('A'side) / Strong enough (live) / No one said it would be easy (live) / The na-na song (live).
Oct 95. (c-s) *(581 220-4)* **WHAT I CAN DO FOR YOU / LEAVING LAS VEGAS (live)** | 43 | –
(cd-s) *(581 221-2)* – ('A'side) / D'yer maker / I'm gonna be a wheel someday / No one said it would be easy.
(cd-s) *(581 885-2)* – ('A'live) / All I wanna do (live) / Strong enough (live) / Can't cry anymore (live).
Sep 96. (c-s) *<1874>* **IF IT MAKES YOU HAPPY / KEEP ON GROWING** | – | 10
Sep 96. (7") *(581 902-7)* **IF IT MAKES YOU HAPPY. / ALL I WANNA DO** | 9 | –
(c-s+=/cd-s+=) *(581 903-4/-2)* – Run, baby, run / Leaving Las Vegas.
(cd-s) *(581 885-2)* – ('A'side) / On the outside / Keep on growing / The book.
Oct 96. (cd/c) *(540 590-2/-4)* **SHERYL CROW** | 5 | 6
– Maybe angels / A change / Home / Sweet Rosalyn / If it makes you happy / Redemption day / Hard to make a stand / Everyday is a winding road / Love is a good thing / Oh Marie / Superstar / The book / Ordinary morning / Free man. *(d-cd-iss. Nov97; 540719-2)*
Nov 96. (c-s/cd-s) *(582 021-4/-2)* **EVERYDAY IS A WINDING ROAD / STRONG ENOUGH / CAN'T CRY ANYMORE / WHAT I CAN DO FOR YOU** | 12 | 11 Mar97
(cd-s) *(582 023-2)* – ('A'side) / If it makes you hapy (live BBC) / All I wanna do (live BBC) / Run, baby, run (live BBC).
Mar 97. (c-s/cd-s) *(582 147-4/-2)* **HARD TO MAKE A STAND / HARD TO MAKE A STAND (alt.) / HARD TO MAKE A STAND (live) / IN NEED** | 22 | ▢
(cd-s) *(582 149-2)* – ('A'side) / Sad sad world / No one said it would be easy (live) / If it makes you hapy (live).
Jul 97. (c-s) *(582 217-4)* **A CHANGE WOULD DO YOU GOOD / EVERYDAY IS A WINDING ROAD (live) / CAN'T CRY ANYMORE (live) / LEAVING LAS VEGAS (live)** | 8 | ▢
(cd-s) *(582 271-2)* – (first 2 tracks) / If it makes you happy / Hard to make a stand.
(cd-s) *(582 209-2)* – ('A'track) / Hard to make a stand (live) / On the outside (live) / ('A'live).
Oct 97. (cd-s) *(582399-2)* **HOME / STRONG ENOUGH / SWEET ROSALYN / I SHALL BELIEVE** | 25 | ▢
(cd-s) *(582401-2)* – ('A'side) / Hard to make a stand / Can't cry anymore / Redemption day.
Dec 97. (c-s) *(582456-4)* **TOMORROW NEVER DIES / ORDINARY MORNING** | 12 | ▢
(cd-s+=) *(582457-2)* – The book / No one said it would be easy.
(cd-rom) *(044067-2)* – ('A'mixes + CD-Rom).
Aug 98. (c-s) *(582761-4/-2) <radio play>* **MY FAVOURITE MISTAKE / SUBWAY RIDE / CRASH & BURN** | 9 | 20
(cd-s) *(582763-2)* – ('A'side) / In need (new remix) / Carolina.
Sep 98. (cd/c) *<(540974-2/-4)>* **THE GLOBE SESSIONS** | 2 | 5
– My favourite mistake / There goes the neighbourhood / Riverwide / It don't hurt / Maybe that's something / Am I getting through (part I & II) / Anything but down / The difficult kind / Mississippi / Members only / Crash & burn / Resuscitation. *(special d-cd Mar99 +=; 541025-2)* – A change would do you good / Riverwide / It don't hurt / Strong enough / Difficult kind / Everyday is a winding road.
Nov 98. (c-s) *(582806-4)* **THERE GOES THE NEIGHBOURHOOD / STRAIGHT TO THE MOON** | 19 | ▢
(cd-s+=) *(582807-2)* – My favourite mistake (live).
(cd-s) *(582809-2)* – ('A'live) / You always get your way / Hard to make a stand (live).
Feb 99. (c-s) *(582826-4) <radio cut>* **ANYTHING BUT DOWN / RUN BABY RUN (live)** | 19 | 49 Mar99
(cd-s+=) *(582829-2)* – Riverwide (live).
(cd-s) *(582827-2)* – ('A'side) / Leaving Las Vegas (live) / Mississippi (live).
Aug 99. (cd-s) **SWEET CHILD O' MINE / LEAVING LAS VEGAS** | 30 | ▢
Dec 99. (cd/c) *<(450574-2/-4)>* **SHERYL CROW AND FRIENDS LIVE FROM CENTRAL PARK (live)** | ▢ | ▢
– Everyday is a winding road / My favourite mistake / Leaving Las Vegas / Strong enough (w/ DIXIE CHICKS) / It don't hurt / A change would do you good / Gold dust woman (w/ STEVIE NICKS) / If it makes you happy (w/ CHRISSIE HYNDE) / All I wanna do / Happy (w/ KEITH RICHARDS & CHRISSIE HYNDE) / Difficult kind (w/ SARAH McLACHLAN) / White room / There goes the neighbourhood / Tombstone blues (w/ KEITH RICHARDS & DIXIE CHICKS).

CROWDED HOUSE

Formed: New Zealand ... virtually as SPLIT ENDS in October '72 by TIM FINN and PHIL JUDD. They slightly altered their name to SPLIT ENZ, stylising their own brand of tongue-in-cheek pop, inspired no doubt, by SPARKS and ROXY MUSIC. In fact, PHIL MANZANERA, guitarist of the latter, produced and remixed their 'SECOND THOUGHTS' album in 1976. They were subsequently joined by TIM's brother NEIL, as a replacement for chief songwriter, JUDD. With TIM's more melodic sensibilities increasingly to the fore, the band enjoyed some belated success with the 'TRUE COLOURS' (1980) album. A single, 'I GOT YOU', even hit the British Top 20, topping the Australian charts for over two months. Despite their pop charm, the band's latter day albums such as 'TIME AND TIDE' (1982) and 'CONFLICTING

EMOTIONS' (1984) sold relatively poorly outside Australia/NZ. They finally split for good in 1985, with NEIL forming CROWDED HOUSE alongside PAUL HESTER and NICK SEYMOUR. Relocating to L.A., the band signed to 'Capitol' and enjoyed massive Stateside success with their eponymous debut album in 1986/87. Taking the popcraft of SPLIT ENZ and injecting it with an aching melody, NEIL FINN proved himself an exquisite songwriter. The standout track was the bittersweet 'DON'T DREAM IT'S OVER' (later a UK hit for PAUL YOUNG), while other near misses were 'SOMETHING SO STRONG' and 'WORLD WHERE YOU LIVE'. Yet they couldn't repeat the formula on follow-up, 'TEMPLE OF LOW MEN' (1988), the album just scraping into the American Top 40 and failing miserably in Britain. There was only one thing for it, TIM had to return; with his additional songwriting and harmony vocals, 'WOODFACE' (1991) was a near masterpiece. If 'WEATHER WITH YOU' was perhaps a little sugary and 'CHOCOLATE CAKE' a mite leaden, there was no denying the swoonsome beauty of 'FALL AT YOUR FEET' and the almost spiritual reverence of 'FOUR SEASONS IN ONE DAY'. The trademark offbeat humour was still bubbling under the surface, rising to the top on the likes of 'THERE GOES GOD'. Although the set was slow to pick up, it deservedly spent more than two years in the British charts, although incredibly it failed to take off in the States. An unlikely pairing with former KILLING JOKE bassist/dance guru, YOUTH, led to CROWDED HOUSE's most experimental, profound and possibly finest effort in 'TOGETHER ALONE' (1993). Recorded at Kare Kare (a remote coastal area in their native New Zealand), the album was shrouded in an atmosphere of mystical calm and resolve, even on the rockier tracks such as 'LOCKED OUT'. 'DISTANT SUN' was a glorious burst of life-affirming, semi-acoustic melody, although it was the hypnotic grace of 'FINGERS OF LOVE' and 'PRIVATE UNIVERSE' which really carried the essence of this masterpiece. Enjoying another extended residence in the UK charts and spawning another string of hit singles, few could have predicted it would be the band's swansong. Yet after a further bout of touring and a UK No.1 compilation, 'RECURRING DREAM' (1996), the band announced a split amid tearful farewell shows. TIM FINN (husband of actress, Greta Scacchi), who had combined a solo career that encompassed a handful of albums (the last of which was the UK Top 30 'BEFORE AND AFTER' in 1993), formed one-off trio, ALT, with ANDY WHITE and LIAM O'MAONLAI. The FINN brothers were awarded OBE's for their services to New Zealand's music industry. • Songwriters: NEIL FINN penned except MR. TAMBOURINE MAN (Bob Dylan) + EIGHT MILES HIGH + SO YOU WANT TO BE A ROCK'N'ROLL STAR (Byrds). SPLIT ENZ; either NEIL or TIM. • Trivia: SIX MONTHS IN A LEAKY BOAT was banned by the BBC in 1982, due to the Argentinian / Falklands conflict. NICK is the brother of HUNTER + COLLECTORS' frontman, MARK SEYMOUR.

Album rating: Split Enz: MENTAL NOTES (*6) / SECOND THOUGHTS (*5) / DIZRHYTHMIA (*7) / FRENZY (*5) / TRUE COLOURS (*7) / WAIATA (*7) / TIME AND TIDE (*6) / SEE YA ROUND (*4) / HISTORY NEVER REPEATS compilation (*7) / Crowded House: CROWDED HOUSE (*5) / TEMPLE OF LOW MEN (*6) / WOODFACE (*8) / TOGETHER ALONE (*7) / RECURRING DREAM – THE VERY BEST OF CROWDED HOUSE compilation (*9) / Tim Finn: ESCAPADE (*5) / BIG CANOE (*5) / TIM FINN (*7) / BEFORE AND AFTER (*6) / ALTITUDE (*6; with Alt:= with Andy White & Liam O'Maonlai) / FINN (*5; as Finn:= Tim & Neil) / Neil Finn: TRY WHISTLING THIS (*6)

SPLIT ENZ

TIM FINN (b.25 Jun'52, Te Awamutu, New Zealand) – vocals, piano / **PHIL JUDD** – vocals, guitar / **JONATHAN CHUNN** – bass / **MILES GOLDING** – violin / **MICHAEL HOWARD** – drums

	Vertigo	not iss.
Apr 73. (7"; as SPLIT ENDS) FOR YOU. /	☐	-

—— **EDDIE RAYNOR** – keyboards repl. MILES / **WALLY WILKINSON** – guitar + **NOEL CROMBIE** – percussion repl. HOWARD

	Mushroom	not iss.
Jun 75. (lp) (L 35588) MENTAL NOTES	-	Austra

– Late last night / Walking down a road / Titus / Lovey dovey / Sweet dreams / Stranger than fiction / Time for a change / Matinee idyll / The woman who loves you / Mental notes. (UK-iss.Aug76 on 'Chrysalis' lp/c; CHR/ZCHR 1131)

Jun 75. (7") TITUS. /	-	Austra
Sep 75. (7") LOVEY DOVEY. /	-	Austra
May 76. (lp) (L 35981) SECOND THOUGHTS (re-mixes of debut)	-	Austra

—— **NEIL FINN** (b.27 May'58, Te Awamutu, New Zealand) – vocals, guitar repl. JUDD / JON and drummer EMLYN CROWTHER were repl. by Englishmen **NIGEL GRIGGS** (b.18 Aug'49) – bass / **MALCOLM GREEN** (b.25 Jan'53) – drums / **ROBERT GILLIE** – saxophone
(next iss. Australia; May77 on 'Mushroom')

	Chrysalis	Mushroom
Nov 76. (7") (CHS 2120) LATE LAST NIGHT. / WALKING DOWN THE ROAD	☐	☐
Feb 77. (7") (CHS 2131) ANOTHER GREAT DIVIDE. / STRANGER THAN FICTION	☐	☐
Oct 77. (7") (CHS 2170) MY MISTAKE. / CROSSWORDS	☐	☐
	(12"+=) (CHS 2170-12) – The woman who loves you.	
Oct 77. (lp/c) (CHR/ZCHR 1145) DIZRHYTHMIA	☐	☐

– Bold as brass / My mistake / Parrot fashion love / Sugar and spice / Without a doubt / Crosswords / Charley / Nice to know / Jambouree. (Aus-iss.; 36347)

—— JUDD re-joined but quit again, while GILLIE also quit

	Mushroom	not iss.
1978. (lp) (L 36921) FRENZY	-	Austra

—— now without WILKINSON

——

	Illegal	not iss.
Nov 79. (7"m) (ILS 0019) I SEE RED. / GIVE IT A WHIRL / HERMIT McDERMITT	☐	-

—— Issued earlier in Australia

—— Initial A&M material iss.Australia 1979 'Mushroom'.

	A&M	A&M
Aug 80. (lp/c) (AMLH/CAM 64822) <4822> TRUE COLOURS	42	40

– Shark attack / I got you / What's the matter with you / I hope I never / Nobody takes me seriously / Missing persons / Poor boy / How can I resist her / The choral sea. (cd-iss. 1988; CDA 3235) (re-iss. Oct92 cd/c; CD/C MID 130)

Aug 80. (7") (AMS 7546) <2252> I GOT YOU. / DOUBLE HAPPY	12	53
Nov 80. (7") (AMS 7574) NOBODY TAKES ME SERIOUSLY. / THE CHORAL SEA	☐	☐
Jan 81. (7") (AMS 8101) POOR BOY. / MISSING PERSON	☐	☐
Jan 81. (7") <2285> I HOPE I NEVER. / THE CHORAL SEA	-	☐
Mar 81. (7") <2293> NOBODY TAKES ME SERIOUSLY. / WHAT'S THE MATTER WITH YOU	-	☐
Mar 81. (lp/c) (AMLH/CAM 64848) <4848> WAIATA		45 May81

– Hard to follow / One step ahead / I don't wanna dance / Iris / Whale / Clumsby / History never repeats / Walking through the ruins / Ships / Ghost girl / Albert of India.

Apr 81. (7"m) (AMS 8128) HISTORY NEVER REPEATS. / SHARK ATTACK / WHAT'S THE MATTER WITH YOU	63	-
Jun 81. (7") (AMS 8146) <2339> ONE STEP AHEAD. / IN THE WARS	☐	☐

—— MALCOLM GREEN left and NOEL now on drums

Apr 82. (7") (AMS 8216) <2411> SIX MONTHS IN A LEAKY BOAT. / MAKE SOME SENSE OF IT	☐	☐
Apr 82. (lp/c) (AMLH/CAM 64894) <4894> TIME AND TIDE	71	58

– Dirty creature / Giant heartbeat / Hello Sandy Allen / Never ceases to amaze me / Lost for words / Small world / Take a walk / Pioneer / Six months in a leaky boat / Haul away / Log cabin fever / Make some sense of it.

Aug 84. (7") (AMS 203) <2652> MESSAGE TO THE GIRL. / BON VOYAGE (KIAKATIA)	☐	☐
Aug 84. (lp/c) (AMLH/CAM 64963) <4963> CONFLICTING EMOTIONS	☐	☐ Jul84

– Strait old line / Bullett brain and cactus head / Message to my girl / Working up an appetite / Our day / No mischief / The devil you know / I wake up every night / Conflicting emotions / Bon voyage. (cd-iss. 1988)

—— Now a quartet (**EDDIE RAYNOR, NEIL FINN, NIGEL GRIGGS + NOEL CROMBIE**) when TIM FINN married actress Greta Saatchi and went solo.

1985. (m-lp) SEE YOU ROUND (live)	☐	☐

—— disbanded 1985; NEIL formed CROWDED HOUSE, which later included TIM. A year later, PHIL JUDD, NOEL CROMBIE, NIGEL GRIGGS and MICHAEL DEN ELZEN formed their own outfit, SCHNELL FENSTER, who released two quirky-funk/jazz sets, 'SOUND OF TREES' (1988) and 'OK ALRIGHT A HUH OH YEAH' (1991).

– compilations, etc. –

Dec 80. (lp) Chrysalis; (CHR 1329) BEGINNING OF THE ENZ	☐	-
Sep 87. (d-lp) Concept; (CCQ 050) COLLECTION: 1973-1984 . . . THE BEST OF SPLIT ENZ	-	Austra
Oct 92. (cd) Chrysalis; (CDMID 175) HISTORY NEVER REPEATS (THE BEST OF SPLIT ENZ)	☐	☐

– I got you / Hard act to follow / Six months in a leaky boat / What's the matter with you / One step ahead / I see red / Message to my girl / History never repeats / I hope I never / Dirty creature / Poor boy.

Feb 94. (cd/c) Chrysalis; (CD/TC CHR 6059) THE BEST OF SPLIT ENZ	☐	☐
Apr 95. (cd) Mushroom; (D 98010) ANNIVERSARY	☐	☐

CROWDED HOUSE

NEIL FINN – vocals, guitar, piano / **NICK SEYMOUR** (b. 9 Dec'58, Benella, Australia) – bass / **PAUL HESTER** (b. 8 Jan'59, Melbourne) – drums, vocals with many guests **TIM PIERCE** – guitar / **MITCHELL FROOM** – keyboards, producer / **JOE SATRIANI** – b.vox / **JORGE BERMUDEZ** – percussion etc.

	Capitol	Capitol
Aug 86. (7") (CL 416) WORLD WHERE YOU LIVE. / THAT'S WHAT I CALL LOVE	☐	☐

(ext.12"+=) (12CL 416) – Can't carry on.
(ext.c-s+=/ext.cd-s+=) (TC/CD CL 416) – Something so strong / Don't dream it's over.

Mar 87. (7") (CL 438) <5614> DON'T DREAM IT'S OVER. / THAT'S WHAT I CALL LOVE	27	2 Jan87

(c-s+=/12"+=) (TC/12 CL 438) – ('A'extended.)

Mar 87. (7") <5634> LOVE YOU 'TIL I DIE. / MEAN TO ME	-	☐
Mar 87. (lp/c)(cd) (EST/TC-EST 2016)(CDP 746693-2) <12485> CROWDED HOUSE		12 Aug86

– World where you live / Now we're getting somewhere / Don't dream it's over / Mean to me / Love you 'til the day I die / Something so strong / Hole in the river / I walk away / Tombstone / That's what I call love. (cd+=) – Can't carry on. (re-iss. Mar94 cd/c; same)

Jun 87. (7") (CL 456) <5695> SOMETHING SO STRONG. / I WALK AWAY		7 Apr87

(12"+=) (12CL 456) – Don't dream it's over (live).

Aug 87. (7") <44033> WORLD WHERE YOU LIVE. / HOLE IN THE RIVER	-	65
Nov 87. (7") <44083> NOW WE'RE GETTING SOMEWHERE. / TOMBSTONE	-	☐
Jun 88. (7") (CL 498) <44164> BETTER BE HOME SOON. / KILL EYE		42

(12"+=/cd-s+=) (12/CD CL 498) – Don't dream it's over (live).

Jul 88. (lp/c)(cd) (EST/TC-EST 2064)(CDP 748763-2) <48763> TEMPLE OF LOW MEN		40

– I feel possessed / Kill eye / Into temptation / Mansion in the slums / When you come / Never be the same / Love this life / Sister madly / In the lowlands / Better be home soon.

Aug 88. (7") <44226> **INTO TEMPTATION. / BETTER BE HOME SOON**　`[ - ]` `[  ]`
Aug 88. (7") (CL 509) **SISTER MADLY. / MANSION IN THE SLUMS**
(12"+=/cd-s+=) (12/CD CL 509) – Something so strong (live).
Nov 88. (12"ep) <44406> **I FEEL POSSESSED. /**　`[ - ]` `[  ]`
────　added **TIM FINN** – vocals, piano, keyboards
Jun 91. (cd)(c)(lp) (CDP 793559-2)(TC+/EST 2144) <93559>
WOODFACE　`[ 34 ]` `[ 83 ]`
– Chocolate cake / It's only natural / Fall at your feet / Tall trees / Four seasons in one day / Weather with you / Whispers and moans / There goes God / Fame is / All I ask / As sure as I am / Italian plastic / She goes on / How will you go. *(album hit UK No.6 in Feb92)*
Jun 91. (c-s/7") (TC+/CL 618) **CHOCOLATE CAKE. / AS SURE AS I AM**　`[ 69 ]` `[  ]`
(12"+=/cd-s+=) (12/CD CL 618) – Anyone can tell.
Oct 91. (c-s) <44747> **FALL AT YOUR FEET / WHISPERS AND MOANS**　`[ - ]` `[ 75 ]`
Oct 91. (c-s/7") (TC+/CL 626) **FALL AT YOUR FEET. / DON'T DREAM IT'S OVER**　`[ 17 ]` `[ - ]`
(cd-s+=) (CDCL 626) – Sister madly / Better be home soon.
(cd-s) (CDCLX 626) – ('A'side) / Six months in a leaky boat (live) / Now we're getting somewhere (live) / Something so strong (lp version).
────　reverted to a trio again, when TIM departed Autumn '91. He was replaced on tour in 1993 by US session keyboard player **MARK HART** (b. 2 Jul'53, Fort Scott, Kansas)
Feb 92. (c-s/7") (TC+/CL 643) **WEATHER WITH YOU. / INTO TEMPTATION**　`[ 7 ]` `[  ]`
(cd-s) (CDCL 643) – ('A'side) / Mr. Tambourine man (live) / Eight miles high (live) / So you want to be a rock'n'roll star (live).
(cd-s) (CDCLS 643) – ('A'side) / Fall at your feet (live) / When you come (live) / Walking on the spot (live).
Jun 92. (c-s/7") (TC+/CL 655) **FOUR SEASONS IN ONE DAY. / THERE GOES GOD**　`[ 26 ]` `[  ]`
(cd-s) (CDCL 655) – ('A'side) / Dr. Livingstone (live) / Recurring dream (live) / Anyone can tell (live).
(cd-s) (CDCLS 655) – ('A'side) / Weather with you (live) / Italian plastic (live) / Message to my girl (live).
Sep 92. (c-s/7") (TC+/CL 661) **IT'S ONLY NATURAL. / CHOCOLATE CAKE**　`[ 24 ]` `[  ]`
(cd-s+=) (CDCL 661) – Medley:- It's only natural – Six months in a leaky boat – Hole in the river / The burglar's song.
Sep 93. (c-s/7") (TC+/CL 697) **DISTANT SUN. / WALKING ON THE SPOT**　`[ 19 ]` `[  ]`
(cd-s+=) (CDCL 697) – Throw your arms around me (live) / One step ahead (live).
(cd-s) (CDCLS 697) – ('A'side) / This is massive (live) / When you come (live).
Oct 93. (cd/c/lp) (CD/TC+/EST-U 2215) <27048> **TOGETHER ALONE**　`[ 4 ]` `[ 73 ]`
– Kare Kare / In my command / Nails in my feet / Black & white boy / Fingers of love / Pineapple head / Locked out / Private universe / Walking on the spot / Distant sun / Catherine wheels / Skin feeling / Together alone.
Nov 93. (c-s/7") (TC+/CL 701) **NAILS IN MY FEET. / ZEN ROXY**　`[ 22 ]` `[  ]`
(cd-s+=) (CDCL 701) – Don't dream it's over (live).
Feb 94. (c-s) (TCCL 707) **LOCKED OUT / DISTANT SUN (live)**　`[ 12 ]` `[  ]`
(cd-s+=) (CDCL 707) – Hole in the river (live) / Sister Madly (live).
(10"+=) (10CL 707) – Private universe (live) / Fall at your feet (live).
(cd-s) (CDCLS 707) – ('A'side) / Private universe (live) / Fall at your feet (live) / Better be home soon (live).
Jun 94. (c-s) (TCCL 715) **FINGERS OF LOVE (live). / NAILS IN MY FEET (live)**　`[ 25 ]` `[  ]`
(cd-s) (CDCL 715) – ('A'side) / Skin feeling / Kare Kare (live) / In my command (live).
(10") (10CL 715) – ('A'side) / Love u till the day I die (live) / Whispers and moans (live) / It's only natural (live).
(cd-s) (CDCLS 715) – ('A'side) / Catherine wheels / Pineapple head (live) / Something so strong (live).
Sep 94. (c-s) (TCCL 723) **PINEAPPLE HEAD (live). / WEATHER WITH YOU**　`[ 27 ]` `[  ]`
(10"+=/cd-s+=) (10/CD CL 723) – Don't dream it's over / Together alone.
────　NEIL and TIM were awarded O.B.E.'s in Queen's birthday honours.
Jun 96. (c-s) (TCCL 774) **INSTINCT / RECURRING DREAM**　`[ 12 ]` `[  ]`
(cd-s+=) (CDCL 774) – Weather with you (live) / Chocolate cake (live).
(cd-s) (CDCLS 774) – ('A'side) / World where you live (live) / In the lowlands (live) / Into temptation (live).
Jun 96. (cd/c/lp) (CD/TC+/EST 2283) **RECURRING DREAM – THE VERY BEST OF CROWDED HOUSE** (compilation)　`[ 1 ]` `[  ]`
– Weather with you / World where you live / Fall at your feet / Locked out / Don't dream it's over / Into temptation / Pineapple head / When you come / Private universe / Not the way you think you are / Instinct / I feel possessed / Four seasons in one day / It's only natural / Distant sun / Something so strong / Mean to me / Better be home soon / Everything is good for you. *(cd w/extra live-cd; CDESTX 2283)* – There goes God / Newcastle jam / Love u till the day I die / Hole in the river / Pineapple head / Private universe / How will you go / Left hand / Whispers and moans / Kill eye / Fingers of love / Don't dream it's over / When you come / Sister madly / In my command.
────　They are now no longer having disbanded June '96.
Aug 96. (c-s) (TCCL 776) **NOT THE GIRL YOU THINK YOU ARE. / BETTER BE HOME SOON (live)**　`[ 20 ]` `[  ]`
(cd-s+=) (CDCL 776) – Private universe (live) / Fingers of love (live).
(cd-s) (CDCLS 776) – ('A'side) / Instinct (live) / Distant sun (live) / Fall at your feet (live).
Oct 96. (7") (CL 780) **DON'T DREAM IT'S OVER. / WEATHER WITH YOU (live)**　`[ 25 ]` `[  ]`
(cd-s+=) (CDCLS 780) – Into temptation (live) / Locked out (live).
(cd-s) (CDCL 780) – ('A'side) / Four seasons in one day (live) / In my command (live) / Pineapple head (live).

– compilations, etc. –

Nov 95. (3xcd-box) E.M.I.; (CDOMB 001) **CROWDED HOUSE / TEMPLE OF LOW MEN / WOODFACE**　`[  ]` `[  ]`

TIM FINN

────　(solo with some SPLIT ENZ members)

		Epic	A&M
Nov 83. (7") <2572> **GRAND ADVENTURE. / THROUGH THE YEARS**		-	
Nov 83. (7") (A 3932) **FRACTION TOO MUCH FRICTION. / BELOW THE PAST**			Apr84
Jan 84. (7") <2597> **MADE MY DAY. / GRAND ADVENTURE**		-	
Jun 84. (lp/c) (EPC/40 25812) **ESCAPADE**			Sep83

– Fraction too much friction / Staring at the embers / Through the years / Not for nothing / In a minor key / Made my day / Wait and see / Below the belt / I only want to know / Growing pains. *(cd-iss. Oct93 on 'Sony Europe';) (re-iss. Jun94 cd/c; 474610-2/-4)*

		Virgin	Virgin
Mar 86. (7") (VS 849) **NO THUNDER NO FIRE NO CAR. / SEARCHING FOR THE STREETS**			-
Apr 86. (lp/c/cd) (V/TCV/CDV 2369) **THE BIG CANOE**			

– Are we one or are we two? / Searching the streets / Hole in my heart / Spiritual hung / Don't bury my heart / Timmy / So into wine / Hyacinth / Big canoe. *(re-iss. cd Mar94; OVED 221)*
Jun 86. (7"/12") (VS 866/+12) **CARVE YOU IN MARBLE. / HOLE IN MY HEART**

		Capitol	Capitol
Apr 89. (lp/c/cd) (EST/TC-EST/CD-EST 2088) **TIM FINN**			-

– Young mountain / Not even close / How'm I gonna sleep / Parihaka / Tears inside / Birds swim fish fly / Suicide on Downing Street / Show a little mercy / Crescendo / Been there, done that. *(re-iss. Oct92; same)*
Jul 89. (7") (CL 542) <44339> **HOW'M I GONNA SLEEP. / CRUEL BLACK CROW**
(12"+=/cd-s+=) (12/CD CL 542) – Six months in a leaky boat.
────　with **RICHARD THOMPSON / ANDY WHITE / LIAM O'MAONLAI**
Jun 93. (c-s) (659248-4) **PERSUASION. / STRANGENESS AND CHARM (version)**　`[ 43 ]`
(cd-s) (659248-2) – ('A'side) / Parihaka / Secret heart / ('A'acoustic).
(cd-s) (659248-5) – ('A'side) / Six months in a leaky boat (live) / Not even close (live) / Protected (live).
Jun 93. (cd/c) (CD/TC EST 2202) **BEFORE AND AFTER**　`[ 29 ]`
– Hit the ground running / Protected / In love with it all / Persuasion / Many's the time in Dublin) / Funny way / Can't do both / In your sway / Strangness in charm / Always never now / Walk you home / I found it *(cd re-iss. Sep94; same)*
Sep 93. (c-s) (TCCL 694) **HIT THE GROUND RUNNING. / NO MORE TEARS**　`[ 50 ]`
(cd-s+=) (CDCL 694) – Not made of stone / You've changed.
(cd-s) (CDCLS 694) – ('A'side) / Walk you home (live) / Charlie (live w / PHIL MANZANERA) / ('A'live).

ALT

TIM FINN / + **ANDY WHITE** – vocals, guitar (former solo artist) / **LIAM O'MAONLAI** – vocals, guitar (ex-HOTHOUSE FLOWERS). ALT (ANDY, LIAM & TIM) recorded in Australia, although initiated in Dublin.

		Parlophone	Cooking Vinyl
Jun 95. (cd/c) (CD/TC PCS 7377) **ALTITUDE**		67	Oct95

– We're all men / Penelope tree / When the winter comes / Favourite girl / Swim / The refugee tree / What you've done / Second swim / Girlfriend guru / Mandala / I decided to fly / The day you were born / Halfway round the world.

FINN

TIM + NEIL duo

		Parlophone	Capitol
Oct 95. (c-s) (TCR 6417) **SUFFER NEVER / WEATHER WITH YOU (demo)**		29	

(cd-s+=) (CDRS 6417) – Prodigal son (demo) / Catherine wheel (demo).
(cd-s) (CDR 6417) – ('A'side) / Strangeness and charm (demo) / In love with it all (demo) / Four seasons in one day.
Oct 95. (cd/c) (CD/TC FINN 1) **FINN**　`[ 15 ]`
– Only talking sense / Eyes of the world / Mood swinging man / Last day of June / Suffer never / Angels heap / Niwhai / Where is my soul / Bullets in my hairdo / Paradise ((wherever you are) / Kiss the road of Rarotonga.
Nov 95. (c-s/cd-s) (TCR/CDR 6421) **ANGELS HEAP / IT'S ONLY NATURAL (demo) / CHOCOLATE CAKE (demo)**　`[ 41 ]`
(cd-s) (CDRS 6421) – ('A'side) / There goes God (demo) / How will you go (demo).

NEIL FINN

────　with augmentation from a host of musicians on a few tracks each
Jun 98. (c-s) (TCR 6495) **SHE WILL HAVE HER WAY / ASTRO**　`[ 26 ]`
(cd-s+=) (CDRS 6495) – 808 song.
(cd-s) (CDR 6495) – ('A'side) / Faster than light / Identical twin.
Jun 98. (cd/c/lp) (72434 95139-2/-4/-1) **TRY WHISTLING THIS**　`[ 5 ]`
– Last one standing / Souvenir / King tide / Try whistling this / She will have her way / Sinner / Twisty bass / Loose tongue / Truth / Astro / Dream date / Faster than light / Addicted.
Oct 98. (c-s/cd-s) (TCR/CDRS 6505) **SINNER / TOKYO / SHE COMES SCATTERED**　`[ 39 ]`
(cd-s) (CDR 6505) – ('A'live) / Not the girl you think you are (live) / Last one standing (live).

CRUNT (see under ⇒ BABES IN TOYLAND)

CRYSTALS

Formed: Brooklyn, New York, USA ... 1961 by BARBARA ALSTON, MARY THOMAS, DEE DEE KENNIBREW, LALA BROOKS and PAT WRIGHT. While the quintet came together after meeting songwriter, LEROY BATES (whose daughter CRYSTAL inspired the group's name), their rise to fame came via PHIL SPECTOR. A legend in the making, the young producer/would-be mogul had just formed his own label, 'Philles', together with Lester Sill. He relocated to New York shortly after, signing The CRYSTALS before taking up a lucrative A&R position at 'Liberty'. In the meantime, the girls hit the US Top 20 with their October '61 debut single, 'THERE'S NO OTHER (LIKE MY BABY)', scoring a similar sized hit early the following year with the Mann/Weill-penned 'UPTOWN'. A controversial third single, 'HE HIT ME (AND IT FELT LIKE A KISS)' was released that summer although an airplay ban – due to the well dodgy subject matter – kept it off the chart. There was no such problem with the Gene Pitney-penned 'HE'S A REBEL', a massive No.1 hit that stands as SPECTOR's first fully realised take on his revolutionary 'Wall Of Sound'. With THOMAS out of the picture on marital duties, SPECTOR had controversially assembled an alternative CRYSTALS line-up (comprising lead singer DARLENE LOVE and a couple of fellow ex-BLOSSOMS) backed by a crew of crack session players. Almost as controversially, he ignored the conventions of record production by packing the sessions with as much musicians, instruments and distortion as possible; the result was a thrillingly visceral racket that took teen-dream pop music to a higher plane and made SPECTOR a millionaire. The formula was repeated on 1963's 'DA DOO RON RON', a transatlantic Top 5 which saw the orignal CRYSTALS (save THOMAS) reinstated with LALA on lead vocals. 'THEN HE KISSED ME' completed the stunning hat trick a few months later, narrowly missing the UK No.1 spot. Yet subsequent US singles, ('LITTLE BOY' and 'ALL GROWN UP') floundered while SPECTOR concentrated his attentions on his latest baby, The RONETTES. A short-lived deal with 'United Artists' provided a further couple of singles to zero success and the girls finally called it a day in mid-'66. Eventually resurfacing in 1971, The CRYSTALS (in various incarnations) would sporadically tour the golden oldie circuit over the forthcoming decades. • **Miscellaneous:** The CRYSTALS appeared on PHIL SPECTOR's seasonal Christmas 1963 lp, 'A CHRISTMAS GIFT FOR YOU', contributing 'Santa Claus Is Coming To Town' and 'Rudolph The Red Nosed Reindeer'.

Best CD compilation: THE BEST OF THE CRYSTALS (*6)

BARBARA ALSTON (b.1945) – vocals / **MARY THOMAS** (b.1946) – vocals / **DEE DEE KENNIBREW** (b.DELORES HENRY, 1945) – vocals / **DOROLES 'LA LA' BROOKS** – vocals / **PATRICIA WRIGHT** (b.1945) – vocals

		Parlophone	Philles	
Feb 62.	(7") (R 4867) <100> **THERE'S NO OTHER (LIKE MY BABY). / OH YEAH, MAYBE BABY**		20	Nov61

―― <above was originally released in US Jul'61 then flipped over>

| Mar 62. | (7") <102> **UPTOWN. / WHAT A NICE WAY TO TURN SEVENTEEN** | - | 13 | |
| May 62. | (lp) <PHLP 4000> **TWIST UPTOWN** | - | | |

– Uptown / Another country, another world / Frankenstein twist / Oh yeah, maybe baby / Please hurt me / There's no other (like my baby) / On Broadway / What a nice way to turn seventeen / No one ever tells you / Gee whiz, look at my eyes / I love you Eddie. (cd-iss. Jun88 on 'Spectrum'; U 4062)

| Jun 62. | (7") <105> **HE HIT ME (AND IT FELT LIKE A KISS). / NO ONE EVER TELLS YOU** | - | | |

―― (Oct'62) now a quartet when MARY left to get married. The next two 45's saw SPECTOR using bogus CRYSTALS (DARLENE LOVE – lead vocals & **FANITA JAMES** and **GRACIA NITZSCHE** – b.vocals ex-BLOSSOMS)

		London	Philles	
Nov 62.	(7") (HLU 9611) <106> **HE'S A REBEL. / I LOVE YOU EDDIE**	19	1	Aug62

(re-iss. Jun75 on 'Phil Spector Int.'; 2010 002)

| Jan 63. | (7") (HLU 9661) <109> **HE'S SURE THE BOY I LOVE. / WALKIN' ALONG (LA LA LA)** | | 11 | Dec62 |
| Mar 63. | (lp) (HA-U 8120) <PHLP 4001> **HE'S A REBEL** | | | |

– He's a rebel / Uptown / Another country, another world / Frankenstein twist / Oh yeah, maybe baby! / He's sure the boy I love / There's no other like my baby / On Broadway / What a nice way to turn seventeen / No one ever tells you / He hit me (and it felt like a kiss) / I love you Eddie.

―― **LALA** now on lead vocals (with other 3 originals)

| Jun 63. | (7") (HLU 9732) <112> **DA DOO RON RON. / GIT' IT** | 5 | 3 | Apr63 |
| Sep 63. | (7") (HLU 9773) <115> **THEN HE KISSED ME. / BROTHER JULIUS** | 2 | 6 | Aug63 |

―― **FRANCES COLLINS** – vocals; repl. PAT who also got married

Jan 64.	(7") <119> **LITTLE BOY. / HARRY (FROM W. Va.) & MILT**	-	92	
Jan 64.	(7"; w-drawn) (HLU 9837) **LITTLE BOY. / UPTOWN**	-	-	
Feb 64.	(7") (HLU 9852) **I WONDER. / LITTLE BOY**	36	-	
Jul 64.	(7") <122> **ALL GROWN UP. / Phil Spector Group: IRVING (JAGGERED SIXTEENTHS)**		98	

		U.A.	U.A.
Oct 65.	(7") (UP 1110) **MY PLACE. / YOU CAN'T TIE A GIRL DOWN**		
Feb 66.	(7") < **ARE YOU TRYING TO GET RID OF ME, BABY? / I GOT A MAN**	-	

―― In 1966 they were discarded by SPECTOR and retired to domesticity. After a few out of retirement gigs, they appeared mid '71 at New York's 'Rock'n'roll revival show'. Depleted somewhat in line-up, they continued throughout the 70's & 80's on the 'Golden Oldies' circuit.

– compilations, others, etc. –

1963.	(7"ep) London; (RE-U 1381) **THE CRYSTALS**		-
1964.	(lp) Philles; <PHLP 4003> **THE CRYSTALS SING THEIR GREATEST HITS VOLUME 1**	-	
	(UK-iss.Oct75 on 'Phil Spector Int.';)		
Jan 69.	(7") London; (HLU 10239) **DA DOO RON RON. / HE'S A REBEL**		
Oct 74.	(7"blue) Warners; (K 19010) **DA DOO RON RON. / THEN HE KISSED ME**	15	-
	(re-iss. 7".Jan76; 2010 011)		
Oct 75.	(lp) Phil Spector Int.; (2307 006) **PHIL SPECTOR WALL OF SOUND VOLUME 3: THE CRYSTALS**		
Apr 77.	(7") Phil Spector Int.; (2010 020) **ALL GROWN UP. / THE TWIST**		
Oct 80.	(7"m) Creole; (CR 182) **DA DOO RON RON. / AND THEN HE KISSED ME / HE'S A REBEL**		
Aug 87.	(7") Raise The Roof; (ROOF 3) **DA DOO RON RON. / THEN HE KISSED ME**		
	(12"+=) (ROOFT 3) – He's a rebel.		
Jun 89.	(cd/c; shared with The SHANGRI-LA'S) Spectrum; (K/U 30152) **THE CRYSTALS MEETS THE SHANGRI-LA'S**		
Sep 92.	(cd/c) Phil Spector Int.; <(PSCD/PSTC 1007)> **THE BEST OF THE CRYSTALS**		

– There's no other (like my baby) / Oh yeah, maybe baby / Uptown / What a nice way to turn seventeen / He hit me (and it felt like a kiss) / No one ever tells you / He's a rebel / I love you Eddie / Another country, another world / Please hurt me / He's sure the boy I love / Look in my eyes / Da doo ron ron / Heartbreaker / Then he kissed me / I wonder / Little boy / Girls can tell / All grown up.

| Apr 93. | (cd) Sixteen; **16 GREATEST HITS** | | - |
| Sep 99. | (cd) Auto Pilot; (ROGER 21) **THEN HE KISSED ME** | | - |

CUD (dig out; Great Alt & Indie ...)

CULT

Formed: Bradford, England ... 1982 as the SOUTHERN DEATH CULT for whom IAN ASTBURY (then going under the name IAN LINDSAY) took on vocal duties. Having spent time in Canada as a kid, ASTBURY had been profoundly influenced by Native American culture and problems soon arose when the singer felt his pseudo hippy/Red Indian philosophy was being compromised by the band set-up. The group split the following year, ASTBURY keeping the name but shortening it to DEATH CULT. Relocating to London, ASTBURY duly recruited a new band (all seasoned hands on the post-punk circuit) and released an eponymous, 4-track 12" single. The band released a further solitary single, 'GOD'S ZOO', before trimming the name further to The CULT. While the band's music still betrayed slight indie/goth tendencies, they were eager to lose the 'gothic' tag. 'DREAMTIME' (1984) sounded confused and directionless, and it wasn't until 'LOVE', the following year, that the band fashioned some kind of distinct identity. Veering from the cascading bombast of the classic singles, 'RAIN' and 'SHE SELLS SANCTUARY' to the mystic schtick of 'BROTHER WOLF, SISTER MOON', the album semi-successfully ploughed a deeper retro furrow than the myriad BYRDS clones of the day. ASTBURY's flowing locks were also something of an anomaly for an 'alternative' band in those dark 80's days, and the band were derided in some areas of the music press. The CULT's response was to throw caution to the wind and do what they'd probably always secretly dreamed of doing, writing massive, anthemic heavy rock songs. With metal guru RICK RUBIN at the production helm, DUFFY's guitar was pushed way up in the mix and the sound generally tightened. The result: any fans clinging to gothic pretensions were aghast while Kerrang readers loved it. Possibly The CULT's finest moment, it spawned the booty-shaking singles 'LOVE REMOVAL MACHINE', 'LI'L DEVIL' and 'WILDFLOWER', hell, it even had a cover of 'BORN TO BE WILD'! 'SONIC TEMPLE' (1989) was another heavy rock effort, if a bit more grandiose in its reach, featuring their tribute to doomed 60's child, EDIE SEDGEWICK, 'EDIE (CIAO BABY)'. This album saw The CULT finally gain major success in America, the US 'big rock' sound evident in the record's grooves. Line-up changes had dogged The CULT throughout their career and by 1991, ASTBURY and DUFFY were the only remaining members from the original line-up. That year's album, 'CEREMONY', sounded somewhat listless, although it was a relative success. 1993 saw a No.1 compilation album, 'PURE CULT' selling like hotcakes, although people weren't quite so eager to shell out for '94's 'THE CULT' album. Their glory days were clearly over, the band remaining a cult (!) phenomenon. In 1996, ASTBURY was in full flight again, fronting a new rock outfit, The HOLY BARBARIANS, although the album, 'CREAM' didn't shift many copies. • **Songwriters:** From '83 onwards, all by ASTBURY / DUFFY. Covered WILD THING (Troggs) / LOUIE LOUIE (Kingsmen) / CONQUISTADOR (Theatre Of Hate) / FAITH HEALER (Alex Harvey).

Album rating: SOUTHERN DEATH CULT (*6; as the Southern Death Cult) / DREAMTIME (*7) / LOVE (*8) / ELECTRIC (*6) / SONIC TEMPLE (*8) / CEREMONY (*6) / PURE CULT compilation (*7) / THE CULT (*5) / Holy Barbarians: CREAM (*6)

SOUTHERN DEATH CULT

IAN LINDSAY (b. ASTBURY, 14 May'62, Heswell, Cheshire, England)– vocals / **BUZZ BURROWS** – guitar / **BARRY JEPSON** – bass / **AKY (NAWAZ QURESHI)** – drums

Dec 82. (7") *(SIT 19)* **FATMAN. / MOYA**   [Situation2: -] [not iss.: -]
(12"+=) *(SIT 19T)* – The girl.

Jun 83. (lp) *(BEGA 46)* **SOUTHERN DEATH CULT**   [Beggars Banquet: 43] [not iss.: -]
– All glory / Fatman / Today / False faces / The crypt / Crow / Faith / Vivisection / Apache / Moya. *(re-iss. Jul88 lp/c/cd; BBL/+C 46/+CD)*

—— (Apr'83) (as BUZZ, AKY and BARRY formed GETTING THE FEAR)

DEATH CULT

with now **IAN ASTBURY** recruited new people– **BILLY DUFFY** (b.12 May'61)– lead guitar (ex-THEATRE OF HATE, ex-NOSEBLEEDS) / **JAMIE STUART** – bass (ex-RITUAL, ex-CRISIS) / **RAY MONDO** (r.n.SMITH)– drums (ex-RITUAL)

Jul 83. (12"ep) *(SIT 23T)* **BROTHERS GRIMM / HORSE NATION. / GHOST DANCE / CHRISTIANS**   [Situation2: -] [not iss.: -]

—— **NIGEL PRESTON** – drums (ex-SEX GANG CHILDREN) repl. MONDO
Nov 83. (7"/12") *(SIT 29/+T)* **GOD'S ZOO. / GOD'S ZOO (THESE TIMES)**   [ ] [ ]
(re-iss. Nov88)

CULT

—— (same line-up)

May 84. (7") *(SIT 33)* **SPIRITWALKER. / A FLOWER IN THE DESERT**   [Situation2: -] [not iss.: -]
(12"+=) *(SIT 33T)* – Bone rag.

Aug 84. (lp/c) *(BEG A/C 57)* **DREAMTIME**   [Beggars Banquet: 21] [Sire: -]
– Horse nation / Spiritwalker / 83rd dream / Butterflies / Go west (crazy spinning circles) / Gimmick / A flower in the desert / Dreamtime / Rider in the snow / Bad medicine waltz. *(free live-lp w/ above, also on c)* **DREAMTIME AT THE LYCEUM** (CULT 1) – 83rd dream / God's zoo / Bad medicine / A flower in the desert / Dreamtime / Christians / Horse nation / Bone rag / Ghost dance / Moya. *(pic-lp iss.Dec84; BEGA 57P) (re-iss. Oct88 lp/c/cd; BBL/+C 57/+CD)* – Bone rag / Sea and sky / Resurrection Joe.

Sep 84. (7"/7"poster) *(BEG 115/+P)* **GO WEST. / SEA AND SKY**   [ ] [-]
(12"+=) *(BEG 115T)* – Brothers Grimm (live).

Dec 84. (7") *(BEG 122)* **RESURRECTION JOE / ('A'-Hep cat mix)**   [74] [-]
(12"+=) *(BEG 122T)* – ('A'extended).

May 85. (7") *(BEG 135)* **SHE SELLS SANCTUARY. / NO.13**   [15] [-]
(12"+=) *(BEG 135T)* – The snake.
(12") *(BEG 135TP)* – ('A'-Howling mix) / Assault on sanctuary.
(c-s) *(BEG 135C)* – ('A'extended) / ('A'-Howling mix) / The snake / Assault on sanctuary.

Jul 85. (7") *<28820>* **SHE SELLS SANCTUARY. / LITTLE FACE**   [-] [ ]

—— **MARK BRZEZICKI** – drums (of BIG COUNTRY) deputised repl. PRESTON
Sep 85. (7") *(BEG 147)* **RAIN. / LITTLE FACE**   [17] [-]
(12"+=) *(BEG 147T)* – (Here comes the) Rain.

Oct 85. (lp/c)(cd) *(BEGA/BEGC 65)(BEGA 65CD) <25359>* **LOVE**   [4] [87]
– Nirvana / Big neon gliter / Love / Brother Wolf, Sister Moon / Rain / The phoenix / The hollow man / Revolution / She sells sanctuary / Black angel. *(cd+=)* – Judith / Little face.

—— **LES WARNER** (b.13 Feb'61) – drums (ex-JOHNNY THUNDERS, etc) repl. MARK
Nov 85. (7") *(BEG 152)* **REVOLUTION. / ALL SOULS AVENUE**   [30] [-]
(d7"+=/c-s+=/12"+=) *(BEG D/C/T 152)* – Judith / Sunrise.
Feb 87. (7") *(BEG 182)* **LOVE REMOVAL MACHINE / WOLF CHILD'S BLUES**   [18] [-]
(12"+=) *(BEG 182T)* – ('A'extended).
(d7"+=) *(BEG 182D)* – Conquistador / Groove Co.
(c-s+=) *(BEG 182C)* – (all above).

Apr 87. (lp/c)(cd) *(BEGA/BEGC 80)(BEGA 80CD) <25555>* **ELECTRIC**   [4] [38]
– Wild flower / Peace dog / Lil' devil / Aphrodisiac jacket / Electric ocean / Bad fun / King contrary man / Love removal machine / Born to be wild / Outlaw / Memphis hip shake. *(gold-pic-lp Aug87; BEGA 80G)*

Apr 87. (7") *(BEG 188)* **LIL' DEVIL. / ZAP CITY**   [11] [-]
(12"+=) *(BEG 188T)* – She sells sanctuary (live) / Bonebag (live).
(d12"+=/c-s+=) *(BEG 188 TD/C)* – She sells sanctuary (live) / The phoenix (live) / Wild thing . . .Louie Louie (live).
(cd-s+=) *(BEG 188CD)* – Love removal machine (live) / The phoenix (live) / She sells sanctuary (live).

May 87. (7") *<29290>* **LIL' DEVIL. / MEMPHIS HIPSHAKE**   [-] [ ]
Aug 87. (7"/7"pic-d) *(BEG 195/+P) <28213>* **WILD FLOWER. / LOVE TROOPER**   [24] [ ]
(12"+=) *(BEG 195T)* – ('A'extended rock mix).
(c-s+++=) *(BEG 195C)* – Horse nation (live).
(d7"+=) *(BEG 195D)* – Outlaw (live) / Horse nation (live).
(cd-s+=) *(BEG 195CD)* – (all 5 above) / She sells sanctuary (live).
(12") *(BEG 195TR)* – ('A'ext.) / ('A'-Guitar dub) / ('B'side).

—— **MICKEY CURRY** – (on session) drums repl. WARNER + KID CHAOS
Mar 89. (7"/c-s) *(BEG 228/+C) <27543>* **FIRE WOMAN. / AUTOMATIC BLUES**   [15] [46 May89]
(12"+=/3"cd-s+=) *(BEG 228 T/CD)* – Messin' up the blues.
(12") *(BEG 228TR)* – ('A'-L.A. rock mix) / ('A'-N.Y.C. rock mix).

Apr 89. (lp/c)(cd) *(BEGA/BEGC 98)(BEGA 98CD) <25871>* **SONIC TEMPLE**   [3] [10]
– Sun king / Fire woman / American horse / Edie (ciao baby) / Sweet soul sister / Soul asylum / New York City / Automatic blues / Soldier blue / Wake up time for freedom. *(c+=/cd+=)* – Medicine train.

—— **ASTBURY, DUFFY + STUART** were joined by **MATT SORUM** – drums / **MARK TAYLOR** – keyboards (on tour)
Jun 89. (7"/7"gf/c-s) *(BEG 230/+G/C)* **EDIE (CIAO BABY). / BLEEDING HEART GRAFFITI**   [32] [-]

(pic-cd+=) *(BEG 230CP)* – Lil' devil (live) / Love removal machine (live).
(12"/12"poster) *(BEG 230 T/TP)* – ('A'side) / Medicine train / Love removal machine (live).
(3"cd-s) *(BEG 230CD)* – ('A'side) / Love removal machine (live) / Revolution (live).

Sep 89. (7") *<22873>* **EDIE (CIAO BABY). / LOVE REMOVAL MACHINE**   [-] [93]
Nov 89. (7"/c-s) *(BEG 235/+C)* **SUN KING. / EDIE (CIAO BABY)**   [39] [-]
(12"+=/12"hologram+=) *(BEG 235T/+H)* – She sells sanctuary.
(cd-s+=) *(BEG 235CD)* – ('A'extended).

Feb 90. (7"/c-s) *(BEG 241/+C)* **SWEET SOUL SISTER. / THE RIVER**   [42] [-]
(12"gf+=) *(BEG 241TG)* – American horse (live).
(cd-s+=) *(BEG 241CG)* – Soul asylum (live).
(cd-s) *(BEG 241CD)* – ('A'rock mix) / American horse (live) / ('A'live).
(12") *(BEG 241TR)* – ('A'rock's mix) / Soul asylum (live).
(12") *(BEG 241TP)* – ('A'rock's mix) / ('A'side) / ('A'live).

Mar 90. (c-s) *<19926>* **SWEET SOUL SISTER. / SOLDIER BLUE**   [-] [-]

—— (Apr-Oct90) **MARK MORRIS** – bass (ex-BALAAM AND THE ANGEL) repl. STUART

—— (1991) **ASTBURY** and **DUFFY** brought in **CHARLIE DRAYTON** – bass / **MICKEY CURRY** – drums / **RICHIE ZITO** – keyboards, producer / **BELMONT TENCH** – piano, mellotron / **TOMMY FUNDERBUCK** – backing vocals
Sep 91. (7"/c-s) *(BEG 255/+C)* **WILD HEARTED SON. / INDIAN**   [40] [-]
('A'ext.12"+=) *(BEG 255T)* – Red Jesus.
(cd-s+++=) *(BEG 255CD)* – ('A'extended version).

Sep 91. (cd)(c/lp) *(BEGA 122CD)(BEGC/BEGA 122) <26673>* **CEREMONY**   [9] [25]
– Ceremony / Wild hearted son / Earth mofo / White / If / Full tilt / Heart of soul / Bangkok rain / Indian / Sweet salvation / Wonderland.

Feb 92. (7"/c-s) *(BEG 260/+C)* **HEART OF SOUL. / EARTH MOFO**   [51] [-]
(12"+=/cd-s+=) *(BEG 260 T/CD)* – Edie (ciao baby) (acoustic) / Heart of soul (acoustic).

Jan 93. (12"ep) *(BEG 263T)* **SANCTUARY 1993 MIXES**   [15] [-]
– She sells sanctuary / ('A'-Dog Star Rising) / ('A'-Slutnostic mix) / ('A'-Sundance mix).
(cd-ep) *(BEG 263CD2)* – ('A'live) repl. above original.
(cd-ep) *(BEG 263CD1)* – (first 2 tracks) / ('A'-Phlegmatic mix) / ('A'-Flusteresqueish mix).

Feb 93. (d-lp/c)(cd/4x12") *(BEGA/BEGC 130)(BEGA 130 CD/B)* **PURE CULT** compilation)   [1] [ ]
– She sells sanctuary / Fire woman / Lil' devil / Spiritwalker / The witch / Revolution / Wild hearted Sun / Love removal machine / Rain / Edie (ciao baby) / Heart of soul / Love / Wildflower / Go west / Ressurection Joe / Sun king / Sweet soul ister / Earth mofo. *(d-lp w/ other d-lp)* LIVE AT THE MARQUEE '91

—— **ASTBURY + DUFFY** now with **CRAIG ADAMS** (b. 4 Apr'62, Otley, England) – bass (ex-MISSION, ex-SISTERS OF MERCY) + **SCOTT GARRETT** (b.14 Mar'66, Washington, D.C.) – drums
Sep 94. (c-s) *(BBQ 40C)* **COMING DOWN. / ('A'remix)**   [50] [-]
(12"+=/cd-s+=) *(BBQ 40 T/CD)* – Gone.
Oct 94. (cd/c/lp) *(BBQ CD/MC/LP 164) <45673>* **THE CULT**   [21] [69]
– Gone / Coming down / Real grrrl / Black Sun / Naturally high / Joy / Star / Sacred life / Be free / Universal you / Emperor's new horse / Saints are down.
Dec 94. (c-s) *(BBQ 45C)* **STAR. / BREATHING OUT**   [65] [-]
(12"+=/cd-s+=) *(BBQ 45 T/CD)* – The witch (extended).

—— In Apr'95, they cancelled tour, due to new guitarist JAMES STEVENSON returning to the re-formed GENE LOVES JEZEBEL.

– compilations, others, etc. –

all on 'Beggars Banquet'
Dec 88. (pic-cd-ep) *(BBP 1CD)* **THE MANOR SESSIONS**   [ ] [ ]
Dec 89. (pic-cd-ep) *(BBP 2CD)* **THE LOVE MIXES**   [ ] [ ]
Dec 89. (pic-cd-ep) *(BBP 3CD)* **THE ELECTRIC MIXES**   [ ] [ ]
Aug 91. (pic-cd-ep) *(BBP 6CD)* **SPIRITWALKER / A FLOWER IN THE DESERT / BONE BAG / GO WEST / SEA AND SKY / BROTHERS GRIMM (live)**   [-] [-]
Aug 91. (pic-cd-ep) *(BBP 7CD)* **RESURRECTION JOE / SHE SELLS SANCTUARY / THE SNAKE / NO.13 / ASSAULT ON SANCTUARY / RESURRECTION JOE (Hep Cat mix)**   [-] [-]
Aug 91. (pic-cd-ep) *(BBP 8CD)* **RAIN / LITTLE FACE / REVOLUTION / ALL SOULS AVENUE / JUDITH / SUNRISE**   [-] [-]
Aug 91. (pic-cd-ep) *(BBP 9CD)* **LOVE REMOVAL MACHINE / CONQUISTADOR / GROOVE CO. / ZAP CITY / LOVE TROOPER / WOLF CHILD'S BLUES / LIL' DEVIL**   [-] [-]
Aug 91. (pic-cd-ep) *(BBP 10CD)* **WILD FLOWER / WILD FLOWER (guitar dub) / HORSE NATION (live) / OUTLAW (live) / SHE SELLS SANCTUARY (live) / PHOENIX (live) / WILD THING . . . LOUIE LOUIE**   [-] [-]
Aug 91. (pic-cd-ep) *(BBP 11CD)* **FIRE WOMAN / AUTOMATIC BLUES / MESSIN' UP THE BLUES / EDIE)CIAO BABY) / BLEEDING HEART GRAFFITI / SUN KING / FIRE WOMAN (L.A. rock mix) / FIRE WOMAN (N.Y.C. rock mix)**   [-] [-]
Aug 91. (pic-cd-ep) *(BBP 12CD)* **SWEET SOUL SISTER / THE RIVER / LOVE REMOVAL MACHINE (live) / LIL' DEVIL (live) / REVOLUTION (live) / SWEET SOUL SISTER (live) / AMERICAN HORSE (live) / SOUL ASYLUM (live) / SWEET SOUL SISTER (Rock's mix)**   [-] [-]
Aug 91. (10x pic-cd-ep) *(CBOX 1)* **SINGLES COLLECTION 1984-1990**   [-] [-]
– (all above)
Jun 92. (video w/free cd-ep) **FAITH HEALER / FULL TILT (live) / LOVE REMOVAL MACHINE (live)**   [ ] [ ]

HOLY BARBARIANS

—— **IAN ASTBURY** plus **PATRICK SUGG** – guitar, vocals (ex-LUCIFER WONG) / **SCOTT GARRETT** – drums / **MATT GARRETT** – bass

		Beggars Banquet	Beggars Banquet
Apr 96.	(7") (BBQ 65) **SPACE JUNKIE. / DOLLY BIRD**	☐	☐
	(cd-s+=) (BBQ 65CD) – Hate you.		
May 96.	(cd/c/lp) (BBQ CD/MC/LP 182) **CREAM**	☐	☐

– Brothers fights / Dolly bird / Cream / Blind / Opium / Space junkie / She / You are there / Magick Christian / Bodhisattva.

CULTURE CLUB (see under ⇒ BOY GEORGE)

CURE

Formed: Crawley, Sussex, England . . . 1976 initially as The EASY CURE by ROBERT SMITH, LAWRENCE TOLHURST and MICHAEL DEMPSEY. In 1978, following a brief liaison with the small 'Hansa' label the previous year, the band recorded a one-off 45, 'KILLING AN ARAB', for indie operation, 'Small Wonder'. Although actually inspired by classic Albert Camus novel, 'The Outsider', the track was met with its fair share of controversy upon its early '79 re-release by Chris Parry's new 'Fiction' imprint. A subsequent debut album, 'THREE IMAGINARY BOYS' (1979) remains among The CURE's finest work, their strangely accessible post-punk snippets lent an air of suppressed melancholy by SMITH's plangent whine. The record almost scraped into the Top 40, while the pop brilliance of accompanying single, 'BOYS DON'T CRY', saw The CURE lauded as one of the UK's most promising young bands. With SIMON GALLUP replacing DEMPSEY (who joined The ASSOCIATES), the group again drew critical plaudits for the insidious 'JUMPING SOMEONE ELSE'S TRAIN'. A track railing against fashion victims, The CURE carved out their own solitary path over the course of the next three albums. Claustrophobic is normally the favoured critical bon mot in getting to grips with The CURE's sound and few would argue that the spiralling disorientation of 'A FOREST' was easy listening. SMITH and CO.'s first Top 40 hit, the track previewed follow-up set, 'SEVENTEEN SECONDS' (1980), an album which took them into the UK Top 20 despite its gloomy sound. Revered by the more pasty faced among the group's fanbase, 'FAITH' (1981) and 'PORNOGRAPHY' (1982) ploughed a similarly grim furrow, although the latter set went Top 10. Internal feuding subsequently led to the departure of GALLUP, SMITH and TOLHURST taking charge and effecting a bit of a stylistic departure on the more flippantly pop-friendly 'LET'S GO TO BED' (not before you take that eyeliner off, BOB) single. Finally, in summer of the following year, The CURE scored a long awaited breakthrough hit with 'THE WALK', the track narrowly missing the Top 10. Nevertheless, SMITH was simultaneously busying himself with SIOUXSIE AND THE BANSHEES, contributing guitar to their Top 5 cover of The Beatles' 'Dear Prudence' and playing on the 'Hyaena' album as well as hooking up with BANSHEES man, STEVE SEVERIN, for side project, The GLOVE. Meanwhile, the flouncing 'LOVECATS' single introduced the group to a whole new audience, a song with an alarmingly high irritability factor that still gets played to death by radio. With SMITH back on board in a full-time capacity by Spring '84, The CURE again managed to take their skewered pop vision into the pop charts with 'THE CATERPILLAR', a track lifted from bizarre new album, 'THE TOP' (1984). More line-up changes occurred prior to the recording of the band's breakthrough set, 'HEAD ON THE DOOR' (1985), including the return of SIMON GALLUP. Trailed by the classic 'IN BETWEEN DAYS', the record spawned a further major hit in the glockenspiel weirdness of 'CLOSE TO ME', its breathy claustrophobia segueing into a sassy, brassy finale. The track was also accompanied by a celebrated video (directed by long standing associate Tim Pope), featuring the whole band, erm, playing inside a wardrobe (honestly!). A subsequent two year lull was punctuated by an impressive singles retrospective, 'STANDING ON A BEACH' (1986), before the band returned with the sprawling 'KISS ME, KISS ME KISS ME' (1987) double set. Hardly an easy ride, the record showcased the many strange faces of The CURE and more, incredibly making the US Top 40 where they'd slowly been building up a cult following. This time around there was no stellar pop to liven up the Stock, Aitken & Waterman-clogged Top 10 although the record did spawn a trio of minor hits in 'WHY CAN'T I BE YOU', 'CATCH' and 'JUST LIKE HEAVEN'. The latter track was later privy to a genius fuzz-pop mangling courtesy of DINOSAUR JR., an interpretation that reportedly impressed SMITH no end. The CURE were now a formidable commercial proposition on both sides of the Atlantic, which probably explains why the ponderous 'DISINTEGRATION' (1989) album made the UK Top 3 and the 'LOVESONG' single almost topped the American Hot 100. The turn of the decade saw major upheaval as TOLHURST finally bailed out after clashing with SMITH, a pared down line up of SMITH, GALLUP, PORL THOMPSON, BORIS WILLIAMS and PERRY BAMONTE seeing the group through most of the following decade. A remix album, 'MIXED UP', appeared in 1990, its sensual dancefloor appeal illustrating just how adaptable the band's music was, bearing in mind that SMITH and Co. were sometimes dismissed as whimsical, goth-pop throwbacks. New material finally arrived in Spring '92 with the 'WISH' album, the huge hit 'FRIDAY I'M IN LOVE' following in their occasional tradition of jangling dreaminess. The album itself became The CURE's first UK No.1, missing the top of the American charts by a whisker; the band were now sufficiently world dominating that they could almost get away with two double live albums, 'SHOW' amd 'PARIS', released

simultaneously in late '93. The remainder of the decade saw the band's profile at its lowest since their shadowy beginnings, a low-key 1996 set, 'WILD MOOD SWINGS' their sole studio output in almost five years. • **Songwriters:** Group compositions, except covers of FOXY LADY + PURPLE HAZE (Jimi Hendrix), HELLO I LOVE YOU (Doors). • **Trivia:** SMITH married childhood sweetheart Mary Poole on the 13th of August '88.

Album rating: THREE IMAGINARY BOYS (*8) / BOYS DON'T CRY exploitation (*7) / SEVENTEEN SECONDS (*6) / FAITH (*6) / PORNOGRAPHY (*6) / JAPANESE WHISPERS mini (*6) / THE TOP (*7) / CONCERT: LIVE (*5) / THE HEAD ON THE DOOR (*7) / STANDING ON THE BEACH / STARING AT THE SEA: THE SINGLES compilation (*9) / KISS ME, KISS ME, KISS ME (*7) / DISINTEGRATION (*8) / MIXED UP (*4) / WISH (*6) / PARIS (*4) / SHOW (*4) / WILD MOOD SWINGS (*5) / GALORE – THE SINGLES 1987-1997 compilation (*6)

ROBERT SMITH (b.21 Apr'59, Blackpool, England) – vocals, lead guitar / **LAWRENCE TOLHURST** (b. 3 Feb'59) – drums, keyboards / **MICHAEL DEMPSEY** – bass

		Small Wonder	not iss.
Aug 78.	(7") (SMALL 11) **KILLING AN ARAB. / 10.15 SATURDAY NIGHT**	☐	–

		Fiction	not iss.
Jan 79.	(7") (FICS 001) **KILLING AN ARAB. / 10.15 SATURDAY NIGHT**	☐	–
May 79.	(lp/c) (FIX/+C 1) **THREE IMAGINARY BOYS**	44	–

– 10.15 Saturday night / Accuracy / Grinding halt / Another day / Object / Subway song / Foxy lady / Meat hook / So what / Fire in Cairo / It's not you / Three imaginary boys. (cd-iss. Apr90; 827 686-2)

May 79.	(7") (FICS 002) **BOYS DON'T CRY. / PLASTIC PASSION**	☐	–

—— **SIMON GALLUP** (b. 1 Jun'60, Surrey, England) – bass, keyboards (ex-MAG-SPYS, ex-LOCKJAW) repl. DEMPSEY who joined The ASSOCIATES

Oct 79.	(7") (FICS 005) **JUMPING SOMEONE ELSE'S TRAIN. / I'M COLD**	☐	–

—— added **MATHIEU HARTLEY** – keyboards, synthesizers

Nov 79.	(7") (FICS 006) **I'M A CULT HERO (as "CULT HERO"). / I DIG YOU**	☐	–

—— (on above they backed FRANK BELL)

Mar 80.	(7"/ext.12") (FICS/+X 10) **A FOREST. / ANOTHER JOURNEY BY TRAIN**	31	–
Apr 80.	(lp/c) (FIX/+C 004) **SEVENTEEN SECONDS**	20	–

– A reflection / Play for today / Secrets / In your house / Three . . . / The final sound / A forest / M / At night / Seventeen seconds. (cd-iss. Jan86; 825 354-2)

—— reverted to trio of **SMITH, TOLHURST & GALLUP** when HARTLEY left to form CRY.

		Fiction	P.V.C.
Mar 81.	(7"/ext.12") (FICS/+X 12) **PRIMARY. / DESCENT**	43	–
Apr 81.	(lp/c) (FIX/+C 6) <2383 605> **FAITH**	14	

– The holy hour / Primary / Other voices / All cats are grey / The funeral party / Doubt / The drowning man / Faith. (cd-iss. Jan86; 827 687-2) (c+=) **CARNAGE VISORS** (film soundtrack)

Oct 81.	(7") (FICS 14) **CHARLOTTE SOMETIMES. / SPLINTERED IN HER HEAD**	44	–

(12"+=) (FICSX 14) – Faith (live).

		Fiction	A&M
Apr 82.	(lp/c) (FIX D/C 7) <4902> **PORNOGRAPHY**	8	☐

– One hundred years / A short term effect / The hanging garden / Siamese twins / The figurehead / A strange day / Cold / Pornography. (cd-iss. Jan86; 827 688-2)

Jul 82.	(7") (FICS 15) **THE HANGING GARDEN. / KILLING AN ARAB** (live)	34	–

(d7"+=) (FICG 15) – One hundred years (live) / A forest (live).

—— **STEVE GOULDING** – bass repl. GALLUP who later joined FOOLS DANCE. (LOL now keyboards)

Nov 82.	(7"/ext.12") (FICS/+X 17) **LET'S GO TO BED. / JUST ONE KISS**	44	–

—— trimmed to duo of **SMITH + TOLHURST**

Jul 83.	(7"/7"pic-d) (FICS/+P 18) **THE WALK. / THE DREAM**	12	–

(12"+=) (FICXT 18) <23928> – The upstairs room / Lament.
(free 12"w/ free 12") (FICSX 17) – Let's go to bed / Just one kiss.

—— added **PHIL THORNALLEY** – bass / **ANDY ANDERSON**-drums (ex-BRILLIANT)

Oct 83.	(7"/7"pic-d) (FICS/+P 19) **THE LOVECATS. / SPEAK MY LANGUAGE**	7	–

(ext.12"+=) (FICSX 19) – Mr. Pink eyes.

Dec 83.	(m-lp/c) (FIXM/+C 8) <25076> **JAPANESE WHISPERS**	26	☐

– Let's go to bed / The dream / Just one kiss / The upstair's room / The walk / Speak my language / Lament / The lovecats. (cd-iss. Apr88; 817 470-2)

Mar 84.	(7"/7"pic-d) (FICS/+P 20) **THE CATERPILLAR. / HAPPY THE MAN**	14	–

(12"+=) (FICSX 20) – Throw your foot.

Apr 84.	(lp/c)(cd) (FIXS/+C 9)(821 136-2) <25086> **THE TOP**	10	☐

– Shake dog shake / Birdmad girl / Wailing wall / Give me it / Dressing up / The caterpillar / Piggy in the mirror / The empty world / Bananafishbones / The top.

—— added **PORL THOMPSON** (b.8 Nov'57, London, England) – guitar, saxophone, keyboards (a member in '77)

Oct 84.	(lp/d-c)(cd) (FIXH/+C 10)(823 682-2) **CONCERT – THE CURE LIVE** (live)	26	–

– Shake dog shake / Primary / Charlotte sometimes / The hanging garden / Give me it / The walk / One hundred years / A forest / 10.15 Saturday night / Killing an Arab. (d-c+=) **CURIOSITY: CURE ANOMALIES 1977-1984** – Heroin face / Boys don't cry / Subway song / At night / In your house / The drowning man / Other voices / The funeral party / All mine / Forever.

—— **SIMON GALLUP** returned to repl. PORL. **BORIS WILLIAMS** (b.24 Apr'57, Versailles, France) – drums (ex-THOMPSON TWINS) repl. ANDERSON who joined JEFFREY LEE PIERCE (of The GUN CLUB)

		Fiction	Elektra
Jul 85.	(7") (FICS 22) **IN BETWEEN DAYS. / EXPLODING BODY**	15	–

(12"+=) (FICSX 22) – A few hours after this.

Aug 85. (lp/c)(cd) *(FIXH/+C 11)(827 231-2) <60435>* **THE HEAD ON THE DOOR** `7` `59`
– In between days / Kyoto song / The blood / Six different ways / Push / The baby screams / Close to me / A night like this / Screw / Sinking.

Sep 85. (7"/7"poster) *(FICS/+G 23)* **CLOSE TO ME (remix). / A MAN INSIDE MY MOUTH** `24` `-`
(12"+=) *(FICSX 23)* – Stop dead.
(10"++=) *(FICST 23)* – New day.

Jan 86. (7") *<69604>* **IN BETWEEN DAYS. / STOP DEAD** `-` `99`
Mar 86. (7") *<69551>* **CLOSE TO ME. / SINKING** `-`
Apr 86. (7") *(FICS 24)* **BOYS DON'T CRY (new mix). / PILLBOX BLUES** `22` `-`
(club-12"+=) *(FICSX 24)* – Do the Hansa.

Apr 87. (7"/ext.12") *(FICS/+X 25) <69474>* **WHY CAN'T I BE YOU? / A JAPANESE DREAM** `21` `54` Jun87
(d7"+=) *(FIGSG 25)* – Six different ways (live) / Push (live).

May 87. (d-lp/c)(cd) *(FIXH/+C 13)(832 130-2) <60737>* **KISS ME KISS ME KISS ME** `6` `35`
– The kiss / Catch / Torture / If only tonight we could sleep / Why can't I be you? / How beautiful you are / Snakepit / Hey you / Just like heaven / All I want / Hot hot hot!!! / One more time / Like cockatoos / Icing sugar / The perfect girl / A thousand hours / Shiver and shake / Fight. *(pic-lp.Dec87; FIXP 13)* *(free-ltd.12"orange / or green,w/cd)* – A Japanese dream / Breathe / Chain of flowers / Sugar girl / Snow in summer / Icing sugar (remix).

—— added on tour **ROBERT O'CONNELL** – keyboards (ex-PSYCHEDELIC FURS)

Jul 87. (7"/7"clear) *(FICS/+P 26)* **CATCH. / BREATHE** `27`
(c-s+=/12"+=) *(FICS C/X 26)* – A chain of flowers.
(7"ep+=) *(FICSE 26)* – Kyoto song (live) / A night like this (live).

Oct 87. (7",7"white/7"pic-d) *(FICS/+P 27)* **JUST LIKE HEAVEN. / SNOW IN SUMMER** `29` `-`
(12"+=/cd-s+=) *(FICSX/FIXCD 27)* – Sugar girl.

Oct 87. (7") *<69443>* **JUST LIKE HEAVEN. / BREATHE** `-` `40`
Feb 88. (12"/cd-s) *(FICSX/FIXCD 28) <69424>* **HOT HOT HOT!!! (extended remix). / HOT HOT HOT!!! (remix) / HEY YOU!!! (extended remix)** `45` `65`

Apr 89. (7"/7"gf/7"clear) *(FICS/+G/P 29)* **LULLABY (remix). / BABBLE** `5` `-`
(ext.12"+=/ext.12"pink+=) *(FIC SX/VX 29)* – Out of mind. (3"cd-s++=) *(FICCD 29)* – ('A'extended).

May 89. (lp/c)(cd) *(FIXH/+C 14)(839 353-2) <60855>* **DISINTEGRATION** `3` `12`
– Plainsong / Pictures of you / Closedown / Lovesong / Lullaby / Fascination street / Prayers for rain / The same deep water as you / Disintegration / Untitled. *(cd+=)* – Last dance / Homesick. *(pic-lp Apr90; FIXHP 14)*

May 89. (7") *<69300>* **FASCINATION STREET. / BABBLE** `-` `46`
Aug 89. (7"/7"box/c-s) *(FIC S/SG/CD 30) <69280>* **LOVESONG. / 2 LATE** `18` `2`
(ext.12"+=) *(FICSX 30)* – Fear of ghosts.
(cd-s++=)(cd-vid++=) *(FICCD 30)(081398-2)* – ('A'-12"mix).

Nov 89. (c-s) *<69249>* **LULLABY / HOMESICK** `-` `74`

—— (Mar'89) reverted to a quintet when TOLHURST left **SMITH, GALLUP, THOMPSON, WILLIAMS + PERRY BAMONTE** (b. 6 Sep'60, London, England) – keyboards

Mar 90. (7"/7"green/c-s) *(FIC A/PA/CA 34)* **PICTURES OF YOU (remix). /** `24` `71`
(ext.12"+=/ext.12"green+=/cd-s+=) *(FICXA/FIXPA/FICDA 34)* – Fascination Street (live).
(7"/7"purple/c-s) *(FIC B/PB/CB 34) <64974>* – PICTURES OF YOU (remix). / PRAYERS FOR RAIN (live)
(12"+=/12"purple+=/cd-s+=) *(FICXB/FIXPB/FICDB 34)* – Disintigration (live).

—— (W.H. Smith's released ENTREAT (May90) a live EP, which featured the 5 tracks +=) – Closedown / Homesick / Untitled.

Sep 90. (7"/c-s) *(FIC S/CS 35)* **NEVER ENOUGH. / HAROLD AND JOE** `13` `72` Oct90
(12"+=/cd-s+=/pic-cd-s+=) *(FICSX/FICCD/FICDP 35)* – Let's go to bed (milk mix).

Oct 90. (7"/c-s) *(FIC S/CS 36) <64911>* **CLOSE TO ME (closet remix). / JUST LIKE HEAVEN (dizzy mix)** `13` `97` Jan91
(12"+=/cd-s+=) *(FIC SX/CD 36)* – Primary (red mix).
(cd-s+=) *(FICDR 36)* – Why can't I be you? (extended).

Nov 90. (cd)(d-lp/c) *(847 009-2)(FIXH/+C 18) <60978>* **MIXED UP (remix album)** `8` `14`
– Lullaby (extended mix) / Close to me (closer mix) / Fascination Street (extended mix) / The walk (everything mix) / Lovesong (extended mix) / A forest (tree mix) / Pictures of you (extended dub mix) / Hot hot hot!!! (extended mix) / The caterpillar (flicker mix) / Inbetween days (shiver mix) / Never enough (big mix).

Apr 91. (cd)(lp/c) *(843 359-2)(FIXH/+C 17)* **ENTREAT (live)** `10`
– (finally nationally released; see above)

Mar 92. (7"/c-s) *(FIC S/CS 39) <64766>* **HIGH. / THIS TWILIGHT GARDEN** `8` `42`
('A'-Higher mix-12"+=) *(FICSX 39)* – Play.
(cd-s+=) *(FICCD 39)* – (all above).

Apr 92. (12"clear) *(FICSX 41)* **HIGH (trip mix). / OPEN (fix mix)** `44` `43`
(cd-s) *(FICCD 41)* – (see last cd-s for 4 tracks).

Apr 92. (cd)(d-lp/c) *(513 261-2)(FIXH/+C 20) <61309>* **WISH** `1` `2`
– Open / High / Apart / From the edge of the deep green sea / Wendy time / Doing the unstuck / Friday I'm in love / Trust / A letter to Elise / Cut / To wish impossible things / End.

May 92. (7"/c-s) *(FIC S/CS 42) <64742>* **FRIDAY I'M IN LOVE. / HALO** `6` `18`
('A'-Strangelove mix-12"colrd+=) *(FICSX 42)* – Scared as you.
(cd-s+=) *(FICCD 42)* – (all above).

Oct 92. (7"/c-s) *(FIC S/CS 46)* **A LETTER TO ELISE. / THE BIG HAND** `28`
(Blue mix-12"+=) *(FICSX 46)* – A foolish arrangement.
(cd-s+=) *(FICCD 46)* – (all above).

Sep 93. (d-cd/d-c/d-lp) *(FIX CD/MC/LP 26) <61551>* **SHOW (live)** `29` `42`
– Tape / Open / High / Pictures of you / Lullaby / Just like heaven / Fascination Street / A night like this / Trust / Doing the unstuck / The walk / Let's go to bed /

Friday I'm in love / In between days / From the edge of the deep green sea / Never enough / Cut / End.

—— PORL departed after the above.

Oct 93. (cd/c/d-lp) *(FIX CD/MC/LP 26) <61552>* **PARIS (live)** `56`
– The figurehead / One hundred years / At night / Play for today / Apart / In your house / Lovesong / Catch / A letter to Elise / Dressing up / Charlotte sometimes / Close to me.

Apr 96. (c-s) *(576468-4)* **THE 13TH (swing radio mix) / IT USED TO BE ME** `15` `-`
(cd-s+=) *(576469-2)* – ('A'-Killer bee mix).
(cd-s) *(576493-2)* – ('A'-Two chord cool mix) / Ocean / Adonais.

Apr 96. (c-s) *<64292>* **THE 13TH / ADONAIS** `44`
May 96. (cd/c/lp) *(FIX CD/MC/LP 28) <61744>* **WILD MOOD SWINGS** `9` `12`
– Want / Club America / This is a lie / The 13th / Strange attraction / Mint car / Jupiter crash / Round & round & round / Gone! / Numb / Trap / Treasure / Bare.

Jun 96. (c-s) *(FICCS 52) <64275>* **MINT CAR / HOME** `31` `58`
(cd-s+=) *(FICCD 52)* – ('A'-buskers mix).
(cd-s) *(FISCD 52)* – ('A'-electric mix) / Waiting / A pink dream.

Nov 96. (c-s) *(FICCS 53)* **GONE! / THIS IS A LIE (ambient mix)** `60`
(cd-s+=) *(FICD 53)* – Strange attraction (strange mix) / The 13th (feels good mix).

Nov 97. (cd/c/lp) *(FIX CD/MC/LP 30)* **GALORE – THE SINGLES 1987-1997** (compilation) `37` `32`
– Why can't you / Catch / Just like Heaven / Hot, hot, hot / Lullaby / Fascination Street / Love song / Pictures of you / Never enough / Close to me / High / Friday I'm in love / Letter to Elise / The 13th / Mint car / Strange attraction / Gone / Wrong number.

Nov 97. (c-s) *(FICMC 54)* **WRONG NUMBER / ('A'-radio mix mix)** `62` `-`
(12"/cd-s+=) *(FIC SX/D 54)* – ('A'mixes).

– compilations, etc. –

Aug 83. (lp/c) *Fiction; (SPE LP/MC 26) / P.V.C.; <7916>* **BOYS DON'T CRY** `71` Aug80
– Boys don't cry / Plastic passion / 10.15 Saturday night / Accuracy / Object * / Jumping someone else's train / Subway song / Killing an Arab / Fire in Cairo / Another day / Grinding halt / World war * / Three imaginary boys. *(cd-iss. Nov86; 815 011-2) (w/ out tracks * +=)* – So what.

May 86. (7") *P.V.C.;* **BOYS DON'T CRY. / LET'S GO TO BED** `-` `-`
May 86. (lp/d-c)(cd) *Fiction; (FIXH/+C 12)(829 239-2) / Elektra; <60477>* **STANDING ON THE BEACH** ('A'45's) / **STARING AT THE SEA** ('B'45's) `4` `48`
– Killing an Arab / Boys don't cry / Jumping someone else's train / A forest / Primary / Charlotte sometimes / The hanging garden / Let's go to bed / The walk / The lovecats / The caterpillar / In between days / Close to me. *(cd+=)* – 10.15 Saturday night / Play for today / Other voices / A night like this. *(re-iss. Feb91; same)*

May 88. (12"ep/cd-ep) *Strange Fruit; (SFPS/+CD 050)* **PEEL SESSIONS** `-` `-`
– Killing an Arab / Boys don't cry / 10:15 Saturday night / Fire in Cairo.

Oct 88. (vid-cd) *Fiction; (080184-2)* **WHY CAN'T I BE YOU (video) / JAPANESE DREAM / HEY YOU / WHY CAN'T I BE YOU** `-` `-`
Oct 88. (vid-cd) *Fiction; (080182-2)* **IN BETWEEN DAYS (video) / SIX DIFFERENT WAYS (live) / PUSH (live)** `-` `-`
Oct 88. (vid-cd) *Fiction; (080186-2)* **CATCH (video) / CATCH / BREATHE / A CHAIN OF FLOWERS / ICING SUGAR (new mix)** `-` `-`

CURLEW (see under ⇒ LASWELL, Bill)

CURVE (dig out; Great Alt & Indie . . .)

CURVED AIR (dig out; Great Psychedelic . . .)

CYPRESS HILL

Formed: Los Angeles, California, USA . . . 1988 by DJ MUGGS, B-REAL and SEN DOG. In the early 90's, after signing to US 'Columbia' label through their own 'Ruffhouse' label, the hard-core rappers cracked the Top 40 with their eponymous debut. The album contained the single, 'I COULD JUST KILL A MAN', alongside the dirty, trippy narcotica of tracks like 'ULTRAVIOLET DREAMS' and 'SOMETHING FOR THE BLUNTED'. With B-REAL's sneering intonation and the bass-heavy production, CYPRESS HILL were instantly recognisable. Tireless advocates of marijuana use (and legalisation), most of the band's music was so claustrophobically heavy it sounded like they'd been stoned since birth. Influenced by the infamous 'Rodney King' incident in L.A., the follow-up album, 'BLACK SUNDAY' (1993) took a decidedly darker turn, gangsta-like bravado ('LICK A SHOT', 'COCK THE HAMMER', 'A TO THE K') interspersing the trademark homages to hash. 'INSANE IN THE BRAIN' (1993) was the first in a string of U.K. hit singles and the band consolidated their success in Britain by playing at a number of predominantly white rock festivals, proving their crossover appeal. 'CYPRESS HILL III (TEMPLES OF BOOM)' (1996) upped the gangsta ante with such subtle fare as 'KILLAFORNIA' and 'KILLA HILL NIGGAS' although the hopelessly stoned vibe was still sufficiently alive and kicking (or head bowed and nodding) to satisfy fans. • **Songwriters:** Group penned. WE AIN'T GOIN' OUT LIKE THAT sampled; THE WIZARD (Black Sabbath) / WHEN THE SH-- GOES DOWN sampled; DEEP GULLY (Outlaw Blues Band) / LIL' PUTOS sampled; ODE TO BILLY JOE (Bobbie Gentry) / etc. • **Trivia:** MUGGS also produced HOUSE OF PAIN, BEASTIE BOYS and ICE CUBE.

Album rating: CYPRESS HILL (*9) / BLACK SUNDAY (*8) / III – TEMPLES OF BOOM (*6) / IV (*6)

B-REAL (b. LOUIS FREESE, 2 Jun'70) – vocals (ex-DVX) / **SEN DOG** (b. SENEN REYES, 20 Nov'65, Cuba) – vocals (ex-DVX) / **DJ MUGGS** (b. LARRY MUGGERUD, 28 Jan'68, Queens, N.Y.) – DJ, producer (ex-7A3)

		Ruffhouse	Ruffhouse
Jan 92.	(cd/c/lp) (468893-2/-4/-1) <47889> **CYPRESS HILL** – Pigs / How I could just kill a man / Hand on the pump / Hole in the head / Ultraviolet dreams / Light another / The phuncky feel one / Break it up / Real estate / Stoned is the way of the walk / Psycobetabuckdown / Something for the blunted / Latin lingo / The funky Cypress Hill shit / Tres equis / Born to get busy. *(cd re-iss. May94 & Feb97; same)*	☐	31 Nov91
Feb 92.	(7") <73930> **HOW I COULD JUST KILL A MAN. / THE PHUNKY FEEL ONE**	–	77 94
Apr 92.	(c-s) <74105> **HAND ON THE PUMP / REAL ESTATE** (cd-s) <74332> – ('A'-Mugg's Blunted mix) / ('A'extended mix) / ('A'-instrumental) / Hand on the glock.	–	☐
Jun 92.	(12"ep/cd-ep) <74478> **LATIN LINGO (Prince Paul mix) / STONED IS THE WAY OF THE WALK (reprise) / HAND ON THE GLOCK**	–	☐
Jul 93.	(c-s) <77135> **INSANE IN THE BRAIN / STONED IS THE WAY OF THE WALK**	–	19
Jul 93.	(c-s) (659533-4) **INSANE IN THE BRAIN (radio version). / WHEN THE SH-- GOES DOWN (radio version)** (12"+=/cd-s+=) (659533-6/-2) – ('A'instrumental).	32	–
Jul 93.	(cd/c/lp) (474075-2/-4/-1) <53931> **BLACK SUNDAY** – I wanna get high / We ain't goin' out like that / Insane in the brain / When the sh-- goes down / Lick a shot / Cock the hammer / Interlude / Lil' putos / Legalize it / Hits from the bong / What go around come around, kid / A to the K / Hand on the glock / Break 'em off some.	13	1
Sep 93.	(c-s) (659670-8) **WHEN THE SH-- GOES DOWN (extended). / LATIN LINGO / HOW COULD I JUST KILL A MAN (the Killer mix)** (12"+=/cd-s+=) (659670-6/-2) – ('A'instrumental) / The phuncky feel one (extended).	19	–
Dec 93.	(c-s) (659690-4) <77307> **WE AIN'T GOIN' OUT LIKE THAT. / HITS FROM THE BONG** (12"+=/cd-s+=) (659690-6/-2) – When the sh-- goes down (Diamond D mix).	15	65
Feb 94.	(c-s) (660176-4) **INSANE IN THE BRAIN. / STONED IS THE WAY OF THE WALK** (12"+=) (660176-6) – Latin lingo (Prince Paul mix). (cd-s) (660176-2) – ('A'side) / Something for the blunted.	21	–
Apr 94.	(c-s) (660319-4) **LICK A SHOT (Baka Boys remix). / I WANNA GET HIGH** (12"+=/cd-s+=) (660319-6/-2) – Scooby Doo.	20	
Sep 95.	(c-s) (662354-4) <78042> **THROW YOUR SET IN THE AIR / KILLA HILL NIGGAS** (12"+=/cd-s+=) (662354-6/-2) – ('A'-Slow roll remix) / ('B'instrumental).	15	45
Oct 95.	(cd/c/d-lp) (478127-2/-4/-1) <66991> **CYPRESS HILL III / TEMPLES OF BOOM** – Spark another owl / Throw your set in the air / Stoned raiders / Illusions / Killa hill niggas / Boom biddy bye bye / No rest for the wicked / Make a move / Killafornia / Funk freakers / Locotes / Red light visions / Strictly hip hop / Let it rain / Everybody must get stoned. *(d-cd+=/t-lp+=; 478127-9/-0)* – DJ MUGGS BUDDHA MIX:- Hole in the head – How could I just kill a man – Insane in the brain – Stoned is the way of the walk – Hits from the bong – Hand on the pump – Real estate – I wanna get high. *(cd re-iss. Jan99; same)*	11	3
Feb 96.	(12"ep) (662905-6) **ILLUSIONS / THROW YOUR SET IN THE AIR (radio version). / ILLUSIONS (harpsicord mix) / ILLUSIONS (harpsicord instrumental)** (cd-ep) (662905-2) –	23	☐
——	SEN DOG went solo (DOGWOOD) and was repl. by DJ SCANDALOUS		
Jun 96.	(c-s) <78339> **BOOM BIDDY BYE BYE / ('A'version)**	–	87
Aug 96.	(m-cd/m-c/m-lp) (485230-2/-4/-1) <67780> **UNRELEASED & REVAMPED EP** – Boom biddy bye bye (Fugees remix) / Throw your hands in the air / Intellectual dons (featuring Call O Da Wild) / Hand on the pump (Muggs' blunted mix) / Whatta you know / Hits from the bong (T-Ray's mix) / Illusions (Q-Tip remix) / Latin lingo (Prince Paul mix) / When the ship goes down (Diamond D remix).	29	21
——	**MUGGS and B-REAL** recruited **BARON** – rapper / **BO-BO** – percussion		
Sep 98.	(c-s,cd-s) <79024> **DR. GREENTHUMB /**	–	70
Sep 98.	(12"/cd-s) (666493-6/-2) **TEQUILA SUNRISE / (mixes)** (cd-s) (666493-5) – ('A'side) / Champions / Can you handle this.	23	☐
Oct 98.	(cd/c/lp) (491604-2/-4/-1) <69037> **IV** – Looking through the eye of a pig / Checkmate / From the window of my room / Prelude to a come up (featuring Mc EIHT) / Riot starter / Audio X (featuring BARRON RICKS) / Steel magnolia (featuring BARRON RICKS) / I remember that freak bitch (from the club) (featuring BARRON RICKS – interlude part 2) / (Goin' all out) Nothin' to lose / Tequila sunrise (featuring BARRON RICKS) / Dead men tell no tales / Feature presentation (featuring BARRON RICKS) / Chance infinite / Dr. Greenthumb / 16 men till there's no men left / High times / Clash of the Titans / Lightning strikes.	25	11
Mar 99.	(c-s/cd-s) (667120-4/-2) **DR. GREENTHUMB (clean radio mix) / DR. GREENTHUMB (Fun Lovin' Criminals clean remix)** (12") (667120-2) – ('A'-version) / ('A'-Fun Lovin' Criminals instrumental remix) / ('A'-Fun Lovin' Criminals remix).	34	☐
Jun 99.	(c-s; JASON NEVINS vs CYPRESS HILL) *(INCRL 17MC)* **INSANE IN THE BRAIN** (cd-s) *(INCRL 17CD)* – ('A' - Jason's Master Blaster mixes) / (Da funky chunky mix) (above issued on 'Incredible')	19	☐

Holger CZUKAY (see under ⇒ CAN)

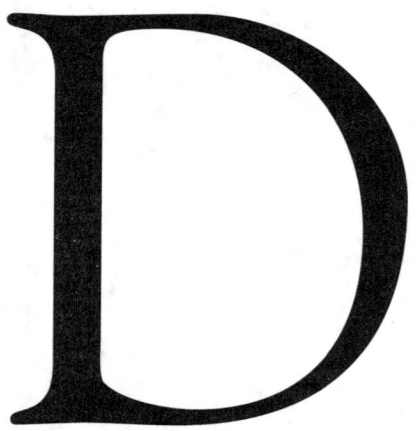

Chuck D (see under ⇒ PUBLIC ENEMY)

D.A.F. (dig out; Great Alt & Indie . . .)

DAFT PUNK

Formed: Paris, France . . . 1992 originally as DARLING, by THOMAS BANGALTER (his father was the man behind such disco gems as 'CUBA' by The GIBSON BROTHERS and 'D.I.S.C.O.' by OTTOWAN) and GUY-MANUEL DE HOMEM CHRISTO. The duo had one track included on a STEREOLAB-compiled various artists album, described as "Daft Punk" by one daft critic. The lads were then daft enough to adopt this moniker as a full-time concern, releasing a clutch of 12"ers in the mid 90's on the Scottish dance label, 'Soma'. The grunge disco classic, 'DA FUNK', was a massive underground club hit, creating a buzz that eventually led to a major label signing race. 'Virgin' subsequently came out on top (oo er!), securing the pleasure of releasing their soon-to be widely acclaimed debut long player, 'HOMEWORK'. Issued in early '97, it hit the UK Top 10 as well as surprisingly breaking new ground in the States on the back of the minimalist 70's trance-funk oddity 'AROUND THE WORLD', which was their second UK Top 10 smash. While 1977 was the year of punk, 1997 was most definitely the year of DAFT PUNK, the duo wowing fans at sold out venues and bulging festival dance tents up and down the country.

Album rating: HOMEWORK (*8)

THOMAS BANGALTER (b. 3 Jan'75) – electronics / GUY-MANUEL DE HOMEM CHRISTO (b. 8 Feb'74) – electronics

	Soma	not iss.
Apr 94. (12"ep) (SOMA 014) **FRENCH TEEN** – The new wave / Alive.	☐	–
May 95. (12"ep) (SOMA 025) **DA FUNK / DA FUNK (version) /** **MUSIQUE**	☐	–

	Virgin	Virgin
Jan 97. (cd/c/d-lp) (CD/TC+/V 2821) **HOMEWORK** – Daftendirekt / Wdpk 83.7 fm / Revolution 909 / Da funk / Phoenix / Fresh / Around the world / Rollin' & scratchin' / Teachers / High fidelity / Rock'n roll / Oh yeah / Burnin' / Indo silver club / Alive / Funk Ad.	8	Mar97
Feb 97. (7"/c-s) (VS LH/C 1625) **DA FUNK. / MUSIQUE** (12"+=/cd-s+=) (VS T/CD 1625) – ('A'original).	7	☐
Apr 97. (7"/c-s) (VS LH/C 1633) **AROUND THE WORLD. / TEACHERS** (12"+=/cd-s+=) (VS T/CD 1633) – ('A'-Motorbass remix).	5	61 Aug97
Sep 97. (c-s/cd-s) (VS C/CD 1649) **BURNIN' / (mixes by Slam &** **Ian Pooley)** (12"+=) (VST 1649) – ('A'remixes by DJ Sneak).	30	☐
Feb 98. (c-s/12"/cd-s) (VS C/T/CDT 1682) **REVOLUTION 909. /** ('A'-Roger Sanchez mix) / ('A'-acappella)	47	☐

THOMAS BANGALTER

	Roule	unknown
Mar 97. (12") (ROULE 301ST) **TRAX ON DA ROCKS EP**	☐	–
Mar 97. (12") (ROULE 302ST) **SPINAL SCRATCH (mixes)** (re-iss. May98; same)	☐	–
Nov 97. (12"; as THOMAS BANGALTER & ALAN BRAXE) (ROULE 303) **VELOCITY EP**	☐	–
Jul 98. (12"; as STARDUST) (ROULE 305ST) <38651> **MUSIC** **SOUNDS BETTER WITH YOU (club mix). / ('A'-Bob** **Sinclair remix)** above with ALAN 'BRAXE' QUEME + BENJAMIN 'DIAMOND' COHEN	2	62 Sep98
Oct 98. (12"ep) (ROULE 306ST) **TRACKS ON DA ROCKS VOL.2** – Club soda / Extra dry / Shuffle / Colossus / Turbo.	☐	☐

DAISY CHAINSAW (dig out; Great Alt & Indie . . .)

Dick DALE

Born: RICHARD MONSOUR, 4 May'37, Boston, Massachusetts, USA. The son of a Lebanese emigrant, DALE formed the DEL-TONES in 1960 and attempted to replicate in sound the visceral thrill of riding whitewater surf. While acts such as Seattle's VENTURES had precipitated the craze for tremelo-soaked instrumental music, it was in sunny Southern California that the surf guitar sound would be pioneered, chiefly by DALE, who was duly christened 'The Pied Piper of Balboa Beach'. Although he had competition in the likes of The BELAIRS, DALE's demon staccato runs electrified audiences while his association with the Fender guitar company allowed him to road-test new equipment. Following the success of his Top 60 debut single, 'LET'S GO TRIPPIN' (widely acknowledged as the first bonafide surf track) in 1961, DALE introduced Fender's new reverb unit on the landmark 'MISIRLOU' the following year. If you didn't already know, you'd never guess that the track had been adapted from a 1940's Greek pop song such was DALE's breakneck, finger-blurring ferocity on his stratocaster (amplified, of course, all the way to 11). Backed up by pummelling drums and bleating sax, the overall effect was intoxicating, inspiring countless imitators (the BEACH BOYS of course, putting their own slant on the surf craze). Drawing on his Middle Eastern heritage, DALE would subsequently incorporate various strands of world music into his studio experiments, making him an unlikely ambassador of global musical unity years before the likes of PAUL SIMON and PETER GABRIEL. A debut album, 'SURFER'S CHOICE' also emerged in 1962 and spawned a further reverb-crazed single, 'SURFBEAT', towards the end of the year. Subsequently snapped up by 'Capitol', DALE released a string of albums including 'KING OF THE SURF GUITAR' (1963), 'CHECKERED FLAG' (1963) and 'MR. ELIMINATOR' (1964), the latter two concentrating on the subsequent hot-rod/dragster craze (alongside the likes of The SCRAMBLERS and RONNIE & THE DAYTONAS). Although DALE preferred his L.A. beach stronghold to touring, a young JIMI HENDRIX – who was stationed at the local San Pedro airbase – was apparently lucky enough to catch his live show on a regular basis. It's fair to say that America went surf mad in the early 60's, the craze becoming so all-pervasive that even JAMES BROWN and ALBERT KING got in on the action! Needless to say, it also burned out just as fast and following 'SUMMER SURF' (1965), DALE bowed out of the spotlight. He next surfaced on vinyl in 1987 with a collaborative (alongside the late STEVIE RAY VAUGHAN) cover of the Chantay's classic 'PIPELINE' for the soundtrack to retro surf film, 'Back To The Beach'. In 1994 – having been invited a year previous – a whole new generation of landlocked kids were treated to the joys of aural surfing when DALE's 'MISERLOU' was used over the opening sequence of Quentin Tarantino's 'Pulp Fiction'. The resulting resurge in interest saw DALE back in the studio for a trio of mid-90's albums – 'TRIBAL THUNDER' (1993), 'UNKNOWN TERRITORY' (1994) and 'CALLING UP SPIRITS' (1996) – and, at long last, a UK tour!

Best CD compilation: KING OF THE SURF GUITAR: THE BEST OF . . . (*8)

DICK DALE and the DEL-TONES

DICK DALE – guitar / with the DEL-TONES

	not iss.	Del-Tone
Aug 59. (7") <5012> **OOH-WHEE-MARIE. / BREAKING HEART**	–	☐
Nov 59. (7") <5013> **STOP TEASIN'. / WITHOUT YOUR LOVE**	–	☐
Aug 60. (7") <5014> **JESSIE PEARL. / ST. LOUIS BLUES**	–	☐
Nov 60. (7"; by DICK DALE) <106> **THE FAIREST OF THEM ALL. /** **WE'LL NEVER HEAR THE END OF IT**	–	☐
——	<above issued on 'Cupid'> <re-iss. 1963 on 'Saturn'; 401> <re-iss. 1963 on 'Yes'; 7014> <re-iss. 1963 on 'Concert Hall'; 371>	
May 61. (7") <5016> **OOH-WHEE-MARIE. / WITHOUT YOUR LOVE**	–	☐
Oct 61. (7") <5017> **LET'S GO TRIPPIN'. / DEL-TONE ROCK**	–	60
Mar 62. (7") <5018> **SHAKE N' STOMP. / JUNGLE FEVER**	–	☐
May 62. (7") <5019> **MISIRLOU. / EIGHT TILL MIDNIGHT**	–	☐
Nov 62. (7") <5020> **SURF BEAT. / PEPPERMINT MAN**	–	☐
Jan 63. (7") <5028> **A RUN FOR LIFE. / LOVIN' ON MY BRAIN**	–	☐

DICK DALE and his DEL-TONES

	Capitol	Capitol
Jan 63. (7") <4939> **MISERLOU. / EIGHT TILL MIDNIGHT**	☐	☐
Mar 63. (lp) <(DT 1886)> **SURFERS' CHOICE** – Surf beat / Sloop John B. / Take it off / Night owl / Fanny Mae / Miserlou twist / Peppermint twist / Surfing drums / Shake n' stomp / Lovey dovey / Death of a gremmie / Let's go trippin'. <orig.rel.Nov62 on 'Del-Tone'; LPM 1001>	☐	Jan63
Mar 63. (7") (CL 15296) <4940> **SURF BEAT. / PEPPERMINT MAN**	☐	☐
Jun 63. (7") <4963> **KING OF THE SURF GUITARS. / HAVA** **NAGILA**	–	☐
Jun 63. (lp) (ST 1930) **KING OF THE SURF GUITAR** – King of the surf guitars / The lonesome road / Kansas City / Dick Dale stomp / What'd I say / Greenback dollar / Hava nagila / You are my sunshine / Mexico / Break time / Riders in the sky / If I never get to Heaven.	☐	☐
Jul 63. (7") <5010> **SECRET SURFIN' SPOT. / SURFIN' AND** **A-SWINGIN'**	–	☐
Oct 63. (7") (CL 15320) <5048> **THE SCAVENGER. / WILD IDEAS**	–	98
Nov 63. (lp) <ST 2002> **CHECKERED FLAG** – The scavenger / Surf buggy / Hot rod racer / Mag wheels / Big black cad / Hodad machine / Grudge run / Motion / 426 – super stock / The wedge / It will grow on you / Night rider.	☐	☐
Dec 63. (7"; as DICK DALE) <5098> **THE WEDGE. / NIGHT** **RIDER**	–	☐
Mar 64. (7") <5140> **THE VICTOR. / MR. ELIMINATOR**	–	☐
Mar 64. (lp) <ST 2053> **MR. ELIMINATOR**	–	☐

– Mr. Eliminator / 50 miles to go / Flashing eyes / Taco wagon / The squirrel / The victor / Blond in the 406 / Firing up / My X-Ke / Nitro fuel / Hot rod alley.

Jun 64. (7") **<5187> GRUDGE RUN. / WILD, WILD MUSTANG**

Jul 64. (lp) *<ST 2111>* **SUMMER SURF**
– Summer surf / Feel so good / Surfin' / Spanish kiss / Star of David / Banzai washout / Glory wave / Surfin' rebel / Never on Sunday / Mama's gone surfin' / Tidal wave / Thunder wave.
(some w/ free 7" by Jerry Cole & His Spacemen)

Aug 64. (7") *<5225>* **GLORY WAVE. / NEVER ON SUNDAY**

Nov 64. (7") *<5290>* **WHO CAN HE BE? / OH MARIE**

Feb 65. (7") *<5389>* **LET'S GO TRIPPIN' '65. / WATUSI JO**

Mar 65. (lp) *<ST 2293>* **ROCK OUT WITH DICK DALE AND HIS DEL-TONES – LIVE AT CIRO'S** (live)
– Peter Gunn / Money honey / Angry generation / Summertime blues / Blowin' in the wind / Don't stop now (movin' and a-groovin') / Let's go trippin' '65 / Bony Moronie / Watusi Jo / Money / What'd I say.

DICK DALE

—— with various session people

			not iss.	Cougar
Jan 67.	(7") *<C-711>* **RAMBLIN' MAN. / YOU'RE HURTIN' NOW**		-	-
May 67.	(7") *<C-712>* **TACO WAGON. / SPANISH KISS**		-	-

			not iss.	Accent
1967.	(lp) *<3536>* **COAST TO COAST**		-	
1968.	(7") *<1243>* **EYES OF A CHILD. / JUST A WAITIN'**		-	

			not iss.	Balboa
1983.	(lp) *<BR 1001>* **THE TIGERS LOOSE 'KING OF THE SURF GUITAR'**		-	

– Peter Gunn / The wedge / Pick and play / Summertime blues / House of the rising sun / Miserlou / Let's go trippin' / Lovey dovey / Firing up / Something on your mind / King of the surf guitar / Jessie Pearl.

			not iss.	Columbia
1987.	(7") *<07340>* **PIPELINE. / (other by Stevie Ray Vaughan)**		-	

—— band:- **PRAIRE PRINCE** – drums (ex-TUBES) / **RON EGLIT** – bass / **SCOTT MATTHEWS** – drums / **VINCE WELNICK** – keyboards

			not iss.	Hightone
May 93.	(cd/c) *<HCD/HC 8046>* **TRIBAL THUNDER**		-	

– Nitro / New victor / Esperanza / Shredded heat / Trail of tears / Caravan / Eliminator / Speardance / Hot links: Caterpillar crawl – Rumble / Long ride / Tribal thunder. *(UK-iss.Mar95; same as US)*

Jun 94. (cd/c) *<HCD/HC 8055>* **UNKNOWN TERRITORY**
– Scalped / Mexico / F groove / Terry Dicktyl / Take it or leave it / Ghost riders in the sky / Fish taco / California sun / Maria Elena / Hava nagila / The beast / Unknown territory / Ring of fire. *(UK-iss.Mar95; same as US)*

			Beggars Banquet	Beggars Banquet
May 96.	(cd/lp) *(BBQ CD/LP 184) <80184>* **CALLING UP SPIRITS**			

– Nitrus / The wedge Paradiso / The pit / Fever / Doom box / Catamount / The window / Calling up spirits / Temple of Gizeh / Bandito / Third stone from the sun / Peppermint man / Gypsy fire.

– compilations, others, etc. –

1975. (lp) *GNP-Crescendo; <GNPS 2095>* **GREATEST HITS**
– Misirlou / Surf beat / Sloop John B. / King of the surf guitar / The wedge / Those memories of you / Let's go trippin' / The victor / Peppermint man / Get back the feelin' / Peter Gunn. *(UK-iss.1988; same)*

1975. (7") *GNP-Crescendo; <804>* **LET'S GO TRIPPIN'. / THOSE MEMORIES OF YOU**

Jun 88. (lp) *Rhino; <(RNLP 70074)>* **KING OF THE SURF GUITAR: THE BEST OF DICK DALE & THE DEL-TONES**   1986
– Let's go trippin' / Shake n' stomp / Miserlou / Peppermint man / Surf beat / Take it off / King of the surf guitar / Hava nagila / Riders in the sky / The wedge / Night rider / Mr. Eliminator / The victor / Taco wagon / Tidal wave / Banzai washout / One double one oh! / Pipeline. *<(cd-iss.Aug89; R2 70074)>*

Oct 88. (7") *Pulchwave;* (PSC 666) **PICK AND PLAY. / THE WEDGE**
(12"+=/3"cd-s) *(12PSC/PSCD 666)* – Hava nagila / King of the surf guitar (remix).

Jun 97. (d-cd) *Rhino; <72631>* **BETTER SHRED THAN DEAD: THE DICK DALE ANTHOLOGY** (1959-1995)

DALI'S CAR (see under ⇒ BAUHAUS)

Roger DALTREY (see under ⇒ WHO)

DAMNED

Formed: London, England ... May 1976 by BRIAN JAMES and RAT SCABIES who soon found The CAPTAIN and former undertaker, DAVE VANIAN. Signed to new UK indie label, 'Stiff', by JAKE RIVERA, they released the classic track, 'NEW ROSE', produced by stablemate, NICK LOWE. The DAMNED became the first "New Wave Punks" to release and chart with an album, namely the enduring 'DAMNED DAMNED DAMNED' (1977). One of the classic punk debuts, the album pogo'd and and thrashed its way through a frenetic set of three-chord wonders, LOWE's garden shed production underlining the riotous pandemonium. The band had also broken into the Top 40, although ironically enough, prolonged chart success would come later in the 80's when The DAMNED had changed almost beyond recognition. Live, the band were also one of the major attractions on the London scene; with VANIAN's proto-goth affectations, SENSIBLE's beret-topped antics and SCABIES' demented drummer persona all competing against each other, The DAMNED were indeed a motley crew. Their musical assault was bolstered later that year by a second guitarist, LU EDMONDS,

who debuted on the flaccid 'MUSIC FOR PLEASURE' (1977). The album was universally derided and SCABIES soon left for pastures new. Although future CULTURE CLUB man, JOHN MOSS was drafted in briefly as a replacement, the band splintered early the following year. After a period of solo work, VANIAN, SENSIBLE and SCABIES regrouped as The DAMNED early in '79 and emerged rejuvenated into the UK Top 20 via the impressive 'LOVE SONG'. With ALGY WARD completing the line-up, the band scored a second chart hit with 'SMASH IT UP', releasing their lauded 'MACHINE GUN ETIQUETTE' album later that year. Sure, they were still as swift and deadly as the title might suggest, but somehow they'd acquired a mastery of pop dynamics; a third single, 'I JUST CAN'T BE HAPPY TODAY', was the closest they'd yet come to a rock solid tune. PAUL GRAY replaced WARD for 1980's 'UNTITLED (THE BLACK ALBUM)', an even more surprising, ambitious double set which flew in the face of punk convention with its rampant experimentalism. The poppy 'STRAWBERRIES' (1982) marked the last stand of CAPTAIN SENSIBLE, who'd scored with the annoying 'HAPPY TALK' earlier that summer, the first fruits of his solo deal with 'A&M'. VANIAN and SCABIES lumbered on with new members ROMAN JUGG and BRYAN GUNN, suprisingly enough enjoying major chart success with a string of overtly commercial, pseudo goth rockers, the biggest of which, a cover of BARRY RYAN's 'ELOISE' made the Top 3. 'PHANTASMAGORIA' (1985) became their biggest selling album to date, catering to a whole new generation of fans. Most critics were agreed, however, that it paled in comparison to their earlier work, the DAMNED finally fading in the late 80's. For any interested parties, the band periodically get together with an amorphous line-up for all-dayer's and one-off gigs; old punks never die, they just tour with The DAMNED. • **Songwriters:** Most written by JAMES, until he left, when group took over. Covered:- HELP! (Beatles) / I FEEL ALRIGHT (Stooges / Iggy Pop) / JET BOY JET GIRL (New York Dolls) / CITADEL (Rolling Stones) / ELOISE (Paul & Barry Ryan) / WHITE RABBIT (Jefferson Airplane) / ALONE AGAIN OR (Love) / WILD THING (Troggs) / LET THERE BE RATS (aka DRUMS) (Sandy Nelson). • **Trivia:** NICK MASON (Pink Floyd drummer) produced disappointing 2nd album MUSIC FOR PLEASURE. CAPTAIN SENSIBLE had UK-No.1 in 1982 with (Rogers-Hammerstein's) HAPPY TALK, and although briefly, became a top disco/pop act abroad.
Album rating: DAMNED DAMNED DAMNED (*8) / MUSIC FOR PLEASURE (*5) / MACHINE GUN ETIQUETTE (*7) / BLACK ALBUM (*6) / BEST OF THE DAMNED compilation (*8) / STRAWBERRIES (*5) / PHANTASMAGORIA (*5) / ANYTHING (*3) THE LIGHT AT THE END OF THE TUNNEL compilation (*7) / FINAL DAMNATION exploitation (*4)

DAVE VANIAN (b. DAVE LETTS) – vocals / **BRIAN JAMES** (b. BRIAN ROBERTSON) – guitar (ex-LONDON S.S.) / **CAPTAIN SENSIBLE** (b. RAY BURNS, 23 Apr'55) – bass, vocals / **RAT SCABIES** (b. CHRIS MILLER, 30 Jul'57) – drums (ex-LONDON S.S.)

		Stiff	Frontier
Nov 76.	(7") *(BUY 6)* **NEW ROSE. / HELP!**		-
Feb 77.	(7") *(BUY 10)* **NEAT NEAT NEAT. / STAB YOR BACK / SINGALONGASCABIES**		-
Feb 77.	(lp) *(SEEZ 1)* **DAMNED DAMNED DAMNED**	36	Apr77

– Neat neat neat / Fan club / I fall / Born to kill / Stab yor back / Feel the pain / New rose / Fish / See her tonite / 1 of the 2 / So messed up / I feel alright. *(re-iss. Apr87 on 'Demon' lp/c/cd; FIEND/+CASS/CD 91) (pic-lp 1988; PFIEND 91)*

—— added (ROBERT) **LU EDMUNDS** – guitar

Sep 77.	(7") *(BUY 18)* **PROBLEM CHILD. / YOU TAKE MY MONEY**		-
Nov 77.	(lp) *(SEEZ 5)* **MUSIC FOR PLEASURE**		-

– Problem child / Don't cry wolf / One way love / Politics / Stretcher case / Idiot box / You take my money / Alone / Your eyes / Creep (you can't fool me) / You know. *(re-iss. Apr88 on 'Demon' lp/c/cd; FIEND/+CASS/CD 108)*

Dec 77. (7",7"purple) *(BUY 24)* **DON'T CRY WOLF. / ONE WAY LOVE**

—— **DAVE BERK** – drums (ex-JOHNNY MOPED) repl. SCABIES who formed various bands

—— **JOHN MOSS** – drums replaced BERK. They split Feb 78. VANIAN joined DOCTORS OF MADNESS. SENSIBLE formed SOFTIES then KING. EDMUNDS & MOSS formed THE EDGE. MOSS later joined ADAM & THE ANTS then CULTURE CLUB. EDMUNDS became part of ATHLETICO SPIZZ 80, The MEKONS, SHRIEKBACK, PIL. etc. BRIAN JAMES formed TANZ DER YOUTH, who released one single, 'I'M SORRY I'M SORRY' for 'Radar', before going solo the following year (1979) to issue his version of 'AIN'T THAT A SHAME'. He subsequently formed another punk supergroup, The HELLIONS, issuing one 1981 single for 'Illegal', 'WHY WHY WHY', before he jointly formed The LORDS OF THE NEW CHURCH. The DAMNED re-formed in Autumn '78 as The **DOOMED** with LEMMY of MOTORHEAD on bass. (1 gig) **HENRY BADOWSKI** – bass (ex-CHELSEA) replaced LEMMY. The group reverted to name The **DAMNED** with originals VANIAN, SENSIBLE (now guitar & keyboards) and SCABIES

—— **ALGY WARD** – bass (ex-SAINTS) replaced BADOWSKI who went solo

		Chiswick	Roadrunner
Apr 79.	(7",7"red) *(CHIS 112)* **LOVE SONG. / NOISE NOISE NOISE / SUICIDE**	20	-

(re-iss. 7"blue Feb82 on 'Big Beat'; NS 75)

Oct 79.	(7") *(CHIS 116)* **SMASH IT UP. / BURGLAR**	35	-

(re-iss. 7"red Mar82 on 'Big Beat'; NS 76)

Nov 79.	(lp) *(CWK 3011)* **MACHINE GUN ETIQUETTE**	31	Dec79

– Love song / Machine gun etiquette / I just can't be happy today / Melody Lee / Anti-Pope / These hands / Plan 9 channel 7 / Noise noise noise / Looking at you / Smash it up (parts 1 & 2). *(re-iss. Jun85 on 'Ace' lp/c; DAM/+MC 3) (cd-iss. 1986 +=; CDWIK 905)* – Ballroom blitz / Suicide / Rabid (over you) / White rabbit.

Nov 79. (7") *(CHIS 120)* **I JUST CAN'T BE HAPPY TODAY. / BALLROOM BLITZ / TURKEY SONG**   46   -

──── **PAUL GRAY** – bass, vocals (ex-EDDIE AND THE HOT RODS) repl. WARD who formed TANK

Jun 80. (7";w-drawn) *(CHIS 130)* **WHITE RABBIT. / RABID (OVER YOU) / SEAGULLS** □ –

Sep 80. (7"m/12"m) *(CHIS/+12 135)* **THE HISTORY OF THE WORLD (part 1). / I BELIEVE THE IMPOSSIBLE / SUGAR AND SPITE** □ –

Nov 80. (d-lp) *(CWK 3015)* **UNTITLED** (THE BLACK ALBUM) (1/2 studio, 1/4 live, 1/4 concept) 〔29〕 –
– Wait for the blackout / Lively arts / Silly kids games / Drinking about my baby / Hit and miss / Doctor Jekyll and Mr. Hyde / 13th floor vendetta / Twisted nerve / Sick of this and that / History of the world (part 1) / Therapy // Curtain call / live side:- Love song / Second time around / Smash it up (parts 1 & 2) / New rose / I just can't be happy today / Plan 9 Channel 7. *(re-iss. Aug82 on 'Ace' as one-lp/d-c; DAM/+MC 3)* *(c-iss.Jun85; TCWIK 3015)* *(cd-iss. Mar90; CDWIK 906)* – (omits live tracks)

Nov 80. (7"m) *(CHIS 139)* **THERE AINT NO SANITY CLAUS. / HIT OR MISS / LOOKING AT YOU (live)** □ –

	N.E.M.S.	not iss.

Nov 81. (d7"ep) *(TRY 1)* **FRIDAY THE 13th** 〔50〕 –
– Disco man / The limit club / Citadel / Billy bad breaks.

	Bronze	not iss.

Jul 82. (7"m/7"pic-d) *(BRO/+P 149)* **LOVELY MONEY. / LOVELY MONEY (disco) / I THINK I'M WONDERFUL** 〔42〕 –

Sep 82. (7"ep) *(BRO 156)* **DOZEN GIRLS. / TAKE THAT / MINE'S A LARGE ONE, LANDLORD / TORTURE ME** □ –

Oct 82. (lp/c) *(BRON 542)* **STRAWBERRIES** 〔15〕 –
– Ignite / Generals / Stranger on the town / Dozen girls / The dog / Gun fury / Pleasure and the pain / Life goes on / Bad time for Bonzo / Under the floor again / Don't bother me. *(re-iss. Mar86 on 'Legacy' red-lp/c; LLM/+K 3000)* *(re-iss. Dec86 on 'Dojo' lp/cd; DOJO LP/CD 46)* *(cd re-iss. Nov92 on 'Dojo'; DOJOCD 46)* *(cd-iss. Apr94 on 'Cleopatra'; CLEO 1029-2)* *(cd re-iss. Mar97 on 'Essential'; ESMCD 473)*

Nov 82. (7"m) *(BRO 159)* **GENERALS. / DISGUISE / CITADEL ZOMBIES** □ –

	Damned	not iss.

Nov 83. (pic-lp/lp) *(P+/DAMU 2)* **LIVE IN NEWCASTLE (live)** – – mail-o
(cd-iss. Jan94 on 'Receiver'; RRCD 181)

	Plus One	not iss.

May 84. (7"colrd/7"pic-d) *(DAMNED 1/+P)* **THANKS FOR THE NIGHT. / NASTY** □ –
(re-iss. 12"-ltd.1985 +=; DAMNED 1T) – Do the blitz.

──── **VANIAN** and **SCABIES** recruited new guys **ROMAN JUGG** – guitar, keyboards / who replaced the CAPTAIN who carried on with solo career. **BRYN GUNN** – bass repl. GRAY

	M.C.A.	Off Beat

Mar 85. (7"/7"pic-d/'A'-Spic'n'Spec mix-12") *(GRIM/+P/T 1)* **GRIMLY FIENDISH. / EDWARD THE BEAR** 〔21〕 –
(12"white+=) *(GRIMX 1)* – ('A'-Bad Trip mix).

Jun 85. (7") *(GRIM 2)* **SHADOW OF LOVE. / NIGHTSHIFT** 〔25〕 –
('A'-Ten Inches Of Hell mix-10"+=) *(GRIMX 2)* – Would you.
(12"+=) *(GRIMT 2)* – Would you.
(d7"+=) *(GRIMY 2)* – Let there be Rats / Wiped out.

Jul 85. (lp/c/pic-lp/white-lp/blue-lp) *(MCF/+C/P/W/B 3275)* **PHANTASMAGORIA** 〔11〕 –
– Street of dreams / Shadow of love / There'll come a day / Sanctum sanctorium / Is it a dream / Grimly fiendish / Edward the bear / The eighth day / Trojans. *(free 7" w.a.)* I JUST CAN'T BE HAPPY TODAY *(re-iss. 1986; same)* – (contains free 12"blue ELOISE) *(cd-iss. Aug89; DMCL 1887)*

Sep 85. (7") *(GRIM 3)* **IS IT A DREAM (Wild West End mix) / STREET OF DREAMS (live)** 〔34〕 □
(12"+=) *(GRIMT 3)* – Curtain call (live) / Pretty vacant (live) / Wild thing (live).

Jan 86. (7") *(GRIM 4)* **ELOISE. / TEMPTATION** 〔3〕 □
(12"blue+=/'A'-No Sleep Until Wednesday mix-12") *(GRIM T/X 4)* – Beat girl.

Nov 86. (7") *(GRIM 5)* **ANYTHING. / THE YEAR OF THE JACKAL** 〔32〕 □
(10"blue+=,10"yellow+=) *(GRIMX 5)* – ('A'mixes).
(12"+=) *(GRIMT 5)* – Thanks for the night.

Nov 86. (lp/c/cd) *(MCG/MCGC/DMCG 6015)* <5966> **ANYTHING** 〔40〕 □
– Anything / Alone again or / The portrait / Restless / In dulce decorum / Gigolo / The girl goes down / Tightrope walk / Psychomania.

Feb 87. (7"colrd/12"clear) *(GRIM/+T 6)* **GIGOLO. / THE PORTRAIT** 〔29〕 –

Apr 87. (7") *(GRIM 7)* **ALONE AGAIN OR. / IN DULCE DECORUM** 〔27〕 –
(12"+=) *(GRIMT 7)* – Psychomania.
(d7"++=) *(DGRIM 7)* – Eloise.

Nov 87. (7") *(GRIM 8)* **IN DULCE DECORUM. / PSYCHOMANIA** 〔72〕 –
(12"+=) *(GRIMT 8)* – ('A'dub).

──── disbanded in the late 80's, although re-union gigs were forthcoming

	Essential	Restless

Aug 89. (green-lp) *(ESCLP 008)* <72385> **FINAL DAMNATION** (live '88 reunion) □ □
– See her tonite / Neat neat neat / Born to kill / I fall / Fan club / Fish / Help / New rose / I feel alright / I just can't be happy today / Wait for the blackout / Melody Lee / Noise noise noise / Love song / Smash it up (parts 1 & 2) / Looking at you / The last time. *(cd-iss. Apr94 on 'Castle'; CLACD 338)*

– compilations, etc. –

1981. (4x7"box) *Stiff; (GRAB 2)* **FOUR PACK** –
– (NEW ROSE / NEAT NEAT NEAT / PROBLEM CHILD / DON'T CRY WOLF)

Nov 81. (lp/c) *Ace; (DAM/+C 1)* **THE BEST OF THE DAMNED** 〔43〕 –
– New rose / Neat neat neat / I just can't be happy today / Jet boy jet girl / Hit or miss / There ain't no sanity claus / Smash it up (parts 1 & 2) / Plan 9 channel 7 / Rabid (over you) / Wait for the blackout / History of the world (part 1). *(cd-iss. Oct87; CDDAM 1)*

May 82. (7"/7"pic-d) *Big Beat; (NS/+P 77)* **WAIT FOR THE BLACKOUT. / Captain Sensible & The Softies: JET BOY, JET GIRL** □ –

Oct 82. (7"green) *Big Beat; (NS 80)* **LIVELY ARTS. / TEENAGE DREAM** □ –

(10"+=) *(NST 80)* – I'm so bored.

Nov 82. (lp) *Ace; (NED 1)* **LIVE SHEPPERTON 1980 (live)** □ –
– Love song / Second time around / I just can't be happy today / Melody Lee / Help / Neat neat neat / Looking at you / Smash it up (parts 1 & 2) / New rose / Plan 9 channel 7. *(also iss.Nov82 on 'Big Beat'; WIKM 27)* *(c-iss.Jun85; WIKC 27)* *(cd-iss. Jun88; CDWIKM 27)*

Nov 85. (12"ep) *Stiff; (BUYIT 238)* **NEW ROSE / NEAT NEAT NEAT. / STRETCHER CASE / SICK OF BEING SICK** □ –

Jan 86. (lp/c/cd) *Dojo; (DOJO LP/TC/CD 21)* **DAMNED BUT NOT FORGOTTEN** □ –
(cd re-iss. Nov92; same) *(cd re-iss. Feb97 on 'Essential'; ESMCD 472)*

Jun 86. (12"ep) *Strange Fruit; (SFPS 002)* **THE PEEL SESSIONS (10.5.77)** □ –
– Sick of being sick / Stretcher case / Feel the pain / Fan club. *(c-ep.1987; SFPSC 002)* *(cd-ep.May88; SFPSCD 002)*

Jul 86. (blue-m-lp) *Stiff; (GET 4)* **THE CAPTAIN'S BIRTHDAY PARTY – LIVE AT THE ROUNDHOUSE** □ –
(cd-iss. Nov91 on 'Demon'; VEXCD 7)

Jul 87. (12"ep) *Strange Fruit; (SFPS 040)* **THE PEEL SESSIONS (30.11.76)** □ –
– Stab yor back / Neat neat neat / New rose / So messed up / I fall.

Oct 87. (cd/lp) *I.D.; (C+/NOSE 18)* **MINDLESS, DIRECTIONLESS, ENEMY (live)** □ –
(re-iss. Jun89 cd/c/lp; CDOSE/KOSE/NOSE 18X)

Dec 87. (d-lp) *M.C.A.; (MCSP 312)* **THE LIGHT AT THE END OF THE TUNNEL** 〔87〕 –

Jun 88. (lp/c) *Big Beat; (WIK/+C 80)* **THE LONG LOST WEEKEND: BEST OF VOL.1/2** □ –

1990. (cd) *Marble Arch; (cd)* **THE DAMNED LIVE (live)** □ –

Dec 90. (cd/c/d-lp) *Castle; (CCS CD/MC/LP 278)* **THE COLLECTION** □ –

Jan 91. (12"blue-ep) *Deltic; (DELT 7T)* **FUN FACTORY ('82). / Captain Sensible: FREEDOM / PASTIES / A RIOT ON EASTBOURNE PIER** □ –

Jun 91. (cd/colrd-lp) *Receiver; (RR CD/LP 159)* **BALLROOM BLITZ – LIVE AT THE LYCEUM (live)** □ –

Dec 91. (cd) *Dojo; (DOJOCD 65)* **TOTALLY DAMNED (live + rare)** □ –

Jan 92. (cd) *Street Link; (AOK 101)* **ALTERNATIVE CHARTBUSTERS** □ –

Feb 92. (clear-lp) *Receiver; (RRLP 159)* **LIVE AT THE LYCEUM (live)** □ –

Aug 92. (cd) *Connoisseur; (VSOPCD 174)* **THE MCA SINGLES A'S & B'S** □ –

Sep 92. (cd) *Demon; (VEXCD 12)* **SKIP OFF SCHOOL TO SEE THE DAMNED (THE STIFF SINGLES A'S & B'S)** □ –

May 93. (cd) *Receiver; (RRCD 179)* **SCHOOL BULLIES** □ –

Jul 93. (cd) *Success; (550 747-2)* **THE DAMNED: FROM THE BEGINNING** □ –

Nov 93. (cd) *Strange Fruit; (SFRSCD 070)* **SESSIONS OF THE DAMNED** □ –

Jun 94. (cd/c) *M.C.I.; (MUS CD/MC 017)* **ETERNALLY DAMNED – THE VERY BEST OF THE DAMNED** □ –

Dec 94. (cd) *Cleopatra; (CLEO 7139-2)* **TALES FROM THE DAMNED** □ –

May 95. (cd) *Spectrum; (550 747-2)* **FROM THE BEGINNING** □ –

Sep 95. (cd/c) *Emporio; (EMPR CD/MC 592)* **NOISE – THE BEST OF: LIVE** □ –

Jun 96. (cd) *Nighttracks; (CDNT 011)* **RADIO 1 SESSIONS** □ –

Oct 96. (cd) *Cleopatra; (CLP 9804)* **FIENDISH SHADOWS** □ –

Feb 97. (3xcd-box) *Demon; (FBOOK 14)* **NEAT NEAT NEAT** □ –

Mar 97. (cd) *Cleopatra; (CLP 9960)* **THE CHAOS YEARS** □ –

Apr 97. (cd/c) *The Record Label; (MOCDR/MOMC 1)* **I'M ALRIGHT JACK AND THE BEANSTALK** □ –

May 97. (d-cd) *Snapper; (SMDCD 143)* **BORN TO KILL** □ –

Jun 97. (lp) *Cleopatra; (CLP 9782)* **SHUT IT** □ –

Nov 97. (7") *Skinnies Cut; (AVL 1077)* **PROKOFIEV. /** □ –

Nov 97. (7") *Marble Orchard; (MOS 2)* **TOUR SINGLE. /** □ –

Oct 98. (7") *Musical Tragedy; (MT 418)* **PRETTY VACANT. / DISCO MAN** □ –

DAMN YANKEES (see under ⇒ NUGENT, Ted)

DANDY WARHOLS

Formed: Portland, Oregon, USA … mid 90's by buzzed-up guys, COURTNEY TAYLOR and PETER HOLMSTROM, who, with rhythm section, ERIC HEDFORD and feisty babe, ZIA McCABE, emerged from their recording basement in 1996. After a one-off double mini-CD, the harmony-fuelled psychedelia of 'DANDYS RULE OK', they inked a deal with 'Capitol', although they riled their bosses by failing to deliver on a promised set of songs; exposure in the Rolling Stone was subsequently mis-timed. Unsurprisingly the band gave themselves a proverbial kick up the ass and rose from their drug ashes with a fine set of songs, two of which ('EVERYDAY SHOULD BE A HOLIDAY' and 'NOT IF YOU WERE THE LAST JUNKIE ON EARTH') were UK Top 30 singles and preceded their Top 20 album, 'COME DOWN' (1998). • **Covers:** THE WRECK OF THE EDMUND FITZGERALD (Gordon Lightfoot) / etc.

Album rating: DANDYS RULE OK (*6) / COME DOWN (*7)

COURTNEY TAYLOR – vocals, guitar / **PETER HOLMSTROM** – guitar / **ERIC HEDFORD** – drums / **ZIA McCABE** – bass

	Tim/Kerr	Tim/Kerr

Dec 95. (2xm-cd) <TK95CD 0091> **DANDYS RULE OK** □ □
– Introduction by young Tom / Dandy Warhol's T.V. theme song / Ride / Best friend / Not your bottle / (Tony, this song is called) Lou Weed / Nothin' to do / Coffee and tea wrecks / Genius / Dick / Just try / Nothing (lifestyle of a tortured artist for sale) / Grunge Betty / Prelude – It's a fast-driving rave-up with the Dandy Warhols sixteen minutes – Finale // Little drummer boy / Dick / (It doesn't take a) Genius / Untitled.

		Capitol	Capitol
Jan 96.	(pic-d-cd) <(TK 95PD 104)> **RIDE / WE LOVE YOU DICK**	☐	☐

Feb 98.	(c-s/7"purple) (TC+/CL 797) **EVERYDAY SHOULD BE A HOLIDAY. / ONE (ULTRA LAM WHITE BOY)** (cd-s+=) (CDCL 797) – Head.	29	☐
Apr 98.	(c-s/7") (CL 800) **NOT IF YOU WERE THE LAST JUNKIE ON EARTH. / GENIUS** (cd-s+=) (CDCLS 800) – Ride. (cd-s) (CDCL 800) – ('A'side) / ('A'live) / It's a fast drivin' rave up with the Dandy Warhols sixteen minutes (live).	13	☐
May 98.	(cd/c) (836505-2/-4) **COME DOWN** – Be in / Boys better / Minnasoter / Orange / I love you / Not if you were the last junkie on earth / Every day should be a holiday / Good morning / Whipping tree / Green / Cool as Kim Deal / Hard on for Jesus / Pete International airport. (d-lp iss.Mar98 on 'Tim/Kerr'; TK 1671)	16	☐
Jul 98.	(7") (CL 805) **BOY'S BETTER. / NOTHIN' TO DO** (cd-s+=) (CDCL 805) – Grunge Betty. (cd-s) (CDCLS 805) – ('A'side) / The wreck of the Edmund Fitzgerald / Free for all.	36	☐

DANNY & DUSTY (see under ⇒ GREEN ON RED)

DANSE SOCIETY　(dig out; Great Alt & Indie . . .)

DANZIG

Formed: Los Angeles, California, USA . . . 1987 out of SAMHAIN, by ex-MISFITS (70's/80's hardcore/punk group) frontman GLENN DANZIG. In 1981, GLENN released his solo debut 45, 'WHO KILLED MARILYN', while still providing the muscle behind The MISFITS. Retaining bassist EERIE VON, GLENN recruited JOHN CHRIST and CHUCK BISCUITS, both seasoned campaigners of the US hardcore scene. Signed by Rick Rubin in 1988 to boost his newly created 'Def American' label, DANZIG (the group) released their eponymous debut the same year. Subtly powerful, DANZIG were essentially a unique combination of primal blues, gothic-metal and darkly rich melody. Akin to a satanic ELVIS PRESLEY (well, he did cover 'TROUBLE'), (GLENN) DANZIG was a constant, brooding presence, his sinister croon/howl and musclebound frame casting a demonic shadow over proceedings. Highlights of the debut included 'TWIST OF CAIN', the Morrison-esque 'SHE RIDES' and the darkly raging 'MOTHER', a transatlantic hit five years later following MTV exposure. 1990 saw the release of their much-anticipated follow-up, 'LUCIFUGE', a more consistent set which garnered sufficient critical plaudits to give it a Top 75 placing. However, it was only with their third set, 'HOW THE GODS KILL' (1992), that DANZIG achieved the commercial success which had long been their due. In 1994, hot on the heels of 'MOTHER's chart action, they scored their second Top 30 album, 'DANZIG IV', the record's more accessible approach bringing accusations of selling out from the group's more hardcore fans. After losing CHUCK and EERIE, their final album to date, 'DANZIG 5: BLACKACIDEVIL' (1996), saw them lose some commercial and critical ground; it also featured a cover of Black Sabbath's 'HAND OF DOOM' – what else?!

Album rating: DANZIG (*7) / LUCIFUGE (*8) / DANZIG III – HOW THE GODS KILL (*7) / DANZIG IV (*6) / DANZIG 5: BLACKACIDEVIL (*4)

SAMHAIN

GLENN DANZIG (b.23 Jun'59, Lodi, New Jersey) – vocals (ex-MISFITS) / **EERIE VON** (b.25 Aug'64, Lodi) – bass (ex-MISFITS) / **PETER 'DAMIEN' MARSHALL** – guitars / a series of drummers; **STEVE ZING, LYLE PRESLAR + LONDON MAY**

		Revolver	Plan 9
1984.	(lp) **INITIUM**	-	☐
1985.	(m-lp) **UNHOLY PASSION**	-	☐
Aug 86.	(lp) (REVLP 82) **NOVEMBER-COMING-FIRE** – Diabolos '88 / In my grip / Mother of mercy / Birthright / To walk the night / Let the day begin / Halloween II / November's fire / Kiss of steel / Unbridled / Human pony girl.	-	☐

—　**JOHN CHRIST** (b.19 Feb'65, Baltimore, Maryland) – guitar ; repl. MARSHALL

– compilations, etc. –

1990.	(cd/lp) Plan 9; <PL9 10-2/-1> **FINAL DESCENT** – Night chill / Descent / Death . . . in its arms / Lords of the left hand / The birthing / Unholy passion / All hell / Moribund / The hungry end / Misery tomb / I am misery.	-	☐

DANZIG

DANZIG, VON + CHRIST plus **CHUCK BISCUITS** (b.17 Apr'??, Calif.) – drums (ex-BLACK FLAG, ex-D.O.A., ex-CIRCLE JERKS)

		Mercury	Def American
Dec 88.	(lp/c/cd) (828124-1/-4/-2) <DEF 24208-1/-4/-2> **DANZIG** – Twist of Cain / Not of this world / She rides / Soul on fire / Am I demon / Mother / Possession / End of time / The hunter / Evil thing. (re-iss.Dec89 lp/c/cd; 838487-1/-4/-2) (cd re-iss. Apr95 on 'American'; 74321 24841-2)	☐	Sep88

		Def American	Def American
Jun 90.	(cd/c/lp) (846375-2/-4/-1) <DEF 24281-2/-4/-1> **DANZIG II – LUCIFUGE** – Long way back from Hell / Snakes of Christ / Killer wolf / Tired of being alive / I'm the one / Her black wings / Devil's plaything / 777 / Blood and tears / Girl / Pain in the world. (cd re-iss. Apr95 on 'American'; 74321 24842-2)	☐	74
Sep 90.	(c-s) <19692> **HER BLACK WINGS /**	-	☐

May 92.	(7") (DEFA 17) **DIRTY BLACK SUMMER. / WHEN DEATH HAD NO NAME** (12"+=)(cd-s+=) (DEFA 17-12)(DEFCD 17) – Bodies.	☐	☐
Jul 92.	(cd/c/lp) (512270-2/-4/-1) <DEF 26914-2/-4/-1> **DANZIG III – HOW THE GODS KILL** – Godless / Anything / Bodies / How the gods kill / Dirty black summer / Left hand black / Heart of the Devil / Sistines / Do you wear the mark / When the dying calls. (cd re-iss. Apr95 on 'American'; 74321 24843-2)	☐	24 Jun92
May 93.	(m-cd/m-c/m-lp) (514876-2/-4/-1) <45286> **THRALL / DEMONSWEATLIVE (live)** – It's coming soon / The violent fire / Trouble / Snakes of Christ / Am I demon / Sistines / Mother. (cd re-iss. Apr95 on 'American'; 74321 24844-2)	☐	54

		American	American
May 94.	(10"sha-pic-d) (MOM 1) <18256> **MOTHER. / MOTHER (live)** (12"+=) (MOMX 1) – When death had no name. (cd-s+=) (MOMCD 1) – How the gods kill.	62	43 Jan94
Oct 94.	(cd/c/lp) (74321 23681-2/-4/-1) <45647> **DANZIG IV** – Brand new god / Little whip / Cantspeak / Going down to die / Until you call on the dark / Dominion / Bringer of death / Sadistikal / Son of the morning star / I don't mind the pain / Stalker song / Let it be captured.	☐	29

—　**JOEY CASTILLO** (b.30 Mar'66, Gardenia, Calif.) – drums; repl. BISCUITS (guest on 3 tracks JERRY CANTRELL)

—　**JOSH LAZIE** – bass repl. EERIE VON

		Hollywood	Hollywood
Oct 96.	(cd/c) <(162084-2/-4)> **DANZIG 5: BLACKACIDEVIL** – 7th house / Blackacidevil / See all you were / Sacrifice / Hint of her blood / Serpentia / Come to silver / Hand of doom: version / Power of darkness / Ashes.	☐	41

—　**TOMMY VICTOR** – guitar (ex-PRONG) was added on tour

Terence Trent D'ARBY

Born: TERENCE TRENT DARBY, 15 Mar'62, New York City, New York, USA. After being raised in Manhattan, he moved to East Orange, Chicago with his preacher father. After enlisting in the army in 1980, he was based in Germany (took up boxing), where in 1982 he joined funk band, TOUCH. After some recordings, he left for London in 1984, where, after two years making demos, etc, he signed to 'C.B.S.' with the help of manager, Klaus Pieter 'KP' Schleinitz. With a promotional push on UK TV Channel 4's 'The Tube', he hit chart land immediately with 'IF YOU LET ME STAY', followed soon by an acclaimed debut MARTYN WARE-produced album, 'INTRODUCING THE HARDLINE ACCORDING TO . . .'. A funk/soul romantic who fashioned himself between PRINCE, STEVIE WONDER and SMOKEY ROBINSON, his debut set ran the gamut of modern R&B, from the smouldering 'SIGN YOUR NAME' to the itchy funk of 'WISHING WELL', a US No.1. The flipside of D'ARBY's good looks and electric charisma was a penchant of not being the most modest of chaps, his attitude not always appealing to everyone. This, together with a wilfully experimental and commercially suicidal follow-up set, 'NEITHER FLESH NOR FISH' (1989), saw D'ARBY's career lose momentum in the late 80's/early 90's. Virtually written off, D'ARBY came storming back in 1993 with 'SYMPHONY OR DAMN', a record that was still stamped with pretentiousness yet redeemed by a breathtaking stylistic diversity and poise that squarely challenged LENNY KRAVITZ. A Top 5 hit with four UK singles, the album put D'ARBY back on track. Although 1995's heavier 'TTD'S VIBRATOR' wasn't quite so successful or alluring, it's safe to say that D'ARBYs chameleon, seer-like musical vision has still to be fully realised.
• **Covered:** HEARTBREAK HOTEL (Elvis Presley) / UNDER MY THUMB and JUMPIN' JACK FLASH (Rolling Stones) / WONDERFUL WORLD (Sam Cooke).

Album rating: INTRODUCING THE HARDLINE ACCORDING TO . . . (*7) / NEITHER FISH NOR FLESH (*3) / SYMPHONY OR DAMN (*5) / TTD'S VIBRATOR (*5)

		C.B.S.	Columbia
Feb 87.	(7"/7"s) (TRENT/+Q 1) <07398> **IF YOU LET ME STAY. / LOVING YOU IS ANOTHER WORD FOR LONELY** (12"w-free 12"+=) (TRENTT 1) – ('A'-Hardline mix).	7	68 Oct87
Jun 87.	(7"/7"s) (TRENT/+G 2) <07675> **WISHING WELL. / ELEVATORS AND HEARTS** (12"+=) (TRENTT 2) – ('A'mix). (12"+=) (TRENTQ 2) – Wonderful world.	4	1 Jan88
Jul 87.	(lp/c/cd) (450911-1/-4/-2) <40964> **INTRODUCING THE HARDLINE ACCORDING TO TERENCE TRENT D'ARBY** – If you all get to Heaven / If you let me stay / Wishing well / I'll never turn my back on you / Dance little sister / Seven more days / Let's go forward / Rain / Sign your name / As yet untitled / Who's loving you?. (pic-lp.Dec87; 450911-0) (re-iss. May95 cd/c; same)	1	4 Oct87
Sep 87.	(7"/7"s) (TRENT/+Q 3) <08023> **DANCE LITTLE SISTER. / (part 2)** (12"+=) (TRENTT 3) – Sunday jam (one woman man). (c-s+=) (TRENTC 3) – Heartbreak hotel.	20	30 Aug88
Dec 87.	(7"/7"s) (TRENT/+Q 4) <07911> **SIGN YOUR NAME. / GREASY CHICKEN (live)** (12"+=/12"pic-d+=) (TRENT T/P 4) – Under my thumb (live) / Jumpin' Jack Flash (live). (10"+=) (TRENTG 4) – Rain (remix) / If you all get to Heaven (remix). (cd-s-pic+=) (TRENTC 4) – Dance little sister.	2	4 May88
Oct 89.	(lp/c/cd) (465809-1/-4/-2) <45351> **NEITHER FLESH NOR FISH** – Declaration / Neither flesh nor fish / I have faith in these desolate times / It feels so good to love someone like you / I'll be alright / Billy don't fall / This side of love / You will pay tomorrow / Roly Poly / I don't want to bring your gods down / And I need to be with someone tonight.	12	61 Nov89

Nov 89. (7"/c-s) *(TRENT/+M 5)* **THIS SIDE OF LOVE. / SAD SONG FOR SISTER SARAH**
(12"+=/12"s) *(TRENT T/Q 5)* – Sign your name (live).
(cd-s+=/pic-cd-s+=) *(TRENT C/P 5)* – Seven more days.

Jan 90. (7"/7"pic-d) *(TRENT/+E 6)* **TO KNOW SOMEONE DEEPLY IS TO LOVE SOMEONE SOFTLY. / LOOSE VARIATIONS ON A DEAD MAN'S VIBE IN CM** | 55 |
(12"+=/cd-s+=) *(TRENT T/C 6)* – ('A'mix) / Rain (live).

—— now with **TIM PIERCE** – guitar / **NEIL STUBENHAUSEN or KEVIN WYATT** – bass plus various guests

| | Columbia | Columbia |

Apr 93. (c-s) *(659 073-4)* **DO YOU LOVE ME LIKE YOU SAY? / READ MY LIPS (I DIG YOUR SCENE) / PERFUMED PAVILLION (THE MOTION OF MY MEMORIES)** | 14 |
(cd-s+=) *(659 073-2)* – ('A'original).
(cd-s) *(659 073-5)* – ('A'side) / Wishing well / If you let me stay / To know someone is to love someone.
(12"/cd-s) *(659 073-6)* – (3 'A'mixes) / Read my lips (I dig your scene).

May 93. (cd/c/lp) *(473 561-2/-4/-1) <53616>* **SYMPHONY OR DAMN** | 4 |
– PART I – CONFRONTATION; Welcome to my monasteryo / She kissed me / Do you love me like you say? / Baby let me share my love / Delicate / Neon messiah / Penelope please / Wet your lips / Turn the page.
– PART II – RECONCILIATION; Castilian blue / "T.I.T.S." – "F & J" / Are you happy? / Succumb to me / I still love you / Seasons / Let her down easy. *(re-iss. Sep96 cd/c; same)*

Jun 93. (7"/c-s) *(659 331-7/-4)* **DELICATE. / SHE'S MY BABY** | 14 |
(cd-s+=) *(659 331-2)* – Dance little sister (extended) / Survivor.

Aug 93. (c-s) *<77128>* **DELICATE / SHE KISSED ME** | - | 74 |

Sep 93. (7"/c-s) *(659 592-7/-4)* **SHE KISSED ME. / DO YOU LOVE ME LIKE YOU SAY? (Masters At Work 12" Mix)** | 16 |
(12"+=/cd-s+=) *(659 592-6/-2)* – (2-'B'mixes).

Nov 93. (7"white/c-s) *(659 864-7/-4)* **LET HER DOWN EASY. / TURN THE PAGE** | 18 |
(12"+=) *(659 864-6)* – Do you love me like you say?
(cd-s) *(659 864-2)* – ('A'side) / Sign your name / Delicate.

—— with **LOUIS METOYER** – guitar / **KEVIN WYATT** – bass / **EPHEN THEARD (STEVO)** – drums / etc.

Mar 95. (c-s) *(661 423-4)* **HOLDING ON TO YOU / ANGELS FLY BECAUSE** | 20 |
(cd-s+=) *(661 423-2)* – Your love is indecipherable / Epilog.
(cd-s) *(661 423-5)* – ('A'side) / Sign your name / Delicate / To know someone deeply is to love someone softly.

Apr 95. (cd/c) *(478 505-2/-4) <67070>* **TTD'S VIBRATOR** | 11 |
– Vibrator / Supermodel sandwich / Holding on to you / Read my lips (I dig your scene) / Undeniably / We don't have that much time together / C.Y.F.M.L.A.Y? / If you go before me / Surrender / TTD's recuring dream / Supermodel sandwich w/cheese / Resurrection / It's been said.

Aug 95. (c-s) *(662 258-4)* **VIBRATOR / SURRENDER (Brooklyn mix)** | 57 |
(cd-s+=) *(662 258-2)* – Surrender (MK mix) / I realy want you.
(cd-s) *(662 258-5)* – ('A'side) / Do you love me like you say? / She kissed me / Attracted to you.

– others, etc. –

Sep 89. (7"; as The INCREDIBLE E.G. O'REILLY) *Polydor; (EGOR 1)* **THE BIRTH OF MAUDIE. / AN CHUILEANN** | | - |

TOUCH

(featuring **TERENCE TRENT D'ARBY** – vocals) **MIKE WILLIAMS, MARK BURTON** – guitar / **FRANK 'Babyface' ITT** – bass / **STEFAN LUPP** – keyboards / **DETLEF VOGEL** – guitar / **BENNY BRACIN** – drums

Aug 89. (lp/cd) *(839 303-1/-2)* **TOUCH** (early works rec.'83) | - | | German
– I want to know (international lady) / Eggs and coffee / Don't call me up / Long way / Weekends / Passion / Immaterial / Somebody else / Get up and run / Cross my heart.

DARLING BUDS (dig out; Great Alt & Indie . . .)

Dave DAVIES (see under ⇒ KINKS)

John DAVIS (see under ⇒ SEBADOH; the FOLK IMPLOSION)

Miles DAVIS

Born: 25 May 1926, Alton, Illinois, USA, but raised in East St. Louis. The single most influential black musician (and certainly jazz musician) ever, next to JAMES BROWN, DAVIS began playing trumpet professionally in the early 40's. In 1944, after a period with bandleader BILLY ECKSTINE, he moved with his new wife to New York, where he briefly attended the Juilliard School Of Music before joining singer, RUBBERLEGS WILLIAMS. Around the same time, DAVIS also recorded and performed with his roommate/mentor, saxophonist CHARLIE PARKER. DAVIS subsequently assembled his own 9-piece ensemble, dubbed The TUBA BAND, which included saxophonists GERRY MULLIGAN and LEE KONITZ. They issued a number of radical 78's (singles), which were later (in 1957) compiled on seminal jazz work, 'THE BIRTH OF THE COOL'. After initially being influenced by bop pioneers such as PARKER and DIZZY GILLESPIE, DAVIS was now beginning to develop his own languid, downbeat style. Through the early to mid-50's, with revolving personnel, DAVIS worked sporadically due to his heroin addiction,

although his reputation as the hippest cat on the jazz block continued to spread. In 1955, after a bout of illness, he formed his now famous MILES DAVIS QUINTET, a groundbreaking formation that numbered JOHN COLTRANE, RED GARLAND, PAUL CHAMBERS and PHILLY JOE JONES. This relatively stable line-up recorded a string of albums including 'WORKIN', 'STEAMIN' and 'COOKIN', while "the man with the horn" subsequently signed for 'Columbia' and put together a new band consisting of JIMMY COBB, BILL EVANS and CANNONBALL ADDERLEY amongst an ever changing cast of others. This period saw the release of the seminal 'KIND OF BLUE' (1959), an album which revolutionised jazz with its substitution of conventional chord structures for modal improvisation. In collaboration with arranger GIL EVANS, DAVIS also recorded career-best works in Gershwin's 'PORGY AND BESS' (1959) and the hauntingly beautiful 'SKETCHES OF SPAIN' (1960). In 1963, he formed a new combo of young musicians, namely HERBIE HANCOCK, RON CARTER, TONY WILLIAMS and WAYNE SHORTER; this line-up produced enough brilliant performances to enthuse a new beatnik buying public, giving the unfashionable trumpet a new lease of life and an unlikely US chart position for the 'SEVEN STEPS TO HEAVEN' set. Five years later, DAVIS shocked both the jazz and rock fraternities, when, like DYLAN, he introduced electric instrumentation into a traditionally acoustic genre with the 'MILES IN THE SKY' album; in other words, DAVIS pioneered jazz-rock fusion. Other new talent to emerge during this transitional period, were JOHN McLAUGHLIN, JOE ZAWINUL and CHICK COREA to name but a few. Their following two albums, 'IN A SILENT WAY' (1969) and the double-set, 'BITCHES' BREW' (1970), saw them universally peaking, both critically and commercially (the latter hit the US Top 40, his only effort ever to do so!). Augmented on the second of these by keyboard wizard, LARRY YOUNG (who had replaced HANCOCK), DAVIS and Co. had created a work of genre-defying genius that explored the outermost limits of jazz, a mission that SUN RA had set out upon some years earlier. After the release of two further, wildly experimental concert sets, 'LIVE AT FILLMORE' (1971) and 'LIVE-EVIL' (1972), DAVIS survived a serious car crash and became increasingly more reclusive, shying away from the mainstream music business. Up until 1975 however, DAVIS continued recording, moving further away from jazz and into electronic funk with albums, 'ON THE CORNER' (1973), 'GET UP WITH IT' (1974) and 'AGHARTA' (1975); the latter set was his last for five years. In the early 80's, his return was heralded with the comeback album, 'THE MAN WITH THE HORN' (1981); a decidedly more commercial affair, it helped the infamously volatile DAVIS reach a new plateau of middleground popularity. In 1986, he broke a 27-year partnership with 'Columbia' after signing with 'Warner Brothers', his umpteenth album, 'TUTU' delivering his smooth interpretation of Scritti Politti's 'PERFECT WAY', having previously challenged his long-standing fans with an elevator-friendly version of Cyndi Lauper's 'TIME AFTER TIME'. Although he continued recording, DAVIS increasingly devoted more of his time to his second love, art. Sadly, just as his recording career might have taken off once more, he died on the 27th of December 1991 after contracting AIDS some years earlier. • **Trivia:** In 1982, he married actress CICELY TYSON.

Album rating (selective): BIRTH OF THE COOL (*9) / WORKIN' / STEAMIN' / COOKIN' / RELAXIN' (all *8) / SKETCHES OF SPAIN (*8) / KIND OF BLUE (*10) / MILESTONES (*8) / SOMEDAY MY PRINCE WILL COME (*7) / E.S.P. (*7) / MILES SMILES (*9) / NEFERTITI (*6) / MILES IN THE SKY (*7) / FILLES DE KILIMANJARO (*7) / IN A SILENT WAY (*7) / BITCHES' BREW (*8) / A TRIBUTE TO JACK JOHNSON (*8) / ON THE CORNER (*7) / PANGAEA (*6) / THE MAN WITH THE HORN (*6) / WE WANT MILES (*6) / STAR PEOPLE (*6) / DECOY (*5) / YOU'RE UNDER ARREST (*6) / AURA (*7) / TUTU (*7) / MUSIC FROM SIESTA (*5) / LIVE AROUND THE WORLD (*6) / AMANDLA (*6) / HOT SPOT (*5) / DINGO (*5) / DOO-BOP (*5) / MILES & QUINCY LIVE AT MONTREUX (*6)

(1948) **MILES DAVIS** – trumpet / **GIL EVANS, GERRY MULLIGAN, LEE KONITZ, JOHN LEWIS, JOHNNY CARISI, GUNTHER SCHULLER, SANDY SIEGELSTEIN** – saxophones / **JAY JAY JOHNSON** – trombone / **JOHN 'Bill' BARBER** – tuba / **MAX ROACH (or) KENNY CLARKE** – drums / with on some **JUNIOR COLLINS** – French horn / **MIKE ZWERIN**

| | Capitol | Capitol |

1950. (78) *(CL 13249)* **BUDO. / MOVE**
1950. (78) *(CL 13255)* **BOPLICITY. / ISRAEL**
1950. (78) *(CL 13429)* **VENUS DE MILO. / DARN THAT DREAM**
1950. (lp) *<DT 1974>* **BIRTH OF THE COOL** | - |
– Move / Jeru / Moon dreams / Venus De Milo / Budo / Deception / Godchild / Boplicity / Rocker / Israel / Rouge.

—— (May52 with) **JOHNSON + CLARKE** plus **JACKIE McLEAN** – alto sax / **GIL COGGINS** – piano / **OSCAR PETTIFORD** – bass

| | not iss. | Blue Note |

Oct 51. (lp) *<6525>* **DIG** | - |
– Dig / It's only a paper moon / Dental / Bluing / Out of the blue. *(UK-iss.1958 on 'Esquire'; 32-062)*

May 52. (lp) **MILES DAVIS VOL.1** | - |
– How deep is the ocean / Dear old Stockholm / Chance it / Yesterdays / Donna / Woody 'n you.

—— (Apr53) **PERCY HEATH** – bass repl. PETTIFORD / **ART BLAKEY** – drums repl. CLARKE / **JIMMY HEATH** – tenor sax repl. McLEAN
Tracks recorded: – Tempes fugit / Kelo / Enigma / Ray's idea / C.T.A. / I waited for you.

Sep 53. (lp) **AT LAST! MILES DAVIS AND THE LIGHTHOUSE ALL STARS** | - |

—— (Mar54) **HORACE SILVER** – piano repl. JIMMY, JAY JAY + GIL

Mar 54. (lp) **MILES DAVIS VOL. 2** | - |
Tracks recorded: – Take-off / Weirdo / Well you needn't / The leap / Lazy Susan / It never entered my mind.
They also recorded tracks: – Four / Old Devil Moon / Blue haze.

—— He formed The MILES DAVIS QUARTET earlier (May53) with **PERCY HEATH** – bass **JOHN LEWIS** – piano / **MAX ROACH** – drums with guest **CHARLIE MINGUS** – piano (1)
Albums issued at this time:- BAGS GROOVE / . . . & HORNS / MILES DAVIS
Tracks recorded: – When lights are low / Tune up / Miles ahead / Smooch.

—— The first incarnation of **MILES DAVIS QUINTET** appeared with **MILES, HORACE, PERCY, KENNY CLARKE** plus **DAVEY SCHILDKRAUT** – alto sax

MILES DAVIS ALL-STARS

—— were **CLARKE, JOHNSON, SILVER, PERCY HEATH & LUCKY THOMPSON**

not iss. / Prestige

Apr 54. (lp) <7078> **WALKIN'**
– Walkin' / Blues 'n' boogie / Solar / You don't know what love is / Love me or leave me. *(UK-iss.1960 on 'Esquire'; 32-098) (cd-iss. Aug93 + Nov93 on 'Jazz Hour')*

—— (Jun55) **MILES** – trumpet + **RED GARLAND** – piano / **PHILLY JOE JONES** – drums / **OSCAR PETTIFORD** – bass
1955. (lp) <7007> **THE MUSING OF MILES**
– I didn't / Will you still be mine? / Green haze / I see your face before me / A night in Tunisia / A gal in Calico. *(UK-iss.1950's on 'Esquire'; 32-012) (re-iss. Jun84)*

—— (Nov55) **JOHN COLTRANE** – tenor sax + **PAUL CHAMBERS** – bass repl. OSCAR

MILES DAVIS QUINTET

Nov 55. (lp) <7014> **MILES**
– Just squeeze me / There is no greater love / How am I to know? / S'posin' / The theme / Stablemates.
(above 2 albums issued as 'MILES' in 1958)
Oct 56. (lp) <7094> **COOKIN'** (live)
– If I were a bell / Stella by starlight / Walkin' / Miles. *(UK-iss.1958 on 'Esquire'; 32-048)*
1958. (lp) <7129> **RELAXIN' WITH THE MILES DAVIS QUINTET**
– You're my everything / I could write a book / Cleo / It could happen to you / Woody'n you. *(UK-iss.195 on 'Esquire'; 32-068)*
1958. (lp) <7166> **WORKIN' WITH THE MILES DAVIS QUINTET**
– It never entered my mind / Four / In your own sweet way / The theme (take 1 + 2) / Treme's blues / Ahmad's blues / Half Nelson. *(UK-iss.1960 on 'Esquire'; 32-108)*
1958. (lp) <7200> **STEAMIN' WITH THE MILES DAVIS QUINTET**
– Surrey with the fringe on top / Salt peanuts / Something I dreamed last night / Diane / Well you needn't / When I fall in love. *(UK-iss.1961 on 'Esquire'; 32-138)*
1959. (lp) <7540> **ODYSSEY**
– Dr. Jackie / Bitty ditty / Minor march / Change.
1959. (lp) <7650> **MODERN JAZZ GIANTS**
– Bag's groove – take 1 & 2 / Bemsha swing – take 1 & 2 / Swing spring.
1959. (lp) <7744> **CONCEPTION**
1959. (lp) <7847> **OLEO**
– Oleo / Doxy / Airegin / But not for me – take 1 & 2 / Vierd blues / In our own sweet way / No line.

—— **BILL EVANS** – piano + **JIMMY COBB** – drums repl. GARLAND + JONES / added **CANNONBALL ADDERLEY** – alto sax

Fontana / Prestige

May 57. (lp) (TFL 5007) <7822> **MILES AHEAD**
– Springsville / Maids of Cadiz / Duke / My ship / Miles ahead / Blues for Pablo / New rhumba / Meaning of the blues / Lament / I don't wanna be kissed.

Fontana / Columbia

Apr 58. (lp) (TFL 5035) <9428> **MILESTONES**
– Doctor Jekyll / Sid's ahead / Two bass hits / Miles / Billy Boy / Straight no chaser. *(cd-iss. 1992)*

—— added on below lp **JOHN COLTRANE** – tenor sax
May 59. (lp) (STFL 513) <8163> **KIND OF BLUE**
– So what / Freddie Freeloader / Blue in green / All blues / Flamenco sketches. *(cd-iss. Sep93)*
Nov 59. (lp) (TFL 5056) <8085> **PORGY AND BESS**
– The buzzard song / Bess, you is my woman / Gone, gone, gone, gone / Summertime / Bess, oh where's my Bess / Prayer / Objector Jesus / Fisherman / Strawberry and Devil crab / My man's gone now / It ain't necessarily so / Here comes de honey man / I love you Porgy / There's a boat that's leaving soon for New York. *(re-iss. Sep82) (re-iss. +cd.Feb88)*
Jan 60. (7") <42069> **IT AIN'T NECESSARILY SO. / I LOVES YOU PORGY**
(above + below lp's credited arranger GIL EVANS ORCHESTRA)
1960. (7") (JAZ 100) **BUDO. / TADD'S DELIGHT**
above issued on 'Philips' at this time.

C.B.S. / Columbia

Apr 60. (lp) (CBS 62327) <8271> **SKETCHES OF SPAIN**
– Concerto de Aranjuez / Will o' the wisp / The pan piper / Saeta / Solea. *(re-iss. Mar81 + Apr88, cd-iss. Dec85 + Apr92)*

—— In Autumn 1960, **SONNY STITT** – saxophone repl. COLTRANE in Sweden. Later in the year **SAM RIVERS** then **WAYNE SHORTER** repl. SONNY
Sep 61. (d-lp) <820> **IN PERSON (AT THE BLACKHAWK)** – 68
– Fran-dance / So what / Cleo / If I were a bell / Neo / Round midnight. *cd-iss. Jun 93 on 'Giants of Jazz')*

—— **HANK MOBLEY** – saxophone repl. COLTRANE
Mar 62. (lp) (TFL 5172) <8456> **SOMEDAY MY PRINCE WILL COME**
– Someday my prince will come / Old folks / Pfrancing / Drad-dog / Teo / I thought about you. *(re-iss. 1964 on 'C.B.S.'; 62104) (re-iss. Jul75 on 'Code-CBS') (cd-iss. Jan86 + Apr92)*
Sep 62. (lp) <8612> **MILES DAVIS AT CARNEGIE HALL 1961** (live) – 59
– So what / Spring is here / No blues / Oleo / Someday my prince will come / The meaning of the blues / Lament / New rhumba. *(cd-iss. Apr93 on 'Sony Europe')*
Oct 62. (7") <42583> **NEW RHUMBA. / SLOW SAMBA**
Dec 62. (lp) (CBS 62323) <8649> **ROUND ABOUT MIDNIGHT**
– Round about midnight / Ah leucha / All of you / Bye bye blackbird / Tadd's delight / Dear old Stockholm. *(cd-iss. Apr92)*
(above recorded 1956)

—— now with **HERBIE HANCOCK** – piano / **TONY WILLIAMS** – drums / **RON CARTER** – bass / **GEORGE COLEMAN** – tenor sax

Sep 63. (lp; stereo/mono) (S+/BPG 62170) <8851> **SEVEN STEPS TO HEAVEN** – 62
– Basin street blues / Seven steps to Heaven / I fall in love too easily / So near so far / Baby won't you please come home / Joshun. *(re-iss. Jul75 on 'Code-CBS')*
Oct 63. (7") <42853> **SEVEN STEPS TO HEAVEN. / THE DEVIL MAY CARE**
Apr 64. (lp; stereo/mono) (S+/BPG 62213) <8906> **QUIET NIGHTS** – 93
– Once upon a summertime / Aos pes da cruz / Song No.1 / Wait till you see her / Corrovado / Summer night. *(re-iss. Jul75 on 'Code-CBS') (cd-iss. Jul89)*
1964. (lp; stereo/mono – MILES DAVIS & THELONIUS MONK) (S+/BPG 62389) <8978> **MILES AND MONK AT NEWPORT**
– Ah-leu-cha / Straight, no chaser / Fran-dance / Two bass hit / Nutty / Blue Monk. *(re-iss. Jul75 on 'Code-CBS')*
Sep 64. (lp; stereo/mono) (S+/BPG 62390) <8983> **DAVIS IN EUROPE** (live)
– Untitled medley:- Agitation / Footprints / Round midnight / No blues / Masquelero / All of you. *(re-iss. Jul75 on 'Code-CBS')*

—— Line-up now **DAVIS, WILLIAMS, HANCOCK, CARTER + SHORTER**
Apr 65. (lp; stereo/mono) (S+/BPG 62510) <9106> **MY FUNNY VALENTINE: MILES DAVIS LIVE IN CONCERT** (live)
– My funny valentine / All of you / Stella by starlight / All blues / I thought about you. *(UK-iss.Jul75 on 'Code-CBS') (cd-iss. May87 on 'CBS')*
Jan 66. (lp; stereo/mono) (S+/BPG 62577) <9150> **E.S.P.**
– E.S.P. / Eighty one / Little one / R.J. / Agitation / Iris / Mood. *(re-iss. Jul75 on 'Code-CBS') (cd-iss. Apr92)*

—— credited his QUINTET, (**SHORTER** repl. COLEMAN)
1967. (lp; stereo/mono) (S+/BPG 62933) <9401> **MILES SMILES**
– Orbits / Circle / Footprints / Dolores / Freedom jazz dance / Ginger bread boy. *(re-iss. Aug75 on 'Code-CBS')*
1968. (lp; stereo/mono) (S+/BPG 63097) <9532> **THE SORCERER**
– Prince of darkness / Vonetta / Limbo / Masquealero / Pee wee / The sorcerer. *(re-iss. Aug76) (re-iss. Jul87) (re-iss. cd Sep93)*
1968. (lp) (CBS 63248) <9594> **NEFERTITI**
– Nefertiti / Fall / Hand jive / Madness / Riot / Pinocchio. *(re-iss. Aug76) (cd-iss. Apr92)*
Nov 68. (lp) (CBS 63352) <9628> **MILES IN THE SKY**
– Stuff / Paraphernalia / Black comedy / Country son. *(re-iss. Aug75 on 'Code-CBS')*
1969. (lp) (CBS 63551) <9750> **FILLES DE KILIMANJARO**
– Frelon burn (Brown hornet) / Tout de suite / Petits machins (little stuff) / Filles de Kilimanjaro (girls of . . .) / Mademoiselle Mabry. *(cd-iss. Apr92)*

MILES DAVIS

—— with past members **HERBIE HANCOCK** – electric piano / **WAYNE SHORTER** – soprano sax / **TONY WILLIAMS** – drums. New:- **DAVE HOLLAND** – bass repl. CARTER / **CHICK COREA** – electric piano / **JOSEF ZAWINUL** – electric piano & organ / **JOHN McLAUGHLIN** – guitar
Aug 69. (lp) (CBS 63630) <9875> **IN A SILENT WAY** – Jul69
– Ssh-Peaceful / In a silent way / It's about that time.
1970. (7") <45090> **GREAT EXPECTATIONS. / LITTLE BLUE FROG**

—— **LARRY YOUNG** – electric piano repl. HANCOCK who cont. solo work / **JACK DeJOHNETTE + LENNY WHITE** – drums repl. WILLIAMS who formed his LIFETIME / added **JIM RILEY** – percussion / **HARVEY BROOKS** – Fender bass / **BENNIE MAUPIN** – clarinet
Jun 70. (d-lp) (CBS 66236) <26> **BITCHES BREW** 71 – 35 May70
– Pharoah's dance / Bitches brew / Spanish key / John McLaughlin / Miles runs the voodoo down / Sanctuary. *(re-iss. Sep87, d-cd-iss. Apr92)*
Jul 70. (7") (CBS 7104) <45171> **MILES RUNS THE VOODOO DOWN. / SPANISH KEY**
Jan 71. (d-lp) (CBS 66257) <30038> **MILES DAVIS AT FILLMORE** (live) – Nov70
– Wednesday Miles / Thursday Miles / Friday Miles / Saturday Miles. *(re-iss. Jul75 on 'Code-CBS')*
Feb 71. (7") <45327> **SATURDAY MILES. / FRIDAY MILES**

—— Other members at this time **BILLY COBHAM** – percussion / **KEITH JARRETT** – keyboards
May 71. (lp) (CBS 70089) <30455> **A TRIBUTE TO JACK JOHNSON (Soundtrack)** – Apr71
– Right off / Yesternow. *(re-imported Jan76) (cd-iss. Sep93)*
May 71. (7") <45350> **RIGHT OFF. / (part 2)**
Dec 71. (d-lp) (CBS 67219) <30954> **LIVE-EVIL**
– Sivod / Little church / Medley: Gemini-Double image / What I say / Nem um talvez / Selim / Funky tonk / Inamorata.
Sep 72. (7") <45709> **MOLESTER. / (part 2)**
Nov 72. (7") <45822> **VOTE FOR MILES. / (part 2)**
Nov 72. (lp) (CBS 65246) <31906> **ON THE CORNER**
– On the corner / New York girl / Thinkin' one thing and doin' another / Vote for Miles / Black satin / One and one / Helen Butte / Mr. Freedom X. *(re-iss. Jan87) (re-iss. Dec88 on 'B.G.O.', cd-iss. Apr92) (re-iss cd Feb94 on 'Sony')*
Apr 73. (d-lp) (CBS 68222) **IN CONCERT** (live) –
Jun 74. (d-lp) (CBS 88024) <32866> **BIG FUN**
– Go ahead, John / Lonely fire / Great expectations / Mulher Laranja / Ife.
Jun 74. (7") <45946> **BIG FUN. / HOLLYWOOD**
Oct 74. (7") <46074> **GREAT EXPECTATIONS. / GO AHEAD JOHN**
Jan 75. (lp) (CBS 88092) <33236> **GET UP WITH IT**
– He loved him madly / Maiysha / Honky tonk / Rated X / Calypso frelimo / Red China blues / Mtume / Billy Preston.
Jan 75. (7") <10110> **RED CHINA BLUES. / MAIYSHA**
Nov 75. (d-lp) (CBS 88159) <33967> **AGHARTA** (live)
– Prelude (pt.1 & 2) / Maiysha / Interlude / Theme from Jack Johnson. *(re-iss. Jan87) (re-iss. d-cd Sep93)*
Jun 76. (d-lp) (36AP 178990) **PANGAEA** (live) – Japan
-Zimbabwe (parts 1-3). *(re-iss. Sep93 on 'Warners')*
In the mid-70's, he suffered from injuries sustained in a car crash. He recuperated, with record co. issuing some recordings/out-takes.
Apr 77. (lp) <34396> **WATER BABIES** (rec.'68-69)
– Water babies / Capricorn / Sweet pea / Two-faced / Dual Mr. Tillman Anthony. *(re-iss. Jul86)*

Nov 77. (lp) *(CBS 82100)* **PARIS FESTIVAL INTERNATIONAL (live)**
– Rifftide / Good bait / Don't blame me / Lady bird / Wah'hoo / Allen's alley / Embraceable you / Ornithology / All the things you are.

Jan 80. (d-lp) *(CBS 88471)* **CIRCLE IN THE ROUND** (recorded 1955-70)
– Two bars hit / Love for sale / Blues No.2 / Circle in the round / Ted's bag / Side car 1 + 2 / Splash / Sanctuary / Guinnevere. *(re-iss. May82)(re-iss. cd Sep93)*

—— DAVIS returned tour/studio with **MARCUS MILLER** – bass / **MIKE STERN** – guitar / **BILL EVANS** – soprano + tenor sax / **AL FOSTER** – drums / **MINO CINELU** – percussion

Jul 81. (7") *<02467>* **FAT TIME. / SHORT**

Jul 81. (lp) *(CBS 84708) <36790>* **THE MAN WITH THE HORN** `53`
– Fat time / Back seat Betty / Short / Aida / The man with the horn / Urasula. *(cd-iss. 1983)(re-iss. cd Sep93)*

Jun 82. (d-lp) *(CBS 88579) <38005>* **WE WANT MILES (live Boston/Tokyo)** `May82`
– Jean Pierre / Back seat Betty / Fast track / My man's gone now / Kix. *(re-iss. cd Sep93)*

—— added **JOHN SCOFIELD** – electric guitar / **TOM BARNEY** – electric bass

May 83. (7") *<03605>* **STAR ON CICELY. / IT GETS BETTER**

May 83. (lp) *(CBS 25395) <38657>* **STAR PEOPLE**
– Come get it / It gets better / Speak / Star people / U'il / Star on Cicely. *(cd-iss. May87) (re-iss. cd Sep93)*

—— **DARYLL 'The Munch' JONES** – electric bass repl. MILLER to SCRITTI POLITTI / **ROBERT IRVING III** – synthesizers, co-composer repl. MIKE STERN + TOM BARNEY / **BRANFORD MARSALIS** shared sax duties with EVANS

Jun 84. (7") *<04564>* **DECOY. / CODE M.D.**

Jun 84. (lp/cd/cd) *(CBS/40/CD 25951)* **DECOY**
– Decoy / Robot 415 / Code M.D. / Freaky Deaky / What it is / That's right / That's what happened. *(re-iss. cd Sep93)*

—— **VINCE WILBURN JR.** – drums + **STEVE THORNTON** – percussion repl. CINELU / **BOB BERG** – soprano sax repl. MARSALIS + EVANS / guest on 2 tracks **JOHN McLAUGHLIN** – guitar

May 85. (7"/12") *(A/TA 4871) <04829>* **TIME AFTER TIME. / KATIA**

Jun 85. (lp/c) *(CBS/40 26447) <40023>* **YOU'RE UNDER ARREST** `88` `May85`
– One phone call – Street scenes / Human nature / Intro: MD1 – Something's on your mind- MD2 / Ms. Morrisine / Katia prelude / Katia / Time after time / You're under arrest medley: Jean Pierre – You're under arrest – Then there were none. *(cd-iss. May87; CD 26447) (re-iss. cd Sep93)*

—— **MILES DAVIS** now with basic line-up of **MILLER, GEORGE DUKE** – multi / **PAULINHO DA COSTA** – synthesizers / plus **JASON MILES** – synth.prog. / **ADAM HOLZMAN** – synth.prog. / **STEVE REID** – percusson / **OMAR HAKIM** – drums, perc / etc.

	Warners	Warners
Oct 86. (lp/c/cd/cd) *(925490-1/-4/-2) <25490>* **TUTU**	`74`	

– Tutu / Tomaas / Portia / Splatch / Backyard ritual / Perfect way / Don't lose your mind / Full Nelson.

Jan 87. (7") *<28501>* **TUTU. / PORTIA**

Mar 87. (7") *<28406>* **FULL NELSON. / TOMAAS**

May 87. (7") *<28309>* **BACKYARD RITUAL. / TOMAAS**

Feb 88. (lp/c/cd/cd) *(925655-1/-4/-2) <25655>* **SIESTA (Soundtrack)**
– Lost in Madrid (pt.1): Siesta – Kitt's kiss / Lost in Madrid (part 2): / Theme for Augustine – Wind – Seduction – Kiss / Submission / Lost in Madrid (pt.3): Conchita – Lament / Lost in Madrid (pt.4): Rat dance – The call / Claire – Lost in Madrid (pt.5): Afterglow / Los Feliz.
In 1988, he appeared on albums by JONI MITCHELL and SCRITTI POLITTI.

—— Next included loads of musicians, including **MILLER, DUKE, CINELU, MILES, FOSTER, DA COSTA, HAKIM, KENNY GARRETT** – soprano sax / **DON ALIAS** – percussion

May 89. (lp/c/cd) *(WX 250/+C)(925873-2) <25873>* **AMANDLA** `49`
– Catembe / Cobra / Big time / Hannibal / Jo Jo / Amandla / Jilli / Mr. Pastorius.

—— due to heroin addiction, MILES lost his battle against AIDS on the 28th September '91. He had already contributed to the 'DINGO' *<7599 26438-2>* soundtrack with MICHAEL LEGRAND.

—— Next was a collaboration with **EAZY MO BEE** – rapper, writer

May 92. (cd/c/lp) *<7599 26938-2/-4/-1>* **DOO-BOP**
– Mystery / The doo-bop song / Chocolate chip / High speed chase / Blow / Sonya / Fantasy / Duke Booty / Mystery (reprise).

– (some) compilations, others, etc. –

on 'CBS' / 'Columbia' records, unless mentioned otherwise

1954. (7"ep) *Capitol; (EAP1 459)* **MILES DAVIS ORCHESTRA**
1954. (7"ep) *Capitol; (EAP2 459)* **MILES DAVIS ORCHESTRA**
1955. (7"ep) *Vogue; (EPV 1075)* **MILES DAVIS SEXTET**
1957. (7"ep) *Vogue; (EPV 1191)* **MILES DAVIS**
1957. (lp) *Capitol; <DT 1974>* **BIRTH OF THE COOL**
– Move / Jeru / Moon dreams / Budo / Deception / Godchild / Boplicity / Rocker / Israel / Rouge. *(UK-iss.Jul78 on 'Capitol'; CAPS 1024) (cd-iss. Apr90+=; CDP 792 862-2) – Darn that dream. (cd-iss. Mar95 on 'Blue Note')*
1950's. (7"ep) *Esquire; (EP 132)* **MILES DAVIS QUARTET**
1950's. (7"ep) *Esquire; (EP 152)* **MILES DAVIS**
1950's. (7"ep) *Esquire; (EP 172)* **MILES DAVIS QUARTET**
1959. (7"ep) *Esquire; (EP 212)* **MILES DAVIS NEW QUARTET**
1959. (7"ep) *Esquire; (EP 222)* **MILES THEME**
1959. (7"ep) *Philips; (BBE 12266)* **MILES DAVIS**
1959. (7"ep) *Fontana; (TFE 17119)* **MILES DAVIS**
1959. (7"ep) *Fontana; (TFE 17195)* **MORE MILES**
1959. (7"ep) *Fontana; (TFE 17197)* **STRAIGHT NO CHASER**
1960. (7"ep) *Fontana; (TFE 17223)* **MILES DAVIS NO.2**
1960. (7"ep) *Fontana; (TFE 17225)* **MILES DAVIS NO>3**
1960. (7"ep) *Fontana; (TFE 17247)* **PORGY AND BESS**
1960. (7"ep) *Esquire; (EP 232)* **BLUE MILES**
1961. (7"ep) *Philips; (BBE 12351)* **MILES DAVIS**
1961. (7"ep) *Philips; (BBE 12418)* **DAVIS CUP**
1960's. (7") *Prestige; <734>* **MORPHEUS. / BLUE ROOM**
1960's. (7") *Prestige; <742>* **DOWN. / WHISPERING**
1960's. (7") *Prestige; <766>* **MY OLD FLAME. / (part 2)**

1960's. (7") *Prestige; <777>* **DIG. / (part 2)**
1960's. (7") *Prestige; <817>* **IT'S ONLY A PAPER MOON. / (part 2)**
1960's. (7") *Prestige; <846>* **BLUING. / (part 2)**
1960's. (7") *Prestige; <868>* **CONCEPTION. / BLUING 3**
1960's. (7") *Prestige; <876>* **OUT OF THE BLUE. / (part 2)**
1960's. (7") *Prestige; <884>* **TASTY PUDDING. / (part 2)**
1960's. (7") *Prestige; <893>* **BLUE HAZE. / (part 2)**
1960's. (7") *Prestige; <898>* **FOUR. / THAT OLD DEVIL THE MOON**
1960's. (7") *Prestige; <902>* **MILES AHEAD. / WHEN LIGHTS ARE LOW**
1960's. (7") *Prestige; <915>* **BUT NOT FOR ME. / (part 2)**
1960's. (7") *Prestige; <103>* **GREEN HAZE. / (part 2)**
1960's. (7") *Prestige; <114>* **A NIGHT IN TUNISIA. / (part 2)**
1960's. (7") *Prestige; <123>* **IF I WERE A BELL. / (part 2)**
1960's. (7") *Prestige; <157>* **WALKIN'. / (part 2)**
1960's. (7") *Prestige; <195>* **WHEN I FALL IN LOVE. / (part 2)**
1960's. (7") *Prestige; <248>* **DIANE. / SURREY WITH THE FRINGE ON TOP**
1960's. (7") *Prestige; <268>* **S'POSIN'. / JUST SQUEEZE ME**
1960's. (7") *Prestige; <321>* **IT'S ONLY A PAPER MOON. / DIG**
1960's. (7") *Prestige; <353>* **SMOOCH. / VALENTINE**
1960's. (7") *Prestige; <395>* **CLEO. / TUNE-UP**
1960's. (7") *Prestige; <413>* **AIREGIN. / 'ROUND MIDNIGHT**
1966. (d-lp) *Transatlantic; (PR 7044)* **COLLECTORS ITEMS** *(re-iss. 1973 on 'Prestige')*
1971. (lp; with LEE KONITZ) *Xtra; (XTRA 5004)* **EZZ THETIC** *<US-iss.Feb86 on 'Fantasy'; 1902119>*
1973. (lp) *(66310)* **THE ESSENTIAL MILES DAVIS**
Aug 74. (lp) **JAZZ AT THE PLAZA (live)**
1976. (d-lp) *(68606)* **LIVE AT THE PLUGGED NICKEL** *(re-iss. Dec82)*
May 76. (lp) *(88138)* **CLASSICS**
1976. (7") *(13-33037)* **ROUND MIDNIGHT. / SOLEA**
1979. (lp) *(88029)* **MILES DAVIS WITH JOHN COLTRANE QUINTET (live)**
Mar 81. (d-lp) *(88514)* **DIRECTIONS**
Feb 83. (d-c) *(40-22146)* **SKETCHES OF SPAIN / IN A SILENT WAY**
May 83. (lp/c) *(CBS/40 21070)* **BLUES AT CHRISTMAS**
Jan 84. (d-lp/d-c) *(CBS 88626)* **HEARD 'ROUND THE WORLD**
Feb 88. (lp/c) *(450 593-2/-4>)* **A PORTRAIT OF MILES DAVIS**
1988. (lp) *(85560)* **FOUR & MORE** *(cd-iss. Apr93 on 'Sony Europe')*
Apr 89. (lp/c/cd) *(461 099-1/-4/-2>)* **BALLADS**
Oct 89. (d-lp/c/cd) *(463 351-1/-4/-2>)* **AURA**
Apr 92. (cd) **MELLOW MILES**
May 93. (d-cd) **COMPLETE CONCERT '64 (live)**
Nov 94. (d-cd) **AT THE FILLMORE**
Nov 94. (d-cd) **IN CONCERT**

– more compilations, etc. –

Jun 76. (lp) *Beppo; (BEP 501)* **AT THE BIRDLAND '51 (live)**
Jun 76. (lp) *Beppo; (BEP 502)* **MILES DAVIS' ALL-STARS & GIL EVANS**
Nov 76. (d-lp) *Vogue; (VKD 5529)* **DAVIS, PARKER & GILLESPIE**
1973. (d-lp) *Prestige; (PR 24012)* **TALLEST TREES**
May 74. (d-lp) *Prestige; (PR 24034)* **WORKIN' AND STEAMIN'** *(re-iss. Oct93, 4xcd)*
Nov 76. (d-lp) *Prestige; (PR 24064)* **GREEN HAZE**
– (lp's:- THE MUSING OF MILES + MILES)
May 79. (d-lp) *Prestige; (PR 24077)* **TUNE UP**
Dec 80. (12xlp-box) *Prestige; (P 012)* **CHRONICLE – THE COMPLETE PRESTIGE RECORDINGS 1951-1956** *(re-iss. Jun92 as 8xcd-box)*
Aug 84. (lp) *Prestige;* **BLUE HAZE** *(cd-iss. Apr93)*
Jul 75. (lp) *Prestige; (PR 7674)* **EARLY MILES**
Nov 76. (lp) *D.J.M.; (DJML 062)* **BIRD AND MILES (with CHARLIE PARKER)**
Jan 91. (cd) *D.J.M.;* **COOKIN' AND RELAXIN'**
May 79. (lp) *Blue Note; (NS 40036)* **SOMETHING ELSE WITH CANNONBALL ADDERLEY**
Jul 82. (lp) *Blue Note; (BLP 1501)* **MILES DAVIS VOLUME 1**
Jul 82. (lp) *Blue Note; (BLP 1502)* **VOLUME 2**
Jun 80. (lp) *Manhattan; (MAN 5022)* **WORLD OF JAZZ**
Jun 80. (lp) *Manhattan; (MAN 5028)* **MILES OF FUN**
1979. (lp) *Joker; <SM 3717>* **MILES DAVIS IN L.A. 1946 (live)**
Apr 81. (lp/c) *Joker; <SJAZZ/+C 2>* **A NIGHT IN TUNISIA (live)**
Apr 81. (lp) *V.G.M.; (VGM 0003)* **MILES AT ST.LOUIS (live with QUINTET 1963)**
Apr 81. (lp) *Jazz Horizons; (BLJ 8003)* **PRE-BIRTH OF THE COOL** (with HIS TUBA BAND 1948)
Apr 81. (lp; with JOHN COLTRANE) *Unique Jazz; <UJ 19>* **LIVE**
Aug 81. (lp) *Kingdom Of Jazz;* **MILES DAVIS & STAN GETZ**
Jul 82. (lp) *Kingdom Of Jazz; <KLJ 20025>* **AT HIS RARE OF ALL RAREST PERFORMANCES VOL.1**
Aug 85. (c) *Deja Vu; (DVMC 2039)* **THE MILES DAVIS COLLECTION** *(cd-iss. Sep87; DVCD 2039)*
Apr 93. (d-cd/d-c) *Deja Vu; ()* **THE GOLD COLLECTION**
May 87. (cd) *J.V.C.; (VDJ 1586)* **ARTISTRY IN JAZZ (GREATEST HITS)**
Jan 89. (cd) *J.V.C.; (VDJ 1605)* **MILES DAVIS & THE MODERN JAZZ GIANTS** *(re-iss. Oct93 on 'Fantasy')*
Sep 87. (lp) *Giants Of Jazz; (LPJT 55)* **1954 – THE MASTERPIECES**
1988. (cd) *Giants Of Jazz; (GOJCD 0221)* **EVOLUTION OF A GENUIS 1945-1954**
Jun 88. (lp/cd) *Black Lion; (BLP/BLCD7 60102)* **BOPPIN' THE BLUES** (rec.Oct'46)

Jun 90. (cd/c/d-lp) *Castle; (CCS CD/MC/LP 243)* **THE COLLECTION** ☐ -

Dec 90. (cd/lp) *Flyright; (EB 418)* **LIVE IN 1958 (live)** ☐ -

Dec 90. (cd) *Regal Jazz; (RJD 514)* **LIVE-NONET 1948 / JAM 1949 (live)** ☐ -

Aug 91. (cd/c/lp) *Magnetic;* **FREE TRADE HALL 1960, VOL.1 & 2** ☐ -

Feb 93. (cd) *O.M.D.;* **LIVE IN EUROPE 1988** ☐ -

Mar 93. (cd) *Original Jazz;* **CONCEPTION** ☐ -

Nov 93. (cd) *Original Jazz; (OJCCD 0432)* **BLUE MOODS** ☐ -

May 93. (cd/c; with FREDDIE HUBBARD) *Royal Collection; (RC 83/82 144)* **SUPER HORNS** ☐ -

Sep 93. (cd) *Natasha;* **WHY DO I LOVE YOU? - RARE BROADCASTS 1947-48** ☐ -

Nov 93. (cd) *Jazz Door;* **MILES IN MONTREUX** ☐ -

Dec 93. (cd) *Sony Europe; (474558-2)* **ESSENTIAL JEAN-PIERRE** ☐ -

—— also QUINCY JONES for release in Aug'93 'LIVE AT MONTREUX'.

Mar 94. (cd) *Le Jazz; (LEJAZZCD 124)* **THE BIRDLAND SESSIONS** ☐ -

May 94. (cd) *J.M.Y.; (JMY 1015-2)* **WHAT I SAY? VOLUME 1** ☐ -

May 94. (cd) *J.M.Y.; (JMY 1016-2)* **WHAT I SAY? VOLUME 2** ☐ -

Aug 94. (cd) *Jazz Roots; (CD 56009)* **MILESTONES 1945-1954** ☐ -

Nov 94. (cd) *Jazz Roots;* **CONCIERTO DE ARANJUEZ (live)** ☐ -

Aug 94. (cd) *Jazz Portrait;* **1954-1955** ☐ -

Aug 94. (cd) *Jazz Portrait;* **1956-1958** ☐ -

Aug 94. (cd) *Jazz Portrait;* **1958-1960** ☐ -

Oct 94. (cd) *Jazz Door; (JD 1242)* **LIVE IN NEW YORK (1957-59 w /JOHN COLTRANE)** ☐ -

Mar 95. (cd) *RTE;* **IN CONCERT (1960)** ☐ -

Jul 95. (cd) *Le Jazz; (LEJAZZCD 45)* **AT THE ROYAL ROOST 1948, AT BIRDLAND 1950/1, 1953** ☐ -

Jul 95. (8xcd-box) *Sony Jazz; (CXK 66955)* **LIVE AT PLUGGED NICKEL 1965** ☐ -

Oct 95. (cd) *Sony Jazz; (481434-2)* **HIGHLIGHTS FROM THE PLUGGED NICKEL** ☐ -

Oct 95. (5xcd-box) *Sony Jazz; (CXK 67397)* **THE COMPLETE COLUMBIA STUDIO SESSIONS (with GIL EVANS)** ☐ -

Oct 95. (d-cd) *Sony Jazz;* **HIGHLIGHTS FROM THE COMPLETE COLUMBIA STUDIO SESSIONS (with GIL EVANS)** ☐ -

Nov 95. (3xcd-box) *Blue Note; (CDOMB 007)* **BIRTH OF THE COOL / VOLUME 1 / VOLUME 3** ☐ -

Dec 95. (cd) *Music De-Luxe; (MSCD 19)* **COOL** ☐ -

Sep 96. (cd/c) *Sony; (SONYTV 17 CD/MC)* **THE VERY BEST OF** 64 ☐

Spencer DAVIS GROUP

Formed: Birmingham, England ... August 1963, DAVIS meeting PETER YORK and the WINWOOD brothers STEVE and MUFF at a local jazz club. It was soon apparent that the veterans (in their early 20's), were being overshadowed by the precocious 15-year old multi-talented STEVE. After a year on the circuit, they signed to 'Fontana' records with the aid of 'Island' owner CHRIS BLACKWELL, who had recommended the act. Their early 45's failed to distinguish them from the R&B pack (having only achieved minor placings) and it was only with the release of JACKIE EDWARDS' 'KEEP ON RUNNING' that the band exploded onto the scene. It topped the chart for one week in January 1966, a year that also saw the rejuvenation of 'THE FIRST LP' (which hit Top 10), a follow-up 45, 'SOMEBODY HELP ME' (another No.1) and STEVE's first self-penned hit, 'WHEN I COME HOME'. A prolific period for the band, they ended the year on a high, having scored with another Top 10 album and their third slice of genius, 'GIMME SOME LOVIN'' (denied pole position by The Four Tops' 'Reach Out I'll Be There'). Still only 17, STEVE's 'Motown'-influenced vocal talent increasingly began to outlive the basic R&B backing the rest of the band were providing. Breaking away from the group, he took a more psychedelic approach with his new outfit, TRAFFIC. SPENCER DAVIS soldiered on with a new line-up, but it was clear the spark had been extinguished and the hits soon dried up. • Other covers: DIMPLES (John Lee Hooker) / EVERY LITTLE BIT HURTS (Brenda Holloway) / etc. • Trivia: Late in 1967, they made a small cameo appearance in the film 'HERE WE GO ROUND THE MULBURRY BUSH'.

Best CD compilation: EIGHT GIGS A WEEK: THE STEVE WINWOOD YEARS (*7)

SPENCER DAVIS (b.17 Jul'42, Swansea, Wales) – guitar, vocals, harmonica (ex-SAINTS) / **STEVE WINWOOD** (b.12 May'48, Birmingham) – vocals, keyboards, guitar / **MUFF WINWOOD** (b.MERVYN, 14 Jun'43) – bass, vocals / **PETER YORK** (b.15 Aug'42, Middlesborough, England) – drums

	Fontana	Fontana
Aug 64. (7") *(TF 471)* **DIMPLES. / SITTIN' AND THINKIN'**	☐	-
Oct 64. (7") *(TF 499) <1960>* **I CAN'T STAND IT. / MIDNIGHT TRAIN**	47	- Mar65
Jan 65. (7") *(TF 530)* **EVERY LITTLE BIT HURTS. / IT HURTS ME SO**	41	-
May 65. (7") *(TF 571)* **STRONG LOVE. / THIS HAMMER**	44	-
Jul 65. (lp) *(TL 5242)* **THEIR FIRST LP (hit-Jan66)**	6	-

– My babe / Dimples / Searchin' / Every little bit hurts / I'm blue (gong gong song) / Sittin' and thinkin' / I can't stand it / Here right now / Jump back / It's gonna work out fine / Midnight train / It hurts me so. *(re-iss. 1968 as 'EVERY LITTLE BIT HURTS' on 'Wing'; WL 1165)*

	Fontana	Atco
Nov 65. (7") *(TF 632) <6400>* **KEEP ON RUNNING. / HIGH TIME BABY**	1	76
Jan 66. (lp) *(TL 5295)* **THE SECOND ALBUM**	2	-

– Look away / Keep on running / This hammer / Georgia on my mind / Please do something / Let me down easy / Strong love / I washed my hands in muddy water / Since I met you baby / You must believe me / Hey darling / Watch your step.

Mar 66. (7") *(TF 679) <6416>* **SOMEBODY HELP ME. / STEVIE'S BLUES**	1	
Aug 66. (7") *(TF 739)* **WHEN I COME HOME. / TRAMPOLINE**	12	☐

Sep 66. (lp) *(TL 5359)* **AUTUMN '66** 4 -
– Together till the end of time / Take this hurt off me / Nobody knows you when you're down and out / Midnight special / When a man loves a woman / When I come home / Mean woman blues / Dust my blues / On the green light / Neighbour, neighbour / High time baby / Somebody help me.

	Fontana	U.A.
Oct 66. (7") *(TF 762) <50108>* **GIMME SOME LOVING. / BLUES IN F**	2	7 Jan67

(above 'A'side was different remix in the States)

Jan 67. (7") *(TF 785) <50144>* **I'M A MAN. / CAN'T GET ENOUGH OF IT**	9	10 Mar67
Mar 67. (lp; mono/stereo) *<UAL3/UAS6 578>* **GIMME SOME LOVIN'**	-	54

– Keep on running / When a man loves a woman / Take this hurt off me / Georgia on my mind / You must believe me / Here right now / When I get home / I'm a man. *(UK-iss 1988 on 'Capitol';)*

Jun 67. (7") *<50162>* **SOMEBODY HELP ME. / ON THE GREEN LIGHT** - 47

—— **EDDIE HARDIN** (b.EDWARD HARDING, 19 Feb'49) – organ, vocals replaced STEVE who joined TRAFFIC and later BLIND FAITH then solo. / **PHIL SAWYER** (b.8 Mar'47) – lead guitar replaced MUFF who became A&R man, / also **CHARLIE McCRACKEN** – bass (guest)

Jul 67. (lp; mono/stereo) *<UAL3/UAS6 589>* **I'M A MAN** - 83
– Dimples / Every little bit hurts / Stevie's blues / On the green light / Searchin' / Midnight train / My babe / Georgia on my mind / I can't get enough of it / I'm a man / I can't stand it / Look away.

Jul 67. (7") *(TF 854) <50202>* **TIME SELLER. / DON'T WANT YOU NO MORE** 30 100

	U.A.	U.A.
Dec 67. (7") *(UP 1203)* **MR. SECOND CLASS. / SANITY INSPECTOR**	35	-
Dec 67. (7") *<50286>* **AFTER TEA. / LOOKING BACK**	-	-
Mar 68. (7") *(UP 2213)* **AFTER TEA. / MOONSHINE**	-	-

Apr 68. (lp; stereo/mono) *(S+/ULP 1192)* **WITH THEIR NEW FACE ON** - -
– With his new face on / Mr. Second class / Alec in transitland / Sanity inspector / Feel your way / Morning sun / Moonshine / Don't want you no more / Time seller / Stop me, I'm fallin'.

—— (Nov68) **DEE MURRAY** – bass / **NIGEL OLSSON** – drums repl. HARDIN & YORK who formed self named duo.

1969. (lp) *<UAS 6691>* **HEAVIES** - -
– Please do something / Waltz for lum umba / I'm blue (gong gong song) / Hey darling / Mean woman blues / Watch your step / Drown in my own tears / Together til' the end of time / Take this hurt off me / Back into my life again.

—— (signed to 'CBS/Columbia' and copies of album 'LETTERS FROM EDITH' surfaced; US title 'FUNKY')

—— Split mid '69. MURRAY and OLSSON joined ELTON JOHN's Band.

1971. (lp; by SPENCER DAVIS & PETER JAMESON) *(UAS 29177)* **IT'S BEEN SO LONG** ☐ ☐
– It's been so long / Crystal river / One hundred years ago / Balkan blues / Brother can you make up your mind / Mountain lick / Jav's tune / King of her / It's too late now.

1972. (lp; by SPENCER DAVIS) *(UAS 29361)* **MOUSETRAP** ☐ ☐
– Rainy season / Listen to the rhythm / What can I be / Tried / Easy rider / Tumbledown tenement row / Sunday walk in the rain / I washed my hands in muddy water / Sailor's lament / Hollywood Joe / In the hills of Tennessee / Ella speed.

1972. (7"; by SPENCER DAVIS) *<50922>* **LISTEN TO THE RHYTHM. / SUNDAY WALK IN THE RAIN** - ☐

1972. (7"; by SPENCER DAVIS) *<50993>* **RAINY SEASON. / TUMBLE-DOWN TENEMENT ROW** - ☐

—— now group re-united w / **HARDIN, YORK, FENWICK + CHARLIE McCRACKEN** – bass

	Vertigo	Vertigo
Mar 73. (7") *(6059 076)* **CATCH YOU ON THE REBOB. / THE EDGE**	☐	-

May 73. (lp) *(6360 088)* **GLUGGO** ☐ ☐
– Catch you on the Moon / Don't it let it bring you down / Alone / Today Gluggo, tomorrow the world / Feeling rude / Legal eagle shuffle / Trouble in mind / Mr.Operator / Tumbledown tenement row.

May 73. (7") *<110>* **DON'T LET IT BRING YOU DOWN. / TODAY GLUGGO, TOMORROW THE WORLD** ☐ -

Jun 73. (7") *(6059 082)* **MR. OPERATOR. / TOUCHING CLOTH** ☐ -

Oct 73. (7") *(6059 087) <112>* **LIVIN' IN A BACK STREET. / SURE NEED A HELPING HAND** ☐ ☐

Jun 74. (lp) *(6360 105)* **LIVIN' IN A BACK STREET** ☐ ☐
– Living in a backstreet / One night / Hanging around / No reason / Fasted thing / On four wheels / Backstreet boys / Another day / Sure need a helping hand / We can give it a try / Let's have a party.

—— SPENCER retired from solo work until 1983.

	Allegience	not iss.
Apr 84. (lp/c) *(ALE/+C 5603)* **CROSSFIRE**	☐	-

– Blood runs hot / Don't want you no more / Love is on a roll / Crossfire / Private number / Just a gigolo / Careless love / A pretty girl is like a melody / When the day is done / Hush-a-bye. *(cd-iss. Dec92 as 'NOW' on 'Kenwest'; SPCD 352)*

May 84. (7"; by SPENCER DAVIS & DUSTY SPRINGFIELD) *(ALES 3)* **PRIVATE NUMBER. / DON'T WANT YOU NO MORE** ☐ -

—— SPENCER became an executive at Island records in the mid 70's. In mid-80's, **SPENCER DAVIS BAND** reformed with others **DON KIRKPATRICK, EDDIE TREE** – guitars / **RICK SERATTE** – keys / **CHARLIE HARRISON** – bass / **BRYAN HITT** – drums (ex-WANG CHUNG)

	In Akustik	not iss.
1988. (cd) *(INAK 8410)* **LIVE TOGETHER**	☐	-

(above recorded 1984) (re-iss. Mar95; same)

1988. (cd) *(INAK 8590)* **24 HOURS – LIVE IN GERMANY** ☐ -
(above recorded 1985) (re-iss. Mar95; same)

– compilations, others, etc. –

1965. (7"ep) *Fontana; (TE 17444)* **SHE PUT THE HURT ON ME**   ☐   –
– She put the hurt on me / I'm getting better / I'll drown in my own tears / Goodbye Stevie.

Aug 65. (7"ep) *Fontana; (TE 17450)* **EVERY LITTLE BIT HURTS**   ☐   –
– Every little bit hurts / It hurts me so / I can't stand it / Midnight train.

Jun 66. (7"ep) *Fontana; (TE 17463)* **SITTIN' AND THINKIN'**   ☐   –
– Sittin' and thinkin' / Jump back / Dimples / Searching.

Mar 68. (lp; mono/stereo) *Island; (ILP/+S 9070)* **THE BEST OF THE
SPENCER DAVIS GROUP FEATURING STEVIE WINWOOD**   ☐   –
(re-iss. Oct86; same) (cd-iss. May88; CID 9070) (re-iss. cd Mar93; IMCD 151)

Mar 68. (lp) *United Artists; <UAS 6641>* **SPENCER DAVIS' GREATEST
HITS**   –   –

1969. (c-ep) *Philips; (MCF 5003)* **THE HITS OF THE SPENCER
DAVIS GROUP**   ☐   –

Aug 76. (7") *Island; (WIP 6318)* **GIMME SOME LOVING. / GIMME
SOME LOVING '76**   ☐   –

May 78. (7"ep) *Island; (IEP 10)* **THE SPENCER DAVIS GROUP**   ☐   –
– Keep on running / Somebody help me / Every little bit hurts / I'm a man.

1985. (cd) *E.M.I.; (CDP 746 598-2)* **THE BEST OF THE SPENCER
DAVIS GROUP**   ☐   –

1986. (lp) *Rhino; <RNLP 70172>* **GOLDEN ARCHIVE SERIES**   ☐   –
Dec 88. (c) *Capitol; (4XLL 9055)* **GIMME SOME LOVIN'**   ☐   –
Mar 91. (cd) *O.N.N. Range; (ONNCD 82)* **SPENCER DAVIS**   ☐   –
May 91. (7") *Island; (IS 487)* **KEEP ON RUNNING. / HIGH TIME
BABY**   ☐   –
(12"+=/cd-s+=) (12IS/CID 487) – Somebody help me / This hammer.

Aug 92. (cd) *Success; (22511CD)* **KEEP ON RUNNING**   ☐   –
May 93. (cd/c) *Royal Collection; (RC 82149)* **KEEP ON RUNNING** ☐   –
Aug 93. (cd) *Pilz; (448215-2)* **I'M A MAN**   ☐   –
Feb 94. (cd) *Javelin; (HADCD 123)* **SPOTLIGHT ON SPENCER DAVIS** ☐   –
Mar 94. (cd-ep) *Pilz; (447523-2)* **I'M A MAN**   ☐   –
– Keep on running / Somebody help me / I'm a man / Gimme some loving / Crossfire.

Apr 94. (cd) *Music De-Luxe; (MSCD 4)* **KEEP ON KEEPING ON**   ☐   –
Jun 94. (cd) *R.P.M.; (RPMCD 127)* **TAKING OUT TIME 1967-69**   ☐   –
Oct 94. (cd) *Charly; (CDCD 1193)* **KEEP ON RUNNING**   ☐   –
Jun 95. (cd) *R.P.M.; (RPMCD 150)* **CATCH YOU ON THE REBOP –
LIVE IN EUROPE 1973**   ☐   –

Mar 96. (d-cd) *Island Chronicles; (CRNCD 5)* **EIGHT GIGS A WEEK –
THE STEVE WINWOOD YEARS**   ☐   –

Jun 97. (cd/c) *Hallmark; (30431-2/-4)* **GIMME SOME LOVIN'**   ☐   –

—— (also look out for STEVE WINWOOD compilations 'KEEP ON RUNNING' & 'THE FINER THINGS', which have a batch of SDG hits.

DAWN OF THE REPLICANTS

Formed: Galashiels, Scotland . . . 1996 by Teeside-raised singer-songwriter, PAUL VICKERS along with guitarist, ROGER SIMIAN, the latter spending the bulk of his student loan on a mail-order debut EP, 'SO FAR SO SPITFIRE' (recorded as The REPLICANTS). Available from early '97, the record's R.E.M.-esque lead track, 'COCAINE ON THE CATWALK', was given airplay by both John Peel and Mark Radcliffe, selling out its initial 500 copies almost immediately. Expanding the line-up with addition of former schoolmates, DONALD KYLE, MIKE SMALL and GRANT PRINGLE, The DAWN OF THE REPLICANTS released a second single, 'HOGWASH FARM' on their 'dumbSULK trigg-er' imprint and after interest from the likes of 'Che', 'Too Pure' and 'Chemikal Underground', they opted to sign on the dotted line for Warner Brothers subsidiary 'eastwest'. Their major label tenure got off to a prolific start with the release of three EP's (namely 'VIOLENT SUNDAYS', 'ALL THAT CHEYENNE CABOODLE' and 'RHINO DAYS' in the latter half of '97, the lead tracks being re-recorded versions of 'COCAINE ON THE CATWALK', 'LISA BOX' and the brand new 'RADARS' respectively. With music press acclaim steadily growing, the Borders lads notched up their first chart entry with the morbidly infectious 'CANDLEFIRE', a song that invoked the ghosts of early 80's Liverpool (i.e. IAN McCULLOCH, JULIAN COPE and The ROOM's DAVE JACKSON). The heavy release schedule continued unabated with the much anticipated Top 75 debut set, 'ONE HEAD, TWO ARMS, TWO LEGS' (1998), a pot-pourri of wilful experimentation and contrasting styles that collected together all of the aforementioned tracks side by side with fresh material such as 'WINDY MILLER' (Trumpton revisited REPLICANTS style), the U2 goes Lo-Fi 'SO SLEEPY' and the lyrically enigmatic (not for the first time) 'SGT GROWLEY'. • **Covered:** BALLAD OF A THIN MAN (Bob Dylan).

Album rating: DAWN OF THE REPLICANTS (*8) / WRONG TOWN, WRONG PLANET, THREE HOURS LATE. (*7)

PAUL VICKERS – vocals, synthesizer / **ROGER SIMIAN** – guitar, keyboards, vocals

	dumbSULK trigg-er	not iss.
Jan 97. (7"ep; as The REPLICANTS) *(DST 7-1)* **SO FAR SO SPITFIRE EP**	–	mail-o
– Cocaine on the catwalk / Digging bear / Lisa box / Bizarre concoction.		

—— added **DONALD KYLE** – bass, guitar / **MIKE SMALL** – guitar, keyboards, vocals / **GRANT PRINGLE** – drums, keyboards, vocals

	eastwest	not iss.
Jun 97. (10") *(SAM 2063)* **HOGWASH FARM. / CHAOS IN AN INKWELL**	☐	–
Aug 97. (d7"ep/cd-ep) *(EW 115/+CD)* **VIOLENT SUNDAYS E.P.**	☐	–
– Cocaine on the catwalk (re-recording) / Non capisco / Only small birds do / Beyond the nest.		
Sep 97. (d7"ep/cd-ep) *(EW 125/+CD)* **ALL THAT CHEYENNE CABOODLE E.P.**	☐	–

– Lisa box (re-recording) / Diggin' bear (re-recording) / Will you ever phone? / Skullcrusher.

Nov 97. (d7"ep/cd-ep) *(EW 134/+CD)* **RHINO RAYS E.P.**   ☐   –
– Radars / Bionic stardust / The wrong turnstile / Seasick odyssey.

Jan 98. (10") *(EW 147 TE/CD1)* **CANDLE FIRE. / SKULLCRUSHER
(David Holmes & Tim Goldsworthy remix)**   52   –
(cd-s+=) (EW 147CD1) – Leaving so soon?
(cd-s) (EW 147CD2) – ('A'side) / Leaving iota / Chesty Morgan.

Feb 98. (cd/c/lp) *(0630 19600-2/-4/-1)* **ONE HEAD, TWO ARMS,
TWO LEGS**   62   –
– Cocaine on the catwalk / Candle fire / Ten sea birds / Lisa box / Return of the board game / Windy Miller / Radars / So sleepy / Let them eat coal / Sgt Growley / Hogwash farm / Sleepy spiders / Float on a raft / Mary Louise / Fatal firework.

Mar 98. (7"ep/cd-ep) *(EW 157/+CD)* **HOGWASH FARM (THE DIESEL
HANDS E.P.)**   65   –
– Hogwash farm (re-built) / Night train to Lichtenstein / The duchess of Surin / Crow valley.

Jun 98. (12"ep/cd-ep) *(EW 166 T/CD)* **I SMELL VOODOO E.P.**   ☐   –
– Mary Louise / Ballad of a thin man / Myrrh tingle / Dual converter.

Aug 98. (7"/cd-s) *(NING 59/+CD)* **BORN IN BASKETS. / Inner
Sleeve: Come Alive**   ☐   –
(above 'GOING DOWN THE TUBES WITH . . . single was on 'Fierce Panda')

Apr 99. (cd/c/lp) *(3984 26474-2/-4/-1)* **WRONG TOWN, WRONG
PLANET, THREE HOURS LATE.**   ☐   –
– Gasoline vine / Love is a curse / Rule the roost / Sub erotic fields / Zulu kites / Wheelie bin drive / Cabin fever / Jack Fanny's gym / Science fiction freak / Big hefty hounds / The soil idea / Tear dog eyes / Get a bright flame / Howlin' in the dark / Hand relief / Fearless vampire hunters.

Apr 99. (12"ep/cd-ep) *(EW 197 T/CD1)* **RULE THE ROOST. / ON
THE RADIO / RUNNING INTO TROUBLE**   –
(cd-s) (EW 197CD2) – ('A'side) / Chaos in an inkwell (original dumb-SULK version) / Sgt Growley (Peel session version).

Jul 99. (7") *(EW 204)* **SCIENCE FICTION FREAK. / YELLOW BEATLE** ☐   –
(cd-s+=) (EW 204CD) – Buffalo ballet.

DAYS OF THE NEW

Formed: Louisville, Kentucky, USA . . . 1996 by TRAVIS MEEKS who sacked his original band before recruiting new members TODD WHITENER, JESSE VEST and MATT TAUL. Described as the new ALICE IN CHAINS or PEARL JAM with the DOORS thrown in for good measure, they carried on the bleak and outdated grunge tradition. Almost immediately signed to Geffen's new 'Outpost' imprint, MEEKS and Co delivered their eponymous set in 1997. Climbing into the US Top 60, the brooding outfit quickly became part of Grunge Mk.II alongside CREED, etc. Two years on, album No.2 fared even better, although it stayed only one week in the Top 40.

Album rating: DAYS OF THE NEW (*7) / DAYS OF THE NEW 2 (*5)

TRAVIS MEEKS – vocals, guitar / **TODD WHITENER** – guitar / **JESSE VEST** – bass / **MATT TAUL** – drums

	Outpost	Outpost
Feb 98. (7"/c-s) *(OPR S/MC 22299)* **TOUCH, PEEL & STAND. / GOT TO BE YOU**	☐	☐
(cd-s+=) (OPRCD 22299) – Independent slave.		
Mar 98. (cd) *<(OPD 30004)>* **DAYS OF THE NEW**	☐	54 Oct97
– Shelf in the room / Touch, peel & stand / Face of the earth / Solitude / The down town / What's left for me? / Freak / Now / Whimsical / Where I stand / How do I know you? / Cling.		
Jan 99. (cd-s) *<22352>* **THE DOWN TOWN / ('A'version)**	–	–
Aug 99. (cd) *<OPD 30037>* **DAYS OF THE NEW 2**	–	40
– Flight response / Real / Enemy / Weapon and the wounded / Skeleton key / Take me back then / Bring yourself / I think / Longfellow / Phobics of tragedy / Not the same / Provider / Last one.		

John DEACON (see under ⇒ QUEEN)

DEACON BLUE

Formed: Glasgow, Scotland . . . 1985 by former remedial teacher, RICKY ROSS, who recruited JAMES PRIME, GRAEME KELLING, EWAN VERNAL and DOUGLAS VIPOND: by sheer accident/inspiration, ROSS invited girlfriend, LORRAINE to sing/accompany his vocals and she soon became the sixth member. Subsequently signed to 'C.B.S.' by their manager, MUFF WINWOOD (ex-SPENCER DAVIS GROUP), the band released their debut single, 'DIGNITY', in Spring '87. A tale of working class pride, the song reflected DEACON BLUE's inherent politicism (although they were hardly The REDSKINS) while the slightly jazzy pop/rock dynamics of the music came as little surprise bearing in mind the group took their name from a STEELY DAN song. The debut album, 'RAINTOWN', followed a few months later, a promising set of soulful Celtic pop which suggested a more solid, less flighty PREFAB SPROUT. The melancholy ebb and flow of 'CHOCOLATE GIRL' was DEACON BLUE at their laidback best, the track a minor hit in summer '88 following similar low-key chart success for a re-issued 'DIGNITY' and 'WHEN WILL YOU (MAKE MY TELEPHONE RING)'. It was the anthemic 'REAL GONE KID', however, which took the band from the fringes of the Scottish scene into the hearts of the mainstream pop market, the song's infectious keyboard hook and girly harmonies seeing it reach the Top 10 in October '88. Trailed by the Top 20 success of 'WAGES DAY', a second album, 'WHEN THE WORLD KNOWS YOUR NAME', topped the UK album charts the following Spring; perhaps they'd been afflicted by SIMPLE MINDS syndrome, as the cool subtlety which had characterised their first release was replaced with a heavy dose of stadium-friendly bombast. Presumably as a reaction to such critical rumblings, DEACON BLUE opted to release an EP of BACHARACH & DAVID covers in summer '90, its Top 5 success closely followed by a B-sides/rarities affair, 'OOH LAS VEGAS' (1990). A follow-up proper, 'FELLOW HOODLUMS' (1991), was another major success although it failed to convince their detractors, and roping in dance bod production duo, Paul Oakenfold/Steve Osbourne, for 'WHATEVER YOU SAY, SAY NOTHING' (1993), smacked of desperation. A split finally came the following year, DEACON BLUE bowing out with a No.1 greatest hits set, and fittingly, with a third-time-lucky success for the superior 'DIGNITY'. While VIPOND went on to be a presenter on STV, ROSS worked with ex-STEELY DAN sessioner, JEFF 'SKUNK' BAXTER amongst others on a debut solo set, 'WHAT YOU ARE' (1996) – (ROSS also played 'T In The Park' that year). • **Songwriters:** All written by ROSS, except covers ANGELIOU (Van Morrison) / TRAMPOLENE (Julian Cope) / I'M DOWN (Beatles).

Album rating: RAINTOWN (*7) / WHEN THE WORLD KNOWS YOUR NAME (*7) / OOH LAS VEGAS collection (*6) / FELLOW HOODLUMS (*5) / WHATVER YOU SAY, SAY NOTHING (*5) / OUR TOWN – THE GREATEST HITS compilation (*8) / WALKING BACK HOME (*4) / Ricky Ross: WHAT YOU ARE (*5)

RICKY ROSS (b.22 Dec'57, Dundee) – vocals / **JAMES PRIME** (b. 3 Nov'60, Kilmarnock) – keyboards (ex-ALTERED IMAGES) / **GRAEME KELLING** (b. 4 Apr'57, Paisley) – guitar / **EWAN VERNAL** (b.27 Feb'64, Glasgow) – bass, keyboard bass / **DOUGLAS VIPOND** (b.15 Oct'66, Johnstone) – drums, percussion / **LORRAINE McINTOSH** (b.13 May'64, Glasgow) – vocals

		C.B.S.	Columbia
Mar 87.	(7") (DEAC 1) <07755> **DIGNITY. / RICHES** (with free c-s+=) – (excerpts 'RAINTOWN' lp) (12"+=) (DEAC T1) – Ribbons and bows.	☐	☐
May 87.	(lp/c/cd) (450549-1/-4/-2) **RAINTOWN** – Born in a storm / Raintown / Ragman / He looks like Spencer Tracy now / Loaded / When will you (make my telephone ring) / Chocolate girl / Dignity / The very thing / Love's great fears / Town to be blamed. (re-dist.Feb88; same); hit UK No.14) (re-packaged Aug88 free with above lp+c) **RICHES** (XPR 1361) – Which side are you on / King of the western world * / Riches * / Angeliou / Just like boys / Raintown / Church / Suffering / Shifting sand / Ribbons and bows / Dignity. (cd+= *)	☐	☐
Jun 87.	(7") (DEAC 2) **LOADED. / LONG DISTANCE FROM ACROSS THE ROAD** (c-s+=/ext.12"+=) (DEAC C/T 2) – Which side of the world are you on / Kings of the western world.	☐	-
Aug 87.	(7") (DEAC 3) **WHEN WILL YOU (MAKE MY TELEPHONE RING). / CHURCH** (12"+=) (DEAC T3) – A town to be blamed (live) / Angeliou (live).	☐	-
Jan 88.	(7") (DEAC 4) **DIGNITY. / SUFFERING** (10"+=) (DEAC Q4) – Shifting sand. (cd-s++=) (CDDEAC 4) – Just like boys. (7"ep+=) (DEAC EP4) – Ronnie Spector / Raintown (piano). (ext.12"+=) (DEAC T4) – Ronnie Spector / Just like boys.	31	-
Mar 88.	(7"/7"box) (DEAC 5) **WHEN WILL YOU (MAKE MY TELEPHONE RING). / THAT BRILLIANT FEELING** (12"+=/cd-s+=/pic-cd-s+=) (DEACT/CDDEAC/CPDEAC 5) – Punch and Judy man / Disneyworld.	34	-
Apr 88.	(7") <07954> **WHEN WILL YOU (MAKE MY TELEPHONE RING). / TOWN TO BE BLAMED**	-	☐
Jul 88.	(7") (DEAC 6) **CHOCOLATE GIRL. / S.H.A.R.O.N.** (12"+=) (DEAC T6) – Love's great fears (live) / Dignity (live). (7"ep+=/cd-s+=) (DEACEP/CDDEAC 6) – The very thing / Love's great fears.	43	-
Oct 88.	(7") (DEAC 7) <068944> **REAL GONE KID. / LITTLE LINCOLN** (12"+=/12"w-poster+=) (DEAC/+Q T7) – ('A'extended). (7"ep+=/cd-s+=) (DEACEP/CDDEAC 7) – Born again / It's not funny anymore.	8	-
Feb 89.	(7"/s7") (DEAC/+Q 8) **WAGES DAY. / TAKE ME TO THE PLACE** (12"+=) (DEAC T8) – ('A'extended). (7"ep+=/cd-s+=) (DEACEP/CDDEAC 8) – Take the saints away / Trampolene.	18	-
Apr 89.	(lp/c/cd) (463321-1/-4/-2) **WHEN THE WORLD KNOWS YOUR NAME** – Queen of the New Year / Wages day / Real gone kid / Love and regret / Circus lights / This changing light / Fergus sings the blues / Sad loved girl / The world is hit by lightning / Silhouette / One hundred things / Your constant heart / Orphans.	1	☐
May 89.	(7"/7"box) (DEAC/+B 9) **FERGUS SINGS THE BLUES. / LONG WINDOW TO LOVE** (12"+=/12"g-f+=) (DEAC/+G T9) – ('A'extended). (ext.c-ep+=) (DEAC C9) – London A to Z. (10"+=/cd-ep+=) (DEAC QT/CD DEAC 9) – London A to Z / Back here in Beano land.	14	-
Sep 89.	(7"/c-s) (DEAC/+M 10) **LOVE AND REGRET. / DOWN IN THE FLOOD** (cd-s+=) (CDDEAC 10) – Undeveloped heart / ('A'extended). (ext.12"+=) (DEAC T10) – Undeveloped heart. (10"/cd-s+=) (DEAC QT/CD DEAC 10) – ('A'live) / Spanish moon – Down in the flood (live) / Dark end of the street (live) / When will you (make my telephone ring) (live).	28	-
Dec 89.	(7"/c-s) (DEAC/+M 11) **QUEEN OF THE NEW YEAR. / MY AMERICA** (12"+=) (DEACT 11) – ('A'extended) / Circus lights (acoustic). (7"ep+=/cd-ep+=) (DEAC EP/CD DEAC 11) – Sad loved girl (extended) / Las Vegas. (c-s/12") (DEAC QM/DEAC QT 11) – ('A'live) / Chocolate girl (live) / Undeveloped heart (live) / A town to be blamed (live).	21	-
Aug 90.	(7"ep/12"ep/cd-ep) (DEAC/+T/CD 12) **FOUR BACHARACH AND DAVID SONGS** – I'll never fall in love again / The look of love / Message to Michael / Are you there (with another girl).	2	-
Sep 90.	(d-cd/c/d-lp) (467 242-2/-4/-1) **OOH LAS VEGAS** (B-sides, sessions)	3	☐

– Disneyworld / Ronnie Spector / My America / S.H.A.R.O.N. / Undeveloped heart / Souvenirs / Born again / Down in the flood / Back here in Beanoland / Love you say / Let your hearts be troubled// Gentle teardrops / Little Lincoln / That country / Is it cold beneath the hill? / Circus lights / Trampolene / Las Vegas / Killing the blues / Long window to love / Christine / Take me to the place / Don't let the teardrops start.

		Columbia	Columbia
May 91.	(7"/-s) (656 893-7/-4) **YOUR SWAYING ARMS. / FOURTEEN YEARS** (cd-s+=) (656 893-2) – Faifley. (12"++=) (656 893-6) – ('A'extended). (10") (656 893-0) – ('A'-12"alternative mix) / ('A'-Drumapella mix) / ('A'-7"mix) / ('A'-dub mix).	23	-
Jun 91.	(cd/c/lp) (468 550-2/-4/-1) **FELLOW HOODLUMS** – James Joyce soles / Fellow hoodlums / Your swaying arms / Cover from the sky / The day that Jackie jumped the jail / The wildness / A brighter star than you will shine / Twist and shout / Closing time / Goodnight Jamsie / I will see you tomorrow / One day I'll go walking.	2	-
Jul 91.	(7"/-s) (657 302-7/-4) **TWIST & SHOUT. / GOOD** (12"+=) (657 302-6) – ('A'extended) / I'm down. (cd-s+=) (657 302-2) – Golden bells.	10	-
Oct 91.	(7"/-s) (657 502-7/-4) **CLOSING TIME. / I WAS LIKE THAT** (cd-s+=) (657 502-2) – Into the good night. (12"++=) (657 502-6) – Friends of Billy the bear.	42	-
Dec 91.	(7"/-s) (657 673-7/-4) **COVER FROM THE SKY. / WHAT DO YOU WANT THE GIRL TO DO / CHRISTMAS (BABY PLEASE COME HOME)** (12"+=) (657 673-6) – Real gone kid / Loaded / One hundred things. (cd-s+=) (657 673-2) – Wild mountain thyme / Silhouette / I'll never fall in love again.	31	-

		Columbia	Sony
Nov 92.	(7"/-s) (658 786-7/-4) **YOUR TOWN. / ALMOST BEAUTIFUL** (cd-s+=) (658 786-2) – I've been making such a fool. (12") (658 786-6) – ('A'-Perfecto mix) / ('A'extended).	14	-
Feb 93.	(7"/-s) (658 973-2/-4) **WILL WE BE LOVERS. / SLEEPER** (cd-s+=) (658 973-2) – Paint it red. (12") (658 973-6) – ('A'side) / (4 other A-mixes).	31	-
Mar 93.	(cd/c/lp) (473 527-2/-4/-1) **WHATEVER YOU SAY, SAY NOTHING** – Your town / Only tender love / Peace and jobs and freedom / Hang your head / Bethlehem's gate / Last night I Dreamed of Henry Thomas / Will we be lovers / Fall so freely down / Cut lip / All over the world.	4	-
Apr 93.	(7"/-s) (659 184-7/-4) **ONLY TENDER LOVE. / RICHES** (cd-s+=) (659 184-2) – Which side are you on? / Shifting sand. (12") (659 184-6) – ('A'side) / Pimp talking / Cracks you up. (cd-s) (659 184-5) – (above / Your town (Perfecto mix).	22	-
Jul 93.	(c-ep/cd-ep) (659 460-4/-2) **HANG YOUR HEAD EP** – Hang your head – freedom train (live) / Here on the wind / Indigo sky. (cd-ep) (659 460-5) – (1st track) / Ribbons & bows / Just like boys / Church.	21	-
Mar 94.	(7"/-s) (660 222-7/-4) **I WAS RIGHT AND YOU WERE WRONG. / MEXICAN RAIN** (cd-s+=) (660 222-2) – Goin' back / Wages day. (cd-s) (660 222-5) – ('A'extended) / Kings of the western world / Suffering / Raintown (piano version).	32	-
Apr 94.	(cd/c/d-lp) (476 642-2/-4/-1) **OUR TOWN – THE GREATEST HITS** (compilation) – Dignity / Wages day / Real gone kid / Your swaying arms / Fergus sings the blues / I was right and you were wrong / Chocolate girl / I'll never fall in love again / When will you (make my telephone ring) / Twist and shout / Your town / Queen of the New Year / Only tender love / Cover from the sky / Love and regrets / Will we be lovers / Loaded / Bound to love / Still in the mood. (d-lp+=) – Beautiful stranger.	1	
May 94.	(7"/-s) (6604485-7/-4) **DIGNITY. / BEAUTIFUL STRANGER** (cd-s+=) (660448-2) – Waves of sorrow / Bethlehem's gate. (cd-s) (660448-5) – ('A'side) / Fergus sings the blues (live) / Loaded (live) / Chocolate girl (live).	20	-

—— Disbanded after above release, as it looks certain ROSS will go solo. VIPOND has already secured a regular spot on a Scottish TV programme.

RICKY ROSS

—— - vocals, guitar, piano; with **JEFF 'Skunk' BAXTER** – guitars / **MARK HARRIS** – bass / **SCOTT CRAGO** – drums / + other guests

		Columbia	Sony
May 96.	(c-s/cd-s) (663 135-4/-2) **RADIO ON / DARK WEATHER / JOE / MY FRIEND TONIGHT** (cd-s) (663 135-5) – ('A'side) / Death work song / Never always / Always alone.	35	-
Jun 96.	(cd/c) (483998-2/-4) **WHAT YOU ARE** – Good evening Philadelphia / Icarus / Cold Easter / What you are / Radio on / When sinners fall / Jack Singer / The lovers / Wake up and dream / Rosie Gordon lies so still / Promise you rain / Love isn't hard it's strong.	36	-
Jul 96.	(c-s) (663 533-4) **GOOD EVENING PHILADELPHIA / ('A'live)** (cd-s) (663 533-5) – ('A'side) / Radio on (live) / Icarus (live) / Rosie Gordon lies so still (demo). (cd-s) (663 533-2) – ('A'side) / In the pines / The river is wide / Shake some action.	58	-

		Internazionalmknown	
Mar 98.	(cd-ep) (INTER 002) **THE UNDEVELOPED HEART EP** – The undeveloped heart ('98 remix) / Ghost Wake up and dream / Passing through / Only love remains.	☐	-

DEACON BLUE

—— re-formed

Oct 99.	(cd/c) (496380-2/-4) **WALKING BACK HOME**	39	☐

DEAD BOYS (dig out; Great Alt & Indie . . .)

DEAD CAN DANCE

Formed: Melbourne, Australia . . . 1981 by multi-instrumentalist, BRENDAN PERRY and vocalist, LISA GERRARD, both of Anglo-Irish parentage. After initially immersing himself in the punk scene, PERRY turned became increasingly intrigued by the possibilities offered by electronic music, subsequently hooking up with GERRARD and two other early members, PAUL ERIKSON and SIMON MONROE. With a solitary homeland recording (very limited for 'Fast Forward' cassette mag) to their name, PERRY and GERRARD decided to take DEAD CAN DANCE to London where they fitted in perfectly among the avant-garde hopefuls at up and coming indie label, '4 a.d.'. At pains to point out that their name symbolised the energy inherent in apparently lifeless matter rather than the goth connotations many assumed, DEAD CAN DANCE were soon mesmerising critics and fans alike with their otherworldly synthesis of classical, ethnic and electronic music. An eponymous debut album emerged in 1984 and although its noisy dissonance only hinted at the sculpted aesthetics to come, highlights included 'A PASSAGE IN TIME', 'THE TRIAL' and 'THE FATAL IMPACT'. However, with a costly 15-piece ensemble in tow, they only selected a few venues for concerts and never toured consistently. 1985's 'SPLEEN AND IDEAL' was a more atmospheric, darkly intoxicating affair, introducing more varied instrumental textures and the wailing Middle Eastern, OFRA HAZA-style vocals of GERRARD on such compulsive tracks as 'THE CARDINAL SIN', 'MESMERISM' and every monk's favourite, 'DE PROFUNDIS (OUT OF THE DEPTHS OF SORROW)'. 'WITHIN THE REALM OF A DYING SUN' (1987) moved towards classical territory with a cast of violin, viola, etc, while 'SERPENT'S EGG' (1988) tackled medieval folk styles of Eastern Europe. PERRY and GERRARD moved even further into the past (or rather brought the past into the future) with their exploration of Renaissance era music – both spiritual and secular – on 1990's 'AION'. The early 90's found PERRY and GERRARD working on a variety of side projects including scoring music for a production of 'Oedipus Rex' and the soundtrack to the movie, 'Baraka'. DEAD CAN DANCE briefly emerged from the realm of cult obscurity and into the Top 50 (also hovered under the US Top 100) in 1993 with their seventh album, 'INTO THE LABYRINTH'. LISA went on to release a few solo outings, one under the pseudonym of ELIJAH'S MANTLE, while DEAD CAN DANCE managed to capture the mystical allure of their studio work on live set, 'TOWARD THE WITHIN' (1994). With 1995's 'SPIRITCHASER', DEAD CAN DANCE nearly cracked the UK Top 40 while making the US Top 75, a mark of burgeoning popular appeal for a band who were already almost universally respected among fellow artists across the musical spectrum. Of late, DEAD CAN DANCE have been keeping uncharacteristically quiet, although LISA GERRARD (who'd debuted solo in 1995 with 'THE MIRROR POOL') released a collaborative set with PETER BOURKE (of SOMA) entitled 'DUALITY' (1998). Towards the end of the decade and with DCD now defunct, it would be BRENDAN's turn to go single-handed. 'EYE OF THE HUNTER' was a marked shift from his earlier goth-meets-baroque style rock in that he chose to virtually mimic his idols, SCOTT WALKER ('ARCHANGEL' & 'SATURDAY'S CHILD) and TIM BUCKLEY ('I MUST HAVE BEEN BLIND' – didn't he do this for '4ad' conglomerate THIS MORTAL COIL). However, the seriousness of his intentions came across quite well, although the world of opera might be getting ready for a new recruit – perhaps not!
• **Songwriters:** GERRARD / PERRY (some w/ others and some trad folk samples). • **Trivia:** They also can be heard on '4 a.d.' amalgam THIS MORTAL COIL and also featured two tracks on various lp, 'Lonely As An Eyesore'.

Album rating: DEAD CAN DANCE (*7) / SPLEEN AND IDEAL (*6) / WITHIN THE REALM OF A DYING SUN (*8) / THE SERPENT'S EGG (*7) / AION (*8) / A PASSAGE IN TIME compilation (*8) / INTO THE LABYRINTH (*7) / TOWARD THE WITHIN (*6) / SPIRITCHASER (*6) / Lisa Gerrard: THE MIRROR POOL (*6) / DUALITY with Peter Bourke (*6) / Brendan Perry: EYE OF THE HUNTER (*6)

BRENDAN PERRY – multi-instrumentalist, vocals / **LISA GERRARD** – vocals, percussion / **PETER ULRICH** – percussion, drums, tapes with **JAMES PINKER** – timpani, mixer / **SIMON RODGER** – trombone; plus **MARTIN McCARRICK + GUY FERGUSON** – cello / **CAROLYN LOSTIN** – violin / **RICHARD AVISON** – trombone / **TONY AYERS** – timpani / **ANDREW NUTTER** – soprano vox

		4 a.d.	Rough Trade
Feb 84.	(lp) *(CAD 404)* **DEAD CAN DANCE**		-

– A passage in time / Threshold / The trial / Frontier / Ocean / Fortune / East of Eden / The fatal impact / Wild in the woods / Musical eternal. *(cd-iss. Feb87; CAD 404CD)* – (includes below EP). *<US-iss.1994 on '4 a.d.-Reprise' cd,c; 45546>*

Sep 84.	(12"ep) *(BAD 408)* **THE GARDEN OF ARCANE DELIGHTS**		-

– Carnival of light / The arcane / Flowers of the sea / In power we entrust the love advocated.

Nov 85.	(lp/c)(cd) *(CAD/+C 512)(CAD 512CD)* **SPLEEN AND IDEAL**		-

– De profundis (out of the depths of sorrow) / Ascension / Circumradiant dawn / The cardinal sin / Mesmerism / Enigma of the absolute / Advent / Avatar / Indoctrination. *(cd+=)* – This tide / A design for living. *<US-iss.1994 on '4 a.d.-Reprise' cd,c; 45547>*

now a basic duo of **BRENDAN + LISA** when ULRICH departed (SIMON + JAMES formed HEAVENLY BODIES). Retained **FERGUSON + AVISON** and recruited **ALISON HARLING + EMLYN SINGLETON** – violin / **PIERO GASPARINI** – viola / **TONY GAMMAGE + MARK GERRARD** (bother) – trumpet / **RUTH WATSON** – oboe, bass trombone / **JOHN + PETER SINGLETON** – trombone / **ANDREW CAXTON** – tuba, bass trombone

Jul 87.	(lp/c)(cd) *(CAD/+C 705)(CAD 705CD)* **WITHIN THE REALM OF A DYING SUN**		-

– Dawn of the Iconoclast / In the wake of adversity / New age / Summoning of the muse / Anywhere out of the world / Cantara / Windfall / Xavier / Persephone (the gathering of flowers). *<US-iss.1994 on '4 a.d.-Reprise' cd,c; 45577>*

LISA + BRENDAN brought in **DAVID NAVARRO SUST** (retained **ALISON + TONY**), new **REBECCA JACKSON** – violin / **SARAH BUCKLEY + ANDREW BEESLEY** – violas

Oct 88.	(lp/c)(cd) *(CAD/+C 808)(CAD 808CD)* **THE SERPENT'S EGG**		-

– The host of Seraphim / Orbis de Ignis / Severance / Chant of the Paladin / The writing on my father's hand / Echolalia / In the kingdom of the blind, the one-eyed are kings / Song of Sophia / Mother tongue / Ullyses. *<US-ss.1994 on '4 a.d.-Reprise' cd,c; 45576>*

Jul 90.	(cd)(lp/c) *(CAD 0007CD)(CAD/+C 0007)* **AION**		-

– The arrival and the reunion / Saltarello / Mephisto / The song of the Sibyl / Fortune presents gifts not according to the book / As the bell rings the maypole spins / The end of the words / Black sun / Wilderness / The promised womb / The garden of Zephirus / Radharc. *<US-iss.1994 on '4 a.d.-Reprise' cd,c; 45575>*

Sep 93.	(cd)(c)(d-lp) *(CAD 3013CD)(CADC 3013)(DAD 3013) <45384>*		
	INTO THE LABYRINTH	47	

– Yulunga (spirit dance) / The ubiquitous Mr. Lovegrove / The wind that shakes the barley / The carnival is over / Ariadne / Saldek / Towards the within / Tell me about the forest (you once called home) / The spider's Stratagem / Emmeleia / How fortunate the man with none. *(d-lp+=)* – Bird / Spirit.

Oct 94.	(cd)(d-lp/c) *(DAD 4015CD)(DAD/+C 4015) <45769>* **TOWARD**		
	THE WITHIN		

– Rakim / Persian love song / Desert song / Yulunga (spirit dance) / Piece for solo flute / The wind that shakes the barley / I am stretched on your grave / I can see now / American dreaming / Cantara / Oman / Song of the Sibyl / Tristan / Sanveen / Don't fade away.

Jun 96.	(c/cd)(d-lp) *(CAD 6008/+CD)(DAD 6008) <46230>*		
	SPIRITCHASER	43	75

– Nierika / Song of the stars / Indus / Song of the dispossessed / Dedicaci outr / The snake and the Moon / Song of the Nile / Devorzhum.

– compilations, etc. –

Oct 91.	(cd)(c) *4 a.d.; (CAD 1010CD)(CADC 1010)* / Rykodisc; *<RCD2/RACS 0215>* **A PASSAGE IN TIME** (part compilation)		

– Salterello / Song of Sophia / Ullyses / Cantara / The garden of Zephirus / Enigma of the absolute / Wilderness / The host of Seraphim / Anywhere out of the world / The writing on my father's hand / Severance / The song of the Sibyl (traditional version; Catalan 16th Century) / Fortune presents gifts not according to the book / In the kingdom of the blind the one-eyed are kings / Bird / Spirit.

Dec 91.	(cd) *Emperion; (IMP 008)* **THE HIDDEN TREASURES** (out-takes, live, rare)		-

– Awakening / Reached from above / In power we entrust the love advocated / To the shore / Alone / Pray for dawn / Lartomento / The night we were lost / Lyndra / Isabella / Tune for Sheba / Cyndrill / The serpent's army / They don't even cry / Eyeless in Gaza / The endless longing of sea doves.

LISA GERRARD

with The VICTORIAN PHILHARMONIC ORCHESTRA. She had worked on the scores for 'Oedipus Rex' and 'Baraku', while sidelining with ELIJAH'S MANTLE.

Aug 95.	(cd)(c) *(CAD 5009CD)(CADC 5009) <45916>* **THE MIRROR POOL**		

– Violina: The last embrace / La Bas: Song of the drowned / Persian love song: The silver gun / Sanvean: I am your shadow / The rite / Ajhon / Glorafin / Majhnavea's music box / Largo / Werd / Laurelei / Celon / Ventelas / Swans / Nilleshna / Gloradin. *(cd re-iss. Jul98; GAD 5009CD)*

next a collaboration with **PETER BOURKE** (of SOMA)

Apr 98.	(cd; by LISA GERRARD & PETER BOURKE) *(CAD 8004CD) <46854>* **DUALITY**		

– Shadow magnet / Tempest / Forest veil / The comforter / The unfolding / Pilgrimage of lost children / The human game / The circulation of shadows / Sacrifice / Nadir (synchronicity).

BRENDAN PERRY

with various musicians

Oct 99.	(lp/cd) *(CAD 9015/+CD)* **EYE OF THE TIGER**		

– Saturday's child / Voyage of bran / Medusa / Sloth / I must have been blind / The captive heart / Death will be my bride / Archangel.

DEAD KENNEDYS

Formed: San Francisco, California, USA . . . early 1978 by JELLO BIAFRA and EAST BAY RAY, who recruited KLAUS FLOURIDE, TED and briefly, the mysterious 6025. Inspired by British punk rock, BIAFRA formed The DEAD KENNEDYS primarily as a vehicle for his raging, razor-sharp satire of America and everything it stood for. Public enemy #1 from the off, major labels steered well clear of the band, BIAFRA and Co. subsequently forming their own label, the legendary 'Alternative Tentacles', releasing 'CALIFORNIA UBER ALLES' as their debut 45 in late '79. A scathing critique of California governor, Jerry Brown, the record introduced the singer's near-hysterical vocal undulations set against a pulverising punk/hardcore musical backdrop. Released on the independent 'Fast' imprint in Britain, the record's initial batch of copies sold like proverbial hotcakes. The 1980 follow-up, 'HOLIDAY IN CAMBODIA' (released on Miles Copeland's 'Faulty' label; 'Cherry Red' in the UK) remains The DEAD KENNEDYS' most viciously realised moment, a dark, twisting diatribe on American middle-class liberal trendies. Later in the year, the group kept up their aural assault with a debut album, 'FRESH FRUIT FOR ROTTING VEGETABLES', an unexpected Top 40 entry in the seemingly "Punk Is Dead" Britain, which contained the aforesaid 45's plus perennial favourites, 'LET'S LYNCH THE LANDLORD', 'DRUG ME' and the forthcoming UK hit, 'KILL THE POOR'. The record also offered a glimpse of BIAFRA's reassuringly twisted sense of humour in such surreal cuts as 'STEALING PEOPLE'S MAIL' and 'VIVA LAS VEGAS' (the latter was a hit for Elvis!). In 1981, drummer D.H. PELIGRO replaced TED, making his debut on the bluntly-titled 'TOO DRUNK TO FUCK', the only UK Top 40 charting single in musical history (up to that point!) to utilise the "f***" word. Once again mocking the inherent hypocrisy of corporate America, The DEAD KENNEDYS released a frenetic 10" mini-set, 'IN GOD WE TRUST INC.' (1981), highlights being the self-explanatory 'NAZI PUNKS FUCK OFF' (a US-only single) and a deadpan version of 'RAWHIDE'. The band then took a brief hiatus, busying themselves with an 'Alternative Tentacles' compilation of promising unsigned American bands, entitled 'Let Them Eat Jellybeans'. That same year (1982), the group released their second album proper, 'PLASTIC SURGERY DISASTERS'; issued on 'Statik' in the UK, it featured the singles 'BLEED FOR ME' and 'HALLOWEEN'. Spending the ensuing few years touring, the band resurfaced in 1985 with 'FRANKENCHRIST', an album that finally saw BIAFRA's upstanding enemies closing in (ie. the PMRC, the US government, etc) due to the album's free "penis landscape" poster by Swiss artist H.R. Giger. Although BIAFRA and Co. (including some senior label staff) were tried in court for distributing harmful material to minors (a revised obscenity law), the case was subsequently thrown out after a hung jury. Nevertheless, the cost of the trial effectively put the band out of business, The DEAD KENNEDYS poignantly-titled finale, 'BEDTIME FOR DEMOCRACY' being issued late in 1986. Although KLAUS and RAY followed low-key solo careers, the ever-prolific BIAFRA vociferously protested against his treatment on spoken-word sets, 'NO MORE COCOONS' (1987) and 'THE HIGH PRIEST OF HARMFUL MATTER' (1989). He subsequently collaborated with a wide range of hardcore/industrial acts such as D.O.A., NO MEANS NO and TUMOR CIRCUS, although it was with LARD (a project with MINISTRY mainmen, AL JOURGENSEN and PAUL BARKER) that BIAFRA really came into his own. A late 80's mini-set, 'THE POWER OF LARD' preceded a full-length album, 'THE LAST TEMPTATION OF LARD', a minor UK hit early in 1990. This demented set included such hilarious BIAFRA monologues as 'CAN GOD FILL TEETH?' and even a rendition of Napolean XIV's 'THEY'RE COMING TO TAKE ME AWAY'. In 1994, he hooked up with another likeminded soul in hillbilly punk, MOJO NIXON, releasing one album, 'PRAIRIE HOME INVASION' (the title possibly a parody of an ICE-T album). BIAFRA continues to work at 'Alternative Tentacles', supplying the country with suitably deranged hardcore and occasionally taking time out for other projects, most recently a second LARD set, 'PURE CHEWING SATISFACTION' (1997). • Trivia: In 1979, BIAFRA stood in the elections for Mayor of San Francisco (he came 4th!).

Album rating: FRESH FRUIT FOR ROTTING VEGETABLES (*9) / IN GOD WE TRUST INC. mini (*5) / PLASTIC SURGERY DISASTERS (*6) / FRANKENCHRIST (*6) / BEDTIME FOR DEMOCRACY (*5) / GIVE ME CONVENIENCE OR GIVE ME DEATH compilation (*8) / Jello Biafra: NO MORE COCOONS spoken (*5) / HIGH PRIEST OF HARMFUL MATTER spoken (*5) / THE LAST TEMPTATION OF LARD with Lard (*6) / THE LAST SCREAM OF THE MISSING NEIGHBORS with D.O.A. (*6) / THE SKY IS FALLING AND I WANT MY MOMMY with No Means No (*5) / I BLOW MINDS FOR A LIVING (*6) / HIGH VOLTAGE CONSPIRACY FOR RADICAL FREEDOM with Tumor Circus (*5) / PRAIRIE HOME INVASION with Mojo Nixon (*6) / BEYOND THE VALLEY OF THE GIFT POLICE (*5) / PURE CHEWING SATISFACTION with Lard (*5)

JELLO BIAFRA (b. ERIC BOUCHER, 17 Jun'58, Boulder, Colorado) – vocals / **EAST BAY RAY** (b. RAY GLASSER, Castro Valley, California) – guitar, (synthesisers-later 80's) / **KLAUS FLUORIDE** (b. Detroit, Michigan) – bass, vocals / **BRUCE SLESINGER** (aka TED) – drums

		Fast	Alternative Tentacles
Oct 79.	(7") (FAST 12) <AT 95-41> **CALIFORNIA UBER ALLES. / MAN WITH THE DOGS**	☐	☐

		Cherry Red	Faulty-IRS
Jun 80.	(7")12" (CHERRY/12CHERRY 13) <IR 9016> **HOLIDAY IN CAMBODIA. / POLICE TRUCK** (re-iss. 7"/cd-s Jun88 & Mar95; same)	☐	☐
Sep 80.	(lp) (B-RED 10) <SP 70014> **FRESH FRUIT FOR ROTTING VEGETABLES**	33	☐ Nov80

– Kill the poor / Forward to death / When ya get drafted / Let's lynch the landlord / Drug me / Your emotions / Chemical warfare / California uber alles / I kill children / Stealing people's mail / Funland at the beach / Ill in my head / Holiday in Cambodia / Viva Las Vegas. (cd-iss. Nov87 & Mar95; CDBRED 10)

| Oct 80. | (7") (CHERRY 16) **KILL THE POOR. / IN SIGHT** (re-iss. Nov87 & Mar95; CDCHERRY 16) | 49 | – |

— **D.H. PELIGRO** (b. DARREN, East St.Louis, Illinois) – drums; repl. BRUCE/TED

		Cherry Red	Alternative Tentacles
May 81.	(7")/12" (CHERRY/12CHERRY 24) <VIRUS 2> **TOO DRUNK TO FUCK. / THE PREY** (re-iss. May88 & Mar95 cd-s; CDCHERRY 24)	36	☐

		Statik	Alternative Tentacles
Nov 81.	(10"ep) (STATEP 2) <VIRUS 5> **IN GOD WE TRUST INC.**	☐	☐

– Religious vomit / Moral majority / Kepone factory / Dog bite / Nazi punks fuck off / We've got a bigger problem now / Rawhide. <US c-ep+= ; VIRUS 5C> – Too drunk to fuck / The prey / Holiday in Cambodia. (re-iss. Jun92 cd-ep; STATEP 2CD)

Dec 81.	(7") <VIRUS 6> **NAZI PUNKS FUCK OFF. / MORAL MAJORITY**	–	☐
Jul 82.	(7")/12" (STAT/+12 22) <VIRUS 23> **BLEED FOR ME. / LIFE SENTENCE** (cd-s Jun92; STAT 22CD)	☐	☐
Nov 82.	(lp) (STATLP 11) **PLASTIC SURGERY DISASTERS**	☐	–

– Government flu / Terminal preppie / Trust your mechanic / Well paid scientist / Buzzbomb / Forest fire / Halloween / Winnebago warrior / Riot / Bleed for me / I am the owl / Dead end / Moon over Marin. (re-iss. Oct85; same) (cd-iss. Nov86 & Jun92 +=; same) – IN GOD WE TRUST INC. (ep)

| Nov 82. | (7"/12") (STAT/+12 27) <VIRUS 28> **HALLOWEEN. / SATURDAY NIGHT HOLOCAUST** (cd-s Jun92; STAT 27CD) | ☐ | ☐ |

— meanwhile KLAUS and EAST BAY released solo singles (see below)

		Alternative Tentacles	Alternative Tentacles
May 82.	(12"; KLAUS FLUORIDE) <(VIRUS 12)> **SHORTNING BREAD. / DROWNING COWBOY**	☐	☐
Jun 84.	(7"; EAST BAY RAY) <VIRUS 34> **TROUBLE IN TOWN. / POISON HEART** (12 re-iss. Apr89 on 'New Rose' France; GMO 40)	☐	☐
Aug 84.	(12"ep; KLAUS FLUORIDE) **CHA CHA CHA WITH MR. FLUORIDE** – Ghost riders / etc.	☐	–
Dec 85.	(lp) <VIRUS 45> **FRANKENCHRIST**	☐	☐

– Soup is good food / Hellnation / This could be anywhere (this could be everywhere) / A growing boy needs his lunch / Chicken farm / Macho-rama (invasion of the beef-patrol) / Goons of Hazzard / At my job / M.T.V. – Get off the air / Stars and stripes of corruption. (cd-iss. 1986; VIRUS 45CD)

| Dec 86. | (lp/c/cd) <(VIRUS 50/+C/CD)> **BEDTIME FOR DEMOCRACY** | ☐ | ☐ |

– Take this job and shove it / Hop with the jet set / Dear Abby / Rambozo the clown / Fleshdunce / The great wall / Shrink / Triumph of the swill / I spy / Macho insecurity / Cesspools in Eden / One-way ticket to Pluto / Do the slag / Gone with the wind / A commercial / Anarchy for sale / Chickenshit conformist / Where do ya draw the line / Potshot heard round the world / D.M.S.O. / Lie detector.

— split Dec '86 when RAY departed (he subsequently turned up in SKRAPYARD). KLAUS FLUORIDE went solo, releasing albums 'BECAUSE I SAY SO' (1988) and 'THE LIGHT IS FLICKERING' (1991) and forming acoustic outfit FIVE YEAR PLAN

– compilations, etc. –

on 'Alternative Tentacles' unless mentioned otherwise

| Jun 87. | (lp/cd) <(VIRUS 57/+CD)> **GIVE ME CONVENIENCE OR GIVE ME DEATH** | 84 | ☐ |

– Police truck / Too drunk to f*** / California uber alles / Man with the dogs / In sight / Life sentence / A child and his lawnmower / Holiday in Cambodia / Night of the living rednecks / I fought the law / Saturday night holocaust / Pull my strings / Short songs / Straight A's / Kinky sex makes the world go round / The prey. (cd+=/free flexi-disc) – BUZZBOMB FROM PASADENA

| Jun 93. | (7"ep) Subterranean; (SUB 24) **NAZI PUNKS **** OFF / ARYANISMS. / ('A'live) / CONTEMPTUOUS** (re-iss. Dec97; same) | ☐ | – |

JELLO BIAFRA

| Nov 87. | (lp) <(VIRUS 59)> **NO MORE COCOONS** (spoken word) (cd-iss. Mar93; VIRUS 59CD) | ☐ | ☐ |
| Jul 89. | (d-lp) <(VIRUS 66)> **HIGH PRIEST OF HARMFUL MATTER (TALES OF THE TRIALS, LIVE)** (spoken word) (cd-iss. Mar93; VIRUS 66CD) | ☐ | ☐ |

LARD

BIAFRA, AL JOURGENSEN + PAUL BARKER (Ministry) / **JEFF WARD** – drums

| Nov 89. | (12"ep/c-ep/cd-ep) <(VIRUS 72 T/C/CD)> **THE POWER OF LARD / HELL FUDGE. / TIME TO MELT (31 mins.)** | ☐ | ☐ |
| Jul 90. | (lp/cd) <(VIRUS 84/+CD)> **THE LAST TEMPTATION OF LARD** | 69 | ☐ |

– Forkboy / Pineapple face / Hate, spawn and die / Drug raid at 4am. / Can God fill teeth? / Bozo skeleton / Sylvestre Matuschka / They're coming to take me away / I am your clock.

JELLO BIAFRA & D.O.A.

— w/ **JOE KEITHLEY + CHRIS PROHOM** – guitar, vocals / **BRIAN GOBLE** – bass, vocals / **JON CARD** – drums

| May 90. | (lp/cd) <(VIRUS 78/+CD)> **THE LAST SCREAM OF THE MISSING NEIGHBORS** | ☐ | ☐ |

– That's progress / Attack of the peacekeepers / Wish I was in El Salvador / Power is boring / We gotta get out of this place / Full metal jackoff.

JELLO BIAFRA & NO MEANS NO

with **TIPPER GORE BOB WRIGHT** – guitar / **JOHN WRIGHT** – drums / **JON CARD** – percussion

| Mar 91. | (lp/c/cd) <(VIRUS 85/+C/CD)> **THE SKY IS FALLING AND I WANT MY MOMMY** | ☐ | ☐ |

– The sky is falling and I want my mommy (falling space junk) / Jesus was a terrorist / Bruce's diary / Sad / Ride the flume / Chew / Sparks in the Gene pool / The myth is real – let's eat.

JELLO BIAFRA

| Jun 91. | (d-lp/c/cd) <(VIRUS 94/+C/CD)> **I BLOW MINDS FOR A LIVING** | ☐ | ☐ |

– Pledge of allegience / Talk on censorship – let us prey / Die for oil, sucker – higher octane version / I was a teenage pacifist / If voting changed anything . . . / Running for mayor / Grow more pot / Lost orgasm / Talk on censorship-Better living through new world orders + Fear of a free planet.

TUMOR CIRCUS

— **DARREN MOR-X / DALE FLAT-UM + MIKE MDRASKOID** (of STEEL POLE BATH TUB) / **KING GRONG CHARLIE (TOLNAY)** (of LUBRICATED GOAT) + **J. BIAFRA**

| Nov 91. | (lp/c/cd) <(VIRUS 087/+C/CD)> **TUMOR CIRCUS – HIGH VOLTAGE CONSPIRACY FOR RADICAL FREEDOM** | ☐ | ☐ |

– Hazing for success / Human cyst / The man with the corkscrew eyes / Fireball /

Calcutta a-go-go / Turn off the respirator. (cd+=) Swine flu / Take me back or I'll drown our dog / Meathook up my rectum.
Feb 92. (7") <*VIRUS 102*> **MEATHOOK UP MY RECTUM. / (etched side)**
(12"+=/cd-s+=) <*VIRUS 102 T/CD*> – Take me back or I'll drown the dog / Swine flu / Fireball.

JELLO BIAFRA & MOJO NIXON

Nov 93. (7") (*VIRUS 136*) **WILL THE FETUS BE ABORTED? / THE LOST WORLD**
(cd-s+=) (*VIRUS 136CD*) – Drinkin' with Jesus / Achey raky heart.
Feb 94. (lp/cd) <*VIRUS 137/+CD*> **PRAIRIE HOME INVASION**
– Buy my snake oil / Where are we gonna work (when the trees are gone) / Convoy in the sky / Atomic power / Are you drinkin' with me Jesus / Love me, I'm a liberal / Burgers of wrath / Nostalgia for an angel that never existed / Hammer chicken plant disaster / Mascot mania / Let's go burn de Nashville down / Will the fetus be aborted? / Plastic Jesus.

JELLO BIAFRA

Oct 94. (d-lp) <*VIRUS 150*> **BEYOND THE VALLEY OF THE GIFT POLICE** (spoken word)
– Message to our sponsor / Experts / Ban everything / I have a dream / Talk on censorship / What we are not being told / President McMuffin tightens the belt / Talk on censorship / What we are not being told / In the belly of the wrong beast / Talk on censorship / Eric meets the moose diarrhea / Virturcrats unreality.

LARD

—— see last line-up + add **BILL RIEFLIN** – drums
May 97. (lp/c/cd) <*VIRUS 199/+MC/CD*> **PURE CHEWING SATISFACTION**
– War pimp renaissance / I wanna be a drug sniffing dog / Moths / Generation execute / Faith hope and treachery / Peeling back the foreskin of liberty / Mangoat / Sidewinder.

JELLO BIAFRA

Oct 98. (t-lp/d-cd) <*VIRUS 201/+CD*> **IF EVOLUTION IS OUTLAWED ONLY OUTLAWS WILL EVOLVE** (spoken word)
– Depends on the drug / Wake up and smell the coffee / The murder of Mumia Abu Jemal / Clinton comes to Long Beach / Half time / Hex flies space shuttle sequel / New Soviet Union / Talk on censorship.

DEADLINE (see under ⇒ LASWELL, Bill)

DEATH CULT (see under ⇒ CULT)

DEATH IN VEGAS

Formed: London, England . . . mid 90's by the production duo of RICHARD FEARLESS and STEVE HELLIER. The former was a public schoolboy and subsequently studied graphic design (and indie-rock for homework!) at art college before getting his act together at the Joy club. By the time DIV came to release distorted breakbeat singles like 'OPIUM SHUFFLE' (as DEAD ELVIS) and 'DIRT', FEARLESS was already a respected DJ at the capital's superhip Heavenly Social club (where The Chemical Brothers also made their name). After the underground success of their early releases, DIV became much in demand remixers for major labels desperate for a bit of street cred. After the techno-noir of their acclaimed debut album, 'DEAD ELVIS' (1997), the re-issues of 'DIRT' and 'ROCCO' managed Top 75 placings. Just prior to these, they had covered a BEAT hit, 'TWIST AND CRAWL', which featured RANKING ROGER of all guests(!). With the older and wiser TIM HOLMES (engineer on their debut LP) now in place of HELLIER, higher profile vocal contributors such as BOBBY GILLESPIE (of PRIMAL SCREAM), JIM REID (of the Jesus & Mary Chain), DOT ALLISON (ex-ONE DOVE) and IGGY POP were called upon – Scotland 3, the USA 1, you could say. 'THE CONTINO SESSIONS' – a name taken from the basement of their Clerkenwell (East London) studios – was unleashed in September '99, rave reviews from every music tabloid creating a stir for the dance-cum-goth album. A UK Top 20 pacesetter, the record and its pieces of 12"-only wonderments (i.e. 'DIRGE', 'NEPTUNE CITY' and 'AISHA') were crafted into shape like NEU! meeting FELT meeting the VELVET UNDERGROUND; a classic!
Album rating: DEAD ELVIS (*8) / THE CONTINO SESSIONS (*9)

RICHARD FEARLESS (b. MAGUIRE, 1972, Zambia, Africa) – DJ, samples / **STEVE HELLIER** – producer / with guest **ANDY VISSER** – flute, sax (also on album)

	Concrete	Time Bomb
May 95. (12"; as DEAD ELVIS) (*HARD 6*) **OPIUM SHUFFLE** (mixes)		-
—— with guests **ANTHONY ANDERSON** – guitar / **MAT FLINT** – bass (both also on album)		
Nov 95. (10") (*HARD 8-10*) **REMATERIALISED** (mixes)		-
—— bass by **NICK 'AVIN IT** (also on album)		
May 96. (10"/12"/cd-s) (*HARD 9-10/-12/-CD*) **DIRT** (mixes)		-
Oct 96. (12"/cd-s) (*HARD 14-12/-CD*) **ROCCO. / CITY RUB / DR. CLEAN / CLAIMING MARION**		-
Feb 97. (12"/cd-s) (*HARD 23-12/-CD*) **REKKIT / (3 mixes) / I SPY**		-
(12") (*HARD 23-12X*) – Death by a thousand cuts (remixes by Two Lone Swordsmen).		

—— other guests **SELAH** – vocals / **SEAMUS BEAGHAN** – hammond organ / **TIM WELLER** – drums / **JONATHAN HAINES** – strings / **PAUL RUTHERFORD** – trombone

Mar 97. (cd/d-lp) (*HARD 22 LPCD/LP12*) <*43511*> **DEAD ELVIS**	52	
– All that glitters / Opium shuffle / GBH / Dirt / Rocco / Rekkit / I spy / Amber / Rematerialised / 68 balcony / Sly.		
Apr 97. (12"/cd-s) (*HARD 26-12/-CD*) **TWIST AND CRAWL (featuring RANKING ROGER). / OPIUM SHUFFLE (Monkey Mafia mix)**		-
Jul 97. (12"/cd-s) (*HARD 27-12/-CD*) **DIRT** (mixes; Slayer / original album / Mullet) / **ROCCO** (Dave Clarke mix)	61	-
Oct 97. (12"/cd-s) (*HARD 29-12/-CD*) **ROCCO. / CITY RUB** (Jim's Rub) / **ROCCO** (Dave Clarke remix)	51	
(cd-s) (*HARD 29CDX*) – ('A'mixes).		

—— **TIM HOLMES** (the engineer) (repl.) HELLIER

Jul 99. (ltd-12") (*HARD 39-12*) **DIRGE. / LUTHER'S FUNK**	-	-
Sep 99. (cd/c/d-lp) (*HARD 41 CD/MC/LP*) **THE CONTINO SESSIONS**	19	
– Dirge (with DOT ALLISON) / Soul auctioneer (with BOBBY GILLESPIE) / Death threat / Flying / Aisha (with IGGY POP) / Lever street / Aladdin's story / Broken little sister (with JIM REID) / Neptune city.		
Oct 99. (ltd-12") (*YAWNING 1*) **BLOOD YAWNING**		
Nov 99. (12"/cd-s) (*HARD 40 12/CD*) **NEPTUNE CITY. / BLOOD YAWNING**	-	

—— 'AISHA' being released in the first month of the new century.

Chris DeBURGH

Born: CHRISTOPHER JOHN DAVIDSON, 15 Oct'50, Buenos Aires, Argentina. The son of British parents who were stationed around the globe (his father was in the diplomatic corps), CHRIS finally settled in Dublin, Ireland. Setting himself up as an ambitious singer-songwriter in a vaguely prog-rock vein, the bushy-browed one's initial break came in 1974 when 'A&M' picked him up midway between tours with HORSLIPS and SUPERTRAMP. A debut album, 'FAR BEYOND THESE CASTLE WALLS', appeared the following year and showcased DeBURGH's predilection for folksy, medieval-style romantic fantasy. Unsurprisingly, perhaps, the record made zero headway in a UK rock scene that was formenting the bile of punk. It did, however, spawn a massive Brazilian No.1 hit in the shape of the double A-side, 'FLYING' / 'TURNING AROUND', DeBURGH's cosmopolitan upbringing possibly filtering through to his music and striking a chord in far-flung audiences. It was a similar story with the rest of the man's 70's output, albums such as 'SPANISH TRAIN & OTHER STORIES' (1975), 'AT THE END OF A PERFECT DAY' (1977) and 'CRUSADER' (1979) garnering scant interest in either Britain or America but racking up healthy sales in other parts of the world. A pairing with producer/arranger Rupert Hine finally brought UK success – albeit minor – in 1982 with Top 30 album, 'THE GETAWAY' and accompanying Top 50 single, 'DON'T PAY THE FERRYMAN'. Further British success came in 1984 when DeBURGH narrowly missed the Top 10 with the 'MAN ON THE LINE' album although it took the finely crafted MOR balladry of 'LADY IN RED' (apparently written after the big man glimpsed his wife in a red dress and was struck dumb by her beauty, awwww!) to make him a bonafide star. Just on the right side of sentimental slush, the record topped the UK charts and even made the US Top 3. It also formed the centrepiece of UK No.1 album, 'INTO THE LIGHT' (1986), a record that saw the singer approach middle age from the middle of the road, mastering the kind of AOR-lite that saw FLEETWOOD MAC rehabilitated the following year. Determined to have a Christmas hit with the trippy 'A SPACEMAN CAME TRAVELLING' (one of the better tracks from DeBURGH's mid-70's sophomore effort, 'SPANISH TRAIN..'), 'A&M' attempted to capitalise on the man's newfound success by releasing the single for the umpteenth time in late '86. Surprisingly, the song still only managed to scrape the Top 40; there's just no pleasing some people. Instead, UK punters looked more favourably upon the schmaltz overload of 1988's 'MISSING YOU' single, a Top 3 hit lifted from a second No.1 album, 'FLYING COLOURS'. While the early 90's found DeBURGH continuing to notch up Top 5 albums – 'POWER OF TEN' (1992) and 'THIS WAY UP' (1994) – he couldn't quite manage another chivalrous ballad to woo the housewives and by 1995's Top 40 'BEAUTIFUL DREAMS' album, his star was beginning to fade.

Album rating: FAR BEYOND THESE CASTLE WALLS (*4) / SPANISH TRAIN & OTHER STORIES (*6) / AT THE END OF A PERFECT DAY (*4) / CRUSADER (*5) / EASTERN WIND (*4) / BEST MOVES compilation (*6) / THE GETAWAY (*6) / MAN ON THE LINE (*5) / THE VERY BEST OF CHRIS DeBURGH compilation (*6) / INTO THE LIGHT (*7) / FLYING COLOURS (*6) / FROM A SPARK TO A FLAME (*4) / THE VERY BEST OF CHRIS DeBURGH compilation (*6) / HIGH ON EMOTION LIVE FROM DUBLIN (*5) / POWER OF TEN (*3) / THIS WAY UP (*4) / BEAUTIFUL DREAMS (*4) / THE LOVE SONGS compilation (*5) / QUIET REVOLUTION (*3)

CHRIS DE BURGH – vocals, piano (with various session people)

	A&M	A&M
Jan 75. (lp) (*AMLH 68284*) <*4516*> **FAR BEYOND THESE CASTLE WALLS**		
– Hold on / The key / Windy night / Sin city / Turning round / New moon / Watching the world / Sat on green shutters / Lonesome cowboy / Goodnight. i(re-iss. 1981 on 'Hallmark'; SHM 3151) (re-iss. Mar82 & Jun85 lp/c; AMID/CMID 119) (re-iss. 1988 lp/c/cd; AMA/AMC/CDA 3287) (re-iss. Oct92 cd/c; CD/C MID 110)		
Feb 75. (7") (*AMS 7148*) **HOLD ON. / SIN CITY**		
Jul 75. (7") (*AMS 7182*) **FLYING (TURNING ROUND). / WATCHING THE WORLD**		
Oct 75. (lp/c) (*AMLH/CAM 68343*) <*4568*> **SPANISH TRAIN & OTHER STORIES**		
– Spanish train / Lonely sky / This song for you / The painter / Patricia the stripper / A spaceman came travelling / I'm going home / Old friend / The tower / Just another poor boy. (cd-dist.Aug85; same) – hit UK No.78 (cd re-iss. Feb89; CDA 3143) (cd re-iss. Oct92; CDMID 111)		

Jan 76. (7") (AMS 7146) **LONELY SKY. / THIS SONG FOR YOU**

Apr 76. (7") (AMS 7224) **PATRICIA THE STRIPPER. / OLD FRIEND**

Nov 76. (7") (AMS 7267) **A SPACEMAN CAME TRAVELLING. / JUST A POOR BOY**　Nov77

Aug 77. (7") (AMS 7305) **SUMMER RAIN. / RAINY NIGHTS IN PARIS**

Aug 77. (lp/c) (AMLH/CAM 64647) <4647> **AT THE END OF A PERFECT DAY**
– Broken wings / Round and around / I will / Summer rain / Discovery / Brazil / In a country churchyard / Rainy nights in Paris / If you love her, let her go / Perfect day. (cd-iss. 1988; CDA 4647) (re-iss. Oct95 cd/c; Cd/C MID 112)

Oct 77. (7") (AMS 7320) **BROKEN WINGS. / I WILL**

Jan 78. (7") (AMS 7336) **DISCOVERY. / ROUND AND AROUND**

Mar 78. (7") (AMS 7347) **PERFECT DAY. / SPANISH TRAIN**

Feb 79. (7") (AMS 7416) **I HAD THE LOVE IN MY EYES. / JUST IN TIME**

Feb 79. (lp/c) (AMLH/CAM 64746) <4746> **CRUSADER**
– Carry on / I had the love in my eyes / Something else again / The girl with April in her eyes / Just in time / The Devil's eyes / It's such a long way home / Old fashioned people / Quiet moments / Crusader: a) The fall of Jerusalem, b) In the court of Saladin, c) The battlefield, d) Finale / You and me. (re-iss. Sep86 lp/c; AMLH/CAM 64746) – hit UK No.72 (cd-iss. 1988; CDA 4746) (cd re-iss. Oct92; CDMID 113)

Feb 79. (7") **CARRY ON. / THE GIRL WITH APRIL IN HER EYES**

Apr 79. (7") (AMS 7430) **THE DEVIL'S EYES. / IT'S SUCH A LONG WAY HOME**

Jul 80. (lp/c) (AMLH/CAM 64815) <4815> **EASTERN WIND**
– The traveller / The record company bash / Tonight / Wall of silence / Flying home / Shadows and lights / Sailor / Some things never change / Tourist attraction / Eastern wind. (cd-iss. 1988; CDA 4815) (re-iss. Oct92 cd/c; CD/C MID 167)

Aug 80. (7") (AMS 7546) **SHADOWS AND LIGHTS. / WALLS OF SILENCE**

Oct 80. (7") (AMS 7562) **THE TRAVELLER. / EASTERN WIND**

Nov 80. (7") **THE TRAVELLER. / WALL OF SILENCE**

Aug 81. (lp/c) (AMLH/CAM 68532) **BEST MOVES** (compilation)　65
– The traveller / Every drop of rain / In a country churchyard / Patricia the stripper / Satin green shutters / Spanish train / Waiting for the hurricane / Broken wings (live) / Lonely sky / A spaceman came travelling / Crusader. (cd-iss. 1988; CDA 5083) (cd/c re-iss. May95; 395083-2/-4)

Sep 81. (7") (AMS 8160) **WAITING FOR THE HURRICANE. / BROKEN WINGS** (live)

Nov 81. (7") (AMS 8182) **A SPACEMAN CAME TRAVELLING. / PATRICIA THE STRIPPER**

Sep 82. (7") (AMS 8256) <2511> **DON'T PAY THE FERRYMAN. / ALL THE LOVE I HAVE INSIDE**　48　34 Apr83

Oct 82. (lp/c) (AMLH/CAM 68549) <4929> **THE GETAWAY**　30　Mar83
– Don't pay the ferryman / Living on the island / Crying and laughing / I'm counting on you / The getaway / Ship to shore / All the love I have inside / Borderline / Where peaceful waters flow / The revolution / Light a fire / Liberty. (cd-iss. Apr84; CDA 68549) (cd re-iss. May95; 394929-2/-4)

Nov 82. (7") (AMS 8268) **THE GETAWAY. / LIVING ON THE ISLAND**

Feb 83. (7") (AMS 8309) **SHIP TO SHORE. / CRYING AND LAUGHING**

Aug 83. (7") <2565> **SHIP TO SHORE. / THE GETAWAY**　-　71

Apr 84. (7"/12") (AM/+X 190) <2643> **HIGH ON EMOTION. / MUCH MORE THAN THIS**　44　44 Jun84

May 84. (lp/c/cd) (AMLX/CXM/CDA 65002) <5002> **MAN ON THE LINE**　11　69 Jun84
– The ecstasy of flight (I love the night) / Sight and touch / Taking it to the top / The head and the heart / The sound of a gun / High on emotion / Much more than this / Man on the line / Moonlight and vodka / Transmission ends. (re-iss. Mar93 cd/c; CD/C MID 188)

Jul 84. (7") (AM 202) **THE ECSTASY OF FLIGHT (I LOVE THE NIGHT). / MOONLIGHT AND VODKA**
(12"+=) (AMX 202) – Don't pay the ferryman / A spaceman came travelling.

Dec 84. (7") (AM 225) **A SPACEMAN CAME TRAVELLING. / BORDERLINE**

Feb 85. (7") (AM 237) **SIGHT AND TOUCH / TAKING IT TO THE TOP**

Mar 86. (7") (AM 317) **FIRE ON THE WATER. / THE VISION**
(12"+=) (AMY 317) – The leader / What about me.

May 86. (lp/c/cd) (<AMA/AMC/CDA 5121>) **INTO THE LIGHT**　1　25 Sep86
– Last night / Fire on the water / The ballroom of romance / The lady in red / Say goodbye to it all / The spirit of man / Fatal hesitation / One word (straight to the heart) / For Rosanna / The leader / The vision / What about me. (re-iss. cd/c May95; 395121-2/-4)

Jun 86. (7") (AM 331) **THE LADY IN RED. / SAY GOODBYE TO IT ALL**　1　-
(12"+=) (AMY 331) – Don't pay the ferryman.

Sep 86. (7") (AM 346) **FATAL HESITATION. / ECSTACY OF FLIGHT (I LOVE THE NIGHT)**　44　-
(12"+=) (AMY 346) – Ship to shore.

Nov 86. (7") (AM 365) **A SPACEMAN CAME TRAVELLING. / THE BALLROOM OF ROMANCE**　40　-
(12"+=) (AMY 365) – The getaway.
(d7"++=) (AMD 365) – Borderline.

Nov 86. (7") **FATAL HESITATION. / THE BALLROOM OF ROMANCE**　-　-

Feb 87. (7") <2848> **THE LADY IN RED. / THE VISION**　-　3

Dec 87. (7") **THE SIMPLE TRUTH (A CHILD IS BORN). / LOVE IS MY DECISION**

Dec 87. (7") (AM 427) **THE SIMPLE TRUTH (A CHILD IS BORN). / THE SPIRIT OF MAN**　55　-
(12"+=) (AMY 427) – The head and the heart (live).

Oct 88. (7"/12") (AM/+Y 474) **MISSING YOU. / THE RISEN LORD**　3　-
(cd-s+=) (CDEE 474) – The last time I cried.

Oct 88. (7") **MISSING YOU. / THE LAST TIME I CRIED**　-　-

Nov 88. (lp/c/cd) (<AMA/AMC/CDA 5224>) **FLYING COLOURS**　1
– Sailing away / Carry me (like a fire in your heart) / Tender hands / A night on the river / Leather on my shoes / Suddenly love / Missing you / I'm not scared anymore / Don't look back / Just a word away / The risen lord / The last time I cried. (cd+=) – The simple truth (A child is born). (re-iss. cd/c May95; 395224-2/-4)

Dec 88. (7") (AM 486) **TENDER HANDS. / A NIGHT ON THE RIVER**　43
(12"+=/cd/c) (AMY/CDEE 486) – The simple truth (a child is born).

Feb 89. (7") (AM 494) **SAILING AWAY. / THE HEAD AND THE HEART**
(12"+=/cd-s+=) (AMY/CDEE 474) – ('A'extended).

Sep 89. (7") (AM 528) **THIS WAITING HEART. / CARRY ME (LIKE A FIRE IN YOUR HEART)**　59
(12"+=/cd-s+=) (AMY/AMCD 528) – The spirit of man.

Oct 89. (lp/c/cd) (CDB LP/MC/CD 100) **FROM A SPARK TO A FLAME – THE VERY BEST OF CHRIS DE BURGH** (compilation)　4
– This waiting heart / Don't pay the ferryman / Much more than this / Sailing away / The lady in red / Borderline / Say goodbye to it all / One word (straight to the heart) / A spaceman came travelling / Ship to shore / Missing you / Diamond in the dark / Tender hands / The getaway / Where peaceful waters flow / High on emotion. (cd+=) – Spanish train / Fatal hesitation.

Nov 89. (7") (AM 537) **DIAMOND IN THE DARK. / LAST NIGHT**
(12"+=/cd-s+=) (AMY/CDEE 537) – Transmission ends.

Sep 90. (cd/c/d-lp) (397-86-2/-4/-1) **HIGH ON EMOTION – LIVE FROM DUBLIN** (live)　15
– Last night / Sailing away / The revolution / I'm not scared anymore / Spanish train / Borderline / The risen Lord / The last time I cried / The lady in red / Lonely sky / A spaceman came travelling / Patricia the stripper / The ballroom of romance / Say goodbye to it all / Don't pay the ferryman / High on emotion. (re-iss. cd/c May95; same)

Apr 92. (7"/-c-s) (AM/+C 863) **SEPARATE TABLES. / MAKING THE PERFECT MAN** (extended)　30　-
(cd-s+=) (AMCD 863) – The Connemara coast (instrumental).

May 92. (cd/c/lp) (397188-2/-4/-1) **POWER OF TEN**　3
– Where we will be good / By my side / Heart of darkness / In your eyes / Separate tables / Talk to me / Brother John / The Connemara coast / Shine on / A celebration / She means everything to me / Making the perfect man. (re-iss. cd/c May95)

Jul 92. (7"/-c-s/cd-s) **MAKING THE PERFECT MAN. / SAY GOODBYE TO IT ALL** (live) / **BORDERLINE** (live)

Sep 92. (7"/-c-s) **SHINE ON. / HEART OF DARKNESS**　-
(12"+=/cd-s+=) – I'm not scared anymore (live).

—— now w/ **VIC MARTIN** – keyboards / **NEIL TAYLOR** – guitar / **PHIL SPALDING** – bass, rhythm guitar, vocals / **JIMMY COPLEY** – drums

May 94. (7"/-c-s) (580592-7/-4) **BLONDE HAIR, BLUE JEANS. / YOU ARE THE REASON**　51
(cd-s+=) (580593-2) – Strangers on a train.

May 94. (cd/c) (540233-2/-4) **THIS WAY UP**　5
– This silent world / This is love / This weight on me / Here is your Paradise / Oh my brave hearts / Blonde hair, blue jeans / The son and the father / The snows of New York / You's got a hold on me / You are the reason / Up here in Heaven.

Jul 94. (7"/-c-s) **THIS SILENT WORLD. / ON MY BRAVE HEARTS**　-
(cd-s+=) – When I see you tonight.

Oct 94. (7"/-c-s) (580812-7/-4) **HERE IS YOUR PARADISE. / THE SNOWS OF NEW YORK**　-
(cd-s+=) (580813-2) – Shine on.

Nov 95. (cd/c) (540432-2/-4) **BEAUTIFUL DREAMS**　33
– Missing you / Carry me / Discovery / The snows of New York / In love forever / Shine on / Lady in red / In dreams / I'm not crying over you / Always on my mind / Say goodbye to it all / One more mile to go.

Dec 95. (c-s/cd-s) (581289-4/-2) **THE SNOWS OF NEW YORK / GIRL / MISSING YOU**　60　-

Oct 96. (c-s) (581995-4) **THAT'S WHAT FRIENDS ARE FOR / RIDING ON A RAINBOW**
(cd-s) (581995-2) – Missing you.

Sep 97. (c-s) (582393-4) **SO BEAUTIFUL / FATAL HESITATION**　29
(cd-s+=) (582393-2) – Suddenly love.

Oct 97. (cd/c) (540794-2/-4) **THE LOVE SONGS** (compilation)　8　-
– Here is your paradise / Missing you / So beautiful / In love forever / Borderline / The lady in red / Much more than this / It's me (and I'm ready to go) / Separate tables / Fatal hesitation / Forevermore / The head and the heart / Lonely sky / Suddenly love / If you really love her let her go / In a country churchyard.

　　　　　　　　　　　　　　　　　　　　　Mercury　Universal

Sep 99. (c-s) (497130-4) **WHEN I THINK OF YOU / I SEE YOU EVERYWHERE**　59　-
(cd-s+=) (497130-2) – Living in the world.

Sep 99. (cd/c) (490446-2/-4) **QUIET REVOLUTION**　23
– When I think of you / Love of the heart divine / Living in the world / Same sun / Nothing ever happens round here / A woman's heart / Last moments of the dawn / I see you everywhere / Saint Peter's gate / You look beautiful / I want it (and I want it now) / Natasha dance / River of Abraham / My lover is / Quiet revolution.

Nov 99. (cd-s) (497179-2) **THE LADY IN RED /**　-

Nov 99. (cd-s) (497193-2) **A WOMAN'S HEART /**　-

– compilations, etc. –

Dec 84. (lp/c/cd) Telstar; (STAR/STAC/TCD 2248) **THE VERY BEST OF CHRIS DE BURGH**　6　-

Aug 88. (cd-ep) A&M; (AMCD 915) **COMPACT HITS**
– The ecstasy of flight (I love the night) / The lady in red / Don't pay the ferryman / High on emotion.

May 90. (d-c) A&M; (AMC 24108) **INTO THE LIGHT / FLYING COLOURS**
(d-cd-iss. Oct93; CDA 24116)

May 91. (7"/-c-s) A&M; (RELF/+C 1) **THE SIMPLE TRUTH (A CHILD IS BORN). / THE SPIRIT OF MAN**　36　-
(12"+=/cd-s+=) (RELF T/CD 1) – The head and the heart (live).

DEEP FOREST

Formed: Paris, France . . . 1992 by keyboard kings MICHEL SANCHEZ and ERIC MOUQUET, who moved to the USA the following year. Initially a hit in Australia, the single 'SWEET LULLABY' took Europe by storm early in '94. Ambient club sounds using haunting voices of the Central

African Pygmies, plus Baka chants of Cameroun, Burundi and Senegal, DEEP FOREST were a little similar in conceptual idea to ENIGMA with the panpipes of INCANTATION thrown in. An eponymous album fully realised their vision and some of the profits from its healthy sales were ploughed back into charities working with indigenous tribes. MOUQUET and SANCHEZ subsequently travelled to Eastern Europe, where they hooked up with Hungarian folk singer, MARTA SEBESTYEN, sampling her vocals for a follow-up album, 'BOHEME' (1995), which also featured ethnic music from the farthest flung corners of the globe. The album spawned 'MARTA'S SONG', which gave the duo another UK Top 30 hit, the track also being included on the soundtrack of Robert Altman's movie, 'Pret-A-Porter'. As well as various film projects, DEEP FOREST's unique talents were in demand as remixers for an eclectic array of artists.

Album rating: DEEP FOREST (*7) / BOHEME (*6) / DEEP FOREST III – COMPARSA (*4)

ERIC MOUQUET – keyboards, claviers, programming / **MICHEL SANCHEZ** – keyboards, claviers, programming; additional vocals **MICHEL VILLAIN**

		Columbia	Epic
Dec 92.	(7"/-c-s) *(658 877-7/-4)* **SWEET LULLABY. /** ('A'mix)		Jun93
	(12"+=) *(658 877-6)* – (2 more remixes).		
	(cd-s++=) *(658 877-2)* – (2 more remixes; now 6 in total).		
Jan 94.	(7"/-c-s) *(659 924-7/-4)* <77095> **SWEET LULLABY. /** ('A'-Round The World mix)	10	78
	(12"+=) *(659 924-6)* – (2 more mixes).		
	(cd-s++=) *(659 924-2)* – (2 more mixes).		
Feb 94.	(cd/c) *(474 178-2/-4)* <53747> **DEEP FOREST**	15	Aug93
	– Deep forest / Sweet lullaby / Hunting / Night bird / The first twilight / Savana dance / Desert walk / White whisper / The second twilight / Sweet lullaby (ambient mix) / Forest hymn. <re-iss. Jan94; 57840> – hit US No.59		
May 94.	(c-s) *(660 411-4)* **DEEP FOREST / SWEET LULLABY**	20	
	(12"/cd-s) *(660 411-6/-2)* – ('A'side) / (5-'A'remixes).		
	(cd-s) *(660 411-5)* – (6-'A'mixes).		
Jul 94.	(c-s) *(660 635-4)* **SAVANNA DANCE /** ('A'mix)	28	
	(cd-s+=) *(660 635-2)* – (4-'A'remixes).		
May 95.	(cd/c) *(478 623-2/-4)* <67115> **BOHEME**	12	62
	– Anathasia / Bohemian ballet / Marta's song / Gathering / Lament / Bulgarian melody / Deep folk song / Freedom cry / Twosome / Cafe Europa / Katharina / Boheme.		
Jun 95.	(c-s) *(662 140-4)* **MARTA'S SONG / SWEET LULLABY**	26	
	(cd-s+=) *(662 140-2)* – ('A'-Into the deep mix) / ('A'-Arnand's Muslim mix).		
	(12") *(662 140-6)* – (6 'A'mixes).		
Jan 98.	(cd/c) *(488725-2/-4)* <68726> **DEEP FOREST III – COMPARSA**	60	
	– Noonday sun / Green and blue / Madazulu / 1716 / Deep weather / Comparsa / Earthquake (transition 1) / Tres Marias / Radio Belize / Ekue ekue / La lune se bat avec etoiles (transition 2) / Forest power / Media luna.		

DEEP PURPLE

Formed: London, England . . . 1968 intially as ROUNDABOUT, by former Searchers sticksman, CHRIS CURTIS. He duly recruited classically trained organist, JON LORD and guitar maestro, RITCHIE BLACKMORE, who was living in Germany at the time. By Spring of that year, the band had become DEEP PURPLE with NICK SIMPER on bass and ROD EVANS on vocals. Their debut single, a cover of JOE SOUTH's 'HUSH', reached the US Top 5 and the band were subsequently furnished with a three album contract, signing with 'Tentagramme' in America (a label run by US comedian Bill Cosby!), 'Parlophone' in Britain. This line-up (known as Mk.I in DEEP PURPLE parlance) recorded three albums, 'SHADES OF DEEP PURPLE' (1968), 'BOOK OF TALIESYN' (1969) and the eponymous 'DEEP PURPLE' (1969), littered with chugging, proto-metal covers of the era's pop hits a la VANILLA FUDGE. Following the collapse of 'Tentagramme', the band signed with 'Warners', drafting in IAN GILLAN and ROGER GLOVER (both ex-EPISODE SIX) to replace EVANS and SIMPER respectively. The revamped line-up's first release was the pseudo-classical drivel of the live 'CONCERTO FOR GROUP AND ORCHESTRA WITH THE ROYAL PHILHARMONIC ORCHESTRA' (1970). Thankfully, after the record failed to sell in any great quantity, common sense prevailed and BLACKMORE steered the group in a heavier direction. 'IN ROCK', released later the same year, announced the arrival of a major contender in the heavyweight arena alongside the likes of BLACK SABBATH and LED ZEPPELIN. Preceded by the lumbering 'BLACK NIGHT' (No.2 in the UK) single, the album was dinosaur rock before the phrase was even coined; the pummelling rhythm section of GLOVER and PAICE driving the beast ever onward while BLACKMORE's razor sharp guitar solos clawed mercilessly at LORD's shuddering organ. 'CHILD IN TIME' was the ballad, the full range of GILLAN's talent on show as he progressed from mellow musings to his trademark glass shattering shriek. While 'FIREBALL' (1971) was competent, if lacking in the songs department, 'MACHINE HEAD' (1972) was the DEEP PURPLE tour de force, the classic album from the classic Mk.II line-up. Cuts like 'HIGHWAY STAR' and 'SPACE TRUCKIN' were relentless, high-octane metal riff-athons which became staples in the DP live set for years to come. 'SMOKE ON THE WATER' probably stands as the band's most famous track, its classic three chord bludgeon and tale of disaster averted, reaching No.4 in America upon its release as a single a year later. This further boosted 'MACHINE HEAD' sales into the millions, DEEP PURPLE now firmly established as a world class act. The band also had a stellar live reputation, the concert double set, 'MADE IN JAPAN' (1972), going on to achieve cult status among metal afficiondos and earning the group a place in the Guinness Book Of Records as loudest band, woaargh!! As the heavy touring and recording schedule ground on, the beast began to stumble, however, recording a further, fairly lacklustre album, 'WHO DO WE THINK WE ARE!' (1973), before disintegrating later that summer among constant in-fighting and personality clashes. BLACKMORE, LORD and PAICE remained, enlisting future WHITESNAKE vocalist DAVID COVERDALE on vocals and GLENN HUGHES (ex-TRAPEZE) in place of GLOVER to create DEEP PURPLE Mk.III. 'BURN' (1974) and 'STORMBRINGER' (1974) were characterised by COVERDALE's bluesy voice, although the new boy and BLACKMORE were not exactly fond of each other, the latter eventually quitting in 1975. His replacement was semi-legendary guitarist TOMMY BOLIN, who graced 'COME TASTE THE BAND' (1975). Less than a year later, however, DEEP PURPLE were no more, the behemoth finally going belly up after the perils of rock'n'roll had finally taken their toll. While BOLIN O.D'd on heroine, of the remaining members, GLENN HUGHES reformed TRAPEZE while COVERDALE formed WHITESNAKE. BLACKMORE, meanwhile, had not been simply sitting around stuffing cucumbers down his pants and turning his amp up to 11, he had formed the rather grandiose sounding RITCHIE BLACKMORE'S RAINBOW. The other key member of DEEP PURPLE, IAN GILLAN, had also been equally prolific during the 70's, initially with the IAN GILLAN BAND. A revamped DEEP PURPLE is where the paths of messrs. BLACKMORE, GILLAN, GLOVER, LORD and PAICE (the latter two had dabbled in solo and group work throughout the 70's-see discography) crossed once more. While the comeback album, 'PERFECT STRANGERS' (1984), was welcomed by fans, it became clear that the ever dominant BLACKMORE was being as dominant as ever. After another relatively successful studio effort, 'HOUSE OF BLUE LIGHT' (1987), and a live album, GILLAN was given the order of the boot. Typically incestuous, DEEP PURPLE then recruited ex-RAINBOW man, JOE LYNN TURNER, for the awful 'SLAVES AND MASTERS' (1990) album. In an increasingly absurd round of musical chairs, GILLAN was then reinstated, consequently clashing once more with BLACKMORE who eventually stomped off to reform RAINBOW. DEEP PURPLE lumbered on, recruiting STEVE MORSE for their last album to date, 'PURPENDICULAR' (1996). If The ROLLING STONES are still rolling, some might say, what's to stop DEEP PURPLE? Well, considering The 'STONES have had around three line-up changes in their whole career while DEEP PURPLE have almost managed the same number for each album, the future doesn't look particularly promising. Then again, is anyone still listening? (my mate Russell, apparently!) • **Songwriters:** Mk.I:-Mostly BLACKMORE / EVANS / LORD. Mk.II:- Group. Mk.III:- BLACKMORE / COVERDALE, adding at times LORD and PAICE. Mk.IV:- Permutate any two of COVERDALE, BOLIN or HUGHES. Covered HUSH (Joe South) / WE CAN WORK IT OUT + HELP (Beatles) / KENTUCKY WOMAN (Neil Diamond) / RIVER DEEP MOUNTAIN HIGH (Ike & Tina Turner) / HEY JOE (Jimi Hendrix) / I'M SO GLAD (Cream). • **Trivia:** To obtain charity monies for the Armenian earthquake disaster late 1989, BLACKMORE, GILLAN and others (i.e. BRUCE DICKINSON, ROBERT PLANT, BRIAN MAY etc.) contributed to Top 40 new version of SMOKE ON THE WATER.

Album rating: SHADES OF DEEP PURPLE (*5) / THE BOOK OF TALIESYN (*4) / DEEP PURPLE (*4) / CONCERTO FOR GROUP AND ORCHESTRA (*1) / IN ROCK (*8) / FIREBALL (*7) / MACHINE HEAD (*9) / MADE IN JAPAN (*8) / WHO DO WE THINK WE ARE (*6) / BURN (*7) / STORMBRINGER (*5) / COME TASTE THE BAND (*6) / DEEPEST PURPLE compilation (*9) / PERFECT STRANGERS (*6) / HOUSE OF BLUE LIGHT (*5) / NOBODY'S PERFECT (*5) / SLAVES AND MASTERS (*4) / COME HELL OR HIGH WATER (*7) / PURPENDICULAR (*5) / ABANDON (*4)

RITCHIE BLACKMORE (b.14 Apr'45, Weston-Super-Mare, Avon, England) – guitar (ex-MANDRAKE ROOT, ex-OUTLAWS, ex-SCREAMING LORD SUTCH, etc.) / **JON LORD** (b.9 Jun'41, Leicester, England) – keyboards (ex-FLOWERPOT MEN) / **NICK SIMPER** (b. 1946, Southall, London) – bass (ex-JOHNNY KIDD & PIRATES) / **ROD EVANS** (b. 1945, Edinburgh, Scotland) – vocals (ex-MAZE, ex-MI5) / **IAN PAICE** (b.29 Jun'48, Nottingham, England) – drums (ex-MAZE, ex-MI5)

		Parlophone	Tetragramme
Jun 68.	(7") *(R 5708)* <1503> **HUSH. / ONE MORE RAINY DAY**		4
Sep 68.	(lp) *(PCS 7055)* <102> **SHADES OF DEEP PURPLE**		24
	– And the address / Hush / One more rainy day / (prelude) Happiness – I'm so glad / Mandrake root / Help / Love help me / Hey Joe. (re-iss. Feb77 on 'EMI Harvest'; SHSM 2016) (cd-iss. Mar89; CZ 170) (cd-iss. Feb95 on 'Fame'; CDFA 3314) (lp re-iss. Nov97 on 'E.M.I.'; LPCENT 25)		
Nov 68.	(7") <1508> **KENTUCKY WOMAN. / HARD ROAD**	-	38
Nov 68.	(7") *(R 5745)* **KENTUCKY WOMAN. / WRING THAT NECK**	-	-
Jan 69.	(7") <1514> **RIVER DEEP – MOUNTAIN HIGH. / LISTEN, LEARN, READ ON**	-	53
Feb 69.	(7") *(R 5763)* **EMMARETTA. / WRING THAT NECK**	-	-
Apr 69.	(7") <1519> **EMMARETTA. / THE BIRD HAS FLOWN**	-	-

		Harvest	Tetragramme
Jun 69.	(lp/c) *(SHVL/TC-SHVL 751)* <107> **BOOK OF TALIESYN**		54 Jan69
	– Listen, learn, read on / Wring that neck / Kentucky woman / Shield / a) Exposition – b) We can work it out / The shield / Anthem / River deep, mountain high. (re-iss. Jun85 on 'EMI';) (cd-iss. Aug89; CDP 792408-2) (cd re-iss. Feb96 on 'Premier'; CZ 171)		
Nov 69.	(lp) *(SHVL 759)* <119> **DEEP PURPLE**		Jul69
	– Chasing shadows / Blind / Lalena: (a) Faultline, (b) The painter / Why didn't Rosemary? / The bird has flown / April. (re-iss. Jun85 on 'EMI';) (cd-iss. Mar89; CZ 172) (re-iss. cd May95 on 'Fame'; CDFA 3317)		

—— (In Jun'69 below two were used on session for 'HALLELUJAH'. They became regular members after the recording of 'DEEP PURPLE' album.) / **IAN GILLAN** (b.19 Aug'45, Hounslow, London) – vocals (ex-EPISODE SIX) replaced EVANS who joined CAPTAIN BEYOND. / **ROGER GLOVER** (b.30 Nov'45, Brecon, Wales) – bass (ex-EPISODE SIX) replaced SIMPER who later formed WARHORSE

Jul 69. (7") *(HAR 5006) <1537>* **HALLELUJAH (I AM THE PREACHER). / APRIL (part 1)**

	Harvest	Warners

Jan 70. (lp/c) *(SHVL/TC-SHVL 767) <1860>* **CONCERTO FOR GROUP AND ORCHESTRA WITH THE ROYAL PHILHARMONIC ORCHESTRA (live)** — `26` May70
– First Movement: Moderato – Allegro / Second Movement: Andante (part 1) – Andante conclusion / Third Movement: Vivace – Presto. *(cd-iss. Aug90 on 'E.M.I.' += ; CZ 342)* – Wring that neck / Child in time.

Jun 70. (7") *(HAR 5020)* **BLACK NIGHT. / SPEED KING** — `2` —

Jun 70. (lp/c) *(SHVL/TC-SHVL 777) <1877>* **DEEP PURPLE IN ROCK** — `4` Sep70
– Speed king / Blood sucker / Child in time / Flight of the rat / Into the fire / Living wreck / Hard lovin' man. *(re-iss. May82 on 'Fame' lp/c; FA/TC-FA 3011) (cd-iss. Apr88; CDFA 3011) (pic-lp.Jun85; EJ 2603430) (purple-lp iss.1995 on 'E.M.I.'; 7243-8-34019-8) (with free-lp)* – Cry free (Roger Glover remix) / Jam stew / Flight of the rat (Roger Glover remix) / Speed king (Roger Glover remix) / Black night (Roger Glover remix).

Jul 70. (7") *<7405>* **BLACK NIGHT. / INTO THE FIRE** — `-` `66`

Feb 71. (7") *(HAR 5033) <7493>* **STRANGE KIND OF WOMAN. / I'M ALONE** — `6` —

Sep 71. (lp/c) *(SHVL/TC-SHVL 793) <2564>* **FIREBALL** — `1` `32` Aug71
– Fireball / No no no / Demon's eye / Anyone's daughter / The mule / Fools / No one came. *(re-iss. Mar84 on 'Fame' lp/c; FA/TC-FA 41-3093-1/-4) (re-iss. Aug87 lp/c; CDFA/TC-ATAK 105) (re-iss. Oct87 on 'E.M.I.' lp/c; EMS/TC-EMS 1255) (cd-iss. Jan88 on 'E.M.I.'; CZ 30) (pic-lp.Jun85 on 'E.M.I.'; EJ 2403440) (lp re-iss. 1996 on 'E.M.I.'; 7243-8-53711-0) (with free lp)* – Strange kind of woman (remix '96) / I'm alone / Freedom (session out-take) / Slow train (session out-take) / Midnight in Moscow – Robin Hood – William Tell – Fireball (the noise abatement) / Backwards piano / No one came (remix '96).

Oct 71. (7") *(HAR 5045)* **FIREBALL. / DEMON'S EYE** — `15` —

Nov 71. (7") *<7528>* **FIREBALL. / I'M ALONE** — `-` —

	Purple	Warners

Mar 72. (7") *(PUR 102) <7572>* **NEVER BEFORE. / WHEN A BLIND MAN CRIES** — `35` —

Apr 72. (lp/c) *(TPSA/TC-TPSA 7504) <2607>* **MACHINE HEAD** — `1` `7`
– Highway star / Maybe I'm a Leo / Pictures of home / Never before / Smoke on the water / Lazy / Space truckin'. *(re-iss. Jun85 on 'E.M.I.' lp/c; ATAK/TC-ATAK 39) (re-iss. Oct86 on 'Fame' lp/c; FA/TC-FA 3158) (cd-iss. Mar87 on 'E.M.I.'; CZ 83) (cd re-iss. Mar89; CDFA 3158) (re-iss. Sep97 on 'E.M.I.' d-cd-lp; CD+/DEEPP 3)*

Jun 72. (7") *<7595>* **LAZY. / WHEN A BLIND MAN CRIES** — `-` —

Oct 72. (7") *<7634>* **HIGHWAY STAR. / (part 2)** — `-` —

Dec 72. (d-lp/d-c) *(TPSP/TC2-TPSP 351) <2701>* **MADE IN JAPAN (live)** — `16` `6` Apr73
– Highway star / Child in time / Smoke on the water / The mule / Strange kind of woman / Lazy / Space truckin'. *(cd-iss. Sep88 on 'E.M.I.'; CDTPS 351) (re-iss. Oct92 on 'Fame' cd/c; CD/TC FA 3268) (re-iss. Jan98 on 'E.M.I.' cd/lp; 857864-2/-4)* – hit No.73

Feb 73. (lp/c) *(TPSA/TC-TPSA 7508) <2678>* **WHO DO YOU THINK WE ARE!** — `4` `15` Jan73
– Woman from Tokyo / Mary Long / Super trouper / Smooth dancer / Rat bat blue / Place in line / Our lady. *(re-iss. Jun85 on 'E.M.I.' lp/c; ATAK/TC-ATAK 127) (cd-iss. Oct87 on 'E.M.I.'; CZ 6)*

Apr 73. (7") *<7672>* **WOMAN FROM TOKYO. / SUPER TROUPER** — `-` `80`

May 73. (7") *<7710>* **SMOKE ON THE WATER. / (part 2)** — `-` `4`

Sep 73. (7") *<7737>* **WOMAN FROM TOKYO. / SUPER TROOPER** — `-` `60`

—— **BLACKMORE, LORD** and **PAICE** brought in new members / **DAVID COVERDALE** (b.22 Sep'49, Saltburn-by-the-sea, Cleveland, England) – vocals replaced GILLAN who later formed own band. / **GLENN HUGHES** (b.Penkridge, England) – bass (ex-TRAPEZE) repl. GLOVER who became top producer.

	Polydor	Mercury

Feb 74. (lp/c) *(TPS/TC-TPS 3505) <2766>* **BURN** — `3` `9`
– Burn / Might just take your life / Lay down stay down / Sail away / You fool no one / What's goin' on here / Mistreated / "A" 200. *(re-iss. Mar84 on 'E.M.I.' lp/c; ATAK/TC-ATAK 11) (cd-iss. Jul89; CZ 203)*

Mar 74. (7") *(PUR 117) <7784>* **MIGHT JUST TAKE YOUR LIFE. / CORONARIAS REDIG** — `91`

May 74. (7") *<7809>* **BURN. / CORONARIAS REDIG** — `-` `20`

Nov 74. (lp/c) *(TPS/TC-TPS 3508) <2832>* **STORMBRINGER** — `6` `20`
– Stormbringer / Love don't mean a thing / Holy man / Hold on / Lady double dealer / You can't do it right (with the one you love) / High ball shooter / The gypsy / Soldier of fortune. *(re-iss. Jun85 on 'E.M.I.' lp/c; ATAK/TC-ATAK 70) (cd-iss. Oct88 on 'E.M.I.'; CZ 142)*

Nov 74. (7") *<8049>* **HIGH BALL SHOOTER. / YOU CAN'T DO IT RIGHT** — `-` —

Jan 75. (7") *<8069>* **STORMBRINGER. / LOVE DON'T MEAN A THING** — `-` —

—— **TOMMY BOLIN** (b.1951, Sioux City, Iowa, USA) – guitar (ex-JAMES GANG, ex-ZEPHYR) repl. BLACKMORE who formed RAINBOW. (see further below)

Oct 75. (lp/c) *(TPSA/TC-TPSA 7515) <2895>* **COME TASTE THE BAND** — `19` `43`
– Comin' home / Lady luck / Gettin' together / Dealer / I need love / Drifter / Love child / This time around – Owed to the 'G' / You keep on moving. *(re-iss. Jun85 on 'E.M.I.' lp/c;) (cd-iss. Jul90 on 'E.M.I.'; CZ 343) (cd re-iss. Jul95 on 'Fame'; CDFA 3318)*

Mar 76. (7") *(PUR 130)* **YOU KEEP ON MOVING. / LOVE CHILD** — `-` `-`

Mar 76. (7") *<8182>* **GETTIN' TIGHTER. / LOVE CHILD** — `-` —

Nov 76. (lp/c) *(TPSA/TC-TPSA 7517) <2995>* **MADE IN EUROPE (live)** `12`
<US title 'DEEP PURPLE LIVE'>
– Burn / Mistreated (interpolating 'Rock me baby') / Lady double dealer / You fool no one / Stormbringer. *(cd-iss. Jul90 on 'E.M.I.'; CZ 344)*

—— split Spring 76, TOMMY BOLIN went solo. He died (of an overdose) 4th Dec'76. HUGHES reformed TRAPEZE. COVERDALE formed WHITESNAKE, he was later joined by LORD and PAICE, after they had been in PAICE, ASHTON and LORD. Remarkably **DEEP PURPLE** reformed 8 years later with early 70's line-up. GILLAN, BLACKMORE, LORD, PAICE and GLOVER.

	Polydor	Mercury

Nov 84. (lp/pic-lp/c) *(POLH/+P/C 16) <824003>* **PERFECT STRANGERS** — `5` `17`
– Knocking at your back door / Under the gun / Nobody's home / Mean streak / Perfect strangers / A gypsy's kiss / Wasted sunsets / Hungry daze. (c+=) – Not responsible. *(re-iss. Mar91 cd/c/lp; 823777-2/-4/-1)*

Jan 85. (7"/7"pic-d) *(POSP/+P 719)* **PERFECT STRANGERS. / SON OF ALERIK** — `48` Mar85
(12"+=) *(POSPX 719)* – Wasted sunsets / Hungry daze.

Jun 85. (7"/12") *(POSP/+X 749) <880477>* **KNOCKING AT YOUR BACK DOOR. / PERFECT STRANGERS** — `68` `61` Jan85

Jan 87. (lp/c)(cd) *(POLH/+C 32)(<831318-2>)* **THE HOUSE OF BLUE LIGHT** — `10` `34`
– Bad attitude / The unwritten law / Call of the wild / Mad dog / Black and white / Hard lovin' woman / The Spanish archer / Strangeways / Mitzi Dupree / Dead or alive. *(re-iss. Mar91 lp/c; 831318-1/-4)*

Jan 87. (7"/7"pic-d) *(POSP/+P 843)* **CALL OF THE WILD. / STRANGEWAYS** — `-` `-`
(12") *(POSPX 843)* – ('A'side) / ('B'-long version).

Jun 88. (7") *(PO 4)* **HUSH (live). / DEAD OR ALIVE (live)** — `62`
(12"+=/cd-s+=) *(PZ/+CD 4)* – Bad attitude (live).

Jun 88. (d-lp/d-c)(cd) *(PODV/+C 10)(<835897-2>)* **NOBODY'S PERFECT (live)** — `38`
– Highway star / Strange kind of woman / Perfect strangers / Hard lovin' woman / Knocking at your back door / Child in time / Lazy / Black night / Woman from Tokyo / Smoke on the water / Hush. *(d-lp has extra tracks) (re-iss. Mar91 d-lp/d-c; 835897-1/-4)*

—— **JOE LYNN TURNER** – vocals (ex-RAINBOW, ex-YNGWIE MALMSTEEN'S RISING FORCE) repl. GILLAN who continued solo.

	R.C.A.	R.C.A.

Oct 90. (7") *<c-s> (PB 49247) <2703>* **KING OF DREAMS. / FIRE IN THE BASEMENT** — `70`
(12"+=/cd-s+=) *(PT/PD 49248)* – ('A'-album version).

Nov 90. (cd/c/lp) *(PD/PK/PL 90535) <2421>* **SLAVES AND MASTERS** — `45` `87`
– King of dreams / The cut runs deep / Fire in the basement / Truth hurts / Breakfast in bed / Love conquers all / Fortuneteller / Too much is not enough / Wicked ways. *(re-iss. cd Apr94; 74321 18719-2)*

Feb 91. (7"/c-s) *(PB/PK 49225)* **LOVE CONQUERS ALL. / TRUTH HURTS** — `57`
(12"+=)(12"pic-d+=)(cd-s+=) *(PT 49212)(PT 49224)(PD 49226)* – Slow down sister.

—— early 70s line-up again after TURNER was sacked.

	R.C.A.	Giant

Jul 93. (cd/c/lp) *(74321 15240-2/-4/-1) <24517>* **THE BATTLE RAGES ON** — `21`
– The battle rages on / Lick it up / Anya / Talk about love / Time to kill / Ramshackle man / A twist in the tale / Nasty piece of work / Solitaire / One man's meat. *(re-iss. cd Oct95; same)*

Nov 94. (cd/c/d-lp) *(74321 23416-2/-4/-1)* **COME HELL OR HIGH WATER (live mid-93)**
– Highway star / Black night / Twist in the tail / Perfect strangers / Anyone's daughter / Child in time / Anya / Speed king / Smoke on the water.

—— **STEVE MORSE** – guitar (ex-DIXIE DREGS) repl. JOE SATRIANI who repl. BLACKMORE on European tour late '93-mid '94

Feb 96. (cd/c) *(74321 33802-2/-4)* **PURPENDICULAR** — `58`
– Vavoom: Ted the mechanic / Loosen my strings / Soon forgotten / Sometimes I feel like screaming / Cascades: I'm not your lover / The aviator / Rosa's cantina / A castle full of rascals / A touch away / Hey Cisco / Somebody stole my guitar / The purpendicular waltz.

May 98. (cd) *(495306-2)* **ABANDON**
– Any fule kno that / Almost human / Don't make me happy / Seventh heaven / Watching the sky / Fingers to the bone / Jack Ruby / She was / Whatsername / 69 / Evil Louie / Bludsucker.

– compilations, exploitation releases, etc. –

Sep 72. (d-lp) *Warners; <2644>* **PURPLE PASSAGES** — `-` `57`

Oct 72. (7") *Warners;* **HUSH. / KENTUCKY WOMAN** — `-` `-`

1972. (lp) *Citation; <CTN 18010>* **THE BEST OF DEEP PURPLE** — `-`

Jun 75. (lp/c) *Purple; (TPSM/TC-TPSM 2002)* **24 CARAT PURPLE (1970-73)** — `14` `-`
– Woman from Tokyo / Fireball / Strange kind of woman / Never before / Black night / Speed king / Smoke on the water / Child in time. *(re-iss. Sep85 on 'Fame' lp/c; FA41 3132-1/-4) (cd-iss. Oct87; CDFA 3132)*

Mar 77. (7"m,7"purple) *Purple; (PUR 132)* **SMOKE ON THE WATER. / CHILD IN TIME / WOMAN FROM TOKYO** — `21`

Sep 77. (7"ep) *Purple; (PUR 135)* **NEW LIVE & RARE** — `31`
– Black night (live) / Painted horse / When a blind man cries.

Jan 78. (lp/c) *Purple; (TPS 3510)* **POWERHOUSE (early 70's line-up)** — `-`

Sep 78. (7"ep) *Purple; (PUR 137)* **NEW LIVE & RARE VOL.2** — `45`
– Burn (edit) / Coronarias redig / Mistreated (live).

Oct 78. (lp/c) *Harvest; (SHSM 2026)* **THE SINGLES A's & B's** — `-`
(re-iss. Nov88 on 'Fame' cd/c/lp; CD/TC+/FA 3212) (cd-iss. Jan93 on 'E.M.I.'; TCEMC 3658)

Apr 79. (lp/c) *Purple; (TPS/TC-TPS 3514)* **THE MARK II PURPLE SINGLES** — `24`

Apr 79. (7"/12") *Harvest; (HAR 5178)* **BLACK NIGHT. / STRANGE KIND OF WOMAN** — `-`

Jul 80. (lp/c) *E.M.I.; (EMTV/TC-EMTV 25) / Warners; <3486>* **DEEPEST PURPLE** — `1` Oct80
– Black night / Speed king / Fireball / Strange kind of woman / Child in time / Woman from Tokyo / Highway star / Space truckin' / Burn / Demon's eye / Stormbringer / Smoke on the water. *(cd-iss. Aug84; CDP 746032-2) (re-iss. 1989 lp/c; ATAK/TC-ATAK 138) (re-iss. Jul90 on 'Fame' cd/c/lp; CD/TC+/FA 3239)*

Jul 80. (7") *Harvest; (HAR 5210)* **BLACK NIGHT. / SPEED KING** — `43` `-`

Oct 80. (7"ep) *Harvest; (SHEP 101)* **NEW LIVE & RARE VOL.3** — `48`
– Smoke on the water (live) / The bird has flown / Grabsplatter.

Dec 80. (lp/c) *Harvest; (SHDW 412)* **IN CONCERT 1970-1972 (live)** — `30`
– Speed king / Wring that neck / Child in time / Mandrake root / Highway star / Strange kind of woman / Lazy / Never before / Space truckin' / Lucille. *(cd-iss. May92;)*

Aug 82. (lp/c) *Harvest; (SHSP/TC-SHSP 4124)* **DEEP PURPLE LIVE IN LONDON (live '74)** — `23`
– Burn / Might just take your life / Lay down, stay down / Mistreated / Smoke on the water / You fool no one.

Jun 85.	(d-lp/d-c) *Harvest; (PUR/TC-PUR 1)* **THE ANTHOLOGY**	**50**
Nov 87.	(lp/c/cd) *Telstar; (STAR/STAC/TCD 2312)* **THE BEST OF DEEP PURPLE**	–
Oct 88.	(d-lp/d-c/d-cd) *Connoisseur; (DPVSOP LP/MC/CD 125)* **SCANDINAVIAN NIGHTS (live)**	–
Mar 91.	(d-cd/d-c/t-lp) *E.M.I.; (CD/TC+/EM 5013)* **THE ANTHOLOGY**	–
Aug 91.	(d-cd/d-c/d-lp) *Connoisseur; (DPVSOP CD/MC/LP 163)* **IN THE ABSENCE OF PINK (KNEBWORTH '85 live)**	–
Sep 91.	(cd/c/lp) *Polygram TV; (845534-2/-4/-1)* **PURPLE RAINBOWS** – (all work including RAINBOW, GILLAN, WHITESNAKE, etc.)	–
Apr 92.	(cd/c) *Polygram; (511438-2/-4)* **KNOCKING AT YOUR BACK DOOR**	–
May 93.	(cd/c) *Spectrum; (550027-2/-4)* **PROGRESSION**	–
Jul 93.	(cd) *Connoisseur; (VSOPCD 187)* **THE DEEP PURPLE FAMILY ALBUM** (associated releases)	–
Nov 93.	(3xcd-box) *E.M.I.; (CDEM 1510)* **LIVE IN JAPAN (live)**	–
Jun 95.	(12"/cd-s) *E.M.I.; (CD/12 EM 382)* **BLACK NIGHT (remix). / SPEED KING (remix)**	**66** –
Sep 95.	(cd) *Spectrum; (551339-2)* **CHILD IN TIME**	–
Nov 95.	(3xcd-box) *E.M.I.; (CDOMB 002)* **BOOK OF TALIESYN / SHADES OF DEEP PURPLE / DEEP PURPLE IN CONCERT**	–
May 96.	(cd) *Premier; (PRMUCD 2)* **CALIFORNIA JAMMING**	–
Jul 96.	(3xcd-box) *Connoisseur; (DPVSOPCD 230)* **THE FINAL CONCERTS (live)**	–
Oct 98.	(cd/c/d-lp) *E.M.I. ; (496807-2/-4/-1)* **THE VERY BEST OF**	**39**

– Hush / Black night / Speed king / Child in time / Strange kind of woman / Fireball / Demon's eye / Smoke on the water / Highway star / When a blind man cries / Never before / Woman from Tokyo / Burn / Stormbringer / Ted the mechanic / Any fule kno that.

DEF LEPPARD

Formed: Sheffield, England . . . 1977 as ATOMIC MASS by RICK SAVAGE, PETE WILLIS and TONY KENNING. Frontman JOE ELLIOT came into the picture not long after and the band adopted the name DEAF LEOPARD, soon altering it to the more rock'n'roll DEF LEPPARD. Additional guitarist STEVE CLARK joined in time for the band's first gigs in July 1978, while FRANK NOON replaced KENNING on drums prior to the band recording their first single. With finance provided by ELLIOT's father, the group issued a debut EP on their own label, 'Bludgeon Riffola', entitled 'GETCHA ROCKS OFF' (was the young BOBBY GILLESPIE a fan, perchance?). Later that year (1979), with RICK ALLEN taking up permanent residence on the drum stool, and following tours supporting AC/DC etc., the band were signed to 'Vertigo'. This prompted a move to London and in 1980, their debut album, 'ON THROUGH THE NIGHT', broke the UK Top 20 although it would be America that would initially embrace the band. They were certainly metal, albeit metal of the most easy listening variety and while the critics hated them, their growing army of fans lapped up their every release. Although 'HIGH 'N' DRY' (1981) marked the beginning of their association with MUTT LANGE and was far more assured in terms of songwriting, DEF LEPPARD's big break came with 1983's 'PYROMANIA'. Legendary for its use of all manner of studio special effects and state-of-the-art technology, the record revolutionised heavy metal and became the benchmark by which subsequent 80's albums were measured. Yet it wasn't a case (as it so often is) of studio flash masking a dearth of genuine talent; DEF LEPPARD were actually capable of turning out finely crafted songs over the course of a whole album. Highly melodic and relentlessly hook-laden, the Americans loved 'PYROMANIA' and its attendant singles, 'PHOTOGRAPH', and 'ROCK OF AGES', the album selling over 7 million copies. Tragedy struck, however, when RICK ALLEN lost his arm in a car crash on New Year's Eve 1984. A true metal warrior, ALLEN soldiered bravely on using a customised drum kit with programmable drum pads and foot pedals. Bearing in mind ALLEN's accident and the band's perfectionist nature, four years wasn't too long to wait for a new album, and for the majority of fans the delay was well worth it. A melodic rock tour de force, the album finally broke the band in their home country with three of its attendant singles reaching the UK Top 10, 'LOVE BITES' giving the band their first No.1. Similarly successful across the Atlantic and worldwide, the album sold a staggering amount, DEF LEPPARD staking their claim as the biggest heavy metal act on the planet. Ironically, just as the group were entering the big league, tragedy struck again as STEVE CLARK was found dead in January 1991 after a prolonged drink/drugs binge. The band recruited elder statesman of rock, VIVIAN CAMPBELL, as a replacement and began work on the 'ADRENALIZE' (1992) album. While the likes of single, 'LET'S GET ROCKED' bordered on the cringeworthy (if only for the awful title), the album's glossy pop-metal once again pulled in the punters in their millions. The next few years saw the release of a B-sides/rarities affair, 'RETRO ACTIVE' (1993) and greatest hits collection, 'VAULT' (1995). A new studio set, 'SLANG', eventually graced the racks in 1996, showcasing a more modern sound (ELLIOT had even traded in his poodle mane for a relatively trendy bobbed haircut). A record executive's wet dream, DEF LEPPARD remain radio friendly unit shifters in the true sense of the phrase. • **Songwriters:** Group compositions, except ONLY AFTER DARK (Mick Ronson) / ACTION (Sweet) / YOU CAN'T ALWAYS GET WHAT YOU WANT (Rolling Stones) / LITTLE WING (Jimi Hendrix) / ELECTED (Alice Cooper) / ZIGGY STARDUST (David Bowie). Roadie STUMPUS MAXIMUS sung; PLEASE RELEASE ME (Engelbert Humperdinck).

Album rating: ON THROUGH THE NIGHT (*5) / HIGH 'N' DRY (*6) / PYROMANIA (*7) / HYSTERIA (*7) / ADRENALIZE (*6) / RETROACTIVE

compilation (*5) / VAULT 1980-1995 – DEF LEPPARD'S GREATEST HITS compilation (*8) / SLANG (*5) / EUPHORIA (*5)

JOE ELLIOT (b. 1 Aug'59) – vocals / **PETE WILLIS** – lead guitar / **STEVE CLARK** (b.23 Apr'60) – guitar / **RICK SAVAGE** (b. 2 Dec'60) – bass / **FRANK NOON** – drums

		Bludgeon Riffola	not iss.
Jan 79.	(7"ep) *(SRT-CUS 232)* **THE DEF LEPPARD EP** – Ride into the sun / Getcha rocks off / The overture.		
Feb 79.	(7"m) *(MSB 001)* **RIDE INTO THE SUN / GETCHA ROCKS OFF / THE OVERTURE**		–

––– **RICK ALLEN** (b. 1 Nov'63) – drums; repl. FRANK who later joined LIONHEART, then WAYSTED

		Vertigo	Mercury
Aug 79.	(7"m) *(6059 240)* **GETCHA ROCKS OFF. / RIDE INTO THE SUN / THE OVERTURE**		
Nov 79.	(7") *(6059 247)* **WASTED. / HELLO AMERICA**	**61**	
Feb 80.	(7") *(LEPP 1)* **HELLO AMERICA. / GOOD MORNING FREEDOM**	**45**	
Mar 80.	(lp)(c) *(9102 040)(7231 028) <3828>* **ON THROUGH THE NIGHT**	**15**	**51**
	– Rock brigade / Hello America / Sorrow is a woman / It could be you / Satellite / When the walls come tumblin' down / Wasted / Rocks off / It don't matter / Answer to the master / Overture. *(re-iss. Jan89 lp/c/cd; 822533-1/-4/-2)*		
Jun 80.	(7") *<76064>* **ROCK BRIGADE. / WHEN THE WALLS COME TUMBLIN' DOWN**	–	
Jul 81.	(lp/c) *(6359/7150 045) <4021>* **HIGH 'N' DRY**	**26**	**38**
	– High 'n' dry (Saturday night) / You got me runnin' / Let it go / Another hit and run / Lady Strange / Mirror, mirror (look into my eyes) / No no no / Bringin' on the heartbreak / Switch 625. *<US re-iss. May84 +=; 818836>* – Bringin' on the heartbreak (remix) / Me and my wine. *(re-iss. Jan89 lp/c/cd+=; 818836-1/-4/-2)* – You got me runnin' (remix) / Me and my wine.		
Aug 81.	(7") *(LEPP 2) <76120>* **LET IT GO. / SWITCH 625**		
Jan 82.	(7") *(LEPP 3)* **BRINGIN' ON THE HEARTACHE (remix). / ME AND MY WINE** (12"+=) *(LEPP 3-12)* – You got me runnin'.		–

––– **PHIL COLLEN** (b. 8 Dec'57) – lead guitar (ex-GIRL) repl. PETE

		Vertigo	Mercury
Jan 83.	(7") *(VER 5) <811215>* **PHOTOGRAPH. / BRINGIN' ON THE HEARTBREAK** (12"+=) *(VERX 5)* – Mirror, Mirror (look into my eyes).	**66**	–
Feb 83.	(7") *<811215>* **PHOTOGRAPH. / ACTION! NOT WORDS**	–	**12**
Mar 83.	(lp/c) *(VERS/+C 2) <810308>* **PYROMANIA**	**18**	**2** Jan83
	– Rock! rock! (till you drop) / Photograph / Stagefright / Too late for love / Die hard the hunter / Foolin around / Rock of ages / Comin' under fire / Action! not words / Billy's got a gun. *(cd-iss. 1988; 810308-2)*		
Jun 83.	(7") *<812604>* **ROCK OF AGES. / BILLY'S GOT A GUN**		**16**
Aug 83.	(7"/7"s/7"sha-pic-d/12") *(VER/+Q/P/X 6)* **ROCK OF AGES. / ACTION! NOT WORDS**	**41**	–
Aug 83.	(7") *<814178>* **FOOLIN'. / COMIN' UNDER FIRE**	–	**28**
Nov 83.	(7") *(VER 8) <814178>* **FOOLIN'. / TOO LATE FOR LOVE** (12"+=) *(VERX 8)* – High'n'dry.	–	–
Jun 84.	(7") *<818779>* **BRINGIN' ON THE HEARTBREAK (remix). / ME AND MY WINE**	–	**61**
Aug 85.	(7"/7"g-f) *(VER/+G 9)* **PHOTOGRAPH. / BRINGIN' ON THE HEARTBREAK** (12"+=) *(VERX 9)* – Mirror, mirror.		

––– Remained a 5-piece although RICK ALLEN lost an arm in a car crash (31st December '84). He now used a specially adapted programmable drum pads and foot pedals.

		Vertigo	Mercury
Jul 87.	(7") *(LEP 1)* **ANIMAL. / TEAR IT DOWN** (12"+=/12"red+=) *(LEP X/C 1)* – ('A'extended). (cd-s++=) *(LEPCD 1)* – Women.	**6**	–
Aug 87.	(lp/pic-lp/c)(cd) *(HYS LP/PD/MC 1)(<830675>)* **HYSTERIA**	**2**	**1**
	– Women / Rocket / Animal / Love bites / Pour some sugar on me / Armageddon it / Gods of war / Don't shoot shotgun / Run riot / Hysteria / Excitable / Love and affection. *(cd+=)* – I can't let you be a memory.		
Aug 87.	(7") *<888757>* **WOMEN. / TEAR IT DOWN**	–	**80**
Sep 87.	(7"/7"sha-pic-d/c-s) *(LEP/+S/MC 2)* **POUR SOME SUGAR ON ME. / I WANNA BE YOUR HERO** (12"+=) *(LEPX 2)* – ('A'extended mix).	**18**	–
Oct 87.	(7") *<888832>* **ANIMAL. / I WANNA BE YOUR HERO**	–	**19**
Nov 87.	(7"/7"s/c-s) *(LEP/+S/MC 3) <870004>* **HYSTERIA. / RIDE INTO THE SUN ('87 version)** (12"+=/12"s+=) *(LEPX 3/+13)* – Love and affection (live). (cd-s++=) *(LEPCD 3)* – I wanna be your hero.	**26**	**10** Jan88
Apr 88.	(7") *<870298>* **POUR SOME SUGAR ON ME. / RING OF FIRE**	–	**2**
Apr 88.	(7"/7"s) *(LEP/+P 4)* **ARMAGEDDON IT! (The Atomic mix). / RING OF FIRE** (12"+=/12"s+=) *(LEPX/+B 4)* – ('A'version). (pic-cd-s++=) *(LEPCD 4)* – Animal / Pour some sugar on me.	**20**	–
Jul 88.	(7"g-f) *(LEP 5) <870402>* **LOVE BITES. / BILLY'S GOT A GUN (live)** (12"+=/12"box+=/cd-s+=) *(LEP X/XB/CD 5)* – Excitable (orgasmic mix).	**11**	**1**
Nov 88.	(7") *<870692>* **ARMAGEDDON IT! / RELEASE ME (STUMPUS MAXIMUS & THE GOOD OL' BOYS)**	–	**3**
Jan 89.	(7"/7"s) *(LEP/+C 6)* **ROCKET. / RELEASE ME (STUMPUS MAXIMUS & THE GOOD OL' BOYS)** ('A'-Lunar mix; 12"+=/12"s+=/12"pic-d+=/cd-s+=) *(LEP X/XC/XP/CD 6)* – Rock of ages (live).	**15**	–
Feb 89.	(7") *<872614>* **ROCKET. / WOMEN (live)**	–	**12**

––– STEVE CLARK was found dead on the 8th of January '91 after drinking/drugs session. Replaced by VIVIAN CAMPBELL (b.25 Aug'62, Belfast, N.Ireland) – guitar (ex-DIO, ex-WHITESNAKE, ex-SHADOWKING)

Mar 92.	(7"/c-s) *(DEF/+MC 7) <866568>* **LET'S GET ROCKED. / ONLY AFTER DARK** (12"pic-d+=) *(DEFXP 7)* – Too late for love (live). (pic-cd-s+=) *(DEFCD 7)* – Women (live).	**2**	**15**

Apr 92. (cd/c/lp) (510978-2/-4/-1) <512185> **ADRENALIZE** |1| |1|
– Let's get rocked / Heaven is / Make love like a man / Tonight / White lightning / Stand up (kick love into motion) / Personal property / Have you ever needed someone so bad / I wanna touch you / Tear it down. (pic-lp iss.Dec92, w / 2 extra tracks; 510978-0)

Jun 92. (7"/c-s) (LEP/+MC 7) <864038> **MAKE LOVE LIKE A MAN. / MISS YOU IN A HEARTBEAT** |12| |36|
(12"+=) (LEPXP 7) – Two steps behind (acoustic).
(cd-s+=) (LEPCD 5) – Action.

Aug 92. (c-s) <864136> **HAVE YOU EVER NEEDED SOMEONE SO BAD / ELECTED (live)** |–| |12|

Sep 92. (7"/c-s) (LEP/+MC 8) **HAVE YOU EVER NEEDED SOMEONE SO BAD. / FROM THE INSIDE** |16| |–|
(12"pic-d+=) (LEPXP 8) – You can't always get what you want.
(cd-s++=) (LEPCD 8) – Little wing.

Dec 92. (c-s) <864604> **STAND UP (KICK LOVE INTO MOTION) / FROM THE INSIDE (THE ACOUSTIC HIPPIES FROM HELL)** |–| |34|

Jan 93. (7"etched/c-s) (LEP/+MC 9) **HEAVEN IS. / SHE'S TOO TOUGH** |13| |–|
(pic-cd-s+=) (LEPCD 9) – Let's get rocked (live) / Elected (live).
(12"pic-d) (LEPX 9) – ('A'side) / Let's get rocked (live) / Tokyo road (live).

Mar 93. (c-s) <862016> **TONIGHT / SHE'S TOO TOUGH** |–| |62|

Apr 93. (7"/c-s) (LEP/+MC 10) **TONIGHT. / NOW I'M HERE (live)** |34| |–|
(12"pic-d+=) (LEPX 10) – Hysteria (live).
(cd-s+=) (LEPCD 10) – Photograph (live).
(cd-s) (LEPCD 10) – ('A'side) / Pour some sugar on me / ('A'demo).

Sep 93. (7"/c-s) (LEP/+MC 12) <77116> **TWO STEPS BEHIND. / TONIGHT (acoustic demo)** |32| |12|
(cd-s+=) (LEPCD 12) – S.M.C.

—— <above single from the film 'Last Action Hero' on 'Columbia' US>

Oct 93. (cd/c/lp) (<518305-2/-4/-1>) **RETRO ACTIVE** |6| |9|
– Desert song / Fractured love / Two steps behind (acoustic) / Only after dark / Action / She's too tough / Miss you in a heartbeat (acoustic) / Only after dark (acoustic) / Ride into the sun / From the inside / Ring of fire / I wanna be your hero / Miss you in a heartbeat / Two steps behind.

Nov 93. (c-s,cd-s) <858080> **MISS YOU IN A HEARTBEAT (acoustic version) / LET'S GET ROCKED (live)** |–| |39|

Jan 94. (7"/c-s) (LEP/+MC 13) **ACTION. / MISS YOU IN A HEARTBEAT (demo)** |14| |–|
(cd-s+=) (LEPCD 13) – She's too tough (demo).
(cd-s+=) (LEPCX 13) – Two steps behind (demo) / Love bites (live).

Oct 95. (c-s) (LEPMC 14) **WHEN LOVE & HATE COLLIDE / POUR SOME SUGAR ON ME (remix)** |2| |–|
(cd-s+=) (LEPCD 14) – Armageddon it! (remix).
(cd-s++=) (LEPDD 14) – ('A'demo).
(cd-s) (LEP 14) – ('A'side) / Rocket (remix) / Excitable (remix).
(cd-s) (LEP 14) – ('A'side) / Excitable (remix) / ('A'demo).

Oct 95. (cd/c/lp) (528652-2/-4/-1>) <528815> **VAULT 1980-1995 DEF LEPPARD GREATEST HITS** (compilation) |3| |15|
– Pour some sugar on me / Photograph / Love bites / Let's get rocked / Two steps behind / Animal / Heaven is / Rocket / When love & hate collide / Action / Make love like a man / Armageddon it / Have you ever needed someone / So bad / Rock of ages / Hysteria / Bringin' on the heartbreak. (cd w/free cd) – LIVE AT DON VALLEY, SHEFFIELD

Nov 95. (c-s) <852424> **WHEN LOVE AND HATE COLLIDE / CAN'T KEEP AWAY FROM THE FLAME** |–| |58|

Apr 96. (c-s) (LEPMC 15) **SLANG / ANIMAL (live acoustic)** |17| |–|
(cd-s+=) (LEPCD 15) – Ziggy Stardust (live acoustic) / Pour some sugar on me (live acoustic).
(cd-s) (LEPDD 15) – ('A'side) / Can't keep the flame away / When love and hate collide (strings and piano version).

May 96. (cd/c/lp) (<532486-2/-4/-1>) **SLANG** |5| |14|
– Truth / Turn to dust / Slang / All I want is everything / Work it out / Breathe a sigh / Deliver me / Gift of flesh / Blood runs cold / Where does love go when it dies / Pearl of euphoria. (cd w/ free cd rec. live in Singapore) – Armageddon it / Two steps behind / From the inside / Animal / When love & hate collide / Pour some sugar on me.

Jun 96. (c-s) (LEPMC 16) **WORK IT OUT / TWO STEPS BEHIND** |22| |–|
(cd-s+=) (LEPCD 16) – Move with me slowly.
(cd-s) (LEPDD 16) – ('A'side) / ('A'demo) / Truth?

Sep 96. (c-s) (LEPMC 17) **ALL I WANT IS EVERYTHING / WHEN SATURDAY COMES** |38| |–|
(cd-s+=) (LEPCD 17) – Jimmy's theme / ('A'radio edit).
(cd-s) (LEPDD 17) – ('A'side) / 'Cause we ended as lovers / Led boots / ('A'radio edit).

Nov 96. (c-s) (578838-4) **BREATHE A SIGH / ROCK! ROCK! (TILL YOU DROP)** |43| |–|
(cd-s+=) (578839-2) – Deliver me (live) / Slang (live).
(cd-s) (578841-2) – ('A'side) / Another hit and run (live) / All I want is everything (live) / Work it out (live).

Jun 99. (cd/c) (<546 244-2/212-4>) **EUPHORIA** |11| |11|
– Demolition man / Promises / Back in your face / Goodbye / All night / Paper sun / It's only love / 21st century sha la la girl / To be alive / Disintigrate / Guilty / Day after day / Kings of oblivion.

Jul 99. (c-s) (562136-4) **PROMISES / BACK IN YOUR FACE – GOODBYE – ALL NIGHT (excerpts)** |41| | |
(cd-s+=) (562137-2) – Under my wheels.
(cd-s) (562136-2) – ('A'side) / World's collide / Immortal.

Sep 99. (c-s) (562288-4) **GOODBYE / IMMORTAL** | | | |
(cd-s+=) (562288-2) – Burnout.
(cd-s) (562289-2) – ('A'side) / Who do you love? / When love and hate collide.

DEFTONES

Formed: Sacramento, California, USA ... 1989, by magnetic frontman CHINO MORENO, plus STEPHEN CARPENTER, CHI CHENG and ABE CUNNINGHAM. One of the more promising acts to have signed to MADONNA's 'Maverick' label (through 'Warners'), The DEFTONES released their debut album, 'ADRENALINE' in 1995. Like a gonzoid cross between JONATHAN DAVIS (KORN) and ZACK DE LA ROCHA, CHINO's incendiary live presence helped the group build up a loyal following. By the release of their next set, 'AROUND THE FUR' (1997), their post-metal noise had reached fruition, from the sonic assault of the album's opener, 'MY OWN SUMMER (SHOVE IT)' to 'HEADUP' (a collaboration with Sepultura's MAX CAVALERA). • **Covered:** THE CHAUFFEUR (Duran Duran).

Album rating: ADRENALINE (*9) / AROUND THE FUR (*8)

CHINO MORENO – vocals / **STEPHEN CARPENTER** – guitar / **CHI CHENG** – bass, vocals / **ABE CUNNINGHAM** – drums

		Maverick	Maverick

Oct 95. (cd/c) <(9362 46054-2/-4)> **ADRENALINE** | | | |
– Bored / Minus blindfold / One weak / Nosebleed / Lifter / Root / 7 words / Birthmark / Engine No.9 / Fireal.

Nov 97. (cd/c) <(9362 46810-2/-4)> **AROUND THE FUR** |56| |29|
– My own summer (shove it) / Lhabia / Mascara / Around the fur / Be quiet and drive / Lotion / Dai the flu / Headup / MX.

Mar 98. (7"/c-s) (W 0432/+C) **MY OWN SUMMER (SHOVE IT). / ROOT (live)** |29| | |
(cd-s+=) (W 0432CD) – Nosebleed (live) / Lifter (live).
(cd-s) (W 0432CDX) – ('A'side) / Lotion (live) / Fireal swords (live) / Bored (live).

Jun 98. (7") (W 0445) **BE QUIET AND DRIVE (FAR AWAY). / ('A'acoustic)** |50| | |
(cd-s+=) (W 0445CD) – Birthmark (live).
(cd-s) (W 0445CDX) – ('A'side) / Engine No.9 (live) / Teething (live).

DEL AMITRI

Formed: Glasgow, Scotland ... 1983 by singer/songwriter JUSTIN CURRIE and IAIN HARVIE, who recruited additional musicians BRYAN TOLLAND and PAUL TYAGI prior to recording their debut single, 'SENSE SICKNESS', for independent label, 'No Strings'. Emerging in the golden era of Scots indie when 'Postcard' was the hippest namedrop on the block, the group's early, acoustic-orientated approach brought inevitable comparisons with ORANGE JUICE and their ilk, while CURRIE's subtly sardonic lyrics marked him out as an aspiring wordsmith. A punishing round of gigging, including a number of prestigious support slots, slowly raised DEL AMITRI's profile and subsequently attracted the interest of 'Chrysalis' records. Signed to a major label deal, the band made their album debut in Spring '85 with 'DEL AMITRI', a competent set which showcased the band's intelligent folk pop/rock. The initial press reaction was encouraging and the future looked bright prior to a subsequent dispute with the company leaving them label-less. Lending new meaning to the term "grassroots following", DEL AMITRI's loyal band of US fans were pivotal in the success of their ensuing American tour, promoting gigs and providing an accommodation alternative to the dreaded tour van. The success of the jaunt led to another major label venture, this time around with 'A&M', who were far more successful in getting DEL AMITRI's career off the ground. Throughout the interim "wilderness" years, CURRIE had been carefully honing his writing skills, the more mature approach paying off when the 'KISS THIS THING GOODBYE' single made the UK Top 60. Released at the same time, a belated follow-up album, 'WAKING HOURS' (1989), eventually made the British Top 10 following the success of 'NOTHING EVER HAPPENS'. A world-weary diatribe on societal inertia, the track's earthy sound – if not its tone of barely concealed bitterness – was characteristic of the more accessible path DEL AMITRI were now cultivating. With his legendary sideburns and windswept good looks, CURRIE also became something of an unlikely early 90's sex symbol, the shag candidate for the more discerning female prior to EVAN DANDO cornering the market with his flowing locks. Whatever, CURRIE was certainly the group's focal point and many fans no doubt scarcely noticed that new boys DAVID CUMMINGS (a replacement for MICK SLAVEN, who himself had succeeded TOLLAND on the previous set) and BRIAN McDERMOTT had been recruited for a third set, 'CHANGE EVERYTHING' (1992). More polished and chart-friendly than any DEL AMITRI release to date, the record narrowly missed the UK No.1 spot, its immaculately crafted (yet often verging on bland) MOR spawning another major hit in 'ALWAYS THE LAST TO KNOW' and a further trio of fairly minor chart encounters with 'BE MY DOWNFALL', 'JUST LIKE A MAN' and 'WHEN YOU WERE YOUNG'. A fourth set, 'TWISTED' (1995), hardly broke new ground, although it did spawn a US Top 10 in 'ROLL TO ME'; that DEL AMITRI appealed to the American market was hardly surprising, their reliably safe, inoffensive coffee-table roots-rock ideal fodder for FM radio. Never being the trendiest of bands, DEL AMITRI never really suffered a backlash, carving out their own little niche with relative success almost guaranteed. • **Songwriters:** CURRIE – HARVIE composed except covers; DON'T CRY NO TEARS (Neil Young) / BYE BYE PRIDE (Go-Betweens) / CINDY INCIDENTLY (Faces). • **Trivia:** DEL AMITRI means 'from the womb' in Greek.

Album rating: DEL AMITRI (*6) / WAKING HOURS (*8) / CHANGE EVERYTHING (*7) / TWISTED (*6) / SOME OTHER SUCKER'S PARADE (*5) / HATFUL OF RAIN – THE BEST OF DEL AMITRI compilation (*8)

JUSTIN CURRIE (b.11 Dec'64) – vocals, bass, acoustic guitar / **IAIN HARVIE** (b.19 May'62) – guitar / **BRYAN TOLLAND** – guitar / **PAUL TYAGIS** – drums, percussion

	No Strings	not iss.
Aug 83. (7") *(NOSP 1)* **SENSE SICKNESS. / THE DIFFERENCE IS**	☐	-
	Chrysalis	Chrysalis

May 85. (lp/c) *(CHR/ZCHR 1499)* **DEL AMITRI**
– Heard through a wall / Hammering heart / Former owner / Sticks and stones girl / Deceive yourself (in ignorant Heaven) / I was here / Crows in a wheatfield / Keepers / Ceasefire / Breaking bread. *(cd-iss. Dec90; CCD 1499)*

Jul 85. (7") *(CHS 2859)* **STICKS AND STONES GIRL. / THIS KING IS POOR**   ☐   -
(12"+=) *(CHS12 2859)* – The difference is.

Oct 85. (7") *(CHS 2925)* **HAMMERING HEART. / LINES RUNNING NORTH**   ☐   -
(12"+=) *(CHS12 2925)* – Brown eyed girl.

—— **MICK SLAVEN** – guitar (ex-BOURGIE BOURGIE) repl. TOLLAND / sessions from **ANDY ALSTON** – keyboards / **ROBERT CAIRNS** – violin / **BLAIR COWAN** – accordion / **STEPHEN IRVINE** – drums / **JULIAN DAWSON** – harmonica / **JAMES O'MALLEY** – bass / **CAROLINE LEVELLE** – cello / **WILL MOWAT** – seq, keyboards

	A&M	A&M
Jul 89. (7") *(AM 515)* **KISS THIS THING GOODBYE. / NO HOLDING ON**	59	☐

(12"+=/3"cd-s+=) *(AMY/CDEE 515)* – Slowly, it's coming back.

Jul 89. (lp/c/cd) *(AMA/AMC/CDA 9006) <5287>* **WAKING HOURS**   ☐   95 Feb90
– Kiss this thing goodbye / Opposite view / Move away Jimmy Blue / Stone cold sober / You're gone / When I want you / This side of the morning / Empty / Hatful of rain / Nothing ever happens. *(re-dist.Feb90 hit UK No.6; same)* *(re-iss. Mar95 cd/c; same)*

Oct 89. (7") *(AM 527)* **STONE COLD SOBER. / THE RETURN OF MAGGIE BROWN**   ☐   ☐
(12"+=/3"cd-s+=) *(AMY/CDEE 527)* – Talk it to death.

Jan 90. (7"/c-s) *(AM/+MC 536)* **NOTHING EVER HAPPENS. / SO MANY SOULS TO CHANGE**   11   ☐
(12"+=/cd-s+=) *(AMY/CDEE 536)* – Don't I look like the kind of guy you used to hate? / Evidence.

Mar 90. (7"/7"g-f/c-s) *(AM/+S/MC 551)* **KISS THIS THING GOODBYE. / NO HOLDING ON**   43   -
(10"+=/12"+=/cd-s+=) *(10AMX/AMY/AMCD 551)* – Slowly, it's coming back.

Apr 90. (c-s) *<1485>* **KISS THIS THING GOODBYE. / THE RETURN OF MAGGIE BROWN**   -   35

Jun 90. (7"/c-s) *(AM/+MC 555)* **MOVE AWAY JIMMY BLUE. / ANOTHER LETTER HOME**   36   ☐
(12"+=) *(AMX 555)* – April the first / This side of the morning (live).
(12"+=/cd-s+=) *(AM Y/CD 555)* – April the first / More than you'd ever know.

Oct 90. (7"/c-s) *(AM/+MC 589)* **SPIT IN THE RAIN. / SCARED TO LIVE**   21   ☐
(12"+=) *(AMY 589)* – The return of Maggie Brown.
(10"++=/cd-s++=) *(AM X/CD 589)* – Talk it to death.

—— **DAVID CUMMINGS** – guitar repl. SLAVEN / **BRIAN McDERMOTT** – drums (who guested on last) repl. TYGANI

Apr 92. (7"/c-s) *(AM/+MC 870) <1604>* **ALWAYS THE LAST TO KNOW. / LEARN TO CRY**   13   -
(cd-s+=) *(AMCD 870)* – Angel on the roof / The whole river is quiet.

Jun 92. (cd/c/lp) *(395385-2/-4/-1) <5385>* **CHANGE EVERYTHING**   2   ☐
– Be my downfall / Just like a man / When you were young / Surface of the Moon / I won't take the blame / The first rule of love / The ones that you love lead you nowhere / Always the last to know / To last a lifetime / As soon as the tide comes in / Behind the fool / Sometimes I just have to say your name. *(re-iss. cd/c Mar95; same)*

Jun 92. (7"/c-s) *(AM/+MC 884)* **BE MY DOWNFALL. / WHISKEY REMORSE**   30   -
(10"+=/cd-s+=) *(AM X/CD 884)* – Lighten up the load / The heart is a bad design.

Jul 92. (c-s) *<1604>* **ALWAYS THE LAST TO KNOW / BE MY DOWNFALL**   -   30

Sep 92. (7"/c-s) *(AM/+MC 0057)* **JUST LIKE A MAN / SPIT IN THE RAIN (remix)**   25   ☐
(cd-s+=) *(AMCDR 0057)* – I won't take the blame (acoustic) / Scared to live.
(cd-s) *(AMCD 0057)* – ('A'side) / Don't cry no tears / Bye bye pride / Cindy incidentally.

Jan 93. (7"/c-s) *(AM/+MC 0132)* **WHEN YOU WERE YOUNG. / LONG JOURNEY HOME THE ONES THAT YOU LOVE LEAD YOU NOWHERE**   20   ☐
(cd-s+=) *(AMCDR 0132)* – The verb to do / Kestral road.
(cd-s) *(AMCD 0132)* – ('A'side) / The ones that you love lead you nowhere (live) / Kiss this thing goodbye (live) / Hatful of rain (live).

Feb 95. (c-s) *(580 959-4)* **HERE AND NOW / LONG WAY DOWN**   21   ☐
(10"+=) *(580 969-1)* – Someone else will / Queen of false alarms.
(cd-s+=) *(580 959-2)* – Queen of false alarms / Crashing down.
(cd-s) *(580 969-2)* – ('A'side) / Always the last to know (live) / When I want you (live) / Stone cold sober (live).

Feb 95. (cd/c/lp) *(540 311-2/-4/-1) <0311>* **TWISTED**   3   ☐
– Food for songs / Start with me / Here and now / One thing left to do / Tell her this / Being somebody else / Roll to me / Crashing down / It might as well be you / Never enough / It's never too late to be alone / Driving with the brakes on. *(re-iss. d-cd Aug95; 540396-2)*

Apr 95. (7"/c-s) *(581 004-7/-4)* **DRIVING WITH THE BRAKES ON. / LIFE BY MISTAKE**   18   ☐
(cd-s+=) *(581 005-2)* – A little luck / In the meantime.
(cd-s) *(581 007-2)* – ('A'side) / Nothing ever happens / Kiss this thing goodbye / Always the last to know.

Jun 95. (c-s) *(581 128-4)* **ROLL TO ME / IN THE FRAME**   22   -
(cd-s+=) *(581 129-2)* – Food for songs (acoustic) / One thing left to do (acoustic).
(cd-s) *(581 131-2)* – ('A'side) / Spit in the rain / Stone cold sober (remix) / Move away Jimmy Blue.

Jun 95. (c-s) *<1114>* **ROLL TO ME / LONG WAY DOWN**   -   10

Oct 95. (c-s) *(581 214-4)* **TELL HER THIS / A BETTER MAN**   32   ☐
(cd-s+=) *(581 215-2)* – The last love song / When you were young.

(cd-s) *(518 217-2)* – ('A'side) / Whiskey remorse / Fred Partington's daughter / Learn to cry.

Jun 97. (c-s) *(582 252-4)* **NOT WHERE IT'S AT / SLEEP INSTEAD OF TEARDROPS**   21   ☐
(cd-s+=) *(582 253-2)* – Spair pair of laces / Before the evening steals the afternoon.
(cd-s+=) *(582 255-2)* – A grimace not a smile / Low friends in high places.

Jul 97. (cd/c/lp) *(540 705-2/-4/-1)* **SOME OTHER SUCKER'S PARADE**   6   ☐
– Not where it's at / Some other sucker's parade / Won't make it better / What I think she sees / Medicine / High times / Mother nature's writing / No family man / Cruel light of day / Funny way to win / Through all that nothing / Life is full / Lucky guy / Make it always be too late.

—— In Sep'97, 'MEDICINE' was due for release but withdrawn; see below single for corresponding b-sides; 582365-2/582367-2/582569-2.

Nov 97. (cd-s) *(582 433-2)* **SOME OTHER SUCKER'S PARADE / DRIVING WITH THE BRAKES ON (live) / MOVE AWAY JIMMY BLUE (live) / THE ONES THAT YOU LOVE LEAD YOU NOWHERE (live)**   46   ☐
(cd-s) *(582 435-2)* – ('A'side) / Roll to me (live) / Here & now (live) / Hatful of rain (live).
(cd-s) *(582 437-2)* – ('A'side) / ('A'live) / Always the last to know (live) / Stone cold sober (live).

Jun 98. (c-s/cd-s) *(582 705-4/-2)* **DON'T COME HOME TOO SOON / THREE LITTLE WORDS / PAPER THIN / DON'T COME HOME TOO SOON (instrumental)**   15   ☐
(cd-s) *(582 707-2)* – ('A'side) / Nothing ever happens / Kiss this thing goodbye / Always the last to know.

Aug 98. (c-s) *(566 347-4)* **CRY TO BE FOUND / CANNED LAUGHTER**   40   ☐
(cd-s+=) *(566 347-2)* – One step at a time.
(cd-s) *(566 349-2)* – ('A'side) / Being somebody else (live) / Not where it's at.

Sep 98. (cd/c) *(540 940-2/-4)* **HATFUL OF RAIN – THE BEST OF DEL AMITRI** (compilation)   5   ☐
– Cry to be found / Roll to me / Kiss this thing goodbye / Not where it's at / Nothing ever happens / Always the last to know / Here & now / Just like a man / Spit in the rain / When we were young / Driving with the brakes on / Stone cold sober / Tell her this / Move away Jimmy Blue / Be my downfall / Some other sucker's parade / Don't come home too soon. *(d-cd includes LOUSY WITH LOVE – THE B-SIDES; 540 941-2)* – Scared to live / The return of Maggie Brown / In the frame / Sleep instead of teardrops / Long journey home / Paper thin / The last love song / Verb to do / In the meantime / Long way down / Whiskey remorse / Before the evening steals the afternoon / So many souls to change.

DELANEY & BONNIE

Formed: Los Angeles, California, USA ... 1967 by married couple DELANEY BRAMLETT and BONNIE LYNN. Hitched within a week of meeting one another, BRAMLETT was part of the transplanted community of Southern musicians (including LEON RUSSELL, J.J. CALE, DAVID GATES, JESSE DAVIS etc,) working sessions in L.A. while LYNN had been the only white 'Ikette' in IKE & TINA TURNER's mid-60's revue. With a shared love of blues, soul, country and gospel, the pair became the first all-white act to sign with Memphis soul bastion, 'Stax'. There, they initiated their hybrid of rootsy country/soul with the 'HOME' (1969) album, pitting LYNN's gritty delivery against BRAMLETT's mean guitar picking and country-inflected vocal to thrilling effect on standout cuts 'IT'S BEEN A LONG TIME COMING', 'THINGS GET BETTER' and 'HARD TO SAY GOODBYE'; even the sleeve was "down home", featuring a shot of BRAMLETT's grandfather's country shack. A further (eponymous) album followed later that year on the 'Independence' label although the DELANEY & BONNIE machine only really started motoring after they'd signed to 'Elektra'. Summer 69's 'ACCEPT NO SUBSTITUTE – THE ORIGINAL DELANEY & BONNIE' (released on the BEATLES' 'Apple' in the UK) caused enough of a stir to see D&B signed up as opening act for the forthcoming US tour by BLIND FAITH (the much hyped blues-rock "supergroup" featuring ERIC CLAPTON amongst others). Even the ROLLING STONES were hooked on DELANEY & BONNIE's sound, so impressed by the album that they relocated to L.A. to complete sessions for their 'Let It Bleed' masterpiece. While the end of the aforesaid tour was to signal the end of the line for the short-lived BLIND FAITH, it was only the beginning for DELANEY & BONNIE who'd struck up a lasting professional and personal friendship with CLAPTON. Eager to duck out of the media circus, the guitar maestro joined D&B's band alongside an incredible line-up that included the likes of BOBBY WHITLOCK, DUANE ALLMAN, BOBBY KEYS, LEON RUSSELL and JIM KELTNER. CLAPTON then brought this trail-blazing southern-fried roots revue to England for a legendary series of dates that saw the likes of DAVE MASON (of TRAFFIC fame) and GEORGE HARRISON joining them on stage. The accompanying vinyl document, 'DELANEY & BONNIE & FRIENDS ON TOUR WITH ERIC CLAPTON' (1971) remains an electrifying listening experience with CLAPTON stealing the show on opening track 'THINGS GET BETTER' and D&B hitting all the right spots on MASON's 'ONLY YOU KNOW AND I KNOW'. Unsurprisingly, the record (which boasted another classic country-rock style sleeve) became the duo's biggest seller, making the UK Top 40 and the US Top 30. After working with JOHN LENNON and touring Europe, the ensemble returned to the US in 1970 as headliners. Yet the whole project went awry (and the tour subsequently cancelled) as various members broke ranks for both CLAPTON's DEREK & THE DOMINOES and JOE COCKER's MAD DOGS & ENGLISHMEN. Unfazed, the duo continued recording, cutting 'TO DELANEY FROM BONNIE' (1970), the acoustic 'MOTEL SHOT' (1971) and 'COUNTRY LIFE' (1971), racking up a couple of Top 20 hits in 'NEVER ENDING SONG OF LOVE' and a re-recorded 'ONLY YOU KNOW AND I KNOW'. Following a final album for 'Columbia', 'D&B

TOGETHER' (1972), the couple dissolved both their musical partnership and their marriage. Both went on to solo careers, DELANEY cutting a couple of albums for 'Columbia' and one for 'M.G.M.' before reuniting with his former sparring partners (RUSSELL, CLAPTON etc.) for 'CLASS REUNION' (1977) on 'Motown's 'Prodigal' offshoot. BONNIE, meanwhile cut 'SWEET BONNIE BRAMLETT' (1973) backed by Scotland's own AVERAGE WHITE BAND(!) before signing to southern rock outlet, 'Capricorn'. She also graced many a session (including LITTLE FEAT's sizzling 'Dixie Chicken') with her sassy vocals. Not a lady to be messed with, BONNIE punched ELVIS COSTELLO in a 1979 incident over alleged racial remarks(!) although by the 90's she had swapped the rock'n'roll lifestyle for acting, regularly appearing in popular US sitcom, 'Roseanne'. • **Songwriters:** Both penned material. Leon Russell wrote 'GROUPIE (SUPERSTAR)', which later became a hit for The CARPENTERS. • **Trivia:** Their Top 20 US hit 'NEVER ENDING SONG OF LOVE' became a UK Top 3 hit for NEW SEEKERS.

Album rating: HOME (*7) / DELANEY & BONNIE (*6) / ACCEPT NO SUBSTITUTE (*6) / DELANEY AND BONNIE AND FRINDS ON TOUR (WITH ERIC CLAPTON) (*8) / TO DELANEY FROM BONNIE (*6) / D&B TOGETHER (*5) / THE BEST OF DELANEY & BONNIE compilation (*7)

DELANEY BRAMLETT (b. 1 Jul'39, Pontotoc Co., Mississippi) – vocals (had released two solo 45's 'HEARTBRREAK HOTEL' and 'LIVERPOOL LOU') / **BONNIE BRAMLETT** (b. BONNIE LYNN, 8 Nov'44, Acton, Illinois) – vocals with back-up from BOOKER T. & THE MG'S / **BOBBY WHITLOCK** – keyboards

			Stax	Stax
Aug 68.	(7") <0003> **IT'S BEEN A LONG TIME COMING. / WE'VE JUST BEEN FEELING BAD**		-	
Feb 69.	(lp) (SXATS 1029) <22026> **HOME**			

– It's been a long time coming / A right now love / We can love / My baby specializes / Everybody loves a winner / Things get better / Just plain beautiful / Hard to say goodbye / Pour your love on me / Piece of my heart. (re-iss. 1974; 2362 001) (cd-iss. May90 on 'Stax-Ace'; CDSXE 029)

Nov 69.	(7") <0057> **JUST PLAIN BEAUTIFUL. / HARD TO SAY GOODBYE**		-	

(UK-iss.1970; same as US)

—— now back-up from future DEREK & THE DOMINOES (see; Eric CLAPTON). Also incl. **WHITLOCK, JERRY McGEE** – guitar / **DAVE MASON, DUANE ALLMAN**, etc.

			Elektra	Elektra
Jul 69.	(lp) <(EKS 74039)> **ACCEPT NO SUBSTITUTE – THE ORIGINAL DELANEY & BONNIE**			

– Get ourselves together / Someday / The ghetto / When the battle is over / Dirty old man / Love me a little bit longer / I can't take it much longer / Do right man – do right man / Soldiers of the cross / The gift of love. (originally w-drawn on 'Apple'; SAPCOR 7) (re-iss. Feb88 on 'Thunderbolt' lp/cd; THBL/CDBL 050)

Oct 69.	(7"; w-drawn UK) <(EKSN 45066)> **GET OURSELVES TOGETHER. / SOLDIERS OF THE CROSS**			
Feb 70.	(7") <(EKSN 45078)> **SOMEDAY. / DIRTY OLD MAN**			

DELANEY & BONNIE & FRIENDS

—— now with **DEREK & THE DOMINOES** plus guest **GEORGE HARRISON**

			Atlantic	Atco
Dec 69.	(7"; as DELANEY & BONNIE & FRIENDS featuring ERIC CLAPTON) (584 308) <6725> **COMIN' HOME. / GROUPIE (SUPERSTAR)**		16	84 Feb70
May 70.	(lp) (2400 029) <326> **DELANEY & BONNIE & FRIENDS ON TOUR WITH ERIC CLAPTON**		39	29 Apr70

– Things get better / Poor Elijah – Tribute to Johnson (medley) / Only you know and I know / I don't want to discuss it / That's what my man is for / Where there's a will, there's a way / Coming home / Little Richard medley: Tutti Frutti – The girl can't help it – Long tall Sally – Jenny Jenny. (re-iss. Jul87; K 30030) (cd-iss. Feb92; 7567 90397-2)

—— the BRAMLETT's brought numerous session people

Jun 70.	(7") (2091 016) <6756> **FREE THE PEOPLE. / SOUL SHAKE**		75	
				43 May70
Oct 70.	(lp) (2400 029) <341> **TO BONNIE FROM DELANEY**		58	

– Hard luck and troubles / God knows I love you / Lay down my burden / Medley: Come on in my kitchen – Mama, he treats your daughter mean – Going down the road feeling bad / The love of my man / They call it rock and roll music / Soul shake / Miss Ann / Alone together / Living on the open road / Let me be your man / Free the people.

—— In 1970, D&B (with ERIC CLAPTON) featured on KING CURTIS style 'TEASIN' / 'SOULIN'

Nov 70.	(7") **MISS ANN. / THEY CALL IT ROCK AND ROLL MUSIC**		-	-
Mar 71.	(7") (2091 065) **MISS ANN. / LET ME BE YOUR MAN**			-
Jun 71.	(7") (2091 115) <6804> **NEVER ENDING SONG OF LOVE. / DON'T DECEIVE ME (PLEASE DON'T GO)**		13 May71	
Jul 71.	(lp) (2400 119) <358> **MOTEL SHOT**		65 Apr71	

– Where the soul never dies / Will the circle be unbroken / Rock of ages / Long road ahead / Faded love / Talkin' about Jesus / Come on in my kitchen / Don't deceive me (please don't go) / Never ending song of love / Sing my way home / Going down the road feeling bad / Lonesome and a long way from home.

DELANEY & BONNIE

—— with session people

Oct 71.	(7") (2091 151) <6838> **ONLY YOU KNOW AND I KNOW. / GOD KNOWS I LOVE YOU**		20 Sep71	
Nov 71.	(lp) (K 40324) <33383> **COUNTRY LIFE**			

– Only you know and I know / Sound of the city / I'm on fire / Superstargroupie song / Well well / I know something good about you / Coming home / Country life / Big change comin' / Wade in the River Jordan / Your kind of kindness / Try a little harder.

Jan 72.	(7") <6866> **MOVE 'EM OUT. / SING MY WAY HOME**		-	59

Mar 72.	(7") <6883> **WHERE THERE'S A WILL THERE'S A WAY. / LONESOME AND A LONG WAY FROM HOME**		-	99
			C.B.S.	Columbia
Jul 72.	(lp) (CBS 64959) <31377> **D & B TOGETHER**			Apr72

– Only you know and I know / Wade in the river Jordan / Sound of the city / Well, well / I know how it feels to be lonely / Comin' home / Move 'em out / Big chance comin' / A good thing (I'm on fire) / Groupie (superstar) / I know something good about you / Country life.

—— divorced and dissolved their partnership after above; both went solo

– compilations, others, etc. –

1971.	(lp) London; (ZGL 113) / Crescendo; <2054> **DELANEY & BONNIE**			

– What the world needs now is love / You've lost that loving feeling / Heartbreak Hotel / Tomorrow never comes / I can't take it much longer / I got a woman / Lonely me / Without your love / Better than me / Liverpool Lou / You never looked sweeter / You have no choice.

Jul 72.	(7"m) Atlantic; (K 10223) **THEY CALL IT ROCK & ROLL. / SOUL SHAKE / WHERE THERE'S A WILL THERE'S A WILL**			-
Jan 73.	(lp) Atlantic; (K 40429) **THE BEST OF DELANEY & BONNIE**			

– When the battle is over / Dirty old man / Only you know and I know / We've got to get ourselves together / Where there's a will, there's a way / Never ending song of love / Coming home / The love of my man / Soul shake / Come on in my kitchen / Mama, he treats your daughter mean / Goin' down the road feeling bad / Free the people. (re-iss. 1987)

1973.	(7") Atco' **WILL THE CIRCLE BE UNBROKEN. / SING MY WAY HOME**		-	

DE LA SOUL

Formed: Amityville, Long Island, New York, USA ... 1987 by DAVID JOLICOEUR (TRUGOY THE DOVE), KELVIN MERCER (POSDNOUS) & VINCENT MASON (PACEMASTER MASE). They quickly set about writing their soon-to-be critically acclaimed cross-Atlantic debut album, '3 FEET HIGH AND RISING', which made the Top 30 in the Spring of '89. Produced by STETSASONIC's PRINCE PAUL, it featured cameos from A TRIBE CALLED QUEST, JUNGLE BROTHERS (their inspiration) and QUEEN LATIFAH. Their much-anticipated but disappointing 1991 follow-up, 'DE LA SOUL IS DEAD,' accurately predicted their fate. Nevertheless, the album sold respectively and on reflection, many critics acknowledged that it contained some disturbing but poignant messages. On '93's 'BUHLOONE MINDSTATE', DE LA SOUL were back on top form once again, firing subtly subversive broadsides at the white middle class ruling system. • **Style:** Psychedelic hip-hop rappers, influenced a little by the mid 80's urban scene. Dressed mostly in baggy sportswear, they infused their lyrics with a pseudo flower-power, visionary attitude, termed as 'daisy-age'. These hip hop gypsies sampled everything from JAMES BROWN (again!) to STEELY DAN, the latter on debut hit 'ME MYSELF AND I'.

Album rating: 3 FEET HIGH AND RISING (*9) / DE LA SOUL IS DEAD (*6) / BUHLOONE MINDSTATE (*6) / STAKES IS HIGH (*7)

TRUGOY THE DOVE (b. DAVID JOLICOEUR, 21 Sep'68, Brooklyn) – vocals / **POSDNOUS** (b. KELVIN MERCER, 17 Aug'69, Bronx) – vocals / **PACEMASTER MASE** (b. VINCENT MASON, 24 Mar'70, Brooklyn) – DJ

			Tommy Boy	Tommy Boy
Jul 88.	(7") **PLUG TUNIN'. / FREEDOM OF SPEAK**		-	
Oct 88.	(7") <(TB 917)> **JENIFA (TAUGHT ME). /**			
			Big Life	Tommy Boy
Mar 89.	(lp/c/cd) (DLS LP/MC/CD 1) <TB/+C/CD 1019> **3 FEET HIGH AND RISING**		13	24

– Intro / The magic number / Change in speak / Cool breeze on the rocks / Can you keep a secret / Jenifa (taught me) / Ghetto thang / Transmitting live from Mars / Eye know / Take it off / A little bit of soap / Tread water / Say no go / Do as De La does / Plug tunin' / De La orgee / Buddy / Description / Me myself and I / This is a recording for living in a fulltime era I can do anything / D.A.I.S.Y. age / Potholes in my lawn. (cd re-iss. Jan96; DLSCD 1) (cd re-iss. Jun97 +=; TBCD 1019) – Plug tunin' (12"mix). (re-iss. Sep99, hit UK No.17)

Mar 89.	(7") (BLR 7) <7926> **ME MYSELF AND I. / BRAIN WASHED FOLLOWER**		22	34 Feb89

(12"+=) (BLR 7T) – Ain't hip to be labelled a hippie / What's more. (re-iss. Sep99 on 'B.C.M.'; BCM 14232)
(cd-s+=) (BLR 7CD) – Ain't hip to be labelled a hippie / ('A'version).
(12"+=) (BLR 7R) – ('A'remixes).

Jun 89.	(7"/7"pic-d) (BLR 10/+P) **SAY NO GO. / THEY DON'T KNOW THAT THE SOUL DON'T GO FOR THAT**		18	

(12"+=/cd-s+=) (BLR 10 T/CD) – ('A'versions).
(12"+=) (BLR 10R) – ('A'remixes). (re-iss. Sep99 on 'B.C.M.'; BCM 12295)

Sep 89.	(7"/7"pic-d/c-s) (BLR 13/+P/C) **EYE KNOW. / THE MACK DADDY ON THE LEFT**		14	

(12"+=/cd-s+=) (BLR 13 T/CD) – ('A'versions).

Dec 89.	(7"/c-s) (BLR 14/+MC) **THE MAGIC NUMBER. / BUDDY**		7	

(12"+=/cd-s+=) (BLR 14 T/CD) – Ghetto thang.
(12"+=) (BLR 14R) – ('A'remixes). (re-iss. Sep99 on 'B.C.M.'; BCM 12387)

—— In Mar'90, DE LA SOUL were credited on QUEEN LATIFAH's UK Top 20 single 'MAMA GAVE BIRTH TO THE SOUL CHILDREN' (Gee Street; GEE 26)

Apr 91.	(7"/c-s) (BLR 42/+MC) **RING RING RING (HA HA HEY). / PILES AND PILES OF DEMO TAPES BI DA MILES**		10	

(12") (BLR 42T) – ('A'extended) / Afro connection of a mis / ('A'-sax version).
(cd-s+=) (BLR 42CD) – ('A'-party mix).

May 91.	(cd/c/d-lp) (BLR CD/MC/LP 8) <TB/+C/CD 1029> **DE LA SOUL IS DEAD**		7	26

– Intro / Oodles of O's / Talkin' bout hey love / Pease porridge / (skit 1) / Johnny's dead aka Vincent Mason (live from the BK lounge) / A roller skating jam named 'Saturdays' (disco fever edit) / WRMS' dedication to the bitty / Bitties in the BK lounge / (skit 2) / Let, let me in / Rap de rap show / Millie pulled a pistol on Santa / (skit 3) / Pass the plugs / Ring ring ring (ha ha hey) / WRMS: Cat's in control / (skit 4) / Shwingalokate / Fanatic of the B word / Keepin' the faith / (skit 5). (*cd re-iss. Jan96; DLSCD 8*)

Jul 91. (7"/c-s) (*BLR 55/+MC*) **A ROLLER SKATING JAM CALLED 'SATURDAYS'. / WHAT YOUR LIFE CAN TRULY BE** | 22 | [ ]
(12"+=/cd-s+=) (*BLR 55 T/CD*) – ('A'-disco mix) / Who's skatin'.

Nov 91. (7"/c-s) (*BLR 64/+MC*) **KEEPIN' THE FAITH (remix). / ('A'instrumental)** | 50 | [ ]
(12"+=) (*BLR 64T*) – Roller skating jam called 'Saturdays' / Ring ring ring (ha ha hey).
(cd-s) (*BLR 64CD*) – (2 'A'versions) / ('A'instrumental) / ('A' funky mix).

Sep 93. (7"/c-s) (*BLR/+C 103*) <7586> **BREAKADAWN. / EN FOCUS (vocal version)** | 39 | 76
(12"+=/cd-s+=) (*BLR T/CD 103*) – ('A'mixes).

Oct 93. (cd/c/lp) (*BLR CD/MC/LP 25*) <1063> **BUHLOONE MIND STATE** | 37 | 40 Sep93
– Intro / Eye patch / En focus / Patti Dooke / I be blowin' / Long Island wildin' / Ego trippin' / Paul Revere / Three days later / Area / I am I be / In the woods / Breakadawn / Dave has a problem . . . seriously / Stone age / Lonely days.

—— In Mar'94. they teamed up with TEENAGE FANCLUB on the single 'FALLIN' (*Epic 660262-4/-2*). From the rap-rock film 'Judgement Night'.

Nov 95. (12"/cd-s) (*BLR T/D 132*) **ME MYSELF & I. /** | Tommy Boy | Tommy Boy

Jun 96. (c-s) (*TBC 7730*) **STAKES IS HIGH / ('A'-UK clean version)** | 55 | [ ]
(cd-s) (*TBCD 7730*) – ('A'side) / ('A'extended) / ('A'-DJ original) / The bizness.
(12") (*TBV 7730*) – ('A'extended) / ('A'-DJ original) / ('A'-album version) / ('A'-acapella).

Jul 96. (cd/c/d-lp) <(*TB CD/C/V 1149*)> **STAKES IS HIGH** | 42 | 13
– Intro / Supa emcees / The bizness (featuring COMMON SENSE) / Wonce again Long Island / Dinninit / Brakes / Dog eat dog / Baby baby baby ooh baby / Long Island degrees / Betta listen / Itsoweezee (featuring HOT) / 4 more (featuring ZHANE) / Big brother beat (featuring MOS DEF) / Down syndrome / Pony ride (featuring TRUTH ENOLA) / Stakes is high / Sunshine. (*cd re-iss. Feb97; same*)

Mar 97. (c-ep/12"ep/cd-ep) (*TB C/V/CD 7779*) **4 MORE / BABY BABY BABY BABY OOH BABY. / ITZSOWEEZEE / SWEET DREAMS** | 52 | [ ]

DELGADOS

Formed: Glasgow, Scotland . . . late 1994 by ex-university graduates, ALUN WOODWARD, EMMA POLLOCK, STEWART HENDERSON and PAUL SAVAGE. Not only did they kickstart Scotland's flagging (nae, virtually dead) indie scene, they did it by initiating their own imprint, 'Chemikal Underground'. The label's debut, 'MONICA WEBSTER', was greatly received by the music press and of course, who else? DJ John Peel, their angular guitar reminiscent of PAVEMENT, although ALUN and EMMA's twee vocal touches called to mind BELLE & SEBASTIAN. Single after single continued to impress until the excellent debut album, 'DOMESTIQUES', surfaced in late '96. Their "difficult" second album, 'PELOTON' (1998), managed to crack the UK Top 60, spurred on by indie hits, 'PULL THE WIRES FROM THE WALL' and 'THE WEAKER ARGUMENT DEFEATS THE STRONGER'. Where would ARAB STRAP, MOGWAI and now majors-tempted BIS be without the DELGADOS and their seminal label?! • **Covers:** THE DIRGE (New Bad Things) / SACRE CHARLEMAGNE (France Gall) / A VERY CELLULAR SONG (Incredible String Band).

Album rating: DOMESTIQUES (*8) / PELOTON (*8)

ALUN WOODWARD – vocals, guitar / **EMMA POLLOCK** – vocals, guitar / **STEWART HENDERSON** – bass / **PAUL SAVAGE** – drums

		Chemikal Underground	not iss.
Jul 95.	(7") (*chem 001*) **MONICA WEBSTER. / BRAND NEW CAR**	[ ]	-
Aug 95.	(7"ep/cd-ep) (*SCAN/+CS 07*) **THE LAZERWALKER EP**	[ ]	-
	(above issued on 'Radarscope') (below on 'Che')		
Dec 95.	(7"; various artists) <*che 47*>	[ ]	-
Mar 96.	(7"ep/cd-ep) (*chem 004/+cd*) **CINECENTRE. / THIRTEEN GLIDING PRICES / MULE EMULATOR**	[ ]	-
Aug 96.	(7"ep/cd-ep) (*chem 006/+cd*) **UNDER CANVAS / EEN TELF. / BEAR CLUB / STRATHCONA**	[ ]	-
Oct 96.	(7"ep/cd-ep) (*chem 008/+cd*) **SUCROSE. / EUROSPRINT / THE DIRGE**	[ ]	-
Nov 96.	(lp/cd) (*chem 010/+CD*) **DOMESTIQUES**	[ ]	-

– Under canvas under wraps / Leaning on a cane / Strathcona slung / Tempered, not tamed / One more question / Big business in Europe / Falling and landing / Akumulator / Sucrose / Pinky / Friendly conventions / Smaller mammals / 4th channel / D'estus morte.

1996.	(ltd-7") (*HISS 4*) **LIQUIDATION GIRL. / (other track by Van Impe)**	[ ]	-
	(above issued on 'Boa' / below release on 'Lissy's')		
Jun 97.	(7") (*LISS 20*) **SACRE CHARLEMAGNE. / (other by The NEW BAD THINGS)**	[ ]	-
Mar 98.	(7") (*chem 022*) **EVERYTHING GOES AROUND THE WATER / BLACKPOOL**	[ ]	-
	(cd-s+=) (*chem 022cd*) – The drowned and the saved.		
May 98.	(7") (*chem 023*) **PULL THE WIRES FROM THE WALL. / MAURON CHANSON**	69	-
	(cd-s+=) (*chem 023cd*) – Mark the day.		
Jun 98.	(cd) (*chem 024cd*) **PELOTON**	56	-

– Everything goes around the water / The arcane model / The actress / Clarinet / Pull the wires from the wall / Repeat failure / And so the talking stopped / Don't stop / Blackpool / Russian orthodox / The weaker argument defeats the stronger.

Sep 98. (7") (*chem 029*) **THE WEAKER ARGUMENT DEFEATS THE STRONGER. / A VERY CELLULAR SONG** | [ ] | -
(cd-s+=) (*chem 029cd*) – The actress – Irian Jaya remix.

– **compilations, etc.** –

Sep 97. (cd) *Strange Fruit*; (*SFRSCD 037*) **BBC SESSIONS** | | -
– Primary alternative / I've only just started to breathe / Lazerwalker / Indian fables / Under canvas under wraps / Sucrose / Teen elf / Thirteen gliding principles / Friendly conventions / Tempered not tamed / Falling and landing.

Sandy DENNY

Born: ALEXANDRA ELENE MacLEAN DENNY, 6 Jan'47, Wimbledon, London, England. From playing guitar and piano from an early age, SANDY, as she would be known all her life, grew up listening to the sounds of her father's collection of classical, jazz and traditional Scottish folk music, before finding her own taste in the sound of 60's pop/folk, especially BOB DYLAN. After a brush with nursing and attending Kensington Art College, she started singing regularly in the folk clubs of London, where she met JOHN RENBOURN and ALEX CAMPBELL. An invitation in late '66 from CAMPBELL to join a folk session for the BBC World Service show, A Cellarfull Of Folk, led to her first recordings on the LP's 'ALEX CAMPBELL AND FRIENDS' and 'SANDY AND JOHNNY'. With a regular spot at The Troubadour, she was heard by DAVE COUSINS of The STRAWBS. Joining the band soon afterwards, she recorded 'SANDY DENNY & THE STRAWBS' in '67 featuring 'WHO KNOWS WHERE THE TIME GOES', one of DENNY's most powerful songs. Meanwhile, through gigs around London's folk scene, she had formulated friendships with DANNY THOMPSON of PENTANGLE fame, and the founder of 'Witchseason' records, JOE BOYD, as well as earning herself a strong reputation as one of the best folk singers in the country. When JUDY DYBLE left FAIRPORT CONVENTION, featuring a young RICHARD THOMPSON, in '68, DENNY auditioned and made an immediate impact, her classy singing and mercurial personality bringing out the best in the musicians around her. 'What We Did On Our Holidays', SANDY's first album with FAIRPORT, was full of highlights, including DENNY's song 'FOTHERINGAY', and a crystal clear rendition of 'SHE MOVES THROUGH THE FAIR'. Whilst rehearsing for their second album, SANDY met TREVOR LUCAS, an Australian singer/songwriter and member of the band ECLECTION. After the two bands shared a bill in Birmingham, she left with him instead of returning to London with FAIRPORT. It proved a fortuitous move, as FAIRPORT's journey ended in tragedy, a crash taking the life of drummer, MARTIN LAMBLE. This event led to a re-think of the band's repertoire, and in the meantime the songs recorded before the crash were compiled by BOYD to form the album, 'UNHALFBRICKING', featuring a re-recording of 'WHO KNOWS WHERE THE TIME GOES' and 'AUTOPSY'. DENNY's vocals throughout the album are stunning, her voice matured and yet containing a purity that is strangely compelling to the listener. After the inclusion of DAVE SWARBRICK on violin, FAIRPORT's next album, 'Liege And Lief', proved groundbreaking, but soon after, SANDY was to leave the band to form FOTHERINGAY, with ex-ECLECTION members, including her husband-to-be TREVOR LUCAS, and recording their only album, simply titled 'FOTHERINGAY', as well as recording a duet with ROBERT PLANT, 'THE BATTLE OF EVERMORE', on 'LED ZEPPELIN IV'. Although the album and the group were well-received by fans, the band dispersed after a misunderstanding between BOYD and DENNY, RICHARD THOMPSON going on to produce SANDY's first of four solo albums, the haphazard 'THE NORTH STAR GRASSMAN AND THE RAVEN'. Her second solo album, 'SANDY' was produced by BOYD, and is her stand-out album, especially her mesmerising singing on 'THE QUIET JOYS OF BROTHERHOOD'. The LP did not live up to expected sales figures, but did earn her many new fans, including DYLAN, FRANK ZAPPA, and PETE TOWNSHEND, who cast her as the nurse in 'Tommy'. After touring America in the Spring of '73, she completed her third solo set, 'LIKE AN OLD FASHIONED WALTZ', a fine example of her timeless singing, and her first album without a trace of folk. During this period, SANDY performed the shows of her life, and married long-time partner, LUCAS, with THOMPSON as best man. By '74, she had returned to FAIRPORT, the line-up having included her husband since '73. The atmosphere within the band was strained as FAIRPORT and DENNY attempted to gel their by now different styles, yet the GLYN JOHNS produced album, 'Rising For The Moon', turned out to be a triumph, SANDY's 'ONE MORE CHANCE' bringing together exceptional instrumental work with singing unprecedented in DENNY's recording career, her voice full of maturity yet also possessing a fragility that gives a real urgency to the song, written as a plea for peace. Although her work kept improving, her career failed to fully take off, and after 'Rising . . .' failed to be the commercial success it should have been, FAIRPORT were dropped by 'Island', and the band drifted apart. '77 saw her final solo offering, 'RENDEZVOUS', including an unfortunate renditioning of 'CANDLE IN THE WIND' and a hint of reggae on 'GOLDDUST'. It did have its fine moments with 'ONE WAY DONKEY RIDE' and 'I'M A DREAMER', but its sales were poor, and DENNY's contract expired at 'Island'. It was to be her final recording. In April '78, SANDY fell down a flight of stairs at a friend's home, lapsing into a coma which led to her death from a brain haemorrhage on the 21st of that month. • **Covered:** TOMORROW IS A LONG TIME (Bob Dylan) / LET'S JUMP THE BROOMSTICK (Brenda Lee) / SILVER THREADS AND GOLDEN NEEDLES (Springfields). FOTHERINGAY covered; TOO MUCH OF NOTHING (Bob Dylan).

Album rating: THE NORTH STAR GRASSMAN AND THE RAVENS (*6) / SANDY (*7) / LIKE AN OLD FASHIONED WALTZ (*5) / RENDEZVOUS (*6) / THE BEST OF SANDY DENNY compilation (*7)

SANDY DENNY – vocals (with below artists **JOHNNY SILVO & ALEX CAMPBELL**) (below a compilation of 'ALEX CAMPBELL & FRIENDS' and 'SANDY & JOHNNY' albums '67)

		Saga	not iss.
1970.	(lp) (EROS 8153) **SANDY DENNY**		

– This train / 3:10 to Yuma / Pretty Polly / You never wanted me / Milk and honey / My ramblin' boy / The last thing on my mind / Make me a pallet on your floor / The false bride / Been on the road so long. (re-iss. 1978 as 'THE ORIGINAL SANDY DENNY' on 'Mooncrest'; CREST 28) (cd-iss. Feb91 cd/c; CREST CD/MC 002)

FOTHERINGAY

SANDY DENNY – vocals (ex-FAIRPORT CONVENTION, ex-STRAWBS) plus **JERRY DONAHUE** – guitar, vocals / **TREVOR LUCAS** – guitar, vocals (ex-ECLECTION) / **GERRY CONWAY** – drums (ex-ECLECTION) / **PAT DONALDSON** – bass

		Island	A&M
Jun 70.	(lp) (ILPS 9125) <4269> **FOTHERINGAY**	18	

– Nothing more / The sea / The ballad of Ned Kelly / Peace in the end / Winter winds / The way I feel / The pond down the stream / Too much of nothing / Banks of the Nile. (re-iss. Jul87 on 'Hannibal' lp/c; HNB L/C 4426) (cd-iss. May89; HNCD 4426)

Jul 70.	(7") (WIP 6085) **PEACE IN THE END. / WINTER WINDS**		
Aug 70.	(7") <1223> **THE BALLAD OF NED KELLY. / THE SEA**	-	

Split early '71. CONWAY, DONALDSON and DONAHUE then backed MICK GREENWOOD with the latter joining LUCAS (now a producer) to FAIRPORTS.

SANDY DENNY

		Island	A&M
Sep 71.	(lp) (ILPS 9165) <4317> **THE NORTH STAR GRASSMAN AND THE RAVENS**	31	

– Late November / Black waterside / The sea captain / Down in the flood / John the gun / Next time around / The optimist / Let's jump the broomstick / Wretched Wilbur / The north star grassman and the ravens / Crazy lady blues. (re-iss. Nov86; ILPM 9165) (re-iss. May89 on 'Carthage' lp/c; CGLP/CGC 4429) (re-iss. Aug91 cd)(c; IMCD 133)(ICM 9165)

Feb 72.	(7") <1331> **CRAZY LADY BLUES. / LET'S JUMP THE BROOMSTICK**	-	
Sep 72.	(7"ep) (WIP 6141) **HERE IN SILENCE. / MAN OF IRON** (soundtrack from 'Pass Of Arms' film)		-
Sep 72.	(lp) (ILPS 9207) <4371> **SANDY**		

– It'll take a long time / Sweet Rosemary / For nobody to hear / Tomorrow is a long time / Quiet joys of brotherhood / Bushes and friars / The lady / Listen listen / It sets me wild / The music weaver. (re-iss. Aug91 cd)(c; IMCD 132)(ICM 9207)

Sep 72.	(7") (WIP 6142) <1410> **LISTEN LISTEN. / TOMORROW IS A LONG TIME**		
Nov 73.	(7") (WIP 6176) **WHISPERING GRASS. / FRIENDS**		-
Jun 74.	(lp) (ILPS 9258) <9340> **LIKE AN OLD FASHIONED WALTZ**		

– Solo / Whispering grass / Like an old fashioned waltz / Friends / Carnival / Dark of the night / At the end of the day / Until the real thing comes along / No end. (re-iss. May88 & Jun96 on 'Carthage'; CGLP 4425) (cd-iss. Nov88 & May95; CGC 4425)

—— SANDY had returned to FAIRPORT CONVENTION between Mar74-Jan76 and after a years rest she was back with solo work in '77.

May 77.	(lp) (ILPS 9433) **RENDEZVOUS**		-

– I wish I was a fool for you / Gold dust / Candle in the wind / Take me away / One way donkey ride / I'm a dreamer / All our days / Silver threads and golden needles / No more sad refrains. (re-iss. Jan87 on 'Hannibal' lp/c; HNBL/HNBC 4423) (cd-iss. Jan89 +=; HNCD 4423) – Full moon.

—— tragically SANDY died on the 21st April '78

– compilations, others, etc. –

1973.	(lp; by SANDY DENNY & THE STRAWBS) Hallmark; (SHM 813) **ALL OUR OWN WORK**		-

(re-iss. Jul91 on 'Hannibal' cd/c; HNCD/HNBC 1361)

1978.	(7") Mooncrest; (MOON 54) **MAKE ME A PALLET ON YOUR FLOOR. / THIS TRAIN**		-
Jan 86.	(4xlp-box) Hannibal; (SDSP 1) **WHO KNOWS WHERE THE TIME GOES?**		-

– (best material from 1967-1977, including live, out-takes, demos, and group work with STRAWBS, FAIRPORT CONVENTION, FOTHERINGAY, & The BUNCH) (re-iss. May89 & Nov91; HNBX 5301)

Aug 87.	(lp) Island; (SDC/CDSC 100) **THE BEST OF SANDY DENNY**		

– Listen, listen / One way donkey ride / It'll take a long time / Farewell, farewell / Tam Lin / The pond and the stream / Late November / The sea / Banks of the Nile / Next time around / For shame of doing wrong / Stranger to himself / I'm a dreamer / Who knows where the time goes? (re-iss. Sep89 on 'Hannibal' cd/c; HNCD/HNBC 1328) (re-iss. Mar96 cd)(c; IMCD 217)(ICM 2084)

Jul 95.	(cd) Special Delivery; (SPDCD 1052) **THE ATTIC TRACKS 1972-1984 (with TREVOR LUCAS & FRIENDS)**		-

John DENVER

Born: JOHN HENRY DEUTSCHENDORF Jnr., 31 Dec'43, Roswell, New Mexico, USA. The son of a record-breaking aviator and US airforce instructor, his childhood was characterised by a rootless existence that saw him shuttled between various states in the American southwest and even a spell in Japan (no doubt a clue to the recurring theme of 'home' – leaving and especially returning – in DENVER's later work). Famously given a Gibson acoustic guitar by his grandmother as he entered his teens, it was only after he was rejected by the airforce for shortsightedness that the budding singer/songwriter began to seek out a career as a musician. Although he attended an architecture course in Texas, DEUTSCHENDORF soon headed for L.A. where he immersed himself in the thriving folk scene. At the suggestion of The NEW CHRISTY MINSTRELS' Randy Sparks, he subsequently changed his name to JOHN DENVER which best suited his passion for the mountains and all things natural. After rumours that he was to join The BYRDS, DENVER enlisted with The CHAD MITCHELL TRIO instead, helping to revitalise their failing fortunes. Finally gaining the confidence to strike out on his own, DENVER signed to 'R.C.A.' in 1969 with the help of veteran folk producer, Milt Okun, who was to have a long and fruitful relationship with the singer. DENVER's exquisite 'LEAVING ON A JET PLANE', originally recorded by the TRIO in 1967, furnished PETER, PAUL & MARY with a US No.1 the same year and suddenly DENVER's name was on the map. His debut album, 'RHYMES AND REASONS' (1969), was released around the same time, featuring a newly recorded version of the hit alongside political satire like 'THE BALLAD OF RICHARD NIXON'. A hangover from his TRIO days, DENVER moved unequivocally into the mould of sensitive, sentimental country-folk balladeer over the course of his next two albums, 'TAKE ME TO TOMORROW' (1970) and 'WHOSE GARDEN WAS THIS' (1970). Yet it was only with the release of the 'POEMS, PRAYERS AND PROMISES' (1971) album and its massive 'TAKE ME HOME COUNTRY ROADS' single that DENVER became a household name. Written in collaboration with folksters BILL and TAFFY DANOFF, the track was a million selling country/MOR anthem that narrowly missed the US No.1 spot before being covered by everyone from OLIVIA NEWTON JOHN to TOOTS & THE MAYTALS (!). Both the album's title track and future hit (1974), 'SUNSHINE ON MY SHOULDERS' were also classic early period DENVER; hardly possessing the strongest of voices and pushing inoffensive lyrics that bordered on mawkishness, he was an obvious target for critics yet his best work resonated with a bittersweet emotional honesty that only the most hardened musical cynic would deny. The 'AERIE' (1971) album wasn't so successful but 'ROCKY MOUNTAIN HIGH' (1972) cemented his position as eco-friendly blonde warrior with the title track (US Top 10) waxing lyrical about his "rebirth" in the surroundings of his beloved Colorado. By 1974/5, DENVER was a bonafide superstar partly as a result of his hugely successful US TV show, 'An Evening With John Denver', partly due to the multi-platinum 'GREATEST HITS' (1973) set and partly down to the No.1 album, 'BACK HOME AGAIN' (1974). The latter set featured the transatlantic No.1 tribute to his wife, 'ANNIE'S SONG', a track that perhaps more than any other is identified with DENVER in his heyday and surprisingly, remains his only UK Top 40 hit. 1975 was another bumper year as both 'AN EVENING WITH JOHN DENVER' and 'WINDSONG' (US No.1) sold in their millions. The fact that the execrable 'THANK GOD I'M A COUNTRY BOY' made No.1 in the States was possibly a sign that DENVER fever was getting out of hand; the governor of Colorado even proclaimed him poet laureate of the state (!). Still, if listening to his music had become akin to watching paint dry, at least the man was doing something constructive with his riches, setting up the ecology-based 'Windstar Foundation' in 1976. He also started his own label ('Windsong') and branched into acting (alongside George Burns in 1977's 'Oh God!'), becoming an all round showbiz personality. He even cut an album with the muppets (1979's 'A CHRISTMAS TOGETHER WITH THE MUPPETS'), oh God right enough. By the early 80's, DENVER had separated from his wife and was focusing his energies on ecological, anti-nuclear and humanitarian causes, even touring the Eastern Bloc and China. Albums such as 'AUTOGRAPH' (1980), 'SOME DAYS ARE DIAMONDS' (1981), 'IT'S ABOUT TIME' (1983) and 'DREAMLAND EXPRESS' (1985) saw his commercial returns progressively diminish while 1990's comeback set, 'THE FLOWER THAT SHATTERED THE STONE' barely scraped the US Top 200. Worse was to come in 1993 when his wholesome image was tarnished with a drunk-driving charge. Nevertheless, the man's basic philosophy remained the same and he picked up the Albert Schweitzer Music Award for lifetime humanitarianism that same year before publishing his autobiography in 1994. In one of rock'n'roll's stranger fatal accidents (and there've been more than a few), DENVER died tragically on October the 12th, 1997 at the age of 53 when the light plane he was flying suddenly dropped out of the sky, killing him instantly. His recorded legacy remains though and anyone with a penchant for wistful country-folk is recommended to bypass the critical barbs and check out his early to mid-period stuff.

Album rating: RHYMES AND REASONS (*5) / TAKE ME TO TOMORROW (*5) / WHOSE GARDEN WAS THIS (*4) / POEMS, PRAYERS AND PROMISES (*7) / AERIE (*5) / ROCKY MOUNTAIN HIGH (*5) / FAREWELL ANDROMEDA (*4) / THE BEST OF or JOHN DENVER'S GREATEST HITS compilation (*8) / BACK HOME AGAIN (*4) / AN EVENING WITH JOHN DENVER (*4) / WINDSONG (*6) / ROCKY MOUNTAIN CHRISTMAS (*4) / LIVE IN LONDON (*5) / SPIRIT (*4) / JOHN DENVER'S GREATEST HITS, VOLUME 2 compilation (*6) / I WANT TO LIVE (*2) / JOHN DENVER (*3) / A CHRISTMAS TOGETHER with The Muppets (*0) / AUTOGRAPH (*3) / SOME DAYS ARE DIAMONDS (*3) / SEASONS OF THE HEART (*4) / IT'S ABOUT TIME (*4) / JOHN DENVER COLLECTION compilation (*7) / JOHN DENVER'S GREATEST HITS VOLUME 3 compilation (*4) / DREAMLAND EXPRESS (*3) / ONE WORLD (*3) / HIGHER GROUND (*4) / THE FLOWER THAT SHATTERED THE STONE (*3) / DIFFERENT DIRECTIONS (*2) / THE WILDLIFE CONSERVATION SOCIETY CONCERT (*6) / THE ROCKY MOUNTAIN COLLECTION compilation (*5)

JOHN DENVER – vocals, acoustic guitar (with session people)

		not iss.	Reprise
1968.	(7"; by DENVER, BOISE & JOHNSON) <0695> **TAKE ME TO TOMORROW. / THE '68 NIXON (THIS YEAR'S MODEL)**	-	

RCA Victor / RCA Victor

Sep 69. (7") <74-0275> **DAYDREAM. / I WISH I KNEW HOW IT WOULD FEEL TO BE FREE** — | —

Oct 69. (lp) <LSP 4207> **RHYMES & REASONS** — | —
– The love of the common people / Catch another butterfly / Daydream / The ballad of Spiro Agnew / Circus / When I'm sixty-four / The ballad of Richard Nixon / Yellow cat / Leaving on a jet plane / You done stomp on my heart / My old man / I wish I knew how I would feel to be free / Today is the first day of the rest of my life (sugacity). (UK-iss.Jun73; SF 8348) – hit No.21

Mar 70. (7") <74-0305> **ANTHEM – REVELATION. / STICKY SUMMER WEATHER** — | —

Apr 70. (lp) <LSP 4278> **TAKE ME TO TOMORROW** — | —
– Take me to tomorrow / Isabel / Follow me / Forest lawn / Aspenglow / Anthem – Revelation / Sticky summer weather / Carolina on my mind / Jimmy Newman / Molly. (UK-iss.Jul73; SF 8354)

May 70. (7") (RCA 1960) <74-0332> **FOLLOW ME. / ISABEL** ☐ | ☐

Aug 70. (7") <74-0376> **SAIL AWAY HOME. / I WISH I WOULD HAVE BEEN THERE (WOODSTOCK)** — | —

Sep 70. (lp) <LSP 4414> **WHOSE GARDEN WAS THIS** — | —
– Tremble if you must / Sail away home / The night they drove old Dixie down / Mr. Bojangles / I wish I could have been there (Woodstock) / Whose garden was this / This game is over / Eleanor Rigby / Old folks: Medley – Golden slumbers / Sweet sweet life / Tremble if you must (2nd version) / Jungle bells. (UK-iss.Jul73; SF 8355)

Oct 70. (7") <74-0391> **WHOSE GARDEN WAS THIS. / MR. BOJANGLES** — | —

Apr 71. (7") (RCA 2118) <74-0445> **TAKE ME HOME, COUNTRY ROADS. / POEMS, PRAYERS AND PROMISES** — | 2 Mar71

Apr 71. (lp) <LSP 4499> **POEMS, PRAYERS AND PROMISES** — | 15
– Poems, prayers and promises / Let it be / My sweet lady / Wooden Indian / Junk / Gospel changes / I guess he'd rather be in Colorado / Sunshine on my shoulders / Around and around / Fire and rain / The box. (UK-iss.May73; SF 8219) – hit No.19 (re-iss.Nov84 lp/c; NL/NK 85189)

Nov 71. (7") (RCA 2156) <74-0567> **FRIENDS WITH YOU. / STARWOOD IN ASPEN** — | 47 Oct71

Nov 71. (lp) <LSP 4607> **AERIE** — | —
– Starwood in Aspen / Everyday / Casey's last ride / City of New Orleans / Friends with you / 60 second song for a bank, with the phrase "May We Help You Today?" / Blow up your T.V. / All of my memories / She won't fly me away / Readjustment blues / The eagle and the hawk / Tools. (UK-iss.Jul73; SF 8252)

Mar 72. (7") <74-0647> **EVERYDAY. / CITY OF NEW ORLEANS** — | 81

Jul 72. (7") <74-0737> **GOODBYE AGAIN. / THE EAGLE AND THE HAWK** — | 88

Sep 72. (7") <74-0801> **LATE WINTER, EARLY SPRING (WHEN EVERYBODY GOES TO MEXICO). / HARD LIFE, HARD TIMES (PROMISES)** — | —

Jan 73. (7") (RCA 2312) <74-0829> **ROCKY MOUNTAIN HIGH. / SPRING** 9 | 9 Nov72

Mar 73. (lp) <SF 8308> <4731> **ROCKY MOUNTAIN HIGH** 11 | 4 Sep72
– Rocky mountain high / Mother Nature's son / Paradise / For baby (for Bobbie) / Darcy Farrow / Prisoners / Goodbye again / Summer / Fall / Winter / Late Winter, early Spring (when everybody goes to Mexico) / Spring. (re-iss.Nov84 lp/c; NL/NK 85190) (cd-iss. Oct88; PD 85190)

May 73. (7") <74-0955> **I'D RATHER BE A COWBOY. / SUNSHINE ON MY SHOULDERS** — | 62

Aug 73. (lp) <SF 8369> <APL1 0101> **FAREWELL ANDROMEDA** — | 16 Jun73
– I'd rather be a cowboy / Berkeley woman / Please, daddy / Angels from Montgomery / River of love / Rocky mountain suite (cold nights in Canada) / Whiskey basin blues / Sweet misery / Zachary and Jennifer / We don't live here no more / Farewell Andromeda (welcome to my morning). (re-iss.Nov84 lp/c; NL/NK 85191) (cd-iss. Feb89; ND 85195)

Sep 73. (7") <APBO 0067> **FAREWELL ANDROMEDA (WELCOME TO MY MORNING). / WHISKEY BASIN BLUES** — | 89

Dec 73. (7") <APBO 0182> **PLEASE, DADDY. / ROCKY MOUNTAIN SUITE (COLD NIGHTS IN CANADA)** — | 69
(UK-iss.Nov75; RCA 2636)

Mar 74. (7") (RCA 2372) <APBO 0213> **SUNSHINE ON MY SHOULDERS. / AROUND AND AROUND** ☐ | 1 Jan74

Mar 74. (lp) <(APL1 0374)> **THE BEST OF JOHN DENVER** (compilation) <US-title 'JOHN DENVER'S GREATEST HITS'> 7 | 1 Nov73
– Take me home, country roads / Follow me / Starwood in Aspen / For baby (for Bobbie) / Rhymes and reasons / Leaving on a jet plane / The eagle and the hawk / Sunshine on my shoulders / Goodbye again / Poems, prayers and promises / Rocky mountain high. (re-iss. Sep81 lp/c; RCA LP/K 3005) (re-iss. Sep84 as 'GREATEST HITS' lp/c/cd; PL/PK/PD 83074) (re-iss. Oct90 cd/c; ND/NK 90523)

Jul 74. (7") <(APBO 0295)> **ANNIE'S SONG. / COOL AN' GREEN AN' SHADY** 1 | 1 May74

Aug 74. (lp) <(APL1 0548)> **BACK HOME AGAIN** 3 | 1 Jun74
– Back home again / On the road / Grandma's feather bed / Matthew / Thank God I'm a country boy / The music is you / Annie's song / It's up to you / Cool an' green an' shady / Eclipse / Sweet surrender / This old guitar. (re-iss. Sep81 lp/c; RCA LP/K 3007) (re-iss. Nov84 lp/c; NL/NK 85193) (cd-iss. Oct87; ND 85193)

Sep 74. (7") <10065> **BACK HOME AGAIN. / IT'S UP TO YOU** — | 5

Oct 74. (7") <APBO 0213> **SUNSHINE ON MY SHOULDERS. / AROUND AND AROUND** ☐ | ☐

Jan 75. (7") (RCA 2509) <10148> **SWEET SURRENDER. / SUMMER** ☐ | 13 Dec74

Mar 75. (d-lp)(d-c) (LSA 32 11-12)(DPTK 5014) <CPL2 0764> **AN EVENING WITH JOHN DENVER** (live) 31 | 2
– The music is you / Farewell Andromeda / Mother Nature's son / Summer / Today / Saturday night in Toledo, Ohio / Matthew / Rocky mountain suite / Sweet surrender / Grandma's feather bed / Annie's song / The eagle and the hawk / My sweet lady / Annie's other song / Boy from the country / Rhymes and reasons / Forest lawn / Pickin' the sun down / Thank God I'm a country boy / Take me home, country roads / Poems, prayers and promises / Rocky mountain high / This old guitar.

Mar 75. (7") <10239> **THANK GOD I'M A COUNTRY BOY. / MY SWEET LADY** — | 1

Aug 75. (7") (RCA 2588) <10353> **I'M SORRY. / CALYPSO** — | 1 | 2

Oct 75. (lp) <(APL1 1183)> **WINDSONG** 14 | 1 Sep75

– Windsong / Cowboy's delight / Spirit / Looking for space / Shipmates and Cheyenne / Late nite radio / Love is everywhere / Two shots / I'm sorry / Fly away / Calypso / Song of Wyoming. (re-iss.Nov84 lp/c; NL/NK 85191) (cd-iss. Jun88; ND 85191)

Nov 75. (lp) <APL11201> **ROCKY MOUNTAIN CHRISTMAS** (festive) — | 14
– Rudolf, the red-nosed reindeer / Silver bells / Silent night, holy night / The Christmas song / Christmas for cowboys / Oh holy night / Please, daddy / A baby just like you / Away in a manger / Coventry carol / What child is this. <re-iss. Dec76; same> (cd-iss. Oct98; 07863 67641-2) (cd re-iss. Oct99 on 'RCA Camden'; 74321 69578-2)

Dec 75. (d-lp) <1263> **JOHN DENVER GIFT PAK** (above 2 sets) — | ☐

Dec 75. (7") <10464> **CHRISTMAS FOR COWBOYS. / SILENT NIGHT, HOLY NIGHT** — | 58

Jan 76. (7") (RCA 2646) <10517> **FLY AWAY. / TWO SHOTS** 13 | Nov75

Feb 76. (7") <10586> **LOOKING FOR SPACE. / WINDSONG** — | 29

Apr 76. (7") <10687> **IT MAKES ME GIGGLE. / SPIRIT** — | 60

May 76. (lp) (RS 1050) **LIVE IN LONDON** (live) 2 | —
– Starwood in Aspen / Sunshine on my shoulders / Back home again / Grandma's feather bed / Pickin' the sun down / Thank God I'm a country boy / The eagle and the hawk / Spirit / Calypso / Amsterdam / Annie's song / Take me home, country roads / Leaving on a jet plane. (re-iss. 1984 lp/c; PL/PK 89225)

Jun 76. (7") (RCA 2712) **LEAVING ON A JET PLANE. / SUNSHINE ON MY SHOULDERS** — | —

Aug 76. (lp) <(APL1 1694)> **SPIRIT** 9 | 7
– Come and let me look in your eyes / Eli's song / Wrangle mountain song / Hitchhiker / In the grand way / Polka dots and moonbeams / It makes me giggle / Baby, you look good to me tonight / Like a sad song / San Antonio rose / Pegasus / The wings that fly us home. (re-iss. Nov84 lp/c; NL/NK 85194)

Sep 76. (7") (RCA 2740) <10774> **LIKE A SAD SONG. / PEGASUS** — | 36

Dec 76. (7") <10854> **BABY, YOU LOOK GOOD TO ME TONIGHT. / WRANGLE MOUNTAIN SONG** — | 65

Mar 77. (7") (PB 9046) <10911> **MY SWEET LADY. / WELCOME TO MY MORNING (FAREWELL ANDROMEDA)** — | 32

Mar 77. (lp) (PL 42120) <2195> **BEST OF JOHN DENVER, VOLUME 2** (compilation) <US-title 'JOHN DENVER'S GREATEST HITS, VOLUME 2'> 9 | 6 Feb77
– Annie's song / Farewell Andromeda (welcome to my morning) / Fly away / Like a sad song / Looking for space / Baby, you look good to me tonight / Grandma's feather bed / I'd rather be a cowboy / I'm sorry / My sweet lady / Calypso / This old guitar. (re-iss. Sep81 lp/c; RCA LP/K 3019) (re-iss. Sep84 as 'GREATEST HITS VOL.2' lp/c/cd; PL/PK/PD 82195) (re-iss. Sep93 cd/c; 74321 15480-2/-4)

Jan 78. (7") (PB 1036) <11036> **HOW CAN I LEAVE YOU AGAIN. / TO THE WILD COUNTRY** 44 | Nov77

Feb 78. (lp/c) (PL/PK 12521) <AFL1 2521> **I WANT TO LIVE** 25 | 45 Nov77
– Singing skies and dancing waters / How can I leave you again / The wild country / Tradewinds / Bet on the blues / Thirsty boots / It amazes me / Ripplin' waters / Dearest Esmeralda / Druthers / I want to live.

Feb 78. (7") <11214> **IT AMAZES ME. / DRUTHERS** — | 59

Apr 78. (7") <11267> **I WANT TO LIVE. / TRADEWINDS** — | 55

Feb 79. (lp/c) (PL/PK 13075) **JOHN DENVER** 68 | 25 Jan79
– Downhill stuff / Sweet Melinda / What's on your mind / Joseph and Joe / Life is so good / Berkeley woman / Johnny B. Goode / You're so beautiful / Southwind / Garden song / Songs of ...

Mar 79. (7") (PB 1479) <11479> **DOWNHILL STUFF. / LIFE IS SO GOOD** ☐ | Jan79

Jun 79. (7") (PB 1535) <11535> **WHAT'S ON YOUR MIND. / SWEET MELINDA** ☐ | Apr79

Sep 79. (7") <11637> **GARDEN SONG. / BERKELEY WOMAN** — | ☐

Nov 79. (7"; as JOHN DENVER & THE MUPPETS) <11767> **HAVE YOURSELF A MERRY LITTLE CHRISTMAS – WE WISH YOU A MERRY CHRISTMAS. / A BABY JUST LIKE YOU** ☐ | ☐

Nov 79. (lp/c; as JOHN DENVER & THE MUPPETS) (PL/PK 13451) <3451> **A CHRISTMAS TOGETHER** (festive) ☐ | 26
(cd-iss. Nov94 on 'Music Club'; MCCDX 007)

Nov 79. (7"; as JOHN DENVER & THE MUPPETS) (PB 9463) **THE PEACE CAROL. / DECK THE HALLS – WE WISH YOU A MERRY CHRISTMAS** ☐ | ☐

Feb 80. (7") <11915> **AUTOGRAPH. / THE MOUNTAIN SONG** — | 52

Feb 80. (lp/c) (PL/PK 13449) <3449> **AUTOGRAPH** — | 39
– Dancing with the mountains / How mountain girls can love / Song for the life / The ballad of St. Anne's reel / In my heart / Wrangle mountain song / Whale bones and crosses / American child / You say that the battle is over / Autograph.

Jun 80. (7") <12017> **DANCING WITH THE MOUNTAINS. / AMERICAN CHILD** — | 97

Jun 81. (7") (RCA 97) <12246> **SOME DAYS ARE DIAMONDS (SOME DAYS ARE STONE). / COUNTRY LOVE** ☐ | 36

Jul 81. (lp/c) (RCA LP/K 5034) <4055> **SOME DAYS ARE DIAMONDS** ☐ | 32 Jun81
– Some days are diamonds (some days are stone) / Gravel on the ground / San Francisco Mabel joy / Sleepin' alone / Easy on easy street / The cowboy and the lady / Country love / Till you opened my eyes / Wild flowers in a mason jar (the farm) / Boy from the country. (re-iss. 1984 lp/c; PL/PK 84055)

Oct 81. (7") <12345> **THE COWBOY AND THE LADY. / TILL YOU OPEN MY EYES** — | 66

—— Late in '81 & early '82, PLACIDO DOMINGO and JOHN DENVER had a mini UK & US hit with 'PERHAPS LOVE', which was the title track of the UK Top 20 album on 'C.B.S.'; 73592

Apr 82. (7") (RCA 218) <13071> **SHANGHAI BREEZES. / WHAT ONE MAN CAN DO** ☐ | 31 Feb82

May 82. (lp/c) (RCA LP/K 6032) <4256> **SEASONS OF THE HEART** ☐ | 39 Mar82
– Seasons of the heart / Opposite tables / Relatively speaking / Nothing but a breeze / What one man can do / Shanghai breezes / Islands / Heart to heart / Perhaps love / Children of the universe. (re-iss. 1984 lp/c/cd; PL/PK/PD 84256)

Jul 82. (7") <13270> **SEASONS OF THE HEART. / ISLANDS** — | 78

Oct 82. (7") <13371> **OPPOSITE TABLES. / RELATIVELY SPEAKING** — | —

Sep 83. (7"; JOHN DENVER & EMMYLOU HARRIS) <13562> **WILD MONTANA SKIES. / I REMEMBER ROMANCE** — | —

Oct 83. (lp/c) *(RCA LP/K 6087)* <4683> **IT'S ABOUT TIME** `90` `61`
– Hold on tightly / The thought of you / Somethin' about / On the wings of a dream / Flight (the higher we fly) / Falling out of love / I remember romance / Wild Montana skies / World game / It's about time. *(re-iss. Nov84 lp/c/cd; PL/PK/PD 84740)*

Nov 83. (7") *(RCA 374)* <13642> **HOLD ME TIGHTLY. / FLIGHT (THE HIGHER WE FLY)**

Jan 84. (7") <13740> **IT'S ABOUT TIME. / WORLD GAME** `-`

Mar 84. (7") <13782> **THE GOLD AND BEYOND. / THE WAY I AM** `-`

Oct 84. (7"; JOHN DENVER and SYLVIE VARTAN) *(RCA 450)* <13931> **LOVE AGAIN. / IT'S ABOUT TIME** `85`

Mar 85. (lp/c/cd) *(PL/PK/PD 85313)* <5313> **JOHN DENVER'S GREATEST HITS, VOLUME 3** (compilation)
– Dancing with the mountains / Wild Montana skies / I want to live / Gold and beyond / Autograph / How can I leave you again / Some days are diamonds / Shanghai breezes / Seasons of the heart / Perhaps love / Love again. *(cd re-iss. Feb96; 74321 15480-2/-4)*

Nov 85. (lp/c/cd) *(PL/PK/PD 85458)* <5458> **DREAMLAND EXPRESS** `90` Jun85
– Dreamland express / Claudette / Gimme your love / Got my heart set on you / Harder they fall / Don't close your eyes tonight / A wild heart looking for a home / Desired / Trail of tears / African sunrise.

Apr 86. (7") *(PB 49961)* <14115> **DON'T CLOSE YOUR EYES TONIGHT. / A WILD HEART LOOKING FOR A HOME** Jan86

Apr 86. (7") <14227> **DREAMLAND EXPRESS. / AFRICAN SUNRISE** `-`

Aug 86. (lp/c/cd) *(PL/PK/PD 85811)* <5811> **ONE WORLD** `91`
– Love is the master / Love again / I remember you / Hey there, Mr. Lonely Heart / Let us begin (what are we making weapons for?) / Flying for me / Along for the ride('56 T-bird) / I can't escape / True love takes time / One world / It's a possibility.

Nov 86. (7") <14406> **ALONG FOR THE RIDE ('56 T-BIRD). / LET US BEGIN (WHAT ARE WE MAKING WEAPONS FOR?)** `-`

Jan 87. (7") <5086-7R> **LET US BEGIN (WHAT ARE WE MAKING WEAPONS FOR?). / LOVE AGAIN** `-`

	R.C.A.	Windstar
Sep 88. (7") *(PB 49497)* **FOR YOU. / ALASKA AND ME**	`-`	
Oct 88. (lp/c/cd) *(PL/PK/PD 90240)* <D1/D4/D2 72850> **HIGHER**		`-`

GROUND
– Higher ground / Home grown tomatoes / Whispering Jesse / Never a doubt / Deal with the ladies / Sing Australia / A country girl in Paris / For you / All this joy / Falling leaves (the refugees) / Bread and roses / Alaska and me. *(cd re-iss. Mar95 on 'Music Club'; MCCD 197)*

	Windstar	Windstar
Nov 88. (7") <75720> **A COUNTRY GIRL IN PARIS. / BREAD AND ROSES**	`-`	
Sep 90. (cd/c) <WR 53334-2/-4> **THE FLOWER THAT SHATTERED THE STONE**	`-`	

– The flower that shattered the stone / Thanks to you / Postcard from Paris / High, wide and handsome / Eagles and horses / A little further north / Raven's child / Ancient rhymes / The gift you are / I watch you sleeping / Stonehaven sunset / The flower that shattered the stone (reprise). *(UK-iss.Feb92 on 'Windstar'; 884900) (re-iss. Feb94 on 'Music Club' cd/c; MCCD/MCTC 154)*

Oct 91. (cd/c) <WR 58888-2/-4> **DIFFERENT DIRECTIONS**
– The foxfire suite):- Spring is alive ... You are ... / Whisper the wind – Spring is alive (reprise) / Potters wheel / Ponies / Chained to the wheel / Two different directions / Hold on to me / The chosen ones / Amazon (let this be a voice) / Tenderly calling. *(re-iss. Mar96 on 'Music Club' cd/c; MCCD/MCTC 035)*

	Columbia	Legacy-Sony
Aug 95. (cd/c) *(480694-2/-4)* <64655> **THE WILDLIFE CONSERVATION SOCIETY CONCERT (live 23-24 February, 1995 at Sony Music Studios, NYC)**		Jul95

– Leaving on a jet plane – Goodbye again (medley) / Rocky mountain high / Rhymes and reasons / Country roads / Back home again / I guess he'd rather be in Colorado / Matthew / Sunshine on my shoulders / You say the battle is over / Eagles and horses / Darcy Farrow / Whispering Jesse / Me and my uncle / Wild mountain skies / Bet on the blues / The harder they fall / Shanghai breezes / Fly away / A song for all / Lovers / Dreamland express / For you / Is it love / Falling out of love / Annie's song / Poems, prayers and promises / Calypso / Amazon / This old guitar.

—— tragically, DENVER was killed on the 12 Oct'97 when his plane crashed

– compilations, etc. –

Nov 84. (lp/c) *Telstar; (STAR/STAC 2253)* **JOHN DENVER COLLECTION** `20` `-`
– Annie's song / Take me home, country roads / Rocky mountain high / Starwood in Aspen / Follow me / I'd rather be a cowboy / Rhymes and reasons / Perhaps love (with PLACIDO DOMINGO) / Calypso / Country love / Leaving on a jet plane / Thank God I'm a country boy / Dancing with the mountains / Baby, you look good to me tonight / Wild Montana skies / Love again (with SYLVIE VARTAN). *(cd-iss. Apr86; TCD 2253)*

Nov 86. (7") *Old Gold; (OG 9633)* **ANNIE'S SONG. / TAKE ME HOME COUNTRY ROAD** `-`

Sep 91. (cd/c) *Music Club; (MCCD/MCTC 035)* **EARTH SONGS**

Oct 95. (d-cd) *Double Platinum; (DBP 102008)* **TWO DIFFERENT DIRECTIONS / GREATEST HITS AND FAVOURITES** `-`

Jan 96. (cd) *Happy Price; (HP 93482)* **IN CONCERT** (live)

Apr 96. (cd) *Country Stars; (CTS 55434)* **TAKE ME HOME**

Sep 96. (cd-ep) *R.C.A.; (7863 66837-2)* **ROCKY MOUNTAINS EP**

Nov 96. (cd) *Column-Universe; (280729)* **THE COLLECTION**

Mar 97. (d-cd/d-c) *R.C.A.; (07863 6683720-2/-4)* **THE ROCKY MOUNTAIN COLLECTION**
(re-dist.Oct97) – hit UK No.55

Jul 97. (cd) *Epic; (487390-2) / Legacy; <65183>* **THE BEST OF JOHN DENVER LIVE** (live)

Sep 97. (5xcd-box) *Laserlight; (15978)* **THE COLLECTION** `-`

Nov 97. (cd) *E.M.I.; <(823137-2)>* **THE UNPLUGGED COLLECTION** Dec98

Dec 97. (cd) *Laserlight; <(12923)>* **TAKE ME HOME, COUNTRY ROADS** Jun97

Dec 97. (cd) *Laserlight; <(12924)>* **ANNIE'S SONG** Jun97

Dec 97. (cd) *Laserlight; <(12925)>* **ROCKY MOUNTAIN HIGH** Jun97

Dec 97. (cd) *Laserlight; <(12926)>* **SUNSHINE ON MY SHOULDERS** Jun97

Dec 97. (cd) *Laserlight; <(12927)>* **CALYPSO** Jun97

Mar 98. (4xcd-box) *R.C.A.; <(07863 67437-2)>* **THE COUNTRY ROADS COLLECTION**

May 98. (cd) *R.C.A.; (07863 66987-2)* **REFLECTIONS (SONGS OF LOVE AND LIFE)**

May 98. (cd) *R.C.A.; <(07863 67604-2)>* **THE GREATEST COUNTRY HITS**

Nov 98. (cd) *RCA Camden; (74321 62804-2)* **LOVE SONGS AND POETRY**

May 99. (cd) *R.C.A.; (74321 15479-2)* <54792> **VOICE OF AMERICA** Sep93

Jun 99. (cd) *RCA Camden; (74321 67442-2)* **THE VERY BEST OF JOHN DENVER**

Oct 99. (d-cd) *R.C.A.; (07863 67783-2)* **PORTRAIT**

DEPECHE MODE

Formed: Basildon, Essex, England . . . 1976 by VINCE CLARKE, MARTIN GORE and ANDY FLETCHER while still at school. The line-up was completed by frontman DAVE GAHAN, and by 1980 they had adopted the DEPECHE MODE moniker, immersing themselves in the London 'New Romantic' scene which spawned the likes of SPANDAU BALLET and VISAGE. After gigging around the capital and having a track, 'PHOTOGRAPHIC', included on the 'Some Bizzare Album' various artists collection, the band were picked up by the fledgling 'Mute' label. While their debut single, 'DREAMING OF ME', scraped the lower regions of the chart in 1981, a follow-up, 'NEW LIFE', almost made the Top 10. Dominated by synthesizers and drum machines, yet retaining a keen sense of melody, the band initially took their cue from KRAFTWERK. As evidenced on their insanely catchy Top 10 breakthrough, 'JUST CAN'T GET ENOUGH' (the first of 24 consecutive Top 30 hits), their lyrics weren't quite as enigmatic as their Teutonic heroes, although they improved with time. The success of the single (which no doubt still gets played ten times a night in French discos!) paved the way for the debut album, 'SPEAK AND SPELL' (1981), a promising collection of catchy synth-pop fare which made the UK Top 10. Chief songwriter VINCE CLARKE quit shortly after, going on to pastures new with YAZOO and then ERASURE, GORE taking up the pensmith chores for the follow-up album, 'A BROKEN FRAME' (1982). Shortly after its release, ALAN WILDER, who had previously toured with the band, was recruited as a full time replacement for CLARKE. Like its predecessor, 'CONSTRUCTION TIME AGAIN' (1983) failed to make any significant leap forward from the debut, musically at least, although it did contain the classic 'EVERYTHING COUNTS', GAHAN's voice summoning up as much portentous doom as he could muster. While the 'PEOPLE ARE PEOPLE' single gave the band valuable exposure in America, their real breakthrough came with 1984's 'SOME GREAT REWARD'. Featuring the likes of 'BLASPHEMOUS RUMOURS' and 'MASTER AND SERVANT', the album was palpably darker, the music more satisfyingly varied. 'BLACK CELEBRATION' (1986) was deliberately darker still, much of the material creeping along at a funereal pace. 'MUSIC FOR THE MASSES' (1987) was the band's biggest Stateside success to date, the material for the live album, '101' (1989) coming from the American leg of their 1988 sell-out world tour. 'VIOLATOR' (1990) was heralded as DEPECHE MODE's best work since 'SOME GREAT REWARD', spawning two of their better singles in 'PERSONAL JESUS' and the uncharacteristically emotional 'ENJOY THE SILENCE'. Never the warmest sounding band, with 'SONGS OF FAITH AND DEVOTION' (1993) their clinical sound was softened somewhat with a move towards more rock-centric territory. That's not to say the music was soft, at least not on the single, 'I FEEL YOU', a dirty great guitar riff grinding away relentlessly. Elsewhere, the album had something of a transcendent, redemptive quality about it on such powerful tracks as 'MERCY IN YOU' and 'ONE CARESS'. The record gave the band their first No.1, UK and US, although some longtime fans were understandably miffed at the band's new direction. • **Covered:** ROUTE 66 (Chuck Berry). • **Trivia:** MARTIN GORE's solo album contained six cover versions incl. NEVER TURN YOUR BACK ON MOTHER EARTH (Sparks). He later covered Leonard Cohen's COMING BACK TO YOU.

Album rating: SPEAK & SPELL (*6) / A BROKEN FRAME (*6) / CONSTRUCTION TIME AGAIN (*7) / SOME GREAT REWARD (*7) / THE SINGLES 1981-1985 compilation (*9) / BLACK CELEBRATION (*8) / MUSIC FOR THE MASSES (*7) / 101 (*5) / VIOLATOR (*7) / SONGS OF FAITH & DEVOTION (*7) / SONGS OF LOVE & DEVOTION LIVE (*3) / ULTRA (*6) / THE SINGLES 86>98 compilation (*7)

VINCE CLARKE (b. 3 Jul'60, South Woodford, England) – keyboards, synthesiser / **DAVID GAHAN** (b. 9 May'62, Epping, England) – vocals / **MARTIN GORE** (b.23 Jul'61) – keyboards, synthesizer, vocals / **ANDY FLETCHER** (b. 8 Jul'61, Nottingham, England) – guitar, synthesiser, drum machine

		Mute	Sire
Mar 81. (7") *(MUTE 013)* **DREAMING OF ME. / ICE MACHINE**		`57`	
Jun 81. (7") *(MUTE 014)* **NEW LIFE. / SHOUT!**		`11`	
(12") *(12MUTE 014)* – ('A'extended) / ('B'-Rio mix).			
Sep 81. (7") *(MUTE 016)* **JUST CAN'T GET ENOUGH. / ANY SECOND NOW**		`8`	`-`
(12") *(12MUTE 016)* – ('A'-Schizo mix) / ('B'-altered).			
Oct 81. (lp/c) *(STUMM/CSTUMM 5)* <3642> **SPEAK & SPELL**		`10`	

– New life / Just can't get enough / I sometimes wish I was dead / Puppets / Boys say go / No disco / What's your name / Photographic / Tora! Tora! Tora! / Big Muff / Any second now. *(cd-iss. Apr88 +=; CDSTUMM 5)* – Dreaming of me / New life (extended) / Shout! (Rio mix) / Any second now (altered mix).

Nov 81. (7") **JUST CAN'T GET ENOUGH. / TORA! TORA! TORA!**   `-` ☐

—— **ALAN WILDER** (b. 1 Jun'59, London, England) – electronics (ex-HITMEN) repl. VINCE who formed YAZOO

Jan 82. (7"/ext.12") *(MUTE/12MUTE 018)* **SEE YOU. / NOW, THIS IS FUN**   `6` ☐ Aug82

Apr 82. (7") *(MUTE 022)* **THE MEANING OF LOVE. / OBERKORN (IT'S A SMALL TOWN)**   `12`
(12") *(12MUTE 022)* – ('A'extended) / ('B'-Fairly odd mix).

Aug 82. (7") *(7BONG 1)* **LEAVE IN SILENCE. / EXCERPT FROM MY SECRET GARDEN**   `18`
(ext.12"+=) *(12BONG 1)* – ('A'quieter version).

Sep 82. (lp/c) *(STUMM/CSTUMM 9)* <23751> **A BROKEN FRAME**   `8`
– Leave in silence / My secret garden / Monument / Nothing to fear / See you / Satellite / The meaning of love / A photograph of you / Shouldn't have done that / The sun and the rainfall. *(cd-iss. Jul88; CDSTUMM 13)*

Feb 83. (7"/ext.12") *(7/12 BONG 2)* **GET THE BALANCE RIGHT. / THE GREAT OUTDOORS**   `13`
(12") *(L12BONG 2)* – ('A'side) / My secret garden (live) / See you (live) / Satellite / Tora! Tora! Tora! (live).

Jul 83. (7") *(7BONG 3)* **EVERYTHING COUNTS. / WORK HARD**   `6`
(12") *(12BONG 3)* – ('A'-larger amounts) / ('B'-East End mix).
(12") *(L12BONG 3)* – ('A'side) / Boys say go (live) / New life (live) / Nothing to fear (live) / The meaning of love (live).

Aug 83. (lp/c) *(STUMM/CSTUMM 13)* **CONSTRUCTION TIME AGAIN**   `6`   `-`
– Love in itself / More than a party / Pipeline / Everything counts / Two minute warning / Shame / The landscape is changing / Told you so / And then . . . *(cd-iss. Jul88; CDSTUMM 13)*

Sep 83. (7") *(BONG 4)* **LOVE IN ITSELF. / FOOLS**   `21`
(12") *(12BONG 4)* – Love in itself (3) / (4) / Fools (bigger).
(12") *(L12BONG 4)* – ('A'side) / Just can't get enough (live) / Photograph (live) / A photograph of you (live) / Shout! (live).

Mar 84. (7") *(7BONG 5)* <29221> **PEOPLE ARE PEOPLE. / IN YOUR MEMORY**   `4`   `13` May85
(12"+=) *(12BONG 5)* – ('A'-On-U-Sound remix).
(12") *(12BONG 5)* – ('A'different mix) / ('B'-Slik mix).

Jul 84. (lp) <25124> **PEOPLE ARE PEOPLE**   `-`   `71`
– People are people / Everything counts / Get the balance right / Love in itself / Now this is fun / Leave in silence / Told you so / Work hard.

Aug 84. (7") *(7BONG 6)* <28918> **MASTER AND SERVANT. / SET ME FREE (RENOVATE ME)**   `9` ☐ Aug85
('A'-Slavery whip mix-12"+=) *(12BONG 6)* – ('A'voxless).
('A'-On-U-Sound mix-12"+=) *(L12BONG 6)* – Are people people?.

Sep 84. (lp/c) *(STUMM/CSTUMM 19)* <25194> **SOME GREAT REWARD**   `5`   `51` Jan85
– Something to do / Lie to me / People are people / It doesn't matter / Stories of old / Somebody / Master and servant / If you want to / Blasphemous rumours. *(cd-iss. Sep87; CDSTUMM 19)*

Nov 84. (7") *(7BONG 7)* **BLASPHEMOUS RUMOURS. / SOMEBODY**   `16`
(7"ep+=) *(7BONG 7E)* – Told you so (live) / Everything counts (live).
(12"+=) *(12BONG 7)* – Ice machine / Two minute warning / Everything counts (live).

May 85. (7"/remix-12") *(7/12 BONG 8)* **SHAKE THE DISEASE. / FLEXIBLE**   `18`
(12") *(L12BONG 8)* – Edit the shake / Master and servant (live) / Flexible (deportation mix) / Something to do (metal mix).

Sep 85. (7"/remix-12") *(7/12 BONG 9)* **IT'S CALLED A HEART. / FLY ON THE WINDSCREEN**   `18`
(ext.d12"+=) *(D12BONG 9)* – ('A'-slow mix) / ('A'-death mix).

Oct 85. (lp/c) *(MUTEL/CMUTEL 1)* <25346> **THE SINGLES 1981-1985** (compilation) <US-title 'CATCHING UP WITH DEPECHE MODE'>   `6`
– People are people / Master and servant / It's called a heart / Just can't get enough / See you / Shake the disease / Everything counts / New life / Blasphemous rumours / Leave in silence / Get the balance right / Love in itself / Dreaming of me. *(c+=)* – (2 extra). *(cd-iss. Sep87; CDMUTEL 1)*

Feb 86. (7") *(7BONG 10)* **STRIPPED. / BUT NOT TONIGHT**   `15`
(ext.12"+=) *(12BONG 10)* – Breathing in fumes / Fly on the windscreen (quiet mix) / Black day.

Mar 86. (lp/c) *(STUMM/CSTUMM 26)* <25429> **BLACK CELEBRATION**   `4`   `90`
– Black celebration / Fly on the windscreen – final / A question of lust / Sometimes / It doesn't matter two / A question of time / Stripped / Here is the house / World full of nothing / Dressed in black / New dress. *(cd-iss. Sep87+=; CDSTUMM 26)* – But not tonight / Breathing in fumes / Black day.

Apr 86. (7") *(7BONG 11)* **A QUESTION OF LUST. / CHRISTMAS ISLAND**   `28`
(free c-s. w/7") *(CBONG 11)* – ('A'-Flood mix) / If you want (live) / Shame (live) / Blasphemous rumours (live).
(ext.12"+=) *(12BONG 11)* – It doesn't matter (instrumental) / People are people (live) / A question of lust (minimal).

Aug 86. (7") *(7BONG 12)* **A QUESTION OF TIME. / BLACK CELEBRATION**   `17`
(ext.12"+=) *(12BONG 12)* – Stripped (live) / Something to do (live).
(12") *(L12BONG 12)* – ('A'-Newtown mix) / ('A'live) / ('B'-Black tulip mix) / More than a party (live).

Apr 87. (7") *(7BONG 13)* <28366> **STRANGELOVE. / PIMPF**   `16`   `76`
('A'-Maximix-12"+=) *(12BONG 13)* – ('A'Midimix).
(cd-s++=) *(CDBONG 13)* – Agent orange.
('A'-Blind mix-12"+=) *(L12BONG 13)* – ('A'-Pain mix) / Agent orange.

Aug 87. (7") *(7BONG 14)* <28189> **NEVER LET ME DOWN AGAIN. / PLEASURE, LITTLE PLEASURE**   `22`   `63`
(12"/c-s) *(12/C BONG 14)* – ('A'-split mix) / ('B'-glitter mix) / ('A'-aggro mix).
(cd-s++=) *(CDBONG 14)* – To have and to hold (Spanish taster).
(12") *(12BONG 14)* – ('A'-Tsangarides mix) / ('B'-join mix) / To have and to hold (Spanish taster).

Sep 87. (cd/d-c/lp,clear-lp) *(CD/C+/STUMM 47)* <25614> **MUSIC FOR THE MASSES**   `10`   `35`
– Never let me down again / The things you said / Strangelove / Sacred / Little 15 / Behind the wheel / I want you now / To have to hold / Nothing / Pimpf. *(cd+=)* – Agent orange / Never let me down again (aggro mix) / To have

and to hold (Spanish) / Pleasure the treasure (glitter mix). *(d-c+=)* – BLACK CELEBRATION (album)

Dec 87. (7") *(7BONG 15)* <27991> **BEHIND THE WHEEL. / ROUTE 66**   `21`   `61`
(c-s+=/cd-s+=) *(C/CD BONG 15)* – ('A'-Shep Pettibone mix) / ('A'-lp version).
(12") *(12BONG 15)* – ('A'-Shep Pettibone mix) / ('B'-Beatmasters mix).
(12") *(L12BONG 15)* – ('A'-Beatmasters mix) / ('B'-Casualty mix).

May 88. (7"import) *(LITTLE 15)* **LITTLE 15. /**   `60`

Sep 88. (7") <27777> **STRANGELOVE. / NOTHING**   `-`   `50`

Feb 89. (7") *(7BONG 16)* **EVERYTHING COUNTS (live). / NOTHING (live)**   `22`
(12"+=/cd-s+=) *(12/CD BONG 16)* – Sacred (live) / A question of lust (live). (remix-cd-s) *(CDLBONG 16)* – Strangelove (remix).
(3"cd-s) *(LCDBONG 16)* – ('A'-Tim Simenon & M. Saunders remix) / ('B'-Justin Strauss remix) / Strangelove (Tim Simenon & M. Saunders remix).
(12") *(L12BONG 16)* - **('A'-Bomb The Bass mix) / ('B'-Hijack mix).**
(10") *(10BONG 16)* – ('A'-Absolute mix) / ('B'-US mix) / ('A'-1983 mix).

Mar 89. (d-cd/d-c/d-lp) *(CD/C+/STUMM 101)* <25853> **101 (live)**   `5`   `45`
– Pimpf / Behind the wheel / Strangelove / Sacred * / Something to do / Blasphemous rumours / Stripped / Somebody / Things you said / Black generation / Shake the disease / Nothing * / Pleasure little treasure / People are people / A question of time / Never let me down again / A question of lust * / Master and servant / Just can't get enough / Everything counts *. *(c+=*/cd+=*)*

Aug 89. (7")<US-c-s> *(BONG 17)* <19941> **PERSONAL JESUS. / DANGEROUS**   `13`   `28` Nov89
(7"g-f+=/12"+=/c-s+=/cd-s+=) *(G/12/C/CD BONG 17)* – ('A'acoustic mix).
('A'pump mix-3"cd-s) *(LCDBONG 17)* – ('A'-Telephone stomp mix).

Feb 90. (c-s/7") *(C+/BONG 18)* <19885> **ENJOY THE SILENCE. / MEMPHISTO**   `6`   `8` Mar90
(cd-s+=) *(LCDBONG 18)* – ('A'-Bassline):- Bassline / Harmonium / Rikki Tick Tick / Mempheto.
(etched-12"/3"cd-s) *(XL12/XLCD BONG 18)* – ('A'-The quad: Final mix).

Mar 90. (cd/c/lp) *(CD/C+/STUMM 64)* <26081> **VIOLATOR**   `2`   `7`
– World in my eyes / Sweetest perfection / Personal Jesus / Halo / Waiting for the night / Enjoy the silence / Policy of truth / Blue dress / Clean.

May 90. (c-s/7") *(C+/BONG 19)* <19842> **POLICY OF TRUTH. / KALEID (remix)**   `16`   `15` Aug90
('A'-Trancentral mix; 12"+=/cd-s+=) *(LCDBONG 19)* – ('A'-Pavlov's dub mix).

Sep 90. (12"/cd-s/7") *(12/CD+/BONG 20)* <19580> **WORLD IN MY EYES / HAPPIEST GIRL / SEA OF SIN**   `17`   `52` Nov90
(12") *(L12BONG 20)* – (first 2 tracks) / ('A'remix).
(c-s+=)(cd-s+=) *(CDLBONG 20)* – Meaning of love / Somebody.

Feb 93. (c-s/7") *(C+/BONG 21)* <18600> **I FEEL YOU. / ONE CARESS**   `8`   `37`
(12"+=/cd-s+=) *(12/CD BONG 21)* – ('A'-Throb mix) / ('A'-Babylon mix).
(12"/cd-s) *(12L/CDL BONG 21)* – ('A'side) / ('A'swamp mix) / ('A'-Renegade Soundwave mix) / ('A'-Helmut mix).

Mar 93. (cd/c/lp) *(CD/C+/STUMM 106)* <45243> **SONGS OF FAITH AND DEVOTION**   `1`   `1`
– I feel you / Walking in my shoes / Condemnation / Mercy in you / Judas / In your room / Get right with me / Rush / One caress / Higher love. *(live version of album iss.Dec93; same)*

May 93. (7"/c-s) *(7/C BONG 22)* <18506> **WALKING IN MY SHOES. / MY JOY**   `14`   `69`
(12"+=/cd-s+=) *(12/CD BONG 22)* – ('A'-Grungy Gonads mix).
(ext;12"/cd-s) *(L12/LCD BONG 22)* – ('A'-Random Carpet mix) / ('A'-Anandamidic mix) / ('A'-Mark Stent 12" Ambient Whale mix).

Sep 93. (7"/c-s) *(7/C BONG 23)* **CONDEMNATION. / DEATH'S DOOR (jazz mix)**   `9`
(cd-s+=) *(CDBONG 23)* – Rush (spiritual mix) / Rush (amylnitrate mix).
(12"+=) *(12BONG 23)* – Rush (mixes).
(12"/cd-s) *(L12/LCD 23)* – ('A'live) / Personal Jesus (live) / Enjoy the silence (live) / Halo (live).

Dec 93. (cd) <45505> **SONGS OF FAITH AND DEVOTION – LIVE (live)**   `-` ☐

Jan 94. (c-s) *(CBONG 24)* **IN YOUR ROOM (Zephyr mix) / HIGHER LOVE (Adrenaline mix)**   `8`
('A'-Jeep Rock mix; cd-s+=) *(XLCDBONG 24)* – ('A'-Apex mix).
(12"++=) *(12BONG 24)* – ('A'-extended Zephyr mix).
(cd-s) *(CDBONG 24)* – ('A'-Zephyr mix) / ('A'extended Zephyr mix) / Never let me down again / Death's door.
(cd-s) *(LCDBONG 24)* – ('A'side) / Policy of truth / World in my eyes / Fly on the windscreen (final).
(12"++=) *(L12BONG 24)* – Never let me down again / Death's door.

—— ANDREW FLETCHER departed to take over groups' business affairs.

—— On the 17th August '95, GAHAN was thought by the music press, to have attempted suicide by cutting at his wrists after his wife left him. His record company however said this had been an accident and was over-hyped by the media. GAHAN is currently being treated for his drug problems and has been charged by US police for similar offences.

Feb 97. (c-s) *(7BONG 25)* **BARREL OF A GUN / PAINKILLER ('A'-Underworld soft mix) / ('A'-One Inch Punch mix)**   `4`   `47`
(12") *(L12BONG 25)* – ('A'-One Inch Punch mix) / ('A'-United mix) / Painkiller (Plastikman mix) / Painkiller.
(cd-s) *(LCDBONG 25)* – ('A'-Underworld hard mix) / ('A'-United mix) / Painkiller (Plastikman mix).
(12") *(12BONG 25)* – ('A'-Underworld hard mix) / ('A'-3 Phase mix) / ('A'-One Inch Punch mix) / ('A'-United mix).

Apr 97. (c-s) *(CBONG 26)* **IT'S NO GOOD / SLOWBLOW**   `5`   `38`
(cd-s+=) *(CDBONG 26)* – ('A'-Bass bounce mix) / ('A'-Speedy J mix).
('A'-Hardfloor mix; cd-s+=) *(LCDBONG 26)* – ('A'-Andrea Parker mix) / ('A'-Motor bass mix).
(12") *(12BONG 26)* – ('A'-Hardfloor mix) / ('A'-Speedy J mix) / ('A'-Motor bass mix) / ('A'-Andrea Parker mix) / ('A'-Dom T mix).

Apr 97. (cd/c/lp) *(CD/C+/Stumm 148)* <46522> **ULTRA**   `1`   `5`
– Barrel of a gun / The love thieves / Home / It's no good / Uselink / Useless / Sister of night / Jazz thieves / Freestate / The bottom line / Insight.

Jun 97. (c-s) *(CBONG 27)* **HOME / IT'S NO GOOD**   `23`   `88` Nov97
('A'-Grantby mix; cd-s+=) *(LCDBONG 27)* – ('A'-Jedi Knights remix: Drowning in time) / Barrel of a gun.

(12") (12BONG 27) – ('A'-Jedi Knights remix: Drowning in time) / ('A'-Grantby mix) / ('A'-Air around the golf remix) / ('A'-LFO mix).

(cd-s) (CDBONG 27) – ('A'side) / ('A'-LFO mix) / ('A'-The Noodles and the damage done mix).

Oct 97.　(cd-s) (CDBONG 28) USELESS / ('A'-Escape From **Wherever parts 1&2)** / ('A'-Cosmic Blues mix) / **BARREL OF A GUN (video)**　　　　| 28 | |

(12") (12BONG 28) – ('A'-The Kruder & Dorfmeister session) / ('A'-CJ Bolland funky sub mix) / ('A-Air 20 mix).

(cd-s) (LCDBONG 28) – ('A'-CJ Bolland ultrasonar mix) / ('A'-The Kruder & Dorfmeister session) / ('A'live) / It's no good (CD-rom).

Sep 98.　(cd-s) (CDBONG 29) <44546> **ONLY WHEN I LOSE MYSELF / SURRENDER / HEADSTAR**　| 17 | 61 |

(12"/cd-s) (12/LCD BONG 29) – ('A'-Subsonic legacy remix) / ('A'-Dan The Automator remix) / Headstar (Luke Slater remix).

(12") (L12BONG 29) – ('A'remixes) / Painkiller / Surrender.

(cd-s+=) (XLCDBONG 29) – World in my eyes.

Sep 98.　(d-cd/c/3x12") (CD/C+/MUTEL 5) <47110> **THE SINGLES 86>98** (compilation)　| 5 | 38 | Oct98

– Stripped / A question of lust / A question of time / Strangelove / Never let me down again / Behind the wheel / Personal Jesus / Enjoy the silence / Policy of truth / World in my eyes / I feel you / Walking in my shoes / Condemnation / In your room / Barrel of a gun / It's no good / Home / Useless / Only when I lose myself / Little 15 / Everything counts (live).

– compilations, others –

on 'Mute' unless otherwise mentioned

Nov 91.　(6xcd-ep-box) (DMBX 1CD) **SINGLES BOX SET**　| | - |
Nov 91.　(6xcd-ep-box) (DMBX 2CD) **SINGLES BOX SET**　| | - |
Nov 91.　(6xcd-ep-box) (DMBX 3CD) **SINGLES BOX SET**　| | - |
Jan 99.　(cd/c) <47298> **THE SINGLES 81>85**　| - | |

MARTIN L. GORE

		Mute	Sire

Jun 89.　(m-cd/m-c/m-lp) (CD/C+/STUMM 67) <25980>
COUNTERFEIT　　| 51 | |
– Smile in the crowd / Never turn your back on Mother Earth / Gone / Motherless child / Compulsion / In a manner of speaking.

DEREK & THE DOMINOES (see under ⇒ CLAPTON, Eric)

Rick DERRINGER (dig out; Great Metal . . .)

DESCENDENTS (dig out; Great Alt & Indie . . .)

dEUS

Formed: Antwerp, Belgium ... 1991 by TOM BARMAN alongside RUDY TROUVE, KLAUS JANZOONS, JULLE DE BORGHER and STEF CARLENS. Beginning life as a VIOLENT FEMMES / VELVET UNDERGROUND covers outfit, this experimental art-rock collective were picked up by 'Island' in 1994, initially making an impact via their appearance at that year's Glastonbury festival. A UK debut single, 'SUDS & SODA' (they had issued 'ZEA' in Belgium), was closely followed by 'VIA', TOM WAITS and CAPTAIN BEEFHEART being the most commonly cited reference points – in fact the latter's right hand man, ERIC DREW FELDMAN produced them. Open-ended in the established tradition of late 60's/early 70's Euro-rock yet pregnant with the potential to be as abrasive as early BIG BLACK or even BLACK FLAG, dEUS' avant-garde pop polarised opinion; you either loved it or hated it. Certainly more challenging than many of the identikit grunge albums doing the rounds at the time, 'WORST CASE SCENARIO' (1994) focused the band's wayward muse into a listenable whole; it also proved that there was more to Belgian music than plastic Europap passed off as "techno". dEUS released a follow-up set, 'IN A BAR, UNDER THE SEA' (1996), an album that contained their only Top 50 single to date, 'LITTLE ARITHMETICS'. • **Songwriters:** Group (BARMAN (words) / CARLENS some with SERGEY) or (TROUVE + JANZOONS with VERMEERSCH + VERVLOESEM) except a sample of FRANK ZAPPA on their 1994 album. In 1996, BARMAN, CARLENS and WARD became the writers.

Album rating: MY SISTER IS MY CLOCK (*6) / WORST CASE SCENARIO (*8) / IN A BAR, UNDER THE SEA (*7) / THE IDEAL CRASH (*8)

TOM BARMAN – vocals / **KLAUS JANZOONS** – violin / **RUDY TROUVE** – guitar / **JULLE DE BORGHER** – drums / **STEF KAMIL CARLENS** – bass

		own label	not iss.

1993.　(cd-ep) **ZEA EP**　| - | - | Belgian

		Island	Polygram

Jul 94.　(7") (IS 598) **SUDS & SODA. / SECRET HELL**
(12"+=/cd-s+=) (12IS/CID 598) – Texan coffee / It. furniture in the far west.

Sep 94.　(7") (IS 599) **VIA. / VIOLINS AND HAPPY ENDINGS**
(12"+=/cd-s+=) (12IS/CID 599) – Great American nude (strip mix) / Niche.

Oct 94.　(cd/c/lp) (CID/ICT/ILPS 8028) <524045> **WORST CASE SCENARIO**　　| | Feb95
– Intro / Suds & soda / W.C.S. (first draft) / Jigsaw you / Morticiahair / Via / Right as rain / Mute / Lets get lost / Hotellounge (be the death of me) / Shake your hip / Great American nude / Secret hell / Divebomb djingle.

Jan 95.　(c-s/7") (C+/IS 603) **HOTELLOUNGE (BE THE DEATH OF ME). / JIGSAW YOU (live)**　| 55 | - |
(cd-s+=/cd-s+=) (CID/+X 603) – Whose Vegas (is it anyway).

Jan 95.　(cd) (IMCD 8031) **MY SISTER IS MY CLOCK**　| - | - | mail-o
– Middlewave / Almost white / Health insurance / Little ghost / How to row a cat / Only a colour to her / Sick sugar / Sweetness / Horror party jokes / Void / Sans titre pour sira / Glovesong / Lorre in the forest.

──── **CRAIG WARD** (b. Scotland) – guitar; repl. TROUVE who formed KISS MY JAZZ

Jul 96.　(7"/10") (IS/10IS 630) **THEME FROM TURNPIKE. / OVERFLOW / MY LITTLE CONTESSA**　| 68 | |
(cd-s+=) (CID 630) – Worried about Satan.

Oct 96.　(c-s/7"pic-d) (C+/IS 643) **LITTLE ARITHMETICS. / MY WIFE JAN**　| 44 | - |
(cd-s+=) (CID 643-854 719-2) – The tugboat / Everything is the same (except no one believes me).

Nov 96.　(cd/c/lp) (CID/ICT/ILPS 8052) <524296> **IN A BAR, UNDER THE SEA**　| | Mar97
– I don't mind what ever happens / Fell off the floor, man / Opening night / Theme from Turnpike / Little arithmetics / Gimme the heat / Serpentine / A shocking lack thereof / Supermarketsong / Memory of a festival / Guilty pleasures / Nine threads / Disappointed in the sun / For the roses / Wake me up before I sleep.

Mar 97.　(7"pic-d) (IS 645) **ROSES. / I SUFFER ROCK**　| 56 | - |
(cd-s+=) (CID 645) – Nine threads (demo) / Difficult day.
(cd-s) (CIDX 645) – ('A'-Vermeersch version) / Via (live) / Hotel lounge (be the death of me) (live) / Jigsaw you (live).

Sep 97.　(c-s/7"pic-d) (C+/IS 663) **LITTLE ARITHMETICS. / FELL OFF THE FLOOR, MAN (Dust Brothers edit)**　| | - |
(cd-s+=) (CID 663) – Me & your mother / Disappointed in the sun.

Mar 99.　(cd/c/lp) (CID/ICT/ILPS 8082) **THE IDEAL CRASH**　| 64 | |
– Put the freaks up front / Silver dew / One advice space / Magic hour / The ideal crash / Instant Street / Magdalena / Everybody's weird / Let's see who goes down first / Dream sequence #1.

Apr 99.　(7") (IS 742) **INSTANT STREET. / DREAM SEQUENCE**　| 49 | |
(cd-s) (CID 742) – ('A'side) / Sam Peckinpah's daughter / You can't deny what you liked as a child.
(cd-s) (CIDX 742) – ('A'side) / There / Everybody's weird (demo).

Jun 99.　(7") (IS 750) **SISTER DEW. / 13 (live)**　| 62 | |
(cd-s+=) (CID 750) – A shocking lack thereof (session).
(cd-s) (CIDX 750) – ('A'side) / Sister dew (enhanced) / Gimme the heat (live) / Little arithmetics (live).

Oct 99.　(7") (IS 760) **THE IDEAL CRASH. / EVERYBODY'S WEIRD (remixed by Soulwerk)**　| | |
(cd-s+=) (CID 760) – Infant street / Sister dew / ('A' video)
(cd-s) (CIDX 760) –

DEVO

Formed: Akron, Ohio, USA ... 1972 by two sets of brothers, MARK and BOB MOTHERSBAUGH together with GERALD and BOB CASALE (drummer, ALAN MYERS completed the line-up). From the early 70's, they had been known as The DE-EVOLUTION BAND, before sensibly abbreviating the name to DEVO. This bunch of lab-coated weirdos (taking up The RESIDENTS' terminally skewed vision) issued two obscure 45's on their own indie label, 'Booji Boy', which were heavily imported into Britain through leading indie outlet, 'Stiff,' late in 1977. Early the following year, both the double A-sided 'MONGOLOID' / 'JOCKO HOMO' and a hilarious electro-fied rendition of The Rolling Stones' '(I CAN'T GET NO) SATISFACTION', were repressed due to popular demand, the singles subsequently becoming minor chart entries. After a third classic, 'BE STIFF' also hit UK Top 75, the flowerpot-headed, potato-faced futurists secured a deal with 'Virgin' ('Warners' in the US) and continued to inject a quirky humour into the po-faced New Wave movement with a fourth hit, 'COME BACK JONEE'. A debut album, inspiringly titled 'Q: ARE WE NOT MEN? A: WE ARE DEVO!' (produced by BRIAN ENO, who else!?), was released a month later to a confused but appreciative audience who helped propel the record into the Top 20 (Top 100 US). However, their follow-up set, 'DUTY NOW FOR THE FUTURE' (1979), suffered a slight backlash, the novelty wearing thin without the impact of a hit single. 1980's 'FREEDOM OF CHOICE' would have suffered a similar fate, but for a freak US Top 20 single, 'WHIP IT'. The rest of their 80's output lacked their early wit, although America embraced such albums as 'DEV-O LIVE' (1981), 'NEW TRADITIONALISTS' (1981), 'OH NO, IT'S DEVO' (1982) and 'SHOUT' (1984). Having disbanded in the middle of the decade, DEVO (with new drummer, DAVID KENDRICK) reformed in 1988, signing to 'Enigma' and releasing one non-event of an album after another. Their days of inspired innovation now behind them, the legacy of DEVO was nevertheless plundered to unusual effect when SOUNDGARDEN, SUPERCHUNK and even ROBERT PALMER!!! covered their 1980 classic, 'GIRL U WANT'. • **Songwriters:** GERALD and MARK wrote most of material, SECRET AGENT MAN (Johnny Rivers) / ARE U EXPERIENCED (Jimi Hendrix) / WORKING IN A COALMINE (Lee Dorsey). • **Trivia:** In 1982, DEVO had contributed services to choreographer TONI BASIL on her debut solo album 'WORD OF MOUTH'. In the late 70's, MARK had appeared on HUGH CORNWALL (of The STRANGLERS) and ROBERT WILLIAMS collaboration 'Nosferatu'.

Album rating: Q: ARE WE NOT MEN? A: WE ARE DEVO! (*8) / DUTY NOW FOR THE FUTURE (*7) / FREEDOM OF CHOICE (*7) / DEV-O LIVE mini (*2) / NEW TRADITIONALISTS (*6) / OH NO! IT'S DEVO (*6) / SHOUT (*4) / E-Z LISTENING DISC collection (*4) / TOTAL DEVO (*4) / NOW IT CAN BE TOLD (DEVO AT THE PALACE 12/9/88) live (*5) / SMOOTH NOODLE MAPS (*4) / HARDCORE DEVO, VOL.1 compilation (*6) / THE GREATEST HITS compilation (*7) / HARDCORE DEVO, VOL.2 compilation (*5) / DEVO LIVE: THE MONGOLOID YEARS compilation (*4) / HOT POTATOES: THE BEST OF DEVO compilation (*8)

BOB MOTHERSBAUGH – vocals, guitar / **MARK MOTHERSBAUGH** – keyboards, synthesizers / **BOB CASALE** – guitar / **JERRY CASALE** – bass, vocals / **ALAN MYERS** – drums repl. JIM MOTHERSBAUGH

		Stiff	Booji Boy
Feb 78.	(7") *(DEV 1)* <*7033-14*> **MONGOLOID. / JOCKO HOMO**	62	1977
Apr 78.	(7")(12") *(DEV 2)(BOY 1)* **(I CAN'T GET ME NO) SATISFACTION. / SLOPPY (I SAW MY BABY GETTING)** <*re-iss. 1978 on 'Bomp'; 72843*>	41	1977

		Stiff	not iss.
Jul 78.	(7"clear,7"lemon) *(BOY 2)* **BE STIFF. / SOCIAL FOOLS**	71	-

		Virgin	Warners
Aug 78.	(7"grey) *(VS 223)* **COME BACK JONEE. / SOCIAL FOOLS**	60	-
Sep 78.	(lp/c) *(V/TCV 2106)* <*3239*> **Q: ARE WE NOT MEN? A: WE ARE DEVO!**	12	78
	– Uncontrollable urge / (I can't get no) Satisfaction / Praying hands / Space junk / Mongoloid / Jocko homo / Too much paranoias / Gut feeling – (slap your mammy) / Come back Jonee / Sloppy (I saw my baby getting) / Shrivel-up. (w/free flexi-7"; VDJ 27) (pic-lp; VP 2106) (re-iss. Mar84 lp/c; OVED/+C 37)		
Jan 79.	(7") <*WB 8745*> **COME BACK JONEE. / PRAYING HANDS**	-	
Jun 79.	(7") *(VS 265)* **THE DAY MY BABY GAVE ME A SURPRIZE. / PENETRATION IN THE CENTREFOLD**	-	-
Jun 79.	(lp/c) *(V/TCV 2125)* <*3337*> **DUTY NOW FOR THE FUTURE**	49	73
	– Devo corporate anthem / Clockout / Timing X / Wiggly world / Blockhead / Strange pursuit / S.I.B. (Swelling Itching Brain) / Triumph of the will / The day my baby gave me a surprize / Pink pussycat / Secret agent man / Smart patrol – Mr. DNA / Red eye. (re-iss. Mar84 lp/c; OVED/+C 38)		
Jul 79.	(7") <*WBS 49028*> **SECRET AGENT MAN. / RED EYE EXPRESS**	-	
Aug 79.	(7") *(VS 280)* **SECRET AGENT MAN. / SOO BAWLS**	-	
May 80.	(7") *(VS 350)* **GIRL U WANT. / TURN AROUND**	-	
May 80.	(lp/c) *(V/TCV 2162)* <*3435*> **FREEDOM OF CHOICE**	47	22
	– Girl u want / It's not right / Whip it / Snowball / Ton o' luv / Freedom of choice / Gates of steel / Cold war / Don't you know / That's Pep! / Mr. B's ballroom / Planet Earth. (re-iss. Mar84 lp/c; OVED/+C 39)		
Jul 80.	(7") <*WBS 49550*> **GIRL U WANT. / MR. B'S BALLROOM**	-	
Aug 80.	(7") <*WBS 49550*> **WHIP IT. / TURN AROUND**		14
Nov 80.	(7") *(VS 383)* **WHIP IT. / SNOWBALL**	51	-
	(12"+=) *(VS 383-12)* – Gates of steel.		
Nov 80.	(7") <*WBS 49621*> **FREEDOM OF CHOICE. / SNOWBALL**	-	
Mar 81.	(7") <*WBS 49711*> **GATES OF STEEL. / BE STIFF (live)**	-	
May 81.	(m-lp/m-c) *(OVED 1)* <*3548*> **DEV-O LIVE (live)**		49 Apr81
	– Freedom of choice (theme song) / Whip it / Girl u want / Gates of steel / Be stiff / Planet Earth.		
Jun 81.	(7") <*WBS >* **THROUGH BEING COOL. / GOING UNDER**	-	
Aug 81.	(7") *(VS 450)* **THROUGH BEING COOL. / RACE OF DOOM**	-	
Aug 81.	(lp/c) *(V/TCV 2191)* <*3595*> **NEW TRADITIONALISTS**	50	24
	– Through being cool / Jerkin' back 'n' forth / Pity you / Soft things / Going under / Race of doom / Love without anger / The super thing / Beautiful world / Enough said. (re-iss. Aug87 lp/c; OVED/+C 73)		
Aug 81.	(7") <*WBS 47204*> **WORKING IN A COALMINE. / PLANET EARTH** <*above issued on 'Full Moon' US*>	-	
Oct 81.	(7") *(VS 457)* **WORKING IN A COALMINE. / ENOUGH SAID**	-	
Oct 81.	(7") <*WBS 49834*> **BEAUTIFUL WORLD. / ENOUGH SAID**	-	
Jan 82.	(7") *(VS 470)* **BEAUTIFUL WORLD. / THE SUPER THING**	-	
Mar 82.	(7") <*WBS 50010*> **JERKIN' BACK 'N' FORTH. / MECHA MANIA BOY**	-	
Oct 82.	(7")<*US-7"/12"*> *(VS 536)* <*WBS 29931/29906*> **PEEK-A-BOO. / FIND OUT**	-	
Oct 82.	(lp/c) *(V/TCV 2241)* <*23741*> **OH NO! IT'S DEVO!**		47
	– Time out for fun / Peek-a-boo / Out of synch / Explosions / That's good / Patterns / Big mess / Speed racer / What I must do / I desire / Deep sleep. (re-iss. Aug88 lp/c; OVED/+C 122)		
Jan 83.	(7") <*WBS 29811*> **THAT'S GOOD. / WHAT MUST I DO**	-	
Jun 83.	(7"/12") *(MCA/+T 822)* <*52215*> **THEME FROM DOCTOR DETROIT. / (track by James Brown)**		59 May83
	(above issued on 'M.C.A.' UK / 'Backstreet' US)		

		Warners	Warners
Oct 84.	(7") <*29133*> **ARE YOU EXPERIENCED?. / GROWING PAINS**	-	
Oct 84.	(lp/c) *(925 097-1/-4)* <*25097*> **SHOUT!**		83
	– Shout / The satisfied mind / Don't rescue me / The 4th dimension / C'mon / Here to go / Jurisdiction of love / Puppet boy / Please please / Are you experienced?		
Mar 85.	(7") *(W 9119)* **SHOUT. / C'MON**		-
	(d7"+=) *(W 9119F)* – Mongoloid / Jocko homo.		

—— **DAVID KENDRICK** – drums; repl. MYERS

		Enigma	Enigma
Jul 88.	(lp/c/cd) *(ENVLP/TCENV/CDENV 503)* <*73303*> **TOTAL DEVO**		Jun88
	– Baby doll / Disco dancer / Some things never change / Plain truth / Happy guy / Don't be cruel / I'd cry if you died / Agitated / Man turned inside out / Blow up. (cd re-iss. Mar95 on 'Restless'; 72756-2)		
Jul 89.	(3 sided-lp/cd) *(ENVLP/CDENV 532)* **NOW IT CAN BE TOLD (DEVO AT THE PALACE 12/9/88) (live)**		
	(cd re-iss. Mar95 on 'Restless';)		
Oct 90.	(7") **POST-POST MODERN MAN. / WHIP IT (live)**		
	(12"+=) – ('A'-Ultra post mix). (cd-s+=) – Baby doll (mix).		
Oct 90.	(cd/c/lp) *(CDENV/TVENV/ENVLP 1006)* <*73526*> **SMOOTH NOODLE MAPS**		Jun90
	– Stuck in a loop / Post-post modern man / When we do it / Spin the wheel / Morning dew / A chance is gonna cum / The big picture / Pink jazz trancers / Devo has feelings too / Jimmy / Danghaus. (re-iss. cd Mar95 on 'Restless'; 72757-2)		

– compilations, etc. –

Jan 79.	(m-lp) *Stiff; (ODD 1)* **BE STIFF** (first 3 singles)		
May 83.	(12"ep) *Virgin; (VS 594-12)* **COME BACK JONEE. / WHIP IT / + 2**		-

---

Aug 87.	(cd) *Warners;* **E-Z LISTENING DISC** (UK-iss.Nov91 on 'Rykodisc'; RACD 0031)	-	
Oct 90.	(cd) *Fan Club; Rykodisc; <RCD/RLP 10188>* **HARDCORE DEVO, VOL.1** (demos 74-77) (re-iss. c Mar94 on 'New Rose'; 422105)		Aug90
Dec 90.	(cd) *Warners;* **THE GREATEST HITS**	-	
Dec 90.	(cd) *Warners;* **THE REST: GREATEST MISSES**	-	
Dec 91.	(cd) *Rykodisc; <(RCD 20208)>* **HARDCORE DEVO, VOL.2: 1974-1977** (re-iss. c Mar94; RACS 0208)		Aug91
Oct 92.	(cd) *Rykodisc; <(RCD 20209)>* **DEVO LIVE: THE MONGOLOID YEARS (live)**		
Jun 93.	(cd) *Virgin; (CDV 2106)* **Q: ARE WE NOT MEN? A: WE ARE DEVO / DEV-O LIVE**		
Jun 93.	(cd) *Virgin; (CDV 2125)* **DUTY NOW FOR THE FUTURE / NEW TRADITIONALISTS**		
Jun 93.	(cd) *Virgin; (CDV 2241)* **OH NO! IT'S DEVO / FREEDOM OF CHOICE**		
Sep 93.	(cd/c) *Virgin; (CDVM/TCVM 9016)* **HOT POTATOES: THE BEST OF DEVO**		
	– Jocko homo / Mongoloid / Satisfaction (I can't get me no) / Whip it / Girl u want / Freedom of choice / Peek-a-boo / Thru being cool / That's good / Working in a coalmine / Devo corporate anthem / Be stiff / Gates of steel / Come back Jonee / Secret agent man / The day my baby gave me a surprise / Beautiful world / Big mess / Whip it (HMS & M remix).		
Oct 94.	(3xcd-box) *Virgin; (TPAK 38)* **THE COMPACT COLLECTION**		
	– (Q: ARE WE NOT MEN / DUTY NOW FOR THE FUTURE / OH NO IT'S DEVO!)		
Aug 96.	(cd-rom) *Discovery:* **ADVENTURES OF SMART PATROL**	-	

Howard DEVOTO (see under ⇒ MAGAZINE)

DEXYS MIDNIGHT RUNNERS

Formed: Birmingham, England . . . July '78 by ex-KILLJOYS members, KEVIN ROWLAND and AL ARCHER, taking the name from pep pill, 'dexedrine'. With a cast of players including PETE SAUNDERS, PETE WILLIAMS, BOBBY JUNIOR (soon replaced with ANDY 'STOKER' GROWCOTT) and the brass section of JIMMY PATTERSON, J.B. BLYTE and STEVE 'BABYFACE' SPOONER, the band set out to emulate their heroes of the mid-60's soul scene. After a minor debut hit with 'DANCE STANCE' (and the replacement of SAUNDERS with ex-MERTON PARKAS/future STYLE COUNCIL man, MICK TALBOT), a brilliant tribute to one such hero, 'GENO' (Washington), saw DEXY's topping the UK charts in Spring 1980. A third single, 'THERE THERE MY DEAR', was issued later that summer, with a debut album, 'SEARCHING FOR THE YOUNG SOUL REBELS', following into the Top 10. Sporting an image inspired by Martin Scorcese's classic 'Mean Streets' movie (i.e. New York dockers) and coupling it with their idiosyncratic 80's take on classic soul, DEXY's were initially the toast of the UK music press. There was dissension in the ranks, however, the bulk of the band leaving in early '81 to form BUREAU; with ROWLAND and PATTERSON the only remaining members, they bolstered the line-up with new recruits, BILLY ADAMS, MICKEY BILLINGHAM, PAUL SPEARE, BRIAN MAURICE, SEB SHELTON and STEVE WYNNE. The resulting single, 'SHOW ME', hit the Top 20 later that summer, although a follow-up, 'LIARS A TO E', failed to chart and the group retired to reconsider their approach. Augmenting the group with The EMERALD EXPRESS (that is, fiddlers HELEN O'HARA, STEVE BRENNAN and ROGER MacDUFF), DEXYS re-emerged in Spring '82 with a revamped Irish folk/soul hybrid (not too dissimilar to 'His Band And The Street Choir'-era VAN MORRISON, a rousing cover of Van The Man's 'JACKIE WILSON SAID' making the Top 5 later that year) and a suitably dishevelled gypsy/romantic vagabond image. 'THE CELTIC SOUL BROTHERS' introduced this new approach and although the track just missed the Top 40, a classic follow-up, 'COME ON EILEEN', was a massive transatlantic No.1 smash; not only were DEXYS big news again in Britain, they'd cracked America (albeit briefly) and the subsequent album, 'TOO-RYE-AY' (1982) was the most successful of their career. Yet again, however, the line-up splintered and the momentum faltered, the brass section of PATTERSON, MAURICE and SPEAR departing in summer '82. It would be a further three years before the release of 'DON'T STAND ME DOWN', a considerably lower-key effort which enjoyed only a brief sojourn in the charts. A solitary hit single, 'BECAUSE OF YOU' (used as a theme for TV sitcom, 'Brush Strokes') followed in 1986, before DEXYS were consigned to history and ROWLAND faded into musical folklore. Despite his revered talent, the maverick Celtic minstrel had only released one solo set, 'THE WANDERER', in the past 12 years, with live performances a rarity. However in early 1997, ROWLAND inked a deal with 'Creation' records and finally came up with some new material (including the wearing of kinky lingerie!) for his er, cumback covers set, 'MY BEAUTY' (1999). Actually, apart from his embarrassing OTT attire, the album might've done quite well, although only the appropriately titled 'I CAN'T TELL THE BOTTOM FROM THE TOP' made it worthwhile. • **Songwriters:** All penned by ROWLAND, except BURNING DOWN THE WALLS OF HEARTACHE (Johnny Johnson & The Bandwagon) / ONE WAY LOVE (Russell-Meade) / SOUL FINGER (Bar-Kays).

Album rating: SEARCHING FOR THE YOUNG SOUL REBELS (*8) / TOO-RYE-AYE (*7) / DON'T STAND ME DOWN (*5) / THE VERY BEST OF DEXYS MIDNIGHT RUNNERS compilation (*8) / Kevin Rowland: THE WANDERER (*4) / MY BEAUTY (*5)

KEVIN ROWLAND – vocals, guitar (b.17 Aug'53, Wolverhampton, England) (ex-KILLJOYS, as KEVIN ROLAND) / AL ARCHER – guitar, vocals (ex-KILLJOYS) / PETE SAUNDERS – keyboards / PETE WILLIAMS – bass, vocals / JIMMY PATTERSON – trombone / J.B. BLYTE – tenor, saxophone / STEVE 'BABYFACE' SPOONER – alto sax / ANDY 'STOKER' GROWCOTT – drums repl. BOBBY JUNIOR

		Parlophone	not iss.
Nov 79. (7") (R 6028) DANCE STANCE. / I'M JUST LOOKING		40	-

—— MICK TALBOT – keyboards (ex-MERTON PARKAS) repl. SAUNDERS

Mar 80. (7") (R 6033) GENO. / BREAKING DOWN THE WALLS OF HEARTACHE		1	-
Jun 80. (7") (R 6038) THERE THERE MY DEAR. / THE HORSE		7	-
Jul 80. (lp/c) (PCS/TCPCS 7213) SEARCHING FOR THE YOUNG SOUL REBELS		6	-

– Burn it down / Tell me when my light turns green / The teams that meet in caffs / I'm just looking / Geno / Seven days too long / I couldn't help it if I tried / Thankfully not living in Yorkshire, it doesn't apply / Keep it / Love (pt.1) / There, there my dear. (re-iss. 1982 on 'Fame' lp/c;) (cd-iss. Jan88; CZ 31)

Nov 80. (7") (R 6042) KEEP IT PART TWO . / ONE WAY LOVE			-
Mar 81. (7") (R 6046) PLAN B. / SOUL FINGER		58	-

—— ROWLAND + PATTERSON recruited new guys BILLY ADAMS – guitar / MICKEY BILLINGHAM – keyboards / PAUL SPEARE – tenor sax / BRIAN MAURICE – alto sax / SEB SHELTON – drums (ex-SECRET AFFAIR) / STEVE WYNNE – bass (replaced ARCHER, GROWCOTT and TALBOT who formed BUREAU)

		Mercury	Mercury
Jun 81. (7") (DEXYS 6) SHOW ME. / SOON		16	
Nov 81. (7") (DEXYS 7) LIARS A TO E. / . . . AND YES, WE MUST REMAIN THE WILDHEARTED OUTSIDERS			

—— retained ADAMS, SHELTON, PATTERSON / + GIORGIO KILKENNY – bass repl. WYNNE

DEXYS MIDNIGHT RUNNERS & The EMERALD EXPRESS

—— added HELEN O'HARA – violin, vocals repl. BILLINGHAM / STEVE BRENNAN – violin / ROGER MacDUFF – violin

Mar 82. (7") (DEXYS 8) THE CELTIC SOUL BROTHERS. / LOVE (part 2)		45	
Jun 82. (7") (DEXYS 9) <76189> COME ON EILEEN. / DUBIOUS		1	1 Jan83
(12"+=) (DEXYS 9-12) – Liars A to E (remix).			
Jul 82. (lp/c) (MERS/+C 8) <4069> TOO-RYE-AY		2	14 Feb83

– The Celtic soul brothers / Let's make this precious / All in all / Jackie Wilson said (I'm in Heaven when you smile) / Old / Plan B – I'll show you / Liars A to E / Until I believe in my soul / Come on Eileen. (cd-iss. Jan83; 810054-2) (re-iss. Jul86 lp/c; PRICE/PRIMC 89) (cd re-mast.Mar96; 514839-2)

KEVIN ROWLAND & DEXYS MIDNIGHT RUNNERS

—— PATTERSON left June '82, MAURICE and SPEARE left July '82

Sep 82. (7") (DEXYS 10) JACKIE WILSON SAID. / LET'S MAKE THIS PRECIOUS		5	
(12"+=) (DEXYS 10-12) – T.S.O.P.			
Nov 82. (7") (DEXYS 11) LET'S GET THIS STRAIGHT FROM THE START. / OLD (live)		17	
(12"+=) (DEXYS 11-12) – Respect (live).			
Mar 83. (7"/7"s) (DEXY S/P 12) <811142> THE CELTIC SOUL BROTHERS. / REMINISCE PART ONE		20	86 May83
(12"+=) (DEXYS 12-12) – Show me.			

DEXYS MIDNIGHT RUNNERS

—— line-up ROWLAND, O'HARA & ADAMS / JIMMY PATTERSON – trombone (returned) + new part-time sessioners / NICKY GATFIELD – saxophone / JULIAN LITTMAN – mandolin / JOHN EDWARDS – steel guitar / TOMMY EVANS – bass / TIM DANCY – drums / ROBERT NOBLE – keyboards, synth / and special guest star VINCENT CRANE – piano (ex-ATOMIC ROOSTER)

Sep 85. (lp/c)(cd) (MERH/+C 56)(822989-2) <> DON'T STAND ME DOWN		22	

– The occasional flicker / This is what she's like / Knowledge of beauty / One of those things / Reminisce part two / Listen to this / The waltz. (cd+=) – This is what she's like (instrumental). (cd re-iss. Jun97 on 'Creation'; CRECD 154)

Nov 85. (7") (DEXYS 13) THIS IS WHAT SHE'S LIKE. / ('A'instrumental)			
(12"+=) (DEXYS 13-12) – Reminisce (part 1).			
(10") (DEXYS 13-10) – ('A'side) / Marguerita time.			
(d7"++=) (DEXYD 13) – ('A'&'B' versions).			
Oct 86. (7") (BRUSH 1) BECAUSE OF YOU. / KATHLEEN MAVOUREEN		13	
(12"+=) (BRUSH 1-12) – Sometimes theme.			

– compilations, etc. –

Mar 83. (lp) E.M.I.; (EMS 1007) GENO		79	
(re-iss. Oct87 lp/c; ATAK/TC-ATAK 72) (cd-iss. Jun88 on 'Fame'; CDFA 3189)			
Mar 84. (7") EMI Gold; (G 455) DANCE STANCE. / THERE THERE MY DEAR			-
1989. (cd-video) Mercury; (080 628-2) COME ON EILEEN / THE CELTIC SOUL BROTHERS / JACKIE WILSON SAID (I'M IN HEAVEN WHEN YOU SMILE) / LIARS TO E			-
Mar 90. (7") Old Gold; (OG 9900) COME ON EILEEN / JACKIE WILSON SAID (I'M IN HEAVEN WHEN YOU SMILE)			-
Sep 92. (cd-s) Old Gold; (126238342-2) GENO / THERE THERE MY DEAR / DANCE STANCE			-
Jun 91. (cd/c/lp) Mercury; (846460-2/-4/-1) THE VERY BEST OF DEXYS MIDNIGHT RUNNERS		12	

– Come on Eileen / Jackie Wilson said (I'm in heaven when you smile) / Let's get this straight (from the start) / Because of you / Show me / The Celtic soul brothers

(more, please, thank you) / Liars a to e / One way love / Old / Geno / There there my dear / Breakin' down the walls of heartache / Dance stance / Plan b / Keep it / I'm just looking / Soon / This is what she's like / Soul finger. (cd+=) – (5 extra tracks) (re-iss. Jul92)

Jun 91. (7") Mercury; COME ON EILEEN. / BECAUSE OF YOU			-
(12"+=/cd-s+=) – Let's get this straight (from the start).			
May 93. (cd/c) Spectrum; (550 003-2/-4) BECAUSE OF YOU			-
Nov 93. (cd) Windsong; (WINCD 047) BBC RADIO 1 LIVE IN CONCERT – NEWCASTLE (live)			-
Jul 95. (cd) Nighttracks; (CDNT 009) 1980-1982 – THE RADIO SESSIONS			-
Aug 95. (d-cd) Mercury; (528608-2) TOO RYE AY / DON'T STAND ME DOWN			-
May 96. (cd) Premier; (PRMUCD 1) IT WAS LIKE THIS			-

KEVIN ROWLAND

Apr 88. (7") (DEXYS 14) WALK AWAY. / EVEN WHEN I HOLD YOU			-
(12"+=/12"box+=) (DEXY S/B 14-12) – ('A'version) / The way you look tonight.			
(cd-s+=) (DEXCD 14) – The way you look tonight / Because of you.			
Jun 88. (lp/c)(cd) (MERH/+C 121)(834488-2) THE WANDERER			

– Young man / Walk away / You'll be the one for me / Heartaches by the number / I am a wanderer / Tonight / When you walk alone / Age can't wither you / I want / Remember me.

Jul 88. (7") (ROW 1) TONIGHT. / KEVIN ROWLAND'S BAND			
(12"+=) (ROW 1T) – Come on Eileen.			
Oct 88. (7") (ROW 2) YOUNG MAN. / ONE WAY TICKET TO PALOOKAHVILLE			
(12"+=) (ROW 2-12) – Jackie Wilson said (I'm in heaven when you smile).			
(cd-s++=) (ROWCD 2) – Show me.			

		Creation	unsure
Sep 99. (c-s/cd-s) (CRE CS/SCD 332) CONCRETE AND CLAY / I CAN'T TELL THE BOTTOM FROM THE TOP			-
Oct 99. (cd) (CRECD 216) MY BEAUTY			

– The greatest love of all / Rag doll / Concrete and clay / Daydream believer / This guy's in love with you / The long and winding road / It's getting better / I can't tell the bottom from the top / Labelled with love (I'll stay with my dreams) / Reflections of my life / You'll never walk alone.

Neil DIAMOND

Born: NOAH KAMINSKY, 24 Jan'41, Brooklyn, New York, USA. By the time he'd graduated from Brooklyn's Erasmus high school and embarked upon a degree at New York University, DIAMOND had already begun writing and recording. As one-half of the duo NEIL & JACK (with Jack Parker), he released a couple of early singles on the small 'Duel' label before cutting a one-off solo track for 'Columbia' in 1963. Upon dropping out of university he began working full-time as a staff writer for various publishers, providing material for the likes of CLIFF RICHARD, JAY & THE AMERICANS and most successfully, The MONKEES, for whom he wrote the 1967 US No.1, 'I'M A BELIEVER'. A year previous, DIAMOND had signed a new recording contract with 'Bang' records and had already scored a Top 10 hit with 'CHERRY, CHERRY' following on from the minor chart success of his definitive 'SOLITARY MAN'. A string of moderate Jeff Barry/Ellie Greenwich-produced hits ensued over the next two years including the classics, 'GIRL, YOU'LL BE A WOMAN SOON' and 'KENTUCKY WOMAN'. Wrapping his ominous baritone around hook-driven, rootsy pop-rock, DIAMOND had created a songwriting formula that was irresistibly populist yet enduring, his success encouraging him to push for full creative control and make it as a credible singer/songwriter in his own right. 'Uni' subsequently offered him the deal he was looking for and despite the relative failure of the experimental 'VELVET GLOVES AND SPIT' (1968) album, the hits began rolling in at the turn of the decade as the anthemic 'SWEET CAROLINE' became his biggest hit to date (US Top 5) in summer '69. The accompanying album, 'TOUCHING YOU TOUCHING ME' (1970), established his credentials/ambitions with a tasteful selection of covers from the likes of FRED NEIL and JONI MITCHELL while also spawning a second major hit in 'HOLLY HOLY'. Later that year he scored his first US No.1 (UK No.3) with 'CRACKLIN' ROSIE', a highlight of the 'TAPROOT MANUSCRIPT' (1971) set wherein he even attempted an ambitious suite, 'THE AFRICAN TRILOGY'. Despite his wish to be recognised as a "serious" singer/songwriter, DIAMOND just couldn't help penning gloriously catchy, future karaoke classics like 'I AM ... I SAID' (transatlantic Top 5) and 'SONG SUNG BLUE' (US No.1) while late 1973's 'HOT AUGUST NIGHT' live set captured his lavish showmanship on vinyl and cemented his superstar status. 'Columbia' were so impressed they stumped up five million dollars for his record-breaking signing later that year, their investment paying off as the 'JONATHAN LIVINGSTON SEAGULL' (1974) soundtrack ended up coining in more cash than the film itself. The BAND's ROBBIE ROBERTSON lent DIAMOND a modicum of street cred by producing 1976's 'BEAUTIFUL NOISE', a concept effort based on NEIL's formative years as a Brill Building protege. Even through the punk era, DIAMOND kept racking up the hits, scoring another US No.1 in 1978 via the BARBRA STREISAND duet, 'YOU DON'T BRING ME FLOWERS'. The album of the same name also spawned another karaoke fave in the shape of country-tinged singalong, 'FOREVER IN BLUE JEANS' (Top 20), cheesy MOR maybe but great stuff all the same. Surprisingly perhaps, the man's biggest success was yet to come, arriving in the shape of his soundtrack to a remake of 1920's movie, 'The Jazz Singer' in which DIAMOND himself starred alongside Laurence Olivier. Released in late 1980, the record went multi-platinum and spawned three US Top 10 singles, 'LOVE ON THE ROCKS', 'HELLO AGAIN' and 'AMERICA'. The polished balladry of 'HEARTLIGHT' (1982) brought further success in the States with its title track becoming an MOR radio staple. Despite a surprise Top 10 placing in the UK, 'PRIMITIVE' (1984) found DIAMOND treading water if not drowning in a stagnant pond of romantic mush. 'HEADED FOR THE FUTURE' (1986) attempted to bring him up to date without much success while 'HOT AUGUST NIGHT II' (1987) was a pale reflection of its predecessor. Signing to 'Columbia' at the dawn of the 90's, DIAMOND revisited the era of the 60's songwriter with the critically mauled 'ON THE ROOF – SONGS OF THE BRILL BUILDING' (1993). More successful was 'TENNESSEE MOON' (1996), DIAMOND's Nashville record. Essentially a singles artist, the man's various greatest hits sets are a worthy addition to even the hippest of record collections and while the likes of UB40 have covered his work to great success in the past, alt-rockers URGE OVERKILL demonstrated his kitsch appeal to brilliant effect with their 'Pulp Fiction' performance of 'GIRL YOU'LL BE A WOMAN SOON'. • Covered: NEW ORLEANS (Gary U.S. Bonds) / UNTIL IT'S TIME FOR YOU TO GO (Buffy Sainte-Marie) / HE AIN'T HEAVY, HE'S MY BROTHER (Hollies) / HEARTLIGHT + FRONT PAGE STORY (Bacharach/Bayer-Sager) / I'M ALIVE (co-with David Foster) / MORNING HAS BROKEN (Cat Stevens) / etc, etc, etc

Album rating: JUST FOR YOU (*5) / VELVET GLOVES AND SPIT (*5) / TOUCHING YOU, TOUCHING ME (*6) / TAPROOT MANUSCRIPT (*6) / STONES (*4) / MOODS (*5) / HOT AUGUST NIGHT (*7) / DOUBLE GOLD compilation (*7) / RAINBOW collection (*5) / JONATHAN LIVINGSTON SEAGULL (*6) / HIS 12 GREATEST HITS compilation (*8) / SERENADE (*4) / BEAUTIFUL NOISE (*6) / LOVE AT THE GREEK (*4) / I'M GLAD YOU'RE HERE WITH ME TONIGHT (*4) / YOU DON'T BRING ME FLOWERS (*5) / SEPTEMBER MORN (*4) / THE JAZZ SINGER (*6) / ON THE WAY TO THE SKY (*3) / 12 GREATEST HITS, VOL.II compilation (*6) / HEARTLIGHT (*3) / PRIMITIVE (*3) / HEADED FOR THE FUTURE (*3) / HOT AUGUST NIGHT II (*4) / THE BEST YEARS OF OUR LIVES (*5) / LOVESCAPE (*3) / THE GREATEST HITS 1966-1992 compilation (*8) / THE CHRISTMAS ALBUM (*2) / UP ON THE ROOF – SONGS FROM THE BRILL BUILDING (*4) / LIVE IN AMERICA (*4) / TENNESSEE MOON (*4) / AS TIME GOES BY – THE MOVIE ALBUM (*3)

NEIL DIAMOND – vocals, acoustic guitar / **JACK PACKER** – vocals, acoustic guitar

			not iss.	Duel
1960.	(7"; as NEIL & JACK) <508> **YOU ARE MY LOVE AT LAST. / WHAT WILL I DO**		-	
1961.	(7"; as NEIL & JACK) **I'M AFRAID. / TILL YOU'VE TRIED LOVE**		-	

—— NEIL now used various session people

			not iss.	Columbia
1963.	(7") <42809> **CLOWN TOWN. / AT NIGHT**		-	

—— He then began writing for JAY & THE AMERICANS, CLIFF RICHARD and later The MONKEES. He returned to the studio early 1966.

		London	Bang
May 66.	(7") (HLZ 10049) <519> **SOLITARY MAN. / DO IT**		55
Sep 66.	(7") (HLZ 10072) <528> **CHERRY, CHERRY. / I'LL COME RUNNING**		6 Aug66
Nov 66.	(7") (HLZ 10092) <536> **I GOT THE FEELIN' (OH NO NO). / THE BOAT THAT I ROW**		16
Jan 67.	(lp; mono/stereo) (HAZ 8307) <BLP/+S 214> **THE FEEL OF NEIL DIAMOND**		Oct66

– Solitary man / Red rubber ball / La bamba / Do it / Hanky panky / Monday Monday / New Orleans / Someday baby / I got the feelin' / I'll come running / Love to love / Cherry, Cherry.

		London	Bang
Feb 67.	(7") (HLZ 10111) <540> **YOU GOT TO ME. / SOMEDAY BABY**		18 Jan67
Apr 67.	(7") (HLZ 10126) <542> **GIRL, YOU'LL BE A WOMAN SOON. / YOU'LL FORGET**		10
Jul 67.	(7") (HLZ 10151) <547> **I THANK THE LORD FOR THE NIGHT. / LONG WAY HOME**		13
Sep 67.	(lp; mono/stereo) <BLP/+S 217> **JUST FOR YOU**	-	80

– Girl, you'll be a woman soon / The long way home / Red red wine / You'll forget / The boat that I row / Cherry, Cherry / I'm a believer / Shilo / You got to me / Solitary man / Thank the Lord for the night time.

		London	Bang
Nov 67.	(7") (HLZ 10161) <551> **KENTUCKY WOMAN. / THE TIME IS NOW**		22 Oct67
Jan 68.	(7") (HLZ 10177) <554> **NEW ORLEANS. / HANKY PANKY**		51 Dec67
Apr 68.	(7") (HLZ 10187) <556> **RED RED WINE. / RED RUBBER BALL**		62

		Uni	Uni
May 68.	(7") (UN 503) <55065> **BROOKLYN ROADS. / HOLIDAY INN BLUES**		58

		M.C.A.	Uni
Jun 68.	(lp) (MUPS 365) <73030> **VELVET GLOVES AND SPIT**		

– Two-bit manchild / A modern day version of love / Honey dripping times / The pot smoker's song / Brooklyn roads / Shilo / Sunday sun / Holiday inn blues / Practically newborn / Knackerffeng / Merry-go-round. (re-iss. 1970 on 'Uni'; UNLS 106) (re-iss. 1974; MCF 2512) (re-iss. Feb82 lp/c; MCL/+C 1640) (re-iss. Apr92 cd/c; MCL D/C 1904-2/-4)

			Uni
Jul 68.	(7") (MU 1033) <55075> **TWO-BIT MANCHILD. / BROAD OLD WOMAN (9 a.m. INSANITY)**		66
Sep 68.	(7") <55084> **SUNDAY SUN. / HONEY DRIPPING TIMES**	-	68
Apr 69.	(7") (MU 1070) <55109> **BROTHER LOVE'S TRAVELLING SALVATION SHOW. / A MODERN DAY VERSION OF LOVE**		22 Mar69
Apr 69.	(lp) (MUPS 382) <73047> **BROTHER LOVE'S TRAVELLING SALVATION SHOW**		82 Mar69

– Brother Love's travelling salvation show / Dig in / River runs, newgrown plums / Juliet / Long gone / And the grass won't pay you no mind / Memphis street / Glory road / Deep in the morning / If I ever knew your name / You're so sweet horseflies

keep hanging round your face / Hurtin' / You don't come easy. (re-iss. 1970 on 'Uni'+=; UNLS 107) – Sweet Caroline. (re-iss. 1974; MCF 2536)

		Uni	Uni
Jul 69.	(7") (MU 198) <55136> **SWEET CAROLINE (GOOD TIMES NEVER SEEMED SO GOOD). / DIG IN**		4
Nov 69.	(7") (UN 512) <55175> **HOLLY HOLY. / HURTIN' YOU DON'T COME EASY**		6 Oct69
Jan 70.	(lp) (UNLS 110) <73071> **TOUCHING YOU TOUCHING ME**		30 Dec69

– Sweet Caroline (good times never seemed so good) / Until it's time for you to go / Everybody's talkin' / Mr. Bojangles / Smokey lady / Holly holy / Both sides now / And the singer sings his song / Ain't no way / New York boy.

		Uni	Uni
Feb 70.	(7") <55204> **UNTIL IT'S TIME FOR YOU TO GO. / AND THE SINGER SINGS HIS SONG**	-	53
May 70.	(7") (UN 522) <55224> **SOOLAIMON (AFRICAN TRILOGY II). / AND THE GRASS WON'T PAY YOU NO MIND**		30
Aug 70.	(7") (UN 529) <55250> **CRACKLIN' ROSIE. / LORDY** (re-iss. Feb74 on 'M.C.A.'; MCA 113)	3	1
Sep 70.	(lp) (UNLS 116) <73084> **GOLD (live at Troubador)**	23	10

– Lordy / Both sides now / Solitary man / Holly holy / Cherry, cherry / Kentucky woman / Sweet Caroline / Thank the Lord for the night time / And the singer sings his songs / Brother Love's travelling salvation show. (re-iss. 1974 on 'M.C.A.'; MCF 2515) (re-iss. Oct87 on 'Music For Pleasure'; MFP 5815)

		Uni	Uni
Nov 70.	(7") <55264> **HE AIN'T HEAVY HE'S MY BROTHER. / FREE LIFE**	-	20
Feb 71.	(7") (UNS 531) **SWEET CAROLINE. / BROTHER LOVE'S TRAVELLING SALVATION SHOW** (re-iss. Jan74 on 'M.C.A.'; MCA 106)	8	-
Mar 71.	(lp) (UNLS 117) <73092> **TAPROOT MANUSCRIPT**	19	13 Nov70

– Cracklin' Rosie / Free life / Coldwater morning / Done too soon / He ain't heavy he's my brother / The African trilogy (a folk ballet: I am the lion / Madrigal / Soolamain / Missa / African smile / Childsong (reprise). (re-iss. 1974 on 'M.C.A.'; MCF 2509) (re-iss. Sep86 lp/c; MCL/+C 1707) (cd-iss. 1987 on 'M.C.A.'; DIDX 273) (cd re-iss. Aug92; MCLD 19119)

		Uni	Uni
Apr 71.	(7") (UN 532) <55278> **I AM . . . I SAID. / DONE TOO SOON**	4	4
			65 Mar71
Nov 71.	(7") (UN 536) <55310> **STONES. / CRUNCHY GRANOLA SUITE**		14
Nov 71.	(lp) (UNLS 121) <93106> **STONES**	18	11

– I am . . . I said / The last thing on my mind / Husbands and wives / Chelsea morning / Crunchy granola suite / Stones / If you go away / Suzanne / I think it's going to rain today / I am . . . I said (reprise). (re-iss. 1974 on 'M.C.A.'; MCF 2530) (cd-iss. Aug90; DMCL 1908) (cd re-iss. Apr92; MCLD 19118)

		Uni	Uni
Apr 72.	(7") (UN 538) <55326> **SONG SUNG BLUE. / GITCHY GOOMY**	14	1
Jul 72.	(lp) (UNLS 128) <93136> **MOODS**	7	5

– Walk on water / Song sung blue / Porcupine pie / High rolling man / Canta libre / Captain Sunshine / Play me / Gitchy goomy / Theme / Prelude in E major / Morningside. (cd-iss. 1985 on 'M.C.A.'; DMCA 115) (cd re-iss. Jul87 on 'M.C.A.'; CDCAD 31061) (cd re-iss. 1988 on 'M.C.A.'; DIDX 272) (re-iss. Sep91 on 'M.C.A.' cd/c; DMCML/MCLC 1759) (re-iss. Apr92 on 'M.C.A.' cd/c; MCL D/C 19043)

		Uni	Uni
Aug 72.	(7") (UNS 546) <55346> **PLAY ME. / PORCUPINE PIE**		11
Nov 72.	(7") (UNS 551) <55352> **WALK ON WATER. / HIGH ROLLING MAN**		17

		Uni	M.C.A.
Mar 73.	(7") (UNS 556) <40017> **CHERRY CHERRY (live). / MORNINGSIDE**		31
Dec 73.	(d-lp) (ULD 1-2) <2-8000> **HOT AUGUST NIGHT (live)**	32	5 Dec72

– Prologue / Crunchy granola suite / Done too soon / Dialogue / Solitary man / Cherry cherry / Sweet Caroline / Porcupine pie / You're so sweet / Red red wine / Soggy pretzels / And the grass won't pay you no mind / Shilo / Girl you'll be a woman soon / Play me / Canta libre / Morningside / Song sung blue / Cracklin' Rosie / Holly holy / I am . . . I said / Soolamain / Brother Love's travelling salvation show / Encore. (re-iss. 1975 on 'M.C.A.'; MCSP 255)

		C.B.S.	Columbia
Nov 73.	(7") (CBS 1843) <45942> **BE. / FLIGHT OF THE GULL**		
Jan 74.	(lp/c) (CBS/40 69047) <KS 32550> **JONATHAN LIVINGSTON SEAGULL (Film Soundtrack)**	35	2 Nov73

– Prologue / Be / Flight of the gull / Dear father / Skybird / Lonely looking sky / The odyssey: Be – Lonely looking sky – Dear father / Anthem / Be / Skybird / Dear father / Be. (cd-iss. 1986)

		C.B.S.	Columbia
Apr 74.	(7") (CBS 2191) <45998> **SKYBIRD. / LONELY LOOKING SKY**	11	75 Feb74
Oct 74.	(lp/c) (CBS/40 69067) <PC 32919> **SERENADE**	11	3

– I've been this way before / Rosemary's wine / Lady Magdalene / The last Picasso / Longfellow serenade / Yes I will / Reggae strut / The gift of song. (re-iss. Jun81; CBS 32050) (cd-iss. May87; CD 69067) (re-iss. Sep89 on 'Pickwick' lp/c/cd; 982195-1/-4/-2) (re-iss. Dec95 on 'Columbia' cd/c; 465012-2/-4)

		C.B.S.	Columbia
Nov 74.	(7") (CBS 2769) <10043> **LONGFELLOW SERENADE. / ROSEMARY'S WINE**		5
Feb 75.	(7") (CBS 3058) <10084> **I'VE BEEN THIS WAY BEFORE. / REGGAE STRUT**		34
Jun 75.	(7") (CBS 3350) <10138> **THE LAST PICASSO. / THE GIFT OF SONG**		
Jun 76.	(7") (CBS 4398) <10366> **IF YOU KNOW WHAT I MEAN. / STREET LIFE**	35	11
Jul 76.	(lp/c) (CBS/40 86004) <PC 33935> **BEAUTIFUL NOISE**	10	4

– Beautiful noise / Stargazer / Lady oh / Don't think . . . feel / Surviving the life / If you know what I mean / Street life / Home is a wounded heart / Jungletime / Signs / Dry your eyes. (re-iss. Apr87 lp/c; 450452-1/-4) (cd-iss. May87; CD 86004) (re-iss. Mar91; 450452-2)

		C.B.S.	Columbia
Sep 76.	(7") <10405> **DON'T THINK . . . FEEL. / HOME IS A WOUNDED HEART**	-	43
Sep 76.	(7") (CBS 4601) **BEAUTIFUL NOISE. / HOME IS A WOUNDED HEART**	13	-
Feb 77.	(d-lp/d-c) (CBS/40 95001) <34402> **LOVE AT THE GREEK (live)**	3	8

– Street life / Kentucky woman / Sweet Caroline (good times never seem so good) / The last Picasso / Longfellow serenade / Beautiful noise / Lady-oh / Stargazer / If you know what I mean / Surviving the life / Glory road / Song sung blue / Holly

holy / Brother Love's travelling salvation show / Jonathan Livingstone Seagull / Be / Dear father / Lonely looking sky / Sanctus / Skybird / Be (encore) / I've been this way before. (*cd-iss. May87*) (*re-iss. cd+c Apr93 on 'Columbia'*)

Dec 76. (7") <10452> **BEAUTIFUL NOISE. / SIGNS** | | -

Mar 77. (7") (*CBS 5115*) **STARGAZER (live). / STREET LIFE (live)** | | -

Jun 77. (7") (*CBS 5350*) **I'VE BEEN THIS WAY BEFORE (live). / SURVIVING THE LIFE (live)** | | -

Jul 77. (7") (*CBS 5440*) **DON'T THINK . . . FEEL. / SIGNS** | | -

Dec 77. (7") (*CBS 5869*) <10657> **DESIREE. / ONCE IN A WHILE** | 39 | 16

Dec 77. (lp/c) (*CBS/40 86044*) <34990> **I'M GLAD YOU'RE HERE WITH ME TONIGHT** | 16 | 6
– God only knows / Let me take you in my arms / Once in a while / Let the little boy sing / I'm glad you're here with me tonight / Lament in D minor / Dance of the sabres / Desiree / As if / Free man in Paris. (*cd-iss. May87; CD 86044*) (*re-iss. Oct90 cd/c/lp; CD/40CBS 32395*)

Feb 78. (7") (*CBS 6064*) **GOD ONLY KNOWS. / ONCE IN A WHILE** | | -

Mar 78. (7") <10720> **I'M GLAD YOU'RE HERE WITH ME TONIGHT. / DANCE OF SABRES** | - | -

Apr 78. (7") (*CBS 6288*) **I'M GLAD YOU'RE HERE WITH ME TONIGHT. / AS IF** | | -

Sep 78. (7") (*CBS 6207*) **LET ME TAKE YOU IN MY ARMS. / AS IF** | | -

Nov 78. (7"; NEIL DIAMOND & BARBRA STREISAND) (*CBS 6803*) <10840> **YOU DON'T BRING ME FLOWERS. / (instrumental)** | 5 | 1

Dec 78. (lp/c) (*CBS/40 86077*) <35625> **YOU DON'T BRING ME FLOWERS** | 15 | 4
– The American popular song / Forever in blue jeans / Remember me / You've got your troubles / You don't bring me flowers / The dancing bumble-bee-bumble boogie / Mothers and daughters, fathers and sons / Memphis flyer / Say maybe / Diamond girls. (*cd-iss. May87; CD 86077*) (*re-iss. Aug91 on 'Columbia' cd/c; 468782-2/-4*)

Feb 79. (7") (*CBS 7047*) <10897> **FOREVER IN BLUE JEANS. / REMEMBER ME** | 16 | 20

May 79. (7") <10945> **SAY MAYBE. / DIAMOND GIRLS** | - | 55

May 79. (7") (*CBS 7408*) **THE AMERICAN POPULAR SONG. / DIAMOND GIRLS** | |

Jan 80. (7") (*CBS 8130*) <11175> **SEPTEMBER MORN. / I'M A BELIEVER** | | 17

Jan 80. (lp/c) (*CBS/40 86096*) <36121> **SEPTEMBER MORN** | 14 | 10 Dec79
– September morn / Mama don't know / That kind / Jazz time / The good Lord loves you / Dancing in the street / The shelter of your arms / I'm a believer / The sun ain't gonna shine anymore / Stagger Lee. (*cd-iss. May87; CD 86096*) (*cd re-iss. Feb97 on 'Columbia'; 484455-2*)

Mar 80. (7") <11232> **THE GOOD LORD LOVES YOU. / JAZZ TIME** | - | 67

Mar 80. (7") (*CBS 8322*) **DANCING IN THE STREET. / JAZZ TIME** | |

Capitol | *Capitol*

Oct 80. (7") (*CL 16173*) <4939> **LOVE ON THE ROCKS. / ACAPULCO** | 17 | 2

Nov 80. (lp/c) <(*EAST/TCEAST 12120*)> **THE JAZZ SINGER (soundtrack)** | 14 | 3
– America / Adon o lume / You baby / Love on the rocks / Amazed and confused / The Robert E. Lee / Summer love / Hello again / Acapulco / Hey Louise / Songs of life / Jerusalem / Kol ridre / My name is Yussef (theme) / America (reprise). (*cd-iss. Jul84; CDEAST 12120*) (*re-iss. Jul98 on 'Columbia' cd/c; 483927-2/-4*)

Jan 81. (7") (*CL 16176*) <4960> **HELLO AGAIN. / AMAZED AND CONFUSED** | 51 | 6

Apr 81. (7") (*CL 16197*) <4994> **AMERICA. / SONGS OF LIFE** | | 8

C.B.S. | *Columbia*

Oct 81. (lp/c) (*CBS/40 85343*) <37628> **ON THE WAY TO THE SKY** | 39 | 17
– Yesterday's songs / On the way to the sky / Right by you / Only you / Save me / Be mine / The drifter / Fear of the market place / Rainy day song / Guitar Heaven / Love burns. (*cd-iss. Jul87; CD 85343*)

Nov 81. (7") (*CBS 1755*) <02604> **YESTERDAY'S SONGS. / GUITAR HEAVEN** | | 11

Jan 82. (7") (*CBS 2033*) **RAINY DAY SONGS. / BE MINE TONIGHT** | | -

Feb 82. (7") <02712> **ON THE WAY TO THE SKY. / SAVE ME** | | 27

Jun 82. (7") (*CBS 2580*) <02928> **BE MINE TONIGHT. / RIGHT BY YOU** | | 35

Sep 82. (7") (*CBS 2814*) <03219> **HEARTLIGHT. / YOU DON'T KNOW ME** | 47 | 5

Oct 82. (lp/c) (*CBS/40 25073*) <38359> **HEARTLIGHT** | 43 | 9
– Heartlight / I'm alive / I'm guilty / Hurricane / Lost amongst the stars / A fool for you / In enserada / Star flight / Front page story / Comin' home / First you have to say you love me. (*cd-iss. May87; CD 25073*) (*re-iss. cd Mar94 on 'Sony'; 982835-2*)

Jan 83. (7") (*CBS 3050*) **FRONT PAGE STORY. / LOVE AMONG THE STARS** | | -

Feb 83. (7") <03503> **I'M ALIVE. / LOST AMONGST THE STARS** | - | 35

Apr 83. (7") <03801> **FRONT PAGE STORY. / I'M GUILTY** | - | 65

Jul 84. (7") (*CBS 4458*) <04541> **TURN AROUND. / BROOKLYN ON A SATURDAY NIGHT** | | 62

Aug 84. (lp/c) (*CBS/40 86036*) <39199> **PRIMITIVE** | 7 | 35
– Turn around / Primitive / Fire on the tracks / Brooklyn on a Saturday night / Sleep with me tonight / Crazy / My time with you / Love's own song / It's a trip (go for the moon) / You make it feel like Christmas / One by one. (*cd-iss. May87; CD 86036*) (*re-iss. Aug91 on 'Sony' cd/c; 982636-2/-4*)

Sep 84. (7") (*CBS 4673*) **PRIMITIVE. / IT'S A TRIP** | | -

Sep 84. (7") <04646> **SLEEP WITH ME TONIGHT. / ONE BY ONE** | - | -

Nov 84. (7") <04719> **YOU MAKE IT FEEL LIKE CHRISTMAS. / CRAZY** | | -

Nov 84. (7") (*CBS 4888*) **YOU MAKE IT FEEL LIKE CHRISTMAS. / ONE BY ONE** | |

May 86. (7") <05889> **HEADED FOR THE FUTURE. / ANGEL** | - | 53

May 86. (lp/c/cd) (*CBS/40/CD 26952*) <40368> **HEADED FOR THE FUTURE** | 36 | 20
– Headed for the future / The man you need / I'll see you in the radio (Laura / Stand up for love / It should have been me / Lost in Hollywood / The story of my life / Angel / Me beside you / Love doesn't live here anymore. (*cd re-iss. Feb98 on 'Columbia'; 489453-2*)

Jul 86. (7"/12") (*A/TA 7225*) **STAND UP FOR LOVE. / THE STORY OF MY LIFE** | | -

Jul 86. (7") <06136> **THE STORY OF MY LIFE. / LOVE DOESN'T LIVE HERE ANYMORE** | | -

Nov 87. (7"/cd-s) (*651201-7/-2*) <07614> **I DREAMED A DREAM. / SWEET CAROLINE** | | -

Dec 87. (d-lp/c/cd) (*460406-1/-4/-2*) <40990> **HOT AUGUST NIGHT II (live)** | 74 | 59 Nov87
– Song of the whales (fanfare) / Headed for the future / September morn / Thank the Lord for the night time / Cherry cherry / Sweet Caroline / Hello again / Love on the rocks / America / Forever in blue jeans / You don't bring me flowers / I dreamed a dream / Back in L.A. / Song sung blue / Crackling Rosie / I am . . . I said / Holly holy / Soolamain / Brother Love's travelling salvation show / Heartlight. (*re-iss. Sep93 on 'Columbia'*)

Jan 88. (7") <07751> **CHERRY CHERRY (live). / AMERICA (live)** | | -

Feb 89. (lp/c/cd) (*463201-1/-4/-2*) <45025> **THE BEST YEARS OF OUR LIVES** | 42 | 46 Jan89
– The best years of our lives / Hard times for young lovers / This time / Everything's gonna be fine / Hooked on a memory of you / Take care of me / Baby can I hold you / Carmelita's eyes / Courtin' disaster / If I couldn't see you again / Long hard climb.

May 89. (7") <08514> **THIS TIME. / IF I COULDN'T SEE YOU AGAIN** | | -

May 89. (7"/c-s) (*654518-7/-4*) **THIS TIME. / BABY CAN I HOLD YOU** | | -
(12"+=) (*654518-6*) – Hooked on the morning of you.
(cd-s+=) (*654518-2*) – Beautiful noise / If you know what I mean.

Sep 89. (7") <08741> **THE BEST YEARS OF OUR LIVES. / CARMELITA'S EYES** | - | -

Columbia | *Columbia*

Oct 91. (cd/c/lp) (*468890-2/-4/-1*) <48610> **LOVESCAPE** | 36 | 44 Sep91
– If there were no dreams / Mountains of love / Don't turn around / Someone who believes in you / When you miss your love / Fortune of the night / One hand, one heart / Hooked on the memory of you / Wish everything was alright / The way / Sweet L.A. days / All I really need is you / Lonely lady 17 / I feel you / Common ground. (*cd re-iss. Apr99; 468890-2*)

Jun 92. (cd/c/d-lp) (*471502-2/-4*) <52703> **THE GREATEST HITS 1966-1992** (compilation) | 1 | 90 May92
– Solitary man / Cherry, Cherry / I get the feelin' (oh no, no) / Thank you Lord for the night time / Girl, you'll be a woman soon / Kentucky woman / Shilo / You got to me / Brooklyn roads / Red, red wine / I'm a believer / Sweet Caroline / Soolaimon / Cracklin' Rose / Song sung blue / lay me / Holly holy / Morningside / Crunchy granola suite / Brother Love's travelling salvation show / I am . . . I said / Be / Longfellow serenade / Beautiful noise / If you know what I mean / Desiree / September morn / You don't bring me flowers (w / BARBRA STREISAND) / Forever in blue jeans / Hello America / Love on the rocks / Yesterday's songs / Heartlight / Headed for the future / Heartbreak Hotel (w / KIM CARNES) / All I really need is you. (*re-iss. Aug98; same*)

Nov 92. (7"/c-s) (*658826-7/-4*) **MORNING HAS BROKEN. / SANTA CLAUS IS COMING TO TOWN** | | 36
(cd-s) (*658826-2*) – ('A'side) / Happy xmas (war is over) / Silver bells / Love on the rocks.

Nov 92. (cd/c/lp) (*472410-2/-4/-1*) <52914> **THE CHRISTMAS ALBUM** | 50 | 8
– O come o come Emmanuel / We three kings of Orient are / Silent night / Little drummer boy / Santa Claus is coming to town / Christmas song / Morning has broken / Happy Xmas (war is over) / White Christmas / God rest ye merry gentlemen / Jingle bells rock / Hark the herald angels sing / Silver bells / You make it feel like Christmas / Holy night.

Sep 93. (cd/c/lp) (*474356-2/-4/-1*) <57529> **ON THE ROOF – SONGS FROM THE BRILL BUILDING** | 28 | 28
– You've lost that lovin' feelin' (duet with DOLLY PARTON) / Up on the roof / Love potion number nine / Will you love me tomorrow/ Don't be cruel / Do wah diddy diddy (with MARY'S DANISH) / I (who have nothing) / Do you know the way to San Jose? / Don't make me over / River deep mountain high / A groovy kind of love / Spanish Harlem / Sweets for my sweet / Happy birthday sweet sixteen / Ten lonely guys / Save the last dance for me.

Aug 94. (d-cd/d-c) (*477211-2/-4*) <66321> **LIVE IN AMERICA (live)** | | 93
– America / Hello again / Kentucky woman / You got to me / Cherry cherry / I'm a believer / Sweet Caroline / Love on the rocks / Hooked on the memory of you (with LINDA PRESS) / Lady oh / Beautiful noise / Play me / Up on the roof / You've lost that lovin' feelin' (with RAVEN KANE) / River deep, mountain high / I (who have nothing) / Missa / Soolaimon / Holly holy / And the grass won't pay you no mind / You don't bring me flowers (with RAVEN KANE) / September morn / Havah nagilah / Solitary man / Red red wine / Song sung blue / Forever in blue jeans / Heartlight / Cracklin' Rose / I am . . . I said / Crunchy Granola suite / Brother Love's traveling salvation show.

Nov 94. (cd/c) (*477598-2/-4*) <66465> **THE CHRISTMAS ALBUM VOLUME II** | | 51
– Joy to the world / Mary's boy child / Deck the halls / We wish you a merry Christmas / Winter wonderland / Have yourself a merry little Christmas / I'll be home for Christmas / Rudolph the red nosed reindeer / Sleigh ride / Candlelight carol / Away in a manger / O come all ye faithful (adesta Fidells) / O little town of Bethlehem / Angels we have heard on high / The first noel / Hallelujah chorus.

Feb 96. (cd/c) (*481378-2/-4*) <67382> **TENNESSEE MOON** | 12 | 14
– Tennessee moon / One good love / Shame / A matter of love / Marry me / Deep inside of you / Gold don't rush / Like you do / Can anybody hear me / Win the world / No limit / Reminisce for a while / Kentucky woman / If I lost my way / Everybody / Talking optimist blues (good day today) / Open wide these prison doors / Blue highway. (*cd re-iss. Jan99; same*)

Nov 98. (cd/c/d-c) (*491655-2/-4*) <69540> **AS TIME GOES BY – THE MOVIE ALBUM** | 68 | 31
– As time goes by / Secret love / Unchained melody / Can you feel the love tonight / The way you look / Love with the proper stranger / Puttin' on the Ritz / When you wish upon a star / Windmills of your mind / Ebb tide / True love / My heart will go on / The look of love / Can't help falling in love / Ruby / I've got you under my skin / Come for my baby / And I love her / Moon river / In the still of the night / As time goes by (reprise).

– compilations, others, etc. –

1968. (7") *Bang*; <561> **SHILO. / LA BAMBA** | - |
<re-iss. Jan70; 575> – hit No.24

Jul 68. (lp) *Bang*; <219> **NEIL DIAMOND'S GREATEST HITS** | - | 100

Jul 70. (7") *Bang*; <578> **SOLITARY MAN. / THE TIME IS NOW** | - | 21

Entry	UK	US
Sep 70. (lp) *Bang; <221>* **SHILO**	-	52
Dec 70. (7") *Bang; <580>* **DO IT! / HANKY PANKY**	-	36
Feb 71. (lp) *Bang; <224>* **DO IT!**	-	100
Feb 71. (7") *President; (PT 324)* **SOLITARY MAN. / HANKY PANKY**		-
Apr 71. (7"m) *President; (PT 335)* **KENTUCKY WOMAN. / CHERRY CHERRY / I THANK THE LORD FOR THE NIGHT TIME**		-
Jun 71. (7") *President; (PT 342) / Bang; <586>* **I'M A BELIEVER. / CROOKED STREET**		51
1971. (lp) *Joy; (JOYS 188)* **GREATEST HITS**		-
1971. (lp) *Joy; (JOYS 210)* **I'M A BELIEVER**		-
Jan 73. (d-lp) *Bang; <227>* **DOUBLE GOLD**	-	36
Aug 73. (7") *London; (HLM 10427) / Bang; <703>* **THE LONG WAY HOME. / MONDAY, MONDAY**		91
1973. (lp) *London; (ZGM 132)* **GOLD DIAMOND**		-
Aug 73. (7") *M.C.A.; <40092>* **THE LAST THING ON MY MIND. / CANTA LIBRE**	-	56
Feb 74. (lp/c) *M.C.A.; (MCF/+C 2529) <2103>* **RAINBOW**	39	35 *Dec73*
May 74. (7") *M.C.A.; (MCA 130)* **SHILO. / BROOKLYN ROADS**		-
Jun 74. (lp/c) *M.C.A.; (MCF/+C 2550) <2106>* **HIS 12 GREATEST HITS** *(cd-iss. May87; DMCA 114)*	13	29 *May74*
Aug 74. (7") *M.C.A.; (MCA 151)* **HOLLY HOLY. / SOOLAIMON (AFRICAN TRILOGY II)**		-
Sep 74. (lp) *London; (ZGM 134)* **GOLD DIAMOND VOL.2**		-
Sep 75. (d-lp) *London; (FOSM 7-8)* **FOCUS ON NEIL DIAMOND**		-
Oct 75. (d-lp/d-c) *M.C.A.; (MCF/+C 273)* **DIAMONDS** *(re-iss. Oct81; MCLD/+C 603)*		-
Mar 76. (7") *C.B.S.; (CBS 3962)* **BE. / LONGFELLOW SERENADE**		-
Nov 76. (lp/c) *M.C.A.; (MCF/+C 2777) <2227>* **AND THE SINGER SINGS HIS SONG** *(re-iss. Aug81; MCF/+C 1629)*		*Sep76*
Jun 77. (7"ep) *M.C.A.; (MCA 304)* **LIVE DIAMONDS EP (live)** – Shilo / Brother Love's travelling salvation show / Cherry Cherry.		-
Nov 77. (7") *M.C.A.; (MCA 357)* **AND THE GRASS WON'T PAY YOU NO MIND. / MERRY-GO-ROUND**		-
Nov 78. (lp/c) *M.C.A.; (MCTV 2)* **20 GOLDEN GREATS** *(re-iss. Feb91 cd/c; D+/MCTV 2) (re-iss. May96 cd/c; MCD/MCC 11452)*	2	-
Sep 79. (lp/c) *Music For Pleasure; (MFP/TC-MFP 50449)* **NEIL DIAMOND**		-
Jan 81. (lp/c) *M.C.A.; (MCF/+C 3092)* **LOVE SONGS** *(re-iss. Apr97 cd/c; MCB D/C 19525)*	43	
Sep 81. (lp/c) *Hallmark; (SHM/HSC 3093)* **SOLITARY MAN**		-
Dec 81. (4xlp-box) *W.R.C.; (ALBUM 91)* **THE BEST OF NEIL DIAMOND**		-
Apr 82. (lp/c) *M.C.A.; (MCF/+C 3137)* **LIVE DIAMONDS (live)**		-
Apr 82. (d-c) *M.C.A.; (MCA2 106)* **TOUCHING ME TOUCHING YOU / MOODS**		-
Jun 82. (lp/c) *C.B.S.; (CBS/40 85844) / Columbia; <38068>* **12 GREATEST HITS VOLUME 2** *(cd-iss. May87; CD 85844)*	32	48 *May82*
Jul 82. (7") *Old Gold; (OG 9205)* **SONG SUNG BLUE. / I AM ... I SAID**		-
Jan 83. (c-ep) *C.B.S.; (CBS40 3065)* **CASSETTE EP** – You don't bring me flowers / If you know what I mean / September morn / Beautiful noise.		-
Apr 83. (7") *Old Gold; (OG 9324)* **CRACKIN' ROSIE. / SWEET CAROLINE**		-
Jun 83. (lp/c) *C.B.S.; (CBS/40 32349) / Columbia; <38792>* **CLASSICS – THE EARLY YEARS** *(cd-iss. May87; CD 25531) (cd re-iss. Apr89; CD 32349) (cd re-iss. May98 on 'Columbia'; 477784-2)*		-
Dec 83. (lp) *K-Tel; (NE 1262)* **THE VERY BEST OF NEIL DIAMOND**	33	-
Sep 84. (d-c) *M.C.A.; (MCA2 119)* **LOVE SONGS / GOLD**		-
Sep 86. (lp/c) *Hallmark; (SHM/HSC 3200)* **THE BEST OF NEIL DIAMOND** *(cd-iss. Jan89 & Feb96; PWKS 510)*		-
Feb 88. (lp/c) *Hallmark; (SHM/HSC 3230)* **RED RED WINE**		-
Oct 88. (lp/c) *BR Music; (BRLP/BRMC 58)* **GREATEST HITS**		-
1989. (cd-ep) *Old Gold; (OG 6149)* **CRACKIN' ROSIE / I AM ... I SAID / SONG SONG BLUE**		-
Aug 93. (3xcd-box) *Columbia; (474143-2)* **I'M GLAD YOU'RE HERE WITH ME TONIGHT / BEAUTIFUL NOISE / YOU DON'T SEND ME FLOWERS**		-
Jul 96. (d-cd) *M.C.A.; (MCD 33005)* **SWEET CAROLINE / MOODS**		-
Aug 96. (cd/c) *Sony TV – MCA; (MOOD CD/C 45)* **THE ULTIMATE COLLECTION**	5	-
Oct 96. (3xcd-box) *Columbia; (C3K 65013)* **IN MY LIFETIME**		-
Nov 97. (3xcd-box) *Columbia; (488676-2)* **BEAUTIFUL NOISE / JONATHAN LIVINGSTONE SEAGULL / THE JAZZ SINGER**		-

---

DIAMOND HEAD (dig out; Great Metal . . .)

DICKIES (dig out; Great Alt & Indie . . .)

Bruce DICKINSON (dig out; Great Metal . . .)

DICTATORS (dig out; Great Alt & Indie . . .)

Bo DIDDLEY

Born: OTHA ELLAS BATES, 30 Dec'28, McComb, Missouri, USA. As a toddler, he was given the surname, McDANIEL, after he was adopted by his mother's cousin, Mrs. Gussie McDaniel. In the early 50's, BO DIDDLEY (named after a one-stringed African guitar) gave up a promising boxing career, moving in 1955 from Chicago street busking to sign for 'Checker' records. His debut recording, 'BO DIDDLEY', sold well enough in R&B circles to give him his first break later in the year on the 'Ed Sullivan Show'. Its flip side, 'I'M A MAN', also became a standard for many 60's beat combos (The WHO, YARDBIRDS, MANFRED MANN and especially The ROLLING STONES), and although DIDDLEY initially failed to score a Billboard Hot 100 hit, the bulk of his output was later embraced by countless rock acts. Songs such as 'BRING IT TO JEROME', 'DIDDY WAH DIDDY', 'WHO DO YOU LOVE' and 'MONA', followed a tried and tested formula which saw the "boss" man fusing R&B and rock'n'roll in drivingly rhythmic style (much like his recording companion, CHUCK BERRY). His umpteenth attempt at commercial success was finally rewarded with a belated minor US hit 45, 'CRACKIN UP' in the summer of '59. This was almost immediately followed by an even bigger hit, 'SAY MAN', which saw BO flaunt his quick witted humour in a taunting match with maracas man, JEROME. DIDDLEY continued in the same fashion throughout the early 60's, scoring low-key hits with 'ROAD RUNNER' and 'YOU CAN'T JUDGE A BOOK BY THE COVER', the momentum of the British beat boom seeing three DIDDLEY long-players ('BO DIDDLEY', ' . . . IS A GUNSLINGER' and ' . . . RIDES AGAIN') gaining a full UK release and subsequent Top 20 success in the Autumn of '63. His fourth album to grace the charts, 'BO DIDDLEY'S BEACH PARTY', surfaced early the following year, although this period represented the pinnacle of his career and as the white R&B/rock took over, DIDDLEY and his ilk were consigned to the margins. Save for a lone Top 40 excursion in 1965 with 'HEY GOOD LOOKIN', DIDDLEY had to settle for cult status in the decades to come, although he was a guest of The CLASH in 1979.

Best CD compilation: HIS BEST (CHESS 50th ANNIVERSARY COLLECTION) (*8)

BO DIDDLEY – vocals, guitar

Entry	London	Checker
Jun 55. (7",78) *<814>* **BO DIDDLEY. / I'M A MAN** *<re-iss. Dec61; 997>*	-	

—— **BILLY BOY ARNOLD** – harmonica / **JEROME GREEN** – bass, maracas, etc. / **FRANK KIRKLAND** – drums / guest **OTIS SPANN** – piano

Entry	London	Checker
Jun 56. (7",78) *<819>* **DIDDLEY DADDY. / SHE'S FINE, SHE'S MINE**	-	-
Jun 56. (7"ep) *(RE-U 1054)* **RHYTHM & BLUES WITH BO DIDDLEY** – (above 4 tracks).		
Sep 56. (7",78) *<827>* **BRING IT TO JEROME. / PRETTY THING**	-	
Dec 56. (7",78) *<832>* **DIDDY WAH DIDDY. / I'M LOOKING FOR A WOMAN**	-	
Mar 57. (7",78) *<842>* **WHO DO YOU LOVE. / IN BAD**	-	
Jul 57. (7",78) *<850>* **COPS AND ROBBERS. / DOWN HOME SPECIAL**	-	
Oct 57. (7",78) *<860>* **HEY! BO DIDDLEY. / MONA**	-	
Feb 58. (7",78) *<878>* **SAY! (BOSS MAN). / BEFORE YOU ACCUSE ME**	-	
Jun 58. (7",78) *<896>* **HUSH YOUR MOUTH. / DEAREST DARLING**	-	
Nov 58. (7",78) *<907>* **WILLIE AND LILLIE. / LET'S MEET THE MONSTER**	-	
Feb 59. (lp) *(HA-M 2230) <1436>* **GO BO DIDDLEY** – Crackin' up / I'm sorry / Bo's guitar / Willie and Lillie / You don't love me (you don't care) / Say! (boss man) / Oh, yea! / Don't let it go / Little girl / Dearest darling / The clock struck twelve.		*Oct58*
Feb 59. (7",78) *<914>* **I'M SORRY. / OH YEA!**	-	
Aug 59. (7",78) *(HLM 8913) <924>* **CRACKIN' UP. / THE GREAT GRANDFATHER**		62 *Jun59*
Nov 59. (7",78) *(HLM 8975) <931>* **SAY MAN. / THE CLOCK STRIKES TWELVE**		20 *Oct59*
Jan 60. (7") *(HLM 9035) <936>* **SAY MAN, BACK AGAIN. / SHE'S ALRIGHT**	-	
Apr 60. (7") *(HLM 9112) <942>* **ROAD RUNNER. / MY STORY**		75
Jun 60. (7") *<951>* **CRAWDADDY. / WALKIN' AND TACKIN'**		
Nov 60. (7") *<965>* **GUNSLINGER. / SIGNIFYING BLUES**		
Mar 61. (7") *<976>* **NOT GUILTY. / AZTEC**		
Jun 61. (7") *<985>* **CALL ME. / PILLS**		

—— added half-sister **THE DUCHESS** – guitar

Entry	London	Checker
Sep 61. (lp) *<2977>* **BO DIDDLEY IS A GUNSLINGER** – Gunslinger / Ride on Josephine / Doing the craw-daddy / Cadillac / Somewhere / Whoa mule / Sixteen tons / Cheyenne / No more lovin' / Diddling. (UK-iss.Nov63 on 'Pye Jazz'; NJL 33) – hit No.20	-	

Entry	Pye Int.	Checker
Oct 62. (7") *(7N 25165) <1019>* **YOU CAN'T JUDGE A BOOK BY THE COVER. / I CAN TELL** *(UK re-iss. Sep63; 7N 25216)*		48 *Jul62*
Nov 62. (lp) *<2984>* **BO DIDDLEY** – You can't judge a book by the cover / Mama don't allow no twistin' / Mr. Khruschev / Sad sack / You all green / Diddling / Who may your lover be / Babes in the wood / Bo's bounce / Bo's twist / I can tell / Give me a break. (UK-iss.Nov63; NPL 28026) – hit No.11 (re-iss. Apr87) (cd-iss. Dec86)	-	
May 63. (lp) *(NPL 28025) <2992>* **HEY! BO DIDDLEY** – Mess around / Somebody's crying / Hong Kong / Can I go home with you / I'm going home / Rhyme song / Cracklin' on. (re-iss. May94 on 'Charly')		
Jun 63. (7") *(7N 25193)* **WHO DO YOU LOVE?. / THE TWISTER**		
Jul 63. (7") *(7N 25210)* **BO DIDDLEY. / DETOUR**		
Sep 63. (7") *(7N 25217)* **PRETTY THING. / ROAD RUNNER**	34	-
Oct 63. (7") *<1045>* **GREATEST LOVER IN THE WORLD. / SURFER'S LOVE CALL**	-	-
Nov 63. (lp) *(NPL 28029)* **BO DIDDLEY RIDES AGAIN** – Bring it to Jerome / Cops and robbers / Mumblin' guitar / Oh, yea! / You don't love me / Down home special / Bo Diddley is loose / Help out / Call me (Bo's blues) / Don't let it go / Nursery rhyme / Dearest darling. (cd-iss. Feb94 on 'See For Miles')	19	-

Nov 63. (7") *(7N 25227)* **BO DIDDLEY IS A LOVER. / DOIN' THE JAGUAR**

Jan 64. (lp) *(NPL 28032)* **BO DIDDLEY'S BEACH PARTY** `13`
– Memphis / Gunslinger / Hey Bo Diddley / Old Smokey / Bo Diddley's dog / I'm all right / Mr.Custer / Bo's waltz / What's buggin' you / Roadrunner. *(re-iss. 1989)*

Feb 64. (7") *(7N 25235)* <1058> **MEMPHIS. / MONKEY DIDDLE**

May 64. (7") *(7N 25243)* **MONA. / GIMME GIMME**

Jun 64. (lp) *(NPL 28034)* <2976> **IN THE SPOTLIGHT**
– Gimme, gimme / Not guilty / Scuttle bug / Say, man / Let me in / Hong Kong / Mississippi / Craw-dad / Bo's a lumber Jack / Walkin' and talkin' / I need you, baby / You're looking good / She's alright.

Aug 64. (7") *(7N 25258)* <1083> **MAMA KEEP YOUR BIG MOUTH SHUT. / JO-ANN**

1964. (lp) <2988> **ROADRUNNER**
– Bo Diddley / I'm a man / Pretty thing / Who do you love / Mona (I need you baby) / Say man / Hush your mouth / Road runner / You can't judge a book by looking at the cover / Cops and robbers / Hey Bo Diddley / Crackin' up / Diddley daddy / Bring it to Jerome. *(UK-iss.Jul84 on 'Black Lion')* *(cd-iss. Nov89 on 'Instant-Charly')*

                                                  Chess   Checker

Mar 65. (7") *(CRS 8000)* <1098> **HEY GOOD LOOKIN'. / YOU AIN'T BAD (AS YOU CLAIM TO BE)** `39`

Mar 65. (lp) *(CRL 4002)* <2992> **HEY GOOD LOOKIN'**
– Mess around / Somebody's crying / King Kong / Can I go home with you / I'm going home / Rhyme song / Crackin' / Rockin' on. *(re-iss. Aug86 on 'Magnum Force')* *(re-iss. +cd.May88 on 'Jazz Life')*

May 65. (7") *(CRS 8014)* **SOMEBODY BEAT ME. / MUSH MOUTH MILLIE**

Sep 65. (7") *(CRS 8021)* **LET THE KIDS DANCE. / LET ME PASS**

Sep 65. (lp) *(CRL 4507)* **LET ME PASS**
– Let me pass / Stop my monkey / Greasy spoon / Tonight is ours / Root hoot / Stinkey / Hey red riding hood / Let the kids dance / He's so mad / Soul food / Corn bread / Somebody beat me / 500% more man / Mama, keep your big mouth shut / We're gonna get married / Easy *(cd-iss. Feb94 on 'See For Miles')*

Nov 65. (7") <1223> **500% MORE MAN. / LET THE KIDS DANCE**

Dec 65. (7") *(CRS 8026)* **500% MORE MAN. / STOP MY MONKEY**

Jan 66. (lp) <2996> **500% MORE MAN**
– 500% more man / Let me pass / Stop my monkey / Greasy spoon / Tonight is ours / Root hoot / Hey Red Riding Hood / Let the kids dance / He's so mad / Soul food / Corn bread / Somebody beat me.

—— JEROME and The DUCHESS left his band

Apr 66. (7") <1142> **WE'RE GONNA GET MARRIED. / DO THE FROG**

Jun 66. (7") *(CRS 8036)* **WE'RE GONNA GET MARRIED. / EASY**

Jan 67. (lp) *(CRL 4525)* <3001> **THE ORIGINATOR**
– Pills / Jo Ann / Two flies / Yakky doodle / What do you know about love / Lazy woman / You ain't bad / Love you baby / Limbo / Background to a music / Puttentang / Africa speaks.

May 67. (7") *(CRS 8053)* <1158> **OOH BABY. / BACK TO SCHOOL** `88` Jan67

Feb 68. (7") *(CRS 8057)* <1168> **WRECKING MY LOVE LIFE. / BOO-GA-LOO BEFORE YOU GO**

Jun 68. (7") *(CRS 8078)* <1200> **ANOTHER SUGAR DADDY. / I'M HIGH AGAIN**

Mar 69. (lp; with MUDDY WATERS & LITTLE MILTON) *(CRL 4529)* <3010> **SUPERBLUES**
– Long distance call / Who do you love? / I'm a man / Bo Diddley / You can't a book by the cover / I just want to make love to you / My babe / You don't love me.

Apr 69. (7") *(CRS 8088)* <1213> **BO DIDDLEY '69. / SOUL TRAIN**

Feb 70. (7") <1238> **THE SHAPE I'M IN. / POLLUTION**

—— BO virtually retired from business, but released comebacks below. He surfaced periodically on live work.

                                             Chess   Chess

Oct 71. (lp) <50001> **ANOTHER DIMENSION**
– The shape I'm in / I love you more than you'll ever know / Pollution / Bad moon rising / Down on the corner / Said shut up woman / Bad side of the moon / Lodi / Go for broke.

1972. (7") <2117> **I SAID SHUT UP WOMAN. / I LOVE YOU MORE THAN YOU'LL EVER KNOW**

1972. (7") <2129> **BO DIDDLEY-ITIS. / INFATUATION**

1972. (7") <2134> **HUSBAND-IN-LAW. / BO-JAM**

1973. (7") <2142> **DON'T WANT NO LYIN' WOMAN. / MAKE A HIT RECORD**

1973. (d-lp) *(6467 304)* <60005> **GOT ANOTHER BAG OF TRICKS**
(compilation)

                                             R.C.A.   R.C.A.

Apr 76. (7") <10618> **DRAG ON. / NOT FADE AWAY**

                                             Magnum   not iss.
                                             Force

Apr 86. (lp) *(MFM 021)* **HEY . . . BO DIDDLEY IN CONCERT** (with MAINSQUEEZE)
– Intro – Bo Diddley vamp / Doctor Jeckyll / Everleen / I don't know where I've been / You can't judge a book by the cover / Road runner / I'm a man / Bubble Bo Diddley.

                                             New Rose   not iss.

Jun 84. (7") **AIN'T IT GOOD TO BE FREE. / BO DIDDLEY PUT THE ROCK IN ROCK'N'ROLL** French

Jun 84. (lp) *(ROSE 34)* **AIN'T IT GOOD TO BE FREE**
– Bo Diddley / Bo Diddley put the rock in rock'n'roll / Gotta be a change / I don't want your welfare / Mona, where's your sister / Stabilize yourself / I don't know where I've been / I ain't gonna force it on you / Evil woman / Let the fox talk. *(re-iss. +cd.Feb88)*

Sep 89. (lp/c/cd) *(ROSE 188/+C/CD)* **LIVING LEGEND**
– Turbo Diddley 2000 / R.U. serious? / Jeanette Jeanette / I broke the chain / Bo-pop quake / The best / I'll lick yo' face / U killed it / Going home to McComb.

– compilations, others, etc. –

on 'Pye International' unless mentioned otherwise

Sep 63. (7"ep) *(NEP 44009)* **CHUCK AND BO**

Nov 63. (7"ep) *(NEP 44012)* **CHUCK AND BO, VOL.2**

Feb 64. (7"ep) *(NEP 44017)* **CHUCK AND BO, VOL.3**

Nov 64. (7") **CHUCK'S BEAT. / BO'S BEAT**

Nov 64. (lp) *(NPL 28047)* **TWO GREAT GUITARS**
(above items credited with CHUCK BERRY)

Nov 63. (7"ep) *(NEP 44014)* **HEY! BO DIDDLEY**

Apr 64. (7"ep) *(NEP 44019)* **THE BO DIDDLEY STORY**

Oct 64. (7"ep) *(NEP 44031)* **BO DIDDLEY IS A LUMBERJACK**

Nov 64. (7"ep) *(NEP 44036)* **DIDDLING**

Dec 64. (lp) *(NPL 28049)* **16 ALL TIME HITS**

Aug 65. (lp) *Marble Arch; (MAL 751)* **SURFIN' WITH BO DIDDLEY**
<above issued in the US earlier on 'Checker'>

Nov 65. (7"ep) *Chess; (CRE 6008)* **I'M A MAN**

Jul 66. (7"ep) *Chess; (CRE 6023)* **ROOSTER STEW**

May 82. (lp/c) *Chess; (CXMD 4003)* **CHESS MASTERS VOLUME 1**
(re-iss. Mar88 on 'Stylus' lp/c/cd; SMR/SMC/SMD 849)

May 83. (lp/c) *Chess; (CXMD 4009)* **CHESS MASTERS VOLUME 2**

Jul 85. (7"ep) *Chess; (CHES 4001)* **BO DIDDLEY / PRETTY THING. / ROAD RUNNER / SAY MAN**

Aug 88. (cd) *Chess; (CDRED 2)* **DIDDLEY DADDY**

Jul 73. (lp) *London; (6499 476)* **THE LONDON BO DIDDLEY SESSIONS**
(cd-iss. Jun90 on 'Chess'; CHD 9296)

Nov 89. (2xcd/2xc/2xlp;box) *(CD/TC+/BOX 257)* **BO DIDDLEY BOX SET**

Feb 89. (cd-ep) *Charly; (CDS 11)* **BO DIDDLEY / ROAD RUNNER / YOU CAN'T JUDGE A BOOK BY THE COVER / MONA (I NEED YOU BABY)**

Feb 93. (cd) *Charly; (CDCD 1019)* **I'M A MAN**

Jul 93. (cd/c) *Charly; (CDBM/TCBM 43)* **SIGNIFYING BLUES**

Nov 93. (12xcd-box) *Charly; (CDREDBOX 8)* **BO DIDDLEY: THE CHESS YEARS**

Jun 85. (12"ep; with BILLY BOY ARNOLD) *Red Lightnin'; (RLEP12 045)* **IT'S GREAT TO BE RICH**

Aug 91. (cd) *Roots; (RTS 33031)* **ROADRUNNER VOL.2**

Jun 91. (lp/c/cd) *See For Miles; (SEE/+K/CD 321)* **THE EP COLLECTION**

1991. (lp/cd) *Edsel; (ED/+CD 318)* **THE 20th ANNIVERSARY OF ROCK'N'ROLL** `1976`

Sep 93. (cd) *Charly; (CDCHD 396)* **BO'S BLUES**

Jul 95. (cd) *Beat Goes On; (BGOCD 287)* **HEY! BO DIDDLEY / BO DIDDLEY**

Aug 95. (cd) *Triple X; (TX 51161CD)* **THE MIGHTY BO DIDDLEY**

DIFFORD & TILBROOK (see under ⇒ SQUEEZE)

Ani DiFRANCO

Born: 23 Sep'70, Buffalo, New York, USA. Having learned to sing and play guitar at an early age, DiFRANCO began playing professionally after a move to the centre of New York. As fiercely independent and enterprising as she was talented, DiFRANCO set up her own 'Righteous Babe' imprint for the release of her eponymous debut album. Issued in 1990 as an American-only release, the album had originally been on sale at live shows before demand soon outstripped supply and necessitated a larger operation. Featuring the cream of the apparently massive catalogue of songs she'd built up throughout her teens, the record's intimate acoustic confessionals went down a storm with both militant lesbians and straight down the line folk/rock fans. Openly bisexual herself, the tattooed, pierced and shaven-headed DiFRANCO steadily built up a diehard following of kindred spirits through a punishing tour schedule. 1991's 'NOT SO SOFT' was another bare bones acoustic affair dealing in heartfelt sexual politics although it wasn't until the release of the more instrumentally rich 'IMPERFECTLY' (1992) and 'PUDDLE DIVE' (1993), that DiFRANCO began to draw attention from major labels. Standing by her DIY ethos, she released her most widely acknowledged album to date in 'OUT OF RANGE' (1994). Again embellishing her rhythmic acoustic guitar playing with eclectic instrumental textures, the record set the scene for her breakthrough opus, 'NOT A PRETTY GIRL'. With girl power very much on the agenda in the mid-90's, DiFRANCO finally gained recognition as one of America's foremost female commentators alongside the likes of LIZ PHAIR, HEATHER NOVA, etc. The one-woman powerhouse also finally clinched a UK deal with 'Cooking Vinyl', while 1996's acclaimed 'DILATE' gave DiFRANCO her first Top 100 US chart placing. Following on from 1997's well received double set, 'LIVING IN CLIP', she scored her biggest success to date with near Top 20 US album, 'LITTLE PLASTIC CASTLES' (1998).

Album rating: ANI DiFRANCO (*6) / NOT SO SOFT (*6) / IMPERFECTLY (*7) / PUDDLE DIVE (*7) / LIKE I SAID – SONGS 1990-1991 compilation (*7) / OUT OF RANGE (*7) / NOT A PRETTY GIRL (*8) / DILATE (*7) / MORE JOY, LESS SHAME (*5) / LIVING IN CLIP (*8) / LITTLE PLASTIC CASTLE (*7) / UP UP UP UP UP UP (*6)

ANI DiFRANCO – vocals, guitar

                                          Haven   Righteous Babe

Nov 89. (cd) *<RBR 001CD>* **ANI DiFRANCO**
– Both hands / Talk to me now / Slant / Work you way out / Dog coffee / Lost woman song / Pale purple / Rush hour / Fire door / The story / Every angle / Out of habit / Letting the telephone ring / Egos like hairdos. *(UK-iss.Jul95; same)* *(re-iss. Jun97 on 'Cooking VInyl'; COOKCD 112)*

1991. (cd) *<RBR 002CD>* **NOT SO SOFT**
– Anticipate / Rockabye / She says / Make me stay / On every corner / Small world / Not so soft / Roll with it / Itch / Gratitude / Whole night / The next big thing / Brief bus stop / Looking at the holes. *(UK-iss.Sep97 on 'Cooking Vinyl'; COOKCD 133)*

1992. (cd) *<RBD 003CD>* **IMPERFECTLY**
– What if no one's watching / Fixing her hair / In or out / Every state line / Circle of light / If it isn't her / Good, bad, ugly / I'm no heroine / Coming up / Make

them apologize / Waiting song / Served faithfully / Imperfectly. *(UK-iss.Jul95; same)*

Jul 93. (cd/c) *(HAVEN CD/MC 002) <RBR 004 CD/C>* **PUDDLE DIVE** ☐ ☐
— Names and dates and times / Anyday / 4th of July / Willing to fight / Egos like hairdos / Back around / Blood in the boardroom / Born a lion / My IQ / Used to you / Pick yer nose / God's country. *(re-iss. Jan95; same)*

Jul 94. (cd) *<(RBR 005CD)>* **LIKE I SAID: SONGS 1990-1991** ☐ ☐
(re-recorded early tracks)
— Anticipate / Rockabye / Not so soft / Roll with it / Work your way out / Fire door / Gratitude / Whole night / Both hands / She says / Rush hour / Out of habit / Lost woman song / Talk to me now / Slant.

		Haven	Righteous Babe

Jan 95. (cd/c) *(HAVEN CD/MC 3) <RBR 006CD>* **OUT OF RANGE** ☐ ☐ Jul94
— Buildings and bridges / Out of range / Letter to a John / Hell yeah / How have you been / Overlap / Face up and sing / Falling is like this / Out of range / You had time / If he tries anything / Diner.

		Righteous Babe	Righteous Babe

Nov 95. (cd) *<(RBR 007CD)>* **NOT A PRETTY GIRL** ☐ ☐ Jul95
— Worthy / Tiptoe / Cradle and all / Shy / Sorry I am / Light of some kind / Not a pretty girl / Million you never made / Hour follows hour / 32 flavors / Asking too much / This bouquet / Crime for crime. *(UK-iss.Jan97 on 'Cooking Vinyl'; COOKCD 113)*

		Cooking Vinyl	Righteous Babe

Jul 96. (cd) *(COOKCD 103) <RBR 008CD>* **DILATE** ☐ 87 May96
— Untouchable face / Outta me, onto you / Superhero / Dilate / Amazing grace / Napoleon / Shameless / Done wrong / Going down / Adam and Eve / Joyful girl.

Jan 97. (cd-s) *(FRYCD 049)* **OUTTA ME ONTO YOU / SHY** ☐ ☐

Apr 97. (cd; UTAH PHILLIPS & ANI DiFRANCO) *(COOKCD 124) <RBR 009CD>* **THE PAST DIDN'T GO ANYWHERE** ☐ ☐
— Bridges / Nevada City, California / Korea / Anarchy / Candidacy / Bum on the road / Enormously wealthy / Mess with people / Natural resources / Heroes / Half a ghost town / Holding on.

Dec 96. (m-cd) *(COOKCD 119) <RBR 010CD>* **MORE JOY, LESS SHAME** ☐ ☐
— Joyful girl / Joyful girl / Joyful girl / Joyful girl / Shameless / Both hands.

Jun 97. (d-cd) *(COOKCD 122) <RBR 011CD>* **LIVING IN CLIP** (live) ☐ ☐ Apr97
— Whatever / Wherever / Gravel / Willing to fight / Shy / Joyful girl / Hide and seek / Napoleon / I'm no heroine / Amazing grace / Anitpate / Tiptoe / Sorry I am / Diner / Slant / 32 flavors / Out of range / Untouchable face / Shameless / Distracted / Adam and Eve / Fire door / Both hands / Out of habit / Every state line / Not so soft / Travel tips / Wrong with me / In or out / We're all gonna blow / Letter to a John / Overleaf.

Feb 98. (cd) *(COOKCD 140) <RBR 012CD>* **LITTLE PLASTIC CASTLE** ☐ 22
— Little plastic castle / Fuel / Gravel / As is / Two little girls / Deep dish / Loom / Pixie / Swan dive / Glass house / Independence day / Pulse.

Jan 99. (cd) *(COOKCD 193) <RBR 013CD>* **UP UP UP UP UP UP** ☐ 29
— Tis of thee / Virtue / Come away from it / Jukebox / Angel food / Angry anymore / Everest / Up up up up up / Know now then / Trickle down / Hat shaped hat.

Mar 99. (cd-s) *(FRYCD 079)* **NOT ANGRY ANYMORE / (mixes; album / extended)** ☐ ☐

– compilations, etc. –

Nov 94. (cd) *Tradition & Moderne; (T&M 105)* **WOMEN IN (E)MOTION FESTIVAL** ☐ ☐
<US-iss.Jun98 on 'Imprint'; 28376>

DIGABLE PLANETS (dig out; 4th edition)

Steve DIGGLE (see under ⇒ BUZZCOCKS)

DIGITAL UNDERGROUND

Formed: Oakland, California, USA . . . 1987 by Queens born GREGORY JACOBS (aka SHOCK G), who had lived in Florida and CHOPMASTER J. Obsessed by P-FUNK (PARLIAMENT / FUNKADELIC), they embarked on lewd and libidinous attacks on the polite society, under the guise of concept albums. The duo were joined by urban rappers 2PAC SHAKUR, KENNY K, DJ GOLDFINGERS and MONEY B, achieving US Top 40 chart success with debut 'Tommy Boy' single 'DOOWUTCHYALIKE'. Americans also lapped up 'THE HUMPTY DANCE', a smutty tribute to SHOCK G's alter ego, EDDIE 'HUMPTY HUMP' HUMPREY, concerning ED's ability to have his wicked way with the ladies despite his false nose. He had sustained severe burns in a kitchen accident, which led him to wear such an object. The innuendo continued with the debut 'SEX PACKETS' in 1990, a comic rap-concept in the true CLINTON fashion, concerning a wonder drug that gave users a wet dream. The following two albums (especially 1991's 'SONS OF THE P'), took the group's P-FUNK fetish to its zenith, resulting in a somewhat extroverted sound. While the prophylactic proselytising of 1993's 'THE BODY-HAT SYNDROME', offered a few laughs, it was obvious DU were running out of ideas. The polished R&B of 'FUTURE RHYTHM' did nothing to improve the situation. 2PAC left in the early 90's to embark on a massively successful solo career only to be gunned down in 1996, a victim of the vicious internecine feuding of the hip hop community. • **Songwriters:** SHOCK G and group, except a plethora of samples; KNEE DEEP (Funkadelic) / etc.

Album rating: SEX PACKETS (*8) / SONS OF THE P (*6) / THE BODY-HAT SYNDROME (*5) / FUTURE RHYTHM (*3)

SHOCK G (b. GREGORY JACOBS) – vocals, keyboards, synthesizers / **KENNY-K** + **MONEY-B** – rappers / **CHOPMASTER J** – samples, percussion / **DJ GOLDFINGERS** – decks

		B.C.M.	Tommy Boy

1989. (7") *(BCM 330)* **DOOWUTCHYALIKE. / HIP-HOP DOLL (vocal)** ☐ ☐

(12"+=/cd-s+=) *(BCM 330 X/CD)* – ('A'-Playhowyalike mix).

Mar 90. (7") *(BCM 364) <7944>* **THE HUMPTY DANCE. / ('A'instrumental)** ☐ 11
(12"+=/cd-s+=) *(BCM 364 X/CD)* – ('A'mixes).

Apr 90. (cd/c/lp) *(BCM 377 CD/MC/LP) <TB CD/MC/LP 1026>* **SEX PACKETS** 59 24
— The Humpty dance / The way we swing / Packet prelude / Sex packets / Street scene / Packet man / Freaks of the industry / Underwater rimes (remix) / The new jazz (one) / Rhymin' on the funk / The danger zone / Packet reprise / Doowutchyalike. *(cd+=)* – Gutfest '89. *(cd re-iss. Jan96 on 'Big Life'; BLRCD 16)*

Jun 90. (12"/cd-s) *(BCM 463 X/CD)* **DOOWUTCHYALIKE (mixes). / PACKET MAN (mixes)** 59 ☐
(re-iss. Nov95 on 'Big Life' 12"ep/cd-ep; BLR T/D 124)

		Big Life	Tommy Boy

Jan 91. (cd-ep) *<964>* **THIS IS AN E.P. RELEASE** - 29
— Same song / Tie the knot / The way we swing / Nuttin' is funky / Packet man / Arguin' on the funk.
(above and below featured 2 tracks from the film 'Nothing But Trouble', in which they appeared)

Mar 91. (7") *(BLR 40)* **SAME SONG. / TIE THE KNOT** 52 ☐
(12"+=) *(BLRT 40)* – Arguin' on the funk / The way we swing.
(cd-s) *(BLRD 40)* – ('A'version; repl. 7"b-side).

—— added **2PAC SHAKUR** – rapping

Nov 91. (7"/c-s) *(BLR/+C 63) <993>* **KISS YOU BACK. / ('A'-Smackapella mix)** 40
(12"/cd-s) *(BLR T/D 63)* – ('A'side) / ('A'-On the jazz trip) / ('A'-full French kiss mix).

Oct 91. (cd/c/lp) *(BLR CD/MC/LP 12) <1045>* **SONS OF THE P** ☐ 44
— The DFLO shuttle / Heartbeat props / No nose job / Sons of the P / Flowin' on the D-line / Kiss you back / Tales of the funky / The higher heights of spirituality / Family of the underground / The D-flowstrumental / Good thing we're rappin'. *(cd re-iss. Jan96; same)*

—— now with guest **TREACH** (of NAUGHTY BY NATURE) – rapper / Also **DJ JAY Z, CLEE + SAAFIR** (SAUCY NOMAD), who all replaced the solo bound 2PAC

Oct 93. (cd) *<1080>* **THE BODY-HAT SYNDROME** - 79
— Return of the crazy one / Doo woo you / Holly Wanstaho / Bran nu swetta / Humpty dumpty awards / The body-hats (part 1) / Dope-a-delic / Intermission / Wussup with the luv / Digital lover / Carry the way / The body-hats (part 2) / Circus entrance / Jerkit circus / Circus exit – the after-nut / Shake & bake / The body-hats (part 3) / Do ya like it dirty? / Bran nu sweat the beat / Wheee!
<cd+=> – <3 extra>.

		Edel	Critique

Jun 96. (12"/cd-s) *(009778-2/-1 RAP)* **ORGEGANO FLOW. / ('A'mix)** ☐ ☐
Jul 96. (cd/lp) *(009778-2/-1 RAP) <15452>* **FUTURE RHYTHM** ☐ Jun96
— Walk real kool / Glooty-us-maximus / Oregano flow / Fool get a clue / Rumpty rump / Food fight / Future rhythm / Hokis pokis (a classic case) / We got more / Hella bump / Stylin' / Midnite snack / Oregano flow / Want it all.

DILLARD & CLARK (see under ⇒ CLARK, Gene)

DIM STARS (see under ⇒ HELL, Richard)

DINOSAUR JR.

Formed: Amherst, Massachusetts, USA . . . 1983 by J. MASCIS. Initially recording hardcore punk under the DEEP WOUND moniker, the band recruited PATRICK MURPHY and metamorphosed into DINOSAUR. Their self-titled debut album appeared in 1985, a raw blueprint for their distinctive candy-coated noise rock that was good enough to secure an American tour support slot with SONIC YOUTH. After protestations from aging West Coast rockers DINOSAUR, J.MASCIS' crew added the JR. to part of their name. Subsequently recording one album for 'SST', 'YOU'RE LIVING ALL OVER ME' (1987), the band further developed their melodic distortion although it was the 'FREAK SCENE' (1988) single, their debut for 'Blast First', which saw DINOSAUR JR. pressed to the cardigan-clad bosoms of the nations pre-baggy indie kids. A wildly exhilarating piece of pristine pop replete with copious amounts of intoxicating noise pollution, MASCIS' go-on-impress-me vocals epitomised the word slacker when that dubious cliche was still gestating in some hack's subconscious. The follow-up album, 'BUG' (1988) was arguably the band's finest moment, perfectly crafted pop spiked with scathing slivers of guitar squall. BARLOW departed soon after the album's release, going off to form SEBADOH while MASCIS' mob came up with a wonderfully skewed cover of The CURE's 'JUST LIKE HEAVEN'. DON FLEMING (of GUMBALL fame) and JAY SPIEGEL featured on DINOSAUR JR.'s major label debut for 'WEA' subsidiary 'Blanco Y Negro', 'THE WAGON' (1991). Another slice of cascading noise-pop, the single raised expectations for the follow-up album 'GREEN MIND' (1991). More or less a MASCIS solo album, it failed to live up to its promise although by the release of 1993's 'WHERE YOU BEEN', MASCIS had found a permanent bassist in MIKE JOHNSON. Their most successful album to date, DINOSAUR JR. at last reaped some rewards from the grunge scene they'd played a major role in creating. With both JOHNSON and MASCIS releasing solo albums in 1996, DINOSAUR JR. have been conspicuous by their absence of late. • **Songwriters:** MASCIS wrote all, except LOTTA LOVE (Neil Young) / QUICKSAND (David Bowie) / I FEEL A WHOLE LOT BETTER (Byrds) / GOIN' BLIND (Kiss) / HOT BURRITO 2 (Gram Parsons). J. MASCIS solo:- EVERY MOTHER'S SON (Lynyrd Skynyrd) / THE BOY WITH THE THORN IN HIS SIDE (Smiths) / ON THE RUN (Wipers) / ANTICIPATION (Carly Simon). MIKE JOHNSON solo:- SECOND LOVERS SONG (Lynyrd Skynyrd) / LOVE AND OTHER CRIMES (Lee Hazlewood) / IF YOU'RE GONE (Gene Clark). • **Trivia:** In

Jun'91, MASCIS moonlighted as a drummer with Boston satanic hard-core group UPSIDE DOWN CROSS, who made one self-titled album Autumn '91 on 'Taang!'. He also wrote songs and made a cameo appearance in the 1992 film, 'Gas, Food, Lodging'.

Album rating: DINOSAUR (*6) / YOU'RE LIVING ALL OVER ME mini (*7) / BUG (*8) / GREEN MIND (*7) / WHERE YOU BEEN (*8) / WITHOUT A SOUND (*5) / HAND IT OVER (*7) / J. Mascis: MARTIN AND ME (*6) / Mike Johnson: YEAR OF MONDAYS (*5)

LOU BARLOW (b.17 Jul'66, Northampton, Mass.) – guitar / **J. MASCIS** (b. JOSEPH, 10 Dec'65) – drums / **CHARLIE NAKAJIMA** – vox / **SCOTT HELLAND** – bass

			not iss.	Radiobeat
Dec 83.	(7"ep; as DEEP WOUND) <RB 002> **I SAW IT**		-	

– I saw it / Sisters / In my room / Don't need / Lou's anxiety song / Video prick / Sick of fun / Deep wound / Dead babies.

J. MASCIS – vocals, guitar, percussion / **LOU BARLOW** – bass, ukelele, vocals / added **MURPH** (b. EMMETT "PATRICK" MURPHY, 21 Dec'64) – drums (ex-ALL WHITE JURY)

			not iss.	Homestead
Jun 85.	(lp; as DINOSAUR) <HMS 015> **DINOSAUR**		-	

– Forget the swan / Cats in a bowl / The leper / Does it float / Pointless / Repulsion / Gargoyle / Several lips / Mountain man / Quest / Bulbs of passion.

Mar 86.	(7"; as DINOSAUR) <HMS 032> **REPULSION. / BULBS OF PASSION**		-	

(UK-iss.Apr97; same)

			S.S.T.	S.S.T.
Mar 87.	(12"ep) <SST 152> **DINOSAUR JR.**		-	

– Little fury things / In a jar / Show me the way. (cd-ep iss.Dec88; SSTCD 152)

Jul 87.	(m-lp/c) <(SST/+C 130)> **YOU'RE LIVING ALL OVER ME**			

– Little fury things / Kracked / Sludgefeast / The lung / Raisans / Tarpit / In a jar / Lose / Poledo / Show me the way. (cd-iss. Oct95; same)

			Blast First	S.S.T.
Sep 88.	(7") (BFFP 30) **FREAK SCENE. / KEEP THE GLOVE**			

(US-iss.7",7"green; SST 220)

Oct 88.	(lp/c/cd) (BFFP 31/+C/CD) <SST/+C/CD 216> **BUG**			

– Freak scene / No bones / They always come / Yeah we know / Let it ride / Pond song / Budge / The post / Don't.

DONNA BIDDELL – bass (ex-SCREAMING TREES) repl. BARLOW who formed SEBADOH

Apr 89.	(7"/etched-12"/cd-s) (BFFP 47 S/T/CD) <SST 244> **JUST LIKE HEAVEN. / THROW DOWN / CHUNKS (A Last Rights Tune)**	78		Feb 90

(US version 12"ep+=/c-ep+=/cd-ep+=) (SST/+C/CD 244) – Freak scene / Keep the glove.

DONNA left and was repl. by **DON FLEMING** – guitar + **JAY SPIEGEL** – drums (both B.A.L.L.)

			Glitterhouse	Sub Pop
Jun 90.	(7"/7"white) (GR 0097) <SP 68> **THE WAGON. / BETTER THAN GONE**			

In Oct 90, J.MASCIS and other ex-DINOSAUR JR member FLEMING + SPIEGEL, made an album 'RAKE' as VELVET MONKEYS (aka B.A.L.L. + friends).

			Blanco Y Negro	Sire
Jan 91.	(7"/c-s) (NEG 48/+C) **THE WAGON. / THE LITTLE BABY**	49	-	

(12"+=/cd-s+=) (NEG 48 T/CD) – Pebbles + weeds / Quicksand.

Feb 91.	(lp/c/cd) (BYN 24/+C/CD) <26479> **GREEN MIND**	36		

– The wagon / Puke + cry / Blowing it / I live for that look / Flying cloud / How'd you pin that one on me / Water / Muck / Thumb / Green mind.

Aug 91.	(7"/c-s) (NEG 52/+C) **WHATEVER'S COOL WITH ME. / SIDEWAYS**			

(12"+=/cd-s+=) (NEG 52 T/CD) – Thumb (live) / Keep the glove (live).

MASCIS + **MURPH** introduced new member **MIKE JOHNSON** (b.27 Aug'65, Grant's Pass, Oregon, USA) – bass (ex-MARK LANEGAN, ex-GEORGE LANE, ex-SNAKEPIT)

Nov 92.	(7") (NEG 60) **GET ME. / HOT BURRITO #2**	44	-	

(c-s+=/12"+=/cd-s+=) (NEG 60 C/T/CD) – Qwest (live).

Jan 93.	(7") (NEG 61) **START CHOPPIN'. / TURNIP FARM**	20	-	

(10"+=/12"+=/cd-s+=) (NEG 61 TEP/T/CD) – Forget it.

Feb 93.	(lp/c/cd) (BYN 28/+C/CD) <45108> **WHERE YOU BEEN?**	10	50	

– Out there / Start choppin' / What else is new? / On the way / Not the same / Get me / Drawerings / Hide / Goin' home / I ain't sayin'.

Jun 93.	(7"/c-s/12") (NEG 63/+C/T) **OUT THERE. / KEEBLIN' (live) / KRACKED (live)**	44		

(10"+=) (NEG 63TE) – Post.
(cd-s+++=) (NEG 63CD) – Quest (live).
(cd-s) (NEG 63CDX) – ('A'side) / Get me / Severed lips / Thumb (radio sessions).

now without MURPH

Aug 94.	(7"/c-s) (NEG 74/+C) **FEEL THE PAIN. / GET OUT OF THIS**	25		

(10"etched+=/cd-s+=) (NEG 74 TE/CD) – Repulsion (acoustic).

Sep 94.	(cd/c/lp) (4509 96933-2/-4/-1) <45719> **WITHOUT A SOUND**	24	44	

– Feel the pain / I don't think so / Yeah right / Outta hand / Grab it / Even you / Mind glow / Get out of this / On the brink / Seemed like the thing to do / Over your shoulder.

Feb 95.	(7"green/c-s) (NEG 77 X/C) **I DON'T THINK SO. / GET ME (live)**	67		

(cd-s+=) (NEG 77CD) – What else is new? / Sludge.

Mar 97.	(c-s/12"/cd-s) (NEG 103 C/T/CD) **TAKE A RUN AT THE SUN. / DON'T YOU THINK IT'S TIME / THE PICKLE SONG**	53		

Mar 97.	(cd/c/lp) (0630 18312-2/-4/-1) <46506> **HAND IT OVER**			

– Take a run at the sun / Never bought it / Nothin's goin' on / I'm insane / Can't we move this alone / Sure not over you / Loaded / Mick / I know yer insane / Gettin' rough / Gotta know.

			Trade 2	not iss.
Sep 97.	(7") (TRDSC 009) **I'M INSANE. / I MISUNDERSTOOD**			-

– compilations, etc. –

1990.	(10"m-lp) S.S.T.; (SST 275) **FOSSILS**		-	

MIKE JOHNSON

with **BARRETT MARTIN, AL LARSEN + DAVID KRUEGER**

			not iss.	Up
Nov 94.	(cd) <8> **WHERE AM I?**		-	

– Overland – Turn back alone / Save today / Separation / Untitled / Second lovers song / Down the line / Love and other crimes / See through / If you're gone / Carry on / 100% off / Atrophy.

now with his wife **LESLIE HARDY** – bass (of JUNED, who he produced) / **J. MASCIS, BARRETT MARTIN + MARK LANEGAN**

			Atlantic	Atlantic
Apr 96.	(cd/c) <(7567 92669-2/-4)> **YEAR OF MONDAYS**			Feb96

– Where am I? / One way out / The way it will be – Too far / Another side / Circle / Eclipse / Left in the dark / Hold the reins / Say it's so / Overdrive.

now with **KRUEGER, JOHN ATKINS, ELI BRADEN, DAN PETERS, TIFFANY ANDERS, CLAUDIA GROOM + BRETT ARNOLD**

			not iss.	Up
Aug 98.	(cd) <UP 057> **I FEEL ALRIGHT**		-	

– All there is / Turn around / I don't love you / Minor aversion / Not over yet / Leaving Greensleeves / I've got to have you / One liner / Message to pretty / Impatient and unwilling / Performer / Tradewinds.

J. MASCIS

			WEA	Warners
May 96.	(cd/c) <(46177)> **MARTIN + ME**			Apr96

– Thumb / So what else is new / Get me / Blowin' it / Repulsion / Goin' home / The boy with the thorn in his side / Not you again / On the run / Keeblin / Flying cloud / Anticipation / Drawerings / Every mother's son.

DIO (dig out; Great Metal . . .)

DION

Born: DION DiMUCCI, 18 Jul'39, The Bronx, New York, USA. Exercising his boyhood tonsils on street corners with fellow Italian-American Doo-Wop devotees, DION had his first taste of professional performing after being picked to appear on the Teen Club TV show in Philadelphia. In 1957, he formed DION & THE TIMBERLAINES, who, after one flop single, became DION & THE BELMONTS. The following year, the group notched up their first US hit when 'I WONDER WHY' made the Top 30. Chart regulars from then on in, the clean-cut DION and crew amassed several further hits including their finest two minutes, 'A TEENAGER IN LOVE', an angst-ridden schoolyard anthem that furnished them with their first Top 5 US hit and a new line in designer college sweat shirts. DION was lucky just to be able to enjoy his success; a few months previous (3rd February, 1959), he narrowly escaped death after declining a ride on the doomed charter plane that killed BUDDY HOLLY, RITCHIE VALENS and BIG BOPPER. Towards the end of 1960, DION, on the advice of his manager, embarked on a successful solo career that spawned two US million sellers, 'RUNAROUND SUE' and 'THE WANDERER' (also major hits in the UK). Although his run of success continued with 'LOVERS WHO WANDER', 'LITTLE DIANE', 'LOVE CAME TO ME' and 'RUBY BABY' (the latter his first effort for new label, 'Columbia'), privately DION was battling with a drugs problem. Like many teen idols of the day, his career took a bit of a battering with the onslaught of the British Invasion during 1964. He subsequently moved through roots-blues before reinventing himself as a mellow folk-protest singer in 1968 with the US Top 5 tribute single, 'ABRAHAM, MARTIN AND JOHN' (a big UK hit for MARVIN GAYE a few years later); he finally kicked his habit to touch the same year. After a further series of misguided cover versions (including 'PURPLE HAZE'!), DION & THE BELMONTS re-formed for a one-off special on the 2nd June, 1972, at Madison Square Garden; the 'REUNION' album quickly followed. For the remainder of the 70's and on into the 80's, DION lingered in the commercial wilderness and subsequently converted to Christianity. However, in 1989, the man returned in fine style with a harder-edged rock'n'roll set, 'YO FRANKIE', masterminded by producer DAVE EDMUNDS. • **Songwriters:** Penned some of own material, except several by ERNIE MARESCA. The group worked in the late 1950's with writers DOC POMUS and MORT SHUMAN. Covered; WHERE OR WHEN (Rodgers & Hart) / WHEN YOU WISH UPON A STAR (?) / IN THE STILL OF THE NIGHT (Cole Porter). DION solo covered RUBY BABY + DRIP DROP (Leiber-Stoller) / COME GO WITH ME (Del Vikings) / I'M YOUR HOOCHIE COOCHIE MAN (Muddy Waters) / JOHNNY B. GOODE (Chuck Berry) / SPOONFUL (Willie Dixon) / ABRAHAM, MARTIN & JOHN (Dick Holler) / PURPLE HAZE (Jimi Hendrix) / FROM BOTH SIDES NOW (Joni Mitchell) / AND THE NIGHT STOOD STILL (Diane Warren) / SAN DIEGO SERENADE (Tom Waits) / etc. • **Trivia:** DION was featured on the sleeve of the BEATLES' 'Sgt. Pepper' album.

Best CD compilation: THE BEST OF DION & THE BELMONTS (*7)

DION & THE BELMONTS

DION DiMUCCI – lead vocals / **CARLO MASTRANGELO** (b. 5 Oct'39) – vocals / **FRED MILANO** (b.26 Aug'40) – vocals / **ANGELO D'ALEO** (b. 3 Feb'41) – vocals

		not iss.	Mohawk
1957.	(7",78; as DION & THE TIMBERLAINES) <105> **THE CHOSEN FEW. / OUT IN COLORADO** <re-iss. 1957 on 'Jubilee'; 5294>	-	
1957.	(7",78; as The BELMONTS) <106> **TEEN-AGE CLEMENTINE. / SANTA MARGUERITA**	-	
1958.	(7",78) <107> **WE WENT AWAY. / TAG ALONG**	-	

		London	Laurie
Jul 58.	(7",78) (HL 8646) <3013> **I WONDER WHY. / TEEN ANGEL**		22 May58
Oct 58.	(7",78) (HL 8718) <3015> **NO ONE KNOWS. / I CAN'T GO ON (ROSALIE)**		19 Aug58
Feb 59.	(7",78) (HL 8799) <3021> **DON'T PITY ME. / JUST YOU**		40 Dec58
Jun 59.	(7",78) (HLU 8874) <3027> **A TEENAGER IN LOVE. / I'VE CRIED BEFORE**	28	5 Apr59
Oct 59.	(lp) (HA-U 2194) <LLP 2002> **PRESENTING DION & THE BELMONTS** – I wonder why / Teen angel / Where or when / You better not do that / Just you / I got the blues / Don't pity me / A teenager in love / Wonderful girl / Funny feeling / I've cried before / That's my desire / No one knows / I can't go on (Rosalie). (UK-iss.1984 on 'Ace'; CH 107) (cd-iss. 1989; CDCHM 107)		

— now a trio when D'ALEO was conscripted to US navy

Nov 59.	(7",78) (7N 25038) <3035> **EVERY LITTLE THING I DO. / A LOVER'S PRAYER**		48 73 Sep59

(above single on 'Pye Int.' UK)

Jan 60.	(7",78) (HLU 9030) <3044> **WHERE OR WHEN. / THAT'S MY DESIRE**		3 Dec59

		Top Rank	Laurie
Apr 60.	(7") <3052> **WHEN YOU WISH UPON A STAR. / WONDERFUL GIRL**	-	30
May 60.	(7") (JAR 368) **WHEN YOU WISH UPON A STAR. / MY PRIVATE JOY**	-	
Jul 60.	(7") <3059> **IN THE STILL OF THE NIGHT. / A FUNNY FEELING**	-	38
Sep 60.	(7") (JAR 503) **IN THE STILL OF THE NIGHT. / SWINGING ON A STAR**	-	-
Dec 60.	(lp; with others) (25-027) **THE TOPPERMOST – VOL.1** – When you wish upon a star / In the still of the night / My private joy / My day begins with you / Swinging on a star / All the things you are / Paper moon / In other words / I'm through with love / When the red, red robin / September song.	-	-

DION

— went solo; The BELMONTS signed to 'Sabina' and issued their own 45's

Nov 60.	(7") (JAR 521) <3070> **LONELY TEENAGER. / LITTLE MISS BLUE**	47	12 96 Oct60
Nov 60.	(lp) <LLP 2004> **ALONE WITH DION** – Lonely teenager / After the dance / P.S. I love you / Save the last dance for me / Little Miss Blue / Havin' fun / Close your eyes / Fools rush in / My one and only love / North east end of the corner / One for my baby / Then I'll be tired of you. (re-iss. 1985 on 'Ace'; CH 115)		-
Feb 61.	(7") (JAR 545) <3081> **HAVIN' FUN. / NORTH-EAST END OF THE CORNER**		42
Apr 61.	(7") <3090> **KISSIN' GAME. / HEAVEN HELP ME**	-	82
May 61.	(lp; as DION & THE BELMONTS) <LLP 2006> **WISH UPON A STAR** (collection) – When you wish upon a star / In the still of the night / A lover's prayer / My private joy / My day / Swinging on a star / All the things you are / It's only a paper moon / In other words / I'm through with love / When the red, red robin comes bob, bob bobbin' along / September song. (re-iss. 1985 on 'Ace'; CH 138)	-	
Jul 61.	(7") <3101> **SOMEBODY NOBODY WANTS. / COULD SOMEBODY TAKE MY PLACE TONIGHT**	-	
Oct 61.	(7") (JAR 586) <3110> **RUNAROUND SUE. / RUNAWAY GIRL** (re-iss. Aug76 on 'Philips') (re-iss. Aug82 on 'EMI Gold')	11	1 Sep61
Dec 61.	(lp) (CLP 1539) <LLP 2009> **RUNAROUND SUE** – Runaround Sue / Somebody wants me / Dream lover / Life is but a dream / The wanderer / Runaway girl / I'm gonna make it somehow / The majestic / Could somebody take my place tonight / Little star / Lonely world / In the still of the night / Kansas City / Take good care of my baby. (re-iss. 1985 on 'Ace'; CH 148) (cd-iss. Aug89; CDCHM 148)		11 Nov61

		H.M.V.	Laurie
Feb 62.	(7") (POP 971) <3115> **THE WANDERER. / THE MAJESTIC**	10	2 36 Nov61
May 62.	(7") (POP 1020) <3123> **LOVERS WHO WANDER. / (I WAS) BORN TO CRY**		3 42 Apr62

		Stateside	Laurie
Aug 62.	(7") (SS 115) <3134> **LITTLE DIANE. / LOST FOR SURE**		8 Jul62
Aug 62.	(lp) (SL 10034) <LLP 2009> **LOVERS WHO WANDER** – Lovers who wander / Come go with me / King without a queen / So long friend / Twist / Little Diane / Mi muchacha / Stagger Lee / Shout / Tonight, tonight / Born to cry / Queen of the hop / Candy man / Sandy / Lost for sure / Love came to me. (UK-iss.Jan86 on 'Ace'; CH 163)		8 Jul62
Nov 62.	(7") (SS 139) <3145> **LOVE CAME TO ME. / LITTLE GIRL**		10

		C.B.S.	Columbia
Jan 63.	(7") (AAG 133) <42662> **RUBY BABY. / HE'LL ONLY HURT YOU**		2
Mar 63.	(7"; stereo/mono) (S+/BPG 62137) <CS 8810> **RUBY BABY** – Ruby baby / The end of the world / Go away little girl / Gonna make it alone / Fever / My mammy / Will love ever come my way / The loneliest man in the world / You made me love you (I didn't want to do it) / He'll only hurt you / You're nobody 'til somebody loves you / Unloved, unwanted me.		20

May 63.	(7") (AAG 145) <42776> **THIS LITTLE GIRL. / THE LONELIEST MAN IN THE WORLD**		21 Apr63
Jul 63.	(7") (AAG 161) <42810> **BE CAREFUL OF STONES THAT YOU THROW. / I CAN'T BELIEVE (THAT YOU DON'T LOVE ME ANYMORE)**		31

DION DiMUCCI

Sep 63.	(7") (AAG 169) <42852> **DONNA THE PRIMA DONNA. / YOU'RE MINE**		6
Sep 63.	(lp; stereo/mono) (S+/BPG 62203) <CS 8907> **DONNA THE PRIMA DONNA** – Donna the prima donna / Can't we be sweethearts / Sweet, sweet baby / This little girl of mine / Flim flam / Troubled man / This little girl / Oh happy days / You're mine / Donna / I can't believe (that you don't love me anymore) / Be careful of stones that you throw.		
Nov 63.	(7") (AAG 177) <42917> **DRIP DROP. / NO ONE'S WAITING FOR ME**		6
Mar 64.	(7") (AAG 188) <42977> **I'M YOUR HOOCHIE COOCHIE MAN. / THE ROAD I'M ON (GLORIA)**		
1964.	(lp; as DION & THE BELMONTS) <LLP 2016> **TOGETHER WITH THE BELMONTS** – We belong together / Every little thing I do / Meant to be / Come take a walk with me / Tag along / Teen angel / Such a long way / We went away / I can't go on / That's how I need you / Will you love me still / Faith.	-	
Oct 64.	(7") (AAG 224) <43096> **JOHNNY B. GOODE. / CHICAGO BLUES**		71
Mar 65.	(7") (201728) <43213> **SWEET SWEET BABY. / UNLOVED, UNWANTED ME**		
Jun 65.	(7"; as DION) (201780) <43293> **SPOONFUL. / KICKIN' CHILD**		

— In 1966, he formed folk-pop outfit

DION & THE WANDERERS

1966.	(7") <43423> **YOU MOVE ME BABE. / TOMORROW WON'T BRING THE RAIN**	-	
1966.	(7") <43483> **TIME IN MY HEART FOR YOU. / WAKE UP BABY**	-	
1966.	(7") <43692> **SO MUCH YOUNGER. / TWO TON FEATHER**	-	

DION & THE BELMONTS

— (see last line-up)

		H.M.V.	ABC Paramount
Nov 66.	(7") (POP 1565) <10868> **BERIMBAU (MY GIRL). / THE MONTH OF MAY**		
Mar 67.	(7") (POP 1585) <10896> **MOVIN' MAN. / FOR BOBBIE**		
May 67.	(lp) (CLP 3618) NANCS 599> **TOGETHER AGAIN** – Movin' man / Berimbau / Come to my side / All I wanna do / But not for me / New York town / Loserville / For Bobbie / Jump back baby / Baby you've been on my mind / My girl / The month of May. (re-iss. 1969 on 'B&C'; CAS 1002)		

DION

		not iss.	Columbia
1968.	(lp) <CS 9773> **WONDER WHERE I'M BOUND** – I can't help but wonder where I'm bound / It's all over now, baby blue / A Sunday kind of love / Knowing I won't go back there / 900 miles / Now / Southern train / The seventh son / Farewell / Wake up baby / Baby, please don't go.		

		London	Laurie
Nov 68.	(7") (HLP 10229) <3463> **ABRAHAM, MARTIN AND JOHN. / DADDY ROLLIN'** (re-iss. Mar75 on 'UK Decca')		4 Oct68
Dec 68.	(lp; mono/stereo) (HA-P/SH-P 8390) <SLP 2047> **DION** – Abraham, Martin and John / Purple haze / Tomorrow is a long time / Everybody's talkin' / Sonny boy / The dolphins / He looks a lot like me / Sun fun song / From both sides now / Sisters of mercy / Loving you is sweeter than ever. (re-iss. Feb87 as 'ABRAHAM, MARTIN & JOHN' on 'Ace'; CH 204)		
Feb 69.	(7") <3478> **PURPLE HAZE. / THE DOLPHINS**	-	63
Apr 69.	(7") <3495> **FROM BOTH SIDES NOW. / SUN FUN SONG**	-	91

		Warners	Warners
Jun 69.	(7") <3504> **LOVING YOU IS SWEETER THAN EVER. / HE LOOKS A LOT LIKE ME**	-	
Jun 69.	(7") (HLP 10277) <3495> **BOTH SIDES NOW. / SONNY BOY**	-	
Jan 70.	(7") <(WB 7356)> **IF WE ONLY HAVE LOVE. / NATURAL MAN**		
Jul 70.	(7") <(WS 1826)> **SIT DOWN OLD FRIEND** – Natural man / I don't believe my race is run / Jammed up blues / Little pink pony / You can't judge a book by the cover / If we only have love / Sweet pea / Just a little girl / Let go, let God / King con man / Sit down old friend.		
Aug 70.	(7") <(WB 7401)> **YOUR OWN BACK YARD / SIT DOWN OLD FRIEND**		75
Apr 71.	(7") <WB 7469> **CLOSE TO IT ALL. / LET IT BE**		
Apr 71.	(7") (WB 6120) **CLOSE TO IT ALL. / WINDOWS**		
Apr 71.	(lp) <(WS 1872)> **YOU'RE NOT ALONE** – Close to it all / Sunniland / Windows / The visitor / Peaceful place / Let it be / The stuff I got / Blackbird / Josie / Attraction works better than promotion.		
Jun 71.	(7") <7491> **JOSIE. / SUNNILAND**	-	
Jul 71.	(7") (K 16100) **SUNNILAND. / PEACEFUL PLACE**	-	
Dec 71.	(lp) (K 46122) <WS 1945> **SANCTUARY** (some live) – Sunshine lady / Sanctuary / Willigo / Harmony sound / Gotta get up / Please be my friend / Take a little time / The wanderer / Abraham, Martin and John / Almond joy / Ruby baby / Brand new morning.		
May 72.	(7") (K 16132) <7537> **SANCTUARY. / BRAND NEW MORNING**		
Nov 72.	(lp) (K 46199) <WS 2642> **SUITE FOR LATE SUMMER**		

– Seagull / Wedding song / Jennifer knew / It all fits together / To dream tomorrow / Didn't you change / Tennessee Madonna / Traveler in the rain / Running close behind you.

Nov 72.	(7") <7663> **RUNNING CLOSE BEHIND YOU. / SEAGULL**	-	

—— On 2nd of Jun'72 DION re-united with The BELMONTS for a live one-off

Feb 73.	(lp) (K 46208) <2664> **REUNION (live at Madison Square Garden)**		

– The wanderer / No one knows / I wonder why / Teenager in love / Ruby baby / That's my desire / Drip drop / Where or when / Runaround Sue / Little Diane.

1973.	(7") <7704> **DOCTOR ROCK AND ROLL. / SUNSHINE LADY**	-	
1973.	(7") <7793> **NEW YORK CITY SONG. / RICHER THAN A RICH MAN**	-	
1974.	(7") <8234> **HEY MY LOVE. / LOVER BOY SUPREME**	-	
1974.	(7") <8258> **LOVER BOY SUPREME. / THE WAY YOU DO THE THINGS YOU DO**	-	
1974.	(7") <8293> **QUEEN OF '59. / OH THE NIGHT**	-	
1975.	(7") <8406> **YOUNG VIRGIN EYES (I'M ALL WRAPPED UP). / OH THE NIGHT**	-	

		Phil Spector Int.	Phil Spector Int.
1975.	(7") <16063> **BORN TO BE WITH YOU. / RUNNING CLOSE BEHIND YOU**		-
Jun 75.	(7") <0403> **MAKE THE WOMAN LOVE ME. / RUNNING CLOSE BEHIND YOU**		-
Oct 75.	(lp) (2307 002) <002> **BORN TO BE WITH YOU**		-

– Born to be with you / ake the woman love me / Your own backyard / He's got the whole world in his hands / Only you know / New York City song / In and out of showers / Good vin' man.

Feb 76.	(7") (2010 012) **BORN TO BE WITH YOU. / GOOD LOVIN' MAN**		-
Aug 76.	(7") (2010 018) **BABY LET'S STICK TOGETHER. / NEW YORK CITY SONG**		-

		Warners.	Warners
Aug 76.	(lp) (K 56279) <BS 2954> **STREETHEART**		

– Runaway man / Streetheart / Hey my love / On the night / Lover boy supreme / Queen of '59 / You showed me what love is / More to you / If I can just get through the night.

Aug 76.	(7") (K 16801) **YOU SHOWED ME WHAT LOVE IS. / LOVER BOY SUPREME**		

		not iss.	Lifesong
1978.	(lp) <35356> **RETURN OF THE WANDERER**	-	

– Lookin' for the heart of Saturday night / Midtown American main street gang / You've awakened something in me / Guitar queen / The pattern of my lifeline / (I used to be a) Brooklyn Dodger / Streetheart theme / The power of love within / Spanish Harlem incident / Do you believe in magic. (cd-iss. Jun90 on 'Ace')

1978.	(7") <1765> **LOOKING FOR THE HEART OF SATURDAY NIGHT. / YOU'VE AWAKENED SOMETHING IN ME**	-	
1978.	(7") <1770> **GUITAR QUEEN. / MIDTOWN AMERICAN MAIN STREET GANG**	-	
1978.	(7") <1785> **(I USED TO BE A) BROOKLYN DODGER. / STREETHEART THEME**	-	

		Dayspring	Dayspring
1982.	(lp/c) <(DAY/TCDAY 4006)> **INSIDE JOB**		-

– I believe / He's the one / Centre of my life / Truth will set you free / Gonna be ready / Old souvenirs / New Jersey wife / Man in the glass / Sweet Surrender.

		Aura	Dayspring
Oct 83.	(7") (AUS 39) **WE DON'T TALK ANYMORE. / MIDNIGHT LOVER**		-
Aug 84.	(7") (AUS 42) **THE WAY YOU DO THE THINGS YOU DO. / HEY MY LOVE**		-

		Dayspring	Dayspring
1984.	(lp/c) <(DAY/TCDAY 4016)> **I PUT AWAY MY IDOLS**		-

– Here is my servant / Trust in my Lord / Day of the Lord / I put away my idols / Daddy / Very soon / He won't tell you / Healing / Give up and surrender / My prayer for you.

1985.	(lp/c) <(DAY/TCDAY 4032)> **KINGDOM IN THE STREETS**		

DION

—— with **DAVE EDMUNDS** – guitar, bass / **JIM HORN** – sax / **PHIL CHEN** – bass / **CHUCK LEAVELL** – keyboards / **DAVE CHARLES** – percussion

		Arista	Arista
Jun 89.	(7") (112 408) <9797> **AND THE NIGHT STOOD STILL. / TOWER OF LOVE**		75 May89

(12"+=/cd-s+=) (612/662 408) – The wanderer.

Jun 89.	(lp/c/cd) (209/409/259 766) <8549> **YO FRANKIE**		May89

– King of the New York streets / And the night stood still / Yo Frankie (she's all right with me) / I've got to get to you / Medley:- Written on the subway wall – Little star / Drive all night / Always in the rain / Loving you is killing me / Tower of love / Serenade.

Jul 89.	(7") (112 556) **KING OF THE NEW YORK STREETS. / THE WANDERER**	74	

(12"+=/cd-s+=) (612/662 556) –

Feb 90.	(7"ep/cd-ep) (112/662 910) **WRITTEN ON THE SUBWAY WALL - LITTLE STAR (medley) / KING OF THE NEW YORK STREETS. / AND THE NIGHT STOOD STILL / TOWER OF LOVE**		

– compilations, etc. –

Dec 62.	(lp) Laurie; <2013> **DION SINGS HIS GREATEST HITS**	-	29
Mar 63.	(7") Stateside; (SS 161) / Laurie; <3153> **SANDY. / FAITH**	-	21 Feb63
Jun 63.	(lp) Laurie; <2017> **DION SINGS TO SANDY (AND ALL HIS OTHER GIRLS)**	-	
Jul 63.	(7") Stateside; (SS 209) / Laurie; <3171> **COME GO WITH ME. / KING WITHOUT A QUEEN**		48 Jun63
1964.	(7") Laurie; <3187> **LONELY WORLD. / TAG ALONG**	-	

1965.	(7") Laurie; <3225> **THEN I'LL BE TIRED OF YOU. / AFTER THE DANCE**	-	
1965.	(7") Laurie; <3240> **SHOUT. / LITTLE GIRL**	-	
1966.	(7") Laurie; <3303> **(I WAS) BORN TO CRY. / I GOT THE BLUES**	-	
Mar 73.	(lp) Columbia; <31942> **DION'S GREATEST HITS** (re-iss. Apr74 & Dec81 on 'R.C.A.'-UK / 'Laurie'-US)	-	
Apr 76.	(7") Philips; (6146 700) **THE WANDERER. / LITTLE DIANE**	16	-
Jul 76.	(lp) Sonic; (SON 001) **PICK HITS OF THE RADIO GOOD GUYS VOL.1**		
Jul 76.	(lp) Sonic; (SON 004) **PICK HITS OF THE RADIO GOOD GUYS VOL.2**		
Jul 76.	(lp) Sonic; (SON 019) **PICK HITS OF THE RADIO GOOD GUYS VOL.3**		
Oct 76.	(7") Philips; (6146 705) **A TEENAGER IN LOVE. / I CAN'T GO ON (ROSALIE)**		
May 79.	(lp) Ensign; (ENGY 8) **DION & THE BELMONTS**		
Mar 80.	(lp) K-Tel; (NE 1057) **DION AND THE BELMONTS' 20 GOLDEN GREATS**	31	-
Oct 80.	(7"m) Philips; **THE WANDERER. / RUNAROUND SUE / I WONDER WHY**		
Aug 81.	(7") RCA-Gold; (GOLD 525) **THE WANDERER. / LOVE COME BACK TO ME**		
Aug 81.	(7") RCA-Gold; (GOLD 526) **RUNAROUND SUE. / RUNAWAY GIRL**		
Aug 81.	(7") RCA-Gold; (GOLD 527) **A TEENAGER IN LOVE. / I WONDER WHY**		
Jun 84.	(7") Old Gold; (OG 9403) **THE WANDERER. / LOVERS WHO WANDER**		
Jun 84.	(7") Old Gold; (OG 9404) **RUNAROUND SUE. / LONELY TEENAGER**		
Jun 84.	(7") Old Gold; (OG 9405) **A TEENAGER IN LOVE. / WHERE OR WHEN**		
Nov 85.	(lp) Ace; (CH 155) **SO WHY DIDN'T YOU DO THAT THE FIRST TIME**		
Aug 86.	(lp/c/cd; as DION & THE BELMONTS) Ace; (CHA/CHC/CDCH 176) **HITS**		
Jan 88.	(cd) Ace; (CDCH 915) **RUNAROUND SUE – THE BEST OF THE REST**		
1988.	(lp/c; as DION & THE BELMONTS) WEA; (K/K4 26049) **ROCK'N'ROLL FOREVER**		
Jul 88.	(lp) Masterpiece; (42917) **DRIP DROP**		-
Oct 88.	(lp/c) B.R. Music; (BRLP/BRMC 19) **20 GREATEST HITS**		-
Feb 89.	(cd-ep) Old Gold; (OG 6112) **THE WANDERER / RUNAROUND SUE / A TEENAGER IN LOVE**		
May 90.	(cd) Ace; (CH 294) **RETURN OF THE WANDERER**		
May 90.	(lp) Ace; (CH 295) **FIRE IN THE NIGHT**		
Jun 90.	(cd) Ace; (CDCHD 936) **RETURN OF THE WANDERER / FIRE IN THE NIGHT**		
Sep 90.	(cd) Ace; (CDCH 945) **WISH UPON A STAR / ALONE WITH DION**		
Feb 91.	(cd) Ace; (CDCHD 943) **LOVERS WHO WANDER / SO WHY DIDN'T YOU DO THAT THE FIRST TIME**		
Mar 91.	(cd) Ace; (CDCHD 966) **PRESENTING DION & THE BELMONTS / RUNAROUND SUE**		
Sep 91.	(cd/c) Ace; (CDFAB/FABC 002) **THE FABULOUS DION & THE BELMONTS**		

– Where or when / A teenager in love / I wonder why / No one knows / Don't pity me / Every little thing I do / A lover's prayer / When you wish upon a star / In the still of the night / I can't go on (Rosalie) / That's my desire / Wonderful girl.

Sep 91.	(cd/c) Ace; (CDFAB/FABC 008) **THE FABULOUS DION**		

– Runaround Sue / The wanderer / Lovers who wander / Little Diane / Love came to me / Lonely teenager / Little Miss Blue / The majestic / (I was) Born to cry / Sandy / Come go with me / Havin' fun.

Apr 92.	(cd/c) Legacy; (469060-2/-4) **BRONX BLUES (THE COLUMBIA RECORDINGS 1962-1965)**		
Oct 92.	(cd) Vision; (VR 3327) **DREAM ON FIRE**		-
May 93.	(cd) Ce De Int.; (CD 66075) **ALL THE HITS**		-
Apr 96.	(cd/c) Music For Pleasure; CD/TC MFP 6218) **THE BEST OF DION & THE BELMONTS**		
Feb 97.	(d-cd) Legacy; (486823-2) **THE ROAD I'M ON (A RETROSPECTIVE)**		
Apr 97.	(cd) Ace; (CDCHD 644) **THE BEST OF THE GOSPEL YEARS**		-
Apr 99.	(d-cd) Collector's Choice; (WSCCM 0071-2) **THE COMPLETE DION AND THE BELMONTS**		

DIRE STRAITS

Formed: Deptford, London, England . . . mid-'77 by ex-teacher and journalist MARK KNOPFLER alongside brother DAVID, JOHN ILLSLEY and PICK WITHERS. After Radio 1 DJ, Charlie Gillett gave their demo an airing later the same year, they were signed to 'Vertigo' by A&R man, John Stainze, releasing a classic debut single, 'SULTANS OF SWING', in Spring '78. A driving but subtle slice of rootsy, bluesy R&B, the song was a wonderfully observed snapshot of the London pub rock scene where they'd initially plied their trade. Although it failed to chart, their eponymous debut album (released later that summer) made the UK Top 40 after rave live reviews and a major deal with 'Warners' in the States. Comparisons with BOB DYLAN's easier going material and the laidback (horizontal, even!) country-blues grooves of J.J. CALE were the favoured choice of salivating critics although KNOPFLER's dry wit and unmistakable guitar lines gave DIRE STRAITS the stamp of authenticity. In fact, DYLAN was so impressed he invited KNOPFLER to augment him on his 1979 set, 'SLOW TRAIN COMING'; by this point, both the debut single and album had amassed transatlantic

Top 10 sales with the help of a sell-out US tour while a follow-up set, 'COMMUNIQUE' (1979), further developed KNOPFLER's narrative skills on the likes of the epic 'ONCE UPON A TIME IN THE WEST'. With HAL LINDES replacing the departing DAVID and ex-E STREET BAND man, ROY BITTAN drafted in on keyboards, 'MAKING MOVIES' (1980) took a harder-edged yet more melodic, accesible and expansive approach; vivid story-songs such as the bittersweet 'ROMEO AND JULIET' saw KNOPFLER compared to SPRINGSTEEN while the heady momentum of 'TUNNEL OF LOVE' effortlessly conjured up the giddy thrills and spills of a trip to the fairground. Opening with another compelling narrative in 'TELEGRAPH ROAD' and boasting the moody 'PRIVATE INVESTIGATIONS', 'LOVE OVER GOLD' (1982) became DIRE STRAITS' first UK No.1 album, the band flying in the face of fashion and selling millions. This was nothing, however, compared to the global phenomenon that was 'BROTHERS IN ARMS'; released in 1985 following the lengthy double live set, 'ALCHEMY' (1984), the record's glossy production and more focused pop-friendly approach saw it breaking UK sales records. Its biggest hit, 'MONEY FOR NOTHING', was an acerbic comment on US MTV domination, the accompanying video ironically caned by the channel in all its innovative, technology-enhanced glory. It was also the closest DIRE STRAITS ever veered towards heavy rock, the bulk of the material going in for coffee table, ear-massaging atmospherics and acoustic textures. The soft-focus minimalism of the title track is arguably DIRE STRAITS' finest moment and, despite the stigma surrounding the album, 'BROTHERS IN ARMS' remains an essential 80's release. Following the attendant mammoth touring commitments, DIRE STRAITS/KNOPFLER took an extended sabbatical with only a 1988 'best of' to keep fans happy. Having already scored soundtracks for 'Local Hero' (1983) and 'Cal' (1984), KNOPFLER was commissioned for both 'The Princess Bride' (1987) and 'Last Exit To Brooklyn' (1989). He also got back to his pub-rock roots with The NOTTING HILLBILLIES, releasing an album, 'MISSING . . . PRESUMED HAVING A GOOD TIME', in 1990. Later that year, he hooked up with country picker, CHET ATKINS, for the 'NECK AND NECK' album. DIRE STRAITS eventually returned in 1991 with 'ON EVERY STREET', an album which couldn't hope to emulate 'BROTHERS . . .' and didn't even try. It made No.1 all the same and sold enough to keep their record company happy in the meantime. With KNOPFLER actually recording a solo set proper, 'GOLDEN HEART', in 1996, the chances of a further DIRE STRAITS release seem slim although a split has yet to be confirmed. • **Songwriters:** KNOPFLER compositions, except The NOTTING HILLBILLIES cover of FEEL LIKE GOING HOME (Charlie Rich). • **Trivia:** MARK penned 'PRIVATE DANCER' for TINA TURNER in 1983, and also produced to name but a few; 'Infidels' for BOB DYLAN and 'Knife' for AZTEC CAMERA.

Album rating: DIRE STRAITS (*8) / COMMUNIQUE (*5) / MAKING MOVIES (*6) / LOVE OVER GOLD (*6) / ALCHEMY – LIVE (*7) / BROTHERS IN ARMS (*8) / MONEY FOR NOTHING compilation (*8) / ON EVERY STREET (*5) / ON THE NIGHT (*5) / Mark Knopfler: LOCAL HERO (*5) / GOLDEN HEART (*4)

MARK KNOPFLER (b.12 Aug'49, Glasgow, Scotland) – vocals, lead guitar / **DAVID KNOPFLER** (b.1951, Glasgow) – guitar / **JOHN ILLSLEY** (b.24 Jun'49, Leicester, England) – bass / **PICK WITHERS** – drums

		Vertigo	Warners
May 78.	(7") (6059 206) <8736> **SULTANS OF SWING. / EASTBOUND TRAIN** (re-iss. Feb79; same) – (hit No.8)		4 Jan79
Jun 78.	(lp)(c) (9102 021)(723 1015) <3266> **DIRE STRAITS** – Down to the waterline / Water of love / Setting me up / Six blade knife / Southbound train / Sultans of swing / Wild west end / Lions / In the gallery. (master edition Apr82; HS 9102 021) (cd-iss. 1987; 800 051-2) (cd re-iss. Jun96; same)	5	2 Oct78
Jul 79.	(7") (6059 230) <49006> **LADY WRITER. / WHERE DO YOU THINK YOU'RE GOING**		45
Aug 79.	(lp)(c) (9102 031)(723 1021) <3330> **COMMUNIQUE** – Once upon a time in the west / News / Where do you think you're going / Communique / Lady writer / Angel of mercy / Portobello belle / Single-handed sailor / Follow me home. (cd-iss. 1987; 800 052-2) (re-iss. Jun96; same)	5	11 Jun79
Oct 79.	(7") <49082> **ONCE UPON A TIME IN THE WEST. / NEWS**	-	

—— **HAL LINDES** (b.30 Jun'53, Monterey, Calif.) – guitar repl. DAVID who later went solo, also added **ROY BITTAN** – keyboards / (ex-E-STREET BAND BRUCE SPRINGSTEEN)

		Vertigo	Warners
Oct 80.	(lp/c) (6359/7150 034) <3480> **MAKING MOVIES** – Tunnel of love / Romeo and Juliet / Skateaway / Expresso love / Hand in hand / Solid rock / Les boys. (master edition Apr82; HS 6359 034) (cd-iss. 1987; 800 050-2) (cd re-iss. Jun96; same)	4	19 Nov80
Nov 80.	(7") (MOVIE 1) <49688> **ROMEO AND JULIET / SOLID ROCK**	8	Mar81
Dec 80.	(7") <49632> **SKATEAWAY. / SOLID ROCK**	-	58
Mar 81.	(7") (MOVIE 2) **SKATEAWAY. / EXPRESSO LOVE**	37	-
Sep 81.	(7") (MOVIE 3) **TUNNEL OF LOVE. / TUNNEL OF LOVE (part 2)**	54	-

—— **ALAN CLARK** (b. 5 Mar'52, Durham, England) – keyboards repl ROY.

		Vertigo	Warners
Aug 82.	(7"/10") (DSTR 1/+10) **PRIVATE INVESTIGATIONS. / BADGES POSTERS STICKERS T-SHIRTS**	2	-
Sep 82.	(lp/c) (6359/7150 109) <23728> **LOVE OVER GOLD** – Telegraph road / Private investigations / Industrial disease / Love over gold / It never rains / If I had you / Twisting by the pool / Two young lovers / Badges, posters, stickers, t-shirts. (cd-iss. 1984; 800 088-2; same)	1	19
Dec 82.	(7") <29880> **INDUSTRIAL DISEASE. / BADGES POSTERS STICKERS T-SHIRT**	-	75
Jan 83.	(7"/10"/12") (DSTR 2/+10/12) **TWISTING BY THE POOL. / TWO YOUNG LOVERS / IF I HAD YOU**	14	-
Mar 83.	(m-lp) <29800> **TWISTING BY THE POOL** – Twisting by the pool / Two young lovers / If I had you / Badges posters stickers T-shirts.	-	53

		Vertigo	Warners
May 83.	(7") <29706> **TWISTING BY THE POOL. / BADGES POSTERS STICKERS T-SHIRTS**	-	-

—— **IOMAR HAKIM** – drums, percussion repl. PICK above was replaced by **TERRY WILLIAMS** – drums ex-MAN, ex-MOTORS, ex-ROCKPILE / (both played on album below alongside **MARK, JOHN, HAL + ALAN**)

		Vertigo	Warners
Feb 84.	(7"/10"/12") (DSRT 6/+10/12) <> **LOVE OVER GOLD (live). / SOLID GOLD (live)**	50	
Mar 84.	(d-lp/c)(cd) (VERY/+C 11)(810243-2) <25085> **ALCHEMY – LIVE (live)** – Once upon a time in the west / Romeo and Juliet / Expresso love / Private investigations / Sultans of swing / Two young lovers / Tunnel of love / Telegraph road / Solid rock / Going home (theme from 'Local Hero'). (c+=/cd+=) – Love over gold (live). (cd re-iss. Jun96; same)	3	46 Apr84

—— added **GUY FLETCHER** – keyboards / also **JACK SONNI** – guitar (on tour)

		Vertigo	Warners
Apr 85.	(7"/10"/12") (DSRT 9/+10/12) **SO FAR AWAY. / WALK OF LIFE**	20	-
May 85.	(lp/c)(cd) (VERH/+C 25)(824499-2) <25264> **BROTHERS IN ARMS** – So far away / Money for nothing / Walk of life / Your latest trick / Why worry? / Ride across the river / The man's too strong / One world / Money for nothing / Brothers in arms. (c+=/cd+=; extended versions) – So far away / Money for nothing / Your latest trick / Why worry? (cd re-iss. Jun96; ame)	1	1
Jun 85.	(7"/10"/12")(7"sha-pic-d) (DSRT 10/+10/12)(DSPIC 10) <28950> **MONEY FOR NOTHING. / LOVE OVER GOLD (live)**	4	1
Oct 85.	(7") <28878> **WALK OF LIFE. / ONE WORLD**	-	7
Oct 85.	(7"sha-pic-d)(10") (DSPIC 11)(DSTR 11-10) **BROTHERS IN ARMS. / GOING HOME – THEME FROM 'LOCAL HERO' (live)**	16	
	(12"+=) (DSTR 11-12) – Why worry. (d7"++=) (DSTRD 11) – Sultans of swing / Eastbound train.		
Jan 86.	(7") (DSRT 12) **WALK OF LIFE. / TWO YOUNG LOVERS (live)**	2	
	(12"+=) (DSRT 12-12) – Sultans of swing. (d7"++=) (DSTRD 12) – Eastbound train (live).		
Feb 86.	(7") <28789> **SO FAR AWAY. / IF I HAD YOU**	-	19
Apr 86.	(7") (DSTR 13) **YOUR LATEST TRICK. / IRISH BOY**	26	
	(12"+=) (DSTR 13-12) – The long road.		
Oct 88.	(lp/c)(cd) (VERH/+C 64)(836419-2) <25794> **MONEY FOR NOTHING** (compilation) – Sultans of swing / Down to the waterline / Portobello belle (live) / Twisting by the pool / Tunnel of love / Romeo and Juliet / Where do you think you're going / Walk of life / Private investigations / Telegraph Road (live) / Money for nothing / Brothers in arms.	1	62 Nov88
Nov 88.	(7") (DSTR 15) **SULTANS OF SWING. / PORTOBELLO BELLE (live)**	62	
	(12"+=)(cd-s+=) (DSTR 15-12)(DSCD 15) – Romeo and Juliet / Money for nothing.		
Aug 91.	(7"/c-s) (DSTR/+C 16) **CALLING ELVIS. / IRON HAND**	21	
	(12"+=)(cd-s+=) (DSTR 16-12)(DSCD 16) – Millionaire blues.		
Sep 91.	(cd/c/lp) (510160-2/-4/-1) <26680> **ON EVERY STREET** – Calling Elvis / On every street / When it comes to you / Fade to black / The bug / You and your friend / Heavy fuel / Iron hand / Ticket to Heaven / My parties / Planet of New Orleans / How long.	1	12
Oct 91.	(7"/c-s) (DSTR/+C 17) <19094> **HEAVY FUEL. / PLANET OF NEW ORLEANS**	55	
	(12"+=)(cd-s+=) (DSTR 17-12)(DSCD 17) – Kingdom come.		
Feb 92.	(7"/c-s) (DSTR/+C 18) **ON EVERY STREET. / ROMEO AND JULIET**	42	-
	(cd-s+=) (DSCD 18) – Private investigations / Sultans of swing.		
Jun 92.	(7"/c-s) (DSTR/+C 19) **THE BUG. / TWISTING BY THE POOL**	67	
	(cd-s+=) (DSCD 19) – ('A'version).		

—— added touring band 91-93 **DANNY CUMMINGS** – percussion / **PHIL PALMER** – guitar / **PAUL FRANKLIN** – pedal steel / **CHRIS WHITE** – sax, flute / **CHRIS WHITTEN** – drums

		Vertigo	Warners
May 93.	(cd/c/lp) (514766-2/-4/-1) <45259> **ON THE NIGHT (live)** – Calling Elvis / Walk of life / Heavy fuel / Romeo & Juliet / Your latest trick / Private investigations / On every street / You and your friend / Money for nothing / Brothers in arms.	4	
May 93.	(c-ep/12"ep/cd-ep) (DSTRC/DSTR12/DSCD 20) **ENCORES LIVE EP (live)** – Your latest trick / The bug / Solid rock / Local hero (wild theme).	31	

—— Oct'93; MARK was credited on HANK MARVIN's single 'Wonderful Land'.

—— DIRE STRAITS looked to have disbanded since it has been five years since a recording.

– compilations, etc. –

		Vertigo	Warners
Oct 88.	(cd-video) Vertigo; (080 128-2) **SULTANS OF SWING / WILD WEST END / DOWN THE WATERLINE**		
Oct 88.	(cd-video) Vertigo; (080 130-2) **MONEY FOR NOTHING (extended) / ONE WORLD / SO FAR AWAY**		
Oct 88.	(cd-video) Vertigo; (080 132-2) **BROTHERS IN ARMS (extended) / YOUR LATEST TRICK / RIDE ACROSS THE RIVER**		
Oct 88.	(cd-video) Vertigo; (080 134-2) **WALK OF LIFE / WHY WORRY / RIDE ACROSS THE RIVER**		
Oct 88.	(cd-video) Vertigo; (080 136-2) **TWISTING BY THE POOL / TWO YOUNG LOVERS / IF I HAD YOU / TWISTING BY THE POOL**		
Jul 95.	(cd/c/lp) Windsong; (WIN CD/MC/LP 072) **LIVE AT THE BBC**	71	
Oct 98.	(cd/c) Warners; (558658-2/-4) <47130> **SULTANS OF SWING – THE VERY BEST OF DIRE STRAITS** – Sultans of swing / Lady writer / Romeo and Juliet / Tunnel of love / Private investigations / Twisting by the pool / Love over gold / So far away / Money for	6	

nothing / Brothers in arms / Walk of life / Calling Elvis / Heavy fuel / On every street / Your latest trick / Local hero – Wild theme. *(also d-cd; 538003-2)*

MARK KNOPFLER

(first with **CLARK, LINDES** plus **MIKE BRECKER** – sax)

	Vertigo	Warners
Feb 83. (7"/12") *(DSTR 4/+12)* <29725> **GOING HOME (THEME OF 'LOCAL HERO'). / SMOOCHING**	56	
Apr 83. (lp/c) *(VERL/+C 4)* **MUSIC FROM THE FILM SOUNDTRACK 'LOCAL HERO'**	14	

– The rocks and the water / Wild theme / Freeway flyer / Boomtown / The way it always starts / The rocks and the thunder / The ceilidh and the northern lights / The mist covered mountains / The ceilidh: Louis' favourite Billy's tune / Whistle theme / Smooching / The rocks and the thunder / Going home (theme from 'Local Hero'). *(cd-iss. Jul84; 811 038-2)*

	Vertigo	Warners
Jul 83. (7") *(DSTR 5)* **THEME FROM LOCAL HERO: WILD THEME. / GOING HOME**		-
Jul 84. (12") *(DSTR 7-12)* **JOY (FROM 'COMFORT AND JOY'). / FISTFUL OF ICE CREAM**		-
Sep 84. (7"/ext.12") *(DSTR 8/+12)* **THE LONG ROAD (THEME FROM CAL'). / IRISH BOY**		-
Oct 84. (lp/c/cd) *(VERH/+C 17)(822 769-2)* **CAL (MUSIC FROM THE FILM)**	65	

– Irish boy / The road / Waiting for her / Irish love / A secret place / Where will you go? / Father and son / Meeting under the trees / Potato picking / in a secret place / Fear and hatred / Love and guilt / The long road.

	Vertigo	Warners
Oct 86. (7") *(DSTR 14)* **GOING HOME. / WILD THEME**		-
(12"+=) *(DSTR 14-12)* – Smooching.		
(cd-s+=) *(DSCD 14)* – Comfort (from 'Comfort And Joy').		
Nov 87. (lp/c)(cd) *(VERH/+C 53)(832 864-2)* **MUSIC FROM THE FILM SOUNDTRACK 'THE PRINCESS BRIDE'**		

– Once upon a time . . . storybook love / I will never love again / Florin dance / Morning ride / The friends' song / The cliffs of insanity / The sword fight / Guide my sword / The fireswamp and the rodents of unusual size / Revenge / A happy ending / Storybook love.

	Vertigo	Warners
Mar 88. (7"-c-s; with WILLY DeVILLE) *(VER/+MC 37)* **THEME FROM 'THE PRINCESS BRIDE': STORYBOOK LOVE. / THE FRIENDS' SONG (with GUY FLETCHER)**		-
(cd-s+=) *(VERCD 37)* – Once upon a time . . . storybook love.		
Nov 89. (lp/c/cd) *(838725-1/-4/-2)* **LAST EXIT TO BROOKLYN (Soundtrack)**		

– Last exit to Brooklyn / Victims / Think fast / A love idea / Tralala / Riot / The reckoning / As low as it gets / Last exit to Brooklyn – finale.

NOTTING HILLBILLIES

MARK KNOPFLER – guitar, vocals, producer / **GUY FLETCHER** – guitar, vocals, producer / **BRENDAN CROKER** – guitar, vocals / **STEVE PHILLIPS** – guitar, vocals / with **PAUL FRANKLIN** – pedal steel guitar

	Vertigo	Warners
Feb 90. (7"-c-s) *(NHB/+MC 1)* **YOUR OWN SWEET WAY. / BEWILDERED**		-
(12"+=)(cd-s+=) *(NHB 1-12)(NHBCD 1)* – That's where I belong.		
Mar 90. (cd/c/lp) *(842 671-2/-4/-1)* <26147> **MISSING . . . PRESUMED HAVING A GOOD TIME**	2	52

– Railroad worksong / Bewildered / Your own sweet way / Run me down / One way gal / Blues stay away from me / Will you miss me / Please baby / Weapon of prayer / That's where I belong / Feel like going home.

	Vertigo	Warners
Apr 90. (7"-c-s) *(NHB/+MC 2)* **FEEL LIKE GOING HOME. / LONESOME WIND BLUES**		-
(12"+=)(cd-s+=) *(NHB 2-12)(NHBCD 2)* – One way gal.		
Jun 90. (7"-c-s) *(NHB/+MC 3)* **WILL YOU MISS ME. / THAT'S WHERE I BELONG**		
(12"+=)(cd-s+=) *(NHB 3-12)(NHBCD 3)* – Lonesome wind blues.		

CHET ATKINS & MARK KNOPFLER

	C.B.S.	Columbia
Oct 90. (7"-c-s) *(656 373-7/-4)* **POOR BOY BLUES. / SO SOFT YOUR GOODBYE**		
(cd-s+=) *(656 373-2)* – There'll be some changes made.		
Nov 90. (cd/c/lp) *(467435-2/-4/-1)* <45307> **NECK AND NECK**	41	Oct90

– Poor boy blues / Sweet dreams / There'll be some changes made / Just one time / So soft / Your goodbye / Yakety axe / Tahitian skies / Tears / I'll see you in my dreams / The next time I'm in town.

MARK KNOPFLER

	Vertigo	Warners
Oct 93. (7"-c-s) *(VER/+MC 81)* **THEMES FROM LOCAL HERO: GOING HOME. / WILD THEME**		-
(cd-s+=) *(VERCD 81)* – Comfort.		

(above was obviously a re-issue. MARK also featured on HANK MARVIN's new version of 'Wonderful Land'; released Oct'93

	Vertigo	Warners
Mar 96. (c-s/cd-s) *(VER MC/CD 88)* **DARLING PRETTY / GRAVY TRAIN**	33	
(cd-s+=) *(VERDD 88)* – My claim to fame.		
Apr 96. (cd/c) *(514732-2/-4)* <46026> **GOLDEN HEART**	9	

– Darling pretty / Imelda / Golden heart / No can do / Vic and Ray / Don't you get it / A night in summer long ago / Cannibals / I'm the fool / Je suis desole / Rudiger / Nobody's got the gun / Done with Bonaparte / Are we in trouble now.

	Vertigo	Warners
May 96. (c-s/cd-s) *(VER MC/CD 89)* **CANNIBAL / THE ORDER BABY**	42	
(cd-s+=) *(VERDD 89)* – What have I got to do		

—— In 1996, a collaboration cd with STEVE PHILIPS, 'JUST PICKIN' was issued by 'Buried Treasure' (TROV 2)

DISCHARGE (dig out; Great Alt & Indie . . .)

DISPOSABLE HEROES OF HIPHOPRISY

Formed: Bay Area, San Francisco, California, USA . . . 1987 as The BEATNIGS, by MICHAEL FRANTI, a 6' 6" rapper (who was adopted by a middle class family), and Oriental partner, RONO TSE. This industrial funk quintet released a few singles and an eponymous album for JELLO BIAFRA's 'Alternative Tentacles' in the late 80's (including the first incarnation of the 'TELEVISION' track), before the pair (along with CHARLIE HUNTER) formed The DISPOSABLE HEROES OF HIPHOPRISY as a more conventional rap vehicle for their highly articulate political commentary. A brilliant dissection of TV's malign influence, the revamped version of the aforementioned 'TELEVISION' introduced their atmospheric slo-mo hip hop; with his portentous half-spoken vocal style and razor-sharp diatribes, FRANTI was acclaimed as the new GIL SCOTT-HERON (although the original version was still out and about). The early 90's saw the release of two further, criminally ignored 12"er's, 'LANGUAGE OF VIOLENCE' and 'FAMOUS AND DANDY LIKE AMOS 'N' ANDY', before '4th & Broadway' took them on and kickstarted their career with a second re-issue of 'TELEVISION: THE DRUG OF THE NATION'. Released in March '92, it grabbed a minor UK chart placing and subsequently reached the Top 50 at the end of the year. In the interim, the DHOH unleashed their debut album, 'HIPHOPRISY IS THE GREATEST LUXURY', a refreshing liberal alternative to the lyrical excesses of much American hip hop. Though it made the UK Top 40, the group were given the cold shoulder by the majority of hardcore rap fans, white middle class indie kids forming the groundswell of their support. Perhaps as a reaction to this (and a low-key set with poet, WILLIAM S. BURROUGHS, entitled 'SPARE ASS ANNIE AND OTHER TALES'), FRANTI left the polemic at home and formed the more laidback and funky SPEARHEAD, releasing two albums for 'Capitol, 'HOME' (1994) and 'CHOCOLATE SUPA HIGHWAY' (1997).
• **Songwriters:** FRANTI penned except; CALIFORNIA UBER ALLES (Dead Kennedys).
Album rating: HIPHOPRISY IS THE GREATEST LUXURY (*8) / SPARE ASS ANNIE AND OTHER TALES (*5) / Spearhead: HOME (*6) / CHOCOLATE SUPA HIGHWAY (*6) / Beatnigs: BEATNIGS (*5)

The BEATNIGS

MICHAEL FRANTI (b.21 Apr'67) – vocals, bass, tapes, industrial percussion / **RONO TSE** (b. 8 Dec'66, Hong Kong) – percussion, industrial percussion / **HENRY FLOOD** – percussion, industrial percussion / **KEVIN** – vocals, tapes, industrial percussion / **ANDRE FLORES** – keyboards, industrial percussion

	Alternative Tentacles	E.F.A.
Oct 88. (7") *(VIRUS 71)* **TELEVISION (extended). / JAZZY BEATS**		
(12"+=) *(VIRUS 71T)* – ('A'dub) / ('A'radio).		
(re-iss. May92; same)		

—— Above remixed by ADRIAN SHERWOOD & TACKHEAD
Dec 88. (lp/c/cd) *(VIRUS 65/+C/CD)* <LP 07779> **BEATNIGS**
– (Welcome) / Television / CIA / (Instructions) / When you wake up in the morning / (The experiences of us all) / Street fulla nigs / (Re classification) / Control / Malcolm X / Nature / Burritos / Rooticus sporaticus / Who is doin' this to all my people / Rules. *(cd-iss. 1992 +=; same)* – Jazzy beats / Pre-war America / Television (radio edit) / Television (remix). *(re-iss. cd Sep95; same)*

DISPOSABLE HEROES OF HIPHOPRISY

FRANTI + TSE + CHARLIE HUNTER – jazz guitar, bass, piano, organ

	not iss.	Island
1989. (12"/cd-s) **TELEVISION IS THE DRUG OF THE NATION. / WINTER OF THE LONG HOT SUMMER**	-	
1990. (12"/cd-s) **LANGUAGE OF VIOLENCE. /**	-	

	Worker's Playtime	Alternative Tentacles
Oct 90. (12"ep; as HIPHOPRISY) *(PLAY 016 T)* **(WHAT WILL WE DO TO BECOME) FAMOUS AND DANDY LIKE AMOS 'N' ANDY**		

– Famous and dandy (extended) / Satanic reverses / Financial leprosy / Famous and dandy (steal our heat mix) / Financial reverses (steal our heat mix). *(cd-s+=) (PLAY 016CD)* – (2 extended title tracks) *(re-iss. Jun92; same)*

	4th & Broad	4th & Broad
Mar 92. (7") *(BRW 241)* **TELEVISION THE DRUG OF THE NATION. / WINTER OF THE LONG HOT SUMMER**	57	

(12"+=) *(12BRW 241)* – Language of violence.
(cd-s++=) *(BRCDY 241)* – ('A'mix).
(cd-s+=) *(BRCDX 241)* – Financial leper (live) / California uber alles (live) / It's a crime to be broke in England / America (live).
(re-iss. Dec92, hit UK No.44; same)

	4th & Broad	4th & Broad
May 92. (cd/c/d-lp) *(BR CD/CA/LP 584)* **HIPHOPRISY IS THE GREATEST LUXURY**	40	

– Satanic reverses / Famous and dandy (like Amos 'n' Andy) / Television the drug of the nation / Language of violence / The winter of the long hot summer / Hypocrisy is the greatest luxury / Everyday life has become a health risk / INS greencard A-19 191 500 / Socio-genetic experiment / Music and politics / Financial leprosy / California uber ales / Water pistol man.

	4th & Broad	4th & Broad
May 92. (cd-s) *(BRCA 248)* **LANGUAGE OF VIOLENCE / FAMOUS AND DANDY (LIKE AMOS 'N' ANDY) (instrumental)**	68	

(12"+=/12"+=/cd-s+=) *(12BRW/12BRZ/BRCD 248)* – Water pistol man (live).
Sep 92. (7"-c-s) *(BRW 259/+C)* **FAMOUS AND DANDY (LIKE AMOS AND ANDY). / POSITIVE**

(12"+=/cd-s+=) *(12/CD BRW 259)* – Language of violence (jazz version).

Oct 93. (cd/c/lp; as WILLIAM S. BURROUGHS & DISPOSABLE
HEROES OF HIPHOPRISY) *(BRCD/BRCA/BRLP 600)*
SPARE ASS ANNIE AND OTHER TALES
– Wrinkled earlobes are a sign of impending heart attacks (interlude) / Spare ass
Annie / This is insane (interlude 2) / The last words of Dutch Schultz (this is
insane) / The vultures are gone and will never come back (interlude 3) / Mildred
Pierce reporting 2 (Old Sarge) / Dr. Benway operates / Warning to young couples
(huntsmen's hounds) / Did I ever tell you about the man who taught his asshole to
talk? / Last words with Ras I. Zulu / A one God universe / Fletch is here (interlude
4) / The junky's Christmas / Words of advice for young people / Last words with
Michael Franti.

SPEARHEAD

——　**MICHAEL FRANTI** / + **MARY HUNTER** – vocals / **KRAVITZ** / **STORCH** (RONO was
to form BLACK CHINA)

	Capitol	Capitol

Oct 94. (cd/c/d-lp) *(CD/TC+/EST 2236)* **HOME**
– People in the middle / Love is da shit / Piece o' peace / Positive / Of course you
can / Hole in my bucket / Home / Dream team / Runfayalife / Crime to be broke in
America / 100,000 miles / Red beans and rice / Caught without an umbrella.

Dec 94. (c-s) *(TCCL 733)* **OF COURSE YOU CAN. / POSITIVE /
WATER PISTOL MAN (acoustic)**　　　　　　　　　`74`
(cd-s+=) *(CDCL 733)* – Booty and the beats.

Apr 95. (12"ep/c-ep) *(12/TC CL 742)* **HOLE IN THE BUCKET /
RUNFAYLIFE (Franti mix). / ('A'-Sensimi Street mix) /
('A'-Adrian Sherwood mix)**　　　　　　　　　`55`
(cd-ep) *(CDCL 742)* – ('A'-Slave ship mix) – (repl. last mix).

Jun 95. (12"/cd-s) *(12/CD CL 752)* **PEOPLE IN THA MIDDLE / ('A'-
Mello madness mix) / ('A'-Angel remix) / ('A'-album
mix) / ('A'-Adrian Sherwood remix)**　　　　　`49`
(cd-s) *(CDCLS 752)* – ('A'side) / Hole in the bucket / 100,000 miles (live) / Positive
(live).

Mar 97. (12"/cd-s) *(12/CD CL 785)* **WHY OH WHY. / FOOD FOR
THA MASSES / HOLE IN THE BUCKET**　　　　`45`
(cd-s+=) *(CDCLS 785)* – ('A'mixes).

Mar 97. (cd/c/lp) *(CD/TC+/EST 2293)* **CHOCOLATE SUPA HIGHWAY**　`68`
– Africa on line / Chocolate supa highway / Keep me lifted / Food for tha masses /
U can't sing R song / Payroll (stay strong) / Madness in the hood (free ride) / Rebel
music (3 o'clock roadblock) / Why oh why / Comin' to gitcha / Life sentence / Ganja
babe.

Jul 97. (12") *(12CL 791)* **U CAN'T SING R SONG. / ('A'-Prince
Charles Urban mix) / WHY OH WHY (K.M.A. hard
step way mix)**
(cd-s) *(CDCL 791)* – (first 2 tracks) / ('A'-Blacksmith late nite mix) / ('A'-Celeb's
soul mix).
(cd-s) *(CDCLS 791)* – (first & third tracks) / ('A'-The Mystro & Esmail's hip hop
mix) / Why oh why (K.M.A. undersea mix).

DIVINATION (see under ⇒ LASWELL, Bill)

DIVINE COMEDY

Formed: Londonderry, Northern Ireland ... 1990 by bishop's son, NEIL
HANNON, JOHN McCULLAGH and KEVIN TRAYNOR. Moving across the
water to London, the three signed to maverick indie label, 'Setanta', releasing
a SEAN O'NEILL (That Petrol Emotion)-produced debut, 'FANFARE FOR
THE COMIC MUSE' (1990). A mini-set, it was followed by two further EP's,
before the extroverted HANNON took over the reins as McCULLAGH and
TRAYNOR bailed out. Free to pursue his own eccentric muse, HANNON
steered The DIVINE COMEDY away from trad indie-rock towards a more
self-consciously cultured approach which suggested the influence of everyone
from SCOTT WALKER to JARVIS COCKER, in a cod-romantic ANDREW
LLOYD-WEBBER-esque fashion of course! His first step towards educating
the alternative pop scene came in the shape of 1993's 'LIBERATION'
album, his debonair charisma in full effect on tracks such as 'EUROPOP',
'BERNICE BOBS HER HAIR' and 'I WAS BORN YESTERDAY'. His
next set of songs, 'PROMENADE' (1994), was a loose concept affair and
featured the Irish comedian, SEAN HUGHES, who provided verbal support
on the track, 'THE BOOKLOVERS'. The name, DIVINE COMEDY, came
to the attention of 'Father Ted'-loving music fans after the instrumental,
'SONGS OF LOVE', was used as the theme tune to the popular Channel 4
programme. HANNON also co-wrote another ditty for the second series of
the show; the downright silly 'My Beautiful Horse' was the singing priests'
(Ted and Dougal) entry for the Eurovision Song Contest!!! In 1996, HANNON
(together with his new DIVINE COMEDY recruits) released his most perfectly
conceived pop masterpiece to date in 'CASANOVA', the Roger Moore of rock
crooning his way through a dapper set of richly orchestrated diamonds. Duly
encrusted into the Top 50, the album contained such memorably tongue-in-
cheek hits as 'SOMETHING FOR THE WEEKEND', 'BECOMING MORE
LIKE ALFIE' and 'THE FROG PRINCESS'. Now a firm critical fave, The
DIVINE COMEDY (well, HANNON) had two more Top 20 successes with 'A
SHORT ALBUM ABOUT LOVE' (a mini-set) and 'EVERYBODY KNOWS
(EXCEPT YOU)' (a single). In August '98, "the Leslie Thomas" of indie-
pop/rock, HANNON/DIVINE COMEDY had his first Top 10 album, 'FIN DE
SIECLE', a record that boasted three further hits including 'GENERATION
SEX' and 'NATIONAL EXPRESS'; a stop-gap UK Top 3 'best of' package,
'A SECRET HISTORY', was delivered the following year. • Covered: THERE
IS A LIGHT THAT NEVER GOES OUT (Smiths) / MIRANDA + LAST
STAND IN METROLAND (Michael Nyman).

Album rating: FANFARE FOR THE COMIC MUSE mini (*4) / LIBERATION (*6) /
PROMENADE (*7) / CASANOVA (*8) / A SHORT ALBUM ABOUT LOVE (*7) / FIN
DE SIECLE (*7) / A SECRET HISTORY – THE BEST OF THE DIVINE COMEDY
(*7)

NEIL HANNON (b. 7 Nov'70) – vocals, guitar, bass, piano, etc. / **JOHN McCULLAGH** –
bass, vocals / **KEVIN TRAYNOR** – drums

	Setanta	Setanta

Aug 90. (m-cd/m-lp) *(SET CDM/LPM 002)* **FANFARE FOR THE COMIC
MUSE**　　　　　　　　　　　　　　　　□　-
– Ignorance is bliss / Indian rain / Bleak landscape / Tailspin / Rise and fall / Logic
vs. emotion / Secret garden.

Nov 91. (12"ep) *(SET 008)* **TIMEWATCH. / JERUSALEM / THE RISE
AND FALL**　　　　　　　　　　　　　　　　□　-

Feb 92. (12"ep) *(SET 011)* **EUROPOP EP**　　　　　□　□
– New wave / Intifada / Monitor.
(cd-ep+=) *(SET 011CD)* – Timewatch / Jerusalem / The rise and fall.

——　now **HANNON** solo after the other two departed

Jul 93. (7"ep) *(CAO 008)* **LUCY. / THE POP SINGER'S FEAR OF
THE POLLEN COUNT / I WAS BORN YESTERDAY**　□　-

Aug 93. (cd/c/lp) *(SET CD/MC/LP 011)* **LIBERATION**　　□　-
– Festive road / Death of a supernaturalist / Bernice bobs her hair / I was born
yesterday / Your daddy's car / Europop / Timewatching / The singer's fear of the
pollen count / Queen of the south / Victoria Falls / Three sisters / Europe by train /
Lucy. *(re-iss. Aug96; same)*

Oct 93. (7"pic-d-ep) *(DC 001)* **INDULGENCE No.1**　　□　-
– Untitled melody / Hate my way / Europe by train.

Mar 94. (cd/c/lp) *(SET CD/MC/LP 013)* **PROMENADE**　　□　-
– Bath / Going downhill / The booklovers / A seafood song / Geronimo / Don't
look down / When the lights go out all over Europe / The summerhouse / Neptune's
daughter / A drinking song / Ten seconds to midnight / Tonight we fly. *(re-iss. Aug96
& Aug97; same)*

Aug 94. (7"ep) *(DC 002)* **INDULGENCE No.2**　　　　□　-
– A drinking song / Tonight we fly (live) / When the lights go out all over Europe.

——　now one-man band **NEIL HANNON** and a large ensemble of musicians including
main band; **STUART 'PINKIE' BATES** – hammond organ / **JOBY TALBOT** – piano,
arranger / **IVOR TALBOT** – guitar / **BRYAN MILLS** – bass / **MIGUEL 'MIGGY'
BARRADAS** – drums

Apr 96. (cd/c/lp) *(SET CD/MC/LP 025) <36863>* **CASANOVA**　`48`
– Something for the weekend / Becoming more like Alfie / Middle-class heroes / In
& out of Paris & London / Charge / Songs of love / The frog princess / A woman of
the world / Through a long & sleepless night / Theme from Casanova / The dogs &
the horses.

——　<above issued on 'Tristar' in the US>

Jun 96. (c-s) *(SETMC 026)* **SOMETHING FOR THE WEEKEND /
SONGS OF LOVE (theme from 'Father Ted')**　`14`
(cd-s+=) *(SETCD 026)* – Birds of Paradise farm / Love is lighter than air.

Aug 96. (7"/c-s) *(SET/+MC 027)* **BECOMING MORE LIKE ALFIE. /
YOUR DADDY'S CAR (live)**　　　　　　`27`　-
(cd-s+=) *(SETCD 027)* – Untitled melody (acoustic) / The dogs & the horses
(acoustic).

Nov 96. (c-s) *(SETMC 032)* **THE FROG PRINCESS / MOTORWAY
TO DAMASCUS**　　　　　　　　　　`15`　-
(cd-s+=) *(SETCD 032)* – A woman of the world / Lucy (demo).
(cd-s) *(SETCDL 032)* – ('A'side) / Something before the weekend / Neptune's
daughter / Tonight we fly.

Feb 97. (m-cd/m-c) *(<SET CD/MC 036>)* **A SHORT ALBUM ABOUT
LOVE**　　　　　　　　　　　　　　`13`
– In pursuit of happiness / Everybody knows (except you) / Someone / If . . . / If I
were you (I'd be through with me) / Timewatching / I'm all you need.

Mar 97. (cd-ep) *(SETCDA 038)* **EVERYBODY KNOWS (EXCEPT
YOU) / MAKE IT EASY ON YOURSELF (live) / A
DRINKING SONG (live) / SOMETHING FOR THE
WEEKEND (live)**　　　　　　　　　　`14`
(cd-ep) *(SETCDB 038)* – ('A'side) / Johnny Mathis' feet (live) / Your daddy's car
(live) / Europe by train (live).
(cd-ep) *(SETCDC 038)* – ('A'side) / Bath (live) / Tonight we fly (live) / Middle class
heroes (live).

——　In April '98, The DIVINE COMEDY were part of a NOEL COWARD tribute album
in which a single, 'I'VE BEEN TO A MARVELLOUS PARTY' was taken. It hit
No.28 and was backed with a Shola Ama & Craig Armstrong track

——　added **ROB FARRER** – percussion

	Setanta	Imprint

Aug 98. (cd/c) *(SET CD/MC 057) <111813>* **FIN DE SIECLE**　`9`　□ Dec98
– Generation sex / Thrillseeker / Commuter love / Sweden / Eric the gardener /
National express / Life on Earth / The certainty of chance / Here comes the flood /
Sunrise. *(also ltd-cd; SETCDL 057)*

Sep 98. (7") *(SET 050)* **GENERATION SEX. / POSTCARD TO ROSIE**　`19`　□ Nov98
(cd-s) *(SETCDA 050) <114195>* – ('A'side) / London Irish / Time lapse.
(cd-s) *(SETCDB 050) <114197>* – ('A'side) / Chasing sheep is best left to shepherds /
Little acts of kindness.

	Setanta	Setanta

Nov 98. (c-s) *(SETMC 067)* **THE CERTAINTY OF CHANCE /
MARYLAND ELECTRIC RAINSTORM**　　`49`　□ Mar99
(cd-s) *(<SETCDA 067>)* – ('A'side) / Last stand in Metroland / Miranda.
(cd-s) *(<SETCDB 067>)* – ('A'side) / Dead only quickly / Knowing the ropes.

Jan 99. (c-s) *(SETMC 069)* **NATIONAL EXPRESS / THE HEART OF
ROCK AND ROLL**　　　　　　　　　`8`
(cd-s) *(SETCDA 069)* – ('A'side) / Going downhill fast / Radioactivity.
(cd-s) *(SETCDB 069)* – ('A'side) / Famous / Overstrand.

Aug 99. (c-s) *(SETMC 070)* **THE POP SINGER'S FEAR OF THE
POLLEN COUNT / JACKIE**　　　　　　`17`
(cd-s) *(SETCDA 070)* – ('A'side) / With whom to dance / Eric the gardener.
(cd-s) *(SETCDB 070)* – ('A'side) / This side of paradise / Vapour trail.

Aug 99. (cd/c) *(SET CD/MC 100)* **A SECRET HISTORY – THE BEST OF
THE DIVINE COMEDY** (compilation)　　`3`

– National express / Something for the weekend / Everybody knows (except you) / Generation sex / Becoming more like Alfie / Summerhouse / Your daddy's car / The pop singer's fear of the pollen count / The frog princess / Gin soaked boy / Lucy / Songs of love / In pursuit of happiness / I've been to a marvellous city / Certainty of chance / Too young to die / Tonight we fly.

Nov 99. (c-s) *(SETMC 071)* **GIN SOAKED BOY / EUROPOP (live)**   [38]   ☐
(cd-s) *(SETCDA 071)* – ('A'side) / Songs of love / I am.
(cd-s) *(SETCDB 071)* – ('A'side) / Geronimo / My lovely horse.

Willie DIXON

Born: 1st July 1915, Vicksburg, Mississippi, USA. Interested in words and music from an early age and admiring the playing of LITTLE BROTHER MONTGOMERY, this 6 and a half foot, 250lb mountain of a man started singing with local gospel groups in his teens. After numerous scrapes with the law he decided to hitch-hike his way to Chicago, taking up boxing and winning the Golden Gloves Heavyweight title in 1936. DIXON became a professional musician on meeting BABY DOO CASTON in 1937 and together they formed the FIVE BREEZES, recording a blend of blues, jazz and vocal harmonies in the 40's. CASTON taught the young DIXON how to play bass and guitar although his progress was halted when he resisted the World War II draft and was imprisoned for 10 months. After the war he formed FOUR JUMPS OF JIVE before reuniting with CASTON in the BIG THREE TRIO, who went on to record for 'Columbia'. DIXON subsequently signed to 'Chess' as a recording artist but as he became more involved with the label his live performance work took a back seat and by 1951 he was a full time employee of the company with duties including producer, A&R man, session musician, talent scout and songwriter. He stayed with 'Chess', apart from an interlude with 'Cobra' (in a similar capacity, only reluctantly returning to 'Chess' when the label folded), until 1971 although his relationship with the label wasn't always a happy one and he once had to take them to court to regain copyright control of his songs. DIXON eventually left 'Chess' in 1957 because he felt that he was being underpaid and also because the label had rejected OTIS RUSH who DIXON thought was an exceptional talent. He subsequently set up 'Cobra' with ELI TOSCANO and signed OTIS RUSH, although TOSCANO gambled away the company's profits and DIXON returned to 'Chess', taking OTIS and BUDDY GUY with him. He was, on the whole, responsible for the sound of Chicago blues on both the aforementioned labels (furnishing MUDDY WATERS and HOWLIN' WOLF with most of their best known repertoire) with the black rock'n'roll of CHUCK BERRY and BO DIDDLEY also benefitting from his touch. DIXON teamed up with MEMPHIS SLIM in the early 60's to play folk festivals, also operating as a booking agent and manager, a role which proved crucial to the American Folk Blues Festival Tours of Europe. Many British R&B bands subsequently recorded his songs including The ROLLING STONES, JEFF BECK, CREAM and LED ZEPPELIN, all in their own inimitable style. On leaving 'Chess', DIXON went into independent production with his own labels, 'Yambo' and 'Spoonful', resuming his personal recording and performing career while also administering the Blues Heaven Foundation, a charity which promoted the awareness of the blues and offered support to old performers who had fallen on hard times. He once claimed "I am the blues", and although that may sound a bit arrogant, you can't take it away from the man that he was one of the major influences on the genre through his songwriting, production and performing. His songs, 'BACK DOOR MAN', 'MY BABE', 'HOOCHIE COOCHIE MAN', 'LITTLE RED ROOSTER', 'I JUST WANT TO MAKE LOVE TO YOU', 'I CAN'T QUIT YOU BABY', 'YOU NEED LOVE', 'YOU SHOOK ME', 'BRING IT ON HOME', 'I AIN'T SUPERSTITIOUS', 'SPOONFUL', 'WANG DANG DOODLE' and 'YOU CAN'T JUDGE A BOOK BY THE COVER' and hundreds more are a lasting legacy to his brilliance and may well make him the most recorded blues composer ever. His health suffered in the 70's and 80's, when he contracted diabetes and eventually had a leg amputated. He died of heart failure in California on the 29th of January 1992. • **Legacy:** Wrote for other blues artists MUDDY WATERS (I'm Ready / I Just Want To Make Love To You / Walking Blues / I'm Your Hoochie Coochie Man / Don't Go No Further / I Love The Life I Live, I Live The Life I Love / Close To You / My Captain / Same Thing / When The Eagle Flies); HOWLIN' WOLF (Spoonful / Wang Dang Doodle / Little Baby / The Red Rooster / Shake For Me / Built For Comfort / Do The Do / I Ain't Superstitious / Evil); LITTLE WALTER (My Babe); OTIS RUSH (I Can't Quit You Baby); LITTLE MILTON (I Can't Quit You Baby / Country Style / Too Late); BO DIDDLEY (You Can't Judge A Book By The Cover); KOKO TAYLOR (I Got What It Takes / Don't Mess With The Messer / Whatever I Am, You Made Me / Blue Heaven / (I Got) All You Need / Wang Dang Doodle / What Came First: The Egg Or The Hen? / Fire / Insane Asylum / I Don't Know Who Cares / Separate Or Integrate / Yes, It's Good For You); BUDDY GUY (co:-I Dig Your Wig / Crazy Love (Crazy Music) / Too Many Ways / Goin' Home / I Cry And Sing The Blues / Every Girl I See (DIXON-MURPHY); ETTA JAMES (Fire); EDDIE BOYD (Third Degree); JIMMY WITHERSPOON (Everything But You / Crazy Mixed Up World); ALBERT KING (Howlin' For My Darling / Down In The Bottom); SONNY BOY WILLIAMSON (co:- BUDDY GUY- I Dig Your Wig);

Best CD compilation: THE ORIGINAL WANG DANG DOODLE – THE CHESS RECORDINGS AND MORE (*8)

WILLIE DIXON & THE ALL-STARS

WILLIE DIXON – vocals, bass / **LAFAYETTE LEAKE** – piano / **FRED BELOW** – drums / **HAROLD ASHBY** – tenor sax

		London	Checker
Aug 55.	(7",78) <822> **WALKING THE BLUES. / IF YOU'RE MINE**	-	
Jan 56.	(7",78) <828> **CRAZY FOR MY BABY. / I AM THE LOVER MAN**	-	
Jul 56.	(7",78) *(HLU 8297)* **WALKING THE BLUES. / CRAZY FOR MY BABY**	-	-
	(re-iss. & flipped over Oct64 on 'Pye International'; 7N 25270)		
Aug 57.	(7",78) <851> **TWENTY NINE WAYS. / THE PAIN IN MY HEART**	-	-

WILLIE DIXON

—— now with **MEMPHIS SLIM** – piano / **WALLY RICHARDSON** – guitar / **HAROLD ASHBY** – tenor sax / **GUS JOHNSON** – drums

		Bluesville	Prestige
Feb 60.	(7") <803> **NERVOUS. / SITTIN' AND CRYIN' THE BLUES**	-	
1962.	(lp) *(BV 1003)* <1003> **WILLIE'S BLUES**		

– Nervous / Good understanding / That's my baby / Slim's thing / That's all I want baby / Don't you tell nobody / Youth to you / Sittin' and cryin' the blues / Built for comfort / I got a razor / Go easy / Move me. *<re-iss. Feb84 on 'O.B.C.'; OB 501> (cd-iss. Jun92 on 'Charly'; CDCHD 349)*

—— now with – LUCKY THREE TRIO – (DIXON / **LEAKE + CLIFTON JAMES** – drums)

		not iss.	Tuba
1962.	(7") **BACK HOME IN INDIANA. / WRINKLES**	-	-

WILLIE with drummer – **PHILIPPE COMBELLE**

		Polydor	not iss.
1963.	(lp) *(LPHM 46131)* **WILLIE DIXON & PHILIPPE COMBELLE**		-

– African hunch with a boogie beat / Baby, baby, baby / Cold blooded / Do de do / Just you and I / New way to love / Shame, pretty girls / The way she loves a man. now with The CHICAGO ALL-STARS: **WALTER HORTON** (aka SHAKY JAKE) – harmonica / **SUNNYLAND SLIM** – piano / **JOHNNY SHINES** – guitar / **CLIFTON JAMES** – drums

		not iss.	Columbia
1969.	(lp) <9987> **I AM THE BLUES**		

– Back door man / I can't quit you, baby / The seventh son / Spoonful / I ain't superstitious / You shook me / I'm your hoochie coochie man / The little red rooster / The same thing. *<cd-iss. 1986 on 'Mobile Fidelity'; MFCD 872>*

—— now with **BUSTER BENTON + DENNIS MILLER** – guitar / **LAFAYETTE LEAKE** – piano / **FREDDIE DIXON** – bass / **CLIFTON JAMES** – drums / **CARRIE BELL HARRINGTON** – harmonica

		Ovation	not iss.
1976.	(lp; w-drawn) *(HA-O 8465)* **CATALYST**	-	-
1978.	(lp) *(QD 1441)* **WHAT HAPPENED TO MY BLUES**	-	

– Moon cat / What happened to my blues / Pretty baby / Got to love you baby / Shakin' the shack / Hold me baby / It's so easy to love you / Oh Hugh baby / Put it all in there / Hey hey pretty mama.

		not iss.	Spivey
1970's.	(lp) **WILLIE DIXON AND THE CHICAGO BLUES BAND**	-	-
1980's.	(lp) **MIGHTY EARTHQUAKE AND HURRICANE**		-

		not iss.	Spoonful
1980's.	(lp) **BACKSTAGE ACCESS (live)**	-	-

		Varese Sarabande Colosseum	Varese Sarabande Colosseum
Oct 89.	(lp/c/cd) <(VS/+C/CD 5234)> **GINGER ALE AFTERNOON** (soundtrack)	☐	☐

– Miseries of memories / Wigglin' worm / I don't trust nobody / Earthquake and hurricane / The real thing / Move me baby / Save my child / I just want to make love to you / Sittin' and cryin' the blues / Save my child II / Shakin' the shake / That's my baby / Ginger ale blues / Save my child III / Good understanding.

		Silvertone	Silvertone
Apr 91.	(cd/c) *(ORE CD/C 515)* **HIDDEN CHARMS** (rec.1988)	☐	☐

– Blues you can't lose / I don't trust myself / Jungle swing / Don't mess with the messer / Study war no more / I love the life I live / I cry for you / Good advice / I do the job. *(re-iss. cd/c Mar94 & Apr95; same)*

—— On 29th Jan'92, WILLIE died of heart failure at St.Thomas' Hospital, California.

– compilations, etc –

Jan 87.	(lp/c) *Deja Vu; (DVLP/DVMC 2092)* **WILLIE DIXON: 20 BLUES GREATS**	☐	-

– Little red rooster / Built for comfort / Wang dang doodle / Ain't superstitious / Evil / Walking the blues / Fiery love / Alone / Mannish boy / All aboard / Rock me / I love the life I live / Sugar sweet / Thunderbird / One more / Teenage beat / Snake dancer / Temperature / Rock bottom / Black angel blues.

Sep 90.	(d-cd/d-c/t-lp; various artists) *Chess-MCA; (CHD 216500)* **THE CHESS BOX**	☐	☐
	(d-cd re-iss. Apr97; MCD 16500)		
Nov 92.	(cd) *Chess; (CDRED 37)* **TRIBUTE TO WILLIE DIXON**		-
Mar 93.	(cd) *Blues Encore; (CD 52026)* **I'M THE BLUES**		-
	Note; Below releases on 'Roots' were his songs by various artists		
Jun 93.	(c) *Roots; (RTS 43045)* **THE BLUES DIXONARY VOL.1**	☐	☐
Jun 93.	(c) *Roots; (RTS 43046)* **THE BLUES DIXONARY VOL.2**	☐	☐
Jun 93.	(c) *Roots; (RTS 43047)* **THE BLUES DIXONARY VOL.3**	☐	☐
Jun 93.	(c) *Roots; (RTS 43048)* **THE BLUES DIXONARY VOL.4**	☐	☐
Jun 93.	(c) *Roots; (RTS 43049)* **THE BLUES DIXONARY VOL.5**	☐	☐
Mar 95.	(cd; WILLIE DIXON & JOHNNY WINTER) *Thunderbolt; (CDTB 166)* **CRYING THE BLUES (LIVE AT LIBERTY HALL)**	☐	-

DJ SHADOW

Born: JOSH DAVIS, Hayward, San Francisco, California, USA. While hip hop continued to stagnate in a vicious circle of violence, recrimination and manicured beats, a handful of individuals are making leaps and bounds off the musical map. One such character is the aptly named DJ SHADOW, an elusive figure who entranced and beguiled the music world in 1996 with his groundbreaking debut album, 'ENDTRODUCING . . .' Eschewing rapping altogether, SHADOW took the form back to its roots in samples, scratching, beats, breaks and ingenious creativity, employing an obsessive knowledge of hip hop and vinyl culture to create something as funky and compulsive as it was cerebral, dark and complex. Working around a haunting central theme, the turntable guru moves in and out of musical focus, manipulating sounds and juxtaposing strings, creeping/rampaging beats, twilight zone organ and obscure samples with ever impressive cohesion. Located somewhere in the no-man's land between hip hop, trip-hop and avante-garde experimentalism, DJ SHADOW thankfully bypasses the head-nodding tendencies of much 'Mo-Wax' fodder while continuing to be feted by a wide cross-section of both the dance and rock communities. 1997's live 'Q-BERT MIX' was a scratch-athon taster of DJ SHADOW live in the flesh, an occurence which remains, on UK shores at least, about as rare as . . . A few years earlier, DJ SHADOW had teamed up with label boss, JAMES LAVELLE on the UNKLE project, a mini-album, 'TIME HAS COME' (1996) surfaced, although it was 1998's 'PSYENCE FRICTION', that broke them into the UK Top 10. 'RABBIT IN YOUR HEADLIGHTS' – co-written and sung by RADIOHEAD's THOM YORKE – was certainly the highlight, although amongst others, stars such as The Verve's RICHARD ASHCROFT and the Beastie Boys' MIKE D also contributed greatly to the classic.

Album rating: ENTROPY (*6) / IN/FLUX mini (*7) / LOST AND FOUND (*6) / WHAT DOES YOUR SOUL LOOK LIKE (*7) / ENTRODUCING (*7) / Unkle: PSYENCE FICTION (*8)

		not iss.	Sole Sides
1993.	(cd) **ENTROPY**	-	-
		Mo'Wax	Mo'Wax
Sep 94.	(12"/cd-s) <(MW 014/+CD)> **IN FLUX. / HINDSIGHT**		Dec93
Mar 95.	(12"/cd-s) <(MW 027/+CD)> **WHAT DOES YOUR SOUL LOOK LIKE? / (3-'A'mixes)**	59	
	(cd-s) (MW 027CDL) – ('A'mixes).		
May 95.	(12"; DJ SHADOW & DJ KRUSH) <(MW 024)> **LOST AND FOUND. / DJ Krush: KEMURI**		1994
Sep 96.	(12"/cd-s) <(MW 057/+CD)> **MIDNIGHT IN A PERFECT WORLD (mixes). / MUTUAL SLUMP**	54	-
Sep 96.	(d-lp/c/cd) <(MW 059/+MC/CD)> **ENTRODUCING**		Nov96
	– Best foot forward / Building steam with a grain of salt / The number song / Changeling / (transmission #1) / What does your soul look like (part 4) / (untitled) / Stem – Long stem / (transmission #2) / Mutual slump / Organ donor / Why hip hop sucks in '96 / Midnight in a perfect world / Napalm brain – Scatter brain / What does your soul look like (part 1 – Blue sky revisit) / (transmission #3). *(d-lp re-iss. Jan98; same)*		
Oct 96.	(12"/cd-s) <(MW 058/+CD)> **STEM / RED BUS NEEDS TO LEAVE. / LONG STEM / SOUP**	74	
Jun 97.	(12"; DJ SHADOW & XCEL) (SS 005) **HARDCORE HIP HOP. /**		-
	(above issued on 'Solesides')		
Sep 97.	(7"/c-s) <(MW 063 S/MC)> **HIGH NOON. / ORGAN DONOR (extended overhaul)**	22	
	(12"+=/cd-s+=) <(MW 063/+CD)> – The Devil's advocate (Heaven and Hell bonus beats) / Hypnotize spoken word intro – outro.		
Dec 97.	(m-lp/m-cd) <(MW 084/+CD)> **"Q-BERT MIX-LIVE!!":- CAMEL BOBSLED RACE (mixed by Q-BERT)**	62	
Jan 98.	(cd/c) <540867> **PREEMPTIVE STRIKE**	-	
	– Strike one / In – Flux / Hindsight / Strike two / What does your soul look like (part 2) / What does your soul look like (part 3) / What does your soul look like (part 4) / What does your soul look like (part 1) / Strike three (and I'm out) / High noon / Organ donor (extended overhaul).		
Jan 98.	(12") <(MW 087)> **WHAT DOES YOUR SOUL LOOK LIKE (part 1). / (part 2)**	54	
Feb 98.	(ltd-12") (MW 086DJ) **NUMBER SONG (Cut Chemist mix). / PAINKILLER (DJ Shadow Vs. Depeche Mode)**		-

U.N.K.L.E.

aka DJ SHADOW + JAMES LAVELLE plus TIM GOLDSWORTHY + MASAYUKI KUDO (Major Force West)

Jan 95.	(12"/12"pic-d) <(MW 028/+P)> **THE TIME HAS COME (mixes)**		-
	(re-iss. May96 w/cd-ep; MW 028CD)		
Feb 97.	(12"/cd-s) <(MW 069/+CD)> **BERRY MEDITATION (mixes)**		-
	(12"clear) (MW 069L) – ('A'remixes).		
Mar 97.	(12") <(MW 070/+CD)> **ROCK ON (mixes)**		-
	—	DJ SHADOW + LAVELLE with guests vocalists **THOM YORKE** (Radiohead) / **RICHARD ASHCROFT** (Verve) / **MIKE D** (Beastie Boys) / **MARK HOLLIS** (ex-Talk Talk) / **ALICE TEMPLE** (Eg And Alice) / **BADLY DRAWN BOY + KOOL G RAP**		
Aug 98.	(lp/c/cd) (MW 085/+MC/CD) <540970> **PSYENCE FICTION**	4	-
	– Guns blazing / UNKLE main title theme / Bloodstain / Unreal / Lonely soul / Getting ahead in the field of artistic management / Nursery rhyme / Celestial annihilation / Knock / Chaos / Rabbit in your headlights. *(also ltd;d-cd/d-lp; MW 085 CDS/S)*		
Oct 98.	(12"ep/cd-ep) (MW 103/+CD) **RABBIT IN YOUR HEADLIGHTS (instrumental) / (Underdog mix) / (Underdog instrumental) / (30 mix 'reverse light') / (30 mix 'reverse light' instrumental) / (Suburban hell remix)**	-	- nochart

---

Feb 99.	(12"/cd-s; UNKLE featuring IAN BROWN) (MW 108/+CD1) **BE THERE (mixes; original / Underdog / Underdog instrumental)**	8	-
	(cd-s) (MW 108CD2) – ('A'side) / The knock (drums of Zep) (Noel Gallagher mix) / Rabbit in your headlights (video).		

DMX

Born: EARL SIMMONS, 18 Dec'70, New York, USA. As a troubled teen, with a chequered past, the apprehensive MC began his quest from the gutter and into rap stardom when he struck a deal with 'Columbia'; an unsigned talent show had panned the spotlight on the unknown 21-year-old. His debut, 'BORN LOSER' (1996), flopped unceremoniously when released in the States, most likely due to the fact that 2PAC and NOTORIOUS B.I.G. were stealing the show with their very own brand of humourless hardcore rap. It wasn't until 'Def Jam' were dumbfounded by a lost demo tape and the aforemetioned rap martyrs were all dead that DMX and his RUFF RIDERS (a collection of friends and producers from his hood) could stand alone as the most outstanding artists of their generation. He cameo'd on songs by MA$E, LL COOL J and JAY-Z before issuing the haunting 'IT'S DARK AND HELL IS NOT' in 1998. Through subsequent months, the set began to slowly climb its way up the American Billboard charts before selling a whopping 3 million copies, gaining the talented gothic rapper the title "The Dawg". From its outset, the album was a bleak study into the underworld of hopelessness in the ghettos and the unforgotten suburban neighborhoods, where anything could and would happen. 'DAMIEN', the album's strongest moment, was a reflection from the point of view of a crazy murderer, commanded by his alter-ego to kill. The track began with a sinister orchestral riff accompanied by a beatbox before DMX began with the line: "Why is it that every move I make turns out to be a bad one, where's my guardian angel, need one, wish I had one . . ." which then segued into a biblical chorus: it was the most disturbing rap song since 2PAC's enraged 'HIT 'EM UP'. Other tracks induced DMX's disturbed imagery: in 'PRAYER', he pleads with God, questioning him about the decisions he could have helped the rapper make in his vexatious years; in 'X IS COMING' he fantasises about the rape and subsequent murder of a 15-year-old (and to think that he's MARIAH CAREY's favourite rapper!). SIMPSON surfaced again in the same year with the major label sophomore set, 'FLESH OF MY FLESH, BLOOD OF MY BLOOD' and it was much weaker than its heavyweight contender. DMX, "The Dawg", seemed to be barking phrases instead of rapping, loosening false pretentions with his overpowering ego. MARILYN MANSON and MARY J BLIGE were among the performers included on the album which had our anti-hero soaked in blood on the cover. His worst came in the form of ' . . .AND THEN THERE WAS X' (1999), a sloppy, inadequate fourth album, where The 'X droned on about his reign as the best rapper in the world. However, at this time of writing, he still remains the most successful, having had three US No.1 chartbusters. • **Note:** Not to be confused with the DMX CREW.

Album rating: IT'S DARK AND HELL IS NOT (*8) / FLESH OF MY FLESH BLOOD OF MY BLOOD (*7) / . . .AND THEN THERE WAS X (*6)

EARL SIMMONS – rapper, etc

		not iss.	Sony
Jul 93.	(c-s/12"/cd-s) <74908> **BORN LOSER**	-	-
		not iss.	Metropolitan
Nov 94.	(12"; by DMX & STEPHANIE MARANO) <1034> **SECRET GARDEN. /**	-	-
		Def Jam	Def Jam
Feb 98.	(c-s/12"/cd-s; DMX featuring SHEEK of The LOX) <568523> **GET AT ME DOG /**	-	39
Jun 98.	(cd/lp) <(558227-2/-1)> **IT'S DARK AND HELL IS NOT**	1	May98
	– Intro / Ruff ryders / Fuckin' wit D / Storm / Look thru my eyes / Get at me dog / Let me fly / X-is coming / Damien / How's it goin' down / Mickey / Crime story / Stop being greedy / Ate / For my dogs / I can feel it / Prayer / Convo / Niggaz done started something.		
	—	DMX also featured on two V/A 12"ep's, 'SURVIVAL OF THE ILLEST' (Vols. 1 & 2) along with FAITH EVANS, ONYX and The DEF SQUAD		
Aug 98.	(cd-s) **STOP BEING GREEDY /**	-	79
Oct 98.	(12"; by DMX & FAITH EVANS) <566217> **HOW'S IT GOIN' DOWN. /**	-	
Jan 99.	(cd/d-lp) <(538640-2/-1)> **FLESH OF MY FLESH BLOOD OF MY BLOOD**	1	Dec98
	– My niggas / Bring your whole crew / Pac man / Ain't no way / We don't give a fuck / Keep your shit the hardest / Coming from / It's all good / Omen / Slippin' / No love 4 me / Dogs for life / Blackout / Flesh of my flesh blood of my blood / Heat / Ready to meet him.		
Feb 99.	(c-s/cd-s) <566217> **RUFF RYDERS' ANTHEM**	-	94
May 99.	(12") <(563867-1) <870755> **SLIPPIN'. / RUFF RYDERS' ANTHEM / STOP BEING GREEDY**	30	Apr99
	(cd-s) (870755-2) – (first 2 tracks) / How's it goin' down.		
	(cd-s) (870755-2) – ('A'side) / No love for me / Get at me dog (2 versions).		
Nov 99.	(12") <562540> **WHAT'S MY NAME**	-	
Dec 99.	(cd/lp) <(546933-2/-1) **. . .AND THEN THERE WAS X**		1
	– Kennel / One more road to cross / The professional / Fame / Alot to learn / Here we go again / Party up / Make a move / What these bastards want / What's my name? / More 2 a song / Don't you ever / Shakedown / D-X-L / Comin' for ya / Prayer III / Angel / Good girls, bad guys.		

DNA / Arto LINDSAY (dig out; Great Alt & Indie . . .)

DOCTORS OF MADNESS (dig out; Great Alt & Indie . . .)

DODGY

Formed: Hounslow, London, England . . . early 1990 by vocalist/bassist NIGEL CLARK, guitarist ANDY MILLER and drummer MATTHEW PRIEST. With DJ, CHRIS SLADE, they set up The Dodgy Club in a London bar, where they cultivated a grassroots fanbase over the course of the summer. Just over a year later, DODGY embarked upon their first national jaunt, christened the 'Word Of Mouth' tour in recognition of its unconventional nature; their fans had to phone up prospective promoters and venues to find out where they were playing (well dodgy!). After initial 7" singles on their own 'Bostin' label, they were snapped up by 'A&M', the major releasing two quickfire follow-ups in Spring '93, 'WATER UNDER THE BRIDGE' and 'LOVEBIRDS', the latter a Top 75 entry. The TURTLES to Oasis's BEATLES, DODGY's hazy shade of peace-pipe pop also incorporated the songwriting quality of SQUEEZE or CROWDED HOUSE. 'THE DODGY ALBUM' bounced onto the shelves that summer, although their spliff-friendly spirituality wasn't an immediate success and charming singles such as 'I NEED ANOTHER' and 'HOMEGROWN' went virtually unnoticed. A year later, DODGY's camper-van sound made inroads into the Top 50; two hit singles, 'MELODIES HAUNT YOU' and the evocative 'STAYING OUT FOR THE SUMMER' preceded a second set, 'HOMEGROWN', although the critics remained unconvinced. 'SO LET ME GO FAR' and 'MAKING THE MOST OF' both broke their Top 30 duck and were followed by a re-issue of 'STAYING OUT FOR THE SUMMER', actually released in the summer this time around and a deserved Top 20 smash as Brit-pop gripped the nation. Now summer festival specialists, DODGY had finally found their sunkissed niche and a third album, 'FREE PEACE SWEET' (1996) was released to critical acclaim and major Top 10 success; the record also spawned four Top 20 singles, the pick of the bunch being the Top 5, 'GOOD ENOUGH'. However, after 'EVERY SINGLE DAY' hit the Top 40 in Autumn '98 and an accompanying 'best of' package failed to meet sales expectations, NIGEL bailed out. MILLER and PRIEST carried on regardless and by Spring the following year a new singer DAVE BASSEY was found. Augmented by NICK ABNETT and CHRIS HALLAM, DODGY were one of the first bands to release a single through the internet (yes, the music industry was indeed getting a major shake-up). • **Covered:** I CAN'T MAKE IT (Small Faces) / REVOLUTION (Beatles) / BACK INTO YOUR LIFE (Love Affair).

Album rating: THE DODGY ALBUM (*7) / HOMEGROWN (*6) / FREE PEACE SWEET (*8) / ACE A'S AND KILLER B'S compilation (*7)

NIGEL CLARK (b.18 Sep'66, Redditch, England) – vocals, bass, guitars / **ANDY MILLER** (b.18 Dec'68) – lead guitar, vocals / **MATTHEW PRIEST** (b. 3 Apr'70) – drums, vocals, percussion

		Bostin	not iss.
Sep 91.	(7") *(BTN 001)* **SUMMER FAYRE. / ST. LUCIA**		-
Nov 91.	(7") *(BTN 002)* **EAST WAY. / SEEMS LIKE A BAD DAY**		-
	(cd-s+=) *(BTN 002CD)* – Groove song (St. Lucia demo) / See the way.		
Apr 92.	(7"black & white) *(BTN 003)* **THE BLACK AND WHITE SINGLE:- black side: WORTH THE BLOOD. / white side: THE ELEPHANT**		-
	(12"black & white+=) *(BTN 003X)* – Worth the blood (full).		
	(cd-s++=) *(BTN 003CDS)* – The D-Club versions; See the way / Jungle dark dance bath / Elevators goin' up / 4am nocturnal / Watch the sun go down.		

—— added 4th member **CHRIS SLADE** – DJ, keyboards

		A&M	A&M
Mar 93.	(7"/c-s) *(AM/+MC 196)* **WATER UNDER THE BRIDGE. / IT'S BEEN SO LONG**		-
	(12"+=/cd-s+=) *(AM Y/CD 196)* – She wants my loving / Valuable fool.		
Apr 93.	(7"/c-s) *(AM/+MC 0177)* **LOVEBIRDS. / BIG BROWN MOON**	65	
	(12"+=/cd-s+=) *(AM Y/CD 0177)* – Sylvia's bedroom / Smashed up in a flat.		
Jun 93.	(cd/c/lp) *(<540 082-2/-4/-1>)* **THE DODGY ALBUM**	75	
	– Water under the bridge / I need another / Lovebirds / Satisfied / Grand old English oak tree / Stand by yourself / As my time goes by / Never again / Cold tea / We're not going to take this anymore.		
Jun 93.	(7"mustard/c-ep/c-ep) *(580 317-7/-)* **I NEED ANOTHER. / IF I FALL / HENDRE DHU**	67	-
	(12"ep+=/cd-ep+=) *(580 317-1/-2)* – Never again (campfire version).		
Oct 93.	(7"ep/c-ep) *(580 414-7/-4)* **HOMEGROWN E.P.**		-
	– Don't go back (to the beaten track) / Home grown / Let's wait till we get there.		
	(10"ep+=/cd-ep+=) *(580 415-0/-2)* –		

—— now without CHRIS and back to trio

Jul 94.	(7"ep/c-ep) *(580 676-7/-4)* **THE MELOD-E.P.: MELODIES HAUNT YOU. / THE SNAKE**	53	-
	(12"+=) *(580 676-1)* – Don't go back (to the beaten track).		
	(cd-s++=) *(580 676-2)* – Summer fayre. *(re-iss. Jul97; same)*		
Sep 94.	(7"blue/c-s) *(580 788-7/-4)* **STAYING OUT FOR THE SUMMER. / LOVEBIRDS (original)**	38	-
	(cd-s+=) *(580 797-2)* – As time goes by (demo) / Back to life.		
	(cd-s) *(580 789-2)* – ('A'side) / A summer's day in mid-January / Don't you think / Colour me with paints. *(re-iss. Jul97; same)*		
Oct 94.	(cd/c/lp) *(<540 282-2/-4/-1>)* **HOMEGROWN**	43	-
	– Staying out for the summer / Melodies haunt you / So let me go far / Crossroads / One day / We are together / Whole lot easier / Making the most of / Waiting for the day / What have I done wrong? / Grassman. *(re-iss. Jun95, hit No.28)*		
Dec 94.	(7"/c-s) *(580 903-4)* **SO LET ME GO FAR / DON'T GET LOW, DON'T LET GO (U.K. R.I.P.)**	30	-
	(12"+=/cd-s+=) *(580 905-1/-2)* – So let me Wobble Jah / The elephant (the Balaphon-a-bing bong immigrant mix).		

	(cd-s) *(580 903-2)* – ('A'side) / I need another (live) / Satisfied (live) / Melodies haunt you (live). *(re-iss. Jul97; same)*		
	(above featured JAH WOBBLE – bass) (below featured The KICK HORNS)		
Feb 95.	(7"pic-d/c-s) *(580 986-7/-4)* **MAKING THE MOST OF. / FAISONS AU MIEUX (YES, IT'S IN FRENCH)**	22	-
	(cd-s+=) *(580 987-2)* – The Ludlow sessions part 1: Spent all my time running / All the time in the world.		
	(cd-s) *(580 989-2)* – ('A'extended) / The Ludlow sessions part 2: Watch out watcha doin' / This is ours / (Get off your) High horse. *(re-iss. Jul97; same)*		
Jun 95.	(c-s) *(581 092-4)* **STAYING OUT FOR THE SUMMER (mixed up in 95) / SATISFIED (live)**	19	-
	(cd-s) *(581 093-2)* – ('A'side) / (Your love keeps lifting me) Higher and higher / Crossroads (live) / Melodies haunt you (live).		
	(cd-s) *(581 095-2)* – ('A'side) / Waiting for the day (live) / One day (live) / (Get off your) High horse (live). *(re-iss. Jul97; same)*		

—— now with guest (4th member) **RICHARD PAYNE** – keyboards

May 96.	(7"white/c-s) *(581 624-7/-4)* **IN A ROOM. / OUTCLUBBING**	12	-
	(cd-s) *(581 625-2)* – ('A'side) / Self doubt / Long life (acoustic) / Jungle UK (no rest in peace). *(re-iss. Jul97; same)*		
Jun 96.	(cd/c/lp) *(<540 573-2/-4/-1>)* **FREE PEACE SWEET**	7	-
	– Intro / In a room / Trust in time / You've gotta look up / If you're thinking of me / Good enough / Ain't no longer asking / Found you / One of those rivers / Prey for drinking / Jack the lad / Long life / U.K.R.I.P. / Homegrown.		
Jul 96.	(7"/c-s) *(581 814-7/-4)* **GOOD ENOUGH. / NUTTERS**	4	-
	(cd-s+=) *(581 815-2)* – Speaking in tongues / Lovebirds on Katovit. *(re-iss. Jul97; same)*		
Nov 96.	(7"/c-s) *(581 998-7/-4)* **IF YOU'RE THINKING OF ME. / IN A ROOM (acoustic)**	11	-
	(cd-s) *(581 998-2)* – ('A'side) / Pebblemilljam / Forever remain / Good enough (version). *(re-iss. Jul97; same)*		
Mar 97.	(7"/c-s) *(582 132-7/-4)* **FOUND YOU. / STAND BY YOURSELF**	19	-
	(cd-s) *(582 133-2)* – ('A'side) / I can't make it / Revolution.		

		Polygram	Polygram
Sep 98.	(c-s) *(MERMC 512) <582737>* **EVERY SINGLE DAY / THE BRIDGE / MOSTAR KEEP SHINING**	32	Nov98
	(cd-s) *(MERCD 512)* – (first two tracks) / Look up.		
	(cd-s) *(MERDD 512)* – (first & third tracks) / Staying out for the summer.		
Oct 98.	(cd/c) *(<541 018-2/-4>)* **ACE A'S AND KILLER B'S** (compilation)	55	Nov98
	– Every single day / Staying out for the summer (summer 95) / Water under the bridge / Good enough / Melodies haunt you / Big brown moon / Found you / Self doubt / In a room / Making the most of / If you're thinking of me / Lovebirds / (Get off your) High horse / So let me go far / Grassman / Ain't no longer asking / The elephant. *(<also d-cd; 541 019-2>)*		

—— **DAVE BASSEY** – vocals (ex-MUSTARD) repl. NIGEL who went solo

—— **NICK ABNETT** – bass + **CHRIS HALLAM** – keyboards (were added)

—— a single, 'BACK INTO YOUR LIFE' was available in August '99 through the internet only:- www.dodgy.co.uk

---

John DOE (see under ⇒ X)

DOG EAT DOG (dig out; Great Metal . . .)

DOGS D'AMOUR (dig out; Great Metal . . .)

DOKKEN (dig out; Great Metal . . .)

DOLPHIN BROTHERS (see under ⇒ JAPAN)

Fats DOMINO

Born: ANTOINE DOMINO, 26 Feb'28, New Orleans, Louisiana, USA. Growing up in a musical family, FATS began playing local honky tonk clubs before he even reached his teens. Nicknamed 'FATS' – for his 16 stone stature – by his bass player, BILLY DIAMOND, he was soon tinkling the ivories alongside Crescent City masters like PROFESSOR LONGHAIR and CHAMPION JACK DUPREE while digging the records of FATS WALLER and LOUIS JORDAN. DOMINO was barely over sixteen when he joined the band of trumpeter/producer/composer extraordinaire, Dave Bartholomew, although the pair would subsequently strike up a long and fruitful partnership. Also working as an A&R man for 'Imperial', Bartholomew helped the youngster sign to the label in 1949, the same year the pair co-penned what would become DOMINO's debut single, 'THE FAT MAN'. A rollicking piano groove oft cited as the first rock'n'roll record (alongside a host of others), the track was release by 'Imperial' in the Spring of 1950 and went on to sell a million copies over the ensuing three years. More importantly, it created a sizeable market for FATS' laid-back, free-rolling take on classic New Orleans R&B and with a crack band consisting of BARTHOLOMEW, RED TYLER and EARL PALMER, DOMINO cut a further succession of R&B hits over the next five years while touring almost constantly. It was only a matter of time before he crossed over to the mainstream pop charts and in summer 1955 FATS took his propulsive boogie-woogie to the masses with 'AIN'T THAT A SHAME', a US Top 10. Along with his appearance in two teen movies, 'Shake, Rattle & Roll' and 'The Girl Can't Help It', this success initiated almost a decade of regular chart action, his best-loved and most well known song, 'BLUEBERRY HILL', making the Top 10 on both sides of the pond in Autumn '56 (its B-side 'ITS KEEPS RAININ', has been cited as a precursor to Jamaican ska/reggae after import copies caused a musical storm – BITTY McLEAN took it to UK No.2 in 1993). This consolidated FATS as one of the most popular and respected performers of the rock'n'roll era, his unique encapsulation of his native city's multicultural musical heritage seeing him rack up more sales than any other American artist save ELVIS PRESLEY. Among the best and biggest of his hits were 'BLUE MONDAY' (sadly not an early version of NEW ORDER's electro classic), 'I'M WALKIN', 'WHOLE LOTTA LOVING' and 'WALKING TO NEW ORLEANS', all million-selling US Top 10's. By the time of FATS' move to 'ABC Paramount' in 1963, the hits were becoming thinner on the ground as the British Invasion heated up. Ironically, The BEATLES were big DOMINO fans and were no doubt both thrilled and amused when the Big Man covered 'LADY MADONNA' in 1968, one of his first singles for 'Reprise' and his last chart entry. Nevertheless, he continued to tour and record right up until the early 80's, when he finally retired from the music business. • **Covered:** WHEN THE SAINTS GO MARCHING IN (trad.) / JAMBALAYA + YOU WIN AGAIN (Hank Williams) / I HEAR YOU KNOCKIN' (Smiley Lewis) / DID YOU EVER SEE A DREAM WALKIN' (Eddy Duchin) / RED SAILS IN THE SUNSET (Platters) / I CAN'T STOP LOVING YOU (Ray Charles) / I LEFT MY HEART IN SAN FRANCISCO (Tony Bennett) / LOVELY RITA + EVERYBODY'S GOT SOMETHING TO HIDE EXCEPT ME AND THE MONKEY (Beatles) / etc. • **Trivia:** He married childhood sweetheart Rosemary in the late 40's, bringing up 8 children in homeland New Orleans.

Best CD compilation: MY BLUE HEAVEN: THE BEST OF FATS DOMINO (*7)

FATS DOMINO – vocals, piano with **DAVE BARTHOLOMEW** – trumpet / **RED TYLER** – bass / **EARL PALMER** – drums

			not iss.	Imperial
Apr 50.	(78) <5058>	THE FAT MAN. / DETROIT CITY BLUES	-	
May 50.	(78) <5065>	BOOGIE WOOGIE BABY. / LITTLE BEE	-	
Jul 50.	(78) <5077>	SHE'S MY BABY. / HIDE AWAY BLUES	-	
Sep 50.	(78) <5085>	HEY LA BAS BOOGIE. / BRAND NEW BABY	-	
Nov 50.	(7",78) <5099>	KOREA BLUES. / EVERY NIGHT ABOUT THIS TIME	-	

—— FATS now finds own musicians

			not iss.	Imperial
Feb 51.	(7",78) <5114>	TIRED OF CRYING. / WHAT'S THE MATTER BABY	-	
May 51.	(7",78) <5123>	DON'T LIE TO ME BABY. / SOMETIMES I WONDER	-	
Aug 51.	(7",78) <5138>	NO NO BABY. / RIGHT FROM WRONG	-	
Nov 51.	(7",78) <5145>	ROCKIN' CHAIR. / CARELESS LOVE	-	
Jan 52.	(7",78) <5167>	YOU KNOW I MISS YOU. / I'LL BE GONE	-	
Mar 52.	(7",78) <5180>	GOIN' HOME. / REELIN' AND ROCKIN'	-	
Jun 52.	(7",78) <5197>	POOR POOR ME. / TRUST IN ME	-	
Sep 52.	(7"red,78) <5209>	HOW LONG. / DREAMING	-	
Jan 53.	(7"red,78) <5220>	NOBODY LOVES ME. / CHEATIN'	-	
May 53.	(7"red,78) <5231>	GOING TO THE RIVER. / MARDI GRAS IN NEW ORLEANS	-	
Jul 53.	(7",78) <5240>	PLEASE DON'T LEAVE ME. / THE GIRL I LOVE	-	

—— added **LEE ALLEN** – saxophone

			London	Imperial
Feb 54.	(7",78) (HL 8007) <5251>	ROSE MARY. / YOU SAID YOU LOVED ME		Oct53
Jul 54.	(7",78) (HL 8063) <5272>	YOU DONE ME WRONG. / (HEY) LITTLE SCHOOL GIRL		Feb54
Nov 54.	(7",78) (HL 8096) <5262>	DON'T LEAVE ME THIS WAY. / SOMETHING'S WRONG		Dec53
Jun 54.	(7",78) <5283>	BABY PLEASE. / WHERE DID YOU STAY	-	
Nov 54.	(7",78) <5301>	YOU CAN PACK YOUR SUITCASE. / I LIVED MY LIFE	-	
Feb 55.	(7",78) (HL 8124) <5313>	LOVE ME. / DON'T YOU HEAR ME CALLIN' YOU		1954
Apr 55.	(7",78) (HL 8133) <5323>	I KNOW. / THINKIN' OF YOU		Jan55
Apr 55.	(7",78) <5340>	DON'T YOU KNOW. / HELPING HAND		

—— now with **WALTER NELSON** – guitar / **CORNELIUS COLEMAN** – drums.

			London	Imperial
Sep 55.	(7",78) (HLU 8173) <5348>	AIN'T THAT A SHAME. / LA-LA-LA		10 Jun55

(above single hit UK chart No.23 in Jan57)

Nov 55. (lp) <9004> **CARRY ON ROCKIN'**
– The fat man / Tired of crying / Goin' home / You said you love me / Going to the river / Please don't leave me / Rose Mary / All by myself / Ain't that a shame / Poor me / Bo Weevil / Don't blame it on me. *<re-iss. Mar57 as 'ROCK AND ROLLIN' WITH FATS DOMINO'; same> (UK-iss.Apr57; HA-P 2041)*

			London	Imperial
Sep 55.	(7",78) <5357>	ALL BY MYSELF. / TROUBLES OF MY OWN	-	
Nov 55.	(7",78) <5369>	POOR ME. / I CAN'T GO ON (ROSALIE)	-	
Mar 56.	(7",78) (HLU 8256) <5375>	BO WEEVIL. / DON'T BLAME IT ON ME		35 Feb56
Jul 56.	(7",78) (HLU 8280) <5386>	I'M IN LOVE AGAIN. / MY BLUE HEAVEN	12	3 / 19
Aug 56.	(7",78) (HLU 8309) <5396>	WHEN MY DREAMBOAT COMES HOME. / SO-LONG		14 / 44 Jul56
Sep 56.	(7",78) <5407>	BLUEBERRY HILL. / HONEY CHILE	-	5
Oct 56.	(7",78) (HLU 8330) <5396>	BLUEBERRY HILL. / I CAN'T GO ON (ROSALIE)	6	-

Oct 56. (lp) (HA-U 2028) <9009> **FATS DOMINO – ROCK AND ROLLIN'**   [Imperial] 18
– The fat man / Tired of crying / Goin' home / You said you love me / Going to the river / Please don't leave me / Rose Mary / All by myself / Ain't that a shame / Poor me / Bo Weevil / Don't blame it on me.

			UK	US
Jan 57.	(7",78) (HLU 8356)	HONEY CHILE. / DON'T YOU KNOW	29	-
Feb 57.	(lp) (HA-P 2073) <9028>	THIS IS FATS DOMINO!		19

– Blueberry hill / Honey chile / What's the reason I'm not pleasing you / Blue Monday / So long / La la / Troubles of my own / You done me wrong / Reeling and rocking / The fat man's hop / Poor poor me / Trust in me.

			UK	US
Mar 57.	(7",78) (HLP 8377) <5417>	BLUE MONDAY. / WHAT'S THE REASON I'M NOT PLEASING YOU	23	5 / 50 Dec56
Apr 57.	(7",78) (HLP 8407) <5428>	I'M WALKIN'. / I'M IN THE MOOD FOR LOVE	19	4 Feb57
Jul 57.	(7",78) (HLP 8449) <5442>	VALLEY OF TEARS. / IT'S YOU I LOVE	25	8 / 6 May58
Aug 57.	(7",78) (HLP 8471) <5454>	WHEN I SEE YOU. / WHAT WILL I TELL MY HEART		29 / 64
Nov 57.	(7",78) (HLP 8519) <5467>	WAIT AND SEE. / I STILL LOVE YOU		23 / 79 Oct57

—— sessions incl. **ALLEN TOUSSAINT** – piano

			UK	US
Mar 58.	(7",78) (HLP 8575) <5477>	THE BIG BEAT. / I WANT YOU TO KNOW	20	26 / 32 Dec57
Feb 58.	(7",78) <5492>	YES, MY DARLING. / DON'T YOU KNOW I LOVE YOU	-	55
May 58.	(lp) (HA-P 2052) <9038>	HERE STANDS FATS DOMINO		

– Detroit City blues / Hide away blues / She's my baby / New baby / Little bee / Every night about this time / I'm walkin' / I'm in the mood for love / Cheatin' / You can pack your suitcase / Hey fat man / I'll be gone.

			UK	US
Jun 58.	(7",78)(HLP 8628) <5515>	SICK AND TIRED. / NO, NO	26	22 / 55
Jun 58.	(lp) (HA-P 2087) <9040>	THIS IS FATS		

– The rooster song / My happiness / As time goes by / Hey la bas / ove me / Don't you hear me calling you / It's you I love / Valley of tears / Where did you stay / Baby please / Thinking of you / You know I miss you. *(re-iss. Apr79 on 'Flyover') (re-iss. US Jan83)*

			UK	US
Jul 58.	(7",78) (HLP 8663) <5526>	LITTLE MARY. / PRISONER'S SONG		48 Jun58
Oct 58.	(7",78) (HLP 8727) <5537>	YOUNG SCHOOL GIRL. / IT MUST BE LOVE		92 Sep58
Nov 58.	(7",78) (HLP 8759) <5553>	WHOLE LOTTA LOVING. / COQUETTE		6 / 92
Sep 58.	(lp) (HA-P 2135) <9055>	THE FABULOUS "MR.D"		

– The big beat / I'll be glad when you're dead you rascal you / What will I tell my heart / Barrelhouse / Little Mary / Sick and tired / I want you to know / "44" / Mardi Gras in New Orleans / I can't go on / Long lonesome journey / Young school girl *(re-iss. US Jan83)*

			UK	US
Mar 59.	(7",78) (HLP 8822) <5569>	WHEN THE SAINTS GO MARCHING IN. / TELLING LIES		50 Feb59
May 59.	(7",78) (HLP 8865) <5585>	MARGIE. / I'M READY	18	51 / 16

(re-iss. Jul76 on 'United Artists')

Jun 59. (lp) (HA-P 2223) <9065> **LET'S PLAY FATS DOMINO**
– You left me / Ain't it good / Howdy podner / Stack & Billy / Would you / Margie / Hands across the table / When the saints go marching in / Ida Jane / Lil' Liza Jane / I'm gonna be a wheel some day / I want to walk you home.

			UK	US
Sep 59.	(7",78) (HLP 8942) <5606>	I WANT TO WALK YOU HOME. / I'M GONNA BE A WHEEL SOMEDAY	14	8 / 17 Jul59
Dec 59.	(7",78) (HLP 9005) <5629>	BE MY GUEST. / I'VE BEEN AROUND	11	8 / 33 Oct59
Dec 59.	(lp) <9062>	FATS DOMINO SWINGS	-	

– The fat man / Blue Monday / Blueberry Hill / I'm in love again / Going to the river / My blue Heaven / Bo Weevil / Goin' home / Please don't leave me / Ain't that a shame / I'm walkin' / Whole lotta lovin'. *(cd-iss. Nov99 on 'Magic'; 523017-2)*

			UK	US
Mar 60.	(7",78) (HLP 9073) <5645>	COUNTRY BOY. / IF YOU NEED ME	19	25 / 98 Jan60
Jun 60.	(7",78) (HLP 9133) <5660>	TELL ME THAT YOU LOVE ME. / BEFORE I GROW TOO OLD		51 / 84 Apr60
Jul 60.	(7",78) (HLP 9163) <5675>	WALKING TO NEW ORLEANS. / DON'T COME KNOCKIN'	19	6 / 21 Jun60
Oct 60.	(7") (HLP 9198) <5687>	THREE NIGHTS A WEEK. / PUT YOUR ARMS AROUND ME HONEY	45	15 / 58 Aug60
Nov 60.	(lp) (HA-P 2312) <9127>	A LOT OF DOMINOES		

– Put your arms around me honey / Three nights a week / Shu rah / Rising sun / My girl Josephine / The sheik of Araby / Walking to New Orleans / Don't come knockin' / Magic isles / You always hurt the one you love / It's the talk of the town / Natural born lover.

			UK	US
Dec 60.	(7") (HLP 9244) <5704>	MY GIRL JOSEPHINE. / NATURAL BORN LOVER	32	14 / 38 Oct60
Mar 61.	(7") (HLP 9301) <5723>	WHAT A PRICE. / AIN'T THAT JUST LIKE A WOMAN		22 / 33 Jan61
Apr 61.	(7") (HLP 9327) <5734>	SHU RAH. / FELL IN LOVE ON MONDAY		32 Mar61
Apr 61.	(lp) (HA-P 2364) <9138>	I MISS YOU SO		

– I miss you so / It keeps rainin' / Ain't that just like a woman / Once in a while / I hear you knockin' / Isle of Capri / What a price / When I was young / Fell in love on Monday / My bleeding heart / Easter parade / I'll always be in love with you.

			UK	US
Jun 61.	(7") (HLP 9374) <5753>	IT KEEPS RAININ'. / I JUST CRY	49	23 May61

Sep 61. (7") *(HLP 9415)* <5764> **LET THE FOUR WINDS BLOW. / GOOD HEARTED MAN** — 15 Jul61

Sep 61. (lp) *(HA-P 2420)* <9153> **LET THE FOUR WINDS BLOW**
– Along the Navajo trail / You win again / One night / I'm alone because I love you / Won't you come on back / Trouble blues / I can't give you anything but love / Good hearted man / Your cheating heart / Let the four winds blow / In a shanty in Old Shanty Town / Am I blue.

Nov 61. (7") *(HLP 9456)* <5779> **WHAT A PARTY. / ROCKIN' BICYCLE** — 22 / 83 Sep61

Nov 61. (lp) *(HA-P 2426)* <9164> **WHAT A PARTY**
– Did you ever see a dream / Walking rockin' bicycle / Before I grow too old ain't gonna do it / Bad luck and trouble / Hold hands / Trouble in mind / Coquette / What a party / I just cry / I've been calling / Tell me that you love me.

Nov 61. (7") <5796> **JAMBALAYA (ON THE BAYOU). / I HEAR YOU KNOCKIN'** — 30 / 67

Feb 62. (7") <5816> **YOU WIN AGAIN. / IDA JANE** — 22 / 90

Mar 62. (7") *(HLP 9520)* **JAMBALAYA. / YOU WIN AGAIN** 41 —

Apr 62. (lp) *(HA-P 2447)* <9170> **TWISTIN' THE STOMP**
– Twistin' the spots / The twist set me free / I know / Every night / Town talk / Wait and see / Twistin' the stomp / Don't deceive me / A long way from home / The girl I love / Do you know what it means to miss New Orleans / South of the border.

Jun 62. (7") *(HLP 9557)* <5833> **MY REAL NAME. / MY HEART IS BLEEDING** — 59 May62

Jul 62. (lp) <9195> **MILLION SELLERS BY FATS** (compilation) —
– You said you love me / I still love you / Be my guest / Country boy / If you need me / I want to walk you home / It's you I love / I've been around / I'm gonna be a wheel some day / I'm ready / Margie / I want you to know.

Aug 62. (7") *(HLP 9590)* <5863> **DANCE WITH MR.DOMINO. / NOTHING NEW (SAME OLD THING)** — 98 / 77 Jun62

Oct 62. (7") *(HLP 9616)* <5875> **STOP THE CLOCK. / DID YOU EVER SEE A DREAM WALKING** — 79 Sep62

Dec 62. (7") <5895> **WON'T YOU COME ON BACK. / HANDS ACROSS THE TABLE** — —

Jan 63. (7") <5909> **THOSE EYES. / HUM-DIDDY-DOO** — —

| | H.M.V. | ABC Paramount |

May 63. (7") *(POP 1164)* <10444> **THERE GOES (MY HEART AGAIN). / CAN'T GO ON WITHOUT YOU** — 59

Jul 63. (7") *(POP 1917)* <10475> **WHEN I'M WALKING (LET ME WALK). / I'VE GOT A RIGHT TO CRY** — —

Sep 63. (7") *(POP 1219)* <10484> **RED SAILS IN THE SUNSET. / SONG FOR ROSEMARY** 34 35

Sep 63. (lp) *(CLP 1690)* <455> **HERE COMES . . . FATS DOMINO**
– When I'm walking / I got a right to cry / There goes (my heart again) / Just a lonely man / Red sails in the sunset / Bye baby, bye, bye / Forever, forever / I'm livin' right / Can't go on without you / Land of 1000 dances / Song for Rosemary / Tell me the truth, baby. *(cd-iss. Sep92 + Jul93 on 'Repertoire')*

Jan 64. (7") *(POP 1265)* <10512> **WHO CARES. / JUST A LONELY MAN** — 63 Dec63

Feb 64. (lp) *(CLP 1740)* <479> **FATS ON FIRE**
– I don't want to set the world on fire / You know I miss you / Fats on fire / Land of make believe / Old man trouble / Love me / Mary, oh Mary / Gotta get a job / The fat man / Valley of tears / Fats shuffle / I'm a fool to care.

Mar 64. (7") *(POP 1281)* <10531> **LAZY LADY. / DON'T WANT TO SET THE WORLD ON FIRE** — 86 Feb64

May 64. (7") *(POP 1303)* <10545> **SOMETHING YOU GOT BABY. / IF YOU DON'T KNOW WHAT LOVE IS** — Apr64

Jul 64. (7") *(POP 1324)* <10567> **MARY OH MARY. / PACKIN' UP** — Jun64

Aug 64. (7") <10584> **SALLY WAS A GOOD OLD GIRL. / FOR YOU** — 99

Nov 64. (7") *(POP 1370)* <10596> **HEARTBREAK HILL. / KANSAS CITY** — 99 Oct64

Apr 65. (7") *(POP 1421)* <10631> **WHY DON'T YOU DO RIGHT. / WIGS** — —

Jun 65. (lp) *(CLP 1821)* <510> **GETAWAY WITH FATS DOMINO**
– When the dreamboat comes home / Wigs / Trouble in mind / Man that's all / Kansas City / Reelin' and rockin' / On a slow boat to China / Monkey business / Heartbreak hill / Girl I'm gonna marry you / Why don't you do right / Ballin' the jack. *(re-iss. Dec83 on 'Ace-Charly'; CH 90)*

| | Mercury | Mercury |

Jul 65. (7") <10644> **LET ME CALL YOU SWEETHEART. / GOODNIGHT SWEETHEART** — —

Sep 65. (7") *(MF 896)* <72463> **I LEFT MY HEART IN SAN FRANCISCO. / I DONE GOT FOR YOU** —

Nov 65. (7") *(MF 873)* <72485> **WHAT'S THAT YOU GOT. / IT'S NEVER TOO LATE** —

Dec 65. (lp; stereo/mono) *(S+/MCL 20070)* <62039> **DOMINO '65 (live)**
– (Introduction) / Blueberry hill / Please don't leave me / Domino twist / Let the four winds blow / I'm gonna be a wheel someday / I'm in the mood for love / Jambalaya (on the bayou) / Oh, what a price / Ain't that a shame / So long.

| | not iss. | Broadmoor |

Dec 67. (7") <104> **THE LADY IN BLACK. / WORK MY WAY UP STEADY** — —

Feb 68. (7") <105> **BIG MOUTH. / WAIT TILL IT HAPPENS TO YOU** —

| | Reprise | Reprise |

Jun 68. (7"; UK w-drawn) *(RS 20696)* <0696> **ONE FOR THE HIGHWAY. / HONEST PAPAS LOVE THEIR MAMAS BETTER** —

Aug 68. (7") *(RS 20763)* <0763> **LADY MADONNA. / ONE FOR THE HIGHWAY** — 100

Sep 68. (lp) *(RSLP 107)* <6304> **FATS IS BACK**
– My old friends / I'm ready / So swell when you're well / Wait till it happens to you / I know / Lady Madonna / Honest papas love their mamas better / Make me

belong to you / One for the highway / Lovely Rita / One more song for you. *(re-iss. Nov81 on 'Mercury' lp/c; 6463/7145 043) (cd-iss. Apr99 on 'Bullseye'; CDBB 9616)*

Nov 68. (7") <0775> **LOVEY RITA. / WAIT TILL IT HAPPENS TO YOU** — —

1969. (7") *(RS 20810)* **EVERYBODY'S GOT SOMETHING TO HIDE EXCEPT ME AND THE DONKEY. / SO SWELL WHEN YOU'RE WELL** — —

1970. (7") <0891> **MAKE ME BELONG TO YOU. / HAVE YOU SEEN MY BABY** — —

1970. (lp) <6439> **FATS**
– I'm going to cross that river / Big mouth / It's a sin to tell a lie / Wait till it happens to you / I'm going to be a friend / The lady in black / Another mule / When you're smiling (the whole world smiles with you) / These old shoes / Lawdy Miss Clawdy / Work my way up steady.

1970. (7") <0944> **NEW ORLEANS AIN'T THE SAME. / SWEET PATOOTIE** — —

| | Atlantic | not iss. |

Jun 74. (lp) *(K 50107)* **LIVE AT MONTREAUX – HELLO JOSEPHINE (live '73)** — —
– Hello Josephine / I'm in love again / Blueberry hill / Jambalaya / Walking to New Orleans / I'm walking / Blue Monday / Mardi Gras in New Orleans / Stagger Lee / I want to walk you home / Let the four winds blow / I'm walking / When the saints go marching in / Sentimental journey.

| | Sonet | Polydor |

May 79. (lp) *(SNTF 793)* <PD 3215> **SLEEPING ON THE JOB**
– Sleeping on the job / After hours / When I lost my baby / Something about you baby / Move with the groove / Any old time / Shame on you / I just can't get the girl I love / Love me.

Nov 78. (7") *(SON 2168)* **SLEEPING ON THE JOB. / AFTER HOURS** — —

| | not iss. | Warners |

Jan 81. (7") <49610> **WHISKEY HEAVEN. / BEERS TO YOU (by the Texas Opera Company)** — —

—— FATS retired from music to spend time with his family, although he made a comeback album in 1985

| | Magnum Force | Toot Toot |

1985. (7"; with DOUG KERSHAW) <1> **MY TOOT TOOT. / MY TOOT TOOT-THREE** — —

Aug 85. (7"; with DOUG KERSHAW) *(MFS 4)* **MY TOOT TOOT. / DIGGY IGGY TO** — —

—— he was now backed by many session men

| | not iss. | M.C.A. |

1986. (lp) **HIS GREATEST HITS (live)**
– My girl Josephine / The fat man / I'm gonna be a wheel someday / Blue Monday / Jambalaya (on the bayou) / Blueberry Hill / Going to the river / I'm ready / I want to walk you home / Whole lotta loving / Poor me / Ain't that a shame / I almost lost my mind / I'm in love again / I'm walkin' / Walking to New Orleans / Let the four winds blow / Shake, rattle and roll / My toot toot / I can't go on.

– compilations, etc. –

1955. (7"ep) *London;* *(RE-P 1022)* **BLUES FOR LOVE**		—
1956. (7"ep) *London;* *(RE-U 1062)* **BLUES FOR LOVE VOL.2**		—
1957. (7"ep) *London;* *(RE-U 1073)* **FATS**		—
1958. (7"ep) *London;* *(RE-P 1079)* **HERE COMES FATS VOL.1**		—
1958. (7"ep) *London;* *(RE-P 1080)* **HERE COMES FATS VOL.2**		—
1958. (7"ep) *London;* *(RE-P 1115)* **CARRY ON ROCKIN' PART 1**		—
1958. (7"ep) *London;* *(RE-P 1116)* **CARRY ON ROCKIN' PART 2**		—
1958. (7"ep) *London;* *(RE-P 1117)* **BLUES FOR LOVE VOL.3**		—
1958. (7"ep) *London;* *(RE-P 1121)* **BLUES FOR LOVE VOL.4**		—
1958. (7"ep) *London;* *(RE-P 1138)* **HERE COMES FATS VOL.3**		—
1959. (7"ep) *London;* *(RE-P 1206)* **THE ROCKIN' "DR.D" VOL.1**		—
1959. (7"ep) *London;* *(RE-P 1207)* **THE ROCKIN' "MR.D" VOL.2**		—
1960. (7"ep) *London;* *(RE-P 1261)* **BE MY GUEST**		—
1960. (7"ep) *London;* *(RE-P 1265)* **THE ROCKIN' "MR.D" VOL.3**		—
1962. (7"ep) *London;* *(RE-P 1340)* **WHAT A PARTY**		—

Jun 63. (7") *London;* *(HLP 9738)* / *Imperial;* <5937> **YOU ALWAYS HURT THE ONE YOU LOVE. / TROUBLE BLUES** —

1963. (lp) *London;* *(HA-P 8084)* / *Imperial;* <9227> **WALKIN' TO NEW ORLEANS** —

1963. (7") *Imperial;* <5959> **ISLE OF CAPRI. / TRUE CONFESSION** —

1963. (7") *Imperial;* <5980> **ONE NIGHT. / I CAN'T GO ON THIS WAY** — —

1963. (lp) *Imperial;* <9239> **LET'S DANCE** — —

1963. (lp) *Imperial;* <9248> **HERE HE COMES AGAIN** — —

1964. (7") *Imperial;* <66005> **I CAN'T GIVE YOU ANYTHING BUT LOVE. / GOIN' HOME** — —

1964. (7"ep) *H.M.V.;* *(7EG 8862)* **RED SAILS IN THE SUNSET** —

1964. (7") *Imperial;* <66016> **YOUR CHEATIN' HEART. / WHEN I WAS YOUNG** — —

Apr 65. (lp) *Liberty;* *(LBY 3033)* **MILLION SELLERS BY FATS VOL.1** *(re-iss. 1967; LBL 83023)* —

Jul 65. (lp) *Liberty;* *(LBY 3046)* **MILLION SELLERS BY FATS VOL.2** *(re-iss. 1967; LBL 83024)* —

1965. (7"ep) *Liberty;* *(LEP 4026)* **MY BLUE HEAVEN** —

1966. (7"ep) *Liberty;* *(LEP 4045)* **ROLLIN'** —

1967. (7") *H.M.V.;* *(POP 1582)* / *ABC-Paramount;* <10902> **I DON'T WANT TO SET THE WORLD ON FIRE. / I'M LIVIN' RIGHT** —

1968. (7") *Liberty;* *(LBF 15098)* **WALKING TO NEW ORLEANS. / BLUEBERRY HILL** —

1968. (lp) *Liberty;* *(LBL 83101)* **MILLION SELLERS BY FATS VOL.3** —

1968. (lp; stereo/mono) *Stateside;* *(S+/SL 10240)* **FANTASTIC FATS** —

1968. (lp; mono/stereo) *Liberty;* *(LBL/LBS 83142E)* **FAT SOUND** —

1969. (7") *Mercury;* *(MF 1104)* **JAMBALAYA / WHAT'S THAT YOU GOT?** —

Apr 70. (lp) *Liberty;* *(LBS 83331)* **THE VERY BEST OF FATS DOMINO: PLAY IT AGAIN FATS** 56 —

1970.	(lp; mono/stereo) *Liberty;* (LBL/LBS 83174E) **RARE DOMINO'S**	
Jun 71.	(7") *United Artists;* (UP 35220) **BLUE MONDAY. / DON'T YOU KNOW I LOVE YOU**	
1971.	(lp) *United Artists;* (UAS 29152) **RARE DOMINO'S VOL.II**	
1972.	(d-lp) *United Artists;* (60015-6) <9958> **LEGENDARY MASTERS**	
May 73.	(7") *United Artists;* (UP 35539) **BLUEBERRY HILL. / PLEASE DON'T LEAVE ME**	
Jul 74.	(6xlp-box) *Liberty;* **THE FATS DOMINO STORY**	
Apr 76.	(7") *United Artists;* (UP 35797) **BLUEBERRY HILL. / WALKIN' TO NEW ORLEANS**	41
Mar 77.	(lp) *United Artists;* (UAS 29667) **20 GREATEST HITS**	
May 77.	(d-lp) *United Artists;* **THE FATS DOMINO STORY VOLS.1 & 2**	
Jul 77.	(d-lp) *United Artists;* **THE FATS DOMINO STORY VOLS.3 & 4**	
Oct 77.	(d-lp) *United Artists;* **THE FATS DOMINO STORY VOLS.5 & 6**	
Mar 78.	(lp) *United Artists;* (30121) **LIVE IN EUROPE** (live)	
May 79.	(7") *United Artists;* (UP 36524) **BLUEBERRY HILL. / IT KEEPS RAININ'**	
May 79.	(7") *United Artists;* (UP 36525) **WALKIN' TO NEW ORLEANS. / THE FAT MAN**	
Dec 79.	(lp) *Hammer;* (HMR 9002) **GOLDEN GREATS**	
Jun 83.	(lp) *Charly;* (CRB 1054) **REELIN' AND ROCKIN'**	
May 84.	(7") *EMI-Gold;* (G45 17) **AIN'T THAT A SHAME. / THE FAT MAN**	
Jun 84.	(7"ep) *S.M.P.;* (SKM 6) **BLUEBERRY HILL / AIN'T THAT A SHAME. / I WANT TO WALK YOU HOME / THE FAT MAN**	
1984.	(lp/c) *Premier;* (CBR/KCBR 1003) **BLUEBERRY HILL**	
Nov 84.	(lp/c) *Astan;* <2/4 0082> **MY BLUE HEAVEN**	-
Nov 84.	(lp/c) *Astan;* <2/4 0083> **JAMBALAYA**	-
Nov 84.	(lp/c) *Topline;* (TOP/KTOP 110) **THE FAT MAN**	
Jan 85.	(lp) *Charly;* (CRB 1053) **LIVE IN CONCERT**	
Sep 85.	(lp) *Charly-Ace;* (CHD 140) **BOOGIE WOOGIE BABY**	
Oct 85.	(lp) *Liberty;* (EG 260762-1) **THE BEST OF FATS DOMINO** (cd-iss. Jul88 on 'Music For Pleasure'; CDMFP 6026)	
Nov 85.	(lp/c/cd) *Deja Vu;* (DV LP/MC/CD 2030) **20 GOLDEN GREATS: THE FATS DOMINO COLLECTION**	
Dec 85.	(pic-lp) *Astan;* <PD 50003> **FATS DOMINO**	-
Mar 86.	(lp) *Magnum Force;* (MFM 023) **THE FAT MAN LIVE**	
Apr 86.	(lp/c) *Music For Pleasure;* (MFP/TC-MFP 5747) **FATS DOMINO**	
May 86.	(lp/c) *Bulldog;* (BDL/BDC 1059) **BE MY GUEST**	
May 87.	(cd) *Bescol;* (Cd 32) **16 GREATEST HITS**	
May 88.	(cd-ep) *Rhino;* (R 373007) **LIL' BIT OF GOLD**	
May 88.	(lp/c/cd) *Black Tulip;* (22/21/24 36012) **BLUEBERRY HILL**	
May 88.	(pic-lp) *Picture Disc;* (PD 50001) **BLUEBERRY HILL**	
Jul 88.	(lp/c) *Knight;* (KNLP/KNMC 11006) **EASYRIDING**	
1988.	(cd) *Pickwick;* (PWK 021) **BLUEBERRY HILL**	
1988.	(lp/c) *Joker;* <SM/MC 3895> **FATS DOMINO VOL.1**	-
1988.	(lp) *Joker;* <SM 3896> **FATS DOMINO VOL.2**	
1988.	(cd) *Spectrum;* (SPEC 85015) **COLLECTION: FATS DOMINO**	
1988.	(cd) *Silver Line;* (SLCD 804) **24 GREATEST HITS**	
Dec 88.	(c) *Capitol;* (4XLL 8347) **BLUEBERRY HITS**	
Jun 89.	(cd/c) *Spectrum;* (K/U 3016-2) **THE BEST OF THE FAT MAN**	
Apr 90.	(cd/c/lp) *Tomato;* <269663-2/-4/-1> **ROLLIN'**	-
Aug 90.	(cd/c) *Graffiti Collection;* (GRCD/GRMC 06) **GRAFFITI COLLECTION**	
Nov 90.	(7") *Liberty;* **MY BLUE HEAVEN. / BLUEBERRY HILL** (12"+=) – Walking to New Orleans. (cd-s++=) – The fat man.	
Feb 91.	(cd/c) *E.M.I.;* (CD/TC EMS 1381) **MY BLUE HEAVEN: THE BEST OF FATS DOMINO**	-

– My blue Heaven / The fat man / Please don't leave me / Ain't that a shame / I'm in love again / When my dreamboat comes home / Blueberry hill / Blue Monday / I'm walkin' / Valley of tears / Big beat / Yes my darling / Whole lotta loving / I'm ready / I'm gonna be a wheel someday / I want to walk you home / Be my guest / Walking to New Orleans (undubbed) / Let the four winds blow / What a party.

Sep 91.	(cd) *Charly;* (CDINS 5043) **BE MY GUEST – LIVE** (live)	-
Nov 91.	(4xcd-box) *E.M.I.;* (CDS 796784-2) **THEY CALL ME THE FAT MAN**	
Mar 92.	(cd) *Entertainers;* (ENTCD 265) **HIS 28 GREATEST HITS**	
Jun 92.	(cd) *Tring;* (CDAA/MCAA 048) **AUDIO ARCHIVE**	
Oct 92.	(cd/c) *Muskateer;* (MU 5/4 015) **HIS GREATEST HITS**	
Feb 93.	(cd) *Charly;* (CDCD 1015) **ROCKIN' WITH FATS**	
Jul 93.	(cd) *Repertoire;* (REP 4160) **KINGS OF FATS**	
Aug 93.	(cd) *Tomato;* (5980063-2) **ANTOINE FATS DOMINO**	
Nov 93.	(cd) *Bear Family;* **OUT OF NEW ORLEANS**	
Nov 93.	(cd) *Koch Int.;* (3/2 99232) **THE BEST OF FATS DOMINO**	
Feb 94.	(cd/c) *Javelin;* (HAD CD/MC 133) **SPOTLIGHT ON . . .**	
Mar 94.	(cd/c) *Spectrum;* (550179-2/-4) **JAMBALAYA**	
May 94.	(cd/c) *Laserlight;* (1/7 2362) **WHEN I'M WALKING**	
Jul 94.	(cd/c) *Success;* **GREATEST HITS LIVE** (live)	
Aug 94.	(cd) *Dynamite;* (LECD 047) **FATS DOMINO**	
Oct 94.	(cd) *Kenwest;* (KWEST 5400) **BLUEBERRY HILL**	
Nov 94.	(cd) *See For Miles;* (SEECD 416) **THE E.P. COLLECTION**	
Feb 95.	(cd/c) *Marble Arch;* (MAT CD/MC 325) **THE BEST OF FATS DOMINO**	
Feb 95.	(d-cd) *Double Platinum;* (DBP 102006) **50 GREATEST HITS**	
Aug 95.	(cd/c) *Prestige;* (CD/CASS GP 0162) **FATS DOMINO IN CONCERT**	
Jun 96.	(cd) *Ace-Charly;* (CDCHD 597) **THE EARLY IMPERIAL SINGLES (1950-1952)**	
Aug 96.	(cd/c) *Autograph;* (MAC CD/MC 148) **THE BEST OF FATS DOMINO**	
Sep 96.	(3xcd-box) *Disky;* (SA 87262-2) **THE FAT MAN**	
Sep 96.	(cd) *Laserlight;* (12661) **THAT'S FATS**	
Sep 96.	(cd) *See For Miles;* (SEECD 455) **THE E.P. COLLECTION VOL.2**	
Nov 96.	(cd) *Tring;* (QED 060) **THE MAGIC OF FATS DOMINO IN CONCERT** (live)	
Feb 97.	(cd/c) *Platinum;* (PLA TCD/C 128) **THE VERY BEST OF FATS DOMINO**	
Apr 97.	(cd) *Ace-Charly;* (CDCHD 649) **THE IMPERIAL SINGLES VOL.2 (1953-1956)**	
May 97.	(cd/c) *A-Play;* (10039-2/-4) **IN CONCERT**	
Jul 97.	(cd) *Charly;* (CPCD 8291-2) **HITS ALIVE** (live)	
Feb 98.	(cd) *Disky;* (LS 88634-2) **20 GREAT LOVE SONGS**	
May 98.	(d-cd) *Charly;* (CPCD 8339-2) **THE DOMINO EFFECT**	
Jun 98.	(cd) *Ace-Charly;* (CDCHD 689) **THE IMPERIAL SINGLES VOL.3**	
Nov 98.	(cd) *Hallmark;* (30219-2) **ROCKIN' AND ROLLIN'**	
Nov 98.	(d-cd) *Disky;* (HR 85389-2) **ORIGINAL GOLD**	
Feb 99.	(d-cd) *Repertoire;* (RR 4737) **THE PARAMOUNT TAPES**	
Mar 99.	(cd) *A.B.M.;* (ABMMCD 1032) **I'M WALKIN'**	
Jun 99.	(cd) *Auto Pilot;* (ROGER 12) **BLUEBERRY HILL**	

Lonnie DONEGAN

Born: ANTHONY JAMES DONEGAN, 29 April'31, Glasgow, Scotland. The son of a classical violinist who played with the Scottish National Orchestra, DONEGAN began playing guitar in his teens. He was also an avid fan of folk, country, blues and jazz, immersing himself in the sounds of FRANK CRUMIT, JOSH WHITE, HANK WILLIAMS, LOUIS ARMSTRONG, LEADBELLY, WOODY GUTHRIE, etc. His musical ambitions eventually led him to London where he auditioned for CHRIS BARBER's band; the pair hit it off immediately and became lifelong friends. Following a stint of national service in Europe (where he was introduced to the musical delights of the American Forces Radio Network), DONEGAN returned to form The KEN COLYER JAZZMEN with BARBER and KEN COLYER. Between sets, DONEGAN took the spotlight and began developing the frantic hybrid of blues, jazz, folk and country that would come to be known as 'Skiffle'. Named – by COLYER's brother – after an old blues combo, the DAN BURLEY SKIFFLE GROUP, this unique sound kicked off a musical revolution almost as far reaching as ELVIS PRESLEY's lip-curling cross of rockabilly, gospel and jump-blues. When COLYER departed the group in 1954, BARBER took the helm and the band soon found themselves in the studio courtesy of 'Decca'. DONEGAN (who now took the stage name LONNIE after a compere confused him with guitarist LONNIE JOHNSON) persuaded the A&R man to let them cut a couple of tracks in his skiffle style, subsequently included on the 10" album, 'NEW ORLEANS JOY' (1955). One of them, 'ROCK ISLAND LINE' (a trad folk song cut by LEADBELLY amongst others), was released as a single – under the LONNIE DONEGAN SKIFFLE GROUP moniker – and proceeded to tear up the charts as well as the musical rule book; six months later it had sold an incredible three million copies, staying on the UK chart for 22 weeks and even making the US Top 10, a feat previously unheard of for a British act. Follow-up track, 'DIGGIN' MY POTATOES', was banned by the BBC for its suggestive title (hmmm . . .), giving old LONNIE (who duly signed to 'Pye') one of the first 'rebel' tags of the era. The ban only served to increase his popularity and over the next decade, an avalanche of hit singles buried the UK chart including No.1s 'CUMBERLAND GAP', 'PUTTING ON THE STYLE' (both 1957) and comic novelty track, 'MY OLD MAN'S A DUSTMAN' (1960). The latter track became the first ever single to go straight in at No.1, reflecting DONEGAN's 'King Of Skiffle' status. Imitators were ten a penny, utilising any DIY instruments they could lay their hands on i.e. washboards, soup spoons, etc. In fact, a young PAUL McCARTNEY was one particularly mad keen fan, an early incarnation of The BEATLES playing at one of DONEGAN's folk appreciation society gigs in 1958. Ironically, though, the fab four's own adaptation of rock's roots steered the course of pop music in a different direction and skiffle mania was all but over by the early 60's. LONNIE's last Top 20 hit came in 1962 with 'PICK A BALE O' COTTON' and after 'THE FOLK ALBUM' (1965) failed to capture the imagination of the new folkies on the block, DONEGAN concentrated on production work for 'Pye'. 1970's flop 'LONNIEPOPS' album marked the end of his tenure with the label and he subsequently worked in Germany where there was a brief skiffle mini-revival. The man's curious brand of humour was showcased once more in 1976 with a one-off single, 'I'VE LOST MY LITTLE WILLIE'. Unfortunately he suffered a heart attack the same year and relocated to California to recuperate in the West Coast sun. 1978 saw the release of 'PUTTING ON THE STYLE', an all-star skiffle affair featuring the likes of RINGO STARR, RON WOOD and ELTON JOHN, all long time fans. The album actually made the UK Top 60 although the C&W follow-up, 'SUNDOWN' (1979) made little headway. 1981, meanwhile found him teaming up with Scots group, SHAKIN' PYRAMIDS for a one-off single although continuing heart problems curtailed him for much of the early-mid 80's. A further one-off single, 'DONEGAN'S DANCING SUNSHINE BAND', appeared in summer '87. In 1995, DONEGAN was presented with an Ivor Novello award, an occasion which saw him singing with longtime fan VAN MORRISON. The pair discussed cutting some tracks together, the results finally emerging in 1999 on 'MULESKINNER BLUES', an 'R.C.A.' set combining old and new material with contributions from the likes of ALBERT LEE, JACQUI McSHEE and even SAM BROWN. Standout tracks, though were the two pairings with VAN MORRISON, on the rabble-rousing title track and the brilliant remake of 'I'M ALABAMMY BOUND'. Clearly, DONEGAN (or VAN for that matter) hasn't reached the end of the rock island line just yet;

he recently added Glastonbury to his already packed gig diary while his fans straddle both the generation gap and geographical boundaries (from Land's End to Falkirk, at least!). Basically DONEGAN IS SKIFFLE and we are not worthy.

Best CD collection: TALKING GUITAR BLUES – THE VERY BEST OF . . . (*7)

LONNIE DONEGAN – vocals, guitar, banjo with his Skiffle Group: **DENNY WRIGHT** – lead guitar / **MICKY ASHMAN** – upright bass / **NICK NICHOLS** – drums

		Decca	London
Nov 55.	(7"/78; as The LONNIE DONEGAN SKIFFLE GROUP) (F/FJ 10647) <1650> **ROCK ISLAND LINE. / JOHN HENRY**	8	8 Feb56
Feb 56.	(7"/78; as The LONNIE DONEGAN SKIFFLE GROUP) (F/FJ 10695) **DIGGIN' MY POTATOES. / BURY MY BODY**		–

		Pye Nixa	Mercury
Apr 56.	(7"/78) (7N/N 15036) <70872> **LOST JOHN. / STEWBALL**	2	58 May56
Jun 56.	(7"ep) (NJE 1017) **SKIFFLE SESSION EP** – Railroad Bill / Stackalee / Ballad of Jessie James / Ol' Riley.	20	
Aug 56.	(7"/78) (7N/N 15071) **BRING A LITTLE WATER, SYLVIE. / DEAD OR ALIVE** (below lp hit the singles chart due to non-existence of UK lp chart)	7	
Dec 56.	(10"lp) (NPT 19012) **LONNIE DONEGAN SHOWCASE LP** – Wabash cannonball / How long how long blues / Nobody's child / I shall not be moved / I'm Alabammy bound / I'm a rambling man / Wreck of the old '97 / Frankie and Johnny. (re-iss. 1968 on 'Marble Arch'; MAL 797)	26	
Dec 56.	(lp) <M 920229> **AN ENGLISHMAN SINGS AMERICAN FOLK SONGS**	–	
Jan 57.	(7"/78) (7N/N 15080) **DON'T YOU ROCK ME, DADDY-O. / I'M ALABAMMY BOUND**	4	
Mar 57.	(7"/78) (7N/N 15087) **CUMBERLAND GAP. / LOVE IS STRANGE**	1	
May 57.	(7"/78) (7N/N 15093) **GAMBLIN' MAN. / PUTTING ON THE STYLE (live)**	1	
Sep 57.	(7"/78) (7N/N 15108) **MY DIXIE DARLING. / I'M JUST A ROLLING STONE**	10	
Nov 57.	(10"lp) (NPT 19027) **LONNIE** – Lonesome traveller / The sunshine of his love / Ain't no more cane on the Brazos / Ain't you glad you've got religion / Times are getting hard, boys / Lazy John / Light from the lighthouse / I've got my rocks in my bed / Long summer day.	–	
Dec 57.	(7"/78) (7N/N 15116) **JACK O'DIAMONDS. / HAM 'N' EGGS**	14	
Apr 58.	(7"/78) (7N/N 15129) **THE GRAND COOLEE DAM. / NOBODY LOVES LIKE AN IRISHMAN**	6	
Jun 58.	(7"/78) (7N/N 15148) **SALLY, DON'T YOU GRIEVE. / BETTY, BETTY, BETTY**	11	
Sep 58.	(7"/78) (7N/N 15158) **LONESOME TRAVELLER. / TIMES ARE GETTING HARD BOYS**	28	
Sep 58.	(lp) (NPL 18034) **TOPS WITH LONNIE** – Don't you rock me, daddy-o / Putting on the style / Gamblin' man / My Dixie darling / Bring a little water, Sylvie / Cumberland gap / Saly, don't you grieve / Nobody loves likes an Irishman / Lost John / Does your chewing gum lose it's flavour / Tom Dooley.	–	
Nov 58.	(7"/78) (7N/N 15165) **LONNIE'S SKIFFLE PARTY (medley part 1: LITTLE LIZA JANE – PUTTING ON THE STYLE – CAMPTOWN RACES – KNEES UP MOTHER BROWN. / (medley part 2: SO LONG – ON TOP OF OLD SMOKEY – DOWN IN THE VALLEY – SO LONG**	23	–
Nov 58.	(7"/78) (7N/N 15172) **TOM DOOLEY. / ROCK O' MY SOUL**	3	–

		Pye-Nixa	Dot
Dec 58.	(lp) n<DLP 3159> **LONNIE DONEGAN**	–	
Jan 59.	(7"/78) (7N/N 15181) <15911> **DOES YOUR CHEWING GUM LOSE ITS FLAVOUR. / AUNT RILEY** <US re-iss. Jul61; same> – hit No.5	3	Feb59
Apr 59.	(7"/78) (7N/N 15198) **FORT WORTH JAIL. / WHOA BUCK**	14	
May 59.	(lp) (NPL 18043) **LONNIE RIDES AGAIN** – Fancy talking tinker / Miss Otis regrets / Jimmie Brown the newsboy / Mr. Froggy / Take this hammer / The gold rush is over / You pass me by / Talking guitar blues / John Hardy / House of the rising sun / San Miguel. (re-iss. 1969 on 'Marble Arch'; MAL 1153)		

		Pye	Atlantic
Jun 59.	(7"/78) (7N/N 15206) **BATTLE OF NEW ORLEANS. / DARLING COREY**	2	
Aug 59.	(7"/78; Irish-only) (7N/N 15219) **KEVIN BARRY. / MY LAGAN LOVE**	–	
Sep 59.	(7"/78) (7N/N 15223) **SAL'S GOT A SUGAR LIP. / CHESAPEAKE BAY**	13	
Nov 59.	(7"/78) (7N/N 15237) **SAN MIGUEL. / TALKING GUITAR BLUES**	19	
Dec 59.	(lp) <8038> **SKIFFLE FOLK MUSIC**	–	
Mar 60.	(7"/78) (7N/N 15256) **MY OLD MAN'S A DUSTMAN. / THE GOLDEN VANITY**	1	
May 60.	(7"/78) (7N/N 15267) **I WANNA GO HOME (THE WRECK THE THE JOHN). / JIMMY BROWN THE NEWSBOY**	5	
Aug 60.	(7"/78) (7N/N 15275) **LORELEI. / IN ALL MY WILDEST DREAMS**	10	
Nov 60.	(7") (7N 15312) **LIVELY. / BLACK CAT (CROSS MY PATH TODAY)**	13	
Dec 60.	(7") (7N 15315) **VIRGIN MARY. / BEYOND THE SUNSET**	27	
Mar 61.	(7") (7N 15330) **(BURY ME) BENEATH THE WILLOW. / LEAVE MY WOMAN ALONE**		
Apr 61.	(lp) (NPL 18063) **MORE! TOPS WITH LONNIE** – Battle of New Orleans / Lorelei / Lively! / Sal's got a sugar lip / I wanna go home / Leave my woman alone / My old man's a dustman / Fort Worth jail / Have a drink on me / (Bury me) Beneath the willow / Little Liza Jane / Puttin' on the style / Camptown races / Knees up, Mother Brown / On top of Old Smokey / Down in the valley / So long.		
May 61.	(7") (7N 15354) **HAVE A DRINK ON ME. / SEVEN DAFFODILS**	8	

		Pye	A.B.C.
Aug 61.	(7") (7N 15371) **MICHAEL ROW THE BOAT. / LUMBERED**	6	
Jan 62.	(7") (7N 15410) **THE COMMANCHEROS. / RAMBLIN' ROUND**	14	
Mar 62.	(7") (7N 15424) **THE PARTY'S OVER. / OVER THE RAINBOW**	9	
Jun 62.	(7") (7N 15446) **I'LL NEVER FALL IN LOVE AGAIN. / KEEP ON THE SUNNYSIDE**		
Aug 62.	(7") (7N 15455) **PICK A BALE OF COTTON. / STEAL AWAY**	11	–
Dec 62.	(7") **THE MARKET SONG. / TIT-BITS (with MAX MILLER & The LONNIE DONEGAN GROUP)**		
Dec 62.	(lp) (NPL 18073) **SING HALLELUJAH** – Sing hallelujah / We shall walk through the valley / No hiding place / Good news, chariot's a-comin' / Noah found grace in the eyes of the Lord / Joshua fit the battle of Jericho / His eye is on the sparrow / Born in Bethlehem / This train / New burying ground / Steal away / Nobody knows the trouble I've seen.		
Apr 63.	(7") (7N 15514) **LOSING BY A HAIR. / TRUMPET SOUNDS**		
Jun 63.	(7") (7N 15530) **IT WAS A VERY GOOD YEAR. / RISE UP**		
Sep 63.	(7") (7N 15564) **LEMON TREE. / I'VE GOTTA GIRL SO FINE**		
Nov 63.	(7") (7N 15579) **500 MILES AWAY FROM HOME. / THIS TRAIN**		
Jul 64.	(7") (7N 15669) **BEANS IN MY EARS. / IT'S A LONG ROAD TO TRAVEL**		
Sep 64.	(7") (7N 15679) **FISHERMAN'S LUCK. / THERE'S A BIG WHEEL**		
Mar 65.	(7") (7N 15803) **GET OUT OF MY LIFE. / WON'T YOU TELL ME**		
Jul 65.	(7") (7N 15893) **LOUISIANA MAN. / BOUND FOR ZION**		
Aug 65.	(lp) (NPL 18126) **THE LONNIE DONEGAN FOLK ALBUM** – I'm gonna be a bachelor / Interstate forty / After taxes / Where in the world are we going / Diamonds of dew / Bound for Zion / She was T-bone talking woman / Wedding bells / Reverend Mr. Black / The doctor's daughter / Blistered / Farewell. (re-iss. 1967 on 'Golden Guinea'; GGL 0382)		
Jan 66.	(7") (7N 15993) **WORLD CUP WILLIE. / WHERE IN THIS WORLD ARE WE GOING**		
May 66.	(7") (7N 17109) **I WANNA GO HOME. / BLACK CAT (CROSS MY PATH TODAY)**		
Jan 67.	(7") (7N 17232) **AUNT MAGGIE'S REMEDY. / MY SWEET MARIE**		

		Columbia	not iss.
Mar 68.	(7") (DB 8371) **TOYS. / RELAX YOUR MIND**		

		Decca	not iss.
Nov 69.	(7") (F 12984) **MY LOVELY JUANITA. / WHO KNOWS WHERE THE TIME GOES**		
1970.	(lp) (SKL 5068) **LONNIEPOPS – LONNIE DONEGAN TODAY** – Little green apples / Hey! hey! / First of May / Both sides now / If you go away / Love song to a princess / Who knows where the times goes / What the world needs now is love / My lovely Juanita / Windmills of your mind / Long haired lover from Liverpool / And you need me.		

		Pye	not iss.
Feb 70.	(7") (7N 45009) **BURNING BRIDGES. / 'TIL I CAN'T TAKE NO MORE**		–

		R.C.A.	not iss.
Nov 71.	(7") (RCA 2128) **COME TO AUSTRALIA. / DON'T BLAME THE CHILD**		–

		Pye	not iss.
Oct 72.	(7") (7N 45184) **SPEAK TO THE SKY. / GET OUT OF MY LIFE**		–
Jun 73.	(7"; with KENNY BALL & THE JAZZMEN) (7N 45252) **WHO'S GONNA PLAY THIS OLD PIANO. / SOUTH**		

		Philips	
1974.	(lp) (6305 227) **LONNIE DONEGAN MEETS LEINEMANN** – Casey's last ride / Bottle of wine / Dixie darling / Frankie and Johnny / Tops at loving you / Gloryland / Leinemann's potatoes / Me and Bobby McGee / Does your chewing gum lose its flavour / Becky Deen / Jack o' diamonds.		German
1976.	(lp) (6305 288) **COUNTRY ROADS** – Country roads / Rock island line / Keep on the sunny side / Dixie Lily / Louisiana man / Dead or alive / Midnight special / Muleskinner blues / Roll in my sweet baby's arms / Lost John / Have a drink on me / Dublin O'Shea.	–	– German

		Black Lion	not iss.
Jul 76.	(7") (BSP 45105) **LOST JOHN. / JENNY'S BALL**		

		Decca	not iss.
Aug 76.	(7") (FR 13669) **I'VE LOST MY LITTLE WILLIE. / CENSORED**		–

		Chrysalis	U.A.
Jan 78.	(7") (CHS 2205) **ROCK ISLAND LINE. / HAM 'N' EGGS**		–
Feb 78.	(lp/c) (CHR/ZCHR 1158) <UALA 827> **PUTTIN' ON THE STYLE** – Rock island line / Have a drink on me / Ham 'n' eggs / I wanna go home / Diggin' my potatoes / Nobody's child / Puttin' on the style / Frankie and Johnny / Drop down baby / Lost John.		51
Apr 78.	(7") (CHS 2211) **PUTTIN' ON THE STYLE. / DROP DOWN BABY**		–
May 79.	(lp/c) (CHR/ZCHR 1205) **SUNDOWN** – I'm all out and down / Home / Streamline train / Sundown / Mama's got the know how / Morning light / Louisiana sun / The battle of New Orleans / Cajun / Dreaming my dreams with you.		–

		Cuba Libre – Virgin	not iss.
Nov 81.	(7"ep; with the SHAKIN' PYRAMIDS) (VS 460) **CUMBERLAND GAP / WABASH CANNONBALL / DON'T YOU ROCK ME DADDY-O / ONLY MY PILLOW / GRAB IT AND GROWL**		–

—— next with guests MONTY SUNSHINE, CHRIS BARBER, KEN COLYER, etc

		Dakota	not iss.
Dec 81.	(d-lp/d-c) (ICSD/ZCICSD 2001) **JUBILEE CONCERT (live Autumn 1981)**		–

– Ace in the hole / Isle Of Capri / Going home / Shine / Jenny's ball / One sweet letter from you / Hush-a-bye / Bugle call march / Ice cream / John Henry / Take this hammer / Railroad Bill / Tom Dooley / New burying ground / Grand Coulee Dam / New York town / Miss Otis Regrets / Does your chewing gum lose its flavour on the bedpost overnight / One night of love / Rock island line / Gloryland / Corrina Corrina / Goodnight Irene.

	Rosie's Records	not iss.
Jul 87. (7"; with MONTY SUNSHINE) (RR 015) **DONEGAN'S DANCING SUNSHINE BAND. / LEAVING BLUES**		-

—— In 1987 he turned actor, noteably in TV series 'Rockcliffe's Babies'

—— LONNIE returned with more stars as backing

	Capo-RCA	Capo-RCA
Jan 99. (cd) (<CAPO 501>) **MULESKINNER BLUES**		

– Muleskinner blues (with VAN MORRISON) / Please don't call me in the morning / Rock island line / When I get off this feeling / Fancy talking tinker / I'm Alabamma bound (with VAN MORRISON) / Stewball / Skiffle / Welfare line / All together now / I don't wanna lose you / Poker club / Spanish nights / Always from the heart.

– compilations, others, etc. –

Jan 56. (78) Nixa-Jazz; (NJS 2006) **MIDNIGHT SPECIAL. / WHEN THE SUN GOES DOWN**		-
1956. (7"ep) Jazz Today; (JTE 107) **BACKSTAIRS SESSION**		-

– Midnight special / When the sun goes down / New burying ground / Worried man blues. (re-iss. 1956 on 'Pye-Nixa'; NJE 1014)

Nov 56. (78) Oriole; (CB 1329) **THE PASSING STRANGER. / (B-side by Tommy Reilly)**		-
Dec 56. (7",78) Columbia; (DB 3850) **ON A CHRISTMAS DAY. / TAKE MY HAND PRECIOUS LORD**		-
1957. (7"ep) Pye-Nixa; (NEP 24031) **HIT PARADE**		-

– Lost John / Stewball / Bring a little water / Dead or alive.

1957. (7"ep) Pye-Nixa; (NEP 24040) **HIT PARADE VOL.2**		-

– Cumberland gap / Love is strange / Don't you rock me, daddy-o / I'm Alabammy bound.

1958. (7"ep) Pye-Nixa; (NEP 24067) **HIT PARADE VOL.3**		-

– Putting on the style / My Dixie darling / Gamblin' man / I'm just a rolling stone.

1958. (7"ep) Pye-Nixa; (NEP 24075) **DONEGAN ON STAGE (live)**		-

– Mule skinner blues / Old Hannah / On a Monday / Glory.

1958. (7"ep) Pye-Nixa; (NEP 24081) **HIT PARADE VOL.4**		-

– Grand Coolee Dam / Ham 'n' eggs / Nobody loves like an Irishman / Jack O'Diamonds.

1959. (7"ep) Pye-Nixa; (NEP 24104) **HIT PARADE VOL.5**		-

– Tom Dooley / Rock o' my soul / Sally don't you grieve / Betty, Betty, Betty.

1959. (7"ep) Pye-Nixa; (NEP 24107) **RELAX WITH LONNIE**		-

– Bewildered / Kevin Barry / It's no secret / My lagan love.

1959. (7"ep) Pye-Nixa; (NEP 24114) **HIT PARADE VOL.6**		-

– The battle of New Orleans / Fort Worth jail / Does your chewing gum lose the flavour (on the bedpost overnight) / Darling Corey.

1960. (7"ep) Pye-Nixa; (NEP 24127) **YANKEE DOODLE DONEGAN**		-

– Corrine Corrina / Junko partner / Nobody understands me / Sorry but I'm gonna have to pass.

1961. (7"ep) Pye-Nixa; (NEP 24134) **HIT PARADE VOL.7**		-

– My old man's a dustman / The golden vanity / Sal's got a sugar lip / Talking guitar blues.

1961. (7"ep) Pye-Nixa; (NEP 24149) **HIT PARADE VOL.8**		-

– Michael row the boat / I wanna go home / Lumbered / Have a drink on me.

Aug 62. (lp) Golden Guinea; (GGL 0135) **A GOLDEN AGE OF DONEGAN**	3	-

(re-iss. 1966 on 'Marble Arch'; MAL 636)

Jan 63. (lp) Golden Guinea; (GGL 0170) **A GOLDEN AGE OF DONEGAN VOL.2**	15	-

(re-iss. 1967 on 'Marble Arch'; MAL 698)

1970. (lp) Hallmark; (HM 204) **MY OLD MAN'S A DUSTMAN**		-
1971. (lp/c) Golden Hour; (GH/ZCGH 514) **A GOLDEN HOUR OF LONNIE DONEGAN**		-

(re-iss. Sep90 on 'Knight' cd/c; KGH CD/MC 129)

1973. (lp) Golden Hour; (GH 565) **A GOLDEN HOUR OF LONNIE DONEGAN VOL.2**		-
1973. (lp) Hallmark; (HMA 252) **LONNIE DONEGAN**		-
Jan 76. (7") Pye; (7N 45548) **BATTLE OF NEW ORLEANS. / PUTTIN' ON THE STYLE**		-
1976. (lp) Ronco; (RTL 2017) **GREATEST HITS**		-
1977. (12"ep) Pye; (BD 108) **DOES YOUR CHEWING GUM LOSE ITS FLAVOUR / MY OLD MAN'S A DUSTMAN / BATTLE OF NEW ORLEANS / TOM DOOLEY**		-
Nov 77. (d-lp/d-c) Pye; (FILD/ZCFLD 011) **THE LONNIE DONEGAN FILE**		-
Jul 78. (7") Pye; (7N 46096) **MY OLD MAN'S A DUSTMAN. / I WANNA GO HOME**		-
Jul 78. (7") Pye; (7N 46107) **TOM DOOLEY. / BATTLE OF NEW ORLEANS**		-
Jul 78. (lp/c) Music For Pleasure; (MFP 50389) **THE HITS OF LONNIE DONEGAN**		-
May 79. (7") Flashback; (FBS 10) **MY OLD MAN'S A DUSTMAN. / DOES YOUR CHEWING GUM LOSE ITS FLAVOUR**		-
Feb 80. (c) Bravo; (BRC 2530) **GREATEST HITS**		-
Jul 82. (7") Old Gold; (OG 9131) **GAMBLIN' MAN. / PUTTING ON THE STYLE**		-
Mar 83. (lp) Ditto; (DTO 10048) **GREATEST HITS**		-
Jun 85. (lp) Bear Family; (BFX 15170) **RARE AND UNISSUED GEMS**		-
Oct 85. (lp/c) Flashback; (FBLP/ZCFBL 8071) **ROCK ISLAND LINE**		-
Sep 87. (d-lp/d-c/d-cd) P.R.T.; (PYL/PYM/PYC 7003) **THE HIT SINGLES COLLECTION**		-
Jan 89. (cd) Pickwick; (PWK 076) **THE BEST OF LONNIE DONEGAN**		-
1989. (7") Old Gold; (OG 9902) **ROCK ISLAND LINE. / LAST TRAIN TO SAN FERNANDO**		-
Sep 89. (lp/c/cd) Castle; (CCS LP/MC/CD 223) **LONNIE DONEGAN: THE COLLECTION**		-

1991. (cd) Music For Pleasure; (MFP 5917) **LONNIE DONEGAN AND HIS SKIFFLE GROUP**		-
Apr 92. (cd) See For Miles; (SEECD 331) **LONNIE DONEGAN – THE ORIGINALS**		-
May 92. (cd/c) See For Miles; (SEE CD/K 346) **THE EP COLLECTION**		-
Jul 92. (cd) Kaz; (KAZCD 21) **BEST OF LONNIE DONEGAN**		-
Dec 92. (3xcd-box) Sequel; (NXTCD 233) **PUTTIN' ON THE STYLES**		-
Oct 93. (cd) See For Miles; (SEECD 382) **THE EP COLLECTION VOL.2**		-
Oct 93. (4xcd-box) Bear Family; (BCD 15700) **MORE THAN PIE IN THE SKY**		-
May 94. (cd) Disky; (GOLD 213) **THE BEST OF LONNIE DONEGAN**		-
1994. (d-cd) Timeless; (CDTTD 586) **40 YEARS JUBILEE**		-
Mar 95. (cd/c) Spectrum; (550761-2/-4) **FAVOURITE FLAVOURS**		-
Nov 95. (cd-s) Old Gold; (12623 6343-2) **DOES YOUR CHEWING GUM LOSE ITS FLAVOUR ON THE BEDPOST OVERNIGHT / CUMBERLAND GAP**		-
Feb 96. (cd-s) Old Gold; (12623 6343-2) *GRAND COLUEE DAM / BRING A LITTLE WATER, SYLVIE*		-
May 96. (cd-s) Old Gold; (12623 6370-2) **GAMBLIN' MAN / LOST JOHN**		-
May 96. (cd-s) Old Gold; (12623 6371-2) **MY OLD MAN'S A DUSTMAN / PUTTING ON THE STYLE**		-
Aug 96. (cd/c) Autograph; (MAC 165) **KING OF SKIFFLE**		-
Jul 97. (cd) Laserlight; (21040) **ROCK MY SOUL**		-
Oct 98. (cd) Castle Select; (SELCD 539) **SKIFFLE SENSATION**		-
Jun 99. (cd) Zircon; (ZIRC 1002) **LIVE 1957 – THE COMPLETE CONWAY HALL CONCERT (live)**		-
Jun 99. (d-cd) Jasmine; (JASCD 352/3) **LONNIE DONEGAN MEETS LEINEMANN / COUNTRY ROADS**		-
Aug 99. (cd) Castle Pie; (PIESD 121) **KING OF SKIFFLE**		-
Sep 99. (d-cd) Sequel; (NEECD 325) **TALKING GUITAR BLUES – THE VERY BEST OF LONNIE DONEGAN**		-

– Lost John / Stewball / Railroad Bill / Bring a little water, Sylvie / Dead or alive / Wabash cannonball / Nobody's child / Frankie and Johnny / Don't you rock me, daddy-o / Cumberland gap / Gamblin' man / Putting on the style / My Dixie darling / Jack O'Diamonds / On a Monday / Muleskinner blues / Grand Coulle Dam / Sally don't you grieve / Lonnie's skiffle (Little Liza Jane – Putting on the style – Camptown races – Little Liza Jane / Knees up mother Brown) / Tom Dooley / Does your chewing gum lose its flavour / Fort Worth jail / Battle of New Orleans / Sal's got a sugar lip / Take this hammer / You pass me by / San Miguel / Talking guitar blues / My old man's a dustman / I wanna go home / Lorelei / Sorry but I'm gonna have to pass / Lively / Virgin Mary / Have a drink on me / Michael row the boat ashore / Lumbered / The commancheros / The party's over / I'll never fall in love again / Pick a bale of cotton / This train / Noah found grace in the eyes of the Lord / Beans in my ears / She was T-bone talking woman / Farewell (fare thee well) / World Cup Willie.

Tanya DONELLY (see under ⇒ BELLY)

DONOVAN

Born: DONOVAN PHILIP LEITCH, 10 May'46, Maryhill, Glasgow, Scotland. At the age of 10, his family moved to Hatfield, England. In 1964, while playing small gigs in Southend, he was spotted by Geoff Stephens and Peter Eden, who became his managers. Later that year, after performing on the 'Ready Steady Go!' pop show over three consecutive weeks, the denim-clad beatnik signed to 'Pye'. His debut single, 'CATCH THE WIND' (issued the same time as DYLAN's 'The Times They Are A-Changin'), saw him break into the Top 5, later reaching Top 30 in America where he was enjoying the fruits of a burgeoning career. His follow-up, 'COLOURS', also made the Top 5 in the summer of '65, as did the debut album, 'WHAT'S BIN DID AND WHAT'S BIN HID'. Later in the year, the 'UNIVERSAL SOLDIER' EP saw DONOVAN begin to develop his uncompromising anti-war stance, a theme which he touched on with his second album, 'FAIRYTALE'. Initially heralded as Britain's answer to BOB DYLAN, he began to build on his folk/pop roots, progressing into flower-power with 'SUNSHINE SUPERMAN' in 1966. The album of the same name (issued only in the States) saw DONOVAN hit a creative high point and included the much revered, 'SEASON OF THE WITCH'. At the beginning of '67, the single 'MELLOW YELLOW' was riding high in the American hit parade, and 'EPISTLE TO DIPPY' soon followed suit. In the meantime, 'MELLOW YELLOW', was given a belated UK release (making Top 10), while its similarly titled parent album (again only issued in the US), hit No.14. 'SUNSHINE SUPERMAN', a UK compilation lp of both aforementioned albums, made the Top 30 in the middle of '67. His label, 'Pye', followed the same marketing strategy with his next UK album, the double 'A GIFT FROM A FLOWER TO A GARDEN', which was in actual fact, two US-only lp's in one. During this highly prolific period, which saw him inspired by the transcendental meditation of guru Maharishi Mahesh Yogi, he released two sublime pieces of acid-pop in 'THERE IS A MOUNTAIN' and 'JENNIFER JUNIPER'. The momentum continued with, 'HURDY GURDY MAN', another classic sojourn into psychedelia which hit Top 5 on both sides of the Atlantic. In 1969, he collaborated with The JEFF BECK GROUP on 'GOO GOO BARABAJAGAL', although this was his final 45 to make a major chart appearance. An album, 'OPEN ROAD' (1970), named after his new band, surprised many by cracking the US & UK charts. In 1971, he recorded a double album of children's songs 'H.M.S. DONOVAN', which led to a critical backlash from the music press. After a 3-year exile in Ireland for tax reasons, he set up home in California with his wife Linda Lawrence and daughters Astrella and Oriole. He has fathered two other children with his new American wife, Enid; DONOVAN LEITCH JNR. (star of the film 'Gas, Food, Lodging') and IONE SKYE, the latter said to be none too bothered about her famous father. DONOVAN enjoyed something of a renaissance in the early 90's when HAPPY MONDAYS' mainman SHAUN RYDER (now of BLACK GRAPE) sang his praises, leading to a comeback album, 'DONOVAN RISING'. He is still going strong today, releasing a well-received album, 'SUTRAS', for the RCA affiliated 'American' label in 1996. • **Songwriters:** Self-penned except, UNIVERSAL SOLDIER (Buffy Sainte-Marie) / LONDON TOWN (Tim Hardin) / REMEMBER THE ALAMO (Jane Bowes) / CAR CAR (Woody Guthrie) / GOLDWATCH BLUES (Mick Softley) / DONNA DONNA (Kevess-Secunda-Secanta-Schwartz-Zeitlin) / OH DEED I DO+ DO YOU HEAR ME NOW (Bert Jansch) / CIRCUS OF SOUR (Paul Bernath) / LITTLE TIN SOLDIER (Shawn Phillips / LORD OF THE DANCE (Sydney Carter) / ROCK'N'ROLL WITH ME (David Bowie-Warren Peace) / MY SONG IS TRUE (Darell Adams) / NO MAN'S LAND (Eric Bogle) / WIND IN THE WILLOWS (Eddie Hardin) / NEWEST BATH GUIDE + MOIRA McCAVENDISH (John Betjeman) / THE SENSITIVE KIND (J. J. Cale) / traditional:- KEEP ON TRUCKIN' + YOU'RE GONNA NEED SOMEBODY + CANDY MAN + THE STAR + COULTER'S CANDY + HENRY MARTIN + THE HEIGHTS OF ALMA + YOUNG BUT GROWING + STEALIN'. He also put music to words/poetry by; William Shakespeare (UNDER THE GREENWOOD TREE) / Gypsy Dave (A SUNNY DAY) / Lewis Carroll (WALRUS AND THE CARPENTER + JABBERWOCKY) / Thora Stowell (THE SELLER OF STARS + THE LITTLE WHITE ROAD) / Fifida Wolfe (LOST TIME) / Lucy Diamond (THE ROAD) / Agnes Herbertson (THINGS TO WEAR) / Edward Lear (THE OWL AND THE PUSSYCAT) / Eugene Field (WYNKEN, BLYNKEN AND NOD) / W. B. Yeats (THE SONG OF WANDERING AENGUS) / Natalie Joan (A FUNNY MAN) / Thomas Hood (QUEEN MAB) / Astella Leitch (MEE MEE I LOVE YOU) / Warwick Embury (ONE NIGHT IN TIME) / Note; HURLEY GURDY MAN originally had a verse by GEORGE HARRISON but this was not recorded and he only added this for live appearances. • **Trivia:** Sang co-lead on title track from ALICE COOPER's 1973 lp 'Billion Dollar Babies'.

Album rating: WHAT'S BIN DID AND WHAT'S BIN HID (*7) / CATCH THE WIND (*6) / FAIRYTALE (*7) / SUNSHINE SUPERMAN (US version; *7) / MELLOW YELLOW (*6) / A GIFT FROM A FLOWER TO A GARDEN (*7; WEAR YOUR LOVE LIKE HEAVEN; *5 – FOR LITTLE ONES; *4) / DONOVAN IN CONCERT (*4) / HURDY GURDY MAN (*6) / DONOVAN'S GREATEST HITS compilation (*7) / BARABAJAGAL (*7) / OPEN ROAD (*5) / H.M.S. DONOVAN (*5) / COSMIC WHEELS (*5) / ESSENCE TO ESSENCE (*5) / 7-TEASE (*5) / SLOW DOWN WORLD (*4) / DONOVAN (*4) / NEUTRONICA (*4) / LADY OF THE STARS (*4) / GREATEST HITS AND MORE compilation (*8) / TROUBADOUR: THE DEFINITIVE COLLECTION compilation (*8) / SUTRAS (*5)

DONOVAN -- vocals, acoustic guitar, harmonica with **BRIAN LOCKING** – bass / **SKIP ALLEN** – drums / **GYPSY DAVE** (b. DAVID MILLS) – kazoo, etc.

		Pye	Hickory
Mar 65.	(7") (7N 15801) <1309> **CATCH THE WIND. / WHY DO YOU TREAT ME LIKE YOU DO**	4	23 Apr65
May 65.	(7") (7N 15866) <1324> **COLOURS. / TO SING FOR YOU**	4	61 Jun65
May 65.	(lp) (NPL 18117) <123> **WHAT'S BIN DID AND WHAT'S BIN HID** <US title 'CATCH THE WIND'>	3	30

– Josie / Catch the wind / Remember the Alamo / Cuttin' out / Car car * (riding in my car) / Keep on truckin' / Goldwatch blues / To sing for you / You're gonna need somebody on your bond / Tangerine puppet / Donna Donna * / Ramblin' boy (re-iss. Jul68 on 'Marble Arch';) – (omitted *)

Sep 65.	(7") <1338> **UNIVERSAL SOLDIER. / DO YOU HEAR ME**	-	53
Sep 65.	(7"ep) (NEP 24219) **THE UNIVERSAL SOLDIER EP**	13	-

– Universal soldier / The ballad of a crystal man / Do you hear me now* / The war drags on.

Oct 65.	(lp) (NPL 18128) **FAIRYTALE**	20	85 Dec 65

– Colours * / To try for the sun / Sunny Goodge street / Oh deed I do / Circus of sour / The summer day reflection song / Candy man / Jersey Thursday / Belated forgiveness plea / Ballad of a crystal man / Little tin soldier * / Ballad of Geraldine. (re-iss. Mar69 on 'Marble Arch';) – (omitted *). (re-iss. Feb91 on 'Castle' cd/c; CLA CD/MC 226)

Nov 65.	(7") (7N 15984) **TURQUOISE. / HEY GYP (DIG THE SLOWNESS)**	30	-
Nov 65.	(7") <1375> **YOU'RE GONNA NEED SOMEBODY ON YOUR BOND. / THE LITTLE TIN SOLDIER**	-	-
Jan 66.	(7") <1402> **TO TRY FOR THE SUN. / TURQUOISE**	-	-
Feb 66.	(7") (7N 17067) **JOSIE. / LITTLE TIN SOLDIER**	-	-
Apr 66.	(7") (7N 17088) **REMEMBER THE ALAMO. / THE BALLAD OF A CRYSTAL MAN**	-	-

---

DONOVAN plus **JOHN CAMERON** – piano, harpsichord / **HAROLD McNAIR** – flute

		Pye	Epic
Jul 66.	(7") (7N 17241) <10045> **SUNSHINE SUPERMAN. / THE TRIP**	2	1 Jun66
Sep 66.	(lp; mono)<stereo> <LN 24217> <BN 26217> **SUNSHINE SUPERMAN**	-	11

– Sunshine superman / Legend of a girl child Linda / The observation / Guinevere / Celeste / Writer in the Sun / Season of the witch / Hampstead incident / Sand and foam / Young girl blues / Three kingfishers / Bert's blues. (UK-iss.Feb91 on 'Beat Goes On' cd/c; BGO CD/MC 68) (cd re-iss. Oct96 on 'EMI Gold'; CDGOLD 1066)

Nov 66.	(7") <10098> **MELLOW YELLOW. / SUNNY SOUTH KENSINGTON**	-	2
Jan 67.	(7") <10127> **EPISTLE TO DIPPY. / PREACHIN' LOVE**	-	19
Feb 67.	(7") (7N 17267) **MELLOW YELLOW. / PREACHIN' LOVE**	8	-
Feb 67.	(lp; mono)<stereo> <LN 24239> <BN 26239> **MELLOW YELLOW**	-	14

– Mellow yellow / Writer in the Sun / Sand and foam / The observation / Bleak city woman / House of Jansch / Young girl blues / Museum / Hampstead incident / Sunny South Kensington. (cd-iss. Oct93 on 'Sony Europe';)

Jun 67.	(lp) (NPL 18181) **SUNSHINE SUPERMAN** -(compilation of last 2 US albums)	25	-

Oct 67.	(7") (7N 17403) <10212> **THERE IS A MOUNTAIN. / SAND AND FOAM**	8	11 Sep67

---- **DONOVAN** retained **HAROLD** and in came **TONY CARR** – percussion / **CANDY JOHN CARR** – bongos **CLIFF BARTON** – bass / **KEITH WEBB** – drums / **MIKE O'NEIL** – keyboards / **MIKE CARR** – vibraphone / **ERIC LEESE** – electric guitar

Dec 67.	(7") <10253> **WEAR YOUR LOVE LIKE HEAVEN. / OH GOSH**	-	23
Dec 67.	(lp; mono)<stereo> <LN 24349> <BN 26349> **WEAR YOUR LOVE LIKE HEAVEN**	-	60

– Wear your love like Heaven / Mad John's escape / Skip-a-long Sam / Sun / There was a time / Oh gosh / Little boy in corduroy / Under the greenwood tree / The land of doesn't have to be / Someone's singing / Song of the naturalist's wife / The enchanted gypsy.

---- **KEN BALDOCK** – bass repl. BARTON, LEESE, WEBB, O'NEIL + MIKE CARR

Dec 67.	(lp; mono)<stereo> <LN 24350> <BN 26350> **FOR LITTLE ONES**	-	-

– Voyage into the golden screen / Isle of Islay / The mandolin man and his secret / Lay of the last tinker / The tinker and the crab / Widow with shawl (a portrait) / The lullaby of spring / The magpie / Starfish-on-the-toast / Epistle to Derroll.

Feb 68.	(7") (7N 17457) <10300> **JENNIFER JUNIPER. / POOR COW**	5	26
Apr 68.	(d-lp-box; mono/stereo) (NPL/NSPL 20000) <L2N6/B2N 171> **A GIFT FROM A FLOWER TO A GARDEN**	13	19

– (contains 2 US Dec67 albums boxed) (cd-iss. Jul93 & Jun97 on 'Beat Goes On'; BGOCD 194)

May 68.	(7") (7N 17537) <10345> **HURDY GURDY MAN. / TEEN ANGEL**	4	5
Sep 68.	(lp; mono/stereo) (NPL/NSPL 18237) <BN 26420> **DONOVAN IN CONCERT (live)**		18 Jul68

– Isle of Islay / Young girl blues / There is a mountain / Poor cow / Celeste / The fat angel / Guinevere / Widow with shawl (a portrait) / Preachin' love / The lullaby of Spring / Writer in the Sun / Rules and regulations / Mellow yellow. (re-iss. May91 & Apr97 on 'Beat Goes On' cd/c/lp; BGO CD/MC/LP 90) (cd-iss. Nov94 on 'Start';) (re-iss. cd Jan96 on 'Happy Price'; HP 93432)

Oct 68.	(7") <10393> **LALENA. / AYE, MY LOVE**	-	33
Oct 68.	(lp) <BN 26420> **HURDY GURDY MAN**	-	20

– Jennifer Juniper / Hurdy gurdy man / Hi, it's been a long time / Peregrine / The entertaining of a shy girl / Tangier / As I recall it / Get thy bearings / West Indian lady / Teas / The river song / The Sun is a very magic fellow / A sunny day.

Nov 68.	(7") (7N 17660) **ATLANTIS. / I LOVE MY SHIRT**	23	-
Feb 69.	(7") <10434> **ATLANTIS. / TO SUSAN ON THE WEST COAST WAITING**	-	7 / 35
Mar 69.	(lp) (NPL/NSPL 18283) <BXN 26439> **DONOVAN'S GREATEST HITS** (compilation)		4

– Epistle to Dippy / Sunshine Superman / There is a mountain / Jennifer Juniper / Wear your love like Heaven / Season of the witch / Colours / Hurdy gurdy man / Catch the wind / Lalena. <re-iss. 1972; PE 26439> <re-iss. 1973; BN 26836> (re-iss. Sep79 on 'CBS-Embassy' lp/c; CBS/40 31759) (cd-iss. Aug90 on 'Epic';)

Jun 69.	(7"; DONOVAN with The JEFF BECK GROUP) (7N 17778) **GOO GOO BARABAJAGAL (LOVE IS HOT). / BED WITH ME**	12	-
Sep 69.	(7"; DONOVAN with The JEFF BECK GROUP) <10510> **GOO GOO BARABAJAGAL (LOVE IS HOT). / TRUDI**	-	36
Sep 69.	(lp; DONOVAN with The JEFF BECK GROUP) <BN 26481> **BARABAJAGAL**		-

– Barabajagal / Superlungs my supergirl / I love my shirt / The love song / To Susan on the West Coast waiting / Atlantis / Trudi / Pamela Jo / Happiness runs. (cd-iss. Oct93 on 'Sony Europe';)

---- with **JOHN CARR** – drums, vocals / **MIKE THOMPSON** – bass, vocals / **MIKE O'NEILL** – piano

		Dawn	Epic
Sep 70.	(lp) (DNLS 3009) <30125> **OPEN ROAD**	30	16 Jul70

– Changes / Song for John / Curry land / Joe Bean's theme / People used to / Celtic rock / Riki tiki tavi / Clara clairvoyant / Roots of oak / Season of farewell / Poke at the Pope / New Year's resovolution.

Sep 70.	(7"; DONOVAN with OPEN ROAD) (DNS 1006) <10649> **RIKI TIKI TAVI. / ROOTS OF OAK**		55

---- (DANNY – double bass)

Dec 70.	(7"; DONOVAN with DANNY THOMPSON) (DNA 1007) **CELIA OF THE SEALS. / MR.WIND**		-
Feb 71.	(7") <10694> **CELIA OF THE SEAS. / THE SONG OF THE WANDERING AENGUS**		84
Jul 71.	(d-lp) (DNLD 4001) **H.M.S. DONOVAN**		-

– The walrus and the carpenter / Jabberwocky / The seller of the stars / Lost time / The little white road / The star / Coulter's candy / The road / Things to wear / The owl and the pussycat / Homesickness / Fishes in love / Mr.Wind / Wynken, Bylnken and Nod / Celia of the seas / The pee song / The voyage to the Moon / The unicorn / Lord of dance / Little Ben / Can ye dance / In an old fashioned picture book / The song of the wandering Aengus / A funny man / Lord of the reedy river / Henry Martin / Queen Mab / La moor.

---- with guests **CHRIS SPEDDING** – guitar / **JOHN 'RABBIT' BUNDRICK** – keyboards / **JIM HORN** – bass / **COZY POWELL** – drums

		Epic	Epic
Mar 73.	(lp) (SEPC 65450) <32156> **COSMIC WHEELS**	15	25

– Cosmic wheels / Earth sign man / Maria Magenta / Wild witch lady / Sleep / The music makers / The intergallactic laxative / I like you / Only the blues / Appearances. (cd-iss. Sep94 on 'Epic-Rewind'; 477378-2)

Apr 73.	(7") (EPC 1471) <10983> **I LIKE YOU. / EARTH SIGN MAN**		66
Jun 73.	(7") (EPC 1644) <11023> **MARIA MAGENTA. / THE INTERGALLACTIC LAXATIVE**		-

---- now with **STEVE MARRIOT, PETER FRAMPTON** and **NICKY HOPKINS**

Nov 73.	(7") (EPC 1960) **SAILING HOMEWARD. / LAZY DAZE**		-
Dec 73.	(lp) (SEPC 69050) <32800> **ESSENCE TO ESSENCE**		-

– Operating manual for spaceship Earth / Lazy daze / Life goes on / There is an ocean / Dignity of man / Yellow star / Divine daze of deathless delight / Boy for every girl / Saint Valentine's angel / Life is a merry-go-round / Sailing homeward.

Jan 74. (7") <11108> **SAILING HOMEWARD. / YELLOW STAR**

—— Mainly used session musicians from now on.

Sep 74. (7") (EPC 2661) <50016> **ROCK'N'ROLL WITH ME. / THE DIVINE DAZE OF DEATHLESS DELIGHT**   Nov74

Nov 74. (lp) (SEPC 69104) <33245> **7-TEASE**
– Rock and roll souljer / Your broken heart / Salvation stomp / The ordinary family / Ride-a-mile / Sadness / Moon rok / Love of my life / The voice of protest / How silly / The great song of the sky / The quest.

Jan 75. (7") <50077> **ROCK AND ROLL SOULJER. / HOW SILLY**

Feb 75. (7") (EPC 3037) **ROCK AND ROLL SOULJER. / LOVE OF MY LIFE**

Jun 76. (lp) (SEPC 86011) <33945> **SLOW DOWN WORLD**
– Dark-eyed blue jean angel / Cryin' shame / The mountain / Children of the world / My love is true (love song) / A well known has-been / Black widow / Slow down world / Liberation rag.

Jun 76. (7") <50237> **A WELL-KNOWN HAS-BEEN. / DARK EYED BLUE JEAN ANGEL**

    Rak   **Arista**

Aug 77. (7") <0280> **DARE TO BE DIFFERENT. / THE INTERNATIONAL MAN**

Oct 77. (lp) (SRAK 528) **DONOVAN**
– Brave new world / Local boy chops wood / Kalifornia kids / International man / Lady of the stars / Dare to be different / Mijah's dance / The light / Astral angel.

Nov 77. (7") (RAK 265) **THE LIGHT. / THE INTERNATIONAL MAN**

Feb 78. (7") (RAK 269) **DARE TO BE DIFFERENT. / SING MY SONG**

—— (note:- on above US singles [Jan 73, Jan 75, Jun 76, Aug 77] the 'B' side was mono version on 'A').

    Luggage-R.C.A.   **Allegiance**

Aug 80. (lp) (PL 28429) **NEUTRONICA**
– Shipwreck / Only to be expected / Comin' to you / No hunger / Neutron / Mee Mee I love you / The heights of Alma / No man's land / We are one / Madrigalinda / Harmony.

—— with **DANNY THOMPSON** – double bass / **JOHN STEPHENS** – drums / **TONY ROBERTS** – multi-wind instruments / and his 9 year-old daughter **ASTELLA** – dual vocals

Oct 81. (lp) (PL 28472) **LOVE IS ONLY FEELING**
– Lady of the flowers / Lover o lover / The actor / Half Moon bay / The hills of Tuscany / Lay down Lassie / She / Johnny Tuff / Love is only feeling / Marjorie Margerine.

Oct 81. (7") (7-LUG 03) **LAY DOWN LASSIE. / LOVE IS ONLY FEELING**

Jan 84. (lp) (PL 70060) <72857> **LADY OF THE STARS**
– Lady of the stars / I love you baby / Seasons of the witch / Bye bye girl / Every reason / Boy for every girl / Local boy chops wood / Sunshine superman / Til I see you again / Living for the lovelight.
After nearly 7 years in the wilderness, he returned on new label

    Permanent Permanent

Nov 90. (cd/c/lp) (PERM CD/MC/LP 2) **DONOVAN RISING**
– Jennifer Juniper / Catch the wind / The hurdy gurdy man / Sunshine superman / Sadness / Universal soldier / Cosmic wheels / Atlantis / Wear your love like heaven / Colours / To Susan on the west coast waiting / Young girl blues / Young but growing / Stealing / Sailing homeward / Love will find a way / Lalena.

—— He had also credited on The SINGING CORNER's (Nov90) single version of his JENNIFER JUNIPER.

    Silhouette   **not iss.**

Apr 92. (cd-ep) (MDCDKR 3) **NEW BATH GUIDE / MOIRA McCAVENDISH / BROTHER SUN, SISTER MOON**

    American-RCA   **American**

Oct 96. (cd) (74321 39743-2) **SUTRAS**
– Please don't bend / Give it all up / Sleep / Everlasting sea / High your love / The clear-browed one / The way / Deep peace / Nirvana / Eldorado / Be mine / Lady of the lamp / The evernow / Universe am I.

– compilations, others, etc. –

on 'Pye' UK / 'Hickory' (70's 'Epic') US unless otherwise mentioned

Dec 65. (7"ep) (NEP 24229) **COLOURS**
– Catch the wind / Why do you treat me like you do / Colours / To sing for you.

Mar 66. (7"ep) (NEP 24239) **DONOVAN VOL.1**
– Sunny Goodge Street / Oh deed I do / Jersey Thursday / Hey Gyp (dig the slowness).

Jul 66. (7") <1417> **HEY GYP (DIG THE SLOWNESS). / THE WAR DRAGS ON**

Oct 66. (7") <1470> **SUNNY GOODGE STREET. / SUMMER DAY REFLECTION SONG**

Sep 66. (lp) <135> **THE REAL DONOVAN**   96

Jan 67. (7") <193> **CATCH THE WIND. / UNIVERSAL SOLDIER**

Oct 67. (lp) Marble Arch; (MAL 718) **UNIVERSAL SOLDIER**   5
(re-iss. Feb83 on 'Spot'; SPR/SPC 8514)

Feb 68. (7"ep) (NEP 24287) **CATCH THE WIND**
– Catch the wind / Remember the Alamo / Josie / Rambling Rose.

Apr 68. (lp) <143> **LIKE IT IS, WAS AND EVERMORE SHALL BE**

1968. (7") <1492> **DO YOU HEAR ME NOW. / WHY DO YOU TREAT ME LIKE YOU DO**

Aug 68. (7"ep) (NEP 24299) **HURDY GURDY DONOVAN**
– Jennifer juniper / Hurdy gurdy man / Mellow yellow / There is a mountain. (re-iss. Nov71; PMM 104)

Jun 69. (lp) United Artists; (UAS 29044) **IF IT'S TUESDAY IT MUST BE BELGUIM (Soundtrack)**

Nov 69. (lp) <149> **THE BEST OF DONOVAN**

1970. (lp) Marble Arch; (MAL 1168) **THE WORLD OF DONOVAN**

Oct 70. (7") Janus; <A-501> **COLORS. / JOSIE**

Oct 70. (7") Janus; <A-502> **CATCH THE WIND. / WHY DO YOU TREAT ME LIKE YOU DO**

Oct 70. (7") Janus; <A-503> **CANDY MAN. / HEY GYP (DIG THE SLOWNESS)**

Nov 70. (d-lp) Janus; <3022> **DONOVAN P.LEITCH** (early work)

1971. (lp) Golden Hour; (GH 506) **THE GOLDEN HOUR OF DONOVAN**

1971. (lp) Hallmark; (HMA 200) **CATCH THE WIND**
(re-iss. Apr86 on 'Showcase' lp/c; SH LP/TC 133)

1972. (lp) Hallmark; (HMA 241) **COLOURS**
(re-iss. Oct87 on 'P.R.T.' lp/c/cd; PYL/PYM/PYC 7004)

1972. (7") Memory Lane; <15-2251> **SUNSHINE SUPERMAN. / MELLOW YELLOW**

1972. (7") Memory Lane; <15-2280> **JENNIFER JUNIPER. / HURDY GURDY MAN**

1973. (4xlp-set) (11PP 102) **FOUR SHADES OF DONOVAN / OPEN ROAD / DONOVAN'S GREATEST HITS/ / H.M.S. DONOVAN**

Nov 77. (d-lp/c) (FILD/ZCFLD 004) **THE DONOVAN FILE**

Jul 78. (7") **COLOURS. / UNIVERSAL SOLDIER**

Jul 80. (7"ep) Flashback; (FBEP 107) **EP**
– Catch the wind / Turquoise / Colours / Universal soldier.

Oct 81. (lp/c) P.R.T.; (SPOT/ZCSPT 1017) **SPOTLIGHT ON DONOVAN**

Jul 82. (7") Old Gold; (OG 9134) **CATCH THE WIND. / COLOURS**

Jul 83. (10"lp/c) P.R.T.; (DOW/ZCDOW 13) **MINSTREL BOY**

Feb 85. (7") EMI Gold; (G 4545) **MELLOW YELLOW. / SUNSHINE SUPERMAN**

Aug 89. (7") E.M.I.; (EM 98) **SUNSHINE SUPERMAN. / JENNIFER JUNIPER**
(ext.12"+=) (12EM 98) – Wear your love like Heaven.
(cd-s++=) (CDEM 98) – Mellow yellow.

Sep 89. (cd)(c/lp) E.M.I.; (CZ 193)(TC+/EMS 1333) **GREATEST HITS AND MORE**
– Sunshine Superman / Wear your love like Heaven / Jennifer Juniper / Barabajagal (love is hot) / Hurdy gurdy man / Epistle to Dippy / To Susan on the West Coast waiting / Catch the wind / Mellow yellow / There is a mountain / Happiness runs / Season of the witch / Colours / Superlungs – My Supergirl / Lalena / Atlantis. (cd+=) – Preachin' love / Poor cow / Teen angel / Aye my love.

1990. (cd) Marble Arch; **JOSIE**
(re-iss. Jul94 on 'Success')

Oct 90. (lp/c/cd) See For Miles; (SEE/+K/CD 300) **THE EP COLLECTION**

Dec 90. (cd/c) Castle; (CCS CD/MC 276) **THE COLLECTION**

Feb 91. (d-cd/d-c/d-lp) E.M.I.; (CD/TC+/EM 1385) **THE TRIP** (1964-1968 material)

Mar 91. (7") Gulf Peace Team; (GPT 1) **UNIVERSAL SOLDIER. / CATCH THE WIND**
(12"+=) (GPT 001T) – I'll try for the sun.

Jun 91. (cd)(c) Mammoth; (MMCD 5717)(MMMC 4717) **THE HITS**

Jul 91. (cd) The Collection; (ORO 155) **TILL I SEE YOU AGAIN**
(re-iss. Jul94 on 'Success')

Mar 93. (cd) Dojo-Castle; (EARLD 13) **THE EARLY YEARS**

Sep 93. (cd/c) Remember; (RMB 7/4 5059)

Dec 93. (cd) Disky; (GOLD 206) **GOLD: GREATEST HITS**

May 94. (cd) Music DeLuxe; (MDCD 6) **COLOURS**

Oct 94. (cd) Charly; (CDCD 1206) **SUNSHINE SUPERMAN**

Nov 94. (4xcd-box) E.M.I.; (DONOVAN 1) **ORIGINALS**

Jan 95. (cd/c) Spectrum; (550 721-2/-4) **UNIVERSAL SOLDIER**

Dec 95. Javelin; (cd) **SUNSHINE SUPERMAN**

Aug 96. (cd/c) Hallmark; (30501-2/-4) **SUNSHINE TROUBADOR**

Nov 96. (cd) Experience; (EXP 013) **DONOVAN**

Apr 97. (cd) Artful; (ARTFULCD 5) **THE VERY BEST OF**

May 97. (cd) C.M.C.; (100082) **SUNSHINE SUPERMAN**

DOOBIE BROTHERS

Formed: San Jose, California, USA . . . 1970 by JOHN HARTMAN, TOM JOHNSTON (who had both played in an earlier incarnation of The DOOBIE BROTHERS, PUD, along with GREGG MURPHY) and DAVE SHOGREN. Starting out playing bar room boogie that was popular with local bikers, they signed to 'Warner Bros.' in 1971 and released an unsuccessful eponymous Ted Templeman produced album. Their second effort, 'TOULOUSE STREET', gave them their first gold disc and set the musical blueprint for the first half of their career. Coming on like an easy-listening ALLMANS, all crystal clear harmonies and laidback strumming, the band were quintessential Californian 70's rock. 'LISTEN TO THE MUSIC' was akin to an aural massage, while 'LONG TRAIN RUNNIN' from 'THE CAPTAIN AND ME' (1973) repeated the formula, its insidious chorus and foot shuffling groove taking it into the US Top 10. By now the DOOBIE's were selling millions, the country-rock of 'BLACK WATER', giving the band their No.1 in 1974. Its parent album, 'WHAT WERE ONCE VICES ARE NOW HABITS', and the follow-up, 'STAMPEDE' (1975) showed, however, that the sound was becoming tired. Thanks to JEFF BAXTER and MICHAEL McDONALD (both ex-STEELY DAN), the band underwent a timely, if subtle transformation from country boogie to polished, AOR funk. The former had joined before the band recorded 'STAMPEDE' while McDONALD arrived in late '75, initially to fill JOHNSTON's place on tour, the frontman giving up live commitments due to medical problems. McDONALD subsequently reworked the DOOBIE's back catalogue on stage, while writing most of the band's new material. Although many old fans were probably none too happy with the change, it certainly breathed new life into the band and while 'TAKIN' IT TO THE STREETS' (1976) was a marked improvement, the band were back at the top of the charts in 1978 with the multimillion selling 'MINUTE BY MINUTE'. The album also spawned a No.1 single in 'WHAT A FOOL BELIEVES', McDONALD's rich baritone now the essential ingredient in the DOOBIE BROTHERS sound (JOHNSTON having eventually left the previous year). The band then underwent a number of line-up changes before their final studio effort, 'ONE STEP CLOSER' (1980), although by this point McDONALD basically was the DOOBIE BROTHERS and it was inevitable he'd pack the band in for a solo career. The group officially split in March '82, recording a final farewell live album later that year. While McDONALD went on to a major solo success, The DOOBIE BROTHERS reformed in 1988 with a-near original line-up, JOHNSTON back in his role as frontman. The comeback album, 'CYCLES' (1989) went gold, spawning a Top 10 single with 'THE DOCTOR', although the follow-up set, 'BROTHERHOOD' (1991) was virtually ignored. • **Songwriters:** JOHNSTON or SIMMONS penned until MICHAEL McDONALD contributed on his 1975 arrival. JESUS IS JUST ALRIGHT (Byrds) / TAKE ME IN YOUR ARMS (Holland-Dozier-Holland) / LITTLE DARLIN' (I NEED YOU) (Marvin Gaye) / etc. WHAT A FOOL BELIEVES was co-written by McDONALD and KENNY LOGGINS. • **Trivia:** They took the name 'DOOBIE' from the slang for a joint.

Album rating: THE DOOBIE BROTHERS (*5) / TOULOUSE STREET (*6) / THE CAPTAIN AND ME (*7) / WHAT WERE ONCE VICES ARE NOW HABITS (*6) / STAMPEDE (*5) / TAKIN' IT TO THE STREETS (*7) / BEST OF THE DOOBIES compilation (*8) / LIVIN' ON THE FAULT LINE (*5) / MINUTE BY MINUTE (*7) / ONE STEP CLOSER (*6) / BEST OF THE DOOBIES, VOLUME II compilation (*6) / THE DOOBIE BROTHERS FAREWELL TOUR (*4) / CYCLES (*3) / BROTHERHOOD (*3) / LISTEN TO THE MUSIC – THE VERY BEST OF THE DOOBIES compilation (*7) / ROCKIN' DOWN THE HIGHWAY – THE WILDLIFE CONCERT (*4)

TOM JOHNSTON (b. Visalia, California) – vocals, guitar / **PAT SIMMONS** (b.23 Jan'50, Aberdeen, Washington) – guitar, vocals / **DAVE SHOGREN** (b. San Francisco, California) – bass / **JOHN HARTMAN** (b.18 Mar'50, Falls Church, Virginia) – drums

			Warners	Warners
Apr 71.	(lp) (K 46090) <1919> THE DOOBIE BROTHERS			

– Nobody / Slippery St. Paul / Greenwood creek / It won't be right / Travellin' man / Feelin' down farther / The master / rowin' a litle each day / Beehive state / Closer every day / Chicago. (cd-iss. May95; 7599 26215-2)

Apr 71.	(7") <7495> NOBODY. / SLIPPERY ST. PAUL		-	
Jul 71.	(7") <7527> TRAVELIN' MAN. / FEELIN' DOWN FARTHER		-	
Sep 71.	(7") <7544> BEEHIVE STATE. / CLOSER EVERY DAY		-	

—— **TIRAN PORTER** (b. Los Angeles) – bass, vocals repl. SHOGREN.
added 2nd drummer **MICHAEL HOSSACK** (b.18 Sep'50, Paterson, New York, USA)

| Jul 72. | (lp) (K 46183) <2634> TOULOUSE STREET | | | 21 |

– Listen to the music / Don't start me talkin' / Mamaloi / Toulouse street / Rockin' down the highway / Jesus is just alright / White sun / Cotton mouth / Disciple / Snake man. (quad-lp 1976) (cd-iss. Jul88; K2 46183) (cd-iss. May93; 7599 27263-2)

| Aug 72. | (7") <7619> LISTEN TO THE MUSIC. / TOULOUSE STREET | - | 11 |

(UK-iss.Feb74; K 16208) – hit No.29

| Dec 72. | (7") <7661> JESUS IS JUST ALRIGHT. / ROCKIN' DOWN THE HIGHWAY | - | 35 |
| Mar 73. | (lp) (K 46217) <2694> THE CAPTAIN AND ME | | 7 |

– Natural thing / Long train runnin' / China Grove / Dark-eyed Cajun woman / Clear as the driven snow / Without you / South city midnight lady / Evil woman / Busted down around O'Connelly corners / Ukiah / The captain and me. (cd-iss. Oct87 & Feb95; K2 46217)

| Apr 73. | (7") <7698> LONG TRAIN RUNNIN'. / WITHOUT YOU | - | 8 |

(UK-iss.Apr74; K 16267)

| Aug 73. | (7") <7728> CHINA GROVE. / EVIL WOMAN | - | 15 |

(UK-iss.Aug74; K 16310)

—— **KEITH KNUDSON** (b.18 Oct'52, Ames, Iowa) – drums (ex-MANDELBAUM); repl. HOSSACK / added **BILL PAYNE** – keyboards (ex-LITTLE FEAT)

| Feb 74. | (lp/c) (K/K4 56026) <2750> WHAT WERE ONCE VICES ARE NOW HABITS | 19 | 4 |

– Song to see you through / Spirit / Pursuit on 53rd street / Black water / Eyes of silver / Road angel / You just can't stop it / Tell me what you want / Down in the track / Another park, another Sunday / Flying cloud. (quad-lp US 1976) (cd-iss. Jul88; K2 56026) (cd re-iss. May93; 7599 2780-2)

Apr 74.	(7") <7795> ANOTHER PARK, ANOTHER SUNDAY. / BLACK WATER	-	32
Aug 74.	(7") (K 16450) <7832> EYES OF SILVER. / YOU JUST CAN'T STOP IT	52	58	Jul74
Oct 74.	(7") <8041> NOBODY. / FLYING CLOUD	-	58
Dec 74.	(7") <8062> BLACK WATER. / SONG TO SEE YOU THROUGH	-	1

—— **JEFF BAXTER** (b.13 Dec'48, Washington, D.C.) – guitar (ex-STEELY DAN) repl. PAYNE who rejoined LITTLE FEAT

| Apr 75. | (lp/c) (K/K4 56094) <2835> STAMPEDE | 14 | 4 |

– Sweet Maxine / Neal's fandango / Texas lullaby / Music man / Slat key sequel rag / Take me in your arms / I cheat the hangman / Precis / Rainy day crossroad blues / I've been workin' on you / Double dealin' four flusher. (cd-iss. Jun89; 927289-2) (cd-iss. May93; 7599 27289-2)

Apr 75.	(7") (K 16559) <8092> TAKE ME IN YOUR ARMS. / SLAT KEY SEQUEL RAG	29	
Jul 75.	(7") (K 16601) <8126> SWEET MAXINE. / DOUBLE DEALIN' FOUR FLUSHER	-	40
Nov 75.	(7") <8161> I CHEAT THE HANGMAN. / MUSIC MAN	-	60

—— **MICHAEL McDONALD** (b.12 Feb'52, St.Louis, Missouri) – keyboards, vocals (ex-STEELY DAN) repl. JOHNSTON who fell ill

| Mar 76. | (lp/c) (K/K4 56196) <2899> TAKIN' IT TO THE STREETS | 42 | 8 |

– Wheels of fortune / Takin' it to the streets / 8th Avenue shuffle / Losin' end / Rio / For someone special / It keeps you runnin' / Turn it loose / Carry me away. (cd-iss. Jun89 & Jul93; 927289-2)

Mar 76.	(7") (K 16559) <8196> TAKIN' IT TO THE STREETS. / FOR SOMEONE SPECIAL		13
Aug 76.	(7") <8233> WHEELS OF FORTUNE. / SLAT KEY SEQUEL RAG	-	87
Nov 76.	(7") <8282> IT KEEPS YOU RUNNIN'. / TURN IT LOOSE	-	37
Nov 76.	(lp/c) (K/K4 56308) <2978> THE BEST OF THE DOOBIES (compilation)		5

– China Grove / Long train runnin' / Takin' it to the streets / Listen to the music / Black water / Rockin' down the highway / Jesus is just alright / It keeps you runnin' /

South city midnight lady / Take me in your arms (rock me a little while) / Without you. (cd-iss. 1988; K2 56308)

| Jan 77. | (7") (K 16835) LISTEN TO THE MUSIC. / LONG TRAIN RUNNIN' | | - |

—— **TOM JOHNSTON** returned but left again early '77 to go solo

| Jul 77. | (7") (K 16989) <8408> LITTLE DARLING (I NEED YOU). / LOSING END | | 48 |
| Aug 77. | (lp/c) (K/K4 56383) <3045> LIVIN' ON THE FAULT LINE | 25 | 10 |

– You're made that way / Echoes of love / Little darling (I need you) / You belong to me / Livin' on the fault line / Nothin' but a heartache / Chinatown / There's a light / Need a lady / Larry the logger two-step. (cd-iss. Jun89; 927315-2)

Sep 77.	(7") (K 17044) <8471> ECHOES OF LOVE. / THERE'S A LIGHT		66
Mar 78.	(7") <8500> LIVIN' ON THE FAULT LINE. / NOTHIN' BUT A HEARTACHE	-	
Dec 78.	(lp/c) (K/K4 56486) <3193> MINUTE BY MINUTE		1

– Sweet feelin' / Open your eyes / Here to love you / Minute by minute / You never change / What a fool believes / Steamer lane breakdown / How do the fools survive? / Don't stop to watch the wheels. (cd-iss. 1988; K2 56486)

Feb 79.	(7") (K 17314) <8725> WHAT A FOOL BELIEVES. / DON'T STOP TO WATCH THE WHEELS	31	1	Jan79
Apr 79.	(12") (K 17362) WHAT A FOOL BELIEVES. / DON'T STOP TO WATCH THE WHEELS / IT KEEPS YOU RUNNIN'	72	-
Apr 79.	(7") <8828> MINUTE BY MINUTE. / SWEET FEELIN'	-	14
Jul 79.	(7") (K 17411) MINUTE BY MINUTE. / HOW DO THE FOOLS SURVIVE?	47	
Jul 79.	(7") <49029> DEPENDIN' ON YOU. / HOW DO THE FOOLS SURVIVE?	-	25
Aug 79.	(7") (K 17461) OPEN YOUR EYES. / STEAMER LANE BREAKDOWN		-

—— **JOHN McFEE** (b.18 Nov'53, Santa Cruz, California) – guitar, vocals; repl. BAXTER / **CHET McCRACKEN** (b.17 Jul'52, Seattle, Washington) – drums, vibes (ex-session man) repl. HARTMAN / added **CORNELIUS BUMPUS** (b.13 Jan'52) – keyboards, sax (ex-MOBY GRAPE) / (now septet alongside SIMMONS, McDONALD, PORTER + KNUDSEN)

| Aug 80. | (7") <49503> REAL LOVE. / THANK YOU LOVE | - | 5 |
| Oct 80. | (lp/c) (K/K4 56824) <3452> ONE STEP CLOSER | 53 | 3 |

– Dedicate this heart / Real love / No stoppin' us now / Thank you love / One step closer / Keep this train a-rollin' / Just in time / South bay strut / One by one. (cd re-iss. Jan96; 7599 26628-2)

| Nov 80. | (7") (K 17707) <49622> ONE STEP CLOSER. / SOUTH BAY STRUT | | 24 |
| Jan 81. | (7") <49642> WYNKEN, BLYNKEN AND NOD. / IN HARMONY | - | 76 |

(above credited w/ KATE + SIMON TAYLOR)

| Jan 81. | (7") <49642> KEEP THIS TRAIN A-ROLLIN'. / JUST IN TIME | - | 62 |
| Nov 81. | (lp/c) (K/K4 56956) <3612> THE BEST OF THE DOOBIES VOLUME II (compilation) | | 39 |

– Little darlin' / Echoes of love / You belong to me / One step closer / What a fool believes / Dependin' on you / Here to love you / One by one / Real love / Minute by minute.

| Jan 82. | (7") <50001> HERE TO LOVE YOU. / WYNKEN, BLYNKEN AND NOD | - | 65 |

—— **WILLIE WEEKS** – bass repl. PORTER

—— split Mar'82, recorded final concert album Sep'82

			WEA	WEA
Jun 83.	(d-lp/d-c) (923 772-1/-4) <23772> THE DOOBIE BROTHERS FAREWELL TOUR (live)		79

– Slippery St. Paul / Takin it to the streets / Jesus is just alright / Minute by minute / Can't let it get away / Listen to the music / Echoes of love / What a fool believes / Black water / You belong to me / Slat key sequel rag / Streamer lane breakdown / South city / Midnight lady / Olana / Don't start me to talking / Long train runnin' / China grove.

| Jul 83. | (7") <29552> YOU BELONG TO ME (live). / SOUTH CITY MIDNIGHT LADY (live) | - | 79 |

—— By this time MICHAEL McDONALD had gone solo, as did PATRICK SIMMONS. DOOBIE BROTHERS reformed mid'88. (JOHNSTON, HARTMAN, SIMMONS, PORTER) plus **MICHAEL HOSSACK** – drums / **BOBBY LaKIND** (b.1945) – percussion

			Capitol	Capitol
Jul 89.	(7") (CL 536) <44376> THE DOCTOR. / TOO HIGH A PRICE	73	9	May89

(12"+=/cd-s+=) (12/CD CL 536) – Anything for love.

| Jul 89. | (cd/c/lp) (CD/TC+/EST 2100) <90371> CYCLES | | 17 | Jun89 |

– The doctor / One chain (don't make no prison) / Take me to the highway / South of the border / Time is here and gone / Need a little taste of love / I can read your mind / Wrong number / Tonight I'm coming through (the border) / Too high a price.

| Sep 89. | (7") (CL 552) <44441> NEED A LITTLE TASTE OF LOVE. / I CAN READ YOUR MIND | | 45 | Aug89 |

(12"+=/cd-s+=) (12/CD CL 552) – The doctor.

| May 91. | (cd/c/lp) (CD/TC+/EST 2141) <94623> BROTHERHOOD | | 82 |

– Something you said / Is love enough / Dangerous / Our love / Divided highway / Under the spell / Excited / This train I'm on / Showdown / Rollin' on.

—— On the 24th December '92, LaKIND died of cancer

—— vocalists now **TOM JOHNSTON, MICHAEL McDONALD + PATRICK SIMMONS**

			Columbia	Sony
Aug 96.	(d-cd) (484452-2) ROCKIN' DOWN THE HIGHWAY – THE WILDLIFE CONCERT (live)		-	Jul96

– China grove / What a fool believes / Dangerous / Jesus is just alright / Rockin' down the highway / Dependin' on you / Eyes of silver / Another park another Sunday / Slack key sequel rag (instrumental) / South city midnight lady / Clear as the driven snow / Black water / Wild ride / Slow burn / The doctor / Take me in your arms (rock me) / Long train runnin' / Without you / Excited / Dark eyed Cajun woman / Neal's fandango / Listen to the music / Minute by minute / Takin' it to the streets.

– compilations etc. –

on 'Warners' unless mentioned otherwise

Nov 84. (d-c) (K4 66117) **TAKIN' IT TO THE STREETS / LIVIN' ON THE FAULT LINE** ☐ –

Mar 86. (7") Old Gold; (OG 9573) **LISTEN TO THE MUSIC. / WHAT A FOOL BELIEVES** ☐ –

Jan 87. (7") (W 8451) **WHAT A FOOL BELIEVES. / MINUTE BY MINUTE** 57 –
(12"+=) (W 8451T) – Real love.

May 93. (cd) F.N.A.C.; () **INTRODUCING . . .** ☐ –

May 93. (cd/c) (9548 31094-2/-4) **LISTEN TO THE MUSIC – THE VERY BEST OF THE DOOBIE BROTHERS** ☐ –
(re-iss. May94 cd/c; 9548 32803-2/-4)

Nov 93. (7"/c-s) (W 0217/+C) **LONG TRAIN RUNNIN'. / ('A'mix)** 7 –
(12"+=/cd-s+=) (W 0217 T/CD) – ('A'mix).

Apr 94. (7"/c-s) (W 0228/+C) **LISTEN TO THE MUSIC ('94 remix). / ('A'mix)** 37 –
(12"+=/cd-s+=) (W 0228 T/CD) – ('A'remixes by MOTIV8 / RAMP . . . / DEVELOPMENT CORPORATION).

Feb 96. (cd) B.A.M.; (KLMCD 055) **THE EARLY YEARS** ☐ –

May 97. (cd) Experience; (EXP 014) **THE DOOBIE BROTHERS** ☐ –

—— JOHN HARTMAN who was a reserve fireman /policeman was refused promotion by his home state court, due to his alleged drug-taking past

DOORS

Formed: Los Angeles, California, USA . . . July 1965 by RAY MANZAREK and JIM MORRISON. In 1966, after some personnel changes, they soon settled with JOHN DENSMORE and ROBBY KRIEGER and became The DOORS. They were released from a 'Columbia' recording contract, when ARTHUR LEE (of LOVE), recommended them to his 'Elektra' label boss Jac Holzman. Early in 1967, their eponymous debut album was issued, which soon climbed to US No.2 after an edited version of 'LIGHT MY FIRE' hit No.1 in July '67. The single and album showcased MORRISON's overtly sexual vocal theatrics against a backdrop of organ-dominated, avant-garde blues. The classic debut also contained two cover versions (see below), the lucid psychedelia of 'THE CRYSTAL SHIP', plus the extremely disturbing 11-minute epic, 'THE END' (which was later used on the soundtrack for the 1979 Francis Ford Coppola film, 'Apocalypse Now'). While other bands of the era were into peace and love, The DOORS found their salvation in a much darker vision, again in evidence on the follow-up (also in '67), 'STRANGE DAYS'. This was another classic, tracks like, 'LOVE ME TWO TIMES', 'YOU'RE LOST LITTLE GIRL' and 'PEOPLE ARE STRANGE' further enhancing the band's powerful mystique. As MORRISON's drink and drugs antics became increasingly problematic, he was arrested many times (on stage and off), mostly for lewd simulation of sexual acts and indecent exposure. Nevertheless, in the late summer of '68, they found themselves at the top of the US charts again with the 45, 'HELLO I LOVE YOU' and the album, 'WAITING FOR THE SUN'. A disappointing 4th album, 'THE SOFT PARADE' (1969), did, however, contain a classic US Top 3 hit, 'TOUCH ME'. More controversy was generated, when, in November '69, MORRISON was accused of interfering with an airline stewardess while a flight was in progress. He was later acquitted, but the following year, was given eights months hard labour after being found guilty of indecent exposure and profanity. He was freed on appeal and began work on 1970's, 'MORRISON HOTEL / HARD ROCK CAFE', a return to rawer, more basic rock'n'roll. After the recording of 'L.A. WOMAN', he relocated to Paris in the Spring of '71 with his girlfriend Pamela, amid rumours of an imminent split from the group. The aforementioned album was delivered in June, a masterpiece that carried on the re-evaluation of their blues roots. His over-indulgence in drugs and booze, had given his vocal chords a deeper resonance, showcased on such classics as, 'RIDERS ON THE STORM' (a Top 30 hit), 'LOVE HER MADLY', the JOHN LEE HOOKER cover 'CRAWLING KING SNAKE' and the freewheeling title track. Ironically, just as the band seemed to have found their feet again, JIM MORRISON was found dead in his bathtub on the 3rd of July 1971. Speculation was rife at the time, but it later became apparent he had died from a drugs/drink induced heart attack. He was also buried in Paris, his grave becoming a shrine to all but his parents, who disowned him in 1967. The others continued as a trio for the next two years, but sadly the public refused to acknowledge them as the real DOORS. The "god-like" cult of MORRISON has mushroomed to incredible proportions in the years following his death, rumours continuing, Elvis-like, to circulate that he is still alive. There have been many imitators over the last quarter of a century, although none have matched his/their dark majesty. • **Songwriters:** MORRISON – words/poetry (under the influence of explorative narcotics), Group/MANZAREK compositions. Covered; ALABAMA SONG (Brecht-Weill) / BACK DOOR MAN (Howlin' Wolf) / WHO DO YOU LOVE (Bo Diddley) / LITTLE RED ROOSTER (Willie Dixon) / BEEN DOWN SO LONG (J.B. Lenoir). • **Trivia:** In 1968, they featured on a UK TV documentary 'The Doors Are Open', which was later issued on video. In 1991, Oliver Stone released a feature film 'THE DOORS', with Val Kilmer playing the role of MORRISON.

Album rating: THE DOORS (*9) / STRANGE DAYS (*8) / WAITING FOR THE SUN (*6) / THE SOFT PARADE (*5) / MORRISON HOTEL – HARD ROCK CAFE (*8) / ABSOLUTELY LIVE (*6) / 13 compilation (*8) / L.A. WOMAN (*9) / OTHER VOICES (*4) / WEIRD SCENES INSIDE THE GOLDMINE compilation (*8) / FULL CIRCLE (*4) / AN AMERICAN PRAYER – JIM MORRISON exploitation (*4) / GREATEST HITS compilation (*8) / ALIVE, SHE CRIED exploitation (*4) / BEST

OF THE DOORS compilation (*8) / LIVE AT THE HOLLYWOOD BOWL exploitation (*4) / THE DOORS soundtrack (*5) / IN CONCERT exploitation (*5) / GREATEST HITS compilation (*9) / THE COMPLETE STUDIO RECORDINGS boxed-set (*8)

JIM MORRISON (b. 8 Dec'43, Melbourne, Florida) – vocals / **RAY MANZAREK** (b.12 Feb'35, Chicago, Illinois) – keyboards, bass pedal / **ROBBY KRIEGER** (b. 8 Jan'46) – guitar / **JOHN DENSMORE** (b. 1 Dec'45) – drums / also guest **DOUG LUBAHN** – bass (of CLEAR LIGHT)

		Elektra	Elektra
Feb 67.	(7") (EKSN 45009) <45611> **BREAK ON THROUGH (TO THE OTHER SIDE). / END OF THE NIGHT**	☐	Jan67
Mar 67.	(lp; mono/stereo) <(EKL/EKS 74007)> **THE DOORS** – Break on through (to the other side) / Soul kitchen / The crystal ship / Twentieth century fox / Alabama song (whiskey song) / Light my fire / Back door man / I looked at you / End of the night / Take it as it comes / The end. (re-iss. Nov71 lp/c; K/K4 42012) (cd-iss. Jan84; K2 42012) (re-iss. cd Feb89; 974007-2) (re-hit UK No.43 in Apr91)	☐	Mar 67
Apr 67.	(7") (EKSN 45012) **ALABAMA SONG (WHISKEY BAR). / TAKE IT AS IT COMES**	☐	–
Jul 67.	(7") (EKSN 45014) <45615> **LIGHT MY FIRE (edit). / THE CRYSTAL SHIP** (re-iss. Jul71; same)	49	1 Jun67
Sep 67.	(7") (EKSN 45017) <45621> **PEOPLE ARE STRANGE. / UNHAPPY GIRL**	☐	12
Dec 67.	(lp; mono/stereo) <(EKL/EKS 74014)> **STRANGE DAYS** – Strange days / You're lost little girl / Love me two times / Unhappy girl / Horse latitudes / Moonlight drive / People are strange / My eyes have seen you / I can't see your face in my mind / When the music's over. (re-iss. Nov71 lp/c; K/K4 42016) (cd-iss. Jan86; K2 42016) (cd re-iss. Feb89; 974014-2)	☐	3 Nov67
Dec 67.	(7") (EKSN 45022) <45624> **LOVE ME TWO TIMES. / MOONLIGHT DRIVE**	☐	25
Apr 68.	(7") (EKSN 45030) <45628> **THE UNKNOWN SOLDIER. / WE COULD BE SO GOOD TOGETHER** (re-iss. Jun71; K 12004)	☐	39 Mar68
Aug 68.	(7") (EKSN 45037) <45635> **HELLO, I LOVE YOU. / LOVE STREET**	15	1 Jul68
——	**LEROY VINEGAR** – acoustic bass repl. LABAHN		
Sep 68.	(lp; mono/stereo) <(EKL/EKS 74024)> **WAITING FOR THE SUN** – Hello I love you / Love street / Not to touch the Earth / Summer's almost gone / Wintertime love / The unknown soldier / Spanish caravan / My wild love / We could be so good together / Yes, the river flows / Five to one. (re-iss. Nov71 lp/c; K/K4 42041) (cd-iss. Jan86; K2 42041) (cd re-iss. Feb89; 974024-2)	16	1 Aug68
Dec 68.	(7") (EKSN 45050) <45646> **TOUCH ME. / WILD CHILD**	☐	3
May 69.	(7") (EKSN 45059) <45656> **WISHFUL SINFUL. / WHO SCARED YOU**	☐	44 Mar69
Aug 69.	(7") (EKSN 45065) <45663> **TELL ALL THE PEOPLE. / EASY RIDE**	☐	57 Jun69
Sep 69.	(lp) <(EKS 75005)> **THE SOFT PARADE** – Tell all the people / Touch me / Shaman's blues / Do it / Easy ride / Wild child / Runnin' blue / Wishful sinful / The soft parade. (re-iss. Nov71 lp/c; K/K4 42079) (cd-iss. Feb89; 975005-2)	☐	6 Aug69
Sep 69.	(7") <45675> **RUNNIN' BLUE. / DO IT**	–	64
——	guest **LONNIE MACK** – bass repl. LUBAHN		
Apr 70.	(7") <45685> **YOU MAKE ME REAL. / ROADHOUSE BLUES**	–	50
Apr 70.	(7") (2101 004) **YOU MAKE ME REAL. / THE SPY**	☐	–
Apr 70.	(lp) <(EKS 75007)> **MORRISON HOTEL / HARD ROCK CAFE** – Land ho! / The spy / Queen of the highway / Indian summer / Maggie McGill / Roadhouse blues / Waiting for the sun / You make me real / Peace frog / Blue Sunday / Ship of fools. (re-iss. Nov71 lp/c; K/K4 42080) (cd-iss. Apr86; K2 42080) (re-iss. cd.Feb89; 975007-2)	12	4 Mar70
Jul 70.	(7") (2101 008) **ROADHOUSE BLUES. / BLUE SUNDAY**	☐	–
Sep 70.	(d-lp) (2665 002) <9002> **ABSOLUTELY LIVE (live)** – Who do you love medley: Alabama song – Back door man – Love hides – Five to one / Build me a woman / When the music's over / Close to you / Universal mind / Break on through (to the other side) / The celebration of the lizard / Soul kitchen. (re-iss. Nov71 d-lp; K 62005) (d-cd-iss. Mar87 w-drawn; 2665 002)	69	8 Aug70
Oct 70.	(7") <45708> **UNIVERSAL MIND. / THE ICEWAGON FLEW**	–	–
Mar 71.	(lp/c) (K/K4 42062) <74079> **13** (compilation) – Light my fire / People are strange / Back door man / Moonlight drive / The crystal ship / Roadhouse blues / Touch me / Love me two times / You're lost little girl / Hello, I love you / Land ho / Wild child / The unknown soldier.	☐	25 Dec70
——	guest **JERRY SCHEFF** – bass repl. MACK		
May 71.	(7") <(EK 45726)> **LOVE HER MADLY. / (YOU NEED MEAT) DON'T GO NO FURTHER**	☐	11 Apr71
Jun 71.	(lp/c) (K/K4 42090) <75011> **L.A. WOMAN** – The changeling / Love her madly / Been down so long / Cars hiss by my window / L.A. woman / L'America / Hyacinth house / Crawling King Snake / The wasp (Texas radio and the big beat) / Riders on the storm. (cd-iss. 1984; K2 42090) (cd re-iss. Feb89 & Apr91; 975011-2)	26	9 May71
Jul 71.	(7") (K 12021) <45738> **RIDERS ON THE STORM (edit). / THE CHANGELING**	22	14
——	**RAY** – vocals, ROBBIE and JOHN carried on when JIM MORRISON died 3rd Jul'71 of a mysterious heart attack. The trio continued (MANZAREK now on vox). Used guest session bassmen **WILLIE RUFF**, **WOLFGANG MERTZ** and **JACK CONRAD**		
Nov 71.	(7") (K 12036) <45757> **TIGHTROPE RIDE. / VARIETY IS THE SPICE OF LIFE**	☐	71
Dec 71.	(lp/c) (K/K4 42104) <75017> **OTHER VOICES** – In the eye of the sun / Variety is the spice of life / Ships w.sails / Tightrope ride / Down on the farm / I'm horny, I'm stoned / Wandering musician / Hang on to your life	☐	31 Nov71
May 72.	(7") (K 12048) <45768> **SHIP W. SAILS. / IN THE EYE OF THE SUN**	☐	☐
——	bass sessions **J. CONRAD, CHARLES LARKEY, LEE SKLAR** and **CHRIS ETHRIDGE.**		
Aug 72.	(7") (K 12059) <45793> **GET UP AND DANCE. / TREETRUNK**	☐	☐
Aug 72.	(lp/c) (K/K4 42116) <75038> **FULL CIRCLE**	☐	68

– Get up and dance / Four billion souls / Verdilac / Hardwood floor / Good rockin' / The mosquito / The piano bird / It slipped my mind / The Peking king and the New York queen.

Sep 72.	(7") <45807> **THE MOSQUITO. / IT SLIPPED MY MIND**	-	85
Dec 72.	(7"w-drawn) **THE PIANO BIRD. / GOOD ROCKIN'**	-	-

—— They finally split 1973. MANZAREK went solo and KRIEGER & DENSMORE formed The BUTTS BAND. With JESS RODEN as lead singer / **PHILIP CHEN** – bass / **ROY DAVIS** – keyboards, they made 2 albums for ~'Blue Thumb' records; 'THE BUTTS BAND' (1974) / 'HEAR AND NOW' (1975).

– compilations, etc. –

Note; All on 'Elektra' until mentioned otherwise

Mar 72.	(d-lp/d-c) (K/K4 62009) <6001> **WEIRD SCENES INSIDE THE GOLD MINE**	50	55 Feb72

– Break on through (to the other side) / Strange days / Shaman's blues / Love street / Peace frog / Blue Sunday / The wasp (Texas radio and the big beat) / End of the night / Love her madly / Ship of fools / The spy / The end / Take it as it comes / Running blue / L.A. woman / Five to one / Who scared you? / Don't go no further / Riders on the storm / Maggie McGill / Horse latitudes / When the music's over.

Sep 74.	(lp/c) (K/K4 42143) <5035> **THE BEST OF THE DOORS**		
Feb 76.	(7") (K 12203) **RIDERS ON THE STORM. / L.A. WOMAN**	33	-
Sep 76.	(7") (K 12227) **LIGHT MY FIRE. / THE UNKNOWN SOLDIER**		-
Sep 76.	(7") (K 12228) **LOVE HER MADLY. / TOUCH ME**		-
Nov 78.	(lp/c; by JIM MORRISON) (K/K4 52111) <502> **AN AMERICAN PRAYER** (poetry recorded 8 Nov'70 with some DOORS tapes)	54	

– Awake / Ghost song / Dawn's highway / Newborn awakening / To come of age / Black polished chrome / Latino chrome / Angels and sailors / Stoned immaculate / The poet's dreams / The movie / Curses invocations / World on fire / American night / Roadhouse blues / Lament / The hitchhiker / An American prayer. (re-iss. May95 cd/lp;)

Jan 79.	(7") (K 12215) **LOVE ME TWO TIMES. / HELLO I LOVE YOU** (w/ free 7"+=) (SAM 94) – GHOST SONG. / ROADHOUSE BLUES		
Jan 79.	(7") **ROADHOUSE BLUES. / AN AMERICAN PRAYER**	-	
Jan 80.	(7")<12"> (K 12400) <ELK 22032> **THE END. / (b-side 'Delta' not by The DOORS)**	-	
Oct 80.	(lp/c) (K/K4 52254) <515> **GREATEST HITS**	17	

– Hello, I love you / Light my fire / People are strange / Love me two times / Riders on the storm / Break on through / Roadhouse blues / Touch me / L.A. woman / Love her madly / The ghost song / The end. (cd-iss. Oct95 cd/c; 7559 61860-2/-4)

Oct 80.	(7") **PEOPLE ARE STRANGE. / NOT TO TOUCH THE EARTH**	-	
Oct 82.	(d-c) (K4 62034) **MORRISON HOTEL / L.A. WOMAN**	-	
Oct 83.	(7") <60269> **GLORIA (live). / MOONLIGHT DRIVE (live)**	-	71
Oct 83.	(12") (E 9774T) **GLORIA (live). / LOVE ME TWO TIMES (live)**		-
Oct 83.	(lp/c) (960269-1/-4) <60269> **ALIVE SHE CRIED (live)**	36	23

– Gloria / Light my fire / You make me real / The wasp (Texas radio and the big beat) / Love me two times / Little red rooster / Moonlight drive. (cd-iss. Jul84; 960269-2)

Aug 84.	(d-c) (K4 62040) **THE SOFT PARADE / AN AMERICAN PRAYER**		
Jun 85.	(lp/c) (EKT 9/+C) <60417> **CLASSICS**		
Sep 85.	(7") Old Gold; (OG 9520) **RIDERS ON THE STORM. / LIGHT MY FIRE**		
Nov 85.	(d-lp/c/c/cd) (EKT 21/+C/CD) <60345> **BEST OF THE DOORS**		

– Break on through (to the other side) / Light my fire / The crystal ship / People are strange / Strange days / Love me two times / Five to one / Waiting for the Sun / Spanish caravan / When the music's over / Hello, I love you / Roadhouse blues / L.A. woman / Riders on the storm / Touch me / Love her madly / The unknown soldier / The end. (cd+=) – Alabama song (whiskey bar). (re-iss. Apr91 hit UK No.17 & US No.32) (re-iss. Mar98, hit UK No.37)

Jun 87.	(m-lp/c)(cd) (EKT 40/+C)(960741-2) <60741> **LIVE AT THE HOLLYWOOD BOWL (live)**		

– Wake up / Light my fire / The unknown soldier / A little game / The hill dwellers / Spanish caravan.

Mar 91.	(lp/c)(cd) (EKT 85/+C)(961047) <61047> **THE DOORS: A FILM BY OLIVER STONE – MUSIC FROM THE ORIGINAL SOUNDTRACK**	11	8
Apr 91.	(7") (EKR 121) **BREAK ON THROUGH. / LOVE STREET** (12"+=/cd-s+=) (EKR 125 TW/CD) – Hello I love you / Touch me.	64	
May 91.	(7") (EKR 125) **LIGHT MY FIRE. / PEOPLE ARE STRANGE** (ext; 12"+=/cd-s+=) (EKR 125 TW/CD) – Soul kitchen.	7	
May 91.	(t-lp/d-c)(d-cd) (EKT 88/+C)(7559 61082) <61082> **THE DOORS: IN CONCERT (live)**	24	50
Jul 91.	(7") (EKR 131) **RIDERS ON THE STORM. / LOVE ME TWO TIMES (live)** (12"+=/cd-s+=) (EKR 131 TW/CD) – Roadhouse blues (live).	68	
Jun 95.	(c-s; by JIM MORRISON & THE DOORS) (EKR 205C) **THE GHOST SONG. / (interview)** (cd-s+=) (EKR 205CD) – Love me two times (live) / Roadhouse blues (live).		
Oct 97.	(4xcd-box) <(7559 62123-2)> **THE DOORS BOX SET**		65
Nov 99.	(cd) <(7559 62475-2)> **STONED IMMACULATE**		
Nov 99.	(7xcd-box) <(7559 62434-2)> **THE COMPLETE STUDIO RECORDINGS**		

Ray DORSET (see under ⇒ MUNGO JERRY)

DOWN (see under ⇒ PANTERA)

Nick DRAKE

Born: 19 Jun'48, Burma. He moved to Britain in the mid 50's, first to Tamworth-in-Ardon then Stratford. Already a budding singer-songwriter by the time he reached Cambridge University, he was discovered playing a gig by ASHLEY HUTCHINGS of Fairport Convention, who, in turn, introduced him to Witchseason Productions head JOE BOYD. Bowled over by his talent, BOYD helped him sign to 'Island', who released debut album 'FIVE LEAVES LEFT' in '69. The album highlighted his precocious talent and painful sensitivity, the music possessing a remarkable maturity not in keeping with DRAKE's young years. The melancholic resonance of DRAKE's voice and his crystalline guitar playing were complemented by delicate string arrangements, the effect one of understated intensity. After moving to London, DRAKE recorded the classic 'BRYTER LAYTER' in 1970 with BOYD again producing a cast of musicians that included RICHARD THOMPSON and JOHN CALE. The album boasted a jazzier flavour which saw DRAKE in a slightly more positive frame of mind. Ironically, like its predecessor, the album failed to sell in any great quantity. Due to his crippling shyness, DRAKE found live work too difficult, passing up the opportunity to promote his music. He fell into a deep depression, no doubt frustrated at his lack of success and inability to do something about it. After a spell in Europe he returned to record his tortured masterpiece, 'PINK MOON'. Recorded in just two nights, its spare, haunting songs were cloaked in regret and dissillusionment. The bleak tone only let up occasionally as DRAKE attemted to exorcise his demons over a skeletal acoustic backing. Once again, the album was a commercial failure and DRAKE's mood blackened further, although he did begin work on a new album in 1973. He spent time in France with singer/friend FRANCOISE HARDY and his bouts of depression diminished when he decided to live there permanently. However, this didn't last long and he sadly overdosed on anti-depressants on 25th November 1974, a tragic end to a troubled but brilliant career. A questionable coroner's verdict was "Death By Suicide". The subsequent interest in DRAKE's work led to various compilations being released, including the excellent 'FRUIT TREE' boxed set. His music entrances more listeners with each passing year, a belated recognition that recently saw him grace the cover of 'Mojo' magazine. • **Trivia:** His sister Gabrielle was a TV actress in the 70's/80's 'Crossroads' soap.

Album rating: FIVE LEAVES LEFT (*8) / BRYTER LAYTER (*9) / PINK MOON (*8) / HEAVEN IN A WILD FLOWER posthumous (*7) / FRUIT TREE – THE COMPLETE RECORDED WORKS collection (*9) / TIME OF NO REPLY (*7) / WAY TO BLUE – AN INTRODUCTION TO NICK DRAKE compilation (*9)

NICK DRAKE – vocals, guitar, piano with **RICHARD THOMPSON** – guitar / **DANNY THOMPSON** – double bass / **PAUL HARRIS** – keyboards / **CLAIRE LOWTHER** and **ROCKY DZIDZORNU**, plus 15-piece orchestra.

		Island	Antilles
Sep 69.	(lp) (ILPS 9105) <AN 7010> **FIVE LEAVES LEFT**		

– Time has told me / River man / Three hours / Day is done / Way to blue / Cello song / The thoughts of Mary Jane / Man in a shed / Fruit tree / Saturday sun. (cd-iss. Feb87; CID 9195) (re-iss. cd May89; IMCD 8)

—— retained **RICHARD** bringing in other (FAIRPORT CONVENTION members: **DAVE PEGG** – drums / **DAVE MATTACKS** – bass. Also sessioned **PAUL HARRIS, RAY WARLEIGH, CHRIS McGREGOR**.

Nov 70.	(lp) (ILPS 9134) <7028> **BRYTER LAYTER**		

– Introduction / Hazey Jane II / At the chime of a city clock / One of these things first / Hazey Jane I / Bryter layter / Fly / Poor boy / Northern sky / Sunday. (cd-iss. May87; CID 9134) (re-iss. cd Oct89; IMCD 71)

—— **NICK DRAKE** – vocals, guitar (totally solo)

Feb 72.	(lp) (ILPS 9184) <AN 9184> **PINK MOON**		

– Pink moon / Place to be / Road / Which will / Horn / Things behind the sun / Know / Parasite / Ride / Harvest breed / From the morning / Voice from the mountain / Rider on the wheel / Black eyed dog / Hanging on a star. (cd-iss. Apr90; IMCD 94)

—— He had put down some tracks for new album, when on 25th Nov'74, he overdosed on medication/drugs.

– compilations, others, etc. –

1972.	(lp) Island; <9307> **NICK DRAKE** (69-70 material)	-	
Apr 79.	(3xlp-box) Island; (NDSP 100) **FRUIT TREE – THE COMPLETE RECORDED WORKS** – (contains all 3 albums)	-	-
May 85.	(lp/c) Island; (ILPS 9826) **HEAVEN IN A WILD FLOWER** (cd-iss. Apr90; IMCD 91)		
Aug 86.	(4xlp-box) Hannibal / Rykodisc; (HNBX 5502) **FRUIT TREE** – (all 3 lp's, plus 1987 album) (4xcd-box-iss.Dec91; HNCD 5402)(+=) – TIME OF NO REPLY / Fruit tree / Fly / Man in a shed / Thoughts of Mary Jane.		
Mar 87.	(lp/cd) Hannibal / Rykodisc; (HN BL/CD 1318) **TIME OF NO REPLY**		
Jun 94.	(cd)(c/lp) Island; (IMCD 196)(ICM/ILPM 2082) **WAY TO BLUE – AN INTRODUCTION TO NICK DRAKE**		

DR. DRE (see under ⇒ N.W.A.)

DREADZONE (dig out; 4th edition)

DREAM SYNDICATE

Formed: Los Angeles, California, USA . . . 1981 by STEVE WYNN and KENDRA SMITH. The former had previously cut his teeth with SID GRIFFIN in an embryonic LONG RYDERS. They soon completed the line-up with KARL PRECODA and DENNIS DUCK. After an untitled mini-lp back home, they caught the interest of UK indie, 'Rough Trade', in 1983, who released their debut full-length album 'THE DAYS OF WINE AND ROSES'. Cut from a distinctly rougher-hewn cloth than most of the band's 'Paisley Underground' contemporaries, the album's dark intensity caused enough of a stir to eventually get them snapped up by 'A&M'. By the release of their major label debut, 'MEDICINE SHOW' (1984), KENDRA SMITH had been replaced by DAVE PROVOST. Although more mainstream than its predecessor, the album still showed the ragged influence of NEIL YOUNG and THE VELVET UNDERGROUND and while it didn't accrue the success it was probably due, its critical acclaim paved the way for other majors to give them a shot at the big league. After a final album for 'A&M', the compilation of early live material, 'IT'S NOT THE NEW DREAM SYNDICATE ALBUM' (1985), the band released their next studio offering on 'Chrysalis', 1986's 'OUT OF THE GREY'. Despite the more commercial, straight ahead rock sound of the record, success continued to elude the band and they split in early 1989 after releasing a final well-received album for 'Enigma', 'GHOST STORIES'. • **Songwriters:** Most written by WYNN, except covers CINNAMON GIRL (Neil Young) / MR. SOUL (Buffalo Springfield). WYNN covered KOOL THING (Sonic Youth) / BOY IN THE BUBBLE (Paul Simon) / GUTTERBALL mainly WYNN with HARVEY or McCARTHY. • **Trivia:** Early '85, STEVE WYNN was also in DANNY & DUSTY duo alongside old cohort DAN STUART (of GREEN ON RED).

Album rating: THE DAYS OF WINE AND ROSES (*7) / THE MEDICINE SHOW (*7) / THIS IS NOT THE NEW DREAM SYNDICATE ALBUM (*4) / OUT OF THE GREY (*5) / 50 IN A 25 ZONE (*4) / GHOST STORIES (*5) / LIVE AT RAJI'S (*7) / TELL ME WHEN IT'S OVER: THE BEST OF DREAM SYNDICATE compilation (*8) / Steve Wynn: KEROSENE MAN (*6) / DAZZLING DISPLAY (*6) / TAKE YOUR FLUNKY AND DANGLE (*5) / FLUORESCENT (*5) / MELTING IN THE DARK (*6)

STEVE 'DUSTY' WYNN (b.21 Feb'60, Santa Monica, Calif.) – vocals / **KARL PRECODA** (b.1961) – guitar / **DENNIS DUCK** (b.25 Mar'53) – drums / **KENDRA SMITH** (b.14 Mar'60, San Diego, Calif.) – bass / guest on below; **TOM ZVONCHECK** – keyboards

	not iss.	Down There
Dec 82. (m-lp) <VEX 10> **THE DREAM SYNDICATE**	-	☐

– Sure thing / Some kinda itch / That's what you always say / When you smile. *(UK-iss.Jun85 on 'Zippo'; ZANE 001; cd-iss. Aug92; VEXCD 10)*

	Rough Trade	Ruby
Nov 83. (lp) *(ROUGH 53)* **THE DAYS OF WINE AND ROSES**	☐	☐

– Tell me when it's over / Definitely clean / That's what you always say / Then she remembers / Halloween / When you smile / Until lately / Too little, too late / The days of wine and roses. *(re-iss. Jan87 on 'Slash'; 23844-1) (cd-iss. Jan95 on 'Normal'; NORMAL 176CD)*

Dec 83. (12"ep) *(RTT 121)* **TELL ME WHEN IT'S OVER. / SOME KINDA ITCH (live) / MR. SOUL (live) / SURE THING (live)** ☐ ☐

—— **DAVE PROVOST** – bass repl. KENDRA (she joined RAINY DAY then OPAL) (appeared on live album early '84) and later went solo

	A&M	A&M
Jun 84. (lp/c) *(AMLX/CXM 64990)* **MEDICINE SHOW**	☐	☐

– Still holding on to you / Daddy's girl / Burn / Armed with an empty gun / Bullet with my name on it / The medicine show / John Coltrane stereo blues / Merrittville.

Feb 85. (lp) *(AMLH 12511)* **IT'S NOT THE NEW DREAM SYNDICATE ALBUM (live)** ☐ ☐

– Tell me when it's over / Bullet with my name on it / Armed with an empty gun / The medicine show / John Coltrane stereo blues.

—— **PAUL B. CUTLER** (b. 5 Aug'54, Phoenix, Arizona) – lead guitar + **MARK WALTON** (b. 9 Aug'59, Fairfield, Calif.) – bass; repl. PRECODA + PROVOST

	Chrysalis	Big Time
Jun 86. (lp/c) *(CHR/ZCHR 1539)* **OUT OF THE GREY**	☐	☐

– Out of the grey / Forest for the trees / 50 in a 25 zone / Boston / Slide away / Dying embers / Now I ride alone / Dancing blind / You can't forget. *(cd-iss. 1987; CCD 1539) (re-iss. Oct87 on 'Big Time' lp/c; ZL/ZK 71457X)*

Sep 87. (12"ep) *(ZT 41420)* **50 IN A 25 ZONE. / DRINKING PROBLEM / BLOOD MONEY / THE LONELY BULL** ☐ ☐

	Enigma-Virgin	Enigma
Sep 88. (lp/c/cd) *(ENVLP/TCENV/CDENV 506)* <73341-1/-4/-2> **GHOST STORIES**	☐	☐

– The side I'll never show / My old haunts / Loving the sinner, hating the sin / Whatever you please / Weathered and torn / See that my grave is kept clean / I have faith / Some place better than this / Black / When the curtain calls. *(cd re-iss. Sep95 on 'Restless'; 72758-2)*

Nov 88. (7") *(ENV 6)* **I HAVE FAITH. / NOW I RIDE ALONE** ☐ ☐
(12"+=) *(ENVT 6)* – I ain't living long like this.

—— split early 1989, when WYNN decided to venture solo. He released a number of albums, the first two being 'KEROSENE MAN' and 'DAZZLING DISPLAY'. He also formed GUTTERBALL with Long Ryder; STEPHEN McCARTHY. WALTON would subsequently form The CONTINENTAL DRIFTERS.

– compilations etc. –

Jun 89. (lp/cd) *Enigma-Virgin; (ENVLP/CDENV 531) / Restless; <72293-2>* **LIVE AT RAJI'S (live in Hollywood January '85)** ☐ ☐
– Still holding on to you / Forest for the trees / Until lately / That's what you always say / Burn / Merrittville / The days of wine and roses / The medicine show / Halloween / Boston / John Coltrane stereo blues. *(re-iss. Jun90 on 'Demon' lp/cd; DFIEND/FIENDCD 176)*

Sep 89. (lp) *Another Cowboy; (ANOTHER 1)* **IT'S TOO LATE TO STOP NOW** ☐ ☐
Apr 90. (d-lp/cd) *Demon; (FIEND/+CD 170)* **LIVE AT RAJI'S / GHOST STORIES** ☐ ☐
Jun 92. (cd) *Rhino;* **TELL ME WHEN IT'S OVER: THE BEST OF DREAM SYNDICATE** ☐ ☐
Nov 93. (cd) *Normal; (NORMAL 156CD)* **THE LOST TAPES 1985-1988** ☐ ☐

STEVE WYNN

	World Service	Rhino
May 90. (lp/c/cd) *(SERV 011/+MC/CD)* <8122 70969-2> **KEROSENE MAN**	☐	☐ Apr90

– Tears won't help / Carolyn / The blue drifter / Younger / Under the weather / Here on Earth as well / Something to remember me by / Killing time / Conspiracy of the heart / Kerosene man / Anthem. *(cd re-iss. Feb93 on 'Rhino'; same as US)*

1991. (cd-ep) **KEROSENE MAN EP** - ☐
– Kerosene man / Something to remember me by / Boy in the bubble / Kool thing / etc.

	Rhino	Rhino
Dec 91. (cd-ep) **DRAG**	-	
Mar 93. (cd) <(8122 02832-2)> **DAZZLING DISPLAY**		☐ Nov91

– Drag / Tuesday / When she comes around / A dazzling display / Halo / Dandy in disguise / Grace / As it should be / Bonnie and Clyde / 405 / Close your eyes / Light of hope.

—— next with an array of backing musos including JOHN WESLEY HARDING

	Brake Out	Mute
Nov 94. (cd) *(OUT 1162)* <61652> **FLUORESCENT**	☐	☐ Mar94

– Follow me / Collision course / Carelessly / Carry a torch / Open the door / Older / Layer by layer / That's why I wear black / Wedding bells / The sun rises in the west / Look both ways / Never ending rain.

—— next with the group, COME

	Brake Out	Zero Hour
Jul 96. (cd) *(OUT 1242)* <ZEROCD 1160> **MELTING IN THE DARK**	☐	☐

– Why / Sheeley's blues / What we call love / Drizzle / Angels / Epilogue / Silence is our only friend / Stare it down / Smooth / For all I care / The way you punish me / Down / Melting in the dark.

	Zero Hour	Zero Hour
Sep 97. (cd) <(ZEROCD 2160)> **SWEETNESS AND LIGHT**	☐	☐

– Silver lining / Black magic / Sweetness and light / This strange effect / This deadly game / How's my little girl / Ghosts / Blood from a stone / In love with everyone / Great divide / That's the way love is / If my life was an open book.

– his compilations, etc. –

Nov 94. (cd) *Return To Sender; <(RTS 13)>* **TAKE YOUR FLUNKY AND DANGLE** (unissued material rec.1987-1993) ☐ ☐ Nov93
– Animation / Gospel #1 / How's my little girl / Counting the days / The subject was roses / Closer / Woodshed blues / Boxing song / AA / Gospel #2 / It only comes out at night.

GUTTERBALL

STEVE WYNN – vocals, guitar / **BRYAN HARVEY** – guitar, vocals (ex-HOUSE OF FREAKS) / **STEPHEN McCARTHY** – guitar, vocals (ex-LONG RYDERS) / **JOHNNY HOTT** – drums, vocals (ex-HOUSE OF FREAKS) / **BOB RUPE** – bass, vocals (ex-SILOS)

	Brake Out	Mute
Jan 94. (cd) *(OUT 113-2)* <61510> **GUTTERBALL**	☐	☐ Jun93

– Trial separation blues / Top of the hill / Lester Young / Motorcycle boy / One by one / When you make up your mind / Think it over / Falling from the sky / Please don't hold back / The preacher and the prostitute / Patent leather shoes / Blessing in disguise.

—— **ARMISTEAD WELLFORD** – bass, vocals; repl. RUPE

	Brake Out	Brake Out
Apr 95. (cd/lp) <(OUT 119-2/-1)> **WEASEL**	☐	☐

– Transparency / Your best friend / Black and gold / Is there something I should know? / Hesitation / The firefly / Sugar fix / Maria / One-eyed dog / Tarzana, pt.2 / Angelene / California / Everything / Over 40 / Mickey's big mouth.

– compilations, etc. –

Aug 95. (cd) *Return To Sender; <(RTS 17)>* **TURNYOR HEDINKOV** ☐ ☐

DR. FEELGOOD

Formed: Canvey Island, Essex, England . . . mid-'71 by LEE BRILLEAUX and WILKO JOHNSON alongside JOHN B. SPARKS and JOHN MARTIN aka The BIG FIGURE, taking their name from a 50's bluesman. After an initial period spent gigging in Southend-on-Sea, the group made a name for themselves in the capital, where their lean n' mean brand of revivalist R&B was going down a storm on the pub-rock circuit. While the band's mean faced assault was best sampled in the sweaty confines of a packed public house, DR. FEELGOOD secured a recording contract with 'United Artists' and proceeded to release an enjoyable series of albums beginning with 'DOWN BY THE JETTY' (1974). The band's JOHNNY KIDD & The PIRATES' influenced originals (stand out track being the piledriving 'KEEP IT OUT OF SIGHT') jostled for elbow room alongside covers material like 'BONY MORONIE' (Larry Williams) and 'TEQUILA' (The Champs). It was the follow-up set, 'MALPRACTICE' (1975), however, that saw the band make their break into the UK Top 20, the record's success a gauge of the changing musical climate; with their drainpipe suits, short hair (well, shorter than your average rock band of the day), stripped down sound and surly demeanour, DR. FEELGOOD were as influential as any band in the onset of punk. Their mushrooming popularity was confirmed when live set, 'STUPIDITY' (1976), topped the British charts. During the recording of subsequent set, 'SNEAKIN' SUSPICION' (1977), the band were dealt a potentially fatal blow with the departure of guitarist, co-writer and focal point, WILKO. Bearing up, they recruited JOHN 'GYPIE' MAYO as a replacement and, with NICK LOWE producing, introduced a slicker sound on 'BE SEEING YOU'. This was commercially rewarded when 1978's 'PRIVATE PRACTICE' spawned a Top 10 hit single (the only one of their career) in the classic 'MILK AND ALCOHOL'. Though their short period of chart grace was more or less over, the band remained a hot live ticket, releasing two concert sets in the space of three years, 'AS IT HAPPENS' (1979) and 'ON THE JOB' (1981). This marked the end of MAYO's tenure with the band, SPARKS and The BIG FIGURE departing around the same time and leaving BRILLEAUX as the sole constant in an ever changing line-up throughout the 80's. DR. FEELGOOD continued to record and perform to a loyal audience right up until BRILLEAUX's untimely death from throat cancer on 7th April '94, the band subsequently continuing with new singer PETE GAGE. • **Songwriters:** BRILLEAUX and JOHNSON, and later MAYO. Covered:- BONY MORONIE (Larry Williams) / TEQUILLA (Champs) / ROUTE 66 (Nelson Riddle) / DUST MY BROOM (Elmore James) / MAD MAN BLUES + DIMPLES (John Lee Hooker) / ROCK ME BABY (B.B. King) / MY BABY (Willie Dixon) / SOMETHING YOU GET (Kenner) / CAN'T FIND THE LADY (Larry Wallis) / GOING DOWN (Don Nix) / NO TIME (JJ Cale) / STANDING AT THE CROSSROADS AGAIN (Mickey Jupp) / BEEN DOWN SO LONG (Doors) / DON'T WORRY BABY (Ritchie Valens) / YOU'VE GOT MY NUMBER (Undertones) / GET RHYTHM (Johnny Cash) / I'M A REAL MAN (John Hiatt) / AS LONG AS THE PRICE IS RIGHT (Larry Wallis) / GREAT BALLS OF FIRE (Jerry Lee Lewis) / etc. • **Trivia:** In 1977, NICK LOWE produced and co-wrote some material.

Album rating: DOWN BY THE JETTY (*7) / MALPRACTICE (*7) / STUPIDITY (*6) / SNEAKIN' SUSPICION (*6) / BE SEEING YOU (*6) / PRIVATE PRACTICE (*5) / AS IT HAPPENS (*5) / LET IT ROLL (*4) / A CASE OF THE SHAKES (*5) / ON THE JOB (*4) / CASEBOOK compilation (*6) / FAST WOMEN AND SLOW HORSES (*4) / DOCTOR'S ORDERS (*5) / MAD MAN BLUES (*6) / BRILLEAUX (*5) / CASE HISTORY – THE BEST OF DR. FEELGOOD compilation (*7) / SINGLES – THE UA YEARS compilation (*7) / LIVE IN LONDON (*4) / DOWN AT THE DOCTOR'S (*5) / ON THE ROAD AGAIN (*3)

LEE BRILLEAUX (b. LEE GREEN, 1953, Durban, S. Africa) – vocals, harmonica / **WILKO JOHNSON** (b. JOHN WILKINSON, 1947) – guitar (ex-ROAMERS) / **JOHN B.SPARKS** – bass / **THE BIG FIGURE** (aka. JOHN MARTIN, 1947) – drums (ex-ROAMERS)

		U.A.	Columbia
Nov 74.	(7"; mono) (UP 35760) **ROXETTE. / (GET YOUR KICKS ON) ROUTE 66**		-
Dec 74.	(lp; mono) (UAS 29727) **DOWN BY THE JETTY**		-

– She does it right / Boom boom / The more I give / Roxette / One weekend / That ain't the way to behave / I don't mind / Twenty yards behind / Keep it out of sight / All through the city / Cheque book / Oyeh / Bonie Moronie / Tequila. *(re-iss. May82 on 'Fame' lp/c; FA/TC-FA 3029) (re-iss. Oct85 on 'Edsel'; ED 160) (re-iss. Jan90 on 'Grand' lp/cd; GRAND/+CD 05)*

Mar 75.	(7") (UP 35815) **SHE DOES IT RIGHT. / I DON'T MIND**		-
Jul 75.	(7") (UP 35857) **BACK IN THE NIGHT. / I'M A MAN**		-
Oct 75.	(lp) (UAS 29880) **MALPRACTICE**	17	

– I can tell / Going back home / Back in the night / Another man / Rolling and tumbling / Watch your step / Don't let your daddy know / Don't you just know it / Riot in cell block No.9 / Becaue you're mine / You shouldn't call the doctor (if you can't afford the bill). *(re-iss. Aug90 on 'Grand' lp/cd; GRAND/+CD 09)*

| Sep 76. | (lp) (UAS 29990) **STUPIDITY** (live) | 1 | |

– I'm talking about you / Twenty yards behind / Stupidity / All through the city / I'm a man / Walking the dog / She does it right / Going back home / I don't mind / Back in the night / I'm a hog for you baby / Checkin' up on my baby / Roxanne. *(free 7"-w.a.)* **RIOT IN CELL BLOCK NO.9. / JOHNNY B. GOODE** *(re-iss. Aug85 on 'Liberty'; lp/c; ED 260634-1/-4) (re-iss. Apr91 as 'STUPIDITY PLUS (LIVE 1976-1990)' on 'Liberty' d-lp/c)(d-cd; CDP 795934-2)*

Sep 76.	(7") (UP 36171) **ROXETTE (live). / KEEP IT OUT OF SIGHT (live)**		-
May 77.	(7") (UP 36255) **SNEAKIN' SUSPICION. / LIGHTS OUT**	47	-
May 77.	(lp) (UAS 30075) **SNEAKIN' SUSPICION**	10	

– Sneakin' suspicion / Paradise / Nothin' shakin' (but the leaves and trees) / Walking on the edge / Lights out / Lucky 7 / All my love / You'll be mine / Time and the Devil / Hey mama / Keep your big mouth shut. *(re-iss. May87 on 'Fame' lp/c; FA/TC-FA 3179) (cd-iss. Jun91 on 'Grand' lp/cd; GRAND/+CD 13)*

—— (Mar77) **JOHN 'GYPIE' MAYO** (b. JOHN CAWTHRA) – guitar replaced HENRY McCULLOCH who had for 2 months repl. WILKO JOHNSON who went solo.

| Sep 77. | (7") (UP 36304) **SHE'S A WINDUP / HI-RISE** | 34 | |

(12"+=) (12UP 36304) – Homework (live).

| Sep 77. | (lp) (UAS 30123) **BE SEEING YOU** | 55 | |

– Ninety-nine ana a half (won't do) / She's a windup / I thought I had it made / I don't wanna know / That's it, I quit / As long as the price is right / Hi-rise / My buddy buddy friends / Baby Jane / The blues had a baby, and they named it rock'n'roll / Looking back / 60 minutes of our love. *(re-iss. Oct87 on 'Edsel'; ED 238) (cd-iss. Sep91 on 'Grand' lp/cd; GRAND/+CD 14)*

| Nov 77. | (7") (UP 36332) **BABY JANE / LOOKING BACK** | | |

(12"+=) (12UP 36332) – You upset me baby (live).

| Sep 78. | (7") (UP 36444) **DOWN AT THE DOCTORS. / TAKE A TIP** | 48 | |
| Oct 78. | (lp) (UAG 30184) **PRIVATE PRACTICE** | 41 | |

– Down at the doctors / Every kind of vice / Things get better / Milk and alcohol / Night time / Let's have a party / Take a tip / It wasn't me / Greaseball / Sugar shaker. *(re-iss. Oct88 on 'Grand' lp/cd; GRAND/+CD 01)*

Jan 79.	(7",7"milky,7"beer-colrd) (UP 36468) **MILK AND ALCOHOL. / EVERY KIND OF VICE**	9	
Apr 79.	(7"blue/7"brown/7"purple/7") (X/Y/Z+/UP 36506) **AS LONG AS THE PRICE IS RIGHT (live). / DOWN AT THE DOCTORS (live)**	40	-
May 79.	(lp) (UAK 30239) **AS IT HAPPENS** (live)	42	-

– Take a tip / Every kind of vice / Down at the doctors / Baby Jane / Sugar shaker / Things get better / She's a windup / Ninety-nine and a half (won't do) / My buddy buddy friends / Milk and alcohol / Matchbox / As long as the price is right / Night time. *(free live 7"ep)* **ENCORE EP** *(FEEL 2)* – Riot In Cell Block No.9 / Blues Had A Baby And They Named It Rock'n' Roll / Lights Out / Great Balls Of Fire. *(cd-iss. Dec92 on 'Grand' lp/cd+=; GRAND/+CD 15)* – (EP tracks).

| Aug 79. | (7") (BP 306) **PUT HIM OUT OF YOUR MIND. / BEND YOUR EAR** | 73 | - |

| Sep 79. | (lp/c) (UAG/TCK 30269) **LET IT ROLL** | | - |

– Java blue / Feels good / Put him out of your mind / Bend your ear / Hong Kong money / Keeka smeeka / Shotgun blues / Pretty face / Riding on the L & N / Drop everything and run.

Jan 80.	(7") (BP 338) **HONG KONG MONEY. / KEEKA SMEEKA**		-
Aug 80.	(7") (BP 366) **NO MO DO YAKAMO. / BEST IN THE WORLD**		-
Sep 80.	(lp/c) (UAG/TC-UAG 30311) **A CASE OF THE SHAKES**		-

– Jumping from love to love / Going some place else / Best in the world / Punch drunk / King for a day / Violent love / No mo do Yakamo / Love hound / Coming to you / Who's winning / Drives me wild / A case of the shakes. *(re-iss. Aug86 on 'Edsel'; ED 189) (re-iss. Oct90 on 'Grand' lp/cd; GRAND/+CD 10)*

| Nov 80. | (7") (BP 374) **JUMPING FROM LOVE TO LOVE. / LOVE HOUND** | | - |
| Jan 81. | (7") (BP 386) **VIOLENT LOVE. / A CASE OF THE SHAKES** | | - |

		Liberty	not iss.
Aug 81.	(lp) (LBG 30328) **ON THE JOB** (live)		-

– Drives me wild / Java blue / Jumping from love to love / Pretty face / No mo do Yakomo / Love hound / Shotgun blues / Best in the world / Who's winning / Riding on the L' & 'N / Shotgun blues / Goodnight Vienna. *(cd-iss. Dec92 on 'Grand' lp/cd; GRAND/+CD 16)*

—— (early'81) **JOHNNY GUITAR** – guitar (ex-COUNT BISHOPS) repl. MAYO

| Oct 81. | (7") (BP 404) **WAITING FOR SATURDAY NIGHT. / EILEEN** | | - |

—— **LEE & JOHNNY** recruited **PAT McMULLEN** – bass (ex-COUNT BISHOPS) repl. SPARKS / **BUZZ BARWELL** – drums (ex-LEW LEWIS BAND) repl. THE BIG FIGURE

		Chiswick	not iss.
Sep 82.	(7") (DICE 16) **TRYING TO LIVE MY LIFE WITHOUT YOU. / MURDER IN THE FIRST DEGREE**		-
Oct 82.	(lp) (TOSS 4) **FAST WOMEN AND SLOW HORSES**		-

– She's the one / Monkey / Sweet sweet lovin' (gone sour on me) / Trying to live my life without you / Rat race / Baby Jump / Crazy about girls / Sugar bowl / Educated fool / Bum's rush / Baby why do you treat me this way / Beautiful Delilah. *(re-iss. May89 on 'Grand' lp/c/cd; GRAND/+C/CD 03)*

| Mar 83. | (7") (DICE 18) **CRAZY ABOUT GIRLS. / SOMETHING OUT OF NOTHING** | | - |

—— (1983) **GORDON RUSSELL** – guitar repl. JOHNNY GUITAR —— **PHIL MITCHELL** – bass repl. McMULLEN

—— (1984) **KEVIN MORRIS** – drums repl. BUZZ

		Demon	not iss.
Sep 84.	(7") (D 1030) **DANGEROUS. / CAN'T FIND THE LADY**		-
Oct 84.	(lp) (FIEND 29) **DOCTOR'S ORDERS**		-

– Close but no cigar / So long / You don't love me / My way / Neighbour, neighbour / Talk of the Devil / Hit git and split / I can't be satisfied / Saturday night fish fry / Drivin' wheel / It ain't right / I don't worry about a thing / She's in the middle / Dangerous. *(re-iss. Jan90 on 'Grand' lp/cd; GRAND/+CD 06)*

| Dec 84. | (7") (D 1032) **MY WAY. / SHE'S IN THE MIDDLE** | | - |

		I.D.	not iss.
Oct 85.	(lp) (NOSE 5) **MAD MAN BLUES**		-

– Dust my broom / Something you got / Dimples / Living on the highway / Tore down / Mad man blues / I've got news for you / My babe / Can't find the lady / Rock me baby. *(re-iss. Oct88 on 'Grand' lp/cd; GRAND/+CD 02)*

		Stiff	not iss.
Aug 86.	(7") (BUY 253) **DON'T WAIT UP. / SOMETHING GOOD**		-

(w/free 7") (FBUY 56) – Back in the night / Milk and alcohol. (12"+=) (BUYIT 253) – Rockin' with somebody new.

| Aug 86. | (lp/c) (SEEZ/ZSEEZ 65) **BRILLEAUX** | | - |

– I love you, so you're mine / You've got my number / Big enough / Don't wait up / Get rhythm / Here is the next one? / Play dirty / Grow too old / Rough ride / I'm a real man / Come over here / Take what you can get. *(re-iss. May89 on 'Grand' lp/c/cd; GRAND/+C/CD 04)*

| Nov 86. | (7") (BUY 255) **SEE YOU LATER ALLIGATOR. / I LOVE YOU SO YOU'RE MINE** | | - |

(12"+=) (BUYIT 255) – What do you think of that.

| Jun 87. | (7") (BUY 259) **HUNTING SHOOTING FISHING. / BIG ENOUGH** | | - |

(12"+=) (BUYIT 259) – Don't underestimate your enemy. (c-s+=) (CRASH 1) – Crash Your Car Megamix.

| Sep 87. | (lp/c) (SEEZ/ZSEEZ 67) **CLASSIC** | | - |

– Hunting shooting fishing / Break these chains / Heartbeat / (I wanna) Make love to you / Hurricane / See you later alligator / Quit while you're behind / Nothing like it / Spy vs. spy / Highway 61 / Crack me up. *(re-iss. Oct90 on 'Grand' lp+=/cd+=; GRAND/+CD 11)*

		E.M.I.	not iss.
Apr 89.	(7") (EM 89) **MILK AND ALCOHOL (new recipe). / SHE'S GOT HER EYES ON YOU**		-

(12"+=) (12EM 89) – Mad man blues.

—— **BRILLEAUX + MITCHELL + MORRIS** recruited **STEVE WALWYN** – guitar (ex-STEVE MARRIOTT group)

		Grand	not iss.
Apr 90.	(lp/c/cd) (GRAND/+C/CD 08) **LIVE IN LONDON** (live)		-

– King for a day / You upset me baby / As long as the price is right / Mad man blues / She does it right / Baby Jane / Quit while you're behind / Back in the night / Milk and alcohol / See you later alligator / Down at the doctors / Route 66 / Going back home / Bony Moronie / Tequila.

| Jun 91. | (lp/cd) (GRAND/+CD 12) **PRIMO** | | - |

– Heart of the city / My sugar turns to alcohol / Going down / No time / World in a jug / If my baby quit me / Primo blues / Standing at the crossroads again / Been down so long / Don't worry baby / Down by the jetty blues / Two times nine.

—— **DAVE BRONZE** – bass repl. MITCHELL

| Jul 93. | (lp/cd) (GRAND/+CD 17) **THE FEELGOOD FACTOR** | | - |

– The feelgood factor / Tranqueray / Tell me no lies / Styrofoam / I'm in the mood for you / Double crossed / Lying about the blues / She moves me / Wolfman calling / One step forward / One to ten / Fool for you.

—— On 7th Apr'94; LEE BRILLEAUX died of throat cancer.

May 94. (lp/cd) *(GRAND/+CD 18)* **DOWN AT THE DOCTORS (live early '94)** ☐ -

—— veteran **PETE GAGE** took over the role of singer and the group was reborn. Others in line-up **PHIL MITCHELL / DAVE BRONZE + STEVE WALWYN**

Aug 96. (cd) *(GRAND 19)* **ON THE ROAD AGAIN** ☐ -

– compilations, others, etc. –

Nov 81. (lp) *United Artists; (LBG 30341)* **CASEBOOK** ☐ -

Apr 87. (cd) *E.M.I.; (CDP 746 711-2)* **CASE HISTORY – THE BEST OF DR.FEELGOOD** ☐ -

May 89. (cd/c/d-lp) *Liberty; (CD/TC+/EM 1332)* **SINGLES (THE U.A. YEARS)** ☐ -
– Roxette / She does it right / Back in the night / Going back home / Riot in cell block 9 / Sneakin' suspicion / She's a wind-up / Baby Jane / Down at the doctors / Milk and alcohol / As long as the price is right / Put him out of your mind / Hong Kong money / No modo Yakama / Jumping from love to love / Violent love / Waiting for Saturday night / Monkey / Trying to live my life without you / Crazy about girls / My way / Mad man blues / See you later alligator / Hunting shooting fishing. *(d-lp+=/c+=)* – Don't wait up / Milk and alcohol (new recipe).

Oct 95. (5xcd-box) *Liberty; (ACDFEEL 195)* **LOOKING BACK** ☐ -

Apr 97. (d-cd) *Grand; (GRAND 20)* **TWENTY FIVE YEARS OF DR FEELGOOD** ☐ -

---

┌─────────────────────────────────────┐
│ **DRIVE LIKE JEHU (see under ⇒** │
│ **ROCKET FROM THE CRYPT)** │
└─────────────────────────────────────┘

DR. JOHN

Born: MALCOLM REBENNACK, 20 Nov'42, New Orleans, Louisiana, USA. He became a noted session man in 1957 and soon branched out on his own the same year, taking up the piano after one of his fingers was shot off in a bar room brawl. Drawn to L.A. in the mid-60's, he continued his session work and began to assume his alter ego, DR. JOHN (CREAUX) THE NIGHT TRIPPER. Taking the name from a 19th Century New Orleans witchdoctor type, the character was a hybrid of psychedelic mysticism and deep South voodoo. 'GRIS GRIS' (1968) was the first DR. JOHN release on 'Atco', a sinister series of voodoo funk meditations that combined New Orleans R&B, creole soul and psychedelia. The next three releases, 'BABYLON' (1968), 'REMEDIES' (1970) and 'THE SUN, MOON AND HERBS' (1971) carried on in much the same vein without achieving quite the same foreboding effect. The JERRY WEXLER-produced 'GUMBO' (1972) saw DR. JOHN (by this time, he'd given up his nocturnal tripping) return to his bayou roots. A deeply satisfying journey through New Orleans' rich musical heritage, the record saw the good doctor belting out some spirited updates of standards like 'IKO IKO' and 'JUNKO PARTNER'. With impeccable credentials (produced by ALLEN TOUSSAINT, recorded with The METERS) 1973's 'IN THE RIGHT PLACE' concentrated on downhome funk. 'DESITIVELY BONNAROO' (1974) offered similar rhythmical remedies, spawning the rump shaking single '(EVERYBODY WANNA GET RICH) RITE AWAY'. Seemingly abandoning the New Orleans (black) magic, DR. JOHN made a misguided attempt at more rocking fare on the live 'HOLLYWOOD BE THY NAME' (1975). 'CITY LIGHTS' (1978) and 'TANGO PALACE' (1979) sounded confused and it was only with 1981's 'DR. JOHN PLAYS MAC REBENNACK' that he regained his focus. The album found him alone at his piano, effortlessly reeling off inspired tributes to New Orleans past masters. 'THE BRIGHTEST SMILE IN TOWN' (1983) proved that his return to form was no fluke although 'IN A SENTIMENTAL MOOD' (1989) sounded overwrought. DR. JOHN returned to his old stamping ground on funky 90's releases like 'GOIN' BACK TO NEW ORLEANS' (1992) and 'TELEVISION' (1994) while his far reaching influence was illustrated by his guesting on one of 1997's best albums, SPIRITUALIZED's 'LADIES AND GENTLEMEN WE ARE FLOATING IN SPACE BP'. • **Songwriters:** REBENNACK compositions except; IKO IKO (Dixie Cups) / THE WAY YOU DO THE THINGS YOU DO (Smokey Robinson) / YESTERDAY (Beatles) / IT'S ALL RIGHT WITH ME (Cole Porter) / BLUE SKIES (Irving Berlin) / etc. • **Trivia:** His organ playing featured heavily on ARETHA FRANKLIN's 1971 single 'Spanish Harlem'.

Album rating: GRIS GRIS (*7) / BABYLON (*6) / REMEDIES (*5) / SUN, MOON AND HERBS (*6) / DR. JOHN'S GUMBO (*7) / IN THE RIGHT PLACE (*6) / DESITIVELY BONAROO (*6) / HOLLYWOOD BE THY NAME (*4) / CUT ME WHILE I'M HOT (*5) / CITY LIGHTS (*6) / TANGO PALACE (*4) / DR. JOHN PLAYS MAC REBENNACK (*7) / THE BRIGHTEST SMILE IN TOWN (*6) / I BEEN HOODOOD compilation (*6) / IN THE NIGHT exploitation (*6) / SUCH A NIGHT – LIVE IN LONDON (*5) / IN A SENTIMENTAL MOOD (*5) / BLUESIANA TRIANGLE with Art Blakely & David 'Fathead' Newman (*4) / GOIN' BACK TO NEW ORLEANS (*5) / ANTHOLOGY compilation (*7) / TELEVISION (*4) / AFTERGLOW (*5) / THE VERY BEST OF DR. JOHN compilation (*7)

MAC REBENNACK

		not iss.	Rex
1958.	(lp) *<2020>* **DR.JOHN AND HIS NEW ORLEANS CONGREGATION**	-	☐
1959.	(7") *<1008>* **STORM WARNING. / FOOLISH LITTLE GIRL**	-	☐

		not iss.	A.F.O.
1962.	(7") *<309>* **THE POINT. / ONE NAUGHTY FLAT**	-	☐

—— He became a session man in the early 60's. He also formed numerous bands, including ZU ZU. Around 1963 he adopted the name of DR. JOHN THE NIGHT TRIPPER.

---

		not iss.	Trip
1965.	(lp) *<9518>* **ZU ZU MAN** (demos ?)	-	☐

– Cat and mouse game / She's just a square / Bald headed / In the night / Helpin' hand / Zu zu man / Mean cheatin' woman / Woman's the root of all evil / Trader John / Shoo-ra / Tipatina / One night late. *(cd-iss. Apr87 on 'Topline'; TOPCD 504) (re-iss. May89 on 'Thunderbolt' lp/cd; THBL/CDTB 069) (re-iss. Jul93 on 'Charly' cd/c; CDCD/CDCM 1090)*

DR. JOHN

– vocals, piano with various sessioners

		Atlantic	Atco
1968.	(7"; as DR. JOHN THE NIGHT TRIPPER) *<6607>* **I WALK ON GUILDED SPLINTERS. / (part 2)**	-	☐
1968.	(lp; as DR. JOHN THE NIGHT TRIPPER) *(588 147) <33234>* **GRIS GRIS**		☐

– Gris gris gumbo ya ya / Danse kalinda ba boom / Mama roux / Danse fambeaux / Croker court bullion / Jump steady / I walk on gilded splinters. *(re-iss. Aug87 on 'Sonet'; AL 3904) (cd-iss. Nov93; 7567 80437-2)*

Feb 69.	(7"; as DR. JOHN THE NIGHT TRIPPER) *<6635>* **MAMA ROUX. / JUMP STEADY**		☐
Apr 69.	(7") *<6697>* **PATRIOTIC FLAG WAVER. / ('A'-long version)**		☐
Apr 69.	(lp) *(228 018) <33-270>* **BABYLON**		☐

– Babylon / Glowin' / Black Widow spider / Barefoot lady / Twilight zone / The patriotic flag-waver / The lonesome guitar strangler. *(cd-iss. Nov93; 7567 80438-2)*

May 70.	(7"; as DR.JOHN THE NIGHT TRIPPER) *<6755>* **WASH MAMA WASH. / LOUP GAROO**		☐
Jun 70.	(7") *(2091 019)* **WASH MAMA WASH. / MAMA ROUX**		☐
Aug 70.	(lp) *(2400 015) <33-316>* **REMEDIES**		☐

– Loup garoo / What goes around comes around / Wash, mama, wash / Chippy, chippy / Mardi Gras day / Angola anthem. *(cd-iss. Nov93; 7567 80439-2)*

Nov 71.	(lp; as DR. JOHN THE NIGHT TRIPPER) *(2400 161) <33-362>* **SUN, MOON AND HERBS**		☐ Oct71

– Black John the conqueror / Where ya at mule / Cranet crow / Familiar reality (opening) / Pots on fiyo / Zu Zu mama / Familiar reality (reprise). *(re-iss. 1971; K 40250) (cd-iss. Nov93; 7567 80440-2)*

Apr 72.	(7") *(K 10158) <6882>* **IKO IKO. / HUEY SMITH MEDLEY**		☐ 71
Jul 72.	(lp) *(K 40384) <7006>* **DR. JOHN'S GUMBO**		☐ May71

– Iko iko / Blow wind blow / Big chief / The lock / Mess around / Let the good times roll / Junko partner / Stack-a-lee / Tipitina / Those lonely lonely nights / Huey Smith medley / High blood pressure / Don't you just know it / Well I'll be John Brown / Little Liza Jane. *(re-iss. Nov87 on 'Alligator'; AL 3901) (cd-iss. Feb95; 7567 80398-2)*

Jul 72.	(7") *(K 10214)* **WANG DANG DOODLE. / BIG CHIEF**		☐
Nov 72.	(7") *<6900>* **LET THE GOOD TIMES ROLL. / STACK-A-LEE**	-	☐
Mar 73.	(7") *(K 10291) <6914>* **RIGHT PLACE, WRONG TIME. / I BEEN HOODOOED**		9
Mar 73.	(lp) *(K 50017) <7018>* **IN THE RIGHT PLACE**		24

– Right place, wrong time / Same old same old / Just the same / Qualified / Travelling mood / Peace brother peace / Life / Such a nite / Shoo fly marches on / I been hoodooed / Cold cold cold. *(cd-iss. Jun93; 7567 80360-2)*

Jun 73.	(7") *(K 10329)* **SUCH A NITE. / LIFE**		-
Jun 73.	(7") *<6937>* **SUCH A NITE. / COLD COLD COLD**		42

—— In Aug'73 he was credited on album TRIUMVIRATE with JOHN HAMMOND and MIKE BLOOMFIELD.

Mar 74.	(lp) *(K 50035) <7043>* **DESITIVELY BONNAROO**		☐

– Quitters never win / Stealin' / What comes around / Me-You-Loneliness / Mos'scocious / Rite away / Let's make a better world / Ru four real / Sing along song / Can't git enuff / Go tell the people / Desitively Bonnaroo. *(cd-iss. Nov93; 7567 80441-2)*

Apr 74.	(7") *(K 10445) <6957>* **(EVERYBODY WANNA GET RICH) RITE AWAY. / MOS'SCOCIOUS**		92
Aug 74.	(7") *(K 10501) <6971>* **LET'S MAKE A BETTER WORLD. / ME, YOU = LONELINESS**		☐

		D.J.M.	not iss.
Sep 75.	(lp) *(22019)* **CUT ME WHILE I'M HOT (ANYTIME ANYPLACE)**	☐	-

– Woman is the root of all evil / Shoo ra / Tipatina / One night late / Cat and mouse game / She's just a square / Bald headed / In the night / Helpin' hand / Mean cheatin' woman. *(cd-iss. Feb95 on 'Thunderbolt'; CDTB 158)*

		U.A.	U.A.
Dec 76.	(lp) *(UAG 29902) <UALA 552>* **HOLLYWOOD BE THY NAME (live)**	☐	☐

– New island soiree / Reggae doctor / The way you do the things you do / Swanee river boogie / Yesterday / Babylon / Back by the river / Medley: It's all right with me – Blue skies – Will the circle be unbroken / Hollywood be thy name / I wanna rock. *(re-iss. Oct89 on 'Beat Goes On' lp/cd; BGO LP/CD 62) (cd re-iss. Aug98; same)*

—— In 1977, he joined The R.C.O. ALL STARS with LEVON HELM and others.

—— now with **STEVE GADD** – drums / **WILL LEE** – bass / **RICHARD TEE** – keyboards / **JOHN TROPEA** – guitar / **HUGH McCRACKEN** – guitar / **ARTHUR JENKINS** – percussion

		not iss.	R.C.A.
1978.	(7") *<11285>* **SWEET RIDER. / TAKE ME HIGHER**	-	☐

		Horizon	A&M
Oct 78.	(lp) *(AMLJ 732) <SP 732>* **CITY LIGHTS**	☐	☐

– Dance the night away with you / Street side / Wild honey / Rain II snake eyes / Fire of love / Senata – he's a hero / City lights.

1979.	(lp) *<SP 740>* **TANGO PALACE**		☐

– Keep the music simple / Discotherapy / Renegade / Fonky side / Bon steps rouler / Something you got / I thought I heard New Orleans say / Tango palace / Louisiana lullabye.

—— Early in 1981, DR. JOHN w/ LUBBY TITUS & AL JARREAU released 'Warner Bros' single, SAILOR AND THE MERMAID. / ONE GOOD TURN.

		Demon	Clean Cuts
Sep 82.	(7") *(D 1015)* **THE NEARNESS OF YOU. / MAC'S BOOGIE**	☐	☐
Oct 82.	(lp) *(FIEND 1) <705>* **DR. JOHN PLAYS MAC REBENNACK**	☐	☐

– Dorothy / Mac's boogie / Memories of Professor Longhair / The nearness of you /

Delicato / Honeydripper / Big Mac / New island midnight / Saints / Pinetop. *(re-iss. Jan90 c/cd +=; FIEND CASS/CD 1)* – Silent night / Dance a la Negras / Wade in the water.

Nov 83. (lp/c) *(FIEND/+CASS 9)* **THE BRIGHTEST SMILE IN TOWN**   ☐   –
– Saddled the cow / Boxcar boogie / The brightest smile in town / Waiting for a train / Monkey puzzle / Average kind of guy / Pretty Libby / Marie Le Veau / Come rain or shine / Suite home New Orleans. *(cd-iss. 1992 +=;)* – Didn't he ramble / Touro infirmary / Closer walk with thee.

		Beggars Banquet	Streetwise

Mar 84. (7"/12") *(BEG/+T 107)* **JET SET.** / ('A'dub)

		Spindrift	not iss.

Jun 84. (lp) *(SPIN 107)* **SUCH A NIGHT – LIVE IN LONDON** (live)

		Topline	not iss.

Jan 85. (lp/c) *(TOP/KTOP 118)* **IN THE NIGHT**   ☐   –
– Bald head / Bring your love / Did she mention my name / Go ahead / Grass is greener / I pulled the cover off you two lovers / In the night / Just like America / Tipitina / Zuzu man / Mean cheatin' woman / New Orleans / Shoo-ra / The time has come / Noe night late / The ear is on strike.

		Warners	Warners

Apr 89. (lp/c/cd) *(925889-2/-4/-1)* <25889> **IN A SENTIMENTAL MOOD**   ☐   ☐
– Makin' whoopee / Candy / Ac-cent-tchu-ate the positive / My buddy / In a sentimental mood / Black night / Don't let the Sun catch you cryin' / Love for sale / More than you know.

Jun 89. (7") *(W 2976)* **MAKIN' WHOOPEE. / MORE THAN YOU KNOW**   ☐   ☐
(12"+=) *(W 2976T)* – In a sentimental mood.
(above 'A'side featured RICKIE LEE JONES)

Jul 92. (cd/c) <(7599 26940-2/-4)> **GOIN' BACK TO NEW ORLEANS**   ☐   ☐
– Litanie des saints / Careless love / My red Indian / Milneburg joys / I thought I heard Buddy Bolden say / Basin Street blues / Didn't he ramble / Do you call that a buddy? / How come my dog don't bark (when you come around) / Good night, Irene / Fess up / Since I fell for you / I'll be glad when you're dead, you rascal you / Cabbage head / Goin' home tomorrow / Blue Monday / Scald dog medley – I can't go on – Goin' back to New Orleans.

—— next with **HUGH McCRACKEN** – guitar, harmonica / **GEORG WADENIUS** – guitar / **DAVID BARARD** – bass / **FREDDIE STAHLE** – drums

		GRP-MCA	GRP-MCA

Apr 94. (cd/c) <(GRM 4025-2/-4)> **TELEVISION**   ☐   ☐
– Television / Lissen / Limbo / Witchy red / Only the shadow knows / Shut d. fonk up / Thank you / Spaceship relationship / Hold it / Money / U lie too much / Same day service. *(cd re-iss. May98; same)*

Jul 95. (cd/c) <(GRB 7000-2/-4)> **AFTERGLOW**   ☐   ☐
– I know what I've got / Gee baby, ain't I good to you / I'm just a lucky so and so / Blue skies / So long / New York City blues / Tell me you'll wait for me / There must be a better world somewhere / I still think about you / I'm confessin' (that I love you).

		Parlophone	Parlophone

Jun 98. (cd/c/lp) *(495490-2/-4/-1)* **ANUTHA ZONE**   33   ☐
– Zonata / Ki ya gris gris / Voices in my head / Hello God / Party hellfire / I don't wanna know about evil / Anutha zone / I like ki yoka / Olive tree / Soulful warrior / The stroke / Sweet home New Orleans.

– compilations, others, etc. –

1975. (lp) *Rare Earth;* <8014> **NIGHT TRIPPER AT HIS BEST**   –   ☐
(UK-iss.Jul88 on 'Bellaphon'; BID 8014)
Jan 77. (7") *Atlantic;* (K 10877) **RIGHT PLACE, WRONG TIME.** / **SUCH A NIGHT**   ☐   ☐
1970's. (lp) *Trip;* <TOP 16-1> **16 GREATEST HITS**   –   ☐
1970's. (lp) *Trip;* <4018> **DR. JOHN SUPERPAH**   –   ☐
1982. (lp) *Fontana;* (80023) **LOSER FOR YOU BABY** (1960's material)   ☐   ☐
– The time had come / Loser for you baby / The ear is on strike / A little closer to my home / I pulled a cover off you two lovers / New Orleans / Go ahead on / Just like a mirror / Bring your love / Bald head. *(re-iss. Nov88 on 'Thunderbolt' lp/cd+=; THBL/CDTB 66)* – (2 extra tracks). *(cd-iss. Jun98 on 'MagMid'; MM 006)*
Jul 84. (lp) *Edsel;* (ED 128) **I BEEN HOODOOED** ('73 + '74)   ☐   ☐
Feb 86. (d-c) *Demon;* (FIENDCASS 9) **MAC REBENNACK / BRIGHTEST SMILE IN TOWN**   ☐   –
Jun 88. (cd) *Warners;* (WSP 2761-2) **THE ULTIMATE DR.JOHN**   ☐   ☐
Feb 94. (d-cd) *Rhino;* <(8122 71450-2)> **MOS'SCOCIOUS – THE DR. JOHN ANTHOLOGY**   ☐   ☐
– Bad neighborhood (RONNIE & DELINQUENTS) / Morgus The Magnificent (MORGUS & THE 3 GHOULS) / Storm warning (MAC REBENNACK) / Sahara (MAC REBENNACK & HIS ORCHESTRA) / Down the road (ROLAND STONE) / Gris-gris gumbo ya ya / Mama Roux / Jump sturdy / I walk on guilded splinters / Black widow spider / Loop garoo / Wash, mama, wash / Mardi Gras day / Familiar reality – opening / Zu zu mamou / Mess around / Somebody changed the lock / / Iko iko / Junko partner / Tipitina / Huey Smith medley; a) High blood pressure, b) Don't you just know it, c) Well I'll be John Brown / Right place wrong time / Traveling mood / Life / Such a night / I been hoodooed / Cold cold cold / Quitters never win / What comes around (goes around) / Mos'scocious / Let's make a better world / Back by the river / I wanna rock / Memories of Prof. Longhair / Honey dripper / Pretty Libby / Makin' whoopee! / Accentuate the positive / More than you know.
May 95. (cd) *Rhino;* <(9548 33553-2)> **THE VERY BEST OF DR.JOHN**   ☐   ☐
May 97. (cd) *Aim;* (AIMA 4CD) **CRAWFISH SAUCE**   ☐   –
Mar 98. (cd) *Eagle;* (EABCD 077) **THE MASTERS**   ☐   –
Apr 98. (cd/c) *Hallmark;* (30598-2/-4) **VOODOO BLUES**   ☐   –
Apr 98. (d-cd) *Dressed To Kill;* (AOP 64) **DR. JOHN**   ☐   –

DR. STRANGELY STRANGE
(dig out; Great Psychedelic . . .)

DRUGSTORE (dig out; Great Alt & Indie . . .)

DUBSTAR (dig out; 4th edition & Great Alt & Indie . . .)

DUB WAR (dig out; Great Metal . . .)

Anne DUDLEY & Jaz COLEMAN (see under ⇒ ART OF NOISE)

Stephen DUFFY / LILAC TIME
(dig out; Great Alt & Indie . . .)

DUKES OF STRATOSPHEAR (see under ⇒ XTC)

DURAN DURAN

Formed: Birmingham, England . . . 1978 by NICK RHODES, JOHN TAYLOR, STEPHEN DUFFY and clarinet player, SIMON COLLEY, taking their name from a character in cult space-kitsch movie, 'Barbarella'. The following year, ANDY WICKETT and ROGER TAYLOR replaced DUFFY (who went on to a briefly successful solo career as STEPHEN 'TIN TIN' DUFFY) and COLLEY respectively, while SIMON LE BON finally entered the fray as frontman in Spring '80. After a UK tour supporting HAZEL 'Breaking Glass' O'CONNOR, the band were snapped up by 'E.M.I.', initiating their manicured career in early '81 with 'PLANET EARTH'. The toast of the London cognoscenti, extravagantly coiffured (and even more outlandishly attired) poseurs ensured DURAN DURAN a near Top 10 hit as the scene that perpetrated one of the worst fashion crimes in history (i.e. legwarmers) was stepped up a gear. Later that summer, an eponymous debut album and a suitably po-faced follow-up single, 'GIRLS ON FILM', confirmed the band's synth-powered, post-ROXY MUSIC/BOWIE pretensions with lashings of attitude and mascara. Riding in on the floppy fringe of the New Romantic zeitgeist, the album made the UK Top 3 and, with the help of heavy MTV rotation for the 'HUNGRY LIKE THE WOLF' video, eventually the US Top 10. The latter track was a transatlantic Top 5 and previewed the follow-up set, 'RIO' (1982). By this point the band's fanbase had grown from an arty clique to hordes of screaming girlies, ensuring massive success for the sub-panoramic warbling of 'SAVE A PRAYER', the streamlined aquatic rush of the title track and the whining 'IS THERE SOMETHING I SHOULD KNOW', youth centre dancefloor fillers the lot. Although the latter track wasn't included on the album, it did give the band their first UK No.1; with continuing support from MTV in the States, DURAN DURAN were also churning out ever more flamboyant videos to keep the Americans happy. A vague concept affair, 'SEVEN AND THE RAGGED TIGER' (1983) came in for a bit of a critical pasting, although the hits continued apace with the dodgy 'UNION OF THE SNAKE' and transatlantic No.1, 'THE REFLEX' (a quintessentially 80's effort complete with stuttering vocals, while the video was famous for five minutes with its water-coming-out-of-the-screen trickery, brilliant!). The zenith of DURAN DURAN's bombastic heyday came with 'THE WILD BOYS', a classic slice of white nouveau-funk with added rhythmic oomph courtesy of ex-CHIC man/producer in demand, NILE RODGERS, the accompanying video setting the boys in a storm-drenched, sub-Mad Max style netherworld. The single made No.2 in Britain and America, preceding the universally panned live effort, 'ARENA' (1984). A James Bond theme tune, 'VIEW TO A KILL' (another US No.1) nicely rounded off the first chapter in the band's career as the various members took time out to indulge themselves in solo projects. The less said about ARCADIA (LeBON, NICK RHODES and ROGER TAYLOR) the better, while the marginally more entertaining POWER STATION (ANDY/JOHN TAYLOR, ROBERT PALMER and ex-CHIC sticksman, TONY THOMPSON) released an eponymous album (1985) of sterile funk-rock, hitting the UK Top 10 with 'SOME LIKE IT HOT' and a cover of T.Rex's 'GET IT ON'. DURAN DURAN eventually returned in late '86 (minus ANDY and ROGER, the former setting out on a solo career while the latter quit the music business) with 'NOTORIOUS' (1986), the RODGERS-masterminded title track narrowly missing the top of the American charts. Gone were the hedonistic pop thrills of old, however, successive albums, 'BIG THING' (1988) and 'LIBERTY' (1990) being indescribably bland. Nevertheless, ageing fans ensured continuing chart action, the latter album still making the UK Top 10, while 1993 saw them make something of a mini-comeback with 'ORDINARY WORLD', their best single for years and US Top 5 to boot. A second single, 'COME UNDONE', also made the grade, while the accompanying eponymous album gave a hint as to what was in store with an unlikely cover of The Velvet Underground's 'FEMME FATALE'. Even more unlikely was a cover of hip hop/electro landmark, 'WHITE LINES (DON'T DO IT)', just one of the many erm, 'interpretations' on the 'THANK YOU' (1995) album. Incredibly, GRANDMASTER FLASH actually had a hand in this sacrilege, although what CHUCK D thought of the ridiculous rendition of '911 IS A JOKE' is anyone's guess. A well meant attempt at reinventing their heroes perhaps, but please, a cover of 'LAY LADY LAY'?! Of late, DURAN DURAN have plundered the past to regain some cred, a new (but old-sounding) American-only set, 'MEDAZZALAND' (1997) followed by a 'GREATEST HITS' package (again!) and worse still, a remix album in '99, entitled 'STRANGE BEHAVIOUR' (strange behaviour, indeed!). • **Songwriters:** LE BON – lyrics / RHODES – music. Covered; MAKE ME SMILE (Steve Harley & Cockney Rebel) / I WANNA TAKE

YOU HIGHER (Sly & The Family Stone) / PERFECT DAY (Lou Reed) / WATCHING THE DETECTIVES (Elvis Costello) / SUCCESS (Iggy Pop) / CRYSTAL SHIP (Doors) / BALL OF CONFUSION (Temptations) / THANK YOU (Led Zeppelin). • Trivia: SIMON LE BON married top-model, Yasmin Parvanah, on the 27th of December '85, while a year previously, the other two, ROGER and NICK, had also married cosmopolitan models.

Album rating: DURAN DURAN (*7) / RIO (*7) / SEVEN AND THE RAGGED TIGER (*5) / ARENA (*4) / NOTORIOUS (*6) / BIG THING (*4) / DECADE compilation (*8) / LIBERTY (*2) / DURAN DURAN (THE WEDDING ALBUM) (*5) / THANK YOU (*4) / MEDAZZALAND (*3) / GREATEST compilation (*7) / STRANGE BEHAVIOUR (*2) / Power Station: THE POWER STATION (*5) / Arcadia: SO RED THE ROSE (*4)

SIMON LE BON (b.27 Oct'58, Bushley, Hertfordshire, England) – vocals / **ANDY TAYLOR** (b.16 Feb'61, Newcastle, England) – guitar / **NICK RHODES** (b. NICHOLAS BATES, 8 Jun'62) – keyboards / **JOHN TAYLOR** (b.20 Jul'60, Solihull, England) – bass / **ROGER TAYLOR** (b.26 Apr'60) – drums.

		E.M.I.	Harvest
Jan 81.	(7") (EMI 5137) **PLANET EARTH. / LATE BAR** (12"+=) (12EMI 5137) – Planet earth (night version). (re-iss. Aug83; same)	12	
Apr 81.	(7"/12") (EMI/12EMI 5168) **CARELESS MEMORIES. / KHANDA** (re-iss. Aug83, 7"+=/12"+=; same) – Fame.	37	
Jun 81.	(lp/c) (EMC/TC-EMC 3372) <12158> **DURAN DURAN** – Girls on film / Planet Earth / Anyone out there / To the shore / Careless memories / (Waiting for the) Night boat / Sound of thunder / Friends of mine / Tel Aviv. <re-dist.Feb83, hit US No.10> (re-iss. Aug83; same) (cd-iss. Sep87 on 'Fame' cd/c/lp; CD/TC+/FA 3185) (re-iss. Aug95 cd/c; CD/TC PRG 1003)	3	
Jul 81.	(7") (EMI 5206) **GIRLS ON FILM. / FASTER THAN LIGHT** (12"+=) (12EMI 5206) – ('A'instrumental). (re-iss. Aug83, 7"/12"; same)	5	
Nov 81.	(7") (EMI 5254) **MY OWN WAY. / LIKE AN ANGEL** (12"+=) (12EMI 5254) – ('A'night version). (re-iss. Aug83, 7"/12"; same)	14	
May 82.	(7"/12") (EMI/12EMI 5295) <5134> **HUNGRY LIKE THE WOLF. / CARELESS MEMORIES (live)** (re-iss. Aug83, 7"/12"; same) <re-iss. Dec82 with diff.B-side; 5195> – hit No.3.	5	

		E.M.I.	Capitol
May 82.	(lp/c) (EMC/TC-EMC 3411) <12211> **RIO** – Rio / My own way / Lonely in your nightmare / Hungry like the wolf / Hold back the rain / New religion / Last chance on the stairway / Save a prayer / The chauffeur. (cd-iss. Aug83; CZ 291) (re-iss. Mar90 lp/c; ATAK/TC-ATAK 149) (re-iss. Sep93 cd/c; CD/TC PRG 1004)	2	6 Jan83
Aug 82.	(7"/12") (EMI/12EMI 5327) **SAVE A PRAYER. / HOLD BACK THE RAIN (remix)** (re-iss. Aug83, 7"/12"; same)	2	–
Sep 82.	(m-lp) (Harvest; <15006>) **CARNIVAL** – My own way / Hold back the rain / Girls on film / Hungry like the wolf.	–	98
Nov 82.	(7") (EMI 5346) <5175> **RIO. / THE CHAUFFEUR (BLUE SILVER)** (12") (12EMI 5346) – ('A'side) / Rio / (pt.2) / My own way. (re-iss. Aug83, 7"/12"; same)	9	–
Mar 83.	(7") <5215> **RIO. / HOLD BACK THE RAIN**	–	2
Mar 83.	(7"/12") (EMI/12EMI 5371) **IS THERE SOMETHING I SHOULD KNOW. / FAITH IN THIS COLOUR** (re-iss. Aug83, 7"/12"; same)	1	–
May 83.	(7") <5233> **IS THERE SOMETHING I SHOULD KNOW. / CARELESS MEMORIES**	–	4
Oct 83.	(7") (EMI 5429) <5290> **UNION OF THE SNAKE. / SECRET OKTOBER** (12"+=) (12EMI 5429) – ('A'-Monkey remix).	3	3
Nov 83.	(lp/c) (EMC/TC-EMC 1654) <12310> **SEVEN AND THE RAGGED TIGER** – The reflex / New Moon on Monday / (I'm looking for) Cracks in the pavement / I take the dice / Of crime and passion / Union of the snake / Shadows on your side / Tiger tiger / The seventh stranger. (cd-iss. Mar84; CZ 36) (re-iss. Aug88 on 'Fame' cd/c/lp; CD/TC+/FA 3205) (re-iss. Sep93 cd/c; CD/TC PRG 1005)	1	8
Jan 84.	(7"/12") (DURAN/12DURAN 1) <5309> **NEW MOON ON MONDAY. / TIGER TIGER**	9	10
Apr 84.	(7"/7"s) (DURAN/+P 2) **THE REFLEX. / MAKE ME SMILE (COME UP AND SEE ME) (live)** (12"+=/12"pic-d+=) (12DURAN/+P 2) – ('A'dance mix).	1	–
Apr 84.	(7") <5345> **THE REFLEX. / NEW RELIGION**	–	1
Oct 84.	(7"/12") (DURANC/12DURANC 3) <5417> **THE WILD BOYS. / (I'M LOOKING FOR) CRACKS IN THE PAVEMENT**	2	2
Nov 84.	(lp/c) (DD/TC-DD 2) <12374> **ARENA (live)** – Is there something I should know / Hungry like the wolf / New religion / Save a prayer / The wild boys / The seventh stranger / The chauffeur / Union of the snake / Planet Earth / Careless memories. (cd-iss. Dec84; CZ 79) (re-iss. Oct89 on 'Fame' cd/c/lp; CD/TC+/FA 3225)	6	4
Jan 85.	(7") <5438> **SAVE A PRAYER. / ('A'live version)**	–	16

		Parlophone	Capitol
May 85.	(7"/7"white) (DURAN/+G 007) <5475> **A VIEW TO A KILL. / ('A'instrumental)**	2	1

— took time off for own solo projects

The POWER STATION

(ANDY & JOHN TAYLOR) / **ROBERT PALMER** – vocals (solo artist see under own listing) / **TONY THOMPSON** – drums (ex-CHIC)

		Parlophone	Capitol
Mar 85.	(7"/7"pic-d) (R/+P 6091) <5444> **SOME LIKE IT HOT. / THE HEAT IS ON** (12"+=/12"pic-d+=) (12R/+P 6091) – ('A'extended).	14	6
Apr 85.	(lp/c) (POST/TC-POST 1) <12380> **THE POWER STATION**	12	6

— Some like it hot / Murderess / Lonely tonight / Communication / Get it on (bang a gong) / Go to zero / Harvest for the world / Still in your heart. (cd-iss. Jul85; CDP 746127-2) (re-iss. Sep88 on 'Fame' cd/c/lp; CD/TC+/FA 3206) (cd re-iss. Aug93; CDPRG 1011)

May 85.	(7")(12") <5479> **GET IT ON. / GO TO ZERO**	22	9
Nov 85.	(7")(12") <5511> **COMMUNICATION. / MURDERESS**	75	34

— **MICHAEL DES BARNES** – vocals; repl. PALMER on tour

ARCADIA

SIMON LE BON – vocals / **NICK RHODES** – keyboards / **ROGER TAYLOR** – drums / with session people

Oct 85.	(7") (NSR 1) <5501> **ELECTION DAY. / SHE'S MOODY AND GREY SHE'S MEAN AND SHE'S RESTLESS** (12"+=) (12NSR 1) – ('A'-Consensus mix). (12") (12NSRA 1) – ('A'-Cryptic Cut No Voice mix) / ('A'mix) / ('A'-Consensus mix).	7	6
Dec 85.	(lp/c) (PCSD/TC-PCSD 101) <12428> **SO RED THE ROSE** – Election day / Keep me in the dark / Goodbye is forever / The flame / Missing / Rose Arcana / The promise / El Diablo / Lady Ice. (re-iss. Aug93 cd/c; CD/TC PRG 1010)	30	23
Dec 85.	(7") <5542> **GOODBYE IS FOREVER. / MISSING**	–	33
Feb 86.	(7") (NSR 2) **THE PROMISE. / ROSE ARCANE** (12"+=) (12NSR 2) – ('A'extended).	37	
Jul 86.	(7") (NSR 3) **THE FLAME. / FLAME AGAIN** (12") (12NSR 3) – ('A'extended) / ('B'-Homeboy mix) / Election day (Early Rough mix).	58	

JOHN TAYLOR

Mar 86.	(7") (R 6125) <5551> **I DO WHAT I DO . . . (theme from 9 1/2 weeks). / JAZZ (instrumental)** (12"+=) (12R 6125) – ('A'-Film mix).	42	23

DURAN DURAN

— ANDY went solo and subsequently released a handful of singles including a US Top 30 smash, 'TAKE IT EASY' (from the movie, 'American Anthem') and an album, 'THUNDER', a US Top 50 breaker in '87. (ROGER quit the music business)

— now down to SIMON, NICK + JOHN

Oct 86.	(7") (DDN 45) <5648> **NOTORIOUS. / WINTER MARCHES ON** (c-s+=/12"+=) (TC/12 DDNX 45) – ('A'-Latin Rascals mix).	7	2
Nov 86.	(lp/c/cd) (DDN/TCDDN 331)(CDP 746 415-2) <12540> **NOTORIOUS** – Notorious / American science / Skin trade / A matter of feeling / Hold me / Vertigo (do the demolition) / So misled / Meet el Presidente / Winter marches on / Proposition. (re-iss. Sep93 cd/c; CD/TC PRG 1004)	16	12
Feb 87.	(7"/7"w-poster) (TRADE/+X 1) <5670> **SKIN TRADE. / WE NEED YOU** (c-s+=) (TCTRADE 1) – ('A'-Stretch mix).	22	39
Apr 87.	(7") (TOUR 1) **MEET EL PRESIDENTE. / VERTIGO (DO THE DEMOLITION)** (ext.cd-s+=) (CDTOUR 1) – ('A'-Meet el Beat mix).	24	70

— added **WARREN CUCCURULLO** – guitar (ex-FRANK ZAPPA, ex-MISSING PERSONS) / **STEVE FERRONE** – drums (ex-BRIAN AUGER, ex-AVERAGE WHITE BAND) (both on last lp)

Sep 88.	(7") (YOUR 1) <44237> **I DON'T WANT YOUR LOVE. / ('A'-lp version)** (etched/cd-s+=) (12/CD YOURS 1) – ('A'Big Mix version).	14	4
Oct 88.	(cd/c/lp) (CD/TC+/DDB 33) <90958> **BIG THING** – Big thing / I don't want your love / All she wants is / Too late Marlene / Drug (it's just a state of mind) / Do you believe in shame? / Palomino / Interlude one / Land / Flute interlude / The edge of America / Lake shore driving. (re-iss. Mar90 on 'E.M.I.' lp/c; ATAK/TC-ATAK 148) (cd-iss. Mar90 on 'E.M.I'; CZ 290) (re-iss. Sep93 cd/c; CD/TC PRG 1007)	15	24
Dec 88.	(7") (DD 11) <44287> **ALL SHE WANTS IS. / I BELIEVE – ALL I NEED TO KNOW (medley)** (12"+=) (12DD 11) <44287> – ('A'-US master mix). (3"cd-s+=) (CDDD 11) – Skin trade (Parisian mix).		22
Apr 89.	(7"/7"pic-d) (DD/+PD 12) <44337> **DO YOU BELIEVE IN SHAME? / ('A'-Krush Brothers LSD mix)** (10"+=) (10DD 12) – Notorious (live). (3"cd-s++=) (CDDD 12) – God (London) / This is how a road gets made. (3x7"box) (DD A/B/C 12) – Do you believe in shame? / God (London) // Palomino / This is how a road gets made // Do you believe in shame? / Drugs – it's just a state of mind.	30	72 Mar89
Nov 89.	(cd/c/lp) (CD/TC+/DDX 10) <93178> **DECADE** – Planet Earth / Girls on film / Hungry like the wolf / Rio / Save a prayer / Is there something I should know / Union of the snake / The reflex / Wild boys / A view to a kill / Notorious / Skin trade / I don't want your love / All she wants is.	5	67
Dec 89.	(c-s/7") (TC+/DD 13) **BURNING THE GROUND. / DECADENCE** (12"+=/cd-s+=) (12/CD DD 13) – Decadence (extended).	31	–

— **STERLING CAMPBELL** – drums repl. FERRONE

Jul 90.	(c-s/7") (TC+/DD 14) **VIOLENCE OF SUMMER (LOVE'S TAKING OVER). / ('A'mix)** (12"+=) (12DD 14) – ('A'extended). (cd-s+=) (CDDD 14) – Throb.	20	–
Aug 90.	(c-s) <44608> **VIOLENCE OF SUMMER (LOVE'S TAKING OVER) / YO BAD AZIZI**	–	64
Aug 90.	(cd/lp) (CD/TC+/PCSD 112) <94292> **LIBERTY** – Violence of summer (love's taking over) / Liberty / Hothead / Serious / All along the water / My Antarctica / Read my lips / First impression / Can you deal with it / Venice drowning / Downtown. (re-iss. Sep93 cd/c; CD/TC RG 1009)	8	46
Nov 90.	(c-s/7") (TC+/DD 15) **SERIOUS. / YO BAD AZIZI** (12"+=/cd-s+=) (12/CD DD 15) – Water babies.	48	–
Jan 93.	(c-s) <44908> **ORDINARY WORLD / ('A'acoustic) / SAVE A PRAYER (live)**	–	3

Jan 93. (c-s/7")(7"pic-d) *(TC+/DD 16)(DDP 16)* **ORDINARY WORLD. / MY ANTARTICA** | 6 | - |
(cd-s+=) *(CDDDS 16)* – Save a prayer / Skin trade.
(cd-s) *(CDDDP 16)* – ('A'side) / The reflex / Hungry like the wolf / Girls on film.

Feb 93. (cd/c/lp) *(CD/TC+/CD 34) <98876>* **DURAN DURAN (THE WEDDING ALBUM)** | 4 | 7 |
– Too much information / Ordinary world / Love voodoo / Drowning man / Shotgun / Come undone / Breath after breath / UMF / Home of the above / Femme fatale / Shelter / To whom it may concern. *(cd-box Jan94; CDDDB 35)*

Mar 93. (c-s/7") *(TC+/DD 17)* **COME UNDONE. / ORDINARY WORLD (acoustic)** | 13 | - |
(cd-s+=) *(CDDD 17)* – ('A'mixes).
(cd-s) *(CDDDS 17)* – ('A'side) / ('A'version) / Rio / Is there something I should know / A view to a kill.

Apr 93. (c-s) *<44918>* **COME UNDONE / ('A'-mix 2 master) / TIME FOR TEMPTATION** | - | 7 |

Aug 93. (c-s/12") *(TC/12 DD 18)* **TOO MUCH INFORMATION. / COME UNDONE (live)** | 35 | - |
(12"+=) *(12DD 18)* – Come undone (12"mix Coming together) / Notorious (live).
(cd-s) *(CDDD 18)* – ('A'side) / Drowning man.

Aug 93. (cd-s) *<44955>* **TOO MUCH INFORMATION / FIRST IMPRESSION / COME UNDONE (new mix)** | - | 45 |
(with live free c-ep) **NO ORDINARY EP** – Hungry like the wolf / Notorious / Come undone.

Mar 95. (c-s/7") *(TC+/DD 20)* **PERFECT DAY. / FEMME FATALE (alt.mix)** | 28 | - |
(cd-s+=) *(CDDDS 20)* – Make me smile (come up and see me) / Perfect day (acoustic).
(cd-s) *(CDDDP 20)* – ('A'side) / Love voodoo / Needle and the damage done / 911 is a joke (alternative mix).

Mar 95. (cd/c) *(CD/TC DDB 36) <29419>* **THANK YOU** | 12 | 19 |
– White lines / I wanna take you higher / Perfect day / Watching the detectives / Lay lady lay / 911 is a joke / Success / Crystal ship / Ball of confusion / Thank you / Drive by / I wanna take you higher again.
below actually featured GRANDMASTER FLASH

Jun 95. (c-s) *(TCDD 19)* **WHITE LINES (DON'T DO IT) / SAVE A PRAYER / NONE OF THE ABOVE (Drizabone mix)** | 17 | |
(cd-s+=) *(CDDD 19)* – Ordinary world (acoustic).
(12") *(12DD 19)* – ('A'side) / ('A'-Junior Vasquez mix) / ('A'-Oakland fonk mix) / ('A'-70's club mix).

	Virgin	Capitol

May 97. (7"/c/cd-s) *(VS LH/C/CDT 1639)* **OUT OF MY MIND / SILVA HALO** | 21 | - |
(cd-s+=) *(VSCDX 1639)* – Sinner or saint / ('A'remix).

Sep 97. (c-s,cd-s) *<58674>* **ELECTRIC BARBARELLA /** | - | 52 |

Oct 97. (cd,c) *<33876>* **MEDAZZALAND** | - | 58 |
– Medazzaland / Big bang generation / Electric Barbarella / Out of my mind / Who do you think you are? / Silva halo / Be my icon / Buried in the sand / Michael you've got a lot to answer for / Midnight sun / So long suicide / Undergoing treatment.

Jan 99. (c-s) *(TCELEC 2000)* **ELECTRIC BARBARELLA / GIRLS ON FILM (Tin Tin Out mix)** | 23 | - |
(cd-s+=) *(CDELEC 2000)* – ('A'-Tee's club mix).
(12"+=) *(12ELEC 2000)* – ('A'-Electric sex mix).

– compilations, etc. –

Nov 98. (cd/c) *E.M.I.; (496239-2/-4)* **GREATEST** | 15 | |
– Is there something I should know? / The reflex / A view to a kill / Ordinary world / Save a prayer / Rio / Hungry like the wolf / Girls on film / Planet Earth / Union of the snake / New moon on Monday / Wild boys / Notorious / I don't want your love / All she wants is / Electric Barbarella / Serious / Skin trade / Come undone.

Mar 99. (d-cd) *(493972-2)* **STRANGE BEHAVOIR** (remixes) | 70 | |

POWER STATION

—— re-grouped (**PALMER / TAYLOR / TAYLOR / THOMPSON**)

	Chrysalis	Chrysalis

Oct 96. (c-s) *(TCCHS 5039)* **SHE CAN ROCK IT / ('A'mix)** | 63 | |
(cd-s+=) *(CDCHS 5039)* – Power trippin' / Charanga.

Oct 96. (cd/c) *(CD/TC CHR 6117)* **LIVING IN FEAR** | | |
– Notoriety / Scarred / She can rock it / Let's get it on / Life forces / Fancy that / Living in fear / Shut up / Dope / Love conquers all / Taxman.

DURUTTI COLUMN

Formed: Manchester, England ... early 1978 by VINI REILLY, CHRIS JOYCE and DAVE ROWBOTHAM. That year, they signed to TONY WILSON's indie label, 'Factory', although they dramatically split in mid-'79 leaving skinny VINI to pick up the pieces. Taking their name from the 1930's art-terrorists, Situationiste Internationale, and given free time by label boss, WILSON, under the wing of producer MARTIN HANNETT, the guitarist finally came up with DURUTTI's debut 'THE RETURN OF . . .' (1980). This was a brilliant introduction to his minimalist yet picturesque guitar improvisations, although its gimmick sandpaper sleeve was not exactly the toast of the record retailers who had to protect the rest of their stock from its glassy debris. He subsequently supported on tour fellow Mancunian, JOHN COOPER CLARKE, PAULINE MURRAY and even JOHN MARTYN, while recording the follow-up, 'L.C.' (1981), another masterpiece that fused light jazz into barren but dreamy landscapes. However, not for the first time, ill-health was to dog VINI, and it took a few years to record 'ANOTHER SETTING' (1983). All the above albums featured eccentric percussionist BRUCE MITCHELL, he of former parody-rock outfit, ALBERTOS Y LOST TRIOS PARANOIAS, the man becoming a stalwart on all VINI/DURUTTI's further work. In 1986, VINI took a trip to California, where he invited punkette,

DEBI DIAMOND, to sing on a version of JEFFERSON AIRPLANE's 'White Rabbit'. After the release of the 1987 album, 'GUITAR AND OTHER MACHINES', REILLY was invited by old fellow-NOSEBLEEDS chum, MORRISSEY, to play guitar pieces on his 1988 solo debut, 'VIVA HATE'. In 1990, DURUTTI COLUMN returned in fine style with 'OBEY THE TIME', although this was the last for Factory, as the label went bankrupt in '92. Under the control of 'Polygram', the imprint was once again under way in 1994 as 'Factory Too', and a happier VINI unleashed another textured beauty, 'SEX AND DEATH'. • **Songwriters:** All composed by REILLY, except cover; I GET ALONG WITHOUT YOU VERY WELL (Hoagy Carmichael). • **Note:** On the 8th of November '91, original member, DAVE ROWBOTHAM, was axed to death.

Album rating: THE RETURN OF THE DURUTTI COLUMN (*9) / L.C. (*7) / ANOTHER SETTING (*6) / WITHOUT MERCY (*6) / DOMO ARIGATO (*7) / CIRCUSES AND BREAD (*5) / THE GUITAR AND OTHER MACHINES (*6) / VALUABLE PASSAGES compilation (*8) / VINI REILLY (*7) / OBEY THE TIME (*5) / SEX AND DEATH (*7) / FIDELITY (*5)

VINI REILLY (b. Aug'53) – guitar (ex-NOSEBLEEDS, ex-V2) / **DAVE ROWBOTHAM** – guitar / **CHRIS JOYCE** – drums / **BRUCE MITCHELL** – percussion / also **TONY BOWERS** – bass / **PHIL RAINFORD** – vocals (left Jul78)

—— recorded for Various Artists EP – A FACTORY SAMPLER. Split mid'79, DAVE, CHRIS and TONY joined The MOTHMEN. **VINI REILLY** now brought in **MARTIN HANNETT** – switches, producer (ex-INVISIBLE GIRLS (JOHN COOPER CLARKE) with **PETER CROOKS** – bass / **TOBY** (b.PHILIP TOMANOV) – drums / **GAMMER** – melody

	Factory	not iss.

Feb 80. (lp) *(FACT 14)* **THE RETURN OF THE DURUTTI COLUMN** | | - |
– Sketch for Summer / Requiem for a father / Katherine / Conduct / Beginning / Jazz / Sketch for winter / Collette / In "D". *(w/ free testcard flexi by MARTIN HANNETT)* **FIRST ASPECT OF THE SAME THING. / SECOND ASPECT OF THE SAME THING.**
(re-iss. Jul80 lp/c; FACT 14/+C)

—— **VINI** on his own, featured **PHIL RAYNHAM** – vocals

Nov 80. (12") *Factory Benelux; (FACBN 2)* **LIPS THAT WOULD KISS (FORM PRAYERS TO BROKEN STONE). / MADELEINE** | - | - | Belgium
(re-iss. Mar81; FACBN 2-005) (re-iss. cd-ep Mar91; FBN 2CD)

Mar 81. (7"ltd) *Sordide Sentimentale; (SS 45-005)* **ENIGMA. / DANNY** | - | - | Italy

—— now just a duo when **VINI** – guitars, now on extra vocals & keyboards / added **BRUCE MITCHELL** – percussion (ex-ALBERTOS Y LOST TRIOS PARANOIAS)

Sep 81. (lp/c) *(FACT 44/+C)* **LC** | | - |
– Sketch for dawn 1 / ~Portrait for Frazier / Jacqueline / Messidor / Sketch for dawn 2 / Never known / The act committed / Detail for Paul / The missing boy / The sweet cheat gone.

—— VINI now completely solo

1982. (7"ltd) *Factory Benelux; (FBN 100)* **FOR PATTI. / WEARINESS AND FEVER** | | - | Belgium

Mar 82. (12"ep) *Factory Benelux; (FBN 10)* **DEUX TRIANGLES** | | - | Belgium
– Favourite painting / Zinni / Piece for out of tune grand piano.

—— added guests **LINDSAY WILSON** – vocals / **MAUNAGH FLEMING** – cor anglais

Aug 82. (7") *(FAC 64)* **I GET ALONG WITHOUT YOU VERY WELL. / PRAYER** | | - |

—— **VINI** now augmented by **MERVYN FLETCHER** – saxophone / **TONY BOWERS** – bass / **CHRIS JOYCE** – drums / **TIM KELLETT** – trumpet (all ex-MOTHMEN)

Aug 83. (lp/c) *(FACT 74/+C)* **ANOTHER SETTING** | | - |
– Prayer / Bordeaux / The beggar / The response / For a western / Francesca / Smile in the crowd / Dream of a child / Spent time / You've heard it before / Second family.

—— **VINI** retained **MERVYN** and **TIM**. (TONY & CHRIS later joined SIMPLY RED with TIM). **BRUCE MITCHELL** rejoined (he had always been part of live set-up) / **MAUNAGH FLEMING** rejoined with new guests **CAROLINE LAVELLE** – cello / **RICHARD HENRY** – trombone / **BLAINE REININGER** – viola/violin (of TUXEDO MOON)

Dec 84. (lp/c) *(FACT 84/+C)* **WITHOUT MERCY** | | - |
– Face 1 / Face 2.

—— Now just basically **VINI** with **BRUCE** with old friends augmenting

Mar 85. (12"ep) *(FAC 114)* **SAY WHAT YOU MEAN, MEAN WHAT YOU SAY** | | - |
– Goodbye / The room / E.E. / A little mercy / Silence / Hello.

Aug 85. (video-cd) *(FACD 144)* **DOMO ARIGATO (live Japan)** | | - |
– Sketch for Summer / Mercy theme / Sketch for dawn / E.E. / Little mercy / Jacqueline / Dream of a child / Mercy dance / The room / Blind elevator girl / Tomorrow / Belgian friends / Missing boy / Self-portrait / (audience noise).

Mar 86. (7") *Factory Benelux; (FBN 51)* **TOMORROW. / TOMORROW (live)** | - | - | Belgium
(12"+=) *(FBN 51)* – All that love and maths can do.

Mar 86. (lp)(cd) *(FBN 36)(FACD 154)* **CIRCUSES AND BREAD** | | - |
– Pauline / Tomorrow / Dance 2 / For Hilary / Street fight / Royal infirmary / Black horses / Dance 1 / Blind elevator girl – Osaka. *(cd+=)* – (last 45). *(cd-iss. Nov93 on 'Crepescule';)*

—— **VINI** with **MITCHELL, KELLETT, JOHN METCALFE**

Oct 86. (12") *Materiali Sonori; (MASO 70003)* **GREETINGS THREE** | - | - | Italy
– Florence sunset / All that love and maths can do / San Giovanni dawn / For friends in Italy.

Aug 87. (12"ep; w/ DEBI DIAMOND) *(FAC 184)* **THE CITY OF OUR LADY** | | - |
– Our lady of the angels / White rabbit* / Catos con guantes.

Dec 87. (cd-ep) *(FACD 194)* **OUR LADY OF THE ANGELS / CATOS CON GUANTAS / WHEN THE WORLD (Newson mix)** | | - |

—— **VINI + BRUCE** were joined by guests **TIM KELLETT** (of SIMPLY RED) (1 track.) / **STANTON MIRANDA** – vocals (solo artist – 2 tracks.) **POL** – vocals (3 tracks.) / **STEPHEN STREET** – bass (1 track.) **JOHN METCALFE** – viola (1 track.) / **ROB GREY** – mouth organ

Nov 87. (lp/cd)(c/dat) *(FAC T/D 204)(FACT 204 C/D)* **THE GUITAR AND OTHER MACHINES** | | - |
– When the world / Arpeggiator / What is it to me (woman) / U.S.P. / Red shoes /

Jongleur grey / Bordeaux sequence / Miss Haynes / Don't think you're funny / English tradition landscape / Pol in 'B'. *(cd+=)* – Dream topping / You won't feel out of place / 28 Oldham Street.

Dec 87. (7"flexi) *(FAC 214)* **THE GUITAR AND OTHER MARKETING DEVICES** ☐ ☐ -
– Jongleur grey / Bordeaux sequence / English landscape tradition / U.S.P.

―― added **ROBERT NEWTON** plus **DV8 PHYSICAL THEATRE**

Apr 88. (cd-s-video) *(FACDV 194)* **WHEN THE WORLD (soundtrack) / WHEN THE WORLD** (lp) / **FINAL CUT / WHEN THE WORLD** (video) ☐ ☐ ☐ ☐ -

Dec 88. (3"cd-ep) *(FACD 234)* **WOMAD LIVE** (live) ☐ ☐ -
– Otis / English landscape tradition / Finding the sea / Bordeaux.

Mar 89. (lp/cd)(dat) *(FAC T/CD 244)(FACT 244D)* **VINI REILLY** ☐ ☐
– Homage to Catalonea / Opera II / People's pleasure park / Pol in G / Love no more / Opera I / Finding the sea / Otis / They work every day / Requiem again / My country. *(lp w/ free 7" with MORRISSEY)* *(FAC 244+)* – **I KNOW VERY WELL HOW I GOT MY NOTE WRONG** *(cd w/ free 3"cd-ep)* *(FAC 244+)* – (above) / Red square / William B.

―― Included sampled voices of OTIS REDDING, ANNIE LENNOX and TRACY CHAPMAN. **VINI** added **PAUL MILLER**

Dec 90. (cd/lp)(c/dat) *(FAC D/T 274)(FACT 274 C/D)* **OBEY THE TIME** ☐ ☐
– Vino della easa Bianco / Fridays / Home / Art and freight / Spanish reggae / Neon / The warmest rain / Contra-indications / Vino della casa rosso.

Feb 91. (12"ep/cd-ep) *(FAC/+D 284)* **THE TOGETHER MIX. / CONTRA INDICATIONS** (version) / **FRIDAYS** (up-person mix)

Jun 91. (cd)(lp) *Materiali Sonori; (CDMASO 90024)(33-065)* **DRY** ☐ - ☐ - Italy
– Dry / Paradise passage road / Rope around my neck / Short / Boat people / Boat people / Our lady / Grade 2 duet / Octaves / Out of the blue / Otis / English language tradition / Finding the sea / Bordeaux / Beggar. *(cd+=)* – WOMAD LIVE (tracks).

―― **VINI, BRUCE** w / guests **PETER HOOK** – bass (of NEW ORDER) + **MARTIN JACKSON** – keyboards (ex-/of-SWING OUT SISTER)

		Factory Too	not iss.

Nov 94. (cd) *(FACD 201)* **SEX AND DEATH** ☐ -
– Anthony / The rest of my life / For Colette / The next time / Beautiful lies / My irasable friend / Believe in me / Fermina / Where I should be / Fado / Madre mio / Blue period.

	Crepescule	not iss.

May 96. (cd) *(TWI 9762)* **FIDELITY** ☐ -

– compilations, etc. –

Jun 83. (lp) *V.U.; (VINI 1)* **LIVE AT THE VENUE** (live VINI & BRUCE) ☐ -
– Sketch for summer / Conduct / Never known / Jacqueline / Party / etc.

Dec 85. (lp) *Fundacao Atlantica; (1652071)* **AMIGOS EM PORTUGAL / DEDICATIONS FOR JACQUELINE** ☐ - Portu
– Friends in Portugal / Small girl by a pool / Crumpled dress / Sara and Tristana / Nighttime Estoril / Lisbon / To end with / Wheels turning / Favourite descending intervals / Saudade / Games of rhythm / Lies of mercy.

Dec 86. (lp/cd)(d-c) *Factory; (FAC T/D 164)(FACT 164C)* **VALUABLE PASSAGES** ☐ -
– Sketch for summer / Conduct / Sketch for winter / Lips that would kiss / Belgian friends / Danny / Piece for out-of-tune piano / Never know / Jacqueline / Missing boy / Prayer / Spent time / Without mercy stanzas 2-8 & 12-15 / Room / Blind elevator girl / Tomorrow / LFO MOD.

Nov 87. (c) *R.O.I.R.; (A-152)* **THE DURUTTI COLUMN LIVE AT THE BOTTOM LINE, NEW YORK** (live) ☐ ☐
(re-iss. May93 & Feb95 cd/c; A-152 CD/C)

Mar 88. (4xcd-box) *Factory; (FACD 224)* **THE DURUTTI COLUMN – THE FIRST FOUR ALBUMS** ☐ ☐

Dec 89. (ltd-cd) *Spore; (CD 1)* **THE SPORADIC RECORDINGS** ☐ ☐

Sep 94. (cd) *Materiali Sonori; (90037)* **RED SHOES** ☐ ☐

Ian DURY

Born: 12 May'42, Upminster, Essex, England. At age seven he became partially crippled from contracting polio. In 1970, he was employed as a teacher / lecturer at Canterbury College. The following year, he formed KILBURN & THE HIGH ROADS, who embarked on pub/college circuit in London. After 1 album in the mid-70's and many line-up changes, they disbanded, leaving DURY and manager DAVE ROBINSON to create solo deal for the singer. Signing to Jake Riviera's new indie label, 'Stiff', he soon raced up album charts in 1977 with the new wave favourite 'NEW BOOTS AND PANTIES!!!'. DURY's articulate patter and intelligent lyrics fused well with funky/jerky group backing which alternated between rock'n'roll and disco. He also developed many areas of Cockney rhyme-slang into rude but clever lyrics. The album made the UK Top 5, preceded by the brilliant 'SEX AND DRUGS AND ROCK AND ROLL', DURY's typically wry comment on the excesses of the music business. The following year, the singer's cast of sidemen became The BLOCKHEADS, the line-up of CHAZ JANKEL, NORMAN WATT-ROY, CHARLEY CHARLES, MICKEY GALLAGHER, JOHN TURNBULL and DAVY PAYNE playing on DURY's first hit single, 'WHAT A WASTE'. However, it was the follow-up, 'HIT ME WITH YOUR RHYTHM STICK' which really earned DURY a smutty place in the annals of pop history, its half-spoken narrative style breaking into a gloriously demented chorus. The track sat astride the UK singles chart for a few weeks, while the attendant album, 'DO IT YOURSELF' (1979) made No.2. The DURY/JANKEL writing partnership was to end soon after, however, the latter embarking on solo work and freeing up a position for ex-DR. FEELGOOD guitarist, WILKO JOHNSON. The resulting album, 'LAUGHTER' (1980), met with limited success, prompting a musical Spring clean from DURY; signing to 'Polydor', securing the esteemed services of SLY & ROBBIE and reuniting with JANKEL, the cheeky cockney released the acclaimed 'LORD UPMINSTER'. Commercial success continued

to elude him, however, and DURY semi-retired in the mid-80's following the '4,000 WEEKS HOLIDAY' (1984) opus. He eventually resurfaced in 1989 with the 'APPLES' soundtrack, although he proved his inimitable sense of humour hadn't deserted him on 1992's 'THE BUS DRIVERS PRAYER & OTHER STORIES'. Having been diagnosed with cancer of the colon in 1995 (it was soon to spread into his liver), IAN DURY wanted to bow out with a bang not a whimper. In the summer of '98, the man did just that (with the help of his ever faithful BLOCKHEADS). His comeback album, 'Mr LOVE PANTS', even returned him back into the charts, but sadly, this was IAN's last lyrical message – he died on the 27th March, 2000; they said he died with a smile on his face. • **Songwriters:** DURY – words / JANKEL – music, until his departure from The BLOCKHEADS. • **Trivia:** After he semi-retired in the mid-80's, he started an acting career in films:- NUMBER ONE (1985) / PIRATES (1986) / HEARTS OF FIRE (1987), and TV plays:- KING OF THE GHETTOS (1986) / TALK OF THE DEVIL (1986) / NIGHT MOVES (1987). His other work on TV was mainly for commercials, etc.

Album rating: NEW BOOTS AND PANTIES!! (*8) / DO IT YOURSELF (*7) / LAUGHTER (*6) / JUKEBOX DURY compilation (*6) / LORD UPMINSTER (*6) / 400 WEEKS HOLIDAY (*5) / SEX AND DRUGS AND ROCK AND ROLL compilation (*7) / APPLES (*5) / THE BUS DRIVER'S PRAYER AND OTHER STORIES (*6) / Mr LOVE PANTS (*6)

KILBURN & THE HIGH ROADS

IAN DURY – vocals / **KEITH LUCAS** – guitar / **DAVEY PAYNE** – sax / **CHARLIE SINCLAIR** – bass repl. HUMPHREY OCEAN who had repl. CHARLIE HART / **LOUIS LAROSE** then **GEORGE BUTLER** – drums

―― Early 1974, recorded lp for 'Raft', which was shelved after 'Warners' took over label. It was later issued by them in Oct'78 as 'WOTABUNCH', after DURY was top of the charts.

―― (mid-74) **DAVID ROHOMAN** – drums repl. BUTLER / **ROD MELVIN** – piano repl. HARDY

		Dawn	not iss.

Nov 74. (7") *(DNS 1090)* **ROUGH KIDS. / BILLY BENTLEY** ☐ -

Feb 75. (7") *(DNS 1102)* **CRIPPLED WITH NERVES. / HUFFETY PUFF** ☐ -

Jun 75. (lp) *(DNLS 3065)* **HANDSOME** ☐ -
– The roadette song / Pam's mood / Crippled with nerves / Broken skin / Upminster kid / Patience / Father / Thank you mum / Rough kids / The badger and the rabbit / The mumble rumble and the cocktail rock / The call up. *(re-iss. Nov85 on 'Flashback' lp/c; FBLP/ZCFBL 8094)*

―― Disbanded mid-75, although IAN gigged at times with a new line-up as IAN DURY & THE KILBURNS. KEITH LUCAS was later to become NICK CASH and form 999. There were also other KILBURN material re-released after DURY's success.

1977. (lp) *Warners; (K 56513)* **WOTABUNCH** ☐ -

Sep 78. (7") *Warners; (K 17225)* **BENTLEY. / PAM'S MOODS** ☐ -

Jul 83. (lp/c) *P.R.T.; (DOW/ZCDOW 17)* **UPMINSTER KIDS** ☐ -

IAN DURY

―― - vocals solo with **CHAZ JANKEL** – guitar, keyboards (ex-BYZANTIUM) plus session men that became The BLOCKHEADS (see below)

		Stiff	Stiff

Aug 77. (7",7"orange) *(BUY 17)* **SEX AND DRUGS AND ROLL. / RAZZLE IN MY POCKET** ☐ -

Sep 77. (lp/gold-lp/c) *(SEEZ/SEEZG/ZSEEZ 4) <0002>* **NEW BOOTS AND PANTIES!!!** ☐ 5 ☐ Apr78
– Sweet Gene Vincent / ake up and make love with me / I'm partial to your abracadabra / My old man / Billericay Dickie / Clevor Trever / If I was with a woman / Plainstow Patricia / Blockheads / Blackmail man. *(re-iss. Sep86 on 'Demon' lp/c/cd+=; FIEND/+CASS/CD 63)* – (interview). *(re-iss. cd May95 on 'Disky';)* *(cd re-iss. Aug98 on 'Hit'; AHLCD 57)*

Nov 77. (7") *(BUY 23)* **SWEET GENE VINCENT. / YOU'RE MORE THAN FAIR** ☐ -

IAN DURY AND THE BLOCKHEADS

―― with **JANKEL** plus **NORMAN WATT-ROY** – bass (ex-LOVING AWARENESS, ex-GLENCOE) / **CHARLEY CHARLES** – drums (ex-LOVING AWARENESS, ex-GLENCOE) / **MICKEY GALLAGHER** – keyboards (ex-LOVING AWARENESS, ex-FRAMPTON'S CAMEL) / **JOHN TURNBULL** – guitar (ex-LOVING AWARENESS) / **DAVEY PAYNE** – saxophone (ex-WRECKLESS ERIC)

Apr 78. (7"/12") *(BUY 27/+12)* **WHAT A WASTE. / WAKE UP AND MAKE LOVE WITH ME** 11 ☐

Nov 78. (7"; as IAN & THE BLOCKHEADS) *(BUY 38)* **HIT ME WITH YOUR RHYTHM STICK. / THERE AIN'T HALF BEEN SOME CLEVER BASTARDS** 1 ☐

May 79. (lp/c) *(SEEZ/ZSEEZ 14) <36104>* **DO IT YOURSELF** 2 ☐ Jul79
– Inbetweenies / Quiet / Don't ask me / Sink my boats / Waiting for your taxi / This is what we find / Uneasy sunny hotsy totsy / Mischief / Dance of the screamers / Lullaby for Francies. *(re-iss. Feb90 on 'Demon' lp/c/cd; FIEND/+CASS/CD 133)* *(re-iss. cd May95 on 'Disky';)* *(cd re-iss. Aug98 on 'Hit'; AHLCD 58)*

Jul 79. (7") *(BUY 50)* **REASONS TO CHEERFUL (pt.3). / COMMON AS MUCK** 3 ☐

Aug 80. (7") *(BUY 90)* **I WANT TO BE STRAIGHT. / THAT'S NOT ALL HE WANTS** 22 ☐

―― **WILKO JOHNSON** – guitar (ex-DR. FEELGOOD, solo artist) repl. JANKEL who went solo

Oct 80. (7") *(BUY 100)* **SUEPERMAN'S BIG SISTER. / F***ING ADA** 51 ☐
(12"+=) *(BUYIT 100)* – You'll see glimpses.

Nov 80. (lp/c) *(SEEZ/ZSEEZ 30) <36998>* **LAUGHTER** 48 ☐ Jan81
– Sueperman's big sister / Pardon / Delusions of grandeur / Yes and no (Paula) / Dance of the crackpots / Over the points / (Take your elbow out of the soup you're

sitting on the chicken) / Uncoolohol / Hey, hey, take me away / Manic depression / Oh, Mr. Peanut / F***ing Ada. *(cd-iss. May95 on 'Disky';) (cd re-iss. Aug98 on 'Hit'; AHLCD 59)*

—— IAN DURY now brought in the services of rhythm boys **SLY & ROBBIE** plus **JANKEL + TYRONE DOWNIE** – keyboards

	Polydor	Polydor
Aug 81. (7"/12") *(POSP/+X 285)* **SPASTICUS AUSTICIOUS. /** ('A'instrumental)		
Sep 81. (lp/c) *(POLD/+C 5042) <16337>* **LORD UPMINSTER**	53	

– Funky disco pops / Red letter / Girls watching / Wait for me / The body song / Lonely town / Trust is a must / Spasticus austicious. *(re-iss. Dec89 on 'Great Expectations' lp/cd; PIP LP/CD 005)*

IAN DURY & THE MUSIC STUDENTS

—— with many musicians including **JANKEL, PAYNE + RAY COOPER**

Nov 83. (7"/12") *(POSP/+C 646)* **REALLY GLAD YOU CAME. /** INSPIRATION		
Jan 84. (lp/c) *(POLD/+C 5112)* **4,000 WEEKS HOLIDAY**	54	-

– (You're my) Inspiration / Friends / Tell your daddy / Peter the painter / Ban the bomb / Percy the poet / Very personal / Take me to the cleaners / The man with no face / Really glad you came. *(re-iss. Dec89 on 'Great Expectations' lp/cd; PIP LP/CD 004)*

Feb 84. (7") *(POSP 673)* **VERY PERSONAL. / BAN THE BOMB**		

(12"+=) *(POSPX 673)* – The sky's the limit.

IAN DURY

—— solo, with **PAYNE, GALLAGHER, COOPER** plus **STEVE WHITE** – drums / **MICHAEL McEVOY** – bass, synth / **MERLIN RHYS-JONES** – guitar / **FRANCES RUFELLE** – vocals / etc.

	E.M.I.	not iss.
Oct 89. (7"/7"pic-d) *(EMI/+P 5534)* **PROFOUNDLY IN LOVE WITH PANDORA. / EUGENIUS (YOU'RE A GENIUS)**	45	-

(above from the TV series, 'Adrian Mole')

	WEA	WEA
Oct 89. (7") *(YZ 437)* **APPLES. / BYLINE BROWN**		-
Oct 89. (lp/c)(cd) *(WX 326/+C)(246355-2)* **APPLES** (soundtrack)		-

– Apples / Love is all / Byline Browne / Bit of kit / Game on / Looking for Harry / England's glory / Bus driver's prayer / P.C. Honey / The right people / All those who say okay / Riding the outskirts of fantasy.

—— In Sep'90 he reformed IAN DURY & THE BLOCKHEADS for two reunion gigs

IAN DURY

	Demon	not iss.
Apr 91. (lp/cd) *(FIEND/+CD 777)* **WARTS 'N' AUDIENCE** (live 22 December 1990)		-

– Wake up / Clever Trevor / Billericay Dickie / Quiet / My old man / Spasticus autisticus / Plaistow Patricia / Clever bastards / Sweet Gene Vincent / What a waste / Hit me with your rhythm stick / Blockheads. (cd+=) – If I was with a woman.

Nov 92. (cd/c) *(FIEND CD/CASS 702)* **THE BUS DRIVERS PRAYER & OTHER STORIES**		-

– That's enough of that / Bill Haley's last words / Poor Joey / Quick quick slow / Fly in the ointment / O'Donegal / Poo-poo in the prawn / Ave a word / London talking / D'orine the cow / Your horoscope / No such thing as love / Two old dogs without a name / Bus driver's prayer.

IAN DURY & THE BLOCKHEADS

—— with **CHAZ JANKEL, MICKEY GALLAGHER, DAVEY PAYNE, JOHN TURNBULL, NORMAN WATT-ROY, STEVEN MONTI** (drums) / The **BREEZEBLOCKS** – backing vocals

	Ronnie Harris	unknown
Jun 98. (cd) *(DUR 1)* **Mr LOVE PANTS**	57	

– Jack shit George / The passing show / You're my baby / Honeysuckle highway / Itinerant / Geraldine / Cacka boom / Bed 'o' roses No.9 / Heavy living / Mash it up Harry.

– compilations etc. –

Nov 81. (lp/c) *Stiff; (SEEZ/ZSEEZ 41)* **JUKE BOX DURY**		-

(re-iss. Sep82 as 'GREATEST HITS' on 'Fame' lp/c; FA/TC-FA 3031)

May 85. (7") *Stiff; (BUY 214)* **HIT ME WITH YOUR RHYTHM STICK (Paul Hardcastle mix). / SEX AND DRUGS AND ROCK AND ROLL**	55	-

(12"+=) *(BUYIT 214)* – Reasons to be cheerful / Wake up and make love to me (Paul Hardcastle mix).

Apr 87. (lp/c/cd) *Demon; (FIEND/+CASS/CD 69)* **SEX AND DRUGS AND ROCK AND ROLL**		-

– Hit me with your rhythm stick / I want to be straight / There ain't half been some clever bastards / What a waste! / Common as muck / Reasons to be cheerful (pt.3) / Sex and drugs and rock and roll / Sueperman's big sister / Razzle in my pocket / You're more than fair / Inbetweenies / You'll see glimpses.

Jul 91. (7"/c-s) *Flying; (FLYR 1/+C)* **HIT ME WITH YOUR RHYTHM STICK '91 (The Flying Remix Version) / HIT ME WITH YOUR RHYTHM STICK**	73	-

(12"+=/cd-s+=) *(FLYR 1 T/CD)* – ('A'mix).

Aug 91. (3xcd-box) *Demon; (IAN 1)* **IAN DURY & THE BLOCKHEADS**		-

– (NEW BOOTS AND PANTIES / DO IT YOURSELF / SEX AND DRUGS AND ROCK AND ROLL)

Aug 96. (cd) *Disky; (DC 88975-2)* **THE BEST OF IAN DURY**		-
Sep 99. (cd) *E.M.I.; (522888-2)* **REASONS TO BE CHEERFUL – THE VERY BEST OF IAN DURY & THE BLOCKHEADS**	40	-

—— The BLOCKHEADS also released their own singles and lp early 80's

---

DUST BROTHERS
(see under ⇒ CHEMICAL BROTHERS)

DUST JUNKYS   (dig out; Great Alt & Indie . . .)

Bob DYLAN

Born: ROBERT ALLAN ZIMMERMAN, 24 May'41, Duluth, Minnesota, USA. In 1960 he left his local university, changing his name to BOB DYLAN. He also began a trek to New York where he played his first gig supporting JOHN LEE HOOKER on 11 April '61 at Gerde's Folk City. Soon after, he enjoyed harmonica session work for folk songstress Caroline Hester. Her employers 'Columbia' records, through John Hammond Snr., signed him in October '61. His eponymous debut album in 1962 gained sparse attention, although his live work created critical appraisal. In 1963 he unleashed 'THE FREEWHEELIN' BOB DYLAN', and after PETER, PAUL & MARY lifted a million-seller from it, 'BLOWIN' IN THE WIND', the record gained enough respect to give him a US Top 30 album. The record also saw a pronounced development in DYLAN's songwriting dexterity on tracks like the cutting 'MASTERS OF WAR'. While his untrained, nasal vocals could be something of an acquired taste, they communicated the lyrics in a way that lent them greater depth and resonance. But DYLAN really hit his stride with 'THE TIMES THEY ARE A-CHANGIN' the following year, an album that represented his most pointed protest writing. On subsequent albums, DYLAN shied away from direct missives like 'WITH GOD ON OUR SIDE' and 'ONLY A PAWN IN THEIR GAME'. 'ANOTHER SIDE OF BOB DYLAN' (1964) was contrastingly personal in tone, 'I DON'T BELIEVE IN YOU' and 'IT AIN'T ME BABE' venting DYLAN's spleen on matters of the heart rather than the soapbox. The lyrics also began to assume an air of enigmatic suggestiveness, 'MY BACK PAGES' and 'CHIMES OF FREEDOM' boasting striking, lucid imagery which The BYRDS would later complement with their incandescent, chiming guitars and ringing harmonies. Influenced by the British R&B boom (especially The BEATLES), DYLAN stunned folk purists with the half electric/half acoustic 'BRINGING IT ALL BACK HOME' (1965). The newly plugged-in DYLAN was a revelation and with the likes of the stream-of-consciousness 'SUBTERRANEAN HOMESICK BLUES', the album influenced in turn the bands DYLAN had taken his cue from. The acoustic tracks on the second side such as 'MR. TAMBOURINE MAN' and 'IT'S ALL OVER NOW BABY BLUE' rank among DYLAN's finest, the former giving The BYRDS their breakthrough hit. While the folk faithful hissed DYLAN at that summer's Newport Festival, he wowed the rock world with the masterful 'LIKE A ROLLING STONE' single and followed it up with the seminal 'HIGHWAY 61 REVISITED' (1965). A free flowing hybrid of blues, folk and R&B that used such esteemed musicians as AL KOOPER and PAUL BUTTERFIELD, rock music had never been graced with such complex, expansive lyrics. Backed by members of The HAWKS (who'd supported DYLAN on his recent tour and later become The BAND) and a posse of crack Nashville sessioneers, DYLAN recorded another rock milestone with 'BLONDE ON BLONDE' (1966). 'VISIONS OF JOHANNA' was DYLAN at his most lysergic, casting surreal lyrical spells with hypnotic ease. After a motorcycle accident that summer he sustained severe neck injuries and went into semi-retirement, looking after his family and holing up in Woodstock with The BAND. These sessions eventually saw the light of day in 1975 as 'THE BASEMENT TAPES', a classic double album of experimental roots rock. Upon his return to the music scene, DYLAN's vocals were slightly altered and his music had taken a distinct turn towards country-rock on 'JOHN WESLEY HARDING' (1968). The following year's 'NASHVILLE SKYLINE' was stone country, even featuring a bittersweet duet with JOHNNY CASH. After a lean spell, DYLAN returned with two harder-edged rock classics, 'BLOOD ON THE TRACKS' (1975) and 'DESIRE' (1975), providing him with a much needed boost in credibility both with the critics and the buying public. From 1979 on through the 80's his work mellowed into more spiritual themes as a result of his new found Christianity. Only the DANIEL LANOIS-produced 'OH MERCY' (1989) came close to capturing the magic of old, the outtakes/rarities compilations 'BIOGRAPH' (1985) and 'THE BOOTLEG SERIES' (1991) of more interest to DYLAN fans than much of his new material. • **Songwriters:** 99% DYLAN compositions except; HOUSE OF THE RISING SUN + IN MY TIME OF DYIN' (trad.) / TAKE A MESSAGE TO MARY (Everly Brothers) / THE BOXER (Simon & Garfunkel) / EARLY MORNIN' RAIN (Gordon Lightfoot) / A FOOL SUCH AS I + CAN'T HELP FALLING IN LOVE (hits; Elvis Presley) / BIG YELLOW TAXI (Joni Mitchell) / MR.BOJANGLES (Jerry Jeff Walker) / LET'S STICK TOGETHER (Wilbert Harrison) / SPANISH IS THE LOVING TONGUE + SHENANDOAH (trad.) / ANGELS FLYING TOO CLOSE TO THE GROUND (Willie Nelson) / etc. **Writing credits/hits:** BLOWIN' IN THE WIND + DON'T THINK TWICE, IT'S ALRIGHT (Peter, Paul & Mary; 1963) / ALL I REALLY WANT TO DO (Cher; 1965) / IT AIN'T ME BABE (Turtles; 1965) / MR. TAMBOURINE MAN + ALL I REALLY WANT TO DO + MY BACK PAGES (Byrds; 1965-1967) / IT'S ALL OVER NOW, BABY BLUE + FAREWELL ANGELINA (Joan Baez; 1965) / IF YOU GOTTA GO, GO NOW + JUST LIKE A WOMAN + MIGHTY QUINN (Manfred Mann; 1965/66/68) / TOO MUCH OF NOTHING (Peter, Paul & Mary; 1967) / THIS WHEEL'S ON FIRE (Julie Driscoll, Brian Auger & The Trinity; 1968) / ALL ALONG THE WATCHTOWER (Jimi Hendrix; 1968) / IF NOT FOR YOU (Olivia Newton-John; 1971) / A HARD RAIN'S A-GONNA FALL (Bryan

Ferry; 1973) / KNOCKIN' ON HEAVEN'S DOOR (Eric Clapton; 1975 / Guns n' Roses; 1992) / I'LL BE YOUR BABY TONIGHT (UB40 & Robert Palmer; 1990) / & some minor hits. **Filmography:** DON'T LOOK BACK (1965 documentary) / EAT THE DOCUMENTARY (1971 docu-film) / PAT GARRETT & BILLY THE KID (1973) / RENALDO AND CLARA (1978) / HEARTS OF FIRE (1987). • **Trivia:** On the 22 Nov'65, BOB married Sara Lowndes, but she divorced him in 1977. (Band members in discography are selective)

Album rating: BOB DYLAN (*7) / THE FREEWHEELIN' BOB DYLAN (*9) / THE TIMES THEY ARE A-CHANGIN' (*7) / ANOTHER SIDE OF BOB DYLAN (*8) / BRINGING IT ALL BACK HOME (*9) / HIGHWAY 61 REVISITED (*10) / BLONDE ON BLONDE (*10) / GREATEST HITS compilation (*10) / JOHN WESLEY HARDING (*6) / NASHVILLE SKYLINE (*6) / SELF PORTRAIT (*4) / NEW MORNING (*6) / MORE GREATEST HITS compilation (*7) / PAT GARRETT AND BILLY THE KID (*5) / PLANET WAVES (*6) / BEFORE THE FLOOD (*7) / BLOOD ON THE TRACKS (*10) / DESIRE (*10) / THE BASEMENT TAPES early recordings (*9) / HARD RAIN (*6) / SLOW TRAIN COMING (*5) / STREET LEGAL (*5) / AT BUDOKAN (*5) / SLOW TRAIN COMING (*5) / SAVED (*4) / SHOT OF LOVE (*4) / INFIDELS (*6) / REAL LIVE (*5) / EMPIRE BURLESQUE (*6) / BIOGRAPH boxed-set (*9) / KNOCKED OUT LOADED (*4) / DOWN IN THE GROOVE (*5) / DYLAN AND THE DEAD with Grateful Dead (*3) / OH MERCY (*6) / UNDER THE RED SKY (*5) / GOOD AS I BEEN TO YOU (*5) / WORLD GONE WRONG (*5) / 30th ANNIVERSARY CONCERT (*5) / GREATEST HITS, VOL.3 compilation (*6) / MTV UNPLUGGED (*5) / TIME OUT OF MIND (*7)

BOB DYLAN – vocals, guitar, harmonica

		C.B.S.	Columbia
Mar 62.	(7") *<42656>* **MIXED UP CONFUSION. / CORRINA CORRINA**	–	
Jun 62.	(lp; stereo/mono) *(S+/BPG 62022) <8579>* **BOB DYLAN**		Mar62

– She's no good / Talkin' New York / In my time of dyin' / Man of constant sorrow / Fixin' to die blues / Pretty Peggy-o / Highway 51 blues / Gospel plow / Baby, let me follow you down / House of the risin' sun / Freight train blues / Song to Woody / See that grave is kept clean. *(re-dist.May65, hit No.13) (re-iss. Mar81 lp/c; CBS/40 32001) (cd-iss. Nov89; CD 32001)*

—— added musicians **HOWARD COLLINS** – guitar / **GEORGE BARNES** – bass / **HERB LOVELL** – drums / **LEONARD GASKIN** – bass / etc.

| Nov 63. | (lp; stereo/mono) *(S+/BPG 62193) <8786>* **THE FREEWHEELIN' BOB DYLAN** | 16 | 22 May63 |

– Blowin' in the wind / Girl from the North Country / Masters of war / Down the highway / Bob Dylan's blues / A hard rains a-gonna fall / Don't think twice, it's all right / Bob Dylan's dream / Oxford Town / Talking World War III blues / Corrina, Corrina / Honey, just allow me one more chance / I shall be free. *(re-dist.Apr65, hit No.1) (re-iss. Mar81 lp/c; CBS/40 62193) (cd-iss. Nov89; 32390)*

| Jan 64. | (7") *<42856>* **BLOWIN' IN THE WIND. / DON'T THINK TWICE IT'S ALRIGHT** | – | |
| Jun 64. | (lp; stereo/mono) *(S+/BPG 62251) <8905>* **THE TIMES THEY ARE A-CHANGIN'** | 20 | 20 Mar64 |

– The times they are a-changin' / Ballad of Hollis Brown / With God on our side / One too many mornings / North country blues / Only a pawn in their game / Boots of Spanish leather / When the ship comes in / The lonesome death of Hattie Carroll / Restless farewell. *(re-dist.Apr65, hit No.4) (re-iss. Mar81 lp/c; CBS/40 32021) (cd-iss. Nov89; CD 32021)*

| Nov 64. | (lp; stereo/mono) *(S+/BPG 62429) <8993>* **ANOTHER SIDE OF BOB DYLAN** | 8 | 43 Sep64 |

– All I really want to do / Black crow blues / Spanish Harlem incident / Chimes of freedom / I shall be free No.10 / To Ramona / Motorpsycho nitemare / I don't believe you / Ballad in plain D / It ain't me babe. *(re-iss. Mar81 lp/c; CBS/40 32034) (cd-iss. Nov89; CD 32034)*

| Mar 65. | (7") *(201751)* **THE TIMES THEY ARE A-CHANGIN'. / HONEY, JUST ALLOW ME ONE MORE CHANCE** | 9 | – |

(re-iss. May82; 1751)

—— with **BOBBY GREGG** – drums / **JOHN SEBASTIAN** – bass / **BRUCE LANGHORNE** – guitar

| Apr 65. | (7") *(201753) <43242>* **SUBTERRANEAN HOMESICK BLUES. / SHE BELONGS TO ME** | 9 | 39 Mar65 |
| May 65. | (lp; stereo/mono) *(S+/BPG 62515) <9128>* **BRINGING IT ALL BACK HOME** | 1 | 6 Apr65 |

– Subterranean homesick blues / She belongs to me / Maggie's farm / Love minus zero – No limit / Outlaw blues / On the road again / Bob Dylan's 115th dream / Mr. Tambourine man / Gates of Eden / It's alright, ma (I'm only bleeding) / It's all over now, baby blue. *(re-iss. Jul83 lp/c; CBS/40 32344) (cd-iss. Jul87; CD 62515) (cd re-iss. Jul89 as 'SUBTERRANEAN HOMESICK BLUES'; CD 32344)*

| Jun 65. | (7") *(201781)* **MAGGIE'S FARM. / ON THE ROAD AGAIN** | 22 | – |

—— now with **AL KOOPER** – organ / **PAUL BUTTERFIELD** – guitar / **PAUL GRIFFIN** – keyboards / **CHARLIE McCOY** – guitar / **RUSS SAVAKUS** – bass

| Aug 65. | (7") *(201811) <43346>* **LIKE A ROLLING STONE. / GATES OF EDEN** | 4 | 2 Jul65 |

(re-iss. May82; 1811)

| Sep 65. | (lp; stereo/mono) *(S+/BPG 62572) <9189>* **HIGHWAY 61 REVISITED** | 4 | 3 |

– Like a rolling stone / Tombstone blues / It takes a lot to laugh, it takes a train to cry / From a Buick 6 / Ballad of a thin man / Queen Jane approximately / Highway 61 revisited / Just like Tom Thumb's blues / Desolation row. *(re-iss. Dec85 lp/c; CBS/40 62572) (cd-iss. Nov89; CD 62572)*

Oct 65.	(7") *(201824) <43389>* **POSITIVELY 4th STREET. / FROM A BUICK 6**	8	7 Sep65
Jan 66.	(7") *(201900) <43477>* **CAN YOU PLEASE CRAWL OUT YOUR WINDOW? / HIGHWAY 61 REVISITED**	17	58 Dec65
Apr 66.	(7") *(202053) <43541>* **ONE OF US MUST KNOW (SOONER OR LATER). / QUEEN JANE APPROXIMATELY**	33	Feb66

—— Now augmented by members of The **BAND:-** ROBBIE ROBERTSON – guitar / **RICHARD MANUEL** – keyboards / **LEVON HELM** – drums / **RICK DANKO** – bass / **GARTH HUDSON** – keyboards plus also **KENNY BUTTREY** – drums

| May 66. | (7") *(202307) <43592>* **RAINY DAY WOMEN NOS.12 & 35. / PLEDGING MY TIME** | 7 | 2 Apr66 |

| Jul 66. | (7") *(202258) <43683>* **I WANT YOU. / JUST LIKE TOM THUMB'S BLUES (live)** | 16 | 20 Jun66 |
| Aug 66. | (d-lp; stereo/mono) *(S+/66012) <841>* **BLONDE ON BLONDE** | 3 | 9 Jul66 |

– Rainy day women Nos.12 & 35 / Pledging my love / Visions of Johanna / One of us must know (sooner or later) / Most likely you go your way (and I'll go mine) / Temporary like Achilles / Absolutely sweet Marie / 4th time around / Obviously 5 believers / I want you / Stuck inside of Mobile with the Memphis blues again / Leopard-skin pill-box hat / Just like a woman / Sad eyed lady of the lowlands. *(re-iss. May82 d-lp/d-c; CBS 22130) (d-cd re-iss. Jul87; CD 66012) (d-cd re-iss. Jun89; CD 22130) (d-cd re-iss. Feb95; CK 64411)*

| Sep 66. | (7") *<43792>* **JUST LIKE A WOMAN. / OBVIOUSLY 5 BELIEVERS** | – | 33 |
| Jan 67. | (lp; stereo/mono) *(S+/BPG 62847) <9463>* **BOB DYLAN'S GREATEST HITS** (compilation) *<US diff.tracks>* | 6 | 10 Apr67 |

– Blowin' in the wind / It ain't me babe / The times they are a-changin' / Mr. Tambourine man / She belongs to me / It's all over now, baby blue / Subterranean homesick blues / One of us must know (sooner or later) / Like a rolling stone / Just like a woman / Rainy day women Nos. 12 & 35. *(re-iss. Mar88; 460907) (cd-iss. Nov89; 450882-2) (re-iss. Feb91 & Apr97 on 'Columbia'; 460907-2) (re-iss. cd Oct94 as 'BEST OF...';)*

| May 67. | (7") *(202700) <44069>* **LEOPARD-SKIN PILL-BOX HAT. / MOST LIKELY YOU GO YOUR WAY (AND I'LL GO MINE)** | | 81 |

—— now with **BUTTREY, McCOY** and **PETE DRAKE** – sitar, guitar

| Feb 68. | (lp; stereo/mono) *(S+/BPG 63252) <9604>* **JOHN WESLEY HARDING** | 1 | 2 Jan68 |

– John Wesley Harding / As I went out one morning / I dreamed I saw St. Augustine / All along the watchtower / The ballad of Frankie Lee and Judas Priest / Drifter's escape / Dear landlord / I am a lonesome hobo / I pity the poor immigrant / The wicked messenger / Down along the cove / I'll be your baby tonight. *(re-iss. Nov89 lp/c/cd; 463359-1/-4/-2)*

—— next featured **CHARLIE DANIELS** – bass, guitar / **etc.**

| May 69. | (7") *(4219) <44826>* **I THREW IT ALL AWAY. / DRIFTER'S ESCAPE** | 30 | 85 |
| May 69. | (lp) *(63601) <9825>* **NASHVILLE SKYLINE** | 1 | 3 Apr69 |

– Girl from the North country (with JOHNNY CASH) / Nashville skyline rag / To be alone with you / I threw it all away / Peggy Day / Lady lady lay / One more night / Tell me that it isn't true / Country pie / Tonight I'll be staying here with you. *(re-iss. May87 lp/c; CBS/40 32675) (cd-iss. Jan86; CD 63601)*

Sep 69.	(7") *(4434) <44926>* **LAY LADY LAY. / PEGGY DAY**	5	7 Jul69
Dec 69.	(7") *(4611) <45004>* **TONIGHT I'LL BE STAYING HERE WITH YOU. / COUNTRY PIE**		50 Oct69
Jul 70.	(d-lp) *(66250) <30050>* **SELF PORTRAIT**	1	4 Jun70

– All the tired horses / Alberta #1 / I forgot more than you'll ever know / Days of 49 / Early mornin' rain / In search of little Sadie / Let it be me / Little Sadie / Woogie boogie / Belle isle / Living the blues / Like a rolling stone (version) / Copper kettle (the pale moonlight) / Gotta travel on / Blue Moon / The boxer / The mighty Quinn (Quinn, the eskimo) / Take me as I am / Take a message to Mary / It hurts me too / Minstrel boy / She belongs to me / Wigwam / Alberta #2. *(re-iss. Sep87 d-lp/c; 460112-1/-4) (re-iss. Feb91 on 'Columbia' cd/c; 460112-2/-4)*

| Jul 70. | (7") *(5122) <45199>* **WIGWAM. / COPPER KETTLE (THE PALE MOONLIGHT)** | | 41 |
| Nov 70. | (lp) *(69001) <30290>* **NEW MORNING** | 1 | 7 |

– If not for you / Day of the locusts / Time passes slowly / Went to see the gypsy / Winterlude / If dogs ran free / New morning / Sign on the window / One more weekend / The man in me / Three angels / Father of the night. *(re-iss. Sep83 lp/c; CBS/40 32267) (re-iss. Feb91 & Feb94 on 'Columbia' cd/c; CD 32267)*

Mar 71.	(7") *(7092)* **IF NOT FOR YOU. / NEW MORNING**	–	–
Jun 71.	(7") *(7329) <45409>* **WATCHING THE RIVER FLOW. / SPANISH IS THE LOVING TONGUE**	24	41
Dec 71.	(7") *(7688) <45516>* **GEORGE JACKSON (acoustic). / GEORGE JACKSON (big band version)**		33 Nov71
Dec 71.	(d-lp/c) *(CBS/40 67239) <31120>* **MORE BOB DYLAN GREATEST HITS** <US-title 'BOB DYLAN'S GREATEST HITS, VOL.II'> (compilation)	12	14

– Watching the river flow / Don't think twice, it's alright / Lay lady lay / Stuck inside Mobile with the Memphis blues again / I'll be your baby tonight / All I really want to do / My back pages / Maggie's farm / Tonight I'll be staying here with you / Positively 4th Street / All along the watchtower / The mighty Quinn (Quinn, the eskimo) / Just like Tom Thumb's blues / A hard rain's a-gonna fall / If not for you / New morning / Tomorrow is a long time / When I paint my masterpiece / I shall be released / You ain't goin' nowhere / Down in the flood. *(cd-iss. Oct87; CD 67239) (cd re-iss. Aug92 on 'Columbia'; 467851-2) (re-iss. Mar93 on 'Columbia' cd/c; 471243-2/-4)*

| Sep 73. | (lp/c) *(CBS/40 69042) <32460>* **PAT GARRETT AND BILLY THE KID (Soundtrack)** | 29 | 16 Jul73 |

– Main title theme / Cantina theme (working for the law) / Billy 1 / Bunkhouse theme / River theme / Turkey chase / Knockin' on heaven's door / Final theme / Billy 4 / Billy 7. *(re-iss. Mar82 lp/c; CBS/40 32098) (re-iss. Feb91 on 'Columbia' cd/c;)*

| Sep 73. | (7") *(1762) <45913>* **KNOCKIN' ON HEAVEN'S DOOR. / TURKEY CHASE** | 14 | 12 Aug73 |
| Dec 73. | (lp/c) *(CBS/40 69049) <32747>* **DYLAN** (rec.1970) | | 17 |

– Lily of the west / Can't help falling in love / Sarah Jane / The ballad of Ira Hayes / Mr. Bojangles / Mary Ann / Big yellow taxi / A fool such as I / Spanish is the loving tongue. *(re-iss. Mar83) (cd+c-iss.Feb91 on 'Columbia')*

| Jan 74. | (7") *(2006) <45982>* **A FOOL SUCH AS I. / LILY OF THE WEST** | | 55 Dec73 |

		Island	Asylum
Feb 74.	(lp/c) *(ILPS/ICT 9261) <1003>* **PLANET WAVES**	7	1

– On a night like this / Going going gone / Tough mama / Hazel / Something there is about you / Forever young / Dirge / You angel you / Never say goodbye / Wedding song. *(re-iss. Sep82 lp/c; CBS/40 32154) (cd-iss. Nov89 on 'C.B.S.'; CD 21154)*

Feb 74.	(7") *(11033)* **ON A NIGHT LIKE THIS. / YOU ANGEL YOU**	–	44
Feb 74.	(7") *(WIP 6168)* **ON A NIGHT LIKE THIS. / FOREVER YOUNG**	–	
Apr 74.	(7") **SOMETHING THERE IS ABOUT YOU. / GOING GOING GONE**	–	

Jul 74. (d-lp/d-c; as BOB DYLAN & THE BAND) (IBD 1) <201>
BEFORE THE FLOOD (tracks by The BAND) [Asylum **8**] [Asylum **3**]
– Most likely you go your way (and I'll go mine) / Lay lady lay / Rainy day women Nos.12 & 35 / Knockin' on Heaven's door / It ain't me babe / The ballad of a thin man / Up on Cripple Creek * / I shall be released / Endless highway * / The night they drove old Dixie down * / Stage fright * / Don't think twice, it's all right / Just like a woman / It's alright ma (I'm only bleeding) / The shape I'm in * / When you awake * / The weight * / All along the watchtower / Highway 61 revisited / Like a rolling stone / Blowin' in the wind. (re-iss.Sep80 on 'C.B.S.' d-lp/d-c; CBS/40 22137) (cd-iss. Jul87 + Nov89 + Jun96; CD 22137)

—— The BAND had been his backing group from the mid '60's.

Aug 74. (7") <11043> **MOST LIKELY YOU GO YOUR WAY (AND I'LL GO MINE) (live). / STAGE FRIGHT** (The BAND live) [–] [**66**]

Nov 74. (7") **ALL ALONG THE WATCHTOWER (live). / IT AIN'T ME BABE** (live) [–] []

[C.B.S.] [Columbia]

Feb 75. (lp/c) (CBS/40 69097) <32235> **BLOOD ON THE TRACKS** [**4**] [**1**]
– Tangled up in blue / Simple twist of fate / You're a big girl now / Idiot wind / You're gonna make me lonesome when you go / Meet me in the morning / Lily, Rosemary and the Jack of Hearts / If you see her, say hello / Shelter from the storm / Buckets of rain. (cd-iss.Dec85; CD 69097) (re-iss.Sep93 on 'Columbia' cd/c; 467842-2/-4)

Mar 75. (7") (3160) <10106> **TANGLED UP IN BLUE. / IF YOU SEE HER, SAY HELLO** [] [**31**]

Jul 75. (d-lp/c) (CBS/40 88147) <33682> **THE BASEMENT TAPES** (rec.1967) [**8**] [**7**]
– Odds and ends / Orange juice blues (blues for breakfast) / Million dollar bash / Yazoo street scandal / Goin' to Acapulco / Katie's been gone / Lo and behold / Bessie Smith / Clothes line saga / Apple suckling tree / Please Mrs. Henry / Tears of rage / Too much of nothing / Yea! heavy and a bottle of wine / Ain't no more Cane / Crash on the levee (down in the flood) / Ruben Remus / Tiny Montgomery / You ain't goin' nowhere / Don't ya tell Henry / Nothing was delivered / Open the doors, Homer / Long distance operator. (cd-iss.Nov89; 466137-2)

Oct 75. (7") (3665) **MILLION DOLLAR BASH. / TEARS OF RAGE** [] []

—— next featured **EMMYLOU HARRIS** – vocals / **SCARLET RIVIERA** – violin / **RONNE BLAKELY** – vocals / **HOWIE WYTHE** – drums / **ROB STONER** – bass / **STEVEN SOLES** – guitar

Jan 76. (7") (3879) <10245> **HURRICANE (part 1). / HURRICANE (full version)** [**43**] [**33** Nov75]

Jan 76. (lp/c) (CBS/40 86003) <33893> **DESIRE** [**3**] [**1**]
– Hurricane / Isis / Mozambique / One more cup of coffee / Oh, sister / Joey / Romance in Durango / Black diamond bay / Sara. (re-iss.Apr85 lp/c; CBS/40 32570) (cd-iss. Jul87; 86003) (cd re-iss. Jun89; CD 32470)

Apr 76. (7") (4113) <10298> **MOZAMBIQUE. / OH, SISTER** [] [**54** Mar76]

—— His HARD RAIN tour added **MICK RONSON** – guitar / **DAVID MANSFIELD** – keyboards

Sep 76. (lp/c) (CBS/40 86016) <34349> **HARD RAIN (live)** [**3**] [**17**]
– Maggie's farm / One too many mornings / Stuck inside of Mobile with the Memphis blues again / Lay lady lay / Shelter from the storm / You're a big girl now / I threw it all away / Idiot wind. (re-iss.Apr83 lp/c; CBS/40 32308) (cd-iss. Nov89; CD 32308)

Feb 77. (7") (4859) <10454> **RITA MAY. / STUCK INSIDE OF MOBILE WITH THE MEMPHIS BLUES AGAIN** (live) [] []

May 78. (7"/12") (7/12 6499) <10805> **BABY STOP CRYING. / NEW PONY** [**13**] []

Jun 78. (lp/c) (CBS/40 86067) <35453> **STREET-LEGAL** [**2**] [**11**]
– Changing of the guards / New pony / No time to think / Baby stop crying / Is your love in vain / Senor (tales of Yankee power) / True love tends to forget / We better talk this over / Where are you tonight (journey through dark heat). (cd-iss.Mar86; CD 86087) (re-iss.May95 cd/c; 403289)

Oct 78. (7"/12") (7/12 6718) **IS YOUR LOVE IN VAIN. / WE BETTER TALK THIS OVER** [**56**] []

Dec 78. (7") (6935) <10851> **CHANGING OF THE GUARDS. / SENOR (TALES OF YANKEE POWER)** [] []

1978. (7"ep) **4 SONGS FROM "RENALDO AND CLARA"** [–] []
– People get ready / Never let me go / Isis / It ain't me babe.

May 79. (d-lp/d-c) (CBS/40 96004) <36067> **BOB DYLAN AT BUDOKAN** (live) [**4**] [**13**]
– Mr. Tambourine man / Shelter from the storm / Love minus zero – No limit / Ballad of a thin man / Don't think twice, it's all right / Maggie's farm / One more cup of coffee / Like a rolling stone / I shall be released / Oh sister / Is your love in vain? / Going going gone / Blowin' in the wind / Just like a woman / Simple twist of fate / All along the watchtower / I want you / I all really want to do / Knockin' on Heaven's door / It's alright ma (I'm only bleeding) / Forever young / The times they are a-changin'. (cd-iss.Jul87; CD 96004)

Jun 79. (7"m) (7473) **FOREVER YOUNG (live). / ALL ALONG THE WATCHTOWER (live). / I WANT YOU** (live) [] []

Aug 79. (7") (7828) **PRECIOUS ANGEL. / TROUBLE IN MIND** [] []

Sep 79. (lp/c) (CBS/40 86095) <36120> **SLOW TRAIN COMING** [**2**] [**3**]
– Gotta serve somebody / Precious angel / I believe in you / Slow train / Gonna change my way of thinking / Do right to me baby (do unto others) / When you gonna wake up / Man gave names to all the animals / When he returns. (re-iss.Nov85 lp/c; CBS/40 32524) (cd-iss.Mar86; CD 86095) (cd re-iss. Apr89; CD 32524)

Sep 79. (7") (11072) **GOTTA SERVE SOMEBODY. / TROUBLE IN MIND** [–] [**24**]

Oct 79. (7") (7970) **MAN GAVE NAMES TO ALL THE ANIMALS. / WHEN HE RETURNS** [] [–]

Jan 80. (7") (11168) **MAN GAVE NAMES TO THE ANIMALS. / WHEN YOU GONNA WAKE UP** [] []

Jan 80. (7") (8134) **GOTTA SERVE SOMEBODY. / GONNA CHANGE MY WAY OF THINKING** [] []

Mar 80. (7") (11235) **SLOW TRAIN. / DO RIGHT TO ME BABY (DO UNTO OTHERS)** [] [–]

May 80. (7") (11318) **SOLID ROCK. / COVENANT WOMAN** [] [–]

Jun 80. (lp/c) (CBS/40 83113) <36553> **SAVED** [**3**] [**24**]
– A satisfied mind / Saved / Covenant woman / What can I do for you? / Solid rock / Pressing on / In the garden / Saving Grace / Are you ready. (reiss.Sep86 lp/c; CBS/40 32742) (re-iss. Feb91 & Mar93 on 'Columbia' cd/c; 403274-2/-4)

Jun 80. (7") (8743) <11370> **SAVED. / ARE YOU READY** [] []

Jun 81. (7") <02510> **HEART OF MINE. / THE GROOM'S STILL WAITING AT THE ALTAR** [–] [–]

Jul 81. (7") (A 1406) **HEART OF MINE. / LET IT BE ME** [–] []

Aug 81. (lp/c) (CBS/40 85178) <37496> **SHOT OF LOVE** [**6**] [**33**]
– Shot of love / Heart of mine / Property of Jesus / Lenny Bruce / Watered down love / Dead man, dead man / In the summertime / Trouble / Every grain of sand. (re-iss. Feb91 on 'Columbia' cd+=/c+=; 467839-2/-4) – The groom's still waiting at the altar. (re-iss. cd Jun94 on 'Sony Europe'; 983338-2)

Sep 81. (7") (A 1460) **LENNY BRUCE. / DEAD MAN, DEAD MAN** [] []

Oct 83. (7") (A 3916) **UNION SUNDOWN. / I AND I** [] []

Nov 83. (lp/c) (CBS/40 25539) <38819> **INFIDELS** [**9**] [**20**]
– Jokerman / Sweetheart like you / Neighbourhood bully / License to kill / Man of peace / Union sundown / I and I / Don't fall apart on me tonight. (cd-iss.Jul87; Cd 25539) (re-iss. Dec89 lp/c/cd; 460727-1/-4/-2)

Dec 83. (7") <04301> **SWEETHEART LIKE YOU. / UNION SUNDOWN** [–] [**55**]

May 84. (7") <04425> **JOKERMAN. / ISIS** [–] []

Jun 84. (7") (A 4055) **JOKERMAN. / LICENSE TO KILL** [] []

Dec 84. (lp/c/cd) (CBS/40/CD 26334) <39944> **REAL LIVE (live)** [**54**] []
– Highway 61 revisited / Maggie's farm / I and I / License to kill / It ain't me babe / Tangled up in blue / Masters of war / Ballad of a thin man / Girl from the North country / Tombstone blues. (re-iss.Feb91 on 'Columbia' cd/c; 467841-2/-4)

Jan 85. (7"/7"g-f) (A/GA 5020) **HIGHWAY 61 REVISITED (live). / IT AIN'T ME BABE** (live) [] []

Jun 85. (7") (A 6303) <04933> **TIGHT CONNECTION TO MY HEART. / WE'D BETTER TALK THIS OVER** [] []

Jun 85. (lp/c/cd) (CBS/40/CD 86313) <40110> **EMPIRE BURLESQUE** [**11**] [**33**]
– Tight connection to my heart (has anybody seen my love) / Seeing the real you at last / I'll remember you / Clean cut kid / Never gonna be the same again / Trust yourself / Emotionally yours / When the night comes falling from the sky / Something's burning, baby / Dark eyes. (re-iss. cd.1988; Cd 86313) (re-iss. Feb91 on 'Columbia' cd/c; 467840-2/-4)

Aug 85. (7"/ext.12") (A/TA 6469) **WHEN THE NIGHT COMES FALLING FROM THE SKY. / DARK EYES** [] [–]

—— In Apr'86, he was credited next on the TOM PETTY ⇒ single 'BAND OF THE HAND'.

Oct 85. (7") <05697> **WHEN THE NIGHT COMES FALLING FROM THE SKY. / EMOTIONALLY YOURS** [–] [–]

Jul 86. (lp/c/cd) (CBS/40/CD 86326) <40439> **KNOCKED OUT LOADED** [**35**] [**53**]
– You wanna ramble / They killed him / Driftin' too far from shore / Precious memories / Maybe someday / Brownsville girl / Got my mind made up / Under your spell. (re-iss.Feb91 & Mar93 on 'Columbia' cd/c; 467040-2/-4)

Oct 86. (7") (651148-7) **THE USUAL. / GOT MY MIND MADE UP** [] []
(12"+=) (651148-6) – Precious memories / Driftin' too far from shore.

Jun 88. (lp/c/cd) (460267-1/-4/-2) <40957> **DOWN IN THE GROOVE** [**32**] [**61**]
– Let's stick together / When did you leave Heaven? / Sally Sue Brown / Death is not the end / Had a dream about you, baby / Ugliest girl in the world / Silvio / Ninety miles an hour (down a dead end street) / Shenandoah / Rank strangers to me.

Jul 88. (7") **SILVIO. / DRIFTIN' TOO FAR FROM SHORE** [] [–]

Jul 88. (7") (651406-7) **SILVIO. / WHEN DID YOU LEAVE HEAVEN?** [] [–]
(12"+=) (651406-6) – Driftin' too far from shore.

—— Later in '88 & onwards, he was also part of supergroup TRAVELING WILBURYS

Feb 89. (lp/c/cd; BOB DYLAN & GRATEFUL DEAD) (463381/-1/-4/-2) <45056> **DYLAN & THE DEAD (live July '87)** [**38**] [**37**]
– Slow train / I want you / Gotta serve somebody / Queen Jane approximately / Joey / All along the watchtower / Knockin' on Heaven's door. (re-iss. May94 on 'Columbia' cd/c; 463381-2/-4)

Oct 89. (lp/c/cd) (465800-1/-4/-2) <45281> **OH MERCY** [**6**] [**30**]
– Political world / Where teardrops fall / Everything is broken / Ring them bells / Man in the long black coat / Most of the time / What good am I? / Disease of conceit / What was it you wanted / Shooting star.

Oct 89. (7") **EVERYTHING IS BROKEN. / DEAD MAN, DEAD MAN** [–] [–]

Oct 89. (7") (655358-7) **EVERYTHING IS BROKEN. / DEATH IS NOT THE END** [] [–]
(12"/12"w-print) (655358-6/-8) – ('A'side) / Dead man, dead man / I want you (live).
(cd-s) (655358-2) – ('A'side) / Where the teardrops fall / Dead man, dead man (live) / Ugliest girl in the world (live).

Feb 90. (7") (655643-7) **POLITICAL WORLD. / RING THEM BELLS** [] []
(12"+=/cd-s+=) (655643-6/-2) – Silvio / All along the watchtower (live).
(cd-s) (655643-5) – ('A'side) / Caribbean wind / You're a big girl now / It's all over now, baby blue.

Sep 90. (cd/c/lp) (467188-2/-4/-1) <46794> **UNDER THE RED SKY** [**13**] [**38**]
– Wiggle wiggle / Under the red sky / Unbelievable / Born in time / TV talkin' time / 10,000 men / 2x2 / God knows / Handy Dandy / Cat's in the well.

Sep 90. (7") (656304-7) **UNBELIEVABLE. / 10,000 MEN** [] []
(cd-s+=) (656304-2) – In the summertime / Jokerman.

Feb 91. (7"/c-s) (656707-7/-4) **SERIES OF DREAMS / SEVEN CURSES** [] []
(cd-s+=) (656707-5) – Tangled up in blue / Like a rolling stone.

—— totally solo DYLAN

[Columbia] [Columbia]

Nov 92. (cd/c/lp) (472710-2/-4/-1) <53200> **GOOD AS I BEEN TO YOU** [**18**] [**51**]
– Frankie & Albert / Jim Jones / Blackjack Davey / Canadee-i-o / Sittin' on top of the world / Little Maggie / Hard times / Step it up and go / Tomorrow night / Arthur McBride / You're gonna quit me / Diamond Joe / Froggie went a courtin'.

—— In Aug93, a host of artists released a live tribute d-cd,d-c 'ANNIVERSARY CONCERT', which hit US No.30. Below all traditional tunes.

Nov 93. (cd/c) (474857-2/-4) <57590> **WORLD GONE WRONG** [**35**] [**70**]
– World gone wrong / Ragged and dirty / Love Henry / Blood in my eyes / Delia / Broke down engine / Two soldiers / Stack A Lee / Jack A Roe / Love pilgrim.

—— with **TONY GARNIER** – bass / **JOHN JACKSON** – guitar / **BUCKY BAXTER** – pedal steel, dobro / **WINSTON WATSON** – drums / **BRENDAN O'BRIEN** – hammond organ

Apr 95. (cd/c/lp) (478374-2/-4/-1) <67000> **MTV UNPLUGGED** [**10**] [**23** May95]
– Tombstone blues / Shooting star / All along the watchtower / The times they are a-changin' / John Brown / Desolation row / Rainy day women #12 & 35 / Love minus

zero – No limit / Dignity / Knockin' on Heaven's door / Like a rolling stone / With God on our side.

May 95. (c-s) *(662076-4)* **DIGNITY / JOHN BROWN**   `33`   ☐
(cd-s+=) *(662076-5)* – It ain't me babe (live).
(cd-s) *(662076-2)* – ('A'side) / A hard rain's a-gonna fall.

—— To end '96, 'KNOCKIN' ON HEAVEN'S DOOR' hit UK No.1 for DUNBLANE; Scottish musicians and children of the town where psycho Thomas Hamilton murdered 16 children and a teacher earlier in the year. This added another verse, highlighting the need to outlaw guns in Britain.

Oct 97. (cd/c) *(486936-2/-4)* *<68556>* **TIME OUT OF MIND**   `10`   `10`
– Love sick / Dirt road blues / Standing in the doorway / Million miles / Tryin' to get to Heaven / 'Til I fell in love with you / Not dark yet / Cold irons bound / Make you feel my love / Can't wait / Highlands.

Jun 98. (cd-s) *(665997-2)* **LOVE SICK / COLD IRONS BOUND (live) / COCAINE (live) / BORN IN TIME (live)**   `64`   ☐
(cd-s) *(665997-5)* – ('A'side) / Can't wait (live) / Roving gambler (live) / Blind Willie McTell (live).

– compilations, others, etc. –

on 'CBS / Columbia' unless otherwise mentioned

Nov 65. (7"ep) *(EP 6051)* **DYLAN**   ☐   –
Apr 66. (7"ep) *(EP 6070)* **ONE TOO MANY MORNINGS**   ☐   –
– One too many mornings / Spanish Harlem incident / Oxford town / She belongs to me.
Jun 66. (7"ep) *(EP)* **DON'T THINK TWICE IT'S ALRIGHT**   ☐   –
– Don't think twice it's alright / Blowin' in the wind / Corrina, Corrina / When the ship comes.
Oct 66. (7"ep) *(EP 6078)* **MR. TAMBOURINE MAN**   ☐   –
– Mr. Tambourine man / Subterranean homesick blues / It's all over now, baby blue.
Mar 73. (7") *(1158)* **JUST LIKE A WOMAN. / I WANT YOU**   ☐   –
Feb 76. (7") *(3945)* **LAY LADY LAY. / I THREW IT ALL AWAY**   ☐   –
Oct 83. (lp/c) *Go International; (GLP/GMC 1)* **HISTORICAL ARCHIVES VOL.1**   ☐   –
Oct 83. (lp/c) *Go Internationals; (GLP/GMC 2)* **HISTORICAL ARCHIVES VOL.2**   ☐   –
Nov 85. (5xlp-box/3xc-box/3xcd-box) *(CBS/40/CD 66509)* *<38830>* **BIOGRAPH**   ☐   `33`

—— (above contains 16 unreleased tracks)

Sep 87. (cd) *Compact Collection; (76025)* **THE GASLIGHT TAPES**   ☐   –
1988. (lp) *Joker; (SM 4123)* **THE BEST OF BOB DYLAN**   ☐   –
May 88. (lp/c) *Big Time; (22/21 15531)* **DON'T THINK TWICE, IT'S ALRIGHT**   ☐   –
May 88. (lp/c) *Big Time; (22/21 15551)* **BLOWIN' IN THE WIND**   ☐   –
1988. (d-c) *(CDBD 241)* **DESIRE / BLOOD ON THE TRACKS**   ☐   –
Apr 91. (3xcd/3xc/6xlp) *(468086-2/-4/-1)* *<47382>* **THE BOOTLEG SERIES VOLUMES 1-3 (RARE & UNRELEASED) 1961-1991**   `32`   `49`
Aug 92. (d-cd) *(466831-2)* **HIGHWAY 61 REVISITED / JOHN WESLEY HARDING**   ☐   –
Oct 93. (3xcd-box) *(471621-2)* **BLONDE ON BLONDE / JOHN WESLEY HARDING / SELF PORTRAIT**   ☐   –
Nov 94. (cd/c/d-lp) *Columbia; (477805-2/-4/-1)* *<66783>* **GREATEST HITS VOLUME III**   ☐
– Tangled up in blue / Changing the guards / The groom's still waiting at the altar / Hurricane / Forever young / Jokerman / Dignity / Silvio / Ring them bells / Gotta serve somebody / Series of dream / Brownsville girl / Under the red sky / Knockin' on Heaven's door.
Jun 97. (d-cd/d-c) *Sony; (SONYTV 28 CD/MC)* **THE BEST OF BOB DYLAN**   `8`   ☐
– Blowin' in the wind / The times they are a-changin' / Don't think twice, it's alright / Mr. Tambourine man / Like a rolling stone / Just like a woman / All along the watchtower / Lay lady lay / If not for you / Knockin' on Heaven's door / Forever young / Tangled up in blue / Shelter from the storm / I shall be released / Oh sister / Gotta serve somebody / Jokerman / Everything is broken.
Oct 98. (d-cd/d-c) *Legacy-Columbia; (491485-2/-4)* *<65759>* **LIVE AT THE ROYAL ALBERT HALL** <US title 'BOB DYLAN LIVE 1966: THE 'ROYAL ALBERT HALL' CONCERT>   `19`   `31`
– She belongs to me / Fourth time around / Visions of Johanna / It's all over now, baby blue / Desolation row / Just like a woman / Mr. Tambourine man / Tell me momma / I don't believe you (she acts like we never met) / Baby let me follow you down / Just like Tom Thumb's blues / Leopard-skin pillbox hat / One too many mornings / Ballad of a thin man / Like a rolling stone.

EAGLES

Formed: Los Angeles, California, USA . . . 1971, by GLENN FREY and DON HENLEY who had previously been part of LINDA RONSTADT's backing band on her 'SILK PURSE' (1970) album. They duly recruited BERNIE LEADON and RANDY MEISNER (both seasoned hands; see discography) and gave birth to The EAGLES. The very name spelled out their musical ambitions; like The BYRDS they wanted to fly high with heavenly country harmonies although they wanted a tougher, more predatory sound. Signed to 'Asylum' records that year, they stormed the charts from the off with the FREY / JACKSON BROWNE-penned, open-road classic, 'TAKE IT EASY'. The eponymous debut album followed soon after, hitting the US Top 30. Not exactly groundbreaking, it contained more than a few duffers although 'PEACEFUL EASY FEELING' still sounds gorgeous. Considered by many to be the band's finest hour, 'DESPERADO' (1973) was a Wild West concept album. While the idea sounds too awful to contemplate on paper, they somehow managed to pull it off. Amid the twists and turns of the plot lay such goose-bump masterpieces as 'TEQUILA SUNRISE' and the elegiac title track, although no major hit singles were forthcoming. With the addition of guitarist DON FELDER and BILL SZYMCZYK on production duties, 'ON THE BORDER' (1974) introduced a more robust sound, spawning the US No.1, 'BEST OF MY LOVE'. The breakthrough came with 'ONE OF THESE NIGHTS' (1975), featuring three Top 5 hits in 'LYIN' EYES', 'TAKE IT TO THE LIMIT' and the hard-edged title track. LEADON was not a happy chappy however, his country boy sensibilities displeased at The EAGLES' increasing predilection for "rawk". Maybe it was for the best, however, as he'd no doubt have been horrified by 'HOTEL CALIFORNIA' (1976), a decidedly harder affair with nary a hint of country to be found. In its place was a set of immaculately crafted, quintessentially Californian soft rock that was the stuff of radio programmer's dreams. Up there with 'Rumours' and 'Thriller' in terms of legendary and commercial status, its slow burning title track was an epic metaphor for that crazy, frozen-nosed Californian lifestyle that mere mortals could only dream of. Even punk champion JOHN PEEL was a fan (hipper-than-thou detractors take note!), playing the classic closing track, 'THE LAST RESORT', another song dealing with the jaded, faded City Of Angels. Guitarist JOE WALSH was partly responsible for the heavier sound, having replaced LEADON, while 1977 saw another line-up change with TIMOTHY B. SCHMIT taking the place of the departing MEISNER. The band's parting shot, 'THE LONG RUN' (1979) was another massive seller although it lacked the staying power of their previous efforts. After a live album in 1980, the band drifted apart with solo careers beckoning. HENLEY's career was set back somewhat in Nov'80, however, when a 16 year-old female was found naked and drugged in his Californian home (he was fined and ordered to attend a drug counselling scheme). The following year, he recorded his debut album, 'I CAN'T STAND STILL', with DANNY KORTCHMAR and GREG LADANYI, although this lay dormant until late 1982. In the meantime, he was credited on a US Top 10 single by STEVIE NICKS 'Leather And Lace'. Upon its release, his debut hit the US Top 30, helped by an appropriately titled Top 3 single, 'DIRTY LAUNDRY'. In '84, he moved to the 'Geffen' label, and secured a cross-Atlantic Top 20 single with the atmospheric 'THE BOYS OF SUMMER' and subsequent album, 'BUILDING THE PERFECT BEAST' (1985). Four years later, HENLEY garnered further critical acclaim with 'THE END OF THE INNOCENCE' album, his last solo work to date. FREY meanwhile, still contracted to 'Asylum' records, issued the US Top 40 album, 'NO FUN ALOUD', an easy-going set that found little sympathy with the British buying public. In 1984, his next Top 40 effort, 'THE ALLNIGHTER', prompted NBC TV to feature the sax-driven 'SMUGGLER'S BLUES' and FREY himself, on their 'Miami Vice' cop series. This gave him a cross-Atlantic Top 30 hit in 1985, and was followed by another hit song from the series, 'YOU BELONG TO THE CITY'. After a quiet two years, FREY returned to business with 1988's 'SOUL SEARCHIN' album. They had always insisted it would never happen, yet in 1994 a line-up of HENLEY, FREY, WALSH,

FELDER and SCHMITT reformed for an MTV performance and tour. They even released an album, 'HELL FREEZES OVER', featuring material culled from the MTV show, together with four new cuts. Their Wembley Stadium show was eagerly anticipated although some of the new material was dodgy, 'ORDINARY AVERAGE GUY' springs to mind. The EAGLES have always been an easy and predictable target for the fashion police, yet their back catalogue contains some of the finest harmonies in rock history.
• **Songwriters:** All took turns writing and also covered; OL'55 (Tom Waits) / PLEASE COME HOME FOR CHRISTMAS (Charles Brown). HENLEY covered EVERYBODY KNOWS (Leonard Cohen). • **Trivia:** In 1979, FREY, HENLEY and WALSH appeared on RANDY NEWMAN's 'Little Criminals'. In 1990, FREY was honoured by the Rock'n'charity foundation for his work to prevent against AIDS and cancer.

Album rating: EAGLES (*5) / DESPERADO (*8) / ON THE BORDER (*6) / ONE OF THESE NIGHTS (*8) / THEIR GREATEST HITS 1971-1975 compilation (*10) / HOTEL CALIFORNIA (*10) / THE LONG RUN (*6) / THE EAGLES LIVE (*4) / EAGLES GREATEST HITS, VOL.2 compilation (*6) / BEST OF THE EAGLES compilation (*7) / HELL FREEZES OVER (*5) / Glenn Frey: NO FUN ALOUD (*5) / THE ALLNIGHTER (*6) / SOUL SEARCHIN' (*5) / Don Henley: I CAN'T STAND STILL (*6) / BUILDING THE PERFECT BEAST (*7) / THE END OF THE INNOCENCE (*6) / ACTUAL MILES: HENLEY'S GREATEST HITS compilation (*6)

GLENN FREY (b. 6 Nov'48, Detroit, Mich.) – guitar, vocals (ex-LINDA RONSTADT Band, ex-LONGBRANCH PENWHISTLE) / **BERNIE LEADON** (b.19 Jul'47, Minneapolis, Minnesota) – guitar, vocals (ex-LINDA RONSTADT Band, ex-FLYING BURRITO BROTHERS) / **RANDY MEISNER** (b. 8 Mar'47, Scottsbluff, Nebraska) – bass, vocals (ex-LINDA RONSTADT Band, ex-POCO, ex-RICK NELSON) / **DON HENLEY** (b.22 Jul'47, Gilmer, Texas) – drums, vocals (ex-LINDA RONSTADT Band, ex-SHILOH)

			Asylum	Asylum
Jun 72.	(7") (AYM 505) <11005> **TAKE IT EASY. / GET YOU IN THE MOOD**			12 May72
Sep 72.	(7") (AYM 508) <11008> **WITCHY WOMAN. / EARLY BIRD**			9
Oct 72.	(lp/c) (SYLA/SYTC 101) <5054> **EAGLES**			22 Jun 72
	– Take it easy / Witchy woman / Chug all night / Nightingale / Train leaves here this morning / Take the Devil / Early bird / Peaceful easy feeling / Tryin'. (re-iss. Jun76 lp/c; K/K4 53009) (cd-iss. Feb87; K2 53009)			
Dec 72.	(7") <11013> **PEACEFUL EASY FEELING. / TRYIN'**		–	22
Feb 73.	(7") (AYM 512) **TRYIN'. / CHUG ALL NIGHT**			–
Apr 73.	(lp/c) (SYLA/SYTC 9011) <5068> **DESPERADO**			41
	– Doolin-Dalton / Twenty-one / Out of control / Tequila sunrise / Desperado / Certain kind of fool / Outlaw man / Saturday night / Bitter creek. (re-iss. Aug75 lp/c; K/K4 53008) – hit UK No.39 (re-iss. Jun76; K/K4 53008) (cd-iss. 1989; K 253008)			
Jul 73.	(7") <11017> **TEQUILA SUNRISE. / TWENTY-ONE**			64 Jun73
Oct 73.	(7") (AYM 523) **OUTLAW MAN. / CERTAIN KIND OF FOOL**			59 Sep73
—	added **DON FELDER** (b.21 Sep'47, Gainsville, Florida) – guitar, vocals (ex-FLOW)			
Apr 74.	(lp/c) (SYLA/SYTC 9016) <7E 1004> **ON THE BORDER**		28	17
	– Already gone / You never cry like a lover / Midnight flyer / My man / On the border / James Dean / Ol' 55 / Is it true / Good day in Hell / Best of my love. (re-iss. Jun76 lp/c; K/K4 43005) (quad-lp 1977) (cd-iss. 1989; K2 43005)			
Apr 74.	(7") <11036> **ALREADY GONE. / IS IT TRUE**		–	32
May 74.	(7") (AYM 527) **JAMES DEAN. / IS IT TRUE**			–
Jul 74.	(7") (AYM 530) **ALREADY GONE. / OL' 55**			–
Sep 74.	(7") <45202> **JAMES DEAN. / GOOD DAY IN HELL**		–	77
Nov 74.	(7") <45218> **BEST OF MY LOVE. / OL' 55**		–	1
Dec 74.	(7") (AYM 538) **BEST OF MY LOVE. / MIDNIGHT FLYER**			
May 75.	(7"m) (AYM 542) **MY MAN. / TAKE IT EASY / TEQUILA SUNRISE**			–
Jun 75.	(lp/c) (SYLA/SYTC 8759) <1039> **ONE OF THESE NIGHTS**		8	1
	– One of these nights / Too many hands / Hollywood waltz / Journey of the sorceror / Lyin' eyes / Take it to the limit / Visions / After the thrill is gone / I wish you peace. (re-iss. Jun76 lp/c; K/K4 53014) (quad-lp 1977) (cd-iss. 1989; K2 53014)			
Jun 75.	(7") (AYM 543) <45257> **ONE OF THESE NIGHTS. / VISIONS**		23	1 May75
Oct 75.	(7") (AYM 548) **LYIN' EYES. / JAMES DEAN**		23	–
Dec 75.	(7") (K 13025) <45279> **LYIN' EYES. / TOO MANY HANDS**			2 Sep75
Dec 75.	(7") <45293> **TAKE IT TO THE LIMIT. / AFTER THE THRILL IS GONE**		–	4
Feb 76.	(7") (K 13029) **TAKE IT TO THE LIMIT. / TOO MANY HANDS**		12	–
Feb 76.	(lp/c) (K/K4 53017) <1052> **THEIR GREATEST HITS 1971-1975** (compilation)		2	1
	– Take it easy / Witchy woman / Lyin' eyes / Already gone / Desperado / One of these nights / Tequila sunrise / Take it to the limit / Peaceful easy feeling / Best of my love. (cd-iss. May87; 253 017-2)			
—	**JOE WALSH** (b.20 Nov'47, Wichita, Kansas) – guitar, vocals (ex-Solo artist, ex-JAMES GANG),repl. LEADON who formed own duo band			
Dec 76.	(lp/c) (K/K4 53051) <1084> **HOTEL CALIFORNIA**		2	1
	– Hotel California / New kid in town / Life in the fast lane / Wasted time / Wasted time (reprise) / Victim of love / Pretty maids all in a row / Try and love again / The last resort. (cd-iss. May87; 253 051)			
Jan 77.	(7") (K 13069) <45373> **NEW KID IN TOWN. / VICTIM OF LOVE**		20	1 Dec76
Apr 77.	(7") (K 13079) <45386> **HOTEL CALIFORNIA. / PRETTY MAIDS ALL IN A ROW**		8	1 Feb77
Jun 77.	(7") (K 13085) <45403> **LIFE IN THE FAST LANE. / THE LAST RESORT**			11 May77
—	**TIMOTHY B. SCHMIT** (b.30 Oct'47, Sacramento, Calif.) – bass, vocals (ex-POCO) repl. MEISNER who went solo.			
—	(SCHMIT now alongside FREY, HENLEY, WALSH and FELDER)			
Dec 78.	(7") (K 13415) <45555> **PLEASE COME HOME FOR CHRISTMAS. / FUNKY NEW YEAR**		30	18
—	added p/t **JOE VITALE** – keyboards			
Sep 79.	(7") (K 12394) <46545> **HEARTACHE TONIGHT. / TEENAGE JAIL**		40	1
Sep 79.	(lp/c) (K/K4 52181) <508> **THE LONG RUN**		4	1

– The long run / I can't tell you why / In the city / The disco strangler / King of Hollywood / Heartache tonight / Those shoes / Teenage jail / The Greeks don't want no freaks / The sad cafe. *(cd-iss. 1986; 252 181)*

Nov 79.	(7") *(K 12404)* <46569> **THE LONG RUN. / THE DISCO STRANGLER**	66	8
Jan 80.	(7") *(K 12418)* <46608> **I CAN'T TELL YOU WHY. / THE GREEKS DON'T WANT NO FREAKS**		8 –
May 80.	(7") *(K 12424)* **THE SAD CAFE. / THOSE SHOES**		
Jul 80.	(7") <47004> **LYIN' EYES. / Johnny Lee: LOOKIN' FOR LOVE**	–	–
Sep 80.	(7") <47073> **LYIN' EYES. / Jimmy Buffet: HELLO TEXAS**	–	–
Nov 80.	(d-lp/d-c) *(K/K4 62032)* <705> **EAGLES LIVE (live)**	24	6

– Hotel California / Heartache tonight / I can't tell you why / The long run / New kid in town / Life's been good / Seven bridges road / Wasted time / Take it to the limit / Doolin-Dalton / Desperado / Saturday night / All night long / Life in the fast lane / Take it easy. *(d-cd-iss. Feb93; 7559 60591-2)*

Dec 80.	(7") <47100> **SEVEN BRIDGES ROAD (live). / THE LONG RUN (live)**	–	21
Jan 81.	(7") *(K 12504)* **TAKE IT TO THE LIMIT (live). / SEVEN BRIDGES ROAD (live) / TAKE IT EASY (live)**		–

not iss.   Full Moon

Mar 81.	(7") <49654> **I CAN'T TELL YOU WHY. / Ambrosia: OUTSIDE**		–

—— By this time they had all mutually agreed to disband. All five went on to individual solo careers.

DON HENLEY

WEA   Asylum

Sep 82.	(7") *(K 13200)* <69971> **JOHNNY CAN'T READ. / LONG WAY HOME**		42 Aug82

Elektra   Asylum

Dec 82.	(7") *(E 9849)* <69894> **DIRTY LAUNDRY. / LILAH**	59	3 Oct82

(12"+=) *(E 9849T)* – Them and us. *(re-iss. Jun85, 7"/12"; EKR 6/+T)*

Jan 83.	(7") <69931> **I CAN'T STAND STILL. / THEM AND US**	–	48

Asylum   Asylum

Feb 83.	(lp/c) *(K/K4 52365)* <60048> **I CAN'T STAND STILL**		24 Aug82

– I can't stand still / You better hang up / Long way home / Nobody's business / Talking to the Moon / Dirty laundry / Johnny can't read / Them and us / La Eile / Lilah / The unclouded day. *(cd-iss. Jun89; 960 048-2)*

May 83.	(7") *(E 9876)* **THE UNCLOUDED DAY. / LONG WAY HOME**		–

(12"+=) *(E 9876T)* – I can't stand still.

Jul 83.	(7") <69831> **NOBODY'S BUSINESS. / LONG WAY HOME**	–	

Geffen   Geffen

Dec 84.	(7"/12") *(A/TA 4945)* <29141> **THE BOYS OF SUMMER. / A MONTH OF SUNDAYS**	12	5 Nov84
Feb 85.	(lp/c) *(GEF/GEC 25939)* <24026> **BUILDING THE PERFECT BEAST**	14	13 Dec84

– The boys of summer / You can't make love / Man with a mission / You're not drinking enough / Not enough love in the world / Building the perfect beast / All she wants to do is dance / Sunset grill / Drivin' with your eyes closed / Land of the living. *(cd+=)* – A month of Sundays. *(re-iss. Sep86 lp/c; 924026-1/-4) (cd-iss. Feb87; 924026-2) (cd re-iss. 1988; CD 25939) (re-iss. Jan91 lp/c/cd; GEF/+C/D 24026) (cd re-iss. Mar95; GFLD 19267)*

Feb 85.	(7") <29065> **ALL SHE WANTS TO DO IS DANCE. / BUILDING THE PERFECT BEAST**	–	9
Apr 85.	(7") *(A 6161)* **SUNSET GRILL. / BUILDING THE PERFECT BEAST**		–
Jul 85.	(7") *(A 6419)* <29012> **NOT ENOUGH LOVE IN THE WORLD. / MAN WITH A MISSION**	–	34 May85
Aug 85.	(7") <28906> **SUNSET GRILL. / MAN WITH A MISSION**		22

—— his basic back-up consisted of **DANNY KORTCHMAR** – guitar, keyboards / **STAN LYNCH** – drums / **PINO PALLADINO** – bass / **JAI WINDING** – keyboards / **MIKE CAMPBELL** – keyboards

Jun 89.	(lp/c)(cd) *(WX 253/+C)(924217-2)* <24217> **THE END OF THE INNOCENCE**	17	8

– The end of the innocence / How bad do you want it? / I will not go quietly / The last worthless evening / New York minute / Shangri-la / Gimme what you got / If dirt were dollars / The heart of the matter. *(re-iss. Jan91 lp/c/cd; GEF/+C/D 24217) (cd re-iss. Oct95; GFLD 19285)*

Jul 89.	(7"/c-s) *(GEF/+C 57)* <22925> **THE END OF THE INNOCENCE. / IF DIRT WERE DOLLARS**	48	8 Jun89

(12"+=/cd-s+=) *(GEF 57 T/CD)* – The boys of summer.

Oct 89.	(7"/c-s) *(GEF 66)* **NEW YORK MINUTE. / GIMME WHAT YOU GOT**		–

(10"+=/12"+=/cd-s+=) *(GEF 66 TE/T/CD)* – Sunset grill (live).

Oct 89.	(7") <22771> **THE LAST WORTHLESS EVENING. / GIMME WHAT YOU GOT**	–	21
Feb 90.	(7"/c-s) *(GEF 71)* **THE LAST WORTHLESS EVENING. / ALL SHE WANTS TO DO IS DANCE**		

(12"+=) *(GEF 71T)* – You can't make love.
(cd-s++=) *(GEF 71CD)* – ('A'version).

Feb 90.	(c-s) <19898> **THE HEART OF THE MATTER / LITTLE TIN GOD**	–	21
Jun 90.	(c-s) <19699> **HOW BAD DO YOU WANT IT? / NEW YORK MINUTE**	–	48
Oct 90.	(c-s) <19660> **NEW YORK MINUTE / THE HEART OF THE MATTER (acoustic)**	–	48

—— In Sep'92, HENLEY and PATTY SMYTH charted US No.2 / UK No.22 with 'SOMETIMES LOVE JUST AIN'T ENOUGH' on 'M.C.A.' <54403>

—— In Mar'93, DON featured on TRISH YEARWOOD's single 'Walkaway Joe'.

Nov 95.	(cd/c) <(GED/GEC 24834)> **ACTUAL MILES: HENLEY'S GREATEST HITS (compilation + 2 new *)**		48

– Dirty laundry / The boys of summer / All she wants to do is dance / Not enough love in the world / Sunset grill / The end of the innocence / The last worthless evening / New York minute / The heart of the matter /

The garden of Allah * / You don't know me at all *. *(cd+=)* – I get the message.

Jul 98.	(c-s/cd-s) *(GFS C/TD 22350)* **THE BOYS OF SUMMER / ALL SHE WANTS TO DO IS DANCE / SOMETIMES LOVE JUST AINT ENOUGH**	12	

GLENN FREY

Asylum   Asylum

Jun 82.	(lp/c) *(K/K4 52395)* <60129> **NO FUN ALOUD**		32

– I found somebody / The one you love / Party town / I volunteer / I've been born again / Sea cruise / That girl / All those lies / She can't let go / Don't give up.

Jul 82.	(7") *(K 13812)* <47466> **I FOUND SOMEBODY. / SHE CAN'T LET GO**		31 Jun82
Oct 82.	(7") <69974> **THE ONE YOU LOVE. / ALL THOSE LIES**	–	15
Jan 83.	(7") <69857> **ALL THOSE LIES. / THAT GIRL**		41

M.C.A.   M.C.A.

Jul 84.	(lp/c) *(MCF/+C 3232)* <5501> **THE ALLNIGHTER**		37

– The allnighter / Sexy girl / I got love / Somebody else / Lover's moon / Smuggler's blues / Let's go home / Better in the U.S.A. / The heat is on / New love. *(re-act.Jun85, hit UK No.31) (cd-iss. Jul85; DMCF 3232) (cd re-iss. Aug89; DMCL 1893) (re-iss. Apr92 cd/c; MCL D/C 19009)*

Sep 84.	(7") *(MCA 911)* <52413> **SEXY GIRL. / BETTER IN THE U.S.A.**		20 Aug84
Oct 84.	(7") <52461> **THE ALLNIGHTER. / SMUGGLER'S BLUES**	–	54
Jan 85.	(7"/12") *(MCA/+T 941)* <52513> **THE HEAT IS ON. / Harold Faltermeyer: SHOOT OUT**	12	2 Dec84

above was used for the film 'Beverly Hills Cop' starring Eddie Murphy

Mar 85.	(7") <52546> **SMUGGLER'S BLUES. / NEW LOVE**		12

below was issued on 'BBC' records in Britain only.

Jun 85.	(7") *(RESL 170)* **SMUGGLER'S BLUES. / NEW LOVE**	22	–

(12"+=) *(12RSL 170)* – Living in darkness.

Jul 85.	(7") *(MCA 965)* **SEXY GIRL. / BETTER IN THE U.S.A.**		–

(12"+=) *(MCAT 965)* – The heat is on (dub) / New love.

Sep 85.	(7") <52651> **YOU BELONG TO THE CITY. / SMUGGLER'S BLUES**		2
Oct 85.	(7") *(MCA 1008)* **YOU BELONG TO THE CITY. / I GOT LOVE**		–

(12"+=) *(MCAT 1008)* – ('A'version).

Sep 88.	(7") *(MCA 1284)* <53363> **TRUE LOVE. / WORKING MAN**		13 Aug88

(12"+=/cd-s+=) *(MCAT/DMCA 1284)* – The heat is on.

Oct 88.	(lp/c/cd) *(MCF/MCFC/DMCF 3429)* <6239> **SOUL SEARCHIN'**		36 Aug88

– Soul searchin' / Livin' right / True love / I did it for your love / Working man / Two hearts / Some kind of blue / Can't put out this fire / Let's pretend we're still in love / It's your life.

Jan 89.	(7") *(MCA 1294)* <53452> **SOUL SEARCHIN'. / IT'S COLD DOWN HERE**		

(12"+=/cd-s+=) *(MCAT/DMCA 1294)* – True love.

Mar 89.	(7") <53497> **LIVIN' RIGHT. / SOUL SEARCHIN'**	–	90
May 89.	(7") <53684> **TWO HEARTS. / SOME KIND OF BLUE**		

—— now writes with keyboard player **JAY OLIVER** or **JACK TEMPCHIN**

Apr 91.	(c-s) <54060> **PART OF ME, PART OF YOU**	–	55

above taken from the film 'Thelma And Louise'

Jul 92.	(c-s) <54429> **I'VE GOT MINE / A WALK IN THE DARK**		91
Jul 92.	(7"/c-s) <54429> **I'VE GOT MINE. / PART OF ME, PART OF YOU**	–	–

(cd-s+=) – A walk in the dark.

Aug 92.	(cd/c) *(MCA D/C 10599)* **STRANGE WEATHER**		

– Silent spring / Long hot summer / Strange weather / Agua tranquillo / Love in the 21st century / He took advantage / River of dreams / Before the ship goes down / I've got mine / Rising sun / Brave new world / Delicious / A walk in the dark / Big life / Part of me, part of you.

Sep 92.	(c-s) <54461> **RIVER OF DREAMS / HE TOOK ADVANTAGE**		
May 93.	(cd/c) *(MCD/MCC 10826)* **LIVE (live)**		

– Peaceful easy feeling / New kid in town / The one you love / Wild mountain thyme / Strange weather / I've got mine / Lyin' eyes – Take it easy (medley) / River of dreams / True love / Love in the 21st century / Smuggler's blues / The heat is on / Heartache tonight / Desperado.

Apr 95.	(cd) *(MCD 11227)* **SOLO CONNECTION**		

– This way to happiness / Who's been sleeping in my bed / Common ground / Call on me / The one you love / Sexy girl / Smuggler's blues / The heat is on / You belong to the city / True love / Soul searchin' / Part of me, part of you / I've got mine / River of dreams / Brave new world.

– compilations, etc. –

Jul 96.	(d-cd) M.C.A.; *(MCD 33727)* **SOUL SEARCHIN' / STRANGE WEATHER**		

EAGLES

re-formed **HENLEY / FREY / WALSH / FELDER + SCHMIDT**

Geffen   Geffen

Nov 94.	(cd/c) <(GED/GEC 24725)> **HELL FREEZES OVER**	28	1

– Get over it / Love will keep us alive / The girl from yesterday / Learn to be still / Tequila sunrise / Hotel California / Wasted time / Pretty maids all in a row / I can't tell you why / New York minute / The last resort / Take it easy / In the city / Life in the fast lane / Desperado.

Nov 94.	(c-s) <19376> **GET OVER IT** / ('A'live version)	–	31
Jul 96.	(c-s) *(GFSC 21980)* **LOVE WILL KEEP US ALIVE / HELP ME THROUGH THE NIGHT**	52	–

(cd-s+=) *(GFSTD 21980)* – New York minute.

– compilations etc. –

Note; All releases on 'Asylum' unless mentioned otherwise

Sep 76.	(7") *(K 13044)* **TAKE IT EASY. / WITCHY WOMAN**	–	–
Sep 76.	(7") *(K 13045)* **PEACEFUL EASY FEELING. / OL' 55**	–	–
Sep 76.	(7") *(K 13046)* **TEQUILA SUNRISE. / ON THE BORDER**	–	–
Oct 82.	(lp/c) Elektra; *(E 205-1/-4)* / Asylum; <60205> **EAGLES GREATEST HITS – VOLUME 2**		52

– Hotel California / Heartache tonight / Life in the fast lane / Seven bridges road / The sad cafe / I can't tell you why / New kid in town / The long run / Victim of love / After the thrill is gone. *(cd-iss. Dec82; 960 205-2)*

Oct 83.	(d-c) *(K4 62033)* **DESPERADO / ONE OF THESE NIGHTS**	☐ -
Nov 83.	(d-c) *(960 275-4)* **HOTEL CALIFORNIA / THE LONG RUN**	☐ -
May 85.	(lp/c) *(EKT 5/+C)* **THE BEST OF THE EAGLES**	10 -

– Tequila sunrise / Lyin' eyes / Take it to the limit / Hotel California / Life in the fast lane / Heartache tonight / The long run / Take it easy / Peaceful easy feeling / Desperado / Best of my love / One of these nights / New kid in town. *(re-hit.Aug88 made UK No.8)*

Sep 85.	(7") *Old Gold; (OG 9510)* **TAKE IT TO THE LIMIT. / BEST OF MY LOVE**	☐ -
Sep 85.	(7") *Old Gold; (OG 9511)* **HOTEL CALIFORNIA. / DESPERADO**	☐ -
Oct 85.	(7") *Old Gold; (OG 9526)* **LYIN' EYES. / ONE OF THESE NIGHTS**	☐ -
Jun 88.	(7") *(EKR 10)* **HOTEL CALIFORNIA. / PRETTY MAIDS ALL IN A ROW**	☐ -
	(12"+=) *(EKRT 10)* – The sad cafe.	
	(cd-s+=) *(EKRCD 10)* – Hotel California (live).	
Jun 89.	(cd-ep) **TAKE IT EASY / ONE OF THESE NIGHTS / DESPERADO / LYIN' EYES**	
Jul 94.	(cd/c) *(9548 32375-2/-4)* **THE VERY BEST OF EAGLES**	5 -

– Take it easy / Witchy woman / Peaceful easy feeling / Doolin Dalton / Desperado / Tequila sunrise / Best of my love / James Dean / I can't tell you why / Lyin' eyes / Take it to the limit / One of these nights / Hotel California / New kid in town / Life in the fast lane / Heartache tonight / The long run.

Steve EARLE

Born: 17 Jan'55, Fort Monroe, Virginia, USA. The son of an air traffic controller, EARLE was raised in Schertz, Texas where his youth was spent immersed in guitar playing and rebelling against the authorities. At the age of 16, the long-haired would-be troubadour left home and eventually wound up in Houston where he befriended a coterie of songwriters that numbered the likes of TOWNES VAN ZANDT, JERRY JEFF WALKER and GUY CLARK. Subsequently relocating to Nashville, EARLE scraped by with a series of day jobs while playing in CLARK's backing band at night. A burgeoning talent for songwriting and a growing network of music biz contacts eventually saw him land a job as staff writer for a Nashville publishing company, his songs placed with PATTY LOVELESS and even ELVIS PRESLEY. Following a brief foray into acting (a bit part in Robert Altman's 'Nashville'), EARLE set about bringing together a backing band, The DUKES, who survived numerous incarnations over the first decade of EARLE's career. By this point (1980), he was already on his third wife, Carol, who temporarily helped put the brakes on his wilder instincts. EARLE took out a new job with publishers, 'DEA & CLARK', issuing a debut EP, 'PINK AND BLACK' on their small 'L.S.I.' label in 1982. A Nashville music journalist, John Lomax, was quick to spot EARLE's talent and offered his services as manager before helping net him a deal with 'Epic'. Unfortunately, the major label bods were at odds with EARLE over his musical direction, rejecting an album's worth of songs and demanding that he recut them in a more commercial style. A number of US-only tracks were eventually released in the space of a year or two including 'NOTHING BUT YOU', 'SQUEEZE ME IN' (featuring an early version of the scorching 'DEVIL'S RIGHT HAND') 'WHAT'LL YOU DO ABOUT ME' and 'A LITTLE BIT IN LOVE'. None were successful, however, and after a mutual split, EARLE moved on to 'M.C.A.' with the help of producer Tony Brown. Finally, with the backing of a revamped DUKES (BUCKY BAXTER, RICHARD BENNETT, KEN MOORE, HARRY STINSON, EMORY GORDY JR., JOHN JARVIS, STEVE NATHAN and PAUL FRANKLIN), the self-styled Nashville renegade released a debut album, 'GUITAR TOWN' (1986). Walking the country line between threadbare folk, blues and rockabilly, the record found an audience with the 'new country' brigade looking for the next DWIGHT YOAKAM while commanding the respect of rock critics who praised his blue collar sentiments and gravel-throated troubadour approach. 'EXIT 0' (1987) continued in a similar, if slightly more countrified vein, featuring signature tune 'I AIN'T EVER SATISFIED' alongside the track he penned for Farm Aid, 'THE RAIN CAME DOWN'. Neither of these albums, however, hinted at the hard-bitten roots-rock of 'COPPERHEAD ROAD', EARLE's landmark 1988 effort that firmly established him within the mainstream rock community while simultaneously alienating many of his core country fans. From the epic grit of the title track to the frenetic POGUES collaboration, 'JOHNNY COME LATELY', EARLE never sounded so visceral. Neither had his lyrics been so vividly realised, bringing to life a motley cast of moonshiners, Vietnam vets and petty criminals. The record's success made EARLE a popular live attraction in Europe especially and he subsequently spent a large amount of time in London. His chaotic personal life was also catching up with him and besides coping with spiralling alcohol and drug dependency, he had to contend with an assault conviction (on a security guard at his own show) and the bankruptcy of 'Uni', the 'M.C.A.' subsidiary that'd handled his album. 'THE HARD WAY' (1990) then, was his dark night of the soul, a downbeat, introspective record that ironically furnished him with his highest UK chart placing (Top 30). Yet its relative commercial failure signalled the end of EARLE's tenure with his label and, burned out after a punishing few years of touring, he finally disbanded The DUKES. Things hardly improved for the beleaguered singer over the ensuing five years as he struggled with cocaine and heroin addiction, avoiding a one-year jail term by agreeing to enter a detox centre. Like the proverbial phoenix rising from the ashes, EARLE released what many critics considered his most accomplished

record to date in 1995 with 'TRAIN A-COMIN'. Issued via the Nashville indie label, 'Winter Harvest' (the rejuvenated 'Transatlantic' in the UK), the album was an acoustic affair going back to EARLE's country roots and utilising such talents as EMMYLOU HARRIS. Critically, commercially and creatively reborn, EARLE subsequently signed a new contract with 'Warners' and released another winner in 1996's 'I FEEL ALRIGHT'. Older and wiser, EARLE has become one of the most respected elder statesmen in the country-roots field, going on to release the acclaimed 'EL CORAZON' (1997) and record and tour with the DEL McROURY BAND with whom he delivered his latest set, 'THE MOUNTAIN' (1999). • **Covered:** THE DEVIL'S RIGHT HAND (Waylon Jennings) / DEAD FLOWERS (Rolling Stones) / TECUMSEH VALLEY (Townes Van Zandt) / RIVERS OF BABYLON (trad.) / WHAT'S YOUR NAME (Lynyrd Skynyrd) / etc. MARIA McKEE (ex-LONE JUSTICE) co-wrote two songs on his 1990 album.

Album rating: GUITAR TOWN (*7) / EXIT '0' (*6) / COPPERHEAD ROAD (*8) / THE HARD WAY (*6) / SHUT UP AND DIE LIKE AN AVIATOR (*7) / TRAIN A COMIN' (*7) / I FEEL ALRIGHT (*5) / EL CORAZON (*7) / THE MOUNTAIN with the Del Coury Band (*8) / EARLY TRACKS compilation (*5) / THE ESSENTIAL STEVE EARLE compilation (*7)

STEVE EARLE – vocals, guitar + session players

		not iss.	L.S.I.
1982.	(7"ep) **PINK AND BLACK**	-	☐

—— **STEVE EARLE** – vocals, guitar (with The **DUKES**) **BUCKY BAXTER** – steel guitar, vocals / **RICHARD BENNETT** – guitars / **KEN MOORE** – organ, synthesizer, vocals / **HARRY STINSON** – drums, vocals / **EMORY GORDY JR.** – bass, mandolin / plus **JOHN JARVIS** – piano / **STEVE NATHAN** – synthesizer / **PAUL FRANKLIN** – pedal steel

		not iss.	Epic
Aug 83.	(7") *<04070>* **NOTHING BUT YOU. / CONTINENTAL TRAILWAY BLUES**	-	
Feb 84.	(7") *<04307>* **SQUEEZE ME IN. / THE DEVIL'S RIGHT HAND**	-	
Jun 84.	(7") *<04666>* **WHAT'LL YOU DO ABOUT ME. / CRY MYSELF TO SLEEP**	-	
Oct 84.	(7") *<04784>* **A LITTLE BIT IN LOVE. / THE CRUSH**	-	

		M.C.A.	M.C.A.
Aug 86.	(7") (MCA 1083) *<52920>* **SOMEDAY. / HILLBILLY HIGHWAY**	☐	
Aug 86.	(lp/c) *(MCF/+C 3335) <5713>* **GUITAR TOWN**		89

– Guitar town / Goodbye's all we've got left / Hillbilly highway / Good ol' boy (gettin' tough) / My old friend the blues / Someday / Think it over / Fearless heart / Little rock'n'roller / Down the road. *(cd-iss. Apr87; DMCF 3335) (cd re-iss. Jan90 +=; DMCL 1888)* – Good ol' boy (gettin' tough) (live).

Feb 87.	(7") *(MCA 1123)* **SOMEDAY. / GUITAR TOWN**	☐
	(12"+=) *(MCAT 1123)* – Good ol' boy (gettin' tough).	
	(cd-s++=) *(MCACD 1123)* – Goodbye's all we've got left.	
Feb 87.	(7") *<53011>* **GOODBYE'S ALL WE'VE GOT LEFT. / GOOD OL' BOY (GETTIN' TOUGH)**	-

—— credited on sleeve to "STEVE EARLE & THE DUKES" (EARLE, BAXTER, MOORE, STINSON plus **RENO KING** – bass / **MIKE McADAM** – guitars. Others included BENNETT, GORDY JR., JARVIS and **K-MEAUX BOUDIN** – accordion

Apr 87.	(7") *(MCA 1141)* **FEARLESS HEART. / LITTLE ROCK'N'ROLLER**	-
	(12"+=) *(MCAT 1141)* – ('A'long version).	
May 87.	(7"/12") *(MCA/+T 1162)* **I AIN'T EVER SATISFIED. / NOWHERE ROAD**	-
Jun 87.	(lp/c/cd) *(MCF/MCFC/DMCF 3379) <5998>* **EXIT 'O'**	77 90

– Nowhere road / Sweel little '66 / No.29 / Angry young man / San Antonio girl / The rain came down / I ain't ever satisfied / The week of living dangerously / I love you too much / It's all up to you. *(cd re-iss. Oct92; MCLD 19070)*

Sep 87.	(7") *<53182>* **SWEET LITTLE '66. / ANGRY YOUNG MAN**	-
Nov 87.	(d7") *(MCA 1209)* **THE RAIN CAME DOWN. / GUITAR TOWN (live) // I LOVE YOU TOO MUCH (live). / No.29 (live)**	-
Feb 88.	(7") *<53249>* **THE WEEK OF LIVING DANGEROUSLY. / SIX DAYS ON THE ROAD**	-
Jun 88.	(7") **I AIN'T EVER SATISFIED. / MY OLD FRIEND THE BLUES**	-
	(12"+=) – I love you too much.	

		M.C.A.	Uni
Sep 88.	(7") *(MCA 1280)* **COPPERHEAD ROAD. / LITTLE SISTER**	45	-
	(12"+=) *(MCAT 1280)* – No.29.		
	(cd-s+=) *(DMCA 1280)* – San Antonio girl / I ain't ever satisfied.		
Oct 88.	(lp/c/cd) *(MCF/MCFC/DMCF 3426) <7>* **COPPERHEAD ROAD**	44	56

– Copperhead road / Snake oil / Back to the wall / You belong to me / Devil's right hand / Johnny come lately / Even when I'm blue / Waiting on you / Once you love / Nothing but a child. *(cd re-iss. Aug93; MCLD 19213)*

Dec 88.	(7") *(MCA 1301)* **JOHNNY COME LATELY. / NOTHING BUT A CHILD**	75 -
	(12"+=) *(MCAT 1301)* – Nebraska (live).	
	(cd-s++=) *(DMCA 1301)* – Copperhead Road (live).	
Feb 89.	(7") *(MCA 1319)* **BACK TO THE WALL. / SNAKE OIL**	☐ -
	(12"+=/cd-s+=) *(MCAT/DMCA 1319)* – State trooper.	

STEVE EARLE AND THE DUKES

—— he retained **BAXTER, MOORE** and p/t **JARVIS** / newcomers = **ZIP GIBSON** – guitar, vocals / **KELLY LEONEY** – bass, vocals / **CRAIG WRIGHT** – drums / plus **PATRICK EARLE** – percussion and other guests

May 90.	(7") *(MCA 1426)* **THE OTHER KIND. / WEST NASHVILLE BOOGIE**	☐ -
	(12"+=/cd-s+=) *(MCAT/DMCA 1426)* – Guitar town (live) / Dead flowers (live).	
Jun 90.	(cd/c/lp) *(MCG/MCGC/DMCG 6095) <6430>* **THE HARD WAY**	22 100 Jul90

– The other kind / Promise you anything / Hopeless romantics / Esmeralda's Hollywood / This highway's mine (roadmaster) / Billy Austin / Justice in Ontario /

Have mercy / Country girl / When the people find out / Regular guy / Close your eyes / West Nashville boogie.

Sep 90. (7"/c-s) **JUSTICE IN ONTARIO. / THIS HIGHWAY'S MINE (ROADMASTER)** `[ ]` `[ - ]`
(12"+=/cd-s+=) – Copperhead road (live) / I ain't ever satisfied (live).

—— **STACEY EARLE-MIMS** – backing vocals, percussion; repl. JARVIS

Sep 91. (d-lp/c/cd) *(MCA/+C/D 10315)* **SHUT UP AND DIE LIKE AN AVIATOR (live)** `[ 62 ]` `[ ]`
– Good ol' boy (gettin' tough) / Devil's right hand / I ain't ever satisfied / Someday / West Nashville boogie / Snake oil / Blue yodel #9 / The other kind / Billy Austin / Copperhead road / Fearless heart / Guitar town / I love you too much / The rain came down / She's about a mover / Dead flowers. *(cd re-iss. Sep96; same)*

—— now with PETER ROWAN / NORMAN BLAKE / ROY HUSKEY + EMMYLOU HARRIS

	Transatla.	Winter Harvest
Jul 95. (cd/c) *(TRA CD/MC 111)* **TRAIN A COMIN'**	`[ ]`	`[ ]`

– Mystery train part II / Hometown blues / Sometimes she forgets / you / Mercenary song / Goodbye / Tom Ames' prayer / Nothin' without you / Angel is the Devil / I'm looking through you / Northern winds / Ben McCulloch / Rivers of Babylon / Tecumseh Valley.

—— now with The V-ROYS: **RICHARD BENNETT** – guitar, harmonium, percussion / **RAY KENNEDY** – guitar / **KELLEY LOONEY + GARRY TALLENT + ROY HUSKEY + RIC KIPP** – bass / **KEN MOORE** – organ / **CUSTER + GREG MORROW + RICK SCHELL** – drums / **DUB CORNETT** – percussion

	Transatla.	Warners
Mar 96. (cd/c) *(TRA CD/MC 227)* <46201> **I FEEL ALRIGHT**	`[ 44 ]`	`[ ]`

– Feel alright / Hard-core troubadour / More than I can do / Hurtin' me, hurtin' you / Now she's gone / Poor boy / Valentine's day / The unrepentant / CCKMP / Billy and Bonnie / South Nashville blues / You're still standin' there (with LUCINDA WILLIAMS).

Jun 96. (12") *(TRAT 1026)* **JOHNNY TOO BAD. / STRAIGHT HIGHWAY** `[ ]` `[ - ]`
(cd-s+=) *(TRAX 1026)* – Ellis unit one.

	Sub Pop	Sub Pop
Jul 97. (cd-ep) <(PSCD 388)> **STEVE EARLE & THE SUPERSUCKERS**	`[ ]`	`[ ]`

– Creepy Jackalope eye / Angel is the Devil / Before they make me run / Creepy Jackalope eye (SUPERSUCKERS) / Angel is the Devil (STEVE EARLE).

	Warners	Warners
Oct 97. (cd/c) <(9362 46789-2/-4)> **EL CORAZON**	`[ 59 ]`	`[ ]`

– Christmas in Washington / Taneytown / If you fall / I still carry you around / Telephone road / Someone out there / You know the rest / NYC / Poison lovers / The other side of town / Here I am / Fort Worth blues.

STEVE EARLE and the DEL McCOURY BAND

	Grapevine	E-Squared
Feb 99. (cd) *(GRACD 252)* <1064> **THE MOUNTAIN**	`[ 51 ]`	`[ ]`

– Texas eagle / Yours forever blue / Carrie Brown / I'm still in love with you / Graveyard shift / Harlan man / The mountain / Outlaw's honeymoon / Connemara breakdown / Leroy's dustbowl blues / Dixieland / Paddy on the beat / Long lonesome highway blues / The pilgrim.

May 99. (cd-s) *(CDGPS 256)* **DIXIELAND /** `[ ]` `[ ]`
Oct 99. (cd-s) *(CDGPS 270)* **THE MOUNTAIN / COPPERHEAD ROAD (live) / I AIN'T EVER SATISFIED (live)** `[ ]` `[ - ]`

– compilations etc. –

Jul 87. (lp/c) *Epic; (450873-1/-4)* **EARLY TRACKS** `[ ]` `[ Oct86 ]`
– Nothin' but you / If you need a fool / Continental trailway blues / Open up your door / Breakdown lane / Squeeze me in / Annie, is tonight the night / My baby worships me / Cadillac / Devil's right hand. *(cd-iss. Jul91 on 'Pickwick'; 982597)* *(cd re-iss. Feb98 on 'Koch'; 7903)*
(above was to have been released in '83 as 'CADILLAC')

Jun 92. (cd/c) *Windsong; (WIN CD/MC 020)* **BBC RADIO 1 IN CONCERT (live)** `[ ]` `[ ]`
Oct 93. (cd/c) *Pickwick; (PWK S/MC 4178)* **THIS HIGHWAY'S MINE** `[ ]` `[ ]`
Aug 96. (cd) *Nectar; (NTMCD 532)* **ANGRY YOUNG MAN (THE VERY BEST OF STEVE EARLE)** `[ ]` `[ - ]`
Sep 96. (cd) *M.C.A.; (MCLD 19325)* **THE ESSENTIAL STEVE EARLE** `[ ]` `[ - ]`
– Guitar town / Hillbilly highway / The Devil's right hand / Goodbye's all we've got left / Six days on the road / Someday / Good ol' boy (gettin' tough) / Copperhead road / The rain came down / I ain't ever satisfied / Nowhere road / The week of living dangerously / Continental trailway blues.

EARTHLING (dig out; 4th edition)

EARTH, WIND & FIRE

Formed: Chicago, Illinois, USA ... 1969 as The SALTY PEPPERS by ex-'Chess' session man, MAURICE WHITE, who gathered together a jazz/fusion/funk ensemble of VERDINE WHITE, WADE FLEMONS, DON WHITEHEAD, MICHAEL BEAL, SHERRY SCOTT, YACKOV BEN ISRAEL, CHET WASHINGTON and ALEX THOMAS. Changing their name to EARTH, WIND & FIRE the following year, the band signed to 'Warners' and released their eponymous debut set in Spring '71. A further set, 'THE NEED OF LOVE', appeared in early '72, prior to a major personnel upheaval (and a change of labels to 'Columbia') which saw the induction of the silky voiced PHILIP BAILEY as frontman; by the release of 1973's 'HEAD TO THE SKY', the line-up had stabilised around VERDINE, LARRY DUNN, RALPH JOHNSON, AL McKAY, ANDREW WOODFOLK, JESSICA CLEAVES and JOHNNY GRAHAM. While that album gave the group their first major US chart success, it was 'OPEN OUR EYES' (1974), which began to encompass WHITE's pseudo mystical concepts into a more commercially

viable proposition. A laidback, creamy rich blend of soul/funk with a finely polished pop sensibility, 'THAT'S THE WAY OF THE WORLD' (1975) and its flagship single, 'SHINING STAR' both topped the US charts, beginning an extended run of chart success. 'GRATITUDE' (1975), 'SPIRIT' (1976) and 'ALL 'N' ALL' (1978) made the American Top 3 while EARTH, WIND & FIRE got to grips with disco on the enduring glitter-ball favourite, 'BOOGIE WONDERLAND'. Recorded with female backing group, The EMOTIONS, the track was one of their bigger British hits, culled from 1979 album, 'I AM' (1979). Though their success continued into the early 80's, the group's creative and commercial flame began to dampen and they split in '84. Three years later, a core of the WHITE brothers, BAILEY and WOODFOLK reformed the band and continued to release and record material into the 90's with mixed results.
• **Songwriters:** WHITE penned with others, except covers MAKE IT WITH YOU (Bread) / WHERE HAVE ALL THE FLOWERS GONE (Pete Seeger) / GOT TO GET YOU INTO MY LIFE (Beatles) / AFTER THE LOVE HAS GONE (c.David Foster, Bill Champlin + Jay Graydon).
Album rating: EARTH, WIND & FIRE (*4) / THE NEED OF LOVE (*4) / LAST DAYS AND TIME (*4) / HEAD TO THE SKY (*6) / OPEN OUR EYES (*6) / THAT'S THE WAY OF THE WORLD (*7) / GRATITUDE (*6) / SPIRIT (*7) / ALL 'N ALL (*6) / THE BEST OF EARTH, WIND & FIRE, VOL.1 compilation (*8) / I AM (*6) / FACES (*6) / RAISE! (*5) / POWERLIGHT (*4) / ELECTRIC UNIVERSE (*4) / TOUCH THE WORLD (*5) / THE BEST OF EARTH, WIND & FIRE, VOL.II compilation (*6) / HERITAGE (*3) / MILLENNIUM (*4) / LIVE AND UNPLUGGED (*3) / IN THE NAME OF LOVE (*4)

MAURICE WHITE (b.19 Dec'41, Memphis, USA) – vocals, drums, percussion, etc (ex-RAMSEY LEWIS TRIO, also sessioned for IMPRESSIONS / JACKIE WILSON) / **VERDINE WHITE** (b.25 Jul'51) – bass, **WADE FLEMONS** – keyboards, vocals / **DON WHITEHEAD** – piano, vocals / **MICHAEL BEAL** – guitar, etc. / **SHERRY SCOTT** – vocals / **YACKOV BEN ISRAEL** – congas, etc. / **CHET WASHINGTON** – tenor sax / **ALEX THOMAS** – trombone

	not iss.	Capitol
Feb 69. (7"; as the SALTY PEPPERS) <2433> **LA LA TIME. / (part II)**	`[ - ]`	`[ ]`
Sep 69. (7"; as the SALTY PEPPERS) <2568> **YOUR LOVE IS LIFE. / UH HUH YEAH**	`[ - ]`	`[ ]`

	Warners	Warners
Jan 71. (7") <7480> **THIS WORLD TODAY. / FAN THE FIRE**	`[ - ]`	`[ ]`
Mar 71. (7") <7492> **LOVE IS LIFE. / THIS WORLD TODAY**	`[ - ]`	`[ 93 ]`
Mar 71. (lp) <(WS 1905)> **EARTH, WIND AND FIRE**	`[ ]`	`[ ]`

– Help somebody / Moment of truth / Love is life / Fan the fire / C'mon children / The world today / Bad tune. *(cd-iss. Jan96; 7599 26861-2)*

May 71. (7") <(WB 6125)> **HELP SOMEBODY. / LOVE IS LIFE**	`[ ]`	`[ - ]`
Nov 71. (7") <7549> **C'MON CHILDREN. / I THINK ABOUT LOVIN' YOU**	`[ - ]`	`[ ]`
Jan 72. (lp) <WS 1958> **THE NEED OF LOVE**	`[ ]`	`[ 89 ]`

– Energy / Beauty / I can feel it in my bones / I think about lovin' you / Everything is everything. *(cd-iss. Jan96; 7599 26862-2)*

—— WHITE retains only brother **VERDINE**, and recruited/**employed new line-up PHILIP BAILEY** (b. 8 May'51, Denver, Colorado) – vocals, percussion / **LARRY DUNN** (b.19 Jun'53, Colorado) – keyboards, clavinet / **RALPH JOHNSON** (b. 4 Jul'51, California) – drums, percussion / **ROLAND BAUTISTA** – guitar / **RONALD LAWS** – saxophone, flute / **JESSICA CLEAVES** (b.1943) – vocals

	C.B.S.	Columbia
Oct 72. (lp/c) *(CBS/40 65208)* <31702> **LAST DAYS AND TIME**	`[ ]`	`[ 87 ]`

– Time is on your side / They don't see / Make it with you / Power / Remember the children / Where have all the flowers gone / I'd rather have you / Mom. *(re-iss. Oct79 lp/c; CBS/40 31761) (cd-iss. Feb92 on 'Columbia'; 982736-2)*

—— **AL McKAY** (b. 2 Feb'48, Louisiana) – guitar repl. BAUTISTA / **ANDREW WOODFOLK** (b.11 Oct'50, Texas) – horns repl. LAWS who went solo / added **JOHNNY GRAHAM** (b. 3 Aug'51, Kentucky)

May 73. (lp/c) *(CBS/40 65604)* <32194> **HEAD TO THE SKY**	`[ ]`	`[ 27 ]`

– Evil / Keep your head to the sky / Build your nest / The world's masquerade / Clover / Zanzibar. *(quad-lp 1975; CBSQ 65604) (re-iss. Mar81 lp/c; CBS/40 32017) (cd-iss. Sep93 on 'Sony Collectors'; 982997-2)*

Oct 73. (7") *(CBS 1792)* <45888> **EVIL. / CLOVER**	`[ ]`	`[ 50 ]` Jul73
Feb 74. (7") *(CBS 2033)* <45953> **KEEP YOUR HEAD TO THE SKY. / BUILD YOUR NEST**	`[ ]`	`[ 53 ]` Nov73

—— now w/out JESSICA

May 74. (7") *(CBS 2284)* <46007> **MIGHTY MIGHTY. / DRUM SONG**	`[ ]`	`[ 29 ]` Mar74
Jun 74. (lp/c) *(CBS/40 65844)* <32712> **OPEN OUR EYES**	`[ ]`	`[ 15 ]` Mar74

– Mighty mighty / Devotion / Fair but so uncool / Feelin' blue / Kalimba story / Drum song / Tee nine chee bit / Spasmodic mood / Caribou / Open our eyes. *(re-iss. Mar81; 32033)*

Sep 74. (7") <10026> **DEVOTION. / FAIR BUT SO UNCOOL**	`[ - ]`	`[ 33 ]`
Nov 74. (7") *(CBS 2782)* <46070> **KALIMBA STORY. / TEE NINE CHEE BIT**	`[ ]`	`[ 55 ]` Jul74

—— added other brother **FRED WHITE** (b.13 Jan'55, Chicago) – drums

—— Early 1975, EARTH WIND & FIRE were credited on two US Top 50 singles by RAMSEY LEWIS; 'Hot Dawgit' <10056> and 'Sun Goddess' <10103>.

Apr 75. (lp/c) *(CBS/40 80575)* <33280> **THAT'S THE WAY OF THE WORLD**	`[ ]`	`[ 1 ]` Mar75

– Shining star / That's the way of the world / Happy feelin' / All about love / Yearnin', learnin' / Reasons / Africano / See the light. *(re-iss. Nov81 on 'CBS-Embassy'; 32054) (cd-iss. May87; CD 80575) (cd re-iss. Feb97 on 'Columbia'; 484467-2)*

Apr 75. (7") *(CBS 3137)* <10090> **SHINING STAR. / YEARNIN', LEARNIN'**	`[ ]`	`[ 1 ]` Feb75
Jul 75. (7") *(CBS 3519)* <10172> **THAT'S THE WAY OF THE WORLD. / AFRICANO**	`[ 12 ]`	`[ ]` Jun75
Nov 75. (7") *(CBS 3847)* **SHININ' STAR (live). / HAPPY FEELIN'**	`[ ]`	`[ ]`
Dec 75. (d-lp) *(CBS 88160)* <33694> **GRATITUDE (most live)**	`[ ]`	`[ 1 ]` Nov75

– (introduction) / Sing a song / Gratitude / Celebrate / Can't hide love / Sunshine / Shining star / Sun Goddess / reasons / Sing a message to you / Devotion / Medley:

Africano – Power / Yearnin', learnin'. *(re-iss. May82; CBS 22129) (cd-iss. 1987; CD 88160)*

Date	Details	UK	US
Feb 76.	(7") *(CBS 3859)* <10251> **SING A SONG (live). / (instrumental)**		5 Nov75
Mar 76.	(7") <10309> **CAN'T HIDE LOVE. / GRATITUDE**	-	39
May 76.	(7") *(CBS 4240)* **REASONS (live). / GRATITUDE**		
Aug 76.	(7") *(CBS 4532)* <10373> **GETAWAY. / (instrumental)**		12 Jul76
Nov 76.	(lp/c) *(CBS/40 81451)* <34241> **SPIRIT**		2 Sep76

– Getaway / On your face / Imagination / Spirit / Saturday nite / Earth, wind and fire / Departure / Biyo / Burnin' bush. *(re-iss. Apr84 on 'Pickwick'; SHM 3133)*

Jan 77.	(7") *(CBS 4835)* <10439> **SATURDAY NITE. / DEPARTURE**	17	21 Nov76
Apr 77.	(7") <10492> **BIYO. / ON YOUR FACE**		
Jun 77.	(7") <10512> **ON YOUR FACE. / SATURDAY NITE (live)**	-	
Dec 77.	(7") *(CBS 5778)* <10625> **SERPENTINE FIRE. / (instrumental)**		13 Oct77
Jan 78.	(lp/c) *(CBS/40 86051)* <34905> **ALL 'N' ALL**	13	3 Nov77

– Serpentine fire / Fantasy / In the market place / Jupiter / Love's holiday / Brazillian rhyme / I'll write a song for you / Master mind / Runnin' / Be ever wonderful. *(re-iss. Mar83 lp/c; CBS/40 32266) (cd-iss. May87; CD 82238) (re-iss. Apr94 on 'Sony Collectors' cd/c; 982842-2/-4)*

Jan 78.	(7") <10688> **FANTASY. / RUNNIN'**	-	32
Feb 78.	(7") *(CBS 6056)* **FANTASY. / BOOGIE WONDERLAND**	14	-
Apr 78.	(7") *(CBS 6267)* **JUPITER. / RUNNIN'**	41	-
Jul 78.	(7") *(CBS 6490)* **MAGIC MIND. / LOVE'S HOLIDAY**	54	-
Sep 78.	(7") *(CBS 6553)* <10796> **GOT TO GET YOU INTO MY LIFE. / I'LL WRITE A SONG FOR YOU**	33	9 Jul78
Oct 78.	(7") <10854> **SEPTEMBER. / LOVE'S HOLIDAY**	-	8
Nov 78.	(7") *(CBS 6922)* **SEPTEMBER. / CAN'T HAVE LOVE**	3	
Dec 78.	(lp/c) *(CBS/40 83284)* <35647> **THE BEST OF EARTH, WIND & FIRE, VOL.1** (compilation)	6	6 Nov78

– Got to get you into my life / Fantasy / Can't hide love / Saturday night / Love music / Getaway / That's the way of the world / September / Shining star / Reasons / Sing a song. *(re-iss. Nov84 lp/c; CBS/40 32536) (cd-iss. Jun89; CD 32536) (cd re-iss. Oct94 on 'Columbia'; 477508-2)*

May 79.	(7"/12"; EARTH, WIND & FIRE WITH THE EMOTIONS) *(CBS 7292)* <10956> **BOOGIE WONDERLAND. / (instrumental)**	4	6
Jun 79.	(lp/c) *(CBS/40 86084)* <35730> **I AM**	5	3

– In the stone / Can't let go / After the love has gone / Let your feelings show / Boogie wonderland / Star / Wait / Rock that / You and I. *(re-iss. Jun85 lp/c; CBS/40 32656) (cd-iss. May87; CD 86084)*

Jul 79.	(7") *(CBS 7721)* <11033> **AFTER THE LOVE HAS GONE. / ROCK THAT**	4	2
Sep 79.	(7") *(CBS 7902)* <11165> **STAR. / YOU AND I**	16	64 Dec79
Oct 79.	(7") <11093> **IN THE STONE. / YOU AND I**	-	58
Dec 79.	(7") *(CBS 8077)* **CAN'T LET GO. / LOVE MUSIC**	46	-
Feb 80.	(7") *(CBS 8252)* **IN THE STONE. / AFRICAN BIYO**	53	-
Sep 80.	(7") *(CBS 8982)* <11366> **LET ME TALK. / (instrumental)**	29	44
Oct 80.	(d-lp/c) *(CBS/40 88498)* <36795> **FACES**	10	10

– Let me talk / Turn it into something good / Pride / You / Sparkle / Back on the road / Song in my heart / You went away / And love goes on / Sail away / Take it to the sky / Win or lose / Share your love / In time / Faces. *(cd-iss. Mar94 on 'Sony Collectors'; 983316-2) (cd-iss. Feb97 on 'Columbia'; 474679-2)*

Nov 80.	(7") <11407> **YOU. / SHARE YOUR LOVE**	-	
Dec 80.	(7") *(CBS 9377)* **BACK ON THE ROAD. / TAKE IT TO THE SKY**	63	-
Jan 80.	(7") <11434> **AND LOVE GOES ON. / WIN OR LOSE**	-	59
Feb 81.	(7") *(CBS 9521)* **AND LOVE GOES ON. / FACES**		
May 81.	(7") *(A 1204)* **YOU. / PRIDE**		

—— **ROLAND BAUTISTA** – guitar rejoined repl. McKAY who went into production.

Oct 81.	(7") *(A 1679)* <02536> **LET'S GROOVE. / (instrumental)**	3	3
Nov 81.	(lp/c) *(CBS/40 85272)* <37548> **RAISE!**	14	5

– Let's groove / Lady Sun / My love / Evolution orange / Kalimba tree / You are a winner / I've had enough / Wanna be with you / The changing times. *(cd-iss. Aug86; CD 85272)*

Jan 82.	(7") *(A 1959)* **I'VE HAD ENOUGH. / KALIMBA TREE (instrumental)**	29	-
Jan 82.	(7") <02688> **WANNA BE WITH YOU. / KALIMBA TREE (instrumental)**	-	51
Mar 82.	(7") *(A 2074)* **WANNA BE WITH YOU. / MY LOVE**	-	-
Jan 83.	(7"/12") *(A/+12 2927)* <03375> **FALL IN LOVE WITH ME. / LADY SUN**	47	17
Feb 83.	(lp/c) *(CBS/40 25120)* <38367> **POWERLIGHT**	22	12

– Fall in love with me / Spread your love / Side by side / Straight from the heart / The speed of love / Freedom of choice / Something special / Heart to heart / Miracles. *(cd-iss. 1988; CD 25120) (cd re-iss. Oct93 on 'Sony Europe')*

Mar 83.	(7") *(A 3211)* **SPREAD YOUR LOVE. / HEART TO HEART**		
May 83.	(7") <03814> **SIDE BY SIDE. / SOMETHING SPECIAL**	-	76
Jul 83.	(7"/12") <04002/04008> **SPREAD YOUR LOVE. / FREEDOM OF CHOICE**	-	

—— Still a member, PHIL BAILEY also takes on solo career.

Nov 83.	(7"/12") *(A/TA 3887)* <04210/04211> **MAGNETIC. / SPEED OF LOVE**		57
Dec 83.	(lp/c) *(CBS/40 25775)* <38980> **ELECTRIC UNIVERSE**		40

– Magnetic / Touch / Moonwalk / Could it be right / Spirit of a new world / Sweet sassy lady / We're living in our own time / Electic nation. *(cd-iss. 1988; CD 25772)*

Feb 84.	(7") *(A 4164)* **TOUCH. / SEPTEMBER**	-	-
	(12"+=) *(TA 4164)* – After the love has gone / Boogie wonderland.		
Feb 84.	(7") <04329> **TOUCH. / SWEET SASSY LADY**	-	
May 84.	(7") <04427> **MOONWALK. / WE'RE LIVING IN OUR OWN TIME**	-	-

—— disbanded March '84; both MAURICE and PHILIP continued solo

—— they re-formed with (**MAURICE WHITE, VERDINE WHITE, PHILIP BAILEY, ANDREW WOODFOLK**)plus new man **SHELDON REYNOLDS** – guitar + loads of session people

Oct 87.	(7") *(EWF 1)* <07608> **SYSTEM OF SURVIVAL. / WRITING ON THE WALL**	54	60
	(12"+=) *(EWFT 1)* – ('A'acappella) / ('A'dub).		

Date	Details	UK	US
	(12"+=/cd-s+=) *(EWFQT/CDEWF 1)* – ('A'-12"version).		
Nov 87.	(lp/c/cd) *(460409-1/-4/-2)* <40596> **TOUCH THE WORLD**		33

– System of survival / Evil boy / Thinking of you / You and I / Musical interlude: new horizons / Money tight / Every now and then / Touch the world / Here today and gone tomorrow / Victim of the modern heart.

Dec 87.	(7") <07687> **MUSICAL INTERLUDE: NEW HORIZONS. / YOU AND I**	-	
Feb 88.	(7") *(EWF 2)* <07695> **THINKING OF YOU. / MONEY TIGHT**		67
	(12"+=) *(EWFT 2)* – ('A'version).		
	(12"+=/cd-s+=) *(EWFQT/CDEWF 2)* – ('A'-House mix).		
Feb 88.	(7") <07687> **EVIL BOY. / (part 2)**		
Nov 88.	(7") <08107> **TURN ON (THE BEAT BOX). / (part 2)**		
Dec 88.	(lp/c/cd) <45013> **THE BEST OF EARTH, WIND & FIRE, VOL.1** (compilation)	-	

– Turn on (the beat box) / Let's groove / After the love has gone / Fantasy / Devotion / Serpentine fire / Love's holiday / Boogie wonderland / Saturday nite / Mighty mighty. *(UK-iss.May91 on 'Columbia' cd/c; 463200-2/-4)*

—— added **RALPH JOHNSON** – percussion / **SONNY EMORY** – drums / **+ session people**

Feb 90.	(7"/c-s) *(EWF/+M 3)* <73205> **HERITAGE. / GOTTA FIND OUT**		
	(12"+=) *(EWFT 3)* – ('A'acappella) / Let's groove (extended).		
	(cd-s+=) *(CDEWF 3)* – Fantasy / September / ('A'extended).		
	(12"+=) *(EWFQT 3)* – Brazillian rhyme (interlude) / Got to get you into my life / I've had enough.		
Mar 90.	(cd/c/lp) *(466242-2/-4/-1)* <45268> **HERITAGE**		70 Feb90

– Soweto / Takin' chances / Heritage / Good time / Body wrap / Anything you want / Bird / Wanna be the man / Close to home / Daydreamin' / King of the groove / I'm in love / For the love of you / Gotta find out / Motor / Faith / Welcome / Soweto (reprise).

Apr 90.	(c-s) <73344> **FOR THE LOVE OF YOU / MOTOR**	-	-
Sep 90.	(7"/c-s) <73436> **WANNA BE THE MAN. / WELCOME**	-	-
	(ext.12"+=/cd-s+=) <73396> – ('A'dub version).		

		Reprise	Reprise
Sep 93.	(cd/c) <(9362 45274-2/-4)> **MILLENNIUM**		39

– Even if you wonder / Sunday morning / Blood brothers / Kalimba interlude / Spend the night / Divine / Two hearts / Honor the magic / Love is the greatest story / The L word / Just another lonely night / Super hero / Wouldn't change a thing about you / Love across the wire / Chicago (Chitown) blues / Kalimba blues.

Oct 93.	(7"/c-s) *(W 0205/+C)* <18461> **SUNDAY MORNING. / THE L WORD**		53 Aug93
	(cd-s+=) *(W 0205CD)* – Just another lonely heart.		

		Avex	Avex
Nov 95.	(cd/c) *(AVEX CD/MC 20)* **LIVE AND UNPLUGGED (live)**		

		Eagle	Rhino
Jul 97.	(cd/c) *(EAG CD/MC 002)* **IN THE NAME OF LOVE**		

– Revolution / Rock it / In the name of love / Revolution / When loves goes wrong / Fill you up / The right time / Round and round / Keep it real / Cruising / Love is life / Avatar (interlude).

– compilations, others, etc. –

on 'C.B.S.' UK / 'Columbia' US unless mentioned otherwise

Sep 74.	(d-lp) *Warners;* <2798> **ANOTHER TIME** (first 2 albums)	-	97
1975.	(7") *(13-33247)* **KEEP YOUR HEAD TO THE SKY. / EVIL**	-	-
Apr 77.	(7") *(CBS 5198)* **SING A SONG. / BIYO**	-	-
Oct 79.	(t-lp-box) *(CBS 66350)* **EARTH, WIND & FIRE** – (3 early albums)		
Aug 80.	(7") *(CBS 8848)* **AFTER THE LOVE HAS GONE. / THAT'S THE WAY OF THE WORLD**		-
Aug 80.	(7") *(CBS 8876)* **FANTASY. / BOOGIE WONDERLAND**		-
Oct 80.	(lp) *Pickwick; (SSP 3078)* **EARTH, WIND & FIRE**		
1982.	(c-ep) **SING A SONG / BIYO / SHINING STAR / THAT'S THE END OF THE WORLD**		
Sep 85.	(7") *Old Gold; (OG 9556)* **FANTASY. / SEPTEMBER**		
Sep 85.	(7") *Old Gold; (OG 9558)* **BOOGIE WONDERLAND. / LET'S GROOVE**		
Feb 86.	(12"ep) *Old Gold; (OG 4008)* **STAR / SATURDAY NITE. / AFTER THE LOVE HAS GONE / I'VE HAD ENOUGH**		
May 86.	(lp)(c)(cd) *K-Tel; (NE1/CD2/NCD3 322)* **THE COLLECTION**		
Jun 86.	(7"/12") *(A/TA 7253)* **BOOGIE WONDERLAND. / LET'S GROOVE**		
May 88.	(cd) *Arcade; (ADEHCD 821-0)* **THE VERY BEST OF . . . VOL.1**		
May 88.	(cd) *Arcade; (ADEHCD 821-1)* **THE VERY BEST OF . . . VOL.2**		
Dec 90.	(3xcd-box) *Columbia; (467388-2)* **I AM / ALL 'N' ALL / RAISE**		
Jan 93.	(3xcd-box/3xc-box) *Columbia; (472614-2/-4)* **THE ETERNAL DANCE**		
Jul 94.	(3xcd-box) *Columbia; (468804-2)* **POWERLIGHT / ELECTRIC UNIVERSE / SPIRIT**		
Dec 95.	(cd/c) *Columbia; (467768-2/-4)* **THE LOVE SONGS**		
Sep 96.	(cd/c) *Telstar; (TCD/STAC 2879)* **BOOGIE WONDERLAND – THE BEST OF . . .**	35	
Mar 97.	(cd/lp) *Stax; (CDSXE/SXD 103)* **SWEET SWEETBACK'S BAADASSS SONG** (original soundtrack)		
Jul 99.	(12"/c-s/cd-s) *Incredible; (INCR 24/+MC/CD)* **SEPTEMBER 99** (mixes)	25	
Jul 99.	(cd/c) *Sony TV; (SONYTV 66 CD/MC)* **THE ULTIMATE COLLECTION**	34	

EASYBEATS (dig out; Great Psychedelic . . .)

EAZY-E (see under ⇒ N.W.A.)

ECHO & THE BUNNYMEN

Formed: Liverpool, England . . . Autumn 1978 by IAN McCULLOCH, WILL SERGEANT and LES PATTINSON. McCULLOCH had once been in The CRUCIAL THREE alongside future stars, JULIAN COPE and PETE WYLIE, the former two starting up another low key act, A SHALLOW MADNESS, together writing 'READ IT IN BOOKS' (the b-side of E&TB's debut single, 'PICTURES ON MY WALL'). The BUNNYMEN, complete with drum machine ECHO, released the aforementioned 45 as a one-off for the local 'Zoo' label, before signing to 'WEA/Warners' subsidiary, 'Korova', late in '79. By the following year, they'd had a Top 20 album, 'CROCODILES', and were soon breaking into the singles chart with 'RESCUE'. Overtly melancholy and DOORS-influenced, their material contained a fresher up-tempo feel which combined powerful melodrama and McCULLOCH's ego-fuelled attitude. From 1981-84, their albums 'HEAVEN UP HERE', 'PORCUPINE' and 'OCEAN RAIN', solidified a Merseyside revival that even crossed successfully over the Atlantic. They split after their last gig on the 26th April '88, and it surprised everyone, not least the solo bound McCULLOCH (he had issued a single in '84, Kurt Weill's 'SEPTEMBER SONG'), when The BUNNYMEN decided to carry on without him. However, in June '89, PETE DE FREITAS was tragically killed in a motorcycle accident. In the early 90's, The BUNNYMEN (SERGEANT, PATTINSON, plus NOEL BURKE – vocals, JACK BROCKMAN – keyboards and DAMON REECE – drums) struggled without their moody frontman. A disappointing album, 'REVERBERATION' (1990), did little to excite the public, the group forming their own 'Euphoric' label after 'Korova/WEA' dropped them. McCULLOCH meanwhile, had been continuing his search for glory, releasing two albums, the Top 20 'CANDLELAND' (1989) and the Top 50, 'MYSTERIO' (1992), the last of which was poorly received. Late in '94, McCULLOCH and SERGEANT were back with a new rock-driven tour de force, ELECTRAFIXION, their solo album, 'BURNED' (1995), was well received by the music press, went Top 40 and enjoyed moderate sales. There was considerably more media interest over the reformation of the original ECHO & THE BUNNYMEN line-up in 1997. A strong comeback single, 'NOTHING LASTS FOREVER', and album, 'EVERGREEN', both made the UK Top 10, while the band proved they could still cut it live with a tour and a series of summer festival appearances.
• **Songwriters:** Mainly group compositions, except covers PEOPLE ARE STRANGE (Doors) / PAINT IT BLACK (Rolling Stones) / ALL YOU NEED IS LOVE (Beatles) / FRICTION (Television) / RUN RUN RUN (Velvet Underground) / SHIP OF FOOLS (John Cale). McCULLOCH covered: RETURN TO SENDER (hit; Elvis Presley) / LOVER, LOVER, LOVER (Leonard Cohen). • **Trivia:** DAVE BALFE (of DALEK I LOVE YOU) played keyboards on their first JOHN PEEL session in August 1979.

Album rating: CROCODILES (*9) / HEAVEN UP HERE (*9) / PORCUPINE (*7) / OCEAN RAIN (*7) / SONGS TO LEARN AND SING compilation (*9) / ECHO & THE BUNNYMEN (*5) / REVERBERATION (*3) / BALLYHOO: THE BEST OF ECHO & THE BUNNYMEN compilation (*8) / EVERGREEN (*7) / WHAT ARE YOU DOING WITH YOUR LIFE? (*8) / Ian McCulloch: CANDLELAND (*7) / MYSTERIO (*5) / Electrafixion: BURNED (*6) / Will Sergeant: THEMES FOR GRIND (*3)

IAN McCULLOCH (b. 5 May'59) – vocals, guitar (ex-CRUCIAL THREE) **WILL SERGEANT** (b.12 Apr'58) – lead guitar / **LES PATTINSON** (b.18 Apr'58) – bass (& 'ECHO' a drum machine)

			Zoo	not iss.
Mar 79.	(7") (CAGE 004) **PICTURES ON MY WALL. / READ IT IN BOOKS**		▢	–
	(re-iss. Mar91 on 'Document' 12"/cd-s; DC 3/+CD)			

—— **PETE DE FREITAS** (b. 2 Aug'61, Port Of Spain, Trinidad) – drums repl. 'ECHO'

			Korova	Sire
Apr 80.	(7") (KOW 1) **RESCUE. / SIMPLE STUFF** (12"+=) (KOW 1T) – Pride.		62	–
Jul 80.	(lp/c) (KODE/CODE 1) <6096> **CROCODILES** – Going up / Stars are stars / Pride / Monkeys / Crocodiles / Rescue / Villier's terrace / Pictures on my wall / All that jazz / Happy death men. (re-iss. Nov80 w/ free 7"; SAM 128) DO IT CLEAN. / READ IT IN BOOKS (re-iss. 1989 on 'WEA' lp/c/cd; same/same/2423162)		17	▢
Sep 80.	(7") (KOW 11) **THE PUPPET. / DO IT CLEAN**		▢	▢
Apr 81.	(12"ep)(c-ep) (ECHOZ 1)(ECHO 1M) **SHINE SO HARD** (live) – Crocodiles / Zimbo / Over the wall / All that jazz.		37	–
May 81.	(lp/c) (KODE/CODE 3) <3569> **HEAVEN UP HERE** – Show of strength / With a hip / Over the wall / It was a pleasure / A promise / Heaven up here / The disease / All my colours / No dark things / Turquoise days / All I want. (cd-iss. Jul88 on 'WEA'; 2432173)		10	▢
Jul 81.	(7"/12") (KOW 15/+T) **A PROMISE. / BROKE MY NECK**		49	–
May 82.	(7") (KOW 24) **THE BACK OF LOVE. / THE SUBJECT** (12"+=) (KOW 24T) – Fuel.		19	–
Jan 83.	(7") (KOW 26) **THE CUTTER. / WAY OUT AND UP WE GO** (w/ free c-ep+=) (KOW 26C) – The cutter / Villier's terrace / Ashes to ashes (stars are stars) / Monkeys / Read it in books. (12"+=) (KOW 26T) – Zimbo (live).		8	–
Jan 83.	(lp/c)(cd) (KODE/CODE 6) <23770> **PORCUPINE** – The cutter / The back of love / My white devil / Clay / Porcupine / Heads will roll / Ripeness / Higher hell / Gods will be gods / In bluer skies. (free ltd.c-ep w/ above lp) – 'JOHN PEEL SESSIONS' (re-iss. Jul88 on 'WEA' lp/c/cd; same/same/K 400 272)		2	▢
Feb 83.	(7") **THE CUTTER. / GODS WILL BE GODS**		▢	▢
Jul 83.	(7") (KOW 28) **NEVER STOP. / HEADS WILL ROLL** (12"+=) (KOW 28T) – ('A'-Discotheque) / ('B'-Summer version) / The original cutter (A drop in the ocean).		15	–
Jan 84.	(7") (KOW 32) **THE KILLING MOON. / DO IT CLEAN** (12"+=) (KOW 32T) – ('A'-All night version).		9	–

Jan 84.	(m-lp) <23987> **ECHO AND THE BUNNYMEN** – Back of love / Never stop / Rescue / The cutter / Do it clean.		–	▢
Apr 84.	(lp/c)(cd) (KODE/CODE 8)(K 240388-2) <25084> **OCEAN RAIN** – Silver / Nocturnal me / Crystal days / The yo yo man / Thorn of crowns / The killing moon / Seven seas / My kingdom / Ocean rain.		4	87 Jun84
Apr 84.	(7") (KOW 34) **SILVER. / ANGELS AND DEVILS** (12"+=) (KOW 34T) – Silver (Tidal wave).		30	▢
Jun 84.	(7") (KOW 35) **SEVEN SEAS. / ALL YOU NEED IS LOVE** (12"+=/d7"+=) (KOW 35 T/F) – The killing Moon / Stars are stars (acoustic) / Villier's terrace (acoustic).		16	–
Oct 85.	(7"/7"pic-d) (KOW 43/+P) **BRING ON THE DANCING HORSES. / OVER MY SHOULDER** (ext.12"+=) (KOW 43T) – Beds, bugs and ballyhoo. (d7"+=) (KOW 43F) – Villier's terrace / Monkeys.		21	▢
Nov 85.	(lp/c)(pic-lp)(cd) (KODE/CODE 13)(KODE 13P)(240 767-2) <25360> **SONGS TO LEARN AND SING** (compilation) – Rescue / The puppet / Do it clean / The promise / The back of love / The cutter / Never stop / The killing moon / Silver / Seven seas / Bring on the dancing horses. (c+=/cd+=) – Pride / Simple stuff / Read it in books / Angels and devils. (free ltd.c-s w/ same extra tracks)		6	▢

—— (Feb86) temp. **MARK FOX** – drums (ex-HAIRCUT 100) repl. DE FREITAS until return Sep'86.

			WEA	Sire
Jun 87.	(7") (YZ 134) **THE GAME. / SHIP OF FOOLS** (12"+=/12"w poster+=) (YZ 134T/+W) – Lost and found.		28	–
Jul 87.	(lp/c)(cd) (WX 108/+C)(242 137-2) <25597> **ECHO AND THE BUNNYMEN** – The game / Over you / Bedbugs and ballyhoo / All in your mind / Bombers bay / Lips like sugar / Lost and found / New direction / Blue blue ocean / Satellite / All my life. (re-iss. cd Nov94)		4	51
Jul 87.	(7"/7"gf/7"box) (YZ 144/+V/B) **LIPS LIKE SUGAR. / ROLLERCOASTER** (12"+=) (YZ 144T/+X) – People are strange.		36	▢
Feb 88.	(7"/c-s) (YZ 175/+C) **PEOPLE ARE STRANGE. / RUN RUN RUN** (live) (12"+=) (YZ 175T) – Paint it black / Friction. (re-iss. Feb91 7"/c-s; YZ 567/+C /12"/cd-s; YZ 567 T/CD) – hit UK No.34)		29	▢

—— They split some unofficial time in '88. Re-formed after McCULLOCH went solo. PETE DE FREITAS joined SEX GODS. He died in motorcycle accident 14 Jun '89.

—— **SERGEANT** and **PATTINSON** reformed group early 1990, with newcomers **NOEL BURKE** (b.Belfast, N.Ireland) – vocals (ex-St.VITAS DANCE) / **JACK BROCKMAN** – keyboards / **DAMON REECE** – drums

			Korova	Sire
Oct 90.	(7"/c-s) (9031 72796-7/-4) **ENLIGHTEN ME. / LADY, DON'T FALL BACKWARDS** (12"+=/cd-s+=) (9031 72796-1/-2) – ('A'extended).		▢	▢
Nov 90.	(cd)(c/lp) (9031 72553-2)(CODE/KODE 14) <26388> **REVERBERATION** – Freaks dwell / Cut and dried / Revilement / Flaming red / Salvatore / Fine thing / Gone, gone, gone / Enlighten me / King of your castle / Senseless / Thick skinned world. (cd+=) – False goodbyes.		▢	Dec90

			Euphoric	not iss.
Oct 91.	(12"ep/cd-ep) (E 001 T/CDS) **PROVE ME WRONG. / FINE THING / REVERBERATION** (live)		▢	–
Mar 92.	(12"/cd-s) (K 002 T/CD) **INSIDE ME, INSIDE YOU. / WIGGED OUT WORLD**		▢	–

—— The BUNNYMEN disbanded soon after the above and LES joined TERRY HALL'S backing group.

WILL SERGEANT

			WEA	not iss.
Jul 82.	(7") (K 19238) **FAVOURITE BRANCHES. / (b-side by Ravi Shankar & Bill Lovelady)**		▢	–

			92 Happy C.	not iss.
Mar 83.	(lp) (HAPLP 1) **THEMES FOR "GRIND"** – Grind starts the generator / The wheel turns / The small screen flickers. (cd-iss. Jan98 +=; HAPSCD 1) – Theme / Favourite branches / Aquarius dub.		▢	–

			Ochre	not iss.
1995.	(7"orange) (OCH 003) **COSMOS. / VENUS IN FLARES**		▢	–

Ian McCULLOCH

IAN McCULLOCH – vocals while still a member of The BUNNYMEN

			Korova	not iss.
Nov 84.	(7"/10") (KOW 40/+L) **SEPTEMBER SONG. / COCKLES & MUSSELS** (12"+=) (KOW 40T) – ('A'extended).		51	–

—— Now solo his back-up came from **RAY SHULMAN** – keyboards, programmer, bass, producer / plus guests **MICHAEL JOBSON** – bass / **BORIS WILLIAMS** – drums / **OLLE REMO** – drum programmer / **LIZ FRASER** – vox (of COCTEAU TWINS)

			WEA	Sire
Aug 89.	(7"/7"box/c-s) (YZ 417/+B/C) **PROUD TO FALL. / POTS OF GOLD** (12") (YZ 417T) – ('A'extended) / ('A'side) / The dead end. (cd-s) (YZ 417CD) – (above 3 tracks) / ('A'version). (12") (YZ 417TX) – ('A'side / Everything is real / The circle game.		51	–
Sep 89.	(lp/c)(cd) (WX 303/+C)(2292 46225-2) <26012> **CANDLELAND** – The flickering wall / The white hotel / Proud to fall / The cape / Candleland / Horse's head / Faith and healing / I know you well / In bloom / Start again.		18	▢
Nov 89.	(7"/c-s) (YZ 436/+C) **FAITH AND HEALING (remix). / TOAD** ('A'mix-12"+=) (YZ 436T) – Fear of the known.		▢	▢

(cd-s++=) *(YZ 436CD)* – Rocket ship.
(12") *(YZ 436TX)* – ('A'side) / Fear of the known / Rocket ship.
Apr 90. (7"/c-s) *(YZ 436/+C)* **CANDLELAND (THE SECOND
COMING). / THE WORLD IS FLAT** | 75 | – |
(12"+=/12"gf+=/cd-s+=) *(YZ 452 T/TG/CD)* – Big days / Wassailing in the night.

—— His backing band from late '89, were The PRODIGAL SONS; **MIKE MOONEY** –
guitar / **JOHN McEVOY** – guitar, keyboards / **EDGAR SUMMERTIME** – bass / **STEVE
HUMPHRIES** – drums

	East West	Warners
Feb 92. (7"/c-s) *(YZ 643/+C)* **LOVER, LOVER, LOVER. / WHITE
HOTEL (acoustic) / THE GROUND BELOW** | 47 | – |
('A'-Indian Dawn remix-12"+=/cd-s+=) *(YZ 643T)* – Vibor blue (acoustic).
Apr 92. (lp/c)(cd) *(WX 453/+C)(<9031 76264-2>)* **MYSTERIO** | 46 | – |
– Mayreal world / Close your eyes / Dug for love / Honeydrip / Damnation / Lover,
lover, lover / Webbed / Pomegranate / Vibor blue / Heaven's gate / In my head.
Apr 92. (7"/c-s) *(YZ 660/+C)* **DUG FOR LOVE. / POMMEGRANITE
(live)** | | – |
(12"+=)(cd-s+=) *(YZ 660 T/CD)* – Do it clean (live) / In my head (live).

ELECTRAFIXION

—— **IAN McCULLOCH** – vocals, guitar / **WILL SERGEANT** – guitar / **LEON DE SYLVA** –
bass / **TONY McGUIGAN** – drums

	WEA	Warners
Nov 94. (c-ep/12"ep/cd-ep) *(YZ 865 C/T/CD)* **THE ZEPHYR EP** | 47 | – |
– Zephyr / Burned / Mirrorball / Rain on me.
Sep 95. (7"red/c-s) *(YZ 977 X/C)* **LOWDOWN. / HOLY GRAIL** | 54 | – |
(cd-s+=) *(YZ 977CD)* – Land of the dying sun / Razors edge.
Sep 95. (cd/c) *(0630 11248-2/-4) <61793>* **BURNED** | 38 | Oct95 |
– Feel my pulse / Sister pain / Lowdown / Timebomb / Zephyr / Never / Too far
gone / Mirrorball / Who's been sleeping in my head? / Hit by something / Bed of
nails.
Oct 95. (c-s) *(WEA 022C)* **NEVER / NOT OF THIS WORLD** | 58 | – |
(cd-s+=) *(WEA 022CD)* – Subway train / Lowdown (rest of the trash mix).
(cd-s) *(WEA 022CDX)* – ('A'side) / Lowdown / Work it on out / Never (Utah Saints
blizzard on mix) / Sister pain.
Mar 96. (cd-ep) *(WEA 037CD1)* **SISTER PAIN / FEEL MY PULSE /
ZEPHYR / LOWDOWN (live)** | 27 | – |
(cd-ep) *(WEA 037CD2)* – ('A'side) / Burned / Loose (live) / Who's been sleeping
in my head (acoustic).
(cd-ep) *(WEA 037CD3)* – ('A'live) / Holy grail (live) / Never (live) / Too far gone
(live).

—— the last set-up issued a very limited gold-7" in Sep'97, 'BASEBALL BILL' released
on 'Phree' (PHREE 1)

ECHO & THE BUNNYMEN

—— the original trio (**McCULLOCH, SEARGEANT + PATTINSON**) re-formed

	London	Polygram
Jun 97. (7") *(LON 396)* **NOTHING LASTS FOREVER. /
WATCHTOWER** | 8 | – |
(cd-s+=) *(LONCD 396)* – Polly / Colour me in.
(cd-s) *(LONCDP 396)* – ('A'side) / Antelope / Hurracaine / Jonny.
Jul 97. (cd/c/lp) *(<828905-2/-4/-1>)* **EVERGREEN** | 8 | – |
– Don't let it get you down / In my time / I want to be there (when you come) /
Evergreen / I'll fly tonight / Nothing lasts forever / Baseball Bill / Altamont / Just a
touch away / Empire state halo / Too young to kneel / Forgiven. *(d-cd-iss. Nov97;
828980-2) (cd re-iss. Sep99; 3984 29642-2)*
Aug 97. (7") *(LON 399)* **I WANT TO BE THERE (WHEN YOU COME). /
KILLING MOON (session)** | 30 | – |
(cd-s+=) *(LONCD 399)* – Nothing lasts forever (session)
(cd-s) *(LOCDP 399)* – ('A'side) / Sense of life / Beyond the green.
Oct 97. (7") *(LON 406)* **DON'T LET IT GET YOU DOWN. / OVER
THE WALL** | 50 | – |
(cd-s+=) *(LONCD 406)* – Back of love.
(cd-s) *(LONCDP 406)* – ('A'side) / Rescue / Altamont.

—— In Jun'98, McCULLOCH provided ENGLAND UNITED with their World Cup
song, '(HOW DOES IT FEEL TO BE) ON TOP OF THE WORLD' which hit Top
10.

—— a few months later, a joint single, 'GET IN THE CAR' with The FUN LOVIN'
CRIMINALS, was withdrawn from release

Mar 99. (7") *(LON 424)* **RUST. /** | 22 | |
(cd-s+=) *(LONCD 424)* –
(cd-s) *(LONCDP 424)* –
Apr 99. (cd/c) *(556080-2/-4)* **WHAT ARE YOU DOING WITH YOUR
LIFE?** | 21 | |
– What are you doing with your life? / Rust / Get in the car / Baby rain / History
chimes / Lost on you / Morning sun / When it all blows over / Fools like us.

– compilations, others, etc. –

Nov 88. (12"ep/cd-ep) *Strange Fruit; (SFPS/+CD 060)* **THE PEEL
SESSIONS** (15.8.79) | | – |
– Read it in books / Stars are stars / I bagsy yours / Villier's terrace. *(re-iss. cd-ep
Dec94; same)*
Jul 90. (7") *Old Gold; (OG 9939)* **THE KILLING MOON. / SEVEN
SEAS** | | – |
Jul 90. (7") *Old Gold; (OG 9941)* **THE CUTTER. / THE BACK OF
LOVE** | | – |
Nov 91. (cd/lp) *Windsong; (WIN CD/LP 006)* **BBC RADIO 1 LIVE IN
CONCERT (live)** | | – |
Mar 93. (cd/c) *Pickwick-WEA; (4509-91886-2/-4)* **THE CUTTER**
(re-iss. Sep95 on 'Warners'; same) | | – |
Jun 97. (cd/c) *W.E.A.; (0630 19103-2/-4)* **BALLYHOO – THE BEST OF
ECHO & THE BUNNYMEN** | 59 | – |
– Rescue / Do it clean / Villier's terrace / All that jazz / Over the wall / A promise /

The disease / The back of love / The cutter / Never stop / The killing moon / Silver /
Seven seas / Bring on the dancing horses / People are strange / The game / Lips like
sugar / Bedbugs & ballyhoo.

ECHOBELLY

Formed: London, England . . . 1992 by Anglo-Asian, SONYA AURORA
MADAN, alongside co-writer and guitarist, GLENN JOHANSSON, ALEX
KEYSER and ANDY HENDERSON. With MADAN's BLONDIE-esque
vocals set to a SMITHS-style musical backdrop, ECHOBELLY were one of
Brit-pop's early leading lights, debuting in late '93 with the 'BELLYACHE'
EP. Adding former CURVE guitar abuser, DEBBIE SMITH (who had
initially filled in for the injured JOHANSSON on a tour of the States with
MORRISSEY, one of their biggest fans apparently!) and signing to the
independent 'Fauve' label, the band released a debut album, 'EVERYONE'S
GOT ONE' (as in EGO), in summer '94. Its jagged indie pop and intelligent,
aware lyrics drew considerable critical acclaim and, combining studied cool
with a vaguely PC agenda, MADAN became something of a female figurehead
for the genre along with LOUISE WENER (SLEEPER) and JUSTINE
FRISCHMANN (ELASTICA). A Top 10 UK hit, the album's success spurred
them on to greater things as the Britpop phenomena reached its zenith in
the summer of '95. That year's follow-up set, 'ON', was a bigger budget
affair which nevertheless still managed to capture ECHOBELLY's abrasive
immediacy, the record making the UK Top 5. The songwriting was as caustic
as ever, singles 'KING OF THE KERB' and 'DARK THERAPY', making the
Top 30. By the release of 1997's 'LUSTRA', however, the Britpop bubble had
long since burst and, along with acts such as SLEEPER, ECHOBELLY seemed
to be at the sharp end of the backlash.

Album rating: EVERYONE'S GOT ONE (*6) / ON (*5) / LUSTRA (*4)

SONYA AURORA MADAN – vocals / **GLENN JOHANSSON** – guitar / **ALEX KEYSER** –
bass, piano / **ANDY HENDERSON** – drums

	Pandemonium	not iss.
Nov 93. (12"ep/cd-ep) *(PANN/+CD 001)* **BELLYACHE** | | – |
– Give her a gun / Call me names / England swings.
Jan 94. (12"ep/cd-ep) *(PANN/+CD 002)* **BELLYACHE / SLEEPING
HITLER. / GIVE HER A GUN / I DON'T BELONG HERE** | | – |
(re-iss. May94; PANN/+CD 003)

	Fauve-Epic	Epic
Mar 94. (7"/c-s) *(FAUV 001/+C)* **INSOMNIAC. / TALENT** | 47 | – |
(12"+=) *(FAUV 001T)* – ('A'mix).
(cd-s++=) *(FAUV 001CD)* – Centipede.

—— added **DEBBIE SMITH** – guitar noise

Jun 94. (7"/c-s) *(FAUV 002/+C)* **I CAN'T IMAGINE THE WORLD
WITHOUT ME. / VENUS WHEEL** | 39 | – |
(12"+=/cd-s+=) *(FAUV 002 T/CD)* – Sober.
Aug 94. (cd/c/lp) *(FAUV 3 CD/C/LPS) <66775>* **EVERYONE'S GOT
ONE** | 8 | Oct94 |
– Today tomorrow sometime never / Father, ruler, king, computer / Give her a gun /
I can't imagine the world without me / Bellyache / Taste of you / Insomniac / Call
me names / Close . . . but / Cold feet warm heart / Scream.
Oct 94. (7"/c-s/12") *(FAUV 004/+C/T)* **CLOSE . . . BUT. / SO LA DI
DA** | 59 | – |
(cd-s+=) *(FAUV 004CD)* – I can't image the world without me (live) / Cold feet
warm heart (live).

	Fauve-Epic	Work–Columbia
Aug 95. (c-s) *(FAUV 5C)* **GREAT THINGS / HERE COMES THE SCENE** | 13 | – |
(cd-s+=) *(FAUV 5CD)* – God's guest list / On turn off.
(cd-s) *(FAUV 5CDX)* – ('A'side) / On turn on / Bunty / One after 5 a.m.
Sep 95. (cd/c/lp) *(FAUV 6 CD/C/LP) <67368>* **ON** | 4 | Oct95 |
– Oar fiction / King of the kerb / Great things / Natural animal / Go away / Pantyhose
and roses / Something hot in a cold country / Four letter word / Nobody like you /
In the year / Dark therapy / Worms are angels.
Oct 95. (c-s) *(FAUV 7C)* **KING OF THE KERB / CAR FICTION
(French)** | 25 | – |
(cd-s+=) *(FAUV 7CD)* – On turn on (acoustic) / Natural animal (acoustic).
(cd-s) *(FAUV 7CDX)* – ('A'live) / I can't imagine the world without me (live) /
Insomniac (live) / Great things (live).
Feb 96. (7"blue-ep/c-ep/cd-ep) *(FAUV 8/+C/CD)* **DARK THERAPY /
WE KNOW BETTER. / ATOM / ALOHA LOLITA** | 20 | – |

—— (Aug'95) **JAMES HARRIS** – bass; repl. KEYSER

	Epic	Epic
Aug 97. (c-s/cd-s) *(664815-4/-2)* **THE WORLD IS FLAT / HOLDING
THE WIRE / THE WORLD IS FLAT (mix)** | 31 | – |
(cd-s+=) *(664815-5)* – Drive myself distracted / Falling flame.
Oct 97. (c-s) *(665245-4)* **HERE COMES THE BIG RUSH / MOUTH
ALMIGHTY** | 56 | – |
(cd-s+=) *(665245-2)* – Tesh.
(cd-s) *(665245-5)* – ('A'mixes).
Nov 97. (cd/c) *(<488967-2/-4>)* **LUSTRA** | 47 | |
– Bulldog baby / I'm not a saint / Here comes the big rush / Iris art / The world is
flat / Everyone knows better / Wired on / O / Bleed / Paradise / Angel B / Lustra.

EDDIE & THE HOT RODS (dig out; Great Alt & Indie . . .)

Duane EDDY

Born: 26 Apr'38, Corning, New York, USA. Moving with his family to Phoenix, Arizona, in his early teens, DUANE began getting seriously involved in the local music scene after dropping out of high school. Crucial to the development of his famous guitar twang was LEE HAZLEWOOD, a local DJ and all-round music biz hustler who signed EDDY's band, The REBELS (comprising AL CASEY, BUDDY WHEELER, DONNIE OWENS, CORKY CASEY, MIKE BERMANI and PIAS JOHNSON) to 'Jamie', a label he co-ran with 'American Bandstand' host, Dick Clark. Soon DUANE was touring with Clark's Caravan of Stars and following a one-off single for the small 'Ford' label, 'RAMROD' (released as The REBELS), the group released their debut single (now trading as DUANE EDDY & THE REBELS) for 'Jamie' in the shape of 'MOVIN 'N' GROOVIN'. EDDY's unique guitar sound was created by feeding the sound from the bass strings of his beloved Gretsch through a storage tank echo chamber in HAZLEWOOD's Ramco studio. The resulting grimy reverberation laid the basis for a string of transatlantic Top 40 hits beginning with 1958's definitive 'REBEL ROUSER', a single which narrowly missed the US Top 5 and established EDDY's instrumental guitar/honking sax sound at the forefront of the era's rapidly evolving pop/rock scene. The track was featured (alongside subsequent hits 'CANNONBALL', 'THE LONELY ONE' and a re-issued 'RAMROD') on his brilliantly titled debut album, 'HAVE TWANGY GUITAR WILL TRAVEL' (1959). That summer also saw EDDY score his biggest hit to date, narrowly missing the Top 5 in Britain with the classic Henry Mancini-penned 'PETER GUNN THEME'. While EDDY's sound was pivotal in the development of America's massive surf craze via his influence on the likes of The VENTURES and DICK DALE, he was also extremely influential and indeed more popular in the UK where The SHADOWS approximated their own take on instrumental twang; EDDY narrowly missed the UK No.1 spot with sophomore album, 'THE TWANG'S THE THANG' (1960) as well as singles, 'BECAUSE THEY'RE YOUNG' and 'PEPE'. In 1962 DUANE signed to 'R.C.A.' and embarked on a solo career, roaring back into the UK Top 10 after a lean spell with the 'TWISTIN' 'N' TWANGIN' album and glorious high noon cheesiness of 'THE BALLAD OF PALADIN'. He even hooked up with a gaggle of female backing singers (THE REBELETTES) for '(DANCE WITH THE) GUITAR MAN', another UK Top 5 smash later that year. Yet ironically it was to be the success of British Invasion acts like The BEATLES (whose GEORGE HARRISON was also clearly influenced by the twang) that would finally put paid to EDDY's five year chart run. His last Top 40 hit came in the shape of Spring 63's 'LONELY BOY, LONELY GUITAR', although the likes of the haunting DAVID GATES-penned 'BLOWIN' UP A STORM' (from the 1963 album, 'TWANGIN' UP A STORM') stands up against his best work. Thereafter a series of theme albums failed to cut the mustard ('DUANE GOES BOB DYLAN'?! c'mon!). A subsequent move to 'Reprise', more ridiculously-titled albums and a final brace of independent singles later, EDDY took a sabbatical from the recording front, taking time out during which he produced PHIL EVERLY's 1973 solo album, 'Star Spangled Springer'. Back with The REBELETTES in 1975, he scored a one-off UK Top 10 hit for the 'G.T.O.' label with 'PLAY ME LIKE YOU PLAY YOUR GUITAR' although subsequent material for 'Elektra' and 'Capitol' failed to make any headway. More recently (1986), EDDY re-appeared on 'Top Of The Pops' alongside 80's electronic types, ART OF NOISE, who'd covered 'PETER GUNN' in suitably idiosyncratic style. This encouraged him to record an eponymous comeback album, released by 'Capitol' in 1987 and featuring the not inconsiderable production talents of PAUL McCARTNEY, JEFF LYNNE, GEORGE HARRISON and RY COODER. • **Trivia:** His photogenic appearance gained him acting experience in the 1960 film 'Because They're Young' (EDDY also cut the title track). A few years later he appeared in the films 'The Savage Seven' and 'Kona'.

Best CD compilation: TWANG THANG: ANTHOLOGY (*8)

The REBELS

featuring **DUANE EDDY** – guitar / **AL CASEY** – guitar, piano / **BUDDY WHEELER** – bass / **DONNIE OWENS** – guitar / **CORKY CASEY** – guitar / **MIKE BERMANI** – drums / **PIAS JOHNSON** – saxophone

	not iss.	Ford
Jan 58. (7",78) <500> RAMROD. / CARAVAN	-	

DUANE EDDY & THE REBELS

	London	Jamie	
Apr 58. (7",78) <1101> MOOVIN' N' GROOVIN'. / UP AND DOWN	-	72	
Aug 58. (7",78) (HL 8669) <1104> REBEL-ROUSER. / STALKIN'	19	6	Jun58
Oct 58. (7",78) (HL 8723) <1109> RAMROD. / WALKER		27	Aug58
Dec 58. (7",78) (HL 8764) <1111> CANNONBALL. / MASON-DIXON LINE	22	15	Nov58
Mar 59. (7",78) (HLW 8821) <1117> THE LONELY ONE. / DETOUR		23	Jan59
Apr 59. (7",78) (HLW 8879) <1122> YEP! / THREE-30 BLUES	-	30	
Jun 59. (lp) (HA-W 2160) <3000> HAVE "TWANGY" GUITAR – WILL TRAVEL	6	5	Jan59
	– Lonesome road / I almost lost my mind / Rebel-rouser / Three-30-blues / Cannonball / The lonely one / Detour / Stalkin' / Ramrod / Anytime / Movin' n' Groovin' / Loving you. (cd-iss. Feb90 on 'Motown'; WD 72688) (cd re-iss. Aug99 on 'Jamie'; JAMIE 4007-2)			
Jun 59. (7",78) (HLW 8879) PETER GUNN THEME. / YEP!	6	-	
Aug 59. (7",78) (HLW 8929) <1126> FORTY MILES OF BAD ROAD. / THE QUIET THREE	11	9 46	

Jun59 Oct 59.	(lp) (HA-W 2191) <3006> ESPECIALLY FOR YOU	6	24 Aug59
	– Peter Gunn / Only child / Lover / Fuzz / Yep! / Along the Navajo trail / Just because / Quiniela / Trouble in mind / Tuxedo Junction / Hard times / Along came Linda.		
Dec 59.	(7",78) (HLW 9007) SOME KIND-A EARTHQUAKE. / FIRST LOVE, FIRST TEARS	12	37 59 Oct59
Dec 59.	(7",78) <1144> BONNIE CAME BACK. / LOST ISLAND	-	26
Feb 60.	(7",78) (9050) BONNIE CAME BACK. / MOVIN' & GROOVIN'	12	-
Apr 60.	(lp) (HA-W 2236) <3009> THE "TWANGS" THE "THANG"	2	18 Jan60
	– My blue Heaven / Tiger love and turnip greens / The last minute of innocence / Route No.1 / You are my sunshine / St.Louis blues / Night train to Memphis / The battle / Trombone / Blueberry hill / Rebel walk / Easy.		

—— His touring REBELS were now **AL CASEY** – bass / **JIM HORN** – sax / **LARRY KNECHTEL** – piano / **JIMMY TROXEL** – drums

Apr 60.	(7",78) (HLW 9104) <1151> SHAZAM! / THE SECRET SEVEN	4	45 Mar60
Jul 60.	(7",78) (HLW 9162) <1156> BECAUSE THEY'RE YOUNG. / REBEL WALK	2	4 May60
Sep 60.	(7") <1158> (WHY MUST I DIE) THE GIRL ON DEATH ROW. / WORDS MEAN NOTHING	-	
Oct 60.	(7") (HLW 9225) <1163> KOMMOTION. / THEME FOR MOON CHILDREN	13	78 Aug60
Oct 60.	(7") <1168> PETER GUNN. / ALONG THE NAVAJO TRAIL	-	27
Dec 60.	(lp) (HA-W 2285) <3011> SONGS OF OUR HERITAGE	13	
	– Cripple Creek / Riddle song / John Henry / Streets of Laredo / Prisoner's song / In the pines / Ole Joe Clark / Wayfarin' stranger / Top of Old Smokey / Mule train / Scarlet ribbons.		
Jan 61.	(7") (HLW 9257) <1175> PEPE. / LOST FRIEND	2	18 Dec60
Feb 61.	(lp) (HA-W 2325) <3021> A MILLION DOLLARS' WORTH OF TWANG (compilation)	5	11 Dec60
	– Up and down / Lost island / The quiet three / Bonnie came back / Because they're young / Moon children / Shazam! / The secret seven / Forty miles of bad road / Some kinda earthquake / First love, first tears / Kommotion. (cd-iss. Feb90 on 'Motown'; WD 72687)		
Apr 61.	(7") (HLW 9324) THEME FROM DIXIE. / THE BATTLE	7	-
Mar 61.	(7") <1183> THEME FROM DIXIE. / GIDGET GOES HAWAIIAN	-	39
May 61.	(7") <1187> RING OF FIRE. / BOBBY	-	84
Jun 61.	(7") (HLW 9370) RING OF FIRE. / GIDGET GOES HAWAIIAN	17	-
Aug 61.	(7") <1195> DRIVIN' HOME. / TAMMY	-	87
Aug 61.	(7") (HLW 9406) DRIVIN' HOME. / MY BLUE HEAVEN	30	-
Aug 61.	(7") <1200> MY BLUE HEAVEN. / ALONG CAME LINDA	-	50
Aug 61.	(lp) (HA-W 2373) <3019> GIRLS GIRLS GIRLS		93 Jul61
	– Brenda: I want to be wanted that's all you gotta do / I'm sorry / Sioux City Sue / Tommy / Big 'liza / Mary Ann / Annette / Tuesday / Sweet Cindy / Patricia / Mona Lisa / Connie / Carol.		

DUANE EDDY

		Parlophone Gregmark	
Sep 61.	(7") (R 4826) <5> CARAVAN. / (part 2)	42	
		London	Jamie
Jan 62	(7") (HLW 9477) <1206> THE AVENGER. / LONDONDERRY AIR		
Feb 62	(7") <1209> THE BATTLE. / TROMBONE	-	
Apr 62	(7") <1224> RUNAWAY PONY. / JUST BECAUSE	-	
		R.C.A.	R.C.A.
May 62.	(7") (RCA 1288) <7999> DEEP IN THE HEART OF TEXAS. / SAINTS AND SINNERS	19	78 Apr62
Aug 62.	(lp) (RD 27264) <LSP 2525> TWISTIN' N' TWANGIN'	8	82 May62
	– The peppermint twist / Twistin' 'n' twangin' / Let's twist again / Miss Twist / Sugartime twist / Exactly like you / Walkin' 'n' twistin' (I'm walkin') / Dear lady twist / Moanin' 'n' twistin' / Country twist / The twist / Twisting off a cliff.		
Aug 62.	(7") (RCA 1300) <8047> THE BALLAD OF PALADIN. / THE WILD WESTERNER	10	33 Jul62

DUANE EDDY & THE REBELETTES

(REBELETTES were female singers)

Oct 62.	(7") (RCA 1316) <8087> (DANCE WITH THE) GUITAR MAN. / STRETCHIN' OUT	4	12
Nov 62.	(lp; mono/stereo) (RD/SF 7510) <LSP 2576> TWANGY GUITAR – SILKY STRINGS	13	72 Oct62
	– High noon / Born to be with you / Secret love / Unchained melody / When I fall in love / Mirriam / Moon river / Bali Ha'l / Hi-lili, hi-lo / Angel on my shoulder / Memories of Madrid / Love me tender. (re-iss. 1970 on 'RCA-Camden'; CDS 1072)		
Jan 63.	(lp; mono/stereo) (RD/SF 7545) <LSP 2648> DANCE WITH THE GUITAR MAN	47	
	– Dance with the guitar man / Limbo rock / Wild Watusi / The scrape / New Hully Gully / Popeye (the hitchhiker) / Spanish twist / The climb / Loco-locomotion / Nashville stomp / Creamy mashed potatoes / Waltz of the wind. (cd-iss. Apr93)		
Feb 63.	(7") (RCA 1329) <8131> BOSS GUITAR. / THE DESERT RAT	27	28

DUANE EDDY

May 63.	(7") (RCA 1344) <8180> LONELY BOY, LONELY GUITAR. / JOSHIN'	35	82
Aug 63.	(7") (RCA 1357) <8214> YOUR BABY'S GONE SURFIN'. / SHUCKIN'	49	93
Aug 63.	(lp; mono/stereo) (RD/SF 7560) <LSP 2681> TWANG A COUNTRY SONG		
	– Sugar foot rag / Weary blues / Fireball mail / Please help me I'm falling / Wildwood flower / Precious memories / Crazy arms / Have you ever been lonely / The window up above / A satisfied mind / Making believe / Peace in the valley.		
Oct 63.	(7") (RCA 1369) MY BABY PLAYS THE SAME OLD SONG ON HIS GUITAR ALL NIGHT. / GUITAR'D AND FEATHERED		-
Oct 63.	(lp; mono/stereo) (RD/SF 7568) <LSP 2700> TWANGIN' UP A STORM		93

– Guitar child / All you gave to me / Giddy goose / Walk right in / He's so fine / Beach bound / Mr.Guitar man / Blowin' up a storm / My baby plays the same old song on his guitar all night long / Guitar'd and feathered / Soldier boy / Soul twist.

Nov 63. (7") *(RCA 1389)* <8276> **THE SON OF REBEL ROUSER. / THE STORY OF THREE LOVERS**   `-` `97`

Dec 63. (7") <8335> **GUITAR CHILD. / JERKY JALOPY**

Apr 64. (lp; mono/stereo) *(RD/SF 7621)* <LSP 2798> **LONELY GUITAR**
– I'm so lonesome I could cry / Long lonely days of winter / Along came Linda / Someday the rainbow / Gunsmoke / A home in the meadow / Danny boy / Shenandoah / Summer kiss / My destiny / Cryin' happy tears / Annie Laurie.

Jan 64. (7") <8376> **THEME FROM A SUMMER PLACE. / WATER SKIING**   `-`

Jul 64. (lp; mono/stereo) *(RD/SF 7656)* <LSP 2918> **WATER SKIING**   `-`
– Water skiing / Slalom rooster tail / The backward swan / Whip off / Jitterboard / Deep-water start / The wake ballet / Toe-hold side slide / Banana peels / In gear / Jumping the wake.

Oct 64. (7") *(RCA 1425)* <8442> **GUITAR STAR. / THE IGUANA**

Jan 65. (7") <8507> **MOONSHOT. / ROUGHNECK**

                                Colpix   *Colpix*

Aug 65. (7") <(PX 779)> **TRASH. / SOUTH PHOENIX**

Oct 65. (lp) <(PXL 490)> **DUANE A-GO-GO-GO!**
– Trash / Puddin' / Movin'n'groovin' / Choo choo a go go – toot toot! / Just to satisfy you / Around the block in 80 days (march in 'A') / Cottonmouth / If you've seen one, you've seen them all! / South Phoenix / Dream lover / Busted / I'm blue.

Dec 65. (7") <(PX 788)> **THE HOUSE OF THE RISING SUN. / DON'T THINK TWICE IT'S ALRIGHT**

Mar 66. (lp) <(PXL 494)> **DUANE GOES BOB DYLAN**
– Don't think twice / House of the rising sun / It ain't me babe / Not the loving kind / She belongs to me / All I really want to do / Houston / Love minus zero – no limit / Mr.Tambourine man / Blowin' in the wind / Swing low sweet chariot / Eve of destruction.

                                Reprise   *Reprise*

1966. (7") <795> **EL RANCHO GRANDE. / POPPA'S MOVIN' ON (I'M MOVIN' ON)**   `-`

1966. (7") *(RS 20504)* <0504> **DAYDREAM. / THIS GUITAR WAS MADE FOR TWANGIN'**

1967. (7") *(RS 20557)* <0557> **MONSOON. / ROARIN'**

1967. (7") <0622> **GUITAR ON MY MIND. / WICKED WOMAN FROM WICKENBURG**   `-`

1967. (lp; mono/stereo) <(RLP/RSLP 6218)> **THE BIGGEST TWANG OF THEM ALL**
– This guitar was / Made for twangin' / Batman / Monday Monday / Strangers in the night / Night train / Ballad of the green berets / Daydream / What now my love / Younger girl / Where were you when I needed you / A groovy kind of love / Mame.

1967. (7") <0662> **THIS TOWN. / THERE IS A MOUNTAIN**   `-`

1967. (7") *(RS 20690)* <0690> **NIKI HOEKY. / VELVET NIGHTS**

1967. (lp) *(RLP 6240)* <6240> **THE ROARING TWANGIES**
– Bye bye blues / Roarin' / A happy girl / Goofus / American patrol / Out on the town / Undecided / Born free / St.Louis blues march / Hello, Dolly / A string of pearls / Wicked woman from Wickenburg.

                                C.B.S.   *Columbia*

1969. (7") *(CBS 3962)* **BREAK MY MIND. / LOVING BIRD**

                                not iss.   *Uni*

1970. (7") <55237> **THE FIVE-SEVENTEEN. / SOMETHING**

                                not iss.   *Big Tree*

1970. (7") <157> **RENEGADE. / NIGHTLY NEWS**

                                not iss.   *Congress*

1970. (7") <6010> **PUT A LITTLE LOVE IN YOUR HEART. / FREIGHT TRAIN**   `-`

DUANE EDDY & THE REBELETTES

                                G.T.O.   *not iss.*

Feb 75. (7") *GT 11* **PLAY ME LIKE YOU PLAY YOUR GUITAR. / BLUE MONTANA SKY**   `9` `-`

Apr 75. (lp) *(GTLP 002)* **GUITAR MAN**   `-`
– Rock'n'roll guitar man / Night prowler / Son of a guitar man / Love theme from Romeo & Juliet / Play me like you play your guitar / Mark of Zorro / The man with the gold guitar / (Last night) I didn't get to sleep at all / Cannon ball rag / Blue Montana sky / Dance with the guitar man. (re-iss.Apr78 on 'Hallmark'; SHM 947)

Jun 75. (7") *(GT 25)* **THE MAN WITH THE GOLDEN GUITAR. / MARK OF ZORRO**

                                Target   *Target*

Oct 75. (7") <(101)> **LOVE CONFUSION. / LOVE IS A WARM EMOTION**

                                Elektra   *Elektra*

Nov 78. (7") <44018> **SPIES. / ROCKABILLY HOLIDAY**   `-` `-`

Mar 79. (7") <45359> **YOU ARE MY SUNSHINE. / 7 TO 8**   `-` `-`

—— made his live comeback in 1983 and In May '86 he featured on the ART OF NOISE single version of 'PETER GUNN' (this hit UK No.8 / US No.50 enabling him to return to solo work)

                                Capitol   *Capitol*

Sep 87. (7") *(CL 463)* **ROCKESTRA THEME. / BLUE CITY**   `-`
(12"+=) *(12CL 463)* – ('A'version).

Sep 87. (lp/c/cd) <EST/TCEST/CDEST 2034> **DUANE EDDY**   `-`
– Kickin' asphalt / Rockestra theme / Theme for something reading important / Spies / Blue city / The trembler / Los campaneros / Lost innocence / Rockabilly holiday / Last look back.

– compilations, others, etc. –

on 'London' UK / 'Jamie' US – unless otherwise mentioned

1958. (7"ep) *(RE 1175)* **REBEL ROUSER**   `-`

1959. (7"ep) *(RE-W 1216)* **THE LONELY ONE**

1959. (7"ep) *(JEP 100)* **MOVIN' N' GROOVIN'**   `-`

1959. (7"ep) *(RE-W 1217)* <JEP 300> **YEP!**

1959. (7"ep) *(JEP 301)* **DETOUR**

1960. (7"ep) <JEP 303> **SHAZAM!**   `-`

1960. (7"ep) *(RE-W 1252)* <JE 304> **BECAUSE THEY'RE YOUNG**   `-`

1960. (7"ep) *(RE-W 1257)* **TWANGY**   `-`

1961. (7"ep) *(RE-W 1287)* **PEPE**   `-`

1961. (7"ep) *(RE-W 1303)* **DUANE EDDY PLAYS MOVIE THEMES**   `-`

1961. (7"ep) *(RE-W 1341)* **TWANGY No.2**   `-`

Jun 62. (lp) *(HA-W 2435)* <3021> **A MILLION DOLLARS' WORTH OF TWANG VOL.2**   `18`
– The walker / Pepe / Lost friend / Theme from Dixie / Gidget goes Hawaiian / Ring of fire / Bobbie / Drivin' home / Tammy / The avenger / Londonderry air / Liza Jane.

1963. (7"ep) *R.C.A.; (RCX 7115)* **A COUNTRY TWANG**

1963. (7"ep) *R.C.A.; (RCX 7129)* **MR. TWANG**

1963. (7"ep) *R.C.A.; (RCX 7146)* **TWANGIN' UP A SMALL STORM**

1965. (7"ep) *Colpix; (PE 304)* **COTTONMOUTH**

1965. (lp; mono/stereo) *R.C.A.; (RD/SF 7689)* <LSP 2993> **TWANGIN' THE GOLDEN HITS**

Nov 65. (lp; mono/stereo) *R.C.A.; (RD/SF 7754)* / <LSP 3432> **TWANGSVILLE**

May 68. (7") *(HLW 1091)* **PETER GUNN. / REBEL ROUSER**

May 70. (lp) *(ZGW 105)* **MOVIN' 'N' GROOVIN'**
– Peter Gunn / Rebel rouser / Thirty three blues / Movin' 'n' groovin' / Forty miles of bad road / Shazam! / Some kinda earthquake / Only child / Blueberry hill / Hard times / The avenger / Because they're young.

May 75. (d-lp) *Deram; (DLL 5003-4)* **LEGEND OF ROCK**   `-`

Aug 78. (d-lp) *Pickwick; (PDA 043)* **THE COLLECTION**   `-`

Jan 79. (lp) *R.C.A.; (NL 12671)* **DUANE EDDY**   `-`

Oct 80. (7"m) *Creole; (CR 185)* **REBEL ROUSER. / ROCKIN' ROBIN / PONY TIME**   `-`

Oct 80. (7"m) *Creole; (CR 194)* **FORTY MILES OF BAD ROAD. / RAINDROPS / HONKY TONK**   `-`

Nov 80. (lp/c) *R.C.A.; (INT S/K 5056)* **20 TERRIFIC TWANGIES**   `-`

May 83. (d-lp/d-c) *Cambra; (CR/+T 065)* **THE FABULOUS DUANE EDDY**   `-`

Sep 84. (lp/c) *Nouveaux; (NML/ZCNML 1012)* **THE BEST OF DUANE EDDY**   `-`

Nov 84. (lp) *Magnum Force; (MFLP 031)* **REBEL ROUSIN'**   `-`

Jul 86. (d-lp/d-c) *R.C.A.; NL/NK 89246)* **FOREVER**   `-`

Sep 86. (lp/c) *Music For Pleasure; (MFP/TC-MFP 5777)* **GUITAR MAN**   `-`

Feb 87. (lp/c) *Arena; (ARA/+C 1004)* **DANCE WITH THE GUITAR MAN**   `-`

Feb 88. (cd) *Motown; (WD 72547)* **COMPACT COMMAND PERFORMANCES (21 GREATEST HITS)**   `-`

Apr 88. (cd) *Diamond; (CD 90119)* **DUANE EDDY**   `-`

May 89. (lp/c/cd) *Performance; (PF P/C/CD 1000)* **THE GUITAR MAN (20 CLASSIC TRACKS)**   `-`

Jun 91. (cd)(c) *R.C.A.; (CZ 425)(TCEMS 1405)* **TWANGY PEAKS**   `-`
– (DUANE A GO-GO / DUANE GOES DYLAN)

Mar 93. (cd) *R.C.A.; (74321 12699-2)* **2GETHER ON ONE**   `-`

May 94. (cd) *Bear Family; (BCD 15702)* **THAT CLASSIC TWANG**   `-`

May 94. (cd) *Bear Family; (BCD 15799)* **ESPECIALLY FOR YOU / GIRLS GIRLS GIRLS**   `-`

May 94. (cd) *Bear Family; (BCD 15807)* **THE "TWANGS" THE "THANG" / SONGS OF OUR HERITAGE**   `-`

Aug 94. (cd/c) *Ariola; (2/4 95041)* **ROCKIN' ME GUITAR**   `-`

Dec 94. (7xcd-box) *Bear Family; (BCD 15778)* **TWANGIN' FROM PHOENIX TO L.A. (THE JAMIE YEARS)**   `-`

May 94. (cd/c) *B.R. Music; (BR/+MC 149-2/-4)* **BECAUSE THEY'RE YOUNG**   `-`

Jun 94. (cd/c) *Ronco; (CD/TC SR 049)* **20 TWANGY HITS**   `-`
(re-iss. Jun99; CDSR 9006)

Nov 94. (cd/c) *See For Miles; (SEECD 417)* **HIS TWANGY GUITAR AND THE REBELS**   `-`
(re-iss. Nov96 & Sep99; same)

Apr 96. (cd/c) *Music; (CD6/MC7 010)* **SHAZAM!**   `-`

Jun 96. (cd) *R.C.A.; (74321 12701-2)* **THE R.C.A. YEARS**   `-`

Nov 96. (cd) *Hit; (CURCD 032)* **GHOSTRIDER**   `-`

Mar 97. (cd/c) *K-Tel; (ECD3/EMC2 314)* **THE BEST OF DUANE EDDY**   `-`

Sep 97. (cd) *Summit; (SUMCD 4146)* **THE BEST OF DUANE EDDY**   `-`

Sep 97. (cd) *Camden; (74321 51198-2)* **BOSS GUITAR**   `-`

Nov 97. (cd) *Eagle; (EABCD 024)* **THE MASTERS**   `-`

Dec 97. (cd) *World; (WR 31108)* **GREATEST HITS**   `-`

Apr 98. (cd) *Hallmark; (30859-2)* **PETER GUNN**   `-`

Jun 98. (cd) *One Way; (OW 34541)* **THE BEST OF DUANE EDDY / LONELY GUITAR**   `-`

Jun 98. (cd) *One Way; (OW 34542)* **DANCE WITH THE GUITAR MAN / TWISTIN' AND TWANGIN'**   `-`

Jun 98. (cd) *One Way; (OW 34543)* **TWANGIN' (THE GOLDEN HITS)**   `-`

Jun 98. (cd) *One Way; (OW 34545)* **TWANGY GUITAR / WATER SKI**   `-`

Feb 99. (cd/c) *Pulse; (PLS CD/MC 309)* **MR. TWANGY GUITAR**   `-`

The EDGE (see under ⇒ U2)

Dave EDMUNDS

Born: 15 Apr'44, Cardiff, Wales. After being in two local bands: The 99'ers and The RAIDERS in the mid-60's, he joined The IMAGE in 1966, breaking away with their drummer the following year to form The HUMAN BEANS. In 1968, this bunch evolved into LOVE SCULPTURE and smashed into the UK Top 5 with 'SABRE DANCE'. Two years on and now solo, EDMUNDS topped the UK charts with his version of Smiley Lewis's 'I HEAR YOU KNOCKIN', which also broke the US Top 10. EDMUNDS scored a further couple of UK Top 10 hits in a similar vein with The Ronettes' 'BABY I LOVE YOU' and The Chordettes 'BORN TO BE WITH YOU'. As well as appearing in the 1974 film, 'Stardust' (alongside DAVID ESSEX and KEITH MOON), EDMUNDS also had his hands full with his Rockfield studio in Wales, a perennially popular operation where he first met NICK LOWE; then bass player for BRINSLEY SCHWARZ, LOWE would subsequently collaborate with EDMUNDS on a number of occasions, The BRINSLEY's initially helping out on 1975's 'SUBTLE AS A FLYING MALLET'. Signing to LED ZEPPELIN's 'Swan Song' label shortly after, EDMUNDS formed a semi-permanent backing band, ROCKPILE, consisting of LOWE, guitarist BILLY BREMNER (no, not the wee Scottish footballer!) and drummer TERRY WILLIAMS, this formation making their debut on 'GET IT' (1977). With LOWE also co-writing, his knack for clever pop combined with EDMUNDS' instinctive rhythm and feel resulted in such enduring tracks as 'I KNEW THE BRIDE', a Top 30 hit in summer '77. Despite critical acclaim and the major success of the 'GIRLS TALK' (penned by ELVIS COSTELLO) and 'QUEEN OF HEARTS' singles in 1979, the accompanying album, 'REPEAT WHEN NECESSARY', only just scraped into the Top 40. Recorded under the ROCKPILE moniker, 1980's 'SECONDS OF PLEASURE' was EDMUNDS' first album under his new American contract with 'Columbia', the album achieving a healthy Top 30 US chart position on the back of a Stateside tour with BAD COMPANY. The singer fulfilled his obligations to 'Swan Song' with the following year's 'TWANGIN', his first without LOWE and Co. (LOWE continued to enjoy a relatively successful solo career, while WILLIAMS went on to join DIRE STRAITS). Recruiting a new band and signing to 'Arista' in the UK, EDMUNDS released the sturdy 'D.E. 7th' in 1982, before hooking up with ELO man, JEFF LYNNE for 'INFORMATION' (1983) and 'RIFF RAFF' (1984). He continued to produce an eclectic variety of acts throughout the 80's, the respect afforded him in this area a mark of the man's adaptability and musical intuition. The 90's meanwhile, saw EDMUNDS return with the star studded 'CLOSER TO THE FLAME' and his contribution to the MTV 'Unplugged' era, 'PLUGGED IN'. • Covers: The HUMAN BEANS covered MORNING DEW (Tim Rose). LOVE SCULPTURE covered WANG DANG DOODLE (Willie Dixon) / SABRE DANCE (Khachaturian) / ON THE ROAD AGAIN (Wilbert Harrison) / SUMMERTIME (Gershwin). EDMUNDS solo; BLUE MONDAY (Fats Domino) / GET OUT OF DENVER (Bob Seger) / HEY GOOD LOOKIN' (Hank Williams) / GIRLS TALK (Elvis Costello) / CRAWLING FROM THE WRECKAGE (Graham Parker) / SINGING THE BLUES (Guy Mitchell) / WRONG WAY (Difford-Tilbrook of Squeeze) / ALMOST SATURDAY NIGHT (John Fogerty) / FROM SMALL THINGS BIG THINGS COME (Bruce Springsteen) / OUTLAW BLUES (Bob Dylan) / etc. • Trivia: EDMUNDS produced many artists, including SHAKIN' STEVENS & THE SUNSETS in 1970, BRINSLEY SCHWARZ (1974) / FLAMIN' GROOVIES (1976) / FABULOUS THUNDERBIRDS (1980-81) / EVERLY BROTHERS (1983-86) / k.d.LANG (1988) / NICK LOWE (1989) / DION (1989) / STRAY CATS (1980 + 1989).

Album rating: Love Sculpture: BLUES HELPING (*4) / FORMS AND FEELINGS (*4) / ROCKPILE (*5; as Dave Edmunds' Rockpile) / SUBTLE AS A FLYING MALLET (*5) / GET IT (*6) / TRACKS ON WAX (*6) / REPEAT WHEN NECESSARY (*7) / SECONDS OF PLEASURE (*7; as Rockpile) / THE BEST OF DAVE EDMUNDS compilation (*7) / TWANGIN' (*5) / D.E. 7th (*5) / INFORMATION (*4) / RIFF RAFF (*4) / I HEAR YOU ROCKIN' (*5; as Dave Edmunds Band) / CLOSER TO THE FLAME (*4) / THE ANTHOLOGY (1968-1990) compilation (*7) / PLUGGED IN (*5)

HUMAN BEANS

DAVE EDMUNDS – vocals, guitar / **TOMMY RILEY** – drums / **JOHN WILLIAMS** – bass

			Columbia	not iss.
Jul 67.	(7")	(DB 8230) **MORNING DEW. / IT'S A WONDER**	□	–

LOVE SCULPTURE

(same line-up)

			Parlophone	Rare
Feb 68.	(7")	(R 5664) **RIVER TO ANOTHER DAY. / BRAND NEW WOMAN**	□	□
——		**BOB 'CONGO' JONES** – drums repl. RILEY		
Sep 68.	(7")	(R 5731) **WANG-DANG-DOODLE. / THE STUMBLE**	□	–
Nov 68.	(7")	(R 5744) **SABRE DANCE. / THINK OF LOVE**	5	–
Dec 68.	(lp; mono/stereo)	(PMC/PCS 7059) <505> **BLUES HELPING**		

– The stumble / 3 o'clock blues / I believe to my soul / Blues helping / Summertime (from Porgy and Bess) / Don't answer the door / So unkind / On the road again / Wang-dang-doodle / Come back baby / Shake your hips.

			Parlophone	Parrot
Feb 69.	(7")	(R 5807) **FARENDOLE. / SEAGULL**		–
Jan 70.	(lp)	<PCS 7090> <71035> **FORMS AND FEELINGS**		

– In the land of the few / Seagull / Nobody's talking / People people / Why (how now) / Sabre dance (from 'Gayaneh-Ballet') / You can't catch me / Farandole.

Feb 70.	(7")	(R 5831) **IN THE LAND OF THE FEW. / PEOPLE PEOPLE**	□	–

—— **TERRY WILLIAMS** – drums (ex-DREAM) repl. JONES who joined SASSAFRASS / added **MICKEY GEE** – guitar (ex-JOE COCKER'S GREASE BAND ex-TOM JONES)

—— split soon after; GEE and WILLIAMS later joined MAN

DAVE EDMUNDS' ROCKPILE

EDMUNDS – multi-instrumentalist; retained **JOHN WILLIAMS**

			M.A.M.	M.A.M.
Nov 70	(7")	(MAM 1) <3601> **I HEAR YOU KNOCKING. / BLACK BILL**	1	4

			Regal Zonophone	M.A.M.
Mar 71.	(7")	(RZ 3032) <3608> **I'M COMING HOME. / COUNTRY ROLL**	□	75

Jul 71.	(7")	(RZ 3037) **BLUE MONDAY. / I'LL GET ALONG**	□	□

—— guests included **TERRY WILLIAMS** – drums / **B.J. COLE** – pedal steel guitar / **ANDY FAIRWEATHER-LOW** – guitar (ex-AMEN CORNER)

Jun 72.	(lp)	(SLRZ 1026) <MAM 3> **ROCKPILE**		

– Down down down / It ain't easy / I hear you knockin' / Hell of a pain / You can't catch me / Dance dance dance / Outlaw blues / Egg or the hen.

Jul 72.	(7")	(RZ 3059) **DOWN DOWN DOWN. / IT AIN'T EASY**	□	□

DAVE EDMUNDS

went solo playing nearly every instrument himself

			Rockfield	R.C.A.
Dec 72.	(7")	(ROC 1) **BABY I LOVE YOU. / MAYBE**	8	
May 73.	(7")	(ROC 2) **BORN TO BE WITH YOU. / PICK AXE BLUES**	5	
Sep 74.	(7")	(ROC 4) **NEED A SHOT OF RHYTHM AND BLUES. / LET IT BE ME**	□	□
Feb 75.	(7")	(ROC 6) **I AIN'T NEVER. / SOME OTHER GUY**	□	□

—— **EDMUNDS** added guests **BRINSLEY SCHWARTZ** – guitar and some of his band **NICK LOWE** – bass / **BOB ANDREWS** – keyboards / **IAN GOMM** – guitar / **PICK WITHERS, TERRY WILLIAMS and BILLY RANKIN** – drums

Apr 75.	(lp)	(RRL 101) <APL-1 5003> **SUBTLE AS A FLYING MALLET**		

– Baby I love you / Leave my woman alone / Maybe / Let it rock / Let it be me / Da doo ron ron / No money down / I ain't never / Billy the kid / Shot of rhythm and blues / She's my baby / Born to be with you. (re-iss. 1978 on 'R.C.A.' lp/c; RCA LP/K 5129) (re-iss. Oct81 on 'R.C.A.')

			Swan Song	Swan Song
Aug 76.	(7")	(SSK 19408) **HERE COMES THE WEEKEND. / AS LOVERS DO**	□	□
Oct 76.	(7")	(SSK 19409) **WHERE OR WHEN. / NEW YORK'S A LONELY TOWN**	□	□

—— Now DAVE's band was **LOWE, T. WILLIAMS** and **BILLY BREMNER** – guitar plus session people as guests

Apr 77.	(lp/c)	(SSK/SK4 59404) <8418> **GET IT**	□	□

– Get out of Denver / Back to schooldays / Hey good lookin' / I knew the bride (when she used to rock'n'roll) / Get it / Here comes the weekend / Worn out suits and brand new pockets / Where or when / Ju ju man / Let's talk about us / What did I do last night? / My baby left me / Little darlin'.

Apr 77.	(7")	(SSK 19410) **JU JU MAN. / WHAT DID I DO LAST NIGHT?**	□	□
Jun 77.	(7")	(SSK 19411) **I KNEW THE BRIDE. / BACK TO SCHOOLDAYS**	26	□
Aug 78.	(7")	(SSK 19413) **DEBORAH. / WHAT LOOKS BEST ON YOU**	□	□
Sep 78.	(lp)	(SSK/SK4 59407) <8505> **TRACKS ON WAX**	□	□

– Trouble boys / Never been in love / Not a woman, not a child / Television / What looks best on you / Readers wives / Deborah / Thread your needle / A.1 on the jukebox / It's my own business / Heart of the city.

Oct 78.	(7")	(SSK 19414) **TELEVISION. / NEVER BEEN IN LOVE**	□	□
Feb 79.	(7")	(SSK 19417) **A-1 ON THE JUKEBOX. / IT'S MY OWN BUSINESS**	□	□
Jun 79.	(7"clear)	(SSK 19418) **GIRLS TALK. / BAD IS BAD**	4	–
Jun 79.	(lp/c)	(SSK/SK4 8507) **REPEAT WHEN NECESSARY**	39	54

– Girls talk / Crawling from the wreckage / Sweet little Lisa / The creature from the black lagoon / Home in my hand / Take me for a little while / Queen of hearts / We were both wrong / Bad is bad / Dynamite / Goodbye Mr Good Guy. (cd-iss. Jan93 on 'Warners'; 7567 90337-2)

Aug 79.	(7")	<71001> **GIRLS TALK. / THE CREATURE FROM THE BLACK LAGOON**	–	65
Sep 79.	(7")	(K 19419) **QUEEN OF HEARTS. / CREATURE FROM THE BLACK LAGOON**	11	□
Nov 79.	(7")	(K 19420) **CRAWLING FROM THE WRECKAGE. / AS LOVERS DO**	59	□
Jan 80.	(7")	(K 19422) **SINGIN' THE BLUES. / BOYS TALK**	28	□

—— In Aug'80, EDMUNDS collaborated on a single, 'BABY RIDE EASY' with CARLENE CARTER (XX 8)

ROCKPILE

(EDMUNDS, LOWE, BREMNER and T. WILLIAMS)

			F-Beat	Columbia
Sep 80.	(7"/7"yellow)	(XX 9/+C) **WRONG WAY. / NOW AND ALWAYS**	□	□
Oct 80.	(lp/c)	(XX LP/C 7) <36886> **SECONDS OF PLEASURE**	34	27

– Teacher teacher / If sugar was as sweet as you / Wrong way / Now and always / Knife and fork / When I write the book / Pet you and hold you / Oh what a thrill / Play that fast thing (one more time) / For too long / Heart / (You ain't nothing but) Fine fine fine. (free 7"ep w/ above) (BEV 1) NICK LOWE & DAVE EDMUNDS SING THE EVERLY BROTHERS (re-iss. Jun84 on 'Demon'; FIEND 28) (cd-iss. 1989 on 'Line'; LICD 0005)

Nov 80.	(7")	(XX 11) <11388> **TEACHER TEACHER. / FOOL TOO LONG**	□	51
Mar 81.	(7")	<60503> **TAKE A MESSAGE TO MARY. / ROCKPILE HEART**	–	□

DAVE EDMUNDS

—— solo again. NICK LOWE continued his solo career also WILLIAMS later joined DIRE STRAITS. **EDMUNDS** now used session people including past friends

			Swan Song	Swan Song
Mar 81.	(7")	(SSK 19424) <72000> **ALMOST SATURDAY NIGHT. / YOU'LL NEVER GET ME UP (IN ONE OF THOSE)**	58	54
Apr 81.	(lp/c)	(SSK/SK4 59411) <16034> **TWANGIN'**	37	48

– (I'm gonna start) Living again if it kills me / The race is on / Almost Saturday night / Singin' the blues / Something happens / It's been so long / Cheap talk, patter and jive / You'll never get me up (in one of those) / I'm only human / Baby let's play house.

	Arista	Columbia

Jun 81. (7"; DAVE EDMUNDS & THE STRAY CATS) *(SSK 19425)* **THE RACE IS ON. / (I'M GONNA START) LIVING AGAIN IF IT KILLS ME** — 34 / —

—— His touring band consisted of **MICKEY GEE** – guitar / **JOHN DAVID** – bass and **DAVID CHARLES** – drums. (They appear on album alongside sessioners)

Feb 82. (7") *(ARIST 439)* **WARMED OVER KISSES (LEFT OVER LOVE). / LOUISIANA MAN** — / —

Mar 82. (lp/c) *(SPART/TC-SPART 1184) <37930>* **D.E. 7th** — 60 / 46
– From small things big things come / Dear dad / Me and the boys / Bail you out / Generation number / Other guy's girls / Warmed over kisses (left over love) / Paula meet Jeanne / One more night / Deep in the heart of Texas / Louisiana man. *(free 7"ep w/a)* *(JUKE 1)* **LIVE AT THE VENUE** (live) *(re-iss. Mar84 on 'Fame' lp/c; FA41/TC-FA 41 3090-1/-4)*

Apr 82. (7") *(ARIST 471)* **ME AND THE BOYS. / QUEEN OF HEARTS** (live) — / —

Jul 82. (7") *(ARIST 478)* **FROM SMALL THINGS BIG THINGS COME. / YOUR TRUE LOVE** (live) — / —

Jul 82. (7") **FROM SMALL THINGS BIG THINGS COME. / WARMED OVER KISSES (LEFT OVER LOVE)** — / —

—— plus **JEFF LENNY** – bass, synthesizers and production

Mar 83. (7"/12") *(ARIST/+12 522) <03877>* **SLIPPING AWAY. / DON'T CALL ME TONIGHT** — 60 / 39

Apr 83. (lp/c) *(205/405 348) <38651>* **INFORMATION** — 92 / 51
– Slipping away / Don't you double / I want you bad / Wait / The watch on my wrist / The shape I'm in / Feels so right / What have I got to do to win / Have a heart / Information / Don't call me tonight.

May 83. (7"/12") *(ARIST/+12 532) <04080>* **INFORMATION. / WHAT HAVE I GOT TO DO TO WIN** — / —

—— **DAVE EDMUNDS** retained **JOHN DAVID /RICHARD TANDY** – keyboards (ex-ELECTRIC LIGHT ORCHESTRA) repl. GEE **TERRY WILLIAMS** – drums returned to repl. DAVID CHARLES

Jul 84. (7") *(ARIST 562) <04585>* **SOMETHING ABOUT YOU. / CAN'T GET ENOUUGH** — / —
(12"+=) *(ARIST12 562)* – Slipping away / Warmed over kisses (left over love) / From small things big things come.

Sep 84. (7") *<04700>* **BREAKING OUT. / HOW COULD I BE SO WRONG** — / —

Sep 84. (lp/c) *(206/406 396) <39273>* **RIFF RAFF** — / —
– Something about you / Breaking out / Busted loose / S.O.S. / Far away / Rules of the game / Steel claw / Can't get enough / How could I be so wrong / Hang on.

Sep 84. (7") *(ARIST 583)* **STEEL CLAW. / HOW COULD I BE SO WRONG** — / —

Apr 85. (7") *<04923>* **DO YOU WANT TO DANCE. / DON'T CALL ME TONIGHT** — / —

Jul 85. (7") *(A 6277) <04762>* **HIGH SCHOOL NIGHTS. / PORKY'S REVENGE** — / 91 Apr85

—— (above from film 'Porky's Revenge', lp featured 3 more EDMUNDS tracks) 'RUN RUDOLPH RUN' appeared on 2 various comps. 'CHRISTMAS AT THE PATTI (live) and 'PARTY PARTY' soundtrack. They also appeared on 'STARDUST' soundtrack on 'CBS'/'Columbia'.

Jan 87. (lp/c/cd) *(208/408/258 228) <40603>* **I HEAR YOU ROCKIN' – LIVE: DAVE EDMUNDS BAND** (live) — / —
– I hear you knocking / Down down down / Hell of a pain / I'll get along / It ain't easy / Country roll / Blue monday / The promised land / Dance, dance, dance / Lover not a fighter / Egg or the hen / Sweet little rock and roller / Black bill / Outlaw blues / Sabre dance.

Apr 87. (7") *<06599>* **THE WANDERER** (live). **/ INFORMATION** (live) — / —

—— next featured **LEE ROCKER / BRIAN SETZER** (Stray Cats)

	Capitol	Capitol

Mar 90. (7") *(CL 568)* **KING OF LOVE. / STAY WITH ME TONIGHT** — 68 / —
(12"+=/cd-s+=) *(12/CD CL 568)* – Everytime I see her.
(10"+=) *(10CL 568)* – King of love (at 78 rpm).

Apr 90. (cd/c/lp) *(CD/TC+/EST 2113) <90372>* **CLOSER TO THE FLAME** — / —
– King of love / Don't talk to me / Everytime I see her / Test of love / Closer to the flame / Stockholm / Fallin' through a hole / Never take the place of you / I got your number / Sincerely.

	Columbia	Columbia

Aug 94. (cd/c/lp) *(477333-2/-4/-1)* **PLUGGED IN** — / —
– Chutes and ladders / New step back / I love music / Halfway down / Beach Boy blood (in my veins) / The claw / I got the will / Better word for love / Standing at the crossroads / It doesn't really matter / Sabre dance.

– compilations, etc. –

May 80. (7"ep) *R.C.A.; (PE 5243)* **BABY I LOVE YOU / DA DOO RON RON. / BORN TO BE WITH YOU / SHOT OF RHYTHM AND BLUES** — / —

Aug 80. (lp/c) *Harvest; (SHAM/TC-SHAM 2032)* **THE SINGLES A's & B's** — / —
(re-iss. 1989 on 'See For Miles' lp/cd; SEE/+CD 282)

Nov 81. (lp/c) *Swan Song; (SSK/SK4 59413) <8510>* **THE BEST OF DAVE EDMUNDS** — / —
– Deborah / Girls talk / I knew the bride / A.1. on the jukebox / The race is on / I hear you knockin' / Almost Saturday night / Sabre dance / Queen of hearts / Crawling from the wreckage / Here comes the weekend / Trouble boys / Ju ju man / Singing the blues / Born to be with you. *(cd-iss. Mar97 on 'Warners'; 7567 90338-2)*

May 82. (7") *RCA Gold; (GOLD 548)* **BABY I LOVE YOU. / BORN TO BE WITH YOU** — / —

Oct 83. (7") *Old Gold; (OG 9368)* **SABRE DANCE. / (track by other artist)** — / —

Aug 87. (lp/c) *E.M.I.; (EMS/TC-EMS 1126)* **THE ORIGINAL ROCKPILE VOL.II** — / —

Aug 87. (7") *Old Gold; (OG 9711)* **I HEAR YOU KNOCKIN'. / SHE'S ABOUT A MOVER / SABRE DANCE** — / —

Jul 91. (d-cd) *E.M.I.; (CDEM 1406)* **THE COMPLETE EARLY EDMUNDS** — / —

Sep 93. (cd) *Arista; (74321 12540-2)* **THE BEST OF DAVE EDMUNDS** — / —
– Something about you / I hear you knockin' (live) / Deep in the heart of Texas / Information / Breaking out / From small things big things come (live) / The shape I'm in / Some other guy / Bail you out / S.O.S. / Slipping away / Generation rumble / Your true love (live) / Steel claw / Queen of hearts / How could I be so wrong.

Dec 94. (cd) *Connoisseur; (VSOPCD 209)* **CHRONICLES** — / —

Feb 97. (cd) *RCA Camden; (74321 45192-2)* **ROCKIN' (THE BEST OF DAVE EDMUNDS)** — / —

Feb 97. (cd) *EMI Gold; (CDGOLD 1083)* **I HEAR YOU KNOCKING** — / —

Mar 97. (cd) *Disky; (DC 87862-2)* **THE COLLECTION** — / —

EELS

Formed: Los Angeles, California, USA . . . 1995 by E (MATT EMERSON), who had previously released two solo albums under this rather minimalist moniker (only in America). Hooking up with fellow slippery characters TOMMY WALTER and BUTCH NORTON, they set free their electric debut album, 'BEAUTIFUL FREAK'. Lyrically grim, The EELS packaged their tales of dysfunctional Americana in deceptively effervescent indie melodies, the UK Top 10 singles 'NOVOCAINE FOR THE SOUL' and 'SUSAN'S HOUSE' being prime examples of post-NIRVANA lo-fi rock. 1998's 'ELECTRO-SHOCK BLUES' was a more private and personal exploration of life's darker side, E exorcising the demons of his sister's suicide and his mother's death from cancer. • **Songwriters:** Most songs by E, some with JIM JACOBSEN, JIM WEATHERLY, MARK GOLDENBERG, JON BRION or JILL SOBULE.

Album rating: E: A MAN CALLED E (*7) / BROKEN TOY SHOP (*5) / Eels: BEAUTIFUL FREAK (*7) / ELECTRO-SHOCK BLUES (*6)

(E)

E (b. MATT EMERSON, Virginia, USA) – vocals, piano, multi

	not iss.	Polydor

Dec 91. (cd-s) *<CDP 654>* **HELLO CRUEL WORLD** — / —

Feb 92. (cd/c) *<511570-2/-4>* **A MAN CALLED (E)** — / —
– Hello cruel world / Fitting in with the misfits / Are you and me gonna happen / Looking out the window with a blue / Nowheresville / Symphony for toy piano in G minor / Mockingbird Franklin / I've been kicked around / Pray / E's tune / You'll be the scarecrow.

—— now with various personnel incl. **PARTHENON HUXLEY + SEAB COLEMAN**

Dec 93. (cd/c) *<519976-2/-4>* **BROKEN TOY SHOP** — / —
– Shine it all on / Standing at the gate / The only thing I care about / Manchester girl / L.A. river / Most unpleasant man / Mass / Tomorrow I'll be nine / The day I wrote you off / Someone to break the spell / She loves a puppet / My old raincoat / Permanent broken heart / Eight lives left.

Dec 93. (cd-ep) *<SACD 772>* **NOT FOR AIRPLAY** — / —
– Shine it all on / L.A. river / Tomorrow I'll be nine / Everything's gonna be cool this summer.

EELS

—— E with **TOMMY WALTER** – bass, vocals / **BUTCH NORTON** – drums, vocals

	Dreamworks	Dreamworks

Feb 97. (cd/c) *<(DRD/DRC 50001)>* **BEAUTIFUL FREAK** — 5 / Aug96
– Novocaine for the soul / Susan's house / Rags to rags / Beautiful freak / Not ready yet / My beloved monster / Flower / Guest list / Mental / Spunky / Your lucky day in Hell / Manchild.

Feb 97. (7"/c-s) *(DRM S/C 22174)* **NOVOCAINE FOR THE SOUL. / GUEST LIST** — 10 / —
(cd-s+=) *(DRMCD 22174)* – Fucker / My beloved monster (live).

May 97. (7"/c-s) *(DRM S/C 22238)* **SUSAN'S HOUSE. / STEPMOTHER** — 9 / —
(cd-s+=) *(DRMCD 22238)* – Manchester girl.

Sep 97. (7"/c-s) *(DRM S/C 22277)* **YOUR LUCKY DAY IN HELL. / SUSAN'S APARTMENT** — 35 / —
(cd-s+=) *(DRMCD 22277)* – Alter boy.

Sep 98. (7"/c-s) *(DRM S/C 22346) <5112>* **LAST STOP: THIS TOWN. / ('A'mix)** — 23 / —
(cd-s+=) *(DRMCD 22346)* – ('A'mix).

Sep 98. (cd/c) *<(DRD/DRC 50052)>* **ELECTRO-SHOCK BLUES** — 12 / —
– Elizabeth on the bathroom floor / Going to your funeral part 1 / Cancer for the cure / My descent into madness / 3 speed / Hospital food / Electro-shock blues / Efils' god / Going to your funeral part II / Last stop: this town / Baby genius / Climbing to the moon / Ant farm / Dead of winter / The medication is wearing off / P.S. you rock my world.

Nov 98. (7"/c-s) *(DRM S/C 22373)* **CANCER FOR THE CURE. / EVERYTHING'S GONNA BE COOL THIS XMAS** — 60 / —
(cd-s+=) *(DRMCD 22373)* – Exodus III.

EGGMAN (see under ⇒ BOO RADLEYS)

---

808 STATE

Formed: Manchester, England . . . 1987 by MARTIN PRICE and GRAHAM MASSEY, along with programmer GERALD SIMPSON (aka A GUY CALLED GERALD). All met while working next to, and frequenting MARTIN PRICE's 'Eastern Bloc' record shop. After two albums on indie label, 'Creed', they signed to 'Island' off-shoot 'ZTT' in 1989. 808 STATE's first single, 'PACIFIC STATE' breached the UK Top 10 and initially their onslaught around Europe. Techno-dance rave-rock using sampling and sparse anthemic vocals, they were once described as TANGERINE DREAM on speed. A further succession of early 90's Top 10 hits followed in 'THE ONLY RHYME THAT BITES' (a collaboration with Manc rapper, MC TUNES, who later formed The DUST JUNKYS), 'IN YER FACE' and the dancefloor shredding 'CUBIK'. Icelandic pop pixie, BJORK, guested on their Top 5 'EX:EL' (1991), a tougher set which also featured NEW ORDER's BERNARD SUMNER on the track, 'SPANISH HEART'. PRICE departed later that year; however, 808 STATE surfaced briefly in 1992 with an ill-advised UB40 collaboration, 'ONE IN TEN', before releasing the more textured 'GORGEOUS' album in early '93. Having already worked on QUINCY JONES and DAVID BOWIE material, the group remain increasingly dramatic and atmospheric, as evidenced on their 'DON SOLARIS' set in 1996. • Trivia: In 1990, they composed the theme tune for TV pop/chat programme 'The Word'.

Album rating: NEWBUILD (*7) / 808:90 (*6) / EX:EL (*7) / GORGEOUS (*6) / DON SOLARIS (*5) / 808:88:98 compilation (*7)

GRAHAM MASSEY (b. 4 Aug'60) – programmer, engineer, keyboards (ex-BITING TONGUES) / **MARTIN PRICE** (b.26 Mar'55, Farnworth, England) – programmer, keyboards, engineer / **GERALD SIMPSON** (b.16 Feb'64) – programmer, engineer, keyboards

				Creed	not iss.
Sep 88.	(lp) (STATE 002) **NEWBUILD**			☐	☐

– Sync – Swim / Flow coma / Dr Lowfruit (4am mix) / Headhunters / Narcossa / E talk / Compulsion. (re-iss. Apr99 on 'Rephlex' cd/3x12"; CAT 080 CD/LP)

Nov 88. (12") (STATE 003) **LET YOURSELF GO (303 mix). / LET YOURSELF GO (D50 mix) / DEEPVILLE** ☐ —

—— **ANDREW BARKER** (b. 9 Mar'68) – DJ, drum programmer, keyboards + **DARREN PARTINGTON** (b. 1 Nov'69 – DJ, drum programmer repl. SIMPSON who became A GUY CALLED GERALD and had hit single 'Voodoo Ray'.

Jul 89. (m-lp) (STATE 004) **QUADRASTATE** ☐ —

– Pacific state / 106 / State ritual / Disco state / Fire cracker / State to state.

		Z.T.T.	Tommy Boy

Oct 89. (7"/c-s) (ZANG 1/+C) <TB 949> **PACIFIC STATE. / PACIFIC B** 10 ☐ Mar90

(12"/3"cd-s) (ZANG 1 T/CD) – Pacific 202 / Pacific state origin / Pacific 303 / Cobra bora shortcut. <US 12"version; TB 949>

(12") (ZANG 1TX) – Pacific 909 (mellow birds mega edit) / Bonus bird beats / Cobra bora.

Dec 89. (lp/c)(cd) (ZTT 2/+C)(246 461-2) <TC/+C/CD 1033> **808:90** 57 ☐ Jun90

– Magical dream / Ancodia / Cobra bora / Pacific 202 / Donkey doctor / Sunrise / 808080808 / The fat shadow (pointy head mix). <US-title 'UTD. STATE 90'; TB/+C/CD 1033> (cd re-iss. Jun98; ZTT 102CD)

Mar 90. (12"ep) (ZANG 2T) **THE EXTENDED PLEASURE OF DANCE** 56 —

– Cobra bora (call the cops mix) / Ancodia (taters deep nit funky beat mix) / Cubik.

—— The below two singles and album were credited to "MC TUNES VERSUS 808 STATE". (MC TUNES = **NICHOLAS LOCKETT** – English rapper)

May 90. (7"/c-s/12") (ZANG 3/+C/T) **THE ONLY RHYME THAT BITES. / THE ONLY RHYME THAT BYTES** 10 —

(ext.cd-s+=) (ZANG 3CD) – (other version).

Sep 90. (7"/c-s/+C) (ZANG 6/+C) **TUNES SPLIT THE ATOM (rap). / DANCE YOURSELF TO DEATH (bassless)** 18 —

('B'-Marley mix-12"+=) (ZANG 6T) – ('A'-Zero gravity mix).

(cd-s++=) (ZANG 6CD) – ('A'-original rap mix).

(12") (ZANG 6TX) – ('A'-Creamatomic mix) / ('A'-Creamatomic instrumental) / ('A'-Cool atom mix) / ('A'-Cool atom instrumental).

Oct 90. (lp/c/cd) (ZTT 3/+C/CD) **NORTH AT ITS HEIGHTS** 26 —

– The only rhyme that bites / This ain't no fantasy / Dance yourself to death / Own worst enemy / The north at it's heights / Tunes splits the atom / Mancunian blues / The sequel / Primary rhyming / Dub at it's heights.

—— MC TUNES also released own single (7"/c-s12"/cd-s/s12") in November 'PRIMARY RHYMING'; (ZANG 10/+C/T/CD/TW), with 808 STATE still in tow. It hit UK No.67.

Oct 90. (7"/c-s) (ZANG 5/+C) <TB 959> **CUBIK (original mix). / OLYMPIC (flutey mix)** 10 —

(12"+=/cd-s+=) (ZANG 5 T/CD) – ('A'-Pan-Am mix) / Olympic (Euro-bass mix). <US version 12"ep/cd-ep; TB 959>

(12") (ZANG 5TX) – Cubik (tomix) / Olympic (August '90) / Lambrusco cowboy (mix).

Feb 91. (7"/c-s/12") (ZANG 14/+C/T) **IN YER FACE. / LEO LEO (featuring Raagman)** 9 —

(cd-s+=) (ZANG 14CD) – ('A'-In yer face mix).

(12") (ZANG 14TX) – ('A'-Facially yours remix) / ('B'-Poonchanting instrumental).

—— next featured **BJORK** (Sugarcubes) – vocals (*)

Mar 91. (cd)(lp/c) (9031 73755-2)(ZTT 6/+C) <1042> **EX:EL** 4 ☐ May91

– San Francisco / Spanish heart / Leo Leo / Qwart * / Nephatiti / Lift / Ooops * / Empire / In yer face / Cubik / Lambrusco cowboy / Techno ball. (cd+=) – Olympic. (cd re-iss. Jan97; same) (cd re-iss. Jun98; ZTT 102CD)

Apr 91. (7"/c-s) (ZANG 19/+C) <TB 986> **OOOPS. / THE SKI FAMILY** 42 ☐

(12"+=/cd-s+=) (ZANG 19 T/CD) – 808091 (live).

(12") (ZANG 19TX) – ('A'-Utsula mix) / ('A'-Mellow Birds mix). <US version 12"ep/cd-ep; TB 986>

Aug 91. (7"/c-s) (ZANG 20/+C) **LIFT. / OPEN YOUR MIND** 38 ☐

(12"+=/cd-s+=) (ZANG 20 T/CD) – ('A'-heavy mix) / ('B'-sound galore mix). <US version 12"ep/c-ep/cd-ep; ZANG 989>

—— MARTIN PRICE departed Oct'91 and formed label 'Sun Text'.

In Feb'92, they collaborated with DAVID BOWIE on a version of 'SOUND AND VISION'. Below single as "808 STATE featuring BJORK".

Aug 92. (7"/c-s) (ZANG 33/+C) <TB 540> **TIME BOMB. / NIMBUS** ☐ ☐

('Fon'mix-12"+=/cd-s+=) (ZANG 33 T/CD) – Reaper repo (short mix) / Reaper repo.

Nov 92. (7"/c-s/+C) (ZANG 39/+C) <TB 553> **ONE IN TEN 808. / ONE IN TEN UB40 VOCAL** 17 ☐

(cd-s+=) (ZANG 39CD) <TB12 553> – ('A'-808 original mix) / ('A'-Fast Fon mix) / ('A'instrumental) / ('A'-Forcable Labotomy mix).

(12") (ZANG 39T) <TBCD 553> – ('A'-original mix) / ('A'-Fast Fon mix) / ('A'side) / ('A'-Forcable Labotomy mix).

(12") (ZANG 39TX) – ('A'-UB 40 vocal) / ('A'-UB40 full instrumental).

Jan 93. (7"/c-s) (ZANG 38/+C) **PLAN 9. / OLYMPIC '93 (The Word mix)** 50 —

('A'-Choki Galaxy mix-12"+=) (ZANG 38T) – ('A'-Guitars on fire mix).

(cd-s++=) (ZANG 38CD) – Nbambi (the April showers mix).

Feb 93. (cd)(lp/c) (4509 91100-2)(ZTT 12/+C) <TBCD 1067> **GORGEOUS** 17 —

– Plan 9 / Moses / Contrique / 10 x 10 / Timebomb / One in ten / Europa / Orbit / Black morpheus / Southern cross / Nimbus / Colony. (cd re-iss. Jan97; same) (cd re-iss. Jun98; ZTT 104CD)

Jun 93. (c-s) (ZANG 42C) **10 x 10 (radio mix). / LA LUZ (chunky funky mix)** 67 —

(12"+=) (ZANG 42T) – ('A'-black eye mix) / ('A'-trance mix).

('A'-hit man's club-10"+=) (ZANG 42X) – ('A'instrumental).

(cd-s) (ZANG 42CD) – (3 'A'mixes above) / ('A'-Rockathon mix) / ('A'vox mix) / ('A'beats mix) / ('A'hit man's acapella mix).

		Z.T.T.	Z.T.T.

Aug 94. (c-s/12"/cd-s) (ZANG 54 C/T/CD) <TB 629> **BOMBADIN. / MARATHON** 67 —

		Z.T.T.	Z.T.T.

Jun 96. (12") (ZANG 80T) **BOND. / CHISLER** 57 —

(c-s/cd-s) (ZANG 80 C/CD) – ('A'side) / Bonded.

Jun 96. (cd/c/lp) (0630 14356-2/-4/-1) <14356> **DON SOLARIS** ☐ —

– Intro / Bond / Bird / Azura / Black Dartangnon / Joyrider / Lopez / Balboa / Kohoutek / Mooz / Jerusahat / Banacheq. (re-iss. Feb97; same) <US version on 'Hypnotic'> (cd re-iss. Jun98; ZTT 105CD)

below featured LOUISE (from LAMB) on vocals

Aug 96. (12"/cd-s) (ZANG 84 T/CD2) **AZURA. / JOYRIDER / GOA** ☐ —

(cd-s) (ZANG 84CD1) – ('A'-4 mixes).

Jan 97. (c-s; as 808 STATE featuring JAMES DEAN BRADFIELD) (ZANG 87C) **LOPEZ / ('A'mix)** 20 —

(cd-s) (ZAND 87CD) – ('A'mixes).

(12") (ZANG 87T) – ('A'mixes).

		Z.T.T.	ZTT-Universal

May 98. (12"/cd-s) (ZTT 98 T/CD1) **PACIFIC. / CUBIK** 21 —

(cd-s) (ZTT 98CD2) – ('A'mixes).

May 98. (cd/c) (ZTT 100 CD/C) <53139> **808:88:98 (compilation)** 40 ☐ Jun98

– Pacific 707 / Cubik / In yer face / The only rhyme that bites / Olympic / Ooops / Lift / One in ten / Plan 9 / Bombadin / Bond / Azura / Lopez / Crash / Pacific 808:98 / Cubik:98.

		Slut Smalls	not iss.

Jan 99. (7") (SMALL 002) **QUINCY'S LUNCH. / Jega: MOVE U.R. BODY** ☐ —

		All Saints	not iss.

Oct 99. (cd-ep; as 808 STATE & JON HASSELL) (ASCD 017) **VOICEPRINT (mixes) / STREETFAXX** ☐ —

		Bellboy	not iss.

Nov 99. (12") (BL 043) **INVADERS** ☐ ☐

EINSTURZENDE NEUBAUTEN

(dig out; Great Alt & Indie . . .)

Mark EITZEL (see under ⇒ AMERICAN MUSIC CLUB)

ELASTICA

Formed: London, England . . . October '92 by JUSTINE FRISCHMANN, who had been an embryonic member of SUEDE, with then boyfriend, BRETT ANDERSON. Signing for the new 'Deceptive' label in 1993, JUSTINE and Co (namely DONNA MATTHEWS, ANNIE HOLLAND and JUSTIN WELSH) collected critical acclaim from the music press for their debut 45, 'STUTTER'. Their (early '94) follow-up, 'LINE UP', gave them a UK Top 20 and made American labels take note. 'Geffen' soon took up the option for worldwide sales as all awaited 1995's tip for the top and their first album. New wave of the new wave featuring fuzzgun WIRE-like guitars, their blatant plagiarism didn't go without notice when they had to settle out of court with WIRE for the use of 'Three Girl Rhumba' riff on the 'CONNECTION' hit. Soon after this, The STRANGLERS were paid out of court for 'No More Heroes'-esque backing on another hit, 'WAKING UP' (however bassist, JEAN-JAQUES BURNEL, is said to be a great fan). Finally released in Spring '95, their eponymous debut album went straight into the UK charts at No.1, ELASTICA's spkiy, punk-inspired sound the toast of Brit-pop's golden year with FRISCHMANN as the scene's uncrowned ice queen. Although HOLLAND departed in summer '95, it was almost a year before replacements were found in SHEILA CHIPPERFIELD. Conspicuous by their absence from the recording front, FRISCHMANN subsequently refused any more press interviews following the media circus surrounding her relationship with BLUR frontman, DAMON ALBARN. The only action from the ELASTICA camp of late was the ME ME ME project (featuring STEPHEN DUFFY, Blur's ALEX JAMES and CHARLIE BLOOR) who scored a UK Top 20 hit in summer '96 with 'HANGING AROUND'. Early in '99 and despite rumours of their demise, ELASTICA were still around in one way or another. By that summer, JUSTINE, JUSTIN, 1996 acquisition DAVID BUSH, new players PAUL JONES and MEW (who took DONNA's place) plus the returning ANNIE (who replaced SHEILA CHIPPERFIELD) made up the 6-piece that were back in August '99. To coincide with a new EP/mini-set release (recorded between

1996-99) entitled, er, 'ELASTICA', the band were more than happy to return to the limelight playing the Leeds and Reading festivals. Of the six tracks (which were incidently not eligible for the charts!), probably the highlight was the number 'HOW WE WROTE ELASTICA MAN', a FALL song with MARK E. on guesting vocals. As the century came to a close, ELASTICA were in the studio polishing off a long-awaited sophomore set scheduled for release in 2000 or whenever. • **Songwriters:** FRISCHMANN lyrics / group compositions.
• **Trivia:** DAMON ALBARN (as DAN ABNORMAL – anagram) played keyboards on their debut album and featured with them on Top Of The Pops.

Album rating: ELASTICA (*8) / ELASTICA mini (*5)

JUSTINE FRISCHMANN (b.1968, Twickenham) – vocals, rhythm guitar (ex-SUEDE) / DONNA MATTHEWS (b. Newport, Wales) – vocals, guitar / ANNIE HOLLAND (b. Brighton, England) – bass / JUSTIN WELCH – drums (ex-SUEDE)

			Deceptive	Sub Pop
Oct 93.	(7") *(BLUFF 003)* <SB 275> **STUTTER. / PUSSYCAT**			
Aug94				
Jan 94.	(7") *(BLUFF 004)* **LINE UP. / VASELINE**		20	
	(12"+=/cd-s+=) *(BLUFF 004 T/CD)* – Rockunroll / Annie (both John Peel sessions).			
			Deceptive	D.G.C.
Oct 94.	(7"/c-s) *(BLUFF 010/+C)* **CONNECTION. / SEE THAT ANIMAL**		17	-
	(12"+=/cd-s+=) *(BLUFF 010 T/CD)* – Blue (demo) / Spastica.			
Feb 95.	(7"/c-s) *(BLUFF 011/+C)* **WAKING UP. / GLORIA**		13	-
	(12"+=/cd-s+=) *(BLUFF 011 T/CD)* – Car wash / Brighton rock.			
Mar 95.	(cd/c/lp) *(BLUFF 014 CD/C/LP)* <24728> **ELASTICA**		1	66
	– Line up / Annie / Connection / Car song / Smile / Hold me now / S.O.F.T. / Indian song / Blue / All-nighter / Waking up / 2:1 / Vaseline / Never here / Stutter.			
Mar 95.	(c-s) <19385> **CONNECTION / GLORIA**		-	53

—— In Jul'95, they guested on 'Sub Pop' 4x7"box-set 'HELTER SHELTER'.

| Jun 95. | (10"cd-ep/cd-ep) *<DGC 10/CD 22001>* **STUTTER / ROCKUNROLL. / 2:1 (1 F.M. evening session) / ANNIE (John Peel session)** | | - | 67 |

—— ANNIE departed in August '95, and was replaced nearly a year later by SHEILA CHIPPERFIELD – bass / DAVID BUSH – keyboards (ex-FALL)

—— ELASTICA were back in '99; JUSTINE, JUSTIN, DAVID and the returning ANNIE recruited PAUL JONES – guitar (ex-LINOLEUM) who repl. DONNA + MEW – keyboards (ex-HEAVE)

Aug 99.	(12"ep/cd-ep) *(BLUFF 071 T/CD)* **ELASTICA EP**		-	
	– How we wrote Elastica man / Nothing stays the same / Miami nice / KB / Operator / Generator.			
	(above was ineligible for the singles chart)			

ME ME ME

JUSTIN WELCH + ALEX JAMES (Blur), STEPHEN DUFFY + CHARLIE BLOOR

		Indolent	not iss.
Aug 96.	(c-s/cd-s) *(DUFF 005 C/CD)* **HANGING AROUND / HOLLYWOOD WIVES / TABITHA'S ISLAND**	19	-

ELECTRAFIXION
(see under ⇒ ECHO & THE BUNNYMEN)

ELECTRIC FLAG

Formed: San Francisco, California, USA ... April '67 by MIKE BLOOMFIELD, an ex-session man for the likes of BOB DYLAN, OTIS REDDING and WILSON PICKETT. With BUDDY MILES, NICK GRAVENITES, BARRY GOLDBERG, HARVEY BROOKS, MARCUS DOUBLEDAY, PETER STAZZA and HERBIE RICH completing the formidable line-up, they made their live debut at the seminal Monterey Pop Festival the same year. After laying down tracks (as The AMERICAN MUSIC BAND) for cult movie, 'The Trip' (directed by Jack Nicholson and starring Peter Fonda), they subsequently signed to 'Columbia'. The following year, the 'FLAG finally released their much-anticipated debut album, 'A LONG TIME COMIN', the outfit's brassy blues excursions best sampled on 'GROOVIN' IS EASY' and 'SITTIN' IN CIRCLES'. Later in the year, BLOOMFIELD jumped ship to form the collaborative (and hugely popular) 'SUPER SESSIONS' project with AL KOOPER and STEVE STILLS. With BUDDY MILES now at the helm, The ELECTRIC FLAG limped on for a further six months, finally disbanding in '69 after the release of an eponymous follow-up. BLOOMFIELD released a few low-key solo albums (including a collaborative 1973 set, 'TRIUMVRATE', with DR. JOHN and JOHN HAMMOND) in the early 70's, before taking up the opportunity to reform the 'FLAG for a one-off 1974 set, 'THE BAND KEPT PLAYING'. In the mid 70's, BLOOMFIELD teamed up once more with GOLDBERG, forming the workmanlike KGB, before he delivered a string of trad blues sets later in the 70's. Tragically, the guitarist was to meet with an untimely death via a drug overdose on the 15th of February '81. • **Covered:** KILLING FLOOR (Howlin' Wolf) / YOU THREW YOUR LOVE ON ME TOO STRONG (Albert King) / IT TAKES A LOT TO LAUGH, IT TAKES A LOT TO CRY (Bob Dylan) / etc. KGB covered I'VE GOT A FEELING (Beatles).

Album rating: THE TRIP soundtrack (*4) / A LONG TIME COMIN' (*7) / THE ELECTRIC FLAG (*4) / THE BAND KEPT PLAYIN' (*3) / OLD GLORY: THE BEST OF ELECTRIC FLAG compilation (*7) / Michael Bloomfield: SUPER SESSION (*8; by Mike Bloomfield, Al Kooper & Steve Stills) / THE LIVE ADVENTURES OF MIKE BLOOMFIELD AND AL KOOPER (*4; with Al Kooper) / IT'S NOT KILLING ME (*4) / LIVE AT BILL GRAHAM'S FILLMORE EAST (*5) / TRIUMVIRATE (*6; with John Paul Hammond & Dr.John) / TRY IT BEFORE YOU BUY IT (*4) / KGB (*4;

with KGB) / MOTION (*3; with KGB) / IF YOU LOVE THESE BLUES, PLAY 'EM AS YOU PLEASE (*5) / ANALINE (*4) / COUNT TALENT AND THE ORIGINALS (*4) / MICHAEL BLOOMFIELD (*4) / MICHAEL BLOOMFIELD & WOODY HARRIS (*4) / BETWEEN A HARD PLACE AND THE GROUND (*4) / CRUISIN' FOR A BRUISIN' (*4) / LIVIN' IN THE FAST LANE (*4) / BLOOMFIELD – A RETROSPECTIVE compilation (*6) / DON'T SAY THAT I AIN'T YOUR MAN compilation (*7)

MICHAEL BLOOMFIELD (b.28 Jul'44, Chicago, Illinois) – guitar, percussion (ex-PAUL BUTTERFIELD BLUES BAND) / NICK GRAVENITES (b. Chicago) – vocals, guitar / BARRY GOLDBERG – keyboards (ex-MITCH RYDER, ex-duo w/ STEVE MILLER) / BUDDY MILES (b. 5 Sep'46, Omaha, Nebraska) – drums, percussion / HARVEY BROOKS – bass, guitar / MARCUS DOUBLEDAY – trumpet, percussion / plus PETER STRAZZA – tenor sax / HERBIE RICH – guitar, saxophone

		not iss.	Sidewalk
Jun 67.	(lp; The ELECTRIC FLAG, AN AMERICAN MUSIC BAND) *<ST 5908>* **THE TRIP (soundtrack)**	-	
	– Peter's trip / Joint passing / Psyche soap / M-23 / Synethesia / A little head / Hobbit / Inner pocket / Fewghh / Green and gold / The other Ed Norton / Flash, bam pow / Home room / Peter gets off / Practice music / Fine jung thing / Senior citizen / Gettin' hard. *(UK-iss.Mar87 on 'Edsel'; ED 211)*		
Jul 67.	(7") *<929>* **PETER'S TRIP. / GREEN AND GOLD**	-	
		C.B.S.	Columbia
Jul 68.	(lp) *(CBS 62394)* <9597> **A LONG TIME COMIN'**		31 Apr68
	– Killing floor / Groovin' is easy / Over-lovin' you / She should have just / Wine / Texas / Sittin' in circles / You don't realise / Another country / Easy rider. *(re-iss. Aug74 on 'Embassy-CBS'; 31061)*		
Jul 68.	(7") *(CBS 3584)* <44307> **GROOVIN' IS EASY. / OVER-LOVIN' YOU**		
Jan 69.	(lp) *(CBS 63462)* <9714> **THE ELECTRIC FLAG**		76
	– Soul searchin' / Sunny / With time there is change / Nothing to do / See to your neighbor / Qualified / Hey, little girl / Mystery / My woman that hangs around the house.		
Mar 69.	(7") *(CBS 4066)* <44376> **SUNNY. / SOUL SEARCHIN'**		

—— Disband '69, GOLDBERG went solo and BROOKS joined FABULOUS RHINESTONES. BUDDY MILES formed his own EXPRESS and joined JIMI HENDRIX's BAND OF GYPSIES.

MIKE BLOOMFIELD, AL KOOPER & STEVE STILLS

(AL KOOPER ex-BLUES PROJECT) / (STEVE STILLS of-CROSBY, STILLS & NASH)

Sep 68.	(lp) *(63396)* <CS 9701> **SUPER SESSION**		12 Aug68
	– Albert's shuffle / Stop / Man's temptation / His holy modal majesty / Really / It takes a lot to laugh, it takes a train to cry / Seasons of the witch / You don't love me / Harvey's tune. *(quad-lp 1973; Q 63396) (cd-iss. 1988; CD 63396) (re-iss. cd Aug91 on 'Essential'; ESSCD 951)*		
Oct 68.	(7") *(3770)* <44657> **SEASON OF THE WITCH. / ALBERT'S SHUFFLE**		

MIKE BLOOMFIELD & AL KOOPER

—— also featured ELVIN BISHOP + CARLOS SANTANA

Feb 69.	(d-lp) *(66216)* <PG 6> **THE LIVE ADVENTURES OF MIKE BLOOMFIELD AND AL KOOPER (live)**		18 Jan69
	– The 59th Street Bridge song / I wonder who / Her holy modal highness / The weight – Mary Ann / Together 'til the end of time / That's all right – Green onions / Sonny Boy Williamson / No more lonely night / Dear Mr.Fantasy / You threw your love on me so strong / Finale – Refugee. *(re-iss. May88 on 'Edsel'; DED 261) (d-cd-iss. Jun94 & Mar97 on 'Legacy'; 485151-2)*		
Feb 69.	(7") *<44678>* **THE WEIGHT. / MAN'S TEMPTATION**	-	
Mar 69.	(7") *(CBS 4094)* **THE WEIGHT. / THE 59th STREET BRIDGE SONG**		-

—— BLOOMFIELD then (Apr69) appeared on MUDDY WATERS live album 'Fathers And Sons'.

MICHAEL BLOOMFIELD

—— solo NICK GRAVENITES – vocals / JOHN KAHN – bass / MARK NAFTKAN – keyboards / IRA KAMIN – keyboards / BOB JONES – drums

Nov 69.	(lp) *(CBS 63652)* <9883> **IT'S NOT KILLING ME**		Oct69
	– If you see my baby / For anyone you meet / Good old guy / Far too many nights / It's not killing me / Next time you see me / Michael's lament / Why must my baby / The ones I loved are gone / Don't think about it, baby / Goofers.		
Nov 70.	(lp) *(CBS 63816)* <9893> **LIVE AT BILL GRAHAM'S FILLMORE EAST (live)**		
	– It takes time / Oh mama / Love got me / Blues on a westside / One more mile to go / It's about time / Carmelita skiffle.		

—— MIKE back into session work, until helping out NICK GRAVENITES on his soundtrack album 'Steelyard Blues' 1973. The same year he collaborated with HAMMOND – vocals / DR. JOHN – piano, vocals

Aug 73.	(lp; by MIKE BLOOMFIELD, JOHN PAUL HAMMOND & DR. JOHN) *(CBS 65659)* <32172> **TRIUMVRATE**		Jun73
	– Cha-dooky-doo / Last night / I yi yi / Just to be with you / Baby let me kiss you / Sho bout to drive me wild / It hurts me too / Rock me baby / Ground hog blues / Pretty thing. *(re-iss. May87 on 'Edsel'; ED 228) (cd-iss. Jun94 on 'Sony Europe')*		

ELECTRIC FLAG

BLOOMFIELD with GRAVENITES, GOLDBERG + MILES, plus new man ROGER 'Jellyroll' TROY – bass, vocals

		Atlantic	Atlantic
Nov 74.	(lp) *(K 50090)* <18112> **THE BAND KEPT PLAYING**		
	– Sweet soul music / Every now and then / Sudden change / Earthquake country / Doctor oh doctor / Lonely song / Make your love / Inside information / Talkin' won't get it / The band kept playing.		

Nov 74. (7") <3222> **SWEET SOUL MUSIC. / EVERY NOW AND THEN**

Feb 75. (7") <3237> **THE BAND KEPT PLAYING. / DOCTOR OH DOCTOR**

—— Broke-up again in 1975

– compilations, etc. –

Nov 71. (lp) C.B.S.; (64337) / Columbia; <10169> **THE BEST OF THE ELECTRIC FLAG**

Nov 83. (lp) Thunderbolt; (THBL 1.006) **GROOVIN' IS EASY (live)**
(cd-iss. Nov88; CDTB 1.006)

Jul 95. (cd) Columbia; (CK 57629) **OLD GLORY (THE BEST OF THE ELECTRIC FLAG)**

KGB

BLOOMFIELD + GOLDBERG with **RAY KENNEDY** – vocals / **RICK GRECH** – bass / **CARMINE APPICE** – drums

	M.C.A.	M.C.A.

Jun 76. (lp) (MCF 2749) <2166> **KGB** | | Mar76
– Let me love you / Midnight traveler / I've got a feeling / High roller / Sail on sailor / Workin' for the children / You got the notion / Baby should I stay or go / It's gonna be a hard night / Magic in your touch.

Jun 76. (7") <40544> **MIDNIGHT TRAVELER. / MAGIC IN YOUR TOUCH**

Sep 76. (7") <40573> **SAIL ON SAILOR. / WORKIN' FOR THE CHILDREN**

—— **GREG SUTTON** – bass repl. GRECH **BEN SCHULTZ** – guitar repl. BLOOMFIELD who went solo again (see further below)

Jan 77. (lp) (MCF 2773) <2221> **MOTION**
– Woman, stop watcha doin' / I only need a next time / My serene Coleene / Lookin' for a better way / Lay it all down / Treading water / Goin' through the motions / Je t'aime / Determination.

MICHAEL BLOOMFIELD

—— with **NICK GRAVENITES** – guitar, vocals / **ROGER TROY + DOUG KILMER** – bass / **IRA KAMIN** – keyboards / **TOM DONLINGER + DAVE NEDITCH** – drums / **ERIC KRISS** – piano

	Sonet	Guitar Player

Aug 77. (lp) (SNTF 726) <3002> **IF YOU LOVE THESE BLUES, PLAY 'EM AS YOU PLEASE**
– If you love these blues / Hey foreman / India / Death cell rounder blues / City girl / Kansas City / Mama lion / Thrift shop rag / Death in the family / East Colorado blues / Blue ghost blues / The train is gone / The alter song.

—— now w / **GRAVENITES / TROY + BOB JONES** – drums / **MARCIA ANN TAYLOR + ANNA RIZZO** – vocals

	Sonet	Takoma

Dec 77. (lp) (SNTF 749) <1059> **ANALINE**
– Peepin' an a moanin' / Mr. Johnson & Mr. Dunn / Frankie and Johnny / At the cross / Big 'C' blues / Hilo waltz / Effionna rag / Mood indingo / Analine.

1978. (lp) (82516) **COUNT TALENT AND THE ORIGINALS**
– Love walk / You was wrong / Peach tree man / Sammy knows how to party / When I need you / I need your loving / Bad man / Saturday night / You're changin' / Let the people dance.
(above was issued on 'T.K.' in the UK)

—— **DAVID SHOREY** – bass, vocals repl. TROY

Nov 78. (lp) <1063> **MICHAEL BLOOMFIELD**
– Guitar king / Knockin' myself out / My children, my children / Women loving each other / Sloppy drunk / You took my money / See that my grave is kept clean / The gospel truth.

—— **ROGER TROY** – bass returned to replace SHOREY

Nov 79. (lp) <7070> **BETWEEN THE HARD PLACE AND THE GROUND**
– Lights out / Between the hard place and the ground / Big chief from New Orleans / Kid man blues / Orphans blues / Juke joint / Your friends. (re-iss. Sep90 on 'Thunderbolt' cd/lp; CDTB/THBL 076) (cd re-iss. Dec99 on 'MagMid'; MM 041)

—— now w/ **HENRY ODEN** – bass / **TOM RIZZO** – drums / **JONATHAN CRAMER** – keyboards / **HART McNEE** – baritone sax / **KING PERKOFF + DERRICK WALKER** – tenor sax

Jun 81. (lp) (SNTF 860) <7091> **CRUISIN' FOR A BRUISIN'**
– Cruisin' for a bruisin' / Linda Lu / Papa mama rompah stompah / Jurker's blues / Midnight / It'll be me / Motorized blues / Mathilda / Winter bird / Snowblind.

—— He brought back a near 1977 line-up.

	Waterhouse	not iss.

Apr 82. (lp) (DAMP 100) **LIVING IN THE FAST LANE**
– Maudie / Shine on love / Roots / Let them talk / Watkin's rag / Andy's bad / When I get home / Used to it / Big "C" blues / The dizz rag. (cd-iss. May91 on 'Line'; LICD 900395)

—— Above was his last album, recorded just before his death of a drug overdose on the 15th of February '81.

– (MIKE BLOOMFIELD) compilations –

Apr 80. (lp; MIKE BLOOMFIELD & WOODY HARRIS) Kicking Mule; <(KM 164)> **BLOOMFIELD & HARRIS – INITIAL SHOCK (live)**
– Eyesight to the blind / Woman lovin' each other / Linda Lu / Kansas City / Blues in B-flat / Medley: Darktown strutters ball – Mop top – Call me a dog / I'm glad I'm Jewish / Great gifts from Heaven / Lo, though I am thee / Jockey blues / Between the hard place and the ground / Don't lie to me / Cherry red / Uncle Bob's barrelhouse blues / Wee wee hours / Vamp in C / One of these days.

Jan 84. (d-lp/d-c) C.B.S.; (CBS/40 22164) **BLOOMFIELD – (A RETROSPECTIVE)**

—— I've got my mojo working / Born in Chicago / Texas / Groovin' is easy / Killing floor / You don't realise / Wine / Albert's shuffle / Stop / I wonder who / You're killing my love / Goofers / It hurts me too / Relaxin' blues / Blues for Jimmy Yancey / Sunnyland Slim and Otis Spann / Woodyard street / Midnight on my radio / Why Lord, oh why? / Easy rider.

Apr 84. (lp) Thunderbolt; (THBL 1.009) **AMERICAN HERO**
(cd-iss. Mar88; CDTB 1.009)

Jun 87. (lp) Demon; (FIEND 92) **I'M WITH YOU ALWAYS** (rare)
(cd-iss. Aug90; FIENDCD 92)

Nov 92. (cd) Skyranch; (SR 652328) **THE LOST WORKS**

Mar 94. (cd/c) Shanachie; (SHCD/SHMC 99007) **BLUES, GOSPEL AND RAGTIME GUITAR INSTRUMENTALS**

Jun 94. (cd/c) Columbia; (476721-2/-4) **DON'T SAY THAT I AIN'T YOU MAN (ESSENTIAL BLUES 1964-69)**

Mar 96. (cd) Prestige; (CDSGP 0216) **KNOCKIN' MYSELF OUT**

May 96. (cd) Affinity; (840089-2) **A TRUE SOUL BROTHER**

Oct 96. (cd) Thunderbolt; (CDTB 179) **GOSPEL TRUTH**

ELECTRIC LIGHT ORCHESTRA

Formed: Birmingham, England . . . 1968 by ROY WOOD, as an alternative to his other group The MOVE who were drifting into cabaret circuit decline. In 1969, he offered close friend JEFF LYNNE a place in The MOVE, although the singer resisted and waited until ROY came up with ELO in 1971. Gathering in an array of outlandish but highly talented musicians (namely BEV BEVAN, RICHARD TANDY, BILL HUNT, WILF GIBSON, HUGH McDOWELL and ANDY CRAIG), the two outfits co-existed at this period, the eponymous ELECTRIC LIGHT ORCHESTRA debut, finally hitting the shops later that year. Much lauded by the critics, it didn't hit the UK Top 40 until the single, '10538 OVERTURE', made the Top 10 in August 1972. WOOD subsequently departed both ELO and The MOVE to form glam/flash rockers, WIZZARD, which left JEFF LYNNE as the group's main man. A creative BEATLES-influenced rock/pop outfit who relied heavily on string-laden themes and a romanticised lyrical future, the new line-up (without WIZZARD-bound HUNT and McDOWELL) rejuvenated a past Chuck Berry classic 'ROLL OVER BEETHOVEN' to the heights of the Top 10. The accompanying follow-up album, 'II' (1973), again made the British Top 40 and ELO enjoyed a further major chart hit with the infectious 'SHOWDOWN' single later that year. The track's more pop-friendly approach indicated the direction LYNNE would steer the band over the coming decade; both 'ON THE THIRD DAY' (1973) and 'EL DORADO . . .' (1974) saw him hone his songwriting skills, something which paid off when 'CAN'T GET IT OUT OF MY HEAD' became a surprise US Top 10 hit, boosting Statside sales of the latter album and taking it into the American Top 20. Subsequent album, 'FACE THE MUSIC' (1975), established the band as a major concert attraction across the Atlantic, where they spent much of their time touring. Though that album's 'EVIL WOMAN' had made the UK Top 10, they finally re-established themselves in their home country with 'A NEW WORLD RECORD' (1976). ELO reached a commercial peak towards the end of the decade with their finely crafted, harmony-laden songs represented everything the thriving punk scene set out to destroy; both 'OUT OF THE BLUE' (1977) and 'DISCOVERY' (1979) were massive transatlantic successes, while the band scored a formidable run of chart hits including 'MR. BLUE SKY', 'SWEET TALKIN' WOMAN', 'SHINE A LITTLE LOVE' and the classic 'DON'T BRING ME DOWN'. In summer 1980, a collaboration with OLIVIA NEWTON JOHN on the dreamy 'XANADU' provided the band with their only No.1 hit, the track taken from the soundtrack to the film of the same name. The hits continued to roll in with the inimitable cheesiness of 'TICKET TO THE MOON', 'HOLD ON TIGHT' and 'ROCK'N'ROLL IS KING', the latter track being their last Top 40 hit. As their chart success dried up in the mid-80's, LYNNE helped form The TRAVELING WILBURYS alongside BOB DYLAN, GEORGE HARRISON, ROY ORBISON and TOM PETTY. BEVAN eventually emerged in the early 90's with an ELO Mk.II, although their material inevitably lacked LYNNE's songwriting spark. The bearded one had produced DAVE EDMUNDS (1981-84), BRIAN WILSON (1988) and TOM PETTY (1989), to name just a few and released a solo album, 'ARMCHAIR THEATER' in 1990 which hit the UK Top 30.

Album rating: ELECTRIC LIGHT ORCHESTRA (aka 'NO ANSWER' US) (*5) / ELECTRIC LIGHT ORCHESTRA II (*4) / ON THE THIRD DAY (*6) / THE NIGHT THE LIGHTS WENT ON IN LONG BEACH (*4) / ELDORADO (*7) / FACE THE MUSIC (*6) / OLE ELO compilation (*6) / A NEW WORLD RECORD (*6) / OUT OF THE BLUE (*8) / DISCOVERY (*5) / ELO'S GREATEST HITS compilation (*8) / XANADU with Olivia Newton-John (*4) / TIME (*4) / SECRET MESSAGES (*4) / BALANCE OF POWER (*4) / PART II (*2; as Electric Light Orchestra Part II) / MOMENT OF TRUTH (*3; as Electric Light Orchestra Part II) / STRANGE MUSIC: THE BEST OF ELECTRIC LIGHT ORCHESTRA compilation (*7)

ROY WOOD (b. 8 Nov'46) – cello, vocals, multi (ex-The MOVE) / **JEFF LYNNE** (b.30 Dec'47) – vocals guitar (ex-The MOVE, ex-IDLE RACE) / **BEV BEVAN** (b. BEVERLEY, 24 Nov'46) – drums, vocals (ex-The MOVE) / **RICHARD TANDY** (b.26 Nov'48) – bass, keyboards, vocals (ex-BALLS, ex-UGLYS) / **BILL HUNT** – keyboards, French horn / **WILF GIBSON** – violin / **HUGH McDOWELL** (b.31 Jul'53, London, England) – cello / **ANDY CRAIG** – cello

	Harvest	U.A.

Dec 71. (lp) (SHVL 797) <5573> **THE ELECTRIC LIGHT ORCHESTRA**
<US-title 'NO ANSWER'> | 32 |
– 10538 overture / Look at me now / Nellie takes her bow / The battle of Marston Moor (July 2nd, 1644) / First movement (jumpin' biz) / Mr. Radio / Manhattan rumble (49th Street massacre) / Queen of the hours / Whisper in the night. (re-iss. Nov83 on 'Fame' lp/c; FA/TCFA 4130841)

Jul 72. (7") (HAR 5053) **10538 OVERTURE. / FIRST MOVEMENT (JUMPIN' BIZ)** — `9` / `-`

Sep 72. (7") <50914> **10538 OVERTURE. / THE BATTLE OF MARSTON MOOR (JULY 2ND, 1644)** — `-` / `☐`

──── **MIKE EDWARDS** – cello repl. ROY WOOD who formed WIZZARD (also went solo) / **MICHAEL DE ALBUQUERQUE** – bass repl. HUNT and McDOWELL who joined WIZZARD / **COLIN WALKER** – cello repl. ANDY CRAIG

Jan 73. (7") (HAR 5063) <173> **ROLL OVER BEETHOVEN. / QUEEN OF THE HOURS** — `6` / `42` Apr73

Feb 73. (lp) (SHVL 806) <040> **ELECTRIC LIGHT ORCHESTRA II** — `35` / `62`
– In old England town (boogie £2) / Momma / Roll over Beethoven / From the sun to the world (boogie £1) / Kuiama. (re-iss. May82 on 'Fame' lp/c; FA/TCFA 3003)

Sep 73. (7") (HAR 5077) <337> **SHOWDOWN. / IN OLD ENGLAND TOWN** — `12` / `53` Nov73

──── **MIK KAMINSKI** (b. 2 Sep'51, Harrogate, England) – violin repl. GIBSON / **HUGH McDOWELL** – cello returned to repl. WALKER (above 2 in septet with LYNNE, BEVAN, TANDY, WALKER ALBUQUERQUE and EDWARDS.

	Warners	U.A.
Dec 73. (lp/c) (K/K4 56021) <188> **ON THE THIRD DAY**		`52`

– Ocean breakup – King of the universe / Daybreaker / Bluebird is dead / Oh no, not Susan / New world rising / Ocean breakup (reprise) / Showdown / Daybreaker / Ma-Ma-Ma belle / Dreaming of 4000 / In the hall of the Mountain King. (re-iss. 1977 on 'United Artists' lp/c; UAG/UAC 30091) (re-iss. Jun77 on 'Jet' clear-lp/c; JET LP/CA 202)

Mar 74. (7") (K 16349) **MA-MA-MA BELLE. / CAN'T FIND THE TITLE** — `22` / `-`

Mar 74. (lp) <UALA 318> **THE NIGHT THE LIGHT WENT OUT IN LONG BEACH (live)** — `-` / `☐`
– Daybreaker / Showdown / Daytripper / 10538 overture / Mik's solo / Orange blossom special / Medley: In the hall of the mountain king – Great balls of fire / Roll over Beethoven. (UK-iss.Nov85 on 'Epic' lp/c; EPC/40 32700)

Apr 74. (7") <405> **DAYBREAKER (live). / MA-MA-MA BELLE (live)** — `-` / `87`

Jun 74. (7") (K 16510) <573> **CAN'T GET IT OUT OF MY HEAD. / ILLUSIONS IN G MAJOR** — `☐` / `9` Dec74

Oct 74. (lp/c) (K/K4 56090) <339> **ELDORADO – A SYMPHONY BY THE ELECTRIC LIGHT ORCHESTRA** — `☐` / `16`
– Eldorado – overture / Can't get it out of my head / Boy blue / Larendo tornado / Poor boy (the greenwood) / Mister Kingdom / Nobody's child / Illusions in G major / Eldorado – finale. (re-iss. 1977 on 'United Artists' lp/c; UAG/UAC 30092) (re-iss. Jun77 on 'Jet' yellow-lp/c; JET LP/CA 203) (re-iss. 1986; JETLP 32397)

Nov 74. (7") **ELDORADO. / BOY BLUE**

──── **KELLY GROUCUTT** (b. 8 Sep'45, Coseley, England) – bass, vocals repl. ALBUQUERQUE / **MELVYN GALE** (b.15 Jan'52, London) – cello repl. EDWARDS

	Jet	Jet
Oct 75. (lp/c) (JET LP/TC 11) <546> **FACE THE MUSIC**		`8`

– Fire on high / Waterfall / Evil woman / Night rider / Poker / Strange magic / Down home town / One summer dream. (re-iss. Oct76 on 'Jet-United Artists' lp/c; UAG/UAC 30034) (re-iss. Mar77 green-lp/c; JET LP/CA 201) (re-iss. Jun85 on 'Epic'; lp/c; (EPC/40 32544) (cd-iss. Nov91 on 'Pickwick'; 9825962) (re-iss. cd Mar94 on 'Sony Collectors')

Dec 75. (7") (JET 764) <JET 729> **EVIL WOMAN. / 10538 OVERTURE (live)** — `10` / `10` Oct75

Mar 76. (7") (JET 769) **NIGHT RIDER. / DAYBREAKER** — `-` / `-`

Mar 76. <JET 770> **STRANGE MAGIC. / NEW WORLD RECORD** — `-` / `14`

Jun 76. (7") (JET 779) **STRANGE MAGIC. / SHOWDOWN (live)** — `38` / `-`

Jul 76. (7") <JET 842> **SHOWDOWN. / DAYBREAKER (live)** — `-` / `59`

	U.A.	Jet
Oct 76. (7",7"blue) (UP 36184) **LIVIN' THING. / FIRE ON HIGH**	`4`	`-`
Oct 76. (7") <JET 888> **LIVIN' THING. / MA-MA-MA BELLE**	`-`	`13`

Nov 76. (lp/c) (UAG/UAC 30017) <679> **A NEW WORLD RECORD** — `6` / `5` Oct76
– Tightrope / Telephone line / Rockaria! / Mission (a new world record) / So fine / Livin' thing / Above the clouds / Do ya / Shangri-la. (re-iss. Jun77 red-lp/c; JET LP/CA 200) (re-iss. 1985 on 'Epic' lp/c; JET LP/CA 32545) (cd-iss. Mar87; CDJET 200) (re-iss. cd Apr89; JETCD 32545) (re-iss. Sep89 on 'Pickwick' lp/c/cd; 902198-1/-4/-2)

Jan 77. (7") <JET 939> **DO YA. / NIGHTRIDER** — `-` / `24`

Feb 77. (7") (UP 36209) **ROCKARIA!. / POKER** — `9` / `-`
(re-iss. May78; SJET 100)

May 77. (7"m) (UP 36254) **TELEPHONE LINE. / POORBOY (THE GREENWOOD) / KING OF THE UNIVERSE** — `8` / `-`
(re-iss. May78; SJET 101)

May 77. (7") <+=> (UP 36209) **TELEPHONE LINE. / POORBOY (THE GREENWOOD)** — `-` / `7`

Oct 77. (7") (UP 36313) <1099> **TURN TO STONE. / MISTER KINGDOM** — `18` / `13` Nov77
(re-iss. May78; SJET 103)

Nov 77. (d-lp/d-c) (UAR/UAC 100) <823> **OUT OF THE BLUE** — `4` / `4`
– Turn to stone / It's over / Sweet talkin' woman / Across the border / Night in the city / Starlight / Jungle / Believe me now / Steppin' out / Standing in the rain / Summer and lightning / Mr. Blue Sky / Sweet is the night / The whale / Wild west hero / Birmingham Blues. (re-iss. 1978 on double-blue-lp; JETDP 400) (re-iss. May87 on 'Epic' d-lp/d-c/d-cd; 450885-1/-4/-2) (re-iss. cd Jun91 on 'Epic')

Jan 78. (7") (UP 36342) <5050> **MR. BLUE SKY. / ONE SUMMER DREAM** — `6` / `35` Jun78
(re-iss. May78 in 7"blue; SJET 104)

	Jet	Jet
Feb 78. (7") <1145> **SWEET TALKIN' WOMAN. / FIRE ON HIGH**	`-`	`17`

Jun 78. (7"/12"yellow) (SJET/+12 109) **WILD WEST HERO. / ELDORADO** — `6` / `-`

Oct 78. (7") <5052> **IT'S OVER. / THE WHALE** — `-` / `75`

Sep 78. (7",7"mauve/12"mauve) (SJET/+12 121) **SWEET TALKIN' WOMAN. / BLUEBIRD IS DEAD** — `6` / `-`

May 79. (7"/12",12"white) (SJET/+12 144) <5057> **SHINE A LITTLE LOVE. / JUNGLE** — `6` / `8`

Jun 79. (lp/c) (JET LX/CX 500) <35769> **DISCOVERY** — `1` / `5`
– Shine a little love / Confusion / Need her love / The diary of Horace Wimp / Last train to London / Midnight blue / On the run / Wishing / Don't bring me down. (re-

iss. Nov86 on 'Epic' lp/c; EPC/40 450083-1/-4) (cd-iss. Apr87; CDJET 500) (re-iss. cd Jun91 on 'Epic'; 450083-2)

Jul 79. (7") (JET 150) **THE DIARY OF HORACE WIMP. / DOWN HOME TOWN** — `6` / `-`

Aug 79. (7"/12") (JET/+12 153) <5060> **DON'T BRING ME DOWN. / DREAMING OF 4000** — `3` / `4`

Oct 79. (7") <5064> **CONFUSION. / POKER** — `-` / `37`

Nov 79. (7") (JET 166) **CONFUSION. / LAST TRAIN TO LONDON** — `8` / `-`

Nov 79. Jet; (lp/c) (JET LX/CX 525) <36310> **ELO'S GREATEST HITS** (compilation) — `7` / `30`
– Telephone line / Evil woman / Livin' thing / Can't get it out of my head / Showdown / Turn to stone / Rockarai / Sweet talkin' woman / Ma-ma-ma belle / Strange magic / Mr. Blue sky. (re-iss. Jan87 on 'Epic' lp/c; 450357-1/-4) (cd-iss. Dec86 on 'Epic; CDJET 525)

Jan 80. (7") <5067> **LAST TRAIN TO LONDON. / DOWN HOME TOWN** — `-` / `39`

──── Now trimmed basic quartet of **LYNNE, BEVAN, TANDY** and **GROUCUTT** (KAMINSKI formed VIOLINSKI) (McDOWELL and GALE also departed). For below album / singles they shared billing with OLIVIA NEWTON-JOHN

	Jet	M.C.A.
May 80. (7") (JET 179) <41246> **I'M ALIVE. / DRUM DREAMS**	`2`	`16`

Jun 80. (7"/10"pink; by OLIVIA NEWTON-JOHN and ELECTRIC LIGHT ORCHESTRA) (JET/+10 185) **XANADU. / FOOL COUNTRY** — `1` / `-`

Jun 80. (7") <41285> **XANADU. / (other track by GENE KELLY & OLIVIA NEWTON JOHN)** — `-` / `8`

Jul 80. (lp/c) (JET LX/CX 526) <6100> **XANADU** (film soundtrack) — `2` / `4`

Jul 80. (7"/10"blue) (JET/+10 195) **ALL OVER THE WORLD. / MIDNIGHT BLUE** — `11` / `-`

Jul 80. (7") <41289> **ALL OVER THE WORLD. / DRUM DREAMS** — `-` / `13`

Nov 80. (7") (JET 7004) **DON'T WALK AWAY. / ACROSS THE BORDER** — `21` / `-`

Jul 81. (7") (JET 7011) <02408> **HOLD ON TIGHT. / WHEN TIME STOOD STILL** — `4` / `10`

Aug 81. (lp/c) (JET LP/CA 236) <37371> **TIME** — `1` / `16`
– Prologue / Twilight / Yours truly, 2095 / Ticket to the Moon / The way life's meant to be / Another heart breaks / Rain is falling / From the end of the world / The lights go down / Here is the news / 21st century man / Hold on tight / Epilogue. (re-iss. Feb88 on 'Epic'; 460212) (cd-iss. May88 on 'Jet'; ZK 37371) (re-iss. cd Jun91; 460212-2)

Oct 81. (7") (JET 7015) <02559> **TWILIGHT. / JULIE DON'T LIVE HERE** — `30` / `33`

Dec 81. (7"/12"pic-d) (JET/+P12 7018) **TICKET TO THE MOON. / HERE IS THE NEWS** — `24` / `-`

Jan 82. (7") <02693> **RAIN IS FALLING. / ANOTHER HEART BREAKS** — `-` / `-`

Mar 82. (7") (JET 7021) **THE WAY LIFE'S MEANT TO BE. / WISHING** — `-` / `-`

	Jet-Epic	Jey-CBS
Jun 83. (7") (JETA 3500) <03964> **ROCK'N'ROLL IS KING. / AFTER ALL**	`13`	`19`

(12"+=) (JETTA 3500) – Time after time.

Jun 83. (lp/c) (JET LX/CX 527) <38490> **SECRET MESSAGES** — `4` / `36`
– Secret messages / Loser gone wild / Bluebird / Take me on and on / Four little diamonds / Stranger / Danger ahead / Letter from Spain / Train of gold / Rock'n'roll is king. (cd-iss. May87; CDJET 527) – Time after time. (re-iss. Jun91 cd/c; 462487-2/-4) (re-iss. Mar93 cd/c)

Aug 83. (7"/7"pic-d) (JET A/WA 3720) **SECRET MESSAGES. / BUILDINGS HAVE EYES** — `48` / `-`

Oct 83. (7") (JETA 3869) <04130> **FOUR LITTLE DIAMONDS. / LETTER FROM SPAIN** — `-` / `86` Sep83
(12"+=) (JETTA 3869) – The bouncer.

Jan 84. (7") <04208> **STRANGER. / TRAIN OF GOLD** — `-` / `☐`

──── after a brief spell in BLACK SABBATH, **BEVAN** rejoined ELO with others **JEFF LYNNE** and the returning **MICK KAMINSKI**

	Epic	C.B.S.
Feb 86. (7") (A 6844) <05766> **CALLING AMERICA. / CAUGHT IN A TRAP**	`28`	`18` Jan86

(12"+=) (QTA 6844) – Destination unknown.

Mar 86. (lp/c) (EPC/40 26467) <40048> **BALANCE OF POWER** — `9` / `49` Feb86
– Heaven only knows / So serious / Getting to the point / Secret lives / Is it alright? / Sorrow about to fall / Without someone / Calling America / Endless lies / Send it. (cd-iss. May87; CD 26467) (re-iss. Jun91 cd/c; 468576-2/-4) (re-iss. Mar93 cd/c)

Apr 86. (7") (A 7090) **SO SERIOUS. / A MATTER OF FACT** — `☐` / `-`
(12"+=) (TA 7090) – ('A'-alternative mix).

May 86. (7") <05892> **SO SERIOUS. / ENDLESS LIES** — `-` / `☐`

Jul 86. (7") (A 7317) **GETTING TO THE POINT. / SECRET LIVES** — `☐` / `-`
(12"+=) (TA 7317) – Elo megamix.

──── continued without LYNNE! who went solo and joined TRAVELING WILBURYS

ELECTRIC LIGHT ORCHESTRA PART II

──── now with **BEVAN, KAMINSKI, McDOWELL, GROUCUTT, LOUIS CLARK, PETE HAYCOCK** – vocals (ex-CLIMAX BLUES BAND) / session **NEIL LOCKWOOD, ERIC TROYER**

	Telstar	Scotti Bros
Apr 91. (7"/c-s) (ELO 100/+C) **HONEST MAN. / LOVE FOR SALE**	`60`	

(12"+=/cd-s+=) (ELO 100 T/CD) – ('A'extended).

May 91. (cd/c/lp) (TCD/STAC/STAR 2503) **PART II** — `34` / `☐`
– Hello / Honest man / Every night / Once upon a time / Heartbreaker / Thousand eyes / For the love of a woman / Kiss me red / Heart of hearts / Easy street.

──── **ERIC TROYER + PHIL BATES** – guitar, vocals repl. HAYCOCK (now solo again)

	Ultrapop	Ultrapop
Aug 94. (c-s/cd-s) (9612-4/-5 ULT) **POWER OF A MILLION LIGHTS**		
Oct 94. (cd/c) (9610 – 2/4 ULT) **MOMENT OF TRUTH**		

– Moment of truth (overture) / Breakin' down the walls / Power of a million lights / Interlude / One more tomorrow / Don't wanna / Voices / Interlude 2 / Vixen / The fox / Love or money / Blue violin / Whiskey girls / Interlude / Twist of the knife / So glad you said goodbye / Underture / The leaving.

Oct 94. (c-s/cd-s) **BREAKIN' DOWN THE WALLS / DON'T WANNA** / ('A'version)

☐	-

– compilations, etc. –

on 'Harvest' unless mentioned otherwise

Oct 74.	(lp/c) (SHSP/TC-SHSP 4037) **SHOWDOWN**	☐	-
Apr 77.	(lp/c) (SHSM/TC-SHSM 2015) **THE LIGHT SHINES ON**	☐	-
Dec 77.	(7"/12") (HAR/+12 5121) **SHOWDOWN. / ROLL OVER BEETHOVEN**	☐	-
Jun 76.	(lp) Jet; (JETLP 19 w/drawn) <35528> **OLE ELO**	-	32
Dec 78.	(7"ep) Jet; (ELO 1) **E.L.O. EP**	34	
	– Can't get it out of my head / Strange magic / Evil woman / Ma-ma-ma-belle.		
Dec 78.	Jet; (3xlp-box) (JETBX 1) **THREE LIGHT YEARS**	38	
	– (ON THE THIRD DAY / ELDORADO / FACE THE MUSIC)		
Mar 79.	(lp/c) (SHSM/TC-SHSM 2027) **THE LIGHT SHINES ON (VOL.2)**	☐	-
Nov 80.	(4xlp-box) Jet; (JETBX 2) **FOUR LIGHT YEARS**	☐	-
	– (A NEW WORLD RECORD / OUT OF THE BLUE / DISCOVERY)		
May 84.	(7") EMI Gold; (G45 22) **ROLL OVER BEETHOVEN. / 10538 OVERTURE**	☐	-
Apr 86.	(lp/c) (EMS/EMC 1128) **FIRST MOVEMENT** (cd-iss. Oct87; CZ 14)	☐	-
1988.	(cd) Jet; (JETCD 24043) **A PERFECT WORLD OF MUSIC**	☐	-
May 88.	(cd) Arcade; (01024661) **ALL OVER THE WORLD**	☐	-
Dec 89.	(lp/c/cd) Telstar; (STAR/+T/CD 2370) **THE VERY BEST OF ELO**	23	-
	– Evil woman / Livin' thing / Can't get it out of my head / Showdown / Turn to stone / Rockaria! / Sweet talkin' woman / Telephone line / Ma ma ma belle / Strange magic / Mr blue sky (re-iss. Oct90 as 'THE VERY BEST OF THE ELECTRIC LIGHT ORCHESTRA'; same) – hit UK No.28		
Aug 91.	(cd/c/d-lp) E.M.I.; (CD/TC/LP EM 1419) **EARLY ELO** (– first 2 albums, plus bonus tracks)	☐	-
Sep 92.	(cd/c) Collection; (R 450357-2/-4) **GREATEST HITS VOL.2**	☐	-
Oct 92.	Epic; (3xcd-box) (EPC 472267 123) **BOXED SET**	☐	-
	– (OUT OF THE BLUE / ELDORADO / A NEW WORLD RECORD)		
Dec 92.	(3xcd-box) Epic; (472267-2) **ELDORADO / A NEW WORLD RECORD / OUT OF THE BLUE**	☐	-
Jun 94.	Dino; (cd/c) (DIN CD/C 30) **THE VERY BEST OF THE ELECTRIC LIGHT ORCHESTRA**	4	-
Jul 94.	(3xcd-box) Legacy-Epic; (CD 46090) **AFTERGLOW**	☐	-
Oct 94.	(3xcd-box) Epic; (477526-2) **TIME / SECRET MESSAGES / DISCOVERY**	☐	-
May 96.	(cd/c) EMI Gold; (CD/TC GOLD 1002) **THE GOLD COLLECTION**	☐	-
Oct 97.	(cd/c) Epic; (3013-2/-4) **ONE NIGHT IN AUSTRALIA LIVE VOL.1** (live)	☐	-
Oct 97.	(cd/c) Epic; (3014-2/-4) **ONE NIGHT IN AUSTRALIA LIVE VOL.2** (live)	☐	-
Nov 97.	(cd/c) Epic; (489039-2/-4) **LIGHT YEARS – THE VERY BEST OF**	60	-
Nov 97.	(3xcd-box) Epic; (485340-2) **DISCOVERY / OUT OF THE BLUE / TIME**	☐	-

—— JEFF LYNNE released two solo 45's while a ELO member. These were 'DOIN' THAT CRAZY THING'. / 'GOIN' DOWN TO RIO' in 1977 and 'VIDEO'. / 'SOONER OR LATER' in 1984 (US only). BEV BEVAN issued a single in 1976, 'LET THERE BE DRUMS'. / 'HEAVY HEAD'.

ELECTRIC PRUNES

(dig out; 4th edition or Great Psychedelic . . .)

ELECTRONIC (see under ⇒ NEW ORDER)

Cass ELLIOT (see under ⇒ MAMAS & THE PAPAS)

E.L.O. (see under ⇒ ELECTRIC LIGHT ORCHESTRA)

EMBRACE

Formed: Bradford/Huddersfield, England . . . 1993 by Irish-ancestry songwriting brothers, DANNY (lyrics) and RICHARD McNAMARA (the music), who enlisted the rhythm team of STEVE FIRTH and MIKE KEATON. After the stunning OASIS-esque grandeur of the early '97 debut, 'ALL YOU GOOD GOOD PEOPLE', for the 'Fierce Panda' set-up, they signed to Virgin offshoot, 'Hut'. The band made an immediate impact on the singles chart with the EP, 'FIREWORKS', increasing their chart exposure with the summer '97 follow-up, 'ONE BIG FAMILY'. However, the pop nation finally clutched them to their proverbial bosom with the re-issue of 'ALL YOU GOOD GOOD PEOPLE', which cracked the Top 10 in the Autumn. The following year, the much vaunted songwriting siblings scored a further two Top 10 hits, 'COME BACK TO WHAT YOU KNOW' and 'MY WEAKNESS IS NONE OF YOUR BUSINESS', both taken from their chart-topping debut album, 'THE GOOD WILL OUT'. Towards the end of the decade and with part-timer MICKEY DALE now their official 5th member, EMBRACE previewed their forthcoming sophomore set (released in 2000) via a Top 20 hit, 'HOOLIGAN'.
Album rating: THE GOOD WILL OUT (*8)

DANNY McNAMARA – vocals / **RICHARD McNAMARA** – guitar, vocals / **STEVE FIRTH** – bass / **MIKE KEATON** – drums, vocals

		Fierce Panda	not iss.
Feb 97.	(ltd-7") (NING 29) **ALL YOU GOOD GOOD PEOPLE.** /	-	-
		Hut	Geffen
May 97.	(c-ep/12"ep/cd-ep) (HUT C/T/CD 84) **FIREWORKS EP**	34	-
	– The last gas / Now you're nobody / Blind / Fireworks. (12"ep re-iss. Nov98; same)		
Jul 97.	(c-ep/12"ep/cd-ep) (HUT C/T/CD 86) **ONE BIG FAMILY EP**	21	-
	– One big family / Dry kids / You've only got to stop to get better / Butter wouldn't melt. (12"ep re-iss. Nov98; same)		
Oct 97.	(c-ep/12"ep/cd-ep) (HUT C/T/DX 90) **ALL YOU GOOD GOOD PEOPLE EP**	8	-
	– All you good good people (extended) / You won't amount to anything – this time / The way I do / Free ride. (12"ep re-iss. Nov98; same)		
	(cd-ep) (HUTCD 90) – ('A'radio edit) / One big family (Perfecto mix) / ('A'-Fierce Panda version) / ('A'-orchestral mix).		
May 98.	(c-s) (HUTC 93) <95132> **COME BACK TO WHAT YOU KNOW / LOVE IS BACK**	6	Jul98
	(12"+=/cd-s+=) (HUT T/DX 93) – If you feel like a sinner / Perfect way.		
	(cd-s) (HUTCDX 93) – ('A'side) / Butter wouldn't melt (live) / Dry kids (live) / ('A'orchestral).		
Jun 98.	(cd/c/d-lp) (CDHUT/HUTMC/HUTDLP 46) <25165> **THE GOOD WILL OUT**	1	Jul98
	– Intro / All you good good people / My weakness is none of your business / Come back to what you know / One big family / Higher sights / Retread / I want the world / You've got to say yes / Fireworks / The last gas / That's all changed forever / Now you're nobody / The good will out.		
Aug 98.	(7") (HUT 103) **MY WEAKNESS IS NONE OF YOUR BUSINESS. / FEELINGS I THOUGHT YOU SHARED**	9	-
	(c-s+=/cd-s+=) (HUT C/CD 103) – Don't turn your back on love.		
	(cd-s) (HUTDX 103) – ('A'live) / Higher sights (live) / Retread (live). (12"ep re-iss. Nov98; HUTT 103)		
Nov 98.	(12"ep) (HUTT 107) **THE GOOD WILL OUT. / BUTTER WOULDN'T MELT (live) / DRY KIDS (live) / BLIND**	☐	-

—— added p/t (now f/t) 5th member **MICKEY DALE** – keyboards

Nov 99.	(c-s/cd-s) (HUT C/CD 123) **HOOLIGAN / I'VE BEEN RUNNING / I CAN'T FEEL BAD ANYMORE**	18	☐
	(cd-s) (HUTDX 123) – ('A'side) / Like a believer / With the one who got me here.		

EMERSON, LAKE & PALMER

Formed: London, England . . . mid-1970 by KEITH EMERSON, GREG LAKE and CARL PALMER, who had all cut their teeth in late 60's acts/combos (see below). After an aborted collaboration with HENDRIX (just prior to his death) and an appearance at the Isle Of Wight festival on the 29th August '70, they signed to 'Island'. Later in the year, they unleashed their eponymous debut, which immediately established the band as one of the leading purveyors of 70's prog-rock. In fact, they focused more on the classical side of things, proving that rock could be adapted for more high-brow tastes (EMERSON had previously explored this field while with The NICE). Next-up was 'TARKUS' (1971), a misguided concept piece which was based around a battle between a Manticore (a mythical beast) and a mechanized armadillo (!). Riding on the coat-tails of their debut success, it nevertheless reached No.1 (Top 10 in the States). Their third album was a live adaptation of Mussorgsky's 'PICTURES AT AN EXHIBITION', a fine effort which was let down by the closing track, a pointless cover of B.BUMBLE & THE STINGERS' early 60's hit 'NUTROCKER'. In 1972, they fulfilled their early potential with 'TRILOGY', an album that also made the Top 3, showcasing their most accomplished work to date on tracks such as 'THE ENDLESS ENIGMA', 'LIVING SIN' and 'ABADDON'S BOLERO'. The following year, ELP created the label 'Manticore', its first release being the 'BRAIN SALAD SURGERY' album which consolidated their position as one of the 70's leading bands, at least in commercial terms. Once again, former part-time KING CRIMSON member PETE SINFIELD was drafted in to collaborate on the lyrics. Tracks like the romantic 'STILL . . . YOU TURN ME ON' and the grandiose epic, 'KARN EVIL 9' were skillfully placed side by side with an arresting re-working of the hymn 'JERUSALEM'. While the band took a 2-year hiatus, they released a stop-gap triple live set entitled, 'WELCOME BACK MY FRIENDS' that was a little too overblown, pricey and pretentious for many. In 1975, the fans cringed when a solo GREG LAKE returned with the festive 'I BELIEVE IN FATHER CHRISTMAS' which hit No.2. The multi-talented keyboard maestro, KEITH EMERSON, also had a solo outing, a surprisingly basic rock'n'roll cover of Meade Lux Lewis' 'HONKY TONK TRAIN BLUES'. In 1977, ELP eventually returned with the double album, 'WORKS 1', a patchy affair which nevertheless spawned an inspired cover of Aaron Copeland's 'FANFARE FOR THE COMMON MAN'. In its edited form, the track gave the band a near No.1 in the UK. This however, was to be the last real work of any relevance. All went solo in the 80's, and when PALMER formed PM, ELP conveniently found a replacement (P) in the guise of Cozy POWELL. This set-up was short-lived although the original EMERSON, LAKE & PALMER re-formed once more in 1991. They were found floundering on past glories with the mediocre 'BLACK MOON' album the following year. • **Trivia:** 'Manticore', the label they formed in 1973, also signed PETE SINFIELD, P.F.M. and LITTLE RICHARD!

Album rating: EMERSON, LAKE & PALMER (*6) / TARKUS (*5) / PICTURES AT AN EXHIBITION (*6) / TRILOGY (*8) / BRAIN SALAD SURGERY (*8) / WELCOME BACK MY FRIENDS TO THE SHOW THAT NEVER ENDS – LADIES AND GENTLEMEN . . . EMERSON, LAKE & PALMER (*5) / WORKS 1 (*5) / WORKS 2 (*3) / LOVE BEACH (*3) / IN CONCERT (*4) / THE BEST OF EMERSON, LAKE & PALMER compilation (*5) / EMERSON, LAKE & POWELL (*4) / TO THE POWER OF THREE (er . . . *3; by 3) / BLACK MOON (*4) / THE ATLANTIC YEARS compilation (*7) / LIVE AT THE ROYAL ALBERT HALL (*4) / IN THE HOT SEAT (*4)

KEITH EMERSON (b. 2 Nov'44. Todmorden, England) – keyboards (ex-NICE, ex-GARY FARR & THE T-BONES / **GREG LAKE** (b.10 Nov'48, Bournemouth, England) – vocals, guitar, bass (ex-KING CRIMSON) / **CARL PALMER** (b.20 Mar'47, Birmingham, England) – drums, percussion (ex-ATOMIC ROOSTER, ex-CRAZY WORLD OF ARTHUR BROWN)

		Island	Cotillion
Nov 70.	(lp/c) (ILPS/ILPC 9132) **EMERSON, LAKE & PALMER** – The barbarian / Take a pebble / Knife edge / The three fates:- Clotho – Lachesis – Acropus / Tank / Lucky man. (re-iss. Dec73 on 'Manticore' lp/c; K/K4 43503) (cd-iss. 1988 on 'Cotillion')	4	18
Mar 71.	(7") <44106> **LUCKY MAN. / KNIFE EDGE** <US re-iss. Jan73 on 'Atlantic'; 13153> hit No.51>	–	48
Jun 71.	(lp/c) (ILPS/ILPC 9155) **TARKUS** – Tarkus:- Eruption – Stones of years – Iconoclast – The mass – Manticore – Battlefield – Aquatarkus – (conclusion) / Jeremy Bender / Bitches crystal / The only way / Infinite space / A time and a place / Are you ready Eddy?. (re-iss. Dec73 on 'Manticore' lp/c; K/K4 43504) (cd-iss. Sep89 on 'WEA') (re-iss. cd Dec93 on 'Victory')	1	9
Sep 71.	(7") <44131> **STONES OF YEARS. / A TIME AND A PLACE**	–	–
Nov 71.	(lp/c) (HELP/HELC 1) **PICTURES AT AN EXHIBITION** – Promenade: The gnome – Promenade – The sage – The old castle – Blues variation – Promenade – The hut of Baba Yaga – The curse of Baba Yaga – The hut of Baba Yaga – The great gates of Kiev – Nutrocker. (re-iss. Dec73 on 'Manticore' lp/c; K/K4 33501) (cd-iss. 1988 on 'Cotillion' & Sep89 on 'WEA') (re-iss. Dec93 on 'Victory')	3	10
Mar 72.	(7") <44151> **NUTROCKER. / THE GREAT GATES OF KIEV**	–	70
Jul 72.	(lp/c) (ILPS/ILPC 9186) **TRILOGY** – The endless enigma (part 1) – Fugue – The endless enigma (part 2) / From the beginning / The sheriff / Hoedown / Trilogy / Living sin / Abaddon's bolero. (re-iss. Dec73 on 'Manticore' lp/c; K/K4 43505) (cd-iss. Jun89 on 'Atlantic') (re-iss. cd Dec93 on 'Victory')	2	5
Aug 72.	(7") <44158> **FROM THE BEGINNING. / LIVING SIN**	–	39

		Manticore	Manticore
Dec 73.	(lp/c) (K/K4 53501) **BRAIN SALAD SURGERY** – Jerusalem / Toccata / Still . . .you turn me on / Benny the bouncer / Karn evil 9. 1st impression – part 1 & 2 – 2nd impression – 3rd impression. (cd-iss. Jun89 on 'WEA') (re-iss. cd Dec93 on 'Victory')	2	11
Dec 73.	(7") (K 13503) **JERUSALEM. / WHEN THE APPLE BLOSSOM BLOOMS IN THE WINDMILLS OF YOUR MIND, I'LL BE YOUR VALENTINE**	–	–
Dec 73.	(7") <2003> **BRAIN SALAD SURGERY. / STILL YOU TURN ME ON**	–	–
Aug 74.	(t-lp/d-c) (K/K4 63500) **WELCOME BACK MY FRIENDS, TO THE SHOW THAT NEVER ENDS – LADIES AND GENTLEMEN . . . EMERSON, LAKE & PALMER (live)** – Hoedown / Jerusalem / Toccata / Tarkus:- Eruption – Stones of years – Iconoclast – The mass – Manticore – Battlefield – Epitaph – Aquatarkus – (conclusion) / Take a pebble – Piano improvisations – Take a pebble (conclusion) / Jeremy Bender / The sheriff / Karn evil 9. 1st impression – 2nd impression – 3rd impression. (re-iss. cd Dec93 on 'Victory')	5	4
Nov 75.	(7"; by GREG LAKE) (K 13511) <3305> **I BELIEVE IN FATHER CHRISTMAS. / HUMBUG** (re-iss. Nov82, hit No.72 – Dec83 hit No.65) (re-iss. Nov92 on 'Atlantic'; A 7393)	2	95
Apr 76.	(7"; by KEITH EMERSON) (K 13513) **HONKY TONK TRAIN BLUES. / BARREL HOUSE SHAKE DOWN**	21	–

		Atlantic	Atlantic
Mar 77.	(d-lp/d-c) (K/K4 80009) **WORKS 1** – Piano concerto No.1 – 1st movement: Allegro giojoso / 2nd movement: Andante molto cantabile / 3rd movement: Toccata con fuoco / Lend your love to me tonight / C'est la vie / Hallowed by thy name / Nobody loves you like I do / Closer to believing / The enemy God dances with the black spirits / L.A. nights / New Orleans / Bach: Two part invention in D minor / Food for your soul / Tank / Fanfare for the common man / Pirates. (re-iss. Jun89) (re-iss. d-cd Dec93 on 'Victory')	9	12
Jun 77.	(7"/12") (K 10946/+T) <3398> **FANFARE FOR THE COMMON MAN (edit). / BRAIN SALAD SURGERY**	2	
Aug 77.	(7"; A-side by GREG LAKE) (K 10990) <3405> **C'EST LA VIE. / JEREMY BENDER**		91
Nov 77.	(lp/c) (K/K4 50422) **WORKS 2** (compilation of rare and demo work) – Tiger in a spotlight / When the apple blossoms bloom in the windmills of your mind, I'll be your valentine / Bullfrog / Brain salad surgery / Barrel house shake down / Watching over you / So far to fall / Maple leaf rag / I believe in Father Christmas / Close but not touching / Honky tonk train blues / Show me the way to go home. (cd-iss. Jun89) (re-iss. cd Dec93 on 'Victory')	20	37
Jan 78.	(7"; A-side by GREG LAKE) **WATCHING OVER YOU. / HALLOWED BE THY NAME**		
Nov 78.	(lp/c) (K/K4 50552) **LOVE BEACH** – All I want is you / Love beach / Taste of my love / The gambler / For you / Canario / Memoirs of an officer and a gentleman – Prologue – The education of a gentleman / Love at first sight / Letters from the front / Honourable company. (cd-iss. Jun89) (re-iss. cd Dec93 on 'Victory')	48	55
Nov 78.	(7") (K 11225) **ALL I WANT IS YOU. / TIGER IN A SPOTLIGHT**		

— (disbanded Dec78)

		Atlantic	Atlantic
Oct 79.	(lp/c) (K/K4 50652) **EMERSON, LAKE & PALMER IN CONCERT (live 1978)** – (introductory fanfare) / Peter Gunn / Tiger in a spotlight / C'est la vie / The enemy god dances with the black spirits / Knife edge / Piano concerto No.1 / Pictures at an exhibition.		73
Dec 79.	(7") (K 11416) **PETER GUNN (live). / KNIFE EDGE (live)**		

KEITH EMERSON

		Atlantic	Atlantic
Sep 80.	(7") (K 11612) **TAXI RIDE (ROME). / MATER TENEBRARUM**		

		Atlantic	Cinevox
Dec 80.	(lp) (K 50753) **INFERNO (Soundtrack)** – Inferno / Rose's descent into a cellar / The taxi ride / The library / Sarah in the library vaults / Bookbinder's delight / Rose leaves the apartment / Rose gets it /		

Elisa's story / A cat attic attack / Kazanian's tarantella / Mark's discovery / Matter tenebarum / Inferno (finals) / Ices, cigarettes, etc. (re-iss. Mar90 on 'Cinevox'; CIA 5022)

— added **NEIL SYMONETTE** – drums / **TRISTAN FRY** – percussion / **GREG BOWEN** – trumpet / **JEROME RICHARDSON** – sax / **PAULETTE McWILLIAMS** – vocals

		M.C.A.	Backstreet
Apr 81.	(7") (MCA 697) **I'M A MAN. / NIGHTHAWKS MAIN TITLE THEME**		
Apr 81.	(lp) (MCF 3107) **NIGHTHAWKS (Soundtrack)** – Nighthawks – main title theme / Mean stalkin' / The bust / Nighthawking / The chase / I'm a man / The chopper / tramway / I'm comin' in / Face to face / The flight of the hawk. (re-iss. Jan89; MCA 1521)		

		Red Bus	not iss.
Dec 83.	(7") (RBUS 85) **UP THE ELEPHANT AND ROUND THE CASTLE. / ('A'instrumental)** (above featured comedian JIM DAVIDSON)		–

		Chord	not iss.
Apr 85.	(lp) (ESP 1) **THE BEST OF KEITH EMERSON** (compilation)		–
Apr 85.	(lp/cd) (CHORD/+CD 001) **BEST REVENGE (Soundtrack with JOHN COLEMAN)** – Dream runner / The runner / Wha 'dya mean / Straight between the eyes / Orchestral suite to "Best Revenge" / Playing for keeps (main title theme). (re-iss. Nov86)		–

— **MOTT** – guitar / **DICK MORRISSEY + ANDREW BRENNAN + PETE KING** – saxophone

| Apr 85. | (lp/cd) (CHORD/+CD 002) **HONKY** – Hello sailor / Bach before the mast / Salt cay / Green ice / Intro-juicing / Big horn breakdown / Yancey special / Rum-a-thing / Jesus loves me. (re-iss. May86) | | |
| Apr 85. | (lp) (CHORD 003) **HARMAGEDON / CHINA FREE FALL (Soundtracks; b-side by DEREK AUSTIN)** – Theme from Floi / Joe and Micheko / Children of the light / Funny's skate state / Zamedy stomp / Challenge of the psonic fighters. (re-iss. Feb87) | | |

— Some with **DOREEN CHANTER** – vocals / **MIKE SEBBAGE** – vocals / **TOM NICOL + DEREK WILSON** – drums / **MICHAEL SHEPPARD** – bass, guitar, co-producer

| May 86. | (lp/cd) (CHORD/+CD 004) **MURDEROCK (soundtrack)** – Murderock / Tonight is your night / Streets to blame / Not so innocent / Prelude to Candice / Don't go in the shower / Coffee time / Candice / New York dash / Tonight is not your night / The spill one. | | |

— next with The National Philharmonic Orchestra, plus **BRAD DELP, LEVON HELM**.

		Priority	not iss.
Dec 86.	(cd) (CDCOLL 1) **THE EMERSON COLLECTION** (compilation)		–
Nov 88.	(lp/c/cd) (KEITH LP/MC/CD 1) **EMERSON – THE CHRISTMAS ALBUM** (cd-iss. Jun93 & Dec95 on 'Amp'; AMPCD 018)		–

		Emerson	not iss.
Dec 88.	(7") (KEITH 1) **WE THREE KINGS OF ORIENT ARE. / CAPTAIN STARSHIP HOPKINS**		–

		Amp	not iss.
Apr 95.	(cd) (AMPCD 026) **CHANGING STATES**		–
Dec 95.	(cd-s) **TROIKA (THE CHRISTMAS SINGLE). /**		

GREG LAKE BAND

GREG LAKE – vocals, guitar, bass with **TOMMY EYRE** – keyboards / **GARY MOORE** – guitar (ex-solo artist ex-THIN LIZZY ex-COLOSSEUM) / **TRISTRAM MARGETTS** – bass / **TED McKENNA** – drums (ex-SENSATIONAL ALEX HARVEY BAND)

		Chrysalis	Chrysalis
Sep 81.	(7") (CHS 2553) **LOVE YOU TOO MUCH. / SOMEONE**	62	62
Oct 81.	(lp/c) (<CHR/ZCHR 1357>) **GREG LAKE** – Nuclear attack / Love you too much / It hurts / One before you go / Loving goodbye / Retribution drive / Black and blue / Let me love you once / The lies / For those who dare.		
Dec 81.	(7") <2571> **LET ME LOVE YOU ONCE. / RETRIBUTION DRIVE**	–	48
Feb 82.	(7") (CHS 2567) **IT HURTS. / RETRIBUTION DRIVE**		
Jul 83.	(lp/c) (<CHR/ZCHR 1392>) **MANOEUVRES** – Manoeuvres / Too young to love / Paralysed / A woman like you / I don't want to lose your love tonight / It's you, you've got to believe / Famous last words / Slave to love / Haunted / I don't know why I still love you.		

— LAKE joined ASIA with PALMER

PM

CARL PALMER with **TODD COCHRAN** – keyboards / **BARRY FINNERTY** – guitar, vocals / **JOHN NITZINGER** – guitar, vocals / **ERIK SCOTT** – bass, vocals

		Ariola	Ariola
May 80.	(lp/c) (ARL/ZCARL 5048) **1 PM** – Dynamite / You've got me rockin' / Green velvet splendour / Dreamers / Go on carry on / D'ya go all the way / Go for it / Madeleine / You're too much / Children of the air age.		
Apr 80.	(7") (ARO 217) **YOU GOT ME ROCKIN'. / GO FOR IT**		–
Jul 80.	(7") (ARO 234) **DYNAMITE. / D'YA GO ALL THE WAY**		–

— (Jan81) PALMER joined ASIA

EMERSON, LAKE & POWELL

— are the new set up **COZY POWELL** (b.29 Dec'47, Cirencester, England) – drums, (ex-solo artist, ex-RAINBOW, etc.)

		Polydor	Polydor
Jul 86.	(lp/c)(cd) (POLD/+C 5191)(<829 297-2>) **EMERSON, LAKE & POWELL** – Mars, the bringer of war / The score / Learning to fly / Touch and go / Miracle / Love blind / Step aside / Lay down your guns.	35	23 Jun86
Jul 86.	(7") (POSP 804) <885101> **TOUCH AND GO. / LEARNING TO FLY**		60 Jun86

(12"+=) *(POSPX 804)* – The locomotion.
Sep 86. (7") **LAY DOWN YOUR GUNS.** /　　　　　　 - □
—— (1987 originals reformed but disbanded Oct87)

3

was the unit formed by **EMERSON, PALMER** and American **ROBERT BERRY** – vocals (ex-HUSH)

		Geffen	Geffen
Feb 88. (lp/c/cd) *(924181-1/-4/-2)* <24181> **TO THE POWER OF THREE**			

– Talkin' about / Lover to lover / Chains / Desde la vida / Eight miles high / Runaway / You do or you don't / On my way home.
Feb 88. (7") **TALKIN' ABOUT.** / **LA VISTA**　　　　 - □

EMERSON, LAKE & PALMER

—— re-formed 1992

	Victory-London	Victory
Apr 92. (cd/c/lp) *(828 318-2/-4/-2)* <480003> **BLACK MOON**		78

– Black Moon / Paper blood / Affairs of the heart / Romeo and Juliet / Farewell to arms / Changing states / Burning bridges / Close to home / Better days / Footprints in the snow. *(cd re-iss. Apr97 on 'Essential'; ESMCD 506)*

	London	London
May 92. (7") *(LON 320)* **BLACK HOLE.** / **MILES IZ DEAD**	□	-

(12"+=/cd-s+=) *(LON X/CD 320)* – A blade of grass.
Nov 92. (7"/c-s) *(LON/+C 327)* **AFFAIRS OF THE HEART.** / **BETTER DAYS**　　□ -
(cd-s+=) *(LONCD 327)* – A blade of grass / Black moon.
(cd-s) *(LOCDP 327)* – ('A'side) / Black moon (radio) / Fanfare for the common man / Jerusalem.
Feb 93. (cd/c) *(828 933-2/-4)* **LIVE AT THE ROYAL ALBERT HALL (live)**　　□ □
– 1st impression part 2 / Tarkus: Eruption – Stones of years – Iconoclast / Knife edge / Paper blood / Romeo & Juliet / Creole dance / Still . . . you turn me on / Lucky man / Black moon / The pirates / Finale / Fanfare for the common man / America / Blue rondo a la Turk. *(cd re-iss. Apr97 on 'Essential'; ESMCD 504)*
Nov 93. (4xcd-box) *(828 459-2)* **RETURN OF THE MANTICORE** (old & new material)　　□ □
Dec 93. (cd) *(828 477-2)* **WORKS LIVE** (live)　　□ □
Sep 94. (cd/c) *(828 554-2/-4)* **IN THE HOT SEAT**　　□ □
– Hand of truth / Daddy / One by one / Heart on ice / Thin line / Man in the long black coat / Change / Give me a reason to stay / Gone too soon / Street war. *(cd+=)* – Pictures at an exhibition: a) Promenade – b) The gnome – c) Promenade – d) The sage – e) The hut of Baba Yaga – f) The great gates of Kiev.

– compilations, others, etc. –

Nov 80. (lp/c) *Atlantic; (K/K4 50757)* **THE BEST OF EMERSON, LAKE & PALMER**　　□ □
– Hoedown / Lucky man / Karn evil 9 / Trilogy / Fanfare for the common man / Still . . .you turn me on / Tiger in a spotlight / Jerusalem / Peter Gunn. *(cd-iss. 1983; K2 50757)*
Jul 92. (cd/c/lp) *Atlantic; (<7567 82403-2/-4>)* **THE ATLANTIC YEARS**　　□ □
Apr 97. (d-cd; GREG LAKE) *Essential; (ESDCD 522)* **FROM THE BEGINNING: THE GREG LAKE RETROSPECTIVE**　　□ -

EMF

Formed: Cinderford / Forest of Dean, Gloucestershire, England . . .late '89 by Oxford graduate IAN DENCH and JAMES ATKIN, DERRY BROWNSON, ZAC FOLEY, MARK DE CLOEDT and scratcher/DJ, MILF. After their 4th gig, they were spotted by ABBO (from former goth punks, UK DECAY) and his girlfriend, LINDA, who helped get them signed to 'E.M.I.' subsidiary, 'Parlophone' in March '90. Late that year, their debut single, 'UNBELIEVABLE', broke into the UK Top 3 and early the following year, they set about taking both sides of the Atlantic by storm. Similar in style to, say, JESUS JONES, or an uptempo DEPECHE MODE, EMF's brattish blend of indie dance and funky pop saw them hailed as the great white hopes of British music for as long as it took their teenybop fanbase to find someone new (i.e. not that long!). ATKIN's posh-accented whine was a bit much to take over the stretch of a whole album, although, spurred by the success of further singles, 'I BELIEVE' and 'CHILDREN', 'SCHUBERT DIP' (1991) was one of the year's biggest selling sets; it even did well in American where 'UNBELIEVABLE' had topped the charts. Touted as spearheading a second "British Invasion" along with JESUS JONES and Co., EMF's assault soon surrendered to the machinations of the music business as follow-up album, 'STIGMA' (1992) saw them making an ill-advised attempt at big boys' rock. Its heavier approach only succeeded in alienating their original fanbase, the band's apparent attempt to lighten up their image with a VIC REEVES and BOB MORTIMER collaboration (a Top 3 cover of The Monkees 'I'M A BELIEVER') not enough to prevent 'CHA CHA CHA' from virtually stiffing. Subsequently dropped by their label, EMF faced the inevitable and jacked it in. However, the story didn't quite finish there as DENCH resurfaced a few years later with his new trio, WHISTLER. • **Covered:** LOW SPARK OF THE HIGH HEELED BOYS (Traffic) / SHADDAP YOU, FACE (Joe Dolce) / I'M A BELIEVER (Monkees) / STRANGE BREW (Cream). / WHISTLER:- AT SEVENTEEN (Janis Ian) / I JUST DON'T KNOW WHAT TO DO WITH MYSELF (hit; Dusty Springfield) / BLUE, RED AND GREY / ALL APOLOGIES (Nirvana). • **Trivia:** EMF was rumoured to stand for ECSTASY MOTHER FUCKERS, but later claimed to be EPSOM MAD FUNKERS.

Album rating: SCHUBERT DIP (*5) / STIGMA (*7) / CHA CHA CHA (*4) / Whistler: WHISTLER (*6)

JAMES ATKIN (b.28 Mar'67) – vocals / **IAN DENCH** (b. 7 Aug'64) – guitar, keyboards (ex-APPLE MOSAIC) / **DERRY BROWNSON** (b. DERRAN, 10 Nov'70) – samples, percussion (ex-LAC's) / **ZAC FOLEY** (b. ZACHARY, 9 Dec'70) – bass (ex-IUC's) / **MARK DE CLOEDT** (b.26 Jun'67) – drums (ex-ZU) / plus **MILF** – DJ scratcher

	Parlophone	E.M.I.
Oct 90. (c-s/7") *(TC/+R 6273)* **UNBELIEVABLE.** / **EMF** (live)	3	-

(12"+=/cd-s+=) *(12R/CDR 6273)* – ('A'-Cin City sex mix).
Jan 91. (c-s/7") *(TC/+R 6279)* **I BELIEVE.** / **WHEN YOU'RE MINE**　　6 -
(12"+=/cd-s+=) *(12R/CDR 6279)* – Unbelievable (funk mix).
Mar 91. (c-s) <50350> **UNBELIEVABLE** / ('A'-Cin City Sex mix)　　- 1
Apr 91. (c-s/7") *(TC/+R 6288)* **CHILDREN.** / **STRANGE BREW** (live remix)　　19 □
(12"+=) *(12R 6288)* – Children (mix).
(cd-s+=) *(CDR 6288)* – Children – Battle for the minds of North Amerika.
(7"ep+=) *(RX 6288)* – (live versions).
May 91. (cd/c/lp) *(CD/TC+/PCS 7353)* <96238> **SCHUBERT DIP**　　3 12
– Children / Long summer days / When you're mine / Travelling not running / I believe / Unbelievable / Girl of an age / Admit it / Lies / Long time. *(re-iss. Mar94 cd/c; same)*
Aug 91. (c-s/7") *(TC/+R 6295)* **LIES.** / **HEAD THE BALL**　　28 -
(12"+=/cd-s+=) *(12R/CDR 6295)* – ('A'mix).
Sep 91. (c-s) <50363> **LIES** / **STRANGE BREW** (live)　　- 18
Apr 92. (7"ep) *(SGE 2026)* **UNEXPLAINED**　　18 -
– Getting through / Far from me / The same.
(12"ep+=/cd-ep+=) *(12/CD SGE 2026)* – Search and destroy.
Sep 92. (c-s/7") *(TC/+R 6321)* **THEY'RE HERE.** / **PHANTASMAGORIC**　　29 -
(12"+=) *(12R 6321)* – ('A'remix).
(cd-s+=) *(CDR 6321)* – Low spark of the high heeled boys.
Sep 92. (cd/c/lp) *(CD/TC+/PCSD 122)* <80348> **STIGMA**　　19 -
– They're here / Arizona / It's you that leaves me dry / Never know / Blue highs / Inside / Getting through / She bleeds / Dog / The light that burns twice as bright . . .
Nov 92. (c-s/7") *(TC/+R 6327)* **IT'S YOU.** / **DOF** (Foetus mix)　　23 -
(cd-s+=) *(CDR 6327)* – (2 other 'A' Butch Vig mixes).
(cd-ep) *(CDRS 6327)* – It's you (Orbital mix) / The light that burns twice as bright . . . (mix) / They're here (mix).

	Parlophone	Parlophone
Feb 95. (c-s) *(TCR 6401)* **PERFECT DAY** / **ANGEL**	27	□

(cd-s+=) *(CDR 6401)* – I won't give into you / Kill for you (lo-fi mix).
(12"+=) *(12R 6401)* – ('A'-Temple of boom remix) / ('A'-Chris & James epic).
(cd-s) *(CDRS 6401)* – ('A'side) / ('A'-Chris & James mix) / ('A'-Black One mix) / ('A'-Toytown mix).
Mar 95. (cd/c) *(<CD/TC PCSD 165>)* **CHA CHA CHA**　　30 □
– Perfect day / La plage / The day I was born / Secrets / Shining / Bring me down / Skin / Slouch / Bleeding you dry / Patterns / When will you come / West of the Cox / Ballad o' the bishop / Glass smash Jack.
Apr 95. (c-s) *(TCR 6407)* **BLEEDING YOU DRY** / **TOO MUCH** / **EASY** / **PERFECT DAY** (acoustic)　　□ -
(cd-s) *(CDRS 6407)* – (first 3 tracks) / Shining (acoustic).
(cd-s) *(CDR 6407)* – ('A'side) / I pushed the boat out so far it sank / Patterns (acoustic).
Jun 95. (c-s/7"; EMF and REEVES & MORTIMER) *(TC/+R 6412)* **I'M A BELIEVER.** / **AT LEAST WE'VE GOT OUR GUITARS**　　3 -
(cd-s) *(CDR 6412)* – ('A'side) / At this stage I couldn't say / ('A'-Unbelievable mix) / La plage (mix).
Oct 95. (c-s) *(TCR 6416)* **AFRO KING** / **UNBELIEVABLE**　　51 -
(cd-s+=) *(CDR 6416)* – Children / I believe.
(cd-s) *(CDRS 6416)* – ('A'side) / Too much / Easy / Bring me down.
—— split not long after the relative failure of the above single. DENCH returned in 1998 with a new outfit (see further below)

– compilations, etc. –

1998. (cd,c; shared with JESUS JONES) *EMI Capitol special; <19641>* **BACK 2 BACK**　　- □

WHISTLER

IAN DENCH – multi-instruments / **KERRY SHAW** – vocals / **JAMES TOPHAM** – viola (ex-BRIAN ENO)

	Wiiija	not iss.
May 98. (7") *(WIJ 084)* **RARE AMERICAN SHOES.** / **THINGS YOU NEVER SAY**	□	-

(cd-s+=) *(WIJ 084CD)* – Thinking it's over.
Sep 98. (7") *(WIJ 091)* **IF I GIVE YOU A SMILE.** / **GOT WHAT YOU WANTED**　　□ -
(cd-s+=) *(WIJ 091CD)* – Song about you.
Feb 99. (7") *(WIJ 096)* **DON'T JUMP IN FRONT OF MY TRAIN.** / **FOR REAL**　　□ -
(cd-s+=) *(WIJ 096CD)* – Tender years.
Mar 99. (cd/lp) *(WIJ CD/LP 1087)* **WHISTLER**　　□ -
– If I give you a smile / Don't jump in front of my train / Closing time / Emily / End / Rare American shoes / Heaven help me / Pulling the strings / Natalie's song / Please don't love me anymore.
Sep 99. (10"ep/cd-ep) *(WIJ 104 T/CD)* **INTERMISSION e.p.**　　□ -
– At seventeen / I just don't know what to do with myself / Blue, red and grey / All apologies.

EMINEM

Born: MARSHALL MATHERS, 1975, Kansas City, USA. Spending his childhood roaming from one State to the next, the gifted rapper and one time SOUL INTENT member began freestyling in his friend's basement at the age of fifteen. Five years (and, apparently, a lot of mushrooms and NWA albums) later, the white MC decided to try his luck in the increasing world of hip hop. He debuted with the poorly distributed album 'INFINITE' (1996) and failed blindly at attracting attention from any major labels. Legend DR DRE apparently discovered EMINEM (a word play on his initials) when he found a demo tape on Interscope's Jimmy Iovines' garage floor. To be fully convinced by the rapper, DRE travelled to watch him perform in the 1997 Rap Olympics before rushing over and signing him on the spot. His major label debut, 'THE SLIM SHADY LP', appeared in the Spring of '99, sales boosted after the rather offensive massive hit single, 'MY NAME IS'. The aforementioned platter rocketed to the top spot in America and sent parents into a fit of rage over the filth and obscenities our white chump was slobbering about on tape. The American media, senseless rock stars and a few bad words about his dear old momma were all mentioned in the single, that had such an infectious chorus it made listeners fall under the spell of EMINEM's crazy, high-speed, nasal-pinching slur. The sophomore album did not do so bad either, selling nearly a million copies in its first week and a further million in the months prior to its release. But the raging battle between him and the general public continued, when songs that depicted rape, murder, violence, excessive drug taking, child molesting and, erm, his poor old mother were all raised in frequent "morality" debates. The second single (and to some, his finest), 'GUILTY CONSCIENCE', featured DRE as his alter ego, who pops up to discuss EMINEM's relationship problems when he finds his wife in bed with another man. Not surprising to see then, that EMINEM returned the favour by contributing to DRE's '2001' LP on the brilliant and humorous track 'IT'S ALL ABOUT DRE'.

Album rating: INFINITE (*4) / THE SLIM SHADY LP (*7)

EMINEM – vocals / with **MARKY** and **JEFF BASS**

		not iss.	Indep ...
1996.	(cd-s; as SOUL INTENT) **FUCKING BACKSTABBER / BITERPHOBIA**	-	
1997.	(cd) **INFINITE**	-	

– Infinite / W.E.G.O. (interlude) / It's ok / 313 / Tonite / Maxine / Open mic / Never 2 far – Searchin' / Backstabber / Jealousy.

		Interscope	Interscope
Mar 99.	(c-s) (INC 95638) <95040> **MY NAME IS** / ('A'mix)	2	36 Feb99
	(cd-s) (IND 95638) – ('A'mixes).		
	(12") (INT 95638) – ('A'mixes).		
Apr 99.	(cd/c-d-lp)(clean;cd/c) <(IND/INC/INT 90287)><(IND/INC 90321)> **THE SLIM SHADY LP**	12	2

– Public service announcement / My name is / Guilty conscience / Brain damage / Paul / If I had / '97 Bonnie & Clyde / Zoe / Role model / Lounge / My fault / Ken Kaniff / Come on everybody / Rock bottom / Just don't give / Soap / As the world turns / I'm shady / Bad meets evil / Still don't give.

May 99.	(12") (RWK 193) **ANY MAN.** / ('A'mix)		
	(above issued on 'Rawkus')		
Aug 99.	(c-s; by EMINEM & DR.DRE) (497129-4) **GUILTY CONSCIENCE** / ('A'mix)	5	
	(cd-s) (497128-2) – ('A'side) / ('A'video).		
	(cd-s) (497129-2) – ('A'side) / My name is (video).		

Alec EMPIRE (see under ⇒ ATARI TEENAGE RIOT)

Scott ENGEL (see under ⇒ WALKER BROTHERS / Scott WALKER)

ENIGMA

Formed: By the German-based duo of MICHAEL CRETU and wife SANDRA who almost immediately found themselves with an unusual worldwide hit in 'SADENESS', early in 1991. Born in Bucharest, Rumania (18th of May '57), CRETU had been trained as a classical pianist in Paris, although he subsequently moved to Frankfurt's Academy Of Music and to conducting. In the late 70's, he worked as a session musician and became a key figure for the European disco scene. Around the same period, CRETU released his debut album, 'MOON, LIGHT AND FLOWERS', for the German side of 'Polydor'. A few years later, his outfit, MOTI SPECIAL, hit the top of the German charts with a single, 'COLD DAYS HOT NIGHTS' (Carrere; 7"/12" CAR/+T 364) taken from the album 'MOTI VATION'. He subsequently left MOTI members, NILS TUXEN and DICKY TARRACH, when he discovered, then produced his wife's massive Euro hit, 'I'LL NEVER BE MARIA MAGDALENA'. The electronic wizard went on to produce several albums by SANDRA and work with MIKE OLDFIELD, whom he had met at his Ibiza residence. With three albums, 'MCMXC a.D.' (1990), 'THE CROSS OF CHANGES' (1994) and 'LE ROI EST MORT, VIVE LE ROI!' (1996), now safely under their belt, ENIGMA have now sold nearly 20 million, their Gregorian chant musak (initially sampled from Munich's Kapelle Antiqua Choir) over a hip-hop dance beat, the toast of the coffee-table sect. • **Sampled:** SONGS FROM THE VICTORIOUS CITY (Anne Dudley & Jaz Coleman) + THE CALLING (Mind Over Rhythm).

Album rating: MCMXC a.D. (*6) / THE CROSS OF CHANGES (*5) / LE ROI EST MORT, VIVE LE ROI! (*4)

MICHAEL CRETU

with various session people

		Polydor	not iss.
1979.	(lp) (827834-1) **MOON, LIGHT AND FLOWERS**	-	- German

– '57 (the year I was born) / Fire and rain / Wild river / Shadows over my head / Love me / Moonlight flower / Sparks of imagination / Streets of time / Song for unknown heroes.

		Virgin	not iss.
1983.	(lp) (205290) **LEGIONAIRE**	-	- German

– Legionaire / Total normal / Spiel af zeit / Frau aus Stein / Goldene Jahre / Zeitlose Reise / Data-alpha-4 / Karawanen / Der planet der verlornen Zeit.

Aug 83.	(7") (VS 621) **TODAY, TODAY.** / **I OBEY**	-	-
1985.	(lp) (206884) **DIE CHINESISCHE**	-	- German

– Intro / Mikado / Coda / Amazonen / Chinesische Mauer / Samurai / Carte blanche / Schwarzer engel / Zinnsoldat.

Jul 85.	(7"/ext.12") (VS 774/+12) **SILVER WATER.** / **CARTE BLANCHE**	-	
Jul 85.	(lp/c) (V/TCV 2354) **THE INVISIBLE MAN**	-	

– Amurai / Carte blanche / Silver water / Your favourite toy / Intro / Mikado / Coda / Heavy traffic / The invisible man.

Sep 85.	(7"/12") (VS 823/+12) **SAMURAI.** / **SWORD OF FEAR**	-	
1988.	(lp; as CRETU & THEIRS) (208578) **BELLE EPOQUE**	-	- German

– Mona Lisa / Crazy life / When love is the missing word / Waterfall / Captain Right / 200 ways to Heaven / Don't say you love me (let me feel it) / Snowin' under my skin.

ENIGMA

CURLY M.C. (MICHAEL CRETU) – electronics / **F. GREGORIAN** (b. SANDRA, France) – vocals / **DAVID-FAIRSTEIN** – etc.

		Virgin Int	Charisma
Nov 90.	(7"/c-s) (DINS/+C 101) <98864> **SADENESS (part 1).** / ('A'-Meditation mix)	1	5
	(12"+=/cd-s+=) (DINS T/D 101) – ('A'extended) / ('A'violent US mix).		
Dec 90.	(cd/c/lp) (CD/MC+/VIR 11) <91642> **MCMXC a.D.**	1	6

– The voice of Enigma / Principles of lust (a) Sadeness (b) Find love (c) Sadeness-(reprise) / Callas went away / Mea culpa / The voice & the snake / Knocking on-forbidden doors / Back to the rivers of belief (a) Way to eternity (b) Hallelujah (c) The rivers of belief. (re-iss. Nov91)

Mar 91.	(7"/c-s) (DINS/+C 104) **MEA CULPA (part II).** / ('A'-Catholic mix)	55	-
	(12"+=/cd-s+=) (DINS T/D 104) – ('A'-fading shades mix).		
Sep 91.	(7"/c-s) (DINS 110) **PRINCIPLES OF LUST.** / **SADENESS (pt.2 radio mix)**	59	-
	(12"+=) (DINST 110) – ('A'extended) / ('A'-Owen mix).		
	(cd-s+=) (DINSD 110) – ('A-jazz mix) / ('A'-Owen mix).		
Jan 92.	(7"/c-s) (DINS/+C 112) **THE RIVERS OF BELIEF.** / **KNOCKING ON FORBIDDEN-DOORS**	68	
	(12"/cd-s) (DINS T/CD 112) – ('A'mixes).		
Jan 94.	(7"/c-s) (DINS/+C 123) <38423> **RETURN TO INNOCENCE.** / ('A'-380 midnight mix)	3	4
	(12"+=) (DINST 123) – ('A'extended mix).		
	(cd-s++=) (DINSD 123) – ('A'mix).		
Feb 94.	(cd/c/lp) (CD/MC+/VIR 20) <39236> **THE CROSS OF CHANGES**	1	9

– Second chapter / The eyes of truth / Return to innocence / Love you . . . I'll kill you / Silent warrior / The dream of the dolphin / Age of loneliness (Carly's song) / Out from the deep / The cross of changes. (gold-cd-iss. Nov94; CDVIRX 20)

May 94.	(7"/c-s) (DINS/+C 126) **THE EYES OF TRUTH.** / ('A'mix)	21	-
	(cd-s+=) (DINSD 126) – (2 other 'A'mixes).		
	(cd-s) (DINSDX 126) – ('A'side) / Sadeness (part I) / Mea culpa (part II) / Principles of lust.		
Aug 94.	(12"/c-s) (DINS T/C 135) **AGE OF LONELINESS.** / ('A'-Jam & Spoon mix)	21	
	(cd-s+=) (DINSDX 135) – Return to innocence (mix) / Sadeness part 1 (mix) / Principles of lust (everlasting lust).		
	(cd-s) (DINSD 135) – (5-'A'mixes).		

		Virgin	Virgin
Nov 96.	(cd/c) (CD/MC VIR 60) **LE ROI EST MORT, VIVE LE ROI!**	12	25 Dec96

– Le roi est mort, vive le roi / Morphing thru time / Third of its kind / Beyond the invisible / Why / Shadows in silence / Child in us / TNT for the brain / Almost full moon / Roundabout / Prism of life / Odyssey of the mind.

Jan 97.	(c-s) (DINSC 155) <38572> **BEYOND THE INVISIBLE** / **ALMOST FULL MOON**	26	81 Nov96
	(cd-s+=) (DINSD 155) – Light of your smile.		
Apr 97.	(c-s) (DINSC 161) **TNT FOR THE BRAIN** / ('A'mix)	60	
	(cd-s) (DINSD 161) – ('A'mixes).		

Brian ENO

Born: BRIAN PETER GEORGE ST.JOHN LE BAPTISTE DE LA SALLE ENO, 15 May'48, Suffolk, England. After leaving art school, where he fronted heavy group MAXWELL DEMON, he joined ROXY MUSIC in 1971. Contributing greatly to their image and sound on the albums, 'ROXY MUSIC' & 'FOR YOUR PLEASURE', he left due to a dispute over their increasingly pop-rock orientated direction. His first post-ROXY venture was '(NO PUSSYFOOTING)' in 1973 with ROBERT FRIPP (of KING CRIMSON). This was nothing more than extreme experimentation of synth-electronics and treated guitar. However, it did provide art lovers with a photo-shot of ENO & FRIPP in a multi-mirrored room. His first solo work in early 1974, 'HERE COME THE WARM JETS', disappointed the critics, who gave it the thumbs down, bar one gem, 'BABY'S ON FIRE'. He released two more greatly improved efforts for 'Island' before he formed his own label in 1975, appropriately titled 'Obscure'. Preceding this, in a fit of depression, he joined The WINKIES for a short tour during Feb-Mar'74, but departed after being diagnosed with a collapsed lung. He recovered to find himself on an 'Island records' concert bill on '1st JUNE, 1974', alongside stablemates KEVIN AYERS, NICO and JOHN CALE. The following year, he was hit by a car, which caused slight but not lasting brain damage. 1975's 'ANOTHER GREEN WORLD' represented the fruition of ENO's aural experimentation, sculpting instrumental, insidiously melodic soundscapes while the title track was subsequently used as the theme tune for the BBC TV arts series, 'Arena'. 'BEFORE AND AFTER SCIENCE' (1977) was an equally brilliant, if colder sounding, tapestry of sonic delights. Around this time, ENO began working with DAVID BOWIE on a trilogy of lp's that included 'LOW' (1977) and 'HEROES' (1977), while the following year he hooked up with TALKING HEADS, producing three of their albums during the period 1978-'80. He also collaborated with DAVID BYRNE on the ethnic-flavoured 'MY LIFE IN THE BUSH OF GHOSTS' (1981). With 'AMBIENT 1: MUSIC FOR AIRPORTS' (1978), ENO created an innovative classic while 'APOLLO: ATMOSPHERS AND SOUNDTRACKS' (1983) was a beguiling fusion of country and ambient, the gorgeous 'DEEP BLUE DAY' belatedly cropping up on the 'TRAINSPOTTTING' (1996) soundtrack. After initially collaborating with Canadian producer/engineer DANIEL LANOIS for production duties on such early 80's projects as 'THE PEARL' (a HAROLD BUDD/ENO album), the two worked wonders on U2's seminal 'UNFORGETTABLE FIRE' (1984). ENO clocked up further U2 production credits on 'THE JOSHUA TREE' (1987) and 'ACHTUNG BABY' (1991), scooping a joint Grammy (with LANOIS) in 1992 for the latter. The same year saw the release of a long awaited ENO solo album, 'NERVE NET', which took its cue from the burgeoning ambient techno scene. Throughout the 90's, this electronic auteur has continued to work on a dizzying array of music and other multi media projects, even publishing a volume of diaries in 1996, 'A YEAR WITH SWOLLEN APPENDICES'. The balding genius once described himself as a non-musician who just turned dials and switches. Maybe, but he happens to turn the right dials and switches, and this technically brilliant ambient experimentalist's obscure new musak will possibly have a direct link to what listeners will appreciate in the 21st century. • **Songwriters:** All composed by ENO. • **Trivia:** His 1977 song 'KING'S LEAD HAT' was in fact an anagram of TALKING HEADS. ENO has also done session and production work for JOHN CALE (1974-75), ROBERT WYATT (1975), ROBERT CALVERT (1975), DAVID BOWIE (1977) / DEVO (1978) / TALKING HEADS (1978-80) / U2 (1985-91 with Daniel Lanois) / etc.

Album rating: NO PUSSYFOOTIN' with Fripp (*2 at the time – *6 now!?) / HERE COME THE WARM JETS (*7) / TAKING TIGER MOUNTAIN (BY STRATEGY) (*7) / ANOTHER GREEN WORLD (*9) / DISCREET MUSIC (*6) / EVENING STAR with Fripp (*2 at the time – *5 now!?) / BEFORE AND AFTER SCIENCE (*8) / CLUSTER AND ENO with Cluster (*6) / AFTER THE HEAT with Moebius & Roedelius (*6) / MUSIC FOR FILMS (*6) / AMBIENT 1: MUSIC FOR AIRPORTS (*7) / AMBIENT 2: THE PLATEAUX OF MIRROR with Harold Budd (*5) / FOURTH WORLD VOL.1: POSSIBLE MUSICS with Jon Hassell (*6) / MY LIFE IN THE BUSH OF GHOSTS with David Byrne (*8) / AMBIENT 4: ON LAND (*7) / APOLLO, ATMOSPHERES & SOUNDTRACKS with Daniel Lanois & Roger Eno (*8) / THE PEARL with Harold Budd & Daniel Lanois (*5) / THURSDAY AFTERNOON (*6) / HYBRID with Michael Brook & Daniel Lanois (*5) / VOICES with Roger Eno (*5) / MORE BLANK THAN FRANK compilation (*7) / DESERT ISLAND SELECTION compilation (*7) / MUSIC FOR FILMS 2 (*6) / WRONG WAY UP with JOHN CALE (*7) / NERVE NET (*6) / THE SHUTOV ASSEMBLY (*6) / :NEROLI: (*5) / SPANNER with Jah Wobble (*6) / THE DROP (*5)

FRIPP & ENO

ROBERT FRIPP – guitar of KING CRIMSON / **BRIAN ENO** – synthesizers, instruments

	Island-Help	Antilles
Nov 73. (lp) (HELP 16) <7007> **NO PUSSYFOOTING**		

– The heavenly music corporation / Swastika girls. (re-iss. Oct77 on 'Polydor'; 2343 095) (re-iss. Jan87 on 'E.G.' lp/cd; EGED/EEGCD 2)

ENO

now solo with guest session people, including ROXY MUSIC musicians and ROBERT FRIPP, CHRIS SPEDDING, PAUL RUDOLPH and others.

	Island	Island
Jan 74. (lp/c) (ILPS/ICT <9268>) **HERE COME THE WARM JETS**	26	

– Needles in the camel's eye / The paw paw Negro blowtorch / Baby's on fire / Cindy tells me / Driving me backwards / On some faraway beach / Black frank / Dead finks don't talk / Some of them are old / Here come the warm jets. (re-iss. Mar77 on 'Polydor'; 2302 063) (re-iss. Jan87 on 'E.G.' lp/c/cd; EG LP/MC/CD 11) (cd re-iss. Mar91; same)

Mar 74. (7") (WIP 6178) **SEVEN DEADLY FINNS. / LATER ON**

—— guests incl. PORTSMOUTH SINFONIA ORCHESTRA, PHIL COLLINS – drums / etc.

Nov 74. (lp/c) (ILPS/ICT <9309>) **TAKING TIGER MOUNTAIN (BY STRATEGY)**

– Burning airlines give you so much more / Back in Judy's jungle / The fat lady of Limbourg / Mother whale eyeless / The great pretender / Third uncle / Put a straw under baby / The truth wheel / China my China / Taking tiger mountain. (re-iss. Mar77 on 'Polydor'; 2302 068) (re-iss. Jan87 on 'E.G.' lp/c/cd; EG LP/MC/CD 17) (cd re-iss. Mar91; same)

Aug 75. (7") (WIP 6233) <036> **THE LION SLEEPS TONIGHT (WIMOWEH). / I'LL COME RUNNING**

—— now with **FRIPP** (3) / **COLLINS** (3) / **JOHN CALE** – viola (2) / **PAUL RUDOLPH** (3) / **PERCY JONES** – bass (3) / **ROD MELVIN** – piano (3) / **BRIAN TURRINGTON** – bass, piano (1)

Sep 75. (lp/c) (ILPS/ICT <9351>) **ANOTHER GREEN WORLD**

– Sky saw / Over Fire Island / St. Elmo's fire / In dark trees / The big ship / I'll come running / Another green world / Sombre reptiles / Little fishes / Golden hours /

Becalmed / Zawinul – Lava / Everything merges with the night. (re-iss. Mar77 on 'Polydor'; 2302 069) (re-iss. Jan87 & Mar91 on 'E.G.' lp/c/cd; EG LP/MC/CD 21)

	Obscure	Antilles
Nov 75. (lp) (OBS 3) <7030> **DISCREET MUSIC**		

– Discreet music 1 & 2 / Three Variations on canon in D major; a) Fullness of wind – b) French catalogues – c) Brutal ardour. (re-iss. Jan87 on 'EG-Editions' lp/c/cd; EGED/EGEDC/EEGCD 23)

FRIPP & ENO

collaborate again.

	Help-Island	Antilles
Dec 75. (lp) (HELP 22) <7018> **EVENING STAR**		

– Wind on water / Evening star / Evensong / Wind on wind / An index of metals. (re-iss. Oct77 on 'Polydor'; 2343 094) (re-iss. Jan87 on 'E.G.' lp/cd; EGED/EEGCD 3)

—— For the next couple of years he worked with 801 (PHIL MANZANERA's band). He also produced his own 'Obscure' label, discovering people including PENGUIN CAFE ORCHESTRA, MICHAEL NYMAN, MAX EASTLEY & DAVID TOOP, HAROLD BUDD plus JAN STEELE / JOHN CAGE. More commercially he also played on and produced 1977 albums by DAVID BOWIE, TALKING HEADS, ULTRAVOX.

BRIAN ENO

	Polydor	Island
Dec 77. (lp) (2302 071) <9478> **BEFORE AND AFTER SCIENCE**		May78

– No one receiving / Backwater / Kurt's rejoiner / Energy fools the magician / King's lead hat / Here he comes / Julie with ... / By this river / Through hollow lands / Spider and I. (re-iss. Jan87 on 'E.G.' lp/c/cd; EG LP/MC/CD 32) (cd re-iss. Mar91; same)

Jan 78. (7") (2001 762) **KING'S LEAD HAT. / R.A.F. (by "ENO & SNATCH")**

	Polydor	E.G.
Sep 78. (lp) (2310 623) <EGS 105> **MUSIC FOR FILMS**	55	

– M386 / Aragon / From the same hill / Inland sea / Two rapid formations / Slow water / Sparrowfall 1 / Sparrowfall 2 / Sparrowfall 3 / Quartz / Events in dense fog / There is nobody / A measured room / Patrolling wire borders / Task force / Alternative 3 / Strange light / Final sunset. (privately pressed 1976 on 'EG'; EGM 1) (re-iss. Jan87 on 'E.G.' lp/c/cd; EGED/EGEDC/EEGCD 5)

	Ambient	P.V.C.
Mar 79. (lp/c) (AMB/+C 001) <7908> **AMBIENT 1: MUSIC FOR AIRPORTS**		

– 1'1 / 2'1 / 1'2 / 2'2. (re-iss. Jan87 on 'E.G.' lp/c/cd; EGED/EGEDC/EEGCD 17)

—— Early in '79, ENO and MOEBIUS & ROEDILIUS (from CLUSTER) released album 'AFTER THE HEAT' (Sky 021)

—— Late in 1979, ENO collaborated with trumpeter JON HASSELL on album 'FOURTH WORLD VOL.1: POSSIBLE MUSICS' on 'E.G.'; EGED 007)

—— next with **HAROLD BUDD** – piano

	E.G.-Ambient	E.G.
Apr 80. (lp; ENO & BUDD) (EGAMB 002) <EGS 107> **AMBIENT 2: THE PLATEAUX OF MIRRORS**		

– First light / Steal away / The plateau of mirror / Above Chiangmai / An arc of doves / Not yet remembered / The chill air / Among fields of crystal / Wind in lonely fences / Failing light. (re-iss. Jan87 on 'EG')

—— next with DAVID BYRNE, vocalist and instrumentalist w/ TALKING HEADS

	E.G.	Sire
Feb 81. (lp/c; BRIAN ENO & DAVID BYRNE) (EG LP/MC 48) <6093> **MY LIFE IN THE BUSH OF GHOSTS**	29	44

– America is waiting / Mea culpa / Regiment / Help me somebody / The Jezebel spirit / Qu'ran / Moonlight in glory / The carrier / A secret life / Come with us / Mountain of needles. (re-iss. Jan87 on 'E.G.' lp/c/cd; EG LP/MC/CD 48)

May 81. (7"; BRIAN ENO & DAVID BYRNE) (EGO 1) **THE JEZEBEL SPIRIT. / REGIMENT**

(12"+=) (EGOX 1) – Very very hungry (Qu'ran).

Mar 82. (lp/c) ('EG-Editions'; EGED/+C 20) **AMBIENT (4): ON LAND**	93	-

– Lizard point / The lost day / Tal coat / Shadow / Unfamiliar wind / A clearing / Dunwich Beach, Autumn 1960. (cd-iss. Jan87 on 'E.G.'; EEGCD 20)

Jul 83. (lp; BRIAN ENO with DANIEL LANOIS & ROGER ENO) (EGLP 53) **APOLLO: ATMOSPHERES & SOUNDTRACKS**		-

– Under stars / The secret place / Matta / Signals / An ending (ascent) / Under stars II / Drift / Silver morning / Deep blue day / Weightless / Always returning / Stars. (re-iss. Jan87 & Mar91 on 'E.G.' lp/c/cd; EG LP/MC/CD 53)

	EG-Editions	not iss.
Aug 84. (lp; HAROLD BUDD & BRIAN ENO with DANIEL LANOIS) (EGED 37) **THE PEARL**		

– Late October / A stream with bright fish / The silver ball / Against the sky / Lost in the humming air / Dark-eyed sister / Their memories / The pearl / Foreshadowed / An echo of night / Still return. (re-iss. Jan87 on 'E.G.' lp/c/cd; EG LP/MC/CD 37)

—— In 1984, he released 2 albums 'BEGEGNUNGEN I & II' with MOEBIUS, ROEDILUS & PLANK.

Aug 85. (lp/c; MICHAEL BROOK with BRIAN ENO & DANIEL LANOIS) ('EG-Editions'; EGED/+C 41) **HYBRID**		-

– Hybrid / Distant village / Mimosa / Pond life / Ocean motion / Midday / Earth floor / Vacant. (re-iss. Nov86 on 'E.G.' lp/c/cd; EG LP/MC/CD 41)

Aug 85. (lp; ROGER ENO with BRIAN ENO) ('EG-Editions'; EGED 42) **VOICES**		-

– A place in the wilderness / The day after / At the water's edge / Grey promenade / A paler sky / Through the blue / Evening tango / Recalling winter / Voices / The old dance / Reflections on I.K.B. (re-iss. Jan87 on 'E.G.' lp/c/cd; EG LP/MC/CD 42)

Jan 87. (lp/cd) (EG LP/CD 64) **THURSDAY AFTERNOON**		-

– Thursday afternoon. (1 track only) (re-iss. cd Mar91; same)

ENO / CALE

—— (collaboration **JOHN CALE** – vocals, multi-)with **ROBERT AHWAI** – rhythm guitar / **DARYL JOHNSON** – bass / **NEIL CATCHPOLE** – violin / **RONALD JONES** – drums, tabla / **DAVE YOUNG** – guitars, bass

		Land	Opal-Warner
Oct 90.	(lp/c/cd) *(AS/+C/CD 12)* **WRONG WAY UP**	☐	☐

– Lay my love / One word / In the backroom / Empty frame / Cordoba / Spinning away / Footsteps / Been there done that / Crime in the desert / The river. *(re-iss. Jul92; same)*

| Nov 90. | (12"ep/cd-ep) **ONE WORLD. / GRANDFATHER'S HOUSE / PALAQUIN** | ☐ | - |

BRIAN ENO

		Opal-WEA	Opal-Warner
Jul 92.	(7") **FRACTIAL ZOOM.** / ('A'-Moby mix)	☐	☐

(12"+=) – (4 mixes).
(cd-s++=) – (another mix) / The roil, the choke.

| Sep 92. | (cd/c) *(9362 45033-2/-4)* **NERVE NET** | 70 | ☐ |

– Fractial zoom / Wire shock / What actually happened? / Pierre in mist / My squelchy life / Decentre / Juju space jazz / The roil, the choke / Ali click / Distributing being / Web.

| Oct 92. | (7") **ALI CLICK (Beirut mix).** / ('A'-Rural mix) | ☐ | ☐ |

(12"+=) – ('A'-Markus Draws + Grid mixes).
(cd-s) – ('A'side) / ('A'-Markus Draws + Grid mixes) / ('A'-trance long darkly mad mix) / ('A'-trance instrumental).

| Nov 92. | (cd/c) *(9362 45010-2/-4)* **THE SHUTOV ASSEMBLY** | ☐ | ☐ |

– Triennale / Alhondiga / Markgraph / Lanzarote / Francisco / Riverside / Innocenti / Stedelijk / Ikebukero / Cavallino.
(above music inspired by Moscow painter Sergei Shutov)

—— Around the same time as above, he lectured at Sadler's Wells, and is the brunt of NME jokes as Professor Eno.

		All Saints	Gyroscope
Jun 93.	(cd) *(ASCD 015)* **:NEROLI:**	☐	☐

– :Neroli:.
above's long piece of music was used in hospitals for childbirth!

—— Sep 94; he was credited on JAMES' ltd.album 'WAH WAH'.

| Oct 95. | (lp/c/cd; BRIAN ENO & JAH WOBBLE) *(AS/+C/CD 023)* **SPANNER** | 71 | ☐ |

– Where we lived / Like organza / Steam / Garden recalled / Marine radio / Unusual balance / Space diary 1 / Spinner / Transmitter and trumpet / Left where it fell.

| Jun 97. | (cd) *(ASCD 032)* **THE DROP** | ☐ | |

– Slip dip / But if / Belgiam drop / Cornered / Black drop / Out-out / Swanky / Coasters / Blissed / M.C. Organ / Boomcubist / Hazard / Rayonism / Dutch blur / Back clack / Dear world / Iced world.

– his compilations, others, etc. –

on 'E.G.' unless mentioned otherwise

| Apr 82. | (d-c; FRIPP & ENO) *(EGDC 2)* **NO PUSSYFOOTIN' / EVENING STAR** | ☐ | - |
| Nov 83. | (10xlp-box) *(EGBS 002)* **WORKING BACKWARDS 1983-1973** | ☐ | - |

– (first 9 lp's, plus MUSIC FOR FILMS VOL.2 / + RARITIES m-lp:- Seven deadly finns / The lion sleeps tonight / Strong flashes of light / More volts / Mist rhythm)

| Mar 86. | (lp/c) *(EG LP/MC 65)* **MORE BLANK THAN FRANK** | ☐ | - |

(cd-iss. Jun87 & Mar91; EGCD 65)

| Jan 87. | (cd) *(EGCD 65)* **DESERT ISLAND SELECTION** | | - |

– Here he comes / Everything merges with the night / I'll come running (edit) / On some faraway beach (edit) / Spirits drifting / Back in Judy's jungle / St. Elmo's fire / No one receiving / Julie with . . . / Taking tiger mountain (edit) / 1'1.

| Jan 87. | (lp/c) *EG-Editions; (EGED/+C 35)* **MUSIC FOR FILMS 2** | | - |

– The dove / Roman twilight / Matta / Dawn, marshland / Climate study / The secret place / An ending (ascent) / Always returning 1 / Signals / Under stars / Drift / Study / Approaching Taidu / Always returning 2.

| Mar 89. | (cd-s) *(CDT 41)* **ANOTHER GREEN WORLD / DOVER BEACH / DEEP BLUE DAY / 2'1** | ☐ | - |
| Dec 89. | (3xc-box)(3xcd-box) *(EG BM/BC 7)* **ISLAND VARIOUS ARTISTS** | ☐ | - |

– (ANOTHER GREEN WORLD / BEFORE AND AFTER SCIENCE / APOLLO)

Nov 93.	(3xcd-box) *Virgin; (ENOBX 1)* **BRIAN ENO** (collaborations)	☐	-
Nov 93.	(3xcd-box) *Virgin; (ENOBX 2)* **BRIAN ENO 2** (collaborations)	☐	-
Feb 94.	(cd/c) *Venture; (CD/TC VE 920)* **THE ESSENTIAL FRIPP AND ENO**	☐	-
Oct 94.	(3xcd-box) *Virgin; (TPAK 36)* **THE COMPACT COLLECTION**	☐	-

—— ENO contributed 2 tracks on live lp 'JUNE 1st, 1974' with KEVIN AYERS, NICO and JOHN CALE. He also with brother ROGER and DANIEL LANOIS provided one track to DUNE film (1984). For albums by CLUSTER & ENO; see CLUSTER.

JOHN ENTWISTLE (see under ⇒ WHO)

ENUFF Z'NUFF (dig out; Great Metal . . .)

ENYA

Born: EITHNE NI BHRAONAIN, 17 May'61, Gweadore, County Donegal, Ireland. Classically trained as a pianist, she made her first inroads into the music business via contributions to her family's (CLANNAD) early 80's album, 'FUAIM', although her first solo project was a soundtrack for 'Island' records, 'The Frog Prince', in 1985. She had already been commissioned by the BBC to write the TV score to the cultural documentary, 'The Celts'. Built around new age synths, piano, wailing bagpipes and washes of ambient atmospherics, with ENYA singing in Irish, the record was different enough to attract interest from the mainstream music press and a subsequent Top 70 UK chart placing. Signed to 'Warners', ENYA began collaborating on the songwriting front with backing musicians, ROMA and NICKY RYAN, the latter also becoming her producer. Together they penned the acclaimed 'WATERMARK' (1988) opus, the hypnotic, aquatic orchestrations of 'ORINOCO FLOW' giving ENYA her first UK No.1 and bringing her worldwide recognition. The lavish arrangements and choral-like effects transported the singer's crystal pure vocals into an ethereal new dimension, the bulk of the album alternating between hymn-like grace and more expansively sublime sound collages. Spawning a further two singles in 'EVENING FALLS' and 'STORMS IN AFRICA', the record went on to become a multi-million seller, more of a landmark than a watermark. A subsequent follow-up, 'SHEPHERD MOONS' (1991), stuck more or less to the same formula if not quite capturing the otherworldly allure of its predecessor. Nevertheless, it became ENYA's first UK No.1 album, selling even more copies around the world and spending a staggering four years in the American charts. Though the demand was intense, the reclusive star once again chose not to tour, instead ensconcing herself in the studio once more to begin work on a third album, 'THE MEMORY OF TREES' (1995). The record deviated little from her previous output although if anything, it was more accessible, the positively jaunty 'ANYWHERE IS' coming as close to conventional pop music as ENYA has yet strayed. The single provided her with another Top 10 hit, while the album itself was another transatlantic success story. A compilation album, 'PAINT THE SKY WITH STARS – THE BEST OF ENYA' was released late in '97, filling in some time before her next effort, probably released at the turn of the century. • **Trivia:** Her father LED BRENNAN was a member of showband SLIEVE FOY BAND.

Album rating: ENYA (*4; + THE CELTS) / WATERMARK (*7) / SHEPHERD MOONS (*6) / MEMORY OF TREES (*6) / PAINT THE SKY WITH STARS – THE BEST OF ENYA compilation (*7)

ENYA – vocals, keyboards, percussion (ex-CLANNAD)

		Island	not iss.
Oct 85.	(lp/c) *(ISTA/ICT 10)* **THE FROG PRINCE** (soundtrack)	☐	☐

		B.B.C.	Atlantic
Feb 87.	(lp/c/cd) *(REB/ZCF/BBCCD 605) <81842>* **ENYA** (rec.1980)	69	☐

– The Celts / Aldebaran / I want tomorrow / March of the Celts / Deireadh on tuath / The Sun in the stream / To go beyond (1) / Epona / Fairytale / Epona Triad: St. Patrick Cu Chulainn-oisin / Boadicea / Bard dance / Dan y dur / To go beyond (II). *(re-iss. Nov92 as 'THE CELTS' on 'WEA' hit UK No.10 – cd+=)(lp/c; 450991167-2)(WX 498/+C) – Portrait (out of the blue).*

| Feb 87. | (7") *(RESL 201)* **I WANT TOMORROW.** / THE CELTS THEME | | - |

(12"+=/cd-s+=) *(RESL)* – To Go Beyond I + II. *(re-iss. Nov88; same)*

		W.E.A.	Geffen
Sep 88.	(lp/c)(cd) *(WX 199/+C)(246006-2) <24233>* **WATERMARK**	5	25 Jan89

– Watermark / Cursum perficio / On your shore / Storms in Africa / Exile / Miss Clare remembers / Orinoco flow / Evening falls / River / The longships / Na laetha geal m'oige / Storms in Africa (part II).

| Oct 88. | (7") *(YZ 312) <27633>* **ORINOCO FLOW.** / OUT OF THE BLUE | 1 | 24 Jan89 |

(12"+=/cd-s+=) *(YZ 312 T/CD)* – Smaotin.

| Dec 88. | (7") *(YZ 356)* **EVENING FALLS.** / OICHE CHIUN (SILENT NIGHT) | 20 | ☐ |

(12"+=/cd-s+=) *(YZ 356 T/CD)* – Morning glory.

| Feb 89. | (7"/c-s) *(YZ 368/+C)* **STORMS IN AFRICA (pt.II).** / STORMS IN AFRICA | 41 | ☐ |

(12"+=/cd-s+=/3"cd-s+=) *(YZ 368 T/CD/CDX)* – The Celts / Aldebaran.

| May 91. | (7"/c-s) *(YZ T/CD)* **EXILE.** / ON YOUR SHORE | ☐ | ☐ |

(12"+=/cd-s+=) *(YZ T/CD)* – Watermark / River.

		W.E.A.	Reprise
Oct 91.	(7"/c-s) *(YZ 604/+C) <19089>* **CARIBBEAN BLUE.** / ORINOCO FLOW	13	79 Feb92

(cd-s+=) *(YZ 604CD)* – Angels.
(cd-s++=) *(YZ 604CDX)* – As baile / Oriel window.

—— album guests **ROMA RYAN** – percussion / **STEVE SIDWELL** – cornet / **NICKY RYAN** and **ANDY DUNCAN** – perc. / **LIAM O'FLIONN** – vulcan pipes / **ROY JEWITT** – clarinet

| Nov 91. | (cd)(lp/c) *(903175572-2)(WX 431/+C) <26775>* **SHEPHERD MOONS** | 1 | 17 |

– Shepherd moons / Caribbean blue / How can I keep from singing? / Ebudae / Angeles / No holly for Miss Quinn / Book of days / Evacuee / Lothlorien / Marble halls / Afer Ventus / Smaonte . . .

| Dec 91. | (7"/c-s) *(YZ 365/+C)* **HOW CAN I KEEP FROM SINGING? / ORCHE CHIUN (SILENT NIGHT)** | 13 | ☐ |

(12"+=/cd-s+=) *(YZ 365 T/CD)* – 'S Fagain mo baile.

| Jul 92. | (7"/c-s) *(YZ 640/+C)* **BOOK OF DAYS. / AS BAILE** | 10 | ☐ |

(cd-s+=) *(YZ 640CD)* – ('A'side) / Watermark / On your shoe / Exile.

| Nov 92. | (7"/c-s) *(YZ 705/+C)* **THE CELTS. / OFCHE CHIUN** | 29 | ☐ |

(cd-s+=) *(YZ 705 T/CD)* – S'fagain mobhaile.

| Nov 95. | (c-s) *(WEA 023C)* **ANYWHERE IS / BOADICEA** | 7 | ☐ |

(cd-s+=) *(WEA 023CD)* – Oriel window.
(cd-s) *(WEA 023CDX)* – ('A'side) / Book of days / Caribbean blue / Orinoco flow.

| Nov 95. | (cd/c) *(0630 12879-2/-4) <46106>* **THE MEMORY OF TREES** | 5 | 9 |

– The memory of trees / Anywhere is / Pax deorum / Athair ar neamh / From where I am / China roses / Hope has a place / Tea-house moon / Once you had gold / La sonadora / On my way home.

| Nov 96. | (c-s) *(WEA 047C)* **ON MY WAY HOME / BOADICEA** | 26 | - |

(cd-s+=) *(WEA 047CD)* – Eclipse / Storms in Africa (part 2).
(cd-s) *(WEA 047CDX)* – ('A'side) / Morning glory / I may not awaken.

| Nov 97. | (cd/c) *(3984 20895-2/-4) <46835>* **PAINT THE SKY WITH STARS – THE BEST OF ENYA** (compilation) | 4 | 38 |

– Orinoco flow / Caribbean blue / Book of days / Anywhere is / Only if . . . / The

Celts / China roses / Shepherd moons / Ebudae / Storms in Africa / Watermark / Paint the sky with stars / Marble halls / On my way home / Memory of trees / Boadicea.

Dec 97. (c-s/cd-s) *(WEA 143 C/CD)* **ONLY IF . . . / OICHE CHUIN (SILENT NIGHT Gaelic version)** | 43 | - |
(cd-s+=) *(WEA 143CDX)* – Willows on the water.

EPMD (dig out; 4th edition)

ERASURE

Formed: London, England . . . 1985 by VINCE CLARKE and one-time choirboy ANDY BELL, who answered a Melody Maker "vocalist wanted" ad. CLARKE's lucrative past had included spearheading other outfits; DEPECHE MODE ('81), YAZOO (82-83) and the one-off ASSEMBLY ('84) with FEARGAL SHARKEY and E.C.RADCLIFFE. In June 1985, he teamed up with PAUL QUINN (ex-Bourgie Bourgie) on another one-off, 'ONE DAY'. All were released on Daniel Miller's indie label 'Mute', as were his new outfit. ERASURE's debut single in September '85, 'WHO NEEDS LOVE LIKE THAT', only found a No.55 placing and things looked bleak when both of their follow-ups only managed to scrape into the Top 100 (one of them, 'OH L'AMOUR', later became a Top 10 hit in late '87 for pop duo, DOLLAR). ERASURE finally broke through from the indie scene in October '86, when 'SOMETIMES' made UK No.2. BELL's vocal theatrics were almost as distinctive as his Liberace meets Sylvester stage persona, although the comparisons with ALISON MOYET were inevitable if a little unfair. The fact that CLARKE and BELL were successful in Europe before breaking in Britain speaks volumes. Basically, ERASURE was the shiny, happy, extrovert young pop kid to the sullen, rather aloof older brother of DEPECHE MODE and if you're looking for someone to blame for the 90's Euro-pop overload (SCATMAN, CULTURE BEAT, LA BOUCHE etc.), this dastardly duo are your men. Still, any group capable of such swoonful pop genius as 'BLUE SAVANNAH' and 'STAR', deserves leniency (and besides, 'Rhythm Of The Night' was a top tune!). Yet these were but two of ERASURE'S rather impressive run of 18 consecutive hits throughout the late 80's and early 90's, while 'THE INNOCENTS' (1988), 'WILD!' (1989) and 'CHORUS' (1991) were all No.1 albums. In the summer of '92, the band were again at the top of the charts, this time with the 'ABBA-ESQUE' EP; no prizes for guessing what this was all about. A fairly unoriginal, if charming tribute/parody to everybody's favourite Swedish popsters, it goes without saying that the boys did a brilliant ANNA/FRIDA for the video. A greatest hits collection, 'POP! THE FIRST 20 HITS' (1992), flew off the shelves that Christmas, with the group taking a well-earned break. Returning to the scene in 1994, they found the going a little tougher; The PRODIGY were charting with much harder electronic sounds and the dance scene in general was becoming less pop-centric (and conversely, the pop scene was becoming more dance-centric). Perhaps bearing this in mind, then, the group duly drafted in the likes of ORBITAL and old hands KRAFTWERK to give 'ERASURE' (1995), their last effort to date more of an electro sheen. • **Songwriters:** CLARKE writes all material except covers; RIVER DEEP MOUNTAIN HIGH (Phil Spector) / GIMME GIMME GIMME + ABBA-ESQUE EP (Abba) / TOO DARN HOT (Cole Porter). • **Trivia:** In 1991, 'BLUE SAVANNAH' was named as Most Performed Song at the Ivor Novello awards.

Album rating: WONDERLAND (*7) / THE CIRCUS (*6) / THE INNOCENTS (*7) / WILD! (*5) / CHORUS (*5) / POP! THE FIRST 20 HITS compilation (*8) / I SAY I SAY I SAY (*6) / COWBOY (*4)

VINCE CLARKE (b. 3 Jul'60, South Woodford, England) – keyboards / **ANDY BELL** (b.25 Apr'64, Peterborough, England) – vocals (ex-The VOID)

		Mute	Sire

Sep 85. (7") *(MUTE 40)* **WHO NEEDS LOVE LIKE THAT. / PUSH ME SHOVE ME** | 55 | |
(diff.mix-12"+=) *(12MUTE 40)* – ('A'instrumental work-out mix).
(12") *(L12MUTE 40)* – ('A'-Mexican mix) / ('B'-Tacos mix).
(re-iss. cd-s Sep93; CDMUTE 40)

Nov 85. (7") *(MUTE 42)* **HEAVENLY ACTION. / DON'T SAY NO** | 100 | |
(12"+=) *(12MUTE 42)* – My heart . . . so blue (Incidental mix).
(d12"+=) *(D12MUTE 42)* – Who needs love like that (Mexican mix) / Push me shove me (Tacos mix).
(12") *(L12MUTE 42)* – ('A'-Yellow Brick mix) / ('B'-Ruby Red mix).
(re-iss. cd-s Sep93; CDMUTE 42)

Apr 86. (7") *(MUTE 45)* **OH L'AMOUR. / MARCH ON DOWN THE LINE** | 85 | |
(12"+=) *(12MUTE 45)* – Gimme gimme gimme (a man after midnight).
('A-Funky Sister mix-12"+=) *(L12MUTE 45)* – Gimme gimme gimme..
(re-iss. cd-s Sep93; CDMUTE 45)

Jun 86. (cd/c/lp) *(CD/C+/STUMM 25)* **WONDERLAND** | 71 | |
– Who needs love like that / Reunion / Cry so easy / Push me shove me / Heavenly action / Say what / Love is a loser / My heart . . . so blue / Oh l'amour / Pistol. *(ltd-12"-w/lp)*– OH L'AMOUR / MARCH ON DOWN THE LINE / GIMME GIMME GIMME. *(cd+=)* – (remixes); Say what / Senseless / March on down the line.

Oct 86. (7") *(MUTE 51)* **SOMETIMES. / SEXUALITY** | 2 | |
(ext-12"+=) *(12MUTE 51)* – Say what.
(diff.mix-12"+=) *(L12MUTE 51)* – Say what.
(d7"+=) *(DMUTE 51)* – Push me shove me / Who needs love like that.
(c-s+=) *(CDMUTE 51)* – Who needs love like that / Heavenly action / Oh l'amour.
(re-iss. cd-s Sep93; CDMUTE 51)

Feb 87. (7") *(MUTE 56)* **IT DOESN'T HAVE TO BE. / IN THE HALL OF THE MOUNTAIN KING** | 12 | |
('A'-diff.mix-12"+=) *(12MUTE 56)* – Who needs love like that.
('A'-diff.mix-12"+=) *(L12MUTE 56)* – Heavenly action.

(d7"+=) *(DMUTE 56)* – Sometimes / Sexuality.
(cd-s++=) *(CDMUTE 56)* – Sometimes / Oh l'amour / Heavenly action / Who needs love like that / Gimme gimme gimme.
(re-iss. cd-s Sep93; same)

Apr 87. (cd/c/lp) *(CD/C+/STUMM 35)* <25554> **THE CIRCUS** | 6 | |
– It doesn't have to be / Hideaway / Don't dance / If I could / Sexuality / Victim of love / Leave me to bleed / Sometimes / The circus / Spiralling. *(ltd.d-c+=)* – WONDERLAND *(cd+=)* – Sometimes (remix) / It doesn't (mix) / In the hall of the mountain king.

May 87. (7"/7"pic-d) *(MUTE/+P 61)* **VICTIM OF LOVE (remix). / THE SOLDIER'S RETURN** | 7 | |
('A'ext-12"+=/12"pic-d+=) *(12MUTE 61)* – ('A'dub).
(12"+=) *(L12MUTE 61)* – If I could help (Japanese mix).
(cd-s+=) *(CDMUTE 61)* – ('A' dub) / Safety in numbers (live) / Don't dance (live) / Leave me to bleed (live).

Sep 87. (7") *(1MUTE 66)* **THE CIRCUS (remix). / THE CIRCUS (version)** | 6 | |
(12") *(1MUTE 66T)* – ('A'live) / Victim of love (live) / If I could (live) / Spiralling (live).
(12") *(2MUTE 66T)* – ('A'-Bareback Rider mix) / It doesn't have to be (live) / Who needs love like that (live) / Gimme gimme gimme (live).
(12") *(3MUTE 66T)* – ('A'-Gladiator mix) / Sometimes (live) / Say what (live) / Oh l'amour (live).
(re-iss. cd-s Sep93; CDMUTE 66)

Dec 87. (2x12"lp/cd) *(L/LCD STUMM 35)* <25667> **THE TWO RING CIRCUS** *(re-iss. last lp)* | | |
(cd+=) – Victim of love / The Circus / Spiralling / Sometimes / Gimme gimme gimme / Oh l'amour / Who needs love like that.

Feb 88. (7") *(MUTE 74)* **SHIP OF FOOLS / WHEN I NEEDED YOU** | 6 | |
(diff.mix;12"+=/3"cd-s+=) *(12/CD MUTE 74)* – River deep mountain high (mix).
(diff.mix-12"+=) *(L12MUTE 74)* – River deep mountain high (dance).

Apr 88. (cd/c/lp) *(CD/C+/STUMM 55)* <25730> **THE INNOCENTS** | 1 | 49 |
– A little respect / Ship of fools / Phantom bride / Chains of love / Sixty-five thousand / Heart of stone / Yahoo! / Imagination / Witch in the ditch / Weight of the world. *(cd+=)* – River deep mountain high (mix) / When I needed you (mix).

May 88. (7") *(MUTE 83)* <27844> **CHAINS OF LOVE. / DON'T SUPPOSE** | 11 | 12 Jul88 |
(diff.mixes;12"+=/cd-s+=) *(12/CD MUTE 83)* – The good, the bad and the ugly (mix).
(diff.mix-12"+=) *(L12MUTE 83)* – (extra track as above).

Sep 88. (s7"/7") *(P+/MUTE 85)* <27738> **A LITTLE RESPECT. / LIKE ZSA ZSA GABOR** | 4 | 14 Dec88 |
(diff.mix;12"+=/cd-s+=) *(12/CD MUTE 85)* – Love is cooler than death.
(diff.mix;12"+=/cd-s+=) *(L12/LCD MUTE 85)* – (extra track as above).

Dec 88. (12"ep/cd-ep/7"ep) *(12/CD+/MUTE 93)* <25904> **CRACKERS INTERNATIONAL: EP** | 3 | 73 Apr89 |
– Stop / Knocking on your door / She won't be home / The hardest part.
(d3"cd-ep+=/12"+=) *(L12/LCD MUTE 93)* – Stop (Mark Saunders remix) / Knocking on your door (Mark Saunders remix) / God rest ye merry gentlemen.

Jul 89. (c-s) <22879> **STOP! / SHIP OF FOOLS** | - | 97 |

Sep 89. (c-s/7") *(C+/MUTE 89)* **DRAMA! / SWEET SWEET BABY** | 4 | |
(diff.mixes;12"+=/3"cd-s+=) *(12/CD MUTE 89)* – Paradise (mix).

Oct 89. (cd/c/lp) *(CD/C+/STUMM 75)* <26026> **WILD!** | 1 | 57 |
– You surround me / Drama! / How many times? / Crown of thorns / Piano song (instrumental) / Blue savannah / Star / La Gloria / Brother and sister / 2,000 miles / Piano song.

Dec 89. (c-s/7") *(C+/MUTE 99)* **YOU SURROUND ME. / 91 STEPS** | 15 | |
(diff.mixes;12"+=/3"cd-s+=) *(12/CD MUTE 99)* – Supernature.
(diff.mixes;12"+=/cd-s+=) *(L12/LCD MUTE 99)* – Supernature (William Orbit mix).
(12") *(XL12MUTE 99)* – ('A'-Gareth Jones remix) / Supernature (Mark Saunders remix) / Supernature (Daniel Miller & Phil Legg dub mix).

Mar 90. (c-s/7") *(C+/MUTE 109)* **BLUE SAVANNAH. / NO G.D.M. (unfinished mix)** | 3 | |
(12"+=/cd-s+=) *(12/CD MUTE 109)* – Runaround on the underground.
(extra-12") *(XL12MUTE 109)* – ('A'-Der Deutche mix 1 & 2).

May 90. (c-s/7") *(C+/MUTE 111)* **STAR. / ('A'soul mix)** | 11 | |
(12"+=/cd-s+=) *(12/CD MUTE 111)* – ('A'-Dreamlike state 24 hour technicolour mix).

Jun 91. (c-s/7") *(C+/MUTE 125)* **CHORUS. / ('A'mix)** | 3 | 83 |
(12"+=) *(12MUTE 125)* <19202> – (2-'A'mixes) / Snappy.
(cd-s+=) *(CDMUTE 125)* – Over the rainbow.

Sep 91. (c-s/7") *(C+/MUTE 131)* **LOVE TO HATE YOU. / VITAMIN C** | 4 | |
(12"+=) *(12MUTE 131)* – La la la.
(cd-s++=) *(CDMUTE 131)* – ('A'version).

Oct 91. (cd/c/lp) *(CD/C+/STUMM 95)* <26668> **CHORUS** | 1 | 29 |
– Chorus / Waiting for the day / Joan / Breath of life / Am I right? / Love to hate you / Turns the love to anger / Siren song / Perfect stranger / Home.

Nov 91. (cd-ep/12"ep/7"ep) *(CD/12+/MUTE 134)* **AM I RIGHT?** | 15 | |
– Am I right? / Carry on clangers / Let it flow / Waiting for sex.

Jan 92. (7"ep-ltd.15,000) *(LMUTE 134)* **AM I RIGHT? (EP) (re-mix)** | 22 | |
– Am I right? (The Grid remix) / Love to hate you (Mark Saunders remix) / Chorus (Moby remix).
(12"+=) *(12MUTE 134)* – B3.
(cd-s+=) *(CDMUTE 134)* – Perfect stranger.

Mar 92. (c-s/7") *(C+/MUTE 142)* **BREATH OF LIFE. / ('A'version)** | 8 | |
(12"+=/cd-s+=) *(12/CD MUTE 142)* – (3 other 'A'versions).

		Mute	Elektra

Jun 92. (12"ep/c-ep/cd-ep/7"ep) *(12/C/CD+/MUTE 144)* <61386> **ABBA-ESQUE** | 1 | 85 |
– Lay your love on me / S.O.S. / Take a chance on me / Voulez vous.

Oct 92. (12"/c-s/cd-s) *(12/CD/MUTE 150)* **WHO NEEDS LOVE LIKE THAT (Hanbury mix). / SHIP OF FOOLS (Orb mix) / SOMETIMES (remix)** | 10 | |
(cd-s) *(LCDMUTE 150)* – ('A'side) / Don't say no / Soldier's return / The circus (remix).

Nov 92. (cd/c/d-lp) *(CD/C+/MUTEL 2)* <45153> **POP! THE FIRST 20 HITS** (compilation) | 1 | |
– Who needs love like that / Heavenly action / Oh l'amour / Sometimes / It dooesn't have to be like that / Victim of love / The circus / Ship of fools / Chains of love / A

little respect / Stop! / Drama! / You surround me / Blue Savannah / Star / Chorus / Love to hate you / Am I right? / Breathe of life / Take a chance on me. (c+=) – Who needs love like that (Hamburg mix).

Apr 94. (c-s/cd-s/7") (C/CD+/MUTE 152) **ALWAYS.** / ('A'mix)　　`4`　`-`
(12"+=/cd-s+=) (L12/LCD MUTE 152) – (2 more 'A'mixes).

Apr 94. (c-s) <64552> **ALWAYS / TRAGIC**　　`-`　`20`

May 94. (cd/c/lp) (CD/C+/STUMM 115) <61633> **I SAY I SAY I SAY**　`1`　`18`
– Take me back / I love Saturday / Man in the moon / So the story goes / Run to the sun / Always / All through the years / Blues away / Miracle / Because you're so sweet.

Jul 94. (c-s/7"yellow) (C+/MUTE 153) **RUN TO THE SUN. /**
TENDEREST MOMENT　　`6`　`-`
(12"+=/cd-s+=) (12/CD MUTE 153) – ('A'-Beatmasters mix).
(cd-s++=) (LCDMUTE 153) – ('A'-Andy Bell remix).

Nov 94. (c-s) (CMUTE 166) **I LOVE SATURDAY / DODO / BECAUSE**
YOU'RE SO SWEET　　`21`　`-`
(cd-s) (EPCDMUTE 166) – ('A'side) / Ghost / Truly, madly, deeply / Tragic (vocal version).
(cd-s) (CDMUTE 166) – ('A'side) / ('A'radio mix) / ('A'-JX mix) / ('A'-Beatmasters dub mix) / Dodo.
(cd-s) (LCDMUTE 166) – ('A'-Beatmasters club mix) / ('A'-Andy Bell mixes) / Always (x cut dub).

Sep 95. (c-s/cd-s) (C/CD MUTE 174) **STAY WITH ME / TRUE LOVE**
WARS　　`15`　`-`
(12"+=/cd-s+=) (12/LC MUTE 174) – ('A'-Flow mix) / ('A'guitar mix) / ('A'-Castaway mix).

Oct 95. (cd/c/d-lp) (CD/C+/STUMM 145) <61852> **ERASURE**　`14`　`82`
– Guess I'm into feeling / Rescue me / Sono luminous / Fingers & thumbs (cold summer's day) / Rock me gently / Grace / Stay with me / Love the way you do so / Angel / I love you / A long goodbye.

Nov 95. (c-s/cd-s) (C/CD MUTE 178) **FINGERS & THUMBS (COLD**
SUMMER'S DAY) / HI NRG　　`20`　`-`
(cd-s+=) (LCDMUTE 178) – ('A'-Tin Tin Out mix) / ('A'-Francois Kevorkian mix) / ('A'-Wire mix).

Jan 97. (c-s) (CMUTE 190) **IN MY ARMS / RAPTURE**　`13`　`55` May97
(12"+=/cd-s+=) (12/CD MUTE 190) – ('A'mixes).
(cd-s) (LCDMUTE 190) – ('A'mixes).

Mar 97. (c-s) (CMUTE 195) **DON'T SAY YOUR LOVE IS KILLING**
ME / HEART OF GLASS (live)　　`23`　`-`
(cd-s+=) (CDMUTE 195) – ('A'-Jon Pleased Wimmin flashback mix) / ('A'-Tall Pall mix).
(12"+=) (12MUTE 195) – Oh l'amour: Groove terminator.
(cd-s) (LCDMUTE 195) – ('A'-Jon Pleased Wimmin flashback mix) / Oh l'amour (Matt Darey mix) / Oh l'amour (Tin Tin Out mix).

Apr 97. (cd/c) (CD/C STUMM 155) **COWBOY**　　`10`　`43`
– Rain / Worlds on fire / Reach out / In my arms / Don't say your love is killing me / Precious / Treasure / Boy / How can I say / Save me darling / Love affair.

Roky ERICKSON
(see under ⇒ 13th FLOOR ELEVATORS)

Melissa ETHERIDGE

Born: 29 May '61, Leavenworth, Kansas, USA. A budding singer/songwriter by the time she'd reached her teens, ETHERIDGE went on to study at Boston's Berklee College Of Music. Relocating to California after graduating, she was spotted by 'Island' executive CHRIS BLACKWELL who signed her to a long term deal. Spring '88 saw the release of an eponymous debut album, her grainy blues-soaked vocals, angry, tough-talking lyrics and bar-band style attracting a loyal following which helped place the record in the US Top 30 and eventually saw it go gold. Subsequent albums, 'BRAVE AND CRAZY' (1989) and 'NEVER ENOUGH' (1992) attained similar chart positions although virtually all her singles failed to make a mark. This situation was rectified in 1993 when she scored a US Top 10 hit with 'I'M THE ONLY ONE', the track lifted from accompanying multi-platinum album, 'YES I AM'. ETHERIDGE had only recently "come out", appearing alongside other members of music's gay community at a concert organised to celebrate the election of Bill Clinton. By the release of 1995's 'YOUR LITTLE SECRET', her profile had been raised to the point that the album narrowly missed the Top 5 despite a mixed reaction from critics. ETHERIDGE's BONNIE TYLER-influenced vocals and rootsy, BRUCE SPRINGSTEEN-influenced songs continue to appeal to an adult, album oriented market, setting her apart somewhat from the new breed of young female singer/songwriters such as ALANIS MORISSETTE and JEWEL. Now signed to 'Mercury', ETHERIDGE saw out the decade with her long-awaited sixth album, 'BREAKDOWN' (1999), although it failed to build on her past successes. • **Trivia:** After writing for the 'Weeds' film in 1988, she provided backing vox for DON HENLEY's 'New York Minute'. BONO of U2 guested on her second album 'BRAVE AND CRAZY'.

Album rating: MELISSA ETHERIDGE (*6) / BRAVE AND CRAZY (*5) / NEVER ENOUGH (*6) / YES I AM (*6) / YOUR LITTLE SECRET (*3) / BREAKDOWN (*4)

MELISSA ETHERIDGE – vocals, guitar, piano / **KEVIN McCORMICK** – bass / **CRAIG KRAMPF** – drums, percussion / **WADDY WACHTEL + JOHNNY LEE SCHELL** – guitars / **SCOTT THURSTON + WALLY BADAROU** – keyboards

		Island	Island
Apr 88.	(7") (IS 356) **SIMILAR FEATURES.** / **I WANT YOU** (12"+=/cd-s+=) (12IS/CID 356) – Don't you need.		
May 88.	(lp/c/cd) (ILPS/ICT/CID 9879) <90875> **MELISSA ETHERIDGE** – Similar features / Chrome plated heart / Like the way I do / Precious pain / Don't you need / The late September dogs / Occasionally / Watching you / Bring me some water / I want you.		`22`
Jun 88.	(7") (IS 376) **DON'T YOU NEED. / PRECIOUS PAIN**		

(12"+=) (12IS 376) – ('A'live).
(cd-s++=) (CID 376) – Similar features.

Feb 89. (7") (IS 393) **BRING ME SOME WATER. / OCCASIONALLY**　　`-`　`-`
(12"+=/cd-s+=) (12IS/CID 393) – I want you.

Mar 89. (7") <99251> **SIMILAR FEATURES. / BRING ME SOME**
WATER　　`-`　`94`

— **MAURICIO FRITZ LEWAK** – drums + **BERNIE LARSEN** – guitar; repl. SCHELL + BADAROU

Jul 89. (7") (IS 431) <99176> **NO SOUVENIRS.** / ('A'live)　`-`　`95`
(12"+=/cd-s+=) (12IS/CID 431) – Brave and crazy (live).

Sep 89. (lp/c/cd) (ILPS/ICT/CID 9939) <91285> **BRAVE AND CRAZY**　`63`　`22`
– No souvenirs / Brave and crazy / You used to love to dance / The angels / You can sleep while I drive / Testify / Let me go / My back door / Skin deep / Royal Station 4-16. (cd re-iss. Mar97; IMCD 241)

Nov 89. (7") (IS 440) **THE ANGELS.** / ('A'live)　　`-`　`-`
(12"+=/cd-s+=) (12IS/CID 440) – Chrome plated heart (live). (re-iss. May90; same)

Mar 90. (7") **YOU CAN SLEEP WHILE I DRIVE. / THE LATE**
SEPTEMBER DOGS (live)　　`-`　`-`
(12"+=) – ('A'live).

— **STUART SMITH + MARK GOLDENBERG** – guitars; repl. LARSEN + WACHTEL

Feb 92. (c-s/7") **DANCE WITHOUT SLEEPING. / AIN'T IT HEAVY**　`-`　`-`
(12"+=/cd-s+=) – Similar features.

Apr 92. (cd/c/lp) (CID/ICT/ILPS 9990) <512120> **NEVER ENOUGH**　`56`　`21` Mar92
– Ain't it heavy / 2001 / Dance without sleeping / Place your hand / Must be crazy for me / Meet me in the back / The boy feels strange / Keep it precious / The letting go / It's for you. (cd re-iss. Mar96; IMCD 214)

Apr 92. (7") **AIN'T IT HEAVY. / THE BOYS FEEL STRANGE**　`-`　`-`
(12"+=/cd-s+=) – Royal station 4-16 (live).

Jul 92. (c-s/7") **2001.** / ('A'remix)　　`-`　`-`
(12"+=) – Meet me in the back / Testify.
(cd-s+=) – Meet me in the back / ('A'-12"remix).

Sep 93. (cd/c/lp) (CID/ICT/ILPS 8010) <848660> **YES I AM**　`-`　`15`
– I'm the only one / If I wanted to / Come to my window / Silent legacy / I will never be the same / All American girl / Yes I am / Resist / Ruins / Talking to my angel. (re-dist.Apr94)

Nov 93. (c-s/7") (C+/IS 579) **I'M THE ONLY ONE.** / ('A'version)　`-`　`-`
(cd-s) (CID 579) – ('A'side) / Bring me some water / Yes I am (live).

Feb 94. (c-s) <858028> **COME TO MY WINDOW / AIN'T IT HEAVY**
(live)　　`-`　`25`

Jul 94. (c-s) <854068> **I'M THE ONLY ONE / MAGGIE MAY (live)**　`-`　`-`

Oct 94. (c-s/cd-s) (CIS/CID 604) **COME TO MY WINDOW / AIN'T**
IT HEAVY (live) / THE LETTING GO (live) / I'M THE ONLY
ONE (live)　　`-`　`-`

Feb 95. (c-s) <854238> **IF I WANTED TO / LIKE THE WAY I DO**　`-`　`16`
`42`

Oct 95. (c-s) (CIS 608) **YOUR LITTLE SECRET / ALL AMERICAN**
GIRL　　`-`　`-`
(cd-s+=) (CID 608) – Bring me some water / Skin deep.

Nov 95. (cd/c) (CID/ICT 8042) <524154> **YOUR LITTLE SECRET**　`-`　`6`
– Your little secret / I really like you / Nowhere to go / An unusual kiss / I want to come over / All the way to Heaven / I could have been you / Shriner's Park / Change / This war is over.

Feb 96. (c-s) (CIS 627) <854528> **I WANT TO COME OVER / YOUR**
LITTLE SECRET　　`-`　`22`
(cd-s+=) (CID 627) – Must be crazy for me (live) / Let me go (live).

Jul 96. (c-s) (CIS 642) <854664> **NOWHERE TO GO / BRING ME**
SOME WATER　　`-`　`40` Sep96
(cd-s+=) (CID 642) – Like the way I do.

Sep 99. (c-s/cd-s) <562345> **ANGELS WOULD FALL**　　`-`　`51`

Oct 99. (cd/c) <(546518-2/-4)> **BREAKDOWN**　　`-`　`12`
– Breakdown / Angels would fall / Stronger than me / Into the dark / Enough of me / Truth of the heart / Mama I'm strange / Scarecrow / How would I know / My lover / Sleep. (some w/ extra cd+=; CDL 546608-2) – Touch and go / Cherry avenue / Beloved.

EUROPE　(dig out; Great Metal . . .)

EURYTHMICS

Formed: London, England . . . 1976, by Aberdonian, ANNIE LENNOX and Sunderland-born, DAVE STEWART. They formed The CATCH in 1977 with PETE COOMBES, which, by 1979, had evolved into The TOURISTS. Signing to 'Logo' records, they scored with some Top 10 pop hits, namely 'I ONLY WANT TO BE WITH YOU' and 'SO GOOD TO BE BACK HOME', before they broke with COOMBES late in 1980. The duo, now The EURYTHMICS, began recording their debut at Conny Plank's Cologne studio. Featuring contributions from the likes of CAN's HOLGER CZUKAY and JAKI LIEBEZEIT as well as MARCUS STOCHHAUSEN (son of KARLHEINZ), 'IN THE GARDEN' (1981) was a radical musical departure. Icy synth-pop with avant-garde tendencies, the band's closest musical compadres were the lipstick 'n' legwarmers 'New Romantic' crowd, although The EURYTHMICS vision was unique. So unique, in fact, that the record languished in relative obscurity, given scant support by 'R.C.A.'. Undeterred, the band recorded 'SWEET DREAMS (ARE MADE OF THIS)' (1983), the title track giving the band an international breakthrough. This time around, the sculpted synth soundscapes were fashioned with a studied pop nous, LENNOX's mournful vocals heavy with dark implications. Visually striking, the band's image was also highly marketable and ANNIE became the chameleon queen of the new video generation, leading to overnight success in the States. 'TOUCH' (1983) consolidated the EURYTHMICS' position as pop frontrunners, the single 'HERE COMES THE RAIN AGAIN' going Top 10 on both sides of the Atlantic. While their next project, the soundtrack for the film '1984 – For The Love Of Big Brother' was a relative success in Britain, it stiffed big time in the

US amid recriminations from both parties; the director, MICHAEL RADFORD and The EURYTHMICS themselves. 'BE YOURSELF TONIGHT' (1985) saw LENNOX in soul diva mode, belting out the likes of 'SISTERS ARE DOIN' IT FOR THEMSELVES' and putting in a breathtaking feat of vocal histrionics on the No.1 hit, 'THERE MUST BE AN ANGEL (PLAYING WITH MY HEART)'. Perhaps playing all those stadiums was beginning to affect the band, as 'REVENGE' saw the band veering towards big-rock, tracks like 'MISSIONARY MAN' sounding downright clumsy. By the release of 'WE TOO ARE ONE', (1989) the band were clearly on their last legs and it was obvious, on listening to the record, that the working relationship between LENNOX and STEWART had finally broken down. LENNOX went on to do charity work before releasing 'DIVA' in 1992, her multi-platinum-selling solo debut. She also released a collection of covers, 'MEDUSA', in 1995. STEWART, meanwhile, recorded the soundtrack 'LILY WAS HERE' with sax-diva, CANDY DULFER, before going on to form his SPIRITUAL COWBOYS and generally receive a bit of a pasting from the critics. • **Songwriters:** COOMBES penned songs in The TOURISTS, except I ONLY WANT TO BE WITH YOU (Dusty Springfield). DAVE and ANNIE wrote together in The EURYTHMICS. Now a solo writer, ANNIE LENNOX covered KEEP YOUNG AND BEAUTIFUL (Al Dubin-Harry Warren) / FEEL THE NEED (Detroit Emeralds) / RIVER DEEP MOUNTAIN HIGH (Phil Spector) / DON'T LET ME DOWN (Beatles) / NO MORE "I LOVE YOU'S" (The Lover Speaks) / TAKE ME TO THE RIVER (Al Green) / A WHITER SHADE OF PALE (Procol Harum) / DON'T LET IT BRING YOU DOWN (Neil Young) / TRAIN IN VAIN (Clash) / I CAN'T GET NEXT TO YOU (Strong-Whitfield) / DOWNTOWN LIGHTS (Blue Nile) / THE THIN BLUE LINE BETWEEN LOVE AND HATE (Pretenders; hit) / WAITING IN VAIN (Bob Marley) / SOMETHING SO RIGHT (Paul Simon) / LADIES OF THE CANYON (Joni Mitchell) / I'M ALWAYS TOUCHED BY YOUR PRESENCE DEAR (Blondie). DAVE STEWART's VEGAS covered SHE (Charles Aznavour). • **Trivia:** In March '84 ANNIE, now not involved intimately with DAVE, married German Hare Krishna RADHA RAMAR, although this only lasted six months. She married again in the early 90's and gave birth to her first child in the Spring of '93. On the 1st of August '84, DAVE married SHAKESPEAR'S SISTER/ex-BANANARAMA singer, SIOBHAN FAHEY. The bearded one has also produced many artists including FEARGAL SHARKEY, MARIA McKEE, DARYL HALL, BOB GELDOF, BOB DYLAN, TOM PETTY, MICK JAGGER, BORIS GREBENSHIKOV (Russian rocker) and LONDONBEAT. Just a wee note to say, DAVE was not the DAVE STEWART that had a No.1 hit with BARBARA GASKIN.

Album rating: Tourists: THE TOURISTS (*4) / REALITY EFFECT (*4) / LUMINOUS BASEMENT (*5) / Eurythmics: IN THE GARDEN (*5) / SWEET DREAMS (ARE MADE OF THIS) (*8) / TOUCH (*7) / TOUCH DANCE mini remix (*3) / 1984 (FOR THE LOVE OF BIG BROTHER) (*4) / BE YOURSELF TONIGHT (*7) / REVENGE (*6) / SAVAGE (*6) / WE TOO ARE ONE (*6) / EURYTHMICS' GREATEST HITS compilation (*8) / EURYTHMICS LIVE 1983-1989 collection (*4) / Dave Stewart: LILY WAS HERE (*5) / DAVE STEWART & THE SPIRITUAL COWBOYS (*6) / HONEST (*5) / GREETINGS FROM THE GUTTER (*5) / Annie Lennox: ANNIE LENNOX – DIVA (*7) / MEDUSA (*5) / Eurythmics: PEACE (*5)

CATCH

ANNIE LENNOX (b.25 Dec'54, Aberdeen, Scotland) – vocals, keyboards, flute / **DAVE STEWART** (b. 9 Sep'52, Sunderland, England) – guitar, keyboards (ex-LONGDANCER) / **PETE COOMBES** – guitar, vocals

		Logo	not iss.
Nov 77.	(7") *(GO 103)* **BORDERLINE. / BLACK BLOOD**		–

TOURISTS

added **EDDY CHIN** – bass / **JIM TOOMEY** – drums

		Logo	Epic
May 79.	(7") *(GO 350)* **BLIND AMONG THE FLOWERS. / HE WHO LAUGHS LAST LAUGHS LONGEST** (d7"+=) *(GOD 350)* – The golden lamp / Wrecked.	52	
Jun 79.	(lp) *(LOGO 1018)* **THE TOURISTS** – Blind among the flowers / Save me / Fool's paradise / Can't stop laughing / Don't get left behind / Another English day / Deadly kiss / Ain't no room / The loneliest man in the world / Useless duration of time / He who laughs last laughs longest / Just like you. (re-iss.Jun81 on 'RCA Int.' lp/c; INT S/K 5096)	72	
Aug 79.	(7"/7"pic-d) *(GO/+P 360)* **THE LONELIEST MAN IN THE WORLD. / DON'T GET LEFT BEHIND**	32	
Oct 79.	(lp/c) *(LOGO/KLOGO 1019)* **REALITY EFFECT** – It doesn't have to be this way / I only want to be with you / In the morning / All life's tragedies / Everywhere you look / So good to be back home / Nothing to do / Circular fever / In my mind / Something in the air tonight / Summers night.	23	
Oct 79.	(7") *(GO 370)* <50850> **I ONLY WANT TO BE WITH YOU. / SUMMER NIGHT**	4	83 Apr80
Jan 80.	(7") *(TOUR 1)* **SO GOOD TO BE BACK HOME. / CIRCULAR SAW**	6	

		R.C.A.	R.C.A.
Sep 80.	(7") *(TOUR 2)* **DON'T SAY I TOLD YOU SO. / STRANGE SKY**	40	
Oct 80.	(lp/c) *(RCA LP/K 5001)* **LUMINOUS BASEMENT** – Walls and foundations / Don't say I told you so / Week days / So you want to go away now / One step nearer the edge / Angels and demons / Talk to me / Round round blues / Let's take a walk / Time drags so slow / I'm going to change my mind. (free-7"yellow) *(FREE 5001)* – FROM THE MIDDLE ROOM. / INTO THE FUTURE	75	

— The TOURISTS split late '80.

EURYTHMICS

— were formed by **ANNIE LENNOX + DAVE STEWART** with guests **ROBERT GORL** and **GABI DELGADO** of D.A.F. / **JAKI LIEBEZEIT** – percussion and **HOLGER CZUKAY** – bass (both ex-CAN)

		R.C.A.	R.C.A.
Jun 81.	(7"/ext.12") *(RCA/+T 68)* **NEVER GONNA CRY AGAIN. / LE SINISTRE**	63	
Aug 81.	(7") *(RCA 115)* **BELINDA. / HEARTBEAT, HEARTBEAT**		
Oct 81.	(lp/c) *(RCA LP/K 5061)* **IN THE GARDEN** – English summer / Belinda / Take me to your heart / She's invisible now / Your time will come / Caveman head / Never gonna cry again / All the young (people of today) / Sing sing / Revenge. (re-iss.Mar84 lp/c; PL/PK 70006) (cd-iss.Jan87; PD 70006) (re-iss.Sep91 cd/c/lp; ND/NK/ND 75036)		

— **ANNIE** and **DAVE** now augmented with synthesisers, also guests **CLEM BURKE** – drums (ex-BLONDIE, who later joined RAMONES in '87)

Mar 82.	(7") *(RCA 199)* **THIS IS THE HOUSE. / HOME IS WHERE THE HEART IS** (12") *(RCAT 199)* – ('A'side) / Your time will come (live) / 4-4 In leather (live) / Never gonna cry again (live) / Take me to your heart (live).		
Jun 82.	(7"m) *(RCA 230)* **THE WALK. / STEP ON THE BEAST / THE WALK (part 2)** (12"+=) *(RCAT 230)* – Invisible hands / Dr. Trash.		
Sep 82.	(7"/7"pic-d) *(DA 1)* **LOVE IS A STRANGER. / MONKEY, MONKEY** (12"+=) *(DAT 1)* – Let's just close our eyes. (re-iss.Apr83, hit No.6) <US re-iss. Sep83; 13618; hit No.23>	54	
Jan 83.	(7"/7"pic-d) *(DA/+P 2)* <13533> **SWEET DREAMS (ARE MADE OF THIS). / I COULD GIVE YOU (A MIRROR)** (12"+=) *(DAT 2)* – Baby's gone blue.	2	1 Apr83
Feb 83.	(lp/pic-lp/c) *(RCA LP/LPP/K 6063)* <4681> **SWEET DREAMS (ARE MADE OF THIS)** – Sweet dreams (are made of this) / Jennifer / This city never sleeps / This is the house / Somebody told me / The walk / I've got an angel / Love is a stranger / Wrap it up / I could give you (a mirror). (re-iss.Aug84 lp/c; PL/PK 70014) (cd-iss.Jan84; RCD 25447) (re-iss.Oct87 lp/c/cd; NL/NK/ND 71471)	3	15 May83
Jul 83.	(7"/7"pic-d) *(DA/+P 3)* **WHO'S THAT GIRL?. / YOU TAKE SOME LENTILS . . . AND YOU TAKE SOME RICE** (12"+=) *(DAT 3)* – ABC (freeform).	3	–
Oct 83.	(7"/7"pic-d) *(DA/+P 4)* <13695> **RIGHT BY YOUR SIDE. / ('A'party mix)** (7"w/ free-c-s) *(DA 4-EUC 001)* – Intro speech / Step on the beast / Invisible hands / Angel (dub) / Satellite of love. (12"+=) *(DAT 4)* – Plus something else.	10	29 Jul84

— **ANNIE** and **DAVE** were augmented on album by **CLEM** – drums plus **DICK CUTHELL** – brass MARTIN DOBSON – horns / **DEAN GARCIA** – bass(above 3 also went on tour adding) **VIC MARTIN** – synthesizers / **PETE PHIPPS** – drums / and backing singers **GILL O'DONOVAN, SUZIE O'LISZT** and **MAGGIE RYDER**

Nov 83.	(lp/pic-lp/c) *(PL/PLP/P 70109)* <4917> **TOUCH** – Here comes the rain again / Regrets / Right by your side / Cool blue / Who's that girl? / The first cut / Aqua / No fear, no hurt, no pain (no broken hearts) / Paint a rumour. (cd-iss. Sep84; PD 70109) (re-iss.Sep89 lp/c/cd; NL/NK/ND 90369)	1	7 Jan84
Jan 84.	(7"/7"pic-d) *(DA/+P 5)* <13725> **HERE COMES THE RAIN AGAIN. / PAINT A RUMOUR** (ext.12"+=) *(DAT 5)* – This city never sleeps (live).	8	4
Apr 84.	(7") <13800> **WHO'S THAT GIRL? / AQUA**	–	21
Jun 84.	(m-lp/c) *(PG/PH 70354)* <5086> **TOUCH DANCE** (remixes) – The first cut (instrumental) / Cool blue (instrumental) / Paint a rumour (instrumental) / The first cut / Cool blue / Paint a rumour / Regrets. (cd-iss.Dec91; ND 75151)	31	
Oct 84.	(7") *(VS 728)* <13956> **SEXCRIME (NINETEEN EIGHTY-FOUR). / I DID IT JUST THE SAME** (12"/12"pic-d) *(VS 728-12)* – ('A'extended).	4	81
Nov 84.	(lp/c) *(V/TCV 1984)* <5349> **1984 – FOR THE LOVE OF BIG BROTHER** (soundtrack) – I did it just the same / Julia / Sexcrime (nineteen eighty-four) / Doubleplusgood / For the love of big brother / Ministry of love / Winston's diary / Room 101 / Greetings from a dead man. (re-iss.Jan88 lp/c; OVED/+C 207) (cd-iss.Apr89; CDV 1984) (re-iss.cd.Dec95;)	23	93
Jan 85.	(7"/7"pic-d) *(VS 734)* **JULIA. / MINISTRY OF LOVE** (12"+=) *(VS 734-12)* – ('A'extended). (above album & two singles were issued UK on 'Virgin')	44	
Apr 85.	(7",7"red,7"yellow,7"blue) *(PB 40101)* <14078> **WOULD I LIE TO YOU? / HERE COMES THAT SINKING FEELING** (ext.remix; 12",12"red,12"yellow,12"blue;+=) *(PT 40102)* – ('A'-E.T.mix).	11	5
May 85.	(lp/c/cd) *(PL/PK/PD 70711)* <5429> **BE YOURSELF TONIGHT** – It's alright (baby's coming back) / Would I lie to you / There must be an angel (playing with my heart) / I love you like a ball and chain / Sisters are doin' it for themselves / Conditioned soul / Adrian / Here comes that sinking feeling / Better to have lost in love (than never to have loved at all). (re-iss.May90 cd/c/lp; ND/NK/NL 74602)	3	9
Jun 85.	(7")(12"/dance mix-12") *(PB 40247)(PT 40248/+R)* <14160> **THERE MUST BE AN ANGEL (PLAYING WITH MY HEART). / GROWN UP GIRLS**	1	22
Oct 85.	(7"; as EURYTHMICS & ARETHA FRANKLIN) *(PB 40339)* <14214> **SISTERS ARE DOIN' IT FOR THEMSELVES. / I LOVE YOU LIKE A BALL AND CHAIN** (12"+=) *(PT 40340)* – ('A'-E.T. remix with ARETHA).	9	18
Jan 86.	(7") *(PB 40375)* <14284> **IT'S ALRIGHT (BABY'S COMING BACK). / CONDITIONED SOUL** (d7"+=/d12"+=) *(PB/PB 40375/40376; 2nd-free in yellow, blue or red)* – Would I lie to you? / Here comes that sinking feeling. (12"+=) *(PT 40376)* – Tous les garcons et les filles.	12	78
Jun 86.	(7") *(DA 7)* **WHEN TOMORROW COMES. / TAKE YOUR PAIN AWAY** (ext.12"+=) *(DAT 7)* – ('A'-orchestral).	30	
Jul 86.	(lp/c/cd) *(PL/PK/PD 71050)* <5847> **REVENGE**	3	12

– Let's go / Take your pain away / A little of you / Thorn in my side / In this town / I remember you / Missionary man / The last time / When tomorrow comes / The miracle of love. (cd re-iss. Sep93; 74321 12529-2)

Jul 86. (7"/12") <14414> **MISSIONARY MAN. / TAKE YOUR PAIN AWAY**   – | 14

Aug 86. (7") (DA 8) <5058> **THORN IN MY SIDE. / IN THIS TOWN**   5 | 68 Oct86
(12"+=) (DAT 8) – ('A'extended or Houston mix).

Nov 86. (7"/7"sha-pic-d) (DA/+P 9) **THE MIRACLE OF LOVE. / WHEN TOMORROW COMES** (live)   23 |
(12"+=) (DAT 9) – Who's that girl? (live).

Feb 87. (7"/ext.12") (DA/+T 10) **MISSIONARY MAN. / THE LAST TIME** (live)   31 | –

Oct 87. (7"/7"w-poster) (DA 11/+P) **BEETHOVEN (I LOVE TO LISTEN TO). / HEAVEN**   25 |
(ext.12"+=)(cd-s+=) (DAT 11)(DA 11CD) – ('A'dance mix).

Nov 87. (lp/c/cd) (PL/PK/PD 71555) <6794> **SAVAGE**   7 | 41
– Beethoven (I love to listen) / I've got a lover (back in Japan) / Do you want to break up? / You have placed a chill in my heart / Shame / Savage / I need a man / Put the blame on me / Heaven / Wide eyed girl / I need you / Brand new day. (re-iss. cd May93; 74321 13440-2)

Dec 87. (7") (DA 14) **SHAME. / I'VE GOT A LOVER (BACK IN JAPAN)**   41 |
(12"+=/12"s+=) (DAT 14/+P) – ('A'dance mix).
('A'dance mix-cd-s+=) (DA 14CD) – There must be an angel (playing with my heart).

Dec 87. (7") <5361> **I NEED A MAN. / HEAVEN**   – | 46

Mar 88. (7") (DA 15) **I NEED A MAN. / I NEED YOU**   26 |
(12"+=) (DAT 15) – ('A'-macho mix).
(cd-s++=) (DA 15CD) – Missionary man (live).
(10"+=) (DA 15X) – There must be an angel (playing with my heart).
(7"m+=) (DA 15R) – I need a man (live).

May 88. (7") (DA 16) **YOU HAVE PLACED A CHILL IN MY HEART. / ('A'acoustic mix)**   16 | 64
(12"+=) (DAT 16) – ('A'dance).
(cd-s++=) (DA 16CD) – Do you want to break up / Here comes the rain again (live).

—— In Oct'88, ANNIE was credited with AL GREEN on single 'PUT A LITTLE LOVE IN YOUR HEART' on 'A&M' 7"/12"; (AM/+Y 484)

	R.C.A.	Arista

Aug 89. (7"/c-s) (DA/+K 17) **REVIVAL. / PRECIOUS**   26 |
(12"+=/cd-s+=) (DAT/DACD 17) – ('A'dance mix).
(12"+=/12"s+=) (DAT 18/+P) – ('A'-extended E.T. dance mix).

Sep 89. (lp/c/cd) (PL/PK/PD 74251) <8606> **WE TOO ARE ONE**   1 | 34
– We two are one / The King and Queen of America / (My my) Baby's gonna cry / Don't ask me why / Angel / Revival / You hurt me (and I hate you) / Sylvia / How long? / When the day goes down. (re-iss. cd Jun94; 74321 20898-2)

Oct 89. (7"/c-s) (DA/+K 19) <9880> **DON'T ASK ME WHY. / RICH GIRL**   25 | 40 Sep89
(12"+=/12"pic-d+=/cd-s+=) (DA T/P/CD 19) – Sylvia.
(12"+=/cd-s+=) (DA T/CD 20) – ('A'acoustic) / When the day goes down.

Jan 90. (7"/c-s) (DA/+K 23) **KING AND QUEEN OF AMERICA (remix). / SEE NO EVIL**   29 | –
(cd-s+=) (DACD 23) – There must be an angel (playin' with my heart) (live) / I love you like a ball and chain (live) / ('A'dub).
(12") (DAT 23) – ('A'dance mix) / ('B'side) / ('A'dub mix).
(12"+=/cd-s+=) (DA T/CD 24) – (as extra above except 'A'dub).

Apr 90. (7"/c-s) (DA/+K 21) **ANGEL. / ANGEL (choir version)**   23 | –
(12"+=/cd-s+=) (DA T/CD 21) – Missionary man (acoustic).
(12") (DAT 25) – ('A'remix) / Sweet dreams (are made of this) (Nightmare mix).

Apr 90. (c-s) <9917> **ANGEL / PRECIOUS**   – |

Jun 90. (c-s) <9939> **(MY MY) BABY'S GONNA CRY / ('A'acoustic)**   – |

—— split after the above release

– compilations, others, etc. –

on 'RCA' UK / 'Arista' US unless otherwise stated

Nov 88. (3"cd-ep/5"cd-ep) Virgin; (CDT/CDF 22) **SEXCRIME (1984 extended mix) / JULIA (extended) / I DID IT JUST THE SAME** | –

Mar 89. (3"cd-ep) (PD 42651) **SWEET DREAMS (ARE MADE OF THIS) / I COULD GIVE YOU (A MIRROR) / HERE COMES THE RAIN AGAIN / PAINT A RUMOUR** | –

Mar 91. (cd/c/lp) (PD/PK/PL 74856) <8680> **EURYTHMICS' GREATEST HITS**   1 | 72
– Love is a stranger / Sweet dreams (are made of this) / Who's that girl? / Right by your side / Here comes the rain again / There must be an angel (playing with my heart) / Sisters are doin' it for themselves / It's alright (baby's coming back) / When tomorrow comes / You have placed a chill in my heart / Sexcrime (nineteen eighty-four) / Thorn in my side Don't ask me why. (cd+=/c+=) – Miracle of love / Angel / Would I lie to you? / Missionary man / I need a man.

Mar 91. (7"/c-s) (PB/PK 44265) **LOVE IS A STRANGER. / JULIA**   46 | –
(12"+=/cd-s+=) (PT/PD 44266) – ('A'obsession mix) / There must be an angel (playin' with my heart).
(12") (PT 44268) – ('A'-JC meets the Obsessor mix) / ('A'instrumental) / ('A'-Coldcut mix).

Nov 91. (7"/c-s) (PB/PK 45031) <2243> **SWEET DREAMS (ARE MADE OF THIS) '91. / KING AND QUEEN OF AMERICA**   48 |
(12") (PT 45032) – ('A'side) / ('A'-house mix) / ('A'-nightmare mix) / ('A'-hot remix).
(cd-s) (PD 45032) – ('A'side) / Beethoven (I love to listen to) / Shame / This city never sleeps.

Nov 93. (d-cd/d-c) (74321 17145-2/-4) **EURYTHMICS LIVE 1983-1989 (live)**   22 | –
– Never gonna cry again / Love is a stranger / Sweet dreams (are made of this) / This city never sleeps / Somebody told me / Who's that girl? / Right by your side / Here comes the rain again / Sex crime / Love you like a ball and chain / There must be an angel (playing with my heart) / Thorn in my side / Let's go / Missionary man / The last time / Miracle of love / I need a man / We two are one / (My my) Baby's gonna cry / Don't ask me why / Angel. (cd includes free 7 track EP) (re-iss. Oct95; same)

Apr 95. (d-cd) (74321 26442-2) **BE YOURSELF TONIGHT / REVENGE** | –

ANNIE LENNOX

in 1992 with **STEPHEN LIPSON** – guitars, prog., keyboards / **PETER-JOHN VITTESE** – keyboards, recorder / **MARIUS DE VRIES** – programming, keyboards/ also **LOUIS JARDIM** – percussion / **ED SHEARMUR** – piano / **KEITH LeBLANC** – drums / **DOUG WIMBUSH** – bass / **KENJI JAMMER** – guitar / **STEVE JANSON** – drum pro / **DAVE DeFRIES** – trumpet / **GAVON WRIGHT** – violin / **PAUL MOORE** – keyboards (co-writer on 1)

	R.C.A.	Arista

Mar 92. (7"/c-s) (PB/PK 45317) <12419> **WHY. / PRIMITIVE**   5 | 34
(12"+=) (PT 45317) – Keep young and beautiful.
(cd-s+=) (PD 45317) – ('A'instrumental).

Apr 92. (cd/c/lp) (PL/PK/PD 75326) <18704> **ANNIE LENNOX – DIVA**   1 | 27
– Why / Walking on broken glass / Precious / Legend in my living room / Cold / Money can't buy it / Little bird / Primitive / Stay by me / The gift. (cd+=) – Keep young and beautiful. (re-iss. Feb96 cd/c; 74321 33102-2/-4)

May 92. (7"/c-s) (74321 10025-7/-4) **PRECIOUS. / ('A'version)**   23 |
(cd-s+=) (74321 10025-2) – Step by step / Why.

Aug 92. (7"/c-s/cd-s) (74321 10722-7/-4/-2) **WALKING ON BROKEN GLASS. / LEGEND IN MY OWN LIVING ROOM**   8 | –
(12"+=/cd-s+=) (74321 28483-1/-2) – Don't let me down.

Aug 92. (c-s) <12452> **WALKING ON BROKEN GLASS / DON'T LET ME DOWN**   – | 14

Oct 92. (7") (74321 11688-7) **COLD. / ('A'live)**   26 |
(c-s) (74321 11688-4) – River deep mountain high / You have placed a chill in my heart / Why.
(cd-s) (74321 11690-2) – ('A'side) / River deep mountain high / Feel the need in me / Don't let me down.
(cd-s) (74321 11689-2) – ('A'side) / Why / The gift / Walking on broken glass.
(cd-s) (74321 11688-2) – ('A'side) / It's alright / Here comes the rain again / You have placed a chill in my heart.

Jan 93. (7"/c-s/12") (74321 123383-7/-4/-1) <12508> **LITTLE BIRD. / LOVE SONG FOR A VAMPIRE**   3 | 49
(cd-s+=) (74321 12383-2) – Feel the need (live).
(cd-s+=) (74321 12383-3) – River deep mountain high (live).
(cd-s+=) (74321 12383-8) – Don't let me down (live).

—— with **STEPHEN LIPSON** – programmer, guitar, keyboards, bass

Feb 95. (7"/c-s) (74321 25716-7/-4) <12804> **NO MORE "I LOVE YOU'S". / LADIES OF THE CANYON**   2 | 23
(cd-s) (74321 25551-2) – Love song for a vampire.
(cd-s) (74321 25716-2) – ('A'side) / Why (acoustic) / Cold (acoustic) / Walking on broken glass (acoustic).

Mar 95. (cd/c/lp) (<74321 25717-2/-4/-1>) **MEDUSA**   1 | 11
– No more "I love you's" / Take me to the river / A whiter shade of pale / Don't let it bring you down / Train in vain / I can't get next to you / Downtown lights / The thin line between love and hate / Waiting in vain / Something so right. (re-iss. d-cd Dec95; 74321 33163-2) – w/ free 'LIVE IN CENTRAL PARK')

May 95. (c-s) (74321 28482-4) **A WHITER SHADE OF PALE / HEAVEN**   16 |
(cd-s+=) (74321 28482-2) – I'm always touched by your presence dear / Love song for a vampire.
(cd-s) (74321 28483-2) – ('A'side) / Don't let it bring you down / You have placed a chill in my heart / Here comes the rain again.

Sep 95. (c-s) (74321 31612-4) **WAITING IN VAIN. / NO MORE "I LOVE YOU'S"**   31 |
(cd-s+=) (74321 31613-2) – (interview) / ('A'-Strong body mix).
(cd-s) (74321 31612-2) – ('A'side) / Train in vain (3 mixes).
(12") (74321 31612-1) – ('A'-Strong body mix) / ('A'-Howie B mix).
(below featured PAUL SIMON)

Nov 95. (cd-s) (74321 33238-2) **SOMETHING SO RIGHT / SWEET DREAMS (ARE MADE OF THIS)** (live)   44 |
(c-s+=) (74321 33238-4) – Who's that girl (live) / Waiting in vain (live).
(cd-s) (74321 33239-2) – ('A'side) / I love you like a ball and chain / Money can't buy it.

DAVID A. STEWART

—— as DAVID A. STEWART he recorded single 'AVENUE D' with ETTA JAMES (May89) next with (CANDY solo artist and ex-PRINCE)

	Anxious-RCA	Arista

Feb 90. (7"/c-s) (ZB/ZK 43045) <2187> **LILY WAS HERE. / LILY ROBS THE BANK**   7 | 11 Apr91
(12"+=/cd-s+=) (ZT/ZD 43046) – ('A'space centre medical unit mix).

Apr 90. (cd/7"/ZK/ZL 74233) **LILY WAS HERE** (Soundtrack)   35 |
– Lily was here / The pink building / Lily robs the bank / Toyshop robbery / Toys on the sidewalk / The good hotel / Second chance / Here comes the rain again / Alone in the city / Toyshop (part one) / The coffin / Teletype / Inside the pink building / Percussion jam / Peaches / Lily was here (reprise).

	R.C.A.	Arista

Oct 91. (cd/c/lp) (ZD/ZK/ZL 75187) **JUTE CITY** (BBC Soundtrack) |
– Jute City / Dead planets / Last love / In Duncan's arms / Black wedding / Jute City revisited / Contaminated / See no evil / Jigula / The lords theme / Hats off to Hector / Deep waters / Dark wells.

Oct 91. (7"/c-s) (ZB/ZK 45043) **JUTE CITY. / JUTE CITY (Caroline's mix)** | –
(cd-s+=) (ZD 45044) – Dead planet / Black wedding.
(12") (ZT 45043) – ('A'-Waddell's remix) / (above extra 2).

DAVE STEWART AND THE SPIRITUAL COWBOYS

with **IZZY MAE DOORITE** – guitar, vocals / **WILD MONDO** – keyboards, vocals / **CHRISTOPHER D.JAMES** – bass, vocals / **MARTIN O'DALE** – drumwarp, vocals / **ZAC BARTEL** – drum prog. / **JOHN TEXAS TURNBULL** – electric bow semi-acoustic

Aug 90. (7"/c-s) (PB/PK 43907) **JACK TALKING. / SUICIDE SID**   69 | –
(12"+=) (PT 43908) – Love calculator.
(cd-s++=) (PD 43908) – Jack talking.

Sep 90. (cd/c/lp) *(PD/PK/PL 74710)* **DAVE STEWART AND THE SPIRITUAL COWBOYS**   [38] [ ]
– Soul years / King of the hypocrites / Diamond avenue / This little town / On fire / Heaven and Earth / Love shines / Party town / Mr.Reed / Fashion bomb / Jack talking / Hey Johnny / The Devil's just been using you / Spiritual love.

Oct 90. (7"/c-s)(12") *(PB/PK 44009)(PT 44010)* **LOVE SHINES. / MARIANNE** [ ] [-]
(10"+=) *(PJ 44010)* – Instant karma (live).
(cd-s+=) *(PD 44010)* – Victim of fate.

Jan 91. (c-s) *<2046>* **PARTY TOWN (party on down mix). / PARTY TOWN (politico mix)** [ ] [-]
(cd-s+=) *(2073)* – Love calculator / Suicidal Sid.

May 91. (c-s) *<2112>* **LOVE SHINES. / INSTANT KARMA** [ ] [-]

Sep 91. (7"/c-s) *(PB/PK 44823)* **CROWN OF MADNESS. / FRUSTRATION** [ ] [ ]
(12"+=)(cd-s+=) *(PT/PD 4482 3/4)* – If that's love.
(cd-s) *(PD 44866)* – ('A'side) / Honest (live) / On fire (live) / Motorcycle mystics (live).

Oct 91. (cd/c/lp) *(PD/PK/PL 75081)* **HONEST** [ ] [ ]
– Honest / Whole wide world / Count of madness / Out of reach / You've lost / Fool's parradise / Motorcycle mystery / Impossible / Here we go again / Here she comes / Fade away / Cat with a tale / R U satisfied

Nov 91. (7"/c-s) *(PB/PZ 45001)* **OUT OF REACH. / DAY OF THE DEAD** [ ] [ ]
(12"+=/cd-s+=) *(PT/PD 45002)* – The ballad of Michael Pain.

—— DAVE STEWART teamed up with TERRY HALL to form VEGAS.

DAVE STEWART

with **BOOTSY COLLINS** – bass, space bass / **BERNIE WORRELL** – keyboards / **JEROME 'BIG FOOT' BRAILEY** – drums + guests **LAURIE ANDERSON** (electric violin, vox on 'Kinky Sweetheart') / **LOU REED** (guitar solo on 'You Talk a lot' w /saxophone **DAVE SANBORN**) / **CARLY SIMON** (argumented w/**SANBORN**; last track) / **TERRY DISLEY** – keyboards

	East West	Warners
Aug 94. (c-s) *(YZ 845C)* **HEART OF STONE / PEACE IN WARTIME**	36	
(cd-s+=/12"+=) *(YZ 845 CD/T)* – ('A'mix).		
(cd-s+=) *(YZ 845CDX)* – ('A'-Sure is Pure remixes).		
Sep 94. (cd/c) *<(4509 97546-2/-4)>* **GREETINGS FROM THE GUTTER**		

– Heart of stone / Greetings from the gutter / Jealousy / St.Valentine's day / Kinky sweetheart / Damien save me / Crazy sister / You talk a lot / Tragedy Street / Chelsea lovers / Oh no, not you again.

Apr 95. (c-s) *(YZ 898C)* **JEALOUSY / BLIND LEADING THE BLIND** [ ] [ ]
(cd-s+=) *(YZ 898CD)* – Tragedy Street.

Oct 95. (c-s) *(EW 009C)* **SECRET / ('A'-SPS vocal mix)** [ ] [ ]
(cd-s+=) *(EW 009CD)* – Kinky sweetheart.
(12"+=) *(EW 009T)* – ('A'-Posterity mix) / ('A'-SPS mad club mix).

	Edel	unknown
Oct 98. (c-s) *(0039969ERE)* **HAPPY TO BE HERE / ('A'mix)**		
(cd-s) *(0039965ERE)* – ('A'mixes).		

EURYTHMICS

—— re-formed in 1999 after a decade split

	Arista	Arista
Oct 99. (c-s/cd-s) *(74321 69563-4/-2)* **I SAVED THE WORLD TODAY / LIFTED**	11	
(cd-s) *(74321 69564-2)* – ('A'side) / You have placed a chill in my heart / There must be an angel playing with my heart.		
Oct 99. (cd/c) *(74321 69582-2/-4 <14617>)* **PEACE**	4	25

– Seventeen again / I saved the world today / Beautiful child / I want it all / Peace is just a word / Power to the meek / Forever / Anything but strong / I've tried everything / True love / Lifted.

EVERCLEAR

Formed: Portland, Oregon, USA . . . 1991 by former teenage junkie, ART ALEXAKIS (he gave up alcohol, drugs and nicotine in June '84). Coming from a broken home, he was also dogged by the drug deaths of his girlfriend and older brother, George. Another founder member, CRAIG MONTOYA (other two, STEVEN BIRCH and SCOTT CUTHBERT) helped produce their debut indie album, 'WORLD OF NOISE', in 1994 and after rave reviews they were whisked away by 'Capitol' A&R man PERRY WATTS-RUSSELL. It was alleged that they were released from the indie only when the gun-toting ALEXAKIS convinced the boss to let them go. By Spring '96 (and now with GREG EKLUND who had replaced CUTHBERT and BIRCH), their second album, 'SPARKLE AND FADE', had climbed into the US Top 30, a stylish anti-drug affair, it was described as ELVIS COSTELLO fused with LED ZEPPELIN, HUSKER DU or NIRVANA! ALEXAKIS and Co. returned in 1998 with a third set proper (the previous year's 'WHITE TRASH HELL' consisted of outtakes), 'SO MUCH FOR THE AFTERGLOW', the US Top 40 album almost spawning another UK Top 40 single, 'EVERYTHING TO EVERYONE'. • **Trivia:** The cover of the 1996 album featured snapshots of the trio as young children.

Album rating: WORLD OF NOISE (*8) / SPARKLE AND FADE (*7) / SO MUCH FOR THE AFTERGLOW (*6)

ART ALEXAKIS (b.12 Apr'62) – vocals, guitar / **STEVEN BIRCH** – guitar / **CRAIG MONTOYA** (b.14 Sep'70) – bass, vocals / **SCOTT CUTHBERT** – drums, vocals

	Fire	Tim/Kerr
Feb 95. (cd/lp) *(FIRE CD/LP 46) <TK 59>* **WORLD OF NOISE**		Nov93

– Your genius hands / Sick & tired / Laughing world / Fire maple song / Pennsylvania is . . . / Nervous and weird / Malevolent / Sparkle / Trust fund / Loser makes good / Invisible / Evergleam. *<US re-iss. Nov94 on 'Capitol' cd/c; 30562-2/-4>*

	Fire	Capitol
Feb 95. (cd-s) *(BLAZE 77CD) <58255>* **FIRE MAPLE SONG /**		Nov94

—— **GREG EKLUND** (b.18 Apr'70) – drums, vocals; repl. CUTHBERT + BIRCH

	Capitol	Capitol
Nov 95. (cd-ep) *<23261-2>* **HEROIN GIRL / ANNABELLA'S SONG / NAHALEM / AMERICAN GIRL**	-	
Mar 96. (cd/c/lp) *(CD/TC-/EST 2257) <30929>* **SPARKLE AND FADE**	25	May95

– Electra made me blind / Heroin girl / You make me feel like a whore / Santa Monica / Summerland / Strawberry / Heartspark dollar / The twistinside / Her brand new skin / Nahalem / Queen of the air / Pale green stars / Chemical smile / My sexual life. *(d-cd=Jun98) (CDESTX 2257)* – (other tracks).

Apr 96. (cd-ep) *<58538>* **HEARTSPARK DOLLARSIGN / HEROIN GIRL / HAPPY HOUR / SIN CITY** [-] [85]

May 96. (7"clear) *(CL 773)* **HEARTSPARK DOLLARSIGN. / LOSER MAKES GOOD (live)** [48] [-]
(cd-s+=) *(CDCL 773)* – Sparkle (live).
(cd-s) *(CDCLS 773)* – ('A'side) / Pennsylvania is (live) / Nervous & weird (live).

Aug 96. (7") *(CL 775)* **SANTA MONICA (WATCH THE WORLD DIE). / AMERICAN GIRL** [40] [ ] Feb96
(cd-s+=) *(CDCL 775)* – Strawberry / Fire maple song.
(cd-s) *(CDCLS 775)* – ('A'side) / Heroin girl / Summerland / Sin city.

—— added **CHRIS BIRCH** – guitar

Mar 98. (cd/c) *<(36503-2/-4/-1)>* **SO MUCH FOR THE AFTERGLOW** [63] [33] Nov97
– So much for the afterglow / Everything to everyone / Ataraxia / Normal like you / I will buy you a new life / Father of mine / One hit wonder / El distorto de melodica / Amphetamine / White men in black suits / Sunflower / Why don't I believe in God / Like a California king.

Apr 98. (7") *(CL 799)* **EVERYTHING TO EVERYONE. / OUR LIPS ARE SEALED** [41] [ ]
(cd-s+=) *(CDCL 799)* – What do I get / ('A'-CD-Rom video).
(cd-s) *(CDCLS 799)* – ('A'side) / Walk don't run / Search and destroy / Santa Monica heroin (CD-Rom video).

Jul 98. (cd-s) *<85592>* **I WILL BUY YOU A NEW LIFE** [-] [ ]
Nov 98. (cd-s) *<86181>* **FATHER OF MINE** [-] [70]

– compilations, etc. –

Apr 97. (m-cd) *Fire; (MCD 45)* **WHITE TRASH HELL** [ ] [ ]
Aug 95. (cd) *Imprint; <97633>* **LIVE FROM TORONTO** (live) [-] [-]

EVERLAST (see under ⇒ HOUSE OF PAIN)

EVERLY BROTHERS

Formed: Kentucky, USA . . . 1955 by brothers DON and PHIL EVERLY, the offspring of country singing parents, IKE and MARGARET. No strangers to the music scene (the boys having appeared on numerous radio shows alongside their folks), they went to Nashville later that year hoping that hillbilly artists would buy their close harmony songs. The following year, they secured a deal with 'Columbia' records, the label releasing one country-style single, 'KEEP A LOVIN' ME', before opting out as the rock'n'roll era began to kick in. After a short struggle in an attempt to find another label, their father contacted old friend, star picker CHET ATKINS, who got them signed as writers for the legendary Roy Acuff/Wesley Rose songsmith team. ROSE subsequently became the siblings' manager, persuading Archie Bleyer of 'Cadence' records to take them on as recording artists in 1957. Adopting a new style combining their vocal harmonies with easy going pop'n'roll strumming, The EVERLY BROTHERS made an immediate impact with 'BYE BYE LOVE', a million-selling single which peaked at No.2 that summer. Their profile heightened by a handful of TV appearances (i.e. the Ed Sullivan and Perry Como shows), the brothers' clean-cut apple-pie good looks and teen heartbreak appeal saw further singles, 'WAKE UP LITTLE SUSIE', 'ALL I HAVE TO DO IS DREAM' and 'BIRD DOG' fare equally well over the ensuing three years. In 1960, they signed to 'Warners', scoring a transatlantic chart topper with their label debut, 'CATHY'S CLOWN', a 45 that had to battle for chart supremacy against reissued 'Cadence' material. The lads were now also relying on their own material, having left the Felice & Boudleaux Bryant songwriting duo behind when they switched stables. A further clutch of major hits, 'SO SAD (TO WATCH GOOD LOVE GO BAD)', 'WALK RIGHT BACK', 'TEMPTATION', 'CRYIN' IN THE RAIN' etc, saw them dominate the pre-BEATLES pop charts in both America and Britain, although it would be the UK who stood by the duo when the onslaught of 1963-64 British Invasion took hold. In 1965, as their American profile was on the wane, they scored considerable critical and commercial success as the classic, 'THE PRICE OF LOVE' hit No.2 in Britain (criminally ignored in their homeland). Their records continued to sell moderately throughout the latter half of the 60's, although a dalliance with country rock in the early 70's brought little commercial reward; the increasingly estranged brothers finally parted company on less than amicable terms during a disastrous gig on 14th of July '73. Over the next ten years, the brothers followed sporadically successful solo careers (PHIL, together with CLIFF RICHARD, had a 1983 UK Top 10 hit 'SHE MEANS NOTHING TO ME'), eventually coming together again for a reunion concert in '83; they were back on speaking terms after attending the funeral of their father. The resulting live album put The EVERLY BROTHERS back in the UK Top 50 as did the following year's eponymous (PAUL McCARTNEY-produced) comeback set, and although they maintained their working relationship they failed to keep up the momentum. • **Covered:** CLAUDETTE (Roy Orbison) / LET IT BE ME (Gilbert Becaud) / BE-BOP-A-LULA (Gene Vincent) / LUCILLE (Little Richard) / WALK RIGHT

BACK (Sonny Curtis; of Crickets) / EBONY EYES + IT'S MY TIME (John D. Loudermilk) / TEMPTATION (Bing Crosby) / CRYING IN THE RAIN (Carole King & Howard Greenfield) / BOWLING GREEN (Terry Slater) / ABANDONED LOVE (Bob Dylan) / THE GIRL SANG THE BLUES + LOVE HER (Mann-Weill) / YVES (Scott McKenzie). After an inter-label rift between Wesley Rose was rectified, The BRYANTS returned on late 1964's 'GONE GONE GONE'. The album 'ROCK'N'SOUL' featured many classic rock'n'roll oldies. • **Trivia:** Many famous musicians have passed through their ranks, including FLOYD CHANCE – bass (1957) / JOEY PAGE – guitar (1962) / JIM GORDON and BILLY PRESTON. Other 60's sessioners stemmed from The BYRDS, The HOLLIES and LED ZEPPELIN!

Best CD compilation(s): CADENCE CLASSICS: THEIR 20 GREATEST HITS (*9) / WALK RIGHT BACK: THE EVERLY BROTHERS ON WARNER BROS. (*8)

DON EVERLY (b.ISAAC DONALD EVERLY, 1 Feb'37, Brownie, Kentucky, USA) – vocals, guitar / **PHIL EVERLY** (b.19 Jan'39, Chicago, Illinois, USA) – vocals, guitar

		not iss.	Columbia	
		London	Cadence	

Feb 56.	(7") <21496> **KEEP A LOVIN' ME. / THE SUN KEEPS SHINING**	– / –
Jun 57.	(7",78) (HLA 8440) <1315> **BYE BYE LOVE. / I WONDER IF I CARE AS MUCH** (re-iss. Jul82 on 'Old Gold'; OG 9060)	6 / 2 May57
Oct 57.	(7",78) (HLA 8498) <1337> **WAKE UP LITTLE SUSIE. / MAYBE TOMORROW** (re-iss. Jul82 on 'Old Gold'; OG 9061)	2 / 1 Sep57
Feb 58.	(7",78) (HLA 8554) <1342> **THIS LITTLE GIRL OF MINE. / SHOULD WE TELL HIM**	26 / 16 Jan58
Mar 58.	(lp) (HA-A 2081) <3003> **THE EVERLY BROTHERS** – This little girl of mine / Maybe tomorrow / Bye bye love / Brand new Heartache / Keep a knockin' / Be-bop-a-lula / Rip it up / I wonder if I care as much / Wake up little Susie / Leave my woman alone / Should we tell him / Hey doll baby.	
May 58.	(7",78) (HLA 8554) <1348> **ALL I HAVE TO DO IS DREAM. / CLAUDETTE** <re-iss. Jul61, A-side hit No.96> (re-iss. Jul82 on 'Old Gold'; OG 9062)	1 / 1 / 30 Apr58
Sep 58.	(7",78) (HLA 8685) <1350> **BIRD DOG. / DEVOTED TO YOU** (re-iss. Apr79 on 'Lightning; LIG 9018)	2 / 1 / 10 Jul58
Nov 58.	(lp) (HA-A 2150) <3016> **SONGS OUR DADDY TAUGHT US** – Roving gambler / Down in the willow garden / Longtime gone / Lightning express / That silver haired daddy of mine / Who's gonna shoe your pretty little feet / Barbara Allen / Oh so many years / I'm here to get my baby out of jail / Rockin' alone (in an old rocking chair) / Kentucky / Put my little shoes away. (re-iss. Aug83 on 'Charly' CH 75)	Sep58
Jan 59.	(7",78) (HLA 8781) <1355> **PROBLEMS. / LOVE OF MY LIFE** (re-iss. Jul82 on 'Old Gold'; OG 9063)	6 / 2 / 40 Nov58
May 59.	(7",78) (HLA 8863) <1364> **POOR JENNY. / TAKE A MESSAGE TO MARY** (re-iss. Jul82 on 'Old Gold'; OG 9064)	14 / 22 / 16 Apr59
Sep 59.	(7",78) (HLA 8934) <1364> **TILL I KISSED YOU. / OH WHAT A FEELING** (re-iss. Jul82 on 'Old Gold'; OG 9065)	2 / 4 Aug59
Feb 60.	(7",78) (HLA 9039) <1376> **LET IT BE ME. / SINCE YOU BROKE MY HEART** (re-iss. Jul82 on 'Old Gold'; OG 9066)	13 / 7 Jan60

		Warners	Warners

Apr 60.	(7",78) (WB 1) <5151> **CATHY'S CLOWN. / ALWAYS IT'S YOU**	1 / 1 / 56
Jun 60.	(lp) (WM 4012) <1381> **IT'S EVERLY TIME!** – So sad / Just in case / Memories are made of this / That's what you do to me / Sleepless nights / What kind of girl are you / Oh true love / Carol Jane / Some sweet day / Nashville blues / You thrill me / I want you to know. (re-iss. May85 on 'Rollercoaster'; ROLI 313)	2 / 9 May60
Sep 60.	(7",78) (WB 19) <5163> **LUCILLE. / SO SAD (TO WATCH GOOD LOVE GO BAD)**	4 / 21 / 7 Aug60
Jan 61.	(7") (WB 33) <5199> **WALK RIGHT BACK. / EBONY EYES**	1 / 7 / 8
Feb 61.	(lp) (WM 4028) <1395> **A DATE WITH THE EVERLY BROTHERS** – Made to love / That's just too much / Stick with me baby / Baby what you want me to do / Sigh cry almost die / Always it's you / Love hurts / Lucille / So how come / Donna Donna / A change of heart / Cathy's clown. (re-iss. May85 on 'Rollercoaster'; ROLI 314)	3 / 9 Nov60
Jun 61.	(7") (WB 42) <5199> **TEMPTATION. / STICK WITH ME BABY**	1 / 27 / 41
Sep 61.	(7") (WB 50) <5501> **DON'T BLAME ME. / MUSKRAT**	20 / 20 / 82
1961.	(lp) (WM 4052) <1418> **BOTH SIDES OF AN EVENING** – My mamma / Muskrat / My gal Sal / My grandfather's clock / Bully of the town / Chloe / Mention my name in Sheboygan / Hi Lili hi lo / Wayward wind / Don't blame me / Now is the hour / Little old lady / When I grow too old to dream / Love is where you find it.	
Jan 62.	(7") (WB 56) <5250> **CRYIN' IN THE RAIN. / I'M NOT ANGRY**	6 / 6
May 62.	(7") (WB 67) <5273> **HOW CAN I MEET HER. / THAT'S OLD FASHIONED (THAT'S THE WAY LOVE SHOULD BE)**	12 / 75 / 9
Jul 62.	(lp) (WM 4061) <1430> **INSTANT PARTY**	20

– Jezebel / Oh my papa / Step it up and go / True love / Bye bye blackbird / Trouble in mind / Love makes the world go round / Long lost John / Autumn leaves / Party's over / Ground hawg / When it's night time in Italy. (re-iss. Oct86 on 'Rollercoaster'; ROLI 321)

Sep 62.	(lp; mono/stereo) (WM/WS 8108) <1471> **THE GOLDEN HITS OF THE EVERLY BROTHERS** (compilation) – That's old fashioned (that's the way love should be) / How can I meet her? / Crying in the rain / I'm not angry / Don't blame me / Ebony eyes / Cathy's clown / Walk right back / Lucille / So sad (to watch good love go bad) / Muskrat / Temptation. (re-iss. Dec65 mono/stereo; W/WS 1471) (cd+c-iss 1991 on 'WEA')	35
Oct 62.	(7") (WB 79) <5297> **NO ONE CAN MAKE MY SUNSHINE SMILE. /**	11 / 48 B-side
Dec 62.	(lp; mono/stereo) (WM/WS 8116) <1483> **CHRISTMAS WITH THE EVERLY BROTHERS AND THE BOYS TOWN CHOIR** (trad Xmas songs)	
Mar 63.	(7") (WB 94) <5346> **SO IT WILL ALWAYS BE. / NANCY'S MINUET**	23
May 63.	(lp; mono/stereo) (WM/WS 8138) <1513> **... SING GREAT COUNTRY HITS** – Oh lonesome me / Born to lose / Just one time / Send me the pillow you dream on / Release me / Please help me I'm falling / I walk the line / Lonely street / Silver threads and golden needles / I'm so lonesome I could cry / Sweet dreams / This is the last song I'm ever going to sing. (re-iss. Dec85 on 'Rollercoaster'; ROLI 329)	
Jun 63.	(7") (WB 99) <5362> **IT'S BEEN NICE. / I'M AFRAID**	26
Oct 63.	(7") (WB 109) <5389> **THE GIRL SANG THE BLUES. / LOVE HER**	25
Apr 64.	(7") (WB 129) <5422> **AIN'T THAT LOVIN' YOU BABY. / HELLO AMY**	
Jun 64.	(7") (WB 135) <5441> **THE FERRIS WHEEL. / DON'T FORGET TO CRY**	22 / 72
Jan 65.	(lp; mono/stereo) (WM/WS 8163) <1554> **THE VERY BEST OF THE EVERLY BROTHERS** (re-recorded hits) – Bye bye love / (Til) I kissed you / Wake up little Susie / Crying in the rain / Walk right back / Cathy's clown / Bird dog / All I have to do is dream / Devoted to you / Lucille / So sad (to watch good love go bad) / Ebony eyes. (re-iss. May74 lp/c; K/K4 46008) – hit UK No.43	Jul64
1964.	(7") <5466> **RING AROUND MY ROSIE. / YOU'RE THE ONE I LOVE**	– / –
Nov 64.	(7") (WB 146) <5478> **GONE GONE GONE. / TORTURE**	36 / 31
Dec 64.	(lp; mono/stereo) (WM/WS 8169) <1585> **GONE GONE GONE** – Donna, Donna / Lonely island / The facts of life / Ain't that lovin' you baby / Love is all I need / The drop out / Radio and TV / Honolulu / It's been a long dry spell / The ferris wheel / Gone gone gone. (re-iss. 1970 on 'Valient'; VS 109) (re-iss. May85 on 'Rollercoaster'; ROLI 316)	
Feb 65.	(7") (WB 154) <5600> **YOU'RE MY GIRL. / DON'T LET THE WHOLE WORLD KNOW**	
Apr 65.	(7") (WB 158) <5611> **THAT'LL BE THE DAY. / GIVE ME A SWEETHEART**	30
May 65.	(lp; mono/stereo) (WM/WS 8171) <1578> **ROCK'N'SOUL** – That'll be the day / So fine / Maybelline / Dancing in the street / Kansas City / I got a woman / Love hurts / Slippin' and slidin' / Susie Q / Hound dog / I'm gonna move to the out-skirtsd of town / Lonely weekends. (re-iss. May85 on 'Rollercoaster'; ROLI 317)	
May 65.	(7") (WB 161) <5628> **THE PRICE OF LOVE. / IT ONLY COSTS A DIME**	2
Aug 65.	(7") (WB 5539) <5639> **I'LL NEVER GET OVER YOU. / FOLLOW ME**	35
Sep 65.	(lp) <(WS 1605)> **BEAT AND SOUL** – Love is strange / Money / What am I living for / High heel sneakers / C.C. rider / Lonely avenue / Man with money / People get ready / My babe / Walking the dog / I almost lost my mind / The girl can't help it. (re-iss. Dec85 on 'Rollercoaster'; ROLI 319)	
Oct 65.	(7") <(WB 5649)> **LOVE IS STRANGE. / MAN WITH MONEY**	11
Mar 66.	(7") (WB 5743) <5808> **THE POWER OF LOVE. / LEAVE MY GIRL ALONE**	
Mar 66.	(lp) <(WS 1620)> **IN OUR IMAGE** – Leave my girl alone / Chained to a memory / I'll never get over you / The doll house is empty / Glitter and gold / The power of love / The price of love / It's all over / I used to love you / Lonely Kravezit / June is as cold as December / It only cost a dime. (re-iss. May85 on 'Rollercoaster'; ROLI 318)	
Mar 66.	(7") <5682> **I USED TO LOVE YOU. / IT'S ALL OVER**	– / –
1966.	(7") <5698> **THE DOLL HOUSE IS EMPTY. / LONELY KRAVEZIT**	
Jul 66.	(lp) <(WS 1646)> **TWO YANKS IN ENGLAND** – Somebody help me / So lonely / Kiss your man goodbye / Signs that will never change / Like everytime before / Pretty flamingo / I've been wrong before / Have you ever loved somebody / The collector / Don't run and hide / Fifi the flea / Hard, hard year. (re-iss. Feb89 on 'Edsel'; ED 297)	
Aug 66.	(7") (WB 5754) **I'VE BEEN WRONG BEFORE. / HARD, HARD YEAR**	
Sep 66.	(7") <5833> **SOMEBODY HELP ME. / HARD, HARD YEAR**	– / –
Dec 66.	(7") <5857> **FIFI THE FLEA (by "DON"). / LIKE EVERYTIME BEFORE (by "PHIL")**	
Feb 67.	(lp) <(WS 1676)> **THE HIT SOUND OF THE EVERLY BROTHERS** – Blueberry Hill / Movin' on / Devil's child / Trains and boats and planes / Sea of heartbreak / Oh boy / (I'd be a) Legend in my time / Let's go get stoned / Sticks and stones / The house of the rising Sun / She never smiles anymore / Good golly Miss Molly.	
Mar 67.	(7") <5901> **THE DEVIL'S CHILD. / SHE NEVER SMILES ANYMORE**	
Mar 67.	(7") (WB 6074) **OH BOY. / GOOD GOLLY MISS MOLLY**	– / –
Jun 67.	(7") <(WB 7020)> **BOWLING GREEN. / I DON'T WANT TO LOVE YOU**	40
Sep 67.	(7") <(WB 7062)> **MARY JANE. / TALKING TO THE FLOWERS**	
Nov 67.	(7") <(WB 7088)> **LOVE OF THE COMMON PEOPLE. / A VOICE WITHIN**	

Apr 68. (7") <(WB 7192)> **IT'S MY TIME. / EMPTY BOXES**	**39**	
Aug 68. (7") <(WB 7226)> **MILK TRAIN. / LORD OF THE MANOR**		

Nov 68. (lp) <(WS 1752)> **ROOTS** (new & re-old material)
– Introduction: The Everly family / Mama tried / Less of me / T for Texas / I wonder if I care as much / Ventura boulevard / Shady grove / Illinois / Living too close to the ground / You done me wrong / Turn around / Sing me back home / Montage : The Everly family-Shady grove-Kentucky. *(re-iss. 1971; K 46128) (re-iss. Sep86 on 'Rollercoaster'; ROLI 322) (re-iss. 1987 on 'Edsel'; ED 203) (cd-iss. May95)*

Apr 69. (7") <7290> **I'M ON MY WAY HOME AGAIN. / THE CUCKOO BIRD**	**-**	
1969. (7") <7262> **T – FOR TEARS. / I WONDER IF I CARE AS MUCH**	**-**	
1969. (7") <7290> **CAROLINA ON MY MIND. / MY LITTLE YELLOW BIRD**	**-**	

Feb 70. (d-lp) <(WS 1858)> **THE EVERLY BROTHERS SHOW** (live at The Grand Hotel)
– Mama tried / Kentucky / Bowling green / Till I kissed you / Wake up little Susie / Cathy's clown / Bird dog / Maybelline / Lord of the manor / I wonder if I care as much / Love is strange / Let it be me / Give peace a chance / Rock and roll music / The end / Aquarius / If I were a carpenter / The price of love / The thrill is gone / Games people play / Baby what you want me to do / All I have to do is dream / Walk right back / Susie Q / Hey Jude.

Oct 70. (7") <(WB 7425)> **YVES. / HUMAN RACE**		Feb70
	RCA Victor	RCA Victor
1972. (7") (RCA 2232) <74-0717> **RIDIN' HIGH. / STORIES WE COULD TELL**		

Jun 72. (lp) (SF 8270) <4620> **STORIES WE COULD TELL**
– All we really want to do / Breakdown / Green river / Mandolin wind / Up in Mabel's room / Del Rio Dan / Ridin' high / Brand new Tennessee waltz / Stories we can tell / Christmas eve can kill you / I'm tired of singing my songs in Las Vegas.

1972. (7") <74-0849> **PARADISE. / LAY IT DOWN**	**-**	
1973. (7") <74-0901> **NOT FADE AWAY. / LADIES LOVE OUTLAWS**		
1973. (7") (RCA 2286) **NOT FADE AWAY. / LAY IT DOWN**	**-**	

Feb 73. (lp) (SF 8332) <4781> **PASS THE CHICKEN AND LISTEN**
– Lay it down / Husbands and wives / Woman don't you try to tie me down / Sweet memories / Ladies love outlaws / Not fade away / Watchin' it go / Paradise / Somebody nobody knows / Good-hearted woman / A nickel for the fiddler / Rocky top. *(re-iss. +cd.Jul91 on 'Edsel')*

—— Announced their break-up at a 14 Jul'73 concert. PHIL went solo later.

DON EVERLY

with one lp under his belt, also continued with solo career.

	A&M	Ode
1971. (7") <66009> **TUMBLIN' TUMBLEWEEDS. / ONLY ME**	**-**	

1971. (lp) (AMLS 2007) <77005> **DON EVERLY**
– Don't drink the water / Eyes of Asia / February 15th / My baby / My friend / Omaha / Safari / Sweet dreams of you / Tumbling tumbleweed / Thinking it over / When I stop dreaming.

—— His next album featured group HEADS, HANDS & FEET

	Ode	Ode
Aug 74. (7") <(ODS 66046)> **WARMIN' UP THE BAND. / EVELYN SWING**		

Oct 74. (lp) <(ODE 77023)> **SUNSET TOWERS**
– Melody train / Jack Daniels Old No.7 / Warmin' up the band / Helpless when you're gone / Did it rain / Brand new rock and roll band / Takin' shots / The way you remain / Evelyn swing / Southern California.

	D.J.M.	Hickory
Jul 76. (7") (DJS 10692) <368> **YESTERDAY JUST PASSED MY WAY AGAIN. / NEVER LIKE THIS**		
Mar 77. (7") (DJS 10760) **SO SAD TO WATCH GOOD LOVE GO BAD. / LOVE AT LAST SIGHT**		
1976. (7") <54002> **OH, I'D lIKE TO GO AWAY. / LOVE AT LAST SIGHT**	**-**	
1976. (7") <54005> **DEEP WATER. / SINCE YOU BROKE MY HEART**	**-**	

Mar 77. (lp) (20501) <44003> **BROTHER JUKE BOX**
– Brother juke box / Love at last sight / So sad to watch good love go bad / Lettin' go / Since you broke my heart / Never like this / Deep water / Yesterday just passed my way again / Oh I'd like to go away / Oh what a feeling / Turn the memories back again. *(re-iss. May88 on 'Sundown' lp/c; SDLP/SDC 002) (cd-iss. Aug94)*

	Polydor	Polydor
Mar 78. (7") (DJS 10842) <54012> **BROTHER JUKE BOX. / OH, WHAT A FEELING**		
	Sundown	Sundown
Aug 81. (7") (POSP 315) **LET'S PUT OUR HEARTS TOGETHER. / SO SAD TO WATCH GOOD LOVE GO BAD**	**-**	**-**
Nov 85. (7") (SDS 1) **BROTHER JUKE BOX. / NEVER LIKE THIS**		

PHIL EVERLY

solo with **JAMES BURTON / WARREN ZEVON, JIM HORN** and **EARL PALMER**

	R.C.A.	R.C.A.
Sep 73. (7") (RCA 2409) **THE AIR THAT I BREATHE. / GOD BLESS OLD LADIES**		**-**

Sep 73. (lp) (SF 8370) <APL-1 0092> **STAR SPANGLED SPRINGER**
– The air that I breathe / Sweet grass country / God bless older ladies (for they made rock and roll) / It pleases me to please you / Lady Anne / Red, white and blue / Our song / Poisonberry pie / La divorce / Snowflake bombadier.

	Pye	Pye
Mar 74. (7") <71014> **OLD KENTUCKY RIVER. / SUMMERSHINE**	**-**	
Jun 74. (7") <71036> **NEW OLD SONG. / BETTER THAN NOW**	**-**	
Aug 74. (7") (7N 45398)) **INVISIBLE MAN. / IT'S TRUE**		
Nov 74. (7") (7N 45415) **SWEET MUSIC. / GOODBYE LINE**		**-**

Jan 75. (lp) (NSPL 18448) <12104> **THERE'S NOTHING TOO GOOD FOR MY BABY** <US-title 'PHIL'S DINER'>

— Sweet music / Goodbye line / Feather bed / Summershine / Too blue / There's nothing too good for my baby / Invisible man / Caroline / We're running out / It's true / New old song. *(US title – 'PHIL'S DINER')*

Oct 75. (7") (7N 45544) **BETTER THAN NOW. / YOU AND I ARE A SONG**		

Nov 75. (lp) (NSPL 18473) <12121> **MYSTIC LINE**
– Patiently / Lion and the lamb / Mystic line / Jammy butterfly / You and I are a song / Worlds in your eyes / Better than now / When will I be loved / Back when the bands played in ragtime / Friends.

1976. (7") <71055> **WORLDS IN YOUR EYES. / BACK WHEN THE BAND PLAYED IN RAGTIME**	**-**	
1976 (7") (APBO 0064) **GOD BLESS OLDER LADIES. / SWEET GRASS COUNTRY**	**-**	
	not iss.	Elektra
1979. (lp) <6E 213> **LIVING ALONE**	**-**	

– It was too late for the party / Ich bin dein (I am yours) / You broke it / Living alone / Buy me a beer / California gold / Love will pull us through / I just don't feel like dancing / Charleston guitar / The fall of '59.

—— guested on SANDRA LOCKE single 'Don't Say You Don't Love Me No More'

1979. (7") <46519> **LIVING ALONE. / I JUST DON'T FEEL LIKE DANCING**	**-**	
	Epic	Curb
1979. (7") <46556> **YOU BROKE IT. / BUY ME A BEER**	**-**	
Mar 81. (7") (EPCA 9575) <5401> **DARE TO DREAM AGAIN. / LONELY DAYS LONELY NIGHTS**		
1981. (7") <ZS6 02116> **SWEET SOUTHERN LOVE. / IN YOUR EYES**	**-**	
	Capitol	Capitol
Oct 82. (7") (CL 266) **LOUISE. / SWEET SUZANNE**	**47**	**-**
Jan 83. (7"; PHIL EVERLY & CLIFF RICHARD) (CL 276) **SHE MEANS NOTHING TO ME. / A WOMAN AND A MAN**	**9**	**-**
1983. (7") <5197> **WHO'S GONNA KEEP ME WARM. / ONE WAY LOVE ON A TWO WAY STREET**	**-**	
Apr 83. (lp/c) (EST/TC-EST 27670) **PHIL EVERLY**	**61**	

– She means nothing to me / I'll mend your broken heart / God bless older ladies / Sweet pretender / Never gonna dream again / Better than now / A woman and a man / Louise / When I'm dead and gone / Sweet Suzanne / Oh baby oh (you're the star). *(re-iss Aug87 as 'LOUISE' on 'Magnum Force' lp/c; MFLP/MFC 053) (cd-iss. Jan88; CDMF 053) (cd-iss. Oct93 & Feb95 on 'B.G.O.')*

Apr 83. (7") (CL 285) **SWEET PRETENDER. / BETTER THAN NOW**		**-**
Jun 83. (7") (CL 294) **OH BABY OH (YOU'RE THE STAR). / GOD BLESS OLDER LADIES**		**-**

EVERLY BROTHERS

re-united.

	Impression	Passport
Nov 83. (7"ep)(12"ep) (IMS 1) **DEVOTED TO YOU / EBONY EYES. / LOVE HURTS / THE PRICE OF LOVE (all live)**		**-**
Dec 83. (lp/c) (IMDP/IMDK 1) <11001> **EVERLY BROTHERS' REUNION CONCERT** (Royal Albert Hall – Sep'83)	**47**	

– The price of love / Walk right back / Claudette / Crying in the rain / Love is strange / Live medley / Take a message to mary / Maybe tomorrow / I wonder if I care as much / When will I be loved / Bird dog / Live medley; Devoted to you – Ebony eyes – Love hurts / Barbara Allen / Lightning Express / Put my little shoes away / Long time gone / Down in the willow garden / Step it up and go / Cathy's clown / Gone, gone, gone / You send me / So sad (to watch good love go bad) / Blues (stay away from me) / Bye bye love / All I have to do is dream / Wake up little Susie / ('Til) I kissed you / Temptation / Be-bop-a-lula / Lucille / Let it be me / Good golly Miss Molly. *(cd-iss. May86 on 'Mercury') (re-iss. cd in 2 parts Jul95 on 'Charly') (re-iss. cd/c Sep95 on 'Emporio')*

	Mercury	Mercury
Aug 84. (7") (MER 170) <880 213-7> **ON THE WINGS OF A NIGHTINGALE. / ASLEEP**	**41**	**50**
Oct 84. (d-lp/c)(cd) (MERH/+C 44)<(822431-2)> **THE EVERLY BROTHERS** <US-title 'EB 84'>	**36**	**38**

– Danger, danger / The first in line / On the wings of a nightingale / The story of me / I'm taking my time / Lay lady lay / Following the Sun / You make it seem so easy / More than I can handle / Asleep. *(re-iss. Jun87 lp/c; REICE/PRIMC 110)*

Nov 84. (7") (MER 180) **THE STORY OF ME. / FOLLOWING THE SUN**	**-**	
Nov 84. (7") <880 423-7> **THE STORY OF ME. / THE FIRST IN LINE**	**-**	
Oct 85. (7") (MER 206) **AMANDA RUTH. / BORN YESTERDAY**	**-**	
Oct 85. (7") <884 428-7> **BORN YESTERDAY. / DON'T SAY GOODNIGHT**		**83**
Nov 85. (lp/c)(cd) (MERH/+C 80)<(826142-2)> **BORN YESTERDAY**		

– Amanda Ruth / I know love / Born yesterday / These shoes / Arms of Mary / That uncertain feeling / Thinkin' about you / Why worry / Abandoned love / Don't say goodnight / Always drive a Cadillac. *(c-cd+=) – You send me.*

Feb 86. (7") <884 694-7> **I KNOW LOVE. / THESE SHOES**	**-**	
Nov 88. (7"; EVERLY BROTHERS & The BEACH BOYS) (MER 280) **DON'T WORRY BABY. / BORN YESTERDAY**		**-**
(cd-s+=) (MERCD 280) – On the wings of a nightingale.		
Apr 89. (lp/c/cd) <(832520-1/-4/-2)> **SOME HEARTS**		Nov88

– Some hearts / Ride the wind / Can't get it over / Brown eyes / Julianne / Don't worry baby / Be my love again / Angel of the darkness / Three bands of steel / Any single – solitary heart.

Apr 89. (7") <872 098-7> **DON'T WORRY BABY. / RIDE THE WIND**	**-**	

– compilations, others, etc. –

Note; on 'Warners' unless mentioned otherwise
EP's on 'London' / US 'Cadence' unless stated otherwise

1958. (7"ep) (RE-A 1113) **THE EVERLY BROTHERS**		
1958. (7"ep) (RE-A 1148) **THE EVERLY BROTHERS No.2**		
1958. (7"ep) (RE-A 1149) **THE EVERLY BROTHERS No.3**		
Jan 59. (7"ep) (RE-A 1195) **SONGS OUR DADDY TAUGHT US (Part 1)**		

Feb 59.	(7"ep) *(RE-A 1196)* **SONGS OUR DADDY TAUGHT US (Part 2)**		
Mar 59.	(7"ep) *(RE-A 1197)* **SONGS OUR DADDY TAUGHT US (Part 3)**		
1959.	(7"ep) *(RE-A 1174)* **THE EVERLY BROTHERS No.4**		
1960.	(7"ep) *(RE-A 1229)* **THE EVERLY BROTHERS No.5**		
Jul 60.	(7") *(HLA 9157) <1380>* **WHEN WILL I BE LOVED. / BE-BOP-A-LULA**	4	8 / 74 Jun60
	(re-iss. Oct80 on 'Old Gold'; OG 9067)		
1960.	(m-lp) *London; <CLLP 333>* **ROCKIN' WITH THE EVERLY BROTHERS**	-	
Oct 60.	(lp) *London; (HA-A 2266) / <25040>* **THE FABULOUS STYLE OF THE EVERLY BROTHERS**	4	23 Aug60
	<re-iss. Jan86 on 'Rhino'; RNLP 213> (cd-iss. Dec91 on 'Ace')		
Nov 60.	(7") *Cadence; <1388>* **LIKE STRANGERS. / BRAND NEW HEARTACHE**	-	22
Dec 60.	(7") *London; (HLA 9250)* **LIKE STRANGERS. / LEAVE MY WOMAN ALONE**	11	-
1961.	(7"ep) *(RE-A 1311)* **THE EVERLY BROTHERS No.6**		
Oct 62.	(7") *Cadence; <1429>* **I'M HERE TO GET MY BABY OUT OF JAIL. / LIGHTNING EXPRESS**	-	76
1961.	(7"ep) *Warners; (WEP 6034)* **ESPECIALLY FOR YOU**		
1961.	(7"ep) *Warners; (WEP 6049)* **FOR EVERLY YOURS**		
1962.	(7"ep) *Warners; (WEP 6056)* **IT'S EVERLY TIME!**		
1962.	(7"ep) *Warners; (WEP 6107)* **A DATE WITH THE EVERLY BROTHERS Vol.1**		
1962.	(7"ep) *Warners; (WEP 6109)* **A DATE WITH THE EVERLY BROTHERS Vol.2**		
1962.	(7"ep) *Warners; (WEP 6111)* **INSTANT PARTY (Vol.1)**		
1962.	(7"ep) *Warners; (WEP 6113)* **INSTANT PARTY (Vol.2)**		
1963.	(7"ep) *Warners; (WEP 6115)* **BOTH SIDES OF AN EVENING – FOR DANCING**		
1963.	(7"ep) *Warners; (WEP 6117)* **BOTH SIDES OF AN EVENING – FOR DREAMING**		
1964.	(7"ep) *Warners; (WEP 6128)* **... SING GREAT COUNTRY HITS Vol.1**		
1964.	(7"ep) *Warners; (WEP 6131)* **... SING GREAT COUNTRY HITS Vol.2**		
1964.	(7"ep) *Warners; (WEP 6132)* **... SING GREAT COUNTRY HITS Vol.3**		
1964.	(7"ep) *Warners; (WEP 6138)* **BOTH SIDES OF AN EVENING – FOR FUN**		
1965.	(7"ep) *Warners; (WEP 604)* **THE PRICE OF LOVE**		
1965.	(7"ep) *Warners; (WEP 608)* **ROCK'N'SOUL Vol.1**		
1965.	(7"ep) *Warners; (WEP 609)* **ROCK'N'SOUL Vol.2**		
1966.	(7"ep) *Warners; (WEP 610)* **LOVE IS STRANGE**		
1966.	(7"ep) *Warners; (WEP 612)* **PEOPLE GET READY**		
1966.	(7"ep) *Warners; (WEP 618)* **WHAT AM I LIVING FOR**		
1967.	(7"ep) *Warners; (WEP 622)* **LEAVE MY GIRL ALONE**		
1967.	(7"ep) *Warners; (WEP 623)* **SOMEBODY HELP ME**		
May 69.	(7") *(WB 6056)* **CATHY'S CLOWN. / WALK RIGHT BACK**		
	(re-iss. Jul81; K 16002)		
1974.	(7") *(WB 727)* **CATHY'S CLOWN. / CRYIN' IN THE RAIN**		
1974.	(7") *(WB 747)* **WAKE UP LITTLE SUSIE. / BYE BYE LOVE**		
1975.	(7") *(K 16562)* **CATHY'S CLOWN. / ALL I HAVE TO IS DREAM**		
Oct 75.	(lp/c) *(K/K4 56168)* **WALK RIGHT BACK WITH THE EVERLYS**	10	-
1976.	(7") *(K 16163)* **WALK RIGHT BACK. / FERRIS WHEEL**		
Mar 76.	(7") *(K 16709)* **EBONY EYES. / WAKE UP LITTLE SUSIE**		
Mar 77.	Warwick; (lp) *(WW 5027)* **LIVING LEGENDS** ('Cadence' hits)	12	
Sep 77.	(lp/c) *(K/K4 56415)* **THE NEW ALBUM** (from vaults)		
Sep 77.	(7") *(K 17004)* **SILENT TREATMENT. / DANCING ON MY FEET**		
Nov 83.	(lp/c) *(923 994-1/-4)* **THE BEST OF THE EVERLY BROTHERS**		
May 93.	(cd/c) *(9548 31992-2/-4)* **THE GOLDEN YEARS OF THE EVERLY BROTHERS – THEIR 24 GREATEST HITS**	26	
Sep 70.	(d-lp) *C.B.S.; (66255) / Barnaby; <6006>* **THE EVERLY BROTHERS ORIGINAL GREATEST HITS**	7	
Dec 70.	(lp) *C.B.S.; (66259) / Barnaby; <30260>* **END OF AN ERA**		
Jun 75.	(7") *Janus; (6146200)* **ALL I HAVE TO DO IS DREAM. / WAKE UP LITTLE SUSIE**	-	-
Dec 82.	(lp/c) *K-Tel; (NE1/CD2 197)* **LOVE HURTS**	31	-
	(re-iss. Sep84; same)		
Jul 82.	(7") *Revival; (BONUS 1)* **YOU'RE JUST WHAT I WAS LOOKING FOR. / WHATEVER HAPPENED TO JUDY**		-
Jul 80.	(14x7"box) *Old Gold; (SET 1)* **(14 singles boxed)**		-
Jul 82.	(7") *Old Gold; (OG 9068)* **LIKE STRANGERS. / SHOULD WE TELL HIM**		-
Jul 82.	(7") *Old Gold; (OG 9069)* **CATHY'S CLOWN. / TEMPTATION**		-
Jul 82.	(7") *Old Gold; (OG 9072)* **THE PRICE OF LOVE. / CRYING IN THE RAIN**		-
Nov 87.	(7") *Old Gold; (OG 9734)* **TILL I KISSED YOU. / BIRD DOG**		-
Feb 89.	(cd-ep) *Old Gold; (OG 6111)* **ALL I HAVE TO DO IS DREAM / BYE BYE LOVE / WAKE UP LITTLE SUSIE**		-
Mar 90.	(7") *Old Gold; (OG 9071)* **WALK RIGHT BACK. / EBONY EYES**		-
Sep 83.	(7"ep/c-ep) *(7SR/7SC 5000)* **6 TRACK HITS**		-
	– All I have to do is dream / Wake up little Susie / Bye bye love / Bird dog / Problems / Till I kissed you.		
Sep 84.	(lp) *Magnum Force; (MFLP 1028)* **NICE GUYS**		-
Jul 87.	(lp/c) *Magnum Force; (MF LP/C 052)* **SUSIE Q**		-
	(cd-iss. Jun88; CDMF 052)		
Feb 85.	(lp/c) *Hallmark; (SHM/HSC 3161)* **GREATEST HITS Vol.1**		-
May 85.	(lp/c) *Hallmark; (SHM/HSC 3168)* **GREATEST HITS Vol.2**		-
Oct 88.	(lp/c) *Hallmark; (SHM/HSC 3246)* **THE VERY BEST OF THE EVERLY BROTHERS**		-

	– Bye bye love / This little girl of mine / Should we tell him / Claudette / Devoted to you / Problems / Love of my life / Poor Jenny / Since you broke my heart / Let it be me / Wake up little Susie / I wonder if I care as much / Maybe tomorrow / All I have to do is dream / Bird dog / Brand new heartache / Take a message to Mary / ('Til I kissed you) / When will I be loved / Like strangers. *(cd-iss. Oct88 on 'Pickwick'; PWKS 515)*		
1988.	(cd) *Neon; (NCD 833 300-7)* **GREATEST HITS**		-
Feb 83.	(lp) *Ace-Charly; (CH 64)* **RIP IT UP**		-
Oct 84.	(lp) *Ace-Charly; (CH 118)* **PURE HARMONY**		-
Nov 85.	(lp) *Ace-Charly; (CH 159)* **IN THE STUDIO**		-
Feb 86.	(lp/c) *Crown; ; (GEM/+C 002)* **ROCKIN' IN HARMONY**		-
May 86.	(lp/c/cd) *Ace-Charly; (CHA/CHC/CDCH 194)* **GREAT RECORDINGS**		-
1989.	(d-c) *Ace-Charly; (CHC 804)* **RIP IT UP / PURE HARMONY**		-
Sep 89.	(lp) *Ace-Charly;* **HIDDEN GEMS**		-
May 89.	(lp) *Ace-Charly; (CH 272)* **THE WARNER BROTHERS YEARS Vol.1**		-
Oct 89.	(lp) *Ace; (CH 281)* **THE WARNER BROTHERS YEARS Vol.2**		-
Apr 90.	(cd) *Ace; (CDCH 932)* **THE EVERLY BROTHERS (debut) / THE FABULOUS STYLE OF . . .**		-
Jan 85.	(c) *V.F.M.; (VCA 110)* **BYE BYE LOVE**		-
	(re-iss. Sep87 on 'Entertainers' lp/c; ENT LP/MC 13025)		
Dec 85.	(pic-lp) *Astan; (AR 30046)* **GREATEST HITS**		-
Jan 86.	(lp) *Rhino; (RNLP 214)* **ALL THEY HAVE TO DO IS DREAM**	-	-
Jan 87.	(lp) *Muskateer; (LSP 1056)* **IN GERMANY & ITALY (live)**		-
May 86.	(lp/c) *Castle; (CCS LP/MC 139)* **THE COLLECTION**		-
	(cd-iss. 1988; CCSCD 139)		
1986.	(cd) *Creole; (RNCD 5258)* **CADENCE CLASSICS – 20 GREATEST HITS**		-
May 88.	(cd-ep) *Rhino; (R 373008)* **LIL' BIT OF GOLD**		-
	– Wake up little Susie / Bird dog / Let it be me / All I have to do is dream.		
Jul 86.	(cd) *Spectrum; (SPEC 85010)* **20 GREATEST HITS**		-
Jul 86.	(cd) *Spectrum; (SPEC 85016)* **20 GOLDEN LOVE SONGS**		-
May 93.	(cd/c) *Spectrum; (550056-2/-4)* **DREAMING**		-
May 88.	(d-lp) *Mercury; (832173-1)* **EB 84 / BORN YESTERDAY**		-
Feb 90.	(cd/c/lp) *Mainline; (260 471-2/-4/-1)* **SO MANY YEARS**		-
Jun 91.	(cd) *Sequel; (NEXCD 164)* **THE LONDON SESSIONS (PHIL EVERLY)**		-
Apr 92.	(3xcd-box) *Bear Family; (BCD 15618)* **CLASSIC EVERLY BROTHERS**		-
Jun 93.	(3xcd-box) *Sequel; (NXT 245)* **THE PERFECT HARMONY**		-
Dec 93.	(cd) *Disky;* **GOLD: GREATEST HITS**		-
Jan 94.	(cd) *Disky; (DCD 5324)* **THE BEST OF THE EVERLY BROTHERS**		-
Oct 94.	(cd) *Woodford; (WMCD 5704)* **SIMPLY THE BEST**		-
Dec 94.	(cd) *Ace; (CHM 544)* **THE ORIGINAL BRITISH HIT SINGLES**		-
Feb 95.	(cd/c) *More Music; (MO CD/MC 3002)* **RE-UNION AT THE ROYAL ALBERT HALL (live)**		-
Apr 95.	(cd) *Mercury; (514726-2)* **GREATEST HITS**		-
May 95.	(cd/c) *Spectrum; (570762-2/-4)* **WILL I BE LOVED? (PHIL EVERLY)**		-
May 95.	(cd/c) *Pickwick; (PWK S/MC 4259)* **THE BEST OF THE EVERLY BROTHERS – RARE SOLO CLASSICS**		-
Jul 95.	(cd) *Music Club; (MC 209)* **THE BEST OF THE EVERLY BROTHERS**		-

EVERYTHING BUT THE GIRL

Formed: Hull, England ... mid-1982 by ex-Hull university graduates TRACEY THORN (ex-MARINE GIRLS) and BEN WATT. They both had recorded solo efforts ('A DISTANT SHORE' and 'NORTH MARINE DRIVE' respectively) for indie label 'Cherry Red', before venturing onto 'WEA' (in 1983) subsidiary 'Blanco Y Negro' (run by Geoff Travis & Mike Alway). They almost immediately struck gold, with 'EACH AND EVERY ONE' (1984), making the UK Top 30, while its parent album, 'EDEN', hit the Top 20. A publicly shy, melancholy duo, EBTG blended together light jazz, folk and agitpop, their influences ranging from COLE PORTER to the modern day JOHN MARTYN. The following years' 'LOVE NOT MONEY', however, was a more conventional indie affair which breached the UK Top 10, although the band went for an orchestrated country sound on 'BABY THE STARS SHINE BRIGHT' (1986), having been influenced by America's grassroots music scene while touring there. Thus far, EBTG's career had been grounded in album sales, their loyal student following ensuring a respectable placing for each successive release; no one really expected their tender cover of Danny Whitten's heartbreaking 'I DON'T WANT TO TALK ABOUT IT' to make the Top 3 in summer '88. The attendant album, 'IDLEWILD' (1988), considered by many to be their finest hour, made the Top 20, although no further singles were forthcoming. Employing yet another ensemble of classy musicians, the band cut the more overtly jazzy 'THE LANGUAGE OF LIFE' (1990) at the turn of the decade. The early 90's saw the pair scoring with covers of The Everly Brothers' 'LOVE IS STRANGE' and Simon & Garfunkel's 'THE ONLY LIVING BOY IN NEW YORK', although WATT was still recovering from a rare, life-threatening illness (something he later documented in his book). THORN, meanwhile, found a perfect vehicle for her languorous vocal stylings with trip hop pioneers, MASSIVE ATTACK, the singer's contribution resulting in two of the best songs on their 1994 set, 'Protection' i.e. 'Better Things' and the title track. With contributions from such stalwarts as RICHARD THOMPSON, DAVE MATTACKS and the ubiquitous DANNY THOMPSON, 'AMPLIFIED HEART' (1994) was a return to form, showing the duo more willing to experiment with sound and atmosphere. One of the album's tracks, 'MISSING', was given an unlikely remix by house DJ, TODD TERRY; the result was a stunning combination of dancefloor dynamics and raw emotion which captured the imagination of record buyers around the world

in late '95 (also a transatlantic Top 5). Suddenly, EBTG were big news, a hip name to drop in dance circles; the following year's 'WALKING WOUNDED' album took the logical next step and paired the duo's stripped down melancholy with cutting edge drum 'n' bass textures. Critically acclaimed by both dance critics and the mainstream rock media, the record became one the biggest selling EBTG albums to date, spawning two Top 10 singles in 'WRONG' and the title track. Where the duo go from here is anybody's guess – like TEXAS, a single with WU-TANG CLAN perhaps?!! However, BEN and TRACEY were cutting the rug once more with a fresh set of songs courtesy of 1999's 'TEMPERAMENTAL', this critically lambasted bedsit musak for the New Labour yuppie becoming a bit trite for the more discerning rock ear. • Songwriters: Most written by duo or individually, except the covers; NIGHT AND DAY (Cole Porter) / KID (Pretenders) / ALFIE (hit; Cilla Black) / DOWNTOWN TRAIN (Tom Waits) / I FALL TO PIECES (Patsy Cline) / TAKE ME (Womack And Womack) / ON MY MIND (?) / NO PLACE LIKE HOME (from 'Wizard Of Oz') / LOVE IS STRANGE (Everly Brothers) / TOUGHER THAN THE REST (Bruce Springsteen) / TIME AFTER TIME (Cyndi Lauper) / ALISON (Elvis Costello) / MY HEAD IS MY ONLY HOUSE UNLESS IT RAINS (Jackson Browne) / THESE DAYS (Jackson Browne) / CORCOVADO (Antonio Carlos Jobim) / SINGLE contains a sample of Tim Buckley's (SONG TO THE SIREN). TRACEY THORN solo:- FEMME FATALE (Velvet Underground). • Trivia: EVERYTHING BUT THE GIRL was the name of a local second-hand store in Hull.
Album rating: Tracey Thorn: A DISTANT SHORE mini (*6) / Ben Watt: NORTH MARINE DRIVE (*6) / Everything But The Girl: EDEN (*7) / LOVE NOT MONEY (*5) / BABY, THE STARS SHINE BRIGHT (*5) / IDLEWILD (*6) / THE LANGUAGE OF LIFE (*7) / WORLDWIDE (*5) / AMPLIFIED HEART (*6) / HOME MOVIES – THE BEST OF EVERYTHING BUT THE GIRL compilation (*8) / WALKING WOUNDED (*7) / TEMPERAMENTAL (*4)

TRACEY THORN

		Cherry Red	not iss.
Aug 82. (m-lp) (MRED 35) **A DISTANT SHORE**			–

– Smalltown girl / Simply couldn't care / Seascape / Femme fatale / Dreamy / Plain sailing / New opened eyes / Too happy. (cd-iss. Jun87 + Aug93; MRED 35CD)

Dec 82. (7") (CHERRY 53) **PLAIN SAILING. / GOODBYE JOE**			–

BEN WATT

		Cherry Red	not iss.
Jun 81. (7"m) (CHERRY 25) **CANT. / AUBADE / TOWER OF SILENCE**			–
Apr 82. (12"ep; by BEN WATT & ROBERT WYATT) (12CHERRY 36) **SUMMER INTO WINTER**			–

– Walter and John / Aquamarine / Slipping slowly / Another conversation with myself / A girl in winter.

Feb 83. (7") (CHERRY 55) **SOME THINGS DON'T MATTER. / ON BOX HILL**			–
Feb 83. (lp) (BRED 40) **NORTH MARINE DRIVE**			–

– On Box hill / Some things don't matter / Lucky one / Empty bottles / North Marine Drive / Waiting like mad / Thirst for knowledge / Long time no sea / You're gonna make me lonesome when you go. (cd-iss. Jun87 + Jul93 w/ SUMMER INTO WINTER EP; BRED 40CD)

EVERYTHING BUT THE GIRL

TRACEY THORN (b.26 Sep'62) – vocals, guitar / **BEN WATT** (b. 6 Dec'62, London, England) – vocals, guitar, piano

Jun 82. (7"m) (CHERRY 37) **NIGHT AND DAY. / FEELING DIZZY / ON MY MIND**			–

(12"-iss.Dec85; 12CHERRY 37) (cd-s-iss.Mar89; CDCHERRY 37) (re-iss. Jul93)

with **SIMON BOOTH** – guitar (of WORKING WEEK, ex-WEEKEND) / **CHUCHO MERCHAN** – double bass / **CHARLES HAYWARD** – drums / **BOSCO DE OLIVEIRA** – percussion / **PETER KING** – alto saxophone / **NIGEL NASH** – tenor saxophone / **DICK PEARCE** – flugel trumpet

		Blanco Y Negro	Sire
Apr 84. (7") (NEG 1) **EACH AND EVERY ONE. / LAUGH YOU OUT THE HOUSE**		28	–

(12"+=) (NEG 1T) – Never could have been worse.

Jun 84. (lp/c)(cd) (BYN/+C 2)(<240-395-2>) **EDEN**		14	

– Each and every one / Bittersweet / Tender blue / Another bridge / The spice of life / The dustbowl / Crawbulk / Even so / Frost and fire / Fascination / I must confess / Soft touch. (US-title 'EVERYTHING BUT THE GIRL'; 7599-25212-1>

Jul 84. (7") (NEG 3) **MINE. / EASY AS SIN**		58	–

(12"+=) (NEG 3T) – Gun cupboard love.

Sep 84. (7") (NEG 6) **NATIVE LAND. / RIVERBED DRY**		73	–

(12"+=) (NEG 6T) – Don't you go.
(12"++=) (NEG 6TX) – Easy as sin / Gun cupboard love.

now with **NEIL SCOTT** – guitars / **PHIL MOXHAM** – bass (ex-The GIST ex-YOUNG MARBLE GIANTS) / **JUNE MILES KINGSTON** – drums, vocals (ex-MODETTES, ex-FUN BOY THREE) and the wind section

Mar 85. (7") (NEG 7) **WHEN ALL'S WELL. / HEAVEN HELP ME**			–

(12"+=) (NEG 7T) – Kid.

Apr 85. (lp/c)(cd) (BYN 3/+C)(<240-657-2>) **LOVE NOT MONEY**		10	

– When all's well / Ugly little dreams / Shoot me down / Are you trying to be funny / Sean / Ballad of the times / Anytown / This love (not for sale) / Trouble and strife / Angel. (c+=) – Heaven help me / Kid.

May 85. (7"m) (NEG 15) **ANGEL. / PIGEONS IN THE ATTIC ROOM / CHARMLESS, CALLOW WAYS**			–

(12"+=) (NEG 15T) – Easy as sin.

now **BEN + TRACEY** used new session people below plus an orchestra **CARA TIVEY** – keyboards / **MICKEY HARRIS** – bass / **PETER KING** – alto sax / **ROBERT PETERS** – drums (ex-DANGEROUS GIRLS)

Jul 86. (7") (NEG 21) **COME ON HOME. / DRAINING THE BAR**		44	–

(12"+=) (NEG 21T) – I fall to pieces.

Aug 86. (lp/c)(cd) (BYN/+C 9)(<240-966-2>) **BABY, THE STARS SHINE BRIGHT**		22	

– Come on home / Don't leave me behind / A country mile / Cross my heart / Don't let the teardrops rust your shining heart / Careless / Sugar Finney / Come hell or high water / Fighting talk / Little Hitler.

Sep 86. (7") (NEG 23) **DON'T LEAVE ME BEHIND. / ALFIE**		72	–

(12"+=) (NEG 23T) – Where's the playground, Susie?.
(d7"+=) (NEG 23F) – Come on home (acoustic) / Always on my mind (live).

Feb 87. (7") **DON'T LEAVE ME BEHIND. / DRAINING THE BAR**		–	–

BEN and TRACEY now with **PETER KING / IAN FRASER** – tenor saxophone / **STEVE PEARCE** – bass / **JAMES McMILLAN** – trumpet / **DAMON BUTCHER** – piano, synth.

Feb 88. (7") (NEG 30) **THESE EARLY DAYS. / DYED IN THE GRAIN**		75	–

(12"+=) (NEG 30T) – No place like home.
(12"ep+=/3"cd-ep+=) (NEG 30TX) – ('A'original demo) / Another day another dollar.

Mar 88. (lp/c)(cd) (BYN/+C 14)(<242-288-2>) **IDLEWILD**		13	

– Love is here where I live / These early days / I always was your girl / Oxford Street / The night I heard Caruso sing / Goodbye Sunday / Shadow on a harvest moon / Blue moon rose / Tears all over town / Lonesome for a place I know / Apron strings. (re-iss. Jul88, hit UK No.21- lp/c/cd; BYN/+C 16)(243-840-2) (+=) – I don't want to talk about it. (re-iss. 2nd version cd Nov94)

Mar 88. (7") (NEG 33) **I ALWAYS WAS YOUR GIRL. / HANG OUT THE FLAGS**			–

(12"+=) (NEG 33T) – Home from home.
(3"cd-s++=) (NEG 33CD) – Almost blue.

Jun 88. (7") (NEG 34) **I DON'T WANT TO TALK ABOUT IT. / OXFORD STREET**		3	–

(12"+=) (NEG 34T) – ('A'instrumental) / Shadow on a harvest moon.
(3"cd-s+=) (NEG 34CD) – ('A'instrumental) / Come on home.

Sep 88. (7") (NEG 37) **LOVE IS HERE WHERE I LIVE. / LIVING ON HONEYCOMB**			–

(12"+=) (NEG 37T) – How about me?.
(3"cd-s++=) (NEG 37CD) – Each and every one.

Dec 88. (7") (NEG 39) **THESE EARLY DAYS (Dave Bascombe remix). / DYED IN THE GRAIN**			–

(12"+=) (NEG 39T) – No place like home.
(3"cd-s++=) (NEG 39CD) – Another day another dollar.

duo now with **OMAR HAKIM** – drums / **JOHN PATITUCCI** – bass / **LARRY WILLIAMS** – synth, piano / **LENNY CASTRO** – percussion / **MICHAEL LANDAU** – guitar / etc.

		Blanco Y Negro	Atlantic
Jan 90. (7"/c-s) (NEG 40/+C) **DRIVING. / ME AND BOBBY D**		54	

(12"+=/cd-s+=) (NEG 40 T/CD) – Downtown train / ('A'extended).
(ext.12"gf+=) (NEG 40TG) – Easy as sin / I don't want to talk about it.

Feb 90. (cd)(lp/c) (246-260-2)(BYN/+C 21) <82057> **THE LANGUAGE OF LIFE**		10	77

– Driving / Get back together / Meet me in the morning / Take me / Me and Bobby D / The language of life / Imagining America / My baby don't love me / Letting love go / The road. (re-iss. cd Feb95)

Mar 90. (7"/c-s) (NEG 44/+C) **TAKE ME. / DRIVING (acoustic)**			–

(12"+=/cd-s+=) (NEG 44 T/CD) – ('A'-Hamblin remix).

now with **GEOFF GISCOYNE** and **STEVE PEARCE** – bass / **DICK OATTS** – saxophone / **RALPH SALMINS** – drums, percussion

Aug 91. (7"/c-s) (NEG 51/+C) **OLD FRIENDS. / APRON STRINGS (live)**			–

(12"+=) (NEG 51T) – Politics aside (instrumental).
(cd-s+=) (NEG 51CD) – Back to the old house (live).

Sep 91. (cd)(lp/c) (9031-75308-2)(BYN/+C 25) **WORLDWIDE**		29	

– Old friends / Understanding / You lift me up / Talk to me like the sea / British summertime / Twin cities / Frozen river / One place / Politics aside / Boxing and pop music / Feel alright. (re-iss. cd Feb92 +=; 9031-76583-2) – Love is strange.

Nov 91. (7"/c-s) (NEG 53/+C) **TWIN CITIES (Wildwood remix). / MEET ME IN THE MORNING (live)**			–

(12"+=) (NEG 53T) – ('A'-The green plains a cappella mix). (cd-s+++=) (NEG 53CD) – Mine.

Feb 92. (7"ep/c-ep/12"ep/cd-ep) (NEG 54/+C/T/CD) **COVERS EP**		13	–

– Love is strange / Tougher than the rest / Time after time / Alison. (above issued in the US as 'ACOUSTIC' w/ extra; 7567-82395-2>

Apr 93. (7"ep/c-ep/12"ep/cd-ep) (NEG 62/+C/T/CD) **THE ONLY LIVING BOY IN NEW YORK EP**		42	–

– The only living boy in New York / Gabriel / Birds / Horses in the room.

May 93. (cd)(lp/c) (4509-92319-2)(BYN/+C 29) **HOME MOVIES – THE BEST OF EVERYTHING BUT THE GIRL** (compilation)		5	

– Each and every one / Another bridge / Fascination / Native land / Come on home / Cross my heart / Apron strings / I don't want to talk about it / The night I heard Caruso sing / Driving / Imagining America / Understanding / Twin cities / Love is strange / I didn't know I was looking for love / The only living boy in New York.

Jun 93. (7"ep/c-ep/cd-ep) (NEG 64/+C/CD) **I DIDN'T KNOW I WAS LOOKING FOR LOVE EP**		72	–

– I didn't know I was looking for love / My head is my only house unless it rains / Political science / A piece of my mind.

with **DAVE MATTACKS** – drums / **DANNY THOMPSON** – double bass (both ex-FAIRPORT CONVENTION) / **MARTIN DITCHAM** – percussion / (guests) **RICHARD THOMPSON** – guitar / **PETER KING** – alto sax / **KATE St.JOHN** – cor anglais

May 94. (7"ep/c-ep/cd-ep) (NEG 69/+C/CD) **THE ROLLERCOASTER EP**		65	–

– Rollercoaster / Straight back to you / Lights of Te Touan / I didn't know I was looking for love (demo).

Jun 94. (cd/c) (4509-96482-2/-4) <82605> **AMPLIFIED HEART**		20	46

– Rollercoaster / Troubled mind / I don't understand anything / Walking to you / Get me / Missing / Two star / We walk the same line / 25th December / Disenchanted. (re-iss. Nov95; 0603-10453-2)

Aug 94. (c-ep/cd-ep) (NEG 71 C/CD1) **MISSING – THE LIVE EP**		69	–

– Missing / Each and every one (live) / I don't want to talk about it (live) / These days (live).
(12"ep/cd-ep) (NEG 71 T/CD2) **THE (FULL) REMIX EP** – ('A'side) / ('A'-Chris & James remix) / ('A'-Little Joey remix) / ('A'-Ultramarine remix).

Oct 95. (c-s) *(NEG 84C)* <87124> **MISSING (Todd Terry club mix) /**
('A'-Amplified Heart album mix) | **3** | **2** Jul95
(cd-s+=) *(NEG 84CD)* – ('A'-radio edit) / ('A'-Rockin' blue mix) / ('A'-Chris &
James full on club mix) / ('A'-Todd Terry's piece).
(12") *(NEG 84T)* – (all above except 'B'side).

	Virgin	Atlantic
Apr 96. (c-s/12"/cd-s) *(VS C/T/CDT 1577)* **WALKING WOUNDED**		
(mixes; Spring Heel Jack / Omni Trio / Dave Wallace)	**6**	**–**
May 96. (cd/c/lp) *(CD/TC+/V 2803)* <82912> **WALKING WOUNDED**	**4**	**37**

– Before today / Wrong / Single / The heart remains a child / Walking wounded /
Flipside / Big deal / Mirrorball / Good cop bad cop / Wrong (Todd Terry remix) /
Walking wounded (Omni Trio remix).

Jun 96. (c-s/12"/cd-s) *(VS C/T/CDT 1589)* <87059> **WRONG (mixes;**		
original / Todd Terry / Deep Dish / Mood II Swing)	**8**	**68** May96
Sep 96. (c-s) *(VSC 1600)* **SINGLE / CORCOVADO**	**20**	**–**

(cd-s+=) *(VSCDT 1600)* – ('A'-Photek remix) / ('A'-Brad Wood Memphis remix).
(12"+=) *(VST 1600)* – (above except 'Corcovado') / Wrong (Todd Terry remix).

| Feb 97. (c-s/cd/s) *(VSC/+DT 1624)* **BEFORE TODAY (mixes; album /** | | |
| **Adam F / Darren Emerson 1 & 2 / Dilinja / Chicane)** | **25** | **–** |

—— in Sep'98, EBTG were credited on the DEEP DISH hit single, 'The Future Of The
Future (Stay Gold)'.

Sep 99. (c-s/cd-s) *(VSC/+DT 1742)* **FIVE FATHOMS / FIREWALL**	**27**	
(12"/cd-s) *(VST/VSCDX 1742)* – ('A'mixes).		
Sep 99. (cd/c/lp) *(CD/TC+/V 2892)* <83214> **TEMPERAMENTAL**	**16**	**65**

– Five fathoms / Low tide of the night / Hatfield 1980 / Blame / Temperamental /
Compression / Downhill racer / Lullaby of clubland / No difference / Future of the
future (stay gold).

| Dec 99. (12"/cd-s) *(VST/VSCDT 1752)* **BLAME (mixes; album /** | | |
| **Grooverider Jeep dub / Fabio / J Majik VIP)** | | **–** |

– compilations, etc. –

Oct 96. (cd/c) *Blanco Y Negro; (0630 16637-2/-4)* **THE BEST OF**		
EVERYTHING BUT THE GIRL	**23**	
Nov 96. (c-s) *Blanco Y Negro; (NEG 99C)* **DRIVING (remix) /**	**36**	

(cd-s) *(NEG 99CD1)* – ('A'remixes).
(cd-s) *(NEG 99CD2)* – ('A'remixes).

EVE6

Formed: Los Angeles, California, USA . . . 1993 by 15 year-old bassist/singer
MAX COLLINS and 13 year old guitarist JON SIEBELS. They spent their
High School years trying to develop their own brand of high velocity punk
pop, although the end result gives more than just a nod to GREEN DAY and
OFFSPRING. With drummer TONY FAGENSEN now on board, 'R.C.A.'
signed them in '96, releasing the remarkably well received first album, 'EVE6'
(1998), two years later. The preceding single, 'INSIDE OUT' was snapped
up by a large portion of the US adolescent public hungry for a fresh anti-
establishment sound. It topped the new Billboard rock chart and the album's
release date was brought forward. Lyrically ambitious, 'EVE6' (which has
now sold over half a million copies) showed the trio attempting an ELVIS
COSTELLO-esque edge; on tracks such as 'INSIDE OUT' and 'LEECH' they
showed that they were capable of playing with a rare gusto but more often
than not found themselves held back by a severe naivety in the songwriting
department. Standout track, 'JESUS NITELITE' relied more on talent than
pace, giving a very brief insight into what this band could achieve should they
choose this direction for the future.

Album rating: EVE6 (er . . . *6)

MAX COLLINS – vocals, guitar / **JON SIEBELS** – guitar, vocals / **TONY FAGENSON** –
drums

	R.C.A.	R.C.A.
Sep 98. (ltd-7"red) *(74321 60569-7)* <radio play> **INSIDE OUT. /**		
SATURDAY NIGHT		**28**
(cd-s+=) *(74321 60569-2)* – Showerhead.		
Oct 98. (cd) <(07863 67617-2)> **EVE6**		**33** Apr98

– How much longer / Inside out / Leech / Showerhead / Open road song / Jesus
nitelite / Superhero girl / Tongue tied / Saturday night / There's a face / Small town
trap.

Feb 99. (7") *(74321 63918-7)* **LEECH. / INSIDE OUT (acoustic)**		**–**
(cd-s+=) *(74321 63918-2)* – Open road song (acoustic).		
Jun 99. (7") *(74321 67985-7)* **OPEN ROAD SONG.** /		**–**
(cd-s+=) *(74321 67985-2)* –		

EXPLOITED (dig out; Great Alt & Indie . . .)

EXTREME

Formed: Boston, Massachusetts, USA . . . 1988 initially as The DREAM, by
GARY CHERONE and PAUL GEARY. After the band split, CHERONE began
collaborating with Portuguese-born axe wizard, NUNO BETTENCOURT (the
main songwriter), who recruited bassist PAT BADGER. Naming themselves
EXTREME (a self-deprecating jape, perhaps?) they were picked up by
'A&M' in 1987, releasing their eponymous debut two years later. Drawing
its influences from QUEEN, KISS and CHEAP TRICK, it was a fairly
unremarkable affair although it did give an indication of where they were
headed. Coming on like a neutered CHILI PEPPERS, 'GET THE FUNK
OUT' surprisingly made the UK Top 20, but it was the acoustic ballad,
'MORE THAN WORDS', which propelled the band to stadium status.
No.1 in America, No.2 in Britain, the single boosted sales of the album,

---

'PORNOGRAFFITTI' (1991), which eventually went double platinum.
Another ballad, 'HOLE HEARTED', made Top 5 in the States and the band
toured with big guns like ZZ TOP. 'III SIDES TO EVERY STORY' (1992) was
a wildly ambitious affair, echoes of dodgy 70's prog-rock concepts evident in
their use of musical 'suites'. The album was a relative success nevertheless,
although by the release of 'WAITING FOR THE PUNCHLINE' (1995),
interest in the band was dwindling. BETTENCOURT delivered a solo album,
'SCHIZOPHONIC', early in '97, an improvement on the aforesaid EXTREME
finale, although nothing startling. • **Covers:** LOVE OF MY LIFE (Queen) /
STRUTTER (Kiss).

Album rating: EXTREME (*5) / PORNOGRAFFITTI (*7) / III SIDES TO
EVERY STORY (*6) / WAITING FOR THE PUNCHLINE (*4) / Nuno Bettencourt:
SCHIZOPHONIC (*5)

GARY CHERONE (b.26 Jul'61, Malden, Mass.) – vocals / **NUNO BETTENCOURT** (b.20
Sep'66, Azores, Portugal) – guitar, keyboards, vocals / **PAT BADGER** (b.22 Jul'67, Boston)
– bass, vocals / **PAUL GEARY** (b.24 Jul'61, Medford, Mass.) – drums, percussion

	not iss.	Toppe
1985. (lp; as The DREAM) **THE DREAM**	**–**	**–**

– Take your time / The tender touch / Makes no sense / All over again / Tipsy on
the brink of love / You / Here is the love / Desires / Suzanne / Wonderful world /
Last Monday.

	A&M	A&M
Mar 89. (lp/c/cd) (<AMA/AMC/CDA 5238>) **EXTREME**		**80**

– Little girls / Wind me up / Kid ego / Watching, waiting / Mutha (don't wanna go to
school today) / Teachers pet / Big boys don't cry / Smoke signals / Flesh 'n' blood /
Rock a bye bye. *(cd+=)* – (1 track).

Apr 89. (7") <1415> **KID EGO. / SMOKE SIGNALS**	**–**	**–**
Apr 89. (7";w-drawn) *(AM 504)* **KID EGO. / FLESH 'N' BLOOD**	**–**	**–**
(12"+=) *(AMY 504)* – Smoke signals.		
Jun 89. (7") <1438> **LITTLE GIRLS. / NICE PLACE TO STAY**	**–**	**–**
Aug 89. (7") <1444> **TEACHER'S PET. / MUTHA (DON'T WANNA**		
GO TO SCHOOL TODAY)	**–**	**–**
Mar 91. (7") <1552> **MORE THAN WORDS. / ('A'remix)**		**1**
May 91. (7"/c-s) *(AM/+MC 737)* **GET THE FUNK OUT. / LI'L JACK**		
HORNY	**19**	**–**

(12"+=) *(AMX 737)* – Little girls (edit).
(12"pic-d+=) *(AMP 737)* – Nice place to visit.
(cd-s+=) *(AMCD 737)* – Mutha (don't wanna go to school) (remix).

| May 91. (cd/c/lp) *(395313-2/-4/-1)* <5313> **PORNOGRAFFITTI** | **12** | **10** Aug90 |

– Decadence dance / Li'l Jack Horny / When I'm president / Get the funk out / More
than words / Money (in God we trust) / It ('s a monster) / Pornograffitti / When I
first missed you / Suzi (wants her all day what?) / He-man woman hater / Song for
love. *(originally released UK Sep90)*

Jul 91. (7"/c-s) *(AM/+MC 792)* **MORE THAN WORDS. / NICE**		
PLACE TO VISIT	**2**	**–**
(cd-s+=) *(AMCD 792)* – Little girls.		
(12"++=) *(AMX 792)* – Mutha (don't wanna go to school) (remix).		
Jul 91. (c-s) <1564> **HOLE HEARTED. / SUZI (WANTS HER ALL**		
DAY WHAT?)	**–**	**4**
Sep 91. (7"/c-s) *(AM/+MC 773)* **DECADENCE DANCE. / MONEY**		
(IN GOD WE TRUST)	**36**	Mar91

(12"+=/cd-s+=) *(AM Y/CD 773)* – ('A'version) / More than words (acappella with
congas).

| Nov 91. (7"/c-s) *(AM/+MC 839)* **HOLE HEARTED. / GET THE FUNK** | | |
| **OUT (remix)** | **12** | **–** |

(12"box+=/cd-s+=) *(AM Y/CD 839)* – Suzi (wants her all day what?) / Sex and love.

Apr 92. (7"/c-s/12"/cd-s) *(AM/+MC/Y/CD 698)* **SONG FOR LOVE. /**		
LOVE OF MY LIFE (featuring BRIAN MAY)	**12**	
Aug 92. (7"/c-s) *(AM/+MC 0055)* <0055> **REST IN PEACE. /**		
PEACEMAKER DIE	**13**	**96** Oct92

(etched-12"+=) *(AMY 0055)* – ('A'-lp version).
(cd-s++=) *(AMCD 0055)* – Monica.

| Sep 92. (cd/c/d-lp) *(540006-2/-4/-1)* <40006> **III SIDES TO EVERY** | | |
| **STORY** | **2** | **10** |

– Warheads / Rest in peace / Politicalamity / Color me blind / Cupid's dead /
Peacemaker die/ Seven Sundays / Tragic comic / Our father / Stop the world / God
isn't dead// Everything under the Sun (I) Rise'n shine / (II) Am I ever gonna change /
(III) Who cares?

| Nov 92. (7"/c-s) *(AM/+MC 0096)* **STOP THE WORLD. / CHRISTMAS** | | |
| **TIME AGAIN** | **22** | **–** |

(12"+=) *(AMY 0096)* – Warheads / ('A'version).
(cd-s++=) *(AMCD 0096)* – Don't leave me alone.

| Jan 93. (7"etched/c-s) *(AM/+MC 0156)* **TRAGIC COMIC. /** | | |
| **HOLEHEARTED (horn mix)** | **15** | |

(12"pic-d+=/cd-s+=) *(AM Y/CD 0156)* – ('A'version) / Rise'n'shine (acoustic).
(cd-s) *(AMCDR 0156)* – ('A'side) / Help! / When I'm president (live).

| Feb 93. (c-s) <0120> **STOP THE WORLD / WARHEADS** | **–** | **95** |
| Feb 95. (cd/c) *(540305-2/-4)* <0327> **WAITING FOR THE PUNCHLINE** | **10** | **40** |

– There is no God / Cynical / Tell me something I don't know / Hip today / Naked /
Midnight express / Leave me alone / No respect / Evilangelist / Shadow boxing /
Unconditionally / Fair-weather friend.

| Mar 95. (7"sha-pic-d) *(580099-7)* **HIP TODAY. / THERE IS NO GOD** | **44** | |

(cd-s+=) *(580099-2)* – Better off dead / Kid ego (live).
(cd-s+=) *(580099-5)* – Never been funked / When I'm president (live) / Strutter.
(12") *(580099-6)* – ('A'side) / Wind me up (1987 demo).

| Jul 95. (cd-s; w-drawn) **UNCONDITIONALLY** | | |

—— Disbanded after above. CHERONE joined VAN HALEN late '96 while
BETTENCOURT released a solo album, 'SCHIZOPHONIC', in '97.

EXTREME NOISE TERROR (dig out; Great Metal . . .)

FABULOUS THUNDERBIRDS (dig out; 4th edition)

FACES (see under ⇒ SMALL FACES)

Donald FAGEN (see under ⇒ STEELY DAN)

FAIRGROUND ATTRACTION
(see under ⇒ READER, Eddi)

FAIRPORT CONVENTION

Formed: Muswell Hill, London, England . . . mid-1967 by RICHARD THOMPSON, SIMON NICOL, ASHLEY HUTCHINGS, JUDY DYBLE and original drummer SHAUN FRATER. By the end of the year, FRATER was superseded by MARTIN LAMBLE, and after a debut 45 for 'Polydor', they added IAIN MATTHEWS. This new sextet with Joe Boyd on production, recorded their 1968 eponymous debut lp, although after its release, JUDY left and was replaced by SANDY DENNY. They signed to 'Island' around the same time and issued a second album, 'WHAT WE DID ON OUR HOLIDAYS' which was the last to feature MATTHEWS (a year later, he was at the UK No.1 spot with his SOUTHERN COMFORT version of 'Woodstock'). After the completion of their third set, 'UNHALFBRICKING', and while on tour, tragedy struck on the 14th of May '69, when MARTIN LAMBLE was killed as their van crashed. With the help of their Top 30 French version of a Dylan song ('IF YOU GOTTA GO, GO NOW'), 'SI TU DOIS PARTIR', the aforementioned album was the first of four consecutive UK Top 20 entries. At this stage, the band were Britain's answer to US West Coast folk-rock, although they increasingly adopted a more traditional folk sound in the 70's and subsequently influenced many other acts. After the classic, 'LIEGE AND LIEF' (1969), HUTCHINGS left for STEELEYE SPAN and DENNY formed FOTHERINGAY, both outfits enjoying their own bit of fame. Recruiting DAVE PEGG on bass, the band recorded another album, 'FULL HOUSE' (1970), before RICHARD THOMPSON departed for an acclaimed solo career which stretched a quarter of a century (plus). While 'ANGEL DELIGHT' (1971), hit the UK Top 10, the concept album 'BABBACOMBE LEE' (1971) stiffed and throughout the 70's, FAIRPORT underwent a dizzying series of personnel changes (DENNY eventually rejoining for 'LIVE CONVENTION' in '74). SANDY's stunning vocals made it one of the band's best releases of the 70's and she stayed for one further studio album, 'RISING FOR THE MOON' (1975), before going solo once more. Tragedy struck on the 21st of April 1978, when SANDY died from a brain haemorrhage after falling down a flight of stairs. Despite cutting a farewell live album in 1979, the band continued recording throughout the 80's and 90's amid constantly changing line-ups. In the early 80's, they limited their live appearances to an annual bash at Cropredy in Oxfordshire, an event which has now become something of a mini-festival attracting thousands of folk/roots fans each year. • **Songwriters:** Mainly group compositions, with numerous renditions of traditional English folk tunes. Other writers:- IF I HAD A RIBBON BOW (Maxine Sullivan) / NOTTAMUN TOWN + SHE MOVED THROUGH THE FAIR + loads more (trad.) / MILLION DOLLAR BASH (Bob Dylan) / GOLD (Peter Blegvad). The 1972 album as The BUNCH was full of covers (see below). • **Trivia:** In 1970, their B-side, 'SIR B. McKENZIE'S DAUGHTER . . .' entered The Guinness Book Of Records for having the longest song title ever.

Album rating: FAIRPORT CONVENTION (*6) / WHAT WE DID ON OUR HOLIDAYS (*8) / UNHALFBRICKING (*8) / LIEGE AND LIEF (*8) / FULL HOUSE (*7) / ANGEL DELIGHT (*6) / BABBACOMBE LEE (*6) / THE HISTORY OF FAIRPORT CONVENTION compilation (*8) / ROSIE (*5) / FAIRPORT NINE (*5) / LIVE CONVENTION (*5) / RISING FOR THE MOON (*5) / GOTTLE O' GEER (*3) / BONNY BUNCH OF ROSES (*4) / TIPPLER'S TALES (*4) / FAREWELL, FAREWELL (*6) / MOAT ON THE LEDGE (*5) / GLADYS' LEAP (*6) / EXPLETIVE

DELIGHTED (*5) / IN REAL TIME: LIVE '87 (*4) / RED AND GOLD (*4) / FIVE SEASONS (*5) / JEWEL IN THE CROWN (*5) / OLD NEW BORROWED BLUE (*7) / CLOSE TO THE WIND (*5)

RICHARD THOMPSON (b. 3 Apr'49) – guitar, vocals / **SIMON NICOL** (b.13 Oct'50) – guitar, banjo, dulcimer, bass, viola, vocals / **JUDY DYBLE** (b.1948) – vocals, autoharp / **ASHLEY HUTCHINGS** (b.Jan'45) – bass / **MARTIN LAMBLE** (b.Aug'49) – drums repl. SHAUN FRATER

			Polydor	Cotillion
Nov 67.	(7") *(604 020)* **IF I HAD A RIBBON BOW. / IF (STOMP)**		☐	☐

―――― added **IAIN MATTHEWS** (b.IAN MATTHEW MacDONALD, 16 Jun'46, Scunthorpe, England) – vocals, guitar, percussion (ex-PYRAMIDS)

Jun 68.	(lp) *(583 035)* <SD 9024> **FAIRPORT CONVENTION**	

– Time will show the wiser / I don't know where I stand / If (stomp) / Decameron / Jack O'Diamonds / Portfolio / Chelsea morning / Sun shade / The lobster / It's alright ma, it's only witchcraft / One sure thing / M1 breakdown. *(re-iss. Jul75; 238 4047) (re-iss. Aug90 cd/c; 835 230-2/-4)*

―――― **SANDY DENNY** (b. 6 Jan'47) – vocals (ex-STRAWBS, etc) repl. JUDY who joined GILES, GILES and FRIPP

			Island	A&M
Nov 68.	(7") *(WIP 6047)* **MEET ON THE LEDGE. / THROWAWAY STREET PUZZLE**		☐	-
Jan 69.	(lp) *(ILPS 9092)* **WHAT WE DID ON OUR HOLIDAYS**		☐	-

– Fotheringay / Mr. Lacey / Book song / The Lord is in his place / No man's land / I'll keep it with mine / Eastern rain / Nottamun town / Tale in hard time / She moves through the fair / Meet on the ledge / End of a holiday. *(re-iss. May89 on 'Carthage' lp/c; CG LP/C 4430) (cd-iss. Feb90; IMCD 97)*

1969.	(7") <1108> **FOTHERINGAY. / I'LL KEEP IT WITH MINE**		-	☐

―――― Trimmed to a quintet when IAIN formed MATTHEW'S SOUTHERN COMFORT

Jul 69.	(7") *(WIP 6064)* <1155> **SI TU DOIS PARTIR. / GENESIS HALL**		**21**	☐
Jul 69.	(lp) *(ILPS 9102)* <4206> **UNHALFBRICKING**		**12**	☐

– Genesis Hall / Si tu dois partir / Autopsy / A sailor's life / Cajun woman / Who knows where the time goes / Percy's song / Million dollar bash. *(cd-iss. Feb87; CID 9102) (re-iss. May89 on 'Carthage' lp/c; CG LP/C 4418) (cd-iss. Nov89; IMCD 61)*

―――― **DAVE MATTACKS** (b.Mar'48, London) – drums repl. MARTIN LAMBLE who died 14 May'69 in tour bus crash / also added **DAVE SWARBRICK** (b. 5 Apr'41) – fiddle, vocals

Dec 69.	(lp) *(ILPS 9115)* <4257> **LIEGE & LIEF**		**17**	☐

– Come all ye / Reynardine / Matty Groves / Farewell farewell / The deserter / The lark in the morning / Tamlin / Crazy man Michael / Rakish Paddy / Foxhunters jigs / Toss the feathers. *(re-iss. Sep86 lp/c/cd; ILPM/ICM/CID 9115) (cd re-iss. Oct89; IMCD 60)*

―――― **DAVE PEGG** (b. 2 Nov'47, Birmingham, England) – bass, vocals (ex-UGLYS) repl HUTCHINGS who joined STEELEYE SPAN (**PEGG** now in quintet with **THOMPSON, NICOL, MATTACKS** and **SWARBRICK** because SANDY DENNY also departed to form FOTHERINGAY)

Jul 70.	(lp) *(ILPS 9130)* <4265> **FULL HOUSE**		**13**	☐

– Walk awhile / Dirty linen / Sloth / Sir Patrick Spens / Flatback caper / Doctor of physick / Flowers of the forest. *(re-iss. Jul87 on 'Hannibal'; HNBL 4417) (c-iss.May89; HNBC 4417) (re-iss. Jan92 cd/c; HNCD/HNBC 4417)*

Oct 70.	(7") *(WIP 6089)* **NOW BE THANKFUL. / SIR B. McKENZIE'S DAUGHTER'S LAMENT FOR THE 77th MOUNTED LANCERS' RETREAT FROM THE STRAITS OF LOCH KOMBE IN THE YEAR OF OUR LORD 1727, ON THE LAIRD OF KINLEAKIE**

Nov 70.	(7") <1195> **WALK AWHILE. / SIR PATRICK SPENS**		-	-

―――― Now a quartet when RICHARD THOMPSON left to go solo

Jun 71.	(7") <1333> **THE JOURNEYMAN'S GRACE. / THE WORLD HAS SURELY LOST IT'S HEAD**		-	☐
Jun 71.	(lp) *(ILPS 9162)* <4319> **ANGEL DELIGHT**		**8**	☐

– Lord Marlborough / Sir William Gower / Bridge over the River Ash / Wizard of the worldly game / The journeyman's grace / Angel delight / Banks of the sweet primroses / Instrumental medley:- Cuckoo's nest – Hardiman the fiddler – Papa stoor / The bonny black hare / Sickness and diseases. *(cd-iss. Mar93; IMCD 166)*

Sep 71.	(7") *(WIP 6128)* **JOHN LEE. / THE TIME IS NEAR**
Nov 71.	(lp) *(ILPS 9176)* <4333> **BABBACOMBE LEE**

– John Babbacombe Lee: (John's reflection of his boyhood / His struggle with his family / Then the happiest period of his life, the Navy / Returning reluctantly to his job after being invalided out of the service / And the senseless murder of his mistress and the three attempts to hang him – Hanging song). *(cd-iss. Aug92; IMCD 153)*

―――― **ROGER HILL** – guitar, vocals repl. NICOL who joined ALBION COUNTRY BAND / **TOM FARNAL** – drums repl. MATTACKS who joined ALBION COUNTRY BAND

―――― In Jun72, **DAVID REA** – guitar repl. ROGER HILL until Aug72 when **MATTACKS** returned to repl. FARNALL / **TREVOR LUCAS** (b.25 Dec'43, Bungaree, Australia) – guitar, vocals (ex-FOTHERINGAY) repl. REA / **adding JERRY DONAHUE** (b.24 Sep'46, New York City, N.Y.) – guitar, vocals (ex-FOTHERINGAY)

Mar 73.	(7") *(WIP 6155)* **ROSIE. / KNIGHTS OF THE ROAD**		☐	-
Mar 73.	(lp) *(ILPS 9208)* <4386> **ROSIE**		☐	-

– Rosie / Matthew, Mark, Luke and John / Knights of the road / Peggy's pub / The plainsman / Hungarian rhapsodie / My girl / Me with you / The hen's march through the midden & the four-poster bed / Furs and feathers. *(cd-iss. Aug92; IMCD 152)*

Oct 73.	(lp) *(ILPS 9246)* <4407> **FAIRPORT NINE**

– The Hexamshire lass / Polly on the shore / The brilliancy medley and Cherokee shuffle / To Althea from prison / Tokyo / Bring 'em down / Big William / Pleasure and pain / Possibly Parsons Green. *(cd-iss. Aug92; IMCD 154)*

―――― added the returning **SANDY DENNY** – vocals (from solo career)

Oct 74.	(lp) *(ILPS 9285)* **LIVE CONVENTION (live)**		☐	-

– Matty Groves / Rosie / Fiddlestix / John the gun / Something you got / Sloth / Dirty linen / Down in the flood / Sir B. MacKenzie . . . *(cd-iss. Feb90; IMCD 95)*

―――― **PAUL WARREN** – drums repl. MATTACKS who rejoined ALBION DANCE BAND

―――― **BRUCE ROWLANDS** – drums (ex-RONNIE LANE, ex-JOE COCKER) repl. WARREN

			Island	Island
Jul 75.	(7") (WIP 6241) **WHITE DRESS. / TEARS**			–
Jul 75.	(lp) (ILPS <9313>) **RISING FOR THE MOON**		52	–

– Rising for the moon / Restless / White dress / Let it go / Stranger to himself / What is true? / Iron lion / Dawn / After halloween / Night-time girl / One more chance. (cd-iss. Aug92; IMCD 155)

—— FAIRPORT Basic trio SWARBRICK, PEGG and ROWLANDS recruited new folks **DAN AR BRAS** – guitar repl. SANDY DENNY who went solo again. (She later died of a brain haemorrage on 21 Apr78 after falling down her stairs) **BOB BRADY** – piano (ex-WIZZARD) repl. LUCAS who became producer. **ROGER BURRIDGE** – mandolin, fiddle repl. DONAHUE who became session man

			Island	not iss.
May 76.	(lp; as FAIRPORT) (ILPS 9389) **GOTTLE O'GEER**			–

– When first into this country / Our band / Lay me down easy / Cropedy capers / The frog up the pump / Don't be late / Sandy's song / Come and get it / Limey's lament.

—— **FAIRPORT CONVENTION** again because founder member **SIMON NICOL** – guitar returned to repl. BRADY, BRAS and BURRIDGE

			Vertigo	not iss.
Feb 77.	(lp) (9102 015) **BONNY BUNCH OF ROSES**			–

– James O'Donnell's jig / The Eynsham poacher / Adieu adieu / The bonny bunch of roses / The poor ditching boy / General Taylor / Run Johnny run / The last waltz / Royal Selection No.13. (re-iss. Oct88 on 'Woodworm' lp/c/cd; WR/+C/CD 011)

May 78.	(lp) (9102 022) **TIPPLER'S TALES**			–

– Ye mariner's all / Three drunken maidens / Jack O'rion / Reynard the fox / Lady of pleasure / Bankruptured / The widow of Westmorland / The hair of the dogma / As bitme / John Barleycorn. (re-iss. 1989 on 'Beat Goes On' lp/c/cd; BGO LP/MC/CD 72)

			Simons	not iss.
Oct 79.	(7") (PMW 1) **RUBBER BAND. / BONNY BLACK HARE**			–
Nov 79.	(lp) (GAMA 1) **FAREWELL FAREWELL (live)**			–

– Matty Groves / Orange blossom special / John Lee / Bridge over the River Ash / Sir Patrick Spens / Mr. Lacey / Walk awhile / Bonny black hare / Journeyman's grace / Meet on the ledge. (re-iss. Apr80 on 'Woodworm'; BEAR 22) (cd-iss. May96 on 'Red Steel'; SIXCD 0002)

			Woodworm	Varrick
1982.	(lp) (WR 001) **MOAT ON THE LEDGE – LIVE 1981 (live)**			–

– Walk awhile / Country pie / Rosie / Matty Groves / Both sides now / Poor Will and the hangman / The brilliancy medley – Cherokee shuffle / Woman or man / High school confidential. (c-iss.1985 on 'Stoney Plain'; SP5 1052)

—— **DAVE MATTACKS** and **DAVE PEGG** returned to repl. SWARBRICK and ROWLAND NICOL also recruited sessioners **MARTIN ALLCOCK** (b. 5 Jan'57, Manchester, England) – strings / **RIC SAUNDERS** – violin (ex-SOFT MACHINE)

				1988
Aug 85.	(lp/c/cd) (WR/+C/CD 007) <V/VRC/CDVR 023> **GLADYS LEAP**			

– How many times / Bird from the mountain / Honour and praise / The hiring fair / Instrumental medley '85: The riverhead – Glady's leap – The wise maid / My feet are set for dancing / Wat Tyler / Head in a sack. (cd-iss. Aug94 on 'Terrapin Truckin'; TRUCKCD 015) (cd re-iss. May96 on 'Red Steel'; SIVCD 0003)

				1988
1986.	(lp/c/cd) (WR/+C/CD 009) <CDVR 029> **EXPLETIVE DELIGHTED!**			

– Medley; The Rutland reel – Sack the juggler / Medley; The cat on the mixer – Three left feet / Bankruptured / Portmeirion / James O'Donnell's jig / Expletive delighted / Sigh beg sigh mor / Innstuck / The gas almost works / Hanks for the memory; Shazam – Pipeline – Apache / Peter Gunn. (re-iss. Aug94 on 'Terrapin Truckin' cd/c; TRUCK CD/MC 016) (cd re-iss. Jun96 on 'Red Steel'; SIVCD 0004)

			Island	not iss.
Nov 87.	(lp/c/cd) (ILPS/ICT/CID 9883) **IN REAL TIME: LIVE '87 (live)**			–

(cd re-iss. 1989; IMCD 10) (c re-iss. Jul93; ICM 2026)

—— now 7-piece of ALLCOCK, SAUNDERS, PEGG, MATTACKS, NICOL, DONAHUE and **RICHARD THOMPSON**

			New Routes	Rough Trade
Jan 89.	(lp/c/cd) (RUE/+MC/CD 002) **RED AND GOLD**		74	

– Set me up / The noise club / Red and gold / The beggars song / The battle / Dark eyed Molly / The rose hip / Summer before the war / Open the door Richard. (cd re-iss. Dec95 on 'H.T.D.'; HTDCD 47)

Dec 90.	(lp/c/cd) (RUE/+MC/CD 005) **THE FIVE SEASONS**			

– Cloudy beats: medley – Cup of tea! – A loaf of bread – Miss Monahan's / All your beauty / Sock it in! / Gold / Ginnie / Mock Morris '90:- The green man – The cropedy badger – Molly on the jetty / Medley:- The card song – Shuffle the pack – The wounded whale. (cd re-iss. Jan96 on 'H.T.D.'; HTDCD 48)

—— NICOL, ALLCOCK, PEGG, MATTACKS + SAUNDERS

			Woodworm	Green Linnet
Jan 95.	(c/cd) (WRC/+D 023) **JEWEL IN THE CROWN**			

– Jewel in the crown / Slip jigs and reels / A surfeit of lampreys / Kind of fortune / Diamonds and gold / The naked highwayman / The islands / The youngest daughter / London Danny / Summer in December / Travelling by steam / (Travel by steam) / She's like the swallow / Red tide / Home is where the heart is / Closing time.

—— In Jun'96, they featured on DAVE SWARBRICK's '50th Birthday Concert' on 'Cooking Vinyl'; MASHCD 001)

Jun 96.	(cd) (WRCD 024) <3114> **OLD NEW BORROWED BLUE**			

– Woodworm swing / Men / Aunt Sally shuffle / There once was love – Innstuck / Frozen man / Mr. Sands is in the building / Lalla rookh / Foolish you / Crazy man Michael / Widow of Westmorland's daughter / Genesis hall / Deserter / Swimming song / Struck it right / Hiring fair / Matty Groves – Dirty linen.

– compilations etc. –

on 'Island' unless mentioned otherwise

Jul 70.	(7") Polydor; (2058 014) **IF (STOMP). / CHELSEA MORNING**			
Nov 72.	(d-lp) (ICD 4) **THE HISTORY OF FAIRPORT CONVENTION**			

– Meet on the ledge / Fotheringay / Mr.Lacey / Book song / Sailor's life / Si tu dois partir / Who knows where the time goes / Matty Groves / Crazy man Michael / Now be thankful (medley) / Walk awhile / Sloth / The bonny black hare / Angel delight / Bridge over the river Ash / John Lee / Breakfast in Mayfair / Hanging song / The hen's march through the midden / The four-poster bed. (cd-iss. Apr88; CIDD 4) – (omits 2 tracks). (re-iss. Jul91 cd)(c; IMCD 128)(ICM 2073)

1976.	(lp) A&M; <3530> **FAIRPORT CHRONICLES**		–	
Dec 76.	(lp) Help-Island; (HELP 28) **LIVE AT THE L.A. TROUBADOUR 1970 (live)**			–

	(re-iss. Jan87 as 'HOUSE FULL' on 'Hannibal' lp/c; HN BL/BC 1319) (re-iss. Jan92 cd/c; HNCD/HNBC 1319)			
1982.	(c) Woodworm; (none) **THE AIRING CUPBOARD TAPES**			–
Sep 84.	(c) Woodworm; (WRC 1) **AT 2 (THE AIRING CUPBOARD TAPES)**			–
1985.	(d-c) Woodworm; (none) **THE BOOT**			–
1987.	(d-c) Woodworm; (none) **THE OTHER BOOT**			–
May 87.	(7") (IS 324) **MEET ON THE LEDGE (re-recorded). / SIGH BHEG SIGH MHOR (live)**			–
	(12"+=) (12IS 324) – John Barleycorn (live).			
Sep 87.	(lp/c/cd) Hannibal; (HN BL/BC/CD 1329) **HEYDAY (BBC sessions '68-'69)**			
Apr 88.	(cd) (CIDD 4) **THE BEST OF FAIRPORT CONVENTION**			
Aug 89.	(d-c) Woodworm; (none) **THE THIRD LEG**			–
Jan 92.	(cd/c) Woodworm; (WR CD/C 015) **THE WOODWORM YEARS**			–
Aug 92.	(4xcd-box) Island; (FCBX 1) **25th ANNIVERSARY PACK**			–

– (ROSIE / JOHN BABBACOMBE LEE / NINE / RISING FOR THE MOON)

The BUNCH

TREVOR LUCAS (his idea), **SANDY DENNY, RICHARD THOMPSON, ASHLEY HUTCHINGS, DAVE MATTACKS** and session people

			Island	A&M
Apr 72.	(lp) (ILPS 9189) **ROCK ON**			

– That'll be the day / Love's made a fool of you / When will I be loved / Willie and the hand jive / Learning the game / My girl in the month of May / Don't be cruel / The locomotion / Jambalaya (on the bayou) / Sweet little rock'n'roller / Nadine / Crazy arms. (7"flexi w/a) (WI 4002) **LET THERE BE DRUMS** (re-iss. May88 on 'Carthage' lp/c; CG LP/C 4424)

Apr 72.	(7") (WIP 6130) **WHEN WILL I BE LOVED. / WILLIE AND THE HAND JIVE**			–

Marianne FAITHFULL

Born: 29 Dec'46, Hampstead, London, England, daughter of a university lecturer and an Austrian baroness, who sent her to St. Joseph's convent school in Reading, Berkshire. At the age of 17, while attending a party with her artist boyfriend, JOHN DUNBAR, she was spotted by ANDREW LOOG OLDHAM (the ROLLING STONES' manager), who signed her to 'Decca' records. MARIANNE's debut 45, 'AS TEARS GO BY' (from the pen of JAGGER and RICHARDS), soon careered into the UK Top 10 and the US Top 30; however, her follow-up, Dylan's 'BLOWIN' IN THE WIND', flopped. Early in '65, 'COME AND STAY WITH ME' gave MARIANNE her biggest hit to date (and subsequently ever) and this was followed by two simultaneously issued folk/pop albums, 'COME MY WAY' and the eponymous, 'MARIANNE FAITHFULL' (both of which hit the Top 20). Later the same year, she gave birth to a son, Nicholas, although she was soon to separate from DUNBAR. The sultry blonde bombshell then began a much-publicised affair with MICK JAGGER after allegedly bedding the other three! (not WATTS). Busted for drugs with JAGGER and Co. on many occasions, the couple visited the Maharishi Yogi in '68, although her career in the flower-power years had taken a sharp nosedive. Around the same time, she also began acting and starred in 'The Three Sisters' (a Chekhov play) and in the film, 'Girl On A Motorcycle', with Alain Delon. Later in '68, she miscarried with JAGGER's baby and six months later, both were arrested in their London home for possession of marijuana. A single, 'SISTER MORPHINE' (written with JAGGER and RICHARDS), was withdrawn and it looked like her music career was about to end. In the summer of '69, while on the set of the movie, 'Ned Kelly', alongside JAGGER, she was found in a coma after overdosing on barbituates (100+ Tuinal). MARIANNE was sadly dropped from the film and subsequently went into hospital to try and cure her heroin addiction and depression. A year later, after a season playing Ophelia in 'Hamlet' (alongside Nicol Williamson), much was made out of her suspected suicide bids which were reported by the press, her divorce from DUNBAR and split with JAGGER, also in the dailys. After five years in the proverbial wilderness, MARIANNE returned with a new contract on 'Nems', the single, 'DREAMING MY DREAMS' a pleasant if not brilliant comeback. Two albums appeared for the label, 'DREAMIN' MY DREAMS' (1977) and 'FAITHLESS' (1978), before she signed to 'Island', returning to the UK Top 50 in 1979 with her rendition of Shel Silverstein's, 'THE BALLAD OF LUCY JORDAN' (once a hit by DR. HOOK). On the 23rd of November '79, she married BEN BRIERLY (of punk rock band, The VIBRATORS), although her future seemed always to be dogged by her drug intake. Her last album's unfruitful attempt at C&W was soon forgotten when she unleashed what was to become her greatest achievement, the 'BROKEN ENGLISH' album. Released nearing the end of, what was for her, a torturous 70's, it marked a pinnacle in her up and down career and was helped in the writing department by her long-time guitarist, BARRY REYNOLDS. Highlighted by her explicit, 'WHY D'YA DO IT' track, the leather-clad mistress was in full swing using sex as her vocal weapon backed by "the in-thing" electro/new wave; her cover of John Lennon's 'WORKING CLASS HERO' also a must-hear. Two albums followed in relatively quick succession, 'DANGEROUS ACQUAINTANCE' (1981) and 'A CHILD'S ADVENTURE' (1983), showing too desperately for some, that she wanted to retain her new "rock" street cred. In 1987, still surprisingly contracted to 'Island' and now living in Cambridge, Massachusetts with new husband and writer, Giorgio Della, she issued a comeback album of sorts, 'STRANGE WEATHER'. It delivered some powerful and poignant messages, showing her once croaky voice to shining effect; EDITH PIAF would have been proud of her. However, the following year, MARIANNE was deported from the States, the singer subsequently choosing to settle in Ireland to finish off her autobiography, simply titled 'Faithfull'. In the mid-90's, she released a handful of albums (including 1995's 'A SECRET LIFE' and 1996's '20th CENTURY BLUES'). She even took time out to appear with the likes of The CHIEFTAINS. Like a 'BROKEN ENGLISH' part II, in the sense that it was just as lyrically intriguing, 'VAGABOND WAYS' (1999) delivered her back into the critical limelight. Tracks such as 'ELECTRA' (accounting all the infamous women of history), 'INCARCERATION OF A FLOWER CHILD' (a late 60's number written by ROGER WATERS about SYD BARRETT) and a cover of Leonard Cohen's 'TOWER OF SONG' were excellent by today's high standards – FAITHFULL was indeed the saving grace amongst her contemporary divas. • **Songwriters:** Penned some herself, although she initially covered others; I'LL BE YOUR BABY TONIGHT (Bob Dylan) / GREENSLEEVES + HOUSE OF THE RISING SUN + SCARBOROUGH FAIR (trad.) / COME AND STAY WITH ME (Jackie DeShannon) / GREEN ARE YOUR EYES (Bert Jansch) / THE LAST THING ON MY MIND (Tom Paxton) / THE FIRST TIME EVER I SAW YOUR FACE (Ewan MacColl) / SALLY FREE AND EASY (. . . Tannery) / COCKLESHELLS (. . . Taylor) / THIS LITTLE BIRD (John D.Loudermilk) / SUNNY GOODGE STREET + THE MOST OF WHAT IS LEAST (Donovan) / YESTERDAY (Beatles) / SOMETHING BETTER (Goffin-King) / IS THIS WHAT I GET FOR LOVING YOU (Ronettes) / DREAMING MY DREAMS (Waylon Jennings) / STRANGE WEATHER (Tom Waits) / MADAME GEORGE (Van Morrison) / GHOST DANCE (Patti Smith), etc. • **Trivia:** In 1967, she appeared and supplied backing vocals for The BEATLES on their 'All You Need Is Love', single & TV video.

Album rating: COME MY WAY (*4) / MARIANNE FAITHFULL (*6) / GO AWAY FROM MY WORLD (*5) / NORTH COUNTRY MAID (*4) / FAITHFULL FOREVER (*4) / LOVE IN A MIST (*4) / DREAMING MY DREAMS (*3) / FAITHLESS (*4) / BROKEN ENGLISH (*8) / DANGEROUS ACQUAINTANCES (*6) / A CHILD'S ADVENTURE (*5) / THE VERY BEST OF MARIANNE FAITHFULL compilation (*7) / STRANGE WEATHER (*7) / BLAZING AWAY (*6) / FAITHFULL: A COLLECTION OF HER BEST RECORDINGS compilation (*6) / A SECRET LIFE (*5) / 20th CENTURY BLUES (*4) / VAGABOND WAYS (*7)

MARIANNE FAITHFULL – vocals (with session people)

			Decca	London	
Jul 64.	(7")	(F 11923) <9697> **AS TEARS GO BY. / GREENSLEEVES**	9	22	Oct64
Oct 64.	(7")	(F 12007) **BLOWIN' IN THE WIND. / THE HOUSE OF THE RISING SUN**			
Feb 65.	(7")	(F 12075) <9731> **COME AND STAY WITH ME. / WHAT HAVE I DONE WRONG**	4	26	
Apr 65.	(7")	(F 12162) <9759> **THIS LITTLE BIRD. / MORNING SUN**	6	32	May65
May 65.	(lp)	(LK 4688) **COME MY WAY**	12		

  – Come my way / Jabberwock / Portland town / The house of the rising sun / Spanish is a loving tongue / Fare thee well / Lonesome traveller / Down in the Salley garden / Mary Ann / Full fathom five / Four strong winds / Black girl / Once I had a sweetheart / Bells of freedom. (re-iss. Sep91 on 'Deram' lp/cd+=; 820 629-2) – Blowin' in the wind / Et maintenant (what now my love) / That's right baby / Sister Morphine.

			Decca	London	
May 65.	(lp)	(LK 4689) <3423> **MARIANNE FAITHFULL**	15	12	

  – Come and stay with me (UK-only) / / They will never leave you / What have they done to the rain / In my time of sorrow / What have I done wrong / I'm a loser / As tears go by / If I never get to love you / Time takes time / He'll come back to me / Paris bells / Plaisir d'amour. (re-iss. Aug84; DOA 3) (cd-iss. Jun89 on 'London'+=; 820 630-2) – Can't you hear my heartbeat? / Downtown.

			Decca	London	
Jul 65.	(7")	(F 12193) <9780> **SUMMER NIGHTS. / THE SHA LA LA SONG**	10	24	Aug65
Oct 65.	(7")	(F 12268) **YESTERDAY. / OH LOOK AROUND YOU**	36		
Nov 66.	(7")	<9802> **GO AWAY FROM MY WORLD. / OH, LOOK AROUND YOU**	–	89	
Dec 65.	(lp)	<3452> **GO AWAY FROM MY WORLD**	–	81	

  – Go away from my world / Yesterday / Come my way / Last thing on my mind / How should my true love know / Wild mountain time / Summer nights / Mary Ann / Scarborough Fair / Lullabye / North country maid / Sally free and easy.

			Decca	London	
Apr 66.	(lp)	(LK 4778) **NORTH COUNTRY MAID**		–	

  – Green are your eyes / Scarborough fair / Cockleshells / The last thing on my mind / The first time ever I saw your face / Sally free and easy / Sunny Goodge Street / How should your true love know / She moved through the fair / North country maid / Lullaby / Wild mountain thyme. (cd-iss. Aug90+=; 820 631-2) – The most of what is least / Come my way / Mary Ann.

			Decca	London	
May 66.	(7")	(F 12408) **TOMORROW'S CALLING. / THAT'S RIGHT BABY**			
Jul 66.	(7")	(F 12443) **COUNTING. / I'D LIKE TO DIAL YOUR NUMBER**			
Nov 66.	(lp)	<3482> **FAITHFULL FOREVER**	–		

  – Counting / Tomorrow's calling / The first time / With you in mind / In the night time / Ne me quitte pas (love theme from Umbrellas of Cherbourg) / Monday Monday / Some other Spring / That's right baby / Lucky girl / I'm the sky / I have a love.

			Decca	London	
Feb 67.	(7")	(F 22524) **IS THIS WHAT I GET FOR LOVING YOU?. / TOMORROW'S CALLING**	43		
Feb 67.	(lp; mono/stereo)	(LK/SKL 4854) **LOVEINAMIST**		–	

  – Yesterday / You can't go where the roses go / Our love has gone / Don't make promises / In the night time / This little bird / Ne me quite pas / Counting / Reason to believe / Conquillage / With you in mind / Young girl blues / Good guy / I love a love. (cd-iss. Oct88+=; 820 632-2) – Rosie, Rosie.

			Decca	London	
Feb 69.	(7"; w-drawn)	(F 12889) **SOMETHING BETTER. / SISTER MORPHINE**			

—— She retired from music business for around half a decade

			NEMS	not iss.	
Nov 75.	(7")	(NES 004) **DREAMIN' MY DREAMS. / LADY MADELAINE**		–	

			NEMS	not iss.	
Sep 76.	(7")	(NES 013) **ALL I WANNA DO IN LIFE. / WRONG ROAD AGAIN**		–	
Jan 77.	(lp)(c)	(NEL 6007) **DREAMIN' MY DREAMS**			

  – Fairy tale hero / This time / I'm not Lisa / he way you want me to be / Wrong road again / All I wanna do in life / I'm looking for blue eyes / Somebody loves you / Vanilla O'lay / Dreamin' my dreams / Lady Madelaine / Sweet little sixteen.

			NEMS	not iss.	
Jan 77.	(7")	(NES 014) **WRONG ROAD AGAIN. / THE WAY YOU WANT ME TO BE**		–	

—— she was now backed by **The GREASE BAND**

			NEMS	not iss.	
Mar 78.	(lp)	(NEL 6012) **FAITHLESS**			

  – Dreamin' my dreams / Vanilla O'Lay / Wait for me down by the river / I'll be your baby tonight / Lady Madelaine / All I wanna do in life / The way you want me to be / Wrong road again / This was the day (Nashville) / This time / I'm not Lisa / Honky tonk angels. (re-iss. Apr89 on 'Castle' lp/c/cd; CLA LP/MC/CD 148) (cd re-iss. Apr99 on 'Essential'; ESSCD 713)

			NEMS	not iss.	
Mar 78.	(7")	(NES 117) **THE WAY YOU WANT ME TO BE. / THAT WAS THE DAY (NASHVILLE)**		–	

—— now with **BARRY REYNOLDS** – guitar, co-producer / **STEVE YORK** – bass / **TERRY STANNARD** – drums / **JOE HAVETY** – keys / etc.

			Island	Island
Oct 79.	(7")	(WIP 6491) **THE BALLAD OF LUCY JORDAN. / BRAIN DRAIN**	48	
Oct 79.	(lp)	(M 1) <ILPS 9570> **BROKEN ENGLISH**	57	82

  – Broken English / Witches song / Brain drain / Guilt / The ballad of Lucy Jordan / What's the hurry / Working class hero / Why d'ya do it? (c-iss.May81; ICT 9570) (re-iss. Sep86 lp/c; ILPM/ICM 9570) (cd-iss. May89; IMCD 11) (re-iss. May94; ILPS 9570)

			Island	Island
Jan 80.	(7")	<49121> **BROKEN ENGLISH. / BRAIN DRAIN**	–	
Jan 80.	(7")	(WIP 6542) **BROKEN ENGLISH. / WHAT'S THE HURRY** (12") (12WIP 6542) – ('A'side) / Why d'ya do it?.		
Oct 81.	(7")	(WIP 6737) **INTRIGUE. / FOR BEAUTY'S SAKE**		
Oct 81.	(lp/c)	(ILPS/ICT 9648) **DANGEROUS ACQUAINTANCE**	45	

  – Sweetheart / Intrigue / Easy in the city / Strange one / Tenderness / For beautie's sake / So sad / Eye communication / Truth bitter truth. (cd-iss. May95; IMCD 205)

			Island	Island
Nov 81.	(7")	(WIP 6752) **SWEETHEART. / OVER HERE**		
Jan 82.	(7")	**SWEETHEART. / FOR BEAUTIE'S SAKE**	–	
May 82.	(7")	(MF 100) **BROKEN ENGLISH. / SISTER MORPHINE**	–	

—— **BEN BRIERLEY** + **MIKEY CHUNG** – guitar repl. MAVETY **FERNANDO SAUNDERS** – bass / **WALLY BADAROU** – keyboards repl. YORK

			Island	Island
Feb 83.	(lp)	(ILPS 9734) **A CHILD'S ADVENTURE**	99	

  – Times Square / The blue millionaire / Falling from grace / Morning come / Ashes in my hand / Running for our lives / Ireland / She's got a problem. (re-iss. Apr87 lp/c; ILPM/ICM 9734) (cd-iss. May95; IMCD 206)

			Island	Island
Mar 83.	(7")	(IS 105) **RUNNING FOR OUR LIVES. / SHE'S GOT A PROBLEM**		

—— now w/ **many on session, incl. SAUNDERS.**

			Island	Island
Jun 87.	(7")	(IS 323) **AS TEARS GO BY. / TROUBLE IN MIND (THE RETURN)** (12"+=) (12IS 323) – This hawk el Galvion.		
Jul 87.	(lp/c/cd)	(ILPS/ICT/CID 9874) **STRANGE WEATHER**	78	

  – Stranger intro / Boulevard of broken dreams / I ain't goin' down to the well no more / Yesterdays / Sign of judgement / Strange weather / Love, life and money / I'll keep it with mine / Hello stranger / Penthouse serenade / As tears go by / A stranger on Earth. (cd re-iss. May89; IMCD 12)

—— now with **BARRY REYNOLDS** – guitar / **MARC RIBOT** / **LEW SOLOFF** / **GARTH HUDSON**

			Island	Island
May 90.	(cd/c/lp)	(CID/ICT/ILPS 9957) **BLAZING AWAY (live + 1 studio)**		

  – Les prisons du roi / Guilt / Sister morphine / Why d'ya do it? / The ballad of Lucy Jordan / Blazing away / Broken English / Strange weather / Working class hero / As tears go by / When I find my life / Times Square / She moved through the fair. (re-iss. cd May95; IMCD 207) (c re-iss. May95; same)

			Island	Island
Sep 94.	(cd/c)	(DID/ICT 8023) **FAITHFULL – A COLLECTION OF HER BEST RECORDINGS** (compilation)		

  – Broken English / The ballad of Lucy Jordan / Working class hero / Guilt / Why d'ya do it / Ghost dance / Trouble in mind (the return) / Times Square (live) / Strange weather / She / As tears go by.

below from a VAN MORRISON tribute album on 'Exile-Polydor' / 'M.C.A.'

			Island	Island
Sep 94.	(c-s)	**MADAME GEORGE.** / ('b'side by Brian Kennedy) (cd-s+=) – (other by Brian Kennedy + Shana Morrison).		

below with composer ANGELO BADALEMENTI

			Island	Island
Apr 95.	(cd/c)	(CID/ICT 8038) **A SECRET LIFE**		

  – Prologue / Sleep / Love in the afternoon / Flaming September / She / Bored by dreams / Losing / The wedding / The stars line up / Epilogue.

			RCA Victor	RCA Victor
Sep 96.	(cd)	(74321 38656-2) **20th CENTURY BLUES**		

  – Alabama song / Want to buy some illusions / Pirate Jenny / Salomon song / Boulevard of broken dreams / Complainte de la Seine / Ballad of the soldier's wife / Intro / Mon ami, my friend / Falling in love again / Mack the knife / 20th century blues / Don't forget me / Surabaya Johnny / Outro (street singers farewell).

			EMI Disc	not iss.
Aug 97.	(cd-ep)	(CDDISC 10) **HANG IT ON YOUR HEART / (TV theme version) / (instrumental)**		–

			ITR	Virgin
Jun 99.	(cd)	(ITRCD 1) **VAGABOND WAYS**		

  – Vagabond ways / Incarceration of a flower child / File it under fun from the past / Electra / Wilder shores of love / Marathon kiss / For wanting you / Great expectations / Tower of song / After the ceasefire.

			ITR	Virgin
Nov 99.	(cd-s)	**ELECTRA**		–

– compilations, etc. –

on 'Decca' unless mentioned otherwise

May 65.	(7"ep)	(DFE 8624) **MARIANNE FAITHFULL**		

  – Go away from my world / The most of what is least / El main tenant (what now my love) / The sha la la song.

Feb 69.	(lp)	(SPA 17) **THE WORLD OF MARIANNE FAITHFULL**		
Apr 69.	(lp)	London; <3547> **MARIANNE FAITHFULL'S GREATEST HITS** (same tracks as above)	–	

Jul 80.	(7"ep) *(F 13890)* **AS TEARS GO BY / COME AND STAY WITH ME. / THIS LITTLE BIRD / SUMMER NIGHTS**	☐	-
Feb 81.	(lp) *(TAB 13)* **AS TEARS GO BY**	☐	-
Apr 83.	(7") *Old Gold; (OG 9335)* **AS TEARS GO BY. / COME AND STAY WITH ME**		-
Mar 84.	(lp) *(TAB 78)* **SUMMER NIGHTS**	☐	-
Nov 85.	(d-lp/c/cd) *Castle; (CCS LP/MC/CD 107)* **RICH KID BLUES**	☐	-
Mar 87.	(cd) *London; (820 482-2)* **THE VERY BEST OF MARIANNE FAITHFULL**		-

– As tears go by / Come and stay with me / Scarborough Fair / Monday, Monday / Yesterday / The last thing on my mind / What have they done to the rain / This little bird / Something better / In my time of sorrow / Is this what I get for loving you? / Tomorrow's calling / Reason to believe / Sister Morphine / Go away from my world / Summer nights *(re-iss. Sep87 lp/c; 820 482-1/-4)*

Oct 87.	(lp) *Hannibal;* **HEYDAY** (BBC sessions 1968-69)	☐	-
Nov 92.	(d-cd) *Island; (IRSCD 10)* **BROKEN ENGLISH / STRANGE WEATHER**	☐	-
Oct 93.	(cd/c) *Spectrum; (550 097-2/-4)* **THIS LITTLE BIRD**	☐	-
Nov 99.	(cd) *Spectrum; (544 180-2)* **THE BEST OF MARIANNE FAITHFULL**	☐	-

FAITHLESS

Formed: London, England . . . early '96 by veterans of the hip-hop dance scene MAXI JAZZ and ROLLO. The former had founded "The Soul Food Cafe Sound System" in 1984, later spending time at the 'Acid Jazz' label before forming his own imprint in '92; 'Namu'. He released three solo outings under various guises and toured the world supporting SOUL II SOUL and JAMIROQUAI. The man also worked with JAH WOBBLE on his 'INVADERS OF THE HEART', just prior to meeting ROLLO in the studio. ROLLO (a member of Mensa), worked on FELIX's massive seller 'DON'T YOU WANT ME', before remixing the likes of SIMPLY RED, GABRIELLE, LIVIN' JOY, M-PEOPLE and The PET SHOP BOYS. One of the top producers/mixers in the world, he also worked on GLOWORM's 'Lift My Cup' among others on his own 'Cheeky' records. JAMIE CATTO was a singer/songwriter, who became frontman for BIG TRUTH BAND, while SISTER BLISS had outings as a solo singer. FAITHLESS revived 'Cheeky' records and had a Top 10 hit with the house dramatics of 'INSOMNIA' at the end of '96, pushing their album into the big league. ROLLO's ascendance from the narrow confines of the dance scene to muso acceptance was confirmed with FAITHLESS' appearance on Jools Holland's 'Later With . . .' show.
• **Songwriters:** Permutation of quartet, some with DIDO. • **Trivia:** ROLLO had four hits:- 'Get Off Your High Horse' (CHEKCD 003) by ROLLO GOES CAMPING, which hit the UK Top 50 twice in 1994, while 'Love Love Love – Here I Come' (CHEKCD 007) by ROLLO GOES MYSTIC hit No.32 in the summer of '95. His final effort, 'Let This Be A Prayer' (CHEKCD 013) hit No.26 around a year later and was as ROLLO GOES SPIRITUAL WITH PAULINE TAYLOR.

Album rating: REVERENCE (*7) / SUNDAY 8PM (*6)

MAXI JAZZ – vocals / **JAMIE CATTO** – vocals / **SISTER BLISS** – keyboards, vocals / **ROLLO** – programming / with others **DIDO** – vocals / **PAULINE TAYLOR** – vocals / + more musicians

				Cheeky	Intercord
Jul 95.	(c-s) *(CHEKK 008)* **SALVA MEA (SAVE ME) / ('A'mix)**			30	-
	(12"+=/cd-s+=) *(CHEK 12/CD 008)* – ('A'mixes).				
Nov 95.	(c-s) *(CHEKK 010)* **INSOMNIA / ('A'mix)**			27	-
	(12"+=/cd-s+=) *(CHEK 12/CD 010)* – ('A'mixes).				
Mar 96.	(c-s) *(CHEKK 012)* **DON'T LEAVE / ('A'mix)**			34	-
	(12"+=/cd-s+=) *(CHEK 12/CD 012)* – ('A'mixes).				
Apr 96.	(cd/c/d-lp) *(CHEK CD/K/LP 500)* **REVERENCE**			63	

– Reverence / Don't leave / Salva Mea / If lovin' you is wrong / Angeline / Insomnia / Dirty ol' man / Flowerstand man / Baseball cap / Drifting away. *(re-dist.Nov96 hit UK No.26; same)* *(free cd w/cd)* *(CHEKXCD 500)* **IRREVERENCE** – Flowerstand man (Matty's remix) / Angeline (The Innocents mix) / Reverence (Tamsin's refix) / Soundcheck jam / Salva Mea (Way Out West remix) / Don't leave (Floating remix) / Drifting away (Paradiso mix) / Insomnia (Moody mix) / Baseball dub (Cheeky All Stars remix).

Jun 96.	(12") *(VENMX 07ST)* **SALVA MEA (mixes)**			☐	-
	(above issued on 'Vendetta')				
Oct 96.	(c-s) *(CHEKK 017)* **INSOMNIA / ('A'mix)**			3	62 Mar97
	(12"+=/cd-s) *(CHEK 12/CD 017)* – ('A'mixes; CEC / monster).				
	(cd-s) *(CHEKXCD 017)* – ('A'mixes; moody / tuff).				
Dec 96.	(c-s) *(CHEKK 018)* **SALVA MEA / ('A'mix)**			9	
	(12"/cd-s) *(CHEK 12/CD 018)* – ('A'mixes).				
	(cd-s) *(CHEKXCD 018)* – ('A'mixes).				
Apr 97.	(c-s) *(CHEKK 019)* **REVERENCE / INSOMNIA**			10	
	(12"/cd-s) *(CHEK 12/CD 019)* – ('A'mixes).				
	(cd-s) *(CHEKXCD 019)* – ('A'mixes).				
Nov 97.	(c-s) *(CHEKK 024)* **DON'T LEAVE / ('A'mix)**			21	
	(cd-s) *(CHEKXCD 024)* – ('A'mixes).				
	(cd-s) *(CHEKXCD 024)* – ('A'mixes).				

—— **DAVE RANDALL** – guitar; repl. ROLLO (still producer, etc)

Aug 98.	(c-s) *(CHEKK 028)* **GOD IS A DJ / ('A'mix)**			6	
	(12"+=/cd-s+=) *(CHEK 12/CD 028)* – ('A'mixes).				
Sep 98.	(cd/c/d-lp) *(CHEK CD/K/LP 503)* **SUNDAY 8PM**			10	

– The garden / Bring my family back / Hour of need / Postcards / Take the long way home / Why go? / She's my baby / God is a DJ / Hem of his garment / Sunday 8 pm / Killer's lullaby.

Nov 98.	(c-s) *(CHEKK 031)* *<INT 886486-6>* **TAKE THE LONG WAY HOME / ('A'-Rollin' mix)**			15	☐ Dec98
	(cd-s+=) *(CHEKCD 031)* – ('A'-Epic mix) / ('A'-16c+ mix).				
	(12") *(CHEK12 031)* – ('A'mixes).				

Apr 99.	(12") *(CHEK12 035)* **BRING MY FAMILY BACK (mixes; Boombastic / Robbie Rivera's Phat Funked up mix)**	14	☐
	(cd-s) *(CHEKCD 035)* – ('A'side) / ('A'-Paul Van Dyk mix) / ('A'-Jan Driver boombastic mix) / ('A'-Rollo & Sister Bliss monster mix).		
	(cd-s) *(CHEKXCD 035)* – ('A'side) / God is a DJ (first ever mix) / Insomnia (Armand's unreleased mix).		
Oct 99.	(d-cd) *(CHEKCD 503)* **SATURDAY 3AM** (remixes)	☐	☐
Nov 99.	(12"/cd-s; by FAITHLESS & BOY GEORGE) *(CHEK 12/CD 038)* **WHY GO? (mixes)**	☐	☐
	(cd-s) *(CHEKXCD 038)* – ('A'mixes).		

FAITH NO MORE

Formed: Los Angeles & San Francisco, California, USA . . . 1980 by BILL GOULD and MIKE BORDIN, although they only started gigging in 1982. With CHUCK MOSELEY and JIM MARTIN completing the line-up, the band began to carve out their innovative fusion of funk, rap, hardcore and metal. In 1985, they issued their eponymous debut album on local indie label, 'Mordan', the single, 'WE CARE A LOT' drawing the attention of 'Slash' records, who unleashed 'INTRODUCE YOURSELF' the same year. In 1988, due to musical differences and off-beat stage humour, MOSELEY was discharged from the band. His replacement was magnetic, Kyle Mclachlan-alike, MIKE PATTON who immediately became a focal point, his impressive vocal theatrics and commanding stage presence transforming FAITH NO MORE into a formidable live act. PATTON also penned the bizarre, enigmatic lyrics for the band's breakthrough record, 'THE REAL THING' (1989). Arguably the best metal album of the decade, if you could call it metal, it veered from the stuttering rap-rock of 'EPIC' to the sublimely aquatic 'UNDERWATER LOVE' and on to a searing cover of BLACK SABBATH's 'WAR PIGS. The record went on to sell over a million copies, gave a tired heavy metal scene a much needed boot up the arse and more importantly, gave FAITH NO MORE the convenience of a bigger budget for their next album. 'ANGEL DUST' (1992) wreaked aural havoc, a mish mash of styles even more diverse than its predecessor. By turns defiantly inaccessible ('MALPRACTICE') and pop-friendly ('MIDLIFE CRISIS'), the record was characterised by a fractured, schizophrenic sound that seemed to tally with PATTON's increasingly outrageous antics. Following on from their live TECHNOTRONIC/NEW KIDS ON THE BLOCK (ironic? Americans? nah) medley, the band released their rather uninspired cover of The COMMODORES' 'I'M EASY'. It became their biggest selling UK single to date, while the album also sold by the truckload following a world tour with GUNS N' ROSES. By the release of 'KING FOR A DAY . . . FOOL FOR A LIFETIME' (1995), MARTIN had been replaced with TREY SPRUANCE, who played alongside PATTON in his part-time side project, MR. BUNGLE. The record was as uncompromising as ever, venom-spewing hardcore rage sitting side by side with wilful weirdness. A blistering headlining set at that year's Phoenix festival (almost topping PUBLIC ENEMY's poignant farewell slot earlier that day) proved once more that live, FAITH NO MORE have few peers and even less scruples. While the group maintain they're simply a rock band and nothing more, they remain one of the genre's quintessential outsiders, image-unfriendly and maverick to the last, as evidenced on their most recent effort to date, 'ALBUM OF THE YEAR' (1997). If not quite living up to the rather presumptuous title, the record illustrated that FAITH NO MORE still have their collective finger in more than one pie, 'LAST CUP OF SORROW' being their most affecting single for years. Unfortunately, it would also be their epitaph as the band split up the following April.
• **Covered:** THE RIGHT STUFF (Edwin Starr) / MIDNIGHT COWBOY (John Barry) / MALPRACTICE (sampled: Kronos Quartet No.8) / LET'S LYNCH THE LANDLORD (Dead Kennedys) / I'M EASY (Commodores) / I STARTED A JOKE (Bee Gees) / GREENFIELDS (Gilykson-Dehr-Miller) / SPANISH EYES (hit; Al Martino) / THIS GUY'S IN LOVE WITH YOU (Burt Bacharach) / HIGHWAY STAR (Deep Purple). IMPERIAL TEEN covered SHAYLA (Blondie).

Album rating: FAITH NO MORE (*5) / INTRODUCE YOURSELF (*8) / THE REAL THING (*8) / LIVE AT BRIXTON ACADEMY (*6) / ANGEL DUST (*8) / KING FOR A DAY – FOOL FOR A LIFETIME (*7) / ALBUM OF THE YEAR (*6) / WHO CARES A LOT? compilation (*9) / Mr. Bungle: MR. BUNGLE (*4) / DISCO VOLANTE (*4) / CALIFORNIA (*6) / Imperial Teen: SEASICK (*4)

CHUCK MOSELEY – vocals / **BILLY GOULD** (b.24 Apr'63, L.A.) – bass / **RODDY BOTTUM** (b. 1 Jul'63, L.A.) – keyboards / **JIM MARTIN** (b.JAMES, 21 Jul'61, Oakland, Calif.) – guitar / **MIKE BORDIN** (b.27 Nov'62) – drums

			not iss.	Mordan
1985.	(lp) *<MDR 1>* **FAITH NO MORE**		-	☐

– We care a lot / The jungle / Mark Bowen / Jim / Why do you bother / Greed / Pills for breakfast / As the worm turns / Arabian disco / New beginnings. *(imported into UK.Feb88 as 'WE CARE A LOT'; same)*

			Slash	Slash
Oct 87.	(lp/c)(cd) *(SLAP/SMAC 21)<(828051-2)>* **INTRODUCE YOURSELF**		☐	☐

– Faster disco / Anne's song / Introduce yourself / Chinese arithmetic / Death march / We care a lot / R'n'r / Crab song / Blood / Spirit.

Jan 88.	(7") *(LASH 17)* *<28287>* **WE CARE A LOT. / SPIRIT**		53	☐
	(12"+=) *(LASHX 17)* – Chinese Arithmetic (radio mix).			
Apr 88.	(7"/7"pic-d/12") *(LASH/+P/X 18)* **ANNE'S SONG (remix). / GREED**		☐	☐

—— **MIKE PATTON** (b.27 Jan'68, Eureka, Calif.) – vocals (of-MR. BUNGLE) repl. CHUCK who later (1991) joined BAD BRAINS

Jul 89.	(lp/c/cd) *(828154-1/-4/-2)* *<25878>* **THE REAL THING**		30	11

– From out of nowhere / Epic / Falling to pieces / Surprise, you're dead / Zombie eaters / The real thing / Underwater love / The morning after / Woodpecker from Mars. *(cd+=)* – Edge of the world / War pigs. *(actually hit charts early 1990) (re-iss. Sep92 cd/c; same)*

Oct 89.	(7") *(LASH 19)* **FROM OUT OF NOWHERE. / COWBOY SONG**				
	(12"+=) *(LASHX 19)* – The grave.				
Jan 90.	(7"/7"sha-pic-d) *(LASH/LASPD 21)* **EPIC. / WAR PIGS** (live)		37	-	
	(7"m+=) *(LASHG 21)* – Surprise you're dead (live).				
	(12"++=/cd-s++=) *(LASHX/LASCD 21)* – Chinese arithmetic.				
Apr 90.	(7") *(LASCS 24)* **FROM OUT OF NOWHERE. / WOODPECKER FROM MARS** (live)		23		
	(7"m+=) *(LASHG 24)* – Epic (live).				
	(12"++=/12"pic-d++=/cd-s++=) *(LASHX/LASPX/LASCD 24)* – The real thing (live).				
Jun 90.	(c-s) *<19813>* **EPIC / EDGE OF THE WORLD**		-	9	
Jul 90.	(7") *(LASHP 25)* **FALLING TO PIECES. / WE CARE A LOT** (live)		41	-	
	(7"m+=)(c-s+=) *(LASHG/LASCS 25)* – Underwater love (live).				
	(12"++=/12"w-poster++=/cd-s++=) *(LASHX/LASPX/LASCD 25)* – From out of nowhere (live).				
Sep 90.	(7"sha-pic-d) *(LASPD 26)* **EPIC. / FALLING TO PIECES** (live)		25	-	
	(7"m+=/c-s+=) *(LASH/LASCS 26)* – Epic (live).				
	(12"++=/cd-s++=) *(LASHX/LASCD 26)* – As the worm turns.				
Oct 90.	(c-s) *<19563>* **FALLING TO PIECES / ZOMBIE EATERS**		-	92	
Feb 91.	(cd/c/lp) *(828238-2/-4/-1)* **LIVE AT BRIXTON ACADEMY** (live)		20		
	– Falling to pieces / The real thing / Pump up the jam / Epic / War pigs / From out of nowhere / We care a lot / The right stuff / Zombie eaters / Edge of the world. *(cd+=/c+=)* – The grade / Cowboy song.				
May 92.	(7"/7"colrd/c-s) *(LASH///LASCS 37)* **MIDLIFE CRISIS. / JIZZLOBER / CRACK HITLER**		10		
	(12"pic-d+=/pic-cd-s+=) *(LASHX/LASCD 37)* – Midnight cowboy.				
Jun 92.	(cd/c/lp) *(828321-2/-4/-1)* *<26785>* **ANGEL DUST**		2	10	
	– Land of sunshine / Caffeine / Midlife crisis / RV / Smaller and smaller / Everything's ruined / Malpractise / Kindergarten / Be aggressive / A small victory / Crack Hitler / Jizzlober / Midnight cowboy. *(lp w/ free-12"ep)* – MIDLIFE CRISIS (remix) / (2). *(re-iss. Feb93)* *(+=)* – I'm easy.				
Aug 92.	(7"/c-s) *(LASH/LASCS 39)* **A SMALL VICTORY. / LET'S LYNCH THE LANDLORD**		29		
	(12"+=)(12"pic-d+=) *(LASHX 39)* – Malpractise.				
	(cd-s++=) *(LASCD 39)* – ('A'extended).				
Sep 92.	(12"ep/cd-ep) *(LASHX/LASCD 40)* **A SMALL VICTORY (Youth remix) / R-EVOLUTION 23 (Full Moon mix) / SUNDOWN (mix) / SUNDOWN (instrumental)**		55	-	
Nov 92.	(7"/c-s) *(LASH/LASCS 43)* **EVERYTHING'S RUINED. / MIDLIFE CRISIS** (live)		28		
	(cd-s+=) *(LASCD 43)* – Land of sunshine (live).				
	(cd-s+=) *(LASHCD 43)* – Edge of the world (live) / RV (live).				
Jan 93.	(7"/c-s/12"/cd-s) *(LASH/LASCS/LASHX/LACDP 44)* **I'M EASY. / BE AGGRESSIVE**		3	-	
Mar 93.	(c-s) *<18569>* **EASY / DAS SCHUTENFEST**		-	58	
Oct 93.	(12"ep/c-ep/cd-ep; by FAITH NO MORE & BOO-YAA TRIBE) *(659794-6/-4/-2)* **ANOTHER BODY MURDERED. / Just Another Victim (by "HELMET / HOUSE OF PAIN")**		26		

—— (above from the film 'Judgement Day', released on 'Epic')

—— **DEAN MENTA** – guitar repl. JIM MARTIN (TREY SPRUANCE played on below album)

Mar 95.	(7"/c-s) *(LASH/LASCS 51)* **DIGGING THE GRAVE. / UGLY IN THE MORNING**		16		
	(12"blue+=) *(LASHX 51)* – Absolute zero / Get out.				
	(cd-s+=) *(LASCD 51)* – Absolute zero / Cuckoo for Caca.				
	(cd-s) *(LASHCD 51)* – I started a joke / Greenfields.				
Mar 95.	(cd/c/lp) *(828 560-2/-4/-1)* *<45723>* **KING FOR A DAY – FOOL FOR A LIFETIME**		5	31	
	– Get out / Ricochet / Evidence / The great art of making enemies / Star A.D. / Cuckoo for Caca / Caralho Voador / Ugly in the morning / Digging the grave / Take this bottle / King for a day / What a day / The last to know / Just a man. *(7"box-set)* – (interviews). *(re-iss. Sep97 cd/c; same)*				
May 95.	(c-s) *(LASCS 53)* **RICOCHET / SPANISH EYES**		27		
	(cd-s+=) *(LASCD 53)* – I wanna f**k myself.				
	(cd-s) *(LACDP 53)* – ('A'side) / Midlife crisis (live) / Epic (live) / We care a lot (live).				
Jul 95.	(c-s) *(LASCS 54)* **EVIDENCE / EASY** (live)		32		
	(cd-s+=) *(LASCD 54)* – Digging the grave (live) / From out of nowhere (live).				
	(cd-s) *(LACDP 54)* – ('A'side) / Das schutzenfest / (interview).				

—— **JON HUDSON** – guitar; repl. MENTA

May 97.	(cd-ep) *(LASCD 61)* **ASHES TO ASHES / LIGHT UP AND LET GO / COLLISION / ASHES TO ASHES (DJ Icey & Mystero mix)**		15		
	(cd-ep) *(LASCDP 61)* – ('A'side) / The big Kahuna / Mouth to mouth / ('A'-Hard Knox alternative mix).				
	(12"ep) *(LASX 61)* – ('A'side) / ('A'-Hard Knox alternative mix) / ('A'-DJ Icey & Mystero mix) / ('A';-DJ & Mystero dub mix).				
Jun 97.	(cd/c/lp) *(828 797-2/-4/-1)* **ALBUM OF THE YEAR**		7	41	
	– Collision / Strip search / Last cup of sorrow / Naked in front of the computer / Helpless / Mouth to mouth / Ashes to ashes / She loves me not / Got that feeling / Paths of glory / Home sick home / Pristina. *(cd with free cd Jan98; 828902-2)*				
Jul 97.	(cd-ep) *(LASCD 62)* **LAST CUP OF SORROW / LAST CUP OF SORROW (Bonehead mix) / SHE LOVES ME NOT (Spinna main mix) / SHE LOVES ME NOT (Spinna crazy dub)**			-	
	(cd-ep) *(LASDP 62)* – ('A'side) / Pristina (Billy Gould mix) / Last cup of sorrow (Roli Mosimann mix) / Ashes to ashes (Dillinja remix).				

—— In Nov'97, they teamed up with 70's popsters SPARKS on a combined version of 'THIS TOWN AIN'T BIG ENOUGH FOR BOTH OF US'.

Jan 98.	(cd-s) *(LASCD 63)* **ASHES TO ASHES / LAST CUP OF SORROW (Rammstein mix) / LAST CUP OF SORROW (Sharam Vs FNM club mix)**		29		

	(cd-s) *(LASCX 63)* – ('A'side) / ('A'-Dillinja remix) / The gentle art of making enemies / ('A'live).				
	(12") *(LASHX 63)* – ('A'-Dillinja mix) / ('A'-Hardknox mix).				

—— the band had already split in April '98

Oct 98.	(cd-s) *(LONCD 65)* **I STARTED A JOKE / THE WORLD IS YOURS / THEME FROM MIDNIGHT COWBOY**		49		
	(cd-s) *(LASCX 65)* – ('A'side) / This guy's in love with you / We care a lot (CD-rom).				
Nov 98.	(d-cd/d-c) *(556 057-2/-4)* **WHO CARES A LOT? – THE GREATEST HITS** (compilation)		37		
	– We care a lot (original) / Introduce yourself / From out of nowhere / Epic / Falling to pieces / Midlife crisis / A small victory / Easy / Digging the grave / The gentle art of making enemies / Evidence / I started a joke / Last cup of sorrow / Ashes to ashes / Stripsearch // The world is yours / Hippie jam song / Instrumental / I won't forget you / Introduce yourself (4-track demos) / Highway star / Theme from Midnight Cowboy / This guy's in love with you.				

MR. BUNGLE

PATTON + **TREY DUNN** – bass / **WILLIAM WINANT** – percussion, etc /

			Slash	Warners
Sep 91.	(cd/c/lp) *(828267-2/-4/-1)* **MR. BUNGLE**		57	
	– Quote unquote / Slowly growing deaf / Squeeze me macaroni / Carousel / Egg / Stubb (a dub) / The girls of porn / Love is a fist / Dead goon.			

—— **PATTON, TREY, THEO, UNCOOKED MEAT PRIOR TO STATE VECTOR COLLAPSE / CLINTON McKINNON + I QUIT**

Jan 96.	(cd/c) *(828 694-2/-4)* *<45963>* **DISCO VOLANTE**			Oct95
	– Everyone I went to high school with is dead / Chemical marriage / Sleep / Desert search for techno Allah / Violenza domestica / After school special / Sleep / Ma meeshka mow skwoz / Bends / Backstrokin' / Platypus / Merry go bye bye – Nothing.			
Nov 99.	(cd) *(3984 29829-2)* *<47447>* **CALIFORNIA**			Jul99
	– Sweet charity / None of them knew they were robots / Retrovertigo / Air conditioned nightmare / Ars moriendi / Pink cigarette / Golem II: the bionic vapour boy / Holy filament / Vanity fair / Goodbye sober day.			

IMPERIAL TEEN

RODDY BOTTUM – vocals, guitar, etc / **WILL SCHWARTZ** – vocals, etc / **JONE STEBBINGS** – bass, etc / **LYNN PERKO** – drums, etc

			Custom	Custom
Jun 96.	(7") *(CUSTOM 001)* **IMPERIAL TEEN. /**			
			Slash	Slash
Aug 96.	(7") *(LASH 57)* **YOU'RE ONE. / SHAYLA**		69	
	(12"c-s/cd-s) *(LAST/LASCS/LASCD 57)* – ('A'side) / Waterboy / Pretty.			
Sep 96.	(cd/c) *(828 728-2/-4)* **SEASICK**			
	– Imperial / Water boy / Butch / Pig Latin / Blaming the baby / You're one / Balloon / Tippy tap / Copafeelia / Luxury / Eternity.			
Oct 96.	(7") *(LASH 59)* **BUTCH. / HELPFUL**			
	(cd-s+=) *(LASCD 59)* – Pig Latin.			

FALL

Formed: Salford, Manchester, England . . . late '76 by vocalist MARK E. SMITH, guitarist MARTIN BRAMAH and bassist TONY FRIEL. Completing the line-up with UNA BAINES (electric piano) and KARL BURNS (drums), the unusual punk band completed a 1977 session for Radio One's John Peel show, before signing to indie outlet, 'Step Forward'. In summer of the following year, The FALL released their debut, the 'BINGO-MASTERS BREAK-OUT! EP'. Sharp-witted right from the outset, the shrieking MARK E traversed the minefield of punk sterotypes, the last track, 'REPETITION' a slow teaser to the other quickfire numbers, 'PSYCHO MAFIA' and 'BINGO-MASTER'. The first of many personnel changes was to occur soon after, MARC RILEY and YVONNE PAWLETT coming in for the departing FRIEL (to The PASSAGE) and BAINES (to The BLUE ORCHIDS) respectively. A weird, disappointing follow-up, 'IT'S THE NEW THING' was thankfully not on their glorious Bob Sergeant-produced debut album, 'LIVE AT THE WITCH TRIALS'. Unleashed to an ever-changing alternative rock audience (who were probably now holding down office jobs while daydreaming of their pogoing dancefloor days of yore!?), the studio set (recorded in two days) packed a lyrical angst not heard since the days of The VELVET UNDERGROUND (one of MARK E's inspirators). Quirky punk tracks such as 'FUTURES AND PASTS' and 'REBELLIOUS JUKEBOX' fitted in nicely with longer excursions into experimentation, 'FRIGHTENED' and 'MUSIC SCENE', making this a classic debut worthy of more listeners. MARK E was now in full control after the remaining founding members, BRAMAH and BURNS bailed out (also joining BLUE ORCHIDS and The PASSAGE) to be subsequently replaced by STEVE HANLEY and MIKE LEIGH respectively. What came next was a piece of punk rock genius, the single 'ROWCHE RUMBLE' ditching conventional rhythms in mindblowing style. PAWLETT left the band soon after and was replaced by guitarist, CRAIG SCANLON, just in time for yet another masterful set that year, 'DRAGNET' (1979). A darker, even more experimental affair, MARK E's twisted tales of life's stranger characters were summed up best on tracks such as 'MUZOREWI'S DAUGHTER', 'A FIGURE WALKS', 'SPECTRE VS. RECTOR' and the "rockabilly" 'PSYKICK DANCEHALL'. The FALL kickstarted the 80's in fine fashion with another punkabilly classic, 'FIERY JACK', an ever better version appearing on 'THE FALL LIVE – TOTALE'S TURNS', their first for 'Rough Trade' a couple of months later. With PAUL HANLEY taking over the vacant drum stool, Mark and Co. delivered two more classic 45's, 'HOW I WROTE ELASTIC MAN' and 'TOTALLY WIRED', their third studio set, 'GROTESQUE (AFTER THE GRAMME)', being released later in 1980. An impressive if not brilliant album, it featured such acidic, "Mancabilly" screechers, 'THE CONTAINER DRIVERS', 'PAY YOUR RATES' and 'NEW FACE IN HELL', the kazoo backing provided by the group's manager and MARK E's girlfriend, KAY CARROLL. Next up was another unusual concept, the 10" mini-set that was 'SLATES' (1981), a patchy affair that nevertheless contained another gem, 'AN OLDER LOVER ETC'. With founder member KARL BURNS (the second drummer! and extra keyboard player) now back in tow, The FALL signed to 'Kamera', releasing another diamond of a single, 'LIE DREAM OF A CASINO SOUL' (backed by 'FANTASTIC LIFE' on the B-side; like all 45's at this time, not from the accompanying album). They finally found some degree of commercial success when 1982's 'HEX ENDUCTION HOUR' broke silently into the Top 75. Recorded in Iceland, it was sixty minutes of lyrical abandon, excellent songs, however confusing, came in the shape of 'THE CLASSICAL', 'WHO MAKES THE NAZIS?', 'HIP PRIEST' and their most commercial tune to date, 'JAW-BONE AND THE AIR-RIFLE'. Later that year, the most prolific band on earth issued yet another long-player, 'ROOM TO LIVE', a more self-indulgent delivery that disappointed their growing college/uni fanbase. In 1983, they lost the talents of MARC RILEY, who formed his own outfit, The CREEPERS (another great band!), KAY also leaving after she split (not for the first time!) with the grumpy one. Returning to 'Rough Trade', The FALL excelled once more with two splendid singles, 'THE MAN WHOSE HEAD EXPANDED' and 'KICKER CONSPIRACY', before MARK E's new Californian girlfriend, BRIX, came into the fold. She immediately made her mark, augmenting on vocals, playing guitar and co-writing a few numbers on The FALL's late 1983 album, 'PERVERTED BY LANGUAGE'. This set was another to whet the appetite of the faithful (and another illustrious indie chart topper), MARK's mental execution of tracks like 'EAT Y'SELF FITTER' and 'TEMPO HOUSE' the pick of a bizarre bunch. Advancing to 'Beggars Banquet', MARK E, BRIX E and Co. delivered a couple of odd pop singles in the shape of 'OH BROTHER' and 'C.R.E.E.P.', the records not featuring on their forthcoming eighth set, 'THE WONDERFUL AND FRIGHTENING WORLD OF . . .' (1984). Their buoyant rockabilly was back in full flow on two numbers, 'LAY OF THE LAND' and '2 x 4', while GAVIN FRIDAY of The VIRGIN PRUNES guested on a couple of tracks. A month later, a 12"ep, 'CALL FOR ESCAPE ROUTE', saw The FALL experimenting once more, although this was their last with PAUL HANLEY, who was superseded by the numerous talents of SIMON ROGERS (he had been a member of panpipes afficionados, INCANTATION!). With STEVE HANLEY on summer vacation in 1985, the band released the disappointing 'COULDN'T GET AHEAD' single, its flipside containing their first cover, Gene Vincent's 'ROLLIN DANY'. STEVE was back in time to record their most accessible recording to date, 'THIS NATION'S SAVING GRACE' (1985). Regarded as their best work since their debut, the UK Top 60 album housed the excellent 'PAINTWORK', 'MY NEW HOUSE' and 'I AM DAMO SUZUKI', the latter track MARK E's tribute (sort of!) to the CAN singer. BURNS jumped ship after the obligatory set of singles, SIMON WOOLSTENCROFT taking his place for The FALL's first hit (well, No.75), a cover version of The Other Half's 'MR. PHARMACIST'. This seemed to pay off commercially, especially when the accompanying (for once) 'BEND SINISTER' album reached the dizzy heights of the Top 40 in 1986. Another minor hit 45, 'HEY! LUCIANI' (Top 60 this time), preceded the following year's Top 30 embarrassment coming in the shape of R. Dean Taylor's 'THERE'S A GHOST IN MY HOUSE'. Some time later in 1987, BRIX brought in her old friend, MARSHA SCHOFIELD (both were in BANDA DRATSING together), the keyboard player and vocalist arriving in time for two more hits, 'HIT THE NORTH' and 'VICTORIA' (the latter from the pen of Ray Davies). Now without SIMON, who stayed on as their producer, MARK E and Co. hit the charts (Top 20!) with 'THE FRENZ EXPERIMENT' (1988), a confused set that nevertheless contained one standout song, 'CARRY BAG MAN'. Having also been a friend of ballet dancer, MICHAEL CLARK (who used FALL tapes as his backing soundtrack), MARK E and The FALL collaborated with the bare-arsed performer on the band's next ambitious concept, 'I AM KURIOUS ORANJ' (1988). It was indeed, curious, although the Top 60 album did have its moments, especially in 'CAB IT UP!' and a tongue-in-cheek rendition of William Blake's 'JERUSALEM' (segued with the 'DOG IS LIFE' poem). A concert set, 'SEMINAL LIVE' (1989) filled in time during which MARK and BRIX split up, the blonde (who had initiated her own band, ADULT NET, some time ago) eventually becoming the girlfriend of posh/cockney (you choose) classical violinist, NIGEL KENNEDY. He had previously guested on an earlier FALL album (she stunned many after appearing on 'This Is Your Life', which looked back over NIGEL's short career). BRAMAH was now back in the fold, enrolling in time for their umpteenth long-player, 'EXTRICATE' (1990), their first album jointly controlled by the group's new imprint, 'Cog Sinister' and major 'Fontana' label. Premiered by a hit version of Cold Cut's 'TELEPHONE THING', the cynical but accessible set featured other acidic attacks, 'SING! HARPY', 'THE LITTLEST REBEL' and two more obscure covers, 'POPCORN DOUBLE FEATURE' (Searchers) and 'BLACK MONK THEME' (Monks). MARK then trimmed the band down to a quartet, retaining only CRAIG, STEVE and JOHN to record an excellent SID VICIOUS-esque version of Big Bopper's 'WHITE LIGHTNING'. This minor hit was followed by an uncharacteristic flop, 'HIGH TENSION LINE', although both tracks appeared on the follow-up album, 'SHIFT-WORK' (1991), which added a fifth member, violinist KENNY BRADY. Split into two, titled sides, the UK Top 20 record was highlighted by two more excellent pieces of wordplay,

'EDINBURGH MAN' (still makes me sad) and their umpteenth rockabilly delivery, 'A LOT OF WIND' (as in, you talk . . .). BRADY was let go soon after, DAVID BUSH coming in as a more permanent fixture on their next set, 'CODE: SELFISH' (1992). The album disappointed many of the faithful, although some FALL diehards regard it as one of the best (I'm in the former, I'm afraid), its re-working of Hank Williams' 'JUST WAITING' not the MARK E of old, although the hit single, 'FREE RANGE' gets back to grips. Moving to 'Permanent' records (not the most appropriate label title for them), MARK and the lads released their biggest seller to date, 'THE INFOTAINMENT SCAN', which went Top 10 in 1993. Short of a classic MARK E song, it collected together another bunch of covers, this time in the shape of Sister Sledge's 'LOST IN MUSIC', S. Bent's (who?!) 'I'M GOING TO SPAIN' and Lee Perry's 'WHY ARE PEOPLE GRUDGEFUL?' (a Top 50 hit). For many, The FALL "lost it" from then on, their formula of sticking several good (not brilliant) songs together with a few obscure covers saw their fanbase dwindle dramatically. Early in '94, a collaboration between MARK and The INSPIRAL CARPETS on the brilliant 'I WANT YOU' single gave him another hit, the mainman subsequently being invited to do similar things for other acts (notably, COLD CUT and DOSE). The return of KARL BURNS for the disappointing 'MIDDLE CLASS REVOLT' (Top 50, 1994) and BRIX for the bittersweet 'CEREBRAL CAUSTIC' (Top 75, 1995), did little to rectify this change in commercial climate. Now signed to 'Jet' records (once home to ELO!), they added JULIA NAGLE and a few guest members to the fold for their next effort, 'THE LIGHT USER SYNDROME' (1996), gaining some critical respect once again, as well as brief chart action. Returning early '98 on 'Artful' records with 'LEVITATE', MARK E and his crew seemed a tad "lost in music", the album being under par for once. Evidently, their had been friction between him and his "employees", three of them (STEVE HANLEY, KARL BURNS and guitarist TOMMY CROOKS) subsequently bailing out after the frontman became "impossible" to work with. Unperturbed, MARK E talked about a spoken-word album, 'THE POST NEARLY MAN', while the DOSE track, 'INCH' (a No.7 in John Peel's 1997 Festive 50), finally hit the shops early in '99. The FALL (Mk.1998/99) were back soon after, NAGLE standing by her man while newcomers NEVILLE WILDING, TOM HEAD and ADAM HALAL (the former two both session men on the last set – ADAM replaced KAREN LATHAM) were beginning to "fall" into place. That Spring, album number thirty odd, 'THE MARSHALL SUITE', was dispatched to the shops and although it was a slight improvement the record found no new fans in the way of sales. Never far from the music biz tabloids, MARK E appeared (as a janitor!) in the low-budget movie, 'Glow Boys', while he collaborated with the CLINT BOON EXPERIENCE (ex-INSPIRAL CARPETS man) on the track, 'I Wanna Be Your Dog'. • Other covers: A DAY IN THE LIFE (Beatles) / LEGEND OF XANADU (Dave Dee, Beaky, Mick and Tich) / SHUT UP! (Monks) / JUNK MAN (McFree) / WAR (Slapp Happy) / I'M NOT SATISFIED (Frank Zappa) / JUST WAITING (Hank Williams) / ROADHOUSE (John Barry) / STAY AWAY (OLD WHITE TRAIN) (Johnny Paycheck) / LAST CHANCE TO TURN AROUND (hit; Gene Pitney) / JUNGLE ROCK (Hank Mizell) / THIS PERFECT DAY (Saints) / F-'OLDIN' MONEY (Tommy Blake). • Trivia: MARK E. featured on TACKHEAD b-side of 'Dangerous Sex' in mid 1990, alongside ADRIAN SHERWOOD and GARY CLAIL. Just previous to this, he had a solo track 'ERROR-ORROR I' for the Various Artists compilation 'HOME'.

Album rating: LIVE AT THE WITCH TRIALS (*9) / DRAGNET (*8) / THE FALL LIVE – TOTALE'S TURNS (IT'S NOW OR NEVER) (*6) / GROTESQUE (AFTER THE GRAMME) (*7) / SLATES (*6) / EARLY YEARS 77-79 compilation (*7) / HEX ENDUCTION HOUR (*7) / ROOM TO LIVE (*6) / PERVERTED BY LANGUAGE (*7) / THE WONDERFUL AND FRIGHTENING WORLD OF . . . (*7) / HIP PRIESTS & KAMERADS compilation (*6) / THIS NATION'S SAVING GRACE (*8) / BEND SINISTER (*7) / IN PALACE OF SWORDS REVERSED collection (*6) / THE FRENZ EXPERIMENT (*6) / I AM KURIOUS, ORANJ (*7) / SEMINAL LIVE (*4) / 458489 A-SIDES compilation (*8) / 458489 B-SIDES compilation (*7) / EXTRICATE (*8) / SHIFT-WORK (*8) / CODE: SELFISH (*7) / THE INFOTAINMENT SCAN (*8) / MIDDLE CLASS REVOLT (*6) / CELEBRAL CAUSTIC (*6) / THE TWENTY-SEVEN POINTS (*5) / THE LIGHT USER SYNDROME (*7) / LEVITATE (*6) / THE MARSHALL SUITE (*7)

MARK E. SMITH (b. MARK EDWARD SMITH, 5 Mar'57) – vocals / **TONY FRIEL** – bass / **MARTIN BRAMAH** – guitar / **UNA BAINES** – electric piano / **KARL BURNS** – drums

		Step Forward	I.R.S.
Jun 78.	(7"ep) (SF 7) **BINGO-MASTERS BREAK-OUT!** – Psycho Mafia / Bingo-Master / Repitition.	☐	-

`——` **MARC RILEY** – bass repl. (ERIC AND JOHNNIE BROWN) who had repl. FRIEL (He formed The PASSAGE) / **YVONNE PAWLETT** – keyboards repl. BAINES who formed BLUE ORCHIDS

Nov 78.	(7") (SF 9) **IT'S THE NEW THING. / VARIOUS TIMES**	☐	-
Jan 79.	(lp) (SFLP 1) <SP 003> **LIVE AT THE WITCH TRIALS** – Frightened / Crap rap 2 – Like to blow / Rebellious jukebox / No Xmas for John Quays / Mother-sister! / Industrial estate / Underground medecin / Two steps back / Live at the Witch Trials / Futures and pasts / Music scene. (cd-iss. Jun97 on 'Cog Sinister – Voiceprint'; COGVP 103CD) <US cd-iss. 1997 on 'Resurgent'; 4107>	☐	☐

`——` **MARK E.** (now sole founder), RILEY (now guitar) and **PAWLETT** recruited **STEVE HANLEY** (b.20 May'59, Dublin, Ireland) – bass repl. BRAMAH who also joined BLUE ORCHIDS / **MIKE LEIGH** – drums repl. BURNS who also joined The PASSAGE and P.I.L.

Jul 79.	(7") (SF 11) **ROWCHE RUMBLE. / IN MY AREA**	☐	-

`——` **CRAIG SCANLON** (b. 7 Dec'60) – guitar (RILEY now guitar, keyboards) repl. PAWLETT

Oct 79.	(lp) (SFLP 4) **DRAGNET** – Psykick dancehall / A figure walks / Printhead / Dice man / Before the Moon	☐	-

falls / Your heart out / Muzorewi's daughter / Flat of angles / Choc-stock / Spectre vs. rector / Put away. (re-iss. Dec90 lp/cd; SFAL/SPLPCD 4)

Jan 80. (7") (SF 13) **FIERY JACK. / SECOND DARK AGE / PSYKICK DANCEHALL II**

Rough Trade | not iss.

May 80. (lp) (ROUGH 10) **THE FALL LIVE – TOTALE'S TURNS (IT'S NOW OR NEVER) (live)**
– (intro) / Fiery Jack / Rowche rumble / Muzorewi's daughter / In my area / Choc-stock / Spectre vs. rector 2 / That man / New puritan / No Xmas for John Quays. (cd-iss. Nov92 on 'Dojo'; DOJOCD 83)

—— **PAUL HANLEY** – drums repl. LEIGH

Jun 80. (7") (RT 048) **HOW I WROTE ELASTIC MAN. / CITY HOBGOBLINS**

Sep 80. (7") (RT 056) **TOTALLY WIRED. / PUTTA BLOCK**

—— **KAY CARROLL** their manager augmented p/t on backing vocals, kazoo

Nov 80. (lp) (ROUGH 18) **GROTESQUE (AFTER THE GRAMME)**
– Pay your rates / English scheme / New face in Hell / C'n'c Smithering / The container drivers / Impression of J. Temperance / In the park / W.M.C. – Blob 59 / Gramme Friday / The N.W.R.A. (<cd-iss. Sep93 on 'Castle'; CLACD 391>) (cd re-iss. Jun98 on 'Essential'; ESMCD 640)

Apr 81. (10"m-lp) (RT 071) **SLATES**
– Middle mass / An older lover etc. / Prole art threat / Fit and working again / Slates, slags, etc. / Leave the capitol.

—— **KARL BURNS** – drums returned now alongside **SMITH, RILEY, SCANLON, S and P HANLEY**

Kamera | not iss.

Nov 81. (7") (ERA 001) **LIE DREAM OF A CASINO SOUL. / FANTASTIC LIFE**

Mar 82. (lp) (KAM 005) **HEX ENDUCTION HOUR** `71`
– The classical / Jaw-bone and the air-rifle / Hip priest / Fortress – Deer park / Mere psued mag. ed / Winter / Winter 2 / Just step s'ways / Who makes the Nazis? / Iceland / And this day. (re-iss. 1987 on 'Line'; LILP 400126) (<cd-iss. Sep89 & Mar98; LICD 900126>)

Apr 82. (7") (ERA 004) **LOOK KNOW. / I'M INTO C.B.**

Nov 82. (lp) (KAM) **ROOM TO LIVE**
– Joker hysterical face / Marquee cha-cha / Hard life in the country / Room to live / Detective instinct / Solicitor in studio / Papal visit. (re-iss. Oct87 on 'Line'; LILP 400109) (cd-iss. Apr98 on 'Cog Sinister'; COGVP 105CD) <US cd-iss. 1998 on 'Resurgent'; 4257>

—— reverted to quintet when RILEY left to form MARC RILEY & THE CREEPERS (note that their manager and p/t member KAY CARROLL also departed)

Rough Trade | not iss.

Jun 83. (7") (RT 133) **THE MAN WHOSE HEAD EXPANDED. / LUDD GANG**

Oct 83. (d7") (RT 143) **KICKER CONSPIRACY. // WINGS / CONTAINER DRIVERS (live) / NEW PURITANS (live)**

—— added **LAURA-ELISE** (now BRIX E. SMITH) (b. California, USA) – guitar, vocals (ex-BANDA DRATSING) P. HANLEY added keyboards and BURNS added lead bass to their repertoire

Dec 83. (lp/c) (ROUGH/+C 62) **PERVERTED BY LANGUAGE**
– Eat y'self fitter / Neighbourhood of infinity / Garden / Hotel Bloedel / I feel voxish / Tempo house / Hexen definitive / Strife knot. (re-iss. Oct87 on 'Line'; LILP 400116) (cd-iss. Sep89+=; LICD 900116) – Oh! brother / God-box / C.R.E.E.P. / Pat-trip dispenser. (<cd re-iss. Sep93 on 'Castle'; CLACD 392>) (cd re-iss. Feb98 on 'Cog Sinister – Voiceprint'; COGVP 104CD) (cd re-iss. Jun98 on 'Essential'; ESMCD 639)

Beggars Banquet | Beggars Banquet

Jun 84. (7") (BEG 110) **OH BROTHER. / GOD-BOX**
(12"+=) (BEG 110T) – ('A'instrumental).

Aug 84. (7") (BEG 116) **C.R.E.E.P. / PAT-TRIP DISPENSER**
(12"green+=/12"s (BEG 116T/+P) – ('A'extended).

—— added **GAVIN FRIDAY** – some vocals (of VIRGIN PRUNES) (on next 2 releases)

Sep 84. (lp/c) (<BEGA/+C 58>) **THE WONDERFUL AND FRIGHTENING WORLD OF . . .** `62`
– Lay of the land / 2 x 4 / Copped it / Elves / Slang king / Bug day / Stephen song / Craigness / Disney's dream debased. (re-iss. Jul88 on 'Beggars Banquet' lp/c)(cd+= (BBL/+C 58)(BBL 58CD) – Oh! brother / Draygo's guilt / God-box / Clear off! / C.R.E.E.P. / Pat-trip dispenser / No bulbs.

Oct 84. (12"ep) (BEG 120E) **CALL FOR ESCAPE ROUTE**
– Draygo's Guilt / No bulbs / Clear Off!.
(with free-7") **NO BULBS 3. / SLANG KING**

—— **SIMON ROGERS** – bass, keyboards repl. P. HANLEY (he cont. with KISS THE BLADE) (GAVIN returned to VIRGIN PRUNES and S. HANLEY took a holiday)

Jul 85. (7") (BEG 134) **COULDN'T GET AHEAD. / ROLLIN' DANY**
(12"+=) (BEG 134T) – Petty (thief) lout.

—— **STEVE HANLEY** returned to join **MARK E., BRIX, CRAIG, KARL and SIMON**

Sep 85. (lp/c/cd) (<BEGA/BEGC 47)(BEGA 67CD)) **THIS NATION'S SAVING GRACE** `54`
– Mansion / Bombast / Barmy / What you need / Spoilt Victorian child / L.A. / Out of the quantifier / My new house / Paintwork / I am Damo Suzuki / To nkroachment: yarbles. (re-iss. Feb90 lp/c/(cd+=; BBL/+C 67)(BBL 67CD) – Vixen / Couldn't get ahead / Pretty (thief) lout / Rollin' Dany / Cruiser's creek.

Oct 85. (7") (BEG 150) **CRUISER'S CREEK. / L.A.**
(12"+=) (BEG 150T) – Vixen.

Jul 86. (7") (BEG 165) **LIVING TOO LATE. / HOT AFTER-SHAVE BOP**
(12"+=) (BEG 165T) – Living too long.

—— **JOHN SIMON WOOLSTENCROFT** (b.19 Jan'63, Altringham, England) – drums (ex-WEEDS) repl. BURNS who formed THIRST

Sep 86. (7") (BEG 168) **MR. PHARMICIST. / LUCIFER OVER LANCASHIRE** `75`
(12"+=) (BEG 168T) – Auto-tech pilot.

Oct 86. (lp/c) (BEGA/BEGC 75) **BEND SINISTER** `36`
– R.O.D. / Dktr. Faustus / Shoulder pads #1 / Mr. Pharmicist / Gross chapel – British grenadiers / U.S. 80's-90's / Terry Waite sez / Bournemouth runner / Riddler /

Shoulder pads #2. (cd-iss. Jan88+=; BEGA 75CD) – Living too late / Auto-tech pilot.

Nov 86. (7") (BEGA 176) **HEY! LUCIANI. / ENTITLED** `59`
(12"+=) (BEG 176T) – Shoulder pads.

Apr 87. (7") (BEG 187) **THERE'S A GHOST IN MY HOUSE. / HAF FOUND, BORMAN** `30`
(12"+=/c-s+=) (BEG 187 T/C) – Sleepdebt / Snatches / Mark'll sink us.

—— added **MARSHA SCHOFIELD** (b.1963, Brooklyn, N.Y.) – keyboards, vocals of ADULT NET, (ex-BANDA DRATSING)

Oct 87. (7"/7"pic-d/+P) **HIT THE NORTH. / (part 2)** `57`
(12"+=) (BEG 200T) – Australians in Europe.
(cd-s+=) (BEG 200C) – Northerns in Europe / (Hit the north versions).

—— reverted back to sextet of **MARK E., BRIX, CRAIG, JOHN S., STEVE** and **MARSHA** when **SIMON** became their producer and studio guitarist only

Jan 88. (7") (BEG 206) **VICTORIA. / TUFF LIFE BOOGIE** `35`
(12"+=) (BEG 206T) – Guest informant / Twister.

Mar 88. (lp/c)(cd) (BEGA/BEGC 91)(BEGA 91CD) <6987> **THE FRENZ EXPERIMENT** `19`
– Frenz / Carry bag man / Get a hotel / Victoria / Athlete cured / In these times / The steak place / Bremen nacht / Guest informant (excerpt) / Oswald defence lawyer. (c/cd+=) – Tuff life boogie / Guest informant / Twister / There's a ghost in my house / Hit the north (part 1).

Oct 88. (lp/c)(cd) (BEGA/BEGC 96)(BEGA 96CD) <9582> **I AM KURIOUS, ORANJ** `54`
– New big prinz / Overture from 'I Am Curious, Orange' / Dog is life – Jerusalem / Wrong place, right time / C.D. win fall 2088 ad / Yes, o yes / Van plague? / Bad news girl / Cab it up! / Last nacht * / Big new priest *. (c+=/cd+= *)

Nov 88. (d7"ep/d3"cd-ep) (FALL 2 B/CD) **JERUSALEM / ACID PRIEST 2088. / BIG NEW PRINZ / WRONG PLACE, RIGHT TIME** `59`

Jun 89. (7") (BEG 226) **CAB IT UP. / DEAD BEAT DESCENDENT (out take from ballet**
(12"+=) (BEG 226T) – Kurious oranj (live) / Hit the north (live).

Beggars Banquet – Lowdown | not iss.

Jun 89. (lp/c)(cd) (BBL/+C 102)(BBL 102CD) <9807> **SEMINAL LIVE (some studio)** `40`
– Dead beat descendant / Pinball machine / H.O.W. / Squid law / Mollusc in Tyrol / 2 x 4 / Elf prefix – L.A. / Victoria / Pay your rates / Cruiser's creek. (c+=/cd+=) – Kurious oranj / Hit the north / In these times / Frenz.

—— **MARTIN BRAMAH** – guitar returned to repl. BRIX E. who continued with ADULT NET.

Cog Sinister-Fontana | Fontana

Jan 90. (7"/c-s) (SIN/+MC 4) **TELEPHONE THING. / BRITISH PEOPLE IN HOT WEATHER** `58`
(12"+=)(cd-s+=) (SIN 4-12)(SINCD 4) – Telephone (dub).

Feb 90. (cd/c/lp) (<842204-2/-4/-1->) **EXTRICATE** `31`
– Sing! Harpy / I'm Frank / Bill is dead / Black monk theme part 1 / Popcorn double feature / Telephone thing / Hilary / Chicago, now! / The littlest rebel / British people in hot weather / And therein. (c+cd+=) – Arms control poseur / Black monk theme part II / Extricate.

Mar 90. (7"/c-s) (SIN/+MC 5) **POPCORN DOUBLE FEATURE. / BUTTERFLIES 4 BRAINS**
(12"+=) (SIN 5-12) – Arms control poseur.
(cd-s+=) (SINCD 5) – Zandra / Black monk theme part II.

—— trimmed to basic quartet of **MARK E, CRAIG, STEVE and JOHN.**

Aug 90. (7") (SIN 6) **WHITE LIGHTNING. / BLOOD OUTTA STONE** `56`
(12"+=) (SINR 6-12) – Zagreb.
(12"ep+=)(cd-ep+=) **THE DREDGER EP** (SIN 6-12)(SINCD 6) – Life just bounces.

Dec 90. (7") (SIN 7) **HIGH TENSION LINE. / XMAS WITH SIMON**
(12"+=)(cd-s+=) (SIN 7-12)(SINCD 7) – Don't take the pizza.

—— added guest **KENNY BRADY** – violin

Apr 91. (cd/c/lp) (<848594-2/-4/-1->) **SHIFT-WORK** `17`
– EARTH'S IMPOSSIBLE DAY :-So what about it? / Idiot joy showland / Edinburgh man / Pittsville direkt / The book of lies / High tension line / The war against intelligence! / NOTEBOOKS OUT PLAGIARISTS :-Shift-work / You haven't found it yet / The mixer / White lightning / A lot of wind / Rose / Sinister waltz.

—— **DAVID BUSH** (b. 4 Jun'59, Taplow, England) – keyboards, machines repl. BRADY

Mar 92. (7") (SINS 8) **FREE RANGE. / EVERYTHING HURTZ** `40`
(12"+=)(pic-cd-s+=) (SIN 8-12)(SINCD 8) – Dangerous / Return.

Mar 92. (cd/c/lp) (<512162-2/-4/-1->) **CODE: SELFISH** `21`
– The Birmingham school of business school / Free range / Return / Time enough at last / Everything hurtz / Immorality / Two-face! / Just waiting / So-called dangerous / Gentlemen's agreement / Married, 2 kids / Crew filth. (cd re-iss. Aug93)

Jun 92. (12"ep)(cd-ep) (SIN 9-12)(SINCD 9) **ED'S BABE / PUMPKIN HEAD XSCAPES / THE KNIGHT, THE DEVIL AND DEATH / ARID'S AL'S DREAM / FREE RANGER**

Permanent | Matador

Apr 93. (7") (SPERM 9) <OLE 053> **WHY ARE PEOPLE GRUDGEFUL? / GLAM-RACKET** `43`
(12"+=/cd-s+=) (12/CD SPERM 9) <OLE 054> – The re-mixer / Lost in music.

Apr 93. (cd/c/lp) (PERM CD/MC/LP 12) <OLE 055> **THE INFOTAINMENT SCAN** `9` May93
– Ladybird (green grass) / Lost in music / Glam-racket / I'm going to Spain / It's a curse / Paranoia man in cheap sh*t room / Service / The league of bald-headed men / A past gone mad / Light fireworks / League Moon monkey mix. (cd+=) – Why are people grudgeful?

—— added the returning **KARL BURNS** – percussion(now 6-piece yet again)

Dec 93. (d-cd-ep/d12"ep) (CD/12 SPERM 13) **BEHIND THE COUNTER EP** `75`
– Behind the counter / War / M5 / Happy holiday / Cab driver / (1).

—— Feb 94; MARK guested for INSPIRAL CARPETS on their single 'I Want You.'

Apr 94. (10"clear-ep/12"ep/cd-ep) (10/12/CD SPERM 14) <OLE 094> **15 WAYS. / HEY! STUDENT / THE $500 BOTTLE OF WINE** `65` May94

May 94. (cd/c/lp) *(PERM CD/MC/LP 18)* <OLE 095> **MIDDLE CLASS REVOLT (aka THE VAPOURISATION OF REALITY** [48] | Jul94
– 15 ways / The reckoning / Behind the counter / M5#1 / Surmount all obstacles / Middle class revolt! / You're not up to much / Symbol of Mordgan / Hey! student / Junk man / The $500 bottle of wine / City dweller / War / Shut up!.

—— added on tour the returning **BRIX SMITH**– guitar, vocals

Permanent Permanent

Feb 95. (cd/c/lp) *(<PERM CD/MC/LP 30>)* **CEREBRAL CAUSTIC** [67] | May95
– The joke / Don't call me darling / Rainmaster / Feeling numb / Pearl city / Life just bounces / I'm not satisfied / The aphid / Bonkers in Phoenix / One day / North west fashion show / Pine leaves.

Aug 95. (d-cd/d-c/d-lp) *(<PERM CD/MC/LP 36>)* **THE TWENTY-SEVEN POINTS (live)** | Sep95
– Mollusc in Tyrol / Return / Lady bird (green grass) / Idiot – Walk-out / Ten points / Idiot – Walk-out / Big new prinz / Intro: Roadhouse / The joke / ME's jokes / The British people in hot weather / Free range / Hi-tension line / The league of the bald headed men / Glam racket: Star / Lost in music / Mr. Pharmacist / Cloud of black / Paranoia man in cheap shit room / Bounces / Outro / Passable / Glasgow advice / Middle class revolt: Simon, Dave and John / Bill is dead / Strychnine / War! / Noel's chemical effluence / Three points – Up too much.

—— added **JULIA NAGLE** – keyboards, guitar / + 7th member **LUCY RIMMER** – vocals / **MIKE BENNETT** – vocals, co-producer (to MARK E., BRIX, SIMON, STEPHEN + KARL)

Jet   Jet

Feb 96. (12"ep/c-ep/cd-ep) *(JET/+MC/SCD 500)* **THE CHISELERS / CHILINIST. / INTERLUDE / CHILINISM** [60] | -

—— MARK E. worked with DOSE on their single 'PLUG MYSELF IN', released on Pete Waterman's new label 'Coliseum'!

Jun 96. (cd/c/lp) *(<JET CD/MC/LP 1012>)* **THE LIGHT USER SYNDROME** [54] |
– D.I.Y. meat / Das vulture ans ein nutter-wain / He Pep! / Hostile / Stay away (old white train) / Spinetrak / Interlude – Chilinism / Powder keg / Oleano / Cheetham Hill / The Coliseum / Last chance to turn around / The ballard of J. Drummer / Oxymoron / Secession man.

Artful   Artful

Feb 98. (10"ep/cd-ep) *(10/CD ARTFUL 1)* **MASQUERADE. / IVANHOES TWO PENCE / SPENCER MUST DIE / TEN HOUSES OF EVE** [69] | -
(cd-ep) *(CXARTFUL 001)* – ('A'side) / Calendar / Scareball / Ol' gang (live)

Feb 98. (cd/c/lp) *(<ARTFUL CD/MC/LP 9>)* **LEVITATE**
– Ten houses of Eve / Masquerade / Hurricane Edward / I'm a mummy / Quartet of Doc Shanley / Jap kid / 4 1/2 inch / Spencer must die / Jungle rock / Ol' gang / Tragic days / I come and stand at your door / Levitate / Everybody but myself.

—— **SMITH** retained **NAGLE** and recruited **NEVILLE WILDING** – guitar + **TOM HEAD** – drums

—— **ADAM HALAL** – bass; repl. temp. KAREN LATHAM

Mar 99. (12"/cd-s) *(12/CD ARTFUL 2)* **TOUCH SENSITIVE. /** | -
Apr 99. (cd/c/lp) *(<ARTFUL CD/MC/LP 17>)* **THE MARSHALL SUITE** | Oct99
– Touch sensitive / F-'oldin' money / Snake-off / This perfect day / (Jung Nev's) Antidotes / Inevitable / Anecdotes + anecdotes in B# / Early life of crying Marshal / Birthday song / Mad. men-eng, dog / On my own.

Aug 99. (cd-s) *(CDARTFUL 3)* **F-'OLDIN' MONEY / THIS PERFECT DAY (remix) / BIRTHDAY SONG (remix)** | -
(cd-s) *(CDXARTFUL 3)* – ('A'side) / The early life of the crying marshal (remix) / Tom Raggazzi (remix).

– compilations, etc. –

Sep 81. (lp) *Step Forward; (ROUGH 18)* **77-EARLY YEARS-79** | -
Mar 82. (c) *Chaos; (LIVE 006)* **LIVE AT ACKLAM HALL, LONDON 1980** | -
(cd-iss. Jan96 as 'THE LEGENDARY CHAOS TAPES'; SAR 1005) (cd re-iss. Jul97 on 'Cog Sinister – Voiceprint'; COGVP 101CD)
Nov 82. (lp) *Cottage;* **A PART OF AMERICA THEREIN** | -
Nov 83. (7") *Kamera; (KAM 014)* **MARQUEE CHA-CHA. / ROOM TO LIVE // (PAPAL VISIT original b-side)** | -
Mar 85. (lp/c) *Situation 2; (SIT U/C 13)* **HIP PRIESTS AND KAMERADS** | -
(81-82 material)
(c+=) – (has 4 extra tracks) (cd-iss. Mar88+= same 4; SITU 13CD) (re-iss. 1988 on 'Situation 2-Lowdown' lp/c)(cd+=; SITL/+C 13)(SITU 13CD) (cd re-iss. Sep95 on 'Beggars Banquet')
May 87. (12"ep/c-ep) *Strange Fruit; (<SFPF/SFPSC 028>)* **THE PEEL SESSIONS (28.11.78)** | 1991
– Put away / No Xmas for John Quay / Like to blow / Mess of my.
Nov 87. (cd/c/lp) *Cog Sinister; (CD/C+/COG 1)* **IN PALACE OF SWORDS REVERSED (80-83)** | -
Sep 90. (cd)(lp/c) *Beggars Banquet; (BEGA 111CD)(BEGA/+C 111)* <2430> **458489** ('A'sides; 1984-89) [47] |
– Oh! brother / C.R.E.E.P. / No bulbs 3 / Rollin' Dany / Couldn't get ahead / Cruiser's creek / L.A. / Living too late / Hit the north (part 1) / Mr. Pharmacist / Hey! Luciani / There's a ghost in my house / Victoria / Big new prinz / Wrong place, right time No.2 / Jerusalem / Dead beat descendant. // God-box / Pat-trip dispenser / Slang king 2 / Draygo's guilt / Clear off! / No bulbs / Petty thief lout / Vixen / Hot aftershave bop / Living too long / Lucifer over Lancashire / Auto tech pilot / Entitled / Shoulder pads #1 / Sleep debt snatches / Mark'll sink us / Haf found Bormann / Australians in Europe / Northerns in Europe / Hit the north (part 2) / Guest informant / Tuff life boogie / Twister / Acid priest 2088 / Cab it up. <US cd re-iss. 1994 on 'Atlantic'; 92380>
Dec 90. (cd)(d-lp/c) *Beggars Banquet; (BEGA 116CD)(BEGA/+C 116)* <2430> **458489** (B'sides; 1984-89) |
– God-box / Pat-trip dispenser / Slang king 2 / Draygo's guilt / Clear off! / No bulbs / Petty thief lout / Vixen / Hot aftershave bop / Living too long / Lucifer over Lancashire / Auto tech pilot / Entitled / Shoulder pads £1 / Sleep debt snatches / Mark'll sink us / Haf found Bormann / Australians in Europe / Northerns in Europe / Hit the north (part 2) / Guest informant / Tuff life boogie / Twister / Acid priest 2088 / Cab it up. (cd+=) – Bremen nache run out / Mark'll sink us (live) / Kurious oranj. <US cd re-iss. 1994 on 'Atlantic'; 92474>

Mar 93. (7"ep/cd-ep) *Strange Fruit; (SFPS/SFPCD 087) / Dutch East India; <8355>* **KIMBLE** | -
– Kimble / C'n'c hassle schmuk / Spoilt Victorian child / Words of expectation.
Apr 93. (cd) *Castle; (CCSCD 365)* **THE COLLECTION** | -
Aug 93. (m-cd) *Windsong; (WINCD 038) / Griffin; <404>* **BBC RADIO 1 LIVE IN CONCERT** | -
Feb 94. (cd) *Loma; (LOMACD 10)* **SLATES / PART OF AMERICA IN THERIN 1981** | -
Aug 94. (cd) *Matador; <62>* **THE LEAGUE OF BALD HEADED MEN** | -
Feb 96. (cd) *Receiver; (<RRCD 209>)* **SINISTER WALTZ** | -
Apr 96. (cd) *Receiver; (<RRCD 211>)* **FIEND WITH A VIOLIN** | -
Apr 96. (cd/lp) *Receiver; (<RRCD/RRLP 213>)* **OSWALD DEFENCE LAWYER** | -
Oct 96. (3xcd-box) *Receiver; (<RRXCD 506>)* **THE OTHER SIDE OF THE FALL** (above 3 albums) | -
Apr 97. (d-cd) *Cog Sinister – Voiceprint; (COGVP 102CD)* **FALL IN A HOLE** | -
(was originally a New Zealand release on 'Flying Nun') (re-iss. Nov97 on 'Resurgence'; RSG 4016)
Jun 97. (d-cd) *Snapper; (<SMDCD 132>)* **THE LESS YOU LOOK THE MORE YOU FIND** | -
Aug 97. (cd) *Receiver; (RRCD 239)* **15 WAYS TO LEAVE YOUR MAN (live)** | -
Nov 97. (cd) *Receiver; (<RRCD 246>)* **OXYMORON** | -
Nov 97. (cd) *Rialto; (<RMCD 214>)* **THE FALL ARCHIVES** | -
Dec 97. (cd) *Receiver; (<RRCD 247>)* **CHEETHAM HILL** | -
Mar 98. (cd) *Strange Fruit; (SFRSCD 048)* **THE PEEL SESSIONS** | -
Mar 98. (cd) *Castle; (CCSCD 823)* **SMILE . . . IT'S THE BEST OF THE FALL** | -
Apr 98. (cd) *Cog Sinister – Voiceprint; (COGVP 108CD)* **LIVE ON AIR IN MELBOURNE 1982 (live)** | -
Jun 98. (cd) *M.C.I.; (MCCD 350)* **NORTHERN ATTITUDE** | -
Jun 98. (cd) *Artful; (ARTFULCD 3)* **IN THE CITY (live in Manchester 1995)** | -
Aug 98. (cd) *Cog Sinister – Voiceprint; (COGVP 111CD)* **LIVE VARIOUS YEARS (live)** | -

FAMILY

Formed: Leicester, England . . . 1967 by CHARLIE WHITNEY, ROGER CHAPMAN, JIM KING and RIC GRECH. They had stemmed from The FARINAS, a band who existed for 5 years and who issued one single in 1964 for 'Fontana'; 'YOU'D BETTER STOP / I LIKE IT LIKE THAT'. After moving to London, the band made their debut at The Royal Albert Hall in July '67 supporting TIM HARDIN. Signing to 'Reprise' in 1968, following a one-off 7" for 'Liberty', TRAFFIC's DAVE MASON & JIMMY MILLER produced the debut album, 'MUSIC FROM A DOLL'S HOUSE', which made the UK Top 40. CHAPMAN's unmistakable, frog-in throat vocal style, complemented by WHITNEY's distinctive guitar and GRECH's violin, created an enduring classic and soon marked the band out as cult favourites. The follow-up, 'ENTERTAINMENT', included 'WEAVER'S ANSWER', a song which went on to become a staple of the band's infamous live show. Soon after the album's release, GRECH departed for BLIND FAITH, being replaced by JOHN WEIDER. The band also recruited POLI PALMER on keyboards in place of saxophonist KING before releasing two Top 10 albums within a year, 'A SONG FOR ME' & 'ANYWAY'. Unusually for a prog-rock outfit, FAMILY were no strangers to hit singles, the classic 'IN MY OWN TIME' (from 'ANYWAY') reaching No.4, following on from the memorable successes 'NO MULES FOOL' and 'STRANGE BAND'. During the next three years the band went through yet more personnel shifts, perhaps accounting for the inconsistency of their last two albums. While 'FEARLESS' was quite impressive, 'BANDSTAND' was patchy, although it did spawn one of their last hits, 'BURLESQUE'. FAMILY then moved to the 'Raft' label where they recorded their final, slightly disappointing effort, 'IT'S ONLY A MOVIE', in 1973. The album was a complete flop and the band broke up, CHAPMAN and WHITNEY going on to form the more basic STREETWALKERS. CHAPMAN has released numerous solo albums, beginning with 'CHAPPO' in '79. Included on these albums were a number of covers:- LET'S SPEND THE NIGHT TOGETHER (Rolling Stones) / I'M YOUR HOOCHIE COOCHIE MAN + THAT SAME THING (Willie Dixon) / KEEP A KNOCKIN' (Little Richard) / I'M A KING BEE (Sam Moore) / STONE FREE (Jimi Hendrix) / LOVE LETTERS IN THE SAND (Pat Boone?) / SLOW DOWN (Hank Williams) / BUSTED LOOSE (Paul Brady) / KEEP FORGETTING (Leiber-Stoller) / TALKING ABOUT YOU (Chuck Berry).

Album rating: MUSIC IN A DOLL'S HOUSE (*8) / ENTERTAINMENT (*7) / A SONG FOR ME (*6) / ANYWAY (*6) / OLD SONGS NEW SONGS remixes (*7) / FEARLESS (*7) / BANDSTAND (*6) / IT'S ONLY A MOVIE (*4) / THE BEST OF FAMILY compilation (*9) / Streetwalkers: STREETWALKERS (*4) / DOWNTOWN FLYERS (*4) / RED CARD (*5) / VICIOUS BUT FAIR (*4) / LIVE (*4) / THE BEST OF STREETWALKERS compilation (*5) / Roger CHAPMAN: CHAPPO (*5) / LIVE IN HAMBURG (*5) / MAIL ORDER MAGIC (*4) / HYENAS ONLY LAUGH FOR FUN (*4) / HE WAS SHE WAS YOU WAS WE WAS (*4) / MANGO CRAZY (*4) / THE SHADOW KNOWS (*5) / ZIPPER (*4) / TECHNO-PRISONERS (*4) / WALKING THE CAT (*5) / HYBRID AND LOWDOWN (*5) / UNDER NO OBLIGATION (*4) / KICK IT BACK compilation (*6) / KISS MY SOUL (*4)

ROGER CHAPMAN (b. 8 Apr'44) – vocals / **CHARLIE WHITNEY** (b. 4 Jun'44) – guitar, vocals / **JIM KING** (b.1945) – saxophone, flute / **RICK GRECH** (b. 1 Nov'46, Bordeaux, France) – bass / **HARRY OVENALL** – drums

		Liberty	not iss.
Sep 67.	(7") *(LBF 15031)* **SCENE THRU THE EYE OF A LENS. / GYPSY WOMAN**	☐	-

—— **ROB TOWNSEND** (b. 7 Jul'47) – drums repl. HARRY

		Reprise	Reprise
Jun 68.	(7") *(RS 23270)* **ME AND MY FRIEND. / HEY MR. POLICEMAN**	☐	☐
Jul 68.	(7") *<0786>* **OLD SONGS NEW SONGS. / HEY MR. POLICEMAN**	-	☐
Jul 68.	(lp; mono/stereo) *(<RLP/RSLP 6312>)* **MUSIC IN A DOLL'S HOUSE**		35

– The chase / Mellowing grey / Never like this / Me and my friend / Variation on a theme of Hey Mr. Policeman / Winter / Old songs new songs / Variation on a theme of the breeze / Hey Mr. Policeman / See through windows / Variation on a theme of me and my friend / Peace of mind / Voyage / The breeze / 3 x time. *(re-iss. Sep87 on 'See For Miles' lp/c/cd; SEE/+K/CD 100)*

| Nov 68. | (7") *(RS 23315)* *<0809>* **SECOND GENERATION WOMAN. / HOME TOWN** | ☐ | ☐ |
| Mar 69. | (lp; mono/stereo) *(<RLP/RSLP 6340>)* **FAMILY ENTERTAINMENT** | | 6 |

– The weaver's answer / Observations from a hill / Hung up down / Summer '67 / How-hi-the-li / Second generation woman / From past archives / Dim / Processions / Face in the crowd / Emotions. *(re-iss. Sep87 on 'See For Miles' lp/c/cd; SEE/+K/CD 200)*

—— **JOHN WEIDER** (b.21 Apr'47) – bass, violin (ex-ERIC BURDON & ANIMALS) repl. GRECH who joined BLIND FAITH

| Oct 69. | (7") *(RS 27001)* *<0881>* **NO MULE'S FOOL. / GOOD FRIEND OF MINE** | 29 | ☐ |

—— **POLI PALMER** (b. JOHN, 25 May'43) – keyboards, vibes (ex-ECLECTION) repl. KING who joined RING OF TRUTH

| Jan 70. | (lp) *(RSLP 9001)* *<6384>* **A SONG FOR ME** | 4 | |

– Drowned in wine / Some poor soul / Love is a sleeper / Stop for the traffic (through the heart of me) / Wheels / Song for sinking lovers / Hey let it rock / The cat and the rat / 93's ok J. / A song for me. *(re-iss. Nov88 on 'See For Miles' lp/cd; SEE/+CD 240) (cd re-iss. Nov93 on 'Castle'; CLACD 376)*

| Apr 70. | (7") *(RS 27005)* **TODAY. / SONG FOR SINKING LOVERS** | ☐ | ☐ |
| Aug 70. | (7"m) *(RS 27009)* **STRANGE BAND. / THE WEAVER'S ANSWER / HUNG UP DOWN** | 11 | |

		Reprise	U.A.
Nov 70.	(lp) *(RSX 9005)* *<5527>* **ANYWAY . . .** (half live)	7	☐

– Good news bad news / Holding the compass / Strange band / Willow tree / Part of the load / Anyway / Normans / Lives and Ladies. *(re-iss. Nov88 on 'See For Miles' lp/cd; SEE/+CD 245) (re-iss. cd May94 on 'Castle'; CLACD 375)*

| Mar 71. | (lp) *(RMP 9007)* *<6413>* **OLD SONGS NEW SONGS** (compilation remixed) | ☐ | ☐ |

– Hung up down / Today / Observations from a hill / Good friend of mine / Drowned in wine / Peace of mind / Home town / The cat and the rat / No mule's fool / See through windows / The weaver's answer. *(cd-iss. Mar92 on 'See For Miles' SEECD 334)*

| Jun 71. | (7") *(K 14090)* *<50832>* **IN MY OWN TIME. / SEASONS** | 4 | ☐ |

—— **JOHN WETTON** (b.12 Jul'49, Derby, England) – bass, vocals (ex-MOGUL THRASH) repl. WEIDER who joined STUD

| Oct 71. | (lp) *(K 54003)* *<5562>* **FEARLESS** | 14 | ☐ |

– Between blue and me / Sat'd'y barfly / Larf and sing / Spanish tide / Save some for thee / Take your partners / Children / Crinkly grin / Blind / Burning bridges. *(re-iss. cd May94 on 'Castle';)*

Nov 71.	(7") *<50882>* **BETWEEN BLUE AND ME. / LARF & SING**	-	☐
Sep 72.	(7") *(K 14196)* *<50951>* **BURLESQUE. / THE ROCKIN' R's**	13	☐
Sep 72.	(lp) *(K 54006)* *<5644>* **BANDSTAND**	15	☐

– Burlesque / Bolero babe / Coronation / Dark eyes / Broken nose / My friend the sun / Glove / Ready to go / Top of the hill. *(re-iss. Nov88 on 'See For Miles' lp/cd; SEE/+CD 241) (cd re-iss. Mar94 on 'Castle'; CLACD 322)*

| Jan 73. | (7") *(K 14218)* *<171>* **MY FRIEND THE SUN. / GLOVE** | ☐ | ☐ |

—— CHAPMAN, WHITNEY and TOWNSEND were joined by **JIM CREGAN** – bass, guitar (ex-STUD) repl. WETTON who joined KING CRIMSON / **TONY ASHTON** (b. 1 Mar'46, Blackburn, England) – keyboards (ex-ASHTON, GARDNER and DYKE) repl. PALMER

		Raft	U.A.
Apr 73.	(7") *(RA 18501)* **BOOM BANG. / STOP THIS CAR**	☐	☐
Sep 73.	(7") *(RA 18503)* **SWEET DESIREE. / DRINK TO YOU**	☐	☐
Sep 73.	(lp) *(RA 58501)* *<UALA 181>* **IT'S ONLY A MOVIE**	30	☐

– It's only a movie / Leroy / Buffet tea for two / Boom bang / Boots 'n' roots / Banger / Sweet Desiree / Suspicion / Check out.

| Oct 73. | (7") *<416>* **IT'S ONLY A MOVIE. / SUSPICION** | - | ☐ |

—— They split late '73 with TOWNSEND joining MEDICINE HEAD and CREGAN went to COCKNEY REBEL, ASHTON went into production. ROGER and CHARLIE formed CHAPMAN / WHITNEY STREETWALKERS, who released a number of albums before ROGER went solo in 1979 (see GREAT ROCK DISCOGRAPHY)

– compilations, etc. –

on 'Reprise' UK, or 'United Artists' in the States

| Sep 74. | (lp) *Reprise; (K 54023)* **THE BEST OF FAMILY** | ☐ | - |

– Burlesque / My friend the Sun / The chase / Old songs, new songs / Part of the load / In my own time / It's only a movie / Sweet desiree / Sat'd'y barfly / Children / No mule's fool / The weaver's answer. *(re-iss. Nov91 on 'See For Miles' lp/cd+=; SEE/+CD 330) (cd re-iss. Jul94 on 'Line'; CRCD 901238)*

Nov 74.	(7") *(K 14378)* **MY FRIEND THE SUN. / BURLESQUE**	☐	-
May 78.	(7"ep) *(K 14487)* **BURLESQUE. / IN MY OWN TIME / THE WEAVER'S ANSWER**	☐	☐
Oct 81.	(lp) *Rebecca; (BEC 777)* **RISE . . . VERY BEST OF FAMILY**	☐	
Jan 82.	(7") *Rebecca; (BECS 77)* **BURLESQUE. / MY FRIEND THE SUN**	☐	
Nov 88.	(12"ep/cd-ep) *Strange Fruit; (SFPS/+CD 061)* **THE PEEL SESSIONS** (8.5.73)	☐	☐
Aug 89.	(d-lp/d-c/d-cd) *That's Original; (TFO LP/MC/CD 22)* **IT'S ONLY A MOVIE / FEARLESS**	☐	

Oct 91.	(cd) *Windsong; (WINCD 001)* **BBC RADIO 1 LIVE IN CONCERT**	☐	-
Nov 92.	(cd) *Castle; (CCSCD 354)* **THE COLLECTION – THE SINGLES A's & B's**	☐	☐
Mar 93.	(cd/c) *Castle; (CCS CD/MC 374)* **THE BEST OF FAMILY**	☐	☐
Mar 93.	(cd) *Dutch East India; (DEI 8333-2)* **THE PEEL SESSIONS**	☐	☐

STREETWALKERS

ROGER CHAPMAN – vocals / **CHARLIE WHITNEY** – guitar / **BOBBY TENCH** – guitar, vocals (ex-JEFF BECK) / **PHILIP CHEN** – bass / **TIM HINKLEY** – keyboards / **MEL COLLINS** – saxophone, flute / **IAN WALLACE** – drums (both ex-KING CRIMSON)

		Reprise	Mercury
May 74.	(lp) *(K 54017)* *<SRMI 1060>* **STREETWALKERS**	☐	☐

– Parisienne high heels / Roxianna / Systematic stealth / Call ya / Creature feature / Sue and Betty Jean / Showbiz Joe / Just four men / Tokyo rose / Hangman.

| Jun 74. | (7") *(K 14357)* **ROXIANNA. / CRACK** | ☐ | - |

—— **JON PLOTEL** – bass (ex-CASABLANCA) repl. CHEN & HINKLEY (to sessions) / **NICKO McBAIN** – drums repl. WALLACE & COLLINS (to ALVIN LEE ⇒ TEN YEARS AFTER)

		Vertigo	Mercury
Oct 75.	(lp) *(6360 123)* **DOWNTOWN FLIER**	☐	☐

– Downtown flyers / Toenail draggin' / Raingame / Miller / Crawfish / Walking on waters / Gypsy moon / Burn it down / Ace o'spades.

| Oct 75. | (7") *(6059 130)* **RAINGAME. / MILLER** | ☐ | ☐ |
| May 76. | (red-lp) *(9102 010)* *<SRMI 1083>* **RED CARD** | 16 | |

– Run for cover / Me an' me horse an' me rum / Crazy charade / Daddy rolling stone / Roll up, roll up / Between us / Shotgun messiah / Decadence code. *(cd-iss. Aug91 on 'Repertoire'; REP 4147WP)*

| Jun 76. | (7") *(6059 144)* **DADDY ROLLING STONE. / HOLE IN YOUR POCKET** | ☐ | - |

—— CHAPMAN, WHITNEY + TENCH were joined by **MICKY FEAT** – bass / **DAVID DOWLE** – drums / **BRIAN JOHNSON** – keyboards (McBAIN joined PAT TRAVERS and later IRON MAIDEN

| Jan 77. | (lp) *<SRMI 1135>* **VICIOUS BUT FAIR** | ☐ | |

– Mama was mad / Chili con carne / Dice man / But you're beautiful / Can't come in / Belle star / Sam (maybe he can come to some arrangement) / Cross time woman. *(cd-iss. Aug92 on 'See For Miles'+=; SEECD 352)* – Downtown flyers / Gypsy Moon / Crawfish / Raingame / Crazy charade / Shotgun Messiah / Decadence code / Daddy rolling stone.

| Dec 77. | (d-lp) *(6641 703)* **LIVE** (live) | ☐ | - |

– Chilli con carne / Crazy charade / Walking on waters / Dice man / My friend the Sun / Toenail draggin' / Mama was mad / Me an' me horse an' me rum / Run for cover / Burlesque / Can't come in.

—— Had already split, TENCH and FEAT joined VAN MORRISON. JOHNSON and DOWLE joined DAVID COVERDALE'S WHITESNAKE.

– compilations, etc. –

| Dec 90. | (cd/c/lp) *Vertigo; (846661-2/-4/-1)* **THE BEST OF STREETWALKERS** | ☐ | - |
| Jun 94. | (cd) *Windsong; ()* **BBC RADIO 1 LIVE IN CONCERT** | ☐ | ☐ |

ROGER CHAPMAN

went solo, augmented by MICKEY JUPP

		Arista	Arista
Mar 79.	(lp/c) *(SPART/TC-SPART 1083)* **CHAPPO**	☐	☐

– Midnite child / Moth to a flame / Keep forgettin' / Shape of things / Face of stone / Who pulled the nite down / Always gotta pay in the end / Hang on to a dream / Pills / Don't give up. *(re-iss. 1988 on 'Maze' lp/cd; 604620/764630) (cd-iss. Jul92 on 'Castle' cd/c; CLACD/CLAMC 299) (cd re-iss. Mar99 on 'Essential'; ESMCD 678)*

| Mar 79. | (7") *(ARIST 244)* **MIDNITE CHILD. / MOTH TO A FLAME** | ☐ | ☐ |

		Acrobat	not iss.
May 79.	(7") *(BAT 5)* **WHO PULLED THE NIGHT DOWN. / SHORTLIST**	☐	-
Jul 79.	(7") *(BAT 9)* **LET'S SPEND THE NIGHT TOGETHER. / SHAPE OF THINGS**	☐	-
Dec 79.	(lp/c) *(ACT/TC-ACT 6)* **LIVE IN HAMBURG** (live w/ The SHORTLIST)	☐	-

– Moth to a flame / Keep forgettin' / Midnite child / Who pulled the nite down / Talking about you / Shortlist / Can't get in / Keep a knockin' / I'm your hoochie coochie man / Let's spend the night together. *(re-iss. 1988 on 'Maze' lp/cd; 604627/764635) (cd re-iss. Nov92 on 'Castle'; CLACD 320) (cd re-iss. Mar99 on 'Essential'; ESMCD 692)*

		B.B.C.	not iss.
Oct 80.	(7") *(RESL 85)* **SPEAK FOR YOURSELF. / SWEET VANILLA**	☐	-

—— with PALMER / HINKLEY / WHITEHORN

		Kamera	not iss.
Sep 81.	(lp) *(KAM 001)* **MAIL ORDER MAGIC**	☐	-

– Unknown soldier (can't get to Heaven) / He was, she was / Barman / Right to go / Duelling man / Making the same mistake / Another little hurt / Mail order magic / Higher ground / Ground floor. *(re-iss. 1988 on 'Maze' lp/cd; 604627/764636) (cd re-iss. Dec92 on 'Castle' cd/c; CLA CD/MC 301) (cd re-iss. Mar99 on 'Essential'; ESMCD 564)*

		Teldec	not iss.
Dec 81.	(lp) *(AS6/HCT4 24850)* **HYENAS ONLY LAUGH FOR FUN**	-	- German

– Prisoner / Hyenas only laugh for fun / Killing time / Want's nothing chained / The long goodbye / Goodbye (reprise) / Hearts on the floor / Step up – Take a bow / Jukebox mama. *(UK-iss.1988 on 'Maze' lp/cd; 604625/764626) (cd re-iss. Jun92 on 'Castle'; CLACD 305)*

		Polydor	not iss.
Oct 82.	(d-lp) *(2646 106)* **HE WAS SHE WAS YOU WAS WE WAS** (live)	-	- German

– Higher ground / Ducking down / Making the same mistake / Blood and sand / Medley:- I'm a king bee – That same thing – Face of stone / Hyeanas only laugh for fun / Prisoner / Medley:- Slow down – Common touch / Jukebox mama No.3 / He was, she was / Stone free / Bitches brew / Unknown soldier. *(UK-iss. 1988 on 'Maze' lp/cd; 084 624/854633) (cd re-iss. Apr94 on 'Castle'; CLACD 373)*

Mar 83. (lp) (on 'Instant'; 28532) **MANGO CRAZY** [-] [-] German
– Mango crazy / Toys: Do you? / I read your file / Los dos Bailadores / Blues breaker / Turn it up loud / Let me down / Hunt the man / Rivers run dry / I really can't go straight / Room service / Hegoshegoyougoamigo. *(re-iss. 1988 on 'Maze' lp/cd; 604623/764634) (cd-iss. Jun92 on 'Castle'; CLACD 304)*

—— (CHAPMAN provided vocals for MIKE OLDFIELD on single 'Shadow On The Wall')

Apr 84. (7") (POSP 683) **HOW HOW HOW. / HOLD THAT TIDE BACK** [ ] [-]
　　　　　R.C.A.　not iss.

May 85. (lp/c) (ZL/ZK 70482) **THE SHADOW KNOWS**
– Busted loose / Leader of men / Ready to roll / I think of you now / The shadow knows / How how how / Only love is in the red / Sweet vanilla / I'm a good boy now. *(cd-iss. 1988; ZD 70482) (cd-iss. cd Mar94 on 'Castle'; CLACD 370)*

1986. (lp/c/cd) (PL/PK/PD 70989) **ZIPPER** [-] [-] German
– Zipper / Running with the flame / On do die day / Never love a rolling stone / Let the beat get heavy / It's never too late to do-ron-ron / Woman of destiny / Hoodoo me up.

1987. (lp/cd) (PL/PD 71516) **TECHNO-PRISONERS** [-] [-] German
– The drum / Wild again / Techno-prisoner / Black forest / We will touch again / Run for your love / Slap bang in the middle / Who's been sleeping in my bed / Ball of confusion. *(re-iss. cd Mar94 on 'Castle'; CLACD 371)*
　　　　　Maze　not iss.

1989. (cd) (854632) **WALKING THE CAT** [-] [-] German
– Kick it back / Son of Red moon / Stranger than strange / Just a step away (let's go) / The fool / Walking the cat / J & D / Come the dark night / Hands off / Jivin' / Saturday night kick back. *(UK cd-iss. Nov93 on 'Castle'; CLACD 372)*

Nov 89. (m-lp) (604639) **LIVE IN BERLIN (live)**
– Shadow on the wall / Let me down / How how how / Mango crazy. *(cd-iss. Dec92 on 'Castle'; CLACD 313)*
　　　　　Essential　not iss.

1992. (cd/c) (ESM CD/MC 175) **KICK IT BACK** (compilation)
– Walking the cat / Cops in shades / House behind the sun / Chicken fingers / Kick it back / Son of red Moon / Someone else's clothes / Hideaway / Toys: Do you? / Hot night to rhumba / Stranger than strange / Just a step away (let's go) / Jesus and the Devil. *(re-iss. Aug96; same)*

May 96. (cd) (ESSCD 382) **KISS MY SOUL** [ ] [-]

– compilations, etc. –

Oct 98. (d-cd) *Essential; (ESDCD 665)* **THE BEST OF ROGER CHAPMAN** [ ] [-]

FAMILY CAT (dig out; Great Alt & Indie . . .)

FANATICS (see under ⇒ OCEAN COLOUR SCENE)

FARM

Formed: Liverpool, England . . . early '83 by PETE HOOTEN and STEVE GRIMES. They appeared on BBC2 TV's 'Oxford Road Show' where they met MADNESS frontman, SUGGS McPHERSON, who subsequently produced their 1984 debut 45, 'HEARTS AND MINDS'. The group struggled early on and ultimately suffered tragedy when drummer, ANDY McVANN, died in a car crash late in '86. Replacing him initially with MICK HANRATTY and later ROY BOULTER (KEITH MULLEN and CARL HUNTER also replaced MELVIN and PHILIP respectively), the group ploughed on, moving away from their overtly political, brassy DEXYS/REDSKINS fixation and adopting an ill-advised synth-orientated sound with the addition of keyboard player, BEN LEACH. The resulting single, 'BODY AND SOUL', was another flop and the band decided drastic measures were needed; initiating their own label, 'Produce', and securing the services of house guru TERRY FARLEY, they score a sizeable club hit (and a Top 60 chart placing) with a dancefloor friendly makeover of The Monkees' 'ALL TOGETHER NOW'. Finally, everything clicked into place; The FARM found themselves at the epicentre of the indie/dance "baggy" scene in 1990 with the unstoppable momentum of 'GROOVY TRAIN' and penned one of the scene's anthems in 'ALL TOGETHER NOW', both becoming massive UK Top 10 hits (even heartthrob, Mike Dixon – from scouse soap, Brookside, was seen sporting a FARM T-shirt!). By the release of a belated debut album proper, 'SPARTACUS', the following year, the scene was fading fast; hardly the most glamorous band in the world, The FARM had always been a favourite target for music press jibes, and the continual criticism certainly didn't help reverse the band's swift fall from grace. Though the album had gone straight in at No.1, surplus copies were to be found propping up record store bargain bins for the next three years. Despite a new deal with 'Sony' and a further UK Top 20 hit (an awful cover of The Human League's 'DON'T YOU WANT ME'), the insipid songwriting on 'LOVE SEE NO COLOUR' (1992) saw the album sink without trace. Even a third-time-lucky deal with 'Sire' couldn't halt the decline and the band after the failure of 1994's 'HULLABALOO' (which contained another cover, The Flamin' Groovies 'SHAKE SOME ACTION'). • **Miscellaneous:** In 1990, their live technician RAY TOOMEY, was jailed for 30 months for his part in the Risley Remand Centre rooftop protest.

Album rating: SPARTACUS (*6) / LOVE SEE NO COLOUR (*5) / HULLABALOO (*4) / PASTURES OLD AND NEW early compilation (*5)

PETE HOOTEN (b.28 Sep'62) – vocals / **STEVE GRIMES** (b. 4 Jun'62) – guitar / **JOHN MELVIN** – guitar / **PHILIP STRONGMAN** – bass / **ANDY McVANN** – drums / plus **TONY EVANS** – trombone / **GEORGE MAHER** – trumpet / **STEVE 'SNOWY' LEVY** – saxophone / **and occasional live JOE MUSKER** – percussion

Nov 84. (12"ep) (END 1) **HEARTS AND MINDS. / ('A'dub version) / INFORMATION MAN / SAME OLD STORY**
　　　　　Skysaw　not iss.
　　　　　[-]

Nov 85. (7") (PRA 1) **STEPS OF EMOTION. / MEMORIES**
(12") (PRAT 1) – ('A'side) / Power over me / No man's land / Better / Living for tomorrow.
　　　　　Admiralty　not iss.
　　　　　[-]

Sep 86. (7") (BLAZE 13) **SOME PEOPLE. / STANDING TOGETHER**
(12") (BLAZE 13T) – Sign of the times / The Moroccan.
　　　　　Fire　not iss.
　　　　　[ ] [-]

Oct 86. (lp) (REFIRE 3) **PASTURES OLD AND NEW** (compilation of sessions) [-]
– Hearts and minds / Information man / Same old story / Hearts and minds (dub) / Steps of emotion / Power over me / No man's land / Better / Worn out sayings / Some people / Little ol' wine drinker me. *(re-iss. Aug89;)*

—— (early '87) MICK HANRATTY – drums (on tour) repl. ANDY McVANN who died in a crash Dec86. Late 1987; ROY BOULTER (b. 2 Jul'64) – drums repl. HANRATTY and the horn section / KEITH MULLEN (DR. KEITH LOVE) (b.Bootle) – guitar repl. MELVIN / CARL HUNTER (b.14 Apr'65, Bootle, England) – bass repl. PHILLIP

—— (early '89) HOOTEN, GRIMES, HUNTER, MULLEN + BOULTER added BEN LEACH (b. 2 May'69) – keyboards
　　　　　Foresight　not iss.

Jul 89. (7") (FR 2301) **BODY AND SOUL. / COLONELS** [-]
(12") (FR 2301-12) – ('A'side) / Colonels and heroes / Stuck on you.
　　　　　Produce　Sire

Apr 90. (7"/ext.12") **STEPPING STONE (ghost dance mix). / FAMILY OF MAN** [58] [-]

Sep 90. (7"/c-s) (MILK 102/+C) **GROOVY TRAIN. / ('A'-3:30 a.m. mix)** [6] [-]
(ext.12"+=)(cd-s+=) (MILK 102T)(CDMILK 102) – ('A'-Bootle mix). (below featured PETE WYLIE; WAH!)

Nov 90. (7"/c-s) (MILK 103/+C) **ALL TOGETHER NOW. / ('A'-Terry Farley mix)** [4] [ ]
(12"+=)(cd-s+=) (MILK 103T)(CDMILK 103) – ('A'-Rocky & Diesel mix).

—— added guest backing vocalist PAULA DAVID

Mar 91. (cd/c/lp) (MILK CD/MC/LP 1) <26600> **SPARTACUS** [1] [ ] Apr91
– Hearts and minds / How long / Sweet inspiration / Groovy train / Higher and higher / Don't let me down / Family of man / Tell the story / Very emotional / All together now. *(initial copies, incl.free remix lp)*

Apr 91. (7"/c-s) (MILK 104/+C) **DON'T LET ME DOWN. / ('A' Terry Farley mix)** [36] [-]
(12"+=)(cd-s+=) (MILK 104T)(CDMILK 104) – ('A'-Rocky & Diesel mix).

Aug 91. (7"/c-s) (MILK 105/+C) **MIND. / STEPPING STONE** [31] [-]
(12"+=)(cd-s+=) (MILK 105T)(CDMILK 105) – ('A'new mix).

Sep 91. (c-s) <19209> **GROOVY TRAIN / STEPPING STONE** [-] [41]

Dec 91. (7"/c-s) (MILK 106/+C) **LOVE SEE NO COLOUR (Suggs mix). / ('A' Noel Watson mix)** [58] [-]

Perry FARRELL (see under ⇒ JANE'S ADDICTION)

FASTBALL

Formed: Austin, Texas, USA . . . 1995 by former punks, MILES ZUNIGA, JOEY SHUFFIELD and TONY SCALZO. The former two had been members of the short-lived alt-rock act, BIG CAR, who only managed one album, 'NORMAL', for the 'Giant' label in '92. After performing under the moniker MAGENTO U.S.A., the scuzzy country-pop merchants, FASTBALL's first album, 'MAKE YOUR MAMA PROUD', hit the bargain bins in '96. A second long-player, 'ALL THE PAIN MONEY CAN BUY' (1998) was a much zanier affair and surprised many by hitting the US Top 30, helped by the fact 'THE WAY' (imagine ABBA's 'Fernando' backwoods style) received an MTV playlisting and later became a minor UK hit.

Album rating: MAKE YOUR MAMA PROUD (*5) / ALL THE PAIN MONEY CAN BUY (*5)

BIG CAR

MILES ZUNIGA – vocals, guitar / **JOEY SHUFFIELD** – drums / + 2
　　　　　Giant-RCA Giant-RCA

May 92. (cd/c) <(7599 24443-2/-4)> **NORMAL** [ ] [ ]
– Tunnel of love / Rosalita / Venus / Get started / Mad all the world / Amazing contradictions / Cats / Day by day / Shut up / Easy street.

FASTBALL

—— ZUNIGA + SHUFFIELD added TONY SCALZO – vocals, bass
　　　　　Polydor　Hollywood

Apr 96. (cd/c) <162045-2/-4> **MAKE YOUR MAMA PROUD** [ ] [ ]
– Human torch / She come 'round / Make your mama proud / Back door / Are you ready for the fastball? / Nothing / Boomerang / Eater / Knock it down / Lender / Altamont / Emily / Telephone calls.

Sep 98. (7"/c-s) (569946-7/-4) **THE WAY. / ARE YOU READY FOR THE FALLOUT** [21] [-]
(cd-s+=) (569947-2) – Freeloader Freddy.
　　　　　Hollywood Hollywood

Oct 98. (cd/c) <(162130-2/-4)> **ALL THE PAIN MONEY CAN BUY** [29] Mar98
– The way / Fire escape / Better than it was / Which way to the top? / Sooner or later / Warm fuzzy feeling / Slow drag / G.O.D. (Good Old Days) / Charlie, the methadone man / Out of my head / Damaged goods / Nowhere road / Sweetwater, Texas.

Jun 99. (-) <radio cut> **OUT OF MY HEAD** [-] [20]

Jul 99. (c-s) *(0100949HWR)* <*567951*> **FIRE ESCAPE / THE WAY** (unpaved) (cd-s+=) *(0103385HWR)* – ('A'-versions).	☐	**86** Dec98

FATBOY SLIM (see under ⇒ COOK, Norman)

FAUST

Formed: Hamburg, Germany . . . 1970 by producer UWE NETTELBECK, who was given money to assemble a collective of musicians in his Wumme studios. These numbered RUDOLF SOSNA, HANS JOACHIM IRMLER, JEAN HERVE PERON, GUNTHER WUSTHOFF and ARNULF MEIFERT; the latter being replaced by RICHARD DIERMAYER in 1971. Following in the footsteps of CAN, TANGERINE DREAM and AMON DUUL II, they became an integral part of the burgeoning underground "krautrock" scene. Early recordings for 'Polydor', although strikingly innovative, failed to gain any widespread commercial appeal outside Germany. However, 'THE FAUST TAPES' (a 'Virgin' sampler of unreleased tunes) introduced them to the UK and sold a respectable quantity due to its 49p price-tag. This unfortunately disqualified it from chart returns. Inspired by a myriad of influences that took in everything from KARL-HEINZ STOCKHAUSEN to The BEATLES to The MOTHERS OF INVENTION, they left conventional song structures at the starting gate. Instead they opted for a continuous collage of musical set pieces which nevertheless had the potential to be great 3-minute songs. Alternately delighting and disgusting audiences, they were prone to playing pinball machines and wielding pneumatic drills on stage. They toured this bizarre spectacle around Europe after Richard Branson's 'Virgin' issued 'FAUST IV' while in 1974, they recorded an album with American minimalist TONY CONRAD (he had earlier been in The DREAM SYNDICATE; part of JOHN CALE's pre-VELVET days). Eventually FAUST faded away into obscurity but were re-called for a one-off gig at London's Marquee on the 25th of October '92. Their comeback albums, 'RIEN' and 'YOU KNOW faUSt', were issued between 1996-1997 and they were lined up for another rare live appearance at the Edinburgh Festival. • **Trivia:** UWE also produced for SLAPP HAPPY. Were and still are one of JULIAN COPE's (ex-TEARDROP EXPLODES) fave bands.

Album rating: FAUST (*7) / FAUST SO FAR (*8) / THE FAUST TAPES (*5 at the time – *8 now!?) / FAUST IV (*5) / MUNICH & ELSEWHERE collection (*5) / 71 MINUTES OF FAUST compilation (*7) / RIEN (*4) / YOU KNOW faUSt (*6) / LIVE IN EDINBURGH – AUGUST 1997 (*6) / FAUST WAKES NOSFERATU (*5) / RAVVIVANDO (*7)

RUDOLF SOSNA – guitar / **HANS JOACHIM IRMLER** – guitar / **WERNER DIERMAIER** – drums; repl. **ARNULF MEIFERT** / **JEAN HERVE PERON** – bass / **GUNTHER WUSTHOFF** – saxophone

	Polydor	not iss.
Jul 72. (lp) *(2310 142)* **FAUST** – Why don't you eat carrots / Meadow meal / Miss Fortune. *(re-iss. Oct79 as 'FAUST ONE' on 'Recommended'; RRA 1) (cd-iss. Nov96 on 'Klangbad'; KLANG 01)*	☐	–

—— MEIFERT departed around same time, but still contributed later

1972. (lp) *(2310 196)* **FAUST SO FAR** – It's a rainy day, sunshine girl / On the way to Abamae / No harm / So far / Mamie is blue / I've got my car and my T.V. / Picnic on a frozen river / Me back space . . . / . . . In the spirit. *(re-iss. Oct79 on 'Recommended'; R.R.TWO)*	☐	–
	Caroline	not iss.
1972. (7") *(2001 299)* **SO FAR**	☐	–
1972. (lp; by TONY CONRAD & FAUST) *(C 1501)* **OUTSIDE THE DREAM SYNDICATE** – From the side of man and womankind / From the side of the machine / From the side of woman and mankind. *(cd-iss. Feb94 on 'Southern'; LITHIUM 2) <(cd re-iss. Apr98 on 'Table Of Elements'; LITHIUM 6)>*	☐	–

—— added **PETER BLEGVAD** – guitar, clarinet, vocals

	Virgin	not iss.
1973. (lp) *(V 2004)* **FAUST IV** – Krautrock / The sad skinhead / Jennifer / Just a second / Picnic on a picnic river / Deuxieme tableux / Giggy smile / Laeuft . . . heisst dass ie laeuft oder es kommt bald . . . laeuft / It's a bit of a pain. *(cd-iss. Oct92; CDV 2004)*	☐	–
1973. (lp) *(VC 501)* **THE FAUST TAPES** (rec.1971-73) – (no song titles) *(re-iss. 1980 on 'Recommended'; RRA 6) (cd-iss. Apr91 as 'THE LAST ALBUM' + Feb94 + Jun 96 on 'Recommended'; RERF 2CD)*	☐	–

—— disbanded in 1973 and PETER BLEGVAD went solo. However, they (**IRMLER, DEIRMAIER + PERON**) did re-form for a London Marquee gig on 25th October '92

	Recommended	Recommended
Jan 97. (cd) *(<RERF 3CD>)* **YOU KNOW faUSt** – Hurricane / Tenne laufen / C pluus / Irons / Cendre / Sixty sixty / Winds / Liebeswehen 2 / Elektron 2 / Ella / Men from the Moon / Der pfad / Noizes from Pythagoras / Na sowas / L'oiseau / Huttenfreak / Teutonentango. *(lp-iss.Feb98 on 'Klangbad'; KLANGBAD 1) (re-iss. Oct98 on 'Recommended'; F 4CD)*	☐	Feb97
	Table Of Elements	Table Of Elements
Jun 97. (cd) *(<CHROMIUM 24>)* **RIEN** – Eroberung der stille, teil I / Fin / O / Rien / ? / Long distance calls in the desert / Eroberung der stille, teil II.	☐	1996
	Klangbad	EFA
Nov 97. (cd) *(FAUSTLIVECD 1)* <*KLANGF 2*> **LIVE IN EDINBURGH – AUGUST 1997** (live) *(re-iss. Dec97 on 'Think Progressive'; EFA 03560-2) (re-iss. Mar99; C 8326)*	☐	
Mar 98. (cd)(lp) *(C 8173)(FL 15)* <*3558*> **FAUST WAKES NOSFERATU** – Aufbruch nach Rumanien / Verwirrung / Telepathia / Kampf der machte / Unheil breitet sich aus / Die entscheidung.	☐	☐
Apr 99. (cd) *(EFA 36000-2)* **RAVVIVANDO**	☐	☐

– compilations, others, etc. –

on 'Recommended' unless mentioned otherwise

Mar 80. (7"ep) *(RRI 15)* **EXTRACTS FROM FAUST PARTY 3**	☐	–
1980. (lp) *(RR 5)* **CASABLANCA MOON**	☐	–
Sep 86. (lp) *(RR 25)* **MUNICH AND ELSEWHERE** (live)	☐	–
Nov 92. (cd) *(RERF 1CD)* **71 MINUTES OF FAUST** *(re-iss. Feb94 + Jun96; same)*	☐	–
Oct 96. (cd) *(RERHCD 2)* **KIRK**	☐	–
Jun 97. (cd) *(RER 25)* **RETURN OF A LEGEND**	☐	–
Dec 97. (cd) *Table of Elements; (265584-2)* **FAUST CONCERTS VOL.1**	☐	–
Dec 97. (cd) *Table Of Elements; (58933-2)* **FAUST CONCERTS VOL.2**	☐	–
Jun 98. (lp) *(RERFV 3)* **THE BBC SESSIONS**	☐	–

FEAR FACTORY

Formed: Los Angeles, California, USA . . . 1991 by BURTON C. BELL, the very-large DINO CAZARES and RAYMOND HERRERA. The group completed two BILL GOULD (Faith No More)-produced tracks for compilation album, 'L.A. Death Metal' before being snapped up by 'Roadrunner'. Instrumental in ushering in the current era of fertile cross-breeding between extreme metal and extreme techno, FEAR FACTORY debuted with the COLIN RICHARDSON-produced album, 'SOUL OF A NEW MACHINE' (1992), the record indicating expansive new possibilities for a flagging death-metal scene. Following US live work with BIOHAZARD and SICK OF IT ALL, they teamed up with veteran Canadian industrialists, FRONT LINE ASSEMBLY, who remixed their debut as 'FEAR IS THE MINDKILLER', NIN style. 1995 saw them grow into frontrunners of the new electronic-industrial death-metal brigade with the groundbreaking 'DEMANUFACTURE' set, a brutally uncompromising album which continued their obsession with technology and the darker side of the human psyche. The record broke the UK Top 30, while another follow-up remix project, 'REMANUFACTURE (CLONING TECHNOLOGY)' (1997), made an even bigger dent in the UK charts. Featuring rhythmic (ranging from the funky to the synapse shattering) reworkings from the likes of JUNKIE XL and DJ DANO, the album further blurred the fine line between organic and electronic music. CAZARES, with the help of BELL and FAITH NO MORE's BILL GOULD, were the mysterious members (although they denied this) behind BRUJERIA, a mock death-metal (pseudo-Mexican) septet, who released two albums, 'MATANDO GUEROS' (1993) and 'RAZA ODLADA' (1995). In 1999, FEAR FACTORY took on Gary Numan's 'CARS' and released it as a single. • **Songwriters:** BELL / CAZARES / HERRERA, except DOG DAY SUNRISE (Head Of David).

Album rating: SOUL OF A NEW MACHINE (*6) / FEAR IS THE MINDKILLER mini (*5) / DEMANUFACTURE (*6) / REMANUFACTURE (CLONING TECHNOLOGY) (*8) / OBSOLETE (*7)

BURTON C. BELL – vocals / **DINO CAZARES** – guitar (also of BRUJERIA) / **ANDREW SHIVES** – bass / **RAYMOND HERRERA** – drums

	Roadrunner	Roadrunner
Sep 92. (cd) *(RR 9160-2)* **SOUL OF A NEW MACHINE** – Martyr / Leechmaster / Scapegoat / Crisis / Crash test / Flesh hold / Lifeblind / Scumgrief / Natividad / Big god – Raped souls / Arise above oppression / Self immolation / Suffer age / W.O.E. / Desecrate / Escape confusion / Manipulation.	☐	–
Apr 93. (m-cd) *(RR 9082-2)* **FEAR IS THE MINDKILLER** – Martyr (suffer bastard mix) / Self immolation (vein tap mix) / Scapegoat (pigf*** mix) / Scumgrief (deep dub trauma mix) / Self immolation (liquid sky mix) / Self immolation (album version).	☐	–

—— **CHRISTIAN OLDE WOLBERS** – bass; repl. SHIVES

Jun 95. (cd/c/lp) *(RR 8956-2/-4/-1)* **DEMANUFACTURE** – Demanufacture / Self bias resistor / Zero signal / Replica / New breed / Dog day sunrise / Body hammer / H-K (Hunter-Killer) / A therapy for pain / Flashpoint / Pisschrist. *(d-lp+=)* – Resistancial! / New breed (revolutionary designed mix).	**27**	
Nov 95. (12"ep/cd-ep) *(RR 2330-6/-3)* **DOG DAY SUNRISE** ('A'version) / **CONCRETO** / **REPLICA** (electric sheep mix) (12"/cd-s) *(NRR 2330-6/-3)* – ('A'remixes).	☐	
Jun 97. (cd/c/lp) *(RR 8834-2/-4)* **REMANUFACTURE (CLONING TECHNOLOGY)**	**22**	
Jul 97. (12"ep) **THE BABBER MIXES** – New breed (Steel gun mix) / Flashpoint (Chosen few mix) / T-1000 (DJ Dano mix) / Manic cure.	☐	–
Oct 97. (cd-ep) *(RR 2271-3)* **BURN / CYBERDYNE / TRANSGENIC / REFUELLED**	☐	–
Jul 98. (cd/c) *(RR 8752-2/-4)* **OBSOLETE** – Shock / Edgecrusher / Smasher – Devourer / Securiton (Police state 2000) / Descent / Hi-tech hate / Freedom or fire / Obsolete / Resurrection / Timelessness.	**20**	**77**
Dec 98. (cd-ep) *(RR 2232-5)* **RESURRECTION / 0-0 (WHERE EVIL DWELLS) / SOULWOUND**	☐	
Sep 99. (cd-s) *(RR 2189-3)* **CARS / DESCENT** (Falling Deeper mix) / **EDGECRUSHER** (Urban Assault mix)	☐	

BRUJERIA

JUAN BRUJO – vocals / **GUERO SIN FE + FANTASMA + HONGO** – bass / **ASESINO** – guitar / **GRENUDO** – drums / **JR HOZICON/DIRECTOR DIABOLICO** (aka CAZARES, BELL + BILL GOULD, etc.)

	Roadrunner	Roadrunner
Jul 93. (cd) *(RR 9061-2)* **MATANDO GUEROS** – Pura de venta / Leves narcos / Sacrificio / Santa Lucia / Matando gueros / Seis seis seis / Cruza la frontera / Grenudos locos / Chingo de mecos / Narcos – Satanicos / Desperado / Culeros / Misas negras (sacrifico lo) / Chinga tu madre / Verga del		

Brujo – Estan chingados / Moestando ninos muertos / Machetazos (sacrifico II) / Castigo del Brujo / Cristo de la Roca. *(re-iss. Sep96; same)*

Sep 95. (cd) *(RR 8923-2)* **RAZA ODLADA** ☐ ☐
(re-iss. Sep96; same)

FEEDER

Formed: London, England ... 1993 by Newport-born frontman GRANT NICHOLAS, fellow Welshman JON HENRY LEE on bass and through many auditions, Japanese bassist TAKA HIROSE, the group now set to become the British answer to The SMASHING PUMPKINS. After slogging around the toilet circuit, the band signed to 'Echo' (home of JULIAN COPE and BABYBIRD), releasing their debut single 'TWO COLOURS' at the end of '95. The mini-album, 'SWIM' (mid '96), consolidated their pop-metal/grunge credentials, while an appearance at the CMJ music business conference in New York, led them to sign for 'Elektra'. Following on from the glistening dynamics and sonic confetti of their well-received debut album, 'POLYTHENE' (1997), they scored a number of minor UK chart successes culminating in the Top 30, 'HIGH'.

Album rating: POLYTHENE (*6) / YESTERDAY WENT TOO SOON (*6)

GRANT NICHOLAS (b.1967) – vocals, guitar / **TAKA HIROSE** – bass / **JON HENRY LEE** – drums

		Echo	Elektra
Oct 95.	(7"/cd-s) *(ecs +cd 13)* **TWO COLOURS. / PICTURES OF PAIN**	☐	–
May 96.	(m-cd/m-c/m-lp) *(ech cd/mc/lp 9)* **SWIM**	☐	–
	– Sweet 16 / Stereo world / W.I.T. / Descend / World asleep / Swim. *(m-cd re-iss. Oct98; same)*		
Oct 96.	(7") *(ecs 27)* **STEREO WORLD. / MY PERFECT DAY**	☐	–
	(cd-s+=) *(ecscd 27)* – World asleep / Change.		
Feb 97.	(7") *(ecs 32)* **TANGERINE. / RHUBARB**	60	☐
	(cd-s+=) *(ecscd 32)* – Rain.		
	(cd-s+=) *(ecscx 32)* – ('A'side) / TV me / Elegy.		
Apr 97.	(7") *(ecs 36)* **CEMENT. / PICTURES OF PAIN**	53	☐
	(cd-s+=) *(ecscd 36)* – Undivided.		
	(cd-s) *(ecscx 36)* – ('A'live) / Tangerine (live) / Shade (live) / Stereo world (live).		
May 97.	(cd/c/lp) *(ech/mc/lp 15)* <62085> **POLYTHENE**	65	☐
	– Polythene girl / My perfect day / Cement / Crash / Radiation / Suffocate / Descend / Stereo world / Tangerine / Waterfall / Forgive / Twentieth century trip. *(re-iss. Oct97 & Oct99 cd/c; ech cd/mc 19)*		
Aug 97.	(7") *(ecs 42)* **CRASH. / HERE IN THE BUBBLE**	48	☐
	(cd-s+=) *(ecscd 42)* – Forgive (acoustic) / Stereo world (video).		
	(cd-s) *(ecscx 42)* – ('A'side) / Undivided / Swim (version) / Tangerine (video).		
Oct 97.	(7"colrd) *(ecs 44)* **HIGH. / WHEN THE MORNING COMES**	24	☐
	(cd-s+=) *(ecscd 44)* – Women in towels / Cement (video cd-rom).		
	(cd-s) *(ecscx 44)* – ('A'side) / ('A'acoustic) / Sweet 16 / Crash (video cd-rom).		
Feb 98.	(7"purple) *(ecs 52)* **SUFFOCATE. / ECLIPSE**	37	☐
	(cd-s+=) *(ecscd 52)* – Cockroach / High (video – live).		
	(cd-s) *(ecscx 52)* – ('A'side) / Dry (acoustic) / Teddy bear / Descend (live).		
Mar 99.	(7") *(ecs 75)* **DAY IN DAY OUT. / CAN'T DANCE TO DISCO / HONEYFUZZ**	31	☐
	(cd-s) *(ecscd 75)* – ('A'side) / I need a buzz / Fly.		
	(cd-s) *(ecscx 75)* – ('A'side) / Can't dance to disco / Don't bring me down.		
May 99.	(c-s/cd-s) *(ecs mc/cd 77)* **INSOMNIA / SPACE AGE HERO / LIVING IN PARANOID**	22	☐
	(cd-s) *(ecscx 77)* – ('A'side) / Divebomb / Fly.		
Aug 99.	(c-s) *(ecsmc 79)* **YESTERDAY WENT TOO SOON / OXIDISE / TOMORROW SHINE**	20	☐
	(cd-s) *(ecscd 79)* – ('A'side) / Getting to know you well / Tomorrow shine.		
	(cd-s) *(ecscx 79)* – ('A'side) / Rubberband / Slide.		
Aug 99.	(cd/c/lp) *(ech cd/mc/lp 28)* **YESTERDAY WENT TOO SOON**	8	☐
	– Anaesthetic / Insomnia / Picture of perfect youth / Yesterday went too soon / Waiting for changes / Radioman / Day in day out / Tinsel town / You're my evergreen / Dry / Hole in my head / So well / Paperfaces. *(d-cd; echcx 28)* – Bubble head.		
Nov 99.	(c-s) *(ecsmc 85)* **PAPERFACES / WHOOEY / WAITING FOR CHANGES (session)**	41	☐
	(cd-s) *(ecscd 85)* – (first two tracks) / Tinsel town (session).		
	(cd-s) *(ecscx 85)* – ('A'side) / Crash mat / You're my evergreen (session).		

FEELIES (dig out; Great Alt & Indie . . .)

FELT / DENIM (dig out; Great Alt & Indie . . .)

Bryan FERRY (see under ⇒ ROXY MUSIC)

FEVER TREE (dig out; Great Psychedelic . . .)

FFWD (see under ⇒ ORB)

FIELDS OF THE NEPHILIM (dig out; Great Alt & Indie . . .)

FILTER

Formed: Cleveland, Ohio, USA ... 1995 by RICHARD PATRICK and BRIAN LIESEGANG (once both of NINE INCH NAILS). With the addition of GENO LENARDO, FRANK CAVANAH and MATT WALKER, the group scraped into the lower regions of the US chart with their debut album, 'SHORT BUS' (1995). A basement industrial outfit utilising dense Euro-rock

sounds, the group eventually secured some widespread exposure when they hit the UK Top 40 via a collaboration with The CRYSTAL METHOD, '(CAN'T YOU) TRIP LIKE I DO', featured on the soundtrack to 'The Spawn'. Mixing a cocktail of metal and goth once again (the kids just loved it, didn't they!), FILTER resurfaced with that difficult second album. Entitled confusingly enough, 'TITLE OF RECORD' (1999), the set made it all the way into the US Top 30 (UK Top 75), 'WELCOME TO THE FOLD' and 'TAKE A PICTURE' were worthy specimens. • **Note:** Don't let yourself buy the different house/club act, FILTER, who released a single, 'RUNNING AWAY', in '97.

Album rating: SHORT BUS (*8) / TITLE OF RECORD (*6)

RICHARD PATRICK (b.1967) – vocals, guitar, bass / **BRIAN LIESEGANG** (b.1970) – keyboards, drums / with **KEVIN HANLEY** – guitars / **SCOTT KERN + MIKE PEFFER** – drums

		Warners	Reprise
May 95.	(cd/c) <(9362 45864-2/-4)> **SHORT BUS**	☐	59
	– Hey man, nice shot / Dose / Under / Spent / Take another / Stuck in here / It's over / Gerbil / White like that / Consider this / So cool.		

`——` basic duo now with **GENO LENARDO** – guitar / **FRANK CAVANAGH** – bass / **MATT WALKER** – drums

Aug 95.	(12"/cd-s) *(W 0299 T/CD1)* <43531> **HEY MAN NICE SHOT (sober mix) / ('A'-1/2oz mix) / ('A'-1/4lb mix) / ('A'-Big Mac mix)**	☐	76 Jul95
	(cd-s) *(W 0299 CD2)* <43531> – ('A'-Bud gets the lead out mix) / ('A'-Sawed off edit) / ('A'-Nickel bag mix) / White like that.		
	(re-iss. May96; same)		
Nov 95.	(cd-s) **DOSE**	–	☐

`——` WALKER joined the SMASHING PUMPKINS in '96

In Sep'97, FILTER & The CRYSTAL METHOD hit UK Top 40 with '(CAN'T YOU) TRIP LIKE I DO' from the film 'The Spawn'.

Aug 99.	(9362 47519-2/-4) <47388> **TITLE OF RECORD**	75	30
	– Sand / Welcome to the fold / Captain Bligh / It's gonna kill me / Best things / Take a picture / Skinny / I will lead you / Cancer / I'm not the only one / Miss Blue.		
Sep 99.	(cd-s) *(W 502CD)* **WELCOME TO THE FOLD / ONE (IS THE LONELIEST NUMBER) / ('CAN'T YOU) TRIP LIKE I DO**	☐	–
	(cd-s) *(W 502CDX)* – ('A'-Freaq Nasty remix) / ('"-Militant Moving Fusion remix) / ('A'-video).		
Nov 99.	(c-s) <44788> **TAKE A PICTURE**	–	34

FINE YOUNG CANNIBALS

Formed: Birmingham, England ... late '83 by ex-(ENGLISH) BEAT men, ANDY COX and DAVID STEELE. They pair subsequently discovered vocalist, ROLAND GIFT, wielding his trademark falsetto for a London blues group; he'd previously blown sax for Humberside-based act, The AKRYLYXX. Signing to 'London' Records early in '85, the trio lifted their moniker from a 1960 movie title and premiered their soon-to-be released UK Top 10 debut single, 'JOHNNY COME HOME', on Channel 4's 'The Tube'. Although the anti-Tory follow-up, 'BLUE', narrowly missed the Top 40, the COX/STEELE-penned debut album, 'FINE YOUNG CANNIBALS' (1985), became a permanent fixture in the chart over the next year or so. At their best interpreting other artists' work, the multi-racial trio scored their biggest hit to date (No.8) with a classy pop-soul cover of Elvis' 'SUSPICIOUS MINDS' (featuring JIMMY SOMERVILLE on backing vox). In April '87, they applied their tried and tested formula to the soundtrack of Jonathan Demme's 'Something Wild', subsequently netting another Top 10 hit with an arrangement of the Buzzcocks' 'EVER FALLEN IN LOVE'. ROLAND himself branched further into the movie world when he made his acting debut in that year's cult UK production, 'Sammy And Rosie Get Laid'. He put in another competent performance in 1989's controversial 'Scandal' film, while his erstwhile bandmates reached the Top 20 (under the one-off pseudonym of TWO MEN, A DRUM MACHINE & A TRUMPET) with the dancefloor friendly 'I'M TIRED OF GETTING PUSHED AROUND'. Also towards the end of the decade, FYC finally got around to a fresh single, 'SHE DRIVES ME CRAZY', a rock/dance-fusion effort which surprisingly topped the American charts (UK Top 5) and served as an appetiser for their long-time-coming but mouth-watering second helping, 'THE RAW AND THE COOKED' (1989). Reaching No.1 on both sides of the Atlantic, the album was milked for all it was worth with a further four chart hits (including a second US chart-topper, 'GOOD THING') and an obligatory but predictable remix set. Save for a one-off contribution (Cole Porter's 'LOVE FOR SALE') to AIDS benefit album, 'Red Hot + Blue', FYC kept a low profile throughout the first half of the 90's. In October '96, they returned with a new song, 'THE FLAME', a UK Top 20 entry which was collected together with all their hits to date (and a further couple of recent recordings!) on the retrospective, 'THE FINEST'. A minor hit re-issue of 'SHE DRIVES ME CRAZY' the following year suggested FYC were treading water; much more interesting was the TOM JONES / ZUCCHERO re-working on the Welshman's 1999 comeback covers set, 'Reload'.

Album rating: FINE YOUNG CANNIBALS (*6) / THE RAW AND THE COOKED (*7) / THE RAW & THE REMIX (*3) / THE FINEST compilation (*7)

ROLAND GIFT (b.28 Apr'61) – vocals (ex-AKRYLYKX) / **ANDY COX** (b.25 Jan'60) – rhythm guitar (ex-BEAT) / **DAVID STEELE** (b. 8 Sep'60, Isle Of Wight, England) – bass, keyboards (ex-BEAT) / with **MARTIN PARRY** – percussion / **GRAEME HAMILTON** – trumpet

		London	I.R.S.
May 85.	(7"/7"pic-d/12") *(LON/+P/X 68)* <52760> **JOHNNY COME HOME. / GOOD TIMES AND BAD**	8	76 Mar86
Oct 85.	(7"/s7") *(LON/+C 79)* **BLUE. / WADE IN THE WATER**	41	–
	(12"+=) *(LONX 79)* – ('A'remix).		

(d7"+=) *(LONDP 79)* – ('A'version) / Love for sale.

Nov 85.	(7") **BLUE. / LOVE FOR SALE**		-	
Dec 85.	(lp/c)(cd) *(LON LP/C 16)(828004-2) <5683>* **FINE YOUNG** **CANNIBALS**		11	49

– Johnny come home / Couldn't care more / Don't ask me to choose / Funny how love is / Suspicious minds / Blue / Move to work / On a promise / Time isn't kind / Like a stranger.

Dec 85.	(7"/7"pic-d) *(LON/+P 82)* **SUSPICIOUS MINDS. / PRICK** **UP YOUR EARS**		8	

(12"+=) *(LONX 82)* – ('A'live) / Time isn't kind.
(12") *(LONXE 82)* – (US remix) / ('A'-Shakedown mix) / ('A'live).

Mar 86.	(7"/7"pic-d) *(LON/+P 88)* **FUNNY HOW LOVE IS. /** **MOTHERLESS CHILD**		58	

(12"+=) *(LONX 88)* – Johnny come home (live).

Apr 87.	(7") *(LON 121)* **EVER FALLEN IN LOVE. / COULDN'T CARE** **MORE**		9	-

(12"+=) *(LONX 121)* – ('A'dub mix).
(c-s+=)(cd-s+=) *(LONC 121)(886115-2)* – ('A'-club senseless mix) / Blue (live).
(12") *(LONX 121)* – ('A'-club senseless mix) / ('A'-rare groove bootleg mix).

May 87.	(7") **EVER FALLEN IN LOVE. / MOVE TO WORK**		-	
Jan 89.	(7"/7"box) *(LON/+T 199) <53483>* **SHE DRIVES ME CRAZY. /** **PULL THE SUCKER OFF**		5	1

(12"+=)(cd-s+=) *(LONXE 199)(886361-2)* – ('A'-Monie Love remix).
(12") *(LONX 199)* – ('A'-David Z mix) / ('B'side).

Feb 89.	(lp/c/cd) *(828069-1/-4/-2) <6273>* **THE RAW AND THE** **COOKED**		1	1

– She drives me crazy / Good thing / I'm not the man I used to be / I'm not satisfied / Tell me what / Don't look back / It's OK (it's alright) / Don't let it get you down / As hard as it is / Ever fallen in love.

Apr 89.	(7"/7"box/10") *(LON/+B/T 218) <53639>* **GOOD THING. /** **SOCIAL SECURITY**		7	1

(cd-s+=) *(LONCD 218)* – ('A'remix) / She drives me crazy (Monie Love remix).
(12") *(LONX 218)* – ('A'side) / ('A'-different mix) / ('A'-instrumental).

Aug 89.	(7"/7"box/c-s) *(LON/+T/CD 220) <53695>* **DON'T LOOK** **BACK. / YOU NEVER KNOW**		34	11

(12"+=)(cd-s+=) *(LONX/+3D 220)* – ('A'remix).
(12") *(LONXG 220)* – ('A'-special mix) / ('A'side) / ('A'instrumental).

Nov 89.	(7"/7"s7") *(LON/+T 244) <53686>* **I'M NOT THE MAN I USED** **TO BE. / MOTHERLESS CHILD**		20	

(12"/cd-s) *(LON X/CD 244)* – ('A'side) / She drives me crazy / Good thing / Don't look back.
(12") – ('A' 3 versions) / ('A'instrumental).

Feb 90.	(7"/s7"/c-s) *(LON/+T/CS 252)* **I'M NOT SATISFIED. /** **('A'-Nicci mix)**		46	

(12"+=)(cd-s+=) *(LON X/CD 252)* – ('A'-New York mixes).

Dec 90.	(cd/c/lp) *(828221-2/-4/-1)* **THE RAW & THE REMIX** ('89 album remixed)		61	
Oct 96.	(c-s) *(LONCS 389)* **THE FLAME / I'M NOT THE MAN I USED** **TO BE**		17	

(cd-s+=) *(LONCD 389)* – Trust.
(pic-cd-s) *(LONCDP 389)* – ('A'mixes).

Nov 96.	(cd/c) *(828854-2/-4)* **THE FINEST** (part compilation)		10	

– She drives me crazy / The flame / Johnny come home / Good thing / Suspicious minds / Blue / Ever fallen in love / Don't look back / Tell me what / I'm not the man I used to be / Couldn't care more / Funny how love is / Take what I can get / Since you've been gone. *(cd w/ free cd) (828855-2)* – She drives me crazy / Motherless child / Wade in the water / Love for sale / Prick up your ears / Pull the sucker off / You never know.

Dec 96.	(c-s) *(LONCS 391)* **SHE DRIVES ME CRAZY / JOHNNY** **COME HOME**		36	

(12"/cd-s+=) *(LON X/CD 391)* – ('A'mixes).

TWO MEN, A DRUM MACHINE & A TRUMPET

—— **COX + STEEL** one-off

			London	I.R.S.
Jan 88.	(7"/12") *(LON/+X 144)* **I'M TIRED OF GETTING PUSHED** **AROUND. / MAKE IT FUNNY**		18	

Neil / Tim FINN (see under ⇒ CROWDED HOUSE)

FIRM (see under ⇒ LED ZEPPELIN)

FISH

Born: DEREK WILLIAM DICK, 25 Apr'58, Dalkeith, Midlothian, Scotland. After leaving top progsters, MARILLION, in less than agreeable circumstances in September '88, he finally released a debut single, 'STATE OF MIND', a year later. This hit the UK Top 40, as did his early 1990 follow-up, 'BIG WEDGE'. A Top 5 album, 'VIGIL IN A WILDERNESS OF MIRRORS' was soon in the charts, FISH solo following a more commercial yet ambitiously diverse guitar-based sound while retaining the PETER GABRIEL-esque vocal theatrics. Through an ever changing cast of backing musicians, FISH recorded another two major label albums for 'Polydor', 'INTERNAL EXILE' (1991) and a covers set, 'SONGS FROM THE MIRROR' (1993), the latter of which stalled outside the Top 40. Moving back to Scotland after living in London, the singer then set up his own label, 'Dick Bros.', proceeding to maintain a prolific recording schedule over the ensuing four years as well as producing and releasing other low-key Scottish-based projects. Much of the material consisted of concert recordings, FISH retaining a loyal live following, especially in Europe. Studio wise, he released the 'SUITS' set in 1994, another Top 20 hit despite crticisms from the usual quarters. The Caledonian maverick even recorded a duet with forgotten 80's starlet SAM BROWN although predictably

it failed to make the chart. 1995 saw the release of two complementary best of/live affairs, 'YIN' and 'YANG', while the singer's most recent release was the 1997 set, 'SUNSETS ON EMPIRE'. • **Songwriters:** He co-wrote most of material with MICKEY SIMMONDS. He covered; THE FAITH HEALER (Sensational Alex Harvey Band). In early 1993, he released full covers album with tracks: QUESTION (Moody Blues) / BOSTON TEA PARTY (Sensational Alex Harvey Band) / FEARLESS (Pink Floyd) / APEMAN (Kinks) / HOLD YOUR HEAD UP (Argent) / SOLD (Sandy Denny) / I KNOW WHAT I LIKE (Genesis) / JEEPSTER (T.Rex) / FIVE YEARS (David Bowie) / ROADHOUSE BLUES (Doors). In October '86, FISH was credited on TONY BANKS (Genesis) single 'Short Cut To Nowhere'.

Album rating: VIGIL IN A WILDERNESS OF MIRRORS (*6) / INTERNAL EXILE (*5) / SONGS FROM THE MIRROR (*3) / SUSHI (*5) / ACOUSTIC SESSION (*5) / SUITS (*4) / YIN collection (*6) / YANG collection (*6) SUNSETS ON EMPIRE (*6) / RAINGODS WITH ZIPPOS (*4)

FISH – vocals (ex-MARILLION) with guest musicians on debut album **FRANK USHER** – guitar / **HAL LINDES** – guitar / **MICKEY SIMMONDS** – keyboards / **JOHN GIBLIN** – bass / **MARK BRZEZICKI** – drums / **CAROL KENYON** – backing vocals / plus **LUIS JARDIM** – percussion / **JANICK GERS** – guitar

			E.M.I.	E.M.I.
Oct 89.	(c-s/7") *(TC+/EM 109)* **STATE OF MIND. / THE VOYEUR** **(I LIKE TO WATCH)**		32	

(12"+=/cd-s+=) *(12/CD EM 109)* – ('A'-Presidential mix).

Dec 89.	(7"/7"s)(c-s) *(EM/+S 125)(TC 125)* **BIG WEDGE. / JACK** **AND JILL**		25	

(12"+=/12"pic-d)(cd-s+=) *(12EM/+PD 125)(CDEM 125)* – Faith healer (live).

Feb 90.	(lp/c/cd)(pic-lp) *(CD/C+/EMD 1015)(EMPD 1015)* **VIGIL IN** **A WILDERNESS OF MIRRORS**		5	

– Vigil / Big wedge / State of mind / The company / A gentleman's excuse me / The voyeur (I like to watch) / Family business / View from the hill / Cliche. *(cd re-iss. Nov98 on 'Roadrunner'+=; RR 8687-2)* – Jack and Jill / Internal exile / A gentleman's excuse me / Whiplash.

Mar 90.	(7"/7"red/7"sha-pic-d)(c-s) *(EM/+S/PD 135)(TCEM 135)* **A** **GENTLEMAN'S EXCUSE ME. / WHIPLASH**		30	

(12"+=/12"pic-d+=)(cd-s+=) *(12EM/+PD 135)(CDEM 135)* – ('A'demo version).

—— retained SIMMONDS and USHER, and brought in **ROBIN BOULT** – lead guitar, vocals / **DAVID PATON** – bass / **ETHAN JOHNS** – drums, percussion / guest drummer **TED McKENNA**

			Polydor	Polydor
Sep 91.	(7") *(FISH Y/C 1)* **INTERNAL EXILE. / CARNIVAL MAN**		37	

(12"+=) *(FISHS 1)* – ('A'-Karaoke mix).
(cd-s++=) *(FISCD 1)* – ('A'remix).

Oct 91.	(cd/c/lp) *(511049-2/-4/-1)* **INTERNAL EXILE**		21	

– Shadowplay / Credo / Just good friends (close) / Favourite stranger / Lucky / Dear friend / Tongues / Internal exile. *(re-iss. cd Apr95; same) (cd re-iss. Nov98 on 'Roadrunner'+=; RR 8683-2)* – Poet's moon / Something in the air / Carnival man.

Dec 91.	(7"/c-s) *(FISH Y/C 2)* **CREDO. / POET'S MOON**		38	

(12"box+=/cd-s+=) *(FISHS/FISCD 2)* – ('A'mix).
(12"+=) *(FISHX 2)* – (the 2 'A'versions) / Tongues (demo).

Jun 92.	(7"/c-s) *(FISH Y/C 3)* **SOMETHING IN THE AIR. / DEAR** **FRIEND**		51	

(12"+=) *(FISHX 3)* – ('A'-Teddy bear mix).
(cd-s++=) *(FISHP 3)* – ('A'radio mix).
(cd-s) *(FISHL 3)* – ('A'side) / ('A'-Christopher Robin mix) / Credo / Shadowplay.

—— **FOSTER PATTERSON** – keyboards, vocals repl. SIMMONS / **KEVIN WILKINSON** – drums, percussion repl. JOHNS.

Jan 93.	(cd/c/lp) *(517249-2/-4/-1)* **SONGS FROM THE MIRROR**		46	

– Question / Boston tea party / Fearless / Apeman / Hold your head up / Solo / I know what I like (in your wardrobe) / Jeepster / Five years. *(re-iss. cd Apr95; same) (cd re-iss. Nov98 on 'Roadrunner'; RR 8682-2)*

			Dick Bros	not iss.
Mar 94.	(d-cd) *(DDICK 002CD)* **SUSHI** (live)			-

– Fearless / Big wedge / Boston tea party / Credo / Family business / View from a hill / He knows you know / She chameleon / Kayleigh / White Russian / The company / Just good friends / Jeepster / Hold your head up / Lucky / Internal exile / Cliche / Last straw / Poet's Moon / Five years. *(re-iss. Sep96 on 'Blueprint'; DDICK 2CD) (re-iss. Nov98 on 'Roadrunner'; RR 8680-2)*

Apr 94.	(c-s/ext-12"pic-d/cd-s) *(DDICK 3 CAS/PIC/CD1)* **LADY LET** **IT LIE / OUT OF MY LIFE. / BLACK CANAL**		46	

(cd-s) *(DDICK 3CD2)* – ('A'extended) / ('B'live) / Emperors song (live) / Just good friends.

May 94.	(cd/c/lp/pic-lp) *(DDICK 004 CD/MC/LP/PIC)* **SUITS**		18	

– 1470 / Lady let it lie / Emperor's song / Fortunes of war / Somebody special / No dummy / Pipeline / Jumpsuit city / Bandwagon / Raw meat. *(cd re-iss. Sep96 on 'Blueprint'; DDICK 4CD) (cd re-iss. Nov98 on 'Roadrunner'; RR 8686-2)*

Sep 94.	(cd-ep) *(DDICK 008CD1)* **FORTUNES OF WAR** (edit) / **SOMEBODY SPECIAL** (live) / **STATE OF MIND** (live) / **LUCKY** (live)		67	

(cd-ep) *(DDICK 008CD2)* – ('A'live) / Warm wet circles / Jumpsuit city / The company (all live).
(cd-ep) *(DDICK 008CD3)* – ('A'acoustic) / Kayleigh (live) / Internal exile (live) / Just good friends (acoustic).
(cd-ep) *(DDICK 008CD4)* – ('A'acoustic) / Sugar mice (live) / Dear friend (live) / Lady let it lie (acoustic).

—— Above 4-cd single (nearly 90 mins.) (can be fitted in together as 1 package.

Aug 95.	(c-s; FISH featuring SAM BROWN) *(DDICK 014MC)* **JUST** **GOOD FRIENDS / SOMEBODY SPECIAL**		63	

(cd-s+=) *(DDICK 014CD1)* – State of mind.
(cd-s) *(DDICK 014CD2)* – ('A'side) / Raw meat (live) / Roadhouse blues (live).

Sep 95.	(cd/c) *(DDICK 011 CD/MC)* **YIN** (THE BEST OF FISH & '95 remixes)		58	-

– Incommunicado / Family business / Just good friends / Pipeline / Institution waltz / Tongues / Favourite stranger / Boston tea party / Raw meat / Time & a word / Company / Incubus / Solo. *(cd re-iss. Sep96 on 'Blueprint'; DDICK 11CD)*

Sep 95. (cd/c) *(DDICK 012 CD/MC)* **YANG** (THE BEST OF FISH
& '95 remixes)　　　　　　　　　　**52**　　–
– Lucky / Big wedge / Lady let it lie / Lavender / Credo / A gentleman's excuse
me / Kayleigh / State of mind / Somebody special / Sugar mice / Punch & Judy /
Internal exile / Fortunes of war. *(cd re-iss. Sep96 on 'Blueprint'; DDICK 12CD)*

May 97. (cd-s) *(DDICK 24CD1)* **BROTHER 52 / BROTHER 52
(Stateline mix) / DO NOT WALK OUTSIDE THIS AREA /
BROTHER 52 (album version)**　　　　　　□　　–
(cd-s) *(DDICK 24CD2)* – (first 2 tracks) / ('A'-4 am dub mix).

May 97. (cd) *(DDICK 25CD)* **SUNSETS ON EMPIRE**　　**42**　　–
– Perception of Johnny punter / Goldfish and clowns / Change of heart / What colour
is God / Tara / Jungle ride / Worm in a bottle / Brother 52 / Sunsets on empire /
Say it with flowers / Do not walk outside this area. *(other cd; DDICK 26CD)* (re-iss.
Nov98 on 'Roadrunner'; RR 8679-2)

Aug 97. (cd-s) *(DDICK 27CD)* **CHANGE OF HEART /**　　　　　–
　　　　　　　　　　　　　　　　Roadrunner Roadrunner
Apr 99. (7"pic-d/cd-s; as FISH with ELIZABETH ANTWI) *(RR
2185-7/-3)* **INCOMPLETE. / MAKE IT HAPPEN (acoustic
mix) / INCOMPLETE (castle demo)**　　　　　　□　　–

Apr 99. (cd) *(RR 8677-2)* **RAINGODS WITH ZIPPOS**　　**57**　　–
– Tumbledown / Mission statement / Incomplete / Tilted cross / The faith healer /
Rites of passage / Plague of ghosts (Old haunts) / Digging deep / Chocolate frogs /
Waving at stars / Raingods dancing / Wake-up call (make it happen).

– compilations, others, etc. –

Sep 96. (cd) *Blueprint; (DDICK 6CD)* **ACOUSTIC SESSIONS**　□　　–
Sep 96. (d-cd) *Blueprint; (DDICK 16CD)* **PIGPENS BIRTHDAY**　□　　–
　　(re-iss. Nov98 on 'Roadrunner'; RR 8684-2)
Nov 98. (cd) *Roadrunner; (RR 8678-2)* **KETTLE OF FISH 88-98**　□　　–
– Big wedge / Just good friends (with SAM BROWN) / Brother 52 / Chasing Miss
Pretty / Credo / A gentleman's excuse me / Goldfish and clowns / Lady let it lie /
Lucky / State of mind / Mr Buttons / Fortunes of war / Internal exile. *(also w/
CD-ROM; RR 8678-8)*
Nov 98. (d-cd) *Roadrunner; (RR 8681-2)* **KRAKOW** (live)　□　　–
Nov 98. (d-cd) *Roadrunner; (RR 8685-2)* **UNCLE FISH AND THE CRYPT
CREEPERS**　　　　　　　　　　　　□　　–
Nov 98. (d-cd) *Roadrunner; (RR 8688-2)* **TALES FROM THE BIG BUS**
(live)　　　　　　　　　　　　　　□　　–
Nov 98. (d-cd) *Roadrunner; (RR 8689-2)* **FORTUNES OF WAR**　□　　–
May 99. (cd) *Blueprint; (BP 297CD)* **THE BBC SESSIONS**　□　　–

FISHBONE (dig out; Great Alt & Indie)

FLAG OF CONVENIENCE / F.O.C.
(see under ⇒ BUZZCOCKS)

FLAMIN' GROOVIES

Formed: Bay Area, San Francisco, California, USA ... 1965 originally as
The CHOSEN FEW and then The LOST AND FOUND, by CYRIL JORDAN,
ROY LONEY, GEORGE ALEXANDER and TIM LYNCH. In 1967, they
issued a self-financed debut lp, the 10" 'SNEAKERS', which resulted in a
deal with 'Epic'. After one poorly promoted lp, 'SUPERSNAZZ', they left to
join the roster of the 'Kama Sutra' label, aided by producer Richard Robinson
in 1970. There, they issued two well-received albums, 'FLAMINGO' and
'TEENAGE HEAD', before again moving stables to 'United Artists' in '72.
Critically acclaimed, the albums highlighted The 'GROOVIES' characteristic
high-energy rock'n'roll, updating 50's material into 60's-style garage punk.
The following years resulted in many personnel changes, and after touring
Europe in 1976, they finally released the DAVE EDMUNDS-produced 'Sire'
comeback, 'SHAKE SOME ACTION' (he had previously worked on their
1972 album, 'SLOW DEATH'). Although the band were associated with
the embryonic new wave/punk movement, the album's power-pop harmonies
found little credibility with this scene. The band released a further two albums
in the same vein before splitting then re-forming for the live comeback lp,
'ONE NIGHT STAND' (1987). • **Songwriters:** JORDAN-LONEY, until the
latter's departure in '71. Recorded many covers including; SOMETHIN' ELSE
(Eddie Cochran) / PISTOL PACKIN' MAMA (Gene Vincent) / SHAKIN' ALL
OVER (Johnny Kidd) / THAT'LL BE THE DAY (Buddy Holly) / KEEP A
KNOCKIN' (Little Richard) / MOVE IT (Cliff Richard) / FEEL A WHOLE
LOT BETTER (Byrds) / PAINT IT BLACK + JUMPIN' JACK FLASH +
19th NERVOUS BREAKDOWN (Rolling Stones) / MARRIED WOMAN
(Frankie Lee Sims) / TEENAGE CONFIDENTIAL (Jerry Lee Lewis) /
WEREWOLVES OF LONDON (Warren Zevon) / ABSOLUTELY SWEET
MARIE (Bob Dylan) / TALLAHASSEE LASSIE (Freddy Cannon) / KICKS
(Mann-Weill) / CALL ME LIGHTNING (Who) / MONEY (Barrett Strong) /
PLEASE PLEASE ME + MISERY + THERE'S A PLACE (Beatles) / etc.
• **Trivia:** Long-time fan GREG SHAW, issued 1975 single 'YOU TORE ME
DOWN', for his own 'Bomp' magazine label.

Album rating: SNEAKERS (*5) / SUPERSNAZZ (*6) / FLAMINGO (*7) / TEENAGE
HEAD (*7) / SHAKE SOME ACTION (*8) / FLAMIN' GROOVIES NOW! (*7) /
JUMPIN' IN THE NIGHT (*6) / ONE NIGHT STAND (*4) / GROOVIES GREATEST
GROOVES compilation (*8)

ROB LONEY (b.13 Apr'46) – vocals / **CYRIL JORDAN** (b. 1948) – lead guitar / **TIM LYNCH**
(b.18 Jul'46) – rhythm guitar / **GEORGE ALEXANDER** (b.18 May'46, San Mateo, Calif.)
– bass / **DANNY MIHM** – drums (ex-WHISTLING SHRIMP) repl. RON GRECO

　　　　　　　　　　　　　　　　not iss. Snazz
1967. (10"m-lp) *<2371>* **SNEAKERS**　　　　　–　　–
– The slide / I'm drowning / Babes in the sky / Love time / My yada / Golden clouds /
Prelude in A flat to afternoon of a plad. *<US re-iss. 1975 on 'Skydog'; FGG 803>*

---

　　　　　　　　　　　　　　　　not iss. Epic
1968. (7") *<10501>* **ROCKIN' PNEUMONIA AND THE BOOGIE
WOOGIE FLU. / THE FIRST ONE'S FREE**　　–　　□
1968. (7") *<10564>* **SOMETHIN' ELSE. / LAURIE DID IT**　–　□
1970. (lp) *<26487>* **SUPERSNAZZ**　　　　　　　□　　□
– Love have mercy / The girl can't help it / Laurie did it / Apart from that / Rockin'
pneumonia and the boogie woogie flu / The first one's free / Pagan Rachel / a)
Somethin' else, b) Pistol packin' mama / Brushfire / Bam balam / Around the corner.
(UK-rel.Feb86 on 'Edsel'; ED 173) (cd-iss. Aug93 on 'Columbia'; 467073-2)

　　　　　　　　　　　　　　　Kama　Kama
　　　　　　　　　　　　　　　Sutra　Sutra
1971. (lp) *<KSBS 2021>* **FLAMINGO**　　　　　□　　□
– Roadhouse / Headin' for the Texas border / Gonna rock tonite / Comin' after
you / Sweet roll me on down / Keep a knockin' / Second cousin / Childhood's
end / Jailbait. *(UK cd-iss. Jan90 on 'Big Beat'+=; CDWIK 925)* – Walkin' the dog /
Somethin' else / My girl Josephine / Louie Louie / Rockin' pneumonia and the
boogie woogie flu / Going out theme (version 2).
1971. (d-lp) *<KSBS 2031>* **TEENAGE HEAD**　　　　□　　□
– Teenage head / Whiskey women / Yesterday's numbers 32:20 / High flyin'
baby / City lights / Have you seen my baby / Evil-hearted Ada / Doctor Boogie /
Rumble / Shakin' all over / That'll be the day / Round and round / Going out theme.
*('FLAMINGO' + 'TEENAGE HEAD' iss.UK as 'FLAMIN' GROOVIES' on 'Kama
Sutra' d-lp; 2683 003) (UK re-iss. 1989 on 'Dojo' lp/cd; DOJO LP/CD 58) (cd re-iss.
Jan90 on 'Big Beat'; CDWIK 926)*
Aug 71. (7") *(2013 031)* **TEENAGE HEAD. / EVIL-HEARTED ADA**　□　□
Mar 72. (7"ep) *(2013 042)* **GONNA ROCK TONITE / KEEP
A-KNOCKIN'. / (3 others by 'Sha Na Na')**　　　□　□

—— **CHRIS WILSON** (b.10 Sep'52, Waltham, Massachusetts, USA) – vocals (ex-LOOSE
GRAVEL) repl. LONEY / **JAMES FARRELL** – guitar (ex-LOOSE GRAVEL) repl.
LYNCH who formed HOT KNIVES. —— changed to The DOGS for a short while,
before returning to same

　　　　　　　　　　　　　　　　U.A.　U.A.
Jun 72. (7") *(UP 35392)* **SLOW DEATH. / TALAHASSIE LASSIE**　□　□
Jun 72. (lp) **SLOW DEATH**
– Sweet little rock'n'roller / Doctor Boogie / Walking the dog / Roadhouse / Teenage
head / Slow death / Shakin' all over / Louie Louie / Have you seen my baby / Can't
explain.
Jan 73. (7") *(UP 35464)* **MARRIED WOMAN. / GET A SHOT OF
RHYTHM & BLUES**　　　　　　　　　□　　□

—— **JORDAN, WILSON, FARRELL** and **ALEXANDER** recruited new member **DAVID
WRIGHT** – drums repl. TERRY RAE who had repl. MIHM (to HOT KNIVES)

　　　　　　　　　　　　　　Skydog　not iss.
1974. (7") *()* **JUMPIN' JACK FLASH. / BLUES FROM PHILLYS**　–　– France
(re-iss. '77 on 12";)
1974. (7"ep) *<>* **GREASE**　　　　　　　　　–　– France
– Let me rock / Dog meat / Sweet little rock'n'roller.

　　　　　　　　　　　　　　Philips　not iss.
1975. (7") *()* **LET THE BOY ROCK'N'ROLL. / YES IT'S TRUE**　□　– France
　　　　　　　　　　　　　　not iss.　Bomp
1975. (7") *<101>* **YOU TORE ME DOWN. / HIM OR ME**　–　□
　　　　　　　　　　　　　　Sire　Sire
Jun 76. (lp) *(9103 251)* **SHAKE SOME ACTION**　　　□　□
– Shake some action / Sometimes / Yes it's true / St. Louis blues / You tore me
down / Please please girl / Let the boy rock'n'roll / Don't you lie to me / She said
yeah / I'll cry alone / Misery / I saw her / Teenage confidential / I can't hide. *(re-iss.
Sep78; SRK 6021) (cd-iss. Sep93 on 'Aim'; AIMCD 1017)*
Jul 76. (7"m) *(6198 086)* **DON'T YOU LIE TO ME. / SHE SAID
YEAH / SHAKE SOME ACTION**　　　　　□　□
Nov 76. (7") *(6078 602)* **SHAKE SOME ACTION. / TEENAGE
CONFIDENTIAL**　　　　　　　　　□　□
Nov 76. (7") *<731>* **TEENAGE CONFIDENTIAL. / I CAN'T HIDE**　–　□

—— **MIKE WILHELM** – guitar repl. FARRELL who joined PHANTOM MOVERS
Apr 78. (lp) *(9103 333)* **THE FLAMIN' GROOVIES NOW!**　　□　□
– Feel a whole lot better / Bewteen the lines / Ups and downs / There's a place / Take
me back / Reminiscing / Good laugh man / Yeah my baby / House of blue lights /
All I wanted / Blue turns to grey / When I heard your name / Move it / Don't put
me on. *(re-iss. Sep78; SRK 7059)*
Apr 78. (7"m,12"m) *(6078 619)* **FEEL A WHOLE LOT BETTER. /
PAINT IT BLACK / SHAKE SOME ACTION**　　□　□
Aug 78. (7") *(SIR 4002)* **MOVE IT. / WHEN I HEARD YOUR NAME**　□　□
Jun 79. (lp) *(SRK 6067)* **JUMPING IN THE NIGHT**　　　□　□
– Please please girl / Next one crying / Down down down / Tell me again / Absolutely
sweet Marie / (Yes he my) Wonderful one / Jumpin' in the night / 19th nervous
breakdown / Boys / 5D / First plane home / Lady friend / In the U.S.A. *<US-different
tracks>*
1979. (7"m) *(SIR 4018)* **ABSOLUTELY SWEET MARIE. /
WEREWOLVES OF LONDON / NEXT ONE CRYING**　□　□

—— **DANNY MIHM** – drums (ex-PHANTOM MOVERS) re-repl. WRIGHT before
split CHRIS WILSON joined BARRACUDAS in '82, **CYRIL JORDAN** re-formed
FLAMIN' GROOVIES in 1986

—— **JACK JOHNSON** – guitar + **PAUL ZAHL** – drums repl.WILSON, WRIGHT +
WILHELM

　　　　　　　　　　　　　　A.B.C.　not iss.
Jul 87. (7") *(ABCS 015)* **SHAKE SOME ACTION (live). / ?**　□　□
Jul 87. (lp) *(ABCLP 10)* **ONE NIGHT STAND (live)**　　　□　□
– Kicks / Bittersweet / I can't hide / Money / Call me lightning / Shake some action /
Slow death / Teenage head / Slow down / Tallahassie lassie. *(cd-iss. Apr89; ABCD
10) (re-iss. Sep93 on 'Aim' cd/c; AIM CD/C 1008)*

– compilations etc. –

Jun 76. (7") *Kama Sutra; (KSS 707)* **TEENAGE HEAD. / HEADIN'
FOR TEXAS BORDER**　　　　　　　□　□
Nov 76. (7"ep) *United Artists; (REM 406)* **SLOW DEATH EP**　□　□
– Slow death / Talahassie lassie / Married woman / Get a shot of rhythm & blues.
May 84. (lp) *Skydog; (SK 12226)* **SUPERGREASE**　　　–　– France
1980's. (7") *Skydog;* **I CAN'T EXPLAIN. / LITTLE QUEENIE**　–　– France

---

Nov 84. (lp) *Eva; (12044)* **'68 (live)**	-	- France
Nov 84. (lp) *Eva; (12045)* **'70 (live)**	-	- France
Jul 85. (lp/c) *Buddah; (252262-1/-4)* **STILL SHAKIN'**	-	-
May 86. (lp/c) *Edsel; (ED/CED 183)* **ROADHOUSE**	-	-
– (compilation of 'FLAMINGO' + 'TEENAGE HEAD').		
Aug 88. (lp) *Voxx; (200009)* **BUCKET OF BRAINS**	-	
(UK cd-iss. Apr95 on 'E.M.I.'; CZ 542)		
Aug 89. (lp/c/cd) *Sire; (K 925948-1/-4/-2)* **GROOVIES GREATEST**		-
GROOVES		

– Shake some action / Teenage head / Slow death / Tallahassie lassie / Yeah my baby / Yes it's true / First plane home / In the U.S.A. / Between the lines / Don't you lie to me / Down down down / I'll cry alone / You tore me down / Please please girl / Yes I am / Teenage confidential / I can't hide / Absolutely sweet Marie / Don't put me on / I saw her / All I wanted / Jumpin' in the night / There's a place / River deep, mountain high. *(cd re-iss. Jan96 on 'Warners'; 7599 25948-2)*

Nov 89. (lp) *Aim; (COLLECT 2)* **ROCKFIELD SESSIONS**	-	-
Apr 93. (cd/lp) *Marilyn;* **RARE DEMOS & LIVE RECORDINGS**	-	-
Sep 93. (cd/c) *Ain; (AIM CD/C 1030)* **STEP UP**	-	-
Oct 93. (cd) *Aim; (COLLECT 1-2)* **SNEAKERS / ROCKFIELD**	-	-
SESSIONS		
Nov 93. (cd) *Mystery;* **ROCKIN' AT THE ROUNDHOUSE – LIVE IN**	-	-
LONDON 1976/78 (live)		
May 94. (cd) *Eva; (842070)* **LIVE 68/70 (live)**		-
Nov 94. (10"lp) *Bomp;* **EP**		-
Apr 95. (cd) *Aim; (AIM 1051CD)* **LIVE AT THE FESTIVAL OF THE**		-
SUN BARCELONA (live)		
Apr 97. (cd) *Aim; (AIM 2001CD)* **OLDIES BUT GOLDIES: BEST OF**		-

FLAMING LIPS

Formed: Oklahoma City, Oklahoma, USA . . . 1983 by the COYNE brothers WAYNE and MARK, who reputedly stole instruments from a church hall to get their act off the ground. After a rare and weird EP in 1985, MARK left brother WAYNE to recruit new members for the 'Enigma' album, 'HEAR IT IS'. Their next, 'OH MY GAWD!!!', in '87, saw them strike with many poetic assaults, including the near 10-minute track 'ONE MILLION BILLIONTH OF A MILLISECOND ON A SUNDAY MORNING'. Their reputation grew, with wild, climactic live appearances, highlighting albums 'TELEPATHIC SURGERY' and 'IN A PRIEST-DRIVEN AMBULANCE (WITH SILVER SUNSHINE STARES)'. Phew!!!. Signed to 'Warners' in 1992, and between appearing at the Reading Festival, they released 'HIT TO DEATH IN THE MAJOR HEAD' and the US No.108 (!) album 'TRANSMISSIONS FROM THE SATELLITE HEART'. By the mid-90's, they had secured weirdo posterity, after giving birth to the drug-orientated, narrative track, 'WATERBUG'. Their avant-garde psychedelic (BARRETT / FLOYD) approach was now well behind them, their barrage of sound, once described as The JESUS & MARY CHAIN meeting BLACK FLAG or The DEAD KENNEDYS, took a sharp detour and ended up in DAVE FRIDMANN's (of MERCURY REV) up-state New York studio, where the LIPS (now consisting of only three; WAYNE COYNE, STEVE DROZD and MICHAEL IVINS) recorded the spooky but highly commercial 'THE SOFT BULLETIN' (1999) for 'Warners'. The album spawned two hit singles, 'RACE FOR THE PRIZE' and the echo fronted 'WAITIN' FOR A SUPERMAN', which was their most pop orientated work since the 1995 release 'BAD DAYS'. 'THE SOFT BULLETIN' marked the work of a band who had matured in age and in sound. Adding the FRIDMANN formula, the album sounded similar to MERCURY REV's 'Deserter's Songs', although relying largely on its YES-type chord changes/structures and BEACH BOYS harmonies with COYNE attempting to sing in tune (possibly for the very first time). • **Songwriters:** Group except; SUMMERTIME BLUES (Eddie Cochran) / WHAT'S SO FUNNY 'BOUT PEACE, LOVE & UNDERSTANDING (Brinsley Schwarz) / THAN YOU (Led Zeppelin) / DEATH VALLEY '69 (Sonic Youth & Lydia Lunch) / STRYCHNINE (Sonics) / AFTER THE GOLD RUSH (Neil Young) / ALL THAT JAZZ + HAPPY DEATH MEN (Echo & The Bunnymen) / LIFE ON MARS (David Bowie) / WHAT A WONDERFUL WORLD (Nat King Cole) / ICE DRUMMER (Suicide) / CHOSEN ONE + LITTLE DRUMMER BOY (Smog).

Album rating: HEAR IT IS (*5) / OH MY GAWD!!! . . . THE FLAMING LIPS (*7) / TELEPATHIC SURGERY (*5) / IN A PRIEST-DRIVEN AMBULANCE (*6) / HIT TO DEATH IN THE FUTURE HEAD (*6) / TRANSMISSIONS FROM THE SATELLITE HEART (*8) / CLOUDS TASTE METALLIC (*7) / ZAIREEKA (*7) / THE SOFT BULLETIN (*9)

MARK COYNE – vocals / **WAYNE COYNE** – guitar / **MICHAEL IVINS** – bass / **RICHARD ENGLISH** – drums

	not iss.	Lovely Sorts Of Death
1985. (7"green-ep) *<L-19679>* **THE FLAMING LIPS E.P.**	-	

– Bag full of thoughts / Out for a walk / Garden of eyes – Forever is a long time / Scratching the door / My own planet. *(re-iss. 1986 red-ep; same) (re-iss. 1987 on 'Pink Dust' 7"ep/c-ep; 731881-1/-4)*

— **WAYNE** now on vox, when MARK departed

	Enigma	Restless
Nov 86. (white-lp,lp/c/cd) *<72173-1/-4/-2>* **HEAR IT IS**		

– With you / Unplugged / Trains, brains and rain / Jesus shootin' heroin / Just like before / She is death / Charles Manson blues / Man from Pakistan / Godzilla flick / Staring at sound – With you. *(cd+=)* – Bag full of thoughts / Out for a walk / Garden of eyes – Forever is a long time / Scratching the door / My own planet / Summertime blues. *(cd re-iss. Jul99; same)*

Nov 87. (clear-lp,lp/c/cd) *<72207-1/-4/-2>* **OH MY GAWD!!! . . .**	-	
THE FLAMING LIPS		

– Can't exist / Can't stop the spring / Ceiling is bending / Everything's explodin' / Love yer brain / Maximum dream for Evil Knievel / Ode to CC / One million billionth / Prescription: Overkill / Thank.

Feb 89. (lp/c/cd) *(ENVLP/TCENV/CDENV 523)* *<72350-1/-4/-2>*		
TELEPATHIC SURGERY		

– Drug machine / Michael time to wake up / Miracle on 42nd Street / UFO story / Shaved gorilla / Begs and achin' / Right now / Hare Krishna stomp wagon / Chrome plated suicide / Redneck school of technology / Spontaneous combustion of John / The last drop of morning dew. *(cd re-iss. Jul99 on 'Restless'; same as US)*

— **JONATHAN PONEMANN** – guitar + **JOHN DONAHUE** – guitar

	City Slang	Sub Pop
Jun 89. (7"m) *(EFA 40153)* *<SP-28>* **DRUG MACHINE /**		Jan89
STRYCHNINE. / (WHAT'S SO FUNNY ABOUT) PEACE,		
LOVE AND UNDERSTANDING		

— **NATHAN ROBERTS** – drums repl. ENGLISH

	City Slang	Atavistic
Jan 91. (12"ep) *(EFA 04063-05)* **UNCONSCIOUSLY SCREAMIN' EP**		

– Unconsciously screamin' / Lucifer rising / Ma, I didn't notice / Let me be it.

	City Slang	Restless
Feb 91. (pink-lp,lp/c/cd) *(SLANG 005/+C/CD)* *<72359>* **IN A**		Sep90
PRIEST-DRIVEN AMBULANCE (WITH SILVER SUNSHINE		
STARES)		

– Shine on sweet Jesus – Jesus song No.5 / Unconsciously screamin' / Rainin' babies / Take me ta Mars / Five stop Mother Superior rain / Stand in line / God walks among us now / Jesus song No.6 / There you are / Jesus song No.7 / Mountain song / What a wonderful world. *(cd re-iss. Sep96 on 'Restless'; 72359-2)*

	Warners	Warners
Jul 92. (cd-ep) *<40244>* **. . . WASTIN' PIGS IS STILL RADICAL**	-	-

– Talkin' 'bout the smiling deathporn immorality blues (everyone wants to live forever) / All that jazz – Happy death men / Jets (Cupid's kiss vs. the psyche of death).

Aug 92. (cd/c/lp) *<(7599 26838-2/-4/-1)>* **HIT TO DEATH IN THE**		
MAJOR HEAD		

– Talkin' about the smiling deathporn immorality blues (everyone wants to live forever) / Hit me like you did the first time / The Sun / Felt good to burn / Gingerale afternoon (the astrology of a Saturday) / Halloween on the Barbary Coast / The magician vs. the headache / You have to be joking (autopsy of the Devil's brain) / Frogs / Hold your head. *(re-iss. Apr95; same)*

— **RONALD JONES** – guitar repl. JOHN who joined MERCURY REV

— **STEVEN DROZD** – drums repl. NATHAN

Jun 93. (cd/c/lp) *<(9362 45334-2/-4/-1)>* **TRANSMISSIONS FROM**		
THE SATELLITE HEART		

– Turn it on / Pilot can at the queer of God / Oh my pregnant head (labia in the sunlight) / She don't use jelly / Chewin' the apple of your eye / Superhumans / Be my head / Moth in the incubator / Plastic Jesus / When yer twenty-two / Slow nerve action.

Aug 94. (7"/c-s) *(W 0246/+C)* *<18131>* **SHE DON'T USE JELLY. /**		55 Nov94
TURN IT ON (bluegrass version)		
(cd-s+=) *(WO 246CD)* – Translucent egg.		
(cd-s) *(WO 246CD)* – ('A'side) / The process / Moth in the incubator.		
Apr 95. (cd-s) *<43509>* **TURN IT ON**	-	
Jul 95. (m-cd) *<45748>* **PROVIDING NEEDLES FOR YOUR**	-	
BALLOONS		

– Bad days / Jets part 2 (my two days as an ambulance driver) / Ice drummer / Put the waterbug in the policeman's ear / Chewin the apple of yer ear / Chosen one / Little drummerboy / Slow nerve action.

Sep 95. (cd/c) *<(9362 45911-2/-4)>* **CLOUDS TASTE METALLIC**		

– The abandoned hospital ship / Psychiatric explorations of the fetus with needles / Placebo headwound / This here giraffe / Brainville / Guy who lost a headache and accidentally saves the world / When you smile / Kim's watermelon gun / They punctured my yolk / Lightning strikes the postman / Christmas at the zoo / Evil will prevail / Bad days (aurally excited version).

Dec 95. (c-s) *(W 0322C)* **BAD DAYS / GIRL WITH HAIR LIKE AN**		-
EXPLOSION		
(cd-s+=) *(W 0322CD)* – She don't use jelly / Giraffe (demo).		
(cd-s) *(W 0322CDX)* – ('A'side) / Ice drummer / When you smiled I lost my only idea / Put the water bug in the policeman's ear.		
Mar 96. (cd-s) *(W 0335CD)* **THIS HERE GIRAFFE / JETS pt.2 (MY**		
TWO DAYS AS AN AMBULANCE DRIVER) / LIFE ON		
MARS	72	-
(c-s/cd-s) *(W 0335 C/CDX)* – ('A'side) / The sun / Hit me like you did the first time.		

above was the first ever shaped cd single.

Aug 96. (3D-cd-s) *(W 0370CD)* **BRAINVILLE / EVIL WILL PREVAIL**		
(live) / WATERBUG (live)		
(c-s/cd-s) *(W 0370 C/CDX)* – ('A'side) / Brainville (live) / Raindrops keep falling on my head.		
Oct 97. (4xcd-box) *<(9362 46804)>* **ZAIREEKA**		

– Okay I'll admit that I really don't care / Riding to work in the year 2025 (your invisible now) / Thirty-five thousand feet of despair / Machine in India / The train runs over the camel but is . . . / How will we know? (futuristic crashendos) / March of the rotten vegetables / Big ol' bug is the new baby now.

(above was an unusual concept in that you needed 4 separate CD players to hear the simultaneous recordings at its full potential)

— now down to a trio of **WAYNE COYNE, STEVEN DROZD + MICHAEL IVINS**

May 99. (cd/c) *<(9362 47393-2/-4)>* **THE SOFT BULLETIN**		39

– Race for the prize / A spoonful weighs a ton / The spark that bled / Slow motion / What is the light? / The observer / Waitin' for a superman / Suddenly everything has changed / The gash / Feeling yourself disintegrate / Sleeping on the roof / Race for the prize (remix) / Waitin' for a superman (remix) / Buggin' (remix).

Jun 99. (cd-s) *(W 494CD1)* **RACE FOR THE PRIZE / RIDING TO**		
WORK IN THE YEAR 2025		39
(cd-s) *(W 494CD2)* – ('A'side) / You're invisible / Thirty thousand feet of despair.		
Nov 99. (c-s/cd-s) *(W 505 C/CD2)* **WAITIN' FOR A SUPERMAN /**		
RIDING TO WORK IN THE YEAR 2025 / YOU'RE		
INVISIBLE / 35,000 FEET OF DESPAIR		
(cd-s) *(W 505CD1)* – ('A'mixes).		

– compilations, etc. –

Oct 98. (cd) *Restless*; <(RST 72963)> **A COLLECTION OF SONGS REPRESENTING AN ENTHUSIASM FOR RECORDING . . . BY AMATEURS** (1984-1990) ☐ ☐ Sep98
– Bag full of thoughts / Jesus shootin' heroin / One million billionth / Chrome plated suicide / Michael time to wake up / Hell's angels cracker factory / Unconsciously screamin' / God walks among us now / Stychnini – Peace, love and understanding / Death valley '69 / Thank you / Ma, I didn't notice / After the gold rush / I want to kill my brother: The cymbal.

FLEETWOOD MAC

Formed: London, England . . . July 1967, by MICK FLEETWOOD, PETER GREEN and BOB BRUNNING. They quickly inducted JEREMY SPENCER and made their live debut at the prestigious Windsor Jazz & Blues Festival on the 12th of August '67. Replacing BRUNNING with another ex-BLUESBREAKERS member, JOHN McVIE, they signed to 'Blue Horizon'. Initially billed as PETER GREEN'S FLEETWOOD MAC, the group made little impact in late '67 with their first 45, 'I BELIEVE MY TIME AIN'T LONG'. Around the same time, they became the in-house band for blues artists like OTIS SPANN and DUSTER BENNETT. Early in '68, the debut album, 'PETER GREEN'S FLEETWOOD MAC' hit the Top 5, a fairly derivative set of white-boy blues which nevertheless introduced GREEN's incredibly instinctive feeling for the music, both in his guitar playing and his bruised, soulful vocals. The promise was fully realised with 'BLACK MAGIC WOMAN', a classic slice of brooding voodoo blues with a lean, blistering GREEN solo. Another single, 'NEED YOUR LOVE SO BAD', followed into the lower regions of the chart soon after, while the follow-up album, 'MR. WONDERFUL', again made the Top 10 album charts. But the real breakthrough came with the billowy wistfulness of the GREEN instrumental, 'ALBATROSS', which made No.1 and saw the band melding their blues fixation into something more original. Listening to 'MAN OF THE WORLD', arguably GREEN's most affecting composition (presumably included for those who found the single too sensitive, was the charmingly titled B-side, 'SOMEBODY'S GONNA GET THEIR HEAD KICKED IN TONIGHT'!) , it was clear that all was not well with the band's frontman, and indeed he abruptly left the band the following year. Taking LSD had seriously affected GREEN and he began giving all his money away in line with his newly acquired religious beliefs, his last recording with the band, 'GREEN MANALISHI (WITH THE TWO PRONGED CROWN)', giving light to his demons in chilling style. Truly one of the most tragic cases in the history of rock, GREEN never really recovered from his mental problems and at one particularly low ebb in the 80's, was even sleeping rough around Richmond, Surrey. Despite his difficulties, GREEN did record a couple of solo albums in the 70's and more recently, the man undertook a 1997 comeback tour under the moniker PETER GREEN & THE SPLINTER GROUP. Rarely has a white man played the blues with such feeling (legendary bluesman BB.KING was one of his biggest fans) and it was inevitable that with his departure, FLEETWOOD MAC would be a radically different proposition. The remaining quartet of FLEETWOOD, McVIE, SPENCER and (DANNY) KIRWAN (who had joined a couple of years previous) cut a further album, 'KILN HOUSE' (1970), before recruiting CHRISTINE PERFECT (ex-CHICKEN SHACK) on keyboards/vocals. The next casualty to depart from FLEETWOOD MAC in bizarre circumstances was JEREMY SPENCER, who, in an infamous incident, went AWOL while the band were on tour in Los Angeles. When they eventually tracked him down, he was living with a religious cult, the Children Of God, and informed the band he was staying put. Surprisingly, GREEN returned briefly to fill in on the remainder of the tour although SPENCER was eventually replaced with session pro BOB WELCH. The addition of WELCH saw the band move ever further into the melodic rock vein which PERFECT and KIRWAN had been steering the band since GREEN's departure. KIRWAN was next to leave, however, DAVE WALKER (ex-SAVOY BROWN) and BOB WESTON (ex-LONG JOHN BALDRY) briefly joining up. When the band cancelled a US tour, manager CLIFFORD DAVIS formed a 'new' FLEETWOOD MAC around WALKER and WESTON, the real FLEETWOOD MAC not unreasonably slapping an injunction on the imposters. Amid much legal wrangling, the band severed themselves from DAVIS and moved to California in 1974, only FLEETWOOD and JOHN and CHRISTINE McVIE (the pair had since been hitched) remaining. And so began the second chapter in the marathon MAC saga, as the band hooked up with studio maestro LINDSEY BUCKINGHAM and the sexiest woman to ever walk the planet, STEVIE NICKS. This girlfriend/boyfriend team had previously released an album on 'Polydor', 'BUCKINGHAM-NICKS', and FLEETWOOD was suitably impressed. For once, the band line-up gelled and by the following year, in an incredible reversal of fortunes, FLEETWOOD MAC were sitting pretty at the top of the US charts with the eponymous 'FLEETWOOD MAC' album. Highly melodic, airbrushed pop/rock was the order of the day while in NICKS, the band had a singer of a distinctiveness to match the likes of EMMYLOU HARRIS. The classic 'RHIANNON' found NICKS at her most alluring, fuelling the fantasies of clean cut American boys the country over with her breathy purr. While creatively the band were reaching for the stars, personally they were hitting the depths; JOHN and CHRISTINE divorced the following year, while BUCKINGHAM and NICKS had split acrimoniously. To top it all, FLEETWOOD was in the process of divorcing his wife, JENNY. Instead of imploding, the band chanelled the emotional turmoil into writing songs, creating one of the most phenomenally successful records ever released.

'RUMOURS' (1977) remains the quintessential break-up record, every track, from 'GO YOUR OWN WAY' to 'GOLD DUST WOMAN' giving a different perspective on the situation. The songwriting was impeccable, not a duffer in sight, and in terms of AOR the record has yet to meet its match. 'TUSK' (1979), meanwhile, was a completely different kettle of fish; expensive, often experimental and bloody long. A double album, it was hard going in places yet there were moments of genius, notably NICKS' 'SARA', a beautifully melancholic ballad which arguably stands as the highlight of her career. Come 1980, various members began work on solo projects, FLEETWOOD recording 'THE VISITOR' (1981) with African musicians while NICKS started out on a successful solo career with 'BELLADONNA' (1981). The next MAC project was 'MIRAGE' (1982), a pleasant but ultimately unsatisfying attempt to recreate their winning 70's formula. It was relatively successful nevertheless, reaching No.1 in the States, although it would be the last ditch effort for five years. In the interim, BUCKINGHAM released his well-received 'GO INSANE' (1984) album (he'd made his solo debut three years earlier with 'LAW AND ORDER') while CHRISTINE McVIE released a self-titled album in 1984. Eventually regrouping in 1985, the band began working on what would become 'TANGO IN THE NIGHT' (1987). Basically the MAC sound translated into modern musical currency, the record surprisingly made more of an impact in Britain than the States. Like 'RUMOURS', the record was characterised by varying moods and textures, from BUCKINGHAM's clever, insistent 'BIG LOVE' to the cascading 'LITTLE LIES', and spawned a number of major chart hits. This marked the end of the classic line-up, however, as BUCKINGHAM departed the following summer after escalating tension with NICKS. RICK VITO and BILLY BURNETT were drafted in as replacements but on the showing of 'BEHIND THE MASK' (1990), BUCKINGHAM's midas touch was sorely missed. While the record made No.1 in the States, it failed to produce any singles, more calamity befalling the band later that year as NICKS bailed out following allegations in MICK FLEETWOOD's recently published biography. While BUCKINGHAM and NICKS played with the band at Bill Clinton's inauguration in 1993, there was no question of them rejoining, and ex-TRAFFIC man, DAVE MASON was hired along with BEKKA BRAMLETT (daughter of the legendary DELANEY & BONNIE). The resultant album, 'TIME' (1995), was released to general indifference although it was competent enough. Maybe the album should've been titled 'TIME, GENTLEMEN' as the band seemed something of an irrelevance in the 1990's. Then again, given their chequered history, anything is possible; an album of drum 'n' bass remixes, anyone? • **Songwriters:** GREEN compositions, except early covers; NEED YOUR LOVE SO BAD (Little Willie John) / NO PLACE TO GO (Howlin' Wolf) / DUST MY BROOM (Robert Johnson) / etc. • **Trivia:** Late 1973, their manager Clifford Davis, put together a bogus FLEETWOOD MAC, which resulted in a legal court battle, in which they won. The bogus group became STRETCH, and had a late '75 UK Top 20 hit with 'Why Did You Do It'.

Album rating: PETER GREEN'S FLEETWOOD MAC (*7) / MR. WONDERFUL (*6) / ENGLISH ROSE (*7) / PIOUS BIRD OF GOOD OMEN compilation (*7) / THEN PLAY ON (*7) / KILN HOUSE (*6) / FLEETWOOD MAC IN CHICAGO exploitation (*5) / FUTURE GAMES (*6) / GREATEST HITS compilation on 'CBS' (*9) / BARE TREES (*5) / PENGUIN (*4) / MYSTERY TO ME (*5) / HEROES ARE HARD TO FIND (*6) / FLEETWOOD MAC (*8) / RUMOURS (*10) / TUSK (*7) / FLEETWOOD MAC LIVE (*5) / MIRAGE (*6) / TANGO IN THE NIGHT (*6) / GREATEST HITS compilation on 'Warners' (*8) / BEHIND THE MASK (*5) / TIME (*3) / THE DANCE (*4) / Mick Fleetwood: THE VISITOR (*4) / I'M NOT ME with Zoo (*3) / SHAKIN' THE CAGE with Zoo (*3) / Lindsey Buckingham: LAW AND ORDER (*6) / GO INSANE (*5)

JEREMY SPENCER (b. 4 Jul'48, Hartlepool, England) – guitar, vocals / **PETER GREEN** (b. PETER GREENBAUM, 29 Oct'49) – guitar, vocals (ex-JOHN MAYALL'S BLUESBREAKERS, ex-SHOTGUN EXPRESS) / **MICK FLEETWOOD** (b.24 Jun'42, Redruth, England) – drums (ex-JOHN MAYALL'S BLUESBREAKERS) / **JOHN McVIE** (b.26 Nov'45) – bass (ex-JOHN MAYALL'S BLUESBREAKERS) repl. BOB BRUNNING who formed SUNFLOWER BLUES BAND after recording B-side

		Blue Horizon	Epic
Nov 67.	(7"; as PETER GREEN'S FLEETWOOD MAC) (57-3051) **I BELIEVE MY TIME AIN'T LONG. / RAMBLING PONY** *(re-iss. 1969 on 'C.B.S.'; 3051)*	☐	-
Feb 68.	(lp; stereo/mono) (S+/7-63200) <26402> **PETER GREEN'S FLEETWOOD MAC** <US-title 'FLEETWOOD MAC'> – My heart beat like a hammer / Merry go round / Long grey mare / Shake your moneymaker / Looking for somebody / No place to go / My baby's good to me / I love another woman / Cold black night / The world keep on turning / Got to move. *(re-iss. Oct73 on 'CBS-Embassy'; EMB 31036) (re-iss. Jul77 on 'CBS' lp/c; CBS/40 31494) (cd-iss. Aug94 as 'FLEETWOOD MAC' on 'Columbia Rewind'; 477 358-2)*	4	☐ Aug68
Mar 68.	(7") (57-3138) **BLACK MAGIC WOMAN. / THE SUN IS SHINING**	37	-
Apr 68.	(7") <10351> **BLACK MAGIC WOMAN. / LONG GREY MARE**	-	☐
Jul 68.	(7") (57-3139) <10386> **NEED YOUR LOVE SO BAD. / STOP MESSIN' ROUND**	31	☐
Aug 68.	(lp) (7-63200) **MR. WONDERFUL** – Stop messin' round / Coming home / Rollin' man / Dust my broom / Love that burns / Doctor Brown / Need your love tonight / If you be my baby / Evenin' boogie / Lazy poker blues / I've lost my baby / Trying so hard to forget. *(re-iss. Nov89 on 'Essential' lp/c/cd; ESS LP/MC/CD 010) (re-iss. cd on 'Castle'; CCSCD 368)*	10	
	added **DANNY KIRWAN** (b.13 Mar'50) – guitar, vocals (ex-BOILERHOUSE)		
Nov 68.	(7") (57-3145) <10436> **ALBATROSS. / JIGSAW PUZZLE BLUES** *(re-iss. Nov71 on 'C.B.S.'; CBS 3145)*	1	☐
Feb 69.	(lp) (BN 26446) **ENGLISH ROSE** – Stop messin' round / Jigsaw puzzle blues / Doctor Brown / Something inside of		

me / Evenin' boogie / Love that burns / Black magic woman / I've lost my baby / One sunny day / Without you / Coming home / Albatross.

	Immediate	not iss.
Apr 69. (7"; b-side by EARL VINCE & THE VALIENTS) (IM 080) **MAN OF THE WORLD. / SOMEBODY'S GONNA GET THEIR HEAD KICKED IN TONIGHT** (re-iss. Feb83; same)	2	-

	Reprise	Reprise
Sep 69. (7") <0860> **RATTLESNAKE SHAKE. / COMING YOUR WAY**	-	-
Sep 69. (7") (RS 27000) <0883> **OH WELL (part 1). / OH WELL (part 2)**	2	55 Jan70

—— (note that SPENCER, for some reason did not play on the below album)

Sep 69. (lp) (RSLP 9000) <6368> **THEN PLAY ON**	6	

– Coming your way / Closing my eyes / Showbiz blues / Underway / Oh well / Although the sun is shining / Rattlesnake shake / Searching for Madge / Fighting for Madge / Closing my eyes / When you say / One sunny day / Although the sun is shining / Like crying / Before the beginning. (re-iss. Jul71 lp/c; K/K4 44103) ;re-iss. Apr77) (re-iss. Jun88 with extra tracks; 927 448-2)

May 70. (7") (RS 27007) <0925> **THE GREEN MANALISHI (WITH THE TWO-PRONG CROWN). / WORLD IN HARMONY**	10	

—— Now a quartet of **FLEETWOOD, McVIE, SPENCER and KIRWAN** when GREEN went solo

Sep 70. (lp) (RSLP 9004) <6408> **KILN HOUSE**	39	69

– This is the rock / Station man / Blood on the floor / Hi ho silver / Jewel eyed Judy / Buddy's song / Earl Grey / One together / Tell me all the things you do / Mission bell. (re-iss. Jul71 lp/c; K/K4 54001) (cd-iss. Feb93 on 'Warners'; 7599 27453-2)

Jan 71. (7") <0984> **JEWEL EYED JUDY. / STATION MAN**	-	-

—— added **CHRISTINE (PERFECT) McVIE** (b.12 Jul'43, Birmingham, England) – keyboards, vocals (ex-CHICKEN SHACK) (she had already guested on 'MR. WONDERFUL' album)

Mar 71. (7") (RS 27010) **DRAGONFLY. / PURPLE DANCER**	-	-

—— **BOB WELCH** (b.31 Jul'46, Los Angeles, Calif.) – guitar, vocals (ex-HEAD WEST) repl. SPENCER who formed CHILDREN OF GOD

Sep 71. (lp/c) (K/K4 44153) <6465> **FUTURE GAMES**	-	91

– Women of 1000 years / Morning rain / What a shame / Future games / Sands of time / Sometimes / Lay it all down / Show me a smile. (re-iss. Apr77; same) (cd-iss. Feb93 on 'Warners'; 7599 27458-2)

Sep 71. (7") <1057> **SANDS OF TIME. / LAY IT ALL DOWN**	-	-
Apr 72. (lp/c) (K/K4 44181) <2080> **BARE TREES**	-	70

– Child of mine / The ghost / Homeward bound / Sunny side of Heaven / Bare trees / Sentimental lady / Danny's chant / Spare me a little of your love / Dust / Thoughts on a grey day. (re-iss. Apr77; same) (cd-iss. Feb93 on 'Warners'; 7599 27240-2)

Aug 72. (7") <1093> **SENTIMENTAL LADY. / SUNNY SIDE OF HEAVEN**	-	-
Aug 72. (7") (K 14194) **SPARE ME A LITTLE OF YOUR LOVE. / SUNNY SIDE OF HEAVEN**	-	-

—— **DAVE WALKER** – vocals (ex-SAVOY BROWN) repl. KIRWAN who went solo / added **BOB WESTON** – guitar, vocals (ex-LONG JOHN BALDRY) (above two now with FLEETWOOD, J. McVIE, C. McVIE and WELCH)

May 73. (7") <1157> **REMEMBER ME. / DISSATISFIED**	-	-
May 73. (lp/c) (K/K4 44235) <2138> **PENGUIN**	-	49 Apr73

– Remember me / Bright fire / Dissatisfied / (I'm a) Road runner / The derelict / Revelation / Did you ever love me / Night watch / Caught in the rain. (re-iss. Apr77; same) (cd-iss. Feb93 on 'Warners'; 7599 26178-2)

Jun 73. (7") <1172> **DID YOU EVER LOVE ME. / REVELATION**	-	-
Jun 73. (7") (K 14280) **DID YOU EVER LOVE ME. / THE DERELICT**	-	-

—— Reverted to a quintet when WALKER departed forming HUNGRY FIGHTER

Jan 74. (lp/c) (K/K4 44248) <2158> **MYSTERY TO ME**	-	67 Nov73

– Emerald eyes / Believe me / Just crazy love / Hypnotized / Forever / Keep on going / The city / Miles away / Somebody / The way I feel / Good things come to those who wait / Why / For your love. (re-iss. Apr77; same) (cd-iss. Feb93 on 'Warners'; 7599 25982-2)

Mar 74. (7") (K 14315) <1188> **FOR YOUR LOVE. / HYPNOTIZED**	-	-

—— Trimmed to quartet when WESTON also left

Sep 74. (lp/c) (K/K4 54026) <2196> **HEROES ARE HARD TO FIND**	-	34

– Heroes are hard to find / Coming home / Angel / The Bermuda Triangle / Come a little bit closer / She's changing me / Bad loser / Silver heels / Prove your love / Born enchanter / Safe harbour. (cd-iss. Feb93 on 'Warners'; 7599 27216-2)

Feb 75. (7") (K 14388) <1317> **HEROES ARE HARD TO FIND. / BORN ENCHANTER**	-	-

—— **LINDSEY BUCKINGHAM** (b. 3 Oct'47. Palo Alto, Calif.) – guitar, vocals (as below; ex-BUCKINGHAM-NICKS) repl. WELCH / added **STEVIE NICKS** (b. STEPHANIE NICKS, 26 May'48, Phoenix, Arizona) – vocals

Aug 75. (lp,white-lp/c) (K/K4 54043) <2225> **FLEETWOOD MAC**	23	1

– Monday morning / Warm ways / Blue letter / Rhiannon / Over my head / Crystal / Say you love me / Landslide / World turning / Sugar daddy / I'm so afraid. (Nov76 hit UK No.23) (cd-iss. 1983; 2281-2) (cd-iss. Dec85 on 'Warners'; K2 54043) (re-iss. Feb93 cd/c/lp; 7599 27241-2/-4/-1)

Oct 75. (7") (K 14403) **WARM WAYS. / BLUE LETTER**	-	-
Feb 76. (7") (K 14411) <1339> **OVER MY HEAD. / I'M SO AFRAID**	-	20 Nov75
Apr 76. (7") (K 14430) <1345> **RHIANNON. / SUGAR DADDY** (re-iss. Feb78 reached UK-No.46)	-	11 Feb76
Sep 76. (7") (K 14447) <1356> **SAY YOU LOVE ME. / MONDAY MORNING**	40	11 Jun76

	Warners	Warners
Jan 77. (7") (K 16872) <8304> **GO YOUR OWN WAY. / SILVER SPRINGS**	38	10
Feb 77. (lp,white-lp/c) (K/K4 56344) <3010> **RUMOURS**	1	1

– Second hand news / Dreams / Never going back again / Don't stop / Go your own way / Songbird / The chain / You make loving fun / I don't want to know / Oh daddy / Gold dust woman. (cd-iss. Dec83; K2 56344) (re-iss. Jun88 lp/c; K/K4 56344) (re-iss. Feb93 cd/c/lp; 7599 27313-2/-4/-1) (re-hit No.18 UK in Sep'97)

Apr 77. (7") (K 16930) <8413> **DON'T STOP. / GOLD DUST WOMAN**	32	3 Jul77
Jun 77. (7") (K 16969) <8371> **DREAMS. / SONGBIRD**	24	1 Apr77

Sep 77. (7") (K 17013) **YOU MAKE LOVING FUN. / NEVER GOING BACK AGAIN**	45	-
Oct 77. (7") <8483> **YOU MAKE LOVING FUN. / GOLD DUST WOMAN**	-	9
Sep 79. (7") (K 17468) <49077> **TUSK. / NEVER MAKE ME CRY**	6	8
Oct 79. (d-lp/c) (K/K4 66088) <3350> **TUSK**	1	4

– Over & over / The ledge / Think about me / Save me a place / Sara / What makes you think you're the one / That's all for everyone / Not that funny / Sisters of the Moon / Angel / That's enough for me / Brown eyes / Never make me cry / I know I'm not wrong / Honey hi / Beautiful child / Walk a thin line / Tusk / Never forget. (cd-iss. Mar87; K2 66088) (re-iss. Feb93 cd/c/d-lp; 7599 27395-2/-4/-1)

Dec 79. (7") (K 17533) <49150> **SARA. / THAT'S ENOUGH FOR ME**	37	7
Feb 80. (7") (K 17577) **NOT THAT FUNNY. / SAVE ME A PLACE**	-	-
Mar 80. (7") <49196> **THINK ABOUT ME. / SAVE ME A PLACE**	-	20
Mar 80. (7") (K 17614) **THINK ABOUT ME. / HONEY HI**	-	-
Jun 80. (7") <49500> **SISTERS OF THE MOON. / WALK A THIN LINE**	-	86
Nov 80. (d-lp/c) (K/K4 66097) <3500> **FLEETWOOD MAC LIVE (live)**	31	14

– Monday morning / Say you love me / Dreams / Oh well / Over & over / Sara / Not that funny / Never going back again / Landslide / Fireflies / Over my head / Rhiannon / Don't let me down again / One more night / Go your own way / Don't stop / I'm so afraid / The farmer's daughter.

Jan 81. (7") <49660> **FIREFLIES. / OVER MY HEAD**	-	60
Feb 81. (7") (K 17746) **THE FARMER'S DAUGHTER (live). / DREAMS (live)**	-	-
Mar 81. (7") <49700> **THE FARMER'S DAUGHTER (live). / MONDAY MORNING (live)**	-	-
Jul 82. (7") (K 17965) <29966> **HOLD ME. / EYES OF THE WORLD**	-	4 Jun82
Jul 82. (lp/c) (K/K4 56952) <23607> **MIRAGE**	5	1

– Love in store / Can't go back / That's alright / Book of love / Gypsy / Only over you / Empire state / Straight back / Hold me / Oh Diane / Eyes of the world / Wish you were here. (cd-iss. Dec83; K2 56952) (re-iss. Feb93 cd/c/lp; 7599 23607-2/-4/-1)

Sep 82. (7") (K 17997) <29918> **GYPSY. / COOL WATER**	46	12 Aug82
Nov 82. (7") <29848> **LOVE IN STORE. / CAN'T GO BACK**	-	22
Dec 82. (7"/7"pic-d) (FLEET 1/+P) **OH DIANE. / ONLY OVER YOU** (12"+=) (FLEET 1T) – The chain.	9	-
Feb 83. (7") <29698> **OH DIANE. / THAT'S ALRIGHT**	-	-
Apr 83. (7") (W 9848) **CAN'T GO BACK. / THAT'S ALRIGHT** (12") (W 9848T) – ('A'side) / Rhiannon / Tusk / Over and over.	-	-
Mar 87. (7"/ext.12"/ext.12"pic-d) (W 8398/+T/TP) <28398> **BIG LOVE. / YOU AND I, PART 1** (d7"+=) (W 8398F) – The chain / Go your own way.	9	5
Apr 87. (lp/c)(cd) (WX 65/+C)(925 471-2) <25471> **TANGO IN THE NIGHT**	1	7

– Big love / Seven wonders / Everywhere / Caroline / Tango in the night / Mystified / Little lies / Family man / Welcome to the room . . . Sara / Isn't it midnight / When I see you again / You and I, part II.

Jun 87. (7") (W 8317) <28317> **SEVEN WONDERS. / BOOK OF MIRACLES (instrumental)** (ext-remix.12"+=/ext-remix.12"pic-d+=) (W 8317T/+P) – ('A'dub)	56	19
Aug 87. (7") (W 8291) <28291> **LITTLE LIES. / RICKY** (ext.c-s+=/ext.12"+=/12"pic-d+=) (W 8291/+C/T/TP) – ('A'dub).	5	4
Nov 87. (7") (W 8114) <28114> **FAMILY MAN. / DOWN ENDLESS STREET** (7"box/12") (W 8114 B/T) – ('A'extended vocal remix) / Family party bonus beats / You and I, part II.	54	90 Mar88
Feb 88. (7") (W 8143) <28143> **EVERYWHERE. / WHEN I SEE YOU AGAIN** (12"+=) (W 8143T) – ('A'extended) / ('A'dub version). (3"cd-s+=) (W 8143CD) – Rhiannon / Say you love me.	4	14 Nov 87
Jun 88. (7") (W 7860) **ISN'T IT MIDNIGHT. / MYSTIFIED** (12"+=/3"cd-s+=) (W 7860 T/CD) – Say you love me / Gypsy.	60	-
Nov 88. (7") (W 7644) <27644> **AS LONG AS YOU FOLLOW. / OH WELL (live)** (12"+=/3"cd-s+=) (W 7644 T/CD) – Gold dust woman.	66	43
Nov 88. (lp/c)(cd) (WX 221/+C)(925 838-2) <25801> **FLEETWOOD MAC'S GREATEST HITS (compilation)**	3	14

– As long as you follow / No questions asked / Rhiannon / Don't stop / Go your own way / Hold me / Everywhere / Gypsy / Say you love me / Dreams / Little lies / Sara / Tusk. (c+=/cd+=) – Oh Diane / Big love / You making loving fun / Seven wonders.

Feb 89. (7") (W 7528) **HOLD ME. / NO QUESTIONS ASKED** (12"+=/3"cd-s+=) (W 7528 T/CD) – I loved another woman (live).	-	-

—— (Jul'88) when BUCKINGHAM departed, he was repl. by **RICK VITO** (b.13 Oct'49, Darby, Pennsylvania) – guitar / **BILLY BURNETT** (b. 8 May'53, Memphis, Tenn.) – guitar (ex-MICK FLEETWOOD'S ZOO)

Apr 90. (7"/c-s) (W 9866/+C) <19866> **SAVE ME. / ANOTHER WOMAN** (12"+=/cd-s+=/s-cd-s+=) (W 9866 T/CD/CDX) – Everywhere (live).	53	33
Apr 90. (cd)(lp/c) (<7599 26111-2>)(WX 335/+C) **BEHIND THE MASK**	1	18

– The skies the limit / In the back of my mind / Do you know / Save me / Affairs of the heart / When the Sun goes down / Behind the mask / Stand on the rock / Hard feelings / Freedom / When it comes to love / The second time. (also cd-box; 7599 26206) (cd re-iss. Feb95; same)

Aug 90. (7"/c-s) (W 9739/+C) **IN THE BACK OF MY MIND. / LIZARD PEOPLE** (12"/cd-s) (W 9739 T/CD) – ('A'side) / Little lies (live) / The chain (live). (s-cd-s+=) (W 9739CDX) – Lizard people.	58	-
Nov 90. (7"/c-s) (W 9740/+C) **THE SKIES THE LIMIT. / LIZARD PEOPLE** (12"/cd-s) (W 9740 T/CD) – ('A'side) / Little lies (live) / The chain (live).	-	-
Feb 91. (7") **SKIES THE LIMIT. / THE SECOND TIME**	-	-

—— (late 1990) STEVIE NICKS left to go solo, and CHRISTINE departed due to MICK's new book allegations.

Jan 93. (7"/c-s) (W 0145/+C) **LOVE SHINES. / THE CHAIN (alt.mix)** (cd-s+=) (W 0145CD) – The chain (Not That Funny live version) / Isn't it midnight (alt.version).	-	-

—— **MICK FLEETWOOD, JOHN McVIE, CHRISTINE McVIE** (departed in '94, but on below) + **BILLY BURNETTE** added **DAVE MASON** (b.10 May'46, Worcester, England) – vocals, guitars (ex-TRAFFIC, ex-solo artist)/ **BEKKA BRAMLETT** (b.19 Apr'68, Westwood, Calif.) – vocals (daughter of DELANEY & BONNIE)

Oct 95. (cd/c) (<9362 45920-2/-4>) **TIME**   `47` `-`
– Talkin' to my heart / Hollywood (some other kind of town) / Blow by blow / Winds of change / I do / Nothing without you / Dreamin' the dream / Sooner or later / I wonder why / Nights in Estoril / I got it in for you / All over again / These strange times.

—— the famous mid-late 70's line-up reformed for one-off MTV performance below (complete with orchestra/band!)

Aug 97. (cd/c) (<9362 46702/-2/-4>) **THE DANCE**   `15` `1`
– The chain / Dreams / Everywhere / Rhiannon / I'm so afraid / Temporary one / Bleed to love her / Big love / Landslide / Say you love me / My little demon / Silver springs / You make loving fun / Sweet girl / Go your own way / Tusk / Don't stop.

Jul 98. (12"ep/cd-ep) <44540> **LANDSLIDE /**   `-` `51`

– (with PETER GREEN) compilations, others, etc. –

Note all 'Blue Horizon' releases were on 'Epic' US.

Jul 69. (7") Blue Horizon; (57-3157) **NEED YOUR LOVE SO BAD. / NO PLACE TO GO**   `32` `-`

Aug 69. (lp) Blue Horizon; (7-63215) **PIOUS BIRD OF GOOD OMEN**   `18` `-`
– Need your love so bad / Coming home / Rambling pony / The big boat / I believe my time ain't long / The sun is shining / Albatross / Black magic woman / Just the blues / Jigsaw puzzle blues / Looking for somebody / Stop messin' around. (re-iss. Jun81 on 'C.B.S.'; CBS 32050) (cd-iss. Jun95 on 'Columbia-Rewind'; 480 524-2)
Note all CBS releases were on 'Epic' US.

May 71. (lp) C.B.S.; (63875) **THE ORIGINAL FLEETWOOD MAC BEFORE THE SPLIT**
(re-iss. +c/cd.Jun90 on 'Castle')

Jun 71. (d-lp) Blue Horizon; <3801> **FLEETWOOD MAC IN CHICAGO**   `-`
<US-iss.Nov75 on 'Sire'; SASH 37152> <re-iss. 1977; 2XS 6009>

Oct 71. (d-lp) Epic; <KE 30632> **BLACK MAGIC WOMAN**   `-`
(US lp's; 'FLEETWOOD MAC' (1968) & 'ENGLISH ROSE')

Nov 71. (lp/c) C.B.S.; (CBS/40 69011) **GREATEST HITS**   `36`
– The green Manalishi (with the two-pronged crown) / Oh well (part 1 & 2) / Shake your moneymaker / Need your love so bad / Rattlesnake shake / Dragonfly / Black magic woman / Albatross / Man of the world / Stop messin' around / Love that burns. (re-iss. Feb88 lp/c; CBS 460 704-1/4) (cd-iss. Apr89; 460 704-2) (re-iss. cd Dec94 on 'Columbia-Rewind'; 477 512-2)

May 72. (7") Reprise; (K 14174) **THE GREEN MANALISHI (WITH THE TWO-PRONG CROWN). / OH WELL (Pt.1)**
(re-iss. Mar73 & Nov76; same)

May 73. (7") C.B.S.; (CBS 8306) **ALBATROSS. / NEED YOUR LOVE SO BAD**   `2`
(re-iss. Feb78; CBS 5957) (re-iss. Nov90 on 'Old Gold'; OG 9955)

Aug 73. (7") C.B.S.; (CBS 1722) **BLACK MAGIC WOMAN. / STOP MESSIN' ROUND**

Jun 75. (lp) C.B.S.; (CBS 22025) **THE ORIGINAL FLEETWOOD MAC / ENGLISH ROSE**
(re-iss. Jun76; 81308-9) (re-iss. Jun90 on 'Essential' cd/c/lp; ESS CD/MC/LP 026) (re-iss. cd May94 on 'Castle'; CLACD 344)

Oct 75. (7"; b-side by DANNY KIRWAN) D.J.M.; (DJS 10620) **MAN OF THE WORLD. / SECOND CHAPTER**   `-`
(re-iss. Feb76 & Jun78 on 'Epic'; EPC 6466)

Mar 77. (d-lp/c) C.B.S. / Sire; (CBS 40 88227) <3706> **VINTAGE YEARS**
(re-iss. May82 as 'THE VINTAGE YEARS: HISTORY OF FLEETWOOD MAC'; CBS 22122)

Aug 77. (lp) Embassy; (EMB 31569) **ALBATROSS** (1 side by 'CHRISTINE PERFECT')   `-`
(cd-iss. Feb91 on 'Columbia'; CD 31569)

Sep 78. (lp/c) C.B.S.; (CBS/40 83110) **MAN OF THE WORLD**   `-`

Feb 80. (lp) C.B.S.; (CBS 31798) **BLACK MAGIC WOMAN**   `-`

Aug 83. (c) C.B.S.; (40-22163) **FLEETWOOD MAC / THE PIOUS BIRD OF GOOD OMEN**

Jul 84. (7") C.B.S.; (A 4578) **ALBATROSS. / MAN OF THE WORLD**

Jan 85. (lp) Shanghai; (HAI 107) **LIVE IN BOSTON** (live)
(re-iss. May88 on 'Line'; IMLP 400129) (cd-iss. Oct85 on 'Shanghai'; HAI 400) (cd-iss. Oct89 on 'Castle')

Aug 85. (d-lp/c) Shanghai; (HAI/HAC 300) **CERULEAN (LIVE IN BOSTON Part II)**

Sep 85. (7") Old Gold; (OG 9529) **MAN OF THE WORLD. / ('Natural Born boogie' by Humble Pie)**   `-`

Oct 85. (lp) Platinum; (24076) **RATTLESNAKE SHAKE**   `-`

Oct 85. (lp) Platinum; (24077) **MADISON BLUES**   `-`

Dec 85. (lp) Platinum; (24082) **OH WELL**   `-`

Apr 86. (lp) Commander; (LP 39006) **RATTLESNAKE SHAKE LIVE**   `-`

Apr 86. (lp) Commander; (LP 39007) **OH WELL LIVE**   `-`

Apr 86. (lp) Commander; (LP 39008) **GREEN MANALISHI LIVE**   `-`

Nov 86. (cd) Commander; (CD 99011) **FLEETWOOD MAC LIVE (live 1968)**   `-`
(re-iss. May88; same) (re-iss. May94//Nov94 on 'Arc'; MEC 949020//MO 3016) (re-iss. Aug95 on 'Abracadabra'; AB 3017)

Nov 86. (lp/c/cd) Thunderbolt; (THBL/THBC/CDTB 1.038) **LONDON LIVE '68** (live)

Jul 87. (d-lp/c/cd) Castle; (CCS LP/MC/CD 157) **THE COLLECTION**   `-`
(re-iss. cd Jan94)

Sep 87. (lp) Commander; (224 821-7) **GREATEST HITS LIVE**   `-`
(re-iss. Dec89 lp/c/cd; 264 821-7/-4/-2) (re-iss. cd Apr93 on 'Zillion'; 261 0992)

1988. (lp) Varrick; <VR 020> **JUMPING AT SHADOWS**   `-` `-`
– (same as above)

Feb 89. (7") C.B.S.; (654 613-7) **ALBATROSS. / MAN OF THE WORLD**   `-`
(12"+=/cd-s+=) (654 613-6/-2) – Black magic woman / Love that burns.

Apr 89. (lp/c/cd) Castle; (CCS LP/MC/CD 216) **THE BLUES COLLECTION**   `-`

1989. (3"cd-ep) C.B.S.; (655 171-3) **ALBATROSS / BLACK MAGIC WOMAN / NEED YOUR LOVE SO BAD / I'D RATHER GO BLIND**   `-`

Oct 89. (lp/c/cd) Castle; (CLA LP/MC/CD 152) **BOSTON LIVE**

Nov 89. (lp/c/cd) Mainline; (264 824-1/-4/-2) **OH WELL**

Nov 89. (lp/c) Hallmark; (SHM/HSC 3268) **LOOKING BACK ON FLEETWOOD MAC**
(cd-iss. May90 on 'Pickwick'; PWKS 533)

Jul 90. (cd) Marble Arch; (CMACD 125) **FLEETWOOD MAC LIVE** (live)

Feb 91. (3xcd/5xlp) Essential; (ESB CD/LP 138) **THE BLUES YEARS**

Jun 91. (cd/c) Elite; (ELITE 008 MC/CD) **LIKE IT THIS WAY**
(re-iss. Sep93; same)

Mar 92. (cd/lp; as PETER GREEN'S FLEETWOOD MAC) Reciever; (RR CD/LP 157) **LIVE AT THE MARQUEE** (live)   `-`
(re-iss. cd Jun92 on 'Sunflower'; SF-CD 104)

Sep 92. (cd; as PETER GREEN'S FLEETWOOD MAC) Dojo Early Years; (EARLD 5) **THE EARLY YEARS**

Feb 93. (cd) Castle; (SSLCD 207) **LIVE**

Jun 93. (cd) Point; (261 0202) **21 GREATEST HITS LIVE**

Mar 94. (cd) Castle; (MACCD 187) **MADISON BLUES LIVE**

May 94. (cd) Castle; (MATCD 266) **THE BLUES YEARS**

Jul 94. (cd/c) Success; **LIVE** (live)

Jun 95. (cd) Renaissance; (551 776-2) **FLEETWOOD MAC**

Sep 95. (d-cd/d-c; as PETER GREEN'S FLEETWOOD MAC) Fleetwood; (EDF CD/MC 297) **LIVE AT THE BBC**   `48` `-`

– (without GREEN) compilations, others, etc

on 'Warners' unless mentioned otherwise

1978. (lp/c) Reprise; (K/K4 44138) **THE BEST OF FLEETWOOD MAC**

Oct 82. (c) (K4 66103) **RUMOURS / FLEETWOOD MAC**

Nov 92. (4xcd-box/4xc-box) (<9362 45129-2/-4>) **25 YEARS – THE CHAIN**

Feb 93. (d-cd) (<9362 45188-2>) **25 YEARS – SELECTIONS FROM THE CHAIN**

FLOWERED UP (dig out; Great Alt & Indie . . .)

FLUKE

Formed: Beaconsfield, Buckinghamshire, England . . . mid 1989 by the trio of MIKE BRYANT, MICHAEL TOURNIER and JONATHAN FUGLER. They emerged with the white label 12", 'THUMPER!', before creating a stir via club favourite, 'JONI', which sampled JONI MITCHELL's 'Big yellow taxi' single. In 1990, after a debut gig at a 'Boy's Own' label rave, they signed to 'Creation'. Early the following year saw the release of their first album, 'THE TECHNO ROSE OF BLIGHTY', paving the way for a major signing to Virgin subsidiary, 'Circa'. 1993's 'SIX WHEELS ON MY WAGON' cemented the band's reputation as critical darlings of intelligent electronica, spawning dancefloor hits 'GROOVY FEELING' and 'ELECTRIC GUITAR'. Crossover success finally came with the 'BULLET' EP, reaching No.23 in the summer of '95. This was later consolidated by their first top 20 hit, the throbbing 'ATOM BOMB', at the tail end of 1996. With the success of acts like UNDERWORLD and LEFTFIELD, it remains to be seen whether FLUKE (often courted by the same indie press that fawned over the aforementioned bands) can break out of the dance margins (similar to the CABS or YELLO). • **Songwriters:** Group – sampled many including TALK TALK's 'Life's What You Make It'/ STEVE HILLAGE's 'Hello Dawn'/ BILL NELSON's 'When Your Dream Of Perfect Beauty Comes True'/ etc. • **Trivia:** Have been house remixers for the likes of TEARS FOR FEARS, TALK TALK, WORLD OF TWIST, etc.

Album rating: THE TECHNO ROSE OF BLIGHTY (*6) / SIX WHEELS ON MY WAGON (*7) / OTO (*6) / RISOTTO (*6)

MIKE BRYANT (b. 1 May'60, High Wycombe) – synthesizer/ **MICHAEL TOURNIER** (b.24 May'63, High Wycombe) – synthesizer/ **JONATHAN FUGLER** (b.13 Oct'2, St.Austell, Cornwall, England) – synthesizer

	Fluke	not iss.
Sep 89. (12") (FLUKE 001T) **THUMPER!. / COOL HAND FLUTE**		`-`

	Taxi	not iss.
May 90. (12") **JONI** (mixes)		

	Creation	not iss.
Oct 90. (7") (CRE 090) **PHILLY. / TAXI**		

(12"/cd-s) (CRE 090T)(CRESCD 090) – ('A'side) / ('A'-amorphous mix) / ('A'-Jamoeba mix) / ('A'-Jameteur mix).

Feb 91. (cd/lp)(c) (CRE CD/LP 072)(C-CRE 072) **THE TECHNO ROSE OF BLIGHTY**
– Philly / Glorious / Cool hand Fluke / Joni / Easy peasy / Phin / Jig / Taxi / Coolest.

	Virgin	not iss.
Nov 91. (12"ep/cd-ep) **THE BELLS. / (other mixes)**		`-`

Nov 91. (cd/lp) (FLUKD/FLUKE 1) **OUT (IN ESSENCE)**
– Pan Am into Philly / Pearls of wisdom / The bells:- Heresy – Garden of Blighty.

—— added **JULIAN NUGENT** – synthesizer

	Circa	Virgin
Mar 93. (12"ep/cd-ep) (YR T/CD 103) **SLID (glid) / (4 other mixes); No guitars / Glidub / PDFMIX / Scat and sax frenzy mix)**	`59`	

Jun 93. (12"ep/c-ep) (YR T/C 104) **ELECTRIC GUITAR (vibrochamp). / ('A'-superhound mix) / ('A'-headstock mix)**   `58`
(cd-ep+=) (YRCD 104) – ('A'-sunburst mix) / ('A'-hot tube mix).
(12"ep) (YRTX 104) – ('A'side) / (above 2 mixes).

Sep 93. (7"ep/c-ep) (YR/+C 106) **GROOVY FEELING** (Toni Bell's single scoop) / ('A'-Make mine a 99 mix) / ('A'-Nutty chip cornet mix) `45` ☐
(12"ep+=/cd-ep+=) (YR T/CD 106) – ('A'-Lolly gobble choc bomb') / ('A'-screwball mix).

Oct 93. (cd/c/d-lp) (CIR CDX/C/CA 27) **SIX WHEELS ON MY WAGON** `41` ☐
– Groovy feeling – Make mine a 99 / Letters / Glidub / Electric guitar – Humbucker / Top of the world / Slid – PDFMONE / Slow motion / Spacey (Catch 22 dub) / Astrosapiens / Oh yeah / Eko / Life support. (cd/d-lp w/free cd/lp) – THE TECHNO ROSE OF BLIGHTY

Apr 94. (c-ep/cd-ep) (YR C/CD 110) **BUBBLE** (speakbubble). / ('A'-stuntbubble mix) / ('A'-burstbubble mix) `37` ☐
(12"+=) (YRT 110) – ('A'-Braillbubble mix).

Jul 95. (12"ep/cd-ep) (YR T/CD 121) **BULLET** / ('A'-Dust Brothers (US) mix) / ('A-Empirion mix) / ('A'-Atlas space odyssey mix) `23` ☐
(cd-ep+=) (YRCDX 121) – ('A'-Bullion mix) / ('A'-percussion cap mix) / ('A'-cannonball mix) / ('A'-bitter mix).

Aug 95. (cd/c/lp) (CIR CD/C/CA 31) **OTO** `44` ☐
– Bullet / Tosh / Cut / Freak / Wobbler / Squirt / O.K. / Setback.

Nov 95. (12"ep) (YRT 122) **TOSH** / (mixes; gosh / mosh / cosh / posh) `32` ☐
(cd-ep) (YRCD 122) – ('A'mixes; Nosh / Dosh / Josh / Shriekbackwash).
(cd-ep) (YRCDX 122) – ('A'mixes; Mosh / Gosh / Nosh / Dosh).

Oct 96. (12"/cd-s; as LUCKY MONKEYS) (575713-1/-2) **BJANGO.** / ('A'mixes) `50` –
(above issued on 'Hi-Life')

Nov 96. (12"ep/cd-ep) (YR T/CD 125) **ATOM BOMB** / ('A'mixes) `20` ☐
(cd-ep) (YRCDX 125) – ('A'mixes).

May 97. (12"/cd-s) (YR T/CD 126) **ABSURD.** / ('A'mixes) `25` ☐
(cd-s) (YRCDX 126) – ('A'mixes; Reeferendrum / Whitewash / Mighty Dub Katz dub / Headrillaz vox).

Sep 97. (7") (YRT 127) **SQUIRT.** / ('A'mix) `46` ☐
(cd-s+=) (YRCD 127) – Slid (mixes).
(cd-s) (YRCDX 127) – ('A'mixes; Reeferendrum / Whitewash / eMighty dub Katz dub – Headrillaz vox).

Oct 97. (c/cd/d-lp) (CIRC/+D/A 33) **RISOTTO** `45` ☐
– Absurd / Atom bomb / Kitten moon / Mosh / Bermuda / Setback / Amp / Reeferendrum / Squirt / Goodnight lover.

– compilations, etc. –

Dec 94. (cd/lp) Strange Fruit; (SFMCD/SFPMA 215) **THE PEEL SESSIONS** ☐ –
– Thumper / Taxi / Jig / Our definition of jazz / The bells / The allotment of Blighty / Time keeper.

FLYING BURRITO BROTHERS

Formed: Los Angeles, California, USA ... late 1968 by ex-BYRDS members GRAM PARSONS and CHRIS HILLMAN. While PARSONS had left The BYRDS on the eve of their South African tour, HILLMAN departed upon their return, the pair duly hooking up to realise GRAM's long held vision of a 'Cosmic American Music'. Recruiting pedal steel maestro, SNEAKY PETE KLEINOW, bassist CHRIS ETHRIDGE and drummer JON CORNEAL (who'd played with GRAM previously in The INTERNATIONAL SUBMARINE BAND), this troupe of musical outlaws recorded one of the all-time great country records and one of the first country-rock records in 'THE GILDED PALACE OF SIN' (1969). Equal parts country soul/rock/R&B, alongside the poignant 'HOT BURRITO No.1' (GRAM's fragile voice eternally on the point of cracking) and 'JUANITA', the album featured sublime versions of standards 'DO RIGHT WOMAN' and 'DARK END OF THE STREET' (both written by the legendary DAN PENN). On more uptempo numbers like 'CHRISTINE'S TUNE', the BURRITO's cut a swaggering country rug like no-one else. Onstage and image-wise, the band were just as vivid, custom made Nudie suits and foxy hippy chicks the order of the day. Clearly, playing the Grand Ole Opry as The BYRDS had done before them, was out of the question, PARSONS no doubt past caring about the head-in-the-sand opinion of the country establishment. Yet the rock establishment was equally blinkered in its outlook, the band making little impact outside their native L.A., despite a slot at The ROLLING STONES' ill-fated Altamont gig. MICK JAGGER and KEITH RICHARDS were big fans of the band, RICHARDS especially, building up a close friendship with GRAM. As the pair spent more and more time together, however, GRAM's interest in The BURRITO's began to dwindle. By the release of the follow-up, 'BURRITO DELUXE' (1970), MICHAEL CLARKE and BERNIE LEADON had been drafted in to replace the departed ETHERIDGE and CORNEAL. The album was more upbeat than the debut, but despite such enduring PARSONS/HILLMAN material as 'CODY, CODY', the record lacked the focus and sense of purpose of its predecessor. In spirit, GRAM was only half there, his mind on thoughts of solo stardom, and he left soon after the album's release. In effect, the FLYING BURRITO BROTHERS was GRAM's baby, the band failing to grow, creatively or otherwise after its founding father's departure. They made a further eponymous album with RICK ROBERTS taking PARSONS' place, but by late '71, HILLMAN had split (he joined STEPHEN STILLS in MANASSAS, later going on to C&W success with the DESERT ROSE BAND) and the band were verging on a parody of their former selves. While LEADON went on to success with The EAGLES and ROBERTS (to a lesser degree) with FIREFALL, through various line-ups and label changes, The FLYING BURRITO BROTHERS continued as a kind of clearing house for aging country-rockers, still releasing albums as recently as

1993. • **Songwriters:** PARSONS wrote most, until his premature departure after the second LP. The rest of group took over writing credits from then on. Covered; WILD HORSES (Rolling Stones) / IF YOU GOTTA GO, GO NOW (Bob Dylan) / etc. • **Trivia:** DAVID CROSBY guested his harmonies on their 1969 track 'DO RIGHT WOMAN'.
Album rating: THE GILDED PALACE OF SIN (*9) / BURRITO DELUXE (*7) / THE FLYING BURRITO BROTHERS (*6) / THE LAST OF THE RED HOT BURRITOS (*6) / CLOSE UP THE HONKY TONKS compilation (*8) / FLYING AGAIN (*4) / SLEEPLESS NIGHTS some by Gram Parsons solo (*5) / AIRBORNE (*4) / LIVE IN TOKYO (*4) / DIM LIGHTS, THICK SMOKE AND LOUD MUSIC collection (*6) / FARTHER ALONG: BEST OF compilation (*8) / BACK TO THE SWEETHEARTS OF THE RODEO (*5) / SOUTHERN TRACKS (*5) / ENCORE – LIVE IN EUROPE (*4) / EYE OF THE HURRICANE (*4) / CALIFORNIA JUKEBOX (*4)

GRAM PARSONS (b. INGRAM CECIL CONNOR, 5 Nov'46, Winter Haven, Florida) – vocals, guitar (ex-BYRDS) / **CHRIS HILLMAN** (b. 4 Dec'42) – guitar, vocals (ex-BYRDS) / **SNEAKY PETE KLEINOW** (b.1935, South Bend, Indiana) – pedal steel guitar (ex-BYRDS part-time) / **CHRIS ETHERIDGE** – bass / **JON CORNEAL** – drums (half) / other guest drummers **POPEYE PHILLIPS** / **EDDIE HOH** + **SAM GOLDSTEIN**

		A&M	A&M

Apr 69. (lp) (AMLS 931) <4175> **THE GILDED PALACE OF SIN** ☐ ☐ Mar69
– Christine's tune / Sin city / Do right woman / Dark end of the street / My uncle / Wheels / Juanita / Hot burrito #1 / Hot burrito #2 / Do you know how it feels / Hippie boy. (re-iss.Jul86 on 'Edsel' lp/c; ED/CED 191) (cd-iss. 1988; EDCD 191)

Jun 69. (7") (AMS 756) <1067> **THE TRAIN SONG.** / **HOT BURRITO #1** ☐ ☐

—— **BERNIE LEADON** (b.19 Jul'47, Minneapolis, Minnesota) – guitar, vocals (ex-DILLARD & CLARK) repl. ETHERIDGE / **MICHAEL CLARKE** (b. 3 Jun'44, New York City) – drums (ex-DILLARD & CLARK) repl. CORNEAL (exchanged to D&C) (HILLMAN now switched to bass, vocals)

Apr 70. (7") <1166> **IF YOU GOTTA GO, GO NOW.** / **CODY, CODY** – –

May 70. (lp) (AMLS 983) <4258> **BURRITO DELUXE** ☐ ☐
– Lazy day / Image of me / High fashion queen / If you gotta go, go now / Man in the fog / Further along / Older guys / Cody, Cody / God's own singer / Down in the churchyard / Wild horses. (re-iss.Jul86 on 'Edsel'; ED 194) (cd-iss. Jun90; EDCD 194)

Jul 70. (7") (AMS 794) <1189> **OLDER GUYS.** / **DOWN IN THE CHURCHYARD** ☐ ☐

—— **RICK ROBERTS** (b.1950, Florida) – guitar, vocals repl. PARSONS (went solo, died 19 Sep'73)

Dec 70. (7") (AMS 816) **TRIED SO HARD.** / **LAZY DAY** ☐

Jun 71. (lp) (AMLS 64295) <SP 4295> **THE FLYING BURRITO BROTHERS** ☐
– White line fever / Colorado / Hand to mouth / Tried so hard / Just can't be / To Romana / Four days of rain / Can't you hear me calling / All alone / Why are you crying.

Jul 71. (7") <1277> **COLORADO.** / **WHITE LINE FEVER** – –

—— **HILLMAN, ROBERTS, CLARKE** bring in new members **AL PERKINS** – pedal steel (ex-SHILOH) repl. SNEAKY PETE who went into sessions / **KENNY WERTZ** – guitar, vocals (ex-DILLARD & CLARK) repl. LEADON (later EAGLES) / added **ROGER BUSH** – bass / **BYRON BERLINE** – drums (both ex-COUNTRY GAZETTE)

Jul 72. (lp) (AMLS 74343) <SP 4343> **LAST OF THE RED HOT BURRITOS** (live) ☐ ☐ Feb72
– Devil in disguise / Six days on the road / My uncle / Dixie breakdown / Don't let your deal go down / Orange blossom special / Ain't that a lot of love / High fashion queen / Don't fight it / Hot burrito #2 / Losing game. (cd-iss. Apr89; CDA 4343)

—— Had already split late '71. HILLMAN and PERKINS joined STEPHEN STILLS band. ROBERTS Enlisted BUSH, BERLINE, WERTZ, DON BECK, ALAN MUNDE + ERIC DALTON. They tour Europe and the Netherlands release 2 live albums for 'Ariola'; 'LIVE IN AMSTERDAM' (d-lp; Feb73) & 'BLUEGRASS SPECIAL' (1974). KLEINOW returned but they made no recordings.

—— **SNEAKY PETE + ETHERIDGE** re-formed band with **FLOYD 'GIB' GUILBEAU** – fiddle / **GENE PARSONS** – drums (ex-BYRDS) / **JOEL SCOTT HILL** – bass (ex-CANNED HEAT) ROBERTS & CLARKE later formed FIREFALL

		C.B.S.	Columbia

Nov 75. (7") (CBS 3724) <10229> **BUILDING FIRES.** / **HOT BURRITO #3** ☐ ☐

Dec 75. (lp) (CBS 61984) <33817> **FLYING AGAIN** ☐ ☐ Oct75
– Easy to get on / Wind and rain / Why baby why / Dim lights, thick smoke (and loud, loud music) / You left the water running / Building fires / Desert childhood / Bon soir blues / River road / Hot burrito #3.

Feb 76. (7") <10287> **BON SOIR BLUES.** / **HOT BURRITO #3** – –

—— **SKIP BATTIN** – bass (ex-BYRDS, ex-NEW RIDERS OF THE PURPLE SAGE) repl. ETHERIDGE

Jul 76. (lp) (CBS 81433) <34222> **AIRBORNE** ☐ ☐ Jun76
– Waitin' for love to begin / Out of control / Big bayou / Toe tappin' music / Linda Lu / Walk on the water / Northbound bus / Jesus broke the wild horse / She's a sailor / Quiet man / Border town.

Aug 76. (7") <10389> **BIG BAYOU.** / **WAITIN' FOR LOVE TO BEGIN** – ☐

—— disbanded when BATTIN re-joined NEW RIDERS ... / His replacement ED PONDERS also departed as did PARSONS.

SIERRA

—— were formed by **GUILBEAU, KLEINOW + HILL** plus **THAD MAXWELL** – bass / **MICKEY McGEE** – drums / **BOBBY COCHRAN**

		not iss.	Mercury

1977. (lp) <SRM-1 1179> **SIERRA** – ☐
– Gina / Farmer's daughter / Honey dew / I found love / Strange here in the night / I'd rather be with you / If I could only get to you / She's the tall one / Don't plant roses / You give me lovin' / Let me live.

1977. (7") <73966> **GINA.** / **STRANGE HERE IN THE NIGHT** – ☐

FLYING BURRITO BROTHERS

were once again with **GUILBEAU, KLEINOW + GREG HARRIS** – guitar / **ED PONDER + SKIP BATTIN**

		Sundown	Regency
Jun 79.	(lp) <79001> **LIVE IN TOKYO** (live)	-	

– Big bayou / White line fever / Dim lights, thick smoke / There'll be no teardrops tonight / Roll in my sweet baby's arms / Hot burrito #2 / Colorado / Rocky top / Six days on the road / Truck drivin' man. *(UK-iss.Jan86 on 'Sundown' lp/cd; SDLP/CDSD 025)*

Dec 79.	(7") <45001> **WHITE LINE FEVER** (live). / **BIG BAYOU** (live)	-	

The BURRITO BROTHERS

—— **JOHN BELAND** – vocals, guitar (ex-SWAMPWATER) repl. HARRIS + PONDER

		not iss.	Curb
Dec 80.	(7") <5402> **SHE'S A FRIEND OF A FRIEND. /**	-	
Jan 81.	(lp) <JZ 37004> **HEARTS ON THE LINE**	-	

– That's the way you know it's over / She's a friend of a friend / Isn't that just like love / She belongs to everyone but me / Why must the ending be so sad / Family tree / Damned if I'll be lonely tonight / Does she wish she was single again / Too much honky tonkin' / Oh lonesome me.

Apr 81.	(7") <01011> **DOES SHE WISH SHE WAS SINGLE AGAIN. /** **OH LONESOME ME**	-	
Jul 81.	(7") <02243> **SHE BELONGS TO EVERYONE BUT ME. /** **WHY MUST THE ENDING ALWAYS BE SO SAD**	-	

—— Trimmed to a duo of **BELAND + GUILBEAU**

Dec 81.	(7") <02641> **IF SOMETHING SHOULD COME BETWEEN US (LET IT BE LOVE). / DAMNED IF I'LL BE LONELY TONIGHT**	-	
Jan 82.	(lp) <FZ 37705> **SUNSET SUNDOWN**	-	

– If something should come between us / Louisiana / I'm drinkin' Canada dry / When you're giving yourself to a stranger / What's one more time / Run to the night / How'd we ever get this way / Coast to coast / Closer to you / Save the wild life.

Apr 82.	(7") <02835> **CLOSER TO YOU. / COAST TO COAST**	-	
Jul 82.	(7") <03023> **I'M DRINKIN' CANADA DRY. / HOW'D WE EVER GET THAT WAY**	-	
Nov 82.	(7") <03314> **BLUE AND BROKEN HEARTED ME. / OUR ROOTS ARE COUNTRY MUSIC**	-	

		M.C.A.	Curb
1983.	(7";with EARL SCRUGGS) **COULD YOU LOVE ME ONE MORE TIME. / ROLLER COASTER**	-	

—— The duo cut another lp for 'Curb' but this was shelved.

Jan 84.	(7") *(MCA 868)* <52329> **ALMOST SATURDAY NIGHT. / JUKEBOX KIND OF NIGHT**		
May 84.	(7") <52379> **MY KIND OF LADY. / DREAM CHASER**	-	

—— Signed to LEON RUSSELL's 'Paradise', but album was shelved until '95.

The FLYING BROTHERS

—— with **SNEAKY PETE, SKIP BATTIN, GREG HARRIS + JIM GOODALL**

		not iss.	Relix
Oct 85.	(lp) <RRLP 2008> **CABIN FEVER** (live)	-	

– Wheels / Hot burrito #2 / Hickory wind / Do right woman / Uncle Penn / Louisiana man / She belongs to me / Six days on the road / Mr. Spaceman / Bugles.

Sep 86.	(lp) <RRLP 2022> **LIVE FROM EUROPE** (live)	-	

– Streets of Baltimore / Cash on the barrelhead / Help is on it's way / Roll on brother / Come a little closer / Star of the show / Spitting image / Sin city / Christin's tune / Foggy mountain breakdown / Steam-powered airplane / Mystery train.

The FLYING BURRITO BROTHERS

reformed by **GUILBEAU + BELAND**

		Disky	Disky
Dec 87.	(d-lp/c/cd) <DLP2/DC4/DCD5 025)> **BACK TO THE SWEETHEARTS OF THE RODEO**		

– Back to the sweethearts of the rodeo / Burning embers / Red shoes / Shoot for the Moon / Moonlight raider / Gold guitar / True true love / I'm impressed / Let's do something crazy / Like a shadow / I don't believe you met my baby / My heart stops a beat / Take a message to Mary / Last call / You're running wild / This could be the night / My shoes keep walking back to you / You should know my name by now / I've got a new heartace / Roadmaster. *(re-iss. d-cd Jul95 as The BURRITO BROTHERS on 'Appalosa' += ; AP 05455-2)* – Carry me / Baby won't you let me be the one / You're a fool to love / Mean streets / Burn the midnight oil / Should we tell him / One man woman / Do you know Mary Lou. *(cd re-iss. Feb96 on 'Sundown'; SDCD 502)*

—— **KLEINOW, GUILBEAU & BELAND** added **GEORGE GRANTHAM** – bass (ex-POCO)

		Voodoo	not iss.
1990.	(cd) <VD 103> **SOUTHERN TRACKS**	-	– France

– Crazy horses / Born for honky tonkin' / Armed and dangerous / Shelly's little girl / Thunder road / Matchbox / She's your lover now / Love minus zero / They want to hang a bad boy / My believing heart / Christine's tune (live) / My bucket's got a hole in it (live). *(UK-iss.Oct93; same)*

—— **LARRY PATTON + RICK LANOW** – bass + drums repl.GRANTHAM

		Sundown	not iss.
May 91.	(cd) <CDSD 069> **ENCORE – LIVE IN EUROPE** (live)	-	

– Dim lights, thick smoke / You ain't goin' nowhere / Hickory wind / White line fever / Sweet little Colette / Big bayou / Sweet Suzanna / Wild horses / Silverwings / Help wanted / Cannonball rag / When it all comes down to love / Wheels.

—— **CHRIS ETHERIDGE / BRIAN CADD** (b.Australia) – keyboards / **RONNIE TUTT** – drums; repl. PATTON + LANOW

Oct 93.	(cd) <CDSD 075> **EYE OF THE HURRICANE**		-

– Wheel of love / Like a thief in the night / Bayou blues / Angry words / Rosetta

---

knows / Heart highway / I sent your saddle home / Jukebox Saturday night / Arizona moon / Wild wild west / Eye of a hurricane / Sunset boulevard / Smile. *(re-iss. Jul94 on 'One Way'; OW 30030)*

– compilations, etc. –

1972.	(lp; shared with DILLARD & CLARK) *Mayfair; (AMLB 51038)* **GRASS ROOTS**		-
1973.	(lp) *Bumble; (GEXD 301)* **SIX DAYS ON THE ROAD – LIVE IN AMSTERDAM**		-
Jul 74.	(d-lp) *A&M; (AMLH 63631)* <SD 3631> **CLOSE UP THE HONKY TONKS** (out-takes)		-
Mar 87.	(lp/cd) *Edsel; (ED/+CD 197)* **DIM LIGHTS, THICK SMOKE AND LOUD, LOUD MUSIC**		-

– Train song / Close up the honky tonks / Sing me back home / Tonight the bottle let me down / Your angel steps out of Heaven / Crazy arms / Together again / Honky tonk women / Green, green grass of home / Dim lights / Bony Moronie / To love somebody / Break my mind / Dim lights, thick smoke and loud music.

1989.	(cd) *A&M;* **FARTHER ALONG**		
May 90.	(cd/lp) *Sundown; (CDSD/CDSD 067)* **HOLLYWOOD NIGHTS** (demos 1979-81)		-
May 91.	(cd) *Sundown; (CDSD 072)* **FROM ANOTHER TIME** (live 1975)		-
1992.	(cd) *Relix;* **SIN CITY** (live 1976)	-	
Mar 93.	(cd) *Castle; (CCSCD 366)* **THE COLLECTION**	-	
Nov 94.	(cd) *Start; (HP 9342-2)* **IN CONCERT**	-	
Dec 95.	(cd) *Sundown; (CDSD 079)* **DOUBLE BARREL** (rec.1984)	-	

– She's single again / New shade of blue / Price of love / Ain't love just like the rain / One more time / Sailor / No easy way out / Tonight / Hearts in my eyes / Ain't worth the powder / Late in the night / I'm confessing / Let your heart do the talking.

Apr 96.	(d-cd) *A&M; (540408-2)* **OUT OF THE BLUE**		-
May 96.	(cd) *Country Stars; (CTS 55439)* **TOO MUCH HONKY TONIK'**		-
Mar 97.	(cd) *A&M; (540704-2)* **GUILDED PALACE OF SIN / BURRITO DELUXE**		-

---

FLYING SAUCER ATTACK   (dig out; Great Alt & Indie . . .)

FLY PAN AM (see under ⇒ GODSPEED YOU BLACK EMPEROR!)

FOCUS

Formed: Amsterdam, Netherlands . . . late 1969 by THIJS VAN LEER, HANS CLEUVER and MARTIN DRESDEN, who became backing band for the Dutch version of the musical 'HAIR'. In 1970, they enlisted virtuoso guitarist JAN AKKERMAN, who had previously departed from BRAINBOX. Signing to the 'Bovema' label in Holland, their first lp, 'IN AND OUT OF FOCUS', hit the shelves. Following the European success of the 'HOUSE OF THE KING' track, 'Blue Horizon' picked it up for release in the UK and it subsequently provided the theme tune for many a British TV documentary. Their 2nd album, 'MOVING WAVES', was a more progressively innovative set, containing the extended version of 'HOCUS POCUS', furnishing them with a surprise UK Top 20 hit for new label 'Polydor'. It was described by some as a novelty single due to LEER's strangulated yodel intermittently punctuating AKKERMAN's blistering guitar-work. Fairly unrepresentative of the FOCUS sound, the majority of the band's material was characterised by more pronounced neo-classical and jazz-rock leanings. They consolidated this early chart success with 'SYLVIA', a less frantic, more melodic piece, which fared even better than its predecessor. The single was gleaned from the 1972 double-set, 'FOCUS 3', another album which surprised many by also hitting the charts Stateside. However, after a stop-gap live album recorded at The Rainbow, the band disappointed critics and fans alike with the more conventional 'HAMBURGER CONCERTO' in 1974. From then on the band chose jazz-fusion as their raison d'etre, leading to a sharp commercial decline and inevitable split. AKKERMAN and VAN LEER had already moonlighted with solo outings, going full-time after FOCUS's demise. • **Songwriters:** AKKERMAN & VAN LEER, except TOMMY (Tom Barlage). • **Trivia:** On Apr'90, FOCUS of late'72 re-formed for Dutch TV special.

Album rating: IN AND OUT OF FOCUS (*5) / MOVING WAVES (*7) / FOCUS III (*6) / LIVE AT THE RAINBOW (*4) / HAMBURGER CONCERTO (*4) / MOTHER FOCUS (*3) / SHIP OF MEMORIES exploitation (*4) / FOCUS CON PROBY with P.J. Proby (*4) / HOCUS POCUS – THE BEST OF FOCUS compilation (*7)

BRAINBOX

JAN AKKERMAN – guitar, organ / **KAZIMIRZ LUX** – vocals, percussion / **ANDRE REYNEN** – bass / **PIERRE VAN DER LINDEN** – drums

		Parlophone	Elektra
Jun 69.	(7") (R 5775) <45673> **WOMAN'S GONE. / DOWN MAN**		

		Parlophone	Capitol
1969.	(lp) (PCS 7094) <ST 596> **BRAINBOX**		1970

– Dark rose / Reason to believe / Baby, what you want me to do / Scarborough Fair / Summertime / Sinner's prayer / Sea of delight. *(cd-iss. Jun97 by BRAINBOX & JAN AKKERMAN on 'Oseudonym'; CDP 1033DD)*

May 70.	(7") (R 5842) **TO YOU. / SO HELPLESS**		-

FOCUS

THIJS VAN LEER (b.31 Mar'48) – organ, flute, some vocals / **JAN AKKERMAN** (b.24 Dec'46) – lead guitar, lute (ex-HUNTERS) / **MARTIN DRESDEN** – guitar / **HANS CLEUVER** – drums

				Polydor	Sire
Jan 71.	(lp)	*(2344 003)*	<97027> **IN AND OUT OF FOCUS**	☐	☐

– Focus (instrumental) / Why dream / Happy nightmare (mescaline) / Anonymous / Black beauty / Sugar Island / House of the king / Focus (vocal). *<US re-iss. Jun73; 7404> (re-iss. Dec73; same as above)*

| Jan 71. | (7") | *(2001 134)* | <352> **HOUSE OF THE KING. / BLACK BEAUTY** | ☐ | ☐ |

—— **PIERRE VAN DER LINDEN** (b.19 Feb'46) – drums (ex-BRAINBOX, ex-HUNTERS) repl. CLEUVER / **CYRIL HAVERMANS** – bass, vocals repl. DRESDEN

				Blue Horizon	Sire
Oct 71.	(lp)	*(2931 002)*	<7401> **MOVING WAVES**	☐	☐

– Hocus pocus / Le clochard ("bread") / Janus / Moving waves / Focus II / Eruption: Orpheus – Pupilla – Tommy – Pupilla – Answer – The bridge – Euridice – Dayglow – Endless road – Answer – Orfeus – Euridice. *(re-dist.Nov72 by 'Polydor' lp/c; same); hit No.2) <US re-dist.Nov72; same>*

| Oct 71. | (7") | *(2094 006)* | **HOCUS POCUS. / JANIS** | ☐ | – |
| Jan 72. | (7") | *(2094 008)* | **TOMMY. / FOCUS II** | ☐ | – |

				Polydor	Sire
Oct 72.	(7")	*(2001 211)*	**HOCUS POCUS. / JANIS**	20	–

—— **BERT RUITER** (b.26 Nov'46) – bass, vocals repl. CYRIL who went solo

| Nov 72. | (d-lp/c) | *(2659/ 016)* | <3901> **FOCUS III** | 6 | 35 | Mar73 |

– Round goes the gossip / Love remembered / Sylvia / Carnival fugue / Focus III / Answers? questions! questions? answers! / Anonymous II (part 1) / Elspeth of Nottingham / House of the king.

Dec 72.	(7")	*(2001 422)*	**SYLVIA. / HOUSE OF THE KING**	4	–
Feb 73.	(7")	<704>	**HOCUS POCUS (pt.1). / HOCUS POCUS (pt.2)**	–	9
Jul 73.	(7")	<708>	**SYLVIA. / LOVE REMEMBERED**	–	89
Oct 73.	(lp/c)	*(2443/ 118)*	<7408> **FOCUS AT THE RAINBOW (live)**	23	–

– Focus III / Answers? questions! questions? answers! / Focus II / Eruption: Orfeus – Answer – Pupilla – Tommy – Pupilla / Hocus pocus / Sylvia / Hocus pocus (reprise). *(cd-iss. Apr97 on 'E.M.I.'; REPLAYCD 40)*

—— (Oct73) **COLIN ALLEN** – drums (ex-STONE THE CROWS, ex-JOHN MAYALL) repl. LINDEN (He later briefly returned)

				Polydor	Atco
Apr 74.	(7")	*(2058 466)*	**HAREM SCAREM. / EARLY BIRTH**	☐	☐
May 74.	(lp/c)	*(2442/ 124)*	<36-100> **HAMBURGER CONCERTO**	20	66

– Delitiae musicae / Harem scarem / La cathedrale de Strasbourg / Birth / Hamburger concerto:- Starter – Rare – Medium I – Medium II – Well done – One for the road.

| Jul 75. | (lp) | *(2384 070)* | **FOCUS** (compilation) | 23 | – |

—— (mid'75) **DAVID KEMPER** (b.USA) – drums repl. ALLEN

| Oct 75. | (lp/c) | *(2302/ 036)* | <36-117> **MOTHER FOCUS** | ☐ | ☐ |

– Mother Focus / I need a bathroom / Bennie Helder / Soft vanilla / Hard vanilla / Tropic bird / Focus IV / Someone's crying . . .what! / All together . . .oh that! / No hang ups / My sweetheart / Father Bach. *(cd-iss. Apr97 on 'E.M.I.'; REPLAYCD 41)*

| Mar 76. | (7") | *(2001 640)* | **HOUSE OF THE KING. / O AVENDROOD** | ☐ | ☐ |

—— (Mar76) **PHILIP CATHERINE** (b.27 Oct'42, London) – guitar (ex-JEAN LUC PONTY, ex-JOHN McLAUGHLIN) repl. JAN AKKERMAN who went solo / **STEVE SMITH** – drums (ex-JEAN LUC PONTY) repl. VAN DER LINDEN / added **EEF ALBERS** – guitar

				Harvest	Sire
Sep 77.	(lp)	*(SHSP 4068)*	<7531> **SHIP OF MEMORIES** (rare 1973)	☐	☐

– P's march / Can't believe my eyes / Focus V / Out of Vesuvius / Glider / Red sky at night / Spoke the Lord Creator / Crackers / Ship of memories.

| Jan 78. | (lp) | *(SHSP 11721)* | **FOCUS CON PROBY** | ☐ | – |

– Wingless / Orion / Night flight / Eddy / Sneezing bull / Brother / Tokyo Rose / Maximum / How long.

—— They split around the same time but managed to leave a collaboration with 60's pop star **P.J.PROBY** above

—— **RICHARD JAMES** – drums repl. SMITH who joined JOURNEY. THIJS VAN LEER continued his solo career, further below.

—— **AKKERMAN + VAN LEER** re-formed for Dutch gigs and album (with **TATO GOMEZ + RUUS JACOBS** – bass / **ED STARING** – synthesizers / **SERGIO CASTILLO** – drums / **USTAD ZAMIR AHMED KHAN** – tabla

				Vertigo	not iss.
Aug 85.	(lp/cd)	*(824 524-1/-2)*	**FOCUS**	☐	–

– Russian roulette / King Kong / Le tango / Indian summer / Beethoven's revenge / Ole Judy / Who's calling.

—— In April 1990, the 1972/73 line-up were back again

– compilations, others, etc. –

| Feb 75. | (lp) | *Sire; <7505>* **DUTCH MASTERS – A SELECTION OF THEIR FINEST RECORDINGS 1969-1973** | – | – |
| Sep 84. | (lp/c) | *Fame; (FA 41 3112-1/-4)* **GREATEST HITS OF FOCUS** | ☐ | – |

– Focus / Moving waves / Focus II / Tommy / Hocus pocus / House of the king / Sylvia / Janis.

Feb 85.	(7")	*Golden 45's; (G 4539)* **SYLVIA. / HOCUS POCUS**	☐	–
Apr 87.	(7")	*Old Gold; (OG 9696)* **SYLVIA. / HOCUS POCUS**	☐	–
May 94.	(cd)	*E.M.I.; (CDP 828162-2)* **HOCUS POCUS – THE BEST OF FOCUS**	☐	–

FOETUS (dig out; Great Alt & Indie . . .)

John FOGERTY (see under ⇒ **CREEDENCE CLEARWATER REVIVAL)**

FOGHAT (dig out; 4th edition)

Ben FOLDS FIVE

Formed: Chapel Hill, North Carolina, USA . . . 1994 by songwriter/singer/pianist BEN FOLDS, bassist ROBERT SLEDGE and drummer DARREN JESSEE. Taking his cue from the likes of SUPERTRAMP and RANDY NEWMAN, self-confessed rather uncool fellow FOLDS eventually formed his unconventional guitarless, lo-fi piano combo after years of dallying with classical orchestras. Putting a new slant on nerd-rock, FOLDS' inspired ivory-bashing/tinkling tales of life's losers won him a cult following upon the release of his self-titled debut album in Spring '96. Further exposure came with a slot on the Lollapolooza touring festival later that summer, FOLDS gaining a reputation for instrument (piano) abuse not seen since JIMI HENDRIX shagged his axe and set it on fire. Surprisingly then, perhaps, the band's early '97 follow-up, 'WHATEVER AND EVER AMEN' was a more laid back affair, albeit with a darkly caustic undercurrent, the likes of 'SONG FOR THE DUMPED' and 'ONE ANGRY DWARF AND 200 SOLEMN FACES' not without a hint of bitterness. • **Covered:** CHAMPAGNE SUPERNOVA (Oasis) / SHE DON'T USE JELLY (Flaming Lips).

Album rating: BEN FOLDS FIVE (*8) / WHATEVER AND EVER AMEN (*7) / THE UNAUTHORIZED BIOGRAPHY OF REINHOLD MESSNER (*7)

BEN FOLDS – piano / **ROBERT SLEDGE** – bass / **DARREN JESSEE** – drums

				Caroline	Passenger
Apr 96.	(cd/c/lp)	*(CAROL 002 CD/MC/LP)*	<9501> **BEN FOLDS FIVE**	☐	Aug95

– Jackson cannery / Philosophy / Julianne / Where's summer B.? / Alice Childress / Underground / Sports & wine / Uncle Walter / Best imitation of myself / Video / The last polka / Boxing. *(cd re-iss. Oct96 on 'Epic'; 7243.8.41629-2/-4)*

				Caroline	Alex
Apr 96.	(7")	*(7CAR 002)*	<5620> **UNDERGROUND. / JACKSON CANNERY (live)** / **('A'live)**	☐	May96

(cd-s) *(CDCAR 002)* – ('A'side) / Sports & wine / Boxing.

| Jun 96. | (7"/c-s) | *(7/MC CAR 005)* | <5673> **WHERE'S SUMMER B. / TOM AND MARY (live)** | ☐ | ☐ |

(cd-s+=) *(CDCAR 005)* – Emaline (live).

| Sep 96. | (7") | *(7CAR 008)* | **UNDERGROUND. / SATAN IS MY MASTER** | 37 | – |

(cd-s+=) *(CDCAR 008)* – Video (live).
(cd-s) *(CDCAR 008X)* – ('A'side) / Jackson Cannery.

				Epic	Sony
Feb 97.	(7")	*(664230-7)*	**BATTLE OF WHO COULD CARE LESS. / CHAMPAGNE SUPERNOVA (live)**	26	–

(cd-s+=) *(664230-2)* – Theme from Dr. Pyser.
(cd-s) *(664230-5)* – ('A'side) / Hava nagila / For those of ya'll who wear fannie packs.

| Mar 97. | (cd/c/lp) | *(486698-2/-4/-1)* | <67762> **WHATEVER AND EVER AMEN** | 30 | 42 |

– One angry dwarf and 200 solemn faces / Fair / Brick / Song for the dumped / Selfless, cold and composed / Kate / Smoke / Cigarette / Steven's last night in town / Battle of who could care less / Missing the war / Evaporated.

| May 97. | (cd-s) | *(664536-2)* | **KATE / BAD IDEA / FOR ALL THE PRETTY PEOPLE** | 39 | – |

(cd-s) *(664536-5)* – ('A'side) / Mitchell Lane / All shook up.

| Jan 98. | (cd) | *<(CAR 7554)>* | **NAKED BABY PHOTOS** (rare & live) | 65 | 94 |

– Eddie Walker / Jackson Cannery / Emaline / Alice Childress / Dick Holster / Tom and Mary / For those of ya'll who wear fannie packs / Bad idea / Underground / Ultimate sacrifice / Satan is my master / Julianne / Song for the dumped / Philosophy / Twin falls / Boxing.
(above also issued on 'Caroline' in the UK & US) <below on 'Alex' US>

| Apr 98. | (c-s) | *(665661-4)* | <6019> **BRICK / SMOKE (live)** | 26 | |

(cd-s+=) *(665661-2)* – Song for the dumped (Japanese version).
(cd-s) *(665661-5)* – ('A'side) / Missing the war (live) / She don't use jelly.

| Apr 99. | (c-s) | *(667218-4)* | **ARMY / AIR** | 28 | |

(cd-s+=) *(667218-2)* – Theme from "Dr Pyser".
(cd-s) *(667218-5)* – ('A'side) / Leather jackets / Birds.

| Apr 99. | (cd/c) | *(493312-2/-4)* | <69808> **THE UNAUTHORIZED BIOGRAPHY OF REINHOLD MESSNER** | 22 | 35 |

– Don't change your plans / Mess / Magic / Hospital song / Army / Narcolepsy / Your redneck past / Jane / Your most valuable possession / Regrets / Lullabye.

FOLK IMPLOSION (see under ⇒ **SEBADOH)**

FOO FIGHTERS

Formed: Seattle, Washington, USA . . . April/May '94, after the death of KURT COBAIN (Nirvana), by drummer turned singer/guitarist DAVE GROHL. He subsequently brought in COBAIN stand-in, PAT SMEAR, along with NATE MANDEL and WILLIAM GOLDSMITH, taking the group name from the mysterious lights reported by pilots during World War II. Continuing the UFO concept, the group founded their own 'Roswell' label, (funded by 'Capitol') and debuted in the summer of '95 with UK Top 5 single, 'THIS IS A CALL'. More harmonic and positively life-affirming than NIRVANA (comparisons were inevitable), The FOO FIGHTERS' offered up one of the most exciting debuts of the year; while the lyrics may have been somewhat cryptic, the obvious grunge influences were tempered with an infectious, pop-hardcore rush that was impossible to resist. The album sold well on both sides of the Atlantic, with GROHL & Co heading out on a successful series of festival dates. Work on the Gil Norton-produced follow-up, 'THE COLOUR AND THE SHAPE', got off to a difficult start with initial sessions in Seattle being scrapped. Further problems arose with the departure of sticksman GOLDSMITH halfway through recording, although GROHL subsequently completed the drum parts and the record was finally released in Spring '97 to rave reviews. Outpacing even the debut, The FOO FIGHTERS had come on leaps and bounds in the songwriting department, their rich post-grunge tapestry markedly more diverse. With good old romantic love as the driving theme of the record, the likes of the heart-rending (UK Top 20) 'EVERLONG' took starry-eyed, melodic distortion-pop to new (neck) hair-raising limits (complete with 'Evil Dead'-style video for that true-love atmosphere!). More mellow musings like 'WALKING AFTER YOU' (used on the movie 'X-Files: Fight The Future') and 'DOLL' suggested GROHL was gaining enough confidence in his writing to chill out and reflect rather than continually going for the jugular. The group's growing self-belief was confirmed by some storming festival sets, while the album later came out top in rock 'bible', 'Kerrang!'s yearly critic's poll. After GROHL's brief expedition into film-score work (with soundtrack 'TOUCH' being issued mid-'98), the band inked a deal with 'R.C.A.' and were ready to unleash a third album. 'THERE IS NOTHING LEFT TO LOSE' (1999), disappointed no one with its melodic, HUSKER DU/PIXIES-inspired rock tunes, especially the hit 'LEARN TO FLY' (although I hear RUSH's 'Finding My Way' every time). • **Covers:** OZONE (Kiss) / GAS CHAMBER (Angry Samoans) / BAKER STREET (Gerry Rafferty). • **Trivia:** GREG DULLI (Afghan Whigs) played guitar on 'X-static'.

Album rating: FOO FIGHTERS (*8) / THE COLOUR AND THE SHAPE (*9) / TOUCH soundtrack by Dave Grohl (*6) / THERE IS NOTHING LEFT TO LOSE (*8)

DAVE GROHL (b.14 Jan'69, Warren, Ohio) – vocals, guitar / **PAT SMEAR** – guitar (ex-GERMS) / **NATE MANDEL** – bass / **WILLIAM GOLDSMITH** – drums (both of SUNNY DAY REAL ESTATE)

			Roswell	Roswell
Jun 95.	(7",7"red) (CL 753) **THIS IS A CALL. / WINNEBAGO** (12"luminous+=/cd-s+=) (12/CD CL 753) – Podunk.		5	-
Jun 95.	(cd/c/lp) (CD/TC+/EST 2266) <34027> **FOO FIGHTERS** – This is a call / I'll stick around / Big me / Alone + easy target / Good grief / Floaty / Weenie beenie / Oh, George / For all the cows / X-static / Wattershed / Exhausted.		3	23
Sep 95.	(c-s/7"red) (TC+/CL 757) **I'LL STICK AROUND. / HOW I MISS YOU** (12"+=/cd-s+=) (12/CD CL 757) – Ozone.		18	-
Nov 95.	(c-s/7"blue) (TC+/CL 762) **FOR ALL THE COWS. / WATTERSHED (live at Reading)** (cd-s+=) (CDCL 762) – ('A'-live at Reading).		28	-
Mar 96.	(c-s/7"white) (TC+/CL 768) **BIG ME. / FLOATY (BBC session) / GAS CHAMBER (BBC session)** (cd-s+=) (CDCL 768) – Alone + easy target (BBC session).		19	-

—— **TAYLOR HAWKINS** – drums (of-ALANIS MORISSETTE) repl. GOLDSMITH

Apr 97.	(7") (CL 788) **MONKEY WRENCH. / THE COLOUR AND THE SHAPE** (cd-s+=) (CDCLS 788) – Up in arms (slow version). (cd-s) (CDCL 788) – ('A'side) / Down in the park / See you (acoustic).		12	-
May 97.	(cd/c/lp) (CD/TC+/EST 2295) <58530> **THE COLOUR AND THE SHAPE** – Doll / Monkey wrench / Hey Johnny Park / My poor brain / Wind up / Up in arms / My hero / See you / Enough space / February stars / Everlong / Walking after you / New way home.		3	10
Aug 97.	(7"blue) (CL 792) **EVERLONG. / DRIVE ME WILD** (cd-s+=) (CDCL 792) – See you (live). (cd-s) (CDCLS 792) – ('A'side) / Requiem / I'll stick around (live).		18	-

—— now without SMEAR who was repl. by **FRANZ STAHL** (ex-SCREAM)

Jan 98.	(7"red) (CL 796) **MY HERO. / DEAR LOVER** (cd-s+=) (CDCL 796) – Baker Street (BBC session). (with enhanced cd+=) – Everlong (video) / Monkey wrench (video).		21	-
Jun 98.	(cd; by DAVE GROHL) <(7243 855632-25)> **TOUCH** (music from the motion picture) – Bill Hill theme / August Murray theme / How do you do / Richie Baker's miracle / Making popcorn / Outrage / Saints in love / Spinning newspapers / Remission my ass / Scene 6 / This loving thing / Final miracle / Touch. above featured guests LOUISE POST + JOHN DOE plus BARRETT JONES keyboards + ERIC RICHARDS slide guitar			
Aug 98.	(7"/c-s/pic-d) (E 4100/+CD) **WALKING AFTER YOU (remix). / (Ween: Beacon Light)** (above from the movie, 'X-Files: Fight The Future' on 'Elektra')		20	-

—— now trio of **GROHL, MANDEL + HAWKINS**/ added on tour **CHRIS SHIFLETT** – guitar (ex-NO USE FOR A NAME)

			R.C.A.	R.C.A.
Oct 99.	(c-s) (74321 71308-4) <album cut> **LEARN TO FLY / HAVE A CIGAR** (cd-s+=) (74321 71308-2) – Iron and stone. (cd-s+=) (74321 71310-2) – Make a bet.		21	22
Nov 99.	(cd/c/lp) <(07863 67892-2/-4/-1)> **THERE IS NOTHING LEFT TO LOSE** – Stacked actors / Breakout / Learn to fly / Gimme stitches / Generator / Aurora / Live-in skin / Next year / Headwires / Ain't it the life / M.I.A.		10	10

FOR CARNATION (see under ⇒ SLINT)

Lita FORD (dig out; Great Metal . . .)

FOREIGNER

Formed: New York, USA ... early 1976 by English expatriot MICK JONES, who was already the owner of a rather chequered music biz CV. After beginning his career in England with 60's outfit NERO & THE GLADIATORS, he later worked with French singer JOHNNY HALLIDAY as well as undergoing a stint in SPOOKY TOOTH before moving to New

York and securing a job as an A&R man. Eventually hooking up with Englishmen, IAN McDONALD and DENNIS ELLIOTT alongside New Yorkers, LOU GRAMM, AL GREENWOOD and ED GAGLIARI, JONES formed FOREIGNER. After a year in the studio, the group unleashed an eponymous debut album for 'Atlantic'. Although the record failed to chart in the UK, it hit Top 5 in the States, becoming a multi-million seller and staying on the chart for a year. Its success was boosted by two hit singles, 'FEELS LIKE THE FIRST TIME' and 'COLD AS ICE', FOREIGNER rapidly established as prime staples for American FM radio. Though their material was harder-edged than the likes of REO SPEEDWAGON etc., FOREIGNER captured the middle ground perfectly, their AOR/hard-rock straddling sound gaining them massive sales for subsequent releases such as 'DOUBLE VISION' (1978) and 'HEAD GAMES' (1979), the former's title track narrowly missing the US top spot. Depsite the group headlining the 1978 Reading Festival, the latter album (which saw another seasoned player, RICK WILLS, replacing GREENWOOD) failed to chart in the UK. FOREIGNER would have to wait until the release of the huge, Mutt Lange-produced '4' (1981) album, before they enjoyed transatlantic success. This was secured on the back of the UK/US Top 10, 'WAITING FOR A GIRL LIKE YOU'. It would be another histrionic AOR ballad, 'I WANT TO KNOW WHAT LOVE IS' (featuring the gospel talents of the New Jersey Mass Choir), that would become the group's best known song, its success even furnishing the band with a UK No.1 album. Released after a lengthy sabbatical, 'AGENT PROVOCATEUR' (1984), gave FOREIGNER yet another multi-million selling set, the success of the single making the band a household name. While LOU GRAMM cut a successful solo set in 1987, 'READY OR NOT', MICK JONES flopped with an eponymous set in '89, GRAMM eventually leaving the band for a time at the beginning of the 90's. While FOREIGNER had enjoyed reasonable success with the 1987 set, 'INSIDE INFORMATION', their first GRAMM-less set (with JOHNNY EDWARDS on vocals) was a relative commercial failure. GRAMM finally returned in 1994 although it was clear FOREIGNER's glory days were over. • **Songwriters:** JONES penned some with GRAMM, until his 1987 departure.

Album rating: FOREIGNER (*5) / DOUBLE VISION (*6) / HEAD GAMES (*6) / 4 (*7) / RECORDS compilation (*8) / AGENT PROVOCATEUR (*6) / INSIDE INFORMATION (*5) / UNUSUAL HEAT (*5) / THE VERY BEST OF FOREIGNER or THE VERY BEST . . . AND BEYOND compilations (*7) / MR MOONLIGHT (*4)

LOU GRAMM (b. 2 May'50, Rochester, New York) – vocals (ex-BLACK SHEEP) / **MICK JONES** (b.27 Dec'47, London, England) – guitar (ex-SPOOKY TOOTH) / **IAN McDONALD** (b.25 Jun'46, London) – guitar, keyboards (ex-KING CRIMSON) / **AL GREENWOOD** (b. New York) – keyboards / **ED GAGLIARI** (b.13 Feb'52, New York) – bass (ex-STORM) / **DENNIS ELLIOTT** (b.18 Aug'50, London) – drums (ex-IAN HUNTER BAND)

			Atlantic	Atlantic
Apr 77.	(7") (K 10917) <3394> **FEELS LIKE THE FIRST TIME. / WOMAN OH WOMAN**		-	4 Mar77
Apr 77.	(lp/c) (K/K4 50356) <18215> **FOREIGNER** – Feels like the first time / Cold as ice / Starrider / Headknocker / The damage is done / Long, long way from home / Woman oh woman / At war with the world / Fool for the anyway / I need you. (cd-iss. Apr85; 250356) (re-iss. cd Oct95;)		-	4 Mar77
Jul 77.	(7",7"clear) (K 10986) <3410> **COLD AS ICE. / I NEED YOU** (hit UK No.24 in Jul'78)			6
Dec 77.	(7") <3439> **LONG, LONG WAY FROM HOME. / THE DAMAGE IS DONE**		-	20
Apr 78.	(7"m) (K 11086) **FEELS LIKE THE FIRST TIME. / LONG, LONG WAY FROM HOME / COLD AS ICE**		39	-
Aug 78.	(lp/c) (K/K4 50476) <19999> **DOUBLE VISION** – Back where you belong / Blue morning, blue day / Double vision / Hot blooded / I have waited so long / Lonely children / Spellbinder / Tramontane / You're all I am. (cd-iss. 1988 & Oct95)		32	3 Jul78
Oct 78.	(7",7"red) (K 11167) <3488> **HOT BLOODED. / TRAMONTANE**		42	3 Jun78
Dec 78.	(7") (K 11199) <3514> **DOUBLE VISION. / LONELY CHILDREN**			2 Sep78
Feb 79.	(7",7"pic-d) (K 11236) <3543> **BLUE MORNING, BLUE DAY. / I HAVE WAITED SO LONG**		45	15 Dec78

—— **RICK WILLS** – bass (ex-ROXY MUSIC, ex-SMALL FACES) repl. AL (he joined The SPYS)

Sep 79.	(7") (K 11373) <3618> **DIRTY WHITE BOY. / REV ON THE RED LINE**			12
Sep 79.	(lp/c) (K/K4 50651) <29999> **HEAD GAMES** – Dirty white boy / Love on the telephone / Women / I'll get even with you / Seventeen / Head games / The modern day / Blinded by science / Do what you like / Rev on the red line. (cd-iss. Feb93 on 'Atco'; 7567 81598-2) (re-iss. cd Nov95; 250651)			5
Feb 80.	(7") (K 11417) <3633> **HEAD GAMES. / DO WHAT YOU LIKE**			14 Nov79
Apr 80.	(7") (K 11456) <3651> **WOMEN. / THE MODERN DAY**			41 Feb80
Sep 80.	(7") (K 11602) **I'LL GET EVEN WITH YOU. / BLINDED BY SCIENCE**			-

—— Trimmed to quartet, when GAGLIARI and McDONALD left

Jul 81.	(7") (K 11665) <3831> **URGENT. / GIRL ON THE MOON**		54	4 Jun81
Jul 81.	(lp/c) (K/K4 50796) <16999> **4** – Night life / Juke box hero / Break it up / Waiting for a girl like you / Luanne / Urgent / I'm gonna win / Woman in black / Urgent / Girl on the Moon / Don't let go. (cd-iss. Aug85; 250796) (re-iss. cd Feb91; 7567 82795-2)		5	1
Sep 81.	(7") (K 11678) <4017> **JUKE BOX HERO. / I'M GONNA WIN**		48	26 Feb82
Oct 81.	(7") <3868> **WAITING FOR A GIRL LIKE YOU. / I'M GONNA WIN**		-	2
Nov 81.	(7"m) (K 11696) **WAITING FOR A GIRL LIKE YOU. / FEELS LIKE THE FIRST TIME / COLD AS ICE**		8	-
Mar 82.	(7") (K 11718) **DON'T LET GO. / FOOL FOR YOU ANYWAY**		-	-

Apr 82.	(7") <4044> **BREAK IT UP. / LUANNE**	–	26
Apr 82.	(7") (K 11728) **URGENT. / HEAD GAMES (live)**	45	–
	(12") (K 11728T) – ('A'side) / Hot blooded (live).		
Jul 82.	(7") <4072> **LUANNE. / FOOL FOR YOU ANYWAY**	–	75
Dec 82.	(lp/c)(cd) (A 0999/+4)(780 999-2) <80099> **RECORDS (THE BEST OF . . .)** (compilation)	58	10
	– Cold as ice / Double vision / Head games / Waiting for a girl like you / Feels like the first time / Urgent / Dirty white boy / Jukebox hero / Long, long way from home / Hot blooded. (re-iss. cd Oct95; 7567 82800-2)		
Nov 84.	(7",7"sha-pic-d) (A 9596) <89596> **I WANT TO KNOW WHAT LOVE IS. / STREET THUNDER**	1	1
	(12"+=) – A 9596T) – Urgent.		
Dec 84.	(lp/c/cd) (781999-1/-4/-2) <81999> **AGENT PROVOCATEUR**	1	4 Nov84
	– Tooth and nail / That was yesterday / I want to know what love is / Growing up the hard way / Reaction to action / Stranger in my own house / A love in vain / Down on love / Two different worlds / She's too tough. (re-iss. cd Oct95;)		
Mar 85.	(7") (A 9571) <89571> **THAT WAS YESTERDAY (remix). / TWO DIFFERENT WORLDS**	28	12
	(12"+=) (A 9571T) – ('A'-orchestral version).		
May 85.	(7") <89542> **REACTION TO ACTION. / SHE'S TOO TOUGH**	–	54
Jun 85.	(7") (A 9539) **COLD AS ICE (remix). / REACTION TO ACTION**	64	–
	(12"+=) (A 9539T) – Head games (live).		
	(d7"++=) (A 9539/SAM 247) – Hot blooded (live).		
Aug 85.	(7") <89493> **DOWN ON LOVE. / GROWING UP THE HARD WAY**	–	54
——	LOU GRAMM left to go solo		
Jul 87.	(7") (A 9169) <89169> **SAY YOU WILL. / A NIGHT TO REMEMBER**	71	6 Nov87
	(7"box+=/12"+=/cd-s+=) (A 9169 B/T/CD) – Hot blooded (live).		
Dec 87.	(lp/c)(cd) (WX 143/+C)(781808-2) <81808> **INSIDE INFORMATION**	64	15
	– Heart turns to stone / Can't wait / Say you will / I don't want to live without you / Counting every minute / Inside information / The beat of my heart / Face to face / Out of the blue / A night to remember.		
May 88.	(7") (A 9101) <89101> **I DON'T WANT TO LIVE WITHOUT YOU. / FACE TO FACE**		5 Mar88
	(12"+=/cd-s+=) (A 9101 T/CD) – Urgent.		
Jul 88.	(7") <89046> **HEART TURNS TO STONE. / COUNTING EVERY MINUTE**	–	56
——	(1990) added JOHNNY EDWARDS – vocals to join JONES + THOMAS		
Jun 91.	(7"/c-s) **LOWDOWN AND DIRTY. / FLESH WOUND**	☐	☐
	(12"+=/cd-s+=) – No hiding place.		
Jul 91.	(cd)(lp/c) <(7567 82299-2)>(WX 424/+C) **UNUSUAL HEAT**	56	☐
	– Only Heaven knows / Lowdown and dirty / I'll fight for you / Moment of truth / Mountain of love / Ready for the rain / When the night comes down / Safe in my heart / No hiding place / Flesh wound / Unusual heat. (cd-iss. Nov93;)		
Aug 91.	(7"/c-s) (A 7608/+MC) **I'LL FIGHT FOR YOU / MOMENT OF TRUTH**	☐	☐
	(12"+=/cd-s+=) (A 7608 T/CD) – Dirty white boy (live).		
Apr 92.	(cd)(lp/c) (7597 80511-2)(WX 469/+C) <89999> **THE VERY BEST OF FOREIGNER** (compilation)	19	
	– Feels like the first time / Cold as ice / Starrider / Hot blooded / Blue morning, blue day / Double vision / Dirty white boy / Women / Head games / Juke Box hero / Waiting for a girl like you / Urgent / That was yesterday / I want to know what love is / Say you will / I don't want to live without you. (re-iss. Dec92 as 'THE VERY BEST. . . AND BEYOND' cd; 7567 89999-2)(+=) – (3 extra tracks).		
Apr 92.	(7"/c-s) **WAITING FOR A GIRL LIKE YOU. / COLD AS ICE**	☐	☐
	(12"+=/cd-s+=) – That was yesterday / Feels like the first time.		
Dec 93.	(cd/c) <(7567 82525-2/-4)> **CLASSIC HITS LIVE (live)**	☐	☐
	– Double vision / Cold as ice / Damage is done / Women / Dirty white boy / Fool for you anyway / Head games / Not fade away – Mona / Waiting for a girl like you / Juke box hero / Urgent / Love maker / I want to know what love is / Feels like the first time.		
——	JONES + GRAMM recruited MARK SCHULMAN – drums / JEFF JACOBS – keyboards / BRUCE TURGON – bass		

		B.M.G.	Rhythm Safari
Oct 94.	(7"/c-s) (74321 23286-7/-4) **WHITE LIE. / UNDER THE GUN**	58	☐
	(cd-s+=) (74321 23286-2) – ('A'-alternate version).		
Nov 94.	(cd/c) (74321 23285-2/-4) **MR. MOONLIGHT**	59	☐
Mar 95.	(c-s) <53183> **UNTIL THE END OF TIME / UNDER THE GUN**	–	42
Mar 95.	(c-s) (74321 25457-4) **UNTIL THE END OF TIME / HAND ON MY HEART**		–
	(cd-s+=) (74321 25457-2) – ('A'mix).		

FORMINX (see under ⇒ VANGELIS)

Robert FORSTER (see under ⇒ GO-BETWEENS)

FOTHERINGAY (see under ⇒ DENNY, Sandy)

FOUNTAINS OF WAYNE

Formed: New York City, New York, USA . . . 1995 by the songwriting team of ADAM SCHLESINGER and CHRIS COLLINGWOOD, who met at Williams College in Massachusetts in 1987. ADAM, also of the revered outfit IVY, helped form the 'Scratchie' label with D'ARCY of The SMASHING PUMPKINS, the former having already recorded under the moniker of PINNWHEEL alongside CHRIS. Other moonlighting shenanigans included penning 'THAT THING YOU DO' for mock outfit The WONDERS, which featured in the movie of the same name starring Tom Hanks. FOW signed

to 'Atlantic' in '96 and achieved some degree of success with debut single, 'RADIATION VIBE', a taste of retro 60's BEACH BOYS-esque pop with an edgy 90's slant. Their eponymous debut followed later that summer, a fine collection of power-pop akin to a heavier LEMONHEADS. The slightly wanton, 'UTOPIA PARKWAY' (1999), was too clean-cut and all-American for some, their Modern Rock tunes, 'DENISE' and 'RED DRAGON TATTOO' (both singles), pop puree for college kids into 'Happy Days' nostalgia.

Album rating: FOUNTAINS OF WAYNE (*7) / UTOPIA PARKWAY (*5)

ADAM SCHLESINGER (b.1968) – vocals, guitars / **CHRIS COLLINGWOOD** (b.1968) – vocals, guitar / live work:- **JODY PORTER** – bass (ex-BELLTOWER) / **BRIAN YOUNG** – drums (of The POSIES)

		Atlantic	Atlantic
Mar 97.	(7"/c-s) (A 5626/+C) **RADIATION VIBE. / KARPET KING**	32	–
	(cd-s+=) (A 5626CD) – Janice's party / Imperia.		
Apr 97.	(7"/c-s) (A 5612/+C) **SINK TO THE BOTTOM. / CAN'T GET IT OUT OF MY HEAD**		–
	(cd-s+=) (A 5612CD) – Kid gloves.		
May 97.	(cd/c) <(7567 92725-2/-4)> **FOUNTAINS OF WAYNE**	67	
	– Radiation vibe / Sink to the bottom / Joe Rey / She's got a problem / Survival car / Barbara H. / Sick day / I've got a flair / Leave the biker / You curse all girls / Please don't rock me tonight / Everything's ruined.		
Jul 97.	(7"/c-s) (AT 0004/+C) **SURVIVAL CAR. / COMEDIENNE**	53	–
	(cd-s+=) (AT 004CD) – I want you around (4-track demo).		
Oct 97.	(7"/c-s) (AT 0016/+C) **BARBARA H. / PLACES**		–
	(cd-s+=) (AT 0016CD) – She's got a problem (live).		
Dec 97.	(7"-c-s/cd-s) (AT 0020/+C/CD) **I WANT AN ALIEN FOR CHRISTMAS. / THE MAN IN THE SANTA SUIT**	36	☐
Mar 99.	(7"/c-s) (AT 0053/+C) **DENISE. / I KNOW YOU WELL**	57	
	(cd-s+=) (AT 0053CD) – I'll do the driving.		
May 99.	(7"/c-s) (AT 0067/+C) **RED DRAGON TATTOO. / TODAY'S TEARDROPS**		
	(cd-s+=) (AT 0067CD) – Nightlight.		
May 99.	(cd/c) <(7567 83177-2/-4)> **UTOPIA PARKWAY**		
	– Utopia parkway / Red dragon tattoo / Denise / Hat and feet / The valley of malls / Troubled times / Go, hippie / A fine day for a parade / Amity gardens / Laser show / Lost in space / Prom theme / It must be summer / The senator's daughter.		
Sep 99.	(7"/c-s) (AT 0074/+C) **TROUBLED TIMES. / YOU'RE JUST NEVER SATISFIED**		
	(cd-s+=) (AT 0074CD) – These days.		

4 HERO

Formed: North London, England, 1990 . . . by DEGO McFARLANE, MARC MAC and his 'Reinforced' crew, IAN and GUS LAWRENCE. Run collectively as a pioneering dance imprint, the latter label was the outlet for 4 HERO's Star Trek-sampling debut single, 'MR. KIRK', (and all subsequent releases by the group until their deal with 'Talkin' Loud' in the late 90's) as well as many other cutting edge practitioners on the underground hardcore scene. GOLDIE also became a member of the 'Reinforced' posse for a period, undertaking an A&R role and cutting sought-after tracks under the RUFIGE CRU moniker before going on to major success in his own right. By the release of '94's 'PARALLEL UNIVERSE' set, 4 HERO and their label were becoming synonymous with the burgeoning ambient techno/drum'n'bass scene which GOLDIE brought to worldwide attention with his landmark 'Timeless' album. As well as breaking such acclaimed artists/DJ's as PESHAY, 4 HERO were busy working on their own elaborate take on intelligent dance music. Breaking the mould and employing a cast of "real" musicians (playing acoustic guitar, sax, double bass etc.), the group worked on material which would eventually surface in the shape of the critically acclaimed double set, 'TWO PAGES' (1998). A deeply soulful, consciousness-raising journey of jazz-inflected drum'n'bass, the record segued smoothly from spoken word pleas to space age electronic vistas and sax honking freakouts. Hot on the heels of old mucker GOLDIE and fellow pioneer RONI SIZE, 4 HERO can now boast a Top 40 album under their belts as well as remix work that ranges from NUYORICAN SOUL to PULP's 'This Is Hardcore' single.

Album rating: PARALLEL UNIVERSE (*6) / TWO PAGES (*9)

DEGO McFARLANE – vocals, DJ / **MARC MAC** (b.MARK CLAIRE) – vocals, vibes / **IAN** – / **GUS LAWRENCE** – / plus guests

		Smile	not iss.
1990.	(cd-ep) **MR. KIRK**		
	– Energize (radio version) / Spanergize (radio version) / Energize (club mix) / Spanergize (club mix) / original / jungle. (re-iss. Dec95 as 'MR. KIRK'S NIGHTMARE' some as d10"orange; same)		
——	joined at times by GOLDIE until he went solo		

		Reinforced	unknown
Jul 91.	(lp/c) (RIV LP/MC 1) **IN ROUGH TERRITORY**	☐	☐
	– Genesis / No sleep raver (Tired eyes mix) / Mr Kirks nightmare (live mix) / Reachin / Can' strain my brain / Put your thinkin' cap on / May the wicked perish in the fire of Hell / The last ever bleep track (used to death) / Risin' sun (instrumental) / Mad dogs (feeding propaganda) / Massacre / 4 hero (featuring R-Solution) / Mr Kirks nightmare (original 12th mix).		
Jan 93.	(12") (RIVET12 35) **JOURNEY FROM THE LIGHT (mixes)**	☐	–
Sep 93.	(12"ep) (RIVET12 50) **GOLDEN AGE E.P.**	☐	–
Jun 94.	(cd/lp) (RIV CD/LP 4) **PARALLEL UNIVERSE**	☐	Mar95
	– Universal love / No imitation / Parallel universe / Talk around town / Follow your heart / Wrinkles in time / Terraforming / People always criticise us / Follow your heart (pt.2) / Shadow run / Sunspots / Sounds from the black hole / Power to move the stars / Solar emissions.		
——	In Jun'97, 4 HERO were credited on CHRIS BOWDEN's 12"single, 'HERO BACKED WITH LULLABY' for 'Satellite' (STL 002).		

—— the duo of **DEGO + MARC** added a plethora of singers & musicians including **URSULA RUCKER** – spoken word / **ISH aka 'BUTTERFLY'** – rap / **FACE** – vocals / **CAROL CROSBY** – vocals / **ANDY HAMILL** – double bass / **LUKE PARKHOUSE** – drums, percussion / **LEON MARR** – bass, acoustic guitar / **CHRIS BOWDEN** – saxophone / **BRAD MUNN** – piano, percussion / **EVERTON NELSON + BRIAN WRIGHT** – violins / **SALLY WARD** – viola / **GAY-YEE WESTERHOFF** – cello / **ANDY ROGERS** – trombone / **JUDITH GOODMAN** – french horn / etc.

	Talkin Loud – Mercury	Mercury
Oct 97. (12"ep/cd-ep) *(TL /+CD 24)* **EARTH PIONEERS EP**	☐	☐
– Hal's chicken / Grand river / Planetaria / Dauntless / Loveless.		
Jul 98. (cd/4x12"lp) *(558 465-2/-1)* **TWO PAGES**	38	☐
– Loveless / Golden age of life / Planetaria / Third stream / Wormholes / Escape that / Mother solar / Spirits in transit / Greys / The action / Star chasers / Wishful thinking / Normal changing world / Universal reprise / We who are not as others / Humans / Pegasus 51 / (9 symbols) / De-sci-fer. *(Re-interpretations version Feb99 d-cd/t-lp; 538824-2/-1)*		
Aug 98. (12"/cd-s) *(TL X/CD 36)* **STAR CHASERS. / STAR CHASERS (Masters At Work main mix)**	41	☐
(cd-s) *(TLDD 36)* – ('A'-The Photek remix) / ('A'-DJ Spinna remix) / The action (Shawn J Period remix).		
Feb 99. (12"/cd-s) *(TLX/TLCD 38)* **ESCAPE THAT. / (mixes)**	☐	-
(12") *(TLXX 38)* – ('A'mixes).		

4 NON BLONDES

Formed: San Francisco, California, USA ... 1990 by singer/songwriter, LINDA PERRY, and friend CHRISTA HILLHOUSE. Graduating from the acoustic troubadour circuit, PERRY's hook-up with HILLHOUSE was consolidated with the recruitment of SHANA HALL and WANDA DAY to create a bonafide all-female rock outfit. Having built up a strong local following and having come up trumps in a "best unsigned band" competition, 4 NON BLONDES were rewarded with a major label deal via 'Atlantic'-offshoot, 'Intercord'. Except that 4 NON BLONDES were now three girls and a guy, LOUIS METOYER replacing HALL while DAWN RICHARDSON came in for DAY. 'WHAT'S UP' surpassed all expectations for a debut single, a soul-searching grunge-lite classic with PERRY's paint-stripping, GRACE SLICK-like vocals (described as the female equivalent of AXL ROSE) carrying the song along on a tide of 20-something hippy/rock-chick angst. The track narrowly missed the UK No.1 and suddenly PERRY was a role model for a nation of disaffected teeny grunge girls. Across the pond the picture was even rosier, the debut album, 'BIGGER, BETTER, FASTER, MORE!' (1993) neatly summing up the Stateside mentality and ironically shifting more than half a million units. Yet in Britain at least, the band proved one-hit wonders. Critics remained dubious of the band's talents and a follow-up single, 'SPACEMAN', struggled into the Top 60. A third track, 'DEAR MR. PRESIDENT', didn't even register and the 4 NON BLONDES hype deflated almost as rapidly as it had sprung up, DJ MIKO further trouncing the band's credibility by releasing a gorgonzola-strength Euro-pop version of their defining moment. PERRY later resurfaced in 1996 with a solo set, 'IN FLIGHT', a reasonable collection which nevertheless failed to crack the charts.

Album rating: BIGGER, BETTER, FASTER, MORE! (*5) / Linda Perry: IN FLIGHT (*5)

LINDA PERRY – vocals / **ROGER ROCHA** – guitar repl. LOUIS METOYER after 1st lp / **CHRISTA HILLHOUSE** – bass, vocals / **DAWN RICHARDSON** – drums / and track guests on 1

	Interscope	Interscope
Jun 93. (7"/c-s) *(A 8412/+C)* <98430> **WHAT'S UP. / TRAIN**	2	14 Apr93
(12"+=/cd-s+=) *(A 8412 T/CD)* – ('A'mixes).		
Jun 93. (cd/c) <(7567 92112-2/-4)> **BIGGER, BETTER, FASTER, MORE!**	4	13 Mar93
– Train / Superfly / What's up / Pleasantly blue / Morphine & chocolate / Spaceman / Old Mr. Heffer / Calling all the people / Dear Mr. President / Drifting / No place like home. *(cd re-iss. Aug96 & Sep97; IND 92112)*		
Oct 93. (7"/c-s) *(A 8349/+C)* **SPACEMAN. / STRANGE**	53	☐
(12"+=) *(A 8349T)* – What's up (remix or piano version).		
(cd-s+=) *(A 8349CD)* – Pleasantly blue.		
Dec 93. (7"/c-s) *(A 8333/+C)* **DEAR MR. PRESIDENT. / SUPERFLY**	☐	☐
(12"+=/cd-s+=) *(A 8333 T/CD)* – Drifting.		

—— In Aug '94, 'WHAT'S UP' was ripped up and started again by charting dance/pop terrorist DJ MIKO. The group split after PERRY went solo.

LINDA PERRY

	Interscope	Interscope
Aug 96. (cd) <(IND 90061)> **IN FLIGHT**	☐	☐
– In my dreams / Freeway / Uninvited / Success / Life in a bottle / Fill me up / Knock me out / Too deep / Taken / Fruitloop / Daydream / Machine man / In flight.		

FOUR TOPS

Formed: Detroit, Michigan, USA ... 1953 as vocal quartet, The FOUR AIMS by LEVI STUBBS, RENALDO 'OBIE' BENSON, LAWRENCE PAYTON and ABDUL 'DUKE' FAKIR. In order to avoid confusion with the AMES BROTHERS, the group subsequently changed their name to The FOUR TOPS and cut a one-off single, 'KISS ME BABY', for the 'Chess' label in 1956. 'AIN'T THAT LOVE' and 'WHERE ARE YOU' followed on 'Columbia' and 'Riverside' respectively in the early 60's before the boys were picked up by long-time acquaintance, Berry Gordy, for his new 'Tamla

Motown' operation. As astute as ever, Gordy paired them up with his crack writing team of Holland/Dozier/Holland, the resultant 'BABY I NEED YOUR LOVING' (reputedly the inspiration for the Mann/Weil-penned RIGHTEOUS BROTHERS classic, 'You've Lost That Lovin' Feelin') narrowly missing the Top 10 in 1964. This served notice that 'Motown' had yet another ace up their sleeve in their bid for total domination of the pop/soul scene as the 60's began to swing. It also unveiled the emotionally fired-up tour de force that was STUBBS in full vocal flight, singing his pain against the towering harmonies of messrs BENSON, PAYTON and FAKIR. Summer '65 found them at No.1 with 'I CAN'T HELP MYSELF' while follow-up, 'IT'S THE SAME OLD SONG', made the Top 5 a few months later. The FOUR TOPS reached their dramatic peak in 1966 with transatlantic No.1, 'REACH OUT I'LL BE THERE', a soul symphony of epic proportions that remains their signature tune. The formula was repeated early the following year with 'STANDING IN THE SHADOWS OF LOVE', again achieving similar sales on both sides of the pond (Top 10). The hits kept coming – 'BERNADETTE', '7 ROOMS OF GLOOM', 'YOU KEEP RUNNING AWAY' – but towards the end of the year, Holland/Dozier/Holland departed 'Motown' to form their own label. Divorced from their songwriting/production team, The FOUR TOPS fell back on covers, making the US Top 20 (UK Top 10) with such seemingly incongruous material as The Left Banke's 'WALK AWAY RENEE' and Tim Hardin's 'IF I WERE A CARPENTER'. Although they continued to hit the UK Top 20 with the likes of 'WHAT IS A MAN?', 'DO WHAT YOU GOTTA DO' and 'I CAN'T HELP MYSELF', it'd be 1970 before they were back in the US Top 40 with 'IT'S ALL IN THE GAME' (Top 5 in the UK). 'STILL WATER (LOVE)' finally put them back in the American Top 20 while a duet with The SUPREMES on the Phil Spector classic, 'RIVER DEEP MOUNTAIN HIGH' was a similar-sized hit in 1971. That year's album, 'CHANGING TIMES', couldn't have been more aptly named with The FOUR TOPS struggling to find their place amid a radically altered 'Motown' set-up (the label had relocated its main operation to L.A.) wherein the likes of STEVIE WONDER and MARVIN GAYE (although OBIE actually co-wrote GAYE's seminal 'What's Goin' On') were making massive steps as "serious" artists in their own right and 60's stalwarts (GLADYS KNIGHT, The ISLEY BROTHERS etc.) were defecting in droves. STUBBS and Co themselves parted company with Gordy in 1972, signing with 'Dunhill' ('Probe' in the UK) and initially enjoying something of a mini revival with major hits like 'KEEPER OF THE CASTLE', 'AIN'T NO WOMAN (LIKE THE ONE I'VE GOT)' and 'ARE YOU MAN ENOUGH?', the latter The FOUR TOPS' token contribution to blaxploitation mania with the film in question being 'Shaft In Africa'. From that point on the hits dried up with R&B Top 10 'CATFISH' being their last (very minor i.e. Top 75) pop hit of the decade in 1976. Veterans of the supper club circuit, the FOUR TOPS continued to sell out both nightclubs and major tour venues despite their lack of commercial recording success. The inevitable comeback came at the dawn of the 80's courtesy of a new deal with 'Casablanca', the group scoring a UK Top 3 (US Top 20) hit with 'WHEN SHE WAS MY GIRL' and again hitting the Top 20 in Britain with 'DON'T WALK AWAY'. A brief mid-80's reunion with 'Motown' failed to provide any hits although a double header tour with The TEMPTATIONS packed the crowds in and The FOUR TOPS enjoyed another one-off hit (UK Top 10) in 1988 with 'LOCO IN ACAPULCO' after signing to 'Arista'. While their enduring popularity ensures they're always a hot live ticket, it seems unlikely that the longest-running (and most stable) group of the 'Motown' golden period will grace the charts in the near future. • **Covered:** DO WHAT YOU GOTTA DO + MacARTHUR PARK (Jimmy Webb) / IT'S ALL IN THE GAME (Tommy Edwards) / A SIMPLE GAME + SO DEEP WITHIN YOU (Moody Blues) / WONDERFUL BABY (Smokey Robinson) / LAST TRAIN TO CLARKSVILLE (Boyce-Hart) / I'M A BELIEVER (Neil Diamond) / etc. • **Trivia:** BILLY BRAGG made one Four Top famous again, after singing about LEVI STUBBS' TEARS on a 1986 single. That year LEVI also provided the voice for the man-eating plant in the film musical 'Little Shop Of Horrors'.

Best CD compilation: THE SINGLES COLLECTION (*8)

LEVI STUBBS (b. LEVI STUBBLES) – lead vocals (ex-ROYALS) / **RENALDO 'OBIE' BENSON** – vocals / **LAWRENCE PAYTON** – vocals / **ABDUL 'DUKE' FAKIR** (b.26 Dec'35) – vocals

	not iss.	Chess
Jul 56. (7") <1623> **KISS ME BABY. / COULD IT BE YOU**	-	☐
	not iss.	Columbia
Oct 60. (7") <41755> **AIN'T THAT LOVE. / LONELY SUMMER**	-	☐
<re-iss. Jul65; 43356> – hit No.93		
	not iss.	Riverside
1962. (7") <4534> **WHERE ARE YOU? / PENNIES FROM HEAVEN**	-	☐
	Stateside	Motown
Sep 64. (7") *(SS 336)* <1062> **BABY I NEED YOUR LOVING. / CALL ON ME**	☐	11 Jul64
Jan 65. (7") *(SS 371)* <1069> **WITHOUT THE ONE YOU LOVE (LIFE'S NOT WORTH WHILE). / LOVE HAS GONE**	☐	43 Nov64
	Tamla Motown	Motown
Mar 65. (7") *(TMG 507)* <1073> **ASK THE LONELY. / WHERE DID YOU GO?**	☐	24 Jan65
Jun 65. (7") *(TMG 515)* <1076> **I CAN'T HELP MYSELF (SUGAR PIE, HONEY BUNCH). / SAD SOUVENIRS**	23	1 May65
Jun 65. (lp) *(TML 11010)* <622> **FOUR TOPS**	☐	63 Feb65
– Baby I need your loving / Without the one you love / Where did you go / Ask the lonely / Your love is amazing / Sad souvenirs / Don't turn away / Tea house in Chinatown / Left with a broken heart / Love has gone / Call on me. *(re-iss. Mar77 & Feb82)*		

Aug 65. (7") *(TMG 528) <1081>* **IT'S THE SAME OLD SONG. / YOUR LOVE IS AMAZING** | 34 | 5 Jul65

Nov 65. (7") *(TMG 542) <1084>* **SOMETHING ABOUT YOU. / DARLING I HUM OUR SONG** | 19 |

Mar 66. (lp; mono/stereo) *(TML/STML 11021) <647>* **FOUR TOPS SECOND ALBUM** | 20 Nov65
– Baby I need your loving / Without the one you love / Where did you go / Ask the lonely / Your love is amazing / Sad souvenirs / Tea house in China / Left with a broken heart / Love has gone / Call on me / I can't help myself / Love feels like fire / Is there anything that I can do / Something about you / It's the same old song. *(re-iss. Jan80 + Oct82)*

Mar 66. (7") *(TMG 568) <1090>* **SHAKE ME, WAKE ME (WHEN IT'S OVER). / JUST AS LONG AS YOU NEED ME** | 18 Feb66

Jul 66. (7") *(TMG 568) <1096>* **LOVING YOU IS SWEETER THAN EVER. / I LIKE EVERYTHING ABOUT YOU** | 21 | 45 May66

Oct 66. (7") *(TMG 5790) <1098>* **REACH OUT I'LL BE THERE. / UNTIL YOU LOVE SOMEONE** | 1 | 1 Aug66

Nov 66. (lp; mono/stereo) *(TML/STML 11037) <634>* **4 TOPS ON TOP** | 9 | 32 Aug66
– I got a feeling / Brenda / Loving you is sweeter tha ever / Shake me, wake me (when it's over) / Until you love someone / There's no one left / Matchmaker / Michelle / In the still of the night / Bluesette / Quiet nights of quiet stars / Then.

Jan 67. (7") *(TMG 589) <1102>* **STANDING IN THE SHADOWS OF LOVE. / SINCE YOU'VE BEEN GONE** | 6 | 6 Dec66

Feb 67. (lp; mono/stereo) *(TML/STML 11041) <654>* **FOUR TOPS LIVE!** (live) | 4 | 17 Dec66
– (Introduction) / It's the same old song / It's not unusual / Baby I need your loving / Reach out I'll be there / I'll turn to stone / I left my heart in San Francisco / You can't hurry love / Ask the lonely / Climb ev'ry mountain / The girl from Ipanema / If I had a hammer / I can't help myself / I like everything about you. *(re-iss. Apr85)*

Mar 67. (7") *(TMG 601) <1104>* **BERNADETTE. / I GOT A FEELING** | 8 | 4

Apr 67. (lp; mono/stereo) *(TML/STML 11046) <657>* **4 TOPS ON BROADWAY** | 79

Jun 67. (7") *(TMG 612) <1110>* **7 ROOMS OF GLOOM. / I'LL TURN TO STONE** | 12 | 14 / 76 May66

Oct 67. (lp; mono/stereo) *(TML/STML 11056) <660>* **FOUR TOPS REACH OUT** | 4 | 11 Aug67
– What else is there to do (but think about you?) / If I were a carpenter / Reach out, I'll be there / Walk away Renee / 7 nights of gloom / Last train to Clarksville / I'll turn to stone / I'm a believer / Standing in the shadows of love / Cherish / Wonderful baby. *(cd-iss. Sep95)*

Oct 67. (7") *(TMG 623) <1113>* **YOU KEEP RUNNING AWAY. / IF YOU DON'T WANT MY LOVE** | 26 | 19 Sep67

Dec 67. (7") *(TMG 634)* **WALK AWAY RENEE. / MAME** | 3 | -

Jan 68. (lp; mono/stereo) *(TML/STML 11061) <662>* **THE FOUR TOPS GREATEST HITS** (compilation) | 1 | 4 Sep67
– Baby i need your loving / It's the same old song / Reach out i'll be there / Ask the lonely / Standing in the shadows of love / Loving you is sweeter than ever / I can't help myself / Without the one you love (life's not worthwhile) / 7 rooms of gloom / Something about you / Bernadette / Shake me, wake me (when it's over).

Jan 68. (7") *<1119>* **WALK AWAY RENEE. / YOUR LOVE IS WONDERFUL** | - | 14

Mar 68. (7") *(TMG 647)* **IF I WERE A CARPENTER. / YOUR LOVE IS WONDERFUL** | 7 | -

Apr 68. (7") *(TMG 647) <1124>* **IF I WERE A CARPENTER. / WONDERFUL BABY** | - | 20

Aug 68. (7") *(TMG 665) <1127>* **YESTERDAY'S DREAMS. / FOR ONCE IN MY LIFE** | 23 | 49 Jul68

Nov 68. (7") *(TMG 675) <1132>* **I'M IN A DIFFERENT WORLD. / REMEMBER WHEN** | 27 | 51 Sep68

Jan 69. (lp; mono/stereo) *(TML/STML 11087) <669>* **YESTERDAY'S DREAMS** | 37 | 91 Sep68
– Yesterday's dreams / Can't seem to get you out of my mind / I'm in a different world / We've got a strong love (on our side) / By the time I get to Phoenix / Remember when / Sunny / Never my love / Daydream believer / Once upon a time / The sweetheart tree / A place in the sun.

May 69. (7") *(TMG 698) <1147>* **WHAT IS A MAN. / DON'T BRING BACK MEMORIES** | 16 | 53

Sep 69. (lp; mono/stereo) *(TML/STML 11113) <675>* **FOUR TOPS NOW!** | 74 Jun69
– The key / What is a man / My past just crossed my future / Don't let him take your love from me / Eleanor Rigby / Little green apples / Do what you gotta do / MacArthur Park / Don't bring back memories / Wish I don't love you so / Opportunity knock (for me) / The fool on the hill.

Sep 69. (7") *(TMG 710)* **DO WHAT YOU GOTTA DO. / CAN'T SEEM TO GET YOU OUT OF MY MIND** | 11 | -

Sep 69. (7") *<1159>* **DON'T LET HIM TAKE YOUR LOVE FROM ME. / THE KEY** | - | 45

Feb 70. (lp; mono/stereo) *(TML/STML 11138) <695>* **SOUL SPIN** | Dec69
– Look out your window / Barbara's boy / Lost in a pool of red / Got to get you into my life / Stop the world / Nothing / This guy's in love with you / Light my fire / Honey / The look of love / California dreamin'.

Mar 70. (7") *(TMG 732)* **I CAN'T HELP MYSELF. / BABY I NEED YOUR LOVING** | 10 | -

May 70. (7") *(TMG 736) <1164>* **IT'S ALL IN THE GAME. / LOVE IS THE ANSWER** | 5 | 24 Apr70

Jun 70. (lp)(c) *(STML 11149) <704>* **STILL WATERS RUN DEEP** | 29 | 21 Apr70
– Still water (love and peace) / Reflections / It's all in the game / Everybody's talkin' / Love is the answer / I wish I were your mirror / Elusive butterfly / Ring me together / L.A. (my town) / I'm a believer / Standing in the shadows of love / Cherish / Bernadette / Wonderful baby. *(re-iss. Jun82) (re-iss. Mar91)*

Sep 70. (7") *(TMG 752) <1170>* **STILL WATER (LOVE). / STILL WATER (PEACE)** | 10 | 11 Aug70

—— (with The SUPREMES ⇒, they release (Nov'70) album THE MAGNIFICENT 7, this was issued UK May71 hit No.6. At same time 7" – RIVER DEEP MOUNTAIN HIGH hit US No.14, and UK No.11 in Jun71.

Jan 71. (lp) *(STML 11173) <721>* **CHANGING TIMES** | Oct70
– In these changing times / Just seven numbers / Raindrops keep fallin' on my head / Right before my eyes / I almost had her / Try to remember / Something's tearing at the edges of time / Sing a song of yesterday / The long and winding road.

May 71. (7") *(TMG 770) <1175>* **JUST SEVEN NUMBERS (CAN STRAIGHTEN OUT MY LIFE). / I WISH I WERE YOUR MIRROR** | 36 | 40 Jan71

Jun 71. (7") *<1185>* **IN THESE CHANGING TIMES. / RIGHT BEFORE MY EYES** | - | 70

—— again with The SUPREMES, they issued (Jun71) album RETURN OF THE MAGNIFICENT 7 and single YOU GOTTA HAVE LOVE IN YOUR HEART

Sep 71. (7") *<1189>* **MACARTHUR PARK (part II). / (part 1)** | - | 38

Sep 71. (7") *(TMG 785)* **A SIMPLE GAME. / YOU STOLE MY LOVE** | 3 | -

Nov 71. (lp) *(STML 11195) <740>* **FOUR TOPS GREATEST HITS VOL.2** (compilation) | 25 | Sep71
– In these changing times / Still water (love) / Still water (peace) / Don't let him take your love from me / It's all in the game / I'm in a different world / If I were a carpenter / Walk away Renee / You keep running away / Yesterday's dreams / Just seven numbers.

Jan 72. (7") *<1196>* **A SIMPLE GAME. / L.A. (MY TOWN)** | - | 90

Feb 72. (7"m) *(TMG 803)* **BERNADETTE. / I GOT A FEELING / IT'S THE SAME OLD SONG** | 23 | -

—— final collaborations with The SUPREMES, came out (US Jan72 / UK Apr72) with DYNAMITE lp. Singles WITHOUT THE ONE YOU LOVE + REACH OUT AND TOUCH (SOMEBODY'S HAND) were issued May72 + Nov72 respectively.

May 72. (7") *<1198>* **I CAN'T QUIT YOUR LOVE. / HAPPY (IS A BUMPY ROAD)** | -

Jun 72. (lp) *(STML 11206) <748>* **NATURE PLANNED IT** | 50 May72
– I am your man / (It's the way) Nature planned it / I'll never change / She's an understanding woman / I can't quit your love / Walk with me, talk with me, darling / Medley: Hey man – We got to get you a woman / You got to forget him darling / If you let me / Happy (is a bumpy road) / How will I forget you.

Jul 72. (7") *(TMG 823)* **WALK WITH ME, TALK WITH ME DARLING. / L.A. (MY TOWN)** | 32 | -

Sep 72. (7") *<1210>* **(IT'S THE WAY) NATURE PLANNED IT. / I'LL NEVER CHANGE** | - | 53

Sep 72. (7") *(TMG 829)* **I'LL TURN TO STONE. / LOVE FEELS LIKE FIRE** | - |
(Probe / Dunhill)

Nov 72. (7") *(PRO 575) <4330>* **KEEPER OF THE CASTLE. / JUBILEE WITH SOUL** | 18 | 10

Nov 72. (lp) *(SPB 1064) <50129>* **KEEPER OF THE CASTLE** | 33
– Keeper of the castle / Ain't no woman / Put a little love away / Turn on the light of your love / When tonight meets tomorrow / Love music / Remember what I told you to forget / Love makes you human / Dreaming / The good Lord knows / Jubilee with soul / Keeper of the castle (reprise). *(re-iss. Oct74 on 'A.B.C.'; ABCL 5023)*

Jan 73. (7") *<4339>* **AIN'T NO WOMAN (LIKE THE ONE I'VE GOT). / THE GOOD LORD KNOWS** | - | 4

Jul 73. (7") *(PRO 596) <4354>* **ARE YOU MAN ENOUGH?. / PEACE OF MIND** | 15 Jun73
(above from the soundtrack 'Shaft In Africa' issued on 'Probe-ABC')

Oct 73. (7") *(PRO 604) <4366>* **SWEET UNDERSTANDING LOVE. / MAIN STREET PEOPLE** | 33

Dec 73. (lp)(c) *(SPBA 6277) <50144>* **MAIN STREET PEOPLE** | 66 Sep73
– Main street people intro / I just can't get you out of my mind / It won't be the first time / Sweet understanding love / Am I my brother's keeper / Are you man enough? / Whenever's there's blue / Too little, too late / Peace of mind / One woman man / Main street people. *(re-iss. Oct74 on 'A.B.C.') (cd-iss. Jun86 on 'Charly'; CRB 1129)*

Feb 74. (7") *(PRO 612) <4377>* **I JUST CAN'T GET YOU OUT OF MY MIND. / AM I MY BROTHER'S KEEPER** | 62 Jan74

Apr 74. (7") *<4386>* **ONE CHAIN DON'T MAKE A PRISON. / TURN ON THE LIGHT OF YOUR LOVE** | - | 41

Jul 74. (lp) *(SPBA 6283) <50166>* **MEETING OF THE MINDS** | Apr74
– One chain don't make no prison / Midnight flower / The well is dry / Love ain't easy to come by / No sad songs / Right on, brother / Tell me you love me / All my love / I found the spirit / Meeting of the minds. *(re-iss. Oct74 on 'A.B.C.')*

Aug 74. (7") *<15005>* **MIDNIGHT FLOWER. / ALL MY LOVE** | 55
(A.B.C. / A.B.C.)

Oct 74. (7") *(ABC 4013)* **THE WELL IS DRY. / MIDNIGHT FLOWER** | -

Oct 74. (lp) *(ABCL 5062) <50188>* **LIVE & IN CONCERT** (live) | 92
– Intro and countdown / Are you man enough / Love ain't easy to come by / Medley / Love music / Reach out I'll be there / Standing in the shadow of love / Midnight flower / Baby I need your loving / Keeper of the castle / I am your man / Ain't no woman (like the one I've got) / One chain don't make no prison / I can't help myself (sugar pie honey bunch). *(cd-iss. Aug89 on 'M.C.A.'; DMCL 1890)*

Jun 75. (7") *(ABC 4057) <120960>* **SEVEN LONELY NIGHTS. / I CAN'T HOLD ON MUCH LONGER** | 71 May75

Jul 75. (lp) *(ABCL 5132) <862>* **NIGHT LIGHTS HARMONY** | Jun75
– Seven lonely nights / Is this the price / We all gotta stick together / I've got what you need / I can't hold on much longer / Drive me out of my mind / I'm glad you walked into my life / Let me know the truth.

Dec 75. (7") *<12123>* **WE ALL GOTTA STICK TOGETHER. / (IT WOULD ALMOST) DRIVE ME OUT OF MY MIND** | - | 97

Sep 76. (7") *(ABC 4143) <12214>* **CATFISH. / LOOK AT ME BABY** | 71

Nov 76. (lp) *(ABCL 5197) <968>* **CATFISH**
– Catfish / Feel free / You can't hold back on love / I know you like it / Strung out for your love / Love don't come easy / Disco daddy / Look at me baby.

Nov 76. (7") *<12236>* **FEEL FREE. / I KNOW YOU LIKE IT** | -

Feb 77. (7") *<12267>* **STRUNG OUT FOR YOUR LOVE. / YOU CAN'T HOLD BACK ON LOVE** | -

Jan 78. (7") *(ABC 4199)* **FOR YOUR LOVE. / YOU'LL NEVER A BETTER MAN** | -

Nov 77. (lp) *(ABCL 5223) <1014>* **THE SHOW MUST GO ON**
– The show must go on / I can't live without you / Save it for a rainy day / Runnin' from your love / See the real me / Love is a joy / You'll never find a better man / Candy.

Jan 78. (7") *<12315>* **THE SHOW MUST GO ON. / RUNNIN' FROM YOUR LOVE** | - | -

Oct 78. (7") *<12427>* **H.E.L.P. / INSIDE A BROKEN HEARTED MAN** | - | -

Oct 78. (7") *(ABC 4235)* **PUT IT ON THE NEWS. / WINGS** | | | – |

Jan 79. (lp) *(ABCL 5262)* **AT THE TOP** | | | Nov78 |
    – H.E.L.P. / Bits and pieces / Seclusion / Put it on the news / This house / Just in time / Inside a broken hearted man / When your dreams take wings and fly.

Jan 79. (7") *<12457>* **JUST IN TIME. / THIS HOUSE** | – | | – |
       not iss.   Reliant

1980. (7") *<1691>* **I'M HERE AGAIN. / ('A'instrumental)** | | | |
       Casablanca Casablanca

Sep 81. (7"/12") *(CAN/+X 1005) <2338>* **WHEN SHE WAS MY GIRL. / SOMETHING TO REMEMBER** | 3 | | 11 | Aug81

Nov 81. (lp/c) *(6480/7190 058) <7258>* **TONIGHT!** | | | 37 | Sep81
    – When she was my girl / Don't walk away / Tonight / I'm gonna love you / Who's right, who's wrong / Let me set you free / Something to remember / From a distance / All I do / I'll never leave again. *(cd-iss. Feb89; 836967-2)*

Nov 81. (7") *<2344>* **LET ME SET YOU FREE. / FROM A DISTANCE** | – | | – |

Dec 81. (7"/12") *(CAN/+X 1006)* **DON'T WALK AWAY. / I'LL NEVER EVER LEAVE AGAIN** | 16 | | – |

Jan 82. (7") *<2345>* **TONIGHT I'M GONNA LOVE YOU ALL OVER. / I'LL NEVER EVER LEAVE AGAIN** | – | | – |

Feb 82. (7"/12") *(CAN/+X 1008)* **TONIGHT I'M GONNA LOVE YOU ALL OVER. / FROM A DISTANCE** | 43 | | – |

May 82. (7") *(RSO 89) <1069>* **BACK TO SCHOOL AGAIN. / (B-side by the 'Grease' cast)** | 62 | | 71 |
    (above from the film 'Grease' and issued on 'R.S.O.')

Jul 82. (7"/12") *(CAN/+X 1012) <2353>* **SAD HEARTS. / I BELIEVE IN YOU AND ME** | | | 84 | Aug82

Aug 82. (lp/c) *(CANS/+C 3)* **ONE MORE MOUNTAIN** | | | |
    – Sad hearts / One more mountain to climb / Givin' it up / I believe in you and me / I'm the one / Keep on lightin' my fire / Nobody's gonna love you like I do / Dream on / Whatever it is.

       Motown   Motown

Oct 83. (7"/12") *(TMG/+T 1321) <1706>* **I JUST CAN'T WALK AWAY. / HANG** | | | 71 |

Nov 83. (lp/c) *(STML/CSTML 12197)* **BACK WHERE I BELONG** | | | |
    – Make yourself right at home / I just can't walk away / Sail on / Back where I belong / What have we got to lose / The masquerade is over / Body and soul / Hang.

Jan 84. (7") *<1718>* **MAKE YOURSELF RIGHT AT HOME. / SING A SONG OF YESTERDAY** | – | | – |

Jun 85. (7") *<1790>* **SEXY WAYS. / BODY AND SOUL** | – | | – |

Jul 85. (lp/c) *)ZL/ZK 72301)* **MAGIC** | | | Jun85
    – I can feel the magic / Don't tell me that it's over / Sexy ways / Easier said than done / Don't turn away / I'm ready for love / Again / Maybe tomorrow / Remember me.

Oct 85. (7") *<1811>* **I'M READY FOR LOVE. / DON'T TELL ME THAT IT'S OVER** | – | | – |

Sep 86. (7") *<1854>* **HOT NIGHTS. / AGAIN** | – | | – |

Oct 86. (lp/cd) *(ZL/ZD 72480)* **HOT NIGHTS** | – | | – |
    – Hot nights / Red hot love / I believe in you and me / Let's jam / We got bus'ness / This is love / 80 up for you / Livin' it up too much / The four of us.

       Arista   Arista

Aug 88. (7") *(111 717) <9706>* **INDESTRUCTIBLE. / ARE YOU WITH ME** | 55 | | 35 |
    (12"+=/cd-s+=) *(611/661 717)* – ('A'version).

Sep 88. (lp/c/cd) *(208/408/258 840) <8492>* **INDESTRUCTIBLE** | | | |
    – Indestructible / Change of heart / If ever a love there was / The Sun ain't gonna shine / Next time / Loco in Acapulco / Are you with me / I'm only wounded / When you dance / Let's jam. *(re-iss. Jun91 cd/c/lp; 261/411/211 567)*

Oct 88. (7") *<9801>* **LOVE IN ACAPULCO. / CHANGE OF HEART** | – | | – |

Nov 88. (7") *(111 850)* **LOCO IN ACAPULCO. / THE FOUR OF US** | 9 | | – |
    (12"+=/cd-s+=) *(611/661 850)* – ('A'-Body mix).

Feb 89. (7"; by FOUR TOPS featuring ARETHA FRANKLIN) *<9850>* **IF EVER A LOVE THERE WAS. / LET'S JAM** | – | | – |

Feb 89. (7"; by FOUR TOPS featuring SMOKEY ROBINSON) *(112 074)* **INDESTRUCTIBLE. / ARE YOU WITH ME** | 30 | | – |
    (12"+=/cd-s+=) *(612/662 074)* – ('A'versions).
    (7"pic-d) *(112 151)* – ('A'side) / Next time.

Jul 89. (7") *(112 252)* **THE SUN AIN'T GONNA SHINE (The Ben Liebrand Remix) / LOCO IN ACAPULCO** | | | – |
    (12"+=/cd-s+=) *(612/662 252)* – ('A'versions).

—— retired to the cabaret circuit for the rest of the 90's

– compilations, etc. –

on 'Tamla Motown' unless stated otherwise

Feb 66. (7"ep) *(TME 2012)* **THE FOUR TOPS** | | | – |
    – I can't help myself / Ask the lonely / Something about you.

Mar 67. (7"ep) *(TME 2018)* **FOUR TOPS HITS** | | | – |
    – Reach out, I'll be there / Bernadette / Standing in the shadows of love / If I were a carpenter.

Mar 73. (7") *(TMG 850)* **SO DEEP WITHIN YOU. / HAPPY (IS A BUMPY ROAD)** | | | – |

Jun 73. (7") *(TMG 858)* **I CAN'T QUIT YOUR LOVE. / I AM YOUR MAN** | | | – |

Oct 73. (d-lp) *(TMSP 11241-2) <764>* **THE FOUR TOPS STORY 1964-72** <US-title 'THE BEST OF THE FOUR TOPS'> | 35 | | |

Oct 75. (7") *(TMG 1011)* **WALK AWAY RENEE. / YOU KEEP RUNNING AWAY** | | | – |

Sep 76. (7") *(TMG 1049)* **REACH OUT I'LL BE THERE. / STANDING IN THE SHADOWS OF LOVE** | | | – |

Nov 76. (lp) *(STML 8028)* **SUPER HITS** | | | – |
    (re-iss. Oct81 lp/c; STMA/CSTMA 8024)

Sep 78. (7") *(TMG 1120)* **I CAN'T HELP MYSELF (SUGAR PIE, HONEY BUNCH). / IT'S THE SAME OLD SONG** | | | – |

Jan 79. (lp/c) Music For Pleasure; *(MFP/TC-MFP 50416)* **IT'S ALL IN THE GAME** | | | – |

Jun 80. (lp/c) EMI-TV; *(EMTV/CMTV 26)* **20 GOLDEN GREATS** | | | – |

Feb 82. (lp/c) K-Tel; *(NE1/CE2 160)* **THE BEST OF THE FOUR TOPS** | 13 | | – |

Apr 82. (lp) M.C.A.; *(MCL 1675)* **GREATEST HITS** | | | |

Jun 82. (lp/c) *(TMS/TMC 3502)* **THE FABULOUS FOUR TOPS** | | | – |

Sep 82. (d-lp/d-c) *(TMSP/CTMSP 6013)* **ANTHOLOGY** | | | – |
    (cd-iss. Apr89; WD 72528)

Oct 82. (lp/c) *(TMS/TMC 3514)* **HITS OF GOLD** | | | – |

Feb 83. (7") *(TMG 958)* **IF I WERE A CARPENTER. / 7 ROOMS OF GLOOM** | | | – |

Apr 83. (7") *(TMG 978)* **BABY I NEED YOUR LOVING. / YESTERDAY'S DREAMS** | | | – |

Jul 83. (c-ep) *(CTME 2032)* **FLIP HITS** | | | – |
    – It's all in the game / Bernadette / Standing in the shadows of love / If I were a carpenter.

Sep 83. (7") *(TMG 972)* **STILL WATER (LOVE). / SIMPLE GAME** | | | – |

Jun 84. (7"/12") Calibre; *(CAB 124)* **YOUR SONG. / I'M HERE AGAIN** | | | – |

Apr 85. (7"/12") *(TMG/+T 995)* **BERNADETTE. / IT'S ALL IN THE GAME** | | | – |

Oct 86. (d-cd) *(ZD 72472)* **FOUR TOPS REACH OUT / STILL WATERS RUN DEEP** | | | – |

Oct 86. (d-cd) *(ZD 72491)* **FOUR TOPS / FOUR TOPS SECOND ALBUM** | | | – |

Oct 87. (cd) *(WD 72220)* **19 GREATEST HITS: COMPACT COMMAND PERFORMANCES** | | | – |

May 88. (7") *(ZB 41943)* **REACH OUT I'LL BE THERE. / STANDING IN THE SHADOWS OF LOVE** | 11 | | – |
    (12"+=/cd-s+=) *(ZT/ZD 41944)* – ('A'instrumental).

Jul 90. (cd) E.M.S.; *(295 704)* **LEGEND** | | | – |

Jan 91. (cd/c/lp) Telstar; *(TCD/STAC/STAR 2437)* **THEIR GREATEST HITS** | 47 | | – |

Jul 91. (cd/c) Knight; *(KNCD/KNMC 12055)* **HEART AND SOUL** | | | – |

Jan 92. (cd/c/lp) *(530016-2/-4/-1)* **MOTOWN'S GREATEST HITS** | | | – |

Jul 92. (cd) Castle; *(CCS CD/MC 344)* **THE COLLECTION** | | | – |

Jul 92. (cd) Raven-Topic; **SHAKE ME WAKE ME: 25 GREATEST HITS 1964-1973** | – | | |

Sep 92. (cd/c/lp) Polygram; *(515710-2/-4/-1)* **THE SINGLES COLLECTION** | 11 | | |
    – Reach out I'll be there / Standing in the shadows of love / Bernadette / Walk away Renee / If i were a carpenter / Simple game / 7 Rooms of gloom / Loving you is sweeter than ever / You keep running away / Yesterday's dreams / I'm in a different world / What is a man / Loco in Acapulco / Indestructible / When she was my girl / It's all in the game / Still water (love) / I can't help myself / Do what you gotta do / Keeper of the castle / Don't walk away.

May 93. (cd/c) Spectrum; *(550077-2/-4)* **THE LOOK OF LOVE** | | | – |

Jun 93. (cd/c) WEA; *<(8122 71183-2/-4)>* **UNTIL YOU LOVE SOMEONE – MORE BEST OF THE FOUR TOPS (1965-1970)** | | | |

Oct 93. (cd/c) Spectrum; *(550135-2/-4)* **WITH LOVE** | | | |

Jul 96. (cd/c) Spectrum; *(552119-2/-4)* **MOTOWN EARLY CLASSICS** | | | |

Apr 97. (cd) Spectrum; *(530791-2)* **REACH OUT I'LL BE THERE** | | | |
    (re-iss. Aug99; same)

Feb 98. (cd) Disky; *(WB 88552-2)* **THE VERY BEST OF THE FOUR TOPS LIVE** | | | – |

Apr 98. (cd) Music Club; *(MCCD 340)* **THE FOUR TOPS** | | | – |

Aug 98. (cd) *(530825-2)* **THE ULTIMATE COLLECTION** | | | – |

Mar 99. (cd) Platinum; *(PLA TCD/C 446)* **THE COLLECTION** | | | – |

Mar 99. (d-cd) Laserlight; *(24638)* **THE FOUR TOPS** | | | – |

John FOXX (dig out; Great Alt & Indie . . .)

Roddy FRAME (see under ⇒ AZTEC CAMERA)

Peter FRAMPTON

Born: 22 Apr'50, Beckenham, Kent, England. After leaving HUMBLE PIE late in '71, FRAMPTON signed a solo deal with 'A&M', a debut album, 'WINDS OF CHANGE', was subsequently supported by a US tour with headliners The J. GEILS BAND. In 1973, his next album, 'FRAMPTON'S CAMEL' (as FRAMPTON'S CAMEL), failed to make any substantial commercial impact and it was decided to drop the CAMEL part of the name to avoid confusion with the British band of same name. A year later, FRAMPTON gained his first US Top 40 entry with his third set, 'SOMETHIN'S HAPPENING' and followed the next year with another hit album, 'FRAMPTON'. In 1976, his live double-lp, 'FRAMPTON COMES ALIVE' (recorded live at Winterland, California), soon topped the US chart, becoming a multi-million seller in the process. Its sales were boosted by three smash hits, 'SHOW ME THE WAY', 'BABY, I LOVE YOUR WAY' and 'DO YOU FEEL LIKE WE DO', the former seeing the singer/guitarist trademarking his new "Voxbox" guitar sound. His 1977 studio follow-up, 'I'M IN YOU', became an even greater success (Top 3 US and Top 20 UK), its title track hit US Top 3, while his version of Stevie Wonder's 'SIGNED, SEALED, DELIVERED (I'M YOURS)' made the Top 20. A 1979 effort, 'WHERE I SHOULD BE', proved to be his last major success as he all but faded commercially in the 80's. A very talented guitarist, FRAMPTON established himself as the "Golden boy of US mainstream AOR". His curly locks and youthful face were still all the rage in the 70's having been idolized as a kid with 60's outfit, The HERD. • **Songwriters:** Self-penned numbers, except; JUMPING JACK FLASH (Rolling Stones) / (I'M A) ROADRUNNER (Junior Walker) / FRIDAY ON MY MIND (Easybeats) / etc. • **Trivia:** Late in 1988, the group, WILL TO POWER, hit US No.1 with a segue of his 'BABY I LOVE YOUR WAY' and LYNYRD SKYNYRD's 'Freebird'.

Album rating: WIND OF CHANGE (*5) / FRAMPTON'S CAMEL (*6) / SOMETHIN'S HAPPENING (*4) / FRAMPTON (*5) / FRAMPTON COMES ALIVE! (*8) / I'M IN YOU (*5) / WHERE I SHOULD BE (*4) / BREAKING ALL THE RULES

(*4) / THE ART OF CONTROL (*3) / PREMONITION (*2) / WHEN ALL THE PIECES FIT (*3) / SHINE ON – A COLLECTION compilation (*5) / PETER FRAMPTON (*5) / FRAMPTON COMES ALIVE II (er . . . *II)

PETER FRAMPTON – vocals, guitar (ex-HUMBLE PIE, ex-HERD) with **MIKE KELLIE** – drums (ex-SPOOKY TOOTH) / **RICK WILLS** – bass (ex-COCHISE) / & guests **BILLY PRESTON** – keyboards (solo artist) / **RINGO STARR** – drums, vox (solo artist) / **ANDY BOWN** – keyboards (ex-HERD) / **KLAUS VOORMAN** – keyboards (ex-MANFRED MANN)

Release		A&M	A&M
May 72.	(7") <1379> **JUMPING JACK FLASH. / OH FOR ANOTHER DAY**	-	
May 72.	(lp) (AMLH 68099) <4348> **WIND OF CHANGE** – Fig tree bay / Wind of change / Lady lie right / Jumping Jack Flash / It's a plain shame / Oh for another day / All I want to be (is by your side) / The lodger / Hard / Alright.	-	
Sep 72.	(7") (AMS 7025) **IT'S A PLAIN SHAME. / OH FOR ANOTHER DAY**		-

—— FRAMPTON retained only WILLS and brought in **MICKEY GALLAGHER** – keyboards (ex-BELL & ARC) / **JOHN SIOMES** (b. USA) – drums (ex-MITCH RYDER)

Release			
May 73.	(lp) (AMLH 68150) <4389> **FRAMPTON'S CAMEL** – I got my eyes on you / All night long / Lines on my face / Which way the wind blows / I believe (when I fall in love with you it will be forever) / White sugar / Don't fade away / Just the time of your / Do you feel like we do. (above lps & below 45s, credited to "FRAMPTON'S CAMEL")		
May 73.	(7") (AMS 7069) <1456> **ALL NIGHT LONG. / DON'T FADE AWAY**		
Jul 73.	(7") <1470> **WHICH WAY THE WIND BLOWS. / I BELIEVE (WHEN I FALL IN LOVE IT WILL BE FOREVER)**	-	

—— disbanded, bringing in session people

Release			
May 74.	(lp) (AMLH 63619) 3619> **SOMETHIN'S HAPPENING** – Doobie wah / Golden goose / Underhand / I wanna go to the sun / Baby (somethin's happening) / Waterfall / Magic Moon / Sail away.		25 Mar74
May 74.	(7") <1506> **BABY (SOMETHIN'S HAPPENING). / I WANNA GO TO THE SUN**	-	

—— **ANDY BOWN** – keyboards, bass returned to repl. GALLAGHER (to GLENCOE) and WILLS (to ROXY MUSIC)

Release			
Mar 75.	(lp) (AMLH 64512) <4512> **FRAMPTON** – Day's dawning / Show me the way / One more time / The crying clown / Fanfare / Nowhere's too far (for my baby) / Nassau / Baby, I love your way / Apple of your eye / Penny for your thoughts / (I'll give you) Money.		32
Jun 75.	(7") (AMS 7174) <1693> **SHOW ME THE WAY. / THE CRYING CLOWN**		
Aug 75.	(7") <1738> **BABY, I LOVE YOUR WAY. / (I'LL GIVE YOU MONEY)**	-	
Oct 75.	(7") <1763> **(I'LL GIVE YOU) MONEY. / NOWHERE'S TOO FAR (FOR MY BABY)**	-	

—— Still with SIOMOS, also now w / **STANLEY SHELDON** – bass / **BOB MAYO** – keyboards

Release			
Apr 76.	(d-lp/d-c) (AMLH/CLM 63703) <3703> **FRAMPTON COMES ALIVE!** (live) – Somethin's happening / Doobie wah / Show me the way / It's a plain shame / All I want to be (is by your side) / Wind of change / Baby, I love your way / I wanna go to the sun / Penny for your thoughts / (I'll give you) Money / Shine on / Jumping Jack Flash / Lines on my face / Do you feel like we do. <US pic-lp 1978> (re-iss. Feb85 as 'THE BEST OF FRAMPTON COMES ALIVE' on 'Hallmark' lp/c; SHM/HSC 3165) (cd-iss. 1988; CDA 6505) (re-iss. Jun91 cd/c; CD/C MID 164)	6	1 Jan76
Apr 76.	(7") (AMS 7218) <1795> **SHOW ME THE WAY (live). / SHINE ON (live)**	10	6 Feb76
Jun 76.	(7") <1832> **BABY, I LOVE YOUR WAY (live). / IT'S A PLAIN SHAME (live)**	-	12
Aug 76.	(7") (AMS 7246) **BABY, I LOVE YOUR WAY (live). / (I'LL GIVE YOU) MONEY (live)**	43	-
Oct 76.	(7") (AMS 7260) <1867> **DO YOU FEEL LIKE WE DO (live). / PENNY FOR YOUR THOUGHTS (live)**	39 / 19	10 Sep76 / 2
Jun 77.	(lp/c) (AMLK/CAM 64039) <4704> **I'M IN YOU** – I'm in you / (Putting my) Heart on the line / St.Thomas (don't you know how I feel) / Won't you be my friend / You don't have to worry / Tried to love / Rocky's hot club / (I'm a) Roadrunner / Signed, sealed, delivered (I'm yours).		
Jul 77.	(7") (AMS 7298) <1941> **I'M IN YOU. / ST.THOMAS (DON'T YOU KNOW HOW I FEEL)**	41	2 May77
Sep 77.	(7") (AMS 7312) <1972> **SIGNED, SEALED, DELIVERED (I'M YOURS). / ROCKY'S HOT CLUB**		18 Aug77
Dec 77.	(7") <1988> **TRIED TO LOVE. / YOU DON'T HAVE TO WORRY**	-	41
May 79.	(7") <2148> **I CAN'T STAND IT NO MORE. / WHERE SHOULD I BE**	-	14
Jun 79.	(7") (AMS 7449) **I CAN'T STAND IT NO MORE. / MAY I BABY**		-
Jun 79.	(lp/c) (AMLK/CAM 63701) <3710> **WHERE I SHOULD BE** – I can't stand it no more / Got my feet back on the ground / Where I should be / Everything I need / May I baby / You don't know like I know / She don't reply / We've just begun / Take me by the hand / It's a sad affair.		19
Aug 79.	(7") <2174> **SHE DON'T REPLY. / ST. THOMAS (DON'T YOU KNOW HOW I FEEL)**		
Jun 81.	(lp/c) (AMLK/CAM 63722) <3722> **BREAKING ALL THE RULES** – Dig what I say / I don't wanna let you go / Rise up / Wasting the night away / Going to L.A. / You kill me / Friday on my mind / Lost a part of you / Breaking all the rules.		43
Aug 81.	(7") (AMS 8154) <2350> **BREAKING ALL THE RULES. / NIGHT TOWN**		
Nov 81.	(7") <2362> **WASTING THE NIGHT AWAY. / YOU KILL ME**		
Aug 82.	(7") <2442> **SLEEPWALK. / THEME FROM NIVRAM**	-	
Sep 82.	(lp/c) (AMLH/CAM 64905) <4905> **THE ART OF CONTROL** – I read the news / Sleepwalk / Save me / Back to Eden / An eye for an		Aug82

eye / Don't think about me / Heart in the fire / Here comes Caroline / Barbara's vacation.

—— PETER now used guitar & synthesizers, etc. plus band **TONY LEVIN** – guitar / **STEVE FERRONE + OMAR HAKIM** – drums / **PETE SOLLEY** – piano / **RICHARD COTTLE** – keys / **RICHIE PUENTE** – percussion

Release		Virgin	Atlantic
Nov 85.	(7") <89463> **LYING. / INTO VIEW**	-	74
Dec 85.	(7"pic-d/12") (VS 827/+12) **LYING. / YOU KNOW SO WELL**		80
Jan 86.	(lp/c/cd) (C/TCV/CDV 2365) <81290> **PREMONITION** – Stop / Hiding from a heartache / You know so well / Premonition / Lying / Moving a mountain / All eyes on you / Into view / Call of the wild. (re-iss. Jul87 lp/c; OVED/+C 220)		
Feb 86.	(7") <89426> **ALL EYES ON YOU. / SO FAR AWAY**	-	
Apr 86.	(7"/12") (VS 847/+12) **ALL EYES ON YOU. / INTO VIEW**	-	
May 86.	(7") <89395> **HIDING FROM A HEARTACHE. / INTO VIEW**		-

—— He became guitarist for DAVID BOWIE in 1987. The following year he sessioned for KARLA BONOFF and returned to solo work in 1989.

Release		Atlantic	Atlantic
Sep 89.	(7") <88820> **HOLDING ON TO YOU. / GIVE ME A LITTLE LOVE THAT'S REAL**	-	
Oct 89.	(lp,c,cd) <82030> **WHEN ALL THE PIECES FIT** – More ways than one / Holding on to you / My heart goes out to you / Hold tight / People all over the world / Back to the start / Mind over matter / Now and again / Hard earned love / This time around.	-	

—— His new back-up band now featured **DAVE MENIKETTI** – guitar (ex-Y&T) after signing to 'Geffen' (no releases)

Release		Relativity	Relativity
Apr 94.	(cd/c/lp) <(475876-2/04/-1)> **PETER FRAMPTON** – Day in the Sun / You can be sure / It all comes down to you / You can't take that away / Young island / Off the hook / Waiting for your love / So hard to believe / Out of the blue / Shelter through the night / Changing all the time.		

Release		I.R.S.	I.R.S.
Oct 95.	(cd/c) (EIRS CD/TC 1074) **FRAMPTON COMES ALIVE II** (live) – (intro) / Day in the sun / Lying / For now / Most of all / You / Waiting for your love / I'm in you / Talk to me / Hang on to a dream / Can't take that away / More ways than one / Almost said goodbye / Off the hook. (cd with free live cd; EIRSCDX 1074) – Show me the way / Baby I love your way / Lines on my face / Do you feel like we do.	-	

Release		In-Akustik	not iss.
Oct 96.	(cd) (INAK 11004) **MOON'S TRAIN**	-	- German

– compilations, others –

Release			
Jun 79.	(lp) Flyover; **THE SUPER DISC OF PETER FRAMPTON**		-
Oct 83.	(7") Old Gold; (OG 9363) **SHOW ME THE WAY. / BABY I LOVE YOUR WAY**		-
Jun 84.	(7"ep/c-ep) Scoop; (7SR/7SC 5039) **6 TRACK HITS** – Show me the way / Baby, I love your way / Penny for your thoughts / I'm in you / Wind of change / Signed, sealed, delivered (I'm yours).		
Dec 92.	(d-cd) A&M; (CDMID 174) **SHINE ON – A COLLECTION** – Wind of change / It's a plain shame / Jumping Jack Flash / All I want to be (is by your side) / The lodger / I got my eyes on you / All night long / Lines on my face / Don't fade away / I wanna go to the sun / Baby (somethin's happening) / Nowhere's too far (for my baby) / Nassau – Baby I love your way / The crying clown / Penny for your thoughts / (I'll give you) Money / Show me the way / Shine on / Do you feel like we do / I'm in you / (Putting my) Heart on the line / Signed sealed delivered (I'm yours) / I can't stand it no more / Breaking all the rules / Theme from Nivram / Lying / More ways than one / Holding on to you / The bigger they come / I won't let you down.		
Mar 94.	(cd/c) Spectrum; (550 103-2/-4) **PETER FRAMPTON SHOWS THE WAY**		-
Dec 95.	(cd; PETER FRAMPTON & FRIENDS) Javelin; (HADCD 199) **LOVE TAKER**		-
Feb 96.	(cd) Prestige; (CDSGP 0243) **PACIFIC FREIGHT**		-

FRANK & WALTERS (dig out; Great Alt & Indie . . .)

FRANKIE GOES TO HOLLYWOOD

Formed: Liverpool, England . . . August '80 (initially as HOLLYCAUST) by HOLLY JOHNSON, who had issued two solo singles, 'YANKEE ROSE' and 'HOBO JOE', after once being part of punk experimentalists, BIG IN JAPAN. Taking their name from a news headline concerning singer, FRANKIE VAUGHAN going into the movies, FGTH enjoyed some TV exposure in late 1982. After a session on David Jensen's Radio One show, they were invited onto Channel 4's 'The Tube', where they sang an embryonic, 'RELAX'. This led to 'Z.T.T.' (Zang Tumb Tumm) label, run by PAUL MORLEY and TREVOR HORN (ex-BUGGLES) signing them in Autumn 1983. With HORN's clever production, the song 'RELAX' soon climbed to the top in the UK, aided by another Radio One DJ, Mike Read, who helped it get banned from airplay due to its risque lyrics. In June '84, with 'RELAX' still in the chart, the follow-up, 'TWO TRIBES', went straight in at No.1, and gave a new lease of life to the debut (it resurged back up to No.2, while 'TWO TRIBES' was at No.1!). This well-produced, power-disco/rock outfit were always at the front end of controversy (so to speak!), their gay/S&M sex themes (provided by leather clad HOLLY and boyfriend/dancer, PAUL RUTHERFORD) were the toast of the burgeoning mid-80's dance scene. Their debut (a double!) album in October '84, 'WELCOME TO THE PLEASURE DOME', also hit peak position, as did their third consecutive No.1 single, 'THE POWER OF LOVE' (a feat only previously achieved by another Mersey group, GERRY & THE PACEMAKERS). In March '85, their fourth single, the title track from the album, spoiled the run when it stalled at No.2. The group returned in late summer '86 after over a year off, their fifth single, 'RAGE HARD', only just scraping into the UK Top 5. Poor reviews of their follow-up album, 'LIVERPOOL', saw the group fading into a sharp commercial decline with each subsequent single release. HOLLY JOHNSON was back early in 1989. Having signed a contract with 'M.C.A.', the singer subsequently charted high with the singles, 'LOVE TRAIN' and 'AMERICANOS', which previewed his No.1 album, 'BLAST'. In mid-1990, HOLLY was asked by friend RICHARD O'BRIEN, to act as FRANK 'N' FURTER in the 'Rocky Horror Picture Show'. HOLLY's second solo album, 'DREAMS THAT MONEY CAN'T BUY' (1991), failed miserably, its sales so poor that the set didn't achieve a Top 75 placing. Sadly, HOLLY was subsequently diagnosed with the AIDS virus and was HIV positive as he wrote his autobiography, entitled 'A Bone In My Flute' (1994). • **Songwriters:** All group compositions except; FERRY ACROSS THE MERSEY (Gerry & The Pacemakers) / BORN TO RUN (Bruce Springsteen) / WAR (Edwin Starr) / SUFFRAGETTE CITY (David Bowie) / GET IT ON (T.Rex) / SAN JOSE (Bacharach-David). HOLLY solo covered; LOVE ME TENDER (Elvis Presley). The track 'ACROSS THE UNIVERSE' was not The BEATLES original. • **Trivia:** The 'TWO TRIBES' video (directed by GODLEY & CREME) featured Ronald Reagan & Chernenko lookalikes fighting in a wrestling ring.

Album rating: WELCOME TO THE PLEASURE DOME (*7) / LIVERPOOL (*5) / Holly Johnson: BLAST (*5) / DREAMS THAT MONEY CAN'T BUY (*3) / SOULSTREAM (*3)

HOLLY JOHNSON (b. WILLIAM JOHNSON, 9 Feb'60, Khartoum, Sudan) – vocals (ex-solo artist, ex-BIG IN JAPAN) / **PAUL RUTHERFORD** – vocals (ex-SPITFIRE BOYS) / **BRIAN NASH** (b.20 Mar'63) – guitar repl. GED O'TOOLE / **MARK O'TOOLE** (b. 6 Jan'64) – bass / **PETER GILL** (b. 8 Mar'64) – drums

		ZTT-Island	Island
Oct 83.	(7"pic-d/7") (P+/ZTAS 1) <99805> **RELAX. / ONE SEPTEMBER MORNING**	1	67 Mar84
	(12"/12"pic-d) (12/+P ZTAS 1) – ('A'version) / Ferry across the Mersey.		
	(c-ep) (CTIS 102) – "Relax's Greatest Bits" – (various mixes).		
Jun 84.	(7"pic-d/7") (P+/ZTAS 3) <99695> **TWO TRIBES. / ONE FEBRUARY MORNING**	1	43 Oct84
	(12"/12"pic-d) (12/+P ZTAS 3) – ('A'version) / War (hide yourself).		
	(12"pic-d) (XZTAS 3) – (all 3 tracks above).		
	(c-ep) (CTIS 103) – "Two Tribes (Keep The Peace)" – (various mixes).		
Nov 84.	(d-lp/c/cd) (ZTTIQ/ZCIQ/CDIQ 1) <90232> **WELCOME TO THE PLEASURE DOME**	1	33
	– Well . . . / The world is my oyster / Snatch of fury / Welcome to the pleasure dome / Relax / War / Two tribes / Ferry / Born to run / San Jose / Wish the lads were here (inc. 'Ballad of 32') / Black night white light / The only star in Heaven / The power of love / Bang . . . (also d-pic-lp; NEAT 1) (re-iss. May94 & Feb95 cd/c; same) (re-hit No.16 in Jun99)		
Nov 84.	(7"pic-d/7") (P+/ZTAS 5) **THE POWER OF LOVE. / THE WORLD IS MY OYSTER**	1	
	(12"+=) (12XZTAS 5) – ('A'-Pleasurefix mix) / ('A'-Starfix mix).		
	(12"pic-d)(c-s) (12PZTAS 5)(CTIS 105) – ('A'side) / Trapped and scrapped / Holier than thou.		
Mar 85.	(7"sha-pic-d/7") (P+/ZTAS 7) <99653> **WELCOME TO THE PLEASURE DOME. / HAPPY HI / GET IT ON**	2	48
	(12"+=) (XTAS 7) – Born to run (live).		
	(c-s+=) (CTIS 107) – How to remake the world.		
Aug 86.	(7") (ZTAX 22) **RAGE HARD. / (DON'T LOSE WHAT'S LEFT) OF YOUR LITTLE MIND**	4	
	(12"+=) (12ZTAQ 22) – Suffragette City.		
	(12"+=/12"box+=) (12ZTAX/+B 22) – Roadhouse blues.		
	(cd-s+=) (ZCID 22) – Suffragette city / Roadhouse blues.		
Sep 86.	(lp/c/cd) (ZTT/ZC/ZCD IQ 8) <90546> **LIVERPOOL**	5	88
	– Warriors of the wasteland / Rage hard / Kill the pain / Maximum joy / Watching the wildlife / Lunar bay / For Heaven's sake / Is anybody out there?. (re-iss. 1989 on 'Island'; IMCD 13) (re-iss. May94 cd/c;)		
Nov 86.	(7") (ZTAS 25) **WARRIORS OF THE WASTELAND. / WARRIORS (instrumental)**	19	
	(12"+=/c-s+=/cd-s+=) (12ZTAS/CTIS/ZCID 25) – Warriors (lots of different mixes).		
Feb 87.	(7") (ZTAS 26) **WATCHING THE WILDLIFE. / THE WAVES**	28	
	(12"+=) (12ZTAX 26) – Wildlife (Bit 3 & 4).		
	(c-s+=/cd-s+=) (CTIS/ZCID 26) – (various mixes, etc.).		

—— They split after legal contractual problems. RUTHERFORD went solo.

– compilations, etc. –

releases on 'ZTT'.

Sep 93.	(7"/c-s) (FGTH 1/+C) **RELAX. / RELAX MCMXCIII**	5	
	(12"+=/cd-s+=) (FGTH 1 T/CD) – ('A'mixes; Jam & Spoon, etc.).		
Oct 93.	(cd/c/lp) (4509 93912-2/-4/-1) **BANG! . . . THE GREATEST HITS OF . . .**	4	
	– Relax / Two tribes / War / Ferry / Warriors of the wasteland / For Heaven's sake / The world is my oyster / Welcome to the Pleasure dome / Watching the wildlife / Born to run / Rage hard / The power of love / Bang . . . (re-iss. Jun94 cd/c)		
Nov 93.	(7"/c-s) (FGTH 2/+C) **WELCOME TO THE PLEASURE DOME. / ('A'-Elevatorman's non-stop top floor mix)**	18	
	(12"+=/cd-s+=) (FGTH 2 T/CD) – ('A'mixes; Brothers In Rhythm, etc.).		
Dec 93.	(7"/c-s) (FGTH 3/+C) **THE POWER OF LOVE. / ('A'mix)**	10	
	(cd-s+=) (FGTH 3CD) – Rage hard (original DJ mix) / Holier than thou.		
Feb 94.	(7"/c-s) (FGTH 4/+C) **TWO TRIBES (Fluke's minimix). / ('A'mix)**	16	
	(12"+=/cd-s+=) (FGTH 4 T/CD) – ('A'mixes).		
May 94.	(cd/c/lp) (4509 95292-2/-4/-1) **RELOAD – THE WHOLE 12 INCHES**		-

---

—— In Spring of '93, HOLLY revealed he was HIV positive (AIDS).

HOLLY JOHNSON

had earlier returned to a solo career

		M.C.A.	M.C.A.
Jan 89.	(7") (MCA 1306) **LOVE TRAIN. / MURDER IN PARADISE**	4	
	(12"+=/cd-s+=) (MCAT/DMCA 1306) – ('A'mix).		
Mar 89.	(7"/c-s) (MCA/+C 1323) **AMERICANOS. / ('A'dub version)**	4	
	(cd-s+=/12"+=) (D+/MCAT 1323) – ('A'-Liberty mix).		
	(12") (MCAX 1323) – ('A'remixes).		
Apr 89.	(lp/c/cd) (DMCG/MCGC/MCG 6042) **BLAST**	1	
	– Atomic city / Heaven's here / Americanos / Deep in love / S.U.C.C.E.S.S. / Love train / Got it made / Love will come / Perfume / Feel good.		
Jun 89.	(12"/c-s) (MCA T/C 1342) **ATOMIC CITY. / BEAT THE SYSTEM**	18	
	(12"+=/cd-s+=) (MCAX/DMCAT 1342) – ('A'extended).		
Sep 89.	(7"/7"pic-d/c-s) (MCA/+P/C 1365) **HEAVEN'S HERE. / HALLELUJAH**	62	-
	(cd-s+=/12"+=) (D+/MCAT 1365) – ('A'version).		
Jul 90.	(cd/c/lp) (DMCL/MCLC/MCL 1902) **HALLELUJAH, THE REMIX ALBUM** (BLAST remixed)		-
Nov 90.	(7"/c-s) (MCA/+C 1460) **WHERE HAS LOVE GONE. / PERFUME**	73	
	(cd-s+=/12"+=) (D+/MCAT 1460) – ('A'version).		
Mar 91.	(7"/c-s) (MCA/+C) **ACROSS THE UNIVERSE. / FUNKY PARADISE**		
	(cd-s+=/12"+=) (D+/MCAT) – ('A'-Space a-go-go mix).		
May 91.	(lp/c/cd) (MCA/+C/D 10278) **DREAMS THAT MONEY CAN'T BUY**		-
	– Across the universe / When the party's over / The people want to dance / I need your love / Boyfriend '65 / Where has love gone? / Penny arcade / Do it for love / You're a hit / The great love story.		
Aug 91.	(7"/c-s) **PEOPLE WANT TO DANCE. / ('A'-Apollo 440 mix)**		
	(12"+=/cd-s+=) – Love train (anxious big beat version).		

		Club Tool	not iss.
Sep 94.	(12"ep/cd-ep) **LEGENDARY CHILDREN (ALL OF THEM QUEER). / (4-'A'mixes)**		-

		Pleasuredome	not iss.
Aug 99.	(12"/cd-s) (PLD/+CD1 004) **DISCO HEAVEN (mixes; Sicario club radio / Daz & Andy's Heavenly / Sicario club)**		-
Oct 99.	(cd/c) (PLD CD/MC 001) **SOULSTREAM**		-
	– Lady luck / Slipstream / Disco heaven / Don't give up / Hope / Best invention / Haalelujah / All U need is love / Legendary children / The power of love / Urban jungle / In the house of the rising sun.		
Dec 99.	(c-s/cd-s) (PLD MC/CD1 005) **THE POWER OF LOVE (mix) / IN THE HOUSE OF THE RISING SUN (mixes; 12" & Doggs House)**	56	-
	(cd-s) (PLCD 2005) – ('A'-Millennium mix) / In the house of the rising sun (DNA instrumental) / All U need is love (demo).		

HOLLY

early solo

		Eric's	not iss.
Dec 79.	(7"m) (ERIC'S 003) **YANKEE ROSE. / TREASURE ISLAND / DESPERATE DAN**		-
Jun 80.	(7") (ERIC'S 007) **HOBO JOE. / STARS OF THE BARS**		-

Aretha FRANKLIN

Born: 25 Mar'42, Memphis, Tennessee, USA. She was one of six children (future recording artists ERMA and CAROLYN among them) raised by her well-to-do preacher father, Rev. C.L. Franklin (a much revered figure, who himself had released a catalogue of recordings of his famous sermons) after they moved to Detroit, Michigan. In the early 50's, ARETHA was given singing lessons by family friends, MAHALIA JACKSON and CLARA WARD, who influenced her early career. ARETHA's initial recordings (included in the recently re-released 'Chess Masters' CD series) were primarily gospel releases, the celebratory, acappella black religious singing style that had developed from the old time spirituals and which went on to form a cornerstone of popular music. Inspired by the secular success of SAM COOKE, ARETHA subsequently moved to New York where she found manager, Joe King. There, she was spotted by music biz legend, JOHN HAMMOND, and in 1960 she signed to 'Columbia', releasing her debut single, 'TODAY I SING THE BLUES' In the autumn. After a minor hit, 'WON'T BE LONG', the gospel diva scored her first US Top 40 entry in 1961 with the standard, 'ROCK-A-BYE YOUR BABY WITH A DIXIE MELODY'. She continued to break the Hot 100 many times but FRANKLIN's wild creative spirit was essentially stifled by record company attempts to market her as a mainstream blues torch singer. Things really took off when she signed to 'Atlantic' in late '66, veteran producer Jerry Wexler relocating FRANKLIN to the legendary 'Muscle Shoals' studio in Alabama, the combination of WEXLER's experience and the "down home" style of the resident musicians, allowing FRANKLIN's formidable talents to flower in a manner that previous producer, Mitch Miller, hadn't touched on. With a team of WEXLER, engineer TOM DOWD and arranger ARIF MARDIN behind her, ARETHA was unstoppable and in the ensuing two years notched up a staggering run of hit singles, every one a timeless classic. 'I NEVER LOVED A MAN (THE WAY I LOVE YOU)' heralded her creative rebirth, FRANKLIN marking her territory with a seductive, primal femininity. The flip side was a sensitive cover of the DAN PENN/SPOONER OLDHAM classic, 'DO RIGHT WOMAN, DO RIGHT MAN', a potential hit in its own right. The same could be said of the follow-up, a blistering interpretation of Otis Redding's 'RESPECT', released with FRANKLIN's slow burning 'DR. FEELGOOD' in America and backed with the equally impressive 'SAVE ME' in Britain. The single was a US chart topper, the album 'I NEVER LOVED A MAN (THE WAY I LOVE YOU)' (1967) arguably her magnum opus and certainly a landmark soul release. More hits followed in the shape of the GOFFIN/KING-penned, '(YOU MAKE ME FEEL LIKE) A NATURAL WOMAN (No.8 US), a cover of Don Covay's 'CHAIN OF FOOLS' (No.2 US) and 'SINCE YOU'VE BEEN GONE (SWEET SWEET BABY)'. All were included on 'LADY SOUL' (1968), another essential album which could've conceivably been titled 'FIRST LADY OF SOUL', ARETHA consolidating her position as the most talented female soul vocalist in the world as well as a highly accomplished piano player. 'THINK' was next up, a sexy soul juggernaut of a record and arguably the most uplifting call to feminist arms in the history of recorded music, while 'I SAY A LITTLE PRAYER', a beautifully sweet cover of the BACHARACH & DAVID number, was another million selling single, backed with the insidiously funky 'HOUSE THAT JACK BUILT' on the American release. As the decade drew to a close however, FRANKLIN began to lose her focus, splitting with her husband and sometime songwriting partner, TED WHITE. Nevertheless, 1970 saw a masterful gospel set, 'SPIRIT IN THE DARK', which contained the brilliant 'DON'T PLAY THAT SONG'. 'LIVE AT FILLMORE WEST' (1971) was a smoking concert set, while 'YOUNG GIFTED AND BLACK' (1972) featured the gritty funk of FRANKLIN's 'ROCK STEADY', proving that the 'Queen Of Soul' could compete with the Godfather, JAMES BROWN. 1972 also saw the release of 'AMAZING GRACE', Aretha's spellbinding double gospel set recorded with JAMES CLEVELAND & THE SOUTHERN CALIFORNIA COMMUNITY CHOIR. 'UNTIL YOU COME BACK TO ME (THAT'S WHAT I'M GONNA DO)', partly composed by STEVIE WONDER, was FRANKLIN's last major hit of the 70's and despite a reunion in 1974 with WEXLER and MARDIN, she couldn't match the depth and power of her late 60's heyday. Following a move to 'Arista' at the turn of the decade, FRANKLIN teamed up with LUTHER VANDROSS, releasing a string of slicker and poppier, if equally bland albums, the best of which, 'WHO'S ZOOMIN' WHO' (1985), providing her with her last Top 10 hit to date in the title track (excluding her smash hit duets with ANNIE LENNOX snd GEORGE MICHAEL). More interesting was the 1987 gospel album, 'ONE LORD, ONE FAITH, ONE BAPTISM', her voice still a revelation on a set which included contributions from the likes of MAVIS STAPLES and JESSE JACKSON. More's the pity then, that ARETHA seems to be lost without some kind of guiding hand, her wonderful voice wasted on uninspired projects. All her records from the golden period of '67-'72 are worth shelling out for, as is the Grammy Award-winning 4CD Box Set, covering the cream of the 'Atlantic' years. • **Songwriters:** Although ARETHA wrote many songs herself, her greatest success came with 'Atlantic' covers: SEE SAW (Don Covay) / YOU SEND ME (Sam Cooke) / SATISFACTION (Rolling Stones) / THE WEIGHT (Band) / TRACKS OF MY TEARS (Miracles) / GENTLE ON MY MIND (John Hartford) / ELEANOR RIGBY + LET IT BE (Beatles) / SON OF A PREACHER MAN (Dusty Springfield) / BRIDGE OVER TROUBLED WATER (Simon & Garfunkel) / DON'T PLAY THAT SONG + SPANISH HARLEM (Ben E. King) / WHOLY HOLY (Marvin Gaye) / YOU'RE ALL I NEED TO BE GOT BY + AIN'T NOTHING LIKE THE REAL THING (Marvin Gaye & Tammi Terrell) / ANGEL (Jimi Hendrix) / WHEN YOU GET RIGHT DOWN TO IT (Ronnie Dyson) / WHAT A FOOL BELIEVES (Doobie Brothers) / EVERYDAY PEOPLE (Staple Singles) / etc. • **Trivia:** On her 1969 recordings, DUANE ALLMAN played slide guitar. She had been produced by many greats including QUINCY JONES (1973) / CURTIS MAYFIELD (1976) / LAMONT-DOZIER (1977) / ARIF MARDIN (1980) / LUTHER VANDROSS (1982-83) / NARADA MICHAEL WALDEN (1985-87). In 1980, she appeared as a waitress in the film, 'The Blues Brothers'.

Album rating: ARETHA (*4) / THE ELECTRIFYING ARETHA FRANKLIN (*4) / THE TENDER, THE MOVING, THE SWINGING (*5) / LAUGHING (ON THE OUTSIDE) (*4) / UNFORGETTABLE: A TRIBUTE TO DINAH WASHINGTON (*4) / SONGS OF FAITH gospel (*4) / RUNNIN' OUT OF FOOLS (*5) / YEAH!!! (*4) / SOUL SISTER (*4) / I NEVER LOVED A MAN (THE WAY I LOVE YOU) (*9) / ARETHA FRANKLIN'S GREATEST HITS exploitation compilation (*6) / ARETHA ARRIVES (*7) / ARETHA: LADY SOUL (*9) / ARETHA NOW (*8) / ARETHA IN PARIS (*6) / ARETHA FRANKLIN: SOUL '69 (*7) / ARETHA'S GOLD compilation (*8) / THIS GIRL'S IN LOVE WITH YOU (*6) / SPIRIT IN THE DARK (*6) / ARETHA LIVE AT FILLMORE WEST (*6) / AERTHA'S GREATEST HITS compilation (*7) / YOUNG, GIFTED & BLACK (*5) / AMAZING GRACE (*7) / HEY NOW HEY (THE OTHER SIDE OF THE SKY) (*5) / LET ME IN YOUR LIFE (*6) / WITH EVERYTHING I FEEL IN ME (*5) / YOU (*4) / SPARKLE (*5) / SWEET PASSION (*4) / ALMIGHTY FIRE (*4) / LA DIVA (*3) / ARETHA (*5) / LOVE ALL THE HURT WAY (*4) / JUMP TO IT (*5) / GET IT RIGHT (*5) / WHO'S ZOOMIN' WHO (*6) / ARETHA [1986] (*7) / ONE LORD, ONE FAITH, ONE BAPTISM (*4) / THROUGH THE STORM (*5) / WHAT YOU SEE IS WHAT YOU SWEAT (*4) / QUEEN OF SOUL – THE VERY BEST OF ARETHA FRANKLIN compilation (*9)

ARETHA FRANKLIN – vocals(with session people)

		not iss.	Checker
1960.	(7") <861> **NEVER GROW OLD. / YOU GROW CLOSER**	-	
1960.	(7") <941> **PRECIOUS LORD. / (part 2)**	-	

		Fontana	Columbia
Jan 61.	(7") (H 271) <41793> **LOVE IS THE ONLY THING. / TODAY I SING THE BLUES** <re-iss. 1970>		Oct60
Feb 61.	(7") <41923> **WON'T BE LONG. / RIGHT NOW**	-	76

Jul 61.	(7") <41985> **MAYBE I'M A FOOL. / ARE YOU SURE**	-	
Oct 61.	(7") (H 343) <42157> **ROCK-A-BYE YOUR BABY WITH A DIXIE MELODY. / OPERATION HEARTBREAK**		37
Jan 62.	(lp) (TFL 5173) <8412> **ARETHA**		Oct61

– Won't be long / Over the rainbow / Love is the only thing / Sweet lover / All night long / Who needs you? / Right now / Are you sure / Maybe I'm a fool / It ain't necessarily so / Blue by myself / Today I sing the blues. (re-iss. Jan84 on 'Cameo-CBS')

		C.B.S.	Columbia
Jan 62.	(7") <42266> **I SURRENDER, DEAR. / ROUGH RIDER**	-	87 / 94
Apr 62.	(lp) <8561> **THE ELECTRIFYING ARETHA FRANKLIN**	-	

– You made me love you / I told you so / Rockabye your baby with a Dixie melody / Nobody like you / Exactly like you / It's so heartbreakin' / Rough lover / Blue holiday / Just for you / That lucky old sun / I surrender, dear / Ac-cent-tchu-ate the positive.

Jun 62.	(7") <42456> **DON'T CRY BABY. / WITHOUT THE ONE YOU LOVE**	-	92
Sep 62.	(7") <42520> **TRY A LITTLE TENDERNESS. / JUST FOR A THRILL**	-	100
Nov 62.	(lp) <8676> **THE TENDER, THE MOVING, THE SWINGING ARETHA FRANKLIN**	-	69

– Don't cry baby / Try a little tenderness / I apologize / Without the one you love / Look for the silver lining / I'm sitting on top of the world / Just for a thrill / God bless the child / I'm wandering / How deep is the ocean / I don't know you anymore / Lover come back to me.

Dec 62.	(7") <42625> **TROUBLE IN MIND. / GOD BLESS THE CHILD**	-	86
Jan 63.	(lp) <8897> **LAUGHING (ON THE OUTSIDE)**		

– Skylark / For all we know / Make someone happy / I wonder / Solitude / Laughing on the outside / Say it isn't so / Until the real thing comes along / If ever I would leave you / Where are you / Mr.Ugly / I wanna be around.

1963.	(7") <42796> **SAY IT ISN'T SO. / HERE'S WHERE I CAME IN**	-	
1963.	(7") <42874> **SKYLARK. / YOU'VE GOT HER**	-	
1963.	(7") <42933> **JOHNNY. / KISSIN' BY THE MISTLETOE**	-	
1964.	(7") <43009> **SOULVILLE. / EVIL GAL BLUES**	-	
Sep 64.	(7") <43113> **RUNNIN' OUT OF FOOLS. / IT'S JUST A MATTER OF TIME**		57
Oct 64.	(lp) <8963> **UNFORGETTABLE: A TRIBUTE TO DINAH WASHINGTON**	-	

– Unforgettable / Cold cold heart / What a difference a day made / Drinking again / Evil gal blues / Nobody knows the way I feel this morning / Don't say you're sorry again / This bitter Earth / If I should lose you / Soulville. (cd-iss. Jun95)

Nov 64.	(7") <43177> **WINTER WONDERLAND. / THE CHRISTMAS SONG**		
Dec 64.	(lp) <9081> **RUNNIN' OUT OF FOOLS**	-	84

– Mockingbird / How glad I am / Walk on by / My guy / Every little bit hurts / Shoop shoop song / You'll lose a good thing / I can't wait until I see my baby's face / It's just a matter of time / Runnin' out of fools / Two sides of love / One room Paradise.

Mar 65.	(7") <43203> **CAN'T YOU JUST SEE ME. / LITTLE MISS RAGGEDY ANNE**		96 Jan65
May 65.	(7") <43241> **I CAN'T WAIT UNTIL I SEE MY BABY'S FACE. / ONE STEP AHEAD**	-	
Nov 65.	(lp; stereo/mono) (S+/BPG 62566) <9151> **YEAH!!! – IN PERSON**		Jul65

– This could be the start of something / Once in a lifetime / Misty / More / There is no greater love / Muddy water / If I had a hammer / Impossible / Today I love everybody / Without the one you love / Trouble in mind / Love for sale.

Jul 66.	(7") <4333> **SWEET BITTER LOVE. / I'M LOSING YOU**	-	
Aug 66.	(lp; stereo/mono) (S+/BPG 62744) <9321> **SOUL SISTER**	-	

– Until you were gone / You made me love you / Follow your heart / Ol' man river / Sweet bitter love / Mother's love / Swanee / I'm losing you / Take a look / Can't just see me / Cry like a baby.

1966.	(7") <43442> **THERE IS NO GREATER LOVE. / YOU MADE ME LOVE YOU**	-	
1966.	(7") <43515> **HANDS OFF. / TIGHTEN UP YOUR TIE, BUTTON UP YOUR JACKET**	-	
1967.	(7") <43637> **UNTIL YOU WERE GONE. / SWANEE**	-	

		Atlantic	Atlantic
Apr 67.	(7") (584 084) <2386> **I NEVER LOVED A MAN (THE WAY I LOVE YOU). / DO RIGHT WOMAN, DO RIGHT MAN**	-	9 Mar67
Apr 67.	(7") <2403> **RESPECT. / DR. FEELGOOD**	-	1
May 67.	(7") (584 115) **RESPECT. / SAVE ME**	10	-
Jul 67.	(lp; mono/stereo) (587/588 066) <8139> **I NEVER LOVED A MAN (THE WAY I LOVE YOU)**	36	2 Apr67

– Respect / Drown in my own tears / I never loved a man (the way I loved you) / Soul serenade / Don't let me lose this dream / Baby, baby, baby / Dr. Feelgood / Good times / Do right woman – do right man / Save me / A change is gonna come. (re-iss. 1972) (cd-iss. Jun93)

Aug 67.	(7") (584 127) <2427> **BABY I LOVE YOU. / GOING DOWN SLOW**	39	4 Jul67
Sep 67.	(7") <2441> **A NATURAL WOMAN (YOU MAKE ME FEEL LIKE). / BABY BABY BABY**	-	8
Oct 67.	(lp; mono/stereo) (587/588 085) <8150> **ARETHA ARRIVES**		5 Aug67

– Satisfaction / You are my sunshine / Never let me go / 96 tears / Prove it / Night life / That's life / I wonder / Ain't nobody (gonna turn me around) / Going down slow / Baby, I love you. (re-iss. 1972) (cd-iss. Aug93 on 'Rhino')

Oct 67.	(7") (584 141) **(YOU MAKE ME FEEL LIKE A) NATURAL WOMAN. / NEVER LET ME GO**	-	-
Nov 67.	(7") <2464> **CHAIN OF FOOLS. / PROVE IT**	-	2
Dec 67.	(7") (584 157) **CHAIN OF FOOLS. / SATISFACTION**	37	-
Mar 68.	(7") (584 172) <2486> **(SWEET SWEET BABY) SINCE YOU'VE BEEN GONE. / AIN'T NO WAY**	47	5 / 16 Feb68
Mar 68.	(lp; mono/stereo) (587/588 099) <8176> **ARETHA: LADY SOUL**	25	2 Feb68

– Chain of fools / Money won't change You / Peopie get ready / Niki Hoeky / (You make me feel like) A natural woman / Since you've been gone (sweet sweet baby) / Good to me as I am to you / Come back baby / Groovin' / Ain't no way. (re-iss. Jun88, cd-iss. Sep89) (cd-iss. Jun93)

May 68. (7") (584 186) <2518> **THINK. / YOU SEND ME**   `26`   `7` / `56`

Jul 68. (7") (584 206) **I SAY A LITTLE PRAYER. / SEE-SAW**   `4`   `-`

Aug 68. (7") <2546> **THE HOUSE THAT JACK BUILT. / I SAY A LITTLE PRAYER**   `-`   `6` / `10`

Sep 68. (7") (584 239) **THE HOUSE THAT JACK BUILT. / DON'T LET ME LOSE THIS DREAM**

Sep 68. (lp; mono/stereo) (587/588 114) <8186> **ARETHA NOW**   `6`   `3` Jul68
– Think / I say a little prayer / See saw / Night time is the right time / You send me / You're a sweet sweet man / I take what I want / Hello sunshine / A change / I can't see myself leaving you (cd-iss. Aug93 on 'Rhino')

Nov 68. (7") <2574> **SEE SAW. / MY SONG**   `-`   `14` / `31`

Dec 68. (lp; mono/stereo) (587/588 149) <8207> **ARETHA IN PARIS – LIVE AT THE OLYMPIA** (live)   `13` Nov68
– (I can't get no) Satisfaction / Don't let me lose this dream / Soul serenade / Night life / Baby I love you / Groovin' / Natural woman / Come back baby / Dr. Feelgood / Since you've been gone / I never loved a man (the way I love you) / Chain of fools / Respect. (re-iss. cd Dec94 on 'Rhino-Atlantic')

Mar 69. (7") (584 252) <2603> **THE WEIGHT. / THE TRACKS OF MY TEARS**   `19` / `71` Feb69

Mar 69. (lp) (588 169) <8212> **SOUL '69**   `15` Feb69
– Ramblin' / Today I sing the blues / River's invitation / Pitiful / Crazy he calls me / Bring it on home to me / Tracks of my tears / If you gotta make a fool of somebody / Gentle on my mind / So long / I'll never be free / Elusive butterfly (cd-iss. Feb94 on 'Rhino-Atlantic')

Apr 69. (7") <2619> **I CAN'T SEE MYSELF LEAVING YOU. / GENTLE ON MY MIND**   `-`   `28` / `76`

Aug 69. (7") (584 285) <2650> **SHARE YOUR LOVE WITH ME. / PLEDGING MY LOVE / THE CLOCK**   `13` Jul69

Nov 69. (7") (584 306) <2683> **ELEANOR RIGBY. / IT AIN'T FAIR**   `17` Oct69

Mar 70. (7") (584 322) <2706> **CALL ME. / SON OF A PREACHER MAN**   `13` Feb70

Apr 70. (lp) (2400 004) <8248> **THIS GIRL'S IN LOVE WITH YOU**   `17` Feb70
– Son of a preacher man / Share your love with me / The dark end of the street / Let it be / Eleanor Rigby / This girl's in love with you / It ain't fair / The weight / Call me / Sit down and cry (cd-iss. Feb94 on 'Rhino-Atlantic')

May 70. (7") (2091 008) **LET IT BE. / MY SONG**   `-`

May 70. (7") <2731> **SPIRIT IN THE DARK. / THE THRILL IS GONE**   `-`   `23`

—— Her new band comprised **KING CURTIS** – saxophone / **CORNELL DUPREE** – guitar / **RICHARD TEE** – piano / **JERRY JEMMOTT** – bass / **BERNARD PURDIE** – drums

Jul 70. (7") <2751> **DON'T PLAY THAT SONG. / LET IT BE**   `11`

Aug 70. (7") (2091 027) **DON'T PLAY THAT SONG. / THE THRILL IS GONE**   `13`   `-`

Sep 70. (lp) (2400 021) <8265> **DON'T PLAY THAT SONG** <US-title 'SPIRIT IN THE DARK'>   `25`
– Don't play that song / The thrill is gone / Pullin' / You and me / Honest I do / Spirit in the dark / When the battle is over / One way ticket / Try Matty's / That's all I want from you / Oh no, not my baby / When I sing the blues. (cd-iss. Feb94 on 'Rhino-Atlantic')

Dec 70. (7") (2091 044) **OH NO NOT MY BABY. / YOU AND ME**   `-`

Dec 70. (7") <2772> **BORDER SONG (HOLY MOSES). / YOU AND ME**   `-`   `37`

Feb 71. (7") <2787> **YOU'RE ALL I NEED TO GET BY. / PULLIN'**   `-`   `19`

Mar 71. (7") (2091 063) **YOU'RE ALL I NEED TO GET BY. / BORDER SONG**

May 71. (7") (2091 090) <2796> **BRIDGE OVER TROUBLED WATER. / A BRAND NEW ME**   `6` Apr71

Jul 71. (lp) (2400 136) <7205> **LIVE AT FILLMORE WEST** (live)   `7` May71
– Respect / Love the one you're with / Bridge over troubled water / Eleanor Rigby / Make it with you / Don't play that song / Dr. Feelgood / Spirit in the dark / Spirit in the dark (reprise with RAY CHARLES) / Reach out and touch (somebody's hand). (cd-iss. Feb94 on 'Rhino-Atlantic')

Jul 71. (7"m) (2091 111) **I SAY A LITTLE PRAYER (live). / (I CAN'T GET NO) SATISFACTION (live)**   `-`

Aug 71. (7") (2091 127) **A BRAND NEW ME. / SPIRIT IN THE DARK**   `-`

—— On the 13th August '71, her legendary sax player and soloist, KING CURTIS, was stabbed to death on the street. She and her father sang and gave sermon at funeral. She attended another funeral 6 months later of her friend/mentor Mahalia Jackson.

Sep 71. (7") (2091 138) <2817> **SPANISH HARLEM. / LEAN ON ME**   `14`   `2` Jul71

Oct 71. (7") <2838> **ROCK STEADY. / OH ME OH MY (I'M A FOOL FOR YOU BABY)**   `-`   `9` / `73`

Mar 72. (7") (K 10154) <2866> **DAYDREAMING. / I'VE BEEN LOVING YOU TOO LONG**   `5`

Mar 72. (lp) (K 40323) <7213> **YOUNG, GIFTED AND BLACK**   `11` Feb72
– Oh me oh my (I'm a fool for you baby) / Daydreaming / Rock steady / Young, gifted and black / All the king's horses / A brand new me / April fools / I've been loving you too long / First snow in Kokomo / The long and winding road / Didn't I (blow your mind this time) / Border song. (cd-iss. Feb94 on 'Rhino-Atlantic')

May 72. (7") <2883> **ALL THE KING'S HORSES. / APRIL FOOLS**   `-`   `26`

Aug 72. (7") <2901> **WHOLY HOLY. / GIVE YOURSELF TO JESUS**   `-`   `81`

Sep 72. (7") (K 10224) **ALL THE KING'S HORSES. / ROCK STEADY**   `-`

Sep 72. (d-lp) (K 60023) <906> **AMAZING GRACE (live)**   `7` Jun72
– Mary don't you weep / Medley / Precious Lord, Take my hand / You've got a friend / Old landmark / Give yourself to Jesus / How I got over / What a friend we have in Jesus / Amazing grace / Precious memories / Climbing higher mountains / Remarks by Reverend C L Franklin / God will take care of you / Wholy holy / You'll never walk alone / Never grow old. (re-iss. Nov87)(cd-iss. Aug93)

Mar 73. (7") (K 10288) <2941> **MASTER OF EYES (THE DEEPNESS OF YOUR EYES). / MOODY'S MOOD FOR LOVE**   `33` Feb73

Aug 73. (7") (K 10346) <2969> **ANGEL. / SISTER FROM TEXAS**   `37`   `20` Jul73

Aug 73. (lp/c) (K/K4 40504) <7265> **HEY NOW HEY (THE OTHER SIDE OF THE SKY)**   `30` Jul73
– Hey now hey / Somewhere / So well when you're well / Angel / Sister from Texas / Mister Spain / That's the way I feel about cha / Moody's mood / Just right tonight. (re-iss. cd Dec94 on 'Rhino-Atlantic')

Jan 74. (7") (K 10399) <2995> **UNTIL YOU COME BACK TO ME (THAT'S WHAT I'M GONNA DO). / IF YOU DON'T THINK**   `26`   `3` Nov73

Apr 74. (lp/c) (K/K4 50031) <7292> **LET ME IN YOUR LIFE**   `14` Mar74
– Let me in your life / Every natural thing / Ain't nothing like the real thing / I'm in love / Until you come back to me (that's what I'm gonna do) / The masquerade is over / With pen in hand / Oh baby / Eight days on the road / If you don't think / A song for you. (re-iss. cd Dec94 on 'Rhino-Atlantic')

Jun 74. (7") (K 10447) <2999> **I'M IN LOVE. / OH BABY**   `19` Apr74

Aug 74. (7") <3200> **AIN'T NOTHING LIKE THE REAL THING. / EIGHT DAYS A WEEK**   `-`   `47`

Jan 75. (7") (K 10543) <3224> **WITHOUT LOVE. / DON'T GO BREAKING MY HEART**   `45` Nov74

Feb 75. (lp/c) (K/K4 50093) <18116> **WITH EVERYTHING I FEEL IN ME**   `57` Jan75
– Without love / Don't go breaking my heart / When you get right down to it / You'll never get to Heaven / With everything I feel in me / I love every little thing about you / Sing it again – say it again / All of these things / You move me.

Mar 75. (7") (K 10577) **WHEN YOU GET RIGHT DOWN TO IT. / SING IT AGAIN – SAY IT AGAIN**

Apr 75. (7") <3249> **SING IT AGAIN – SAY IT AGAIN. / WITH EVERYTHING I FEEL IN ME**   `-`

Oct 75. (7") (K 10669) <3289> **MR. D.J. (5 FOR THE D.J.). / AS LONG AS YOU ARE THERE**   `53` Sep75

Dec 75. (7") <3311> **YOU. / WITHOUT LOVE**   `-`   `83` Nov75

Dec 75. (lp/c) (K/K4 50159) <18151> **YOU**   `-`
– Mr D.J. / It only happens / I'm not strong enough to love you again / Walk softly / You make my life / Without you / The sha-la bandit / You / You got all the aces / As long as you are there.

Jun 76. (7") (K 16765) <3326> **SOMETHING HE CAN FEEL. / LOVING YOU BABY**   `28`

Jun 76. (lp/c) (K/K4 56248) <18176> **SPARKLE (Soundtrack)**   `18`
– Sparkle / Giving him something he can feel / Hooked on your love / Look into your heart / I get high / Jump / Loving you baby / Rock with me.

Sep 76. (7") <3358> **JUMP. / HOOKED ON YOUR LOVE**   `-`   `72`

Jan 77. (7") <3373> **LOOK INTO YOUR HEART. / ROCK WITH ME**   `-`   `82`

May 77. (7") (K 10938) <3393> **BREAK IT TO ME GENTLY. / MEADOWS OF SPRINGTIME**   `85`

Jun 77. (lp/c) (K/K4 50368) <19102> **SWEET PASSION**   `49`
– Break it to me gently / When I think about you / What I did for love / No one could ever love you more / Tender touch / Touch me up / Sunshine will never be the same / Meadows of Springtime / Mumbles / I've got the music in me / Passion.

Sep 77. (7") (K 11007) <3418> **WHEN I THINK ABOUT YOU. / TOUCH ME**   `-`

Jun 78. (lp/c) (K/K4 50445) <19161> **ALMIGHTY FIRE**   `63` May78
– Almighty fire (woman of the future) / Lady day / More than just a joy / Keep on loving you / I needed you baby / Close to you / No matter who you love / This you can believe / I'm your speed.

Jun 78. (7") <3468> **ALMIGHTY FIRE. / I'M YOUR SPEED**   `-`

Nov 78. (7") <3495> **THIS YOU CAN BELIEVE. / MORE THAN JUST A JOY**   `-`

Oct 79. (7") (K 11390) <3605> **LADIES ONLY. / WHAT IF I SHOULD EVER NEED YOU**

Oct 79. (lp/c) (K/K4 50637) <19248> **LA DIVA**   `-`
– Ladies only / It's gonna get a bit better / What if I should ever need you / Honey I need your love / I was made for you / Only star / Reasons why / You brought me back to life / Half a love / The feeling.

Jan 80. (7") <3632> **HALF A LOVE. / ONLY STAR**   `-`

Arista   Arista

Oct 80. (7"/12") (ARIST/+12 377) **WHAT A FOOL BELIEVES. / SCHOOLDAYS**   `46`   `-`

Oct 80. (lp/c) (SPART/TCART 1147) <9538> **ARETHA**   `47`
– Come to me / I can't turn you loose / United together / Take me with you / Whatever it is / What a fool believes / Together / Love me forever / Schooldays. (re-iss. May88 lp/c/cd; 208/408/258 883)

Mar 81. (7") (ARIST 395) <0569> **UNITED TOGETHER. / I CAN'T TURN YOU LOOSE**   `56` Dec80

May 81. (7") <0600> **COME TO ME. / SCHOOL DAYS**   `-`   `84`

Aug 81. (7"/12"; ARETHA FRANKLIN & GEORGE BENSON) (ARIST/+12 428) <0624> **LOVE ALL THE HURT AWAY. / HOLD ON I'M COMING**   `49`   `46`

Sep 81. (lp/c) (SPART/TCART 1170) <9552> **LOVE ALL THE HURT AWAY**   `36`
– Hold on I'm coming / You can't always get what you want / It's my turn / Living in the streets / Love all the hurt away / There's a star for everyone / Truth and honesty / Search on / Whole lot of man (cd-iss. 1988; 253 913)

Jan 82. (7") <0646> **IT'S MY TURN. / KIND OF MAN**   `-`

Feb 82. (7"/12") (ARIST/+12 442) **HOLD ON I'M COMING. / KIND OF MAN**

Apr 82. (7") <0665> **LIVIN' IN THE STREETS. / THERE'S A STAR FOR EVERYONE**   `-`

Aug 82. (7"/12") (ARIST/+12 479) <0699> **JUMP TO IT. / JUST MY DAYDREAM**   `42`   `24`

Aug 82. (lp/c) (204/404 742) <9602> **JUMP TO IT**   `23`
– Love me right / 16 she don't want your love / This is for real / (It's just) Your love / I wanna make it up to you / It's your thing / Just my day dream. (re-iss. May88 lp/c/cd; 209/409/259 060)

Jan 83. (7"/12") (ARIST/+12 500) <1023> **LOVE ME RIGHT. / (IT'S JUST) YOUR LOVE**

Mar 83. (7") <1043> **THIS IS FOR REAL. / I WANT TO MAKE IT UP TO YOU**   `-`

Jul 83. (7"/12") (ARIST/+12 537) **GET IT RIGHT. / JUMP TO IT**   `74`   `-`

Jul 83. (7") <9034> **GET IT RIGHT. / GIVING IN**   `61`

Jul 83. (lp/c) (205/405 544) <8019> **GET IT RIGHT**   `36`
– Get it right / Pretender / Every girl (wants my guy) / When you love me like that / I wish it would rain / Better friends than lovers / I got your love / Giving in.

Oct 83. (7") <9095> **EVERY GIRL (WANTS MY GIRL). / I GOT YOUR LOVE**   `-`

—— In Jul'85, while attending a civil rights campaign, her father C.L. is shot and went into a coma. He never recovered fully and died in Jul'87.

Jul 85. (7") (ARIST 624) <9354> **FREEWAY OF LOVE. / UNTIL YOU SAY YOU LOVE ME** `68` `3` Jun85
(12"+=) (ARIST12 624) – Jump to it.
(d7"+=) (ARIST22 624) – Zoomin' to the freeway.
(7"/12" – re-dist.Apr86, hit UK No.51)

—— (Oct85) She duets with EURYTHMICS on her 'SISTERS ARE DOIN' IT FOR THEMSELVES'. It hit UK No.9 + US No.18.

Nov 85. (lp/c/cd) (207/407 202) <8286> **WHO'S ZOOMIN' WHO?** `49` `13` Jul85
– Who's zoomin' who / Freeway of love / Another night / Sweet bitter love / Sisters are doin' it for themselves / Until you say love me / Push / Ain't nobody ever loved you / Integrity. *(re-iss. Jul88 lp/c/cd; 259/409/259 053)*

Nov 85. (7") (ARIST 633) <9410> **WHO'S ZOOMIN' WHO. / SWEET BITTER LOVE** `11` `7` Sep85
(12"+=) (ARIST12 633) – ('A'dub version) / ('A'acappella mix).

Feb 86. (7")(12") (ARIST 657) <9453> **ANOTHER NIGHT. / KIND OF MAN** `54` `22`
(12"+=) (ARIST12 657) – School days / Together again.
(d7"++=) (ARIST22 657) – ('A'-Nightlife mix).

Aug 86. (7") (ARIST 667) <9474> **AIN'T NOBODY EVER LOVED YOU. / INTEGRITY**
(12"+=) (ARIST12 667) – ('A'dub mix) / ('A-Percappella mix).

Oct 86. (lp/c/cd) (208/408/258 020) <8442> **ARETHA** `51` `32`
– Jimmy Lee / I knew you were waiting (for me) / Do you still remember / Jumpin' Jack Flash / Rock-a-lott / An angel cries / He'll come along / If you need my love tonight / Look to the rainbow. *(cd re-iss. Nov93 on 'Entertainers')*

Oct 86. (7") (ARIST 678) <9528> **JUMPIN' JACK FLASH. / INTEGRITY** `58` `21` Sep86
(12"+=) (ARIST12 678) – Who's zoomin' who / Sweet bitter love.

Nov 86. (7") <9546> **JIMMY LEE. / IF YOU NEED MY LOVE TONIGHT** `-` `28`

—— She hit No.1 UK/US with GEORGE MICHAEL duet 'I KNEW YOU WERE WAITING (FOR ME)', This was released 'Epic' UK / 'Arista' US.

Feb 87. (7") (RIS 6) <9557> **JIMMY LEE. / AN ANGEL CRIES** ` ` Apr87
(12"+=/cd-s+=) (RIST/RICD 6) – ('A'dub version) / Aretha megamix.

Jun 87. (7") (RIS 20) <9574> **ROCK-A-LOTT. / LOOK TO THE RAINBOW** ` ` `82`
(12") (RIST 20) – ('A'side) / ('A'dub) / ('A'cappella mix).

Oct 87. (7") <9623> **IF YOU NEED MY LOVE TONIGHT. / HE'LL COME ALONG** `-`

Nov 87. (lp/c/cd) (208/408/258 715) <8497> **ONE LORD, ONE FAITH, ONE BAPTISM**
– Walking in the light / Prayer invitation by Cecil Franklin / Introduction by Rev. Jesse Jackson / Jesus hears every prayer / Surely God is able / The Lord's prayer / Oh happy day / We need prayer / Speech by Rev. Jesse Jackson / Ave Maria / Introduction by Rev. Jasper Williams / Higher ground / Prayer by Rev. Donald Person / I've been in the storm too long / Waking up ready to go.

Feb 88. (7"/12") (109780/610978) <9672> **OH HAPPY DAY. / THE LORD'S PRAYER**

—— (above featured MAVIS STAPLES)

Apr 89. (7"-c-s/7"pic-d; ARETHA FRANKLIN & ELTON JOHN) (112 185/409957/112377) <9809> **THROUGH THE STORM. / COME TO ME** `41`
(12"+=/cd-s+=) (612/162 185) – Oh happy day.

May 89. (lp/c/cd) (209/409/259 842) <8572> **THROUGH THE STORM** `46` `55`
– Through the storm / Gimme your love / He's the boy / It ain't never gonna be / Think / Mercy / It isn't, it wasn't, it ain't never gonna be / If ever a love there was.

Jun 89. (7"; ARETHA FRANKLIN & WHITNEY HOUSTON) <9850> **IT ISN'T, IT WASN'T, IT AIN'T NEVER GONNA BE. / IF EVER A LOVE THERE WAS** `-` `41`

Sep 89. (7"/c-s; ARETHA FRANKLIN & WHITNEY HOUSTON) (112545/410093) **IT ISN'T, IT WASN'T, IT AIN'T NEVER GONNA BE. / THINK '89** `29` `-`
(12"+=) (612545) – ('A'extended remix).
(cd-s+=) (662545) – ('A'-Hip hop remix).

Nov 89. (7") (112728) <9884> **GIMME YOUR LOVE. / HE'S THE BOY**
(12"+=/cd-s+=) (612/662 727) – ('A'parts 1 & 2 versions).

Jul 91. (7") (114420) <2239> **EVERYDAY PEOPLE. / YOU CAN'T TAKE ME FOR GRANTED** `69`
(12") (114420) <2340> – ('A'side) / ('A'people remix) / ('A'people dub).
(cd-s+=) (114420) – ('A'remixed).

Aug 91. (cd/c/lp) (261/411/211 724) <8628> **WHAT YOU SEE IS WHAT YOU SWEAT**
– Everyday people / Everchanging times (with MICHAEL McDONALD / What you see is what you sweat / Mary goes round / I dreamed a dream / Someone' else's eyes / Doctor's orders / You can't take me for granted / What did you give / Everyday people (remix). *(cd re-iss. Feb94; same)*

Sep 91. (c-s) <2350> **SOMEONE ELSE'S EYES / WHAT DID YOU GIVE** `-`

Nov 91. (c-s) <2380> **WHAT YOU SEE IS WHAT YOU SWEAT /** `-`

Feb 92. (c-s) <2394> **YOU CAN'T TAKE ME FOR GRANTED / EVERCHANGING TIMES** `-`

Jan 94. (c-s) (74321 18702-4) <12657> **A DEEPER LOVE. / ('A'-Tribesman mix)** `5` `63`
(12"+=/cd-s+=) (74321 18702-1/-2) – (2 other mixes).

Mar 94. (cd/c) (74321 16202-2/-4) <18722> **GREATEST HITS 1980-1994** (compilation) `27` `85`
– Freeway of love / I knew you were waiting (for me) (w/ GEORGE MICHAEL) / Jump to it / Willing to forgive / Doctor's orders / United together / Who's zoomin' who / A deeper love / Honey / Get it right / Another night / Ever changing times / Jimmy Lee / (You make me fee like) A natural woman / I dreamed a dream / Jumpin' Jack Flash.

Jun 94. (c-s) (74321 21334-4) <12680> **WILLING TO FORGIVE / JUMP TO IT** `17` `26`
(12"+=/cd-s+=) (74321 21334-1/-2) – ('A'mix).

Apr 98. (c-s/cd-s) (74321 56974-4/-2) <13465> **A ROSE IS STILL A ROSE / ('A'mix)** `22` `26` Mar98
(cd-s) (74321 58035-2) – ('A'mixes).

May 98. (cd/c) <(0782 2 18987-2/-4)> **A ROSE IS STILL A ROSE** `30` Apr98
– A rose is still a rose / Never leave you again / In case you forgot / Here we go again / Every lil' bit hurts / In the morning / I'll dip / How many times / Watch my back / Love pang / Woman.

Sep 98. (c-s/cd-s) (74321 61274-4/-2) <13502> **HERE WE GO AGAIN / (mixes)** `68` `76` Jul98
(cd-s) (74321 61275-2) – ('A'side) / Who's zoomin' who / Everyday people.

– compilations, etc. –

on 'CBS' / 'Columbia' unless mentioned otherwise

1967. (7") (202468) <42827> **CRY LIKE A BABY. / SWANEE**
1967. (lp) (CBS 52562) <11274> **QUEEN OF SOUL**
Jun 67. (7") <44181> **LEE CROSS. / UNTIL YOU WERE GONE** `-`
Jun 67. (lp) (CBS 64536) <9473> **GREATEST HITS: ARETHA FRANKLIN 1960-65** `94`
(re-iss. Apr87 lp/c;)
Aug 67. (7") <44270> **TAKE A LOOK. / FOLLOW YOUR HEART** `56`
Oct 67. (7") (CBS 3059) **LEE CROSS. / TAKE A LOOK** `-`
Oct 67. (lp) (SBPG 62969) **TAKE IT LIKE YOU GIVE IT**
Nov 67. (lp) (63160) **LEE CROSS**
Dec 67. (7") <44381> **MOCKINGBIRD. / A MOTHER'S LOVE** `-` `94`
Jan 68. (lp) (63269) <9554> **TAKE A LOOK** Oct67
Feb 68. (7") <44441> **SOULVILLE. / EVIL GAL BLUES** `83`
1968. (lp) (CBS 63064) **GREATEST HITS VOL.2**
1968. (lp) <9776> **SOFT & BEAUTIFUL**
1969. (lp) Chess; (SCRL 54550) **SONGS OF FAITH**
(cd-iss. Oct88 on 'Vogue'; VGCD 600168)
1969. (7") <44550> **TONIGHT I SUNG THE BLUES. / CAN'T YOU JUST SEE ME** `-`
1969. (7") <44851> **FRIENDLY PERSUASION. / JIM** `-`
1969. (lp) <9956> **TODAY I SING THE BLUES** `-`
1969. (7") <44951> **TODAY I SING THE BLUES. / LOVE IS THE ONLY THING** `-`
Apr 83. (d-lp) (CBS 22112) **THE LEGENDARY QUEEN OF SOUL**
Jun 85. (d-lp) (CBS 22188) **THE ELECTRIFYING ARETHA FRANKLIN / SOUL SISTER**
Aug 98. (cd) (491454-2) **SOUL SISTER (THE BEST OF ARETHA FRANKLIN)**

– more compilations, etc. –

on 'Atlantic' unless mentioned otherwise

1968. (lp) <8212> **THE BEST OF ARETHA FRANKLIN**
(re-iss. Jun84 lp/c; 780169-1/-4) (cd-iss. 1986; K2 50840)
Jul 69. (lp) (588 182) <8227> **ARETHA'S GOLD** `18`
(re-iss. 1972) (cd-iss. Aug93)
1970. (lp) (2464 007) **I SAY A LITTLE PRAYER** `-`
Sep 71. (lp) (K 40279) <8295> **ARETHA'S GREATEST HITS** `19`
(re-iss. 1982) (cd-iss. Aug93)
1973. (lp) **THE COLLECTION**
1975. (d-lp) **TWO ORIGINALS OF ARETHA FRANKLIN**
Dec 76. (lp/c) (K/K4 50328) **TEN YEARS OF GOLD**
1977. (d-lp) (K 60030) **ARETHA'S MOST BEAUTIFUL SONGS**
1978. (lp) (K 20017) **STAR COLLECTION VOL.1**
1978. (lp) (K 20079) **STAR COLLECTION VOL.2**
Apr 80. (7") (K 11614) **THINK. / RESPECT**
Apr 84. (7") **I SAY A LITTLE PRAYER. / ROCK STEADY**
May 86. (7") (A 9409) **(YOU MAKE ME FEEL LIKE A) NATURAL WOMAN. / NEVER LOVED A MAN (THE WAY I LOVE YOU)**
(12"+=) (TA 9409) – Do right woman, do right man.
Jan 87. (lp/c; ARETHA FRANKLIN & REVEREND FRANKLIN) Chess; (GCH/+K7 8014) **NEVER GROW OLD**
Jun 87. (7") (YZ 121) **RESPECT. / DO RIGHT WOMAN, DO RIGHT MAN**
(12"+=) (YZ 121T) – Rock steady.
May 93. (cd) <(7567 81230)> **ARETHA'S JAZZ**
Jun 93. (d-cd) <(7567 81668-2)> **30 GREATEST HITS**
Oct 94. (cd/c) <(7567 80606-2/-4)> **QUEEN OF SOUL – THE VERY BEST OF . . .** `23`

– even more compilations, etc. –

1973. (lp) Embassy-CBS; (CBS/40 65482) **FIRST 12 SIDES**
May 86. (d-lp/d-c) Stylus; (SMR/SMC 8506) **THE FIRST LADY OF SOUL** `89` `-`
Jul 81. (7") Old Gold; (OG 9102) **I SAY A LITTLE PRAYER. / RESPECT**
1988. (12") Old Gold; (OG 4057) **JUMP TO IT. / GET IT RIGHT**
Apr 89. (12") Old Gold; (OG 4511) **IT'S JUST YOUR LOVE. / LOVE ME RIGHT**
Sep 86. (d-lp/c/cd) Castle; (CCS LP/MC/CD 152) **THE COLLECTION VOL.1 & 2** `-`
(re-iss. Jul87; same)
Jul 87. (cd) WEA; (K 2 41135) **20 GREATEST HITS**
– I never loved a man (the way I loved you) / Respect / Do right woman – do right man / Dr Feelgood / (You make me feel like) a natural woman / Chain of fools / Save me / The house that Jack built / Think / I say a little prayer / See saw / Daydreaming / Call me / Don't play that song / You're all I need to get by / I'm in love / Spanish Harlem / Rock steady / Angel / Until you come back to me (that's what I'm gonna do).
Dec 87. (c/cd; shared PERCY SLEDGE) Blue Moon; (BMDC/CDBM 001) **SOUL SENSATION**
May 88. (lp/c/cd) Streetlife; (226/216/246 2525) **SO SWELL** `-`
Mar 90. (cd) Collector's; (902291-2) **THE GREAT ARETHA FRANKLIN** `-`
Mar 90. (7") East West; (A 7951) **THINK. / (b-by Blues Brothers)** `31` `-`
(12"+=/cd-s+=) (TA/CDA 7951) – ('A'mixes).
Nov 93. (d-cd) Legacy; (CD 48515) **JAZZ TO SOUL**

Apr 94.	(cd) *That's Soul; (TS 009)* **RESPECT**			-	
Jul 94.	(cd) *Charly; (CDCD 1164)* **GOSPEL ROOTS**			-	
Nov 98.	(d-cd/d-c) *Global TV; (RAD CD/MC 110)* **GREATEST HITS**	38			

FRANTIC ELEVATORS (see under ⇒ SIMPLY RED)

FREAK POWER (see under ⇒ COOK, Norman)

FREE

Formed: London, England . . . Spring 1968 by PAUL RODGERS (vocals), PAUL KOSSOFF (guitar) and SIMON KIRKE (drums). The latter two had been members of blues combo BLACK CAT BONES before poaching RODGERS from another blues outfit, BROWN SUGAR. With the addition of young ex-BLUESBREAKER, ANDY FRASER, on bass, this precocious line-up was complete, adopting the name FREE at the suggestion of blues grandaddy ALEXIS KORNER. KORNER also tipped off 'Island' supremo CHRIS BLACKWELL, and after resisting an extremely misguided BLACKWELL attempt to rename them The HEAVY METAL KIDS, FREE duly signed to his label and began work on their debut album, 'TONS OF SOBS' (1968). Emerging from the shadow of CREAM, the album was an impressive set of heavy, organic blues, KOSSOFF stealing the show with his emotionally charged, liquid gold guitar style, in full effect on BOOKER T's 'THE HUNTER'. By the release of 'FREE' (1969), RODGERS' soulful voice was developing into one of the best in rock, while FRASER had taken on joint songwriting duties with RODGERS. The band also had a blistering live reputation and had already built up a sizeable following by the time 'ALL RIGHT NOW' was a massive worldwide hit. Its gritty R&B stomp paved the way for FREE's magnum opus, 'FIRE AND WATER' (1970), a No.3 UK album that boasted such enduring fare as the introspective ballads, 'OH I WEPT' and 'HEAVY LOAD' while RODGERS' wonderfully evocative vocals lent 'REMEMBER' a mellow resonance. That summer, cresting the wave of their popularity, the band played to over half a million people at the Isle Of Wight festival. With pressure to come up with a successful follow-up to 'ALL RIGHT NOW', FREE were confident that 'THE STEALER' would do the business. When it stiffed completely things started to go seriously awry, the 'HIGHWAY' (1970) album receiving a similarly lukewarm reception. This relative commercial failure increased tensions in what was already a perilously fraught inter-band relationship, the group deciding to call it a day after fulfilling touring commitments in Japan and Australia. The split eventually came in May '71, ironically almost coinciding with their biggest hit since 'ALL RIGHT NOW', a FACES-style romp entitled 'MY BROTHER JAKE'. Solo projects by RODGERS (PEACE) and FRASER (TOBY) came to little, although KOSSOFF and KIRKE's eponymous collaboration with Texan keyboard player, JOHN 'RABBIT' BUNDRICK, and Japanese bassist TETSU YAMAUCHI, was released to relative critical and commercial success, KOSSOFF relishing the opportunity to realise his ideas outwith the confines of FREE. The band subsequently regrouped in early 1972 and recorded the 'FREE AT LAST' album, a reasonable effort which spawned a Top 20 hit with the 'LITTLE BIT OF LOVE' single, a highly melodic slice of rock, the sort of thing RODGERS would go on to perfect with BAD COMPANY. While the album made the Top 10, KOSSOFF was spiralling into serious drug dependence, and following a disastrous American tour, the band's stability received a further blow when FRASER departed for the group SHARKS (he subsequently released a few melodic rock albums in the mid 70's). With TETSU and RABBIT filling in, FREE undertook a Japanese tour prior to recording a final album, 'HEARTBREAKER' (1973). Although KOSSOFF was too ill to make much of a contribution, the album stands among FREE's best, boasting RODGERS' desperate plea to KOSSOFF, 'WISHING WELL', and the superb, BEATLES-esque 'COME TOGETHER IN THE MORNING'. Following a final tour of America with TRAFFIC, FREE finally split in summer '73, RODGERS and KIRKE going on to form BAD COMPANY. KOSSOFF, meanwhile, had already begun his ill-fated solo career, forming BACK STREET CRAWLER. After a handful of relatively well-received albums, KOSSOFF finally succumbed to heroin addiction, dying in his sleep on the 19th March '76. It was a tragic end for a guitarist that was once destined to be remembered in the same breath as the likes of ERIC CLAPTON and JIMI HENDRIX.

Album rating: TONS OF SOBS (*5) / FREE (*6) / FIRE AND WATER (*8) / HIGHWAY (*6) / FREE LIVE (*4) / FREE AT LAST (*5) / HEARTBREAKER (*5) / THE FREE STORY compilation (*8) / COMPLETELY FREE compilation (*7) / THE BEST OF FREE – ALL RIGHT NOW compilation (*8) / MOLTEN GOLD: THE ANTHOLOGY compilation (*8) / KOSSOFF, KIRKE, TETSU & RABBIT (*4)

PAUL RODGERS (b.12 Dec'49, Middlesbrough, England) – vocals (ex-BROWN SUGAR) / **PAUL KOSSOFF** (b.14 Sep'50, Hampstead, London, England) – guitar (ex-BLACK CAT BONES) / **SIMON KIRKE** (b.28 Jul'49, Shrewsbury, England) – drums (ex-BLACK CAT BONES) / **ANDY FRASER** (b. 7 Aug'52, Shropshire, England) – bass (ex-JOHN MAYALL'S BLUESBREAKERS)

			Island	A&M	
Nov 68.	(lp) *(ILPS 9089)* <4198> **TONS OF SOBS**				Aug69

– Over the green hills (part 1) / Worry / Walk in my shadow / Wild Indian woman / Goin' down slow / I'm a mover / The hunter / Moonshine / Sweet tooth / Over the green hills (part 2). *(cd-iss. Jun88; CID 9089)* *(cd re-iss. 1989; IMCD 62)*

Mar 69.	(7") <1099> **I'M A MOVER. / WORRY**		-	-
Mar 69.	(7") *(WIP 6054)* **BROAD DAYLIGHT. / THE WORM**		-	-

Jul 69.	(7") *(WIP 6062)* **I'LL BE CREEPIN'. / SUGAR FOR MR. MORRISON**			-
Aug 69.	(7") *(WIP 6062)* **I'LL BE CREEPIN'. / MOUTHFUL OF GRASS**			-
Oct 69.	(lp) *(ILPS 9104)* <4204> **FREE**	22		

– I'll be creepin' / Songs of yesterday / Lying in the sunshine / Trouble on double time / Mouthful of grass / Woman / Free me / Broad daylight / Mourning sad morning. *(cd-iss. Jun88; CID 9104)*

May 70.	(7") *(WIP 6082)* <1206> **ALL RIGHT NOW. / MOUTHFUL OF GRASS**	2	4	Jul70

(re-iss. Jul73 hit UK No.15)

Jun 70.	(lp) *(ILPS 9120)* <4268> **FIRE AND WATER**	2	17	Aug70

– Fire and water / Oh I wept / Remember / Heavy load / Mr. Big / Don't say you love me / All right now. *(re-iss. Sep86 lp/c/cd; ILPM/ICM/CID 9120)* *(cd-iss. Apr90; IMCD 80)* *(re-iss. lp Jan94 + May94; ILPS 9120)*

Nov 70.	(7") *(WIP 6093)* **THE STEALER. / LYING IN THE SUNSHINE**		-	
Nov 70.	(7") <1230> **THE STEALER. / BROAD DAYLIGHT**	-	49	
Dec 70.	(lp) *(ILPS 9138)* <4287> **HIGHWAY**	41		Feb71

– The highway song / The stealer / On my way / Be my friend / Sunny day / Ride on pony / Love you so / Bodie / Soon I will be gone. *(cd-iss. Jun88; CID 9138)* *(cd re-iss. 1989; IMCD 63)*

Jan 71.	(7") <1248> **THE HIGHWAY SONG. / LOVE YOU SO**	-		
Mar 71.	(7") <1266> **I'LL BE CREEPIN'. / MR. BIG**	-		
Apr 71.	(7") *(WIP 6100)* <1276> **MY BROTHER JAKE. / ONLY MY SOUL**	4		
Jun 71.	(lp) *(ILPS 9160)* <4306> **FREE LIVE! (live)**	4	89	Aug71

– All right now / I'm a mover / Be my friend / Fire and water / Ride on pony / Mr. Big / The hunter / Get where I belong (studio). *(cd-iss. Jun88; CID 9160)* *(cd re-iss. 1989; IMCD 73)*

—— They had already split May'71. FRASER formed TOBY, while RODGERS formed the short-lived PEACE.

KOSSOFF, KIRKE, TETSU & RABBIT

were formed by the other two plus **TETSU YAMAUCHI** (b.21 Oct'47, Fukuoka, Japan) – bass / **JOHN 'RABBIT' BUNDRICK** – keyboards, vocals / and guest **B.J. COLE** – steel guitar

Nov 71.	(lp) *(<ILPS 9188>)* **KOSSOFF, KIRKE, TETSU & RABBIT**			-

– Blue grass / Sammy's alright / Just for the box / Colours / Hold on / Yellow house / Dying fire / Fool's life / Anna / I'm on the run. *(re-iss. Aug91 cd)(c; IMCD 139)(ICM 9188)*

FREE

—— re-formed originals Feb'72 (**RODGERS, KOSSOFF, FRASER + KIRKE**)

May 72.	(7") *(WIP 6129)* <1352> **LITTLE BIT OF LOVE. / SAIL ON**	13		
Jun 72.	(lp/c) *(ILPS/ICT 9192)* <4349> **FREE AT LAST**	9	69	

– Catch a train / Soldier boy / Magic ship / Sail on / Travelling man / Little bit of love / Guardian of the universe / Child / Goodbye. *(cd-iss. Jun88; CID 9192)* *(cd re-iss. Feb90; IMCD 82)*

—— **TETSU YAMAUCHI** – bass (see above); repl. FRASER who joined SHARKS / added **JOHN 'RABBIT' BUNDRICK** – keyboards (see above) / **RODGERS** – also added guitar

Dec 72.	(7") *(WIP 6146)* **WISHING WELL. / LET ME SHOW YOU**	7		
Jan 73.	(lp/c) *(ILPS 9217)* <9324> **HEARTBREAKER**	9	47	

– Wishing well / Come together in the morning / Travellin' in style / Heartbreaker / Muddy water / Common mortal man / Easy on my soul / Seven angels. *(cd-iss. Jun88; CID 9217)* *(cd re-iss. Feb90; IMCD 81)*

Mar 73.	(7") *(WIP 6160)* **TRAVELLIN' IN STYLE. / EASY ON MY SOUL**			-

(re-iss. Mar74; WIP 6223)

—— **WENDELL RICHARDSON** – guitar of OSIBISA, on UK & US tour early '73 repl. KOSSOFF who formed BACK STREET CRAWLER. He died in his sleep 19 Mar'76 after years of drug abuse. FREE split early '73. RABBIT went solo before joining (KOSSOFF's) CRAWLER. TETSU joined The FACES. RODGERS and KIRKE formed BAD COMPANY.

– compilations, etc. –

on 'Island' UK / 'A&M' US unless mentioned otherwise

Mar 74.	(d-lp) *(ISL D4)* **THE FREE STORY**	2		

– I'm a mover / I'll be creepin' / Mourning sad morning / All right now / Heavy load / Fire and water / Be my friend / The stealer / Soon I will be gone / Mr. Big / The hunter / Get where I belong / Travelling man / Just for the box / Lady / My brother Jake / Little bit of love / Sail on / Come together in the morning. *(re-iss. Oct89 lp/c/cd; ILPS/ICT/CID 9945)* *(cd re-iss. Sep96; IMCD 226)*

1974.	(7") <1629> **LITTLE BIT OF LOVE. / THE STEALER**	-		
1974.	(7") <1720> **ALL RIGHT NOW. / THE STEALER**	-		
Apr 75.	(lp) <3663> **THE BEST OF FREE**	-		
Nov 76.	(lp) *(ILPS 9453)* **FREE AND EASY, ROUGH AND READY**		-	
Nov 76.	(7") *(WIP 6351)* **THE HUNTER. / WORRY**		-	
Feb 78.	(7"ep) *(IEP 6)* **THE FREE EP**	11		

– All right now / My brother Jake / Wishing well. *(re-iss. Oct82 as 12"pic-d; PIEP 6)* – hit UK No.57.

Oct 82.	(lp/c) *(ILPS/ICT 9719)* **COMPLETELY FREE**			
May 85.	(7") *(IS 221)* **WISHING WELL. / WOMAN**			

(12"+=) (12IS 221) – Walk in my shadow.

Feb 91.	(c-s/7") *(C+/IS 486)* **ALL RIGHT NOW. / I'M A MOVER**	8		

(12"+=/cd-s+=) (12IS/CID 486) – Get where I belong.

Feb 91.	(cd/c/lp) *(CID/IC/ILP TV 2)* **ALL RIGHT NOW – THE BEST OF FREE**	9		

– Wishing well / All right now / Little bit of love / Come together in the morning / The stealer / Sail on / Mr. Big / My brother Jake / The hunter / Be my friend / Travellin' in style / Fire and water / Travelling man / Don't say you love me.

Apr 91.	(c-s/7") *(C+/IS 495)* **MY BROTHER JAKE (remix). / WISHING WELL (remix)**			

(12"+=/cd-s+=) (12IS/CID 495) – The stealer (extended) / Only my soul (extended).

Nov 92.	(d-cd) *(ITSCD 3)* **FIRE AND WATER / HEARTBREAKER**		-	
May 94.	(d-cd) *(CRNCD 2)* **MOLTEN GOLD: THE ANTHOLOGY**		-	

PAUL KOSSOFF

with all of FREE as guests; plus **TREVOR BURTON** – bass / **ALAN WHITE** – drums

	Island	Island
Dec 73. (lp) *(ILPS 9264)* **BACK STREET CRAWLER**	□	□

– Tuesday morning / I'm ready / Time away / Molten gold / Back street crawler. *(re-iss. Apr87, lp/c; ILPM/ICM 9264) (cd-iss. Feb90; IMCD 84) (cd-iss. Jul92; IMCD 144)*

BACK STREET CRAWLER

KOSSOFF – lead guitar with **TERRY WILSON-SLESSER** – vocals / **TERRY WILSON** – bass / **TONY BRAUNAGEL** – drums / **MIKE MONTGOMERY** – keyboards / plus **PETER VAN DER PUIJE** – sax / **EDDIE QUANSAH** – horns / **GEORGE LEE LARNYOH** – flute, saxes

	Atlantic	Atco
Aug 75. (lp) *(K 50173)* <36125> **THE BAND PLAYS ON**	□	□

– Who do women / New York, New York stealing my way / Survivor / It's a long way down to the top / All the girls are crazy / Jason blue / Train song / Rock & roll junkie / The band plays on.

—— **GEOFF WHITEHORN** – guitar repl. wind section

May 76. (lp) *(K 50267)* **2ND STREET**	□	-

– Selfish lover / Blue soul / Stop doing what you're doing / Raging river / Some kind of happy / Sweet beauty / Just for you / On your life / Leaves the wind.

—— Tragedy had already struck when on the 19th March '76, KOSSOFF died in his sleep, suffering from drug abuse.

—— The rest carried on as CRAWLER and released 4 singles as well as 2 albums on 'Epic'; 'CRAWLER' (1977) & 'SNAKE, RATTLE & ROLL' (1978).

– his compilations, etc. –

Oct 77. (d-lp) *D.J.M.; (29002)* <300> **KOSS** (1974/75)	□	□

(re-iss. Aug83 on 'Street Tunes'; SDLP 1001) (cd-iss. Jul87 on 'Castle' lp/c/cd; CLA LP/MC/CD 127)

May 83. (lp) *Street Tunes; (STLP 001)* **THE HUNTER** (1969-75)	□	-
Aug 83. (lp) *Street Tunes; (STLP 002)* **LEAVES IN THE WIND** (1975/76)	□	-
Sep 83. (d-lp) *Street Tunes; (SDLP 1002)* **CROYDON – JUNE 15th 1975 (live)**	□	-
Nov 83. (c) *Street Tunes; (STC 0012)* **MR. BIG**	□	-
Apr 86. (lp/c) *Island; (PKSP/PKC 100)* **BLUE SOUL**	□	-
May 95. (cd) *The Hit Label; (AHLCD 31)* **THE COLLECTION**	□	-
Mar 97. (cd/c) *Carlton; (303600095-2/-4)* **STONE FREE**	□	-

---

FREE KITTEN (see under ⇒ **SONIC YOUTH**)

FREUR (see under ⇒ **UNDERWORLD**)

Glenn FREY (see under ⇒ **EAGLES**)

Robert FRIPP (see under ⇒ **KING CRIMSON**)

Edgar FROESE (see under ⇒ **TANGERINE DREAM**)

FRONT 242   (dig out; Great Alt & Indie . . .)

FUGAZI

Formed: Arlington, Virginia, USA . . . 1987 by IAN MacKAYE (now of Washington DC), who had the previous year featured on an album by EMBRACE (not the more recent outfit!). MacKAYE and drummer JEFF NELSON subsequently founded the 'Dischord' label, a bedrock of the Washington DC hardcore scene and an outlet for a pair's new band, MINOR THREAT. Completing the line-up with LYLE PRESLAR and BRIAN BAKER, this highly influential outfit releasing two singles in 1981, before they added STEVE HANSEN to boost their minimalist sound on the album, 'OUT OF STEP' (1983). A further album, the eponymous 'MINOR THREAT', contained the track 'STRAIGHT EDGE', a term which would be adopted by a generation of fans who followed MacKAYE and Co.'s example of abstinence and individual responsibility. Following their split, mainman MacKAYE formed FUGAZI, sharing vocal and songwriting duties with GUY PICCOTTO (ex-leader of RITES OF SPRING and INSURRECTION – the latter outfit having released a self-titled effort for 'Peaceville'). With the FUGAZI line-up crystallising around BRENDAN CANTY and JOE LALLY, they released two HENRY ROLLINS-produced mini-sets, the eponymous 'FUGAZI' and 'MARGIN WALKER' (1989), before fully realising their aggressively economical sound on the acclaimed 'REPEATER' (1990) album. Bringing to mind the once wilfully obscure vocals of DAVID THOMAS (PERE UBU) backed by the hardcore of NO MEANS NO, FUGAZI delivered a fourth set, 'STEADY DIET OF NOTHING' (1991), their perseverance paying off with a minor placing in the UK charts. Two years later, 'IN ON THE KILLTAKER' scored a deserved UK Top 30 and dominated the indie charts for months; despite persistent major label interest, FUGAZI have admirably refused to play the corporate game (how many bands can you say that about?). The mid 90's saw the release of the last FUGAZI album to date, 'RED MEDICINE', taking the staunchly independent hardcore crusaders into previously uncharted territory, i.e. the UK Top 20 (appropriately enough, the commercial behemoth that is the American music industry has so far prohibited the band's domestic success). MacKAYE, PICCIOTTO and crew were back in '98, although 'END

HITS' (not a compilation) suffered a little commercially due to their long absence. Unperturbed, FUGAZI worked on a soundtrack album. Jem Cohen's docu-film, 'INSTRUMENT', was delivered the following Spring, the music (with sparse vocals!) a return of sorts to their abrasive best. • **Covered:** 12XU (Wire). • **Trivia:** MacKAYE produced the early '89 BEEFEATER single, 'House Burning Down'.

Album rating: 13 SONGS compilation (*8) / REPEATER (*8) / STEADY DIET OF NOTHING (*7) / IN ON THE KILLTAKER (*7) / RED MEDICINE (*6) / END HITS (*6) / INSTRUMENT soundtrack (*7) / Minor Threat: COMPLETE DISCOGRAPHY compilation (*8)

MINOR THREAT

IAN MacKAYE (b.1963) – vocals, guitar / **LYLE PRESLAR** – guitar / **BRIAN BAKER** – bass (ex-GOVERNMENT ISSUE) / **JEFF NELSON** – drums

	Dischord	Dischord
Jun 81. (7"ep) *<Dischord 3>* **MINOR THREAT EP**	-	□
Dec 81. (7",7"red) *<Dischord 5-Limp 41>* **IN MY EYES**	-	□

—— added **STEVE HANSEN** – bass (BAKER now on second guitar)

1983. (lp/c) *<(DISCHORD 10/+C)>* **OUT OF STEP**	□	□

– Betray / It follows / Think again / Look back and laugh / Sob story / No reason / Little friend / Out of step / Stand up / 12XU.

1984. (lp/c) *<(DISCHORD 12/+C)>* **MINOR THREAT**	□	□

– Filler / I don't wanna hear it / Seeing red / Straight edge / Small man, big mouth / Screaming at a wall / Bottled violence / Minor threat / In my eyes / Out of step (with the world) / Guilty of being white / Steppin' stone.

Aug 85. (7"ep) *<(DISCHORD 15)>* **SALAD DAYS / GOOD GUYS. / STUMPED / CASHING IN**	□	□
Mar 90. (cd) *<(DISCHORD 40)>* **COMPLETE DISCOGRAPHY** (compilation)	□	□

FUGAZI

IAN MacKAYE – vocals, guitar (ex-MINOR THREAT, ex-TEEN IDES, ex-EMBRACE) / **GUY PICCIOTTO** (b.1966) – vocals (ex-INSURRECTION, ex-RITES OF SPRING, ex-ONE LAST WISH) / **JOE LALLY** (b.1964, Rockville, Maryland) – bass / **BRENDAN CANTY** (b.1967) – drums

	Dischord	Dischord
Dec 88. (m-lp/m-c) *<(DISCHORD 30/+C)>* **FUGAZI**	□	□

– Waiting room / Bulldog front / Bad mouth / Burning / Give me the cure / Suggestion / Glue man. *(re-iss. Apr98; same)*

Jul 89. (m-lp/m-c) *<(DISCHORD 35/+C)>* **MARGIN WALKER**	□	□

– Margin walker / And the same / Burning too / Provisional / Lockdown / Promises. *(cd-iss. Oct89 as '13 SONGS'+=; DIS 36)* – FUGAZI *(re-iss. Apr98; same)*

Feb 90. (7",7"green) *<(DISCHORD 43)>* **JOE #1. / BREAK IN / SONG #1**	□	□
Mar 90. (lp/c/cd) *<(DISCHORD 44/+C/CD)>* **REPEATER**	□	□

– Turnover / Repeater / Brendan /1 / Merchandise / Blueprint / Sieve-fisted grind / Greed / Two beats off / Styrofoam / Reprovisional / Shut the door. *(cd+=)* – Song #1 / Joe /1 / Break in. *(re-iss. Apr98; same)*

Aug 91. (lp/c/cd) *<(DISCHORD 60/+C/CD)>* **STEADY DIET OF NOTHING**	63	□

– Exit only / Reclamation / Nice new outfits / Stacks / Latin roots / Steady diet / Long division / Runaway return / Polish / Dear justice letter / K.Y.E.O. *(re-iss. Apr98; same)*

Jun 93. (m-lp/m-c/m-cd) *<(DIS 70/+C/D)>* **IN ON THE KILLTAKER**	24	□

– Facet squared / Public witness program / Returning the screw / Smallpox champion / Rend it / 23 beats off / Sweet and low / Cassavetes / Great cop / Walken's syndrome / Instrument / Last chance for a slow dance. *(re-iss. Apr98; same)*

May 95. (lp/cd) *<(DIS 90/+CD / EFA 17990-2)>* **RED MEDICINE**	18	□

– Do you like me / Bed for the scraping / Latest disgrace / Birthday pony / Forensic scene / Combination lock / Fell, destroyed / By you / Version / Target / Back to base / Downed city / Long distance runner. *(re-iss. Apr98; same)*

—— FUGAZI were put in backburner until their return below

Apr 98. (cd/c/lp) *<(DIS 110 CD/C/V)>* **END HITS**	47	□

– Break / Place position / Recap modotti / No surprise / Five corporations / Caustic acrostic / Closed captioned / Floating boy / Foreman's dog / Arpeggiation / Guilford fall / Pink frosty / F/D.

Apr 99. (cd/c/lp) *<(DIS 120 CD/C/V)>* **INSTRUMENT** (soundtrack)	□	□

– Pink frosty (demo) / Lusty scripps / Arpeggiator (demo) / Afterthought / Trio's / Turkish disco / Me and Thumbelina / Floating boy (demo) / Link track / Little Debbie / H.B. / I'm so tired / Rend it (demo) / Closed caption (demo) / Guildford fall (demo) / Swingset / Shaken all over / Slo crostic.

FUGEES

Formed: New Jersey, USA . . . early 90's by expatriate Haitian (hence the name FUGEES, as in refugees) cousins, PRAKAZREL 'PRAS' MICHEL and WYCLEF JEAN, who recruited sweet-voiced vocalist, LAURYN HILL; she had previously scored a bit part in US comedy, 'Sister Act II', and had just completed a degree at Columbia university. Signed to 'Ruffhouse' (part of 'Columbia'), The FUGEES' debut set, 'BLUNTED ON REALITY' (1994), reflected their more intelligent, socially conscious approach to hip hop while musically they were also more enlightened, fusing reggae and African folk-style acoustic guitar parts over their laidback rapping. Although the debut garnered critical acclaim, the group would have to wait a further two years for any real commerical rewards. Fuelled by the massive success (UK No.1) of their intuitive, innovative cover of Lori Lieberman's 'KILLING ME SOFTLY', Bob Marley's 'NO WOMAN, NO CRY' and the tough but soulful 'READY OR NOT', 'THE SCORE' (1996) became a multi-million worldwide seller, The FUGEES possibly one of the most commercially successful hip hop acts to make it in recent years. After the excitement of 1996, JEAN released a solo project under the moniker, WYCLEF JEAN & THE REFUGEE ALLSTARS the following year as well as a charming collaborative single with HILL, 'THE SWEETEST THING'. While PRAS worked on his solo set, entitled 'GHETTO SUPASTAR' (featuring the massive hit of the same name) and released in November '98, LAURYN HILL was conjuring up some magic of her own. 'THE MISEDUCATION OF . . .' (1998), pushed all the right buttons and was a massive success all over the world, especially America where it won a plethora of Grammy's the following year. Its everso cool songs – segued with a "back-in-time" LAURYN in the classroom – grooved high and mighty above any of today's soul and hip hop, tracks such as 'DOO WOP (THAT THING)' (also a chart-topper), 'EX-FACTOR' and 'EVERYTHING IS EVERYTHING', giving her top marks all round. • **Trivia:** FUGEE is a slang American term for a Haitian refugee, thus the suffix of REFUGEE CAMP on 'THE SCORE' after their group name.

Album rating: BLUNTED ON REALITY (*5) / THE SCORE (*8) / THE SCORE – BOOTLEG VERSIONS (*5) / Wyclef Jean & The Refugee All-Stars: THE CARNIVAL (*6) / Pras: GHETTO SUPASTAR (*6) / Lauryn Hill: THE MISEDUCATION OF LAURYN HILL (*8)

LAURYN HILL (b.19 Oct'75, East Orange, New Jersey, USA) – vocals, guitar / **PRAS MICHEL** (b. SAMUEL PRAKAZREL MICHEL, 19 Oct'72, Haiti) – vocals / **WYCLEF JEAN** (b. JEANNEL WYCLEF JEAN, 17 Oct'72, Haiti) – vocals

		Ruffhouse– Columbia	Ruffhouse– Columbia	
Mar 94.	(cd/c) <(474713-2/-4)> **BLUNTED ON REALITY** – (Introduction) / Nappy heads / (Blunted interlude) / Recharge / (Freestyle interlude) / Vocab / (Special news bulletin interlude) / Boof baf / Temple / How hard is it? / (Harlem chit chat interlude) / Refugees on the mic / Living like there ain't no tomorrow / Shouts out from the block. *(cd+=)* – Nappy heads (remix). *(re-iss. Oct96; same)*			
May 94.	(c-s) (660421-4) **BOOF BAF / NAPPY HEADS** (12"s+=/cd-s+=) (660421-6/-2) – ('A'mixes).			
Jun 94.	(c-s; as FUGEES – Tranzlator Crew) <77431> **NAPPY HEADS / ('A'instrumental)** (cd-s+=) <77432> – (4-'A'versions) / Some seek stardom.	–	49	
Oct 94.	(c-s; as FUGEES – Tranzlator Crew) **VOCAB / (mixes)** (cd-s+=) – ('A'mixes; Refugees hip hop / Refugees acoustic) / Refugees on the mic / ('A'mixes; instrumental / Salaam's acoustic / Vibey) / Nappy heads (Mad Spider mix).	–		
Jan 95.	(c-s) **TEMPLE / (mixes)**	–		
Mar 96.	(cd/c) (483549-2/-4) <67147> **THE SCORE** – Red intro / How many mics / Ready or not / Zealots / The beast / Fu-gee-la / Family business / Killing me softly / The score / The mask / Cowboys / No woman, no cry / Manifest – outro / Fu-gee-la (Refugee Camp remix) / Fu-gee-la (Refugee Camp global remix) / Mista mista. *(cd+=)* – Fu-gee-la (Refugee Camp global remix).	2	1 Feb96	
Mar 96.	(c-s) (663066-4) <78195> **FU-GEE-LA / HOW MANY MICS** (cd-s+=) (663066-2) – ('A'mixes; instrumental / Refugee Camp / Refugee Camp instrumental). (12") (663066-6) – ('A'mixes; North Side / Sly & Robbie).	21	29	
Jun 96.	(c-s) (663343-4) **KILLING ME SOFTLY / ('A'mix)** (cd-s+=) (663343-2) – ('A'mix). (cd-s) (663343-5) – ('A'mixes).	1	–	
Sep 96.	(c-s) (663721-4) **READY OR NOT / THE SCORE** (cd-s+=) (663721-2) – ('A'mix). (12") (663721-6) – ('A'side) / Killing me softly / Cowboys.	1	–	
Nov 96.	(c-s) (6639224-4) **NO WOMAN, NO CRY / ('A'mix)** (cd-s) (6639224-2) – ('A'mixes). (cd-s) (6639224-5) – ('A'mixes).	2	–	
Nov 96.	(cd/c) (486824-2/-4) **THE SCORE . . . BOOTLEG VERSIONS** – Ready or not / Nappy heads / Don't cry, dry your eyes / Vocab / Killing me softly / No woman no cry.	55	–	

—— In Mar'97, FUGEES featured on BOUNTY KILLER's US hit, 'Hip-Hopera'.

| Mar 97. | (c-s) (574069-4) **RUMBLE IN THE JUNGLE / ('A'mix)**
(cd-s) (574069-2) – ('A'mix).
(above featured A TRIBE CALLED QUEST & BUSTA RHYMES and was issued on 'Mercury' records) | 3 | – | |

WYCLEF JEAN

Jun 97.	(c-s/cd-s; WYCLEF JEAN & THE REFUGEE ALL STARS) (664681-4/-2) **WE TRYING TO STAY ALIVE / FLAVOR FROM THE CARNIVAL** (cd-s+=) (664681-5) – Anything can happen / Imagio.	13	46	
Jun 97.	(cd/c; WYCLEF JEAN featuring THE REFUGEE ALL STARS) (487442-2/-4/-1) <67974> **THE CARNIVAL** – Intro-Court-Clef-Intro / Apocalypse / Guantanamera / Pablo Diablo / Bubblegoose / Prelude to all the girls / Down to ho / Anything can happen / Gone till November / Words of wisdom / Year of the dragon / Sang Fezi / Fresh interlude / Mona Lisa / Street jeopardy / Killer MC / We trying to stay alive / Gunpowder / Closing arguments / Enter the carnival / Jaspora / Yele / The carnival. *(re-iss. May98; same)*	40	16	
Aug 97.	(c-s; REFUGEE ALL STARS & LAURYN HILL) (664978-4) **THE SWEETEST THING / ('A'mix)** (cd-s+=) (664978-2) – ('A'mixes).	18		
Sep 97.	(c-s,12"/cd-s; REFUGEE CAMP ALL STARS featuring PRAS – with KY-MANI) <13411> **AVENUES / ('A'mix)** (above from the film, 'Money Talks'; issued on 'Arista' records)	–	35	
Sep 97.	(c-s) (665085-4) **GUANTANAMERA / ROXANNE ROXANNE** (cd-s+=) (665085-2) – Trying to stay alive. (cd-s) (665085-5) – ('A'side) / Bubble goose bakin' cake / No airplay men in blue.	25		

—— LAURYN HILL featured on the PAID & LIVE single 'All The Time', which hit UK Top 60 in Dec'97.

| May 98. | (c-s,12"/cd-s; WYCLEF JEAN) (665871-6/-4) <78752> **GONE TILL NOVEMBER (The Makin' Runs remixes; original / instrumental / acappella) / NO AIRPLAY / NO AIRPLAY (instrumental)**
(cd-s+=) (665871-5) – ('A'mixes) / Bubblegoose / Guantanamera. | 3 | 9 Jan98 | |

| Jul 98. | (c-s,12",cd-s) <78993> **CHICKENHEAD / WHAT'S CLEF / CHEATED (R&B mix) / CHEATED (rock remix) / TO ALL THE GIRLS**
(above featured SPRAGGA BENZ) | – | 61 | |
| Oct 99. | (c-s/cd-s; WYCLEF JEAN featuring BONO) (668212-4/-2) **NEW DAY / NEW DAY (clean mix)**
(cd-s) (668212-5) – ('A'mix) / Gone till November / To all the girls. | 23 | Sep99 | |

PRAS

		Interscope	Interscope
Jun 98.	(c-s/12"/cd-s; PRAS MICHEL featuring OL' DIRTY BASTARD & introducing MYA) *(INC/INT/IND 95593)* <95021> **GHETTO SUPASTAR (THAT IS WHAT YOU ARE) / ('A'instrumental) / DON'T BE AFRAID**	2	15

		Columbia	Columbia
Oct 98.	(c-s/cd-s) (666621-4/-2) **BLUE ANGELS / (mixes)** (cd-s) (666621-5) – ('A'side) / Ghetto supastar / M.Y.A. / Murder death.	6	
Nov 98.	(cd/c) <69516> **GHETTO SUPASTAR** – Hallelujah / Ghetto supastar (that is what you are) / 1st phone interlude / What'cha wanna do / For the love of this / Blue angels / Can't stop the shinning (RIP rock part 2) / Get your groove on / Frowsey (part 2) / Dirty cash / For the love of this / Wha'wha'wha'what / 2nd phone interlude / Lowriders / Yeah 'eh yeah 'eh / Murder dem / 3rd phone interlude / Final interlude / Amazing Grace / Avenues / Another one bites the dust.	44	55

—— In Nov'98, QUEEN and WYCLEF JEAN (featuring PRAS & FREE) hit UK No.5 with a re-working of, 'ANOTHER ONE BITES THE DUST' (from the movie, 'Small Soldiers')

LAURYN HILL

		Columbia	Columbia
Sep 98.	(c-s/cd-s) (666515-4/-2) <78868> **DOO WOP (THAT THING) / (Gordon's mix) / (instrumental)** (cd-s) (666515-5) – ('A'side) / Lost ones / Forgive them father.	3	1 Nov98
Sep 98.	(cd/c) (489843-2/-4) <69035> **THE MISEDUCATION OF LAURYN HILL** – Intro / Lost ones / Ex-factor / To Zion / Doo wop (that thing) / Superstar / Final hour / When it hurts so bad / I used to love him / Forgive them father / Every ghetto, every city / Nothing even matters / Everything is everything / The miseducation of Lauryn Hill. *(cd hidden+=)* – Can't take my eyes off you / Tell him.	2	1
Feb 99.	(c-s/cd-s) (666945-4/-2) <radio cut> **EX-FACTOR / ('A'mix)** (cd-s) (666945-5) – ('A'mixes).	4	21 Jan99
Jun 99.	(c-s/cd-s) (667574-4/-2) <79206> **EVERYTHING IS EVERYTHING / EX-FACTOR (a simple mix)** (cd-s+=) (667574-5) – ('A'radio & instrumental) / Ex-fator (a simple breakdown).	19	35

FUGS (dig out; Great Psychedelic . . .)

FUN BOY THREE (see under ⇒ HALL, Terry)

FUNHOUSE (see under ⇒ WATERBOYS)

FUNKADELIC (see under ⇒ CLINTON, George)

FUN LOVIN' CRIMINALS

Formed: Manhattan, New York, USA . . . 1993 by former marine HUEY (of Puerto-Rican/Irish decent), FAST and STEVE. This hard-bitten NY hip hop-rock posse, took on the mantle of early BEASTIE BOYS, fusing it together with "acid"-ic jazz and the mandatory drug references. The slow-rollin' CHEECH & CHONG-esque 'SCOOBY SNACKS' and 'SMOKE 'EM', were highlights from their much touted debut album, 'COME FIND YOURSELF'. Initally unleashed in '96, it was virtually ignored in the States, although it created quite a stir in Britain almost a year on, when 'SCOOBY SNACKS' (sampling 'Movement Of Fear' by TONES ON TAILS), 'THE FUN LOVIN' CRIMINAL' and 'THE KING OF NEW YORK' all had Top 30 success. In the summer of '97, they played major festivals including Scotland's 'T In The Park', while HUEY (was it him or FAST who was seeing SAFFRON of REPUBLICA?) chilled out on the Various Artists/LOU REED No.1 smash 'Perfect Day'. The following year, FLC were back in fine suggestive form with their sophomore long-player, '100% COLOMBIAN' (1998), a UK Top 3 entry. Premiered by the – Barry White saved my life – single/tribute, 'LOVE UNLIMITED', the record was indeed laid back, laid back enough to bury yourselves between the sheets for a marathon session and hope rigor mortis or viagra take hold (a bucket of water has just been poured over my head, thank-you!). • **Songwriters:** Group, except WE HAVE ALL THE TIME IN THE WORLD (Hal David & John Barry) / I'M NOT IN LOVE (10cc). Sampled LYNYRD SKYNYRD's 'Freebird' on 'BOMBIN' THE L' and the soundtracks from QUENTIN TARANTINO's 'Reservoir Dogs' & 'Pulp Fiction' on 'SCOOBY SNACKS'. 'KING OF NEW YORK' used pieces of 'Insensatez' (Ray Brown Trio) & 'Also Sprach Zarathestra' (Deodato).

Album rating: COME FIND YOURSELF (*8) / 100% COLOMBIAN (*7) / MIMOSA (THE LOUNGE ALBUM) (*5)

HUEY – vocals, guitar / **FAST** – bass, keyboards, trumpet / **STEVE** – drums

		not iss.	Silver Spotlight
Nov 95.	(cd-ep) <36515> **ORIGINAL SOUNDTRACK FOR HI-FI LIVING**	–	

– Passive – Aggressive / Blues for suckers / I can't get with that / Coney Island girl.

		Chrysalis	Capitol

Jun 96. (7") (CHS 5031) **THE GRAVE AND THE CONSTANT. /**
BOMBIN' THE L / BLUES FOR SUCKERS `72` `-`
(12"+=/cd-s+=) (12/CD CHS 5031) – King of New York.

Jul 96. (cd/c/lp) (CD/TC+/CHR 6113) <35703> **COME FIND**
YOURSELF `7` Feb96
– The fun lovin' criminal / Passive – Aggressive / The grave and the constant / Scooby snacks / Smoke 'em / Bombin' the L / I can't get with that / King of New York / We have all the time in the world / Bear hug / Come find yourself / Crime and punishment / Methadonia / I can't get with that (schmoove version) / Coney Island girl.

Aug 96. (7") (CHS 5034) **SCOOBY SNACKS. / I'LL BE SEEING YOU** `22` `-`
(cd-s) (CDCHS 5034) – ('A'side) / Smoke 'em (live) / Come find yourself (live) / I can't get with that (live).
(cd-s) (CDCHS 5034) – ('A'mixes).

Nov 96. (7"pic-d) (CHSPD 5040) <58581> **THE FUN LOVIN'**
CRIMINAL. / COME FIND YOURSELF (live BBC session) `26` Feb97
(cd-s+=) (CDCHSS 5040) – ('A'-Hee Haw version) / The grave and the constant (Stephen Lironi 12"mix).
(cd-s) (CDCHS 5040) – ('A'side) / The grave and the constant (live) / Coney Island girl (live) / Scooby snacks.

Mar 97. (7"colrd) (CHS 5049) **KING OF NEW YORK. / SCOOBY**
SNACKS (Schmoove version) `28` `-`
(cd-s+=) (CDCHS 5049) – ('A'-Jack Dangers complex mix).
(cd-s) (CDCHS 5049) – ('A'side) / ('A'-Jack Dangers complex mix) / Blues for suckers / ('A'instrumental).

Jun 97. (7"m) (CHS 5060) **SCOOBY SNACKS. / I'M NOT IN LOVE /**
CONEY ISLAND GIRL (Schmoove version) `12` `-`
(cd-ep) (CDCHS 5060) – (first 2 tracks) / Scooby snacks (live) / I can't get with that (live).
(cd-ep) (CDCHSS 5060) – (2nd & 3rd tracks) / Scooby snacks (Schmoove version) / Bombin the L (Schmoove version).

		Chrysalis	Virgin

Aug 98. (c-s/cd-s) (TC/CD CHS 5096) **LOVE UNLIMITED / SHINING**
STAR / 10th STREET `18` `-`
(cd-s) (CDCHS 5096) – ('A'side) / ('A'mix) / ('A'instrumental).

Aug 98. (cd-s) <97463> **100% COLOMBIAN (mixes)** `-`

Aug 98. (cd/c/lp) (497056-2/-4/-1) <23140> **100% COLOMBIAN** `3`
– Up on the hill / Love unlimited / The view belongs to everyone / Korean bodega / Back on the block / 10th street / Sugar / South side / We are all very worried about you / All for self / All my time is gone / Big night out / Mini bar blues.

Oct 98. (cd-s) (TC/CD CHS 5101) **BIG NIGHT OUT / SUMMER**
WIND (with IAN McCULLOCH) / LOVE UNLIMITED `29` `-`
(cd-s) (CDCHSS 5101) – ('A'side) / We are all very worried about you / My D (slight return).

Apr 99. (c-s) (TCCHS 5108) **KOREAN BODEGA / KOREAN BODEGA**
(Aero Mexicana mix) `15` `-`
(cd-s) (CDCHS 5108) – ('A'side) / The ballad of Larry Davis / Sleepyhead.
(cd-s) (CDCHSS 5108) – ('A'side) / The fun lovin' criminal / Big night out (full length video).

Nov 99. (cd) (523459-2) **MIMOSA (THE LOUNGE ALBUM)** `37`
– Couldn't get it right / Scooby snacks (schmoove) / Shining star / Bombin' the L (circa 1956 version) / I'm not in love / Summer wind / Crazy wind / I can't get with that (schmoove) / We have all the time in the world (Copa Capana version) / Coney Island girl (schmoove) / I'll be seeing you.

FUSE (see under ⇒ CHEAP TRICK)

FUTURE SOUND OF LONDON

Formed: London, England . . . 1991 initially as HUMANOID by Manchester dance duo of GARY COCKBAIN and BRIAN DOUGANS, who created one of the all-time great acid-house records with the 1988 UK Top 20 hit, 'STAKKER HUMANOID'. This outfit spawned other projects; SEMI REAL, YAGE, METROPOLIS + ART SCIENCE TECHNOLOGY before 'Virgin' signed the duo as FUTURE SOUND OF LONDON in 1991. Early the following year, their fourth effort, the seminal 'PAPUA NEW GUINEA', was very reminiscent of ENO & DAVID BYRNE's proto-ambient work, although it possessed an overtly commercial appeal. 'LIFEFORMS', in 1994, was a 90 minute gothic soundscape epic which careered into the Top 10 and featured a guest vocal spot from LIZ FRASER (Cocteau Twins). To complete the year, they conducted a pioneering experiment by playing gigs down a ISDN line, issuing the results as a cd-album. In 1996, prior to the 'DEAD CITIES' double-album, they returned to the singles charts with the moody classic, 'MY KINGDOM'. • **Songwriters:** DOUGANS / COCKBAIN except FLAK; co-written w / ROBERT FRIPP plus WILLIAMS / GROSSART / THOMPSON / NIGHTINGALE. OMNIPRESENCE co-wriiten with KLAUS SCHULZE. MY KINGDOM sampled VANGELIS & ENNIO MORRICONE. • **Trivia:** Augmented on NOMAD's single 'Your Love Has Lifted Me', SYLVIAN-FRIPP's album 'Darshan' and APOLLO 440's 'Liquid Cool'.

Album rating: ACCELERATOR (*7) / ISDN (*7) / LIFEFORMS (*8) / DEAD CITIES (*7)

HUMANOID

GARRY COCKBAIN (b. Bedford, England) – keyboards / **BRIAN DOUGANS** (b.Scotland) – keyboards

		Westside	not iss.

Oct 88. (7") (WSR 7) **STAKKER HUMANOID. / (part 2)** `6` `-`
(12"+=/3"cd-s+=) (WSR T/CD 12) – ('A'-Omen mix).
(re-iss. 8 mixes Jul92 on 'Jumpin' & Pumpin' 12"ep/cd-ep; 12/CD TOT 27); hit No.40 (note 7"+c-s+cd-s; original part 2 was repl. by 'A'-Smart Systems remix)

Apr 89. (7") (WSR 14) **SLAM. / BASS INVADERS** `54` `-`
(12"+=/cd-s+=) (WSR T/CD 14) – ('A'dub mix) / ('A'-hip house).

		Humanoid	not iss.

Aug 89. (7"; HUMANOID featuring SHARON BENSON) (HUM
1) **TONIGHT. / ('A'mix)**
(12"+=/cd-s+=) (HUM/+T/CD 1) – (3-'A'mixes).

Oct 89. (lp/c/cd) (HUMAN/ZCHUM/CDHUM 1989) **GLOBAL**

Apr 90. (12"ep) (HUMT 2) **THE DEEP (3 mixes). / CRY BABY**

		Debut	not iss.

1990. (12"; as ART SCIENCE TECHNOLOGY) (DEBTX 3100)
A.S.T. / ESUS FLOW

FUTURE SOUND OF LONDON

—— same line-up as above.

		Jumpin' & Pumpin'	not iss.

1991. (12"ep) (12TOT 11) **PULSE EP**
– Bring on the pulse / In the mind of a child / Hardhead / Pulse state.

1991. (12"ep) (12TOT 15) **PRINCIPLES OF MOTION EP**

1991. (12"ep) (12TOT 16) **PULSE 3 EP**
– Tingler / Owl / Bite the bullet / Calcium.

Feb 92. (12"ep) (TOT 17) **PAPUA NEW GUINEA (Dali mix) /**
('A'-Dumb child of a Q mix) / ('A'-Qube mix) `22`
(12"ep/c-ep/cd-ep) (12/TC/CD TOT 17) – (the remixes by Andy Weatherall & Graham Massey). (re-iss. May95 12"cd-s; 12TOT/CDSTOT 17) (12" re-issjun97; 12TOT 17R)

1992. (12"ep) (12TOT 18) **SMART SYSTEMS EP**

1992. (12") (12TOT 2S) **PULSE 4**
– I'm not gonna let you do it / The creator / Shrink / 18 space virus.

Jun 92. (cd/c/lp) (CD/MC/LP TOT 2) **ACCELERATOR** `75`
– Expander / Stolen documents / While others cry / Calcium / It's not my problem / Papau New Guinea / Moscow / 1 in 8 / Pulse state / Central industrial. (cd re-iss. Aug94 +=; CDTOT 2R) – Expander (remix) / Moscow (remix).
above featured **BASIL CLARKE** – vocals (ex-YARGO)

1992. (12"ep) **EXPANDER (remix). / MOSCOW (remix) /**
CENTRAL INDUSTRIAL (remix)
(cd-ep+=) – ('A'radio remix). (re-iss. Jul94 12"cd-s; 12/CDS TOT 37); hit UK 72)

		Quigly	not iss.

Jun 93. (lp/c; as AMORPHOUS ANDROGYNOUS) (LP/TC EBV
1) **TALES OF EPHIDRINA** `-`
– Swab / Mountain goat / In mind / Ephidrina / Auto pimp / Pod room / Fat cat.

Aug 93. (12"ep/cd-ep; as AMORPHOUS ANDRONGYNOUS)
ENVIRONMENTS `-`

		Virgin	Astralwerks

Oct 93. (12"/c-s) (VS T/C 1478) **CASCADE. / ('A'-parts 2-5)** `27` `-`
(cd-s+=) (VSCDT 1478) – ('A'-short form mix).

May 94. (d-cd/d/cd-lp) (CD/TC+/V 2722) **LIFEFORMS** `6`
– Cascade / Ill flower / Flak / Bird wings / Dead skin cells / Lifeforms / Eggshell / Among myselves / / Domain / Spineless jelly / Interstat / Vertical pig / Cerebral / Life form ends / Vit / Omnipresence / Room 208 / Elaborate burn / Little brother.

Aug 94. (7"/c-s) (VS P/C 1484) **LIFEFORMS. / ('A'alternative mix)** `14` `-`
(12"+=/cd-s+=) (VS/+T/CDT 1484) – ('A'-paths 1-7).
(above featured LIZ FRASER (of COCTEAU TWINS) on vocals)

Dec 94. (cd/c/d-lp) (CD/TC+/VX 2755) **I.S.D.N.** `62` `-`
– Just a f***in' idiot / Far out son of lung and the ramblings of a madman / Appendage / Slider / Smokin' Japanese babe / You're creeping me out / Eyes-pop-skin-explodes-everybody's dead / It's my mind that works / Dirty shadows / Tired of bugs / Egypt / Are they fighting us? / Hot knives. (re-iss. Jun95 with 3 new remixed tracks, hit No.44)

—— (In 1994, they were also at times, abbreviated to F.S.O.L.)

May 95. (12"ep/c-ep/cd-ep) (VS T/C/CDT 1540) **FAR OUT SON OF**
LUNG AND THE RAMBLINGS OF A MADMAN. / SNAKE
HIPS / SMOKIN' JAPANESE BABE / AMOEBA `22` `-`

Oct 96. (12") (VST 1605) **MY KINGDOM (parts 1-4)** `13`
(c-s+=/cd-s+=) (VS C/CDT 1605) – (part 5).

Oct 96. (cd/c) (CD/TC+/V 2814) **DEAD CITIES** `26` `-`
– Herd killing / Dead cities / Her face forms in summertime / We have explosive / Everyone in the world is doing something without me / My kingdom / Max / Antique toy / Quagmire / In a state of permanent abyss / Glass / Yage / Vit drowning / Through your gills I breathe / First death in the family. (d-cd-iss. ; CDVX 2814)

Apr 97. (12"/cd-s) (VST/VSCDT 1616) **WE HAVE EXPLOSIVE (pt.1-5)** `12` `-`
(cd-s) (VSCDX 1616) – ('A'mixes; Oil Funk / Mantronik / Oil dub / radio).

		Arista	Restless
Oct 99.	(c-s; as WARREN G featuring MACK 10) <73721> I **WANT IT ALL**	–	23
Oct 99.	(cd/c) <74321 69374-2/-4> <63710> **I WANT IT ALL**		21

– (intro) / Gangsta love / Why oh why / Dollars make sense / I want it all / Havin' it all / You never know / My momma / G-spot / We got that / Dope beat / World wider riders / We can groove / The game don't wait / I want it all / (outro).

Peter GABRIEL

Born: 13 May '50, Cobham, Surrey, England. After 8 years as leader of GENESIS, he left in May '75 to pursue a solo career, releasing the first of his four self-titled studio albums in 1977. Produced by BOB EZRIN (more often found working with heavy-rock acts), the album's overwrought feel found GABRIEL struggling for a musical identity despite including such enduring songs as the classic 'SOLISBURY HILL', a Top 20 hit single, and its creepy flipside, 'MORIBUND THE BURGERMEISTER'. 1978's follow-up boasted ROBERT FRIPP at the production helm, and a somewhat pared-down sound, GABRIEL illustrating his admiration for the punk ethos on 'D.I.Y.' and rocking out on the raging 'ON THE AIR'. His third, in 1980, moved towards a radically different style of songwriting, based around rhythm rather than chord sequences. With the use of a pioneering sampler, the Fairlight CMI, GABRIEL was able to construct tracks around the rhythm, adding instrumentation to enhance the sound. With STEVE LILLYWHITE producing and a cast of collaborators including FRIPP, KATE BUSH and PHIL COLLINS, he created a compelling set of minimalistic songs, the hypnotic anti-war single 'GAMES WITHOUT FRONTIERS', taking GABRIEL into the Top 5. The album also included his inspired tribute to murdered black South African activist (STEVE) 'BIKO'. This introduced GABRIEL's growing interest in world music, an area he would explore further on his fourth album (released in the States as 'SECURITY'). Incorporating ethnic sounds and rhythms into his distinctive songwriting technique, GABRIEL discovered a new found artistic freedom, creating one of his most accomplished and inventive albums in the process. Highlights included the single, 'SHOCK THE MONKEY', the African tribal drumming of 'RHYTHM OF THE HEAT', and the exotic 'THE FAMILY AND THE FISHING NET'. His increasing immersion in all things ethnic saw him become involved with the newly conceived WOMAD festival in 1982, highlighting music from the furthest flung corners of the globe. After a shaky start, the festival has now become an annual event with an affiliated world music label, 'Real World'. The 80's also saw GABRIEL record two soundtrack albums, Alan Parker's 'BIRDY' (1985) and Martin Scorsese's 'THE LAST TEMPTATION OF CHRIST' (1989). The former was made up largely of revamped tracks from his earlier work, the original songs transformed into atmospheric mood pieces to impressive effect, while the latter was an eerily affecting collage of folksy, world music stylings. Sandwiched between these two was the album which finally marked his arrival as a major league rock star. 'SO', released in 1986, saw GABRIEL incorporating his ethnic experimentation into the pop format with remarkable dexterity. The track, 'SLEDGEHAMMER', with its polished funk and famous, award winning video, shot into the upper regions of the charts, propelling the album to No.1 in the UK (No.2 in America). The record was a free-ranging world trip, showcasing strong melodies ('DON'T GIVE UP' with KATE BUSH) against exotic backdrops, the culmination of his work to date. The long awaited "proper" follow-up, 'US' was eventually released in 1992, just held off the top spot on both sides of the Atlantic. The album was a markedly more downbeat, introspective affair, the single, 'DIGGING IN THE DIRT', highlighting GABRIEL's return to more personal songwriting. It was also inspired by his mid-80's divorce from childhood sweetheart JILL MOORE and the split with his girlfriend, actress ROSANNA ARQUETTE. GABRIEL continued to devote much of his time to the 'Real World' label, although he did find some time for a tour and a live album, 'SECRET WORLD' in 1994. • **Covered;** STRAWBERRY FIELDS FOREVER (Beatles) / SUZANNE (Leonard Cohen). • **Trivia:** In 1982, he co-wrote & produced 'Animals Have More Fun' for JIMMY PURSEY (ex-SHAM 69). He has also guested for ROBBIE ROBERTSON (his 1987 album) & JONI MITCHELL (her 1991 album).

Album rating: PETER GABRIEL [1] (*7) / PETER GABRIEL [2] (*6) / PETER GABRIEL [3] (*7) / PETER GABRIEL (SECURITY) (*6) / PETER GABRIEL – PLAYS LIVE (*5) / BIRDY soundtrack (*5) / SO (*8) / PASSION: MUSIC FOR THE LAST TEMPTATION OF CHRIST (*6) / SHAKIN' THE TREE: SIXTEEN GOLDEN GREATS compilation (*8) / US (*6) / SECRET WORLD LIVE (*5)

PETER GABRIEL – vocals, keyboards (ex-GENESIS, ex-GARDEN WALL) with **TONY LEVIN** – bass / **STEVE HUNTER** – guitar / **LARRY FAST** – keyboards / **JIMMY MAELEN** – percussion / **ALAN SCHWARTZBERG** – drums / **ROBERT FRIPP** – guitar

		Charisma	Atco
Feb 77.	(lp/c) (CDS/+MC 4006) <36-147> **PETER GABRIEL**	7	38

– Moribund the burgermeister / Solisbury Hill / Modern love / Excuse me / Humdrum / Slowburn / Waiting for the big one / Down the Dolce Vita / Here comes the flood. (cd-iss. May83; CDSCD 4006) (re-iss. Aug88 lp/c; CHC/+MC 38) (cd re-iss. May87; PGCD 1)

Mar 77.	(7") (CB 301) <7079> **SOLISBURY HILL. / MORIBUND THE BURGERMEISTER**	13	68
Jun 77.	(7") (CB 302) **MODERN LOVE. / SLOWBURN**		

——— now with **FRIPP**, plus **JERRY MAROTTA** – drums / **ROY BITTAN** – piano / **SID McGINNIS** – guitar / **BAYETE** – keyboards

May 78.	(7") (CB 311) **D.I.Y. / PERSPECTIVE**		–

(12"w-drawn) (CB 319) – ('A'remix) / Mother of violence / Teddy bear.

Warren G

Born: WARREN GRIFFIN III, c.1971, Long Beach, California, USA. Being the half-brother of the notorious DR DRE, it was probably inevitable that WARREN would take the hip hop path. What was more surprising was the consistent chart success the rapper enjoyed following a Transatlantic Top 5 placing for his debut single, 'REGULATE'. The track initially appeared on the soundtrack to the movie, 'Above The Rim', a clever MICHAEL McDONALD sample creating an evocative, downbeat but funky backing for G's mellow rapping style. This, together with debut album, 'REGULATE . . . G FUNK ERA' (1994), and the work of brother DRE and mates like SNOOP DOGGY DOGG, helped imprint the G-funk sound on the nation's musical consciousness. More crossover/pop than "gangsta", the album narrowly missed the US top spot, becoming one of the biggest selling hip hop albums of the year. Following a quiet '95, WARREN signed to 'Def Jam' and promptly hooked up with ADINA HOWARD for a hip hop cover of Tina Turner's 'WHAT'S LOVE GOT TO DO WITH IT'. Only slightly more cheesy than a follow-up makeover of Bob Marley's 'I SHOT THE SHERIFF', these singles seemed to open the floodgates for a slew of similar dulloids, most notably Puff Daddy's 'MISSING YOU', an artless take-off of The Police's 'EVERY BREATH YOU TAKE'. Still, the singles furnished WARREN with his biggest UK success to date, ensuring a Top 20 placing for his second album, 'TAKE A LOOK OVER YOUR SHOULDER (REALITY)' (1997). Of late, the G man has found it hard to keep up with the plethora of rap stars that are around today, his third album, the patchy 'I WANT IT ALL' (1999), just failing to hit its G-spot and the US Top 20.

Album rating: REGULATE . . . G FUNK ERA (*6) / TAKE A LOOK OVER YOUR SHOULDER (REALITY) (*7) / I WANT IT ALL (*5)

WARREN G – vocals; with various crew

		Death Row	Death Row
Jul 94.	(7"/c-s) (A 8290/+C) **REGULATE. / PAIN**	5	2

(12"+=/cd-s+=) (A 8290 T/CD) – Mi Monie rite / Loyal to the game.

		R.A.L.	R.A.L.
Jul 94.	(cd/c/lp) (523 335-2/-4/-1) <523364> **REGULATE . . . G FUNK ERA**	25	2

– Regulate (WARREN G & NATE DOGG) / Do you see / Gangsta sermon / Recognize / Super soul sis / '94 ho draft / So many ways / This DJ / This is the shack / What's next / And ye don't stop / Runnin' with no breaks.

Oct 94.	(7"/c-s) (RAL/+MC 1) <853236> **THIS DJ. / ('A'mix)**	12	9

(12"+=/cd-s+=) (12RAL/RALCD 1) – Regulate.

Mar 95.	(c-s) (RALMC 3) **DO YOU SEE / ('A'mix)**	29	42

(12"+=) (12RAL 3) – ('A'mix).
(cd-s++=) (RALCD 3) – What's next.

		Interscope	Interscope
Nov 96.	(c-s; WARREN G & ADINA HOWARD) <(INC 97008)> **WHAT'S LOVE GOT TO DO WITH IT /**	2	32 Sep96

(12"+=/cd-s+=) <(INT/IND 97008)> –

		Def Jam	Def Jam
Feb 97.	(c-s) (DEFMC 31) **I SHOT THE SHERIFF / REGULATE**	2	20

(12"+=/cd-s+=) (12DEF/DEFCD 31) – What's love got to do with it (with ADINA HOWARD) / Relax your mind.

Feb 97.	(cd/c/lp) (533 484-2/-4/-1) **TAKE A LOOK OVER YOUR SHOULDER (REALITY)**	20	11

– Intro / Annie Mae / Smokin' me out (featured RON ISLEY) / Reverend Eazy Dick / Reality / Interlude / Young fun / When we go through / We bring heat / Can you feel it / Transformers / Reel light intro / Relax your mind / To all the DJ's / Back up / What's love got to do with it (WARREN G & ADINA HOWARD) / I shot the sheriff.

May 97.	(c-s; WARREN G featuring RON ISLEY) (574 442-4) **SMOKIN' ME OUT / WHAT WE GO THROUGH**	14	35

(12"+=/cd-s+=) (574 443-1/-2) – I shot the sheriff (mix).

Melanie G (see under ⇒ SPICE GIRLS)

		Charisma	Atlantic

Jun 78. (lp/c) (CAS/+MC 4013) <19181> **PETER GABRIEL** — `10` `45`
– On the air / D.I.Y. / Mother of violence / A wonderful day in a one-way world / White shadow / Indigo / Animal magic / Exposure / Flotsam and jetsam / Perspective / Home sweet home. (re-iss. Mar84 lp/c; CHC/+MC 24) (cd-iss. May87; PGCD 2)

Jun 78. (7") **D.I.Y. / MOTHER OF VIOLENCE** — `-` `☐`

		Charisma	Mercury

Feb 80. (7"m) (CB 354) **GAMES WITHOUT FRONTIERS. / THE START / I DON'T REMEMBER** — `4` `-`

May 80. (7") (CB 360) **NO SELF CONTROL / LEAD A NORMAL LIFE** — `33` `☐`

Jul 80. (7") <76086> **GAMES WITHOUT FRONTIERS. / LEAD A NORMAL LIFE** — `-` `48`

Sep 80. (7") <76086> **I DON'T REMEMBER. /** — `-` `☐`

—— now with **FRIPP, LEVIN + MAROTTA** plus guests **PHIL COLLINS** – drums / **KATE BUSH + PAUL WELLER** – vocals

May 80. (lp/c) (CAS/+Mc 4019) <3848> **PETER GABRIEL** — `1` `22`
– Intruder / No self control / Start / I don't remember / Family snapshot / And through the wire / Not one of us / Lead a normal life / Biko. (re-iss. Sep83 lp/c; CDS/+MC 4019) (cd-iss. May87; PGCD 3)

Aug 80. (7"/12") (CB 370/+12) **BIKO. / SHOSHOLOZA / JETZT KOMMT DIE FLUT** — `38` `☐`

—— guests on next incl. **DAVID LORD** – synthesizers, co-producer / **JOHN ELLIS** – guitar / + some of last line-up

		Charisma	Geffen

Sep 82. (lp/c) (PG/+MC 4) <2011> **PETER GABRIEL** <US-title 'SECURITY'> — `6` `28`
– The rhythm of the heat / San Jacinto / I have the touch / The family and the fishing net / Shock the monkey / Lay your hands on me / Wallflower / Kiss of life. (re-iss. Sep83 lp/c; same) (cd-iss. 1986; PGCD 4)

Sep 82. (7"/7"pic-d/12") (SHOCK 1/+22/12) <29883> **SHOCK THE MONKEY. / SOFT DOG (instrumental)** — `58` `29`
(7"/12") (SHOCK 1/350) – ('A'side) / ('B'-instrumental).

Dec 82. (7") (CB 405) **I HAVE THE TOUCH. / ACROSS THE RIVER** — `-` `☐`

Jun 83. (d-lp/c) (PGD L/MC 1) <4012> **PETER GABRIEL PLAYS LIVE (live)** — `8` `44`
– The rhythm of the heat / I have the touch / Not one of us / Family snapshot / D.I.Y. / The family and the fishing net / Intruder / I go swimming / San Jacinto / Solisbury Hill / No self control / I don't remember / Shock the monkey / Humdrum / On the air / Biko. (cd-iss. Jun85; PGDLD 1) (cd re-iss. 1988; CDPGD 100) – (omits 4 tracks).

Jun 83. (7") (GAB 1) **I DON'T REMEMBER (live). / SOLISBURY HILL (live)** — `62` `-`
(12"+=) (GAB 12) – Kiss of life (live).
(free-12"w- 12") (GAB 122) – GAMES WITHOUT FRONTIERS (live). / SCHNAPPSCHUSS (EIN FAMILIENFOTO)

		Virgin	Geffen

Nov 83. (7") <29542> **SOLISBURY HILL (live). / I GO SWIMMING (live)** — `-` `84`

May 84. (7") (VS 689) **WALK THROUGH THE FIRE. / THE RACE (by Larry Carlton)** — `69` `☐`
(12"+=) (VS 689-12) – I have the touch (remix).

Mar 85. (lp/c/cd) (CAS/+MC/CD 1167) <24070> **BIRDY – MUSIC FROM THE FILM (soundtrack)** — `51` `☐`
– At night / Floating dogs / Quiet and alone / Close up / Slow water / Dressing the wound / Birdy's flight / Slow marimbas / The heat / Sketchpad with trumpet and voice / Under lock and key / Powerhouse at the foot of the mountain. (re-iss. Apr90 on 'Virgin' lp/c; OVED/+C 283)

—— with **MAROTTA, LEVIN** plus **DANIEL LANOIS** – guitar, co-producer / **MANU KATCHE** – percussion / **YOUSSOU N'DOUR + KATE BUSH** – guest vocals / **STEWART COPELAND** – drums /etc.

Apr 86. (7") (PGS 1) **SLEDGEHAMMER / JOHN HAS A HEADACHE** — `4` `-`
(12"+=) (PGS 112) – Don't break this rhythm / ('A'dance mix).
('A'dance-12"+=) (PGS 113) – Biko (extended) / I have the touch ('85 remix).

May 86. (7") <28718> **SLEDGEHAMMER. / DON'T BREAK THIS RHYTHM** — `-` `1`

May 86. (lp/c/cd) (PG/+MC/CD 5) <24088> **SO** — `1` `2`
– Red rain / Sledgehammer / Don't give up / That voice again / In your eyes / Mercy street / Big time / We do what we're told. (pic-cd.Dec88+=; PGCDP 5) – This is the picture (excellent birds). (re-iss. Feb97 on 'E.M.I.'; LPCENT 16)

Sep 86. (7") <28622> **IN YOUR EYES. /** ('A'-Special mix) — `-` `26`

Oct 86. (7"; PETER GABRIEL & KATE BUSH) (PGS/+P 2) **DON'T GIVE UP. / IN YOUR EYES (special mix)** — `9` `-`
(12"+=) (PGS 2-12) – This is the picture (excellent birds).

Jan 87. (7") <28503> **BIG TIME. / WE DO WHAT WE'RE TOLD** — `-` `8`

Mar 87. (7") (PGS 3) **BIG TIME. / CURTAINS** — `13` `-`
(12"+=) (PGS 312) – ('A'extended).
('A'ext-c-s) (PGT 312) – Across the river / No self control (live). (re-iss. 3"cd-s.1989; GAIL 312)

Mar 87. (7"; PETER GABRIEL & KATE BUSH) <28463> **DON'T GIVE UP / CURTAINS** — `-` `72`

Jun 87. (7") (PGS 4) **RED RAIN / GA GA (I GO SWIMMING)** — `46` `-`
(12"+=/c-s+=) (PGS/+C 412) – Walk through the fire.

Jan 88. (7") (PGS/+C 6) **BIKO (live). / NO MORE APARTEID** — `49` `-`
(12"+=/cd-s+=) (PGS/CDPGS 6-12) – I have the touch ('85 remix).

—— In May 89, PETER ws credited with YOUSSOU N'DOUR on minor hit single 'SHAKIN THE TREE' (VS/+T/CD 1167)

		Real World	Geffen

Jun 89. (d-lp/c/cd) (RW LP/MC/CD 1) <24206> **PASSION (music for the Last Temptation Of Christ)** — `29` `60`
– The feeling begins / Gethsemane / Of these, hope / Lazarus raised / Of these, hope – reprise / In doubt / A different drum / Zaar / Troubled / Open* / Before night falls / With this love / Sandstorm / Stigmata** / Passion / With this love – choir / Wall of breath / The promise of shadows / Disturbed / It is accomplished / Bread and wine. (*= with SHANKAR) (**= with MAHMOUD TABRIZI ZADEH)

Sep 92. (7"/c-s) (PGS/+C 7) <19136> **DIGGING IN THE DIRT. / QUIET STEAM** — `24` `52`
(cd-s+=) (PGSDG 7) – ('A'instrumental).
(cd-s++=) (PGSCD 7) – Bashi-bazouk.

Oct 92. (lp/c/cd) (PG/+MC/CD 7) <24473> **US** — `2` `2`
– Come talk to me / Love to be loved / Blood of Eden / Steam / Digging in the dirt / Fourteen black paintings / Kiss that frog / Secret world.

Dec 92. (c-s) <19145> **STEAM / GAMES WITHOUT FRONTIERS (live)** — `-` `32`

Jan 93. (7"/c-s) (PGS/+C 8) **STEAM. /** ('A'-Carter mix) — `10` `☐`
(cd-s) (PGSDG 8 / PGSDX 8) – ('A' mix) / Games without frontiers (mix) / (2 'A' extended + dub mix or Games (other mix)

Mar 93. (7"/c-s) (PGS/+C 9) **BLOOD OF EDEN. / MERCY STREET** — `43` `☐`
(cd-s+=) (PGSDG 9) – ('A'-special mix)
(cd-s+=) (PGCDX 9) – Sledgehammer.

Sep 93. (7"/c-s) (PGS/+C 10) **KISS THAT FROG. /** ('A'- mindblender mix) — `46` `☐`
(cd-s+=) (PGSDG 10) – Digging in the dirt.
(cd-s+=) (PGSDX 10) – Across the river / Shaking the tree (Bottrill remix).

—— Below single, another from 'Philadelphia' film on 'Epic' records.

Jun 94. (7"/c-s) (660480-7/-4) **LOVE TOWN. / LOVE TO BE LOVED** — `49` `☐`
(cd-s+=) (660480-2) – Different drum.

—— live with **TONY LEVIN** – bass, vocals / **DAVID RHODES** – guitar, vocals / **MANU KATCHE** – drums / **PAULA COLE** – vocals / **JEAN CLAUDE NAIMRO** – keyboards, vocals / **RAVI SHANKAR** – violin, vocals / **LEVON MINASSIAN** – doudouk

Aug 94. (c-s) (PGSC 11) **SECRET WORLD (live). / COME TALK TO ME** — `39` `☐`
(cd-ep) (PGSCD 11) – ('A'live) / Red rain (live) / San Jacinto (live) / Mercy Street (live).

Sep 94. (d-cd/d-c) (PG DCD/MC 8) <24722> **SECRET WORLD LIVE (live)** — `10` `23`
– Come talk to me / Steam / Across the river / Slow marimbas / Shaking the tree / Red rain / Blood of Eden / Kiss that frog / Washing of the water / Solisbury Hill / Digging in the dirt / Sledgehammer / Secret world / Don't give up / In your eyes.

– compilations, etc. –

on 'Virgin' UK / 'Geffen' US, unless mentioned otherwise

Jan 83. (7") Old Gold; (OG 9265) **SOLISBURY HILL. / GAMES WITHOUT FRONTIERS** — `☐` `-`

Mar 83. (d-c) Charisma; (CASMC 102) **PETER GABRIEL 1 / PETER GABRIEL 2** — `☐` `-`

1988. (3"cd-ep) (CDT 33) **SOLISBURY HILL / MORIBUND THE BURGERMEISTER / SOLISBURY HILL (live)** — `☐` `-`
(re-iss. Apr90; VVCS 8)

Jun 88. (cd) XCDSD 4018) **PETER GABRIEL 3 (German version)** — `☐` `-`

May 89. (7") W.T.G.; <68936> **IN YOUR EYES. /** (track by Fishbone) — `-` `41`
(above from the film, 'Say Anything')

Oct 90. (3xcd-box) (TPAK 9) **PETER GABRIEL 1 / 2 / 3** — `☐` `-`

Nov 90. (lp/c/cd) (PGTV/+CD 6) <24326> **SHAKING THE TREE – SIXTEEN GOLDEN GREATS** — `11` `48`
– Solisbury Hill / I don't remember / Sledgehammer / Family snapshot / Mercy Street / Shaking the tree / Don't give up / Here comes the flood / Games without frontiers / Shock the monkey / Big time / Biko. (cd+=/c+=) – San Juanito / Red rain / I have the touch / Zaar.

Dec 90. (7"/c-s) (VS/+C 1322) **SOLISBURY HILL. / SHAKING THE TREE (w/ YOUSSOU N'DOUR)** — `57` `-`
(12"+=/cd-s+=) (VS T/CD 1322) – Games without frontiers.

GADGETS (see under ⇒ THE THE)

Serge GAINSBOURG

Born: LUCIEN GINZBERG, 2 Apr'28, Paris, France. The son of Russian Jewish immigrants, GAINSBOURG attended art college and initially tried to scrape a living as a painter. To supplement his income, he worked nights as a bar pianist before being snapped up for an unwilling singing role in the musical 'Milord L'Arsoille'. Reluctant to take to the stage himself (partly due to his less than conventionally handsome appearance), GAINSBOURG felt more comfortable as a songwriter, composing for major-league French stars such as SACHA DISTEL and JOHNNY HALLIDAY. Nevertheless, he ventured into the studio himself in the late 50's for debut album, 'LE POINCONNEUR DES LILAS' (1958), following it up with 'NO.2' (1960), 'L'ETONNANT SERGE GAINSBOURG' (1961), 'NO.4' (1962), 'GAINSBOURG CONFIDENTIEL' (1964) and 'GAINSBOURG PERCUSSIONS' (1964). Although these weren't great successes (outside France) in their own right, his material was exposed to English audiences via the likes of DIONNE WARWICK and PETULA CLARK. A close association with French actress/sex symbol BRIGITTE BARDOT inspired some of GAINSBOURG's finest work, the pair cutting a series of celebrated duets including 'BONNIE & CLYDE' and 'HARLEY DAVIDSON'. Even the infamous 'JE T'AIME … MOI NON PLUS' was penned for BARDOT who subsequently declined to perform it. Instead, the increasingly wayward Frenchman duetted on the track with another actress-cum-sex-kitten, JANE BIRKIN. Released as a single on 'Fontana' in July 1969, this breathy ode to sweaty love was banned by the BBC although it crowned the UK chart all the same (in October '69 the 'Major Minor' re-issue was No.1 while its identical counterpart was still in the charts having made No.2!); it even made the Top 60 in the USA. 1971's 'HISTOIRE DE MELODY NELSON' album found GAINSBOURG preoccupied with life's darker side (MELODY was a 14-year-old girl with whom the writer – as narrator – was having an affair!), a trait which would become more pronounced as his reputation grew ever more lecherous and provocative. His concept-type sets in the the mid-

70's were weird to say the least. From 1973's 'VU DE L'EXTERIEUR' – with its fart joke song ('DES VENTS DES PETS DES POUM') – to 75's Adolf Hitler concept! 'ROCK AROUND THE BUNKER' and 'L'HOMME A TETE DE CHOU' ('THE MAN WITH A CABBAGE HEAD'), all were extremely shocking and OTT; LOU REED meeting 50's rock'n'roll was how one could describe it. 1979's cod-reggae 'AUX ARMES ET CAETERA' (his only UK release) was also diverse, SLY & ROBBIE giving it their Jamaican dub treatment. SERGE even recorded a concept album about male prostitutes, 'LOVE ON THE BEAT' (1984), which updated 'HARLEY...' as 'HARLEY DAVID SON OF A BITCH'. Also guaranteed to shock was a duet with his daughter (actress Charlotte Gainsbourg), 'LEMON INCEST'; the Gallic Jew going a little astray even by his standards. Controversy was SERGE's middle name, while appearances on French chat shows were often accompanied by outrageous comments and remarks; actor Oliver Reed must have been watching. A pillar of the French anti-establishment, GAINSBOURG's hard-drinking lifestyle eventually caught up with him on 2nd March 1991 when he died of heart complications.

Album rating: LE POINCONNEUR DES LILAS (*5) / NO.2 (*5) / L'ETONNANT SERGE GAINSBOURG (*5) / NO.4 (*5) / GAINSBOURG CONFIDENTIEL (*5) / GAINSBOURG PERCUSSIONS (*5) / ANNA soundtrack (*6) / INITIALES B.B. (*7) / BONNIE AND CLYDE with Brigitte Bardot (*6) / JANE BIRKIN & SERGE GAINSBOURG – JE T'AIME (*6) / HISTORIE DE MELODY NELSON (*7) / VU DE L'EXTERIEUR (*6) / ROCK AROUND THE BUNKER (*7) / L'HOMME A TETE DE CHOU (*6) / AUX ARMES ET CAETERA (*4) / MAUVAISES NOUVELLES DES ETOILES (*4) / LOVE ON THE BEAT (*3) / YOU'RE UNDER ARREST (*3) / LE ZENITH DE GAINSBOURG (*3) / COMIC STRIP compilation (*7) / DE GAINSBOURG A GAINSBARRE boxed-set collection (*9)

SERGE GAINSBOURG – vocals, piano, guitar / (with sessioners)

		Philips	not iss.	
1958.	(lp) **LE POINCONNEUR DES LILAS**	-	-	French

– Le poincooneur des lilas / Le poinconneur de lilas / Recette de l'amour fou / Douze belles dans la peau / Ce mortel ennui / Ronsard / Femmes des uns sous le corps des autres / L'alcool / Du jazz dans le ravin / Charleston des demenageurs de piano / Jambe de bios "Friedland" / Claquer de doigts.

| 1960. | (lp) **NO.2** | - | - | French |

– Nuit d'Octobre / Adieu creature / L'anthracite / Mambo miam miam / Indifferente / Jeunes femmes et vieux messieurs / L'amour a la papa / Cha cha cha du loup / Sois belle et tais toi / Laissez-moi tranquille / Judith / L'eau a la bouche.

| 1961. | (lp) **L'ETONNANT SERGE GAINSBOURG** | - | - | French |

– Chanson de prevert / En relisant ta lettre / Rock de nerval / Oubliettes / Chanson de Maglia / Viva villa / Amours perdues / Femmes c'est du chinois / Personne / Sonnet d'Arvers.

| 1962. | (lp) **NO.4** | - | - | French |

– Goemons / Black trombone / Baudelaire / Intoxicated man / Quand tu t'y mets / Cigarillos / Requiem pour un twister / Ce grand mechant vous / L'appareil a sous.

| 1963. | (7"ep) **VILAINES FILLES, MAUVAIS GARCONS** | - | - | French |

– Vilaines filles, mauvais garcons / Violin, un jambon / La Javanaise.

| 1964. | (lp) **GAINSBOURG CONFIDENTIEL** | - | - | French |

– Chez le ye-ye / Sait-on jamais ou va une femme quand elle . . . . / Le talkie-walkie / Fille au rasoir / Saison des pluies / Alaeudania teiteia / Scenic railway / Tempes de yoyos / Amour sans amour / No no thanks no / Maxim's / Negative blues.

| 1964. | (lp) **GAINSBOURG PERCUSSIONS** | - | - | French |

– Joanna / La-bas c'est naturel / Pauvre Lola / Quand mon 6.35 me fait les yeux doux / Machins choses / Sambassadeurs / New York City U.S.A. / Couleur cafe / Marabout / Ces petits riens / Tatoue Jeremie / Coco and Co / Comment trouvez vous ma soeur?

| 1967. | (lp; V/A soundtrack) **ANNA** | - | - | French |

– Soul le soleil exactement / Sous le soleil exactement II / C'est la cristallisation comme dit / Pas mal'pas mal du tout / J'etais fait pour le sympathies / Photographes et religieuses / Rien rien j'disais ca comme ca / Jour comme un autre / Boomerang / Poison violent, c'est ca l'amour / De plus en plus, de moins en moins / Roller girl / Ne dis risen / Pistolet Jo / G.I. Jo / Je n'avais qu'un seul mot a lui dire. *(UK cd-iss. Oct98 on 'Mercury'+=; 558 837-2) – JE T'AIME MOI NON PLUS "BALLADE DE JOHNNY-JANE" soundtrack + others.*

| 1968. | (lp) **INITIALES B.B.** | - | - | French |

– Chanson du forcat / Chanson du forcat II / Manon / Requiem pour un con / L herbe tendre / Initiales B.B. / Comic strip / Bloody Jack / Docteur Jeckyll et Monsieur Hyde / Torrey canyon / Shu ba du ba loo ba / Ford Mustang.
(above featured BRIGITTE BARDOT)

| 1968. | (lp; by BRIGITTE BARDOT ET SERGE GAINSBOURG) **BONNIE AND CLYDE** | - | - | French |

– Bonnie and Clyde / Bubble gum / Comic strip / Un jour comme un autre / Pauvre Lola / L'eau a la bouche / La Javanaise / Madrague / Intoxicated man / Everybody loves my baby / Baudelaire / Docteur Jekyll et Monsieur Hyde.

		Fontana	Fontana	
1969.	(lp; as JANE BIRKIN & SERGE GAINSBOURG) **JANE BIRKIN & SERGE GAINSBOURG**	-	-	French

– Chanson de slogan / L'anamour / Orang outan / Souse le soleil exactement / 18-39 / 69 Annee erotique / Jane B / Elisa / Canari est sur la balc / Manon. *(UK-iss.Jun88 as 'JE T'AIME . . . MOI NON PLUS' on 'Bam Caruso'; DN 2002) (cd-iss. Oct98 as 'JE T'AIME . . . MOI NON PLUS' on 'Mercury'; 558 774-2)*

| Jul 69. | (7"; by JANE BIRKIN & SERGE GAINSBOURG) (TF 1042) **JE T'AIME . . . MOI NON PLUS. / Jane Birkin: JANE B** | 2 | 58 | Nov69 |

(re-iss. Sep69 on 'Major Minor'; MM 645) – hit UK No.1 (re-iss. Nov74 on 'Atlantic'; K 11511) – hit No.31

		Philips	not iss.	
1971.	(lp) **HISTORIE DE MELODY NELSON**	-	-	French

– Melody (extrait de Melody Nelson) / Ballade de Melody Nelson / Valse de Melody / Ah! Melody / L'hotel particulier (extrait de bof Melody) / Un Melody / Cargo culte. *(UK cd-iss. 1988; 812826-2) (<cd re-iss. Oct98 on 'Mercury'; 532 073-2)*

1973.	(7") **SEX SHOP. /**	-	-	French
1973.	(7") **LA DECADANSE. /**	-	-	French
1973.	(lp) **VU DE L'EXTERIEUR**	-	-	French

– Je suis venu te dire que j'm en vais / Vu de l'exterieur / Panpan cucul / Par hasard et pas rase / Des vents des pets des poums / Titicaca / Pamela popo / Poupee qui fait / L'hippopodame / Sensuelle et sans suite. *<US cd-iss. Oct98 on 'Mercury'; 532 075-2>*

| 1975. | (lp) **ROCK AROUND THE BUNKER** | - | - | French |

– Nazi rock / Tata teutonne / J'entends des voix off / Eva / Smoke gets in your eyes / Zig zag avec toi / Est-ce est-ce si bon / Yellow star / Rock around the bunker / S.S. in Uruguay. *<US cd-iss. Oct98 on 'Mercury'; 532 074-2>*

| 1976. | (lp) **L'HOMME A TETE DE CHOU"** | - | - | French |

– L'homme a tete de chou / Chez max coiffeur pour hommes / Marilou reggae / Transit a Marilou / Flash-forward / Aeroplanes / Premiers symptomes / Ma Lou Marilou / Variations sur Marilou / Meurtre a l'extincteur / Marilou sous la neige / Lunatic asylum. *(UK cd-iss. 1988; 812825-2) <US cd-iss. Oct98 on 'Mercury'; 532 076-2>*

| 1976. | (lp; soundtrack) **JE T'AIME MOI NON PLUS "BALLADE DE JOHNNY-JANE"** | - | - | French |

– Ballade de Johnny-Jane / Camion Jane / Banjo au bord du Styx / Rock'n'roll autor de Johnny / L'abominable strip-tease / Joe Banjo / Je t'aime moi non plus / Je t'aime moi non plus au lac vert / Je t'aime moi non plus au motel / Ballade de Johnny-Jane (finale).

| 1977. | (lp; soundtrack) **MADAME CLAUDE** | - | - | French |

– Diapositivisme / Discophoteque / Mi corasong / Ketchup in the night / Fish-eye blues / Teleobjectivisme / Putain que ma joie demeure / Burnt island / Yesterday yes a day / Dusty lane / First class ticket / Long focal rock / Arabysance / Passage a tobacco / Yesterday on Fender.

| Jan 79. | (7") (6042 412) **SEA, SEX & SUN. / MISTER ICEBERG** | - | - | |

—— next with **SLY & ROBBIE** – rhythm, etc / **ANSEL COLLINS** – organ / **I-THREES** :- MARCIA GRIFFITHS, RITA MARLEY + JUDY MOWATT

		Island	Polydor	
Aug 79.	(7") (WIP 6518) **AUX ARMES ET CAETERA. / DAISY TEMPLE**			
Aug 79.	(lp) (ILPS 9581) **AUX ARMES ET CAETERA**			

– La Javanaise remake / Aux armes et caetera / Les cocataires / Des laids des laids / Brigade des stups / Vielle canaille / Lola rastaquourere / Relax baby be cool / Daisy temple / Eau et gaz a tous le etages / Pas long feu / Marilou reggae dub. *US cd-iss. Oct98 on 'Mercury'; 532 077-2>*

		Philips	Mercury	
1981.	(lp) **MAUVAISES NOUVELLES DES ETOILES**	-	-	French

– Overseas telegram / Ecce homo / Mickey Maosse / Juif et dieu / Shush shush Charlotte / Toi mourir / Nostalgie camarade / Bana basadi balalo / Eugenie Sokolov / Negusa nagast / Strike / Bad news from the stars. *(UK cd-iss. 1988; 812823-2) <US cd-iss. Oct98 on 'Mercury'; 532 078-2>*

| 1984. | (lp/c) (822 849-1/-4) **LOVE ON THE BEAT** | - | - | French |

– Love on the beat / Sorry angel / Hmm hmm hmm / Kiss me Hardy / No comment / I'm the boy / Harley David son of a bitch / Lemon incest.

| 1987. | (cd) (834 034-2) **YOU'RE UNDER ARREST** | - | - | French |

– You're under arrest / Five easy pisseuses / Baille baille Samantha / Suck baby suck / Gloomy Sunday / Aux enfants de la chance / Shotgun / Glass securit / Dispatch box / Mon legionnaire.

| 1989. | (cd) (838 162-2) **LE ZENITH DE GAINSBOURG** (live 1988) | - | - | French |

—— sadly, SERGE was to die (2nd March, 1991) of heart complications

– compilations, etc. –

1988.	(cd) Philips; (812 877-2) **1958 – 25 ANS – 1983**		
Oct 96.	(cd) Philips; (<522 629-2>) **DU JAZZ DANS LE RAVIN**		

– Angoisse / Du jazz dans le ravin / Requiem pour un twisteur / Chez les ye-yes / Black march / Black trombone / Ce mortel ennui / Generique / Coco and Co / Intoxicated man / Le talkie-walkie / Some small chance / Quend tu t'y mets / La fille au rasor / Quand mon 6.35 me fait les yeux doux / Fugue / Machins choses / Negative blues / Wake me at five.

Oct 96.	(cd) Philips; (<528 949-2>) **COULEUR CAFE** (the 1964 albums)		
Feb 97.	(cd) Philips; 528 951-2> **COMIC STRIP** (1966-1969)	-	Feb97
Apr 98.	(10xcd-box) Polygram; <532 130-2> **DE GAINSBOURG A GAINSBARRE**		

– (LE POINCONNEUR DES LILAS; collection of first 2 albums / LA JAVANAISE; collection of second 2 albums / COULEUR CAFE; collection of 1964 albums / ANNA; collection of 1967 lp and BALLADE DE JOHNNY-JANE soundtrack / INITIALES B.B.; collection of 1968 album and BRIGITTE BARDOT duets / JE T'AIME MOI NON PLUS; collection of the JANE BIRKIN duets / JE SUIS VENU TE DIRE QUE JE M'EN VAIS; collection of 2 singles, the albums VU DE L'EXTERIEUR and ROCK AROUND THE BUNKER / L'HOMME A TETE DE CHOU; collection of the album and a 70's singles compilation / AUX ARMES ET CAETERA; collection of the album and MAUVAISES NOUVELLES DES ETOILES / LOVE ON THE BEAT; collection of the album and YOU'RE UNDER ARREST).

| Apr 98. | (cd) Polygram; **DE GAINSBOURG A GAINSBARRE VOL.1** | - | |

– Le poinconneur des lilas / Le sucettes / La javanaise / Chez les ye-ye / Couleur cafe / New York U.S.A. / Je t'aime . . . moi non plus / Elisa / Ballade de Melody Nelson / Je suis venu te dire que je m'en vais / L'ami caouette / Sea, sex and sun / Sorry angel / Aux enfants de la chance.

| Apr 98. | (cd) Polygram; <830 599-2> **LE PALACE 80** (live) | | |
| Aug 98. | (cd) Mercury; <558 842-2> **CLASSE X** | | |

– Je t'aime . . . moi non plus / Sucettes / Sex shop / Decadanse / Raccrochez c'est une horreur / Sea, sex and sun / Je pense queue / Good bye Emmanuelle / Vu de l'exterieur / Chez max coiffeur pour hommes / Panpan cucul / Des vents des pets des poums / Variations sur Marilou / Lola rastaquouere / Eau et gaz a tous le etages / Mickey Maousse / Eugenie Sokolov / Love on the beat / No comment / Suck baby suck.

GALAXIE 500 / LUNA / DAMON & NAOMI / etc

(dig out; Great Alt & Indie . . .)

Rory GALLAGHER

Born: 2 Mar'49, Ballyshannon, Donegal, Ireland. After playing in various school bands in Cork, RORY formed The FONTANA SHOWBAND, who subsequently became The IMPACT. By 1965, they'd secured residencies in Hamburg, mostly playing CHUCK BERRY songs to post-BEATLES audiences. A year later, just as the British blues revival was gathering steam, he formed TASTE with NORMAN DAMERY and ERIC KITTERINGHAM, although the latter two were eventually replaced by CHARLIE McCRACKEN and JOHN WILSON. After an eponymous debut album failed to break through, TASTE hit the UK Top 20 in 1970 with the follow-up set, 'ON THE BOARDS'. The album established GALLAGHER as Ireland's ambassador of the blues guitar, setting the stage for his forthcoming solo career. A self-titled debut appeared in 1971, the record selling enough initial copies to give it a Top 40 placing. Worshipping at the altar of blues KING-s; B.B., FREDDIE and ALBERT that is, GALLAGHER was revered by loyal fans for his musical integrity and down-to-earth approach (described as the working man's guitarist, due to his unconformist attire – i.e. lumberjack shirt, jeans and ruffled hair – GALLAGHER could also drink many a rock star under the table, eventually into the grave). After another blistering studio set in 1971, 'DEUCE', he scored a massive UK Top 10 with the concert album, 'LIVE IN EUROPE' (1972). Recorded at the peak of GALLAGHER's powers, 'BLUEPRINT' (1972) and 'TATTOO' (1973) stand among the Irishman's most overlooked albums, although the former nearly hit the UK Top 10. To coincide with the projected release of an in-concert rockumentary, GALLAGHER released yet another live set, the electrifying double set, 'IRISH TOUR '74'. Moving to 'Chrysalis' records soon after, GALLAGHER's form slumped slightly just as the new, leaner breed of guitar acts were up and coming, his commercial appeal subsiding under this pressure with each successive release. Nevertheless he continued to record some worthwhile material and perform live for a hardcore following, persevering with the rock industry well into the 90's. Death was the only thing that could prise GALLAGHER away from his guitar, the Irishman passing away on the 14th June '95 after suffering complications with a liver transplant. • Covers: SUGAR MAMA + DON'T START ME TALKING (Sonny Boy Williamson) / I'M MOVING ON (Hank Snow) / I TAKE WHAT I WANT (Hayes-Porter-Hedges) / ALL AROUND MAN (Davenport) / OUT ON THE WESTERN PLAINS (Leadbelly) / RIDE ON RED, RIDE ON (Levy-Glover-Reid) / I WONDER WHO (. . . Boyle) / AS THE CROW FLIES (Josh White) / JUST A LITTLE BIT (Dexter Gordon) / MESSING WITH THE KID (Julie London) / PISTOL SLAPPER BLUES (. . . Allen) / etc. • Trivia: VINCENT CRANE of ATOMIC ROOSTER guested on RORY's debut lp in '71. GALLAGHER also sessioned on albums by MUDDY WATERS (London Sessions) / JERRY LEE LEWIS (London Sessions) / LONNIE DONEGAN (Putting On The Style) / etc.

Album rating: Taste: TASTE (*6) / ON THE BOARDS (*7) / LIVE TASTE (*4) / LIVE AT THE ISLE OF WIGHT exploitation (*4) / Rory Gallagher: RORY GALLAGHER (*6) / DEUCE (*5) / LIVE IN EUROPE (*6) / BLUEPRINT (*7) / TATTOO (*7) / IRISH TOUR '74 (*8) / SINNER . . . AND SAINT early stuff (*5) / AGAINST THE GRAIN (*5) / THE STORY SO FAR compilation (*4) / CALLING CARD (*7) / PHOTO FINISH (*5) / TOP PRIORITY (*5) / STAGE STRUCK (*5) / JINX (*5) / DEFENDER (*4) / THE BEST OF RORY GALLAGHER & TASTE compilation (*6) / EDGED IN BLUE (*7)

TASTE

RORY GALLAGHER – vocals, guitar / **CHARLIE McCRACKEN** (b.26 Jun'48) – bass repl. ERIC KITTERINGHAM / **JOHN WILSON** (b. 3 Dec'47) – drums (ex-THEM) repl. NORMAN DAMERY

		Major Minor	not iss.
Apr 68.	(7") *(MM 560)* **BLISTER ON THE MOON. / BORN ON THE WRONG SIDE OF TIME** *(re-iss. Jul70; MM 718)*		–

		Polydor	Atco
Mar 69.	(7") *(56313)* **BORN ON THE WRONG SIDE OF TIME. / SAME OLD STORY**		–
Apr 69.	(lp) *(583 042)* **TASTE** – Blister on the moon / Leaving blues / Sugar mama / Hail / Born on the wrong side of time / Dual carriageway pain / Same old story / Catfish / I'm moving on. *(re-iss. 1977; 2384 076) (cd-iss. Aug92; 841 600-2)*		
Jan 70.	(lp) *(583 083)* **ON THE BOARDS** – What's going on / Railway and gun / It's happened before, it'll happen again / If the day was any longer / Morning sun / Eat my words / On the boards / If I don't sing I'll cry / See here / I'll remember. *(cd-iss. Apr94; 841 599-2)*	18	
Feb 71.	(lp) *(2310 082)* **LIVE TASTE (live)** – Sugar mama / Gamblin' blues / Feel so good (part 1) / Feel so good (part 2) / Catfish / Same old story.		–

—— GALLAGHER went solo. The other two formed STUD. McCRACKEN also joined SPENCER DAVIS GROUP

RORY GALLAGHER

solo – vocals, guitar with **GERRY MacAVOY** – bass (ex-DEEP JOY) / **WILGAR CAMPBELL** – drums (ex-METHOD)

		Polydor	Atlantic
May 71.	(lp) *(2383 044)* <33368> **RORY GALLAGHER** – Laundromat / Just the smile / I fall apart / Wave myself goodbye / Hands up / Sinner boy / For the last time / It's you / I'm not surprised / Can't believe it's true. *(re-iss. 1979 on 'Chrysalis' lp/c; CHR/ZCHR 1258)*	32	
Jun 71.	(7"m) *(2814 004)* **IT'S YOU. / JUST THE SMILE / SINNER BOY**		
Nov 71.	(lp) *(2383 076)* <7004> **DEUCE** – Used to be / I'm not awake yet / Don't know where I'm going / Maybe I will / Whole lot of people / In your town / Should've learn't my lesson / There's a light / Out of my mind / Crest of a wave. *(re-iss. 1979 on 'Chrysalis' lp/c; CHR/ZCHR 1254)*	39	

		Polydor	Polydor
May 72.	(lp) *(2383 112)* <5513> **LIVE! IN EUROPE (live)** – Messin' with the kid / Laundromat / I could've had religion / Pistol slapper blues /	9	

Going to my home town / In your town / Bullfrog blues. *(re-iss. 1979 on 'Chrysalis' lp/c; CHR/ZCHR 1257) (cd-iss. Mar95 on 'Castle'; CLACD 406)*

—— **ROD DE'ATH** – drums (ex-KILLING FLOOR) repl. CAMPBELL / added **LOU MARTIN** – keyboards, mandolin (ex-KILLING FLOOR)

Feb 73.	(lp) *(2383 189)* <5522> **BLUEPRINT** – Walk on hot coals / Daughter of the Everglades / Banker's blues / Hands off / Race the breeze / The seventh son of a seventh son / Unmilitary two-step / If I had a reason. *(re-iss. 1979 on 'Chrysalis' lp/c; CHR/ZCHR 1253) (cd-iss. Feb94 on 'Castle'; CLACD 316)*	12	
Aug 73.	(lp) *(2383 230)* <5539> **TATTOO** – Tattoo'd lady / Cradle rock / 20:20 vision / They don't make them like you anymore / Livin' like a trucker / Sleep on a clothes-line / Who's that coming / A million miles away / Admit it. *(re-iss. 1979 on 'Chrysalis' lp/c; CHR/ZCHR 1259) (cd-iss. Jan94 on 'Castle'; CLACD 315)*	32	
Jul 74.	(d-lp) *(2659 031)* <9501> **IRISH TOUR '74 (live)** – Cradle rock / I wonder who (who's gonna be your sweet man) / Tattoo'd lady / Too much alcohol / As the crow flies / A million miles away / Walk on hot coals / Who's that coming / Back on my (stompin' ground) / Just a little bit. *(re-iss. 1979 on 'Chrysalis' lp/c; CTY/ZCTY 1256) (re-iss. May88 on 'Demon' d-lp)(d-c/d-cd; DFIEND 120)(FIEND CASS/CD 120)*	36	

		Chrysalis	Chrysalis
Oct 75.	(lp/c) *(<CHR/ZCHR 1098>)* **AGAINST THE GRAIN** – Let me in / Cross me off your list / Ain't too good / Souped-up Ford / Bought and sold / I take what I want / Lost at sea / All around man / Out on the western plain / At the bottom. *(re-iss. May91 on 'Castle' cd/c/lp; CLA CD/MC/LP 223)*		
Nov 75.	(7") *(CDV 102)* **SOUPED-UP FORD. / I TAKE WHAT I WANT**		
Oct 76.	(lp/c) *(<CHR/ZCHR 1124>)* **CALLING CARD** – Do you read me / Country mile / Moonchild / Calling card / I'll admit you're gone / Secret agent / Jack-knife beat / Edged in blue / Barley and grape rag. *(re-iss. Apr91 on 'Essential' cd/c/lp; ESS CD/MC/LP 143) (re-iss. cd Mar94 on 'Castle'; CLACD 352)*	32	

—— **TED McKENNA** – drums (ex-SENSATIONAL ALEX HARVEY BAND) repl.DE'ATH and MARTIN (to RAMROD)

Oct 76.	(lp/c) *(<CHR/ZCHR 1170>)* **PHOTO FINISH** – Shin kicker / Brute force and ignorance / Cruise on out / Cloak and dagger / Overnight bag / Shadow play / The Mississippi sheiks / The last of the indepenents / Fuel to the fire.		
Jan 79.	(7"m) *(CHS 2281)* **SHADOW PLAY. / SOUPED UP FORD / BRUTE FORCE AND IGNORANCE** (10"+=) *(CXP 2281)* – Moonchild		–
Aug 79.	(7",7"colrd) *(CHS 2364)* **PHILBY. / HELLCAT / COUNTRY MILE**		
Sep 79.	(lp/c) *(<CHR/ZCHR 1235>)* **TOP PRIORITY** – Follow me / Philby / Wayward child / Keychain / At the depot / Bad penny / Just hit town / Off the handle / Public enemy No.1. *(re-iss. May88 on 'Demon' lp/c/cd; FIEND/+CASS/CD 123)*	56	
Aug 80.	(7",7"colrd) *(CHS 2453)* **WAYWARD CHILD (live). / KEYCHAIN**		
Sep 80.	(lp/c) *(<CHR/ZCHR 1280>)* **STAGE STRUCK (live)** – Shin kicker / Wayward child / Brute force and ignorance / Moonchild / Follow me / Bought and sold / The last of the independents / Shadow play. *(cd-iss. Mar95 on 'Castle'; CLACD 407)*	40	
Dec 80.	(7") *(CHS 2466)* **HELLCAT. / NOTHIN' BUT THE DEVIL**		

—— (May'81) **GALLAGHER** with **McAVOY** brought in **BRENDAN O'NEILL** – drums; repl. McKENNA who joined GREG LAKE BAND then MSG

		Chrysalis	Mercury
Apr 82.	(lp/c) *(CHR/ZCHR 1359)* <SRMI 4051> **JINX** – Signals / The Devil made me do it / Double vision / Easy come, easy go / Big guns / Jinxed / Bourbon / Ride on Red, ride on / Loose talk. *(re-iss. May88 on 'Demon' lp/c/cd; FIEND/+CASS/CD 126)*	68	
Jun 82.	(7") *(CHS 2612)* **BIG GUNS. / THE DEVIL MADE ME DO IT**		
1983.	(10"ep) *(CXP 2281)* **SHADOW PLAY / BRUTE FORCE AND IGNORANCE. / MOONCHILD / SOUPED UP FORD**		

		Capo-Demon	Intercord
Jul 87.	(lp)(c/cd) *(XFIEND 98)(FIEND CASS/CD 98)* **DEFENDER** – Kickback city / Loanshark blues / Continental op / I ain't no saint / Failsafe day / Road to Hell / Doing time / Smear campaign / Don't start me talkin' / Seven days. *(c+=/cd+=) (free-7")* – SEEMS TO ME. / NO PEACE FOR THE WICKED		

—— guests **MARK FELTHAM** – harmonica / **LOU MARTIN** – piano / **JOHN EARL** – saxophones / **GERAINT WATKINS** – accordion / **JOHN COOKE** – keyboards / **RAY BEAVIS** – tenor sax / **DICK HANSON** – trumpet

		Capo	Intercord
Jun 90.	(cd/c/lp) *(CAPO CD/MC/LP 14)* **FRESH EVIDENCE** – 'Kid' gloves / The king of Zydeco (to: Clifton Chenier) / Middle name / Alexis / Empire state express / Ghost blues / Heaven's gate / The loop / Walkin' wounded / Slumming angel. *(re-iss. cd Oct92 on 'Essential'; ESSCD 155)*		

—— on the 14th June 1995, RORY died after complications from a liver transplant operation

– compilations etc. –

1974.	(c) *Emerald-Gem;* (GES 1110) / *Springboard;* <SPB 4056> **IN THE BEGINNING (VOCAL AND GUITAR)** (rec.'67) <US-title 'TAKE IT EASY BABY'>		1976
Aug 72.	(lp; by TASTE) *Polydor;* (2383 120) **TASTE – LIVE AT THE ISLE OF WIGHT (live)** *(cd-iss. Apr94; 841 601-2)*	41	–
Feb 75.	(lp) *Polydor;* (2383 315) <6510> **SINNER . . . AND SAINT** (1971 material)		
Oct 82.	(7"ep/12"ep) *Polydor;* (POSP/+X 609) **BLISTER ON THE MOON / SUGAR MAMA. / CATFISH / ON THE BOARDS**		–
Feb 76.	(lp) *Polydor;* (2383 376) <6519> **THE STORY SO FAR**		–
1977.	(lp) *Polydor;* (2384 079) **LIVE**		
May 80.	(lp) *Hallmark;* (HSC 3041) **RORY GALLAGHER**		
Feb 88.	(cd) *Razor;* (MACH 10D) **THE BEST OF RORY GALLAGHER & TASTE** – Blister on the moon / Hail / Born on the wrong side of time / Dual carriageway		–

pain / Same old story / On the boards / See here / I'll remember / Sugar mama (live) / Sinner boy (live) / I feel so good (live) / Catfish / I'm movin' on / What's going on / Ralway at sun / Morning Sun / Eat my words.

May 89. (d-lp/d-c/d-cd) *That's Original; (TFO LP/MC/CD 20)* **LIVE! IN EUROPE / STAGE STRUCK** ☐ –
Jul 89. (d-lp/d-c/d-cd) *That's Original; (TFO LP/MC/CD 21)* **TATTOO / BLUEPRINT** ☐ –
May 91. (4xcd-box) *Demon; (RORY G1)* **RORY GALLAGHER** ☐ –
– (IRISH TOUR '74 / DEFENDER / TOP PRIORITY / JINX)
Jun 92. (lp/c/cd) *Demon; (FIEND/+C/CD 719)* **EDGED IN BLUE** ☐ –
Nov 92. (3xcd-box) *Essential; (ESBCD 187)* **G-MEN: BOOTLEG SERIES VOLUME ONE** ☐

GALLIANO (dig out; 4th edition)

GALLON DRUNK (dig out; Great Alt & Indie . . .)

GANG OF FOUR
(dig out; 4th edition or Great Alt & Indie . . .)

GANG STARR

Formed: Brooklyn, New York, USA . . . 1988. One part organic turntable negotiator DJ PREMIER aka CHRIS MARTIN, one part worthy wordsmith GURU (Gifted Unlimited Rhymes Universal) aka KEITH ELAM, GANG STARR shook up a potent cocktail of Afro-centric hip hop and jazz far removed from the gangsta rap cliches their name might suggest. Although ELAM had initiated the GANG STARR project some years before in his hometown of Boston, the blue juice only really started flowing after the rapper hooked up with PREMIER, having earlier heard his demo tape. Signed to local label 'Wild Pitch', the duo's debut album, 'NO MORE MR. NICE GUY' appeared in 1989, film director Spike Lee sufficiently impressed to offer GANG STARR the opportunity of recording with saxophonist BRANFORD MARSALIS. The result was 'JAZZ THING', a funky, free-flowing history lesson on the finer points of the genre used in LEE's seminal 'Mo' Better Blues'. Ensuing interest helped secure a major label deal (with 'Chrysalis' off-shoot, 'Cooltempo') and 'STEP IN THE ARENA' (1991) announced the arrival of a vibrant figurehead in the emerging rap/jazz fusion movement. One of the few acts to favour vinyl and live mixing on stage, GANG STARR's experimental sound – personified by the moog-sampling 'JUST TO GET A REP' – gripped the imagination of the hip hop community and DJ PREMIER soon became a producer in demand, going on to work with the likes of JERU THE DAMAJA and NAS. GURU, in turn, was developing into one of the most articulate and socially aware commentators on the scene, initiating the acclaimed 'JAZZMATAZZ' project after GANG STARR's third album, 'DAILY OPERATION' (1992). Having already collaborated with The BRAND NEW HEAVIES, GURU rounded up an impressive posse of respected musicians/vocalists including MARSALIS, DONALD BYRD, COURTNEY PINE, SHARA NELSON and DC LEE, an achievement in itself. Conceived with GURU's pro-positive vision of black music, 'JAZZMATAZZ VOLUME 1' (1993) proved to be much more than just another superstar jam session, more a stylish, sophisticated marriage of street and studio and a perfect companion piece to US 3's 'Blue Note' homage, 'Hand On The Torch'. Blessed with the inimitable guitar groove of RONNY JORDAN, 'NO TIME TO PLAY' was a definite highlight and one of summer 93's best singles. Back on GANG STARR duty, GURU and PREMIER came up with their most focused album to date, 'HARD TO EARN' (1994), both obviously having honed their respective disciplines in the interim. While a second instalment of 'JAZZMATAZZ VOLUME 2: THE NEW REALITY' (1995) didn't meet with the same dizzy heights as its predecessor, GURU remains something of an, erm . . . guru for the hip hop scene, a willing spokesman on the ever controversial issues affecting the genre. It was to be another four years before the return of GANG STARR proper, 1998's hugely successful 'MOMENT OF TRUTH' breaking the duo big time in the States.

Album rating: STEP IN THE ARENA (*6) / DAILY OPERATION (*6) / HARD TO EARN (*6) / MOMENT OF TRUTH (*6) / FULL CLIP: A DECADE OF GANG STARR compilation (*7) / Guru: JAZZMATAZZ VOLUME 1 (*7) / JAZZMATAZZ VOLUME 2: THE NEW REALITY (*6)

GURU (b. KEITH ELAM, 18 Jul'66, Boston, Mass.) – rapper / **DJ PREMIER** (b. CHRISTOPHER MARTIN) – turntables, etc

	S.B.K.	Wild Pitch
Nov 89. (12"ep) *<(SBK 004)>* **THE MANIFEST EP** ☐ ☐
Dec 89. (lp/cd) *<98709>* **NO MORE MR NICE GUY** – ☐
– Premier & the Guru / Jazz music / Gotch U / Manifest / Gusto / DJ Premier in deep concentration / Postivity / Manifest / Conscience be free / Cause and effect / 2 steps ahead / No more Mr. nice guy / Knowledge / Postivity. (re-iss. Jul99 on 'Wild Pitch'; WPL 2001-2/-1)

	C.B.S.	Columbia
Sep 90. (7") *(356377-7)* **JAZZ THING. /** 66 ☐
(12"+=/cd-s+=) *(356377-6/-2)* –
(above from the Spike Lee movie, 'Mo Better Blues')

	Cooltempo	Chrysalis
Jan 91. (cd)(c/lp) *(CCD 1798)(Z+/CTLP 21) <21798>* **STEP IN THE ARENA** 36 ☐
– Game plan / Take a rest / What you want this time? / Street ministry / Just to get a rep / Say your prayers / As I read my S-A / Precisely the right rhymes / The meaning of the name / Name tag (Premier & the Guru) / Step in the arena / Form of intellect / Execution of a chump (no more Mr. Nice Guy pt.2) / Who's gonna take

the weight? / Beyond comprehension / Check the technique / Lovesick / Here today, gone tomorrow.

Feb 91. (7") *(COOL 230)* **TAKE A REST (remix). /** 63 ☐
(12"+=/cd-s+=) *(12/CD COOL 230)* – Just to get a rep / Who's gonna take the weight.
May 91. (7") *(COOL 234)* **LOVESICK. /** 50 ☐
(12"+=/cd-s+=) *(12/CD COOL 234)* –
Apr 92. (7") *(COOL)* **TAKE IT PERSONAL. /** ☐ ☐
(12"+=/cd-s+=) *(12/CD COOL)* –
May 92. (cd)(c/lp) *(CCD 1910)(Z+/CTLP 27) <21910>* **DAILY OPERATION** 65 ☐
– Intro / The place where we dwell / Flip the script / Ex girl to next girl / Soliloquy of chaos / I'm the man / 92 interlude / Take it personal / 2 deep / 24-7/365 / No shame in my game / Conspiracy / The illest brother / Hardcore composer / B.Y.S. / Much too much (mack a mil) / Take two and pass / Stay tuned (interlude).
Jun 92. (7") *(COOL 256)* **2 DEEP. / TAKE IT PERSONAL** 67 ☐
(12"+=/cd-s+=) –

	Cooltempo	Chrysalis
Feb 94. (cd-s) *<58111>* **MASS APPEAL / (versions)** – 67
Feb 94. (cd/c/lp) *(CT CD/TC/LP 38) <28435>* **HARD TO EARN** 29 25
– Intro – The first steps / ALONGWAYTOGO / Code of the streets / Brainstorm / Tonz 'O' gunz / The planet / Aiiight chill / Speak ya clout / DWYCK / Words from the nutcracker / Mass appeal / Blowin' up the spot / Suckas need bodyguards / Now you're mine / Mostly the voice / F.A.L.A. / Comin' for the datazz.
Oct 94. (12") *(Y 58265)* **SUCKAS NEED BODYGUARDS. /** ☐ ☐

—— during the mid 90's, GURU and PREMIER concentrated more on their own label 'Illkid' and production work noteably for a part-time GANG STARR collaborator, JERU THE DAMAJA on his US Top 40 set, 'The Sun Rises In The East'.

Nov 97. (ltd-12") *(12COOL 330)* **YOU KNOW MY STEEZ. /** 76
Mar 98. (cd/c/lp) *(845585-2/-4/-1)* **MOMENT OF TRUTH** 43 6
– BI and friendship / Rep growz bigga / Above the clubs / You know what she wantz / In memory of / JFK 2 / LAX / She knows what she wants / Militia / Robbin hood theory / Royalty / Itz a set up / My advice 2 you / Mall / What I'm here for / Betrayal / Next time / Pause mixin'.
Jul 98. (12"/cd-s) *(12/CD COOL 337)* **YOU KNOW MY STEEZ. /** ☐ –

– compilations, etc. –

Mar 99. (12") *Wild Pitch; (DRI 2004)* **DWYCK. /** ☐ ☐
Jul 99. (d-cd/q-lp) *Cooltempo; (521189-2/-1) / Noo Trybe; <47279>* **FULL CLIP: A DECADE OF GANG STARR** 47 33
– Intro / Full clip / Discipline / Words (manifest mix) / Ex girl to the next girl / I'm the man / Full clip / Mass appeal / Jazz think / Militia / Freddie Foxxx / Tonz o' gunz / Royalty / Who's gonna take the weight / You know my steez / Above the clouds / Just to get a rep / DWYCK / All 4 the ca$h / Step in the arena / Work / Sililoquy of chaos / Take it personal / Speak ya clout / Lil dap / Gotta get over (taking loot) / 1/2 and 1/2 / The question remains / Code of the streets / So wassup / Now you're mine / Betrayal / BYS / Credit is due / Militia II / You know my steez (mix).

GURU

with **DONALD BYRD, ROY AYERS, LONNIE LISON SMITH, CARLEEN ANDERSON, N'DEA DAVENPORT, RONNY JORDAN, DC LEE, COURTNEY PINE + MC SOLAAR**

	Cooltempo	Chrysalis
May 93. (cd/c/lp) *(CT CD/TC/LP 34) <21998>* **JAZZMATAZZ VOLUME 1** ☐ 94
– Introduction / Loungin' / When you're near / Transit ride / No time to play / Down the backstreets / Respectful dedications / Take a look (at yourself) / Trust me / Slicker than most / Le bien, le mal / Sights in the city.

—— now with **CHAKA KHAN, ME'SHELL NDEGEOCELLO, PATRA, DONALD BYRD, MICA PARIS, SHARA NELSON, RAMSEY LEWIS, JAMIROQUAI, RONNY JORDAN, FREDDIE HUBBARD, COURTNEY PINE, DC LEE, IN KAMOZE** etc.

Jul 95. (cd/c/lp) *(CT CD/TC/LP 47) <34290>* **JAZZMATAZZ VOLUME II: THE NEW REALITY** ☐ 71
– Intro / Lifesaver / Living in this world / Looking through darkness / Watch what you say / Defining purpose / For you / Medicine / Lost souls / Nobody knows / Hip hop as a way of life / Respect the architect / Feel the music / Young ladies / The traveller / Count your blessings / Maintaining focus / Choice of weapons / Something in the past / Revelation.
Jul 96. (d-cd) *(CTCD 54)* **JAZZMATAZZ VOLUMES ONE & TWO** ☐ ☐
(collection above 2)

GARBAGE

Formed: Madison, Wisconsin, USA . . . 1994 by BUTCH VIG, DUKE ERIKSON and STEVE MARKER, out of the ashes of FIRE TOWN and SPOONER. BUTCH's ham-pop/rock act had been on the go since early 1978 and released their debut EP 'CRUEL SCHOOL', a year later *<Boat; SP 4001>*. Another soon followed, 'WHERE YOU GONNA RUN?' *<Boat; SP 3001>*, before an album, 'EVERY CORNER DANCE' surfaced in '82; *<Mountain Railroad; HR 8005>*. BUTCH then set up his own studio and produced KILLDOZER, before giving SPOONER another outing with the album 'WILDEST DREAMS' *<Boat; SP 1004>*. In 1986, their final flop 45, 'MEAN OLD WORLD' *<Boat; SP 1018>*, made BUTCH form FIRE TOWN with old buddy STEVE MARKER and co-songwriter DOUG ERIKSON. A few singles, 'CARRY THE TORCH' *<7-89242>* and 'RAIN ON YOU' *<7-89204>*, appeared from the 'Atlantic' stable alongside albums 'IN THE HEART OF THE HEART COUNTRY' *<Boat; 1013 / re-iss. Atlantic; 81754>* & 'THE GOOD LIFE' cd/lp; *<781945-2/-1>*. In 1989/90, BUTCH re-formed with the original line-up of SPOONER, DUKE ERIKSON, DAVE BENTON, JEFF WALKER and JOEL TAPPERO, to release one-off comeback cd 'THE FUGITIVE DANCE' *<Dali-Chameleon; 89026>*. He was then to find fame in production work for greats like NIRVANA, SONIC YOUTH, SMASHING PUMPKINS, NINE INCH NAILS and U2, before coming across Edinburgh-born vixen SHIRLEY MANSON fronting the band ANGELFISH on MTV. The new-look GARBAGE contributed the electro-goth of 'VOW' to a 'Volume' various artists compilation and this ended up as their limited edition debut 45 in 1995. By that year's summer, they had signed to Geffen's 'Almo Sounds' (UK 'Mushroom') records, which helped them break into the UK Top 50 with 'SUBHUMAN'. Success finally came with the 'ONLY HAPPY WHEN IT RAINS' single, a grungey, more tuneful affair that retained the goth overtones, MANSON weaving her deep-throat vocals around the melody like a spider's web. She was an obvious focal point for the group; on their Top Of The Pops debut the singer made like a brooding, 90's incarnation of CHRISSIE HYNDE while the rest of the band remained comfortably anonymous in uniform black. The eponymous debut album, released later that year, was a mixed bag of styles that worked fairly effectively. Subsequent single, 'QUEER', kind of summed up the GARBAGE ethos, a deceptively poppy number featuring a MANSON vocal positively dripping with loathing, self or otherwise. GARBAGE continued their rise to the top of the pile with a UK chart-topping second set, 'VERSION 2.0', masterfully treading the finest of lines between alternative credibility and outright mainstream success; the hits kept on coming with 'PUSH IT', 'I THINK I'M PARANOID' and 'SPECIAL' all making the UK Top 20. • Covered: KISS MY ASS (Vic Chesnutt) / sampled the CLASH's 'Train In Vain' on 'STUPID GIRL'.

Album rating: GARBAGE (*8) / VERSION 2.0 (*7)

SHIRLEY MANSON (b. Edinburgh, Scotland) – vocals, guitar (ex-GOODBYE MR MACKENZIE) / **STEVE MARKER** – guitar, samples, loops / **DUKE ERIKSON** (b. DOUG) – guitar, keyboards, bass / **BUTCH VIG** (b. BRYAN VIG, Viroqua, Wisconsin) – drums, loops, efx

				Discordant AlmoSounds	
Mar 95.	(7") (CORD 001) <89000> **VOW. / VOW (Torn Apart version)**				97 Jul95
				Mushroom AlmoSounds	
Aug 95.	(s7"/7") (SX/S 1138) <89001> **SUBHUMAN. / £1 CRUSH** (cd-s+=) (D 1138) – Vow.			50	
Sep 95.	(7"/c-s/cd-s) (SX/C/D 1199) <89002> **ONLY HAPPY WHEN IT RAINS. / GIRL DON'T COME / SLEEP**			29	55 Feb96
Oct 95.	(cd/c/2x45rpm-lp/6x7"box) (D/C/L/LX 31450) <80004> **GARBAGE**			6	20 Aug95

– Supervixen / Queer / Only happy when it rains / As Heaven is wide / Not my idea / A stroke of luck / Vow / Stupid girl / Dog new tricks / My lover's box / Fix me now / Milk. (d-lp re-iss. Sep99 on 'Simply Vinyl' +=; SVLP 123) – Dumb (live) / Stupid girl (live) / Temptation waits (live) / Vow (live).

―――― on above **MIKE KASHAN** – bass / **PAULI RYAN** – percussion

Nov 95.	(7") (SX 1237) <89003> **QUEER. / QUEER (Adrian Sherwood remix)**			13	Mar96

(silver-cd-s) (<89004>) – ('A'side) / Trip my wire / ('A'-The very queer dub-bin mix) / ('A'-The most beautiful girl in town mix).
(gold-cd-s) (DX 1237) – ('A'side) / Butterfly collector / ('A'-Rabbit in the Moon remix) / ('A'-Danny Saber remix).

Mar 96.	(7") (SX 1271) **STUPID GIRL. / DOG NEW TRICKS (pal mix)**			4	-

(red-cd-s+=) (D 1271) – Driving lesson / ('A'-Red Snapper mix).
(blue-cd-s) (DX 1271) – ('A'side) / Alien sex fiend / ('A'-Dreadzone dub) / ('A'-Dreadzone vox).

Jul 96.	(c-s) <89004> **STUPID GIRL / DRIVING LESSON**			-	24
Nov 96.	(7") (SX 1494) <89007> **MILK (The wicked mix). / MILK (the Tricky remix)**			10	

(cd-s) (D 1494) – Milk (the wicked mix featuring TRICKY) / ('A'-Goldie's completely trashed remix) / ('A'-original version) / Stupid girl (Tees radio mix by TODD TERRY).
(cd-s) (DX 1494) – Milk (the wicked mix featuring TRICKY) / ('A'-Massive Attack classic remix) / ('A'-Rabbit in the moon udder remix) / Stupid girl (the Danny Saber remix).

May 98.	(c-s) (MUSH 28MCS) <89014> **PUSH IT / LICK THE PAVEMENT**			9	52

(cd-s+=) (MUSH 28CDS) – ('A'-Boom Boom Satellites remix).
(3"cd-s) (MUSH 28CDSX) – ('A'side) / Thirteen.

May 98.	(cd/c/lp) (74321 55410-2/-4/-1) <80018> **VERSION 2.0**			1	13

– Temptation waits / I think I'm paranoid / When I grow up / Medication / Special / Hammering in my head / Push it / The trick is to keep breathing / Dumb / Sleep together / Wicked ways / You look so fine. (d-cd-iss. Jun99; MUSH 29CDX)

Jul 98.	(c-s) (MUSH 35MCS) <40035> **I THINK I'M PARANOID / DEADWOOD**			9	

(cd-s+=) (MUSH 35CDS) – Afterglow.
(cd-s) (MUSH 35CDX) – ('A'side) / ('A'extended) / ('A'-Purity mix).
(3"cd-ep+=) (MUSH 35CDXXX) – (all of the above).

Oct 98.	(c-s) (MUSH 39MCS) <827> **SPECIAL / THIRTEEN X FOREVER**			15	52 Nov98

(cd-s+=) (MUSH 39CDS) – ('A'-Brothers In Rhythm mix).
(cd-s) (MUSH 39CDSX) – ('A'side) / Medication (acoustic) / Push it (Victor Calderone remix).
(3"cd-s) (MUSH 39CDSXXX) – (all 5 above).

Jan 99.	(c-s) (MUSH 43MCS) **WHEN I GROW UP / CAN'T SEEM TO MAKE YOU MINE**			9	

(cd-s+=) (MUSH 43CDS) – ('A'-Danny Tenaglia club mix).
(cd-s+=) (MUSH 43CDSXXX) – Tornado / ('A'-Danny Tenaglia club).
(cd-s) (MUSH 43CDSX) – ('A'side) / Tornado / Special (Rickidy raw mix).

May 99.	(c-s) (MUSH 49MCS) **YOU LOOK SO FINE / SOLDIER THROUGH THIS**			19	

(cd-s+=) (MUSH 49CDS) – ('A'-Fine Young Cannibals remix).
(cd-s) (MUSH 49CDSX) – ('A'side) / Get busy with the fizzy / ('A'-Eric Kupper mix).
(3"cd-s) (MUSH 49CDSXXX) – ('A'side) / ('A'-Fine Young Cannibals mix) / ('A'-Eric Kupper mix) / ('A'-Plaid mix).

Nov 99.	(c-s/cd-s) (RAX C/TD 40) **THE WORLD IS NEVER ENOUGH (mixes; original / UNKLE / Ice Bandits)**			11	

(above from the Bond movie of the same name – issed on 'Radioactive')

―――――――――――――――――――――――――――――――――

Jerry GARCIA (see under ⇒ GRATEFUL DEAD)

Art GARFUNKEL (see under ⇒ SIMON & GARFUNKEL)

GASTR DEL SOL (see under ⇒ SQUIRREL BAIT)

David GATES (see under ⇒ BREAD)

GAY DAD

Formed: Sunninghill, Berkshire, England . . . 1995 by CLIFF JONES and BAZ CROWE, who had been playing in a group together since their pre-pubescent days. Experimenting with progressive and psychedelic rock in the beginning, the two protagonists parted ways as adulthood beckoned. JONES became a regular contributor to ~~'The Face' and 'Mojo~' while CROWE set up his own publication cult 'Creator'. It wasn't until 1995 that the duo put the plan into action and debuted on a London stage (with a line-up that comprised JONES, CROWE and former medical drop-out NIGEL HOYLE on vocals); however, the gig was so shambolic that HOYLE leapt off stage in embarrassment and ran out of the hall . . . the manager proceeded to put the disco back on for the bewildered crowd. Despite this laughable inauguration, JONES marked the occasion, claiming it to be a turning point for the group, and took to some intensive re-shaping, recruiting JAMES RISEBORO on keyboards. In late '97, the new GAY DAD entered a London studio to record three new tracks: 'DESIRE', 'OH JIM' and 'TO EARTH WITH LOVE'; all were later included on the debut album. When the three-track demo was unleashed into A&R hands, many believed it to be the work of an obscure 70's pop/rock outfit. The press, however, were slightly sceptical about the demo and had convinced themselves that a troupe of session musicians were generating a premeditated joke at their expense! This theory was dampened when GAY DAD signed to 'London' records in September 1998 and released the Glam pop rock-out single 'TO EARTH WITH LOVE~' early the following year. Radio stations couldn't get enough of this new arrival and would give any excuse to play the record. Its spacey keyboards and "fab" guitars weren't of the esoteric kind; on the other hand, its poignant piano break remained as the only true delightful aspect of the song. But as the public were catching a glimpse of the trademark 'Walking Man' posters that had been littered all over the major cities, the more the GAY DAD hype was overflowing. Frontman, JONES, who looked and sounded like a soap opera bad guy, received attention from closet indie kids who hailed him as their new guitar hero pin-up. A spot in the Top 10, hyperbolised reviews and a controversial name all prompted the looming success of the group. But, the cheesy first album proper, 'LEISURE NOISE', only reached a disappointing Top 20. Even worse, singles 'JOY!' and 'OH JIM' virtually bombed, forcing the band to blame their failure on lack of airplay. The pretentious JONES reckoned that this hadn't phased the band. In September 1999, the group returned to the studio to work on the follow-up and set their sights upon a publicity stunt that included a giant Wicker Man, a load of bad reviews and the "Cleansing of GAY DAD".

Album rating: LEISURE NOISE (*5)

CLIFF JONES – vocals / **JAMES RISEBORO** – keyboards, guitar / **BAZ CROWE** (b. NICHOLAS) – drums / +2

				London	London
Jan 99.	(10"/c-s) (LON T/CS 413) **TO EARTH WITH LOVE. / US ROACH**			10	-

(cd-s+=) (LONCD 413) – 51 Pegasus.
(cd-s) (LOCDP 413) – ('A'extended) / How it might end / Soft return.

May 99.	(10") (LONT 428) **JOY! / DESIRE**			22	-

(cd-s+=) (LONCD 428) – Sly.
(cd-s) (LOCDP 428) – ('A'extended) / Electrogeist / Twelve.
(c-s) (LONCS 428) – ('A'side) / Electrogeist / Sly.

Jun 99.	(cd/c/lp) (<556103-2/-4/-1>) **LEISURE NOISE**			14	

– Dimstar / Joy! / Oh jim / My son Mystic / Black ghost / To Earth with love / Dateline / Pathfinder / Different kind of blue / Jesus Christ.

Aug 99.	(c-s) (LONCS 437) **OH JIM / BINGO NATION**			47	-

(cd-s+=) (LONCD 437) – Uva.
(cd-s) (LOCDP 437) – ('A'side) / To Earth with love (demo) / Lieb ist fur immer.

―――― now without STONE who might've been repl. by ANDY BELL (ex-HURRICANE #1) had he not been poached by OASIS

Marvin GAYE

Born: MARVIN PENTZ GAY JR., 2 Apr'39, Washington, D.C., USA, son of an apostolic minister. In 1957, after being discharged from the army, MARVIN joined doo-wop outfit The MARQUEES, releasing two singles ('HEY LITTLE SCHOOL GIRL', produced by Bo Diddley, + 'BABY YOU'RE THE ONLY ONE') for the 'Okeh' label. The following year, HARVEY FUQUA invited them to become his new MOONGLOWS, and after moving to 'Chess' land, Chicago, they recorded the 'ALMOST GROWN' and 'MAMA LOOCIE' singles. In 1960, FUQUA, who accompanied GAY to the motor city of Detroit with the intention of becoming a solo artist, helped arrange for GAY to play session drums on 45's by The MIRACLES. In 1961, after more session work for 'Motown' artists such as The MARVELETTES, he signed as a solo artist to 'Tamla Motown' as well as marrying boss BERRY GORDY's younger sister, ANNA. Suffixing his surname with an E, MARVIN initially had his heart set on becoming a jazz balladeer, although an album, 'THE SOULFUL MOODS OF MARVIN GAYE' (1961), flopped and he was eventually cajoled into recording R&B/soul. The result was the rawer, 'STUBBORN KIND OF FELLOW' single, an immediate success which provided MARVIN with his first R&B Top 10 hit in 1962. 'HITCH HIKE', 'PRIDE AND JOY' and 'CAN I GET A WITNESS' followed in quick succession, all charting in the US Top 50 and establishing GAYE as one of Motown's foremost talents. Like most artists on the label, GAYE was assigned material by various writers (mainly the in-house team of HOLLAND-DOZIER-HOLLAND) although even in those early days, many of his songs were self-penned, including the classic 'WHEREVER I LAY MY HAT (THAT'S MY HOME)' (later made famous again by PAUL YOUNG). In 1964, although still mainly a credible solo artist, Berry Gordy teamed him up with MARY WELLS, and later KIM WESTON with whom he recorded the Top 20 soul-pop brilliance of 'IT TAKES TWO' as well as recording a whole album of duets under a similar title. The mid-60's also saw him developing the super-smooth vocal prowess that would become his trademark on such hits as 'HOW SWEET IT IS (TO BE LOVED BY YOU)' and 'ONE MORE HEARTACHE'. The WESTON alliance was dissolved in mid-67 when GAYE found Philadelphia-born singer, TAMMI TERRELL, their charmed partnership yielding a three-year run of hits on both sides of the Atlantic and producing some of the most sublime duets in the history of soul ('AIN'T NO MOUNTAIN HIGH ENOUGH', 'YOU'RE ALL I NEED TO GET BY', 'AIN'T NOTHING LIKE THE REAL THING' etc.). Tragically, to the obvious dismay of MARVIN, TAMMI died of a brain tumour in March 1970, aged only 24. The previous year, MARVIN had scored his biggest hit to date when 'I HEARD IT THROUGH THE GRAPEVINE' hit No.1 in America and Britain, a brooding, experimental epic that became Motown's biggest selling record in the label's history. But TERRELL's death hit MARVIN hard and his subsequent work was to take on a considerably more introspective bent. Although MARVIN didn't write it, the melancholy 'ABRAHAM, MARTIN AND JOHN' single (released in Spring '70) was an indicator of the direction GAYE was headed. Taking his cue from STEVIE WONDER, MARVIN decided to take complete control of his career, from the writing to the recording, making his first major artistic statement with 'WHAT'S GOING ON' (1971). A radical departure, the album (along with WONDER's early 70's material) changed the way soul music was made and challenged people's perceptions of the genre. Like a black 'Astral Weeks' (in feeling if not lyrically), the album was a lush, orchestral stream of consciousness collage, GAYE gazing into the ether and pleading for some kind of redemption for mankind. Addressing such pertinent issues as war, environmental disaster and God, 'Motown' were extremely reluctant to release the album, only relenting when GAYE threatened to leave the label. The singer was vindicated when the record became his biggest seller to date, as well as being recognised as one of the greatest albums in recording history. GAYE solved the problem of following up such a milestone by recording the soundtrack to blaxploitation flick, 'TROUBLE MAN'. Largely instrumental, the album was an enjoyable collection of jazz-funk grooves, a stop-gap rather than a step forward. A bona fide successor came with 1973's steamy 'LET'S GET IT ON', the title track providing GAYE with the second No.1 of his career. The album itself reached No.2, becoming the most commercially successful release of his career. Like all truly transcendent artists, GAYE embraced both the profane and the sacred, his best work both overtly sexual and deeply spiritual; for GAYE, spiritual healing was sexual healing. Yet, ironically, GAYE's marriage to ANNA GORDY foundered in 1975, with MARVIN detailing the break-up in his under-rated double album, 'HERE MY DEAR' (1979), its title a sarcastic reference to the fact that GORDY was to receive all royalties from the disc as part of the divorce settlement. Despite having scored a third No.1 single two years previously with the disco epic, 'GOT TO GIVE IT UP', GAYE's personal life was a mess. As well as a second failed marriage, GAYE was constantly hounded by the taxman and fell into heavy cocaine use. Escaping to Europe, GAYE worked on another concept album, 'IN OUR LIFETIME'. Following its release in 1981, GAYE accused 'Motown' of tampering with both the sound of the album and the artwork prior to release. This marked the bitter end to his long-standing relationship with the label, and he subsequently signed with 'Columbia'. 'MIDNIGHT LOVE' (1982) was a resounding return to form, the seminal 'SEXUAL HEALING' going Top 5 in Britain and America. Lyrically, the album explored familiar GAYE themes on the nature of God and love, but while the singer was still actively following some kind of spiritual path, he was also sinking deeper into drug dependence and depression. Retreating to his parent's home in L.A., MARVIN's depression and mood swings brought him into continual conflict with his father and after one particularly violent argument on the 1st of April 1984, MARVIN GAYE SNR. shot his son dead. It was a tragic end to the life of one of the most pivotal figures soul music has produced. • **Covered:** . . . GRAPEVINE (Whitfield-Strong) / ABRAHAM, MARTIN AND JOHN (c.Dick Holler). MARVIN's songs have been recorded by many international stars including ROBERT PALMER (Mercy Mercy Me) / CYNDI LAUPER (What's Going On).

Album rating: THE SOULFUL MOODS OF MARVIN GAYE (*5) / THAT STUBBORN KINDA FELLA (*6) / RECORDED LIVE ON STAGE (*4) / WHEN I'M ALONE I CRY (*4) / TOGETHER with Mary Wells (*6) / MARVIN GAYE GREATEST HITS compilation (*7) / HOW SWEET IT IS TO BE LOVED BY YOU (*5) / HELLO BROADWAY THIS IS MARVIN (*5) / A TRIBUTE TO THE GREAT NAT KING COLE (*4) / MOODS OF MARVIN GAYE (*5) / TAKE TWO with Kim Weston (*5) / MARVIN GAYE GREATEST HITS, VOL.2 compilation (*6) / UNITED with Tammi Terrell (*6) / YOU'RE ALL I NEED (*6) / IN THE GROOVE (*6) / M.P.G. (*6) / MARVIN GAYE AND HIS GIRLS collection (*6) / EASY with Tammi Terrell (*6) / THAT'S THE WAY LOVE IS (*5) / MARVIN GAYE & TAMMI TERRELL GREATEST HITS compilation (*6) / MARVIN GAYE SUPER HITS exploitation (*6) / WHAT'S GOING ON (*10) / TROUBLE MAN soundtrack (*5) / LET'S GET IT ON (*9) / ANTHOLOGY compilation (*8) / MARVIN GAYE LIVE! (*4) / I WANT YOU (*6) / MARVIN GAYE'S GREATEST HITS compilation (*7) / MARVIN GAYE LIVE AT THE LONDON PALLADIUM (*5) / HERE, MY DEAR (*7) / IN OUR LIFETIME (*6) / MIDNIGHT LOVE (*7) / DREAM OF A LIFETIME posthumous (*5)

MARVIN GAYE – vocals, drums, etc. (ex-MOONGLOWS, etc.) with Motown session people

		not iss.	Tamla Motown
May 61.	(lp) <221> **THE SOULFUL MOODS OF MARVIN GAYE**	-	
	– The masquerade is over / Love for sale / My funny valentine / Let your conscience be your guide / etc.		
May 61.	(7") <54041> **LET YOUR CONSCIENCE BE YOUR GUIDE. / NEVER LET YOU GO (SHA LA BOP)**	-	
1962.	(7") <54055> **I'M YOURS, YOU'RE MINE. / SANDMAN**	-	
1962.	(7") <54063> **TAKING MY TIME. / SOLDIER'S PLEA**	-	
Nov 62.	(7") <239> **THAT STUBBORN KINDA FELLA**	-	
	– That stubborn kinda fella / Pride and joy / Hitch hike / Get my hands on some lovin' / Soldier's plea / I'm yours, you're mine / Wherever I lay my hat (that's my home) / Taking my time / It hurt me too / Hello there angel		

		Oriole	Tamla
Dec 62.	(7") <54075> **HITCH HIKE. / HELLO THERE ANGEL**	-	30
Feb 63.	(7") (CBA 1803) <54068> **STUBBORN KIND OF FELLOW. / IT HURT ME TOO**		46 Jul62
Jul 63.	(7") (CBA 1846) <54079> **PRIDE AND JOY. / ONE OF THESE DAYS**		10 Apr63
Jul 63.	(lp) <242> **RECORDED LIVE ON STAGE (live)**	-	
	– That stubborn kinda fella / Hitch hike / One of these days / Days of wine and roses / You are my sunshine / etc.		

		Stateside	Tamla
Nov 63.	(7") (SS 243) <54087> **CAN I GET A WITNESS. / I'M CRAZY 'BOUT MY BABY**		22 / 77 Oct63
1964.	(lp) <251> **WHEN I'M ALONE I CRY**	-	
	– You've changed / I was telling her about you / I wonder / I'll be around / Because of you / I don't know why / I've grown accustomed to her face / When your lover has gone / When I'm alone I cry / If my heart could sing.		
Apr 64.	(7") (SS 284) <54093> **YOU'RE A WONDERFUL ONE. / WHEN I'M ALONE I CRY**		15 Feb64

—— Apr64, saw MARVIN duet with MARY WELLS on hit single ONCE UPON A TIME and album TOGETHER. (see further below and for collaborations/duets with **KIM WESTON** and **TAMMI TERRELL**.

		Stateside	Tamla
Aug 64.	(7") (SS 326) <54095> **TRY IT BABY. / IF MY HEART COULD SING**		15 May64
Sep 64.	(7") <54101> **BABY DON'T YOU DO IT. / WALK ON THE WILD SIDE**	-	27
Nov 64.	(lp) (SL 10100) **MARVIN GAYE** (compilation from '63 & '64 lp's)		-
	– You're a wonderful one / Get my hands on some lovin' / Taking my time / Soldier's plea / Hello there, angel / I'm crazy 'bout my baby / Try it, baby / I'm yours, you're mine / Sandman / Hitch hike / Wherever I lay my hat / Can I get a witness.		
Nov 64.	(7") (SS 360) <54107> **HOW SWEET IT IS TO BE LOVED BY YOU. / FOREVER**	49	6

		Tamla Motown	Tamla
Apr 65.	(lp) (STML 11004) <258> **HOW SWEET IT IS TO BE LOVED BY YOU**		Feb65
	– How sweet it is to be loved by you / Try it baby / Baby don't you do it / You're a wonderful one / Now that you've won me / Me and my lonely room / Stepping closer to your heart / No good without you / One of these days / Need your lovin' (want you back) / Forever. <US-tracks slightly different> (cd-iss. Mar91; WD 72732)		
Apr 65.	(7") (TMG 510) <54112> **I'LL BE DOGGONE. / YOU'VE BEEN A LONG TIME COMING**		8 Feb65
Aug 65.	(7") (TMG 524) <54117> **PRETTY LITTLE BABY. / NOW THAT YOU'VE WON ME**		25 Jun65
Sep 65.	(lp) (STML 11015) <259> **HELLO BROADWAY THIS IS MARVIN**		
	– Walk on the wild side / What kind of fool am I / Party's over / Days of wine and roses / People / My way / On the street where you live / Hello Dolly / Hello Broadway / My kind of town / This is the life.		
Nov 65.	(7") (TMG 539) <54122> **AIN'T THAT PECULIAR. / SHE'S GOT TO BE REAL**		8 Sep65
Feb 66.	(lp) (STML 11022) <261> **A TRIBUTE TO GREAT NAT KING COLE**		
	– Nature boy / Ramblin' Rose / Too young / Pretend / Straighten up and fly right / Mona Lisa / Unforgettable / To the ends of the Earth / Sweet Lorraine / It's only a paper Moon / Send for me / Calypso blues. (re-iss. Jul82 lp/c; WL/WK 72210) (cd-iss. Jul92; 530054-2)		
Mar 66.	(7") (TMG 552) <54129> **ONE MORE HEARTACHE. / WHEN I HAD YOUR LOVE**		29 Feb66
Jun 66.	(7") (TMG 563) <54132> **TAKE THIS HEART OF MINE. / NEED YOUR LOVIN' (WANT YOU BACK)**		44 May66
Sep 66.	(7") (TMG 574) <54138> **LITTLE DARLING (I NEED YOU). / HEY DIDDLE DIDDLE**	50	47 Aug66
Aug 67.	(7") (TMG 618) <54153> **YOUR UNCHANGING LOVE. / I'LL TAKE CARE OF YOU**		33 Jul67
Jan 68.	(7") (TMG 640) <54160> **YOU. / CHANGE WHAT YOU CAN**		34
Nov 68.	(7") (TMG 676) <54170> **CHAINED. / AT LAST (I FOUND A LOVE)**		32
Nov 68.	(7") <54176> **I HEARD IT THROUGH THE GRAPEVINE. / YOU'RE WHAT'S HAPPENING (IN THE WORLD TODAY)**	-	1

Jan 69. (lp) *(STML 11091)* <285> **IN THE GROOVE** ☐ | 63 Oct68
– You / Tear it on down / Chained / I heard it through the grapevine / At last (I found a love) / Some kind of wonderful / Loving you is sweeter than ever / Change what you can / It's love I need / Every now and then / You're what's happening (in the world today) / There goes my baby. *(re-iss. Apr85 as 'I HEARD IT THROUGH THE GRAPEVINE' lp/c; WL/WK 72374) (cd-iss. Jun89; WD 72374)*

Feb 69. (7") *(TMG 686)* **I HEARD IT THROUGH THE GRAPEVINE. / NEED SOMEBODY** | 1 | –

Jul 69. (7") *(TMG 705)* <54181> **TOO BUSY THINKING ABOUT MY BABY. / WHEREVER I LAY MY HAT** | 5 | 4 Apr69
(re-iss. Oct81 on 'Motown'; same)

Nov 69. (lp) *(STML 11119)* <292> **M.P.G.** ☐ | 33 Jun69
– Too busy thinking about my baby / This magic moment / I got to get to California / That's the way love is / The end of our road / Seek and you shall find / It's a bitter pill to swallow / Only a lonely man would know / Try my true love / Memories / More than a heart can stand / It don't take too much to keep me. *(re-iss. Jul82 lp/c; STMS/CSTMS 5064) (cd-iss. Aug93; 530210-2)*

Nov 69. (7") *(TMG 718)* <54185> **THAT'S THE WAY LOVE IS. / GONNA KEEP TRYIN' TILL I WIN YOUR LOVE** ☐ | 7 Aug 69

Jan 70. (7") <54190> **HOW CAN I FORGET. / GONNA GIVE HER ALL THE LOVE I'VE GOT** | – | 41 / 67

Apr 70. (lp) *(STML 11136)* <299> **THAT'S THE WAY LOVE IS** ☐ | Oct69
– Gonna give her all the love i've got / Yesterday / Groovin' / I wish it would rain / That's the way love is / How can I forget / Abraham, Martin and John / Gonna keep on tryin' till I win your love / No time for tears / Cloud nine / Don't you miss me a little bit baby / So long. *(cd-iss. Apr91; WD 72736) (cd re-iss. Aug93; 530214-2)*

Apr 70. (7") *(TMG 734)* **ABRAHAM, MARTIN AND JOHN. / HOW CAN I FORGET** | 9 | –

Jun 70. (7") <54195> **THE END OF OUR ROAD. / ME AND MY LONELY ROOM** | – | 40

Jun 71. (7") *(TMG 775)* <54201> **WHAT'S GOING ON. / GOD IS LOVE** ☐ | 2 Feb71
(re-iss. Mar83 on 'Motown')

Oct 71. (lp) *(STML 11190)* <310> **WHAT'S GOING ON** ☐ | 6 Jun71
– What's going on / What's happening brother / Flyin' high (in the friendly sky) / Save the children / God is love / Mercy mercy me (the ecology) / Right on / Wholy holy / Inner city blues (make me wanna holler). *(re-iss. Apr88 lp/c/cd; WL/WK/WD 72611) (re-iss. Jul94; 530022-2/-4)*

Nov 71. (7") *(TMG 796)* **SAVE THE CHILDREN. / LITTLE DARLING** | 41 | ☐
Feb 72. (7") *(TMG 802)* **MERCY MERCY ME. / SAD TOMORROWS** ☐ | 4 Jul71
May 72. (7") *(TMG 817)* <54209> **INNER CITY BLUES (MAKE ME WANNA HOLLER). / WHOLY HOLY** ☐ | 9 Oct71

May 72. (7") <54221> **YOU'RE THE MAN. / (part 2)** | – | 50
Feb 73. (lp) *(STML 11225)* <322> **TROUBLE MAN** ☐ | 14 Dec72
– Main theme from "Trouble Man" / "T" plays it cool / Poor Abbey Walsh / The break-in (police shoot big) / Cleo's apartment / Trouble man / Theme from "Trouble Man" / "T" stands for trouble / Life is a gamble / Deep in it / Don't mess with Mister "T" / There goes Mister "T". *(re-iss. Jul82 lp/c; STMS/CSTMS 5065) (re-iss. 1986 lp/c; WL/WK 72215) (cd-iss. Sep91; WD 72215) (cd re-iss. Apr93; 530097-2)*

Mar 73. (7") *(TMG 846)* <54228> **TROUBLE MAN. / DON'T MESS WITH MISTER "T"** ☐ | 7 Dec72
Aug 73. (7") *(TMG 868)* <54234> **LET'S GET IT ON. / I WISH IT WOULD RAIN** | 31 | 1 Jul73
Nov 73. (lp) *(STMA 8013)* <329> **LET'S GET IT ON** | 39 | 2 Sep73
– Let's get it on / Please don't stay (once you go away) / If I should die tonight / Keep gettin' it on / Come get to this / Distant lover / You sure love to ball / Just to keep you satisfied. *(re-iss. Mar82 lp/c; STMS/XSTMS 5034) (re-iss. Apr84 on 'Motown' lp/c; WL/WK 72085) (cd-iss. Apr88; WD 72085) (cd-iss. Jul92; 530055-2)*

——— Around this time MARVIN teams up with DIANA ROSS, on album DIANA AND MARVIN. Many hits were lifted from it including YOU ARE EVERYTHING.

Jan 74. (7") *(TMG 882)* <54241> **COME GET TO THIS. / DISTANT LOVER** ☐ | 21 Nov73
Jan 74. (7") <54244> **YOU SURE LOVE TO BALL. / JUST TO KEEP YOU SATISFIED** | – | 50
Sep 74. (lp) *(STMA 8018)* <333> **MARVIN GAYE LIVE! (live)** ☐ | 8 Jul74
– (the beginning: introduction & overture) / Trouble man – Inner city blues – Distant lover / Jan / Fossil medley: I'll be doggone – Try it baby – Can I get a witness – Subborn kind of fellow – How sweet it is to be loved by you / Now: Let's get it on – What's going on. *(re-iss. Mar82; same) (cd-iss. Feb88) (cd-iss. Sep93 on 'Stardust'; STAMCD 536)*

Sep 74. (7") <54253> **DISTANT LOVER. / TROUBLE MAN** | – | 28
Apr 76. (7") *(TMG 1026)* <54264> **I WANT YOU. / I WANT YOU (instrumental)** ☐ | 15
May 76. (lp) *(STML 12025)* <342> **I WANT YOU** | 22 | 4 Mar76
– I want you / Come live with me angel / After the dance (instrumental) / Feel all my love inside / I wanna be where you are / I want you / All the way around / Since I had you / Soon I'll be loving you again / I want you (intro jam) / After the dance. *(re-iss. Oct81; same) (re-iss. 1986 on 'Motown'; WL 72027) (cd-iss. Mar90; WD 72027)*

Aug 76. (7") *(TMG 1035)* <54273> **AFTER THE DANCE. / FEEL ALL MY LOVE INSIDE** ☐ | 74

| | Motown | Motown |
Apr 77. (7") *(TMG 1069)* <54280> **GOT TO GIVE IT UP (part 1). / GOT TO GIVE IT UP (part 2)** | 7 | 1

——— next d-lp, * – duets with FLORENCE LYLES

May 77. (d-lp) *(TMSP 6006)* <352> **LIVE AT THE LONDON PALLADIUM (live)** ☐ | 3 Mar77
– (intro theme) / All the way around / Since I had you / Come get to this / Let's get it on / Trouble man / Ain't peculiar / You're a wonderful one / Stubborn kind of fellow / Pride and joy / Little darling (I need you) / I heard it through the grapevine / Hitch hike / You / You busy thinking about my baby / How sweet it is to be loved by you / Inner city blues (make me wanna holler) / God is love / What's going on / Save the children / You're all I need to get by * / Ain't nothing like the real thing * / Your precious love * / It takes two * / Ain't no mountain high enough * / Distant lover / (closing theme) / Got to give it up. *(re-iss. Aug86 lp/c; WL/WK 72213) (cd-iss. Mar87; ZD 72213) (cd re-iss. May89; WD 72213)*

Jan 79. (d-lp) *(TMSP 6008)* <364> **HERE, MY DEAR** ☐ | 26
– Here, my dear / I met a little girl / When did you stop loving me, when did I stop loving you / Anger / Is that enough / Everybody needs love / Time to get it together /

Sparrow / Anna's song / When did you stop loving me, when did I stop loving me (instrumental) / A funky space reincarnation / You can leave, but it's going to cost you / Falling in love again / When did you stop loving me, when did I stop loving you (reprise). *(re-iss. Oct81 lp/c; TMSP/CTMSP 6008) (cd-iss. Nov93; 530253-2)*

Feb 79. (7") <54298> **A FUNKY SPACE REINCARNATION (part 1). / (part 2)** ☐ | ☐
(12"+=) *(TMGT 1138)* – ('A'disco).

——— Around this a collaboration with SMOKEY ROBINSON, DIANA ROSS and STEVE WONDER gave them a minor hit single 'POPS WE LOVE YOU'.

Nov 79. (7") *(TMG 1168)* <54305> **EGO TRIPPING OUT. / 'A' instrumental)** ☐ | ☐
(12") *(TMGT 1168)* – ('A'side) / What's going on / What's happening brother.

Feb 81. (lp) *(TMG 12149)* <374> **IN OUR LIFETIME** | 48
– Praise / Life is for learning / Love party / Funk me / Far cry / Love me now or love me later / Heavy love affair / In our lifetime. *(cd-iss. Oct94; 530274-2)*

Feb 81. (7") *(TMG 1225)* <54322> **PRAISE. / FUNK ME** ☐ | ☐
Oct 81. (7") *(TMG 1232)* <54326> **HEAVY LOVE AFFAIR. / FAR CRY** ☐ | ☐

——— MARVIN now played all instruments (or most of anyway)

| | C.B.S. | Columbia |
Oct 82. (lp/c) *(CBS/40 85977)* <38197> **MIDNIGHT LOVE** | 10 | 7
– Midnight lady / Sexual healing / Rockin' after midnight / 'Til tomorrow / Turn on some music / Third world girl / Joy / My love is waiting. *(re-iss. Apr86 lp/c; CBS/40 32776) (cd-iss. Jul94; CD 85977)*

Oct 82. (7"/12") *(A/TA 2855)* <03302> **SEXUAL HEALING. / ('A'instrumental)** | 4 | 3
Nov 82. (7") <03589> **ROCKIN' AFTER MIDNIGHT. / 'TIL TOMORROW** | – | –
Jan 83. (7"/12") *(A/TA 3048)* **MY LOVE IS WAITING. / ROCKIN' AFTER MIDNIGHT** | 34 | –
Jan 83. (7") <03860> **JOY. / ('A' instrumental)** | – | –
Feb 83. (7") <03870> **STAR SPANGLED BANNER. / TURN ON SOME MUSIC** | – | –
Mar 83. (7") *(A 3242)* <03935> **JOY. / TURN ON SOME MUSIC** | – | –

——— On the 1st April 1984, MARVIN was shot dead by his father.

May 85. (7"/12") *(A/TA 4894)* (04861) **SANCTIFIED LADY. / ('A'instrumental)** | 51
(d7"+=) *(DA 4894)* – Sexual healing / Rockin' after midnight.

Jun 85. (lp/c) *(CBS/40 26239)* <39916> **DREAM OF A LIFETIME (2 new & recordings from the 70's)** | 46 | 41
– Sanctified lady / Savage in the sack / Masochistic beauty / It's madness / Ain't it funny (how things turn around) / Symphony / Life's opera / Dream of a lifetime. *(cd-iss. Jun91 on 'Pickwick'; 982591-2)*

Jul 85. (7") *(A 6462)* <05542> **IT'S MADNESS. / AIN'T IT FUNNY (HOW THINGS TURN AROUND)** ☐ | ☐
(12"+=) *(TA 6462)* – Joy.

Dec 85. (lp/c) *(CBS/40 26744)* <40208> **ROMANTICALLY YOURS** ☐ | ☐
– More / Why did I choose you? / Maria / The shadow of your smile / Fly me to the Moon (in other words) / I won't cry anymore / Just like / Walkin' in the rain / I live for you / Stranger in my life / Happy go lucky. *(cd-iss. Jul89 on 'Pickwick' 902121-2) (re-iss. Jun94 on 'Sony Collectors' cd/c; 463158-2/-4)*

Jan 86. (7") <05791> **JUST LIKE. / MORE** | – | –
Jun 86. (7") *(ZB 40758)* **THE WORLD IS RATED X. / LONELY LOVER** | – | –
(12"+=) *(ZT 40758)* – ('A'instrumental).
Jun 86. (7") <1836> **THE WORLD IS RATED X. / NO GREATER LOVE** | – | ☐

– compilations etc. –

Note all below on 'Tamla Motown' unless mentioned otherwise

Mar 64. (lp) <252> **GREATEST HITS** | – | 72
Oct 66. (lp) *(STML 11033)* <266> **THE MOODS OF MARVIN GAYE** | – | – Jul66
Mar 67. (7"ep) *(TME 2016)* **MARVIN GAYE** | –
Mar 67. (7"ep) *(TME 2019)* **ORIGINALS FROM MARVIN GAYE** | –
Sep 67. (lp) <278> **GREATEST HITS VOL. 2** | –
Feb 68. (lp) *(STML 11065)* **MARVIN GAYE'S GREATEST HITS** | 40 | –
Feb 72. (lp) *(STML 11201)* **THE HITS OF MARVIN GAYE** ☐ | ☐
(re-iss. Oct81. on 'Motown')
Jun 74. (d-lp) *(TMSP 1128)* **ANTHOLOGY** | 61
(d-cd-iss. Oct86) (d-cd re-iss. Apr93)
Nov 74. (7") *(TMG 923)* **I HEARD IT THROUGH THE GRAPEVINE. / CHAINED** ☐ | ☐
Sep 76. (7") *(TMG 953)* **I HEARD IT THROUGH THE GRAPEVINE. / (b-side by The Supremes/Temptations)** ☐ | ☐
Nov 76. (lp) *(STML 12042)* <348> **THE BEST OF MARVIN GAYE** | 56
(re-iss. Oct81)
Feb 80. (7") *(TMG 1165)* **ABRAHAM, MARTIN & JOHN. / (track by Michael Jackson)** ☐ | ☐
Oct 80. (lp) *(STML 9004)* **EARLY YEARS 1961-1964** ☐ | ☐
Oct 83. (lp) <6058> **EVERY GREAT MOTOWN HIT OF MARVIN GAYE** | – | 80
Nov 83. (7") *(TMG 984)* **WHAT'S GOING ON. / I HEARD IT THROUGH THE GRAPEVINE** ☐ | ☐
(12"+=) *(TMGT 984)* – Wherever I lay my hat.
May 84. (cd) *(TCD 06069)* **15 GREATEST HITS** ☐ | ☐
Apr 85. (7") *(TMG 1381)* **GOT TO GIVE IT UP (Pt.1). / HOW SWEET IT IS** ☐ | ☐
(12"+=) *(TMGT 1381)* – ('A'version – Pt.2).
Apr 85. (lp/c) *(WK/WL 72374)* **I HEARD IT THROUGH THE GRAPEVINE** ☐ | ☐
(cd-iss. Nov86; ZD 72457) (cd re-iss. Jun89; WD 72374)
Mar 86. (cd) *(ZD 72422)* **COMPACT COMMAND PERFORMANCES VOL.1** ☐ | ☐
Apr 86. (7") *(ZB 40701)* **I HEARD IT THROUGH THE GRAPEVINE. / CAN I GET A WITNESS** | 8 | ☐
(ext; 12"/c-s) *(ZT/ZV 40702)* – ('A'side) / That's the way love is / You're a wonderful one.

Jun 86. (lp/c) *(ZL/ZK 72463)* *<6172>* **MOTOWN REMEMBERS MARVIN GAYE** ☐ | ☐ Apr86

Jul 86. (c) *(TCD 2234)* **THE VERY BEST OF MARVIN GAYE** ☐ | -

Nov 86. (d-cd) *(ZD 72456)* **WHAT'S GOING ON / LET'S GET IT ON** ☐ | -

Feb 87. (d-cd) *(ZD 72500)* **TROUBLE MAN / M.P.G.** ☐ | -

Mar 87. (cd) *(ZD 72508)* **COMPACT COMMAND PERFORMANCES – VOL.2** ☐ | -

Jul 87. (d-cd) *(ZD 72562)* **THAT STUBBORN KINDA FELLA / HOW SWEET IT IS** ☐ | -

Jan 88. (7") *Old Gold; (OG 9749)* **(SEXUAL) HEALING. / MY LOVE IS WAITING** ☐ | -
(re-iss. 12"- Aug88; OG 4075)

Apr 88. (7") *(ZB 41909)* **AIN'T THAT PECULIAR. / I'LL BE DOGGONE** ☐ | -

Jul 88. (d-lp/c/cd) *(ZL/ZK/ZD 72639)* **MUSICAL TESTAMENT 1964-1984** ☐ | -

Sep 88. (lp/c/cd) *(WL/WK/WD 72645)* **18 GREATEST HITS** ☐ | -
(re-iss. Feb92 as 'MOTOWN'S GREATEST HITS';) – (2 tracks)

Sep 73. (lp) *Music For Pleasure; (MFP 50423)* **HOW SWEET IT IS** ☐ | -
(re-iss. Jan79; same)

Jun 82. (lp) *(TMS/TMC 3508)* **THE MAGIC OF MARVIN GAYE** ☐ | -

Nov 83. (lp/c) *Telstar; (STAR/STAC 2234)* **GREATEST HITS** 13 | -
– I heard it through the grapevine / Let's get it on / Too busy thinking about my baby / How sweet it is to be loved by you / You're all I need to get by / Got to give it up / You are everything / Midnight lady / Sexual healing / What's going on / Abraham, Martin & John / It takes two / Stop, look, listen (to your heart) / My love is waiting / The onion song / Wherever I lay my hat.

Nov 88. (lp/c/cd; shared with SMOKEY ROBINSON) *Telstar; (STAR/STAC/TCD 2331)* **LOVE SONGS** 69 | -

Oct 90. (cd/c/lp) *Telstar; (TCD/STAC/STAR 2427)* **LOVE SONGS** 39 | -

Oct 92. (cd/c) *Muskateer; (MU 3003/2003)* **DISTANT LOVER** ☐ | -
(cd re-iss. Nov93 on 'Star'; ST 5001) (cd re-iss. May94 on 'Javelin' cd/c; HAD CD/MC 165)

Oct 92. (cd/c) *Columbia; (461017-2)* **MIDNIGHT LOVE / DREAM OF A LIFETIME** ☐ | -

May 93. (cd/c) *Spectrum; (550072-2/-4)* **NIGHT LIFE** ☐ | -

Jul 93. (cd/c) *Wisepack; (STA CD/MC 082)* **MARVIN GAYE LIVE** ☐ | -

Jan 94. (cd-video) *Magnum; (MDCD 1)* **FOR THE VERY LAST TIME** ☐ | -

Mar 94. (cd/c) *(530292-2/-4)* **THE VERY BEST OF MARVIN GAYE** 3 | -

May 94. (7"/c-s) *(TMG/+C 1426)* **LUCKY LUCKY ME.** / **('A'extended)** 67
(12"+=/cd-s+=) (TMG T/CD 1426) – ('A'instrumental mix) / ('A'jazz mix) / ('A'ragga vibe mix).

Jun 94. (4xcd-box) **THE CLASSIC COLLECTION** ☐ | -

Oct 94. (3xcd-box) *Columbia; (477525-2)* **DREAM OF A LIFETIME / ROMANTICALLY YOURS / MIDNIGHT LOVE** ☐ | -

Apr 95. (cd/c) *Prestige; (CD/CAS SGP 0152)* **IN CONCERT** ☐ | -

Apr 95. (cd) *Top Masters; (530292-2/-4)* **IN CONCERT** ☐ | -

May 95. (4xcd-box) *(530492-2)* **THE MASTER 1961-1984** ☐ | -

Nov 95. (3xcd-box) **HOW SWEET IT IS / TRIBUTE TO NAT KING COLE / M.P.G.** ☐ | -

– duets –

MARVIN GAYE & MARY WELLS

		Stateside	Tamla
Jul 64. (7") *(SS 316)* *<1057>* **ONCE UPON A TIME. / WHAT'S THE MATTER WITH YOU BABY**		50	19
			17 Apr64
Oct 64. (lp) *(SL 10097)* *<613>* **TOGETHER**			42 May64

– Once upon a time / What's the matter with you baby / Deed I do / Until I met you / After the lights go down low / Together / Squeeze me / For sentimental reasons / You came a long way from St. Louis / Late late show.

MARVIN GAYE & KIM WESTON

		Tamla	
Dec 64. (7") *(SS 363)* *<54104>* **WHAT GOOD AM I WITHOUT YOU. / I WANT YOU AROUND**		☐	61 Oct64

		Tamla Motown	Tamla
Jan 67. (7") *(TMG 590)* *<54141>* **IT TAKES TWO. / IT'S GOT TO BE A MIRACLE**		16	14
May 67. (lp) *(STML 11049)* *<270>* **TAKE TWO**			

– It takes two / I love you, yes I do / Baby I need your loving / It's got to be a miracle / Baby say yes / What good am I without you / Till there was you / Love fell on me / Secret love / I want you 'round / Heaven sent you I know / When.

MARVIN GAYE & TAMMI TERRELL

		Tamla Motown	Tamla
Jun 67. (7") *(TMG 611)* *<54149>* **AIN'T NO MOUNTAIN HIGH ENOUGH. / GIVE A LITTLE LOVE**		☐	19 May67
Sep 67. (7") *(TMG 625)* *<54156>* **YOUR PRECIOUS LOVE. / HOLD ME OH MY DARLING**		☐	5
Dec 67. (7") *(TMG 635)* *<54161>* **IF I COULD BUILD MY WHOLE WORLD AROUND YOU. / IF THIS WORLD WERE MINE**		41	10
			68
Jan 68. (lp) *(STML 11062)* *<277>* **UNITED**			69 Oct67

– Ain't no mountain high enough / Hold me oh my darling / You got wht it takes / If I could build my whole world around you / Somethin' stupid / Your precious love / Two can have a party / Little ole boy, little ole girl / Give a little love / If this world were mine / Sad wedding / Oh how I'd miss you. *(re-iss. Mar82 on 'Motown' lp/c; STMS/CSTMS 5036) (re-iss. Feb88 lp/c/cd; WL/WK/WD 72211)*

Apr 68. (7") *(TMG 655)* *<54163>* **AIN'T NOTHING LIKE THE REAL THING. / LITTLE OLE BOY LITTLE OLE GIRL** 34 | 8

Jul 68. (7") *(TMG 668)* *<54169>* **YOU'RE ALL I NEED TO GET BY. / TWO CAN HAVE A PARTY** 19 | 7

Oct 68. (7") *<54173>* **KEEP ON LOVING ME HONEY. / YOU AIN'T LIVIN' TIL YOU'RE LOVIN'** - | 28

Nov 68. (lp) *(STML 11084)* *<284>* **YOU'RE ALL I NEED** ☐ | 60 Sep68
– Ain't nothing like the real thing / Keep on loving me honey / You're all I need to get by / Baby don'tcha worry / Give in you can't win / You ain't livin' till you're lovin' / That's how it is (since you've been gone) / I'll never stop loving you / When love comes knockin' at my heart / Memory chest / I can't help but love you. *(re-iss. Oct81 lp/c; STMS/CSTMS 5005) (re-iss. May91 cd/c; WD/WK 72208) (cd-iss. Sep93; 530216-2)*

Jan 69. (7") *(TMG 681)* **YOU AIN'T LIVIN' TILL YOU'RE LOVIN'. / OH HOW I MISS YOU** 21 | -

May 69. (7") *(TMG 697)* *<54173>* **GOOD LOVIN' AIN'T EASY TO COME BY. / SATISFIED FEELIN'** 26 | 30 Jan69

Nov 69. (7") *(TMG 715)* **THE ONION SONG. / I CAN'T BELIEVE YOU LOVE ME** 9 | -

Nov 69. (7") *<54187>* **WHAT YOU GAVE ME. / HOW YOU GONNA KEEP IT (AFTER YOU GET IT)** - | 49

Feb 70. (lp) *(STML 11132)* *<294>* **EASY** ☐ | Oct69
– Good lovin' ain't easy to come by / California soul / Love wake me up this morning / This poor heart of mine / I'm your puppet / Onion song / What you gave me / Baby I need your loving / I can't believe you love me / How you gonna keep it / More, more, more / Satisfied feeling. *(re-iss. Sep86 lp/c; WL/WK 72507)*

Apr 70. (7") *<54192>* **THE ONION SONG. / CALIFORNIA SOUL** - | 50

—— Aged 23, TAMMI from a brain tumor after collapsing in the Autumn of '69. A few exploitation releases were forthcoming.

Aug 70. (lp) *(STML 11153)* *<302>* **MARVIN GAYE & TAMMI TERRELL'S GREATEST HITS** ☐ | -
(re-iss. Jul82 lp/c; STMS/CSTMS 5066) (re-iss. Sep86 lp/c/cd; WL/WK/WD 72103)

Apr 85. (7"/12") *(TMG/+T 993)* **THE ONION SONG. / YOU AIN'T LIVIN' TIL YOU'RE LOVIN'** ☐ | -

Mar 74. (lp) *Music For Pleasure;* **THE ONION SONG** ☐ | -

– more duet compilations –

Nov 69. (lp) *(STML 11123)* *<293>* **MARVIN GAYE & HIS GIRLS** ☐ | -
(re-iss. Feb83 on 'Motown' lp/c; STMS/CSTMS 5088) cd-iss. Oct87; WD 72115)

Jan 86. (cd) *(WD 72397)* **MARVIN GAYE & HIS WOMEN** ☐ | -

GAYE BYKERS ON ACID (dig out; Great Alt & Indie . . .)

J. GEILS BAND

Formed: Boston, Massachusetts, USA . . . 1967, initially as The J. GEILS BLUES BAND, by JEROME GEILS and DANNY KLEIN, who soon recruited PETER WOLF, MAGIC DICK and STEPHEN JO BLADD. In 1970, after turning down a Woodstock Festival appearance the year previous, they signed to 'Atlantic'. Their eponymous debut early in '71 was well received by the critics, although the album sold only moderately. A year on, the band had their first of many Top 40 US hits with 'LOOKING FOR A LOVE'. Written by BOBBY WOMACK, the track was included on their follow-up set, 'THE MORNING AFTER' (1972), continuing the formula of combining covers with their own brand of high-energy, no frills R&B. However, it was live that this band made its name, WOLF's "jive" patter (he'd previously been a DJ) and boorish charisma providing an onstage visual focus for their rolling grooves. 1972's 'LIVE – FULL HOUSE' was the first of many concert sets, although the following year's 'BLOODSHOT' made the US Top 10, one of their biggest selling albums of the 70's. Towards the end of the decade, the group began honing their songwriting and aiming more accurately at the pop charts; this approach paid off in late '81/early '82 when they enjoyed a massive transatlantic hit with the anthemic 'CENTERFOLD'. The accompanying synth-enhanced album (they were now signed to 'E.M.I.'), 'FREEZE-FRAME' (1982), topped the American chart and became the biggest selling set of their career. All wasn't well in the ranks, however, WOLF unhappy with his share of the songwriting and subsequently departing for a relatively fruitful solo career. The remaining members stumbled on for a further album before quitting in the mid-80's; GEILS later resurfaced with MAGIC DICK in BLUESTIME and released a couple of blues albums on 'Rounder'.
• **Songwriters:** JUSTMAN contributed most alongside GEILS and WOLF, etc. Covered: IT AIN'T WHAT YOU DO . . . (Juke Joint Jimmy) / FIRST I LOOK AT THE PURSE (Smokey Robinson) / HOMEWORK (Otis Rush) / SERVES YOU RIGHT TO SUFFER (John Lee Hooker) / etc. • **Trivia:** On the 7th of August '74, WOLF married actress Faye Dunaway, although they were to later divorce.

Album rating: THE J. GEILS BAND (*6) / THE MORNING AFTER (*6) / "LIVE" FULL HOUSE (*6) / BLOODSHOT (*5) / LADIES INVITED (*6) / NIGHTMARES . . . AND OTHER TALES FROM THE VINYL JUNGLE (*5) / HOTLINE (*4) / LIVE – BLOW YOUR FACE OUT (*5) / MONKEY ISLAND (*7) / SANCTUARY (*6) / BEST OF THE J. GEILS BAND compilation (*7) / LOVE STINKS (*6) / FREEZE FRAME (*7) / SHOWTIME! (*5) / YOU'RE GETTIN' EVEN WHILE I'M GETTIN' OLD (*4) / FLASHBACK – THE BEST OF J. GEILS BAND compilation (*6)

PETER WOLF (b. PETER BLANKFIELD, 7 Mar'46, New York City) – vocals / **J. GEILS** (b. JEROME, 20 Feb'46, New York City) – guitar / **DANNY KLEIN** (b.13 May'46, Worcester, Massachusetts) – bass / **MAGIC DICK** (b. RICHARD SALWITZ, 13 May'45, New London, Connecticut) – harmonica / **STEPHEN JO BLADD** (b.13 Jul'45, Boston) – drums, vocals / **SETH JUSTMAN** (b.27 Jan'51, Washington, D.C.) – keyboards, vocals

		Atlantic	Atlantic
Jan 71. (7") *<2784>* **HOMEWORK. / FIRST I LOOK AT THE PURSE**		-	☐
Feb 71. (lp) *(K 40108)* *<8275>* **THE J. GEILS BAND**		☐	Jan71

– Wait / Ice breaker (for the big "M") / Cruisin' for a love / Hard drivin' man / Serves you right to suffer / Homework / First I look at the purse / What's your hurry / On borrowed time / Pack fair and square / Sno-cone. *(re-iss. 1974; K 40108) (re-iss. Jul89 on 'Edsel' lp/cd; ED/+CD 300)*

Feb 71. (7") *<2802>* **WAIT. / CRUISIN' FOR A LOVE** - | ☐

Oct 71. (7") <2843> **I DON'T NEED YOU NO MORE. / DEAD PRESIDENTS** – / –

Jan 72. (lp) (K 40293) <8297> **THE MORNING AFTER** 64 Oct71
– I don't need you no more / Whammer Jammer / So sharp / The usual place / Gotta have your love / Looking for a love / Gonna find me a new love / Cry one more time / Floyd's hotel / It ain't what you do (it's how you do it!).

Mar 72. (7") (K 10099) <2844> **LOOKING FOR A LOVE. / WHAMMER JAMMER** 33 Nov71

Oct 72. (lp) (K 40426) <7241> **LIVE – FULL HOUSE (live)** 54
– First I look at the purse / Homework / Pack fair and square / Whammer jammer / Hard drivin' man / Serves you right to suffer / Cruisin' for a love / Looking for a love.

Oct 72. (7") (K 10266) **HARD DRIVIN' MAN (live). / WHAMMER JAMMER (live)** – / –

Apr 73. (lp) (K 40479) <7260> **BLOODSHOT** 10
– (Ain't nothin' but a) House party / Make up your mind / Back to get ya / Struttin' with my baby / Don't try to hide it / Southside shuffle / Hold your loving / Start all over again / Give it to me.

May 73. (7") (K 10295) <2953> **GIVE IT TO ME. / HOLD YOUR LOVING** 30 Mar73

Aug 73. (7") <2974> **MAKE UP YOUR MIND. / SOUTHSIDE SHUFFLE** 98

Jan 74. (lp) (K 40536) <7286> **LADIES INVITED** 51 Nov73
– Did you no wrong / I can't go on / Lay your good thing down / That's why I'm thinking of you / No doubt about it / The lady makes demands / My baby don't love me / Diddyboppin' / Take a chance / Chimes. (cd-iss. Feb95 on 'Warners')

Jan 74. (7") <3007> **DID YOU NO WRONG. / THAT'S WHY I'M THINKING OF YOU** – / –

Nov 74. (7") <3214> **MUST OF GOT LOST. / FUNKY JUDGE** 12

Nov 74. (lp) (K 50073) <18107> **NIGHTMARES . . . AND OTHER TALES FROM THE VINYL JUNGLE** 26 Oct74
– Detroit breakdown / Givin' it all up / Must of got lost / Look me in the eye / Nightmares / Stoop down 39 / I'll be coming home / Funky judge / Gettin' out.

Jan 75. (7") <3251> **GETTIN' OUT. / GIVIN' IT ALL UP** – / –
Jan 75. (7") (K 10550) **GETTIN' OUT. / FUNKY JUDGE** –
Mar 75. (7") (K 10581) **GIVIN' IT ALL UP. / LOOK ME IN THE EYES** –

Oct 75. (lp) (K 50175) <18147> **HOTLINE** 36 Sep75
– Love-itis / Easy way out / Think it over / Be careful / Jealous love / Mean love / Orange driver / Believe in me / Fancy footwork.

Oct 75. (7") <3301> **LOVE-ITIS. / THINK IT OVER** – / –

May 76. (7") (K 10744) <3320> **WHERE DID OUR LOVE GO. / WHAT'S YOUR HURRY** 68 Apr76

Jun 76. (d-lp) (K 60115) <507-2> **LIVE – BLOW YOUR FACE OUT (live)** 40 May76
– Southside shuffle / Back to get ya / Shoot your shot / Musta got lost / Where did our love go / Truck drivin' man / Love-itis / (Ain't nothin' but a) House party / So sharp / Detroit breakdown / Chimes / Sno-cone / Wait / Raise your hand / Start all over / Give it to me. (cd-iss. Oct93; 8122 71278-2)

Oct 76. (7") <3350> **(AIN'T NOTHIN' BUT A) HOUSE PARTY (live). / GIVE IT TO ME (live)** – / –

Feb 77. (7") <3378> **PEANUT BUTTER. / MAGIC'S MOOD** –

Jul 77. (lp; as J. GEILS) (K 50381) <19130> **MONKEY ISLAND** 51
– Surrender / You're the only one / I do / Somebody / I'm falling / Monkey island / I'm not rough / So good / Wreckage.

Jul 77. (7"; as GEILS) <3411> **YOU'RE THE ONLY ONE. / WRECKAGE** – / 83

Sep 77. (7") <3438> **SURRENDER. / MONKEY ISLAND (part 1)** –

	EMI America	EMI America
Nov 78. (7") <8007> **ONE LAST KISS. / REVENGE**		35
Jan 79. (lp/c) (AMS/TC-AMS 2004) <17006> **SANCTUARY**	49 Dec78	

– I could hurt you / One last kiss / Take it back / Sanctuary / Teresa / Wild man / I can't believe you / I don't hang around much anymore / Jus' can't stop me. (cd-iss. May95 on 'Beat Goes On'; BGOCD 262)

Apr 79. (7") (AM 506) <8012> **TAKE IT BACK. / I CAN'T BELIEVE YOU** 67 Mar79

Jun 79. (7") (AM 507) **ONE LAST KISS. / I CAN'T BELIEVE YOU** 74 / –
Aug 79. (7") (EA 12) <8016> **WILD MAN. / I CAN'T STOP ME** – / –

—— MAGIC now added saxophone. (might have been earlier)

Feb 80. (lp/c) (AML/TC-AML 3004) <17106> **LOVE STINKS** 18
– Just can't wait / Come back / Takin' you down / Night time / No anchovies, please / Love stinks / Tryin' not to think about it / Desire (please don't turn away) / Till the walls come tumblin' down. (cd-iss. Dec94 on 'Beat Goes On'; BGOCD 254)

Feb 80. (7") (EA 105) <8032> **COME BACK. / TAKIN' YOU DOWN** 32 Jan80
May 80. (7"/7"pic-d) (EA/+P 111) <8039> **LOVE STINKS. / TILL THE WALLS COME TUMBLIN' DOWN** 38 Apr80
Jul 80. (7") <8047> **JUST CAN'T WAIT. / NO ANCHOVIES, PLEASE** – / 78
Nov 81. (7") <8102> **CENTERFOLD. / RAGE IN THE CAGE** – / 1
Jan 82. (7") (EA 135) **CENTERFOLD. / FLAMETHROWER** 3 / –
Jan 82. (lp/c) (AML/TC-AML 3020) <17062> **FREEZE-FRAME** 12 / 1 Nov81
– Freeze-frame / Rage in the cage / Centerfold / Do you remember when / Insane, insane again / Flamethrower / River blindness / Angel in blue / Piss on the wall. (cd-iss. Mar84; CDP 746551-2) (cd-iss. Aug93 on 'Beat Goes On'; BGOCD 195)

Feb 82. (7") <8108> **FREEZE-FRAME. / FLAMETHROWER** – / 4
Apr 82. (7"/7"pic-d) (EA/+P 134) **FREEZE-FRAME. / RAGE IN THE CAGE** 27 / –
May 82. (7") <8100> **ANGEL IN BLUE. / RAGE IN THE CAGE** – / 40
Jun 82. (7") (EA 138) **ANGEL IN BLUE. / RIVER BLINDNESS** 55 / –
Dec 82. (lp/c) (AML/TC-AML 3028) <SO 17087> **SHOWTIME! (live)** 23
– Jus' can't stop me / Just can't wait / Till the walls come tumblin' down / Sanctuary / I'm falling / Love rap / Love stinks / Stoop down 39 / I do / Centerfold / Land of a thousand dances. (cd-iss. Dec95 on 'Beat Goes On'; BGOCD 264)

Mar 83. (7") (EA 149) <8148> **I DO (live). / SANCTUARY (live)** 24 Nov82
Feb 83. (7") <8156> **LAND OF A THOUSAND DANCES (live). / JUS' CAN'T STOP ME (live)** – / 60

—— Trimmed to a quintet, when WOLF left for semi-successful solo career.

Oct 84. (7") <8242> **CONCEALED WEAPONS. / TELL 'EM JONESY** – / 63
Dec 84. (lp) (EJ 240240-1) <17137> **YOU'RE GETTIN' EVEN WHILE I'M GETTIN' ODD** 80 Nov84
– Concealed weapons / Heavy petting / Wasted youth / Eenie meenie minie moe /

Tell me Jonesy / You're gettin' even while I'm gettin' old / The bite from inside / Californicating / I will carry you home.

	not iss.	Private I
Apr 85. (7") **OO-EE-DIDDLEY-BOP!** /	–	
Jul 85. (7") <05462> **FRIGHT NIGHT. / (track by The Fabulous Fontaines)**	–	91

(above from the film of same name)

– compilations, others, etc. –

Jul 79. (lp) Atlantic; <19284> **THE BEST OF THE J. GEILS BAND** – / –
Apr 87. (cd) EMI America; (CDP 746551-2) **FLASHBACK – (THE BEST OF J.GEILS)** – / –
– Love stinks / Freeze frame / Flamethrower / Just can't wait / I do / Centerfold / Come back / Wild man / One last kiss / Land of a 1000 dances.
Jan 93. (cd) Warners; <(7567 81557-2)> **THE J. GEILS BAND ANTHOLOGY: HOUSE PARTY** – / –
Apr 97. (cd) Connoisseur; (VSOPCD 234) **CENTERFOLD** – / –

Bob GELDOF (see under ⇒ BOOMTOWN RATS)

GENE

Formed: Watford, England . . . Summer 1993 by MARTIN ROSSITER and three ex-members of GO HOLE and then SP!N (STEVE MASON, MATT WINGLEY (JAMES) and KEVIN MILES). SP!N were indie raves (mixing style of STONE ROSES and JIMI HENDRIX) for three years from 1988, before (on the 23rd March '91) a motorway accident left them shattered and unable to continue as a group for some time. Their tour manager, their soundman and their bassman, JOHN MASON (STEVE's older brother) were all seriously injured, with the latter having to be replaced by KEVIN MILES. In 1992, they found ROSSITER from gay disco group, DROP, finally debuting with 'FOR THE DEAD' in the Spring of '94. Both they and their label, 'Costermonger', were then picked up by 'Polydor', who issued Top 60 single, 'BE MY LIGHT, BE MY GUIDE'. Another couple of singles, 'SLEEP WELL TONIGHT' and 'HAUNTED BY YOU' followed, before the band finally released their debut album, 'OLYMPIAN' in Spring '95. With ROSSITER's effete tales of bedsit angst, alienation and despair and SMITHS-style musical approach, GENE polarized opinion. Fans found much to savour in the record's grooves, the vitality of singles giving way to a more reflective, downbeat ambience that characterised much of the album. It went Top 10 in the UK, spawning further singles with the title track and the re-released, 'FOR THE DEAD'. The latter was accompanied by an odds and sods compilation, 'TO SEE THE LIGHTS' (The SMITHS did the same a decade earlier), while a follow-up set proper, 'DRAWN TO THE DEEP END', hit the shelves about a year later. • **Songwriters:** Group penned except DON'T LET ME DOWN (Beatles) / I SAY A LITTLE PRAYER (Burt Bacharach) / WASTELANDS (Jam) / NIGHTSWIMMING (R.E.M.).

Album rating: Sp!n: IN MOTION (*5) / Gene: OLYMPIAN (*7) / TO SEE THE LIGHTS (*6) / DRAWN TO THE DEEP END (*6) / REVELATIONS (*5)

GO HOLE

LEE CLARKE (b.20 Jan'63, Cleethorpes, England) – vocals, guitar / **STEVE MASON** (b.17 Apr'71, Pontypridd, Wales) – guitar / **JOHN MASON** (b. 8 Aug'67, Bristol, England) – bass / **MATT WINGLEY** (b. MATT JAMES, 20 Sep'65) – drums

	Big Pot	not iss.
Aug 87. (7") (GONE 1) **FLIGHT OF ANGELS. / SPANISH FLY**		–

SP!N

	Foundation	not iss.
Aug 90. (12"ep) **SCRATCHES IN THE SAND. / SHAFTED / EAST** (cd-ep+=) – ('A'radio edit).		–
Feb 91. (12"ep) **LET'S PRETEND / (part 2). / MANIFESTO OF LOVE / LET'S PRETEND (JIMI'S DEAD)** (cd-ep+=) – ('A'radio edit).		–
Jul 91. (lp/c/cd) (FOUND 3/+MC/CD) **IN MOTION**		–

– Many sides of you / Let's pretend / Everything / Ask me / Shafted / Sweet / Colour of your eyes / Mary / Scratches (in the sand) / Sister Pearl.

—— **KEV MILES** – bass repl. JOHN who after transit accident left and travelled around the country and then France as a bohemian poet.

Nov 91. (12"ep/cd-ep) **HOT BLOOD** – / –
– Fifteen minutes / I'm getting out / Landslide / My worst nightmare.

—— **MARTIN T. FALLS** (b.15 May'70, Cardiff, Wales) – vocals repl. LEE

—— disbanded 1992 after new member bailed out.

GENE

MARTIN ROSSITER (b.1970, Cardiff, Wales) – vocals, keyboards / **STEVE MASON** – guitars / **KEVIN MILES** – bass / **MATT JAMES** – drums, percussion

	Costermonger-Polydor	Polydor
Apr 94. (7") (COST 1) **FOR THE DEAD. / CHILD'S BODY**	76	–
Aug 94. (7") (COST 2) **BE MY LIGHT, BE MY GUIDE. / THIS IS NOT A CRIME** (cd-s+=) – I can't help myself.	54	–
Oct 94. (7"/c-s/cd-s) (COST 3/+MC/+CD) **SLEEP WELL TONIGHT. / SICK, SOBER AND SORRY / HER FIFTEEN YEARS**	36	–
Feb 95. (7"/c-s/cd-s) (COST 4/+MC/+CD) **HAUNTED BY YOU. / DO YOU WANT TO HEAR IT FROM ME / HOW MUCH FOR LOVE**	32	

Mar 95. (cd/c/lp) *(GENE 1CD/1MC/1LP)* <52-7662> **OLYMPIAN**   `8`   `Jun95`
– Haunted by you / Your love, it lies / Truth, rest your head / A car that sped / Left-handed / London, can you wait? / To the city / Still can't find he phone / Sleep well tonight / Olympian / We'll find our own way. *(cd re-iss. Mar99; 527446-2)*

Jun 95. (7"blue) *(SP 294)* **BE MY LIGHT, BE MY GUIDE. / I CAN'T HELP MYSELF**
(above on 'Sub Pop' UK & feat. on 'HELTER SHELTER' box-set)

Jul 95. (7"/c-s) *(COST 5/+MC)* **OLYMPIAN. / I CAN'T DECIDE IF SHE REALLY LOVES ME / TO SEE THE LIGHTS**   `18`   `-`
(cd-s+=) *(COST 5CD)* – Don't let me down.

Nov 95. (m-cd) <31457 9247-2> **GENE**   `-`
– Sleep well tonight / I can't help myself / This is not my crime / Child's body / The olympian.

Jan 96. (7") *(7COST 6A)* **FOR THE DEAD (version). / CHILD'S BODY**   `14`   `-`
(7"+=/c-s+=) *(COST 6/+MC)* – Sick, sober & sorry (live).
(cd-s) *(COST 6CD)* – ('A'side) / Sick, sober & sorry (live) / Truth rest your head (live).

Jan 96. (cd/c/d-lp) *(GENE 2LP/2MC/2CD)* <8249> **TO SEE THE LIGHTS**   `11`
(compilation of rare, live & bootleg material)
– Be my light, be my guide / Sick, sober & sorry / Her fifteen years / Haunted by you (live – Helter Skelter) / I can't decide if she really loves me / To see the lights / I can't help myself / A car that sped (Radio 1 session) / For the dead (version) / Sleep well tonight (live – Forum) / How much for love / London, can you wait? (Radio 1 session) / Child's body / Don't let me down (Radio 1 session) / I say a little prayer (live – Glastonbury) / Do you want to hear it from me / This is not my crime / Olympian (live – Forum) / Child's body (live – Forum). *(cd re-iss. Mar99; 529807-2)*

	Polydor	A&M
Oct 96. (7"/c-s) *(575689-7/-4)* **FIGHTING FIT. / DRAWN TO THE DEEP END**	`22`	`-`

(cd-s+=) *(575689-2)* – Autumn stone.

Jan 97. (7"/c-s) *(COS TS/MC 10)* **WE COULD BE KINGS. / DOLCE / GABBANA OR NOWT**   `17`   `-`
(cd-s+=) *(COSCD 10)* – Wastelands.

Feb 97. (cd/c/d-lp) *(GENE CD/M/L 3)* <537104> **DRAWN TO THE DEEP END**   `8`   `Mar97`
– New amusements / Fighting fit / Where are they now? / Speak to me someone / We could be kings / Whi I was born / Long sleeves for the summer / Save me, I'm yours / Voice of the father / Accidental / I love you, what are you? / Sub rosa.

May 97. (7") *(COSTS 11)* **WHERE ARE THEY NOW? / CAST OUT IN THE SEVENTIES**   `22`   `-`
(cd-s+=) *(COSCD 11)* – Nightswimming.
(cd-ep) **LIVE AT THE ROYAL ALBERT HALL EP** *(COSDD 11)* – ('A') / Save me, I'm yours / Voice of the father / Sub Rosa.

Jul 97. (7"/c-s) *(COS TS/MC 12)* **SPEAK TO ME SOMEONE. / AS THE BRUISES FADE**   `30`   `-`
(cd-s) *(COSCD 12)* – ('A'side) / Ship song / Drawn to the deep end.
(cd-s) *(COSDD 12)* – ('A'side) / New amusements / Olympian.

Feb 99. (7") *(COSTS 14)* **AS GOOD AS IT GETS. / TOASTING THE UNION**   `23`   `-`
(cd-s+=) *(COSCD 14)* – Man on Earth.
(cd-s) *(COSDD 14)* – ('A'side) / All night / To all who sail on her.

Mar 99. (cd/c/lp) *(GENE C/M/L 4)* **REVELATIONS**   `25`
– As good as it gets / In love with love / Love won't work / British diseases / Fill her up / Something in the water / Mayday / Angel / Looker / Little child / Stop / The police will never find you / You'll never walk again.

Apr 99. (7") *(COSTS 15)* **FILL HER UP. / PASS ON TO ME**   `36`   `-`
(cd-s+=) *(COSCD 15)* – Touched by the hand of havoc.
(cd-s) *(COSDD 15)* – ('A'side) / Common as air / Slice.

– compilations, etc.

1996. (cd) *Hispanolo; <040>* **IF THE DRESS FITS: THE UNOFFICIAL COMPILATION**   `-`

GENE LOVES JEZEBEL (dig out; Great Alt & Indie . . .)

GENERATION X (see under ⇒ **IDOL, Billy**)

GENESIS

Formed: Godalming, Surrey, England . . . early 1967 by Charterhouse public school boys PETER GABRIEL and TONY BANKS (both ex-The GARDEN WALL). They teamed up with former members of The ANON; MICHAEL RUTHERFORD, ANTHONY PHILLIPS and CHRIS STEWART. Still at school, they signed to 'Decca', having sent demos to solo artist and producer JONATHAN KING. Their first 2 singles flopped, as did their 1969 MOODY BLUES-styled album, 'FROM GENESIS TO REVELATION', which only sold around 500 copies. Early in 1970, they were seen live by TONY STRATTON-SMITH, who became their manager after signing them to his 'Charisma' label. Their second album, 'TRESPASS', failed to break through, although it contained the live favourite and edited 45, 'THE KNIFE'. After its release, they found new members PHIL COLLINS and STEVE HACKETT, who replaced recent additions JOHN MAYHEW and ANTHONY PHILLIPS. Late in '71, they issued their set, 'NURSERY CRYME', which featured another two gems, 'THE MUSICAL BOX' and 'THE RETURN OF THE GIANT HOGWEED'. At this point the band transformed into one of the leading purveyors of progressive rock, bizarre extrovert GABRIEL proving a compelling, theatrical focus for the critically-lauded group. It was also the brief debut on lead vox for COLLINS, who sang on the track, 'FOR ABSENT FRIENDS'. A year later, with many gigs behind them, they had their first taste of chart success when 'FOXTROT' hit the UK Top 20. This contained the excellent concept piece, 'SUPPER'S READY', which lasted all

of 23 minutes. In 1973, a live album of their best work so far hit the Top 10, as did their studio follow-up, 'SELLING ENGLAND BY THE POUND'. This boasted another epic track, 'THE BATTLE OF EPPING FOREST', plus another COLLINS lead vocal in 'MORE FOOL ME'. Lifted from it was a near Top 20 single, 'I KNOW WHAT I LIKE (IN YOUR WARDROBE)'. Late in 1974, they again made Top 10 with the concept double album, 'THE LAMB LIES DOWN ON BROADWAY', which was their first US Top 50 placing, the band performing the album in its entirety as part of a worldwide live show. Shortly after a last concert in May '75, GABRIEL left for a solo career, COLLINS taking over the vocal duties. Surprisingly, this did not harm the commercial appeal of the group when they returned in 1976 with the Top 3 album, 'A TRICK OF THE TAIL'. His drum-stool was filled for live gigs by the seasoned BILL BRUFORD, then CHESTER THOMPSON, who appeared on the 1977 live double album, 'SECONDS OUT'. This was also the last album to feature STEVE HACKETT, who also left for a lucrative solo career. In 1978, their next album, appropriately titled ' . . . AND THEN THERE WERE THREE' (COLLINS, BANKS & RUTHERFORD), hit No.3 and also climbed into the US Top 20. The 80's were even more fruitful for the band, as they hit the top spot in the UK with each successive album, also amassing a number of hit singles over the same period. During this era, PHIL COLLINS (who had moonlighted in his own BRAND X) scored a number of easier-listening hit singles and albums. Although they remain one of the stadium rock circuit's largest grossing bands, the band have lost all trace of their pioneering 70's sound. With PHIL COLLINS now out of the picture, BANKS and RUTHERFORD took on the relatively younger Scotsman, RAY WILSON, who had previously fronted chart-toppers, STILTSKIN. TONY BANKS also released some solo work, as did RUTHERFORD, who made coffee-table pop/rock with his outfit, MIKE + THE MECHANICS. • **Songwriters:** GABRIEL lyrics and group compositions. From 1978, the trio collaborated on all work.

Album rating: FROM GENESIS TO REVELATION (*5) / TRESPASS (*6) / NURSERY CRYME (*8) / FOXTROT (*9) / GENESIS LIVE (*7) / SELLING ENGLAND BY THE POUND (*8) / THE LAMB LIES DOWN ON BROADWAY (*8) / A TRICK OF THE TAIL (*7) / WIND & WUTHERING (*6) / . . . AND THEN THERE WERE THREE (*6) / DUKE (*6) / ABACAB (*6) / THREE SIDES LIVE (*5) / GENESIS (*5) / INVISIBLE TOUCH (*6) / WE CAN'T DANCE (*5) / THE WAY WE WALK VOLUME 1: THE SHORTS (*5) / LIVE – THE WAY WE WALK VOLUME 2: THE LONGS (*4) / CALLING ALL STATIONS (*4) / TURN IT ON AGAIN – THE HITS compilation (*8) / Tony Banks: A CURIOUS FEELING (*5) / THE FUGITIVE (*4) / SOUNDTRACKS (*5) / BANKSTATEMENT (*5; by Bankstatement) / STILL (*4) / Mike Rutherford: SMALLCREEP'S DAY (*5) / ACTING VERY STRANGE (*5) / Mike + The Mechanics: MIKE + THE MECHANICS (*4) / THE LIVING YEARS (*5) / WORD OF MOUTH (*5) / BEGGAR ON A BEACH OF GOLD (*4) / HITS compilation (*6)

PETER GABRIEL (b.13 May'50, London, England) – vocals / **TONY BANKS** (b.27 Mar'51, East Heathly, Sussex, England) – keyboards, vocals / **ANTHONY PHILLIPS** (b.Dec'51, Putney, England) – guitar, vocals / **MICHAEL RUTHERFORD** (b. 2 Oct'50, Guildford, Surrey, England) – bass, guitar / **CHRIS STEWART** – drums

	Decca	Parrot
Feb 68. (7") *(F 12735)* <3018> **THE SILENT SUN. / THAT'S ME**	``	``
May 68. (7") *(F 12775)* **A WINTER'S TALE. / ONE-EYED HOUND**	``	`-`

―― **JOHN SILVER** – drums repl. CHRIS

Mar 69. (lp; mono/stereo) *(LK/SKL 4990)* **FROM GENESIS TO REVELATION**   `` ``
– Where the sour turns to sweet / In the beginning / Fireside song / The serpent / Am I very wrong? / In the wilderness / The conqueror / In hiding / One day / Window / In limbo / The silent sun / A place to call my own. *(re-iss. 1974 as 'IN THE BEGINNING'; same) (re-iss. Oct93 on 'Music Club' cd/c;)*

Jun 69. (7") *(F 12949)* **WHERE THE SOUR TURNS TO SWEET. / IN HIDING**   `` `-`

―― (Jul69) **JOHN MAYHEW** – drums repl. JOHN SILVER

	Charisma	Impulse
Oct 70. (7"w-drawn) *(GS 1)* **LOOKING FOR SOMEONE. / VISIONS OF ANGELS**	`-`	`-`
Oct 70. (lp) *(CAS 1020)* <9295> **TRESPASS**	`-`	``

– Looking for someone / White mountain / Visions of angels / Stagnation / Dusk / The knife. <US re-iss. 1974 on 'ABC'; 816> *(re-iss. Mar83; CHC/+MC 12)(hit 98; Apr84) (cd-iss. Jun88; CASCD 1020) (cd re-iss. Aug94; CASCDX 1020)*

Jun 71. (7") *(CB 152)* **THE KNIFE (part 1). / THE KNIFE (part 2)**   `` `-`

―― (Dec70) **GABRIEL, BANKS + RUTHERFORD** recruited new members **PHIL COLLINS** (b.31 Jan'51, Chiswick, London, England) – drums, vocals (ex-FLAMING YOUTH) repl. MAYHEW / **STEVE HACKETT** (b.12 Feb'50, London) – guitar (ex-QUIET WORLD) repl. ANTHONY PHILLIPS who went solo

	Charisma	Charisma
Nov 71. (lp)(c) *(<CAS 1052>)(7208 552)* **NURSERY CRYME**	``	``

– The musical box / For absent friends / The fountain of Salmacis / Seven stones / Harold the barrel / Harlequin / The return of the giant hogweed. *(hit UK No.39 May74) (re-iss. Feb84 lp/c; CHC/+MC 22; hit 68) (cd-iss. Sep85; CASCD 1052) (cd re-iss. Aug94; CASCDX 1052)*

May 72. (7") *(CB 181)* **HAPPY THE MAN. / SEVEN STONES**   `` ``

Oct 72. (lp)(c) *(<CAS 1058>)(7208 553)* **FOXTROT**   `12`
– Get 'em out by Friday / Time-table / Watcher of the skies / Can-utility and the coastliners / Horizon / Supper's ready: (i) Lover's leap, (ii) The guaranteed eternal sanctuary man, (iii) Ikhaton and Itsacon and their band of merry men, (iv) How dare I be so beautiful, (v) Willow farm, (vi) Apocalypse in 9/8 co-starring the delicious talents of Gabble Ratchet, (vii) As sure as eggs is eggs (aching men's feets). *(re-iss. Sep83 lp/c; CHC/+MC 38) (cd-iss. Jul86; CASCD 1058) (cd re-iss. Aug94; CASCDX 1058)*

Feb 73. (7") *<103>* **WATCHER OF THE SKIES. / WILLOW FARM**   `-` `-`

Jul 73. (lp)(c) *(CLASS 1)(7299 288)* <1066> **GENESIS LIVE (live)**   `9`   `May74`
– Watcher of the skies / Get 'em out by Friday / The return of the giant hogweed / The

musical box / The knife. *(re-iss. Feb86 lp/c; CHC/+MC 23) (cd re-iss. Jul87; CLACD 1) (cd re-iss. Aug94; CLACDX 1)*

Oct 73. (lp)(c) *(CAS 1074)(7208 554) <6060>* **SELLING ENGLAND BY THE POUND** `3` `70`
– Dancing with the moonlit knight / I know what I like (in your wardrobe) / Firth of fifth / More fool me / The battle of Epping Forest / After the ordeal / The cinema show / Aisle of plenty. *(re-iss. Oct86 lp/c; CHC/+MC 46) (cd-iss. Feb86; CASCD 1074) (cd re-iss. Aug94; CLACDX 1074) (re-iss. Feb97 on 'E.M.I.'; LPCENT 17)*

Mar 74. (7") *(CB 224) <26002>* **I KNOW WHAT I LIKE (IN YOUR WARDROBE). / TWILIGHT ALEHOUSE** `21` ☐

                                                               Charisma Atco

Nov 74. (d-lp)(d-c) *(CGS 101)(7599 121) <401>* **THE LAMB LIES DOWN ON BROADWAY** `10` `41`
– The lamb lies down on Broadway / Fly on a windshield / Broadway melody of 1974 / Cuckoo cocoon / In the cage / The grand parade of lifeless packaging / Back in N.Y.C. / Hairless heart / Counting out time / Carpet crawlers / The chamber of 32 doors / Lilywhite Lilith / The waiting room / Anyway / Here comes the supernatural anaesthetist / The lamia / Silent sorrow in empty boats / The colony of Slippermen (The arrival – A visit to the doktor – Raven) / Ravine / The light dies down on Broadway / Riding the scree / It. *(re-iss. Sep83 d-lp/c; CGS/+MC 101) (d-cd-iss. Feb86; CGSCD 1) (cd re-iss. Aug94; CGSCDX 1)*

Nov 74. (7") *(CB 238)* **COUNTING OUT TIME. / RIDING THE SCREE** ☐ `-`
Dec 74. (7") *<7013>* **COUNTING OUT TIME. / THE LAMB LIES DOWN ON BROADWAY** `-` `-`
Apr 75. (7") *(CB 251)* **CARPET CRAWLERS. / THE WAITING ROOM (evil jam) (live)** ☐ `-`

—— Now just a quartet when PETER GABRIEL left to go solo.

Feb 76. (lp)(c) *(CDS 4001) <129>* **A TRICK OF THE TAIL** `3` `31`
– Dance on a volcano / Entangled / Squonk / Mad mad Moon / Robbery, assault and battery / Ripples / A trick of the tail / Los endos. *(re-iss. Sep83 lp/c; CDS/+MC 4001) (cd-iss. Apr86; CDSCD 4001) (re-iss. Apr90 on 'Virgin' lp/c; OVED/+C 306) (cd re-iss. Oct94; CDSCDX 4001)*

Mar 76. (7") *(CB 277)* **A TRICK OF THE TAIL. / RIPPLES** `-` `-`
Mar 76. (7") *<7050>* **RIPPLES. / ENTANGLED** `-` `-`
Jan 77. (lp)(c) *(CDS 4005)(7208 611) <144>* **WIND AND WUTHERING** `7` `26`
– Eleventh Earl of Mar / One for the vine / Your own special way / Wot gorilla? / All in a mouse's night / Blood on the rooftops / Unquiet slumbers for the sleepers . . .In that quiet Earth / Afterglow. *(re-iss. Sep83 lp/c; CDS/+MC 4005) (cd-iss. Apr86; CDSCD 4005) (re-iss. Apr90 on 'Virgin' lp/c; OVED/+C 332) (cd re-iss. Oct94; CDSCDX 4005)*

Feb 77. (7") *(CB 300)* **YOUR OWN SPECIAL WAY. / IT'S YOURSELF** `43` `-`
Feb 77. (7") *<7076>* **YOUR OWN SPECIAL WAY. / . . .IN THAT QUIET EARTH** `-` `62`
May 77. (7"ep) *(GEN 001)* **SPOT THE PIGEON** `14` `-`
– Match of the day / Inside and out / Pigeons. *(cd-ep-iss.1988 on 'Virgin'; CDT 40)*

—— added **BILL BRUFORD** – drums (ex-YES, ex-KING CRIMSON) **CHESTER THOMPSON** – drums (ex-FRANK ZAPPA) they were both used on live album below, with CHESTER augmenting on tours.

Oct 77. (d-lp)(d-c) *(GE 2001)(7649 067) <9002>* **SECONDS OUT (live)** `4` `47`
– Sqounk / Carpet crawlers / Robbery, assault and battery / Afterglow / Firth of fifth / I know what I like (in your wardrobe) / The lamb lies down on Broadway / The musical box / Supper's ready / The cinema show / Dance on a volcano / Los endos. *(re-iss. Sep83 d-lp/d-c; GE/+MC 2001) (d-cd-iss. Nov85; GECD 2001) (d-cd re-iss. Oct94; GECDX 2001)*

—— (Jun77) Now a trio of **COLLINS, BANKS & RUTHERFORD** when STEVE HACKETT continued solo career.

                                                          Charisma Atlantic

Mar 78. (7") *(CB 309)* **FOLLOW YOU FOLLOW ME. / BALLAD OF BIG** `7` `-`
Mar 78. (7") *<3474>* **FOLLOW YOU FOLLOW ME. / INSIDE AND OUT** `-` `23`
Apr 78. (lp)(c) *(CDS 4010)(7208 619) <19173>* **. . .AND THEN THERE WERE THREE** `3` `14`
– Down and out / Undertow / Ballad of big / Snowbound / Burning rope / Deep in the motherlode / Many too many / Scene from a night's dream / Say it's alright Joe / The lady lies / Follow you follow me. *(re-iss. Sep83 lp/c; CDS/+MC 4010) (cd-iss. May83; 800 059-2) (re-iss. Aug91 on 'Virgin' lp/c; OVED/+C 368) (cd re-iss. Oct94; CDSCDX 4010)*

Jun 78. (7") *(CB 315)* **MANY TOO MANY. / THE DAY THE LIGHT WENT OUT IN VANCOUVER** `43` `-`
Jul 78. (7") *<3511>* **SCENE FROM A NIGHT'S DREAM. / DEEP IN THE MOTHERLODE** `-` `-`
Mar 80. (7") *(CB 356)* **TURN IT ON AGAIN. / BEHIND THE LINES (part 2)** `8` `-`
Mar 80. (lp/c) *(CBR/+C 101) <16014>* **DUKE** `1` `11`
– Behind the lines / Duchess / Guide vocal / Man of our time / Misunderstanding / Heathaze / Turn it on again / Alone tonight / Cul-de-sac / Please don't ask / Duke's end / Duke's travels. *(re-iss. Sep83 lp/c; CBR/+C 101) (cd-iss. Apr85; CBRCD 101) (re-iss. Mar91 on 'Virgin'; OVED/+C 345) (cd re-iss. Oct94; CBRCDX 101)*

May 80. (7") *(CB 363)* **DUCHESS. / OPEN DOOR** `46` `-`
May 80. (7") *<3662>* **MISUNDERSTANDING. / BEHIND THE LINES** `-` `14`
Sep 80. (7") *(CB 369)* **MISUNDERSTANDING. / EVIDENCE OF AUTUMN** `42` `-`
Sep 80. (7") *<3751>* **TURN IT ON AGAIN. / EVIDENCE OF AUTUMN** `-` `58`
Aug 81. (7") *(CB 388)* **ABACAB. / ANOTHER RECORD** `9` `-`
Sep 81. (lp/c) *(CBR/+C 102) <19313>* **ABACAB** `1` `7`
– Abacab / No reply at all / Me and Sarah Jane / Keep it dark / Dodo / Lurker / Who dunnit? / Man on the corner / Like it or not / Another record. *(cd-iss. May83; 800 044-2) (re-iss. Mar91 on 'Virgin' lp/c; OVED/+C 344) (cd re-iss. Oct94; CBRCDX 102)*

Oct 81. (7") *(CB 391)* **KEEP IT DARK. / NAMINANU** `33` `-`
(12"+=) *(CB 391-12)* – Abacab (long version).
Oct 81. (7") *<3858>* **NO REPLY AT ALL. / HEAVEN LOVE MY LIFE** `-` `29`
Jan 82. (7") *<3891>* **ABACAB. / WHO DUNNIT?** `-` `26`
Feb 82. (7") *(CB 393) <4025>* **MAN IN THE CORNER. / SUBMARINE** `41` `40` Mar82
May 82. (7") *<4053>* **PAPERLATE / YOU MIGHT RECALL** `-` `32`

May 82. (7"ep) *(GEN 1)* **3 X 3 E.P.** `10` `-`
– Paperlate / You might recall / Me and Virgil.
Jun 82. (d-lp)(d-c) *(GE/+MC 2002) <2000>* **THREE SIDES LIVE (live except ***)** `2` `10`
– Turn it on again / Dodo / Abacab / Behind the lines / Duchess / Me and Sarah Jane / Follow you follow me / Misunderstanding / In the cage / Afterglow / One for the vine * / Fountain of Salmacis * / Watcher of the skies * / It * / Paperlate *** / You might recall *** / Me and Virgil *** / Evidence of Autumn *** / Open door *** / You might recall II ***. *(cd-iss. Apr85; GECD 2002) <US-cd.repl.* w/ The cinema show + The colony of Slippermen> (re-iss. Apr92 d-lp/c; DOVD/+C 2) (cd re-iss. Oct94; GECDX 2002)*

                                                         Virgin Atco

Aug 83. (7"/ext.12") *(MAMA 1/+12) <89770>* **MAMA. / IT'S GONNA GET BETTER** `4` `73`
(cd-ep.iss.Jun88; CDT 5)
Oct 83. (lp/c/cd) *(GEN LP/MC/CD 1) <80116>* **GENESIS** `1` `9`
– Mama / That's all / Home by the sea / Second home by the sea / Illegal alien / Taking it all too hard / Just a job to do / Silver rainbow / It's gonna get better. *(re-iss. Jul87; same)*

Nov 83. (7") *(TATA 1)* **THAT'S ALL. / TAKING IT ALL TOO HARD** `16` `-`
(12"+=) *(TATAY 1)* – Firth of fifth (live).
Nov 83. (7") *<89724>* **THAT'S ALL. / SECOND HOME BY THE SEA** `-` `6`
Feb 84. (7"/7"sha-pic-d) *(AL/+S 1) <89698>* **ILLEGAL ALIEN. / TURN IT ON AGAIN (live)** `46` `44`
(12"+=) *(AL 1-12)* – ('A'extended).
Jun 84. (7") *<89656>* **TAKING IT ALL TOO HARD. / SILVER RAINBOW** `-` `50`
May 86. (7",7"clear) *(GENS 1)* **INVISIBLE TOUCH. / THE LAST DOMINO** `15` `1`
(12"+=) *(GENS 1-12)* – ('A'extended).
Jun 86. (lp/c/cd) *(GEN LP/MC/CD 2) <81641>* **INVISIBLE TOUCH** `1` `3`
– Invisible touch / Tonight, tonight, tonight / Land of confusion / In too deep / Anything she does / Domino:- In the glow of the night – The last domino / Throwing it all away / The Brazilian. *(pic-cd.Dec88; GENCDP 2)*

Aug 86. (7"/12") *(GENS 2/+12)* **IN TOO DEEP. / DO THE NEUROTIC** `19` `-`
Aug 86. (7") *<89372>* **THROWING IT ALL AWAY. / DO THE NEUROTIC** `-` `4`
Nov 86. (7") *(GENS 3) <89336>* **LAND OF CONFUSION. / FEEDING THE FIRE** `14` `4` Oct86
(12"+=) *(GENS 3-12)* – Dance the neurotic.
(cd-s+=) *(SNEG 3-12)* – ('A'extended).
Mar 87. (7"/12") *(GENS 4/+12)* **TONIGHT, TONIGHT, TONIGHT. / IN THE GLOW OF THE NIGHT (part 1)** `18` `3` Feb87
(12"+=/cd-s+=) *(GENS/DRAW 4-12)* – Paperlate / ('A'ext.remix).
(cd-s+=) *(CDEP 1)* – Invisible touch (extended) / ('A'-John Potoker remix).
Apr 87. (7") *<89316>* **IN TOO DEEP. / I'D RATHER BE WITH YOU** `-` `3`
Jun 87. (7") *(GENS 5)* **THROWING IT ALL AWAY. / I'D RATHER BE WITH YOU** `22` `-`
(12"+=/c-s+=) *(GENS/+C 5-12)* – Invisible touch (live).
Oct 91. (7"/c-s) *(GENS/+C 6) <87571>* **NO SON OF MINE. / LIVING FOREVER** `6` `13`
(12"+=/cd-s+=) *(GENS/GENCD 6)* – Invisible touch (live).
Nov 91. (cd/c/d-lp) *(GEN CD/MC/LP 3) <82344>* **WE CAN'T DANCE** `1` `4`
– No son of mine / Jesus he knows me / Driving the last spike / I can't dance / Never a time / Dreaming while you sleep / Tell me why / Living forever / Hold on my heart / Way of the world / Since I lost you / Fading lights.
Jan 92. (7"/c-s) *(GENS/+C 7) <87532>* **I CAN'T DANCE. / ON THE SHORELINE** `7` `7`
(cd-s+=) *(GENDG 7)* – In too deep (live) / That's all (live).
(cd-s+=) *(GENDX 7)* – ('A'-sex mix).
Apr 92. (7"/c-s) *(GENS/+C 8) <87481>* **HOLD ON MY HEART. / WAY OF THE WORLD** `16` `12`
(cd-s+=) *(GENDG 8)* – Your own special way (live).
(cd-s+=) *(GENDX 8)* – Home by the sea.
Jul 92. (7"/c-s) *(GENS/+C 9) <87454>* **JESUS HE KNOWS ME. / HEARTS OF FIRE** `20` `23`
(cd-s+=) *(GENDG 9)* – I can't dance (mix).
(cd-s+=) *(GENDX 9)* – Land of confusion (rehearsal version).
Nov 92. (cd/c/d-lp) *(GEN CD/MC/LP 4) <82452>* **THE WAY WE WALK VOLUME 1: THE SHORTS (live)** `3` `35`
– Land of confusion / No son of mine / Jesus he knows me / Throwing it all away / I can't dance / Mama / Hold on my heart / That's all / In too deep / Tonight, tonight, tonight / Invisible touch.
Nov 92. (7"/c-s) *(GENS/+C 10)* **INVISIBLE TOUCH (live). / ABACAB (live)** `7` `-`
(cd-s+=) *(GENDG 10)* – The Brazilian.
Nov 92. (c-s) *<87411>* **NEVER A TIME / TONIGHT, TONIGHT, TONIGHT (live) / INVISIBLE TOUCH (live)** `-` `21`
Jan 93. (cd/c/lp) *(GEN CD/MC/LP 5)* **LIVE / THE WAY WE WALK VOLUME 2: THE LONGS (live)** `1` ☐
– Old medley: Dance on a volcano – Lamb lies down on Broadway – The musical box – Firth of fifth – I know what I like . . . / Driving the fast spike / Domino: part I – In the glow of the night, part II – The last domino / Home by the sea – Second home by the sea / Drum duet.
Feb 93. (7"/c-s) *(GENS/+C 11)* **TELL ME WHY. / DREAMING WHILE YOU SLEEP** `40` ☐
(cd-s+=) *(GENDG 11)* – Tonight, tonight, tonight.

—— **RAY WILSON** – vocals (ex-STILTSKIN) repl. COLLINS who continued his solo career (see own entry ⇒)

Sep 97. (cd/c/lp) *(GEN CD/MC/LP 6)* **CALLING ALL STATIONS** `2` `54`
– Calling all stations / Congo / Shipwrecked / Alien afternoon / Not about us / If that's what you need / Uncertain weather / Small talk / There must be some other way / One man's fool.
Sep 97. (c-s/cd-cs) *(GENS C/D 12)* **CONGO / PAPA HE SAID / BANJO MAN** `29` ☐
(cd-s+=) *(GENSDX 12)* – Second by the sea.
Dec 97. (c-s/cd-s) *(GENS C/D 14)* **SHIPWRECKED / NO SON OF MINE / LOVERS LEAP / TURN IT ON AGAIN** `54` ☐
(cd-s) *(GENSDX 14)* – ('A'side) / Phret / 7-8.

Feb 98. (cd-s) (GENS C/D 15) **NOT ABOUT US / DANCING WITH THE MOONLIT KNIGHT (live) / FOLLOW YOU FOLLOW ME (live) / ('A'live)** — 66
(cd-s) (GENSDX 15) – ('A'side) / Anything new / Sign your life away / Run out of time.

Oct 99. (cd) (GENMD 8) <83244> **TURN IT ON AGAIN – THE HITS** (compilation) — 4 / 65
– Turn it on again / Invisible touch / Mama / Land of confusion / I can't dance / Follow you follow me / Hold on my heart / Abacab / I know what I like (in your wardrobe) / Tonight tonight tonight / In too deep / Congo / Jesus he knows me / That's all / Misunderstanding / Throwing it all away / Carpet crawlers (1999).

– compilations etc. –

on 'Charisma' unless mentioned otherwise

May 74. (d-lp-box) (CGS 102) **GENESIS COLLECTION VOLUME ONE** — / -
– (TRESPASS / NURSERY CRYME)

May 74. (d-lp-box) (CGS 103) **GENESIS COLLECTION VOLUME TWO** — / -
– (FOXTROT / SELLING ENGLAND BY THE POUND)

May 76. (lp/c) Decca; (ROOTS/KRTC 1) **ROCK ROOTS: GENESIS** — / -
– (debut lp + early 45's)

Mar 83. (d-c) (CASMC 112) **FOXTROT / SELLING ENGLAND BY THE POUND** — / -

Apr 86. (lp/pic-lp) Metal Masters; (MACHM/+P 4) **WHEN THE SOUR TURNS TO SWEET** — / -
(cd-iss. Oct87; MACD 4) (re-iss. Jul91;)

Mar 87. (cd) London; (820496-2) **AND THE WORLD WAS** (early) — / -

Jun 88. (7") Old Gold; (OG 9263) **I KNOW WHAT I LIKE (IN YOUR WARDROBE). / COUNTING OUT TIME** — / -

Jun 88. (7") Old Gold; (OG 9264) **FOLLOW YOU FOLLOW ME. / A TRICK OF THE TAIL** — / -

Nov 90. Virgin; (pic-cd-box) (TPAK 1) **GENESIS CD COLLECTORS EDITION** — / -
– (TRESPASS / NURSERY CRYME / FOXTROT)

Jun 98. (4xcd-box) (CDBOX 6) **ARCHIVE 1967-1975** — 35 / -

TONY BANKS

	Charisma	Charisma
Oct 79. (7") (CB 344) **FOR A WHILE. / FROM THE UNDERTOW**	-	-
Oct 79. (lp/c) (CAS/+MC 1148) <2207> **A CURIOUS FEELING**	21	-

– From the undertow / Lucky me / The lie / After the lie / A curious feeling / Forever morning / You / Somebody else's dream / The waters of Lethe / For a while / In the dark. (re-iss. Oct86 lp/c; CHC/+MC 42) (cd-iss. 1988; CASCD 1148)

Jul 80. (7") (CB 365) **A CURIOUS FEELING. / FOR A WHILE**	-	-
Apr 83. (7"/12") (BANKS 1/+12) **THIS IS LOVE. / CHARM**	-	-
May 83. (7") (A 9825) **THE WICKED LADY. / (part 2)**	-	-

(above from the film soundtrack 'THE WICKED LADY; on 'WEA')

Jun 83. (lp/c) (TB/+MC 1) **THE FUGITIVE** — 50
– This is love / Man of spells / And the wheels keep turning / Say you'll never leave me / Thirty three's / By you / At the edge of night / Charm / Moving under. (re-iss. Oct86 lp/c; CHC/+MC 43) (cd-iss. 1988; TBCD 1)

Aug 83. (7") (BANKS 2) **AND THE WHEELS KEEP TURNING. / MAN OF SPELLS** — -
(12"+=) (BANKS 2/+12) – Sometime never.

(below with JIM DIAMOND and TOYAH on vocals)

Sep 85. (7"ep) (CBEP 415) **TONY BANKS** — -
– Red wing (instrumental) / You call this victory / Line of symmetry.

Oct 86. (7"; by FISH & TONY BANKS) (CB 426) **SHORT CUT TO NOWHERE. / SMILIN JACK CASEY** — -
(12"+=) (CB 426-12) – K.2.

Jul 87. (cd) (CASCD 1173) **SOUNDTRACKS** ('Quicksilver' // 'Lorca And The Outlaws') — -
– Short cut to nowhere / Smilin' Jack Casey / Quicksilver suite: Rebirth – Gypsy – Final chase // You call this victory / Lion of symmetry / Redwing suite: Redwing – Lorca – Kid and Detective Droid – Lift off – Death of Abby. (re-iss. Nov89 lp/c; CHC/+MC 82)

BANKSTATEMENT

TONY BANKS with friends, etc.

	Virgin	Atlantic
Jul 89. (7") (VS 1200) **THROWBACK. / THURSDAY THE 12th**	-	-

(12"+=/cd-s+=) (VS T/CD 1200) – This is love.

Aug 89. (lp/c/cd) (V/TCV/CDV 2600) **BANKSTATEMENT** — / -
– Throwback / I'll be waiting / Queen of darkness / That night / Raincloud / he border / Big man / A house needs a roof / The more I hide it. (cd+=) – Diamonds aren't so bad / Thursday the 12th.

Oct 89. (7") (VS 1208) **I'LL BE WAITING. / DIAMONDS AREN'T SO BAD** — -
(12"+=/cd-s+=) (VS T/CD 1208) – And the wheels keep turning.

TONY BANKS

solo, with guest vocals **ANDY TAYLOR, FISH, JAYNEY KLIMEK**

May 91. (7"/c-s) **I WANNA CHANGE THE SCORE. / HERO FOR AN HOUR** — -
(12"+=) – Big man (BANKSTATEMENT).
(cd-s++=) – The waters of Lethe.

Jun 91. (cd/c/lp) (CD/TC+/V 2658) **STILL** — -
– Red day on blue street / Angel face / The gift / Still it takes me by surprise / Hero for an hour / I wanna change the score / Water out of wine / Another murder of a day / Back to back / The final curtain.

MIKE RUTHERFORD

	Charisma	Passport
Jan 80. (7") (CB 353) **WORKING IN LINE. / COMPRESSION**	-	-
Feb 80. (lp) (CAS 1149) <9843> **SMALLCREEP'S DAY**	13	-

– Smallcreep's day: Between the tick and the tock – Working in line – After hours – Cats and rats in the neighbourhood – Smallcreep alone – Out into the daylight – At the end of the day / Moonshine / Time and time again / Romani / Every road / Overnight job. (re-iss. Oct86 lp/c; CHC/+MC 53) (cd-iss. Jun89; CASCD 1149)

| Mar 80. (7") **WORKING IN LINE. / MOONSHINE** | - | - |
| Jul 80. (7") (CB 364) **TIME AND TIME AGAIN. / AT THE END OF THE DAY** | - | - |

	W.E.A.	Atlantic
Aug 82. (7") (K 79331) <89976> **HALFWAY THERE. / A DAY TO REMEMBER**	-	Nov82
Aug 82. (7") <89981> **A DAY TO REMEMBER. / MAXINE**	-	-
Sep 82. (lp/c) (K/K4 99249) <80015> **ACTING VERY STRANGE**	23	-

– Acting very strange / A day to remember / Maxine / Halfway there / Who's fooling who / Couldn't get arrested / I don't wanna know / Hideaway.

| Oct 82. (7"/12") (RUTH 1/+T) **ACTING VERY STRANGE. / COULDN'T GET ARRESTED** | - | - |
| Jan 83. (7") (U 9967) **HIDEAWAY. / CALYPSO** | - | - |

—— MIKE then formed the pop outfit MIKE + THE MECHANICS (see book GREAT ROCK DISCOGRAPHY)

MIKE + THE MECHANICS

RUTHERFORD with **PAUL CARRACK** (b.22 Apr'51, Sheffield, England) – vocals, keyboards (ex-ACE, ex-SQUEEZE, ex-Solo artist) / **PAUL YOUNG** (b.17 Jun'47, Manchester, England) – vocals (ex-SAD CAFE) / **PETER VAN HOOKE** (b. 4 Jun'50, London) – drums / **ADRIAN LEE** (b. 9 Sep'47) – keyboards

	WEA	Atlantic
Oct 85. (lp/c/+C) (WX 49/+C) <81287> **MIKE + THE MECHANICS**	78	26

– Silent running (on dangerous ground) / All I need is a miracle / Par Avion / Hanging by a thread / I get the feeling / Take the reins / You are the one / A call to arms / Taken in. (cd-iss. Jul86; 252496-2)

| Nov 85. (7") <89488> **SILENT RUNNING (ON DANGEROUS GROUND). / PAR AVION** | - | 6 |
| Feb 86. (7") (U 8908) **SILENT RUNNING (ON DANGEROUS GROUND). / I GET THE FEELING** | 21 | - |

(12"+=) (U 8908T) – Too far gone.

| May 86. (7") (U 8765) <89450> **ALL I NEED IS A MIRACLE. / YOU ARE THE ONE** | 53 | 5 Mar86 |

(12"+=) (U 8908T) – A call to arms.

| Jun 86. (7") <89404> **TAKEN IN. / A CALL TO ARMS** | - | 32 |

—— added **TIM RENWICK** – guitar (ex-SUTHERLAND BROTHERS & QUIVER)

| Nov 88. (7") (U 7789) <88990> **NOBODY'S PERFECT. / NOBODY KNOWS** | - | 63 Oct88 |

(12"+=/3"cd-s+=) (U 7789 T/CD) – All I need is a miracle.

| Nov 88. (lp/c)(cd) (WX 203/+C)(256004-2) <81923> **THE LIVING YEARS** | 2 | 13 |

– Nobody's perfect / The living years / Seeing is believing / Nobody knows / Poor boy down / Blame / Don't / Black and blue / Beautiful day / Why me?.

| Feb 89. (7") (U 7717) <88964> **THE LIVING YEARS. / TOO MANY FRIENDS** | 2 | 1 Dec88 |

(12"+=/cd-s+=) (U 7717 T/CD) – I get the feeling (live).

| Apr 89. (7") (U 7602) **NOBODY KNOWS. / WHY ME?** | - | - |

(c-s+=/12"+=/cd-s+=) (U 7602 C/T/CD) – The living years / ('A'edit).

| Apr 89. (c-s) <88921> **SEEING IS BELIEVING / DON'T** | - | 62 |

	Virgin	Atlantic
Mar 91. (7"/c-s/12"/cd-s) (VS/+C/T/CD 1345) <87714> **WORD OF MOUTH. / LET'S PRETEND IT DIDN'T HAPPEN**	13	78

(cd-s+=) (VSCDG 1345) – Taken in (live).

| Apr 91. (cd/c/lp) (CD/TC+/V 2662) <82233> **WORD OF MOUTH** | 11 | - |

– Get up / Word of mouth / A time and place / Yesterday, today, tomorrow / The way you look at me / Everybody gets a second chance / Stop baby / My crime of passion / Let's pretend it didn't happen / Before (the next heartache falls).

| May 91. (7"/c-s) (VS/+C 1351) **A TIME AND A PLACE. / GET UP** | 58 | - |

(12"+=/cd-s+=) (VS T/CD 1351) – I think I've got the message.
(cd-s) (VSCDG 1351) – ('A'side) / I think I've got the message / My crime of passion (acoustic).

| Sep 91. (7"/c-s) **STOP BABY. / GET UP** | - | - |

(cd-s+=) – Before the heartache falls.

| Feb 92. (7"/c-s) (VS/+C 1396) **EVERYBODY GETS A SECOND CHANCE. / THE WAY YOU LOOK AT ME** | 56 | - |

(cd-s+=) (VSCD 1396) – At the end of the day (MIKE RUTHERFORD).

—— now without RENWICK, who was repl. by guests **B.A. ROBERTSON / GARY WALLIS / WIX / CLEM CLEMPSON**

| Feb 95. (7"/c-s) (VS/+C 1526) **OVER MY SHOULDER. / SOMETHING TO BELIEVE IN** | 12 | - |

(cd-s+=) (VSCDG 1526) – Always the last to know.
(cd-s+=) (VSCDX 1526) – Word of mouth / ('A'version).

| Mar 95. (cd/c) (CD/TC V 2772) **BEGGAR ON A BEACH OF GOLD** | 9 | - |

– Beggar on a beach of gold / Another cup of coffee / You've really got a hold on me / Mea culpa / Over my shoulder / Someone always hates someone / The ghost of sex and you / Web of lies / Plain & simple / Something to believe in / A house of many rooms / I believe (when I fall in love it will be forever) / Going going . . .home.

| Jun 95. (c-s/cd-s) (VSC/+DT 1535) **BEGGAR ON A BEACH OF GOLD / HELP ME / NOBODY TOLD ME** | 33 | - |

(cd-s) (VSCDX 1535) – ('A'side) / Boys at the front / Little boy / ('A'acoustic).

| Aug 95. (c-s) (VSC 1554) **ANOTHER CUP OF COFFEE / YOU NEVER CHANGE** | 65 | - |

(cd-s+=) (VSCDG 1554) – You don't know what love is.
(cd-s+=) (VSCDX 1554) – ('A'side) / Everyday hurts / How long.

| Feb 96. (c-s) (VSC 1576) **ALL I NEED IS A MIRACLE '96 (remix) / THE WAY YOU LOOK AT ME** | 27 | - |

(cd-s) (VSCDG 1576) – Don't / Over my shoulder (live).

Mar 96. (cd/c) *(CD/TC V2797)* **HITS** (compilation)   `3`
– All I need is a miracle '96 / Over my shoulder / Word of mouth / The living years / Another cup of coffee / Nobody's perfect / Silent running / Nobody knows / Get up / A time and place / Taken in / Everybody gets a second chance / A beggar on a beach of gold.

May 96. (c-s) *(VSC 1585)* **SILENT RUNNING / PLAIN & SIMPLE**
(cd-s+=) *(VSCDT 1585)* – Stop baby.

May 99. (c-s) *(VSC 1732)* **NOW THAT YOU'VE GONE / WORD OF MOUTH / BEGGAR ON A BEACH OF GOLD** (live)   `35`
(cd-s) *(VSCDT 1732)* – (first & third tracks) / Silent running (live).
(cd-s) *(VSCDX 1732)* – (first two tracks) / I believe when I fall in love it will be forever.

May 99. (cd/c) *(CDV/TCV 2885)* **MIKE & THE MECHANICS**   `14`
– Whenever I stop / Now that you've gone / Ordinary girl / All the light I need / What will you do / My little island / Open up / When I get over you / If only / Asking for the last time / Did you see me coming / Look across at dreamland.

Aug 99. (c-s/cd-s) *(TCV/CDV 1743)* **WHENEVER I STOP / NOW THAT YOU'VE GONE** (live)   `73`
(cd-s) *(VSCDX 1743)* – ('A'side) / Ordinary girl (unplugged) / My little island (live).

GENEVA

Formed: Aberdeen, Scotland ... late 1992 (briefly as SUNFISH) by DOUGLAS CASKIE, STEVEN DORA, STUART EVANS, KEITH GRAHAM and ex-journalist ANDREW MONTGOMERY (with The Sunday Post!). Eventually after only a few gigs, they were spotted by 'Nude' records (home to the likes of SUEDE), where they released their stunning debut, 'NO ONE SPEAKS', which bubbled under the Top 30 singles chart late '96. Around the same time, they secured a support slot on a BLUETONES' tour, exposing the angelic, high-pitched vox of MONTGOMERY, a hybrid of BILLY MacKENZIE, THOM YORKE, IAN ASTBURY or even, God forbid, an 80's style alternative rock version of MORTEN HARKET! During the first half of '97, the singles, 'INTO THE BLUE' and 'TRANQUILIZER', both went Top 30 and featured on their soaringly spiritual Top 20 album, 'FURTHER'. • **Songwriters:** Most by DORA and MONTGOMERY, a few by MONTGOMERY, GRAHAM and one with EVANS.

Album rating: FURTHER (*8)

ANDREW MONTGOMERY – vocals / **STEVEN DORA** – guitar / **STUART EVANS** – guitar / **KEITH GRAHAM** – bass / **DOUGLAS CASKIE** – drums

	Nude	Sony
Oct 96. (7"/c-s) *(NUD 22 S/MC)* **NO ONE SPEAKS. / WHAT YOUR SHRINK SAYS**	32	–

(cd-s) *(NUD 22CD)* – ('A'side) / Closer to the stars / Keep the light on.

| Jan 97. (7"/c-s) *(NUD 25 S/MC)* *<78594>* **INTO THE BLUE. / AT THE CORE** | 26 | Jun97 |

(cd-s) *(NUD 25CD)* – ('A'side) / Riverwatching / Land's End.

| May 97. (7") *(NUD 28S)* **TRANQUILLIZER. / DRIFTWOOD** | 24 | – |

(cd-s) *(NUD 28CD1)* – ('A'side) / Dead give away / Strung out on you.
(cd-s) *(NUD 28CD2)* – ('A'side) / Michaelmas / Compulsive love disorder.

| Jun 97. (cd/c/lp) *(NUDE 7 CD/MC/LP)* *<68156>* **FURTHER** | 20 | Aug97 |

– Temporary wings / Into the blue / The god of sleep / Best regrets / Tranquillizer / Further / No one speaks / Worry beads / Fall apart button / Wearing off / Nature's whore / In the years remaining.

| Aug 97. (7") *(NUD 31S)* **BEST REGRETS. / SELFBELIEF** | 38 | – |

(cd-s) *(NUD 31CD1)* – ('A'side) / Feel the joy / Raymond Chandler.
(cd-s) *(NUD 31CD2)* – ('A'side) / Last orders / The god of sleep (demo).

| Nov 99. (7") *(NUD 46S)* **DOLLARS IN THE HEAVENS. / ECHO CHAMBER** | 59 | – |

(cd-s) *(NUD 46CD1)* – ('A'side) / Faintest tremor in the weakest heart / She's so familiar.
(cd-s) *(NUD 46CD2)* – ('A'side) / When you close your eyes / Museum mile (Dave Fridmann mix).

–––– a new album, 'WEATHER UNDERGROUND', issued in Mar'2000

GENIUS / GZA (see under ⇒ WU-TANG CLAN)

GENTLE GIANT

Formed: Portsmouth, England ... 1966 as SIMON DUPREE & THE BIG SOUND, by SHULMAN brothers DEREK, RAY and PHIL. Early in '67, they had a UK Top 50 hit with 'I SEE THE LIGHT'. By the end of the year, 'KITES' gave them a Top 10 smash, although they soon opted out of the psychedelic pop market in favour of the burgeoning prog-rock scene. Late in 1969, the three brothers, with three new recruits (KERRY MINEAR, GARY GREEN and MARTIN SMITH), re-launched themselves as the more experimental GENTLE GIANT. A year later, they appeared on the pivotal 'Vertigo' label, their eponymous debut album regaining support from stalwart Radio One DJ, ALAN 'Fluff' FREEMAN. Their fourth album, 'OCTOPUS' (1972), although not a major success in Britain, hit the Top 200 in North America. They might have built upon this Stateside interest, but for Columbia's decision not to release their next project, 'IN A GLASS HOUSE'. However, in 1974, they finally cracked the Top 100 with their much-improved, 'THE POWER AND GLORY'. Signing a new deal in Britain with 'Chrysalis' records, their seventh album, 'FREE HAND', again only found a paying audience across the water. However, it did contain more impressive vocal gymnastics, much in evidence on the opening two tracks, 'JUST THE SAME' and 'ON REFLECTION'. The band was subsequently crushed under the jack-booted heels of punk rock, although they did soldier on until 1980. DEREK moved

to New York, becoming an A&R executive and going on to sign hard-rock acts, CINDERELLA and KINGDOM COME. • **Songwriters:** MINNEAR and the SHULMANS collaborated on most recordings. SIMON DUPREE covered; DAY TIME, NIGHT TIME (Mike Hugg of Manfred Mann). • **Trivia:** MINNEAR had graduated from the Royal Academy Of Music in the late 60's.

Album rating: Simon Dupree & The Big Sound: WITHOUT RESERVATIONS (*5) / Gentle Giant: GENTLE GIANT (*6) / ACQUIRING THE TASTE (*6) / THREE FRIENDS (*6) / OCTOPUS (*5) / IN A GLASS HOUSE (*5) / THE POWER AND THE GLORY (*5) / FREE HAND (*6) / GIANT STEPS ... THE FIRST FIVE YEARS compilation (*7) / INTERVIEW (*5) / THE OFFICIAL "LIVE" GENTLE GIANT – PLAYING THE FOOL (*6) / THE MISSING PIECE (*4) / GIANT FOR A DAY (*4) / CIVILIAN (*4)

SIMON DUPREE & THE BIG SOUND

DEREK SHULMAN (b. 2 Feb'47, Glasgow, Scotland) – vocals / **RAY SCHULMAN** (b. 8 Dec'49, Portsmouth, England) – lead guitar / **PHIL SCHULMAN** (b.27 Aug'37, Glasgow) – saxophone, trumpet / **ERIC HINE** – keyboards / **PETE O'FLAHERTY** – bass / **TONY RANSLEY** – drums

	Parlophone	Tower
Dec 66. (7") *(R 5542)* **I SEE THE LIGHT. / IT IS FINISHED**	45	–
Feb 67. (7") *(R 5574)* *<347>* **RESERVATIONS. / YOU NEED A MAN**		
May 67. (7") *(R 5594)* *<427>* **DAY TIME, NIGHT TIME. / I'VE SEEN IT ALL BEFORE**		
Aug 67. (lp; mono/stereo) *(PCM/PCS 7029)* *<T 5097>* **WITHOUT RESERVATIONS**	39	

– Medley: Sixty minutes of your love – A lot of love / Love / Get off my Bach / There's a little playhouse / Day time, night time / I see the light / What is soul / Teacher, teacher / Amen / Who cares / Reservations. (re-dist.1969; same)

Oct 67. (7") *(R 5646)* **KITES. / LIKE THE SUN LIKE THE FIRE**	9	
Mar 68. (7") *(R 5670)* **FOR WHOM THE BELL TOLLS. / SLEEP**	43	
May 68. (7") *(R 5697)* **PART OF MY PAST. / THIS STORY NEVER ENDS**		
Sep 68. (7") *(R 5727)* **THINKING ABOUT MY LIFE. / VELVET AND LACE**		
Nov 68. (7"; as The MOLES) *(R 5743)* **WE ARE THE MOLES (part 2) / (part 2)**		–
Feb 69. (7") *(R 5757)* **BROKEN HEARTED PIRATES. / SHE GAVE ME THE SUN**		

–––– **GERRY KENWORTHY** – keyboards repl. HINE

| Nov 69. (7") *(R 5816)* **THE EAGLE FLIES TONIGHT. / GIVE IT ALL BACK** | | |

–––– Split late '69. The SHULMAN's formed GENTLE GIANT while the others left the business.

– compilations etc. –

| Nov 78. (7"ep) *E.M.I.; (EMI 2893)* **SIMON DUPREE & THE BIG SOUND** | | – |

– Kites / For whom the bells toll / Reservations / I see the light.

| Mar 82. (lp/c) *See For Miles; (CM/+K 109)* **AMEN** | | – |

– Kites / Like the sun like the fire / Sleep / For whom the bells toll / Broken hearted pirates / 60 Minutes of your love / A lot of love / Love / Get off my Bach / There's a little picture playhouse / Day time, night time / I see the light / What is soul / Amen / Who cares / She gave me the sun / Thinking about my life / I've seen it all before / You need a man / Reservations. (re-iss. Dec86 as 'KITES'; same) (cd-iss. May93 & May97 as 'KITES' on 'See For Miles'; SEECD 368)

| Mar 87. (7") *Old Gold; (OG 9655)* **KITES. / (b-side by other artist)** | | – |

GENTLE GIANT

DEREK SHULMAN – vocals, bass, saxophone / **RAY SHULMAN** – guitar, bass, violin, keyboards, drums / **PHIL SHULMAN** – saxophone, trumpet / **KERRY MINNEAR** (b.2 Apr'48, Salisbury, England) – keyboards, vocals (ex-RUST) / **GARY GREEN** (b.20 Nov'50, Stroud Green, England) – guitar, vocals / **MARTIN SMITH** – drums (ex-MOJOS)

	Vertigo	Vertigo
Nov 70. (lp) *(6360 020)* **GENTLE GIANT**		–

– Giant / Funny ways / Alucard / Isn't it quiet and cold / Nothing at all / Why not? / The Queen. (cd-iss. Aug89 on 'Line'; LICD 900722;) (cd re-iss. Nov94 on 'Repertoire';) (cd re-iss. Feb97 on 'Mercury'; 842624-2)

| Aug 71. (lp) *(6360 041)* *<1005>* **ACQUIRING THE TASTE** | | |

– Pantagruel's nativity / Edge of twilight / The house, the street, the room / Acquiring the taste / Wreck / The Moon is down / Black cat / Plain truth. (cd-iss. Oct89 on 'Line'; LICD 900726) (cd re-iss. Aug90; 842917-2) (cd re-iss. Feb97 on 'Mercury'; 842917-2)

–––– **MALCOLM MORTIMER** – drums repl. MARTIN

	Vertigo	Columbia
Jul 72. (lp) *(6360 070)* *<31649>* **THREE FRIENDS**		

– (prologue) / Schooldays / Working all day / Peel the paint / Mister Class and quality? / Three friends. (cd-iss. Oct89 on 'Line'; LICD 900730)

–––– **JOHN WEATHERS** (b.Wales) – drums (ex-GRAHAM BOND, ex-EYES OF BLUE, ex-ANCIENT GREASE, ex-PETE BROWN, etc.) repl. MALCOLM

| Dec 72. (lp) *(6360 080)* *<32022>* **OCTOPUS** | | |

– The advent of Panurge / Raconteur troubadour / A cry for everyone / Knots / The boys in the band / Dog's life / Think of me with kindness / River. (cd-iss. Oct89 on 'Line'; LICD 900736) (cd re-iss. Nov94 on 'Repertoire';) (cd re-iss. Feb97 on 'Mercury'; 842694-2)

–––– now quintet of **DEREK, RAY, KERRY, GARY + JOHN** when PHIL left.

	W.W.A.	Capitol
Dec 73. (lp) *(WWA 002)* **IN A GLASS HOUSE**		

– The runaway / An inmate's lullaby / Way of life / A reunion / Experience / In a glass house / Index. (cd-iss. Dec92 on 'Road Goes On Forever'; RGFCD 1001) (cd re-iss. Jul94 on 'Terrapin Truckin'; TRUCKCD 1)

| Jan 74. (7") *(WWP 1001)* **IN A GLASS HOUSE. / AN INMATE'S LULLABY** | | – |
| Oct 74. (lp) *(WWA 010)* *<11337>* **THE POWER AND THE GLORY** | | 78 |

– Proclamation / So sincere / Aspirations / Playing the game / Cogs in cogs / No god's a man / The face / Valedictory. (cd-iss. Dec92 on 'Road Goes On Forever'; RGFCD 1002)

			Chrysalis	Capitol
Nov 74.	(7") (WWS 017) **THE POWER AND THE GLORY. / PLAYING THE GAME**		☐	–

Aug 75. (lp/c) (CHR/ZCHR 1093) <11428> **FREE HAND**   ☐   48
– Just the same / On reflection / Free hand / Time to kill / His last voyage / Talybont / Mobile. (cd-iss. Aug93 on 'Road Goes On Forever'; RGFCD 1004) (cd-iss. Jul94 on 'Terrapin Truckin'; TRUCKCD 4)

Apr 76. (lp/c) (CHR/ZCHR 1115) <11532> **INTERVIEW**   ☐   –
– Interview / Give it back / Design / Another show / Empty city / Timing / I lost my head. (cd-iss. Mar93 on 'Road Goes On Forever'; RGFCD 1005) (cd-iss. Jul94 on 'Terrapin Truckin'; TRUCKCD 5) (cd re-iss. Oct95 on 'One Way';)

Jan 77. (d-lp/d-c) (CTY/ZCTY 1133) <11592> **PLAYING THE FOOL – LIVE (live)**   ☐   89
– Just the same / Proclamation / On reflection / Excerpts from Octopus (Boys in the band, etc) / Funny ways / In a glass house / So sincere / Free hand / Sweet Georgia Brown (breakdown in Brussels) / Peel the paint / I lost my head. (re-iss. May89 on 'Essential' d-lp/cd; ESS LP/CD 006) (cd re-iss. Dec94 on 'Terrapin Truckin'; TRUCKCD 9)

Aug 77. (lp/c) (CHR/ZCHR 1152) <11696> **THE MISSING PIECE**   ☐   81
– Two weeks in Spain / I'm turning around / Betcha thought we couldn't do it / Who do you think you are? / Mountain time / As old as you're young / Memories of old days / Winning / For nobody. (cd re-iss. Aug93 on 'Road Goes On Forever'; RGFCD 1006) (cd-iss. Jul94 on 'Terrapin Truckin'; TRUCKCD 6)

Aug 77. (7") (CHS 2160) **I'M TURNING AROUND. / JUST THE SAME (live)**   ☐   –

Sep 77. (7") <4484> **I'M TURNING AROUND. / COGS IN COGS**   –   ☐

Oct 77. (7") (CHS 2181) **TWO WEEKS IN SPAIN. / FREE HAND**   ☐   –

Sep 78. (7") (CHS 2245) **THANK YOU. / SPOOKY BOOGIE**   ☐   –

Sep 78. (lp/c) (CHR/ZCHR 1186) <11813> **GIANT FOR A DAY**   ☐   –
– Word from the wise / Thank you / Giant for a day / Spooky boogie / Take me / Little brown bag / Friends / No stranger / It's only goodbye / Rock climber. (cd-iss. Aug93 on 'Road Goes On Forever'; RGFCD 7) (cd-iss. Jul94 on 'Terrapin Truckin'; TRUCKCD 7)

Jan 79. (7") (CHS 2270) **WORD FROM THE WISE. / NO STRANGER**   ☐   –

Jan 79. (7") <4652> **WORD FROM THE WISE. / SPOOKY BOOGIE**   –   ☐

| | | Chrysalis | Columbia |

Aug 80. (lp/c) (CHR/ZCHR 1285) **CIVILIAN**
– Convenience / All through the night / Shadows on the street / Number one / Underground / I'm a camera / Inside out / It's not imagination. (cd-iss. Jul94 on 'Terrapin Truckin'; TRUCKCD 8)

—— Split 1980. RAY SHULMAN went into production. WEATHERS joined MAN.

– compilations, others, etc. –

on 'Vertigo' unless otherwise mentioned

Nov 75. (d-lp) (6641 334) **GIANT STEPS . . . (THE FIRST FIVE YEARS) 1970-75**   ☐   –
– Giant / Alucard / Nothing at all / Plain truth / Prologue / A cry for everyone / Why not / Peel the paint / Mister Class and quality? / River / The face / The runaway / Power and the glory / Playing the game / In a glass house.

Oct 77. (lp) (6641 629) **PRETENTIOUS (FOR THE SAKE OF IT)**   ☐   –

Aug 81. (lp/c) (6381/7215 045) **GREATEST HITS**   ☐   – Dutch

Apr 94. (cd) Terrapin Truckin'; (TRUCKCD 1010) **THE LAST TIME (LIVE 1980)**   ☐   –

Dec 94. (cd) Windsong; (WINCD 066) **IN CONCERT (live)**   ☐   –

Jul 96. (cd) Strange Fruit; (BOJCD 018) **LIVE IN CONCERT (live)**   ☐   –

Sep 96. (cd) Red Steel; (RMCCD 0205) **LAST STEPS (live 1980)**   ☐   –

GENTLE WAVES (see under ⇒ BELLE & SEBASTIAN)

Lowell GEORGE (see under ⇒ LITTLE FEAT)

GEORGIA SATELLITES (dig out; 4th edition)

GERMS (dig out; Great Alt & Indie . . .)

Lisa GERRARD (see under ⇒ DEAD CAN DANCE)

GERRY & THE PACEMAKERS

Formed: Liverpool, England . . . 1959 as The MARS BARS by GERRY MARSDEN, his brother FREDDIE, LES CHADWICK and ARTHUR MACK. Following objections from the confectionary manufacturers, GERRY and Co rather sensibly renamed themselves as they began building up a fanbase at famous Merseyside haunts like The Cavern. MACK was replaced by LES MAGUIRE prior to a stint in Hamburg; there they were spotted by BEATLES manager, Brian Epstein who in turn, secured them a contract with 'Columbia'. Incredibly, perhaps, the quartet were initially more successful than Epstein's other Merseybeat proteges, The BEATLES (with whom they also shared producer George Martin), scoring three UK No.1 hits in a row with their first three single releases. 'HOW DO YOU DO IT?' kicked off their career in Spring '63, a Mitch Murray-penned tune originally intended for The BEATLES. Murray also penned 'I LIKE IT', another moronically cheery ditty that scaled the chart a few months later. Best of the three was 'YOU'LL NEVER WALK ALONE', a cover of the Rogers & Hammerstein standard that at least had some substance to it (the track was later adopted as a terrace anthem by Liverpool football fans). By the close of 1963, GERRY & THE PACEMAKERS had set an unlikely chart record that stood for 21 years before it was equalled by another – decidedly more risque – Merseyside outfit, FRANKIE GOES TO

HOLLYWOOD (HOLLY JOHNSON's mob actually cut 'FERRY ACROSS THE MERSEY' as a B-side to the infamous 'Relax'). MARSDEN took over on the songwriting front with early 64's 'I'M THE ONE' (No.2) while the group joined The BEATLES, The ROLLING STONES, The ANIMALS, etc., in the frontline of the British Invasion when 'DON'T LET THE SUN CATCH YOU CRYING' hit the US Top 5 a few months later. The end of that vintage year saw the release of GERRY & THE PACEMAKERS' most enduring song, 'FERRY ACROSS THE MERSEY', also the title of 'A Hard Day's Night'-style film and soundtrack aired in early '65. While the band's string of UK singles became American hits all over again, their sound was becoming outmoded in the rapidly evolving British music scene. A final UK hit, 'WALK HAND IN HAND' made the Top 30 in late '65 and they carried on for a further year before disbanding in October '66. MARSDEN cut a number of low-key solo singles over the next decade although he was more well known for his work in children's TV. He re-formed the 'PACEMAKERS in the mid-70's for a USA revival tour, the group reuniting sporadically thereafter for dates on the golden oldie circuit. 1985 saw GERRY back at the top of the UK singles chart when he sang on a charity re-make of 'YOU'LL NEVER WALK ALONE', the track credited to The CROWD with proceeds going towards the Bradford FC Disaster Fund (after a tragic fire). Another 'PACEMAKERS nugget, 'FERRY ACROSS THE MERSEY', was dusted down for No.1 reinterpretation in 1989 courtesy of STOCK, AITKEN & WATERMAN together with The CHRISTIANS, PAUL McCARTNEY, GERRY himself, etc.

Best CD compilation: BEST OF GERRY & THE PACEMAKERS: THE DEFINITIVE COLLECTION (*7)

GERRY MARSDEN (b.24 Sep'42) – vocals, lead guitar / **LES CHADWICK** (b.JOHN LESLIE CHADWICK, 11 May'43) – bass / **FREDDIE MARSDEN** (b.23 Oct'40) – drums / **LES MAGUIRE** (b.27 Dec'41, Wallasey, England) – piano, saxophone (ex-UNDERTAKERS) repl. ARTHUR MACK

		Columbia	Laurie
Mar 63.	(7") (DB 4987) <3162> **HOW DO YOU DO IT? / AWAY FROM YOU**	1	☐ Apr63
May 63.	(7") (DB 7041) <3196> **I LIKE IT. / IT'S HAPPENED TO ME**	1	☐ Sep63
Oct 63.	(7") (DB 7126) <3218> **YOU'LL NEVER WALK ALONE. / IT'S ALRIGHT**	1	☐ Dec63
Oct 63.	(lp) (33SX 1546) **HOW DO YOU LIKE IT?**	2	–

– A shot of rhythm and blues / Jambalaya / Where have you been / Here's hoping / Pretend / Maybellene / You'll never walk alone / The wrong yo yo / You're the reason / Chills / You can't fool me / Don't you ever / Summertime / Slow down. (re-iss. 1967 as 'YOU'LL NEVER WALK ALONE' on 'Music For Pleasure'; MPF 1153) (re-iss. Sep89 on 'Beat Goes On'; BGOLP 57) (cd-iss. Aug94 on 'Repertoire';)

Jan 64.	(7") (DB 7189) <3233> **I'M THE ONE / YOU'VE GOT WHAT I LIKE**	2	82 Feb64
Apr 64.	(7") (DB 7268) **DON'T LET THE SUN CATCH YOU CRYING. / SHOW ME THAT YOU CARE**	6	–
May 64.	(7") <3251> **DON'T LET THE SUN CATCH YOU CRYING. / AWAY FROM YOU**	–	4
Jul 64.	(lp) <2024> **DON'T LET THE SUN CATCH YOU CRYING**	–	29

– Don't let the sun catch you crying / I'm the one / Away from you / Jambalaya / Maybellene / You'll never walk alone / How do you do it / You're the reason / Don't you ever / Summertime / Slow down / Show me that you care.

Jul 64.	(7") <3261> **HOW DO YOU DO IT? / YOU'LL NEVER WALK ALONE**	–	9
Aug 64.	(7") (DB 7353) **IT'S GONNA BE ALRIGHT. / IT'S JUST BECAUSE**	24	–
Oct 64.	(7") <3271> **I LIKE IT. / JAMBALAYA**	–	17
Nov 64.	(lp) <2027> **GERRY & THE PACEMAKERS' SECOND ALBUM**	–	–

– I like it / A shot of rhythm and blues / Where have you been / Here's hoping / Pretend / The wrong yo-yo / Chills / You can't fool me / It happened to me / It's all right / Slow down / Jambalaya.

Dec 64.	(7") (7437) **FERRY CROSS THE MERSEY. / YOU YOU YOU**	8	–
Dec 64.	(7") <3279> **I'LL BE THERE. / YOU YOU YOU**	–	14
Jan 65.	(lp) (33SX 1693) <6387> **FERRY CROSS THE MERSEY (live Film Soundtrack on 'United Artists' US)**	19	13 Feb65

– How do you do it? / Ferry cross the Mersey / It's still rock & roll to me / I'm the one / Unchained melody / Roll over Beethoven / Imagine / Running man / Just the way you are / (3 songs not by them). (re-iss. Mar88 on 'Beat Goes On'; BGOLP 10) (cd-iss. Aug94 on 'Repertoire';)

| Jan 65. | (7") <3284> **FERRY CROSS THE MERSEY. / PRETEND** | – | 6 |
| Feb 65. | (lp) <2030> **I'LL BE THERE!** | – | – |

– I'll be there / What'd I say / Rip it up / You win again / You you you / Now I'm alone / My babe / Reelin' and rockin' / I count the tears / Whole lotta shakin' goin' on / It'll be me / Skinny Minnie.

Mar 65.	(7") (DB 7504) **I'LL BE THERE. / BABY YOU'RE SO GOOD TO ME**	15	–
Apr 65.	(7") <3293> **IT'S GONNA BE ALRIGHT. / SKINNY MINNIE**	–	23
May 65.	(lp) <2031> **GERRY AND THE PACEMAKERS' GREATEST HITS** (compilation)	–	44
Aug 65.	(7") <3313> **GIVE ALL YOUR LOVE TO ME. / YOU'RE THE REASON**	–	68
Nov 65.	(7") (DB 7738) **WALK HAND IN HAND. / DREAMS**	29	–
Feb 66.	(7") (DB 7835) <3337> **LA LA LA. / WITHOUT YOU**	–	90
May 66.	(7") <3370> **LOOKING FOR MY LIFE. / BRIGHT GREEN PLEASURE MACHINE**	–	–
Sep 66.	(7") (DB 8044) <3354> **GIRL ON A SWING. / FOOL TO MYSELF**	☐	28

—— Disbanded Oct'66. MARSDEN went solo in 1967 (see GREAT ROCK DISCOG.)

GERRY MARSDEN

		C.B.S.	Columbia
Jun 67.	(7") (2784) **PLEASE LET THEM BE. / I'M NOT BLUE**	☐	☐
1967.	(7") (2946) **GILBERT GREEN. / WHAT MAKES ME LOVE YOU**	☐	☐

—— In 1968, GERRY landed leading role in stage play 'Charlie Girl'.

Jun 68. (7"; by GERRY MARSDEN & DEREK NIMMO) (3575) **LIVERPOOL. / CHARLIE GIRL**

	NEMS	not iss.
	□	-

1968. (7") (56-3831) **IN THE YEAR OF APRIL. / EVERY DAY**

May 69. (7") (56-4229) **EVERY LITTLE MINUTE. / IN DAYS OF OLD**

	Decca	not iss.
	□	-

May 71. (7") (F 13172) **I'VE GOT MY UKELELE. / WHAT A DAY**

	Phoenix	not iss.
	□	-

1972. (7") (SNIX 129) **AMOCREDO. / ('A'version)**

GERRY MARSDEN & THE PACEMAKERS

(with new line-up)

Apr 74. (7") D.J.M.; (DJS 298) **REMEMBER (THE DAYS OF ROCK AND ROLL). / THERE'S STILL TIME**

	□	-

GERRY MARSDEN

went solo again.

		D.J.M.	not iss.

Aug 74. (7") (DJS 10314) **THEY DON'T MAKE DAYS LIKE THAT. / CAN'T YOU HEAR THE SONG**

Apr 75. (7") (DJS 10362) **YOUR SONG. / DAYS I SPENT WITH YOU**

Sep 76. (7") (DJS 10708) **MY HOMETOWN. / LOVELY LADY**

—— GERRY semi-retired from biz, until his vocal contribution May '85 on Disaster Fund (Bradford F.C. fire) No.1 re-indition of YOU'LL NEVER WALK ALONE by 'The CROWD'. The band are still regulars on the cabaret circuit.

– compilations, etc. –

on 'Columbia' unless stated otherwise

Jun 63.	(7"ep) (SEG 8257) **HOW DO YOU DO IT?**		34	-
Dec 63.	(7"ep) (SEG 8295) **YOU'LL NEVER WALK ALONE**			-
Feb 64.	(7"ep) (SEG 8311) **I'M THE ONE**			-
May 64.	(7"ep) (SEG 8346) **DON'T LET THE SUN CATCH YOU CRYING**			-
Dec 64.	(7"ep) (SEG 8367) **IT'S GONNA BE ALRIGHT**			-
Feb 65.	(7"ep) (SEG 8388) **GERRY IN CALIFORNIA (live)**			-
Mar 65.	(7"ep) (SEG 8397) **HITS FROM 'FERRY ACROSS THE MERSEY**			-
Jun 65.	(7"ep) (SEG 8426) **RIP IT UP**			-
Nov 73.	(7"m) E.M.I.; (EMI 2086) **YOU'LL NEVER WALK ALONE. / HOW DO YOU DO IT? / I LIKE IT**			-
Oct 77.	(lp/c) E.M.I.; (NUT/TC-NUT 10) **THE BEST OF GERRY & THE PACEMAKERS**			-
Nov 77.	(7"m) E.M.I.; (EMI 2689) **I LIKE IT. / HOW DO YOU DO IT? / CHILLS**			-
Jun 78.	(7") E.M.I.; (EMI 2814) **FERRY CROSS THE MERSEY. / DON'T LET THE SUN CATCH YOU CRYING**			-
1982.	(7") Creole; (CR 195) **FERRY CROSS THE MERSEY. / YOU'LL NEVER WALK ALONE**			-
Apr 82.	(7") Deb; (DEB 105) **UNCHAINED MELODY. / GIRL WHAT YOU DOIN'**			-
1983.	(7") Deb; (DEB 107) **OH MY LOVE. / IF**			-
Oct 83.	(7") Old Gold; (OG 9373) **FERRY CROSS THE MERSEY. / DON'T LET THE SUN CATCH YOU CRYING**			-
Oct 83.	(7") Old Gold; (OG 9377) **YOU'LL NEVER WALK ALONE. / HOW DO YOU DO IT?**			-
Dec 83.	(lp/c) Deb; (DEB/+C 1101) **THE 20 YEAR ANNIVERSARY ALBUM**			-
May 84.	(7") EMI Gold; (G45 25) **I LIKE IT. / HOW DO YOU DO IT?**			-
May 84.	(lp/c) Music For Pleasure; (MFP 41-5654-1/-4) **THE VERY BEST OF GERRY & THE PACEMAKERS** (cd-iss. Mar93; CDMFP 5654)			-
Jun 84.	(7"m) S.M.P.; (SKM 8) **FERRY CROSS THE MERSEY. / HOW DO YOU DO IT? / I'M THE ONE**			-
Jan 86.	(lp/c) E.M.I.; (EMS/TC-EMS 1125) **HIT SINGLES ALBUM** (cd-iss. May87 as 'THE SINGLES PLUS'; CDP 746 602-2)			-
Apr 86.	(lp/c) Showcase; (SH LP/TC 102) **FERRY CROSS THE MERSEY** (different)			-
Jul 86.	(c) Timeless Treasures; (807) **GERRY AND THE PACEMAKERS**			-
Jun 87.	(lp/c) See For Miles; (SEE/+K 95) **THE EP COLLECTION** (cd-iss. Sep89 & May95; SEECD 95)			-
Jun 90.	(cd/c/lp) Castle; (CCS CD/MC/LP 247) **THE COLLECTION**			-
Jul 91.	(cd) The Collection; (ORO 144) **FERRY CROSS THE MERSEY**			-
Jun 92.	(cd/c) E.M.I.; (CD/TC EMS 1443) **THE BEST OF THE EMI YEARS**			-

– How do you do it / Maybellene / I like it / Chills / Pretend / Jambalaya / You're the reason / Hello little girl / You'll never walk alone / A shot of rhythm and blues / Slow down / It's all right / I'm the one / Don't let the sun catch you crying / You've got what I like / It's just because / You you you / It's gonna be all right / Ferry cross the Mersey / I'll wait for you / Hallelujah I love her so / Reelin' & rockin' / Why oh why / Baby you're so good to me / Walk hand in hand / Dreams / Give all your love to me / I'll be there / La la la / Fool to myself / Girl on a swing.

Jun 92.	(cd-s) Old Gold; (OG 6169) **HOW DO YOU DO IT? / I LIKE IT / I'M THE ONE**		-
Jul 92.	(cd-s) Old Gold; (OG 6172) **YOU'LL NEVER WALK ALONE / FERRY CROSS THE MERSEY / DON'T LET THE SUN CATCH YOU CRYING**		-
Jan 93.	(cd) Tring; (GRF 191) **GERRY & THE PACEMAKERS**		-
May 93.	(cd/c) Royal Collection; (RC 83136) **THE BEST OF GERRY & THE PACEMAKERS** (re-iss. Apr96 on 'Pulse' cd/c; PLS CD/MC 129)		-
Dec 94.	(cd/c) D Sharp; (DSH CD/MC 7011) **50 NON STOP PARTY HITS**		-
Feb 95.	(cd) B.A.M.; (KLMCD 045) **PEARLS OF THE PAST**		-

Nov 95.	(cd-s) Old Gold; (12623 6329-2) **YOU'LL NEVER WALK ALONE. / FERRY 'CROSS THE MERSEY**	□	-
Jun 96.	(cd) Music-De-Luxe; (MSCD 033) **YOU'LL NEVER WALK ALONE**	□	-

(Per) GESSLE (see under ⇒ ROXETTE)

GETO BOYS / SCARFACE (dig out; 4th edition)

G-FORCE (see under ⇒ MOORE, Gary)

GHOSTFACE KILLAH (see under ⇒ WU-TANG CLAN)

GIANT SAND (dig out; Great Alt & Indie . . .)

GIGOLO AUNTS (dig out; Great Alt & Indie . . .)

GILES, GILES & FRIPP (see under ⇒ KING CRIMSON)

GILLAN (dig out; Great Metal . . .)

David GILMOUR (see under ⇒ PINK FLOYD)

GIN BLOSSOMS
(dig out; 4th edition or Great Alt & Indie . . .)

GIRLS AT OUR BEST (dig out; Great Alt & Indie . . .)

GIRLSCHOOL (dig out; Great Metal . . .)

GLASS ONION (see under ⇒ TRAVIS)

Gary GLITTER

Born: PAUL GADD, 8 May '40, Banbury, Oxfordshire, England. His musical career was launched in the late 50's, when film producer and manager, Robert Hartford Davis, secured a deal with 'Decca'. His first 45, 'ALONE IN THE NIGHT' (under the moniker of PAUL RAVEN) flopped, although he found success in the Middle East with a follow-up, 'WALK ON BOY'. After another unlucky miss in '61, the singer all but disappeared from studio sessions, until 1968, that is, when MIKE LEANDER invited him to sing one of his songs, 'MUSICAL MAN', as PAUL MONDAY. More singles followed, mostly under pseudonyms before he joined the cast of 'JESUS CHRIST SUPERSTAR' at the turn of the decade. In 1972, he re-surfaced as GARY GLITTER, and smashed the charts for the first time with 'ROCK'N'ROLL PART 2'. This footstompin', glam-rock phenomenon brightened up the pop music world, while summer '73's No.1 'I'M THE LEADER OF THE GANG (I AM)' upped the terrace-chant ante to a lip-curlingly feverish degree. Though he was arguably one of the more ridiculous looking glam icons (platform heels, 50's rock'n'roll style hairdo and middle age spread), GLITTER attracted a rabid following, its more hardcore element still selling out his gigs twenty years on. Commercially, however, GLITTER-mania faded with the demise of glam. Nevertheless, the star-spangled gent returned to the UK Top 10 in 1984 with the inimitable Yuletide fave, 'ANOTHER ROCK'N'ROLL CHRISTMAS', while echoes of the pioneering GLITTER band sound could be heard in acts like ADAM & THE ANTS and BOW WOW WOW. Four years later, he was back at No.1 again (kind of), when he featured on The TIMELORDS (aka KLF) No.1 hit, 'Doctorin' The Tardis', unashamedly based on GLITTER's 'ROCK'N'ROLL PART 2'. Though he remains something of a minor celebrity, fans were rocked late in 1997 by allegations that child porn had been found in his computer; he had given it to PC World to be repaired. GLITTER was subsequently charged with several sexual offences against a girl and was given a jail sentence for the pornography part. Released from prison but with his reputation in tatters (his seedy private life having been read in every tabloid), GARY GLITTER, or indeed the bald PAUL GADD, will find it hard to return to showbusiness – in this country at least. • **Songwriters:** GLITTER penned, except many covers including; TOWER OF STRENGTH (Bacharach-Hilliard) / HERE COMES THE SUN (Beatles) / STAND (Sly & The Family Stone) / PAPA OOM MOW MOW (Rivingtons) / • **Trivia:** His GLITTER BAND (without him), also scored a run of seven consecutive UK hits, including their biggest early 1975 No.2 'GOODBYE MY LOVE'.

Best CD compilation: MANY HAPPY RETURNS – GARY GLITTER THE HITS (*7)

PAUL RAVEN

			Decca	not iss.
Jan 60.	(7") (F 11205) **ALONE IN THE NIGHT. / TOO PROUD**		□	-

			Parlophone	not iss.
Aug 61.	(7") (R 4812) **WALK ON BOY. / ALL GROWN UP**		□	-
Nov 61.	(7") (R 4842) **TOWER OF STRENGTH. / LIVIN' THE BLUES**		□	-

—— (Unluckily FRANKIE VAUGHAN'S version of above hits No.1, and he was dropped by label. He briefly joined MIKE LEANDER ORCHESTRA, but soon became vocalist for (soon-to-be-called) The BOSTONS. The next half-decade saw them tour Germany, etc, but with no record contract. In 1968, through LEANDER, he signed to . . .

	M.C.A.	not iss.
Jun 68. (7"; some as PAUL MONDAY) *(MU 1024)* **MUSICAL MAN.** / **WAIT FOR ME**	☐	-
Aug 68. (7") *(MU 1035)* **SOUL THING.** / **WE'LL GO WHERE THE WORLD CAN'T FIND US**	☐	-
Sep 69. (7"; as RUBBER BUCKET) *(MK 5006)* **WE ARE LIVING IN ONE PLACE.** / **TAKE ME AWAY**	☐	-
Oct 69. (7"; as PAUL MONDAY) *(MK 5008)* **HERE COMES THE SUN.** / **MUSICAL MAN**	☐	-

—— Later in the year he appeared on the Soundtrack for 'JESUS CHRIST SUPERSTAR'

Jun 70. (7") *(MKS 5053)* **STAND.** / **SOUL THING**	☐	-

GARY GLITTER

backed by **The GLITTER BAND**

	Bell	Bell
Mar 72. (7") *(BELL 1216)* <45237> **ROCK'N'ROLL (part 1).** / **ROCK'N'ROLL (part 2)**	2	7 Jul72
Sep 72. (7") *(BELL 1259)* <45276> **I DIDN'T KNOW I LOVE YOU (TILL I SAW YOU ROCK'N'ROLL).** / **HARD ON ME**	4	35 Nov72
Oct 72. (lp/c) *(BELL S/C 216)* <1108> **GLITTER**	8	

– Rock and roll (part 1) / Baby please don't go / The wanderer / I don't know I loved you / Ain't that a shame / School day / Rock on Donna / The famous instigator / The clapping song / Shakey Sue / Rock and roll (part 2). *(cd-iss. Jul96 on 'Dojo'; DOJOCD 100)*

Jan 73. (7") *(BELL 1280)* <45326> **DO YOU WANNA TOUCH ME (OH YEAH).** / **I WOULD IF I COULDBUT I CAN'T**	2	
Mar 73. (7") *(BELL 1299)* <45345> **HELLO HELLO, I'M BACK AGAIN.** / **I.O.U.**	2	
May 73. (7") <45375> **HAPPY BIRTHDAY.** / **COME ON, COME IN, GET ON**	-	
Jun 73. (lp/c) *(BELL S/C 222)* **TOUCH ME**	2	

– Hello hello I'm back again / Sidewalk sinner / Didn't I do it right / Lonely boy / Hold on to what you got / I.O.U. / Do you wanna touch me / Come on, come in, get on / Happy birthday / Hard on me / To know you is to love you / Money honey. *(cd-iss. Jul96 on 'Dojo'; DOJOCD 200)*

Jul 73. (7") *(BELL 1321)* <45398> **I'M THE LEADER OF THE GANG (I AM).** / **JUST FANCY THAT**	1	
Nov 73. (7") *(BELL 1337)* <45438> **I LOVE YOU LOVE ME LOVE.** / **HANDS UP! IT'S A STICK UP**	1	
Mar 74. (7") *(BELL 1349)* **REMEMBER ME THIS WAY.** / **IT'S NOT A LOT**	3	
Jun 74. (7") *(BELL 1359)* **ALWAYS YOURS.** / **I'M RIGHT, YOU'RE WRONG, I WIN**	1	
Jun 74. (lp/c) *(BELL S/C 237)* **REMEMBER ME THIS WAY (live)**	5	

– I'm the leader of the gang (I am) / Sidewalk sinner / Baby please don't go / Do you wanna touch me / The wanderer / Rock and roll (parts 1 & 2) / Hello hello, I'm back again / I didn't know I loved you (till you rock'n'roll) / I love you love me love / Remember me this way.

Nov 74. (7") *(BELL 1391)* **OH YES! YOU'RE BEAUTIFUL.** / **THANK YOU BABY FOR MYSELF**	2	
Apr 75. (7") *(BELL 1423)* **LOVE LIKE YOU AND ME.** / **I'LL CARRY YOUR PICTURE EVERYWHERE**	10	
Jun 75. (7") *(BELL 1429)* **DOING ALRIGHT WITH THE BOYS.** / **GOOD FOR NO GOOD**	6	
Oct 75. (lp/c) *(BELL S/C 257)* **G.G.**	-	

– Too late to put it down / Satan's daughters / Easy evil / Baby I love your way / Papa oom mow mow / Finder's keepers / Basic lady / Cupid / I'll carry your picture / Personality.

Nov 75. (7") *(BELL 1451)* **PAPA OOM MOW MOW.** / **SHE CAT, ALLEY CAT**	38	-
Mar 76. (7") *(BELL 1473)* **YOU BELONG TO ME.** / **ROCK'N'ROLL PART 1**	40	-

	Arista	not iss.
Jan 77. (7") *(ARIST 85)* **IT TAKES ALL NIGHT LONG.** / **(Part 2)**	25	
Jun 77. (7") *(ARIST 112)* **A LITTLE BOOGIE WOOGIE IN THE BACK OF MY MIND.** / **LAY IT ON ME**	31	
Sep 77. (7") *(ARIST 137)* **OH WHAT A FOOL I'VE BEEN.** / **365 DAYS**	☐	-
Dec 77. (7") *(ARIST 154)* **I DARE YOU TO LAY ONE ON ME.** / **HOOKED ON HOLLYWOOD**	☐	-
Jan 78. (lp) *(SPARTY 1020)* **SILVER STAR**	☐	-

– You belong to me / Haven't I seen you somewhere before / I dare you to lay one on me / Roll of the dice / etc.

	G.T.O.	not iss.
Apr 79. (7"/12") *(GT/+12 247)* **SUPERHERO.** / **SLEEPING BEAUTY**	☐	-

	Eagle	not iss.
Nov 80. (7") *(ERS 004)* **WHATCHA MOMMA DON'T SEE (YOUR MOMMA DON'T KNOW).** / **I'M NOT JUST ANOTHER PRETTY FACE**	☐	-
Jul 81. (7") *(ERS 009)* **WHEN I'M ON I'M ON.** / **WILD HORSES**	☐	-

—— (He guested on BEF's (HEAVEN 17) album MUSIC OF QUALITY . . .)

	Bell	not iss.
Sep 81. (7") *(BLL 1497)* **AND THEN SHE KISSED ME.** / **I LOVE HOW YOU LOVE ME**	39	-
Nov 81. (7") *(BLL 1498)* **ALL THAT GLITTERS (segued hits medley).** / **REACH FOR THE SKY**	48	-
Aug 82. (7") *(BLL 1503)* **BE MY BABY.** / **IS THIS WHAT DREAMS ARE MADE OF**	☐	-

	Arista	not iss.
Jun 84. (7"/7"pic-d) *(ARIST/ARISD 570)* **DANCE ME UP.** / **TOO YOUNG TO DANCE**	25	-

(12"+=) *(ARIST12 570)* – All that glitters.

	Arist	not iss.
Sep 84. (7"/7"mirror-pic-d/12") *(ARIST/ARICV/ARIST12 586)* **SHOUT! SHOUT! SHOUT!** / **HAIR OF THE DOG**	☐	-
Nov 84. (lp/c) *(206/406 687)* **BOYS WILL BE BOYS**	☐	-

– Crash crash / Let's get sexy / Dance me up / When I'm on, I'm on / Another rock'n'roll Christmas / Shout shout shout / If you want me / Hair of the dog / Boys will be boys. *(cd-iss. Dec84; 822 571-2)*

Nov 84. (7"/7"sha-pic-d/12") *(ARIST/ARISD/ARIST12 592)* **ANOTHER ROCK'N'ROLL CHRISTMAS.** / **('A'instrumental)**	7	-

(re-iss. Nov85 on 'M.M.'; MLMRT 1)

Apr 85. (7"/7"pic-d) *(ARIST/ARISD 615)* **LOVE COMES.** / **BOYS WILL BE BOYS**	☐	-

(12"+=) *(ARIST12 615)* – ('A'extended) / Megastarmix (hits medley).

—— Retired from recording, but still managed some live work, due to increasing revival of 'glam-pop'. In 1988, he featured on TIMELORDS (KLF's) No.1 (DOCTORIN' THE TARDIS) a near rendition of ROCK'N'ROLL PART 2

	Altitude	not iss.
Oct 91. (cd/c/lp) *(OY CD/MC/LP 1)* **THE LEADER II**	☐	-

– Ready to rock / Tonight / Why do you do it / Wild women / The only way to survive / Let's go party / Are you hard enough / Shake it up / It's enough / Am I losing you.

Nov 96. (c-s/cd-s) *(OYMC/OYCD 02)* **HOUSE OF THE RISING SUN** /	☐	-

– compilations, etc. –

Sep 75. (lp) *Music For Pleasure; (SPR 90076)* **ALWAYS YOURS**	☐	-

(re-iss. Apr86 on 'Dojo' lp/c; DOJO LP/TC 20)

Mar 76. (lp/c) *Bell; (BELL S/C 262)* **GREATEST HITS**	33	-

(re-iss. Jun92 on 'Tring'; TTMC 065)

Feb 77. (lp) *Hallmark; (SHM 916)* **I LOVE YOU LOVE**	☐	-
Mar 77. (lp) *G.T.O.; (GTLP 021)* **GARY GLITTER'S GOLDEN GREATS**	☐	-
Aug 77. (7") *G.T.O.; (GT 103)* **BABY PLEASE DON'T GO.** / **THE WANDERER**	☐	-
Sep 80. (7"ep) *G.T.O.; (GT 282)* **GARY GLITTER (EP)**	57	

– I'm the leader of the gang (I am) / Rock and roll (Part 2) / Hello hello I'm back again / Do you wanna touch me (oh yeah).

Nov 80. (lp) *G.T.O.; (GTLP 046)* **THE LEADER**	☐	-

(re-iss. Nov83 on 'Epic' lp/c; EPC/40 32200)

Sep 83. (7"ep/c-ep) *Scoop; (7SR/7SC 5002)* **6 TRACK HITS**	☐	-

– Rock'n'roll (Part 2) / Always yours / I'm the leader of the gang (I am) / I didn't know I loved you (till I saw you rock'n'roll) / Remember me this way / I love you love me love.

Mar 85. (lp/c) *A.P.K.; (APK/+C 7)* **ALIVE AND KICKING (live)**	☐	-
Apr 85. (7") *Illuminated; (ILL 60)* **ROCK'N'ROLL.** / **OH NO**	☐	-

(12"+=) *(ILL 60-12)* – Not just a pretty face.

Aug 87. (cd) *Object; (OR 0018)* **GARY GLITTER – COLLECTION**	☐	-
Nov 87. (lp/c/cd) *Telstar; (STAR/STAC/TCD 2310)* **C'MON C'MON – THE GARY GLITTER PARTY ALBUM**	☐	-
Dec 87. (7") *R.C.A.; (GLIT 1)* **ROCK'N'ROLL (Part 3).** / **ROCK'N'ROLL (Part 4)**	☐	-

(12") *(12GLIT 1)* – ('A'side) / ('A'-Part 5) / ('A'-Part 6 instrumental).
(12"+=) *(12GLITX 1)* – Rock'n'roll (Part 1).
(cd-s+=) *(CDGLIT 1)* Do you wanna touch me . . .

Jan 89. (7") *Old Gold; (OG 9850)* **ROCK'N'ROLL (Part 2).** / **I DIDN'T KNOW I LOVED YOU (TILL I SAW YOU ROCK'N'ROLL)**		-
Apr 89. (7") *Old Gold; (OG 9880)* **OH YES! YOU'RE BEAUTIFUL.** / **REMEMBER ME THIS WAY**		-
Nov 89. (lp/c/cd) *Castle; (CCS LP/MC/CD 234)* **GARY GLITTER'S GANGSHOW**		-
Dec 89. (7"/12") *Castle; (GARY/+T 001)* **MEGA GLITTER ROCK-A-LIVE (medley)**		-
Mar 90. (7") *Old Gold; (OG 9875)* **I LOVE YOU LOVE ME LOVE.** / **I'M THE LEADER OF THE GANG**		-
Apr 91. (cd/c; some tracks by The GLITTER BAND) *Pickwick; (PWKS/+S 4052)* **BACK AGAIN – THEIR VERY BEST**		-
Oct 92. (c-s/7") *E.M.I.; (TC+/EM 252)* **AND THE LEADER ROCKS ON – Medley:- I'M THE LEADER OF THE GANG – COME ON, COME IN, GET ON – ROCK ON – I DIDN'T KNOW I LOVE YOU – DIDN'T I DO IT RIGHT – DO YOU WANNA TOUCH ME – HELLO HELLO, I'M BACK AGAIN – I'M THE LEADER OF THE GANG (I AM).** / **LET'S GO PARTY**	58	-

(cd-s+=) *(CDEM 252)* – ('A'extended).

Nov 92. (cd/c/d-lp) *E.M.I.' CD/TC+/EMTV 68)* **MANY HAPPY RETURNS – GARY GLITTER THE HITS** (compilation)	35	-

– Rock and roll (part 1) / Rock and roll (part 2) / I didn't know I loved you (till I saw you rock and roll) / Ready to rock / Rock on / Doin' alright with the boys / I'm the leader of the gang (I am) / The wanderer / Do you wanna touch me (oh yeah) / Hello, hello, I'm back again / I love you love me love / If it takes all night long / Oh yes, you're beautiful / Love like you and me / Little boogie woogie in the back of my mind / Dance me up / Through the years / Remember me this way / And the leader rocks on / Another rock and roll Christmas / Always yours. *(re-iss. Dec93 on 'Fame' cd/c; CD/TC FA 3303)*

Nov 92. (c-s/7") *(TC+/EM 256)* **THROUGH THE YEARS.** / **ANOTHER ROCK AND ROLL CHRISTMAS**	49	-

(12"/cd-s) *(12/CD EM 256)* – ('A'side) / Rock & roll (part 1 & 2).

Nov 92. (4xc-box/4xcd-box) *Tring; (MC+/TFP 026)* **THE LEADER**		-
Dec 95. (c-ep/12"ep/cd-ep) *Carlton; (3036 00019-4/-9/-2)* **BY PUBLIC DEMAND EP**	50	-

– Hello, hello, I'm back again (again!) / etc.

Jun 96. (cd/c) *Essential Gold; (30359 0021-2/-4)* **THE VERY BEST OF GARY GLITTER**		-

GLOVE (see under ⇒ SIOUXSIE AND THE BANSHEES)

GO-BETWEENS

Formed: Brisbane, Australia ... 1978 by ROBERT FORSTER (guitar, vocals) and GRANT McLENNAN (vocals, lead guitar, bass) with DENNIS CANTWELL on drums. After a debut Australian-only 7" single, 'LEE REMICK', CANTWELL was replaced with TIM MUSTAFA while organist MALCOLM KELLY was brought in briefly for the early classic, 'PEOPLE SAY', the band's second and final domestic release (they were also on the books of 'Beserkley' UK for a few months). Finally settling with LINDY MORRISON on drums, The GO-BETWEENS recorded two singles for seminal Scottish indie label, 'Postcard', before settling in London and signing with 'Rough Trade'. Their debut, 'SEND ME A LULLABY' (1982), drew comparisons with The TALKING HEADS, although their root influences remained the classic songwriting of BOB DYLAN and The VELVET UNDERGROUND. Following the addition of ROBERT VICKERS on bass, allowing McLENNAN to switch to guitar, 'BEFORE HOLLYWOOD' (1983) was a marked improvement. The twin songwriting and singing strength of McLENNAN and FORSTER was developing apace, the former's 'CATTLE AND CANE' a yearning, melancholy highlight. Rave reviews abounded and the band were soon signed to the Warner Brothers-affiliated 'Sire' label. 'SPRING HILL FAIR' (1984) marked the GO-BETWEENS major label debut, their swooning melodies enhanced by a superior production on classics like 'BACHELOR KISSES'. Again the band were heralded by the press and adored by a cult following yet a commercial breakthrough proved elusive. The group switched labels yet again (moving to 'Beggar's Banquet') for 'LIBERTY BELLE AND THE BLACK DIAMOND EXPRESS' (1986), the band's most accessible, and probably finest effort of their career; it remains a mystery why the lush guitar-pop of 'SPRING RAIN' failed to breach the charts. With the addition of AMANDA BROWN (guitar, violin, oboe, keyboards), the band cut the more ambitious 'TALLULAH' (1987) and, despite a couple of strong singles, were still confined to the indie margins. Understandably, the group were miffed at their lack of any real success and '16 LOVERS LANE' (1988), another sterling set of consummate, painstakingly crafted songs, proved to be their final effort. The record reached a lowly No.81 on the UK chart, The GO-BETWEENS finally going their own way with McLENNAN and FORSTER both embarking on solo careers. FORSTER's 1991 debut, 'DANGER IN THE PAST' was a fine effort, its sound not much of a departure from the later GO-BETWEENS albums. 'CALLING FROM A COUNTRY PHONE' (1993) was rootsier, employing such traditional instrumentation as banjo and mandolin. McLENNAN initially worked on the more avant-garde project, JACK FROST, with STEVE KILBEY of The CHURCH, before releasing 'WATERSHED' in 1991 as G.W. McLENNAN. Another two fine albums followed with 'FIREBOY' (1993) and 'HORSEBREAKER STAR' (1994), FORSTER releasing an album of covers the same year, 'I HAD A NEW YORK GIRLFRIEND'.
• **Songwriters:** All compositions by FORSTER and McLENNAN, with LINDY MORRISON contributing some. McLENNAN covered BALLAD OF EASY RIDER (Byrds). FORSTER covered; NATURE'S WAY (Spirit) / BROKEN HEARTED PEOPLE (...Clarke) / ECHO BEACH (Martha & The Muffins) / TELL ME THAT IT ISN'T TRUE (Bob Dylan) / 2541 (Bob Mould) / ANYTIME (... Nelson) / LOCKED AWAY (Richards-Jordan) / LOOK OUT HERE COMES TOMORROW (Neil Diamond) / ALONE (Kelly-Steinberg) / BIRD (...Hansoms) / FRISCO DEPOT (... Newbury) / 3 A.M. (Anderson-Todd). • **Trivia:** In 1991, FORSTER and McLENNAN did support slot to LLOYD COLE on a Toronto gig, which prompted GO-BETWEENS reformation rumours.

Album rating: SEND ME A LULLABY (*7) / BEFORE HOLLYWOOD (*8) / SPRING HILL FAIR (*7) / LIBERTY BELLE AND THE BLACK DIAMOND EXPRESS (*7) / TALULAH (*7) / 16 LOVERS LANE (*8) / The GO-BETWEENS 1979-1990 compilation (*9) / Robert Forster: DANGER IN THE PAST (*6) / CALLING FROM A COUNTRY PHONE (*6) / I HAD A NEW YORK GIRLFRIEND (*5) / WARM NIGHTS (*5) / G.W. McLennan: WATERSHED (*7) / FIREBOY (*6) / HORSEBREAKER STAR (*7) / IN YOUR BRIGHT RAY (*6)

GRANT McLENNAN (b.12 Feb'58, Rock Hampton, Australia) – vocals, lead guitar, bass /
ROB FORSTER (b.29 Jun'57) – guitar, vocals / **DENNIS CANTWELL** – drums

			Abel	not iss.	
Oct 78.	(7") *(AB 001)* **LEE REMICK. / KAREN**		-	-	Austra

—— added **TIM MUSTAFA** – drums + **MALCOLM KELLY** – organ to repl. CANTWELL

Oct 79.	(7") *(AB 004)* **PEOPLE SAY. / DON'T LET HIM COME BACK**		-	Austra
	(above released UK Nov86 as 12"ep on 'Situation 2'; *SIT 44T*)			

—— **LINDY MORRISON** (b. 2 Nov'51) – drums (ex-ZERO) repl. TIM + MALCOLM

			Postcard	not iss.
Nov 80.	(7") *(80-4)* **I NEED TWO HEADS. / STOP BEFORE YOU SAY IT**			-
Jul 81.	(7") *(81-9)* **YOUR TURN, MY TURN. / WORLD WEARY**			-
	(possibly not issued in UK, released on their Australian label, 'Missing Link'; MISS 29)			

			Rough Trade	not iss.
Jun 82.	(lp) *(ROUGH 45)* **SEND ME A LULLABY**			-
	– Your turn, my turn / One thing can hold us / Eight pictures / People know / The girls have moved / Midnight to neon / Ride / Caress / All about strength / Hold your horses / It could be anyone / Arrow in a bow. *<US cd-iss. 1990 on 'Beggars Banquet'; 92702>*			
Jul 82.	(7") *(RT 108)* **HAMMER THE HAMMER. / BY CHANCE**			-

—— added **ROBERT VICKERS** (b.25 Nov'59) – bass

Feb 83.	(7") *(RT 124)* **CATTLE AND CANE. / HEAVEN SAYS**			-
Sep 83.	(lp) *(ROUGH 54)* **BEFORE HOLLYWOOD**			-

– A bad debt follows you / Two steps step out / Before Hollywood / Dusty in here / Ask / Cattle and cane / By chance / As long as that / On my block / That way. *(cd-iss. Jun90; LCD 54) <US cd-iss. 1990 on 'Beggars Banquet'; 92703>*

			Sire	not iss.
Oct 83.	(7") *(RT 114)* **MAN O' SAND TO GIRL O' SEA. / THIS GIRL BLACK GIRL**			-
Jul 84.	(7") *(W 9211)* **PART COMPANY. / JUST A KING IN MIRRORS**			-
	(12"+=) *(W 9211T)* – Newton told me.			
Sep 84.	(lp) *(925 179-1)* **SPRING HILL FAIR**			-
	– Bachelor kisses / Five words / The old way out / You've never lived / Part company / Slow slow music / Man o' sand girl o' sea. *<US cd-iss. 1990 on 'Beggars Banquet'; 82003>*			
Sep 84.	(7") *(W 9156)* **BACHELOR KISSES. / RARE BREED**			-
	(12"+=) *(W 9156T)* – Unkind and unwise (instrumental).			

			Beggars Banquet	Big Time
Feb 86.	(7") *(BEG 155)* **SPRING RAIN. / LIFE AT HAND**			-
	(12"+=) *(BEG 155T)* – Little Joe.			
Mar 86.	(lp/c) *(BEGA/BEGC 72) <6010>* **LIBERTY BELLE AND THE BLACK DIAMOND EXPRESS**			
	– Spring rain / The ghost and the black hat / The wrong road / To reach me / Twin layers of lightning / In the core of the flame / Head full of steam / Palm Sunday (on board the S.S.Within) / Apology accepted. *(re-iss. Feb89 on 'Beggars Banquet-Lowdown' lp/c)(cd; BBL/+C 72)(BBL 72CD)*			
May 86.	(7") *(BEG 159)* **HEAD FULL OF STEAM. / DON'T LET HIM COME BACK**			
	(12"+=) *(BEG 159T)* – The wrong road.			

—— added **AMANDA BROWN** (b.17 Nov'65) – keyboards, violin, guitar, oboe

Feb 87.	(7") *(BEG 183)* **RIGHT HERE. / WHEN PEOPLE ARE DEAD**			-
	(12"+=) *(BEG 183T)* – Don't call me gone.			
	(d7"++=) *(BEG 183D)* – A little romance (live).			
May 87.	(7") *(BEG 190)* **CUT IT OUT. / TIME IN DESERT**			-
	(12"+=) *(BEG 190T)* – Doo wop in "A".			
Jun 87.	(lp/c)(cd) *(BEGA/BEGC 81)(BEGA 81CD) <6042>* **TALLULAH**	91		
	– Right here / You tell me / Someone else's wife / I just get caught out / Cut it out / The house that Jack Kerouac built / Bye bye pride / Spirit of a vampyre / The Clarke sisters / Hope then strife. *(re-iss. Feb90 on 'Beggars Banquet-Lowdown' cd)(c/lp; BEGA 81CD)(BEGC/BEGA 81)*			
Aug 87.	(7"/12") *(BEG 194/+T)* **BYE BYE PRIDE. / THE HOUSE THAT JACK KEROUAC BUILT**			-

—— **JOHN WILSTEED** (b.13 Feb'57) – bass repl. VICKERS

			Beggars Banquet	Capitol
Jul 88.	(7") *(BEG 218) <4BX 44262>* **STREETS OF YOUR TOWN. / WAIT UNTIL JUNE**			
	(12"+=) *(BEG 218T)* – Casanova's last words.			
	(cd-s++=) *(BEG 218CD)* – Spring rain / Right here.			
Aug 88.	(lp/c)(cd) *(BEGA/BEGC 95)(BEGA 95CD) <91230>* **16 LOVERS LANE**	81		
	– Love goes on / Quiet heart / Love is a sign / You can't say no forever / The Devil's eye / Streets of your town / Clouds / Was there anything I could do? / I'm alright / Dive for your memory.			
Oct 88.	(7") *(BEG 219)* **WAS THERE ANYTHING I COULD DO. / ROCK'N'ROLL FRIEND**			-
	(12"+=) *(BEG 219T)* – Mexican postcard.			
	(cd-s++=) *(BEG 219CD)* – Bye bye pride.			

—— Split on the day we moved into the 90's. FORSTER and McLENNAN went solo. The latter also being part of JACK FROST with STEVE KILBEY of The CHURCH. AMANDA formed CLEOPATRA WONG.

– compilations, others, etc. –

1982.	(lp) *Man Made;* **VERY QUICK ON THE EYE – BRISBANE 1981 (demo)**			-
1985.	(lp) *P.V.C.; <PVC 8942>* **METAL AND SHELLS**		-	-
Oct 89.	(12"ep/cd-ep) *Strange Fruit; (SFPS/+CD 074) / Dutch East India; <8339>* **THE PEEL SESSIONS**			1991
	– The power that I have now / Second hand furniture / Fire woods / Rare breed.			
Mar 90.	(cd)(c/d-lp) *Beggars Banquet; (BEGA 104CD)(BEGC/BEGA 104) / Capitol; <94681>* **THE GO-BETWEENS 1979-1990**			
	– Hammer the hammer / I need two heads / Cattle and cane / When people are dead / Man o' sand to girl o' sea / Bachelor kisses / People say / Draining the pool for you / World weary / Spring rain / Rock and roll friend / Dusty in here / The Clarke sisters / Right here / Second-hand furniture / Bye bye pride / This girl, black girl / The house that Jack Kerouac built / Don't call me gone / Streets of our own town / Love is a sign / You won't find it again. *(c++=/d-lp+=)* – Karen / 8 pictures / The sound of rain / The wrong road / Mexican postcard.			

ROBERT FORSTER

—— (solo, with MICK HARVEY – producer)

			Beggars Banquet	Beggars Banquet
Sep 90.	(7") **BABY STONES. /**			-
	(12"+=/cd-s+=) -			
Oct 90.	(cd)(c/lp) *(BEGA 113CD)(BEGA/BEGC 113) <3028>* **DANGER IN THE PAST**			
	– Baby stones / The river people / Leave here satisfied / Heart out to tender / Is this what you call change / Dear black dream / Danger in the past / I've been looking for somebody / Justice.			
Apr 93.	(cd/c) *(BBQ CD/MC 127)* **CALLING FROM A COUNTRY PHONE**			-
	– Atlanta lie low / 121 / The circle / Falling star / I want to be quiet / Cats life / Girl to a world / Drop / Beyond theit law / Forever & time. *(cd re-iss. Sep95 on 'Beggars Banquet-Lowdown'; BBL 127CD)*			

—— with **JOHN KEANE** – guitars, banjos, keyboards, bass, etc / **JOEL MORRIS** – drums / **STEVE VENZ** – bass / **ANDY CARLSON** – guitars, mandolin / **TIM WHITE & BILL HOLMES** – porga & piano / **DWIGHT MANNING** – oboe / **SYD STRAW** – backing vocals

		Beggars Banquet	Atlantic
Jul 94.	(cd-ep) *(BBQ 38CD)* **25-41 / 3 a.m. / FREDDIE FENDER / DANGER IN THE PAST (live)**	☐	-
Aug 94.	(cd/c) *(BBQ CD/MC 161)* <92482> **I HAD A NEW YORK GIRLFRIEND**	☐	☐
	– Nature's way / Broken hearted people / Echo beach / Tell me that it isn't true / 2541 / Anytime / Locked away / Look out loves comes tomorrow / Alone / Bird / Frisco depot / 3 a.m.		

		Beggars Banquet	Beggars Banquet
Jul 96.	(cd-ep) *(BEG 300CD)* **CRYIN' LOVE**	☐	☐
Aug 96.	(cd)(lp) *(BEGL 185CD/BEGA 185)* <80185> **WARM NIGHTS**	☐	☐ Sep96
	– I can do / Warn nights / Cryin' love / Snake skin lady / Loneliness / Jug of wine / Fortress / Rock-n-roll friend / On a street corner / I'll jump.		

G.W. McLENNAN

		Beggars Banquet	Beggars Banquet
Mar 91.	(12"ep)(cd-ep) **WHEN WORD GETS AROUND / BLACK MULE / SHE'S SO STRANGE / THE MAN WHO DIED IN RAPTURE**	☐	-
May 91.	(7") **EASY COME EASY GO. / MAKING IT RIGHT FOR HER**	☐	-
	(12"+=)(cd-s+=) – Stones for you.		
Jun 91.	(cd)(c)(lp) *(BEGACD 118)(BEG/BEGC 118)* **WATERSHED**	☐	☐
	– When word gets around / Haven't I been a fool / Haunted house / Stones for you / Easy come easy go / Black mule / Rory the weeks back on / You can't have everything / Sally's revolution / Broadway bride / Just get that straight / Dream about tomorrow.		

		Beggars Banquet	Atlantic
Jan 93.	(cd-ep) **FINGERS / WHOSE SIDE ARE YOU ON / WHAT WENT WRONG**	☐	-
Feb 93.	(cd-ep) **LIGHTING FIRES / DARK SIDE OF TOWN / IF I SHOULD FALL BEHIND**	☐	-
Mar 93.	(cd/c) *(BBQ CD/MC 127)* <92387> **FIREBOY**	☐	☐ Jun94
	– Lighting fires / Surround me / One million miles from here / The dark side of town / Things will change / The pawnbroker / Whose side are you on? / Fingers / Signs of life / The day my eyes Came back / Bathe (in the water) / When I close my eyes / Riddle in the rain.		
Aug 94.	(cd-ep) **DON'T YOU CRY / COMING UP FOR AIR / GIRL IN A BERET / PUT YOU DOWN / NO PEACE IN THE PALACE / THAT'S THAT**	☐	-
Nov 94.	(d-cd/c) *(BBQ CD/MC 162)* **HORSEBREAKER STAR**	☐	-
	– Simone & Perry / Ice in Heaven / What went wrong / Race day rag / Don't you cry for me no more / Put you down / Late afternoon in early August / Coming up for air / Ballad of Easy Rider / Open invitation / Open my eyes / From my lips / Dropping you / Hot water / Keep my word / Do your own thing / That's that / If I was a girl / Head over heels / Girl in a beret / All her songs / No peace in the palace / I'll call you wild / Horsebreaker star. *(re-iss. d-cd Sep95 on 'Beggars Banquet-Lowdown'; BEGA 162CD)*		
Jun 95.	(cd-ep) *(BBQ 57CD)* **SIMONE & PERRY / DON'T YOU CRY FOR ME NO MORE / BALLAD OF EASY RIDER / WHAT WENT WRONG (original)**	☐	-
Jul 97.	(cd) *(BBQCD 192)* **IN YOUR BRIGHT RAY**	☐	☐
	– In your bright ray / Cave in / One plus one / Sea breeze / Malibu '69 / Who said love was dead / Room for skin / All them pretty angels / Comet scar / Down here / Lamp by lamp / Do you see the lights / Parade of shadows.		

Vic GODARD / SUBWAY SECT

(dig out; Great Alt & Indie . . .)

GODFATHERS   (dig out; Great Alt & Indie . . .)

GODLEY & CREME (see under ⇒ 10cc)

GODSMACK

Formed: Boston, Massachusetts, USA ... 1996 by frontman SULLY ERNA and his musical mates, TONY ROMBOLO, ROBBIE MERRILL and TOMMY STEWART, who named themselves after an ALICE IN CHAINS track. If you were to put the aforementioned ALICE IN CHAINS, METALLICA and the rest of the Grunge crew together – and without getting too sarcy – you would probably come up with GODSMACK. This dour 4-piece got their break from none other than PAUL GEARY (former sticksman with EXTREME), who sorted out a contract with 'Universal' in 1998. By the following year, their self-titled debut album was high in the US Top 30, with an invite to Woodstock and Ozzfest to boot. Heralded by young trendy Americans into "that sort of thing", the band also had a surprise alternative rock hit with probably their finest five minutes, 'WHATEVER'.

Album rating: GODSMACK (*3)

SULLY ERNA – vocals / **TONY ROMBOLO** – guitar / **ROBBIE MERRILL** – bass / **TOMMY STEWART** – drums; repl. JOE D'ARCO (although he did return)

		Universal	Universal
Aug 99.	(cd) *(UND 53190)* <153190> **GODSMACK**	☐	22 Aug98
	– Moon baby / Whatever / Keep away / Time bomb / Bad religion / Immune / Someone in London / Get up, get out! / Now or never / Stress / Situation / Voodoo. *<clean version as 'ALL WOUND UP'; UND 53183>*		

GODSPEED YOU BLACK EMPEROR!

Formed: Mile End district, Montreal, Canada ... 1994 by EFRIM and MAURO (the original pair issuing a very limited 33 copy cassette, 'ALL LIGHTS FUCKED ON THE HAIRY AMP DROOLING'). Enlarging the outfit to a 9-piece collective and enlisting DAVE, AIDAN, BRUCE, THIERRY, NORSOLA, SOPHIE and ROGER TELLIER-CRAIG... with STEPH, SYLVIA, COLIN, CRISTOPHE, JESSE, DAN C, SHANEABERG, PETER and AMANDA making up contributors at various times. Revolting against the "pay to play" system that many of the local establishments employed, the ensemble took to playing empty warehouses and other such venues, enabling them to gain popularity among the more alternative-centred individuals in their town. In 1996, GYBE! retreated to Hotel2Tango (a mythological apartment in which certain members of the band were said to occupy), putting down material with the assistance of Chemical Daryl at his Chemical Sound studio. Broke again, they obtained free reel-to-reel tape from a friend and remixed their old material, adding two tracks and sequencing their efforts at Mile End studio. The result was the devastatingly bleak 'F#A#oo' album, issued in limited numbers in the summer of '98 for 'Constellation', harbouring the attention of Chicago-based cult experimental imprint, 'Kranky' for UK and US release. From its post-apocalyptic opener 'THE DEAD FLAG BLUES' (with the memorable spoken dialogue of 'The Car's On Fire And There's No Driver At The Wheel And The Sewers Are All Muddied With A Thousand Lonely Suicides And A Dark Wind Blows . . .') segued together with the eerie rumbling effects on the self-explanatory 'SLOW MOVING TRAINS' cruising into the epic tour de force of 'THE COWBOY' (a landscape of spiralling David Lynch-esque peaks that quite literally tickle the ears into orgasmic proportions on headphone experience!) and uplifted by the bright and folky denouement of its 'OUTRO'. The album's second piece, 'EAST HASTINGS', fades into the broken ramblings of a distressed street anarchist (see below) complaining "NOTHING'S ALRITE IN OUR LIFE" lamented by distant bagpipes and overlapped with soft vibrato acoustics and paranoid MOGWAI meets TANGERINE DREAM (their cinematic period!) slow burning crescendo culminating with ear-bashing orchestral avant-metal. Section two of this lengthy piece, 'THE SAD MAFIESE', navigated the psyche into further headbusting headphone gymnastics with its plucking harmonics swaying continuously like a rocking chair uneasy in a derelict porch. The track's third instalment, 'DRUGS IN TOKYO – BLACK HELICOPTER', was arguably the most disturbing piece of the set, its Oriental chimes festooned between sounds of bees trapped in a generator. Song(!) number three, 'PROVIDENCE', begins with a doubtful riddle lecturing about the current state of America and linking that with the end of time, waking up to a sunrise owned by (BRIAN) ENO. Each of its four pieces were like a homage to late 60's/early 70's experimental rock (i.e. PINK FLOYD) battling on a stranger plateau of military percussion and space-age guitars. The following Spring, the group returned with 'SLOW RIOT FOR NEW ZER0 KANADA E.P.' an unusual two-track mini-set that again stunned audiences and critics alike. Soft violins, rattling guitars, orchestrated crescendoes and bizarre vox-pops were all the standard on opening track, 'MOYA', while the deeply negative 'BBF3' (named eponymously after the aforementioned street/soapbox anarchist, Mister Blaise Bailey Finnegan the third) attacks world society and all its corruptive forces. Arguably this band are the most promising act to hit the year 2000, ironically it's everything that they rebel against. During all the hype and journo commotion, ROGER'S side-project, FLY PAN AM, took off on their campaign of climax-induced minimalist (s)Lo-Fi, the result being a well-received eponymous album in October '99.

Album rating: F#A#oo (*9) / SLOW RIOT FOR NEW ZER0 KANADA mini (*8) / Fly Pan Am: FLY PAN AM (*7)

EFRIM – guitar, tape loops / **MAURO** – bass

		not iss.	not listed
Dec 94.	(ltd-c) <*none*> **ALL LIGHTS FUCKED ON THE HAIRY AMP DROOLING**	-	- Canada
	– Perfumed pink corpses from the lips of Ms. Celine Dion / Revisionist alternatif wounds to the haircut-hit head / Loose the idiot dogs / etc		

—— added **DAVE** – guitar, tape loops / **AIDAN** – percussion / **BRUCE** – percussion, glockenspiel / **THIERRY** – bass / **NORSOLA** – cello / **ROGER TELLIER-CRAIG** – guitar / **SOPHIE** – violin

		Kranky	Kranky
Jun 98.	(cd)(lp) <*(KRANKY 27CD)*><*cst 003*> **F#A#oo**	☐	☐
	– The dead flag blues: 1. The dead flag blues, 2. Slow moving trains, 3. The cowboy, 4. (; Outro) / East Hastings: 1. "Nothing's alrite in our life" – Dead flag blues (reprise), 2. The sad Mafiese, 3. Drugs in Tokyo – Black helicopter / Providence: 1. Divorce and fever, 2. Dead mothery, 3. Kicking horse on broken hill, 4. String loop manufacturer during downpour.		
Apr 99.	(m-lp/m-cd) <*(KRANKY 34/+CD)*><*cst 006*> **SLOW RIOT FOR NEW ZER0 KANADA E.P.**	☐	☐ Mar99
	– Moya / BBF3 (voice by Mister Blaise Bailey Finnegan the third).		

—— <above releases also on 'Constellation' in Canada>

Sep 99.	(7",7"white) <*MAZE 01*> **SUNSHINE & GASOLINE. / Fly Pan Am: L'ESPACE AU SOL EST REDESSINE PAR DES IMMENSES PANNEAUX BLEUS**	-	☐

—— <above issued for 'aMAZEzine!' fanzine>

FLY PAN AM

ROGER TELLIER-CRAIG – guitar

	Constellation	Constellation

Oct 99. (cd) *<(cst 008)>* **FLY PAN AM**
– L'espace au sol est redesine par d'immeses panneaux bleus / Et aussi L'eclairge de plastique au centre de tout ces compartiments lateraux / Dans ses cheveux soixante circuits / Bibi a nice, 1921 / Nice est en feu!

GO-GO'S

Formed: Hollywood, California, USA ... May '78 as all-girl band The MISFITS by BELINDA CARLISLE, CHARLOTTE CAFFEY, JANE WIEDLIN, MARGOT OLAVERRA and ELISA BELLO (subsequently replaced by GINA SHOCK). An integral part of the punk/new wave scene centred on Hollywood's 'Masque' club and nearby 'Canterbury Arms' apartment building, the group subsequently adopted the GO-GO'S moniker. Although they'd later project a more wholesome image, the earliest incarnation of the band lived the drug-taking punk lifestyle to the full, one of their shows even ending in an infamous 1979 riot. Yet their sound gradually lost its early rawness and mutated into a more commerical power-pop style at the turn of the decade; British ska revival nutters MADNESS were sufficiently impressed to offer the girls a support slot on their 1980 UK tour. The resultant exposure led to interest from premier UK indie label, 'Stiff', who released the ladettes' debut single, 'WE GOT THE BEAT', in Spring of the same year. Back in the States, POLICE manager Miles Copeland signed the group to his burgeoning 'I.R.S.' roster and helped put them in the US Top 20 with summer 81's pink vinyl classic 'OUR LIPS ARE SEALED' (co-written by SPECIALS man, TERRY HALL). Debut album, 'BEAUTY AND THE BEAT' (1981) followed hot on its heels, a frothy, surf-influenced set which couched occasionally hard-bitten lyrics in a buoyant, typically Californian veneer. The record topped the charts and suddenly The GO-GO'S were hot property. A more overtly commercial, polished follow-up, 'VACATION' (1982), made the Top 10 and spawned a similarly paced, cheesy summer single in its title track. Yet the band's fast-living ethos had taken its toll and after a third album, 'TALK SHOW' (1984), and final Top 20 single, 'HEAD OVER HEELS', the various members split to do their own thing. While WIEDLIN would go on to have a couple of 80's hits (the biggest and best being 'RUSH HOUR'), it was the cutesy CARLISLE (incredibly a brief member of legendary L.A. punks, The GERMS) who'd emerge as a typically airbrushed 80's pop/rock clone with big hair and even bigger songs. Following on from the Stateside success of her 1986 eponymous debut album and its Top 3 hit, 'MAD ABOUT YOU', she scored a massive transatlantic No.1 towards the end of '87 with the anthemic schlock of 'HEAVEN IS A PLACE ON EARTH'. Now signed to 'Virgin' in the UK, she became one of Britain's biggest late 80's female pop stars, churning out Top 5 doe-eyed dross like 'CIRCLE IN THE SAND' and 'LEAVE A LIGHT ON'. Although she began the new decade on a commercial high with the huge 1990 hit, '(WE WANT) THE SAME THING', her singles increasingly only scraped the Top 30. Nevertheless, the strength of her British following was illustrated by the No.1 success of a 1992 greatest hits set (which didn't even chart in America) while the following year's 'REAL' album made the Top 10. Having already reunited in 1990 to promote a retrospective set (during which time they played a naked but discreet anti-fur campaign benefit), The GO-GO'S got back together again in late '94. This time around they cut a handful of fresh tracks for an anthology of earlier material, 'RETURN TO THE VALLEY OF THE GO-GO'S' (1995), incredibly scoring their first ever UK Top 30 hit with 'THE WHOLE WORLD LOST ITS HEAD'. • **Songwriters:** WIEDLIN or CARLISLE; when the latter went solo, her songs were largely written by producer RICK NOWELS and ELLEN SHIPLEY. In 1992, she collaborated on some with new producer RICHARD FELDMAN. Others writers; I GET WEAK + WORLD WITHOUT YOU (Dianne Warren) / SUMMER RAIN (Seidman-Vidal) / I FEEL FREE (Cream) / THE AIR YOU BREATHE (Weiss-White) / JEALOUS GUY (John Lennon) / ALWAYS BREAKING MY HEART (Per Gessle; Roxette).

Album rating: BEAUTY AND THE BEAT (*6) / VACATION (*5) / TALK SHOW (*4) / GREATEST compilation (*6) / RETURN TO THE VALLEY OF THE GO-GO'S compilation (*5) / Belinda Carlisle: BELINDA (*5) / HEAVEN ON EARTH (*6) / RUNAWAY HORSES (*5) / LIVE YOUR LIFE BE FREE (*4) / THE BEST OF BELINDA CARLISLE compilation (*6) / REAL (*4) / A WOMAN AND A MAN (*3) / ...A PLACE ON EARTH – THE GREATEST HITS compilation (*5)

BELINDA CARLISLE (b.17 Aug'58) – vocals (ex-GERMS) / **CHARLOTTE CAFFEY** (b.21 Oct'53, Santa Monica, Calif.) – lead guitar, vocals / **JANE WIEDLIN** (b.20 May'58, Oconomowoc, Wisconsin) – rhythm guitar, vocals / **MARGOT OLAVERRA** – bass / **GINA SHOCK** (b.31 Aug'57, Baltimore, Maryland) – drums (ex-EDDIE MASSEY & HER EGGS) repl. ELISA BELLO

	Stiff	not iss.
May 80. (7") *(BUY 78)* **WE GOT THE BEAT. / HOW MUCH MORE**		–

—— **KATHY VALENTINE** (b. 7 Jan'59, Austin, Texas) – bass (ex-TEXTONES) repl. MARGOT.

	I.R.S.	I.R.S.
Jul 81. (7"pink) *(PFP 1007)* <9901> **OUR LIPS ARE SEALED. / SURFING AND SPYING**		20
Aug 81. (lp/c) *<(SP/CS 70021)>* **BEAUTY AND THE BEAT**		1 Jul 81

– Our lips are sealed / This town / How much more / Fading fast / We got the beat / Tonite / Skidmarks on my heart / Lust to love / Automatic / You can't walk in your sleep (if you can't sleep) / Can't stop the world. *(cd-iss. 1988; CD 70021)*

Nov 81. (7",7"pic-d) *(PFP 1010)* **WE GOT THE BEAT. / SKIDMARKS ON MY HEART**		–

Jan 82. (7") <9903> **WE GOT THE BEAT. / CAN'T STOP THE WORLD**	–	2
Feb 82. (7",7"pic-d) *(GON 101)* **AUTOMATIC. / TONITE**	–	2
Apr 82. (7") *(GON 102)* **OUR LIPS ARE SEALED. / WE GOT THE BEAT**	47	–
Aug 82. (7") *(GON 103)* <9907> **VACATION. / BEATNIK BEACH**	–	8 Jul82
Aug 82. (lp/c) *<(SP/CS 70031)>* **VACATION**	75	8

– Vacation / This old feeling / He's so strange / Girl of 100 lists / It's everything but partytime / Get up and go / Beatnik beach / I think it's me / The way you dance / We don't get along / Worlds away / Cool jerk.

Sep 82. (7") <9910> **GET UP AND GO. / SPEEDING**	–	50
Nov 82. (7") *(GON 104)* **GIRL OF 100 LISTS. / I THINK IT'S ME**	–	–
Dec 82. (7") **IT'S EVERYTHING BUT PARTYTIME. / THIS OLD FEELING**	–	
Nov 83. (7") **BELONG TO ME. / DON'T YOU LOVE ME**	–	
Apr 84. (7") *(104)* <9926> **HEAD OVER HEELS. / GOOD FOR GONE**		11 Mar84
May 84. (lp/c) *<(IRS A/C 70041)>* **TALK SHOW**		18 Apr84

– Turn to you / You thought / Capture the light / I'm the only one / Mercenary / I'm with you / Yes or no / Head over heels / Forget that day / Beneath the blue sky. *(cd-iss. 1988; CD 70041)*

Jun 84. (7") <9928> **TURN TO YOU. / I'M WITH YOU**	–	32
Sep 84. (7") <9933> **YES OR NO. / MERCENARY**	–	84

—— **PAULA JEAN BROWN** – rhythm guitar repl. JANE WIEDLIN who went solo. They disbanded May 1985 when CAFFEY and CARLISLE left.

BELINDA CARLISLE

—— went solo initially taking with her; **CHARLOTTE CAFFEY**

	I.R.S.	I.R.S.
Jun 86. (7") *(IRM 118)* <52815> **MAD ABOUT YOU. / I NEVER WANTED A RICH MAN**		3 May86

(12"+=) *(IRMT 118)* – ('A'extended). *(re-iss. Jan88; same)* – hit UK No.67 *(re-iss. Jul88; DIRM 118)*

Jul 86. (lp/c) *(MIRF/+C 1012)* <5741> **BELINDA**		13

– Mad about you / I need a disguise / Since you've gone / I feel the magic / I never wanted a rich man / Band of gold / Gotta get to you / From the heart / Shot in the dark / Stuff and nonsense. *(cd-iss. 1988; DMIRF 1012) (cd re-iss. Jan90 & Apr92 cd/c; IRLD/IRLC 19002)*

Sep 86. (7") <52889> **I FEEL THE MAGIC. / FROM THE HEART**	–	82

	Virgin	M.C.A.
Nov 87. (7") *(VS 1036)* <53181> **HEAVEN IS A PLACE ON EARTH. / WE CAN CHANGE**	1	1 Sep87

(12"+=) *(VST 1036)* – ('A'-heavenly version).
(cd-s++=) *(VSCD 1036)* – ('A'-acappella version).

Dec 87. (cd/c/lp) *(CD/TC/+V 2496)* <42080> **HEAVEN ON EARTH**	4	13 Oct87

– Heaven is a place on Earth / Circle in the sand / I feel free / Should I let you in? / World without you / I get weak / We can change / Fool for love / Nobody owns me / Love never dies ... *(pic-cd-iss. Nov88; CDVP 2496) (re-iss. Jan91; OVED/+C 330); hit No.46)*

Feb 88. (7") *(VS 1046)* <53242> **I GET WEAK. / SHOULD I LET YOU IN**	10	2 Jan88

(12"+=/c-s+=/pic-cd-s+=) *(VS T/TC/CD 1046)* – ('A'extended).

Apr 88. (7") <53308> **CIRCLE IN THE SAND. / WE CAN CHANGE**	–	7
Apr 88. (7") *(VS 1074)* **CIRCLE IN THE SAND. / ('A'-seaside mmod groove mix)**	4	

(12"+=/12"pic-d+=) *(VST/+Y 1074)* – ('A'-beach party mix).
(c-s+=/cd-s+=) *(VS TC/CD 1074)* – ('A'-sandblast multi-mix).

Jul 88. (c-s) <53308> **I FEEL FREE. / SHOULD I LET YOU IN**	–	88
Aug 88. (7") *(VS 1114)* **WORLD WITHOUT YOU (remix). / NOBODY OWES ME**	34	

(12"+=) *(VST 1114)* – ('A'extended worldwide mix).
(cd-s) *(VSCD 1114)* – ('A'extended worldwide mix) / ('A'side) / ('A'-pana-vision mix).

Nov 88. (7") *(VS 1150)* **LOVE NEVER DIES. / I FEEL FREE (live)**	54	

(12"+=) *(VST 1150)* – Heaven is a place on Earth (live).
(cd-s++=) *(VSCD 1150)* – Circle in the sand (live).

Sep 89. (7"/c-s) *(VS/+C 1210)* <53706> **LEAVE A LIGHT ON. / SHADES OF MICAELANGELO**	4	11

(12"+=) *(VST 1210)* – ('A'extended).
(cd-s+++=) *(VSCD 1210)* – ('A'-acappella).

Oct 89. (cd/c/lp) *(CD/TC+/V 2599)* <6339> **RUNAWAY HORSES**	4	37

– Leave a light on / Runaway horses / Vision of you / Summer rain / La Luna / (We want) The same thing / Deep deep ocean / Valentine / Whatever it takes / Shades of Michaelangelo. *(re-iss. Jan91 hit No.6).*

Nov 89. (7"/7"g-f/c-s) *(VS/+X/C 1230)* **LA LUNA. / WHATEVER IT TAKES**	38	

(12"/12"g-f/3"cd-s) *(VS T/TP/CD 1230)* – ('A'side) / ('A'extended dance mix) / ('A'extended dub).

Dec 89. (7") <53783> **SUMMER RAIN. / SHADES OF MICHAELANGELO**	–	30
Mar 90. (7"/c-s) *(VS/+C 1244)* **RUNAWAY HORSES. / HEAVEN IS A PLACE ON EARTH (live)**	40	

(12"+=/3"cd-s+=/cd-s+=) *(VS T/TD/CD 1244)* – Circle in the sand (beach party mix).

May 90. (7"/c-s) *(VS/+C 1264)* **VISION OF YOU. / LEAVE A LIGHT ON (kamikaze mix)**	41	

(12"+=/cd-s+=) *(VS T/CD 1264)* – I feel free (extended). *(re-iss. Apr91; same); hit UK No.71)*

Oct 90. (7"/c-s) *(VS 1291)* **(WE WANT) THE SAME THING (summer remix). / SHADES OF MICHAELANGELO**	6	

(12"+=) *(VSTA 1291)* – Heaven is a place on Earth / I get weak.
(pic-cd+=) *(VSCDP 1291)* – Circle in the sand (sandblast multi).

Dec 90. (7"/c-s) *(VS/+C 1323)* **SUMMER RAIN. / LEAVE A LIGHT ON (mix)**	23	–

(12"+=/cd-s+=) *(VS T/CDX 1323)* – ('A'-Justin Strauss mix).

Sep 91. (7"/c-s) *(VS/+C 1370)* **LIVE YOUR LIFE BE FREE. / LONELINESS GAME**	12	

(12"pic-d+=/cd-s+=) *(VS T/CD 1370)* – ('A'club version).

Oct 91. (cd/c/lp) *(CD/TC+/V 2680)* **LIVE YOUR LIFE BE FREE** [7] [ ]
– Live your life be free / Do you feel like I feel? / Half the world / You came out of nowhere / You're nothing without me / I plead insanity / Emotional highway / Little black book / Love revolution / World of love / Loneliness game.

Nov 91. (7"/7"pic-d) *(VS/+P 1383) <54183>* **DO YOU FEEL LIKE I FEEL. / WORLD OF LOVE** [29] [73]
(12"+=) *(VST 1383)* – ('A'dance version).
(cd-s+=) *(VSCD 1383)* – Live your life be free (dance instrumental).

Jan 92. (7"/c-s) *(VS/+C 1388)* **HALF THE WORLD. / ONLY A DREAM** [35] [ ]
(cd-s+=) *(VSCDT 1388)* – Live your life be free (original).
(cd-s) *(VSCDX 1388)* – ('A'side) / Vision of you ('91 remix) / Circle in the sand / Love never dies.

Aug 92. (7"/c-s) *(VS/+C 1428)* **LITTLE BLACK BOOK. / ONLY A DREAM** [28] [–]
(cd-s+=) *(VSCDT 1428)* – The air you breathe.
(cd-s+=) *(VSCDG 1428)* – ('A'mix) / ('A'house mix).

Sep 92. (cd/c/lp) *(BEL CD/MC/TV 1)* **THE BEST OF BELINDA CARLISLE VOLUME 1** (compilation)
– Heaven is a place on Earth / (We want) The same thing / Circle in the sand / Leave a light on / Little black book / Summer rain / Vision of you / Live your life be free / I get weak / La Luna / I plead insanity / World without you / Do you feel like I feel? / Half the world / Runaway horses.

—— with writers **CAFFEY** + brothers **THOMAS** + **RICHARD**, plus **JEFFREY McDONALD** & **STEVEN McDONALD** / and a host of musicians

Sep 93. (7"/c-s) *(VS/+C 1472)* **BIG SCARY ANIMAL. / WINDOWS OF THE WORLD** [12] [–]
(cd-s+=) *(VSCDT 1472)* – Change (demo) / Too much water (demo).
(cd-s+=) *(VSCDX 1472)* –

Oct 93. (cd/c/lp) *(CD/TC+/V 2725)* **REAL** [9] [ ]
– Goodbye day / Big scary animal / Too much water / Lay down your arms / Where love hides / One with you / Wrap my arms / Tell me / Windows of the world / Here comes my baby.

Nov 93. (7"/c-s) *(VS/+C 1476)* **LAY DOWN YOUR ARMS. / TELL ME** [27] [–]
(cd-s+=) *(VSCDX 1476)* – Wrap my arms (demo).
(cd-s+=) *(VSCDG 1476)* – Here comes my baby (demo).

Chrysalis   Chrysalis

Jul 96. (7"pic-d/c-s) *(CHSPD/TCCHS 5033)* **IN TOO DEEP. / (WE WANT) THE SAME THING** [6] [–]
(cd-s+=) *(CDCHS 5033)* – I see no ships / Jealous guy.

Sep 96. (c-s) *(TCCHS 5037)* **ALWAYS BREAKING MY HEART / HEAVEN IS A PLACE ON EARTH** [8] [–]
(cd-s+=) *(CDCHS 5037)* – Circle in the sand / I get weak.
(cd-s) *(CDCHSS 5037)* – ('A'side) / Love walks in / The ballad of Lucy Jordan.

Sep 96. (cd/c) *(CD/TC CHR 6115)* **A WOMAN AND A MAN** [12] [–]
– In too deep / California / A woman and a man / Remember September / Listen to love / Always breaking my heart / Love doesn't live here anymore / He goes on / Kneel at your feet / Love in the key of C / My heart goes out to you.

Nov 96. (c-s) *(TCCHS 5044)* **LOVE IN THE KEY OF C / HEAVEN IS A PLACE ON EARTH / CIRCLE IN THE SAND** [20] [–]
(cd-s) *(CDCHS 5044)* – ('A'side) / Don't cry (demo) / Watcha doin' to me (demo) / Too much water (demo).
(cd-s) *(CDCHSS 5044)* – ('A'side) / Kneel at your feet / In too deep (acoustic) / Circle in the sand (acoustic).

Feb 97. (c-s) *(TCCHS 5047)* **CALIFORNIA / LEAVE A LIGHT ON (live)** [31] [–]
(cd-s+=) *(CDCHSS 5047)* – Live your life be free (live) / Heaven is a place on earth (live).
(cd-s) *(CDCHS 5047)* – ('A'side) / Big scary animal (live) / In too deep (live) / I get weak (live).

Virgin   Virgin

Nov 99. (cd/c) *(CDVX/TCV 2901)* **... A PLACE ON EARTH – THE GREATEST HITS** (compilation) [15] [ ]
– Heaven is a place on Earth / I get weak / Circle in the sand / Leave a light on / La Luna / We want the same thing / Summer rain / Live your life be free / Do you feel like I feel / Little black book / Big scary animal / In too deep / California / Always breaking my heart / Love in the key of C / Feels like I've known you forever / Prayer for everyone / All God's children.

Nov 99. (c-s/cd-s) *(VSC/+DT 1756)* **ALL GOD'S CHILDREN / RUNAWAY HORSES / ONLY A DREAM** [66] [–]

GO-GO'S

—— had briefly re-united in 1990 and late in '94

A&M   A&M

Jan 91. (12") *(AM 712)* **COOL JERK. / WE GOT THE BEAT** [60] [ ]
Feb 91. (cd/c/lp) *(395333-2/-4/-1)* <*447797*> **GO-GO'S GREATEST** (compilation) [ ] [Nov90]
– Our lips are sealed / Cool jerk / We got the beat / Head over heels / Get up and go / Vacation / Beatnik beach / You thought / I'm the only one / This town / Lust to love / Mercenary / How much more / Turn to you. (re-iss. cd Mar93 on 'A&M'; CDMID 184)

I.R.S.   I.R.S.

Feb 95. (7"/c-s) *(EIRS/+C 190)* **THE WHOLE WORLD LOST ITS HEAD. / OUR LIPS ARE SEALED** [29] [ ]
(cd-s+=) *(CDEIRS 190)* – Automatic / Lust to love.

Mar 95. (cd/c) *(EIRS CD/MC 1071)* **RETURN TO THE VALLEY OF THE GO-GO'S** (compilation) [52] [ ]
– Living at the Canterbury – Party pose / Fashion seekers (live) / He's so strange / London boys / Beatnik beach (live) / Cool jerk / We got the beat / Our lips are sealed / Surfing and spying / Vacation / Speeding / Good for gone / Head over heels / Can't stop the world (live) / Mercenary (acoustic) / Good girl / Beautiful / The whole world lost its head.

GO HOLE (see under ⇒ GENE)

GOLDEN EARRING

Formed: The Hague, Netherlands . . . 1961 as The TORNADO'S by RINUS GERRITSEN and GEORGE KOOYMANS, who subsequently added JAAP EGGERMONT, FRANS KRASSENBURG and PETER DE RONDE. In August '65, as EARRING (as they were known then) they scored a domestic Top 10 hit with the single, 'PLEASE GO'. Throughout the latter half of the 60's, the group continued to hit the Dutch charts with a string of quasi-bubblegum psychedelic pop ditties. At the turn of the decade they followed the nascent trend towards hard and heavy rock, a support tour in '72 with newfound friends The WHO resulting in a deal with Kit Lambert & Chris Stamp's 'Track'. By this juncture, several changes had taken place, the most notable being in 1967, when the enigmatic BARRY HAY took over the vocals. Though their first release for the label, 'HEARRING EARRING' was a compilation of their previous two Dutch lp's, a new single, 'RADAR LOVE', finally gave the band a deserved breakthrough in 1973. This highly distinctive tarmac-scorching classic virtually came to define the band's hard-drivin' sound and they found it difficult to create a worthy successor. The accompanying album, 'MOONTAN', also sold by the barrowload, the group enjoying a brief honeymoon period of success in the States in addition to their European standing. Not exactly one hit wonders, the band nevertheless enjoyed only minimal success (outside Holland) with subsequent albums, 'SWITCH' (1975), 'TO THE HILT' (1976), 'MAD LOVE' (1977), etc, etc. The albatross round their necks was briefly lifted late '82/early '83 with the freak US success of the single, 'TWILIGHT ZONE', which engendered a return to the album charts with 'CUT'. GOLDEN EARRING continued to chip away at the American market throughout the 80's, WHITE LION's successful cover of 'RADAR LOVE' in 1991 generating renewed interest in the group. • **Songwriters:** KOOYMANS, GERRITSEN and HAY. • **Trivia:** Early member JAAP EGGERMONT went on to become man behind the fruitful 80's pop STARSOUND medleys.

Album rating: JUST EARRINGS (*6) / WINTER HARVEST (*6) / MIRACLE MIRROR (*6) / EIGHT MILES HIGH (*6) / GOLDEN EARRING (WALL OF DOLLS) (*6) / SEVEN TEARS (*6) / TOGETHER (*6) / HEARING EARRING collection (*6) / MOONTAN (*7) / SWITCH (*6) / TO THE HILT (*6) / CONTRABAND (*5) / MAD LOVE (*5) / GOLDEN EARRING LIVE (*6) / GRAB IT FOR A SECOND (*5) / PRISONER OF THE NIGHT <US= LONG BLOND ANIMAL> (*5) / SECOND LIVE (*4) / CUT (*7) / N.E.W.S. (*6) / SOMETHING HEAVY GOING DOWN – LIVE FROM THE TWILIGHT ZONE (*4) / THE HOLE (*3) / THE CONTINUING STORY OF RADAR LOVE compilation (*8) / KEEPER OF THE FLAME (*5) / BLOODY BUCCANEERS (*5) / THE NAKED TRUTH (*3) / FACE IT (*4) / NAKED II (*3) / PARADISE IN DISTRESS (*3)

GOLDEN EARRINGS

GEORGE KOOYMANS (b.11 Mar'48) – vocals, guitar / **RINUS GERRITSEN** (b.9 Aug'46) – bass, keyboards / **FRANS KRASSENBURG** (b.24 Feb'44) – vocals / **PETER DE RONDE** (b.11 Jul'48) – guitar / **JAAP EGGERMONT** (b.31 Oct'46) – drums (early TORNADO'S members also included HANS VAN HERWERDEN + FREDDIE VAN DER HILST)

Polydor   not iss.

Aug 65. (7") *(S 1181)* **PLEASE GO. / CHUNK OF STEEL** [–] [–] Dutch
Nov 65. (7"; w-drawn) *(S 1185)* **LONELY EVERYDAY. / NOT TO FIND** [–] [–] Dutch
Nov 65. (lp) *(736 007)* **JUST EARRINGS** [–] [–] Dutch
– Nobody but you / I hate saying these words / She may be / Holy witness / No need to worry / Please go / Sticks and stones / I am a fool / Don't stay away / Lonely everyday / When people talk / Now I have.

Jan 66. (7") *(421 023)* **THAT DAY. / THE WORDS I NEED** [–] [–] Dutch
(above imported into UK in 1970; BM 56514)

—— trim slightly when PETER departed

1966. (lp) *(736 068)* **WINTER HARVEST** [–] [–] Dutch
– Another man in town / Smoking cigarettes / In my house / Don't wanna lose that girl / Impecable / Tears and lies / There will be a tomorrow / You've got the intention to hurt me / You break my heart / Baby don't make me nervous / Call me / Happy and young together / Lionel the mission. <US-iss.1967 as 'THE GOLDEN EARRINGS' on 'Capitol'; ST 2823>

Jun 66. (7") *(421 036)* **IF YOU LEAVE ME. / WAITING FOR YOU** [–] [–] Dutch
Aug 66. (7") *(SL 3004)* **THINGS GO BETTER. / RUM AND COCA COLA** [–] [–] Dutch
(above issued for the Coca Cola company!)
Oct 66. (7") *(421 050)* **DADDY BUY ME A GIRL. / WHAT YOU GONNA TELL** [–] [–] Dutch
Dec 66. (7") *(421 056)* **DON'T RUN TOO FAR. / WINGS** [–] [–] Dutch
Apr 67. (7") *(S 1223)* **IN MY HOUSE. / SMOKING CIGARETTES** [–] [–] Dutch
Jul 67. (7") *(S 1244)* **SOUND OF THE SCREAMING DAY. / SHE WON'T COME TO ME** [–] [–] Dutch
Oct 67. (7") *(S 1250)* **TOGETHER WE LIVE, TOGETHER WE LOVE. / I WONDER** [–] [–] Dutch

Capitol   Capitol

May 68. (lp) *<ST 164>* **MIRACLE MIRROR** [–] [–]
– Truth about Arthur / Circus will be in town in time / Crystal heaven / Sam & Sue / I've just lost somebody / Mr. Fortune's wife / Who cares / Born a second time / Magnificent magistral / Nothing can change this world of mine / Gipsy rhapsody.

Jun 68. (7") *(CL 15552)* **I'VE JUST LOST SOMEBODY. / THE TRUTH ABOUT ARTHUR** [–] [–]

—— (late 1967) added **BARRY HAY** (b.16 Aug'48, Faizabad) – vocals, occasional guitar flute, saxophone

Nov 68. (7") *(CL 15567)* **DONG-DONG-DIKI-DIGI-DONG. / WAKE UP BREAKFAST!** [ ] [–]

—— (were still signed to 'Polydor' in Holland)

—— **SIEB WARNER** – drums; repl. JAAP; he re-emerged in medley outfit STARSOUND

		Major Minor	Polydor
Mar 69.	(7") *(MM 601)* **JUST A LITTLE BIT OF PEACE IN MY HEART. / REMEMBER MY FRIEND**		-
Aug 69.	(7") *(MM 633)* **IT'S ALRIGHT BUT I ADMIT IT COULD BE BETTER. / WHERE WILL I BE**		-
Sep 69.	(7") *<2-14001>* **IT'S ALRIGHT I ADMIT IT COULD BE BETTER. / SONG OF A DEVIL'S SERVANT**	-	

GOLDEN EARRING

		Major Minor	Atlantic
Jan 70.	(lp) *(SMLP 65)* *<SD 8244>* **EIGHT MILES HIGH** – Landing / Song of a Devil's servant / One high road / Everyday's torture / Eight miles high. *(cd-iss. 1987; 825 371-2)*		
Feb 70.	(7") *(MM 679)* **ANOTHER FORTY-FIVE MILES. / I CAN'T GET HOLD OF HER**		
Feb 70.	(7") *<45-2710>* **EIGHT MILES HIGH. / ONE HIGH ROAD**	-	

—— **CESAR ZUIDERWIJK** (b.18 Jul'48) – drums; repl. SIEB

		Polydor	Perception
1970.	(lp) *(2310 049)* *<PDLP 2000>* **GOLDEN EARRING (WALL OF DOLLS)** – Yellow and blue / The loner / This is the time of the year / As long as the wind blows / Wall of dolls / Back home / See see / I'm going to send my pigeons to the sky / Big tree blue sea.		
Sep 70.	(7") *(2001 073)* **BACK HOME. / THIS IS THE TIME OF THE YEAR**		-
Feb 71.	(7") *(2001 135)* **HOLY HOLY LIFE. / JESSICA**	-	- Dutch
Oct 71.	(7") *(2001 237)* **SHE FLIES ON STRANGE WINGS. / (part 2)**	-	- Dutch
Oct 71.	(lp) *(2310 135)* **SEVEN TEARS** – Silver ships / The road / Swallowed her name / Hope / Don't worry / She flies on strange wings / This is the other side of fire / You're better off free.		
May 72.	(7") *(2050 184)* **BUDDY JOE. / AVALANCHE OF LOVE**	-	- Dutch
Jun 72.	(lp) *(2310 210)* **TOGETHER** – All day watcher / Avalanche of love / Cruising Southern Germany / Brother wind / Buddy Joe / Jangalene / From Heaven to Hell / Thousand feet below.	-	-
Sep 72.	(7") *(2050 216)* **STAND BY ME. / ALL DAY WATCHER**		- Dutch

		Track	Track
1973.	(lp) *(2406 109)* **HEARING EARRING** (compilation of last 2 lp's) – Jangeline / All day watcher / She flies on strange wings / Avalanche of love / Silver ships / Brother wind / Hope / Thousand feet below.		-
Aug 73.	(7") *(2050 262)* **RADAR LOVE. / THE SONG IS OVER**	-	- Dutch
Nov 73.	(7") *(2094 116)* *<40202>* **RADAR LOVE. / JUST LIKE VINCE TAYLOR**	7	13 Apr74
Dec 73.	(lp) *(2406 112)* *<396>* **MOONTAN** – Radar love / Candy's going bad / Vanilla queen / Big tree, blue sea / Are you receiving me? *<US cd-iss. Jun88 on 'M.C.A.'; 31014>*	24	12 Apr74
May 74.	(7") *(2094 121)* **INSTANT POETRY. / FROM HEAVEN, FROM HELL**		
Nov 74.	(7") *(2094 126)* *<40309>* **CANDY'S GOING BAD. / SHE FLIES ON STRANGE WINGS**		91 Oct74

—— added **ROBERT-JAN STIPS** (b.4 Feb'50) – keyboards

		Track	M.C.A.
Mar 75.	(7") *(2094 130)* *<40369>* **CE SOIR. / LUCKY NUMBERS**		
Apr 75.	(lp) *(2406 117)* *<2139>* **SWITCH** – (intro) / Plus minus absurdio / Love is a rodeo / Switch / Kill me, ce soir / Tons of times / Daddy's gonna save my soul / Troubles and hassles / Lonesome D.J.		
Jun 75.	(7") *<40412>* **SWITCH. / LONESOME D.J.**	-	

		Polydor	M.C.A.
Jan 76.	(7") *(2001 626)* *<40513>* **SLEEP WALKIN'. / BABYLON**		
Mar 76.	(lp) *(2430 330)* *<2183>* **TO THE HILT** – Why me / Facedancer / To the hilt / Nomad / Sleep walkin' / Latin lightnin' / Violins.		Feb76

—— **EELCO GELLING** – guitar (ex-guest) repl. STIPS (remained guest)

		Polydor	
Feb 77.	(7") *(2121 312)* **BOMBAY. / FADED JEANS**		-
Mar 77.	(lp/c) *(2310 491/3100 340)* *<2254>* **CONTRABAND** <US-title 'MAD LOVE'> – Bombay / Sueleen (Sweden) / Con man / Mad love's comin' / Fightin' windmills / Faded jeans / Time's up.		May77
Sep 77.	(d-lp) *(2625 034)* **GOLDEN EARRING LIVE** (live) – Candy's going bad / She flies on strange wings / Mad love's comin' / Eight miles high / The vanilla queen / To the hilt / Fightin' windmills / Con man / Radar love / Just like Vince Taylor. *(re-iss. Oct93; SPELP 44)*		
Sep 77.	(12") *(2121 335)* **RADAR LOVE (live). / JUST LIKE VINCE TAYLOR (live)**	44	-
Oct 77.	(7") *<40802>* **RADAR LOVE (live). / RADAR LOVE (studio)**	-	

		Polydor	Polydor
Jan 79.	(lp) *(2310 639)* *<1-6223>* **GRAB IT FOR A SECOND** <US-title 'NO PROMISES'> – Movin' down life / Against the grain / Grab it for a second / Cell 29 / Roxanne / Leather / Temptin' / U-turn time.		
1980.	(lp) *(2344 161)* *<1-6303>* **PRISONER OF THE NIGHT** <US-title 'LONG BLOND ANIMAL'> – Long blond animal / No for an answer / My town / Prisoner of the night / I don't wanna be nobody else / Cut 'em down to size / Will & Mercy / Come in Outerspace / Going crazy again.	-	- Dutch
Sep 81.	(7") *<14581>* **WEEKEND LOVE. / TIGER BAY**	-	-
Sep 81.	(d-lp)(c) *(2625 042/3500 130)* **SECOND LIVE** (live) – Don't stop the show / My town / No for an answer / Heartbeat / Save your skin / I don't wanna be nobody else / Long blond animal / Prisoner of the night / Weekend love / Sleepwalkin' / I do rock'n'roll / Slow down / Buddy Joe / Back home.	-	- Dutch

		Mercury	21 Records
Jan 83.	(7"/12") *(MER/+X 122)* *<103>* **TWILIGHT ZONE. / KING DARK**		10 Nov82

		Philips	21 Records
Apr 83.	(lp/c) *(6302/7144 224)* *<9004>* **CUT** – The Devil made me do it / Future / Baby dynamite / Last of the Mohicans / Lost and found / Twilight zone / Chargin' up my batteries / Secrets.		24 Nov82
Apr 83.	(7") *<108>* **THE DEVIL MADE ME DO IT. / CHARGIN' UP MY BATTERIES**	-	79

		Carrere	21 Records
Apr 84.	(7"/12") *(CAR/+T 321)* *<112>* **WHEN THE LADY SMILES. / ORWELL'S YEAR**		76 Mar84
Apr 84.	(lp/c) *(CAL/CAC 204)* *<9008>* **N.E.W.S.** – Clear night moonlight / When the lady smiles / Enough is enough / Fist in love / N.E.W.S. / I'll make it all up to you / Mission impossible / It's over now. *(cd-iss. 1988;)*		Mar84

		21 Records	21 Records
Feb 85.	(lp) *(21-0022)* *<823717>* **SOMETHING HEAVY GOING DOWN – LIVE FROM THE TWILIGHT ZONE** (live) – Long blond animal / Twilight zone / When the lady smiles / Future / Something heavy going down / Enough is enough / Mission impossible / Clear night moonlight.		Nov84
Apr 86.	(7") *(21-043)* **QUIET EYES. / GIMME A BREAK**	-	- Dutch
Jun 86.	(lp) *(21-0022)* *<90514>* **THE HOLE** – They dance / Quiet eyes / Save the best for later / Have a heart / Love in motion / Jane Jane / Jump and run / Why do I / Shout in the dark.	-	- German
Jun 86.	(7") *<7-99533>* **QUIET EYES. / LOVE IN MOTION**	-	-
Nov 86.	(7") *<7-99515>* **WHY DO I. / LOVE IN MOTION**	-	-
Dec 86.	(7") *(21-049)* **THEY DANCE. / LOVE IN MOTION**	-	- Dutch

GEORGE KOOYMANS

—— Note:- GEORGE was first to moonlight solo with the 7", 'LOVIN' AND HURTIN'' / 'FOR GAIL' on 'Polydor' (2050 156); both from the Dutch-only LP, 'JOJO' (2925 004)

		Ring	not iss.
1987.	(7") *(108 814)* **LOST FOR LOVE. / THE DEVIL RIDES AGAIN TONIGHT**	-	- Dutch
1987.	(lp) *(258 167)* **SOLO** – Lost for love, give it all you got / World of our own / I'll never give in / To you / The Devil rides again tonight / The beat goes on / Shoot the man down / Lonely hearts / Again.	-	- Dutch
1987.	(7") *(108 814)* **LOST FOR LOVE. / THE DEVIL RIDES AGAIN TONIGHT**	-	- Dutch
1987.	(7") *(109 095)* **THE BEAT GOES ON. / AGAIN**	-	- Dutch
1988.	(7") *(109 260)* **WORLD OF OUR OWN. / ALL THINGS ARE LIGHT**	-	- Dutch

—— Also:- GERRITSEN delivered a one-off US-only single in 1980 for 'Atco', 'ROCK AND BEAST' / 'SUZY'S SONG' <7213> (from the set 'DE G.V.D. BAND' with MICHEL VAN DIK), while ZUIDERWIJK issued two in the mid-80's, 'GIVE ME BACK MY FEELINGS' / 'BETWEEN DUSK AND DAYLIGHT' (21 Records; 039) and 'HELP ME OUT' / 'GRIMACE' (041); taken from the LP, 'LABYRINTH' <90477-1>

BARRY HAY

—— Note:- BARRY had issued a single in '72, 'DID YOU REALLY MEAN IT' / 'ROLL ANOTHER ROCK' for 'Polydor' (2050 193); taken from the Dutch-only LP, 'ONLY PARROTS, FROGS AND ANGELS' (2925 006).

Nov 87.	(7") *(109 460)* **DRAGGIN' THE LINE. / WHAT KINDA LOVE**	-	- Dutch
Dec 87.	(lp) *(208 498)* **VICTORY OF BAD TASTE** – Draggin' the line / I'd lie to you for your love / Jezebel / My favourite spot / Firewater / Did you really mean it / She's here / Girl / Going blind.	-	- Dutch
Feb 88.	(7") *(109 672)* **JEZEBEL. / GOING BLIND**	-	- Dutch

GOLDEN EARRING

—— re-formed in the late 80's, with HAY, GERRITSEN, KOOYMANS + ZUIDERWIJK

Feb 88.	(7") *(21-055)* **MY KILLER, MY SHADOW. / (version)** (12"+=)(cd-s+=) *(2-155)(100.142)* – ('A'extended).	-	-

		Music Box	not iss.
Apr 89.	(7") *(559-7)* **TURN THE WORLD AROUND. / YOU GUN MY LOVE** (cd-s+=) *(559-3)* – Say my prayer.	-	- Dutch
Apr 89.	(lp) *(40402)* *(Dutch; JAWS 5542)* **KEEPER OF THE FLAME** – Can do that / Too much woman / One word / Keeper of the flame / Turn the world around / Circles / My killer, my shadow / Distant love.	-	-
Jun 89.	(7") *(5512-7)* **DISTANT LOVE. / NIGHTHAWKS** (cd-s+=) *(5512-3)* – Can't do that.	-	- Dutch

—— (basically same line-up for over 20 years)

		Columbia	First Quake
Apr 91.	(7"/3"cd-s) *(656802-7/-1)* **GOING TO THE RUN. / TIME WARP** (12"+=/cd-s+=) *(656802-6/-2)* – Steam roller.	-	- Dutch
Jun 91.	(7"/3"cd-s) *(657283-7/-1)* **TEMPORARY MADNESS. / ONE SHOT AWAY FROM PARADISE** (12"+=/cd-s+=) *(657283-6/-2)* – Madame Zou Zou.	-	- Dutch
Aug 91.	(cd/c/lp) *(468093-2/-4/-1)* *<FQCD 4482-2>* **BLOODY BUCHANEERS** – Making love to yourself / Temporary madness / When love turns to pain / Joe / Planet blue / Going to the run / Bloody buchaneers / One shot away from Paradise / In a bad mood / Pouring my heart out again.		
Dec 91.	(7") *(657545-7)* **POURING MY HEART OUT AGAIN. / PLANET BLUE** (d7"+=/cd-s+=) *(657545-0/-2)* – When the lady smiles (live) / Back home (live).	-	- Dutch
Feb 92.	(7") *(657809-7)* **MAKING LOVE TO YOURSELF. / IN A BAD MOOD** (cd-s+=) *(657809-2)* – When love turns to pain.	-	- Dutch
Apr 92.	(7") *(658025-7)* **RADAR LOVE. / BLOODY BUCHANEERS**	-	- Dutch

(cd-s+=) *(658025-2)* – Joe.

1993. (12") *(658952-1)* **ANOTHER 45 MILES (live-acoustic). / WHEN THE LADY SMILES (live-acoustic)** | - | - | Dutch

(cd-s+=) *(658952-2)* – Going to the run (live-acoustic).

1993. (d-cd) *(472619-2) <4481>* **THE NAKED TRUTH** (live-acoustic) | - | | Dutch
– (introduction) / Jangalene / Another 45 miles / Mad love's comin' / Why do I / I can't sleep with you / Weekend love / Vanilla queen / Twilight zone / One shot away from paradise / Long blond animal / Pouring my heart out again / Radar love / Eight miles high / The naked truth.

1993. (cd-ep's) *(659333-2'5)* **LONG BLOND ANIMAL (live-acoustic) / TWILIGHT ZONE (live-acoustic) / JANGALENE (live-acoustic) / DON'T STOP THE SHOW (live-acoustic)** | - | - | Dutch

1993. (cd-s) *(659719-1)* **AS LONG AS THE WIND BLOWS (live-acoustic) / PLEASE GO (live-acoustic) / SOUND OF THE SCREAMING DAY (live-acoustic)** | - | - | Dutch

(cd-s+=) *(659719-2)* – Murdock 9-6182 (live-acoustic).

1994. (cd-s) *(660761-1)* **HOLD ME NOW / LIVIN' WITH ME (AIN'T THAT EASY)** | - | - | Dutch

(cd-s+=) *(660761-2)* – Freedom don't last forever.

1994. (cd-s) *(661150-1)* **JOHNNY MAKE BELIEVE / MINUTE BY MINUTE** | - | - | Dutch

(cd-s+=) *(661150-2)* – Spaceship (remix) / Hold me now (remix).

1995. (cd-s) *(661380-1)* **ANGEL / THE UNFORGETTABLE DREAM** | - | - | Dutch

(cd-s+=) *(661380-2)* – Yellow and blue (live-acoustic) / The Devil made me do it (live-acoustic).

Jun 95. (cd/c) *(477650-2/-4)* **FACE IT** | | |
– Angel / Hold me now / Liquid soul / Minute by minute / Johnny make believe / Spaceship / The unforgettable dream / I can't do without your kiss / Freedom don't last forever / Maximum make up / Legalize telepathy.

Nov 95. (cd) *(481122-2)* **LOVESWEAT** (covers) | - | - | Dutch

1996. (cd-s) *(662831-1)* **THIS WHEEL'S ON FIRE / MY LITTLE RED BOOK** | - | - | Dutch

(cd-s+=) *(662831-2)* – So you want to be a rock'n'roll star – L.A. woman.

1996. (cd-s) *(663224-1)* **GOTTA SEE JANE / TRY A LITTLE TENDERNESS** | - | - | Dutch

                                             C.N.R.   not iss.

1997. (c-s) *(200340-4)* **BURNING STUNTMAN / BOMBAY** | - | - | Dutch

(cd-s+=) *(200340-5)* – When I was young (live) / This wheel's on fire (live).

1997. (cd) *(2003 447)* **NAKED II** (live-acoustic(| | |

1998. (cd-s) *(2003 607)* **THE DEVIL MADE ME DO IT / MOOD INDIGO** | - | - | Dutch

(cd-s) *(200360-8)* – ('A'side) / Holy holy life / Kill me (ce soir) / ('A'version).

Mar 99. (cd) *(48003)* **PARADISE IN DISTRESS** | - | - | Dutch

– compilations, others, etc. –

on Polydor' unless mentioned otherwise

Oct 76. (lp) *(2482 329)* **GOLDEN EARRING** | | -

Nov 80. (d-lp)(c) *(2664 440)(3578 487)* **GREATEST HITS** | | -

Mar 86. (7") *Old Gold; (OG 9582)* **RADAR LOVE. / TWILIGHT ZONE** | | -

May 88. (cd) *Arcade; (01290161)* **THE VERY BEST OF GOLDEN EARRING VOLUME 1** | | -

May 88. (cd) *Arcade; (01290261)* **THE VERY BEST OF GOLDEN EARRING VOLUME 2** | | -

1989. (cd) *M.C.A.; <MCAD 6355>* **THE CONTINUING STORY OF RADAR LOVE** | - | |

Jul 92. (cd) *Connoisseur; (VSOPCD 171)* **THE BEST OF GOLDEN EARRING** | | -
– Radar love / She flies on strange wings / Kill me / Mission impossible / Vanilla queen / Sleepwalkin' / Long blonde animal / Weekend love / When the lady smiles / Quiet eyes / Twilight zone / Turn the world around / Eight miles high.

GOLDEN PALOMINOS (dig out; Great Alt & Indie . . .)

GOLDIE

Born: 1965, Wolverhampton, England. After a rough'n'ready childhood spent in foster homes, GOLDIE was a streetwise dude with a penchant for electro, hip hop and graffiti art. After a spell in Miami with his father, he returned to Britain and met up with DJ duo KEMISTRY and STORM, who took him to the hardcore rave club "Rage" in London's Charing Cross. He worked with Mancunian (A GUY CALLED) GERALD ('Voodoo Ray' man) on his 'ENERGY' single. GOLDIE was hooked and soon became one of the prime movers at 'Reinforced', a small hardcore label which had grown out of the embryonic rave scene and flourished under the entrepreneurial spirit of the time. In the early 90's, GOLDIE (named so, due to his gold-plated molars) released his first recorded music under the RUFIGE KRU moniker. Along with other cutting-edge releases of the day, the records heralded a move away from the smiley sounds of rave culture, replacing the uplifting piano breaks with disturbing sound effects, razor-sharp breakbeats and way-deep sub-basslines. Then, in 1993, under the alias METALHEADZ, a name he'd later use for his own label, GOLDIE recorded the pivotal 'TERMINATOR'. With its deconstructed fluid beats and futuristic samples, the record saw jungle coming of age. The follow-up 'ANGEL' took the blueprint and pushed the parameters ever further. Haunting female vocals and 'Tomorrow Never Knows'-like squawls melted into amphetamine-rush snares, creating music of exquisite beauty and dark grace. After signing to 'Ffrr', GOLDIE released the lush 'INNER CITY LIFE' towards the end of '94. Already a godfather-like figure within the tight-knit breakbeat community, GOLDIE was a charismatic character with a talent for off-the-cuff soundbites and was duly adopted by the music press as the drum'n'bass spokesman. His high media profile helped propel his landmark opus, 'TIMELESS', to the upper reaches of the album charts. Beloved of the inky press as well as the dance mags, the album

went on to sell more than 100,000 copies, inspiring a slew of ambient-jungle imitators and even galvanising Radio One into covering the burgeoning breakbeat movement. In addition to live work at home and abroad, GOLDIE has continued to release pioneering material on his 'Metalheadz' label, anticipating the move towards more jazz-infected rhythms evident in the work of contemporaries like RONI SIZE. The Metalheadz club night in London also continues to pack in the crowds, all of which will ensure that, for the time being at least, GOLDIE will remain as the larger-than-life spokesperson for one of the most innovative musical developments of the last decade. Along with LTJ BUKEM's 'Logical Progression' collection, GOLDIE's epochal 'TIMELESS' album is one of the few jungle releases you'd be likely to see on the well-heeled CD buyers's coffee table. His love life too, became more fodder for the gossip columns, when he became the beau of Icelandic pixie BJORK around 1996.

Album rating: TIMELESS (*8) / SATURNZRETURN (*7)

METALHEADZ

GOLDIE – vocals / with

		Reinforced	not iss.
1992.	(12"ep) **KILLERMUFFIN EP**		-
		Synthetic	not iss.
Nov 92.	(12"ep/c-ep/cd-ep) *(SYNTH/+K/CD 003)* **TERMINATOR EP**		-
	– Terminator / Kemistry / Knowledge / Sinister. *(re-iss. Oct93; SYNTH 3 /+C/CD)*		
Aug 93.	(12"ep) *(SYNTH 7)* **ANGEL EP**		-
	(12") *(SYNTH 7R)* – Angel (remixes).		
1994.	(12"ep) **ENFORCERS EP**		-

GOLDIE

		Ffrr-London	London
Nov 94.	(12"/c-s/cd-s; as GOLDIE PRESENTS METALHEADZ) *(FX/FCS/FCD 251)* **INNER CITY LIFE / ('A'mixes)**	49	
	(12") *(FXX 251)* – ('A'mixes; Roni Size / Nookie remix).		
Mar 95.	(c-s/cd-s) **TIMELESS / INNER CITY LIFE**		
Jul 95.	(d-cd/d-c/d-lp) *(828 646-2/-4/-1)* **TIMELESS**	7	
	– Timeless / Saint Angel / State of mind / This is a bad / Sea of tears / Jah the seventh / State of rage (sensual V.I.P. mix) / Still life / Angel / Adrift / Kemistry / You & me. *(d-lp+=)* – (2 other mixes). *(cd re-iss. Feb98; 828614-2)*		
Aug 95.	(12"/c-s) *(FX/FCS 266)* **ANGEL / SAINT ANGEL / YOU AND ME (THE BEAUTY – THE BEAST)**	41	
	(cd-s+=) *(FCD 266)* – Angel (Peshay back from Narm mix). (above vocals by D. CHARLEMAGNE)		
Nov 95.	(c-s) *(FCS 267)* **INNER CITY LIFE / ('A'-Peshay mix)**	39	
	(cd-s+=) *(FCD 267)* – Kemistry (Doc Scott mix).		
	(12") *(FX 267)* – ('A'radio mix) / ('A'extended) / ('A'-4 Hero part 1 mix) / ('A'-Roni Size instrumental).		

—— following album featured an orchestra arranged by GAVYN WRIGHT

Oct 97.	(12"/cd-s; GOLDIE feat KRS ONE) *(FX/FCD 316)* **DIGITAL / ('A'-original mix) / ('A'-V.I.P. mix)**	13	
	(cd-s) *(FXX/FCDP 316)* – ('A'remixes).		
Jan 98.	(12"/cd-s) *(FX/FCD 325)* **TEMPERTEMPER – (short temper). / TEMPERTEMPER / TEMPERTEMPER – (vipmix)**	13	
	(cd-s) *(FCDP 325)* –		
Feb 98.	(d-cd/c/t-lp) *(828990-2/-4/-1) <828983>* **SATURNZRETURN**	15	
	– MOTHER: Mother / Truth // SATURN: Tempertemper / Digital / I'll be there for you / Believe / Dragonfly / Chico-death of a rockstar / Letter of fate / Fury – the origin / Crystal clear / Demonz.		
Mar 98.	(12"/cd-s) *(FX/FCD 332)* **BELIEVE. / ('A'mixes)**	36	
	(cd-s) *(FCDP 332)* – ('A'mixes).		

GOLLIWOGS (see under ⇒ CREEDENCE CLEARWATER REVIVAL)

GOMEZ

Formed: Southport, Yorkshire, England . . . 1997 originally as GOMEZ, KILL, KILL THE VORTEX by college lads BEN OTTERWELL, TOM GRAY, IAN BALL, PAUL BLACKBURN and OLLY PEACOCK. A home-recorded tape of the band found its way into the hands of record shop worker and former COMSAT ANGELS member, STEVE FELLOWS, who almost immediately became their manager. He in turn set up time in a Sheffield rehearsal studio to which he invited a plethora of A&R men to witness the unique talent of the band. After a fortnight, over thirty record labels were showing signs of interest, although FELLOWS and his protegees opted for Virgin offshoot, 'Hut'. Their early 70's to early 90's sound – like a hybrid of LOWELL GEORGE, GRATEFUL DEAD and BECK – was much in debt to the bluesy whisky-throated chords of lead singer, BEN, whose boyish, bespectacled look stunned an unsuspecting but appreciative audience on their debut single, '78 STONE WOBBLE'. It was their first UK Top 50 entry and was pursued a month later – in April '98 – by their classic debut album, 'BRING IT ON'. A critical and soon-to-be commercial success, its highlights were the tracks, 'GET MILES' (gruffly reminiscent of The BEATLES' 'Come Together'), 'WHIPPIN' PICCADILLY' and 'GET MYSELF ARRESTED', all of which helped it win the much lauded Mercury prize early in '99. Later that year, two brand-new GOMEZ tracks 'BRING IT ON' (surprisingly not a part of the debut!) and 'RHYTHM & BLUES ALIBI' hovered around the Top 20, while parent follow-up set, 'LIQUID SKIN' (1999), smashed in at No.2. On reflection, the band might've been better to wait a little longer. Good on

GOMEZ though, as it says a lot for a band who release a fresh set of songs every year – here's hoping America could be their next prize.

Album rating: BRING IT ON (*9) / LIQUID SKIN (*7)

BEN OTTERWELL – vocals / **IAN BALL** – guitar, vocals, harmonica (ex-SEV) / **TOM GRAY** – keyboards, vocals, guitar, multi / **PAUL BLACKBURN** – bass / **OLLY PEACOCK** – percussion

		Hut	Virgin
Mar 98. (cd-s) *(HUTCD 95)* **78 STONE WOBBLE / WHO'S GONNA GO TO THE BAR / STEVE McCROSKI** (12"+=/cd-s+=) *(HUT T/C 95)* – Wham bam.		44	-
Apr 98. (cd-c/d-lp) *(CDHUT/HUTMC/HUTDLP 49)* <45592> **BRING IT ON**		11	May98

– Get miles / Whippin' Piccadilly / Make no sound / 78 stone wobble / Tijuana lady / Here comes the breeze / Love is better than a warm trombone / Get myself arrested / Free to run / Bubble gum years / Rie's wagon / The comeback.

| Jun 98. (c-s) *(HUTC 97)* **GET MYSELF ARRESTED / THE COWBOY SONG** (12"+=/cd-s+=) *(HUT T/CD 97)* – Flavours / Old school shirt. | | 45 | - |

		Hut	E.M.I.
Aug 98. (c-s) *(HUTC 105)* <95293> **WHIPPIN' PICCADILLY / PUSSYFOOTIN'** (12"+=/cd-s+=) *(HUT T/CD 105)* – Pick up the pieces.		35	Nov98
Jun 99. (c-s/cd-s) *(HUT C/CD 112)* **BRING IT ON / DIRE TRIBE / M57** (cd-s) *(HUTDX 112)* – ('A'side) / Chicken bones / Step inside. (12"+=) *(HUTT 112)* – (all 5 tracks above).		21	
Aug 99. (c-s/cd-s) *(HUT C/CD 114)* **RHYTHM & BLUES ALIBI / THE BEST IN THE TOWN / SO** (cd-s) *(HUTDX 114)* – ('A'-Pre-mellotron version) / ZYX / Tijuanalaska (Tijuana lady – live version). (12"+=) *(HUUT 114)* – (all 6 tracks above).		18	
Sep 99. (cd/c/d-lp) *(CDHUT/HUTMC/HUTDLP 54)* **LIQUID SKIN**		2	

– Hangover / Revolutionary kind / Bring it on / Blue moon rising / Las Vegas dealer / We haven't turned around / Fill my cup / Rhythm & blues alibi / Rosalita / California / Devil will ride.

| Nov 99. (c-s/cd-s) *(HUT C/CD 117)* **WE HAVEN'T TURNED AROUND / FLIGHT / ROSEMARY** (cd-s/12") *(HUT DX/T 117)* – ('A'mix) / Gomez in a bucket (a seaside town made of ice cream slowly melting) / Emergency surgery. | | 38 | |

GONG

Formed: Paris, France . . . c.1970 by Australian DAEVID ALLEN, who had been part of the embryonic Canterbury beatnik scene in England since the mid-60's. Previous to this, he had hung out with the likes of WILLIAM BURROUGHS and ALLEN GINSBERG at the famous Beat Hotel in Paris, cultivating his bohemian leanings and free-form poetry skills. He hitched back to England and soon met a young ROBERT WYATT while lodging at his parents' house. Through WYATT, he was introduced to MIKE RATLEDGE and HUGH HOPPER, with whom he subsequently formed the jazz-influenced WILDE FLOWERS. A prototype SOFT MACHINE, they also numbered another youngster, KEVIN AYERS. ALLEN remained for a one-off 45, 'Love Makes Sweet Music', in 1967, but was subsequently refused re-entry into Britain after a gig in St. Tropez. This effectively ended his tenure with the group, providing the impetus to set up his own commune of hippies who later evolved into GONG. A flexible outfit at this stage, they provided the backing for two albums, 'MAGICK BROTHER, MYSTIC SISTER' and 'BANANA MOON', the latter being credited to ALLEN. Theirs was an enchanting blend of whimsical, unconventional psychedelia that combined spaced-out rock and weird experimentation. 1971 produced the excellent 'CAMEMBERT ELECTRIQUE', which crystalised their innovative sound, the album finally being issued in the UK when Richard Branson's newly formed 'Virgin' label virtually gave it away for 49p (new money!). Titles like 'SQUEEZING SPONGES OVER POLICEMEN'S HEADS', 'WET CHEESE DELIRIUM' and the not-so ridiculously named 'TRIED SO HARD', were perfect examples of GONG's acid-fried humour. They had been part of the Glastonbury scene following a slot at the 1971 festival, although ALLEN broke up the band soon after. A year later, they reformed with a slightly altered line-up; GILLI SMYTH, DIDIER MALHERBE, LAURIE ALLEN, CHRISTIAN TRITSCH and FRANCIS MOZE, along with new space-cadets STEVE HILLAGE and TIM BLAKE. Now on 'Virgin', the band began work on a trilogy of albums entitled 'RADIO GNOME INVISIBLE', beginning with 'THE FLYING TEAPOT'. The second and third of these, 'ANGEL'S EGG' and 'YOU', came out the following year, ALLEN later decamping to Majorca. With their leading light gone, the band went through a dizzying series of personnel changes; HILLAGE went solo, while MOERLEN left a couple of times before he finally took control of the reins in 1976. This resulted in the creatively poor NICK MASON-produced set, 'SHAMAL'. Another, 'GAZEUSE!', was just as bad, the group taking some time to recover from the stagnant jazz-rock they peddled during the MOERLEN period. Meanwhile, ALLEN was carving out his own solo career, the punk-rock number, 'OPIUM FOR THE PEOPLE', in 1978 introducing a harder edge, while PLANET GONG and MOTHER GONG (GILLI's outfit) were as zany as anything the original GONG had ever produced. By the late 80's, GONG (and occasionally GONG MAISON) was again under the control of ALLEN, who had (predictably!) set up home in Glastonbury.

Album rating (selective): MAGICK BROTHER, MYSTIC SISTER (*5) / CONTINENTAL CIRCUS (*6) / BANANA MOON (*5; by Daevid Allen) / CAMEMBERT ELECTRIQUE (*8) / THE FLYING TEAPOT (*7) / ANGEL'S EGG

(*6) / YOU (*6) / SHAMAL (*4) / GOOD MORNING! (*4; by Daevid Allen & Euterpe) / NOW IS THE HAPPIEST TIME OF YOUR LIFE (*5; by Daevid Allen) / LIVE FLOATING ANARCHY 77 (*7; as Planet Gong) / GAZEUSE! (*4) / LIVE, ETC (*4) / EXPRESSO II (*4) / DOWNWIND (*3) / TIME IS THE KEY (*3) / PIERRE MOERLEN'S GONG (*3) / LEAVE IT OPEN (*3) / BREAKTHROUGH (*3) / SECOND WIND (*2) / SHAPESHIFTER (*6) / THE BEST OF GONG compilation (*8) / 25th BIRTHDAY PARTY (*6)

DAEVID ALLEN (b.Australia) – guitar, vocals (ex-SOFT MACHINE) / **GILLI SMYTH** (b.France) – whispered vocals / **DIDIER MALHERBE** – sax, flute / **RACHID HOUARI** – drums, tabla / **DIETER GEWISSLER** – contrabass / **CARL FREEMAN** – contrabass / **BARE PHILLIPS** – contrabass / **BURTON GREEN** – piano, piano harp / **TASMIN SMYTH** (Gilli's daughter) – vocals

		Byg Actuel	not iss.
Feb 70. (lp) *(5-529 029)* **MAGICK BROTHER, MYSTIC SISTER**		-	- France

– Mystick sister, Magick brother / Glad to say to say / Rational anthem / Chainstore chant – Pretty Miss Titty / Fable of a Fredfish – Hope you feel o.k.? / Ego / Gong song / Princess dreaming / 5 & 20 schoolgirls / Cos you got green hair. *(UK-iss.Nov77 on 'Charly'; CRL 5052) (cd-iss. Nov86 on 'Decal'; CDLIK 31)*

| 1970. (7") *(129021)* **EST-CE-QUE JE SUIS. / HIP HIPNOTIZE YOU** | | - | - France |

—— now with Englishmen **PIP PYLE, CHRISTIAN TRITSCH + ROBERT WYATT**

| 1971. (lp; by DAEVID ALLEN) *(45 529 345)* **BANANA MOON** | | - | - France |

– Time of our life / Memories / All I want is out of here / Fred the fish / White rock blues and cabin code / Stoned innocent / Frankenstein, and his adventures in the land of Flip / I am a bowl. *(UK-iss.Jul75 on 'Caroline'; C 1512) (re-iss. May79 on 'Charly'; CR 30165) (cd-iss. May90 on 'Decal'; CDLIK 63) (lp re-iss. Aug99 on 'Get Back'; GET 557)*

—— **CHRISTIAN TRITSCH** – bass / **GERRY FIELDS** – violin / **DANIEL LALOU** – multi horns, percussion repl. FREEMAN, GREEN, PHILLIPS and T. SMYTH

| 1971. (lp) *(45 529 533)* **CAMEMBERT ELECTRIQUE** | | - | - France |

– Radio gnome / You can't kill me / I've bin stone before / Mister long shanks: O mother – I am your fantasy / Dynamite: I am your animal / Wet cheese delirium / Squeezing sponges over policemen's heads / Fohat digs holes in space / Tried so hard / Tropical fish: Selene / Gnome the second. *(UK-iss.Jun74 on 'Caroline'; VC 502) (re-iss. 1982 on 'Charly'; CRM 2003) (cd-iss. Mar86 on 'Decal'; CDLIK 11) (re-iss. cd 1988 on 'Caroline'; C 1520) (re-iss. cd Mar90 on 'Decal'; CDLIK 64) (cd-iss. Nov94 on 'Gas'; AGASCD 001) (re-iss. Sep95 on 'Spalax';)*

| Jan 71. (lp; Philips UK) *(6332 033)* **CONTINENTAL CIRCUS** (Soundtrack) | | | - |

– Blues for Findlay / Continental circus world / What do you want / Blues for Findlay (instrumental). *(cd-iss. May96 on 'Mantra'; 642089)*

—— **LAURIE ALLEN** (b.England) – drums repl. PYLE who joined HATFIELD + THE NORTH / added **FRANCIS MOZE** – bass (ex-MAGMA)

—— Disbanded early '72 after Glastonbury Fayre, but re-formed by end of year. Added **STEVE HILLAGE** (b. 2 Aug'51, England) – guitar (ex-KEVIN AYERS, ex-KHAN, ex-URIEL) / **TIM BLAKE** (b.England) – synthesizers

		Virgin	Virgin
May 73. (lp) *(V 2002)* **FLYING TEAPOT (RADIO GNOME INVISIBLE PART 1)**			-

– Radio gnome invisible / Flying teapot / The pot head pixies / The octave doctors and the crystal machine / Zero to hero and the witch's spell / Witch's song / I am your pussy. *(re-iss. Jan82 on 'Charly'; CR 30202) (re-iss. Mar84; OVED 14) (cd-iss. May91 on 'Decal'; CDLIK 67) (re-iss. cd Sep95 on 'Spalax';)*

—— Although DAEVID and GILLI moved to Majorca, Spain, they returned mid 1973. / **PIERRE MOERLEN** (b.Colmar, France) – drums repl. LAURIE / **MIKE HOWLETT** (b.Fiji) – bass, vocals repl. MOZE

| Dec 73. (lp) *(V 2007)* **ANGEL'S EGG (RADIO GNOME INVISIBLE PART 2)** | | | - |

– Other side of the sky / Sold to the highest Buddha / Castles in the clouds / Prostitute poem / Givin' my luv to you / Selene / Flute salad / Oily way / Outer temple – Inner temple / Percolations / Love is how you make it / I never glid before / Eat that phonebook coda. *(re-iss. Aug82 on 'Charly'; CR 30219) (re-iss. Mar84; OVED 15) (cd-iss. 1989; CDV 2007) (re-iss. cd Apr91 on 'Decal'+=; CDLIK 75)* – Ooby-Stooby doomsday or The D-Day DJs got the DDT blues.

—— **MIQUETTE GIRAUDY** – keyboards repl. GILLI

| Oct 74. (lp) *(V 2019)* **YOU** | | | - |

– Thoughts for nought / A.P.H.P.'s advice / Magick mother invocation / Master builder / A sprinkling of clouds / Perfect mystery / The isle of everywhere / You never blow your trip forever. *(re-iss. Aug82 on 'Charly'; CR 30220) (re-iss. Mar84; OVED 16) (cd-iss. 1989; CDV 2019) (re-iss. cd Aug91 on 'Decal'; CDLIK 76)*

—— Virtually break-up, when DAEVID and GILLI move to Spain again. In May'76, DAEVID continued solo career and re-formed GONG in the late 80's. Meanwhile back in 1975, after he recorded solo FISH RISING album, STEVE HILLAGE also became solo artist using most of GONG!.

GONG

re-formed with only one original **DIDIER MALHERBE**. He recruited **JORGE PINCHEVSKY** – violin / **MIQUETTE GIRAUDY** – keyboards / **MIKE HOWLETT** – drums / **MIREILLE BAUER** – percussion, xylophone, etc. / **PATRICE LEMOINE** – keyboards

—— (HOWLETT went on to become producer of A FLOCK OF SEAGULLS, etc)

| Feb 76. (lp) *(V 2046)* **SHAMAL** | | | |

– Wingful of eyes / Chandra / Bambooji / Cat in Clark's shoes / Mandrake / Shamal. *(re-iss. Mar84; OVED 17) (cd-iss. 1989; CDV 2046)*

—— **PIERRE MOERLEN** returned to repl. BRIAN DAVISON (ex-REFUGEE) who had toured with them in 1976 after BILL BRUFORD left to join GENESIS, etc. / **ALLAN HOLDSWORTH** – guitar (ex-SOFT MACHINE, etc) / **FRANCIS MOZE** – bass returned / **BENOIT MOERLEN** – keyboards / **MINO CINELOU** – percussion / **DIDIER & MIREILLE** also

| Feb 77. (lp) *(V 2074)* **GAZEUSE!** (US title 'EXPRESSO') | | | |

– Expresso / Night illusion / Percolations part 1 & 2 / Shadows of Mireille. *(re-iss. Mar84; OVED 18) (cd-iss. Jun90; CDV 2074)*

—— Disbanded again Spring 1977 (aargghh!!!). Left behind retrospective below (all line-ups).

| Aug 77. (d-lp) *(VGD 3501)* **LIVE! ETC.** (live) | | | - |

– You can't kill me / Zero the hero and the witches spell / Flying teapot / Dynamite:

I am your animal / 6/8 (coit) / Est ce que je suis / Ooby Scooby doomsday or the D-day DJ's got the DDT blues / Radio gnome invisible / Oily way / Outer temple – Inner temple / Where have all the flowers gone / Isle of everywhere / Get it inner / Master builder / Flying teapot. *(cd-iss. Jun90; CDVM 3501)*

—— **PIERRE MOERLEN** retained group name with **HOLDSWORTH, BENOIT MOERLEN, BAUER** (on next lp only), plus **DARYL WAY** – violin (ex-CURVED AIR) / **HANNY ROWE** – bass / **FRANCOISE CHAUSSE** – percussion / **BON LOZANGA** – percussion

Feb 78. (lp) *(V 2099)* **EXPRESSO II**
– Heavy tune / Golden dilemma / Sleepy / Soli / Burning / Three blind mice. *(re-iss. 1986; OVED 65)* *(cd-iss. Jun90; CDV 2099)*

PIERRE MOERLEN'S GONG

	Arista	Arista

Feb 79. (lp) *(SPART 1080)* **DOWNWIND**
– Aeroplane / Crooscurrents / Downwind / Jin go la ba / What you know / Emotions / Xtasea. *(re-iss. Jul91 on 'Great Expectations' cd/lp; PIP CD/LP 025)*

Oct 79. (lp) *(SPART 1105)* **TIME IS THE KEY**
– And na greine / Earthrise / Supermarket / Faerie steps / An American in England / The organ grinder / Sugar street / The bender / Arabesque intro / Esnuria two / Time is the key. *(re-iss. Nov90 on 'Great Expectations' cd/lp; PIP CD/LP 018)*

Jul 80. (lp) *(SPART 1130)* **PIERRE MOERLEN'S GONG LIVE** (live)
– Downwind / Mandrake / Golden dilemma / Soli / Drum solo / Esnurio / Crosscurrents. *(re-iss. Nov90 on 'Great Expectations' cd/lp; PIP CD/LP 019)*

—— (featured **MIKE OLDFIELD** – guitar)

—— **BRIAN HOLLOWAY** – guitar repl. HOLDSWORTH (to various groups)

	Eulenspiegel	not iss.

1981. (lp) *(202955)* **LEAVE IT OPEN** — Dutch
– Leave it open / How much better it has become / I woke up this morning felt like playing the guitar / It's about time / Stok stok stok sto-gak / Adrien.

1986. (lp/c/cd) *(EU LP/MC/CD 1053)* **BREAKTHROUGH** — Dutch
– Breakthrough / Spaceship disco / Rock in seven / Six 8 / Poitou / Children's dreams / Portrait / The road out / Romantic punk / Far east.

	Line	not iss.

1988. (lp) *(LIDLP 5.0003)* **SECOND WIND**
– Second wind / Time and space / Say no more / Deep end / Crystal funk / Exotic / Beton / Alan Key / Crash and co. *(cd-iss. Nov92 on 'Line'+=; LICD 900698)* – Crash and co. (# 2 & 3).

– compilations, others –

Jan 87. (cd) Virgin; *(COMCD 1)* **A WINGFUL OF EYES**
(re-iss. Jan96; CDOVD 462)

Apr 89. (lp) Demi-Monde; *(DMLP 018)* **THE MYSTERY AND THE HISTORY OF THE PLANET GONG** (rarities 1971-72)
(cd-iss. 1989 & 1993 on 'Thunderbolt'; CDTL 010 & CDTB 116) *(cd-iss. Jun97 on 'Spalax'; 14518)*

Nov 95. (cd) Nectar; *(NTMCD 517)* **THE BEST OF GONG**

Dec 95. (3xcd-box) Spalax; **THE RADIO GNOME TRILOGY**

Dec 95. (cd) Strange Fruit; *(SFRCD 137)* **PRE MODERNIST WIRELESS ON RADIO**

May 96. (cd) Mantra; *(890025)* **LIVE AU BATACLAN 1973** (live)

May 96. (cd) Mantra; *(890042)* **LIVE AT SHEFFIELD 1974** (live)

Jun 96. (cd; as GONG MAISON) Gas; *(AGASCD 004)* **GLASTONBURY 1989** (live)

Jun 96. (cd) Summit; *(SUMCD 4117)* **THE VERY BEST OF GONG**

Mar 97. (cd) Gas; *(AGASCD 001)* **CAMEMBERT ELECTRIQUE (Not What You Think . . . Unreleased studio tracks)**

May 97. (cd) Sound & Media; *(SUMCD 4117)* **THE VERY BEST OF GONG**

DAEVID ALLEN

DAEVID + PEPSI MILAN – guitar, mandolin / **ANA CAMPS** – vocals / **TONI PASCUAL** – synths, keyboards / **TONI ARES** – bass / **TONI FREE FERNANDEZ** – guitar / with GONG guests; **MIKE HOWLETT** – bass / **PIERRE MOERLEN** – percussion

	Virgin	not iss.

May 76. (lp; by DAEVID ALLEN & EUTERPE) *(V 2054)* **GOOD MORNING!**
– Children of the new world / Good morning! / Spirit / Song of satisfaction / Have you seen my friend / French garden / Wise man in your heart / She doesn't she. *(cd-iss. Jun90; CDV 2054)* (+=) – Euterpe gratitude piece.

DAEVID + PEPSI + JUAN BIBLIONI – guitar / **SAM GOPAL** – percussion, synthesizers / **VICTOR PERAINO** – synth, keyboards / **MARIANNE OBERASCHER** – harp

	Affinity	not iss.

Nov 77. (lp) *(AFF 3)* **NOW IS THE HAPPIEST TIME OF YOUR LIFE**
– Flamenco zero / Why do we treat ourselves like we do / Tally & Orlando / Meet the cockpit pixie / See you on the moontower / Poet for sale / Crocodile nonsense poem / Only make love if you want to / I am / Deya goddess. *(cd-iss. Nov90 on 'Decal'; CDLIK 69)* *(re-iss. cd Dec95 on 'Spalax'; 542825)*

PLANET GONG

DAEVID ALLEN + HERE AND NOW (London musicians); **GILLIE SMYTH** – vocals / **PROF. S.SHARPSTRINGS** – guitar, vocals / **KEITH MISSILE** – bass / **KIF KIF LE BATTEUR** – drums / **GAVIN DA BLITZ** – synthesizers / **SUZA DA BLOOZ + ANNI WOMBAT** – vocals

Feb 78. (7") *(AF 5101)* **OPIUM FOR THE PEOPLE. / POET FOR SALE**

	Charly	not iss.

Apr 78. (10") *(CYX 202)* **OPIUM FOR THE PEOPLE. / STONED INNOCENT FRANKENSTEIN**

Apr 78. (lp) *(CRM 2000)* **LIVE FLOATING ANARCHY 77** (live)
– Psychological overture / Floating anarchy / Stoned innocent Frankenstein / New age transformation / Try no more sages / Opium for the people / Allez Ali Baba blacksheep have you any bullshit – Mama mya mantram. *(cd-iss. Oct90 on 'Decal'; CDLIK 68)* *(re-iss. cd Dec95 on 'Spalax';)*

—— with **PEPSI + CHRIS CUTLER** – percussion / **GEORGE BISHOP** – sax, clarinet / **ANGEL ADUANO** – banjo / **BRIAN DAMAGE** – drums / **RONALD WALTHERN** – pipes

May 79. (lp; by DAEVID ALLEN) *(CRL 5015)* **N'EXISTE PAS!**
– Professor Sharpstrings says / The freedom of the city in a suitable box / The say the say / Something tells me / H's a fine air for fliss / But it's really not real / Because barroom philoshers / 333 / No other than the mother is my song / Theme from hashish to ashes / The turkeybirds breakfast / Rajneesh with thanks / No God will not go on or the wrong way to be right / O man you.

NEW YORK GONG

DAEVID ALLEN + MATERIAL; BILL LASWELL – bass / **MICHAEL BEINHORN** – synthesizers / **DON DAVIS** – alto sax / **FRED MAHER** – drums / **CLIFF CULTRERI** – guitar / + **BILL BACON** – drums / **MARK KRAMER** – organ / **GARY WINDO** – tenor sax

Jan 80. (7") *(CY 51056)* **MUCH TOO OLD. / I AM A FREUD**

Apr 80. (lp) *(CRL 5021)* **ABOUT TIME**
– Preface / Much too old / Black September / Materialism / Strong woman / I am a freud / O my photograph / Jungle windo(w) / Hours gone. *(cd-iss. Dec90 on 'Decal'; CDLIK 73)*

1980. (10")ep *(CYX 203)* **JUNGLE WINDO(W). / MUCH TOO OLD / MATERIALISM**

DAEVID ALLEN

HARRY WILLIAMSON – bass, sax (repl.DAVIS, WINDO + KRAMER)

1981. (lp) *(CR 30218)* **DIVIDED ALIEN PLAYBAX '80**
– When / Well / Bell / Boon / Dab / Gray / Rude / Disguise / Pearls / Bodygas / Froghello / Fastfather / Smile. *(cd-iss. Dec95 on 'Spalax'; 14837)*

May 83. (12")ep *(CY 2101)* **ALIEN IN NEW YORK**
– Bananareggae / Are you ready / Oo lala / Side windo.

—— with **MARK KRAMER** – piano / **ELIZABETH MIDDLETON** – piano, vocals / **W.S. BURROUGHS**

	Shanghai	not iss.

Nov 82. (m-lp) *(HAI 201)* **THE DEATH OF ROCK AND OTHER ENTRANCES**
– Death of rock / Poet for sale / Tally's birthday song / You never existed at all / Afraid. *(cd-iss. Jan93 on 'Voiceprint'+=; VP 114CD)* – Radio Gnome concert intro loop / the switch doctor / Gong ORFT invasion 1971. *(cd re-iss. Aug96 on 'Blueprint'; BP 114CD)*

—— He returned to Australia and teamed up with DAVID TOLLEY

Aug 86. (m-lp; as The EX) *(HAI 202)* **DON'T STOP**
– Do / Eat / Work / Dinosaur / What they say.

	Invisible	not iss.

1987. (7"; as INVISIBLE OPERA COMPANY OF TIBET) *(INV 001)* **TRIAL BY HEADLINE. / TRIAL BY HEADLINE** — Aust.

	Demi Monde	not iss.

Oct 89. (lp/cd) *(DM LP/CD 1019; one-side by MOTHER GONG)* **THE OWL AND THE TREE**
– The owly song / I am my own lover / I am a tree / Lament for the future of the forest / Hands / Unseen alley / La dee Madri.

GONG

DAEVID + GRAHAM CLARKE – violin / **DIDIER MALHERBE** / **KEITH MISSILE** – bass

Dec 89. (cd/lp; as GONG MAISON) *(DM CD/LP 1022)* **GONG MAISON**
– Flying teacup / 1989 / Titti-caca / Tatlas Logorythique / Negotiate / We circle around. *(cd+=)* – (1 track).

—— In 1991, their touring line-up of GONG MAISON was **DAEVID ALLEN, DIDIER MALHERBE, GRAHAM CLARKE** – violin / **SHYAMAL MAITRA** / **KEITH MISSILE**

	Celluloid	not iss.

Oct 92. (cd) *(66914-2)* **SHAPESHIFTER** — France
– Flying teacup / 1989 / Titti-caca / Tatlas Logorythique / Negotiate / We circle around. *(re-iss. Jan97 on 'Viceroy'; VIC 80392)*

	Code 90	not iss.

Mar 93. (cd) *(NINETY 2)* **LIVE ON TV 1990** (live)
– Planetary introduction / You can't kill me / I've bin stoned before – Long Shanks – Omotha / Radio gnome invisible / Pot-head pixies / Voix lactee / Outer vision / Inner vision / Gorbachev cocktail – I am your animal / Flying teacup / I am you.

Sep 95. (d-cd) *(VPGAS 101CD)* **25th BIRTHDAY PARTY – OCTOBER 8-9, 1994, THE FORUM** (live)
– Thom intro / Floating into a birthday gig / You can't kill me / adio gnome 25 / I am your pussy / ot head pixies / Never glid before / Eat that phonebook / Gnomic address / Flute salad / Oily way. *(re-iss. Mar97; same)*

Sep 95. (m-cd; as GONG GLOBAL FAMILY) *(VPGASCD 102)* **HOW TO NUKE THE EIFFEL TOWER**
– Away away (South Pacific version) / Away away (twelve selves version) / Nuclear megawaste / Chernobyl rain.

	Gliss	not iss.

Aug 97. (12") *(GLISS12 001)* **A SPRINKLING OF CLOUDS**

DAEVID ALLEN

	Demi Monde	not iss.

Feb 90. (cd/lp) *(DM CD/LP 1025)* **AUSTRALIA AQUARIA / SHE**
– Gaia / Peaceful warrior / Australia aquaria / She / Isis is calling / Slave queen / Voice of Om / Voice of Om dub. *(re-iss. cd Feb91 as 'THE AUSTRALIAN YEARS' on 'Voiceprint'+=; VP 101)* – Don't stop. *(cd re-iss. Oct97 on 'Demi-Monde'; DMCD 1025)*

	Amp	not iss.

1990. (cd; by DAEVID ALLEN, HARRY WILLIAMSON & GILLI SMYTH) *(CD 011)* **STROKING THE TAIL OF THE BIRD**
– Stroking the tail of the bird (part 1 & 2) / Moonpeople gliss / Deep sea / Rainbow meditation. *(re-iss. Nov99 on 'Voiceprint'; VP 207CD)*

	Voiceprint	not iss.

Feb 91. (cd) *(VPCD 102)* **THE SEVEN DRONES**
– C drone (muladhara) / D drone (swadhishthana) / E drone (manipura) / F drone (anahata) / G drone (visuddha) / A drone (njna) / B drone (sahaiara) / Hello me.

1991. (cd; as INVISIBLE OPERA COMPANY OF TIBET) *(VP 106CD)* **JEWEL IN THE LOTUS**   ☐ –
(re-iss. Apr96 on 'Gas'; AGASCD 006)

—— Next with; **GRAHAM CLARK + MARK ROBSON**
1992. (cd; by DAEVID ALLEN & THE MAGICK BROTHERS) *(VP 107CD)* **LIVE AT THE WITCHWOOD 1991 (live)**   ☐ –
– Wise man in your heart / etc.

	Shimmy Disc	Shimmy Disc

Nov 92. (lp/cd; by DAEVID ALLEN & KRAMER) *(SHIMMY 060/+CD)* **WHO'S AFRAID**   ☐ ☐
(above was augmented by label boss & BONGWATER man MARK KRAMER)

	Voiceprint	not iss.

Nov 93. (cd) *(VP 111CD)* **TWELVE SELVES**   ☐ –
– Introdrone / Mystico fanatico / Away away away / Colage – Bellyphone of telephone / She – Isis is calling / Colage patafisico – Divided alien manifesto / I love sex but / Wargasm / Children of the new world / O Wichito / Sexual blueprint / Gaia / My heart's song.

Mar 97. (cd; as INVISIBLE OPERA COMPANY OF TIBET) *(VP 147CD)* **GLISSANDO SPIRIT**   ☐ –
– Landing / Uluwatu / Electric bird / Baliman energy / Cosmic dancer / Inner voice / High mountains dance / Dreaming / Moon in the sky / Mirage / Distant shore / Stars can frighten you / 7 keys / Wizard's garden / Eastside.

	G.A.S.	not iss.

May 96. (cd) *(AGASCD 007)* **DREAMING A DREAM**   ☐ –
– Dear friends / High points / Brothers / Big daddy / Wotsa use / Garden song / Came to find you / Rapist / Sittin' in a teashop / Fire becomes her / No one's slave / For song / Dear friends. (re-iss. Oct97 on 'Cleopatra'; CLP 0106)

Jan 99. (cd) *(cd)* *(AGASCD 016)* **EAT ME BABY, I'M A JELLY BEAN**   ☐ –
– So what / Gold top / I can't get started / Slow boat / It ain't necessarily so / My funny valentine / Au privave / St. Petersburg cafe / Salt peanuts.

	Gliss	not iss.

May 99. (cd; by DAEVID ALLEN & HARRY WILLIAMSON) *(GLISSCD 005)* **22 MEANINGS**   ☐ –

	Innerstate	not iss.

Sep 99. (cd; as DAEVID ALLEN & THE UNIVERSITY OF ERRORS) *(INNER 7707)* **MONEY DOESN'T MAKE IT**   ☐ –
– Money doesn't make it / Prince of sidewalk scooter / False teacher / Involve me / Mullumbimby mother / Submarine of salt / Professor Improbable's preamble / Cunning style construct / Talkwind upswerve / Wedding music / Burn your money (remix) / Can't buy me sex.

	Voiceprint	not iss.

Dec 99. (cd; by DAEVID ALLEN & RUSSELL HIBBS) *(VP 206CD)* **NECTAN'S GLEN**   ☐ –
– Ring the bells / Turn / Leshy / We came down / Nectan's glen / Spring song / Watching / Brother / Envirolament / Spirit / Man in the green / Avalon / Queen of hearts / She and I / Bees / Sonic tonic.

– his compilations, etc. –

Feb 94. (m-cd) *Voiceprint; (VPR 012CD)* **VOICEPRINT RADIO SESSION**   ☐ –
Mar 94. (cd; DAEVID ALLEN TRIO) *Voiceprint; (VP 122CD)* **LIVE 1963 (live)**   ☐ –
Mar 95. (cd) *Legend; (KZLM 1505-1)* **BANANA MOON GONG** (late 60's material)   ☐ –
Oct 97. (cd) *Blueprint; (BP 269CD)* **DIVIDED ALIEN CLOCKWORK BAND – LIVE AT SQUAT THEATRE NEW YORK AUGUST 1980 (live)**   ☐ –
(re-iss. Nov97 on 'Gas'; AGASCD 005)

MOTHER GONG

with **DAEVID ALLEN** – producer, guitar, vocals / **DIDIER MALHERBE** – sax, flute / **PIP PYLE** – drums / **PEPSI MILAN** – guitar / **VERA BLUM** – violin / **TONY PASCUAL** – keyboards / etc

	Charly	not iss.

Jun 78. (lp; by GILLI SMYTH) *(CRL 5007)* **MOTHER**   ☐ –
– I am a fool / Back to the womb / Mother / Shakti Yoni / Next time ragtime / Time of the goddess / Taliesin / Keep the children free / Prostitute poem (street version) / O.k. man / This is your world.

—— **GILLI + HARRY WILLIAMSON** – guitar (+ others)
Nov 79. (lp) *(CRL 5018)* **FAIRY TALES**   –
– Wassilissa: Three riders / The Baba Yaga's collage / The forbidden room / Time machine / Flying / Wassilissa returns home / Through the machine again / The Baba Yaga / The three tongues: The shoemaker's son / Land of dogs / The frog / An Irish inn in Rome / The arena / Turtles / Birds / The feast / The Pied Piper: Hamelin / Rats amok / An angry crowd / Rat-rock / A thousand guilders / Children / Magic land.

—— settled line-up; **GILLI, HARRY, DIDIER / + GUY EVANS** – drums (ex-VAN DER GRAAF) / **DAYNE CRANENBURG** – bass / **YAN EMERIC** – slide guitar / **HUGH HOPPER** – bass

	Butt	not iss.

Jan 81. (lp) *(BUTT 003)* **ROBOT WOMAN**   ☐ –
– Disco at the end of the world / Womans place / Robot woman / Machine song / The sea / Listen . . . / Searching the airwaves / Billi Bunker's blues / Military procession / Customs man / Red alert / Stars / Australia.

—— **DAVE SAWYER** – percussion (repl.EMERIC + HOPPER)

	Shanghai	not iss.

Sep 84. (lp) *(HAI 100)* **ROBOT WOMAN II**   ☐ –
– Suggestive station / This train / I wanna be with you / The moving walkway / The upwardly mobile song / Tigers or elephants / Mirror / You can touch the sky / 1999 / Crazy town / Angry song / Looking for / Leotards.

Dec 86. (lp) *(HAI 109)* **ROBOT WOMAN III**   ☐ –
– It's you and me baby / Faces of woman / Desire / War / Children's song / Lady's song / Woman of streams / I'm sorry / Men cry / Solutions / Magenta part one.

—— **GILLI + HARRY / + ROBERT CALVERT** – sax (ex-CATAPILLA)

	Mothermusic	not iss.

1992. (cd) *(MM 101CD)* **LIVE 1991**   – – Aust.

	Voiceprint	not iss.

May 93. (cd) *(VP 134CD)* **SHE MADE THE WORLD – MAGENTA**   ☐ –
– Magenta / Water / She made the world / Weather / Malicious sausage / Sea horse / Spirit calling / Tattered jacket / Warm / When the show is over / I am a witch / Spirit of the bush / Blessed be.

Jun 93. (cd; by GILLI SMYTH) *(VP 139CD)* **EVERY WITCHES WAY**   ☐ –
– Simple / Bold and brazen / Show is over / We who were raging / Beltaine / Four horsemen / Medicine woman / Animal / Magic / Llammas / I am witch / Lady Wise / Simples.

	Demi Monde	not iss.

Feb 94. (cd) *(DMCD 1026)* **WILD CHILD**   ☐ –

	Voiceprint	not iss.

Sep 94. (cd) *(VP 176CD)* **EYE**   ☐ –
– Fanfare / She's the mother of / Sunday / Beds / Time is a hurrying dog / Ancient / Zen / Quantum / Spirit canoe / What if we were gods and godesses / Auction / Little boy / Magic stories / Excuses / Sax canoe / Fairy laughter / Virtual relity.

– her compilations, etc. –

Oct 94. (cd) *Voiceprint; (VP 007CD)* **THE VOICEPRINT RADIO SESSIONS**   ☐ –
—— In France, DIDIER MALHERBE issued 1979 lp 'BLOOM' (Sonopresse) and 1980 single 'DANSEKORLA. / BONG' (Sonopresse). In 1987 'Cryonic' of France released 'FATON BLOOM'. In 1990 'Mantra' issued 'FETISH'. Sep92; 'Tangram' issued 'ZEFF'.

GOODBYE MR MACKENZIE (dig out; Great Alt & Indie . . .)

GOO GOO DOLLS

Formed: Buffalo, New York, USA . . . 1986 by ROBBY TAKAC (a former DJ), JOHNNY RZEZNIK and GEORGE TUTUSKA. Like a grunge-punk fusion of CHEAP TRICK, The LEMONHEADS and The DESCENDENTS, they debuted the following year with a low-rent eponymous album thankfully not given a release in Britain. A follow-up, 'JED' (1989), was also sprinkled with the odd cover version, a reading of Creedence Clearwater Revival's 'DOWN ON THE CORNER' presided over by guest crooner, LANCE DIAMOND. In the early 90's, 'Metal Blade' took over the reins, their powerful metal-punk winning new audiences after the release of their third set, 'HOLD ME UP' (1990). Three years on, the GOO GOO DOLLS returned with 'SUPERSTAR CARWASH', a transitional set preceding their break for the big time. GEORGE had now been replaced by MIKE MALININ, the sticksman coming in for the band's LOU GIORDANO-produced set, 'A BOY NAMED GOO' (1995), a US Top 30 success that featured Top 5 smash, 'NAME'. However, unlike many of their peers (GREEN DAY, OFFSPRING, etc), the 'DOLLS didn't really translate to the saturated British market despite having another two radio airplay hits in the States, both taken from 1998 album, 'DIZZY UP THE GIRL'. • Covered: I WANNA DESTROY YOU (Soft Boys) / DON'T FEAR THE REAPER (Blue Oyster Cult) / SUNSHINE OF YOUR LOVE (Cream) / I COULD NEVER TAKE THE PLACE OF YOUR MAN (Prince) / GIMME SHELTER (Rolling Stones) / I DON'T WANNA KNOW (Fleetwood Mac) / etc.
Album rating: GOO GOO DOLLS (*4) / JED (*4) / HOLD ME UP (*5) / SUPERSTAR CARWASH (*5) / A BOY NAMED GOO (*7) / DIZZY UP THE GIRL (*5)

JOHNNY RZEZNIK (b. 5 Dec'65) – vocals, guitar / **ROBBY TAKAC** (b.30 Sep'64) – bass, vocals / **GEORGE TUTUSKA** – drums

	Celluloid	Mercenary

1987. (lp) *(2211)* <97292-2> **GOO GOO DOLLS**   – ☐ French
– Torn apart / Messed up / Livin' in a hut / I'm addicted / Sunshine of your love / Hardsores / Hammering eggs (the metal song) / (Don't fear) The reaper / Beat me / Scream / Slaughterhouse / Different light / Come on / Don't beat my ass (with a baseball bat). (re-iss. Nov95 on 'Metal Blade'; 14079-2)

	Roadracer	Death-Enigma

Apr 89. (lp/cd) *(RO 9477-1/-2)* <847859> **JED**   ☐ ☐
– Out of sight / Up yours / No way out / 7th of last month / Love dolls / Sex maggot / Down on the corner / Had enough / Road to Salinas / Em Elbmuh / Misfortune / Artie / Gimme shelter / James Dean. (cd re-iss. Feb94 on 'Metal Blade'; CDZORRO 70)

	Fun After All	Metal Blade

Nov 90. (lp/cd) *(AFTER 8/+CD)* <26259-1/-2> **HOLD ME UP**   ☐ ☐
– Laughing / Just the way you are / So outta line / There you are / You know what I man / Out of the red / I could never take the place of your man / Hey / On your side / 22 seconds / Kevin's song / Know my name / Million miles away / Two days in February. (cd re-iss. May96 on 'Metal Blade'; 3984 17018CD)

	Warners	Warners

1993. (cd/c) <9362 45206-2/-4> **SUPERSTAR CARWASH**   ☐ ☐
– Fallin' down / Lucky star / Cuz you're gone / Don't worry / Girl right next to me / Domino / We are the normal / String of lies / Another second time around / Stop the world / Already there / On the lie / Close your eyes / So far away. (UK-iss.Aug99 on 'Edel'; 0102702HWR)

—— **MIKE MALININ** (b.10 Oct'67, Washington, DC) – drums, vocals; repl. GEORGE

Apr 95. (cd/c) <(9362 45750-2/-4)> **A BOY NAMED GOO**   ☐ 27
– Long way down / Burnin' up / Naked / Flat top / Impersonality / Name / Only one / Somethin' bad / Ain't that unusual / So long / Eyes wide open / Disconnected / Slave girl. (cd re-iss. Aug99 on 'Edel'; 0103122HWR)

May 95. (c-s) *(W 0293C)* **ONLY ONE / IMPERSONALITY**   ☐ ☐
(cd-s+=) *(W 0293CD)* – Hit or miss.

		Hollywood	Imprint-Warners	

Sep 95. (c-s) <17758> **NAME / BURNIN' UP / HIT OR MISS** — | 5

Feb 96. (c-s) (W 0333C) **NAME / NOTHING CAN CHANGE YOU** — | -
(cd-s+=) (W 0333CD) – I wanna destroy you.

Jul 96. (c-s) (W 0362C) **LONG WAY DOWN / NAME (live)** — | -
(cd-s+=) (W 0362CD) – Don't change (live).

Jul 98. (c-s) (W 0449C) <44525> **IRIS / LAZY EYE** 50 | 9 Sep98
(cd-s+=) (W 0449CD) – I don't want to know.

		Hollywood	Imprint-Warners	

Mar 99. (c-s) (010239HWR) <1763> **SLIDE / ACOUSTIC #3** 43 | 8 Nov98
(cd-s+=) (010205HWR) – Nothing can change you.

Jul 99. (c-s) (01024 89/42 HWR) **IRIS / IRIS (acoustic)** 26 | -

Jul 99. (cd/c) (0102042HWR) <47058-2/-4> **DIZZY UP THE GIRL** 47 | 15 Sep98
– Dizzy / Slide / Broadway / January friend / Black balloon / Bullet proof / Amigone / All eyes on me / Full forever / Acoustic #3 / Iris / Extra pale / Hate this place.

Jul 99. (c-s/cd-s) <16946> **BLACK BALLOON** — | 16

Nov 99. (c-s/cd-s) (010535 9/5 HWR) **DIZZY / SLIDE (acoustic)** — | -

Martin L. GORE (see under ⇒ DEPECHE MODE)

GORKY'S ZYGOTIC MYNCI

Formed: Camarthen, South Wales . . . early 1991 by EUROS CHILD, RICHARD JAMES and JOHN LAWRENCE. Naming themselves after the Russian writer, MAXIM GORKY, they were signed to the Bangor-based 'Ankst' label by owner ALUN LLWYD and issued their 1992 debut 45, 'PATIO'. Two years later, their first album 'TATAY', found favour in the indie circuit, while they toured supporting The FALL (The GORKY's were banned in some Welsh clubs for combining the Welsh and English language!). A youthful Welsh-language psychedelic/folk/pop-rock outfit, they were largely influenced by the likes of The INCREDIBLE STRING BAND, early SOFT MACHINE, or the even medieval, GRYPHON. Two brilliant singles were released in 1995; 'MISS TRUDY' (from 'LLANFROG' EP) and the classic 'IF FINGERS WERE XYLOPHONES', while they progressed with their second album proper, 'BWYD TIME', in 1995 (another in 1994; 'PATIO' was demos, etc from '91-93). Early in '96, they inked a deal with the major 'Fontana' label, through A&R man Steve Greenberg. Their first single for the label, the excellent 'PATIO SONG', was their initial breakthrough into the UK Top 50. In April '97, this song and 15 others were featured on their best offering to date, the trippy 'BARAFUNDLE' which included the excellently folky 'SOMETIMES THE FATHER IS THE SON'. The following year, with cult glory seemingly at their feet, the GORKY'S released their fifth proper album, 'GORKY 5', a comparatively disappointing effort which, with mediocre reviews, only managed one week in the Top 75. After being dropped by Mercury in '99, they hooked up with Beggars Banquet subsidiary 'Mantra', only for JOHN LAWRENCE to become disillusioned just days before signing. However, a new-line (with RHODRY PUGH in tow) promoted the much-improved 'SPANISH DANCE TROUPE' (1999), the Catalonian-inspired title track scraping into the Top 50. • **Songwriters:** Mostly EUROS CHILDS, some by or with JOHN LAWRENCE (until his departure) and RICHARD JAMES, and a few by MEGAN. Covered; A DAY IN THE LIFE (Beatles) / WHY ARE WE SLEEPING? (Soft Machine) / O CAROLINE (Matching Mole).

Album rating: TATAY (*6) / PATIO (*5) / BWYD TIME (*6) / INTRODUCING . . . compilation US (*6) / BARAFUNDLE (*9) / GORKY 5 (*6) / SPANISH DANCE TROUPE (*7)

EUROS CHILDS – vocals, keyboards, synthesizer / **RICHARD JAMES** – guitars, bass / **JOHN LAWRENCE** – bass, guitars, keyboards / **SION LANE** – keyboards / **STEFFAN** – violin

		Mynci	not iss.

1991. (c) (001) **ALLUMETTE** — | -

—— **OSIAN EVANS** – drums; repl. SION + STEFFAN

		G.Z.M.	not iss.

1992. (c) (none) **PEIRIANT PLESER** — | -

—— added **MEGAN CHILDS** – violin

		Ankst	not iss.

1993. (10"lp;ltd) (ANKST 40) **PATIO** — | -
– Peanut dispenser / Lladd eich gwraig / Dafad yn sirad / Mr Groovy / Ti! Moses / Barbed wire / Miriam o Farbel / Oren, mefus a chadno / Gwallt rhegi Pegi / Sally Webster / Diamonds o Monte Carlo / Siwt nofio. (re-iss. Jan95 & Apr97 cd+=/c+=; ANKST 055 cd/c) – Blessed are the meek / Reverend Oscar Marzaroli / Oren, mefus a chadno / Dean ser / Siwmper heb grys / Llenni al gloi / Anna apera / Siwf nofio / Hi ar gan.

Mar 94. (cd/c) (ANKST 047 cd/c) **TATAY** — | -
– Thema o cartref (Theme from home) / Beth sy'n digwydd i'r fwuch (What happens to the cow?) / Tatay / Y ffordd oren (Orange way) / Gwres prynhawn (Afternoon heat) / Amsermaemaiynddod (When May comes) / Cinema / O, Caroline / Naw.e.pimp (Nine for a pimp) / Kevin Ayers / When you hear the captain sing / O, Caroline II / Tatay (moog mix) / Anna apera:- a. Anna apera – b. Gegin nos (Night kitchen) – c. Silff ffenest (Window sill) – d. Backward dog. (re-iss. Apr97; same)

Jun 94. (7") (ANKST 048) **MERCHED YN GWALLT EI GILYDD. / BOCS ANGELICA / WHEN YOU LAUGH AT YOUR OWN GARDEN IN A BLAZER** — | -
(cd-s+=) (ANKST 048cd) – Mewn. (re-iss. Apr97; same)

Nov 94. (7") (ANKST 053) **THE GAME OF EYES. / PENTREF WRTH Y MOR** — | -
(cd-s+=) (ANKST 053cd) – Cwpwrdd sadwrn. (re-iss. Apr97; same)

—— **EUROS ROWLANDS** – percussion, drums; repl. EVANS

Mar 95. (10"ep/cd-ep) (ANKST 056/+cd) **LLANFWROG EP** — | -
– Miss Trudy / Eira / Methu aros tan haf / Why are we sleeping? (re-iss. Apr97; same)

Jun 95. (7"w-drawn) (ANKST 058) **GEWN NI GORFFEN. / 12 IMPRESSIONISTIC SOUNDSCAPES** — | -

Jul 95. (lp/c/cd) (ANKST 059/+c/cd) **BWYD TIME** — | -
– Bwyd time / Miss Trudy / Paid cheto ar Pam (Don't cheat on Pam) / Oraphis yndelphie / Eating salt is easy / Gewn ni gorffen (Let's finish) / Iechyd da (Good health) / Ymwelwyr a gwrachod (Visitors and witches) / The telescope and the bonfire / The man with salt hair / The game of eyes / Blood chant / Ffarm-wr. (re-iss. Apr97; same)

Nov 95. (7") (ANKST 064) **IF FINGERS WERE XYLOPHONES. / MOON BEATS YELLOW** — | -
(cd-s+=) (ANKST 064cd) – Pethau. (re-iss. Apr97; same)

Jul 96. (10"ep/cd-ep) (ANKST 068/+cd) **AMBLER GAMBLER EP** — | -
– Lucy's hamper / Heart of Kentucky / Sdim yr adar yn canu / 20. (re-iss. Apr97; same)

		Fontana	Polygram

Aug 96. (cd) <532818-2> **INTRODUCING . . .** (compilation) — | -
– Merched ya neod gwalt eu gilydd / If fingers were xylophones / PenTree WRTH Y mor / Games of eyes / Kevin Ayers / Miss Trudy / Why are we sleeping? / Y ffordd oren / Meth aros tan haf / Era / Iechyd da / The moon beats yellow.

Oct 96. (7") (GZM 1) **PATIO SONG. / NO ONE LOOKED AROUND** 41 | -
(cd-s+=) (GZMCD 1) – Morwyr o hyd in lladd eu hun ar y tir.

Mar 97. (7"/c-s/cd-s) (GZM/+MC/CD 2) **DIAMOND DEW. / QUEEN OF GEORGIA / TEARS IN DISGUISE** 42 | -

Apr 97. (cd/c) (534 769-2/-4) <536122> **BARAFUNDLE** 46 | -
– Diamond dew / The barafundle bumbler / Starmoonsun / Patio song / Better rooms . . . / Heywood lane / Pen gwag glas / Bola bola / Cursed, coined and crucified / Sometimes the father is the son / Meirion Wylit / The wizard and the lizard / Miniature kingdoms / Dark night / Hwyl fawr i pawb / Wordless song.

Jun 97. (7"/c-s) (GZM/+MC 3) **YOUNG GIRLS & HAPPY ENDINGS. / DARK NIGHT** 49 | -
(cd-s) (GZMCD 3) – Marching ants.

May 98. (7") (GZM 4) **SWEET JOHNNY. / UN HOGYN UN HOGAN DRIST** 60 | -
(cd-s+=) (GZMCD 4) – Mifi Mihafan.

Aug 98. (7") (GZM 5) **LET'S GET TOGETHER (IN OUR MINDS) . / TONIGHT** 43 | -
(cd-s) (GZMCD 5) – ('A'side) / Billy and the sugarloaf mountain / Hwiangerdd mair.

Aug 98. (cd/c/lp) (558 822-2/-4/-1) **GORKY 5** 67 | -
– The tidal wave / Dyle fi / Let's get together (in our minds) / Tsunami / Not yet / Only the sea makes sense / Softly / Frozen smile / Sweet Johnny / Theme from Gorky 5 (Russian song) / Hush the warmth / Catrin.

		Mantra	Beggars Banquet

Sep 99. (7") (MNT 047) **SPANISH DANCE TROUPE. / (DO THE) CHICKEN IN THE JUNGLE** 47 | -
(cd-s+=) (MNT 047CD) – The Johnny Cash lawsuit song.

Oct 99. (cd/c/lp) (MNT CD/MC/LP 1015) **SPANISH DANCE TROUPE** — | -
– Hallway / Poodle rockin' / She lives on a mountain / Drws / Over and out / Don't you worry / Faraway eyes / Fool / Hair like monkey / Spanish dance troupe / Desolation blues / Murder ballad / Freckles / Christmas eve / Humming song.

—— (Jun'99) now without JOHN who formed the INFINITY CHIMPS (after partly recording with GZM on above) **RHODRY PUGH** (took his place)

GRACES (see under ⇒ BROOKS, Meredith)

GRADUATE (see under ⇒ TEARS FOR FEARS)

GRANDADDY

Formed: Modesto, California, USA . . . 1992 by ex-skater, JASON LYTLE, who, with the help of HOWE GELB (of GIANT SAND), found a sympathetic ear at 'Big Cat' records. The line-up around this time also included JIM FAIRCHILD, TIM DRYDEN, KEVIN GARCIA and AARON BURTCH, although it took time aplenty to finally emerge with debut release, the 'THE MACHINES ARE NOT SHE' EP. The mini-set, 'A PRETTY MESS BY THIS ONE BAND', followed it a year later in '95. 'UNDER THE WESTERN FREEWAY' followed in '98, another based on classic West Coast Americana, their BRIAN WILSON/MERCURY REV-esque sound marking them out as the Sunday drivers of the alt-country brigade.

Album rating: A PRETTY MESS BY THIS ONE BAND mini (*6) / UNDER THE WESTERN FREEWAY (*8) / THE BROKEN DOWN COMFORTER COLLECTION compilation (*8)

JASON LYTLE – vocals / **JIM FAIRCHILD** – guitar / **TIM DRYDEN** – keyboards / **KEVIN GARCIA** – bass / **AARON BURTCH** – drums

		Big Cat	Will

1994. (12"ep) **MACHINES ARE NOT SHE E.P.** — | -
– Levitz / For the dishwasher / Lava kiss / Wretched songs / Sikh in a Baja VW bug / Fentry.
<re-iss. 1998 on 'Big Cat'; ABB 128P>

1995. (m-cd) <041> **A PRETTY MESS BY THIS ONE BAND** — | -
– Away birdies with special sounds / Taster / Peeano / Kim you bore me to death / Pre Merced / Gentle spike resort / Egg hit and Jack too.

Feb 98. (7") (ABB 157S) **EVERYTHING BEAUTIFUL IS FAR AWAY. / FOR THE DISHWASHER** — | -
(cd-s+=) (ABB 157SCD) – Glassy-dusty.

Mar 98. (7"/cd-s) (ABB 161S/+CD) **LAUGHING STOCK. / G.P.C. / 12-PAK 599** — | -

Apr 98. (lp/cd) (ABB 152/+CD) <33646> **UNDER THE WESTERN FREEWAY** — | - Oct97
– Nonphenomenal lineage / A.M. 180 / Collective dreamwish of upper class / Summer here kids / Laughing stock / Under the western freeway / Everything beautiful is far away / Poisoned at Hartsy Thai food / Go progress chrome / Why took your advice / Lawn and so on.

May 98. (7"/cd-s) (ABB 162S/+CD) **SUMMER HERE KIDS / LEVITZ (BIRDLESS) / MY SMALL LOVE** — | -

Oct 98.	(7"/cd-s) (ABB 500350-7/-2) **A.M. 180. / GLASSY-DUSTY /** **FOR THE DISHWASHER**	☐	-

– compilation, etc. –

Jun 99.	(cd) Big Cat; (ABB 100569-2) **THE BROKEN DOWN** **COMFORTER COLLECTION** (first 2 releases)	☐	☐

GRAND FUNK RAILROAD

Formed: Flint, Michigan, USA . . . 1964 as TERRY KNIGHT & THE PACK, by RICHARD KNAPP, MARK FARNER and DON BREWER. A few years into their career, the soulful rock trio scored a US Top 50 hit with 'I (WHO HAVE NOTHING)'. KNIGHT subsequently became their manager in 1969, FARNER (now on vocals and guitar) and BREWER (drums) recruiting bass player MEL SCHACHER, the revamped threesome adopting the GRAND FUNK RAILROAD moniker. Along with STEPPENWOLF, MOUNTAIN, etc, they formulated their own brand of populist proto-heavy metal/rock with an emphasis on extreme volume. Having signed to 'Capitol' around the same time as their Atlanta Pop Festival appearance (mid '69), they immediately hit the US Top 50 with the single, 'TIME MACHINE', a track from their debut Top 30 album, 'ON TIME'. From that point on, the group proceeded to enjoy increasing and extremely profitable popularity with each successive release despite regular critical derision. Highly prolific, GFR delivered an album approximately every six months, the American public seemingly never tiring of their formulaic approach (in June '71, they broke The BEATLES' box-office record, selling out New York's Shea Stadium). By Spring '72, the group had split from the management of TERRY KNIGHT, hiring John Eastman (brother-in-law of PAUL McCARTNEY) to control their finances. The following year, with their moniker clipped to GRAND FUNK, the group enjoyed their finest three minutes with the US chart-topping, 'WE'RE AN AMERICAN BAND'. The similarly-titled, TODD RUNDGREN-produced parent album also shifted millions of copies, although British rock fans were more interested in prog rock or glam. In 1974, they fleshed out their sound with the brief addition of keyboard player, CRAIG FROST, who graced their second US No.1, a rock version of Little Eva's 'LOCOMOTION'. The group proceeded to churn out the inevitable hard rockin' pop hits and patchy albums, culminating in FRANK ZAPPA's disastrous 1976 attempt to redefine the band's sound with 'GOOD SINGIN', GOOD PLAYIN'. This release finally saw GRAND FUNK RAILROAD hitting the buffers at the end of the commercial line. MARK FARNER subsequently took off on a solo sojourn, returning in 1981 with some more below par GRAND FUNK material. • **Covers:** WE'VE GOTTA GET OUT OF THIS PLACE (Animals) / GIMME SHELTER (Rolling Stones) / etc.

Album rating: ON TIME (*6) / GRAND FUNK (*6) / CLOSER TO HOME (*6) / LIVE ALBUM (*6) / SURVIVAL (*6) / E PLURIBUS FUNK (*5) / PHOENIX (*5) / WE'RE AN AMERICAN BAND (*6) / SHININ' (*5) / ALL THE GIRLS IN THE WORLD BEWARE!!! (*5) / CAUGHT IN THE ACT (*4) / BORN TO DIE (*4) / GOOD SINGIN' GOOD PLAYIN' (*6) / GRAND FUNK HITS compilation (86) / GRAND FUNK LIVES (*3) / WHAT'S FUNK? (*3) / CAPITOL COLLECTORS SERIES compilation (*7) / MORE OF THE BEST compilation (*6)

TERRY KNIGHT & THE PACK

TERRY KNIGHT (b. RICHARD KNAPP) – vocals / **MARK FARNER** (b. 29 Sep'48) – vocals, bass (guitar from 1969) / **DONALD BREWER** (b. 3 Sep'48) – drums (ex-JAZZ MASTERS)

		not iss.	A&M
1965.	(7") <769> **YOU LIE. / THE KIDS WILL BE THE SAME**	☐	☐

		Cameo Parkway	Lucky 11
1966.	(7") <225> **I'VE BEEN TOLD. / HOW MUCH MORE?**	-	
1966.	(7") <226> **BETTER MAN THAN I. / I GOT LOVE**	-	
1966.	(7") <228> **LOVIN' KIND. / LADY JANE**	-	
1966.	(7") <229> **WHAT'S ON YOUR MIND? / A CHANGE ON THE WAY**	-	
Nov 66.	(lp) <S-8000> **TERRY KNIGHT & THE PACK** – Numbers / What's on your mind / Where do you go / Better man than I / Lovin' kind / The shut-in / Got love / A change on the way / Lady Jane / Sleep talkin' / I've been told / I (who have nothing).	-	
Jan 67.	(7") (C 102) <230> **I (WHO HAVE NOTHING). / NUMBERS**		46
Apr 67.	(7") <235> **THIS PRECIOUS TIME. / LOVE, LOVE, LOVE, LOVE**	-	
Jul 67.	(7") <236> **ONE MONKEY DON'T STOP NO SHOW. / THE TRAIN**	-	
1968.	(7"; as MARK FARNER & DON BREWER) **WE GOTTA HAVE LOVE. / DOES IT MATTER TO YOU GIRL**	-	☐

GRAND FUNK RAILROAD

KNIGHT became their manager. Added **MEL SCHACHER** (b. 3 Apr'51, Owosso, Michigan) – bass (ex-? AND THE MYSTERIANS)

		Capitol	Capitol
Sep 69.	(7") <2567> **TIME MACHINE. / HIGH ON A HORSE**	-	48
Sep 69.	(lp) <(E-ST 307)> **ON TIME** – Are you ready / Anybody's answer / Time machine / High on a horse / T.N.U.C. / Into the sun / Heartbreaker / Call yourself a man / Can't be too long / Ups and down.		27
Nov 69.	(7") <2691> **MR. LIMOUSINE DRIVER. / HIGH FALOOTIN' WOMAN**	-	97
Jan 70.	(lp) <(E-ST 406)> **GRAND FUNK** – Got this thing on the move / Please don't worry / High falootin' woman / Mr. Limousine driver / In need / Winter and my soul / Paranoid / Inside looking out.	-	11
Mar 70.	(7") (CL 15632) <2732> **HEARTBREAKER. / PLEASE DON'T WORRY**		72 Jan70

Jun 70.	(7") <2816> **NOTHING IS THE SAME. / SIN'S A GOOD MAN'S BROTHER**	-	-
Jul 70.	(lp) <(E-ST 471)> **CLOSER TO HOME.** – Sin's a good man's brother / Aimless lady / Nothing is the same / Mean mistreater / Get it together / I don't have to sing the blues / Hooked on love / I'm your captain.		6
Oct 70.	(7") <2877> **CLOSER TO HOME. / AIMLESS LADY**		22 Aug70
Dec 70.	(7") <2996> **MEAN MISTREATER. / MARK SAYS ALRIGHT**	-	47
Jan 71.	(d-lp) <SWDW 1-2> **LIVE ALBUM** (live) – (introduction) / Are you ready / Paranoid / In need / Heartbreaker / Inside looking out / Words of wisdom / Meam mistreater / Mark says alright / T.N.U.C. / Into the sun.	-	5 Nov70
Jan 71.	(7";33rpm) (CL 15668) **INSIDE LOOKING OUT. / PARANOID**	40	-
Apr 71.	(7") (CL 15683) <3095> **FEELIN' ALRIGHT. / I WANT FREEDOM**		54
Apr 71.	(lp) <(E-SW 764)> **SURVIVAL** – Country road / All you've got is money / Comfort me / Feelin' alright / I want freedom / I can feel him in the morning / Gimme shelter.		6
Jul 71.	(7"m;B-33rpm) (CL 15689) **I CAN FEEL HIM IN THE MORNING. / ARE YOU READY / MEAN MISTREATER**		-
Aug 71.	(7") <3160> **GIMME SHELTER. / I CAN FEEL HIM IN THE MORNING**	-	61
Sep 71.	(7") (CL 15694) **GIMME SHELTER. / COUNTRY ROAD**	-	
Dec 71.	(7") (CL 15705) **PEOPLE, LET'S STOP THE WAR. / SAVE THE LAND**	-	
Jan 72.	(lp) (EA-SW 853) <E-AS 853> **E PLURIBUS FUNK** – Footstompin' music / People, let's stop the war / Upsetter / I come tumblin' / Save the land / No lies / Loneliness.		5 Nov71
Mar 72.	(7") (CL 15709) <3255> **FOOTSTOMPIN' MUSIC. / I COME TUMBLIN'**		29 Dec71
May 72.	(7") (CL 15720) <3316> **UPSETTER. / NO LIES**		73 Apr72
Nov 72.	(7") (CL 15738) <3363> **ROCK'N'ROLL SOUL. / FLIGHT OF THE PHOENIX**		29 Sep72
Jan 73.	(lp) <E-AST 11099> **PHOENIX** – Flight of the phoenix / Trying to get away / Someone / She got to move me / Rain keeps fallin' / I just gotta know / So you won't have to die / Freedom is for children / Gotta find me a better day / Rock'n roll soul.		7 Oct72

GRAND FUNK

Aug 73.	(7")<7"US-pic-d> (CL 15760) <3660> **WE'RE AN AMERICAN BAND. / CREEPIN'**		1 Jul73
Aug 73.	(lp) <(E-AST 11027)> **WE'RE AN AMERICAN BAND** – We're an American band / Stop lookin' back / Creepin' / Black licorice / The railroad / Ain't got nobody / Walk like a man / Loneliest rider.		2
Nov 73.	(7") (CL 15770) <3760> **WALK LIKE A MAN. / RAILROAD** added **CRAIG FROST** (b.20 Apr'48) – keyboards		19
May 74.	(7") (CL 15780) <3840> **THE LOCO-MOTION. / DESTITUTE & LOSIN'**		1 Mar74
Jun 74.	(lp) <(SWAE 11278)> **SHININ' ON** – Shinin' on / To get back in / The loco-motion / Carry me through / Please me / Mr. Pretty boy / Gettin' over you / Little Johnny Hooker.		5 Mar74
Jul 74.	(7") (CL 15789) <3917> **SHININ' ON. / MR. PRETTY BOY**		11
	reverted back to trio.		
Dec 74.	(lp) <E-ST 11356> <SO 11356> **ALL THE GIRLS IN THE WORLD BEWARE!!!** – Responsibility / Runnin' / Life / Look at granny run run / Memories / All the girls in the world beware / Wild / Good & evil / Bad time / Some kind of wonderful.		10
Feb 75.	(7") (CL 15805) <4002> **SOME KIND OF WONDERFUL. / WILD**		3 Dec74
Apr 75.	(7") (CL 15816) <4046> **BAD TIME. / GOOD AND EVIL**		4 Mar75

GRAND FUNK RAILROAD

Dec 75.	(d-lp) (E-STSP 15) <11445> **CAUGHT IN THE ACT** (live) – Footstompin' music / Rock'n roll soul / Closer to home / Some kind of wonderful / Heartbreaker / Shinin' on / The locomotion / Black licorice / The railroad / We're an American band / T.N.U.C. / Inside looking out / Gimme shelter.		21 Sep75
Dec 75.	(7") <4199> **TAKE ME. / GENEVIEVE**	-	53
Mar 76.	(7") <4235> **SALLY. / LOVE IS DYIN'**		69
Apr 76.	(lp) <(E-ST 11482)> **BORN TO DIE** – Born to die / Duss / Sally / I fell for your love / Talk to the people / Take me / Genevieve / Love is dying / Politician / Good things.		47 Jan76

		EMI Inter.	M.C.A.
Aug 76.	(7") (INT 523) <40590> **CAN YOU DO IT. / 1976**		45
Aug 76.	(lp) (EMC 1503) <2216> **GOOD SINGIN' GOOD PLAYIN'** – Just couldn't wait / Can you do it / Pass it around / Don't let 'em take your gun / Miss my baby / Big buns / Out to get you / Crossfire / 1976 / Release your love / Goin' for the pastor.		52
Jan 77.	(7") (INT 528) **PASS IT AROUND. / DON'T LET 'EM TAKE YOUR GUN**	☐	☐
Jan 77.	(7") <40641> **JUST COULDN'T WAIT. / OUT TO GET YOU**	-	-

Disbanded when the rest formed FLINT. FARNER went solo for a while.

GRAND FUNK

re-formed with **FARNER, BREWER + DENNIS BELLINGER** – bass, vocals / (FROST had joined BOB SEGER)

		Full Moon	Full Moon
Nov 81.	(7") <49823> **Y-O-U. / TESTIFY**	-	-
Jan 82.	(lp) (K 99251) <3625> **GRAND FUNK LIVES** – Good times / Queen bee / Testify / Can't be with you tonight / No reason why / We gotta get out of this place / Y.O.U. / Stuck in the middle / Greed of man / Wait for me.		Oct81
Feb 82.	(7") <49866> **STUCK IN THE MIDDLE. / NO REASON WHY**	-	-
Jan 83.	(lp) (K 99251) <923750-1> **WHAT'S FUNK?**	-	German

– Rock & roll American style / Nowhere to run / Innocent / Still waitin' / Borderline / El Salvador / It's a man's world / I'm so true / Don't lie to me / Life in Outer Space.

—— Disbanded again after appearing on 'Heavy Metal' soundtrack. BREWER joined BOB SEGER'S SILVER BULLET BAND. FARNER went solo again in 1988, releasing an album 'JUST ANOTHER INJUSTICE' for 'Frontline'.

– compilations, others, etc. –

on 'Capitol' unless mentioned otherwise

May 72. (d-lp) (E-STSP 10) <11042> **MARK, DON & MEL 1969-1971**		17
Oct 72. (lp) **MARK, DON AND TERRY 1966-67**	-	
Nov 76. (lp) <11579> **GRAND FUNK HITS**	-	
May 89. (c-s) <44394> **WE'RE AN AMERICAN BAND. / THE LOCO-MOTION**	-	
Mar 91. (cd) (CDP 790608-2) **CAPITOL COLLECTORS**		-

– Time machine / Heartbreaker / Inside looking out / Medley / Closer to home / I'm your captain / Mean mistreater / Feelin' alright / Gimme shelter / Footstompin' music / Rock & roll soul / We're an American band / Walk like a man / The Loco-motion / Shinin' on / Some kind of wonderful / Bad time.

Sep 91. (cd) Rhino; **MORE OF THE BEST**	-	
May 92. (cd/c) Castle; (CCS CD/MC 332) **THE COLLECTION**	-	

– The loco-motion / Gimme shelter / Inside looking out / Closer to home / I'm your captain / We're an American band / Into the Sun / Loneliness / Paranoid / Walk like a man / Shinin' on / Creepin' / Sally.

GRANDMASTER FLASH

Born: 1 Jan'58, Barbados, West Indies as JOSEPH SADDLER, although he moved to the Bronx district of New York at an early age. Taking his cue from pioneering DJ's like KOOL HERC, a teenage SADDLER began spinning records at local block parties, eventually developing the complex technique of "cutting" between records on two separate turntables, creating a continuous flow of beats punctuated by repetitive rhythmic "breaks". While these tricks later proved to be one of the most revolutionary and money-spinning developments in the evolution of popular music, for the time being SADDLER aka DJ GRANDMASTER FLASH (so called for his lightning speed turntable techniques) was content to demonstrate his considerable skills at local hip hop events. Enlisting a cast of rappers to complement his spinning, FLASH created The FURIOUS FIVE, originally consisting of GRANDMASTER MELLE MEL (born MELVIN GLOVER), brother KID CREOLE (born NATHANIEL GLOVER and no, not THAT KID CREOLE!), COWBOY (born KEITH WIGGINS), DUKE BOOTEE (born EDWARD FLETCHER) and KURTIS BLOW. The latter was subsequently replaced by RAHIEM (born GUY TODD WILLIAMS), the crew creating a buzz around New York and finally making their vinyl debut in 1979 for 'Enjoy' records with the track 'SUPERRAPPIN'. Like its follow-up, 'WE RAP MORE MELLOW', the track was a massive underground hit, although the band failed to grab the attention of the wider music community. It was only after signing to Sylvia and Joe Robinson's 'Sugar Hill' records that FLASH and his FURIOUS FIVE began to make major waves. With the addition of SCORPIO (born ED MORRIS), the group released the 'FREEDOM' single which hit the American R&B Top 20, closely followed by 'BIRTHDAY PARTY', but it was 'THE ADVENTURES OF GRANDMASTER FLASH ON THE WHEELS OF STEEL' (1981) that really set the hip hop world alight. A revolutionary cut'n'paste of sampling, scratching, breaks and boisterous rapping, the record used Chic's 'GOOD TIMES' and Queen's 'ANOTHER ONE BITES THE DUST' as its base material. Another precedent was set almost a year later with the SYLVIA ROBINSON/DUKE BOOTEE-penned 'THE MESSAGE', as powerful a record as has ever emerged from hip hop. With its hard-hitting account of inner city life, the record pre-empted Gangsta-rap with half the bluster and twice the effectiveness, topping the charts on both sides of the Atlantic in 1982. Financial and personal squabbling led to a split in the ranks the following year during the recording of 'WHITE LINES (DON'T DO IT)', FLASH heading off with RAHIEM and KID CREOLE, eventually securing a contract with 'Elektra'. The latter track, released under the moniker GRANDMASTER FLASH & MELLE MEL, was another revelatory piece of old skool electro-hip hop, all reverberating bass and apocalyptic vocals warning of the dangers of drug addiction. It was a warning that FLASH would've done well to heed, now a freebase cocaine addict himself, and although he eventually won a court battle with MELLE MEL over the use of the group name, his major label records made little impact, FLASH fading into obscurity as the 80's wore on, while young bucks like ERIC B and PUBLIC ENEMY took over. MELLE MEL, meanwhile, who had remained with COWBOY and SCORPIO, continued to record for 'Sugarhill' although he too was afforded about as much interest with his later work as his estranged colleague. FLASH, MELLE MEL and THE FURIOUS FIVE eventually re-united in 1987 for a New York charity concert organised by PAUL SIMON. Tragically, it was the last time the original line-up would be on the same stage together as COWBOY died on the 8th of September '89 as a result of crack addiction. More recently, FLASH played at the 1997 Essential Music Festival in Brighton, England, while MELLE MEL released a solo album the same year. • **Songwriters:** All written by FLASH and MELLE (VAUGHAN), except loads of sampling and covers, including WHO'S THAT LADY (Isley Brothers).

Album rating: THE MESSAGE (*7) / GREATEST MESSAGES compilation (*6) / THEY SAID IT COULDN'T BE DONE (*4) / THE SOURCE (*5) / BA-DOP-BOOM-BANG (*4) / ON THE STRENGTH (*3) / THE GREATEST HITS compilation (*7)

GRANDMASTER FLASH & THE FURIOUS FIVE

GRANDMASTER FLASH (b. JOSEPH SADDLER, 1 Jan '58, Barbados) – turntables / **MELLE MEL** (b. MELVIN GLOVER) – vocals / **COWBOY** (b. KEITH WIGGINS, 20 Sep'60) – vocals / **KID CREOLE** (b. NATHANIEL GLOVER) – vocals / added **MR. NESS** (b. EDDIE MORRIS) – rapper / and **RAHEIM** (b. GUY WILLIAMS) – vocals repl. KURTIS BLOW who went solo

	not iss.	Enjoy
1979. (7") **SUPERRAPPIN'**. / ('A'instrumental)	-	□
	not iss.	Brass
1979. (7"; as The YOUNGER GENERATION) **WE RAP MORE MELLOW**. / ('A' instrumental)	-	□

—— added **SCORPIO** – electronics

	Sugar Hill	Sugar Hill
Apr 81. (7") (SH 555) <759> **BIRTHDAY PARTY**. / ('A'instrumental)	□	□
Jul 81. (7") **FREEDOM**. / ('A'instrumental)	-	□
Dec 81. (12") (SHL 557) **THE ADVENTURES OF GRANDMASTER FLASH ON THE WHEELS OF STEEL**. / THE BIRTHDAY PARTY		
Dec 81. (7") **FLASH TO THE BEAT**. / ('A'instrumental) (originally issued 1979 on 'Bozo Meko')		Oct81
Mar 82 (7"/12") (SH/+L 111) **IT'S NASTY (GENIUS OF LOVE)**. / BIRTHDAY PARTY		
May 82. (7"/12") (SH/+L 117) <584> **THE MESSAGE**. / THE MESSAGE (part 2)	8	62 Sep82
Oct 82. (lp/c) (SHLP/ZCSH 1007) <268> **THE MESSAGE**	77	53

– She's fresh / It's nasty (genius of love) / Scorpio / It's a shame / Dreamin' / You are / The message / Adventures of Grandmaster Flash on the wheels of steel.

Dec 82. (7"/12") (SH/+L 118) <790> **SCORPIO**. / IT'S A SHAME		
Jan 83. (7"/12"; by MELLE MEL & DUKE BOOTEE) (SH/+L 119) <792> **MESSAGE II (SURVIVAL)**. / ('A'instrumental)	74	□
May 83. (7"/12"; by The FURIOUS FIVE) (SH/+L 125) **NEW YORK, NEW YORK**. / ('A'instrumental)		

GRANDMASTER FLASH & MELLE MEL

	Sugarhill	Sugarhill
Nov 83. (7"/12") (SH/+L 130) <465> **WHITE LINES (DON'T DO IT)**. / ('A'version)	7	□

(Jul84; 12"pic-d+=) (SHLX 130) – White lines (New York remix) / ('A'original) / ('A'-US mix). (re-iss. Oct84 as 'CONTINUOUS WHITE LINES'; SHLM 130) (re-iss. Jun87 on 'Blatant' 7"/12"; BLAT 7/12 1)

—— GRANDMASTER FLASH, MELLE MEL & THE FURIOUS FIVE split Nov83. FLASH and MEL split two ways, and went to court to use full group name. MEL adopted

GRANDMASTER MELLE MEL & THE FURIOUS FIVE

—— taking with him **SCORPIO** and **COWBOY**. He recruited new members **LEWIS GLOVER** (MEL's brother) / **TOMMY GUN CHEV** / **LES DE LA CRUZ**

	Sugar Hill	Sugar Hill
1984. (7"/12") (SH/+L 133) **JESSE**. / ('A' instrumental)	□	-

—— (below from the film 'Beat Street' on 'Atlantic')

Jun 84. (7") (A 9659) <89659> **BEAT STREET BREAKDOWN**. / (part II)	42	86
(12"+=) (TA 9659) – Internationally known.		
Jun 84. (lp/c) (SHLP/ZCSH 5552) **GREATEST MESSAGES** (compilation)	41	-

– The message / Survival (The message II) / Freedom / Flash to the beat / Jesse / White lines (don't do it) / New York New York / Internationally known / Birthday party / Adventures on the wheels of steel / Scorpio / It's nasty (genius of love).

Sep 84. (7"/12") (SH/+L 136) <92011> **WE DON'T WORK FOR FREE**. / ('A'instrumental)	45	□
Oct 84. (lp/c) (SHLP/ZCSH 5553) **WORK PARTY**	45	

– Rustler's convention / Yesterday / At the party / The truth / White lines (new UK master mix) / We don't work for free / World war III / Can't keep running away / The new adventures of Grandmaster.

Nov 84. (7") (SH 139) **STEP OFF (part 1)**. / STEP OFF (part 2)	8	□
(12"+=) (SHL 139) – The message.		
(12"+=) (SHLX 139) – Continuous white lines.		
Mar 85. (7") (SH 141) **PUMP ME UP**. / ('A' instrumental)	45	-
(12"+=/12"pic-d+=) (SHL/+X 141) – ('A'version).		
May 85. (lp/c) (SHLP/ZCSH 5555) **STEPPING OFF** (compilation)	□	-

– Pump me up / Step off / The message / We don't work for free / White lines (don't do it) / Jesse / Survival (the message II) / The megaMelle mix.

Jul 85. (7") (SH 143) **WORLD WAR III**. / THE TRUTH		
(12"+=) (SHL 143) – Step off / The message (version).		
Nov 85. (7") (SH 146) <92015> **VICE (from 'Miami Vice' TV)**. / KING OF THE STREET		

GRANDMASTER FLASH

—— went solo, taking **RAHEIM** and **KID CREOLE** plus new people **LEVON, BROADWAY** and **LARRY LOVE**

	Elektra	Elektra
Feb 85. (7") (E 9677) <69677> **SIGN OF THE TIMES**. / LARRY'S DANCE THEME	72	□
(12"+=) (E 9677T) – ('A'instrumental).		
Feb 85. (lp/c) (960389-1/-4) <60389> **THEY SAID IT COULDN'T BE DONE**		95

– Girls love the way he spins / The joint is jumpin' / Rock the house / Jailbait / Sign of the times / Larry's dance theme / Who's that lady / Alternative groove / Paradise.

May 85. (7") <69643> **GIRLS LOVE THE WAY HE SPINS**. / LARRY'S DANCE THEME	-	□
Jul 85. (7") <69617> **WHO'S THAT LADY**. / ALTERNATIVE GROOVE	-	□

Apr 86. (lp/c) *(960476-1/-4) <60476>* **THE SOURCE** ☐ ☐
– Street scene / Style (Peter Gunn theme) / Ms. Thang / P.L.U. (Peace, Love and Unity) / Throwin' down / Behind closed doors / Larry's dance theme (part 2) / Lies / Fastest man alive / Freelance.
May 86. (7") *(EKR 39) <69552>* **STYLE (PETER GUNN THEME). /** ☐ ☐
('A'instrumental)
(12"+=) *(EKR 39T)* – ('A'remix).
Jul 86. (7") *<69530>* **LIES. / BEHIND CLOSED DOORS** - ☐
Mar 87. (7"/12") *(EKR 54/+T) <69490>* **U KNOW WHAT TIME IT** ☐ ☐
IS? / BUS DIS (WOO)
Mar 87. (lp/c/cd) *(960723-1/-4/-2) <60723>* **BA-DOP-BOOM-BANG** ☐ ☐
– Ain't we funkin' now / U know what time it is? / Underarms / Kid named Flash / Get yours / Then jeans / We will rock you / All wrapped up / Tear the roof off / Big black caddy / House that rocked / Bus dis / I am somebody / Ain't we funkin' now (reprise).
May 87. (7") *<69459>* **ALL WRAPPED UP. / KID NAMED FLASH** - ☐

GRANDMASTER FLASH & THE FURIOUS FIVE

(originals re-formed for 'Elektra')
Feb 88. (7") *(EKR 70) <69416>* **GOLD. / BACK IN THE OLD DAYS** ☐ ☐
OF HIP HOP
(12"+=) *(EKR 70T)* – ('A'acappella) / ('A'acappella dub).
Mar 88. (lp/c/cd) *(960769-1/-4/-2) <60769>* **ON THE STRENGTH** ☐ ☐
– Gold / Cold in effect / Yo baby / On the strength / The king / Fly girl / Magic carpet ride / Leave here / This is where you got it from / The boy is dope. *(cd+=)* – Back in the old days of hip-hop. *(cd re-iss. Jan97; 7559 60769-2)*
May 88. (7") *<69400>* **COLD IN EFFECT. / FLY GIRL** - ☐
Jul 88. (7") *<69380>* **ON THE STRENGTH. / MAGIC CARPET RIDE** - ☐

GRANDMASTER MELLE MEL

	Edel	unknown
Jul 97. (12") *(0098470 RAP)* **MR. BIG STUFF. / CHINA WHITE**	☐	-

– compilations, etc. –

1988. (3"cd-ep) *Special Edition; (CD3-1)* **WHITE LINES (DON'T** ☐ -
DO IT). / JESSE / THE MESSAGE II
1988. (3"cd-ep) *Special Edition; (CD3-2)* **THE ADVENTURES OF** ☐ -
GRANDMASTER FLASH ON THE WHEELS OF STEEL. /
THE MESSAGE / IT'S NASTY (GENIUS OF LOVE)
Mar 89. (d-c) *Sugar Hill; (IED 33)* **THE BEST OF GRANDMASTER** ☐ -
FLASH & THE FURIOUS FIVE
Nov 89. (12") *Old Gold; (OG 4152)* **THE MESSAGE. / THE** ☐ -
ADVENTURES ON THE WHEELS OF STEEL
Jul 90. (7") *Castle;* **WHITE LINES (DON'T DON'T DO IT) (freestyle** ☐ -
Ben Legrand mix). / (Part 2)
Jul 91. (cd/c) *Kwest; (KWEST 5/4 193)* **WHITE LINES & OTHER** ☐ -
MESSAGES – THE SILVER COLLECTION
May 92. (cd) *Sequel; (NEMCD 622)* **THE GREATEST HITS** ☐ -
– White lines (don't do it) / Step off / Pump me up / Jesse / Beat Street / Vice / Freedom / Birthday party / Flash to the beat / It's nasty (genius of love) / The message / Scorpio / Survival (Message II) / New York, New York.
Dec 93. (12"/cd-s) *W.G.A.F.; (WGAF/+CD 103)* **WHITE LINES (DON'T** 59 -
DO IT) (D&S 7" Remix) / HEY HEY (D&S 7" Remix)
Mar 94. (12"/cd-s) *W.G.A.F.; (WGAF/+T)* **THE MESSAGE. /** ☐ -
('A'remixes)
Aug 95. (cd-s) *Old Gold; (OG 6314)* **WHITE LINES (DON'T DO IT) /** ☐ -
PUMP ME UP
Sep 95. (cd-s) *Old Gold; (12623 6300-2)* **THE MESSAGE / SURVIVAL** ☐ -
(MESSAGE II)
Nov 96. (cd/lp) *Deep Beats; (DEEP M/X 004)* **MORE HITS** ☐ -
Jul 97. (12"/cd-s) *Deep Cuts; (DEEP 12/CD 001)* **THE MESSAGE** ☐ -
(mixes)
Jul 97. (d-cd; shared with SUGARHILL GANG) *Snapper; (SMDCD* ☐ -
164) **GRANDMASTER FLASH VS THE SUGARHILL GANG**
Mar 99. (12") *Sugarhill-Sequel; (NEET 1003)* **THE MESSAGE. /** ☐ -
THE ADVENTURES OF GRANDMASTER FLASH ON THE
WHEELS OF STEEL
Mar 99. (12") *Sugarhill-Sequel; (NEET 1007)* **WHITE LINES (DON'T** ☐ -
DO IT). / SCORPIO
Mar 99. (3xcd-box) *Sequel; (NXTCD 305)* **BACK TO THE OLD** ☐ -
SCHOOL
Oct 99. (12") *Hot Classics; (HCL 2261)* **THE MESSAGE. / IT'S NASTY** ☐ -
Oct 99. (12") *Hot Classics; (HCL 2262)* **WHITE LINES. / THE** ☐ -
MESSAGE II

GRANT LEE BUFFALO

Formed: North Hollywood, California, USA . . . 1991 by GRANT LEE PHILLIPS (vocals, guitar), PAUL KIMBLE (bass, piano, vocals) and JOEY PETERS (drums, percussion) who had all played together in SHIVA BURLESQUE before splitting the group to concentrate on a new project, GRANT LEE BUFFALO, partly named after lead singer PHILLIPS. After BOB MOULD released 'FUZZY' as a one-off 7" on his own label, the band came to the attention of 'London'-offshoot, 'Slash', making their major label debut with an album, 'FUZZY' (1993). A compelling hybrid of country-rock, folk and feedback hum, the set was lauded by the press, PHILLIPS' incisive lyrics cutting at the heart of America's broken dreams and drawing comparisons with NEIL YOUNG, The WATERBOYS and The DOORS. The album was also praised by MICHAEL STIPE of R.E.M. (spiritual forebears), who pronounced it his favourite release of the year. After a mini album, 'BUFFALONDON EP' (1993), featuring live versions of some of the debut's most sublime tracks ('JUPITER AND TEARDROP', 'THE SHINING

HOUR'), the band released 'MIGHTY JOE MOON' (1994), a set that employed a richer sonic tapestry without losing the raw impact of the debut. At times, PHILLIPS sounded like a more organic EDDDY VEDDER while on songs like 'IT'S THE LIFE', the effect was akin to a countryfied JAMES (decidedly more palatable in reality than on paper!) The breezy melancholy of 'HONEY DON'T THINK' was a highlight, as was 'ROCK OF AGES', rolling the final credits to the album's widescreen sweep. The band's third effort, 'COPPEROPOLIS' (1996), was even more ambitious, embellishing the sound with strings and mellotron amongst other instrumental exotica. The lyrics were more entrenched in threadbare Americana than ever, PHILLIPS invoking the spirit of WOODY GUTHRIE in his sensitive portraits of his country's often tragic past. • **Covered:** BURNING LOVE (hit; Elvis Presley).

Album rating: FUZZY (*8) / MIGHTY JOE MOON (*7) / COPPEROPOLIS (*6) / JUBILEE (*5)

GRANT LEE PHILLIPS – vocals, guitars / **PAUL KIMBLE** – bass, piano, vocals, producer / **JOEY PETERS** – drums, percussion

	Singles Only Label	not iss.
Dec 91. (7") *(227)* **FUZZY. / WE'RE COMING DOWN**		-

	Slash – London	Slash – Reprise
Jun 93. (cd/lp) *(828 389-2/-1) <45217>* **FUZZY**	74	☐ Feb93

– The shining hour / Jupiter and teardrop / Fuzzy / Wish you well / The hook / Soft wolf tread / Stars n' stripes / Dixie drug store / America snoring / Grace / You just have to be crazy. *(cd re-iss. Sep97; same)*
Aug 93. (7") *(LAS 45)* **AMERICA SNORING. / WISH YOU WELL** ☐ -
(12"+=/cd-s+=) *(LAS H/CD 45)* – The hook / Burning love.
Sep 93. (7") *(LAS 46)* **FUZZY. / STARS & STRIPES** ☐ -
(12"+=/cd-s+=) *(LAS H/CD 46)* – Dixie drugstore (Ju Ju mix) / I will take him.
Nov 93. (12"ep/cd-ep) *(LAS H/CD 47)* **BUFFALONDON EP** ☐ -
– Jupiter and teardrop / Wish you well / Soft wolf tread / The shining hour.
Sep 94. (cd/c) *(828 541-2/-4) <45714>* **MIGHTY JOE MOON** 24 ☐
– Lone star song / Mockingbirds / It's the life / Sing along / Mighty Joe Moon / Demon called Deception / Lady Godiva and me / Drag / Last days of Tecumseh / Happiness / Honey don't think / Side by side / Rock of ages.
Oct 94. (cd-ep) *(LASHCD 49)* **MOCKINGBIRDS / ORPHEUS /** ☐ -
GOODNIGHT JOHN DEE
(12"ep+=) *(LASHX 49)* – Let go of my hand.
(cd-ep) *(LASPD 49)* – (first track) / Let go of my hand / We're coming down.
May 96. (12"ep/cd-ep) *(LAS H/CD 55)* **HOMESPUN / ARMCHAIR. /** ☐ -
COMES TO BLOWS / CRASHING AT CORONA
Jun 96. (cd/c/lp) *(828 760-2/-4/-1) <46250>* **COPPEROPOLIS** 34 ☐
– Homespun / The bridge / Arousing thunder / Even the oxen / Crackdown / Armchair / Bethlehem steel / All that I have / Two and two / Better for us / Hyperion and sunset / Comes to blows / Only way down.

—— 3rd member **DAN ROTHCHILD** – bass; repl. KIMBLE

—— additional **JON BRION** – keyboards / **RAMI JAFFE** – organ

—— guests included ROBYN HITCHCOCK, MICHAEL STIPE & E (of The EELS)
Jun 98. (cd) *(556 048-2) <46879>* **JUBILEE** ☐ -
– APB / Seconds / Change your tune / Testimony / Truly, truly / Superslomotion / Fine how'd ya do / Come to mama, she say / 8 mile road / Everybody needs a little sanctuary / My, my, my / Crooked dice / Jubilee / The shallow end.

GRASSHOPPER & THE GOLDEN CRICKETS
(see under ⇒ MERCURY REV)

GRATEFUL DEAD

Formed: San Francisco, California, USA . . . 1965 by JERRY GARCIA, who had spent 9 months of 1959 in the army before finding lyricist extrordinaire ROBERT HUNTER and forming folk outfit The THUNDER MOUNTAIN TUB THUMPERS. Along the way, this loose collective of musicians included soon-to-be GRATEFUL DEAD members BOB WEIR and RON McKERNAN (aka PIGPEN), JERRY going on to make demos in 1963 as duo JERRY & SARAH GARCIA. It wasn't until 1965 that the earliest incarnation of The GRATEFUL DEAD, The WARLOCKS, set out on their "golden road to unlimited gigging", when they took centre stage as house band for KEN KESEY's (author of 'One Flew Over The Cuckoo's Nest') legendary acid tests. Created by KESEY and his band of merry pranksters, the main objective of these psychedelic shindigs was to bombard the tripping hordes with as much sensory overload as posible; flashing lights, pre-recorded chants, hidden speakers hissing subversive messages and of course, the ear splitting racket of The WARLOCKS. With crowd and band liberally dosed with LSD courtesy of acidmeister AUGUSTUS STANLEY III, the events were clearly a formative part of their career. By this time, the band had gone electric, inspired by the raucous rock'n'roll of The BEATLES, bolstering the sound with drummer BILL KREUTZMANN and bassist PHIL LESH. Changing their name to the equally hoary sounding GRATEFUL DEAD (picked at random from a dictionary), the band toured California alongside JEFFERSON AIRPLANE. In 1966, they issued a one-off 45, 'DON'T EASE ME IN', for 'Fantasy' off-shoot label 'Scorpio', which led to 'Warners' signing them up in 1967. Recorded in three amphetamine-fuelled days, 'THE GRATEFUL DEAD' was released to the expectant hippy faithful in December of the same year, an admirable but ultimately doomed attempt to recreated their fabled live sound in the studio. After an impromptu guest spot at one of their early shows, drummer MICKEY HART augmented the band's rhythm section, creating a more subtly complex rather than powerful sound. The group also recruited keyboardist TOM CONSTANTEN, whose avant-garde influences included JOHN CAGE and STOCKHAUSEN. Adding to the DEAD's psychedelic stew, these two further inspired the band's live improvisation, partly captured on 'ANTHEM OF THE SUN' in 1968. An ambitious collage of live and studio pieces, the album was another flawed attempt to seize the essence of the elusive beast that was the band's live show. It did, however, contain bizarrely experimental sections with wonderful cod-hippy titles like, 'CRYPTICAL ENVELOPMENT' and 'THE FASTER WE GO, THE ROUNDER WE GET', these worth the admission price alone. The experimentation continued with 'AOXOMOXOA' in 1969, GARCIA's old mate ROBERT HUNTER marking his first collaboration with the band and helping to contain the explorations inside defined song structures. Highlights included 'MOUNTAINS OF THE MOON', with its celestial harpsicord and 'ST STEPHEN', a song that would go on to become a staple of the band's live set. With the release of 'LIVE DEAD' in 1970, The GRATEFUL DEAD finally did itself justice on vinyl, silencing the critics of their previous output who couldn't understand why the band were held in such high esteem by their fiercely loyal San Franciscan fanbase. On the track 'DARK STAR', the band crystallised their free-flowing improvisation in breathtaking style, while the celebratory 'TURN ON YOUR LOVE LIGHT', was also a standard of the band's now legendary live shows. Attracting multitudes of tie-dyed freaks, affectionately nicknamed "Deadheads", the band's gigs became communal gatherings, where both the crowd and band could lose themselves in the spaced-out jams which would often stretch songs over an hour or more. Forget 15 minutes of fame (as ANDY WARHOL once gave us all), the DEAD needed 15 minutes just for the intro! Ironically the band's next two studio albums marked a radical new direction with pared-down sets of harmony-laden country-folk. With CONSTANTEN out of the picture by early 1970 and mounting debts, the group went for a simpler sound, clearly influenced by CROSBY, STILLS and NASH and GARCIA's part-time dabblings with The NEW RIDERS OF THE PURPLE SAGE. 'WORKINGMAN'S DEAD' was symptomatic of the times as bands began to move away from the psychedelic claustrophobia of the late 60's (note 'NEW SPEEDWAY BOOGIE' about the end of the hippy dream, the Altamont Festival where a ROLLING STONES fan was killed by a drug-crazed Hell's Angel). 'AMERICAN BEAUTY' carried on where the previous album left off, 'SUGAR MAGNOLIA' and 'RIPPLE' being the highlights of this highly regarded piece of roots rock. By 1971, HART had departed and the band were reduced to five core members. Two live albums followed, the double 'GRATEFUL DEAD' and 'EUROPE 72', the latter stretching to three slabs of vinyl. 1972 also saw the release of WEIR's solo album, 'ACE', actually a GRATEFUL DEAD album in all but name. It included the glorious tongue-in-cheek romp, 'MEXICALI BLUES', and also saw WEIR begin writing with JOHN PERRY BARLOW, a partnership that would see HUNTER's input diminish over the following years. Years of alcohol abuse led to PIGPEN dying on 8th May '73 and he was replaced by KEITH GODCHAUX, who had toured with them the previous year. His wife DONNA also joined, taking up vocal duties. Around this time the band set up their own label, imaginatively titled 'Grateful Dead Records', releasing 'WAKE OF THE FLOOD' in July '73. The album was their most successful to date, containing the melancholy 'STELLA BLUE', although ironically, profits were lost to bootleggers. 'BLUES FOR ALLAH', from 1975, signalled a jazzier, fuller sound, though by this juncture the band were in financial deep water and signed with 'United Artists'. The source of much of their money problems was a concert movie which ate up most of their resources. 'STEAL YOUR FACE' was next in line and was intended for the movie, although it remained in the can due to the album's relative critical failure. Signing to 'Arista' and drafting in KEITH OLSEN on production duties, they released 'TERRAPIN STATION' in 1977, an album which showcased a lusher, fuller sound. For '78's 'SHAKEDOWN STREET', the band collaborated with LOWELL GEORGE, and what could have been an interesting pairing came out sounding limp and uninspiring; a pale reflection of what the DEAD were capable of. Despite the inconsistent quality of their studio work, the DEAD were always a safe live bet and they played the gig to surely top all gigs with their series of dates at the Pyramids in Egypt. Still carrying a hippy torch (even through the punk days), they filled large venues wherever they played and became a multi-million-dollar industry in their own right. However, as they concentrated on live work, their studio outings suffered, their 1980 album 'GO TO HEAVEN' being particularly disappointing athough it spawned their first success in the US singles chart with 'ALABAMA GETAWAY'. Another two live sets followed in 1981, 'DEAD SET' and 'RECKONING'. The latter was an acoustic album featuring classics like 'RIPPLE' and 'CASSIDY'. Soon after their release, GARCIA became a full-blown heroin addict, narrowly escaping death when he fell into a diabetic coma in 1986. Once he rehabilitated, the DEAD came back to life with 'IN THE DARK', a spirited set that reached the Top 10 in the US chart, even resulting in top-selling 45, 'TOUCH OF GREY'. Their tribute to growing old with pride, it was a first when the band agreed to make a video for MTV. The awful 'DYLAN & THE DEAD' (yes with Mr. Zimmerman) was muted and dull, as was the 1989 studio offering, 'BUILT TO LAST'. Tragedy hit the band yet again, when keyboardist BRENT MYDLAND (who himself had replaced KEITH GODCHAUX in '79) was killed by a hard-drugs cocktail. BRUCE HORNSBY (yes that geezer) was drafted in temorarily for touring commitments, while VINCE WELNICK joined full-time. The band released yet another live album the same year, the hardly dangerous 'WITHOUT A NET' and also started issuing the DICK'S PICKS series of archive recordings from great days of yore. On 9th August, 1995, the ailing JERRY GARCIA died of heart failure in a rehab unit after his arteries clogged up. It seemed inevitable that the long strange trip of The GRATEFUL DEAD had come to an end, GARCIA's guiding light relocating to find his "Dark Star" once again. The DEAD left behind a rich musical legacy, including numerous solo outings

and off-shoot projects, but will always be remembered, by the Deadheads at least, for their transcendental live performances. Stop press:- WEIR, HART and LESH formed a new 'Dead' outfit, The OTHER ONES (along with BRUCE HORNSBY, DAVE ELLIS, MARK KARAN, JOHN MOLO and STEVE KIMOCK, etc), delivering a surprise oddity set, 'ONLY THE STRANGE REMAIN' (1999). • **Songwriters:** Most by HUNTER-GARCIA or WEIR, LESH and some by others, including JOHN BARLOW. Covered; GOOD MORNING LITTLE SCHOOLGIRL (Don & Bob) / NEW MINGLEWOOD BLUES + SAMSON AND DELILAH (trad.) / JOHNNY B. GOODE (Chuck Berry) / NOT FADE AWAY (Buddy Holly) / ME AND BOBBY McGEE (Kris Kristofferson) / BIG BOSS MAN (Bo Diddley) / DANCING IN THE STREET (hit; Martha & The Vandellas) / STAGGER LEE (Lloyd Price) / LITTLE RED ROOSTER (Willie Dixon) / DEAR MR. FANTASY (Traffic) / WALKIN' BLUES (Robert Johnson) / NEXT TIME YOU SEE ME (Junior Parker) / etc. GARCIA covered; IT TAKES A LOT TO LAUGH + POSITIVELY 4TH STREET + KNOCKIN' ON HEAVEN'S DOOR (Bob Dylan) / LET'S SPEND THE NIGHT TOGETHER + WILD HORSES (Rolling Stones) / HE AIN'T GIVE YOU NONE (Van Morrison) / THAT'S ALL RIGHT MAMA (Arthur Crudup) / MY FUNNY VALENTINE / WHEN THE HUNTER GETS CAPTURED BY THE GAME (Smokey Robinson) / LET IT ROCK (Chuck Berry) / RUSSIAN LULLABY (Irving Berlin) / MIDNIGHT TOWN (Kahn-Hunter) / I SAW HER STANDING THERE (Beatles) / etc. • **Trivia:** An edited 'DARK STAR', was used as theme in the US 70's series of 'Twilight Zone'.

Album rating: THE GRATEFUL DEAD (*5) / ANTHEM OF THE SUN (*7) / AOXOMOXOA (*8) / LIVE/DEAD (*7) / WORKINGMAN'S DEAD (*8) / AMERICAN BEAUTY (*10) / GRATEFUL DEAD live double (*6) / EUROPE '72 (*6) / HISTORY OF THE GRATEFUL DEAD, VOL.1 (BEAR'S CHOICE) / WAKE OF THE FLOOD (*5) / SKELETON'S FROM THE CLOSET: THE BEST OF ... compilation (*5) / GRATEFUL DEAD FROM THE MARS HOTEL (*5) / BLUES FOR ALLAH (*5) / STEAL YOUR FACE (*4) / TERRAPIN STATION (*6) / WHAT A LONG STRANGE TRIP IT'S BEEN compilation (*8) / SHAKEDOWN STREET (*4) / GO TO HEAVEN (*1) / RECKONING (*5) / DEAD SET (*5) / IN THE DARK (*7) / BUILT TO LAST (*4) / WITHOUT A NET (*4) / ONE FROM THE VAULT early concert (*5) / INFRARED ROSES concert (*4) / TWO FROM THE VAULT early concert (*5) / DICK'S PICK, VOL.1 early concert (*5) / DICK'S PICK, VOL.2 early concert (*5) / HUNDRED YEAR HALL early concert (*5) / DICK'S PICK, VOL.3 early concert (*6) / DICK'S PICK, VOL.4 early concert (*8) / Jerry Garcia: HOOTEROLL (*5) / GARCIA (*7) / LIVE AT THE KEYSTONE (*4) / GARCIA on 'Round' (*6) / OLD & IN THE WAY (*4) / REFLECTIONS (*5) / CATS UNDER THE STARS (*6) / RUN FOR THE ROSES (*6) / ALMOST ACOUSTIC (*6) / JERRY GARCIA BAND (*6) / JERRY GARCIA & DAVID GRISMAN (*6) / NOT FOR KIDS ONLY with David Grisman (*5) / HOW SWEET IT IS early gig (*5) / Other Ones: ONLY THE STRANGE REMAIN (*5)

JERRY GARCIA (b. JEROME JOHN GARCIA, 1 Aug'42) – vocals, lead guitar / **BOB WEIR** (b. ROBERT HALL, 6 Oct'47) – rhythm guitar / **RON 'PIGPEN' McKERNAN** (b. 8 Sep'45, San Bruno, Calif.) – keyboards, vocals, mouth harp / **PHIL LESH** (b. PHILIP CHAPMAN, 15 Mar'40, Berkeley, Calif.) – bass / **BILL KREUTZMANN** (b. 7 Apr'46, Palo Alto, Calif.) – drums (DAN MORGAN left before recording)

	not iss.	Scorpio
Jun 66. (7") <003-201> **DON'T EASE ME IN. / STEALIN'**	-	Scorpio
	Warners	Warners

Feb 67. (7") <7016> **THE GOLDEN ROAD (TO UNLIMITED DEVOTION). / CREAM PUFF WAR**   [-]
Dec 67. (lp; mono/stereo) (<W/+S 1689>) **THE GRATEFUL DEAD**   [73] Feb67
   – The golden road (to unlimited devotion) / Cold rain and snow / Good morning little schoolgirl / Beat it on down / Sitting on top of the world / Cream puff war / Morning dew / New, new Minglewood blues / Viola Lee blues. (re-iss. Mar87 on 'Edsel'; ED 221) <US cd-iss. 1987; 2-1689> (cd-iss. Jul88 on 'Atlantic'; K 259302) (cd-iss. Feb93 & Oct95)

—— added **TOM CONSTANTEN** – keyboards / **MICKEY HART** (b.1950, Long Island, N.Y.) – percussion and returning lyricist **ROBERT HUNTER**

Oct 68. (7") (WB <7186>) **BORN CROSS-EYED. / DARK STAR**   [ ]
Nov 68. (lp) (<WS 1749>) **ANTHEM OF THE SUN**   [87] Aug 68
   – That's it for other one:- Cryptical envelopment – Quadlibet for tender feet – The faster we go, the rounder we get – We leave the castle / Born cross-eyed / Alligator / Caution (do not stop on the tracks). (re-iss. Jul71; K 46021) <US cd-iss. 1987; 2-1749> (re-iss. Jul88 on 'WEA' lp/cd; K2 4602-1/2) (re-iss. cd 1992; 7599 27173-2)

Oct 69. (lp) (<WS 1790>) **AOXOMOXOA**   [73] Jun 69
   – St. Stephen / Dupree's diamond blues / Rosemary / Doin' the rag / Mountains of the Moon / China cat sunflower / What's become of the baby / Cosmic Charlie. (re-iss. Jul71; K 46027) ;re-iss. Jan77) <US cd-iss. 1987; 2-1790> (re-iss. Jun89 on 'WEA' c/cd; K4 46027/ K927 128-2)

Oct 69. (7") <7324> **DUPREE'S DIAMOND BLUES. / COSMIC CHARLIE**   [-]
Feb 70. (d-lp) <2(WS 1830)> **LIVE/DEAD (live in the studio)**   [64] Dec 69
   – Dark star / Death don't have no mercy / Feedback / And we bid you goodnight / St. Stephen / The eleven / Turn on your love light. (re-iss. Jul71; K 66002) <US cd-iss. 1987; 2-1830> (cd-iss. Jun89 on 'WEA'; K927 181-2)

—— **DAVID NELSON** – acoustic guitar repl. CONSTANTEN / added guest **JOHN DAWSON** – guitar, vocals (on some)
   above pairing also formed off-shoot band The NEW RIDERS OF THE PURPLE SAGE, who initially toured as support to DEAD, with GARCIA in their ranks.

Sep 70. (lp) (<WS 1869>) **WORKINGMAN'S DEAD**   [27] Jun 70
   – Uncle John's band / High time / Dire wolf / New speedway boogie / Cumberland blues / Black Peter / Easy wind / Casey Jones. (re-iss. Jul71; K 46049) <US cd-iss. 1987; 2-1889> (re-iss. 1988 lp/c) (cd-iss. Jun89 on 'WEA' K2 46049)

Aug 70. (7") (WB <7410>) **UNCLE JOHN'S BAND. / NEW SPEEDWAY BOOGIE**   [69]

—— added guest **DAVID TORBERT** – bass (1)
Dec 70. (lp) (<WS 1893>) **AMERICAN BEAUTY**   [30]
   – Box of rain / Friend of the Devil / Sugar magnolia / Operator / Candyman / Ripple / Brokedown palace / Till the morning comes / Attics of my life / Truckin. (re-iss. Jul71; K 46074) ;re-iss. Jan77) <US cd-iss. 1987; 2-1893> (re-iss. Jun89 on 'WEA' c/cd; K2/K4 46074)

Jan 71. (7") <7464> **TRUCKIN. / RIPPLE**　　- 　64

───── Now **GARCIA, WEIR, LESH, KREUTZMANN** and **'PIGPEN'** with new members **MERL SAUNDERS** – keyboards (repl. PIGPEN for a while when he was ill) all guests had departed, incl. HART and NELSON.

Oct 71. (d-lp) (K 66009) <2WS 1935> **GRATEFUL DEAD** (SKULL & ROSES) (live)　　25
– Bertha / Mama tried / Big railroad blues / Playing in the band / The other one / Me & my uncle / Big boss man / Me & Bobby McGhee / Johnny B. Goode / Wharf rat / Not fade away / Goin' down road feeling bad. <US re-iss. 1987; 2-1935> (cd-iss. 1988; 927 192-2) (re-iss. cd 1992; 7599 27192-2)

Jan 72. (7") **JOHNNY B. GOODE. / SO FINE (by 'Elvin Bishop')**　　-

───── added on tour **KEITH GODCHAUX** (b.14 Jul'48) – keyboards (ex-DAVE MASON band) and **DONNA GODCHAUX** (b.22 Aug'47) – vocals (They both repl. SAUNDERS)

Dec 72. (t-lp) (K 66019) <3WS 2668> **EUROPE '72 (live)**　　24　Nov 72
– Cumberland blues / He's gone / One more Saturday night / Jack Straw / You win again / China cat sunflower / I know you rider / Brown-eyed woman / Hurts me too / Ramble on Rose / Sugar magnolia / Mr. Charlie / Tennessee Jed / Truckin' / (epilog) / (prelude) / (Walk me out in the) Morning dew. (cd-iss. Oct95;)

Dec 72. (7") <7667> **SUGAR MAGNOLIA (live). / MR. CHARLIE (live)**　　-　91

───── Now just basic 4 of **GARCIA, WEIR, LESH, KREUTZMANN** and both **GODCHAUX'S**. ('PIGPEN' sadly died 8 May'73 after a long and threatening bout of illness) note that ROBERT HUNTER was still writing their lyrics, next 2 albums also included ten or more session people.

	Warners	**Grateful Dead**

Jul 73. (lp/c) (K/K4 49301) <GD 01> **WAKE OF THE FLOOD**　　18　Oct 73
– Mississippi half-step uptown toodeloo / Let me sing your blues away / Row Jimmy / Stella blue / Here comes sunshine / Eyes of the world / Weather Report suite (part 1; Prelude – part 2; Let it grow). (re-iss. Jan76 on 'United Artists'; UAS 29903) (<re-iss. Apr89 on 'Grateful Dead' lp/c/cd; GDV/GDTCGDCD 4002>) (pic-cd Feb90; GDPD 4002)

Nov 73. (7") (K 19301) <01> **LET ME SING YOUR BLUES AWAY. / HERE COMES SUNSHINE**

Jan 74. (7") <02> **EYES OF THE WORLD. / WEATHER REPORT SUITE (part 1; PRELUDE)**　　-

Jul 74. (lp/c) (K/K4 59302) <GD 102> **FROM THE MARS HOTEL**　　47　16
– Scarlet begonias / Ship of fools / Pride of Cucamonga / Loose Lucy / U.S. blues / Unbroken chain / China doll / Money money. (re-iss. Jan76 on 'United Artists'; UAS 29904) <US cd-iss. Dec85 on 'Mobile Fidelity'; MFCD 830> (re-iss. Mar89 on 'Grateful Dead' lp/c/cd; GDV/GDTCGDCD 4007) (pic-cd Feb90; GDPD 4007)

Aug 74. (7") (UP 36030) <03> **U.S. BLUES. / LOOSE LUCY**

───── added the returning **MICKEY HART** – percussion

	U.A.	**Grateful Dead**

Oct 75. (lp) (UAS 29895) <LA 494> **BLUES FOR ALLAH**　　45　12　Sep75
– Help on the way / Slipknot / Franklin's tower / Stronger than dirt or milkin' the turkey / The music never stopped / Crazy fingers / Sage & spirit / Blues for Allah / Sand castles & glass camels / Unusual occurances in the desert. (<re-iss. Mar89 on 'Grateful Dead' lp/c/cd; GDV/GDTCGDCD 4001>) (pic-cd Feb90; GDPD 4001)

Oct 75. (7") <718> **THE MUSIC NEVER STOPPED. / HELP IS ON THE WAY**　　-　81

Jun 76. (d-lp) (UAD 60131-2) <LA 620> **STEAL YOUR FACE (live)**　　42　56
– The promised land / Cold rain and snow / Around and around / Stella blue / Mississippi half-step uptown toodeloo / Ship of fools / Beat it down the line / Big river / Black-throated wind / U.S. blues / El Paso / Sugaree / It must have been the roses / Casey Jones. (re-iss. Mar89 on 'Grateful Dead' lp/c/cd; GDV2/GDTCGDCD2 4006) (pic-cd Feb90; GDPD2 4006)

1976. (7") <762> **FRANKLIN'S TOWER. / HELP IS ON THE WAY**　　-

	Arista	**Arista**

Aug 77. (lp/c) (SPART/TC-ARTY 1016) <AL 7001> **TERRAPIN STATION**　　28
– Estimated prophet / Samson and Delilah / Passenger / Dancing in the street / Sunrise / Terrapin station. (re-iss. 1983; Jan87 lp/c; 201/401 190) <US cd-iss. 1986; ARCD 8065> (cd-iss. Nov90; 260175)

Oct 77. (12")<7"> (DEAD 1) <0276> **DANCING IN THE STREETS. / TERRAPIN STATION**

Feb 78. (7") <0291> **PASSENGER. / TERRAPIN STATION**　　-

Dec 78. (lp/c) (ARTY/TC-ART 159) <AB 4198> **SHAKEDOWN STREET**　　41
– Good lovin' / France / Shakedown street / Serangetti / Fire on the mountain / I need a miracle / From the heart of me / Stagger Lee / New, new Minglewood blues / If I had the world to give. <US cd-iss. 1986; ARCD 4198> (cd-iss. Jun91; 251 133)

Dec 78. (7") (ARIST 236) <0383> **GOOD LOVIN'. / STAGGER LEE**

Mar 79. (7") <0410> **SHAKEDOWN STREET. / FRANCE**　　-

───── **BRENT MYDLAND** (b.1953, Munich, Germany) – keyboards repl. both GODCHAUX'S (KEITH was killed in car crash 23 Jul'80)

May 80. (lp/c) (SPART/TCART 1115) <AL 9508> **GO TO HEAVEN**　　23
– Far from home / Althea / Feel like a stranger / Alabama getaway / Don't ease you in / Easy to love you / Lost sailor / Saint of circumstance. <US cd-iss. 1986; ARCD 9508>

Jun 80. (7") <0519> **ALABAMA GETAWAY. / FAR FROM ME**　　-　68

Jan 81. (7") <0546> **DON'T EASE ME IN. / FAR FROM ME**　　-

Apr 81. (d-lp) (DARTY 9) <A2L 8604> **RECKONING (live)** (all line-ups)　　43
– Dire wolf / The race is on / Oh babe it ain't no lie / It must have been the roses / Dark hollow / China doll / Been all around the world / Monkey and the engineer / Jack-a-roe / Deep Elam blues / Cassidy / To lay me down / Rosalie McFall / On the road again / Bird song / Ripple.

1981. (7") <116> **ALABAMA GETAWAY. / SHAKEDOWN STREET**　　-

Sep 81. (d-lp) (DARTY 11) <A2L 8606> **DEAD SET (live)**　　29
– Samson and Delilah / Friend of the Devil / New, new Minglewood blues / Deal / Candyman / Little red rooster / Loser / Passenger / Feel like a stranger / Franklin's tower / Fire on the mountain / Rhythm devils / Greatest story ever told / Brokedown palace. <US cd-iss. 1986; ARCD 8112>

Sep 87. (7"/12") <cds-s/7",7"grey> (RIS/+T 35) <ASCD+/9606> **TOUCH OF GREY. / MY BROTHER ESAU**　　9　Jul87

Oct 87. (lp/c/cd) (208/408/258 564) <AL/AC/ARCD 8452> **IN THE DARK**　　57　6　Jul87
– Touch of grey / Hell in a bucket / When push comes to shove / West L.A. fadeaway /

Tons of steel / Throwing stones / Black muddy river. (re-iss. Nov90 cd/lp; 261/211 145)

Nov 87. (cd-s/7") <ASCD+/9643> **THROWING STONES. / WHEN PUSH COMES TO SHOVE**　　-

───── Late '87, they recorded live album 'DYLAN AND THE DEAD' with BOB DYLAN, which was released early 1989, and hit US No.37.

Nov 89. (lp/c/cd) (210/410/260 326) <AL/AC/ARCD 875> **BUILT TO LAST**　　27
– Foolish heart / Just a little light / Built to last / Blow away / Standing on the Moon / Victim or the crime / We can run / Picasso moon / I will take you home.

Nov 89. (cd-s/7") <ASCD+/9899> **FOOLISH HEART. / WE CAN RUN**　　-

Oct 90. (d-cd/t-lp) (303/353 935) <ACD2 8634> **WITHOUT A NET (live)**　　43
– Feel like a stranger / Mississippi half-step uptown toodeloo / Walkin' blues / Althea / Cassidy / Let it grow / China cat sunflower – I know you rider / Looks like rain / Eyes of the world / Victim or the crime / Help on the way – Slipknot! – Franklin's tower / Bird song / One more Saturday night / Dear Mr. Fantasy.

───── BRETT MYDLAND died 26 Jul'90 of a drug overdose. Replaced by **VINCE WELNICK** (b.22 Feb'52, Phoenix, Arizona) – keyboards (ex-TUBES, ex-TODD RUNDGREN)

– compilations etc. –

on 'Grateful Dead' records unless mentioned otherwise

Apr 72. (lp) Polydor; (2310 171) / Sunflower; <SNF 5004> **HISTORIC DEAD** (rare '66)　　Jun71

Apr 72. (lp) Polydor; (2310 172) / Sunflower; <SUN 5001> **VINTAGE DEAD** (live '66)　　Oct70

1972. (lp) Pride; <PRD 0016> **THE HISTORY OF GRATEFUL DEAD**　　-

Sep 73. (lp) Warners; (K 46246) <BS 2721> **HISTORY OF THE DEAD – BEAR'S CHOICE** (live rarities)　　60　Jul73
<US cd-iss. 1988; 2721-2>

Mar 74. (lp) Warners; (K 56024) <BS 2674> **SKELETONS FROM THE CLOSET**　　75
(re-iss. Oct86 on 'Thunderbolt' lp/c/cd; THBL/THBCCDTB 018) <US cd-iss. 1988; 2764-2>

Apr 74. (7") Warners; <WB 21988> **SUGAR MAGNOLIA. / MR. CHARLIE**　　-

───── All below on 'Grateful Dead' US records, unless otherwise mentioned.

Feb 77. (d-lp) United Artists; (UDM 103-4) **WAKE OF THE FLOOD / FROM MARS HOTEL**

Feb 78. (d-lp) Warners; (K 66073) **WHAT A LONG STRANGE TRIP IT'S BEEN: THE BEST OF GRATEFUL DEAD**　　Nov 77
– New, new Minglewood blues / Cosmic Charlie / Truckin' / Black Peter / Born cross-eyed / Ripple / Doin' that rag / Dark star / High time / New speedway boogie / St. Stephen / Jack Straw / Me & my uncle / Tennessee Jed / Cumberland blues / Playing in the band / Brown-eyed woman / Ramble on Rose. <US cd-iss. 1989; 3091-2>

1987. (6xcd-box) Arista; <ACD6 8530> **DEAD ZONE: THE GRATEFUL DEAD CD COLLECTION 1977-1987**　　-
– (Arista albums from 77-87)

1987. (cd) Pair; <ARP2 1053> **FOR THE FAITHFUL**　　-

Jun 91. (d-cd/d-c/t-lp) (GDCD2/GDTC2/GDV2 4015) **ONE FROM THE VAULT** (live 13 Aug'75, Great American Music Hall, San Francisco)　　May91
– (introduction) / Help on the way / Franklin's tower / Music never stopped / It must have been the roses / Eyes of the world – drums / King Solomon's marbles / Around and around / Sugaree / Big river / Crazy fingers – drums / The other one / Sage and spirit / Goin' down the road feeling bad / U.S. blues / Blues for Allah.

Jan 92. (cd) (GDCD 4016) **INFRARED ROSES (live)**
– Crowd sculpture / Parallelogram / Little Nemo in Lightland / Riverside rhapsody / Post-modern highrise table top stomp / Infrared roses / Silver apples of the Moon / Speaking in swords / Magnesium night light / Sparrow hawk row / River of nine sorrows / Apollo at the Ritz.

Aug 92. (d-cd/d-lp) (GDCD2/GDV2 4018) **TWO FROM THE VAULT** (live 23/24 Aug'68, Shrine Auditorium, L.A.)　　May92
– Good morning little schoolgirl / Dark star / St. Stephen / The eleven / Death don't have no mercy / The other one / New potato caboose / Turn on your lovelight / Morning dew.

Dec 93. (d-cd) (GDCD 4019) **DICK'S PICK VOL.ONE: TAMPA, FLORIDA 12/19/73 (live)**
– Here comes sunshine / Big river / Mississippi half-step uptown toodeloo / Weather report suite (Prelude – part 1, Let it grow – part 2) / Big railroad blues / Playing in the band / He's gone / Truckin' / Nobody's fault but mine / Jam / The other one / Jam / Stella blue / Around and around.

Jan 94. (cd/c) Dare International; (DIL CD/C 1001) **RISEN FROM THE VAULTS**

Jun 95. (cd) (GDCD 4020) **DICK'S PICKS VOL.TWO: COLUMBUS, OHIO 10/3/71 (live)**
– Dark star / Jam / Sugar magnolia / St. Stephen / Not fade away / Going down the road feeling bad / Not fade away.

Oct 95. (d-cd/d-c) (GD CD/MC 24021) **HUNDRED YEAR HALL** (live 26th April 1972, Jahrhundert Halle, Frankfurt)　　26
– Bertha / Me & my uncle / The next time you see me / China cat sunflower / I know you rider / Jack Straw / Big railroad blues / Playing in the band / Turn on your love light / Going down the road feeling bad / One more Saturday night / Truckin' / Cryptical envelopment / Comes a time / Sugar magnolia.

Oct 96. (d-cd/d-c) Arista; <(07822 18934-2/-4)> **THE ARISTA YEARS 1977-95**　　95

Jan 97. (3xcd-box) <(GDCD 34024)> **DOZIN' AT THE KNICK**　　74　Nov96

Jan 97. (3xcd-box) <(GDCD 34026)> **DICK'S PICKS VOL.6**

Apr 97. (3xcd-box) <(GDCD3 4027)> **DICK'S PICKS VOL.7 (Alexandra Palace 9-11 Sep'74)**

May 97. (d-cd) Metro; (OTR 1100024) **NIGHT OF THE GRATEFUL DEAD**　　-

Jun 97. (d-cd) <(GDCD2 4052)> **FALLOUT FROM THE PHIL ZONE**　　83

Jun 97. (d-cd; with JOHN OSWALD) Swell Artifact; (SA 1969) **GRAYFOLDED**
(re-iss. Aug99 on 'Snapper'; SMDCD 215)

Jun 97. (cd; MICKEY & THE HEARTBEATS) *Anthology*; *(ANT 2912)* **HARTBITS VOL.2**

Nov 97. (cd) **FILLMORE EAST 2-11-69 (live)** — | 77

Nov 99. (cd-box) *<14066>* **SO MANY ROADS (1965-1995) (live)** — | —

Dec 99. (pic-lp) *Ugo*; *(UGO 2)* **THE DEAD LIVE IN CONCERT (live)** — | —

JERRY GARCIA

solo used session men from the DEAD plus others

		C.B.S.	Douglas

Jul 71. (lp; by HOWARD WALES & JERRY GARCIA) *(69013)* *<KZ 30859>* **HOOTEROLL?**
– South side strut / A trip to what next / Up from the desert / DC-502 / One a.m. approach / Uncle Martin's / Da bird song. *(cd-iss. Oct87 & Jul92 on 'Rykodisc'; <RCD 10052>) <US cd+=>* – Morning in Marin / Evening in Marin.

Jan 72. (7"; by HOWARD WALES & JERRY GARCIA) *<7-6501>* **SOUTH SIDE STRUT. / UNCLE MARTIN'S** — |

		Warners	Warners

Jan 72. (lp) *(K 46139)* *<BS 2582>* **GARCIA** (aka 'The Wheel') | | | 35
– Deal / Bird song / Sugaree / Loser / Late for supper / Spiderdawg / Eep hour / To lay me down / An odd little place / The wheel. *(<re-iss. Feb89 as 'THE WHEEL' on 'Grateful Dead' lp/c/cd; GDV/GDTC/<GDCD 4003>)*

1973. (7") *<7551>* **THE WHEEL. / DEAL** — |

1973. (7") *<7569>* **SUGAREE. / EEP HOUR** — |

		not iss.	Fantasy

Dec 73. (d-lp) *<F 79002>* **LIVE AT THE KEYSTONE (live with MERLE SAUNDERS)** — |
– Let's spend the night together / It takes a lot to laugh, it takes a train to cry / The harder they come / That's all right mama / He ain't give you none / Positively 4th street / My funny valentine / etc.

		Round	Round

Jun 74. (lp) *(RX 59301)* *<RX 102>* **GARCIA** (aka 'Compliments Of Garcia') | | | 49
– Let it rock / When the hunter gets captured by the game / That's what love will make us do / Russian lullabye / Turn on the bright lights / He ain't give you none / What goes around / Let's spend the night together / Mississippi moon / Midnight town. *(<re-iss. Apr89 as 'COMPLIMENTS OF GARCIA' on 'Grateful Dead' lp/c/cd; GDV/GDC/<GDCD 4011>)*

Jul 74. (7") *<4504>* **LET IT ROCK. / MIDNIGHT TOWN** — |

—— **GARCIA, DAVID GRISMAN, PETER ROWAN, JOHN KAHN, VASSAR CLEMENTS**

Mar 75. (lp; by OLD & IN THE WAY) *<RX 103>* **OLD AND IN THE WAY** — |
– Pig in a pen / Midnight moonlight / Old and in the way / Knockin' on your door / The hobo song / Panama red / Wild horses / Kissimmee kid / White dove / Land of the Navajo. *(UK-iss.Feb85 on 'Sugarhill' lp/c; SH/+CD 3746) <US cd-iss. 1987 on 'Rykodisc'; RCD 1009> (re-iss. cd 1990 on 'Grateful Dead'; GDCD 4014)*

		U.A.	Round

Feb 76. (lp) *(UAG 29921)* *<RX 107>* **REFLECTIONS** | | | 42
– Might as well / Mission in the rain / They love each other / I'll take a melody / It must have been the roses / Tore up over you / Catfish John / Comes a time. *(re-iss. Feb89 on 'Grateful Dead' lp/cd; GDV/GDTC/GDCD 4008)*

		Arista	Arista

Apr 78. (lp; by JERRY GARCIA BAND) *(SPART 1053)* *<AB 4160>* **CATS UNDER THE STARS**
– Rubin and Cherise / Love in the afternoon / Palm Sunday / Cats under the stars / Rhapsody in red / Rain / Down home / Gomorrah. *<US cd-iss. 1988; ARCD 8535>*

Nov 82. (lp) *(1204973)* *<AL 9603>* **RUN FOR THE ROSES**
– Run for the roses / I saw her standing there / Without love / Midnight getaway / Leave the little girl alone / Valerie / Knockin' on Heaven's door. *<US cd-iss. 1986; ARCD 8557>*

		not iss.	Fantasy

1988. (lp) *<MPF 4533>* **KEYSTONE ENCORES VOLUME 1** — |

1988. (cd) *<FCD 7701-2>* **LIVE AT KEYSTONE VOLUME 1** — |

1988. (lp) *<MPF 4534>* **KEYSTONE ENCORES VOLUME 2** — |

1988. (cd) *<FCD 7702-2>* **LIVE AT KEYSTONE VOLUME 2** — |

1988. (cd) *<FCD 7703-2>* **KEYSTONE ENCORES** (compilation of above) — |
(above credited with MERLE SAUNDERS; lp/cd's with diff.titles)

		Grateful Dead	Grateful Dead

Mar 89. (lp/c/cd; as JERRY GARCIA ACOUSTIC BAND) *(GDV/GDC/GDCD 4005)* **ALMOST ACOUSTIC**
– Swing low, sweet chariot / Deep Elam blues / Blue yodel £9 (standing on the corner) / Spike driver blues / I've been all around this world / I'm here to get my baby out of jail / I'm troubled / Oh, the wind and the rain / The girl at the Crossroads bar / Oh babe it ain't no lie / Casey Jones / Diamond Joe / Gone home / Ripple.

—— with **JOHN KAHN** – bass / **DAVID KEMPER** – drums / **MARVIN SEALS** – keyboards / and backing vocalists **JACKIE LA BRANCH** and **GLORIA JONES**

		Arista	Arista

Sep 91. (d-cd) *(354284)* *<18690-2>* **JERRY GARCIA BAND (live)** | | | 97
– The way you do the things you do / Waiting for a miracle / Simple twist of fate / Get out of my life / My sister and brothers / I shall be released / Dear Prudence / Deal / Stop that train / Senor (tales of Yankee power) / Evangeline / The night they drove old Dixie down / Don't let go / That lucky old Sun / Tangled up in blue.

		not iss.	Acoustic Disc

1993. (cd; by DAVID GRISMAN / JERRY GARCIA) *<ACD-9>* **NOT FOR KIDS ONLY** — |

Apr 97. (cd; JERRY GARCIA & DAVID GRISMAN) *<(ACD-21)>* **SHADY GROVE** — |

		Grateful Dead	Grateful Dead

May 97. (cd; JERRY GARCIA BAND) *(GDCD 4051)* **HOW SWEET IT IS** | | | 81 Apr97

OTHER ONES

—— (see biog for line-up)

		not iss.	Arista

Feb 99. (cd) **ONLY THE STRANGE REMAIN** — |
– St. Stephen – The eleven / Jack Straw / Sugaree / Corrina / Only the strange remain / White-wheeled limosine / Estimated prophet / Playing in the band / The other one / Banyan tree / Rainbow's cadillac / Mountains of the moon / Friend of the Devil / Baba jingo / China cat sunflower – I know you rider.

GRAVEDIGGAZ (dig out; 4th edition)

David GRAY

Born: Manchester, England. As a young man, GRAY moved to Wales (Solva) with his family where he found the joys of guitar playing while taking in the local punk and folk scene. In 1992 (through manager/A&R man Rob Holden, he signed to Virgin offshoot, 'Hut' and issued his debut set 'A CENTURY ENDS' (1993), which brilliantly displayed his tender and sparse songwriting skills. 'FLESH' (1994) appeared one year later, and by now GRAY had made a promising name for himself, attracting a huge cult following around Britain and Europe. The aforementioned album was not bad for somebody who was still learning his trade; comparisons to DYLAN, EDDIE VEDDER and MIKE SCOTT were bandied about like confetti at a wedding. The acoustic guitars, bouncing pedal steel and occasional piano made stand-out tracks 'WHAT ARE YOU NOW', 'FALLING FREE' and 'NEW HORIZONS' levitate above some recent attempts at melancholic music, proving GRAY to be one of Britain's best kept secrets and filing him along with assets THOM YORKE and RICHARD ASHCROFT. 'SELL, SELL, SELL' (1996) was perhaps too proverbial for its own good and thus it didn't gain enough exposure to hit the shops in the UK. Nevertheless, it still received some airplay from Radio One's Steve Lamaque and went on to sustain GRAY's reputation in the alt-music world. It was 1999's 'WHITE LADDER' (on new imprint 'iht' through 'eastwest') which caught the attention of music critics and audiences alike. A fine album in every sense, GRAY took us into the underworld of his soul . . . and deeper, with tracks 'SAIL AWAY' and Soft Cell's 'SAY HELLO WAVE GOODBYE' bringing something delicate and strangely human to the work. Easily the highlight from the set was 'BABYLON', a chart flop first time around (but later a UK No.5), although album opener 'PLEASE FORGIVE ME' slightly compensated for this, clocking in at No.72.

Album rating: A CENTURY ENDS (*6) / FLESH (*6) / SELL, SELL, SELL (*6) / WHITE LADDER (*7)

DAVID GRAY – vocals, guitar, keyboards / with **NEILL MacCOLL** – guitar, mandolin, vocals / **ROBIN MILLAR** – guitar / **"FAMOUS DAVE" ANDERSON** – keyboards / **STEVE SIDELNYK** – programming

		Hut	Caroline

Mar 93. (12"/cd-s) *(HUT T/CD 27)* **SHINE. /** | | | —

Apr 93. (cd/c/lp) *(CDHUT/HUTMC/HUTLP 9)* *<1739>* **A CENTURY ENDS**
– Shine / A century ends / Debauchery / Let the truth sting / Gathering dust / Wisdom / Lead me upstairs / Living room / Birds without wings / It's all over.

Jun 93. (12"/cd-s) *(HUT T/CD 32)* **WISDOM. /** | | | —

—— with MacCOLL plus **ANDY METCALFE** – hammond organ / **SIMON EDWARDS + DAVID NOLTE** – bass / **ROY DODS** – drums / **CLUNE** – drums, vocals, keyboards, bass, co-writer

		Hut	Vernon Yard

Sep 94. (cd/c) *(CDHUT/HUTMC 17)* *<39770>* **FLESH**
– Flesh / What are you? / The light / Coming down / Falling free / Mystery of love / Lullaby / New horizons / Love's old song / Flesh.

—— now with different session people

		E.M.I.	not iss.

Apr 96. (cd) *(37357)* **SELL, SELL, SELL** | | | — Europe
– Faster, sooner, now / Late night radio / Sell, sell, sell / Hold on to nothing / Everytime / Magdalena / Smile / Only the lonely / What am I doing wrong? / Gutters full of rain / Forever is tomorrow is today / Folk song.

—— GRAY with **(Mc)CLUNE** + 3rd p/t co-writer/producer, **POLSON**

		Iht – eastwest	A.T.O.

Mar 99. (cd) *(ihtcd 001)* *<21539>* **WHITE LADDER** | | | 2000
– Please forgive me / Babylon / My oh my / We're not right / Nightblindness / Silver lining / White ladder / This years love / Sail away / Say hello wave goodbye.

Mar 99. (cd-s) *(ihtcds 001)* **THIS YEARS LOVE** | | | —

Jul 99. (cd-s) *(ihtcds 002)* **BABYLON / LEAD ME UPSTAIRS (live) / NEW HORIZONS (live) MY HEAD** | | | —
(above single will hit the Top 5 UK nearly a year on!)

Nov 99. (12")(cd-s) *(ihtv 001)(ihtcds 003)* **PLEASE FORGIVE ME / ('A' remix)** | | | 72 | —

Macy GRAY

Born: NATALIE McINTYRE, 1969, Canton, Ohio, USA. An exceptionally accomplished pianist, MACY began to sing one afternoon (her voice had been established after a bout of bronchitis!) when a former vocalist had failed to show at a band practice she had organised in the University of Southern California. While studying screenwriting in L.A., MACY soon became involved with a local jazz group and made extra money singing as a session musician. She signed to 'Epic' records in 1998 and issued her first release, 'DO SOMETHING', a hit song subsequently lifted from her debut Top 3 album, 'ON HOW LIFE IS', the following summer. The CD soared through a collection of influences such as hip-hop, R&B and soul, all backed with MACY's uniquely chocolate-coated, croaky style (BILLIE HOLIDAY and JANIS JOPLIN come to mind). A Top 10 hit single, 'I TRY', was a classy 'Motown'-esque breakup song set to modern times and cleverly produced by Andrew Slater, of FIONA APPLE fame.

Album rating: ON HOW LIFE IS (*7)

MACY GRAY – vocals / with session people incl. co-writers **JEREMY RUZUMNA** – keyboards / **MILES OM TACKETT** – guitar / **KILU BECKWITH** – programming

			Epic	Sony
Jun 99.	(c-s) (667593-4) <79209> **DO SOMETHING / I'VE COMMITTED MURDER**		51	Jul99
	(cd-s) (667593-2) <79241> – ('A'mixes; album / Jay's subliminal funk / King Britt)			
	(cd-s) (667593-5) – ('A'mixes).			
Jul 99.	(cd/c) (494423-2/-4) <69490> **ON HOW LIFE IS**		3	97
	– Why didn't you call me / Do something / Caligula / I try / Sex-o-matic Venus freak / I can't wait to meetchu / Still / I've committed murder / Moment to myself / Letter.			
Sep 99.	(c-s) (668193-4) **I TRY / RATHER HAZY**		6	
	(cd-s) (668193-2) – ('A'full crew mix – extended II – no vocoder).			
	(cd-s) (668193-5) – ('A'side)('A' re-mixes; Grand style / Jay Dee / Bob Power).			

GREAT SOCIETY (dig out; Great Psychedelic . . .)

GREAT WHITE (dig out; Great Metal . . .)

AL GREEN

Born: AL GREENE, 13 Apr '46, Forrest City, Arkansas, USA. AL got off to an early start when, at the age of nine, he formed his first group, The GREEN BROTHERS, a gospel outfit which included siblings ROBERT, WALTER and WILLIAM. After touring throughout the South, AL was dropped from the group after his dad caught him listening to the sweet sounds of JACKIE WILSON, and in doing so instilled an instant love for soul music. By the time AL was sixteen, he had formed his own outfit, AL GREEN & THE CREATIONS, who performed R&B tracks before drifting more into soul. Two members of the group, meanwhile, had formed their own label, 'Hot Line Music Journal', recording the newly-renamed AL GREENE & THE SOUL MATES. Their one and only hit, 'BACK UP TRAIN', was the sole measure of success until 1969 when AL met WILLIE MITCHELL, then bandleader and vice-president of 'Hi' Records. After hearing GREEN sing, MITCHELL immediately signed him to the label, where the soul brother recorded his most soulful and funky tracks. The debut album, 'GREEN IS BLUES', released in early '70, proved MITCHELL had made the right move. GREEN's incredible falsetto voice, blended with the MITCHELL-arranged horn and strings, punctuated a sexy groove that led to the trademark "love man" persona in the early 70's. Although no hits were forthcoming, his second set, 'AL GREEN GETS NEXT TO YOU', proved more accessible, spawning the classic 'TIRED OF BEING ALONE'; this benchmark was to precede four further hits in the next two years. Lifted from his next album, 'LET'S STAY TOGETHER', the title track became the first No.1 of GREEN's glorious career, his alluring voice subsequently gracing the heart-stopping 'I'M STILL IN LOVE WITH YOU' and the spicy 'HERE I AM (COME AND TAKE ME)'. By this point in his career, GREEN was widely recognised as a commercial and critical success, an artist at the pinnacle of his singing career who scored with six consecutive Top 10 singles between '72-'73. His life and career took a dramatic change of course when, on the 25th of October '74, his former girlfriend inflicted second-degree burns on his back by pouring boiling grits over him before killing herself with the singer's gun. This led GREEN to follow a life in the Church, believing that the assault was a sign from God; by 1976 he had become pastor of the Full Gospel Tabernacle in Memphis. Though still making albums with MITCHELL, his sound had become too formulaic and he began to record solely self-produced religious music through his own studio ('American Music') to mixed critical acclaim and significantly smaller sales. The '80s saw GREEN releasing Gospel sets on the 'Myrrh' label, as well as the curious duet with ANNIE LENNOX, 'PUT A LITTLE LOVE IN YOUR HEART'. Now primarily a Gospel artist, the 90's have seen GREEN recording the occasional R&B number, the best of the bunch being 1995's 'YOUR HEART IN GOOD HANDS'. Over the years, his songs have been interpreted by many top artists; TAKE ME TO THE RIVER (Talking Heads) / L.O.V.E. (Orange Juice) / LET'S STAY TOGETHER (Tina Turner) / HERE I AM (UB 40), to name but a few. • Covered: I WANT TO HOLD YOUR HAND + GET BACK (Beatles) / CAN'T GET NEXT TO YOU (Temptations). • Trivia: On the 13th of February '78, L.A. declared this the 'Al Green Day'.

Album rating: BACK UP TRAIN (*5) / GREEN IS BLUES (*6) / AL GREEN GETS NEXT TO YOU (*7) / LET'S STAY TOGETHER (*8) / I'M STILL IN LOVE WITH YOU (*8) / LIVIN' FOR YOU (*8) / AL GREEN EXPLORES YOUR MIND (*7) / AL GREEN'S GREATEST HITS compilation (*9) / AL GREEN IS LOVE (*6) / FULL OF FIRE (*5) / HAVE A GOOD TIME (*5) / AL GREEN'S GREATEST HITS, VOLUME II compilation (*7) / THE BELLE ALBUM (*7) / TRUTH 'N' TIME (*6) / THE LORD WILL MAKE A WAY (*6) / HIGHER PLANE (86) / TOKYO LIVE (*7) / TRUST IN GOD (*5) / HE IS THE LIGHT (*6) / GOING AWAY (*5) / SOUL SURVIVOR (*5) / I GET JOY (*6) / LOVE IS REALITY (*5) / THE SUPREME AL GREEN: THE GREATEST HITS compilation (*8) / YOUR HEART'S IN GOOD HANDS (*4)

AL GREEN – vocals with **CURTIS ROGERS** + **PALMER JONES**

		Stateside	Bell
Jan 68.	(7"; by AL GREEN & The SOUL MATES) (SS 2079) <1188> **BACK UP TRAIN. / DON'T LEAVE ME**		41 Oct67
		Action	Hot Line
Feb 69.	(7"; as AL GREENE) (ACT 4540) **DON'T HURT ME NO MORE. / GET YOURSELF TOGETHER**		-
Mar 69.	(lp) (ACLP 6008) <1500> **BACK UP TRAIN**		
	– Back up train / Hot wire / Stop and check myself / Let me help you / I'm reaching out / Don't hurt me no more / Lovers hideaway / Don't leave me / What's it all about / I'll be good to you / Guilty / That's all it takes (lady) / Get yourself together.		

—— now using 'Hi' records house band THE MEMPHIS HORNS who were WAYNE JACKSON – trumpet / JAMES MITCHELL – baritone sax. / ANDREW LOVE – tenor sax. / JACK HALE – trombone / ED LOGAN – tenor sax. / plus LEROY HODGES – bass / MABON HODGES – guitar. / CHARLES HUGHES – organ and HOWARD GRIMES – drums who repl. AL JACKSON who joined BOOKER T.

		London	Hi
1969.	(7") <2159> **I WANT TO HOLD YOUR HAND. / WHAT AM I TO DO WITH MYSELF**	-	
1969.	(7") <2164> **ONE WOMAN. / TOMORROW'S DREAM**	-	
1969.	(lp) <32055> **GREEN IS BLUES**	-	
	– One woman / Talk to me / My girl / I stand accused / Gotta find a new world / What am I gonna do with myself / Tomorrow's dream / What am I gonna do with myself / Get back baby / Get back / Summertime. <re-iss.Jan73, hit No.19> (UK-iss.Apr86 on 'Hi'; HIUKLP 401)		
Feb 70.	(7") (HLU 10300) <2172> **YOU SAY IT. / GOTTA FIND A NEW WORLD**		
Apr 70.	(7") <2177> **RIGHT NOW RIGHT NOW. / ALL BECAUSE I'M A FOOLISH ONE**	-	
Jan 71.	(7") (HLU 10324) <2182> **I CAN'T GET NEXT TO YOU. / RIDE SALLY RIDE**		60 Nov70
Apr 71.	(7") <2188> **DRIVIN' WHEEL. / TRUE LOVE**	-	
Jul 71.	(7") <2194> **TIRED OF BEING ALONE. / GET BACK BABY**	-	11
Aug 71.	(7") (HLU 10337) **TIRED OF BEING ALONE. / RIGHT NOW RIGHT NOW**	4	-
Nov 71.	(lp) (SHU 8424) <32062> **AL GREEN GETS NEXT TO YOU**		58 Aug71
	– I can't get next to you / Are you lonely for me baby / God is standing by / Tired of being alone / I'm a ram / Drivin' wheel / Light my fire / You say it / Right now right now / All because. (re-iss.Apr86 on 'Hi' lp/cd; HIUK LP/CD 403)		
Dec 71.	(7") (HLU 10348) <2202> **LET'S STAY TOGETHER. / TOMORROW'S DREAM**	7	1 Nov71
Mar 72.	(lp) (SHU 8430) <32070> **LET'S STAY TOGETHER**	8	Feb72
	– Let's stay together / La-la for you / So you're leaving / What is this feeling / Old time lovin' / I've never found a girl / How can you mend a broken heart / Judy / It ain't no fun to me. (re-iss.Jul86 on 'Hi' lp/cd; HIUK LP/CD 405)		
Mar 72.	(7") <2211> **LOOK WHAT YOU DONE FOR ME. / LA-LA FOR YOU**	-	4
May 72.	(7") (HLU 10369) **LOOK WHAT YOU DONE FOR ME. / I'VE NEVER FOUND A GIRL**	44	-
Jul 72.	(7") (HLU 10382) <2216> **I'M STILL IN LOVE WITH YOU. / OLD TIME LOVIN'**	35	3 Jun72
Oct 72.	(7") (HLU 10393) <2227> **YOU OUGHT TO BE WITH ME. / WHAT IS THIS FEELING**		3
Dec 72.	(lp) (SHU 8443) <32074> **I'M STILL IN LOVE WITH YOU**		4 Oct72
	– I'm still in love with you / I'm glad you're mine / Love and happiness / What a wonderful thing love is / Simply beautiful / Oh, pretty woman / For the good times / Look what you done for me / One of these good old days. (re-iss.Jul86 on 'Hi'; HIUKLP 407)		
Feb 73.	(7") (HLU 10406) <2235> **CALL ME (COME BACK HOME). / WHAT A WONDERFUL THING LOVE IS**		10
Apr 73.	(7") (HLU 10419) **LOVE AND HAPPINESS. / SO YOU'RE LEAVING**		-
Jul 73.	(7") (HLU 10426) <2247> **HERE I AM (COME AND TAKE ME). / I'M GLAD YOU'RE MINE**		10 Jun73
Nov 73.	(lp) (SHU 8457) <32077> **CALL ME**		10 May73
	– Call me (come back home) / Have you been making out o.k. / Stand up / I'm so lonesome I could cry / Your love is like the morning sun / Here I am (come and take me) / You ought to be with me / Jesus is waiting. (re-iss.Jul86 on 'Hi'; HIUKLP 409)		
Jan 74.	(7") (HLU 10443) <2257> **LIVIN' FOR YOU. / IT AIN'T NO FUN TO ME**		19 Dec73
Apr 74.	(lp) (SHU 8464) <32082> **LIVIN' FOR YOU**		24 Dec73
	– Livin' for you / Home again / Free at last / Let's get married / So good to be here / My sweet sixteen / Unchained melody / My God is real / Beware. (re-iss.Jul86 on 'Hi'; HIUKLP 411)		
Apr 74.	(7") (HLU 10452) <2262> **LET'S GET MARRIED. / SO GOOD TO BE HERE**		32 Mar74
Oct 74.	(7") (HLU 10470) <2274> **SHA-LA-LA (MAKE ME HAPPY). / SCHOOL DAYS**	20	7 Sep74
Dec 74.	(lp) (SHU 8479) <32087> **AL GREEN EXPLORES YOUR MIND**		15 Nov74
	– Sha-la-la (make me happy) / Take me to the river / God blessed our love / The city / One nite stand / Stay with me forever / Hangin' on / School days. (re-iss.Sep86 on 'Hi' lp/cd; HIUK LP/CD 413)		
Feb 75.	(7") (HLU 10482) <2282> **L-O-V-E. (LOVE). / I WISH YOU WERE HERE WITH ME**	24	13
Jul 75.	(7") (HLU 10493) <2288> **OH ME, OH MY (DREAMS IN MY ARMS). / STRONG AS DEATH (SWEET AS LIFE)**		48
Oct 75.	(lp) (SHU 8488) <32092> **AL GREEN IS LOVE**		28 Sep75
	– L.O.V.E. (love) / Rhymes / The love sermon / There is love / Could I be the one / Love ritual / I didn't know / Oh me, oh my (dreams in my heart) / I wish you were here. (re-iss.Jul86 on Hi'; HIUKLP 415)		
Nov 75.	(7") (HLU 10511) <2300> **FULL OF FIRE. / COULD I BE THE ONE**		28
Mar 76.	(lp) (SHU 8493) <32097> **FULL OF FIRE**		59
	– Glory glory / That's the way it is / Always / There's no way / I'd fly away / Full of fire / Together again / Soon as I get home / Let it shine. (re-iss.Sep86 on 'Hi'; HIUKLP 417)		

May 76. (7") *(HLU 10527)* <2306> **LET IT SHINE. / THERE'S NO WAY**

Oct 76. (7") *(HLU 10542)* <2319> **KEEP ME CRYIN'. / THERE IS LOVE** `37`

Dec 76. (lp) *(SHU 8505)* <32103> **HAVE A GOOD TIME** `93` Nov76
– Keep on cryin' / Smile a little bit more / I tried to tell myself / Something / The truth marches on / Have a good time / Nothing takes the place of you / Happy / Hold on forever. *(re-iss. Jul86 on 'Hi'; HIUKLP 419)*

Apr 77. (7") <2322> **I TRIED TO TELL MYSELF / SOMETHING**

May 77. (7"ep) **I TRIED TO TELL MYSELF / SOMETHING. / WHAT AM I GONNA DO WITH MYSELF / SUMMERTIME**

Nov 77. (7") <2324> **LOVE AND HAPPINESS. / GLORY GLORY**

Jan 78. (lp) <6009> **TRUTH 'N' TIME**
– Blow me down / Lo and behold / Wait here / To sir with love / Truth 'n' time / King of all / Say a little prayer / Happy days.

—— AL GREEN completely changed his backing musicians recruiting **JAMES BASS** – guitar / **RUEBEN FAIRFAX** – bass / **JOHNNY TONEY** – drums / **FRED JORDAN** – trumpet / **BUDDY JARRETT** – alto sax. / **RON ECHOLS** – baritone sax

	Hi-Cream	Hi
Jan 78. (7") <77505> **BELLE. / CHARIOTS OF FIRE**	-	83
Aug 78. (7") <78511> **FEELS LIKE SUMMER. / I FEEL GOOD**	-	
Nov 78. (7") <78522> **TO SIR WITH LOVE / WAIT HERE**	-	
Aug 79. (7") *(HCS 101)* **BELLE. / TO SIR WITH LOVE**		-

Sep 79. (lp) <(6004)> **THE BELLE ALBUM** Dec77
– Belle / Loving you / Feels like summer / Georgia boy / I feel good / Chariots of fire / All in all / Dream. *(re-iss. Nov86 on 'Hi'; HIUKLP 421)*

Jul 81. (d-lp/d-c) *(HCD/ZHCD 5001)* <6005> **TOKYO LIVE (live)**
– L.O.V.E. (love) / Tired of being alone / Let's stay together / How can you mend a broken heart / All n all / Belle / Sha-la-la (make me happy) / Let's get married / God blessed our love / You ought to be with me / For the good times / Dream / I feel good / Love and happiness. *(re-iss. Aug87; 8302 ML2) (cd-iss. Mar90; HIUKCD 104)*

—— The Rev. now used mainly session people and gospel backing singers.

	Hi	Hi
Feb 82. (lp/c) <(HLP/ZCHLP 6006)> **HIGHER PLANE**		

– Where love rules / Amazing grace / His name is Jesus / Battle hymn of the republic / Higher plane / People get ready / By my side / Amazing grace / The spirit might come – on and on. *(re-iss. Nov86; HIUKLP 431)*

Nov 82. (lp) <(HLP 6007)> **PRECIOUS LORD**
– Glory to his name / Rock of ages / In the garden / Hallelujah (I just want to praise the Lord) / Precious Lord / What a friend we have in Jesus / The old rugged cross / Morningstar / How great thou art. *(re-iss. Nov86; HIUKLP 429)*

Feb 85. (lp) *(HIUKLP 423)* **TRUST IN GOD**
– Don't it make you wanna go home / Trust in God / Holy Spirit / Up the ladder to the roof / Ain't no mountain high enough / No not one / Lean on me / Never met anybody like you / Trust in God (reprise) / All we need is a little more love. *(cd-iss. Jul86; HIUKCD 423)*

	A&M	A&M
Feb 85. (7") *(UK45 7003)* **NEVER MET NOBODY LIKE YOU. / HIGHER PLANE**		-
Nov 85. (7") <2786> **GOING AWAY. / BUILDING UP**	-	

Nov 85. (lp/c) <(AMA/AMC 5120)> **GOING AWAY**
– Going away / True love / He is the light / I feel like going on / Be with me Jesus / You brought the sunshine / Power / Building up / Nearer my God to thee.

Jan 86. (7") *(AM 302)* **TRUE LOVE. / YOU BROUGHT THE SUNSHINE** -
(12"+=) *(AMY 302)* – Going away.

Jan 86. (7") <2807> **TRUE LOVE. / HE IS THE LIGHT** -

Feb 87. (7") <2919> **EVERYTHING'S GONNA BE ALRIGHT. / SO REAL TO ME** -

Apr 87. (lp/c) <(AMA/AMC 5150)> **SOUL SURVIVOR**
– Everything's gonna be alright / Jesus will fix it / You know and I know / Yield not to temptation / So real to me / Soul survivor / You've got a friend / He ain't heavy / 23rd psalm.

Jun 87. (7") <2952> **YOU KNOW AND I KNOW. / TRUE LOVE** -

Sep 87. (7") <2962> **SOUL SURVIVOR. / JESUS WILL FIX IT** -

Nov 88. (7"; ANNIE LENNOX & AL GREEN) *(AM 484)* <1255> **PUT A LITTLE LOVE IN YOUR HEART. / Spheres Of Celestial Influence: A GREAT BIG PIECE OF LOVE** `28` `9`
(12"+=/cd-s+=) *(AMY/CDEE 484)* – (2-'A'versions).

	Breakout-A&M	Brreakout-A&M
Jun 89. (7") *(USA 654)* **AS LONG AS WE'RE TOGETHER. / BLESSED**		

(12"+=) *(USAT 654)* – ('A'other mix).

Jun 89. (lp/c/cd) *(395228-1/-4/-2)* **I GET JOY**
– You're everything to me / All my praise / The end is near / Mighty clouds of joy / I get joy / As long as we're together / Praise him / Blessed / Tryin' to do the best I can / Tryin' to get over you.

—— He provided the vocals on ARTHUR BAKER + BACKSTREET DISCIPLES Oct89 single THE MESSAGE IS LOVE.

—— Co-writes w / **DAVID STEELE** (ex-BEAT). **ANDY COX** also appears and is co-producer. The song 'DON'T LOOK BACK' was written by SMOKEY ROBINSON, and featured CURTIS STIGERS. JOE ROBERTS + A.GLASS wrote 'Fountain of love'. LOVE IN MOTION was a cover, as was his single below, which was penned by S.SWIRSKY.

	Word	Word
Apr 92. (cd/c) *(7019271 60X/502)* **LOVE IS REALITY**		

– Just can't let you go / Just can't let it / Love is reality / Positive attitude / Again / Sure feels good / I like it / You don't know me / A long time / A lone time / Why (with DON BYAS).

	Arista	R.C.A.
Sep 93. (7"/c-s) *(74321 16269-7/-4)* **LOVE IS A BEAUTIFUL THING. / ('A'mix)**	56	

(12"+=/cd-s+=) *(74321 16269-6/-2)* – ('A'mixes).

Sep 93. (cd/c/lp) *(74321 16310-2/-4/-1)* **DON'T LOOK BACK**
– Best love / Love is a beautiful thing / Waiting on you / What does it take / Keep on pushing love / You are my everything / One love / People in the world (keep on lovin' you) / Give it everything / Your love (is more than I ever hoped

for) / Fountain of love / Don't look back / Love in motion. *(cd re-iss. Feb97; same)*

Mar 94. (7"/c-s) *(74321 19694-7/-4)* **KEEP ON PUSHING LOVE. / ('A'mix)**
(12"+=/cd-s+=) *(74321 19694-1/-2)* – ('A'mix).

—— In May 94, AL did duet 'Funny How Time Slips Away' with LYLE LOVETT on 'Geffen' c-s/cd-s; (MCS C/TD 1974). Originally a 1962 hit for JIMMY ELLEDGE.

Jul 94. (c-s) *(74321 19349-4)* **WAITING ON YOU. / ('A'mix)**
(12"+=/cd-s+=) *(74321 19349-1/-2)* – (2-'A'mixes).

	not iss.	M.C.A.
Nov 95. (cd) <11350> **YOUR HEART'S IN GOOD HANDS**	-	-

– Your heart's in good hands / Keep on pushing love / Could this be love / Love is a beautiful thing / On love / Don't look back / The best love / Your love (is more than I ever hoped for) / What does it take / People in the world (keep on lovin' you).

– compilations, etc. –

on 'Hi' unless mentioned otherwise

Sep 72. (lp) *Bell;* <6076> **AL GREEN** (early recordings)	-	
Sep 72. (7") *Bell;* <45258> **GUILTY. / LET ME HELP YOU**	-	69
Jan 73. (7") *Bell;* <45305> **HOT WIRE. / DON'T LEAVE ME**	-	71
Mar 75. London; *(SHU 8481)* / Hi; <32089> **AL GREEN'S GREATEST HITS**	18	17 Mar75

– Let's stay together / I can't get next to you / You ought to be with me / Look what you done to me / Let's get married / Tired of being alone / Call me / I'm still in love with you / Here I am (come and take me) / How can you mend a broken heart? *(re-iss. Jul86 on 'Hi' lp/c/cd; HIUK LP/CASS/CD 425)*

Jul 77. (lp) <32105> **GREATEST HITS VOL.2** -
(UK-iss.Oct87 as 'TAKE ME TO THE RIVER – GREATEST HITS VOL.2' on 'Hi' lp/c/cd; HIUK LP/CASS/CD 438)

Jan 80. (lp/c) *Cream; (HLPC/ZCHLP 101)* **THE CREAM OF AL GREEN** -

Jan 80. (7"/12") *Cream; (HCS/12HCS 102)* **TIRED OF BEING ALONE. / HOW CAN YOU MEND A BROKEN HEART** -

May 81. (lp) *Myrrh; (MYR 1109)* **THE LORD WILL MAKE A WAY**
– Highway to heaven / Pass me not / The Lord will make a way / Too close / None but the righteous / I have a friend above all others / Saved / In the holy name of Jesus. *(re-iss. Jul86 on 'Hi' lp/c; HIUKLP 433)*

Oct 81. (d-lp/d-c) *P.R.T.; (SPOT/ZCSPT 1016)* **SPOTLIGHT ON AL GREEN** -

1984. (7") *Cream; (HCS 107)* **TIRED OF BEING ALONE. / LET'S STAY TOGETHER** -
(12"+=) *(12HCS 107)* – How can you mend a broken heart.

Sep 85. (7") *(HIUK45 7001)* **LET'S STAY TOGETHER. / I'M STILL IN LOVE WITH YOU**
(12"+=) *(HIUK45T 7001)* – You ought to be with me.

Jul 86. (lp) *(HIUKLP 425)* **THE BEST OF AL GREEN**

Jul 86. (lp) *(XHIUKLP 437)* **WHITE CHRISTMAS**
(cd-iss. Nov95 +=; HILOCD 21) – (extra tracks).

Sep 88. (lp/c/cd) *K-Tel; (NE1/CD2/NCD3 420)* **HI LIFE – THE BEST OF AL GREEN** `34`

Mar 89. (lp/c/cd) *(HIUK LP/CASS/CD 443)* **LOVE RITUAL – RARE AND PREVIOUSLY UNRELEASED (1968-76)**

Jun 90. (lp) *(HIUK 444)* **YOU SAY IT!**

1990. (cd) *Word;* **ONE IN A MILLION** -

Apr 91. (cd/c) *(HIUK CD/CASS 107* **COVER ME GREEN**

May 91. (cd) *(HIUKCD 113)* **LIVIN' FOR YOU / AL GREEN EXPLORES YOUR MIND**

May 91. (cd) *(HIUKCD 114)* **AL GREEN IS LOVE / FULL OF FIRE**

Sep 91. (cd) *(HIUKCD 119)* **HAVE A GOOD TIME / THE BELLE ALBUM**

Jul 92. (cd/c) *(HIUK CD/CASS 130)* **THE SUPREME AL GREEN: THE GREATEST HITS** -
– Tired of being alone / I can't get next to you / Let's stay together / How can you mend a broken heart / Love & happiness / I'm still in love with you / Simply beautiful / What a wonderful thing love is / Call me (come back home) / My God is real / Let's get married / Sha-la-la (make me happy) / Take me to the river / Love ritual / L-O-V-E / I didn't know / Full of fire / Belle.

Oct 92. (cd; AL GREEN & ACE CANNON) *(HIUKCD 126)* **CHRISTMAS CHEERS**

Nov 92. (cd/c/lp) *Beechwood; (AGREE CD/MC/LP 1)* **AL** `41` -

Jul 93. (cd) *(HIUKCD 141)* **THE FLIP SIDE OF AL GREEN**

Feb 97. (3xcd-box) *(HIBOOK 12)* **A DEEP SHADE OF GREEN**

Peter GREEN

Born: 29 Oct'46, Bethnal Green, London, England. Early in 1966, he joined PETER B'S LOONERS (aka with PETER BARDENS; future CAMEL), who cut one 'Columbia' 45, 'IF YOU WANNA BE HAPPY' / 'JODRELL BLUES', before evolving into SHOTGUN EXPRESS (who boasted a young ROD STEWART on vocals) in May '66. GREEN's tenure only lasted a few months, the guitarist however subsequently replacing ERIC CLAPTON in JOHN MAYALL's BLUESBREAKERS. GREEN appeared on the album, 'A Hard Road', but by summer 1967 he was on the move again, forming FLEETWOOD MAC along with MICK FLEETWOOD. Initially going under the moniker PETER GREEN'S FLEETWOOD MAC, the group gained considerable credibility in both the blues field and the charts with a string of Top 10 albums and Top 3 singles. GREEN was the chief songwriter and his early 'MAC compositions remain among the most enduring of that band's long and pockmarked career, songs like 'BLACK MAGIC WOMAN', 'ALBATROSS', 'OH WELL' and 'MAN OF THE WORLD'. The guitarist's spare, incredibly intuitive interpretation of the blues was almost unique to a skinny white kid and the latter track was all the more poignant for its portrayal of GREEN's precarious emotional state. Like many great artists before him, it seemed that GREEN's genius traversed a parallel borderline with mental fragmentation and, following a final howl at his demons (real or imagined) with the spine-chilling 'GREEN MANALISHI', the guitarist left FLEETWOOD MAC in early 1970 (and, in line with his new religious beliefs, stated his intention to give away all royalties to charity). While many rockstars have been flippantly written off as "acid casualties", the devastating effect of LSD on GREEN was all too real and has been well documented over the years, one of the most tragic tales in rock that ultimately saw PETER alternating between the street and a mental home. Following his departure from FLEETWOOD MAC, he deliberately distanced himself from the machinations of the music industry, refusing press interviews etc., although he did release a lacklustre solo debut effort, 'END OF THE GAME', later that year. This stodgy collection of blues jams gained little support from the critics or buying public and, following a brief reunion with FLEETWOOD MAC on an American tour, GREEN went to ground. Details of the subsequent six years are hazy to say the least, with rumours abounding as to GREEN's activites and whereabouts. It seems he gave away his guitar as well as growing his fingernails and beard, working on a kibbutz in Israel for a while, before taking up various menial jobs in England (i.e. grave-digger, hospital porter, etc.), but little was heard of his low-key activities until . . . early in 1977, he was tragically committed to a mental hospital after returning an unwanted royalty cheque with rifle in hand, to his accountant. (No doubt subtlly wanting to re-form SHOTGUN EXPRESS). This signalled the beginning of GREEN's intermittent periods of hospital treatment for his mental problems although he enjoyed a brief flurry of recording activity at the turn of the decade; in 1978 he signed a new solo contract with 'P.V.K.', surprisingly hitting the UK Top 40 with albums 'IN THE SKIES' (1979) and 'LITTLE DREAMER' (1980). After a final effort in 1983, 'KOLORS', little was heard from GREEN bar the odd insensitive tabloid feature centering on his haggard, unkempt appearance, the guitarist seemingly having hit rock bottom (with rumours that he was sleeping rough in Richmond). More positively, GREEN has made something of a comeback recently with his SPLINTER BAND, apparently the first time he's picked up a guitar in years, having to relearn many parts from scratch. He even toured with the outfit in 1996, playing to fans who'd literally waited decades to see him. One of those fans was veteran bluesman B.B. KING with whom GREEN subsequently enjoyed an onstage jam. Less encouraging was the great man's current musical preferences, MICHAEL JACKSON and BILLY RAY CYRUS, apparently. Oh Well.

Album rating: THE END OF THE GAME (*4) / IN THE SKIES (*5) / LITTLE DREAMER (*5) / WHATCHA GONNA DO (*4) / BLUE GUITAR (*4) / WHITE SKY (*4) / KOLORS (*4) / LEGEND (*4) / PETER GREEN 'Backtrackin' compilation (*6) / Peter Green Splinter Group: SPLINTER GROUP (*6) / THE ROBERT JOHNSON SONGBOOK with Nigel Watson (*5) / SOHO SESSION (*5) / DESTINY ROAD (*5)

PETER GREEN – guitar, vocals / with **ZOOT MONEY** – piano / **NICK BUCK** – keyboards / **ALEX DMOCHOWSKI** – bass / **GODFREY MacLEAN** – drums

	Reprise	Reprise
Nov 70. (lp) (RSLP 9006) **THE END OF THE GAME**	☐	☐

– Bottoms up / Timeless time / Descending scales / Burnt foot / Hidden depths / The end of the game. (re-iss. 1972; K 44106) (cd-iss. Jan96; 7599 26758-2)

Jun 71. (7") (RS 27012) **HEAVY HEART. / NO WAY OUT**	☐	☐

(re-iss. Nov71; K 14092)

Jan 72. (7"; by PETER GREEN & NIGEL WATSON) (K 14141) **BEASTS OF BURDEN. / UGANDA WOMAN**		☐

— Between 1971-78 PETER concentrated on religious activities, and after a time recovering in a mental hospital in 1977, he was gladly making a come-back with **SNOWY WHITE** – guitar / **PETER BARDENS** – keyboards / **KUMA HARADA** – bass and **REG ISADORE** – drums (all mainly on following album) (first 45 below quickly withdrawn)

	P.V.K.	Sail
Jun 78. (7"w-drawn) (PV 16) **THE APOSTLE. / TRIBAL DANCE**	☐	–
May 79. (lp,green-lp) (PVLS 101) **IN THE SKIES**	32	–

– In the skies / Slaybo day / A fool no more / Tribal dance / Seven stars / Funky chunk / Just for you / Proud Pinto / The apostle. (cd-iss. 1988 on 'Creole'; 823793) (cd re-iss. Jun96 on 'Rhino'; RNCD 1001)

Jun 79. (7") (PV 24) **IN THE SKIES. / PROUD PINTO**	☐	☐

— Continued to work with noted session people, too numerous to mention

Apr 80. (lp) (PVLS 102) <0112> **LITTLE DREAMER**	34	☐ Oct80

– Loser two times / Momma don'tcha cry / Born under a bad sign / I could not ask for more / Baby when the sun goes down / Walkin' the road / One woman love / Cryin' won't bring you back / Little dreamer. (cd-iss. Jun96 on 'Rhino'; RNCD 1002)

Apr 80. (7") (PV 36) **WALKIN' THE ROAD. / WOMAN DON'T**	☐	–
Jun 80. (7"w-drawn) (PV 41) **LOSER TWO TIMES. / MOMMA DONTCHA CRY**	–	–
Mar 81. (lp) (PET 1) **WHATCHA GONNA DO**	☐	–

– Gotta see her tonight / Promised land / Bullet in the sky / Give me back my freedom / Last train to San Antone / To break your heart / Bizzy Lizzy / Lost my love / Like a hot tomato / Head against the wall. (cd-iss. Feb93 on 'Rhino';)

Mar 81. (7") (PV 103) **GIVE ME BACK MY FREEDOM. / LOST MY LOVE**	☐	–
Jul 81. (7") (PV 112) **PROMISED LAND. / BIZZY LIZZY**	☐	–

	Headline	not iss.
Jun 82. (lp/c) (HED/+C 1) **WHITE SKY**	☐	–

– Time for me to go / Shining star / The clown / White sky (love that evil woman) / It's gotta be me / Born on the wild side / Fallin' apart / Indian lover / Just another guy. (cd-iss. Nov92 & Jun96 on 'Rhino'; RNCD 1004)

Jun 82. (7") (LIN 2) **THE CLOWN. / TIME FOR ME TO GO**	☐	–
Nov 83. (lp/c) (HED/+C 2) **KOLORS**		

– What am I doing here / Bad bad feelings / Big boy now / Black woman / Bandit / Same old blues / Liquor and you / Gotta do it with me / Funky jam. (cd-iss. Nov92 on 'Rhino'; RNCD 1005)

	Creole	not iss.
1984. (7") (614035) **BIG BOY. / BANDIT**	☐	–

— Virtually retired from the biz in '86 after a recording session with MICK GREEN (ex-PIRATES)

	Disky	Disky
Feb 93. (cd/c) (PACD/PAMC 7013) **ONE WOMAN LOVE**	☐	☐

PETER GREEN SPLINTER GROUP

— **PETER GREEN** – guitar, vocals; with **NIGEL WATSON** – guitars, vocals / **ROGER COTTON** – keyboards, vocal / **NEIL MURRAY** – bass / **LARRY TOLFREE** – drums

	Snapper	Snapper
May 97. (d-cd/d-c) (SAR CD/MC 101) **SPLINTER GROUP**	71	☐

– Hitch hiking woman / Travelling riverside blues / Look on yonder wall / Homework / Stumble / Help me / Watch your stepm / From 4 till late / Steady rolling man / It takes time / Dark end of the street / Going down.

May 98. (cd; with NIGEL WATSON) (SARCD 002) **THE ROBERT JOHNSON SONGBOOK**	57	☐

– When you got a good friend / 32-20 blues / Phonograph blues / Last fair deal gone down / Stop breakin' down blues / Terraplane blues / Walkin' blues / Love in vain blues / Ramblin' on my mind / Stones in my passway / Me and the Devil blues / Honeymoon blues / Kind hearted woman blues / I believe I'll dust my broom / If I had possession over judgement day / Sweet home Chicago.

Mar 99. (d-cd) (SDDCD 816) **SOHO SESSION (live)**	☐	☐

– It takes time / Homework / Black magic woman / Indians / Hey mama keep your big mouth shut / The supernatural / Rattlesnake shake / Shake your hips / Albatross // Travelling Riverside blues / Steady rollin' man / Terraplane blues / Honeymoon blues / Last fair deal gone down / If I had possession over judgement day / Green manalishi / Goin' down / Help me / Look over yonder wall.

Jun 99. (cd) (SMACD 817) **DESTINY ROAD**	☐	☐

– A big change is gonna come / Say that you want to / Heart of stone / Tribal dance / Burglar / Turn your love away / Madison blues / I can't help myself / Indians / Hiding in shadows / There's a river / You'll be sorry someday.

– compilations, etc. –

Nov 81. (lp/c) Creole; (CRX/+C 5) **BLUE GUITAR**	☐	–

– Gotta see her tonight / Last train to San Antone / Woman don't / Whatcha gonna do / Walking in the road / The apostle / A fool no more / Loser two times / Slaybo day / Cryin' won't bring you back. (cd-iss. Jun96 on 'Rhino'; RNCD 1003)

Feb 86. (lp) Homestead; <HMS 031> **COME ON DOWN**	–	☐
Aug 87. (lp/cd) Nightflite; (NTFL 2001) **A CASE FOR THE BLUES**	☐	–

(cd-iss. Sep87 on 'Compact Company'; 74001) (cd re-iss. Jun99 on 'Saraja'; SARCD 007)

Jan 88. (lp/c/cd) Creole; (CRX/+C/CD 12) **LEGEND**	☐	–

– Touch my spirit / Six string guitar / Proud Pinto / The clown / You won't see me anymore / Long way from home / In the skies / Rubbing my eyes / What am I doing here? / Corner of my mind / Carry my love / Bandit / White skies. (cd+=) – Little dreamer. (re-iss. cd Feb93 on 'Rhino'; RNCD 1009)

Jan 90. (cd/c/d-lp) Backtrackin'; (TRK CD/MC/LP 101) **PETER GREEN**	☐	–

– In the skies / A fool no more / Tribal dance / Just for you / Born on the wild side / Proud Pinto / Shining star / Slaybo day / Indian lover / Carry my love / Corner of my mind / Cryin' won't bring you back / Little dreamer / Momma dontcha cry / Baby when the sun goes down / Born under a bad sign / Walkin' the road / Loser two times / What am I doing here / Big boy now / Time for me to go now / It's gonna be me / You won't see me anymore / Bad bad feeling.

Apr 91. (cd; by MICK GREEN with PETER GREEN & THE ENEMY WITHIN) Red Lightnin'; (RLCD 0087) **TWO GREENS MAKE A BLUES**	☐	–

(re-iss. Mar97 on 'Castle'; CLACD 426)

Jun 92. (cd/c/lp) Creole; (FG 2/4/1 802) **LAST TRAIN**	☐	–
Jun 96. (cd/c) Music Club; (MC CD/TC 244) **GREEN AND GUITAR (BEST OF PETER GREEN)**	☐	–
Apr 97. (cd) Milan; (74321 47464-2) **BANDIT**	☐	–
May 97. (cd) C.M.C.; (10064-2) **KATMANDU**	☐	–
Jun 97. (cd) Appaloosa; (APCD 052) **RARITIES**	☐	–
Jul 98. (cd/c) K-Tel; (ECD2/EMC3 356) **BORN ON THE WILD SIDE**	☐	–
Nov 98. (cd) Laserlight; (CD 21064) **IN THE SKIES / LITTLE DREAMER**	☐	–

Norman GREENBAUM (dig out; Great Psychedelic . . .)

GREEN DAY

Formed: Rodeo, nr. Berkeley, California, USA . . . early 90's out of The SWEET CHILDREN by BILLY JOE and MIKE. When TRE COOL replaced BILLY JOE's sister ANA on drums, they became GREEN DAY, this line-up releasing their debut lp, '39 / SMOOTH', which was recorded in under 24 hours. Their third album, 'DOOKIE' (their first for 'Reprise'), was a surprise US smash in 1994 due to its college/MTV favourite, 'BASKET CASE'. Retro punk-rock for young Americans (and now older Brits) who missed out on BUZZCOCKS, DICKIES, RAMONES (and even earlier 60's pop outfit, the MONKEES), GREEN DAY became a phenomenon in the States; like the SEX PISTOLS' revolution all over again, without the danger, unpredictability and raw excitement. Instead we got formulaic, annoyingly and, yes, inanely catchy punk retreads that took you way back to '77. Still, the multi-millions who bought the record ensured that GREEN DAY were indeed radio-friendly unit shifters. A follow-up set, 'INSOMNIAC' (1995), was another massive seller, although it had to compete with the hordes of equally faceless acts clogging up the charts with similar material. A fifth set, 'NIMROAD' (1997), made sure they were still in touch with their fanbase, the tried and tested formula again getting them into the Top 10. • **Songwriters:** Lyrics; BILLY JOE, group songs except TIRED OF WAITING FOR YOU (Kinks). • **Trivia:** DIRNT guested on The SCREAMING WEASEL album, 'How to Make Enemies And Irritate People'. BILLIE JOE was also a member of PINHEAD GUNPOWDER, who released an album, 'Jump Salty', plus a few EP's (also for 'Lookout').

Album rating: 39/SMOOTHED OUT SLAPPY HOUR compilation (*5) / KERPLUNK! (*5) / DOOKIE (*7) / INSOMNIAC (*6) / NIMROD (*6)

BILLY JOE ARMSTRONG (b.17 Feb'72, San Pablo, Calif.) – vocals, guitar / **MIKE DIRNT** (b. PRITCHARD, 4 May'72) – bass, vocals / **TRE COOL** (b. FRANK EDWIN WRIGHT III, 9 Dec'72, Germany) – drums repl. JOHN KIFTMEYER who had repl. AL SOBRANTE

		not iss.	Lookout
1989.	(7"ep) <LOOKOUT 17> **1000 HOURS EP**	-	

– 1000 hours / Dry ice / Only of you / The one I want. *(UK-iss.Dec94; as above)*

1990.	(lp) <LOOKOUT 22> **39 / SMOOTH**	-	

– At the library / Don't leave me / I was there / Disappearing boy / Green day / Going to Pasalacqua / 16 / Road to exceptance / Rest / The judge's daughter / Paper lanterns / Why do you want him? / 409 in your coffeemaker / Knowledge / 1000 hours / Dry ice / Only of you / The one I want / I want to be alone. *(re-iss. Nov91 lp/cd; LOOKOUT 22/+CD) (UK-iss.Sep94 as '1,039 / SMOOTHED OUT SLAPPY HOURS'; as above) (cd re-iss. Aug97 on 'Epitaph'; 6522-2)*

1991.	(7"ep) <LOOKOUT 35> **SLAPPY EP**	-	

– Paper lanterns / Why do you want him? / 409 in your coffeemaker / Knowledge. *(UK-iss.Sep94; as above)*

Dec 91.	(lp) <LOOKOUT 46> **KERPLUNK!**	-	

– 2000 light years away / One for the razorbacks / Welcome to Paradise / Christie Road / Private ale / Dominated love slave / One of my lies / 80 / Android / No one knows / Who wrote Holden Caulfield? / Words I might have ate. *(UK-iss.Sep94 on 'Lookout' lp/cd+=; LOOKOUT 46/+CD) – Sweet children / Best thing in town / Strangeland / My generation. (by SWEET CHILDREN and released US 1990 on 'Skene') (cd re-iss. Aug97 on 'Epitaph'; 6517-2)*

		Reprise	Reprise
Feb 94.	(cd/c) <(9362 45529-2/-4)> **DOOKIE**		2

– Burnout / Having a blast / Chump / Longview / Welcome to Paradise / Pulling teeth / Basket case / She / Sassafras roots / When I come around / Coming clean / Emenius sleepus / In the end / F.O.D. *(cd+=)* – (hidden track). *(re-dist.Jun94)* – *re-iss. Oct94 on green-lp soon hit UK No.13; 9362 45795-2/-4)*

Jun 94.	(7") (W 0247) **LONGVIEW. / ON THE WAGON**		-

(10"/cd-s) (W 0247 T/CD) – ('A'side) / Going to Pasalaqua / F.O.D. (live) / Christy Road (live).

Aug 94.	(7"green/c-s) (W 0257/+C) **BASKET CASE. / TIRED OF WAITING FOR YOU**	55	-

(cd-s+=) (W 0257CD) – On the wagon / 409 in your coffeemaker.

Oct 94.	(12"green/c-s/cd-s) (W 0269 T/C/CDX) **WELCOME TO PARADISE. / CHUMP (live) / EMENIUS SLEEPUS**	20	-

Jan 95.	(7"green/c-s) (W 0279/+C) **BASKET CASE. / 2,000 LIGHT YEARS AWAY (live)**	7	-

(cd-s+=) (W 0279CD) – Burnout (live) / Longview (live).

Mar 95.	(7"/c-s) (W 0278/+C) **LONGVIEW. / WELCOME TO PARADISE (live)**	30	-

(cd-s+=) (W 0278CD) – One of my lies (live).

May 95.	(7"pic-d/c-s) (W 0294/+C) **WHEN I COME AROUND. / SHE (live)**	27	-

(cd-s+=) (W 0294CD) – Coming clean (live).

Sep 95.	(7"red/c-s) (W 0320/+C) **GEEK STINK BREATH. / I WANNA BE ON T.V.**	16	-

(cd-s+=) (W 0320CD) – Don't wanna fall in love.

Oct 95.	(cd/c/lp) <(9362 46046-2/-4/-1)> **INSOMNIAC**	8	2

– Armatage Shanks / Brat / Stuck with me / Geek stink breath / No pride / Bab's Uvula who? / 86 / Panic song / Stuart and the Ave. / Brain stew / Jaded / Westbound sign / Tight wad hill / Walking contradiction.

Dec 95.	(7") (W 0327X) **STUCK WITH ME. / WHEN I COME AROUND (live)**	24	-

(c-s+=) (W 0327C) – Jaded (live).
(cd-s) (W 0327CD) – ('A'side) / Dominated love slave (live) / Chump (live).

Jun 96.	(c-s) (W 0339C) **BRAIN STEW / JADED / GOOD RIDDANCE**	28	-

(cd-s+=) (W 0339CD) – Do da da.
(brain-shaped cd-s++=) (W 0339CDX) – Brain stew (radio).

Sep 97.	(c-s) (W 0424C) <43945> **HITCHIN' A RIDE / SICK**	25	Jun98

(cd-s+=) (W 0424CD) – Espionage.

Oct 97.	(cd/c) <(9362 46794-2/-4)> **NIMROD**	11	10

– Nice guys finish last / Hitchin' a ride / The grouch / Redundant / Scattered / Worry rock / Desensitized / All the time / Platypus (I hate you) / Last ride in / Jinx / Haushinka / Walking alone / Suffocate / Uptight / Take back / King for a day / Good riddance / Prosthetic head.

Jan 98.	(c-s) (W 0430C) <43974> **TIME OF YOUR LIFE (GOOD RIDDANCE) / DESENSITIZED**	11	Jun98

(cd-s+=) (W 0430CD1) – Rotting.
(cd-s) (W 0430CD2) – ('A'side) / Suffocate / You lied.

Apr 98.	(7"/cd-s) (W 0438/+CD1) **REDUNDANT. / THE GROUCH (live) / PAPER LANTERN (live)**	27	

(cd-s) (W 0438CD2) – ('A'side) / Reject all American (live) / She (live).

GREEN ON RED

Formed: Tucson, Arizona, USA ... 1979 by DAN STUART, CHRIS CACAVAS, JACK WATERSON and VAN CRISTIAN. The latter was replaced by ALEX MacNICOL prior to the release of their eponymous mini-lp for STEVE WYNN's 'Down There' label. Their debut album, 'GRAVITY TALKS' (1984), drew comparisons with NEIL YOUNG's more rocky outings, moving away from the ramshackle garage of their earlier releases. This influence was even more evident on their 1985 offering 'GAS FOOD LODGING', which featured the distinctive guitar style of the newly recruited CHUCK PROPHET. Signing to 'Mercury' the same year, they released the disappointing 'NO FREE LUNCH', an album that saw the band attempting a BYRDS-like country sound, and even included a WILLIE NELSON cover 'AIN'T IT FUNNY NOW'. After the similarly poor 'THE KILLER INSIDE ME' in 1987, the group disbanded although DAN and CHUCK re-formed, using session players to flesh out the sound. Always on the verge of a commercial breakthrough, they were dogged by label failures and by the time

of 1989's 'HERE COME THE SNAKES', the band had signed to 'China' in the UK although the record, which showcased a bolshier, heavy guitar sound, was previously to have been issued in August '88 by the soon-to-be bust 'Red Rhino' records. Undaunted, the band played a blinding live set in London, documented on 'LIVE AT THE TOWN AND COUNTRY' (1989). The band issued another three albums (including AL KOOPER-produced 'SCAPEGOATS') to no commercial success and after the ironically titled 'TOO MUCH FUN' (1992), PROPHET and STUART went on to release well-received solo albums. • **More covers:** KNOCKIN' ON HEAVEN'S DOOR (Bob Dylan) / SMOKESTACK LIGHTNIN' (Howlin' Wolf) / RAINY DAYS AND MONDAYS (Carpenters).

Album rating: GREEN ON RED mini (*6) / GRAVITY TALKS (*7) / GAS FOOD LODGING (*8) / NO FREE LUNCH mini (*4) / THE KILLER INSIDE ME (*5) / HERE COME THE SNAKES (*7) / LIVE AT THE TOWN AND COUNTRY (*4) / THIS TIME AROUND (*6) / SCAPEGOATS (*5) / ROCK'N'ROLL DISEASE – THE BEST OF GREEN ON RED compilation (*7) / TOO MUCH FUN (*4) / Danny & Dusty: THE LOST WEEKEND (*5) / Dan Stuart: RETRONEUVO (*5) / CANO'WORMS (*5)

DAN STUART – vocals, guitar / **CHRIS CACAVAS** – keyboards / **JACK WATERSON** – bass / **ALEX MacNICOL** – drums, repl. VAN CRISTIAN

		not iss.	Private
1981.	(12"ep) <none> **TWO BIBLES**	-	

		not iss.	Down There
1982.	(m-lp) <71026> **GREEN ON RED (UNTITLED)**	-	

– Death and angels / Hair and skin / Black night / Illustrated crawling / Aspirin / Lost world / Apartment 6. *(UK-iss.Jun85 on 'Zippo'; ZANE 002)*

		Slash	Slash
Aug 84.	(lp) (SR 207) <23964-1> **GRAVITY TALKS**		1983

– Gravity talks / Old chief / 5 easy pieces / Deliverance / Over my head / Snake bite / Blue parade / That's what you're here for / Brave generation / Abigail's ghost / Cheap wine / Narcolepsy. *(re-iss. Jan87 lp/c; SLM P/C 16)*

—— added **CHUCK W. PROPHET** – steel guitar, vocals

		Zippo	Enigma
May 85.	(lp/c) (ZONG/+CASS 005) <ST/4XT 73249> **GAS FOOD LODGING**		1986

– That's what dreams / Black river / Hair of the dog / This I know / Fading away / Easy way out / Sixteen ways / The drifter / Sea of Cortez / We shall overcome. *(cd-iss. 1990 on 'Enigma'; D2-73249)*

—— **KEITH MITCHELL** – percussion repl. ALEX

		Mercury	Mercury
Oct 85.	(m-lp/m-c) (MERM/+C 78) <82646-1> **NO FREE LUNCH**	99	

– Time ain't nothing / Honest man / Ballad of Guy Fawkes / No free lunch / Funny how time slips away / Jimmy boy / Keep on moving. *(c+=)* – Smokestack lightning.

Nov 85.	(7") (MER 202) **TIME AIN'T NOTHING. / NO FREE LUNCH**		
Feb 87.	(7") (GOR 1) **CLARKSVILLE. / NO DRINKIN'**		

(12"+=) (GOR 1-12) – Broken.

Mar 87.	(lp/c)(cd) (GOR LP/MC 1)(839122-2) <830912-2> **THE KILLER INSIDE ME**		

– Clarksville / Mighty gun / Jamie / Whispering wind / Ghost hand / Sorry Naomi / No man's land / Track you down (his master's voice) / Born to fight / We ain't feee / The killer inside me. *(cd+=)* – NO FREE LUNCH (m-lp)

Jun 87.	(7") (GOR 2) **BORN TO FIGHT. / DON'T SHINE YOUR LIGHT ON ME**		

(ext.12"+=) (GOR 2-12) – While the widow weeps.

—— Disbanded late 1987, DAN and CHUCK reformed and brought in new sessioners. WATERSON released an album 'WHOSE DOG' in 1988, while CHRIS CACAVAS & THE JUNKYARD LOVE released self-titled one in 1989.

		China	Restless
Apr 89.	(7") (CHINA 16) **KEITH CAN'T READ. / THAT'S THE WAY THE WORLD GOES ROUND / VAYA CON DIOS**		-

(12") (CHINX 16) – (1st & 3rd tracks) / Tenderloin.

Apr 89.	(lp/c/cd) (839294-1/-4/-2) <72351-1> **HERE COME THE SNAKES**		

– Keith can't read / Rock and roll disease / Morning blue / Zombie for love / Broken radio / Change / Tenderloin / Way back home / We had it all / D.T. blues.

Aug 89.	(ltd; 10"lp/c) (841013-0/-4) **LIVE AT THE TOWN & COUNTRY CLUB (live)**		

– 16 ways / Change / DT blues / Fading away / Morning blue / Are you sure Hank done it this way / Zombie for love / Hair of the dog. *(c+=)* – Rock and roll disease / We had it all.

—— duo now with **RENE COMAN** – upright bass, bass / **MIKE FINNEGAN** – keyboards / **DAVID KEMPER** – drums, percussion / plus **BERNIE LEADON** – mandolin, acoustic guitar (4) / **PAT DONALDSON** – bass (4) / **SPOONER OLDHAM** – piano (3)

		China	Catalina
Oct 89.	(7") (CHINA 21) **THIS TIME AROUND. / FADING AWAY (live)**		

(12"+=/cd-s+=) (CHINX/CHICD 21) – 16 ways (live).

Nov 89.	(lp/c/cd) (841720-1/-4/-2) <841519-2> **THIS TIME AROUND**		-

– This time around / Cool million / Rev. Luther / Good patient woman / You couldn't get arrested / The quarter / Foot / Hold the line / Pills and booze / We're all waiting. *(free-7"w.a.)* – MORNING BLUE / ROCK AND ROLL DISEASE. / (interview) *(re-iss. Jul91 cd/c; WOL CD/MC 1019)*

Dec 89.	(7") (CHINA 22) **YOU COULDN'T GET ARRESTED. / BROKEN RADIO**		

(ext.12"/ext.cd-s) (CHINX/CHICD 22) – Hair of the dog.

—— DAN and CHUCK recruit **MICHAEL RHODES** – bass / **DAREN HESS** – drums

		China	China
Mar 91.	(7") **LITTLE THINGS IN LIFE. / CHERRY KIND**		-

(12"+=/cd-s+=) – Sun goes down / Waiting for love.

Mar 91.	(cd/c/lp) <(WOL CD/MC/LP 1001)> **SCAPEGOATS**		

– A guy like me / Little things in life / Two lovers (waitin' to die) / Gold in the graveyard / Hector's out / Shed a tear (for the lonesome) / Blowfly / Sun goes down / Where the rooster crows / Baby loves her gun.

Jun 91.	(7") **TWO LOVERS (WAITIN' TO DIE). / KEITH CAN'T READ**	☐	-	
Sep 91.	(cd/c/lp) *(WOL/+MC/CD 1021)* **THE BEST OF GREEN ON RED** (compilation)	☐	-	

– Time ain't nothing / Born to fight / Hair of the dog / Keith can't read / Morning blue / This time around / Little things in life / You couldn't get arrested / That's what dreams / Zombie for love / Baby loves her gun.

―― added **J.D. FOSTER**

Oct 92.	(lp/c/cd) <*(WOL/+MC/CD 1029)*> **TOO MUCH FUN**	☐	-	

– She's all mine / Frozen in my headlights / Love is insane / Too much fun / The getaway / I owe you one / Man needs woman / Sweetest thing / Thing or two / Hands and knees / Wait and see / Rainy days and Mondays.

– compilations, others, etc. –

Sep 91.	(cd/c) *Music Club*; <*(MC CD/TC 037)*> **THE LITTLE THINGS IN LIFE**	☐	☐
May 92.	(cd) *Mau Mau*; <*(MAUCD 612)*> **GAS FOOD LODGING / GREEN ON RED**	☐	☐ Jan96
Jun 94.	(cd) *China*; <*(WOLCD 1047)*> **ROCK'N'ROLL DISEASE – THE BEST OF . . .**	☐	☐ 1995

―― DAN STUART also had appeared on album below.

DANNY & DUSTY

DUSTY being STEVE WYNN of DREAM SYNDICATE. Augmented by LONG RYDERS:- SYD GRIFFIN, TOM STEVENS + STEVE McCARTHY, plus DENNIS DUCK of DREAM SYNDICATE + CHRIS CACAVAS of GREEN ON RED

		Zippo	A&M
Nov 85.	(lp) *(ZONG 007)* <*5075*> **THE LOST WEEKEND**		

– Down to the bone / The word is out / Song for the dreamers / Miracle mile / Baby, we all gotta go down / The king of the losers / Send me a postcard / Knockin' on Heaven's door. <*cd-iss. 1996 on 'Prima'; 6*>

―― DAN was also guest on two of NAKED PREY albums. CHRIS guested on the GIANT SAND album 'VALLEY OF RAIN' in Mar'86. In Sep'90, CHUCK PROPHET issued solo album 'BROTHER ALDO' for 'Fire'. In 1993 for 'China', he issued 'BALINESE DANCER' foolowed by in '95; 'FEAST OF HEARTS'. Meanwhile CACAVAS on 'Normal' released 'PALE BLONDE HELL' (1994) & 'NEW IMPROVED PAIN' (1995).

DAN STUART

―― (on 1995 set) with **J.D. FOSTER, JON DEE GRAHAM, RANDY McREYNOLDS, JAMES VALENCIA, FERNANDO VALENCI, DAREN HESS + CRAIG SCHUMACHER**

		Normal	Monkey Hill
Jul 94.	(cd; by AL PERRY & DAN STUART) *(NORMAL 169CD)* **RETRONEUVO**		-

– Daddy's girl / Hermit of Jerome / I could run / Little slant 6 / Sick and tired / Better than I did / Mamcita / Eyes of a fool / Empty chair / Lone wolf.

Jul 95.	(cd) *(NORMAL 189CD)* <*8131*> **CANO'WORMS**	☐	☐

– Panhandler / Home after dark / La pasionara / Who needs more / What a day / Expat blues / Waterfall / In Madrid / Filipina stripped / Can't get through / The greatest.

GREEN RIVER (see under ⇒ PEARL JAM)

GREENSLADE (dig out; Great Psychedelic . . .)

GRID (dig out; 4th edition or Great Psychedelic . . .)

Sid GRIFFIN (see under ⇒ LONG RYDERS)

Nanci GRIFFITH

Born: 6 Jul'53, Seguin, Texas, USA. This self-styled 'folkabilly' poet/singer began performing from an early age, initially with her parents in the region's honky tonks and later on the Texas folk circuit, her pure, girly cute voice and girl-next-door appeal gaining her a sizeable following. After completing a degree in education at the University of Texas, GRIFFITH focused wholly on music, making her recording debut a year later in 1978 with 'THERE'S A LIGHT BEYOND THESE WOODS'. Released on the small independent label, 'B.F. Deal', the album was largely self-penned, introducing her talent for vivid storytelling and snapshot vignettes. It was another four years before she recorded a follow-up, 1982's 'POET IN MY WINDOW', released on another small label, 'Featherbed'. However, it wasn't until GRIFFITH signed with folk/country label, 'Philo', that her highly original singing/songwriting style began to develop significantly. Backed by established musicians like Irish (electric) lead guitarist PHIL DONNELLY and acoustic maestros such as LLOYD GREEN, ROY HUSKEY JR. and BELA FLECK, GRIFFITH cut her acclaimed 'ONCE IN A VERY BLUE MOON' (1985). Again the album consisted mainly of her own compositions, although there were a few fine covers including LYLE LOVETT's 'IF I WAS THE WOMAN YOU WANTED' and the exceptional PAT ALGER-penned title track after which NANCI would subsequently name the backing band she formed the following year, The BLUE MOON ORCHESTRA. 1986 also saw the release of the Grammy Award winning (Best Folk Album) 'LAST OF THE TRUE BELIEVERS', KATHY MATTEA subsequently scoring a US country smash with one its tracks, the GRIFFITH-penned 'LOVE AT THE FIVE AND DIME'. The album was the first to be released in the UK through the independently distributed 'Demon' and, the same year, 'Philo' re-released

GRIFFITH's first two albums, her star firmly in the ascendant as she inked a new deal with 'M.C.A.' The singer made her major label debut with 'LONE STAR STATE OF MIND' (1987), the most successful release of her career thus far and an album featuring two of her most famous tracks, the bittersweet reminiscence of the PAT ALGER/GENE LEVINE/FRED KOLLER-penned title track (a minor hit) and the crystal-clear, definitive reading of JULIE GOLD's 'FROM A DISTANCE'. Other highlights numbered the re-recorded 'THERE'S A LIGHT BEYOND THESES WOODS (MARY MARGARET)' from the debut, and ROBERT EARL KEEN JNR.'s 'SING ONE FOR SISTER'. 'LITTLE LOVE AFFAIRS' (1988) marked a new songwriting maturity, GRIFFITH creating a thematic continuity on the subject of love in various contexts, over the course of the album. After the live 'ONE FAIR SUMMER EVENING' (1988), GRIFFITH moved into more AOR-esque territory with 'STORMS' (1989), recorded in L.A. and produced by GLYN JOHNS, a man who's had a hand in some of the best albums in rock history. His midas touch gave NANCI her commercial breakthrough, in the UK at least, where the record made the Top 40. 'LATE NIGHT GRANDE HOTEL' (1991) continued in a similar vein, employing PETER VAN HOOKE and ROD ARGENT on production duties and adding strings to her primarily acoustic-based sound. Already a major star in Ireland (she's also contributed to a number of CHIEFTAINS releases) where she regularly has sell-out tours, GRIFFITH finally made the UK Top 20 in 1993 with 'OTHER VOICES, OTHER ROOMS', an album that saw a return to her folk/country roots. A tribute to her favourite songwriters, among the album's many highlights was a plaintive reading of JOHN PRINE's 'SPEED OF THE SOUND OF LONELINESS' as well as a sensitive cover of the late TOWNE VAN ZANDT's 'TECUMSHEH' valley, the record seeing GRIFFITH renewing her partnership with her early producer JIM ROONEY. More recently, 'THE FLYER' (1994) and 'BLUE ROSES FROM THE MOONS' (1997) have seen GRIFFITH consolidate her position as one of the most respected artists in the singer/songwriter/interpretor genre, alongside EMMYLOU HARRIS. • **Covered:** DEADWOOD, SOUTH DAKOTA (Eric Taylor) / ROSEVILLE FAIR (Bill Staines) / HEAVEN (Julie Gold) / NEVER MIND (Harlan Howard) / BALLAD OF ROBIN WINTERSMITH (Richard Dobson) / LET IT SHINE ON ME (P.Kennerly) / NICKEL DREAMS (M.McAnally-D.Lowery) / THE SUN, MOON, AND STARS (Vince Bell) / SAN DIEGO SERENADE (Tom Waits). OTHER VOICES, OTHER ROOMS covers album; ACROSS THE GREAT DIVIDE (Kate Wolf) / WOMAN OF THE PHOENIX (Vince Bell) / TECUMSEH VALLEY (Townes Van Zandt) / THREE FLIGHTS UP (Frank Christian) / BOOTS OF SPANISH LEATHER (Bob Dylan) / FROM CLARE TO HERE (Ralph McTell) / CAN'T HELP BUT WONDER WHERE I'M BOUND (Tom Paxton) / DO RE MI (Woody Guthrie) / THIS OLD TOWN (Janis Ian) / COMIN' DOWN IN THE RAIN (Buddy Mondlock) / TEN DEGREES AND GETTING OLD (Gordon Lightfoot) / MORNING SONG FOR SALLY (Jerry Jeff Walker) / NIGHT RIDER'S LAMENT (Michael Burton) / ARE YOU TIRED OF ME DARLING (G.P.Cook & Ralph Roland) / TURN AROUND (Harry Belafonte) / WIMOWEH (c.Paul Campbell) / GRAVITY OF THE SITUATION with Hootie & The Blowfish (Vic Chesnutt) / etc.

Album rating: THERE'S A LIGHT BEYOND THESE WOODS (*4) / POET IN MY WINDOW (*4) / ONCE IN A VERY BLUE MOON (*6) / LAST OF THE TRUE BELIEVERS (*7) / LONE STAR STATE OF MIND (*7) / LITTLE LOVE AFFAIRS (*7) / ONE FAIR SUMMER EVENING (*7) / STORMS (*8) / LATE NIGHT GRANDE HOTEL (*7) / OTHER VOICES, OTHER ROOMS (*7) / THE BEST OF NANCI GRIFFITH compilation (*8) / FLYER (*7) / BLUE ROSES FROM THE MOON (*6) / OTHER VOICES, OTHER ROOMS 2 (*6)

NANCI GRIFFITH – vocals, acoustic guitar

		not iss.	B.F. Deal
Feb 78.	(lp) <*6*> **THERE'S A LIGHT BEYOND THESE WOODS**	-	☐

– I remember Joe / Alabama soft spoken blues / Michael's song / Song for remembered heroes / West Texas sun / There's a light beyond these woods / Dollar matinee / Montana backroads / John Philipp Griffith. <*re-iss. 1982 on 'Featherbed'; FB 903*> <*re-iss. Aug87 on 'Philo' lp/c/cd; PH 1097/+C/CD*> (UK-iss.Jul89 on 'M.C.A.'; MCG/MCGC/DMCG 6052)

		not iss.	Featherbed
May 82.	(lp) <*FB 902*> **POET IN MY WINDOW**	-	☐

– Marilyn Monroe – Neon and waltzes / Heart of a miner / Julie Ann / You can't go home again / October reasons / Wheels / Workin' in corners / Trouble with roses / Tonight I think I'm gonna go downtown / Poet in my window. <*re-iss. Aug87 on 'Philo' lp/c/cd; PH 1098/+C/CD*> (UK-iss.Jul89 on 'M.C.A.' lp/c/cd; MCG/MCGC/DMCG 6053) (re-iss. Oct91 cd/c; DMCL /MCLC 1911)

		not iss.	Philo
Jul 85.	(7") **ONCE IN A VERY BLUE MOON.** /	-	☐
Dec 85.	(lp) <*PH 1096*> **ONCE IN A VERY BLUE MOON**	-	☐

– Ghost in the music / Love is a hard waltz / Mary & Omie / Roseville fair / Friend out in the madness / Time alone / I'm not drivin' these wheels / Spin on a red brick floor / Ballad of Richard Wintersmith / If I were a woman you wanted. (UK-iss.Jul89 on 'M.C.A.' lp/c/cd; MCG/MCGC/DMCG 6054)

Dec 86.	(cd/c/lp) <*CD/C+/PH 1109*> **LAST OF TRUE BELIEVERS**	-	☐

– Last of the true believers / Love at the Five & Dime / St. Olav's gate / More than a whisper / Banks of the Pontchatrain / Looking for the time / Goin' gone / One of these days / Love's found a shoulder / Fly by night / The wing and the wheel. (UK-iss.Jun88 on 'Rounder' lp/c/cd; REU/+C/CD 1013)

		M.C.A.	M.C.A.
Apr 87.	(7") <*53008*> **LONE STAR STATE OF MIND. / THERE'S A LIGHT BEOND THE WOODS (MARY MARGARET)**	-	☐
Apr 87.	(lp/c) *(MCF/+C 3364)* **LONE STAR STATE OF MIND**	☐	☐

– Lone star state of mind / Cold hearts – closed minds / From a distance / Beacon Street / Nickel dreams / Sing one for sister / Ford Econoline / Trouble in the fields / Love in a memory / Let it shine on me / There's a light beyond these woods (Mary Margaret). (cd-iss. Jul87; MCAD 5927)

Jun 87. (7") <53082> **LOVE IN A MEMORY. / TROUBLE IN THE FIELDS**
       — / —

Jul 87. (7") (MCA 1169) **FROM A DISTANCE. / SING ONE FOR SISTER**
       — / —
(cd-s) (DMCA 1169) – ('A'side) / De Lejos / Gulf Coast highway.

Nov 87. (7"ep) (MCA 1221) <53147> **COLD HEARTS**
– Cold hearts, closed minds / Ford Econoline / Lone star state of mind.

Jan 88. (7") <53184> **FROM A DISTANCE. / NEVER MIND**
       — / —

Feb 88. (7") (MCA 1230) **OUTBOUND PLANE. / SO LONG AGO**
       — / —
(12"+=) (MCAT 1230) – Trouble in the fields.

Mar 88. (lp/c/cd) (MCF/MCFC/DMCF 3413) **LITTLE LOVE AFFAIRS** [78]
– Anyone can be somebody's fool / I knew love / Never mind / Love wore a halo (back before the war) / So long ago / Gulf Coast highway / Little love affairs / I wish it would rain / Outbound plane / I would change my life / Sweet dreams will come.

Mar 88. (7") <53306> **I KNEW LOVE. / SO LONG AGO**

Apr 88. (7") (MCA 1240) **I KNEW LOVE. / NEVER MIND**
(12"+=) (MCAT 1240) – Lone star state of mind.

Sep 88. (7") <53374> **ANYONE CAN BE SOMEBODY'S FOOL. / LOVE WORE A HALO (BACK BEFORE THE WAR)**
   — / —

Sep 88. (7") (MCA 1282) **FROM A DISTANCE. / LOVE WORE A HALO (BACK BEFORE THE WAR)**
   — / —
(cd-s+=) (DMCA 1282) – There's a light beyond these woods (Mary Margaret).

  —— with musicians **JAMES HOOKER** – keyboards / **DENNY BIXBY** – bass

Nov 88. (lp/c/cd) (MCF/MCFC/DMCF 3435) **ONE FAIR SUMMER EVENING** (live)
– Once in a very blue moon / Looking for the time (workin' girl) / Deadwood, South Dakota / More than a whisper / I would bring you Ireland / Roseville fair / Workin' in corners / Trouble in the fields / The wing and the wheel / From a distance / Love at the Five & Dime / Spin on a red brick floor.

Jun 89. (7") <53700> **IT'S A HARD LIFE WHEREVER YOU GO. / FROM A DISTANCE**
   — / —

Jul 89. (7") (MCA 1358) **IT'S A HARD LIFE WHEREVER YOU GO. / GULF COAST HIGHWAY**
   — / —
(cd-s+=/12"+=) (D+/MCAT 1358) – If wishes were changes.

Sep 89. (lp/c/cd) (MCG/MCGC/DMCG 6066) <6319> **STORMS** [38] [99]
– I don't wanna talk about love / Drive-in movies and dashboard lights / You made this love a teardrop / Brave companion of the road / Storms / It's a hard life wherever you go / If wishes were changes / Listen to the radio / Leaving the harbor / Radio Fragile.

Sep 89. (7") <53761> **I DON'T WANT TO TALK ABOUT LOVE. / DRIVE-IN MOVIES AND DASHBOARD LIGHTS**
   — / —

Sep 89. (7") **I DON'T WANT TO TALK ABOUT LOVE. / SPIN ON A RED BRICK FLOOR**
   — / —

Nov 89. (7") (MCA 1379) **YOU MADE THIS LOVE A TEARDROP. / MORE THAN A WHISPER**
(cd-s+=/12"+=) (D+/MCAT 1379) – Little love affairs.

Sep 91. (7"/c-s) **LATE NIGHT GRANDE HOTEL. / IT'S JUST ANOTHER MORNING HERE**
(12"+=) – Wooden heart.
(cd-s++=) – From a distance.

Sep 91. (lp/c/cd) <(MCA/+C/D 10306)> **LATE NIGHT GRANDE HOTEL** [40]
– It's just another morning here / Late night Grande Hotel / It's too late / Fields of summer / Heaven / The power lines / Hometown streets / Down'n'outer / One blade shy of a sharp edge / The Sun, Moon, and stars / San Diego serenade. (re-iss. cd Oct95; MCLD 10304)

Nov 91. (7"/c-s) **HEAVEN. / DOWN 'N' OUTER**
(12"+=) – Tumble and fall.
(cd-s+=) – Love at the Five And Dime (live).

Feb 93. (c-s) (MCSC 1743) **SPEED OF THE SOUND OF LONELINESS / FROM CLARE TO HERE**
(cd-s+=) (MCSTD 1743) – Boots of Spanish leather.

Feb 93. (cd/c) (MCD/MCC 10796) **OTHER VOICES, OTHER ROOMS** [18] [54]
– Across the great divide / Woman of the Phoenix / Tecumseh Valley / Three flights up / Boots of Spanish leather / Speed of the sound of loneliness / From Clare to here / Can't help but wonder where I'm bound / Do re mi / This old town / Comin' down in the rain / Ten degrees and getting colder / Morning song to Sally / Night rider's lament / Are you tired of me darling / Turn around / Wimoweh.

May 93. (c-s) (MCSC 1771) **FROM CLARE TO HERE / CRADLE OF THE INTERSTATE**
(cd-s+=) (MCSTD 1771) – De Lejos (From a distance) (Spanish version) / ('A'extended).

Nov 93. (cd/c) (MCD/MCC 10966) **THE BEST OF NANCI GRIFFITH** (compilation) [27]
– Trouble in the fields / From a distance / Speed of the sound of loneliness / Love at the five and dime / Listen to the radio / Gulf Coast highway / I wish it would rain / Ford Econoline / If wishes were changes / The wing and the wheel / Late night Grande hotel / From Clare to here / It's just another morning here / Trouble and fall / There's a light beyond these woods (Mary Margaret) / Outbound plane / Lone star state of mind / It's a hard life wherever you go / The road to Aberdeen.

                   M.C.A.   Elektra

Sep 94. (cd/c) (MCD/MCC 11155) **FLYER** [20] [48]
– The flyer / Nobody's angel / Say it isn't so / Southbound train / These days in an open book / Time of inconvenience / Don't forget about me / Always will / Going back to Georgia / Talk to me while I'm listening / Fragile / On Grafton Street / Anything you need but me / Goodnight to a mother's dream / This heart.

Sep 94. (c-s) **ON GRAFTON STREET / THIS HEART**
(cd-s+=) – These days in an open book.

                   Warners   Warners

Mar 97. (cd/c) <(7559 962015-2/-4)> **BLUE ROSES FROM THE MOONS** [64]
– Everything's coming up roses / Two for the road / Wouldn't that be fine / Battlefield / Saint Teresa of Avila / Gulf Coast highway / I fought the law / Not my way home / Is this all there is / Maybe tomorrow / Waiting for love / I'll move along / Morning train / She ain't goin' nowhere.

                   Elektra   Elektra

Jul 98. (cd/c) <62235> **OTHER VOICES, TOO (A TRIP TO THE BOUNTIFUL)** [— / 85]

GRIN (see under ⇒ LOFGREN, Nils)

GROUNDHOGS

Formed: New Cross, London, England . . . 1963 by TONY McPHEE, who named them after a JOHN LEE HOOKER track. In 1964, they signed with Mickie Most's Anglo-American agency, soon having their debut 45, 'SHAKE IT', issued on 'Interphon'. Around the same time, they recorded an lp, 'LIVE AT THE AU-GO CLUB, NEW YORK', with their hero, HOOKER. They returned to England in 1965 and subsequently went through a series of false starts before finally stablising their line-up in 1968. Just prior to this, McPHEE had teamed up with The JOHN DUMMER BLUES BAND, who released two singles for 'Mercury'. However, with advice from Andrew Lauder of 'United Artists', the new GROUNDHOGS took-off with (their) debut, 'SCRATCHING THE SURFACE'. In 1969, the single 'BDD' (Blind Deaf Dumb) flopped in the UK, although it bizarrely hit the top spot in Lebanon! In the early 70's, they scored with two UK Top 10 lp's, 'THANK CHRIST FOR THE BOMB' (which caused controversy with its sarcastic praise of the nuclear deterrent) and 'SPLIT' (which they always seemed to do, from then on). One of the tracks from the latter, 'CHERRY RED', featured on Top Of The Pops (22nd of April '71). Although they had lost none of their white-boy Chicago blues elements, the aforementioned couple of albums moved towards a more mellotron-based prog-rock sound. Two albums in 1972, 'WHO WILL SAVE THE WORLD?' and 'HOGWASH', revisited their blues roots. 1974's 'SOLID' album, meanwhile, saw a return to the charts, a feat TONY McPHEE and his GROUNDHOGS couldn't emulate with further releases. They were still going strong well into the 90's, releasing albums for the discerning blues connoisseur. • **Songwriters:** McPHEE penned except; EARLY IN THE MORNING (Sonny Boy Williamson) / STILL A FOOL (Muddy Waters) / MISTREATED (Tommy Johnson) / etc. • **Trivia:** TONY McPHEE appeared on JOHN DUMMER BAND releases between 1968-69. Around the same time he guested on BIG JOE WILLIAMS recordings.

Album rating: SCRATCHING THE SURFACE (*5) / BLUES OBITUARY (*6) / THANK CHRIST FOR THE BOMB (*8) / SPLIT (*7) / WHO WILL SAVE THE WORLD? THE MIGHTY GROUNDHOGS? (*6) / HOGWASH (*5) / SOLID (*4) / CROSSCUT SAW (*4) / BLACK DIAMOND (*4) / RAZOR'S EDGE (*4) / BACK AGAINST THE WALL (*4) / HOGS ON THE ROAD (*4) / NO SURRENDER (*4) / FOOLISH PRIDE (*4) / DOCUMENT SERIES PRESENTS . . . THE GROUNDHOGS (*8) /

TONY McPHEE (b.22 Mar'44, Lincolnshire, England) – guitar, vocals, keyboards / **JOHN CRUIKSHANK** – vocals, mouth harp / **PETE CRUIKSHANK** (b. 2 Jul'45) – bass / **DAVID BOORMAN** – drums / on session **TOM PARKER** – piano repl. BOB HALL

              not iss.   Interphon

Jan 65. (7") <7715> **SHAKE IT. / ROCK ME** [— /]

JOHN LEE'S GROUNDHOGS

HOOKER – solo blues guitarist **TERRY SLADE** – drums repl. BOORMAN + added 3-piece brass section

              Planet   Planet

Jan 66. (7") (<PLF 104>) **I'LL NEVER FALL IN LOVE AGAIN. / OVER YOU BABY**

  —— TONY McPHEE joined The TRUTH for a short stint before sessioning for CHAMPION JACK DUPREE on his '66 single 'Get Your Head Happy'

T.S. McPHEE

– solo with **PETE CRUICKSHANK / BOB HALL / and VAUGHN REES** – drums / **NEIL SLAVEN** – guitar

              Purdah   not iss.

Aug 66. (7") (45-3501) **SOMEONE TO LOVE ME. / AIN'T GONNA CRY NO MO'** [/ —]

  —— This band also backed JO-ANN KELLY. In summer McPHEE formed HERBAL MIXTURE around the same time he joined JOHN DUMMER BLUES BAND on two 1966 singles.

GROUNDHOGS

re-formed (**TONY McPHEE** and **PETE CRUICKSHANK**) recruited **STEVE RYE** – vocals, mouth harp / **KEN PUSTELNIK** – drums

              Liberty   World Pacific

Nov 68. (lp; mono/stereo) (LBL/LBS 83199E) <21892> **SCRATCHING THE SURFACE** (live in the studio)
– Man trouble / Married men / Early in the morning / Come back baby / You don't love me / Rocking chair / Walkin' blues / No more daggin' / Still a fool. (re-iss. Sep88 & Apr97 on 'Beat Goes On' lp/cd+=; BGO LP/CD 15) – Oh death / Gasoline / Rock me / Don't pass the hat around.

Dec 68. (7") (LBF 15174) **YOU DON'T LOVE ME. / STILL A FOOL**

  —— trimmed to a trio when RYE left due to illness

              Liberty   Imperial

Jul 69. (lp) (LBS 83253) <12452> **BLUES OBITUARY**
– B.D.D. / Daze of the weak / Times / Mistreated / Express man / Natchez burning / Light was the day. (re-iss. Jan89 on 'Beat Goes On' lp/cd; BGO LP/CD 6)

Aug 69. (7") (LBF 15263) **BDD. / Tony McPhee: GASOLINE**

              Liberty   Liberty

May 70. (lp) (LBS 83295) <7644> **THANK CHRIST FOR THE BOMB** [9]
– Strange town / Darkness is no friend / Soldier / Thank christ for the bomb / Ship on the ocean / Garden / Status people / Rich man, poor man / Eccentric man. (re-iss.

1975 on 'Sunset'; 50376) (re-iss. May86 on 'Fame' lp/c; FA41/TCFA 3152) (re-iss. Dec89 on 'Beat Goes On' lp/cd; BGO LP/CD 67)

1970.	(7") *(LBF 15346)* **ECCENTRIC MAN. / STATUS PEOPLE**	□	-
1970.	(7") *<56205>* **SHIP ON THE OCEAN. / SOLDIER**	-	-

Liberty   U.A.

Mar 71.	(lp) *(LBS 83401) <UA 5513>* **SPLIT**	5	-

– Split (parts 1-4) / Cherry red / A year in the life / Junkman / Groundhog. *(re-iss. Aug80; LBR 1017) (re-iss. Mar86 on 'E.M.I.' lp/c; ATAK/TC-ATAK 73) (re-iss. Dec89 on 'Beat Goes On'; BGO LP/CD 76)*

U.A.   U.A.

Mar 72.	(lp) *(UAG 29237) <UA 5570>* **WHO WILL SAVE THE WORLD? THE MIGHTY GROUNDHOGS**	□	□

– Earth is not room enough / Wages of peace / Body in mind / Music is the food of thought / Bog roll blues / Death of the sun / Amazing Grace / The grey maze. *(re-iss. Dec89 & Apr91 on 'Beat Goes On' lp/cd; BGO LP/CD 77)*

—— **CLIVE BROOKS** – drums (ex-EGG) repl. PUSTELNIK

Oct 72.	(lp) *(UAG 29419) <UA 008>* **HOGWASH**	□	□

– I love Miss Ogyny / You had a lesson / The ringmaster / 3744 James Road / Sad is the hunter / S'one song / Earth shanty / Mr. Hooker, Sir John. *(re-iss. Apr89 on 'Beat Goes On' lp/cd; BGO LP/CD 44) (cd re-iss. May91;)*

W.W.A.   W.W.A.

Oct 73.	(lp; T.S. McPHEE; solo) *(WWA 1)* **THE TWO SIDES OF TONY (T.S.) McPHEE**	□	-

– Three times seven / All my money, alimoney / Morning's eyes / Dog me, bitch / Take it out / The hunt. *(cd-iss. Dec92 on 'Castle';)*

Nov 73.	(7") *(WWS 006)* **SAD GO ROUND. / OVER BLUE**		
Jun 74.	(lp) *(WWA 004)* **SOLID**	31	

– Light my light / Free from all alarm / Sins of the father / Sad go round / Corn cob / Plea sing plea song / Snowstorm / Jokers grave. *(cd-iss. Oct91 on 'Castle'; CLACD 266)*

Aug 74.	(7") *(WWS 012)* **PLEA SING – PLEA SONG. / Tony McPhee: DOG ME BITCH**	□	□

—— **McPHEE** brought back **PETE CRUIKSHANK** – rhythm guitar, / plus new members **DAVE WELLBELOVE** – guitar / **MARTIN KENT** – bass / **MICK COOK** – drums

U.A.   U.A.

Feb 76.	(lp) *(UAG 29917) <LA 603>* **CROSSCUT SAW**	□	□

– Crosscut saw / Promiscuity / Boogie withus / Fulfilment / Live a little lady / Three way split / Mean mistreater / Eleventh hour.

Mar 76.	(7") *(UP 36095)* **LIVE A LITTLE LADY. / BOOGIE WITHUS**	□	□

—— **RICK ADAMS** – rhythm guitar repl. PETE

Oct 76.	(lp) *(UAG 29994) <LA 680>* **BLACK DIAMOND**	□	□

– Body talk / Fantasy partner / Live right / Country blues / Your love keeps me alive / Friendzy / Pastoral future / Black diamond.

Oct 76.	(7"; as TONY McPHEE & GROUNDHOGS) *(UP 36177)* **PASTORAL FUTURE. / LIVE RIGHT**	□	□

—— split '77. **McPHEE** formed **TERRAPLANE**, with **ALAN FISH** – bass / **WILGUR CAMPBELL** – drums. They appeared on album CHECKIN' IT OUT by 'BILLY BOY ARNOLD'. (1979 split) **TONY** formed **TURBO** ('79-'83) with **CLIVE BROOKS** – drums / **PAUL RAVEN**

TONY McPHEE BAND

with **MICK MIRTON** – drums / **STEVE TOWNER** – bass

T.S.   not iss.

May 83.	(7"; sold at gigs) *(TS 001)* **TIME OF ACTION. / BORN TO BE WITH YOU**	□	-

GROUNDHOGS

McPHEE with **ALAN FISH** – bass / **MICK MIRTON** – drums

Conquest   not iss.

May 85.	(lp) *(QUEST 1)* **RAZOR'S EDGE**	□	-

– Razor's edge / I confess / Born to be with you / One more chance / The protector / Superseded / Moving fast, standing still / I want you to love me. *(re-iss. Nov89 on 'Landslide'; BUTLP 005) (cd-iss. Oct92; BUTCD 005)*

—— (Early '86) **DAVE THOMPSON** – bass repl. FISH who joined DUMPY'S RUSTY NUTS / **KEN PUSTELNIK** – drums returned to repl. MIRTON who joined DUMPY'S RUSTY NUTS. They gigged several times and appeared on Radio 2's 'Rhythm and Blues'.

—— **DAVE ANDERSON** – bass (ex-AMON DUUL II, ex-HAWKWIND) repl. THOMPSON / **MIKE JONES** – drums repl. PUSTELNIK

Demi-Monde   not iss.

May 87.	(lp) *(DMLP 1014)* **BACK AGAINST THE WALL**	□	-

– Back against the wall / No to submission / Blue boar blues / Waiting in shadows / Ain't no slaver / Stick to your guns / In the meantime / 54156. *(cd-iss. Jul87 on 'The CD Label'; CDTL 005)*

—— ANDERSON re-formed AMON DUUL II, taking with him McPHEE as guest

TONY McPHEE and the GROUNDHOGS

recorded album below

Apr 88. (d-lp) *(DMLP 1016)* **HOGS ON THE ROAD (live)** □ □
– Express man / Strange town / Eccentric man / 3744 James Road / I want you to love me / Split IV / Soldier / Back against the wall / Garden / Split I / Waiting in shadows / Light my light / Me and the Devil / Mistreated / Groundhogs blues / Split II / Cherry red. *(cd-iss. Aug88 on 'The CD Label'; CDTL 008) (cd re-iss. Mar94 on 'Thunderbolt'; CDTB 114)*

H.T.D.   not iss.

Aug 89. (lp/cd) *(HTD LP/CD 2)* **NO SURRENDER** □ □
– Razor's edge / 3744 James Road / Superseded / Light my light / One more chance / Garden. *(cd+=)* – Split (pt.2) / Eccentric man / Strange town / Cherry red. *(re-iss. Dec90 cd/lp; same)*

Feb 93. (cd; TONY McPHEE) *(HTDCD 10)* **FOOLISH PRIDE** □ □
– Foolish pride / Every minute / Devil you know / Masqueradin' / Time after time / On the run / Took me by surprise / Whatever it takes / Been there done that / I'm gonna win. *(re-iss. Sep96; same)*

Dec 94. (cd; as TONY (T.S.) McPHEE) *(HTDCD 26)* **SLIDE T.S. SLIDE** □ □
– Reformed man / Mean dispostion / Slide to slide / From a pawn to a king / Tell me baby / Hooker & the hogs / Someday, baby / Driving duck / No place to go / Me & the Devil / Death letter / Can't be satisfied / Still a fool / Write me a few short lines / Down in the bottom. *(re-iss. Sep96; same)*

Apr 97. (cd) *(HTDCD 72)* **BLEACHING THE BLUES** □ □
– When you're down / All your women / There's a light / Went in like a lamb / When your man has gone / Many times / All last night / When you're walking down the street / Meeting of the minds / Bleaching the blues / If I had possession / Love in vain / Floatin' bridge / Terraplane blues / Little red rooster.

– compilations etc. –

Sep 74. (d-lp) *United Artists; (UDF 31) <60063-4>* **GROUNDHOGS' BEST 1969-1972** □ □
– Groundhog / Strange town / Bog roll blues / You had a lesson / Express man / Eccentric man / Earth is not room enough / BDD / Split part 1 / Cherry red / Mistreated / 3744 James Road / Soldier / Sad is the hunter / Garden / Split part 4 / Amazing grace. *(re-iss. Mar88 on 'Beat Goes On' d-lp/cd; BGO DLP/MC 1) (cd-iss. Mar90 on 'E.M.I.'; CDP 7-90434-2)*

Apr 84. (d-lp) *Psycho; (PSYCHO 24)* **HOGGIN' THE STAGE** □ -
(with free 7") *(cd-iss. Nov95 on 'Receiver'; RRCD 207)*

May 86. (d-lp/c) *Raw Power; (RAW LP/TC 021)* **MOVING FAST, STANDING STILL** □ □
– RAZOR'S EDGE & 'THE TWO SIDES OF T.S. McPHEE', incl. 4 extra 'Immediate' 45's)

Jun 92. (cd) *Beat Goes On; (BGOCD 131)* **CROSSCUT SAW / BLACK DIAMOND** □ □

Dec 92. (cd/c) *Connoisseur; (CSAP CD/MC 112)* **DOCUMENT SERIES PRESENTS (CLASSIC ALBUM CUTS 1968-1976)** □ □
– Still a fool / Walking blues / Mistreated / Express man / Eccentric man / Status people / Cherry red / Split (part IV) / Wages of peace / Amazing Grace / Love you Miss Ogyny / Earth shanty / Live a little lady / Boogie with us / Pastoral future / Live right.

Jul 93. (d-cd) *H.T.D.; (HTDCD 12)* **GROUNDHOG NIGHT – GROUNDHOGS LIVE (live)** □ □

Sep 94. (cd) *Windsong; (WINCD 064)* **BBC RADIO 1 LIVE IN CONCERT** □ □

Feb 96. (4xcd-box) *E.M.I.; (CDHOGS 1)* **FOUR GROUNDHOGS ORIGINALS** □ □
– (SCRATCHING THE SURFACE / BLUES OBITUARY / THANK CHRIST FOR THE BOMB / SPLIT)

Oct 96. (cd; as TONY McPHEE'S GROUNDHOGS) *Indigo; (IGOCD 2058)* **WHO SAID CHERRY RED?** □ □

Feb 97. (cd) *EMI Gold; (CDGOLD 1074)* **THE BEST OF** □ □

Jun 97. (cd; with HERBAL MIXTURE) *Distortions; (D 1012)* **PLEASE LEAVE MY MIND** □ □

TONY McPHEE

also released other solo work.

1968. (lp) *Liberty; (LBS 83190)* **ME AND THE DEVIL** □ □
(contributed some tracks to below compilation)

1969. (lp) *Liberty; (LBS 83252)* **I ASKED FOR WATER, SHE GAVE ME GASOLINE** □ □

—— Next credited with **JO-ANN KELLY**

1971. (lp) *Sunset; (SLS 50209)* **SAME THING ON THEIR MINDS** □ □

Apr 98. (cd) *Beat Goes On; (BGOCD 332)* **ME AND THE DEVIL / I ASKED FOR WATER SHE GAVE ME GASOLINE** □ □

David GRUBBS (see under ⇒ SQUIRREL BAIT)

G.T.R. (see under ⇒ HACKETT, Steve)

GUESS WHO

Formed: Winnipeg, Canada . . . as AL & THE SILVERTONES in 1959 by CHAD ALLAN. After a few singles with CHAD as credited leader, they became The GUESS WHO? in 1965, the line-up being completed by RANDY BACHMAN, BOB ASHLEY, JIM KALE and GARY PETERSON. Almost immediately, the band had their first taste of US success with the Top 30 single, 'SHAKIN' ALL OVER' (once the property of JOHNNY KIDD & THE PIRATES). ALLAN subsequently quit the band to go to university, although they had already enlisted BURTON CUMMINGS in their quartet, ASHLEY too, having departed. The group eventually established themselves in the more lucrative American market with the 'WHEATFIELD SOUL' (1969) album and its two Top 10 singles, 'THESE EYES' and 'LAUGHING', although their greatest success came with 'AMERICAN WOMAN' (1970). Its raucous title track topped the American Hot 100, a juddering behemoth of a record fuelled by guitar distortion and a testosterone-saturated verve; CUMMINGS sounded like JIM MORRISON after a particularly heavy night on the whisky and cigs. The same year, The GUESS WHO were unlikely guests at the White House, where they performed for President Richard Nixon, as well as Prince Charles and Princess Anne. It wasn't all celebrations, though, as BACHMAN (who had recently become a Mormon) found the band's rock'n'roll lifestyle incompatible with his newfound beliefs and promptly left. While he later went on to major success with BACHMAN TURNER OVERDRIVE, the hits began to dry up after the successful 'SHARE THE LAND' (1971) set and the Top 20 'RAIN DANCE' single. Line-up changes dogged the band as they trundled on towards the mid-70's, a one-off return to the Top 10 coming with 1974's novelty hit, 'CLAP FOR THE WOLFMAN', the hirsute creature in question being radio DJ, Wolfman Jack (apparently!). When GUESS WHO finally disbanded in Autumn 1975, CUMMINGS and TROIANO both went solo, while PETERSON formed DELPHIA. The former's career, in particular, got off to an auspicious start, CUMMINGS' debut solo single, 'STAND TALL', almost as successful as 'AMERICAN WOMAN', while his eponymous debut made the Top 30. When the band have reformed on occasion, interest has been minimal; nevertheless, they remain one of the biggest selling acts in Canadian music history.

Album rating: SHAKIN' ALL OVER (*3) / WHEATFIELD SOUL (*6) / CANNED WHEAT PACKED BY THE GUESS WHO (*7) / AMERICAN WOMAN (*5) / SHARE THE LAND (*6) / THE BEST OF THE GUESS WHO compilation (*7) / SO LONG, BANNATYNE (*5) / ROCKIN' (*4) / LIVE AT THE PARAMOUNT (SEATTLE) (*3) / ARTIFICIAL PARADISE (*4) / #10 (*4) / THE BEST OF THE GUESS WHO, VOLUME II compilation (*5) / ROAD FOOD (*5) / FLAVOURS (*3) / POWER IN THE MUSIC (*4) / THE GREATEST HITS OF THE GUESS WHO compilation (*6) / LONELY ONE (*3) / THE ULTIMATE COLLECTION compilation (*7)

CHAD ALLAN & THE REFLECTIONS

CHAD ALLAN (b. ALLAN KOBEL, 1945) – vocals, guitar / **BOB ASHLEY** – piano / **RANDY BACHMAN** (b.27 Sep'43) – guitar / **JIM KALE** (b.11 Aug'43) – bass / **GARY PETERSON** (b.26 May'45) – drums

	not iss.	Quality
Mar 63. (7") <802> **BACK AND FORTH. / I JUST DON'T HAVE THE HEART**	-	- Canada
——— (above initially released in 1962 'Canadian-American' label)		
Dec 63. (7") **SHY GUY. /**	-	- Canada
Jun 64. (7"; as CHAD ALLAN & THE ORIGINAL REFLECTIONS) **A SHOT OF RHYTHM & BLUES. /**	-	- Canada
	not iss.	Mala
1964. (7") <12033> **THROUGH THE LOOKING GLASS. / RAMONA'S HOURGLASS**	-	

——— now as CHAD ALLAN & THE EXPRESSIONS, although due to their label, 'Quality', doing a silly publicity stunt they were credited on the following 45 as . . .

GUESS WHO?

	Pye Inter.	Scepter
May 65. (7") (7N 25305) <1295> **SHAKIN' ALL OVER. / TILL WE KISSED**		22
Jul 65. (lp; as GUESS WHO? CHAD ALLAN & THE EXPRESSIONS) <533> **SHAKIN' ALL OVER**	-	

– Shakin' all over / Seven long years / And she's mine / Clock in the wall / Baby's birthday / I want you to love me / I'd rather be alone / I've been away / Turn around and walk away. <US re-iss. 1968 under name "GUESS WHO">

——— **BURTON CUMMINGS** (b.31 Dec'47) – vocals, keyboards repl. ASHLEY

GUESS WHO

——— name adopted as their own

Aug 65. (7") <12108> **HEY HO, WHAT YOU DO TO ME. / GOODNIGHT, GOODNIGHT**	-	
Nov 65. (7") <12118> **HURTING EACH OTHER. / BABY'S BIRTHDAY**	-	
Feb 66. (7") <12131> **BABY FEELIN'. / BELIEVE IN ME**	-	
Jun 66. (7") <12144> **CLOCK ON THE WALL. / ONE DAY**	-	

——— A quartet, when ALLAN departed. (He was briefly subbed by BRUCE DECKER)

	King	Amy
Oct 66. (7") <967> **SHE'S ALL MINE. / ALL RIGHT**	-	
Dec 66. (7") (KG 1044) <976> **HIS GIRL. / IT'S MY PRIDE**	45	
	Fontana	not iss.
May 67. (7") (TF 831) **THIS TIME LONG AGO. / THERE'S NO GETTING AWAY FROM YOU**		-
Sep 67. (7") (TF 861) **MISS FELICITY GREY. / FLYING ON THE GROUND IS WRONG**		-

——— In 1968, ALLAN returned but left as they signed to 'Nimbus 6' in Canada.

	R.C.A.	R.C.A.
Apr 69. (7") (RCA 1832) <74-0102> **THESE EYES. / LIGHTFOOT**		6
May 69. (lp) (SF 8037) <LSP 4171> **WHEATFIELD SOUL**		45

– These eyes / Pink wine sparkles in the glass / I found her in a star / Friends of mine / When you touch me / A Wednesday in your garden / Lightfoot / Love and a yellow rose / Maple fudge / We're coming to dinner.

Jul 69. (7") (RCA 1832) <74-0195> **LAUGHING. / UNDUN**		10
		22
Sep 69. (lp) <LSP 4157> **CANNED WHEAT PACKED BY THE GUESS WHO**	-	91

– No time / Minstrel boy / Laughing / Undun / 6 a.m. or nearer / Old Joe / Of a dropping pin / Key fair warning.

Oct 69. (7") <74-0223> **FRIENDS OF MINE. / (part 2)**	-	
Feb 70. (7") (RCA 1925) <74-0300> **NO TIME. / PROPER STRANGER**	-	5 Dec69
Feb 70. (lp) (SF 8107) <LSP 4266> **AMERICAN WOMAN**		9

– American woman / No time / Talisman / No sugar tonight / New Mother Nature / 969 (the oldies man) / When friends fall out / 8:15 / Proper stranger / Humpty's blues / American woman – epilogue.

Mar 70. (7") (RCA 1943) <74-0325> **AMERICAN WOMAN. / NO SUGAR TONIGHT**	19	1

——— **CUMMINGS, PETERSON & KALE** brought in newcomers **KURT WINTER** (b. 2 Apr'46) – guitar (ex-BROTHER) + **GREG LESKIW** (b. 5 Aug'47) – guitar (ex-WILD RICE) repl. RANDY BACHMAN who formed BRAVE BELT, later BACHMAN-TURNER OVERDRIVE.

Jul 70. (7") (RCA 1994) <74-0367> **HAND ME DOWN WORLD. / RUNNIN' DOWN THE STREET**		17
Oct 70. (7") (RCA 2026) <74-0388> **SHARE THE LAND. / BUS RIDER**		10
Jan 71. (lp) (RCA 2026) <LSP 4359> **SHARE THE LAND**		14 Oct70

– Bus rider / Do you miss me darlin' / Hand me down world / Moan for you Joe / Share the land / Hang on to your life / Coming down off the money bag – Song of the dog / Three more days.

Mar 71. (7") (RCA 2065) <74-0414> **HANG ON TO YOUR LIFE. / DO YOU MISS ME DARLIN'**		43 Jan71
Apr 71. (7") <74-0458> **ALBERT FLASHER. / BROKEN**	-	29
		55
Apr 71. (lp) (AFLI 2594) <LSPX 1004> **THE BEST OF THE GUESS WHO** (compilation)		12

– These eyes / Laughing / Undun / No time / American woman / No sugar tonight / New Mother Nature / Hand me down world / Bus rider / Share the land / Do you miss me darlin' / Hang on to your life.

Aug 71. (7") <74-0522> **RAIN DANCE. / ONE DIVIDED**	-	19
Sep 71. (lp) (SF 8216) <LSP 4574> **SO LONG, BANNATYNE**	-	52 Aug71

– Rain dance / She might have been a nice girl / Goin' a little crazy / Fiddlin' / Pain train / One divided / Grey day / Life in the bloodstream / One man army / Sour suite / So long, Bannatyne.

Nov 71. (7") <74-0578> **SOUR SUITE. / LIFE IN THE BLOODSTREAM**	-	50
Mar 72. (7") <74-0659> **HEARTBROKEN BOPPER. / ARRIVEDERCI GIRL**	-	47
Mar 72. (lp) (SF 8269) <LSP 4602> **ROCKIN'**	-	79

– Heartbroken bopper / Get your ribbons on / Smoke big factory / Arrivederci girl / Guns, guns, guns / Running bear / Back to the city / Your Nashville sneakers / Herbert's a loser / Sea of love – Heaven only moved once yesterday / Don't you want me.

May 72. (7") <74-0708> **GUNS, GUNS, GUNS. / HEAVEN ONLY MOVED ONCE YESTERDAY**	-	

——— **DON McDOUGALL** (b. 5 Nov'47) – guitar repl. LESKIW who formed MOOD JGA JGA

Sep 72. (7") <74-0803> **RUNNIN' BACK TO SASKATOON. / NEW MOTHER NATURE**	-	
Sep 72. (lp) (SF 8329) <LSP 4779> **LIVE AT THE PARAMOUNT, SEATTLE (live)**		39 Aug72

– Albert Fletcher / New Mother Nature / Glace Bay blues / American woman / Runnin' back to Saskatoon / Pain train / Truckin' off across the sky.

——— **BILL WALLACE** (b.18 May'49) – bass (ex-BROTHER) repl. KALE who formed own band

Feb 73. (lp) (SF 8349) <LSP 4830> **ARTIFICIAL PARADISE**		Jan 73

– Bye bye baby / Samantha's living room / Rock and roller steam / Follow your daughter home / Those showbiz shoes / All hashed out / Orly / Lost and found town / Hamba gahle-usalang gahle / The watcher.

Apr 73. (7") (RCA 2361) <74-0880> **FOLLOW YOUR DAUGHTER HOME. / BYE BYE BABY**		Jan73
Jun 73. (7") <74-0926> **THE WATCHER. / ORLY**	-	
Aug 73. (7") <74-0977> **GLAMOUR BOY. / LIE DOWN**	-	
Aug 73. (lp) <APL-1 0130> **#10**		Jan73

– Take it off my shoulders / Musicione / Miss Frizzy / Glamour boy / Self pity / Lie down / Cardboard empire / Just let me sing.

Jan 74. (lp) <APLI 0269> **THE BEST OF THE GUESS WHO, VOLUME II** (compilation)	-	
Feb 74. (7") <0217> **STAR BABY. / MUSICIONE**	-	39
May 74. (lp) <APL-1 0405> **ROAD FOOD**	-	60

– Star baby / Attila's blues / Straight out / Don't you want me / One way road to Hell / Clap for the Wolfman / Pleasin' for a reason / Road food / Ballad of the last five years.

Jul 74. (7") (RCA 2455) <0324> **CLAP FOR THE WOLFMAN. / ROAD FOOD**		6

——— **DOMENIC TROIANO** – guitar (ex-JAMES GANG) repl. WINTER and McDOUGALL

Feb 75. (7") (RCA 2502) <10075> **DANCIN' FOOL. / SEEMS LIKE I CAN'T LIVE WITHOUT YOU**		28 Nov74
Feb 75. (lp) (SF 8399) <APL-1 0636> **FLAVOURS**		48 Jan75

– Dancin' fool / Hoe down time / Nobody knows his name / Diggin' yourself / Seems like I can't live without you / Dirty eye / Loves me like a brother / Long gone.

May 75. (7") <10216> **HOE DOWN TIME. / LOVES ME LIKE A BROTHER**	-	
Aug 75. (lp) (RS 1017) <APL-1 0995> **POWER IN THE MUSIC**		87 Jul75

– Down and out woman / Women / When the band was singin' "Shakin' All Over" / Dreams / Rich world – poor world / Shopping bag lady / Coors for Sunday / Rosanne / Power in the music.

Aug 75. (7") <10360> **DREAMS. / ROSANNE**	-	
Nov 75. (7") <10410> **WHEN THE BAND WAS SINGIN' "SHAKIN' ALL OVER". / WOMEN**	-	

——— disbanded Autumn '75; TROIANO went solo and PETERSON formed DELPHIA. CUMMINGS had the most success, breaking the Top 30 with his eponymous debut

GUESS WHO

——— re-formed in 1978 without CUMMINGS. Line-up **JIM KALE** – bass / **DON McDOUGALL** – guitar / plus **ALAN McDOUGALL** – vocals / **DAVID INGLIS** – guitar / **VINCE MASTERS** – drums / **DAVIS PARASZ** – horns

	not iss.	Elektra
1978. (7") <45698> **TRULY GOOD SONG. / EVERY DAY'S A LOVELY DAY**	-	
	not iss.	Hilltak
Jan 79. (lp) <19299> **ALL THIS FOR A SONG**	-	

– C'mon little mama / That's the moment / It's getting pretty bad / Raisin' hell on the prairies / Moon wave maker / Taxman / Sharin' love / Sweet young thing / All this for a song / Plastic Paradise.

Jan 79. (7") <7603> **C'MON LITTLE MAMA. / MOON WAVE MAKER**	-	
Apr 79. (7") <7803> **SWEET YOUNG THING. / C'MON LITTLE MAMA**	-	
Jun 79. (7") <7808> **SWEET YOUNG THING. / IT'S GETTING PRETTY BAD**	-	

——— disbanded soon after above release

——— late 60's line-up re-formed (**CUMMINGS, BACHMAN, KALE + PETERSON**)

	not iss.	Ready
1984. (lp) <LR 049> **TOGETHER AGAIN (live)**	-	

– What's gonna happen to the kids / Let's watch the Sun go down / No time / Those eyes / Creepin' peepin' baby blues / C'mon and dance / Undun / Love grows / No sugar tonight – New mother nature / American woman.

—— mid-90's line-up:- **KALE + PETERSON** alongside **TERRY HATTY** – vocals (repl. late 80's member KEN CARTER) / **DALE RUSSELL** – vocals, guitar / **LEONARD SHAW** – keyboards (repl. late 80's member MIKE HANFORD)

		not iss.	Intersound
1995.	(cd) <9158> **LONELY ONE**	-	-

– Lonely one / Love's all that matters / Sweet liberty / Haunted heart / Anything for love / Still feels like love / Razor's edge / I feel your pain / Amy / Rock'n'roll classic.

– compilations, etc. –

1973.	(lp) *Pride*; <0012 **HISTORY OF THE GUESS WHO**	-	
1974.	(d-lp) *Trip*; <TSX 3502> **BORN IN CANADA (1965-68)**	-	
1976.	(lp) *R.C.A.*; (APL-1 1778) **THE WAY THEY WERE**	-	
May 77.	(lp) *R.C.A.*; (APL-1 2253) **GREATEST HITS OF THE GUESS WHO**		Apr77

– These eyes / Laughing / Undun / No time / American woman / Hand me down world / Stay baby / Clap for the Wolfman / Dancin' fool / Glamour boy / Albert Flasher / When the band was singing "Shaking All Over".

1977.	(7") *R.C.A.*; <10716> **SILVERBIRD. / RUNNIN' DOWN THE STREET**	-	
1987.	(7") *Old Gold*; (OG) **AMERICAN WOMAN. / (other artist)**	-	-

---

GUIDED BY VOICES (dig out; Great Alt & Indie . . .)

GULLIVER (see under ⇒ HALL, Daryl)

GUN

Formed: Glasgow, Scotland . . . 1986 by BABY STAFFORD and MARK RANKIN. Originally called HAIRSPRAY TO HEAVEN then PHOBIA, before opting simply for GUN, the band's line-up was completed by guitarist GUILIANO GIZZI, his brother DANTE on bass and SCOTT SHIELDS on drums. In late 1987, they signed to 'A&M', soon making the UK Top 50 lists with their debut 1989 album, 'TAKING ON THE WORLD'. Along with TEXAS (whose SHARLEEN SPITERI guested on their debut) and SLIDE (anyone remember them?), the band were hailed as the saviours of the Scottish rock scene although in truth, if any group was up to that mammoth task then it was PRIMAL SCREAM, GUN essentially another bunch of workmanlike grafters in the mode of DEL AMITRI or DEACON BLUE, if a bit heavier. Their debut single, the pop/rock of 'BETTER DAYS', was a minor Top 40 hit, the album lingering on the fringes of the chart. The songwriting was competent enough and the band did have a certain cocksure swagger that caught the eye of MICK JAGGER and KEITH RICHARDS, who duly invited GUN to support them on the UK leg of their 'Urban Jungle' tour. STAFFORD quickly became disillusioned, however, departing soon after. Replacing him with ALEX DICKSON, the band began work on a new album, 'GALLUS' (1992), a more organic, harder-hitting affair that almost made the Top 10 and spawned the group's first Top 30 single, 'STEAL YOUR FIRE'. By 1994's 'SWAGGER', DICKSON had left and MARK KERR had replaced SHIELDS on the drum stool. The first single from the album was a horrendous, club-footed re-hash of CAMEO's funk classic, 'WORD UP', although ironically/predictably, the song gave them a Top 10 hit at long last. Buoyed by the single's success (and to be fair, it wasn't wholly representative of the album), the album went Top 5. In 1997, G.U.N. (as they were now called) disappointed many of their fans with their new pop/rock-orientated material, which sounded more like a poor man's INXS. • **Songwriters:** RANKIN-GIZZI-GIZZI except; LET'S GO CRAZY (Prince) / DON'T BELIEVE A WORD (Thin Lizzy) / CHILDREN OF THE REVOLUTION (T.Rex) / SUFFRAGETTE CITY (David Bowie) / PANIC (Smiths) / KILLING IN THE NAME (Rage Against The Machine) / SO LONELY (Police) / ARE YOU GONNA GO MY WAY (Lenny Kravitz).
Album rating: TAKING ON THE WORLD (*6) / GALLUS (*5) / SWAGGER (*5) / 0141 632 6326 (*5)

MARK RANKIN – vocals / **BABY STAFFORD** – guitar / **GUILIANO GIZZI** – guitar / **DANTE GIZZI** – bass / **SCOTT SHIELDS** – drums

		A&M	A&M
May 89.	(lp/c/cd) (AMA/AMC/CDA 7007) <5285> **TAKING ON THE WORLD**	44	

– Better days / The feeling within / Inside out / Shame on you / Money (everybody loves her) / Taking on the world / Shame / Can't get any lower / Something to believe in / Girls in love / I will be waiting. (re-iss. Mar95 cd/c; 397007-2/-4)

Jun 89.	(7") (AM 505) <1482> **BETTER DAYS. / WHEN YOU LOVE SOMEBODY**	33	
	(12"+=/cd-s+=) (AMY/CDEE 505) – Coming home.		
Aug 89.	(7") (AM 520) **MONEY (EVERYBODY LOVES HER). / PRIME TIME**	73	-
	(12"+=/12"pic-d+=/cd-s+=) (AMY/AMP/CDEE 520) – Dance.		
Oct 89.	(7"/7"s/7"pic-d) (AM/+S/P 531) **INSIDE OUT. / BACK TO WHERE WE STARTED**	57	-
	(12"+=/cd-s+=/d7"+=) (AMY/CDEE/AMB 531) – Where do we go?		
Jan 90.	(7"/7"s) (AM/+S 541) **TAKING ON THE WORLD. / DON'T BELIEVE A WORD**	50	-
	(12"+=/cd-s+=) (AMY/CDEE 541) – Better days (extended).		
Jun 90.	(7"/c-s) (AM/+MC 573) **SHAME ON YOU. / BETTER DAYS (live)**	33	-
	(12"+=/12"s+=/cd-s+=) (AM X/T/CD 573) – Money (everybody loves her).		
	(12") (AMY 573) – ('A'remixes).		

—— **ALEX DICKSON** – guitar repl. BABY STAFFORD

Mar 92.	(7"/c-s) (AM/+MC 851) **STEAL YOUR FIRE. / DON'T BLAME ME**	24	-
	(12"+=/cd-s+=) (AM Y/CD 851) – Burning down the house / Reach out for love.		
Apr 92.	(7"/c-s) (AM/+MC 869) **HIGHER GROUND. / RUN**	48	-
	(12"+=/pic-cd-s+=) (AM Y/CD 869) – One desire.		
Apr 92.	(cd/c/lp) (395383-2/-4/-1) **GALLUS**	14	

– Steal your fire / Money to burn / Long road / Welcome to the real world / Higher ground / Borrowed time / Freedom / Won't break down / Reach out for love / Watching the world go by. (re-iss. Mar95 cd/c; 395383-2/-4)

Jun 92.	(7"/c-s) (AM/+MC 885) **WELCOME TO THE REAL WORLD. / STEAL YOUR FIRE (live)**	43	-
	(12"pic-d+=) (AMY 885) – Standing in your shadow.		
	(cd-s+=) (AMCD 885) – Better days / Shame on you (acoustic).		

—— **MARK KERR** – drums; repl. SHIELDS + DICKSON

Jul 94.	(7"/c-s) (580 664-7/-4) **WORD UP. / STAY FOREVER**	8	
	(cd-s+=) (580 665-2) – The man I used to be / Stranger.		
	(cd-s) (580 667-2) – ('A'mixes).		
	(12") (580 665-1) – ('A'mixes).		
Aug 94.	(cd/c) (540 254-2/-4) **SWAGGER**	5	

– Stand in line / Find my way / Word up / Don't say it's over / The only one / Something worthwhile / Seems like I'm losing you / Crying over you / One reason / Vicious heart.

Sep 94.	(7") (580 754-7) **DON'T SAY IT'S OVER. / STEAL YOUR FIRE**	19	
	(cd-s+=) (580 755-2) – Shame on you.		
	(cd-s) (580 752-2) – ('A'side) / Better days / Money (everybody loves her).		
Feb 95.	(c-s) (580 953-4) **THE ONLY ONE / WORD UP (mix) / WORD UP (Tinman remix)**	29	
	(12"+=) (580 953-1) – Inside out – So lonely.		
	(cd-s++=) (580 953-2) – Time.		
	(cd-s) (580 955-2) – ('A'side) / Killing in the name / Panic / Are you gonna go my way.		
Apr 95.	(cd-ep) (581 043-2) **SOMETHING WORTHWHILE / SUFFRAGETTE CITY / CHILDREN OF THE REVOLUTION / WORD UP**	39	
	(cd-ep) (581 045-2) – ('A'side) / One reason / ('A'-Mac attack mix) / ('A'-Priory mix).		
	(12"pic-d-ep) (581 043-1) – ('A'side) / ('A'-Mac attack mix) / ('A'-King Dong mix) / ('A'-Breakdown mix).		

G.U.N.

Apr 97.	(cd-s) (582 191-2) **CRAZY YOU / SOME THINGS NEVER CHANGE / A WOMAN LIKE YOU**	21	
	(c-s/cd-s) (582 193-4/-2) – ('A'side) / ('A'-K.M. mix) / ('A'instrumental) / ('A'demo).		
May 97.	(cd/c/lp) (540 723-2/-4/-1) **0141 632 6326**	32	

– Rescue you / Crazy you / Seventeen / All my love / My sweet Jane / Come a long way / All I ever wanted / I don't mind / Going down / Always friends.

Jun 97.	(c-s) (582 279-4) **MY SWEET JANE / GOING DOWN (Mizzy Hog mix)**	51	
	(cd-s+=) (582 279-2) – Crazy you / Word up (Tinman mix).		
	(cd-s) (582 277-2) – ('A'side) / Don't cry / Sometimes.		

GUN CLUB / Jeffrey Lee PIERCE

(dig out; Great Alt & Indie . . .)

GUNS N' ROSES

Formed: Los Angeles, California, USA . . . early 1985 by AXL ROSE, IZZY STRADLIN and moonlighting L.A. GUNS member TRACII GUNS, who was soon to return to said outfit. With the addition of SLASH, DUFF McKAGAN and STEVEN ADLER, the seminal G N' R line-up was complete, the ramshackle collection of petty thieves and drug addicts subsequently embarking on the 'hell' tour of the US. Although this outing was a disaster, the band created a major buzz with their residency at L.A.'s Troubadour club and in the summer of '86 unleashed their debut recording, a 7"ep entitled 'LIVE ?!*' LIKE A SUICIDE'. A short, sharp shock of visceral rock'n'raunch, the record struck a major chord with critics and fans alike, quickly selling out of its limited 10,000 pressing. Snapped up by 'Geffen', the band released their debut album, 'APPETITE FOR DESTRUCTION', the following year. A head-on collision of AC/DC, AEROSMITH and The SEX PISTOLS, what the record lacked in originality, it made up for with sheer impact. The opening unholy trinity ('WELCOME TO THE JUNGLE', 'IT'S SO EASY', 'NIGHTRAIN') alone laid the rest of the L.A. hairspray pack to waste, while with 'PARADISE CITY' and 'SWEET CHILD O' MINE', the band staked their claim to chart domination and stadium stardom. In spite of its controversial cover art featuring a robot raping a woman (later withdrawn), the record went on to sell a staggering 20 million copies worldwide and remains one of metal's defining moments. It also remains one of the most vivid portrayals of the claustrophobic seediness of the L.A. metal scene in much the same way as N.W.A. captured the fuck-you nihilism of the city's black ghetto with 'Straight Outta Compton'. Live, GUNS N' ROSES were caustic and volatile, as likely to produce tabloid headlines as blistering performances. Image wise, they had SLASH as an unmistakable focal point; his trademark top hat perched on a nest of thick curls that all but obscured his face, fag constantly hanging from his lips a la KEITH RICHARDS. Controversy turned into tragedy the following summer, however, when two fans were crushed to death during a G N' R set at the 1988 Castle Donington Monsters Of Rock festival. Later that year, the band released 'G N' R LIES', a half live/ half studio affair that combined their earlier EP with four new acoustic numbers. On the lovely 'PATIENCE', ROSE was transformed from sneering vocal acrobat to mellow songsmith, although by 'ONE IN A MILLION', he was back to his old ways with a vengeance. While the song was performed with undeniable passion, it was all the more worrying given the subjects he was railing against. The track was basically an unforgivable tirade of abuse aimed at 'niggers', 'faggots' and 'immigrants', hmmm.. ironic? Yeah, right. Still, the good citizens of America snapped up the record and it peaked at No.2. in the US, No.22 in Britain. Come 1990, the band were supporting The ROLLING STONES on a world tour, their star status rapidly assuming the same magnitude as their drug habits. ADLER's heroin problems eventually saw him kicked out later that summer, CULT drummer MATT SORUM taking his place on the drum stool. The band also recruited a keyboard player, DIZZY REED, a sure sign they were beginning to lose the plot. A terminally dull cover of DYLAN's 'KNOCKIN' ON HEAVEN'S DOOR' (included on the 'Days Of Thunder' soundtrack) seemed to confirm this although 'CIVIL WAR', their contribution to Romanian orphan project, 'Nobody's Child', was more encouraging. When it eventually surfaced, the band's next studio project, 'USE YOUR ILLUSION' (1991), was a resounding disappointment. The very fact they released the disc in 2 volumes showed a severe lack of objectivity and needless to say, the quality control was non-existent. A sprawling, unfocused jumble, the collection nevertheless included a few inspired moments (notably the classic 'NOVEMBER RAIN') and both albums reached Nos. 1 and 2 respectively in both Britain and America. During the subsequent world tour, STRADLIN walked out, finally leaving the band soon after for a solo career (his replacement was GILBY CLARKE). Among the dates on the record breaking 28-month world tour was a performance at AIDS benefit concert, The Freddie Mercury Tribute, rather ironic in light of ROSE's lyrical homophobic tendencies. The bandana'ed one courted further outrage when the group included a CHARLES MANSON song on their 1993 covers album, 'THE SPAGHETTI INCIDENT', a record that also saw the band rework their faves from NAZARETH to The UK SUBS. They also massacred 'SYMPATHY FOR THE DEVIL' for the 'Interview With The Vampire' soundtrack, their last studio recording to date. CLARKE has subsequently left the band following a solo release, 'PAWNSHOP GUITARS', while SLASH also released a side project, 'IT'S FIVE O'CLOCK SOMEWHERE', in 1995 under the moniker SLASH'S SNAKEPIT. • **Songwriters:** All written by AXL except; MAMA KIN (Aerosmith) / NICE BOYS DON'T PLAY ROCK'N'ROLL (Rose Tattoo) / WHOLE LOTTA ROSIE (Ac-Dc) / LIVE AND LET DIE (Paul McCartney & Wings). Punk covers album; SINCE I DON'T HAVE YOU (Skyliners) / NEW ROSE (Damned) / DOWN ON THE FARM (UK Subs) / HUMAN BEING (New York Dolls) / RAW POWER (Iggy & The Stooges) / AIN'T IT FUN (Dead Boys) / BUICK MAKANE (T.Rex) / HAIR OF THE DOG (Nazareth) / ATTITUDE (Misfits) / BLACK LEATHER (Sex Pistols) / YOU CAN'T PUT YOUR ARMS AROUND A MEMORY (Johnny Thunders) / I DON'T CARE ABOUT YOU (Fear) / WHAT'S YOUR GAME! (Charles Manson). McKAGAN covered CRACKED ACTOR (David Bowie) • **Trivia:** On 28 Apr'90, AXL was married to ERIN, daughter of DON EVERLY (Brothers), but a couple of months later, they counterfiled for divorce. BAILEY was AXL's step-father's surname, and he found out real surname ROSE in the 80's.

Album rating: APPETITE FOR DESTRUCTION (*9) / G N' R LIES (*7) / USE YOUR ILLUSION I (*7) / USE YOUR ILLUSION II (*6) / THE SPAGHETTI INCIDENT (*5) / LIVE ERA – 1987-1993 exploitation (*6) / Izzy Stradlin: JU JU HOUNDS (*6) / Slash's Snakepit: IT'S FIVE O'CLOCK SOMEWHERE (*5) / Duff McKagan: BELIEVE IN ME (*5)

W. AXL ROSE (b. WILLIAM BAILEY, 6 Feb'62, Lafayette, Indiana, USA) – vocals / **SLASH** (b. SAUL HUDSON, 23 Jul'65, Stoke-On-Trent, England) – lead guitar / **IZZY STRADLIN** (b.JEFFREY ISBELL, 8 Apr'62, Lafayette) – guitar / **DUFF McKAGAN** (b. MICHAEL, 5 Feb'64, Seattle, Wash.) – bass (ex-10 MINUTE WARNING, ex-FASTBACKS) / **STEVE ADLER** (b.22 Jan'65, Ohio) – drums repl. ROB to L.A. GUNS again.

		not iss.	Uzi Suicide
Aug 86.	(7"ep) <USR 001> **LIVE ?!*' LIKE A SUICIDE**	-	-

– Mama kin / Reckless life / Move to the city / Nice boys (don't play rock'n'roll).
<re-iss. Jan87 on 'Geffen'; >

		Geffen	Geffen
Jun 87.	(7") (GEF 22) **IT'S SO EASY. / MR. BROWNSTONE**		

(12"+=/12"pic-d+=) (GEF 22T/+P) – Shadow of your love / Move to the city.

Aug 87.	(lp/c/cd) (WX 125/+C)(924148-2) <24148> **APPETITE FOR DESTRUCTION**	5	1

– Welcome to the jungle / It's so easy / Nightrain / Out ta get me / Mr. Brownstone / Paradise city / My Michelle / Think about you / Sweet child o' mine / You're crazy / Anything goes / Rocket queen. (peaked UK-No.5 in 1989) (re-iss. Nov90 lp/c/cd; GEF/+C/D 24148) (re-iss. Oct95 cd/c;)

Sep 87.	(7") (GEF 30) **WELCOME TO THE JUNGLE. / WHOLE LOTTA ROSIE (live)**	67	

(12"+=/12"w-poster/12"pic-d+=) (GEF 30 T/TW/P) – It's so easy (live) / Knockin' on Heaven's door (live).

Aug 88.	(7") (GEF 43) <27963> **SWEET CHILD O' MINE. / OUT TA GET ME**	24	1 Jun88

(12"+=/12"s+=/10"+=) (GEF 43T/+V/E) – Rocket queen.

Oct 88.	(7") (GEF 47) <27759> **WELCOME TO THE JUNGLE. / NIGHTRAIN**	24	7

(12"+=/12"w-poster+=/12"w-patch+=/12"pic-d+=/cd-s+=) (GEF 47 T/TW/TV/TP/CD) – You're crazy.

Dec 88.	(lp/c/cd) (WX 218/+C)(924198-2) <24198> **G N' R LIES (live)**	22	2

– Reckless life / Nice boys (don't play rock'n'roll) / Move to the city / Mama kin / Patience / I used to love her / You're crazy / One in a million. (re-iss. Nov90 lp/c/cd; GEF/+C/D 24198) (re-iss. Oct95 cd/c;)

Mar 89.	(7"/7"sha-clear/7"white-pic-d) (GEF 50/+P/X) <27570> **PARADISE CITY. / I USED TO LOVE HER**	6	5 Jan89

(c-s+=)(12"+=) (9275 704)(GEF 50T) – Anything goes.
(cd-s++=) (GEF 50CD) – Sweet child o' mine.

May 89.	(7"/7"s/c-s) (GEF 55/+W/C) **SWEET CHILD O' MINE (remix). / OUT TA GET ME**	6	-

(7"sha-pic-d+=) (GEF 55P) – Rocket queen.
(12"/3"cd-s) (GEF 55 T/CD) – ('A'side) / Move to the city / Whole lotta Rosie (live) / It's so easy (live).

Jun 89.	(7"/c-s) (GEF 56/+C) <22996> **PATIENCE. / ROCKET QUEEN**	10	4 Apr89

(12"+=/3"cd-s+=) (GEF 56 T/CD) – (W. Axl Rose interview).

Aug 89.	(7"/7"sha-pic/d/c-s) (GEF 60/+P/C) <22869> **NIGHTRAIN. / RECKLESS LIFE**	17	93 Jul89

(12"+=/3"cd-s+=) (GEF 60 T/CD) – Knockin' on Heaven's door (live '87).

—— (Aug90) **MATT SORUM** (b.19 Nov'60, Long Beach, Calif.) – drums (ex-CULT) repl. ADAM MARPLES (ex-SEA HAGS) who repl. ADLER due to bouts of drunkeness. added **DIZZY REED** (b. DARREN REED, 18 Jun'63, Hinsdale, Illinois) – keyboards

Jul 91.	(7"/c-s/12"clear-pic-d/cd-s) (GFS/+C/TP/TD 6) <19039> **YOU COULD BE MINE. / CIVIL WAR**	3	29

Sep 91.	(d-lp/c/cd) <GEF/+C/D 24415> **USE YOUR ILLUSION I**	2	2

– Right next door to Hell / Dust n' bones / Live and let die / Don't cry (original) / Perfect crime / You ain't the first / Bad obsession / Back off bitch / Double talkin' jive / November rain / The garden / Garden of Eden / Don't damn me / Bad apples / Dead horse / Coma.

Sep 91.	(d-lp/c/cd) <GEF/+C/D 24420> **USE YOUR ILLUSION II**	1	1

– Civil war / 14 years / Yesterdays / Knockin' on Heaven's door / Get in the ring / Shotgun blues / Breakdown / Pretty tied up / Locomotive / So fine / Estranged / You could be mine / Don't cry (alt.lyrics) / My world.

Sep 91.	(7"/c-s) (GFS/+C 9) <19027> **DON'T CRY (original). / DON'T CRY (alternate lyrics)**	8	10

(12"+=/cd-s+=) (GFST/+D 9) – ('A'demo).

Dec 91.	(7"/c-s/12") (GFS/+C/X 17) <19114> **LIVE AND LET DIE. / ('A'live)**	5	33

(cd-s+=) (GFSTD 17) – Shadow of your love.

—— (Sep'91) **DAVID NAVARRO** – guitar (of JANE'S ADDICTION) repl. IZZY who walked out on tour. **GILBY CLARKE** (b.17 Aug'62, Cleveland, Ohio) – guitar finally repl. IZZY who formed IZZY STRADLIN & THE JU JU HOUNDS

Feb 92.	(7"/c-s) (GFS/+C 18) <19067> **NOVEMBER RAIN. / SWEET CHILD O' MINE (live)**	4	3 Jun92

(12"+=/pic-cd-s+=) (GFST/+D 18) – Patience.

May 92.	(7"/c-s/12") (GFS/+C/T/TD 21) **KNOCKIN' ON HEAVEN'S DOOR (live '92 at Freddie Mercury tribute). / ('A'studio)**	2	-

Oct 92.	(7"/c-s) (GFS/+C 27) **YESTERDAYS. / NOVEMBER RAIN**	8	-

(12"pic-d+=/cd-s+=) (GFST/+D 27) – ('A'live) / Knockin' on Heaven's door (live '87).

Nov 92.	(c-s) <19142> **YESTERDAYS / ('A'live)**	-	72

May 93.	(cd-ep) (GFSTD 43) **CIVIL WAR EP**	11	-

– Civil war / Garden of Eden / Dead horse / (interview with Slash).

Nov 93.	(c-s) (GFSC 62) **AIN'T IT FUN. / DOWN ON THE FARM**	9	-

(cd-s+=) (GFSTD 62) – Attitude.

Nov 93.	(cd/c/lp) <(GED/GEC/GEF 24617)> **THE SPAGHETTI INCIDENT**	2	4

– Since I don't have you / New rose / Down on the farm / Human being / Raw power / Ain't it fun / Buick Makane / Hair of the dog / Attitude / Black leather / You can't put your arms around a memory / I don't care about you / What's your game!.

May 94.	(7"colrd/c-s) (GFS/+C 70) <19266> **SINCE I DON'T HAVE YOU. / YOU CAN'T PUT YOUR ARMS AROUND A MEMORY**	10	69 Feb94

(cd-s+=) (GFSTD 70) – Human being.
(cd-s) (GFSXD 70) – ('A'side) / Sweet child o' mine / Estranged.

—— **PAUL HUGE** – guitar; repl. the sacked and solo bound GILBY (below from the movie 'Interview With A Vampire')

Jan 95.	(c-s) (GFSC 86) **SYMPATHY FOR THE DEVIL / LIVE AND LET DIE**	9	55 Dec94

(cd-s) (GFSTD 86) <19381> – ('A'side) / (track by Elliot Goldenthal).

—— DUFF and MATT teamed up with STEVE JONES (Sex Pistols) and JOHN TAYLOR (Duran Duran) to form mid '96 supergroup, The NEUROTIC OUTSIDERS; released an eponymous album and single, 'JERK', for 'Maverick' records. In early November, SLASH quit, citing ill feeling between him and AXL.

– compilations, etc. –

Nov 99.	(d-cd/d-c) Geffen; <(490514-2/-4)> **LIVE ERA 87-93 (live)**	45	45

– Nighttrain / Mr. Brownstone / It's so easy / Welcome to the jungle / Dust n' bones / My Michelle / You're crazy / Used to love her / Patience / It's alright / November rain / Out to get me / Yesterdays / Move to the city / Rocket queen / Sweet child o' mine / Knockin' on Heaven's door / Don't cry / Estranged / Paradise city.

GURU (see under ⇒ GANG STARR)

Woody GUTHRIE

Born: WOODROW WILSON GUTHRIE, 14 July 1912, Okemah, Oklahoma, USA. The son of a professional boxer, GUTHRIE first began performing in public in his teens before landing a job as a DJ in Los Angeles. By the time musicologist Alan Lomax made his first field recordings of GUTHRIE in 1940, the self-confessed ramblin' man had amassed a staggering catalogue of songs, many based on his experiences as a travelling hobo living on his wits, talent and staunch political beliefs. While he was refused membership of the US communist party after refusing to give up his religious beliefs, socialist ideals permeated much of his work nevertheless; with the now famous message 'This machine kills fascists' (imitated countless times since) emblazoned across his battered acoustic guitar, few were left in doubt as to where his heart lay. 'THIS LAND IS YOUR LAND', perhaps his best known track, remains a populist anthem and an unofficial alternative to 'The Star Spangled Banner', although this message of equality somehow rings hollow in the corporate miasma of modern-day America. GUTHRIE's views had been shaped by years of struggling on the breadline and huddling in boxcars, watching his people leaving their homes to escape the 'dustbowl' of Oklahoma, only to arrive in sunny California and be turned back, beaten up or worse. Songs like 'I AIN'T GOT NO HOME', 'TALKIN' DUST BOWL BLUES' and 'HARD TRAVELIN', sung by GUTHRIE in his weatherbeaten, heavily accented husk of a voice evoke the trials of the migrants just as vividly as Steinbeck's 'Grapes Of Wrath'. Lomax's Library Of Congress recordings were subsequently issued commercially by 'R.C.A.' although GUTHRIE's work wasn't afforded any significant recognition in his own lifetime. Suffering from alcohol problems, he was consigned to a mental institution before being diagnosed with the genetic degenerative disease, Huntington's Chorea. Confined to a hospital bed for the later stages of his life, the illness finally claimed him on October 3rd, 1967. By this time, a young BOB DYLAN had already been crowned America's king of cool, his inspiration (particularly his earlier work and indeed the whole Greenwich Village folk revival) taken largely from GUTHRIE; during the ailing troubadour's final years, DYLAN had been a regular visitor at his bedside, including tribute 'SONG TO WOODY' on his 1962 debut set. Aside from the obvious influence of his work on artists like DYLAN, PETE SEEGER and his own son ARLO, everyone from U2 to BRUCE SPRINGSTEEN paid tribute to the man on 1988's 'Folkways: A Vision Shared'. Round about the same time, 'Folkways' the label released a split album of GUTHRIE and LEADBELLY material. More recently, GUTHRIE's wife unearthed and submitted some of his unfinished 'work in progress' to the combined talents of US roots rockers WILCO & English protest bard, BILLY BRAGG. The results were issued in 1998 in the shape of the critically acclaimed 'Mermaid Avenue', a highly entertaining and often moving collection of songs interpreted with surprising senitivity and intuition. It also sounded utterly relevant, some thirty years after the man's death. A veritable cornerstone of popular music, both GUTHRIE's fame and the continuing influence of his music grow with each passing year.

Album rating (selective): MORE SONGS BY GUTHRIE (*8) / BOUND FOR GLORY (*8) / DUST BOWL BALLADS (*9) / LIBRARY OF CONGRESS RECORDINGS (*8) / THIS IS YOUR LAND (*8) / STRUGGLE (*7) / BALLADS OF SACO & VANZETTI (*5) / SONGS TO GROW ON FOR MOTHER AND CHILD (*6)

WOODY GUTHRIE – vocals, acoustic guitar

		Melodisc	not iss.
1951.	(78) (1141) **RAMBLIN' BLUES. / TALKIN' COLUMBIA BLUES**		-
1955.	(7"ep) (EPM7 84) **RANGER'S COMMAND**		-
	– Ranger's command / Hard, ain't it hard / Ain't gonna be treated this way / Buffalo skinners.		
1955.	(7"ep) (EPM7 85) **WORRIED MAN BLUES**		-
	– Worried man blues / Poor boy / Gypsy Davie / More pretty girls than one.		
1955.	(7"ep) (EPM7 91) **HEY LOLLY LOLLY**		-
1955.	(lp) (MLP12 106) **MORE SONGS BY GUTHRIE**		-
	– Columbus Georgia stockade / Johnny hard / Foggy mountain top / Bury me beneath the willow / Skip to meet Lou / Ezekiel saw the wheel / Take a whiff on me / Bad Lee Brown / The golden vanity / Cumberland gap / Sourwood mountain / Old time religion.		

		Topic	Folkways
1958.	(lp) (12T 31) **BOUND FOR GLORY**		
	– Stagolee / Little stack of sugar / Ship in the sky / Swim swim swimmy / Pastures of plenty / Grand Coulee Dam / This land is your land / Talking fish blues / The sinking of the Reuben James / Jesus Christ / There's a better world.		
1960.	(lp) <5485> **BALLADS OF SACCO & VANZETTI**	-	
	– The flood and the storm / Two good men / I just want to sing your name / Red wine / Suassos lane / You souls of Boston / Old Judge Thayer / Vanzetti's rock / Vanzetti's letter / Root hog and die / We welcome to Heaven / Sacco's letter to his son. <cd/c-iss.Apr96 on 'Smithsonian Folkways'; SFW CD/MC 40060)>		

—— WOODY died in hospital on the 3rd of October, 1967, having been ill and inactive for over a decade

– compilations & posthumous, etc. –

1964.	(lp) R.C.A.; (RD 7642) / Folkways; <FH 5212> **DUST BOWL BALLADS** (rec.1940)		
	– The great dust storm / I ain't got no home / Talkin' dust bowl blues / Vigilante man / Dust can't kill me / Pretty boy Floyd / Dust pneumonia blues / Blowin' down this road / Tom Joad / Dust bowl refugee / Do re mi / Dust bowl blues / Dusty old dust. (re-iss.Jul78 as 'A LEGENDARY PERFORMER' lp/c; PL/PK 12099) <re-iss. 1988 on 'Rounder' lp/c/cd; ROUNDER 1040/+C/CD)> <cd-iss. Feb96 as 'A LEGENDARY PERFORMER'; 74321 31774-2)>		

—— next also featured SONNY TERRY, CISCO HOUSTON & LEADBELLY

1965.	(lp) Xtra; (XTRA 1012) / Everest; **WOODY GUTHRIE**		1964
	– Lindburgh / Hard travellin / Jiggy jiggy bum bum / Hey little water boy / Chisholm trail / Rubber dolly / I ain't got nobody / Philadelphia lawyer / Springfield mountain / Put my little shoes / Ida red / Yeller gal. (re-iss. 1966; XTRA 1064)		
1966.	(t-lp) Elektra; <(EKL 27 1/2/3)> **LIBRARY OF CONGRESS RECORDINGS** (rec.1940)		
	– Lost train blues / Railroad blues / Rye whiskey / Old Joe Clark / Beaumont rag / Greenback dollar / The boll weevil song / So long, it's been so good to know you / Talking dustbowl blues / Do re mi / Hard times / Pretty boy Floyd / They laid Jesus Christ in his grave / Jolly banker / I ain't got no home / Dirty overalls / Chain around my leg / Worried man blues / Lonesome valley / Walking down that railroad line / Goin' down the road feelin' bad / Dust storm disaster / Foggy mountain top / Dust pneumonia blues / California blues / Dust bowl refugees / Will Rogers' highway / Los Angeles New Year's flood. <t-cd-box-iss.1988 on 'Rounder'; CD 1041/2/3> (iss.separately 1988 as VOL.1 & VOL.3; ROUNDER 1041/+C/CD & ROUNDER 1042/+C/CD & ROUNDER 1043/+C/CD)>		
1966.	(lp) Xtra; (XTRA 1065) **POOR BOY**		-
	– Baltimore to Washington / Little black train / Who's going to shoe your little feet / Slip knot / Poor boy / Mean talking blues / Stepstone / Bed on the floor / Little		

darling / Miner's song / Train blues / Danville girl No.2 / Ride old paint. (re-iss. Oct81 on 'Transatlantic'; TRS 113)

1967.	(lp) Xtra; (XTRA 1067) **SONGS TO GROW ON VOL.1**		-
1967.	(lp) Folkways; <FTS 31001> **THIS LAND IS YOUR LAND**		-
	– Talking Columbia blues / Pastures of plenty / New found land / Oregon trail / End of my line / Miner's song / This land is your land / Grand Coulee Dam / Ramblin' round / Goin' down the road / Little black train / Slip knot.		
1968.	(lp) Ember; (CW 129) **WOODY GUTHRIE – IN MEMORIAM**		-
	– Gypsy Dave / More perty galz / Pretty boy Floyd / Poor boy / Hey lolly lolly / Lonesome day – John Henry / Ranger's command / Ain't gonna be treated this way / Buffalo skinners / Hard, ain't it hard / Worried man blues.		
1968.	(lp) Ember; (CW 135) **CISCO HOUSTON AND WOODY GUTHRIE**		-
1968.	(lp) Ember; (CW 136) **BLIND SONNY TERRY & WOODY GUTHRIE**		-
1976.	(lp) Folkways; <FA 2485> **STRUGGLE**	-	
	– Struggle blues / Dollar down / Get along little doggies / Hang knot / Waiting at the gate / The dying miner / Union burying ground / Lost John / Buffalo skinners / Pretty boy Floyd / Ludlow massacre / 1913 massacre. <re-iss.Aug90 on 'Special Delivery' lp/c/cd; SPD/+C/CD 1034)>		
Jun 77.	(lp) Folkways; <(K 56335)> **SONGS FROM 'BOUND FOR GLORY'** (original recordings 1940-1946)		
	– Gypsy Dave / Jesus Christ / Columbus Georgia stockade / So long (it's been good to know ya) / Howdido / Pretty boy Floyd / Hard travellin' / Better world / This land is your land.		
Jan 88.	(lp/cd) Topic; (12T/TSCD 448) / Rounder; <ROUNDER 1036/+CD> **COLUMBIA RIVER COLLECTION**		Aug88
1988.	(lp/c) Joker; (lp/c) <SM/MC 3960> **VOLUME 1**	-	
1988.	(lp) Folkways; <FA 2483> **WOODY GUTHRIE SINGS FOLKSONGS OF LEADBELLY**	-	
1988.	(lp) Folkways; <FA 2484> **WOODY GUTHRIE SINGS FOLKSONGS OF LEADBELLY VOL.2**	-	
	(above also featured CISCO HOUSTON & SONNY TERRY)		
1988.	(cd; by Various Artists) Vanguard; <VMD 73105> **THE GREATEST SONGS OF WOODY GUTHRIE** <re-iss. Jan96; same)>	-	
Jun 88.	(lp/c) Deja Vu; (DVLP/DVMC 2128) **THE WOODY GUTHRIE COLLECTION: 20 GOLDEN GREATS**		-
Jun 92.	(cd/c) Music Club; (MCCD/MCTC 067) **THE VERY BEST OF WOODY GUTHRIE**		
Jun 94.	(cd/c) Smithsonian Folkways; <(SFW CD/MC 40046)> **LONG WAYS TO TRAVEL: UNRELEASED FOLKWAYS MASTERS 1944-1949**		
Dec 94.	(cd/c) Smithsonian Folkways; <(SFW CD/MC 45036)> **NURSERY DAYS – GROW BIG SONGS VOL.1**		1993
Mar 95.	(cd/c) Smithsonian Folkways; <(SFW CD/MC 45035)> **SONGS TO GROW ON FOR MOTHER AND CHILD**		1993
May 96.	(cd) Tradition; <(TCD 1017)> **EARLY MASTERS**		
May 97.	(cd) Smithsonian Folkways; <(SFWCD 40100)> **THIS LAND IS YOUR LAND – THE ASCH RECORDINGS VOL.1**		
Aug 97.	(cd) Collectables; <(COLCD 5095)> **GOLDEN CLASSICS VOL.1 – WORRIED MAN BLUES**		
Aug 97.	(cd) Collectables; <(COLCD 5098)> **GOLDEN CLASSICS VOL.2 – THE IMMORTAL**		
Aug 97.	(cd) Collectables; <(COLCD 5605)> **WOODY GUTHRIE & CISCO HOUSTON VOL.1**		1995
Nov 97.	(cd) Smithsonian Folkways; <(SFWCD 40101)> **MULESKINNER BLUES – THE ASCH RECORDINGS VOL.2**		
Jun 98.	(cd) Smithsonian Folkways; <(SFWCD 40102)> **HARD TRAVELLIN' – THE ASCH RECORDINGS VOL.3**		
Jan 99.	(cd) Prism; <427> **PASTURES OF PLENTY**	-	
Feb 99.	(cd) United Audio . . .; (UAE 30242) **WOODY GUTHRIE – MEMBERS EDITION**		-
May 99.	(cd) Smithsonian Folkways; <(SFW 40103)> **BUFFALO SKINNERS – THE ASCH RECORDINGS VOL.4**		
Jun 99.	(cd) Hallmark; (31172-2) **THIS IS YOUR LAND – THE BEST OF WOODY GUTHRIE**		-
Aug 99.	(4xcd-box) Smithsonian Folkways; <(SFW CD/MC 40112)> **THE ASCH RECORDINGS VOLS.1-4**		
Nov 99.	(4xcd-box) Chrome Dreams; (ABCD 016) **THE WOODY GUTHRIE STORY**		

Arlo GUTHRIE

Born: 10 Jul'47, Coney Island, New York, USA, son of legendary folk singer, WOODY GUTHRIE, who bought him his first electric guitar. ARLO went to school in Stockbridge, Massachusetts, where he sang his father's songs (his father was the inspiration behind DYLAN). In the mid-60's, ARLO met school librarian, ALICE, and they opened a restaurant after which he named his debut album, 'ALICE'S RESTAURANT', late 1967. This renovated old church became a meeting place for mainly middle-class hippies, who were radically opposed to the US involvement in Vietnam; he had earlier been refused induction into the army due to a petty criminal charge. With help from his father's agent and friend, Harold Leventhal, he gained tour work (i.e, Newport Festival), which helped his finely crafted debut reach the US Top 20. Sadly, prior to its success, his father passed away on the 3rd of October '67, the victim of chronic Huntingdon's Chorea disease. In 1970, an Arthur Penn movie, 'ALICE'S RESTAURANT', was made, ARLO playing himself alongside some intentionally amateurish actors. A year previous, after playing Woodstock (August 1969), he bought a 250-acre farm where he settled with wife-to-be, Jackie Hyde. A political but satirical folk-singer, in the mould of early BOB DYLAN, ARLO never quite emerged from the towering shadow of his father, although he did release a series of fine albums including 'RUNNING DOWN THE ROAD' (1969), 'WASHINGTON

COUNTY' (1969), 'HOBO'S LULLABY' (1972) and the eclectic 'LAST OF THE BROOKLYN COWBOYS' (1973). His only singles chart success came with a version of Steve Goodman's 'THE CITY OF NEW ORLEANS' in 1972 and as the decade wore on, ARLO became more of a cult artist. In 1974, he wrote an attack on President Nixon, 'PRESIDENTIAL RAG', which understandably didn't sell in great heaps. 1976's 'AMIGO' brought further critical acclaim but no chart success, while 'ONE NIGHT' (1978), was the first in a series of albums recorded with folk/country act, SHENANDOAH. In the interim, he became a Catholic and appeared on 'The Muppet Show', as well as touring alongside JOE COCKER and JOHN SEBASTIAN on a 'Woodstock reunion' European tour. GUTHRIE remained a staunch social activist throughout, playing all manner of benefit gigs, while in the late 80's, he set up his own label, 'Rising Son'. • **Covered:** DON'T THINK TWICE, IT'S ALRIGHT + PERCY'S SONG + WHEN THE SHIP COMES IN (Bob Dylan) / 1913 MASSACRE (Woody Guthrie) / LIGHTNIN' BAR BLUES + SOMEBODY TURNED ON THE LIGHT (Hoyt Axton) / WHEN I GET TO THE BORDER (Richard Thompson) / etc.

Album rating: ALICE'S RESTAURANT (*8) / ARLO (*4) / ALICE'S RESTAURANT soundtrack with Various Artists (*5) / RUNNING DOWN THE ROAD (*6) / WASHINGTON COUNTY (*6) / HOBO'S LULLABY (*7) / THE LAST OF THE BROOKLYN COWBOYS (*5) / ARLO GUTHRIE (*4) / TOGETHER IN CONCERT (*6; with Pete Seeger) / AMIGO (*7) / THE BEST OF ARLO GUTHRIE compilation (*7) / ONE NIGHT (*4; with Shenandoah) / OUTLASTING THE BLUES (*5; with Shenandoah) / POWER OF LOVE (*5) / PRECIOUS FRIEND (*5; with Pete Seeger) / SOMEDAY (*5) / ALL OVER THE WORLD (*5) / SON OF THE WIND (*5) / MORE TOGETHER AGAIN (*4; with Pete Seeger) / MYSTIC JOURNEY (*6) / ALICE'S RESTAURANT VOL.2: THE MASSACRE REVISITED (*4)

ARLO GUTHRIE – vocals, guitar (with various session people)

			Reprise	Reprise
Dec 67.	(lp) <(RLP 6267)> **ALICE'S RESTAURANT**		☐	17 Nov67

– Alice's restaurant massacre / Chilling of the evening / Ring-a-round-rosy rag / Now and then / I'm going home / Motorcycle song / Highway in the wind. (re-iss. 1972; K 44045) <cd-iss. Jul88; K2 44045>

		Reprise	Reprise
Mar 68.	(7") (RS 20644) **MOTORCYCLE SONG. / NOW AND THEN**	☐	–
Sep 68.	(7") <0793> **MOTORCYCLE SONG. / (part 2)**	–	–
Oct 68.	(lp) <(RSLP 6269)> **ARLO** (live)		100

– Motorcycle song / Wouldn't you believe it / Try me one more time / John looked down / Meditation / Standing at the threshold / The pause of Mr. Claus. (re-iss. 1972; K 44052)

Oct 69.	(lp) <(RSLP 6346)> **RUNNING DOWN THE ROAD**		54

– Running down the road / Oklahoma hills / Every hand in the land / Living in the country / Wheel of fortune / Creole belle / Coming in to Los Angeles / Oh, in the morning / Stealin' / My front pages. (re-iss. 1972; K 44071)

Dec 69.	(lp) <(RSLP 6411)> **WASHINGTON COUNTY**		33

– (introduction) / Fence post blues / Gabriel's mother's hiway ballad #16 blues / Washington County / Valley to pray / Lay down little doggies / I could be singing / If you would just drop by / Percy's song / I want to be around. (re-iss. 1972; K 44049)

Jan 70.	(7") (RS 20877) <0877> **ALICE'S ROCK'N'ROLL RESTAURANT. / COMING IN TO LOS ANGELES**		97 Nov69
May 70.	(7") <0951> **GABRIEL'S MOTHER'S HIWAY BALLAD #16 BLUES. / VALLEY TO PRAY**	–	
May 71.	(7") (RS 20994) <0994> **THE BALLAD OF TRICKY FRED. / SHACKLES AND CHAINS**	☐	–
Jul 72.	(7") (K 14188) **UKELELE LADY. / WHEN THE SHIP COMES IN**	☐	–
Jun 72.	(lp) (K 44169) <2060> **HOBO'S LULLABY**		52

– Anytime / The city of New Orleans / Lightning bar blues / Shackles and chains / 1913 massacre / Somebody turned on the light / Ukelele lady / When the ship comes in / Mapleview (20%) rag / Days are short / Hobo's lullabye.

Sep 72.	(7") (K 14202) <1103> **THE CITY OF NEW ORLEANS. / DAYS ARE SHORT**		18 Jul72
Nov 72.	(7") <1137> **UKELELE LADY. / COOPER'S LAMENT**	–	–
Feb 73.	(7") (K 14257) **LOVESICK BLUES. / FARREL O'GALA**	☐	–
Apr 73.	(7") <1158> **GYPSY DAVE. / WEEK ON THE RAG**	–	–
Apr 73.	(lp) (K 44236) <2142> **LAST OF THE BROOKLYN COWBOYS**		87

– Farrell O'Gara / Gypsy Davy / This troubled mind of mine / Week of the rag / Miss the Mississippi and you / Lovesick blues / Uncle Jeff / Gates of Eden / Last train / Cowboy's song / Sailor's bonnett / Cooper's lament / Ramblin' round. (re-iss. Aug77 +quad)

Aug 74.	(7") (K 14365) <1211> **PRESIDENTIAL RAG. / NOSTALGIA RAG**	☐	☐
Jul 74.	(lp) (K 54019) <2183> **ARLO GUTHRIE**		Jun74

– Won't be long / Presidential rag / Deportee (plane wreck at Los Gatos) / Children of Abraham / Nostalgia rag / When the cactus is in bloom / Me and my goose / Bling blang / Go down Moses / Hard times / Last to leave.

May 75.	(d-lp; with PETE SEEGER) (K 64023) <2214> **TOGETHER IN CONCERT** (live)	☐	☐

– Way out there / Yodelling / Roving gambler / Declaration of independence / Don't think twice, it's alright / Get up and go / City of New Orleans / Estradio Chile / Guantanamera / On a Monday / Presidential rag / Walkin' down the line / Well may the world go / Henry my son / Mother, the queen of my heart / Deportee (plane wreck at Los Gatos) / Joe Hill / May there always be sunshine / Three rules of discipline and the eight rules of attention / Stealin' / Golden vanity / Lonesome valley / Quite early morning / Sweet Rosyanne.

Sep 76.	(lp) (K 54077) <2239> **AMIGO**	☐	☐

– Guabi, Guabi / Darkest hour / Massachusetts / Victor Jara / Patriot's dream / Grocery blues / Walking song / My love / Manzanillo Bay / Ocean crossing / Connection.

Sep 76.	(7") <1363> **PATRIOT'S DREAM. / OCEAN CROSSING**	–	–
Nov 76.	(7") <1376> **GUABI, GUABI. / GROCERY BLUES**	–	–
Mar 77.	(7") <1388> **MASSACHUSETTS. / MY LOVE**	–	–
Feb 78.	(lp) (K 56431) <3117> **THE BEST OF ARLO GUTHRIE** (compilation)	☐	☐

– Alice's restaurant massacre / Gabriel's mother's hiway ballad £16 blues / Cooper's lament / The motorcycle song / Coming in to Los Angeles / Last train / City of New Orleans / Darkest hour / Last to leave. (re-iss. 1984 lp/c; K/K4 56431) (cd-iss. Feb93; 7599 27340-2)

			Warners	Warners
1978.	(lp; with SHENANDOAH) <3232> **ONE NIGHT**		–	☐

– One nite / I've just seen a face / Tennessee stud / Anytime / Little beggar man / Buffalo skinners / St.Louis tickle / The story of Reuben Clamzo and his strange daughter / In the hey of A / Strangest dream.

Jul 79.	(lp; with SHENANDOAH) (K 56658) <3336> **OUTLASTING THE BLUES**	☐	☐

– Weddding song / Epilogue / Sailing down this golden river / Evangelina / Prologue / Which side / World away from me / Telephone / Carry me over / Drowning man / Underground.

Nov 79.	(7"; with SHENANDOAH) <49037> **WEDDING SONG. / PROLOGUE**	☐	☐
Jul 81.	(lp) (K 56910) <3558> **POWER OF LOVE**	☐	Jun81

– Power of love / Oklahoma nights / If I could only touch your life / Waimanalo blues / Living like a legend / Give it all you got / When I get to the border / Jamaica farewell / Slow boat / Garden song.

Aug 81.	(7") <49796> **IF I COULD ONLY TOUCH YOUR LIFE. / SLOW BOAT**	☐	☐
Feb 82.	(7") <49889> **POWER OF LOVE. / OKLAHOMA NIGHTS**	☐	☐
1982.	(d-lp; with SHENANDOAH & PETE SEEGER) **PRECIOUS FRIEND**	☐	☐

– Wabash cannonball / Circles / Hills of Glenshee / Ocean crossing / Celery-time / Run, come see Jerusalem / Sailin' up, sailin' down / How can I keep from singing / Old time religion / Pretty Boy Floyd / Ladies auxiliary / Please don't talk about me / When I'm gone / Precious friend you will be there / Do re mi / Tarantella / The neutron bomb / I'm changing my name to Chrysler / St.Louis tickle / Wimoweh / Will the circle be unbroken? / Garden song / Kisses sweeter than wine / Raggedy raggedy / In dead earnest / If I had a hammer / Amazing Grace.

			Rising Sun	Rising Sun
1989.	(cd) <RSR 0001> **SOMEDAY**		–	☐

– All over the world / Russian girls / Here we are – way out in the country / Someday / Satellite / Oh mom / Unemployment line / Eli / Major blues / You and me.

1991.	(cd) <RSR 0002> **ALL OVER THE WORLD**	–	☐

– All over the world / Oklahoma nights / Massachusetts / Ukelele lady / Manzanillo Bay / Miss the Mississippi and you / When I get to the border / City of New Orleans / Russian girls / Guabi, Guabi / Waimanalo blues / Evangelina / (Last night I had the) Strangest dream.

1992.	(cd) <RSR 0003> **SON OF THE WIND**	–	☐

– Buffalo gals / Dead or alive / Streets of Laredo / Ridin' down the canyon / South coast / Shenandoah / Gal I left behind / When the cactus is in bloom / Woody's rag (hard work) / I ride an old paint / Utah Carroll / Red river valley.

Oct 94.	(d-cd; by ARLO GUTHRIE & PETE SEEGER) <(RSR 0007-8)> **MORE TOGETHER AGAIN IN CONCERT** (live)	☐	☐

– Midnight special / Abiyoyo / Where have all the flowers gone? / Mooses come walking / When the ship comes in / Guantanamera / Ross Perot guide to answering embarrassing / Sailing down this golden river / If I had a hammer (the hammer song) / When a soldier makes it home / Can't help falling in love // De Colores / Solo le pido a dios / Wake up dead / Gabriel's mother highway ballad No.16 / Hills of Glenshee / Little a this 'n that / City of New Orleans / Jacob's ladder / Wimoweh (Mbube) / Amazing grace / This land is your land.

Feb 96.	(cd) <RSR 0009> **MYSTIC JOURNEY**	–	☐

– Moon song / Face of time / Mystic journey / Under cover of night / You are the song / Doors to Heaven / Wake up dead / When a soldier makes it home / Stairs / All this stuff takes time / I'll be with you tonight.

Dec 97.	(cd) <RSR 0010> **ALICE'S RESTAURANT VOL.2: THE MASSACRE REVISITED**	–	☐

– compilations, others, etc. –

Mar 70.	(lp) United Artists; (UAS 29061) <5195> **ALICE'S RESTAURANT** (Soundtrack)	44	63 Oct69

– Travelin' music / Alice's restaurant massacre – 1 / The let down / Songs to aging children (by TIGGER OUTLAW) / Amazing Grace (by The GARRY SHERMAN CHORUS) / Trip to the city / Alice's restaurant massacre – 2 / Crash pad improvs / You're a fink (by AL SCHACKMAN) / Harps and marriage.

—— Also contributed to various albums including 'Woodstock'.

GUTTERBALL (see under ⇒ DREAM SYNDICATE)

Buddy GUY (dig out; 4th edition)

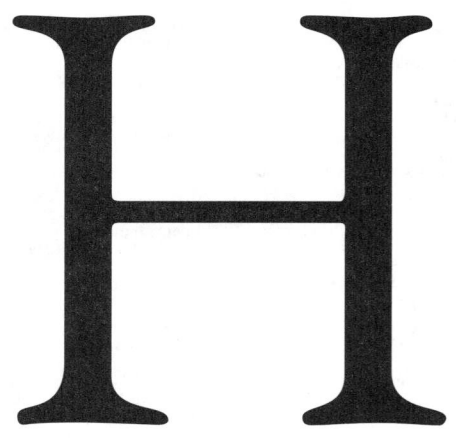

Steve HACKETT

Born: 12 Feb'50, London, England. In the late 60's, after periods with CANTERBURY GLASS and SARABANDE, he formed QUIET WORLD, making one album in 1970, 'THE ROAD'. By the end of the year, he had taken up guitar duties for GENESIS, playing on a string of albums from 'NURSERY CRYME' (1971) to 'SECONDS OUT' (1977). While still part of GENESIS in 1975, he released the first in a long series of solo albums, 'VOYAGE OF THE ACOLYTE', which reached the UK Top 30. By the time of his follow-up, 'PLEASE DON'T TOUCH', HACKETT had left GENESIS to concentrate on his solo career. The album broke away from its predecessor's neo-classical conceptualism, opting for a more accomplished rock set. He continued to score with successive albums until he signed a deal with 'Lambourghini' in '83. The resulting album, 'BAY OF KINGS', was a more acoustic-based affair, going down none too well with a large section of his fanbase. In 1986, he once again saw some chart action with the pomp-rock supergroup, GTR, which also numbered STEVE HOWE of YES. In 1988, HACKETT was back on the solo trail with another classical guitar set, 'MOMENTUM'. In the 90's, he combined some of these styles, even incorporating a blues element on the 1994 album, 'BLUES WITH A FEELING'. • **Covered;** BORN IN CHICAGO (Nick Gravenites) / THE STUMBLE (King-Thompson) / BLUES WITH A FEELING (. . .Jacobs).

Album rating: VOYAGE OF THE ACOLYTE (*8) / PLEASE DON'T TOUCH (*5) / SPECTRAL MORNINGS (*6) / DEFECTOR (*7) / CURED (*6) / HIGHLY STRUNG (*5) / BAY OF KINGS (*5) / TILL WE HAVE FACES (*5; with G.T.R.) / MOMENTUM (*4) / THE UNAUTHORISED BIOGRAPHY compilation (*7) / GUITAR NOIR (*5) / TIME LAPSE (*4) / BLUES WITH A FRIEND (*4) / A MIDSUMMER NIGHT'S DREAM (*2) / GENESIS REVISITED (*5) / THERE ARE MANY SIDES TO THE NIGHT (*4)

STEVE HACKETT – guitar, vocals, keyboards (ex-GENESIS, ex-QUIET WORLD) with **JOHN HACKETT** – flute, synthesizer / **JOHN ACOCK** – keyboards / **SALLY OLDFIELD** – vocals / **NIGEL WARREN-GREEN** – cello / **ROBIN MILLER** – oboe, cor anglais / guests **MIKE RUTHERFORD** – bass, fuzz 12-string / **PHIL COLLINS** – drums, vocals

			Charisma	Chrysalis
Oct 75.	(lp)(c) *(CAS 1111)(7208 555)* <*1112*> **VOYAGE OF THE ACOLYTE**	26	
— Ace of wands / Hands of the priestess part I / A tower struck down / Hands of the priestess part II / The hermit / Star of Sirius / The lovers / Shadow of the Hierophant. *(re-iss. Oct86; CHC 47) (cd-iss. May88; CASCD 1111)*

———— STEVE left GENESIS (deciding on full-time career). Retained only his brother JOHN and friend JOHN ACOCK. Guest vocalists were **RICHIE HAVENS, RANDY CRAWFORD** and **STEVE WALSH**, also **CHESTER THOMPSON** – drums, percussion / **JAMES BRADLEY** – percussion / **PHIL EHART** – percussion / **TOM FOWLER** – bass / **DAVE LEBOLT** – keyboards / **GRAHAM SMITH** – violin.

Apr 78.	(lp)(c) *(CDS 4012)(7208 620)* <*1176*> **PLEASE DON'T TOUCH**	38	
— Narnia / Carry on up the vicarage / Racing in A / Kim / How can I? / Hoping love will last / Land of a thousand autumns / Please don't touch / The voice of Necam / Icarus ascending. *(cd-iss. May88; CDSCD 4012)*

| May 78. | (7") *(CB 312)* **HOW CAN I?. / KIM** | | - |
| Oct 78. | (7") *(CB 318)* **NARNIA. / PLEASE DON'T TOUCH** | | |

———— Steve and brother with **PETER HICKS** – vocals / **DICK CADBURY** – bass / **NICK MAGNUS** – keyboards / **JOHN SHEARER** – drums

May 79.	(lp) *(CDS 4017)* <*1223*> **SPECTRAL MORNINGS**	22	
— Every day / The virgin and the gypsy / The red flower of Tachai blooms everywhere / Clocks – the angel of Mons / The ballad of the decomposing man / Lost time in Cordoba / Tigermoth / Spectral mornings. *(re-iss. Sep83; same) (re-iss. Aug88 lp/c; CHC/+MC 67) (cd-iss. 1987; CDSCD 4017)*

| Jun 79. | (7") *(CB 334)* **EVERY DAY. / LOST TIME IN CORDOBA** | | |
| Sep 79. | (7") *(CB 341)* **CLOCKS – THE ANGELS OF MONS. / ACOUSTIC SET** | | |
(12"+=) *(CB 341-12)* – Tigermoth.

			Charisma	Charisma
Mar 80.	(7") *(CB 357)* **THE SHOW. / HERCULES UNCHAINED**		
Jun 80.	(lp/c) *(CDS/+MC 4018)* <*3103*> **DEFECTOR**	9	
— The Steppes / Time to get out / Slogans / Leaving / Two vamps as guests / Jacuzzi / Hammer in the sand / The toast / The show / Sentimental

institution. *(re-iss. Mar83 lp/c; CHC/+MC 15) (cd-iss. Apr89 on 'Virgin'; CDSCD 4018)*

| Aug 80. | (7") *(CB 368)* **SENTIMENTAL INSTITUTION. / THE TOAST** | | |

———— added **KIM POOR** – vocals / **BIMBO ACOCK** – sax

			Charisma	Epic
Aug 81.	(7") *(CB 385)* **HOPE I DON'T WAKE. / TALES OF THE RIVERBANK**		-
Aug 81.	(lp)(c) *(CDS 4021)(7144 153)* <*37632*> **CURED**	15	
— Hope I don't wake / Picture postcard / Can't let go / The air-conditioned nightmare / Funny feeling / A cradle of swans / Overnight sleeper / Turn back time. *(re-iss. Mar84 lp/c; CHC/+MC 21) (cd-iss. Apr89 on 'Virgin'; CDSCD 4021)*

| Oct 81. | (7") *(CB 390)* **PICTURE POSTCARD. / THEME FROM "SECOND CHANCE"** | | |
| Nov 81. | (7") <*02609*> **HOPE I DON'T WAKE. / A CRADLE OF SWANS** | - | |

———— **CHRIS LAWRENCE** – bass / **NIGEL WARREN GREEN** – cello / **IAN MOSLEY** – drums (returned)

Apr 83.	(7") *(CELL 1)* **CELL 151. / TIME LAPSE AT MILTON KEYNES**	66	
(12"+=) *(CELL 12)* – Air conditioned nightmare.
(free ltd-12" w/a *(CELL 13)* **CLOCKS – THE ANGEL OF MONS. / ACOUSTIC SET / TIGERMOTH**

Apr 83.	(lp/c) *(HACK/HAKC 1)* <*38515*> **HIGHLY STRUNG**	16	
— Camino royale / Cell 151 / Always somewhere else / Walking through walls / Give it away / Weightless / India rubber man / Hackett to pieces. *(re-iss. Aug88 lp/c; CHC/+MC 40) (cd-iss. Apr89 on 'Virgin'; HAKCD 1) (cd re-iss. Mar94 on 'Virgin')*

———— **STEVE HACKETT** now totally solo on guitars

			Lambourghini	not iss.
Nov 83.	(lp/c) *(LMGLP/ZCLGP 3000)* **BAY OF KINGS**	70	-
— Bay of kings / The journey / Kim / Marigold / St.Elmo's fire / Petropolis / Second chance / Cast adrift / Horizons / Black light / The barren land / Calamaria. *(re-iss. Jun89 on 'Start' lp/c/cd; STL/STC/SCD 10) (cd re-iss. Jun94 on 'Permanent'; PERMCDL 20) (cd re-iss. Sep97 on 'Camino'; CAMCD 8)*

———— now with **NICK MAGNUS + FERNAND MOURA** – keyboards / **IAN MOSLEY** – drums / **KIM POOR** – vocals / **RONALDO DIAMANTE** – bass / etc

Aug 84.	(7") *(LMG 16)* **A DOLL THAT'S MADE IN JAPAN. / A DOLL THAT'S MADE IN JAPAN (instrumental)**		
(12") *(12LMG 16)* – ('A'side) / Just the bones.

Sep 84.	(lp/c/cd) *(LMGLP/ZCLMG/CDLMG 4000)* **TILL WE HAVE FACES**	54	-
— Duel / Matilda Smith-Williams' home for the aged / Let me count the ways / A doll that's made in Japan / Myopia / What's my name / The Rio connection / Taking the easy way out / When you wish upon a star. *(re-iss. Oct89 on 'Start' lp/c; STL/STC/SCD 11) (cd re-iss. Jun94 on 'Permanent'; PERMCDL 19) (cd re-iss. Sep97 on 'Camino'; CAMCD 9)*

G.T.R.

formed by **STEVE HACKETT** – guitar / **STEVE HOWE** – guitar (YES) / **MAX BACON** – vocals (ex-NIGHTWING, ex-BRONZ) / **PHIL SPALDING** – bass / **JONATHAN MOVER** – drums (ex-MARILLION, ex-S.O.S.)

			Arista	Arista
May 86.	(7"/7"pic-d) *(GTR/+SD 1)* <*9470*> **WHEN THE HEART RULES THE MIND. / REACH OUT (NEVER SAY NO)**		14
(12"+=) *(GTR12 1)* – Sketches in the sun / Hackett to bits.

Jul 86.	(lp/c/cd) *(207/407/257 716)* <*8400*> **G.T.R.**	41	11
— When the heart rules the mind / The hunter / Here I wait / Sketches in the sun / Jeckyl and Hyde / You can still get through / Reach out (never say no) / Toe the line / Hackett to bits / Imagining. *(re-iss. Apr88 lp/c/cd; 208/408/258 980)*

Aug 86.	(7") <*9512*> **THE HUNTER. / SKETCHES IN THE SUN**	-	85
(12") – ('A'side) / Hackett to bits.

STEVE HACKETT

returned to solo work, retained **JOHN HACKETT** – flute, + brought in **FUDGE SMITH** – drums / **JULIAN COLBECK** – keyboards, bass

			Start	not iss.
Apr 88.	(lp/c/cd) *(STL/STC/SCD 15)* **MOMENTUM**		-
— Cavalcanti / The sleeping sea / Portrait of a Brazilian lady / When the bells break / A bed, a chair & a guitar / Concert for Munich / Last rites of innocence / Troubled spirit / Variations on theme by Chopin / Pierrot / Momentum. *(cd re-iss. Jun94 on 'Permanent'; PERMCDL 21) (cd re-iss. Sep97 on 'Camino'; CAMCD 10)*

			Permanent	not iss.
May 93.	(cd/c) *(PERM CD/MC 13)* **GUITAR NOIR**		-
— Take these pearls / Dark as the grave / Paint your picture / There are many sides to the night / Like an arrow / Walking away from rainbows / Sierra quemada / Lost in your eyes / Little America / In the heart of the city / Vampyre with a healthy appetite / Tristesse. *(cd re-iss. Sep97 on 'Camino'; CAMCD 12)*

Jun 94.	(cd) *(PERMCDL 22)* **TIME LAPSES (live)**		
— Camino royale / Please don't touch / Everyday / In that quiet earth / Depth charge / Jacuzzi / Steppes / Ace of swans / Hope I don't wake / Red flower of Tachai blooms everywhere / Tigermoth / A tower struck down / Spectral mornings / Clocks / Angel of Mons. *(re-iss. Oct97 on 'Camino'; CAMCD 11)*

———— now w / **SINCLAIR / DEGENHARDT / COLBECK** (co-writer some)

			Virgin	Virgin
Oct 94.	(cd/c) *(PERM CD/MC 27)* **BLUES WITH A FEELING**		
— Born in Chicago / The stumble / Love of another kind / Way down south / A blue part of town / Footloose / Tombstone roller / Blues with a feeling / Big Dallas sky / The 13th floor / So many roads / Solid ground. *(cd re-iss. Sep97 on 'Camino'; CAMCD 13)*

			EMI Classics	not iss.
Apr 97.	(cd; STEVE HACKETT & THE ROYAL PHILHARMONIC ORCHESTRA) *(CDC 556348-2)* **A MIDSUMMER NIGHT'S DREAM**		-

———— next with guests JOHN WETTON, BILL BRUFORD, TONY LEVIN, JULIAN COLBECK, CHESTER THOMPSON, ALPHONSO JOHNSON, WILL BATES, NICK MAGNUS, JERRY PEAL, HUGO DEGENHARDT, PAUL CARRACK,

PINO PALLADINO, ROGER KING, BEN FENNER, COLIN BLUNSTONE, ARON FRIEDMAN, JOHN HACKETT, IAN McDONALD, TARQUIN BOMBAST and The Royal Philharmonic Orchestra

	Snapper	not iss.
Sep 97. (cd) *(SRECD 704)* **GENESIS REVISITED**	☐	-

– Watcher of the skies / Dance on a volcano / Valley of the kings / Deja vu / Firth of fifth / For absent friends / Your own special way / Fountain of Salmacis / Waiting room only / I know what I like / Los endos.

	Camino	not iss.
Oct 97. (cd) *(CAMCD 14)* **THERE ARE MANY SIDES TO THE NIGHT**	☐	-

– Horizons / Blood on the rooftops – Cuckoo cocoon / Black light / The Sky boat song / Time lapse at Milton Keynes / Beja flor / Kim / Second chance / Oh how I love you / Journey / Baroque / Walking away from rainbows / Cavalcanti / Tales of the Riverbank / Vivaldi guitar concerto / Blue part of town / Ace of wands / Cinema paradiso / End of day.

– compilations, etc. –

Mar 83. (d-c) *Charisma; (CASMC 105)* **VOYAGE OF THE ACOLYTE / PLEASE DON'T TOUCH** ☐ -

Oct 92. (cd) *Virgin; (CDVM 9014)* **THE UNAUTHORISED BIOGRAPHY** ☐ -

– Narnia / Hackett to pieces / Don't fall away from me / Spectral mornings / The steppes / The virgin and the gypsy / The air-conditioned nightmare / Cell 151 / Slogans / Icarus ascending / Prayers and dreams / Star of Sirius / Hammer in the sand / Ace of wands / Hoping love will last. *(with 2 new songs);* – Players and dreams / Don't fall away from me)

Sammy HAGAR

Born: 13 Oct'47, Monterey, California, USA. Honing his inimitably hoary vocal style in a number of local bands, including FABULOUS CASTILLAS and The JUSTICE BROTHERS, HAGAR subsequently joined MONTROSE in 1973. A prototype 80's hair-metal band, MONTROSE recorded two lauded albums with HAGAR as frontman, 'MONTROSE' (1973) and 'PAPER MONEY' (1974). These sets featured a clutch of classy HAGAR numbers, namely 'SPACE STATION No.5', 'ROCK THE NATION' and 'BAD MOTOR SCOOTER', the singer resurrecting these tracks as the core of his feted stage show. After parting company with MONTROSE, he formed a few short-lived outfits (i.e. DUST COWBOYS and SAMMY WILD), before inking a deal with 'Capitol' records and releasing a solo debut album, 'NINE ON A TEN SCALE' in 1976. Initially he struggled to break through commercially, that is, until 1979's triumphant 'STREET MACHINE', an album that hit the UK! Top 40. Crossover success followed with the more overtly commercial (but hard-rockin' nonetheless) 'DANGER ZONE' (1980) set, although HAGAR only really came into his own in the live arena. Signing to 'Geffen', he delivered a further handful of workmanlike albums, before stunning the rock community by joining VAN HALEN in 1985. Faced with the nigh-on impossible task of replacing the charismatic DAVE LEE ROTH, HAGAR nonetheless won over the fans with his solid and dependable style on such massive 80's albums as '5150' (1986) and 'OU812' (1988). He fulfilled his contractual obligations to 'Geffen', by delivering an eponymous set in 1987. HAGAR continued to enjoy worldwide stardom with VAN HALEN right up until the mid 90's, when he left to resume his solo career. • **Covers:** THE DOCK OF A BAY (Otis Redding) / A WHITER SHADE OF PALE (Procol Harum). • **Trivia:** BETTE MIDLER covered his 'KEEP ON ROCKIN'', in the film 'The Rose'.

Album rating: NINE ON A TEN SCALE (*5) / SAMMY HAGAR (*5) / MUSICAL CHAIRS (*5) / ALL NIGHT LONG (aka LOUD AND CLEAR) (*7) / STREET MACHINE (*5) / DANGER ZONE (*6) / STANDING HAMPTON (*6) / THREE LOCK BOX (*6) / REMATCH compilation (*6) / THROUGH THE FIRE (*5; by HAGAR, SCHON, AARONSON, SHRIEVE) / VOA (*6) / SAMMY HAGAR on 'Geffen' (*5) / THE BEST OF SAMMY HAGAR compilation (*6) / MARCHING TO MARS (*5) / RED VOODOO (*5)

SAMMY HAGAR – vocals (ex-MONTROSE) / with **GARY PIHL** – guitar / **BILL CHURCH** – bass (ex-MONTROSE) / **ALAN FITZGERALD** – keyboards / plus session drummers, etc.

	Capitol	Capitol
May 76. (lp) *<(E-ST 11489)>* **NINE ON A TEN SCALE**	☐	☐

– Keep on rockin' / Urban guerilla / Flamingos fly / China / Silver lights / All American / Confession / Please come back / Young girl blues / Rock'n'roll Romeo. *(re-iss.Jun81 on 'Greenlight'; GO 2017) (re-iss. May83 on 'Fame' lp/c; FA/TC-FA 3068) (cd-iss. May93 on 'Beat Goes On'; BGOCD 182)*

Jun 76. (7") *(CL 15872)* **FLAMINGOS FLY. / URBAN GUERILLA** ☐

SCOTT MATTHEWS – drums (repl. session people)

Mar 77. (red-lp) *<(E-ST 11599)>* **SAMMY HAGAR** ☐ Feb77

– Red / Catch the wind / Cruisin' and boozin' / Free money / Rock'n'roll weekend / Fillmore shuffle / Hungry / The pits / Love has found me / Little star – Eclipse. *(re-iss. May81 on 'Greenlight'; GO 2007) (cd-iss. May93 as 'RED' on 'Beat Goes On'; BGOCD 181)*

Mar 77. (7") *<4388>* **CATCH THE WIND. / RED** - ☐

Mar 77. (7") *(CL 15913)* **CATCH THE WIND. / ROCK'N'ROLL WEEKEND** ☐ -

Jun 77. (7") *<4411>* **CRUISIN' AND BOOZIN'. / LOVE HAS FOUND ME** - ☐

DENNY CARMASSI – drums repl. SCOTT / added **DAVID LEWARK** – guitar

Jan 78. (7") *(CL 15960) <4502>* **YOU MAKE ME CRAZY. / RECKLESS** 62 Nov77

Jan 78. (lp) *<(E-ST 11706)>* **MUSICAL CHAIRS** 100

– Turn up the music / It's gonna be alright / You make me crazy / Reckless / Try (try to fall in love) / Don't stop me now / Straight from the hip kid / Hey boys / Someone out there / Crack in the world. *(re-iss. Jul81 on 'Greenlight'; GO 2021) (cd-iss. May94 on 'Beat Goes On'; BGOCD 183)*

Apr 78. (7") *<4550>* **TURN UP THE MUSIC. / HEY BOYS** - ☐

May 78. (7") *(CL 15983)* **TURN UP THE MUSIC. / STRAIGHT FROM THE HIP KID** ☐ -

May 78. (7") *<4596>* **SOMEONE OUT THERE. / I'VE DONE EVERYTHING FOR YOU** - ☐

GARY PIHL – guitar repl. LEWARK

Aug 78. (lp) *<E-ST 11812>* **ALL NIGHT LONG (live)** - 89

– Red / Rock'n'roll weekend / Make it last – Reckless / Turn up the music / I've done everything for you / Young girl blues / Bad motor scooter. *(UK-iss.Mar80 as 'LOUD & CLEAR' red-lp +=; E-ST 25330) –* Space station No.5. *(hit No.12) (cd-iss. Aug92 as 'LOUD & CLEAR' on 'Beat Goes On'; BGOCD 149)*

Sep 78. (7") *(CL 160010)* **I'VE DONE EVERYTHING FOR YOU (live). / BAD MOTOR SCOOTER (live)** ☐ -

Jun 79. (7") *(CL 16083) <4699>* **(SITTIN' ON) THE DOCK OF THE BAY. / I'VE DONE EVERYTHING FOR YOU** 65 Mar79

CHUCK RUFF – drums repl. DENNY / **NEAL SCHON** – guitar (of JOURNEY) repl. FITZGERALD

Sep 79. (7") *(CL 16101) <4757>* **PLAIN JANE. / WOUNDED IN LOVE** 77

Sep 79. (lp) *<(E-ST 11983)>* **STREET MACHINE** 38 71

– Growing pains / Child to man / Trans am (highway wonderland) / Feels like love / Plain Jane / Never say die / This planet's on fire (burn to hell) / Wounded in love / Falling in love / Straight to the top. *(re-iss. Jun86 on 'Revolver'; REVLP 72) (cd-iss. Dec92 on 'Beat Goes On'; BGOCD 150)*

Nov 79. (7") *<4825>* **GROWING PAINS. / STRAIGHT TO THE TOP** - ☐

Nov 79. (7") *(CL 16114)* **THIS PLANET'S ON FIRE (BURN IN HELL). / SPACE STATION No.5 (live)** 52 -

Jan 80. (7") *(CL 16120)* **I'VE DONE EVERYTHING FOR YOU. / RED** 36 -

added **GEOFF WORKMAN** – keyboards

May 80. (lp) *<(E-ST 12069)>* **DANGER ZONE** 25 85

– Love or money / 20th century man / Miles from boredom / Mommy says, daddy says / In the night (entering the danger zone) / The iceman / Bad reputation / Heartbeat / Run for your life / Danger zone. *(cd-iss. Jul95 on 'Beat Goes On'; BGOCD 261)*

May 80. (7") *(RED 1)* **HEARTBEAT. / LOVE OR MONEY** 67 -

May 80. (7") *<4893>* **HEARTBEAT. / MILES FROM BOREDOM** - ☐

DAVID LAUSER – drums repl. CHUCK

	Epic	Epic
Sep 81. (7"/12") *(EPCA/+13 1600)* **HEAVY METAL. / SATISFIED** (above from film 'Heavy Metal')		

	Geffen	Geffen
Dec 81. (7"/7"pic-d) *(GEFA/+11 1884)* **PIECE OF MY HEART. / BABY'S ON FIRE**	67	-

Dec 81. (7") *<49881>* **I'LL FALL IN LOVE AGAIN. / SATISFIED (by Journey)** - 43

(also issued on 'B'side of CRAZY FOR YOU by 'Madonna' Jun85 hit)

Jan 82. (lp) *(GEF 85456) <GHS 2006>* **STANDING HAMPTON** 84 28

– There's only one way to rock / Baby's on fire / Can't get loose / I'll fall in love again / Heavy metal / Baby it's you / Surrender / Inside looking in / Sweet hitchhiker / Piece of my heart. *(re-iss. Sep86 lp/c; 902006-1/-4)*

May 82. (7") *<50059>* **PIECE OF MY HEART. / SWEET HITCHHIKER** - 73

Jan 83. (lp)(c) *(GEF 25454)(402425-4) <GHS 2021>* **THREE LOCK BOX** 17 Dec82

– Three lock box / Remote love / Remember the heroes / Your love is driving me crazy / In the room / Rise of the animal / I wouldn't change a thing / Growing up / Never give up / I don't need love. *(re-iss. Sep96 lp/c; 902021-1/-4)*

Jan 83. (7") *(GEF 3043) <29816>* **YOUR LOVE IS DRIVING ME CRAZY. / I DON'T NEED LOVE** 13 Dec82

Mar 83. (7") *<29718>* **NEVER GIVE UP. / FAST TIMES AT RIDGEMONT HIGH** - 46

SCHON – guitar / **AARONSON** – bass / **SHRIEVE** – drums

May 84. (lp/c; by HAGAR, SCHON, AARONSON, SHRIEVE) *(GEF/GEC 25893) <4023>* **THROUGH THE FIRE** 92 42 Mar84

– Top of the rock / Missing you / Animation / Valley of the kings / Giza / Whiter shade of pale / Hot and dirty / He will understand / My home town. *(cd-iss. Jan96 on 'Retroactive'; RETRO 50059CD)*

May 84. (7"; by HAGAR, SCHON, AARONSON, SHRIEVE) *<29280>* **A WHITER SHADE OF PALE. / HOT AND DIRTY** - 94

added to 1982 line-up **JESSE HARMS** – keyboards, vocals

Aug 84. (7") *(GEF 4696) <29246>* **TWO SIDES OF LOVE. / BURNING DOWN THE CITY** 38 Jul84

Sep 84. (7") *<29173>* **I CAN'T DRIVE 55. / PICK IN THE DIRT** - 26

Sep 84. (lp/c) *(GEF/GEC 26054) <24043>* **VOA (Voice Of America)** 32 Aug84

– I can't drive 55 / Swept away / Rock is in my blood / Two sides of love / Dick in the dirt / VOA / Don't make me wait / Burnin' down the city. *(re-iss. Sep86 lp/c/cd; GEF/GEC/GED 924043-1/-4/-2)*

It was around this time he replaced DAVE LEE ROTH in VAN HALEN

Apr 87. (7") *(650407-7) / Columbia; <06647>* **WINNER TAKES ALL. / THE FIGHT (by Giorgio Moroder)** - 54 Feb87

(above from the 'Columbia' movie, 'Over The Top')

EDDIE VAN HALEN – bass, vocals repl. CHURCH + PIHL

Jul 87. (lp/c)(cd) *(WX 114/+C)(924144-2) <24144>* **SAMMY HAGAR** 86 14

– When the hammer falls / Hands and knees / Give to live / Boy's night out / Returning home / Standin' at the same old crossroads / Privacy / Back into you / Eagles fly / What they gonna say now. *(some w/ free conversation disc)*

Aug 87. (7") *(GEF 23) <28314>* **GIVE TO LIVE. / WHEN THE HAMMER FALLS** 23 Jun87

(12"+=) *(GEF 23T)* – Standing at the same old crossroads.

Oct 87. (7") *<28185>* **EAGLES FLY. / HANDS AND KNEES** - 82

Mar 94. (cd/c) *(GED/GEC 24702)* **UNBOXED** (compilation) 51

– High hopes / Buying my way into Heaven / I'll fall in love again / There's only one way to rock / Heavy metal / Eagles fly / Baby's on fire / Three lock box / Two sides of love / I can't drive / Give to live / I don't need love.

	Track Factory	M.C.A.
May 97. (cd) *(TRD 11627)* **MARCHING TO MARS**		18

– Little white lie / Salvation on Sand Hill / Who has the right / Would you do it for free / Leaving the warmth of the womb / Kama / On the other hand / Both sides now / Yogi's so high (I'm stoned) / Amnesty is granted / Marching to Mars.

Mar 99. (cd/c; as SAMMY HAGAR AND THE WABORITAS)
<11872> **RED VOODOO**   `-` | 22 |
– Mas tequila / Shag / Sympathy for the human / Red voodoo / Lay your hand on me / High and dry again? / Revival / Don't fight it (feel it) / Love / Right on right / Returning of the wish.

– compilations, etc. –

1979. (7"m) Capitol; (SPSR 441) **TURN UP THE MUSIC. / RED / BAD MOTOR SCOOTER**   `-`

Oct 82. (lp/c) Capitol; (EST/TC-EST 26882) **RED ALERT – DIAL NINE (THE VERY BEST OF SAMMY HAGAR)**   `-`

Jan 83. (lp) Capitol; (12238) **REMATCH** (some live)   `-`
– Trans am (highway wonderland) / Love or money / Plain Jane / 20th century man / This planet's on fire (burn in Hell) / In the night / Danger zone / Space Station No.5.

Jan 87. (lp/c) Geffen; (924127-1/-4) **LOOKING BACK**   `-`

Aug 89. (lp/c)(cd) Warners; (WX 291/+C)(K 924255-2) **THE BEST OF SAMMY HAGAR**
– Red / (Sittin' on) The dock of the bay / I've done everything for you / Rock'n'roll weekend / Cruisin' and boozin' / Turn up the music / Reckless / Trans am (highway wonderland) / Love or money / This planet's on fire (burn in Hell) / Plain Jane / Bad reputation / Bad motor scooter / You make me crazy.

Nov 94. (cd) Connoisseur; (VSOPCD 207) **THE ANTHOLOGY**   `-`

Jun 97. (cd) EMI Gold; (CPD 780262-2) **THE BEST OF SAMMY HAGAR**   `-`

Bill HALEY

Born: WILLIAM HALEY, 6 Jul'25, Highland Park, Detroit, USA. After leaving school in Pennsylvania, BILL became a travelling musician and yodeller for country bands, The DOWN HOMERS and The RANGE DRIFTERS. In 1948, he was hired as a DJ for the local W-PWA station in Chester, taking up the opportunity to air recordings of his new outfit, The FOUR ACES. He subsequently abandoned them in the early 50's, recruiting new backers, The SADDLEMEN, whose reputation was beginning to spread around the hillbilly community. In 1952, HALEY signed to 'Essex' and issued the 78, 'ICY HEART' / 'ROCK THE JOINT', although this was only a minor seller. Renaming the outfit BILL HALEY & HIS COMETS, they hit upon a winning combination of rockabilly fused with their own interpretation of black R&B, scoring their first US Top 20 hit with 'CRAZY MAN CRAZY'. In 1954, the group shifted stables to 'Decca', where they cut 'THIRTEEN WOMEN' as a single, although this was to initially flop. The record's flip side, 'ROCK AROUND THE CLOCK', began to garner airplay from some of the more non-conformist radio stations and their next single, 'SHAKE, RATTLE AND ROLL' became a Top 20 hit (on both! sides of the Atlantic). Due to unprecedented public demand, 'ROCK AROUND THE CLOCK' was reissued, this landmark track eventually becoming a transatlantic chart topper. It was undeniably the birth of popular rock'n'roll, the youth culture transforming virtually overnight (parents hated its rebellious overtones, their offspring bopping uninhibitedly around the nation's dancehalls). HALEY was now giving legendary performances up and down the States, although his clean-cut and well-dressed appearance disappointed his newfound British following who were looking for a thinner, unmarried figurehead to portray this hip new sound. The formula was repeated on subsequent 45's/78's throughout the mid-late 50's, songs such as 'ROCK-A-BEATIN' BOOGIE', 'SEE YOU LATER, ALLIGATOR', 'THE SAINTS ROCK'N'ROLL' and 'ROCKIN' THROUGH THE RYE' dominating the charts prior to the advent of rock'n'roll as an image industry for fresh-faced youngsters (i.e. ELVIS, EDDIE, and even CLIFF). The 60's were virtually a non-starter for HALEY, although his revival concerts of the following decade saw obligatory reissues of 'ROCK AROUND THE CLOCK' hit the UK Top 20. Sadly, after a year spent in and out of hospital with a brain tumour, he died of a heart attack at his home in Harlingen, Texas on the 9th of February, 1981. • **Songwriters:** HALEY adapted songs from obscure originals, writing many himself. Covered ROCK THE JOINT (Jimmy Preston) / ROCKET 88 (hit. Jackie Brenston) / RIP IT UP (Little Richard) / WHEN THE SAINTS GO MARCHING IN (trad.) / ROCKIN' THROUGH THE RYE (Scot. trad) / etc.

Best CD compilation: THE VERY BEST OF BILL HALEY & HIS COMETS (*7)

BILL HALEY and the 4 ACES OF WESTERN SWING

BILL HALEY – vocals, guitar; and unknown backers

		not iss.	Cowboy
1948.	(78) <1201> **TOO MANY PARTIES, TOO MANY PALS. / FOUR LEAF CLOVER BLUES**	`-`	
1948.	(78) <1202> **CANDY KISSES. / TENNESSEE BORDER**	`-`	

JOHNNY CLIFTON & HIS STRING BAND

		not iss.	Center
1949.	(78) <102> **STAND UP AND BE COUNTED. / LOVELESS BLUES**	`-`	

—— In 1950, BILL HALEY's vocals were credited on RENO BROWNE and her BUCKAROOS single, 'MY SWEET LITTLE GIRL FROM NEVADA' <1701>

BILL HALEY and his SADDLEMEN

—— with **JOHNNY GRANDE** – piano / **BILLY WILLIAMSON** – steel guitar

		not iss.	Keystone
1950.	(78) <5101> **DEAL ME A HAND (I PLAY THE GAME ANYWAY). / TEN GALLON STETSON (WITH A HOLE IN THE CROWN)**		
1950.	(78) <5102> **SUSAN VAN DUREN. / I'M NOT TO BLAME** (below was backing for **LOU GRAHAM**	`-`	

		not iss.	Atlantic
1950.	(78) <727> **WHY DO I CRY OVER YOU. / I'M GONNA DRY EVERY TEAR WITH A KISS**	`-`	

		not iss.	Holiday
1951.	(78) <105> (TU 103) **ROCKET 88. / TEARSTAINS ON MY HEART**	`-`	

(UK-iss.Feb81 on 'Thumbs Up')

1951.	(78) <108> **GREEN TREE BOOGIE. / DOWN DEEP IN MY HEART**	`-`	
1951.	(78) <110> **I'M CRYING. / PRETTY BABY**	`-`	
1951.	(78) <111> **A YEAR AGO THIS CHRISTMAS. / I DON'T WANT TO ALONE THIS CHRISTMAS**	`-`	
1952.	(78) <113> **JUKEBOX CANNONBALL. / SUNDOWN BOOGIE**	`-`	

		not iss.	Essex
1952.	(78) <303> **ICY HEART. / ROCK THE JOINT**	`-`	
1952.	(78) <305> **ROCKING CHAIR ON THE MOON. / DANCE WITH THE DOLLY (WITH A HOLE IN HER STOCKING)**	`-`	

BILL HALEY and his COMETS

—— with **GRANDE + WILLIAMSON** plus **DANNY SEDRONE** – lead guitar / **MARSHALL PINGATORE** – up.bass / **DICK RICHARDS** – drums / **JOEY D'AMBROSIA** – tenor sax.

		London	Essex
1952.	(78) <310> **STOP BEATIN' ROUND THE MULBURRY BUSH. / REAL ROCK DRIVE**	`-`	
Aug 53.	(78) (L 1190) <321> **CRAZY MAN, CRAZY. / WHATCHA GONNA DO**		Feb53
Nov 53.	(78) (L 1216) <327> **PAT-A-CAKE. / FRACTURED**		Apr53
1953.	(78) <332> **LIVE IT UP. / FAREWELL, SO LONG, GOODBYE**	`-`	
1953.	(78) <340> **I'LL BE TRUE. / TEN LITTLE INDIANS**	`-`	
1953.	(78) <348> **STRAIGHT JACKET. / CHATTANOOGA CHOO-CHOO**	`-`	
1954.	(78) <374> **SUNDOWN BOOGIE. / JUKEBOX CANNONBALL**	`-`	
1954.	(78) <381> **ROCKET 88. / GREEN TREE BOOGIE**	`-`	
1954.	(lp) <LP 202> **ROCK WITH BILL HALEY & THE COMETS** (re-iss. 1954 on 'Trans World'; same)	`-`	

—— **BILLY GUSACK** – session drums (only 1)

		Brunswick	Decca
Sep 54.	(7",78) (05317) <29124> **ROCK AROUND THE CLOCK. / THIRTEEN WOMEN**		May54

(re-dist.UK Dec54 hit No.17, Oct55 hit No.1, Sep56 hit No.5, stayed Top 30 until early next year) (re-dist.US Apr55, after 'Blackboard Jungle' film appearance, hit No.1, stayed in Top 50 for 1/2 a year)

—— **FRANNY BEECHER** – lead guitar repl. CEDRONE who died of heart attack / **RUDY POMPILLI** – saxophone / **AL POMPILLI** – bass / **RALPH JONES** – drums repl. others

		Brunswick	Decca
Nov 54.	(7",78) (05338) <29204> **SHAKE, RATTLE AND ROLL. / ABC BOOGIE**	4	12 Jul54
Jan 55.	(7",78) (05373) <29317> **DIM, DIM THE LIGHTS (I WANT SOME ATMOSPHERE). / HAPPY BABY**		11 Nov54
Mar 55.	(7",78) (05405) <29418> **MAMBO ROCK. / BIRTH OF THE BOOGIE**	14	18 / 17 Feb55
Jul 55.	(7",78) (05405) <29552> **RAZZLE-DAZZLE. / TWO HOUND DOGS**		15

(UK re-dist.Sep56; hit No.13)

Sep 55.	(10"lp) <DL 5560> **SHAKE RATTLE AND ROLL**		`-`
Nov 55.	(7",78) (05509) <29713> **ROCK-A-BEATIN' BOOGIE. / BURN THAT CANDLE**	4	9 / 23
Feb 56.	(7",78) (05530) <29791> **SEE YOU LATER, ALLIGATOR. / THE PAPER BOY**	7	6 Jan56

(re-dist.UK Sep56; hit No.12)

| May 56. | (7",78) (05565) <29870> **THE SAINTS ROCK'N'ROLL. / R-O-C-K** | 5 | 18 Mar56 / 16 |
| Jun 56. | (lp) (LAT 8117) <DL 8225> **ROCK AROUND THE CLOCK** | | 12 Jan56 |

– (virtually a compilation, didn't make it in UK due to no lp chart until Nov'58)
– Rock around the clock / Shake rattle and roll / ABC boogie / (You hit the wrong note) Billy goat / Thirteen women (and only one man in town) / Tonight's the night / Razzle dazzle / Two hound dogs / Dim dim the lights / Happy baby / Birth of the boogie / Rockin' rollin' Rover / Mambo rock / Hide and seek / Burn that candle / Rock-a-beatin' boogie. (re-iss. 1961 on 'Ace Of Hearts', re-iss. May68, hit UK No.34) (re-iss. Jan71 on 'Coral') (re-iss. Sep81 on 'M.C.A.')

Aug 56.	(7",78) (05582) <29948> **ROCKIN' THROUGH THE RYE. / HOT DOG BUDDY BUDDY**	3	78 / 60
Nov 56.	(7",78) (05615) <30028> **RIP IT UP. / TEENAGER'S MOTHER (ARE YOU RIGHT?)**	4	25 / 68 Aug56
Nov 56.	(lp) (LAT 8139) <DL 8345> **ROCK'N'ROLL STAGE SHOW** (hit singles chart=)	30	18 Sep56

– Calling all comets / Rockin' through the rye / A rocking little tune / Hide and seek /

Hey then there now / Goofin' around / Hook line and sinker / Rudy's rock / Choo choo ch'boogie / Blue comet blues / Hot dog buddy buddy / Tonight's the night. *(re-iss. Aug83 on 'Charly')*

Date	Release		
Nov 56.	(7",78) *(05615)* *<30085>* **RUDY'S ROCK. / BLUE COMET BLUES**	26	34
Dec 56.	(7") *<30148>* **DON'T KNOCK THE ROCK. / CHOO CHOO CH'BOOGIE**	–	45
Feb 57.	(7",78) *(05640)* **DON'T KNOCK THE ROCK. / CALLING ALL COMETS**	7	–
Feb 57.	(7",78) *(05641)* **HOOK, LINE AND SINKER. / GOOFIN' AROUND**	–	–
Mar 57.	(7") *<30214>* **FORTY CUPS OF COFFEE. / HOOK, LINE AND SINKER**	–	70
Apr 57.	(7",78) *(05658)* **FORTY CUPS OF COFFEE. / CHOO CHOO CH'BOOGIE**	–	–

—— **FRANKIE SCOTT** – saxophone repl. RUDY (He was to die 5 Feb'76)

Date	Release		
Jul 57.	(7",78) *(05688)* *<30314>* **(YOU HIT THE WRONG NOTE) BILLY GOAT. / ROCKIN' ROLLIN' ROVER**		
Oct 57.	(7",78) *(05719)* *<30394>* **MISS YOU. / THE DIPSY DOODLE**		
Dec 57.	(lp) *(LAT 8219)* *<DL 8569>* **ROCKIN' THE OLDIES**		

– The dipsy doodle / You can't stop me from dreamin' / (I'll be with you) In apple blossom time / Moon over Miami / Is it true what they say about Dixie / Carolina in the morning / Miss you / Please don't talk about me when I'm gone / Ain't misbehavin' (I'm savin' my love for you) / One sweet letter from you / I'm gonna sit right down and write myself a letter / Somebody else is taking my place. *(re-iss. Oct62 on 'Ace Of Hearts')*

Date	Release		
Feb 58.	(7",78) *(05735)* *<30530>* **MARY, MARY LOU. / IT'S A SIN**		
Apr 58.	(7",78) *(05742)* *<30592>* **SKINNY MINNIE. / HOW MANY**		22
Aug 58.	(7",78) *(05753)* *<30681>* **LEAN JEAN. / DON'T NOBODY MOVE**		67
Nov 58.	(lp) *(LAT 8268)* *<DL 8775>* **ROCKIN' THE JOINT**		

– Rock the joint / Rockin' chair on the Moon / Farewell – So long – Goodbye / Real rock drive / Fractured / Stop beatin' around the mulberry bush / Crazy man, crazy / Pat-a-cake / Live it up / Watcha gonna do / I'll be true to you / Dance with a dolly (with a hole in her stockin').

Date	Release		
Nov 58.	(7",78) *(05766)* *<30741>* **WHOA MABEL! / CHIQUITA LINDA**		
Jan 59.	(7",78) *(05781)* **CORRINE, CORRINA. / B-B-BETTY**	–	
Mar 59.	(7",78) *(05788)* *<30844>* **I GOT A WOMAN. / CHARMAINE**	–	
Jun 59.	(lp) *(LAT 8295)* *<DL 8821>* **BILL HALEY'S CHICKS**		

– Whoa Mabel! / Ida, sweet as apple cider / Eloise / Dinah / Skinny Minnie / Mary, Mary Lou / Sweet Sue – Just you / B-B-Betty / Charmaine / Corrine Corrina / Marie / Lean Jean. *(re-iss. 1960 stereo; STA 3011); (re-iss. Jan64 on 'Ace Of Hearts'; AH 66)*

Date	Release		
Jun 59.	(7") *<30873>* **WHERE DID YOU GO LAST NIGHT? / (NOW AND THEN THERE'S) A FOOL SUCH AS I**	–	
Aug 59.	(7",78) *(05805)* *<30926>* **SHAKY. / CALEDONIA**	–	
Jan 60.	(7",78) *(05810)* *<30956>* **JOEY'S SONG. / LOOK-A-THERE, AIN'T SHE PRETTY**		46 Sep59
Feb 60.	(7") *(05818)* *<31030>* **SKOKIAAN. / PUERTO RICAN JUGGLER**		70 Dec59
Apr 60.	(7") *<31080>* **MUSIC! MUSIC! MUSIC!. / STRICTLY INSTRUMENTAL**	–	
Apr 60.	(lp) *(LAT 8326)* *<DL 8964>* **STRICTLY INSTRUMENTAL**		

– Joey's song / (Put another nickel in) Music, music, music / Mack the knife / In a little Spanish town ('twas on a night like this) / Two shadows / Shaky / Strictly instrumental / Skokiaan (South African song) / Puerto Rican peddlar / Drowsy waters / Chiquita Linda (un poquito de tu amor) / The catwalk.

		Warners	Warners
May 60.	(7") *(WB 6)* **CANDY KISSES. / TAMIAMI**	–	
1960.	(7") *(5154)* **CHUCK SAFARI. / HAWK**	–	
1960.	(7") *(5171)* **SO RIGHT TONIGHT. / LET THE GOOD TIMES ROLL, CREOLE**	–	
Nov 60.	(lp) *(W 1391)* **HALEY'S JUKE BOX**		

– Sing the blues / Candy kisses / No letter today / This is the thanks I get / Bouquet of roses / There's a new Moon over my shoulder / Cold, cold heart / Wild side of life / Any time / Afraid / I don't hurt anymore.

		London	Gone
1960.	(7") *(5228)* **FLIP, FLOP AND FLY. / HONKY TONK**	–	

		not iss.	Orfeon
Dec 61.	(7") *(HLU 9471)* *<5111>* **SPANISH TWIST. / MY KIND OF WOMAN**	–	
1962.	(7") *(5116)* **RIVIERA. / WAR PAINT**	–	

		not iss.	Logo
1962.	(7") **FLORIDA TWIST. / NEGRA CONSENTIDA**	–	– Mexico
1962.	(7") **PURE DE PAPAS. / ANOCHE**	–	– Mexico

		Columbia	Columbia
1962.	(7") *<7005>* **YAKETY SAX. / BOOTS RANDOLPH – BOOTS BLUES**	–	
Oct 62.	(lp) *(33SX 1460)* **TWISTIN' KNIGHTS AT THE ROUNDTABLE (LIVE!)**		

– Lullaby of Birdland twist / Twist Marie / One two three twist / Down by the riverside twist / Queen of the twisters / Caravan twist / I want a little girl / Whistlin' and walkin' twist / Florida twist / Eight more miles to Louisville. *(re-iss. May81 on 'P.R.T.')*

		Stateside	Newtown
Jun 63.	(7") *(SS 196)* *<5013>* **TENOR MAN. / UP GOES MY LOVE**		
1963.	(7") *<5014>* **MIDNIGHT IN WASHINGTON. / WHITE PARAKEET**		–
1963.	(7") *<5024>* **DANCE AROUND THE CLOCK. / WHAT CAN I SAY AFTER I SAY I'M SORRY**		–
1963.	(7") *<5025>* **TANDY. / YOU CALL EVERYBODY DARLING**		–

		Brunswick	Decca
Aug 64.	(7") *(05910)* **HAPPY BABY. / BIRTH OF THE BOOGIE**		–
Oct 64.	(7") *(05917)* *<31650>* **GREEN DOOR. / (YEAH!) SHE'S EVIL**		

		not iss.	Apt
1965.	(7") *<25051>* **BIG DADDY. / ST. LOUIS**	–	
1965.	(7") *<25081>* **BURN THAT CANDLE. / STOP, LOOK AND LISTEN**	–	
1965.	(7") *<25087>* **HALEY A GO-GO. / TONGUE TIED TONY**	–	

		not iss.	U.A.
1969.	(7") *<50483>* **THAT'S HOW I GOT TO MEMPHIS. / AIN'T LOVE FUNNY, HA! HA! HA!**	–	

		not iss.	Kama Sutra
1970.	(7") *<508>* **ROCK AROUND THE CLOCK. / FRAMED**	–	

		Sonet	GNP Cres
1971.	(lp) *(SNTF 623)* *<2097>* **ROCK AROUND THE COUNTRY**		

– Dance around the clock / Games people play / A little piece at a time / I wouldn't have missed it for the world / Bony Moronie / There's a new Moon over my shoulder / Me and Bobby McGee / How many / Who'll stop the rain / Pink eyed pussycat / Travelin' band / No letter today. *(re-iss. Jun74 on 'Hallmark')*

Date	Release		
1972.	(7") *<162>* **A LITTLE PIECE AT A TIME. / TRAVELIN' BAND**		
May 73.	(7") *(SON 2016)* **ME AND BOBBY McGEE. / I WOULDN'T HAVE MISSED IT FOR THE WORLD**		
1973.	(lp) *(SNTF 645)* **JUST ROCK AND ROLL MUSIC**		

– I'm walkin' / High-heel sneakers / Blue suede shoes / Tossin' and turnin' / Flip, flop and fly / Whole lotta shakin' goin' on / CC rider / Lawdy Miss Clawdy / Bring it on home to me / Personality / Crazy man crazy / Rock'n'roll music.

Date	Release		
1974.	(lp) **LIVE IN SWEDEN** (live)		–
Jun 74.	(7") *(SON 2043)* **CRAZY MAN CRAZY** (live). **/ LAWDY MISS CLAWDY** (live)		

		Atlantic	Atlantic
Jun 74.	(lp) *(K 51501)* **LIVE IN LONDON '74** (live)		

– Shake, rattle & roll / Rudy's rock / Rip it up / Spanish eyes / Razzle dazzle / Rock-a-beatin' boogie / Caravan / See you later alligator / Saints rock and roll / Rock around the clock / Rock the joint.

—— HALEY became ill, leading him into retirement. Although in England, he had given final appearance at Royal Variety Show, Nov79. In 1980, now at age 55, he was diagnosed with brain tumor. On 9 Feb'81 he died of a heart attack.

– compilations, others, etc. –

Date	Release		
1953.	(7") *Transworld;* *<718>* **YES INDEED. / REAL ROCK DRIVE**	–	–
Jun 55.	(7"ep) *Brunswick;* *(OE 9129)* **DIM DIM THE LIGHTS**		
Jun 56.	(7"ep) *Brunswick;* *(REF 1031)* **ROCK AND ROLL**		
Jun 56.	(7"ep) *Brunswick;* *(OE 9250)* **ROCK AROUND THE CLOCK**		
Dec 56.	(7"ep) *Brunswick;* *(OE 9278)* **ROCK'N'ROLL STAGE SHOW (PART 1)**		
Dec 56.	(7"ep) *Brunswick;* *(OE 9279)* **ROCK'N'ROLL STAGE SHOW (PART 2)**		
Dec 56.	(7"ep) *Brunswick;* *(OE 9280)* **ROCK'N'ROLL STAGE SHOW (PART 3)**		
Feb 58.	(7"ep) *Brunswick;* *(OE 9349)* **ROCKING THE OLDIES (PART 1)**		
Feb 58.	(7"ep) *Brunswick;* *(OE 9350)* **ROCKING THE OLDIES (PART 2)**		
Feb 58.	(7"ep) *Brunswick;* *(OE 9351)* **ROCKING THE OLDIES (PART 3)**		
Apr 59.	(7"ep) *Brunswick;* *(OE 9446)* **ROCKING AROUND THE WORLD**		
Jul 59.	(7"ep) *Brunswick;* *(OE 9459)* **BILL HALEY AND HIS COMETS**		
Jun 55.	(7") *London;* *(HL 8142)* **GREEN TREE BOOGIE. / SUNDOWN BOOGIE**		
Aug 55.	(10"ep) *London;* *(H-APB 1042)* **LIVE IT UP**		
Aug 55.	(7") *London;* *(HLF 8161)* **FAREWELL, SO LONG, GOODBYE. / I'LL BE TRUE**		
Oct 55.	(7") *London;* *(HLF 8194)* **TEN LITTLE INDIANS. / ROCKING CHAIR ON THE MOON**		
Dec 55.	(7"ep) *London;* *(REF 1031)* **ROCK AND ROLL**		
Feb 56.	(7"ep) *London;* *(REF 1049)* **LIVE IT UP (PART ONE)**		
Feb 56.	(7"ep) *London;* *(REF 1050)* **LIVE IT UP (PART TWO)**		
Oct 56.	(7"ep) *London;* *(REF 1058)* **LIVE IT UP (PART THREE)**		
Feb 57.	(7") *Decca;* *<30461>* **ROCK THE JOINT. / HOW MANY?**	–	
Feb 57.	(7") *London;* *(HLF 8371)* **ROCK THE JOINT. / YES INDEED**	20	
Mar 57.	(lp) *London;* *(HA-F 2037)* **ROCK THE JOINT** ('Essex' work)		

(re-iss. May64 on 'Golden Guinea'; 0282) (re-iss. 1966 on 'Marble Arch'; 817) (re-iss. May79 on 'Rollercoaster' 10"lp; 2002) (re-iss. 1985, 12"lp; ROLL 2009) (cd-iss. Nov89; CDROLL 3001)

Date	Release		
Nov 56.	(7") *Melodisc;* *(1036)* **I'M GONNA DRY EVERY LITTLE TEAR WITH A KISS. / WHY DO I CRY OVER YOU**		
Jun 60.	(7"ep) *Warners;* *(WEP 6001)* **HALEY AND HIS COMETS**		–
May 61.	(7"ep) *Warners;* *(WEP 6025)* **HALEY'S JUKEBOX**		–
Aug 64.	(7") *Warners;* *(WB 133)* **ROCK AROUND THE CLOCK. / LOVE LETTERS IN THE SAND**		–
Oct 64.	(7"ep) *Warners;* *(WEP 6133)* **BILL HALEY VOLUME 1**		–
Nov 64.	(7"ep) *Warners;* *(WEP 6136)* **BILL HALEY VOLUME 2**		–
Jun 81.	(lp/c) *Warners;* *(K 40555)* **ROCK'N'ROLL FOREVER**		–
1961.	(7") *Ksey;* **ABC BOOGIE. / (other artist)**		–
1965.	(lp) *Xtra;* *(XTRA 1027)* **BILL HALEY AND THE COMETS**		

(re-iss. 1970 on 'Valient'; VS 103)

Date	Release		
1967.	(lp) *Ember;* **REAL LIVE ROCK AND ROLL**		–
Jun 68.	(lp) *Ember;* *(EMB 3396)* **KING OF ROCK'N'ROLL**		–
Jan 69.	(lp) *Ember;* *(EMB 3041)* **MR. ROCK'N'ROLL**		–
Apr 68.	(7") *Pye Int.;* *(7N 25455)* **CRAZY MAN CRAZY. / LAWDY MISS CLAWDY**		–
Mar 68.	(lp) *M.C.A.;* *(MU 1013)* **ROCK AROUND THE CLOCK. / SHAKE RATTLE AND ROLL**	20	
May 68.	(lp) *M.C.A.;* *(MUP 318)* **RIP IT UP**		
Mar 74.	(7") *M.C.A.;* *(MCA 128)* **ROCK AROUND THE CLOCK. / RIP IT UP**	12	–
Mar 74.	(7") *M.C.A.;* *(60025)* **(WE'RE GONNA) ROCK AROUND THE CLOCK. / THIRTEEN WOMEN (AND ONLY ONE MAN IN TOWN)**	–	39
Jun 74.	(lp/c) *M.C.A.;* *(MCL/+C 1778)* **GOLDEN HITS**		

Jun 74.	M.C.A.; (7") *(MCA 142)* **SEE YOU LATER ALLIGATOR. /** **RUDY'S ROCK**	☐ ☐
Nov 76.	(7"m) *M.C.A.; (MCA 263)* **SHAKE RATTLE AND ROLL. /** **RAZZLE DAZZLE / ROCK-A-BEATIN' BOOGIE**	☐ -
Jul 78.	(lp/c) *M.C.A.; (MCF 2838)* **ARMCHAIR ROCK'N'ROLL**	☐ -
Sep 78.	(10"ep) *(MCEP 2)* **THE SAINTS ROCK'N'ROLL**	☐ -
Apr 81.	(7") *M.C.A.; (MCA 694)* **HALEY'S GOLDEN MEDLEY. / ABC** **BOOGIE**	50 ☐
May 81.	(d-lp/c) *M.C.A.; (MCL /+C 1770)* **A TRIBUTE TO BILL HALEY**	☐ -
Feb 85.	(cd) *M.C.A.; (120 104)* **GREATEST HITS**	☐ -
Jul 85.	(lp/c) *M.C.A.; (MCL /+C 19184)* **GOLDEN GREATS**	☐ -
Sep 85.	(cd) *M.C.A.; (MCA 5539)* **FROM THE ORIGINAL MASTER** **TAPES**	☐ -
Jun 70.	(lp/c) *Hallmark; (SHM /HSC 668)* **ROCK AROUND THE CLOCK** *(re-iss. Feb83 on 'Spot' lp/c; SPR /SPC 8502)*	☐ -
Sep 70.	(lp) *Hallmark; (SHM 694)* **ON STAGE** (live)	☐ -
Sep 72.	(lp) *Hallmark; (SHM 773)* **GOLDEN KING OF ROCK**	☐ -
Mar 87.	(lp/c) *Hallmark; (SHM /HSC 3207)* **THE ORIGINAL HITS** **'54-'57** *(cd-iss. Mar90 on 'Pickwick'; PWKS 575)*	☐ -
Mar 76.	(d-lp) *Pickwick; (PDA 006)* **THE BILL HALEY COLLECTION**	☐ -
Feb 79.	(lp) *Bulldog; (BDL 2002)* **20 GOLDEN PIECES OF BILL HALEY** *(cd-iss. Nov89 as 'GOLDEN CD COLLECTION'; BDCD 2002)*	☐ -
May 79.	(7") *Rollercoaster; (RRC 2004)* **ROCK THE JOINT. /** **FRACTURED** *(re-iss. 1984)*	☐ -
May 79.	(lp) *Rollercoaster; (ROLL 1300)* **GOLDEN COUNTRY ORIGINS**	☐ -
Feb 80.	(7"ep) *Rollercoaster; (RCEP 102)* **REAL ROCK DRIVE**	☐ -
Nov 84.	(lp) *Rollercoaster; (ROLL 2007)* **HILLBILLY HALEY**	☐ -
Oct 76.	(lp) *Sonet; (SMTF 710)* **R.O.C.K.**	☐ -
Aug 79.	(7") *Sonet; (SON 2188)* **HAIL HAIL ROCK'N'ROLL. / LET** **THE GOOD TIMES ROLL**	☐ -
Nov 79.	(7") *Sonet; (SON 2194)* **EVERYONE CAN ROCK AND ROLL. /** **I NEED THE MUSIC**	☐ -
Jun 80.	(lp) *Sonet; (SNTF 808)* **EVERYONE CAN ROCK AND ROLL**	☐ -
Feb 81.	(7") *Sonet; (SON 2202)* **GOD BLESS ROCK AND ROLL. /** **SO RIGHT TONIGHT**	☐ -
Jul 82.	(7") *Old Gold; (OG 9221)* **SHAKE RATTLE AND ROLL. / SEE** **YOU LATER ALLIGATOR**	☐ -
Jul 90.	(12"ep) *Old Gold;* **ROCK-A-BEATIN' BOOGIE / RAZZLE** **DAZZLE. / BURN THAT CANDLE / DIM DIM THE LIGHTS**	☐ -
Jul 82.	(7") *Revival; (REV 6016)* **RUDY'S ROCK. / ABC BOOGIE**	☐ -
Sep 82.	(5xlp-box) *Bear Family; <BFX 15068-5>* **ROCK ROLLIN'** **BILL HALEY** *(UK-iss.Sep84 on 'Rollercoaster'; same)*	- ☐
Sep 83.	(7"ep/c-ep) *Scoop; (7SR /7SC 5012)* **SIX-TRACK HITS** – Whole lotta shakin' goin' on / Rock around the clock / Shake rattle and roll / Kansas City / Me and Bobby McGee / Rip it up.	☐ -
1984.	(d-lp) *Charly;* **MR. ROCK'N'ROLL / THE ESSENTIAL BILL** **HALEY**	☐ -
Jan 85.	(lp) *Topline; (TOP /KTOP 114)* **BOOGIE WITH BILL HALEY**	☐ -
Jul 85.	(lp/c) *Buddah; (252261-1 /-4)* **BILL HALEY'S ROCK'N'ROLL** **SCRAPBOOK** *(cd-iss. Apr90 on 'Sequel')*	☐ -
Oct 87.	(lp/c) *Music For Pleasure;* **BILL HALEY & HIS COMETS**	☐ -
1988.	(d-lp) *Connoisseur;* **GREATEST HITS**	☐ -
1988.	(d-lp/c/cd) *Connoisseur; (VSOP LP /MC /CD 116)* **RIP IT UP** **ROCK'N'ROLL**	☐ -
Jul 92.	(cd/c) *Music Club; (MC CD /TC 068)* **THE VERY BEST OF BILL** **HALEY & HIS COMETS** – Rock around the clock / Shake, rattle and roll / See you later alligator / The saints rock and roll / Rock-a beatin' boogie / Rockin' thru the rye / Rip it up / Don't knock the rock / Mambo rock / Rudy's rock / Razzle dazzle / Skinny Minnie / R.O.C.K. / Thirteen women / ABC boogie / Birth of the boogie / Forty cups of coffee / Two hound dogs / Burn that candle / Calling all Comets.	☐ -
Oct 93.	(cd) *See For Miles;* **THE EP COLLECTION**	☐ -
Jul 94.	(7"ep) *Rollercoaster;* **REAL ROCK DRIVE / LIVE IT UP. /** **DANCE WITH A DOLLY / ROCKING CHAIR ON THE** **MOON**	☐ -
Aug 94.	(cd) *Dynamite; (LECD 034)* **BILL HALEY**	☐ -
Feb 95.	(cd/c) *More Music; (MOCD /MOMC 3015)* **ROCK AROUND** **THE CLOCK**	☐ -
Mar 95.	(cd) *Laserlight; (12396)* **BILL HALEY & HIS COMETS**	☐ -
Sep 95.	(cd/c) *Hallmark;* **CRAZY MAN CRAZY**	☐ -

HALF MAN HALF BISCUIT   (dig out; Great Alt & Indie . . .)

HALF NELSON (see under ⇒ SPARKS)

Terry HALL

Born: 19 Mar'59, Coventry, England. Having been part of ska revival outfit, The SPECIALS between '78-'81, TERRY HALL broke away with two other SPECIALS; NEVILLE STAPLES and LYNVAL GOULDING to form The FUN BOY THREE, a racially-mixed politically-motivated trio. Still contracted to 'Chrysalis', they issued their debut UK Top 20 single 'THE LUNATICS HAVE TAKEN OVER THE ASYLUM'. Early the next year, they teamed up with new all-girl trio BANANARAMA, to have a UK Top 5 hit with 30's standard 'IT AIN'T WHAT YOU DO IT'S THE WAY THAT YOU DO IT'. It was soon trailed by a Top 10 eponymous album, and four more Top 20 singles. After the release of a DAVID BYRNE (Talking Heads)-produced Top 10 album in 1983, they soon split two ways. While NEVILLE and LYNVAL formed SUNDAY BEST, TERRY HALL formed The COLOUR FIELD, a smoother romance'n'roll affair which nevertheless failed to repeat HALL's

previous commercial success. With a line-up completed by KARL SHALE and TOBY LYONS, The COLOUR FIELD got off to a less than impressive start in early '84, their first two singles stiffing; it would be a full year on before they enjoyed Top 20 success with the elegant schmooze-pop of 'THINKING OF YOU'. A subsequent album, 'VIRGINS AND PHILISTINES' (1985), confirmed HALL's infatuation with 'classic' songwriting and arranging, yet despite some encouraging reviews, his subtle approach seemed doomed to cult appeal. A follow-up, 'DECEPTION' (1987), failed to make any impression and HALL disbanded the project later that year. He then went on to record a one-off album with BLAIR BOOTH and ANOUCHKA GROOCE, 'ULTRA MODERN NURSERY RHYMES' (1990), before collaborating with ex-EURYTHMICS man, DAVE STEWART, in the short-lived VEGAS. Recruiting fellow 80's veterans, CRAIG GANNON, LES PATTINSON and CHRIS SHARROCK, HALL released a solo set, 'HOME', in 1994, while more recently he worked with TRICKY (a massive SPECIALS fan) on the latter's NEARLY GOD (1996) project as well as releasing a live version of 'GHOST TOWN' (on '95's 'RAINBOWS' EP) featuring the Bristolian maverick. • **Songwriters:** HALL/group penned except; SUMMERTIME (Gershwin). 'OUR LIPS ARE SEALED' was composed by HALL and GO-GO's singer BELINDA CARLISLE. The COLOUR FIELD covered; RUNNING AWAY (Sly & The Family Stone) / SHE (Charles Aznavour) / LOVE WILL KEEP US TOGETHER (Neil Sedaka) / THREE COOL CATS (Leiber-Stoller) / GOD ONLY KNOWS (Beach Boys) / THIS GUY'S IN LOVE WITH YOU (Herb Alpert). • **Trivia:** The COLOUR FIELD's 'THINKING OF YOU' single featured the dual vox of KATRINA PHILLIPS, who later joined GHOST DANCE.

Album rating: Fun Boy Three: FUN BOY THREE (*7) / WAITING (*5) / Colour Field: VIRGINS & PHILISTINES (*6) / DECEPTION (*5) / Terry, Blair & Anouchka: ULTRA MODERN NURSERY RHYMES (*5) / Vegas: VEGAS (*5) / Terry Hall: THE COLLECTION compilation 1979-1990 (*7) / HOME (*6) / LAUGH (*5)

FUN BOY THREE

TERRY HALL – vocals (ex-SPECIALS) / **NEVILLE STAPLES** – vocals, percussion (ex-SPECIALS) / **LYNVAL GOULDING** – guitar (ex-SPECIALS)

		Chrysalis	Chrysalis
Oct 81.	(7"/12") *(CHS /+12 2563)* **THE LUNATICS (HAVE TAKEN** **OVER THE ASYLUM). / FAITH, HOPE & CHARITY**	20	☐
Jan 82.	(7"; by FUN BOY THREE & BANANARAMA) *(CHS 2570)* **T'AIN'T WHAT YOU DO (IT'S THE WAY THAT YOU DO IT). / THE FUNRAMA THEME** *(12"+=)* *(CHS12 2570)* – Funrama theme (extended).	4	☐

—— now with **NICKY HOLLAND** – keyboards / **JUNE MILES-KINGSTON** – drums

Mar 82.	(lp/c) *(CHR /ZCHR 1383)* **THE FUN BOY THREE** – Sanctuary / Way on down / The lunatics have taken over the asylum / Life in general / Faith, hope and charity / Funrama 2 / Best of luck mate / T'ain't what you do (it's the way that you do it) / The telephone always rings / I don't believe it / Alone. *(re-iss. Nov84 on 'Fame' lp/c; FA 413115-1 /-4)*	7	☐

—— Mar82 teamed up with BANANARAMA again on 45, 'REALLY SAYING SOMETHING'.

May 82.	(7"/7"pic-d,7"pic-d/12") *(CHS /+P/12 2609)* **THE TELEPHONE** **ALWAYS RINGS. / THE ALIBI**	17	☐
Jul 82.	(7"/7"pic-d/12") *(CHS /+P/12 2629)* **SUMMERTIME. /** **SUMMER OF '82**	18	☐

—— with **BOTHAN PETERS**– bass / **INGRID SCHROEDER**– vocals / **DICK CUTHILL** – coronet / **CAROLINE LEVELLE** – cello / **ANNIE WHITEHEAD**– trombone / **GERALDO D'ARBUY**– percussion

Dec 82.	(7"/12") *(CHS /+12 2664)* **THE MORE I SEE (THE LESS I** **BELIEVE). /**	68	☐
Jan 83.	(7"/7"pic-d/12") *(CHS /+P/12 2678)* **THE TUNNEL OF LOVE. /** **THE LUNACY LEGACY**	10	☐
Feb 83.	(lp/c) *(CHR /ZCHR 1417)* **WAITING** – The tunnel of love / Our lips are sealed / The pressure of life (takes weight off the body) / Things we do / Well fancy that! / Murder she said / The more I see (the less I believe) / Going home / We're having all the fun / The farm yard connection.	14	☐
Apr 83.	(7"/12") *(FUNB /+X 1)* **OUR LIPS ARE SEALED. /** ('A'instrumental) *(d7"+=)* *(FUNXP /FBFRE 1)* – We're having all the fun / Going home.	7	☐

—— (split mid'83) **NEVILLE AND LYNVAL to SUNDAY BEST.**

– compilations, etc. –

Jun 84.	(lp/c) *Chrysalis; (CHR /ZCHR 1459)* **THE BEST OF THE FUN** **BOY THREE** – T'ain't what you do (it's the way that you do it) / Really saying something / Summertime / The lunatics (have taken over the asylum) / The more I see (the less I believe) / The telephone always rings / Our lips are sealed / The tunnel of love / We're having all the fun / The farm yard connection / The pressure of life (takes weight off the body). *(cd-iss. Jun87; CPCD 1469)*	☐ ☐
Jan 88.	(12") *Old Gold; (OG 4038)* **OUR LIPS ARE SEALED. / THE** **TUNNEL OF LOVE / THE LUNATICS (HAVE TAKEN OVER** **THE ASYLUM)**	☐ -
May 94.	(cd) *Connoisseur; (VSOPCD 196)* **THE SINGLES (FUN BOY** **THREE / COLOUR FIELD)**	☐ -
Jun 94.	(cd) *Windsong; (cd) (WHISCD 003)* **LIVE ON THE TEST** (live)	☐ -

COLOUR FIELD

TERRY HALL – vocals / **KARL SHALE** – bass / **TOBY LYONS** – guitar, keyboards (ex-SWINGING CATS) / guest drummer ?

		Chrysalis	Chrysalis
Jan 84.	(7") *(COLF 1)* **THE COLOUR FIELD. / SORRY** *(12"+=)* *(COLFX 1)* – ('A'-special mix).	43	☐

—— added guest **PETE DE FREITAS** – drums (of ECHO & THE BUNNYMEN)

Jul 84. (7") *(COLF 2)* **TAKE. / PUSHING UP THE DAISIES**   `70`
(12"+=) *(COLFX 2)* – Windmills of your mind.

—— added **PAUL BURGESS** – drums

Jan 85. (7") *(COLF 3)* **THINKING OF YOU. / MY WILD FLAME**   `12`
(12"+=) *(COLFX 3)* – ('A'instrumental).
(d7"++=) *(COLFD 3)* – Little things.

Apr 85. (lp/c) *(CHR/ZCHR 1480)* **VIRGINS AND PHILISTINES**   `12`
– Thinking of you / Faint hearts / Castles in the air / Take / Cruel circus / Hammond song / Virgins and Philistines / Armchair theatre / Yours sincerely / Sorry.

Apr 85. (7") *(COLF 4)* **CASTLES IN THE AIR. / LOVE STRINGS**   `51`
(12") *(COLFX 4)* – ('A'side) / ('A'extended) / Your love was smashing.
(d7") *(COLFD 4)* – ('A'side) / I can't get enough of you baby / ('A'instrumental mix) / Your love was smashing.

—— **GARY DWYER** – drums (ex-TEARDROP EXPLODES) repl. BURGESS

Jan 86. (7") *(COLF 5)* **THINGS COULD BE SO BEAUTIFUL. / FROSTY MORNINGS**
(12"+=) *(COLFX 5)* – Pushing up the daisies (live) / Yours sincerely (live).

Feb 87. (7") *(COLF 6)* **RUNNING AWAY. / DIGGING IT DEEP**
(12"+=) *(COLFX 6)* – ('A'long version).
(12"+=) *(COLFR 6)* – ('A'vocal mix) / ('A'dub version).

Mar 87. (lp/c/cd) *(CDL/ZCDL/CCD 1546)* **DECEPTION**   `95`
– Badlands / Running away / From dawn to distraction / Confession / Miss Texas 1967 / She / Heart of America / She / Digging it deep / Monkey in winter / Goodbye Sun valley.

Jul 87. (7") *(COLF 7)* **SHE. / MONKEY IN WINTER**
(12"+=) *(COLFX 7)* – ('A'remix).

—— disbanded 1987.

TERRY, BLAIR & ANOUCHKA

(TERRY HALL, BLAIR BOOTH & ANOUCHKA GROOCE)(BLAIR also co-wrote songs)

Oct 89. (7"/c-s) *(CHS/+MC 3381)* **MISSING. / HAPPY FAMILIES**   `75`
(12"+=/cd-s+=) *(CHS 12/CD 3381)* – Beautiful people.

Jan 90. (7"/c-s) *(CHS/+MC 3478)* **ULTRA MODERN NURSERY RHYMES. / HUSH HUSH BALLOO**
(12"+=/cd-s+=) *(CHS 12/CD 3478)* – Love will keep us together.

Feb 90. (cd/c/lp) *(CD/Z+/CHR 1701)* **ULTRA MODERN NURSERY RHYMES**
– Ultra modern nursery rhyme / Missing / Fishbones and scaredy cats / Lucky in luv' / Day like today / Sweet September sacrifice / Beautiful people / Three cool cats / Happy families / Just go.

—— In 1992, TERRY HALL partnered with DAVE STEWART (ex-EURYTHMICS) in VEGAS.

VEGAS

(aka **DAVE STEWART & TERRY HALL**)

		R.C.A.	R.C.A.

Sep 92. (7"/c-s) *(74321 1043-7/-4)* **POSSESSED. / THE DAY IT RAINED FOREVER**   `32`
(cd-s+=) *(74321 1043-2)* – Infectious.
(cd-s+=) *(74321 1053-2)* – Lying in bed barefoot.

Oct 92. (cd/c) *(74321 11044-25/-??)* **VEGAS**
– Possessed / Walk into the wind / She's alright / Take me for what I am / The trouble with lovers / Nothing alas alack / The thought of you / Anthem / Wise guy / The day it rained forever / She.

Nov 92. (7"/c-s) *(74321 12465-7/-4)* **SHE. / ('A'disco mix)**   `43`
(12"+=) *(74321 12465-1)* – ('A'-Rapino Brothers mix) / ('A'-disco instrumental).
(cd-s+=) *(74321 12465-2)* – Tip of my tongue / If you kill my cat, I'll kill your dog.

Mar 93. (7"/c-s) *(74321 12246-7/-4)* **WALK INTO THE WIND. / WISE GUY**
(cd-s+=) *(74321 12246-2)* – Truth is stranger than fiction / Art blind.

TERRY HALL

with **CRAIG GANNON** – guitar (ex-SMITHS, ex-AZTEC CAMERA, etc) / **LES PATTINSON** – bass (ex-ECHO & THE BUNNYMEN) / **CHRIS SHARROCK** – drums (ex-ICICLE WORKS)

		Anxious	R.C.A.

Aug 94. (c-ep/cd-ep) *(4509 97289-4/-2)* **FOREVER J / FOREVER J (Pulp mix) / SUBURBAN CEMETERY / GUESS IT'S NOT A GREAT DAY TO BE ME**   `67`

Sep 94. (cd/c) *(4509 97269-2/-4)* **HOME**
– Forever J / Grief disguised as joy / First attack of love / I don't got you / No no no / I drew a lemon / Moon on your dress / What's wrong with me / You / Sense.
(re-iss. Nov95; same)

Nov 94. (7"/c-s) *(ANX 1027/+C)* **SENSE / GOD ONLY KNOWS**   `54`
(12"+=/cd-s+=) *(ANX 1037 T/CD)* – This guy's in love with you.
below with DAMON ALBARN (co-writer A), TRICKY and IAN BROUDIE.

Oct 95. (c-ep/cd-ep) *(ANX 1033 C/CD1)* **RAINBOWS e.p.**   `62`
– Chasing a rainbow (with DAMON ALBARN) / Ghost town (live with TRICKY) / Thinking of you (live) / Our lips are sealed (live).
(cd-s) *(ANX 1033CD2)* – (first 2 tracks) / Mistakes (with IAN BROUDIE) / See no evil (live).

		South Sea Bubble	not iss.

Jun 97. (7") *(7BUBBLE 1)* **BALLAD OF A LANDLORD. / BANG WENT FOREVER / (interview)**   `50` –
(cd-s) *(CDBUBBLE 1)* – ('A'side) / Music to watch girls by / Close to you.
(cd-s) *(CXBUBBLE 1)* – ('A'side) / Working class hero (live) / ('A'acoustic).

Oct 97. (cd/c) *(CD/CA BUBBLE 3)* **LAUGH**   `50`
– Love to see you / Room full of nothing / Sonny and his sister / Happy go lucky / Ballad of a landlord / For the girl / Take it forever / Summer follows Spring / Misty water / I saw the light.

– compilations, etc. –

Oct 92. (cd/c) *Chrysalis; (CD/TC CHR 1974)* **THE COLLECTION**
– (best material SPECIALS / FUN BOY THREE / COLOUR FIELD / TERRY, BLAIR, etc.)

Daryl HALL & John OATES

Formed: Philadelphia, Pennsylvania, USA . . . 1972 by the duo, who signed to 'Atlantic', following their work with the band, GULLIVER. They had originally met in 1967, while attending local Temple University; HALL had undergone classical training as a boy, and progressed to doo-wop groups while also featuring on a single recorded by future producer KENNY GAMBLE & THE ROMEOS. He then sessioned for many including THE TEMPTONES and SMOKEY ROBINSON, before forming GULLIVER with TIM MOORE, TOM SELLERS and JIM HELMER. They released one self-titled lp in 1969 for 'Elektra', before being joined by OATES, although they broke up before OATES could cut any songs with them. The duo's debut album, 'WHOLE OATS', was produced by Arif Mardin, and was followed in 1974 by 'ABANDONED LUNCHEONETTE', the latter set containing the first of HALL & OATES chartbound torch ballads in 'SHE'S GONE'. Though not a hit upon its original release, the single made the US Top 10 two years later. The latter track featured on 'WAR BABIES' (1974), a heavier, more experimental set (produced by TODD RUNDGREN) whose commmercial failure marked the end of their ill-fated tenure with 'Atlantic'. Moving to 'R.C.A.', the group concentrated on developing their white soul-rock/R&B, scoring almost immediately when their eponymous 1975 set climbed into the US Top 20 following the massive success of the infectious 'SARA SMILE' (co-written by HALL's sometime collaborator and girlfriend, Sara Allen). A follow-up set, 'BIGGER THAN BOTH OF US' (1976) was even more successful, spawning the duo's first No.1 hit, 'RICH GIRL'. Though their profile took a bit of a battering towards the end of the decade, HALL & OATES emerged with a gleaming new synth/pop-soul sound on 'VOICES' (1980), making the Top 20 with a cover of The Righteous Brothers' 'YOU'VE LOST THAT LOVIN' FEELIN' and scoring a belated second No.1 with 'KISS ON MY LIST' (it also included the original version of 'EVERY TIME YOU GO AWAY', later a hit for PAUL YOUNG). Vaguely akin to a two-headed American version of PHIL COLLINS (granted, a disturbing thought), HALL & OATES cleaned up in both the singles and albums market with a string of MOR hits including 'PRIVATE EYES', 'I CAN'T GO FOR THAT' (NO CAN DO)', 'MANEATER' and 'SAY IT ISN'T SO'; 'PRIVATE EYES' (1981) and 'H2O' (1982) remain among their best-selling albums. The mid-80's concert set, 'LIVE AT THE APOLLO', saw them hooking up with TEMPTATIONS heroes, DAVID RUFFIN and EDDIE KENDRICKS, after which they took time out to work on side projects. Returning in 1988, they scored with the Top 5 hit, 'EVERYTHING YOUR HEART DESIRES', although subsequent albums, 'OOH YEAH!' (1988) and 'CHANGE OF SEASON' (1990) failed to scale the commercial heights of yesteryear. • **Songwriters:** HALL-OATES except; THE WAY YOU DO THE THINGS YOU DO – MY GIRL (Temptations) / CAN'T HELP FALLING IN LOVE (Elvis Presley) / LOVE TRAIN (O'Jays) / etc. HALL covered; WRITTEN IN STONE (J.Allen-S.Dubin-K.Savigar) / ME AND MRS.JONES (Billy Paul). • **Trivia:** ROBERT FRIPP (of KING CRIMSON) produced HALL's solo outing 'SACRED SONGS'.

Album rating: WHOLE OATS (*5) / ABANDONED LUNCHEONETTE (*7) / WAR BABIES (*4) / DARYL HALL & JOHN OATES (*6) / BIGGER THAN BOTH OF US (*5) / NO GOODBYES copilation (*4) / BEAUTY ON A BACK STREET (*6) / LIVETIME (*4) / ALONG THE RED LEDGE (*6) / X-STATIC (*4) / SACRED SONGS (*4; by Daryl Hall) / VOICES (*6) / PRIVATE EYES (*7) / H2O (*7) / ROCK'N'SOUL PART 1 compilation (*8) / BIG BAM BOOM (*6) / LIVE AT THE APOLLO with David Ruffin & Eddie Kendrick (*5) / THREE HEARTS IN A HAPPY ENDING MACHINE (*4; by Daryl Hall) / OOH YEAH! (*4) / CHANGE OF SEASON (*4) / THE BEST OF HALL & OATES – LOOKING BACK compilation (*8) / SOUL ALONE (*4; by Daryl Hall) / MARIGOLD SKY (*3)

DARYL HALL (b.DARYL HOHL, 11 Oct'48, Pottstown, Philadelphia) – vocals, keyboards (ex-TEMPTONES, ex-solo artist, ex-CELLAR DOOR, ex-EXECUTIVE SUITE, ex-GULLIVER) / **JOHN OATES** (b. 7 Apr'49, New York, USA) – vocals, guitar (ex-MASTERS) with various personnel session players.

		Atlantic	Atlantic

Sep 72. (7"; as WHOLE OATS) *<2922>* **GOODNIGHT AND GOOD MORNING. / ALL OUR LOVE**   –

Nov 72. (lp) *<7242>* **WHOLE OATS**   –
– I'm sorry / All our love / Georgie / Fall in Philadelphia / Water wheel / Lazy man / Good night & good morning / They needed each other / Southeast city window / Thank you for . . . / Lily (are you happy). *(UK-iss.Sep76; K 50306) (cd-iss. Feb93; 7567 81423)*

Nov 72. (7") *<2939>* **I'M SORRY. / LILY (ARE YOU HAPPY)**   –

Jan 74. (lp) *(K 40534) <7269>* **ABANDONED LUNCHEONETTE**
– I'm just a kid (don't make me feel like a man) / Laughing boy / She's gone / Las Vegas turnaround / Had I known you better then / Lady rain / When the morning comes / Abandoned luncheonette / Everytime I look at you. *<US re-iss. Oct76 hit No.33> (cd-iss. Jun93; 7567 81537-2)*

Jan 74. (7") *(K 19422)* **LAS VEGAS TURNAROUND. / I'M JUST A KID**

Feb 74. (7") *<2993>* **SHE'S GONE. / I'M JUST A KID (DON'T MAKE ME FEEL LIKE A MAN)**   –   `60`

Jul 74. (7") *(K 10459) <3026>* **WHEN THE MORNING COMES. / LADY RAIN**

Sep 74. (7") *(K 10502)* **SHE'S GONE. / ABANDONED LUNCHEONETTE**   –

Nov 74. (lp) *(K 50086) <18109>* **WAR BABIES**   `86` Oct74

– Can't stop the music (he played it much too long) / Is it a star / Beanie G and the rose tattoo / You're much too soon / 70's scenario / War baby son of Zorro / I'm watching you (a mutant romance) / Better watch your back / Screaming through December / Johnny Gone and the "C" eaters. *(cd-iss. Jul96; 7567 81489-2)*

Nov 74. (7") <3239> **CAN'T STOP THE MUSIC (HE PLAYED IT MUCH TOO LONG). / 70'S SCENARIO** | - | - |

R.C.A. / R.C.A.

Sep 75. (lp) <(APL-1 1144)> **DARYL HALL & JOHN OATES** | 56 | 17 |
– Camelia / Sara smile / Alone too long / Out of me, out of you / Nothing at all / Gino (the manager) / (You know) It doesn't matter anymore / Ennui on the mountain / Grounds for separation / Soldering. *(re-iss. Apr80; INTS 5010)*

Sep 75. (7") (2614) <10373> **CAMELIA. / ENNUI ON THE MOUNTAIN** | - | - |
Nov 75. (7") <10436> **ALONE TOO LONG. / NOTHING AT ALL** | - | - |
Jan 76. (7") (2656) <10530> **SARA SMILE. / SOLDERING** | - | 4 |
May 76. (7") (2684) **GINO (THE MANAGER). / SOLDERING** | - | - |
Sep 76. (lp) <(APL-1 1467)> **BIGGER THAN BOTH OF US** | 25 | 13 | Aug76
– Back together again / Rich girl / Crazy eyes / Do what you want, be what you are / Kerry / London luck and love / Room to breathe / You'll never learn / Falling.

Oct 76. (7") <10808> **DO WHAT YOU WANT, BE WHAT YOU ARE. / YOU'LL NEVER LEARN** | - | 39 |

—— late in '76 DARYL duetted with RUTH COPELAND on single 'Heaven'.

Jan 77. (7") <10860> **RICH GIRL. / LONDON LUCK & LOVE** | - | 1 |
Jan 77. (7") (2757) **RICH GIRL. / YOU'LL NEVER LEARN** | - | - |
May 77. (7") <10970> **BACK TOGETHER AGAIN. / ROOM TO BREATHE** | - | 28 |
May 77. (7") (PB 9053) **BACK TOGETHER AGAIN. / ENNUI ON THE MOUNTAIN** | - | - |
Oct 77. (lp/c) (PL/PK 12300) <2300> **BEAUTY ON A BACK STREET** | 40 | 30 | Sep77
– Don't change / Why do lovers (break each other's heart?) / You must be good for something / The emptyness / Love hurts (love heals) / Bigger than both of us / Bad habits and infections / Winged bull / The girl who used to be. *(re-iss. Jul84; NL 82300)*

Oct 77. (7") (PB 1132) <11132> **WHY DO LOVERS (BREAK EACH OTHER'S HEART?). / THE GIRL WHO USED TO BE** | - | 73 |
Jan 78. (7") <11181> **DON'T CHANGE. / THE EMPTYNESS** | - | - |

—— **CHARLES DE CHANT** – saxophone, keyboards, perc. repl. TOM SCOTT / **KENNY PASSARELLI** – bass repl. LEE SKLAR & SCOTT EDWARDS / **ROGER POPE** – drums repl. JEFF PORCARO / **CALEB QUAYE** – lead guitar / **DAVID KENT** – keyboards repl. other sessioners.

Jun 78. (lp/c) (PL/PK 12802) <2802> **LIVE TIME (live)** | - | 42 | May78
– Rich girl / The emptyness / Do what you want, be what you are / I'm just a kid / Sara smile / Abandoned luncheonette / Room to breathe. *(re-iss. Jun83; INTS 5252)*

Aug 78. (7") <111371> **IT'S A LAUGH. / SERIOUS MATTER** | - | 20 |
Sep 78. (7") (PB 9324) **THE LAST TIME. / SERIOUS MATTER** | - | - |
Sep 78. (lp/c) (PL/PK 12804) <2894> **ALONG THE RED LEDGE** | - | 27 |
– It's a laugh / Melody for a memory / The last time / I don't wanna lose you / Have I been away too long / Alley katz / Don't blame it on love / Serious matter / Pleasure beach / August day. *(re-iss. Jun83; INTS 5258) (re-iss. 1987 lp/c; NL/NK 84231)*

Jan 79. (7") (PB 1424) <11424> **I DON'T WANNA LOSE YOU. / AUGUST DAY** | - | 42 | Dec78

—— They retained DECHANT, PASSARELLI (on next only), and brought in **TOM 'T-Bone' WOLK** – bass, synthe / **G.E. SMITH** – guitar / **MICKEY CURRY** – drums

Nov 79. (7") (PB 9466) **PORTABLE RADIO. / NUMBER ONE** | - | - |
Nov 79. (lp/c) <(AFL-1 3494)> **X-STATIC** | - | 33 | Oct79
– The woman comes and goes / Wait for me / Portable radio / All you want is Heaven / Who said the world was fair / Running from Paradise / Number one / Bebop – Drop / Hallofon / Intravino.

May 80. (7") (PB 1747) <11747> **WAIT FOR ME. / NO BRAIN NO PAIN** | - | 18 | Oct79
May 80. (7") <11920> **WHO SAID THE WORLD WAS FAIR. / ALL YOU WANT IS HEAVEN** | - | - |
Jun 80. (7") (RUN 1) **RUNNING FROM PARADISE. / BEBOP – DROP** | 41 | - |
Jul 80. (7") <12048> **HOW DOES IT FEEL TO BE BACK. / UNITED STATE** | - | 30 |
Aug 80. (lp/c) (PL/PK 13646) <AQL-1 3646> **VOICES** | - | 17 |
– How does it feel to be back / Big kids / United state / Hard to be in love with you / Kiss on my list / Gotta lotta nerve (perfect perfect) / You've lost that lovin' feelin' / You make my dreams / Everytime you go away / Africa / Diddy doo wop (I hear the voices). *(re-iss. Sep81; RCALP 3044) (re-iss. Oct87 lp/c/cd; NL/NK/ND 90078)*

Sep 80. (7") <12103> **YOU'VE LOST THAT LOVIN' FEELIN' / DIDDY DOO WOP (I HEAR THE VOICES)** | - | 12 |
Sep 80. (7") (RCA 1) **YOU'VE LOST THAT LOVIN' FEELIN'. / UNITED STATE** | 55 | - |
Nov 80. (7") (RCA 15) <12142> **KISS ON MY LIST. / AFRICA** | 33 | 1 | Jan81
Jun 81. (7") (RCA 86) <12217> **YOU MAKE MY DREAMS. / GOTTA LOTTA NERVE (PERFECT PERFECT)** | - | 5 | Apr81
Sep 81. (7"/12") (RCA/+T 134) <12296> **PRIVATE EYES. / TELL ME WHAT YOU WANT** | - | 1 | Aug81
(re-promoted.Mar82; hit UK No.32)
Sep 81. (lp/c) (RCA LP/K 6001) <AFL-1 4028> **PRIVATE EYES** | 8 | 5 |
– Private eyes / Loking for a good gun / I can't go for that (no can do) / Mama a mano / Did it in a minute / Head above water / Tell me what you want / Friday let me down / Ungaurded minute / Your imagination / Some men. *(cd-iss. Dec84; PD 84028) (re-iss. Oct87 lp/c/cd; NL/NK/ND 90079)*

Jan 82. (7"/12") (RCA/+T 172) <12361> **I CAN'T GO FOR THAT (NO CAN DO). / UNGUARDED MINUTE** | 8 | 1 | Nov81
Mar 82. (7") <13065> **DID IT IN A MINUTE. / HEAD ABOVE WATER** | - | 9 |
Jun 82. (7"/12") (RCA/+T 239) <13252> **YOUR IMAGINATION. / SARA SMILE** | - | 33 |
Oct 82. (7"/12") (RCA/+T 290) <13354> **MANEATER. / DELAYED REACTION** | 6 | 1 |
Oct 82. (lp/c) (RCA LP/K 6056) <4383> **H2O** | 24 | 3 |
– Maneater / Crime pays / One on one / Art of heartbreak / Open all night / Family man / Italian girls / Guessing games / Delayed reaction / At tension / Go solo. *(cd-iss. 1985; PD 84383)*

Jan 83. (7"/12") (RCA/+T 305) <13421> **ONE ON ONE. / ART OF HEARTBREAK** | 63 | 7 |

(US 12") <13421> – ('A'club) / I can't go for that (no can do) (extended).
Apr 83. (7") <13507> **FAMILY MAN. / OPEN ALL NIGHT** | - | 6 |
Apr 83. (7") (RCA 323) **FAMILY MAN. / CRIME PAYS** | 15 | - |
(12") (RCAT 323) – Open All Night.
Sep 83. (7") <13654> **SAY IT ISN'T SO. / KISS ON MY LIST** | - | 2 |
Oct 83. (7"/12") (RCA/+T 375) **SAY IT ISN'T SO. / DID IT IN A MINUTE** | 69 | - |
Oct 83. (lp/c) (PL/PK 84858) <4858> **ROCK'N SOUL, PART 1 (compilation)** | 16 | 7 |
– Sara smile / She's gone / Rich girl / Kiss on my list / You make my dreams / Private eyes / I can't go for that (no can do) / Maneater / One on one / Wait for me (live) / Adult education / Say it isn't so. *(cd-iss. Oct84; PD 84858)*

Feb 84. (7") <13714> **ADULT EDUCATION. / MANEATER** | - | 8 |
Feb 84. (7") (RCA 396) **ADULT EDUCATION. / SAY IT ISN'T SO** | 63 | - |
(12"+=) (RCAT 396) – I can't go for that (no can do).
Oct 84. (7"/12") (RCA/+T 449) <13916> **OUT OF TOUCH. / COLD DARK AND YESTERDAY** | 48 | 1 | Sep84
Oct 84. (lp/c/cd) (PL/PK/PD 85309) <5309> **BIG BAM BOOM** | 28 | 5 |
– Going thru the motions / Cold dark and yesterday / All American girl / Possession obsession / Dance on your knees / Out of touch / Method of modern love / Bank on your love / Some things are better left unsaid.

Jan 85. (7"/12") (RCA/+T 472) <13960> **METHOD OF MODERN LOVE. / BANK ON YOUR LOVE** | 21 | 5 | Dec84
(d7"+=) (RCAD 472) – I can't go for that (live) / Maneater (live).
Mar 85. (7") <14035> **SOME THINGS ARE BETTER LEFT UNSAID. / ALL AMERICAN GIRL** | - | 18 |
May 85. (7") (PB 49967) **OUT OF TOUCH (remix). / DANCE ON YOUR KNEES** | 62 | - |
(12"+=) (PT 49968) – Every time you go away.
May 85. (7") <14098> **POSSESSION OBSESSION. / DANCE ON YOUR KNEES** | - | 30 |
Aug 85. (7") <14178> **A NITE AT THE APOLLO! (live medley:- THE WAY YOU DO THE THINGS YOU DO – MY GIRL). / EVERY TIME YOU GO AWAY** | - | 20 |
Sep 85. (7"/12") (PB 49935)(PT 49936) **A NITE AT THE APOLLO LIVE! (live medley: – THE WAY YOU DO THE THINGS YOU DO – MY GIRL). / ADULT EDUCATION** | 58 | - |
(above & below credited eith DAVID RUFFIN & EDDIE KENDRICKS; ex-Temptations)
Sep 85. (lp/c/cd) (PL/PK/PD 87035) <7035> **LIVE AT THE APOLLO (WITH DAVID RUFFIN & EDDIE KENDRICKS)** | 32 | 21 |
– Get ready – Ain't too proud to beg – The way you do the things you do – My girl / When something is wrong with my baby / Everytime you go away / I can't go for that (no can do) / One by one / Possession obsession / Adult education. *(cd-iss. Sep93; 74321 16003-2)*

—— In 1986, they split for a while, HALL made solo album

Arista / Arista

Apr 88. (7"/12") (109/609 869) <9684> **EVERYTHING YOUR HEART DESIRES. / REALOVE** | - | 3 |
Jun 88. (lp/c/cd) (208/408/258 895) <8539> **OOH YEAH!** | 52 | 24 | May88
– Downtown life / Everything your heart desires / I'm in pieces / Missed opportunity / Talking all night / Rockability / Rocket to God / Soul love / ReaLove / Keep on pushin' love.

Jul 88. (7") <9727> **MISSED OPPORTUNITY. / SOUL LOVE** | - | 29 |
Sep 88. (7") <9753> **DOWNTOWN LIFE. / ('A'-Urban mix)** | - | 31 |
Sep 90. (7") <2085> **SO CLOSE. / SO CLOSE (unplugged version)** | - | 11 |
Sep 90. (c-s) (113600/411050) **SO CLOSE. / CAN'T HELP FALLING IN LOVE** | 69 | - |
(12"+=)(cd-s+=) (613600)(663600) – She's gone (live).
Nov 90. (cd/c/lp) (210/410/260 548) <8614> **CHANGE OF SEASON** | 44 | 61 | Oct90
– So close / Starting all over again / Sometimes a mind changes / Change of season / I ain't gonna take it this time / Everywhere I look / Give it up (old habits) / Don't hold back your love / Halfway there / Only love / Heavy rain / So close – unplugged.

Dec 90. (c-s) <2157> **DON'T HOLD BACK YOUR LOVE / CHANGE OF SEASON** | - | 41 |
Jan 91. (7")(c-s) (113980/411329) **EVERYWHERE I LOOK. / SOMETIMES A MIND CHANGES** | 74 | - |
(12"+=)(cd-s+=) (613980)(663980) – I can't go for that (Ben Liebrand mix).
Oct 91. (cd/c) (PD/PK 90388) **LOOKING BACK – THE BEST OF DARYL HALL & JOHN OATES (compilation)** | 9 | - |
– She's gone / Sara smile / Rich girl / You've lost that lovin' feelin' / Kiss on my list / Every time you go away / Private eyes / I can't go for that (no can do) / Maneater / One on one / Family man / Adult education / Out of touch / Method of modern love / Starting all over again. *(cd+/c+=)* – Back together again / So close / Everything your heart desires.

– compilations, etc. –

on 'Atlantic' unless mentioned otherwise
Jul 76. (7") <3332> **SHE'S GONE. / I'M JUST A KID (DON'T MAKE ME FEEL LIKE A MAN)** | - | - |
Sep 76. (7"ep) (K 10828) **SHE'S GONE / WAR BABY SON OF ZORRO / LAZY MAN** | 42 | - |
Jan 77. (7") (K 10887) **LAS VEGAS TURNAROUND. / HAD I KNOWN YOU BETTER THEN** | - | - |
Mar 77. (lp) (K 50347) <18213> **NO GOODBYES** | - | 92 |
(cd-iss. Jul96; 7567 80430-2)
Apr 77. (7") (K 10915) **IT'S UNCANNY. / BEANIE G. & THE ROSE TATTOO** | - | - |
Apr 77. (lp) Chelsea; (CHL 547) **PAST TIMES BEHIND** (71-72) | - | - |
May 77. (7") Chelsea; <3063> **THE REASON WHY (Daryl Hall & GULLIVER). / IF THAT'S WHAT MAKES YOU HAPPY (Hall & Oates)** | - | - |
Jun 77. (7") <3397> **IT'S UNCANNY. / LILY (ARE YOU HAPPY)** | - | 80 |
Jul 81. (7") (K 11597) **SHE'S GONE. / WHEN THE MORNING COMES** | - | - |
May 82. (7") RCA Gold; (GOLD 547) **KISS ON MY LIST. / RUNNING FROM PARADISE** | - | - |
May 83. (c-ep) R.C.A.; (RCXK 007) **CASSETTE EP** | - | - |

– I can't go for that (no can do) / Maneater / Private eyes / Kiss on my list.

Jun 84.	(lp) *Magnum Force; (THBM 003)* **THE PROVIDER**	☐	–
Oct 85.	(lp) *Thunderbolt; (THBL 035)* **REALLY SMOKIN'** (cd-iss. Jul93; CDTB 122)	☐	–
Apr 86.	(lp/c) *Showcase; (SHLP/SHTC 134)* **THE EARLY YEARS**	☐	–
Nov 86.	(7") *Old Gold; (OG9658)* **MANEATER. / I CAN'T GO FOR THAT (NO CAN DO)**	☐	–
Nov 86.	(lp/c/cd) *Meteor; (SMT/SMTC/CDSM 006)* **20 CLASSIC TRACKS**	☐	–
Nov 88.	(lp/c/cd) *Big Time; (221/211/241 5012)* **FIRST SESSIONS**	☐	–
Oct 92.	(cd-ep) *Old Gold; (OG 6184)* **I CAN'T GO FOR THAT (NO CAN DO) / PRIVATE EYES / KISS IS ON MY LIST**	☐	–
Oct 92.	(cd-ep) *Old Gold; (OG 6188)* **MANEATER / FAMILY MAN / METHOD OF MODERN LOVE**	☐	–
Feb 94.	(cd/c) *Javelin; (HAD CD/MC 107)* **SPOTLIGHT ON HALL & OATES**	☐	–
Sep 94.	(cd) *Wisepack; (LECD 084)* **LEGENDS IN MUSIC**	☐	–
Sep 94.	(cd) *Prestige; (CDSGP 0128)* **A LOT OF CHANGES COMIN'**	☐	–
Feb 95.	(cd) *B.A.M.;* **PEARLS OF THE PAST**	☐	–
Oct 95.	(cd) *R.C.A.; (74321 28983-2)* **ROCK'N'SOUL PART 2 (GREATEST HITS)**	☐	–
Jul 96.	(cd) *(812272205-2)* **ATLANTIC COLLECTION – THE BEST OF HALL & OATES**	☐	–
Feb 98.	(cd) *R.C.A.; (74321 43662-2)* **WITH LOVE FROM HALL & OATES (THE BEST OF THE BALLADS)**	☐	–

GULLIVER

with **DARYL HALL**

		Elektra	Elektra
1969.	(7") *<45689>* **EVERY DAY'S A LOVELY DAY / ANGELINA**	–	
1970.	(lp) *(2410 006) <EKS 74070>* **GULLIVER** – Every day's a lovely day / I'm really smokin' / Christine / Rose come home / Enough – Over the mountain / Angelina / Flogene / Lemon road / Seventy / Truly good song.		1969
1970.	(7") *<45698>* **A TRULY GOOD SONG. / EVERY DAY'S A LOVELY DAY**	–	☐

DARYL HALL

		not iss.	Parallex
1968.	(7") *<404>* **A LONELY GIRL / VICKY, VICKY**	–	

		not iss.	Amy
1968.	(7") *<11049>* **THE PRINCESS & THE SOLDIER. / (part 2)**	–	

		R.C.A.	R.C.A.
Apr 80.	(lp/c) *(PL/PK 13573) <3573>* **SACRED SONGS** (rec.1977) – Sacred songs / Something in 4/4 time / Babs and Babs / Urban landscape / NYNCY / The farther away (I am) / Why was it so easy / Don't leave me alone with her / Survive / Without tears. (re-iss. Jul84; NL 83573)		58
Apr 80.	(7") *<12001>* **SACRED SONGS. / SOMETHING IN 4-4 TIME**	–	
Jul 86.	(7"/12") *(HALL/+T 1) <14387>* **DREAMTIME. / LET IT OUT**	28	5
Aug 86.	(lp/c/cd) *(PL/PK/PD 87196) <7196>* **THREE HEARTS IN THE HAPPY ENDING MACHINE** – Dreamtime / Only a vision / I wasn't born yesterday / Someone like you / Next stop / For you / Foolish pride / Right as rain / Let it out / What's going to happen to us. (re-iss. May88)	26	29
Oct 86.	(7") *<5038-7>* **FOOLISH PRIDE. / WHAT'S GOING TO HAPPEN TO US**	–	33
Nov 86.	(7") *(HALL 2)* **I WASN'T BORN YESTERDAY. / WHAT'S GONNA HAPPEN TO US** (12"+=) *(HALLT 2)* – Dreamtime.	–	–
Jan 87.	(7") *<5105-7>* **SOMEONE LIKE YOU. / ('A'sax solo version)**	–	57

—— writes with **PETER LORD MORELAND** – keyboards / **V. JEFFREY SMITH** – synth.bass / **ALAN GORRIE** – bass / other musicians **TOMMY EYRE** – keyboards / **MEL WESSON** – programming / **TREVOR MURRELL** – drums / **BOB BITSAND** – bass / **MYLES BOULD** – percussion

		Epic	Epic
Sep 93.	(7"/c-s) *(659 555-7/-4) <77139>* **I'M IN A PHILLY MOOD (Edit) / MONEY CHANGES EVERYTHING** (cd-s+=) *(659 555-2)* – I've finally seen the light. (cd-s) *(659 555-5)* – ('A'side) / Love T.K.O. (live) / Me and Mrs. Jones (live). (re-iss. Mar94, hit UK 52)	59	82
Oct 93.	(cd/c/lp) *(473921-2/-4/-1) <53937>* **SOUL ALONE** – Power of seduction / This time / Love revelation / I'm in a Philly mood / Borderline / Stop loving me, stop loving you / Help me find a way to your heart / Send me / Wildfire / Money changes everything / Written in stone. (re-dist.Jan94)	57	
Jan 94.	(c-s) *(659 999-4)* **STOP LOVING ME, STOP LOVING YOU. / MONEY CHANGES EVERYTHING** (12"+=/cd-s+=) *(659 998-6/-2)* – (4 more 'A'mixes).	30	
May 94.	(7"/c-s) *(660 410-7/-4)* **HELP ME FIND A WAY TO YOUR HEART. / POWER OF SEDUCTION** (cd-s+=) *(660 410-2)* – Stop loving me, stop loving you (live) / I'm in a Philly mood (live).	70	

—— Below on 'Mercury' & the theme from USA soccer World Cup Finals.

Jun 94.	(7"pic-d/c-s/cd-s; DARYL HALL & SOUNDS OF BLACKNESS) *(662 059-7/-4/-2)* **GLORYLAND. / ('A'mixes)**	36	☐
Aug 94.	(c-s) *(660 719-4)* **WILDFIRE / THIS TIME** (cd-s+=) *(660 719-2)* – ('A'extended).	☐	☐

—— DARYL surfaced again when credited in May95 on DUSTY SPRINGFIELD's UK Top 50 hit single 'WHEREVER WOULD I BE'.

DARYL HALL & JOHN OATES

—— reformed in 1997

		Eagle	Push
Nov 97.	(cd/c) *(EAG CD/MC 011) <90200>* **MARIGOLD SKY** – Romeo is bleeding / Marigold sky / The sky is falling / Out of the blue / Want to / Love out loud / Throw the roses away / I don't think so / Promise ain't enough / Time won't pass me by / Hold on to yourself / War of words / Hold on to yourself (remix).	☐	95 Oct97
Feb 98.	(c-s) *(EAGCS 011)* **THE SKY IS FALLING / SHE'S GONE (live)** (cd-s+=) *(EAGXA 011)* – Sara smile (live) / Out of touch (live).	☐	☐

> **Pete HAM (see under ⇒ BADFINGER)**

> **HAMILTON POOL (see under ⇒ MATTHEWS, Iain)**

> **Peter HAMMILL (see under ⇒ VAN DER GRAAF GENERATOR)**

Herbie HANCOCK

Born: 12 Apr'40, Chicago, Illinois, USA. While at Iowa college in the late 50's, HANCOCK formed a 17-piece band/ensemble to play local gigs. At the turn of the 60's, he was invited to play piano in DONALD BYRD's combo, the trumpeter inspiring HANCOCK to issue his 1962 debut solo lp, 'TAKIN' OFF'; an interpretation of 'WATERMELON MAN' by MONGO SANTAMARIA became a surprise Top 10 hit the following year. HANCOCK's classically-trained, confident delivery was noted by legendary trumpeter, MILES DAVIS, who swiftly poached him for his own quintet. The pianist remained an integral part of MILES' pioneering jazz outfit, HANCOCK taking the group's fusion experiments in his own direction following his departure in 1968. Although he had made several albums for 'Blue Note' during the mid 60's (as well as scoring the soundtrack for MGM's cult classic, 'BLOW-UP'), HANCOCK moved on to 'Warner Bros', releasing the highly acclaimed set, 'MWANDISHI' (1971). After relocating to L.A., he signed to 'Columbia' and assembled The HEADHUNTERS (who scored a massive mid-70's dancefloor hit in their own right with the classic 'GOD MADE ME FUNKY') backing group, achieving Top 20 crossover success early in 1974 with an album of the same name. A seminal release, the record found HANCOCK flirting with funk and initiating the most critical and commercial period of his career to date. Subsequent HANCOCK albums such as 'THRUST' (1974), 'MAN-CHILD' (1975), 'SECRETS' (1976), 'SUNLIGHT' (1978) and 'FEETS DON'T FAIL ME NOW' (1979), all made the mainstream US charts, while the man had two UK Top 20 hits (from the last two sets), 'I THOUGHT IT WAS YOU' and 'YOU BET YOUR LOVE'. Two live collaborations in 1979 with CHICK COREA kept his jazz roots intact, while he also got back to basics with 'V.S.O.P.' (1977), an acoustic formation featuring TONY WILLIAMS, RON CARTER, FREDDIE HUBBARD and WAYNE SHORTER. In 1980, HANCOCK delivered his umpteenth set, 'MONSTER', which, like its studio predecessor, utilized his new toy, an electronic vocoder (voice-box). Just as he'd anticipated the jazz-funk scene of the mid-70's, HANCOCK was in at the frontline of the electro/hip-hop explosion with his groundbreaking, BILL LASWELL-produced 'ROCKIT' single in 1983. Lifted from his best-selling album, 'FUTURE SHOCK', the track became a Top 10 hit in Britain (only Top 75 in the States), and although HANCOCK dabbled in further experimentation, it was to be his only major crossover success of the decade. During the latter half of the 80's, he became more noted for his soundtrack work (he had previously worked on 'DEATH WISH' in '75), scoring for such box-office smashes as 'Colors' and 'Round Midnight'.

Album rating: TAKIN' OFF (*8) / MY POINT OF VIEW (*7) / INVENTIONS AND DIMENSIONS (*6) / EMPYREAN ISLES (*8) / MAIDEN VOYAGE (*9) / BLOW-UP soundtrack (*6) / SPEAK LIKE A CHILD (*6) / THE PRISONER (*5) / FAT ALBERT ROTUNDA (*5) / MWANDISHI (*7) / CROSSINGS (*7) / SEXTANT (*5) / HEADHUNTERS (*7) / THRUST (*5) / DEATH WISH soundtrack (*4) / FLOOD (*6) / MAN-CHILD (*6) / SECRETS (*5) / V.S.O.P. – THE QUINTET (*7) / SUNLIGHT (*5) / FEETS DON'T FAIL ME NOW (*5) / AN EVENING WITH HERBIE HANCOCK & CHICK COREA (*6) / MONSTER (*4) / MR. HANDS (*5) / MAGIC WINDOWS (*5) / LITE ME UP (*4) / FUTURE SHOCK (*7) / SOUND SYSTEM (*5) / VILLAGE LIFE (*7) / PERFECT MACHINE (*5) / DIS IS DA DRUM (*4) / THE COLLECTION compilation (*7)

HERBIE HANCOCK – keyboards, etc. (ex-DONALD BYRD Band) with **DEXTER GORDON** – tenor sax / **FREDDIE HUBBARD** – trumpet / **BUTCH WARREN** – bass / **BILLY HIGGINS** – drums

		Blue Note	Blue Note
May 62.	(lp) *<(BLP 4109)>* **TAKIN' OFF** – Watermelon man / Three bags full / Empty pockets / The maze / Driftin' / Alone and I. (re-iss. Sep84; BST 84109) (cd-iss. May86; CDP 746506-2) (cd re-iss. Jun96; CDP 837643-2)	☐	☐
Jun 62.	(7") *<45-1862>* **WATERMELON MAN. / THREE BAGS FULL**	–	☐
Aug 62.	(7") *<45-1863>* **DRIFTIN'. / ALONE AND I**	–	☐

—— In 1963, he joined MILES DAVIS until 1968. Carried on solo career).

—— Now a septet w/ **DONALD BYRD** – trumpet / **GRACKEN MONCUR** – trombone / **HANK MOBLEY** – tenor sax / **GRANT GREEN** – guitar / **CHUCK ISRAELS** – bass / **ANTHONY WILLIAMS** – drums

Mar 63.	(lp) *<(BLP 4126)>* **MY POINT OF VIEW**	☐	1963

– Blind man, blind man / A tribute to someone / King Cobra / The pleasure is mine / And what if I don't. *(re-iss. Oct84; same) (cd-iss. Apr88; BNZ 44)*
Apr 63. (7") <(45-1887)> **BLIND MAN, BLIND MAN. /** (part 2)

— with **PAUL CHAMBER** – bass / **WILLIE BOBO** – percussion / **OSVALDO MARTINEZ** – percussion
1964. (lp) <(BLP 4147)> **INVENTIONS AND DIMENSIONS** ... Aug63
– Sucotash / Triangle / Jack rabbit / Mimoson / Jump ahead. *(cd-iss. Apr89 on 'Blue Note'; CDP 784147-2)*

— now with **FREDDIE HUBBARD / RON CARTER** – bass / **TONY WILLIAMS** – drums
1965. (lp) <(BLP 4175)> **EMPYREAN ISLES** ... Jul64
– One finer snap / Oliloqui valley / Cantaloupe Island / The egg. *(re-iss. Oct85; BST 84175) (cd-iss. Aug89; CDP 784175-2)*

— added **GEORGE COLEMAN** – tenor sax
1966. (lp) <(BLP 4195)> **MAIDEN VOYAGE** ... Mar65
– Maiden voyage / The eye of the hurricane / The little one / Survival of the fittest / Dolphin dance. *(re-iss. May85; BST 84195) (cd-iss. Jul87; CDP 746339-2) (cd re-iss. Mar95)*
May 67. (lp) <4447> **BLOW-UP** (soundtrack on 'M.G.M.') ... Oct66
– Blow up / The bed / Bring down the birds / Curiosity / Jane's theme / The kiss / Verushka (part I & II) / The thief / Thomas studies photos / Naked camera / Stroll on (by The YARDBIRDS)

— with **RON CARTER** – bass / **MICKEY ROKER** – drums / **THAD JONES** – flugelhorn / **JERRY DODGION** – flute / **PETER PHILLIPS** – trombone
Mar 68. (lp) <(BST 84279)> **SPEAK LIKE A CHILD**
– Riot / Speak like a child / First trip / Toys / Goodbye to childhood / The sorcerer. *(cd-iss. Jul87; CDP 746136-2)*
Apr 69. (lp) <(BST 84321)> **THE PRISONER**
– I have a dream / The prisoner / Firewater / He who lives in fear / Promise of the Sun. *(cd-iss. Sep87; CDP 746845-2)*

— Set up new sextet **BERNIE MAUPIN** – reeds / **BUSTER WILLIAMS** – bass, percussion / **BILLY HART** – drums, percussion / **LEON NDUGU CHANCLER** – drums / **JULIAN PRIESTER** – trombone / **EDDIE HENDERSON** – trumpet

		Warners	Warners
1971. (lp) (WS 1834) <56293> **FAT ALBERT ROTUNDA**
– Wiggle-waggle / Fat mama / Tell me a bedtime story / Oh! oh! here he comes / Jessica / Fat Albert Rotunda / Lil' brother. *(re-iss. 1974; K 46039)*
1971. (7") <(WB 7358)> **FAT MAMA. / WIGGLE-WAGGLE**
1971. (lp) (K 46077) <1898> **MWANDISHI**
– Ostinato (suite for Angela) / You'll know when you get there / Wondering spirit song.
Feb 72. (lp) (K 46164) <2617> **CROSSINGS**
– Sleeping giant (part 1-5) / Quasar / Water torture / Crossings.
Mar 72. (7") <WB 7598> **WATER TORTURE. / CROSSINGS**

		C.B.S.	Columbia
May 73. (lp/c) (CBS/40 65582) <32212> **SEXTANT**
– Rain dance / Hidden shadows / Hornets.
Jan 74. (lp/c) (CBS/40 65928) <32731> **HEAD HUNTERS** ... 13
– Chameleon / Watermelon man / Sly / Vein melter. *(re-iss. Mar84; 32008) (cd-iss. Jul84; CD 65928)*
Jan 74. (7") <46073> **WATERMELON MAN (edit). / SLY (edit)**
Apr 74. (7") (CBS 2329) <46002> **CHAMELEON (edit). / VEIN METER (edit)** ... 42 Mar74
Oct 74. (lp/c) (CBS/40 80193) <32965> **THRUST** ... 13 Sep74
– Spank-a-lee / Butterfly / Actual proof / Palm grease.
Feb 75. (7") (CBS 3059) <10050> **PALM GREASE. / BUTTERFLY** ... Nov74
Feb 75. (7") <10094> **SPANK-A-LEE. / ACTUAL PROOF**
1975. (lp) (CBS 80546) <33199> **DEATH WISH (Soundtrack)**
– Death wish / Joanna's theme / Do a thing / Paint her mouth / Rich country / Suite revenge: (a) Striking back – (b) Riverside Park – (c) The alley – (d) Last stop – (e) 8th Avenue Station – Ochoa knose – Party people – Fill your hand.
1975. (d-lp) (98-99) **FLOOD** (live in Japan) ... Japan
– Introduction – Maiden voyage / Actual proof / Spank-a-Lee / Watermelon man / Butterfly / Chameleon / Hang up your hang ups.
Oct 75. (lp) (CBS 69185) <33812> **MAN-CHILD** ... 21
– Hang up your hang ups / Sun touch / The traitor / Bubbles / Steppin' in it / Heartbeat.
Oct 75. (7") <10239> **HANG UP YOUR HANG UPS. / SUNTOUCH**
Sep 76. (lp/c) (CBS/40 81591) <34280> **SECRETS**
– Doin' it / People music / Cantalope Island / Spider / Gentle thoughts / Swamp rat / Sansho Shima.
Sep 76. (7") <10408> **DOIN' IT. / PEOPLE MUSIC**

— His quintet:- **WAYNE SHORTER, RON CARTER, TONY WILLIAMS, FRED HUBBARD**
May 77. (lp/c) (CBS/40 88235) <34976> **V.S.O.P.** (live Newport) ... 79
– (piano introduction) / Maiden voyage / Nefertiti / (introduction of players) / The eye of the hurricane / Toys / (introductions) / You'll know when you get there / Hang up your hang ups / Spider.
Jun 77. (7") <10563> **SPIDER. / MAIDEN VOYAGE**

— HANCOCK now introduced his voice, incorporated into music.
Jul 78. (lp/c) (CBS/40 82240) <34907> **SUNLIGHT** ... 27 58
– I thought it was you / Come running to me / Sunlight / No means yes / Good question.
Aug 78. (7") (CBS 6530) <10781> **I THOUGHT IT WAS YOU. / NO MEANS YES** ... 15
Oct 78. (7") <10835> **SUNLIGHT. / COME RUNNING TO ME**
Jan 79. (7") (CBS 7010) <10894> **YOU BET YOUR LOVE. / KNEE DEEP** ... 18
Feb 79. (lp/c) (CBS/40 83491) <35764> **FEETS DON'T FAIL ME NOW** ... 28 38
– You bet your love / Trust me / Ready or not / Tell everybody / Honey from the jar / Knee deep. *(cd-iss. Sep85; CD 83491) (cd re-iss. Oct93 on 'Sony Collectors'; 983311-2)*
Apr 79. (7") <10936> **READY OR NOT. / TRUST ME**
Apr 79. (7") (CBS/+12 7229) **TELL EVERYBODY. / TRUST ME**
Jun 79. (7") <11019> **TELL EVERYBODY. / HONEY FROM THE JAR**
Jun 79. (d-lp) (CBS 88329) <35663> **AN EVENING WITH HERBIE HANCOCK & CHICK COREA IN CONCERT (live)** ... 100 Mar 79
– Someday my Prince will come / Liza / Button up / February moment / Maiden voyage / La fiesta. *(d-cd-iss. Nov94 on 'Columbia'; 477296-2)*

Dec 79. (7") <11122> **DOIN' IT. / HONEY FROM THE JAR**
Apr 80. (7") <11227> **GO FOR IT. / TRUST ME**
Apr 80. (7") (CBS 8529) **GO FOR IT. / MAKING LOVE**
May 80. (lp/c) (CBS/40 84237) <36415> **MONSTER** ... 94 Apr80
– Saturday night / Stars in your eyes / Go for it / Don't hold it in / Making love / It all comes round.
Sep 80. (7") <11310> **GO FOR IT. / STARS IN YOUR EYES**
Nov 80. (7") <11323> **MAKING LOVE. / IT ALL COMES ROUND**
Nov 80. (lp/c) (CBS/40 84638) <36578> **MR. HANDS**
– Spiralling prism / Calypso / Just around the corner / 4 a.m. / Shiftless shuffle / Textures.

— on next with **RAY PARKER JNR.** – guitar, drums / **GEORGE JOHNSON** – rhythm guitar / **ADRIAN BELEW** – lead guitar / **FREDDIE WASHINGTON & LOUIS JOHNSON** – bass / **JOHN ROBINSON & ALPHONSE MOUZON** – drums / guest vocalists **SYLVESTER / VICKI RANDLE / GAVIN CHRISTOPHER**
Oct 81. (lp/c) (CBS/40 85144) <37387> **MAGIC WINDOWS**
– Magic number / Tonight's the night / Everybody's broke / Help yourself / Satisfied with love / The twilight clone.
Oct 81. (7") <02404> **EVERYBODY'S BROKE. / HELP YOURSELF**
(12") <02461> – ('A'side) / Magic number.
Jan 82. (7") <02615> **MAGIC NUMBER. / HELP YOURSELF**
Apr 82. (7") (A 2222) <02824> **LITE ME UP. / SATISFIED WITH LOVE**
May 82. (lp/c) (CBS/40 32474) <37928> **LITE ME UP**
– Lite me up / The bomb / Gettin' to the good part / Paradise / Can't hide your love / The fun tracks / Motor mouth / Give it all your heart.
Jul 82. (7") (A 2563) **THE FUN TRACKS. / GIVE IT ALL YOUR HEART**
Jul 82. (7") <03004> **THE FUN TRACKS. / GETTIN' TO THE GOOD PART**
Jan 83. (7") <03318> **PARADISE. / THE FUN TRACKS**

— with **RON CARTER** – bass / **TONY WILLIAMS** – drums / **WYNSTON MARSALIS** – trumpet
Jan 83. (d-lp) (CBS 22219) **HERBIE HANCOCK QUARTET (live)**
– Well you needn't / 'Round midnight / Clearways / A quick sketch / The eye of the hurricane / Parade / The sorcerer / Pee Wee / I fall in love too easily. *(cd-iss. Dec93 on 'Columbia'; 465626-2)*
Jul 83. (7")(12") <03978> <04200> **ROCKIT. /** (part 2) ... 71
Jul 83. (7")/12") (A/TA 3577) **ROCKIT. / ROUGH** ... 8
Aug 83. (lp/c) (CBS/40 25540) <38814> **FUTURE SHOCK** ... 27
– Rockit / Future shock / TFS / Earthbeat / Autodrive / Rough. *(re-iss. Apr87 lp/c; 450625-1/-4) (cd-iss. CD 25540)*
Sep 83. (7") <04268> **AUTODRIVE. / CHAMELEON**
Sep 83. (7") (A 3802) **AUTODRIVE. / THE BOMB** ... 33
(12"+=) (TA 3802) – Chameleon.
Jan 84. (7") (A 4075) <04473> **FUTURE SHOCK. / EARTHBEAT** ... 54
(12"+=) (TA 4075) – Herbie Hancock megamix; Rockit – Autodrive – Future shock – TFS – Rough – Chameleon.

— with **WAYNE SHORTER** – lyricon / **HENRY KAISER + NICKY SKOPELITIS** – guitar / **BILL CASWELL** – bass, synth. / **WILL ALEXANDER + BOB STEVENS** – electronics / **JOHNNY ST CYR** – turntables / **ANTON FIER** – drums, percussion / **HAMID DRAKE + DANIEL PONCE + AIYB DIENE** – percussion / **JALI FODAY MUSA SUSO** – balafon / **BERNARD FOWLER + TOSHINORI KONDO** – vocals
Jul 84. (7") <04565> **HARDROCK. /** ('A'version)
Jul 84. (7") (A 4616) **HARDROCK. / TFS** ... 65
(12"+=) (TA 4616) – ('A'-US megamix).
Aug 84. (lp/c) (CBS/40 26062) <39478> **SOUND-SYSTEM** ... 71
– Hardrock / Metal beat / Karabali / Junkie / People are changing / Sound-system. *(c+=)* – (extra mixes).
Sep 84. (7")(ext-12") <04633> <04637> **METAL BEAT. / KARABALI** (below w / FODAY MUSA SUSO)
May 85. (lp/c) (CBS 23697) <39870> **VILLAGE LIFE**
– Moon – Light / Ndan Ndan Nyaria / Early warning / Kanatente.
1986. (lp) <40464> **ROUND MIDNIGHT (Soundtrack)**
– Round midnight / Body and soul / Berangeres nightmare / Fair weather / Una noche con Francis / The peacocks / How long has this been going on / Rhythm-a-ning / Still time / Minuit aux champs – Elysees / Chan's song (never said).
May 88. (7"/12") (651432-7/-8) **VIBE ALIVE. / MAIDEN VOYAGE**
(cd-s+=) (651432-9) – ('A'extended) / ('A'bonus beats).
Jun 88. (lp/c/cd) (460679-1/-4/-2) <40025> **PERFECT MACHINE**
– Perfect machine / Obsession / Vibe alive / Beat wise / Maiden voyage – P bop / Chemical residue.
Sep 88. (7") <07987> **BEAT WISE. / CHEMICAL RESIDUE**

— HERBIE featured on 'Yanarete' cd with MILTON NASCIMENTO early 1992.

		Mercury	Mercury
Jun 95. (cd/c) <(528185-2/-4)> **DIS IS DA DRUM**
– Call it '94 / Dis is da drum / Shooz / The melody (on the deuce by 44) / Mojuba / Butterfly / Juju / Hump / Come and see me / Rubber soul / Bo ba be ba.

		Verve	Verve
Mar 96. (cd) (527715-2) **THE NEW STANDARD**
– Mercy street / Norwegian wood / You've got it bad girl / Thieves in the temple / All apologies.

– compilations, etc. –

1970. (lp) Blue Note; (33199) / <80546> **THE BEST OF HERBIE HANCOCK**
Oct 74. (d-lp) Warners; <2-2807> **TREASURE CHEST** (rare 69-70)
1975. (lp) Blue Note; <LA 152> **SUCOTASH**
1975. (lp) Blue Note; <LA 399> **HANCOCK**
Apr 81. (lp; HERBIE HANCOCK & ALPHONSE MOUZON) MPS Jazz; (MPS 68266) **BY ALL MEANS** *(cd-iss. Apr84 on 'Verve'; 817485-2)*
Nov 84. (lp) C.B.S.; (CBS/40 32526) **THE BEST OF HERBIE HANCOCK**
Nov 84. (lp/c) Premier; (CBR/KCBR 1030) Chase; <SJAZC 4> **HOT AND HEAVY** <re-iss. Apr86 on 'Star Jazz' lp/c; SJAZZ/+C 4>

Sep 85. (7") *Old Gold; (OG 9561)* **YOU BET YOUR LOVE / I THOUGHT IT WAS YOU**

Feb 91. (cd/c) *Castle; (CCS CD/MC 283)* **THE COLLECTION**
– Chameleon / Watermelon man / Maiden voyage / I thought it was you / No means yes / You bet your love / Tell everybody / Lite me up / Rockit / Auto drive / Hardrock / Round midnight.

Jul 91. (cd) *Jazz Collection; (ORO 153)* **HOT PIANO**

Jul 94. (cd) *Blue Note; (CDP 829331-2)* **CANTALOUPE ISLAND**

Nov 94. (cd) *Jazz Door; (JD 1274)* **LIVE IN NEW YORK (TRIO live)**

Nov 94. (d-cd) *Warners; (9362 45732-2)* **MWANDISHI – THE COMPLETE WARNER BROS. RECORDINGS**

Jul 95. (cd) *Jazz Collection; (CK 64665)* **SINGLES COLLECTION**

Nov 95. (3xcd-box) *Blue Note; (CDOMB 009)* **TAKIN' OFF / INVENTIONS & DIMENSIONS / EMPRYEAN ISLES**

HANDSOME FAMILY

Formed: Chicago, Illinois, USA . . . 1993 by songwriter BRETT SPARKS, his wife and co-conspirator RENNIE SPARKS plus third bespectacled member, drummer MIKE WERNER. The husband and wife team were the Gomez and Morticia of alt-country (or even a distorted, updated version of TIMBUK 3!) to the GEORGE JONES and TAMMY WYNETTE of classic Nashville, although BRETT and RENNIE's sound was, well . . . er . . . miles apart. Born of acute personal difficulties, The HANDSOME FAMILY's music was set against a background of strife; BRETT suffered a mental breakdown attempting to write his own bible!, while RENNIE was the "school freak" who immersed herself in literature (Greek classic, 'The Iliad', is apparently her favourite). From the onset, the trio toured extensively promoting their early releases, 'ODESSA' (1995), 'MILK AND SCISSORS' (1996) and 'INVISIBLE HANDS' (1997), dark country tales and lifesize plastic animals unsettling audiences in both America and Europe. Initially aided by co-producer DAVE TRUMFIO, the band of renegade "true country" folk were augmented on the aforesaid releases by studio helpers, et al. Recorded on collaborator JEFF TWEEDY's (WILCO/UNCLE TUPELO) mobile studio, 1998's pioneering (in every sense of the word!) 'THROUGH THE TREES' kicked off with the delightfully disturbing 'WEIGHTLESS AGAIN'. These peerless lyrics describe their 'Dead Man' emotions; "This is why people O.D. on pills, And jump . . . from the Golden Gate Bridge, Anything to feel weightless again". Cloaked in the gothic NEIL YOUNG/BILLY BRAGG-esque vocals of BRETT, The HANDSOME FAMILY's mournful tales of tragic 19th century Wild West folklore conjure up cinematic images of barren canyons and Red Indian ghosts dancing on General Custer's grave.

Album rating: ODESSA (*5) / MILK AND SCISSORS (*5) / INVISIBLE HANDS mini (*5) / THROUGH THE TREES (*8) / DOWN IN THE VALLEY compilation (*8)

BRETT SPARKS – vocals, guitar, keyboards / **RENNIE SPARKS** – bass, vocals / **MIKE WERNER** – drums / with additional musicians DAVE TRUMFIO – acoustic guitar, keyboards, co-producer / MICHAEL HAGLER – guitar / STEVE THOMAS – pedal steel

not iss. Carrot Top

Jan 95. (cd) *<SR 1004>* **ODESSA**
– Here's hopin' / Arlene / Pony / One way up / Water into wine / Giant ant / Everything that rises must converge / Gorilla / The last / Claire said / Moving furniture around / Big bad wolf / She awoke with a jerk / Happy harvest. *(German-iss.Jan96 on 'Scout'; RTD 306-1004-2) (UK-iss.Oct99; same as US)*

—— the trio's guests included MICHAEL, DAVE, HARRY TRUMFIO, DARRELL SPARKS and MARK STRUZYNSKI

Feb 96. (cd) *<SR 1011>* **MILK AND SCISSORS**
– Lake Geneva / Winnebago skeletons / Drunk by noon / The house carpenter / The Dutch boy / The king who wouldn't smile / Emily Shore 1819-1839 / 3-legged dog / #1 country song / Amelia Earhart vs. the dancing bear / Tin foil / Puddin' fingers. *(German-iss.Sep96 on 'Scout'; RTD 306-1011-2) (UK-iss.Oct99; same as US)*

Sep 97. (m-cd) *<RTD 306-1012-2>* **INVISIBLE HANDS**   German
(lp-iss.Oct99 on 'Carrot Top'; SR 016CD)

—— now without WERNER, the husband and wife duo added guests DAVE, JEFF TWEEDY, JESSICA BILLEY, DAVE SMITH and DAVE WINER

Loose   Carrot Top

Apr 98. (cd) *(VJCD 105) <SR 1020>* **THROUGH THE TREES**   Jan98
– Weightless again / My sister's tiny hands / Stalled / Where the birch trees lean / Cathedrals / Down in the ground / The giant of Illinois / Down in the valley of hollow logs / I fell / The woman downstairs / Last night I went out walking / Bury me here / My ghost.

May 99. (7") *(MAG 025)* **split w/ SACKVILLE**
(above issued on 'Mag Wheel')

Vinyl
Junkie   Loose

Oct 99. (cd) *<(VJCD 110)>* **DOWN IN THE VALLEY** (compilation)
– Tin foil / My sister's tiny hands / Lake Geneva / Weightless again / No.1 country song / Giant of Illinois / Drunk by noon / Don't be scared / House carpenter / Arlene / Woman downstairs / Cathedrals / Moving furniture around / Dutchboy.

HANOI ROCKS   (dig out; Great Metal . . .)

HAPPY MONDAYS

Formed: Salford, Manchester, England . . . 1984 by brothers SHAUN and PAUL RYDER. In 1985, with the help of A&R man and producer Mike Pickering, they signed a contract with Tony Wilson's 'Factory' records, issuing a debut 12", 'FORTY-FIVE'. With the addition of MARK BERRY aka BEZ on 'percussion', the band released the 'FREAKY DANCIN' single, as good a description as any for BEZ's onstage contortions. A JOHN CALE-produced debut album followed in 1987, the acclaimed mutant indie funk of 'SQUIRREL AND G-MAN . . .' winning the band many converts in the music press and the beginnings of a cult following. The early live shows have been elevated to almost mythical status, SHAUN & Co. allegedly giving away drugs on the door to their own fans in true scally style. Despite sounding like it'd been recorded in a shed, the Martin Hannett-produced 'BUMMED' (1988) was a classic, a freewheeling groovy noise, punctuated intermittently by RYDER's stoned Mancunian slur. 'MAD CYRIL', 'LAZYITIS' and 'WROTE FOR LUCK' were all brilliant singles, the latter given a dance remix treatment by VINCE CLARKE (Erasure). 'Factory' supremo WILSON decided to take this a step further and set the band to work with the DJ/production team of PAUL OAKENFOLD and STEVE OSBORNE. The result was the pivotal 'MADCHESTER RAVE ON EP', a druggy mash-up of dance, indie, pop and funk that acted as a catylyst for the "Baggy" scene alongside The STONE ROSES' 'FOOL'S GOLD' single (spookily released exactly the same month), inspiring a whole string of bands in Manchester and beyond, some good, some not so good (just don't mention The FARM). Early the following year, The 'MONDAYS hit the Top 5 with their anthemic remake of JOHN KONGOS' 'He's Gonna Step On You Again', retitled 'STEP ON' and injected with typically laissez faire funk. 'KINKY AFRO' also made the Top 5, preceding the band's biggest success of their career, the 'PILLS 'N' THRILLS AND BELLYACHES' (1990) album. This time around there was a cleaner production and a melodic accessibilty coating the trademark melange of dirty 'STONES'-style guitar, raggedy-assed funk and cheesy disco. In addition to the singles, the album's highlights included a tribute to 60's folk-popster DONOVAN, a leering piece of porn-funk, 'BOB'S YER UNCLE' and the classic 'GOD'S COP' (featuring the timeless RYDER line "God laid his E's all on me"). While much of the band's music sounded continuously on the point of collapse and, live, The HAPPY MONDAYS often seemed as if they'd arrived onstage purely by accident, RYDER was no space cadet, his inimitable lyrical couplets sussed, sharp and dryly witty. Almost inevitably though, the backlash began in earnest with an NME interview painting RYDER and BEZ as dim-witted homophobes. Whatever RYDER actually said, it's likely that his tongue was planted firmly in cheek, and besides, to expect The HAPPY MONDAYS to stand up as right-on, PC role models for student NME readers displays a naivety that begs belief. Retreating to the Bahamas with Talking Heads' CHRIS FRANTZ and TINA WEYMOUTH at the production helm, the band struggled through sessions for the ' . . .YES PLEASE!' album, amid tales of general strife, severe drug abuse and obligatory debauchery. The album, an expensive disaster (critically and commercially) that reputedly bankrupted 'Factory', eventually emerged in late '92. Generally ignored and panned by the press, the album nevertheless contained some stellar 'MONDAYS moments, not least the low-key brilliance of 'STINKIN' THINKIN' and the darkly hypnotic 'ANGEL', both tracks using female backing vocals to impressive effect. After a washout of a tour, The HAPPY MONDAYS drifted apart, a messy end for a band that were capable of true musical genius against all the odds. The loose-limbed spirit of The 'MONDAYS lived on, though, in BLACK GRAPE, the band RYDER formed along with rapper KERMIT and JED from the RUTHLESS RAP ASSASSINS and a host of extras. SHAUN's brilliant return from oblivion was complete by summer 1995 when the storming 'REVEREND BLACK GRAPE' launched him back into the Top 10. The mouthiest, grooviest low-slung Manc rave-up to grace the charts since the 'MONDAYS peak, the record pointed squarely in the direction where the party was really happening, bypassing completely the tedious Brit-pop posturing. As ever, RYDER and entourage were never far from controversy, both the song and video subsequently banned from TV as the Catholic church alleged the lyrics condoned Venezuelan terrorist, Carlos The Jackal (which also angered the New York based ADL – Anti-Defamation League). Another classic single, 'IN THE NAME OF THE FATHER', followed into the Top 10, funk rhythms and a sitar-tinged intro previewing the eclecticism of the accompanying No.1 album, 'IT'S GREAT WHEN YOU'RE STRAIGHT . . . YEAH!'. Its title a reference to RYDER's clean living new ways (his inimitable cut 'n' paste lyrics apparently fuelled solely by Guinness!?), the record was compared favourably against The HAPPY MONDAYS' best work and the second coming-style fuss over RYDER's critical rebirth seemed at least partly justified. Loping through a dayglo musical smarty pack of hip-hop, rock, indie-dance, soul and indeed, anything close to hand, RYDER proved his subversive genius was well intact, while KERMIT's hyperactive rapping assaults were a perfect foil for his stoned immaculate drawl. During this time, they were one of the successes at Hamilton Park's 'T In The Park' 2-day festival (near Glasgow), even though KERMIT broke his leg and had to sit out most of the gig on a speaker! During an eventful 1996 of regular touring and high profile press coverage, BEZ and RYDER finally parted ways, while KERMIT embarked on a side project, MAN MADE, the following year. A follow-up album, 'STUPID, STUPID, STUPID' finally emerged at the end of '97 amid furious interband disputes, claims and counter-claims. The feuding saw the band cancel their New Year's Eve show at London's Alexandra Palace. SHAUN resurrected The HAPPY MONDAYS and, in the meantime, BEZ was up to all sorts, including a TV spot on the Lee & Herring Sunday brunch show (dedicated to strange scientific happenings, mad for it, man). He also began writing an autobiography, no really man! The HAPPY MONDAYS (i.e. SHAUN, his brother PAUL, GAZ, 'WAGS', 'NUTS', ROWETTA and of course a reluctant BEZ!) were "smokin'" once again when a new single, 'THE BOYS ARE BACK IN TOWN' (described as only inspired by the THIN LIZZY number!) hit the Top 30. However, after all the hype, the promise and the fuss, only an accompanying 'GREATEST HITS' package was supplied as a stop-gap to feed their fans; PAUL RYDER left on the 11th of August after the Eclipse '99 festival in Cornwall. By this time, SHAUN had paid off the taxman (and child maintenance) from his royalties, but really what did the 'MONDAYS give us during this spell apart from another chance to see the bleary-eyed singer trying to read a cue card on a stage monitor; your answers please on the back of a postage stamp. Stop press:- I've just witnessed (July 2000) the most embarrassing sham on TV since the days of Oliver Reed and George Best. A sober-looking SHAUN was a guest on the Jim Davidson Friday show chanting 'BARCELONA' (yes, that one!) side by side with an opera singer. What's worse is that RYDER's released the record and it's now NME Single Of The Week! Is it me at nearly 40, or is Britain going mad? • Songwriters: Group compositions except; DESMOND (Ob-la-di Ob-la-da; Beatles) / LAZYITIS (Ticket To Ride; Beatles) / TOKOLOSHE MAN (John Kongos). For BLACK GRAPE, SHAUN & KERMIT wrote alongside DANNY SABER, although in October '95, INTASTELLA members MARTIN WRIGHT and MARTIN MITTLER served a writ, claiming they co-wrote with SHAUN on early demos before they departed.

Album rating: SQUIRREL AND G-MAN TWENTY FOUR HOUR PARTY . . . (*8) / BUMMED (*8) / PILLS N' THRILLS AND BELLYACHES (*9) / LIVE (BABY BIG HEAD Bootleg album) (*4) / . . .YES PLEASE (*6) / LOADS – THE BEST OF . . . compilation (*8) / Black Grape: IT'S GREAT WHEN YOU'RE STRAIGHT . . . YEAH! (*9) / STUPID, STUPID, STUPID (*7) / Happy Mondays: THE GREATEST HITS compilation (*8)

SHAUN RYDER (b.23 Aug'62) – vocals / **PAUL RYDER** (b.24 Apr'64) – bass / **MARK DAY** (b.29 Dec'61) – guitar / **PAUL DAVIS** (b. 7 Mar'66) – keyboards / **GARY 'GAZ' WHELAN** (b.12 Feb'66) – drums

	Factory	Rough Trade
Sep 85. (12"ep) *(FAC 129)* **FORTY-FIVE EP** – Delightful / This feeling / Oasis.		-

—— added **BEZ** (b. MARK BERRY, 18 Apr'64) – percussion, dancer

Jun 86. (7") *(FAC 142)* **FREAKY DANCIN'. / THE EGG** (ext.12"+=) *(FAC 142)* – ('A'live).		-
Mar 87. (12") *(FAC 176)* **TART TART. / LITTLE MATCHSTICK OWEN'S RAP**		-
Apr 87. (lp) *(FACT 170)* **SQUIRREL & G-MAN TWENTY-FOUR HOUR PARTY PEOPLE PLASTIC FACE CARNT SMILE (WHITE OUT)** – Kuff dam / Tart tart / 'Enery / Russell / Olive oil / Weekends / Little matchstick Owen / Oasis / Desmond * / Cob 20. *(re-iss. Nov88; same)(track * repl. by)* – Twenty four hour party people. *(cd-iss. Mar90 +=; FACD 170)* – Little matchstick Owen's rap. *(cd re-iss. May99 on 'London'; 520012-2)*		-
Oct 87. (12") *(FAC 192)* **TWENTY FOUR HOUR PARTY PEOPLE. / YAHOO / WAH WAH (THINK TANK)**		-
Nov 88. (7") *(FAC 212-7)* **WROTE FOR LUCK. / BOOM** (12"+=/cd-s+=) *(FAC/+D 212)* – ('A'dance mix) / ('A'club mix).		-
Nov 88. (lp/cd)(d/dat) *(FACT/FACD 220)(FACT 220 C/D)* **BUMMED** – Country song / Moving in with / Mad Cyril / Fat lady wrestlers / Performance / Brain dead / Wrote for luck / Bring a friend / Do it better / Lazyitis. *(hit UK 59 UK Jan90) (cd re-iss. May99 on 'London'; 520013-2)*		-
May 89. (12"/7"/c-s; as HAPPY MONDAYS & KARL DENVER) *(FAC 222/+7/C)* **LAZYITIS – ONE ARMED BOXER. / MAD CYRIL – HELLO GIRLS** *(re-iss. May90; same); hit No.46)*	85	-
Sep 89. (12"/7") *(FAC 232/+7)* **WFL (Vince Clarke mix). / WFL – THINK ABOUT THE FUTURE (the Paul Oakenfold mix)** (cd-s+=) *(FACD 232)* – Lazyitis – one armed boxer.	68	-
Nov 89. (7"clear/12"clear) **MAD CYRIL – HELLO GIRLS. / DO IT BETTER**	-	-
Nov 89. (12"ep/cd-ep)(7"ep/c-ep) *(FAC/+D 242)(FAC 242-7/-C)* **MADCHESTER RAVE ON EP** – Hallelujah / Holy ghost / Clap your hands / Rave on. (7") *(FAC 242R-7)* **Hallelujah (the MacColl mix). / Hallelujah (in out mix).** (c-s)(12"/cd-s) *(FAC 242RC)(FAC/+D 242R)* – ('A'club mix) / Rave on (club mix).	19	-

—— added guest **ROWETA** – backing vocals to repl. other guest KIRSTY MacCOLL

	Factory	Elektra
Mar 90. (12"/7") *(FAC 272/+7) <64899>* **STEP ON (stuff it in mix). / ('A'-One louder mix)** (c-s+=)(cd-s+=) *(FAC 272C)(FACD 272)* – ('A'-Twistin' my melons mix).	5	57 Feb91
Oct 90. (12"/7"/c-s) *(FAC 302/+7/C)* **KINKY AFRO. / KINKY AFRO (live)** (cd-s+=) *(FACD 302)* – ('A'radio edit).	5	
Nov 90. (cd/lp)(c) *(FACD/FACT 320)(FAC 320C) <60986>* **PILLS 'N THRILLS AND BELLYACHES** – Kinky Afro / God's cop / Donovan / Grandbag's funeral / Loose fit / Dennis & Lois / Bob's your uncle / Step on / Holiday / Harmony. *(cd re-iss. May99 on 'London'; 828223-2)*	4	89
Feb 91. (12"/7"/c-s) *(FAC 312/+7/C)* **LOOSE FIT. / BOB'S YOUR UNCLE** (cd-s+=) *(FACD 312)* – Kinky Afro (Euro mix).	17	
Sep 91. (cd/d-lp)(c) *(FACD/FACT 322)(FAC 322C)* **LIVE** (live BABY BIG HEAD Bootleg album) – Hallelujah / Donovan / Kinky Afro / Clap your hands / Loose fit / Holiday / Rave on / E / Tokoloshe man / Dennis and Lois / God's cop / Step on / W.F.L. *(d-lp+=)(c+=)* – Bob's your uncle.	21	-
Nov 91. (12"/7"/c-s) *(FAC 332/+7/C)* **JUDGE FUDGE. / TOKOLOSHE MAN** (cd-s+=) *(FACD 332)* – ('A'version).	24	
Sep 92. (7"/c-s) *(FAC 362 7/C)* **STINKIN' THINKIN'. / ('A'-Boys Own mix)** (12"+=/cd-s+=) *(FAC/+D 362)* – ('A'-Terry Farley mix) / Baby bighead.	31	
Oct 92. (cd/lp)(c) *(FACD/FACT 420)(FAC 420C)* **. . . YES PLEASE!** – Stinkin' thinkin' / Monkey in the family / Sunshine & love / Dustman / Angel / Cut 'em loose Bruce / Theme from Netto / Love child / Total Ringo / Cowboy Dave. *(cd re-iss. May99 on 'London'; 520026-2)*	14	

Nov 92. (7"/c-s) *(FAC 372 7/C)* **SUNSHINE & LOVE. / STAYING ALIVE (mix) / TWENTY FOUR HOUR PARTY PEOPLE (remix)** (12"+=/cd-s+=) *(FAC/+D 372)* – ('A'dance mix).	62	

—— they disbanded early '93, with SHAUN and other two briefly forming The MONDAYS which evolved into BLACK GRAPE

– compilations, etc. –

May 90. (12"ep/c-ep/cd-ep) *Strange Fruit; (SFPS/+C/CD 077)* **THE PEEL SESSION** – Tart tart / Mad Cyril / Do it better. *(cd-ep re-iss. Feb92; same)*		-
Nov 91. (cd-ep) *Strange Fruit;* **THE PEEL SESSION (1986)** – Freaky dancin' / Kuff dam / Olive Oil / Cob 20.		-
Sep 93. (cd) *Elektra;* **DOUBLE EASY: THE US SINGLES**		-
Oct 95. (cd/c) *London; (520036-2/-4)* **LOADS** – Step on / W.F.L. / Kinky Afro / Hallelujah – MacColl mix / Mad Cyril / Lazyitis / Tokoloshe man / Loose fit / Bob's yer uncle / Judge fudge / Stinkin' thinkin' / Sunshine & love / Tart tart / Kuff dam / Twenty four hour party people. *(some cd's w/ free cd+=)* **LOADS MORE** – Lazyitis – one armed boxer mix / W.F.L. (Perfecto mix) / Bob's yer uncle (Perfecto mix) / Loose fit (Perfecto mix) / Hallelujah (Deadstock mix) / Freaky dancing / Delightful.	41	

BLACK GRAPE

SHAUN RYDER + BEZ with **KERMIT** (b.PAUL LEVEREDGE) – rapper (ex-RUTHLESS RAP ASSASINS) / **JED BIRTWHISTLE** – rapper (ex-RUTHLESS RAP ASSASSINS) / **WAGS** – guitar (ex-PARIS ANGELS) / **CRAIG GANNON** – guitar (ex-SMITHS) who replaced INTASTELLA guitarists **MARTIN WRIGHT + MARTIN MITTLER**

	Radioactive	Radioactive
May 95. (c-s) *(RAXC 16)* **REVEREND BLACK GRAPE / STRAIGHT OUT OF TRUMPTON (BASEMENT TAPES)** (cd-s+=) *(RAXTD 16)* – ('A'-dark side mix). (12") *(RAXT 16)* – ('A'side) / ('A'-dub collar mix) / ('A'-dark side mix).	9	
Jul 95. (c-s) *(RAXC 19)* **IN THE NAME OF THE FATHER / LAND OF A THOUSAND KAMA SUTRA BABIES** (cd-s+=) *(RAXTD 19)* – ('A'-chopper's mix) / ('A'-chopper's instrumental). (12") *(RAXT 19)* – ('A'side) / (above 2).	8	
Aug 95. (cd/c/lp) *<RAD/RAC/RAR 11224>* **IT'S GREAT WHEN YOU'RE STRAIGHT . . . YEAH** – Reverend Black Grape / In the name of the father / Tramazi party / Kelly's heroes / Yeah yeah brother / Big day in the north / Shake well before opening / Shake your money / Little Bob.	1	
Nov 95. (c-s) *(RAXC 22)* **KELLY'S HEROES / ('A'-The Milky Bar Kid mix)** (cd-s+=) *(RAXTD 22)* – ('A'-The Archibald mix) / Little Bob (live). (cd-s) *(RAXXD 22)* – ('A'live) / In the name of the father (live) / Fat neck.	17	

—— BEZ quit due to argument with SHAUN over his role in the group.

—— On Channel 4's TFI Friday, SHAUN caused more controversy by adding loads of live f words on their version on SEX PISTOLS 'Pretty Vacant'.

May 96. (c-s) *(RAXC 24)* **FAT NECK / PRETTY VACANT (live)** (cd-s+=) *(RAXTD 24)* – Yeah yeah brother (Outlaw Josey Wales mix). (12") *(RAXT 24)* – ('A'-GOLDIE Beat the f*** down mix) / Yeah yeah brother (Clockwork Orange mix) / Yeah yeah brother (Dog day afternoon mix).	10	
Jun 96. (c-s) *(RAXC 25)* **ENGLAND'S IRIE /** (cd-s) *(RAXTD 25)* – ('A'side) / ('A'-Pass The Durazac mix) / ('A'-Suedehead dub) / ('A'-Mel's L.A. Irie mix). (12") *(RAXT 25)* – above featured JOE STRUMMER and KEITH ALLEN	6	

—— In Oct'96, SHAUN moonlighted with The HEADS (ex-TALKING HEADS) on minor hit single 'Don't Take My Kindness For Weakness'.

Oct 97. (c-s/cd-s) *(RAX C/TD 32)* **GET HIGHER / ('A'mixes)** (cd-s) *(RAXXD 32)* – ('A'mixes).	24	
Nov 97. (lp/c/cd) *<RAR/+C/D 11716>* **STUPID STUPID STUPID** – Get higher / Squeaky / Marbles / Dadi was a badi / Rubber band / Spotlight / Tell me something / Money back guaranteed / Lonely / Words.	11	
Feb 98. (cd-s) *(RAXTD 33)* **MARBLES (remixes by R.I.P. and FABIO PARAS) / MARBLES (demo)** (12"+=) *(RAXT 33)* – ('A'-Tricky remix). (cd-s) *(RAXXD 33)* – ('A'-Tricky remix) / Harry the dog / Get higher (uncensored video on CD-ROM).	46	

HAPPY MONDAYS

—— re-formed **SHAUN + PAUL RYDER , GAZ WHELAN, PAUL 'WAGS' WAGSTAFF, 'NUTS', BEZ + ROWETTA**

	London	Elektra
May 99. (12") *(LONX 432)* **THE BOYS ARE BACK IN TOWN. / ('A'-Dirty mix)** (cd-s) *(LONCD 432)* – ('A'side) / Kinky Afro / ('A'extended). (cd-s) *(LOCDP 432)* – ('A'-Dirty mix) / Loose fit (Perfecto mix) / Bob's yer uncle (Perfecto mix).	24	
May 99. (cd/c) *556105-2/-4)* **THE GREATEST HITS** (compilation) – Step on / WFL (Vince Clarke mix) / Kinky Afro (Perfecto mix) / Hallelujah (club mix) / Mad Cyril / Lazyitis (One Armed Boxer mix) / Loose fit (Perfecto mix) / Bob's yer uncle / Judge fudge / Stinkin' thinkin' / 24 hour party people / WFL (Think About The Future mix) / Stayin' alive / The boys are back in town (clean version) / Step on (Twisting My Melon mix).	11	

Tim HARDIN

Born: EUGENE HARDIN, 23 Dec'41, Oregon, U.S.A. After a short-lived and miserable spell in the marines, HARDIN moved to Greenwich village in the early 60's with little financial means and a heroin habit. He briefly attended the American Academy of Dramatic Art before dropping out and heading for the Boston folk scene, his earliest forays into the music world. There, TIM received a call from manager/producer ERIK JACOBSEN asking him back up to New York to record some demos for 'Columbia'. The company were less than impressed with the results; at this point HARDIN had yet to develop his subtle, jazz-inflected folk-style, instead peddling a rather forgettable strain of awkward, white-boy blues. Some of the material from this period later ended up on 'TIM HARDIN IV' (1969), passed off as new work and subsequently enraging HARDIN, not the first time he'd clash with those trying to guide his career. Nevertheless, HARDIN was already possessed of a unique vocal style, the jazz influence apparent in his phrasing and the way he manipulated notes. JACOBSEN, however, showed faith in the singer and eventually HARDIN was signed to the new 'Verve-Forecast' label with the help of producers CHARLES KOPPELMAN and DON RUBIN. 'TIM HARDIN 1' (1966) showcased a marked improvement in TIM's playing, singing and songwriting, the blues pretensions substituted by a meditative, painfully intimate folk-confessional style, exemplified by the likes of 'MISTY ROSES' and 'HOW CAN WE HANG ON TO A DREAM'. The album was also overdubbed with strings, apparently without HARDIN's consent and much to his disgust, although ironically, they added an austere beauty to many of the tracks. The debut also featured 'REASON TO BELIEVE', like many of HARDIN's songs, much covered and made famous by other artists (in this case ROD STEWART) while TIM lingered in obscurity. One cover version that really incensed HARDIN was BOBBY DARIN's reading of 'IF I WERE A CARPENTER', TIM allegedly claiming that DARIN had the original playing on headphones so he could replicate his phrasing. The song was just one of the many classics on 'TIM HARDIN 2' (1967), the singer's most affecting and realised album. Written immediately prior to the birth of his son, DAMION, 'BLACK SHEEP BOY' (later, appropriately enough, covered by SCOTT WALKER) was heart-rending, 'RED BALLOON' bleakly moving, while HARDIN's hesitant, fragile 'TRIBUTE TO HANK WILLIAMS' saw the singer detail his ambiguous feelings about live performance. "Who watched the pain in his heart and then they sat and then they clapped their hands"; for HARDIN, performing (when he deigned to turn up) was more about internal catharsis than pleasing the crowd. Heralded by BOB DYLAN as the greatest songwriter of the decade, the singer is said to have inspired DYLAN's 'John Wesley Harding' (HARDIN often boasted that he was a descendant of the famed outlaw, JOHN WESLEY HARDIN). Yet despite the brilliance of these two albums, his muse increasingly deserted him as he fell deeper into heroin abuse. 'TIM HARDIN 3' (1968) was a jazzy live set that featured reworkings of songs from the first two albums as well as a smattering of new tracks. Shortly after the record's release, it was announced that HARDIN was suffering fom the respiratory disease, pleurisy, making his live appearances even more erratic. After an English tour with Family ended in disaster at the Royal Albert Hall (Hardin fell asleep on stage), the singer made a concerted effort to wean himself off heroin. When this failed he retreated to Woodstock, writing the brutally naked confessional of 'SUITE FOR SUSAN MOORE AND DAMION' (1969), the first fruits of his new deal with 'Columbia'. The SUSAN MOORE of the title was his wife, who eventually left him soon after the record's release, HARDIN subsequently spiralling into despair. He moved to England, registering as an addict in order to procure drugs on the NHS, releasing a further couple of patchy albums, 'BIRD ON A WIRE' (1971) and 'PAINTED HEAD' (1973), the latter a set of covers. Neither sold well and a film role as WOODY GUTHRIE in a proposed biopic, 'Bound For Glory', came to nothing. He recorded a final album, 'TIM HARDIN 9' (1974), before moving back to L.A. where he finally overdosed on the 29th December '80, aged only 39. • **Covers:** HOUSE OF THE RISING SUN (trad) / BO DIDDLEY (Bo Diddley).

Album rating: TIM HARDIN 1 (*6) / TIM HARDIN 2 (*6) / THIS IS TIM HARDIN early stuff (*5) / TIM HARDIN 3 – LIVE IN CONCERT (*6) / TIM HARDIN 4 (*5) / SUITE FOR SUSAN MOORE AND DAMION-WE ARE-ONE, ONE, ALL IN ONE (*5) / THE BEST OF TIM HARDIN compilation (*6) / BIRD ON A WIRE (*4) / PAINTED HEAD (*5) / NINE (*5) / THE SHOCK OF GRACE posthumous (*5) / HANG ON TO A DREAM (THE BEST OF TIM HARDIN) (*8) / SIMPLE SONGS OF FREEDOM – THE TIM HARDIN COLLECTION compilation (*7)

TIM HARDIN – vocals, guitar, piano

		Verve Folkways	Verve Folkways
Oct 66.	(7") <5008> **HANG ON TO A DREAM. / IT'LL NEVER HAPPEN AGAIN**	-	-
Dec 66.	(lp) (5018) <3004> **TIM HARDIN 1**		
	– Don't make promises / Green rocky road / Smugglin' man / While you're on your way / It'll never happen again / Reason to believe / Never too far / Part of the wind / Ain't gonna do without / Misty roses / How can we hang on to a dream. *(cd-iss. Sep92 on 'Line'; LMCD 951113)*		
Dec 66.	(7") (VS 1504) **HANG ON TO A DREAM. / REASON TO BELIEVE**	50	-
Feb 67.	(7") <5017> **DON'T MAKE PROMISES. / MISTY ROSES**	-	-
May 67.	(7") <5031> **HANG ON TO A DREAM. / MISTY ROSES**	-	
Sep 67.	(7") <5042> **NEVER TOO FAR. / GREEN ROCKY ROAD**	-	
Sep 67.	(lp) (6002) <3022> **TIM HARDIN 2**		
	– If I were a carpenter / Red balloon / Black sheep boy / Lady came from Baltimore / Baby close its eyes / You upset the grace of living when you lie / Speak like a child / See where you are and get out / It's hard to believe in love for long / Tribute to Hank Williams. *(cd-iss. Sep92 on 'Line'; LMCD 951069)*		
Nov 67.	(7") <5048> **BLACK SHEEP BOY. / MISTY ROSES**	-	
Nov 67.	(7") (VS 1511) **LADY CAME FROM BALTIMORE. / BLACK SHEEP BOY**		-
Jun 68.	(7") <5059> **TRIBUTE TO HANK WILLIAMS. / YOU UPSET THE GRACE OF LIVING**	-	-
Jun 68.	(lp) (6010) <3049> **TIM HARDIN 3 – LIVE IN CONCERT (live)**		

– Lady came from Baltimore / Reason to believe / You upset the grace of living when you lie / Misty roses / Black sheep boy / Lenny's tune / Don't make promises / Danville dame / If I were a carpenter / Red balloon / Tribute to Hank Williams / Smugglin' man. *(cd-iss. Sep92 on 'Line'; LMCD 951073)*

Jul 68.	(7") (VS 1516) **DON'T MAKE PROMISES. / SMUGGLIN' MAN**		
Apr 69.	(7") <5097> **SMUGGLIN' MAN. / REASON TO BELIEVE** <re-iss. 1970; 5116>	-	-
May 69.	(lp) (6016) <3064> **TIM HARDIN IV**		

– Airmobile / Whiskey whiskey / Seventh son / How long / Danville dame / Ain't gonna do without (part 1 & 2) / House of the rising son / Bo Diddley / I can't slow down / Hello baby. *(cd-iss. Sep92 on 'Line'; LMCD 951091)*

		C.B.S.	Columbia
May 69.	(lp) (63571) <9787> **SUITE FOR SUSAN MOORE AND DAMION – WE ARE – ONE, ONE, ALL IN ONE**		Apr69
	– First love song / Everything good become more true / Question of birth / Once-touched by flame / Last sweet moments / Magician / Loneliness she knows / The country I'm living in / One, one, the perfect sum / Susan.		
May 69.	(7") <44920> **ONE-TOUCHED BY FLAME. / QUESTION OF BIRTH**	-	
Aug 69.	(7") (4441) <44920> **SIMPLE SONG OF FREEDOM. / QUESTION OF BIRTH**	50	Jul69
Aug 71.	(lp) (64335) <30551> **BIRD ON A WIRE**		Jul71
	– Bird on the wire / Moonshiner / Southern butterfly / A satisfied mind / Soft summer breeze / Hoboin' / Georgia on my mind / Andre Johray / If I knew / Love hymn.		
Aug 71.	(7") <45426> **BIRD ON THE WIRE. / SOFT SUMMER BREEZE**	-	
Jan 73.	(lp) (65209) <31764> **PAINTED HEAD**		
	– You can't judge a book by the cover / Midnight caller / Yankee lady / Lonesome valley / Sweet lady / Do the do / Perfection / Till we meet again / I'll be home / Nobody knows you when you're down and out.		
Jan 73.	(7") (1016) <45695> **DO THE DO. / SWEET LADY**		

		G.M.	Antilles
Jan 74.	(lp) (1004) <7023> **NINE**		
	– Shiloh town / Never too far / Rags & old iron / Look our love over / Person to person / Darling girl / Blues on my ceiling / Is there no rest for the weary / Fire and rain / While you're on your way / Judge and jury. *(re-iss. Dec90 on 'Marquee' cd/c/lp; MQC CD/MC/LP 003) (cd-iss. Apr92 on 'See For Miles'; SEECD 335)*		
Feb 74.	(7") (GMS 14) **DARLING GIRL. / PERSON TO PERSON**		-

—— Resided in the UK from 1974. He died in L.A. of drug abuse in 1980.

– compilations, etc. –

Apr 68.	(lp) *Atlantic;* (588 082) / *Atco;* <33210> **THIS IS TIM HARDIN** (rec.1962)		Sep67
	– I can slow down / Blues on the ceilin' / I'm your hoochie coochie man / Stagger Lee / I've been working on the railroad / House of the rising Sun / Fast freight / Cocaine Bill / You got to have more than one woman / Danville dame. *(re-iss. Jul89 on 'Edsel'; ED 309)*		
1970.	(lp) *Verve;* (2317 003) <3078> **THE BEST OF TIM HARDIN**		
1971.	(7") *Verve;* (2009 006) **IF I WERE A CARPENTER. / HANG ON TO A DREAM**		
1973.	(lp) *M.G.M.;* <4952> **ARCHETYPES**	-	
1974.	(d-lp) *Verve;* (2683 048) **TIM HARDIN I & II**	-	
1981.	(lp) *Columbia;* <37164> **THE STATE OF GRACE**	-	
Feb 82.	(lp) *Polydor;* (PD 16333) **TIM HARDIN MEMORIAL ALBUM**		-
May 82.	(lp) *Kamera;* (KAM 004) **HOMECOMING CONCERT** *(cd-iss. 1989 & Aug94 on 'Line'; LICD 90040)*		
May 88.	(cd) *Polydor;* (835706-2) **REASON TO BELIEVE – THE BEST OF TIM HARDIN**		-
Jan 93.	(cd) *Polydor;* (521583-2) **HANG ON TO A DREAM (THE VERVE RECORDINGS)**		-

HARDLINE (see under ⇒ JOURNEY)

Francoise HARDY

Born: 17 Jan'44, Paris, France. Already a competent singer/songwriter by the time she'd graduated from college, HARDY was courted by various French labels before signing for 'Vogue' in late '61. An almost immediate hit in her native country, she first came to international attention the following year with the swaying romanticism of 'TOUS LES GARCONS ET LES FILLES', a classic pop record that made the UK Top 40 and went on to sell in excess of a million copies in Europe. FRANCOISE HARDY's delicate, often hauntingly atmospheric style stood in stark contrast to the showy glitz that characterised the work of many of the day's major domestic artists while reflecting a wider range of influences from French torch balladeers to US girl groups and folk-rock. 1964 saw the release of 'TOUS LES GARCONS . . .' in English (available on a rare eponymous EP), HARDY's cute, girlish phrasing reminiscent of ASTRUD GILBERTO's attempts at translating her native Portuguese. The mid-60's marked her most creatively fertile period with the likes of the chiming 'CE PETITE COEUR', 'ET MEME' and 'ALL OVER THE WORLD' (the English version of 'DANS LE MONDE ENTIER'), the latter marking her first and only UK Top 20 entry. With 'MA JEUNESSE FOUT LE CAMP' (1967), HARDY moved towards a more sophisticated ballad style, the piano/strings arrangement of 'IL N'Y A PAS D'AMOUR HEUREUX' bringing her trademark dreamy melancholy to the fore. Late 60's albums such as 'COMMENT TE DIRE ADIEU' and 'FRANCOISE HARDY EN ANGLAIS' also saw her increasingly concentrating on cover material and – as the title of the latter might suggest – the international market. Stunningly beautiful but often crippled by stage fright, she found a kindred sensitive soul in tragic English singer/songwriter NICK DRAKE with whom she spent some time in Paris in the early 70's. Despite her shyness, HARDY appeared in a handful of Roger Vadim films and has also worked as a fashion model. While her international fame waned in the 70's, HARDY's huge popularity in her native France remained undimmed, releasing several well-quoted albums. In 1994, Brit-pop faves BLUR invited her to back them on the French-version of 'TO THE END'. 1996's indie-orientated 'LE DANGER' (on 'Virgin'), proved she was far from being out of touch.

Best CD compilation: LES CHANSONS D'AMOUR (*6)

FRANCOISE HARDY – vocals, guitar (with various session people)

			French	not iss.	
1962.	(7") **TOUS LES GARCONS ET LES FILLES.** /		-	-	French
1962.	(7") **LE TEMPS DE L'AMOUR.** /		-	-	French
1963.	(7") **LE PREMIER BONHEUR DU JOUR.** /		-	-	French
1964.	(7") **LA TUA MANO.** /		-	-	French

			Pye		
1964.	(lp) *(NPL 18094)* **FRANCOISE HARDY**		-		

– Tous le garcons et les filles / Ca a rate / La fille avec toi / Oh, oh, Cherie / Le temps de l'amour / Il est tout pour moi / On se plait / Ton meilleur ami / J'ai jete mon coeur / Il est part un jour / J'susie d'acoord / C'est a l'amour auquel je pense.

Apr 64.	(7") *(7N 15612)* **CATCH A FALLING STAR.** / **ONLY FRIENDS**	☐	-		
Jun 64.	(7") *(7N 15653)* **TOUS LES GARCONS ET LES FILLES.** / **L'AMOUR S'EN VA**	36	-		
Sep 64.	(7") *(7N 15696)* **POURTANT TU M'AIMES. JALOUX**		-		
1964.	(lp) *(NPL 18099)* **IN VOGUE**				

– Le premier bonheur du jour / Va prende surai-je Toi je ne t'oublierai pas / Avant de t'en aller / Comme tant d'autres / J'aurais voulu / Nous tous / L'amour d'un garcon Le saistu / L'amour ne dure pas toujours / On di de lui (It's gonna take some time).

Dec 64.	(7") *(7N 15740)* **ET MEME.** / **LES TEMPS DE L'AMOUR**	31	-		
Mar 65.	(7") *(7N 15802)* **ALL OVER THE WORLD.** / **ANOTHER PLACE**	16	☐		

			Vogue		
1965.	(7") *(VRS 7001)* **JUST CALL AND I'LL BE THERE.** / **YOU JUST HAVE TO SAY THE WORD**	☐	-		
1966.	(7") *(VRS 7004)* **SO MANY FRIENDS.** / **HOWEVER MUCH**	☐	-		
1966.	(lp) *(VRL 3021)* **FRANCOISE HARDY**	☐	-		

– Ce petit coeur / Il se fait tard / Tout ce qu'on dit / L'amitie / En t'attendant / Je t'aime / Non, ce n'est pas un reve / Quel mal y a-t-il a da (When I get through with you) / Tu peux bien / Le temps des souvenirs / Je pensais / Dis lui non (Say it now).

1966.	(7") *(VRS 7010)* **THIS LITTLE HEART.** / **THE ROSE**	☐	-		
1966.	(7") *(VRS 7011)* **LA MAISON OU J'AI GRANDI.** / **JE NE SUIS LA POUR PERSONNE**	☐	-		
1966.	(lp) *(VRL 3023)* **LE MEILLEUR DE FRANCOISE HARDY**	☐	-		

– Temps de l'amour / Premier bonheur du jour / L'amour s'en va / Je n'attends plus personne / Ton meilleur ami / Je veux qu'il revienne / Mon amie la rose / Et meme / Je pense a lui / Pourtant tu m'aimes / C'est l'amour auquel je pense / Tous les garcons et les filles.

1966.	(7") *(VRS 7014)* **AUTUMN RENDEZVOUS.** / **IT'S MY HEART**	☐	-		
Oct 66.	(7") *(VRS 7020)* **SI C'EST CA.** / **JE SERAI LA POUR TOI**	☐	-		
1966.	(lp) *(VRL 3025)* **... SINGS IN ENGLISH**	☐	-		

– This little heart / All over the world / However much / It's getting late / Only friends / Say it now / Just call and I'll be there / The rose / Only you can do it / It's my heart / Another place / Autumn rendezvous.

1967.	(lp) *(VRL 3028)* **FRANCOISE**	☐	-		
1967.	(7") *(VRS 7025)* **VOILA.** / **QUI PEUT DIRE**	☐	-		
1967.	(lp) *(VRL 3031)* **VOILA – FRANCOISE HARDY**	☐	-		

– Voila / Qui aime-t-il vraiment / On se quitte toujours / C'est la premiere fois / Apprends le moi / Au fond du reve dore / Qui peut dire / Tu verras / Bien longtemps / Tout rame ne a toi / C'est le passe (Once upon a time).

1967.	(7") *(VRS 7026)* **ON SE QUITTE TOUJOURS.** / **LES PETITS GARCONS**	☐	-		

			U.A.	U.A.	
1968.	(7") *(UP 1208)* **NOW YOU WANT TO BE LOVED.** / **TELL HIM YOU'RE MINE**	☐	-		
1968.	(lp) *(ULP 1207)* **EN ANGLAIS**	☐	-		
1968.	(7") *(UP 2253)* **WILL YOU LOVE ME TOMORROW.** / **LOVING YOU**	☐	-		
1969.	(7") *(UP 35011)* **COMMENT TE DIRE ADIEU.** / **LA MER, LES ETOILES ET LE VENT**	☐	-		
1969.	(7") *(UP 35070)* **ALL BECAUSE OF YOU.** / **TIME PASSING BY**	☐	-		
1970.	(7") *(UP 35105)* **SOON IS SLIPPING AWAY.** / **THE BELLS OF AVIGNON**	☐	-		
1970.	(lp) *(UAS 29046)* **ONE-NINE-SEVEN-ZERO**	☐	-		

			C.B.S.	not iss.	
1972.	(lp) *(65057)* **FRANCOISE HARDY**		-	German

– If you listen / Ocean / Until it's time for you to go / The garden of Jane Delaway / Sometimes / Let my name be sorrow / Brulure / Can't get the one I want / I think it's gonna rain today / Take me hand for a while / Bown bown bown / Till the morning comes.

			Sonopresse	not iss.	
1973.	(lp) *(HY 30902)* **FRANCOISE HARDY**		-	-	French

– Viens / La question / Meme sous la pluie / Chanson d'o / Le martien / Mer / Oui je te dis adieu / Doigts / La maison / Si mi caballero / Bati mon nid / Reve.

			Warners	not iss.	
1974.	(lp) *(K 56019)* **MESSAGE PERSONNEL**		-	-	

– Premiere rencontre / Rever le nez en l'air / L'amour en prive / Berceuse / Pouce, au revoir / L'attente / On dirait / L'habitude / Message personnel (part 1 & 2) / Chanson floue.

			E.M.I.	not iss.	
1977.	(lp) *(064-14426)* **STAR**		-	-	German

– Star / Chanson sur toi et nous / Enregistrement / Avannes / Flashbacks / L'impasse / Ton enfance / Je ne suis que moi / Drole de fete / Fatiguee.

1978.	(lp) *(064-14697)* **MUSIQUE SAOULE**		-	-	German

– J'ecoute la musique saoule / Hallucinogene / Occupe / Brouillard dans la rue corvisart / Tu m'vois plus tu m'sens / Nous deux, nous deux et rien d'autre / Swing

---

au pressing / Perdu d'avance / Tip tap t'entends mes pas / Si je le retrouve un jour / Beau boeing belle.

			Pathe Marconi	not iss.	
1980.	(lp) *(2C070 14869)* **GIN TONIC**		-	-	French

– Jazzy retro satanas / Branche cassee / Ame s'trame drame / Si c'est vraiment vrai / Bosse bossez bossa / Gin tonic / Jukebox / Seule comme une pomme / Chanson ouverte / Minuit minuit / Que tu m'enterres.

			Flarenasch	not iss.	
1981.	(lp) *(723623 WE351)* **A SUIVRE**		-	-	French

– Ca va comme ca / L'amour c'est plus fort / Villegiature / Coupure de courant / Tamalou / Vert ouvert / Ca m'suffit / Voyou voyou / Incurablement sentimentale / Plus personne / Reve de starlett / A suivre.

			WEA	not iss.	
1988.	(cd) *(728690)* **DESCALAGES**		-	-	French

– La sieste / / Une miss s'immisce / Laisse moi rever / Vibrations / Descalages / Partir quand meme / Diletante / Dire tout / Arretons / Je suis de trop ici / Avec toute ma sympathie / La vraie vie c'est ou?

―――― In 1994, FRANCOISE augmented BLUR on their French version on 'To The End', which became available on a UK B-side.

			Virgin	Virgin	
Jun 96.	(cd) *(CDVIR 51)* <41661> **LE DANGER**		-	-	

– Mode d'emploi? / Madeleines / Beaute du diable / L'obscur objet / Peu d'eau / Zero partout / Le danger / Dix heures en ete / Tout va bien / Contr-jour / Ici ou la? / Sa merci / Regarde-toi.

– compilations, others, etc. –

1964.	(7"ep) *Pye; (NEP 24188)* **C'EST FAB**	☐			

– L'amour s'en va / Tous les garcons et les filles / Ton meilleur ami / C'est l'amour auquel je pense.

1964.	(7"ep) *Pye; (NEP 24192)* **FRANCOISE SINGS IN ENGLISH**	☐			

– Find me a boy / I wish it were me / Only friends / Catch a falling star.

1964.	(7"ep) *Pye; (NEP 24195)* **C'EST FRANCOISE**	☐			

– J'aurais / Avant de t'en aller / Le premier bonheur du jour / L'amour d'un garcon (the love of a boy).

1966.	(7"ep) *Vogue; (VRE 5003)* **FRANCOISE HARDY**	☐	-		

– Dis lui non (Say it now) / Dans le monde entire / Tue es ve a moi / Son amour c'est endormi.

1966.	(7"ep) *Vogue; (VRE 5008)* **LE TEMPS DES SOUVENIRS**	☐			
1966.	(7"ep) *Vogue; (VRE 5012)* **CHANTE EN ALLEMAND**	☐			

– Wer du bist / Ich hab das gluck (J'aurais voulu) / Die liebe geht (L'amour s'en va) / Peter und Lou (tous les garcons et les filles).

1967.	(7"ep) *Vogue; (VRE 5015)* **L'AMITIE**		-		

– L'amitie / Ce petit coeur / Non, ce n'est pas un reve / En t'attendant.

1967.	(7"ep) *Vogue; (VRE 5017)* **MON AMIE LA ROSE**	☐			
1967.	(7"ep) *Vogue; (VRE 5018)* **AUTUMN RENDEZVOUS**	☐			

– Autumn rendezvous / Another place / Say it now / All over the world.

1970.	(lp) *Vogue; (500761)* **GREATEST HITS**	☐	-	French
1974.	(lp/c) *Golden Hour; (GH/ZCGH 830)* **GOLDEN HOUR PRESENTS . . . THE BEST OF FRANCOISE HARDY**	☐			
Jun 84.	(cd) *Vogue; (VG 600 006)* **GREATEST HITS**	☐			
Dec 84.	(lp/c) *Vogue; (509/707 191)* **THE HIT PARADE OF FRANCOISE HARDY**	☐			
Oct 88.	(cd) *Vogue; (VGCD 670 010)* **LES GRANDS SUCCES DE FRANCOISE HARDY**	☐			
Oct 88.	(lp) *Vogue; (000 318)* **IN VOGUE** (cd-iss. Feb89; VGCD 600 010)	☐			
Jul 89.	(c/cd) *Vogue; (771/670 041)* **ALL OVER THE WORLD**	☐			
Apr 91.	(cd)(c) *Vogue; (600 309)(706 259)* **FRANCOISE HARDY SORY VOL.4 1967-1969**	☐			
May 93.	(cd/c) *Duchesse; (CD2/MC3 52060)* **TOUS LE GARCONS ET LES FILLES**	☐			
Oct 93.	(cd) *Vogue; (VGCD 600 145)* **IN VOGUE VOL.2**	☐			
Apr 94.	(cd) *Vogue-BMG; (74321 14520-2)* **THE COLLECTION**	☐			
May 95.	(cd) *Vogue-BMG; (74321 20391-2)* **GREATEST RECORDINGS**	☐			
May 95.	(cd) *Vogue-BMG; (74321 26470-2)* **THE YEH-YEH GIRL FROM PARIS!**	☐			
Oct 96.	(cd) *Camden; (74321 41502-2)* **LES CHANSONS D'AMOUR**	☐	-		

– Ce petite coeur / Il n'y a pas d'amour heureux / Mon ame la rose / Tous les garcons et les filles / L'amitie / La maison ou j'ai grandi / Le temps de l'amour / Il est des choses / Ma jeunesse fout le camp / Ton meilleur ami / Voila / Parlami di te / J'ai jete mon coeur (I threw away my heart) / Autumn rendezvous (English version of "Rendez-vous d'automne") / La tua mano / C'est a l'amour auquel je pense / Je ne suis pas la pour personne / Le premier bonheur du jour / Comme / This little heart (English version of "Ce petite coeur") / Find me a boy (English version of "Tous les garcons et les filles") / All over the world (English version of "Dans le monde entier").

Feb 97.	(cd) *Flarenasch; (472297)* **LES INOUBLIABLES DE . . .** *(re-iss. Jan99 on 'Wagram'; 304063-2)*	☐	-		

Steve HARLEY

Born: STEVEN NICE, 27 Feb'51, London, England. After an initial stint as a music journalist, HARLEY formed COCKNEY REBEL, recruiting the interestingly named MILTON REAME-JAMES, JEAN-PAUL CROCKER, PAUL AVON JEFFREYS and STUART ELLIOT. Signed to 'E.M.I.', the group's debut album, 'THE HUMAN MENAGERIE' (1973) sank without trace, although their avant-glam stylings were attracting a growing following in the capital and, in Spring '74, they scored a Top 5 hit with 'JUDY TEEN'. HARLEY's affected enunciation backed by the group's quirky pop creations amounted to a distant 70's cousin of prime KINKS, although the frontman lacked the prolific songwriting prowess of RAY DAVIES. A second album, 'THE PSYCHOMODO' (1974), followed into the Top 10 later that summer, while the 'MR. SOFT' single gave them further chart success. Despite these advances, HARLEY's war of words with the music press continued to escalate, eventually prompting the singer to disband the outfit and re-invent his whole approach. Retaining only ELLIOT from this first incarnation, HARLEY recruited a new line-up of JIM CREGAN, DUNCAN MACKAY and GEORGE FORD (now under the slightly revised moniker of STEVE HARLEY & COCKNEY REBEL), almost immediately hitting the UK No.1 spot with the gorgeous 'MAKE ME SMILE (COME UP AND SEE ME)'. Yet despite its lush melody and harmonies, the track was actually a sarcastic rebuff to his sworn critical enemies in the media. The accompanying album, 'THE BEST YEARS OF OUR LIVES' (1975), reached the Top 5 and became the most successful set of HARLEY's career; the DAVIES/IAN HUNTER-esque lyrical flourishes were still in evidence, just wrapped in more conventional tunes. Subsequent albums, 'TIMELESS FLIGHT' (1976) and 'LOVE'S A PRIMA DONNA' (1976), weren't quite so successful although HARLEY scored a surprise Top 10 in summer '76 with an unlikely cover of The Beatles' 'HERE COMES THE SUN'. The latter set was HARLEY's first full solo attempt, the singer relocating to America where he continued to record low-key albums through till the end of the decade. In the mid-80's, HARLEY came to prominence once more when he duetted with SARAH BRIGHTMAN on the Top 10 excerpt from 'PHANTOM OF THE OPERA', although he was surprised when MICHAEL CRAWFORD was chosen for the lead role in the stage version of the musical. A series of singles followed on Mickie Most's 'R.A.K.' label as well as a collaborative effort with JON ANDERSON, and although HARLEY has sporadically reformed COCKNEY REBEL over the years, mainstream success has proved elusive. • Also: An ex-original member JEFFREYS died in the Lockerbie plane crash on the 21st December '88.

Album rating: Cockney Rebel: THE HUMAN MENAGERIE (*5) / THE PSYCHOMODO (*6) / Steve Harley & Cockney Rebel: THE BEST YEARS OF OUR LIVES (*5) / Steve Harley: LOVE'S A PRIMA DONNA (*4) / FACE TO FACE – A LIVE RECORDING (*3) / HOBO WITH A GRIN (*4) / MAKE ME SMILE – THE BEST OF STEVE HARLEY & COCKNEY REBEL compilation (*7) / YES YOU CAN (*4) / LIVE IN THE UK (*4) / POETIC JUSTICE (*4)

COCKNEY REBEL

STEVE HARLEY – vocals, guitar / **MILTON REAME-JAMES** – keyboards / **JEAN-PAUL** (b. JOHN) **CROCKER** – violin / **PAUL AVRON JEFFERIES** – bass / **STUART ELLIOT** – drums

		E.M.I.	E.M.I.
Aug 73.	(7") (EMI 2051) <3846> **SEBASTIAN. / ROCK AND ROLL PARADE**		
Nov 73.	(lp/c) (EMA/TC-EMA 759) <11294> **THE HUMAN MENAGERIE** – Hideaway / What Ruthy said / Loretta's tale / Crazy raver / Sebastian / Mirror freak / My only vice / Muriel the actor / Chameleon / Death trip. (cd-iss. Jul90+=; CDP 794756-2) – Rock and roll parade / Judy Teen / Spaced out.		
Mar 74.	(7") (EMI 2128) **JUDY TEEN. / SPACED OUT**	5	–
Jun 74.	(lp/c) (EMC/TC-EMC 3033) <11330> **THE PSYCHOMODO** – Sweet dreams / Psychomodo / Mr. Soft / Singular band / Ritz / Cavaliers / Bed in the corner / Sling it / Tumbling down. (re-iss. 1983 on 'Fame' lp/c; FA41 3135-1/-4) (cd-iss. Jul90+=; CDP 794755-2) – Big big deal / Such a dream.	8	–
Jul 74.	(7") (EMI 2191) **MR. SOFT. / SUCH A DREAM**	8	–
Nov 74.	(7"; by STEVE HARLEY) (EMI 2233) **BIG BIG DEAL. / BED IN THE CORNER**		
Nov 74.	(7") <4023> **SINGULAR BAND. / TUMBLING DOWN**	–	

STEVE HARLEY & COCKNEY REBEL

—— retained only ELLIOT with JIM CREGAN – guitar (ex-FAMILY)repl. CROCKER / DUNCAN MACKAY – keyboards repl. REAME-JAMES / GEORGE FORD – bass repl. JEFFERIES (he died early '89 in the Lockerbie disaster).

Feb 75.	(7") (EMI 2263) <4070> **MAKE ME SMILE (COME UP AND SEE ME). / ANOTHER JOURNEY**	1	
Mar 75.	(lp/c) (EMC/TC-EMC 3068) <11394> **THE BEST YEARS OF OUR LIVES** – (introducing the best years) / Mad mad moonlight / Mr. Raffles (man it was mean) / It wasn't me / Panorama / Make me smile (come up and see me) / Back to the farm / 49th parallel / The best years of our lives. (re-iss. Mar91 cd/lp; CDP 795926-2/-1)	4	
May 75.	(7") (EMI 2299) **MR. RAFFLES (MAN IT WAS MEAN). / SEBASTIAN (live)**	13	–
——	now a quartet when JIM CREGAN left to join ROD STEWART's band		
Nov 75.	(7") (EMI 2369) **BLACK OR WHITE. / MAD MAD MOONLIGHT (live)**		–
Feb 76.	(7") <4201> **MAKE ME SMILE (COME UP AND SEE ME). / ANOTHER JOURNEY**	–	96
Feb 76.	(7") (EMI 2409) **WHITE WHITE DOVE. / THROW YOUR SOUL DOWN HERE**		–
Feb 76.	(lp/c) (EMA/TC-EMA 775) <11500> **TIMELESS FLIGHT** – Red is a mean, mean colour / White white dove / Understand / All men are hungry / Black or white / Everything changes / Nothing is sacred / Don't go, don't cry. (cd-iss. Mar91; CZ 386)	18	
Jul 76.	(7") (EMI 2505) **HERE COMES THE SUN. / LAY ME DOWN**	10	–
Aug 76.	(7") <4335> **HERE COMES THE SUN. / ALL MEN ARE HUNGRY**		–
Oct 76.	(7") (EMI 2539) **(I BELIEVE) LOVE'S A PRIMA DONNA. / SIDETRACK ONE**	41	–
Oct 76.	(lp/c) (EMC/TC-EMC 3156) <11596> **LOVE'S A PRIMA DONNA** – Seeking a love / G.I. valentine / Finally a card game / Too much tenderness / Love compared with you / (I believe) Love's a prima donna / Seeking a love (pt.2) / (If this is love) Give me more / Carry me again / Here comes the sun / Innocence and guilt / Is it true what they say.	28	
Dec 76.	(7") <4397> **LOVE COMPARED WITH YOU. / TOO MUCH TENDERNESS**	–	
Jun 77.	(lp/c) (EMSP/TC-EMSP 320) <11661> **FACE TO FACE – A LIVE RECORDING (live)** – Here comes the sun / (I believe) Love's a prima donna / Mad, mad moonlight /	40	

Red is a mean, mean colour / The best years of our lives / Love compared with you / Mr. Soft / Sebastian.

Aug 77.	(7"/12") (EMI/12EMI 2673) **THE BEST YEARS OF OUR LIVES (live). / TUMBLING DOWN (live)**		

STEVE HARLEY

Jul 78.	(7") (EMI 2830) <4622> **ROLL THE DICE. / WAITING**		
Jul 78.	(lp/c) (EMC/TC-EMC 3254) <11770> **HOBO WITH A GRIN** – Roll the dice / America the brave / Living in a rhapsody / I wish it would rain / Riding the waves (with Virginia Woolf) / Someone's coming / Hot youth / (I don't believe) God is an anarchist / Faith, hope and charity.		
Sep 79.	(7") (EMI 2994) **FREEDOM'S PRISONER. / ONE MORE TIME**	58	–
Sep 79.	(lp/c) (EMC/TC-EMC 3311) **THE CANDIDATE** – Audience with the man / Woodchopper / Freedom's prisoner / Love on the rocks / Who's afraid / One more time / How good it feels / From here to eternity / Young hearts (the candidate).		

		Chrysalis	not iss.
Mar 82.	(7") (CHS 2594) **I CAN'T EVEN TOUCH YOU. / I CAN'T BE ANYONE** (above featured MIDGE URE of ULTRAVOX)		–

		Stiletto- RCA	not iss.
Jul 83.	(7") (STIL 14) **BALLERINA (PRIMA DONNA). / FACE TO FACE** (12") (STLT 14) – ('A'extended) / Sebastian (new version).	51	–

		Polydor	not iss.
Dec 85.	(7"/ext.12"; by SARAH BRIGHTMAN & STEVE HARLEY) (POSP/+X 800) **PHANTOM OF THE OPERA. / OVERTURE (From the Musical)**	7	–

—— now solo with a backing band.

		R.A.K.	not iss.
Jun 85.	(7") (RAK 383) **IRRESISTIBLE. / SUCH IS LIFE** (12") (RAK 383-12) – ('A'extended) / Sebastian (original).		–
Apr 86.	(7"/ext.12") (RAK 387/+12) **HEARTBEAT LIKE THUNDER. / WARM MY COLD HEART**		–
Jun 86.	(7"/ext.12") (RAK 389/+12) **IRRESISTIBLE. / LUCKY MAN**		–

—— Late in '88, HARLEY teamed up with JON ANDERSON (of YES) and MIKE BATT for single 'WHATEVER YOU BELIEVE' on 'Epic'; PEEPS/+12P 1)

		Vital Vinyl	not iss.
Jun 89.	(7") (VIT 3) **WHEN I'M WITH YOU. / THEME FROM BABBACOMBE LEE**		–

—— In Apr'90, STEVE HARLEY and several ex-COCKNEY REBEL members reformed as RAFFLES UNITED, and played 4 consecutive Sunday nights live in a Sudbury pub.

		Food For Thought	not iss.
May 93.	(cd/c) (CD/T GRUB 28) **YES YOU CAN** – Victim of love / The lighthouse / Star for a week (Dino) / ain in Venice / The alibi / New fashioned way / Promises / Dancing on the telephone / Fire in the night / Irresistable. (re-iss. Dec95 on 'CTE'; 0843180-2/-4)		–

		Realisation	not iss.
Nov 93.	(cd/c) (RLBT C/M 005) **LIVE IN THE UK (live)** – Mr. Soft / Mr. Raffles (man it was mean) / When I'm with you / Star for a week / Riding the waves (for Virginia Woolf) / The lighthouse / The best years of our lives / Sweet dreams / The psychomodo / Sling it! / Sebastian / Make me smile (come up and see me) / Love's a prima donna.		–

		Transatla.	not iss.
Aug 96.	(cd) (TRACD 242) **POETIC JUSTICE**		–

– (COCKNEY REBEL) compilations, etc. –

releases on 'EMI' unless otherwise mentioned

Apr 76.	(lp) Capitol; <ST 11456> **A CLOSER LOOK**	–	
Sep 80.	(lp/c) (EMI/TC-EMI 13345) **THE BEST OF STEVE HARLEY AND COCKNEY REBEL** (re-iss. May82 on 'Fame' lp/c; FA/TC-FA 3007)		
Oct 80.	(7") (EMI 5112) **MAKE ME SMILE (COME UP AND SEE ME). / SEBASTIAN**		
Sep 83.	(d-lp) (EDP 1546-773) **THE HUMAN MENAGERIE / THE PSYCHOMODO**		
Oct 83.	(7") Old Gold; (OG 9375) **MAKE ME SMILE (COME UP AND SEE ME). / JUDY TEEN**		
Feb 88.	(7") (EM 50) **MR. SOFT. / MAD MAD MOONLIGHT**		
May 88.	(lp/c)(cd) (EM/TC-EM 1291)(CDP 746 714-2) **GREATEST HITS: STEVE HARLEY AND COCKNEY REBEL** (cd+=) – (3 extra).		
1988.	(lp) Connoisseur; (VSOP 124) **MR. SOFT**		
1988.	(lp/c) Castle; (CCS LP/MC 197) **THE COLLECTION**		
Apr 92.	(c-s/7") (TC+/EM 5) **MAKE ME SMILE (COME UP AND SEE ME). / MR. SOFT** (cd-s+=) (EMCT 5) – Spaced out / (Love) Compared with you.	46	–
May 92.	(cd) (CDGO 2036) **MAKE ME SMILE – THE BEST OF STEVE HARLEY & COCKNEY REBEL** – Mr. Soft / Riding the waves (for Virginia Woolf) / Irresistable (remix) / Mr. Raffles / Freedoms prisoner / Hideaway / Judy Teen / Best years of our lives (live) / Make me smile (come up and see me) / If this is love (give me more) (live) / Here comes the sun / Sebastian / Roll the dice / Understand / I believe (love's a prima donna) / Tumbling down.		
May 94.	(cd) Magnum; (MCD 5) **MAKE ME SMILE**		
Jul 95.	(cd) Windsong; (WINCD 073) **LIVE AT THE BBC (live)**		
Nov 95.	(cd-s) Old Gold; (12623 6337-2) **MAKE ME SMILE (COME UP AND SEE ME) / JUDY TEEN**		
Dec 95.	(c-s/7") Premier; (TC+/HARLEY 1) **MAKE ME SMILE (COME UP AND SEE ME). / JUDY TEEN** (cd-s+=) (CDHARLEY 1) – Another journey / (I believe) Love's a prima donna.	33	–

HARMONY ROCKETS (see under ⇒ MERCURY REV)

Ben HARPER

Born: 1969, Inland Empire, California, USA. Born to music-loving parents, HARPER was hooked by the blues as a child, subsequently taking up the guitar and graduating from a hands-on apprenticeship that found him playing on the same stage as such respected veterans as TAJ MAHAL. It was MAHAL who "discovered" HARPER, drawing attention to the distinctive sound the young musician would wring from his vintage Weissenborn lap steel guitar and, before long, the lad was added to the roster of 'Virgin America'. Steeped in the essence of the blues but written in a thoroughly modern context, HARPER's songs addressed current events while reflecting age-old themes. Racism for one; released as his debut single, 'LIKE A KING' was a barbed comment on the Rodney King affair. Cloaked in the sparsest of arrangements, HARPER's more personal material on 'WELCOME TO THE CRUEL WORLD' (1994) was equally forthright, succinct and resonant. While many cited him as the new HENDRIX (how many times have we heard that?), more sympathetic comparisons would be GIL SCOTT-HERON (whom he subsequently played and toured with) and, if only for the purity and soulfulness of his slide playing, the late LOWELL GEORGE (of LITTLE FEAT). Yet while his influences were manifold, HARPER was singing the blues in his own style, accumulating gushing critical praise for his cathartic live performances. 1995's follow-up set, 'FIGHT FOR YOUR MIND', saw the addition of a drummer, OLIVER CHARLES, and a bassist, JUAN NELSON, although the songs were as sparingly radical as ever, if even more intense and imbued with a sense of human truth. Incredibly, perhaps, HARPER maintains that he has only written a handful of "blues" songs in his life, with only one ('HOMELESS CHILD') making it into the recording studio. What can't be disputed is that HARPER's music is about as far from the concept of blues as crusty old pub-rock as it is possible to get, a fact borne out by the continuing support of a wide cross-section of the music press, from the dance and style mags to the inkies. While major chart success continues to elude him, HARPER's third full-length release, 'THE WILL TO LIVE' (1997), suggested that, like his mate TAJ MAHAL, the best is yet to come. Now credited as BEN HARPER AND THE INNOCENT CRIMINALS, the man and his 3-piece backing combo had a well-deserved US Top 75 entry with fourth set, 'BURN TO SHINE' (1999).

Album rating: WELCOME TO THE CRUEL WORLD (*6) / FIGHT FOR YOUR MIND (*7) / THE WILL TO LIVE (*6) / BURN TO SHINE (*6)

BEN HARPER – vocals, acoustic guitar

			Virgin	Virgin
Jul 94.	(cd/c) (CDVUS/VUSMC 69) **WELCOME TO THE CRUEL WORLD**			

– The three of us / Whipping boy / Breakin' down / Don't take that attitude to your grave / Waiting on an angel / Mama's got a girlfriend now / Forever / Like a king / Pleasure and pain / Walk away / How many miles must we march / Welcome to the cruel world / I'll rise.

Nov 94. (12"/cd-s) (VUS T/DG 86) **LIKE A KING. / WHIPPING BOY**

—— now with **JUAN NELSON** – bass / **OLIVER CHARLES** – drums

Jul 95. (cd/c/d-lp) (CDVUS/VUSMC/VUSDLP 93) **FIGHT FOR YOUR MIND**
– Oppression / Ground on down / Another lonely day / Please me like you want to / Gold to me / Burn one down / Excuse me Mr. / People lead / Fight for your mind / Give a man a home / By my side / Power of the gospel / God fearing man / One road to freedom.

Mar 96. (c-ep/cd-ep) (VUS C/CD 99) **GROUND ON DOWN EP**
– Ground on down / Not fire not ice / Wicked man / If I could only hear my mother pray again.

May 97. (cd/c/lp) (CDVUS/VUSMC/VUSLP 128) **THE WILL TO LIVE** | | | | 89 |
– Faded / Homeless child / Number three / Roses from my friends / Jah work / I want to be ready / The will to live / Ashes / Widow of a living man / Glory and consequence / Mama's trippin' / I shall not walk alone. (cd re-iss. Apr98; CDVUSX 128)

Oct 97. (c-s) (VUSC 120) **FADED / VOODOO CHILE**
(cd-s+=) (VUS T/CDX 120) – Gold to me (live) / Fight for your mind. (re-iss. Mar98, + 12"w/mixes, hit UK No.54)

Sep 99. (cd/d-lp; as BEN HARPER AND THE INNOCENT CRIMINALS) (CDVUS/VUSLP 160) <48151> **BURN TO SHINE** | | | | 67 |
– Alone / The woman in you / Less / Two hands of a prayer / Please bleed / Suzie blue / Steal my kisses / Burn to shine / Show me a little shame / The forgiven / Beloved one / In the Lord's arms.

Roy HARPER

Born: 12 Jun'41, Manchester, England. He was raised by his father, following his mother's death during childbirth. His step-mother was a Jehovah's Witness, leading to him becoming anti-religious. As a young teenager, he played in a skiffle group with his brother DAVID, but at 15, after leaving school, he joined the R.A.F. Not finding it to his liking, he feigned madness to escape further service. Roy then underwent ECT treatment at a mental hospital, later being institutionalised in Lancaster Moor. He then spent a year in jail at Walton Prison, Liverpool. In 1964, after busking around Europe, he moved to London and gained a solo residency at LES COUSINS' folk club in Soho. In 1966, he was signed by Peter Richards's 'Strike' records, who issued his debut lp, 'THE SOPHISTICATED BEGGAR'. The record encompassed his best pieces of poetry, only using a simple revox machine as backing. The following year,

he signed to 'C.B.S.', issuing a second flop 45, which preceded the album, 'COME OUT FIGHTING, GENGHIS SMITH'. This featured an 11-minute track, 'CIRCLE', another of his highly personal folk/blues confessionals. In the summer of '68, he played free concerts at London's Hyde Park, which brought him a new underground audience. In 1969, he released the album, 'FOLKJOKEOPUS', which also featured a similarly lengthy track, the 15-minute 'McGOOGHAN'S BLUES'. Signing to 'Harvest' early in 1970, he released his fourth album in as many years, 'FLAT, BAROQUE AND BESERK' (it featured an uncredited guest spot from The NICE on the track, 'HELL'S ANGEL'). ROY then embarked on a US tour, but after arriving there drunk and jet-lagged he was arrested for abusive behaviour. He slept on West Coast beaches, while playing many gigs. In 1971, he released the highly regarded 'STORMCOCK' set, which hosted DAVID BEDFORD on orchestration and friend JIMMY PAGE (of LED ZEPPELIN) on the first of many guitar sessions for him. PAGE had already written an ode, 'Hats Off To Harper' for their LED ZEPPELIN III album. In 1972, he made his acting debut in the low-budget British film, 'Made', alongside Carol White. Most of the music from the film appeared in his next project, 'LIFEMASK', which was written as his last will and testament, following a near-fatal, recurring blood disorder. On the 14th of February '74, he released the appropriately titled 'VALENTINE', which gave him his first entry into the UK album chart. It was premiered at a concert on Valentine's Day at London's Rainbow theatre, with backing from PAGE, BEDFORD, KEITH MOON and JOHN BONHAM. Later in 1974, he formed the band TRIGGER (with BILL BRUFORD – drums / CHRIS SPEDDING – guitar & DAVE COCHRAN – bass), and supported PINK FLOYD at Knebworth. In 1975, he sang lead vox on PINK FLOYD's 'Have A Cigar', featured on the album, 'Wish You Were Here'. FLOYD had already guested on his next album, 'HQ', which, like its 1977 follow-up, 'BULLINAMINGVASE', hit the UK Top 40. In between the aforementioned projects, he had briefly resided in the States. In 1982 with MARK THOMPSON, he set up his own 'Public' records, who issued ROY's return to form with the 'WORK OF HEART' album. Early in 1985, he scored his last UK Top 50 album, the JIMMY PAGE collaboration, 'WHATEVER HAPPENED TO JUGULA'. He continued to take an active part in the music scene, the album, 'DEATH OR GLORY' being his last effort in 1992. • **Trivia:** PAUL and LINDA McCARTNEY guested on his 'ONE OF THOSE DAYS IN ENGLAND' album. Meanwhile, KATE BUSH guested on ROY's 'THE UNKNOWN SOLDIER' album, returning the compliment by appearing on her hit 45, 'Breathing'.

Album rating: THE SOPHISTICATED BEGGAR (*8) / COME OUT FIGHTING GENGHIS SMITH (*6) / FOLKJOKEOPUS (*5) / FLAT, BAROQUE AND BESERK (*6) / STORMCOCK (*8) / LIFEMASK (*7) / VALENTINE (*5) / FLASHES FROM THE ARCHIVES OF OBLIVION (*6) / HQ (*7) / BULLINAMINGVASE (*7) / ROY HARPER 1970-75 compilation (*6) / THE UNKNOWN SOLDIER (*4) / WORK OF HEART (*5) / BORN IN CAPTIVITY (*5) / WHATEVER HAPPENED TO JUGULA with Jimmy Page (*5) / IN BETWEEN EVERY LINE (*4) / DESCENDENTS OF SMITH (*6) / LOONY ON THE BUS early/rare (*4) / ONCE (*5) / BURN THE WORLD (*5) / DEATH OR GLORY (*6) / AN INTRODUCTION TO ROY HARPER collection (*6)

ROY HARPER – vocals, guitar (with session people)

			Strike	not iss.
Mar 66.	(7") (JH 304) **TAKE ME IN YOUR EYES. / PRETTY BABY**		–	–
Dec 66.	(lp) (JHL 105) **THE SOPHISTICATED BEGGAR**		–	–

– China girl / Goldfish / Sophisticated beggar / My friend / Big fat silver aeroplane / Blackpool / Legend / Girlie / October the twelfth / Black clouds / Mr. Station master / Forever / Committed. (re-iss. Aug70 & 1972 as 'RETURN OF THE SOPHISTICATED BEGGAR' on 'Youngblood' and 'Birth' respectively; SSYB 7 & RAB 3) (re-iss. 1977 on 'Big Ben'; BBX 502) (re-iss. Jan89 on 'Sundown' lp/cd; SDLP/CDSM 051) (cd re-iss. Oct94 on 'J.H.D.'; JHDCD 064) (cd re-iss. Oct96 on 'Science Friction'; HUCD 007)

			C.B.S.	not iss.
Oct 67.	(7") (CBS 203001) **MIDSPRING DITHERING. / ZENGEM**			
Jan 68.	(lp) (CBS 63184) **COME OUT FIGHTING GHENGIS SMITH**			

– Freak street / You don't need money / Ageing raver / In a beautiful rambling mess / All you need is / What you have / Circle / Highgate Cemetary / Come out fighting Ghengis Smith / Zaney Janey / Ballad of songwriter / Midspring dithering / Zenjem / It's tomorrow and today is yesterday / Francesca / She's the one / Nobody's got any money in the summer. (re-iss. Jun77 as 'THE EARLY YEARS' on 'CBS-Embassy'; EMB 31544) (re-iss. Sep91 on 'Awareness' lp/cd;) (cd re-iss. Nov94 & Oct96 on 'Science Friction'; HUCD 006)

Apr 68.	(7") (CBS 3371) **LIFE GOES BY. / NOBODY'S GOT ANY MONEY IN THE SUMMER**			–

			Liberty	World Pacific
Apr 69.	(lp; mono/stereo) (LBL/LBS 83231) <21888> **FOLKJOKEOPUS**			

– Sergeant Sunshine / She's the one / In the time of water / Composer of life / One for all / Exercising some control / McGoohan's blues / Manana. (re-iss. Sep77 on 'Sunset'; SLS 50373) <US re-iss. 1978 on 'Chrysalis'; 1160> (re-iss. Aug86 & Nov88 on 'Awareness' lp/c; cd-iss. Oct89; AWCD 1003) (cd re-iss. Oct94 & Oct96 on 'Science Friction'; HUCD 009)

			Harvest	Harvest
Jun 70.	(lp) (SHVL 766) <418> **FLAT, BAROQUE AND BESERK**			

– Don't you grieve / I hate the white man / Feelin' all the Saturday / How does it feel / Goodbye / Another day / Davey / East of the sun / Tom Tiddler's ground / Francesca / Song of the ages / Hell's angels. (re-iss. Jul85 lp/c; 260585-1/-4) (cd-iss. 1992 & Jun94 on 'Hard Up' respectively; HUCD 003 & HUP 3LTDCD)

May 71. (lp) (SHVL 789) **STORMCOCK**
– Hors d'oeuvres / The same old rock / One man rock and roll band / Me and my woman. <US-iss.1978 on 'Chrysalis'; 1161> (re-iss. Apr87 on 'Awareness' lp/c; AWL/AWT 2001) (cd re-iss. Oct94 & Oct96 on 'Science Friction'; HUCD 004)

Oct 72.	(7") (HAR 5059) **BANK OF THE DEAD (VALERIE'S SONG). / LITTLE LADY**			–

Feb 73. (lp) *(SHVL 808)* **LIFEMASK** (music from film soundtrack
'MADE') `[ ]` `[-]`
– Highway blues / All Ireland / Little lady / Bank of the dead (Valerie's song) / South
Africa / The Lord's prayer: Poem – Modal song (part 1-4) – Front song – Middle
song – End song – Front song (reprise). *<US-iss.1978 on 'Chrysalis'; 1162> (re-iss.
Apr87 on 'Science Friction'; HUCD 005)*

Feb 74. (7") *(HAR 5080)* **(DON'T YOU THINK WE'RE) FOREVER. /**
MALE CHAUVINIST PIG BLUES `[ ]` `[-]`

Feb 74. (lp) *(SHSP 4027)* **VALENTINE** `[27]` `[-]`
– Forbidden fruit / Male chauvinist pig blues / I'll see you again / Twelve hours of
sunset / Acapulco gold / Commune / Magic woman / Che / North country / (Don't
you think we're) Forever. *<US-iss.1978 on 'Chrysalis'; 1163> (re-iss. Apr89 on
'Awareness' lp/c/cd; AWL/AWT/AWCD 1015)* – Home (studio) / Too many movies /
Home (live). *(cd re-iss. Nov94 & Oct96 on 'Science Friction'; HUCD 015)*

Oct 74. (7") *(HAR 5089)* **HOME (live). / HOME (studio)** `[ ]` `[-]`

Nov 74. (d-lp) *(SHDW 405)* **FLASHES FROM THE ARCHIVES OF**
OBLIVION (live) `[ ]` `[-]`
– Home / Commune / Don't you grieve / Twelve hours of sunset / Kangaroo blues /
All Ireland / Me and my woman / South Africa / Interference / Highway blues / One
man rock and roll band / Another day / M.C.P. blues / Too many movies / Home
(studio version) *<US-iss.1978 on 'Chrysalis'; 1164> (re-iss. Apr89 on 'Awareness'
d-lp/c/cd; AW CD/TD/LD 1012) (cd re-iss. Sep94 & Oct96 on 'Science Friction';
HUCD 010)*

	Harvest	Chrysalis
May 75. (lp) *(SHSP 4046)* **HQ** <US-title 'WHEN AN OLD CRICKETER LEAVES THE CREASE'>	31	Feb 76

– The game (part I-V) / The spirit lives / Grown-ups are just silly children /
Referendum / Forget-me-not / Hallucinating light / When an old cricketer leaves
the crease / Referendum. *(re-iss. Mar86 on 'E.M.I.' lp/c; ATAK/TCATAK 68) (cd-iss.
Aug95 & Oct96 on 'Science Friction'; HUCD 019)*

May 75. (7") *(HAR 5096)* **WHEN AN OLD CRICKETER LEAVES THE**
CREASE. / HALLUCINATING LIGHT (acoustic) `[ ]` `[-]`

Oct 75. (7") *(HAR 5102)* **GROWN-UPS ARE JUST SILLY CHILDREN. /**
REFERENDUM (LEGEND) `[ ]` `[-]`

Feb 77. (lp) *(SHSP 4060)* **BULLINAMINGVASE** `[25]` `[-]`
– One of those days in England / These last days / Cherishing the lonesome / Naked
flame / Watford Gap * / One of those days in England (parts 2-10). (free 7"w/a (PSR
407) REFERENDUM / ANOTHER DAY (live). / TOM TIDDLER'S GROUND
(live) *lp re-iss. Mar77, track * repl. by;* – Breakfast in bed. *(re-iss. Apr87 on
'E.M.I.' lp/c; EMS/TCEMS 1259)*

Mar 77. (7") *(HAR 5120)* **ONE OF THOSE DAYS IN ENGLAND. /**
WATFORD GAP `[ ]` `[-]`

Nov 77. (7"; as ROY HARPER'S BLACK SHEEP) *(HAR 5140)*
SAIL AWAY. / CHERISHING THE LONESOME `[ ]` `[-]`

Mar 80. (7") *(HAR 5203)* **PLAYING GAMES. / FIRST THING IN THE**
MORNING `[ ]` `[-]`

Jun 80. (lp) *(SHVL 820)* **THE UNKNOWN SOLDIER** `[ ]` `[-]`
– Playing games / I'm in love with you / The flycatcher / You / Old faces / Short
and sweet / First thing in the morning / The unknown soldier / Ten years ago / True
story.

Jun 80. (7"m) *(HAR 5207)* **SHORT AND SWEET. / WATER SPORTS**
(live) / UNKNOWN SOLDIER (live) `[ ]` `[-]`

	Public	not iss.
Oct 82. (7") *(PUBS 1001)* **NO ONE EVER GETS OUT ALIVE. / CASUALITY** (live)	`[ ]`	`[-]`

Nov 82. (lp/c) *(PUBLP/TCPUBLP 5001)* **WORK OF HEART** `[ ]` `[-]`
– Drawn to the flames / Jack of hearts / I am a child / Woman / I still care / Work
of heart; (i) No one ever gets out alive – (ii) Two lovers in the Moon – (iii) We
are the people – (iv) All us children (so sadly far apart) – (v) We are the people
(reprise) – (vi) No one ever gets out alive (finale). *(re-iss. Nov86 on 'Awareness'
lp,c; AWL 1002) (lp w/ free 7"x2; PUBS 1001/1002; 2nd very ltd) (cd-iss. Oct89; AWCD
1002)*

	Hardup	not iss.
Mar 83. (7") *(PUBS 1002)* **I STILL CARE. / GOODBYE LADYBIRD**	`[ ]`	`[-]`

1984. (lp; ltd) *(PUB 5002)* **BORN IN CAPTIVITY** (demos) `[ ]` `[-]`
– Stan / Drawn to the flames / Come to bed eyes / No woman is safe / I am a child /
Elizabeth / Work of heart; (i) No one ever gets out alive – (ii) Two lovers on the
Moon – (iii) We are the people – (iv) All children (so sadly far apart) – (v) We are
the people (reprise) – (vi) No one ever gets out alive (finale). *(re-iss. Jul85 &
Nov88 on 'Awareness' lp/c; AWL/AWT 1001) (cd-iss. Apr89; AWCD 1001) (cd re-iss.
Oct96 on 'Blueprint'; HUCD 008)*

ROY HARPER and JIMMY PAGE

with **JIMMY PAGE** – guitar (ex-LED ZEPPELIN)

	Beggars Banquet	P.V.C.
Feb 85. (lp/c) *(BEGA/BEGC 60)* **WHATEVER HAPPENED TO JUGULA**	44	

– Nineteen forty-eightish / Hangman / Elizabeth / Advertisement / Bad speech /
Hope / Twentieth century man. *(re-iss. Aug88 & Jul91 on 'Lowdown – Beggars
Banquet' lp/c/cd; BBL/+C 60/+CD)*

Mar 85. (7") *(BEG 131)* **ELIZABETH. / ADVERTISEMENT** `[ ]` `[-]`
(12"+=) *(BEG 131T)* – (I hate the) White man (live).

ROY HARPER

	E.M.I.	not iss.
Jun 86. (d-lp/c) *(EM/TCEM 5004)* **IN BETWEEN EVERY LINE** (live)	`[ ]`	`[-]`

– One of those days in England / Short and sweet / True story / Referendum /
Highway blues / One man rock and roll band / The game / Hangman. *(cd-iss. Nov94
& Oct96 on 'Science Friction'; HUCD 018)*

Mar 88. (7") *(EM 46)* **LAUGHING INSIDE. / LAUGHING INSIDE**
(acoustic) `[ ]` `[-]`
(above single was also released as 3 promos in the disguise of palindromes;
RORY PHARE / HARRY ROPE / PER YARROH; *(Regal Zonophone; RP 1 / HP 1 /
PY 1)*

Mar 88. (cd/c/lp) *(CD/TC+/EMC 3524)* **DESCENDANTS OF SMITH** `[ ]` `[-]`
– Laughing inside / Garden of uranium / Still life / Pinches of salt / Desert island /
Government surplus / Surplus liquorice / Liquorice alltime / Maile lei / Same shoes /
Descendants of Smith. *(cd+=)* – Laughing inside (rough and ready version).

*(cd-iss. Sep94 & Oct96 as 'GARDEN OF URANIUM' on 'Science Friction'
respectively; HUCD 014)*
below featured DAVE GILMOUR, KATE BUSH & STEVE BROUGHTON

	Awareness	I.R.S.
May 90. (cd/c/lp) *(AW CD/T/L 1018)* **ONCE**	`[ ]`	`[ ]` 1991

– Once / Once in the middle of nowhere / Nowhere to run to / Black cloud of Islam /
If / Winds of change / Berliners / Sleeping at the wheel / For longer than it takes /
Ghost dance. *(cd re-iss. Oct94 on 'Line'; LICD 900892) (cd re-iss. Oct96 on 'Science
Friction'; HUCD 011)*

Nov 90. (cd/c/lp) **BURN THE WORLD** `[ ]` `[-]`
– Burn the world (studio) / Burn the world (live). *(cd re-iss. Oct94 & Oct96 on
'Science Friction'; HUCD 013)*

Nov 92. (cd/c/lp) **DEATH OR GLORY** `[ ]` `[-]`
– Death or glory / War came home / Tonight duty / Waiting for Godot / Part zed next
to me / Man kind / Tallest tree / Miles remains / Fourth world / Why / Cardboard
city / One more tomorrow / Plough / On summer day / If I can. *(cd re-iss. Dec94 &
Oct 96 on 'Science Friction'; HUCD 012)*

– compilations etc. –

May 78. (7") *Harvest; (HAR 5160)* **WHEN AN OLD CRICKETER LEAVES**
THE CREASE. / HOME (studio) `[ ]` `[-]`

May 78. (lp) *Harvest; (SHSM 2025)* **ROY HARPER 1970-75** `[ ]` `[-]`
– Don't you grieve / (I hate the) White man / Tom Tiddler's ground / Me and my
woman / Little lady / South Africa / Forbidden fruit / I'll see you again / Commune /
Another day / When an old cricketer leaves the crease / Home.

Dec 88. (lp/c/cd) *Awareness; (AWL/AWT/AWCD 1011)* **LOONY ON THE**
BUS (rare) `[ ]` `[-]`
– No change (ten years ago) / Sail away / / Playing prison / I wanna be part of the
news / Burn the world / Casuality / Cora / Loony on the bus / Come up and see me /
The flycatcher / Square boxes.

1992. (c) *Hard Up; (HU 2)* **BORN IN CAPTIVITY II (live)** `[ ]` `[-]`

Nov 94. (cd) *Awareness; (cd)* **BORN IN CAPTIVITY / WORK OF**
HEART `[ ]` `[-]`
(re-iss. cd Nov94 on 'Science Friction';)

Dec 94. (cd) *Awareness;* **COMMERCIAL BREAKS** (unreleased from
1977 on 'Harvest'; *SHSP 4077)* `[ ]` `[-]`
– My little girl / I'm in love with you / Ten years ago / Sail away / I wanna be part
of the news / Cora / Come up and see me / The flycatcher / Too many movies /
Square boxes / Burn the world (part 1) / Playing prisons. *(re-iss. Feb95 & Oct96 on
'Science Friction'; HUCD 016)*

Dec 94. (cd) *Awareness;* **AN INTRODUCTION TO ROY HARPER** `[ ]` `[-]`
– Legend / She's the one / Tom Tiddler's ground / Highway blues / Che /
Hallucinating light / One of those days in England / You / Nineteen forty-eightish /
Pinches of salt / Ghost dance / The tallest tree / Miles remains. *(re-iss. Feb95 &
Oct96 on 'Science Friction'; HUCD 017)*

Aug 95. (cd) *Griffin;* **UNHINGED** `[ ]` `[-]`
– Descendants of Smith / Legend / North country / When an old cricketer leaves the
crease / Three hundred words / Hope / Naked flame / Commune / South Africa /
Back to the stones / Frozen moment / Highway blues / The same old rock. *(re-iss.
Oct96 on 'Blueprint'; HUCD 020)*

May 96. (cd) *Blueprint; (BP 220CD)* **LIVE AT LES COUSINS (live)** `[ ]` `[-]`
Apr 97. (cd) *Science Friction; (HUCD 022)* **LIVE AT THE BBC VOL.1** `[ ]` `[-]`
Apr 97. (cd) *Science Friction; (HUCD 023)* **LIVE AT THE BBC VOL.2** `[ ]` `[-]`
Jun 97. (cd) *Science Friction; (HUCD 024)* **LIVE AT THE BBC VOL.3** `[ ]` `[-]`
Jun 97. (cd) *Science Friction; (HUCD 025)* **LIVE AT THE BBC VOL.4** `[ ]` `[-]`
Jun 97. (cd) *Science Friction; (HUCD 026)* **LIVE AT THE BBC VOL.5** `[ ]` `[-]`
Jun 97. (cd) *Science Friction; (HUCD 027)* **LIVE AT THE BBC VOL.6** `[ ]` `[-]`

Emmylou HARRIS

Born: 2 Apr'47, Birmingham, Alabama, USA. She later moved to Washington,
playing sax in a high school band before going to the University of North
Carolina where she made her first forays into the world of folk music, playing
as part of a duo. From here it was but a short step to the folk clubs of
Greenwich Village in New York where she released her debut 1969 album,
'GLIDING BIRD' for the 'Jubilee' label. The record was hardly a resounding
success and after a spell in Nashville in the early 70's, she drifted back with
baby Hallie to Washington following the failure of her first marriage. By a
twist of fate, this apparent setback proved to be the beginning of her career
proper after she was spotted in a local club by the The FLYING BURRITO
BROTHERS. The band informed ex-member and founding father of Cosmic
American Music (country-rock, basically), GRAM PARSONS, who was after a
partner for his forthcoming solo project. The two hit it off immediately, GRAM
schooling her in the ways of classic country. Over the course of two albums,
'G.P.' (1972) and 'GRIEVOUS ANGEL' (1973), the pair recorded some of
the most sublime duets in the history of recorded music ('WE'LL SWEEP
OUT THE ASHES IN THE MORNING', 'LOVE HURTS' etc.), HARRIS's
mournful soprano combining with PARSON's cracked chords to create music
of a fragile beauty. PARSONS was on a crash course in self-destruction,
however, and after he O.D.'d in 1973, HARRIS's career was once again in
limbo. Down but not out, she eventually formed a new backing outfit from the
ashes of GRAM's FALLEN ANGELS, retaining JAMES BURTON (guitar,
previously of ELVIS PRESLEY's band) and GLENN D.HARDIN (piano),
bringing in EMORY GORDY (bass), RODNEY CROWELL (rhythm guitar,
vocals), HANK DE VITO (pedal steel) and JOHN WARE (drums). Remaining
with PARSON's label, 'Reprise', HARRIS released 'PIECES OF THE SKY'
in 1975, a masterful set which included one of her finest compositions,
'BOULDER TO BIRMINGHAM', a lilting eulogy to GRAM, alongside
the beautiful 'SLEEPLESS NIGHTS' and a rousing cover of the LOUVIN
BROTHERS' 'IF I COULD ONLY WIN YOUR LOVE' which became an
American country No.1. HARRIS possessed one of the most haunting and,
alongside STEVIE NICKS, one of the most distinctive, white female voices
in the business. Over a string of excellent albums and consummate choice of

cover material, she built up a reputation as one of country's leading ladies as well as winning over rock and pop fans. Her tonsils much in demand, she even appeared in The BAND's 'Last Waltz', performing ROBBIE ROBERTSON's 'EVANGELINE', and during the 70's provided backing vocals on a number of classic albums, including LITTLE FEAT's 'Dixie Chicken' and BOB DYLAN's 'Desire'. Following her marriage to producer BRIAN AHERN, HARRIS released her second Top 30 album, 'LUXURY LINER' (1977), arguably her strongest set of the decade wherein she performed a spine-tingling run through of the late, great TOWN VAN ZANDT's 'PANCHO AND LEFTY' while covering The CARTER FAMILY's 'HELLO STRANGER' in fine style. With 'QUARTER MOON IN A TEN CENT TOWN' (1978), the singer moved towards straight country, scoring a Top 3 country hit with her touching cover of DOLLY PARTON's 'TO DADDY'. 'BLUE KENTUCKY GIRL' (1979) and 'ROSES IN THE SNOW' (1980) were rootsier, the latter stripped down to bare acoustic guitar. 'EVANGELINE' (1981) once more saw HARRIS at her best covering classic material, GRAM's 'HOT BURRITO No.2' and CREEDENCE CLEARWATER REVIVAL's 'BAD MOON RISING' both given a thorough going-over. Heading back to Nashville in the mid-80's, HARRIS even recorded a country concept album (!), 'THE BALLAD OF SALLY ROSE' (1985). As the decade wore on, HARRIS and her HOT BAND were met with an increasingly cold reception, commercially at least, and she eventually replaced said backing crew with The NASH RAMBLERS, a rootsier acoustic group. The 90's saw HARRIS re-appraising her sound, hip producer DANIEL LANOIS working on her acclaimed 1995 album, 'WRECKING BALL', a set that also saw the likes of a similarly revamped STEVE EARLE guesting. If anyone can keep the spirit of roots country alive and relevant in an increasingly hi-tech musical world, then it's EMMYLOU, whose dedication to the genre through the ever-changing dictats of fashion is admirable. • **Songwriters:** Writes some herself, collaborates with others, except covers I'LL BE YOUR BABY TONIGHT (Bob Dylan) / THE PRICE YOU PAY + MY FATHER'S HOUSE + BORN TO RUN + TOUGHER THAN THE REST (Bruce Springsteen) / YOU NEVER CAN TELL (Chuck Berry) / THE BOXER (Simon & Garfunkel) / MISTER SANDMAN (Chordettes) / TO DADDY (Dolly Parton) / BURN THAT CANDLE (Bill Haley) / TWO MORE BOTTLES OF WINE (Delbert McClinton) / PLEDGING MY LOVE (Johnny Ace) / DIAMONDS ARE A GIRL'S BEST FRIEND (Jule Styne) / WILD MONTANA SKIES (duet w / JOHN DENVER) / HERE, THERE AND EVERYWHERE + FOR NO ONE (Beatles) / NO REGRETS (Tom Rush) / ICY BLUE HEART (John Hiatt) / LOVE IS (Kate McGarrigle) / WHEELS OF LOVE (Marjy Plant) / SAVE THE LAST DANCE FOR ME (Drifters) / JAMBALAYA (Hank Williams) / BAD MOON RISING + LODI (Creedence Clearwater Revival) / ROSE OF CIMARRON (Poco) / HOT BURRITO + SLEEPLESS NIGHTS (Gram Parsons) / BRAND NEW DANCE (Paul Kennerley) / SWEET DREAMS OF YOU (Kennerley-David) / BETTER OFF WITHOUT YOU (Chapman-Walker-Brown) / NEVER BE ANYONE ELSE BUT YOU (Baker Knight) / RED RED ROSE (David Mallett) / GUITAR TOWN (Steve Earle) / ROLLIN' AND RAMBLIN' (Williams-Williams-Clark) / EASY FOR YOU TO SAY (Routh-Sharp) / IN HIS WORLD (Kostas-Reynolds) / ABRAHAM, MARTIN & JOHN (hit; Marvin Gaye) / SCOTLAND (. . . Monroe) / CATTLE CALL (Buck Owens) / THANKS TO YOU (Jesse Winchester) / BALLAD OF A RUNNING HORSE (Leonard Cohen) / etc. • **Trivia:** In 1980, she won a Grammy for her country lp 'BLUE KENTUCKY GIRL'.

Album rating: GLIDING BIRD (*4) / PIECES OF THE SKY (*7) / ELITE HOTEL (*8) / LUXURY LINER (*8) / QUARTER MOON IN A TEN CENT TOWN (*7) / PROFILE – BEST OF . . . compilation (*7) / BLUE KENTUCKY GIRL (*6) / ROSES IN THE SNOW (*7) / LIGHT OF THE STABLE (*6) / EVANGELINE (*7) / CIMARRON (*6) / LAST DATE (*6) / WHITE SHOES (*6) / PROFILE II – BEST OF . . . compilation (*6) / THE BALLAD OF SALLY ROSE (*5) / THIRTEEN (*5) / TRIO with Dolly Parton & Linda Ronstadt (*5) / ANGEL BAND (*5) / BLUEBIRD (*5) / DUETS (*5) / BRAND NEW DANCE (*5) / DUETS AT THE RYMAN (*7) / NASHVILLE COUNTRY DUETS with Carl Jackson (*5) / COWGIRL'S PRAYER (*6) / SONGS OF THE WEST (*6) / WRECKING BALL (*8) / NASHVILLE (*5)

EMMYLOU HARRIS – vocals, acoustic guitar; with session people

		not iss.	Jubilee
1969.	(lp) <JGS 0031> **GLIDING BIRD**	-	

– I'll be your baby tonight / Fugue for the fox / I saw the light / Clocks / Black gypsy / Gliding bird / Everybody's talkin' / Bobbie's gone / I'll never fall in love again / Waltz of the magic man. (UK-iss.Apr79 as 'THE LEGENDARY GLIDING BIRD ALBUM' on 'Pye Special'; PKL 5577)

		-	-
1969.	(7") <5679> **I'LL BE YOUR BABY TONIGHT. / I'LL NEVER FALL IN LOVE AGAIN**	-	-
1969.	(7") <5697> **FUGUE FOR THE FOX. / PADDY**	-	-

—— he then went solo, augmented soon by The HOT BAND:- **JAMES BURTON** – guitar / **GLEN D.HARDIN** – piano / **EMORY GORDY** – bass / **RODNEY CROMWELL** – rhythm guitar, vocals / **HANK DE VITO** – pedal steel guitar / **JOHN WARE** – drums

		Reprise	Reprise
Apr 75.	(lp/c) (L/K4 54037) <2213> **PIECES OF THE SKY**	45	Mar75

– Bluebird wine / Too far gone / If I could only win your love / Boulder to Birmingham / Before believing / Bottle let me down / Sleepless nights / Coat of many colours / For no one / Queen of the silver dollar. (cd-iss.Feb89; 7599 27244-2)

May 75.	(7") <1326> **BOULDER TO BIRMINGHAM. / TOO FAR GONE**	-	-
Jun 75.	(7") (K 14396) **BOULDER TO BIRMINGHAM. / QUEEN OF THE SILVER DOLLAR**	-	
Nov 75.	(7") (K 14404) <1332> **IF I COULD ONLY WIN YOUR LOVE. / QUEEN OF THE SILVER DOLLAR**	58	Aug75
Jan 76.	(7") (K 14410) <1341> **LIGHT OF THE STABLE. / BLUEBIRD WINE**	-	-

Jan 76.	(lp/c) (K/K4 54060) <2213> **ELITE HOTEL**	17	25

– Amarillo / Together again / Feelin' single – seeing double / Sin city / One of these days / Till I gain control again / Here, there and everywhere / Ooh Las Vegas / Sweet dreams / Jambalaya / Satan's jewel crown / Wheels. (re-iss. May89 on 'Edsel'; ED 306)

Feb 76.	(7") (K 14415) **HERE, THERE AND EVERYWHERE. / AMARILLO**	30	-
Mar 76.	(7") <1346> **HERE, THERE AND EVERYWHERE. / TOGETHER AGAIN**		65
May 76.	(7") (K 14439) **TOGETHER AGAIN. / WHEELS**	-	
Jul 76.	(7") <1353> **ONE OF THESE DAYS. / TILL I GAIN CONTROL AGAIN**		-
Sep 76.	(7") <1371> **AMARILLO. / SWEET DREAMS**		-
Nov 76.	(7") <1379> **LIGHT OF THE STABLE. / BOULDER TO BIRMINGHAM**	-	

—— **ALBERT LEE** – guitar (ex-Solo artist) repl. BURTON (returned to ELVIS)

		Warners	Warners
Jan 77.	(lp/c) (K/K4 56334) <3115> **LUXURY LINER**	17	21

– Luxury liner / Pancho & Lefty / Making believe / You're supposed to be feeling good / I'll be your San Antone rose / (You never can tell) C'est la vie / When I stop dreaming / Hello stranger / She / Tulsa queen. (cd-iss. Jun89; 927338-2)

Feb 77.	(7") (K 16888) **(YOU NEVER CAN TELL) C'EST LA VIE. / HELLO STRANGER**	-	-
Feb 77.	(7") <8329> **(YOU NEVER CAN TELL) C'EST LA VIE. / YOU'RE SUPPOSED TO BE FEELING GOOD**	-	
May 77.	(7") <8388> **MAKING BELIEVE. / I'LL BE YOUR SAN ANTONE ROSE**	-	-
Jan 78.	(lp/c) (K/K4 56443) <3141> **QUARTER MOON IN A TEN CENT TOWN**	40	29

– Easy from now on / Two more bottles of wine / To daddy / My songbird / Leavin' Louisiana in the broad daylight / Defying gravity / I ain't livin' long like this / One paper kid / Green rolling hills / Burn that candle. (cd-iss. 1989; 927345-2)

Feb 78.	(7") (K 17095) <8498> **TO DADDY. / TULSA QUEEN**		-
Apr 78.	(7") <8553> **I AIN'T LIVIN' LONG LIKE THIS. / TWO MORE BOTTLES OF WINE**		-
Apr 78.	(7") (K 17133) **I AIN'T LIVIN' LONG LIKE THIS. / ONE PAPER KID**	-	
Jun 78.	(7") <8623> **EVEN FROM NOW ON. / YOU'RE SUPPOSED TO BE FEELING GOOD**		-
May 79.	(7") <8815> **SAVE THE LAST DANCE FOR ME. / EVEN COWGIRLS GET THE BLUES**	-	
Jun 79.	(lp/c) (K/K4 56627) <3318> **BLUE KENTUCKY GIRL**		43 May79

– Sister's coming home / Beneath still waters / Rough and rocky / Hickory wind / Save the last dance for me / Sorrow in the wind / They'll never take his love from me / Everytime you leave / Blue Kentucky girl / Even cowgirls get the blues. (cd-iss. Jan93; 7599 29392-2)

Jul 79.	(7") <49056> **BLUE KENTUCKY GIRL. / LEAVIN' LOUISIANA IN THE BROAD DAYLIGHT**		-
Oct 79.	(7") <49164> **BENEATH STILL WATERS. / TILL I GAIN CONTROL AGAIN**		-
Nov 79.	(lp/c) (K/K4 56757) <3484> **LIGHT OF THE STABLE (THE CHRISTMAS ALBUM)** (festive)		Nov80
Nov 79.	(7") (K 17528) **THE FIRST NOEL. / SILENT NIGHT**	-	
May 80.	(7") <49239> **GREEN PASTURES. / WAYFARING STRANGERS**		-
May 80.	(lp/c) (K/K4 56796) <3422> **ROSES IN THE SNOW**		26

– Roses in the snow / Wayfaring stranger / Green pastures / The boxer / Darkest hour just before dawn / I'll go stepping too / You're learning / Jordan / Miss the Mississippi / Gold watch and chain.

Jul 80.	(7") (K 17649) <49262> **THAT LOVIN' YOU FEELIN' AGAIN. / (b-side by Craig Hindley)**		55 Jun80

(above from the film 'Roadie' and credited with ROY ORBISON)

Jul 80.	(7") <49551> **THE BOXER. / PRECIOUS LOVE**	-	
Nov 80.	(7") <49633> **BEAUTIFUL STAR OF BETHLEHEM. / LITTLE DRUMMER BOY**	-	
Dec 80.	(7") <49645> **LIGHT OF THE STABLE. / LITTLE DRUMMER BOY**	-	
Feb 81.	(7") <49684> **MISTER SANDMAN. / FOOLS THIN AIR**	-	37
Feb 81.	(7") (K 17758) **MISTER SANDMAN. / ASHES BY NOW**	-	
Feb 81.	(lp/c) (K/K4 56880) <3508> **EVANGELINE**	53	22

– I don't have to crawl / How high the Moon / Spanish Johnny / Bad Moon rising / Evangeline / Hot burrito £2 / Millworker / Oh Atlanta / Mister Sandman / Ashes by now.

May 81.	(7") <49739> **COLORS OF YOUR HEART. / I DON'T HAVE TO CRAWL**	-	
May 81.	(7") (K 17804) **BAD MOON RISING. / I DON'T HAVE TO CRAWL**	-	
Nov 81.	(7") <49892> **MAMA HELP. / TENNESSEE ROSE**	-	
Nov 81.	(lp/c) (K/K4 56955) <3603> **CIMARRON**	-	46

– Rose of cimarron / Spanish is a loving tongue / If I needed you / Another lonesome morning / The last cheater's waltz / Born to run / The price you pay / Son of a rotten gambler / Tennessee waltz / Tennessee rose.

Feb 82.	(7") <29993> **BORN TO RUN. / COLORS OF YOUR HEART**	-	
Feb 82.	(7") (K 17896) **BORN TO RUN. / ASHES BY NOW**	-	
Nov 82.	(lp/c) (923740-1/-4) <23740> **LAST DATE**	-	65

– I'm moving on / It's not love (but it's not bad) / So sad (to watch good love so bad) / Grevious angel / Restless / Racing in the streets / Long may you run / Well sweep out the ashes (in the morning) / Juanita / Devil in disguise / (Lost his love) On our last date / Buckaroo / Love's gonna live here.

Nov 82.	(7") <29898> **(LOST HIS LOVE) ON OUR LAST DATE. / ANOTHER POT O' TEA**	-	
Feb 83.	(7") <29729> **I'M MOVIN' ON (live). / MAYBE TONIGHT**	-	
Apr 83.	(7") <29583> **SO SAD (TO WATCH GOOD LOVE GO BAD) (live). / AMARILLO (live)**	-	
Oct 83.	(7") <29443> **DRIVIN' WHEEL. / GOOD NEWS**	-	
Oct 83.	(lp/c) (923961-1/-4) <23961> **WHITE SHOES**	-	

– Drivin' wheel / Pledging my love / In my dreams / White shoes / On the radio / It's only rock'n'roll / Diamonds are a girl's best friend / Good news / Baby, better start turnin' 'em down / Like an old fashoined waltz. *(cd-iss. Jan84; 923961-2) (cd re-iss. Jan96; 7599 23961-2)*

Jan 84. (7") *<29329>* **LIKE AN OLD FASHIONED WALTZ. / IN MY DREAMS**

May 84. (7") *<29218>* **PLEDGING MY LOVE. / BABY, BETTER START TURNIN' 'EM DOWN**

May 84. (7") *(W 9364)* **ON THE RADIO. / GOOD NEWS**

Nov 84. (7") *<29138>* **SOMEONE LIKE YOU. / LIGHT OF THE STABLE**

Feb 85. (7") *<29041>* **WHITE LINE. / LONG TALL SALLY ROSE**

Feb 85. (lp/c/cd) *(925205-1/-4/-2) <25205>* **THE BALLAD OF SALLY ROSE**
 – The ballad of Sally Rose / Rhythm guitar / I think I love him – (instrumental; You are my flower) – Heart to heart / Woman walk the line / Bad news / Timberline / Long tall Sally Rose / White line / Diamond in my crown / The sweetheart of the rodeo / K-S-O-S (instrumental medley; Ring of fire – Wildwood flower – Six days on the road) – Sweet chariot. *(cd re-iss. Jan96; 7599 25205-2)*

May 85. (7") *<28952>* **DIAMOND IN MY CROWN. / RHYTHM GUITAR**

Aug 85. (7") *<28852>* **TIMBERLINE. / SWEET CHARIOT**

Mar 87. (7") *<28770>* **I HAD MY HEART SET ON YOU. / YOUR LONG JOURNEY**

Apr 87. (lp/c/cd) *(925352-1/-4/-2) <25352>* **THIRTEEN**　Mar87
 – Mystery train / You're free to go / Sweetheart of the pines / Just someone in the know / My father's house / Lacassine special / Today I started loving you again / When I was yours / I had my heart set on you / Your long journey.

Jun 87. (7") *<28770>* **TODAY I STARTED LOVING YOU AGAIN. / WHEN I WAS YOURS**

Jul 87. (lp/c/cd) *<25585-1/-4/-2>* **ANGEL BAND**
 – Where could I go to the Lord / Angel band / If I be lifted up / Precious memories / Bright morning stars / When he calls / We shall rise / Drifting too far / Who will sing for me / Someday my ship will sail / The other side of your life / When they ring those golden bells.

Aug 87. (7") *<28302>* **SOMEDAY MY SHIP WILL SAIL. / WHEN HE CALLS**

Feb 89. (7") *<27635>* **HEARTBREAK HILL. / ICY BLUE HEART**

Feb 89. (lp/c/cd) *(925776-1/-4/-2) <25776>* **BLUEBIRD**
 – Heaven only knows / You've been on my mind / Icy blue heart / Love is / No regrets / Lonely street / Heartbreak hill / I still miss someone / A river for him / If you were a bluebird.

　　　　　　　　　　　　　　　　　　　　　　Reprise　Reprise

May 89. (7") *<22999>* **HEAVEN ONLY KNOWS. / A RIVER FOR HIM**

Aug 89. (7") *<22850>* **I STILL MISS SOMEONE. / NO REGRETS**

Jul 90. (cd/c/lp) *Reprise; <(7599 25791-2/-4/-1)>* **DUETS**

Nov 90. (lp/c/cd) *(WX 396/+C/CD)* **BRAND NEW DANCE**
 – Wheels of love / Tougher than the rest / In his world / Sweet dreams of you / Easy for you to say / Rollin' and ramblin' (the death of Hank Williams) / Better off without you / Never be anyone else but you / Brand new dance / Red red rose. *(cd re-iss. Feb95; same)*

Jan 91. (7") *<19870>* **GULF COAST HIGHWAY (w/ WILLIE NELSON). / EVANGELINE**

Apr 91. (7") *<19707>* **RED RED ROSE. / NEVER BE ANYONE ELSE BUT YOU**

Jan 92. (cd/c/d-lp; EMMYLOU HARRIS & The NASH RAMBLERS) *<(7599 26664-2/-4/-1)>* **AT THE RYMAN (live)**
 – Guitar town / Halk as much / Cattle call / Guess things happen that way / Hard times / Mansion on the hill / Scotland / Montana cowboy / Like strangers / Lodi / Calling my children home / If I could be there / Walls of time / Get up John / Medley:- It's a hard life wherever you go / Smoke along the track. *(cd re-iss. Feb95; same)*

　　　　　　　　　　　　　　　　　　　Grapevine　Asylum

Apr 94. (cd-s) *(CDGPS 101)* **HIGH POWERED LOVE. / BALLAD OF A RUNAWAY HORSE**

May 94. (cd/c/lp) *(GRA 101 CD/C) <61541>* **COWGIRL'S PRAYER**
 – A ways to go / The night / High powered love / You don't know me / Prayer in open D / Cresent city / Lovin' you again / Jerusalem tomorrow / Thanks to you / I hear a call / Ballad of a runaway horse.

Sep 94. (c-s/cd-s) *(CS/CD GPS 102)* **YOU DON'T KNOW ME. / A WAYS TO GO**

Oct 95. (cd/c/lp) *(GRA CD/MC/LP 102) <61854>* **WRECKING BALL**　46　94
 – Where will I be / Goodbye / All my tears / Wrecking ball / Goin' back to Harlan / A deeper well / Every grain of sand / Sweet old world / May this be love / Orphan girl / Blackhawk / Waltz across Texas tonight.

Aug 98. (cd) *<(25001)>* **SPYBOY (live)**　57
 – My songbird / Where will I be / I ain't living long like this / Love hurts / Green pastures / A deeper well / Prayer in open D / Calling my children home / Tulsa queen / Wheels / Born to run / Boulder to Birmingham / All my tears / Maker.

──── In Sep'99, she and LINDA RONSTADT released the 'WESTERN WALL – THE TUCSON SESSIONS' set, which scraped into the US Top 75

– compilations, etc. –

on 'Warners' unless mentioned otherwise

Nov 78. (lp/c) *(K/K4 56570)* **PROFILE – THE BEST OF EMMYLOU HARRIS**　81
 – One of these days / Sweet dreams / To daddy / You never can tell (C'est la vie) / Making believe / Easy from now on / Together again / If I could only win your love / Too far gone / Two more bottles of wine / From Boulder to Birmingham / Hello stranger. *(cd-iss. Jul84; 256570)*

Nov 78. (7") *<8732>* **TOO FAR GONE. / TULSA QUEEN**

Mar 80. (7") *(K 17580)* **(YOU NEVER CAN TELL) C'EST LA VIE. / BOULDER TO BIRMIMGHAM**

Mar 80. (lp) *K-Tel; (NE 1058)* **HER BEST SONGS**　36

Oct 82. (d-c) **ELITE HOTEL / LUXURY LINER**

──── In Nov '83, 'Magnum Force' released lp 'LIVE' with GRAM PARSONS

Oct 84. (lp/c) *<25161>* **PROFILE II – THE BEST OF EMMYLOU HARRIS**
 (UK-iss.Feb94; 7599 25161-2)

──── In July '93, 'Magnum Force' released a cd 'NASHVILLE COUNTRY DUETS' with CARL JACKSON

Nov 94. (cd/c) *<(9362 45725-2/-4)>* **SONGS OF THE WEST**

Dec 96. (3xcd-box) *(9362 45308-2)* **PORTRAIT**

DOLLY PARTON, LINDA RONSTADT, EMMYLOU HARRIS

　　　　　　　　　　　　　　　　　　　Warners　Warners

Mar 87. (lp/c/cd) *(925491-1/-4/-1) <25491>* **TRIO**　60　6
 – The pain of lovin' you / Making plans / To know him is to love him / Hobo's meditation / Wildflowers / Telling me lies / My dear companion / These memories of you / I've had enough / Rosewood casket. *(cd+=/c+=)* – Farther along. *(cd re-iss. Feb95; same)*

Apr 87. (7") *(W 8492)* **TO KNOW HIM IS TO LOVE HIM. / FARTHER ALONG**

Jun 87. (7") *<28371>* **TELLING ME LIES. / ROSEWOOD CASKET**

Sep 87. (7") *<28248>* **THOSE MEMORIES OF YOU. / MY DEAR COMPANION**

Nov 87. (7") *<27970>* **WILDFLOWERS. / HOBO'S MEDITATION**

　　　　　　　　　　　　　　　　　　　Asylum　Asylum

Feb 99. (cd/c) *<62275>* **TRIO II**　62

George HARRISON

Born: 25 Feb'43, Wavertree, Liverpool, England. Released in late 1968, HARRISON's 'WONDERWALL' was the first solo release by a BEATLE, although it flopped in the UK. He followed it up with a classic piece of late 60's self-indulgence, the awful 'ELECTRONIC SOUNDS' (released on his own 'Zapple' label). While HARRISON's pioneering sitar work was praise-worthy, the same experimental spirit applied to a Moog synthesizer (strung out over a whole album) was downright dull. Despite being overshadowed by the writing partnership of LENNON and McCARTNEY, HARRISON's songs rank among the BEATLES' best, not least 'SOMETHING' and 'HERE COMES THE SUN'. When the BEATLES officially split in 1969, it was perhaps an opportunity for GEORGE to really go for it and prove his writing skills over a whole album. Not content with two sides of vinyl, he went for six, releasing the triple-set 'ALL THINGS MUST PASS' in 1970. The Herculean task of keeping a consistently high standard over three albums was beyond even the mercurial talent of HARRISON, although the peaks definitely outweigh the troughs. PHIL SPECTOR's legendary production skills enhanced the gorgeous melodies of 'MY SWEET LORD' and DYLAN's 'IF NOT FOR YOU', while HARRISON's well-documented spirituality was given a voice in the title track and 'THE ART OF DYING'. The aforementioned 'MY SWEET LORD' was released as a single in early '71 topping the charts on both sides of the Atlantic. Success was bittersweet though, as BRIGHT TUNES (owners of songwriter RONNIE MACK's estate) claimed the song plagiarised their CHIFFONS song, 'HE'S SO FINE'. Five years later, the court gave 6-figure royalties to the plaintiff. HARRISON helped to organise a huge famine relief benefit gig in New York, playing alongside a cast of musicians that included his old mucker RINGO STARR as well as BOB DYLAN. The gig was released on another triple-set in 1972 as 'CONCERT FOR BANGLADESH'. May '73 saw yet another No.1 US single, 'GIVE ME LOVE (GIVE ME PEACE ON EARTH)', taken from the similarly successful album, 'LIVING IN THE MATERIAL WORLD'. If HARRISON was riding the crest of a wave, then he was soon to be dallying listlessly in a stagnant creative pond. In 1974, he set up his own 'Dark Horse' label, releasing the clueless album of the same name as well as signing up artists like RAVI SHANKAR and SPLINTER. He and his wife PATTI were divorced in June '77 after her much publicised affair with ERIC CLAPTON. In 1979, he founded his own 'Homemade' film productions, which released the 80's movies: 'Life Of Brian', 'The Long Good Friday', 'Time Bandits', 'The Missionary', 'Mona Lisa', 'A Private Function', 'Water', and 'Shanghai Surprise'. Mediocre albums were his forte at the turn of the decade, and even the tribute to LENNON, 'ALL THOSE YEARS AGO', (from 1981's 'SOMEWHERE IN ENGLAND'), seemed uninspired. HARRISON teamed up with ELO's JEFF LYNNE for 1987's 'CLOUD NINE'; his production, along with the hit, 'GOT MY MIND SET ON YOU', helped to make the record HARRISON's most successful of the 80's (and 90's for that matter). In the decade since, HARRISON has been involved in the relatively brief TRAVELING WILBURYS project (with LYNNE, DYLAN, PETTY & ROY ORBISON under various brotherly guises) as well as releasing 'LIVE IN JAPAN' in 1992, culled from a series of Japanese concerts with CLAPTON. In the mid-90's, he was involved in the archive project which saw the release of a BEATLES documentary, rarities/outtakes albums and even a "new" single, 'FREE AS A BIRD'. As ever though, the man remains an enigma, the quintessential rock star hermit content to do his own thing with a minimum of fuss. • **Covered:** I'D HAVE YOU ANYTIME + I DON'T WANT TO DO IT (Bob Dylan) / BYE BYE LOVE (Everly Brothers) / GOT MY MIND SET ON YOU (James Ray) / ROLL OVER BEETHOVEN (Chuck Berry).

Album rating: WONDERWALL MUSIC (*4) / ELECTRONIC SOUND (*3) / ALL THINGS MUST PASS (*9) / THE CONCERT FOR BANGLA DESH with Various Artists (*6) / LIVING IN THE MATERIAL WORLD (*6) / DARK HORSE (*3) / EXTRA TEXTURE (READ ALL ABOUT IT) (*4) / THE BEST OF GEORGE HARRISON compilation (*6) / THIRTY-THREE & 1/3 (*6) / GEORGE HARRISON (*5) / SOMEWHERE IN ENGLAND (*4) / GONE TROPPO (*3) / CLOUD NINE (*7) / THE BEST OF DARK HORSE 1976-89 compilation (*7) / LIVE IN JAPAN (*4) /

GEORGE HARRISON – instruments (no vocals) (of-BEATLES)

	Apple	Apple

Nov 68. (lp; stereo/mono) *(S+/APCOR 1)* <3350> **WONDERWALL MUSIC (Soundtrack)** [ ] [49 Jan69]
– Microbes / Red lady too / Tabla and Pavajak / In the park / Drilling a hole / Guru Vandana / Greasy legs / Ski-ing / Gat Kirwani / Dream scene / Party Seacombe / Love scene / Crying / Cowboy music / Fantasy sequins / On the bed / Glass box / Wonderwall to be here / Singing om. *(cd-iss. Jun92; CDSAPCOR 1)*

––––– **GEORGE** – moog synthesizer (no vocals)

	Zapple	Zapple

May 69. (lp) *(02)* <3358> **ELECTRONIC SOUND** [ ] [ ]
– Under the Mersey wall / No time or space.

––––– He became in-house 'Apple' producer, before gigging with DELANEY & BONNIE late 1969. The BEATLES broke-up and he went solo again. Now with vocals, etc + augmented by **DEREK & THE DOMINOES** (Eric Clapton and his band) / **BADFINGER / BILLY PRESTON** – keyboards / **RINGO STARR, GINGER BAKER** – drums / etc.

	Apple	Apple

Nov 70. (t-box-lp) *(<STCH 639>)* **ALL THINGS MUST PASS** [4] [1]
– I'd have you anytime / My sweet Lord / Wah-wah / Isn't it a pity / What is life / If not for you / Behind that locked door / Let it down / Run of the mill / Beware of darkness / Apple scruffs / Ballad of Frankie Crisp (let it roll) / Awaiting on you all / All things must pass / I dig love / Art of dying / Isn't it a pity / Hear me Lord / Out of the blue / It's Johnny's birthday / Plug me in / I remember Jeep / Thanks for the pepperoni. *(d-cd.iss.May87 on 'E.M.I.'; CDS 746658-2)*

Nov 70. (7") <2995> **MY SWEET LORD. / ISN'T IT A PITY** [-] [1]
Jan 71. (7") *(R 5884)* **MY SWEET LORD. / WHAT IS LIFE** [1] [-]
(re-iss. Nov76; same)
Feb 71. (7") <1828> **WHAT IS LIFE. / APPLE SCRUFFS** [-] [10]
Jul 71. (7") *(R 5912)* <1836> **BANGLA-DESH. / DEEP BLUE** [10] [23]

––––– In Jan72, he with other artists released live triple album 'CONCERT FOR BANGLADESH'; *(<STCX 3385>)*. It hit UK No.1 & US No.2. *(re-iss. Aug91 d-cd/d-c; 468835-2/-4)*

––––– **GEORGE** now with various session people

May 73. (7") *(R 5988)* <1862> **GIVE ME LOVE (GIVE ME PEACE ON EARTH). / MISS O'DELL** [8] [1]
Jun 73. (lp/c) *(PAS 10006)* <3410> **LIVING IN THE MATERIAL WORLD** [2] [1]
– Give me love (give me peace on earth) / Sue me, sue you blues / The light that has lighted the world / Don't let me wait too long / Who can see it / Living in the material world / The Lord loves the one (that loves the Lord) / Be here now / Try some buy some / The day the world gets 'round / That is all. *(cd-iss. Jan92 on 'E.M.I.'; CDPAS 10006)*

Dec 74. (7") *(R 6002)* <1879> **DING DONG; DING DONG. / I DON'T CARE ANYMORE** [38] [36 Jan75]
Dec 74. (lp/c) *(PAS 10008)* <3418> **DARK HORSE** [4]
– Hari's on tour (express) / Simply shady / So sad / Bye bye love / Maya love / Ding dong; ding dong / Dark horse / Far East man / Is it he (Jai Sri Krishna). *(re-iss. Dec80 on 'Music For Pleasure'; MFP 50510) (cd-iss. Jan92 on 'E.M.I.'; CDPAS 10008)*

Feb 75. (7") *(R 6001)* <1877> **DARK HORSE. / HARI'S ON TOUR (EXPRESS)** [15 Nov74]
Sep 75. (7") *(R 6007)* <1884> **YOU. / WORLD OF STONE** [38] [20]
Oct 75. (lp/c) *(PAS 10009)* <3420> **EXTRA TEXTURE (READ ALL ABOUT IT)** [16] [8]
– The answer's at the end / This guitar (can't keep from crying) / You / Ooh baby (you know that I love you) / World of stone / A bit more of you / Can't stop thinking about you / Tired of midnight blue / Grey cloudy lies / His name is legs (ladies & gentlemen). *(cd-iss. Jan92 on 'E.M.I.'; CDPAS 10009)*

Feb 76. (7") *(R 6012)* <1885> **THIS GUITAR (CAN'T KEEP FROM CRYING). / MAYA LOVE**

	Apple	Capitol

Oct 76. (lp/c) *(PAS 10011)* <11578> **THE BEST OF GEORGE HARRISON** (compilation) [ ] [31]
– Something (BEATLES) / If I needed someone (BEATLES) / Here comes the sun (BEATLES) / Taxman (BEATLES) / Think for yourself (BEATLES) / While my guitar gently weeps (BEATLES) / For you blue (BEATLES) / My sweet Lord / Give me love (give me peace on Earth) / You / Bangla-Desh / Dark horse / What is life. *(re-iss. Oct81 on 'Music For Pleasure' lp/c; MFP 50523) (cd-iss. May87 on 'Parlophone'; CDP 746682-2)*

	Dark Horse	Dark Horse

Nov 76. (7") *(K 16856)* <8294> **THIS SONG. / LEARNING HOW TO LOVE YOU** [25]
Nov 76. (lp/c) *(K/K4 56319)* <3005> **THIRTY-THREE AND A THIRD** [35] [11]
– Woman don't you cry for me / Dear one / Beautiful girl / This song / See yourself / It's what you value / True love / Pure Smokey / Crackerbox palace / Learning how to love you.

Jan 77. (7") <8313> **CRACKERBOX PALACE. / LEARNING HOW TO LOVE YOU** [19]
Feb 77. (7") *(K 16896)* **TRUE LOVE. / PURE SMOKEY** [-] [19]
Jun 77. (7") *(K 16967)* **IT'S WHAT YOU VALUE. / WOMAN DON'T YOU CRY FOR ME** [-]
Feb 79. (7") <8763> **BLOW AWAY. / SOFT-HEARTED HANA** [16]
Feb 79. (7") *(K 17327)* **BLOW AWAY. / SOFT TOUCH** [51]
Feb 79. (lp/c) *(K/K4 56562)* <3255> **GEORGE HARRISON** [39] [14]
– Love comes to everyone / Not guilty / Here comes the moon / Soft-hearted Hana / Blow away / Faster / Your love is forever / Dark sweet lady / Soft touch / If you believe.

Apr 79. (7") *(K 17284)* **LOVE COMES TO EVERYONE. / SOFT-HEARTED HANA** [-]
Apr 79. (7") <8844> **LOVE COMES TO EVERYONE. / SOFT TOUCH** [-]
Jul 79. (7"/7"pic-d) *(K 17423/+P)* **FASTER. / YOUR LOVE IS FOREVER** [-]
May 81. (7") *(K 17807)* <49725> **ALL THOSE YEARS AGO. / WRITING'S ON THE WALL** [13] [2]
Jun 81. (lp/c) *(K/K4 56870)* <3492> **SOMEWHERE IN ENGLAND** [13] [11]
– Blood from a clone / Unconsciousness rules / Life itself / All those years ago / Baltimore oriole / Teardrops / That which I have lost / Writing's on the wall / Hong Kong blues / Save the world.

Jul 81. (7") *(K 17837)* <49785> **TEARDROPS. / SAVE THE WORLD** [ ] [ ]
Oct 82. (7") *(929864-2)* <29864> **WAKE UP MY LOVE. / GREECE** [53]
Nov 82. (lp/c) *(K 923734-1/-4)* <23734> **GONE TROPPO**
– Wake up my love / That's the way it really love you / Greece / Gone troppo / Mystical one / Unknown delight / Baby don't run away / Dream away / Circles.
Jan 83. (7") <29744> **I REALLY LOVE YOU. / CIRCLES** [-]

––––– Took long time off from solo career to establish his film production work. Returned after nearly five years with new session people.

Sep 87. (lp/c)(cd) *(WX 123/+C)(925643-2)* <25643> **CLOUD NINE** [10] [8 Nov87]
– Cloud 9 / That's what it takes / Fish on the sand / Just for today / This is love / When we was fab / Devil's radio / Someplace else / Wreck of the Hesperus / Breath away from Heaven / Got my mind set on you.

Oct 87. (7") *(W 8178)* <28178> **GOT MY MIND SET ON YOU. / LAY HIS HEAD** [2] [1]
(12"+=/12"pic-d+=) *(W 8178T/+P)* – ('A'extended).
Feb 88. (7") *(W 8131)* <28131> **WHEN WE WAS FAB. / ZIGZAG** [25] [23]
(12"+=/12"pic-d+=/3"cd-s+=) *(W 8131 T/TX/CD)* – That's the way it goes (remix) / ('A'mix).
Jun 88. (7") *(W 7913)* <27913> **THIS IS LOVE. / BREATH AWAY FROM HEAVEN** [55]
(12"+=) *(W 7913T)* – All those wasted years ago.
(3"cd-s++=) *(W 7913CD)* – Hong Kong blues.

––––– Later in 1988, HARRISON teamed up with BOB DYLAN, ROY ORBISON, JEFF LYNNE and TOM PETTY in The TRAVELLING WILBURYS. He also continued solo work below.

Oct 89. (lp/c)(cd) *(WX 312/+C)(K 925643-2)* <25726> **THE BEST OF DARK HORSE (1976-1989)** (compilation)
– Poor little girl / Blow away / That's the way it goes / Cockamamie business / Wake up my love / Life itself / Got my mind set on you / Here comes the Moon / Gone troppo / When we was fab / Love comes to everyone / All those years ago / Cheer down. *(c+=/cd+=)* – Crackerbox Palace.

Nov 89. (7") *(W 2696)* **CHEER DOWN. / POOR LITTLE GIRL** [ ] [-]
(12"+=/cd-s+=) *(W 2696 T/CD)* – Crackerbox palace.
Jul 92. (cd/c) *(<7599 26964-2/-4>)* **LIVE IN JAPAN (with ERIC CLAPTON AND BAND)**
– I want to tell you / Old brown shoe / Taxman / Give me love (give me peace on Earth) / If I needed someone / Something / What is life / Dark horse / Piggies / Got my mind set on you / Cloud nine / Here comes the Sun / My sweet Lord / All those years ago / Cheer down / Devil's radio / Isn't it a pity / While my guitar gently weeps / Roll over Beethoven.

– compilations etc. –

Oct 82. (d-cd) *Dark Horse; (K 466101)* **THIRTY-THREE AND A THIRD / GEORGE HARRISON** [-] [-]

Jerry HARRISON (see under ⇒ TALKING HEADS)

Deborah / Debbie HARRY (see under ⇒ BLONDIE)

Grant HART (see under ⇒ HUSKER DU)

Alex HARVEY

Born: 5 Feb'35, the Gorbals area, Glasgow, Scotland. Following loads of jobs in the early 50's, he played in various skiffle groups and after winning a local talent contest in 1956, he was dubbed "The TOMMY STEELE Of Scotland". In 1959, his BIG SOUL BAND backed touring American stars, EDDIE COCHRAN and GENE VINCENT, the former subsequently being killed in a car crash a few months later. They soon made their way to Germany, where they played many gigs while signing to 'Polydor' in the process. Recording a few lp's, and several 45's (some solo), HARVEY joined the crew of the 'Hair' musical in London's West End. In 1972, he returned to Scotland and found the group TEAR GAS, who were just about to disband after two poorly received albums. They became The SENSATIONAL ALEX HARVEY BAND, and, after nationwide tours and signature for 'Vertigo', released their debut album 'FRAMED'. HARVEY's solo R&B roots were abandoned for more theatrical and comic book rock'n'roll. With his buccaneer attitude and attire, he was a musical visionary, only matched by his clown-like guitarist, ZAL CLEMINSON (others numbered CHRIS GLEN and brothers HUGH and TED McKENNA). Late in '73, SAHB issued the excellent 'NEXT...', and should have scored with edited cut and fan favourite, 'THE FAITH HEALER'. A year later, they secured their first UK Top 20 album with 'THE IMPOSSIBLE DREAM', which was followed by a Top 10 album in 1975, and a marvellous Top 10 single rendition of 'DELILAH'. They peaked for another year, but found it difficult to maintain mainstream success with the advent of punk rock. Sadly, no longer in the limelight, ALEX died of a heart attack on a Belgian ferry on the 4th of February 1982. • **Songwriters:** Most by himsef and HUGH McKENNA, with additions from either ZAL or producer DAVE BATCHELOR. Covered; FRAMED (Leiber-Stoller) / I JUST WANT TO MAKE LOVE TO YOU (Willie Dixon) / NEXT (Jacques Brel) / GIDDY-UP-A-DING-DONG (Freddie Bell & The Bellboys) / THE IMPOSSIBLE DREAM (Leigh-Darion) / MONEY HONEY (...Stone) / RIVER OF LOVE (??) / TOMORROW BELONGS TO ME (Ebb-Kander) / DELILAH (hit; Tom Jones) / GAMBLIN' BAR ROOM BLUES (Alley-Rodgers) / CHEEK TO CHEEK (Irving Berlin) / LOVE STORY (Jethro Tull) / CRAZY HORSES (Osmonds) / SCHOOL'S OUT (Alice Cooper) / RUNAWAY (Del Shannon) / GOODNIGHT IRENE (Leadbelly) / SHAKIN' ALL OVER (Johnny Kidd). • **Trivia:** HARVEY's 'LOCH NESS' lp, released unusually on 'K-Tel', featured only interviews from sightings of the monster.

Album rating: ALEX HARVEY & HIS SOUL BAND (*5) / THE BLUES (*5) / ROMAN WALL BLUES (*4) / Sensational Alex Harvey Band: FRAMED (*6) / NEXT . . . (*9) / THE IMPOSSIBLE DREAM (*7) / TOMORROW BELONGS TO ME (*7) / THE SENSATIONAL ALEX HARVEY BAND "LIVE" (*7) / PENTHOUSE TAPES (*5) / SAHB STORIES (*5) / FOURPLAY without Alex (*4) / ROCK DRILL (*5) / THE MAFIA STOLE MY GUITAR (*5) / THE SOLDIER ON THE WALL (*5) / THE BEST OF THE SENSATIONAL ALEX HARVEY BAND compilation (*8)

ALEX HARVEY & HIS SOUL BAND

ALEX HARVEY – vocals / **RICKY BARNES** – saxophone, vocals / **ISOBEL BOND** – vocals / **GIBSON KEMP** – drums / **IAN HINDS** – organ / **BILL PATRICK** – guitar

		Polydor	not iss.
Jan 64.	(7"; as ALEX HARVEY) *(NH 52264)* **I JUST WANNA MAKE LOVE TO YOU. / LET THE GOOD TIMES ROLL**		-
Mar 64.	(lp) *(LPHM 46424)* **ALEX HARVEY AND HIS SOUL BAND (live)**		-

– Framed / I ain't worrying baby / Backwater blues / Let the good times roll / Going home / I've got my mojo working / Teensville U.S.A. / New Orleans / Bo Diddley is a gunslinger / When I grow too old to rock / Evil hearted man / I just wanna make love to you / The blind man / Reeling and rocking. *(Germany re-iss. Oct87 lp/c; 831887-1/-4)*

Jun 64.	(7") *(NH 52907)* **GOT MY MOJO WORKING. / I AIN'T WORRIED BABY**		-

—— ALEX HARVEY brought in new soul band, (his brother **LES HARVEY** – guitar / **BOBBY THOMPSON** – bass / **GILSON KEMP** – drums)

Jul 65.	(7") *(BM 56017)* **AIN'T THAT JUST TOO BAD. / MY KIND OF LOVE**		-
Nov 65.	(lp) *(LPHM 46441)* **THE BLUES**		-

– Trouble in mind / Honey bee / I learned about woman / Danger zone / The riddle song / Waltzing Matilda / The blues / The big rock candy mountain / The Michegan massacre / No peace / Nobody knows you when you're down and out / St. James infirmary / Strange fruit / Kisses sweeter than wine / Good God almighty.

ALEX HARVEY

solo with session musicians.

		Fontana	not iss.
Sep 65.	(7") *(TF 610)* **AGENT OO SOUL. / GO AWAY BABY**		-
Nov 66.	(7") *(TF 764)* **WORK SONG. / I CAN'T DO WITHOUT YOUR LOVE**		-

—— HARVEY now backed by **GIANT MOTH:- JIM CONDRON** – guitar, bass / **MOX** – flute / **GEORGE BUTLER** – drums

		Decca	not iss.
Jul 67.	(7") *(F 12640)* **THE SUNDAY SONG. / HORIZON'S**		-
Sep 67.	(7") *(F 12660)* **MAYBE SOME DAY. / CURTAINS FOR MY BABY**		-

—— next with backing from ROCK WORKSHOP which incl. brother LES and loads of others. In 1970/71 for 'CBS', they released two lp's 'ROCK WORKSHOP' *(64075) & not with ALEX, a double 'THE VERY LAST TIME' (64394)*. Taken from first lp was 45; 'YOU TO LOSE'.

		Fontana	not iss.
Oct 69.	(lp; stereo/mono) *(S+/TL 5534)* **ROMAN WALL BLUES**		-

– Midnight Moses / Hello L.A., bye bye Birmingham / Broken hearted fairytale / Donna / Roman wall blues / Jumping Jack Flash / Hammer song / Let my bluebird sing / Maxine / Down at Bart's place / Candy.

Nov 69.	(7") *(TF 1063)* **MIDNIGHT MOSES. / ROMAN WALL BLUES**		-

—— ALEX then formed his trio (**IAN ELLIS** – bass, ex-CLOUDS, **DAVE DUFORT** – drums) This was broken up after the death, by stage electrocution, of his brother LES, who had been part of STONE THE CROWS since '69 (Aug72) ALEX recruited a whole band

—— **TEAR GAS** who had already made two albums – Nov70 'PIGGY GO BETTER' on 'Famous', without the McKENNA brothers. Aug71. 'TEAR GAS' on 'Regal Zonophone', with all the members of below . . .

The SENSATIONAL ALEX HARVEY BAND

ALEX – vocals, guitar / **ZAL CLEMINSON** (b. 4 May'49) – guitar, vocals / **CHRIS GLEN** (b. 6 Nov'50) – bass / **HUGH McKENNA** (b.28 Nov'49) – keyboards / **TED McKENNA** (b.10 Mar'50) – drums

		Vertigo	Vertigo
Dec 72.	(lp)(c) *(6360 081)* **FRAMED**		-

– Framed / Hammer song / Midnight Moses / Isobel Goudie (part 1 – My lady of the night, part 2 – Coitus interruptus, part 3 – The virgin and the hunter) / Buff's bar blues / I just want to make love to you / Hole in her stocking / There's no lights on the Christmas tree, mother, they're burning big Louie tonight / St. Anthony. *(re-iss. Mar79 on 'Mountain';) (re-iss. Jul86 on 'Sahara' lp/c; (SAH 119/+TC) (cd-iss. 1986 on 'Samurai'+=; SAMRCD 00119)* – Smouldering / Chase it into the night.

Dec 72.	(7") *(6059 070)* **THERE'S NO LIGHTS ON THE CHRISTMAS TREE, MOTHER, THEY'RE BURNING BIG LOUIE TONIGHT. / HARP**		-
Feb 73.	(7") *(6059 075)* **JUNGLE JENNY. / BUFF'S BAR BLUES**		-
Nov 73.	(lp)(c) *(6360 103)* <1017> **NEXT . . .**		-

– Swampsnake / Gang bang / The faith healer / Giddy up a ding dong / Next / Vambo marble eye / The last of the teenage idols (part I-III). *(re-iss. Mar79 on 'Mountain';) (re-iss. Nov84 on 'Sahara'; SAH 114) (pic-lp May86; SAH 114CD) (cd-iss. 1986 on 'Samurai'; SAMRCD 00114) (re-iss. Mar87 on 'Fame' lp/c; FA/TC-FA 3169)*

Feb 74.	(7") *(6059 098)* **THE FAITH HEALER (edit). / ST. ANTHONY**		-
Feb 74.	(7") <113> **SWAMPSNAKE. / GANG BANG**	-	-
Aug 74.	(7") *(6059 106)* **SERGEANT FURY / GANG BANG**		-
Sep 74.	(7") <200> **SERGEANT FURY / TOMAHAWK KID**	-	
Sep 74.	(lp)(c) *(6360 112)* <2000> **THE IMPOSSIBLE DREAM**	16	

– The hot city symphony; (part 1 – Vambo, part 2 – Man in the Jar) / River of love / Long hair music / Sergeant Fury / Weights made of lead / Money honey – The impossible dream / Tomahawk kid / Anthem. *(re-iss. Mar79 on 'Mountain';) (re-iss. Jul86 on 'Samurai' lp/c; SAH 116/+TC)*

Nov 74.	(7") *(6059 112)* **ANTHEM. / ANTHEM (version)**		-
Apr 75.	(lp)(c) *(6360 120)* <2004> **TOMORROW BELONGS TO ME**	9	

– Action strasse / Snake bite / Soul in chains / The tale of the giant stoneater / Ribs and balls / Give my compliments to the chef / Sharks teeth / Ribs and balls / Shake that thing / Tomorrow belongs to me / To be continued . . . *(re-iss. Nov84 on 'Sahara'; SAH 111) (cd-iss. Jul86 on 'Samurai'+=; SAMRCD 00111)* – Big boy / Pick it up and kick it.

		Vertigo	Atlantic
Jul 75.	(7") *(ALEX 001)* <3293> **DELILAH (live). / SOUL IN CHAINS (live)**	7	
Sep 75.	(lp)(c) *(9102 007)* <18184> **THE SENSATIONAL ALEX HARVEY BAND "LIVE" (live)**	14	100

– Fanfare (justly, skillfully, magnanimously) / The faith healer / Tomahawk kid / Vambo / Give my compliments to the chef / Delilah / Framed. *(re-iss. Jul86 on 'Sahara' c/lp/pic-lp; TC+/SAH 117/+PD) (re-iss. Oct86 on 'Fame' lp/c; FA/TC-FA 3161) (cd-iss. 1986 on 'Samurai'; SAMRCD 00117)* – I wanna have you back / Jungle Jenny / Runaway / Love story / School's Out.

Nov 75.	(7") *(ALEX 002)* **GAMBLIN' BAR ROOM BLUES. / SHAKE THAT THING**	38	-
Mar 76.	(7") *(ALEX 003)* **RUNAWAY. / SNAKE BITE**		-
Mar 76.	(lp)(c) *(9102 007)* **PENTHOUSE TAPES** (old covers)	14	-

– I wanna have you back / Jungle Jenny / Runaway / Love story / School's out / Goodnight Irene / Say you're mine / Gamblin' bar room blues / Crazy horses / Cheek to cheek. *(re-iss. Mar79 on 'Mountain';) (re-iss. Nov84 on 'Sahara'; SAH 112) (cd-iss. Jul86 on 'Samurai'; SAMRCD 00112)*

		Mountain	not iss.
May 76.	(7") *(TOP 12)* **BOSTON TEA PARTY. / SULTAN'S CHOICE**	13	-
Jul 76.	(lp)(c) *(TOPS 112)* **SAHB STORIES**	11	-

– Boston Tea Party / Sultan's choice / $25 for a massage / Dogs of war / Dance to your daddy / Amos Moses / Jungle rub out / Sirocco. *(re-iss. Nov84 on 'Sahara'; SAH 115)*

Aug 76.	(7") *(TOP 19)* **AMOS MOSES. / SATCHEL AND THE SCALP HUNTER**		-

—— now all 4 members without ALEX HARVEY. (HUGH on vocals)

Jan 77.	(lp; SAHB WITHOUT ALEX) *(TOPC 5006)* **FOURPLAY**		-

– Smouldering / Chase it into the night / Shake your way to Heaven / Outer boogie / Big boy / Pick it up and kick it / Love you for a lifetime / Too much American pie. *(re-iss. Nov84 on 'Sahara'; SAH 113)*

Jan 77.	(7"; SAHB WITHOUT ALEX) **PICK IT UP AND KICK IT. / SMOULDERING**		-

—— In Apr'77, **ALEX HARVEY** released but withdrew, solo narrative lp 'PRESENTS THE LOCH NESS MONSTER' on 'K-Tel'; *NE 984)*

—— re-formed **HARVEY, CLEMINSON, TED McKENNA and GLEN** recruited **TOMMY EYRE** – keyboards who repl. HUGH McKENNA

Aug 77.	(7") *(TOP 32)* **MRS. BLACKHOUSE. / ENGINE ROOM BOOGIE**		-
Mar 78.	(lp)(c) *(TOPS 114)* **ROCK DRILL**		-

– The rock drill suite: Rock drill – The dolphins – Rock and roll – King Kong / Booids / Who murdered sex / Nightmare city / Water beastie / Mrs. Blackhouse. *(re-iss. Nov84 on 'Sahara'; SAH 118)*

—— (had already split late '77) CHRIS and TED joined ZAL in his own named band. ZAL later joined NAZARETH. TED later joined RORY GALLAGHER and then GREG LAKE BAND. TED and CHRIS later moved on to the MICHAEL SCHENKER GROUP.

ALEX HARVEY BAND

with **TOMMY EYRE** – keyboards / **MATTHEW CANG** – guitar / **GORDON SELLAR** – bass / **SIMON CHATTERTON** – drums

		R.C.A.	not iss.
Oct 79.	(7") *(PB 5199)* **SHAKIN' ALL OVER. / WAKE UP DAVIS**		-
Nov 79.	(lp)(c) *(PL/PK 25257)* **THE MAFIA STOLE MY GUITAR**		-

– Don's delight / Back in the depot / Wait for me mama / The Mafia stole my guitar / Shakin' all over / The whalers (thar she blows) / Oh Sparticus / Just a gigolo / I ain't got nobody. *(cd-iss. Sep91 on 'Mau Mau'; MAUCD 608)*

May 80.	(7") *(PB 5252)* **BIG TREE SMALL AXE. / THE WHALERS (THAR SHE BLOWS)**		-

—— ALEX HARVEY died of a heart attack on the 4th of February 1982 while on a ferry to Belgium

– his posthumous releases –

		Power Supply	not iss.
Nov 83.	(7") *(OHM 3)* **THE POET AND I. /**		-
Nov 83.	(c/lp) *(C+/AMP 2)* **SOLDIER ON THE WALL**		-

SENSATIONAL ALEX HARVEY BAND

—— actually re-formed for live gigs without ALEX!

		Meantime	not iss.
Apr 94.	(cd/c) *(JIMBO/JIMMC 001)* **LIVE IN GLASGOW 1993 (live)**		-

– The faith healer / St. Anthony / Framed / Gang bang / Amos Moses / Boston tea party / Midnight Moses / Vambo / Armed and dangerous / Delilah.

– SAHB compilations, etc. –

May 77.	(lp) Vertigo; *(6360 147)* **BIG HITS AND CLOSE SHAVES** (re-iss. Apr79 on 'Mountain')		-
Jun 77.	(7") Vertigo; *(6059 173)* **CHEEK TO CHEEK. / JUNGLE JENNY**		-
Jul 80.	(c/lp) Mountain; *(T+/TOPS 129)* **COLLECTOR'S ITEMS**		-
Jul 80.	(7"m) Mountain; *(HOT 2)* **DELILAH (live). / BOSTON TEA PARTY / THE FAITH HEALER**		-
Aug 82.	(d-lp/d-c) R.C.A.; *(RCA LP/K 9003)* **THE BEST OF THE SENSATIONAL ALEX HARVEY BAND**		-

– Next / Framed / The faith healer / The hot city symphony; part 1 – Vambo, part 2 – Man in the jar / Sergeant Fury / The tale of the giant stoneater /

Action strasse / Delilah / Weights made of lead / Boston Tea Party / Anthem / Runaway / Crazy horses / Big tree small axe / The Mafia stole my guitar / Gang bang / Tomorrow belongs to me. *(re-iss. May84 d-lp/d-c; PL/PK 70276)*

Date			
Nov 85.	(lp/c) *Sahara; (SAH/+TC 041)* **LEGEND** *(cd-iss. 1986 on 'Samurai'; SAMR 041CD)*	☐	-
Jan 86.	(c) *Sahara; (SAH 041TC)* **ANTHOLOGY**	☐	-
Apr 86.	(c) *Aura;* **DOCUMENT**	☐	-
Sep 86.	(d-lp/c/cd) *Castle; (CCS LP/MC/CD 149)* **THE COLLECTION**	☐	-

– $25 for a massage / The tale of the giant stoneater / Action strasse / Gang bang / Next / Give my compliments to the chef / Framed / Tomorrow belongs to me / Dance to your daddy / Sgt.Fury / Sultan's choice / Delilah (live) / Soul in chains / The faith healer / Boston tea party / Vambo (part 1) / Dogs of war / There's no lights on the Christmas tree mother, they're burning big Louie tonight / Giddy up a ding dong.

Jul 87.	(lp/c)(cd) *K-Tel; (NE1/CE2 368)(NCD 5139)* **THE BEST OF THE SENSATIONAL ALEX HARVEY BAND**	☐	-

– Delilah / The faith healer / Framed / Sergeant Fury / Jungle rub out / Love story / School's out / Boston Tea Party / Gamblin' bar room blues / Next / The man in the jar / Snake bite / Give my compliments to the chef / Cheek to cheek.

Sep 87.	(lp/c/cd) *Start; (STF L/C/CD 1)* **PORTRAIT** *(re-iss. Jan91 lp/c/cd; same)*	☐	-
Feb 91.	(lp/c) *Music Club; (MC CD/TC 001)* **THE BEST OF THE SENSATIONAL ALEX HARVEY BAND** *(re-iss. Jul94 on 'Success';)*	☐	-
Oct 91.	(lp) *Windsong; (WINCD 002)* **BBC RADIO 1 LIVE IN CONCERT (live)**	☐	-
Jun 92.	(cd/c) *Vertigo; (512 201-2/-4)* **ALL SENSATIONS**	☐	-
Nov 94.	(cd) *Windsong; (WHISCD 004)* **LIVE ON THE TEST**	☐	-
Sep 94.	(cd/c) *Spectrum; (550 663-2/-4)* **DELILAH**	☐	-

PJ HARVEY

Born: POLLY JEAN HARVEY, 9 Oct'69, Corscombe, nr.Yeovil, England. Born to music-loving hippie parents, HARVEY was acquainted with music and musicians from an early age. Her first songwriting experience was with rootsy outfit The POLEKATS, HARVEY later joining Somerset-based group AUTOMATIC DLAMINI, who had been around for some five years. Numbered in their ranks were ROBERT ELLIS on drums, JOHN PARISH (ex-THIEVES LIKE US) on guitar and vocals (both ex-HEADLESS HORSEMEN) and bassist DAVE DALLIMORE. With bassist JAMIE ANDERSON, they finally released a well-received debut EP, 'THE CRAZY SUPPER', in June '86 on the 'D For Drum' label (DLAM 1). PARISH also went into production work for The CHESTERFIELDS and BRILLIANT CORNERS. Early members of AUTOMATIC DLAMINI included ex-CLEANERS FROM VENUS keyboard man and future rock critic GILES SMITH, and IAN OLLIVER. 1987 was their busiest year, releasing a single, 'I DON'T KNOW YOU BUT . . .' / 'I'VE NEVER BEEN THAT COLOUR ANYWHERE BEFORE' (DLAM 2) / 7"+12" 'ME AND MY CONSCIENCE' for 'Idea' (IDEA+T 009), and album, 'THE D IS FOR DRUM' (on 'Idea' IDEALP 001). ELLIS departed soon after and POLLY finally convinced PARISH to let her play guitar and sax and contribute backing vocals. Unfortunately, recordings (i.e. 12" 'WATER', an album, 'HERE CATCH SHOUTED HIS FATHER') didn't quite reach the retail stage. In August 1992, the group released 'FROM A DIVA TO A DIVER' (BOT/+CD 04), after which PARISH took time out to produce WALL OF VOODOO and play with ENSENADA JOYRIDE, whose 'Hey Lady' POLLY has always wanted to cover. She then turned up on GRAPE's single 'BABY IN A PLASTIC BAG' and two tracks by The FAMILY CAT; 'COLOUR ME GREY' and 'RIVER OF DIAMONDS'. With ELLIS and OLLIVER, she had already formed PJ HARVEY in 1991, signed to 'Too Pure'. With POLLY on vocals, their first release, 'DRESS', immediately caught the attention of JOHN PEEL and achieved the dubious honour of a Melody Maker single of the week. A driving, primal howl of a record, it introduced HARVEY's lyrical preoccupation with the darker corners of female sexuality, a theme continued with 'SHEELA-NA-GIG' (without OLLIVER who was subsequently replaced by STEPHEN VAUGHAN) in early '92. The single hit the UK Top 75 and and there was enough of a buzz around the band for the debut album, 'DRY', to reach the fringes of the Top 10. HARVEY's impact had been immediate, her raw, defiantly individual interpretation of feminism sparking much debate in the music press, especially after an NME cover shot in which she appeared topless, back to the camera. Signing to 'Island', PJ HARVEY began work on the Steve Albini (ex-BIG BLACK)-produced follow-up, 'RID OF ME', which went Top 3 upon its release in the Spring of'93. As one might expect from the man who gave us 'Songs About Fucking', Albini's production didn't exactly make for an easy listen, HARVEY turning in her most ferocious performance to date. With the likes of 'LEGS', 'MAN SIZE' and 'RUB TILL IT BLEEDS', the singer continued to explore the contradictory and unsavoury aspects of sexuality/relationships with unparalleled feminine fury. Following the departure of ROB ELLIS, HARVEY assembled a backing band that includued JOHN PARISH (guitar, ex-AUTOMATIC DLAMINI), NICK BAGNALL (keyboards/bass), JOE GORE (guitar), ERIC FELDMAN (keyboards) and JEAN-MARC BUTTY (drums). In 1995, with FLOOD and BAD SEED, and MICK HARVEY on production duties, she/they unleashed HARVEY's finest work to date, 'TO BRING YOU MY LOVE', which also hit the US Top 40 and was nominated for a UK "Mercury" award. A more balanced affair, HARVEY's dark rage chose to simmer below the surface this time around, creating the feeling of creeping unease that runs through much of NICK CAVE's work (her new acquaintance!?). In 1996, she gave JOHN PARISH a full credit on their dual album 'DANCE HALL AT LOUSE POINT', which sold relatively poorly. • **Songwriters:** POLLY, and covers; HIGHWAY

61 (Bob Dylan) / DADDY (Willie Dixon) / BALLAD OF THE SOLDIER'S WIFE (Kurt Weill).

Album rating: DRY (*9) / RID OF ME (*8) / TO BRING YOU MY LOVE (*9) / DANCE HALL AT LOUSE POINT with John Parish (*5) / IS THIS DESIRE (*6)

POLLY HARVEY – vocals, guitar, cello, violin, organ / **IAN OLLIVER** – bass / **ROBERT ELLIS** (b.13 Feb'62, Bristol, England) – drums, vocals

			Too Pure	Indigo
Oct 91.	(12"ep) *(PURE 5)* **DRESS. / WATER (demo) / DRY (demo)** *(cd-iss. Mar92; PURECD 5)*		☐	-

—— **STEPHEN VAUGHAN** (b.22 Jun'62, Wolverhampton, England) – bass repl. OLLIVER who returned to brief reformation of AUTOMATIC DLAMINI

Feb 92.	(7"ltd.) *(PURE S8)* **SHEELA-NA-GIG. / JOE (demo)** (12"+=/cd-s+=) *(PURE 8/+CD)* – Hair (demo).		69	
Mar 92.	(lp/c/cd-s-lp) *(PURE 10/+CD/D)* <ING 5001> **DRY**		11	Jun92

– Oh my lover / O Stella / Dress / Victory / Happy and bleeding / Sheela-na-gig / Hair / Joe / Plants and rags / Fountain water. *(s-lp w/ free 'Demonstration' lp; PURED 10)*

			Island	Island
Apr 93.	(7"-c-s) *(IS/CIS 538)* **50FT QUEENIE. / REELING / MAN-SIZE (demo)** (12"+=/cd-s+=) *(12IS/CID 538)* – Hook (demo).		27	-
Apr 93.	(cd/c/lp) *(CID/ICT/ILPS 8002)* <514696> **RID OF ME**		3	May93

– Rid of me / Missed / Legs / Rub 'til it bleeds / Hook / Man-size sextet / Highway '61 revisited / 50ft Queenie / Yuri-G / Man-size / Dry / Me-Jane / Snake / Ecstasy.

Jul 93.	(12"ep/cd-ep) *(12IS/CID 569)* **MAN-SIZE. / WANG DANG DOODLE / DADDY**		42	-

—— drummer ELLIS departed after above.

Oct 93.	(cd/c/lp) *(IMCD/ICT/ILPM 2079)* <518450> **4-TRACK DEMOS (demos)**		19	Nov93

– Rid of me / Legs / Reeling / Snake / Hook / 50ft Queenie / Driving / Ecstasy / Hardly wait / Rub 'til it bleeds / Easy / M-bike / Yuri-G / Goodnight.

—— POLLY now with **JOHN PARISH** – drums, guitar / **JOE GORE** (b. San Francisco) – guitar (ex-TOM WAITS) / **NICK BAGNALL** – keyboards, bass / **ERIC FELDMAN** (b. San Francisco) – keyboards (ex-CAPTAIN BEEFHEART) / **JEAN-MARC BUTTY** (b. France) – drums

Feb 95.	(7"ep/12"ep/cd-ep) *(IS/12IS/CID 607)* **DOWN BY THE WATER. / LYING IN THE SUN / SOMEBODY'S DOWN, SOMEBODY'S NAME**		38	-
Feb 95.	(cd/c/lp) *(CID/ICT/ILPS 8035)* <524085> **TO BRING YOU MY LOVE**		12	40

– To bring you my love / Meet ze monsta / Working for the man / C'mon Billy / Teclo / Long snake moan / Down by the water / I think I'm a mother / Send his love to me / The dancer. *(re-iss. d-cd Dec95 w/ extra B-sides; CIDZ 8035)*

Jul 95.	(12"/cd-s) *(12IS/CID 614)* **C'MON BILLY. / DARLING BE THERE / MANIAC** (cd-s+=) *(CIDX 614)* – One time too many.		29	-
Oct 95.	(7"pic-d) *(IS 610)* **SEND HIS LOVE TO ME. / LONG TIME COMING (session)** (cd-s+=) *(CID 610)* – Harder. (cd-s) *(CIDX 610)* – ('A'side) / Hook (live) / Water (live).		34	-

—— Enjoyed more chart success on duet with NICK CAVE; 'Henry Lee' single released early '96.

JOHN PARISH & POLLY JEAN HARVEY

—— with **JEREMY HOGG** – guitar / **ERIC DREW FELDMAN** – bass, keyboards (ex-CAPTAIN BEEFHEART) / **ROB ELLIS** – drums

			Island	Island
Sep 96.	(cd/c/lp) *(CID/ICT/ILPS 8051)* <524278> **DANCE HALL AT LOUSE POINT**		46	-

– Girl / Rope bridge crossing / City of no sun / That was my veil / Urn with dead flowers in a drained pool / Civil war correspondent / Taut / Un cercle autour du soleil / Heela / Is that all there is / Dance hall at Louse Point / Lost fun zone.

Nov 96.	(7") *(IS 648)* **THAT WAS MY VEIL. / LOSING GROUND** (12"+=/cd-s+=) *(12IS/CID 648)* – Who will love me now? / Civil war correspondent (Global Communications mix).		75	-

—— ELLIS joined 'Too Pure' outfit, LAIKA

PJ HARVEY

—— In 1998, she featured with TRICKY on his 'Broken Homes' single.

			Island	Polygram
Sep 98.	(7") *(IS 718)* <572408> **A PERFECT DAY ELISE. / SWEETER THAN ANYTHING / INSTRUMENTAL #3** (cd-s) *(CID 718)* – (first & third tracks) / The Northwood. (cd-s) *(CIDX 718)* – (first two tracks) / The bay.		25	Oct98
Sep 98.	(cd/c/lp) *(CID/ICT/ILPS 8076)* <524563> **IS THIS DESIRE?**		17	54

– Angelene / Sky lit up / Wind / My beautiful Leah / A perfect day Elise / Catherine / Electric light / Garden / Joy / River / No girl so sweet / Is this desire?

Jan 99.	(7") *(IS 730)* **THE WIND. / NINA IN ECSTASY 2** (cd-s+=) *(CID 730)* – The faster I breathe, the further I go. (cd-s) *(CIDX 730)* – ('A'side) / Rebecca / Instrumental No.2.		29	

HATER (see under ⇒ SOUNDGARDEN)

Juliana HATFIELD / BLAKE BABIES

(dig out; 4th edition or Great Alt & Indie . . .)

Richie HAVENS

Born: 21 Jan'41, Brooklyn, New York, USA and raised as the oldest of nine children in the New York ghetto area of Bedford-Stuyvesant. After inclinations of following in his pianist father's footsteps had lost their attraction due to lack of money, he began to busk the street-corners as a young teenager. He also formed The McCREA GOSPEL SINGERS, before he relocated to Greenwich Village, painting portraits of tourists to earn a living. It was now the early 60's and the folk revival was taking hold in the area to the extent that everybody (now even RICHIE) was picking up their guitar again. His unorthodox technique (tuning with an E-chord) helped him quickly adapt and characterise his own style, which he still maintains today. In 1965, having gained notoriety around the underground 'Village' scene, he was picked up by 'Douglas' records, who quickly shifted out copies of his debut lp, 'THE RICHIE HAVENS ALBUM'. It was followed by another, before 'Verve' took over and set free his 'MIXED BAG' album, which contained a remarkable cover of 'ELEANOR RIGBY'. In 1968, he played a benefit gig for dust-bowl folk-hero idol, WOODY GUTHRIE, who had died the year previous. In August of 1969 he opened for the Woodstock Festival, which (overnight) made him into a star. One song, 'FREEDOM', became not only his anthem but the American people's anthem, delivered from the ashes of hippy psychedelia to a hopeful early 70's generation that never quite disappeared. This showed itself to be the case in the Spring of 1971, when he resurrected (into the US Top 20), a GEORGE HARRISON-written BEATLES song, 'HERE COMES THE SUN'. The accompanying album, 'ALARM CLOCK' made it into the Top 30 as a result. Now on the 'Stormy Forest' label, HAVENS continued in his inimitably earnest style throughout the 70's with albums such as 'THE GREAT BLIND DEGREE' (1972) and 'MIXED BAG II' (1975). He also continued to build up his bulging repertoire of BEATLES and BOB DYLAN covers (see below) and develop his knack for covering the most unlikely artists, material which no black artist would ordinarily go near. Although HAVENS' output diminished in the 80's, fans could console themselves (or not) with his TV advertising voiceovers (!). In 1994, he sued 'Time-Warner' for using his opening Woodstock footage for a new version of the film soundtrack. • **Songwriters:** Self-penned except; CHAIN GANG (Sam Cooke) / OXFORD TOWN + BOOTS OF SPANISH LEATHER + JUST LIKE A WOMAN + SAD EYED LADY + IF NOT FOR YOU + LAY LADY LAY + ALL ALONG THE WATCHTOWER + THE TIMES THEY ARE-A CHANGIN' + IT'S ALL OVER NOW, BABY BLUE + LICENSE TO KILL (Bob Dylan) / C.C. RIDER (hit; Chuck Willis) / ELEANOR RIGBY + STRAWBERRY FIELDS FOREVER + LADY MADONNA + SHE'S LEAVING HOME + WITH A LITTLE HELP FROM MY FRIENDS + ROCKY RACCOON + IN MY LIFE + THE LONG AND WINDING ROAD + LET IT BE (Beatles) / WEAR YOUR LOVE LIKE HEAVEN (Donovan) / FIRE AND RAIN (James Taylor) / TOMMY (Who) / TEACH YOUR CHILDREN (Crosby, Stills, Nash & Young) / GOD BLESS THE CHILD (Billie Holiday) / TUPELO HONEY (Van Morrison) / WHERE HAVE ALL THE FLOWERS GONE (hit; Kingston Trio) / THE LONER (Neil Young) / BAND ON THE RUN (Paul McCartney) / IMAGINE + WORKING CLASS HERO (John Lennon) / MY SWEET LORD (George Harrison) / DO IT AGAIN (Steely Dan) / LONG TRAIN RUNNING (Doobie Brothers) / I'M NOT IN LOVE (10 cc) / OL' 55 (Tom Waits) / WE'VE GOT TONIGHT (Bob Seger) / LIVES IN THE BALANCE (Jackson Browne) / THEY DANCE ALONE (Sting) / THE HAWK (Kris Kristofferson) / HOW THE NIGHTS CAN FLY (Bob Lind) / MY FATHER'S SHOES (Eberhardt) / COMING BACK TO ME (Marty Balin) / etc. • **Miscellaneous:** In 1972, he also took part in the stage production of The Who's 'Tommy'.

Album rating: A RICHIE HAVENS RECORD (*4) / ELECTRIC HAVENS (*4) / MIXED BAG (*8) / SOMETHING ELSE AGAIN (*6) / RICHARD P. HAVENS (*7) / STONEHENGE (*4) / ALARM CLOCK (*5) / THE GREAT BLIND DEGREE (*4) / RICHIE HAVENS ON STAGE (*6) / PORTFOLIO (*5) / MIXED BAG II (*4) / THE END OF THE BEGINNING (*4) / MIRAGE (*4) / CONNECTIONS (*4) / COMMON GROUND (*4) / SIMPLE THINGS (*3) / SINGS BEATLES AND DYLAN (*6) / LIVE AT THE CELLAR DOOR (*3) / NOW (*4) / RESUME – BEST OF... compilation (*7) / CUTS TO THE CHASE (*5)

RICHIE HAVENS – vocals, guitar

		not iss.	Douglas
1965.	(lp) <779> **A RICHIE HAVENS RECORD**	-	

– I'm gonna make you glad / It hurts me / Chain gang / Drown in my own tears / I'm on my way / Baby, I'm leavin' / Nora's dove / Daddy roll 'em / The bag I'm in. *(UK-iss.1969 on 'Transatlantic'; TRA 199)*

1966.	(lp) <780> **ELECTRIC HAVENS**	-	

– Oxford Town / 900 miles from home / I'm a stranger here / My own way / Boots of Spanish leather / C.C. rider / 3:10 to Yuma / Shadow town. <re-dist.Nov68> *(UK-iss.1969 on 'Transatlantic'; TRA 187)*

—— added **PAUL HARRIS** – piano, organ / **PAUL WILLIAMS + HOWARD COLLINS** – guitar / **HARVEY BROOKS** – bass / **BILL LA VORGNA** – drums / **JOE PRICE** – tabla

		Verve	Verve Folkways
Feb 67.	(lp) <3006> **MIXED BAG**	-	

– High flyin' bird / I can't make it anymore / Morning morning / Adam / Follow / Three day eternity / Sandy / Handsome Johnny / San Francisco Bay blues / Just like a woman / Eleanor Rigby. <re-dist.Jul68> *(UK-iss.1968; SVLP 6008)* <re-iss. Nov70 on 'M.G.M.'; 4698> *(cd-iss. May88; 835210-2) (cd re-iss. Jul94 on 'Polydor')*

Mar 67.	(7") <5022> **I CAN'T MAKE IT ANYMORE. / MORNING MORNING**	-	
Jun 67.	(7") <5039> **I'VE GOTTA GO. / MORNING MORNING**	-	

—— **DANIEL BEN ZEBULON + DON McDONALD + SKIP PROKOP** – drums / **WARREN BERNHARDT** – keyboards / **JEREMY STEIG** – flute / **ADRIAN GULLEY** – guitar /

EDDIE GOMEZ + DON PAYNE – bass / **JOHN BLAIR** – violin; repl. everyone except WILLIAMS

Feb 68.	(lp) *(SVLP 6005)* <3034> **SOMETHING ELSE AGAIN**		

– No opportunity necessary, no experience needed / Inside of him / The klan / Don't listen to me / Sugarplums / From the prison / New city / Run, shaker life / Maggie's farm / Something else again.

Jan 69.	(7") *(VS 5068)* **NO OPPORTUNITY NECESSARY, NO EXPERIENCE NEEDED. / THREE DAY ETERNITY**		

—— **ERIC OXENDINE** – bass repl. GOMEZ + PAYNE / (added others on session)

May 69.	(d-lp) *(SVLP 6014/5)* <3047> **RICHIE P. HAVENS, 1983** (some live)		**80** Jan69

– Stop pulling and pushing me / For Haven's sake / Strawberry fields forever / What more can I say John? / I pity the poor immigrant / Lady Madonna / Priests / Indian rope man / Cautiously / Just above my hobby horse's head / She's leaving home / Putting out the vibration, and hoping it comes home / The parable of Ramon / With a little help from my friends / Wear your love like Heaven / Run shaker life / Do you feel good?.

May 69.	(7") <5092> **INDIAN ROPE MAN. / JUST ABOVE MY HOBBY HORSES HEAD**		
		Verve	Stormy Forest
May 69.	(7") *(VS 1519)* **LADY MADONNA. / INDIAN ROPE MAN**	-	-
Jul 69.	(7") *(VS 1521)* <650> **ROCKY RACCOON. / STOP PULLING AND PUSHING ME**		
Sep 69.	(7") *(VS 1523)* <651> **THERE'S A HOLE IN THE FUTURE. / MINSTREL FROM GAULT**		
Oct 69.	(7") *(VS 1524)* <652> **HANDSOME JOHNNY. / SANDIE**		
		Polydor	Stormy Forest
Jan 70.	(lp) *(SVLP 6021)* <6001> **STONEHENGE**		

– Open our eyes / Minstrel from Gault / It could be the first day / Ring around the Moon / Baby blue / There's a hole in the future / I started a joke / Prayer / Tiny little blues / Shouldn't all the world be dancing.

Nov 70.	(7") <653> **TO GIVE ALL MY LOVE AWAY. / NOBODY KNOWS**	-	-
Jan 71.	(lp) *(2310 080)* <6005> **ALARM CLOCK**		**29**

– Here comes the Sun / To give all your love away / Younger men grow older / Girls don't run away / End of the seasons / Some will wait / Patient lady / Missing train / Alarm clock.

Apr 71.	(7") <656> **HERE COMES THE SUN. / YOUNGER MEN GET OLDER**	-	**16**
Apr 71.	(7") *(2001 162)* **HERE COMES THE SUN. / SOME WILL WAIT**		
Jul 71.	(7") <658> **MISSING TRAIN. / I'VE GOT TO GET TO KNOW MYSELF**	-	
Jan 72.	(lp) *(2480 049)* <6010> **THE GREAT BLIND DEGREE**		Nov71

– What about me / Fire and rain / Tommy / In these flames / Think about the children / Fathers & sons / Teach your children / What have we done.

Feb 72.	(7") <660> **THINK ABOUT THE CHILDREN. / FIRE AND RAIN**	-	-
Mar 72.	(7") *(2121 098)* **WHAT ABOUT ME. / FIRE AND RAIN**	-	

HAVENS still with WILLIAMS + ZEBULON live BBC, London, 19 Oct'71.

Sep 72.	(d-lp) *(2659 015)* <6012> **RICHIE HAVENS ON STAGE (live)**		**55**

– From the prison / Younger men grow older / God bless the child / High flying bird / Tupelo honey / Just like a woman / Handsome Johnny / Where have all the flowers gone / Rocky raccoon / Teach the children / Minstrel from Gault / Freedom.

Oct 72.	(7") <664> **I'VE GOT TO GET TO KNOW MYSELF (live). / WHERE YOU GONNA RUN TO (live)**		
Feb 73.	(7") <666> **FREEDOM. / HANDSOME JOHNNY**		

—— added **OXENDINE** / **JERRY FRIEDMAN** – guitar / **ERIC WEISBERG** – steel guitar / etc.

Jul 73.	(lp) *(2480 166)* <6013> **PORTFOLIO**		Jun73

– It was a very good year / Dreaming my life away / 23 days in September / I know I won't be there / I don't need nobody / Woman / What's goin' on / Tightrope / Mama loves you.

Aug 73.	(7") <671> **IT WAS A VERY GOOD YEAR. / I KNOW I WON'T BE THERE**	-	-
Oct 73.	(7") <672> **TIGHTROPE. / WOMAN**	-	-
Nov 73.	(7") *(2121 181)* **TIGHTROPE. / IT WAS A VERY GOOD YEAR**		-
Jan 75.	(lp) *(2310 356)* <6201> **MIXED BAG II**		Oct74

– Ooh child / Headkeeper / Wandering Angus / Sad eyed lady (of the lowlands) / Someone suite / Band on the run / The loner / The makings of you / The Indian prayer.

—— now with numerous session including **HERMAN ERNST** – drums / **DARRYL JOHNSON** – guitar / + (on first) **BOOKER T. & THE MG's**

		A&M	A&M
Sep 76.	(7") <1869> **WE CAN'T HIDE IT ANYMORE. / DREAMING AS ONE**		
Nov 76.	(lp) *(AMLH 64598)* <4598> **THE END OF THE BEGINNING**		Sep76

– I'm not in love / We can't hide it anymore / Dreaming as one / You close your eyes / I was educated by myself / Daughter of the night / If not for you / Do it again / Wild night / Long train running.

Nov 76.	(7") *(AMS 7266)* <1882> **I'M NOT IN LOVE. / DREAMING AS ONE**		
Mar 77.	(7") <1901> **YOU CAN CLOSE YOUR EYES. / WE CAN'T HIDE IT ANYMORE**	-	
Oct 77.	(lp) *(AMLH 64641)* <4641> **MIRAGE**		Apr77

– Live it up (one time) / Shadows of the past / I don't complain / Touch the sky / Billy John / We all wanna boogie / Avalon / Aviation man / Nobody left to crown / The end.

Jan 78.	(7") <1984> **WE ALL WANNA BOOGIE. / NOBODY LEFT TO CROWN**	-	

—— Around mid-78, RICHIE guested on STEVE HACKETT's single 'How Can I.' Later that year, he wrote and apeared in film 'Greased Lightning'. He now employed totally new session men incl. on next **JEFF BAXTER + RICHARD TEE**

		Elektra	Elektra
Nov 79.	(7") <46619> **EVERY NIGHT. / HERE'S A SONG**	-	
Mar 80.	(lp) *(K 52186)* <242> **CONNECTIONS**		Nov79

– Mama we're gonna dance / Every night / You send me / We've got tonight / Ol' 55 / Going back to my roots / Dreams / She touched my heart / Fire down below / Here's a song.

Mar 80. (7") <46657> **THE GIRL, THE GOLD WATCH AND EVERYTHING. / TWO HEARTS IN PERFECT TIME**

Jun 83. (lp) (165155-1) **COMMON GROUND**
– Death at an early age / Gay cavalier / Lay ye down boys / This is the hour / Stand up / Dear John / Leave well enough alone / Moonlight rain / Things must change.

Jun 83. (7") (CX 5381) **DEATH AT AN EARLY AGE. / MOONLIGHT RAIN**

Sep 87. (lp/c/cd) <(RB L/C/D 400)> **SIMPLE THINGS**
– Drivin' / Simple things / Songwriter / Passin' by / Wake up and dream / I don't wanna know / Shouldn't we all be having a good time / Arrow through me / Runner in the night.

1990. (cd) <1001> **LIVE AT THE CELLAR DOOR**
– Can't make it anymore / All along the watchtower / Helplessly hoping / God bless the child / The night they drove old Dixie down / No more, no more / Preparation / Here comes the sun / Fire and rain / Superman / The dolphins / Nobody knows the trouble I've seen – My sweet Lord.

1991. (cd) <75325> **NOW**

May 92. (cd) <(RCD 20035)> **SINGS BEATLES AND DYLAN** (rec.1987)
– Here comes the sun / If not for you / Lay lady lay / In my life / Strawberry fields forver / All along the watchtower / Imagine / My sweet Lord / It's all over now, baby blue / Eleanor Rigby / Just like a woman / The long and winding road / Let it be / License to kill / The times they are a-changin' / Working class hero / Rocky raccoon / With a little help from my friends.

—— In Jul'93, HAVENS and FRANCESCO BRUNO (jazz artist) released the single 'THE WORLD IS SO SMALL' from the 'Prestige' album 'EL LUGAR (THE PLACE)'.

Jun 94. (cd/c) (ESS CD/MC 212) **CUTS TO THE CHASE**
– Lives in the balance / They dance alone / My father's shoes / Darkness, darkness / The hawk / Young boy / The times they are a-changin' / Fade to blue medley: Intro – Old love / How the nights can fly / Comin' back to me / Don't pass it up / At a glance.

– compilations, etc. –

Apr 69. (7") Big T; (BIG 119) **OXFORD TOWN. / MY OWN WAY**
Jul 71. (lp) Polydor; (2304 050) **A STATE OF MIND**
Mar 76. (lp) Polydor; (2482 273) **RICHIE HAVENS**

Screamin' Jay HAWKINS

Born: JALACY HAWKINS, 18 Jul'29, Cleveland, Ohio, USA. He decided upon a musical career after being orphaned and fostered as a young boy. Unfortunately he was not suited to the operatic style of performing (he chose at the time) and began his lifelong ambitions in 1951; he was pianist on several tracks by TINY GRIMES. However, a year later, the tables were turned when his solo career was aided with the help of GRIMES AND HIS ROCKING HIGHLANDERS. HAWKINS' delivered his finest 3 minutes in 1956 with the single, 'I PUT A SPELL ON YOU', a meisterwork in its time that has since achieved great things although never a hit for the man. The infamous grunting sections were reputedly recorded while HAWKINS was in a state of severe intoxication. The single, with its tongue very firmly placed in its cheek, fused swinging R&B instrumentation and backing vocals with a then new care-less attitude to the lead vocals, the drum-lines and guitar licks being provided by his motley crew of friends. It could be said that the man achieved little else in his lifetime, although he tried time and time again to breach the unsympathetic charts. HAWKINS was more famous for his onstage antics, shaped around shock-horror voodoo R'n'R, something not practised before but since associated with ARTHUR BROWN and ALICE COOPER. His antics included appearing from a coffin and also carrying HENRY, a macabre flaming skull companion, while shouting his words like a demented preacher man. This eccentric flair saw him being rebuked in the early 60's, with angry parents and God-fearing Americans having a field day due to its banning on radio. It also translated well onto the cinema screen when HAWKINS had minor memorable roles in the films: 'Two Moon Junction', 'Dance With The Devil' and cult director Jim Jarmush's masterpiece 'Mystery Train'. More recently, albums from HAWKINS included 'BLACK MUSIC FOR WHITE PEOPLE' (1991), 'STONE CRAZY' (1993) and 'SOMETHIN' FUNNY GOIN' ON' (1994), although all were nothing short of incoherent ramblings. However, the man did achieve his first hit single (albeit minor) when his version of Tom Waits' 'HEART ATTACK AND VINE' made it into the UK Top 50 in Spring '93; WAITS would subsequently sue the accompanying TV advert. Stop press:- HAWKINS died on the 12th February, 2000 after an operation on his brain (aneurysm) failed.

Best CD compilation: PORTRAIT OF A MAN – A HISTORY OF . . . (*6)

SCREAMIN' JAY HAWKINS – vocals, piano, saxophone

		not iss.	Timely
1954.	(78) <1004> **BAPTIZE ME IN WINE. / NOT ANYMORE**	-	
1954.	(78) <1005> **PLEASE TRY TO UNDERSTAND. / I FOUND MY WAY TO WINE**	-	

		not iss.	Mercury
1955.	(78; as JAY HAWKINS) <70549> **SHE PUT THE WHAMMY ON ME. / THIS IS ALL**	-	
		not iss.	Wing
1955.	(78; as JAY HAWKINS) <90005> **YOU'RE ALL OF MY LIFE TO ME. / WELL I TRIED**	-	
1956.	(78; as JAY HAWKINS) <90055> **EVEN THOUGH. / TALK ABOUT ME**	-	
		not iss.	Grand
1956.	(78) <135> **TAKE ME BACK. / I IS**	-	
		not iss.	Okeh
1956.	(78) <7072> **I PUT A SPELL ON YOU. / LITTLE DEMON**	-	
	(UK-iss.Jan58 on 'Fontana'; H 107) (7"-iss.1969 on 'Direction'; 58-4097) (re-iss. 1975 on 'Epic'; 15-2209)		
1956.	(78) <7084> **YOU MADE ME LOVE YOU. / DARLING, PLEASE FORGIVE ME**	-	
1956.	(78) <7087> **FRENZY. / PERSON TO PERSON**	-	
1957.	(78) <7101> **ALLIGATOR WINE. / THERE'S SOMETHING WRONG WITH YOU**	-	
		not iss.	Epic
1957.	(lp) <3448> **AT HOME WITH SCREAMIN' JAY HAWKINS**	-	
		not iss.	Apollo
1957.	(78) <506> **PLEASE TRY TO UNDERSTAND. / NOT ANYMORE**	-	
1958.	(78) <528> **BAPTIZE ME IN WINE. / NOT ANYMORE**	-	
		not iss.	Enrica
1962.	(7") <1010> **I HEAR VOICES. / JUST DON'T CARE (with the Chicken Hawks)**	-	
	(UK-iss.Jun65 on 'Sue'; WI 379)		
		not iss.	Chancellor
1962.	(7") <1117> **ASHES. / NITTY GRITTY (with PAT NEWBORN)**	-	
		Columbia	Roulette
Jan 65.	(7") (DB 7460) <4579> **THE WHAMMY. / STRANGE**	-	
		not iss.	Providence
Feb 65.	(7") <411> **PO' FOLKS. / MY KIND OF LOVE**	-	
		Planet	not iss.
1966.	(lp) (PLL 1001) **THE NIGHT AND DAY OF SCREAMIN' JAY HAWKINS**		-
		not iss.	Decca
1967.	(7") <32019> **I'M NOT MADE OF CLAY. / ALL NIGHT**		-
1967.	(7") <32100> **I PUT A SPELL ON YOU. / YOU'RE AN EXCEPTION TO THE RULE**		-
		Direction	Epic
1969.	(lp; stereo/mono) (S+/8-63481) <26457> **I PUT A SPELL ON YOU** (compilation)	-	
	– You made me love you / I put a spell on you / Alligator wine / Little demon / There's something wrong with you / Orange-coloured sky / Yellow coat / Give me back my boots and saddle / Hong Kong / Person to person / Frenzy / I love Paris.		

—— now with a back-up session band

		Mercury	Philips
1969.	(7") <40606> **I'M LONELY. / STONE CRAZY**	-	
1969.	(7") <40645> **DO YOU REALLY LOVE ME. / CONSTIPATION BLUES**	-	
1969.	(7") <40668> **MOANIN'. / CONSTIPATION BLUES**	-	
1969.	(lp) (SMCL 20178) <PHS 600-319> **WHAT THAT IS!**	-	
	– What that is / Feast of the Mau Mau / Do you really love me / Stone crazy / I love you / Constipation blues / I'm lonely / Thing called woman / Dig / I'm your man / Ask him / Reprise. (cd-iss. Aug95 on 'Verve'+=; 527490-2)		
1970.	(lp) <PHS 600-336> **SCREAMIN' JAY HAWKINS**	-	
1970.	(7") <40674> **OUR LOVE IS NOT FOR THREE. / TAKE ME BACK**	-	
		not iss.	Sound Of Hawaii
1970.	(lp) <5013> **A NIGHT AT THE FORBIDDEN CITY** (live)	-	Hawaii
1970.	(7") **TOO MANY TEARDROPS. / MAKAHA WAVES**	-	Hawaii
		not iss.	Queen Bee
1971.	(7") **MONKBERRY MOON DELIGHT. / SWEET GINNY**	-	
		not iss.	Hot Line
1972.	(lp) <10024> **PORTRAIT OF A MAN AND HIS WOMAN** (part compilation)	-	
		not iss.	London
1973.	(7") **AFRICA GONE FUNKY. / (part 2)**	-	
		not iss.	R.C.A.
1974.	(7") **VOODOO. / YOU PUT THE SPELL ON ME**	-	
		not iss.	Versatile
1977.	(7") **I PUT A SPELL ON YOU. / AFRICA GONE FUNKY**	-	
		Polydor	not iss.
Sep 80.	(7") (POSP 183) **I PUT A SPELL ON YOU. / ARMPIT #6 (with KEITH RICHARDS)**	-	

—— recorded next set with French musicians

		Paris	not iss.
1983.	(lp) (C 3358) **REAL LIFE**		French
	– Deep in love / Your kind of love / Get down France / All night / Serving time / Feast of the Mau Mau / I feel alright / Poor folks / Mountain jive / Constipation blues. (UK-iss.Feb89 on 'Charly' lp)(cd; CRB 1205)(CDCHARLY 163) (cd re-iss. Feb93 on 'Blues Collection'; 15755-2)		
		Midnight	not iss.
Mar 86.	(m-lp; with The FUZZTONES) (MIRLP 114) **LIVE (live 1985)**	-	
	– Alligator wine / I put a spell on you / It's that time again / Constipation blues.		
		Demon	Rhino
Mar 91.	(cd/c) (FIEND CD/CASS 211) <R2/R4 70556> **BLACK MUSIC FOR WHITE PEOPLE**		
	– Is you is or is you ain't my baby? / I feel alright / I put a spell on you (dance		

version) / I hear you knockin' / Heart attack and vine / Ignant and shit / Swamp gas / Voodoo priestess / Ice cream man / I want your body / Ol' man river / Strokin'. *(cd re-iss. Mar98 on 'Manifesto'; BP 40102CD)*

Mar 93. (7"/c-s/cd-s) *(659109-7/-4/-2)* **HEART ATTACK AND VINE. / I PUT A SPELL ON YOU / ON THE JOB** | 42 |
(above issued on 'Columbia')

Apr 93. (cd) *(FIENDCD 728) <R2 71184>* **STONE CRAZY**
– Strange / I don't know / Who's been talkin' / I believe / Stone crazy / Last Saturday night / Call the plumber / I wanna know / Sherilyn Fenn / Late night Hawkins / On the job / I am the queen.

—— next featured **BUDDY BLUE** – guitar (ex-BEAT FARMERS)

	Demon	Bizarre – Straight
Feb 94. (cd) *(FIENDCD 750) <40105>* **SOMETHIN' FUNNY GOIN' ON**		Apr95

– Somethin' funny goin' on / I am the cool / Whistling past the graveyard / Rock the house / Scream the blues / Brujo / You make me sick / Give it a break / When you walked out the door / Fourteen wives.

	Last Call	Valley
Feb 98. (cd) *(302742-2) <15008>* **AT LAST**		

– Listen / Because of you / Coulda', woulda', shoulda' / Pot luck / You took me / Deceived / I'll be there / I played the fool / Shut your mouth when you sneeze / Life goes on / You want love / Make me happy / I shot the sheriff.

	Last Call	Last Call
Dec 99. (d-cd) *<(305256-2)>* **LIVE – OLYMPIA, PARIS 1998** (live)		

– I feel alright / Don't love you no more / Pretty girls everywhere / I'm lonely / Deceived / I don't know / I want to know / I'll be there / Stand by me / Bite it / Constipation blues / What'd I say / Alligator wine / I put a spell on you / Itty bitty pretty one / Shout / You took me / Please don't leave me / Goodnight sweetheart / Frankly speaking.

—— sadly, HAWKINS was to die the following February

– compilations, etc. –

Sep 79. (lp) *Red Lightnin'; (RL 0025)* **SCREAMIN' THE BLUES** (material from 1953-1970) | - |
(cd-iss. Aug89; RLCD 75)

Oct 82. (lp) *Edsel; (ED 104)* **FRENZY** (the 'Okeh' recordings) | - |
(re-iss. Mar86 cd/c/lp; CD/C+/ED 104)

Mar 88. (d-lp) *Edsel; (DED 252)* **FEAST OF THE MAU MAU** | - |
(re-iss. Mar91 cd/c; ED/C ED 252)

Jun 89. (lp/cd) *Charly; (CRB 1211)(CDCHARLY 181)* **I PUT A SPELL ON YOU** (not the original) | - |
(cd re-iss. Apr93 on 'Instant'; CDINS 5078) (cd re-iss. Jun96; CPCD 8221)

Feb 90. (cd/c) *Rhino; <R2/R4 70947>* **VOODOO JIVE: THE BEST OF SCREAMIN' JAY HAWKINS** | - |

Dec 90. (d-cd) *Bear Family; <(BCD 15530-BH)>* **SPELLBOUND! 1955-1974**

Oct 91. (cd) *(SJHCD 71829)* **SCREAMIN' JAY HAWKINS 1952-1955 – THE COMPLETE GOTHAM & GRAND RECORDINGS** | - |

Jan 92. (cd) *Evidence; <(ECD 26003-2)>* **LIVE & CRAZY** (live)

Mar 92. (cd/c) *Legacy; (471270-2/-4) / Epic; <EK/ET 47933>* **COW FINGERS AND MOSQUITO PIE**

Sep 93. (cd/c) *Aim; (AIM CD/C 1031)* **I SHAKE MY STICK AT YOU** | - |

Jan 95. (cd) *Edsel; (EDCD 414)* **PORTRAIT OF A MAN – A HISTORY OF SCREAMIN' JAY HAWKINS** | - |
– Little demon / I put a spell on you / Baptize me in wine / Not anymore / I hear voices / Just don't care / Ashes / There's something wrong with you / Strange / The whammy / All night / Poor folks / Your kind of love / Mountain jive / Voodoo / You put the spell on me / Portrait of a man / Ol' man river / Heart attack and vine / I don't know / Don't deceive me / Whistling past the graveyard / Armpit #6 / I put a spell on you (1979 version) / Scream the blues.

Nov 97. (cd) *Prestige; (CDSGP 358)* **DON'T FOOL WITH ME**

Nov 97. (cd) *Music Club; (MCCD 322)* **THE BEST OF ALLIGATOR WINE**

Sep 98. (cd) *M.I.L.; <6121>* **SHE PUT THE WAMMEE ON ME** | - |

HAWKWIND

Formed: London, England ... mid-69 as GROUP X, by ex-FAMOUS CURE members DAVE BROCK and MICK SLATTERY, who were joined by NIK TURNER, TERRY OLLIS, DIK MIK and JOHN HARRISON. They subsequently became HAWKWIND ZOO, although SLATTERY opted out for a gypsy lifestyle in Ireland after they signed to 'United Artists' in late '69. Now as HAWKWIND and many free concerts later (mostly at open-air festivals), they released their eponymous debut in late summer 1970. While this album was a melange of bluesy, heavy psychedelic rock, the band added more personnel for the follow-up, 'IN SEARCH OF SPACE' (1971), including synth player DEL DETTMAR and vocalist/poet ROBERT CALVERT. His sci-fi musings featured heavily on the album, while the scattered electronic stabs and saxophone honking merged with the driving rhythm section to create their own tripped-out take on space rock. The record saw HAWKWIND break into the Top 20, while the following summer they smashed into the Top 3 with the classic 'SILVER MACHINE' (1972) single, LEMMY KILMISTER's pile-driving bass fuelling the beast with a turbo-charged power. The track previously featured on the live various artists 'GREASY TRUCKERS' PARTY' album, as well as appearing on the similar 'GLASTONBURY FAYRE' compilation. The success of the single secured the band Top 20 placings on all four of their future albums for 'United Artists', although come 1975, after the semi-classic 'WARRIOR ON THE EDGE OF TIME' album,

LEMMY had departed to form MOTORHEAD, while CALVERT had been replaced by sci-fi writer, MICHAEL MOORCOCK. HAWKWIND signed to 'Charisma' and despite continuing moderate success, were dogged by legal battles over their moniker (HAWKLORDS was used for one album, 1978's '25 YEARS ON'). With a substantially altered line-up, HAWKWIND continued to release albums on their own 'Flicknife' label throughout the 80's. Tragedy struck when CALVERT died from a heart attack on 14 August '88, although yet another line-up saw HAWKWIND into the 90's with the 'SPACE BANDITS' (1990) album. The band continue to attract a loyal following of die-hard hippies and the emergence of the psychedelic/crusty techno scene has done them no harm, many young stoners citing HAWKWIND as a prominent influence.
• **Songwriters:** Mostly by BROCK or CALVERT until the latter's departure, ALAN DAVEY eventually replacing him. Other various personnel over the years also took part in writing.

Album rating (original & group only): HAWKWIND (*6) / IN SEARCH OF SPACE (*8) / DOREMI FASOL LATIDO (*5) / SPACE RITUAL ALIVE (*8) / HALL OF THE MOUNTAIN KING (*6) / WARRIOR ON THE EDGE OF TIME (*7) / ROADHAWKS live collection (*6) / ASTOUNDING SOUNDS AND AMAZING MUSIC (*5) / QUARK, STRANGENESS AND CHARM (*4) / 25 YEARS ON (*4) / PRX 5 (*5) / LIVE 1979 (*4) / LEVITATION (*5) / SONIC ATTACK (*6) / CHURCH OF HAWKWIND (*6) / CHOOSE YOUR MASQUES (*6) / ZONES (*5) / THIS IS HAWKWIND, DO NOT PANIC (*4) / CHRONICLE OF THE BLACK SWORD (*6) / THE XENON CODEX (*6) / STASIS – THE U.A. YEARS 1971-1975 compilation (*8) / SPACE BANDITS (*6) / ELECTRIC TEEPEE (*6) / IT'S THE BUSINESS OF THE FUTURE TO BE DANGEROUS (*6) / THE BUSINESS TRIP (*4) / ALIEN 4 (*5) / LOVE IN SPACE (*5)

DAVE BROCK (b. 20 Aug'41, Isleworth, England) – vocals, guitar / **NIK TURNER** (b. 26 Aug'40, Oxford, England) – vocals, saxophone / **HUW-LLOYD LANGTON** – guitar repl. MICK SLATTERY (Oct69, when as HAWKWIND ZOO) **JOHN HARRISON** – bass / **TERRY OLLIS** – drums / **DIK MIK** (b. S. McMANUS, Richmond, England) – electronics engineer, synthesizers

	Liberty	U.A.
Jul 70. (7") *(LBF 15382)* **HURRY ON SUNDOWN. / MIRROR OF ILLUSION**		
Aug 70. (lp) *(LBS 83348) <5519>* **HAWKWIND**		

– Hurry on sundown / The reason is? / Be yourself / Paranoia (part 1 & 2) / Seeing is as you really are / Mirror of illusion. *(re-iss. Sep75 on 'Sunset'; SLS 50374) (re-iss. Feb80 as 'ROCKFILE' on 'United Artists'; LBR 1012) (re-iss. Feb84 on 'E.M.I.' lp/pic-lp; SLS/+P 1972921) (hit UK 75) (cd-iss. Feb94 on 'Repertoire';)*

—— (Sep'70) **THOMAS CRIMBLE** – bass repl. JOHN HARRISON / **DEL DETTMAR** – synthesizer repl. LANGTON (partway through next album)

—— (May'71) **DAVE ANDERSON** – bass (ex-AMON DUUL II) repl. CRIMBLE On stage they also added on vocals **ROBERT CALVERT** (b. 9 Mar'45, Pretoria, South Africa) – poet, vocals, **MICHAEL MOORCOCK** – sci-fi writer and **STACIA** – exotic dancer

	U.A.	U.A.
Oct 71. (lp) *(UAG 29202) <5567>* **IN SEARCH OF SPACE**	18	

– You shouldn't do that / You know you're only dreaming / Master of the universe / We took the wrong step years ago / Adjust me / Children of the sun. *(re-iss. Jan81 on 'Liberty'; LBG 29202) (re-iss. Jun85 on 'Liberty-EMI' lp/c; ATAK/TCATAK 9) (re-iss. Oct87 on 'Fame' lp/c; FA/TCFA 3192) (cd-iss. May89 & Dec95 on 'Fame'; CDFA 3192)*

—— (Sep'71) **LEMMY** (b. IAN KILMISTER, 24 Dec'45, Stoke-On-Trent, England) – bass, vocals repl. ANDERSON

—— (Jan'72) **SIMON KING** – drums (ex-OPAL BUTTERFLY) repl. OLLIS (group now KING, LEMMY, BROCK, TURNER, DIK MIK, DETTMAR, CALVERT, STACIA and p/t MOORCOCK)

| Jun 72. (7") *(UP 35381) <50949>* **SILVER MACHINE. / SEVEN BY SEVEN** | 3 | |

(re-iss. '76) (re-iss. Oct78, hit UK 34) (re-hit 67 when re-iss. Dec82 7"/7"pic-d/12"; UP/UPP/12UP 35381)

| Nov 72. (lp) *(UAG 29364) <LA 001>* **DOREMI FASOL LATIDO** | 14 | |

– Brainstorm / Space is deep / One change / Lord of light / Down through the night / Time we left this world today / The watcher. *(re-iss. 1979) (re-iss. Jun85 on 'Liberty-EMI') (US cd-iss. Jul91 on 'One Way')*

| May 73. (d-lp) *(UAD 60037-8) <LA 120>* **SPACE RITUAL – RECORDED LIVE IN LIVERPOOL AND LONDON** (live) | 9 | |

– Earth calling / Born to go / Down through the night / The awakening / Lord of light / The black corridor / Space is deep / Electronic No.1 / Orgone accumulator / Upside down / 10 seconds of forever / Brainstorm / 7 by 7 / Sonic attack / Time we left this world today / Master of the universe / Welcome to the future. *(re-iss. 1979;)*

| Aug 73. (7") *(UP 25566) <314>* **URBAN GUERILLA. / BRAINBOX POLLUTION** | 39 | |

—— Now a trim sex/septet when DIK MIK and CALVERT departed. The latter going solo. (Apr74) **SIMON HOUSE** – keyboards, synthesizers, violin (ex-THIRD EAR BAND, ex-HIGH TIDE) repl. DETTMAR who emigrated to Canada

| Aug 74. (7") *(UP 35715)* **PSYCHEDELIC WARLORDS (DISAPPEAR IN SMOKE). / IT'S SO EASY** | | |
| Sep 74. (lp/c) *(UAG/UAC 29672) <LA 328>* **HALL OF THE MOUNTAIN GRILL** | 16 | |

– The psychedelic warlords (disappear in smoke) / Wind of change / D-rider / Web weaver / You'd better believe it / Hall of the Mountain Grill / Lost Johnnie / Goat willow / Paradox. *(re-iss. Jan81 on 'Liberty'; LBG 29672) (re-iss. Jun85 on 'Liberty-EMI';) (re-iss. Sep85 on 'Fame'; FA41 3133-1) (cd-iss. May89 & Dec95; CD-FA 3133)*

—— added **ALAN POWELL** – 2nd drums (ex-STACKRIDGE, ex-CHICKEN SHACK, etc)

	Charisma	Atco
Mar 75. (7") *(UP 35808)* **KINGS OF SPEED. / MOTORHEAD**		
May 75. (lp/c) *(UAG/UAC 29766) <35115>* **WARRIOR ON THE EDGE OF TIME**	13	

– Assault and battery – part one / The golden void – part two / The wizard blew his horn / Opa-Loka / The demented man / Magnu / Standing at the edge / Spiral galaxy 28948 / Warriors / Dying seas / Kings of speed. *(re-iss. 1979; same) (re-*

iss. Jan81 + Jun85 on 'Liberty-EMI'; TCK 29766) (re-iss. Feb94 on 'Dojo'; DOJOCD 84)

—— **PAUL RUDOLPH** – bass (ex-PINK FAIRIES) repl. LEMMY who formed MOTORHEAD **BOB CALVERT** – vocals returned, STACIA the dancer left to get married. CALVERT and RUDOLPH now with BROCK, TURNER, KING, HOUSE and POWELL. note also that MOORCOCK left to form his DEEP FIX

		Charisma	Sire
Jul 76.	(7") *(CB 289)* **KERB CRAWLER. / HONKY DORKY**		-
Aug 76.	(lp/c) *(CDS 4004)* **ASTOUNDING SOUNDS, AMAZING MUSIC EMPORIUM**	33	-

– Reefer madness / Steppenwolf / City of lagoons / The aubergine that ate Rangoon / Kerb crawler / Kadu flyer / Chronoglide skyway. *(re-iss. Mar83; CHC 14) (cd-iss. Apr89 on 'Virgin'; CDSCD 4004)*

Jan 77.	(7") *(CB 299)* **BACK ON THE STREETS. / THE DREAM OF ISIS**		

—— **ADRIAN SHAW** – bass TURNER who formed SPHINX then INNER CITY BLUES

Jun 77.	(lp/c) *(CDS/CDC 4008)* <6047> **QUARK, STRANGENESS AND CHARM**	30	

– Spirit of the age / Damnation alley / Fable of a failed race / Quark, strangeness and charm / Hassan I Sahba / The forge of Vulcan / Days of the underground / Iron dream. *(re-iss. Oct86 lp/c; CHC/MC 50) (cd-iss. Apr89 on 'Virgin'; CDSCD 4008)*

Jul 77.	(7") *(CB 305)* **QUARK, STRANGENESS AND CHARM. / THE FORGE OF VULCAN**		-

—— **PAUL HAYLES** – keyboards repl. HOUSE who joined DAVID BOWIE on tour

HAWKLORDS

BROCK and CALVERT recruiting new members **STEVE SWINDELLS** – keyboards (ex-STRING DRIVEN THING, ex-PILOT) / **HARVEY BAINBRIDGE** – bass / **MARTIN GRIFFIN** – drums

		Charisma	Charisma
Oct 78.	(lp/c) *(CDS/CDC 4014)* <2203> **25 YEARS ON**	48	

– PSI power / Free fall / Automoton / 25 years / Flying doctor / The only ones / (only) The dead dreams of the cold war kid / The age of the micro man. *(re-iss. Aug82; CHC 10) (cd-iss. Apr89 on 'Virgin'; CDS4014)*

Oct 78.	(7") *(CB 323)* **PSI POWER. / DEATH TRAP**		-
Dec 78.	(7") <CAS 701> **PSI POWER.** / ('A'extended)	-	
Mar 79.	(7") *(CB 332)* **25 YEARS. / (ONLY) THE DEAD DREAMS OF THE COLD WAR KID**		

(12"grey+=) *(CB 332-12)* – P.X.R. 5.

HAWKWIND

recorded '78 by **BROCK, TURNER, SHAW, KING / + HAYLES**

May 79.	(lp/c) *(CDS 4016)* **P.X.R. 5**	59	-

– Death trap / Jack of shadows / Uncle Sam's on Mars / Infinity / Life form / Robot / High rise / P.X.R. 5. *(re-iss. Mar84; CHC 25) (cd-iss. Apr89 on 'Virgin'; CDSCD 4016)*

—— HAWKWIND in 1979 were **SIMON KING** – drums returned from QUASAR, to repl. GRIFFITHS in Dec78 (CALVERT left to go solo). **TIM BLAKE** – keyboards (ex-GONG) repl. SWINDELLS who went solo

—— added **HUW-LLOYD LANGTON** – guitar who returned from QUASAR —— now:- BROCK, LANGTON, BAINBRIDGE, KING & BLAKE

		Bronze	not iss.
Jul 80.	(lp/c) *(BRON/TCBRON 527)* **LIVE 1979 (live)**	15	-

– Shot down in the night / Motorway city / Spirit of the age / Brainstorm / Lighthouse / Master of the universe / Silver machine (requiem). *(cd-iss. Feb92 on 'Castle'; CLACD 243)*

Jul 80.	(7") *(BRO 98)* **SHOT DOWN IN THE NIGHT (live). / URBAN GUERILLA (live)**	59	-

—— **GINGER BAKER** – drums (ex-CREAM, ex-BLIND FAITH, ex-AIRFORCE etc) repl. KING who teamed up with SWINDELLS

Nov 80.	(7") *(BRO 109)* **WHO'S GONNA WIN THE WAR. / NUCLEAR TOYS**		-
Nov 80.	(blue-lp/c) *(BRON/TCBRON 530)* **LEVITATION**	21	-

– Levitation / Motorway city / Psychosis / World of tiers / Prelude / Who's gonna win the war / Space chase / The 5th second forever / Dust of time. *(re-iss. Jul87 on 'Castle' lp/cd; CLA/+CD 129)*

—— **MARTIN GRIFFIN** – drums returned to repl. BAKER / **KEITH HALE** – keyboards repl. BLAKE

		RCA Active	not iss.
Oct 81.	(7") *(RCA 137)* **ANGELS OF DEATH. / TRANS-DIMENSIONAL**		-
Oct 81.	(lp/c) *(RCA LP/K 6004)* **SONIC ATTACK**	19	-

– Sonic attack / Rocky paths / Psychosonia / Virgin of the world / Angels of death / Living on a knife edge / Coded languages / Disintigration / Streets of fear / Lost chances.

May 82.	(lp/c) *(RCA LP/K 9004)* **CHURCH OF HAWKWIND**	26	-

– Angel voices / Nuclear drive / Star cannibal / The phenomena of luminosity / Fall of Earth city / The church / The joker at the gate / Some people never die / Light specific data / Experiment with destiny / The last Messiah / Looking in the future. *(cd-iss. Jun94 on 'Dojo')*

—— **NIK TURNER** – vocals, saxophone returned to repl. HALE

Aug 82.	(7"/7"pic-d) *(RCA/+P 267)* **SILVER MACHINE (remix). / PSYCHEDELIC WARLORDS (remix)**		-
Oct 82.	(lp/c) *(RCA LP/K 6055)* **CHOOSE YOUR MASQUES**	29	-

– Choose your masques / Dream worker / Arrival in Utopia / Utopia / Silver machine / Void city / Solitary mind games / Fahrenheit 451 / The scan / Waiting for tomorrow.

		Flicknife	not iss.
Oct 83.	(lp) *(SHARP 014)* **ZONES** (live, with other 80's line-ups)	57	-

– Zones / Dangerous vision / Running through the back brain / The island / Motorway city / Utopia 84 / Society alliance / Sonic attack / Dream worker / Brainstorm. *(re-iss. Mar84 on pic-lp; PSHARP 014)*

Oct 83.	(7") *(FLS 025)* **MOTORWAY CITY (live). / MASTER OF THE UNIVERSE (live)**		-

Jan 84.	(7") *(7FLEP 104)* **NIGHT OF THE HAWKS. / GREEN FINNED DEMON**		-

(12"ep+=) *(FLEP 104)* - **THE EARTH RITUAL PREVIEW** – Dream dancers / Dragons + fables.

Nov 84.	(lp) *(SHARP 022)* **STONEHENGE: THIS IS HAWKWIND, DO NOT PANIC**		

– Psy power / Levitation / Circles / Space chase / Death trap / Angels of death / Shot down in the night / Stonehenge decoded / Watching the grass grow. *(cd-iss. May92 on 'Anagram'; CDM GRAM 54)*

—— **ALAN DAVEY** – bass, vocals repl. BAINBRIDGE and TURNER / **CLIVE DEAMER** – drums repl. GRIFFIN

Nov 85.	(lp/c/cd) *(SHARP 033/+C/CD)* **CHRONICLE OF THE BLACK SWORD**	65	

– Song of the swords / Shade gate / The sea king / The pulsing cavern / Elric the enchanter / Needle gun / Zarozinia / The demise / Sleep of a thousand tears / Chaos army / Horn of destiny. *(cd-iss. w / 3 extra tracks) (re-iss. cd Aug92 on 'Dojo'; DPJPCD 53)*

Nov 85.	(7") *(FLS 032)* **NEEDLE GUN. / ARIOCH**		

(12"+=) *(FLST 032)* – Song of the swords.

Mar 86.	(7") *(FLS 033)* **ZAROZINIA. / ASSAULT AND BATTERY**		

(12"+=) *(FLST 033)* – Sleep of a 1000 tears.

—— HAWKWIND are now **BROCK**, as **DR. HASBEEN** – vocals, guitar, keyboards, synthesizers, **LANGTON, DAVEY, BAINBRIDGE** now vocals, keyboards, synthesizer and **DANNY THOMPSON** – drums, percussion, vocals

		G.W.R.	Roadrunner
May 88.	(lp/c/cd) *(GW/+C/CD 26)* **THE XENON CODEX**	79	1989

– The war I survived / Wastelands of sleep / Neon skyline / Lost chronicles / Tides / Heads / Mutation zone / E.M.C. / Sword of the east / Good evening. *(US-iss. on pic-d)*

—— BROCK, BAINBRIDGE, DAVEY plus **SIMON HOUSE, RICHARD CHADWICK & BRIDGETT WISHART**

Oct 90.	(lp/c/cd) *(GW/+C/CD 103)* **SPACE BANDITS**	70	

– Images / Black elk speaks / Wings / Out of the shadows / Realms / Ship of dreams / TV suicide. *(re-iss. cd Feb92 on 'Castle'; CLACD 282)*

		Essential	not iss.
May 92.	(cd/c/d-lp) *(ESSCD/ESSMC/ESSD 181)* **ELECTRIC TEPEE**	53	-

– LSD / Blue shift / Death of war / The secret agent / Garden pests / Space dust / Snake dance / Mask of the morning / Rites of Netherworld / Don't understand / Sadness runs deep / Right to decide / Going to Hawaii / Electric teepee. *(re-iss. Jul95 on 'Dojo')*

Oct 93.	(cd/c/lp) *(ESD CD/MC/LP 196)* **IT IS THE BUSINESS OF THE FUTURE TO BE DANGEROUS**	75	

– It's the business of the future to be dangerous / Space is their (Palestine) / Tibet is not China (pt.1 & 2) / Let barking dogs lie / Wave upon wave / Letting in the past / The camera that could lie / 3 or 4 erections during the course of the night / Technotropic zone exists / Give me shelter / Avante.

		4 Real	not iss.
Jun 93.	(12"ep/c-ep/cd-ep) *(4R 1 T/CS/D)* **SPIRIT OF THE AGE (The Solstice remixes)**		-

– (Full Vocal / Hard Trance / Cyber Trance / Flesh To Phantasy)

Nov 93.	(12"ep/cd-ep) *(4R 2 T/D)* **DECIDE YOUR FUTURE EP**		-

– Right to decide / The camera that could lie / Right to decide (radio edit mix) / Assassin (Magick Carpet mix).

		Emergency	not iss.
Sep 94.	(12"ep/cd-ep) *(EBT/+D 110)* **QUARK, STRANGENESS AND CHARM**		-

– Uncle Sam's on Mars (Red Planet radio mix) / Quark, strangeness and charm / Black sun / Uncle Sam's on Mars (Martian Conquest mix).

Sep 94.	(cd/c/d-lp) *(EBS CD/MC/LP 111)* **THE BUSINESS TRIP (live)**		-

– Altair / Quark, strangeness and charm / LSD / The camera that would lie / Green finned demon / Do that / The day a wall came down / Berlin axis / Void of golden light / Right stuff / Wastelands / The dream goes on / Right to decide / The dream has ended / The future / Terra mystica.

Sep 95.	(12"ep/cd-ep) *(EB T/CD 107)* **AREA S.4.**		-

– Alien / Sputnik Stan / Medley: Death trap – Wastelands of sleep – Dream has . . . .

Oct 95.	(cd/lp) *(EB SCD/LP 118)* **ALIEN 4**		-

– Abducted / Alien (I am) / Reject your human touch / Blue skin / Beam me up / Vega / Xenomorph / Journey / Sputnik Stan / Kapal / Festivals / Deah trap / Wastelands / Are you losing your mind? / Space sex.

May 96.	(cd/lp) *(EBS CD/LP 120)* **LOVE IN SPACE (live October 1995)**		-

– Abducted / Death trap / Wastelands / Are you losing your mind? / Photo encounter / Blue skin / Robot / Alien I am / Sputnik Stan / Xenomorph / Vega / Love in space / Kapal / Elfin / Silver machine / Welcome.

– compilations, etc. –

1973.	(d7") *United Artists;* **HURRY ON SUNDOWN. / MASTER OF THE UNIVERSE/ / SILVER MACHINE. / ORGONE ACCUMULATOR**	-	
Apr 76.	(lp) *United Artists; (UAK 29919)* **ROADHAWKS**	34	

– Hurry on sundown / Paranoia (excerpt) / You shouldn't do that (live) / Silver machine (live) / Urban guerilla / Space is deep / Wind of change / The golden void. *(re-iss. Apr84 on 'Fame' lp/c; FA 413096-1/-4)*

Feb 77.	(lp) *United Artists; (UAG 30025)* **MASTERS OF THE UNIVERSE**		-

– Master of the universe / Brainstorm / Sonic attack / Orgone accumulator / It's so easy / Lost Johnnie. *(re-iss. May82 on 'Fame' lp/c; FA/C 3008) (re-iss. Jun87 & Dec95 on 'Liberty' lp/c; EMS/TCEMS 1258) (re-iss. May89 on 'Fame' lp/c/cd; FA/TCFA/CDFA 3220) (re-iss. Jul90 on 'Marble Arch' c/cd; CMA/+CD 129) (re-iss. Jul94 on 'Success' cd/c;) (cd-iss. Apr97 on 'Spalax'; 14972)*

Sep 80.	(lp/c) *Charisma; (BG/+C 2)* **REPEAT PERFORMANCE**		-

– Kerb crawler / Back on the streets / Quark strangeness and charm / Spirit of the age / Steppenwolf / 25 years / PSI power / The only ones / High rise / Uncle Sam's on Mars.

May 81.	(12"ep; as HAWKWIND ZOO) *Flicknife; (FLEP 100)* **HURRY ON SUNDOWN. / SWEET MISTRESS OF PAIN / KINGS OF SPEED (live)**		-

(re-iss. Dec83)

Jul 81.	(7"/12") *Flicknife; (FLS/+EP 205)* **MOTORHEAD. / VALIUM TEN**		-

(re-iss. 12" Oct82)

Nov 81. (12"ep; as SONIC ASSASSINS) *Flicknife; (FLEP 101)* **OVER THE TOP. / FREEFALL / DEATH TRAP**

Mar 82. (lp) *Flicknife; (SHARP 001)* **FRIENDS & RELATIONS** (1/2 live '77-78, 1/2 studio '82)
(re-iss. Nov83) (re-iss. Nov94 on 'Emporio' cd/c)

Jun 82. (7"; as HAWKLORDS) *Flicknife; (FLS 209)* **WHO'S GONNA WIN THE WAR. / TIME OFF**

Feb 83. (7") *Flicknife; (FLS 14)* **HURRY ON SUNDOWN. / LORD OF THE HORNETS / DODGEM DUKE**

Mar 83. (d-c) *Charisma; (CASMC 110)* **QUARK, STRANGENESS & CHARM / PXR 5**
(re-iss. '88)

1983. (lp) *Flicknife; (SHARP 107)* **TWICE UPON A TIME: HAWKWIND FRIENDS AND RELATIONS VOL.2**

Jul 83. (d-lp) *Illuminated; (JAMS 29)* **TEXT OF FESTIVAL** (live '70-72)
(1-lp re-iss. Jul85 as 'IN THE BEGINNING' on 'Demi Monde'; DM 005) (re-iss. cd Mar94 on 'Charly') (re-iss. Dec88 on 'Thunderbolt'; THBL 2.068) (cd-iss. first 3 sides) (cd re-iss. Mar97; CDTB 068)

Jun 84. (10"m-lp) *Flicknife; (SHARP 109)* **INDEPENDENTS DAY**
Nov 84. (d-lp/d-c) *A.P.K.; (APK/+C 8)* **SPACE RITUAL 2** (live)
(cd-iss. 1987 on 'The CD Label'; CDTL 003)

Feb 85. (lp) *Demi-Monde; (DM 002)* **BRING ME THE HEAD OF YURI GAGARIN** (live '73 Empire Pool)
(cd-iss. Nov86 on 'Charly'; CDCHARLY 40) (cd-iss. Nov92 on 'Thunderbolt'; CDTB 101) (cd re-iss. Apr97 on 'Spalax'; 14846)

Feb 85. (lp) *Flicknife; (SHARP 024)* **HAWKWIND, FRIENDS AND RELATIONS VOL.3**
(c-iss.Apr84 with VOL.1 on reverse; SHARP C1024) (other c-iss.Apr84 with VOL.2 on reverse; SHARP C2024)

Jul 85. (lp) *Dojo; (DOJOLP 11)* **LIVE 70-73** (live)
May 85. (lp) *Mausoleum; (SKULL 8333369)* **UTOPIA 1984**
Nov 85. (lp) *Mausoleum; (SKULL 83103)* **WELCOME TO THE FUTURE**
Nov 85. (lp) *Obsession; (OBLP 1)* **RIDICULE**
(re-iss. of disc 2 of 'SPACE RITUAL') (re-iss. 1990 cd/lp; OBSESS CD/LP 1)

Nov 85. (lp/pic-lp)(cd) *Samurai; (SAMR 038/+PD)(SAMRCD 038)* **ANTHOLOGY – HAWKWIND VOL.1**
(cd+=) – Silver machine. (re-iss. pic-lp.Nov86 as 'APPROVED HISTORY OF HAWKWIND'; SAMR 046) (re-iss. Apr90 as 'ACID DAZE 1' on 'Receiver'; RR 125)

Mar 86. (lp/cd)(c) *Samurai; (SAMR/+CD 039)(TCSAMR 039)* **ANTHOLOGY – HAWKWIND VOL. 2**
(cd-iss. 1986 extra 4 tracks) (re-iss. Apr90 as 'ACID DAZE 2' on 'Receiver'; RR 126)

May 86. (7"/7"sha-pic-d) *Samurai; (HW 7001/001)* **SILVER MACHINE. / MAGNU**
(12"+=) (HW12-001) – Angels of death.

Jul 86. (7") *Flicknife; (FLS 034-A)* **MOTORHEAD. / HURRY ON SUNDOWN**

Jul 86. (lp/c) *Samurai; (SAMR 040/+TC)* **ANTHOLOGY – HAWKWIND VOL.3**
(re-iss. Apr90 as 'ACID DAZE 3' on 'Receiver'; RR 127)

Jul 86. (lp) *Hawkfan; (HWFB 2)* **HAWKFAN 12**
Sep 86. (d-lp/d-c/cd) *Castle; (CCS LP/MC/CD 148)* **THE HAWKWIND COLLECTION (Pts. 1 & 2)**
(cd-iss. Dec86 omits some tracks)

Nov 86. (lp/c) *Flicknife; (SHARP 036/+C)* **INDEPENDENTS DAY VOL.2**
Jan 87. (lp/c) *R.C.A.; (NL/NK 71150)* **ANGELS OF DEATH**
Apr 87. (lp/c/cd) *Flicknife; (SHARP 040/+C/CD)* **OUT AND INTAKE**
(cd+=) – (2 extra tracks).

Sep 87. (lp/c/cd) *Start; (STF L/C/CD 2)* **BRITISH TRIBAL MUSIC**
Oct 87. (3xbox-pic-lp) *Flicknife; (HWBOX 1)* **OFFICIAL PICTURE LOGBOOK**
– ('STONEHENGE' / 'BLACK SWORD' / 'OUT & INTAKE' / '(interview)' lp
(cd-iss. Nov94 on 'Dojo';)

Dec 87. (lp/c) *Thunderbolt; (THBL/THBC 044)* **EARLY DAZE (THE BEST OF HAWKWIND)**
(cd-iss. Jun88; CDTB CDTB 044)

Sep 88. (cd) *Virgin; (COMCD 8)* **SPIRIT OF THE AGE**
(re-iss. Oct91 on 'Elite'; ELITE 021CD) (re-iss. Sep 93)

Nov 88. (cd) *Flicknife; (SHARP 1422CD)* **ZONES / STONEHENGE**
Nov 88. (cd) *Flicknife; (SHARP 1724CD)* **BEST OF HAWKWIND, FRIENDS & RELATIONS**
Dec 88. (d-lp/cd) *Flicknife; (SHARP 2045/+CD)* **THE TRAVELLERS AID TRUST**

Dec 88. (d-lp/d-c) *That's Original; (TFO 17/+CD)* **LEVITATION / HAWKWIND LIVE**
Mar 89. (cd) *Avanti; (ISTCD 004)* **IRONSTRIKE**
May 89. (lp) *Legacy; (GWSP 1)* **LIVE CHRONICLES**
(re-iss. Feb92 cd/c on 'Castle'; CCS CD/MC 123)

May 89. (lp/c/cd) *Powerhouse; (POW/+C/CD 5502)* **NIGHT OF THE HAWK**
(cd-iss. has 3 extra tracks)

1990. (cd/c) *Action Replay; (ARLC/CDAR 1018)* **BEST AND THE REST OF HAWKWIND**

Mar 90. (2xcd-box)(3xlp-box) *Receiver; (RRDCD 1X)(RRBX 1)* **ACID DAZE (re-issue)**
(3 VOLUMES re-iss. cd Jul93)

May 90. (cd)(c/lp) *E.M.I.; (CDP 746694-2)(TC+/NTS 300)* **STASIS, THE U.A. YEARS 1971-1975**
– Urban guerilla / Psychedelic warlords (disappear in smoke) / Brainbox pollution / 7 by 7 / Paradox / Silver machine / You'd better believe it / Lord of light / The black corridor (live) / Space is deep (live) / You shouldn't do that (live). (re-iss. cd Dec95 on 'Fame')

Dec 90. (12"blue-ep) *Receiver; (REPLAY 3014)* **THE EARLY YEARS LIVE**
– Silver machine / Spirit of the age / Urban guerilla / Born to go.

1990. (c) *Capitol; <4XLL 57286>* **METAL CLASSICS 2: BEST OF HAWKWIND**

1990. (cd/c) *Knight; (KN CD/MC 10017)* **NIGHT RIDING**
Jun 91. (lp/c/cd) *G.W.R.; (GW/+MC/CD 104)* **PALACE SPRINGS**
– (remixed tracks from 'WARRIORS . . . ' & 'XENON . . .) (re-iss. cd Jul92 on 'Castle'; CLACD 303)

Oct 91. (cd/c) *Windsong; (WIN CD/MC 007)* **BBC RADIO 1 LIVE IN CONCERT** (live)

Feb 92. (3xcd-box) *Castle; (CLABX 911)* **3 ORIGINALS**
Feb 92. (cd) *Raw Fruit; (FRSCD 005)* **THE FRIDAY ROCK SHOW SESSIONS** (live '86)

Jun 92. (cd) *Anagram; (GRAM 53)* **MIGHTY HAWKWIND CLASSICS 1980-1985**
Aug 92. (cd) *Dojo; (DOJOCD 71)* **HAWKLORDS LIVE**
Apr 94. (cd) *Cleopatra; (CLEO 57732)* **LORD OF LIGHT**
Apr 94. (cd) *Cleopatra; (CLEO 57412)* **PSYCHEDELIC WARLORDS**
Dec 94. (cd) *Cyclops; (CYCL 021)* **CALIFORNIA BRAINSTORM**
Feb 95. (cd) *Emergency Broadcast; (EMBSCD 114)* **UNDISCLOSED FILES – ADDENDUM**

Mar 95. (cd) *Anagram; (CDMGRAM 91)* **THE RARITIES . . .**
May 95. (cd) *Spectrum; (550764-2)* **SILVER MACHINE**
Oct 95. (cd) *Anagram; (CDGRAM 94)* **INDEPENDENTS DAY VOLUMES 1 & 2**

Mar 97. (cd) *Emporio; (EMPRCD 710)* **ONWARD FLIES THE BIRD – LIVE AND RARE**
Jul 97. (cd-ep) *E.B.S.; (EBCD 106)* **LOVE IN SPACE / LORD OF LIGHT / SONIC ATTACK**

ROBERT CALVERT

	U.A.	U.A.

May 74. (lp) *(UAG 29507)* **CAPTAIN LOCKHEED AND THE STARFIGHTERS**
– Franz Joseph Strauss / The aerospace inferno / Aircraft salesman / The widow maker / Test pilots / The right stuff / Board meeting / The song of the gremlin / Ground crew / Hero with a wing / Ground control to pilot / Ejection / Interview / I resign / The song of the gremlin (part 2) / Bier garten / Catch a falling starfighter (the gremlin). (re-iss. Jan87 on 'Beat Goes On' lp/cd; BGO/+CD 5)

Jun 74. (7"; as CAPTAIN LOCKHEED AND THE STARFIGHTERS) *(UP 35543) <297>* **CATCH A FALLING STARFIGHTER (THE GREMLIN). / EJECTION**

Sep 75. (lp) *(UAG 29852)* **LUCKY LIEF AND THE LONGSHIPS**
– Ship of fools / The lay of the surfers / Brave new world / Voyaging to inland / The making of Midgare / Moonshine in the mountains / Magical potion / Stormchant of the Skraelings / Volstead o vodeo do / Phase locked lopp / Ragna rock. (re-iss. Mar87 on 'Beat Goes On'; BGO 2) (cd-iss. Jan89; BGOCD 2)

	Wake Up	not iss.

Jul 79. (7"green-flexi; as ROBERT CALVERT and the 1st X1) *(WUR 5)* **CRICKET STAR**

	Flicknife	not iss.

1981. (7") *(FLS 204)* **LORD OF THE HORNETS. / THE GREENFLY & THE ROSE**

	A-side	not iss.

Sep 81. (m-lp) *(IF 0311)* **HYPE (THE SONGS OF TOM MAHLER)**
– Over my head / Ambitious / It's the same / Hanging out on the seafront / Sensitive / Evil rock / We like to be frightened / Teen ballad of Deano / Flight 105 / The luminous green glow of the dials of the dashboard (at night) / The greenfly & the rose / Lord of the hornets. (re-iss. Dec89 on 'See For Miles' lp/cd; SEE/+CD 278)

	Flicknife	not iss.

Sep 84. (m-lp) *(SHGARP 021)* **FREQ**
– Ned Ludd / Acid rain / All the machines are quiet / Picket line / The cool courage of the bomb squad / Work song. (cd-iss. Jun92 as 'FREQ REVISITED' on 'Anagram' +=; CDMGRAM 55) – Lord of the hornets / The greenfly & the rose.

	Demi-Monde	not iss.

Apr 86. (lp) *(DM 1010)* **TEST-TUBE CONCEIVED**
– Telekinesis / I hear voices / Fanfare for the perfect race / On line / Save them from the scientists / Fly on the wall / Thanks to the scientists / ? / In vitro / Breed / The rah rah band. (cd-iss. Aug87 on 'The CD Label'; CDTL 007)

—— On 14 Aug'88, ROBERT CALVERT died of a heart attack.

– (CALVERT) posthumous, etc. –

Aug 89. (lp; mail-order) *Clear; (BLACK 1)* **ROBERT CALVERT AT THE QUEEN ELIZABETH HALL** (live)
(cd-iss. May93 on 'Beat Goes On';)
Oct 92. (cd) *Beat Goes On; (BGOCD 135)* **BLUEPRINTS FROM THE CELLAR**

Barry HAY (see under ⇒ GOLDEN EARRING)

Isaac HAYES

Born: 20 Aug'38, Covington, Tennessee, USA. As a teenager he moved to Memphis, where he learned to play sax and piano. He was soon invited to session for the 'Stax' label in the mid-60's, eventually forming a writing partnership with DAVID PORTER. The pair were highly successful, going on to pen for 'Stax' artists such as OTIS REDDING, SAM & DAVE, EDDIE FLOYD and CARLA THOMAS. After a rambling, jazz-based debut album in 1968, the follow-up, 'HOT BUTTERED SOUL' (1969), gave him a US Top 10 placing and gained widespread respect from critics for its highly original interpretations of standards like JIMMY WEBB's 'BY THE TIME I GET TO PHOENIX'. Establishing himself as the original medallion man, self-styled love-God HAYES created sophisticated mood pieces; stretching songs over seemingly unfeasible, elaborately orchestrated lengths, the singer patented a breathy, often spoken, vocal style, his black velvet tones proving a hit with fans of easy listening, jazz, R&B, pop and rock. Subsequent efforts like 'TO BE CONTINUED' (1970) and 'BLACK MOSES' (1972) followed the same formula although, in late '71, his score for blaxploitation movie, 'SHAFT' provided him with an international smash hit in the wah wah-funk of the main theme. Both the single and the soundtrack album itself toppped the American charts, the latter winning an academy award. Its success spawned a glut of similar films such as 'BLACK CAESAR' (scored by JAMES BROWN) and 'SUPERFLY' (scored by CURTIS MAYFIELD), HAYES himself issuing two further soundtracks on 'Stax', 'TOUGH GUYS' (1974) and TRUCK TURNER (1974) as well as releasing a theme from US cop TV series 'The Men' in 1972. The singer left 'Enterprise-Stax' in 1975 following a disagreement over non-payment of royalties, signing to 'A.B.C.' the same year. As he experimented with disco (a genre he'd laid the foundations for), however, his work lost its impact and, amid mediocre album sales and bankruptcy in '77, he shifted to 'Polydor'. The move failed to resurrect his flagging career and in the 80's, after serving a brief jail term for drug offences, he became more interested in film acting. HAYES had previously acted in the likes of 'TRUCK TURNER' as well as appearing in 'The Rockford Files' in 1977 with DIONNE WARWICK (with whom he also recorded an album of duets the same year). 1981 saw him playing a baddie (what else!) in the film 'Escape From New York' while the mid-80's were marked by cameo appearances in TV series 'The A-Team' and 'Hunter'. The HAYES' legend was given a bit of a dusting down in the late 80's when numerous hip hop and house tunes sampled 'THEME FROM SHAFT'. Similarly, in the 90's, trip hop artists like MASSIVE ATTACK, TRICKY and PORTISHEAD borrowed from the singer's back catalogue, coinciding with HAYES' best album since his early 70's heyday, 'BRANDED' (1995). With the singer back on smoking form, he put in typically elaborate readings of STING's 'FRAGILE' and the LOVIN' Spoonful's 'SUMMER IN THE CITY' (not as ridiculous as it appears on paper) as well as updating classics like 'SOULSVILLE' and 'HYPERBOLICSYLLABICSESQUEDALYMYSTIC'. The latter featured a guest spot by PUBLIC ENEMY's CHUCK D, things coming full circle and illustrating the pivotal influence of HAYES on the development of rap. In recent times, HAYES has contributed his deep-throated larynx as CHEF to adult(!?) animation, 'South Park'; he was even back in the charts with the team's 'Chocolate Salty Balls'; who killed ISAAC? • Covers: WALK ON BY (Bacharach-David) / I STAND ACCUSED (Jerry Butler) / THE LOOK OF LOVE (Lesley Gore ;hit?) / NEVER CAN SAY GOODBYE (Jackson 5) / YOU'VE LOST THAT LOVIN' FEELIN' (Righteous Brothers) / LET'S STAY TOGETHER (Al Green) / HEY GIRL (Freddie Scott) / LET'S GO OUT TONIGHT (Blue Nile) / etc.

Album rating: PRESENTING ISAAC HAYES (*5) / HOT BUTTERED SOUL (*9) / THE ISAAC HAYES MOVEMENT (*8) / TO BE CONTINUED (*6) / SHAFT soundtrack (*7) / BLACK MOSES (*5) / LIVE AT THE SAHARA TAHOE (*4) / JOY (*5) / TOUGH GUYS (*4) / TRUCK TURNER (*4) / CHOCOLATE CHIP (*6) / THE BEST OF ISAAC HAYES compilation (*6) / DISCO CONNECTION (*4) / GROOVE-A-THON (*3) / JUICY FRUIT (DISCO FREAK) (*3) / A MAN AND A WOMAN with Dionne Warwick (*3) / NEW HORIZON (*3) / FOR THE SAKE OF LOVE (*3) / DON'T LET GO (*4) / ROYAL RAPPIN'S with Millie Jackson (*4) / AND ONCE AGAIN (*4) / LIFETIME THING (*4) / U-TURN (*4) / LOVE ATTACK (*4) / ISAAC'S MOODS – THE BEST OF ISAAC HAYES compilation (*8) / BRANDED (*6)

ISAAC HAYES – vocals, keyboards, etc. with Stax session men **DUCK DUNN** and **AL JACKSON**

		Stax	Enterprise
1968.	(lp) <13100> **PRESENTING ISAAC HAYES**	-	

– Precious, precious / When I fall in love / I just want to make love to me / Rock me baby / Going to Chicago blues / Misty / You don't know like I know. <re-iss. Mar72 as 'IN THE BEGINNING' on 'Atlantic'; 1599>

| 1968. | (7") <ENA 002> **GOING TO CHICAGO BLUES. / PRECIOUS PRECIOUS** | - | |
| Oct 69. | (lp) (SXATS 1028) <1001> **HOT BUTTERED SOUL** | 8 | Jul69 |

– Walk on by / Hyperbollesyllaciscesquelalymistc / One woman / By the time I get to Phoenix. (re-iss. Aug71; 2325 011) (re-iss. Aug81 lp/c; STAXL/STAXK 5002) (re-iss. Nov87; SXE 005) (cd-iss. Jun91 on 'Stax-Ace')

Sep 69.	(7") (STAX 133) <ENA 9003> **BY THE TIME I GET TO PHOENIX. / WALK ON BY**	37	Aug69
		30	
Nov 69.	(7") <ENA 9006> **THE MISTLETOE AND ME. / WINTER SNOW**	-	Xmas
May 70.	(lp) (SXATS 1032) <1010> **THE ISAAC HAYES MOVEMENT**	8	Apr70

– I stand accused / One big unhappy family / I just don't know what to do with myself / Something. (re-iss. Aug71; 2325 014) (re-iss. Feb90 cd/lp; CD+/SXE 025)

| Aug 70. | (7") (STAX 154) <ENA 9017> **I STAND ACCUSED. / I JUST DON'T KNOW WHAT TO DO WITH MYSELF** | 42 | Jul70 |

<re-iss. US 1975>

<other 45's from early to mid-70's were also re-issued>

| Dec 70. | (lp) (2325 026) <1014> **TO BE CONTINUED** | 11 | Nov70 |

– (monologue) / Ike's rap 1 / Our day will come / The look of love / Ike's mood – You've lost that lovin' feelin' / Runnin' out of fools. (re-iss. Oct81 lp/c; STAX L/K 5008) (cd-iss. Feb91 on 'Stax-Ace')

Feb 71.	(7") <ENA 9028> **THE LOOK OF LOVE. / IKE'S MOOD**	-	79
May 71.	(7") (2025 020) **YOU'VE LOST THAT LOVIN' FEELIN'. / OUR DAY WILL COME**	-	-
Sep 71.	(7") (2025 029) <ENA 9031> **NEVER CAN SAY GOODBYE. / I CAN'T HELP IT IF I'M STILL IN LOVE**	22	May71
Nov 71.	(7") (2025 069) <ENA 9038> **THEME FROM "SHAFT". / CAFE REGIO'S**	4	1	Oct71
Dec 71.	(d-lp) (2659 007) <5002> **SHAFT (Soundtrack)**	17	1	Oct71

– Theme from Shaft * / Bumpy's lament / Walk from Regio's / Ellie's love theme / Shaft's cab ride / Cafe Regio's / Early Sunday morning / Be yourself / A friend's place / Soulsville * / No name bar / Bumpy's blues / Shaft strikes again / Do your thing * / (the end theme). (tracks *= have vocals)
(above has background vocals by **HOT BUTTERED + SOUL**)

| Feb 72. | (d-lp) (2628 004) <5003> **BLACK MOSES** | 38 | 10 | Dec71 |

– Never can say goodbye / (They long to be) Close to you / Nothing takes the place of you / Man's temptation / Part time love / Ike's rap – A brand new me / Going in circles / Gonna give you up / Ike's rap 2 – Help me love / Need to belong / Good love / Ike's rap 3 – Your love is so doggone good / For the good times / I'll never fall in love again. (re-iss. +cd.Sep90 on 'Stax-Ace')

Feb 72.	(7") <ENA 9042> **DO YOUR THING. / ELLIE'S LOVE THEME**	-	30
Apr 72.	(7") **LET'S STAY TOGETHER. / AIN'T THAT LOVING YOU (FOR MORE REASONS THAN ONE)**	-	-
Apr 72.	(7") <ENA 9045> **LET'S STAY TOGETHER. / SOULSVILLE**	-	48
May 72.	(7"; by ISAAC HAYES & DAVID PORTER) <ENA 9049> **AIN'T THAT LOVING YOU (FOR MORE REASONS THAN ONE). / BABY I'M A WANT YOU**		
Nov 72.	(7") (2025 146) <ENA 9058> **THEME FROM THE MEN. / TYPE THANG**	38	Oct72

(above was from US TV cop series, 'The Men')

| Jun 73. | (d-lp) (2659 026) <5005> **LIVE AT SAHARA TAHOE (live)** | 14 | May73 |

– Theme from "Shaft" / The come on / Light my fire / Ike's rap / Never can say goodbye / Windows of the world / The look of love / Ellie's love theme / Use me / Do your thing / Theme from The Men / It's too late / Rock me baby / Stormy Monday blues / Type thang / The first time ever I saw your face / Ike's rap VI / Ain't no sunshine / Feelin' alright. (re-iss. Nov86 lp/c; MPS/+5 88004) (cd-iss. Oct92)

| Nov 73. | (lp) (2325 111) <5007> **JOY** | 16 | Oct73 |

– Joy / I love you that's all / A man will be a man / The feeling keeps on coming / I'm gonna love (without you). (cd-iss. Jun92)

Nov 73.	(7") (2025 177) <ENA 9065> **(IF LOVING YOU IS WRONG) I DON'T WANT TO BE RIGHT. / ROLLING DOWN A MOUNTAINSIDE**		
Dec 73.	(7") (202 5220) <ENA 9085> **JOY (part 1). / JOY (part 2)**	30	
May 74.	(7") <ENA 9095> **WONDERFUL. / SOMEONE MADE YOU FOR ME**	-	71
Jun 74.	(lp) (STXH 5001) <7504> **TOUGH GUYS (Soundtrack)**		

– (title theme) / Randolph & Dearborn / The red rooster / Joe Bell / Hung up on my baby / Kidnapped / Run Fay run / Buns o'plenty / (the end theme).

| Aug 74. | (7") (STXS 2004) <ENA 9104> **TITLE THEM ('TRUCK TURNER'). / HUNG UP ON MY BABY** | | |
| Aug 74. | (d-lp) (STXD 4001-2) <7507> **TRUCK TURNER (Soundtrack)** | | Jul74 |

– Truck Turner / House of beauty / Blue's crib / Driving in the Sun / You're in my arms again / Give it to me / Drinking / Insurance company / Breakthrough / Now we're one / The duke / Dorinda's party / Pursuit of the pimpmobile / We need each other girl / A house full of girls / Hospital shootout / (end theme).

		A.B.C.	A.B.C.
Jun 75.	(lp) (ABCL 5129) <874> **CHOCOLATE CHIP**		18

– That loving feeling / Body language / Chocolate chip / Chocolate chip (instrumental) / I want to make love to you so bad / Come live with me / I can't turn around.

| Jul 75. | (7") (ABC 4076) <12118> **CHOCOLATE CHIP. / ('A'instrumental)** | | 92 |
| Dec 75. | (lp; as ISAAC HAYES MOVEMENT) <923> **DISCO CONNECTION** | - | 85 |

– The first day of forever / St. Thomas Square / Vykkii / Disco connection / Disco shuffle / Choppers / After five / Aruba.

| Feb 76. | (7") (ABC 4100) <12171> **DISCO CONNECTION. / ST. THOMAS SQUARE** | 10 | |
| Feb 76. | (lp) (ABCL 5155) <925> **GROOVE A THON** | | 45 |

– Groove-a-thon / Your loving is much too strong / Rock me easy baby / We've got a whole lot of love / Wish you were here / Make a little love to me.

| Jun 76. | (7") (ABC 4111) <12176> **ROCK ME EASY BABY. / (part 2)** | | |
| Jul 76. | (lp) <953> **JUICY FRUIT (DISCO FREAK)** | - | |

– Juicy fruit (disco freak) / Let's don't ever blow our thing / The storm is over / Music to make love by / Thank you love / Lady of the night / Love me or lose me.

| Aug 76. | (7") (ABC 4136) <12206> **JUICY FRUIT (DISCO FREAK). / (part 2)** | | |
| Mar 77. | (d-lp; by ISAAC HAYES & DIONNE WARWICK) (ABCD 613) <996> **A MAN AND A WOMAN** | 49 | Feb77 |

– Unity / Just don't know what to do with myself / Walk on by / My love / The way I want to touch you – Have you never been mellow – Love will keep us together – I love music – This will be (an everlasting love) – That's the way I like it – Get down tonight / By the time I get to Phoenix / I say a little prayer / Then came you / Feelings / My eyes adored you / Body language / Can't hide love / Come love with me / Once you hit the road / Chocolate chip.

| Aug 77. | (12") (ABE12 007) **DISCO CONNECTION. / CHOCOLATE CHIP** | | - |

		not iss.	Stax
Nov 77.	(7") <3209> **FEEL LIKE MAKIN' LOVE. / (part 2)**	-	-

		Polydor	Polydor
Dec 77.	(lp) <6120> **NEW HORIZON**	-	78

– Stranger in Paradise / Moonlight lovin' / Don't take your love away / Out of the ghetto / It's heaven to me.

Jan 78.	(7") <14446> **OUT OF THE GHETTO. / IT'S HEAVEN TO ME**	-	
May 78.	(7") (2066 904) <14464> **MOONLIGHT LOVIN'. / IT'S HEAVEN TO ME**	-	
Dec 78.	(lp) (2480 475) <6164> **FOR THE SAKE OF LOVE**	75	Nov78

– Just the way you are / Believe in me / If we ever needed peace / Shaft II / Zeke the freak / Don't let me be lonely tonight.

| Jan 79. | (7"/12") (POSP/+X 23) **ZEKE THE FREAK. / IF WE EVER NEEDED PEACE** | | |
| Mar 79. | (7") <14534> **JUST THE WAY YOU ARE. / (part 2)** | - | - |

———— (Later '79, he was credited with MILLIE JACKSON on 'Royal Rappin's' album <6229> which hit US No.80)

———— Also issued 2 US singles with her on 'Polydor'; DO YOU WANNA MAKE LOVE / I CHANGED MY MIND <2036> and YOU NEVER CROSS MY MIND / FEELS LIKE THE FIRST TIME <2063>

| Nov 79. | (lp) (2480 510) <6224> **DON'T LET GO** | 39 | Sep79 |

– Don't let go / What does it take / Few more kisses to go / Fever / Someone who will take the place of you.

| Dec 79. | (7"/12") (STEP/+X 4) <2011> **DON'T LET GO. / YOU CAN'T HOLD YOUR WOMAN** | 18 | Oct79 |

Feb 80. (7") *<2068>* **FEW MORE KISSES TO GO. / WHAT DOES IT TAKE**

May 80. (lp) *(2480 538) <6269>* **AND ONCE AGAIN** — 59
– It's all in the game / Ike's rap VII – This time I'll be sweeter / I ain't ever / Wherever you are / Love has been good to us.

Jun 80. (7") *(2001 965) <2090>* **I AIN'T EVER. / LOVE HAS BEEN GOOD TO US**

Sep 80. (7") *<2102>* **IT'S ALL IN THE GAME. / WHEREVER YOU ARE**

Sep 81. (7") *<2182>* **I'M GONNA MAKE ME LOVE YOU. / I'M SO PROUD**

Sep 81. (lp) *(2311 074)* **LIFETIME THING**
– I'm gonna make you love me / Three times a lady / Fugitive / Summer / I'm so proud / Lifetime thing.

Nov 81. (7") *<2192>* **LIFETIME THING. / FUGITIVE**

—— Took time out to concentrate on spiraling acting career. He had previously acted in own soundtrack films, 'Truck Turner', etc. He also appeared in 'The Rockford Files' with DIONNE WARWICK in 1977. In 1981, he plays a baddie (what else!) in the film 'Escape From New York'. In 85-86, he cameoed in TV for series 'The A-Team' + 'Hunter'.
(Returned in '86, plays everything)

C.B.S.   Columbia

Dec 86. (7") *(650204-7) <06363>* **HEY GIRL. / IKE'S RAP VIII**
(12"+=) *(650236-6)* – Hey Fred (you need a sunbed).

Dec 86. (lp) *(450 155-1) <40316>* **U-TURN**
– If you want my lovin' (do me right) / Flash backs / You turn me on / Ike's rap VIII – Hey girl / Doesn't rain in London / Can't take my eyes off you / Thing for you / Thank God for love.

Mar 87. (7") *<06655>* **THING FOR YOU. / THANK GOD FOR LOVE**

Jun 87. (7") *<07104>* **IF YOU WANT MY LOVIN' (DO ME RIGHT). / (part 2)**

Jul 88. (7") *<07978>* **SHOWDOWN. / (part 2)**

Nov 88. (lp/c) *(462515-1/-4/-2) <FC 40941>* **LOVE ATTACK** — Oct88
– Love attack / Let me be your everything / Showdown / Eye of the storm / Accused rap / I stand accused '88 / She's got a way / Foreplay rap / Love won't let me wait.

Dec 88. (7") *<08116>* **LET ME BE YOUR EVERYTHING. / CURIOUS**

—— He once again appeared in films (i.e. 'Counter Force' + 'The Sofia Conspiracy').

PointBlank Pointblank

May 95. (cd/c/lp) *(VPB CD/TC/LP 24)* **BRANDED**
– Ike's plea / Life's mood / Fragile / Life's mood II / Summer in the city / Let me love you / I'll do anything (to turn you on) / Thanks to the fool / Branded / Soulsville / Hyperbolicsyllabicesquedalymistic.

Jun 95. (c-s/12") *(POB C/T 12)* **FRAGILE. / FRAGILE / BIRTH OF SHAFT**
(cd-s+=) *(POBD 12)* – Let's go out tonight.

Jul 95. (cd/c/lp) *(VPB CD/MC/LP 25)* **RAW AND REFINED**
– Birth of Shaft / Urban nights / Funkalicious / Tahoe Spring / The night before / Memphis trax / Soul fiddle / Funky junky / You make me live / Making love at the ocean / Southern breeze / Didn't know love was so good / 405.

– compilations, others, etc. –

on 'Stax' UK / 'Enterprise' US unless mentioned otherwise

Sep 75. (lp) **THE BEST OF ISAAC HAYES**

Oct 75. (7") *(STX 2035)* **GOOD LOVE 6-9969. / I'M GONNA HAVE TO TELL HER**

Nov 75. (lp) **USE ME**

Mar 76. (lp/c) *Golden Hour; (GH 844)* **THE GOLDEN HOUR OF . . .**

1977. (lp) **MEMPHIS MOVEMENT**

1977. (7") *(STAX 2002)* **THEME FROM SHAFT. / DO YOUR THING**

Nov 77. (7") *(STAX 1009)* **THEME FROM SHAFT. / I DON'T WANT TO BE RIGHT**

1978. (lp) *<4102>* **HOT BED** (rarities)
(cd-iss. Aug94)

Apr 78. (lp) *(STM 7003)* **THE ISAAC HAYES CHRONICLES**

Jan 80. (lp) *(STM 7008)* **LIGHT MY FIRE**

Nov 80. (d-lp)(c) *(STX 88003)* **HIS GREATEST HITS**

Oct 81. (lp/c) *(STAX L/K 5012)* **THE BEST OF SHAFT**
(re-iss. Jun86; 1052504)

Sep 85. (7") *Old Gold; (OG 9528)* **THEME FROM SHAFT. / NEVER CAN SAY GOODBYE**

Apr 88. (lp/c/cd) *(SX/SXC/CDSX 011)* **ISAAC'S MOODS – THE BEST OF ISAAC HAYES**
– Ike's mood / Soulsville / Joy (part 1) / If loving you is wrong I don't want to be right / Never can say goodbye / The theme from Shaft / Ike's rap VI / A brand new me / Do your thing / Walk on by / I stand accused. (cd+=) – Ike's rap I / Hyperbolic-syllabic-sesquedaly-mystic / Ike's rap III / Ike's rap II.

May 89. (7") *Southbound; (SEWS 701)* **THEME FROM SHAFT. / THEME FROM THE MEN**
(12"+=) *(SEWT 701)* – Theme from The Men / Type thang.
(cd-s+=) *(CDSEW 701)* – Walk on by.

Aug 93. (d-cd) **TOUGH GUYS / TRUCK TURNER**

Mar 95. (cd) *Connoisseur; (VSOPCD 210)* **THE COLLECTION**

Lee HAZLEWOOD

Born: BARTON LEE HAZLEWOOD, 9 Jul'29, Mannford, Oklahoma, USA. Brought up in Port Arthur, Texas, he went on to study at the Southern Methodist University and was subsequently drafted into the army for the Korean war. After being discharged, HAZLEWOOD began carving out a music biz career for himself in mid-50's Phoenix, DJ'ing, writing and producing. In 1956, he had his first taste of success when Sanford Clark took 'THE FOOL' into the the US Top 10. The track sold nigh on a million copies and enabled HAZLEWOOD to form the 'Jamie' record label. From his Ramco studio, he set about masterminding the sound of DUANE EDDY, effecting the famous

guitar twang by using a storage-tank echo chamber and scoring a string of instrumental hits in the process including the likes of 'REBEL ROUSER' and 'PETER GUNN'. One fascinated onlooker during these sessions was none other than a young PHIL SPECTOR, who himself went on to pioneer his own inimitable production techniques. After having a finger in the pie of many small labels (including the earliest incarnation of 'East West'), forming The SHACKLEFORDS (with MARTY COOPER) and even quitting the music biz altogether, HAZLEWOOD returned in 1965 to work as a producer for 'Reprise'. There, he began writing for NANCY SINATRA, steering her to the pinnacle of 60's pop kitsch with the international No.1, 'THESE BOOTS ARE MADE FOR WALKIN'. A string of LEE-penned NANCY hits followed over the period '66-'68 including 'SUGAR TOWN', 'SUMMER WINE', 'LADY BIRD' and the sublime pseudo-psychedelic 'SOME VELVET MORNING'. The crowning of the pair's seemingly incongruous musical partnership came with 1968's 'NANCY & LEE' album, collecting togther the cream of their duets and pitting HAZLEWOOD's cigar-chewing baritone against SINATRA's sassy girlishness to humorously tongue-in-cheek and often brilliant effect. HAZLEWOOD had also formed another label, 'LHI' ('Lee Hazlewood Industries') and was quick to notice the talent of a young GRAM PARSONS, then playing with The INTERNATIONAL SUBMARINE BAND. The moustachioed entrepreneur released the band's debut album, 'Safe At Home', in 1968. Often cited as the first bonafide country-rock set, the record was only released once PARSONS had departed for The BYRDS. Controversy ensued as HAZLEWOOD claimed he owned the rights to GRAM's vocal performances and allegedly threatened a lawsuit as 'Columbia' prepared to release The BYRDS landmark 'Sweetheart Of The Rodeo'; in the event, PARSON's vocals were stripped from the record's original release. While never as successful as his LEE & NANCY duets, HAZLEWOOD's own mutant country/pop recordings secured him a cult following; albums such as 'THE VERY SPECIAL WORLD OF LEE HAZLEWOOD' (1966), 'LEE HAZLEWOODISM: ITS CAUSE AND CURE' (1967) and 'LOVE AND OTHER CRIMES' (1968) are almost impossible to get hold of today. NANCY and LEE made a brief return to the pop charts (well, in the UK anyway) in 1971 with 'DID YOU EVER' which found them back at their verbally sparring best. For the rest of the 70's, he retired to Sweden where he released the odd (very odd! indeed) album or two. Fortunately, STEVE SHELLEY (of SONIC YOUTH) has recently re-issued a few of HAZLEWOOD's more interesting efforts via his own 'Smells Like' imprint. Among these was 'COWBOY IN SWEDEN', originally released in 1971 after the wayward mogul had relocated to Stockholm. Though he appeared with NANCY at a one-off reunion gig in 1995, sightings of the elusive HAZLEWOOD are almost rarer than his records. In 1999, 'Smell Like' issued his first new album in more than twenty years, 'FARMISHT, FLATULENCE, ORIGAMI, ARF!!! AND ME . . .', although his songwriting had taken a back seat as these were (very) old standards. A true maverick of the old school variety, HAZLEWOOD's bizarre career and recording legacy is surely ripe for a re-visit. Even a 'Later' (with Jools Holland) appearance, now that really would be something . . .

Album rating: TROUBLE IS A LONESOME TOWN (*5) / THE LEE HAZLEWOOD N.S.V.I.P.'S (*5) / LEE HAZLEWOOD SINGS FRIDAY'S CHILD (*6) / THE VERY SPECIAL WORLD OF LEE HAZLEWOOD (*6) / LEE HAZLEWOODISM: ITS CAUSE AND CURE (*6) / NANCY AND LEE with Nancy Sinatra (*7) / LOVE AND OTHER CRIMES (*7) / THE COWBOY AND THE LADY (*5) / FORTY (*5) / COWBOY IN SWEDEN (*5) / REQUIEM FOR AN ALMOST LADY (*6) / DID YOU EVER with Nancy Sinatra (*5) / 13 (*5) / I'LL BE YOUR BABY TONIGHT (*4) / POET, FOOL OR BUM (*7) / A HOUSE SAFE FOR TIGERS (*3) / 20TH CENTURY LEE (*3) / MOVIN' ON (*2) / BACK ON THE STREET AGAIN (*3) / FAIRY TALES AND FANTASIES: THE BEST OF NANCY & LEE compilation (*7) / THE MANY SIDES OF LEE compilation (*8) / FARMISHT, FLATULENCE, ORIGAMI, ARF!!! AND ME . . . (*5)

LEE HAZLEWOOD – vocals (with session people, etc)

London   Jamie

1958. (7"; as MARK ROBINSON) *<1103>* **PRETTY JANE. / WANTED**

Nov 60. (7"; by LEE HAZLEWOOD with DUANE EDDY) *(HLW 9223) <1158>* **THE GIRL ON DEATH ROW. / WORDS MEAN NOTHING**
not iss.   Smash

1961. (7") *<S-1734>* **DELLA. / DON'T CRY (NO MORE)**
not iss.   Mercury

1963. (lp) *<MG 20860>* **TROUBLE IS A LONESOME TOWN**
– Long black train / Ugly brown / Son of a gun / We all make the flowers grow / Run, boy, run / Six feet of chain / The railroad / Look at that woman / Peculiar guy / Trouble is a lonesome town. (UK-iss.1969 on 'London' mono/stereo; HA-N/SH-N 8398) <(re-iss. Sep99 on 'Smells Like' lp/cd; SLR 037/+CD)>

SHACKLEFORDS

—— **LEE HAZLEWOOD + MARTY COOPER** – vocals
Mercury   Mercury

1963. (7") *(AMT 1204) <72112>* **BIG RIVER. / A STRANGER IN YOUR TOWN**

1963. (7") *<72153>* **GOLDEN BELLS. / OUR LITTLE BOY BLUE**

1963. (7") *<72199>* **(THERE GOES) THE BIG BOSS MAN. / MY NAME IS JIMMY BROWN**

1963. (lp; mono/stereo) *<MG2/SR6 0806>* **UNTIL YOU'VE HEARD THE SHACKLEFORDS, YOU AIN'T HEARD NOTHIN' YET**
Capitol   Capitol

1965. (7") *<5478>* **FIVE FEET HIGH AND RISING. / ONE**

1965. (7") *<5570>* **AIN'T IT, BABE. / THAT OLD FREIGHT TRAIN**

1966.	(7") <5636> **THE BIPLANE EVERMORE. / FIRST STREET BLUES**	- /
1966.	(7"; with SUZI JANE HOKOM) <5713> **MUDDY MUDDY RIVER. / EVERYTHING I TOUCH TURNS TO TEARS**	- /
1966.	(lp; stereo/mono) <S+/2450> **THE SHACKLEFORDS SING**	- /
Dec 66.	(7") (CL 15486) **THE BIPLANE EVERMORE. / FIVE FEET HIGH AND RISING**	/ -

	not iss.	L.H.I.

1967.	(7") <17008> **CALIFORNIA SUNSHINE GIRL. / (instrumental)**	- /
1968.	(7") <17017> **COASTIN'. / (instrumental)**	- /
1968.	(7") <45-1211? **IT'S MY TIME. / ONE MORE TIME, BILLY BROWN**	- /

LEE HAZLEWOOD

—— continued his solo (and duet) career

	not iss.	Reprise

1965. (lp) <RS 6133> **THE LEE HAZLEWOOD N.S.V.I.P.'S**   - /
– First street blues / I had a friend / I'm gonna fly / Go die big city / I ain't gonna be / Have you made any new bombs today? / Everybody calls me something / Save your vote for Clarence Mudd / I might break even / Just bluesin'.

1965. (lp) <RS 6163> **LEE HAZLEWOOD SINGS FRIDAY'S CHILD**   - /
– Friday's child / Hutchinson jail / By the way (I still love you) / Four kinds of lonely / Houston / Sally was a good old girl / Since you're gone / A real live fool / I'm blue / The fool / That old freight train / Me and Charlie. (UK-iss.1968 as 'FRIDAY'S CHILD'; RSLP 6163) <re-iss. 1968 as 'HOUSTON' on 'Harmony'; HS 11290>

	M.G.M.	M.G.M.

Feb 66. (7") <13434> **BUGLES IN THE AFTERNOON. / I MOVE AROUND**   - /

May 66. (7") (MGM 1310) <13490> **SAND. / MY AUTUMN'S DONE COME**   - /
(above & below featured SUZI JANE HOKOM)

1966. (7") (MGM 1323) <13563> **HOME (I'M HOME). / (B-side by SUZI JANE HOKOM)**   - /

1966. (lp) (MGM-CS 8014) <SE 4362> **THE VERY SPECIAL WORLD OF LEE HAZLEWOOD**   - /
– For one moment / When a fool loves a fool / Not the lovin' kind / Your sweet love / Sand / My baby cried all night long / These boots are made for walkin' / I move around / So long, babe / Bugles in the afternoon / My Autumn's done come. <re-iss. 1966 on 'Capitol'; ST 91130>

1967. (7") (MGM 1348) **MY BABY CRIED ALL NIGHT LONG. / THESE BOOTS ARE MADE FOR WALKIN'**   / -

1967. (7"; with SUZI JANE HOKOM) <13605> **SUZI JANE IS BACK IN TOWN. / THE OLD MAN AND HIS GUITAR**   - /

1967. (7"; with SUZI JANE HOKOM) <13716> **SUMMER WINE. / AFTER SIX**   - /

1967. (lp) <SE 4403> **LEE HAZLEWOODISM: ITS CAUSE AND CURE**   - /
– Girl in Paris / Old man and his guitar / The nights / I am a part / Home / After six / Suzi Jane is back in town / In our time / Dark in my heart.

	Reprise	Reprise

Jun 67. (7"; by NANCY SINATRA & LEE HAZLEWOOD) (RS 20595) <0595> **JACKSON. / Nancy Sinatra: YOU ONLY LIVE TWICE**   11 / 14 44

Aug 67. (7") (RS 20613) <R-0613> **ODE TO BILLIE JOE. / CHARLIE BILL NELSON**   /

Oct 67. (7"; by NANCY SINATRA & LEE HAZLEWOOD) (RS 20629) **LADY BIRD. / SAND**   47 / -

Dec 67. (7"; by NANCY SINATRA & LEE HAZLEWOOD) <R-0651> **SOME VELVET MORNING. / OH LONESOME ME**   / 26

1968. (7") (RS 20667) <R-0667> **RAINBOW WOMAN. / I AM, YOU ARE**   / 1967

1967. (7"; by NANCY SINATRA & LEE HAZLEWOOD) (RS 23215) **SOME VELVET MORNING. / TONY ROME**   / -

Jun 68. (lp; by NANCY SINATRA & LEE HAZLEWOOD) <(RSLP 6273)> **NANCY AND LEE**   17 / 13 Apr68
– You've lost that lovin' feelin' / My elusive dreams / Greenwich Village folk song / Summer wine / Storybook children / Sundown, sundown / Jackson / Some velvet morning / Sand / Lady bird / I've been down so long (it looks like up to me). (re-iss. Sep71; K 44126) – hit UK No.42

1968. (7") <R-0699> **THE HOUSE SONG. / MORNING DEW**   /
1968. (lp) <(RSLP 6297)> **LOVE AND OTHER CRIMES**   /
– Love and other crimes / Morning dew / She comes running / Rosacoke street / She's funny that way / The house song / Wait and see / Forget Marie / Pour man / Love and other crimes. (cd-iss. Jun98 on 'L.H.I.'; LHI 97200)

1968. (7"; by NANCY SINATRA & LEE HAZLEWOOD) <R-0726> **JACKSON. / SUMMER WINE**   /

	not iss.	L.H.I.

1968. (7"; by LEE HAZLEWOOD & ANN-MARGRET) <LHI 2> **SLEEP IN THE GRASS. / CHICO**   - /
1968. (7"; by LEE HAZLEWOOD & ANN-MARGRET) <LHI 5> **DARK END OF THE STREET. / VICTIMS OF THE NIGHT**   - /
1969. (7"; by LEE HAZLEWOOD ANN-MARGRET) <LHI 11> **WALK ON OUT OF MIND. / HANGIN' ON**   - /
1969. (lp; by LEE HAZLEWOOD ANN-MARGRET) <LHIS 12007> **THE COWBOY AND THE LADY**   - /
8- Am I that easy to forget / Only mama that'll walk the line / Greyhound bus depot / Walk on out of my mind / Hangin' on / Victims of the night / Break my mind / You can't imagine / Sweet thing / No regrets / Dark end of the street.

1969. (7") <LHI 17> **NO REGRETS. / GREYHOUND BUS DEPOT**   - /
1969. (7") <LHI 20> **GREYHOUND BUS DEPOT. / TROUBLEMAKER**   - /
1969. (lp) <LHIS 12009> **FORTY**   - /
– It was a very good year / What's more I don't need her / The night before / The bed /

Paris bells / Wait till next year / September song / Let's burn down the cornfield / Bye babe / Mary.

1969. (7"; with SUZI JANE HOKOM) <LHI 21> **CALIFIA (STONE RIDER). / NOBODY LIKE YOU**   - /

	not iss.	Bell

1970. (7") <LHI 28> **NO TRAIN TO STOCKHOLM. / WHAT'S MORE I DON'T NEED HER**   - /

1970. (7") <927> **HEY COWBOY. / PRAY THEM BARS AWAY**   - /
(above & below featured NINA LIZELL)

	Reprise	not iss.

1971. (lp) <3101> **COWBOY IN SWEDEN**   - /
<(re-iss. Apr99 on 'Smells Like' lp/cd; SLR 030/+CD)>

1971. (lp) (K 44161) **REQUIEM FOR AN ALMOST LADY**   / -
– I'm glad I never . . . / If it's Monday morning / L.A. lady / Won't you tell your dreams / I'll yesterdays / Little Miss Sunshine (little love Rain) / Stone lost child / Come on home to me / Must have been something I loved / I'd rather be your enemy. <(re-iss. Sep99 on 'Smells Like' lp/cd; SLR 038/+CD)>

	R.C.A.	R.C.A.

Aug 71. (7"; by NANCY AND LEE) (K 44093) **DID YOU EVER. / BACK ON THE ROAD**   2 / -

Jan 72. (lp; by NANCY SINATRA & LEE HAZLEWOOD) (SF 8240) <LSP 4645> **DID YOU EVER** <US title 'NANCY AND LEE AGAIN'>   31 /
– Did you ever / Tippy toes / Back on the road / Arkansas coal (suite) / Congratulations / Down from Dover / Friendship train / Paris summer / Big red balloon / Got it together again.

Jan 72. (7"; by NANCY SINATRA & LEE HAZLEWOOD) (RCA 2185) **BIG RED BALLOON. / DOWN FROM DOVER**   /

1972. (7"; by NANCY SINATRA & LEE HAZLEWOOD) <74-0614> **PARIS SUMMER. / DOWN FROM DOVER**   /

—— around this time, LEE featured on ANN-KRISTIN HEDMARK releases

	Viking	not iss.

1972. (7") (VIS 1001) **DOWN VALHALLAVAGEN. / SMOKE'S THEME (instrumental)**   - / - Sweden
1972. (lp) (VIF 5003) **13**   - / - Sweden
– You look like a lady / Tulsa Sunday / Ten or 11 towns ago / Toocie and the river / She comes running / Rosacoke street / I move around / And I loved you then / Hej, me I'm riding.

1973. (lp) (VIF 5004) **I'LL BE YOUR BABY TONIGHT**   - / - Sweden

	Stateside	Capitol

May 73. (7") <3611> **NANCY AND ME. / KARI**   - /
Oct 73. (7") <3737> **FEATHERS. / THE PERFORMER**   - /
Mar 74. (7") (SS 2225) **POET. / COME SPEND THE MORNING**   /
1974. (lp) (SSL 10315) <ST 11171> **POET, FOOL OR BUM**   / Nov73
– Poet, fool or bum / Heaven is my woman's love / Kari / Feathers / Nancy and me / The performer / Come spend the morning / Wind, sky, sea and sand / Think I'm coming down / Those were the days of roses. (cd-iss. Jun98 on 'L.H.I.'; LHI 97100)

	C.B.S.	not iss.

1974. (lp) (80534) **THE STOCKHOLM KID LIVE AT BERNS (live)**   / - Sweden
1975. (lp) (80383) **A HOUSE SAFE FOR TIGERS**   / - Sweden
– Souls island / A house safe for tigers / Our little boy blue / Absent friends / Sand hill Anna and the Russian mouse / Lars Gunnar and me / Souls island / Las Vegas / The nights / A house safe for tigers (choir).

	RCA Victor	not iss.

1975. (7") (YSPB 0-715) **OLD MILWAUKEE. / PLEASE COME TO BOSTON**   - / - Sweden
1976. (7") (YSPB 0-727) **INDIAN SUMMER (L'ETE INDIEN). / WHOLE LOTTA SHAKIN' GOIN' ON**   - / - Sweden
1976. (lp) (YSPL 1-575) **20TH CENTURY LEE**   - / - Sweden
– Long haired country boy / That's how I got to Memphis / In a young girl's mind / The ballad Of Lucy Jordan / An old lullaby / Indian summer / My girl Bill / Crazy mama / Whole lotta shakin' goin' on / To Ramona / Brevet fan Lillan.

	Polydor	not iss.

1977. (7") (2053 265) **I'VE GOT TO BE MOVIN'. / MOTHER COUNTRY MUSIC**   - / - German
1977. (lp) (2379 147) **MOVIN' ON**   - / - Sweden
– Mother country music / I've got to be movin' / The rising star / Come on home to me / It's for my dad / Let's burn down the cornfield / Hello Saturday morning / Wait till next year / L.A. lady / Paris bells / Kung Fu you / It was a very good year.

	E.M.I.	not iss.

1977. (7") (1C 006-32757) **YOUR THUNDER AND YOUR LIGHTNING. / YOU MAKE IT LOOK SO EASY**   - / - German
1977. (lp) (1C-066 32553) **BACK ON THE STREET AGAIN**   - / - German
– Back on the street again / Save a place for me / Your thunder and your lightning / Suddenly Tennessee / You make it look so easy / A rider on a white horse / Smokey put the weat on me / Dolly and Hawkeye / Beginning to feel like home / New box of people / Dolly Parton's guitar.

	not iss.	M.C.A.

1979. (7") <41003> **DOLLY PARTON'S GUITAR. / A TASTE OF YOU**   /
1980. (7") <41188> **WILLIE JONES. / HOLLYWOOD**   /

—— In 1993, LEE and his songs featured on the ANNA HANSKI Swedish album, 'Gypsies And Indians'.

	Smells Like	Smells Like

Apr 99. (cd) <(SLR 031)> **FARMISHT FLATULENCE ORIGAMI ARF!!! AND ME . . .**   /
– Honeysuckle rose / Ain't misbehavin' / It had to be you / Don't get around much anymore / Makin' whoopee / Gee baby, ain't I good to you / I can't get started / She's funny that way / Try a little tenderness / The very thought of you / Am I blue.

– compilations, etc. –

1967. (7"ep) *Reprise*; (REP 30083) <RDC 57.001BR> **JACKSON**   - /
– Some velvet morning / Jackson / Sundown, sundown / Summer wine.

1968. (7"ep) *Reprise*; <CT 882T> **NANCY & LEE**   - /
– Lady bird / I've been down so long (it looks like up to me) / Greenwich Village folk song / Salesman.

1968. (7"ep) *Reprise; <SR 6273>* **NANCY & LEE**
– Lady bird / Elusive dreams / You've lost that lovin' feelin' / Some velvet morning.
1989. (cd) *Rhino; <R 170166>* **FAIRY TALES & FANTASIES: THE BEST OF NANCY & LEE**
Jul 96. (cd) *Nancy's; (NANCD 101)* **THE HITS OF NANCY AND LEE**
Feb 98. (cd) *Bellaphon; (28807255)* **LEE HAZLEWOOD AND FRIENDS**
Jun 98. (cd) *Request; (CD 13505)* **THE MANY SIDES OF LEE**
Jun 98. (d-cd) *L.H.I.; (LHI 97300)* **THE COWBOY AND THE LADIES**

Michael HEAD (see under ⇒ SHACK)

HEADS (see under ⇒ TALKING HEADS)

HEADSWIM (dig out; Great Metal . . .)

Jeff HEALEY (dig out; 4th edition)

HEART

Formed: Vancouver, Canada . . . 1975 by sisters ANN and NANCY WILSON, who had graduated from Seattle groups The ARMY and WHITE HEART. In these line-ups were brothers ROGER and MIKE FISHER, the respective boyfriends of ANN and NANCY. The latter had arrived from the solo-folk scene to replace MIKE, who became their sound engineer, the group moving to Vancouver to avoid his draft papers. With bassist STEVE FOSSEN completing the line-up, the group named themselves HEART and were duly signed to the local 'Mushroom' label by owner Shelley Siegal, issuing their well-received debut album, 'DREAMBOAT ANNIE', in 1976. With the help of two US Top 40 singles, 'MAGIC MAN' and 'CRAZY ON YOU', the album made the American Top 10, its JEFFERSON STARSHIP meets LED ZEPPELIN folky pop/rock sound sitting well with FM radio. Following the record's success, HEART returned to Seattle in late '76 and inked a new deal with 'CBS-Portrait', Mushroom promptly suing them for breach of contract. Despite the legal hassles, the group ploughed on, adding keyboardist HOWARD LEESE and permanent drummer MICHAEL DEROSIER for the 'LITTLE QUEEN' (1977) album. A heavier affair, the record was another critical and commercial success, spawning the hard rocking single, 'BARRACUDA'. While punk precluded any real UK success, the band were consistently popular in the States, the rock babe glamour of the WILSON sisters and impressive vocal acrobatics of younger sibling ANNE marking them out from the AOR pack. In 1978, a Seattle judge gave Mushroom the rights to issue their out-takes album, 'MAGAZINE', but ruled that the group could re-record it. Inevitably, the record was a patchy affair, although it surprised many, even the band themselves, by making the Top 20. Later that year, their fourth album, 'DOG AND BUTTERFLY', was another Top 20 success, their last for 'Portrait' as the band underwent personal upheavals and signed a new deal with 'Epic'. The FLEETWOOD MAC-style inter-band relationship problems resulted in ROGER FISHER departing, and though 'BEBE LE STRANGE' (1980) wasn't quite 'Rumours', it was an improvement on their previous effort. The line-up remained unsettled, however, as the band went through a kind of mid-period slump, MARK ANDES and DENNY CARMASI having replaced FOSSEN and DEROSIER respectively by the release of 'PASSIONWORKS' (1983). This album signalled the end of their tenure with 'Epic', although HEART's fortunes were given a bit of a boost when ANN WILSON duetted with LOVERBOY's MIKE RENO on the Top 10 hit single, 'ALMOST PARADISE' (used in the film 'Footloose'). Signing a new deal with 'Capitol', the band rose phoenix-like to top the American charts with the eponymous 'HEART' in 1985. Full of gleaming, MTV-friendly power ballads (i.e.'THESE DREAMS', 'WHAT ABOUT LOVE'), the band had practically re-invented themselves and had the leather 'n' lace-style soft-rock market well and truly cornered. 'BAD ANIMALS' was more of the same, ANNE flexing maximum vocal muscle on the 'ALONE' single and duly breaking the band in Britain where the song went Top 3. 'BRIGADE' (1990) was almost as successful though not quite as convincing, the WILSONs taking time out for solo projects after touring the record. HEART returned with an almost original line-up for 1993's 'DESIRE WALKS ON', while 'THE ROAD HOME' showcased a stripped down acoustic sound. • **Songwriters:** ANN WILSON or the group wrote most except; TELL IT LIKE IT IS (Aaron Neville) / I'M DOWN (Beatles) / LONG TALL SALLY (Little Richard) / UNCHAINED MELODY (hit; Righteous Brothers) / I'VE GOT THE MUSIC IN ME (Kiki Dee) / THESE DREAMS (Martin Page & Bernie Taupin) / ALONE (Billy Steinberg & Tom Kelly) / ALL I WANNA DO IS MAKE LOVE TO YOU (Mutt Lange) / etc. • **Trivia:** In 1967, ANN WILSON AND THE DAYBREAKS issued a couple of singles on 'Topaz'; STANDIN' WATCHIN' YOU. / WONDER HOW I MANAGED and THROUGH EYES AND GLASS. / I'M GONNA DRINK MY HURT AWAY.

Album rating: DREAMBOAT ANNIE (*8) / LITTLE QUEEN (*5) / MAGAZINE (*5) / DOG AND BUTTERFLY (*7) / BEBE LE STRANGE (*5) / GREATEST HITS / LIVE live compilation (*5) / PRIVATE AUDITION (*6) / PASSION WORKS (*6) / HEART (*7) / BAD ANIMALS (*7) / BRIGADE (*5) / ROCK THE HOUSE LIVE (*5) / THESE DREAMS – GREATEST HITS compilation (*8)

ANN WILSON (b.19 Jun'51, San Diego, Calif.) – vocals, guitar, flute / **NANCY WILSON** (b.16 Mar'54, San Francisco, Calif.) – guitar, vocals / **ROGER FISHER** (b.1950) – guitar / **STEVE FOSSEN** – bass with session keyboard player and drummer

	Arista	Mushroom
Apr 76. (7") <7021> **CRAZY ON YOU.** / **DREAMBOAT ANNIE** <re-hit US No.62 early 1978>	-	35
Oct 76. (7") (ARISTA 71) <7011> **MAGIC MAN.** / **HOW DEEP IT GOES** <finally climbed to No.9 by mid-'76>		Feb76
Oct 76. (lp/c)<US-pic-lp> (ARTY/TC-ARTY 139) <5005> **DREAMBOAT ANNIE**	36	7 Mar76

– Magic man / Dreamboat Annie (fantasy child) / Crazy on you / Soul of the sea / Dreamboat Annie / White lightning and wine (love me like music) / I'll be your song / Sing child / How deep it goes / Dreamboat Annie (reprise). (re-iss. Oct87 on 'Capitol' cd/c/lp; CD/TC+/EMS 1277)

	Arista	Mushroom
Feb 77. (7") (ARISTA 86) **CRAZY ON YOU.** / **SOUL OF THE SEA**		
Apr 77. (7") (ARISTA 104) <7023> **DREAMBOAT ANNIE.** / **SING CHILD**		42 Dec76

—— added **HOWARD LEESE** (b.13 Jun'51) – keyboards, synthesizer, guitar (appeared as guest on debut album) / **MICHAEL DEROSIER** – drums

	Portrait	Portrait
Jul 77. (lp/c) (PRT 82075) <34799> **LITTLE QUEEN**	34	9 May77

– Barracuda / Love alive / Sylvan song / Dream of the archer / Kick it out / Little queen / Treat me well / Say hello / Cry to me / Go on cry. (re-iss. Aug86; same) (cd-iss. May87; CDPRT 82075) (cd re-iss. Sep93 on 'Sony Collectors';) (cd re-is.Feb97 on 'Columbia'; 474678-2)

	Portrait	Portrait
Aug 77. (7") (PRT 5402) <70004> **BARRACUDA.** / **CRY TO ME**		11 May77
Oct 77. (7") (PRT 5570) **LOVE ALIVE.** / **KICK IT OUT**		-
Nov 77. (7") (PRT 5751) <70008> **LITTLE QUEEN.** / **TREAT ME WELL**		62 Sep77
Nov 77. (7") <70010> **KICK IT OUT.** / **GO ON CRY**	-	79

(The following few releases on 'Arista' UK & 'Mushroom' US were contractual)

	Arista	Mushroom
Sep 77. (7"w-drawn) (ARISTA 140) **HEARTLESS.** / **HERE SONG**	-	-
Mar 78. (7") <7031> **HEARTLESS.** / **JUST THE WINE**		24
Apr 78. (lp)<US-pic-lp> (SPART 1024) <5008> **MAGAZINE**		17

– Heartless / Devil delight / Just the wine / Without you / Magazine / Here song / Mother Earth blues / I've got the music in me (live). (UK-iss.Oct87 on 'Capitol' cd/c/lp; CD/TC+/EMS 1278)

	Arista	Mushroom
May 78. (7") (ARIST 187) **HEARTLESS (version II).** / **HERE SONG**		
May 78. (7") <7035> **WITHOUT YOU.** / **HERE SONG**	-	-
Jul 78. (7") <7043> **MAGAZINE.** / **DEVIL DELIGHT**	-	-
Aug 78. (7") (ARIST 206) **MAGAZINE.** / **JUST THE WINE**	-	-

	Portrait	Portrait
Oct 78. (7") (PRT 6704) <70020> **STRAIGHT ON.** / **LIGHTER TOUCH**		15 Sep78
Dec 78. (lp/c) (PRT 83080) <35555> **DOG & BUTTERFLY**		17 Oct78

– Cook with fire / High time / Hijinx / Straight on / Lighter touch / Dog & butterfly / Nada one / Mistral wind. (re-iss. Aug86; PRT 32803) (cd-iss. May87; CDPRT 32803)

	Portrait	Portrait
Jan 79. (7") <70025> **DOG & BUTTERFLY.** / **MISTRAL WIND**	-	34

—— Now a quartet when Nancy's boyfriend ROGER FISHER left the band

	Epic	Epic
Mar 80. (7") (EPC 8270) **EVEN IT UP.** / **PILOT**		34 Feb 80
Mar 80. (lp/c) (EPC/40 84135) <36371> **BEBE LE STRANGE**		5

– Bebe le strange / Down on me / Silver wheels / Break / Rockin' heaven down / Even it up / Strange night / Raised on you / Pilot / Sweet darlin'. (cd-iss. 1988; CDEPC 84135) (cd re-iss. May93 on 'Sony Collectors' cd/c;)

	Epic	Epic
May 80. (7") <50874> **DOWN ON ME.** / **RAISED ON YOU**	-	-
Jul 80. (7") <50892> **BEBE LE STRANGE.** / **SILVER WHEELS**	-	-
Nov 80. (7") <50950> **TELL IT LIKE IT IS.** / **STRANGE EUPHORIA**	-	8
Jan 81. (7") (EPC 9436) **TELL IT LIKE IT IS.** / **BARRACUDA (live)**	-	-
Mar 81. (lp/c)<US-d-lp> (EPC/40 84829) <36888> **GREATEST HITS / LIVE** (half comp / half live)		13 Nov80

– Tell it like it is / Barracuda / Straight on / Dog & butterfly / Even it up / Bebe le strange / Sweet darlin' / I'm down – Long tall Sally – Unchained melody / Rock and roll. (re-iss. +cd Dec88)

	Epic	Epic
Mar 81. (7") <51010> **UNCHAINED MELODY (live).** / **MISTRAL WIND**	-	83
Jun 82. (7") (EPCA 2436) <02925> **THIS MAN IS MINE.** / **AMERICA**	-	33 May82
Jun 82. (lp/c) (EPC/40 85792) <38049> **PRIVATE AUDITION**	77	25

– City's burning / Bright light girl / Perfect stranger / Private audition / Angels / This man is mine / The situation / Hey darlin' darlin' / One word / Fast times / America. (re-iss. Feb88 on 'C.B.S.' lp/c; 460174-1/-4) (cd-iss. 1988; CDEPC 85792) (re-iss. cd May94)

	Epic	Epic
Sep 82. (7") <03071> **PRIVATE AUDITION.** / **BRIGHT LIGHT GIRL**	-	-

—— **MARK ANDES** (b.19 Feb'48, Philadelphia, Pennsylvania) – bass (ex-SPIRIT, ex-JO JO GUNNE, ex-FIREFALL) repl. FOSSEN / **DENNY CARMASSI** – drums (ex-MONTROSE, ex-SAMMY HAGAR, ex-GAMMA) repl. DEROSIER who formed ORION THE HUNTER

	Epic	Epic
Aug 83. (7") <04047> **HOW CAN I REFUSE.** / **JOHNNY MOON**	-	-
Sep 83. (lp/c) (EPC/40 25491) <38800> **PASSIONWORKS**		39

– How can I refuse / Blue guitar / Johnny Moon / Sleep alone / Together now / Allies / (Beat by) Jealousy / Heavy heart / Love mistake / Language of love / Ambush. (cd-iss. Feb88; CDEPC 25391)

	Epic	Epic
Sep 83. (12"m) (TA 3695) **HOW CAN I REFUSE.** / **BARRACUDA / LITTLE QUEEN**	-	-
Oct 83. (7") <04184> **ALLIES.** / **TOGETHER NOW**	-	83

—— While HEART looked for new contract ANN WILSON teamed up in '84 with MIKE RENO of LOVERBOY on 7" 'ALMOST PARADISE' from the film 'Footloose'.

	Capitol	Capitol
Jul 85. (7") (CL 361) <5481> **WHAT ABOUT LOVE?.** / **HEART OF DARKNESS**		10 May85
Oct 85. (lp/c) (EJ 0372-1/-4) <12410> **HEART**	50	1 Jul85

– If looks could kill / What about love? / Never / These dreams / The wolf / All eyes / Nobody home / Nothin' at all / What he don't know / Shell shock. (cd-iss. Feb86; CDP 746157-2) (re-iss. cd Sep94;)

	Capitol	Capitol
Oct 85. (7") (CL 380) <5512> **NEVER (remix).** / **SHELL SHOCK** (12"+=) (12CL 380) – ('A'extended remix).		4 Sep85
Jan 86. (7") <5541> **THESE DREAMS.** / **SHELL SHOCK**	-	1
Mar 86. (7") (CL 394) **THESE DREAMS.** / **IF LOOKS COULD KILL (live)**	62	-

(12"+=) *(12CL 394)* – Shell shock.
(d7"+=) *(CLD 394)* – What about love? / Heart of darkness.

May 86. (7"/7"sha-pic-d) *(CL/+P 406)* <5572> **NOTHIN' AT ALL (remix). / THE WOLF**   [ ] [1] Apr86
(12"+=) *(12CL 406)* – ('A'extended remix).

Jul 86. (7") <5605> **IF LOOKS COULD KILL. / WHAT HE DON'T KNOW** [-] [54]

Dec 86. (7") <5654> **THE BEST MAN IN THE WORLD. /** [-] [61]
(above from the film 'The Golden Child' starring Eddie Murphy)

May 87. (7") *(CL 448)* <44002> **ALONE. / BARRACUDA (live)** [3] [1]

May 87. (cd/c/lp) *(CD/TC+/ESTU 2032)* <12546> **BAD ANIMALS** [7] [5]
– Who will you run to / Alone / There's the girl / I want you so bad / Wait for the answer / Bad animals / You ain't so tough / Strangers of the heart / Easy target / RSVP. *(re-iss. cd Jul94;)*

Aug 87. (7") <44040> **WHO WILL YOU RUN TO. / MAGIC MAN** [-] [ ]

Sep 87. (7"/7"pic-d) *(CL/+P 457)* **WHO WILL YOU RUN TO. / NOBODY HOME** [30] [-]
('A'-Rock mix-12"+=) *(12CL 457)* – These dreams.
(cd-s++=) *(CDCL 457)* – ('A'-Rock mix).

Nov 87. (7") *(CL 473)* <44089> **THERE'S THE GIRL (remix). / BAD ANIMALS** [34] [12]
(12"+=) *(12CL 473)* – ('A'extended remix).
(c-s++=/cd-s+=) *(TC/CD CL 473)* – Alone.

Jan 88. (7"/7"g-f/7"pic-d) *(CL/+G/P 482)* **NEVER. / THESE DREAMS** [8] [-]
(12"+=) *(12CL 482)* – ('A'extended remix) / These dreams (version).
(etched-12") *(12CLE 482)* – These dreams (remixes & instrumental) / ('A'extended remix).
(ext-remix.cd-s+=) *(CDCL 482)* – Heart of darkness / If looks could kill (live).

Feb 88. (7") <44116> **I WANT YOU SO BAD. / EASY TARGET** [-] [49]

May 88. (7"/7"pic-d) *(CL/+P 487)* **WHAT ABOUT LOVE. / SHELL SHOCK** [14] [-]
(12"+=/12"g-f+=) *(12CL/+G 487)* – ('A'extended remix).
(cd-s+=) *(CDCL 487)* – Crazy on you / Dreamboat Annie.

Oct 88. (7") *(CL 507)* **NOTHIN' AT ALL (remix). / I'VE GOT THE MUSIC IN ME (live)** [38] [-]
(12"+=/12"pic-d+=) *(12CL/+P 507)* – I want you so bad (extended remix).
(cd-s++=) *(CDCL 507)* – ('A'extended).
(below with ZANDER (CHEAP TRICK) and from the film 'Tequila Sunrise')

Feb 89. (7"; ANN WILSON & ROBIN ZANDER) *(CL 525)* <44288> **SURRENDER TO ME. / (B-side by Dave Grusin featuring Lee Ritenour)** [ ] [6]
(12"+=/cd-s+=) *(12/CD CL 525)* – (by Diamond & Cerney).

Dec 89. (7") <44488> **HERE IS CHRISTMAS.** / [-] [ ]

Mar 90. (c-s/7") *(CL 569)* <44507> **ALL I WANNA DO IS MAKE LOVE TO YOU. / CALL OF THE WILD** [8] [2]
(12"+=/12"pic-d+=/12"clear+=/cd-s+=) *(12CL/12CLPD/12CLE/CDCL 569)* – Cruel tears.

Apr 90. (cd/c/lp) *(CD/TC+/ESTU 121)* <91820> **BRIGADE** [2] [3]
– Wild child / All I wanna do is make love to you / Secret / Tall, dark handsome stranger / I didn't want to need you / The night / Fallen from grace / Under the sky / Cruel nights / Stranded / Call of the wild / I want your world to turn / I love you. *(re-iss. Mar94 cd/c; CD/TC ESTU 2121)*

Jul 90. (7") *(CL 580)* <44553> **I DIDN'T WANT TO NEED YOU. / THE NIGHT** [47] [23] Jun90
(c-s+=/12"+=/12"pic-d+=/cd-s+=) *(TCCL/12CL/12CLPD/CDCL 580)* – The will to love.

Nov 90. (c-s/7") *(TC+/CL 595)* <44621> **STRANDED. / UNDER THE SKY** [60] [13] Sep90
(12"+=/12"pic-d+=/cd-s+=) *(12CL/12CLP/CDCL 595)* – I'll never stop loving you.

Feb 91. (c-s/7") *(TC+/CL 603)* <44614> **SECRET. / I LOVE YOU** [ ] [64] Jan91
(12"+=/cd-s+=) *(12/CD CL 603)* – How can I refuse (live).

Sep 91. (cd/c/lp) *(CD/TC+/ESTU 2154)* <95797> **ROCK THE HOUSE (live)** [45] [ ]
– Wild child / Fallen from grace / Call of the wild / How can I refuse / Shell shock / Love alive / Under the sky / The night / Tall, dark, handsome stranger / If looks could kill / Who will you run to / You're the voice / The way back machine / Barracuda.

Sep 91. (c-s/7") *(TC+/CL 624)* **YOU'RE THE VOICE (live). / CALL OF THE WILD (live)** [56] [ ]
(10"colrd+=/cd-s+=) *(10/CD CL 624)* – Barracuda (live).

—— In 1992, the WILSONS were in splinter group **LOVEMONGERS**. The latter (which also included SUE ENNIS + FRANK COX) released a self-titled cd-ep on 'Capitol' w/tracks – Battle of evermore / Love of the common man / Papa was a rollin' stone / Crazy on you.

—— **FERNANDO SAUNDERS** (b.17 Jan'54, Detroit, Mich.) – bass repl. ANDES / **DENNY FONGHEISER** (b.21 Apr'59, Almeda, Calif.) – drums repl. CARMASSI

Nov 93. (7"pic-d/c-s) *(CLPD/TCCL 700)* **WILL YOU BE THERE (IN THE MORNING). / THESE DREAMS** [19] [-]
(cd-s) *(CDCLS 700)* – ('A'side) / What about love? / Risin' suspicion / Who will you run to.

Nov 93. (cd/c) *(CD/TC EST 2216)* <99627> **DESIRE WALKS ON** [32] [48]
– Desire / Black on black II / Back to Avalon / The woman in me / Rage / In walks the night / My crazy head / Ring them bells / Will you be there (in the morning) / Voodoo doll / Anything is possible / Avalon (reprise) / Desire walks on *[UK+=]* / La mujer que hay en mi / Te quedaras (en la manana).

Dec 93. (c-s) <58041> **WILL YOU BE THERE (IN THE MORNING) / RISIN' SUSPICION** [-] [39]

Mar 94. (cd-s) **BACK TO AVALON / WILL YOU BE THERE (IN THE MORNING) / ALL I WANNA DO IS MAKE LOVE TO YOU** [ ] [ ]

Aug 95. (cd/c) *(CD/TC EST 2258)* <30489> **THE ROAD HOME (live)** [ ] [87]
– Dreamboat Annie (fantasy child) / Dog and butterfly / (Up on) Cherry blossom road / Back to Avalon / Alone / These dreams / Love hurts / Straight on / All I wanna do is make love to you / Crazy on you / Seasons / The river / Barracuda / Dream of the archer. *(re-iss. Sep97; same)*

– compilations etc. –

Sep 87. (d-lp/c) *Epic; (460174-1/-4)* **HEART (THE BEST OF . . .)** [ ] [-]

Nov 88. (d-lp-box/d-c-box/d-cd-box) *Capitol; (CD/TC+/LOVE 2)* **WITH LOVE FROM HEART** (HEART / BAD ANIMALS) [ ] [-]

Nov 90. (t-cd-box)(t-lp-box) *Capitol; (795247-2)(HGIFT 1)* **HEART BOX SET** (HEART / BAD ANIMALS / BRIGADE) [ ] [ ]

Nov 91. (d-cd) *Epic; (465222-2)* **DOG & BUTTERFLY / LITTLE QUEEN** [ ] [ ]

May 94. (cd/c) *Columbia; (460174-2/-4)* **GREATEST HITS** [ ] [ ]

Apr 97. (cd) *Capitol; (7243 8 53376 2 8)* **THESE DREAMS – HEART'S GREATEST HITS** [35] [ ]
– Crazy on you / All I wanna do is make love to you / If looks could kill / Never / Alone / Who will you run to / Straight on (acoustic) / Magic man / What about love / Dreamboat Annie / Dog and butterfly (acoustic) / Nothin' at all / Heartless / Stranded / Will you be there (in the morning) / These dreams / Barracuda (live).

HEARTBREAKERS (see under ⇒ THUNDERS, Johnny)

HEATMISER (see under ⇒ SMITH, Elliott)

HEAVEN 17

Formed: Sheffield, England ... Autumn '80 by ex-HUMAN LEAGUE members, IAN CRAIG-MARSH and MARTYN WARE. Recruiting suitably dapper, rich-voiced frontman, GLENN GREGORY, the group remained with 'Virgin' (who they'd been signed to as part of The HUMAN LEAGUE) and released a debut single, '(WE DON'T NEED THIS) FASCIST GROOVE THANG', in Spring '81. Although it narrowly missed the Top 40, its politically pointed electronic funk-pop had the critics in rapture and their debut album, 'PENTHOUSE AND PAVEMENT' (1981), subsequently made the Top 20. Simultaneously, CRAIG-MARSH and WARE had formed a side project, B.E.F. (British Electric Foundation), releasing a debut album of inspired covers (see below), 'MUSIC OF QUALITY AND DISTINCTION', a few months later. A further series of singles flopped and it wasn't until Spring '83's massive 'TEMPTATION' single that HEAVEN 17 began to match their critical acclaim with chart appeal. An epic configuration of climaxing synths and warbling diva vocals, the track narrowly missed the No.1 slot, pushing the follow-up album, 'THE LUXURY GAP' (1983), into the Top 5. A glossier, more hook-laden affair, it nevertheless offered no let-up in the band's social agenda, spawning further hits in the 'COME LIVE WITH ME' and the self-explanatory 'CRUSHED BY THE WHEELS OF INDUSTRY'. 'HOW MEN ARE' (1984) didn't have quite the same focus and the momentum began to flag, subsequent albums, 'PLEASURE ONE' (1986) and 'TEDDY BEAR, DUKE AND PSYCHO' (1988) sinking without trace. While WARE went on to work as a producer, there was renewed interest in HEAVEN 17 upon the reissue of 'TEMPTATION' in the early 90's; remixed by Brothers In Rhythm, the track again reached the Top 5, boosting sales of 'HIGHER AND HIGHER' (1993), the attendant greatest hits package. History repeated itself again, however, when a revamped '(WE DON'T NEED..)' barely scraped into the Top 40. The early 90's also saw the release of a second B.E.F. album, 'MUSIC OF QUALITY AND DISTINCTION VOLUME 2', another round of cover versions. • **Songwriters:** WARE & CRAIG-MARSH through a computer-synth. Their 1981-82 off-shoot project B.E.F. covered; ANYONE WHO HAD A HEART (Cilla Black) / WICHITA LINEMAN (Glen Campbell) / BALL OF CONFUSION (Temptations) / IT'S OVER (Roy Orbison) / YOU KEEP ME HANGIN' ON (Diana Ross & The Supremes) / THE SECRET LIFE OF ARABIA (David Bowie) / THERE'S A GHOST IN MY HOUSE (R.Dean Taylor) / THESE BOOTS WERE MADE FOR WALKING (Nancy Sinatra) / PERFECT DAY (Lou Reed) / SUSPICIOUS MINDS (Elvis Presley). As disaster fund group The HILLSBOROUGH CREW, they covered in 1986; MOVE ON UP (Curtis Mayfield). • **Trivia:** Named themselves after a group in the controversial film 'Clockwork Orange'.

Album rating: PENTHOUSE AND PAVEMENT (*8) / THE LUXURY GAP (*6) / HOW MEN ARE (*5) / ENDLESS mixes collection (*4) / PLEASURE ONE (*5) / TEDDY BEAR, DUKE AND PSYCHO (*4) / HIGHER AND HIGHER – THE BEST OF HEAVEN 17 compilation (*7)

GLENN GREGORY (b.16 May'58) – vocals / **MARTYN WARE** (b.19 May'56) – synthesizers (ex-HUMAN LEAGUE) / **IAN CRAIG-MARSH** (b.11 Nov'56) – synthesizers (ex-HUMAN LEAGUE)

	Virgin	Arista
Mar 81. (7"/12") *(VS 400/+12)* **(WE DON'T NEED THIS) FASCIST GROOVE THANG. / THE DECLINE OF THE WEST**	45	
May 81. (7"/12") *(VS 417/+12)* **I'M YOUR MONEY. / ARE EVERYTHING**		
Jul 81. (7"/12") *(VS 433/+12)* **PLAY TO WIN. / PLAY**	46	
Sep 81. (lp/c) *(V/TCV 2208)* **PENTHOUSE AND PAVEMENT** <US-title 'HEAVEN 17'>	14	68 Feb83

– (We don't need this) Fascist groove thang / Penthouse and pavement / Play to win / Soul warfare / Geisha boys and temple girls / Let's all make a bomb / The height of the fighting / Song with no name / We're going to live for a very long time. *(re-iss. Apr86 lp/c; OVED/+C 157)* *(cd-iss. Jul87; CDV 2208)*

below 45 featured guests **JOHN WILSON** – bass / **JOSIE JONES** – vocals

	Virgin	Arista
Oct 81. (7"/12") *(VS 455/+12)* **PENTHOUSE AND PAVEMENT. / ('A'instrumental)**	57	
Feb 82. (12") *(VS 483-12)* **THE HEIGHT OF THE FIGHTING (HE-LA-HO). / HONEYMOON IN NEW YORK**		
Oct 82. (7"/12") *(VS 532/+12)* **LET ME GO. / ('A'instrumental)**	41	
Feb 83. (7") <1050> **LET ME GO. / I'M YOUR MONEY**	-	74

—— (next single featured **CAROLE KENYON** – dual vocals)

Apr 83. (7"/7"pic-d)(12") *(VS/+P 570)(VS 57012)* **TEMPTATION. /**
WE LIVE SO FAST | 2 | –

May 83. (7",12") **WE LIVE SO FAST. / BEST KEPT SECRET** | – | –

May 83. (lp/c/cd) *(V/TCV/CDV 2253) <8020>* **THE LUXURY GAP** | 4 | 72
– Crushed by the wheels of industry / Who'll stop the rain / Let me go / Key to the world / Temptation / Come live with me / Lady Ice and Mr. Hex / We live so fast / The best kept secret. *(re-iss. Jul87 lp/c; OVED/+C 213)*

Jun 83. (7"/7"pic-d) *(VS/+P 607)* **COME LIVE WITH ME. / LET'S**
ALL MAKE A BOMB | 5 |
(12"+=) *(VS 607-12)* – Song with no name.

Sep 83. (7"/7"pic-d) *(VS/+P 628)* **CRUSHED BY THE WHEELS OF**
INDUSTRY. / ('A' instrumental) | 17 |
(12"+=) *(VS 628-12)* – ('A'dance version).

Aug 84. (7") *(VS 708)* **SUNSET NOW. / COUNTERFORCE** | 24 |
(12"+=) *(VS 708-12)* – Flame down / Counterforce II.

Sep 84. (lp/c) *(V/TCV 2326)* **HOW MEN ARE** | 12 |
– Five minutes to midnight / Sunset now / This is mine / The fuse / Shane is on the rocks / The skin I'm in / Flame down / Reputation / . . . (And that's no lie). *(re-iss. Jul87 lp/c; OVED/+C 2326) (re-iss. cd Mar94)*

Oct 84. (7") *(VS 722)* **THIS IS MINE. / THE SKIN I'M IN** | 23 |
(12"+=) *(VS 722-12)* – That's mine (mixes).

Jan 85. (7"/12") *(VS 740)* **. . . (AND THAT'S NO LIE). / THE FUSE** | 52 |
(d7"+=) *(VSD 740)* – ('A'&'B'versions).
next featured **JIMMY RUFFIN** – dual vocals (ex-60's soul singer)

                                Virgin   Virgin

Apr 86. (7") *(VS 859)* **THE FOOLISH THING TO DO. / MY**
SENSITIVITY | |
(12"+=) *(VS 859-12)* – ('A'version).

Oct 86. (7") *(VS 881)* **CONTENDERS. / DIARY OF A CONTENDER** | |
(d12"+=) *(VS 881-12)* – ('A'extended dance) / Penthouse and pavement.

Nov 86. (cd/c/lp) *(CD/TC+/V 2400) <90569>* **PLEASURE ONE** | 78 | Mar87
– Contenders / Trouble / Somebody / If I were you / Low society / Look at me / Move out / Free.

Jan 87. (7") *(VS 920)* **TROUBLE. / (BIG) TROUBLE** | 51 |
(12"+=) *(VS 920-12)* – ('A'club version).
(d7"+=) *(VSD 920)* – Move out / Contenders (US version).

Aug 88. (7") *(VS 1113)* **THE BALLAD OF GO-GO BROWN. / I SET**
YOU FREE | |
(12"+=) *(VST 1113)* – ('A'version).
(cd-s+=) *(VSCD 1113)* – Slow all over.

Sep 88. (cd/c/lp) *(CD/TC+/V 2547)* **TEDDY BEAR, DUKE AND**
PSYCHO | |
– Big square people / Don't stop for no one / Snake and two people / Can you hear me? / The ballad of Go-go Brown / Dangerous / I set you free / Train of love and motion / Responsibility. *(cd+=)* – Foolish thing to do / East seven days. *(cd++=)* – Work / Giving up / Slow all over.

Oct 88. (7") *(VS 1134)* **TRAIN OF LOVE AND MOTION. / WORK** | |
(12"+=/3"cd-s+=) *(VS T/CD 1134)* – ('A'extended) / Giving up.

—— disbanded by the late 80's until . . .

                          Eternal-
                          WEA   WEA

Nov 96. (c-s) *(WEA 078C)* **DESIGNING HEAVEN /** | |
(cd-s+=) *(WEA 078CD1)* – ('A'side) / ('A'-Motiv-8 remix) / ('A'-Heaven 17 remix) / ('A'-Gregorio remix).
(cd-s) *(WEA 078CD2)* – ('A'side) / ('A'-Giorgio Moroder remix) / ('A'-Chris Cox remix) / ('A'-Gregorio remix).

Apr 97. (c-s) *(WEA 0398C)* **WE BLAME LOVE / ('A'–Giorgio's mimx)** | | –
(12"+=/cd-s+=) *(W 0398 T/CD)* – ('A'–Space baby mix) / ('A'–Matt Darey dub).

– compilations, etc. –

on 'Virgin' unless mentioned otherwise

Jul 86. (cd/d-c) *(CDV/TCV 2383)* **ENDLESS** (compilation of
12"mixes; cass = 17 extra minutes) | 70 |

Jun 88. (3"cd-ep) *(CDT 19)* **TEMPTATION. / WHO'LL STOP THE**
RAIN / WE LIVE SO FAST | |

Jun 88. (3"cd-ep) *(CDT 21)* **(WE DON'T NEED THIS) FASCIST**
GROOVE THANG / I'M YOUR MONEY / THE HEIGHT
OF THE FIGHTING / THE DECLINE OF THE WEST | |

Nov 88. (7") *Old Gold; (OG 9820)* **TEMPTATION. / COME LIVE WITH**
ME | |

Feb 89. (12") *Old Gold; (OG 4105)* **LET ME GO. / PLAY TO WIN** | |

Nov 92. (7"/c-s) *(VS/+C 1446)* **TEMPTATION (Brothers in rhythm**
remix). / ('A' mix) | 4 |
(12"+=/cd-s+=) *(VS T/CD 1446)* – ('A'mixes).

Feb 93. (7"/c-s) *(VS/+C 1451)* **(WE DON'T NEED THIS) FASCIST**
GROOVE THANG (Rapino edit) / ('A'-Democratic edit) | 40 |
(cd-s+=) *(VSCD 1451)* – ('A'mixes).

Mar 93. (cd/c/lp) *(CD/TC+/V 2717)* **HIGHER AND HIGHER – THE**
BEST OF HEAVEN 17 | 31 |
– Temptation (brothers in rhythm remix) / (We don't need this) Fascist groove thang (rapido edit) / Let me go / Come live with me / This is mine / I'm your money / play to win / (And that's no lie) / Contenders / we live so fast / Sunset now / Trouble / Height of the fighting (he-la-hu) / Penthouse and pavement / Crushed by the wheels of industry / (We don't need this) Fascist groove thang (original) / Temptation (original).

Mar 93. (7"/c-s) *(VS/+C 1457)* **PENTHOUSE AND PAVEMENT. /**
('A'mix) | 54 |
(12"+=/cd-s+=) *(VS T/CD 1457)* – ('A'mixes).

Dec 93. (cd/c) *VIP-Virgin; (CD/TC VIP 110)* **THE BEST OF HEAVEN 17** | | –

Apr 95. (cd/c) *VIP-Virgin; (CD/TC VIP 133)* **THE REMIX COLLECTION** | | –

B.E.F.

—— (aka The BRITISH ELECTRIC FOUNDATION)(**IAN** and **MARTIN** with guest vocalists inc. **GARY GLITTER, PAUL JONES** etc.)

                             Virgin   Arista

Mar 81. (c) *(TCV 2888)* **MUSIC FOR STOWAWAYS** | | –

                              Virgin   Arista

Nov 81. (5x7"box) *(VV 2219)* **MUSIC OF QUALITY AND**
DISTINCTION | 25 |
– Anyone who had a heart / It's over / Ball and confusion / You keep me hangin' on / The secret life of Arabia / There's a ghost in my house / These boots are made for walking / Perfect day / Suspicious minds / Wichita lineman. *(cd-iss. Aug92; CDBEF 1) (cd re-iss. Dec98 on 'Virgin-VIP'; CDVIP 227)*

Apr 82. (7"; by SANDIE SHAW) *(VS 484)* **ANYONE WHO HAD**
A HEART. / (part 2) | | –

Apr 82. (7"; by PAULA YATES) *(VS 493)* **THESE BOOTS ARE MADE**
FOR WALKING. / (part 2) | | –

May 82. (7"; by BILLY MacKENZIE) *(VS 498)* **IT'S OVER. / (part 2)** | | –

May 82. (7"; by TINA TURNER) *(VS 500)* **BALL OF CONFUSION. /**
(part 2) | | –
with guests singers (see below)

                            10-Virgin   Arista

Jul 91. (7"/c-s) **FAMILY AFFAIR. / ('A'instrumental)** | |
(cd-s+=) – ('A'party plan mix).

Sep 91. (cd)(c)(lp) **MUSIC OF QUALITY AND DISTINCTION**
VOLUME 2 | |
– (CHAKA KHAN) – Sunday we'll all be free / (LALAH HATHAWAY) – Family affair / (RICHARD DARBYSHIRE) – Early in the morning / (BILLY MacKENZIE) – Free / (TERENCE TRENT D'ARBY) – It's alright ma, I'm only bleeding / (TASHAN) – I want you / (MAVIS STAPLES) – A song for you / (BILLY PRESTON) – Try a little tenderness / (GREEN GARTSIDE) – I don't know why I love you / (TINA TURNER) – A change is gonna come / (GHIDA DE PALMA) – Feel like makin' love.

HEAVY STEREO   (dig out; Great Alt & Indie . . .)

Richard HELL

Born: RICHARD MYERS, 2 Oct'49, Lexington, Kentucky, USA. Raised in Wilmington, Delaware, he later moved to New York in his late teens, where he wrote poetry and experimented with drugs. Along with his sidekicks, TOM MILLER and BILLY FICCA, he formed The NEON BOYS in 1971. By '73, they'd metamorphasized into TELEVISION, MYERS adopting his RICHARD HELL moniker (while MILLER became TOM VERLAINE) and helping to initiate the city's new wave/punk scene. As legend has it, a sharp-eyed MALCOLM McLAREN was rather taken by HELL's dragged-through-a-hedge-backwards attire and mop of spiked hair, initially attempting to secure his services for his new baby, The SEX PISTOLS; when this failed, well, at least he could go back to England with a few ideas . . . HELL subsequently split with VERLAINE and co., briefly joining JOHNNY THUNDERS in The HEARTBREAKERS, where he co-penned (along with a RAMONE!) the seminal 'CHINESE ROCKS'; like THUNDERS, HELL was well acquainted with the pleasures of heroin, which no doubt accounted for his haphazard career. HELL subsequently formed his own outfit, RICHARD HELL & THE VOIDOIDS along with future LOU REED guitarist ROBERT QUINE, IVAN JULIAN and MARC BELL. They hastily recorded an independently released debut EP before signing to 'Sire'; with the resulting 'BLANK GENERATION' (1977) album, HELL had finally succeeded in capturing his brutally nihilistic poetical/musical vision, if only fleetingly. With his drug problems reaching critical levels, HELL's only release over the next five years was 'THE KID WITH THE REPLACEABLE HEAD', a 1978 NICK LOWE-produced single. A belated follow-up album, 'DESTINY STREET' (1982), eventually appeared in Spring '82, although the momentum had long since disippated. HELL was absent from the music scene for the next ten years (although he did star in the film, 'Smithereens' as well as scoring a cameo role as MADONNA's boyfriend in 'Desperately Seeking Susan'), finally re-emerging with art-noise veterans, THURSTON MOORE and DON FLEMING for a solo EP, before adding STEVE SHELLEY and recording an album under the DIM STARS moniker.
• **Songwriters:** HELL penned all, co-writing 'LOVE COMES IN SPURTS' with VERLAINE. DIM STARS covered RIP OFF (Marc Bolan) / NATCHEZ BURNING (Johnny Burnette). • **Trivia:** He also wrote a column for East Village Eye in the 80's. His biography 'Artifact: Notebooks from Hell' was issued by Hanuman in 1990.

Album rating: BLANK GENERATION (*8) / DESTINY STREET (*5) / R.I.P. – THE ROIR SESSIONS collection (*5) / Dim Stars: DIM STARS (*6)

RICHARD HELL & THE VOID-OIDS

RICHARD HELL – vocals, bass / **ROBERT QUINE** (b.30 Dec'42, Akron, Ohio) – guitar, vocals / **IVAN JULIAN** (b.26 Jun'55, Washington, D.C.) – guitar, vocals / **MARC BELL** (b.15 Jul'56, New York City) – drums (ex-WAYNE COUNTY & THE ELECTRIC CHAIRS)

                             Stiff   Ork

Nov 76. (7"ep) *(BUY 7) <81976>* **(I COULD LIVE WITH YOU IN)**
ANOTHER WORLD. / YOU GOTTA LOSE / (I BELONG
TO) BLANK GENERATION | |
(re-iss. Jun94 on 'Overground' 7"ep/cd-ep; OVER 36/+CD)

                             Sire   Sire

Sep 77. (7") *(6078 608) <SRE 1003>* **BLANK GENERATION. / LOVE**
COMES IN SPURTS | |
(12") *(6078 608)* – ('A'side) / Liars beware / Who says.

Sep 77. (lp) *(SR 6037) <6037>* **BLANK GENERATION** | |
– Love comes in spurts / Liars beware / New pleasure / Betrayal takes two / Down at the rock and roll club / Who says / Blank generation / Walking on the water / The plan / Another world. *(cd-iss. Jun90; 7599 26137-2)*

—— **FRED MAURO** – drums repl. BELL who joined RAMONES

—— added **JERRY ANTONIUS** – keyboards, vocals

	Radar	not iss.
Nov 78. (7") *(ADA 30)* **THE KID WITH THE REPLACEABLE HEAD. / I'M YOUR MAN**	☐	☐

—— **HELL** and **JULIAN** recruited **FRED MAHER** – drums repl. MAURO / **NAUX** (b.29 Jul'51, San Jose, Calif.) – guitar repl. QUINE to LYDIA LUNCH

	I.D.	Red Star
May 82. (lp) *(NOSE 2)* **DESTINY STREET**	☐	☐

– The kid with the replaceable head / You gotta move / Going going gone / Lowest common dominator / Downtown at dawn / Time / I can only give you everything / Ignore that door / Staring in her eyes / Destiny street. *(cd-iss. Sep93 & Mar95 on 'Danceteria';)*

—— Split 1982, RICHARD HELL starred in the film 'Smithereens'. MAHER joined SCRITTI POLITTI. In 1986, he made brief cameo in the film 'Desperately Seeking Susan' as Madonna's boyfriend.

RICHARD HELL

—— (solo) with **THURSTON MOORE + DON FLEMING** – guitar (of GUMBALL)

	Overground	not iss.
Feb 92. (7"ep/cd-ep) *(OVER 24/+CD)* **3 NEW SONGS EP**	☐	☐

– The night is coming on / Baby Huey (Baby do you wanna dance?) / Frank Sinatra.

	Codex	Tim Kerr
Apr 95. (cd-ep/10"ep) *(CODE 3/+X)* <TK 9410 080 CD> **GO NOW** (spoken word)	☐	☐ Oct96

– compilations etc. –

Feb 80. (7"ep; The NEON BOYS) Shake; <SHK 101> **DON'T DIE / TIME. / LOVE COMES IN SPURTS ('73) / THAT'S ALL I KNOW (RIGHT NOW)**	☐	☐

(UK-iss.Feb90 as 'TIME EP' on 'Overground' 7"purple; OVER 11)

Dec 84. (c) *R.O.I.R.;* **R.I.P. (live)**	☐	☐

(UK cd-iss. Jun90 on 'Danceteria'; DANCD 040)

Apr 90. (c) *R.O.I.R.;* **FUNHUNT**	☐	

(cd-iss. Jul92;)

Apr 91. (12"clear/cd-ep; A-side as The NEON BOYS) Overground; *(OVER 19/+CD)* **THAT'S ALL I KNOW (RIGHT NOW) / LOVE COMES IN SPURTS / HIGH HEELED WHEELS. / DON'T DIE / TIME**	☐	☐

DIM STARS

RICHARD HELL + DON FLEMING with **THURSTON MOORE + STEVE SHELLEY** (both of SONIC YOUTH)

	Paperhouse	Caroline
Apr 92. (12"ep/cd-ep) *(PAPER 015 T/CD)* <CAROL 1468> **THE PLUG / DIM STAR THEME. / CHRISTIAN RAP ATTACK / YOU GOTTA LOSE**	☐	☐
Jun 92. (cd/lp) *(PAP CD/LP 014)* <CAROL 1724> **DIM STARS**	☐	☐

– She wants to die / All my witches come true / Memo to Marty / Monkey / Natchez burning / Stop breakin' down / Baby Huey (do you wanna dance?) / The night is coming on / Downtown at dawn / Try this / Stray cat generation / Rip off.

HELLOWEEN (dig out; Great Metal . . .)

HELMET (dig out; Great Alt & Indie . . .)

Jimi HENDRIX

Born: JOHNNY ALLEN HENDRIX, 27 Nov'42, Seattle, Washington, USA. He was raised by a part Cherokee Indian mother and black father, who, at age 3, changed his forenames to JAMES MARSHALL and bought him his first guitar. Being left-handed, he turned it upside down and reversed the strings, teaching himself by listening to blues and rock'n'roll artists such as ROBERT JOHNSON, MUDDY WATERS, B.B. KING and CHUCK BERRY. In the early 60's, he enlisted in the paratroopers, thus avoiding the draft into the US army. He was subsequently discharged for medical reasons in 1962, after injuring himself during a jump. Two years later, the young HENDRIX moved to New York and backed acts LITTLE RICHARD, The ISLEY BROTHERS, IKE & TINA TURNER. He soon struck up a partnership with soul singer CURTIS KNIGHT, also obtaining a contract with Ed Chalpin (KNIGHT is said to have written 'The Ballad Of Jimi' in 1965, after JIMI prophecised his own death circa 1970!). Early the following year, HENDRIX's first real band, JIMMY JAMES & THE BLUE FLAMES, were born. With JIMI's reputation now spreading, he was seen by ex-ANIMALS bassman CHAS CHANDLER, who invited him to London. After auditions, they found a rhythm section of NOEL REDDING and MITCH MITCHELL, smashing their way into the UK Top 10 in early '67 with the 'Polydor' one-off 45, 'HEY JOE'. CHANDLER then set up a deal with Kit Lambert's new 'Track' label, and The JIMI HENDRIX EXPERIENCE exploded onto the scene. Their first Hendrix-penned 45, the thundering acid-fever of 'PURPLE HAZE', made the UK Top 3, as did the scintillating debut album, 'ARE YOU EXPERIENCED?'. This was released hot on the heels of their third Top 10 single, 'THE WIND CRIES MARY'. Hendrix was a revelation, a black super-freak whose mastery of the guitar was above and beyond anything previously heard. In fact, he virtually re-invented the instrument, duly illustrating various methods of on-stage abuse (i.e. biting it, playing it with his teeth, shagging it and even setting fire to it!). He was duly booked on the Monterey International Pop Festival bill, where he proceeded to play an orgasmic version of 'WILD THING'. From the sublime to the ridiculous, the following month saw a wholly inappropriate US support tour with The MONKEES, leaving both him and teenybop audiences baffled, but no doubt entertained for seven nights. After another classic UK hit, 'THE BURNING OF THE MIDNIGHT LAMP', he released his second lp, 'AXIS: BOLD AS LOVE', which made the Top 5 early in '68, and was the first to chart and hit the Top 3 in his native America. In the Autumn of '68, JIMI revived and transformed BOB DYLAN's 'ALL ALONG THE WATCHTOWER', a song that broke into the US Top 20 and UK Top 5. It was trailed by a superb British Top 10 (US No.1) double-lp, 'ELECTRIC LADYLAND', the record featuring the now infamous naked women sleeve (much to JIMI's displeasure), which some shops sold in a brown cover! The beginning of the end came in 1969, when he was busted for drugs, leading to his band disintegrating; the trio played together for the last time on the 29th June at the Denver Pop Festival. REDDING had already formed FAT MATTRESS, MITCHELL returning with other musicians BILLY COX and LARRY LEE to make the group a quartet. The new "Experience" played the Woodstock Festival on the 17-18 August '69, performing an excellent version of 'STAR SPANGLED BANNER' that went down in the folklore of rock music. To end the year, JIMI was found not guilty of an earlier charge of heroin and marijuana possession and at the same time, he formed all-black outfit, BAND OF GYPSYS, along with COX and drummer BUDDY MILES. They released the self-titled live set in May '70 (recorded at Fillmore East, New Year's Eve/Day 1969/70). This hit the Top 5 in the States, and, following a court order, he paid ex-manager Ed Chalpin $1m in compensation and a percentage of royalties. Tragically, after a few more open-air festival concerts and some bad drugs trips, he died in London on the 18th of September '70. He was said to have left a phoned message to Chandler saying "I need help bad, man". The official cause of death was an inhalation of vomit, due to barbiturate intoxication, leading to a coroner's decision of an open verdict. To many rock music buffs, he remains the greatest axegrinder of all-time and who knows what he might have become had he survived the heady sixties. • **Songwriters:** HENDRIX except other covers; HEY JOE (William Roberts) / JOHNNY B.GOODE (Chuck Berry) / GLORIA (Them) / SGT. PEPPER (Beatles) / HANG ON SLOOPY (McCoys) / TUTTI FRUTTI + LUCILLE (Little Richard) / BO DIDDLEY (Bo Diddley) / PETER GUNN (Henry Mancini) / HOOCHIE COOCHIE MAN (Muddy Waters) / BLUE SUEDE SHOES (Carl Perkins) / etc. • **Trivia:** In Jan'69, he and band play live tribute of CREAM's 'Sunshine Of Your Love' on The LULU Show, much to annoyance of TV controllers.

Album rating (selective): ARE YOU EXPERIENCED? (*10) / AXIS: BOLD AS LOVE (*9) / SMASH HITS compilation (*8) / ELECTRIC LADYLAND (*10) / BAND OF GYPSYS (*8) / posthumous:- THE CRY OF LOVE (*7) / EXPERIENCE (*3) / AT THE ISLE OF WIGHT (*4) / RAINBOW BRIDGE (*4) / HENDRIX IN THE WEST (*5) / WAR HEROES (*4) / SOUNDTRACK RECORDINGS FROM THE FILM 'JIMI HENDRIX' (*5) / CRASH LANDING (*4) / MIDNIGHT LIGHTNING (*4) / THE JIMI HENDRIX CONCERTS (*5) / THE SINGLES ALBUM (*4) / LIVE AT WINTERLAND (*7) / RADIO ONE (*7) / CORNERSTONES 1967-1970 (*8) / THE ULTIMATE EXPERIENCE (*10) / BLUES (*6) JIMI HENDRIX: WOODSTOCK (*6) / VOODOO SOUP (*5) / FIRST RAYS OF THE NEW RISING SUN (*6)

JIMI HENDRIX – vocals, lead guitar (ex-CURTIS KNIGHT) with **NOEL REDDING** (b.DAVID REDDING, 25 Dec'45, Folkstone, Kent, England) – bass / **MITCH MITCHELL** (b.JOHN MITCHELL, 9 Jun'47, Ealing, London, England) – drums

	Polydor	Reprise
Dec 66. (7"; as JIMI HENDRIX) *(56139)* **HEY JOE. / STONE FREE**	6	☐

(re-iss. Jul84 on 'Old Gold')

	Track	Reprise
Mar 67. (7") *(604 001)* **PURPLE HAZE. / 51ST ANNIVERSARY**	3	☐
Mar 67. (7") <0572> **HEY JOE. / 51st ANNIVERSARY**	–	☐
May 67. (7") *(604 004)* **THE WIND CRIES MARY. / HIGHWAY CHILE**	6	☐
May 67. (lp; mono/stereo) *(612/613 001)* <6261> **ARE YOU EXPERIENCED?**	2	5 Aug67

– Foxy lady / Manic depression / Red house / Can you see me / Love or confusion / I don't live today / May this be love / Fire / Third stone from the sun / Remember / Are you experienced? *(re-iss. Nov70; 2407 010) (re-iss. Nov81; 612 001) (re-iss. Sep85 on 'Polydor' lp/c; SPE LP/MC 97) (cd-iss. Jun91 & Oct93 cd/c; 521036-2/-4) (re-iss. Apr97 on 'MCA' cd/c; MCD/MCC 11608)*

Aug 67. (7") <0597> **PURPLE HAZE. / THE WIND CRIES MARY**	–	65
Aug 67. (7") *(604 007)* **THE BURNING OF THE MIDNIGHT LAMP. / THE STARS THAT PLAY WITH LAUGHING SAM'S DICE**	18	–
Dec 67. (7"; by JIMI HENDRIX) <0641> **FOXY LADY. / HEY JOE**	–	67
Dec 67. (lp; mono/stereo) *(612/613 003)* <6281> **AXIS: BOLD AS LOVE**	5	3 Feb68

– Experience / Up from the skies / Spanish castle magic / Wait until tomorrow / Ain't no telling / Little wing / If six was nine / You've got me floating / Castles made of sand / She's so fine / One rainy wish / Little Miss Lover / Bold as love. *(re-iss. Nov70;) (re-iss. Aug83 on 'Polydor' lp/c; SPE LP/MC 71) (cd-iss. 1987 on 'Polydor'; 813 572-2) (re-iss. Jul91 & Oct93 on 'Polydor' lp/c/cd; 847243-1/-4/-2) (re-iss. Apr97 on 'MCA' cd/c; MCD/MCC 11601)*

Feb 68. (7") <0665> **UP FROM THE SKIES. / ONE RAINY WISH**	–	82
Apr 68. (lp; mono/stereo) *(612/613 004)* <2025> **SMASH HITS** (compilation)	4	6 Jul69

– Purple haze / Fire / The wind cries Mary / Can you see me / 51st anniversary / Hey Joe / Stone free / The stars that play with laughing Sam's dice / Manic depression / Highway chile / The burning of the midnight lamp / Foxy lady. *(re-iss. Jun73 on 'Polydor'; 2310 268) (re-iss. Aug83 on 'Polydor' lp/c; SPE LP/MC 3) (cd-iss. Feb85; 813 572-2)*

May 68. (7") <0728> **FOXY LADY. / PURPLE HAZE**	–	☐
Jul 68. (7") <0742> **ALL ALONG THE WATCHTOWER. / CROSSTOWN TRAFFIC**	–	☐

—— JIMI now brought in old session campaigners **AL KOOPER** and **STEVE WINWOOD** – keyboards plus **JACK CASADY** – bass / **BUDDY MILES** – drums / (to repl. MITCHELL and REDDING)

Sep 68. (7") <0767> **ALL ALONG THE WATCHTOWER. / BURNING OF THE MIDNIGHT LAMP**	–	20

Oct 68. (7") *(604 025)* **ALL ALONG THE WATCHTOWER. / LONG HOT SUMMER NIGHT** — 5 / –

Nov 68. (d-lp) *(613 008-9) <6307>* **ELECTRIC LADYLAND** — 6 / 1 Oct68
 – And the gods made love / (Have you ever been to) Electric Ladyland / Crosstown traffic / Voodoo chile / Rainy day, dream away / 1983 (a merman I should turn to be) / Moon, turn the tide . . . gently gently away / Little Miss Strange / Long hot summer night / Come on / Gypsy eyes / The burning of the midnight lamp / Still raining still dreaming / House burning down / All along the watchtower / Voodoo chile (slight return). *(also iss.lp/lp; 613 010/017) (re-iss. Jun73 on 'Polydor'; 2657 012) (re-iss. Jan84 on 'Polydor'; 350011-2) (re-iss. Jul91 & Oct93 on 'Polydor' lp/c/cd; 847233-1/-4/-2) (re-iss. Apr97 on 'MCA' cd/c; MCD/MCC 11600) (hit UK No.47 in Aug97)*

Apr 69. (7") *(604 029) <0798>* **CROSSTOWN TRAFFIC. / GYPSY EYES** — 37 / 52 Nov68

Oct 69. (7") *(604 033)* **(LET ME LIGHT YOUR) FIRE. / THE BURNING OF THE MIDNIGHT LAMP**

Feb 70. (7") *<0853>* **STONE FREE. / IF 6 WAS 9** — – / –

Apr 70. (7") *<0905>* **STEPPING STONE. / IZABELLA** — – /

JIMI HENDRIX

retained **BUDDY MILES** + recruited **BILLY COX** – bass

	Track	Capitol

Jun 70. (lp) *(2406 002) <472>* **BAND OF GYPSYS (live)** — 6 / 5 Apr70
 – Who knows / Machine gun / Changes / Power of soul / Message to love / We gotta live together. *(re-iss. Aug83 on 'Polydor'; SPELP 16) (cd-iss. May88; 821 933-2) (re-iss. Dec89 & Jul91 on 'Polydor' lp/c/cd; 847 237-1/-4/-2) (re-iss. Apr97 on 'MCA' cd/c; MCD/MCC 11607)*

―― On the 18th September '70, HENDRIX died of a drug overdose.

– compilations, etc. –

Feb 68. (lp; with CURTIS KNIGHT) *London; (HA 8349) / Capitol; <2856>* **GET THAT FEELING (live 1964)** — 39 / 75

Nov 68. (lp) *London; (HA 8369)* **STRANGE THINGS** — / –
 (re-iss. Apr86 on 'Showcase' lp/c; SHLP/SHTC 101)
 Note; All below 'Track' releases were issued on 'Reprise' US.

Sep 67. (7") *Track; (604 009)* **HOW WOULD YOU FEEL. / YOU DON'T WANT ME** — / –

May 70. (lp; shared with The WHO) *Track; (2407 004)* **BACKTRACK:4** — / –

May 70. (lp; shared with The WHO) *Track; (2407 008)* **BACKTRACK:8** — / –

– posthumous releases –

on 'Polydor' unless mentioned otherwise / 'Reprise' US

Oct 70. (7"; JIMI HENDRIX with CURTIS KNIGHT) *London; (HLZ 10321)* **BALLAD OF JIMI. / GLOOMY MONDAY**

Sep 70. (lp) *Reprise; <2029>* **MONTEREY INTERNATIONAL POP FESTIVAL (live soundtrack)** — – / 16

Oct 70. (7"m) *Track; (2095 001)* **VOODOO CHILE (SLIGHT RETURN). / HEY JOE / ALL ALONG THE WATCHTOWER** — 1 / –

Mar 71. (lp) *Track; (2408 101) <2034>* **THE CRY OF LOVE** — 2 / 3
 – Freedom / Drifting / Ezy rider / Night bird flying / My friend / Straight ahead / Astro man / Angel / In from the storm / Belly button window. *(re-iss. Jun73 on 'Polydor' lp)(c; 2302 023)(3194 025) (re-iss. Sep85 on 'Polydor' lp/c; SPE LP/MC 98) (cd-iss. Mar89; 829 926-2) (re-iss. Jul91 & Mar93 on 'Polydor' cd/c/lp; 847242-2/-4/-1)*

Apr 71. (7") *Track; (2094 007)* **NIGHT BIRD FLYING. / FREEDOM** — / –

Mar 71. (7") *Reprise; <1000>* **FREEDOM. / ANGEL** — – / 59

Oct 71. (7") *Reprise; <1044>* **DOLLY DAGGER. / STAR SPANGLED BANNER** — – / 74

Oct 71. (7"ep) *Track; (2094 010)* **GYPSY EYES. / REMEMBER / PURPLE HAZE / STONE FREE** — 35 /

Nov 71. (lp) *(2302 016)* **JIMI HENDRIX AT THE ISLE OF WIGHT (live)** — 17 / –
 – Midnight lightning / Foxy lady / Lover man / Freedom / All along the watchtower / In from the storm. *(re-iss. Apr84 lp/c; SPE LP/MC 71) (cd-iss. Mar89; 831 813-2) (re-iss. Jul91 & Mar93 cd/c/lp; 847 236-2/-4/-1)*

Jan 72. (lp) *(2302 018) <2049>* **HENDRIX IN THE WEST (live)** — 7 / 12
 – Johnny B. Goode / Lover man / Blue suede shoes / Voodoo chile (slight return) / The queen / Sergeant Pepper's lonely hearts club band / Little wing / Red house.

Jan 72. (7") *Reprise; <1082>* **JOHNNY B. GOODE. / LOVERMAN** — / –

Feb 72. (7") *(2001 277)* **JOHNNY B. GOODE. / LITTLE WING** — 35 / –

May 72. (7") *Reprise;* **LITTLE WING. / THE WIND CRIES MARY** — – /

Nov 72. (lp) *(2302 020) <2103>* **WAR HEROES** — 23 / 48
 – Bleeding heart / Highway chile / Tax free / Peter Gunn / Catastrophe / Stepping stone / Midnight / 3 little bears / Beginning / Izabella. *(re-iss. Aug83 on 'Polydor' lp/c; SPE LP/MC 4) (cd-iss. Mar89; 813 573-2) (re-iss. Jul91 cd/c/lp;) (re-iss. cd+c Mar93)*

Oct 73. (d-lp) **ARE YOU EXPERIENCED / AXIS: BOLD AS LOVE** — / –

Feb 74. (lp) *(2310 301)* **LOOSE ENDS** — / –
 – Come down hard on me baby / Blue suede shoes / Jam 292 / The stars that play with laughing Sam's dice / The drifter's escape / Burning desire / I'm your hoochie coochie man / (Have you ever been) To Electric Ladyland. *(cd-iss. Mar89; 837 574-2)*

Mar 75. (lp) *(2343 080)* **JIMI HENDRIX** — 35 / –

Sep 75. (lp) *(2310 398) <2204>* **CRASH LANDING** — 35 / 5 Mar75
 – Message to love / Somewhere over the rainbow / Crash landing / Coming down hard on me / Peace in Mississippi / With the power / Stone free again / Captain Coconut. *(re-iss. Mar83 lp/c; SPE LP/MC 94) (cd-iss. Mar89;) (cd-iss. Jun91 & Mar93 cd/c/lp; 847263-2)*

Nov 75. (lp) *(2310 415) <2229>* **MIDNIGHT LIGHTNING** — 46 / 43
 – Trashman / Midnight lightning / Hear my train a coming / Hey baby (new rising sun) / Blue suede shoes / Machine gun / Once I had a woman / Beginnings. *(re-iss. Mar89 lp/c/cd; 825 166-1/-4/-2)*

Oct 76. (lp) *(2343086)* **JIMI HENDRIX VOL.2** — / –

Jul 78. (d-lp)(d-c) *(261 2034)(350 0122) <2245>* **THE ESSENTIAL JIMI HENDRIX** — / –
 (with free one-sided 33rpm 7" GLORIA)

Jun 80. (lp) *<2299>* **NINE TO THE UNIVERSE** — – / –

Jun 80. (lp) *(2343 114)* **STONE FREE**

 (re-iss. Nov83 lp/c; SPE LP/MC 51)

Sep 80. (7") **VOODOO CHILE. / GLORIA**

Sep 80. (6x7"-box) **6 SINGLES BOXED** (1st 6)

Sep 80. (12xlp-box) *(2625 038)* **10th ANNIVERSARY BOXED SET**

Jan 81. (lp) *(2311 014) <2293>* **THE ESSENTIAL JIMI HENDRIX VOLUME 2** — / Aug79

Nov 81. (12"ep) *(POSPX 401)* **ALL ALONG THE WATCHTOWER. / FOXY LADY / PURPLE HAZE / MANIC DEPRESSION**

Jun 82. (lp) *(234 3115)* **VOODOO CHILE**
 (re-iss. Nov83 lp/c; SPE LP/MC 52)

Sep 82. (12"ep) *(POSPX 608)* **VOODOO CHILE. / GIPSY EYES / HEY JOE / 3RD STONE FROM THE SUN**

Feb 83. (lp/c) *(PODV/+C 6)* **SINGLES ALBUM** — 77 /

Jun 83. (d-c) *(TWOMC 3)* **CRASH LANDING / MIDNIGHT LIGHTNING**

Nov 84. (lp/c/cd) *(823 704-1/-4/-2)* **KISS THE SKY**
 (re-iss. Jun91 cd/c/lp;) (re-iss. Mar93 cd/c)

Feb 86. (lp/c/cd) *(827 990-1/-4/-2)* **JIMI PLAYS MONTEREY (live)**
 (re-iss. Jun91 & Mar93 cd/c/lp; 847 244-2/-4/-1)

1986. Capitol; (lp,cd) *<SJ 12416>* **BAND OF GYPSYS 2** — – /

Jul 87. (lp/c/cd) *(833 004-1/-4/-2) / Rykodisc; <RCD 20038>* **LIVE AT WINTERLAND (live)**
 (re-iss. Jun91 & Mar93 cd/c/lp; 847 238-2/-4/-1)

Jan 89. (7") *(PO 33)* **PURPLE HAZE. / 51ST ANNIVERSARY**
 (12"+=) *(PZ 33)* – All along the watchtower.
 (cd-s+=) *(PZCD 33)* – Hey Joe.

1989. (4xcd-box) **BOXED SET**
 – ARE YOU EXPERIENCED? / WAR HEROES / IN THE WEST / BAND OF GYPSIES

Nov 89. (cd) *Hai Leonard; <HL 00660036>* **FUZZ, FEEDBACK & WAH-WAH (live)** — – /

Nov 89. (cd) *Hai Leonard; <HL 00660038>* **WHAMMY BAR & FINGER GREASE (live)** — – /

Nov 89. (cd) *Hai Leonard; <HL 00660040>* **RED HOUSE: VARIATIONS ON A THEME (live)** — – /

Nov 89. (cd) *Hai Leonard; <HL 00660041>* **OCTAVIA & UNIVIBE (live)** — – /

Mar 90. (7"/c-s) *(PO/+CS 71)* **CROSSTOWN TRAFFIC. / PURPLE HAZE** — 61 /
 (12"+=) *(PZ 71)* – All along the watchtower.
 (cd-s++=) *(PZCD 71)* – Have you ever been (to Electric Ladyland).

1990. (cd) **THE JIMI HENDRIX EXPERIENCE**

Oct 90. (cd/c/lp) *(847 231-2/-4/-1)* **CORNERSTONES (1967-1970, FOUR YEARS THAT CHANGED THE MUSIC) (live)** — 5 /
 – Hey Joe / Foxy lady / Purple haze / The wind cries Mary / Have you ever been to (Electric Ladyland) / Crosstown traffic / All along the watchtower / Voodoo chile (slight return) / Star spangled banner / Stepping stone / Room full of mirrors / Ezy rider / Freedom / Drifting / In from the storm / Angel. *(cd+=/c+=)* – Fire (live).

Oct 90. (7"ep) *(PO 100)* **ALL ALONG THE WATCHTOWER. / VOODOO CHILE / HEY JOE** — 52 /
 (12"+=/c-s+=) *(POCS/PZCD 100)* – Crosstown traffic.

Nov 90. (4xcd-box) *<9-26435-2>* **LIFELINES: THE JIMI HENDRIX STORY (live)**

Feb 91. (4xcd-box) *(847232-2)* **SESSIONS BOX – ARE YOU EXPERIENCED? / AXIS: BOLD AS LOVE / ELECTRIC LADYLAND / CRY OF LOVE**

Mar 91. (4xcd-box) *(847 235-2)* **FOOTLIGHTS (live)**
 – JIMI PLAYS MONTEREY / ISLE OF WIGHT / BAND OF GYPSIES / LIVE AT WINTERLAND

Feb 92. (4xcd-box) *(511 763-2)* **STAGES (live)**
 – (Stockholm 5 Sep'67 / Paris 29 Jan'68 / San Diego 24 May'69 / Atlanta 4 Jul'70)

Nov 92. (cd/c) *Polygram TV; (517235-2/-4) / M.C.A.; <10829>* **THE ULTIMATE EXPERIENCE** — 25 / 72 Jul93
 – All along the watchtower / Purple haze / Hey Joe / The wind cries Mary / Angel / Voodoo chile (slight return) / Foxy lady / Burning of the midnight lamp / Highway chile / Crosstown traffic / Castles made of sand / Long hot summer night / Red house / Manic depression / Gypsy eyes / Little wing / Fire / Wait until tomorrow / Star spangled banner / Wild thing (live). *(re-iss. Sep95; same)*

Feb 94. (cd) *I.T.M.; (ITM 960004)* **PURPLE HAZE IN WOODSTOCK (live)**

Apr 94. (3xcd-box) *Pulsar; (PULSE 301)* **GREATEST HITS**
 'Polydor' (the ones not mentioned), were issued on 'M.C.A.' in US.

Apr 94. (cd/c) *(521037-2/-4) <11060>* **BLUES** — 10 / 45

Aug 94. (cd/c) *(523384-2/-4) <11063>* **AT WOODSTOCK (live)** — 32 / 37

May 94. (cd) *Ramble Tamble; (RATA 002)* **LIVE AT THE 'SCENE' CLUB N.Y., N.Y. (live)**

Aug 94. (cd) *Charly; (CDCD 1172)* **BEFORE THE EXPERIENCE**

Oct 94. (cd) *Charly; (CDCD 1189)* **THE EARLY YEARS**

Apr 95. (cd/c) *(527 520-2/-4) <11236>* **VOODOO SOUP** — / 66
 – The new rising sun / Belly button window / Stepping stone / Freedom / Angel / Room full of mirrors / Midnight / Night bird flying / Drifting / Ezy rider / Pali gap / Message to love / Peace in Mississippi / In from the storm.

– others, etc. –

Oct 70. (7"; with CURTIS KNIGHT) *R.C.A.;* **NO SUCH ANIMAL (part 1). / (part 2)**

Apr 71. (lp) *Saga; (6307)* **JIMI HENDRIX**

1972. (lp) *Saga; (6313)* **JIMI HENDRIX AT HIS BEST VOL.1**

1972. (lp) *Saga; (6314)* **JIMI HENDRIX AT HIS BEST VOL.2**

1972. (lp) *Saga; (6315)* **JIMI HENDRIX AT HIS BEST VOL.3**

Apr 71. (lp; with CURTIS KNIGHT) *Hallmark;* **THE ETERNAL FIRE OF JIMI HENDRIX** — / –

1973. (lp; with CURTIS KNIGHT) *Hallmark; (SHM 791)* **THE WILD ONE**

Aug 71. (lp) *Ember; (NR 5057)* **EXPERIENCE (live)** — 9 /
 – The sunshine of your love / Room full of mirrors / Bleeding heart / Smashing of amps.

(re-iss. Sep79 on 'Bulldog'; BDL 4002) (cd-iss. Jan87 & Nov91; BDCD 40023) (cd-iss. Mar95 on 'Nectar';)

Mar 72. (lp) *Ember; (NR 5061)* **MORE EXPERIENCE (live)** | | - |
(re-iss. Sep79 & Jul82 on 'Bulldog')

Feb 75. (lp) *Ember; (EMB 3428)* **LOOKING BACK WITH JIMI HENDRIX (live)** | | - |

Oct 73. (lp) *Ember; (NR 5068)* **IN THE BEGINNING (live)** | | - |
(re-iss. 1984 on 'Everest'; CBR 1031)

1974. (lp) *Ember;* **FRIENDS FROM THE BEGINNING (with 'LITTLE RICHARD')** | | - |
(re-iss. Jan77)

Nov 71. (lp) *Reprise; (K 44159) <2040>* **RAINBOW BRIDGE (live soundtrack)** | 16 | 15 Oct71 |
– Dolly dagger / Earth blues / Pali gap / Room full of mirrors / Star spangled banner / Look over yonder / Hear my train a comin' / Hey baby. *(cd-iss. Mar87; K2 44159) (cd re-iss. Apr89; 831 312-2)*

Jun 73. (7") *Reprise;* **HEAR MY TRAIN A-COMIN'. / ROCK ME BABY** | | |

Jul 73. (d-lp) *Reprise; (K 64017)* **SOUNDTRACK RECORDINGS FROM THE FILM 'JIMI HENDRIX'** | 37 | |

Jun 82. (7") *Reprise;* **FIRE. / LITTLE WING** | - | |

Jul 72. (lp) *Music For Pleasure; (MFP 5278)* **WHAT'D I SAY (live)** | | - |

Sep 84. (lp) *Music For Pleasure; (MFP 50053)* **THE BIRTH OF SUCCESS (live)** | | - |

Nov 72. (lp) *Enterprise; (ENTF 3000)* **RARE HENDRIX** | | - |

Dec 72. (lp) *Enterprise;* **JIMI HENDRIX IN SESSION** | | - |

1973. (lp) *Enterprise; (ENTF 1030)* **HENDRIX '66** | | - |

1973. (lp) *Boulevard; (41060)* **JIMI HENDRIX 1964** | | - |

Nov 75. (lp) *D.J.M.; (DJLMD 8011)* **FOR REAL** | | - |
(re-iss. Feb82 on 'Audio Fidelity';)

Aug 79. (lp) *Bulldog; (BDL 2010) / Douglas;* **20 GOLDEN PIECES OF JIMI HENDRIX (live)** | | - |

Sep 79. (lp) *Bulldog; (BDL 4003)* **MORE ESSENTIAL** | | - |

Oct 80. (lp) *Red Lightnin'; (RL 0015)* **WOKE UP THIS MORNING AND FOUND MYSELF DEAD (live)** | | - |
(cd-iss. Nov86; RLCD 0068) (pic-lp.Oct88; RLP 0048) (cd-iss. 1992 on 'Point'; 262033-2)

Jun 81. (lp) *Audio Fidelity; (1002) / Nutmeg; <NUT 1002>* **COSMIC TURNAROUND** | | - |

Oct 81. (4xlp-box) *Audio Fidelity;* **THE GENIUS OF HENDRIX** | | - |

Mar 82. (lp) *Audio Fidelity;* **HIGH, LIVE AND DIRTY** | | - |

Dec 82. (cd) *Bulldog; (BDL 2027)* **20 GOLDEN PIECES OF JIMI HENDRIX VOL.2 (live)** | | - |

Oct 84. (c) *Audio Fidelity; (ZCGAS 703)* **JIMI HENDRIX VOL.1** | | - |

Oct 84. (c) *Audio Fidelity; (ZCGAS 704)* **JIMI HENDRIX VOL.2** | | - |

Oct 84. (c) *Audio Fidelity; (ZCGAS 732)* **JIMI HENDRIX VOL.3** | | - |

Nov 81. (lp) *Phoenix; (PHX 1012)* **FREE SPIRIT** | | - |
(re-iss. Jun87 on 'Thunderbolt'; THBM 006)

Sep 82. (lp) *Phoenix; (PHX 1020)* **MOODS** | | - |

Sep 82. (lp) *Phoenix; (PHX 1026)* **ROOTS OF HENDRIX** | | - |

Aug 82. (d-lp) *C.B.S.; (88592) / Reprise; <22306>* **THE JIMI HENDRIX CONCERTS (live)** | 16 | 79 |
– Fire / I don't live today / Red house / Stone free / Are you experienced? / Little wing / Voodoo chile (slight return) / Bleeding heart / Hey Joe / Wild thing / Hear my train a-comin'. *(re-iss. Aug89 on 'Media Motion' lp/c/cd; MEDIA/+C/CD 1) (re-iss. Feb90 on 'Castle' lp+=/c+=/cd+=; CCS LP/MC/CD 235)* – Foxy lady.

Aug 82. (7"/12") *C.B.S.; (A/+13 2749)* **FIRE (live). / ARE YOU EXPERIENCED (live)** | | - |

Oct 82. (lp) *Dakota;* **THE BEST OF JIMI HENDRIX** | | - |

Nov 83. (lp/c) *Contour; (CN/+4 2067)* **THE JIMI HENDRIX ALBUM** | | - |

Jul 84. (7") *Old Gold; (OG 9430)* **PURPLE HAZE. / THE WIND CRIES MARY** | | - |

Jul 84. (7") *Old Gold; (OG 9431)* **VOODOO CHILE (SLIGHT RETURN). / BURNING OF THE MIDNIGHT LAMP** | | - |

Jul 84. (7") *Old Gold; (OG 9432)* **ALL ALONG THE WATCHTOWER. / FOXY LADY** | | - |

Jul 85. (lp/c) *Topline; (TOP/KTOP 124)* **GANGSTER OF LOVE** | | - |

Apr 86. (lp/c) *Arcade; (ADAH/+C 430)* **THE LEGEND** | | - |

May 86. (lp/c) *Sierra; (FEDB/CFEDB 5032)* **REPLAY OF JIMI HENDRIX** | | - |

Aug 86. (lp/c) *Fame; (FA/TC-FA 3160)* **JOHNNY B. GOODE (live)** | | - |

May 87. (cd) *E.M.I.; (CDP 746 485-2)* **THE BEST OF JIMI HENDRIX** | | - |

May 88. (lp/c/cd) *Big Time; (261 525-1/-4/-2)* **16 GREAT CLASSICS** | | - |

Jun 88. (cd; shared with TINA TURNER) *Thunderbolt; (CDTBD 001)* **VOICES IN THE WIND** | | - |

Nov 88. (12"ep/cd-ep) *Strange Fruit; (SFPS/+CD 065)* **THE PEEL SESSIONS** | | - |
– Radio One theme / Day tripper / Wait until tomorrow / Hear my train a'comin' / Spanish castle magic. *(cd re-iss. Apr96; same)*

Feb 89. (d-lp/c/cd) *Castle; (CCS LP/MC/CD 212) / Rykodisc; <RALP 00782>* **THE RADIO ONE SESSIONS** | 30 | |
– Stone free / Radio one theme / Day tripper / Killing floor / Love or confusion / Catfish blues / Drivin' south / Wait until tomorrow / Hear my train a-comin' / Hound dog / Fire / Hoochie coochie man / Purple haze / Spanish castle magic / Hey Joe / Foxy lady / The burning of the midnight lamp.

Nov 89. (5xlp/3xc/3xcd-box) *Castle; (HB LP/MC/CD 100)* **LIVE AND UNRELEASED – THE RADIO SHOWS (live)** | | - |

Feb 89. (cd) *Koine; (K 880 802)* **JAM SESSIONS** | | - |

Jan 90. (cd) *Zeta; (ZET 517)* **THE LAST EXPERIENCE CONCERT (live)** | | - |

Apr 90. (cd/lp) *Thunderbolt; (CDTB/THBL 075)* **NIGHT LIFE** | | - |

Dec 90. (pic-lp) *Discussion; (IFSIXWAS 9)* **WELL I STAND NEXT TO A MOUNTAIN** | | - |

Feb 91. (cd/c) *Action Replay; (CDAR/ARLC 1022)* **THE BEST & THE REST OF JIMI HENDRIX** | | - |

Dec 91. (cd/lp) *U.F.O.;* **IN 1967 (free w/booklet)** | | - |

Nov 92. (7"/c-s) *East West;* **THE WIND CRIES MARY. / FIRE** | | - |
(12"+=/cd-s+=) – Foxy lady / May this be love.

Dec 92. (cd) *Univibes;* **CALLING LONG DISTANCE** | | - |

Apr 93. (d-cd/d-c) *Deja Vu; (R2CD 4003)* **THE GOLD COLLECTION** | | - |
(re-iss. Jun95; same)

Apr 93. (cd) *Pulsar;* **HIS FINAL LIVE PERFORMANCE (live)** | | - |

Sep 93. (cd) *I.T.M.; (ITM 960008)* **JIMI HENDRIX AT THE MONTEREY POP FESTIVAL, 1967 (live)** | | - |

Dec 93. (cd) *Entertainers;* **FIRE** | | - |

Jan 95. (cd) *Collection; (COL 017)* **THE COLLECTION** | | - |

Mar 95. (cd) *Top Masters; (3179)* **THE EARLY JIMI HENDRIX** | | - |

Apr 95. (cd/c) *Muskateer; (MU 5/4 018)* **LIVE IN NEW YORK** | | - |

May 95. (cd) *Thunderbolt; (CDTB 075)* **NIGHT LIFE** | | - |

Jun 95. (cd) *Receiver; (RRCD 200)* **SUNSHINE OF YOUR LOVE** | | - |

Aug 95. (cd) *Voiceprint; (844200-2)* **SUPERSESSION** | | - |

Sep 95. (cd) *Strawbery; (SRCD 115)* **THE LAST EXPERIENCE** | | - |

Nov 95. (3xcd-box) *Pulsar; (PULS 301)* **GREATEST HITS** | | - |

—— On April 5th 1996, JIMI's girlfriend at the time of his death; MONIKA DANNEMAN, committed suicide (carbon monoxide poisoning). In her book 'The Inner Life Of Jimi Hendrix', she had recently broke an injunction, involving a libellous statement made to JIMI's other one-time girlfriend KATHY ETCHINGHAM.

Apr 96. (cd/c) *Hallmark; (30418-2/-4)* **EARLY DAZE** | | - |

Aug 96. (d-cd) *Natural Collection; (TNC 96205)* **REAL ROCK STANDARDS** | | - |

Feb 97. (cd) *S.P.V.; (SPV 0854468-2)* **BALLAD OF JIMI: THE AUTHENTIC PPX RECORDINGS VOLUME 3** | | - |

Feb 97. (cd) *S.P.V.; (SPV 0854469-2)* **LIVE AT GEORGE'S CLUB: THE AUTHENTIC PPX RECORDINGS VOLUME 4** | | - |

Apr 97. (cd) *Arcade; (300455-2)* **THE DIAMOND COLLECTION** | | - |

May 97. (cd/c/d-lp) *M.C.A.; (MCD/MCC/MCA2 11599)* **FIRST RAYS OF THE NEW RISING SUN** | 37 | 49 |

May 97. (d-cd) *Metro; (OTR 1100030)* **IN WORDS AND MUSIC** | | - |

Jun 97. (cd) *BR Music; (RM 1536)* **PSYCHO** | | - |

Sep 97. (cd/c) *Telstar; (TTV CD/MC 2930)* **EXPERIENCE HENDRIX – THE BEST OF** | 21 | |
– Purple haze / Fire / The wind cries Mary / Hey Joe / All along the watchtower / Stone free / Crosstown traffic / Manic depression / Little wing / If six was nine / Foxy lady / Bold as love / Castles made of sand / Red house / Voodoo chile (slight return) / Freedom / Night bird flying / Angel / Dolly dagger / Star spangled banner.

Oct 97. (cd/c/d-lp) *M.C.A.; (MCD/MCC/MCA 11684)* **SOUTH SATURN DELTA** | | 51 |

May 98. (3xcd-box) *Dressed To Kill; (DTKBOX 81)* **GROOVE MAKER** | | - |

Jun 98. (d-cd/d-c/t-lp) *M.C.A.; <(MCD/MCC/MCA 11742)>* **THE BBC SESSIONS** | 42 | 50 |

Feb 99. (d-cd/d-c/t-lp) *M.C.A.; <(MCD/MCC/MCA 11931)>* **LIVE AT FILLMORE EAST** | | 65 |

Jun 99. (cd/c) *M.C.A.; <11671>* **EXPERIENCE HENDRIX: THE BEST OF JIMI HENDRIX** | - | |

Jul 99. (d-cd/d-c) *M.C.A.; <11987>* **JIMI HENDRIX LIVE AT WOODSTOCK (live)** | - | 90 |

Don HENLEY (see under ⇒ EAGLES)

HENRY COW (dig out; Great Psychedelic . . .)

HERD (dig out; Great Psychedelic . . .)

Kristin HERSH (see under ⇒ THROWING MUSES)

John HIATT

Born: 20 Aug'52, Indianapolis, Indiana, USA. In his late teens, HIATT became a staff songwriter for a Nashville publishing house ('Tree'), where he had songs covered by THREE DOG NIGHT and CONWAY TWITTY (the latter took 'HEAVY TEARS' to the top of the country charts). A deal with 'Epic' presented him with the opportunity to record two creatively diverse but commercially unsuccessful albums with producer Norbert Putnam, 'HANGIN' AROUND THE OBSERVATORY' and 'OVERCOATS', seeing the light of day in the mid-70's. In 1978, HIATT was given another chance by 'M.C.A.', who groomed the singer-songwriter as an American answer to ELVIS COSTELLO with the toughened-up and critically acclaimed 'SLUG LINE' and 'TWO BIT MONSTERS' at the turn of the decade. With his songs now being performed by the likes of RICK NELSON, DAVE EDMUNDS, MARIA MULDAUR, etc, etc, HIATT's professional reputation led him to movie soundtrack work ('American Gigolo' and 'Cruising'). This golden early 80's period also saw him strike up a friendship with RY COODER, the roots scholar inviting HIATT to sing and play on two albums 'Borderline' and 'The Slide Area'. In 1982, JOHN switched to 'Geffen', where he released the Tony Visconti-produced set, 'ALL OF A SUDDEN', following it up with the NICK LOWE-produced 'RIDING WITH THE KING' (1983). LOWE in fact, became a close friend of HIATT and the pair would regularly work together over the coming decade. When 'Geffen' dropped HIATT after 1985's soul-tinged 'WARMING UP TO THE ICE-AGE', he subsequently signed to 'A&M' ('Demon'-only in the UK) and formed a backing band comprising LOWE, COODER and session veteran JIM KELTNER. Having finally won a long battle against alcoholism (and the tragedy of his wife's suicide), a rejuvenated HIATT came up with his sharpest set of songs to date in the Glyn Johns-produced 'BRING THE FAMILY' (1987). His commercial and critical rehabilitation continued with 'SLOW TURNING' (1988) and 'STOLEN MOMENTS' (1990), the former featuring BERNIE LEADON (ex-EAGLES) and DENNIS LOCORRIERE (of DR. HOOK). In 1992, HIATT and backing band became a bonafide group, LITTLE VILLAGE. Although these 'Reprise'-signed supertroubs made the UK Top 30 (Top 75 in the States) with their eponymous debut album, the generally critical consensus deemed the record and accompanying tour slightly disappointing. However, a solo HIATT was back in town for 1993's 'PERFECTLY GOOD GUITAR', its title reflecting the rockier grooves contained within (supplied in part by CRACKER and SCHOOL OF FISH). A sardonically titled stop-gap concert set, 'HIATT COMES ALIVE AT BUDOKAN?' (1994), found the singer backed by The GUILTY DOGS. Signing to 'Capitol' for his next set, 'WALK ON' (1995), the man again made the US Top 50, although it failed to provide the chart longevity of previous efforts. While 1997's 'LITTLE HEAD' also performed poorly saleswise, HIATT retains a cult following and his songs have been covered by everyone from IGGY POP to BONNIE RAITT. • Trivia: 1986's 'WARMING UP TO THE ICE-AGE' featured a duet with ELVIS COSTELLO: the Detroit Spinners covered 'LIVING A LITTLE, LAUGHING A LITTLE'.

Album rating: HANGIN' AROUND THE OBSERVATORY (*5) / OVERCOATS (*4) / SLUG LINE (*5) / TWO BIT MONSTERS (*5) / ALL OF A SUDDEN (*5) / RIDING WITH THE KING (*7) / WARMING UP TO THE ICE-AGE (*7) / BRING THE FAMILY (*8) / SLOW TURNING (*7) / Y'ALL CAUGHT compilation (*6) / STOLEN MOMENTS (*7) / PERFECTLY GOOD GUITAR (*6) / HIATT COMES ALIVE AT BUDOKAN (*5) / WALK ON (*5) / LITTLE HEAD (*4) / THE BEST OF JOHN HIATT compilation (*7)

JOHN HIATT – vocals, guitar / with many on session incl. **SHANE KEISTER** – keyboards

	not iss.	Epic
1973. (7") <10990> **BOULEVARD AIN'T SO BAD. / WE MAKE SPIRIT**	-	

1974. (lp) **HANGIN' ROUND THE OBSERVATORY**
 – Maybe baby, say you do / Whistles in my ears / Sure as I'm sittin' here / Rose / Hangin' around the observatory / Full Moon / Wild-eyed gypsies / It's alright with me / Little blue song for you / Ocean. (cd-iss. Jun94 on 'Sony Europe')
1974. (7") <11095> **SURE AS I'M SITTIN' HERE. / OCEAN** [-]
1974. (7") <50022> **FULL MOON. / HANGIN' ROUND THE OBSERVATORY** [-]
1975. (7") <50115> **MOTORBOAT TO HEAVEN. / DOWN HOME (KEEP ON FALLIN')** [-]
1975. (lp) <33190> **OVERCOATS**
 – One more time / Smiling in the rain / I'm tired of your stuff / Distance / Down home / Overcoats / I want your love inside of me / I killed an ant with my guitar / Motorboat to Heaven / The lady of the night. (cd-iss. Jun94 on 'Sony Europe')

	M.C.A.	M.C.A.
Jul 79. (7") (MCA 502) <41019> **SHARON'S GOT A DRUGSTORE. / RADIO GIRL**		Jun79

Aug 79. (lp/c) (MCF/+C 3005) <3088> **SLUG LINE**
 – You used to kiss the girls / The negroes were dancing / Slug line / Madonna road / (No more) Dancin' in the street / Long night / The night that Kenny died / Radio girl / You're my love interest / Take off your uniform / Sharon's got a drugstore / Washable ink.
Oct 79. (7") (MCA 528) <41132> **SLUG LINE. / MADONNA ROAD** [| Aug79]

— now w / **SHANE KEISTER** – keyboards / **HOWARD EPSTEIN** – bass / **DARYL VERDUSCO** – drums
May 80. (7") **I SPY (FOR THE F.B.I.). / IT HASN'T HAPPENED YET** [-]
Jul 80. (7") (MCA 625) **I SPY (FOR THE F.B.I.). / GOOD GIRL, BAD WORLD** [-]
Oct 80. (lp) (MCF 3078) <5123> **TWO BIT MONSTERS**
 – Back to normal / Down in front / I spy (for the F.B.I.) / Pink bedroom / Good girl, bad world / Face the nation / Cop party / Back to the war / It hasn't happened yet / String pull job / New numbers.
Oct 80. (7") (MCA 649) **BACK TO THE WAR. / PINK BEDROOM** [-]
Feb 81. (7") (MCA 664) **BACK TO NORMAL. / STRING PULL JOB** [-]

— **JESSE HARMS** – keyboards + **JAMES ROLLESTON** – bass; repl. KEISTER + EPSTEIN
Apr 82. (7") **LOOK FOR LOVE. / TAKE TIME TO KNOW HER** [-]

	Geffen	Geffen
Apr 82. (lp/c) (GEF/40 85580) <2009> **ALL OF A SUDDEN**		

 – I look for love / The secret life / Overnight story / Forever yours / Some fun now / The walking dead / I could use an angel / Getting excited / Doll hospital / Something happens / Marianne / My edge of the razor.

— now w / **MARTIN BELMONT** – guitar / **PAUL CARRACK** – keyboards / **NICK LOWE** – bass, vocals / **SCOTT MATTHEWS** – drums, bass, sax, guitar / **BOBBY IRWIN** – drums
Feb 84. (7") (A 4086) **SHE LOVES THE JERK. / LOVE LIKE BLOOD** [-]
Apr 84. (lp/c) <(GEF/GEC 25593)> **RIDING WITH THE KING**
 – I don't even try / Death by misadventure / Girl on a string / Lovers will / She loves the jerk / Say it with flowers / Riding with the king / You may already be a winner / Love like blood / Love that harms / Book lovers / Falling up. (re-iss. May91 cd/c; GEF D/C 04017) (re-iss. Apr92 cd/c; GFL D/C 19056) (cd re-iss. Feb99 on 'Mobile Fidelity'; UDCD 740)

— now w / **RANDY McCORMICK** – keyboards / **JESSE BOYCE** – bass / **LARRIE LONDON** – drums
Jan 85. (7"m) (A 5033) **SHE SAID THE SAME THINGS TO ME. / SHE LOVES THE JERK / SOMETHING HAPPENS** [-]
May 85. (7") (A 6121) **LIVING A LITTLE, LAUGHING A LITTLE. / I'M A REAL MAN** [-]
 (12"+=) (X 6121) – When we ran / Everybody's girl.
Apr 86. (7") (A 9461) **THIS IS YOUR DAY. / SNAKE CHARMER** [-]
 (above was issued on 'Atlantic')
Sep 86. (lp/c) <(K9 24055-1/-4)> **WARMING UP TO THE ICE AGE**
 – The usual / Crush / When we ran / She said the same things to me / Living a little, laughing a little / Zero house / Warming up to the ice age / I'm a real man / Number one honest game / I got a gun. (re-iss. May91 cd/c; GEF D/C 24055) (re-iss. Apr92 cd/c; GFL D/C 19057)

— now w / **RY COODER** – guitar, vocals / **NICK LOWE** – bass, vocals / **JIM KELTNER** – drums

	Demon	A&M
May 87. (7") (D 1050) **THANK YOU GIRL. / MY GIRL**		-

May 87. (lp/c/cd) (FIEND/+CASS/CD 100) <5158> **BRING THE FAMILY**
 – Memphis in the meantime / Alone in the dark / A thing called love / Lipstick sunset / Have a little faith in me / Thank you girl / Tip of my tongue / Your dad did / Stood up / Learning how to love you.
Jul 87. (7") <2950> **THANK YOU GIRL. / LIPSTICK SUNSET** [-]
Oct 87. (7") <2970> **HAVE A LITTLE FAITH IN ME. / THANK YOU GIRL** [-]

— now w / **BERNIE LEADON** – guitar, mandolin, banjo / **DAVID RANSON** – bass / **SONNY LANDRETH** – steel guitar / **KEN BLEVINS** – drums / **JAMES HOOKER** – organ

	A&M	A&M
Aug 88. (7") <1245> **SLOW TURNING. / YOUR DAD DID (live)**	-	
Aug 88. (lp/c/cd) <(AMA/AMC/CDA 5206)> **SLOW TURNING**		98

 – Drive south / Trudy and Dave / Tennessee plates / Icy blue heart / Sometime other than now / Georgia Rae / Ride along / Slow turning / It'll come to you / Is anybody there? / Paper thin / Feels like rain. (cd re-iss. Feb99 on 'Mobile Fidelity'; UDCD 741)
Oct 88. (7") (AM 478) **SLOW TURNING. / IS ANYBODY THERE?**
 (12"+=) (AMY 478) – Already love.
Feb 89. (7") (AM 499) **TENNESSEE PLATES. / GEORGIA RAE (live)** [| -]
 (12"+=) (AMY 499) – Thank you girl (live).
Jun 90. (cd/c/lp) <(395310-2/-4/-1)> **STOLEN MOMENTS** [72 | 61]
 – A real fine love / Seven little Indians / Child of the wild blue yonder / Back of my mind / Stolen moments / Bring back your love to me / The rest of the dream / Thirty years of tears / Rock back Billy / Listening to old voices / Through your hands / One kiss. (cd re-iss. May95; same)
Jul 90. (7") **A REAL FINE LOVE. / JUST ENOUGH ASLAND CITY**
 (12"+=/cd-s+=) – Feels like rain.

— In 1992, he joined LITTLE VILLAGE with NICK LOWE, JIM KELTNER + RY COODER.

— solo (vocals, guitar, piano, organ) again w / **MATT WALLACE** – guitar / **MICHAEL WARD** – lead guitar / **JOHN PIERCE** – bass / **BRIAN MacLEOD** – drums, percussion / **RAVI OLI** – electric sitar
Sep 93. (cd/c) (540135-2/-4)> **PERFECTLY GOOD GUITAR** [67 | 47]
 – Something wild / Straight outta time / Perfectly good guitar / Buffalo River home / Angel / Blue telescope / Cross my fingers / Old habits / The wreck of the Barbie Ferrari / When you hold me tight / Permanent hurt / Loving a hurricane / I'll never get over you.
Oct 93. (7"/c-s) (580426-7/-4) **ANGEL. / LITTLE GOODNIGHT**
 (cd-s+=) (580427-2) – Drive south / I'll never get over you.
Nov 94. (cd/c) <(540284-2/-4)> **HIATT COMES ALIVE AT BUDOKAN (live)**
 – Through your hands / Real fine love / Memphis in the meantime / Icy blue heart / Paper thin / Angel eyes / You dad did / Have a little faith in me / Drive south / A thing called love / Perfectly good guitar / Feels like rain / Tennessee plates / Lipstick sunset / Slow turning.

	Capitol	Capitol
Oct 95. (c-s) (TCCL 759) **CRY LOVE / THE OTHER SIDE / TWENTY ONE**		

 (cd-s+=) (CDCL 759) – Your love is my rent.
Nov 95. (cd/c) <(CD/C 33416)> **WALK ON** [74 | 48]
 – Cry love / You must go / Walk on / Good as she could be / The river knows your name / Native son / Dust down a country road / Ethylene / I can't wait / Shedding the document / Wrote it down and burned it / Your love is my rent / Friend of mine / Mile high.

	Parlophone	Capitol
Jun 97. (cd/c) <(CD/TC EST 2296)> **LITTLE HEAD**		

 8- Little head / Pirate radio / My sweet girl / Feelin' again / Graduated / Sure Pinocchio / Runaway / Woman sawwed in half / Far as we go / After all this time.

– compilations, etc. –

Sep 89. (lp/c/cd) Geffen; <(K9 24247-1/-4/-2)> **Y'ALL CAUGHT?**
 – The crush / She said the same things to me / Love like blood / Slug line / She loves the jerk / My edge of the razor / Pink bedroom / It hasn't happened yet / Radio girl / I look for love / Washable ink / Riding with the King / When we ran.
Jul 93. (cd) Beat Goes On; (BGOCD 176) **SLUG LINE / TWO BIT MONSTERS**
Aug 98. (cd) Capitol; (859179-2) **THE BEST OF JOHN HIATT**
 – Have a little faith / A thing called love / Riding with the king / Cry love / Slow turning / The way we make a broken heart / Memphis in the meantime / Child of the wild blue yonder / Drive south / Angel eyes / Buffalo river home / Feels like rain / Love in flames / Perfectly good guitar / Tennessee plates / Take off your uniform / Don't know much.

HI-FI (see under ⇒ MATTHEWS, Iain)

HIGH (dig out; Great Alt & Indie . . .)

HIGH LLAMAS (dig out; Great Alt & Indie . . .)

HIGHWAYMEN (see under ⇒ CASH, Johnny)

Lauryn HILL (see under ⇒ FUGEES)

Steve HILLAGE

Born: 2 Aug'51, London, England. While at school he joined the short-lived URIEL for six months in early 1968. They became EGG after his departure to university, and made two albums in the early 70's, one of which, 'ARACHEZ' (issued on 'Evoluton'), is now worth over £200. After returning to London in the Spring of '71, HILLAGE formed the equally short-lived KHAN with ex-URIEL member DAVE STEWART (who was also leading the aforementioned EGG at the same time). KHAN released one album, 1972's 'SPACE SHANTY', before HILLAGE joined KEVIN AYERS' touring band, playing

alongside French-based uber-hippies GONG. 1973 saw him hooking up with the communal space cadets, helping to focus their freaky meanderings over the course of three albums. When GONG splintered in 1975, HILLAGE went solo with his girlfriend MIQUETTE GIRAUDY, enlisting assorted GONG members for his debut, 'FISH RISING'. The TODD RUNDGREN-produced follow-up, 'L', was a consummate development of his quasi-psychedelic guitar ambience and "New Age" musings while 1977's 'MOTIVATION RADIO' was produced by synthesizer innovator MALCOLM CECIL (ex-TONTO'S EXPANDING HEAD BAND). While "Punk" was telling the kids there was no future, or at least a rather unpleasant one, HILLAGE was bravely pushing on with the hippy tenets of love, peace and spirituality. He released a clutch of trippy ambient rock albums in the late 70's, as well as having a hand in the 1979 revival of The Glastonbury Fayre, now just plain old Glastonbury. The highlight of his recorded output during this period was 1979's 'RAINBOW DOME MUSICK', a dreamy slice of instrumental ambience. Throughout the 80's, HILLAGE was an in-house producer for 'Virgin', working with the likes of SIMPLE MINDS and ROBYN HITCHCOCK, having previously worked with The SKIDS and others. He then teamed up with ALEX PATERSON of The ORB when the dance scene was in its optimistic infancy back in 1989. This meeting led to the formation of SYSTEM 7, a laid-back collective with HILLAGE and GIRAUDY as its prime movers, enlisting the aid of respected players like the aforementioned PATERSON and PAUL OAKENFOLD along the way. SYSTEM 7's self-titled debut was a tentative step towards their new ambient-techno sound, more fully realised on the relatively successful '777' in 1993. The act were perfect for the neo-psychedelic clubs which were emerging, becoming a live favourite at Club Dog and Whirly-Gig events. Like JAM & SPOON'S Tripomatic Fairytales, SYSTEM 7's next album, 'POINT 3', was released in two halves, 'THE FIRE ALBUM', which was a rhythmic trance opus and 'THE WATER ALBUM', an ambient version of the same tracks. Things had come full circle, HILLAGE was back in his element producing soundtracks for people to lose themselves to, chemically or otherwise, a new generation of pseudo-hippies. 1996's 'POWER OF SEVEN' saw SYSTEM 7 work with DERRICK MAY on a harder set of Detroit-influenced techno.
• Covered: NOT FADE AWAY (Buddy Holly) / HURDY GURDY MAN (Donovan) / IT'S ALL TOO MUCH + GETTING BETTER (Beatles).

Album rating: FISH RISING (*6) / L (*6) / MOTIVATION RADIO (*6) / GREEN (*6) / LIVE HERALD (*7) / RAINBOW DOME MUSICK (*7) / OPEN (*5) / FOR TO NEXT (*5) / System 7: SYSTEM 7 (er . . . *7) / 777 (*6) / POINT 3: THE FIRE ALBUM (*7) / POWER OF SEVEN (*7) / SYSTEM EXPRESS (*6) / GOLDEN SECTION compilation (*6)

KHAN

STEVE HILLAGE – guitar, vocals (ex-GONG, ex-URIEL, ex-KHAN) / **DICK HENNINGHAM** – organ (ex-ARTHUR BROWN) / **NICK GREENWODD** – bass (ex-ARTHUR BROWN) / **ERIC PEACHEY** – drums

	Deram	P.V.C.
May 72. (lp) *(DSL 11)* **SPACE SHANTY**		– 1978

– Space shanty / Stranded effervescent psychonovelty No.5 / Mixed up man of the mountains / Driving to Amsterdam / Stargazers / Hollow stone escape of the space pirates. *(re-iss. Feb77; same) (cd-iss 1991 on 'Mantra' France)*

—— **DAVE STEWART** – organ (ex-EGG, ex-URIEL) repl. HENNINGHAM / **NIGEL SMITH** – bass repl. GREENWOOD. (DAVE moved to HATFIELD + THE NORTH) Late 1972, HILLAGE joined KEVIN AYERS Band on tour. In 1973, he joined GONG making 3 lp's **FLYING TEAPOT** (1973), **ANGEL'S EYES** (1973), **YOU** (1974). He guested for EGG on their Nov74 album 'THE CIVIL SURFACE'.

STEVE HILLAGE

went solo with some GONG members.

	Virgin	Atlantic
Apr 75. (lp/c) *(V/TCV 2031)* **FISH RISING**	33	

– Solar musick suite:- (i) Sun song – (ii) Canterbury sunrise – (iii) Hiram afterglid meets the Dervish – (iv) Sun song (reprise) / Fish / Meditation of the snake / The salmon song:- (i) Salmon pool – (ii) Solomon's Atlantis – (iii) Swimming with the salmon – (iv) King of the fishes / Afterglid:- (i) Sun moon surfing – (ii) Great wave and the boat of Hermes – (iii) The silver ladder – (iv) Astral meadows – (v) The Lafta yoga song – (vi) Gliding – (vii) Golden vibe – the outglid. *(re-iss. Mar84; OVED 28) (cd-iss. Jun87; CDV 2031)*

—— Next used TODD RUNDGREN'S UTOPIA as backing alongside others.

Sep 76. (lp/c) *(V/TCV 2066)* **'L'**	10	

– Hurdy gurdy man / Hurdy gurdy glissando / Electrick gypsies / Om nama Shivaya / Luna musick suite / It's all too much. *(re-iss. Mar84; OVED 29) (cd-iss. Jun87; CDV 2066) (cd re-iss. Apr97 on 'Virgin-VIP'; CDVIP 184)*

Oct 76. (7") *(VS 161)* **IT'S ALL TOO MUCH. / SHIMMER**		–
Feb 77. (7") *(VS 171)* <3384> **HURDY GURDY MAN. / OM NAMA SHIVAYA**		
Sep 77. (lp/c) *(V/TCV 2777)* **MOTIVATION RADIO**	28	

– Mellow dawn / Motivation / Light in the sky / Radio / Wait one moment / Saucer surfing / Searching for the spark / Ovtave doctors / Not fade away (glide forever). *(re-iss. Mar84; OVED 32) (cd-iss. Jun88; CDV 2777)*

Dec 77. (7") *(VS 197)* **NOT FADE AWAY (GLIDE FOREVER). / SAUCER SURFING**		
Apr 78. (lp,green-lp/c) *(T/TCV 2098)* **GREEN**	30	–

– Sea nature / Ether ships / Musick of the trees / Palm trees (love guitar) / Unidentified (flying being) / U.F.O. over Paris / Stargazers / Leyliness to Glassdom / Crystal city / Activation meditation / The glorious om riff. *(re-iss. Mar84; OVED 30) (cd-iss. Jun90; CDV 2098)*

May 78. (7") *(VS 212)* **GETTING BETTER. / PALM TREES (LOVE GUITAR)**		
Feb 79. (d-lp/c) *(V/TCV 3502)* **LIVE HERALD (live)**	54	–

– The salmon song / The Dervish riff / Castle in the clouds / Hurdy gurdy man / Light in the sky / Searching for the spark / Electrick gypsies / Radiom / Lunar musick

suite / Meditation of the dragon / It's all too much / The golden vibe / Talking to the sun / 1988 aktivator / New age synthesis (unzipping the zype) / Healing feeling. *(cd-iss. Jun90, omits side 4; CDVM 3502)*

Apr 79. (lp,clear-lp) *(VR 1)* **RAINBOW DOME MUSICK**	52	–

– Garden of Paradise / Four ever rainbow. *(re-iss. 1984; same) (cd-iss. Jun88; CDVR 1)*

—— with main band **ANDY ANDERSON** – drums, percussion / **DAVE STEWART** – slide guitar, voice / **MIQUETTE GIRAUDY** – synthesizers, voice, vocoder / **PAUL FRANCIS** – bass

Sep 79. (lp/c) *(V/TCV 2135)* **OPEN**	71	–

– Day after day / Getting in tune / Open / Definite activity / Don't dither do it / The fire inside / Earthrise. *(re-iss. Mar84; OVED 31) (cd-iss. Jun90 as 'OPEN FEATURING STUDIO HERALD'; CDV 2135)*

Nov 79. (7") *(VS 313)* **DON'T DITHER DO IT. / GETTING IN TUNE**		

—— Took time off for sessions, etc., until his return in 1982

Jan 83. (7"/12") *(VS 574/+12)* **KAMIKAZE EYES. / BEFORE THE WORLD WAS MADE**		
Feb 83. (lp/c) *(V/TCV 2244)* **FOR TO NEXT**	48	–

– These uncharted lands / Kamikaze eyes / Alone / Anthems for the blind / Bright future / Frame by frame / Waiting / Glory. *(free instrumental-lp w/a 'AND NOT OR')* – Before the storm / Red Admiral / Serotonin / And not or / Knights templar / Still golden. *(re-iss. Dec83; OVED 13) (re-iss. Aug88; OVED 123) (cd-iss. Jul90 with free album; CDV 2244) (re-iss. cd Mar94;)*

Apr 83. (7") *(VS 551)* **ALONE. / FRAME BY FRAME**		–

(12"+=) *(VS 551-12)* – Timelines.

—— HILLAGE went more into production for SIMPLE MINDS, ROBYN HITCHCOCK, etc. In the 90's, he guested with ALEX PATERSON in The ORB and founded his own ambient group SYSTEM 7.

– compilations, others, etc. –

1979. (12"pic-ep) *Virgin; (SIXPACK 2)* **SIX PACK**		–

– The salmon song / It's all too much / The golden vibe / Not fade away / Electric gypsies / Radio.

1983. (lp) *Aura; <AURA 1>* **AURA**	–	
Aug 92. (cd) *Windsong; (WINCD 014)* **BBC RADIO 1 LIVE IN CONCERT (live)**		–

SYSTEM 7

—— **STEVE HILLAGE** – guitar / with **ALEX PATERSON** (Orb) / **YOUTH** / **DERRICK MAY** / **STEVE WADDINGTON** (Beloved) / **PAUL OAKENFIELD** / **MICK McNEIL** (ex-Simple Minds) / **MIQUETTE GIRAUDY** (ex-Gong) / **OLU ROWE** – vocals / **ZOE THRASH** (Orb) / **ANDY FALCONER** (engineer)

	Ten-Virgin	Virgin
Nov 90. (12") *(TENX 335)* **SUNBURST (Flutter mix). / SUNBURST (Paradise mix)**		–

—— now w/ **ANIFF COUSINS** (Chapter and the Verse) / + **MONDAY MICHIRU** – vocals

Sep 91. (cd/c/d-lp) *(DIXCD/CDIX/DIX 102)* **SYSTEM 7**		

– Sunburst / Freedom fighters / Habibi / Altitude / Bon humeur / Fractal liaison / Dog / Thunderdog / Listen / Strange quotations / Miracle / Over and out.

Oct 91. (12"/cd-s) *(TEN X/CD 385)* **HABIBI (Another World mix). / MIRACLE / HABIBI (7" edit)**		

(12"clear) *(TENY 385)* – ('A'-Tex mix) / ('A'-Legian Beach mix) / Mia (Ultraworld Colony mix).

Feb 92. (7") *(TEN 394)* **FREEDOM FIGHTERS (new style). / DEPTH DISCO**		

(12"clear+=/cd-s+=) *(TEN X/CD 394)* – ('A'-Praying by the sea mix) / ('A'-Freedom void mix).
(pic-cd-s+=) *(TENCX 394)* – ('A'-Praying by the sea mix) / Mia (the fisherman mix).

Jun 92. (d12"ep) *(TENG 403)* **ALTITUDES** (8 mixes)		

	Big Life	Astralwerks
Feb 93. (12"ep/cd-ep) *(BFL T/X 2)* **7:7 EXPANSION (mixes)**	39	
Feb 93. (cd/c) *(BFL CD/MC 1)* **777**	30	

– 7:7 expansion / A cool dry place / Desire (ghost mix) / On the seventh night / Sinbad / Ship of the desert / Fay deau deau. *(cd-iss. Sep98; same)*

Jul 93. (12"ep/cd-ep) *(BFL T/D 8)* **SINBAD. / QUEST**		
Oct 94. (12"ep/cd-ep) *(BFL T/D 20)* **SIRENES. / ('A'-Marshall Jefferson mix) / ('A'-Laurent Garnier mix) / Coltrane (water mix)**		

(cd-ep+=) – Alpha wave / Gliding in two-tone curves (water edit).

Oct 94. (cd/c/d-lp) *(BFL CA/MA/LA 11)* **POINT 3: THE FIRE ALBUM**		

– Sirenes / Alpha wave (water edit) / Mysterious traveler / Coltrane (remix) / Radiate / Overview / Gliding on duo-tone curves / Jupiter! / Dr. Livingstone I pressume / Batukau. *(cd re-iss. Sep98; same)*

Oct 94. (cd/c) *(BFL CD/MD 11)* **POINT 3: THE WATER ALBUM** (remixes)		–

– Batakau / Sirenes / Coltrane / Mysterious traveller / Dr. Livingstone I pressume / Alpha wave / Liquid sky / Gliding on duo-tone curves / Jupiter! *(cd re-iss. Sep98; same)*

1995. (d-cd) *<ASW 6137-2>* **SYSTEM 7.3 / FIRE AND WATER**	–	

(UK-iss.Jun98; same)

Apr 95. (12"ep/cd-ep) *(BKL T/D 25)* **ALPHA WAVE (Plastikman acid house mix). / ('A'-Alpha mix) / ('A'-That sound mix)**		

	Butterfly	Cleopatra
Jan 96. (12"ep/cd-ep) *(BFL T/D 30)* **INTERSTATE / ('A'-David Holmes mix) / ('A'-Doc Scott mix)**		
Feb 96. (cd/c/lp) *(BFL CD/MC/LP 16)* <9809> **POWER OF SEVEN**		

– Interstate / Civilization / Davy Jones' locker / Big sky city / Good morning / Night owl / To the power of seven / Hangar 84 / Chicago Indian / Mektoub / Europa. *(cd re-iss. Sep98; same)*

Jul 96. (12"ep/cd-ep) *(BFL T/D 38)* **HANGAR 84 (Cox's W.W. Ultimatum mix). / HANGAR 84 (Cox's W.W. Crazy mix) / HANGAR 84 (live mix – the end 7/2/96)**		
Oct 96. (cd/t-lp) *(BFL CD/LP 21)* <9912> **SYSTEM EXPRESS** (remixes)		Nov96

– Alpha wave / D'Esir / Hangar 84 / Coltrane / Altitude / 7"7 expansion / Big city sky / Big city sky / Interstate / Sirenes / Sunburst. *(cd re-iss. Sep98; same)*

Jun 97. (12"/cd-s) *(BFL T/D 42)* **RITE OF SPRING.** / (mixes; radio / Origin / Doc Scott / Dancefloor / Filter).

Jun 98. (12"ep) *(BFLT 47)* **RING OF FIRE – THE ADVENT MIXES**
– The advent touch III / The advent touch I / The advent touch II / Troniq mix / Volcaniq mix.

Sep 98. (cd) *(BFLCD 27)* <108> **GOLDEN SECTION** (compilation)
– Rite of Spring / Don Corleone / Y2K / Ring of fire / Exdreamist / Wave bender / Sinom X-files / Merkaba! / Y2K (back to the future) / Borobudor.

HINDU LOVE GODS (see under ⇒ R.E.M.)

HIS NAME IS ALIVE (dig out; Great Alt & Indie . . .)

Robyn HITCHCOCK

Born: 3 Mar'53, East Grinstead, London, England. Aged 21, he set out for CAMBRIDGE to locate the home of his idol, SYD BARRETT, but ended up busking instead. 1976 found him forming a string of bands including The WORST FEARS, The BEETLES, MAUREEN & THE MEATPACKERS and, finally by the end of the year, DENNIS AND THE EXPERTS, who were the embryonic SOFT BOYS; alongside ROBYN were ALAN DAVIES, ANDY METCALFE and MORRIS WINDSOR. In March '77, they were offered a deal with indie label, 'Raw', who soon issued their debut release, 'GIVE IT TO THE SOFT BOYS' EP. The record included three trash-punk songs, notably 'WADING THROUGH A VENTILATOR'. KIMBERLEY REW replaced DAVIES before the band embarked on a UK tour supporting ELVIS COSTELLO and The DAMNED. This, in turn, led to a contract with 'Radar', although after only one 45 and many disagreements, they parted company. Taking matters into their own hands, the SOFT BOYS set up their own label, 'Two Crabs', and issued a debut album, 'A CAN OF BEES' (1979). The record was a resounding failure although it has since been the subject of many re-issues in different versions. In 1980 – by which time MATTHEW SELIGMAN had replaced METCALFE – they eventually established themselves, critically at least, with the much loved follow-up, 'UNDERWATER MOONLIGHT'. HITCHCOCK and Co. had finally managed to translate their quirky post-punk psychedelia to vinyl, pointing the way towards the direction of the frontman's erratic solo career. By the following year The SOFT BOYS had split, playing their final shows to more appreciative US audiences. HITCHCOCK subsequently completed a solo album, 'BLACK SNAKE DIAMOND ROLE' (1981), featuring the cult classics, 'BRENDA'S IRON SLEDGE' and the single, 'THE MAN WHO INVENTED HIMSELF'. Clearly the man had lost none of his BARRETT-esque lyrical daftness in the interim, his tongue-in-cheek, surreal humour occasionally even outstripping CAPTAIN BEEFHEART. After the disastrous STEVE HILLAGE-produced 'GROOVY DECAY' (1982), however, ROBYN decided enough was enough. Until 1984, that is, when he returned with an affecting acoustic album, 'I OFTEN DREAM OF TRAINS', the record seeing him reinstate the SOFT BOYS rhythm section (MORRIS WINDSOR and ANDY METCALFE) under the guise of ROBYN HITCHCOCK & THE EGYPTIANS. In 1985, their first product, 'FEGMANIA!', hit the shops, songs like 'THE MAN WITH THE LIGHTBULB HEAD' and 'EGYPTIAN CREAM', resurrecting the man's public profile. After a few more albums in the mid-80's, he and his band were signed to 'A&M', the resulting album, 'GLOBE OF FROGS' (1988), worthy of anything he'd previously recorded. It brought recommendations from R.E.M., who were longtime fans of HITCHCOCK. His band became firm faves on the US college circuit, especially when indie idols, MICHAEL STIPE and PETER BUCK, guested on the two mediocre either-side-of-the-decade albums, 'QUEEN ELVIS' and 'PERSPEX ISLAND'. In 1993, he returned to the eccentric brilliance of old with the highly regarded, John Leckie-produced 'RESPECT', a creative renaissance of sorts which even inspired him to re-unite The SOFT BOYS early in 1994 for some Bosnia benefit concerts. A further couple of solo sets appeared in the mid-90's, 'YOU AND OBLIVION' (1995) and 'MOSS ELIXIR' (1996), the latter with a quintessentially HITCHCOCK, engagingly fantastical life-after-death yarn printed on the inner sleeve. Back to the zaniness of his old self, the man was to bow out of the 90's with a low-key effort, 'JEWELS FOR SOPHIA' (1999).

Album rating: A CAN OF BEES (*7) / UNDERWATER MOONLIGHT (*8) / INVISIBLE HITS compilation (*7) / THE SOFT BOYS 1976-81 compilation (*8) / Robyn Hitchcock: BLACK SNAKE DIAMOND ROLE (*6) / GROOVY DECAY (*4) / I OFTEN DREAM OF TRAINS (*7) / FEGMANIA! (*8) / GOTTA LET THIS HEN OUT (*8) / ELEMENT OF LIGHT (*7) / INVISIBLE HITCHCOCK collection (*5) / GLOBE OF FROGS (*7) / QUEEN ELVIS (*7) / EYE (*7) / PERSPEX ISLAND (*4) / RESPECT (*5) / YOU & OBLIVION (*4) / MOSS ELIXIR (*6) / GREATEST HITS compilation (*8) / JEWELS FOR SOPHIA (*5)

SOFT BOYS

ROBYN HITCHCOCK – vocals, guitar, bass / **ALAN DAVIS** – guitar / **ANDY METCALFE** – bass / **MORRIS WINDSOR** (aka **OTIS FAGG**) – drums

	Raw	not iss.
Jul 77. (7"ep) *(RAW 5)* **GIVE IT TO THE SOFT BOYS** – Wading through a ventilator / The face of death / Hear my brane. *(re-iss. Oct79; RAW 37)*	☐	–

— **KIMBERLEY REW** – guitar, harmonica, vocals repl. DAVIS

	Radar	not iss.
May 78. (7") *(ADA 8)* **(I WANT TO BE AN) ANGELPOISE LAMP.** / **FAT MAN'S SON**	☐	–

	Two Crabs	not iss.
Feb 79. (lp) *(CLAW 1001)* **A CAN OF BEES** – Give it to the soft boys / The pigworker / Human music / Leppo and the jooves / The rat's prayer / Do the chisel / Sandra's having her brain out / The return of the sacred crab / Cold turkey / Skool dinner blues / Wading through a ventilator. *(re-iss. Feb80 on 'Aura'; AUL 709) (re-iss. Jun84 on 'Two Crabs'; same) (cd-iss. Feb95 on 'Rhino'+=; RCD 20231)* – Leppo and the jooves / Sandra's having her brain out / Skool dinner blues / Fatman's son / (I want to be an) Angelpoise lamp / Ugly Nora. *(<cd re-iss. May96 on 'Rykodisc'; RCD 20231>)*	☐	–

— In Oct'79, 'Raw' quickly withdrew release of 45 'WHERE ARE THE PRAWNS'; *RAW 41)*

— **MATTHEW SELIGMAN** – bass, keyboards (ex-SW9) repl. ANDY to FISH TURNED HUMAN

	Armageddon	Armageddon
Jun 80. (7"ep) *(AEP 002)* **NEAR THE SOFT BOYS** – Kingdom of love / Vegetable man / Strange.	☐	–
Jul 80. (lp) *(ARM 1)* **UNDERWATER MOONLIGHT** – I wanna destroy you / Kingdom of love / Positive vibrations / I got the job / Insanely jealous / Tonight / You'll have to go sideways / Old pervert / The queen of eyes / Underwater moonlight. *(cd-iss. Feb'80 on 'Rhino'+=;)* – Vegetable man / Strange / Only the stones remain / Where are the prawns / Dreams / Black snake diamond role / There's nobody like you / Song No.4. *(<cd re-iss. May96 on 'Rykodisc'; RCD 20232>)*	☐	–
Aug 80. (7") *(AS 005)* **I WANNA DESTROY YOU.** / **(I'M AN) OLD PERVERT (DISCO)**	☐	–
Oct 81. (7") *(AS 029)* **ONLY THE STONES REMAIN.** / **THE ASKING TREE**	☐	–
Mar 82. (lp) *(BYE 1)* **TWO HALVES FOR THE PRICE OF ONE** (half live) – Only the stones remain / Where are the prawns / The bells of Rhymney / There's nobody like you / Innocent box / Black snake diamond role / Underwater moonlight / Astronomy domine / Outlaw blues / Mystery train. *<US-title; ONLY THE STONES REMAIN>*	☐	Oct81

— Disbanded in 1982, SELIGMAN who joined The THOMPSON TWINS

– compilations, others, etc –

1982. (7"w/mag) *Bucketful Of Brains; (BOB 1)* **LOVE POISONING.** / **WHEN I WAS A KID**	–	–
Nov 83. (7") *Midnight Music; (DING 4)* **HE'S A REPTILE.** / **SONG NO.4**		–
Nov 83. (7") *Midnight Music; (CHIME 0002)* **INVISIBLE HITS** – Wey-wey-hep-uh-hole * / Have a heart Betty (I'm not fireproof) * / The asking tree / Muriel's hoof / The rout of the clones / Let me put it next to you / When I was a kid * / Rock & roll toilet * / Love poisoning * / Empty girl / Blues in the dark / He's a reptile. *(cd-iss. Feb95 on 'Rhino' +=;)* – (alt.takes of *). *(cd re-iss. May96 on 'Rykodisc'; RCD 20233)*		–
Aug 85. (lp/pic-lp) *De Laurean; (SOFT 1/+P)* **WADING THROUGH A VENTILATOR**	☐	–
1987. (7"flexi; w-mag) *Bucketful Of Brains; (BOB 17)* **DECK OF CARDS.** / **Robyn Hitchcock & Peter Buck: FLESH NO.1**	–	–
Dec 87. (lp) *Midnight Music; (MOIST 4)* **LIVE AT THE PORTLAND ARMS** (live)	☐	–
1989. (7"yellow,7"white; ltd) *Overground; (OVER 4)* **THE FACE OF DEATH.** / **THE YODELLING HOOVER**	☐	–
Sep 93. (d-cd) *Rykodisc; (RCD 10234-35)* **1976-81** – (mostly all of their material).	☐	–

ROBYN HITCHCOCK

was already solo, using session people, including most ex-SOFT BOYS

	Armageddon	not iss.
Apr 81. (7") *(AS 008)* **THE MAN WHO INVENTED HIMSELF.** / **DANCING ON GOD'S THUMB** *(free 7"flexi w-above) (4SPURT 1)* IT'S A MYSTIC TRIP. / GROOVING ON AN INNER PLANE	☐	–
May 81. (lp) *(ARM 4)* **BLACK SNAKE DIAMOND ROLE** – The man who invented himself / Brenda's iron sledge / Do policemen sing? / The lizard / Meat / Acid bird / I watch the cars / Out of the picture / City of shame / Love. *(re-iss. May86 on 'Aftermath'; AFT 1) (cd-iss. 1988; AFTCD 1) (cd re-iss. Feb95 on 'Rhino-Sequel'+=; RSACD 819)* – Dancing on God's thumb / Happy the golden prince / I watch the cars / It was the night / Grooving on an inner plane.		–

— now w / **SARA LEE** – bass / **ANTHONY THISTLETWAITE** – sax / **ROD JOHNSON** – drums repl. SELIGMAN to THOMAS DOLBY (and REW who re-joined The WAVES, who added Czech KATRINA; now KATRINA & THE WAVES)

	Albion	not iss.
Mar 82. (7") *(ION 103)* **AMERICA.** / **IT WAS THE NIGHT / HOW DO YOU WORK THIS THING?**	☐	–
Mar 82. (lp) *(ALB 110)* **GROOVY DECAY** – Night ride to Trinidad / Fifty-two stations / Young people scream / The rain / America / The cars she used to drive / Grooving on an inner plane / St. Petersburg / When I was a kid / Midnight fish. *(some with free various 'Albion' artists; RH track '52 STATIONS') (re-iss. Dec85 on 'Midnight Music'; CHIME 00.15) (cd-iss. Nov89 & Oct94 on 'Line'; ALCD 9.000008) (cd-iss. Feb95 as 'GRAVY DECO (THE COMPLETE GROOVY DECAY / DECOY SESSIONS)' on 'Rhino-Sequel'+=; RSACD 820)* – (extra mixes)	☐	–

	Midnight Music	Slash
Nov 82. (7"m) *(DING 2)* **EATEN BY HER OWN DINNER.** / **LISTENING TO THE HIGSONS / Dr. STICKY** *(12"ep; Oct86) (DONG 2)* – ('A'side) / Grooving on an inner plane / Messages of the dark / The abandoned brain / Happy the golden prince.	☐	–

— now w / **WINDSOR + METCALFE / + ROGER JACKSON** – keyboards

Aug 84. (lp) *(CHIME 00.05S)* **I OFTEN DREAM OF TRAINS** – Nocturne / Uncorrected personality traits / Sounds great when you're dead / Flavour of night / This could be the day / Trams of old London / Furry green atom bowl / Heart full of leaves / Autumn is your last chance / I often dream of trains. *(cd-iss. Oct86; CHIME 00.05CD) (cd re-iss. Feb95 on 'Rhino-Sequel'+=; RSACD 821)*	☐	–

– Ye sleeping knights of Jesus / Sometimes I wish I was a pretty girl / Cathedral / Mellow together / Winter love / The bones in the ground / My favourite buildings / I used to say I love you.

Nov 84. (12"m) *(DONG 8)* **THE BELLS OF RHYMNEY / FALLING LEAVES. / WINTER LOVE / THE BONES IN THE GROUND** ☐ ☐ -

ROBIN HITCHCOCK & THE EGYPTIANS

—— same as solo line-up

Mar 85. (lp) *(CHIME 00.08)* *<25316>* **FEGMANIA!** ☐ ☐
– Egyptian cream / Another bubble / I'm only you / My wife and my dead wife / Goodnight I say / The man with the lightbulb head / Insect mother / Strawberry mind / Glass / The fly / Heaven. *(cd-iss. 1986 +=; CHIME 00.08CD)* – The bells of rhymney / Dwarfbeat / Some body. *(re-iss. Mar95 on 'Rhino-Sequel'+=; RSACD 822)* – Egyptian cream (demo) / Heaven (live) / Insect mother (demo) / Egyptian cream (live) / The pit of souls: I) The plateau – II) The descent – III) The spinal dance – IV) Flight of the iron lung.

May 85. (12"m) *(DONG 12)* **HEAVEN. / DWARFBEAT / SOME BODY** ☐ -

Midnight | Relativity

Oct 85. (lp/c) *(CHIME 00.15 S/C)* **GOTTA LET THIS HEN OUT (live)** ☐ -
– Sometimes I wish I was a pretty girl / Kingdom of love / Acid bird / The cars she used to drive / My wife and my dead wife / Brenda's iron sledge / The fly * / Only the stones remain * / Egyptian cream * / Leppo & the Jooves / America / Heaven / Listening to The Higsons / Face of death. *(cd-iss. Oct86 += *; CHIME 00.15CD)* *(re-iss. cd Mar95 on 'Rhino-Sequel'; RSACD 823)*

Feb 86. (12"ep) *(DONG 17)* **BRENDA'S IRON SLEDGE (live). / ONLY THE STONES REMAIN (live) / THE PIT OF SOULS (part I-IV)** ☐ -

Mar 86. (pic-lp)(c) *(BM 80)(BMC 80-4)* *<EMC 8074>* **EXPLODING IN SILENCE** ☐ ☐

Glass Fish | Combat

Jun 86. (lp) *(MOIST 2)* **INVISIBLE HITCHCOCK** (compilation) ☐ ☐
– All I wanna do is fall in love / Give me a spanner, Ralph / A skull, a suitcase, and a long red bottle of wine / It's a mystic trip / My favourite buildings / Falling leaves / Eaten by her own dinner / Pits of souls / Trash / Mr. Deadly / Star of hairs / Messages of dark / Vegetable friend / I got a message for you / Abandoned brain / Point it at gran / Let there be more darkness / Blues in A. *(re-iss. cd Mar95 on 'Rhino-Sequel'+=; RSACD 825)* – Listening to the higsons / Dr. Sticky.

Sep 86. (lp/c/CD) *(MOIST 3/+CD)* *<885618130>* **ELEMENT OF LIGHT** ☐ ☐
– If you were a priest / Winchester / Somewhere apart / Ted, Woody and Junior / The president / Raymond Chandler evening / Bass / Airscape / Never stop bleeding / Lady Waters & the hooded one / The black crow knows / The crawling / The leopard / Tell me about your drugs. *(re-iss. cd Mar95 on 'Rhino-Sequel'+=; RSACD 824)* – The can opener / Raymond Chandler evening (demo) / President (demo) / If you were a priest (demo) / Airscape (live) / The leopard (demo).

Jan 87. (7") *(OOZE 1)* **IF YOU WERE A PRIEST. / THE CRAWLING** ☐ -
(12"+=) *(OOZE 1T)* – Tell me about your drugs / The can opener.

A&M | A&M

Feb 88. (lp/c/cd) *<(AMA/AMC/CDA 5182)>* **GLOBE OF FROGS** ☐ ☐
– Trapped flesh Mandela / Vibrating / Balloon man / Luminous rose / Sleeping with your devil mask on / Unsettled / Flesh number one / Chinese bones / A globe of frogs / Beatle Dennis / The shapes between us / Turn to animals.

Apr 88. (7") **GLOBE OF FROGS. / BALLOON MAN** - ☐

—— still with **METCALFE + WINDSOR** + guest **PETER BUCK** – guitar (of R.E.M.)

Mar 89. (lp/c/cd) *(395241-1/-4/-2)* **QUEEN ELVIS** ☐ ☐
– Madonna of the wasps / The Devils coachman / Wax doll / Knife / Swirling / One long pair of eyes / Veins of the Queen / Freeze / Autumn sea / Superman. *(cd+=)* – Veins of the Queen (royal mix) / Freeze (shatter mix).

Jul 89. (7") **MADONNA OF THE WASPS. / RULING CLASS** - ☐
(12"+=/cd-s+=) – Veins of the queen (royal mix) / Freeze (shatter mix).

ROBIN HITCHCOCK

Glass Fish | Twin/Tone

Nov 90. (lp/cd) *(MOIST 8/CD)* *<89175>* **EYE** ☐ ☐
– Cynthia mask / Certainly clickot / Queen Elvis / Flesh cartoons / Chinese water python / Executioner / Linctus House / Sweet ghosts of light / College of ice / Transparent lover / Beautiful girl / Raining twilight coast / Clean Steve / Agony of pleasure / Glass hotel / Satellite / Aquarium / Queen Elvis II. *(UK cd-iss. Mar95 on 'Rhino-Sequel'+=; RSACD 826)* – Raining twilight coast (demo) / Agony of pleasure (demo) / Queen Elvis III (demo).

Go! Discs | A&M

Oct 91. (cd/c) *(828 292-2/-4)* *<75021 5368-2>* **PERSPEX ISLAND** ☐ Aug91
– Oceanside / So you think you're in love / Birds in perspex / Ultra unbelievable love / Vegetations and dines / Lysander / Child of the universe / She doesn't exist / Ride / If you go away / Earthly Paradise.

Jan 92. (7") *(GOD 65)* **SO YOU THINK YOU'RE IN LOVE. / WATCH YOUR INTELLIGENCE** ☐ ☐
(12"+=/cd-s+=) *(GOD X/CD 65)* – Dark green energy.
(above featured STIPE + BUCK of R.E.M.)

Jun 93. (cd/c; with ARCHIE ROACH) *(RHE CD/MC 1)* *<540064>* **RESPECT** ☐ Feb93
– The yip song / The arms of love / The moon inside / Railway shoes / When I was dead / The wreck of Arthur Lee / Driving aloud (radio storm) / erpnt at the gates of wisdom / Then you're dust / Wafflehead.

Rhino-Sequel | Rhino-Sequel

Mar 95. (cd) *(<RSACD 827>)* **YOU & OBLIVION** ☐ ☐
– You've got / Don't you / Birdshead / She reached for a light / Victorian squid / Captain Dry / Mr. Rock I / August hair / Take your knife out of my back / Surgery / The dust / Polly on the shore / Aether / Fiend before the shrine / Nothing / Into it / Stranded in the future / Keeping still / September clones / Ghost ship / You & me / If I could look.

Feb 95. (cd-ep) *(CDSEQ 2)* **MY WIFE AND MY DEAD WIFE / I SOMETHING YOU / ZIPPER IN MY SPINE / MAN WITH A WOMAN'S SHADOW** ☐ -

—— now with **DENI BONET** – violin / **NITSHUKS BONGA** – sax / **TIM KEEGAN** – guitar / **JAKE KYLE** – bass / **PATCH HANNAN** – drums / **MORRIS WINDSOR** – vocals, percussion / etc

Warners | Warners

Aug 96. (cd/c) *(<9362 46302-2/-4>)* **MOSS ELIXIR** ☐ ☐
– Sinister but she was happy / The Devil's radio / Heliotrope / Alright, yeah / Filthy bird / The speed of things / Beautiful queen / Man with a woman's shadow / I am not me / De Chirico Street / You and oblivion / This is how it feels.

Sep 99. (cd) *(<9362 47433-2>)* **JEWELS FOR SOPHIA** ☐ Jul99
– Mexican God / Cheese alarm / Viva! sea-tac / I feel beautiful / You've got a sweet mouth on you, baby / NASA clapping / Sally was a legend / Antwoman / Elizabeth Jade / No, I don't remember Guildford / Dark princess / Jewels for Sophia.

– compilations, etc. –

May 83. (12"ep) *Albion; (12ION 1036)* **NIGHT RIDE TO TRINIDAD (long version). / KINGDOM OF LOVE / MIDNIGHT FISH** ☐ -

1984. (7"flexi; w-mag) *Bucketful Of Brains; (BOB 8)* **HAPPY THE GOLDEN PRINCE** - -

Jun 94. (cd) *Strange Roots; (ROOTCD 001)* **KERSHAW SESSIONS** - -

Mar 95. (cd) *Rhino-Sequel;* **RARE & UNRELEASED** - -

Sep 96. (cd) *A&M;* **GREATEST HITS** ☐ ☐

Oct 97. (cd) *Warners; <46846>* **STOREFRONT HITCHCOCK: MUSIC FROM DEMME PICTURE** (live) - -
– 1974 / Let's go thundering / I'm only you / Glass hotel / I something you / Yip! song / Freeze / Alright, yeah / Where do you go when you die? / The wind cries Mary / No, I don't remember Guildford / Beautiful queen.

HOLE

Formed: Los Angeles, California, USA . . . late 1989 by COURTNEY LOVE (bizarrely enough, a two-piece indie band of the same moniker – see under LOIS – surfaced with a few 45's a year later!) and six-foot-plus guitarist and Capitol records employee, ERIC ERLANDSON. LOVE, who had previously worked as an exotic dancer and an actress (she appeared in the 1986 punk movie, 'Sid & Nancy') and played alongside JENNIFER FINCH (L7) and KAT BJELLAND (Babes In Toyland) in a band called SUGAR BABY DOLL, was also involved in an early incarnation of FAITH NO MORE. Taking the name HOLE from a line in Euripides' 'Medea', they placed an ad in a local paper, 'Flipside', finding a bassist and drummer, namely JILL EMERY and CAROLINE RUE. In the Spring of 1990, HOLE released the 'RAT BASTARD' EP, subsequently relocating to the burgeoning Seattle area. Early the following year, 'Sub Pop' issued the 'DICKNAIL' EP, the band duly signing to 'Caroline' records for their debut album, 'PRETTY ON THE INSIDE'. Produced by KIM GORDON and DON FLEMING, it hit the lower regions of the US charts, the record being voted album of the year by New York's Village Voice magazine. A harrowing primal howl of a record, LOVE's demons were confronted mercilessly on such psyche-trawling dirges as 'TEENAGE WHORE' and 'GARBAGE MAN'. Around the same time, LOVE's relationship with NIRVANA's KURT COBAIN, was the talk of the alternative rock world, the singer subsequently marrying him in February '92, giving birth to his daughter, Frances Bean, later that summer. The following year, with newcomers PATTY SCHEMEL (drums) and KRISTEN PFAFF (bass), the group secured a deal with the David Geffen Company ('D.G.C.'), much to the dismay of MADONNA who wanted HOLE for her newly formed 'Maverick' label. In Spring 1994, LOVE finally celebrated a UK Top 20 album, 'LIVE THROUGH THIS', although its success was overshadowed by the shocking suicide of KURT on the 8th of April. She subsequently held a memorial two days later, hailing everyone there to call him an asshole. More press coverage followed later that summer, when PFAFF was found dead in her bath on the 16th June (it was believed to be another tragic drug related death). Despite the press circus surrounding LOVE, the band played a rather disappointing Reading Festival stint in August that year, her at times lethargic vox letting some of the more discerning fans down (EVAN DANDO of The LEMONHEADS was rumoured to be her new boyfriend, although a number of lucky people – including DANDO – were privy to her womanly charms – both of them – when she "flashed" at the side of the stage). With a new bassist, MELISSA AUF DER MAUR, the group released two UK hits, 'DOLL PARTS' and 'VIOLET', LOVE certainly back on top form with her incendiary Top Of The Pops performances (LYDIA LUNCH eat your heart out!?). Back in the news again, she was fined for assaulting BIKINI KILL's KATHLEEN HANNA, LOVE and SCHEMEL conversely taking three security guards to court following an alleged assault incident while signing autographs stagefront at a GREEN DAY concert in Lakefront Arena (yet more column inches were devoted to the controversial singer in August '96, when LOVE was acquitted of a stage assault nine months previous on two teenage fans in Florida). More recently, LOVE has played down her wild child character, exchanging the Seattle grunge mantle for a more respectable Hollywood career. This was largely down to her acclaimed roles in the movies, 'Feeling Minnesota' and more so with the controversial, 'The People Vs. Larry Flint'. On the recording front, only a lone version of FLEETWOOD MAC's 'GOLD DUST WOMAN' has surfaced (this was included on the film soundtrack from 'The Crow II: City Of Angels'). In '98, COURTNEY (and HOLE) was once again writing new material, this time with BILLY CORGAN of the SMASHING PUMPKINS, although a dispute over who actually wrote what the public thought were collaborations was subsequent tabloid news. The album in question, 'CELEBRITY SKIN' (1998), was worthy of its Top 10 placing although a little commercialised for some. The following year (in November), MELISSA bailed out of the band and more shocking still was that she joined COURTNEY's old pal CORGAN in The SMASHING PUMPKINS.
• **Covers:** STAR BELLY sampled DREAMS (Fleetwood Mac) + INTO THE BLACK (Neil Young) / DO IT CLEAN (Echo & The Bunnymen) / CREDIT

IN THE STRAIGHT WORLD (Young Marble Giants) / HUNGRY LIKE THE WOLF (Duran Duran) / SEASON OF THE WITCH (Donovan) / HE HIT ME (IT FELT LIKE A KISS) (Goffin-King) / IT'S ALL OVER NOW, BABY BLUE (Bob Dylan). 'I THINK THAT I WOULD DIE' was co-written w / KAT BJELLAND (Babes In Toyland). • **Note:** Not to be confused with band who released in the late 80's; OTHER TONGUES, OTHER FLESH (lp) and DYSKINSIA (12") both on 'Eyes Media'.

Album rating: PRETTY ON THE INSIDE (*7) / LIVE THROUGH THIS (*9) / MY BODY, THE HAND GRENADE collection (*6) / CELEBRITY SKIN (*7)

COURTNEY LOVE (b. MICHELLE HARRISON, 9 Jul'65, San Francisco, Calif.) – vocals, guitars / **ERIC ERLANDSON** (b. 9 Jan'63) – guitars / **JILL EMERY** – bass, vocals / **CAROLINE RUE** – drums

			not iss.	Sympathy F
Jul 90.	(7"white-ep) <SFTRI 53> **RETARD GIRL. / PHONEBILL SONG / JOHNNIES IN THE BATHROOM** (UK-iss.cd-ep Sep97 +=; SFTRI 53CD) – Turpentine.		-	

			not iss.	Sub Pop
Apr 91.	(7"colrd-various) (SP 93) **DICKNAIL. / BURNBLACK**			

			City Slang	Caroline
Aug 91.	(7"colrd-various) (EFA 04070-45) **TEENAGE WHORE. / DROWN SODA** (12"+=/cd-s+=) (EFA 04070-02/-03) – Burnblack.			
Oct 91.	(cd/c/lp-some red) (EFA 0407-2/-C/-1) <SLANG 012> **PRETTY ON THE INSIDE**	59		Jul91

– Teenage whore / Babydoll / Garbage man / Sassy / Goodsister – bad sister / Mrs. Jones / Berry / Loaded / Star belly / Pretty on the inside / Clouds. (re-iss. Sep95; same)

— **LESLEY** – bass repl. JILL / **PATTY SCHEMEL** (b.24 Apr'67, Seattle Washington) – drums repl. CAROLINE

			City Slang	D.G.C.
Apr 93.	(7") (EFA 04916-45) **BEAUTIFUL SON. / OLD AGE** (12"+=/cd-s+=) (EFA 04916-02/-03) – 20 years in the Dakota.	54	-

— **KRISTEN PFAFF** – bass, piano, vocals repl. LESLEY

Mar 94.	(7"some pink) (EFA 04936-7) **MISS WORLD. / ROCK STAR (alternate mix)** (cd-s+=) (EFA 04936-2) – Do it clean (live).	64	
Apr 94.	(cd/c/lp;some white) (EFA 04935-2/-4/-1) <24631> **LIVE THROUGH THIS**	13	52

– Violet / Miss World / Plump / Asking for it / Jennifer's body / Doll parts / Credit in the straight world / Softer, softest / She walks on me / I think that I would die / Gutless / Rock star. (re-iss. cd/lp Mar95 on 'Geffen'; GED/GEF 24631)

— KRISTEN was found dead in her bath 16th June 1994. COURTNEY, ERIC + PATTI continued and later recruited MELISSA AUF DER MAUR (b.17 Mar'72, Montreal, Canada) – bass. As HOLEZ (HOLE + PAT SMEAR of GERMS) they released tribute GERMS cover 'CIRCLE 1' on 'Dutch East India' Mar95.

			Geffen	D.G.C.
Nov 94.	(c-s) <19379> **DOLL PARTS / PLUMP** (live)	-	58
Apr 95.	(7") (GFS 91) **DOLL PARTS. / THE VOID**	16	-

(cd-s+=) (GFSTD 91) – Hungry like the wolf (live).
(cd-s) (GFSXD 91) – ('A'side) / Plump (live) / I think that I would die (live) / Credit in the straight world (live).

Jul 95.	(7") (GFS 94) **VIOLET. / OLD AGE**	17	

(7"colrd) (GFSP 94) – ('A'side) / He hit me (it felt like a kiss).
(cd-s++=) (GFSCD 94) – Who's porno you burn (black).

Nov 96.	(etched-d7") (573164-7) **GOLD DUST WOMAN. / (NY LOOSE: Spit)**	

(above 45 was a limited edition on 'Polydor' UK, 'Hollywood' US)

Sep 98.	(7"/c-s) (GFS/+C 22345) <radio play> **CELEBRITY SKIN. / BEST SUNDAY DRESS**	19	85

(cd-s+=) (GFSTD 22345) – Dying (original demo).

Sep 98.	(cd/c/lp) <GED/GEC/GEF 25164> **CELEBRITY SKIN**	11	9

– Celebrity skin / Awful / Hit so hard / Malibu / Reasons to be beautiful / Dying / Use once & destroy / Northern star / Boys on the radio / Heaven tonight / Playing your song / Petals. (special cd w/tour cd Jun99 +=; IND 90385) – Pretty on the inside / Heaven tonight / Northern star / Awful / Paradise city / Celebrity skin.

Jan 99.	(7") (GFS 22369) <radio cut> **MALIBU. / DRAG**	22	81

(cd-s+=) (GFSTD 22369) – It's all over now, baby blue.
(cd-s) (GFSCX 22369) – ('A'side) / Celebrity skin (live) / Reasons to be beautiful (live).

			Interscope	Interscope
Jun 99.	(7") (INTS7 97098) **AWFUL. / VIOLET** (live)	42	

(cd-s) (INTDE 97099) – ('A'side) / Miss World (live) / Celebrity skin (CD-Rom video).
(cd-s) (INTDE 97098) – ('A'side) / She walks on me (live) / Malibu (CD-Rom video).

– compilations, etc. –

Oct 95.	(m-cd) Caroline; <1470> **ASK FOR IT** (radio session)	-	
Sep 97.	(cd/c/lp) City Slang; <(EFA 04995-2/-4/-1)> **MY BODY, THE HAND GRENADE**		Oct97

– Turpentine / Phonebill song / Retard girl / Burn black / Dicknail / Beautiful son / 20 years in Dakota / Miss World / Old age / Softer softest / He hit me (it felt like a kiss) / Season of the witch / Drown soda / Asking for it.

HOLLIES

Formed: Manchester, England . . . 1961 by ALLAN CLARKE and GRAHAM NASH, who quickly found DON RATHBONE and ERIC HAYCOCK. In 1963, they signed to EMI's 'Parlophone' label, adding a 5th member, TONY HICKS. Their debut 45, '(AIN'T THAT) JUST LIKE ME', made the UK Top 30, being followed by 'SEARCHIN'', their first of 21 consecutive Top 20

hits until 1971's 'LITTLE WILLY' failed to register. During the early part of their career, The HOLLIES were basically a pop industry beat group, jumping on the psychedelic bandwagon in 1968 with the mythical pretentiousness of 'KING MIDAS IN REVERSE'. However, following the departure of NASH, they increasingly moved into the cabaret scene. They regained a bit of credibility in late 1969, however, with the much-loved ballad, 'HE AIN'T HEAVY'. In August '71, CLARKE left for the first time, returning in mid-73 after his Swedish replacement MICHAEL RICKFORS failed to impress the buying public. They immediately reinstated themselves when a Top 30 hit, was followed by near No.1 smash, 'THE AIR THAT I BREATHE'. Although future hits were few and far between, they ploughed on throughout the 70's & 80's. • **Songwriters:** CLARKE-HICKS-NASH, until latter's departure to CROSBY, STILLS & NASH. HOLLIES covered; (AIN'T THAT) JUST LIKE ME + SEARCHIN' (Coasters) / STAY (Maurice Williams & The Zodiacs) / JUST ONE LOOK (Doris Troy) / YES I WILL (Goffin-Titelman) / I'M ALIVE (Clint Ballard Jr.) / LOOK THROUGH ANY WINDOW + BUS STOP (Graham Gouldman) / IF I NEEDED SOMEONE (George Harrison; Beatles) / I CAN'T LET GO + THE BABY (Chip Taylor) / SORRY SUZANNE (T.MacAuley & G.Stephens) / GASOLINE ALLEY BRED (T.MacAuley-R.Cook-R.Greenaway) / WHEN THE SHIP COMES IN (Bob Dylan) / JESUS WAS A CROSSMAKER (Judee Sill) / SANDY (Bruce Springsteen) / STOP IN THE NAME OF LOVE (Supremes) / SOLDIER'S SONG (Mike Batt) / CARRIE (John Miles) / STAND BY ME (Ben E.King) / SHINE SILENTLY (Nils Lofgren) / etc. Also cover albums 'HOLLIES SING (Bob) DYLAN' and 'BUDDY HOLLY'. KENNY LYNCH collaborated on several with HICKS on 1971's 'DISTANT LIGHT'. • **Trivia:** In 1988 after exposure on Miller lite UK TV ad, the 1969 hit 'HE AIN'T HEAVY, HE'S MY BROTHER' re-charted, hitting No.1.

Best CD compilation: THE AIR THAT I BREATHE – THE BEST OF . . . (*8)

ALLAN CLARKE (b. 5 Apr'42, Salford, Manchester, England) – vocals / **TONY HICKS** (b.16 Dec'43, Nelson, Lancashire, England) – lead guitar / **GRAHAM NASH** (b. 2 Feb'42, Blackpool, England) – guitar / **ERIC HAYDOCK** (b. 3 Feb'43) – bass / **DON RATHBONE** – drums

			Parlophone	Liberty
May 63.	(7") (R 5030) **(AIN'T THAT) JUST LIKE ME. / HEY WHAT'S WRONG WITH ME**	25	-
Aug 63.	(7") (R 5052) **SEARCHIN'. / WHOLE WORLD OVER**	12	-

— **BOBBY ELLIOTT** (b. 8 Dec'42, Burnley, England) – drums (ex-SHANE FENTON & THE FENTONES) repl. RATHBONE (still on next single b-side and album track – *)

Nov 63.	(7") (R 5077) <55674> **STAY. / NOW'S THE TIME**	8		Mar64
Jan 64.	(lp) (PMC 1220) **STAY WITH THE HOLLIES**	2	

– Little lover / Memphis / Talkin' 'bout you / It's only make believe / Rockin' Robin / Mr. Moonlight / You better move on / Watcha gonna do 'bout it / What kind of girl are you / Candy man / What kind of boy. (re-iss. Oct87 on 'Beat Goes On'; BGOLP 4) (cd-iss. Oct88; BGOCD 4)

			Parlophone	Imperial
Feb 64.	(7") (R 5104) <66026> **JUST ONE LOOK. / KEEP OFF THAT FRIEND OF MINE**	2	98	Apr64
May 64.	(7") (R 5137) **HERE I GO AGAIN. / BABY THAT'S ALL**	4	-
Jul 64.	(7") <66044> **HERE I GO AGAIN. / LUCILLE**	-	
Sep 64.	(7") (R 5178) <66070> **WE'RE THROUGH. / COME ON BACK**	7		Oct64
Nov 64.	(lp) (PMC 1235) **IN THE HOLLIES STYLE**		-

– The time for love / Don't you know / You'll be mine / It's in her kiss / Come on home / Set me free / Too much monkey business / I thought of you last night / Nitty gritty; something's got a hold of me. (re-iss. Mar88 & Apr97 on 'Beat Goes On' lp/cd; BGO LP/CD 8)

Jan 65.	(7") (R 5232) **YES I WILL. / NOBODY**	9	-
May 65.	(7") (R 5287) **I'M ALIVE. / YOU KNOW HE DID**	1	-
Aug 65.	(7") (R 5322) <66134> **LOOK THROUGH ANY WINDOW. / SO LONELY**	4	32	Nov65
Sep 65.	(lp) (PMC 1261) <12312> **THE HOLLIES**	8		Jun66

– Put yourself in my place / When I come home to you / That's my desire / Mickey's monkey / Very last day / Down the line / Lawdy Miss Clawdy / You must believe me / Too many people / Fortune teller / I've been wrong. (re-iss. Nov69 as 'REFLECTION' on 'Regal Starline'; SRS 5008) (re-iss. Jul88 on 'Beat Goes On'; BGOLP 25) (cd-iss. Apr91; BGOCD 25)

Dec 65.	(7") (R 5392) **IF I NEEDED SOMEONE. / I'VE GOT A WAY OF MY OWN**	20	-
Jan 66.	(lp) <12299> **HEAR! HERE!**	

– I'm alive / Very last day / You must believe me / Put yourself in my place / Down the line / That's my desire / Look through any window / Lawdy Miss Clawdy / When I come home to you / Lonely / I've been wrong / Too many people.

Feb 66.	(7") (R 5409) <66158> **I CAN'T LET GO. / I'VE GOT A WAY OF MY OWN**	2	42	Mar66
Jun 66.	(lp; mono/stereo) (PMC/PCS 7008) <12330> **WOULD YOU BELIEVE?** <US-title 'BUS STOP'>	16	75	Oct66

– Stewball / Take your time / Don't you even care / Oriental sadness / I take what I want / Hard hard year / Fifi the flea / That's how strong my love is / I am a rock / Sweet little sixteen. (re-iss. Oct88 on 'Beat Goes On'; BGOLP 24) (cd-iss. Apr91; BGOCD 24)

— **BERNIE CALVERT** (b.16 Sep'43, Burnley) – bass repl. HAYDOCK who formed HAYDOCK'S ROADHOUSE JOHN PAUL JONES – bass sessioned on the next b-side. (Later to LED ZEPPELIN)

Jun 66.	(7") (R 5469) <66186> **BUS STOP. / DON'T RUN AND HIDE**	5	5	Jul66

— in Aug'66, they teamed up with actor/comedian PETER SELLERS on single 'AFTER THE FOX', from the film on 'United Artists'

Oct 66.	(7") (R 5508) <66214> **STOP! STOP! STOP!. / IT'S YOU**	2	7
Oct 66.	(lp; mono/stereo) (PMC/PCS 7011) <12339> **FOR CERTAIN BECAUSE** <US-title 'STOP! STOP! STOP!'>	23	91	Feb67

– Don't even think about changing / Peculiar situation / Tell me to my face /

Suspicious look in your eyes / Pay you back with interest / Clown / It's you / Crusader / What's wrong with the way I live / What went wrong / High classed. (re-iss. Dec71 as 'STOP! STOP! STOP!' on 'Regal Starline'; SRS 5088) (re-iss. Apr88 on 'Beat Goes On' lp/c; BGO MC/CD 9) (cd-iss. Dec89; BGOCD 9)

Feb 67. (7") (R 5562) <66231> **ON A CAROUSEL. / ALL THE WORLD IS LOVE** — 4 — 11 Mar67

May 67. (7") <66240> **PAY YOU BACK WITH INTEREST. / WHAT'CHA GONNA DO ABOUT IT** — - — 28

—— between 22nd Feb'67 and 16th Jan'68 used session drummer **DOUGIE WRIGHT** to repl. ELLIOT who had taken ill, also CLEM CATTINI guested

		Parlophone	Epic

May 67. (7") (R 5602) <10180> **CARRIE-ANNE. / SIGNS THAT WILL NEVER CHANGE** — 3 — 9 Jun67

Jun 67. (lp; mono/stereo) (PMC/PCS 7022) <26315> **EVOLUTION** — 13 — 43 Jul67
— When your light's turned on / Have you ever loved somebody / Lullaby to Tim / The games we play / Leave me / Rain on the window / Then the heartaches begin / Ye olde coffee shoppe / You need love / Stop right there / Water on the brain / Heading for a fall. (re-iss. Feb72 as 'HOLLIES' on 'Music For Pleasure'; MFP 5252) (re-iss. 1989 on 'Beat Goes On'; BGOLP 80) (cd-iss. Jun93; BGOCD 80)

Sep 67. (7") (R 5637) **KING MIDAS IN REVERSE. / EVERYTHING IS SUNSHINE** — 18 — -

Sep 67. (7") <10234> **KING MIDAS IN REVERSE. / WATER ON THE BRAIN** — - — 51

Oct 67. (lp; mono/stereo) (PMC/PCS 7039) **BUTTERFLY** — - — -
— Try it / Wish you a wish / Step inside / Pegasus the flying horse / Dear Eloise / Away away away / Elevated observations / Would you believe / Butterfly / Maker / Charlie and Fred. (re-iss. 1989 on 'Beat Goes On' lp/cd; BGO LP/CD 79)

Nov 67. (7") <10251> **DEAR ELOISE. / WHEN YOUR LIGHTS TURNED ON** — - — 50

Mar 68. (7") (R 5680) **JENNIFER ECCLES. / OPEN UP YOUR EYES** — 11 — -

Mar 68. (7") <10298> **JENNIFER ECCLES. / TRY IT** — - — 40

Jun 68. (7") <10361> **DO THE BEST YOU CAN. / ELEVATED OBSERVATIONS** — - — 93

Sep 68. (7") (R 5733) **LISTEN TO ME. / DO THE BEST YOU CAN** — 11 — -

Sep 68. (7") <10400> **LISTEN TO ME. / EVERYTHING IS SUNSHINE** — - — -

—— **TERRY SYLVESTER** (b. 8 Jan'45, Liverpool, England) – vocals, guitar (ex-SWINGING BLUE JEANS) repl. NASH who joined CROSBY, STILLS & NASH. (ELLIOT also returned)

Feb 69. (7") (R 5765) <10454> **SORRY SUZANNE. / NOT THAT WAY AT ALL** — 3 — 56

May 69. (lp; mono/stereo) (PMC/PCS 7078) <26447> **HOLLIES SING DYLAN** — 3 — -
— Blowin' in the wind / I shall be released/ / This wheel's on fire / The mighty Quinn / The times they are a-changin' / I want you / Quit your lowdown ways / Just like a woman / When the ship comes in / My back pages / I'll be your baby tonight / All I really want to do. (re-iss. Oct87 on 'Music For Pleasure' lp/c; MFP/TC-MFP 5811) (cd-iss. Jun93 on 'E.M.I.'; CZ 509)

Sep 69. (7") (R 5806) <10532> **HE AIN'T HEAVY, HE'S MY BROTHER. / 'COS YOU LIKE TO LOVE ME** — 3 — 7 Dec69
(re-iss. Aug82)

Nov 69. (lp) (PCS 7092) <26538> **HOLLIES SING HOLLIES** <US-title 'HE AIN'T HEAVY, HE'S MY BROTHER'> — - — 32
— Do you believe in love / Please let your letters / Please let me please / Goodbye tomorrow / My life is over with you / Soldier's dilemma / Marigold; Gloria swansong / You love 'cos you like it / Why didn't you believe / Look at life / Don't give up easily / Reflections of a time gone past. <US version replaced; 'Marigold' with> – He ain't heavy, he's my brother.

Apr 70. (7") (R 5837) <10613> **I CAN'T TELL THE BOTTOM FROM THE TOP. / MAD PROFESSOR BLYTH** — 7 — 82 May70

Sep 70. (7") (R 5862) <10677> **GASOLINE ALLEY BRED. / DANDELION WINE** — 14 — -

Nov 70. (lp) (PCS 7116) <30255> **CONFESSIONS OF THE MIND** <US-title 'MOVING FINGER'> — 30 — -
— I want to shout / Lady please / Separated / Confessions of a mind / Little girl / Survival of the fittest / Isn't it nice / Perfect lady housewife / Too young to be married / Frightened lady / Man without a heart. (re-iss. 1989 on 'Beat Goes On'; BGOLP 96) (cd-iss. Apr91; BGOCD 96)

Jan 71. (7") <10716> **SURVIVAL OF THE FITTEST. / MAN WITHOUT A HEART** — - — -

May 71. (7") (R 5905) **HEY WILLY. / ROW THE BOAT TOGETHER** — - — -

Jun 71. (lp) (PAS 10005) <30958> **DISTANT LIGHT** — - — 21 Jul71
— Long cool woman (in a black dress) / You know the score / Pull down the blind / Promised land / What a life I've led / Cable car / Hold on / To do with love / Look what we got / Long dark road / Don't let a little thing like love. (re-iss. Jul91 on 'Beat Goes On'; BGO LP/CD 97)

Jun 72. (7") <10871> **LONG COOL WOMAN (IN A BLACK DRESS). / LOOK WHAT WE'VE GOT** — - — 2

Aug 72. (7") (R 5939) **LONG COOL WOMAN (IN A BLACK DRESS). / CABLE CAR** — 32 — -

Nov 72. (7") <10920> **LONG DARK ROAD. / INDIAN GIRL** — - — 26

—— (Aug71) **MICHAEL RICKFORS** – vocals (ex-BAMBOO) repl. CLARKE who went solo

		Polydor	Epic

Feb 72. (7") (2058 199) <10842> **THE BABY. / OH GRANNY** — 26 — -

Nov 72. (7") (2058 289) **MAGIC WOMAN TOUCH. / INDIAN GIRL** — - — -

Nov 72. (lp) (2383 144) <31992> **ROMANY** — - — 84
— Touch / Romany / Blue in the morning / Jesus was a crossmaker / Down river / Magic woman touch / Lizzy and the rainman / Slow down / Delaware Taggart and the outlaw boys / Won't we feel good that morning / Words sdon't come easy / Courage of your convictions.

Jan 73. (7") <10951> **MAGIC WOMAN TOUCH. / BLUE IN THE MORNING** — - — 60

Mar 73. (7") <10989> **JESUS WAS A CROSSMAKER. / I HAD A DREAM** — - — -

May 73. (7") <11025> **SLOW DOWN. / WON'T WE FEEL GOOD** — - — -

		not iss.	Polydor

May 73. (lp) **OUT ON THE ROAD** (studio) — - — - German
— Don't leave the child alone / They don't realise I'm down / Transatlantic westbound

jet / Nearer to you / Slow down go down / Pick up the pieces / The last wind / Mr. Heartbreaker / A better place / Out on the road / I was born a man / I had a dream.

—— (Jul73) **ALLAN CLARKE** – vocals returned to repl. RICKFORS (CLARKE now joining others HICKS, SYLVESTER, CALVERT and ELLIOTT)

Oct 73. (7") (2058 403) <11051> **THE DAY THAT CURLY BILLY SHOT CRAZY SAM McGEE. / BORN A MAN** — 24 — -

Jan 74. (7") (2058 435) <11100> **THE AIR THAT I BREATHE. / NO MORE RIDERS** — 2 — 6 Apr74

Mar 74. (lp) (2383 262) <32574> **THE HOLLIES** — 38 — 28 May74
— Out on the road / Pick up the pieces again / It's a shame, it's a game / Transatlantic westbound jet / Don't let me down / Falling calling / Rubber Lucy / Down on the run / Love makes the world go round.

May 74. (7") (2058 476) **SON OF A ROTTEN GAMBLER. / LAYIN' TO THE MUSIC** — - — -

May 74. (7") (50029) **DON'T LET ME DOWN. / LAY INTO THE MUSIC** — - — -

Nov 74. (7") (2058 533) **I'M DOWN. / HELLO LADY GOODBYE** — - — -

Feb 75. (lp) (2441 128) <33387> **ANOTHER NIGHT** — - — -
— Give me time / Lonely hobo lullaby / You gave me life / Lucy / Sandy (4th of July, Asbury Park) / Look out Johnny (there's a monkey on your back) / Another night / Second-hand hang-ups / Time machine jive.

May 75. (7") (2058 595) <50086> **SANDY (FOURTH OF JULY, ASBURY PARK). / SECOND-HAND HANGUPS** — - — 85 Mar75
<US re-iss. Apr76; 50359>

Jun 75. (7") <50110> **ANOTHER NIGHT. / TIME MACHINE JIVE** — - — 71

Aug 75. (7") <50144> **I'M DOWN. / LOOK OUT JOHNNY (THERE'S A MONKEY ON YOUR BACK)** — - — -

—— **ROD ARGENT** – moog, piano (on next album track – *)

Jan 76. (lp) (2442 141) **WRITE ON** — - — -
— Stranger / Narida / My island / Sweet country calling / Write on / Crocodile woman (she bites) / Star * / Love is the thing / There's always goodbye / I won't move over.

Feb 76. (7") <50204> **WRITE ON. / CROCODILE WOMAN (SHE BITES)** — - — -

Feb 76. (7") (2058 694) **BOULDER TO BIRMINGHAM. / CROCODILE WOMAN (SHE BITES)** — - — -

Apr 76. (7") (2058 719) **STAR. / LOVE IS THE THING** — - — -

Aug 76. (7") (2058 779) **DADDY DON'T MIND. / C'MON** — - — -

Oct 76. (7") (2058 799) **WIGGLE THAT WOTSIT. / CORRINE** — - — -

Dec 76. (lp) (2382 421) **RUSSIAN ROULETTE** — - — -
— My love / Russian roulette / Be with you / Lady of the night / Louise / 48 hour people / Thanks for the memories / Wiggle that wotsit / Draggin' my heels.

Dec 76. (7") <50422> **DRAGGIN' MY HEELS. / I WON'T MOVE OVER** — - — -

Mar 77. (lp) (2383 428) **HOLLIES LIVE HITS** — 4 — -
— I can't let go / Just one look / I can't tell the bottom from the top / Another night / Bust stop / Sandy / Star / My island / I'm down / Stop, stop, stop / Long cool woman (in a black dress) / Carrie-Anne / The air that I breathe / Too young to be married / He ain't heavy, he's my brother.

May 77. (7") (2058 880) **HELLO TO ROMANCE. / 48 HOUR PAROLE** — - — -

Jul 77. (7") (2058 906) **AMNESTY. / CROSSFIRE** — - — -

Mar 78. (lp) (2383 474) <3534> **A CRAZY STEAL** — - — -
— Let it pour / Burn out / Amnesty / Caracas / What am I gonna do / Feet on the ground / Writing on the wall / Clown service.

Apr 78. (7") <50522> **BURN OUT. / WRITING ON THE WALL** — - — -

Mar 79. (7") (POSP 35) **SOMETHING TO LIVE FOR. / SONG OF THE SUN** — - — -
(12"+=) (POSPX 35) – The air that I breathe.

Mar 79. (lp) (2442 160) **FIVE THREE ONE – DOUBLE SEVEN O FOUR** — - — -
— When I'm yours / Satellite three / Something to live for / Maybe it's dawn / Song of the sun / Stormy waters / Boys in the band / It's in every one of us / Say it ain't so / Harlequin.

Mar 80. (7") (2059 246) **SOLDIER'S SONG. / DRAGGIN' MY HEELS** — 58 — -

Sep 80. (7") (POSP 175) **HEARTBEAT. / TAKE YOUR TIME** — - — -

Oct 80. (lp/c) (POLTV/+M 12) **BUDDY HOLLY** — - — -
— Take your time / Wishing / Peggy Sue / Heartbeat / Love's made a fool of you / That'll be the day / Think it over / Tell me how / Maybe baby / I'm gonna love you too / What to do / It doesn't matter / Peggy Sue got married / Midnight shift / Everyday.

—— trimmed to a trio of CLARKE, HICKS and ELLIOTT when CALVERT and SYLVESTER left. Latter teamed with JAMES GRIFFIN (ex-BREAD) (next single b-side with **ALAN JONES** – bass)

Nov 81. (7") (POSP 379) **TAKE MY LOVE AND RUN. / DRIVER** — - — -

—— added returning **GRAHAM NASH** – vocals, guitar

		WEA	Atlantic

Jul 83. (7") (U 9888) <89819> **STOP! IN THE NAME OF LOVE. / MUSICAL PICTURES** — - — 29 May83

Jul 83. (lp/c) (250139-1/-4) <80076> **WHAT GOES AROUND** — - — 90
— Something ain't right / Casualty / Say you'll be mine / If the lights go out / Stop! / In the name of love / I got what I want / Just one look / Someone else's eyes / Having a good time / Let her go down.

Aug 83. (7") <89784> **SOMEONE ELSE'S EYES. / IF THE LIGHTS GO OUT** — - — -

Oct 83. (7") <89768> **CASUALTY. / IF THE LIGHTS GO OUT** — - — -

—— basic trio of **CLARKE, HICKS** and **ELLIOTT** plus **ALAN COATES** – harmonies / **STEVE STROUD** – bass / **DENNIS HAYNES** – keyboards

		Columbia	not iss.

May 85. (7") (DB 9110) **TOO MANY HEARTS GET BROKEN. / YOU'RE ALL WOMAN** — - — -
(12"+=) (12DB 9110) – Laughter turns to tears.

Jan 87. (7") (DB 9146) **THIS IS IT. / YOU GAVE ME STRENGTH** — - — -
(12"+=) (12DB 9146) – You're all woman.

Mar 87. (7") (DB 9151) **REUNION OF THE HEART. / TOO MANY HEARTS GET BROKEN** — - — -
(12"+=) (12DB 9151) – Hollidaze (medley).

—— **RAY STILES** – bass (ex-MUD) repl. STROUD

			Coconut	not iss.	
Jan 88.	(7") **STAND BY ME. / FOR WHAT IT'S WORTH**		–	–	German
Jun 88.	(7") **SHINE SILENTLY. / YOUR EYES**		–	–	German

			E.M.I.	not iss.	
Feb 89.	(7") *(EM 86)* **FIND ME A FAMILY. / NO RULES**			–	
Mar 93.	(c-s/7") *(TC+/EM 264)* **THE WOMAN I LOVE. / PURPLE RAIN** (live)		42		

(cd-s+=) *(CDEM 264)* – The air that I breathe / (Ain't) That just like me.

Mar 93. (cd/c/lp) *(CD/TC+/EMTV 74)* **THE AIR THAT I BREATHE (THE BEST OF THE HOLLIES)** (compilation) `15` `–`
– The air that I breathe / Bus stop / Just one look / Yes I will / Look through any window / He ain't heavy, he's my brother / I can't let go / Searchin' / Stay / I'm alive / If I needed someone / Here I go again / Stop stop stop / On a carousel / Carrie Ann / King Midas in reverse / Jennifer Eccles / Listen to me / Sorry Suzanne / I can't tell the bottom from the top / Gasoline alley bred / Hey Willy / The day that Curly Billy shot down Crazy Sam McGee / The woman I love.

– compilations, etc. –

on 'Parlophone' unless mentiond otherwise

1964.	(7"ep) *(GEP 8909)* **THE HOLLIES**		–
1964.	(7"ep) *(GEP 8911)* **JUST ONE LOOK**		–
1964.	(7"ep) *(GEP 8915)* **HERE I GO AGAIN**		–
1964.	(7"ep) *(GEP 8927)* **WE'RE THROUGH**		–
1965.	(7"ep) *(GEP 8934)* **IN THE HOLLIES STYLE**		–
1965.	(7"ep) *(GEP 8942)* **I'M ALIVE**		–
1966.	(7"ep) *(GEP 8951)* **I CAN'T LET GO**		–
Sep 67.	(7") *Imperial; <66258>* **JUST ONE LOOK. / RUNNING THROUGH THE NIGHT**	–	44
Dec 67.	(7") *Imperial; <66271>* **IF I NEED SOMEONE. / I'LL BE TRUE TO YOU (YES I WILL)**	–	–
Aug 68.	(lp) *(7057) <12350>* **HOLLIES' GREATEST HITS** (US version different)	1	11
Nov 72.	(lp) *(7148)* **THE HOLLIES GREATEST HITS VOL.2**		
Oct 74.	(lp) *Music For Pleasure; (MFP 50094)* **I CAN'T LET GO**		
Sep 75.	(7") *E.M.I.; (EMI 2353)* **LONG COOL WOMAN IN A BLACK DRESS. / CARRIE ANNE**		–
Nov 75.	(d-lp/d-c) *E.M.I.; (EMSP/TC2-EMSP 650)* **THE HISTORY OF THE HOLLIES**		–
Jun 78.	(7") *E.M.I.; (EMI 2813)* **LOOK THROUGH ANY WINDOW. / I'M ALIVE / JUST ONE LOOK**		–
Jul 78.	(lp/c) *E.M.I.; (EMTV/TC-EMTV 11)* **20 GOLDEN GREATS**	2	–

– The air that I breathe / Carrie Anne / Bus stop / Listen to me / Look through any window / I can't let go / Long cool woman in a black dress / Here I go again / I can't tell the bottom from the top / I'm alive / Yes I will / Stay / Sorry Suzanne / Gasoline alley bred / We're through / Jennifer Eccles / Stop! stop! stop! / On a carousel / Just one look / He ain't heavy, he's my brother. *(cd-iss. Mar87 & Jan89; CDP 238-2)*

Aug 78.	(lp) *(PMC 7176)* **THE OTHER SIDE OF THE HOLLIES**		–
Aug 78.	(lp) *(PMC 7174)* **THE BEST OF THE HOLLIES EP's** (re-iss. Mar81 on 'E.M.I.' lp/c; NUTM/TC-NUTM 30)		–
Sep 80.	(lp/c) *Music For Pleasure; (MFP/TC-MFP 50450)* **LONG COOL WOMAN IN A BLACK DRESS**		–
Aug 81.	(7") *E.M.I.; (EMI 5229)* **HOLLIEDAZE (MEDLEY). / HOLLIEPOPS**	28	–
Oct 83.	(7") *Old Gold; (OG 9386)* **HE AIN'T HEAVY, HE'S MY BROTHER. / BUS STOP**		–
Mar 84.	(7") *EMI Gold; (G45 11)* **JUST ONE LOOK. / HERE I GO AGAIN**		–
Feb 86.	(lp) *See For Miles; (SEE 63)* **NOT THE HITS AGAIN** (cd-iss. May89; SEECD 63)		–
Sep 87.	(lp/c) *See For Miles; (SEE/+K 94)* **THE EP COLLECTION** (cd-iss. 1989 & Apr95; SEECD 94)		–
Sep 87.	(c) *Hour Of Pleasure; (HR 8153)* **AN HOUR OF THE HOLLIES**		–
May 88.	(cd) *Compacts For Pleasure; (CC 216)* **HOLLIES**		–
Aug 88.	(7") *E.M.I.; (EM 74)* **HE AIN'T HEAVY, HE'S MY BROTHER. / CARRIE**	1	

(12"+=/cd-s+=) *(12/CD EM 74)* – The air that I breathe.

Sep 88.	(d-lp/d-c)(d-cd) *E.M.I.; (EM/TCEM 1301)(CDS 790 850-2)* **ALL THE HITS AND MORE : THE DEFINITIVE COLLECTION**	51	–
Nov 88.	(lp/c)(cd) *E.M.I.; (EMS/TC-EMS 1311)(CDP 791 297-2)* **RARITIES**		–
Nov 88.	(7") *E.M.I.; (EM 80)* **THE AIR THAT I BREATHE. / WE'RE THROUGH**	60	

(12"+=) *(12EM 80)* – King Midas in reverse / Just one look.
(cd-s+=) *(CDEM 80)* – He ain't heavy, he's my brother.

Apr 90.	(cd/c/lp) *Music For Pleasure; (CD/TC+/MFP 5883)* **THE LOVE SONGS**		–
Jun 92.	(cd-s) *Old Gold;* **HE AIN'T HEAVY, HE'S MY BROTHER / CARRIE ANN / ON A CAROUSEL**		–
Jul 92.	(cd-s) *Old Gold;* **I'M ALIVE / JUST ONE LOOK**		–
Apr 93.	(cd/c) *Music For Pleasure; (CD/TC MFP 5980)* **THE SINGLES A's & B's 1970-1979**		–
May 94.	(cd) *B.R. Music; (BR 1302)* **THE AIR THAT I BREATHE**		–
Nov 94.	(cd) *B.R. Music; (BR 1462)* **ALL THE WORLD IS LOVE**		–
Feb 95.	(4xcd-box) *E.M.I.; (HOLLIES 1)* **FOUR HOLLIES ORIGINALS**		–

– (ANOTHER NIGHT / RUSSIAN ROULETTE / 5317704 / BUDDY HOLLY)

Nov 95.	(cd-s) *Old Gold; (126326330-2)* **HE AIN'T HEAVY, HE'S MY BROTHER / CARRIE ANNE**		–
Feb 96.	(4xcd-box) *Premier-EMI; (CDHOLLIES 2)* **FOUR MORE HOLLIES ORIGINALS**		–

– (ROMANY / WRITE ON / THE HOLLIES / A CRAZY STEAL)

Mark HOLLIS (see under ⇒ TALK TALK)

Buddy HOLLY

Born: CHARLES HARDIN HOLLEY, 7 Sep'36, Lubbock, Texas, USA. In the late 40's, the young HOLLY formed a C&W duo with schoolmate, BOB MONTGOMERY. As BUDDY & BOB, they became regulars on a Saturday afternoon TV show (around 1953/54), the pair subsequently putting together a number of demos, later issued as 'HOLLY IN THE HILLS'. With the addition of bassman, LARRY WELBORN and drummer JERRY ALLISON in 1955, the revamped unit began to make a name for themselves locally. After a gig supporting BILL HALEY & HIS COMETS, and through agent Eddie Crandall, BUDDY HOLLY was signed up by 'Decca' early the following year. Rejecting MONTGOMERY (who went on to become a successful producer, etc), the bespectacled HOLLY formed backing band, The THREE TUNES, retaining JERRY and recruiting SONNY CURTIS on guitar, DON GUESS on bass. Following two flop singles, BUDDY and JERRY left the label, travelling to New Mexico in search of producer, NORMAN PETTY, who was soon to become their manager. Early in 1957, the pair were joined by NIKI SULLIVAN (rhythm guitar) and JOE B. MAUDLIN (bass), becoming The CRICKETS. Their debut single, 'THAT'LL BE THE DAY', hit the top of the charts on both sides of the Atlantic, selling a million in the process. As a solo artist (with CRICKETS backing), BUDDY set up a deal with 'Coral', who released 'PEGGY SUE', another transatlantic Top 10 smash. The single also introduced HOLLY's idiosyncratic vocal mannerisms, his exaggerated hiccuping framed by simple but effective arrangements and infectious hooks which influenced many of the biggest 60's rock/pop stars, including DYLAN, The BEATLES and The 'STONES. Over the course of the following year, he balanced a series of CRICKETS hits ('OH BOY', 'MAYBE BABY' and 'THINK IT OVER') with his own solo classics ('LISTEN TO ME', 'RAVE ON' and 'EARLY IN THE MORNING'). His partnership with The CRICKETS was eventually severed in August '58, BUDDY marrying Maria Elena Santiago and moving to New York. His first CRICKETS-less single, 'HEARTBEAT', was surprisingly disappointing in terms of native chart success (i.e. No.82), although it managed to scrape into the UK Top 30. This was certainly a transitional period, things looking promising early the following year when the singer set out as headliner on a winter-long package tour of the States. Tragically, on the morning of the 3rd of February 1959, HOLLY, along with fellow pop stars, RICHIE VALENS and the BIG BOPPER, were killed when their chartered plane crashed just after take-off from Mason City airport in Iowa. A posthumous release (written by PAUL ANKA), 'IT DOESN'T MATTER ANYMORE' – backed by 'RAINING IN MY HEART' – became one of his biggest UK hits, while climbing the US Top 20. With a bulging vault of HOLLY material at his disposal, NORMAN PETTY proceeded to keep the legend's name alive via a series of hit releases during the early 60's. Although fans might have disagreed on what direction HOLLY's career might have taken, their was no disputing the fact that the 22-year-old surely still had a wealth of music inside of him. • **Songwriters:** HOLLY wrote most himself, except EARLY IN THE MORNING + NOW WE'RE ONE (Bobby Darin) / BABY I DON'T CARE (Elvis Presley) / etc. His songs were later covered by Rolling Stones (NOT FADE AWAY) / Mud (OH BOY) / Showaddywaddy (HEARTBEAT) / Leo Sayer (RAINING IN MY HEART). • **Trivia:** In Sep'58, HOLLY produced his new bass player's (WAYLON JENNINGS) debut single 'JOLE BLON'.

Best CD compilation: THE BUDDY HOLLY COLLECTION (*9)

BUDDY HOLLY – vocals, guitar (backed by The **CRICKETS**

		Brunswick	Decca
Jul 56.	(7",78) *(05581) <29854>* **BLUE DAYS BLACK NIGHTS. / LOVE ME**		☐ Apr56
Dec 56.	(7",78) *<30166>* **MODERN DON JUAN. / YOU ARE MY ONE DESIRE**	–	☐

(with The CRICKETS ⇒ , he hit No.1 (May57-US / Sep57-UK) with the single **THAT'LL BE THE DAY. / I'M LOOKING FOR SOMEONE TO LOVE**

		Coral	Coral
Jun 57.	(7",78) *<61852>* **WORDS OF LOVE. / MAILMAN BRING ME NO MORE BLUES**	–	–
Nov 57.	(7",78) *(Q 72293) <61885>* **PEGGY SUE. / EVERYDAY** (re-iss. Jul82 on 'Old Gold')	6	3 Sep57

—— (with The CRICKETS ⇒ again, he hit US No.10 (Nov57) / UK No.3 (Dec57) with single **OH BOY. / NOT FADE AWAY.**

—— An album **THE CHIRPING CRICKETS** was issued Nov57-US / Mar58-UK. Another single **MAYBE BABY. / TELL ME HOW** hit US No.17 (Feb58) / UK No.4 (Mar58).

Mar 58.	(7",78) *(Q 72288) <61947>* **LISTEN TO ME. / I'M GONNA LOVE YOU TOO**	16	
Jun 58.	(7",78) *(Q 72325) <61985>* **RAVE ON. / TAKE YOUR TIME**	5	37 Apr58
Jul 58.	(lp) *(LVA 9085) <57210>* **BUDDY HOLLY**		Mar58

– I'm gonna love you too / Peggy Sue / Look at me / Listen to me / Valley of tears / Ready Teddy / Everyday / Mailman, bring me no more blues / Words of love / Baby I don't care / Rave on / Little baby. *(re-iss. Jul75)* *(re-iss. Mar83 + Nov86 on 'M.C.A.', cd-iss. Nov92 on 'Sequel') (re-iss. Jul68 as 'LISTEN TO ME' on 'MCA', re-iss. Feb74; all UK)*

—— (with The CRICKETS ⇒ again, he hit US No.27 (Jun58) / UK No.11 (Jul58) with single **THINK IT OVER. / FOOL'S PARADISE**

Aug 58.	(7",78) *(Q 72333) <62006>* **EARLY IN THE MORNING. / NOW WE'RE ONE**		32 Jul58

—— (with The CRICKETS ⇒ again, he was heard on their last single collaboration **IT'S SO EASY. / LONESOME TEARS** (which didn't chart US-Sep58 / UK-Oct58)

He had now left The CRICKETS to hop away on their own Oct'58.

Nov 58.	(7",78) *(Q 72346) <62051>* **HEARTBEAT. / WELL ALL RIGHT**	30	82
Feb 59.	(7",78) *(Q 72360) <62074>* **IT DOESN'T MATTER ANYMORE. / RAINING IN MY HEART**	1	13
			88 Jan59

(re-iss. Apr83 on 'Old Gold')

—— On the 3rd of Feb'59, BUDDY was killed in a plane crash alongside other pop stars RICHIE VALENS and BIG BOPPER.

– past early recording releases –

—— (with back-up from The **THREE TUNES** aka **SONNY CURTIS** – guitar / **DON GUESS** – bass / **JERRY ALLISON** – drums

Sep 57. (7") *Decca; <30434>* **ROCK AROUND WITH OLLIE VEE. / THAT'LL BE THE DAY** | | - | |

Nov 57. (7") *Decca;* **THAT'LL BE THE DAY** | | - | |
– That'll be the day / Ting-a-ling / Blue days, black nights / You are my one desire.

Jan 58. (7") *Decca; <30543>* **LOVE ME. / YOU ARE MY ONE DESIRE** | | - | |

Apr 58. (lp) *Decca; <8707>* **THAT'LL BE THE DAY** | | - | |
(UK-iss.Oct61 on 'Ace Of Hearts', hit No.5) (US re-iss. Mar67 as 'THE GREAT BUDDY HOLLY' on 'Vocalion') (UK re-iss. Dec69 + Feb74 on 'Coral')

Jun 58. (7") *Decca; <30650>* **GIRLS ON MY MIND. / TING-A-LING** | | - | |

Sep 58. (7"ep) *Coral; (FEP 2002)* **BUDDY HOLLY** | | - | |
– Listen to me / Peggy Sue / Everyday / I'm gonna love you too.

Dec 58. (7"ep) *Coral; (FEP 2005)* **RAVE ON** | | - | |
– Rave on / Take your time / Early in the morning / Now we're one.

Jan 59. (7"ep) *Coral; (FEP 20015)* **HEARTBEAT** | | - | |
– Heartbeat / Well all right / Baby I don't care / Little baby.

– posthumous compilations, others, etc. –

Jul 59. (7",78) *Brunswick; (05800)* **MIDNIGHT SHIFT. / ROCK AROUND WITH OLLIE VEE** | 26 | - | |

Jul 59. (7"ep) *Brunswick; (OE 9456)* **BUDDY HOLLY NO.1** | | - | |
– You are my one desire / Blue days, black nights / Ting-a-ling / Modern Don Juan.

Jul 59. (7"ep) *Coral; (FEP 2044)* **THE LATE GREAT BUDDY HOLLY** | | - | |
– Look at me / Ready Teddy / Mailman, bring me no more blues / Little baby. *(some below featured CRICKETS' songs)*

Apr 59. (lp) *Coral; (LVA 9105)* **THE BUDDY HOLLY STORY** | 2 | 11 | Mar 59
(UK re-iss. Jul68 as 'RAVE ON' on 'M.C.A.', re-iss. Feb74, also iss.Aug75 on 'M.F.P.')

Jun 59. (7"ep) *Coral;* **THE BUDDY HOLLY STORY** | | | Mar59
– Early in the morning / Heartbeat / Raining in my heart / It doesn't matter anymore.

Aug 59. (7",78) *Coral; (Q 72376) <62134>* **PEGGY SUE GOT MARRIED. / CRYING, WAITING, HOPING** | 13 | | Jul59

Mar 60. (7",78) *Coral; (Q 72392)* **HEARTBEAT. / EVERYDAY** | 30 | - | |

May 60. (7") *Coral; (Q 72397)* **TRUE LOVE WAYS. / MOONDREAMS** | 25 | - | |

Jun 60. (7") *Coral; <62210>* **TRUE LOVE WAYS. / THAT MAKES IT TOUGH** | | - | |

Oct 60. (7") *Coral; (Q 72411)* **LEARNING THE GAME. / THAT MAKES IT TOUGH** | 36 | - | |

Oct 60. (lp) *Coral; (LVA 9127)* **THE BUDDY HOLLY STORY VOL.2** | 7 | | Mar60
(UK re-iss. Jul68 as 'TRUE LOVE WAYS' on 'M.C.A.', re-iss. Feb74)

Jan 61. (7") *Coral; (Q 72419)* **WHAT TO DO. / THAT'S WHAT THEY SAY** | 34 | - | |

Jun 61. (7") *Coral; (Q 72432) <62283>* **BABY I DON'T CARE. / VALLEY OF TEARS** | 12 | | |

Nov 61. (7") *Coral; (Q 72445)* **LOOK AT ME. / MAILMAN BRING ME NO MORE BLUES** | | | |

Feb 62. (7") *Coral; (Q 724490)* **LISTEN TO ME. / WORDS OF LOVE** | 48 | - | |

Jun 62. (7"ep) *Coral;* **PEGGY SUE GOT MARRIED** | | - | |
– Peggy Sue got married / Crying, waiting, hoping / Learning the game / That makes it tough.

Jun 62. (7"ep) *Coral;* **BROWN-EYED HANDSOME MAN** | | - | |
– Brown-eyed handsome man / Bo Diddley / Wishing / True love ways.

Sep 62. (7") *Coral; (Q 72455) <62329>* **REMINISCING. / WAIT TILL THE SUN SHINES NELLIE** | 17 | | Aug62

Mar 63. (7") *Coral; (Q 72459)* **BROWN-EYED HANDSOME MAN. / SLIPPIN' & SLIDIN'** | 3 | - | |
(below album was dubbed in 1962 with musicians The FIREBALLS)

Apr 63. (lp) *Coral; (LVA 9212) <57246>* **REMINISCING** | 2 | 40 | Feb63
– Reminiscing / Slippin' and slidin' / Bo Diddley / Wait till the Sun shines, Nellie / Baby, won't you come out tonight / Brown-eyed handsome man / Because I love you / It's not my fault / I'm gonna set my foot down / Changing all those changes / Rock-a-bye-rock. *(UK re-iss. Nov86 on 'M.C.A.') (UK re-iss. Jul68 as 'BROWN-EYED HANDSOME MAN' on 'M.C.A.', re-iss. Feb74) (re-iss. Feb89) (cd-iss. Nov92 on 'Castle')*

Apr 63. (7") *Coral; <62369>* **BO DIDDLEY. / TRUE LOVE WAYS** | | - | |

May 63. (7") *Coral; (Q 72463)* **BO DIDDLEY. / IT'S NOT MY FAULT** | 4 | - | |

Jul 63. (7") *Coral; <62369>* **BROWN-EYED HANDSOME MAN. / WISHING** | | - | |

Aug 63. (7") *Coral; (Q 72466)* **WISHING. / BECAUSE I LOVE YOU** | 10 | - | |

Dec 63. (7") *Coral; (Q 72469)* **WHAT TO DO. / UMM OH YEAH (DEAREST)** | 27 | - | |

Jan 64. (7") *Coral; <62390>* **ROCK AROUND WITH OLLIE VEE. / I'M GONNA LOVE YOU TOO** | | - | |

Apr 64. (7") *Coral; <62407>* **MAYBE BABY. / NOT FADE AWAY** | | - | |

Apr 64. (7"; BUDDY HOLLY & THE CRICKETS) *Coral; (Q 72472)* **YOU'VE GOT LOVE. / AN EMPTY CUP** | 40 | - | |

Jun 64. (lp) *Coral; (LVA 9222) <57450>* **SHOWCASE** | 3 | | May64
(UK re-iss. Nov86 & Feb89 on 'M.C.A.') (UK re-iss. Jul68 as 'HE'S THE ONE' on 'M.C.A.') (cd-iss Apr 93 on 'Castle')

Sep 64. (7") *Coral; (Q 724750)* **LOVE'S MADE A FOOL OF YOU. / YOU'RE THE ONE** | 39 | - | |

Sep 64. (7"ep) *Coral; (FEP 2065)* **BUDDY BY REQUEST** | | - | |
– Brown-eyed handsome man / Bo Diddley / Umm..oh yeah (dearest) / Slippin' and slidin'.

Sep 64. (7"ep) *Coral; (FEP 2066)* **THAT TEX-MEX SOUND** | | - | |
– I'm gonna set my foot down / It's not my fault / Rip it up / Baby won't you come out tonight.

Oct 64. (7"ep) *Coral; (FEP 2067)* **WISHING** | | - | |
– Wishing / Reminiscing / Valley of tears / Learning the game.

Nov 64. (7"ep) *Coral; (FEP 2068)* **SHOWCASE VOL.1** | | - | |

– Honky tonk / Gone / You're the one / Guess I was just a fool.

Nov 64. (7"ep) *Coral; (FEP 2069)* **SHOWCASE VOL.2** | | - | |
– Blue suede shoes / Come back baby / Shake rattle and roll / Love's made a fool of you.

Jan 65. (7"ep) *Coral; (FEP 2070)* **BUDDY HOLLY SINGS** | | - | |
– Peggy Sue got married / Crying, waiting, hoping / What to do / That makes it tough.

Mar 65. (7") *Coral; <62554>* **WHAT TO DO. / SLIPPIN' AND SLIDIN'** | - | | |

Jun 65. (lp) *Coral; (LVA 9227) <57463>* **HOLLY IN THE HILLS** (1954 demos) | 13 | | Jan65
(some lp's have track 'Reminiscing' instead of 'Wishing') (UK re-iss. Jul86 as 'WISHING' on 'M.C.A.')

Apr 66. (d-lp) *Coral; <CXB 8>* **THE BEST OF BUDDY HOLLY** | | - | |

May 66. (7") *Coral; (Q 72483)* **MAYBE BABY. / THAT'S MY DESIRE** | | - | |

May 70. (lp) *Coral; (CPS 47)* **BUDDY HOLLY'S GREATEST HITS VOL.2** | | | |
(re-iss. Feb74; same)

May 70. (lp) *Coral;* **BUDDY HOLLY'S GREATEST HITS VOL.3** | | | |

Sep 71. (lp) *Coral; (CPS 71)* **REMEMBER BUDDY HOLLY** | | | |
(re-iss. Feb74)

Feb 74. (lp) *Coral;* **GREATEST HITS** | | | |
(re-iss. Jul75, w / 2 extra tracks, hit UK No.42) (UK re-iss. Sep81 + Sep84 on 'M.C.A.')

Oct 74. (d-lp/d-c) *M.C.A.; (CDMSP 802) <MCLD 606>* **LEGEND** | | | |
(re-iss. Mar82 on 'MCA-Coral'. re-iss. +cd.Feb89)

Nov 75. (lp) *Coral; (CDLM 8038)* **THE NASHVILLE SESSIONS** | | | |
(UK re-iss. Mar83 + Nov86 on 'M.C.A.')

Nov 77. (lp/c) *Coral; (CDLM 8055)* **WESTERN AND BOP ("& BOB MONTGOMERY")** | | | |

Mar 79. (6xlp-box/6xc-box) *Coral; ()* **THE COMPLETE BUDDY HOLLY** | | | |
(re-iss. Aug86 on 'M.C.A.')
Note; All releases on 'M.C.A.' were issued on 'Coral' US until '78.

Mar 68. (7") *M.C.A.; (MU 1012)* **PEGGY SUE. / RAVE ON** | 32 | | |

Jul 68. (7") *M.C.A.;* **RAVE ON. / EARLY IN THE MORNING** | - | | |

Jan 69. (7") *M.C.A.; (MU 1059)* **LOVE IS STRANGE. / YOU'RE THE ONE** | | | Mar69

Mar 69. (lp) *M.C.A.; (MUPS 371)* **GIANT** | 13 | | Jan 69
(re-iss. Feb74 + Nov86)

May 69. (7") *M.C.A.; (MU 1081)* **IT DOESN'T MATTER ANYMORE. / MAYBE BABY** | | - | |

Mar 70. (7") *M.C.A.; (MU 1116)* **RAVE ON. / UMM OH YEAH (DEAREST)** | | - | |

May 73. (7"m) *M.C.A.; (MMU 1198)* **THAT'LL BE THE DAY. / WELL ALL RIGHT / EVERYDAY** | | - | |

Feb 74. (7"m) *M.C.A.; (MCA 119) (MCA 119)* **IT DOESN'T MATTER ANYMORE. / TRUE LOVE WAYS / BROWN-EYED HANDSOME MAN** | | - | |

Aug 75. (7") *M.C.A.; (MCA 207) (MCA 207)* **OH BOY!. / EVERYDAY** | | - | |
(above + below singles were credited to "BUDDY HOLLY & THE CRICKETS")

Sep 76. (7"ep) *M.C.A.; (MCA 254)* **MAYBE BABY / THINK IT OVER. / THAT'LL BE THE DAY / IT'S SO EASY** | | - | |

Sep 76. (7"ep) *M.C.A.; (MCA 253)* **PEGGY SUE / RAVE ON. / ROCK AROUND WITH OLLIE VEE / MIDNIGHT SHIFT** | | - | |

Sep 76. (7"ep) *M.C.A.; (MCA 252)* **TRUE LOVE WAYS / MOONDREAMS. / IT DOESN'T MATTER ANYMORE / RAINING IN MY HEART** | | - | |
(re-iss. Aug81)

Jan 78. (7") *M.C.A.; (MCA 344)* **WISHING. / LOVE'S MADE A FOOL OF YOU** | | - | |

Mar 78. (lp/c) *M.C.A.; (MCTV/+C 1)* **20 GOLDEN GREATS** | 1 | 55 | |
– That'll be the day / Peggy Sue / Words of love / Everyday / Not fade away / Oh! boy / Maybe baby / Listen to me / Heartbeat / Think it over / It doesn't matter anymore / It's so easy / Well all right / Rave on / Raining in my heart / True love ways / Peggy Sue got married / Bo Diddley / Brown-eyed handsome man / Wishing. *(re-iss. Jun79) (cd-iss. Feb89)(re-iss. cd+c Aug93)*

1978. (7") *M.C.A.;* **IT DOESN'T MATTER ANYMORE. / PEGGY SUE** | | | |

Aug 81. (lp/c) *M.C.A.;* **LOVE SONGS** | | | |

Mar 83. (lp/c) *M.C.A.; (MCM/+ 1002)* **FOR THE FIRST TIME ANYWHERE** | | | |
(cd-iss. Sep87)

Sep 84. (d-c) *M.C.A.; (NCA 2117)* **GREATEST HITS / LOVE SONGS** | | | |

Jul 85. (lp/c) *M.C.A.; (MCM/+C 5003)* **GOLDEN GREATS** | | | |
(below are a boxed-set of 10 singles)

Aug 85. (7") *M.C.A.; (BH 1)* **THAT'LL BE THE DAY. / ROCK ME MY BABY** | | | |

Aug 85. (7") *M.C.A.; (BH 2)* **PEGGY SUE. / EVERYDAY** | | | |

Aug 85. (7") *M.C.A.; (BH 3)* **OH BOY. / NOT FADE AWAY** | | | |

Aug 85. (7") *M.C.A.; (BH 4)* **MAYBE BABY. / TELL ME NOW** | | | |

Aug 85. (7") *M.C.A.; (BH 5)* **RAVE ON. / READY TEDDY** | | | |

Aug 85. (7") *M.C.A.; (BH 6)* **THINK IT OVER. / IT'S SO EASY** | | | |

Aug 85. (7") *M.C.A.; (BH 7)* **IT DOESN'T MATTER ANYMORE. / RAINING IN MY HEART** | | | |

Aug 85. (7") *M.C.A.; (BH 8)* **TRUE LOVE WAYS. / WORDS OF LOVE** | | | |

Aug 85. (7") *M.C.A.; (BH 9)* **REMINISCING. / BABY I DON'T CARE** | | | |

Aug 85. (7") *M.C.A.; (BH 10)* **BROWN-EYED HANDSOME MAN. / BO DIDDLEY** | | | |

Oct 85. (cd) *M.C.A.; (DIDX 203)* **FROM THE ORIGINAL MASTER TAPES** | | | |

Aug 86. (7") *M.C.A.; (THAT 1)* **THAT'LL BE THE DAY. / I'M LOOKING FOR SOMEONE TO LOVE** | | - | |
(12"+=) (THAT 1) – It doesn't matter anymore / Raining in my heart.

Aug 86. (7"box) *M.C.A.; (BHB 1)* **THAT'LL BE THE DAY. / ROCK ME BABY / PEGGY SUE** | | - | |

Jun 88. (cd) *M.C.A.; (31037)* **THE GREAT BUDDY HOLLY** | - | | |

Nov 88. (7") *M.C.A.; (MCA 1302)* **TRUE LOVE WAYS. / RAINING IN MY HEART** | 65 | - | |
(12"+=/cd-s+=) (MCAT/DMCA 1302) –

Sep 89.	(7") *M.C.A.; (MCA 1368)* **OH BOY. / NOT FADE AWAY** (10"+=/cd-s+=) *(MCAV/DMCA 1368)* –	☐	-
Sep 89.	(lp-box/c-box/cd-box) *M.C.A.; (DCDSP 807)* **THE BUDDY HOLLY BOX SET**	☐	-
Jun 67.	(lp) *Ace Of Hearts; (AH 148)* **BUDDY HOLLY'S GREATEST HITS** (*UK re-iss. Nov69, re-iss. Aug71; hit No.32, on 'Coral'*)	9	-
Nov 75.	(5xlp-box) *World; (SM 3015)* **THE BUDDY HOLLY STORY**	☐	-
Aug 80.	(lp/c) *M&S; (IMP 114)* **HEARTBEAT**	☐	-
Sep 80.	(lp/c) *Pickwick; (SS C/P 3070)* **BUDDY HOLLY**	☐	-
Mar 90.	(lp/c) *Pickwick; (SHM/HSC 3294)* **MOONDREAMS**	☐	-
Dec 92.	(cd-box) *Pickwick;* **SPECIAL LIMITED EDITION**	☐	-
Sep 93.	(cd) *Pickwick; (PWKS 595)* **THE BEST OF BUDDY HOLLY**	☐	-
Oct 80.	(lp/c) *M.F.P.; (MFP 50490)* **ROCK WITH BUDDY HOLLY**	☐	-
Aug 82.	(lp/c) *M.F.P.; (MFP/TCMFP 5570)* **20 LOVE SONGS**	☐	-
Oct 87.	(lp/c) *M.F.P.; (MFP/TCMFP 5806)* **ROCK'N'ROLL GREATS**	☐	-
Sep 86.	(lp/c) *Hallmark; (SHM/HSC 3199)* **THE BEST OF BUDDY HOLLY**	☐	-
Oct 87.	(lp/c) *Hallmark; (SHM/HSC 3221)* **THE LEGENDARY BUDDY HOLLY**	☐	-
Apr 83.	(7") *Old Gold; (OG 9319)* **RAVE ON. / TRUE LOVE WAYS**	☐	-
May 89.	(cd-ep) *Old Gold; (OG 6147)* **THAT'LL BE THE DAY / OH BOY / MAYBE BABY**	☐	-
Nov 84.	(lp/c) *Astan; (20/40 125)* **23 ALL TIME GREATEST HITS**	☐	-
May 85.	(d-lp) *Charly; (CDX 8)* **BUDDY HOLLY ROCKS**	☐	-
1983.	(d-c) *Cambra; (CRT 008)* **BUDDY HOLLY**	☐	-
May 84.	(d-c) *Cambra; (CRT 123)* **ROCK AROUND WITH BUDDY HOLLY & THE CRICKETS** (*re-iss. Sep86*)	☐	-
Sep 86.	(lp/c) *Rollercoaster; (ROLL 2013)* **SOMETHING SPECIAL FROM BUDDY HOLLY**	☐	-
Oct 87.	(7"ep) *Rollercoaster; (RCEP 104)* **GOOD ROCKIN' TONIGHT / RIP IT UP. / AIN'T GOT NO HOME / HOLLY HOP**	☐	-
Oct 87.	(d-lp/c) *Castle; (CCS LP/MC 172)* **BUDDY HOLLY: THE COLLECTION**	☐	-
Feb 89.	(lp/c/cd) *Telstar; (STAR/STAC/TCD 2339)* **TRUE LOVE WAYS**	8	-
May 88.	(cd) *Arcade; (01266061)* **VERY BEST OF BUDDY HOLLY**	☐	-
May 94.	(cd/c) *M.C.A.;* **THAT'LL BE THE DAY / BUDDY HOLLY**	☐	-
Oct 94.	(cd/c) *Music Club;* **COVER TO COVER (w / CRICKETS)**	☐	-
Dec 94.	(3xcd-box) *Pickwick; (BOXD 26T)* **A SPECIAL COLLECTION**	☐	-
May 95.	(cd/c) *Pickwick;* **THE BEST OF BUDDY HOLLY**	☐	-
May 95.	(cd/c) *Pickwick;* **THE LEGENDARY BUDDY HOLLY**	☐	-
May 95.	(3xcd) *Pickwick;* **A SPECIAL COLLECTION**	☐	-
Nov 96.	(cd/c) *Dino; (DIN CD/MC 133)* **THE VERY BEST OF BUDDY HOLLY**	24	-
Aug 99.	(cd/c) *Universal Music TV; (112048-2/-4)* **THE VERY BEST OF BUDDY HOLLY**	25	☐

David HOLMES

Born: Belfast, Northern Ireland. Formerly one third of house/techno outfit, DISCO EVANGELISTS alongside LYNDSAY EDWARDS and the ubiquitous ASHLEY BEEDLE, HOLMES made his solo debut with a one-off 12" for 'Warp' in Spring '94, 'Johnny Favourite'. Together with PETE LATHAM and ANDY ELLISON, he then cut a track, 'CELESTIAL SYMPHONY', under the SCUBADEVILS moniker for the first volume of the 'Trance Europe Express' compilation series. Already something of a 'name' DJ, HOLMES remix work was much in demand, the Irishman working on material by the likes of ROBOTMAN (the seminal 'Do Da Doo'), KRIS NEEDS' SECRET KNOWLEDGE and The SABRES OF PARADISE as well as recording under a number of aliases for different labels. 1995 saw him sign for 'Go! Discs' and release an acclaimed debut solo set, the catchily titled 'THIS FILM'S CRAP LET'S SLASH THE SEATS'. Ranging from brain-numbing bpm assaults to the techno-celt eeriness of 'NO MANS LAND', the record saw HOLMES leave the dance ghetto well behind and even gain plaudits from the 'adult' rock press. He continued to work with big names as well as the hip and the happening (ARAB STRAP and MOGWAI), subsequently releasing a second solo set, 'LETS GET KILLED', in Autumn '97. The record took HOLMES' widescreen fetish one step further, a groovy, atmospheric nightride into the bowels of neon-lit claustrophobia.

Album rating: THIS FILM'S CRAP LET'S SLASH THE SEATS (*7) / LETS GET KILLED (*7)

		Warp	not iss.
Feb 94.	(12"/cd-s) *(WAP 42/+CD)* **JOHNNY FAVOURITE. (exploding plastic inevitable / Ambience mixes)**	☐	-
		Harthouse	not iss.
Jun 95.	(12"ep; DAVID HOLMES VS ALTER EGO) *(HH 073)* **E.P.**	☐	-
		Go! Discs	unknown
Jun 95.	(12"/cd-s) *(GOD X/CD 129)* **MINUS 61 IN DETROIT. /**	☐	-
Jul 95.	(cd/c/lp) *(828631-2/-4/-1)* **THIS FILM'S CRAP LET'S SLASH THE SEATS** – No mans land / Slash the seats / Shake ya brain / Got fucked up along the way / Gone / Atom and you / Minus 61 in Detroit / Inspired by Layburn / Coming home to the sun.	51	
Oct 95.	(12"/cd-s) *(GOD X/CD 133)* **NO MANS LAND. / SMOKED OAK / SLASH THE BOATS**	☐	-
Mar 96.	(12"/cd-s) *(GOD X/CD 140)* **GONE / (mixes); Alter Ego**	75	-
		Harthouse	not iss.
Mar 97.	(12"; DAVID HOLMES & ALTER EGO) *(HH 111)* **THE EVIL NEEDLE (remix). / ('A'mixes)**	☐	-

		Go! Beat	unknown
Aug 97.	(12"/cd-s) *(GOB X/CD 2)* **GRITTY SHAKER. / (mixes)** (cd-s) *(GOLCD 2)* – ('A'mixes).	53	☐
Sep 97.	(cd/c/lp) *(539 100-2/-4/-1)* **LETS GET KILLED** – Listen / My mate Paul / Lets get killed / Gritty shaker / Head rush on Lafayette / Rodney Yates / Radio 7 / The Parcus & Madder show / Slashers revenge / Freaknik / Caddell returns / Don't die just yet / For you.	34	☐
Dec 97.	(12"/cd-s) *(GOB X/CD 6)* **DON'T DIE JUST YET (mixes by Arab Strap & Mogwai)** (cd-s) *(GOLCD 6)* – (mixes by Max 404, La Funk Mob & Delakota). (below given a release for upstairs 'Go Discs!')	33	☐
Mar 98.	(12"/cd-s) *(GOD X/CD 156)* **MY MATE PAUL (mixes; Major Force / Stereo MC's) / LITTLE SHORT ONE** (12") *(GOBX 8)* – ('A'remixes).	39	☐

HOLY BARBARIANS (see under ⇒ CULT)

HONEYCRACK (dig out; Great Alt & Indie . . .)

HONEYDRIPPERS (see under ⇒ LED ZEPPELIN)

HOODOO GURUS (dig out; Great Alt & Indie . . .)

John Lee HOOKER

Born: 22nd of August 1920, Clarksdale, Mississippi, USA. The last of the original bluesmen who travelled north from the Delta, VAN MORRISON once said that HOOKER was "a window into another age". Doubts remain about his actual birth date although HOOKER recently admitted that he lied about his age as a teenager to get into the army. Taught to play guitar by his stepfather (his birth father disapproved of the blues), a popular local blues guitarist by the name of WILL MOORE, HOOKER drifted north during his teens to Memphis, Cincinatti and finally, to Detroit, where he settled in 1943. The budding bluesman was given his first guitar by the legendary T-BONE WALKER in 1947, sitting in on early sessions with Robert Nighthawk. He worked as a janitor in a car factory by day and performed in clubs around Hastings Street (a notorious area known as 'Black Bottom' from which the dance was named) at night, slowly gaining a reputation which paralleled such Chicago masters as MUDDY WATERS, SONNY BOY WILLIAMSON and HOWLIN' WOLF. HOOKER always maintained that he didn't like Chicago because there were too many other blues guitarists there, his relocation to Detroit paying off when he was introduced to local distributor, record store owner and kingpin of the 'Sensation' record label, Bernie Bessman, in 1948. In November that year he undertook his debut recording session (just himself and his guitar, with his distinctive tapping sounds coming from Coca-Cola bottle tops attached to the soles of his shoes), his first single from the set, 'BOOGIE CHILLUN' topping the "race" chart, as it was then known. After Bessman leased the master to 'Modern', it eventually sold more than a million copies (when it broke, HOOKER was still working as a janitor in the Chrysler car factory). As well as a demon guitarist, he was also a wicked womaniser, almost copping it in 1950 when an aggrieved husband poisoned his whisky (12 years after ROBERT JOHNSON had fatally suffered in a similar manner). HOOKER subsequently signed to 'Modern' in 1951, staying with the label for five years; as with other blues artists of the time, he recorded for anyone who was willing to pay him and got round his contractual obligations by recording 70 singles on 21 different labels under 10 pseudonyms, TEXAS SLIM ('BLACK MAN BLUES' for 'King' Records), BIRMINGHAM SAM ('Savoy' Records), JOHN LEE BOOKER ('Chess' Records), JOHN LEE COOKER ('King' Records), DELTA JOHN ('Regent' Records), JOHNNY LEE ('Deluxe' Records), JOHNNY WILLIAMS ('Gotham' Records), LITTLE PORK CHOPS, THE BOOGIE MAN ('Acorn' Records) and JOHN L'HOOKER. During this period, 'I'M IN THE MOOD' became his second major R&B hit and matched the one million sales of 'BOOGIE CHILLUN', while the following year he made his debut as a DJ on a local radio station. Although B.B. KING outshone him in the 50's, HOOKER signed to 'Vee-Jay', who recognised his wider appeal and crafted him into a tighter performer, backing him with seasoned session players including guitarist, EDDIE TAYLOR, and drummer, TOM WHITEHEAD. During a subsequent 1959 session, HOOKER cut new versions of his most successful songs including 'I'M IN THE MOOD', 'BOOGIE CHILLUN', 'HOBO BLUES' and 'CRAWLIN' KINGSNAKE' (all with his distinctive guttural singing). The following year, he was one of only a few (traditional) blues artists to perform at the 2nd Newport Folk Festival (his set was recorded and later released as 'CONCERT AT NEWPORT'), while the following year, BOB DYLAN made his New York debut opening for HOOKER at Gerde's Folk City venue. 1964 saw the British R&B explosion in full flow with 'BOOM BOOM' becoming a US hit for The ANIMALS (they also covered three HOOKER compositions on their debut album) and HOOKER himself entering the UK chart at 23 with 'DIMPLES'. This success led to numerous UK tours backed by the likes of The SPENCER DAVIS GROUP and The GROUNDHOGS (who took their name from HOOKER's, 'GROUNDHOG BLUES'); many other British bands of the time including The YARDBIRDS, The WHO, The SMALL FACES and, in particular, The ROLLING STONES, were inspired by, and recorded many of HOOKER's songs. In America, meanwhile, he influenced many bands from ZZ TOP (whose 'LA GRANGE' is pure HOOKER) to BRUCE SPRINGSTEEN, the latter including 'BOOM BOOM' as part of his set on the 'Tunnel Of Love' tour in 1988. In 1966, the veteran bluesman signed to 'ABC' Records and, over the next eight years, recorded albums for their subsidiaries, 'Impulse' and 'Bluesway', as well as 'ABC' themselves. HOOKER left Detroit in 1970 after a nasty divorce, settling in San Francisco where he met CANNED HEAT; together they recorded the double album, 'HOOKER 'N' HEAT' (1971), which became the guitarist's first US chart success, reaching the Top 75. Unfortunately, CANNED HEAT's ALAN 'Blind Owl' WILSON died before the album was mixed, the sleeve depicting everyone in sombre mood with a black framed picture of WILSON hanging in the background. HOOKER's ABC contract ended in 1974 and, on the verge of quitting to open a motel, he signed a deal with 'Atlantic' Records. He recorded two albums for the major, 'DETROIT SPECIAL' and 'DON'T TURN ME FROM YOUR DOOR', although by 1978's, 'THE CREAM', he had downshifted to 'Tomato' Records. In 1980, he had a cameo role in 'The Blues Brothers' alongside RAY CHARLES, JAMES BROWN and ARETHA FRANKLIN, while his music also featured in another movie, 'The Color Purple'. Later in the 80's, HOOKER starred in the title role of PETE TOWNSHEND's musical, 'The Iron Man' (singing 'I EAT HEAVY METAL' – far removed from his normal style but performed with typical HOOKER panache nonetheless) and at the turn of the decade he paired up with MILES DAVIS for the soundtrack to the Dennis Hopper movie, 'The Hot Spot' (which featured HOOKER's, 'I'M IN THE MOOD'). He's become more popular with age, 'THE HEALER' (1989) attracting a whole new army of fans and breaking him into the mainstream rock world. The project came about because the contributing artists were all fans of "THE HOOK" (they all lived locally), including CARLOS SANTANA on the title track, BONNIE RAITT on 'I'M IN THE MOOD' (a Grammy winner), ROBERT CRAY on 'CUTTIN' OUT' and LOS LOBOS on 'THINK TWICE BEFORE YOU GO', while most of the songs were completed in one or two takes (a hallmark of HOOKER's career). His next album was the stunning 'Charisma' debut, 'MR. LUCKY', which, in reaching Number 3 in Britain (only made Number 101 in the US!), became the highest charting "real" blues album ever, and at the age of 71, it made HOOKER the oldest artist to reach the UK Top 5. This album was another collection of duets, including the collaborations 'CRAWLIN KINGSNAKE' with KEITH RICHARDS, 'MR. LUCKY' with the ROBERT CRAY BAND, 'SUZIE' with JOHNNY WINTER and 'I COVER THE WATERFRONT' with his No.1 fan, VAN MORRISON, although the stand-outs were 'THIS IS HIP' with RY COODER, 'STRIPPED ME NAKED' (on which HOOKER sounds like a man possessed and CARLOS SANTANA is at his wailing best) and the top of the lot, 'I WANT TO HUG YOU' with CHUCK BERRY's former pianist, JOHNNIE JOHNSON. 1992 saw a rare appearance on Top Of The Pops as 'BOOM BOOM' reached the UK Top 20, further singles, 'BOOGIE AT RUSSIAN HILL' and 'GLORIA' (recorded with VAN MORRISON) also reaching the charts. Although clocking in at a remarkable three quarters of a century, HOOKER retains his humour, ability and style, as witnessed on the 1995 release, 'CHILL OUT'.

Album rating (selective): THE FOLK BLUES OF JOHN LEE HOOKER (*8) / I'M JOHN LEE HOOKER (*8) / TRAVELLIN' (*7) / SINGS THE BLUES (*7) / THAT'S MY STORY (*8) / THE FOLKLORE OF JOHN LEE HOOKER (*8) / THE BEST OF JOHN LEE HOOKER compilation (*7) / JOHN LEE HOOKER AT NEWPORT (*7) / REAL FOLK BLUES (*7) / THE HEALER (*10) / MR. LUCKY (*7) / BOOM BOOM (*6) / CHILL OUT (*7) / DON'T LOOK BACK (*6) / THE ULTIMATE COLLECTION compilation (*8)

JOHN LEE HOOKER – vocals, guitars

		not iss.	Modern
Jan 49.	(78) <20-627> **BOOGIE CHILLEN (BOOGIE CHILDREN).** / **SALLY MAE (THERE'S A DAY COMIN' BABY)**	-	

—— now with **JAMES WATKINS** – piano / **CURTIS FOSTER** – drums

		not iss.	King
Mar 49.	(78; as TEXAS SLIM) <4283> **BLACK MAN BLUES.** / **STOMP BOOGIE (FLUB)**	-	

—— now w/ **ANDREW DUNHAM** – guitar / **EDDIE BURNS** – harmonica

—— released many US 78's over the next several years (some with pseudonyms)

		not iss.	Regent
1949.	(78; as DELTA JOHN) <1001> **HELPLESS BLUES.** / **GOIN' MAD BLUES**	-	

		not iss.	Savoy
1949.	(78; as BIRMINGHAM SAM & HIS MAGIC GUITAR) <5558> **LOW DOWN MIDNITE BOOGIE.** / **LANDING BLUES**	-	

		not iss.	Modern
1949.	(78) <20-663> **HOBO BLUES.** / **HOOGIE BOOGIE**	-	
1949.	(78) <20-688> **WEEPING WILLOW (BOOGIE).** / **WHISTLIN' AND MOANIN' BLUES (HUMMIN' THE BLUES)**	-	
1949.	(78) <20-714> **CRAWLING KING SNAKE.** / **DRIFTING FROM DOOR TO DOOR**	-	

		not iss.	Prize
1949.	(78; as JOHNNY WILLIAMS) <704> **MISS ROSIE MAE.** / **HIGHWAY BLUES**	-	

		not iss.	Sensation
Mar 50.	(78) <21> **MISS SADIE MAE.** / **BURNIN' HELL**	-	
Apr 50.	(78) <26> **CANAL STREET BLUES.** / **HUCKLE UP BABY**		
May 50.	(78) <30> **GOIN' ON HIGHWAY 51 (GOIN' DOWN HIGHWAY 51).** / **LET YOUR DADDY RIDE (SLOW DOWN YOUR CHATTER BABY)**	-	
Jun 50.	(78) <33> **MY BABY'S GOT SOMETHIN'.** / **DECORATION DAY BLUES (LORD TAKETH MY BABY AWAY)**	-	
Jul 50.	(78) <34> **BOOGIE CHILLEN 2 (I GOTTA BE COMIN' BACK).** / **MISS ELOISE (MISS ELOISE, MISS ELOISE)**	-	

		not iss.	Acorn
Aug 50.	(78; as JOHN LEE COOKER) <4504> **MOANING BLUES.** / **STOMP BOOGIE (FLUB)**	-	

		not iss.	Chance
1949.	(78; as THE BOOGIE MAN) <308> **DO THE BOOGIE.** / **MORNING BLUES**	-	

		not iss.	King
1949.	(78; as JOHN LEE BOOKER) <1108> **MISS LORRAINE.** / **TALKIN' BOOGIE**	-	
1949.	(78; as JOHN LEE BOOKER) <1110> **GRAVEYARD BLUES.** / **I LOVE TO BOOGIE**	-	
1949.	(78; as JOHN L. BOOKER) <1122> **609 BOOGIE.** / **ROAD TROUBLE**	-	

		not iss.	Modern
1950.	(78; as TEXAS SLIM) <4315> **THE NUMBERS.** / **DEVIL'S JUMP**	-	
1950.	(78; as TEXAS SLIM) <4323> **I'M GONNA KILL THAT WOMAN.** / **NIGHTMARE BLUES**	-	
1950.	(78; as TEXAS SLIM) <4329> **HEART TROUBLE BLUES.** / **SLIM'S STOMP (instrumental)**	-	
1950.	(78; as TEXAS SLIM) <4334> **DON'T GO BABY.** / **WANDERING BLUES**	-	
Oct 50.	(78; as TEXAS SLIM) <4366> **LATE LAST NIGHT.** / **DON'T YOU REMEMBER ME**	-	
Nov 50.	(78; as TEXAS SLIM) <4377> **MOANING BLUES.** / **THINKING BLUES**	-	

		not iss.	Regal
Apr 50.	(78) <20-730> **PLAYIN' THE RACES (DREAM A NUMBER).** / **WELL I GOT TO LEAVE**		
May 50.	(78) <20-746> **NO FRIEND AROUND (T.B.'S KILLIN' ME).** / **WEDNESDAY EVENING (SHE LEFT ME – ON MY BENDED KNEE)**		
Jun 50.	(78) <20-767> **GIMME YOUR PHONE NUMBER (IT'S A CRIME AND A SHAME).** / **ROCK'N'ROLL (I CRIED THE WHOLE NIGHT LONG)**		
Jul 50.	(78) <20-790> **ONE MORE TIME (LET'S TALK IT OVER).** / **LET YOUR DADDY RIDE**	-	

		not iss.	Gone
1950.	(78) <3304> **NEVER SATISFIED (JUST LIKE A WOMAN).** / **NOTORIETY WOMAN (NO PLACE TO STAY)**	-	

		not iss.	Modern
1950.	(78; as JOHN LEE BOOKER) **MAD MAN BLUES.** / **BOOGIE NOW (HEY BOOGIE)**	-	

		not iss.	Staff
1950.	(78) <814> **QUEEN BEE.** / **JOHN L'S HOUSE RENT BOOGIE (OUT THE DOOR I WENT)**	-	

		not iss.	Gotham
1950.	(78; as JOHNNY WILLIAMS) <710> **HOUSE RENT BOOGIE.** / **WANDERING BLUES**	-	
1950.	(78; as JOHNNY WILLIAMS) <718> **PRISON BOUND.** / **BUMBLE BEE BLUES**	-	

		not iss.	Chess
1951.	(78; as JOHNNY WILLIAMS) <509> **REAL GONE GAL.** / **QUESTIONNAIRE BLUES**	-	
1951.	(78; as JOHNNY WILLIAMS) <513> **LITTLE BOY BLUE.** / **MY DADDY WAS A JOCKEY**	-	
1951.	(78' as JOHN LEE) <515> **CATFISH.** / **MEAN OLD TRAIN**	-	

		not iss.	Modern
Jun 51.	(78; as JOHN LEE BOOKER) <1467> **LEAVE MY WIFE ALONE.** / **RAMBLIN' BY MYSELF**		
Jul 51.	(78; as JOHN LEE BOOKER) <1482> **GROUND HOG BLUES.** / **LOUISE**	-	

<above also iss.Jan52 as JOHN L. HOOKER on 'Modern'; 852>

| Aug 51. | (78) <1505> **HIGH PRICED WOMAN.** / **UNION STATION BLUES** | | |
| Jul 52. | (78) <1513> **WALKIN' THE BOOGIE.** / **SUGAR MAMA** | | |

		Vogue	Modern
Sep 51.	(78) <829> **(FOUR) WOMEN IN MY LIFE.** / **TEASE ME BABY (TEASE YOUR DADDY)**		
Nov 51.	(78) <835> **I'M IN THE MOOD.** / **HOW CAN YOU DO IT**		
Dec 51.	(78; as JOHN L. HOOKER) <847> **TURN OVER A NEW LEAF.** / **ANYBODY SEEN MY BABY (JOHNNY SAYS COME BACK)**	-	
Feb 52.	(78) <862> **ROCK ME MAMA (GOOD ROCKIN' MAMA).** / **COLD CHILLS (ALL OVER ME)**	-	
1952.	(78) (V 2102) **HOOGIE BOOGIE.** / **WHISTLIN' AND MOANIN' BLUES**		-
Sep 52.	(78; as JOHN LEE HOOKER & "LITTLE" EDDIE KIRKLAND) <876> **IT HURTS ME SO.** / **I GOT EYES FOR YOU**	-	
Nov 52.	(78) <886> **KEY TO THE HIGHWAY.** / **BLUEBIRD BLUES**	-	
Feb 53.	(78) <897> **IT'S BEEN A LONG TIME BABY.** / **ROCK HOUSE BOOGIE**	-	
Apr 53.	(78) <901> **RIDE 'TIL I DIE.** / **IT'S STORMIN' AND RAININ'**	-	
Jun 53.	(78) <1562> **IT'S MY OWN FAULT (BABY, I PROVE MY LOVE TO YOU).** / **WOMEN AND MONEY**	-	
1953.	(78; as JOHNNY LEE HOOKER) <30> **BOOGIE RAMBLER.** / **NO MORE DOGGIN'**	-	

—— *<above issued on 'J.V.B.'>*

| Jul 53. | (78; as JOHNNY LEE HOOKER) <908> **PLEASE TAKE ME BACK.** / **LOVE MONEY CAN'T BUY** | - | |
| Aug 53. | (78; as JOHNNY LEE HOOKER) <916> **NEED SOMEBODY.** / **TOO MUCH BOOGIE** | - | |

(UK-iss.1954 on 'London'; HL 8037)

| Sep 53. | (78; as JOHNNY LEE HOOKER) <931> **I WONDER (LITTLE DARLING).** / **JUMP ME (ONE MORE TIME)** | - | |

	not iss.	DeLuxe
Sep 53. (78; as JOHN LEE BOOKER) <6004> **BLUE MONDAY (I AIN'T GOT NOBODY). / LOVIN' GUITAR MAN**	-	
Oct 53. (78; as JOHNNY LEE) <6009> **I'M A BOOGIE MAN. / I CAME TO SEE MY BABY**	-	
Dec 53. (78; as JOHN LEE BOOKER) <6046> **MY BABY DON'T LOVE ME. / REAL REAL GONE**	-	

	not iss.	Rockin'
Oct 53. (78; as JOHN LEE BOOKER) <524> **BLUE MONDAY (I AIN'T GOT NOBODY). / LOVIN' GUITAR MAN**	-	
Nov 53. (78; as JOHN LEE BOOKER) <525> **STUTTERIN' BLUES. / POURING DOWN RAIN (WOBBLIN' BABY)**	-	

	not iss.	Chart
1954. (78) <609> **GOIN' SOUTH. / WOBBLIN' BABY**	-	
1954. (78) <614> **BLUE MONDAY (I AIN'T GOT NOBODY). / MISBELIEVING BABY (MY BABY PUT YOU DOWN)**	-	

	not iss.	Modern
1954. (78) <923> **DOWN CHILD. / GOTTA BOOGIE (GONNA BOOGIE)**	-	
1954. (78) <935> **LET'S TALK IT OVER. / I TRIED HARD**	-	
1954. (78) <942> **BAD BOY. / COOL LITTLE CAR**	-	
1954. (78) <948> **SHAKE, HOLLER AND RUN. / HALF A STRANGER**	-	
1955. (78) <958> **TAXI DRIVER. / YOU RECEIVE ME**	-	
1955. (78) <966> **HUG AND SQUEEZE (YOU). / THE SYNDICATOR (SYNDICATE)**	-	
1955. (78) <978> **LOOKIN' FOR A WOMAN. / I'M READY**	-	

	not iss.	Vee Jay
Dec 55. (7") <164> **MAMBO CHILLUN. / TIME IS MARCHING**	-	
Apr 56. (7") <188> **TROUBLE BLUES. / EVERY NIGHT**	-	
Jun 56. (7") <205> **DIMPLES. / BABY LEE**	-	
Sep 56. (7") <233> **I'M SO WORRIED BABY. / THE ROAD IS SO ROUGH**	-	
Apr 57. (7") <245> **I'M SO EXCITED. / I SEE YOU WHEN YOU'RE WEAK**	-	
Aug 57. (7") <255> **LITTLE WHEEL. / ROSIE MAE**	-	
Sep 57. (7") <265> **YOU CAN LEAD ME BABY. / UNFRIENDLY WOMAN**	-	
Jul 58. (7") <293> **I LOVE YOU HONEY. / YOU'VE TAKEN MY WOMAN**	-	
Feb 59. (7") <308> **I'M IN THE MOOD. / MAUDIE**	-	
Apr 59. (7") <319> **BOOGIE CHILLUN. / TENNESSEE BLUES**	-	
Jun 59. (7") <331> **CRAWLIN' KINGSNAKE. / HOBO BLUES**	-	

	Riverside	Riverside
1960. (lp) <321> **THAT'S MY STORY**		

– I need some money / I'm wanderin' / Democrat man / I want to talk about you / Gonna use my rod / Wednesday evening blues / No more doggin' / One of these days, I'll believe I'll go back home / You're leavin' me baby / That's my story / Black snake / How long blues / Wobblin' baby / She's long, she's tall, she weeps like . . . / Peavine special / Tupelo blues / I rowed a little boat / Water boy / Church bell tone / Bundle up and go. (UK-iss.Nov88 on 'Ace')

| 1962. (lp) (RLP 12-838) <838> **THE FOLK BLUES OF JOHN LEE HOOKER** | | 1959 |

– Black snake / How long blues / Wobblin' baby / She's long, she's tall, she weeps like a willow tree / Pea-vine special / Tupelo blues / I'm prison bound / I rowed a little boat / Water boy / Church bell tone / Bundle up and go / Good mornin' lil' school girl / Behind the plow.

—— singles on other labels at the time

	not iss.	Elmor
1959. (7") <303> **609 BOOGIE. / (MISS SADIE MAE) CURL MY BABY'S HAIR**	-	-

	not iss.	Fortune
1960. (7") <853> **CRY BABY. / LOVE YOU BABY**	-	-
1960. (7") <855> **CRAZY ABOUT THAT WALK. / WE'RE ALL GOD'S CHILLUN**	-	-

	not iss.	Hi-Q
1959. (7") <5018> **BIG FINE WOMAN. / BLUES FOR CHRISTMAS**	-	-

	not iss.	Lauren
1960. (7") <361> **BALLAD TO ABRAHAM LINCOLN (HE GOT ASSASSINATED). / MOJO HAND (RISIN' SUN)**	-	-
1960. (7") <362> **I LOST MY JOB (TELL YOU A STORY). / DEEP DOWN IN MY HEART (HOW LONG CAN THIS GO ON)**	-	-

	not iss.	Galaxy
1960. (7") <716> **SHAKE IT UP (JOHNNY LEE & THE THING). / (I) LOST MY JOB (TELL YOU A STORY)**	-	-

	Stateside	Vee Jay
Apr 60. (7") <349> **SOLID SENDER. / NO SHOES**		
Jul 60. (7") <366> **TUPELO (BACKWATER BLUES) / DUSTY ROAD**		
Feb 61. (7") <379> **I'M MAD AGAIN. / I'M GOING UPSTAIRS**	-	
Apr 61. (7") <397> **WANT AD BLUES. / TAKE ME AS I AM**	-	
Feb 62. (7") <438> **BOOM BOOM. / DRUG STORE WOMAN**	-	60
Apr 62. (7") <453> **SHE'S MINE (KEEP YOUR HANDS TO YOURSELF). / A NEW LEAF**	-	
1962. (lp) (SL 10014) **THE FOLK LORE OF JOHN LEE HOOKER**		-

– Tupelo / I'm mad again / I'm going upstairs / Wanted blues / Five years long / I like to see you walk / The hobo / Hard headed woman / Wednesday evening blues / Take me as I am / My first wife left me / You're looking good tonight. (re-iss. 1974 on 'Joy')

Nov 62. (7") <493> **FRISCO BLUES. / TAKE A LOOK AT YOURSELF**		
1963. (7") <538> **I'M LEAVING. / BIRMINGHAM BLUES**		
1963. (7") <575> **DON'T LOOK BACK. / SEND ME YOUR PILLOW**		
1964. (lp) (SL 10053) **THE BIG SOUL OF JOHN LEE HOOKER**		-

– Frisco blues / Take a look at yourself / Send me your pillow / She shot me down / I love her / Old time shimmy / You know I love you / Big soul / Good rocking mama / Onions / No one told me. (re-iss. 1969 + 1974 on 'Joy')

| Jul 63. (7") (SS 203) **BOOM BOOM. / FRISCO BLUES** | | - |

May 64. (7") (SS 297) **DIMPLES. / I'M LEAVING**	23	-
Sep 64. (7") (SS 341) **I LOVE YOU HONEY. / SEND ME YOUR PILLOW**	-	-
1964. (lp) (SL 10074) **I WANT TO SHOUT THE BLUES**		

– I'm leaving / Love is a burning thing / Birmingham blues / I want to shout / Don't look back / I want to hug you / Poor me / I want to ramble / Half a stranger / My grinding mill / Bottle up and go / One way ticket.

| 1964. (7") <670> **YOUR BABE AIN'T SWEET LIKE MINE. / BIG LEGS, TIGHT SHIRT** | - | |
| 1964. (7") <708> **IT SERVES ME RIGHT (TO SUFFER). / FLOWERS ON THE HOUR** | - | |

	Polydor	not iss.
1964. (7") (NH 52930) **SHAKE IT BABY. / LET'S MAKE IT BABY**	-	

	Pye Int.	Chess
Aug 64. (7") (7N 25255) **HIGH PRICED WOMAN. / SUGAR MAMA**	-	
Nov 64. (7"ep) (NEP 44034) **LOVE BLUES**	-	

	Sue	not iss.
Jun 65. (7") (WI 361) **I'M IN THE MOOD. / BOOGIE CHILLUN'**	-	

	Fontana	not iss.
Nov 65. (lp) (FJL 119) **BLUE** (rec.1960)	-	

	not iss.	Impulse
Jan 66. (7") <242> **BOTTLE UP AND GO. / MONEY**	-	

	Planet	Planet
Feb 66. (7"; as JOHN LEE'S GROUNDHOGS) **I'LL NEVER FALL IN LOVE AGAIN. / OVER YOU BABY**	-	
May 66. (7") <(PLF 114)> **MAI LEE. / DON'T BE MESSING WITH MY BREAD**	-	

	Chess	Chess
Aug 66. (7") (CRS 8039) <1965> **LET'S GO OUT TONIGHT. / I'M IN THE MOOD**		
Jan 67. (7") (CRL 4527) **REAL FOLK BLUES**		

– Let's go out tonight / Please lovin' man / Stella Mae / I put my trust in you / I'm in the mood / You know, I know / I'll never trust your love again / One bourbon, one Scotch, one beer / The waterfront. (cd-iss. Feb90 on 'M.C.A.';)

	H.M.V.	Impulse
1968. (lp) (CLP 5032) <9103> **IT SERVES YOU RIGHT TO SUFFER**		Feb66

– Sugar mama / Declaration day / Money (that's what I want) / It serves you right to suffer / Shake it baby / Country boy / Bottle up and go / You're wrong. (re-iss. 1977 on 'Impulse') (re-iss,Feb84 on 'Jasmine')

	H.M.V.	Bluesway
1968. (lp) (CLP 3612) <BLS 6002> **LIVE AT THE CAFE AU GO-GO** (live)		Jul66

– I'm bad like Jesse James / She's long, she's tall / When my first wife left me / Heartaches and misery / One bourbon, on scotch and one beer / I don't want no trouble / I'll never get out of these blues alive / Seven days. (re-iss. 1973 on 'Bluesway') (re-iss. +c+cd.Oct88 on 'B.G.O.')

| Jan 68. (7") <61010> **WANT AD BLUES. / THE MOTOR CITY IS BURNING** | - | |

	Stateside	Bluesway
Mar 68. (7") <61014> **CRY BEFORE I GO. / MR. LUCKY**	-	
1968. (lp) (SSL 10246) <BLS 6012> **URBAN BLUES**		

– Cry before I go / Boom boom / Backbiters & syndicaters / Mr.Lucky / I can't stand to leave you / My own blues / Think twice before you go / I'm standing in line / Hot water springs (pt.1 & 2) / Wand ad blues (re-iss. Oct91 on 'B.G.O.')

| Jun 68. (7") <61017> **THINK TWICE BEFORE YOU GO. / BACKBITERS AND SYNDICATER** | - | - |
| 1969. (lp) (SSL 10208) **SIMPLY THE TRUTH** | | |

– I don't wanna go to Vietnam / I wanna boogaloo / Tantalizing with the blues / I'm just a drifter / Mini skirts / Mean mean woman / One room country shack. (re-iss. +cd.Feb89 on 'B.G.O.')

	Probe	Bluesway
1969. (lp) (SPB 1016) <BLS 6038> **IF YOU MISS 'IM . . . I GET 'IM**		

– Hookers (if you miss 'im . . . I got 'im) / Baby I love you / Lonesome mood / Bang bang bang / If you take care of me, I'll take care of you / Baby, be strong / I wanna be your puppy / I don't care when you go / Have mercy on my soul.

—— next with **PRETTY PURDIE** – drums / **ERNIE HAYES** – mouth harp

| Feb 69. (7") <61023> **MEAN MEAN WOMAN. / I DON'T WANNA GO TO VIETNAM** | - | - |

– below set are exploitation releases

| 1968. (lp) (RLP 008) **BURNIN'** | | |

– Boom boom / Process / Lost a good girl / A new leaf / Blues before sunrise / Let's make it / I got a letter / Thelma / Drug store woman / Keep you hands to yourself / What do you say. (re-iss. 1974 on 'Joy'; JOYS 124) (re-iss. +c.May87 on 'Topline')

	Joy	Vee-Jay
1968. (lp) (JOYS 101) **I'M JOHN LEE HOOKER**		
1969. (lp) (JOYS 129) **TRAVELIN'**		

– No shoes / I wanna walk / Canal Street blues / Keep on / I'm a stranger / Whiskey and wimmen / Solid sender / Sunny land / Goin' to California / I can't believe / I'll know tonight / Dusty road. (re-iss. 1974)

| 1969. (lp) (JOYS 142) <VJS 1078> **CONCERT AT NEWPORT (live 24 Jun'60)** | | |

– I can't quit you now blues / Stop baby don't hold me that way / Tupelo / Bus station blues / Freight train be my friend / Boom boom boom Talk that talk baby / Sometime baby you make me feel so bad / You've got to walk by yourself / Let's make it / The mighty fire.

| 1969. (lp) (JOYS 152) **IN PERSON** | | - |

– I'm leaving Love is a burning thing / Birmingham blues / I want to shout / Don't look back / I want to hug youu / Poor me / I want to ramble / Half a stranger / My grinding mill / Bottle up and go / One way ticket.

—— In 1970, he recorded dual live album 'HOOKER'N'HEAT' with CANNED HEAT

	Probe	A.B.C.
May 71. (7") **KICK HIT 4 HIT KIX U. / DOIN' THE SHOUT**	-	-
May 71. (d-lp) (SPB 1034) <ABCX 720> **ENDLESS BOOGIE**		Mar71

– (I got) A good 'un / Pots on, gas on high / Kick hit 4 hit kix u / I don't need no stream heart / We might as well call it through . . . / Sittin' in my dark room / Endless boogie parts 27 & 28.

—— next with **ROBERT HOOKER** – organ / **LUTHER TUCKER** – guitar / **ELVIN BISHOP + DON 'Sugarcane' HARRIS** – piano / **CHARLIE MUSSELWHITE** – harmonica / **VAN MORRISON**

Apr 72. (lp) (SPB 1057) <ABCX 736> **NEVER GET OUT OF THESE BLUES ALIVE** — Mar72
– Bumblebee bumblebee / Hit the road / Country boy / Boogee with the Hook / If you take care of me (I'll take care of you) / I've got a go / T.B. sheets / Letter to my baby / Never get out of these blues alive / Baby I love you / Lonesome road. (cd-iss. Feb90 on 'See For Miles', 4 extra tracks)

Apr 72. (7") <> **BOOGIE WITH THE HOOK. / NEVER GET OUT OF THESE BLUES ALIVE**

Dec 72. (lp) <ABCX 761> **LIVE AT SOLEDAD PRISON (live)**
– Super lover / I'm your crosscut saw / What's the matter baby Lucille / Boogie everywhere I go / Serve me right to suffer / Bang bang bang bang.

1973. (lp) <ABCX 768> **BORN IN MISSISSIPPI, RAISED UP IN TENNESSEE**
– Born in Mississippi, raised up in Tennessee / How many more years you gonna dog me 'round / Going down ./ Younger stud / King of the world / Tell me you love me.

Nov 74. (lp) (ABCL 5059) **FREE BEER & CHICKEN** A.B.C. A.B.C.
– Make it funky / Five long years / 713 blues / 714 blues / One bourbon one Scotch one beer / Homework / Bluebird / Sittin' on top of the world / (You'l never amount to anything if you don't go to) College (a fortuitous concatenation of events (a) I know how to rock, (b) Nothin' but the best, (c) The scratch. (re-iss. +cd.Oct91 on 'B.G.O.')

1977. (d-lp) <2-7009> **THE CREAM (live)** not iss. Tomato
– Hey hey / Rock steady / Tupelo / You know it ain't right / She's gone / T.B. sheets / Sugar mama / One room country shack / Drug store woman / I want you to roll me / Bar room drinking / Little girl / Louise / When my first wife left me* / Boogie on*. (UK-iss.+c+cd.Jan88 on 'Charly', cd-omits*)(re-iss. cd Jun93)

—— In 1980, he cameos with loads of other stars in the film, 'BLUES BROTHERS'.

Oct 89. (lp/c/cd) (ORE LP/C/CD 508) <74808> **THE HEALER** Silvertone Chameleon 63 62
– The healer / I'm in the mood / Baby Lee / Cuttin' out / Think twice before you go / Sally Mae / That's alright / Rockin' chair / My dream / No substitute.

Dec 89. (7"/12"; JOHN LEE HOOKER & CARLOS SANTANA) (ORE/+T 10) **THE HEALER. / ROCKIN' CHAIR**
(cd-s+=) (ORECD 10) – ('A'mix) / No substitute.

May 90. (7"; JOHN LEE HOOKER & BONNIE RAITT) (ORE 18) **I'M IN THE MOOD. / MY DREAM**
(cd-s+=) (ORECD 18) – ('A'version) / That's alright. (re-iss. Nov92)

Oct 90. (7"/c-s; JOHN LEE HOOKER & ROBERT CRAY) (ORE) **BABY LEE. / CUTTIN' OUT**
(cd-s+=) (ORECD) – ('A'mix). (re-iss. Apr96, hit UK No.65)

—— with **STEVE EHERMAN** – bass / **SCOTT MATTHEWS** – drums + loads on sessions **CARLOS SANTANA / ALBERT COLLINS / VAN MORRISON / KEITH RICHARDS / BOOKER T. / RY COODER** / etc.

Aug 91. (cd/c/lp) (ORE CD/C/LP 519) <91724> **MR. LUCKY** Silvertone Charisma 3
– I want to hug you / Mr. Lucky / Backstabbers / This is hip / I cover the waterfront / Highway 13 / Stripped me naked / Susie / Crawlin' Kingsnake / Father was a jockey.

Aug 91. (7") (ORE 29) **MR. LUCKY. / THIS IS HIP**
(12"+=/cd-s+=) (ORE T/CD 29) –

Oct 92. (7"/c-s) (POB/+C 3) **BOOM BOOM. / HOMEWORK** Pointblank Pointblank 16
(cd-s+=) (POBCD 3) – The blues will never die / Thought I heard.
(cd-s) (POBDX 3) – ('A'version) / Thought I heard.

Nov 92. (cd/c/lp) (VPB CD/TC/LP 12) **BOOM BOOM (new rec.old tunes)** 15
– Boom boom / I'm bad like Jesse James / Same old blues again / Sugar mama / Trick bag (shoppin' for my tombstone) / Boogie at Russian Hill / Hittin' the bottle again / Bottle up and go / Thought I heard / I ain't gonna suffer no more. (re-iss. Oct93)

Jan 93. (7"/c-s) (POB/+C 4) **BOOGIE AT RUSSIAN HILL. / THE BLUES WILL NEVER DIE** 53
(cd-s+=) (POBDX 4) – I'm bad like Jesse James / Driftin' blues (w/ JOHN HAMMOND).

—— In May'93, he teamed up with VAN MORRISON on UK No.31 hit 'GLORIA'.

—— with **ROY ROGERS** – slide guitar / **CHARLES BROWN** – piano / **DANNY CARON** – guitar / **RUTH DAVIS + JIM GYETT** – bass / **GAYLORD BIRCH + BOWEN BROWN** – drums / guests **CARLOS SANTANA + CHESTER THOMPSON** (track 1) / **VAN MORRISON + BOOKER T** (track 4)

Feb 95. (7"/c-s) (POB/+C 10) **CHILL OUT (THINGS GONNA CHANGE). / TUPELO** 45
(cd-s+=) (POBDG 10) – Boom boom.
(cd-s+=) (POBD 10) – Up and down / Thought I heard.

Feb 95. (cd/c/lp) (VPB CD/TC/LP 22) <40107> **CHILL OUT** 23
– Chill out (things gonna change) / Deep blue sea / Kiddio / Medley: Serves me right to suffer – Syndicator / One bourbon, one scotch, one beer / Tupelo / Woman on my mind / Annie Mae / Too young / Talkin' the blues / If you've never been in love / We'll meet again.

Mar 97. (cd/c) (VPB CD/TC 39) **DON'T LOOK BACK** 63
– Dimples / Healing game / Ain't no gig thing / Don't look back / Blues before sunrise / Spellbound / Travellin' blues / I love you honey / Frisco blues / Red house / Rainy day.

– more compilations, etc. –

1964. (lp) Ember; (EMB 3356) **SINGS THE BLUES**
Jul 64. (lp) Pye Int./ US= Chess; (NPL 28042) **HOUSE OF THE BLUES** (50's recordings) 1960

(UK re-iss. Jan67 on 'Marble Arch', hit No.34) (re-iss. Oct87 on 'Chess') (cd-iss. Dec86 on 'Vogue')

Apr 82. (lp) Chess; (CXMD 4005) **CHESS MASTERS** —
1969. (lp) Joy/ US= Vee Jay; (JOYS 156) **THE BEST OF JOHN LEE HOOKER**
(re-iss. 1974 on 'Crescendo', cd,d-c,d-lp re-iss. Jan89)
1969. (lp) Polydor/ US= Riverside; (673020) **TUPELO BLUES**
Jul 71. (lp) Stax; (2362017) **THAT'S WHERE IT'S AT (rec. '61)**
– Teachin' the blues / Goin' to Louisiana / I need you / My love comes down for you / Please don't go / I just don't know / Slow and easy / Two white horses / So bad / Grinder man.
1970. (7") Stax; **SLOW AND EASY. / GRINDER MAN**
1971. (d-lp) Fantasy; **BOOGIE CHILLUN (live 1962)**
(UK-iss.+cd.May86 as 'MAMBO CHILLUN' on 'Charly')
1977. (lp) Fantasy; **BLACK SNAKE**
1971. (lp) United Artists; (UAS 29235) **COAST TO COAST**
1972. (lp/c) Atlantic/ US= Atco; (K 40405) **DETROIT SPECIAL**
Mar 75. (lp/c) Atlantic/ US= Atco; **DON'T TURN ME FROM YOUR DOOR**
1973. (lp) Greenbottle; (GN 4002) **JOHNNY LEE VOL.1**
(re-iss. May81 on 'Cadet-Ace')
1973. (lp) Checker/ US= Chess; (6467305) **MADMEN BLUES**
1971. (lp) Speciality; (SNTF 5005) **ALONE (rec. 48-51)** — 1967
(UK-iss.1981 on 'London') (US re-iss. +cd.Mar90 on 'Tomato')(re-iss. d-cd Oct93)
1973. (lp) Sonet; **HOOKER, HOPKINS & HOGE** (re-iss. 1974)
Feb 77. (d-lp) D.J.M.; (DJD 28026) **DIMPLES**
1972. (lp) New World; (NW 6003) **JOHN LEE HOOKER**
1973. (lp) Polydor; (2310256) **SLIM'S STOMP**
1975. (lp) Code; (ALB 186) **BLACK RHYTHM & BLUES**
(UK iss. Nov 84 on 'Festival')
Jan 76. (lp) Code; **L'ADVENTURE DU JAZZ**
Sep 79. (lp) Jewel; (JEWEL 5005) **I FEEL GOOD**
Oct 79. (d-lp) Gusto; (G 5032) **MOANIN' AND STOMPIN' BLUES**
Aug 79. (lp) Charly; (CR 30170) **NO FRIEND AROUND**
(re-iss. Sep82 on 'Red Lightnin'; cd-iss. Apr95)
Jul 80. (7"m) Charly; **DIMPLES. / BOOM BOOM / ONIONS**
1980. (lp) Charly; (CRB 1004) **THIS IS HIP**
(re-iss. Jan85)
Mar 81. (lp) Charly; (CRB 1014) **EVERYBODY ROCKIN'**
Nov 81. (lp) Charly; (CRB 1029) **MOANING THE BLUES**
Jul 84. (lp) Charly; (CRB 1081) **SOLID SENDER**
Feb 87. (cd) Charly; (CDCHARLY 62) **HOUSE RENT BOOGIE**
Oct 88. (lp/cd) Charly; (CDX 33) **THE BLUESWAY SESSIONS**
Mar 89. (cd) Charly; (CDCHARLY 170) **LET'S MAKE IT**
Feb 93. (cd) Charly; (CDBM 38) **BLUES FOR BIG TOWN**
Feb 93. (cd) Charly; (CDREDBOX 6) **THE VEE-JAY YEARS 1955-1964**
1981. (7") Ace; **SHAKE, HOLLER & RUN. / ?**
1992. (cd) Ace; (CDCHD 421) **GRAVEYARD BLUES.**
May 93. (cd) Ace; (CDCHD 315) **THE LEGENDARY MODERN RECORDINGS 1948-1954**
Jul 93. (cd) Ace; (CDCHD 474) **EVERYBODY'S BLUES**
Apr 81. (lp) Muse; (MR 5205) **SITTIN' HERE THINKIN'** — 1979
(re-iss. Jul83 on 'Happy Bird')
Apr 91. (cd) Muse; (MCD 6009) **SAD AND LONESOME**
1983. (lp) M.C.A.; **LONESOME MOOD**
May 82. (lp/c) M.C.A.; (MCL /+C 1686) **TANTALIZING WITH THE BLUES**
Aug 91. (cd) M.C.A.; (MCAD 10364) **INTRODUCING . . .**
Oct 91. (cd) M.C.A.; (MCAD 18335) **THE COMPLETE CHESS FOLK BLUES SESSIONS**
May 93. (cd/c) M.C.A.; (MCA D/C 10539) **THE BEST OF JOHN LEE HOOKER 1965-1974**
Below was issued in US as 'BLUES BEFORE SUNRISE' in 1976 of early work.
Jul 84. (lp) Bulldog; (B 90165) **DO THE BOOGIE**
(original title re-iss. 1986) (US re-iss. Nov84 on 'Astan')
Aug 85. (lp/c) Deja Vu; (DV LP/MC 2033) **THE COLLECTION: 20 BLUES GREATS**
(cd-iss. Jun88)
Apr 93. (cd/c) Deja Vu; (D2 CD/MC 07) **THE GOLD COLLECTION**
Nov 87. (lp) Krazy Kat; (KK 816) **DETROIT BLUES (1950-51)**
May 88. (lp/c/cd) Blues City; (26522 – 1/-4/-2) **GREATEST HITS**
May 88. (lp/c/cd) Tomato; **LIVE (live)**
Jun 88. (lp) Rhino; (RNDA 71105) **INFINITE BOOGIE**
Aug 89. (cd/c/lp) Instant; (CD/TC INS 5009/INS 5009) **THE BOOGIE MAN**
Feb 90. (lp/cd) Demon; (FIEND/+CD 154) **THE DETROIT LION**
(re-iss. cd Oct93)
Apr 91. (cd/c) Magnum Force; **NUTHIN' BUT THE BLUES**
May 91. (cd) Music Club; (MCCD 020) **THE BEST OF JOHN LEE HOOKER**
– Boom boom / Shake it baby (original) / The right time / Dimples / Boogie chillun / Mambo chillun / Wheel and deal / I'm so excited / Trouble blues / Everybody's rockin' / Unfriendly woman / Time is marchin' / I see you when you're weak / I'm in the mood / Will the circle be unbroken / This is hip / Hobo blues / Solid sender.
Jun 91. (cd) Mainstream; (MDCD 903) **HALF A STRANGER**
Jun 93. (cd) Mainstream; **BOOM BOOM**
Jun 93. (cd) Mainstream; **I'M IN THE MOOD**
Jul 93. (cd) Mainstream; **SHAKE IT BABY**
Mar 93. (cd) O.B.C.; (OBCCD 555) **BURNING HELL**
Apr 93. (cd) Sixteen; **16 GREATEST HITS**
Mar 94. (cd) Ace; (CDCHM 530) **ORIGINAL FOLK BLUES OF JOHN LEE HOOKER**
Apr 94. (cd) Just A Memory; (RSCD 001) **THE RISING SUN COLLECTION**

May 94. (cd/c) *Laserlight; (1/7 2333)* **BOOM BOOM**	☐	☐
Jul 94. (cd) *See For MIles; (SEECD 402)* **THE EP COLLECTION . . .PLUS**	☐	-
May 94. (cd) *Charly; (CDTT 3)* **TWO ON ONE** (w / MUDDY WATERS)	☐	-
Aug 94. (cd) *Charly;* **WHISKEY & WIMMEN** *(re-iss. Aug95 on 'Imp')*	☐	-
Dec 94. (cd/c) *Marble Arch; (MAT CD/MC 320)* **THE BOSS**	☐	-
Feb 95. (cd) *Castle; (CCSCD 410)* **THE COLLECTION**	☐	-
Apr 95. (cd-box+book) *Charly; (CDDIG 5)* **THE BOOGIE MAN**	☐	-
Jul 95. (3xcd-box) *Charly; (VBCD 301)* **THE VERY BEST OF JOHN LEE HOOKER**	☐	-
Sep 95. (cd) *Best;* **JOHN LEE HOOKER**	☐	-
Nov 95. (3xcd-box) *The Collection;* **THE COLLECTION**	☐	-
Dec 95. (cd) *Opal; (OCD 103)* **CRAWLING KINGSNAKE 1948-52**	☐	-

HOOTIE & THE BLOWFISH

Formed: Columbia, South Carolina, USA . . . 1993 by DARIUS RUCKER, MARK BRYAN, DEAN FELBER and JIM 'SONI' SONEFELD. Their debut single 'HOLD MY HAND' (helped by backing vox from DAVID CROSBY) stormed America, as did multi-million selling No.1 album 'CRACKED REAR VIEW'. In Britain, they were lauded by the likes of TV/radio presenter, Danny Baker, which (I suppose) helped gain growing reputation on Virgin FM safe rock music station. Corporate and melodic, MTV adult-orientated rock, with similar vox references of African-American DARIUS, to BRAD ROBERTS (Crash Test Dummies) or EDDIE VEDDER (Pearl Jam), HOOTIE & THE BLOWFISH struck gold again with their second set, 'FAIRWEATHER JOHNSON' (1996). Another massive No.1 hit in the States, the album even cracked the UK Top 10; their appeal wasn't that universal, though, one MAX CAVALERA (ex-SEPULTURA) making his thoughts pretty explicit on the track 'No!' from the SOULFLY debut. • **Covered:** DRIVER 8 (R.E.M.) / I GO BLIND (54:40) / GRAVITY OF THE SITUATION with Nanci Griffith (Vic Chesnutt).

Album rating: CRACKED REAR VIEW (*7) / FAIRWEATHER JOHNSON (*6) / MUSICAL CHAIRS (*5)

DARIUS RUCKER – vocals, acoustic guitar, percussion / **MARK BRYAN** – guitars, vocals, etc / **DEAN FELBER** – bass, clavinet, vocals / **JIM 'SONI' SONEFELD** – drums, vocals, piano, etc.

	Atlantic	Atlantic
Feb 95. (c-s) *(A 7230C)* <87230> **HOLD MY HAND / I GO BLIND**	50	10 Sep94
(cd-s+=) *(A 7230CD)* – Running from an angel.		
Mar 95. (cd/c) <(7567 82613-2/-4)> **CRACKED REAR VIEW**	12	1 Jul94
– Hannah Jane / Hold my hand / Let her cry / Only wanna be with you / Running from an angel / I'm goin' home / Drowning / Time / Look away / Not even the trees / Goodbye.		
Mar 95. (c-s) <87231> **LET HER CRY** / ('A'version)	-	9
May 95. (c-s) *(A 7188C)* **LET HER CRY / FINE LINE**	75	-
(cd-s+=) *(A 7188CD)* – Hannah Jane (live) / Where were you.		
(cd-s) *(A 7188CDX)* – ('A'side) / Goodbye (live) / The ballad of John and Yoko (live) / Hold my hand (live).		
Jul 95. (c-s) <87132> **ONLY WANNA BE WITH YOU / WHERE WERE YOU**	-	6
Aug 95. (c-s) *(A 7138C)* **ONLY WANNA BE WITH YOU / USE ME (live)**		-
(cd-s+=) *(A 7138CD)* – ('A'live).		
Nov 95. (c-s) <87095> **TIME / GOODBYE (live)**	-	14
Apr 96. (c-s) *(A 5513C)* <87074> **OLD MAN & ME (WHEN I GET TO HEAVEN) / BEFORE THE HEARTACHE ROLLS IN**	57	13
(cd-s+=) *(A 5513CD)* – Time (live) / Only wanna be with you (live).		
Apr 96. (cd/c) <(7567 82886-2/-4)> **FAIRWEATHER JOHNSON**	9	1
– Be the one / Sad caper / Tucker's town / She crawls away / So strange / Old man & me / Earth stopped cold at dawn / Fairweather Johnson / Honeyscrew / Let it breathe / Silly little pop song / Fool / Tootie / When I'm lonely.		
Jul 96. (c-s) <87051> **TUCKER'S TOWN / ARABY**	-	38
Jul 96. (c-s) *(A 5498C)* **TUCKER'S TOWN / NOT EVEN THE TREES**	-	
(cd-s) *(A 5498CD)* – ('A'side) / Araby.		
Sep 98. (cd/c) (7567 83136-2/-4) <83136> **MUSICAL CHAIRS**	15	4
– I will wait / Wishing / Las Vegas nights / Only lonely / Answer man / Michelle post / Bluesy revolution / Home again / One by one / Desert mountain showdown / What's going on here / What do you want from me now.		
Oct 98. (c-s/cd-s) *(AT 0048 C/CD)* **I WILL WAIT / DRIVER 8 / I WILL WAIT (acoustic)**	57	☐
(cd-s) *(AT 0048CD2)* – ('A'side) / Hold my hand (live) / Let her cry (live).		
May 99. (c-s/cd-s) *(AT 0059 C/CD)* **ONLY LONELY / MICHELLE POST / FRANCES**	☐	☐

HOPE BLISTER (see under ⇒ THIS MORTAL COIL)

Bruce HORNSBY

Born: 23 Nov'54, Williamsburg, Virginia, USA. In 1978, after studying music at both Miami University and Boston's Berklee School of Music, he formed The BRUCE HORNSBY BAND with older brother BOBBY and drummer JOHN MOLO. In 1980, on the advice of former DOOBIE, MICHAEL McDONALD, he relocated to L.A. where both he and his younger brother, JOHN, picked up work as professional writers for 20th Century Fox. A couple of years later, BRUCE met rising US star HUEY LEWIS, who wanted to

cover one of his song's for the 1983 album, 'Sports'. Around the same time, BRUCE also topped up his CV with some tour backing work to Scots lass, SHEENA EASTON. Yet even LEWIS' enthusiastic patronage couldn't help furnish HORNSBY with his own record deal and it would be 1985 before a demo of acoustic tracks finally persuaded 'R.C.A.' to take him on along with his backup band, The RANGE (featuring DAVID MANSFIELD, GEORGE MARINELLI, JOE PUERTA and veteran MOLO). A year later he finally scored a minor US hit with 'EVERY LITTLE KISS' before hitting paydirt a few months after that in Autumn '86 with signature tune, 'THE WAY IT IS'. A melancholy MOR quasi-ballad carrying a vaguely wistful anti-racism message and highlighting BRUCE's characteristic piano flourishes, the track topped the US singles chart while also making a respectable dent in the UK market. The 1987 album of the same name was filled with similarly well-crafted sophisti-roots-pop/rock efforts and made BRUCE a middling coffee-table star, the record making the US Top 3 and spawning a further US Top 5 single in 'MANDOLIN RAIN'. Even as a remixed version of 'EVERY LITTLE KISS' eventually made the US Top 20, HORNSBY was looking to further his reputation as a songwriter, placing 'JACOB'S LADDER' (a track he'd written earlier with his brother JOHN) with HUEY LEWIS & THE NEWS who took it to the top of the US singles chart in early 1987. Following the replacement of MANSFIELD with PETER HARRIS, BRUCE HORNSBY & THE RANGE were back in Spring of the following year with 'SCENES FROM THE SOUTHSIDE', an album in the familiar ivory-tinkling mould which, while not quite apeing the success of its predecessor, made the US Top 5 and contained a similar sized hit single in 'THE VALLEY ROAD'. Subsequent singles failed to make a mark, however, and 1990's 'NIGHT ON THE TOWN' only just made the US Top 20, spawning a Top 20 single in 'ACROSS THE RIVER'. Yet despite his diminishing returns with The RANGE, HORNSBY's talents were well utilised by the rock aristocracy, everyone from DON HENLEY (BRUCE wrote the title track from his critically lauded 1989 album, 'End Of The Innocence') to BONNIE RAITT and even SQUEEZE requesting the man's services. Following the death of GRATEFUL DEAD keyboard player, BRETT MYLAND, in 1990, HORNSBY even toured with the band over an 18-month period, returning the favour to JERRY GARCIA who'd guested on 'NIGHT . . .'. With the subsequent demise of The RANGE, HORNSBY embarked on a solo career with the moderately successful 'HARBOR LIGHTS' (1993), again assisted in his endeavours by ,the likes of GARCIA and RAITT alongside such distinguished jazz veterans as BUD POWELL and BRANFORD MARSALIS. A sophomore effort, 'HOT HOUSE', followed in 1995, while 1998 saw the release of a third solo set, 'SPIRIT TRAIL'; HORNSBY has since teamed up with his old GRATEFUL DEAD chums in The OTHER ONES. • **Trivia:** He played accordion on albums by KIM CARNES (View From The House) / PATTI AUSTIN (The Real Me) & HUEY LEWIS (Small World).

Album rating: THE WAY IT IS (*7) / SCENES FROM THE SOUTHSIDE (*6) / A NIGHT ON THE TOWN (*5) / HARBOR LIGHTS (*4) / HOT HOUSE (*4) / SPIRIT TRAIL (*4)

BRUCE HORNSBY & THE RANGE

BRUCE HORNSBY – vocals, keyboards, accordion (ex-SHEENA EASTON Band) / **DAVID MANSFIELD** – violin, mandolin, guitar / **GEORGE MARINELLI** – guitar, vocals / **JOE PUERTA** – bass, vocals / **JOHN MOLO** – drums

	R.C.A.	R.C.A.
Jul 86. (7") <14361> **EVERY LITTLE KISS. / THE RED PLAINS**	-	72
Jul 86. (7") *(PB 49805)* **THE WAY IT IS. / THE RED PLAINS**	15	-
(12"+=) *(PT 49806)* – The wild frontier.		
Sep 86. (lp/c/cd) *(PL/PK/PD 89901)* <5904> **THE WAY IT IS**	16	3 Jun86
– On the western skyline / Every little kiss / Mandolin rain / The long race / The way it is / Down the road tonight / The wild frontier / The river runs low / The red plains. *(cd/c re-iss. Feb97; 74321 44421-2/-4)*		
Sep 86. (7") <5023> **THE WAY IT IS. / THE WILD FRONTIER**	-	1
Sep 86. (7") *(PB 49797)* **EVERY LITTLE KISS. / THE RIVER RUNS LOW**	-	1
(12"+=) *(PT 49798)* – The way it is (instrumental).		
Feb 87. (7") *(PB 49769)* <5087> **MANDOLIN RAIN. / THE RED PLAINS (live)**	70	4 Jan87
(12"+=) *(PT 49770)* – Every little kiss (instrumental).		
(cd-s+=) *(PD 49770)* – The way it is (live).		
—— **PETER HARRIS** – guitar, etc; repl. MANSFIELD		
Apr 88. (lp/c/cd) *(PL/PK/PD 86686)* <6686> **SCENES FROM THE SOUTHSIDE**	15	5
– The show goes on / The old playground / Defenders of the flag / Jacob's ladder / Till the dreaming's done / Look out any window / The valley road / I will walk with you / The road not taken. *(re-iss. Nov90 cd/c/lp; ND/NK/NL 90492)*		
May 88. (7") *(PB 49561)* <7645> **THE VALLEY ROAD. / THE LONG RACE (live)**	44	5 Apr88
(12"+=/cd-s+=) *(PT/PD 49562)* – Mandolin rain (live).		
Jul 88. (7") <8678> **LOOK OUT ANY WINDOW. / THE WAY IT IS (live)**	-	35
Jul 88. (7") *(PB 49533)* **LOOK OUT ANY WINDOW. / ON THE WESTERN SKYLINE**	-	-
(12"+=/cd-s+=) *(PT/PD 49534)* – Mandolin rain.		
Nov 88. (7") <8776> **DEFENDERS OF THE FLAG. / ON THE WESTERN SKYLINE**		
Nov 88. (7") *(PB 49511)* **DEFENDERS OF THE FLAG. / LOOK OUT ANY WINDOW**	☐	-
(12"+=) *(PT 49512)* – Look out any window (live).		
(cd-s++=) *(PD 49512)* – Defenders of the flag (live).		

—— trimmed to quartet when PETER HARRIS departed

Jun 90. (cd/c/lp) *(PD/PK/PL 82041) <2041>* **A NIGHT ON THE TOWN** | 23 | 20 |
– A night on the town / Carry the water / Fire on the cross / Barren ground / Stranded on easy street / Stander on the mountain / Lost soul / Another day / Special night / These arms of mine. *(cd re-iss. Sep93; 74321 16001-2)*

Jul 90. (7") *<2621>* **ACROSS THE RIVER. / FIRE ON THE CROSS** | | 18 Jun90 |
(12"+=) – Mandolin rain (live).

Oct 90. (c-s/cd-s) *<2704>* **LOST SOUL / STANDER ON THE MOUNTAIN** | - | 84 |
above single featured SHAWN COLVIN on vocals

May 91. (cd-ep) *<2846>* **SET IN MOTION EP** | - | |
– Carry the water / Barren ground / Another day.

Bruce HORNSBY

—— (solo) with JIMMY HASLIP – bass / JOHN MOLO – drums / plus session people PAT METHENY – guitar / BRANDFORD MARSALIS – saxophone / JOHN BIGHAM – guitar / PHIL COLLINS – percussion, b.vocals / WILL ROSS – rhythm guitar / JERRY GARCIA – guitar / BUD POWELL – piano / BONNIE RAITT – vocals / GLENN WILSON – horns / etc.

Apr 93. (cd/c) *<(07863 66114-2/-4)>* **HARBOR LIGHTS** | 32 | 46 |
– Harbor lights / Talk of the town / Long tall cool one / China doll / Fields of gray / Rainbow's Cadillac / Passing through / The tide will rise / What a time / Pastures of plenty.

May 93. (c-s/cd-s) *(74321 13692-4/-2) <2846>* **HARBOR LIGHTS / THE END OF INNOCENCE (live)** | | |

Jul 93. (c-s) *<62580>* **TALK OF THE TOWN /** | - | |

Oct 93. (c-s/cd-s) *<62618>* **FIELDS OF GRAY / SONG A** | - | 69 |

Jan 94. (c-s/cd-s) *<62624>* **RAINBOW'S CADILLAC /** | - | |

—— now with JERRY CARCIA + PAT METHENY – guitar / DEBBIE HENRY – vocals / J.T. THOMAS – organ / JOHN MOLO – drums / JOHN D'EARTH – trumpet / BOBBY READ – saxophone

Aug 95. (cd/c) *<(07863 66584-2/-4)>* **HOT HOUSE** | | 68 Jul95 |
– Spider fingers / White wheeled Limousine / Walk in the Sun / The changes / The tango king / Big rumble / Country doctor / The longest night / Hot house ball / Swing street / Cruise control.

Aug 95. (c-s/cd-s) *<64382>* **WALK IN THE SUN / CRUISE CONTROL** | - | 54 |

Oct 98. (cd) *<(74321 60186-2)>* **SPIRIT TRAIL** | | |
– Line in the dust / See the same way / Shadow hand / King of the hill / Resting place / Preacher in the ring (part 1) / Preacher in the ring (part 2) / Song C / Sad moon / Pete and Manny / Fortunate son / Sneaking up on Boo Radley / Great divide / Sunflower cat (some dour cat) (down with that) / Song D / Swan song / Variations on swan song and song D.

HOTHOUSE FLOWERS

Formed: Christchurch, Dublin, Ireland . . . 1985 by Gaelic speakers LIAM O'MAONLAI and FIACHNA O'BRAONAIN. Initially part of punk band CONGRESS (which later evolved into MY BLOODY VALENTINE), the pair left college in 1985 and formed The INCOMPARABLE BENZINI BROTHERS. In this incarnation, they won the Street Entertainer Of The Year Award in their native Dublin (a similar British award seems inconceivable, instead we're blessed with the Criminal Justice Bill). With the addition of LEO BARNES (saxophone), PETER O'TOOLE (bass) and JERRY FEHILY (drums), the band evolved into HOTHOUSE FLOWERS and the following year, after being clocked by U2's BONO on TV ('The Late Late Show'), the fledgling group recorded a debut single for his 'Mother' label. The track, 'LOVE DON'T WORK THAT WAY', led to a deal with 'London' records and later that year, the band released the classic 'DON'T GO', an earthy piece of piano-led celtic soul that VAN MORRISON would have been proud to call his own. The single failed to do the business first time around although in 1988, a re-issued 'DON'T GO' scored a near UK Top 10 hit, preceding a No.2 album, 'PEOPLE'. The group's focal point was O'MAONLAI's voice, a powerful, unmistakably Irish burr that occasionally came close to the gospel-like fervour and conviction of MORRISON. A follow-up album, 'HOME', was released in 1990, spawning a fairly uninspired Top 30 cover of Johnny Nash's 'I CAN SEE CLEARLY NOW'. A slightly more traditional-flavoured opus, 'HOME' reached No.5. Following a period of touring and writing, the band eventually re-surfaced with 'SONGS FROM THE RAIN' (1993), another perfectly listenable release, though hardly life-affirming. And herein lies the problem with HOTHOUSE FLOWERS; their instrumental prowess and sturdy songwriting make them eminently worthy but often dull, their music never actually achieving the transcendence that they presumably aim for.
• **Songwriters:** Mostly band compositions except; HARD RAIN (Bob Dylan) / CARRICK FERGUS + BRIGHT SIDE OF THE ROAD (Van Morrison) / KANSAS CITY (Leiber-Stoller) / BETTER DAYS AHEAD (Gil Scott-Heron) / etc. • **Trivia:** In mid-87, they contributed 5 songs to film soundtrack of 'The Courier'.

Album rating: PEOPLE (*7) / HOME (*5) / SONGS FROM THE RAIN (*5) / BORN (*4)

LIAM O'MAONLAI (b. 7 Nov'64) – vocals / **FIACHNA O'BRAONAIN** (b.27 Nov'65) – guitar / **LEO BARNES** (b. 5 Oct'65) – saxophone / **PETER O'TOOLE** (b. 1 Apr'65) – bass / **JERRY FEHILY** (b.29 Aug'63, Bishopstown, Ireland) – drums

		Mother	not iss.
May 87. (7") *(MUM 7)* **LOVE DON'T WORK THIS WAY. / FREEDOM**			-
(ext.12"+=) *(12MUM 7)* – Seeline woman.			

		London	London
Nov 87. (7") *(LON 159)* **DON'T GO. / BETTER AND BETTER**			
(12"+=) *(LONX 159)* – Big fat heart.			

Mar 88. (7") *(LON 172)* **FEET ON THE GROUND. / HARD RAIN** | | |
(12"+=) *(LONX 172)* – Strange feeling.

Apr 88. (7") *(LON 174)* **DON'T GO (remix). / SAVED** | 11 | |
(12"+=) *(LONX 174)* – Hydromat.
(cd-s+=) *(LONCD 174)* – Feet on the ground / Lonely lane (live).

May 88. (lp/c)(cd) *(LON LP/C 58)(<828101-2>)* **PEOPLE** | 2 | 88 |
– I'm sorry / Don't go / Forgiven / It'll be easier in the morning / Hallelujah Jordan / If you go / The older we get / Was I / Love don't work this way / Ballad of Katie / Feet on the ground. *(cd+=)* – Lonely lane / Saved.

Jul 88. (7") *(LON 187)* **I'M SORRY. / MOUNTAINS** | 53 | |
(12"+=/12"pic-d+=) *(LONX 187)* – Seeline woman.
(cd-s+=) *(LONCD 187)* – Don't go (acoustic-live).

Sep 88. (7"/7"box) *(LON/+B 186)* **EASIER IN THE MORNING. / CARRICK FERGUS** | | |
(12"+=) *(LONX 186)* – Feet on the ground (live).
(cd-s+=) *(LONCD 186)* – Better and better.

May 90. (7") *(LON 258)* **GIVE IT UP. / IF YOU'RE HAPPY** | 30 | |
(c-s+=/cd-s+=) *(LON CS/CD 258)* – If you go.
(12"+=/12"pic-d+=) *(LONX/+P 258)* – Bean phaidini.

Jun 90. (cd/c/lp) *(<828197-2/-4/-1>)* **HOME** | 5 | |
– Hardstone city / Give it up / Christchurch bells / Sweet Marie / Giving it all away / Shut up and listen / I can see clearly now / Movies / Eyes wide open / Water / Home / Trying to get through. *(cd+=)* – Dance to the storm / Seoladh na nGamhna.

Jul 90. (7"/c-s) *(LON/+CS 269)* **I CAN SEE CLEARLY NOW. / KANSAS CITY** | 23 | |
(12"+=) *(LONX 269)* – Better days ahead.
(cd-s++=) *(LONCD 269)* – Strange feelin'.

Oct 90. (7"/c-s) *(LON/+CS 276)* **MOVIES. / SWEET MARIE** | 68 | |
(12"+=) *(LONX 276)* – Don't go (live).
(cd-s+=) *(LONCD 276)* – Give it up.
(12") *(LONXP 276)* – ('A'side) / She moves through the fair / Dance to the storm / Hydromat.

Feb 93. (7"/c-s) *(LON/+CS 335)* **EMOTIONAL TIME. / THE SEASONS WHEELS** | 38 | |
(cd-s+=) *(LONCD 335)* – Help us make our peace / Song of Equador.
(cd-s) *(LOCDP 335)* – ('A'side) / Air from the hills / Banished misfortune / Let the rhythm take you home.

Mar 93. (cd/c/lp) *(<828350-2/-4/-1>)* **SONGS FROM THE RAIN** | 7 | |
– This is it (your soul) / One tongue / An emotional time / Be good / Good for you / Isn't it amazing / Thing of beauty / Your nature / Spirit of the land / Gypsy fair / Stand beside me.

Apr 93. (7"/c-s) *(LON/+CS 340)* **ONE TONGUE. / CARRY ON** | 45 | |
(pic-cd-s+=) *(LOCDP 340)* – Thank you for believing / The rebel.
(cd-s) *(LONCD 340)* – ('A'side) / Same song / Wish you everything / The rain.

Jun 93. (7"/c-s) *(LON/+CS 343)* **ISN'T IT AMAZING. / LET HIM KNOW** | 46 | |
(cd-s) *(LOCDP 343)* – ('A'side) / Fi do mhamo I / Of the people / The well.

Nov 93. (c-s/cd-s) *(LON CS/CD 346)* **THIS IS IT (YOUR SOUL) / SWEET MARIE / GIVE IT UP** | 67 | |
(cd-s+=) *(LOCDP 346)* – ('A'side) / Suspicious minds / Forever young / Come together.

—— subsequently split after above, although they returned 5 years later

May 98. (c-s/cd-s) *(LON CS/DP 410)* **YOU CAN LOVE ME NOW / DON'T GO / IT'LL BE EASIER IN THE MORNING** | 65 | |
(cd-s) *(LONCD 410)* – ('A'side) / This is it (your soul) / It's a man's man's man's world / Love don't work this way.

May 98. (cd) *(828966-2)* **BORN** | | |
– You can love me now / Turn up the reverb / Forever more / Born / Pop song / Used to call it love / At last / Find the time / I believe / Learning to walk.

HOTLEGS (see under ⇒ 10cc)

HOT TUNA (dig out;
4th edition or Great Psychedelic . . .)

HOURGLASS (see under ⇒ ALLMAN BROTHERS BAND)

HOUSEMARTINS

Formed: Hull, England . . . late 1983 by PAUL HEATON and STAN CULLIMORE, CHRIS LANG and TED KEY soon completing the line-up. After local gigs, many of them for political causes (i.e. the miners & CND), they signed to Andy McDonald's new 'Go! Discs' label. With HUGH WHITAKER replacing LANG, they released their debut single, 'FLAG DAY', a record that left you in no doubt where the band's political loyalties lay. Although the single failed to chart, with the follow-up, 'SHEEP' (prior to which, NORMAN COOK replaced TED KEY) faring little better, The HOUSEMARTINS imprinted themselves on mid-80's consciousness with 'HAPPY HOUR'. An outrageously catchy single, this was Brit-pop before Brit-pop was even invented; shiny, happy melodies, chiming guitars and nifty footwork, as always with an underlying right-on message. The record reached No.3 in the UK charts, the debut album, 'LONDON 0 HULL 4' (1986), attaining the same position later that summer. An endearing collection of witty, finely crafted songs which, above all, had a big heart and a deep soul, something not exactly at a premium in those dark 80's days with the twin spectres of Thatcher and Stock, Aitken & Waterman never far away. That Christmas, the band became a household name when they scaled the charts with a lovely a cappella cover of ISLEY JASPER ISLEY's 'CARAVAN OF LOVE'. The following Spring, WHITAKER was replaced by DAVE

HEMMINGWAY, the band releasing their follow-up album later that year, 'THE PEOPLE W19HO GRINNED THEMSELVES TO DEATH'. Even more politically pointed than the debut, the record nevertheless delivered its barbs in unerringly melodic packages, its highlight being the gorgeous gospel-pop of penultimate single, 'BUILD'. Yet the band had almost reached the end of their woefully short lifespan, HEATON and CULLIMORE agreeing from the start that it shouldn't exceed three years. Bowing out with a cover of Burt Bacharach's 'THERE'S ALWAYS SOMETHING THERE TO REMIND ME', The HOUSEMARTINS officially split in early '88. While HEATON went on to even greater success with The BEAUTIFUL SOUTH, the pseudo-Christian, Socialist sentiments he propounded in his earlier career seem a little hollow in light of his alleged penchant for soccer hooliganism. Working Class to the bone, eh mate? WHITAKER's subsequent conduct was little better, the man being sentenced to six years in prison in 1993 for assault and arson offences. NORMAN COOK, on the other hand, became a major player on the dance scene under various aliases, including BEATS INTERNATIONAL, PIZZAMAN and more recently the storming FATBOY SLIM. • **Songwriters:** Penned by HEATON-CULLIMORE except covers; HE AIN'T HEAVY, HE'S MY BROTHER (Hollies) / CARAVAN OF LOVE (Isley Jasper Isley). • **Trivia:** LONDON 0 HULL 4, stemmed from group's promotional hometown pride. They often described themselves as Hull's 4th best group. Who were better? RED GUITARS, EVERYTHING BUT THE GIRL and GARGOYLES.

Album rating: LONDON 0 HULL 4 (*8) / THE PEOPLE WHO GRINNED THEMSELVES TO DEATH (*7) / NOW THAT'S WHAT I CALL QUITE GOOD compilation (*8)

PAUL HEATON (b. 9 May'62, Bromborough, England) – vocals / **STAN CULLIMORE** (b.IAN, 6 Apr'62) – guitar, vocals / **TED KEY** – bass / **HUGH WHITAKER** – drums; repl. CHRIS LANG

		Go! Discs	Elektra
Oct 85.	(7") (GOD 7) **FLAG DAY. / STAND AT EASE**	☐	-
	(12"+=) (GODX 7) – Coal train to Hatfield Main.		

—— **NORMAN COOK** (b. QUENTIN COOK, 31 Jul'63, Brighton, England) – bass repl. TED KEY who formed GARGOYLES

Mar 86.	(7"/7"pic-d) (GOD/+P 9) **SHEEP. / DROP DOWN DEAD**	54	-	
	(d7"+=) (GOD 9/+7) – Flag day / Stand at ease.			
	(12"+=) (GODX 9) – I'll be your shelter / Anxious / People get ready.			
May 86.	(7"/7"sha-pic-d) (GOD/+P 11) <69515> **HAPPY HOUR. /**			
	THE MIGHTY SHIP	3		Sep86
	(12"+=) (GODX 11) – Sitting on a fence / He ain't heavy.			
Jun 86.	(lp/c)(cd) (A/Z GOLP 7)(CCD 1537) <60501> **LONDON 0**			
	HULL 4	3		Feb87
	– Happy hour / Get up off our knees / Flag day / Anxious / Reverends revenge / Sitting on a fence / Sheep / Over there / Think for a minute / We're not deep / Lean on me / Freedom. (c+=) – I'll be your shelter. (cd++=) – People get ready / The mighty ship / He ain't heavy. (re-iss. Oct92 cd/c; same)			
Sep 86.	(7"/7"sha-pic-d) (GOD/+P 13) **THINK FOR A MINUTE. /**			
	WHO NEEDS THE LIMELIGHT	18		
	(12"+=) (GODX 13) – I smell winter / Joy joy joy / Rap around the clock.			
Nov 86.	(7"/7"sha-pic-d) (GOD/+P 16) **CARAVAN OF LOVE. /**			
	WHEN I FIRST MET JESUS	1	-	
	(12"+=) (GODX 16) – We shall not be moved / So much in love / Heaven help us all.			
	(7"box-set+=) (GODB 16) **THE HOUSEMARTINS CHRISTMAS BOX SET** – (all 4 singles +=; GOD 9) – I'll be your shelter. – hit No.84			
Feb 87.	(7") <69491> **FLAG DAY. / THE MIGHTY SHIP**	-	-	

—— **DAVE HEMMINGWAY** (b.20 Sep'60) – drums; repl. WHITAKER who joined GARGOYLES full-time

May 87.	(7") (GOD 18) **FIVE GET OVER EXCITED. / REBEL WITHOUT**			
	THE AIRPLAY	11	-	
	(c-s+=/12"+=) (XGOD/GODX 18) – So glad / Hopelessly devoted to them.			
Aug 87.	(7") (GOD 19) **ME AND THE FARMER. / I BIT MY LIP**	15	-	
	(c-s+=/12"+=) (XGOD/GODX 19) – He will find you out / Step outside.			
Sep 87.	(lp/c) (A/Z GOLP 9) <60761> **THE PEOPLE WHO GRINNED**			
	THEMSELVES TO DEATH	9		Jan88
	– The people who grinned themselves to death / I can't put my finger on it / The light is always green / The world's on fire / Pirate aggro / We're not coming back / Me and the farmer / Five get over excited / Johannesburg / Bow down / You better be doubtful / Build. (re-iss. Oct92 cd/c; same)			
Nov 87.	(7") (GOD 21) **BUILD. / PARIS IN FLARES**	15	-	
	(c-s+=)(10"+=/12"+=/cd-s+=) (ZGOD 21)(GOD X/T/CD 21) – Forwards and backwards / The light is always green (cheaper version).			
Apr 88.	(7") (GOD 22) **THERE IS ALWAYS SOMETHING THERE TO**			
	REMIND ME. / GET UP OFF YOUR KNEES (live)	35	-	
	(12"+=/cd-s+=) (GOD X/CD 22) – Five get over excited (live) / Johannesburg (live).			
Apr 88.	(d-lp/d-c/cd) (AGOLP/ZGOLP/AGOCD 11) **NOW THAT'S**			
	WHAT I CALL QUITE GOOD (compilation)	8	-	
	– I smell winter / Bow down / Think for a minute / There is always something there to remind me / The mighty ship / Sheep / I'll be your shelter / Five get over excited / Everybody's the same / Build / Step outside / Flag day / Happy hour / You've got a friend / He ain't heavy / Freedom / The people who grinned themselves to death / Caravan of love / The light is always green / We're not deep / Me and the farmer / Lean on me.			

—— They had already decided to split up late '87. NORMAN COOK developed several solo projects including the unashamedly commercial BEATS INTERNATIONAL. HEATON and HEMMINGWAY formed The BEAUTIFUL SOUTH.

HOUSE OF LOVE

Formed: Camberwell, London, England ... 1986 by vocalist GUY CHADWICK (ex-KINGDOMS), guitarist TERRY BICKERS (ex-COLENSO PARADE), guitarist ANDREA HEUKAMP, bassist CHRIS GROOTHIZEN and drummer PETE EVANS. Their demo tape soon caught the attention of Creation's ALAN McGEE who signed the act and released their debut single, the sublime and enigmatic 'SHINE ON'. The song was well-received although it didn't make the charts until 1990 when it went Top 20 in its remixed form. John Peel, in particular, was a great fan of the record and played it out over the course of the year. The follow-up, 'REAL ANIMAL' was rather underwhelming in comparison although a sample single for the band's PAT COLLIER (Vibrators)-produced debut album, 'CHRISTINE', picked up where 'SHINE ON' left off, all glistening guitar and darkly mysterious vocals. Sick of touring, HEUKAMP had departed the previous year, leaving the band to record the eponymous debut as a four piece. 'THE HOUSE OF LOVE' (1988) succeeded in living up to the band's early promise, a hypnotic VELVET UNDERGROUND/BYRDS/ONLY ONES hybrid that went down with The STONE ROSES' debut as one of the key releases of the decade. Touted as the future of British guitar music by the press, the band released a final single on 'Creation', 'DESTROY THE HEART', before being snapped up by the 'Polygram'-affiliated 'Fontana' label. A prolonged period of delays and problems ensued as the record company released the 'NEVER' single against the band's wishes in 1989 and the recording of the follow-up album went seriously awry. Another single, 'I DON'T KNOW WHY I LOVE YOU', lingered outside the Top 40 and the year ended with BICKERS departing on less than amicable terms to form his own act, LEVITATION. With SIMON WALKER replacing BICKERS, 'FONTANA' eventually emerged early in 1990 to a varied critical reception although it made the Top 10 and produced another minor Top 40 hit in 'BEATLES AND THE STONES'. A further round of touring followed and later that year ANDREA HEUKAMP returned to the fold. It was to be another year before any new material surfaced, 'THE GIRL WITH THE LONELIEST EYES' eventually being released in October '91. It was a classic CHADWICK composition and despite garnering critical favour again languished in the lower reaches of the charts. During the recording of the band's third album, 'BABE RAINBOW' (1992), WALKER departed, various personnel guesting on the album including WARNE LIVESAY (guitar, keyboards), CAROLE KENYON (vocals) and PANDIT DESH (tablas). Despite CHADWICK's pained deliberation in the studio, the album failed to receive resounding critical acclaim and following a similarly underwhelming attempt to revive the band's earlier sound with 'AUDIENCE WITH THE MIND' (1993), CHADWICK called it a day. He eventually resurfaced in 1997, talking to the press about the drink and drug abuse, in-fighting and poor decisions that had marked the downfall of his band, shouldering the lion's share of the blame. Having inked a new deal with 'Setanta', he issued the mellow 'THIS STRENGTH' single in November, lifted from his comeback album, 'LAZY, SOFT AND SLOW' (1998). • **Covered:** I CAN'T STAND IT (Velvet Underground) / PINK FROST (Chills) / IT'S ALL TOO MUCH (Beatles) / STRANGE BREW (Cream) / ROCK YOUR BABY (George McCrae).

Album rating: THE HOUSE OF LOVE (*8) / FONTANA (*7) / BABE RAINBOW (*6) / SPY IN THE HOUSE OF LOVE collection (*5) / AUDIENCE WITH THE MIND (*6) / Guy Chadwick: LAZY SOFT AND SLOW (*6)

GUY CHADWICK (b.21 Mar'56, Hanover, Germany) – vocals, guitar (ex-KINGDOMS) / **TERRY BICKERS** (b. 6 Sep'65) – guitar (ex-COLENSO PARADE) / **ANDREA HEUKAMP** (b.1965, Germany) – guitar, vocals / **CHRIS GROOTHUIZEN** (b. 8 Jul'65, Otahuhu, New Zealand) – bass / **PETE EVANS** (b.22 Oct'57, Swansea, Wales) – drums

		Creation	Creation
May 87.	(12"m) (CRE 043T) **SHINE ON. / LOVE / FLOW**	☐	-
Sep 87.	(12"m) (CRE 044T) **REAL ANIMAL. / PLASTIC / NOTHING**		
	TO ME		-

—— Now a quartet when ANDREA returned to Germany

Apr 88.	(7") (CRE 053) **CHRISTINE. / LONELINESS IS A GUN**	☐	-
	(12"+=) (CRE 053T) – The hill.		
May 88.	(lp/cd) (CRELP 034/+CD) <88561 8245> **THE HOUSE OF**		
	LOVE	☐	☐
	– Christine / Hope / Road / Sulphur / Man to child / Salome / Love in a car / Happy / Fisherman's tale / Touch me. (lp w/ free 7") (CREFRE 01) – CHRISTINE (demo). / SHINE ON (demo) (re-iss. Aug94 cd/c;)		
Aug 88.	(7") (CRE 057) **DESTROY THE HEART. / BLIND**	☐	-
	(12"+=) (CRE 057T) – Mr Jo.		

		Fontana	Polygram
Apr 89.	(7") (HOL 1) **NEVER. / SOFT AS FIRE**	41	-
	(12"+=/cd-s+=) (HOL 1-12/CD1) – Safe.		
Nov 89.	(7") (HOL 2) **I DON'T KNOW WHY I LOVE YOU. / SECRETS**	41	-
	(c-s+=)(12"+=) (HOLMC 2)(HOL 2-12) – I can't stand it.		
	(cd-s++=) (HOLCD 2) – Clothes.		
	(remix.12"+=) (HOLR 2-12) – Clothes / The spy.		
	(7"g-f) (HOLG 2) – ('A'side) / Love II / Clothes.		

—— **SIMON WALKER** – guitar (of DAVE HOWARD SINGERS) repl. BICKERS

Jan 90.	(7"/7"g-f) (HOL/+G 3) **SHINE ON (remix). / ALLERGY**	20	-
	(c-s+=)(12"+=) (HOLMC 3)(HOL 3-12) – Scratched inside.		
	(cd-s+=) (HOLCD 3-2) – Love III.		
	(12"+=) (HOL 3-22) – Rosalyn.		
	(cd-s++=) (HOLCD 3) – Rough.		
Feb 90.	(cd/c/lp) (842 293-2/-4/-1) **FONTANA**	8	-
	– Hannah / Shine on / Beatles and the Stones / Shake and crawl / Hedonist / I don't know why I love you / Never / Somebody's got to love you / In a room / Blind / 32nd floor / Se dest. (re-iss. Mar94; same)		

Mar 90. (7") *(HOL 4)* **BEATLES AND THE STONES. / LOVE IV** `36` `-`
(12"+=) *(HOL 4-22)* – Phone.
(12"+=) *(HOL 4-12)* – Cut the fool down / Glorify me.
(cd-s+=) *(HOLCD 4-22)* – Marble.
(cd-s+=) *(HOLCD 4)* – Phone (extended) / Soft as fire.
(7"pic-d) *(HOLP 4)* – ('A'side) / Love IV / Love V.
Nov 90. (cd/c/lp) *(846 978-2/-4/-1)* **SPY IN THE HOUSE OF LOVE**
(rare material, etc.) `49` `-`
– Safe / Marble / D song '89 / Scratched inside / Phone (full version) / Cut the fool down / Ray / Love II / Baby teen / Love III / Soft as fire / Love IV / No fire / Love V. *(re-iss. cd Aug94; same)*
—— (Sep90) added returning **ANDREA HEUKAMP** – guitar, vocals
Oct 91. (7"/c-s) *(HOL/+MC 5)* **THE GIRL WITH THE LONELIEST EYES. / PURPLE KILLER ROSE** `58` `-`
(12"+=)(cd-s+=) *(HOL 5-12)(HOLCD 5)* – Tea in the sun / Pink frost.
Apr 92. (7") *(HOL 6)* **FEEL / IT'S ALL TOO MUCH** `45` `-`
(10"+=) *(HOL 6-10)* – Let's talk about you / Strange brew.
(cd-s++=) *(HOLCD 6)* – Real animal.
—— During recording of following album, SIMON left. He was succeeded by **SIMON MAWBEY** (b.24 Dec'60, Leicester, England) – guitar + album guests **ANDREA HEUKAMP** – guitar, vox / **WARNE LIVESEY** – guitar, keyboards, etc. / **CAROL KENYON** – vocals / **PANDIT DENESH** – tablas
Jun 92. (7") *(HOL 7)* **YOU DON'T UNDERSTAND. / SWEET ANATOMY** `46` `-`
(10"+=)(cd-s+=) *(HOL 7-10)(HOLCD 7)* – Kiss the mountain / Third generation liquid song.
(cd-s+=) *(HOLCD 7-2)* – Destroy the heart / Blind / Mr Jo.
Jul 92. (cd/c/lp) *(512549-2/-4/-1)* **BABE RAINBOW** `34` `-`
– You don't understand / Crush me / Crue / High in your face / Fade away / Feel / The girl with the loneliest eyes / Burn down the world / Philly Phile / Yer eyes. *(re-iss. cd Aug94; same)*
Nov 92. (7") *(HOL 8)* **CRUSH ME. / LOVE ME** `67` `-`
(10"+=) *(HOL 8-10)* – Last edition of love / Skin 2 phase 2.
(cd-s) *(HOLCD 8)* – ('A'side) / Christine / Ladies is a gun / The hitch.
Jun 93. (cd/c/lp) *(514880-2/-4/-1)* *<3145>* **AUDIENCE WITH THE MIND** `38` `-`
– Sweet anatomy / Audience with the mind / Haloes / Erosion / Call me / Shining on / Portrait in Atlanta / Corridors / Hollow / All night long / Into the tunnel / You've got to feel. *(re-iss. Aug94 cd/c; same)*
—— CHADWICK was left with group name after the rest departed. He went solo in 1997.

– compilations, etc. –

Aug 95. (d-cd) *Fontana; (528602-2)* **HOUSE OF LOVE (FONTANA) / SPY IN THE HOUSE OF LOVE** `` `-`

GUY CHADWICK

	Setanta	Setanta

Nov 97. (cd-ep) *(SETCD 052)* **THIS STRENGTH / WASTED IN SONG / FAR AWAY** `` `-`
Feb 98. (cd) *<SETCD 053>* **LAZY SOFT AND SLOW** `` May98
– Soft and slow / You've really got a hold of me / One of these days / In her heart / Song for Gala / Mirrored in her mind / Wasted in song / Fall in love with me / This strength / Crystal love song / Close your eyes.
Apr 98. (7") *(SET 048)* **YOU'VE REALLY GOT A HOLD OF ME. / QUESTIONAIRE** `` `-`
(cd-s+=) *(SETCD 048)* – Laughter and honey / Slaughterhouse friend.

HOUSE OF PAIN

Formed: Woodland Hills, Los Angeles, California, USA ... 1990 by solo artist/rapper EVERLAST (whose 1990 eponymous 'Warners' debut featured rap don, ICE T), fellow wordsmith DANNY BOY and DJ LETHAL. Signing to 'Tommy Boy', the band hit the American Top 3 with their debut single, 'JUMP AROUND', a hip hop juggernaut of a record that employed thuggish vocal rhyming, a big 'n' bouncy bassline and screeching PUBLIC ENEMY-style noise to create one of the year's most memorable rap tunes. The self-titled debut was released soon after, hitting the US Top 20 although a follow-up single, 'SHAMROCKS AND SHENANIGANS (BOOM SHALOCK LOCK BOOM)' flopped. Once you got past the gimmicky Irish-American facade there really wasn't much substance to this lot (we thought) apart from cliched macho lyrics and gangsta posturing (degrading women, a speciality). But while their success petered out in America, 'JUMP AROUND' was re-released in the UK the following Spring, making the Top 10. This coincided with EVERLAST being arrested at New York's JFK airport, charged with illegal possession of a firearm, the rapper eventually being sentenced to four months house arrest the following year. Controversy continued to dog the group when, in a particularly nasty incident, a HOUSE OF PAIN road crew member was involved in a fight with the security crew at a gig in Manchester. Such publicity obviously did the band's hard-man image and public profile no harm, 1994's follow-up album, 'SAME AS IT EVER WAS' going Top 10 in the UK, Top 20 in America. A marked improvement on the debut, the album was more impassioned with EVERLAST railing against his perceived role as media fall guy. A third set, 'TRUTH CRUSHED TO EARTH SHALL RISE AGAIN' (1996), did little to resurrect the HOUSE OF PAIN of old and it was inevitable that the group would split; meanwhile, Murphy's beer were screeching out 'JUMP AROUND' for a TV commercial. In 1998, the reformed EVERLAST (he's now a Muslim) re-invented himself as a hip-hop troubadour and turned out his best work in years (if not ever!) with the US Top 10 set, 'WHITEY FORD SINGS THE BLUES'. The record contained at least two classic numbers, the US Top 20 hit, 'WHAT IT'S LIKE' and the man's cautionary tale of greed, 'ENDS'. • Songwriters:

Group penned, and partly produced by DJ MUGGS (Cypress Hill). Sampled HARLEM SHUFFLE (Bob Earl) / I COME TO YOU BABY (John Lee Hooker). • Trivia: DANNY BOY's preoccupation with his Irish ancestry made him mark his body with a 'Sinn Fein' tattoo, although he admitted to being more influenced by actor Mickey Rourke than the Irish political party.
Album rating: HOUSE OF PAIN (*8) / SAME AS IT EVER WAS (*7) / TRUTH CRUSHED TO EARTH SHALL RISE AGAIN (*4) / Everlast: FOREVER EVERLAST (*5) / WHITEY FORD SINGS THE BLUES (*8) / TODAY (WATCH ME SHINE) mini (*6)

EVERLAST

w/ **ICE-T** – vocals / **BILAL BASHIR** – keyboards / **CLARENCE METHENY** – synthesizer / **JOHN BREYER** – guitar / **MIKE GREG** – sax

	Warners	Warners

Sep 88. (7") *<27771>* **SYNDICATION. / BUSTIN' LOOSE** `-` `-`
Feb 90. (cd/c/lp) *<(7599 26097-2/-4/-1)>* **FOREVER EVERLAST** `-` `-`
– Syndicate soldier / Speak no evil / Syndication (remix) / What is this? / The rhythm / I got the knack / On the edge / Fuck everyone / Goodbye / Pass it on / Never missin' a beat. *(cd re-iss. Jun99 on 'Rhino'; 8122 75786-2)*
Mar 90. (7") *<22739>* **SYNDICATE SOLDIER. / NEVER MISSIN' A BEAT** `-` `-`
Jun 90. (19973) **PAY THE PRICE / I GOT THE KNACK** `-` `-`

HOUSE OF PAIN

EVERLAST (b. ERIC SCHRODY, 18 Aug'69, Valley Stream, N.Y.) – vocals / **DANNY BOY** (b. DANIEL O'CONNOR, 12 Dec'68) – vocals / **DJ LETHAL** (b. LEOR DiMANT, 18 Dec'72, Latvia) – turntable

	X.L.	Tommy Boy	

Sep 92. (7"/c-s/12") *(XLS/XLC/XLT 32)* *<526>* **JUMP AROUND / HOUSE OF PAIN ANTHEM** `32` `3` Jun92
(cd-s+=) *(XLS 32CD)* – ('A'mixes).
Nov 92. (cd/c) *(XL CD/TC 111)* *<1056>* **HOUSE OF PAIN** `73` `14` Jul92
– Salutations / Jump around / Put your head out / Top o' the morning to ya / House and the rising sun / Shamrocks and shenanigans (boom shalock lock boom) / House of pain anthem / Danny boy, Danny boy / Guess who's back / Put on your shit kickers / Come and get some of this / Life goes on / One for the road / Feel it / All my love.
Nov 92. (7"/c-s/12") *(XLS/XLC/XLT 38)* *<543>* **SHAMROCKS AND SHENANIGANS (BOOM SHALOCK LOCK BOOM). / PUT YOUR HEAD OUT** ` ` `65`
(cd-s+=) *(XLS 38CD)* – (3-'A'versions).
May 93. (c-s) *<556>* **WHO'S THE MAN? / ('A'instrumental) / PUT ON YOUR SHIT KICKERS (2 versions)** `-` `96`
May 93. (12"/c-s) *(XLC/XLT 43)* **JUMP AROUND (remix). / TOP O' THE MORNING TO YA (remix)** `8` `-`
(cd-s+=) *(XLS 43CD)* – ('A'mixes).
Oct 93. (12"/c-s) *(XLC/XLT 46)* **SHAMROCKS & SHENANIGANS. / WHO'S THE MAN** `23` `-`
(cd-s+=) *(XLS 46CD)* – ('A'mixes).
—— early in '94, EVERLAST was sentenced to 3 months – served at home (tagged), for earlier carrying a weapon. 'IT AIN'T A CRIME' sampled UNDER THE BRIDGE (Red Hot Chili Peppers).
Jul 94. (c-s) *(XSC 52)* *<623>* **ON POINT (The Beatminerz mix). / ('A'-DJ Lethal mix)** `19` `85`
(12"+=)(cd-s+=) *(XST 52)(XLS 52CD)* – Word is bond.
Jul 94. (cd/c/d-lp) *(XL CD/MC/LP 115)* *<1089>* **SAME AS IT EVER WAS** `8` `12` Jun94
– Back from the dead / I'm a swing it / All that / On point / Runnin' up on ya / Over the shit / Word is bond / Keep it comin' / Interlude / Same as it ever was / It ain't a crime / Where I'm from / Still got a lotta love / Who's the man? / On point (lethal dose remix).
Oct 94. (12"/c-s) *(XLT/XLC 55)* **IT AIN'T A CRIME (madhouse remix). / LEGEND** `37` ` `
(cd-s) *(XLS 55CD)* – ('A'side) / Word is bond (Diamond D + Darkman remixes).
Jun 95. (12"/c-s) *(XLT/XLC 61)* **OVER THERE (I DON'T CARE). / JUMP AROUND (mastermix)** `20` ` `
(cd-s+=) *(XLS 61CD1)* – Shamrocks and shenanigans / Top o' the morning to ya.
(cd-s) *(XLS 61CD2)* – ('A'side) / Runnin' up on ya (versions incl. House of Pain vs. Kerbdog).

	Tommy Boy	Tommy Boy

Sep 96. (c-s) *(TBC 7744)* **FED UP / ('A'mix)** `68` ` `
(cd-s) *(TBCD 7744)* – ('A'mix).
(12") *(12TC 7744)* – ('A'mix).
Oct 96. (cd/c/lp) *<(TB CD/C/V 1161)>* **TRUTH CRUSHED TO EARTH SHALL RISE AGAIN** ` ` `47`
– Have nots / Fed up / What's that smell / Heart full of sorrow / Earthquake / Shut the door / Pass the Jinn / No doubt / Choose your poison / X-files / Fed up / Killa rhyme klik / While I'm here.
—— when HOUSE OF PAIN broke-up, DJ LETHAL joined metallers, LIMP BIZKIT

EVERLAST

—— solo once more

	Tommy Boy	Tommy Boy

Feb 99. (c-s/cd-s) *(TBC/+D7 470)* *<radio play>* **WHAT IT'S LIKE / WHAT IT'S LIKE (clean) / WHAT IT'S LIKE (original)** `34` `13` Dec98
Mar 99. (cd/c/d-lp) *<(TB CD/C/V 1236)>* **WHITEY FORD SINGS THE BLUES** `65` `9` Sep98
– The white boy is back / Money (dollar bill) feat. SADAT X / Ends / What it's like / Get down / Sen Dog / Tired / Hot to death / Painkillers / Prince Paul / Praise the Lord / Today (watch me shine) feat. BRONX STYLE BOB / Guru / Death comes callin' / Funky beat feat. CASUAL and SADAT X / The letter / 7 years. *(cd+=)* – Next man.
Jun 99. (7") *(TB7 346)* **ENDS / ('A'live)** `47` ` `

(12"/cd-s) *(12TB/TBCD 346)* – ('A'side) / What it's like (live) / Hot to death.
Nov 99. (m-cd) *(<TBCD 2045>)* **TODAY (WATCH ME SHINE)** ☐ ☐
– Today (watch me shine) / Put your lights on (with SANTANA) / Only love can break your heart / What it's like (live) / Jump around (live) / Some nights are better than others / Hot to death (live).

Steve HOWE (see under ⇒ YES)

HOWLIN' WOLF

Born: CHESTER ARTHUR BURNETT, 10 June 1910, West Point, Mississippi, USA. One of the most important of the Southern expatriates who created the 'Chicago Sound' of the 50's, his earliest musical experience, as with many other blues artists, was singing in the local Baptist church choir. Inspired by CHARLEY PATTON (who taught him how to play guitar) and TOMMY JOHNSON, he gleaned much of his showmanship from them, although his powerful voice and "howlin'" were very much his own (further influences were to be ROBERT JOHNSON and SON HOUSE). BURNETT was a farmer to trade until his late 30's when he was introduced by IKE TURNER to SAM PHILLIPS of Sun Records. PHILLIPS, in turn, made deals with 'Modern' Records in California, 'Chess' Records in Chicago issuing WOLF's other recordings. His first single, 'MOANING AT MIDNIGHT', was released by both companies concurrently, although 'Chess' avoided split sales by promoting the b-side, 'HOW MANY MORE YEARS'. This track was by far the heaviest blues song (in rock terms) released in America to date, both versions of the song reaching the R&B Top 20. After much wrangling between the two record companies, he decided to sign exclusively for 'Chess' in 1952, subsequently moving to Chicago and leaving his band behind in the process. The records never sold well after his initial success, although 'Chess' were making plenty of money through CHUCK BERRY and BO DIDDLEY and could afford to keep the WOLF in business to maintain their core ghetto audience. He eventually went back "down home" to pick up some Delta musicians, including a teenage guitarist going by the name of HUBERT SUMLIN. Despite initial conflict, including one incident in which they punched out each other's front teeth, SUMLIN virtually became WOLF's adopted son, remaining by his side for the rest of his career. During the next 10 years, he recorded most of his classic repertoire, including his own compositions 'SMOKESTACK LIGHTNING', 'NO PLACE TO GO', 'SITTING ON TOP OF THE WORLD', 'EVIL', 'KILLING FLOOR', 'I AIN'T SUPERSTITIOUS' and 'WHO'S BEEN TALKING', plus the WILLIE DIXON songs, 'SPOONFUL', 'DOWN IN THE BOTTOM', 'BACK DOOR MAN', 'THE RED ROOSTER' and 'WANG DANG DOODLE'. HOWLIN' WOLF came to Britain in 1961, 'Pye' releasing 'LITTLE BABY' as his first single, although it failed to chart. In 1963, he was recorded live with OTIS SPANN, BUDDY GUY and MUDDY WATERS, the performance being released the following year on the album, 'FOLK FESTIVAL OF THE BLUES'. WOLF was allegedly not easy to work with, being described by some of his associates as "bone stupid", illiterate and slow witted. He was also chronically suspicious that everyone was out to cheat him and convinced that MUDDY WATERS was his most deadly enemy, even though MUDDY had helped him get work when he first came to Chicago. WILLIE DIXON, who wrote and arranged much of WOLF's 'Chess' material, claimed that the only way he could get the WOLF to record a song was to tell him that MUDDY wanted it! His fans in Britain included The ROLLING STONES and The YARDBIRDS, these groups publicising his work both in Europe and in white America, leading to his music becoming a significant influence on the emerging rock music of the day. Many of his songs were covered by a number of diverse artists, although only CAPTAIN BEEFHEART came close to the raucous aggressiveness of the originals. His only pop hit, the magnificent 'SMOKESTACK LIGHTNING', arrived in June 1964, eight years after its original US release. In 1967 he recorded the album, 'SUPER SUPER BLUES BAND' with BO DIDDLEY and MUDDY WATERS, although disappointingly, it only contained reworkings of familiar songs rather than new material. 1969 was a year of dramatic contrasts for him; 'Chess' and WOLF were impressed by the success of MUDDY WATERS' 'ELECTRIC MUD' album and they decided to release the similarly conceived psychedelic opus, 'THE HOWLIN' WOLF ALBUM'. The record was an unmitigated disaster, WOLF himself even commenting that it was "dog-shit". He was back on familiar ground with 'THE LONDON SESSIONS' album, recorded with, among others, ERIC CLAPTON, STEVE WINWOOD, BILL WYMAN and CHARLIE WATTS. During the recording of the album he attempted to teach the correct beat of 'RED ROOSTER' to the musicians (The STONES already having had a worldwide success with the track) by playing bottleneck guitar. He later suffered a heart attack and then a kidney ailment which left him permanently dependent on dialysis. As a result, WOLF did little between 1969 and 1976, although he did have one final bellow at the world with the extraordinary, 'COON ON THE MOON' from the 1971 album, 'MESSAGE TO THE YOUNG'. The album remains unavailable while the song is yet to make it onto any compilation (probably down to our politically correct times). HOWLIN' WOLF died on the 10th of January 1976 in Hines, Illinois, USA and although he was not the first bluesman to call himself HOWLIN' WOLF (that distinction belongs to J.T. SMITH), he will be the only HOWLIN' WOLF to everyone involved with blues music. Delta bluesman or Chicago titan – who knows?, but whatever you think, there's not been anything like him. The blues can boast better guitarists, better composers, better harmonica players and yes, better singers, but no one has produced a better recorded voice or a

more compelling human presence. • **Rock/pop artists to cover his material:** SPOONFUL (Cream) / I AIN'T SUPERSTITIOUS (Savoy Brown) + (Jeff Beck) / BACK DOOR MAN (Doors) / HOW MANY MORE YEARS? (Little Feat) / KILLIN' FLOOR (Electric Flag) / etc.

Album rating (selective): MOANIN' IN THE MOONLIGHT (*8) / HOWLIN' WOLF aka THE ROCKING CHAIR (*7) / THE REAL FOLK BLUES (*8) / EVIL (*6) / MORE REAL FOLK BLUES (*7) / THE BACK DOOR WOLF (*7) / THE GENUINE ARTICLE – THE BEST OF.. compilation (*8)

HOWLIN' WOLF – vocals, guitar with **HUBERT SUMLIN + WILLIE JOHNSON** – guitar / **WILLIE STEZZ** – drums / **IKE TURNER** – piano

		not iss.	R.P.M.
Oct 51.	(78) *<333>* **MOANIN' AT MIDNIGHT. / RIDIN' IN THE MOONLIGHT**	–	☐
Nov 51.	(78; as HOWLING WOLF) *<340>* **CRYING AT DAYBREAK. / PASSING BY BLUES**	–	☐
Dec 51.	(78; as THE HOWLING WOLF) *<347>* **MY BABY STOLE OFF. / I WANT YOUR PICTURE**	–	☐
		London	Chess
Dec 51.	(78) *<1479>* **MOANIN' AT MIDNIGHT. / HOW MANY MORE YEARS**	–	☐
Feb 52.	(78; as THE HOWLING WOLF) *<1497>* **THE WOLF IS AT YOUR DOOR (HOWLIN' FOR MY BABY). / HOWLIN' WOLF BOOGIE**	–	☐
Mar 52.	(78; as THE HOWLING WOLF) *<1510>* **GETTING OLD AND GREY. / MR. HIGHWAY MAN**	–	☐
Jun 52.	(78; THE HOWLING WOLF) *<1515>* **SADDLE MY PONY. / WORRIED ALL THE TIME**	–	☐
Nov 52.	(78) *<1528>* **OH! RED. / MY LAST AFFAIR**	–	☐
Feb 53.	(78) **ALL NIGHT BOOGIE (ALL NIGHT LONG). / I LOVE MY BABY**	–	☐

—— now w / **WILLIE DIXON** – bass / **OTIS SPANN** – piano / **LEE COOPER** – guitar / **FRED BELOW** – drums

May 54.	(78) *<1566>* **ROCKING DADDY. / NO PLACE TO GO (YOU GONNA WRECK MY LIFE)**	–	☐
Jul 54.	(78) *<1575>* **BABY HOW LONG. / EVIL IS GOING ON**	–	☐
Dec 54.	(78) *<1584>* **I'LL BE AROUND. / FORTY FOUR**	–	☐
May 55.	(78; THE HOWLING WOLF) *<1593>* **WHO WILL BE NEXT. / I HAVE A LITTLE GIRL**	–	☐
Jul 55.	(78) *<1607>* **COME TO ME BABY. / DON'T MESS WITH MY BABY**	–	☐

—— now w / **HOSEA LEE KENNARD** – piano / **HUBERT SUMLIN + WILLIE JOHNSON** – guitar / **EARL PHILLIPS** – drums

Mar 56.	(78) *<1618>* **SMOKESTACK LIGHTNIN'. / YOU CAN'T BE BEAT**	–	☐
Sep 56.	(78) *<1632>* **I ASKED FOR WATER (SHE GAVE ME GASOLINE). / SO GLAD**	–	☐
Dec 56.	(7"ep) *(REU 1072)* **RHYTHM & BLUES WITH HOWLIN' WOLF**	☐	–
	– Smokestack lightnin' / You can't be beat / Don't mess with me baby / Come to me baby.		
Mar 57.	(78) *<1648>* **GOING BACK HOME. / MY LIFE**	–	☐
Jul 57.	(78) *<1668>* **NATURE. / SOMEBODY IN MY HOME**	–	☐
Feb 58.	(78) *<1679>* **SITTIN' ON TOP OF THE WORLD. / POOR BOY**	–	☐
May 58.	(78) *<1695>* **MOANIN' FOR MY BABY (MIDNIGHT BLUES). / I DIDN'T KNOW**	–	☐
Oct 58.	(78) *<1712>* **I'M LEAVING YOU. / CHANGE MY WAY**	–	☐
Nov 58.	(78) *<1726>* **I BETTER GO NOW. / HOWLIN' BLUES**	–	☐

—— added **WILLIE DIXON** – bass / **OTIS SPANN** – piano / **EARL PHILLIPS** – drums

—— now used various personnel

Aug 59.	(7") *<1735>* **MR. AIRPLANE MAN. / I'VE BEEN ABUSED**	–	☐
Nov 59.	(7") *<1744>* **THE NATCHEZ BURNING. / YOU GONNA WRECK MY LIFE**	–	☐
Mar 60.	(7") *<1750>* **WHO'S BEEN TALKING. / TELL ME**	–	☐
Jul 60.	(7") *<1762>* **HOWLIN' FOR MY BABY. / SPOONFUL**	–	☐
Nov 60.	(7") *<1777>* **WANG-DANG-DOODLE. / BACK DOOR MAN**	–	☐
		Pye Int.	Chess
Sep 61.	(7") *(7N 25101) <1793>* **LITTLE BABY. / DOWN IN THE BOTTOM**	☐	☐
Nov 61.	(7") *<1804>* **THE RED ROOSTER. / SHAKE FOR ME**	☐	☐
Feb 62.	(7") *<1813>* **GOING DOWN SLOW. / YOU'LL BE MINE**	☐	☐
Nov 62.	(7") *<1844>* **MAMA'S BABY. / DO THE DO**	☐	☐
Sep 63.	(7") *<1870>* **THREE HUNDRED POUNDS OF JOY. / BUILT FOR COMFORT**	☐	☐
Apr 63.	(7") *(7N 25192) <1823>* **JUST LIKE I TREAT YOU. / I AIN'T SUPERSTITIOUS**	☐	Apr62
Nov 63.	(7"ep) *(NEP 44015)* **SMOKESTACK LIGHTNIN'**	☐	
	– Smokestack lightnin' / Howling for my baby / Going down slow / You'll be mine.		
May 64.	(7") *(7N 25244)* **SMOKESTACK LIGHTNIN'. / GOING DOWN SLOW**	42	–
	(re-iss. Jul85 on 'Chess'; CHESS 4008)		
Oct 64.	(7"ep) *(NEP 44032)* **TELL ME**	☐	
	– Tell me / Who's been talking / Shake for me / Back door man.		
Oct 64.	(7") *(7N 25269)* **LITTLE BABY. / TAIL DRAGGER**	☐	–
Dec 64.	(7") *(7N 25283) <1911>* **LOVE ME DARLING. / MY COUNTRY SUGAR MAMA**	☐	☐
		Chess	Chess
Feb 65.	(lp) *(CRL 4006) <1434>* **MOANIN' IN THE MOONLIGHT** (compilation 50's)	☐	☐
	– Moanin' in the moonlight / How many more years / Smokestack lightnin' / Baby how long / No place to go / Evil / I'm leaving you / Moanin' for my baby / I ask for water / Forty-four / Somebody in my home. *(re-iss. Jan67 on 'Marble Arch'; MAL 665) (re-iss. Apr87 on 'Charly')*		

Apr 65. (7") (CRS 8010) <1923> **KILLING FLOOR. / LOUISE**

JUn 65. (lp) (CRL 4508) **POOR BOY**
– Cause of it all / The killing floor / Little red rooster / Built for comfort / Commit a crime / Do the do / Highway 49 / Worried about you / Poor boy / Wang dang doodle.

Jun 65. (7") (CRS 8016) <1928> **OOH BABY. / TELL ME WHAT I'VE DONE**

Aug 65. (7") <1945> **I WALKED FROM DALLAS / DON'T LAUGH AT ME**

1966. (lp) <1502> **REAL FOLK BLUES**
– Killing floor / Lousie / Poor boy / Sittin' on top of the world / Nature / My country / Sugar mama / Tail draggerr / 300 lb. of joy / Natchez burning / Built for comfort / Ooh baby, hold me / Tell me what I've done. (UK cd-iss. Feb90 on 'M.C.A.')

Jun 66. (7") <1968> **NEW CRAWLIN' KING SNAKE. / MY MIND IS RAMBLIN'**

1966. (7"ep) (CRE 6017) **REAL FOLK BLUES**
– Three hundred pounds of joy / My country sugar mama / Oh baby hold me / Louise.

1967. (lp) <1512> **MORE REAL FOLK BLUES** (compilation 1952-56)

Aug 67. (7") <2009> **I HAD A DREAM. / POP IT TO ME**

May 68. (lp; HOWLIN' WOLF, MUDDY WATERS & BO DIDDLEY) (CRL 4537) <4537> **SUPER SUPER BLUES BAND**
– Long distance call / Goin' down slow / You don't love me / I'm a man / Who do you love / The red rooster / Diddley daddy / I just want to make love to you.

	Chess	Cadet
Feb 69. (7") (CRS 8097) <7013> **EVIL. / TAIL DRAGGER**		-

Apr 69. (lp) (CRLS 4543) **THE NEW ALBUM**
– Spoonful / Tail dragger / Smokestack lightning / Moanin' at midnight / Built for comfort / The red rooster / Evil / Down in the bottom / Three hundred pounds of joy / Back door man.

	Chess	Chess
Aug 69. (7") <2081> **MARY SUE. / HARD LUCK**		-
	Syndicate	Syndicate

May 70. (lp) **GOING BACK HOME** (compilation 1948-58)
– Saddle my pony / Worried all the time / Howlin' Wolf boogie / The Wolf is at your door / On red / My last affair / Mr. Highway man / Gettin' old and grey / Come to me baby / Don't mess with me baby / So glad / My life / Going back home / I don't know / Howlin' blues / I better go now. (re-iss. Sep82)

—— In June '70, he and LITTLE WALTER collaborated with MUDDY WATERS on the album, 'WE THREE KINGS' (Syndicate Chapter; SC 005)

Nov 70. (7") <2108> **IF I WERE A BIRD. / JUST AS LONG**

Feb 71. (7") <2118> **DO THE DO. / THE RED ROOSTER**

1971. (lp) (6310 108) **MESSAGE TO THE YOUNG**
– If I were a bird / I smell a rat / Miss James / Message to the young / She's looking good / Just as long / Romance without finance / Turn me on.

—— (Below lp, featured **BILL WYMAN & CHARLIE WATTS** (of The ROLLING STONES) / **ERIC CLAPTON** – guitar / **STEVE WINWOOD** – keyboards / **RINGO STARR** – drums

	Rolling Stones	Chess
Sep 71. (lp) (COC 49101) <60008> **THE LONDON SESSIONS**		79 Aug71

– I ain't superstitious / Poor boy / The red rooster / Worried about my baby / Do the do / Built for comfort / Sittin' on top of the world / Highway 49 / What a woman / Who's been talkin' / Rockin' daddy / Wang dang doodle. (re-iss. Apr82) (re-iss. Dec85 on 'Charly', cd-iss. Jan91)

1972. (lp) <50015> **LIVE & COOKIN' AT ALICES REVISITED** (live)
– When I laid down I was troubled / I don't know / Mean mistreater / I had a dream / Call me The Wolf / Don't laugh at me / Just passing by / Sitting on top of the world.

1973. (7") <2145> **BACK DOOR WOLF. / COME ON THE MOON**

1973. (lp) <50045> **THE BACK DOOR WOLF**
– Movin' / Coon on the Moon / Speak now woman / Trying to fight you / Stop using me / Leave here walking / The back door wolf / You turn slick on me / Watergate blues / Can't stay here. (UK-iss. +c.1989)

1972. (d-lp) <60016> **AKA CHESTER BURNETT** (compilation 1951-65)

1974. (lp) <60026> **LONDON REVISITED**
(re-iss. Jul93 on 'Charly')

—— earlier in the 70's, he suffered two heart attacks and subsequently a car crash in which he acrued kidney damage. After a concert at Chicago Amphitheater Nov'75 with B.B. KING, BOBBY BLAND and LITTLE MILTON, he was re-hospitalized and died there on the 10th January '76 following brain surgery.

– compilations, etc. –

1966. (lp) Ember; US= United; (EMB 3370) **BIG CITY BLUES** (rec. 1950)

1965. (lp) Chess; **HOWLIN' WOLF**

1974. (lp) Chess; <1540> **EVIL** (rec. 1951-59)

1977. (lp) Chess; <CHV 418> **CHANGIN' MY WAY**

1977. (lp) Chess; (2ACBM 201) **BLUES MASTERS**

Jun 81. (d-lp) Chess; (CXMD 4004) **CHESS MASTERS**

Apr 82. (d-lp) Chess; (CXMD 4007) **CHESS MASTERS VOL.2**

May 83. (lp) Chess; (CXMD 4014) **CHESS MASTERS VOL.3**

Dec 88. (lp/c) Chess; (CHX L/T 102) **CHESS MASTERS VOL.4 – MOANIN' AND HOWLIN'**

Jun 76. (lp) Charly; (CR 30102) **SAM'S BLUES (w / LITTLE MILTON)**

1977. (lp) Charly; (CR 30134) **LEGENDARY SUN PERFORMERS**

Aug 86. (lp/c) Charly; (GCH/+K7 8009) **HIS GREATEST HITS VOL.1**

Jan 87. (lp/c) Charly; **OFF THE RECORD – THE ROCKINGHAM ALBUM**

Apr 87. (cd) Charly; (CDCHARLY 66) **HOWLIN' FOR MY BABY**

Nov 89. (c-box/cd-box/lp-box) Charly; (TC/CD BOX 258/BOX 258)) **THE HOWLIN' WOLF BOX SET**

Feb 93. (cd) Charly; (CDCD 1041) **KILLING FLOOR**

Jul 93. (7xcd-box) Charly; (CDREDBOX 7) **THE COMPLETE RECORDINGS 1951-1969**

Aug 81. (lp) Blues Ball; **HEART LIKE A RAILROAD STEEL**

Aug 81. (lp) Blues Ball; (2002) **CAN'T PUT ME OUT**

May 82. (lp) Ace-Chiswick; (CH 52) **RIDIN' IN THE MOONLIGHT**

Jan 92. (cd) Ace; **HOWLIN' WOLF RIDES AGAIN**

Apr 84. (lp) Blue Moon; (CL 32683) **I AM THE WOLF**

Nov 84. (lp) Blue Moon; (BMLP 1019) **ALL NIGHT BOOGIE**

Nov 84. (lp/c) Astan; (2/4 0019) **GOLDEN CLASSICS**

Nov 85. (lp/c) Deja Vu; (DV LP/MC 2032) **COLLECTION: 20 BLUES GREATS**
– Little red rooster / My baby walked off / Killing floor / My country sugar mama / My life / Going back home / Louise / Highway 49 / Hold on to your money / Built for comfort / Ain't superstitious / My last affair / Dorothy Mae / Commit a crime / Moanin' at midnight / Wang dang doodle / Ridin' in the moonlight / Everybody's in the mood / The wolf is at your door / I better go now. (cd-iss. Aug87)

Apr 93. (cd/c) Deja Vu; **THE GOLD COLLECTION**

1988. (lp/c) Joker; (SM/MC 3990) **RED ROOSTER**
(cd-iss. Aug95 on 'Imp')

1988. (lp) Sundown; (CG 70907) **LIVE IN EUROPE – 1964 (live)**

Apr 89. (lp) Rounder; (SS 28) **CADILLAC DADDY (Memphis rec.)**

Apr 89. (cd) Bear Family; (BCD 15460) **MEMPHIS DAYS (THE DEFINITIVE COLLECTION, VOL.1)**

Jan 91. (cd) Bear Family; (BCD 15500) **MEMPHIS DAYS (THE DEFINITIVE COLLECTION, VOL.2)**

1989. (lp) Wolf; (WOLF 120000) **LIVE IN CHICAGO '75 (live)**

Jul 91. (cd) Fan Club; **LIVE IN CAMBRIDGE MA., 1966 (live)**

Jan 92. (d-cd) Fan Club; **THE WOLF IS AT YOUR DOOR**

Feb 93. (cd/c) Roots; (RTS 3/4 3043) **GOING DOWN SLOW VOLUME 4**

Feb 93. (cd/c) Roots; (RTS 3/4 3042) **THE WOLF IS AT YOUR DOOR VOLUME 3**

Mar 93. (5xcd-box) Roots; **GOING DOWN SLOW**

May 94. (cd) Charly; (CDRB 2) **SPOONFUL**

May 94. (c-s/cd-s) M.C.A.; **SMOKESTACK LIGHTNIN'. / ?**

Jun 94. (cd) M.C.A.; (MCD 11073) **THE GENUINE ARTICLE**

Jul 95. (d-cd) Charly; (VBCD 303) **THE VERY BEST OF HOWLIN' WOLF**

Alan HULL (see under ⇒ LINDISFARNE)

HUMAN LEAGUE

Formed: Sheffield, England ... Autumn 1977 by computer operators MARTYN WARE and IAN CRAIG-MARSH. As The FUTURE, with vocalist ADI NEWTON, they recruited former hospital porter PHIL OAKEY, who soon replaced ADI (later to CLOCKDVA). Now as HUMAN LEAGUE, the trio recorded a demo, enthusiastically accepted by Edinburgh-based indie 'Fast', run by Bob Last. Their debut 45, 'BEING BOILED', became NME single of the week in mid-78. They added ADRIAN WRIGHT on visuals and synths, and after a dire instrumental EP 'THE DIGNITY OF LABOUR', they signed to 'Virgin' in Apr'79. Their first 45 for the label, 'I DON'T DEPEND ON YOU', was credited to The MEN, but their credibility was restored later that year when 'EMPIRE STATE HUMAN', nearly gave them a hit. This was duly followed by a debut album, 'REPRODUCTION', which failed to build on their early promise. In Spring 1980, they went into the UK Top 60 with double-7" EP, 'HOLIDAY '80', and Top 20 with the album, 'TRAVELOGUE'. In October '80, OAKEY and WRIGHT brought in teenage girls JOANNE and SUZANNE to replace WARE and CRAIG-MARSH who left to form HEAVEN 17. Twelve months later, with new additions IAN BURDEN and JO CALLIS, they were at No.1 with both the 'DARE' album, and 'DON'T YOU WANT ME' single, which also peaked at the top in the States. By now, the experimental industrial leanings of their early work had given way to a chart-dominating new romantic/pop synth sound which made 'DARE' one of the definitive albums of the era. They were also responsible, or at least OAKEY was, for perhaps the worst 80's haircut of them all (yes, even worse than the mullet), the accident-with-a-pair-of-garden-shears number that featured one side long and, erm ... one side short! Barnet's aside, the hits were consistent ('KEEP FEELING FASCINATION', 'MIRROR MAN', 'THE LEBANON'), if not exactly prolific and, like many similar 80's acts, by the time they got around to releasing a follow-up set, the fuss had died down. Nevertheless, 'HYSTERIA' (1984) made the UK Top 3, while OAKEY teamed up with disco veteran, GIORGIO MORODER, for the soppy but brilliant 'TOGETHER IN ELECTRIC DREAMS', another massive Top 5 hit in Autumn '84 (the pair subsequently recorded a full length album together, 'CHROME'). Produced by the soul/R&B team of Jimmy Jam and Terry Lewis, 'CRASH' (1986) didn't do the band any favours, although it did spawn the melancholy 'HUMAN', a surprise US No.1 and their biggest hit single since the early 80's heyday. Though a 1988 greatest hits album kept the band's profile high, poor sales of 'ROMANTIC' (1990) saw the end of their tenure with 'Virgin', and it looked like permanent relegation was imminent. A new deal with 'East West' and a 1994 Top 10 album, 'OCTOPUS', suggested otherwise, things coming full circle when a remixed version of 'DON'T YOU WANT ME' made the Top 20 in late '95. Conspicuous only by his absence, PHIL OAKEY has since provided some vocals (alongside 60's crooner, TONY CHRISTIE) on the ALL SEEING I album in '99. • **Songwriters:** WARE and CRAIG-MARSH before their departure, and OAKEY and WRIGHT on all since early 80's. The 90's featured OAKEY composing alongside new member NEIL SUTTON. Covered:- YOU'VE LOST THAT LOVIN' FEELIN' (Righteous Brothers) / ROCK'N'ROLL (Gary Glitter) / NIGHTCLUBBIN' (Iggy Pop) / ONLY AFTER DARK (Mick Ronson).

Album rating: REPRODUCTION (*5) / TRAVELOGUE (*5) / DARE (*8) / LOVE AND DANCING mixes set (*4) / HYSTERIA (*5) / CRASH (*5) / GREATEST HITS compilation (*8) / ROMANTIC? (*4) / OCTOPUS (*6) / Phil Oakey & Giorgio Moroder: CHROME (*4)

PHIL OAKEY (b. 2 Oct'55) – vocals / **IAN CRAIG-MARSH** (b.19 Nov'56) – synthesizers / **MARTYN WARE** (b.19 May'56) – synthesizers

		Fast	not iss.
Jun 78.	(7") *(FAST 4)* **BEING BOILED. / CIRCUS OF DEATH**	☐	–
	(re-iss. Jan82 reached No.6 UK; same)		

—— added **ADRIAN WRIGHT** (b.30 Dec'56) – synthesizers, visuals

Apr 79.	(12"ep) *(FAST 10)* **THE DIGNITY OF LABOUR**		–
	– (part 1 / part 2 / part 3 / part 4) *(contains free spoken word flexi; VF 1)*		

		Virgin	A&M
Jul 79.	(7"/12"; as The MEN) *(VS 269/+12)* **I DON'T DEPEND ON YOU. / CRUEL** (instrumental)	☐	–
Sep 79.	(7") *(VS 294)* **EMPIRE STATE HUMAN. / INTRODUCING**	☐	–
Oct 79.	(lp/c) *(V/TCV 2133)* **REPRODUCTION**	☐	–
	– Almost medieval / Circus of death / The path of least resistance / Blind youth / The word before last / Empire state human / Morale / You've lost that lovin' feelin' / Austerity / Girl one / Zero as a limit. *(re-pro.Aug81, hit UK No.49) (re-iss. Jun88 lp/c; OVED/+C 114) (cd-iss. Dec88; CDV 2133)*		
Apr 80.	(d7"ep) *(SV 105)* **HOLIDAY '80**	56	–
	– Rock'n'roll / Being boiled / Nightclubbing / Dancevision. *(re-iss. Nov81 as 12"ep+=)* – Marianne. *(hit UK No.46)*		
May 80.	(lp/c) *(T/TCV 2160)* **TRAVELOGUE**	16	–
	– The black hit of space / Only after dark / Life kills / Dreams of leaving / Toyota city / Crow and a baby / The touchables / Gordon's Gin / Being boiled / WXJL tonight. *(re-iss. Jun88 lp/c; OVED/+C 115)*		
Jun 80.	(7") *(VS 351)* **ONLY AFTER DARK. / TOYOTA CITY**	62	–
	(free 7" w/) – EMPIRE STATE HUMAN. / INTRODUCING		

—— **JO CATHERALL** (b.18 Sep'62) **& SUSANNE SULLEY** (b.22 Mar'63) – b.vocals repl. WARE and MARSH who formed HEAVEN 17. also added **IAN BURDEN** (b.24 Dec'57) – bass, synthesizers

Feb 81.	(7") *(VS 395)* **BOYS AND GIRLS. / TOM BAKER**	48	–
Apr 81.	(7"/ext.12"; as HUMAN LEAGUE RED) *(VS 416/+12)* **THE SOUND OF THE CROWD. / ('A'instrumental)**	12	–

—— added **JO CALLIS** (b. 2 May'55, Glasgow, Scotland) – guitar (ex-REZILLOS, ex-BOOTS FOR DANCING, ex-SHAKE)

Jul 81.	(7"; as HUMAN LEAGUE RED) *(VS 435)* **LOVE ACTION (I BELIEVE IN LOVE). / HARD TIMES**	3	Apr82
	(12"+=) *(VS 435-12)* – ('A'&'B'instrumental).		
	(cd-ep.iss.Jun88; – the four 12"tracks)		
Oct 81.	(7"; as HUMAN LEAGUE BLUE) *(VS 453)* **OPEN YOUR HEART. / NON-STOP**	6	–
	(12"+=) *(VS 453-12)* – ('A'instrumental) / ('B'instrumental).		
Oct 81.	(lp/pic-lp/c) *(T/TP/TCV 2192)* *<4892>* **DARE**	1	3 Feb82
	– Things that dreams are made of / Open your heart / The sound of the crowd / Darkness / Do or die / Get Carter / I am the law / Seconds / Love action (I believe in love) / Don't you want me. *(cd-iss. 1983; OVED 177) (re-iss. Sep90 lp/c; OVED/+C 333)*		
Nov 81.	(7"; as HUMAN LEAGUE 100) *(VS 466)* *<2397>* **DON'T YOU WANT ME. / SECONDS**	1	1 Feb82
	(2"+=) *(VS 466-12)* – ('A'extended).		
Jul 82.	(lp/c; as LEAGUE UNLIMITED ORCHESTRA) *(OVED/OVEC 6)* *<3209>* **LOVE AND DANCING**	6	Sep92
	– (instrumental versions of "DARE" except;) / Get Carter / Darkness. *(cd-iss. Jan86; CDOVED 6)*		
Aug 82.	(7") **THINGS THAT DREAMS ARE MADE OF. / ('A' instrumental)**	–	
Oct 82.	(7"; as LEAGUE UNLIMITED ORCHESTRA) **DON'T YOU WANT ME. / (part 2)**	–	
Nov 82.	(7"/7"pic-d) *(VS/+Y 522)* **MIRROR MAN. / (YOU REMIND ME OF) GOLD**	2	–
	(ext.12"+=) *(VS 522-12)* – Gold (instrumental).		
Apr 83.	(7"; as HUMAN LEAGUE RED) *(VS 569)* *<2547>* **(KEEP FEELING) FASCINATION. / TOTAL PANIC**	2	8 May83
	(ext.12"+=) *(VS 569-12)* – ('A'improvisation).		
Jul 83.	(m-lp) *<12501>* **FASCINATION** (import, recent hits)	–	22
Sep 83.	(7") *<2587>* **MIRROR MAN. / NON-STOP**	–	30
Apr 84.	(7") *(VS 672)* *<2641>* **THE LEBANON. / THIRTEEN**	11	64 Jul84
	(ext.12"+=) *(VS 672-12)* – ('A'instrumental).		
May 84.	(lp/c/cd) *(T/TCV/CDV 2315)* *<4923>* **HYSTERIA**	3	62
	– I'm coming back / I love you too much / Rock me again and again and again and again and again / Louise / The Lebanon / Betrayed / The sign / So hurt / Life on your own / Don't you know I want you. *(re-iss. Feb88 lp/c; OVED/+C 177)*		
Jun 84.	(7") *(VS 688)* **LIFE ON YOUR OWN. / THE WORLD TONIGHT**	16	–
	(12"+=) *(VS 688-12)* – ('A'extended).		
Aug 84.	(7") **DON'T YOU KNOW I WANT TO. / THIRTEEN**	–	
Oct 84.	(7"/7"pic-d)(12") *(VS/+Y 723)(VS 723-12)* **LOUISE. / THE SIGN**	13	–
Oct 84.	(7") **LOUISE. / THE WORLD TONIGHT**	–	

—— Trimmed down to main trio of **PHIL, SUSANNE, JOANNE** plus **ADRIAN / JIM RUSSELL** – synthesizer repl. BURDEN and CALLIS

Aug 86.	(7") *(VS 880)* *<2861>* **HUMAN. / ('A'instrumental)**	8	1
	(ext.12"+=) *(VS 880-12)* – ('A'acappella).		
Sep 86.	(lp/c/cd) *(V/TCV/CDV 2391)* *<5129>* **CRASH**	7	24
	– Money / Swang / Human / Jam / Are you ever coming back? / I need your loving / Party / Love on the run / The real thing / Love is all that matters.		
Nov 86.	(7") *(VS 900)* **I NEED YOUR LOVING. / ('A'instrumental)**	72	–
	(ext.12"+=) *(VS 900-12)* – ('A'dub).		
Nov 86.	(7") *<2893>* **I NEED YOUR LOVING. / ARE YOU EVER COMING BACK**	–	44
Jan 87.	(7") **LOVE IS ALL THAT MATTERS. / ('A'instrumental)**	–	
Apr 87.	(7") **ARE YOU EVER COMING BACK. / JAM**	–	
Oct 88.	(7") *(VS 1025)* **LOVE IS ALL THAT MATTERS. / I LOVE YOU TOO MUCH**	41	
	('B'dub.12"+=/'B'dub.cd-s+=) *(VS T/CD 1025)* – ('A'extended).		
Nov 88.	(lp/c/cd/pic-cd) *(HL TV/MC/CD/CDP 1)* **GREATEST HITS** (compilation)	3	
	– Mirror man / (Keep feeling) Fascination / The sound of the crowd / The Lebanon /		

Human / Together in electric dreams (PHIL OAKEY & GIORGIO MORODER) / Don't you want me? / Being boiled (re-boiled) / Love action (I believe in love) / Louise / Open your heart / Love is all that matters / Life on your own. *(re-iss. Nov95 cd/c;)*

—— The basic trio, added **RUSSELL BENNETT** – guitar / **NEIL SUTTON** – keyboards

Aug 90.	(7"/c-s) *(VS/+C 1262)* *<1520>* **HEART LIKE A WHEEL. / REBOUND**	29	32 Sep90
	(12"+=) *(VST 1262)* – ('A'extended).		
	(cd-s+=) *(VSCDT 1262)* – ('A'remix).		
	(cd-s+=) *(VSCDX 1262)* – A doorway (dub mix).		
Sep 90.	(cd/c/lp) *(V/TCV/CDV 2624)* **ROMANTIC?**	24	
	– Kiss the future / A doorway / Heart like a wheel / Men are dreamers / Mister Moon and Mister Sun / Soundtrack to a generation / Rebound / The stars are going out / Let's get together again / Get it right this time.		
Nov 90.	(7"/c-s) *(VS/+C 1303)* **SOUNDTRACK TO A GENERATION. / ('A'instrumental)**		
	(12"+=) *(VST 1303)* – ('A'-Orbit mix).		
	(cd-s+=) *(VSCDT 1303)* – ('A'-Pan Belgian mix).		
	(cd-s) *(VSCDX 1303)* – ('A'-Pan Belguin dub) / ('A'-808 instrumental mix) / ('A'-Dave Dodd's mix) / ('A'-acapella).		

		East West	East West
Dec 94.	(c-s) *(YZ 882C)* *<64443>* **TELL ME WHEN. / ('A'mix 1)**	6	31 Mar95
	(cd-s+=) *(YZ 882CD1)* – Kimi ni mune kyun / The bus to Crookes.		
	(12"/cd-s) *(YZ 882 T/CD2)* – ('A'side) / ('A'-Overworld mix) / ('A'-Red Jerry mix) / ('A'-Strictly blind dub mix).		
Jan 95.	(cd/c/lp) *(4509 98750-2/-4/-1)* **OCTOPUS**	6	
	– Tell me when / These are the days / One man in my heart / Words / Filling up with Heaven / House full of nothing / John Cleese; is he funny? / Never again / Cruel young lover.		
Mar 95.	(c-s/cd-s) *(YZ 904 C/CD1)* **ONE MAN IN MY HEART / THESE ARE THE DAYS** (Ba ba mix)	13	
	(cd-s+=) *(YZ 904CD2)* – These are the days (sonic radiation) / ('A'version).		
	(12") *(YZ 904T)* – ('B'side) / ('B'-Symphone Ba Ba mix) / ('B'instrumental) / ('A'-T.O.E.C. unplugged).		
Jun 95.	(c-s/cd-s) *(YZ 944 C/CD1)* **FILLING UP WITH HEAVEN / JOHN CLEESE, IS HE FUNNY?**	36	
	(cd-s) *(YZ 944CD2)* – ('A'side) / ('A'-Hardfloor mix) / ('A'-Neil McLellen mix).		
Jan 96.	(c-s) *(EW 020C)* **STAY WITH ME TONIGHT / ('A'mix)**	40	
	(cd-s) *(EW 020CD)* – ('A'mixes).		

– compilations, etc. –

Oct 90.	(3xcd-box) *Virgin; (TPAK 3)* **DARE / HYSTERIA / CRASH**	☐	–
Oct 95.	(c-s) *Virgin; (VSC 1557)* **DON'T YOU WANT ME** (remix) / ('A'-Snap remix) / (2-'A'-Red Jerry mix)	16	☐
	(12") *(VST 1557)* – ('A'-Snap remix extended) / ('A'-Red Jerry remix extended).		
	(cd-s) *(VSCDT 1557)* – (all 6-'A'versions).		

HUMANOID
(see under ⇒ FUTURE SOUND OF LONDON)

HUMBLE PIE

Formed: Essex, England . . . Spring 1969 as a mini-supergroup by STEVE MARRIOT (ex-SMALL FACES, vocals, guitar) and PETER FRAMPTON (ex-HERD, vocals, guitar). Recruiting GREG RIDLEY (bass, ex-SPOOKY TOOTH) and JERRY SHIRLEY (drums, ex-LITTLE WOMEN), the band signed to Andrew Loog Oldham's 'Immediate' label and released their debut album, 'AS SAFE AS YESTERDAY', in the summer of '69. A solid collection of rootsy rock, the record spawned a Top 5 UK single with 'NATURAL BORN BUGIE', MARRIOT ditching the chirpy cockney popster persona he'd developed with the SMALL FACES in favour of an 'authentic' R&B rasp. The more acoustic-based follow-up, 'TOWN AND COUNTRY' (1969), flopped, and HUMBLE PIE returned from an American tour in late '69 to discover that their record label had gone under. Severe financial problems ensued until help came in the form of US lawyer, Dee Anthony, who helped secure the band a new deal with 'A&M'. The eponymous 'HUMBLE PIE' (1970) failed to resurrect their fortunes, as did the harder-edged 'ROCK ON' (1971). Anthony subsequently packing the band off to America on another tour from whence came the US gold-selling live album, 'PERFORMANCE-ROCKIN' THE FILLMORE' (1971). Despite his diminutive size, MARRIOT had a towering stage presence, the singer blazing his way through a fiery set of boogie-based blues-rock, both HUMBLE PIE originals and frenetic covers including Muddy Waters' 'ROLLIN' STONE' and Dr. John's 'I WALK ON GILDED SPLINTERS'. FRAMPTON departed for a solo career later that year, ex-COLOSSEUM man, DAVE CLEMPSON taking his place. While FRAMPTON had proved a melodic acoustic-rock foil to MARRIOT's hard rockin' excess, the new-look 'PIE continued to move in a heavier direction with 'SMOKIN' (1972), the highest charting album in the band's career, reaching No.6 in the States. Augmented by all-girl backing trio, The BLACKBERRIES (CLYDIE KING, BILLIE BARNUM & VANETTA FIELDS), the band attempted a hard rock/soul fusion with the half live/half studio double set, 'EAT IT' (1973). The album was another American Top 20 hit but HUMBLE PIE's popularity was on the wane, a further two efforts, 'THUNDERBOX' (1974) and 'STREET RATS' (1975) barely making the charts and receiving a scathing critical reaction. The group finally split shortly after the release of the latter album, SHIRLEY forming NATURAL GAS with ex-BADFINGER guitarist JOEY MOLLAND while MARRIOT put together the short-lived STEVE MARRIOTT ALL-STARS with MICKEY FINN (guitar, ex-T.REX), IAN WALLACE (drums, ex-KING CRIMSON) and DAMON BUTCHER

(keyboards). CLEMPSON, meanwhile, joined GREENSLADE. After a brief SMALL FACES reunion in the late 70's, MARIOTT reformed HUMBLE PIE along with SHIRLEY and new members BOBBY TENCH (guitar, ex-STREETWALKERS, ex-JEFF BECK GROUP) and ANTHONY JONES (bass). Signed to 'Atco', the band released two generally ignored albums, 'ON TO VICTORY' (1980) and 'GO FOR THE THROAT' (1981) before disbanding finally in 1981. MARRIOT continued to tour, releasing a low key solo album, 'PACKET OF THREE', in 1986. Hopes of a musical reunion between MARIOTT and FRAMPTON were finally dashed on 20th April '91 when MARIOTT was tragically killed in a fire at his Essex cottage.
• **Songwriters:** All took a shot at writing, with MARIOTT the main contributor. Covered; C'MON EVERYBODY + HALLELUJAH I LOVE HER SO (Eddie Cochran) / ROADRUNNER (Junior Walker) / HONKY TONK WOMAN (Rolling Stones) / ROCK'N'ROLL MUSIC (Chuck Berry) / ALL SHOOK UP (Elvis Presley) / etc.

Album rating: AS SAFE AS YESTERDAY (*6) / TOWN AND COUNTRY (*5) / HUMBLE PIE (*5) / ROCK ON (*6) / PERFORMANCE – ROCKIN' THE FILLMORE (*7) / SMOKIN' (*5) / EAT IT (*5) / THUNDERBOX (*5) / STREET RATS (*5) / ON TO VICTORY (*3) / GO FOR THE THROAT (*2) / HOT N' NASTY – THE ANTHOLOGY compilation (*7) / Steve Marriott: MARRIOTT (*4) / PACKET OF THREE (what else . . . *3) / 30 SECONDS TO MIDNIGHT exploitation (*4)

STEVE MARRIOTT (b.30 Jan'47, London, England) – vocals, guitar, keyboards (ex-SMALL FACES) / **PETER FRAMPTON** (b.22 Apr'50, Beckenham, England) – vocals, guitar (ex-HERD) / **GREG RIDLEY** (b.23 Oct'47, Carlisle, England) – bass (ex-SPOOKY TOOTH) / **JERRY SHIRLEY** (b. 4 Feb'52) – drums (ex-LITTLE WOMEN)

			Immediate	Immediate
Jul 69.	(lp) *(IMSP 025)* <101> **AS SAFE AS YESTERDAY**		32	

– Desperation / Stick shift / Buttermilk boy / Growing closer / As safe as yesterday / Bang? / Alabama '69 / I'll go alone / A nifty little number like you / Wrist job. *(cd-iss. Nov89 on 'Line'; LICD 900296) (cd re-iss. Dec92 on 'Repertoire'+=;)* – Natural born bugie / Wrist job.

Sep 69.	(7") *(IM 082)* **NATURAL BORN BUGIE. / WRIST JOB**		4	

(re-iss. Feb83; same)

Oct 69.	(7") <101> **NATURAL BORN BUGIE. / I'LL GO ALONE**		-	
Dec 69.	(lp) *(IMSP 027)* **TOWN AND COUNTRY**			

– Take me back / The sad bag of shaky Jake / The light of love / Cold lady / Down home again / Ollie Ollie / Every mother's son / Heartbeat / Only you can say / Silver tongue / Home and away. *(re-iss. 1978 on 'Charly'; CR 300016) (cd-iss. Nov93; CDIMM 020) (cd-iss. Dec92 on 'Repertoire' +=;)* – Greg's song / 79th Street blues.

			A&M	A&M
Jul 70.	(lp) *AMLS 986)* <4270> **HUMBLE PIE**			

– Live with me / Only a roach / One eyed trouser-snake rumba / Earth and water song / I'm ready / Theme from Skint (see you later liquidator) / Red light mamma / Red hot / Sucking on the sweet vine.

Mar 71.	(lp) *AMLS 203)* <4301> **ROCK ON**			

– Shine on / Sour grain / 79th and sunset / Stone cold fever / Rollin' stone / A song for Jenny / The light / Big George / Strange days / Red neck jump. *(cd-iss. 1988 on 'Mobile Fidelity'; MFCD 847)*

Sep 71.	(7") <1282> **I DON'T NEED NO DOCTOR (live). / SONG FOR JENNY**		-	73
Nov 71.	(d-lp/d-c) *(AMLH/CDM 63506)* <3506> **PERFORMANCE – ROCKIN' THE FILLMORE (live)**		32	21

– Four day creep / I'm ready / Stone cold fever / I walk on guilded splinters / Rollin' stone / Hallelujah (I love her so) / I don't need no doctor. *(re-iss. 1974;)*

– **DAVE CLEMPSON** (b. 5 Sep'45) – guitar (ex-COLOSSEUM) repl. FRAMPTON who went solo

Mar 72.	(lp) *AMLS 64342)* <4342> **SMOKIN'**		28	6

– Hot 'n' nasty / The fixer / You're so good to me / C'mon everybody / Old time feelin' / 30 days in the hole / (I'm a) Road runner / Roadrunner "G" jam / I wonder who / Sweet peace and time.

Apr 72.	(7") <1349> **HOT 'N' NASTY. / YOU'RE SO GOOD FOR ME**		-	52
Sep 72.	(7") <1366> **30 DAYS IN THE HOLE. / SWEET PEACE AND TIME**		-	

– now augmented by all-girl backing trio The BLACKBERRIES (**CLYDIE KING / BILLIE BARNUM + VANETTA FIELDS**)

Jan 73.	(7") *(AMS 7052)* <1406> **BLACK COFFEE. / SAY NO MORE**			
Apr 73.	(d-lp) *(AMLD 6004)* <3701> **EAT IT** (1-side live)		34	13 Mar73

– Get down to it / Good booze and bad women / Is it for love / Drugstore cowboy / Black coffee / I believe to my soul / Shut up and don't interrupt me / That's how strong my love is / Say no more / Oh, Bella (all that's hers) / Summer song / Beckton dumps / Up our sleeve / Honky tonk woman / (I'm a) Road runner.

Jun 73.	(7") *(AMS 7070)* <1440> **GET DOWN TO IT. / HONKY TONK WOMAN (live)**			
Oct 73.	(7") *(AMS 7090)* **OH LA DE DA. / THE OUTCROWD**			
Feb 74.	(lp) *(AMLH 63611)* <3611> **THUNDERBOX**			52

– Thunderbox / Groovin' with Jesus / I can't stand the rain / Anna / No way / Rally with Ali / Don't worry, be happy / Ninety-nine pounds / Every single day / No money down / Drift away / Oh la de da.

May 74.	(7") <1530> **NINETY-NINE POUNDS. / RALLY WITH ALI**		-	
Feb 75.	(lp) *(AMLS 68282)* <4514> **STREET RATS**		-	100

– Street rat / Rock'n'roll music / We can work it out / Scored out / Road hog / Rain / Funky to the bone / Let me be your lovemaker / Countryman / Stomp / Drive my car / Queens and nuns.

Mar 75.	(7") *(AMS 7185)* **ROCK'N'ROLL MUSIC. / SCORED OUT**		-	
Jul 75.	(7") <1711> **ROCK'N'ROLL MUSIC. / ROAD HOG**			

– Disbanded Spring 1975. JERRY SHIRLEY formed NATURAL GAS, and the others joined

STEVE MARRIOTT ALL-STARS

also included **DAMON BUTCHER** – keyboards / **IAN WALLACE** – drums (ex-KING CRIMSON) / **MICKEY FINN** – guitar (ex-T.REX)

			A&M	A&M
May 76.	(lp) *(AMLH 64572)* <4572> **MARRIOTT**			

– Star in my life / Are you lonely for me baby / You don't know me / Late night lady / Early evening light / East side struttin' / Lookin' for love / Help me through the day / Midnight rock'n'rollin' / Wam bam thank you ma'am.

Jun 76.	(7") *(AMS 7230)* **STAR IN MY LIFE. / MIDNIGHT ROCK'N'ROLLIN'**			
Jun 76.	(7") <1825> **STAR IN MY LIFE. / EAST SIDE STRUTTIN'**		-	

– CLEMPSON and BUTCHER joined ROUGH DIAMOND. WALLACE toured with BOB DYLAN. MICKEY FINN joined PHIL MAY'S FALLEN ANGELS. MARRIOTT re-formed The SMALL FACES

HUMBLE PIE

also re-formed in 1979, with **STEVE MARRIOTT** – vocals, guitar / **JERRY SHIRLEY** – drums / **BOBBY TENCH** – guitar (ex-STREETWALKERS, ex-JEFF BECK) / **ANTHONY JONES** – bass

			Jet	Atco
Apr 80.	(7") *(JET 180)* <7216> **FOOL FOR A PRETTY FACE. / YOU SOPPY PRATT**			52
Apr 80.	(lp) *(JET LP/CA 231)* <38122> **ON TO VICTORY**			60

– Fool for a pretty face / You soppy pratt / Get it in the end / Infatuation / Further down the road / My lover's prayer / Take it from here / Baby don't do it.

Jun 81.	(lp) *(38131)* <131> **GO FOR THE THROAT**			May81

– All shook up / Chip away / Driver / Go for the throat / Keep it on the island / Lottie and the charcoal queen / Restless blood / Teenage anxiety / Tin soldier.

– Finally called it a day in '81

– compilations, others –

Sep 72.	(d-lp) *A&M; <3513>* **LOST AND FOUND** (1st-2 lp's)		-	37
Jul 76.	(lp) *Immediate; (IML 1005)* **BACK HOME AGAIN**		-	
Jan 78.	(lp) *Immediate; (IML 2005)* **HUMBLE PIE'S GREATEST HITS**		-	
Sep 85.	(7") *Old Gold; (OG 9529)* **NATURAL BORN BUGIE. / (other artist)**			
Nov 85.	(d-lp/c/cd) *Castle; (CCS LP/MC/CD 104)* **THE COLLECTION**			

– Bang? / Natural born bugie / I'll go alone / Buttermilk boy / Desperation / Nifty little number like you / Wrist job / Stick shift / Growing closer / As safe as yesterday / Heartbeat / Down home again / Take me back / Only you can see / Silver tongue / Every mother's son / The sad bag of Shaky Jake / Cold lady / Home and away / Light of love. *(cd-iss. Apr94;)*

1988.	(cd) *A&M; (393 208-2)* **THE BEST OF HUMBLE PIE**			
Nov 92.	(cd) *Dojo; (EARLD 4)* **THE EARLY YEARS**			
Feb 95.	(cd) *Band Of Joy; (BOJCD 101)* **NATURAL BORN BOOGIE**			
May 95.	(cd) *A&M; (540 179-2)* **A PIECE OF THE PIE**			
Nov 95.	(d-cd) *Charly; (CDIMMBOX 3)* **THE IMMEDIATE YEARS**			

STEVE MARRIOTT

solo again

			Aura	not iss.
Jan 85	(7") *(AUS 145)* **WHAT'CHA GONNA DO ABOUT IT. / ALL SHOOK UP**			-

			Aura	not iss.
Apr 86.	(lp/c; STEVE MARRIOTT'S PACKET OF THREE) *(AUL/AUC 729)* **PACKET OF THREE**			-

– What'cha gonna do about it / Bad moon rising / All shook up / The fixer / All or nothing / Five long years / I don't need no doctor.

– STEVE MARRIOT died 20 Apr'91, after accidentally setting his Essex cottage on fire with a lighted cigarette.

– his compilations, others –

Sep 89.	(lp/c/cd) *Trax; (MOD EM/EMC/CD 1037)* **30 SECONDS TO MIDNIGHT**			

(re-iss. Apr93 on 'Castle' cd/c; CLA CD/MC 386)

Nov 91.	(cd) *Mau Mau; (MAUCD 609)* **DINGWALLS 6.7.84 (live)**			
Feb 92.	(cd) *Maste – Elastic Cat; (SCRUBBERS** (rec.1974; STEVE MARRIOTT / TIM HINKLEY / GREG RIDLEY)			
May 97.	(cd) *Metro; (OTR 1100020)* **LIVE AT THE PALACE (with A PACKET OF THREE)**			
May 97.	(d-cd) *Metro; (OTR 1100021)* **THE MARRIOTT ANTHOLOGY**		-	
May 97.	(cd) *Metro; (OTR 1100023)* **INTEREPRETATIONS**		-	

Ian HUNTER

Born: 3 Jun'46, Shrewsbury, England. After years spent playing clubs in Hamburg, Germany, he joined AT LAST THE 1958 ROCK & ROLL SHOW, who released a one-off 45 for 'CBS' in 1967, 'I CAN'T DRIVE' / 'WORKIN' ON THE RAILROAD'. The following year, he wrote a few songs for the CHARLIE WOLFE demos, which remained unissued until 'Nems' released them in mid-70's ('STAY STAY STAY' / 'HOME'). After answering an ad in the music press, HUNTER successfully auditioned in June '69 for lead singer in MOTT THE HOOPLE. For the next five years, they became one of Britain's best rock acts, until HUNTER decided to opt for a solo career in 1975. His debut 45, 'ONCE BITTEN TWICE SHY', took up where 'THE HOOPLE' left off, making the UK Top 20 in the process. With help from stalwart supporter and guitarist MICK RONSON, he continued to surface either in England or New York. With credible material, they had already toured supporting each other's solo projects, as the HUNTER-RONSON BAND. Following the Top 30 success of the 'ALL AMERICAN ALIEN BOY' (1976) set, the shady (as in dark spectacled) rock'n'roll hero/icon formed touring band, The OVERNIGHT ANGELS featuring EARL SLICK amongst others (RONSON had joined DYLAN's 'Rolling Thunder' tour in mid-'76). The group backed up HUNTER on a one-off eponymous album which the curly-locked frontman was allegedly none too happy with. Signing to 'Chrysalis' at the end of the decade, HUNTER teamed up with RONSON once more on 'YOU'RE NEVER ALONE WITH A SCHIZOPHRENIC' (1979), while 1981's 'SHORT BACK 'N' SIDES' featured such esteemed guests as TODD RUNDGREN, MICK JONES and TOPPER HEADON (the latter two both members of The CLASH; HUNTER also proved his punk credentials by producing GENERATION X's 'VALLEY OF THE DOLLS' album the same year). He subsequently went to ground following 1983's 'ALL THE GOOD ONES ARE TAKEN', eventually re-emerging in 1990 with another RONSON collaboration, 'Y U I ORTA', released on 'Mercury' (his old pal was to die of cancer in '94). Though HUNTER has never quite risen above second division status in his post-HOOPLE career, he remains, especially among his peers, one of the most respected figures in the rock world.

Album rating: IAN HUNTER (*7) / ALL AMERICAN ALIEN BOY (*5) / OVERNIGHT ANGELS (*4) / YOU'RE NEVER ALONE WITH A SCHIZOPHRENIC (*7) / SHADES OF IAN HUNTER compilation (*7) / WELCOME TO THE CLUB (*6) / SHORT BACK AND SIDES (*7) / ALL THE GOOD ONES ARE TAKEN (*6) / YUI ORTA (*6; as Hunter-Ronson) / THE VERY BEST OF IAN HUNTER compilation (*6) / IAN HUNTER'S DIRTY LAUNDRY (*4) / THE ARTFUL DODGER (*4)

IAN HUNTER – vocals, guitar (ex-MOTT THE HOOPLE, ex-AT LAST THE 1958 . . .) with **MICK RONSON** – guitar, vocals (ex-MOTT THE HOOPLE, ex-DAVID BOWIE, Solo artist) / **PETE ARNESEN** – keyboards / **JEFF APPLEBY** – bass / **DENNIS ELLIOTT** – drums

			C.B.S.	Columbia
Mar 75.	(7") (CBS 3194) <10161> **ONCE BITTEN TWICE SHY. / 3,000 MILES FROM HERE**		14	-
Apr 75.	(lp/c) (CBS/40 80710) <33480> **IAN HUNTER**		21	50

– Once bitten twice shy / Who do you love / Lounge lizard / Boy / 3,000 miles from here / The truth, the whole truth, nuthin' but the truth / It ain't easy when you fall / Shades off / I get so excited. <US cd-iss. Jul90; CK 33480> (re-iss. cd Sep94 on 'Sony Rewind'; COL 477359-2)

Jul 75.	(7") (CBS 3486) **WHO DO YOU LOVE. / BOY**			-

HUNTER with RONSON, brought in mainly session people including **AYNSLEY DUNBAR** – drums / **CORNELL DUPREEE** – guitar / **JACO PASTORUS** – bass / **CHRIS STAINTON** – keyboards / guests **BRIAN MAY + FREDDIE MERCURY** – vocals (QUEEN) All replaced PETE and JEFF who went into sessions + DENNIS who joined FOREIGNER

May 76.	(7") (CBS 4268) **ALL AMERICAN ALIEN BOY. / RAPE**			-
May 76.	(lp/c) (CBS/40 81310) <34142> **ALL AMERICAN ALIEN BOY**		29	

– Letter to Brittania from the Union Jack / All american alien boy / Irene Wilde / Restless youth / Rape / You nearly did me in / Apathy 83 / God (take 1). <US cd-iss. Jan90; CK 34142>

Aug 76.	(7") (CBS 4479) **YOU NEARLY DID ME IN. / LETTER TO BRITANNIA FROM THE UNION JACK**			-

HUNTER formed tour band OVERNIGHT ANGELS:- **EARL SLICK** – guitar (ex-BOWIE) / **PETER OXENDALE** – keyboards / **BOB RAWLINSON** – bass / **CURLY SMITH** – drums (MICK RONSON joined BOB DYLAN's Rolling Thunder Tour mid-76)

May 77.	(7"; as IAN HUNTER'S OVERNIGHT ANGELS) (CBS 5229) **JUSTICE OF THE PEACE. / THE BALLAD OF LITTLE STAR**			
May 77.	(lp/c) (CBS/40 81310) <34721> **OVERNIGHT ANGELS**			

– Golden opportunity / Shallow crystals / Overnight angels / Broadway / Justice of the peace / Silver dime / Wild'n'free / The ballad of little star / To love a woman. (re-iss. cd Jun94 on 'Sony Europe'; 474 780-2)

Jul 78.	(7"; as IAN HUNTER'S OVERNIGHT ANGELS) (CBS 5497) **ENGLAND ROCKS. / WILD'N'FREE**			-

now with RONSON plus **ROY BITTAN** – keyboards / **MAX WEINBERG** – drums / **GEORGE YOUNG + LEW DELGATTO** – sax / **GARY TALLENT** – bass / **ELLEN FOLEY** – vocals

			Chrysalis	Chrysalis
Apr 79.	(7"white) (CHS 2324) **WHEN THE DAYLIGHT COMES. / LIFE AFTER DEATH**			-
Apr 79.	(lp/c) (<CHR/ZCHR 1214>) **YOU'RE NEVER ALONE WITH A SCHIZOPHRENIC**		49	35

– Just another night / Wild east / Cleveland rocks / When the daylight comes / Ships / Life after death / Standin' in my light / Bastard / The outsider. <cd-iss. Jun94 on 'Razor & Tie'; RE 2011> (re-iss. cd Mar94; CD 25CR 03)

Jul 79.	(7") (CHS 2346) **SHIPS. / WILD EAST**			-
Aug 79.	(7") <2352> **JUST ANOTHER NIGHT. / CLEVELAND ROCKS**		-	68
Oct 79.	(7") (CBS 2390) **CLEVELAND ROCKS. / BASTARD**			-

MARTIN BRILEY – bass repl. TALLENT / **ERIC PARKER** – drums repl. WEINBERG / **GEORGE MEYER + TOM MANDEL** – keyboards repl. BITTAN also to BRUCE SPRINGSTEEN / **TOMMY MORRONGIELLO** – guitar, bass repl. YOUNG + DELGATTO

Apr 80.	(d-lp/c) (CJT/ZCJT 6) <1269> **WELCOME TO THE CLUB (live)**		61	69

– F.B.I. / Once bitten twice shy / Angelline / Laugh at me / All the way from Memphis / I wish I was your mother / Irene Wilde / Just another night / Cleveland rocks / Standin' in my light / Bastard / Walkin' with a mountain / Rock'n'roll queen / All the young dudes / Slaughter on Tenth Avenue / We gotta get out of here / Silver needles / Man o' war / Sons and daughters. (re-iss. d-cd May94; CDCHR 6075)

Jun 80.	(d7") (2434) **WE GOTTA GET OUT OF HERE (live). / MEDLEY: PNCE BITTEN TWICE SHY – BASTARD – CLEVELAND ROCKS (live) // SONS AND DAUGHTERS (live). / ONE OF THE BOYS (live)**			-

virtualy same band except featured guests **TODD RUNDGREN** – vocals, bass / **MICK JONES** – guitar / **TOPPER HEADON** – drums (both of CLASH) / **TYMON DOGG** – violin

Aug 81.	(7"clear) (CHS 2542) **LISA LIKES ROCK'N'ROLL. / NOISES**			-
Aug 81.	(lp/c) (<CHR/ZCHR 1326>) **SHORT BACK 'N' SIDES**		79	62

– Central Park'n'West / Lisa likes rock'n'roll / I need your love / Old records never

die / Noises / Rain / Gun control / Theatre of the absurd / Leave me alone / Keep on burning. (re-iss. d-cd.May94+=; CDCHR 6074) – LONG ODDS AND OUT TAKES

now with **RONSON + ROBBIE ALTER + JIMMY RIP** – guitar / **MARK CLARKE + DAN HARTMAN** – bass / **MANDAL / JEFF BOVA + BOB MAYO** – keyboards / **CLARENCE CLEMONS + LOU CORTLEZZI** – sax / **HILLY MICHAELS** – drums

			C.B.S.	Columbia
Jul 83.	(7") (A 3855) **ALL THE GOOD ONES ARE TAKEN. / DEATH 'N' GLORY BOYS**			-

(12"+=) (TA 3855) – Traitor.

Aug 83.	(lp/c) (CBS/40 25379) <38628> **ALL THE GOOD ONES ARE TAKEN**			

– All the good ones are taken / Every step of the way / Fun / Speechless / Death 'n' glory boys / Somethin's goin' on / That girl is rock'n'roll / Captain Void 'n' the video jets / Seeing double / All the good ones are taken (reprise). (re-iss. cd Jun94 on 'Sony Europe'; 474780-2)

Oct 83.	(7") (A 3541) **SOMETHIN'S GOIN' ON. / ALL THE GOOD ONES ARE TAKEN**			
Oct 83.	(7") <04166> **SEEING DOUBLE. / THAT GIRL IS ROCK'N'ROLL**		-	

HUNTER retired from public eye until late '89 he and RONSON re-formed

HUNTER-RONSON

IAN HUNTER + MICK RONSON's band, with **PAT KILBRIDE** – bass / **MICKEY CURRY** – drums / **TOMMY MANDEL** – keyboards

			Mercury	Mercury
Jan 90.	(cd/c/lp) (<838 973-2/-4/-1>) **Y U I ORTA**			Oct89

– American music / The loner / Women's intuition / Tell it like it is / Livin' in a heart / Big time / Cool / Beg a little love / Following in your footsteps * / Sons 'n' lovers / Pain * / How much more can I take * / Sweet dreamer. (c+=/cd+= *)

Feb 90.	(7"/c-s) (MER/+MC 315) **AMERICAN MUSIC. / TELL IT LIKE IT IS**			

(12"+=/cd-s+=) (MER X/CD 315) – Sweet dreamer.

			Norsk Plateproduksjomot iss.	
Feb 95.	(cd-s; as IAN HUNTER'S DIRTY LAUNDRY) (IDS 44) **MY REVOLUTION / DANCING ON THE MOON**		-	- Norway
Mar 95.	(cd; as IAN HUNTER'S DIRTY LAUNDRY) (IDCD 44) **IAN HUNTER'S DIRTY LAUNDRY**		-	- Norway
			Polydor	not iss.
Sep 96.	(cd) (531 794-2) **THE ARTFUL DODGER**			

(UK-iss.Sep97 on 'Citadel' pic-cd; CID 1-CD)

			Citadel	not iss.
Apr 97.	(cd-s) (CIT 101) **THE ARTFUL DODGER / NOW IS THE TIME / FUCK IT UP**			-

– compilations, etc. –

Feb 80.	(lp/c) Columbia; (CBS/40 88476) **SHADES OF IAN HUNTER – THE BALLAD OF IAN HUNTER & MOTT THE HOOPLE**	

<US cd-iss. Nov88; VK 41670>

Apr 91.	(cd/c/lp) C.B.S.; (467508-2/-4/-1) **THE VERY BEST OF IAN HUNTER**			
Jul 91.	(cd/c) Castle; (CCS CD/MC 290) **THE COLLECTION**			-

(Includes tracks by MOTT THE HOOPLE)

Oct 95.	(cd) Windsong; (WINCD 078) **THE HUNTER-HONSON BAND BBC LIVE IN CONCERT**			-

HURRICANE #1

(dig out; 4th edition or Great Alt & Indie . . .)

HUSKER DU

Formed: St. Paul, Minnesota, USA . . . 1978 by MOULD, HART and NORTON. In 1980-82, they issued a few 45's and a live lp 'LAND SPEED RECORD', on their own label, 'New Alliance'. The record typified the band's early uncompromising hardcore which was often tediously workmanlike in its adherence to the steadfast confines of the genre. 'EVERYTHING FALLS APART' (1983) was also unflinching in its intensity and it was all the more surprising when the band showed glimmers of noise-pop greatness on their 1983 debut for 'SST', 'METAL CIRCUS'. They consolidated this by cross fertilising the previously polarised worlds of psychedelia and hardcore punk on an electrifying cover of The BYRDS' 'EIGHT MILES HIGH' (1984). The follow-up double set, 'ZEN ARCADE' (1984), was a further giant step for hardcore kind. A concept album no less, the twin songwriting attack of MOULD and HART was becoming sharper and even the sprawling, unfocused feel of the whole affair wasn't enough to blunt the edges of songs like 'WHATEVER' and 'TURN ON THE NEWS'. The songwriting on 'NEW DAY RISING' (1985) was even more trenchant, the band's adrenaline-fuelled pop-core hybrid developing at breakneck speed. 'FLIP YOUR WIG' (1985), the band's last indie release, marked a stepping stone to their major label debut for 'Warners', 'CANDY APPLE GREY' (1986). While HART perfected HUSKER DU's melodic discord on tracks like 'DEAD SET ON DESTRUCTION', MOULD showcased darkly introspective, acoustic elegies 'TOO FAR DOWN' and 'HARDLY GETTING OVER IT'. The more musically-challenged among HUSKER DU's following were none too taken with this new-fangled unplugged business although the album was released to unanimous critical acclaim. The band's swansong, 'WAREHOUSE: SONGS AND STORIES' (1987), was the culmination of a decade's experimentation and possessed an unprecedented depth, clarity and consistency. By the time of its release, though, tension in the band was reaching breaking point and HUSKER DU was disbanded in 1987. While GRANT HART and BOB MOULD went on to solo careers, as well as respectively forming NOVA MOB and SUGAR, they were always better together and the magic of HUSKER DU is inestimable in its influence on a generation of alternative guitar bands. • **Songwriters:** MOULD-HART compositions except; SUNSHINE SUPERMAN (Donovan) / TICKET TO RIDE + SHE'S A WOMAN + HELTER SKELTER (Beatles) / EIGHT MILES HIGH (Byrds). NOVA MOB covered I JUST WANT TO MAKE LOVE TO YOU (Willie Dixon) / SHEENA IS A PUNK ROCKER (Ramones). Solo GRANT HART covered SIGNED D.C. (Love). • **Trivia:** HUSKER DU means DO YOU REMEMBER in Swedish.

Album rating: EVERYTHING FALLS APART (*5) / ZEN ARCADE (*9) / NEW DAY RISING (*9) / FLIP YOUR WIG (*9) / CANDY APPLE GREY (*7) / WAREHOUSE: SONGS & STORIES (*9) / THE LIVING END live compilation (*6) / Grant Hart: INTOLERANCE (*6) / Nova Mob: THE DAYS DAYS OF POMPEII (*6) / NOVA MOB (*6) / ECCE HOMO (*5)

BOB MOULD (b.12 Oct'60, Malone, N.Y.) – vocals, guitar, keyboards, percussion / **GRANT HART** (b. GRANTZBERG VERNON HART, 18 Mar'61) – drums, keyboards, percussion, vocals / **GREG NORTON** (b.13 Mar'59, Rock Island, Illinois) – bass

		not iss.	Reflex
1980.	(7") <38285> **STATUES. / AMUSEMENT** (live)	-	-

		Alternative Tentacles	New Alliance
1982.	(lp) (VIRUS 25) <NAR 007> **LAND SPEED RECORD** (live)		

– All tensed up / Don't try to call / I'm not interested / Big sky / Guns at my school / Push the button / Gilligan's Island / MTC / Don't have a life / Bricklayer / Tired of doing things / You're naive / Strange week / Do the bee / Ultracore / Let's go die / Data control. (re-iss. Nov88 on 'S.S.T.'; SST 195) (re-iss. cd/lp Oct95)

		not iss.	Reflex
1982.	(7"m) <NAR 010> **IN A FREE LAND. / WHAT DO I WANT? / M.I.C.**	-	-
Jul 83.	(lp) <D> **EVERYTHING FALLS APART**	-	

– From the gut / Blah, blah, blah / Punch drunk / Bricklayer / Afraid of being wrong / Sunshine Superman / Signals from above / Everything falls apart / Wheels / Obnoxious / Gravity. (cd-iss. May93 on 'WEA'+=; 8122 71163-2) – In a free land / What do I want / M.I.C. / Statues / Let's go die / Amusement (live) / Do you remember?

		S.S.T.	S.S.T.
Dec 83.	(m-lp) <SST 020> **METAL CIRCUS**		

– Real world / Deadly skies / It's not funny anymore / Diane / First of the last calls / Lifeline / Out on a limb.

Apr 84.	(7"colrd) (SST 025) **EIGHT MILES HIGH. / MASOCHISM WORLD**

(cd-s iss.Dec88; SST 025CD)

Sep 84. (d-lp) <SST 027> **ZEN ARCADE**
– Something I learned today / Broken home, broken heart / Never talking to you again / Chartered trips / Dreams reoccurring / Indecision time / Hare Krishna / Beyond the threshold / Pride / I'll never forget you / The biggest lie / What's going on / Masochism world / Standing by the sea / Somewhere / One step at a time / Pink turns to blue / Newest industry / Monday will never be the same / Whatever / The tooth fairy and the princess / Turn on the news / Reoccurring dreams. (cd-iss. Oct87; SST 027CD) (re-iss. cd/c/d-lp Oct95 & Jun97; same)

Feb 85. (lp) <(SST 031)> **NEW DAY RISING**
– New day rising / Girl who lives on Heaven Hill / I apologize / Folklore / If I told you / Celebrated summer / Perfect example / Terms of psychic warfare / 59 times the pain / Powerline / Books about UFO's / I don't know what you're talking about / How to skin a cat / Watcha drinkin' / Plans I make. (cd-iss. Oct87; SST 031CD) (re-iss. cd/c/lp Oct95; same)

Aug 85. (7") <(SST 051)> **MAKE NO SENSE AT ALL. / LOVE IS ALL AROUND (MARY'S THEME)**

Oct 85. (lp) <(SST 055)> **FLIP YOUR WIG**
– Flip your wig / Every everything / Makes no sense at all / Hate paper doll / Green eyes / Divide and conquer / Games / Find me / The baby song / Flexible flyer / Private plane / Keep hanging on / The wit and the wisdom / Don't know yet. (cd-iss. Oct87; SST 055CD) (re-iss. cd/c/lp Oct95; same)

		Warners	Warners
Feb 86.	(7") (W 8746) **DON'T WANT TO KNOW IF YOU ARE LONELY. / ALL WORK NO PLAY**		

(12"+=) (W 8746T) – Helter skelter (live).

Mar 86. (lp/c) (WX 40/+C) <25385> **CANDY APPLE GREY**
– Crystal / Don't want to know if you are lonely / I don't know for sure / Sorry somehow / Too far down / Hardly getting over it / Dead set on destruction / Eiffel Tower high / No promises have I made / All this I've done for you. (cd-iss. Nov92; 7599 25385-2)

Sep 86. (7") (W 8612) **SORRY SOMEHOW. / ALL THIS I'VE DONE FOR YOU**
(d7+=/12"+=) (W 8612 F/T) – Flexible flyer / Celebrated summer.

Jan 87. (7") (W 8456) **COULD YOU BE THE ONE. / EVERYTIME**
(12"+=) (W 8456T) – Charity, chastity, prudence, hope.

Jan 87. (d-lp/d-c) (925544-1/-4) <25544> **WAREHOUSE: SONGS & STORIES** [72]
– These important years / Charity, chastity, prudence and hope / Standing in the rain / Back from somewhere / Ice cold ice / You're a soldier / Could you be the one? / Too much spice / Friend, you've got to fall / Visionary / She floated away / Bed of nails / Tell you why tomorrow / It's not peculiar / Actual condition / No reservations / Turn it around / She's a woman (and now he is a man) / Up in the air / You can live at home. (cd-iss. Oct92; 7599 25544-2)

Jun 87. (7") (W 8276) **ICE COLD ICE. / GOTTA LETTA**
(12"+=) (W 8276T) – Medley.

–––– Disbanded in 1987 after manager, DAVID SAVOY Jr., committed suicide. GRANT HART went solo in '89, as did BOB MOULD. In 1992 the latter formed SUGAR.

– compilations, etc. –

May 94. (cd/c) Warners; <(9362 45582-2/-4)> **THE LIVING END** (live)
– New day rising / Heaven Hill / Standing in the rain / Back from somewhere / Ice cold ice / Everytime / Friend you're gonna fall / She floated away / From the gut /

Target / It's not funny anymore / Hardly getting over it / Terms of psychic warfare / Powertime / Books about UFO's / Divide and conquer / Keep hangin' on / Celebrated summer / Now that you know me / Ain't no water in the well / What's goin' on / Data control / In a free land / Sheena is a punk rocker.

GRANT HART

		S.S.T.	S.S.T.
Oct 89.	(7"ep/cd-ep) (SST 219/+CD) **2541. / COME HOME / LET'S GO**		-
Nov 89.	(lp/cd) <(SST 215/+CD)> **INTOLERANCE**		

– All of my senses / Now that you know me / The main / Roller risk / Fanfare in D major (come, come) / You're the victim / 2541 / Anything / She can see the angels coming / Reprise.

May 90. (12"ep/cd-ep) (SST 262/+CD) **ALL OF MY SENSES. / THE MAIN** (edit) **/ SIGNED D.C.**

NOVA MOB

(GRANT HART) & his group:- **TOM MERKL** – bass / **MICHAEL CRECO** – drums

		Rough Trade	Rough Trade
Feb 91.	(cd/c/lp) <(R 2081261-2/-4/-1)> **THE LAST DAYS OF POMPEII**		

– Introduction / Woton / Getaway (gateway) in time / Admiral of the sea (79 a.d. version) / Wernher Von Braun / Space jazz / Where you grave land (next time you fall off of yo) / Over my head / Admiral of the sea / Persuaded / Lavender and grey / Medley:- The last days of Pompeii / Benediction.

Feb 91. (12"ep/cd-ep) (RTT/RCD 267) **ADMIRAL OF THE SEA (first avenue mix) / ('A' milk off mix) / THE LAST DAYS OF POMPEII (mix) / GETAWAY IN TIME (instrumental) / I JUST WANT TO MAKE LOVE TO YOU** (live)

–––– **MARK RELISH** – drums repl. CRECO

		Southern	Big Store
Jul 92.	(cd-ep) <EFA 04669CD> **SHOOT YOUR WAY TO FREEDOM / BALLAD NO.19 / OH! TO BEHOLD / CHILDREN IN THE STREET**		

–––– **HART** with **CHRIS HENSLER** – guitar / **TOM MERKL** – bass / **STEVE SUTHERLAND** – drums

		World Service	Restless
May 94.	(cd/lp) (1571744-2/-1) <72762> **NOVA MOB**		

– Shoot your way to freedom / Puzzles / Buddy / See and feel and know / Little Miss Information / I won't be there anymore / Please don't ask / The sins of their sons / Beyond a reasonable doubt / I was afraid – Coda.

Sep 94. (cd-ep) **OLD EMPIRE / PLEASE DON'T ASK / LITTLE MISS INFORMATION / BEYOND A REASONABLE DOUBT**

Dec 95. (cd; GRANT HART) <(RTD 1573096-2)> **ECCE HOMO** (live)
– Ballad No.19 / 2541 / Evergreen / Memorial drive / Come come / Pink turns to blue / She floated away / The girl who lives on Heaven hill / Admiral of the sea / Back somewhere / Last days of Pompeii / Old Empire / Never talking to you again / Please don't ask / The main.

Michael HUTCHENCE (see under ⇒ INXS)

Janis IAN

Born: JANIS EDDY FINK, 7 May'51, New York City, New York, USA. While attending Manhattan High School of Music & Art, she had her first song 'HAIR OF SPUN GOLD' published by Broadside magazine. In 1965, while singing at The Village Gate, she signed as a songwriter to 'Elektra' records, but was soon dropped when she wanted to sing herself!. Early in 1966, after her family moved from New Jersey to New York, she secured another contract, this time with 'M.G.M.'. Her debut single, 'SOCIETY'S CHILD', released while she was still aged 15, broke into the US chart, and finally reached the Top 20 in 1967. At the same time, her eponymous debut album also made Top 30, but she failed to establish herself and subsequently moved to Philadelphia. In 1971, she uprooted again, this time to California (after she married), 'Capitol' records issuing her fifth set, 'PRESENT COMPANY'. In 1974, she resurfaced on 'Columbia' and hit critically with 'STARS', both the album's title track and 'JESSE' enjoying a series of interpretations by leading artists, the latter track covered in heart-renderingly beautiful style by ROBERTA FLACK on her 'Killing Me Softly' album. By now, IAN's angst-ridden folk-rock outpourings had given way to a more contemporary, jazzy and lyrical style, 'BETWEEN THE LINES' (1975) landing her a No.1 US slot amid the singer/songwriter boom (even if its massive hit single, 'AT SEVENTEEN', was about high school trauma). Although the following year's 'AFTERTONES' made the Top 20, her subsequent albums failed to make any commercial impact and IAN retired from studio work in late '81. Though she continued to undertake live work, it would be more than a decade before she recorded another album, 'BREAKING SILENCE' eventually surfacing in 1993. Though it failed to chart, BETTE MIDLER had a hit with one track, 'SOME PEOPLE'S LIVES'. A further album, 'REVENGE', appeared in '95.

Album rating: JANIS IAN (*6) / FOR ALL THE SEASONS OF YOUR MIND (*5) / THE SECRET LIFE OF J. EDDY FINK (*4) / WHO REALLY CARES (*3) / PRESENT COMPANY (*4) / STARS (*6) / BETWEEN THE LINES (*8) / AFTERTONES (*6) / MIRACLE ROW (*5) / JANIS IAN on 'Columbia' (*4) / NIGHT RAINS (*4) / THE BEST OF JANIS IAN compilation (*6) / RESTLESS EYES (*4) / BREAKING SILENCE (*6) / REVENGE (*6) / SOCIETY'S CHILD: THE VERVE RECORDINGS compilation (*7) / HUNGER (*4)

JANIS IAN – vocals, acoustic guitar, piano (w/ session people)

	Verve Folkways	Verve Folkways
Oct 66. (7") (VS 1503) <5027> **SOCIETY'S CHILD (BABY I'VE BEEN THINKING). / LETTER TO JOHN**	☐	☐
(re-iss. May67; VS 1506) <re-iss. May67, hit US No.14>		
Jun 67. (lp; stereo/mono) (S+VLP 6001) <3017> **JANIS IAN**	☐	29
– Society's child (baby I've been thinking) / Too old to go 'way little girl / Hair of spun gold / Then tangles of my mind / I'll give you a stone if you throw it (changing tymes) / Pro-girl / Younger generation blues / New Christ cardiac hero / Lover be kindly / Mrs. McKenzie / Janey's blues. (re-iss. Jun82 on 'Polydor'; PD 6058)		
Oct 67. (7") <5041> **YOUNGER GENERATION BLUES. / I'LL GIVE YOU A STONE IF YOU THROW IT (CHANGING TYMES)**	-	☐
Jan 68. (lp) (SVLP 6003) <FTS 3024> **FOR ALL THE SEASONS OF YOUR MIND**	☐	☐ Dec67
– A song for all the seasons of your mind / And I did ma / Honey d'ya think? / Bahimsa / Queen Merka & me / There are times / Lonely one / Sunflakes fall, snowrays call / Evening star / Shady acres / Insanity comes quietly to the structured mind.		
Nov 68. (7") (VS 1513) <5072> **SUNFLAKES FALL, SNOWRAYS CALL. / INSANITY COMES QUIETLY TO THE STRUCTURED MIND**	☐	☐
Jan 69. (7") <5079> **A SONG FOR ALL THE SEASONS OF YOUR MIND. / LONELY ONE**	-	☐
Feb 69. (lp) (SVLP 6009) <FTS 3048> **THE SECRET LIFE OF J. EDDY FINK**	☐	☐
– Everybody knows / Mistaken identity / Friends again / 42nd St. psycho blues / She's made of porcelain / Sweet misery / When I was a child / What do you think of the dead / Look to the rain / Son of love / Baby's blue.		
Mar 69. (7") <5090> **FRIENDS AGAIN. / LADIES OF THE NIGHT**	-	☐
Jul 69. (7") <5099> **EVERYBODY KNOWS. / JANEY'S BLUES**	-	☐
Nov 69. (7") <5113> **CALLING YOUR NAME. / MONTH OF MAY**	-	☐

Nov 69. (lp) (SVLP 6023) <FTS 3063> **WHO REALLY CARES**	☐	☐
– Time on my hands / Snowbird / Love you more than yesterday / Orphan of the wind / Sea and sand / Galveston / Do you remember / Month of May / Calling your name.		

	Capitol	Capitol
Feb 71. (7") <3107> **HE'S A RAINBOW. / HERE IN SPAIN**	-	☐
May 71. (7") (CL 15685) **HE'S A RAINBOW. / SEE MY GRAMMY RIDE**	☐	☐
Jun 71. (lp) (VMP 1014) <SM 683> **PRESENT COMPANY**	☐	- Feb71
– The seaside / Present company / See my Grammy ride / Here in Spain / On the train / He's a rainbow / Weary lady / Nature's at peace / See the river / Let it run free / Alabama / Liberty / My land / Hello Jerry / Can you reach me / The sunlight. (cd-iss. Nov92 on 'Beat Goes On'; BGOCD 165)		

	C.B.S.	Columbia
May 74. (7") <46034> **JESSE. / THE MAN YOU ARE IN ME**	-	☐
Jun 74. (lp/c) (CBS/40 80224) <32857> **STARS**	☐	83 May74
– Stars / The man you are in me / Sweet sympathy / Page nine / Thankyou / Dance with me / Without you / Jesse / You've got me on a string / Applause. (re-iss. Jun81; CBS 32049) (re-iss. Aug95 on 'Grapevine' cd/c; GRA CD/MC 302)		
Jul 74. (7") (CBS 2501) **WITHOUT YOU. / YOU'VE GOT ME ON A STRING**	☐	-
May 75. (7") <10119> **WHEN THE PARTY'S OVER. / BRIGHT LIGHTS AND PROMISES**	-	☐
Aug 75. (7") (CBS 3498) <10154> **AT SEVENTEEN. / STARS**	-	3 Jun75
Aug 75. (lp/c) (CBS/40 80635) <33394> **BETWEEN THE LINES**	☐	1 Mar75
– When the party's over / At seventeen / From me to you / Brights lights and promises / In the winter / Water colors / Between the lines / The come on / Light a light / Tea or symphony / Lover's lullaby. (re-iss. Aug95 on 'Grapevine' cd/c; GRA CD/MC 303)		
Oct 75. (7") <10228> **IN THE WINTER. / THANKYOUSE**	☐	☐
Nov 75. (7") (CBS 4798) **IN THE WINTER. / WHEN THE PARTY'S OVER**	☐	-
Feb 76. (lp/c) (CBS/40 69220) <33919> **AFTERTONES**	☐	12 Jan76
– Aftertones / I would like to dance / Love is blind / Roses / Belle of the blues / Goodbye to morning / Boy I really tied one on / This must be wrong / Don't cry, old man / Hymn. (re-iss. Mar81; CBS 32018) (re-iss. Aug95 on 'Grapevine' cd/c; GRA CD/MC 304)		
Mar 76. (7") (CBS 4100) <10297> **BOY I REALLY TIED ONE ON. / AFTERTONES**	☐	☐
May 76. (7") <10331> **I WOULD LIKE TO DANCE. / GOODBYE TO MORNING**	☐	☐
Sep 76. (7") <10391> **LOVE IS BLIND. / ROSES**	☐	☐
Jan 77. (7") <10484> **MIRACLE ROW. / TAKE IT TO THE SKY**	☐	☐
Mar 77. (lp/c) (CBS/40 81879) <34440> **MIRACLE ROW**	☐	45 Jan77
– Party lights / I want to make you love me / Sunset of your life / Take to the sky / Candlelight / Let me be lonely / Slow dance romance / Will you dance? / I'll cry tonight / Miracle row – Maria. (re-iss. Aug95 on 'Grapevine' cd/c; GRA CD/MC 305)		
May 77. (7") <10526> **CANDLELIGHT. / I WANT TO MAKE YOU LOVE ME**	☐	-
Sep 78. (7") <10813> **THAT GRAND ILLUSION. / HOPPER PAINTING**	☐	☐
Sep 78. (lp/c) (CBS/40 82700) <35325> **JANIS IAN**	☐	☐
– That grand illusion / Some people / Tonight will last forever / Hotels & one-night stands / Do you wanna dance? / Silly habits / The bridge / My mama's house / Streetlife serenaders / I need to live alone again / Hopper painting. (re-iss. Aug95 on 'Grapevine' cd/c; GRA CD/MC 306)		
Dec 78. (7") <10864> **DO YOU WANNA DANCE?. / THE BRIDGE**	☐	-
Apr 79. (7") <10979> **TONIGHT WILL LAST FOREVER. / HERE COMES THE NIGHT**	☐	-
Oct 79. (7") (CBS 7936) <11111> **FLY TOO HIGH. / NIGHT RAINS**	44	☐
Oct 79. (lp/c) (CBS/40 83802) <36139> **NIGHT RAINS**	☐	☐
– The other side of the sun / Fly too high / Memories / Night rains / Here comes the night / Day by day / Have mercy love / Lay low / Photographs / Jenny (Iowa sunrise). (re-iss. Mar83; CBS 32298) (re-iss. Aug95 on 'Grapevine' cd/c; GRA CD/MC 307)		
Jan 80. (7") (CBS 8136) **HAVE MERCY LOVE. / JENNY (IOWA SUNRISE)**	☐	-
May 80. (7") (CBS 8611) **THE OTHER SIDE OF THE SUN. / PHOTOGRAPHS**	44	-
Jul 80. (7") <11327> **THE OTHER SIDE OF THE SUN. / MEMORIES**	-	☐
Nov 80. (7") (CBS 9324) **HERE COMES THE NIGHT. / MEMORIES**	☐	☐
Mar 81. (7") <02176> **UNDER THE COVERS. / SUGAR MOUNTAIN**	-	71
Jun 81. (7") (A 1324) **UNDER THE COVERS. / PASSION PLAY**	☐	☐
Jul 81. (lp/c) (CBS 85040) <37360> **RESTLESS EYES**	☐	☐
– Under the covers / I remember yesterday / I believe I'm myself again / Restless eyes / Get ready to roll / Passion play / Down and away / Bigger than real / Dear Billy / Sugar mountain. (re-iss. Aug95 on 'Grapevine' cd/c; GRA CD/MC 308)		
Oct 81. (7") (A 1603) <02546> **I REMEMBER YESTERDAY. / RESTLESS EYES**	☐	☐

—— she retired from studio work 1981; although guested on a MEL TORME album in 1982 and continued to appear live throughout the 80's. In 1991, she wrote 'Some People's Lives' which became a hit for BETTE MIDLER. That year she also made an appearance at the Cambridge Folk Festival.

	Sony	Morgan Creek
Jun 93. (cd) (519614-2) <2959 20023-2> **BREAKING SILENCE**	☐	☐
– All roads to the river / Ride me like a wave / Tattoo / Guess you had to be there / What about the love? / His hands / Walking on sacred ground / This train still runs / Through the years / This house / Some people's lives / Breaking silence.		

	Grapevine	Beacon
May 95. (cd/c/lp) (GRA CD/MC/LP 301) <51559> **REVENGE**	☐	☐
– Ready for the war / Take no prisoners / Tenderness / No one else like you / Davy / When the silence falls / Take me walking in the rain / Berlin / Stolen fire / Ruby / The mission / When angels cry.		
Jul 95. (c-s/cd-s) **TENDERNESS / TAKE NO PRISONERS / WHEN ANGELS CRY**	☐	☐
Oct 97. (cd/c) (GRA CD/MC 233) <11274> **HUNGER**	☐	☐ Sep97
– Black and white / On the dark side of town / Might as well be Monday / Getting over you / Hunger / Welcome to Acousticville / Honor them all / Empty / House without a heart / Shadow / Getting over you.		

– compilations, others, etc. –

1975. (7") *Polydor; <14299>* **SOCIETY'S CHILD (BABY I'VE BEEN THINKING). / I'LL GIVE YOU A STONE IF YOU THROW IT (CHANGING TYMES)** [ ] [ ]

Dec 80. (lp/c) *C.B.S.; (CBS/40 84711)* **THE BEST OF JANIS IAN** [–] [ ]
– At seventeen / Have mercy love / Aftertones / When the party's over / In the winter / Stars / Fly too high / The other side of the sun / Without you / Here comes the night / Jesse (Iowa sunrise) / The bridge / Between the lines / Miracle row / Maria.

Aug 83. (d-c) *C.B.S. (40 22158)* **STARS / NIGHT RAINS** [ ] [ ]

Jan 94. (d-cd) *Polydor; (527591-2) <7591>* **SOCIETY'S CHILD – THE VERVE RECORDINGS** [ ] [ ] Aug95

Jun 95. (cd) *Whistle Test; (WHISCD 008)* **LIVE ON THE TEST (live)** [ ] [–]

Jan 96. (cd/c) *Grapevine; (GRA CD/MC 309)* **UNCLE WONDERFUL** (rec.1981-1983) [ ] [–]
– Just a girl / Trigger happy love / Mechanical telephone / Uncle Wonderful / etc. (above was issued in Australia in 1984)

ICE CUBE

Born: O'SHEA JACKSON, 15 Jun'69, Crenshaw, Los Angeles, California, USA. After starting out as a founding member of seminal rap terrorists N.W.A., CUBE took a sabbatical from the band following the release of the first album, going to study architecture at the Phoenix Institute of Technology. Returning in 1988, he worked on the pivotal 'STRAIGHT OUTTA COMPTON' (1989). After touring the record, the rapper had a dispute with manager JERRY HELLER over royalties, eventually settling in court in 1990. Following the incident, CUBE went solo with his backing crew DA LENCH MOB, releasing his debut, 'AMERIKKKA'S MOST WANTED' the same year. Produced by PUBLIC ENEMY's BOMB SQUAD, the album was as uncompromising, both lyrically and musically, as his best work for N.W.A., following the same gangsta rap blueprint and never budging from his old adage that "Life ain't nothing but bitches and money". Consistently controversial and contradictory, ICE CUBE puts down women at every opportunity yet offers female rapper YO YO a chance to have her say on 'IT'S A MAN'S WORLD', and say it she does, in fine style. 'DEATH CERTIFICATE' (1991) was an even more vicious verbal attack, CUBE railing against the usual targets like the police and the media, although the track's 'NO VASELINE' and 'BLACK KOREA' brought the most criticism. The former was an anti-Semitic outburst against his former boss, the jewish JERRY HELLER, while the latter advocated setting fire to Korean-owned grocery stores. He didn't stop there though, going on to include white "devils", middle class blacks and gay men in his litany of hate. Inevitably, the album brought widespread condemnation, the only thanks the rapper received for his troubles was from the Ku Klux Klan. On 'THE PREDATOR' (1992) CUBE's anger was more focused, the record debuting at No.1 in America and becoming a million seller within a month. It also spawned CUBE's biggest UK hit to date in the deceptively mellow 'IT WAS A GOOD DAY'. The rapper's P-Funk preoccupation continued with 'LETHAL INJECTION' (1993), wherein he spars with GEORGE CLINTON on the 'One Nation Under A Groove'-sampling 'BOP GUN (ONE NATION)', a single that almost made the Top 20 in both Britain and America. • **Songwriters:** Co-writes with SADLER or JINX. Sample The ISLEYS, JAMES BROWN, STEELY DAN and MICHAEL JACKSON, OHIO PLAYERS, PUBLIC ENEMY, DAS EFX, MOMENTS + GRANDMASTER FLASH. • **Trivia:** Starred and contributed to soundtracks for the films 'Boyz 'n' The Hood' and 'Trespass' (circa early 90's). In 1991, he co-wrote with JAMES BROWN and produced female hardcore rapper YO-YO on their 'East-West' debut US hit single 'You can't Play With My World'.

Album rating: AMERIKKKA'S MOST WANTED (*8) / DEATH CERTIFICATE (*8) / THE PREDATOR (*6) / LETHAL INJECTION (*5) / BOOTLEGS & B-SIDES collection (*5) / WAR & PEACE, VOL.1 (THE WAR DISC) (*5)

ICE CUBE – vocals (with backing from DA LENCH MOB)

	Ruthless	Priority
May 90. (12") *(VL 7220)* **AMERIKKKA'S MOST WANTED. / ONCE UPON A TIME IN THE PROJECTS**	[ ]	[ ]

	4th & Broad	Priority
Jun 90. (cd/c/lp) *(CR CD/CA/LP 551) <57120>* **AMERIKKKA'S MOST WANTED**	48	19 May90

– Better off dead / The nigga ya love to hate / Amerikkka's most wanted / What they hittin' foe? / You can't fade me / JD's gaffilin / Once upon a time in the projects / Turn off the radio / Endangered species (tales from the darkside) / A gangsta's fairytale / I'm only for the funny / Get off my Dick and tell yo bitch to come here / The drive-by / Rollin' with the Lench Mob / Who's the Mack? / It's a man's world / The bomb. *(cd re-iss. Sep96 on 'Island'; IMCD 230)*

Mar 91. (m-cd/m-c/m-lp) *(BRECD/BRCM/BRLM 572) <7230>* **KILL AT WILL** (above remixes) [66] [34] Dec90
– Endangered species (tales from the darkside) / Jackin' for beats / Get off my Dick and tell yo bitch to come here / The product / Dead Homiez / JD's gaffilin (part 2) / I gotta say what up!!!.

Nov 91. (cd/c/lp) *(BR CD/CA/LP 581) <57155>* **DEATH CERTIFICATE** [ ] [2]
– The funeral / The wrong nigga to fuck wit / My summer vacation / Steady mobbin' / Robin Lench / Givin' up the nappy dug out / Look who's burnin' / A bird in the hand / Man's best friend / Alive on arrival / Death / The birth / I wanna kill Sam / Horny lil' devil / True to the game / Color blind / Doing dumb shit / Us. *(cd+=)* – No Vaseline / Black Korea. *(cd re-iss. Sep96 on 'Island'; IMCD 232)*

Dec 91. (7") *<7247>* **STEADY MOBBIN' / US** [ ]
(12"+=/cd-s+=) – Dead Homrez / Endangered species (tales from the dark side) (remix).

Nov 92. (cd-s) *<53813>* **WICKED (2 versions) / U AIN'T GONNA TAKE MY LIFE (2 versions)** [–] [55]

Nov 92. (7"/c-s) *(BRW/BRCA 282)* **WICKED. / WE HAD TO TEAR THIS MOTHAFUCKA UP** [ ] [–]

(12"+=/cd-s+=) (*12BRW/BRCD 282*) – ('A'instrumental) / The wrong nigga to fuck wit. *(re-iss. Aug93, hit UK 62; same)*

Nov 92. (cd/c/lp) *(BR CD/CA/LP 592) <57185>* **THE PREDATOR** [73] [1]
– (the first day of school intro) / When will they shoot? / (I'm scared) / Wicked / Now I gotta wet 'cha / The predator / It was a good day / We had to tear this mothafucka up / **** 'em / Dirty Mack / Don't trust 'em / Gangsta's fairytale 2 / Check yo self / Who's got the camera? / Integration / Say hi to the bad guy. *(cd re-iss. Sep96 on 'Island'; IMCD 328)*

Feb 93. (c-s) *<53817>* **IT WAS A GOOD DAY / ('A'instrumental)** [–] [15]

Mar 93. (c-s) *(BRCA 270) <53817>* **IT WAS A GOOD DAY. / AIN'T GONNA TAKE MY LIFE** [27] [–]
(12"+=/cd-s+=) (*12BRW/BRCD 270*) – ('A'&'B'instrumentals).

Jul 93. (c-s; as ICE CUBE featuring DAS EFX) *(BRCA 283)* *<53830>* **CHECK YO SELF / IT WAS A GOOD DAY (radio mix)** [36] [20]
(12"+=/cd-s+=) (*12BRW/BRCD 283*) – 24 with an L / ('A'version).
(cd-s+=) (*BRCDX 283*) – It was a good day (instrumental) / Who got the camera.

Dec 93. (cd/c/lp) *(BR CD/LP) <53876>* **LETHAL INJECTION** [52] [5]
– The shot / Really doe / Ghetto bird / You know how we do it / Cave bitch / Bop gun (one nation) / What can I do? / Lil ass gee / Make it ruff, make it smooth / Down for whatever / Enemy / When I get to Heaven. *(cd re-iss. Sep96 on 'Island'; IMCD 229)*

Dec 93. (12") *(12BRW 302) <53843>* **REALLY DOE. / MY SKIN IS MY SKIN** [66] [54]
(cd-s+=) (*BRCD 302*) – ('A'&'B'mixes).

Mar 94. (7"/c-s) *(BRW/BRCA 303) <53847>* **YOU KNOW HOW WE DO IT. / 2 N THE MORNING** [41] [30]
(12"+=/cd-s+=) (*12BRW/BRCD 303*) – ('A'instrumental). *(re-entered UK No.46 Dec94)*
(cd-s+=) (*BRCDX 303*) – D-voidofpopniggafiedmegamix.

Aug 94. (7"/c-s; by ICE CUBE featuring GEORGE CLINTON) *(BR W/CA 308) <53155>* **BOP GUN (ONE NATION). / DOWN FOR WHATEVER** [22] [23] Jul94
(12"+=) (*12BRW 308*) – ('A'-MYR mix) / Ghetto jam.
(cd-s+=) (*BRCD 308*) – Ghetto bird (Dr. Jam's mix).

—— snippets from the FUNKADELIC song 'One Nation Under A Groove'.

Dec 94. (cd/c/d-lp) *(BR CD/CA/LP 616) <53921>* **BOOTLEGS AND B-SIDES** (compilation) [ ] [19]
– Robin Hood (cause it ain't all good) / What can I do (remix) / 24 with an L / You know how we do it (remix) / 2 n the morning / Check yo self (remix) / You don't want to fuck with these (unreleased '93 shit) / Lil piss gee (eerie gumbo mix) / My skin is my sin / It was a good day (remix) / D'voidofpopniggafied – megamix. *(cd re-iss. Sep96 on 'Island'; IMCD 231)*

—— In 1995, ICE CUBE featured on minor hits by SCARFACE ('People Don't Believe') and WC AND THE MAAD CIRCLE 'West Up!'.

	Priority	Priority
Mar 97. (cd-s) *(894176-2)* **WORLD IS MINE / ('A'mixes)**	60	[ ]

—— In Aug'97, ICE CUBE collaborated with KRS-ONE, B-REAL and SHAQUE O'NEILL on minor US hit single, 'Men Of Steel'.

Dec 97. (cd) *<51037>* **FEATURING . . . ICE CUBE** (compilation) [–] [ ]
– Bend a corner with me / Natural born killaz / Bow down / Bop gun (one nation) / Check yo self / Endangered species (tales from the . . . .) / Trespass / It's a man's world / West up! / Game over / Wicked ways / Two to the head.

Oct 98. (c-s,12",cd-s; ICE CUBE featuring MR. SHORT KHOP) *<5345>* **PUSHIN' WEIGHT / (mixes)** [–] [26]

Nov 98. (cd/lp) *(CDPTY/PTYLP 1616) <50700>* **WAR & PEACE VOL.1 (THE WAR DISC)** [ ] [7]
– Ask about me / Pushin weight / Dr. Frankenstein / Fuck dying / War & peace / Ghetto vet / Greed / MP / Cash over ass / Curse of money / Peckin' order / Limos, demos & bimbos / Once upon a time in the projects 2 / If I was fuckin you / X-bitches / Extradition / 3 strikes you in / Penitentiary.

Nov 99. (c-s/cd-s; as ICE CUBE featuring MACK 10 & MS. TOI) *<53562>* **YOU CAN DO IT** [–] [42]

ICE-T

Born: TRACY MORROW, 16 Feb'58, Newark, New Jersey, USA. With a ghetto background that reportedly involved copious amounts of unlawful activity, a name derived from superpimp, ICEBERG SLIM, and a mean line in caustic wit, ICE-T set himself up as the original 'gangsta' rapper. The fact of the matter is he wasn't actually the first gangsta rapper, although he did invent the particularly potent West Coast strain. With backing from AFRIKA ISLAM and DJ ALADDIN, his debut for 'Warners', 'RHYME PAYS' (1987), set out the ICE-T agenda of unashamed criminal glorification over tough, made to measure beats. 'POWER' (1988) thankfully laid off the "I'm mental, me" sentiments to a certain degree, allowing room for more objectively intelligent lyrics, although that obviously couldn't be applied to 'GIRLS L.G.B.N.A.F.' (LET'S GET BUTT NAKED AND FUCK, dummy). Hardly the most offensive or potentially damaging lyrics in the ICE-T canon, the song nevertheless upset those nice people at the PMRC (an American institutionalised neighbourhood watch scheme for bad pop stars), not the first time he'd upset the powers that be (or would be). This storm in a teacup informed much of 1989's 'THE ICEBERG: FREEDOM OF SPEECH . . . JUST WATCH WHAT YOU SAY', a more rock-based, anti-censorship rant that laid the ground work for his subsequent BODY COUNT project. The record that really took ICE-T's dubious message to the masses was the landmark 'O.G. ORIGINAL GANGSTER' (1991), a UK Top 5 album that saw ICE powering his way through a hardcore rap set of unrelenting intensity. As ever, the lyrics were sharp, witty and artfully articulate but ultimately offensive. While ICE-T argues that he tells it like it is, his lame attempts to justify his continual objectification of women are rarely satisfactory. It's one of hip hop's great tragedies that a rapper as charismatic, intelligent and creative as ICE-T continues to reinforce prejudice and stereotyping; for every inch that CHUCK

D advances the black cause, ICE-T drags it back two. The next logical step for ICE was a foray into the world of heavy metal, another genre not exactly noted for its tolerance. Recruiting ERNIE-C (guitar), D-ROC (guitar), MOOSEMAN (bass) and BEATMASTER V (drums), ICE-T debuted his hardcore/speed metal band, BODY COUNT, on the 1991 Lollapalooza tour prior to the release of their eponymous debut the following year. While the record addressed racism on the likes of 'MOMMA'S GOTTA DIE TONIGHT', the rapper's trademark misogyny was ever present, notably on 'KKK BITCH'. However, the track that really hit the fan squarely with the shit was 'COP KILLER', a nasty little ditty about "taking out" some lawmen. While the LAPD were hardly in a position to come over all moral, they perhaps understandably took offence to such sentiments. As did President George Bush and good ol' Ollie North, ICE-T subsequently being given the honour of the biggest threat to American security since McCARTHY flushed out "those damn commies" in the 50's. The final straw for 'Warners' was when record company personnel started receiving death threats, the label finally giving in and removing the offending song from subsequent pressings. While it's arguably one of the functions of art to question the "norm", to go about it in such a club-footed manner ultimately benefits no-one. ICE-T was as defiant as ever, though, moving to 'Virgin' for 'BORN DEAD' (1994), another accomplished collection that wasn't quite so inflammatory. The rapper's solo career continued, meanwhile, with 'HOME INVASION' (1993) upon which, gasp!, the rapper actually admitted to feelings for his fellow man in 'GOTTA LOTTA LOVE' while remaining as unrepentant about his lifestyle as ever, ('THAT'S HOW I'M LIVIN'). It was to be another three years before the next album and in the interim, ICE-T used his not inconsiderable talent to host a Channel 4 documentary on Blaxploitation movies as well as presenting 'Baadaasss TV', a semi-successful attempt at catering for black culture. He also published a book of his forthright opinions which only served to furnish his opponents with yet more ammunition. ICE-T resumed his recording career in typically bigoted fashion with, 'VI: RETURN OF THE REAL' (1996), a cliched gangsta affair that added anti-semitic sentiment to his litany of hate.

Album rating: RHYME PAYS (*5) / POWER (*5) / THE ICEBERG: FREEDOM OF SPEECH . . . JUST WATCH WHAT YOU SAY (*7) / O.G. ORIGINAL GANGSTER (*8) / BODY COUNT (*8; as Body Count) / HOME INVASION (*6) / BORN DEAD (*5; as Body Count) / IV: RETURN OF THE REAL (*5) / VIOLENT DEMISE (THE LAST DAYS (*4; as Body Count) / THE SEVENTH DEADLY SIN (*5)

ICE-T – vocals / w/**AFRIKA ISLAM** – synthesizers

		Sire	Sire
Jul 87.	(12") (YZ 145) **MAKE IT FUNKY. / SEX**		
Jul 87.	(lp/c/cd) (925602-1/-4/-2) <25602> **RHYME PAYS**		93

– (intro) / Rhyme pays / 6 'n the mornin' / Make it funky / Somebody gotta do it (pimpin' ain't easy) / 409 / I love ladies / Sex / Pain / Squeeze the trigger. (cd-iss. Jan93 on 'Warners'; 7599 25602-2)

Nov 87.	(12") <020805> **SOMEBODY GOT DO IT (PIMPIN' AIN'T EASY). / OUR MOST REQUESTED RECORD**		
Jun 88.	(12") <27902> **COLORS. / SQUEEZE THE TRIGGER**	-	10
Sep 88.	(lp/c/cd) (925765-1/-4/-2) **POWER**		35

– (intro) / Power / Drama / Heartbeat / The syndicate / Radio suckers / I'm your pusher / Personal / High rollers / Girls L.G.B.N.A.F. / Grand larceny / Soul on ice / (outro).

Nov 88.	(7") <27768> **I'M YOUR PUSHER. / GIRLS L.G.B.N.A.F.**	-	
	(12"+=) – ('A'instrumental) / ('A'acappella) / ('B'instrumental) / ('B'acappella).		

		Warners	Sire
Mar 89.	(7") (W 7574) <27574> **HIGH ROLLERS. / THE HUNTED CHILD**	63	
	(12"+=/12"s+=) (W 7574T/+W) – Power.		
Sep 89.	(7") (W 2802) <11810> **LETHAL WEAPON. / HEARTBEAT (remix)**		
	(12"+=/cd-s+=) (W 2802 T/CD) – ('A'instrumental).		
Oct 89.	(lp/c)(cd) (WX 316/+C)<926028-2)> **THE ICEBERG: FREEDOM OF SPEECH . . . JUST WATCH WHAT YOU SAY**	42	37

– (intro) / Shut up, be happy / The iceberg / Lethal weapon / You played yourself / Peel their caps back / The girl tried to kill me / Black'n'decker / Hit the deck / This one's for me / The hunted child / What ya wanna do? / Freedom of speech / My word is bond. (cd re-iss. Feb95)

––––– guested on CURTIS MAYFIELD's re-make of classic 'Superfly'.

Feb 90.	(c-s) <19994> **YOU PLAYED YOURSELF / FREEDOM OF SPEECH**	-	
Feb 90.	(7") (W 9994) **YOU PLAYED YOURSELF. / MY WORD IS BOND**	64	-
	(12"+=) (W 9994T) – Freedom of speech (with HENDRIX sample)		
Apr 90.	(c-s) **WHAT DO YOU WANNA DO? / THE GIRL TRIED TO KILL ME**	-	
Apr 91.	(c-s) <19442> **NEW JACK HUSTLER (NINO'S THEME) / ('A'instrumental)**		67

<above from the film of the same name on US label 'Giant-Sire'>

May 91.	(7") **O.G. ORIGINAL GANGSTER. / BITCHES 2**		
	(12"+=/cd-s+=) – Mind over matter / Midnight.		
May 91.	(cd)(lp/c) <(7599 26492-2)>(WX 412/+C) **O.G. ORIGINAL GANGSTER**	38	5

– Home of the bodybag / First impression / Ziplock / Mic contract / Mind over matter / New Jack hustler / Ed / Bitches 2 (incl. sample:- Dr. Funkenstein) / Straight up nigga / O.G. Original Gangster / The house / Evil E – what about sex? / Fly by / Midnight / Fried chicken / M.V.P.'s / Lifestyles of the rich and infamous / Body count / Prepared to die / Escape from the killing fields / Street killer / Pulse of the rhyme / The tower / Ya should killed me last year. (cd re-iss. Feb95; same)

		Rhyme Syndicate	Rhyme Syndicate
Mar 93.	(d-lp/d-c/d-cd) (RSYN/+C/D 1) <53858> **HOME INVASION**	15	14

– Warning / It's on / Ice MFT / Home invasion / G style / Addicted to danger / Question and answer / Watch the ice break / Race war / That's how I'm livin' / I ain't new ta this / Pimp behind the wheels (DJ Evil E the great) / Gotta lotta love /

Hit the fan / Depths of Hell (featuring DADDY NITRO) / 99 problems (featuring BROTHER MARQUIS) / Funky gripsta / Message to the soldier / Ain't a damn thing changed.

Apr 93.	(12"ep/c-ep/cd-ep) (SYND D/C/R 1) **I AIN'T NEW TA THIS. / MIXED UP / MIXED UP (instrumental)**	62	
Dec 93.	(12"ep/c-ep/cd-ep) (SYND T/C/D 2) **THAT'S HOW I'M LIVIN'. / COLOURS – RICOCHET – NEW JACK HUSTLER (film excerpts)**	21	
Mar 94.	(c-s/12"/cd-s) (SYND C/T/D 3) **GOTTA LOTTA LOVE. / (2-'A'mixes) / excerpt from book 'The Ice Opinion (who gives a f***)'**	24	
	(cd-s) (SYNDD 3) – ('A'mix) / Addicted to danger / G style / Raceway (remixes).		

––––– In Dec 94, ICE-T was credited with WHITFIELD CRANE (Ugly Kid Joe) on MOTORHEAD single 'Born To Raise Hell', hit UK No.47

May 96.	(12"/cd-s) (SYND T/D 5) **I MUST STAND. / ('A'mixes)**	41	
May 96.	(d-lp/c/cd) (RSYN/+C/D) <53933> **VI – THE RETURN OF THE REAL**	26	89

– Pimp anthem / Where the goes down / Bouncin' down the strezeet / Return of the real / I must stand / (Alotta niggas) / Rap games hijacked / How does it feel / The lane / (Rap is fake) / Make the loot loop / Syndicate 4 ever / The 5th / (It's goin' down) / They want me back in / Inside of a gangsta / Forced to do dirt / (Haters) / Cramp your style / (Real).

Nov 96.	(12"ep/cd-ep) (SYND T/D 6) **THE LANE / ('A'mixes). / BOUNCIN' DOWN THE STREZEET / GET MY CASH ON**	18	

		Roadrunner	Coroner
Oct 99.	(cd/d-lp) (RR 8614-2/-1) **THE SEVENTH DEADLY SIN**		

– (intro) / Don't hate the playa / Check your game / Get your moneyman / 7th / NY NY / Valuable game / Eye of the storm / Always wanted to be a ho / Brother Marquis (interlude) / Fuck it / CJ Mac (interlude) / Retaliation / Threat / Check your heart / Sondoobiest (interlude) / Hardcore / In common sense / Numbskull (interlude) / God forgive me / Exodus.

Nov 99.	(cd-s) (RR 2137-3) **VALUABLE GAME / VALUABLE GAME (instrumental) / ICE'S EXODUS (clean version)**		

– compilations, etc. –

May 93.	(cd/c) Warners; (8122 71170-2/-4) **THE CLASSIC COLLECTION**

BODY COUNT

ICE-T with **ERNIE C** – lead guitar / **D-ROC** – rhythm guitar / **MOOSEMAN** – bass / **BEATMASTER 'V'** – drums

		Sire	Sire
Jan 92.	(12"/cd-s; w-drawn) **COP KILLER. / (withdrawn)**	-	
Mar 92.	(cd/c) (9362 45139-2/-4) <26876> **BODY COUNT**		26

– Smoked pork / Body Count's in the house / New sports / Body count / A statistic / Bowels of the Devil / The real problem / KKK bitch / C note / Voodoo / The winner loses / There goes the neighborhood / Oprah / Evil Dick / Body Count anthem / Momma's gotta die tonight / Freedom of speech.

Jun 92.	(12") **THERE GOES THE NEIGHBORHOOD. / KKK BITCH**		

		Rhyme Syndicate	Virgin
Sep 94.	(red-lp/c/cd) (RSYN/+C/D 2) <39802> **BORN DEAD**	15	74

– Body M-F Count / Masters of revenge / Killin' floor / Necessary evil / Drive by / Last breath / Hey Joe / Shallow graves / Surviving the game / Who are you / Sweet lobotomy / Born dead.

Sep 94.	(c-s) (SYNDC 4) **BORN DEAD / BODY COUNT'S IN THE HOUSE (live)**	28	
	(12"pic-d+=) (SYNDTP 4) – ('A'live).		
	(cd-s+=) (SYNDD 4) – Body M-F Count (live) / On with the Body Count (live).		

		Virgin	Virgin
Dec 94.	(etched-10"pic-d) (VSA 1529) **NECESSARY EVIL / NECESSARY EVIL (live) / BOWELS OF THE DEVIL (live)**	45	
	(cd-s) (VSCDX 1529) – ('A'side) / Body Count anthem (live) / Drive by (live) / There goes the neighborhood (live).		

––––– **GRIZ** – bass + **O.T.** – drums; repl. MOOSEMAN + BEATMASTER V

Mar 97.	(cd/c/lp) (CD/TC+/V 2813) **VIOLENT DEMISE (THE LAST DAYS)**		

– (interview) / My way (BODY COUNT & RAW BREED) / Strippers intro / Strippers / Truth or death / Violent demise / Bring it to pain / Music business / I used to love her / Root of all evil / Dead man walking / (interview end) / You're fuckin' with BC / Ernie's intro / Dr. K / Last days.

ICICLE WORKS (see under ⇒ McNABB, Ian)

IDLEWILD

Formed: Edinburgh, Scotland . . . late '95 by RODDY WOOMBLE, ROD JONES and COLIN NEWTON, each having a penchant for noise veterans, SONIC YOUTH and FUGAZI. Having met at a party, the erstwhile students whittled away their revision time with ramshackle rehearsals, eventually channelling their frustrations into a debut single, 'QUEEN OF THE TROUBLED TEENS'. Famously financed by a student loan (and issued on their own 'Human Condition' imprint), the track was championed by Radio One DJ Steve Lamacq, duly rescuing the band from eternal toilet gig hell and setting in motion the mechanics of A&R overload. A follow-up single, 'CHANDELIER', appeared on 'Fierce Panda' while an acclaimed mini-album on 'Deceptive', 'CAPTAIN', kickstarted '98 and became their final fully fledged indie release prior to a deal with 'Food'. Somewhere along the way the band also picked up bassist BOB FAIRFOULL and began to coax some melancholic tunefulness from the blizzard of sound and fury that characterised their youthful approach. 'A FILM FOR THE FUTURE' announced their major label arrival in fittingly convulsive style, the first of many minor hits which have cemented the band's reputation as one of Scotland's most talked about and possibly most dedicated sonic abusers. Their highly anticipated first album proper, 'HOPE IS IMPORTANT' (late '98), made the UK Top 60 and the band's steady rise proves that noisy guitars never go out of fashion; Idle? – nah. Wild? – definitely.

Album rating: HOPE IS IMPORTANT (*7)

RODDY WOOMBLE (b.1976) – vocals / **ROD JONES** (b.1976) – guitar / **COLIN NEWTON** (b.1977) – drums / **PAUL TIPLER** (helped out on) bass

		Human Condition	not iss.
Mar 97. (ltd-7") *(HC 0017)* **QUEEN OF THE TROUBLED TEENS. / FASTER / SELF HEALER** *(re-iss.Jan98; same)*		☐	-

—— **BOB FAIRFOULL** (b.1976) – bass; repl. PAUL

		Fierce Panda	not iss.
Dec 97. (ltd-7") *(NING 42)* **CHANDELIER. / I WANT TO BE A WRITER**		☐	-

		Deceptive	not iss.
Jan 98. (m-cd) *(BLUFF 058CD)* **CAPTAIN** – Self healer / Annihilate now / Captain / Last night I missed all the fireworks / Satan polaroid / You just have to be who you are.		☐	-
Feb 98. (7") *(BLUFF 057)* **SATAN POLAROID. / HOUSE ALONE**		☐	-

		Food	not iss.
Apr 98. (7") *(FOOD 111)* **A FILM FOR THE FUTURE. / MINCE SHOWERCAP (part I)** (cd-s+=) *(CDFOOD 111)* – What am I going to do?	53	-	
Jul 98. (7") *(FOOD 113)* **EVERYONE SAYS YOU'RE SO FRAGILE. / MINCE SHOWERCAP (part II)** (cd-s+=) *(CDFOOD 113)* – Theory of achievement.	47	-	
Oct 98. (7") *(FOOD 114)* **I'M A MESSAGE. / MINCE SHOWERCAP (part III)** (cd-s+=) *(CDFOOD 114)* – This is worse. (cd-s) **THE SESSIONS EP** *(CDFOODS 114)* – ('A'live) / Satan polaroid (live) / You've lost your way (live).	41	-	
Oct 98. (cd/c/lp) *(497132-2/-4/-1)* **HOPE IS IMPORTANT** – You've lost your way / A film for the future / Paint nothing / When I argue I see shapes / 4 people do good / I'm happy to be here tonight / Everyone says you're so fragile / I'm a message / You don't have the heart / Close the door / Safe and sound / Low light.	53		
Feb 99. (7") *(FOOD 116)* **WHEN I ARGUE I SEE SHAPES. / (1903-70) / CHANDELIER (10.15 version)** (cd-s) *(CDFOOD 116)* – (first 2 tracks) / Last night I missed all the fireworks (live). (cd-s) *(CDFOODS 116)* – (first & third tracks) / Palace flophouse.	19	-	
Sep 99. (7") *(FOOD 124)* **LITTLE DISCOURAGE. / BROKEN WINDOWS** (cd-s+=) *(CDFOOD 124)* – A-Tone. (cd-s) *(CDFOODS 124)* – ('A'side) / You don't have the heart (live) / 1990 – night-time.	24	-	

Billy IDOL

Born: WILLIAM BROAD, 30 Nov'55, Stanmore, Middlesex, England. In 1976, this aspiring punk formed GENERATION X alongside BOB ANDREWS and ex-CHELSEA members, TONY JAMES and JOHN TOWE (the latter was soon replaced by former SUBWAY SECT man, MARK LAFF). Though they attracted a loyal fanbase, GENERATION X were never considered a dyed-in-the-wool punk band per se, their more commercial, hooky power pop at odds with the genre's inherent nihilism. Signed to 'Chrysalis', the band hit the Top 40 with their first single, 'YOUR GENERATION', following it up with 'WILD YOUTH' and 'READY STEADY GO', the latter track a decidedly un-punk 60's tribute. An eponymous debut album hit the Top 30 in Spring '78, while the band's sound grew increasingly commercial on successive albums, 'VALLEY OF THE DOLLS' (1979; produced by IAN HUNTER) and 'KISS ME DEADLY' (1981; released under the slightly clipped moniker of GEN X). Following their split in '81, JAMES later formed SIGUE SIGUE SPUTNIK, while the bleached-blond IDOL was free to pursue his barely concealed desire for pop stardom. Relocating to New York, he met manager, Bill Aucoin and producer, Keith Forsey, recruiting guitarist STEVE STEVENS and cutting a cover of Tommy James & The Shondells' 'MONY MONY' (along with a few other tracks – including the GENERATION X song, 'DANCING WITH MYSELF' – it formed part of a US-only mini-set, 'DON'T STOP'). A full length eponymous debut album followed in summer '82, the record including many songs which wouldn't hit the UK charts for another five years. The loping 'HOT IN THE CITY', for example, which became IDOL's first major US success; with the not inconsiderable, IDOL transformed himself into a leather-clad, lip-sneering hard rocker, his anthemic, dancefloor-friendly tunes lapped up by American teeny boppers and older fans alike. 'REBEL YELL' (1984) and the attendant 'EYES WITHOUT A FACE' single gave him further Stateside success, while a re-released 'WHITE WEDDING' gave IDOL a belated UK Top 10 hit in summer '85. A remix compilation, 'VITAL IDOL', was rush released the following month to build on the breakthrough, precipitating a rash of re-issued singles; while sales of his 'WHIPLASH SMILE' (1986) opus certainly benefitted, these re-issues were all bigger hits than his new material, not exactly a good sign. Just prior to the release of 'CHARMED LIFE' (1990), IDOL, ironically enough, suffered a near fatal motorbike crash, the climax to a troubled late 80's period which had seen the singer living out the rock'n'roll lifestyle to the full in sunny L.A. Bluesy and confessional, the album's only hit was 'CRADLE OF LOVE', while the less said about IDOL's cover of The Doors' 'L.A. WOMAN', the better. An ill-advised concept album, 'CYBERPUNK' (1993), was even less well received.

fallen IDOL indeed. • **Songwriters:** GENERATION X:- IDOL – JAMES, except GIMME SOME TRUTH (John Lennon) / SHAKIN' ALL OVER (hit; Johnny Kidd & The Pirates). Solo, IDOL & STEVENS collaborated until 1990 when IDOL wrote with WERNER. Solo Covers; HEROIN (Lou Reed) / MOTHER DAWN (McBrook – Youth).

Album rating: Generation X: GENERATION X (*6) / VALLEY OF THE DOLLS (*5) / KISS ME DEADLY (*5) / PERFECT HITS compilation (*7) / Billy Idol: BILLY IDOL (*6) / REBEL YELL (*7) / WHIPLASH SMILE (*5) / VITAL IDOL remixes (*5) / CHARMED LIFE (*6) / CYBERPUNK (*3) / IDOL SONGS – 11 OF THE BEST compilation (*7)

GENERATION X

BILLY IDOL – vocals (ex-CHELSEA, ex-INFANTS) / **BOB 'Derwood' ANDREWS** – guitar / **TONY JAMES** – bass, vocals (ex-CHELSEA, ex-INFANTS) / **MARK LAFF** – drums (ex-SUBWAY SECT) repl. JOHN TOWE (ex-CHELSEA, ex-INFANTS) who joined ALTERNATIVE TV then ADVERTS, etc

	Chrysalis	Chrysalis
Sep 77. (7") *(CHS 2165)* **YOUR GENERATION. / DAY BY DAY**	36	☐
Dec 77. (7") *(CHS 2189)* **WILD YOUTH. / WILD DUB** *(some copies were mispressed with b-side 'NO NO NO')*		☐
Mar 78. (7") *(CHS 2207)* **READY STEADY GO. / NO NO NO**	47	☐
Mar 78. (lp/c) *(CHR/ZCHR 1169)* **GENERATION X** – From the heart / One hundred punks / Listen / Ready steady go / Kleenex / Promises promises / Day by day / The invisible man / Kiss me deadly / Too personal / Youth, youth, youth. *(cd-iss. Jan86; CCD 1169) (re-iss. cd Mar94; CD25CR 14) (cd re-iss. Jul96 on 'EMI Gold'; CDGOLD 1039)*	29	
Jan 79. (7",7"red,7"pink,7"orange,7"yellow) *(CHS 2261)* **KING ROCKER. / GIMME SOME TRUTH**	11	☐
Jan 79. (lp/c) *(CHR/ZCHR 1193)* **VALLEY OF THE DOLLS** – Running with the boss sound / Night of the Cadillacs / Paradise west / Friday's angels / King rocker / Valley of the dolls / English dream / Love like fire / Paradise west / The prime of Kenny Silvers. *(cd-iss. Jan86; CCD 1193)*	51	
Mar 79. (7",7"brown) *(CHS 2310)* **VALLEY OF THE DOLLS. / SHAKIN' ALL OVER**	23	☐
Jun 79. (7",7"pink) *(CHS 2330)* **FRIDAY'S ANGELS. / TRYING FOR KICKS / THIS HEAT**	62	☐

—— **TERRY CHIMES** – drums (ex-CLASH, ex-COWBOYS INTERNATIONAL) repl. LAFF / **JAMES STEPHENSON** – guitar (ex-CHELSEA) repl. 'DERWOOD' (later to WESTWORLD)

GEN X

Sep 80. (7") *(CHS 2444)* **DANCING WITH MYSELF. / UGLY RASH** (12"+=) *(CHS12 2444)* – Loopy dub / What do you want	62	☐
Jan 81. (lp/c) *(CHR/ZCHR 1327)* **KISS ME DEADLY** – Dancing with myself / Untouchables / Happy people / Heaven's inside / Triumph / Revenge / Stars look down / What do you want / Oh mother. *(cd-iss. Jan86; CCD 1327)*		☐
Jan 81. (7"ep,7"clear-ep/12"ep) *(CHS/+12 2488)* **DANCING WITH MYSELF / UNTOUCHABLES. / KING ROCKER / ROCK ON**	60	☐

—— split early '81, when BILLY went solo. CHIMES rejoined The CLASH, TONY JAMES later formed SIGUE SIGUE SPUTNIK. STEPHENSON later joined GENE LOVES JEZEBEL, then The CULT.

– compilations, etc. –

on 'Chrysalis' unless otherwise mentioned

Nov 85. (lp/c) *(CHM/ZCHM 1521)* **THE BEST OF GENERATION X**		☐ ☐
Feb 87. (7") *Old Gold; (OG 9693)* **KING ROCKER. / VALLEY OF THE DOLLS**		-
Jun 87. (lp) *M.B.C.; (JOCKLP 9)* **THE ORIGINAL GENERATION X**		-
Jun 88. (lp) *M.B.C.; (JOCKLP 11)* **GENERATION X LIVE** (live)		-
Oct 91. (cd/c/lp) *(CCD/ZCHR/CHR 1854)* **PERFECT HITS (1975-81)** – Dancing with myself / Your generation / Ready steady go / The untouchables / Day by day / Wild youth / Wild dub / One hundred punks / King rocker / Kiss me deadly / Gimme some truth / New order / English dream / Triumph / Youth, youth, youth.		☐

BILLY IDOL

—— with **STEVE STEVENS** – guitar / **PHIL FEIT** – bass / **STEVE MISSAL** – drums (same label)

Sep 81. (7") *(CHS 2543)* **MONY MONY. / BABY TALK** (12"+=) *(CHS12 2543)* – Untouchables / Dancing with myself (extended). <US-title 'DON'T STOP' m-lp; 4000>; hit No.71.		☐ ☐
Jul 82. (lp/c) *(CHR/ZCHR 1377)* <41377> **BILLY IDOL** – Come on, come on / White wedding (part 1 & 2) / Hot in the city / Dead on arrival / Nobody's business / Love calling / Hole in the wall / Shooting stars / It's so cruel / Congo man. *(cd-iss. Jan86; CCD 1377) (re-iss. Jul94 cd/c;)*		45
Aug 82. (7"/7"pic-d/ext.12") *(CHS/+P/12 2625)* <2605> **HOT IN THE CITY. / DEAD ON ARRIVAL**	58	23 Jun82
Oct 82. (7"/ext.12") *(CHS/+12 2656)* <42697> **WHITE WEDDING. / HOLE IN THE WALL**		36
Sep 83. (7",7"clear) *(IDOL 1)* **WHITE WEDDING. / HOT IN THE CITY** (12"+=) *(IDOLX 1)* – Love calling / Dancing with myself.		-
Jan 84. (lp/c) *(CHR/ZCHR 1450)* <41450> **REBEL YELL** – Rebel yell / Daytime drama / Eyes without a face / Blue highway / Flesh for fantasy / Catch my fall / Crank call / (Do not) Stand in the shadows / The dead next door. *(hit UK No.36 Sep85) (cd-iss. Jan86; CCD 1450) (re-iss. cd Mar94;)*		6 Nov83
Feb 84. (7"/7"square-pic-d) *(IDOL/+P 2)* <42762> **REBEL YELL. / CRANK CALL** (12"+=) *(IDOLX 2)* – White wedding. (d7"++=) *(IDOLD 2)* – Hot in the city.	62	46 Jan84
Jun 84. (7") *(IDOL 3)* <42786> **EYES WITHOUT A FACE. / THE DEAD NEXT DOOR**	18	4 Apr84

(d7"+=/12"+=/12"pic-d+=) *(IDOL D/X/P 3)* – Dancing with myself / Rebel yell.

Sep 84. (7") *(IDOL 4) <42809>* **FLESH FOR FANTASY. / BLUE HIGHWAY** `54` `29` Aug84
(12"+=/12"pic-d+=) *(IDOL X/P 4)* – ('A'extended).

Oct 84. (7") *<42840>* **CATCH MY FALL. /** `-` `50`
Jun 85. (7",7"white) *(IDOL 5)* **WHITE WEDDING. / FLESH FOR FANTASY** `6` `-`
(7"clear/12",12"white/12"pic-d) *(IDOL+X/P 5)* – ('A'-Shotgun mix pts.1 & 2) / Mega-Idol-mix.

Jul 85. (lp/c) *(CUX/ZCUX 1502) <41620>* **VITAL IDOL** (remix compilation) `7` `10` Oct87
– White wedding (part 1 & 2) / Dancing with myself / Flesh for fantasy / Catch my fall / Mony Mony / Love calling (dub) / Hot in the city. *(cd-iss. Jan86; CCD 1502)*

Sep 85. (7"/7"pic-d) *(IDOL/+P 6)* **REBEL YELL. / (DO NOT) STAND IN THE SHADOWS** (live) `6`
(12"+=/12"pic-d+=) *(IDOL X/P 6)* – Blue highway.

Sep 86. (7",7"colrd) *(IDOL 8) <43024>* **TO BE A LOVER. / ALL SUMMER SINGLE** `22` `6`
(12"+=/12"pic-d+=) *(IDOL X/P 8)* – ('A'-Mercy mix).
(d12"++=) *(IDOLD 8)* – White wedding.

Oct 86. (lp/c/cd) *(CDL/ZCDL/CCD 1514) <41514>* **WHIPLASH SMILE** `8` `6`
– Worlds forgotten boy / To be a lover / Soul standing by / Sweet sixteen / Man for all seasons / Don't need a gun / Beyond belief / Fatal charm / All summer single / One night, one chance. *(re-iss. Mar93 cd/c;)*

Feb 87. (7",7"colrd) *(IDOL 9) <43087>* **DON'T NEED A GUN. / FATAL CHARM** `26` `37` Jan87
(12"+=/12"pic-d+=) *(IDOL X/P 9)* – ('A'version).
(d7"+=) *(IDOLD 9)* – (free single).

May 87. (7") *(IDOL 10) <43114>* **SWEET 16. / BEYOND BELIEF** `17` `20` Apr87
(12"+=/12"pic-d+=) *(IDOL X/P 10)* – Rebel yell.

Sep 87. (7") *(IDOL 11) <43161>* **MONY MONY** (live). / **SHAKIN' ALL OVER** (live) `7` `1` Aug87
(12"+=) *(IDOLX 11)* – ('A'-Hung like a pony mix).

Jan 88. (7") *(IDOL 12) <43203>* **HOT IN THE CITY** (remix). / **CATCH MY FALL** (remix) `13` `48` Dec87
(12"+=) *(IDOLX 12)* – Soul standing by.
('A'-Exterminator mix-cd-s++=) *(IDOLCD 12)* – Mony Mony (live).

Jun 88. (lp/c/cd) *(BILTV/ZBILTV/BILCD 1)* **IDOL SONGS – 11 OF THE BEST** (compilation) `2` `-`
– Rebel yell / Hot in the city / White wedding / Eyes without a face / Catch my fall / Mony mony / To be a lover / Sweet sixteen / Flesh for fantasy / Don't need a gun / Dancing with myself.

Aug 88. (7"/12"/cd-s) *(IDOL/+X/CD 13)* **CATCH MY FALL** (the remix fix). / **ALL SUMMER SINGLE** (remix) `63` `-`

—— now with **MARK YOUNGER-SMITH** – guitar, bass / **KEITH FORSEY** – drums, producer **VITO** and **PHIL SOUSSAN** – bass / **ARTHUR BARROW** – keyboards / **MIKE BAIRD** – drums

Apr 90. (7"/c-s) *(IDOL/+C 14) <23509>* **CRADLE OF LOVE. / 311 MAN** `34` `2`
(12") *(IDOLX 14)* – ('A'extended) / Rob the cradle of love.
(cd-s) *(IDOLCD 14)* – (all 3 tracks above).

Apr 90. (cd/c/lp) *(CD/Z+/CHR 1735) <17735>* **CHARMED LIFE** `15` `11`
– The loveless / Pumping on steel / Prodigal blues / L.A. woman / Trouble with the sweet stuff / Cradle of love / Mark of Caine / Endless sleep / Love unchained / The right way / License to thrill.

Jul 90. (7"/c-s) *(IDOL/+C 15) <23571>* **L.A. WOMAN. / LICENSE TO THRILL** `70` `52`
(12"+=/cd-s+=) *(IDOL X/CD 15)* – Love child.

Dec 90. (7"/c-s) *(IDOL/+C 16)* **PRODIGAL BLUES. / MARK OF CAINE** `47`
(12"+=/cd-s+=) *(IDOL X/CD 16)* – Flesh for fantasy.

—— retained co-writer **YOUNGER-SMITH** + recruited **ROBIN HANCOCK** – keyboards, producer / **DOUG WIMBUSH** – bass / **JAMIE MAMOBERAC** – organ / **TAL BERGHAN** – drums

Jun 93. (7"/12") *(CHS/+12 3994)* **SHOCK TO THE SYSTEM. / HEROIN** (overloads mix) / **HEROIN** (durge trance dub) `30`
(cd-s) *(CHSCD1 3994)* – Heroin (original) / Rebel yell.
(cd-s) *(CHSCD2 3994)* – ('A'side) / Heroin (smack attack) / White wedding.

Jun 93. (cd/c/lp) *(CD/Z+/CHR 6000) <26000>* **CYBERPUNK** `20` `48`
– Wasteland / Shock to the system / Tomorrow people / Adam in chains / Neuromancer / Power junkie / Love labours on / Heroin / Shangrila / Concrete kingdom / Venus / Then the night comes / Mother Dawn.

Sep 93. (c-s/7") *(TC+/CHS 5002)* **ADAM IN CHAINS. / SHOCK TO THE SYSTEM / VENUS**
(cd-s) *(CSCHSS 5002)* – (first 2) / Eyes without a face.
(cd-s) *(CDCHS 5002)* – ('A'side) / Tomorrow people / Mony Mony.

Fox-Arista Fox-Arista

Sep 94. (7"/c-s/cd-s) *(74321 22347-7/-4/-2)* **SPEED. / REBEL YELL (acoustic)** `47`
(above from the film of the same name)

James IHA (see under ⇒ SMASHING PUMPKINS)

Natalie IMBRUGLIA

Born: 4 Feb'75, Sydney, Australia. Before becoming one of Europe's biggest selling pop/rock artists in 1998, IMBRUGLIA was just one of the many soap actresses groomed to become a singer/performer. The childlike brunette was born in a small beach community and grew up with her three sisters who had all played a major influence in her ambitions to become an actress. IMBRUGLIA's lucky break came when Australian soap 'Neighbours' offered her a leading part. The role subsequently led to widespread popularity amongst pre-pubescent teenagers, who heralded her as their new pin-up. After becoming tired of her acting life, she flitted to London in 1996 in the hope of becoming

a pop star, hooking up with former CURE guitarist PHIL THORNALLY and signing an album contract with 'R.C.A.'. Her debut single, 'TORN' was launched in October 1997, a track that had previously been a local hit in 1994 for L.A. outfit, EDNASWAP. NATALIE's version became one of the most heavily rotated songs on UK radio, narrowly missing No.1 and spending an amazing 14 weeks in the charts. Few had predicted the runaway success of the single, many critics writing-off IMBRUGLIA as a lightweight ALANIS MORISSETTE impersonator. A month later, her debut set 'LEFT OF THE MIDDLE' (1997) was released in Australia and Britain (the following Spring in the USA) and included follow-up hits 'BIG MISTAKE' and 'WISHING I WAS THERE', the latter displaying more ALANIS traits through its use of heavy distortion and angry, but radio-friendly vocals. Another highlight was 'SMOKE', a soft ballad in the mould of FIONA APPLE or perhaps LISA LOEB. NATALIE returned in 1999 to sing on a Various Superstar charity re-vamp of the Rolling Stones' 'IT'S ONLY ROCK'N'ROLL', while also guesting on TOM JONES' star-studded cover album 'RELOAD' (the track in question being the INXS song, 'Never Tear Us Apart').

Album rating: LEFT OF THE MIDDLE (*6)

NATALIE IMBRUGLIA – vocals / with various session people

                                      R.C.A.   R.C.A.

Oct 97. (c-s) *(74321 52798-4) <radio play>* **TORN / SOMETIMES** `2` `42` 1998
(cd-s+=) *(74321 52798-2)* – Frightened child.
(cd-s) *(74321 52799-2)* – ('A'side) / Contradictions / Diving in at the deep end.

Nov 97. (cd/c) *(74321 54441-21/-45) <67634>* **LEFT OF THE MIDDLE** `5` `10` Mar98
– Torn / One more addiction / Big mistake / Leave me alone / Intuition / Smoke / Pigeons and crumbs / Don't you think? / Impressed / Wishing I was there / City / Left of the middle.

Mar 98. (c-s) *(74321 56678-4)* **BIG MISTAKE /** `2`
(cd-s+=) *(74321 56678-2)* –
(cd-s) *(74321 56679-2)* – ('A'mixes).

May 98. (c-s) *(74321 58506-4)* **WISHING I WAS THERE / WHY** `19`
(cd-s+=) *(74321 58506-2)* – Big mistake (live for MTV).
(cd-s) *(74321 58515-2)* – ('A'side) / Impressed.

Oct 98. (c-s/cd-s) *(74321 62194-4/-2)* **SMOKE / CITY** (live) `5`
(cd-s) *(74321 62149-2)* – ('A'remixes; Way Out West / Dub Pistols / etc.).

IMPERIAL TEEN (see under ⇒ FAITH NO MORE)

IN-BE-TWEENS (see under ⇒ SLADE)

INCREDIBLE STRING BAND

Formed: Glasgow, Scotland ... early 1966 by ROBIN WILLIAMSON, CLIVE PALMER and MIKE HERON. From the early 60's, WILLIAMSON had played London gigs alongside BERT JANSCH (future PENTANGLE), before he returned to Glasgow. In April 1961, he formed a duo with Englishman PALMER, although they found it difficult to establish themselves, that is, until 1965 when PALMER set up the 'Incredible' folk club in Sauchiehall Street. That same year, the pair performed at the Edinburgh Folk Festival, catching the eye of Nathan Joseph of 'Transatlantic' records who recorded them for the concert's Various Artists compilation. After their folk club was shut down by the police, they became a trio, adding MIKE HERON to become The INCREDIBLE STRING BAND. After months tracking them down, American producer JOE BOYD finally found them and duly signed them to 'Elektra'. He subsequently took them to London, where they recorded their eponymous debut album (summer '66). With this well-received record under their belt, PALMER departed for Afghanistan. When he returned he declined to re-join the act, who were now broke but under the management of BOYD. Upon ROBIN's return from Morocco, the duo (augmented by some friends), played an 'Elektra' records package alongside TOM PAXTON and JUDY COLLINS, at The Royal Albert Hall. It helped promote their second album, '5,000 SPIRITS OR THE LAYERS OF THE ONION', which made the UK Top 30 in 1967. Their underground blend of psychedelic folk was crystallised on such charming tracks as, 'CHINESE WHITE', 'FIRST GIRL I LOVED' and 'PAINTING BOX'. In Spring '68, they surprisingly crashed into the UK Top 5 with their third set, 'THE HANGMAN'S BEAUTIFUL DAUGHTER'. The album's witty lyrics (alternately penned by HERON or WILLIAMSON) and ethnic multi-instrumentation was embellished with the vocals of the duo's girlfriends, LICORICE and ROSE. The highlights of this album, arguably the group's finest hour, were 'A VERY CELLULAR SONG', 'THE MINOTAUR'S SONG' and 'KOEEOADDI THERE'. Late that year, they issued 2 single lp's as a double-set, 'WEE TAM' & 'THE BIG HUGE'. However, this brilliant but confused package failed to sell. Over the next two years, they released three UK Top 40 albums ('I LOOKED UP', a collection of baroque eclecticism – 'U' verging on pantomine), but after a move to 'Island' in 1971, they soon faded from the commercial limelight. Nevertheless, the second 'Island' album, 'LIQUID ACROBAT AS REGARDS THE AIR', hit the Top 50, boasting the spine-tingling melancholy of the 11-minute 'DARLING BELLE'. HERON and WILLIAMSON went their separate ways in the mid-70's, the former writing 'DON'T KILL IT CAROL' (later a hit for MANFRED MANN'S EARTH BAND), the latter becoming something of a self-styled cosmic folk story-teller (complete with harp).

Album rating: THE INCREDIBLE STRING BAND (*6) / 5,000 SPIRITS OR THE LAYERS OF THE ONION (*8) / THE HANGMAN'S BEAUTIFUL DAUGHTER (*8) / WEE TAM & THE BIG HUGE (*7) / CHANGING HORSES (*5) / I LOOKED UP (*4) / "U" (*4) / RELICS OF ... compilation (*7) / BE GLAD FOR THE SONG HAS

NO ENDING (*4) / LIQUID ACROBAT AS REGARDS THE AIR (*5) / EARTHSPAN (*4) / NO RUINOUS FEUD (*5) / HARD ROPE AND SILKEN TWINE (*4) / SEASONS THEY CHANGE – THE BEST OF THE INCREDIBLE STRING BAND compilation (*8)

ROBIN WILLIAMSON (b.24 Nov'43, Edinburgh, Scotland) – vocals, guitars, etc. / **CLIVE PALMER** (b. England) – guitar, banjo, vocals / **MIKE HERON** (b.12 Dec'42) – vocals, rhythm guitar, sitar, etc.

		Elektra	Elektra
Jun 66.	(lp) *(EUK 254)* <*EKS 7322*> **THE INCREDIBLE STRING BAND**		

– Maybe someday / October song / When the music starts to play / Schaeffer's jig / Womankind / The tree / Whistle tune / Dandelion blues / How happy am I / Empty pocket blues / Smoke shovelling song / Can't keep me here / Good as gone / Footsteps of the heron / Niggertown / Everything's fine right now. *(re-iss. Jul68; EKL 254); hit No.34) (cd-iss. Jul93; 7559 61547-2) (cd re-iss. Jun94 on 'Hannibal'; HNCD 4437)*

—— Now a duo when PALMER went to Afghanistan. He later formed FAMOUS JUG BAND added **CHRISTINA 'LICORICE' McKENNA** – some vocals, organ (a guest on below) plus guests **DANNY THOMPSON** – double bass (of PENTANGLE) / **JOHN HOPKINS** – piano

Jul 67.	(lp; mono/stereo) *(EUK/+S7 257)* <*EKS 74010*> **THE 5,000 SPIRITS OR THE LAYERS OF THE ONION**	26	

– Chinese white / No sleep blues / Painting box / The Mad Hatter's song / Little cloud / The eyes of fate / Blues for the muse / The hedgehog's song / First girl I loved / You know that you could be / My name is death / Gently tender / Way back in the 1960's. *(re-iss. 1968; EKS 7257) (re-iss. Jan73 + 1976; K 42001) (cd-iss. Mar92; 7559 60913-2) (cd re-iss. Jun94 on 'Hannibal'; HNCD 4438)*

Mar 68.	(7") *(EKSN 45028)* **PAINTING BOX. / NO SLEEP BLUES**		
Mar 68.	(lp; mono/stereo) *(EUK/+S7 258)* <*EKS 74021*> **THE HANGMAN'S BEAUTIFUL DAUGHTER**	5	Jun68

– Koeeoaddi there / The minotaur's song / Witches hat / A very cellular song / Mercy I cry city / Waltz of the new Moon / The water song / Three is a green crown / Swift as the wind / Nightfall. *(re-iss. Jan73 + 1976; K 42002) (cd-iss. Mar92; 7559 60835-2) (cd re-iss. Jun94 on 'Hannibal'; HNCD 4437)*

—— **MIKE, ROBIN** and his girlfriend **LICORICE** introduced MIKE'S girlfriend **ROSE SIMPSON** – some vocals, bass, percussion, violin

Oct 68.	(d-lp; mono/stereo) *(EKL/EKS7 4036-7)* **WEE TAM / THE BIG HUGE**		

(d-cd-iss. Nov94 on 'Hannibal'; HNCD 4802)

Oct 68.	(lp; mono/stereo) *(EKL/*<*EKS7 4036*>) **WEE TAM**		Mar69

– Job's tears / Puppies / Beyond the see / The yellow snake / Log cabin home in the sky / You get brighter / The half-remarkable question / Air / Ducks on a pond. *(re-iss. Jan73 + 1976; K 42021) (cd-iss. Feb92; 7559 60914-2)*

Oct 68.	(lp; mono/stereo) *(EKL/*<*EKS7 4037*>) **THE BIG HUGE**		Mar69

– Maya / Greatest friend / The son of Noah's brother / Lordly nightshade / The mountain of God / Cousin caterpillar / The iron stone / Douglas Traherne Harding / The circle is unbroken. *(re-iss. Jan73 + 1976; K 42022) (cd-iss. Jul93; 7559 61548-2)*

—— LICORICE was now a full-time member

Oct 69.	(7") *(EKSN 45074)* **BIG TED. / ALL WRIT DOWN**		-
Nov 69.	(lp) *(*<*EKS 74057*>) **CHANGING HORSES**	30	

– Big Ted / White bird / Dust be diamonds / Sleepers, awake! / Mr. & Mrs. / Creation. *(cd-iss. Jul93; 7559 61549-2) (cd-iss. Dec94 on 'Hannibal'; HNCD 4439)*

—— added guest **DAVE MATTACKS** – drums of FAIRPORT CONVENTION

Apr 70.	(lp) *(*<*EKS 7401*>) **I LOOKED UP**	30	Jul70

– Black Jack David / The letter / Pictures in a mirror / This moment / When you find out who you are / Fair as you. *(re-prom.1970; 2469 002) (cd-iss. Dec94 on 'Hannibal'; HNCD 4440)*

Apr 70.	(7") *(2101 003)* **THIS MOMENT. / BLACK JACK DAVY**		
May 70.	(7") *(45696)* **THIS MOMENT. / BIG TED**		-

—— augmented by **JANET SHANKMAN** – b.vocals (ROBIN married her Dec70) **PETE GRANT** – banjo / **GREG HART** – sitar (of STONE MONKEY) plus guest **MALCOLM LE MAISTRE** – keyboards, bass (of EXPLODING GALAXY)

Oct 70.	(d-lp) *(2665 001)* <*7E 2002*> **"U"**	34	Jan71

– El wool suite / The juggler's song / Time / Bad Sadie Lee / Queen of love / Partial belated overture / Light in the time of darkness – Glad to see you / Walking along with you / Hirem pawn Itof – Fairies' hornpipe / Bridge theme / Bridge song / Astral plane theme / Invocation / Robot blues / Puppet song / Cutting the strings / I know you / Rainbow. *(re-iss. Jan73; K 62002)*

—— Back to basic duo of **ROBIN + MIKE** plus **LICORICE + ROSE**

		Island	Elektra
Apr 71.	(lp) *(ILPS 9140)* **BE GLAD FOR THE SONG HAS NO ENDING**		-

– Come with me / All writ down / Vishangro / See all the people / Waiting for you / (Be glad for) The song has no ending.

—— **MALCOLM LE MAISTRE** – keyboards, bass, vocals returned to repl. ROSE

Oct 71.	(lp) *(ILPS 9172)* <*74112*> **LIQUID ACROBAT AS REGARDS THE AIR**	46	Feb72

– Talking of the end / Dear old battlefield / Cosmic boy / Worlds they rise and fall / Evloution rag / Painted chariot / Adam and Eve / Red hair / Here till here is there / Tree / Jigs: Eyes like leaves – Sunday is my wedding day – Drops of whiskey – Grumbling old men / Darling Belle. *(re-iss. Aug91 cd)(c; IMCD 130)(ICM 9172)*

—— added **GERARD DOTT** – clarinet, saxophone (he played on HERON's 1972 solo album) and guest on one **STUART GORDON** – viola

Oct 72.	(lp) *(ILPS 9211)* **EARTH SPAN**		-

– My father was a lighthouse keeper / Antoine / Restless night / Sunday song / Black Jack David / Banks of sweet Italy / The actor / Moon hang low / The sailor and the dancer / Seagull. *(cd-iss. Dec92 on 'Edsel'; EDCD 360)*

Nov 72.	(7") *(WIP 6145)* **BLACK JACK DAVID. / MOON HANG LOW**		-

—— **STAN LEE** – bass repl. LICORICE who joined WOODY WOODMANSEY Band **JACK INGRAM** – drums (added to ROBIN, MIKE, MALCOLM, GERARD and STAN)

		Island	Reprise
Feb 73.	(7") *(WIP 6158)* **AT THE LIGHTHOUSE DANCE. / JIGS**		-
Feb 73.	(lp) *(ILPS 9229)* <*2139*> **NO RUINOUS FEUD**		

– Explorer / Down before Cathy / Saturday maybe / Jigs / Old Bouccaneer / At the lighthouse dance / Second fiddle / Circus girl / Turquoise blue / My blue tears / Weather the storm / Little girl. *(cd-iss. Nov92 on 'Edsel'; EDCD 367)*

—— **GRAHAM FORBES** – electric guitar (ex-POWERHOUSE) repl. GERARD / **JOHN GILSTON** – drums repl. INGRAM

Mar 74.	(lp) *(ILPS 9270)* <*2198*> **HARD ROPE & SILKEN TWINE**		

– Maker of islands / Cold February / Glancing love / Dreams of no return / Dumb Kate / Ithkos. *(cd-iss. Feb93 on 'Edsel'; EDCD 368)*

—— WILLIAMSON + HERON went onto solo careers

– compilations etc. –

Mar 71.	(lp) *Elektra; (EKS 74065) / Reprise; <7E 2004>* **RELICS OF THE INCREDIBLE STRING BAND**		
Nov 76.	(d-lp) *Island; (ISLD 9)* **SEASONS THEY CHANGE – BEST OF THE INCREDIBLE STRING BAND**		-

– Black Jack David / Blues for the muse / Nightfall / Puppies / Cold days of February / Worlds they rise and fall / Chinese white / Empty pocket blues / When the music starts to play / Saturday maybe / Red hair / The circle is unbroken / First girl I loved / Cosmic boy / Darling Belle / My father was a lighthouse keeper / Queen Juanita and her fisherman lover.

Oct 91.	(cd/lp) *Band Of Joy; (BOJ CD/LP 004)* **ON AIR (live)**		-
Nov 92.	(cd) *Windsong; (WINCD 029)* **BBC RADIO 1 LIVE IN CONCERT**		-
Jun 97.	(cd) *Blueprint; (PWMD 5003)* **CHELSEA SESSIONS 1967**		-

—— HERON and WILLIAMSON also released solo albums before their split. HERON = 'SMILING MEN WITH BAD REPUTATIONS' and WILLIAMSON = 'MYRRH'. Plus they went onto solo careers in 1975.

INDIGO GIRLS

Formed: Decatur, Georgia, USA ... 1980 by AMY RAY and EMILY SALIERS, who had written and performed together since childhood. The duo made their vinyl debut in summer '85 with an independently released single, 'CRAZY GAME', following up with an eponymous EP and a self-financed debut album, 'STRANGE FIRE' (1987). With the success of such female nu-folk artists as SUZANNE VEGA and TRACY CHAPMAN, The INDIGO GIRLS' folksy, apple-pie college strumming became hot property and the group were signed up by 'Epic'. Featuring contributions from the likes of R.E.M. and HOTHOUSE FLOWERS, 'INDIGO GIRLS' (1989) was a strong major label debut which had no problem crossing over from their loyal grassroots following to the pop market. Similar to British outfits such as EVERYTHING BUT THE GIRL and FAIRGROUND ATTRACTION, if a bit deeper and (socially/environmentally) lyrically aware, The INDIGO GIRLS' harmony-laden folk pop/rock found particular favour with the burgeoning US feminist movement. Again featuring an array of respected names including MARY CHAPIN CARPENTER and JIM KELTNER, 'NOMADS – INDIANS – SAINTS' (1990) wasn't quite so successful although the more adventurous 'RITES OF PASSAGE' (1992) almost made the US Top 20 and was nominated for a Grammy. The latter's more expansive approach was further developed on 'SWAMP OPHELIA' (1994), which employed the violin of LISA GERMANO to similarly impressive results alongside the acoustic bass playing of the ubiquitous DANNY THOMPSON. The record finally took the pair into the American Top 10 and while that achievement was repeated with 'SHAMING THE SUN' (1997), their success in Britain remains minimal.
• **Covered:** ALL ALONG THE WATCHTOWER + TANGLED UP IN BLUE (Bob Dylan) / FREE OF HOPE (Vic Chesnutt) / LAND OF CANAAN (Joni Mitchell) / DOWN BY THE RIVER (Neil Young) / MIDNIGHT TRAIN TO GEORGIA (Gladys Knight & The Pips).

Album rating: STRANGE FIRE (*4) / INDIGO GIRLS (*8) / NOMADS – INDIANS – SAINTS (*7) / LIVE: BACK ON THE BUS Y'ALL (*4) / RITES OF PASSAGE (*6) / SWAMP OPHELIA (*6) / 4.5 THE BEST OF compilation (*6) / 1200 CURFEWS (*7) / SHAMING OF THE SUN (*6) / COME ON NOW SOCIAL (*6)

AMY RAY (b.12 Apr'64) – vocals, guitars / **EMILY SALIERS** (b.22 Jul'63, New Haven, Connecticut) – vocals, acoustic guitar

		not iss.	J Ellis
Jun 85.	(7") *<A 1264>* **CRAZY GAME. / EVERYBODY'S WAITING (FOR SOMEONE TO COME HOME)**	-	

		not iss.	DragonPath
Nov 86.	(12"ep) *<LMM 1>* **INDIGO GIRLS**	-	

		not iss.	Indigo Music
Oct 87.	(lp) *<LMM 11>* **STRANGE FIRE**	-	

– Strange fire / Crazy game / Left me a fool / I don't wanna know / Hey Jesus / Get together / Walk away / Make it easier / You left it up to me / Land of Canaan. *<US re-iss. Nov89 on 'Epic'; EK 45427>*

—— now with **JAY DEE DAUGHERTY** – drums (ex-HOTHOUSE FLOWERS, ex-WATERBOYS, etc.) / **JOHN KEANE** – guitar, bass / **JOHN VAN TONGEREN** – keyboards / **KASIM SULTAN + DEDE VOGT** – bass / **PAULINHO DA COSTA** – percussion / **JAI WINDING** – piano

		Epic	Epic
Jun 89.	(7") *<68912>* **CLOSER TO FINE. / COLD AS ICE**	-	52
Jun 89.	(7") *(654907-7)* **CLOSER TO FINE. / HISTORY OF US**	-	
	(12"+=/cd-s+=) *(654907-5/-2)* – Center stage.		
Jul 89.	(lp/c/cd) *(463491-1/-4/-2)* <*45044*> **INDIGO GIRLS**		22 Apr89

– Closer to fine / Secure yourself / Kid fears / Prince of darkness / Blood and fire / Tried to be true / Love's recovery / Land of Canaan / Center stage / History of us.

Sep 89.	(7") *<73003>* **LAND OF CANAAN. / NEVER STOP**		
Nov 89.	(12"ep/cd-ep) *(655135-8/-2)* **CLOSER TO FINE / CLOSER TO FINE (live). / MONA LISAS AND MAD HATTERS (live) / AMERICAN TUNE (live)**		
Feb 90.	(7") *<73255>* **GET TOGETHER. / FINLANDIA**		-

—— now w / **DAUGHERTY / PETER BUCK** (of R.E.M.) / **SARA LEE** – bass (ex-GANG OF FOUR) / **MARY CHAPIN CARPENTER / KENNY ARONOFF / BENMONT TENCH /**

JIM KELTNER / PETER HOLSAPPLE / JOHN JENNINGS / DA COSTA / CHRIS McGUIRE / CRAIG EDWARDS / etc.

Oct 90. (c-s) <73607> **HAMMER AND NAIL / WELCOME (live)**

Nov 90. (cd/c/lp) (467308-2/-4/-1) <46820> **NOMADS – INDIANS – SAINTS** | | 43 Sep90
– Hammer and nail / Welcome me / World falls / Southland in the springtime / 1,2,3 / Keeper of my heart / Watershed / Hand me downs / You and me of the 10,000 wars / Pushing the needle too far / The girl with the weight of the world in her hands.

Jun 91. (m-cd) (468415-2) **BACK ON THE BUS Y'ALL (live)**

—— now w / SARA LEE – bass / BUDGIE – drums (of SIOUXSIE & THE BANSHEES) / LISA GERMANO – fiddle / JERRY MAROTTA – drums / MARTIN McCARRICK – cello / DONAL LUNNY – bouziki, bodhran / JENNINGS – guitar / KAI WINDING – piano

Jun 92. (cd/c/lp) (471363-2/-4/-1) <48865> **RITES OF PASSAGE** | | 21 Feb92
– Three hits / Galileo / Ghost / Joking / Jonas & Ezekial / Love will come to you / Romeo & Juliet / Virginia Woolf / Chicken man / Airplane / Nashville / Let it be me / Cedar tree.

Aug 92. (cd-s) <74326> **GALILEO / GHOST / JOKING / LOVE WILL COME TO YOU / JONAS & EZEKIAL** | - | 89

Oct 92. (7"/c-s) (658768-7/-4) **GALILEO. / KID FEARS**
(cd-s) (658768-2) – ('A'side) / Closer to fine / Tried to be true / Hammer and a nail.

—— Augmented by SARA LEE – bass (ex-GANG OF FOUR, etc.) / JERRY MAROTTA – drums / JAMES HALL – trumpet / DANNY THOMPSON – acoustic bass / LISA GERMANO – violin / JOHN PAINTER – flugel horn / JANE SCARPANTONI – cello / MICHAEL LORANT – drums, b.vocals

May 94. (cd-ep) (660340-2) **LEAST COMPLICATED / DEAD MAN'S HILL (acoustic) / MYSTERY (acoustic) / KID FEARS**

May 94. (cd/c/lp) (475931-2/-4/-1) <EM 57621> **SWAMP OPHELIA** | 66 | 9
– Fugitive / Least complicated / Language or the kiss / Reunion / Power of two / Touch me fall / The wood song / Mystery / Dead man's hill / Fare thee well / This train revised.

Jun 95. (c-s) (662166-4) **CLOSER TO FINE / ROCKIN' IN THE FREE WORLD**
(cd-s+=) (662166-2) – Dead man's hill (acoustic) / Mystery (acoustic).
(cd-s) (662166-5) – ('A'side) / Kid fears / All along the watchtower (live) / Let me a fool (live).

Jul 95. (cd/c) (480439-2/-4) **4.5 (THE BEST OF THE INDIGO GIRLS)** (compilation) | 43 |
– Joking / Hammer and nail / Kid fears / Galileo / Tried to be true / Power of love / Pushing the needle too far / Reunion / Closer to fine / Three hits / Least complicated / Touch me fall / Love's recovery / Land of Canaan / Ghost.

Oct 95. (d-cd) <67229> **1200 CURFEWS (live)** | - | 40
– Galileo / Back together again / The ghost / Dead man's hill / This train revised / Strange fire / Virginia Wolf / Tangled up in blue / Bury my heart at Wounded Knee / Closer to fine / Chickenman / Down by the river / I don't wanna know / Jonas & Ezekial / Land of Canaan / Least complicated / Mystery / Language or the kiss / Love's recovery / Midnight train to Georgia / Power of two / Pushing the needle to far / The river / World falls.
(above featured a number of cover versions)

May 97. (cd/c) (486982-2/-4) **SHAMING THE SUN** | | 7 Apr97
– Shame on you / Get out the map / Shed your skin / It's alright / Caramia / Don't give that girl a gun / Leeds / Scooter boys / Everything in its own time / Cut it out / Burn all the letters / Hey kind friend.

Oct 99. (cd/c) (495091-2/-4) <69914> **COME ON NOW SOCIAL** | | 34
– Go / Soon to be nothing / Gone again / Trouble / Sister / Peace tonight / Ozilline / We are together / Cold beer and remote control / Compromise / Andy / Faye Tucker.

INFECTIOUS GROOVES (see under ⇒ SUICIDAL TENDENCIES)

INSANE CLOWN POSSE

Formed: Detroit, Michigan, USA . . . 1989 as The INNER CITY POSSE, by SHAGGY 2 DOPE and VIOLENT J, two face-painted rappers with er . . . a wicked sense of fun. They changed their moniker in 1992, releasing their debut album 'CARNIVAL OF CARNAGE' the following year. Championed by the metal press, INSANE CLOWN POSSE are basically nevertheless a dyed-in-the-wool rap duo, albeit an extremely offensive one with a bizarre line in twisted circus trappings. Following a little contretemps with the Walt Disney corporation (and a short-lived spell with 'Jive' records), the gruesome jokers delivered their breakthrough release, 'THE GREAT MILENKO' in 1997, although this initially ran into difficulties with the all-powerful moral majority (the old record company recalling all copies due to its offensive content). Predictably, sales of the album (released by 'Island') soared, culminating in a US Top 75 placing. Just in time for Yuletide festivities, the 'POSSE laid their Christmas gift 45, 'SANTA'S A FAT BITCH' under the tree of hypocritical middle class America.

Album rating: CARNIVAL OF CHANGE (*4) / THE RING MASTER (*4) / RIDDLE BOX (*6) / THE GREAT MILENKO (*5) / THE AMAZING JECKEL BROTHERS (*4)

SHAGGY 2 DOPE (b. CLARK) – rapper / **VIOLENT J** (b. BROWN) – rapper; with guests **SLASH + STEVE JONES** – guitars

		not iss.	Psychopathic
1993.	(12"ep) <PSY 1005> **BEVERLY HILLS 50187**	-	-
1993.	(cd) **CARNIVAL OF CARNAGE**	-	-

– Intro / Carnival of carnage / Juggla / First day out / Red neck hoe / Wizard of the hood / Guts on the ceiling / Is that you / Night of the axe / Psychopathic / Blackin' your eyes / Never had made it / Your ebel flag / Ghetto freak show / Taste.
(UK-iss.Jun98 on 'Island'; 524514-2)

| 1994. | (12"ep) <PSY 1007> **THE TERROR WHEEL** | - | |
| 1994. | (cd) **THE RING MASTER** | - | |

– Wax museum / Murder go round / Chicken huntin' / Mr. Johnson's head / Southwest song / Get off me dog / Who asked who / Dead one / For the maggots /

Wagon wagon / Loons / Love song / Bugz on my nugz / House of mirrors / Ringmaster's world. (UK-iss.Jun98 on 'Island'; 524515-2)

		not iss.	Battery
Oct 95.	(cd) <02141-46001-2> **RIDDLE BOX**	-	

– Riddle box / The show must go on / Chicken huntin' / Toy box / Cemetery girl / 3 rings / Headless boogie / Joker's wild / Dead body man / Lil' somethin' somethin' / Ol' evil eye / 12 / Killing fields / I'm coming home.

		Island	Hollywood
Oct 97.	(cd/c) (CID/ICT 8061) <524442-2> **THE GREAT MILENKO**	63	Jul97

– Intro / The great Milenko / Hokus pokus / Piggy pie / How many times? / Southwest voodoo / Halls of illusion / Under the moon / What is a juggalo? / House of horrors / Boogie woogie wu / Neden game / Hellalujah / Down with the clown / Just like that / Pass me by.

Dec 97. (cd-s) <57219-2> **CARNIVAL CHRISTMAS: SANTA'S A FAT BITCH** | | 67

Jan 98. (7") (IS 685) **HALLS OF ILLUSION. / SMOG** | 56 |
(cd-s+=) (CID 685) – Southwest voodoo / Cotton candy.

May 98. (7"pic-d) (ISP 705) **HOKUS POKUS. / PROM QUEEN** | 53 |
('A'-Headhunta'z mix; cd-s+=) (CID 705) – My kind of bitch / Skitzofrantic.
(cd-s) (CIDX 705) – ('A'-Headhunta'z mix) / ('A'-radio mix) / ('A'-lp version) / 'A'-Headhunta'z instrumental.

May 99. (cd) <(524661-2)> **THE AMAZING JECKEL BROTHERS** | | 4
– Intro / Jake Jeckel / Bring it on / I want my shit / Bitches! / Terrible / I stab people / Another love song / Everyone rize / Play with me / Jack Jeckel / Fuck the world / The Shaggy show / Mad professor / Assassins / Echo side / Nothing left.

– compilations, etc. –

Aug 98. (d-cd,d-c) Island; <524552> **FORGOTTEN FRESHNESS VOL.1 & 2** (first two albums) | - | 46

INSPECTAH DECK (see under ⇒ WU-TANG CLAN)

INSPIRAL CARPETS

Formed: Manchester, England . . . 1980 initially as The FURS, by schoolboy GRAHAM LAMBERT. He was joined in the mid-80's by STEPHEN HOLT, TONY WELSH and CHRIS GOODWIN. In 1986, as The INSPIRAL CARPETS, they replaced GOODWIN and WELSH with CRAIG GILL, DAVE SWIFT and CLINT BOON. Early in '87, they recorded a version of 'GARAGE' for a 7" flexi-disc given free with 'Debris' magazine. After gigs supporting the WEDDING PRESENT, JAMES, STONES ROSES and The SHAMEN, they issued their official debut, the 'PLANE CRASH EP' in mid-'88 for indie, 'Playtime' records. Early in 1989, they set up their own 'Cow' label, after their distributers, 'Red Rhino', went bust. At the same time, HOLT and SWIFT left to form The RAINKINGS, and were replaced by HINGLEY and WALSH. After a late 1988 recording, 'TRAIN SURFING EP', was issued, they recorded the 808 STATE-produced 'JOE' single/EP. A year later, they had their first UK Top 50 entry with 'MOVE', which led to Daniel Miller of 'Mute' records taking on both band and label. In April 1990, they broke into UK Top 20 with the poignant single, 'THIS IS HOW IT FEELS', pushing their debut album, 'LIFE', to No. 3. A heavy, organ-orientated psychedelic-pop group, their music lay somewhere between The DOORS and The FALL. The INSPIRAL CARPETS continued with a run of hit singles that included, 'SHE COMES IN THE FALL', 'CARAVAN' and 'DRAGGING ME DOWN', the latter two featured on the Top 5 album, 'THE BEAST INSIDE' (1991). The following year, with a further clutch of hit singles under their belt, they scraped into the Top 20 with 'REVENGE OF THE GOLDFISH', a weaker effort. A year of reflection in 1993 preceded a return to form with a MARK E. SMITH (The Fall) collaboration 45, 'I WANT YOU' (now featured on a certain TV ad). This helped the album, 'DEVIL HOPPING', reach the Top 10 but when their next single, 'UNIFORM', failed to even dent the Top 50, they were unceremoniously dropped by their label, 'Mute'. The band split soon after, leaving behind the customary cash-in compilation. • **Songwriters:** Group penned except; 96 TEARS (? & The Mysterians) / GIMME SHELTER (Rolling Stones) / TAINTED LOVE (Soft Cell) / PARANOID (Black Sabbath). • **Trivia:** To promote debut album, they employed the services of the Milk Marketing Board who ran a TV ad on their bottles. Early 1990, they penned 'THE 8.15 FROM MANCHESTER' (theme) from children's Saturday morning TV show.

Album rating: LIFE (*8) / THE BEAST INSIDE (*7) / REVENGE OF THE GOLDFISH (*6) / DEVIL HOPPING (*5) / THE SINGLES compilation (*8) / Clint Boon Experience: (THE COMPACT GUIDE TO) POP MUSIC & SPACE TRAVEL (*7)

GRAHAM LAMBERT (b.10 Jul'64, Oldham, England) – guitar / **STEPHEN HOLT** – vocals / **DAVE SWIFT** – bass repl. TONY WELSH / **CRAIG GILL** (b. 5 Dec'71) – drums repl. CHRIS GOODWIN who joined ASIA FIELDS (later BUZZCOCKS F.O.C. and The HIGH) / added **CLINT BOON** (b.28 Jun'59, Oldham) – organ, vocals (ex-INCA BABIES)

		Playtime	not iss.
Jul 88.	(7"ltd.) (AMUSE 2) **KEEP THE CIRCLE AROUND. / THEME FROM COW**		-

(12"ep+=) **PLANE CRASH EP** (AMUSE 2T) – Seeds of doubt / Garage full of flowers / 96 tears.

		Cow	not iss.
Mar 89.	(12"ep) (MOO 2) **TRAIN SURFING**		-

– Butterfly / Causeway / You can't take the truth / Greek wedding song.

—— **TOM HINGLEY** (b. 9 Jul'65, Oxford, England) – vocals (ex-TOO MUCH TEXAS) repl. HOLT who formed RAINKINGS **MARTIN WALSH** (b. 3 Jul'68) – bass (ex-NEXT STEP) repl. SWIFT who formed RAINKINGS

May 89. (12"ep) (MOO 3) **JOE. / COMMERCIAL MIX / DIRECTING TRAFFIK / COMMERCIAL RAIN** | | -

May 89. (c;ltd) *(DUNG 4)* **DEMO CASSETTE** (rec.Dec'87) ☐ –
– Keep the circle around / Seeds of doubt / Joe / Causeway / 26 / Inside my head / Sun don't shine / Theme from Cow / 96 tears / Butterfly / Garage full of flowers.

Aug 89. (7") *(DUNG 5)* **FIND OUT WHY. / SO FAR** ☐ –
(12"+=/cd-s+=) *(DUNG 5 T/CD)* – Plane crash (live).

Oct 89. (7"/s7") *(DUNG 6/+X)* **MOVE. / OUT OF TIME** |49| –
(12"+=/cd-s+=) *(DUNG 6 T/CD)* – Move in.

                                         Cow-Mute   Elektra

Mar 90. (7") *(DUNG 7)* <66581> **THIS IS HOW IT FEELS. / TUNE FOR A FAMILY** |14|
(12"+=/cd-s+=) *(DUNG 7 T/CD)* – ('A'extended) / Seeds of doubt.
(c-s+=) *(DUNG 7MC)* – ('A'extended) / Whiskey.
(12") *(DUNG 7R)* – ('A'-Robbery mix) / ('B'drum mix).

Apr 90. (lp/c/cd) *(DUNG 8/+CD)* <60987> **LIFE** |2| Oct90
– Real thing / Song for a family / This is how it feels / Directing traffik / Besides me / Many happy returns / Memories of you / She comes in the fall / Monkey on my back / Sun don't shine / Inside my head / Move * / Sackville. (cd+= *) <US++=> – Commercial rain / Weakness / Biggest mountain / I'll keep it in mind.

Jun 90. (7") *(DUNG 10)* **SHE COMES IN THE FALL. / SACKVILLE** |27| –
(12"+=/cd-s+=) *(DUNG 10 T/CD)* – Continental reign (version).
(12"+=) *(DUNG 10R)* – ('A'acappella version).

Nov 90. (7"ep/12"ep) *(DUNG 11/+T)* **ISLAND HEAD** |21| –
– Biggest mountain / I'll keep in mind / Weakness / Gold to . . .
(cd-ep+=) *(DUNG 11CD)* – Mountain sequence.

Mar 91. (7") *(DUNG 13)* <66543> **CARAVAN. / SKIDOO** |30| Apr91
(7"/12") *(DUNG 13 R/T)* – ('A'side) / ('B'-Possession mix).
(cd-s) *(DUNG 13CD)* – ('A'-What noise rethink mix) / ('B'side).

Apr 91. (lp/c/cd) *(DUNG 14/+C/CD)* <61089> **THE BEAST INSIDE** |5| May91
– Caravan / Please be cruel / Born yesterday / Sleep well tonight / Grip / Beast inside / Niagara / Mermaid / Further away / Dreams are all we have.

Jun 91. (7"/c-s) *(DUNG/+C 15)* **PLEASE BE CRUEL. / THE WIND IS CALLING YOUR NAME** |50| –
(12"+=/cd-s+=) *(DUNG 15 T/CD)* – St.Kilda (version).

Feb 92. (7") *(DUNG 16)* **DRAGGING ME DOWN. / I KNOW I'M LOSING YOU** |12| –
(12"+=/cd-s+=) *(DUNG 16 T/CD)* – (2 other 'A'mixes).

May 92. (7") *(DUNG 17)* **TWO WORLDS COLLIDE. / BOOMERANG** |32| –
(12"+=/cd-s+=) *(DUNG 17 T/CD)* – ('A'-Mike Pickering remix).

Sep 92. (7") *(DUNG 18)* **GENERATIONS. / ('A'remix)** |28| –
(c-s) *(DUNG 18C)* – Lost in space again.
(12"/cd-s) *(DUNG 18 T/CD)* – ('A'side) / She comes in the fall (live) / Move (live) / Directing traffik (live).
(cd-s) *(DUNG 18CDR)* – ('A'side) / Joe (live) / Commercial rain (live) / Butterfly (live).

Oct 92. (lp/c/cd) *(DUNG 19/+C/CD)* <61397> **REVENGE OF THE GOLDFISH** |17|
– Generations / Saviour / Bitches brew / Smoking her clothes / Fire / Here comes the flood / Dragging me down / A little disappeared / Two worlds collide / Mystery / Rain song / Irresistable force.

Nov 92. (c-ep/12"ep) *(DUNG 20 C/T)* **BITCHES BREW / TAINTED LOVE. / BITCHES BREW (Fortran 5 remix) / IRRESISTABLE FORCE (Fortran 5 mix)** |36| –
(cd-ep+=) *(DUNG 20CD)* – Mermaid (live) / Born yesterday (live) / Sleep well tonight (live).
(cd-ep+=) *(DUNG 20CDR)* – Dragging me down (live) / Smoking her clothes (live) / Fire (live).

—— parted company with 'Cow' co-founder/manager Anthony Boggiano.

May 93. (7"/c-s) *(DUNG 22/+C)* **HOW IT SHOULD BE. / IT'S ONLY A PAPER MOON** |49| –
(12"+=/cd-s+=) *(DUNG 22 T/CD)* – I'm alive.

Jan 94. (7"/c-s) *(DUNG 23/+C)* **SATURN 5. / PARTY IN THE SKY** |20| –
(cd-s+=/12"+=) *(DUNG 23 T/CD)* – ('A'mixes).
(cd-s) *(DUNG 23CDR)* – ('A'side) / Well of seven heads / Two cows / Going down.

Feb 94. (7"/c-s; by INSPIRAL CARPETS featuring MARK E. SMITH) *(DUNG 24/+C)* **I WANT YOU. / I WANT YOU (version)** |18| –
(cd-s+=) *(DUNG 24CD)* – We can do everything / Inside of you.
(cd-s) *(DUNG 24CDR)* – ('A'side) / Dragging me down / Party in the sky / Plutoman.

Mar 94. (lp/c/cd) *(DUNG 25/+C/CD)* <61632> **DEVIL HOPPING** |10|
– I want you / Party in the sky / Plutoman / Uniform / Lovegrove / Just Wednesday / Saturn 5 / All of this and more / The way the light falls / Half way there / Cobra / I don't want to go blind. (w / free ltd-cd of 'BBC SESSIONS' or free ltd.red-10"lp)

Apr 94. (7"/c-s/cd-s) *(DUNG 26/+C/CD)* **UNIFORM. / PARANOID** |51| –
(cd-s) *(DUNG 26 CDR)* – ('A'side) / Paranoid (Collapsed Lung mix).

Aug 95. (7"m) *(DUNG 27L)* **JOE (acoustic). / SEEDS OF DOUBT / WHISKEY** |37| –
(7"m) *(DUNG 27R)* – Joe (live) / Sackville (live) / Saviour (live).
(cd-s) *(DUNG 25CD)* – ('A'side) / I want you / I'll keep in mind / Tainted love.

Sep 95. (cd/c/d-lp) *(CD/C+/MOOTEL 3)* <9010> **THE SINGLES** (compilation) |17|
– Joe / Find out why / Move / This is how it feels / (extended) / She comes in the fall / Commercial reign / Sackville / Biggest mountain / Weakness / Caravan / Please be cruel / Dragging me down / Two worlds collide / Generations / Bitches brew / How it should be / Saturn 5 / I want you / Uniform.

—— Had already been dropped from the 'Mute' roster late in 1994.

– compilations, etc. –

Jul 89. (12"ep/cd-ep) *Strange Fruit; (SFPS/+CD 072) / Dutch East India; <8305>* **THE PEEL SESSIONS** ☐
– Out of time / Directing traffic / Keep the circle around / Gimme shelter.

Aug 92. (cd/10"lp) *Strange Fruit;* **PEEL SESSIONS** ☐ –

—— also released import 7"colrd/12"colrd/pic-cd-s 'GIMME SHELTER'.

CLINT BOON EXPERIENCE!

—— BOON with STUBBSY, SISTA STUBBS, PAPA T, MOOSE + MATT

                                          Rabid Badger   not iss.

Aug 98. (12"/cd-s) *(NANG 004)* **ONLY ONE WAY I CAN GO. / TIGER WOODS, ASTRONAUT / PRESLEY ON OLDHAM STREET** ☐ –

Nov 98. (7") *(NANG 006)* **WHITE NO SUGAR. / NOT ENOUGH PURPLE, TOO MUCH GREY** ☐ –
(cd-s+=) *(NANG 006CD)* – Philip Glass, astronaut.

Apr 99. (7") *(NANG 008)* **COMET THEME NO.1. / 17 . . . AND OVER** ☐ –
(cd-s+=) *(NANG 008CD)* – Andrew Gill, astronaut.

                                          Artful   not iss.

Aug 99. (7") *(7ARTFUL 31)* **CAN'T KEEP A GOOD MAN DOWN. / NOW I WANNA BE YOUR DOG (featuring MARK E. SMITH)** ☐ –
(cd-s+=) *(CDARTFUL 31)* – ('A'–karaoke mix).

Sep 99. (cd/lp) *(ARTFUL CD/LP 25)* **(THE COMPACT GUIDE TO) POP MUSIC & SPACE TRAVEL** ☐ –
– Presley on Oldham Street / White no sugar / Only one way I can go / You can't keep a good man down / Push me back down / Biggest horizon / Comet theme No.1 / Not enough purple too much grey / Tiger Woods astronaut / The night will see me falling / Cool people who know who the cool people are / Andy Gill astronaut.

Oct 99. (7") *(7ARTFUL 32)* **WHITE NO SUGAR. /** |61| –
(cd-s+=) *(CDARTFUL 32)* –
(cd-s) *(CDXARTFUL 32)* – ('A'side) / Not enough purple too much grey (live) / You can't keep a good man down.

INTERNATIONAL SUBMARINE BAND
(see under ⇒ PARSONS, Gram)

INXS

Formed: Sydney, Australia . . . 1977 as The FARRISS BROTHERS by TIM, ANDREW and JON, plus MICHAEL HUTCHENCE, KIRK PENGILLY and GARRY BEERS. After briefly moving to Perth in 1978, they returned the following year as INXS, gigging extensively and eventually landing a deal with 'Deluxe' through 'RCA'. Their second single, 'JUST KEEP WALKING' was a domestic hit in 1980 and after a couple of straightahead rock efforts, 'INXS' (1980) and 'UNDERNEATH THE COLOURS' (1981), the band were eventually picked up by the American-based, 'Atlantic'-affiliated 'Atco' label. Their major label debut, 'SHABOOH SHOOBAH' (1982) eventually reached the lower fringes of the US Top 40 on the strength of single, 'THE ONE THING', which MTV had latched onto, the band's new groove-rock sound and HUTCHENCE's classic rock-god looks making them hot property in the emerging video generation. They caught the eye of top producer and ex-CHIC maestro NILE RODGERS who worked on the 'ORIGINAL SIN' single, a propulsive slice of funk rock that was the highlight of 'THE SWING', the band's 1984 album that once again almost breached the US Top 40. The break eventually came with the 'LISTEN LIKE THIEVES' opus, a Top 20 album in Britain with the single 'WHAT YOU NEED' reaching the UK Top 5. The band also gained valuable exposure by playing the Australian Live Aid that year, rather ironic bearing in mind HUTCHENCE's future relationship with BOB GELDOF. With 'KICK' (1987), the band moved into the mega stardom league, the album a multi-million worldwide success, spawning four international hit singles. 'NEW SENSATION' and 'NEED YOU TONIGHT' (UK No.1) typified the INXS sound; glossy, supple, danceable rock with chunky basslines and HUTCHENCE's breathy vocals magnifying the raunch factor. 'NEVER TEAR US APART', meanwhile, was a rare ballad, uncharacteristically poignant with atmospheric strings. 1987 also saw the frontman's acting debut in Richard Lowenstein's cult movie, 'Dogs In Space'. The following year, after a gruelling world tour, HUTCHENCE recorded an album with IAN OLSEN under the title of 'MAX Q' (named after his dog!), before re-emerging in 1990 with a new INXS album, 'X'. The record trod the same territory as 'KICK' without achieving quite the same effect, only 'SUICIDE BLONDE' and 'DISAPPEAR' making any impact on the singles charts. After packing out London's Wembley Stadium in 1991, an admirable feat for any band, INXS attempted to cast off the stadium rock tag by recording a more ambitious and experimental record, 'WELCOME TO WHEREVER YOU ARE' (1992). As well as a couple of US hits, the album contained the lovely 'BEAUTIFUL GIRL' single, as good as anything the band have recorded to date. With 'FULL MOON, DIRTY HEARTS' (1993), INXS aimed for a rocking return to their earliest recordings, featuring contributions from RAY CHARLES and CHRISSIE HYNDE. The result was only partly successful, the record stiffing completely in the UK. HUTCHENCE had always played the part of the decadent rock star to the max (Q), dating supermodels and allegedly indulging in copious drug use. Although HUTCHENCE had apparently found some sort of stability through a very public romance with PAULA YATES (the final nail in the coffin of her doomed marriage to BOB GELDOF), friends and colleagues were apparently worried about his increasing drug use in recent years. However, no one could have predicted that HUTCHENCE would take his own life, the apparent cause of death after the singer was tragically found hanging from his hotel room door in Sydney, Australia on November 22, 1997. With tabloids speculating that HUTCHENCE was a casualty of a bizarre sex act gone wrong, and PAULA YATES laying the blame firmly at GELDOF's feet (hysterically calling him "the devil"), the official inquest took a more straightforward view. Whatever, the sad fact is that the music world has lost a talented and well loved star, the future of INXS looking decidedly shakey. 'V2' delivered MICHAEL's final solo recordings as his eponymous debut album in October '99, although what critics might have said – had he been still alive – about this basic self-written set (featuring guests BONO and JOE STRUMMER), we'll never know. • **Songwriters:** Most by ANDREW FARRISS and HUTCHENCE, except some B-sides by TIM. Covered; THE LOVED ONE (The Loved One).

Album rating: INXS (*4) / UNDERNEATH THE COLOURS (*5) / SHABOOH SHOOBAH (*5) / THE SWING (*6) / LISTEN LIKE THIEVES (*7) / KICK (*7) / X (*5) / LIVE BABY LIVE (*3) / WELCOME TO WHEREVER YOU ARE (*6) / FULL MOON, DIRTY HEARTS (*5) / INXS – THE GREATEST HITS compilation (*8) / ELEGANTLY WASTED (*5) / Max Q: MAX Q (*5) / Michael Hutchence: MICHAEL HUTCHENCE (*4)

MICHAEL HUTCHENCE (b.12 Jan'60, Lain Cove, Sydney, Australia) – vocals / **ANDREW FARRISS** (b.27 Mar'59, Perth, Australia) – keyboards, guitar / **TIM FARRISS** (b.16 Aug'57, Perth) – guitar / **KIRK PENGILLY** (b. 4 Jul'58) – saxophone, guitar, vocals / **GARRY GARY BEERS** (b.22 Jun'57) – bass, vocals / **JON FARRISS** (b.18 Aug'61, Perth) – drums

		not iss.	Deluxe	
May 80.	(7") **SIMPLE SIMON. / WE ARE ALL VEGETABLES**	-	-	Austra
Oct 80.	(7") **JUST KEEP WALKING. / SCRATCH**	-	-	Austra
	(UK-iss.Sep81 on 'R.C.A.'; RCA 89)			
Oct 80.	(lp) *(790184-1)* **INXS**	-	-	Austra

– On a bus / Doctor / Just keep walking / Learn to smile / Jumping in vain / Roller skating / Body language / Newsreel babies / Wishy washy. *<US-iss.Aug84 on 'Atco' lp/c; 7.90184-1/-4> (UK-iss.Jul89 on 'Vertigo' lp/c/cd; 838776-1/-4/-2) (re-iss. May90 on 'Vertigo' cd/c/lp; 838925-2/-4/-1)*

		R.C.A.	not iss.	
Feb 81.	(7") **THE LOVED ONE. /**	-	-	Austra
Sep 81.	(7") **STAY YOUNG. /**	-	-	Austra
Dec 81.	(7") **NIGHT OF REBELLION. /**	-	-	Austra
Mar 82.	(lp) *(RCALP 3058)* **UNDERNEATH THE COLOURS**	-	-	

– Stay young / Horizons / Big go-go / Underneath the colours / Fair weather ahead / Night of rebellion / What would you do / Follow / Barbarian / Just to learn again. *(re-iss. Jul89 on 'Vertigo' lp/c/cd; 838777-1/-4/-2)*

		Mercury	Atco	
Oct 82.	(lp) *(90072)* **SHABOOH SHOOBAH**	-	46	

– The one thing / To look at you / Spy of love / Soul mistake / Here comes / Black and white / Golden playpen / Jan's song / Old world new world / Don't change. *(UK-iss.Jun87 lp/c; PRICE/PRIMC 94) (cd-iss. May90; 812084-2)*

Jan 83.	(7") **DON'T CHANGE. / GO WEST**	-	-	Austra
Mar 83.	(7") *(99905)* **THE ONE THING. / PHANTOM OF THE OPERA**	-	30	
Jun 83.	(7") *(99874)* **DON'T CHANGE. / LONG IN TOOTH**	-	80	
Jun 83.	(7") *(INXS 1)* **DON'T CHANGE. / YOU NEVER USED TO CRY**		-	

(12"+=) *(INXS 12-1)* – Golden playpen.

Sep 83.	(7") *(INXS 2)* **THE ONE THING. / THE SAX THING**		-	

(12") *(INXS 2-12)* – ('A'extended) / Black and white.
(12") *(INXS 2-22)* – ('A'side) / Black and white / Here comes II.

Sep 83.	(m-lp) *<7.90115>* **DEKADANCE** (remixes)		-	

– Black and white / Here comes / The one thing / To look at you.

Feb 84.	(7") *(INXS 3)* **ORIGINAL SIN. / JAN'S SONG (live) / TO LOOK AT YOU (live)**		-	

(12"+=) *(INXS 3-12)* – ('A'extended).

Apr 84.	(7") *(99766)* **ORIGINAL SIN. / STAY YOUNG**	-	58	
May 84.	(lp/c) *(MERL/+C 39) <90160>* **THE SWING**		52	

– Original sin / Melting in the sun / I send a message / Dancing on the jetty / The swing / Johnson's aeroplane / Love is (what I say) / Face the change / Burn for you / All the voices. *(cd-iss. Jul86; 818 553-2)*

		Philips	Atco	
May 84.	(7") *(PH 2) <99731>* **I SEND A MESSAGE. / MECHANICAL**		77	Jul84

(12"+=) *(PH 2-12)* – ('A'-long distance version).

Oct 84.	(7") **BURN FOR YOU. / JOHNSON'S AEROPLANE**		-	

		Mercury	Atlantic	
Oct 85.	(lp/c)(cd) *(MERH/+C 82)(824 957-2) <81277>* **LISTEN LIKE THIEVES**	48	11	

– What you need / Listen like thieves / Kiss the dirt (falling down the mountain) / Shine like it does / Good and bad times / Biting bullets / Three sisters / Same direction / One x one / Red red sun. *(initial copies cont. 'THE SWING') (re-iss. Apr95 cd/c;)*

Feb 86.	(7") *(INXS 4) <89497>* **THIS TIME. / ORIGINAL SIN (long)**		81	Nov85
	(12"+=/d7"+=) *(INXS 4-12/D4)* – Burn for you / Dancing on the jetty.			
Apr 86.	(7") *(INXS 5) <89460>* **WHAT YOU NEED. / SWEET AS SIN**	51	5	Jan86

(w/ free c-s+=) *(INXSC 5)* – This time / What you need (live) / I'm over you / (lp excerpts).
(remix-12"+=) *(INXS 5-12)* – ('A'live) / The one thing.
(remix-d12"++=) *(INXSD 5-12)* – Don't change / Johnsons aeroplane.

Jun 86.	(7"/7"sha-pic-d) *(INXS/+P 6) <89429>* **LISTEN LIKE THIEVES. / BEGOTTEN**	46	54	May86

(ext.12"+=) *(INXS 6-12)* – ('A'instrumental remix) / ('A'live).
(d7"+=) *(INXSSD 6)* – One x one / Xs verbiage (band interview).

Aug 86.	(7") *(INXS 7)* **KISS THE DIRT. / 6 KNOTS / THE ONE THING (live)**	54	-	

(12"+=) *(INXS 7-12)* – Spy of love.
(d7"+=) *(INXSD 7)* – This time / Original sin.

In Jun'87, INXS were credited with JIMMY BARNES (ex-COLD CHISEL singer), on US single 'GOOD TIMES' <Atlantic; 89237>, which hit No.47 and was lifted from the film 'The Lost Boys'. Early in 1991, it was finally a UK No.18 hit (Atlantic; A 7751).

Oct 87.	(7") *(INXS 8) <89188>* **NEED YOU TONIGHT. / I'M COMING (HOME)**	58	1	

(12"+=/cd-s+=) *(INXS 8-12/CD8)* – Mediate.

Nov 87.	(lp/c)(cd) *(MERH/+C 114)(832 721-2) <81796>* **KICK**	9	3	

– Guns in the sky / New sensation / Devil inside / Need you tonight / Mediate / The loved one / Wild life / Never tear us apart / Mystify / Kick / Calling all nations / Tiny daggers. *(pic-lp.Nov88; MERHP 114)*

Dec 87.	(7"/7"pic-d) *(INXS/+R 9)* **NEW SENSATION. / DO WOT YOU DO**	25	-	

(ext.12"+=) *(INXSR 9-12)* – Love is (what I say).
(12"++=/12"w-poster++=)(c-s++=/cd-s++=) *(INXS/+P 9-12)(INSM/INXSCD 9)* – Same direction.

Feb 88.	(7"/+P 10) *(INXS/+P 10) <89144>* **DEVIL INSIDE. / ON THE ROCKS**	47	2	

(12"+=) *(INXS 10-12)* – ('A'extended).
(cd-s++=) *(INXSCD 10)* – What you need.
(10"+=) *(INXS 10-10)* – Dancing on the jetty / Shine like it does (live).

May 88.	(7") *<89080>* **NEW SENSATION. / GUNS IN THE SKY (kookaburra mix)**	-	3	
Jun 88.	(7"/7"w-poster)(7"pic-d/ext.12") *(INXS/+P 11)(INXS 11+/12/00)* **NEVER TEAR US APART. / GUNS IN THE SKY (Kickass remix)**	24	-	

(12"+=) *(INXSG 11-12)* – Burn for you / One world new world.
(ext.cd-s+=) *(INXSCD 11)* – Different world / This time.
(10"white+=) *(INXS 11-10)* – Need you tonight / Listen like thieves.

Aug 88.	(7") *<89038>* **NEVER TEAR US APART. / DIFFERENT WORLD**	-	7	
Oct 88.	(7"/7"s) *(INXS/+G 12)* **NEED YOU TONIGHT. / MOVE ON**	2	-	

('A'-Mendolsohn mix-cd-s+=) *(INXSCD 12)* – Original sin / Don't change.
(12"+=) *(INXS 12-12)* – Kiss the dirt / ('A'-Mendelsohn mix).
('A'-Ben Liebrand mix-12"+=) *(INXSR 12-12)* – New sensation.

Mar 89.	(7"/7"g-f) *(INXS/+G 13)* **MYSTIFY. / DEVIL INSIDE (extended)**	14	-	

(cd-s+=) *(INXSCD 13)* – What you need (extended) / Listen like thieves.
(12"+=) *(INXS 13-12)* – Never tear us apart (live) / Shine like it does (live).
(12") *(INXS 13-22)* – ('A'side) / Biting bullets / Shine like it does (live) / Never tear us apart (live).

Sep 90.	(7") *(INXS 14) <87860>* **SUICIDE BLONDE. / EVERYBODY WANTS U TONIGHT**	11	9	

(12"+=)(cd-s+=) *(INXS 14-12)(INXSCD 14)* – ('A'-milk mix).

Sep 90.	(cd/c/lp) *(846668-2/-4/-1) <82140>* **X**	2	5	

– Suicide blonde / Disappear / The stairs / Faith in each other / By my side / Lately / Who pays the price / Know the difference / Bitter tears / On my way / Hear that sound. *(re-iss. cd/c Apr95)*

Nov 90.	(7") *(INXS 15) <87784>* **DISAPPEAR. / MIDDLE BEAST**	21	8	

(12"+=)(cd-s+=) *(INXS 15-12)(INXSCD 15)* – What you need (Cold Cut force mix).
(12") *(INXS 15-22)* – ('A'side) / Need you tonight (mix) / New sensation.

Mar 91.	(7"/c-s) *(INX S/MC 16)* **BY MY SIDE. / THE OTHER SIDE**	42	-	

(12"+=) *(INXS 16-12)* – Faith in each other (live).
(cd-s++=) *(INXSCD 16)* – Disappear (mix).

Mar 91.	(c-s) *<87760>* **BITTER TEARS / THE OTHER SIDE**	-	46	
Jul 91.	(7") *(INXS 17)* **BITTER TEARS. / SOOTHE ME**	30	-	

(12"+=) *(INXS 17-12)* – Disappear (mix) / ('A'tears are bitter mix) / ('A'other mix).
(cd-s+=) *(INXSCD 17)* – Original sin / Listen like thieves (extended remix).

Oct 91.	(7"ep/12"ep/cd-ep) *(INXS/+12/CD 18)* **SHINING STAR**	27	-	

– Shining star / Send a message (live) / Faith in each other (live) / Bitter tears (live).

Nov 91.	(cd/c/lp) *(510580-2/-4/-1) <82294>* **LIVE BABY LIVE (live)**	8	72	

– New sensation / Mystify / Never tear us apart / Need you tonight / Suicide blonde / By my side / Mediate / Hear that sound / The stairs / What you need / Shining star (studio).

Jul 92.	(7"/7"pic-d/c-s/12"/cd-s) *(INX S/P/T/D 19)* **HEAVEN SENT. / IT AIN'T EASY**	31	-	
Aug 92.	(c-s) *<87437>* **NOT ENOUGH TIME / DEEPEST RED**	-	28	
Aug 92.	(cd/c/lp) *(512507-2/-4/-1) <82394>* **WELCOME TO WHEREVER YOU ARE**	1	16	

– Questions / Heaven sent / Communication / Taste it / Not enough time / All around / Baby don't cry / Beautiful girl / Wishing well / Back on line / Strange desire / Men and women. *(re-iss. cd/c Apr95)*

Sep 92.	(7"/c-s) *(INX S/MC 20)* **BABY DON'T CRY. / (part 2)**	20	-	

(cd-s+=) *(INXSCD 20)* – Ptar speaks / Question 8 (instrumental) / ('A'acappella mix).

Nov 92.	(7"/c-s) *(INX S/MC 23)* **TASTE IT. / LIGHT THE PLANET**	21	-	

(cd-s+=) *(INXCD 23)* – Youth / Not enough time (mix).

Feb 93.	(7"/c-s) *(INX S/MC 24)* **BEAUTIFUL GIRL. / IN MY LIVING ROOM / ASHTAR SPEAKS**	23	-	

(cd-s) *(INXCD 24)* – ('A'side) / Strange desire.
(cd-s) *(INXCT 24)* – ('A'side) / Underneath my colours / Wishing well.

Feb 93.	(c-s) *<87383>* **BEAUTIFUL GIRL / STRANGE DESIRE**	-	46	
Oct 93.	(7"/c-s) *(INX S/MC 25)* **THE GIFT. / ('A'mix)**	11	-	

(cd-s+=) *(INXCD 25)* – Born to be wild.
(cd-s+=) *(INXCT 25)* – Heaven sent (live).

Nov 93.	(cd/c/lp) *(518637-2/-4/-1) <82541>* **FULL MOON, DIRTY HEARTS**	3	53	

– Days of rust / The gift / Make your peace / Time / I'm only looking / Please (you got that . . .) / Full moon, dirty hearts / Freedom deep / Kill the pain / Cut your roses down / The messenger / Viking juice.
(below single featured RAY CHARLES)

Dec 93.	(12"/c-s) *(INX S/MC 26)* **PLEASE (YOU GOT THAT . . .). / TASTE IT (live)**	50	-	

(cd-s) *(INXCD 26)* – ('A'side) / ('A'edit) / Freedom deep (extended 12"mix) / Communication (live).

Oct 94.	(7"red/c-s) *(INX S/MC 27)* **THE STRANGEST PARTY (THESE ARE THE TIMES). / WISHING WELL**	15	-	

(cd-s+=) *(INXCD 27)* – ('A'mix) / Sing something.
(cd-s) *(INXCT 27)* – ('A'side) / Need you tonight (remix) / I'm only looking (remix).

Nov 94.	(cd/c/lp) *(526230-2/-4/-1) <82622>* **INXS – THE GREATEST HITS** (compilation)	3	-	

– Mystify / Suicide blonde / Taste it / The strangest party (these are the times) / Need you tonight / Original sin / Heaven sent / Disappear / Never tear us apart / The gift / Devil inside / Beautiful girl / Deliver me / New sensation / What you need / Listen like thieves / Bitter tears / Baby don't cry.

From mid-90's, HUTCHENCE and BOB GELDOF's estranged misses PAULA YATES starting living together. In 1996, complete with breast implants, she had HUTCHENCE's baby (another with a long silly Christian name)

Mar 97.	(c-s/cd-s) *(INX MC/CD 28)* **ELEGANTLY WASTED / I'M ONLY LOOKING**	20	-	

Apr 97. (cd/c) (534 613-2/-4) **ELEGANTLY WASTED** `16` `41`
– Show me (cherry baby) / Elegantly wasted / Everything / Don't lose your head / Searching / I'm just a man / Girl on fire / We are thrown together / Shake the tree / She is rising / Building bridges / Shine.

May 97. (c-s) (INXMC 29) **EVERYTHING / BELIEVE** `71`
(cd-s+=) (INXCD 29) – Suicide blonde.
(cd-s) (INXDD 29) – ('A'side) / Never tear you apart / What you need.

Sep 97. (cd-s) (INXCD 30) **SEARCHIN' /** `69`
(cd-s) (INXDD 30) –
(cd-s) (INXSD 30) –

—— On the 22nd November '97, HUTCHENCE committed suicide after a party in his hotel room. Obviously, the band look like calling it a day,

– some other AUSTRALIA only releases –

on 'WEA' unless mentioned otherwise
Oct 83. (7"/12") **ORIGINAL SIN. / IN VAIN / JUST KEEP WALKING** `-` `-`
1984. (7"/12") **BURN FOR YOU. /** `-` `-`
1984. (7"/12") **DANCING ON THE JETTY. /** `-` `-`
MICHAEL HUTCHENCE also released below single
1987. (7") **ROOMS FOR THE MEMORY. / GOLFCOURSE** `-` `-`

MAX Q

(HUTCHENCE with IAN 'OLLIE' OLSEN duo named after his dog!)

	Mercury	Atlantic
Sep 89. (7") (MXQ 1) <88844> **WAY OF THE WORLD. / ZERO 2-0**		

(c-s+=/cd-s+=)(12"+=) (MXQ MC/CD 1)(MXQ 1-12) – Ghost of the year (Todd Terry mix).

Oct 89. (lp/c/cd) (838942-1/-4/-2) <82014> **MAX Q** `69`
– Sometimes / Way of the world / Ghost of the year / Everything / Zero 2-0 / Soul engine / Buckethead / Monday night by satellite / Tight / Ot-ven-rot.

Feb 90. (7"/7"w-poster/c-s) (MXQ/+P/MC 2) **SOMETIMES. / LOVE MAN** `53` `-`
(12"+=) (MXQ 22-12) – ('A'instrumental).
(12"+=/cd-s+=) (MXQ 2-12/CD2) – ('A'-land of Oz mix) / ('A'-rock house mix).

Feb 90. (7") <88754> **SOMETIMES. / GHOST OF THE YEAR** `-` `-`

MICHAEL HUTCHENCE

	V2	V2
Oct 99. (c-s/cd-s) (VVR 501079-5/-3) **A STRAIGHT LINE / STANDING ON THE ROOFTOP / THE PASSENGER**		

Oct 99. (cd) (VVR 100788-2) **MICHAEL HUTCHENCE**
– Let me show you / Possibilities / Get on the inside / Fear / All I'm saying / A straight line / Baby it's alright / Don't save me from myself / She flirts for England / Flesh and blood / Put the back together / Breathe / Slide away.

IRON BUTTERFLY

Formed: San Diego, California, USA ... 1966 by DOUG INGLE, RON BUSHY, DANNY WEIS, JERRY PENROD and DARRYL DeLOACH. They soon moved to Los Angeles and after being spotted at the Whiskey A-Go-Go, they signed to Atlantic subsidiary label, 'Atco'. Early in 1968, they issued the 'HEAVY' album, which bulldozed its way into the lower regions of the US Top 100. Later that summer, WEIS and PENROD departed, superseded by LEE DORMAN and ERIK BRAUN. This line-up subsequently recorded the organ-driven, progressive proto-metal of 'IN-A-GADDA-DA-VIDA' (aka 'The Garden of Life'), a classic album which hit the US Top 5, going on to sell over three million copies. The edited title track (trimmed from 17-minute lp version) gave them additional success in the singles chart. With the aforementioned album still riding high in the charts, their 1969 'BALL' album bounced into the Top 3. In 1970, IRON BUTTERFLY introduced the twin-guitar assault of MIKE PIERA and LARRY REINHARDT, who featured on their Top 20 set, 'METAMORPHOSIS'. They split soon after, only to surface again in 1975 with two poor efforts, 'SCORCHING BEAUTY' and 'SUN AND STEEL'. • **Songwriters:** INGLE and BUSHY were main contributors until the addition/departure of BRAUN and DORMAN. • **Trivia:** In 1968, two tracks, 'POSSESSION' and 'UNCONSCIOUS POWER' were used on the film soundtrack of 'The Savage Seven'.

Album rating: HEAVY (*6) / IN-A-GADDA-DA-VIDA (*9) / BALL (*6) / IRON BUTTERFLY LIVE (*3) / METAMORPHOSIS (*5) / THE BEST OF IRON BUTTERFLY – EVOLUTION compilation (*6) / SCORCHING BEAUTY (*4) / SUN AND STEEL (*3) / LIGHT AND HEAVY – THE BEST OF IRON BUTTERFLY compilation (*7)

DOUG INGLE (b. 9 Sep'46, Omaha, Nebraska) – keyboards, vocals / **JERRY PENROD** – guitar / **DANNY WEIS** – guitar (both ex-DAVID ACKLES band) / **RON BUSHY** (b.23 Sep'45, Washington, D.C.) – drums, vocals / **DARRYL DeLOACH** – bass, vocals

	Atco	Atco
Feb 68. (lp) (2465 015) <33227> **HEAVY**		`78`

– Possession / Unconscious power / Get out of my life, woman / Gentle as it may seem / You can't win / So-lo / Look for the sun / Fields of sun / Stamped ideas / Iron butterfly theme. (cd-iss. 1992 on 'Repertoire'+=;) – I can't help but deceive you little girl / To be alone.

	Atlantic	Atco
Jun 68. (7") (584 188) <6573> **POSSESSION. / UNCONSCIOUS POWER**		`May68`

—— **ERIK BRAUN** (b.11 Aug'50, Boston, Mass.) – lead guitar, vocals repl. WEIS and PENROD who formed RHINOCEROS / **LEE DORMAN** (b.19 Sep'45, St.Louis, Missouri) – bass, multi repl. DeLOACH

Jul 68. (lp; mono/stereo) (587/588 116) <33250> **IN-A-GADDA-DA-VIDA** `4`
– Most anything you want / Flowers and beads / My mirage / Termination / Are you happy / In-a-gadda-da-vida. (re-iss. Jan73; K 40022) (cd-iss. Jul87 & Jun93; K2 40022) (re-iss. cd deluxe version Nov95 on 'Rhino'; 8122 72196-2)

Aug 68. (7") <6606> **IN-A-GADDA-DA-VIDA (edit). / IRON BUTTERFLY THEME** `-` `30`

Feb 69. (lp) (228 011) <33280> **BALL** `3`
– In the time of our lives / Soul experience / Lonely boy / Real fright / In the crowds / It must be love / Her favourite style / Filled with fear / Belda-beast.

Mar 69. (7") (584 254) <6647> **SOUL EXPERIENCE. / IN THE CROWDS** `75` Feb69

Jul 69. (7") <6676> **IN THE TIME OF OUR LIVES. / IT MUST BE LOVE** `-` `96`

Nov 69. (7") <6712> **I CAN'T HELP BUT DECEIVE YOU LITTLE GIRL. / TO BE ALONE** `-` `-`

Apr 70. (lp) (2400 014) <33318> **IRON BUTTERFLY LIVE (live)** `20`
– In the time of our lives / Filled with fear / Soul experience / You can't win / Are you happy / In-a-gadda-da-vida. (re-iss. 1972; K 40086) (re-iss. 1981; K 40088)

Jul 70. (7") (2091 024) **IN-A-GADDA-DA-VIDA (edit). / TERMINATION** `-`

—— **INGLE, BUSHY and DORMAN** recruited new members **MIKE PINERA** (b.29 Sep'48, Tampa, Florida) – guitar, vocals (ex-BLUES IMAGE) repl. BRAUN who later formed FLINTWHISTLE / added **LARRY REINHARDT** (b. 7 Jul'48, Florida) – guitar

Oct 70. (7") <6782> **EASY RIDER (LET THE WIND PAY THE WAY). / SOLDIER IN OUR TOWN** `-` `66`

Feb 71. (7") <6818> **SILLY SALLY. / STONE BELIEVER** `-` `-`

Apr 71. (lp) (2401 003) <33339> **METAMORPHOSIS** `16` Aug70
– Free flight / New day / Shady lady / Best years of our lives / Slower than guns / Stone believer / Soldier in our town / Easy rider (let the wind pay the way) / Butterfly bleu. (re-iss. 1971; K 40294) (cd-iss. Jun92 on 'Repertoire'; RR 4262)

—— Disbanded Spring '71, with DORMAN and REINHARDT forming CAPTAIN BEYOND. PINERA formed RAMATAM before later joining ALICE COOPER (1981-82). Re-formed 1974, as 4-piece with **BUSHY, BRAUN** and newcomers **HOWARD REITZES** (b.22 Mar'51, Southgate, Calif.) – keyboards, vocals / **PHIL KRAMER** (b.12 Jul'52, Youngstown, Ohio) – bass, vocals

	M.C.A.	M.C.A.
Feb 75. (lp) (MCF 2694) <465> **SCORCHING BEAUTY**		

– 1975 overture / Hard miseree / High on a mountain top / Am I down / People of the world / Searchin' circles / Pearly Gates / Lonely hearts / Before you go. (cd-iss. Jun95 on 'Repertoire'; RR 4558)

Feb 75. (7") <40379> **SEARCHIN' CIRCLES. / PEARLY GATES** `-`

—— **BILL DeMARTINES** – keyboards repl. REITZES

Dec 75. (lp) (MCF 2738) <2164> **SUN AND STEEL**
– Sun and steel / Lightnin' / Beyond the Milky Way / Free / Scion / Get it out / I'm right, I'm wrong / Watch the world goin' by / Scorching beauty. (cd-iss. Mar95 on 'Edsel'; EDCD 408)

Jan 76. (7") (MCA 221) <40494> **BEYOND THE MILKY WAY. / GET IT OUT**

—— Broke up again in 1976, BUSHY formed JUICY GROOVE.

—— In May'89, IRON BUTTERFLY reformed w/**DORMAN, BRAUN, REINHARDT** and new men **STEVE FELDMANN** – vocals / **DEREK HILLARD** – keyboards / **KENNY SUAREZ** – drums

– compilations, others, etc. –

on 'Atlantic' UK & 'Atco' US unless mentioned otherwise
Jan 72. (lp) (K 40298) <33369> **EVOLUTION – THE BEST OF IRON BUTTERFLY** `Dec71`
– Iron Butterfly theme / Possession / Unconscious power / Flowers and beads / Termination / In-a-gadda-da-vida / Soul experience / Stone believer / Belda-beast / Easy rider (let the wind pay the way) / Slower than guns.

1973. (lp) (30038) **STAR COLLECTION** `-`

Oct 75. (d-lp) (K 80003) **TWO ORIGINALS OF . . .** `-`
– (BALL / METAMORPHISIS)

Feb 93. (cd) Rhino; (8122 71166-2) **LIGHT AND HEAVY: THE BEST OF IRON BUTTERFLY**

IRONHORSE (see under ⇒ BACHMAN-TURNER OVERDRIVE)

IRON MAIDEN

Formed: Leytonstone, East London, England ... mid 1976 by STEVE HARRIS, DAVE MURRAY, PAUL DiANNO and DOUG SAMPSON, who played their earliest gigs around mid '77 – an embryonic late '75 IRON MAIDEN included HARRIS, PAUL DAY (vocals), DAVE SULLIVAN (guitar), TERRY RANCE (guitar) and RON MATTHEWS (drums). The band's amphetamine-fuelled trad-metal soon procured them a rabid following around the capital and the following year they released a self-financed debut EP, 'THE SOUNDHOUSE TAPES'. The cassette came to the attention of Rock DJ, Neal Kay, who sent them on a 'Heavy Metal Crusade' tour at London's Music Machine, the resultant publicity and increasing interest in the band leading to a deal with 'E.M.I.' in 1979 (this coincided with personnel changes: CLIVE BURR replaced SAMPSON, while DENNIS STRATTON replaced brief member TONY PARSONS). Their debut single, the 100 horsepower outlaw fantasy, 'RUNNING FREE', hit the shops and UK Top 40 early in 1980, soon followed by a self-titled debut album which made the Top 5. IRON MAIDEN were the leading lights of the New Wave Of British Heavy Metal; carrying on where BLACK SABBATH and URIAH HEEP left off, they helped to create and embody the cartoon caricature that the genre would become. Despite production problems, the debut album remains one the most enduring of their career, the material raw and hungry where later efforts have tended towards flabbiness. Masters of the power chord, tracks like 'IRON MAIDEN' and 'CHARLOTTE THE HARLOT' (Politically Correct this band were not, although the phrase could be interpreted in a different way with regards to the 'KILLERS' album sleeve, a depiction of Thatcher meeting an untimely end) were prime headbanging material, DI'ANNO's vocals more gutteral punk than metal warbling. Yet the band were no musical novices, the stop-start exhilaration of 'PHANTOM OF THE OPERA' sounding considered and spontaneous at the same time. A hasty follow-up, the aforementioned 'KILLERS' (1981), lacked the focus of the debut, something which didn't deter metal fans from buying it in droves. By the release of 'THE NUMBER OF THE BEAST' (1982), DI'ANNO had been replaced by BRUCE DICKINSON, more of a vocal acrobat in the traditional metal sense. More accessible and melodic, if not as exciting, the record was a massive success (No.1 in Britain), packed with songs that would go on to form the backbone of the 'MAIDEN live set. 'RUN TO THE HILLS' was a particular favourite, giving the band their first Top 10 placing in the pop singles chart. 'PIECE OF MIND' (1983) and 'POWERSLAVE' (1984) carried on in much the same anthemic vein, the band capitalising on their staggering worldwide popularity with a mammoth touring schedule. With their trademark ghoulish mascot, 'EDDIE', horror fantasy artwork and readily identifiable sound, the band were arguably the very essence of 'Heavy Metal', a phenomenon which traversed all language boundaries in much the same way as dance music in the 90's. 'SOMEWHERE IN TIME' (1986) marked something of a departure, a more ambitious and musically diverse collection both in terms of songwriting and playing. This avenue was further explored on 'SEVENTH SON OF A SEVENTH SON' (1988), a concept affair that piled on the synth and sharpened the harmonies, resulting in four consecutive Top 10 singles. The steadfast reliability of the band's fanbase was amply illustrated when a series of EP's repackaging the band's singles went Top 10 almost without exception. But there was tension in the ranks with HARRIS favouring a return to their chest-beating roots while guitarist ADRIAN SMITH was less than pleased with the prospect. In the event, SMITH was replaced with JANICK GERS and the band released the no-frills 'NO PRAYER FOR THE DYING' (1990), a back to basics effort which spawned IRON MAIDEN's first No.1 single, the side-splittingly titled 'BRING YOUR DAUGHTER . . . TO THE SLAUGHTER'. 'FEAR OF THE DARK' (1992) gave the band yet another No.1 album, the last to feature the tonsils of DICKINSON, who soon departed for a solo career. DICKINSON's eventual replacement was BLAZE BAILEY (ex- WOLFSBANE) who made his debut on 'THE X-FACTOR' (1995), the band's last album to date (and it's lowest chart placing since 'KILLERS'). While IRON MAIDEN are still the band most readily identifiable with the term 'Heavy Metal', they face a radically altered musical climate with old-style metal on the wane generally. • **Songwriters:** All mostly HARRIS and group. In the 90's, HARRIS or DICKINSON + GERS. Covered; COMMUNICATION BREAKDOWN (Led Zeppelin) / KILL ME, CE SOIR (Golden Earring) / SPACE STATION No.5 (Montrose). DICKINSON solo re-hashed; ALL THE YOUNG DUDES (hit; Mott The Hoople). • **Trivia:** Derek Riggs became the groups' artistic designer and created 'EDDIE', an evil skeleton comic-strip character, who appeared on album sleeves, poster bills & theatrical stage shows. Banned in Chile for being interpreted as 'devils and satanists'. First band to play 'live' on Top Of The Pops since The Who.

Album rating: IRON MAIDEN (*9) / KILLERS (*6) / THE NUMBER OF THE BEAST (*7) / PIECE OF MIND (*8) / POWERSLAVE (*6) / LIVE AFTER DEATH (*8) / SOMEWHERE IN TIME (*6) / SEVENTH SON OF A SEVENTH SON (*7) / NO PRAYER FOR THE DYING (*7) / FEAR OF THE DARK (*7) / A REAL LIVE ONE (*5) / A REAL DEAD ONE (*5) / LIVE AT DONINGTON 1992 (*5) / THE X FACTOR (*6) / THE BEST OF THE BEAST compilation (*9) / VIRTUAL XI (*5)

PAUL DI'ANNO (b.17 May'59, Chingford, Essex, England) – vocals / **DAVE MURRAY** (b.23 Dec'58) – guitar / **STEVE HARRIS** (b.12 Mar'57) – bass, vocals / **DOUG SAMPSON** – drums

	Rock Hard	not iss.
Jan 79. (7"ep) (ROK 1) **THE SOUNDHOUSE TAPES**	☐	-
– Invasion / Iron Maiden / Prowler.		

—— (Nov79) **CLIVE BURR** (b. 8 Mar'57) – drums repl. SAMPSON / **DENNIS STRATTON** (b. 9 Nov'54) – guitar repl. TONY PARSONS (brief stay)

	E.M.I.	Harvest
Feb 80. (7") (EMI 5032) **RUNNING FREE. / BURNING AMBITION**	34	-
Apr 80. (lp/c) (EMC/TCEMC 3330) **IRON MAIDEN**	4	
– Prowler / Remember tomorrow / Running free / Phantom of the opera / Transylvania / Strange world / Charlotte the harlot / Iron maiden. (re-iss. May85 on 'Fame' lp/c; FA/TCFA 41-3121-1) – hit 71 (cd-iss. Oct87 on 'Fame'; CDFA 3121) (re-iss. cd Jul94; CDEMS 1538) (re-iss. cd Dec95; CDEM 1570) (cd re-iss. Sep98; 496916-0)		
May 80. (7"m) (EMI 5065) **SANCTUARY. / DRIFTER / I'VE GOT THE FIRE** (live)	29	-
Oct 80. (7") (EMI 5105) **WOMEN IN UNIFORM. / INVASION**	35	-
(12"+=) (12EMI 5105) – Phantom of the opera (live).		

—— **ADRIAN SMITH** (b.27 Feb'57) – guitar (ex-URCHIN) repl. STRATTON who formed LIONHEART

Feb 81. (lp/c) (EMC/TCEMC 3357) <12141> **KILLERS**	12	78
– The ides of march / Wrathchild / Murders in the Rue Morgue / Another life / Ghenghis Khan / Innocent exile / KIllers / Prodigal son / Purgatory / Drifter. (re-iss. May85 on 'Fame' lp/c; FA/TCFA 41-3122-1) (cd-iss. Oct87 on 'Fame'; CDFA 3122) (re-iss. cd Jul94; CDEMS 1539) (re-iss. cd Dec95; CDEM 1571) (cd re-iss. Sep98; 496917-0)		
Mar 81. (7",7"clear,7"red,c-s) (EMI 5145) **TWILIGHT ZONE. / WRATH CHILD**	31	-

Jun 81. (7") (EMI 5184) **PURGATORY. / GHENGIS KHAN**	52	-
Sep 81. (12"ep)<m-lp> (12EMI 5219) <15000> **MAIDEN JAPAN**	43	89
– Remember tomorrow / Killers / Running free / Innocent exile.		

—— **BRUCE DICKINSON** (b. PAUL BRUCE DICKINSON, 7 Aug'58, Sheffield, England) – vocals (ex-SAMSON) repl. DI'ANNO who formed LONE WOLF

Feb 82. (7"/7"pic-d) (EMI/+P 5263) **RUN TO THE HILLS. / TOTAL ECLIPSE**	7	-
Mar 82. (lp/pic-lp)(c) (EMC/EMCP/TCEMC 3400) <12202> **THE NUMBER OF THE BEAST**	1	33
– Invaders / Children of the damned / The prisoner / 22, Acacia Avenue / The number of the beast / Run to the hills / Gangland / Hallowed be thy name. (re-iss. May87 on 'Fame'; FA/TCFA 3178) (cd-iss. Apr88 on 'Fame'; CDFA 3178) (re-iss. cd Jul94; CDEMS 1533) (re-iss. Dec95 on d-cd w/bonus tracks; CDEM 1572) (cd re-iss. Sep98; 496918-0)		
Apr 82. (7"/7"red) (EMI 5287) **THE NUMBER OF THE BEAST. / REMEMBER TOMORROW**	18	-

—— now **HARRIS, MURRAY, DICKINSON** and **SMITH** were joined by **NICKO McBAIN** (b. MICHAEL, 5 Jun'54) – drums (ex-PAT TRAVERS, ex-TRUST, ex-STREETWALKERS) repl. BURR who joined STRATUS

	E.M.I.	Capitol
Apr 83. (7"/12"pic-d)(c-s) (EMI/12EMIP 5378)(TC IM4) <5248> **FLIGHT OF ICARUS. / I'VE GOT THE FIRE**	11	-
May 83. (lp/c) (EMA/TCEMA 800) <12274> **PIECE OF MIND**	3	14
– Where eagles dare / Revelations / Flight of Icarus / Die with your boots on / The trooper / Still life / Quest for fire / Sun and steel / To tame a land. (cd-iss. Dec86; CZ 82) (re-iss. 1989 lp/c; ATAK/CDATAK 139) (re-iss. cd Jun91 on 'Fame'; CDFA 3245) (re-iss. cd Jul94; CDEMS 1540) (re-iss. Dec95 on d-cd w/bonus tracks; CDEM 1573) (cd re-iss. Sep98; 496919-0)		
Jun 83. (7",7"sha-pic-d) (EMI 5397) **THE TROOPER. / CROSS-EYED MARY**	12	-
Aug 84. (7") (EMI 5489) **2 MINUTES TO MIDNIGHT. / RAINBOW'S GOLD**	11	-
(12"pic-d+=) (12EMI 5489) – Mission from 'Arry.		
Sep 84. (lp/pic-lp)(c)(cd) (POWER/+P 1)(TCPOWER 1)(746045-2) <12321> **POWERSLAVE**	2	21
– Aces high / 2 minutes to midnight / Losfer words (big 'orra) / Flash of the blade / The duellists / Back in the village / Powerslave / Rime of the ancient mariner. (re-iss. 1989 lp/c; ATAK/TCATAK 140) (re-iss. Jun91 on 'Fame'; FA 3244) (re-iss. cd Jul94; CDEMS 1539) (re-iss. Dec95 d-cd w/bonus tracks; CDEM 1574) (cd re-iss. Sep98; 496920-0)		
Oct 84. (7") (EMI 5502) **ACES HIGH. / KING OF TWILIGHT**	20	-
(12"+=/12"pic-d+=) (12EMI/+P 5502) – The number of the beast (live).		
Sep 85. (7") (EMI 5532) **RUNNING FREE (live). / SANCTUARY** (live)	19	-
(12"+=/12"pic-d+=) (12EMI/+P 5532) – Murders in the Rue Morgue (live).		
Oct 85. (d-lp/c)(cd) (RIP/TCRIP 1)(746186-2) <12441> **LIVE AFTER DEATH** (live)	2	19
– Aces high / 2 minutes to midnight / The trooper / Revelations / Flight of Icarus / The rime of the ancient mariner / Powerslave / The number of the beast / Hallowed be thy name / Iron maiden / Run to the hills / Running free. (d-lp+=/c+=) – Wrathchild / 22 Acacia Avenue / Children of the damned / Die with your boots on / Phantom of the opera. (re-iss. 1989 lp/c; ATAK/TCATAK 141) (re-iss. Jun91 on 'Fame' w/ less tracks; CDFA 3248) (re-iss. cd Jul94 w/ fewer tracks; CDEMS 1535) (re-iss. Dec95 d-cd w/ bonus tracks; CDEM 1575) (d-cd re-iss. Sep98; 496921-0)		
Nov 85. (7") (EMI 5542) **RUN TO THE HILLS (live). / PHANTOM OF THE OPERA** (live)	26	-
(12"+=/12"pic-d+=) (12EMI/+P 5542) – Losfer words (The big 'orra) (live).		
Aug 86. (7"/7"sha-pic-d) (EMI/+P 5583) **WASTED YEARS. / REACH OUT**	18	-
(12"+=) (12EMI 5583) – The sheriff of Huddersfield.		
Sep 86. (lp/c)(cd) (EMC/TCEMC 3512)(746341-2) <12524> **SOMEWHERE IN TIME**	3	11
– Caught somewhere in time / Wasted years / Sea of madness / Heaven can wait / The loneliness of the long distance runner / Stranger in a strange land / Deja-vu / Alexander the Great. (re-iss. 1989 lp/c; ATAK/TCATAK 142) (re-iss. Jun91 on 'Fame'; CDFA 3246) (re-iss. cd Jul94; CDEMS 1537) (re-iss. Dec95 d-cd w/bonus tracks; CDEM 1576) (cd re-iss. Sep98; 496924-0)		
Nov 86. (7") (EMI 5589) **STRANGER IN A STRANGE LAND. / THAT GIRL**	22	-
(12"+=/12"pic-d+=) (12EMI/+P 5589) – Juanita.		
Mar 88. (7"/7"w sticker & transfer/7"sha-pic-d) (EM/+S/P 49) <44154> **CAN I PLAY WITH MADNESS. / BLACK BART BLUES**	3	
(12"+=/cd-s+=) (12EM/CDEM 49) – Massacre.		
Apr 88. (cd/c/lp)(pic-lp) (TC/CD+/EMD 1006)(EMDP 1006) <90258> **SEVENTH SON OF A SEVENTH SON**	1	12
– Moonchild / Infinite dreams / Can I play with madness / The evil that men do / Seventh son of a seventh son / The prophecy / The clairvoyant / Only the good die young. (re-iss. 1989 lp/c; ATAK/TCATAK 143) (re-iss. Jun91 on 'Fame'; CDFA 3247) (re-iss. cd Jul94; CDEMS 1534) (re-iss. Dec95 d-cd w/bonus tracks; CDEM 1577) (cd re-iss. Sep98; 496864-0)		
Aug 88. (7"/7"g-f/7"sha-pic-d) (EM/+G/P 64) **THE EVIL THAT MEN DO. / PROWLER '88**	5	
(12"+=/12"poster)(cd-s+=) (12EM/+S 64)(CDEM 64) – Charlotte the harlot '88.		
Nov 88. (7"/7"clear/7"sha-pic-d) (EM/+S/P 79) **THE CLAIRVOYANT** (live). / **THE PRISONER** (live)	6	
(12"+=/12"pic-d+=)(cd-s+=) (12EM/+P 79)(CDEM 79) – Heaven can wait (live).		
Nov 89. (7"/7"sha-pic-d)(c-s) (EM/+PD 117)(TCEM 117) **INFINITE DREAMS** (live). / **KILLERS** (live)	6	
(12"+=/cd-s+=)(12"etched+=) (12/CD EM 117) – Still life (live).		

—— (Feb90) **JANICK GERS** – guitar (ex-GILLAN, ex-WHITE SPIRIT, etc.) repl. SMITH who formed A.S.A.P.

	E.M.I.	Epic
Sep 90. (7"/c-s) (EM/TCEM 158) **HOLY SMOKE. / ALL IN YOUR MIND**	3	
(12"+=/12"pic-d+=)(cd-s+=) (12EM/+P 158)(CDEM 158) – Kill me ce soir.		
Oct 90. (cd/c/lp)(pic-lp)<red-lp> (CD/TC+/EMD 1017)(EMPD 1017) <E 46905> **NO PRAYER FOR THE DYING**	2	17

– Tailgunner / Holy smoke / No prayer for the dying / Public enema number one / Fates warning / The assassin / Run silent run deep / Hooks in you / Bring your daughter . . . to the slaughter / Mother Russia. *(re-iss. cd Jul94; CDEM 1541)* *(re-iss. Dec95 d-cd w/bonus tracks; CDEM 1578)* *(cd re-iss. Sep98; 496865-4)*

Dec 90. (7"/7"pic-d)(c-s) *(EM/+PD 171)(TCEM 171)* **BRING YOUR DAUGHTER . . . TO THE SLAUGHTER. / I'M A MOVER** [1] [ ]
(12"+=/12"pic-d+=)(cd-s+=) *(12EM/+P 171)(CDEM 171)* – Communication breakdown.

—— In Summer 1991, HARRIS and McBAIN back up tennis stars McENROE & CASH on their version of LED ZEPPELIN'S 'Rock And Roll'. In Mar'92, BRUCE DICKINSON was to feature on single with Rowan Atkinson's comic character 'MR.BEAN & SMEAR CAMPAIGN' on a version of an Alice Cooper song '(I Want To Be) Elected'.

Apr 92. (7") *(EM 229)* **BE QUICK OR BE DEAD. / NODDING DONKEY BLUES** [2] [ ]
(12"+=/12"pic-d+=)(cd-s+=) *(12EM/+P 229)(CDEM 229)* – Space station No.5.

May 92. (cd/c/d-lp) *(CD/TC+/EMD 1032)* <48993> **FEAR OF THE DARK** [1] [12]
– Be quick or be dead / From here to eternity / Afraid to shoot strangers / Fear is the key / Childhood's end / Wasting love / The fugitive / Chains of misery / The apparition / Judas be my guide / Weekend warrior / Fear of the dark. *(re-iss. cd Jul94; CDEM 1542)* *(re-iss. Dec95 d-cd w/bonus tracks +=; CDEM 1579)* – Nodding donkey blues / Space station No.5 / I can't see my feeling / No prayer for the dying (live) / Public enema No.1 (live) / Hook in you (live). *(cd re-iss. Sep98; 496925-0)*

Jul 92. (7"etched) *(EM 240)* **FROM HERE TO ETERNITY. / ROLL OVER VIC VELLA** [21] [ ]
(12"+=/cd-s+=) *(12/CD EM 240)* – Public enema number one / No prayer for the dying.
(7"sha-pic-d) *(EMPD 240)* – ('A'side) / I can't see my feeling.

E.M.I.   Capitol

Mar 93. (7"/7"sha-pic-d) *(EMP/+D 263)* **FEAR OF THE DARK (live). / TAILGUNNER (live)** [8] [ ]
(cd-s+=) *(CDEM 263)* – Hooks in you (live) *(on some 7"sha-pic-d)* / Bring your daughter . . .to the slaughter (live).

Mar 93. (cd/c/lp) *(CD/TC+/EMD 1042)* <81456> **A REAL LIVE ONE (live)** [3] [ ]
– Be quick or be dead / From here to eternity / Can I play with madness / Wasting love / Tailgunner / The evil that men do / Afraid to shoot strangers / Bring your daughter . . .to the slaughter / Heaven can wait / The clairvoyant / Fear of the dark.

—— DICKINSON had already announced he had departed to go solo in '94.

Oct 93. (7"red) *(EM 288)* **HALLOWED BE THY NAME (live). / WRATHCHILD (live)** [9] [ ]
(12"pic-d+=/cd-s+=) *(12EMP/CDEM 288)* – The trooper (live) / Wasted years (live).

Oct 93. (cd/c/lp) *(CD/TC+/EMD 1048)* <89248> **A REAL DEAD ONE (live)** [12] [ ]
– The number of the beast / The trooper / Prowler / Transylvania / Remember tomorrow / Where eagles dare / Sanctuary / Running free / Run to the hills / 2 minutes to midnight / Iron Maiden / Hallowed be thy name. *(this & last "live" set, re-iss. Sep98; 496926-0)*

Nov 93. (d-cd/d-c/t-lp) *(CD/MC+/DON 1)* **LIVE AT DONINGTON 1992 (live)** [23] [-]
– Be quick or be dead / The number of the beast / Wrathchild / From here to eternity / Can I play with madness / Wasting love / Tailgunner / The evil that men do / Afraid to shoot strangers / Fear of the dark / Bring your daughter . . . to the slaughter / The clairvoyant / Heaven can wait / Run to the hills / 2 minutes to midnight / Iron maiden / Hallowed be thy name / The trooper / Sanctuary / Running free. *(re-iss. Sep98; 496929-0)*

—— BLAZE BAILEY – vocals (ex-WOLFSBANE) now replacement

E.M.I.   CMC Int.

Sep 95. (c-s) *(TCEM 398)* **MAN ON THE EDGE / THE EDGE OF DARKNESS** [10] [ ]
(12"pic-d+=) *(12EM 398)* – I live my way.
(cd-s+=) *(CDEMS 398)* – Judgement day / (Blaze Bailey interview part 1).
(cd-s+=) *(CDEM 398)* – Justice of the peace / (Blaze Bailey interview part 2).

Oct 95. (cd/c/clear-d-lp) *(+CD/TC EMD 1087)* <8003> **THE X FACTOR** [9] [ ]
– Sign of the cross / Lord of the flies / Man on the edge / Fortunes of war / Look for the truth / The aftermath / Judgement of Heaven / Blood on the world's hands / The edge of darkness / 2 a.m. / The unbeliever.

Sep 96. (12") *(12EM 443)* **VIRUS. / PROWLER (the Soundhouse tapes) / INVASION (the Soundhouse tapes)** [16] [ ]
(cd-s) *(CDEM 443)* – ('A'side) / My generation / Doctor, doctor.
(cd-s) *(CDEMS 443)* – ('A'side) / Sanctuary (metal for muthas) / Wrathchild (metal for muthas).

Sep 96. (d-cd/q-lp) *(CDEMDS 1097)* **BEST OF THE BEAST** [16] [ ]
(compilation with all line-ups)
– Virus / Sign of the cross / Afraid to shoot strangers (live) / Man on the edge / Be quick or be dead / Fear of the dark (live) / Holy smoke / Bring your daughter . . . to the slaughter / Seventh son of a seventh son / Can I play with madness / The evil that men do / The clairvoyant / Heaven can wait / Wasted years / 2 minutes to midnight / Running free (live) / Rime of the ancient mariner (live) / Aces high / Where eagles dare / The trooper * / The number of the beast / Revelations * / The prisoner * / Run to the hills / Hallowed be thy name / Wrathchild / Killers * / Remember tomorrow * / Phantom of the opera / Sanctuary / Prowler * / Invasion * / Strange world / Iron maiden. *(q-lp+= *)*

Mar 98. (7"pic-d) *(EM 507)* **THE ANGEL AND THE GAMBLER. / BLOOD ON THE WORLD'S HANDS (live) / THE AFTERMATH (live)** [18] [ ]
(cd-s) *(CDEMS 507)* – (first 2 tracks) / Afraid to shoot strangers (CD-Rom video).
(cd-s) *(CDEM 507)* – (first & third tracks) / The aftermath (live) / Man on the edge (CD-Rom video).

Mar 98. (cd/c/d-lp) *(493915-2/-4/-1)* <86240> **VIRTUAL XI** [16] [ ]
– Futureal / The angel and the gambler / Lightning strikes twice / Clansman / When two worlds collide / Educated fool / Don't look to the eyes of a stranger / Como estais amigos.

Sep 98. (7"pic-d) *(EM 525)* **FUTUREAL. / THE EVIL THAT MEN DO (live) / MAN ON THE EDGE (live)** [-] [-]
(cd-s) *(CDEM 525)* – (first 2) / Futureal (CD-rom).
(cd-s) *(CDEMS 525)* – (first & third) / The angel and the gambler (CD-rom).

(above only available through the internet shopping channel)

—— early in '99, BRUCE DICKINSON was now back at the helm

– compilations, etc. –

on 'E.M.I.' unless otherwise stated

Feb 90. (cd-ep/d12") *(CD+/IRN 1)* **RUNNING FREE / BURNING AMBITION / SANCTUARY / DRIFTER (live) / I'VE GOT THE FIRE (live) / Listen with Nicko (part 1)** [10] [ ]

Feb 90. (cd-ep/d12") *(CD+/IRN 2)* **WOMEN IN UNIFORM / INVASION / PHANTOM OF THE OPERA / TWILIGHT ZONE / WRATHCHILD / Listen with Nicko (part 2)** [10] [ ]

Feb 90. (cd-ep/d12") *(CD+/IRN 3)* **PURGATORY / GENGHIS KHAN / RUNNING FREE / REMEMBER TOMORROW / KILLERS / INNOCENT EXILE / Listen with Nicko (part 3)** [5] [ ]

Mar 90. (cd-ep/d12") *(CD+/IRN 4)* **RUN TO THE HILLS / TOTAL ECLIPSE / THE NUMBER OF THE BEAST / REMEMBER TOMORROW (live) / Listen with Nicko (part 4)** [3] [ ]

Mar 90. (cd-ep/d12") *(CD+/IRN 5)* **FLIGHT OF ICARUS / I'VE GOT THE FIRE / THE TROOPER / CROSS-EYED MARY / Listen with Nicko (part 5)** [7] [ ]

Mar 90. (cd-ep/d12") *(CD+/IRN 6)* **2 MINUTES TO MIDNIGHT / RAINBOW'S GOLD / MISSION FROM 'ARRY / ACES HIGH / KING OF TWILIGHT / THE NUMBER OF THE BEAST (live) / Listen with Nicko (part 6)** [11] [ ]

Apr 90. (cd-ep/d12") *(CD+/IRN 7)* **RUNNING FREE / SANCTUARY / MURDERS IN THE RUE MORGUE / RUN TO THE HILLS / PHANTOM OF THE OPERA / LOSFER WORDS (THE BIG 'ORRA) / Listen with Nicko (part 7)** [9] [ ]

Apr 90. (cd-ep/d12") *(CD+/IRN 8)* **WASTED YEARS / REACH OUT / THE SHERIFF OF HUDDERSFIELD / STRANGER IN A STRANGE LAND / THAT GIRL / JUANITA / Listen with Nicko (part 8)** [9] [ ]

Apr 90. (cd-ep/d12") *(CD+/IRN 9)* **CAN I PLAY WITH MADNESS / BLACK BART BLUES / MASSACRE / THE EVIL THAT MEN DO / PROWLER '88 / CHARLOTTE THE HARLOT '88 / Listen with Nicko (part 9)** [10] [ ]

Apr 90. (cd-ep/d12") *(CD+/IRN 10)* **THE CLAIRVOYANT (live) / THE PRISONER (live) / HEAVEN CAN WAIT (live) / INFINITE DREAMS (live) / KILLERS (live) / STILL LIFE (live) / Listen with Nicko (part 10)** [11] [ ]

—— (all 10 singles above, basically hit peak number before crashing out)

Aug 94. (cd,cd-vid) *(SAV 4913103)* **MAIDEN ENGLAND (live)** [-] [ ]
– Moonchild / The evil that men do / Prisoner / Still life / Die with your boots on / Infinite dreams / Killers / Heaven can wait / Wasted years / The clairvoyant / Seventh son of a seventh son / The number of the best / Iron maiden.

Chris ISAAK

Born: 6 Jun'56, Stockton, California, USA. In 1984, after graduating with a degree in English & Communications, he formed his own rockabilly backing outfit, SILVERTONE, who comprised JAMES CALVIN WILSEY (lead guitar), ROWLAND SALLEY (bass, vocals), and KENNEY DALE JOHNSON (drums, vocals). They were soon spotted by Erik Jacobsen, who became their manager, helping them secure a deal with 'Warners' and subsequently producing the debut album, 'SILVERTONE', in 1985. A moody cross between heroes ELVIS PRESLEY and ROY ORBISON, ISAAK crooned his way through tales of lost love that functioned best as emotive mood pieces. The 1987 eponymous follow-up and 1989's 'HEART SHAPED WORLD' didn't exactly break any new ground although they perfected the ISAAK formula, the understated tragedy of 'WICKED GAME' becoming a trans-Atlantic Top 10 hit in 1990 after featuring on the soundtrack to the David Lynch movie, 'Wild At Heart'. Signing a new contract with 'Reprise', the success of 'WICKED GAME' resurrected sales of 'HEART SHAPED WORLD', propelling the album back into the US Top 10. The singer had already scored a big hit in France with 'BLUE HOTEL' (from 'CHRIS ISAAK'), the song finally making the UK Top 20 when it was re-released in early 1991. ISAAK re-emerged in 1993 with 'SAN FRANCISCO DAYS', a relatively more uptempo collection which nevertheless included a brooding cover of Neil Diamond's 'SOLITARY MAN'. Another highlight was the country-tinged melancholy of 'EXCEPT THE NEW GIRL'. 'FOREVER BLUE' (1995) saw the prince of heartache reverting back to his rockabilly roots with a new band. • **Songwriters:** BAJA SESSIONS included covers SOUTH OF THE BORDER (DOWN MEXICO WAY) (Meleon – Roy Orbison) / I WONDER (hit; Brenda Lee) / TWO HEARTS (hit; Pat Boone) / RETURN TO ME (hit; Dean Martin) / LEILANI (Harry – Dyens). • **Trivia:** CHRIS has also played bit parts in movies, 'Married To The Mob' & 'The Silence Of The Lambs'. In 1987, he appeared for the first time on Channel 4 TV's 'The Last Resort' which was hosted by fan, Jonathan R/W oss (delete as appropriate).

Album rating: SILVERTONE (*5) / CHRIS ISAAK (*5) / HEART SHAPED WORLD (*6) / WICKED GAME (*7) / SAN FRANCISCO DAYS (*6) / FOREVER BLUE (*5) / BAJA SESSIONS (*4) / SPEAK OF THE DEVIL (*4)

CHRIS ISAAK – vocals, guitar with back-up from **SILVERTONE** who feature **JAMES CALVIN WILSEY** – lead guitar / **ROWLAND SALLEY** – bass, vocals / **KENNEY DALE JOHNSON** – drums, vocals

Warners   Warners

Mar 85. (lp) *(925156-1)* <25156> **SILVERTONE** [ ] [ ]
– Dancin' / Talk to me / Livin' for your lover / Back on your side / Voodoo / Funeral in the rain / The lonely one / Unhappiness / Tears / Goin' ridin' / Pretty girls don't cry / Western stars. *(cd-iss. Dec87; 925156-2)*

Apr 85. (7") <29073> **DANCIN'. / HAPPINESS** [-] [ ]

Jul 85. (7") <28971> **TALK TO ME. / LIVIN' FOR YOUR LOVER** | - | |
Oct 85. (7") <28907> **GONE RIDIN' (theme from 'American Flyer'). / TEARS** | - | |
Mar 87. (lp/c)(cd) (WX 138/+C)(925536-2) <25536> **CHRIS ISAAK**
– You owe me some kind of love / Heart full of soul / Blue hotel / Lie to me / Fade away / Wild love / This love will last / You took my heart / Cryin' / Lovers game / Waiting for the rain to fall.
Apr 87. (7"/12") (W 8467/+T) **YOU OWE ME SOME KIND OF LOVE. / WAITING FOR THE RAIN TO FALL** | | - |
Jul 87. (7") (W 8374) **BLUE HOTEL. / WAITING FOR THE RAIN TO FALL** | | - |
(12"+=/12"pic-d+=) (W 8374T) – Wild love.
Jun 89. (lp/c)(cd) (WX 264/+C)(925837-2) <25837> **HEART SHAPED WORLD**
– Heart shaped world / I'm not waiting / Don't make me dream about you / Kings of the highway / Wicked game / Blue Spanish sky / Wrong to love you / Forever young / Nothing's changed / In the heart of the jungle / Diddley daddy. <re-dist.Jan91, hit No.7>

Nov 90. (c-s) <19704> **WICKED GAME / ('A'instrumental)** | - | 6 |
Nov 90. (7"/c-s) (LON/+CS 279) **WICKED GAME. / COOL CAT WALK** | 10 | - |
(12"+=/cd-s+=) (LON X/CD 279) – Dark Spanish symphony / Blue Hawaiian music.
(above from the movie, 'Wild At Heart' on 'London' records)

	Reprise	Reprise
Jan 91. (cd)(lp/c) (7599 26513-2)(WX 406/+C) **WICKED GAME** (compilation) | 3 | - |
– Wicked game / You owe me some kind of love / Blue Spanish sky / Heart shaped world / Funeral in the rain / Blue hotel / Dancin' / Nothing's changed / Voodoo / Lie to me / Wicked game (instrumental).
Jan 91. (7"/c-s) (W 0005/+C) **BLUE HOTEL. / WICKED GAME** | 17 | - |
(12"+=/cd-s+=) (W 0005 T/CD) – Wrong to love you.
Mar 91. (7"/c-s) (W ?/+C) **DANCIN'. / NOTHING'S CHANGED** | | - |
(12"+=/cd-s+=) (W ? T/CD) – Wild love.
Sep 91. (7"/c-s) (W ?/+C) **BLUE SPANISH SKY. / WICKED GAME** (instrumental) | | - |
(12"/cd-s) (W ? T/CD) – ('A'side) / Don't make me dream about you / The lovely ones / Lovers game.
Mar 93. (7"/c-s) (W 0161/+C) **CAN'T DO A THING (TO STOP ME). / BLUE HOTEL** | 36 | - |
(cd-s) (W 0161CD1) – ('A'side) / Tears / Blue Spanish sky / Lonely with a broken heart.
(cd-s) (W 0161CD2) – ('A'side) / Talk to me / Gone ridin' / Waiting for the rain to fall.
Apr 93. (cd/c/lp) <(9362 45116-2/-4)> **SAN FRANCISCO DAYS** | 12 | 35 |
– San Francisco days / Beautiful homes / Round 'n' round / Two hearts / Can't do a thing (to stop me) / Except the new girl / Waiting / Move along / I want your love / 5:15 / Lonely with a broken heart / A solitary man.
Jul 93. (7"/c-s) (W 0182/+C) **SAN FRANCISCO DAYS. / 5:15** | 62 | - |
(cd-s+=) (W 0182CD1) – Shake little sister.
(cd-s) (W 0182CD2) – ('A'side) / Western stars / Suspicion of love.
Sep 93. (7"/c-s) (W 0202/+C) **A SOLITARY MAN. / WICKED GAME** | | - |
(cd-s+=) (W 0202CD) – Lie to me / Lovers game.

—— SILVERTONE band; **MARK GOLDENBERG / GREGG ARREGUIN / FRANK MARTIN / JASON MORGAN / JEFF WATSON / STEPHEN BISHOP / DAVID GRISMAN / DAVID GRISSOM / BRUCE KAPHAN**
May 95. (c-s) (W 0295C) <17872> **SOMEBODY'S CRYING / CHANGED YOUR MIND** | | 45 |
(cd-s+=) (W 0295CD) – Little white cloud that lied.
(re-iss. Oct95; same)
May 95. (cd/c) <(9362 45845-2/-4)> **FOREVER BLUE** | 27 | 31 |
– Baby did a bad bad thing / Somebody's crying / Graduation day / Go walking down there / Don't leave me on my own / Things go wrong / Forever blue / There she goes / Goin' nohere / Changed your mind / Shadows in a mirror / I believe / The end of everything.
Oct 96. (cd/c) <(9362-46325-2/-4)> **BAJA SESSIONS** | | 33 |
– Pretty girls don't cry / Back on your side / Only the lonely / South of the border (down Mexico way) / I wonder / Wrong to love you / Waiting for my lucky day / Yellow bird / Two hearts / Return to me / Dancin' / Sweet Leilani / Think of tomorrow.
Sep 98. (c-s) (W 0454C) **PLEASE / EVERYONE GETS DOWN** | | |
(cd-s+=) (W 0454CD) –
Oct 98. (cd/c) <(9362 46849-2/-4)> **SPEAK OF THE DEVIL** | | 41 Sep98 |
– Please / Flying / Walk slow / Breakin' apart / This time / Speak of the devil / Like the way she moves / Wanderin' / Don't get so down on yourself / Black flowers / I'm not sleepy / 7 lonely nights / Talkin' 'bout a home / Super magic 2000.
Sep 99. (cd-s) (W 0503C) **BABY DID A BAD BAD THING / WICKED GAME** | 44 | |
(cd-s+=) (W 0503CD) – I wonder.
(cd-s) (W 0503CDX) – ('A'side) / ('A'remix) / ('A'acoustic).

ISLEY BROTHERS

Formed: Cincinatti, Ohio, USA ... early 50's by RONALD, RUDOLPH, O'KELLY and VERNON ISLEY, all experienced gospel singers. The subsequent death of VERNON led to the remaining brothers moving from Cincinnati to New York in '56, where they began their recording career. After achieving some early success with 'SHOUT' in '59, the siblings recorded the enduring 'TWIST AND SHOUT' a couple of years later, a song The BEATLES would later cover to significantly greater commercial success. Eager for more creative control, The ISLEY BROTHERS took the unprecedented step of setting up their own label, 'T-Neck' (named after their new location, Teaneck in New Jersey). Their first homegrown recording, 'TESTIFY', was largely ignored although the featured lead guitarist would go on to influence the playing of generations, the axe-man in question one JIMI HENDRIX. In

an effort to achieve a higher profile, the group signed to 'Motown' in '65. Unfortunately, the label insisted on moulding the band to their formulaic 'hit-factory' approach, stifling their creative input and producing only one hit, 1966's 'THIS OLD HEART OF MINE'. The brothers' finest recordings came after they split with Berry Gordy and Co. in '68, relaunching 'T-Neck' the following year. With creative control firmly back in the hands of the outfit, they let rip with funky grooves and even funkier outfits, their evolution complete with the addition of three more members of the ISLEY clan, brothers ERNIE and MARVIN and cousin CHRIS JASPER. The latter contributed the classic single, 'IT'S YOUR THING', a record which became an instant hit and earned the band a Grammy. Touring frequently in the late 60's and early 70's, a distribution deal with 'C.B.S.' in '73 led to the release of '3 + 3', an album which showcased the roots of the "Isley Sound"; ERNIE's Hendrix-influenced guitar work was a vital component in the trademark blend of dance rhythms and funk-laden grooves best sampled on the sexy 'THAT LADY'. Through '73 to '83, the band scored nine consecutive gold or platinum albums, their sound switching back and forth between RONALD's soulfully smooth ballads and the hard and funky stuff. The two styles combined especially well on the 1975 offering, 'THE HEAT IS ON', alternating the furious vocals of 'FIGHT THE POWER' with a song addressing the need for social awareness and global peace in 'HARVEST FOR THE WORLD'. Towards the early 80's the family released a series of songs with a highly erotic content, a sure-fire winner in terms of sales, which produced the hits 'BETWEEN THE SHEETS' and 'CHOOSY LOVER'. There was a certain amount of compromise to their output, however, and in '84, the band split; the original members signed to 'Warner Bros.' while the "youngsters" went on to form the short-lived ISLEY-JASPER-ISLEY unit. The latter outfit penned the hymnal 'CARAVAN OF LOVE' in '85, later a UK No.1 hit for The HOUSEMARTINS. ERNIE ISLEY subsequently recorded a blistering solo album on 'Elektra', while RONALD, together with his future wife ANGELA WINBUSH, topped the R&B charts with 'SPEND THE NIGHT'. Influencing legions of recording artists throughout their four decades, The ISLEY BROTHERS were inducted into the Rock & Roll Hall Of Fame in '92. • **Songwriters:** Producers LEIBER & STOLLER provided them with their 'Atlantic' material in '61, while the following year, producer BERT BERNS wrote 'RIGHT NOW' and their hit 'TWIST AND SHOUT'. In 1966, with 'Tamla Motown', HOLLAND-DOZIER-HOLLAND provided them with some hits. In 1969, their formation of 'T-Neck' saw them writing their own material. During this time they also covered LOVE THE ONE YOU'RE WITH (Stephen Stills) / LAY LADY LAY (Bob Dylan) / SPILL THE WINE (War) / COLD BOLOGNA (Bill Withers) / FIRE AND RAIN (James Taylor) / MACHINE GUN (Jimi Hendrix) / OHIO (Neil Young) / SUMMER BREEZE (Seals & Croft) / IT'S TOO LATE + BROTHER, BROTHER, BROTHER (Carole King) / etc.
Album rating: SHOUT! (*5) / TWIST & SHOUT! (*6) / THE FABULOUS ISLEY BROTHERS TWISTING AND SHOUTING (*4) / THIS OLD HEART OF MINE (*5) / SOUL ON THE ROCKS (*4) / IT'S OUR THING (*7) / THE BROTHERS: ISLEY (*4) / GIVIN' IT BACK (*5) / BROTHER, BROTHER, BROTHER (*6) / THE ISLEYS LIVE (*5) / 3 + 3 (*8) / LIVE IT UP (*6) / THE HEAT IS ON (*7) / HARVEST FOR THE WORLD (*6) / GO FOR YOUR GUNS (*6) / FOREVER GOLD compilation (*7) / SHOWDOWN (*6) / WINNER TAKES ALL (*6) / GO ALL THE WAY (*6) / GRAND SLAM (*6) / INSIDE YOU (*5) / THE REAL DEAL (*5) / BETWEEN THE SHEETS (*6) / MASTERPIECE (*5) / SMOOTH SAILIN' (*5) / Isley Brothers featuring Ronald Isley: SPEND THE NIGHT (*4) / TRACKS OF LIFE (*4) / MISSION TO PLEASE (*6) / ISLEY BROTHERS STORY VOL.1 (THE ROCK'N'ROLL YEARS 1959-68) compilation (*8) / ISLEY BROTHERS STORY VOL.2 (THE T-NECK YEARS 1969-1985) compilation (*8)

RONALD ISLEY (b.21 May'41) – lead vocals / **RUDOLPH ISLEY** (b. 1 Apr'39) – vocal / **O'KELLY ISLEY** (b.25 Dec'37) – vocals

		not iss.	Teenage
1957.	(7") <1004> **THE COW JUMPED OVER THE MOON. / ANGELS CRIED**	-	
		not iss.	Mark-X
1957.	(7") <7003> **ROCKIN' McDONALD. / DON'T BE JEALOUS**	-	
		not iss.	Gone
1958.	(7") <5022> **EVERYBODY'S GONNA ROCK'N'ROLL. / I WANNA KNOW**	-	
1958.	(7") <5048> **THE DRAG. / THE LOVE**	-	
		not iss.	Cindy
1958.	(7") <3009> **THIS IS THE END. / DON'T BE JEALOUS**	-	
		R.C.A.	R.C.A.
1959.	(7") <7537> **TURN TO ME. / I'M GONNA KNOCK ON YOUR DOOR**	-	
Oct 59.	(7") (RCA 1149) <7588> **SHOUT. / SHOUT (Pt.2)**		47 Sep59
	(re-iss. US Mar 62, hit No.94)		
Jun 60.	(lp) (RD 27165) <LSP 2156> **SHOUT!**		Oct59
	– Shout! (part 1 & 2) / Tell me who / How deep is the ocean (part 1 & 2) / Respectable (parts 1 & 2) / Say you love me / Open up your heart / He's got the whole world in his hands / Without a song / Yes indeed / Ring a ling a ling / That lucky old sun / When the saints go marching in / Gypsy love song / St. Louis blues / Rock around the clock / Turn to me / Not one minute more / I'm gonna knock on your door. (re-iss. Nov70; INTS 1098) (cd-iss. DEc88 on 'Bear Family'; BCD 15425) – (extra tracks).		
Feb 60.	(7") <7657> **RESPECTABLE. / WITHOUT A SONG**	-	
Feb 60.	(7") (RCA 1172) **RESPECTABLE. / I'M GONNA KNOCK ON YOUR DOOR**		-
May 60.	(7") (RCA 1190) <7718> **HE'S GOT THE WHOLE WORLD IN HIS HANDS. / HOW DEEP IS THE OCEAN**		
Aug 60.	(7") <7746> **GYPSY LOVE SONG. / OPEN UP YOUR HEART**	-	
Nov 60.	(7") (RCA 1213) <7787> **TELL ME WHO. / SAY YOU LOVE ME TOO**		

		not iss.	Atlantic
1961.	(7") <2092> **TELL ME HOW TO SHIMMY. / JEEPERS CREEPERS**	-	-
1961.	(7") <2100> **SHINE ON HARVEST MOON. / STANDING ON THE DANCE FLOOR**	-	-
1961.	(7") <2110> **WRITE TO ME. / YOUR OLD LADY**	-	-
1961.	(7") <2122> **A FOOL FOR YOU. / JUST ONE MORE TIME**	-	-

		Stateside	Wand
Feb 62.	(7") <118> **RIGHT NOW. / THE SNAKE**	-	
Jun 62.	(7") (SS 112) <124> **TWIST AND SHOUT. / I.B. Special: SPANISH TWIST** (re-act.Jul63 reached UK No.42)		17 May62
Oct 62.	(7") (SS 132) <127> **TWISTING WITH LINDA. / YOU BETTER COME HOME**		54 Sep62
Oct 62.	(lp) <653> **TWIST AND SHOUT**	-	61

– Twist and shout / Don't you feel / Hold on baby / Time after time / Twisting with Linda / I say love / Right now / Spanish twist / The drag / Don't be jealous / This is the end / Rockin' McDonald. (UK-iss.Feb76 on 'D.J.M.'; 2628) (c-iss.Oct82 on 'Orchid'; ORC 009) (cd-iss. 1988 on 'K-Tel'; NCD 5162)

| Aug 63. | (7") (SS 128) <127> **NOBODY BUT ME. / I'M LAUGHING TO KEEP FROM CRYING** | - | |
| Oct 63. | (7") <137> **HOLD ON BABY. / I SAY LOVE** | - | |

		U.A.	U.A.
Oct 63.	(7") (UP 1034) <605> **TANGO. / SHE'S GONE**		
Dec 63.	(7") <638> **SURF AND SHOUT. / WHAT'CHA GONNA DO**	-	
Feb 64.	(7") <659> **YOU'LL NEVER LEAVE HIM. / PLEASE, PLEASE, PLEASE**	-	
Apr 64.	(7") <714> **WHO'S THAT LADY. / MY LITTLE GIRL**	-	
Apr 64.	(7") (UP 1050) **SHAKE IT WITH ME BABY. / STAGGER LEE**		-
May 64.	(lp) (ULP 1064) <6313> **THE FABULOUS ISLEY BROTHERS – TWISTING AND SHOUTING**		

– Surf and shout / Please please please / Do the twist / She's the one / Tango / What'cha gonna do / Stagger Lee / You'll never leave him / Let's go, let's go, let's go / Shake it with me baby / She's gone / Long tall Sally.

		Atlantic	T-Neck
May 64.	(7") <501> **TESTIFY. / (part 2)**	-	-

		Atlantic	Atlantic
Oct 64.	(7") (AT 4010) <2263> **THE LAST GIRL. / LOOKING FOR A LOVE**		
1965.	(7") <2277> **SIMON SAYS. / WILD AS A TIGER**	-	
1965.	(7") <2303> **MOVE OVER AND LET ME DANCE / HAVE YOU EVER BEEN DISAPPOINTED**	-	

		Tamla Motown	Tamla
Mar 66.	(7") (TMG 555) <54128> **THIS OLD HEART OF MINE (IS WEAK FOR YOU). / THERE'S NO LOVE LEFT** (re-act.Oct68 reached UK No.3)	47	12 Jan66
Oct 66.	(lp) (TML 11034) <269> **THIS OLD HEART OF MINE (IS WEAK FOR YOU)**		Jun66

– Nowhere to run / Stop in the name of love / This old heart of mine (is weak for you) / Take some time out for love / I guess I'll always love you / Baby don't you do it / Who could ever doubt my love / Put yourself in my place / Just ain't enough love / I hear a symphony / There's no love left / Seek and you shall find. (re-act.Dec68 hit UK No.23) (re-iss. Jul81 lp/c; STMS/CSTMS 5026)

Jun 66.	(7") (TMG 556) <54133> **TAKE SOME TIME OUT FOR LOVE. / WHO COULD EVER DOUBT MY LOVE** (re-iss. Nov69; TMG 719)		66 May66
Aug 66.	(7") (TMG 572) <54135> **I GUESS I'LL ALWAYS LOVE YOU. / I HEAR A SYMPHONY**	45	61 Jul66
1967.	(lp) <37080> **TAMLA MOTOWN PRESENTS . . . THE ISLEY BROTHERS** (UK-iss.Mar73 on 'Music For Pleasure';)	-	
May 67.	(7") (TMG 606) <54146> **GOT TO HAVE YOU BACK. / JUST AIN'T ENOUGH LOVE**		93
Jan 68.	(7") <54154> **ONE TOO MANY HEARTACHES. / THAT'S THE WAY LOVE IS**	-	
Feb 68.	(lp) (STML 11066) <275> **SOUL ON THE ROCKS**		

– Got to have you back / That's the way love is / Whispers (gettin' louder) / Tell it's just a rumour baby / One too many heartaches / It's out of the question / Why when love is gone / Save me from the misery / Little Miss Sweetness / Good things / Catching up on time / Behind a painted smile.

Apr 68.	(7") (TMG 652) <54164> **TAKE ME IN YOUR ARMS (ROCK ME A LITTLE WHILE). / WHY WHEN LOVE IS GONE**		
1968.	(7") <54175> **BEHIND A PAINTED SMILE. / ALL BECAUSE I LOVE YOU**	-	
1968.	(7") <54182> **TAKE SOME TIME OUT FOR LOVE. / JUST AIN'T ENOUGH LOVE**	-	

		Major Minor	T-Neck
Jun 69.	(7") (MM 621) <901> **IT'S YOUR THING. / DON'T GIVE IT AWAY**		2 Feb69
Jul 69.	(lp) (SMLP 59) <3001> **IT'S OUR THING**		22 Apr69

– This old heart of mine (is weak for you) / Who could ever doubt my love / I guess I'll always love you / That's the way love is / One too many heartaches / Why when love is gone / Just ain't enough love / Got to have you back / There's no love left / I hear a symphony / Take me in your arms (rock me for a while) / Take some time out for love.

Jul 69.	(7") <903> **TURN ON, TUNE IN, DROP OUT. / (part 2)**	-	-
Aug 69.	(7") <906> **BLACK BERRIES. / (part 2)**	-	79
Sep 69.	(7") (MM 631) <902> **I TURNED YOU ON. / I KNOW WHO YOU BEEN SOCKING IT TO**		23 May69

—— RONNIE, RUDOLPH and O'KELLY (who was now just KELLY) with brass section added **ERNIE ISLEY** (b. 7 Mar'52) – guitar, percussion, guitar (later EVERETT COLLINS – drums) / **MARVIN ISLEY** (b.18 Aug'53) – bass, percussion / **CHRIS JASPER** – keyboards

		Stateside	T-Neck
Dec 69.	(7") <912> **BLESS YOUR HEART. / GIVE THE WOMEN WHAT THEY WANT**	-	
Feb 70.	(7") (SS 2162) <908> **WAS IT GOOD TO YOU. / I GOT TO GET MYSELF TOGETHER**		83 Sep69
Feb 70.	(7") <914> **KEEP ON DOIN'. / SAVE ME**		75
Apr 70.	(7") <919> **IF HE CAN, YOU CAN. / HOLDIN' ON**	-	
Jun 70.	(lp) (SSL 10300) **THE BROTHERS: ISLEY**		Oct69

– Black berries / Vacuum cleaner / I turned you on / Was it good to you / She's my girl / Get down off the train / Gotta get myself together / Feel like the world / Holdin' on.

Jul 70.	(7") <921> **GIRLS WILL BE GIRLS, BOYS WILL BE BOYS. / GET DOWN OFF THE TRAIN**	-	75
Sep 70.	(7") <924> **GET INTO SOMETHING. / (part 2)**	-	89
Sep 70.	(lp) <3004> **LIVE AT THE YANKEE STADIUM (live)**		Oct69

– (shared with The Edwin Hawkins Singers + Brooklyn Bridge)

Dec 70.	(7") <927> **FREEDOM. / I NEED YOU SO**	-	72
May 71.	(7") (SS 2188) <929> **WARPATH. / I GOT TO FIND ME ONE**	-	
Sep 71.	(7") <932> **SPILL THE WINE. / TAKE INVENTORY**	-	49
Sep 71.	(lp) **GIVIN' IT BACK** (all covers)	-	71

– Fire and rain / Ohio machine gun / Lay lady lay / etc

Oct 71.	(7") (SS 2193) <930> **LOVE THE ONE YOU'RE WITH. / HE'S GOT YOUR LOVE**	18 Jun71	
Dec 71.	(7") <933> **LAY LADY LAY. / VACUUM CLEANER**	-	71
Mar 72.	(7") <934> **LAY AWAY. / FEEL LIKE THE WORLD**	-	54
Jun 72.	(lp) <3009> **BROTHER, BROTHER, BROTHER**	-	29

– Brother, brother / Put a little love in your heart / Sweet seasons / Keep on walkin' / Work to do / Pop that thang / Lay away / It's too late / Love put me on the corner.

Jun 72.	(7") <935> **POP THAT THANG. / I GOT TO FIND ME ONE**		24
Oct 72.	(7") <936> **WORK TO DO. / BEAUTIFUL**	-	51
Mar 73.	(lp) <3010> **ISLEY BROTHERS LIVE (live)**		

– Work to do / It's too late / It's your thing / Pop that thang / Love the one you're with / Lay lady lay / Lay away / Ohio / Machine gun.

| May 73. | (7") <937> **IT'S TOO LATE. / NOTHING TO DO BUT TODAY** | - | - |

		Epic	T-Neck
Aug 73.	(7") (EPC 1704) <2251> **THAT LADY. / THAT LADY (part 2)**	14	6 Jul73
Nov 73.	(lp) (EPC 65740) <32453> **3 + 3**		Sep73

– That lady / Don't let me be lonely tonight / If you were there / You walk your way / Listen to the music / What it comes down to / Sunshine (go away today) / Summer breeze / The highways of my life. (re-iss. Mar81 lp/c; EPC/40 32039) (cd-iss. Apr94 on 'Sony'; 962615-2)

Nov 73.	(7") <2252> **WHAT IT COMES DOWN TO. / HIGHWAYS OF MY LIFE**	-	55
Dec 73.	(7") (EPC 1980) **THE HIGHWAYS OF MY LIFE. / DON'T LET ME BE LONELY TONIGHT**	25	-
Apr 74.	(7") (EPC 2244) <2253> **SUMMER BREEZE. / SUMMER BREEZE (part 2)**	16	60 Mar74
Aug 74.	(7") (EPC 2578) <2254> **LIVE IT UP. / (part 2)**		52 Jul74
Sep 74.	(lp/c) (EPC/40 80317) <33070> **LIVE IT UP**		14

– Live it up / Brown eyed girl / Need a little taste of love / Lover's eye / Midnight sky / Hello it's me / Ain't I been good to you.

Nov 74.	(7") (EPC 2803) **NEED A LITTLE TASTE OF LOVE. / IF YOU WERE THERE**		-
Feb 75.	(7") (EPC 3034) <2255> **MIDNIGHT SKY. / (part 2)**		73 Nov74
Jul 75.	(7") (EPC 3434) <2256> **FIGHT THE POWER. / (part 2)**		3 Jun75
Jul 75.	(lp/c) (EPC/40 69139) <33536> **THE HEAT IS ON**		1 Jun75

– Fight the power / Hope you feel better love / For the love of you / Sensuality / Make me say it again girl.

Jan 76.	(7") (EPC 3865) <2259> **FOR THE LOVE OF YOU. / YOU WALK YOUR WAY**		22 Nov75
Jun 76.	(7") (EPC 4369) **HARVEST FOR THE WORLD. / LET ME DOWN EASY**	10	-
Jun 76.	(lp/c) (EPC/40 81268) <33809> **HARVEST FOR THE WORLD**	50	9 May76

– Harvest for the world (prelude) / Harvest for the world / People of today / Who loves you better / Let me down easy / (At your best) You are love / So you wanna stay down / You still feel the need. (re-iss. Jun85 lp/c; EPC/40 32652)

Aug 76.	(7") <2260> **HARVEST FOR THE WORLD. / (part 2)**	-	63
Sep 76.	(7") (EPC 4373) <2260> **WHO LOVES YOU BETTER. / WHO LOVES YOU BETTER (part 2)**		47 May76
Apr 77.	(lp/c) (EPC/40 86027) <34432> **GO FOR YOU GUNS**	46	6

– Livin' in the life / Go for your guns / Voyage to Atlantis / Footsteps in the dark (part 1 & 2) / Tell me when you need it again (part1 & 2) / The pride (part 1 & 2). (re-iss. May93 on 'Sony Collectors')

May 77.	(7") <2262> **THE PRIDE. / (part 2)**	-	63
Jul 77.	(7") (EPC 5443) **VOYAGE TO ATLANTIS. / TELL ME WHEN YOU NEED IT AGAIN**	-	
Apr 78.	(7") (EPC 6292) **TAKE ME TO THE NEXT PHASE. / LIVIN' IN THE LIFE**	-	
Apr 78.	(7") <2264> **LIVIN' IN MY LIFE. / GO FOR YOUR GUNS**		40
Apr 78.	(lp/c) (EPC/40 86039) <34930> **SHOWDOWN**	46	4

– Showdown (part 1 & 2) / Groovin' with you / Ain't givin' up no love / Rockin' with fire (part 1 & 2) / Take me to the next phase (part 1 & 2) / Coolin' me out (part 1 & 2) / Fun and games / Love fever (part 1 & 2).

May 78.	(7") <2270> **SO YOU WANNA STAY DOWN. / VOYAGE TO ATLANTIS**	-	
Jun 78.	(7") <2276> **TAKE ME TO THE NEXT PHASE. / TELL ME WHEN YOU NEED IT AGAIN**	-	
Jul 78.	(7") (EPC 6481) <2277> **GROOVE WITH YOU. / FOOTSTEPS IN THE DARK**	-	
Jul 79.	(d-lp/c) (EPC/40 88460) <36077> **WINNER TAKES ALL**		14

– I wanna be with you / Liquid love / Winner takes all / Life in the city / It's a disco night (rock don't stop) / Let's fall in love / (Can't you see) What you do to me / How lucky I am / You're the key to my heart / You're beside me / Love comes and goes / Let me into your life / Go for what you know / Mind over matter.

| Aug 79. | (7") (EPC 7757) **LIFE IN THE CITY. / (part 2)** | - | - |

Oct 79. (7") (EPC 7911) <2287> **IT'S A DISCO NIGHT (ROCK DON'T STOP). / AIN'T GIVIN' UP ON LOVE** `14` `90`
Jan 80. (7") (EPC 7795) <2284> **WINNER TAKES ALL. / FUN AND GAMES** `Aug79`
Apr 80. (lp/c) (EPC/40 65740) <36035> **GO ALL THE WAY** `8`
    – Go all the way / Say you will / Pass it on / The belly dancer / Here we go again / Don't say goodnight (it's time for love).
Jun 80. (7") (EPC 8664) <2290> **DON'T SAY GOODNIGHT (IT'S TIME FOR LOVE). / (part 2)** `39` `Apr80`
Apr 81. (7") (EPCA 1122) **TONIGHT IS THE NIGHT (IF I HAD YOU). / WHO SAID**
Apr 81. (lp/c) (EPC/40 84914) <37080> **GRAND SLAM** `28` `Mar81`
    – Tonight is the night (if I had you) / Hurry up and wait / I once had your love (and I can't let go) / Young girls / Party night / Don't let go / Who said.
Apr 81. (7") <02033> **HURRY UP AND WAIT. / ('A' instrumental)** `-` `58`
Jul 81. (7") <02179> **I ONCE HAD YOUR LOVE (AND CAN'T LET GO). / ('A'instrumental)** `-`
Nov 81. (7") <02531> **INSIDE YOU. / (part 2)** `-`
Nov 81. (7") (EPCA 1741) **INSIDE YOU. / LOVE ZONE** `-`
Nov 81. (lp/c) (EPC/40 85252) <37533> **INSIDE YOU** `45` `Oct81`
    – Inside you (part 1 & 2) / Baby hold on / First love / Welcome into my heart / Don't hold back your love (part 1 & 2) / Love merry-go-round / Love zone.
Jan 82. (7") <02705> **WELCOME INTO MY HEART. / PARTY NIGHT** `-`
Sep 82. (7") <02985> **THE REAL DEAL. / ('A'instrumental)** `-`
Sep 82. (lp/c) (EPC/40 85790) <38047> **THE REAL DEAL** `87` `Aug82`
    – The real deal (part 1 & 2) / Are you with me / I'll do it all for you / Stone cold lover / It's alright with me / All in my lover's eyes / Under the influence.
Nov 82. (7") <03281> **IT'S ALRIGHT WITH ME. / ('A'instrumental)** `-`
Feb 83. (7") <03420> **ALL IN MY LOVER'S EYES. / I'LL DO IT ALL FOR YOU** `-`
Jun 83. (lp/c) (EPC/40 25419) <38674> **BETWEEN THE SHEETS** `19` `May83`
    – Choosey lover / Touch me / I need your body / Let's make love tonight / Between the sheets / Ballad for the fallen soldier / Slow down children / Way out love / Gettin' over you / Rock you.
Jun 83. (7") <03797> **BETWEEN THE SHEETS. / (part 2)** `-`
Jun 83. (7"/12") (A/TA 3513) **BETWEEN THE SHEETS. / THAT LADY** `52` `-`
Aug 83. (7"/12") (A/TA 3690) <03994> **CHOOSEY LOVER. / CHOOSEY LOVER (part 2)**
Nov 83. (7") <04320> **LETS MAKE LOVE TONIGHT. / ('A'instrumental)** `-`

—— Reverted to original trio when others formed ISLEY, JASPER, ISLEY

                                        Warners   Warners
Nov 85. (7") <28860> **COLDER ARE MY NIGHTS. / BREAK THIS CHAIN**
Dec 85. (7"/12") (WB 8860/+T) **COLDER ARE MY NIGHTS. / ('A'instrumental)** `-`
Dec 85. (lp/c) (925347-1/-4/-2) <25347> **MASTERPIECE**
    – May I / My best was good enough / If leaving me is easy / You never know when you're gonna fall in love / Stay gold / Colder are my nights / Come to me / Release your love / The most beautiful girl.
Mar 86. (7") <28764> **MAY I. / ('A'instrumental)** `-`

—— Now a duo of RONNIE and RUDOLF, when O'KELLY died of a heart attack on the 31st of March '86
Jun 87. (7") <28385> **SMOOTH SAILIN' TONIGHT. / (part 2)** `-`
Jul 87. (lp/c/cd) (925586-1/-4/-2) <25586> **SMOOTH SAILIN'** `64` `Jun87`
    – Everything is alright / Pick it out / It takes a good woman / Send a message / Smooth sailin' tonight / Somebody I used to know / Come my way / I wish.
Sep 87. (7") <28241> **COME MY WAY. / (part 2)** `-`
Nov 87. (7") <28129> **I WISH. / ('A'instrumental)** `-`
Feb 88. (7") <27954> **IT TAKES A GOOD WOMAN. / (part 2)** `-`

ISLEY BROTHERS featuring RONALD ISLEY

—— RONALD, ERNIE + MARVIN
Jun 89. (7") <22990> **SPEND THE NIGHT (CE SOIR). / ('A'instrumental)** `-`
Jul 89. (lp/c/cd) (925940-1/-4/-2) <25940> **SPEND THE NIGHT** `89`
    – Spend the night (ce soir) / You'll never walk alone / One of a kind / Real woman / Come together / If you ever need somebody / Baby come back home / One of a kind (reprise).
Oct 89. (7") <22748> **YOU'LL NEVER WALK ALONE. / ONE OF A KIND** `-`
Feb 90. (7") <19910> **IF YOU EVER NEED SOMEBODY. / ONE OF A KIND** `-`
May 90. (c-s) <19814> **COME TOGETHER /** `-`

—— In Mar 90, RONALD ISLEY backed ROD STEWART on a US Top 10 version of THIS OLD HEART OF MINE. ROD, of course, had earlier made UK No.4 with the song. ERNIE released his solo album, 'HIGH WIRE' early in 1990.
Jun 92. (cd/c) <(7559 26620-2/-4)> **TRACKS OF LIFE**
    – Turn on the demon / Bedroom eyes / Morning love / Sensitive lover / Searching for a miracle / No axe to grind / Brazilian wedding song (setembro) / Dedicate this song / Got my licks in / I'll be there 4 u / Koolin' out / Lost in your love / Red hot.
                                        4th & Broad   Island
May 96. (c-s,cd-s) <854586> **LET'S LAY TOGETHER / ('A'instrumental)** `93`
May 96. (cd/c) <(524214-2/-4)> **MISSION TO PLEASE** `31`
    – Floatin' on your love / Whenever you're ready / Let's lay together / Can I have a kiss (for old time's sake)? / Mission to please you / Make your body sing / Let's het intimate / Show us the way / Tears . . . Ron crying alone.
Oct 96. (c-s) (BRAC 338) <854738> **FLOATIN' ON YOUR LOVE / ('A'remix)** `47` `Sep96`
    (12"+=/cd-s+=) (12BRW/BRCD 338) – ('A'remixes by LIL' KIM and 112).

– compilations, etc. –

on 'Tamla Motown' until otherwise mentioned
Jun 64. (7"ep) R.C.A.; (RCX 7149) **THE ISLEY BROTHERS** `-`
Jan 69. (7") (TMG 683) **I GUESS I'LL ALWAYS LOVE YOU. / IT'S OUT OF THE QUESTION** `11`
Feb 69. (lp) Marble Arch; (894) / T-Neck; <552> **TAKE SOME TIME OUT FOR THE ISLEY BROTHERS**
Apr 69. (7") (TMG 693) **BEHIND A PAINTED SMILE. / ONE TOO MANY HEARTACHES** `5`
Aug 69. (7") (TMG 708) **PUT YOURSELF IN MY PLACE. / LITTLE MISS SWEETNESS** `13`
Sep 69. (lp) (STML 1112) **BEHIND A PAINTED SMILE**
    – Behind a painted smile / Got to have you back / Take me in your arms (rock me a little while) / Catching up on a time / Save me from this misery / Little Miss Sweetness / Good things / All because I love you / That's the way love is / Tell me it's just a rumour baby / It's out of the question / Why when love is gone / One too many heartaches / Whispers (gettin' louder).
1970. (lp) T-Neck; <3007> **IN THE BEGINNING: WITH JIMI HENDRIX** `-`
Oct 70. Regal Starline; (lp)(c) **THE ISLEY BROTHERS' GREATEST HITS**
Oct 73. (7") (TMG 877) **TELL ME IT'S JUST A RUMOUR BABY. / SAVE ME FROM THIS MISERY** `-`
Dec 73. (lp) T-Neck; <3011> **THE ISLEY'S GREATEST HITS** `-`
Feb 76. (lp) (STMA 8024) **SUPER HITS** `-`
    (re-iss. Oct81; same)
Feb 76. (7") D.J.M.; (DJS 10640) **TWIST AND SHOUT. / TIME AFTER TIME** `-`
Sep 76. (7") (TMG 1050) **THIS OLD HEART OF MINE. / BEHIND A PAINTED SMILE** `-`
Mar 77. (7") Epic; (EPC 4880) **THAT LADY. / SUMMER BREEZE** `-`
    (re-iss. Apr83 on 'Old Gold'; OG 9317)
Oct 77. (lp) Epic; (EPC 86040) <34452> **FOREVER GOLD** `58`
    (re-iss. Aug84 lp/c; EPC/40 32238)
Jan 79. (d-lp/d-c) Epic; (EPC/40 88327) / T-Neck; <36650> **TIMELESS** `-`
Aug 79. (12"m) R.C.A.; (PB 9411) **SHOUT / RESPECTABLE / RESPECTABLE (version) / TELL ME WHO** `-`
May 82. (7") Epic; (EPC 8863) **HARVEST FOR THE WORLD. / HIGHWAYS OF MY LIFE** `-`
    (re-iss. Apr83 on 'Old Gold'; OG 9311)
Apr 83. (lp/c) Bulldog; (BDL/AJKL 2032) **20 GOLDEN PIECES OF THE ISLEY BROTHERS** `-`
May 83. (7") (TMG 979) **I GUESS I'LL ALWAYS LOVE YOU. / TAKE SOME TIME OUT FOR LOVE** `-`
Jul 83. (c-ep) (CTME 2033) **FLIP HITS** `-`
    – This old heart of mine / I guess I'll always love you / Behind a painted smile / Put yourself in my place.
Sep 83. (7"ep/c-ep) Scoop; (7SR/7SC 5026) **6 TRACK HITS** `-`
    – Listen to the music / Brown eyed girl / Harvest for the world / Under the influence / You still feel the need / Don' let me be lonely tonight.
Jun 84. (lp/c) Epic; (EPC/40 32433) **GREATEST HITS: ISLEY BROTHERS VOL.1**
Jul 84. (7") C.B.S.; (A 4583) **HARVEST FOR THE WORLD. / SUMMER BREEZE** `-`
1986. (lp/c) Stateside; (SSL/TCSSL 6001) **LET'S GO** `-`
Feb 87. (lp/c/cd) (WL/WK/WD 72516) **GREATEST MOTOWN HITS** `-`
Mar 88. (lp/c/cd) Telstar; (STAR/STAC/SCD 2306) **GREATEST HITS** `41`
Nov 88. (7") Epic; (653154-7) **HARVEST FOR THE WORLD. / SUMMER BREEZE** `-`
    (12"+=) (653154-6) – Who loves you better (parts 1 & 2).
Mar 89. (lp/c/cd) Blatant; (BLAT LP/MC/CD 10) **THE SOUND OF SOUL** `-`
Mar 90. (cd) Charly; (CDCH 928) **SHOUT AND TWIST WITH RUDOLPH, RONALD AND O'KELLY** `-`
Apr 91. (cd) E.M.I.; (CZ 421) **THE COMPLETE U.A. SESSIONS** `-`
May 91. (d-cd) Rhino; **ISLEY BROTHERS STORY VOL 1: ROCK'N'SOUL YEARS 1959-68** `-`
May 91. (d-cd) Rhino; **ISLEY BROTHERS STORY VOL.2: THE T-NECK YEARS 1969-85** `-`
Oct 92. (cd) Carlton; (SMS 056) **SOUL KINGS VOL.1** `-`
Sep 93. (cd/c) Elektra; (7559 61538-2/-4) **LIVE** `-`
Nov 93. (cd) B.A.M.; (KLMCD 009) **PEARLS FROM THE PAST** `-`
Nov 94. (cd) Sequel; (NEMCD 691) **BATTLE OF THE BANDS** `-`
Jun 95. (cd) Epic; (480504-2) **BEAUTIFUL BALLADS** `-`
Jun 95. (cd) Epic; (480507-2) **FUNKY FAMILY** `-`

> **IT'S A BEAUTIFUL DAY** (dig out; Great Psychedelic . . .)

> **IVEYS** (see under ⇒ BADFINGER)

Janet JACKSON

Born: 16 May '66, Gary, Indiana, USA. The baby sister of the precocious JACKSON clan, JANET began her showbiz career singing alongside the family in their 70's variety show before securing parts in US TV sitcoms, 'Good Times' and 'Diff'rent Strokes'. Aged only sweet sixteen, JANET signed up to 'A&M' for an eponymous 1982 debut album. Neither this nor its successor, 'DREAM STREET' (1984) made much of an impact on the pop chart although they did spawn a couple of respectable R&B hits. In the meantime she'd also appeared in the TV series of 'Fame' and become hitched to JAMES DeBARGE, a marriage that barely lasted a year. From this point on JACKSON began taking the initiative, hooking up with crack R&B production team Jimmy Jam and Terry Lewis for her definitive 'CONTROL' (1986) album. Boldly underlining her new independent woman stance, the record scaled the US chart and spawned two million-selling singles, 'WHEN I THINK OF YOU' and ~'LET'S WAIT AWHILE' while Jam/Lewis' hard-assed funk production came into its own on the likes of 'WHAT HAVE YOU DONE FOR ME LATELY' and 'NASTY' (both US Top 5). To top the whole package off, the accompanying videos showcased JACKSON's hyperactive, highly choreographed dance moves and sassy new woman-of-the-world image. Encouraged by her success, she saddled a larger share of the writing duties on 'JANET JACKSON'S RHYTHM NATION 1814' (1989). The result was tracks such as 'STATE OF THE WORLD' and 'THE KNOWLEDGE', dealing with topics like racism, inequality etc. While not all critics were convinced by her newfound social conscience, there was no doubting the quality of another Jam/Lewis production and while her vocal prowess mightn't be top flight she made up for it with another gut-busting performance; the slinky pop of 'MISS YOU MUCH' made the US top spot as did 'ESCAPADE' and the throbbing 'BLACK CAT'. A glitzy sell-out tour ensued and JACKSON's lucrative market value was confirmed as 'Virgin' shelled out fifty million dollars on a two album deal in 1991. The resulting 'JANET' (1993) was a somewhat drawn-out affair spliced with interludes and presenting her in a new sexually mature mould. It was massive nevertheless, going straight in at No.1 on both the US and UK chart and featuring the US No.1 weepie, 'AGAIN'. A 1995 retrospective, 'DESIGN OF A DECADE' cemented her superstar position and aired a couple of new tracks, 'RUNAWAY' and 'TWENTY FOREPLAY'. While her early/mid 90's tours upped the ooer, missus . . . factor with raunchy dance routines etc., JANET (now without the JACKSON tag) returned in 1997 with a new Afro-centric image. One of her funkiest, soulful singles to date, 'GOT TIL IT'S GONE' (based on JONI MITCHELL's famous 'Big Yellow Taxi') featured a great video in which JANET looked naturally sexy without trying too hard. • **Style:** Beautiful pop/dance star, similar in music to brother MICHAEL. Her 1986 raunchier image, was helped by urban music director John McLain, and songstress to be, PAULA ABDUL. • **Songwriters:** Her pensmiths and collaborators from 1985 have been producers JIMMY JAM (JAMES HARRIS III) and TERRY LEWIS (both ex-The TIME). In 1989, she began to write and collaborate with both. • **Trivia:** In 1991, she signed new multi-million dollar contract with 'Virgin America'.

Album rating: JANET JACKSON (*4) / DREAM STREET (*3) / CONTROL (*7) / JANET JACKSON'S RHYTHM NATION 1814 (*7) / JANET. (*6) / DESIGN OF A DECADE 1986-1996 compilation (*8) / THE VELVET ROPE (*6)

JANET JACKSON – vocals (with session people)

		A&M	A&M
Nov 82.	(7") <2440> **YOUNG LOVE. / THE MAGIC IS WORKING**	-	64
Jan 83.	(lp/c) (AMLH/+C 64907) <4907> **JANET JACKSON**	-	63 Nov82

– Say you do / You'll never find (a love like mine) / Young love / Love and my best friend / Don't mess up this good thing / Forever yours / The magic is working / Come give your love to me.

		A&M	A&M
Jan 83.	(7") <2522> **COME GIVE YOUR LOVE TO ME. / FOREVER YOURS**	-	58
Feb 83.	(7"/12") (AMS/AMX 8303) **COME GIVE YOUR LOVE TO ME. / THE MAGIC IS WORKING**	[ ]	-
May 83.	(7"/12") (AM/+X 112) **DON'T MESS UP THIS GOOD THING. / YOUNG LOVE**	[ ]	[ ]
Sep 84.	(7"; JANET JACKSON & CLIFF RICHARD) (AM 210) **TWO TO THE POWER OF LOVE. / ROCK'N'ROLL** (12"+=) (AMX 210) – Don't mess up this good thing.	[ ]	[ ]
Oct 84.	(lp/c/cd) <(AMA/AMC/CDA 4962)> **DREAM STREET**	[ ]	

– Don't stand another chance / Two to the power of love / Pretty boy / Dream street / Communication / Fast girls / Hold back the tears / All my love to you / If it takes all night.

		A&M	A&M
Feb 86.	(7") <2812> **WHAT HAVE YOU DONE FOR ME LATELY. / HE DOESN'T KNOW I'M ALIVE**	-	4
Mar 86.	(7") (AM 308) **WHAT HAVE YOU DONE FOR ME LATELY. / YOUNG LOVE** (12"+=) (AMX 308) – ('A'dub).	3	-
Mar 86.	(lp/c/cd) <(AMA/AMC/CDA 5106)> **CONTROL**	8	1

– Control / What have you done for me lately / You can be mine / The pleasure principle / When I think of you / He doesn't know why I'm alive / Let's wait awhile / Funny how time flies / Nasty. (re-iss. Mar93)

		A&M	A&M
May 86.	(7") (AM 316) <2830> **NASTY. / YOU'LL NEVER FIND (A LOVE LIKE MINE)** (12"+=) (AMY 316) – ('A'instrumental).	19	3
Aug 86.	(7") <2855> **WHEN I THINK OF YOU. / PRETTY BOY**	-	1
Aug 86.	(7") (AM 337) **WHEN I THINK OF YOU. / COME GIVE YOUR LOVE TO ME**	10	-
Oct 86.	(7") <2877> **CONTROL. / FAST GIRLS**	-	5
Oct 86.	(7") (AM 359) **CONTROL. / PRETTY BOY** (cd-s+=) (AMS 359) – Nasty (cool summer nix). (12"++=) (AMY/AMX 359) – ('A'dub).	42	-

		Breakout-A&M	Breakout-A&M
Jan 87.	(7") <2906> **LET'S WAIT AWHILE. / PRETTY BOY**	-	2
Mar 87.	(7"/7"pic-d) (USA/+P 601) **LET'S WAIT AWHILE. / NASTY (cool summer mix part 1)** (12"+=) (USAT 601) – Nasty (cool summer mix part 2). (d7"pic-d/clear+=) (USAD 601) – Nasty (original) / Control / ('A'version) / Nasty (cool summer mix part 1 fade).	3	-

—— she guested on HERB ALPERT's 1987 album, 'Diamonds'

		A&M	A&M
May 87.	(7") <2927> **THE PLEASURE PRINCIPLE. / FAST GIRLS**	-	14
Jun 87.	(7") (USA 604) **THE PLEASURE PRINCIPLE (Shep Pettibone mix). / ('A'dub)** (ext;12"+=/c-s+=) (USAT/+C 604) – ('A'-acapella).	24	-
Nov 87.	(7") (USA 613) **FUNNY HOW TIME FLIES (WHEN YOU'RE HAVING FUN). / WHEN I THINK OF YOU** (12"+=) (USAT 613) – Nasty (cool summer part 1).	59	-
Nov 87.	(lp/c/cd) (MIX LP/MC/CD 1 – AMA/AMC/CDA 5169) **CONTROL – THE REMIXES** (remixes)	20	-
Aug 89.	(7"/7"s/c-s) (USA/+S/TC 663) <1445> **MISS YOU MUCH. / YOU NEED ME** (12"+=/cd-s+=) (USA 663 T/CD) – ('A'-Mama extended mix).	25	1
Sep 89.	(lp/c/cd) <(CDA/AMC/AMA 3920)> **JANET JACKSON'S RHYTHM NATION 1814**	4	1

– (Pledge) / Rhythm nation /(TV) / State of the world / Race The knowledge / (Let's dance) Miss you much / (Come back interlude) / Love will never do (without you) / Livin' in a world (they didn't make) / Alright / (Hey baby) / Escapade / (No acid) / Black cat / Lonely / Come back to me / Someday is tonight / (Livin' in . . . complete darkness). (re-iss. Oct90 pic-lp/cd+=; AMAP/AMAD 3920)

		A&M	A&M
Oct 89.	(7"/7"s/c-s) (USA/+S/TC 673) <1455> **RHYTHM NATION. / ('A'-C.H.R. remix)** (12"/12"pic-d/cd-s) (USA T/PD/CD 673) – ('A'mixes; 12" House Nation / 12" United / United dub).	23	2 Nov89
Jan 90.	(7"/7"box/c-s) (USA/+B/MC 681) **COME BACK TO ME. / ALRIGHT** (12"+=/cd-s+=) (USA T/CD 681) – Alright (Hip Hop dub).	20	-
Mar 90.	(7"/7"pic-d/c-s) (USA/+P/MC 684) <1490> **ESCAPADE. / ('A'-Housecapade)** (12"/cd-s) (USA T/D 684) – ('A'mixes; Shep's Housecapade / Housecapade dub / Shep's good time).	17	1 Jan90
Mar 90.	(7") <1479> **ALRIGHT. / (remix)**	-	4
Jun 90.	(7"/7"sha-pic-d/c-s) (USA/+S/MC 693) **ALRIGHT. / VUELVE A MI (COME BACK TO ME)** (12") (USAT 693) – ('A'-hip hop mix) / ('A'extended house mix). (cd-s+=) (USAD 693) – (all 4 tracks above).	20	-
Jun 90.	(7") <1475> **COME BACK TO ME. / VUELVE A MI (COME BACK TO ME)**	-	2

		A&M	A&M
Aug 90.	(7"/c-s) (AM/+MC 587) **BLACK CAT. / 1814 MEGAMIX – ALRIGHT – ESCAPADE – RHYTHM NATION – MISS YOU MUCH** (ext;12"+=/12"s+=/cd-s+=) (AM Y/X/CD 587) – ('A'-3 snaps up mix).	15	-
Sep 90.	(7") <1477> **BLACK CAT.** (remix)	-	1
Oct 90.	(7"/c-s) (AM/+MC 700) <1538> **LOVE WILL NEVER DO (WITHOUT YOU). / ('A'-The Love mix)** (12"/12"s/cd-s) (AM Y/X/CD 700) – ('A'mixes; Shep's work it out / Shep's work it out dub / U.K. funky).	34	1 Nov90

—— in Jun'92, she hit US No.10 with LUTHER VANDROSS on a duet of 'THE BEST THINGS IN LIFE ARE FREE'; it went onto hit No.2 in the UK

		Virgin	Virgin

Apr 93 (7"/c-s) *(VS/+C 1460)* <12650> **THAT'S THE WAY LOVE GOES. / (instrumental)** — `2` `1`
(12"+=/cd-s+=) *(VST/VSCDG 1460)* – ('A'-CJ R&B mixes).

May 93. (cd/c/lp) *(CD/TC+/V 2720)* <87825> **JANET.** — `1` `1`
– Morning / That's the way love goes / You want this / If / Throb / What'll I do / Funky big band / New agenda / Because of love / Again / Another lover / Where are you now / The body that loves you / Any time, any place / Are you still up. *(d-cd-iss. Dec93 w/ 'REMIXED'+=; CDVX 2720)* – Whoops now / That's the way love is / If (medley) / That's the way love goes (we aimsta win mix) / Again (French) / If (Brothers In Rhythm swing yo pants mix) / One more chance / That's the way love goes (CJ Mackintosh mix) / If (Todd Terry & Janet's jeep mix) / Again (piano-vocal). *(re-iss. Mar95; CDVY 2720)*

Jul 93. (7"/c-s) *(VS/+C 1474)* <12676> **IF. / ONE MORE CHANCE** — `14` `4`
(12"/cd-s) *(VST/VSCDT 1474)* – ('A'mixes; Brothers In Rhythm swing yp pants / D&D 12" / extended / Tee's Freeze).

Nov 93. (7"/c-s) *(VS/+C 1481)* <38404> **AGAIN. / AGAIN (vocal/piano mix)** — `6` `1` Oct93
(cd-s+=) *(VSCDG 1481)* – ('A'instrumental) / Funky big band.
(cd-s+=) *(VSCDX 1481)* – ('A'-French) / That's the way love goes (We aimsta win mix).

Jan 94. (c-s,cd-s) <38422> **BECAUSE OF LOVE / FUNKY BIG BAND** — `-` `10`

Mar 94. (7"/c-s) *(VS/+C 1488)* **BECAUSE OF LOVE. / ('A'-Frankie & David mix)** — `19` `-`
(12"+=/cd-s+=) *(VST/VSCDG 1488)* – ('A'mixes; Frankie & David classic / D&D Bentley radio / Muggs 7" w-bass intro / D&D slow).

Jun 94. (c-s/cd-s) *(VSC/VSCDT 1501)* <38435> **ANY TIME, ANY PLACE / THROB (David Morales remix) / AND ON AND ON** — `13` `2` May94
(12") *(VST 1501)* – ('A'-CJ's 12"mix) / Throb / ('A'-D&D house).
(cd-s) *(VSCDG 1501)* – ('A'-R Kelly mix) / ('A'-C.J. Mackintosh mix) / ('A'-D&D mix).

Nov 94. (c-s/cd-s) *(VSC/VSCDG 1519)* <38455> **YOU WANT THIS / 70's LOVE GROOVE / YOU WANT THIS (Mafia & Fluxy dancehall mix) / AND ON AND ON** — `14` `8` Oct94
(12") *(VST 1519)* – ('A'mixes; E-Smoove's house anthem / E-Smoove's anthem dub / underdub / disco theory / smoove soul 7").
(cd-s) *(VSCDT 1519)* – ('A'mixes; remix / E-Smoove's anthem / Mafia & Fluxy dancehall / Spoiled milk / Disco theory / funk extravaganza / Smoove soul 12").

Mar 95. (7"pic-d/c-s) *(VSY/VSC 1533)* **WHOOPS NOW / WHAT'LL I DO** — `9` `-`
(12"pic-d+=/cd-s+=) *(VSTY/CDG 1533)* – ('B'-Dave Navarro mix) / The body that loves you.

—— In Jun'95, JANET teamed up with brother MICHAEL to hit Top 3 with 'SCREAM'. In 1997, she was simply called JANET in the States only.

Sep 97. (7"/c-s; as JANET, Q-TIP & JONI MITCHELL) *(VS HL/C 1666)* **GOT TIL IT'S GONE / ('A'mix)** — `6`
(12"+=/cd-s+=) *(VS T/CDG 1666)* – ('A'mixes).

Oct 97. (cd/c/lp) *(CD/TC+/V 2860)* <44762> **THE VELVET ROPE** — `6` `1`
– Interlude / The velvet rope / You / Got til it's gone / Go deep / Free zone / Memory / Together again / Online / Empty / Full / What about / Every time / Tonight's the night / I get lonely / Rope burn / Anything / Sad / Special / Can't be stopped.

Dec 97. (c-s) *(VSC 1670)* <38623> **TOGETHER AGAIN / ('A'-Tony Hum mix)** — `4` `1`
(cd-s+=) *(VSCDT 1670)* – ('A'mixes; DJ Premier / Jimmy Jam).
(12") *(VST 1670)* – ('A'mixes; Tony Morales / Jimmy Jam).

Mar 98. (c-s) *(VSC 1683)* <38631> **I GET LONELY / ('A'-TNT remix)** — `5` `3` May98
(12"+=/cd-s+=) *(BST/VSCDT 1683)* – ('A'mixes; extended / Jam & Lewis / Jason vs. Janet).
(above was credited in the States to:- JANET featuring BLACKSTREET)

Jun 98. (c-s) *(VSC 1680)* **GO DEEP / ('A'-Teddy Riley funk mix)** — `13`
(12"+=/cd-s+=) *(VST/VSCDT 1680)* – ('A'mixes; Roni Size / Master At Work – 2).

Sep 98. (c-s/cd-s) *(VSC/+DT 1713)* **YOU / ACCEPT ME / GO DEEP** —

Dec 98. (c-s) *(VSC 1720)* **EVERY TIME / ACCEPT ME** — `46`
(12"+=/cd-s+=) *(VST/VSCDT 1720)* – ('A'mixes).

—— in Apr'99, JANET featured on BLACKstreet's hit single, 'Girlfriend – Boyfriend' and also on BUSTA RHYMES chartbuster, 'What's It Gonna Be!?' and SHAGGY's 'Luv Me, Luv Me'.

– compilations, others. –

—— on 'A&M' unless mentioned otherwise

Sep 95. (c-s) *(581 197-4)* <1194> **RUNAWAY / WHEN I THINK OF YOU (extended Morales house mix)** — `6` `3` Aug95
(12"+=/cd-s+=) *(581 209-1/197-2)* – ('A'mixes; Junior's Factory).
(d12"+=) *(581 243-1)* – ('A'mixes; Junior's unplugged) / When I think of you.

Oct 95. (cd/c) *(540 422-2/-4)* <0399> **DESIGN OF A DECADE – 1986-1996** (compilation) — `2` `3`
– Runaway / What have you done for me lately / Nasty / When I think of you / Escapade / Miss you much / Love will never do (without you) / Alright / Control / Pleasure principle / Black cat / Rhythm nation / That's the way love goes / Come back to me / Let's wait awhile / Twenty foreplay.

Dec 95. (c-s; LUTHER VANDROSS & JANET JACKSON) *(581 309-4)* **THE BEST THINGS IN LIFE ARE FREE / ('A'mix)** — `7` `-`
(cd-s+=) *(581 309-2)* – ~('A'mixes).

Mar 96. (c-s) *(581 511-4)* **TWENTY FOREPLAY / ('A'–Slow jam international)** — `22` `-`
(cd-s+=) *(581 511-2)* – Runaway (Jam S Lewis mixes).

Sep 96. (12"/cd-s) *(581 691-1/-2)* **WHEN I THINK OF YOU / (mixes)** — `-`

Joe JACKSON

Born: 11 Aug'54, Burton-On-Trent, Staffordshire, England, although raised from a very early age in Gosport, near Portsmouth. He left school with top grade music honour and enrolled at The Royal College Of Music in 1973. After a spell in JOHNNY DANKWORTH's NATIONAL YOUTH JAZZ ORCHESTRA, he joined pub rock outfit, ARMS & LEGS; they released three

flop singles for 'M.A.M.' between 1976-1977, before he quit. In 1977, he became a musical director for 'Opportunity Knocks' (TV talent show, hosted by Hughie Green) winners, COFFEE AND CREAM (yuk!). The following year, he moved away from the cabaret scene to London, where he recorded demo tape, which A&M's David Kershenbaum approved, producing first solo attempt, 'IS SHE REALLY GOING OUT WITH HIM?' (it took a re-issue of this single in Summer 1979 to break him into UK and US charts). The debut album, 'LOOK SHARP!' (1979), subsequently hit the US Top 20, its jazzy new-wave power-pop and acerbic lyrics inevitably drawing comparisons with ELVIS COSTELLO. 'I'M THE MAN' (1979), and its accompanying UK Top 5 hit single, the sly 'IT'S DIFFERENT FOR GIRLS', carried on in a similar vein although JACKSON veered off into more unsettling, eclectic musical textures with 1980's self-produced 'BEAT CRAZY'. Although credited to The JOE JACKSON BAND, the line-up remained identical to that which had played on the first two releases, namely GRAHAM MABY, GARY SANFORD and DAVE HOUGHTON. For 'JOE JACKSON'S JUMPIN' JIVE' (1981), only the former remained from the original formation, an array of jazz musicians employed in a fairly successful attempt to update the 40's swing style of LOUIS JORDAN and CAB CALLOWAY. The exotic musical landscape of New York was JACKSON's next stop; having relocated to the Big Apple following the breakdown of his marriage, he proceeded to soak up the spicy latin jazz/salsa influences for his 'NIGHT AND DAY' (1982) album. A transatlantic Top 5 hit, it spawned JACKSON's biggest hit single to date in the dancefloor friendly 'STEPPIN' OUT' and eventually went gold. JACKSON recruited another new group of musicians for 'BODY AND SOUL' (1984), while 'BIG WORLD' was an ambitious live double set featuring all-new material recorded over three successive nights. The vocal-free 'WILL POWER' (1987) set saw JACKSON dabbling in classical orchestration and accordingly failed to chart, while the autobiographical 'BLAZE OF GLORY' (1989) covered all JACKSON's stylistic bases to date. A change of label to 'Virgin', saw the man pen his most direct, accessible material in years with 'LAUGHTER AND LUST' (1991), a welcome diversion from his constant experimentation. • **Covered:** OH WELL (Fleetwood Mac) / MAKING PLANS FOR NIGEL (Xtc). • **Trivia:** He also produced The KEYS in '81, and reggae outfits RASSES and The TOASTERS.

Album rating: LOOK SHARP! (*8) / I'M THE MAN (*7) / BEAT CRAZY (*7) / JUMPIN' JIVE (*7) / NIGHT AND DAY (*7) / BODY AND SOUL (*5) / BIG WORLD (*5) / WILL POWER (*4) / LIVE ... 1980-1986 (*6) / BLAZE OF GLORY (*5) / STEPPIN' OUT – THE VERY BEST OF JOE JACKSON compilation (*8) / LAUGHTER AND LUST (*5) / NIGHT MUSIC (*3) / GREATEST HITS compilation (*8) / THIS IS IT! THE A&M YEARS compilation (*8)

ARMS AND LEGS

JOE JACKSON – piano, violin, vocals, harmonica / **MARK ANDREWS** – vocals / **GRAHAM MABY** – bass

		M.A.M.	not iss.

Apr 76. (7") *(MAM 140)* **JANICE. / SHE'LL SURPRISE YOU** — `-`
Aug 76. (7") *(MAM 147)* **HEAT OF THE NIGHT. / GOOD TIMES** — `-`
Feb 77. (7") *(MAM 156)* **IS THERE ANY MORE WINE. / SHE'LL SURPRISE YOU** — `-`

JOE JACKSON

solo – lead vocals, piano with backing band **GRAHAM MABY** – bass / **GARY SANFORD** – guitar / **DAVE HOUGHTON** – drums

		A&M	A&M

Sep 78. (7") *(AMS 7392)* <2132> **IS SHE REALLY GOING OUT WITH HIM? / (DO THE) INSTANT MASH** — `21` May79
Jan 79. (lp/c) *(AMLH/CAM 64743)* <4743> **LOOK SHARP!** — `40` `20`
– One more time / Sunday papers / Is she really going out with him? / Happy loving couples / Throw it away / Baby stick around / Look sharp! / Fools in love / (Do the) Instant mash / Pretty girls / Got the time. *(re-iss. Aug79 on white-lp; same)* *(re-iss. Mar82; AMID 120)* *(re-iss. Sep84 on 'Hallmark' lp/c; SHM/HSC 3154)* *(cd-iss. Nov84; CDA 64743)* *(re-iss. 1988 lp/c; AMA/AMC 3187)* *(cd re-iss. Oct92; CDMID 115)*
Feb 79. (7") *(AMS 7413)* **SUNDAY PAPERS. / LOOK SHARP!** — `-`
May 79. (7"/10"white) *(AMS/+P 7433)* **ONE MORE TIME. / DON'T ASK ME** — `-`
Jul 79. (7") *(AMS 7459)* **IS SHE REALLY GOING OUT WITH HIM?. / YOU GOT THE FEVER** — `13` `-`
Aug 79. (7") <2186> **IT'S DIFFERENT FOR GIRLS. / COME ON** — `-`
Oct 79. (7") *(AMS 7479)* <2209> **I'M THE MAN. / COME ON (live)** — `-`
Oct 79. (lp/c)(5x7"box) *(AMLH/CAM 64794)(none)* <4794> **I'M THE MAN** — `12` `22`
– On your radio / Geraldine and John / Kinda kute / It's different for girls / I'm the man / The band wore blue shirts / Don't wanna be like that / Amateur hour / Get that girl / Friday. *(cd-iss. 1988; CDA 3221)* *(cd re-iss. Oct92; CDMID 117)*
Dec 79. (7") *(AMS 7493)* **IT'S DIFFERENT FOR GIRLS. / FRIDAY** — `5` `-`
Mar 80. (7") *(AMS 7513)* **KINDA KUTE. / GERALDINE AND JOHN** — `-`

JOE JACKSON BAND

Jun 80. (7"/7"w-poster) *(AMS/+P 7536)* **THE HARDER THEY COME. / OUT OF STYLE / TILT** — `-`
Oct 80. (7") *(AMS 7563)* **MAD AT YOU. / ENOUGH IS NOT ENOUGH** — `-`
Oct 80. (lp/c) *(AMLH/CAM 64837)* <4837> **BEAT CRAZY** — `42` `41`
– Beat crazy / One to one / In every dream home (a nightmare) / The evil eye / Mad at you / Crime don't pay / Someone up there / Battleground / Biology / Pretty boys / Fit. *(cd-iss. 1988; CDA 3241)*
Nov 80. (7") <2276> **ONE TO ONE. / ENOUGH IS NOT ENOUGH** — `-`
Jan 81. (7") *(AMS 8100)* **BEAT CRAZY. / IS SHE REALLY GOING OUT WITH HIM?** — `-`
Mar 81. (7") *(AMS 8116)* **ONE TO ONE. / SOMEONE UP THERE** — `-`

JOE JACKSON'S JUMPIN' JIVE

JOE retained GRAHAM MABY plus PETE THOMAS – sax / RAUOL OLIVERA – trumpet / DAVE BITELI – wind instr. NICK WELDON – piano / LARRY TOLFREE – drums / NICK WELDON – piano

Jun 81. (7") (AMS 8145) <2365> JUMPIN' JIVE. / KNOCK ME A
KISS — 43 ☐

Jun 81. (lp/c) (AMLH/CAM 68530) <4871> JOE JACKSON'S JUMPIN'
JIVE — 14 42
– Jumpin' with symphony Sid / Jack, you're dead / Is you or is you ain't my baby / We the cats will help ya / San Francisco fan / Five guys named Moe / Jumpin' jive / You run your mouth (and I'll run my business) / What's the use of getting sober (when you're gonna get drunk again) / You're my meat / Tuxedo junction / How long must I wait for you. (cd-iss. 1988; CDA 3271) (re-iss. May93 on 'Spectrum' cd/c; 550062-2/-4)

Aug 81. (7") (AMS 8161) JACK, YOU'RE DEAD. / FIVE GUYS
NAMED MOE ☐ -

JOE JACKSON

—— SUE HADJOPOULOS – percussion, flute; repl. WELDON + horns

Jun 82. (7"pic-d) (AMS 8231) REAL MEN. / CHINATOWN ☐ -
Jun 82. (lp/c) (AMLH/CAM 64906) <4906> NIGHT AND DAY 3 4
– Another world / Chinatown / T.V. age / Target / Steppin' out / Breaking us in two / Cancer / Real men / A slow song. (cd-iss. 1983; CDA 64906) (re-iss. Oct92 cd/c; CD/C MID 158)

Aug 82. (7") (AMS 8247) BREAKING US IN TWO. / EL BLANCO ☐ -
Aug 82. (7") <2428> STEPPIN' OUT. / CHINATOWN - 6
Oct 82. (7") (AMS 8262) STEPPIN' OUT. / ANOTHER WORLD 6 -
Jan 83. (7") <2510> BREAKING US IN TWO. / TARGET - 18
Feb 83. (7") (AM 101) BREAKING US IN TWO. / EL BLANCO 59 -
(12"+=) (AMX 101) – T.V. age.
May 83. (7") (AM 114) A SLOW SONG. / REAL MEN ☐ -
Jul 83. (7") <2548> ANOTHER WORLD. / ORTO MUNDO - ☐

—— added JOY ASKEW – synthesizers

Aug 83. (7") (AM 134) COSMOPOLITAN. / BREAKDOWN ☐ -
Sep 83. (lp/c) (AMLX/CAM 64931) <4931> MIKE'S MURDER
(soundtrack) 64
– Cosmopolitan / 1-2-3-go (this town's a fairground) / Laundromat Monday / Memphis / Moonlight / Zemeo / Breakdown / Moonlight theme.

Nov 83. (7") <2601> MEMPHIS. / BREAKDOWN - 85

—— retained only MABY and brought in GARY BURKE – drums / VINNIE ZUMMO – guitar / ED ROYNESDAL – keyboards, violin / TONY AIELLO – sax, flute / MICHAEL MORREALE – wind

Mar 84. (lp/c) (AMLX/CXM 65000) <5000> BODY AND SOUL 14 20
– The verdict / Cha cha loco / Not here, not now / You can't get what you want ('till you know what you want) / Go for it / Loisaida / Be my number two / Heart of ice. (cd-iss. Oct84; CXM 65000) (cd re-iss. Oct92; CDMID 118)

Apr 84. (7"/12") (AM/+X 186) <2635> HAPPY ENDING. / LOISAIDA 58 57 Jul84
Jun 84. (7") (AM 200) BE MY NUMBER TWO. / IS SHE REALLY
GOING OUT WITH HIM? 70 -
(7") (AMX 200) – ('A'side) / Heart of ice.
Sep 84. (7") (AM 212) <2628> YOU CAN'T GET WHAT YOU WANT
('TILL YOU KNOW WHAT YOU WANT). / CHA CHA
LOCO 15 Apr84
(12"+=) (AMX 212) – ('A' dub version).

—— RICK FORD – bass, guitar, vox repl. MABY, AIELLO, ROYNESDAL + MORREALE

Mar 86. (3.sided.d-lp/c/cd) (JWA/JWC/JWD 3) <6021> BIG WORLD
(live) 41 34
– Wild west / Right and wrong / (It's a) Big world / Precious time / Tonight and forever / Shanghai sky / Fifty dollar love affair / We can't live together / Forty years / Survival / Soul kiss / The jet-set / Tango Atlantico / Hometown / Man in the street.

Apr 86. (7") (AM 312) <2829> RIGHT OR WRONG. / BREAKING
US IN TWO (live) ☐ ☐
(12"+=) (AMY 312) – I'm the man (live).
Jun 86. (7"/12") (AM/+Y 324) HOME TOWN. / TANGO ATLANTICO ☐ -
Jun 86. (7") <2847> HOME TOWN. / I'M THE MAN (live) - ☐
Apr 87. (lp/c/cd) (<AMA/AMC/CDA 3908>) WILL POWER ☐ ☐
– No Pasaran / Solitude / Will power / Nocturne / Symphony in one movement. (cd re-iss. Apr89 on 'Mobile Fidelity'; UDCD 503)

May 87. (7") <2944> WILL POWER. / NOCTURNE - ☐
Apr 88. (7") (AM 441) JUMPIN' JIVE (live). / MEMPHIS (live) ☐ ☐
(12"+=) (AMY 441) – You can't get what you want (till you know what you want).

May 88. (d-lp/c/cd) (<AMA/AMC/CDA 6706>) LIVE 1980/86 (live) 66 91
– One to one / I'm the man / Beat crazy / Is she really going out with him? / Cancer / Don't wanna be like that / On your radio / Fools in love / Cancer / Is she really going out with him? (acappella version) / Look sharp! / Sunday papers / Real men / Is she really going out with him? (acoustic) / Memphis / A slow song / Be my number two / Breaking us in two / It's different for girls / You can't get what you want ('till you know what you want) / Jumpin' jive / Steppin' out.

Jun 88. (7") <1207> LOOK SHARP (live). / MEMPHIS (live) - ☐
Aug 88. (7") (AM 481) <1228> (HE'S A) SHAPE IN A DRAPE. /
SPEEDWAY ☐ ☐
(12"+=) (AMY 481) – Sometime in Chicago.

Nov 88. (lp/c/cd) (<AMA/AMC/CDA 3917>) TUCKER – A MAN AND
HIS DREAMS (Soundtrack) ☐ ☐
– Captain of industry / Car of tomorrow / No chance blues / (He's a) Shape in a drape / Factory / Vera / It pays to advertise / Tiger rag / Showtime in Chicago / Loan bank loan blues / Speedway / Marilee / Hangin' in Howard Hughes' hangar / The toast of the town / Abe's blues / The trial / Freedom swing / Rhythm delivery.

—— Now with 10-piece line-up, MABY, ZUMMO, BURKE, ASKEW, AIELLO, FORD, ROYNESDAL, HADJOPOULOS + TOM TEELEY – guitar / ANTHONY COX – bass

Apr 89. (lp/c/cd) (<AMA/AMC/CDA 5249>) BLAZE OF GLORY 36 61
– Tomorrow's child / Me and you (against the world) / Down to London / Sentimental thing / Acropolis now / Blaze of glory / Rant and rave / Nineteen forever / The best I can do / Evil empire / Discipline / The uman touch.

May 89. (7") (AM 506) <1404> NINETEEN FOREVER. / ACROPOLIS
NOW (instrumental) ☐ ☐
(cd-s+=) (CDEE 506) – ('A'extended).
Oct 89. (7") (AM 512) DOWN TO LONDON. / YOU CAN'T GET
WHAT YOU WANT (TIL YOU KNOW WHAT YOU WANT) ☐ -
(cd-s+=) (CDEE 512) – Sunday papers.
Aug 90. (7"/c-s) (AM/+MC 583) STEPPIN' OUT (re-mix). /
SENTIMENTAL THING ☐ ☐
(cd-s+=) (AMCD 583) – It's a big worth.
Sep 90. (cd/c/lp) (397052-2/-4/-1) STEPPIN' OUT – THE VERY BEST
OF JOE JACKSON (compilation) 7 ☐
– Is she really going out with him? / Fools in love / I'm the man / It's different for girls / Beat crazy / Jumpin' jive / Breaking us in two / Steppin' out / Slow song (live) / You can't get what you want ('till you know what you want) / Be my number two / Right and wrong / Home town / Down to London / Nineteen forever.

	Virgin America	Virgin America

Apr 91. (7") STRANGER THAN FICTION. / DROWNING ☐ ☐
(12"+=/cd-s+=) – Different for girls (acoustic).
Apr 91. (cd/c/lp) (CDVUS/VUSMC/VUSLP 34) <91628> LAUGHTER
& LUST 41
– Obvious song / Goin' downtown / Stranger than fiction / Oh well / Jamie G / Hit single / It's all too much / When you're not around / The other me / Trying to cry / My house / The old songs / Drowning.

Oct 94. (cd/c) (CDVUS/VUSMS 78) NIGHT MUSIC ☐ ☐
– Nocturne No.1 / Flying nocturne No.2 / Ever after / The man who wrote Danny Boy / Nocturne No.3 / Lullaby / Only the future / Nocturne No.4 / Sea of secrets.

– compilations, etc. –

Oct 93. (d-cd) A&M; (CDA 24121) NIGHT AND DAY / LOOK SHARP! ☐ ☐
May 96. (cd) A&M; GREATEST HITS - -
Feb 97. (d-cd) A&M; (540402-2) THIS IS IT~! THE A&M YEARS ☐ ☐

Michael JACKSON (& The JACKSONS)

Born: 29th August '58, Indiana, USA. Brought up in a family of child prodigies guided by musician father, JOE (no, not that one!), MICHAEL was groomed for a lead vocal spot from an early age, soon taking pole position alongside his brothers (JACKIE, TITO, JERMAINE and MARLON) in the all singing, all dancing JACKSON 5. Musically inspired by legendary 'Godfather' of soul, JAMES BROWN, along with the choreographed moves of Motown's best acts, this youthful posse initially recorded a couple of tracks for small local label, 'Steeltown', having proved themselves in the prestigious talent contests of The Apollo Theater in New York. Inevitably, the group were subsequently signed up by 'Motown' in 1968, the label quick to spot the potential of a group who were perfect for moulding and developing in their established style. Label guru Berry Gordy moved the family en masse to Hollywood, got the crack in-house team of writers on the job (it's rumoured 'Motown' initially refused to use the group's own material) and sharpened up their moves before eventually releasing a debut single in late '69, 'I WANT YOU BACK'. The label had struck gold yet again and the single became the first of four consecutive US No.1 hits, its pre-pubescent naivety and sugary charm a winning formula (and a treasure trove for hip hop samplers) which saw the classic 'ABC', 'THE LOVE YOU SAVE' and 'I'LL BE THERE' all topping the charts in quick succession. Like many soul outfits, The JACKSON 5 were primarily a singles venture and while albums such as 'DIANA ROSS PRESENTS THE JACKSON 5' (1970), 'ABC' (1970) and 'THE THIRD ALBUM' (1971) had more than their fair share of filler, the emotional charge of the early hits can still get a dancefloor grinning ear to ear. After another clutch of Top 20 singles in '71 (including the timeless 'NEVER CAN SAY GOODBYE'), MICHAEL was singled out for a solo career, debuting with the ballad, 'GOT TO BE THERE' early the following year. The single was a transatlantic Top 5 smash, MICHAEL JACKSON the pop star had arrived; the album of the same name hit the American Top 20, while a sassy cover of Bobby Day's 'ROCKIN' ROBIN' repeated the success of the debut. His most famous hit of the era, however, arrived in the shape of the syrupy 'BEN', an unlikely ode to a pet rat! Although the track gave MICHAEL the first No.1 of his illustrious career, the ensuing few years would see commercial fortunes take a bit of a back seat, both for him and his brothers (with whom he was maintaining a parallel career in The JACKSON 5). From the heady heights of starring in their very own cartoon series, The JACKSON 5 began to struggle as they made the transition from using 'Motown'-penned material to writing their own stuff, the proto-disco of the 'DANCING MACHINE' (1974) album rejuvenating them somewhat despite it being their penultimate set for the label. They (all but JERMAINE who stayed with 'Motown' and was replaced by younger brother RANDY) finally jumped ship for 'Epic' in 1975 (presumably procuring a better royalty rate than the whopping 2.7% they'd been getting at 'Motown'), although GORDY sued them for alleged breach of contract the following year and they were obliged to change their name to The JACKSONS; the case was finally settled at the turn of the decade with the siblings paying GORDY a tidy sum and giving up the rights to the JACKSON 5 name. Ensconced at 'Epic', the brothers enjoyed almost instant success in 1976 with Top 10 hit, 'ENJOY YOURSELF', while the second single lifted from the eponymous major label debut album, 'SHOW YOU THE WAY TO GO', became the family's first UK No.1. In line with the burgeoning disco craze, The JACKSON's adopted a tougher, more mature sound as the decade wore on, the 'DESTINY' (1979) album spawning such enduring glitterball favourites as 'BLAME IT ON THE BOOGIE' and 'SHAKE YOUR BODY (DOWN TO THE GROUND)'. MICHAEL was also developing his stunning vocal prowess, his seminal solo set, 'OFF THE WALL' (released the same year) seeing the singer reinvented as a boogie-down pop powerhouse, sophisticated yet gloriously loose limbed. Seasoned producer/arranger QUINCY JONES was JACKSON's creative foil for the project, the pair having met while working on 'The Wiz', a commercially disastrous attempt at revamping the 'Wizard Of Oz' musical in an Afro-American style. JONES' expertise seemingly freed MICHAEL up to put in a career best performance on such electric material as 'DON'T STOP 'TIL YOU GET ENOUGH' (a massive transatlantic hit and a US No.1), 'ROCK WITH YOU' (another to top the American charts) and tear-jerker 'SHE'S OUT OF MY LIFE'. The album itself – a milestone in pop/soul – went on to become a multi-million worldwide seller and secure a place in history as the first record by a solo artist to spawn four consecutive Top 10 hits. Its success also had a knock-on effect for the subsequent JACKSONS album, 'TRIUMPH' (1980), which sold in bucketloads and prompted a huge US tour, wherein MICHAEL took the opportunity to develop his solo material and work on the moves which would eventually flower into his celebrated stage show. The next phase in the singer's solo career came as he and JONES reunited in 1982 to work on an obscure spoken word set based on the 'E.T.' movie (the record was subsequently withdrawn due to legal problems) before beginning work on a follow-up proper, the legendary 'THRILLER'. Quite literally the biggest selling album in the world . . . ever (40-odd million and counting), JACKSON's second masterpiece was released in late '82, and despite its predecessor's plaudits, few could've predicted the stratospheric commercial heights it would scale. Previewed by the PAUL McCARTNEY duet, 'THE GIRL IS MINE' (which almost reached the US Top spot), the 'THRILLER' phenomenon only really kicked into gear with the release of 'BILLIE JEAN' early the following year, a huge UK/US No.1 which set an ice-cool, tightrope disco-pop groove to a blinding visual backdrop of fleet-footed, snake-hipped choreography and revolutionary effects. Next up was the compulsive 'BEAT IT', a throbbing dancefloor killer utilising the guitar wizardry of EDDIE VAN HALEN and, incredibly, the first video by a black artist to be aired on MTV. JACKSON was now at the cutting edge of the all-important video medium (still in relative infancy) as it mushroomed with the all-pervasive influence of the aforementioned MTV; not content with merely recording the greatest selling album in history, JACKSON went ahead and filmed the most popular, the most talked about, and possibly the most hyped video in history. The near quarter of an hour long promo for 'THRILLER' (the single) came with the added kudos of JOHN LANDIS (director) and VINCENT PRICE (spook voice-over), featuring JACKSON strutting his funky stuff (he'd already debuted his legendary 'moonwalk' on American TV) amid a cast of moonlit grotesqueries. The film's mildly controversial content also marked his first, but by no means his last, major encounter with critical pressure (this time around a fairly mild fracas with his fellow Jehovah's Witnesses). Nevertheless, the hits kept on coming, JACKSON scoring a further three hits from the album, the jittering 'WANNA BE STARTIN' SOMETHING', 'HUMAN NATURE' and 'P.Y.T. (PRETTY YOUNG THING)'. At the tail end of '83, he also enjoyed a further extended run at the top of the charts with another PAUL McCARTNEY duet, 'SAY SAY SAY' (from the latter's 'Pipes Of Peace' album), the singer's newfound superstar status netting him a record-breaking sponsorship deal with Pepsi. While recording a commercial for the company, an accident led to JACKSON suffering second-degree burns requiring scalp and facial treatment. Much has since been made of JACKSON's alleged cosmetic surgery, and while the singer has constantly denied it, the evidence that he's become progressively "whiter" is in-your-face as it were, or indeed his face. While a whole book could probably be devoted to JACKSON's more colourful behaviour, surely any sentient being would struggle to cope with the pressure of following up such a colossal artistic and commercial feat. In the immediate aftermath of 'THRILLER's success, JACKSON recorded a further album with his brothers, 'VICTORY' (1984), and reluctantly undertook an ecstatically received, yet turbulent tour, the last time he'd perform/record with The JACKSONS as a group. Although the singer subsequently helped pen the huge USA For Africa famine-relief single, 'WE ARE THE WORLD', more controversy followed as he snapped up the rights to the catalogue of music publishers, ATV. This included the bulk of BEATLES material penned by LENNON/McCARTNEY, and, surprisingly enough, no further JACKSON/McCARTNEY collaborations ensued. Instead, JACKSON once again hooked up with QUINCY JONES to record a belated follow-up album, 'BAD' (1987). Previewed by a duet with SIEDAH GARRETT, 'I JUST CAN'T STOP LOVING YOU' (another transatlantic No.1), the album once again topped the charts in too many countries to mention and spawned a further four US No.1's, 'THE WAY YOU MAKE ME FEEL', 'MAN IN THE MIRROR', 'DIRTY DIANA' and the title track. Inevitably, the record paled in comparison to what had gone before, both commercially and artistically, even though its sales figures would've counted as blockbusting had they been enjoyed by almost any other artist. He did manage to break one record though, with the accompanying world tour, a gargantuan feat of logistical mastery which was touted as the biggest operation of its kind so far. The late 80's also saw the publication of JACKSON's autobiography, 'Moonwalker', though if fans were hoping for any juicy insights into what made the man tick, they were sorely disappointed. More newsworthy was his record-breaking new contract with 'Sony', a multi-media billion dollar deal in which the singer negotiated, amongst other things, a sizable royalty rate, humungous advances and his own label (MJJ) to play around with. The first release under the new agreement was 1991's 'DANGEROUS' opus, JACKSON partially opting for a more

street-smart sound on tracks such as 'WHY YOU WANNA TRIP ON ME' and 'IN THE CLOSET', the pared-back style courtesy of New Jack Swing maestro, Teddy Riley. The biggest hits, however, 'BLACK OR WHITE' (a transatlantic No.1 addressing the controversy over his skin colour), 'HEAL THE WORLD' etc., were in the patented JACKSON style. The resulting world tour was plagued with misfortune and bad press; JACKSON attracted flak for his alleged arrogance during the African leg of the jaunt, while persistent poor health forced the singer to cancel a number of European shows after collapsing onstage at Wembley Stadium in London. The following year proved even worse, the tabloid machine going into overkill following allegations of sexual impropriety with a 13-year old boy. JACKSON strenuously denied the charge, although, bearing in mind the singer's family appeal, the controversy looked set to wreak havoc on his career. His love of children was already well publicised; the singer regularly invited underprivileged kids to his Neverland theme home, while he'd also set up the 'Heal The World Foundation' to tackle child-based issues. Opinion was understandably split although the press had a field day with the reclusive star, endlessly speculating on the reality behind the accusations. The pressure became too much and the exhausted JACKSON subsequently sought help for an addiction to painkillers before returning to the US to face the music; in the event, he reputedly paid off a sum of between 13 and 30 million dollars to the boy and his family, the LAPD also finally dropping a rumoured criminal case. Though some saw the settlement as a tacit admission of guilt, JACKSON emerged relatively unscathed (commercially at least) from the scandal; while he lost his Pepsi sponsorship, sales of 'DANGEROUS' didn't suffer too badly and he signed a new multi-million dollar deal with 'E.M.I' to handle his ATV catalogue. More surprises were in store as JACKSON announced his marriage to Lisa Marie Presley (ELVIS' daughter) in late '94, doubters proved correct when the relationship hit the rocks less than two years later. On the recording front, he was back in the news again by summer '95, an astronomically expensive video for the 'SCREAM' single (a duet with sister JANET) and a semi-retrospective double set, 'HIStory – PAST, PRESENT AND FUTURE, BOOK 1' ensuring media hyperbole. The latter set predictably topped the charts everywhere, while two new tracks, 'YOU ARE NOT ALONE' and 'EARTH SONG' (his best song ever!?) both topped the UK charts, another unprecedented feat for the veteran pop star. While JACKSON, in all his egocentric, asexual eccentricity, continues to be adored by fanatical fans the world over, some remain less impressed; just ask PULP's JARVIS COCKER, who took such a dislike to JACKSON's Christ-like appearance (rather unadvisedly with 'beggar' children in tow) during his 1997 Brit Awards performance that he invaded the stage and caused another press beano, this time with JACKSON as the victim rather than the villain. Despite everything, MICHAEL JACKSON remains a mythic figure, his increasingly rare recorded output unlikely to yield any clues and even more unlikely to match the towering standards of his early 80's heyday. • **Songwriters:** JACKSON 5 singles covered NEVER CAN SAY GOODBYE (Clifton Davis) / LITTLE BITTY PRETTY ONE (Thurston Harris) / DOCTOR MY EYES (Jackson Browne) / FOREVER CAME TODAY (Supremes) / etc. The JACKSONS:- BLAME IT ON THE BOOGIE (Mick Jackson; no relation). MICHAEL covered ROCKIN' ROBIN (Bobby Day) / AIN'T NO SUNSHINE (Bill Withers) / GIRLFRIEND (Paul McCartney; who he also had two Top 3 duets with) / COME TOGETHER (Beatles). • **Miscellaneous:** In the late 80's, the Jackson family was at the centre of a controversial allegation by daughter/singer LaTOYA, who stated in a book and on US TV, that she was beaten as a child by her/their father. This divided the family into either defending their father or saying nothing. LA TOYA, of course had recently shocked them all by baring herself in the centre spread of Playboy magazine.

Album rating: GOT TO BE THERE (*5) / BEN (*6) / MUSIC AND ME (*4) / FOREVER MICHAEL (*4) / THE BEST OF MICHAEL JACKSON compilation (*6) / OFF THE WALL (*8) / THRILLER (*10) / BAD (*7) / DANGEROUS (*6) / HIStory: PAST, PRESENT AND FUTURE – BOOK 1 part compilation (*8) / BLOOD ON THE DANCE FLOOR: HIStory In The Mix (*5) / THE ULTIMATE COLLECTION the best Jackson 5/Jacksons compilation (*8)

JACKSON 5

MICHAEL JACKSON – lead vocals / JACKIE JACKSON (b.SIGMUND, 4 May'51) – vocals / TITO JACKSON (b.TORIANO, 15 Oct'53) – vocals / JERMAINE JACKSON (b.11 Dec'54) – vocals / MARLON JACKSON (b.12 Mar'57) – vocals

		not iss.	Steeltown	
1968.	(7") <681> BIG BOY. / YOU'VE CHANGED	-	☐	
1969.	(7") <684> SOME GIRLS WANT ME FOR THEIR LOVE. / YOU DON'T HAVE TO BE 21 TO FALL IN LOVE <re-iss. 1980s on 'Dynamo'; 146>	-	☐	

		Tamla Motown	Motown	
Jan 70.	(7") (TMG 724) <1157> I WANT YOU BACK. / WHO'S LOVING YOU (re-iss. Oct81)	2	1	Nov69
Mar 70.	(7") <1163> ABC. / IT'S ALL IN THE GAME	-	1	
Apr 70.	(lp) (STML 11142) <700> DIANA ROSS PRESENTS THE JACKSON 5 – Zip-a dee doo-dah / Nobody / I want you back / Can you remember / Standing in the shadows of love / You've changed / My Cherie amour / Who's loving you / Chained / I'm losing you / Stand / Born to save you. (re-iss. Aug81)	16	5	Jan70
May 70.	(7") (TMG 738) ABC. / THE YOUNG FOLKS	8	-	
Jul 70.	(7") (TMG 746) <1166> THE LOVE YOU SAVE. / I FOUND THAT GIRL	7	1	May70
Aug 70.	(lp) (STML 11156) <709> ABC – The love you save / One more chance / ABC / Come round here (I'm the one you need) / Don't know why I love you / Never had a dream come true / True love can	22	4	May70

2222

2222 22222

2222222 2222

2222

222

22222 22222

2

Michael JACKSON (cont) — THE GREAT ROCK DISCOGRAPHY

[Jackson 5 continued]

be beautiful / La la means I love you / I'll bet you / I found that girl / The young folks. (re-iss. Jun82)

Nov 70. (7") (TMG 758) <1171> **I'LL BE THERE. / ONE MORE CHANCE** — 4 / 1 Sep70

Dec 70. <1174> **SANTA CLAUS IS COMING TO TOWN. / CHRISTMAS WON'T BE THE SAME THIS YEAR** — / —

Dec 70. (lp) (STML 11168) <713> **THE JACKSON 5 CHRISTMAS ALBUM** (festive – hit No.1 US Xmas chart) (cd-iss. Nov94 on 'Spectrum')

Feb 71. (lp) (STML 11174) <718> **THE THIRD ALBUM** — 4 Sep70 — I'll be there / Ready or not here I come / Oh how happy / Bridge over troubled water / Can I see you in the morning / Goin' back to Indiana / How funky is your chicken / Mama's pearl / Reach in / The love I saw in you was just a mirage / Darling dear. (re-iss. Mar82) (cd-iss. Sep83)

Apr 71. (7") (TMG 769) <1177> **MAMA'S PEARL. / DARLING DEAR** — 25 / 2 Jan71

Jun 71. (7") (TMG 778) <1179> **NEVER CAN SAY GOODBYE. / SHE'S GOOD** — 33 / 2 Mar71

Jul 71. <1186> **MAYBE TOMORROW. / I WILL FIND A WAY** — / 20

Oct 71. (lp) (STML 11188) <735> **MAYBE TOMORROW** — 11 Apr71 — Maybe tomorrow / She's good / Never can say goodbye / The wall / Petals / 16 Candles / (We've got) blue skies / My little baby / It's great to be here / Honey chile / I will find a way. (cd-iss. Aug93)

Oct 71. (lp) <742> **GOIN' BACK TO INDIANA (TV Soundtrack)** — 16 — (contained live hits from TV show)

Mar 72. (7") (TMG 809) <1194> **SUGAR DADDY. / I'M SO HAPPY** — 10 Dec71

Sep 72. (lp) (STML 11212) <741> **THE JACKSON 5 GREATEST HITS** (compilation) — 26 / 12 Jan72 (re-iss. Mar 82, re-iss. +cd.Feb88)

MICHAEL JACKSON

started solo career as well on same label.

Jan 72. (7") (TMG 797) <1191> **GOT TO BE THERE. / MARIA (YOU WERE THE ONLY ONE)** — 5 / 4 Oct71

May 72. (7") (TMG 816) <1197> **ROCKIN' ROBIN. / LOVE IS HERE AND NOW YOU'RE GONE** — 3 / 2 Mar72

May 72. (lp) (STML STML 11205) <747> **GOT TO BE THERE** — 37 / 14 Feb72 — Ain't no sunshine / I wanna be where you are / Girl don't take your love from me / In our small way / Got to be there / Rockin' robin / Wings of my love / Maria (you were the only one) / Love is here and now / You're gone / You've got a friend. (re-iss. Aug81 & May84) (cd-iss. Jun89) (re-iss. cd Aug93)

May 72. (lp) <1202> **I WANNA BE WHERE YOU ARE. / WE GOT A GOOD THING GOIN'** — / 16

Jul 72. (7") (TMG 826) **AIN'T NO SUNSHINE. / I WANNA BE WHERE YOU ARE** — 8 / — (re-iss. Oct81)

Nov 72. (7") (TMG 834) <1207> **BEN. / YOU CAN CRY ON MY SHOULDER** — 7 / 1 Aug72 (re-iss. Oct81)

Dec 72. (lp) (STML 11220) <755> **BEN** — 17 / 5 Sep72 — Ben / Greatest show on Earth / People make the world go round / We've got a good thing going / Everybody's fool / My girl / What goes around comes around / In our small way / Shoo-be-doo-be-doo-da-day / You can cry on my shoulder. (re-iss. Oct81 + May84) (cd-iss. Feb90)

May 73. (7") <1218> **WITH A CHILD'S HEART. / MORNING GLOW** — / 50

Jul 73. (lp) (STML 11235) <767> **MUSIC AND ME** — / 92 Apr73 — With a child's heart / Up again / All the things you are / Happy / Too young / Doggin' around / Johnny Raven / Euphoria / Morning glow / Music and me. (re-iss. Nov84) (re-iss. cd/c May93 on 'Spectrum')

Jul 73. (7") (TMG 863) **MORNING GLOW. / MY GIRL** — / —

May 74. (7") (TMG 900) **MUSIC AND ME. / JOHNNY RAVEN** — / —

Feb 75. (7") <1341> **WE'RE ALMOST THERE. / TAKE ME BACK** — / 54

Mar 75. (lp) (STMA 8022) <825> **FOREVER MICHAEL** — We're almost there / Take me back / One day in your life / Cinderella stay awhile / We've got forever / Just a little bit of you / You are there / Dapper Dan / Dear Michael / I'll come home to you. (re-iss. Jun83 + Jun88) (cd-iss. Mar90)

Apr 75. (7") (TMG 946) **ONE DAY IN YOUR LIFE. / WITH A CHILD'S HEART** — / —

Oct 75. (7") (TMG 1006) <1349> **JUST A LITTLE BIT OF YOU. / DEAR MICHAEL** — 23 Jun75

Oct 75. (lp) (STML 12005) <851> **THE BEST OF MICHAEL JACKSON** (compilation) (re-iss. Mar80 + May84) (Jul81 saw it hit UK No.11)

JACKSON 5

MICHAEL had continued as the group's main singer

Apr 72. (7") <1199> **LITTLE BIT PRETTY ONE. / IF I HAVE TO MOVE A MOUNTAIN** — / 13

Sep 72. (7") (TMG 825) **LITTLE BITTY PRETTY ONE. / MAYBE TOMORROW** — / —

Oct 72. (lp) (STML 11214) <750> **LOOKIN' THROUGH THE WINDOWS** — 16 / 7 Jun72 — Ain't nothing like the real thing / Lookin' through the windows / Don't let your baby catch our / To know / Doctor my eyes / Little bitty pretty one / E-ne-me-ne-mi-ne-moe / I'll have to move a mountain / Don't want to see you tomorrow / Children of the light / I can only give you love. (re-iss. Feb83)

Oct 72. (7") (TMG 833) <1205> **LOOKIN' THROUGH THE WINDOWS. / LOVE SONG** — 9 / 16 Jul72

Nov 72. (7") <1214> **CORNER OF THE SKY. / TO KNOW** — / 18

Dec 72. (7"m) (TMG 837) **SANTA CLAUS IS COMING TO TOWN. / SOMEDAY AT CHRISTMAS / CHRISTMAS WON'T BE THE SAME THIS YEAR** — 43 / —

Feb 73. (7") (TMG 842) **DOCTOR MY EYES. / MY LITTLE BABY** — 9 / —

Mar 73. (7") <1224> **HALLELUJAH DAY. / YOU MAKE ME WHAT I AM** — / 16

May 73. (7") (TMG 856) **HALLELUJAH DAY. / TO KNOW** — 20 / —

Jul 73. (lp) (STML 11231) <761> **SKYWRITER** — / 44 Apr73 — Skywriter / Hallelujah day / Boogie man / Touch / Corner of the sky / I can't quit your love / Uppermost / World of sunshine / Ooh, I'd

---

love to be with you / You made me what I am. (re-iss. Nov84) (cd-iss. Aug93)

Aug 73. (7") (TMG 865) **SKYWRITER. / AIN'T NOTHING LIKE THE REAL THING** — 25 / —

Nov 73. (7") (TMG 878) <1277> **GET IT TOGETHER. / TOUCH** — / 28 Sep73

Nov 73. (lp) (STML 11243) <783> **GET IT TOGETHER** — / 100 — Dancing machine / Get it together / Don't say goodbye again / Reflections / Hum along and dance / Mama I gotta brand new thing (don't say no) / It's too late to change the time / You need love like I do (don't you).

Apr 74. (7") (TMG 895) **THE BOOGIE MAN. / DON'T LET YOUR BABY CATCH YOU** — / —

Jun 74. (7") (TMG 904) <1286> **DANCING MACHINE. / IT'S TOO LATE TO CHANGE THE TIME** — / 2 Mar74

Nov 74. (lp) (STML 11275) <780> **DANCING MACHINE** — / 16 Oct74 — Dancing machine / I am love / Whatever you got, I want / She's a rhythm child / The life of the party / What you don't know / If I don't love you this way / It all begins and ends with love / The mirrors of my mind.

Nov 74. (7") <1308> **WHATEVER YOU GOT, I WANT. / I CAN'T QUIT YOUR LOVE** — / 38

Nov 74. (7") (TMG 927) **WHATEVER YOU GOT, I WANT. / THE LIFE OF THE PARTY** — / —

Mar 75. (7") (TMG 942) <1310> **I AM LOVE. / (Part 2)** — / 15 Feb75

Jun 75. (7") <1356> **FOREVER CAME TODAY. / ALL I DO IS THINK OF YOU** — / 60

Jul 75. (lp) (STML 11290) <829> **MOVING VIOLATION** — / 36 — Forever came today / Moving violation / (You were made) Especially for me / Honey love / Body language (do the love dance) / All I do is think of you / Breezy / Call of the wild / Time explosion.

Sep 75. (7") (TMG 1001) **FOREVER CAME TODAY. / I CAN'T QUIT YOUR LOVE** — / —

JACKSONS

RANDY JACKSON (b.29 Oct'62) – vocals repl. JERMAINE who is having own solo career. Temporarily added sisters **LaTOYA** (b.29 May'56) – vocals / **REBBIE** (b. MAUREEN, 29 May'50) – vocals. In 1976, another sister **JANET** also appeared on tours.

(Epic / Epic)

Feb 77. (7") (EPC 4708) <50289> **ENJOY YOURSELF. / STYLE OF LIFE** — 42 / 6 Oct76

Feb 77. (lp/c) (EPC/40 86009) <34229> **THE JACKSONS** — 54 / 36 Nov76 — Enjoy yourself / Think happy / Good times / Keep on dancing / Blues away / Show you the way to go / Living together / Strength of one man / Dreamer / Style of life. (also on pic-lp US) (re-iss. cd Jun94 on 'Sony')

May 77. (7") (EPC 5266) <50350> **SHOW YOU THE WAY TO GO. / BLUES AWAY** — 1 / 28 Apr77

Jul 77. (7") (EPC 5458) **DREAMER. / GOOD TIMES** — 22 / —

Oct 77. (7") (EPC 5732) <50454> **GOIN' PLACES. / DO WHAT YOU WANNA** — 26 / 52

Oct 77. (lp/c) (EPC/40 86035) <34835> **GOIN' PLACES** — 45 / 63 — Music's takin' over / Goin' places / Different kind of lady / Even though you're gone / Jump for joy / Heaven knows I love you girl / Man of war / Do you wanna / Find me a girl. (also iss.pic-lp US) (re-iss. cd Jun94 on 'Sony')

Jan 78. (7") <50496> **FIND ME A GIRL. / DIFFERENT KIND OF LADY** — / —

Jan 78. (7") (EPC 5919) **EVEN THOUGH YOU'RE GONE. / DIFFERENT KIND OF LADY** — 31 / —

Apr 78. (7") (EPC 6263) **MUSIC'S TAKING OVER. / MAN OF WAR** — / —

Sep 78. (7") (EPC 6683) **BLAME IT ON THE BOOGIE. / DO WHAT YOU WANNA** — 8 / —

Oct 78. (7") <50595> **BLAME IT ON THE BOOGIE. / EASE ON DOWN THE ROAD** — / 54

Dec 78. (7") (EPC 6983) **DESTINY. / THAT'S WHAT YOU GET** — 39 / — (12"+=) (EPC13 6983) – Blame it on the boogie.

Apr 79. (lp/c) (EPC/40 83200) <35552> **DESTINY** — 33 / 11 Dec78 — Blame it on the boogie / Push me away / Things I do for you / Shake your body (down to the ground) / Destiny / Bless his soul / All night dancin' / That's what you get. (re-iss. 1984)

Mar 79. (7"/12") (EPC/+13 7181) **SHAKE YOUR BODY (DOWN TO THE GROUND). / ALL NIGHT DANCIN'** — 4 / —

Mar 79. (7") <50656> **SHAKE YOUR BODY (DOWN TO THE GROUND). / THAT'S WHAT YOU GET (FOR BEING POLITE)** — / 7

MICHAEL JACKSON

solo again. In Oct78, he duetted with DIANA ROSS ⇒ on 'MCA' Top 50 US/UK single 'EASE ON DOWN THE ROAD'. (re-iss. May84)

(Epic / Epic)

May 79. (7"pic-d/12") (EPC/+13 7135) **YOU CAN'T WIN. / (Part 2)** — / 81 Feb79

Aug 79. (7") (EPC 7763) <50654> **DON'T STOP 'TIL YOU GET ENOUGH. / I CAN'T HELP IT** — 3 / 1

Aug 79. (lp/c) (EPC/40 83458) <35745> **OFF THE WALL** — 5 / 3 — Don't stop 'til you get enough / Rock with you / Working day and night / Get on the floor / Off the wall / Girlfriend / She's out of my life / It's the falling in love / Burn this disco out. (re-dist.1980 w/ free 7" YOU CAN'T WIN) (re-iss. Nov86) (cd-iss. 1983 & Dec95) (re-iss. Aug92, hit UK No.48)

Oct 79. (7") <50797> **ROCK WITH YOU. / WORKING DAY AND NIGHT** — / 1

Nov 79. (7") (EPC 8045) **OFF THE WALL. / WORKING DAY AND NIGHT** — 7 / —

Feb 80. (7") <50838> **OFF THE WALL. / GET ON THE FLOOR** — / 10 (re-iss. Apr82)

Feb 80. (7")(12") (EPC 8206) **ROCK WITH YOU. / GET ON THE FLOOR** — 7 / — (re-iss. Apr82)

Apr 80. (7") (EPC 8384) **SHE'S OUT OF MY LIFE. / Jacksons: PUSH ME AWAY** — 3 / —

Apr 80. (7") <50871> **SHE'S OUT OF MY LIFE. / GET ON THE FLOOR** — / 10

Jul 80. (7") (EPC 8782) **GIRLFRIEND. / Jacksons: BLESS HIS SOUL** — 41 / —

488

JACKSONS

—— returned to the fold

Oct 80. (7") <50938> **LOVELY ONE. / BLESS HIS SOUL** — | 12
Oct 80. (7") (EPC 9302) **LOVELY ONE. / THINGS I DO FOR YOU** 29 | —
Oct 80. (lp/c) (EPC/40 86112) <36424> **TRIUMPH** 13 | 10
– Can you feel it / Lovely one / Your ways / Everybody / Heartbreak hotel / Time waits for no one / Walk right now / Give it up / Wondering who.
Dec 80. (7") <50959> **HEARTBREAK HOTEL. / THINGS I DO FOR YOU** — | 22
Dec 80. (7") (EPC 9391) **HEARTBREAK HOTEL. / DIFFERENT KIND OF LADY** 44 | —
Feb 81. (7") (EPC 9554) **CAN YOU FEEL IT. / WONDERING WHO** 6 | —
Apr 81. (7") <01032> **CAN YOU FEEL IT. / EVERYBODY** — | 77
Jun 81. (7") (EPC 1294) <02132> **WALK RIGHT NOW. / YOUR WAYS** 7 | 73
Sep 81. (7") (EPC 1579) **TIME WAITS FOR NO ONE. / GIVE IT UP** — | —
Nov 81. (7") <02720> **THE THINGS I DO FOR YOU (live). / WORKING DAY AND NIGHT (live)** — | —
Nov 81. (d-lp/d-c) (EPC/40 88562) <37545> **THE JACKSONS – LIVE! (live)** 53 | 30
– Opening: Can you feel it? Things I do for you / Off the wall / Ben / Heartbreak hotel / She's out of my life / Movie and rap medley (a) I want you back, (b) Never can say goodbye, (c) Got to be there / The love you save / I'll be there / Rock with you / Lovely one / Working day and night / Don't stop 'til you get enough / Shake your body (down to the ground).
Nov 81. (7") (EPC 1902) **THINGS I DO FOR YOU (live). / DON'T STOP 'TIL YOU GET ENOUGH (live)** □ | —

MICHAEL JACKSON

returned to solo work again

Epic | Epic

Nov 82. (7"/7"pic-d; by MICHAEL JACKSON & PAUL McCARTNEY) (EPCA/+11 2729) <03288> **THE GIRL IS MINE. / CAN'T GET OUT OF THE RAIN** 10 | 2
—— (Nearly a year later they had another hit, 'SAY SAY SAY' a No.2 UK / No.1 US)
Dec 82. (lp/c/cd) (EPC/40/CD 85930) <38112> **THRILLER** 1 | 1
– Wanna be startin' something / Baby be mine / The girl is mine / Thriller / Beat it / Billie Jean / Human nature / P.Y.T. (Pretty Young Thing) / The lady in my life. (pic-lp Jul83; EPC11 85930) (re-iss. Aug92 hit UK No.17)
Jan 83. (7") <03509> **BILLIE JEAN. / CAN'T GET OUT OF THE RAIN** — | 1
Jan 83. (7") (EPC 3084) **BILLIE JEAN. / IT'S FALLING IN LOVE** 1 | —
(12"+=) (EPC/+13 3084) – ('A'extended).
Mar 83. (7") <03759> **BEAT IT. / GET ON THE FLOOR** — | 1
Mar 83. (7"/12") (EPC/+13 3258) **BEAT IT. / BURN THIS DISCO OUT** 3 | —
May 83. (7") <03914> **WANNA BE STARTIN' SOMETHING. / (part 2)** — | 5
May 83. (7") (A 3427) **WANNA BE STARTIN' SOMETHING. / Jacksons: ROCK WITH YOU** 8 | —
(12"+=) (TA 3427) – ('A'instrumental).
Jul 83. (7") <03914> **HUMAN NATURE. / BABY BE MINE** — | 7
Oct 83. (7") <04165> **P.Y.T. (PRETTY YOUNG THING). / WORKING DAY AND NIGHT** — | 10
Nov 83. (7"/12") (EPCA/TA 3643) **THRILLER. / THE THINGS I DO FOR YOU** 10 | —
Jan 84. (7") <04364> **THRILLER. / CAN'T GET OUTTA THE RAIN** — | 4
Mar 84. (7") (A 4136) **P.Y.T. (PRETTY YOUNG THING). / HEARTBREAK HOTEL** 11 | —
(12"+=) (TA 4136) – Thriller (instrumental).

JACKSONS

—— now 6-piece when **JERMAINE** returned to join the 5 brothers.

Jun 84. (7"pic-d/12") (A/TA 4431) **STATE OF SHOCK. / YOUR WAYS** 14 | 3
(above featured MICK JAGGER on dual vocals with MICHAEL)
Jul 84. (pic-lp/c) (EPC/40 86303) <38946> **VICTORY** 3 | 4
– Torture / Wait / One more chance / Be not always / State of shock / We can change the world / The hurt / Body. (cd-iss. May87) (cd-iss. Dec94)
Aug 84. (7") (A 4675) <04575> **TORTURE. / ('A'instrumental)** 26 | 17
(12"+=) (TA 4675) – Show you the way to go / Blame it on the boogie.
Nov 84. (7"/12") (A/TA 4883) <04673> **BODY. / ('A'instrumental)** □ | 47
Feb 85. (7"/12") (A/TA 6105) **WAIT. / SHE'S OUT OF MY LIFE** — | —

MICHAEL JACKSON

Jul 87. (7"/7"s/12") (650 202-7/-0/-6) <07253> **I JUST CAN'T STOP LOVING YOU. / BABY BE MINE** 1 | 1
(above featured duet with SIEDAH GARRETT)
Sep 87. (7") <07418> **BAD. / I CAN'T HELP IT** — | 1
Sep 87. (7") (651 155-7) **BAD. / ('A'instrumental)** 3 | —
(12"+=) (651 155-6) – ('A'acappella mix) / ('A'dub version).
(c-s+=) (651 155-4) – ('A'extended).
Sep 87. (lp/c/cd) (450 290-1/-4/-2) <40600> **BAD** 1 | 1
– Bad / The way you make me feel / Speed demon / Liberian girl / Just good friends / Another part of me / Man in the mirror / I just can't stop loving you / Dirty Diana / Smooth criminal. (pic-lp Nov87; 450 290-0) (re-iss. Jul88 as 5x7"box; 450 290-9) (re-iss. Aug92, hit UK No.14)
Nov 87. (7") (651 275-7) <07645> **THE WAY YOU MAKE ME FEEL. / ('A'instrumental)** 3 | 1
(12"+=) (651 275-0) – ('A'dance mix) / ('A'dub mix).
(cd-s+=) (651 275-2) – ('A'acappella mix).

Feb 88. (7"/7"sha-pic-d) (651 388-7/-9) <07668> **MAN IN THE MIRROR. / ('A'instrumental)** 21 | 1
(12"+=) (651 388-6/-2) – ('A'mix).
—— (In Apr'88, he did a duet single, 'GET IT', with STEVIE WONDER which hit UK Top40 & US No.80)
Jul 88. (7") (651 546-7) <07739> **DIRTY DIANA. / ('A'instrumental)** 4 | 1
(12"+=) (651 546-6) – Bad (extended dance).
(3"cd-s+=) (651 546-2) – ('A'-album version).
Sep 88. (7"/7"s) (652 844-7/-9) <07962> **ANOTHER PART OF ME. / ('A'instrumental)** 15 | 11
(12"+=/cd-s+=) (652 844-6/-2) – ('A'acappella) / ('A'radio).
(3"cd-s+=) (653 004-2) – ('A'drum mix) / ('A'acappella).
Nov 88. (7"/7"s) (653 026-7/-0) <08044> **SMOOTH CRIMINAL. / ('A'instrumental)** 8 | 7
(12"+=/cd-s+=) (653 026-1/-2) – ('A'extended) / ('A'acappella) / ('A'dance dub).
(cd-s++=) (653 026-2) – ('A'Annie mix).
Feb 89. (7"/7"s) (654 672-7/-0) **LEAVE ME ALONE. / HUMAN NATURE** 2 | —
(c-s+=/3"cd-s+=) (654 672-4/-3) – Don't stop 'til you get enough.
(cd-s+=) (654 672-2) – Wanna be startin' something (extended).
Jul 89. (7"/7"s/c-s) (654 947-7/-0/-4) **LIBERIAN GIRL. / GIRLFRIEND** 13 | —
(3"cd-s+=) (654 947-3) – Get on the floor.
(cd-s++=) (654 947-2) – The lady in my life.

JACKSONS

Apr 89. (7"/c-s) (654 808-7/-4) <68688> **NOTHIN' (THAT COMPARES 2 U). / HEARTBREAK HOTEL / ALRIGHT WITH ME** □ | 77
(12"+=/cd-s+=) (654 808-6/-2) – ('A'choice dub extended).
Jun 89. (lp/c/cd) (463 352-1/-4/-2) <40911> **2300 JACKSON STREET** □ | 59
– Art of madness / Nothin' (that compares 2 U) / Maria / Private affair / 2300 Jackson Street / Harley / She / Alright with me / Play it up / Midnight rendezvous / If you'd only believe.
Aug 89. (7"/c-s) (655 206-7/-4) <69022> **2300 JACKSON STREET. / WHEN I LOOK AT YOU** □ | □
(12"+=) (655 206-6) – Please come back to me.
(cd-s++=) (655 206-2) – ('A'lp version) / Keep her.

MICHAEL JACKSON

Nov 91. (7"/c-s) (657 598-7/-4) <74100> **BLACK OR WHITE. / ('A'instrumental)** 1 | 1
(12"+=) (657 598-6) – Bad / Thriller.
(cd-s+=) (657 598-2) – Smooth criminal.
(12"+=/cd-s+=) – (other mixes by and 1 by C&C MUSIC FACTORY)
Dec 91. (cd/c/lp) (465 802-2/-4/-1) <45400> **DANGEROUS** 1 | 1
– Jam / Why you wanna trip on me / In the closet / She drives me wild / Remember the time / Can't let her get away / Heal the world / Black or white / Who is it / Give in to me / Will you be there / Keep the faith / Gone too soon / Dangerous.
Jan 92. (c-s) <74200> **REMEMBER THE TIME / BLACK OR WHITE (Clivilles & Cole mix)** — | 3
Feb 92. (7"/c-s/12"/cd-s) (657 774-7/-4/-6/-2) **REMEMBER THE TIME. / COME TOGETHER** 3 | —
Apr 92. (7"/c-s) (658 018-7/-4) <74266> **IN THE CLOSET. / ('A'remix)** 8 | 6
(12"+=/cd-s+=) (658 018-6/-2) – (other 'A'mixes).
Jul 92. (7"/c-s) (658 179-7/-4) **WHO IS IT. / ROCK WITH YOU (mix)** 10 | —
(12"+=/cd-s+=) (658 179-6/-2) – Don't stop 'til you get enough (remix).
Jul 92. (c-s) <74333> **JAM / ROCK WITH YOU (remix)** — | 26
Sep 92. (7"/c-s) (658 360-7/-4) **JAM. / BEAT IT (Moby mix)** 13 | —
(12"+=) (658 360-6) – Wanna be starting something (Brothers In Rhythm house mix).
(cd-s) (658 360-2) – ('A'side) / ('A'-Roger's Jeep mix) / ('A'-Atlanta techno mix) / Wanna be startin' something (Brothers In Rhythm house mix).
Nov 92. (7"/c-s) (658 488-7/-4) <74708> **HEAL THE WORLD. / SHE DRIVES ME WILD** 2 | 27 Dec92
(12"+=) (658 488-6) – Man in the mirror.
(cd-s) (658 488-2) – ('A'side) / Wanna be starting something / Don't stop till you get enough / Rock with you.
Feb 93. (7"/c-s) (659 069-7/-4) **GIVE IN TO ME. / DIRTY DIANA** 2 | —
(cd-s+=) (659 069-2) – Beat it.
Apr 93. (c-s) <74406> **WHO IS IT (Oprah Winfrey intro)** — | 14
Jun 93. (7"/c-s) (659 222-7/-4) <77060> **WILL YOU BE THERE. / GIRLFRIEND** 9 | 7
(cd-s+=) (659 222-2) – Keep the faith.
Dec 93. (7"/c-s) (659 976-7/-4) **GONE TOO SOON. / ('A'instrumental)** 33 | —
(12"/cd-s) (659 976-6/-2) – ('A'side) / Human nature / She's out of my life / Thriller.
Jun 95. (7"/c-s/cd-s; MICHAEL JACKSON & JANET JACKSON) (662 022-7/-4/-2) <78000> **SCREAM / CHILDHOOD** 3 | 5
(cd-s/12"/12") (662 022-2/-6/-8) – ('A'album version) / ('A'-Pressurized dub pt.1 & 2) / ('A'-Naughty By Nature pretty-pella mix) / ('A'-N.B.N. acappella).
(12") – ('A'-classic club mix) / ('A'-David Morales R&B extended mix) / ('A'-Def radio mix). / ('A'-Naughty By Nature main mix) / ('A'-Naughty By Nature main mix no rap) / ('A'-Dave "Jam" Hall's extended urban remix). (note the above 4th & 5th formats hit UK No.43)
Jun 95. (d-cd/d-c/t-lp) (474 709-2/-4/-1) <59000> **HIStory: PAST, PRESENT AND FUTURE – BOOK 1** 1 | 1
– Billie Jean / The way you make me feel / Black or white / Rock with you / She's out of my life / Bad / I just can't stop loving you / Man in the mirror / Thriller / Beat it / The girl is mine / Remember the time / Don't stop 'til you get enough / Wanna be startin' somethin' / Heal the world. // Scream / They don't care about us / Stranger in Moscow / This time around / Earth song / DS / Money / Come together / You are not alone / Childhood / Tabloid junkie / 2 bad / History / Little Susie / Smile.
Aug 95. (c-s) (662 310-4) <78002> **YOU ARE NOT ALONE / SCREAM LOUDER (Flyte Tyme mix with JANET JACKSON)** 1 | 1
(cd-s/12") (662 310-2/-8) – ('A'-Frankie Knuckles remix) / ('A'-Jon B remix).
(cd-s) (662 310-5) – ('A'-R Kelly remix) / Rock with you (Masters At work remix) / Rock with you (Frankie Knuckles remix).

Nov 95. (c-s) *(662 695-4)* **EARTH SONG / ('A'-Hani's extended radio experience)** | `1` | `-`
(cd-s) *(662 695-2)* – ('A'side) / ('A'-Hani's club experience) / Michael Jackson DMC megamix.
(cd-s) *(662 695-5)* – ('A'side) / Wanna be startin' somethin' / ('A'-Brothers In Rhythm mix) / ('A'-Tommy D's main mix).

Apr 96. (c-s/cd-s) *(662 950-4/-2)* <78060> **THEY DON'T CARE ABOUT US / ROCK WITH YOU / EARTH SONG** | `4` | `30` Jun96
(662 950-2) – ('A'mixes) / Beat it.

—— In Aug'96, MICHAEL featured on nephews 3T (offspring of TITO) Top 3 hit 'Why'.

Nov 96. (c-s) *(663 787-4)* **STRANGER IN MOSCOW / ('A'-Tee's radio mix)** | `4` | `91` Aug97
(cd-s) *(663 787-2)* – ('A'-side) / ('A'-Todd Terry mix) / ('A'-Charles 'The Mixologist' Roane mix).
(cd-s) *(663 787-5)* – ('A'side) / ('A'-Hani mix) / ('A'-Basement Boys mix).

Apr 97. (c-s/12"/cd-s) *(664 462-4/-0/-2)* **BLOOD ON THE DANCEFLOOR / (mixes)** | `1` | `42`
(12"/12"/cd-s) *(664 462-6/-8/-5)* – ('A'remixes).

May 97. (cd/c) *(487 500-2/-4)* **BLOOD ON THE DANCEFLOOR** (remixes) | `1` | `24`
– Blood on the dancefloor / Morphine / Superfly sister / Ghosts / Is it scary / Scream louder / Money / 2 bad / Stranger in moscow / This time around / Earth song / You are not alone / History.

Jul 97. (c-s/cd-s) *(664 796-4/-2)* **HISTORY / GHOSTS** | `5` | `-`
(cd-s) *(664 796-5)* – ('A'mixes).

– (MICHAEL JACKSON) compilations, others –

Note; All below on 'Motown' unless stated.
Apr 80. (7") **BEN. / ('B'by MARVIN GAYE)**
(re-iss. Oct81)
Oct 80. (7") *(TMG 973)* **GOT TO BE THERE. / ('B'by MARV JACKSON)**
(re-iss. Oct81)
Apr 81. (7") *(TMG 976)* **ONE DAY IN YOUR LIFE. / TAKE ME BACK** | `1` | `55`
(re-iss. Oct81)
Jul 81. (lp/c) *(STML 12158/CSTML 12158)* **ONE DAY IN YOUR LIFE** | `29` |
– One day in your life / We're almost there / You're my best friend, my love / Don't say goodbye again / Take me back / It's too late to change the time / We've got a good thing going / You are there / Doggin' around / Dear Michael / Girl, don't take your love from me / I'll come home to you.
(re-iss. Mar85)
Jul 81. (7"/12") *(TMG/+T 977)* **WE'RE ALMOST THERE. / WE GOT A GOOD THING GOING** | `46` |
Jul 83. (7"pic-d/12"/7") *(TMG P/T 986/TMG 986)* **HAPPY (LOVE THEME FROM 'LADY SINGS THE BLUES'). / WE'RE ALMOST THERE** | `52` |
Jul 83. (c-ep) *(CTME 2035)* **FLIPHITS** | | `-`
– One day in your life / Got to be there / Ben / Ain't no sunshine.
May 84. (7"/12") *(TMG/+T 1342)* **FAREWELL MY SUMMER LOVE. / CALL ME** | `7` | `38`
Aug 84. (lp/c) *(Z L/K 72227)* **FAREWELL MY SUMMER LOVE** | `9` | `46`
– Don't let it get you down / You've really got a hold on me / Melodie / Touch the one you love / Girl you're so together / Farewell my summer love / Call me / Here I am / To make my father proud.
(re-iss. Jun88, cd-iss. Oct89)
Aug 84. (7") *(TMG 1355)* **GIRL YOU'RE SO TOGETHER. / TOUCH THE ONE YOU LOVE**
(12"+=) – Ben / Ain't no sunshine.
Nov 84. (lp/c) *(W L/K 72289)* **THE GREAT LOVE SONGS OF MICHAEL JACKSON**
May 86. (lp/c) *(W L/K 72424)* **LOOKING BACK TO YESTERDAY**
Apr 87. (d-cd) *(ZD 72530)* **MICHAEL JACKSON ANTHOLOGY**
– Got to be there / Rockin' Robin / Ain't no sunshine / Maria (you were the only one) / I wanna be where you are / Girl don't take your love from me / Love is here and now you're gone / Ben / People make the world go 'round / Shoo-be-doo-be-doo-da-day / With a child's heart / Everybody's somebody's fool / In our small way / All the things you are / You can cry on my shoulder / Maybe tomorrow / I'll be there / Never can say goodbye / It's too late to change the time / Dancing machine / When I come of age / Dear Michael / Music and me / You are there / One day in your life / Love's gone bad / That's what love is made of / Who's looking for a lover / Lonely teardrops / We're almost there / Take me back / Just a little bit of you / Melodie / I'll come home to you / If 'n I was God / Happy / Don't let it get you down / Call on me / To make my father proud / Farewell my summer love. – (w / JACKSON 5 tracks) *(re-iss. d-cd Apr93)*
1987. (7") **25 MILES. / UP ON THE HOUSETOP** | `-` |
Feb 92. (cd/c/lp) *(530014 – 2/-4/-1)* **MOTOWN'S GREATEST HITS**
Apr 82. (7") *Epic; (EPC 8046)* **OFF THE WALL. / DON'T STOP 'TIL YOU GET ENOUGH**
Dec 82. (c-ep) *Epic; (EPC 2906)* **GREATEST ORIGINAL HITS** | | `-`
(re-iss. Mar83 as 7"ep)
Nov 83. (9x7"red-pack) *Epic; (MJ 1)* **SINGLES PACK** | `66` |
(re-iss. Jul88)
Sep 86. (c-ep) *Epic; (4501274)* **THE 12" TAPE**
– Billie Jean / Beat it / Wanna be startin' something / Thriller.
Jul 88. (singles pack) *Epic; (MJ 5)* **SOUVENIR SINGLES PACK** | `91` | `-`
Jul 92. (4xpic-cd-ep's) *Epic; (MJ 4)* **TOUR SOUVENIR PACK** | `32` |
– (3 tracks on each disc).
Jul 82. (lp/c) *Pickwick; (2/4 0038)* **AIN'T NO SUNSHINE** | | `-`
(re-iss. Nov84 on 'Astan')
Jul 83. (lp/c/cd) *Telstar; (STA R/C 2232/TCD 2232)* **18 GREATEST HITS (by MICHAEL JACKSON / JACKSON 5)** | `1` |
(re-iss. Jun88)
May 84. (cd) *Motown; (MCD 06070MD)* **COMPACT COMMAND PERFORMANCES: 18 GREATEST HITS**
(re-iss. Oct87)
Nov 86. (d-cd) *Motown; (ZD 72468)* **GOT TO BE THERE / BEN**
Oct 87. (lp/c/cd) *Telstar;* **LOVE SONGS (w / DIANA ROSS)** | `15` |

Nov 87. (lp/c/cd) *Stylus; (SM R/C/D 745)* **THE MICHAEL JACKSON MIX** | `27` |
Nov 95. (3xcd-box) *Motown;* **FOREVER MICHAEL / MUSIC & ME / BEN** | | `-`
Jun 97. (cd/c) *Polygram TV; (530804-2/-4)* **THE BEST OF MICHAEL JACKSON & THE JACKSON 5** | `5` | `-`
– I want you back / ABC / Love you save / I'll be there / Mama's pearl / Never can say goodbye / Got to be there / Rockin' robin / Ain't no sunshine / Looking through the windows / Ben / Doctor my eyes / We're almost there / Farewell my summer love / Girl you're so together.

– (JACKSONS) compilations, others. –

Note; All on 'Motown' unless stated.
Apr 74. (7") *(TMG 895)* **BOOGIE MAN. / DON'T LET YOUR BABY TOUCH YOU**
Dec 76. (lp/c) *(STML 12046/)* **JOYFUL JUKEBOX MUSIC**
Jan 77. (d-lp/d-c) *(TMSP 6004/)* **THE JACKSON 5 ANTHOLOGY** | | `84` Aug 76
(cd-iss. Jun87)(re-iss. d-cd. Apr93)
Mar 77. (lp) *(STMX 6006)* **MOTOWN SPECIAL – JACKSON 5**
Aug 77. (7") **SKYWRITER. / I WANT YOU BACK / THE LOVE YOU SAVE**
Sep 79. (c/lp) *(CSTML 12121/STML 12121)* **20 GOLDEN GREATS**
(re-iss. Oct81 & Apr84)
Mar 82. (c/lp) *(CSTMS 5038/STMS 5038)* **GREATEST HITS**
Jul 83. (c-ep) *(CTME 2034)* **FLIP HITS**
– I want you back / I'll be there / ABC / Lookin' through any window.
Nov 84. (lp/c) *(W L/K 72290)* **GREAT LOVE SONGS OF THE JACKSON 5**
Nov 86. (cd) *(ZD 72483)* **DIANA ROSS PRESENTS . . . / ABC**
Nov 87. (12") *(ZXT 41656)* **I SAW MOMMY KISSING SANTA CLAUS / SANTA CLAUS IS COMING TO TOWN. / UP ON THE HOUSE TOP / FROSTY THE SNOWMAN**
Feb 88. (lp/c/cd) **THE ORIGINAL SOUL OF . . .**
Apr 88. (7"/12") **I WANT YOU BACK ('88 remix – Stock Aitken Waterman). / NEVER CAN SAY GOODBYE** | `8` |
Jan 79. (lp/c) *M.F.P.; (MFP 50418)* **ZIP-A-DEE-DOO-DAH** | | `-`
Aug 80. (7"/12") *Epic;* **SHAKE YOUR BODY (DOWN TO THE GROUND). / BLAME IT ON THE BOOGIE**
1984. (d-c) *Epic;* **GOIN' PLACES / DESTINY**
Jul 84. (7") *Epic;* **SHOW YOU THE WAY TO GO. / BLAME IT ON THE BOOGIE**
Sep 82. (lp/c) *Pickwick; (TM S/C 3503)* **THE JACKSON 5** | | `-`
Mar 90. (lp/cd/c) *S.D.E.G.; (SDE /+CD/+MC 4018)* **BEGINNING YEARS 1965-67**
Mar 90. (cd/c/lp) *S.D.E.G.; (CD/MC SDE 4018/SDE 4018)* **THE JACKSON 5 AND JOHNNY**
May 93. (cd/c) *Spectrum; (550076 – 4/-2)* **CHILDREN OF THE NIGHT ("JACKSON 5")**
Sep 93. (cd) *Stardust; (STACD 081)* **THE JACKSON 5 FEATURING MICHAEL JACKSON ("JACKSON 5")**
Jul 95. (cd) *Charly; (CPCD 8122)* **THE HISTORIC EARLY RECORDINGS** | | `-`
Jul 95. (cd) *Wisepack;* **SOUL LEGENDS** | | `-`
Jul 95. (4xcd-box) *Motown; (5304892)* **SOULSATION** | | `-`
Nov 95. (3xcd-box) *Motown;* **MAYBE TOMORROW / SKYWRITER / THE THIRD ALBUM** | | `-`

—— JERMAINE, JACKIE, LaTOYA and more successfully JANET, had own solo hits.

Mick JAGGER (see under ⇒ ROLLING STONES)

JAM

Formed: Woking, Surrey, England . . . late '73 by PAUL WELLER, BRUCE FOXTON, RICK BUCKLER and 4th member STEVE BROOKS – guitar. This quartet first gigged mid-74, progressing to the likes of London's Marquee, 101 Club & Red Cow in late '76, by which time BROOKS had departed. Peddling amphetamine charged retro R&B, the band rode in on the first wave of punk's brave new musical world. Incendiary live performances had generated a loyal following and considerable record company interest, the band signing with 'Polydor' early the following year via A&R man Chris Parry. In Spring '77, their debut, 'IN THE CITY', cracked the UK Top 40, an album of the same name following a month later. Image wise, the band were kitted out in unashamed allegiance to the mod masterplan of yore; sharp suits, parkas, scooters etc., another factor that set the band apart from the anti-fashion of punk. Something WELLER did share with his glue-sniffing peers was anger; yep, before WELLER the 'red-wedge' soul smoothie and WELLER the patron of 'Dad Rock' came WELLER the angry young man, so angry in fact, that he professed to voting conservative. Politics aside, 'IN THE CITY' was a cut above the average three chord punk thrash, bristling with adolescent fury yet possessed of an irresistible melodic verve. 'THIS IS THE MODERN WORLD' (1977) was a hastily recorded follow-up, and it showed. Only the pounding title track (the single backed with a cover of Arthur Conley's ~'SWEET SOUL MUSIC') really hit the target, the rest of the album pointlessly recycling WHO riffs ad nauseum. With 'ALL MOD CONS' (1978), however, The JAM were onto something big, WELLER's cutting social reportage and songwriting genius translating into such gems as 'DOWN IN THE TUBE-STATION AT MIDNIGHT', a cover of The Kinks' 'DAVID WATTS' indicating the heights he was aiming for. Come 'SETTING SONS' (1979), and with the bile-spewing 'ETON RIFLES', in particular, WELLER came pretty damn close to updating RAY DAVIES' class-conscious agenda for a harsh new age. The single gave the band their first Top 5 success and the album achieved a similar feat upon its release a month later. In February of the following year, the band went straight in at No.1 with 'GOING UNDERGROUND', a snarling critique of the establishment. The band followed this up with 'START!', a virtual remake (well, intro definitely) of George Harrison/Beatles' 'TAXMAN'; quite why there's never been a court case over the matter remains a mystery. Still, the single marked a move into more ambitious musical territory, WELLER penning his most accomplished tune to date in the lilting, understated ennui of 'THAT'S ENTERTAINMENT'. The album, 'SOUND AFFECTS' (1980), confirmed the shift away from powerchord aggression with the use of horns and more obviously black music-derived rhythms. By this point, THE JAM were one of, if not the, biggest band in Britain although, despite repeated attempts, the American market was apparently impossible for the band to crack. Then again, it's not hard to see that their defiantly British sound just didn't translate in the States, in much the same way as, more recently, BLUR's idiosyncratic Englishness has precluded US recognition. Back home though, the band were No.1 again in early 1982 with the heavily Motown-influenced 'TOWN CALLED MALICE', 'THE GIFT' album being released the following month. It was to be the band's swansong as WELLER, at the peak of the band's fame later that summer, announced he was to break the group up to explore his soul fixation with The STYLE COUNCIL. After a final kiss-off with 'THE BITTEREST PILL' and the brilliant 'BEAT SURRENDER', the band were no more. While WELLER went on to a undergo many musical rebirths, there was no such joy for FOXTON, who later joined aging punks STIFF LITTLE FINGERS. BUCKLER, meanwhile, forsook the evils of the music business for furniture restoration. Thankfully, with no reunion so far, and the possibility of one rather slim, the legend of The JAM remains intact. • Songwriters: WELLER penned except; BACK IN MY ARMS AGAIN (Holland-Dozier-Holland) / DAVID WATTS (Kinks) / MOVE ON UP (Curtis Mayfield). • Trivia: In Oct'81, WELLER started own record company 'Respond', and signed acts The QUESTIONS and TRACIE.

Album rating: IN THE CITY (*6) / THIS IS THE MODERN WORLD (*5) / ALL MOD CONS (*8) / SETTING SONS (*8) / SOUND EFFECTS (*8) / THE GIFT (*6) / DIG THE NEW BREED live collection (*6) / SNAP! compilation (*10) / GREATEST HITS compilation (*8) / DIRECTION REACTION CREATION boxed compilation (*9) / THE VERY BEST OF THE JAM compilation (*8)

PAUL WELLER (b. JOHN WELLER, 25 May'58) – vocals, guitar / **BRUCE FOXTON** (b. 1 Sep'55) – bass, vocals / **RICK BUCKLER** (b. PAUL RICHARD BUCKLER, 6 Dec'55) – drums

		Polydor	Polydor
Apr 77.	(7") (2058 866) **IN THE CITY. / TAKIN' MY LOVE** (re-iss. Apr80) – hit No.40 (re-iss. Jan83) – hit No.47	40	
May 77.	(lp) (2383 447) <6110> **IN THE CITY** – Art school I've changed my address / Slow down / I got by in time / Away from the numbers / Batman / In the city / Sounds from the street / Non stop dancing / Time for truth / Takin' my love / Bricks and mortar. (re-iss. Aug83 lp/c; SPE LP/MC 27) (re-iss. Jul90 cd/c/lp; 817124-2/-4/-1) (cd re-iss. Jul97; 537417-2)	20	
Jul 77.	(7") (2058 903) **ALL AROUND THE WORLD. / CARNABY STREET** (re-iss. Apr80) – hit No.43 (re-iss. Jan83) – hit No.38	13	-
Oct 77.	(7"m) (2058 945) **THE MODERN WORLD. / SWEET SOUL MUSIC (live) / BACK IN MY ARMS AGAIN (live) / BRICKS AND MORTAR (live)** (re-iss. Apr80) – hit No.52 (re-iss. Jan83) – hit No.51	36	-
Nov 77.	(lp) (2383 475) <6129> **THIS IS THE MODERN WORLD** – The modern world / London traffic / Standards / Life from the window / The combine / Don't tell them you're sane / In the street today / London girl / I need you / Here comes the weekend / Tonight at noon / In the midnight hour. (re-iss. Aug83 lp/c; SPE LP/MC 66) (re-iss. Jul90 cd/c/lp; 823281-2/-4/-1) (cd re-iss. Jul97; 537418-2)	22	
Feb 78.	(7") (14462) **I NEED YOU. / IN THE CITY**	-	
Mar 78.	(7"m) (2058 995) **NEWS OF THE WORLD. / AUNTIES AND UNCLES / INNOCENT MAN** (re-iss. Apr80) – hit No.53 (re-iss. Jan83) – hit No.39	27	-
Aug 78.	(7") (2059 054) **DAVID WATTS. / 'A' BOMB IN WARDOUR STREET** (re-iss. Apr80) – hit No.54 (re-iss. Jan83) – hit No.50	25	-
Oct 78.	(7"m) (POSP 8) **DOWN IN THE TUBE STATION AT MIDNIGHT. / SO BAD ABOUT US / THE NIGHT** (re-iss. Apr80) (re-iss. Jan83) – hit No.30	15	-
Nov 78.	(lp/c) (POLD/+C 5008) <6218> **ALL MOD CONS** – All mod cons / To be someone (didn't we have a nice time) / Mr. Clean / David Watts / English rose / In the crowd / Billy Hunt / It's too bad / Fly 3.18 / The place I love / 'A' bomb in Wardour Street / Down in the tube station at midnight. (cd-iss. 1989; 823282-2) (cd re-iss. Jul97; 537419-2)	6	
Mar 79.	(7") (POSP 34) <14553> **STRANGE TOWN. / THE BUTTERFLY COLLECTOR** (re-iss. Apr80) – hit No.44 (re-iss. Jan83) – hit No.42	15	
Jun 79.	(7") <14566> **DOWN IN THE TUBE STATION AT MIDNIGHT. / MR. CLEAN**	-	
Aug 79.	(7") (POSP 69) **WHEN YOU'RE YOUNG. / SMITHERS-JONES** (re-iss. Jan83) – hit No.53	17	-
Oct 79.	(7") (POSP 83) **THE ETON RIFLES. / SEE-SAW** (re-iss. Jan83) – hit No.54	3	-
Nov 79.	(lp/c) (POLD/+C 5028) <6249> **SETTING SONS** – Girl on the phone / Thick as thieves / Private hell / Little boy soldiers / Waste land / Burning sky / Smithers-Jones / Saturday's kids / The Eton rifles / Heat wave. (cd-iss. May88; 831314-2) (cd re-iss. Jul97; 537420-2)	4	
Dec 79.	(7") <2051> **THE ETON RIFLES. / SMITHERS-JONES**	-	-
Feb 80.	(7") (POSP 113) **GOING UNDERGROUND. / DREAMS OF CHILDREN** (d7"+=) (POSPJ 113 – 2616 024) – The modern world (live) / Away from the numbers (live) / Down in the tube station at midnight (live). (re-iss. Jan83) – hit No.21	1	-

		Polydor	Polydor
Apr 80.	(7") <2074> **SATURDAY'S KIDS. / (LOVE IS LIKE A) HEATWAVE**	-	
Aug 80.	(7") (2059 266) **START! / LIZA RADLEY** (re-iss. Jan83) – hit No.60	1	-
Sep 80.	(7") <2155> **START! / WHEN YOU'RE YOUNG**	-	
Nov 80.	(lp/c) (POLD/+C 5035) <6315> **SOUND AFFECTS** – Pretty green / Monday / But I'm different now / Set the house ablaze / Start! / That's entertainment / Dreamtime / Man in the cornershop / Music for the last couple / Boy about town / Scrape away. (re-iss. Apr90 cd/c/lp; 823284-2/-4/-1) (cd re-iss. Jul97; 537421-2)	2	72
Jan 81.	(7") (0030 364) **THAT'S ENTERTAINMENT. / DOWN IN THE TUBE STATION AT MIDNIGHT (live)** (above 45, was actually imported into Britain by German 'Metrognome') (re-iss. Jan83 on 'Polydor'; 2059 482) – hit No.60	21	-
May 81.	(7") (POSP 257) **FUNERAL PYRE. / DISGUISES** (re-iss. Jan83)	4	
Oct 81.	(7") (POSP 350) **ABSOLUTE BEGINNERS. / TALES FROM THE RIVERBANK** (re-iss. Jan83)	4	
Dec 81.	(m-lp) <503> **THE JAM** – Absolute beginners / Funeral pyre / Liza Radley / Tales from the riverbank / Disguises.	-	
Feb 82.	(7"/12") (POSP/+X 400) **TOWN CALLED MALICE. / PRECIOUS** (re-iss. Jan83) – hit No.73	1	
Mar 82.	(lp/c) (POLD/+C 5055) <6349> **THE GIFT** – Happy together / Ghosts / Precious / Just who is the 5 o'clock hero? / Trans-global express / Running on the spot / Circus / The planner's dream goes wrong / Carnation / Town called Malice / The gift. (re-iss. Apr90 cd/c/lp; 823285-2/-4/-1) (cd re-iss. Jul97; 537422-2)	1	82
Jun 82.	(7") (2059 504) **JUST WHO IS THE 5 O'CLOCK HERO?. / THE GREAT DEPRESSION** (12"+=) (2141 558) – War.	6	
Sep 82.	(7") (POSP 505) **THE BITTEREST PILL (I EVER HAD TO SWALLOW). / PITY POOR ALFIE / FEVER – PITY POOR ALFIE** <US-iss.Nov82 as 12"m-lp> – Great depression.	2	
Nov 82.	(7") (POSP 540) **BEAT SURRENDER. / SHOPPING** (d7"+=)<m-lp> (POSPJ 540 – JAM 1) <810751> – Move on up / War / Stoned out of my mind.	1	Mar83
Dec 82.	(lp/c) (POLD/+C 5075) <6365> **DIG THE NEW BREED (live 77-82)** – In the city / All mod cons / To be someone / It's too bad / Start! / Big bird / Set the house ablaze / Ghosts / Standards / In the crowd / Going underground / Dreams of children / That's entertainment / Private hell. (re-iss. Jun87 lp/c; SPE LP/MC 107) (re-iss. Jun90 cd/c/lp; 810041-2/-4/-1) (cd re-iss. Sep95)	2	

—— They split late '82. WELLER formed The STYLE COUNCIL, before making it huge as a solo star. FOXTON, meanwhile, went solo, delivering a solitary solo album, 'TOUCH SENSITIVE' (May 1984) for 'Arista'; the Top 75 breaker contained his only Top 30 hit, 'FREAK', released a year earlier. BUCKLER formed TIME UK who had one minor hit, 'THE CABARET' (Sep'83), before he and FOXTON teamed up with TIME UK singer, JIMMY EDWARDS, to become mid-late 80's outfit, SHARP.

– compilations, etc. –

on 'Polydor' unless mentioned otherwise

Sep 80.	(d-lp) (2683 074) **IN THE CITY / THIS IS THE MODERN WORLD** (re-iss. Jan91 cd/c; 847730-2/-4)		
Jan 83.	(d-c) (TWOMC 1) **SOUND AFFECTS / THE GIFT**		
Feb 83.	(d-c) (1574 098) **ALL MOD CONS / SETTING SONS**		
Oct 83.	(d-lp/d-c) (SNAP/+C 1) **SNAP!** – In the city / Away from the numbers / All around the world / The modern world / News of the world / Billy Hunt / English Rose / Mr. Clean / David Watts / 'A' bomb in Wardour Street / Down in the tube station at midnight / Strange town / The butterfly collector / When you're young / Smithers-Jones / Thick as thieves / The Eton rifles / Going underground / Dreams of children / That's entertainment / Start! / Man in the cornershop / Funeral pyre / Absolute beginners / Tales from the riverbank / Town called Malice / Precious / The bitterest pill (I ever had to swallow) / Beat surrender. (d-lp.with free 7"ep) **LIVE AT WEMBLEY (live)** – The great depression / But I'm different now / Move on up / Get yourself together. (cd-iss. Sep84 as 'COMPACT SNAP'; 821712-2) – omits 4 tracks. (re-iss. Jun90 cd/c/lp; 815537-2/-4/-1)	2	-
Mar 90.	(7") Old Gold; (OG 9894) **TOWN CALLED MALICE. / ABSOLUTE BEGINNERS**		-
Mar 90.	(7") Old Gold; (OG 9895) **BEAT SURRENDER. / BITTEREST PILL (I EVER HAD TO SWALLOW)**		-
Mar 90.	(7") Old Gold; (OG 9896) **THE ETON RIFLES. / DOWN IN THE TUBE STATION AT MIDNIGHT**		-
Mar 90.	(7") Old Gold; (OG 9897) **GOING UNDERGROUND. / START!**		-
Sep 90.	(12"ep/cd-ep) Strange Fruit; (SFPS/+CD 080) **THE PEEL SESSIONS** (26.4.77) – In the city / Art school / I've changed my address / The modern world. (cd-ep re-iss. Sep96; same)		
Jun 91.	(7"/c-s) (PO/+CS 155) **THAT'S ENTERTAINMENT. / DOWN IN THE TUBE-STATION AT MIDNIGHT (live)** (12"+=/cd-s+=) (PZ/+CD 155) – Town called Malice (live).	57	
Jul 91.	(cd/c/lp) (849554-2/-4/-1) **GREATEST HITS**	2	
Mar 92.	(7"/c-s) (PO/+CS 199) **THE DREAMS OF CHILDREN. / AWAY FROM THE NUMBERS (live)** (12"+=/cd-s+=) (PZ/+CD 199) – This is the modern world (live).		-
Apr 92.	(cd/c/lp) (513177-2/-4/-1) **EXTRAS: A COLLECTION OF RARITIES**		
Oct 92.	(cd/c) Pickwick; (PWK S/MC 4129P) **WASTELAND**		
Oct 93.	(cd/c/d-lp) (519667-2/-4/-1) **LIVE JAM (live)** – The modern world / Billy Hunt / Thick as thieves / Burning sky / Mr. Clean / Smithers-Jones / Little boy soldiers / The Eton Rifles / Away from the numbers / Down in the tube station at midnight / Strange town / When you're young / 'A' Bomb	28	

In Wardour Street / Pretty green / Boy about town / Man in the cornershop / David Watts / Funeral pyre / Move on up / Carnation / The butterfly collector / Precious / Town called Malice / Heatwave.

Jul 96.	(d-cd/d-c/d-lp) (531493-2/-4/-1) **THE JAM COLLECTION**	58	-
May 97.	(5xcd-box) (537143-2) **DIRECTION REACTION CREATION**	8	-
Sep 97.	(7"/c-s) (571598-7/-4) **THE BITTEREST PILL (I EVER HAD TO SWALLOW). / THE BUTTERFLY COLLECTOR**	30	-
	(cd-s+=) (571598-2) – That's entertainment / ('A'version).		
Oct 97.	(cd/c) (537423-2/-4) **THE VERY BEST OF THE JAM** (all the singles 1977-1982)	9	-

JAMES

Formed: Manchester, England ... 1982 by JIM GLENNIE, TIM BOOTH, LARRY GOTT and GAVAN WHELAN. In 1983 they signed to Tony Wilson's 'Factory' label, issuing a debut 3-track, the 'JIMONE EP'. Their folksy idiosyncrasy and wilful weirdness was beloved of the music press almost from the off and their cult standing increased considerably after their 2nd classic 45, 'HYMN FROM A VILLAGE', topped the indie chart early in '85. They were soon snapped up by Seymour Stein's 'Sire', legendary underground mover and shaker Lenny Kaye producing the debut album, 'STUTTER'. BOOTH's overtly accented vocals were the primary focus of the band's often erratic and unorthodox, cerebral, improvisation-driven indie rock/folk and this bizarre combination made the band a compelling live act. However, financial difficulties led to the band moving label to WEA subsidiary 'Blanco Y Negro', where they released 'STRIP MINE' (1988). In 1990, after a change of personnel and a spell on 'Rough Trade', JAMES had their first Top 40 hit on 'Fontana' with 'HOW WAS IT FOR YOU?'. It was soon followed by a Top 20 album, 'GOLD MOTHER', that when re-promoted early 1991 with No.2 hit, the outrageously anthemic and subsequently tediously annoying 'SIT DOWN', also hit No.2. Suddenly the band were riding on the frayed, flared coat-tails of the baggy scene alongside fellow Manchester bands like The HAPPY MONDAYS and The STONE ROSES. Their obstinately obscure sound of old had now been bolstered by chant-along choruses of almost terracing proportions and the ubiquitous JAMES t-shirt was de rigeur for fresher students up and down the country. The band were now playing to stadium-sized audiences and they made their follow-up, 'SEVEN' (1992), to match, all big production and bombast that went down like a lead balloon with critics. With 'LAID' (1993), the band roped in BRIAN ENO, and went for a more opaque, stripped-down sound that recalled their experimental, earlier work. Lyrically, the album was as complex and as vivid as ever while the gorgeous 'SOMETIMES' gave the band their first Top 20 hit since early '92. The ENO sessions also provided the material for the 'WAH WAH' (1994) album, a collection of ambient improvisations with the aging electronic wizard. Of late, TIM BOOTH teamed up with ANGELO BADALAMENTI (he of 'Twin Peaks' fame) and ex-SUEDE guitarist, BERNARD BUTLER to release one-off set, 'BOOTH AND THE BAD ANGEL' (1996). In 1997, JAMES were again in the UK Top 10, the single 'SHE'S A STAR' & its parent album, 'WHIPLASH', both achieving the feat. Of late, a stop-gap 'best of' package was treated well by the fans (who made it UK No.1) but 'MILLIONAIRES' (1999) fell short of requirements. Although the near chart-topping record featured hit singles, 'I KNOW WHAT I'M HERE FOR' and 'JUST LIKE FRED ASTAIRE', it had none of the zip and lyrical sparkle of old. The year 2000 might just sort a few bands out (one way or another). • **Songwriters:** TIM BOOTH penned, except SUNDAY MORNING (Velvet Underground) / CHINA GIRL (Iggy Pop & David Bowie).

Album rating: STUTTER (*6) / STRIP MINE (*6) / ONE MAN CLAPPING (*6) / GOLD MOTHER (*8) / SEVEN (*8) / LAID (*7) / WAH WAH (*6) / WHIPLASH (*6) / THE BEST OF JAMES compilation (*8) / MILLIONAIRES (*5) / Booth & The Bad Angel: BOOTH & THE BAD ANGEL (*5)

TIM BOOTH (b. 4 Feb'60) – vocals / **LARRY GOTT** (b. JAMES GOTT) – guitar / **JIM GLENNIE** (b.10 Oct'63) – bass / **GAVAN WHELAN** – drums

		Factory	not iss.
Sep 83.	(7") (FAC 78) **JIMONE**		-
	– What's the world / Fire so close / Folklore.		
Feb 85.	(7") (FAC 119) **JAMES II**		-
	– Hymn from a village / If things were perfect.		
Jun 85.	(12"ep) (FAC 138) **VILLAGE FIRE**		-
	– What's the world / Fire so close / Folklore / Hymn from a village / If things were perfect.		

		Sire	Warners
Feb 86.	(7") (JIM 3) **CHAIN MAIL. / HUP STRINGS**		-
	(12"+=) (JIM 3T) **SIT DOWN EP** – Uprising.		
Jul 86.	(7") (JIM 4) **SO MANY WAYS. / WITHDRAWN**		-
	(12"+=) (JIM 4T) – Just hipper.		
Jul 86.	(lp/c) (JIM LP/C 1) **STUTTER**	68	-
	– Skullduggery / Scarecrow / So many ways / Just hip / Johnny Yen / Summer song / Really hard / Billy's shirts / Why so close / Withdrawn / Black hole. (cd-iss. Nov91; 7599 25437-2)		

		Blanco Y Negro	Sire
Sep 87.	(7") (NEG 26) **YAHO. / MOSQUITO**		-
	(12"+=) (NEG 26T) – Left out of her will / New nature.		
Mar 88.	(7") (NEG 31) **WHAT FOR. / ISLAND SWING**		-
	(c-s+=/12"+=) (NEG 31 C/T) – Not there.		
Sep 88.	(lp/c)(cd) (JIM LP/C 2)(925657-2) **STRIP MINE**	90	
	– What for / Charlie Dance / Fairground / Are you ready / Yaho / Medieval / Not there / Riders / Vulture / Strip mining / Refrain. (re-iss. Jul91; same) (cd re-iss. Feb95; 925657-2)		

		Rough Trade	not iss.
Mar 89.	(lp/c/cd) (ONEMAN 001/+C/CD) **ONE MAN CLAPPING (live in Bath)**		-
	– Chain mail / Sandman (hup strings) / Whoops / Riders / Why so close / Leaking / Johnny Yen / Scarecrow / Are you ready / Really hard / Burned / Stutter. (cd+=) – Yaho.		

—— **DAVE BAIGNTON-POWER** – drums repl. WHELAN / added **SAUL DAVIS** – violin, percussion, guitar / **MARK HUNTER** – keyboards

Jun 89.	(7") (RT 225) **SIT DOWN. / SKY IS FALLING**		-
	(12"+=/3"cd-s+=) (RTT 225/+CD) – Goin' away / Sound investment.		

—— added **ANDY DIAGRAM** – trumpet (ex-PALE FOUNTAINS, ex-DIAGRAM BROS)

Nov 89.	(7") (RT 245) **COME HOME. / PROMISED LAND**		-
	(12"+=/cd-s+=) (RTT 245/+CD) – ('A'extended / Slow right down (demo).		

		Fontana	Mercury
May 90.	(7") (JIM 5) **HOW WAS IT FOR YOU? / WHOOPS (live)**	32	-
	(12") (JIM 5-12) – ('A'side) / Hymn from a village (live) / Lazy.		
	(cd-s) (JIMCD 5) – ('A'side) / Hymn from a village (live) / Undertaker.		
	(12") (JIMM 5-12) – ('A'side) / ('A'different mix) / Lazy / Undertaker.		
Jun 90.	(cd/c/lp) (<846189-2/-4/-1>) **GOLD MOTHER**	16	Aug90
	– Come home / Government walls / God only knows / You can tell how much suffering (on a face that's always smiling) / How was it for you? / Crescendo / Hang on / Walking the ghost / Gold mother / Top of the world. (re-iss. Apr91 cd/c/lp; 848595-2/-4/-1); hit No.2) (cd+=) – Sit down / Lose control.		
Jul 90.	(7"/c-s) (JIM/+C 6) **COME HOME (Flood mix). / DREAMING UP TOMORROW**	32	-
	(12") (JIM 6-12) – ('A'extended) / Stutter (live) / Fire away.		
	(cd-s) (JIMCD 6) – ('A'side) / ('A'extended) / Gold mother (remix) / Fire away.		
	(12") (JIMM 6-12) – ('A'live) / Gold mother (Warp remix) / ('A'-Andy Weatherall Boys own remix).		
Nov 90.	(7"/c-s) (JIM/+C 7) **LOSE CONTROL. / SUNDAY MORNING**	38	-
	(ext.12"+=/ext.cd-s+=) (JIM 7-12/CD7) – Out to get you.		
Mar 91.	(7"/c-s) (JIM/+C 8) **SIT DOWN. / ('A'live)**	2	-
	(12"+=/cd-s+=) (JIM 8-12/CD8) – Tonight.		
Nov 91.	(7"/c-s) (JIM/+C 9) **SOUND. / ALL MY SONS**	9	-
	(12"+=/cd-s+=) (JIM 9-12/CD9) – ('A'extended) / Come home (Youth mix).		
Jan 92.	(7"/c-s) (JIM/+C 10) **BORN OF FRUSTRATION. / BE MY PRAYER**	13	
	(12"+=/cd-s+=) (JIM 10-12/CD10) – Sound (mix).		
Feb 92.	(cd/c/lp) (<510932-2/-4/-1>) **SEVEN**	2	Mar92
	– Born of frustration / Ring the bells / Sound / Bring a gun / Mother / Don't wait that long / Live a life of love / Heavens / Protect me / Seven. (cd+=/c+=) – Next lover. (re-iss. Aug98; same)		
Mar 92.	(7"/c-s) (JIM/+C 11) **RING THE BELLS. / FIGHT**	37	
	(12"+=/cd-s+=) (JIM 11-12/CD11) – The skunk weed skank / Come home (live dub version).		
	(12"++=) (11) – Once a friend.		
Jul 92.	(7"ep/c-ep/cd-ep) (JIM/+C/CD 12) **SEVEN (remix) / GOALIES BALL. / WILLIAM BURROUGHS / STILL ALIVE**	46	
Sep 93.	(7"/c-s) (JIM/+C 13) **SOMETIMES. / AMERICA**	18	
	(12"+=/cd-s+=) (JIM 13-12/CD13) – Building a charge.		
Sep 93.	(cd/c/lp) (<514943-2/-4/-1>) **LAID**	3	72 Oct93
	– Out to get you / Sometimes (Lester Piggott) / Dream thru / One of the three / Say something / Five-o / P.S. / Everybody knows / Knuckle too far / Low, low / Laid / Lullaby / Skindiving. (re-iss. Aug98; same)		
Nov 93.	(7"/c-s) (JIM/+C 14) <858217> **LAID. / WAH WAH KITS**	25	61 Jan94
	(cd-s+=) (JIMCD 14) – The lake / Seconds away.		
	(cd-s) (14) – ('A'live) / Five-O / Say something / Sometimes.		
Mar 94.	(c-s) (JIMMC 15) **JAM J / SAY SOMETHING**	24	
	(12"+=)(cd-s+=) (JIMX 15)(JIMCD 15) – Assassin / ('B'-version).		
	(cd-s) (JIMCD 15) – JAM J – James vs The Sabres Of Paradise (i) Arena dub (ii) Amphetamine pulsate / JAM J – James vs The Sabres Of Paradise (i) Sabresonic tremelo dub (ii) Spaghetti steamhammer.		
Sep 94.	(cd/c/d-lp;ltd) (<314 526 408-2/-4/-1>) **WAH WAH** (w / BRIAN ENO)	11	Oct94
	– Hammer strings / Pressure's on / Jam J / Frequency dip / Lay the law down / Burn the cat / Maria / Low clouds (1) / Building a fire / Gospel oak / DVV / Say say something / Rhythmic dreams / Dead man / Rain whistling / Low clouds (2) / Bottom of the well / Honest Joe / Arabic agony / Tomorrow / Laughter / Sayonara.		

—— **ADRIAN OXAAL** – repl. DIAGRAM

Feb 97.	(cd-s) (JIMED 16) **SHE'S A STAR / STUTTER (live) / JOHNNY YEN (live)**	9	-
	(cd-s) (JIMDD 16) – ('A'side) / Chunney chops / Fishknives / Van Gogh's dog.		
	(cd-s) (JIMCD 16) – ('A'-Dave Angel mix) / ('A'-Biosphere mix) / Come home (Weatherall mix).		
Mar 97.	(cd/c/lp) (<534354-2/-4/-1>) **WHIPLASH**	9	
	– Tomorrow / Lost a friend / Waltzing along / She's a star / Greenpeace / Go to the bank / Play dead / Avalanche / Homeboy / Watering hole / Blue pastures.		
Apr 97.	(cd-ep) (JIMCD 17) **TOMORROW / GONE TOO FAR / HONEST PLEASURE / ALL ONE TO ME**	12	-
	(cd-s) (JIMDD 17) – ('A'side) / Lost a friend (session) / Come home (session) / Greenpeace (session).		
	(cd-s) (JIMED 17) – ('A'mixes; Fila Brazilia / Archive / Dirty Beatnik).		
Jun 97.	(cd-s) (JIMCD 18) **WALTZING ALONG / YOUR STORY / WHERE YOU GONNA RUN? / LONG TO BE RIGHT**	23	-
	(cd-s) (JIMED 18) – Homeboy (live) / How was it for you? (live) / Greenpeace (live).		
	(cd-s) (JIMDD 18) – ('A'remixes by; Disco Socks & Flytronix)		
Mar 98.	(cd-ep) (JIMCD 19) **DESTINY CALLING / GOALIE'S BALL / ASSASSIN / THE LAKE**	17	-
	(cd-ep) (JIMDD 19) – ('A'side) / Jam J (live) / Honest Joe (live) / Sound (live).		
	(cd-s) (JIMED 19) – ('A'side) / She's a star (CD-Rom video).		
Mar 98.	(cd/c) (<536898-2/-4>) **THE BEST OF** (compilation)	1	
	– Come home / Sit down / She's a star / Laid / Waltzing along / Say something / Tomorrow / Born of frustration / Destiny calling / Out to get you / Runaground / Lose control / How was it for you? / Seven / Sound / Ring the bells / Sometimes / Hymn from a village. (also d-cd-iss. ; 558173-2)		

May 98. (cd-ep) *(JIMCD 20)* **RUNAGROUND / CRESCENDO / HANG ON / BE MY POWER** `29` –
(cd-ep) *(JIMDD 20)* – ('A'side) / Say something / Laid / Lose control.
(cd-ep) *(JIMED 20)* – ('A'side) / Egoiste / Lost a friend.

Nov 98. (c-s/cd-s) *(JIM MC/CD 21)* **SIT DOWN (1998 remix) / ('A'-Apollo 440 remix)** `7` –
(cd-s) *(JIMDD 21)* – China girl (radio 1 Iggy Pop tribute).

Jul 99. (c-s) *(JIMC 22)* **I KNOW WHAT I'M HERE FOR / ALL GOOD BOYS** `22`
(cd-s+=) *(JIMCD 22)* – Imagine ourselves.
(cd-s) *(JIMDD 22)* – ('A'side) / Downstairs / Stolen horses.

Oct 99. (c-s) *(JIMC 23)* **JUST LIKE FRED ASTAIRE / I DEFEAT** `17`
(cd-s+=) *(JIMCD 23)* – Long to see.
(cd-s) *(JIMDD 23)* – ('A'side) / Mary / Goal goal goal.

Oct 99. (cd/c) *(546386-2/-4)* **MILLIONAIRES** `2`
– Crash / Just like Fred Astaire / I know what I'm here for / Shooting my mouth off / We're going to miss you / Strangers / Hello / Afro lover / Surprise / Dumb jam / Someone's got it in for me / Vervaceous. *(also d-cd+=; 546789-2)* – (live):- I know what I'm here for / Crash / Destiny calling / Someone's got it in for me / Just like Fred Astaire / I know what I'm here for (video) / Just like Fred Astaire (video).

Dec 99. (c-s) *(JIMMC 24)* **WE'RE GOING TO MISS YOU / WISDOM OF THE THROAT** `48`
(cd-s+=) *(JIMCD 24)* – Top of the world (live).
(cd-s) *(JIMDD 24)* – ('A'side) / Pocketful of lemons ('A'-Eno's version).

BOOTH AND THE BAD ANGEL

—— **TIM BOOTH / ANGELO BADALAMENTI / + BERNARD BUTLER** (ex-Suede)

		Fontana	Mercury
Jun 96.	(c-s) *(BBMC 1)* **I BELIEVE (edit) / I BELIEVE (long version)**	`25`	–
	(cd-s+=) *(BBCD 1)* – When you smiled.		
	(cd-s+=) *(BBDD 1)* – Melting away.		
Jul 96.	(cd/c) *(<526 852-2/-4>)* **BOOTH AND THE BAD ANGEL**	`35`	

– I believe / Dance of the bad angels / Hit parade / Fall in love with me / Old ways / Life gets better / Heart / Rising / Butterfly's dream / Stranger / Hands in the rain. (below lifted from the film 'Martha Meet Franky, Daniel & Laurence'.)

Jun 98. (c-s) *(MERMC 503)* **FALL IN LOVE WITH ME (live) / I BELIEVE (live)** `57` –
(cd-s+=) *(MERCD 503)* – Hit parade (live).
(cd-s) *(MERDD 503)* – ('A'side) / Butterfly's dream (live) ('A'live).

Elmore JAMES

Born: 27 Jan'1918, Richland, Mississippi, USA. Although his recording career spanned only ten years, he will always be remembered for his first hit, 'DUST MY BROOM', a bombshell of a song based on a composition by ROBERT JOHNSON, (whom he had met in 1937 and taught him to play bottleneck), featuring his trademark powerful slide guitar. After a stint in the US Navy (between 1943 and 1945), his formative years were spent in the company of RICE MILLER (SONNY BOY WILLIAMSON II), who was a regular on Radio KFFA's 'King Biscuit Time' show (JAMES played on the programme in 1947). They travelled together for several years, JAMES securing his first contract in 1951 with LILLIAN McMURRAY's 'Trumpet' label through MILLER'S contacts, initially appearing on disc as a backing musician on cuts by WILLIAMSON. After these sessions, WILLIAMSON convinced ELMO (as he was credited then) to record the aforementioned 'DUST MY BROOM' (with WILLIAMSON on harmonica), the record subsequently going on to hit the Top 10 in the R&B chart in 1952. JAMES then moved to Chicago where he formed The BROOMDUSTERS and signed to Joe Bihari's 'Modern' label with further recordings (variations on his initial hit) 'I BELIEVE' and 'DUST MY BLUES' building on that success. Other compositions were to prove influential on future artists with 'BLEEDING HEART', 'SHAKE YOUR MONEYMAKER' and 'DONE SOMEBODY WRONG' being taken up by FLEETWOOD MAC, JIMI HENDRIX and DUANE ALLMAN respectively. His bottleneck style of guitar resurfaced in numerous British R&B bands and in particular, JEREMY SPENCER of FLEETWOOD MAC and BRIAN JONES (early stage name ELMO LEWIS in respect of JAMES) of the ROLLING STONES paid homage to him although his greatest recognition came when B.B. KING admitted to adopting areas of JAMES' style. After heavy drinking affected his recording schedules he was dropped by his record company in 1956 and was blacklisted by the American Foundation of Musicians for using non-union backing players. He went into semi-retirement after a mild heart attack which caused him to reflect on his life, returning to Chicago in 1957 to record with Mel London's 'Mel' records (with backing from WAYNE BENNETT, EDDIE TAYLOR, WILLIE DIXON and FRED BELEW). By the end of the 50's, JAMES was tempted to return to club gigs, subsequently spotted by 'Fire' Records boss, Bobby Robinson, who duly signed him and released the single, 'THE SKY IS CRYING' (which became another R&B success) in 1960. JOHN MAYALL's 'MR. JAMES' was a tribute to the man who sadly didn't live to bask in the acclaim; on the 23rd of May 1963, on the verge of a comeback, he suffered a third, and this time fatal, heart attack after a concert at the Copa Cabana in Chicago. ELMORE died at the home of his cousin, HOMESICK JAMES, who along with J.B. HUTTO, took on his mantle of 'King of the slide guitar'. JAMES only released one album during his lifetime, the 1961 offering, 'BLUES AFTER HOURS' although many more were released after his death, including 'THE IMMORTAL ELMORE JAMES: KING OF THE BOTTLENECK BLUES' which is crammed full of JAMES's best with the wonderful, 'IT HURTS ME TOO' along with his own compositions 'DUST MY BROOM', 'THE SKY IS CRYING', 'SHAKE YOUR MONEYMAKER', 'DONE SOMEBODY

WRONG', 'LOOK ON YONDER WALL', 'CAN'T STOP LOVING' and 'BLEEDING HEART'.

Best CD compilation: ROLLIN' AND TUMBLIN': THE BEST OF . . . (*8)

ELMORE JAMES – vocals, acoustic guitar / with **JOHNNY JONES** – piano / **J.T. BROWN** – tenor sax / **ODIE PAYNE** – drums / **RANSOM KNOWLING** – bass

			not iss.	Trumpet
1952.	(78; as ELMO JAMES) *<146>* **DUST MY BROOM.** / Bobo Thomas: **CATFISH BLUES** *<re-iss. 1954 on 'Ace'; 508>*		–	☐
			not iss.	Meteor
1953.	(78) *<5000>* **I BELIEVE.** / **I HELD MY BABY LAST NIGHT**		–	☐
1953.	(78) *<5003>* **BABY WHAT'S WRONG.** / **SINFUL WOMAN**		–	☐
			not iss.	Checker
1953.	(78) *<777>* **COUNTRY BOOGIE.** / **SHE JUST WON'T DO RIGHT**		–	☐
			not iss.	Flair
1953.	(78) *<1011>* **HAWAIIAN BOOGIE.** / **EARLY IN THE MORNING**		–	☐
1953.	(78) *<1014>* **CAN'T STOP LOVIN'.** / **MAKE A LITTLE LOVE**		–	☐
1954.	(78) *<5016>* **SAXONY BOOGIE.** / **DUMB WOMAN BLUES** (above single on 'Meteor')		–	☐
1954.	(78) *<1022>* **PLEASE FIND MY BABY.** / **STRANGE KINDA BABY**		–	☐
1954.	(78) *<1031>* **MAKE MY DREAMS COME TRUE.** / **HAND IN HAND**		–	☐
1954.	(78) *<1039>* **SHO'NUFF I DO.** / **1839 BLUES**		–	☐

—— now with new line-up **WILLARD McDANIEL** – piano / **CHUCK HAMILTON** – bass / **JESSE SAILES** – drums / **MAXWELL DAVIES** – tenor sax / **JAMES PARR** – trumpet / **JEWEL GRANT** – baritone sax

1955.	(78) *<1048>* **DARK AND DREARY.** / **ROCK MY BABY RIGHT**		–	☐
1955.	(78) *<5024>* **SAX SYMPHONY BOOGIE.** / **FLAMING BLUES** (above single on 'Meteor')		–	☐
1955.	(78) *<1057>* **SUNNY LAND.** / **STANDING AT THE CROSSROADS** *<re-iss. 1966 on 'Kent'; 465>*		–	☐
1955.	(78) *<1062>* **LATE HOURS AT MIDNIGHT.** / **THE WAY YOU TREAT ME**		–	☐
1955.	(78) *<1069>* **HAPPY HOME.** / **NO LOVE IN MY HEART**		–	☐
1955.	(78) *<1074>* **DUST MY BLUES.** / **I WAS A FOOL**		–	☐
1955.	(78) *<1079>* **BLUES BEFORE SUNRISE.** / **GOODBYE BABY**		–	☐
			not iss.	Modern
1956.	(7") *<983>* **LONG TALL WOMAN.** / **WILD ABOUT YOU**		–	☐

—— returned to his original line-up + added **HOMESICK JAMES** – guitar

			not iss.	Mel-Chief
1957.	(7") *<7001>* **THE TWELVE-YEAR OLD BOY.** / **COMING HOME**		–	☐
1957.	(7") *<7004>* **IT HURTS ME TOO.** / **ELMORE'S CONTRIBUTION TO JAZZ**		–	☐
1957.	(7") *<7006>* **CRY FOR ME BABY.** / **TAKE ME WHERE YOU GO** (above also on 'S&M' and 'M-Pac')(re-iss. 1966 on 'USA')		–	☐
1958.	(7") *<7020>* **KNOCKING AT YOUR DOOR.** / **CALLING ALL BLUES**		–	☐
			not iss.	Fire
1959.	(7") *<1011>* **MAKE MY DREAMS COME TRUE.** / **BOBBY'S ROCK**		–	☐
1959.	(7"; as ELMORE JAMES and THE BROOM DUSTERS) *<331>* **DUST MY BLUES (I BELIEVE).** / **HAPPY HOME** *<above single issued on 'Kent'; 331> <re-iss. 1963 on 'Kent'; 394> (UK-iss.Oct64 on 'Sue' records; WI 335)*		–	☐
1960.	(7") *<1016>* **THE SKY IS CRYING.** / **HELD MY BABY LAST NIGHT**		–	☐
1960.	(7") *<1756>* **I CAN'T HOLD OUT.** / **THE SUN IS SHINING** (above single on 'Chess')		–	☐
1960.	(7") *<1024>* **ROLLIN' AND TUMBLIN'.** / **I'M WORRIED**		–	☐
1960.	(7") *<1031>* **DONE SOMEBODY WRONG.** / **FINE LITTLE MAMA**		–	☐
1961.	(lp) *<102>* **BLUES AFTER HOURS**		–	☐

– Dust my blues / Sunnyland / Mean and evil / Dark and dreamy / Standing at the crossroads / Happy home / No love in my heart for you / Blues before sunrise / I was a fool / Goodbye baby. *<re-iss. 1963 on 'Crown'; CLP 5168> <re-iss. 1964 as 'THE ORIGINAL FOLK BLUES' on 'Kent'; KLP 522> <re-iss. 1968 as 'ELMORE JAMES' on 'Kent'; KLP 5022> <re-iss. 1969 as 'BLUES IN MY HEART, RHYTHM IN MY SOUL' on 'United'; 7716> <& again on 'Custom'; 1054>*

—— retained **HOMESICK JAMES** + recruited **SPRUCE JOHNSON** – guitar

1961.	(7") *<1503>* **STRANGER BLUES.** / **ANNA LEE**		–	☐
1961.	(7") *<504>* **LOOK ON YONDER WALL.** / **SHAKE YOUR MONEYMAKER** *<re-iss. 1965 on 'Enjoy'; 2022>*		–	☐

—— His 1962 line-up were **JOHNNY ACEY** – piano / **RIFF RUFFIN** – guitar / **DANNY MOORE** – trumpet / **WILLIAMS** – drums

1963.	(7") *<2020>* **PICKIN' THE BLUES.** / **IT HURTS ME TOO**		–	☐

—— ELMORE died of a heart attack on the 23rd of May '63

– posthumous releases –

1965.	(7") Enjoy; *<2020>* **MEAN MISTREATING MAMA (version).** / **BLEEDING**		–	☐
1965.	(7") Enjoy; *<2027>* **EVERYDAY I HAVE BLUES.** / **DUST MY BROOM**		–	☐
Jul 65.	(7") Sue; (WI 335) / Enjoy; *<2015>* **IT HURTS ME TOO.** / **(MY) BLEEDING HEART**		☐	☐ 1964

Sep 65. (7") *Sue; (WI 392)* **CALLING THE BLUES. / KNOCKING AT YOUR DOOR**
(above 'A'side actually by 'JUNIOR WELLS & EARL HOOKER')

1966. (lp) *Sue; (ILP 918)* **THE BEST OF ELMORE JAMES**
– Dust my blues / Fine little mama / The sky is crying / Shake your moneymaker / Anna Lee / I'm worried / Stranger blues / Rollin' and tumblin' / Look on yonder wall / Happy home / Bobby's rock / Held my baby last night / Done somebody wrong / Make my dreams come true. *(re-iss. 1981 on 'Ace'; CH 31)*

Apr 66. (7") *Sue; (WIP 4007)* **I NEED YOU. / MEAN MISTREATING MAMA**

1967. (lp) *Sue; (ILP 927)* **ELMORE JAMES MEMORIAL ALBUM**
– Standing at the crossroads / The twelve year old boy / One way out / It hurts me too (part 1) / Elmore's contribution to jazz / Take me where you go / I can't stop lovin' you / It hurts me too (part 2) / Dust my broom / Knocking at your door / Coming home / Pickin' the blues / Bleeding heart / Cry for me baby.

1965. (7") *Jewel; <764>* **DUST MY BROOM. / ('b' by Arthur Crudup)**

1966. (7"; as ELMER JAMES) *Jewel; <783>* **MAKE A LITTLE LOVE. / (b-side by Bobo Thomas)**

1965. (lp) *Kent; <KLP 9001>* **ANTHOLOGY OF THE BLUES: THE LEGEND OF ELMORE JAMES**
<re-iss. 1970 on 'United'; 7778> (UK-iss.1970 on 'United Artists'; UAS 29109)

1966. (7") *Kent; <465>* **SUNNYLAND. / GOODBYE BABY**

1966. (lp) *Kent; <KLP 9010>* **ANTHOLOGY OF THE BLUES: THE RESURRECTION OF ELMORE JAMES**
<re-iss. 1970 on 'United'; 7787>

1967. (7") *Kent; <719>* **STRANGER BLUES (version). / ANNA LEE**

1968. (7") *Kent; <508>* **I BELIEVE. / 1839 BLUES**
1968. (lp) *Bell; <6037>* **ELMORE JAMES**
1968. (lp) *Bell; (MBLL/SBLL 104)* **SOMETHING INSIDE OF ME**
1968. (lp) *Ember; (EMB 3397)* **THE LATE FANTASTICALLY GREAT ELMORE JAMES**
Note; next 6 releases on 'Sphere Sound'

1969. (lp) *<7002>* **THE SKY IS CRYING**
1969. (7") *<702>* **MY BLEEDING HEART. / ONE WAY OUT**
1969. (7") *<708>* **I NEED YOU (BABY). / SHAKE YOUR MONEYMAKER**
1969. (7") *<712>* **DUST MY BROOM. / ROLLIN' AND TUMBLIN'**
1969. (7") *<713>* **SOMETHING INSIDE OF ME. / SHE DONE MOVED**
1969. (lp) *<70008>* **I NEED YOU**
1969. (7") *Fury; <2000>* **UP JUMPED ELMORE. / EVERYDAY I HAVE THE BLUES**

1969. (lp) *Chess; <1537>* **WHOSE MUDDY SHOES** (with some tracks by JOHN BRIM)
<re-iss. Apr82; CZMP 2007> (UK-iss.1989 on 'Chess' lp/c; GCH/+K7 8097)

1970. (lp) *Blue Horizon; (7-66204)* **TOUGH** (with 4 tracks by JOHN BRIM)
1970. (d-lp) *Blue Horizon; (7-66230)* **TO KNOW A MAN**
1971. (lp) *Trip; <8007>* **THE HISTORY OF ELMORE JAMES VOL.1**
1972. (lp) *Trip; <9511>* **THE HISTORY OF ELMORE JAMES VOL.2**
1972. (lp) *Upfront; <122>* **THE GREAT ELMORE JAMES**
1973. (lp) *Polydor; (2383 200)* **COTTON PATCH HOTFOOTS** (other side by WALTER HORTON)
1975. (d-lp) *D.J.M.; (DJLMD 8008)* **ALL THEM BLUES**
1977. (lp) *Pickwick; <5014>* **SCREAMIN' BLUES**
1978. (lp/c) *Charly; (CRB/TCCRB 1008)* **ONE WAY OUT**
Mar 81. (lp) *Charly; (CRB 1017)* **GOT TO MOVE**
Apr 81. (7"m) *Charly; (CTD 126)* **DONE SOMEBODY WRONG. / PICKIN' THE BLUES / DUST MY BROOM**
Apr 83. (lp,yellow-lp) *(CH 68)* **KING OF THE SLIDE GUITAR**
Nov 83. (lp) *Blue Moon; (BMLP 008)* **RED HOT BLUES**
Aug 84. (lp) *Ace; (CH 112)* **THE ORIGINAL METEOR AND FLAIR SIDES**
1984. (lp) *Charly; (CRB 1212)* **COME GO WITH ME**
(cd-iss. May89; CDCHARLY 180)
Jan 85. (lp/c) *Topline; (TOP/KTOP 120)* **DUST MY BROOM**
Feb 86. (lp/c) *Crown; (GEM/+C 003)* **KING OF THE BOTTLENECK BLUES**
Apr 86. (lp/c) *Showcase; (SHLP/SHTC 140)* **PICKIN' THE BLUES**
Nov 86. (lp/cd) *Ace; (CDCH/CH 192)* **LET'S CUT IT: THE VERY BEST OF ELMORE JAMES**
(re-iss. Nov93)
Dec 86. (cd) *Charly; (CDCHARLY 34)* **SHAKE YOUR MONEYMAKER**
May 88. (lp/c/cd) *Blues City; (265271-1/-4/-2)* **GREATEST HITS**
May 89. (cd/c) *Deja Vu; (DVRE CD/MC 24)* **THE ELMORE JAMES STORY**
Jul 90. (d-cd) *Instant; (CDINS 5030)* **DUST MY BROOM**
Apr 92. (lp/cd) *Muse; (MR/MCD 5087)* **STREET TALKIN'**
Dec 92. (4xcd-box) *Charly; (CDREDBOX 4)* **KING OF THE SLIDE GUITAR**
Oct 93. (3xcd-box) *Ace; (ABOXCD 4)* **THE CLASSIC EARLY RECORDINGS (1951-1956)**
Jun 95. (cd) *Ace; (CDCHD 563)* **THE BEST OF ELMORE JAMES – THE EARLY YEARS**

Wendy JAMES (see under ⇒ TRANSVISION VAMP)

JAMES GANG

Formed: Cleveland, Ohio, USA ... 1967 by JIM FOX, TOM KRISS and GLENN SCHWARTZ, taking the name from the legendary outlaw gang. When the latter left to join the group, PACIFIC GAS & ELECTRIC, he was replaced by guitarist JOE WALSH (future EAGLES strummer). Late in '69, the JAMES GANG debut set, 'YER' ALBUM', was complete, the record breaking into the

US Top 100. A wholesome serving of earthy mid-Western hard-rock revered by PETE TOWNSHEND, the "Pinball Wizard" was so impressed by WALSH's PAGE-esque axe-grinding, he invited them to support The WHO on a European tour. On his return to the States, WALSH witnessed the killings of four students on the campus of his old university of Kent State, Ohio (4th of May, 1970 – he was later to campaign vigorously for a memorial). With DALE PETERS replacing KRISS, they released their follow-up album, 'RIDES AGAIN', which boasted a minor hit single, 'FUNK 49', a sequel to 'FUNK NO.48', from the first album. Two more Top 30 gold-selling sets followed in quick succession, before WALSH took his not inconsiderable talents to an extremely fruitful solo career. It took two people to replace him, Canadians DOMENIC TROIANO on guitar and ROY KENNER on vocals. The resulting WALSH-less output was found lacking, two albums 'STRAIGHT SHOOTER' (1972) and 'PASSIN' THRU' (1973) not a patch on their earlier work. Following the subsequent departure of TROIANO, guitar prodigy TOMMY BOLIN was secured as a replacement on the recommendation of WALSH. Despite BOLIN's talent, a further two lacklustre albums continued to disappoint all but the most loyal fans, the guitarist soon poached by the revamped DEEP PURPLE. This finally brought about the 'GANG's demise, although FOX and PETERS resurrected the band with two newcomers, BUBBA KEITH and RICHARD SHACK for a couple of forgettable albums. • **Songwriters:** WALSH – KRISS to WALSH-PETERS to group compositions. Covered; CAST YOUR FATE TO THE WIND (Guaraldi-Werber) / STOP (Ragavoy-Schean) / YOU'RE GONNA NEED ME (B.B. King) / LOST WOMAN (Yardbirds) / BLUEBIRD (Buffalo Springfield) / etc.

Album rating: YER' ALBUM (*6) / THE JAMES GANG RIDES AGAIN (*8) / THIRDS (*6) / JAMES GANG LIVE IN CONCERT (*5) / STRAIGHT SHOOTER (*4) / PASSIN' THRU (*4) / THE BEST OF THE JAMES GANG FEATURING JOE WALSH compilation (*7) / 16 GREATEST HITS compilation (*7) / BANG (*4) / MIAMI (*4) / NEWBORN (*4) / JESSE COME HOME (*3) / THE TRUE STORY OF THE JAMES GANG compilation (*7)

JOE WALSH (b.20 Nov'47, Wichita, Kansas, USA) – guitar, vocals; repl. GLEN SCHWARTZ who joined PACIFIC GAS & ELECTRIC / **TOM KRISS** – bass, vocals / **JIM FOX** – drums, vocals

	Stateside	Bluesway
Sep 69. (7") *<61027>* **I DON'T HAVE THE TIME. / FRED**	-	
Nov 69. (lp) *(SSL 10295) <6034>* **YER' ALBUM**		83 Oct69

– Tuning part one / Take a look around / Funk #48 / Bluebird / Lost woman / Stone rap / Collage / I don't have the time / a) Wrapcity in English, b) Fred / Stop. *(re-iss. Oct90 on 'Beat Goes On'; BGOCD 60)*

| Jan 70. (7") *(SS 2158) <61030>* **FUNK #48. / COLLAGE** | | Nov69 |
| Jun 70. (7") *(SS 2173) <61033>* **STOP. / TAKE A LOOK AROUND** | | |

—— **DALE PETERS** – bass, vocals repl. KRISS

	Probe	A.B.C.
Aug 70. (7") *(PRO 502) <11272>* **FUNK #49. / THANKS**		59
Oct 70. (lp) *(SPBA 6253) <711>* **JAMES GANG RIDES AGAIN**	20	Jul70

– Funk #49 / Asshtonpark / Woman / The bomber: (a) Closet queen – (b) Cast your fate to the wind / Tend my garden / Garden gate / There I go again / Thanks / Ashes the rain and I. *(re-iss. Oct74; 5009) <cd-iss. Jun88; 31145> (cd-iss. Sep91 on 'Beat Goes On'; BGOCD 121)*

| Apr 71. (7") *(PRO 533) <11301>* **WALK AWAY. / YADIG?** | | 51 |
| Jul 71. (lp) *(SPB 1038) <721>* **THIRDS** | 27 | Apr71 |

– Walk away / Yadig? / Things I could be / Dreamin' in the country / It's all the same / Midnight man / Again / White man – black man / Live my life again. *(cd-iss. Sep91 on 'Beat Goes On'; BGOCD 119)*

| Oct 71. (7") *<11312>* **MIDNIGHT MAN. / WHITE MAN – BLACK MAN** | - | 80 |
| Dec 71. (lp) *(SPB 1045) <733>* **JAMES GANG LIVE IN CONCERT** (live) | 24 | Sep71 |

– Stop / You're gonna need me / Take a look around / Tend my garden / Ashes, the rain and I / Walk away / Lost woman. *(cd-iss. Sep91 on 'Beat Goes On'; BGOCD 120)*

—— **DOMENIC TROIANO** (b. Canada) – guitar, vocals repl. WALSH went solo / added **ROY KENNER** – vocals

| Apr 72. (7") *<11325>* **LOOKING FOR MY LADY. / HAIRY HYPOCHONDRIAC** | - | |
| Jul 72. (lp) *(SPB 1056) <741>* **STRAIGHT SHOOTER** | 58 | Mar72 |

– Madness / Kick back man / Get her back again / Looking for my lady / Getting old / I'll tell you why / Hairy hypochondriac / Let me come home / My door is open.

| Jul 72. (7") *<11336>* **KICK BACK MAN. / HAD ENOUGH** | - | |
| Oct 72. (lp) *(SPB 1065) <760>* **PASSIN' THRU** | | 72 |

– Ain't seen nothin' yet / One way street / Had enough / Up to yourself / Every day needs a hero / Run, run, run / Things I want to say to you / Out of control / Drifting girl.

	Atlantic	Atco
Dec 73. (lp) *(K 50028) <SD 7039>* **BANG**		

– Standing in the rain / The Devil is singing our song / Must be love / Alexis / Ride the wind / Got no time for trouble / Rather be alone with you / From another time / Mystery.

| Jan 74. (7") *(K 10432) <6953>* **MUST BE LOVE. / GOT NO TIME FOR TROUBLES** | | 54 |
| Apr 74. (7") *<6966>* **STANDING IN THE RAIN. / FROM ANOTHER TIME** | - | |

—— **TOMMY BOLIN** (b.1951, Sioux City, Iowa) – guitar (ex-ENERGY, ex-ZEPHYR) repl. TROIANO (to GUESS WHO)

| Aug 74. (7") *<7006>* **CRUISIN' DOWN THE HIGHWAY. / MIAMI TWO-STEP** | - | |
| Sep 74. (lp) *(K 50028) <9739>* **MIAMI** | | 97 |

– Cruisin' down the highway / Do it / Wildfire / Sleepwalker / Miami two-step / Red skies / Spanish lover / Summer breezes / Head above the water.

—— **PETERS + FOX** recruited **RICHARD SHACK** – guitar repl. KENNER **BUBBA KEITH** – vocals, guitar repl. BOLIN who joined DEEP PURPLE, then went solo (he died on the 4th December '76)

— added **DAVID BRIGGS** – keyboards
May 75. (7") <7021> **MERRY GO ROUND. / RED SATIN LOVER**   `-` ☐
May 75. (lp) (K 50148) <36112> **NEWBORN**
– Merry-go-round / Gonna get by / Earthshaker / All I have / Watch it / Driftin' dreamer / Shoulda' seen your face / Come with me / Heartbreak Hotel / Red satin lover / Cold wind.

BOB WEBB – vocals, guitar / **PHIL GIALLOMARDO** – keyboards, vocals / **FLACO PADRON** – percussion repl. BUBBA, RICHARD + DAVID
Feb 76. (7") <7067> **I NEED LOVE. / FEELIN' ALRIGHT**   `-` ☐
Feb 76. (lp) <36141> **JESSE COME HOME**
– I need love / Another year / Feelin' alright / Pleasant song / Hollywood dream / Love hurts / Pick up the pizzas / Stealin' the show / When I was a sailor.
— Disbanded later in 1976.

– compilations, others –

Jan 73. (lp) *Probe; (1070) / A.B.C.; <774>* **THE BEST OF THE JAMES GANG FEATURING JOE WALSH**   ☐ `79`
– Walk away / Funk #49 / Midnight man / The bomber: (a) Closet queen – (b) Cast your fate to the wind / Yadig? / Take a look around / Funk No.48 / Woman / Ashes the rain and I / Stop. *(re-iss.Oct74; 5027) (re-iss.Oct81 on 'M.C.A.'; 1615)*
Dec 73. (d-lp) *A.B.C.; <801-2>* **16 GREATEST HITS**   `-` ☐
Mar 87. (lp) *See For Miles; (SEE 88)* **THE TRUE STORY OF THE JAMES GANG**   ☐ `-`
(cd-iss.Mar93; SEECD 367) – (with . . . PLUS tracks)
— (also some JAMES GANG tracks on May'94 release, 'ALL THE BEST' by JOE WALSH & THE JAMES GANG)

JAMIE WEDNESDAY (see under ⇒ CARTER THE UNSTOPPABLE SEX MACHINE)

JAMIROQUAI

Formed: /based Ealing, London . . . early 1991, by the youthful, JASON KAY (aka JAY K). After scoring a minor hit on Eddie Pillar's 'Acid Jazz' label, with his debut single, 'WHEN YOU GONNA LEARN?', JAMIROQUAI switched labels to 'Sony Soho Square', the label no doubt hoping to cash in on the super-hip Acid Jazz scene which had already seen The BRAND NEW HEAVIES reap financial rewards for 'London' records, especially in the lucrative American market. And cash in on it they did; where Acid Jazz had once been the preserve of a London clique, JAY K sold the concept nationwide. The image was calculated but perfect; Adidas Gazelles, 70's cords, ethnic hats and funky soul-boy footwork. Vocally, the comparisons with STEVIE WONDER were unavoidable, all 'doo-doo-da-doo-doo' flourishes which seemed irreconcilable with a skinny white kid from London. 'TOO YOUNG TO DIE', his first effort for 'Sony', went Top 10, the debut album, 'EMERGENCY ON PLANET EARTH' (1993) reaching No.1 later that summer. Spontaneous, irresistibly funky and musically accomplished, what the record lacked in originality, it made up for with brazen charm. The only thing that indicated the album had been recorded in the 90's was the lavish use of digeridoo, although this added novelty value rather then any real innovation. Lyrically, the record was a platform for JAY's unceasingly positive guide to life and his often naive, if well-meaning, political and ecological diatribes. In interviews and on stage, JAY's charisma was undeniable, rebuffing charges of being contrived with a cocksure cheekiness. By 'THE RETURN OF THE SPACE COWBOY' (1994) the image was still intact, it was just a case of different album, different hat. As well as cornering the money-spinning pop/teen market, the DAVID MORALES mix of the title track was a massive European club hit, further boosting sales of the album. Musically, the record more or less stuck to the same formula although there were signs of a growing maturity in JK's songwriting and lyrics. 'TRAVELLING WITHOUT MOVING' (1996) saw JAMIROQUAI consolidate their position as purveyors of reliable, chart-friendly pop-funk while JK has become as much of a 90's icon as OASIS, if a bit more stylish. Now "lord of the manor" in a Buckinghamshire country estate (he also owns a number of sports cars, etc.) and the beau of Big Breakfast starlet, Denise Van Outen, JASON KAY was back to what he knows best, writing songs; a new song from the 'Godzilla' movie, 'DEEPER UNDERGROUND' was his return to No.1. 'SYNKRONIZED' (1999) was JAMIROQUAI's fourth album in six years, although the slickness of JAY K's retro persona was wearing a little thin. Nevertheless, the album shot to the top of the UK charts (his first since his debut!) and produced three further hits, 'CANNED HEAT', 'SUPERSONIC' and 'KING FOR A DAY'. • **Songwriters:** JAY and TOBY are main writers, although ZENDER, McKENZIE and others contribute. • **Trivia:** Pronounced JAM-EAR-OH-KWAI, they took the name from a tribe of American Indians.
Album rating: EMERGENCY ON PLANET EARTH (*9) / RETURN OF THE SPACE COWBOY (*7) / TRAVELLING WITHOUT MOVING (*7) / SYNKRONIZED (*6)

JAY K (b. JASON KAY, 30 Sep'69, Stretford, Lancashire, England) – vocals / **TOBY SMITH** (b. TOBY GRAFFETY-SMITH, 29 Oct'70) – keyboards / **NICK VAN GELDER** – drums / **STUART ZENDER** (b.18 Mar'74, Philadelphia, Pennsylvania, USA) – bass / **WALLIS BUCHANAN** (b.29 Nov'65) – didgeridoo / plus **KOFI KARIKARI** – percussion / **MAURIZIO RAVALIO** – percussion / **GLENN NIGHTINGALE + SIMON BARTHOLOMEW** – guitars / **D-ZIRE** – DJ / **GARY BARNACLE** – sax, flute / **JOHN THIRKELL** – trumpet, flugel horn / **RICHARD EDWARDS** – trombone

	Acid Jazz	not iss.
Oct 92. (12") *(JAZID 46T)* **WHEN YOU GONNA LEARN (JK mix & instrumental). / WHEN YOU GONNA LEARN (mixes; Cante Hondo / original demo / Digeridoo instrumental)**	`52`	`-`

(re-iss.Feb93 hit No.69)
(cd-s+=) (JAZID 46CD) – ('A'-digeridon't mix).

	Sony S2	Epic
Mar 93. (12") *(659011-6)* **TOO YOUNG TO DIE (mixes; extended / original / instrumental)** *(cd-s+=) (659011-2)* – ('A'edit).	`12`	`-`
May 93. (c-s) *(659297-4)* **BLOW YOUR MIND (part 1) / HOOKED UP** (12"+=) (659297-6) – Blow your mind (part 2). *(cd-s+=) (659297-2)* – When you gonna learn (JK mix).	`10`	`-`
Jun 93. (cd/c/lp) *(474069-2/-4/-2)* **EMERGENCY ON PLANET EARTH**	`1`	

– When you gonna learn (digeridoo) / Too young to die / Hooked up / If I like it, I do it / Music of the mind / Emergency on Planet Earth / Whatever it is, I just can't stop / Blow your mind / Revolution 1993 / Didgin' out.

| Aug 93. (12"/c-s/cd-s) *(659578-6/-4/-2)* **EMERGENCY ON PLANET EARTH. / IF I LIKE IT, I DO IT (MTV acoustic) / REVOLUTION 1993 (demo)** | `32` | |
| Sep 93. (c-s) *(659695-6)* **WHEN YOU GONNA LEARN (Digeridoo). / DIDGIN' OUT (live at the Milky Way, Amsterdam)** | `28` | |

(cd-s+=) (659695-2) – Too young to die (live) / ('A'-Cante Hondo mix).
(12") *(659695-6) <74925>* – ('A'mixes from 'Acid Jazz').

— **DERRICK McKENZIE** (b.27 Mar'62, Islington, London) – drums; repl. VAN GELDER

| Sep 94. (12") *(660851-6)* **SPACE COWBOY. / JOURNEY TO ARNHEMLAND / SPACE COWBOY – STONED AGAIN** | `17` | ☐ |

(cd-s) *(660851-2)* – (first two tracks) / Kids / ('A'demo).
(cd-s/12") <77827+1> – (6-'A'versions).

| Oct 94. (cd/c/d-lp) *(477813-2/-4/-1)* **THE RETURN OF THE SPACE COWBOY** | `2` | ☐ |

– Just another story / Stillness in time / Half the man / Light years / Manifest destiny / The kids / Mr.Moon / Scam / Journey to Arnhemland / Morning glory / Space cowboy.

| Nov 94. (c-s) *(661003-4)* **HALF THE MAN / SPACE CLAV** | `15` | `-` |

(12"+=/cd-s+=) *(661003-6/-2)* – Emergency on Planet Earth.
(cd-s) *(661003-5)* – ('A'side) / Jamiroquai's Greatest Hits: When you gonna learn? / Too young to die / Blow your mind.

| Feb 95. (c-s) *(661256-4)* **LIGHT YEARS / JOURNEY TO ARNHEMLAND (live)** | ☐ | `-` |

(ext-12"+=) *(661256-6)* – Light years (live).
(cd-s+=) *(661256-2)* – Scan / We gettin' down.

| Jun 95. (12"/cd-s) *(662025-6/-2)* **STILLNESS IN TIME. / SPACE COWBOY (mix)** | `9` | |

(cd-s+=) *(662025-5)* – Emergency on Planet Earth / Light years.

— In Jun'96, JAMIROQUAI featured on M-BEAT's No.12 hit version of 'DO U KNOW WHERE YOU'RE COMING FROM'.

| Aug 96. (7") *(663613-7)* **VIRTUAL INSANITY. / ('A'-Unreality mix)** | `3` | `-` |

(c-s+=) *(663613-4)* – ('A'-album mix).
(12"/cd-s) *(663613-6/-2)* – ('A'side) / Do you know where you're coming from / Bullet / ('A'-album version).
(cd-s) *(663613-5)* – ('A'side) / Space cowboy (classic radio) / Emergency on Planet Earth (London-Rican mix) / Do you know where you're coming from.

| Sep 96. (cd/c/lp) *(483999-2/-4/-1) <67903>* **TRAVELLING WITHOUT MOVING** | `2` | `24` |

– Virtual insanity / Cosmic girl / Use the force / Everyday / Alright / High times / Drifting along / Didjerama / Didjital vibrations / Travelling without moving / You are my love / Spend a lifetime. (cd+=) – (bonus track).

| Nov 96. (7"/c-s) *(663829-7/-4)* **COSMIC GIRL / SLIPIN 'N' SLIDIN'** | `6` | |

(cd-s+=) *(663829-2)* – Didjital vibrations / ('A'-classic radio).
(12"/cd-s) *(663829-6/-5) <78501-2>* – ('A'mixes; radio / classic / Quasar / dub).

| May 97. (cd-s) *(664235-2) <78703>* **ALRIGHT (mixes; radio / vocal version / dub vocal / DJ version excursion)** | `6` | `78` Sep97 |

(cd-s) *(664235-5)* – ('A'mixes; extended / Tee's In House / Tee's Digital club / Tee's radio Jay).
(12") *(664235-6)* – ('A'-version vocal & Tee's In House mix) / Space cowboy (classic club) / Cosmic girl (classic mix).
(d12") <786591> – (7 version incl. above stuff).

| Dec 97. (12"/cd-s) *(665370-6/-2)* **HIGH TIMES (mixes; original / Bionic Supachronic / Doobie dub / album or Jamiroquai dub)** | `20` | |

(cd-s+=) *(665370-5)* – ('A'mixes; incl. Sanchez radio edit).

| Jul 98. (c-s) *(666218-4)* **DEEPER UNDERGROUND / DEEPER UNDERGROUND (the metro mix)** | `1` | |

(cd-s+=) *(666218-2)* – ('A'-instrumental).
(cd-s) *(666218-5)* – ('A'side & mixes; Ummah & S-Man Meets Da Northface Killa dub).
(cd-s+=) <79032> – (all above) / High times (album & Doobie dub).

| May 99. (c-s) *(667302-4) <79189-4/-7>* **CANNED HEAT / WOLF IN SHEEP'S CLOTHING** | `4` | |

(cd-s) *(667302-2)* – ('A'radio edit).
(cd-s) *(667302-5)* – ('A'versions) / Deeper underground (Chillington mix).
(cd-s) <79162> – (all above tracks).

| Jun 99. (cd/c/lp) *(494517-2/-4/-1) <69973>* **SYNKRONIZED** | `1` | `28` |

– Canned heat / Planet home / Black Capricorn day / Soul education / Falling / Destitute illusions / Supersonic / Butterfly / Where do we go from here? / King for a day. (cd+=) – Deeper underground.

| Sep 99. (c-s) *(667839-4)* **SUPERSONIC / SUPERSONIC (album version)** | `22` | |

(cd-s) *(667839-32) <79320><12"= 79307>* – ('A'side) / ('A'-Pete Heller – the love mix) / ('A'-Harvey's Fuel altered mix).
(cd-s) *(667839-5)* – ('A'side) / ('A'-Restless Soul main vocal) / ('A'-Sharp Razor remix).

| Nov 99. (c-s) *(667973-4)* **KING FOR A DAY / PLANET HOME (Trabant Brothers Inc. remix)** | `20` | `-` |

(cd-s+=) *(667973-2)* – Supersonic (Dirty Rotten Scoundrels mix).
(cd-s) *(667973-5)* – ('A'side) / Canned heat (Shanks & Bigfoot – extended master mix) / Supersonic (edit) / Supersonic (CD-Rom version).

JANE'S ADDICTION

Formed: Los Angeles, California, USA . . . 1984 by Miami-raised PERRY FARRELL. The band's debut effort was a self-financed eponymous live album on 'Triple XXX', the record's naked intensity going some way towards capturing FARRELL's skewed musical vision. More successful was the band's debut for 'Warner Brothers', 'NOTHING'S SHOCKING' (1988), a wilfully perverse and eclectic blend of thrash, folk and funk that, musically and lyrically, made L.A.'s cock-rock brigade look like school boys. FARRELL's creepy shrill was something of an acquired taste, although it complemented the abrasive, mantra-like music perfectly, from the juddering 'PIGS IN ZEN' to the bleakly beautiful 'JANE SAYS'. The record courted controversy almost immediately, with its cover art depicting naked siamese twins strapped to an electric chair. Live, the band were just as confrontational, FARRELL stalking the stage like some trans-sexual high priest. 'RITUAL DE LO HABITUAL' (1990) was JANE'S' masterstroke, combining the compelling musical dynamics of the debut with more rhythm and melody. The result was a UK Top 40 hit for 'BEEN CAUGHT STEALING', a funky paeon to the delights of shoplifting. Inevitably, JANE'S ADDICTION incurred, yet again, the wrath of America's moral guardians and the record was banned from several US retail chains. The band replied by re-releasing it in a plain white sleeve with only the First Amendment printed on it. The following year, FARRELL organised the first Lollapalooza tour, a travelling festival of indie, rap and alternative acts. It was while headlining this jaunt that the band reached its messy conclusion, FARRELL eventually coming to blows with guitarist NAVARRO and splitting soon after. While NAVARRO subsequently joined the RED HOT CHILI PEPPERS, FARRELL formed PORNO FOR PYROS with PERKINS and a cast of likeminded musicians. The 1993 eponymous debut was like a more aggressive, less mysterious JANE'S ADDICTION, reaching the Top 5. Following personal problems and a drug bust, the band eventually released a follow-up three years later, 'GOOD GOD'S URGE', a more heavy-lidded, narcotic-centric affair which even featured NAVARRO on one track, 'FREEWAY'. JANE'S ADDICTION have since reformed (with the 'CHILI'S FLEA on bass), initially for some live work in 1997, although a handful of new tracks surfaced on the odds'n'sods collection, 'KETTLE WHISTLE'. Towards the end of the millennium, PERRY was back in a solo capacity, the album 'REV' receiving some tender reviews for his er, carnival of sound (see covers below). • **Songwriters:** Group penned, except SYMPATHY FOR THE DEVIL (Rolling Stones). Perry solo covered WHOLE LOTTA LOVE (Led Zeppelin) / TONIGHT (from 'West Side Story') / SATELLITE OF LOVE (lou Reed) / RIPPLE (Grateful Dead).

Album rating: JANE'S ADDICTION (*7) / NOTHING'S SHOCKING (*8) / RITUAL DE LO HABITUAL (*9) / KETTLE WHISTLE part compilation (*6) / Porno For Pyros: PORNO FOR PYROS (*6) / GOOD GOD'S URGE (*8) / Perry Farrell: REV (*7)

PERRY FARRELL (b. PERRY BERNSTEIN, 29 Mar'59, Queens, N.Y.) – vocals / **DAVE NAVARRO** (b. 6 Jun'67, Santa Monica, Calif.) – guitar / **ERIC AVERY** (b.25 Apr'65) – bass / **STEPHEN PERKINS** (b.13 Sep'67) – drums

	not iss.	Triple X
Aug 87. (lp) <XXX 51004> **JANE'S ADDICTION (live)**	-	

– Trip away / Whores / Pigs in Zen / 1% / I would for you / My time / Jane says / Rock'n'roll / Sympathy / Chip away. <re-iss. Dec88 lp/cd; TX 510041 LP/MC/CD> (UK-iss.Dec90 on 'WEA' cd/c/lp; 7599 26599-2/-4/-1)

	Warners	Warners
Sep 88. (lp/c)(cd) (WX 216/+C)(925727-2) <25727> **NOTHING'S SHOCKING**		

– Up the beach / Ocean size / Had a dad / Ted, just admit it . . . / Standing in the shower . . . thinking / Summertime rolls / Mountain song / Idiots rule / Jane says / Thank you boys. (cd+=) – Pigs in Zen.

Mar 89. (7") <27520> **MOUNTAIN SONG. / STANDING IN THE SHOWER . . . THINKING**	-	-
May 89. (7") (W 7520) **MOUNTAIN SONG. / JANE SAYS**	-	-

(12"ep+=) **THE SHOCKING EP** (W 7520T) – Had a dad (live).

—— added guest **MORGAN** (a female) – violin

Aug 90. (cd)(lp/c) (7599 25993-2)(WX 306/+C) <25993> **RITUAL DE LO HABITUAL**	37	19

– Stop / No one's leaving / Ain't no right / Obvious / Been caught stealing / Three days / Then she did . . . / Of course / Classic girl.

Aug 90. (7"/c-s) (W 9584/+C) **THREE DAYS. / (part 2)**		

(12"/cd-s) (W 9584 T/CD) – ('A'side) / I would for you (demo) / Jane says (demo).

Mar 91. (7"/c-s) (W 0011/+C) <19574> **BEEN CAUGHT STEALING. / HAD A DAD (demo)**	34	

(12"+=/12"box+=/cd-s+=) (W 0011 T/TB/CD) – ('A'remix) / L.A. medley:- L.A. woman / Nausea / Lexicon devil.

May 91. (7"/c-s) (W 0031/+C) **CLASSIC GIRL. / NO ONE'S LEAVING**	60	

(12"pic-d+=/cd-s+=) (W 0031 TP/CD) – Ain't no right.

—— Had already disbanded when FARRELL looked liked heading into film acting. NAVARRO had briefly filled in for IZZY STRADLIN in GUNS N' ROSES, before joining RED HOT CHILI PEPPERS.

PORNO FOR PYROS

—— **FARRELL + PERKINS** with **PETER DISTEFANO** (b.10 Jul'65) – guitar, samples, vocals / **MARTYN LE NOBLE** (b.14 Apr'69, Vlaardingen, Netherlands) – bass (ex-THELONIUS MONSTER) / and guest **DJ SKATEMASTER TATE** – keyboards, samples

	Warners	Warners
Apr 93. (cd/c/lp) <(9362 45228-2/-4/-1)> **PORNO FOR PYROS**	13	3

– Sadness / Porno for pyros / Meija / Cursed female – cursed male / Pets / Badshit / Packin' / • 25 / Black girlfriend / Blood rag / Orgasm.

Jun 93. (7"/c-s) (W 0177/+C) <18480> **PETS. / TONIGHT (from 'West Side Story')**	53	67

(12"pic-d+=/cd-s+=) (W 0177 T/CD) – Cursed female – cursed male (medley).

—— **MIKE WATT** – bass (ex-fIREHOSE, ex-MINUTEMEN, ex-CICCONE YOUTH) repl. MARTYN (on most)

—— added **THOMAS JOHNSON** – samples, engineer and co-producer

May 96. (cd/c/lp) <(9362 46126-2/-4/-1)> **GOOD GOD'S URGE**	40	20

– Porpoise head / 100 ways / Tahitian moon / Kimberly Austin / Thick of it all / Good God's:// Urge! / Wishing well / Dogs rule the night / Freeway / Bali eyes.

JANE'S ADDICTION

—— re-formed **PERRY FARRELL / DAVE NAVARRO / STEPHEN PERKINS + FLEA**

Dec 97. (cd/c) <(9362 46752-2/-4)> **KETTLE WHISTLE** (4 new + live, demos & out-takes)	21	Nov97

– Kettle whistle / Ocean size / Maceo / Hadadad / So what / Jane says / Mountain song / Slow divers / Three days / Ain't no right / Up the beach / Stop / Been caught stealing / Whores / City.

PERRY FARRELL

Nov 99. (cd/c) <(9362 47544-2/-4)> **REV**		

– Rev / Whole lotta love / Been caught stealing / Jane says / Stop / Mountain song / Summertime rolls / Kimberley Austin / Tonight / Tahitian moon / Pets / Cursed male / 100 ways / Hard charger / Ripple / Satellite of love.

Bill JANOVITZ (see under ⇒ BUFFALO TOM)

Bert JANSCH (see under ⇒ PENTANGLE)

JANSEN / BARBIERI (see under ⇒ JAPAN)

JAPAN

Formed: Catford / Lewisham, London, England . . . mid-70's by DAVID SYLVIAN, his brother STEVE JANSEN, MICK KARN and RICHARD BARBIERI. In 1977, they added a second guitarist, ROB DEAN, subsequently signing to 'Ariola-Hansa' after winning a talent competition run by the label. They released a debut album, 'ADOLESCENT SEX', in the Spring of '78, followed six months later by 'OBSCURE ALTERNATIVES'. Basically pop music at the more accessible end of the avant-garde spectrum, JAPAN's proto-New Romantic image contrasted with SYLVIAN's (FERRY-esque) monotone croon. The following year, JAPAN scored a major hit in (of all places) Japan, with the GIORGIO MORODER-produced single, 'LIFE IN TOKYO'; a year on they finally gained a UK chart placing with 'QUIET LIFE'. By the turn of the decade, they'd secured a deal with 'Virgin', releasing the John Porter-produced Top 50 album, 'GENTLEMEN TAKE POLAROIDS'. The next year, after three minor hits in Britain, they went overground with a top selling classic album, 'TIN DRUM'. The record subsequently spawned the spectral 'GHOSTS' single in early '82, which hit the UK Top 5 after their former label had initiated a string of re-issues with 'EUROPEAN SON'; these exploitation releases graced the charts over the course of the next eighteen months while JAPAN officially folded. All band members went on to other projects, DAVID SYLVIAN enjoying most success. After a 1982 collaboration with RYUICHI SAKAMOTO ('BAMBOO HOUSES' and 'FORBIDDEN COLOURS' from the movie, 'Merry Xmas Mr. Lawrence'), the immaculately fringed frontman released his debut solo album, 'BRILLIANT TREES' (1984). The Top 5 album utilised the talents of world trumpeter, JON HASSELL, while JAPAN cohorts JANSEN and BARBIERI also helped to sculpt its sophisticated ambience. On future albums such as 'GONE TO EARTH' (1986), 'SECRETS OF THE BEEHIVE' (1987), 'PLIGHT AND PREMONITION' (1988) and 'FLUX AND MUTATION' (1989) – the latter two were collaborations with HOLGER CZUKAY (ex-CAN) – he worked with left-field luminaries like BILL NELSON and ROBERT FRIPP. In 1991, JAPAN re-formed as RAIN TREE CROW, although it became clear this set-up was only temporary, as all members (especially SYLVIAN), continued to pursue solo careers. SYLVIAN briefly returned to the charts in 1993 with the ROBERT FRIPP collaboration, 'THE FIRST DAY', a more accessible yet still inventive set. Although MICK KARN began a solo career at the same time as SYLVIAN (the bassist's work reminiscent of ENO or BILL NELSON), he went on to work as a sculptor; his track, 'TRIBAL DAWN' (from the album, 'TITLES' – 1982), was used on Channel 4's arty TV programme, 'Altered States'. SYLVIAN was still gaining respect in some quarters of the music world when he turned up courtesy of a fresh set of scrumptious solo songs entitled 'DEAD BEES ON A CAKE' (1999), his aura and presence still on show when this returned him to the Top 40 (as did single, 'I SURRENDER'). • **Songwriters:** SYLVIAN lyrics / group compositions except; DON'T RAIN ON MY PARADE (Rogers-Hammerstein) / AIN'T THAT PECULIAR (Marvin Gaye) / I SECOND THAT EMOTION (Smokey Robinson) / ALL TOMORROW'S PARTIES (Velvet Underground).

Album rating: ADOLESCENT SEX (*6) / OBSCURE ALTERNATIVES (*6) / QUIET LIFE (*6) / GENTLEMEN TAKE POLAROIDS (*7) / TIN DRUM (*9) / ASSEMBLAGE compilation (*7) / OIL ON CANVAS live (*6) / EXORCISING GHOSTS compilation (*9) / Rain Tree Crow: RAIN TREE CROW (*4) / David Sylvian: BRILLIANT TREES (*8) / GONE TO EARTH (*6) / SECRETS OF THE BEEHIVE (*7) / PLIGHT AND PREMONITION with Holger Czukay (*7) / FLUX AND MUTABILITY with Holger Czukay (*6) / THE FIRST DAY with Robert Fripp

(*6) / DEAD BEES ON A CAKE (*8) / APPROACHING SILENCE (*5) / Mick Karn: TITLES (*7) / DREAMS OF REASON PRODUCE (*6) / BESTIAL CLUSTER (*5) / POLLYTOWN (*5) / THE TOOTH MOTHER (*5) / Jansen & Barbieri: CATCH THE FALL / STORIES ACROSS THE BORDER (*5) / BEGINNING TO MELT with Karn (*5) / SEED with Karn (*5) / STONE TO FLESH (*5) / OTHER WORLDS IN A SMALL ROOM (*4)

DAVID SYLVIAN (b. DAVID BATT, 23 Feb'58) – vocals, guitar, keyboards / **RICHARD BARBIERI** (b.30 Nov'57) – keyboards, synthesizers / **ROB DEAN** – guitar, mandolin / **MICK KARN** (b. ANTHONY MICHAELIDES, 24 Jul'58) – bass, saxophone / **STEVE JANSEN** (b. STEVE BATT, 1 Dec'59) – drums, percussion

		Ariola Hansa	Ariola
Mar 78.	(7") *(AHA 510)* **DON'T RAIN ON MY PARADE. / STATELINE**		-
Apr 78.	(lp) *(AHAL 8004)* **ADOLESCENT SEX**		

– Transmission / The unconventional / State line / Wish you were black / Performance / Lovers on Main Street / Don't rain on my parade / Suburban love / Adolescent sex / Communist China / Television. *(re-iss. Sep82; same) (re-iss. Sep84 on 'Fame' lp/c; FA41 3108-1/-4) (cd-iss. 1989 on 'Hansa Germany'; VDP 1153)*

| Aug 78. | (7") *(AHA 525)* **THE UNCONVENTIONAL. / ADOLESCENT SEX** | | |
| Nov 78. | (lp) *(AHAL 8007)* **OBSCURE ALTERNATIVES** | | |

– Automatic gun / Rhodesia / Love is infectious / Sometimes I feel so low / Obscure alternatives / Deviation / Suburban Berlin / The tenant. *(re-iss. Sep82; same) (re-iss. Apr84 on 'Fame' lp/c; FA41 3098-1/-4) (cd-iss. 1989 on 'Hansa Germany'; CDP 1154)*

Nov 78.	(7",7"blue) *(AHA 529) <7727>* **SOMETIMES I FEEL SO LOW. / LOVE IS INFECTIOUS**		
May 79.	(7"red/ext.12"red) *(AHA/+D 540)* **LIFE IN TOKYO. / LIFE IN TOKYO** (part 2)		
Jul 79.	(12") *<7756>* **LIFE IN TOKYO. / LOVE IS INFECTIOUS**	-	
Jan 80.	(lp) *(AHAL 8011)* **QUIET LIFE**	53	

– Quiet life / Fall in love with me / Despair / In-vogue / Halloween / All tomorrow's parties / Alien / The other side of life. *(re-iss. Sep82 on 'Fame' lp/c; FA/TCFA 3037) (cd-iss. 1989 on 'Hansa Germany'; VDP 1155)*

| Feb 80. | (7",7"maroon) *(AHA 559)* **I SECOND THAT EMOTION. / QUIET LIFE** | | |

		Virgin	Virgin
Oct 80.	(7") *(VS 379)* **GENTLEMEN TAKE POLAROIDS. / THE EXPERIENCE OF SWIMMING**	60	

(d7"+=) *(VS 379)* – The width of a room / Burning bridges.

| Oct 80. | (lp/c) *(V/TCV 2180)* **GENTLEMEN TAKE POLAROIDS** | 45 | |

– Gentlemen take polaroids / Swing / Some kind of fool / My new career / Methods of dance / Ain't that peculiar / Night porter / Taking islands in Africa. *(re-iss. Aug88 lp/c; OVED/+C 138) (cd-iss. Jun88; CDV 2180)*

—— Trimmed to quartet when ROB DEAN left, to later form ILLUSTRATED MAN

| Apr 81. | (7"/12") *(VS 409/+12)* **THE ART OF PARTIES. / LIFE WITHOUT BUILDINGS** | 48 | - |
| Oct 81. | (7") *(VS 436)* **VISIONS OF CHINA. / TAKING ISLANDS IN AFRICA** | 32 | - |

(12"+=) *(VS 436-12)* – Swing. *(re-iss. Dec84; same)*

| Nov 81. | (lp/c) *(V/TCV 2209)* **TIN DRUM** | 12 | |

– The art of parties / Talking drum / Ghosts / Canton / Still life in mobile homes / Visions of China / Sons of pioneers / Cantonese boy. *(re-iss. Apr86 lp/c; OVED/+C 158) (cd-iss. Jun88; CDV 2209)*

Jan 82.	(7"/7"pic-d/12") *(VS/+Y 472)(VS 472-12)* **GHOSTS. / THE ART OF PARTIES** (version)	5	
Feb 82.	(7") **VISIONS OF CHINA. / CANTON**	-	
May 82.	(d7") *(VS 502)* **CANTONESE BOY. / BURNING BRIDGES // GENTLEMEN TAKE POLAROIDS / THE EXPERIENCE OF SWIMMING**	24	

—— They had earlier in the year quietly branched out into new projects. DAVID SYLVIAN went solo after a brief collaboration with RYUICHI SAKAMOTO. MICK KARN went solo, had one-off single with MIDGE URE, then went into sessions before forming DALI'S CAR with PETE MURPHY in '84. BARBERI and JANSEN produced Swedes LUSTAN LAKEJER. The pair formed their own duo (The DOLPHIN BROTHERS) before joining DAVID SYLVIAN again.

– compilations, exploitation releases etc. –

—— on 'Hansa-Ariola' unless otherwise mentioned

Apr 81.	(7"/12") *(HANSA/+12 4)* **LIFE IN TOKYO. / EUROPEAN SON**		
Aug 81.	(7"/12") *(HANSA/+12 6)* **QUIET LIFE. / A FOREIGN PLACE / FALL IN LOVE WITH ME**	19	
Sep 81.	(lp/c) *(HANLP 1)(ZCHAN 003)* **ASSEMBLAGE**	26	

– Adolescent sex / State line / Communist China / Rhodesia / Suburban Berlin / Life in Tokyo / European son / All tomorrow's parties / Quiet life / I second that emotion. *(c+=) – (12"extended versions). (re-iss. Sep85 on 'Fame' lp/c; FA41 3136-1/-4)*

Jan 82.	(7"/12") *(HANSA/+12 10)* **EUROPEAN SON. / ALIEN**	31	-
Jun 82.	(7"/12") *(HANSA/+12 12)* **I SECOND THAT EMOTION. / HALLOWEEN**	9	-
Sep 82.	(7"/12") *(HANSA/+12 17)* **LIFE IN TOKYO. / THEME**	28	-

—— now on 'Virgin' unless mentioned otherwise

| Nov 82. | (7") *(VS 554)* **NIGHT PORTER. / AIN'T THAT PECULIAR** | 29 | - |

(12"+=) *(VS 554-12)* – Methods of dance.

Feb 83.	(7"/12") *Hansa; (HANSA/+12 18)* **ALL TOMORROW'S PARTIES. / IN VOGUE**	38	-
May 83.	(7") *(VS 581)* **CANTON (live). / VISIONS OF CHINA (live)**	42	-
Jun 83.	(d-lp/c) *(VD/TCVD 2513)* **OIL ON CANVAS (live)**	5	

– Oil on canvas / Sons of pioneers / Gentlemen take polaroids / Swing / Cantonese boy / Visions of china / Ghosts / Voices raised in welcome, hands held in prayer / Night porter / Still life in mobile homes / Methods of dance / Quiet life / The art of parties / Canton / Temple of dawn. *(cd-iss. Apr85; CDVD 2513)*

| Aug 83. | (d-c) *(XTWO 24)* **ADOLESCENT SEX / OBSCURE ALTERNATIVES** | | |
| Nov 84. | (d-lp/c/cd) *(VGD/+C/CD 3510)* **EXORCISING GHOSTS** | 45 | |

– Methods of dance / Swing / Gentlemen take polaroids / Quiet life / A foreign place * / Night porter / My new career / The other side of life / Visions of China /

Sons of pioneers * / Talking drum / The art of parties / Taking islands in Africa / Voices raised in welcome, hands held in prayer / Life without buildings / Ghosts. *(cd-omits *)*

Jun 88.	(3"cd-ep) *(CDT 11)* **GHOSTS / THE ART OF PARTIES / VISIONS OF CHINA**		
Nov 88.	(3"cd-ep) *(CDT 32)* **GENTLEMEN TAKE POLAROIDS / CANTONESE BOY / METHODS OF DANCE**		
Sep 87.	(7") *Old Gold; (OG 9666)* **I SECOND THAT EMOTION. / ALL TOMORROW'S PARTIES**		-

(12"+=) *(OG 4020)* – Life in Tokyo.

Nov 87.	(7") *Old Gold; (OG 4031)* **QUIET LIFE. / LIFE IN TOKYO**		
Nov 88.	(7") *Old Gold; (OG 9817)* **GHOSTS. / CANTONESE BOY**		
Dec 89.	(c/cd) *R.C.A.; (410/260 360)* **A SOUVENIR FROM JAPAN**		
Nov 90.	(3xcd-box) *(TPAK 6)* **COLLECTOR'S EDITION**		

– (GENTLEMEN TAKE POLAROIDS / TIN DRUM / OIL ON CANVAS)

Nov 92.	(cd-ep) *Old Gold; (OG 6187)* **I SECOND THAT EMOTION / QUIET LIFE / LIFE IN TOKYO**		-
Oct 91.	(cd/c) *Receiver; (RR CD/MC 150)* **THE OTHER SIDE OF JAPAN**		-
Aug 96.	(cd) *B.M.G.; (74321 39338-2)* **IN VOGUE**		

DAVID SYLVIAN

—— - vocals, instruments (ex-JAPAN) / **RYUICHI SAKAMOTO** – synthesizers (ex-YELLOW MAGIC ORCHESTRA)

		Virgin	Virgin
Jul 82.	(7"/ext.12"; by SYLVIAN / SAKAMOTO) *(VS 510)* **BAMBOO HOUSES. / BAMBOO MUSIC**	30	

(below from the the film soundtrack 'Merry Christmas Mr.Lawrence')

| Jun 83. | (7"; by DAVID SYLVIAN & RYUICHI SAKAMOTO) *(VS 601)* **FORBIDDEN COLOURS. / THE SEED AND THE SOWER (by RYUICHI SAKAMOTO)** | 16 | |

(12"+=) *(VS 601-12)* – Last regrets. *(3"/5"cd-ep of SYLVIAN tracks was iss.Aug88; CDT 18)*

—— now solo – vocals, keyboards, guitar, percussion, with **RICHARD BARBIERI** and **STEVE JANSEN** (ex-JAPAN) / **RYUICHI SAKAMOTO** – synthesizers / **HOLGER CZUKAY** – tapes / **DANNY THOMPSON** – upright bass / **KENNY WHEELER** – horns

| May 84. | (7"/7"pic-d)(12") *(VS/+Y 633)(VS 633-12)* **RED GUITAR. / FORBIDDEN COLOURS** (version) | 17 | |
| Jun 84. | (lp/c/cd) *(V/TCV/CDV 2290)* **BRILLIANT TREES** | 4 | |

– Pulling punches / The ink in the well / Nostalgia / Red guitar / Weathered wall / Backwaters / Brilliant trees. *(re-iss. Apr90 lp/c; OVED/+C 239)*

| Aug 84. | (7"/12") *(VS 700/+12)* **THE INK IN THE WELL (remix). / WEATHERED WALL** (instrumental) | 36 | |
| Oct 84. | (7"/ext.12") *(VS 717/+12)* **PULLING PUNCHES. / BACKWATERS** (remix) | 56 | |

—— now with **JOHN HASSELL** and **ROBERT FRIPP** – guitar / **HOLGER CZUKAY** – tapes / **KENNY WHEELER** – horns

| Nov 85. | (12"ep) *(VS 835-12)* **WORDS WITH THE SHAMEN** | 72 | |

– Part 1:- Ancient evening / Part 2:- Incantation / Part 3:- Awakening.

| Dec 85. | (c) *(SLY 1)* **ALCHEMY (AN INDEX OF POSSIBILITIES)** | | - |

– WORDS WITH THE SHAMEN / Preparations for a journey / Steel cathedrals.

—— now with **ROBERT FRIPP** and **BILL NELSON** – guitar / **PHIL PALMER** – accoustic guitar / **MEL COLLINS** – soprano sax. / **KENNY WHEELER** – flugel horn

| Jul 86. | (7"/7"sha-pic-d) *(VS/+Y 815)* **TAKING THE VEIL. /** | 53 | |

(remix-12"+=) *(VS 815-12)* – Bird of prey vanishes into a bright blue sky.

| Aug 86. | (d-lp)(c)(cd) *(VDL/TCVDL/CDVDL 1)* **GONE TO EARTH** | 24 | |

– Taking the veil / Laughter and forgetting / Before the bullfight / Gone to earth / Wave / River man / Silver moon / The healing place / Answered prayers * / Where the railroad meets the sea / The wooden cross * / Silver moon over sleeping steeples * / Campfire: Coyote country * / A bird of prey vanishes into a blue cloudless sky * / Sunlight seen through the towering trees * / Upon this Earth. *(cd-omits tracks *)*

| Sep 86. | (7"/s7") *(VS/+P 895)* **SILVER MOON. / GONE TO EARTH** | | |

(12"+=) *(VS 895-12)* – Silver moon over sleeping steeples.

—— DAVID was also credited on VIRGINIA ASTLEY's Feb87 'Some Small Hope'.

—— now with **SAKAMOTO, PALMER, JANSEN** plus **DANNY CUMMINGS** – percussion / **DAVID TORN** – guitar / **DANNY THOMPSON** – d. bass / **MARK ISHAM** – trumpet

| Oct 87. | (lp)(c)(cd) *(V/TCV/CDV 2471)* **SECRETS OF THE BEEHIVE** | 37 | |

– September / The boy with the gun / Maria / Orpheus / The Devil's own / When poets dreamed of angels / Mother and child / Let the happiness in / Waterfront.

| Oct 87. | (7") *(VS 1001)* **LET THE HAPPINESS IN. / BLUE OF MOON** | 66 | |

(12"+=) *(VS 1001-12)* – Buoy (remix).

| Apr 88. | (7") *(VS 1043)* **ORPHEUS. / THE DEVIL'S OWN** | | |

(12"+=) *(VS 1043-12)* – Mother and child.

—— His touring band JANSEN, BARBIERI, TORN, ISHAM plus **IAN MAIDMAN** – bass, percussion / **ROBBY ALEDO** – guitar

DAVID SYLVIAN & HOLGER CZUKAY

with **JAKI LIEBEZEIT** – drums (ex-CAN)

		Venture-Virgin	Venture
Mar 88.	(lp/c/cd) *(VE/TCVE/CDVE 11)* **PLIGHT AND PREMONITION**	71	

– Plight (the spiralling of winter ghosts) / Premonition (giant empty iron vessel).

—— with LIEBEZEIT, MICHAEL KAROLI – guitar / **MARKUS STOCKHAUSEN** – flugel horn / **MICHI** – vocals

| Sep 89. | (lp/c/cd) *(VE/TCVE/CDVE 43)* **FLUX AND MUTABILITY** | | |

– Flux (a big, bright, colourful world) / Mutability ("a new beginning is in the offing").

DAVID SYLVIAN

		Virgin	Virgin
Nov 89.	(7") *(VS 1221)* **POP SONG. / A BRIEF CONVERSATION ENDING IN DIVORCE**		

(12"+=/cd-s+=) *(VST/VSCDX 1221)* – ('A'remix). (cd-s+=) *(VSCD 1221)* – Stigmas of childhood.

Nov 89. (5-cd-box) *(DXCD 1)* **WEATHERBOX**
– (BRILLIANT TREES / GONE TO EARTH / GONE TO EARTH (instrumental) / SECRETS OF THE BEEHIVE / ALCHEMY – AN INDEX OF POSSIBILITIES)

Nov 91. (cd) *(DSRM 1)* **EMBRE GLANCE (THE PERMANENCE OF MEMORY)**
– The beekeeper's apprentice / Epiphany.

—— JAPAN had reformed quartet in 1990, but as . . .

RAIN TREE CROW

	Virgin	Virgin
Mar 91. (7"/c-s) *(VS/+C 1340)* **BLACK WATER. / RAIN TREE CROW / I DRINK TO FORGET**	62	

(12") *(VST 1340)* – (1st + 3rd track) / Red Earth (as summertime ends).
(cd-s) *(VSCD 1340)* – (all above 4).

| Apr 91. (cd/c/lp) *(CD/TC+/V 2659)* **RAIN TREE CROW** | 24 | |

– Big wheels in Shanty town / Every colour you are / Rain tree crow / Red Earth (as summertime ends) / Rocket full of charge / Boat's for burning / New Moon Red Deer wallow / Black water / A reassuringly dull Sunday / Blackcrow hats shoe shine city.

SLYVIAN – SAKAMOTO

—— next with **INGRID CHAVEZ**

	Virgin America	Virgin Am.
Jun 92. (7"/c-s) *(VUS/+C 57)* **HEARTBEAT (TAINAI KAIKI II) RETURNING TO THE WOMB. / NUAGES**	58	

(cd-s+=) *(VUSCD 57)* – The lost emperor.
(cd-s) *(VUSCDG 57)* – ('A'side) / Forbidden colours / Heartbeat.

DAVID SYLVIAN & ROBERT FRIPP

with **FRIPP** – guitar (of-KING CRIMSON & solo artist) / **TREY GUNN** – synthesizers, vocals, co-writer plus band **DAVID BOTTRILL** – synthesizers / **JERRY MAROTTA** – drums, percussion / **MARC ANDERSON** – percussion / **INGRID CHAVEZ** – backing vocals

	Virgin	Virgin
Jul 93. (cd/c/lp) *(CD/TC+/V 2712)* **THE FIRST DAY**	21	

– God's monkey / Jean the birdman / Firepower / Brightness falls / 20th century dreaming (a shaman's song) / Darshan (the road to Graceland).

| Aug 93. (c-ep/cd-ep) *(VSC/DG 1462)* **JEAN THE BIRDMAN / EARTHBOUND – STARBLIND / ENDGAME** | 68 | |

(cd-ep) *(VSCDT 1462)* – ('A'side) / Tallow moon / Dark water / Gone to Earth.

| Dec 93. (cd/c/lp) *(SYL CD/MC/LP 1)* **DARSHAN** (mixes) | | - |

– Darshan (the road to Graceland) (remixed by The GRID & others).

Sep 94. (cd) *(DAMAGE 1)* **DAMAGE** (live)
– Damage / God's monkey / Brightness falls / Every colour you are / Firepower / Gone to Earth / 20th century dreaming (a shaman's song) / Wave / Riverman / Darshan (the road to Graceland) / Blinding light of Heaven / The first day.

—— In 1996, SYLVIAN was credited on soundtrack of 'Marco Polo' film alongside NICOLA ALESINI & PIER LUIGI ANDREONI. It was released on 'Materiali Sonori'; MASOCD 90069)

DAVID SYLVIAN

Mar 99. (cd-s) *(VSCDT 1722)* **I SURRENDER / LES FLEURS DU MAL / STARRED AND DREAMING** | 40 | - |

(cd-s) *(VSCDX 1722)* – ('A'side) / Whose trip is this / Remembering Julia.

| Mar 99. (cd/c) *(CDV/TCV 2876)* **DEAD BEES ON A CAKE** | 31 | |

– I surrender / Dobro / Midnight sun / Thalhelm / Godman / Alphabet angel / Krishna blue / Shining of things / Cafe Europe / Pollen path / All of my mother's name / Wanderlust / Praise / Darkest dreaming.

	Venture	
Sep 99. (cd-s) *(VEND 8)* **GODMAN** (mixes) / **SHADOWLAND** (mixes)		-
Sep 99. (m-cd) *(CDVE 943)* **APPROACHING SILENCE**		-

– The beekeeper's apprentice / Epiphany / Approaching silence.

MICK KARN

– vocals, bass, keyboards, synthesizers (ex-JAPAN) with session

	Virgin	Virgin
Jun 82. (7"/12") *(VS 508/+12)* **SENSITIVE. / THE SOUND OF WAVES**		
Nov 82. (lp/c) *(V/TCV 2249)* **TITLES**	74	

– Tribal dawn / Lost affections in a room / Passion in moisture / Weather the windmill / Saviour, are you with me / Trust me / Sensitive / Piper blue. *(re-iss. Aug88 lp/c; OVED/+C 91)*

—— In Jun83, he teamed up with ULTRAVOX's MIDGE URE, on the single AFTER A FASHION which reached UK No.39. In 1984 KARN formed **DALI'S CAR** with PETE MURPHY (ex-BAUHAUS) and PAUL VINCENT LAWFORD.

—— MICK KARN returned to solo '86

| Jan 87. (lp/c/cd) *(V/TCV/CDV 2389)* **DREAMS OF REASON PRODUCE MONSTERS** | 89 | |

– First impression / Language of ritual / Buoy / Land / The three fates / When love walks in / Dreams of reason / Answer.

| Jan 87. (7"; by MICK KARN featuring DAVID SYLVIAN) *(VS 910)* **BUOY. / DREAMS OF REASON** | 63 | |

(12"+=) *(VST 910)* – Language of ritual.

	C.M.P.	not iss.
Oct 93. (cd) *(CMPCD 1002)* **BESTIAL CLUSTER**		

– Bestial cluster / Back in the beginning / Beard in the letterbox / The drowning dream / The sad velvet breath of Summer & Winter / Saday, Maday / Liver and lungs / Bones of mud.

May 94. (cd; by DAVID TORN, MICK KARN + TERRY BOZZIO) *(CMPCD 1006)* **POLLYTOWN**

– Honey sweating / Palms for Lester / Open letter to the heart of Diaphora / Bandaged by dreams / Warrior horsemen of the spirit thundering over hills of doubt to a place of hope / Snail hair dune / This is the abduction scene / Red sleep / Res Majuko / City of the dead.

—— with **RICHARD BARBIERI** – keyboards / **STEVE JANSEN** – drums / **DAVID TORN** – guitar / **DAVID LIEBMAN** – soprano sax

May 95. (cd) *(CMPCD 1008)* **THE TOOTH MOTHER** | | - |
– Thundergirl mutation / Plaster the magic tongue / Lodge of skins / Gossip's cup / Feat funk / The tooth mother / Little less hope / There was not anything but nothing.

JANSEN / BARBIERI

JANSEN – vocals, etc / **BARBIERI** – keyboards, etc

	Pan-East	not iss.
Oct 86. (lp/c/cd) *(NEW LP/MC/CD 105)* **WORLD IN A SMALL ROOM**		-

—— (at same time JANSEN w/ YUKIHURO TAKAHASHI released 7"; STAY CLOSE. / BETSU-NI on 'Rime'; RIM 1)

—— The JAPAN duo now

The DOLPHIN BROTHERS

—— with **DAVID RHODES** – guitar / **DANNY THOMPSON** – ac. bass / **MATTHEW SELIGMAN + ROBERT BELL** – bass / **PHIL PALMER** – acoustic guitar / **MARTIN DITCHAM** – percussion

	Virgin	Virgin
Jun 87. (7") *(VS 969)* **SHINING. / MY WINTER**		-

(12"+=) *(VS 969-12)* – ('A'-Am-ex mix).

| Jul 87. (lp/c/cd) *(V/TCV/CDV 2434)* **CATCH THE FALL** | | |

– Catch the fall / Shining / Second sight / Love that you need / Real life, real answers / Host to the holy / My winter / Pushing the river. *(cd re-iss. Mar91; same)*

| Aug 87. (7"/12") *(VS 997/+12)* **SECOND SIGHT. / HOST TO THE HOLY** | | - |

STEVE JANSEN & RICHARD BARBIERI

	Venture	Virgin
Sep 91. (cd) *(CDVE 908)* **STORIES ACROSS BORDERS**		

– Long tales, tall shadows / When things dream / Luman / The insomniac's bed / The night gives birth / Celebration 1988 remix (saw) / Nocturnal sightseeing / One more zombie.

	Medium	not iss.
Mar 94. (cd; by STEVE JANSEN, RICHARD BARBIERI & MICK KARN) *(MPCD 1)* **BEGINNING TO MELT**		-

– Beginning to melt / The wilderness / March of the innocents / Human agie / Shipwrecks / Ego dance / The orange asylum. *(re-iss. Oct96; same)*

Oct 94. (cd; by STEVE JANSEN, RICHARD BARBIERI & MICK KARN) *(MPCD 2)* **SEED**
– Beginning to melt / In the black of desire / The insect tribe / Prey.

Oct 95. (cd) *(MPCD 3)* **STONE TO FLESH**
– Mother London / Sleepers awake / Ringing the bell backwards: Siren – Drift / Swim there / Closer than "I" / Everything ends in darkness. *(re-iss. Oct96 & Apr97; same)*

Oct 96. (cd) *(MPCD 4)* **OTHER WORLDS IN A SMALL ROOM** | | - |
– Remains of a fragile illusion / Light years / Disturbed sense of distance / Breaking the silence / Blue lines / Way the lights falls / Distant fire.

Jean-Michel JARRE

Born: 24 Aug'48, Lyon, France. In the late 60's, having played lead guitar for a few rock bands, he enrolled at Pierre Schaeffer's Musical Research Group, studying ethnic music. His love of free-form conflicted with MRG and he left to work in his own studio with a new synthesizer. He released three lp's in France at the turn of the decade, but chose to write jingles for radio and TV etc. In 1971, JARRE had become the youngest composer to appear at the Palais Garnier Opera House, while in 1973, he scored the soundtrack for the film, 'Les Granges Brulee'. In 1977, JEAN-MICHEL was signed to 'Polydor', who issued 'OXYGENE', a record which was earlier released in France on the 'Disques Motors' imprint. The album soon rose to No.2 in the UK charts, helped by a surprise Top 5 single 'OXYGENE (part 4)', JARRE's multi-layered electro-rock/pop muzak was conceptually similar to MIKE OLDFIELD, minus the instrumental dexterity of course. Later the following year, JARRE's next album, 'EQUINOXE', traced the same formulated pattern without quite the same effect. The record nevertheless matched its predecessor's sales, his subsequent works continuing to triumph commercially throughout the world during the 80s. In April '86, he set a record when playing live to over one million people at Houston, Texas. Two and a half years later, JARRE appeared in front of around three million people at Docklands, London, recorded over two separate nights (due to earlier Newham Council objection). HANK MARVIN, guitarist of The SHADOWS, featured on JARRE's 'LONDON KID' hit, the veteran guitar twanger performing the track alongside JARRE at the aforementioned concert. Not exactly the trendiest of the electronic pioneers, JARRE belatedly gained a smattering of instant credibility in the early 90's with the 'CHRONOLOGIE' series of dance remixes. The reworking by Glasgow's SLAM, in particular, was highly sought after on promo, changing hands for ridiculous sums of money. • **Trivia:** He married actress Charlotte Rampling, after meeting her at 1976 Cannes film festival. In 1983, he released a solitary copy of his lp, 'MUSIC FOR SUPERMARKETS', and after auctioning it for around £10,000, destroyed the master disc.

Album rating: OXYGENE (*8) / EQUINOXE (*6) / MAGNETIC FIELDS (*5) / THE

CONCERTS IN CHINA (*4) / THE ESSENTIAL JEAN-MICHAEL JARRE compilation (*6) / ZOOLOOK (*5) / RENDEZ-VOUS (*5) / IN CONCERT: LYON – HOUSTON (*4) / REVOLUTIONS (*5) / JARRE LIVE (*3) / WAITING FOR COUSTEAU (*3) / IMAGES – THE BEST OF JEAN-MICHEL JARRE compilation (*7) / CHRONOLOGIE (*4) / OXYGENE 7-13 (*4) / ODYSSEY THROUGH OXYGEN (*3)

JEAN-MICHEL JARRE – synthesizers, keyboards

		EMI-Pathe	not iss.
1971.	(lp) *(C006-11739)* **LA CAGE / EROS MACHINE**	–	– France
		Disques Motors	**not iss.**
1972.	(lp; unreleased) **DESERTED PALACE**	–	– France
1973.	(7") *(MT 043)* **HYPNOSE. / DESERTED PALACE**	–	– France
		Polydor	**Polydor**
Jul 77.	(lp)(c) *(2310 555)(3100 398)* <6112> **OXYGENE**	2	78

– Oxygene (Parts 1 – 6). *(cd-iss. 1983; 800 015-2)* *(re-iss. Jun97 on 'Epic' cd/c; 487375-2/-4)*

| Aug 77. | (7") *(2001 721)* **OXYGENE (part 4). / OXYGENE (part 6)** | 4 | |
| Dec 78. | (lp/c) *(POLD/+C 5007)* <6175> **EQUINOXE** | 11 | |

– Equinoxe (Parts I – VIII). *(cd-iss. 1983; 800 025-2)* *(re-iss. Jan93;)* *(re-iss. Jun97 on 'Epic' cd/c; 487376-2/-4)*

Dec 78.	(7") *(POSP 20)* **EQUINOXE (part V). / EQUINOXE (part I)**	45	
Jul 79.	(7") *(2001 896)* **EQUINOXE (part IV remix). / EQUINOXE (part III)**		
Feb 80.	(7") *(2001 968)* **EQUINOXE (part VII) (live). / EQUINOXE (part VIII) (live)**		
May 81.	(lp/c) *(POLS/+C 1033)* <6325> **MAGNETIC FIELDS**	6	98

– Magnetic fields (parts 1 – 5) / The last rumba. *(cd-iss. 1983; 800 024-2)* *(re-iss. Jan93;)*

| Jun 81. | (7") *(POSP 292)* **MAGNETIC FIELDS (part 2 remix). / MAGNETIC FIELDS (part 1 excerpt)** | | |
| Nov 81. | (7") *(POSP 363)* **MAGNETIC FIELDS (part 4 remix). / MAGNETIC FIELDS (part 1 excerpt)** | | |

——— added **DOMINIQUE PERRIER + FREDERIC ROUSSEAU** – synthesizers / **ROGER RIZZITELLI** – percussion, drums

| May 82. | (d-lp)(d-c) *(PODV/+C 3)* **THE CONCERTS IN CHINA (live)** | 6 | |

– The overture / Arpegiator / Equinoxe IV / Fishing junks at sunset / Band in the rain / Equinoxe VII / Laser harp / Orient express / Magnetic fields I, III & IV / Night in Shanghai / The last rumba / Magnetic fields II Souvenir of China. *(d-cd-iss. 1983; 811 551-2)* *(re-iss. Jan93;)*

| May 82. | (7") *(POSP 430)* **ORIENT EXPRESS. / FISHING JUNKS AT SUNSET** | | |
| Oct 83. | (lp/c) *(PRO LP/MC 3)* **THE ESSENTIAL JEAN-MICHEL JARRE** (compilation) | 14 | |

– Oxygene 2, 4 & 6 / Equinoxe 1, 3, 4 & 5 / Magnetic fields 1, 2, 4 & 5 / Orient express / Fishing junks at sunset / Overture. *(cd-iss. Sep84; 817 003-2)*

		Polydor	**Dreyfus**
Nov 84.	(lp/c)(cd) *(POLH/+C 15)(823 763-2)* **ZOOLOOK**	47	

– Ethnicolour / Diva / Zoolook / Wooloomooloo / Zoolookologie / Blah-blah cafe / Ethnicolour II. *(cd+=)* – Zoolook (remix) / Zoolookologie (remix).

——— retained **FREDERIC** and recruited **ADRIAN BELEW + IRA SIEGEL** – guitar / **MARCUS MILLER** – bass / **YOGI HORTON** – drums, percussion / **LAURIE ANDERSON** – vocals

| Nov 84. | (7") *(POSP 718)* **ZOOLOOK. / WOOLOOMOOLOO** | | |

(remix.12"+=) *(POSPX 718)* – ('A'-effects) / ('A'extended).

| Mar 85. | (7") *(POSP 740)* **ZOOLOOKOLOGIE (remix). / ETHNICOLOUR** | | |

(12"+=) *(POSPX 740)* – ('A'extended remixed).
(d7"+=) *(POSPG 740)* – Oxygene (part 4) / Oxygene (part 6).

——— w / **PERRIER / MICHEL GEISS** – synth / **JO HAMMER** – electro drums / **DAVID JARRE** – keyboards

| Apr 86. | (lp/c)(cd) *(POLH/+C 27)(829 125-2)* <829125> **RENDEZ-VOUZ** | 9 | 52 |

– First rendez-vous / Second rendez-vous (part I / II / III / IV) / Third rendez-vous / Fourth rendez-vous / Fifth rendez-vous (part I / II / III) / Last rendez-vous – Ron's piece.

| Aug 86. | (7") *(POSP 788)* **RENDEZ-VOUS IV. / FIRST RENDEZ-VOUS** | 65 | |

(12") *(POSPX 788)* – ('A'side) / Rendez-vous (special + original mix) / Moon machine.

——— with **GEISS** – synthesizers / **FRANCIS LIMBERT** – keyboards, synth. / **PASCAL LEBOURG** – keyboards, synth. / **SYLVIAN DURAND** – keyboards, synthesizers / **PERRIER** – keys, synth (HOUSTON only) / **CHRISTINE DURAND** – soprano / **HAMMER** – drums / **KIRK WHALUM** – sax / **GUY DELACROIX** – bass (LYON only) / **DINO LUMBROSO** – percussion (LYON only) / also used choirs & orchestra, etc.

| Jul 87. | (lp/c)(cd) *(POLH/+C 36)(833 170-2)* **IN CONCERT – LYON / HOUSTON (live)** | 18 | |

– Oxygene V / Ethnicolour / Magnetic fields I / Souvenir of China / Equinoxe 5 / Rendez-vous III / Rendez-vous II / Ron's piece / Rendez-vous IV. *(re-iss. Jun97 on 'Epic' cd/c; 487377-2/-4)*

——— with **DOMINIQUE, MICHAEL, JO** and **GUY,** plus guests **SYLVIAN** – synth / & **HANK MARVIN** – guitar (of SHADOWS) on track – *

| Aug 88. | (lp/c)(cd) *(POLH/+C 45)(837 098-2)* **REVOLUTIONS** | 3 | |

– Industrial revolution: (overture – part 1 – part 2 – part 3) / London kid * / Revolutions / Tokyo kid / Computer weekend / September / The emigrant.

| Oct 88. | (7") *(PO 25)* **REVOLUTIONS. / INDUSTRIAL REVOLUTION 2** | 52 | |

(12"+=) *(PZ/+CD 25)* – ('A'extended).

| Dec 88. | (7") *(PO 32)* **LONDON KID. / INDUSTRIAL REVOLUTION 3** | 48 | |

(12"+=/cd-s+=) *(PZ/+CD 32)* – Revolutions (remix).

| Sep 89. | (7") *(PO 55)* **OXYGENE IV (remix). / INDUSTRIAL REVOLUTION OVERTURE** | 65 | |

(12"+=/cd-s+=) *(PZ/+CD 55)* – ('A'live version) / September.

| Oct 89. | (lp/c/cd) *(841 258-1/-4/-2)* **JARRE LIVE (live)** | 16 | |

– Introduction (revolution) / Industrial revolution: (Overture – part I – part II – part III) / Magnetic fields IV / Oxygene IV / Computer weekend / Revolutions / Rendez-vous IV / Rendez-vous II / The emigrant. *(cd+=)* – (2 extra).

——— Retained **PERRIER** and **GEISS,** plus introduced The **AMACO RENEGADES** – steel drums / guests **GUY DELACROIX** – bass / **CHRISTOPHE DESCHAMPS** – drums

| Jun 90. | (cd/c/lp) *(843 614-2/-4/-1)* **WAITING FOR COUSTEAU** | | |

– Calypso / Calypso (pt.2) / Calypso (pt.3, finale side) / Waiting for Cousteau. *(cd+=)* – (extra music).

| May 93. | (cd/c/lp) *(519 373-2/-4/-1)* **CHRONOLOGIE** | 11 | |

– (part.1 – part.4) / (part.5 – part.8). *(re-iss. Jun97 on 'Epic' cd/c; 487379-2/-4)*

| Jun 93. | (cd-s/12"/cd-s) *(POCS/PO/POCD 274)* **CHRONOLOGIE (part 4). / ('A'part)** | 55 | |

(re-mixed re-iss. Oct93; same); hit UK 56)

| May 94. | (cd/c/lp) *(519 373-2/-4/-1)* **CHRONOLOGIE VI** (mixes) | | |

– (slam mix) / (slam mix 2) / (main mix) / (alternative mix) / (original mix).

		Dreyfus-Epic	**Dreyfus-Epic**
Feb 97.	(cd/c) *(EPC 486984-2/-4)* **OXYGENE 7-13**	11	

– Oxygene 7 (part 1 – part 2 – part 3) / Oxygene 8 / Oxygene 9 (part 1 – part 2 – part 3) / Oxygene 10 / Oxygene 11 / Oxygene 12 / Oxygene 13.

| Mar 97. | (c-s) *(664323-4)* **OXYGENE 8 / ('A'mix)** | 17 | |

(12"+=/cd-s+=) *(664 323-6/-2)* – ('A'mixes).

| Jun 97. | (c-s/cd-s) *(664715-4/-2)* **OXYGENE 10 / ('A'mix)** | 21 | |

(cd-s) *(664715-5)* – ('A'side) / Transcengenics 1 & 2.

| May 98. | (cd/c) *(489764-2/-4)* **ODYSSEY THROUGH OXYGEN** | 50 | |

– Odyssey overture / Oxygene 10 / Oxygene 7 / Oxygene 8 / Oxygene (Hani's 303) / Odyssey (phase 2) / Oxygene 8 (Sunday club) / Oxygene 10 (440 dub) / Odyssey 11 / Oxygene 11 / Oxygene 12 / Oxygene 8 (Takkyu Ishino) / Odyssey finale / Rendezvous '98 / Oxygene 13.

| Jun 98. | (c-s; JEAN-MICHEL JARRE & APOLLO 440) *(666110-4)* **RENDEZVOUS (1998 mix) /** | 12 | – |

(cd-s+=) *(666110-2)* – ('A'mixes).

– compilations, etc. –

on 'Polydor' unless mentioned otherwise

| 1981. | (d-c) *(2683 077)* **OXYGENE / EQUINOXE** | | – |
| Dec 87. | (8xcd-box) *(833 737-2)* **CD BOX SET** | | – |

– (OXYGENE / EQUINOXE / MAGNETIC FIELDS / THE CONCERTS IN CHINA / ZOOLOOK / RENDEZ-VOUS / JARRE IN CONCERT; Houston / Lyon)

| Feb 88. | (7") *Old Gold; (OG 9780)* **OXYGENE (part IV). / EQUINOXE (part 5)** | | – |
| Oct 91. | (cd/c/lp) *(511 306-2/-4/-1)* **IMAGES – THE BEST OF JEAN MICHEL JARRE** | 16 | |

– Oxygene 4 / Equinoxe 5 / Magnetic fields 2 / Oxygene 2 / Computer weekend / Equinoxe 4 / Band in the rain / Rendez-vous 2 / London kid / Ethnicolor 1 / Orient express / Calypso 1 / Calypso 3 (fin de siecle) / Rendez-vous 4 / Moon machine / Eldorado / Globe trotter. *(re-iss. Jun97 on 'Epic' cd/c; 487378-2/-4)*

| Jan 93. | (cd/c/lp) *(815 686-2/-4/-1)* **MUSIK AUS ZEIT UND RAUM** | | |
| Oct 95. | (cd) **JARREMIX** (dance mixes compilation) | | – |

JAYBIRDS (see under ⇒ TEN YEARS AFTER)

JAYHAWKS

Formed: Minneapolis, Minnesota, USA ... 1985 by MARK OLSON and GARY LOURIS, who formed the core of the band through an ever changing series of line-ups. After two American-only albums of rough-hewn country rock, 'THE JAYHAWKS' (1986) and 'BLUE EARTH' (1989), the band were taken under the wing of producer GEORGE DRAKOULIAS. In a well-thumbed tale, they were signed to Rick Rubin's 'Def American' label after roots maestro DRAKOULIAS allegedly phoned 'Twintone' mainman DAVE AYERS and heard a JAYHAWKS tape playing in the background. He was immediately spellbound, as were the country rock faithful among the record buying public when they heard the band's debut for 'Def American', the seminal 'HOLLYWOOD TOWN HALL' (1992). While many fans were under the impression this was the band's first album, the pristine harmonies of OLSON and LOURIS suggested otherwise. Like a fine malt whisky, The JAYHAWKS's songwriting and harmonising had been maturing over almost a decade and the result was something to savour. There wasn't a duff track in sight, and with veteran piano player NICKY HOPKINS on board, this was an essential purchase. Following this release, the band embarked on a heavy round of touring, sparking, along with peers like UNCLE TUPELO, a mini country-rock revival. Expectations were high for the follow-up, 'TOMORROW THE GREEN GRASS' (1995), the band bypassing the dilemma of matching 'HOLLYWOOD's perfection by going for a more eclectic approach. The crystal clear harmonising was still intact, the single 'BLUE' perhaps the JAYHAWKS' finest moment, as affecting a piece of resigned melancholy as ever graced a slab of vinyl. After a further tour, OLSON left and, after a long period of uncertainty and personal crisis, The JAYHAWKS re-emerged, albeit in a radically altered form. 'THE SOUND OF LIES' (1997) was a decidedly low-key affair and despite receiving a 'Masterpiece' award from retro music mag Mojo, the record has largely gone unnoticed. Something of a departure musically and lyrically, the album was downbeat and edgy, not as immediate as the older material but well worth persevering with; the likes of 'TROUBLE' and 'DYING ON THE VINE' coming through bruised but wiser. • **Songwriters:** OLSON-LOURIS except; REASON TO BELIEVE (Tim Hardin). In 1996 LOURIS co-wrote with other members after OLSON left. • **Trivia:** OLSON and LOURIS can also be heard on sessions for MARIA McKEE, COUNTING CROWS and former stablemates SOUL ASYLUM. The latter's DAN MURPHY and DAVE PIRNER (latter part-time) were in the offshoot band, GOLDEN SMOG, which featured LOURIS and PERLMAN.

Album rating: THE JAYHAWKS (*6) / BLUE EARTH (*6) / HOLLYWOOD TOWN HALL (*8) / TOMORROW THE GREEN GRASS (*7) / THE SOUND OF LIES (*6)

MARK OLSON – vocals, guitar, harmonica / GARY LOURIS – vocals, electric guitar / KAREN GROTBERG – keyboards / MARC PERLMAN – bass repl. KEN CALLAHAN

		not iss.	Bunkhouse
1986.	(lp) THE JAYHAWKS	-	-

		not iss.	Twin/Tone
1989.	(lp/cd) <TTR 89151-1/-2> THE BLUE EARTH	-	

– Two angels / She's not alone anymore / Will I be married / Dead end angel / Commonplace streets / Ain't no end / Five cups of coffee / The Baltimore sun / Red firecracker / Sioux City / I'm still dreaming now I'm yours / Martin's song. *(UK-iss.cd Jul95; same) (cd re-iss. Sep98 on 'R.C.A.'; 74321 60575-28)*

—— session NICKY HOPKINS – keyboards (ex-JEFF BECK GROUP, etc)

		Def American	Def American
Sep 92.	(cd/c/lp) (512 986-2/-4/-1) <26829> HOLLYWOOD TOWN HALL		

– Waiting for the sun / Crowded in the wings / Clouds / Two angels / Take me with you / Sister cry / Settled down like rain / Witghita / Nevada, California / Martin's song. *(re-iss. cd Apr95 on 'American-RCA'; 74321 23994-2)*

Aug 93.	(7"/-c-s) (DEFA/MC 28) SETTLED DOWN LIKE RAIN. / SISTER CRY		

(cd-s+=) (DEFCD 28) – Live medley: Settled down like rain – Martin's song.

Nov 93.	(7"/-c-s) (DEFA/MC 25) WAITING FOR THE SUN. / MARTIN'S SONG		

(cd-s+=) (DEFCD 25) – Up above my head / Keith & Quentin.
(cd-s+=) (DEFCDX 25) – Reason to believe / Sister cry / Medley: Martin's song – Settled down like rain.
(cd-s) (DEFCDXX 25) – ('A'side) / Up above my head.

—— now on drums DON HEFFINGTON (studio) / TIM O'REAGAN (tour)

		American-RCA	American-RCA
Feb 95.	(cd/c) (74321 23680-2/-4) <43006> TOMORROW THE GREEN GRASS	41	92

– Blue / I'd run away / Miss Williams' guitar / Two hearts / Real light / Over my shoulder / Bad time / See him on the streets / Nothing left to borrow / Ann Jane / Pray for me / Red's song / Ten little kids.

Feb 95.	(7"/-c-s) (74321 25797-7/-4) BLUE. / TOMORROW THE GREEN GRASS		-

(cd-s+=) (74321 25797-2) – Darling today.

Jul 95.	(7"/-c-s) (74321 29163-7/-4) BAD TIME. / LAST CIGARETTE	70	-

(cd-s+=) (74321 29163-2) – Get the load out / Sing me back home.

—— now without OLSON / line-up LOURIS, PERLMAN, GROTBERG + O'REAGAN plus KRAIG JOHNSON + JESSY GREENE

Apr 97.	(cd/c) <(74321 46406-2/-4)> SOUND OF LIES	61	

– The man who loved life / Think about it / Trouble / It's up to you / Stick in the mud / Big star / Poor little fish / Sixteen down / Haywire / Dying on the vine / Bottomless cup / Sound of lies / I hear you cry.

Jun 97.	(c-s) (74321 48755-4) BIG STAR / SLEEPYHEAD		-

(cd-s+=) (74321 48677-2) – Dying on the vine / I'd run away.

Wyclef JEAN & The REFUGEE ALLSTARS
(see under ⇒ FUGEES)

JEFFERSON AIRPLANE

Formed: San Francisco, California, USA . . . early 1965 by MARTY BALIN and PAUL KANTNER. They recruited others and signed to 'RCA' in late '65, releasing a flop debut single, 'IT'S NO SECRET'. In September '66, their first album, ' . . . TAKES OFF', was finally issued, a competent hybrid of folk-rock and blues notable for the powerful singing of second vocalist SIGNE ANDERSON. By the time of the album's release, however, ANDERSON had left to have a baby and was replaced by GRACE SLICK (formerly of The GREAT SOCIETY). SKIP SPENCE also left and the drum stool was filled by SPENCER DRYDEN. The potential of this all-playing, all-writing group was fulfilled on the follow-up lp, 'SURREALISTIC PILLOW' (1967). A psychedelic classic, the record spawned two top 10 singles in the U.S., 'SOMEBODY TO LOVE' (1967) and 'WHITE RABBIT' (1967), SLICK having brought both songs with her from her previous band. Her vocals were even stronger than ANDERSON's and her commanding clarity stamped itself indelibly on every song, particularly 'WHITE RABBIT', a neo classical, lysergic nursery rhyme (inspired by the Lewis Carroll book 'Alice In Wonderland') that managed to sound at once sinister and insidiously catchy. Even KAUKONEN's blistering guitar work and CASSADY's relentlessly inventive bass playing sounded more assured, the album going on to sell half a million copies. The band then took psychedelic experimentation ever further with 'AFTER BATHING AT BAXTER'S' (1968). Comprising a number of free-form song 'suites', the album was hard going; the melodies were still in there, they were just harder to find among the wilful weirdness and extended instrumental jams. 'R.C.A.' must have breathed a sigh of relief when the band came up with the relatively more accessible 'CROWN OF CREATION' (1968). A more conventional set of songs, it featured the scary 'THE HOUSE AT POONEIL CORNERS', SLICK's haunting 'LATHER' and a cover of DAVID CROSBY's menage-a-trois elegy, 'TRIAD'. After a thundering live set, 'BLESS ITS POINTED LITTLE HEAD' (1969), the band recorded the last album to feature the classic JEFFERSON line-up, 'VOLUNTEERS' (1970). It featured the unflinching politicism of 'WE CAN BE TOGETHER' and though the title track was used in the 'Woodstock' movie, the band's own performance wasn't filmed. Soon after the album's release, DRYDEN left to join The NEW RIDERS OF THE PURPLE SAGE and was replaced by JOEY COVINGTON. BALIN also departed around this time after a prolonged period of tension with SLICK, violinist PAPA JOHN CREACH (was this the man

behind MADONNA's 'Papa Don't Preach' we ask ourselves?) taking up the slack. The subsequent 'BARK' (1971) and 'LONG JOHN SILVER' (1972) albums (released on the band's newly formed 'Grunt' label) bore none of the intensity of The 'AIRPLANE's earlier work and the band's final effort, the live 'THIRTY SECONDS OVER WINTERLAND' (1973) was similarly underwhelming. By this point, JOHN BARBATA had replaced sticksman COVINGTON while DAVID FRIEBERG (ex-QUICKSILVER MESSENGER SERVICE) had been recruited on vocals. While CASSADY and KAUKONEN went full-time with their side project, HOT TUNA, SLICK and KANTNER formed JEFFERSON STARSHIP with the remaining 'AIRPLANE members. The name was taken from an earlier, KANTNER sci-fi inspired project that released one album, 1971's '(IT'S A FRESH WIND THAT) BLOWS AGAINST THE NORTH'. The debut JEFFERSON STARSHIP album, 'DRAGONFLY' (1974), was well written and skillfully executed but it was clear the band were headed towards the mainstream and with 'RED OCTOPUS' (1975), the band's sleek sound was crystallised, the album shifting a cool four million copies. MARTY BALIN was also back in the fold by this point and his song, 'MIRACLES', went Top 3 later the same year. Disillusioned with the new direction, SLICK soon left for a low key solo career while JEFFERSON STARSHIP continued to notch up hit albums. She later rejoined, although by 1984 even KANTNER had become tired of the group's commercial sound, leaving and taking the JEFFERSON part of the name with him. As STARSHIP, the SLICK fronted band went on to even bigger success, reeling off hits like 'WE BUILT THIS CITY ON ROCK 'N' ROLL' (1985) and the nauseous pop slush of 'NOTHING'S GONNA STOP US NOW' (1987). Incredibly/inevitably there was a full reunion of the classic JEFFERSON AIRPLANE line-up in 1989 which produced an eponymous album. A pointless exercise in crusty nostalgia, it was almost as dull as the dishwater STARSHIP were peddling.

Album rating: JEFFERSON AIRPLANE TAKES OFF (*5) / SURREALISTIC PILLOW (*8) / AFTER BATHING AT BAXTER'S (*7) / CROWN OF CREATION (*7) / VOLUNTEERS (*6) / THE WORST OF JEFFERSON AIRPLANE compilation (*6) / BLOWS AGAINST THE EMPIRE (*5; as PAUL KANTNER & JEFFERSON STARSHIP) / SUNFIGHTER (*5; by Paul Kantner & Grace Slick) / BARK (*6) / LONG JOHN SILVER (*5) / THIRTY SECONDS OVER WINTERLAND (*5) / BARON VON TOLBOOTH & THE CHROME NUN (*4; by Paul Kantner, Grace Slick & David Frieberg) / EARLY FLIGHT early stuff (*4) / Grace Slick: MANHOLE (*4) / DREAMS (*4) / WELCOME TO THE WRECKING BALL (*5) / Jefferson Starship: DRAGON FLY (*6) / RED OCTOPUS (*7) / SPITFIRE (*6) / FLIGHT LOG 1966-1976 compilation (*6; Jefferson Airplane & Starship) / EARTH (*4) / GOLD compilation (*7) / FREEDOM AT POINT ZERO (*5) / MODERN TIMES (*5) / WINDS OF CHANGE (*4) / NUCLEAR FURNITURE (*4) / Starship: KNEE DEEP IN THE HOOPLA (*4) / 2400 FULTON STREET – AN ANTHOLOGY remastered early collection (*7) / NO PROTECTION (*4) / LOVE AMONG THE CANNIBALS (*4) / JEFFERSON AIRPLANE (*3; as Jefferson Airplane) / DEEP SPACE – VIRGIN SKY (*3) / GREATEST HITS (TEN YEARS AND CHANGE 1979-1991) compilation (*6; by Starship)

MARTY BALIN (b. MARTYN JEREL BUCHWALD, 30 Jan'43, Cincinnati, Ohio, USA) – vocals, guitar (ex-solo) / **PAUL KANTNER** (b.12 Mar'42, San Francisco) – guitar, vocals / **JORMA KAUKONEN** (b.23 Dec'40, Washington, D.C.) – lead guitar / **SIGNE TOLY ANDERSON** (b.15 Sep'41, Seattle, Wash.) – vocals / **JACK CASSADY** (b.13 Apr'44, Washington, D.C.) – bass repl. BOB HARVEY / **SKIP SPENCE** (b.18 Apr'46, Ontario, Canada) – drums (ex-QUICKSILVER MESSENGER SERVICE) repl. JERRY PELOQUIN

		R.C.A.	R.C.A.
Feb 66.	(7") <8679> IT'S NO SECRET. / RUNNIN' ROUND THIS TABLE		-
May 66.	(7") <8848> COME UP THE YEARS. / BLUES FROM AN AEROPLANE		-
Sep 66.	(lp) <LSP 3584> JEFFERSON AIRPLANE TAKES OFF		

– Blues from an airplane / Let me in / It's no secret / Bringing me down / Tobacco road / Coming up the years / Run around / Let's get together / Don't slip away / Chauffeur blues / And I like it. *(UK-iss.Oct71; SF 8195) (re-iss. Jun74;)*

Sep 66.	(7") <8967> BRINGING ME DOWN. / LET ME IN		

—— GRACE SLICK (b. GRACE BARNETT WING, 30 Oct'39, Chicago, Illinois) – vocals (ex-GREAT SOCIETY) repl. SIGNE who left to look after her baby / SPENCER DRYDEN (b. 7 Apr'38, New York City) – drums (ex-PEANUT BUTTER CONSPIRACY, ex-ASHES) repl. SKIP who formed MOBY GRAPE

Dec 66.	(7") <9063> MY BEST FRIEND. / HOW DO YOU FEEL	-	
Sep 67.	(lp; mono/stereo) (RD/SF 7889) <LSP 3766> SURREALISTIC PILLOW		3 Feb67

– She has funny cars / Somebody to love / My best friend / Today / Comin' back to me / How do you feel / 3/5 mile in 10 seconds / D.C.B.A. – 25 / Embryonic journey / White rabbit / Plastic fantastic lover. *(UK-rel.had different tracks) (cd-iss. Sep84; PD 83766) (cd re-iss. Oct87; ND 83738)*

May 67.	(7") (RCA 1594) <9140> SOMEBODY TO LOVE. / SHE HAS FUNNY CARS		5 Feb67
Sep 67.	(7") (RCA 1631) <9248> WHITE RABBIT. / PLASTIC FANTASTIC LOVER		8 Jun67
Nov 67.	(7") (RCA 1647) <9297> BALLAD OF YOU AND ME AND POONEIL. / TWO HEADS		42 Sep67
Jun 68.	(lp; mono/stereo) (RD/SF 7926) <LSP 1511> AFTER BATHING AT BAXTERS		17 Dec67

– (Streetmasse): / Ballad of you and me and Pooneil – A small package of value will come to you, shortly – Young girl Sunday blues / (The war is over): / Martha – Wild thyme / (Hymn to an older generation): / The last wall of the castle – Rejoyce / How sweet it is:- Watch her ride – Spare chaynge / Shizoforest love suite: Two heads – Won't you try – Saturday afternoon. *(re-iss. Dec88 lp/c; NL/NK 84718)*

Jan 68.	(7") <9389> WATCH HER RIDE. / MARTHA	-	61 Dec67
Jun 68.	(7") (RCA 1711) <9496> GREASY HEART. / SHARE A LITTLE JOKE		98 Mar68
Sep 68.	(7") (RCA 1736) IF YOU FEEL LIKE CHINA BREAKING. TRIAD		-

Oct 68. (7") <9644> **CROWN OF CREATION. / TRIAD** [-] [64]
Dec 68. (lp; mono/stereo) (RD/SF 7976) <LSP 4058> **CROWN OF CREATION** [ ] [6] Sep68
– Lather / In time / Triad / Star track / Share a little joke / Chushingura / If you feel / Crown of creation / Ice cream Phoenix / Greasy heart / The house at Pooh Corner. (re-iss. Oct85 lp/c; NL/NK 83797) (cd-iss. Jun88; ND 83660)
Jun 69. (lp; mono/stereo) (RD/SF 8019) <LSP 4133> **BLESS ITS POINTED LITTLE HEAD (live)** [38] [17] Feb69
– Clergy / 3/5 of a mile in 10 seconds / Somebody to love / Fat angel / Rock me baby / The other side of this life / It's no secret / Plastic fantastic lover / Turn out the lights / Bear melt.
Jul 69. (7") <0150> **PLASTIC FANTASTIC LOVER (live). / THE OTHER SIDE OF THIS LIFE (live)** [-] [ ]
Feb 70. (lp) (SF 8164) <LSP 4238> **VOLUNTEERS** [34] [13] Nov69
– We can be together / Good shepherd / The farm / Hey Frederick / Turn my life down / Wooden ships / Eskimo blue day / A song for all seasons / Meadowlands / Volunteers. (re-iss. Oct85)
Mar 70. (7") (RCA 1933) <0245> **VOLUNTEERS. / WE CAN BE TOGETHER** [ ] [65] Nov69

—— **JOEY COVINGTON** – drums repl. DRYDEN who joined NEW RIDERS OF THE PURPLE SAGE (above new with **SLICK, CASADY, BALIN** and **KAUKONEN**) (note also DRYDEN played on below 'A' side)
Aug 70. (7") (RCA 1989) <0343> **MEXICO. / HAVE YOU SEEN THE SAUCERS?** [ ] [ ]

—— At this time various members, mainly KAUKONEN and CASADY side lined HOT TUNA. PAUL KANTNER then recorded album with what was then p/t JEFFERSON STARSHIP (see further below and his late '71 co-credit with GRACE SLICK

—— **PAPA JOHN CREACH** (b.28 May 1917, Beaver Falls, Pennsylvania) – violin (of HOT TUNA) finally repl. BALIN who left earlier.

		Grunt	Grunt
Oct 71. (lp) <(FTR 1001)> **BARK** [42] [11] Sep71
– When the Earth moves again / Feel so good / Crazy Miranda / Pretty as you feel / Wild turkey / Law man / Rock and roll island / Third week in Chelsea / Never argue with a German if you're tired or European song / Thunk / War movie. (re-iss. Jul84; NL 84386)
Oct 71. (7") <(65-0500)> **PRETTY AS YOU FEEL. / WILD TURKEY** [ ] [60]

—— **JOHN BARBATA** – drums (ex-CROSBY & NASH, ex-TURTLES) repl. JOEY
Jun 72. (lp) <(FTR 1007)> **LONG JOHN SILVER** [30] [20]
– Long John Silver / Aerie (gang of eagles) / Twilight double leader / Milk train / Son of Jesus / Easter? / Trial by fire / Alexander the medium / Eat starch mom.
Sep 72. (7") <(65-0506)> **LONG JOHN SILVER. / MILK TRAIN** [ ] [ ]
1972. (7") <(65-0511)> **TWILIGHT DOUBLE DEALER. / TRIAL BY FIRE** [ ] [ ]

—— **DAVID FREIBERG** (b.24 Aug'38, Boston, Mass.) – vocals (ex-QUICKSILVER MESSENGER SERVICE) (They made last album recorded between 71-72)
Apr 73. (lp) <(FTR 0147)> **30 SECONDS OVER WINTERLAND (live)** [ ] [52]
– Have you seen the saucers / Feel so good / Crown of creation / When the Earth moves again / Milk train / Trial by fire / Twilight double leader. (re-iss. Oct85 lp/c; NL/NK 83867)

—— Now non-recording quintet of SLICK, KANTNER, FREIBERG, BARBATA and CREACH. CASADY and KAUKONEN made HOT TUNA their full-time band.

PAUL KANTNER & JEFFERSON STARSHIP

with JERRY GARCIA, DAVID CROSBY, GRAHAM NASH, MICKEY HART

		R.C.A.	R.C.A.
Jan 71. (7") <0426> **A CHILD IS COMING. / LET'S GO TOGETHER** [-] [ ]
Apr 71. (lp) (SF 8163) <LSP 4448> **(IT'S A FRESH WIND THAT) BLOWS AGAINST THE NORTH** [ ] [20] Nov70
– Mau mau (Amerikon) / The baby tree / Let's go together / A child is coming / Sunrise / Hijack / Home / Have you seen the stars tonite / X-M / Starship.

PAUL KANTNER & GRACE SLICK

		Grunt	Grunt
Dec 71. (lp) <(FTR 1002)> **SUNFIGHTER** [ ] [89]
– Silver spoon / Diana (part 1) / Sunfighter / Titanic / Look at the wood / When I was a boy I watched the wolves / Million / China / Earth mother / Diana (part 2) / Universal Copernican mumbles / Holding together. (re-iss. Apr89 on 'Essential' lp/cd; ESS LP/CD 001)
Jan 72. (7") <0503> **SUNFIGHTER. / CHINA** [-] [ ]

—— KANTNER later released a US only album 'THE PLANET EARTH ROCK AND ROLL ORCHESTRA iss.Aug83. After leaving JEFFERSON STARSHIP he formed KBC with BALIN and CASADY (ex-AIRPLANE members). They released a single and album early '83.

PAUL KANTNER, GRACE SLICK, DAVID FREIBERG

with guests **JORMA KAUKONEN** – guitar / **JACK CASADY** – bass / **CHAQUICO** – guitar / **JERRY GARCIA** ('Grateful Dead') / **DAVID CROSBY** ('Crosby, Stills & Nash')

		Grunt	Grunt
Jun 73. (lp) <(BFL 1-0148)> **BARON VON TOLBOOTH & THE CHROME NUN** [ ] [ ]
– Ballad of the chrome nun / Fat / Flowers of the night / Walkin' / Your mind has left your body / Across the board / Harp tree lament / White boy (transcaucasian airmachine blues) / Fishman / Sketches of China.
Jun 73. (7") <0094> **BALLAD OF THE CHROME NUN. / SKETCHES OF CHINA** [-] [ ]

—— For JEFFERSON STARSHIP + STARSHIP recordings (which had nothing whatsoever to do with psychedelia) see The GREAT ROCK DISCOGRAPHY.

JEFFERSON STARSHIP

(new name re-formed) **SLICK, KANTNER, FREIBERG, CREACH + BARBATA** recruited **CRAIG CHAQUICO** (b.26 Sep'54, Sacramento, Calif.) – guitar (ex-STEELWIND) repl. JORMA / **PETE SEARS** (b. England) – bass, keyboards, vocals repl. PETER KAUKONEN, who had repl. JACK

		Grunt	Grunt
Nov 74. (7") <FB 10080> **RIDE THE TIGER. / DEVIL'S DEN** [-] [84]
Dec 74. (lp) <(BFL 1-0717)> **DRAGONFLY** [ ] [11] Oct74
– Ride the tiger / That's for sure / Be young you / Caroline / Devil's den / Come to life / All fly away / Hyperdrive.
1975. (7") <FB 10206> **BE YOUNG YOU. / CAROLINE** [-] [ ]

—— added the returning **MARTY BALIN** – vocals, guitar
Jul 75. (lp) (FTR 2002) <BFL 1-0999> **RED OCTOPUS** [ ] [1]
– Fast buck Freddie / Miracles / Git fiddler / Al Garimasu (there is love) / Sweeter than honey / Play on love / Tumblin' / I want to see another world / Sandalphon / There will be love. (re-iss. Feb81 on 'RCA International' lp/c; INT S/K 5069) (re-iss. Oct84 on 'RCA' lp/c/cd; PL/PK/PD 80999) (re-iss. Jun86 on 'Fame' lp/c; FA/TC-FA 3156) (cd-iss. Oct87 & Jun88; ND 83464 & ND 83660)
Sep 75. (7") <(FB 10367)> **MIRACLES. / AL GARIMASU (THERE IS LOVE)** [ ] [3] Aug75
Nov 75. (7") <FB 10456> **PLAY ON LOVE / I WANT TO SEE ANOTHER WORLD** [-] [49]

—— Trimmed to sextet when PAPA JOHN CREACH then GRACE SLICK went solo
Jul 76. (lp) <(BFL 1-1557)> **SPITFIRE** [30] [3]
– Hot water / Big city / Switchblade / Cruisin' / Love lovely love / St. Charles / Dance with the dragon / St. Charles / With your love / Song to the sun / Ozymandias / Don't let it rain. (cd-iss. Jun97 on 'R.C.A.'; 0786366876-2)
Aug 76. (7") <(FB 10746)> **WITH YOUR LOVE. / SWITCHBLADE** [ ] [12] Jul76
Nov 76. (7") <(FB 10791)> **ST. CHARLES. / LOVE LOVELY LOVE** [-] [64]
Feb 78. (7") <(FB 11196)> **COUNT ON ME. / SHOW YOURSELF** [ ] [8]
Mar 78. (lp/c) <(FB 12515) <2515> **EARTH** [ ] [5]
– Love too good / Count on me / Take your time / Crazy feelin' / Skateboard / Fire / Show yourself / All nite long. (cd-iss. Jun97 on 'R.C.A.'; 0786366878-2)
Jun 78. (7") <(FB 11274)> **RUNAWAY. / HOT WATER** [ ] [12] May 78
Aug 78. (7") <(FB 11374)> **CRAZY FEELIN'. / LOVE TOO GOOD** [-] [54]
Nov 78. (7"/12") <(FB 11426/11469)> **LIGHT THE SKY ON FIRE. / HYPERDRIVE** [-] [66]

—— **MICKEY THOMAS** (b. Cairo, Georgia) – vocals (ex-ELVIN BISHOP) repl. BALIN who went solo / **AYNSLEY DUNBAR** (b.10 Jan'46, Liverpool, England) – drums (ex-JOURNEY ex-KGB) repl. BARBATA (above 2 joining **KANTNER, FREIBERG, CHAQUICO** and **SEARS**) / **GRACE SLICK** also guested uncredited on the next album (she joined full-time Feb81.)
Jan 80. (7") <(FB 11750)> **JANE. / FREEDOM AT POINT ZERO** [21] [14] Nov79
Jan 80. (lp) (FL 13452) <3452> **FREEDOM AT ZERO POINT** [22] [10] Nov79
– Girl with hungry eyes / Freedom at Zero Point / Fadiing lady night / Lightning Rose / Things to come / Just the same / Rock music / Awakening / Jane. (re-iss. Sep81 lp/c; RCA LP/K 3038) (re-iss. Jun89; NL 89912) (cd-iss. Feb90; ND 89912)
Apr 80. (7") <(FB 11921)> **GIRL WITH THE HUNGRY EYES. / JUST THE SAME** [ ] [55]
Jun 80. (7") <(FB 11961)> **ROCK MUSIC. / LIGHTNING ROSE** [ ] [ ]

		R.C.A.	Grunt
May 81. (7"/12") (RCA 66) <FB 1221-1/-3> **FIND YOUR WAY BACK. / MODERN TIMES** [ ] [29] Apr81
Jun 81. (lp) (3050) <BZL 1-3848> **MODERN TIMES** [ ] [26] Apr81
– Find your way back / Stranger / Wild eyes / Save your love / Modern times / Mary / Free / Alien / Stairway to Cleveland. (re-iss. Sep81 lp/c; RCA LP/K 3050)
Jul 81. (7") <12275> **STRANGER. / FREE** [-] [48]
Oct 81. (7"/12") <1233-2/-3> **SAVE YOUR LOVE. / WILD EYES** [-] [ ]
Oct 82. (7") <13350> **BE MY LADY. / OUT OF CONTROL** [-] [28]
Feb 83. (lp/c) (RCA LP/K 6060) <BXL 1-4372> **WINDS OF CHANGE** [ ] [26] Oct82
– Winds of change / Keep on dreamin' / Be my lady / I will stay / Out of control / Can't find love / Black widow / I came back from the jaws of the dragon / Quit wasting time. (re-iss. Oct84 lp/c/cd; FL/FK/FD 84372)
Jan 83. (7") <13439> **WINDS OF CHANGE. / BLACK WIDOW** [-] [38]
Apr 83. (7") <13531> **CAN'T FIND LOVE. / I WILL STAY** [-] [ ]

—— **DON BALDWIN** – drums (ex-ELVIN BISHOP BAND) repl. DUNBAR
Jun 84. (7") (RCA 424) <13811> **NO WAY OUT. / ROSE GOES TO YALE** [ ] [ ] May84
(12"+=) (RCA 424T) <13812> – Be my lady.
Jun 84. (lp/c/cd) (FL/FK/FD 84921) <4921> **NUCLEAR FURNITURE** [ ] [28]
– Layin' it on the line / No way out / Sorry me, sorry you / Live and let live / Connection / Nuclear furniture / Rose goes to Vale / Magician / Assassin / Shining in the moonlight / Showdown / Champion.
Sep 84. (7") <13872> **LAYIN' IT ON THE LINE. / SHOWDOWN** [-] [66]

STARSHIP

was the name they were allowed to use after KANTNER left. Now **GRACE SLICK, MICKEY THOMAS, CRAIG CHAQUICO, PETE SEARS** and **DON BALDWIN**
Oct 85. (7") (FB 49929) <14170> **WE BUILT THIS CITY. / PRIVATE ROOM** [12] [1] Sep85
(12"+=) (FT 49930) – ('A'extended).
Nov 85. (lp/c/cd) (FL/FK/FD 85488) <5488> **KNEE DEEP IN THE HOOPLA** [ ] [7] Oct85
– We built this city / Sara / Tomorrow doesn't matter tonight / Rock myself to sleep / Desperate heart / Private room / Before I go / Hearts of the world (will understand) / Love rusts. (re-iss. Sep89 lp/cd; NL/NK/ND 90367)
Jan 86. (7") (FB 49893) <14253> **SARA. / HEARTS OF THE WORLD (WILL UNDERSTAND)** [ ] [1] Dec85
(12"+=) (FT 49894) – Jane.
May 86. (7") (FB 49855) <14332> **TOMORROW DOESN'T MATTER TONIGHT. / LOVE RUSTS** [ ] [26] Apr86
(12"+=) (FT 49856) – No way out / Layin' it on the line.
Jun 86. (7",12") <14393> **BEFORE I GO. / CUT YOU DOWN** [-] [68]

—— now w/out SEARS

	R.C.A.	RCA-Grunt
Mar 87. (7") *(FB 49757)* <5109> **NOTHING'S GONNA STOP US NOW. / LAYING IT ON THE LINE**	1	1 Jan87

(12"+=) *(FT 49757)* – We built this city / Tomorrow doesn't matter tonight.

| Jul 87. (lp/c/cd) *(FL/FK/FD 86413)* <6413> **NO PROTECTION** | 26 | 12 |

– Beat patrol / Nothing's gonna stop us now / It's not over ('til it's over) / Girls like you / Wings of a lie / The children / I don't know why / Transatlantic / Babylon / Set the night to music.

| Aug 87. (7") *(RCA 5001)* <5225> **IT'S NOT OVER ('TIL IT'S OVER). / BABYLON** | | 9 Jun87 |

(12"+=)<US-cd-s> *(RCAT 5000)* – Jane / Sara.

| Nov 87. (7") *(RCA 5002)* <5308> **BEAT PATROL. / GIRLS LIKE YOU** | | 46 Sep87 |

(cd-s+=) *(RCAT 5002)* – ('A'extended).

| Feb 88. (7") <6964> **SET THE NIGHT TO MUSIC. / I DON'T KNOW WHY** | - | |

(12"+=) <6964> – ('A'dub version) / ('A'instrumental).

—— STARSHIP in the 90's were: – **MICKEY THOMAS, DONNY BALDWIN, CRAIG CHAQUICO** plus **MARK MORGAN** – keyboards / **BRETT BLOOMFIELD** – bass

| Feb 89. (7") *(EKR 88)* <69349> **WILD AGAIN. / LAYIN' IT ON THE LINE** | | 73 Dec88 |

(12"+=) *(EKR 88T)* – Tutti Frutti.
(above was from the film 'Cocktail' on label 'Elektra')

	R.C.A.	R.C.A.
Sep 89. (7"/c-s) *(PB/PK 49357)* <9032> **IT'S NOT ENOUGH. / LOVE AMONG THE CANNIBALS**		12 Jul89

(12"+=) *(PT 49358)* – Wild again.
(cd-s++=) *(PD 49356)* – Nothing's gonna stop us now.

| Sep 89. (lp/c/cd) *(PL/PK/PD 90387)* <9693> **LOVE AMONG THE CANNIBALS** | | 64 Aug89 |

– The burn / It's not enough / Trouble in mind / I didn't mean to stay all night / Send a message / Love among the cannibals / We dream in colour / Healing waters / Blaze of love / I'll be there. *(cd+=)* – Wild again.

Nov 89. (c-s) <9109> **I DIDN'T MEAN TO STAY ALL NIGHT / WE DREAM IN COLOR**	-	75
Apr 91. (c-s) <2796> **GOOD HEART / (3 album excerpts)**	-	81
Aug 91. (cd/c/lp) *(PD/PK/PL 82423)* **GREATEST HITS (TEN YEARS AND CHANGE 1979-1991)** (compilation)		-

– Jane / Find your way back / Stranger / No way out / Layin' it on the line / Don't lose any sleep / We built this city / Sara / Nothing's gonna stop us now / It's not over ('til it's over) / It's not enough / Good heart. *(re-iss. cd Oct95)*

JEFFERSON AIRPLANE

were reformed with **SLICK, KANTNER, KAUKONEN, CASADY** and **BALIN**. Augmented by **KENNY ARONOFF** – drums / **PETER KAUKONEN** and **RANDY JACKSON** – guitar (ex-ZEBRA)

	Epic	Epic
Oct 89. (lp/c/cd) *(465 659-1/-4/-2)* <45271> **JEFFERSON AIRPLANE**		85

– Planes / Solidarity / Summer of love / The wheel / True love / Now is the time / Panda / Freedom / Ice age / Madeleine Street / Common market madrigal / Upfront blues / Too many years.

| Oct 89. (7") <73044> **SUMMER OF LOVE. / PANDA** | - | |
| Jan 90. (c-s) <73080> **TRUE LOVE /** | - | |

—— JEFFERSON STARSHIP ("the next generation") were formed after above.

JEFFERSON STARSHIP ("the next generation")

KANTNER / CASADY / BALIN + SLICK (repl. CREACH) / **TIM GORMAN** – keyboards, vocals (ex-KBC BAND) / **PRAIRIE PRINCE** (b. 7 May'50, Charlotte, New Connecticut) / **MARK AUGUILAR** – guitar, vocals (ex-KBC BAND) / **DARBY GOULD** – vocals

	Essential	Intersound
Jul 95. (cd/c) *(ESM CD/MC 493)* **DEEP SPACE – VIRGIN SKY**		

– Shadowlands / Ganja of love / Dark ages / I'm on fire / Papa John / Women who fly / Gold / The light / Crown of creation / Count on me / Miracles / Intro to lawman / Lawman / Wooden ships / Somebody to love / White rabbit.

– (AIRPLANE) compilations, etc. –

on 'R.C.A.' unless mentioned otherwise

| Jun 70. (7") *(RCA 1964)* **WHITE RABBIT. / SOMEBODY TO LOVE** | | |
| Nov 70. (lp) *(SF 8164)* <4459> **THE WORST OF JEFFERSON AIRPLANE** | | 12 |

(re-iss. Sep86 on 'Fame' lp/c; FA/TC-FA 3167)

Apr 74. (lp) *Grunt;* <*(APL 1-0437)*> **EARLY FLIGHT**		
Apr 76. (7"m) *(RCA 2676)* **WHITE RABBIT. / SOMEBODY TO LOVE / CROWN OF CREATION**		
Dec 76. (d-lp) *(SF 7889)* <1255> **FLIGHT LOG** (1966-76 work)		37
Apr 79. (12") *RCA Gold; (GOLD 4)* **WHITE RABBIT. / SOMEBODY TO LOVE**		-
Jul 80. (lp/c) *(INT S/K 5030)* <42727> **THE BEST OF JEFFERSON AIRPLANE**		

(re-iss. 1984 lp/c; NL/NK 89186)

Nov 86. (7") *Old Gold; (OG 9631)* **WHITE RABBIT. / SOMEBODY TO LOVE**		-
1987. (7") <5156> **WHITE RABBIT. / PLASTIC FANTASTIC LOVER**	-	-
May 87. (7") *Ariola; (JEFF 1)* **WHITE RABBIT. / SOMEBODY TO LOVE**		

(12"+=) *(JEFFT 1)* – She has funny cars / Third week in Chelsea.

| Jul 87. (d-lp/c/d-cd) *(NL/NK/ND 90036)* <5724> **2400 FULTON STREET – AN ANTHOLOGY** | | |

– It's no secret / Come up the years / My best friend / Somebody to love / Comin' back to me / Embryonic journey / She has funny cars / Plastic fantastic lover / Wild tyme / The ballad of you & me & Pooneil – A small package of value will come to you, shortly / White rabbit / Won't you try Saturday afternoon / Lather / We can be together / Crown of creation / Mexico / Wooden ships / Rejoyce / Volunteers / Pretty as you feel / Martha / Today / Third week in Chelsea. *(d-cd+=)* – Let's get together / Blues from an airplane / J.P.P. McStep B. Blues / Fat angel / Greasy heart / We can be together / Have you seen the saucers / Eat starch mom / Good shepherd / Eskimo blue day / The Levi commercials. *(re-iss. d-cd.1992;)*

| Oct 88. (d-lp/c/cd) *Castle; (CCS LP/MC/CD 200)* **THE COLLECTION** | | - |

<US cd-iss. Oct92; >

1989. (3"cd-ep) *(PD 49463)* **WHITE RABBIT / PLASTIC FANTASTIC LOVER / SOMEBODY TO LOVE / SHE HAS FUNNY CARS**		
May 90. (cd/lp) *Thunderbolt; (CDTB/THBL 074)* **LIVE AT THE MONTEREY FESTIVAL** (live)		-
Nov 92. (3xcd-box) **JEFFERSON AIRPLANE LOVES YOU**		-
Apr 93. (cd) *Pulsar;* **WOODSTOCK REVIVAL**		
Sep 93. (cd/c) *Remember; (RMB 7/4 5065)* **WHITE RABBIT** (featuring GRACE SLICK)		
Aug 96. (cd) *B.M.G. Special; <74321 40057-2>* **JOURNEY (THE BEST OF JEFFERSON AIRPLANE)**		
Sep 96. (cd; w-free pic-cd) *Experience; (EXP 021)* **JEFFERSON AIRPLANE LIVE**		
Jan 97. (cd) *Stampa Alternativa; (SB 03)* **WE ARE ALL ONE**		

– (STARSHIP) compilations etc. –

| Mar 79. (lp/c) *Grunt-RCA; (FL/FK 13247)* <3247> **GOLD** | | 20 Feb79 |

(with free 7") – LIGHT THE SKY ON FIRE. / HYPERDRIVE

| 1979. (7") *Grunt-RCA;* **MIRACLES. / WITH YOUR LOVE** | | - |
| Nov 92. (cd-ep) *Old Gold;* **NOTHING'S GONNA STOP US NOW / WE BUILT THIS CITY / SARA** | | - |

GRACE SLICK

solo, all featuring JEFFERSON's and session people

	Grunt	Grunt
Jan 74. (7") <0183> **THEME FROM MANHOLE. / COME AGAIN? TOUCAN**		-
Jan 74. (lp) <*(BFL 1-0347)*> **MANHOLE**		-

– Jay / Theme from 'Manhole' / Come again? Toucan / It's only music / Better lying down / Epic (#38).

	R.C.A.	R.C.A.
May 80. (7") <11939> **SEASONS. / ANGEL OF NIGHT**	-	-
May 80. (7") *(PB 9534)* **DREAMS. / ANGEL OF NIGHT**	50	-
May 80. (lp/c) <*(PL/PK 1-3544)*> **DREAMS**	28	32

– Dreams / El Diablo / Face to the wind / Angel of night / Seasons / Do it the hard way / Full Moon man / Let it go / Garden of man. *(re-iss. Sep81 lp/c; RCA LP/K 3040)* *(re-iss. Sep91 on 'Great Expectations' cd/c/lp; PIP CD/MC/LP 030)*

Jul 80. (7",12") <1204-1/-2> **DREAMS. / DO IT THE HARD WAY**		
Feb 81. (7") *(RCA 33)* **MISTREATER. / FULL MOON MAN**		
Feb 81. (lp/c) *(RCA LP/K 5007)* <3851> **WELCOME TO THE WRECKING BALL**		48

– Wrecking ball / Mistreater / Shot in the dark / Round & round / Shooting star / Just a little love / Sea of love / Lines / Right kind / No more heroes. *(re-iss. Sep91 on 'Great Expectations' cd/c/lp; PIP CD/MC/LP 029)*

| May 81. (7") <12171> **SEA OF LOVE. / FULL MOON MAN** | | - |
| Mar 84. (lp/c) *(PL/PK 84791)* **SOFTWARE** | | - |

– Call it right call it wrong / Me and me / All the machines / Fox face / Through the window / It just won't stop / Habits / Rearrange my face / Bikini Atoll.

| Mar 84. (12") <13708> **ALL THE MACHINES. / ('A'long version)** | - | |
| May 84. (7") <13764> **THROUGH THE WINDOWS. / HABITS** | - | |

—— (see also under GREAT SOCIETY for other SLICK material)

JELLYFISH (dig out; Great Alt & Indie . . .)

JENNIFERS (see under ⇒ SUPERGRASS)

JESUS & MARY CHAIN

Formed: East Kilbride, Scotland . . . 1983, by brothers WILLIAM and JIM REID, who took their name from a line in a Bing Crosby film. After local Glasgow gigs, they moved to Fulham in London, having signed for Alan McGhee's independent 'Creation' label in May'84. Their debut SLAUGHTER JOE-produced 45, 'UPSIDE DOWN', soon topped the indie charts, leading to WEA subsidiary label, 'Blanco Y Negro', snapping them up in early 1985. They hit the UK Top 50 with their next single, 'NEVER UNDERSTAND', and they were soon antagonising new audiences, crashing gear after 20 minutes on set. Riots ensued at nearly every major gig, and more controversy arrived when the next 45's B-side 'JESUS SUCKS', was boycotted by the pressing plant. With a new B-side, the single 'YOU TRIP ME UP', hit only No.55, but was soon followed by another Top 50 hit in October, 'JUST LIKE HONEY'. A month later they unleashed their debut album, 'PSYCHOCANDY', and although this just failed to breach the UK Top 30, it was regarded by many (NME critics especially) as the album of the year. Early in '86, BOBBY GILLESPIE left to concentrate on his PRIMAL SCREAM project and soon after, JAMC hit the Top 20 with the softer single, 'SOME CANDY TALKING'. In 1987 with new drummer JOHN MOORE, the single 'APRIL SKIES' and album 'DARKLANDS' both went Top 10. Later that year, they remixed The SUGARCUBES' classic 'Birthday' single.'BARBED WIRE KISSES' (1988) was a hotch-potch of B-sides and unreleased material, essential if only for the anarchic trashing of The Beach Boys' 'SURFIN' U.S.A.'. By the release of the 'AUTOMATIC' album in 1989, the Reid brothers had become the core of the band, enlisting additional musicians as needed. The record sounded strangely muted and uninspired although the 'ROLLERCOASTER' EP and subsequent tour (alongside MY BLOODY VALENTINE and a pre-'PARKLIFE' BLUR) were an improvement. True to controversial style, the band returned to the singles chart in 1992 with the radio un-friendly, post-industrial mantra, 'REVERENCE'. Perhaps the last great piece of venom-spewing noise the 'MARY CHAIN produced, the follow-up album, 'HONEY'S DEAD', was tame in comparison. No surprise then, that it received mixed reviews although there were a few low key highlights, notably the melodic bubblegum grunge of 'FAR GONE AND OUT'. After 1993's 'SOUND OF SPEED' EP, the band hooked up with MAZZY STAR's Hope Sandoval for 'STONED AND DETHRONED', a mellow set of feedback-free strumming. While still echoing the brooding portent of the THE VELVETS, the style of the record was more 'PALE BLUE EYES' than 'SISTER RAY'. Predictably, the band were seen as having 'sold out' by Indie-Rock dullards and a 1995 single, 'I HATE ROCK'N'ROLL', didn't even scrape the Top 50. 1998's comeback set, 'MUNKI', peaked at only No.47 in the charts; tension had been reported from other band members as WILLIAM and JIM fought out their differences. With the latter working on something solo (and Alan McGhee's label coming to a close) it was inevitable that the brothers would split the 'CHAIN late in '99. • Songwriters: All written by JIM and WILLIAM except; VEGETABLE MAN (Syd Barrett) / SURFIN' USA (Beach Boys) / WHO DO YOU LOVE (Bo Diddley) / MY GIRL (Temptations) / MUSHROOM (Can) / GUITAR MAN (Jerry Lee Hubbard) / TOWER OF SONG (Leonard Cohen) / LITTLE RED ROOSTER (Willie Dixon) / (I CAN'T GET NO) SATISFACTION (Rolling Stones) / REVERBERATION (13th Floor Elevators) / GHOST OF A SMILE (Pogues) / ALPHABET CITY (Prince) / NEW KIND OF KICK (Cramps). • Trivia: Their 1986 single 'SOME CANDY TALKING' was banned by Radio 1 DJ Mike Smith, due to its drug references. The following year in the States, they were banned from a chart show due to their blasphemous name. Although not yet overwhelming, their success in the US has made albums reach between 100 & 200. On 1994's 'STONED AND DETHRONED', they were joined by William's girlfriend HOPE SANDOVAL (of MAZZY STAR).

Album rating: PSYCHOCANDY (*9) / DARKLANDS (*8) / BARBED WIRE KISSES collection (*7) / AUTOMATIC (*7) / HONEY'S DEAD (*8) / THE SOUND OF SPEED compilation (*7) / STONED AND DETHRONED collection (*6) / I HATE ROCK N ROLL (*5) / MUNKI (*5)

JIM REID (b.29 Dec'61) – vox, guitar / **WILLIAM REID** (b.28 Oct'58) – guitar, vox / **MURRAY DALGLISH** – drums (bass tom & snare) / **DOUGLAS HART** – bass

		Creation	not iss.
Nov 84.	(7") (CRE 012) **UPSIDE DOWN. / VEGETABLE MAN**		-
	(12"+=) (CRE 012T) – ('A' demo).		

—— **BOBBY GILLESPIE** – drums (ex-WAKE, of PRIMAL SCREAM) repl. DALGLISH who formed BABY'S GOT A GUN

		Blanco Y Negro	Reprise
Feb 85.	(7") (NEG 8) **NEVER UNDERSTAND. / SUCK**	47	-
	(12"+=) (NEGT 8) – Ambition.		
Jun 85.	(7") (NEG 13) **YOU TRIP ME UP. / JUST OUT OF REACH**	55	-
	(12"+=) (NEGT 13) – Boyfriend's dead.		
Oct 85.	(7") (NEG 017) **JUST LIKE HONEY. / HEAD**	45	-
	(12"+=) (NEGT 17) – Just like honey (demo) / Cracked.		
	(d7"+=) (NEGF 17) – ('A'demo) / Inside me.		
Nov 85.	(lp/c) (BYN/+C 11) <25383> **PSYCHOCANDY**	31	-
	– Just like honey / The living end / Taste the floor / Hardest walk / Cut dead / In a hole / Taste of Cindy / Never understand / It's so hard / Inside me / Sowing seeds / My little underground / You trip me up / Something's wrong. (cd-iss. Aug86 & Jan97 +=; K 242 000-2) – Some candy talking.		

—— **JOHN LODER** – drums (on stage when BOBBY was unavailable)

Jul 86.	(7") (NEG 19) **SOME CANDY TALKING. / PSYCHO CANDY / HIT**	13	-
	(12"+=) (NEGT 19) – Taste of Cindy.		
	(d7"+=) (NEGF 19)(SAM 291) – Cut dead (acoustic) / You trip me up (acoustic) / Some candy talking (acoustic) / Psycho candy (acoustic).		

—— now basic trio of **JIM, WILLIAM** and **DOUGLAS** brought in **JOHN MOORE** (b.23 Dec'64, England) – drums repl. GILLESPIE (who was busy with PRIMAL SCREAM) / **JAMES PINKER** – drums (ex-DEAD CAN DANCE) repl. MOORE now on guitar

Apr 87.	(7") (NEG 24) **APRIL SKIES. / KILL SURF CITY**	8	-
	(12"+=) (NEGT 24) – Who do you love.		
	(d7"+=) (NEGF 24) – Mushroom / Bo Diddley is Jesus.		
Aug 87.	(7") (NEG 25) **HAPPY WHEN IT RAINS. / EVERYTHING IS ALRIGHT WHEN YOU'RE DOWN**	25	-
	(ext.12"+=) (NEGT 25) – Happy place / F-Hole.		
	(ext.10"+=) (NEGTE 25) – ('A'demo) / Shake.		

—— trimmed to basic duo of REID brothers.

Sep 87.	(lp/c)(cd) (BYN/+C 25)(K 242 180-2) <25656> **DARKLANDS**	5	
	– Darklands / Deep one perfect morning / Happy when it rains / Down on me / Nine million rainy days / April skies / Fall / Cherry came too / On the wall / About you. (cd re-iss. Nov94; K 242 180-2)		
Oct 87.	(7"/7"g-f) (NEG/+F 29) **DARKLANDS. / RIDER / ON THE WALL (demo)**	33	-
	(12"+=/12"g-f+=) (NEGTF 29) – Surfin' U.S.A.		
	(10"+=/cd-s+=) (NEG TE/CD 29) – Here it comes again.		

—— **DAVE EVANS** – rhythm guitar repl. MOORE who formed EXPRESSWAY

Mar 88.	(7") (NEG 32) **SIDEWALKING. / TASTE OF CINDY (live)**	30	-
	(12"+=) (NEGT 32) – ('A'extended) / April skies (live).		
	(cd-s++=) (NEGCD 32) – Chilled to the bone.		
Apr 88.	(lp/c)(cd) (BYN/+C 29)(K 242 331-2) <25729> **BARBED WIRE KISSES** (part compilation)	9	
	– Kill Surf City / Head / Rider / Hit / Don't ever change / Just out of reach / Happy place / Psychocandy / Sidewalking / Who do you love / Surfin' USA / Everything's alright when you're down / Upside down / Taste of Cindy / Swing / On the wall. (c+=/cd+=) – Cracked / Here it comes again / Mushroom / Bo Diddley is Jesus. (cd re-iss. Jan97; same)		

—— In Nov'88, DOUGLAS HART moonlighted in The ACID ANGELS, who released 7"promo 'SPEED SPEED ECSTASY' on 'Product Inc.'; FUEL 1)

Nov 88.	(7") <27754> **KILL SURF CITY. / SURFIN' USA (summer mix)**	-	

—— Basically REID brothers, HART and EVANS. (added **RICHARD THOMAS** – drums) / **BEN LURIE** – rhythm guitar repl. EVANS

Sep 89.	(7") (NEG 41) **BLUES FROM A GUN. / SHIMMER**	32	
	(10"+=) (NEG 41TE) – Break me down / Penetration.		
	(12"+=/c-s+=) (NEG 41 T/C) – Penetration / Subway.		
	(3"cd-s+=) (NEG 41CD) – Penetration / My girl.		
Oct 89.	(lp/c)(cd) (BYN/+C 20)(K 246 221-2) <26015> **AUTOMATIC**	11	
	– Here comes Alice / Coast to coast / Blues from a gun / Between planets / UV ray / Her way of praying / Head on / Take it / Halfway to crazy / Gimme hell. (cd re-iss. Jan97; same)		
Nov 89.	(7") (NEG 42) **HEAD ON. / IN THE BLACK**	57	-
	(12"+=) (NEG 42T) – Terminal beach.		
	(3"cd-s++=) (NEG 42CD) – Drop (acoustic re-mix).		
	(7") (NEG 42XB) – ('A'side.) / DEVIANT SLICE		
	(7") (NEG 42Y) – ('A'side.) / I'M GLAD I NEVER		
	(7") (NEG 42Z) – ('A'side.) / TERMINAL BEACH		
Mar 90.	(7") <19891> **HEAD ON. / PENETRATION**	-	-
Aug 90.	(7") (NEG 45) **ROLLERCOASTER. / SILVER BLADE**	46	-
	(12"+=) (NEG 45T) – Tower of song.		
	(7"ep++=/cd-ep+++=) (NEG 45 D/CD) – Low-life.		

—— Trimmed again, when THOMAS joined RENEGADE SOUNDWAVE on U.S.tour. HART became video director. The **REID** brothers and **BEN** recruited **MATTHEW PARKIN** – bass + **BARRY BLACKER** – drums (ex-STARLINGS)

		Blanco Y Negro	American
Feb 92.	(7") (NEG 55) **REVERENCE. / HEAT**	10	
	(12"+=/cd-s+=) (NEG 55 T/CD) – ('A'radio remix) / Guitar man.		
Mar 92.	(cd/c/lp) (9031 76554-2/-4/-1) <26830> **HONEY'S DEAD**	14	
	– Reverence / Teenage lust / Far gone and out / Almost gold / Sugar Ray / Tumbledown / Catchfire / Good for my soul / Rollercoaster / I can't get enough / Sundown / Frequency. (cd re-iss. Jan97; same)		
Apr 92.	(7") (NEG 56) **FAR GONE AND OUT. / WHY'D DO YOU WANT ME**	23	
	(12"+=/cd-s+=) (NEG 56 T/CD) – Sometimes you just can't get enough.		
Jun 92.	(7") (NEG 57) **ALMOST GOLD. / TEENAGE LUST (acoustic)**	41	
	(12"+=) (NEG 57T) – Honey's dead.		
	(gold-cd-s+=) (NEG 57CD) – Reverberation (doubt) / Don't come down.		
Jun 93.	(7"ep/c-ep/10"ep/cd-ep) (NEG 66/+C/TE/CD) **SOUND OF SPEED EP**	30	-
	– Snakedriver / Something I can't have / White record release blues / Little red rooster.		
Jul 93.	(cd/c/lp) (4509 93105-2/-4/-1) **THE SOUND OF SPEED** (part comp '88-'93)	15	-
	– Snakedriver / Reverence (radio mix) / Heat / Teenage lust (acoustic version) / Why'd you want me / Don't come down / Guitar man / Something I can't have / Sometimes / White record release blues / Shimmer / Penetration / My girl / Tower of song / Little red rooster / Break me down / Lowlife / Deviant slice / Reverberation / Sidewalking (extended version). (cd re-iss. Jan97; same)		

—— next album feat. guest vox HOPE SANDOVAL (Mazzy Star) + SHANE MacGOWAN / **STEVE MONTI** – drums repl. BLACKER

Jul 94.	(7"/c-s) (NEG 70/+C) **SOMETIMES ALWAYS. / PERFECT CRIME**	22	-
	(10"+=/cd-s+=) (NEG 70 TE/CD) – Little stars / Drop.		
Aug 94.	(cd/c/lp) (4509 93104-2/-4/-1) <45573> **STONED AND DETHRONED**	13	98
	– Dirty water / Bullet lovers / Sometimes always / Come on / Between us / Hole / Never saw it coming / She / Wish I could / Save me / Till it shines / God help me / Girlfriend / Everybody I know / You've been a friend / These days / Feeling lucky. (cd re-iss. Jan97; same)		
Oct 94.	(c-s) <18078> **SOMETIMES ALWAYS / DROP**	-	96
Oct 94.	(7"/c-s) (NEG 73/+C) **COME ON. / I'M IN WITH THE OUT-CROWD**	52	
	(cd-s+=) (NEG 73CD) – New York City / Taking it away.		
	(cd-s) (NEG 73CD) – ('A'side) / Ghost of a smile / Alphabet city / New kind of kick.		
Jun 95.	(c-ep/12"ep/cd-ep) (NEG 81 C/TEX/CD) **I HATE ROCK N ROLL / BLEED ME. / 33 1-3 / LOST STAR**	61	-
Sep 95.	(cd,c) <43043> **HATE ROCK N ROLL** (compilation of B-sides & rarities)	-	
	– I hate rock'n'roll / Snakedriver / Something I can't have / Bleed me / Thirty three and a third / Lost star / Penetration / New York City / Taking it away / I'm in with the out crowd / Little stars / Teenage lust / Perfect crime.		

—— **JIM, WILLIAM + BEN** were joined by **NICK SANDERSON** – drums / **TERRY EDWARDS** – horns / + guests vocalists HOPE SANDOVAL + SISTER VANILLA

		Creation	Sub Pop
Apr 98.	(7") (CRE 292) **CRACKING UP. / ROCKET**	35	
	(cd-s+=) (CRESCD 292) – Hide myself / Commercial.		
May 98.	(7"/c-s) (CRE/+CS 296) **I LOVE ROCK N ROLL. / EASYLIFE, EASYLOVE**	38	
	(cd-s+=) (CRESCD 296) – 40,000k / Nineteen 666.		
Jun 98.	(cd/c/d-lp) (CRECD/CCRE/CRELP 232) <SP 426> **MUNKI**	47	
	– I love rock n roll / Birthday / Stardust remedy / Fizzy / Moe Tucker / Perfume / Virtually unreal / Degenerate / Cracking up / Commercial / Supertramp / Never understood / I can't find the time for times / Man on the moon / Black / Dream lover / I hate rock n roll.		

—— they disbanded in October '99

– compilations, etc. –

Sep 91.	(m-lp/m-c/m-cd) Strange Fruit; (SFP MA/MC/CD 210) **THE PEEL SESSIONS (1985-86)**		-
	– Inside me / The living end / Just like honey / all / Hapy place / In the rain.		
Jun 94.	(cd+book) Audioglobe; **LIVE (live)**		-

JESUS JONES

Formed: Bradford-Upon-Avon, Wiltshire, England ... late 1986 as CAMOUFLAGE, by MIKE EDWARDS, GEN (aka SIMON MATTHEWS) and AL JAWORSKI, who subsequently found BARRY D and JERRY DE BORG. In August '88, after moving to Walthamstow, London, they became JESUS JONES and signed with Dave Balfe's 'Food' label, fashioning an allegedly radical hybrid of dance, hip-hop and pop/rock, which, with the benefit of hindsight, sounds about as dangerous as The SPICE GIRLS. The CHEMICAL BROTHERS this band were not. Nevertheless, their debut single, 'INFO FREAKO', kicked up a bit of a storm in 1989 just as the indie-dance crossover was taking shape. Two follow-ups, 'NEVER ENOUGH' and 'BRING IT ON DOWN', both hit the Top 50, and premiered the UK Top 40 album, 'LIQUIDIZER'. You could see what the band were trying to do, but somehow the different parts just didn't blend, the sound more salad bowl than melting pot, all colour and no substance. MIKE EDWARD's watery, whey-faced vocals didn't help matters yet incredibly, the single, 'REAL REAL REAL' made the US charts upon its release early the following year. By December, the band had secured their first UK Top 10 with 'INTERNATIONAL BRIGHT YOUNG THING'. The 'difficult' second album, 'DOUBT' (1991) again piled on the information overload and sonic debris to marginal effect, yet buried under the pointless samples and drum loops was an actual song, 'RIGHT HERE, RIGHT NOW'. It had already been a UK hit the previous year, and after numb-brained yanks pounced on it as some kind of Gulf War theme tune, the track hit No.2 in America in April '91. By 'PERVERSE' (1993), fans and critics alike had obviously tired of EDWARDS' tedious knob-twiddling and the record sank without trace.
• **Songwriters:** MIKE EDWARDS penned except; I DON'T WANT THAT KIND OF LOVE (Crazyhead) / VOODOO CHILE (Jimi Hendrix Experience).
• **Trivia:** The song 'NEVER ENOUGH' was inspired by Woody Allen's film, 'Stardust Memories'.

Album rating: LIQUIDIZER (*7) / DOUBT (*7) / PERVERSE (*5) / ALREADY (*3)

MIKE EDWARDS (b.22 Jun'64) – vocals / **JERRY DE BORG** (b.30 Oct'63) – guitar / **AL JAWORSKI** (b. ALAN DOUGHTY, 31 Jan'66, Plymouth, England) – bass / **BARRY D.** (b. IAIN BAKER, 29 Sep'65, Surrey, England) – keyboards, samplers / **GEN** (b. SIMON MATTHEWS, 23 Apr'64, Wiltshire, England) – drums

			Food-EMI	S.B.K.
Feb 89.	(7") (FOOD 18) **INFO FREAKO. / BROKEN BONES**		42	

(12"+=/cd-s+=) (12/CD FOOD 18) – Info sicko.
(12") (12FOODX 18) – Info psycho / Info sicko / ('A'side).

| Jun 89. | (7"/7"s)(c-s) (FOOD/+S 21)(TCFOOD 21) **NEVER ENOUGH. / WHAT'S GOING ON** | | 42 | |

(12"/cd-s) (12/CD FOOD 21) – ('A'side) / Enough – Never enough / It's the winning that counts.

| Sep 89. | (c-s/7") (TC+/FOOD 22) **BRING IT ON DOWN. / CUT AND DRIED** | | 46 | |

(12"+=/12"w-poster+=)(cd-s+=) (12FOOD/+P 22) (CDFOOD 22) – None of the answers / Beat it down.
('A'-Liquidized mix-12"+=) (12FOODX 2) – Info sicko.

| Oct 89. | (lp/c/cd) (FOOD LP/TC/CD 3) **LIQUIDIZER** | | 32 | |

– Move mountains / Never enough / The real world / All the answers / What's going on / Song 13 / Info freako / Bring it on down / Too much to learn / What would you know? / Too much to learn / One for the money / Someone to blame.

—— In Nov'89, the track 'I DON'T WANT THAT KIND OF LOVE' featured on the Various Artists 'FOOD CHRISTMAS EP'; 12/CD+/FOOD 23)

| Mar 90. | (7"/7"s)(c-s) (FOOD/+S 24)(TCFOOD 24) **REAL REAL REAL. / DEAD PEOPLE'S LIVES** | | 19 | - |

(12"[no B-track]+=/12"w-poster+=)(cd-s+=) (12FOOD/+P 24)(CDFOOD 24) – ('A'-12"raw mix) / Info freako.
(12") (12FOODX 24) – ('A'-Luxury mix) / ('A'-Ben Chapman spaced mix) / ('A'side) / Barry D next to cleanliness.

| Sep 90. | (c-s/7") (TC+/FOOD 25) **RIGHT HERE RIGHT NOW. / MOVE ME / DAMN GOOD AT THIS** | | 31 | - |

(10"+=/cd-s+=) (10/CD FOOD 25) – Are you satisfied (Melvyn mix).
(12") (12FOOD 25) – ('A'-Martyn Phillips mix) / Move mountains (Ben Chapman mix) / ('A'-Dean Krexa mix) / Are you satisfied.

| Dec 90. | (c-s/7") (TC+/FOOD 27) **INTERNATIONAL BRIGHT YOUNG THING. / MARYLAND** | | 7 | |

(12"+=) (12FOOD 27) – ('A'-Phil Harding mix).
(12"pic-d) (12FOODPD 27) – ('A'-I.B.Y.T. version) / ('A'-Chaos mix) / Need to know.
(cd-s) (CDFOOD 27) – (all 4 tracks above).

| Feb 91. | (cd/c/lp) (FOOD CD/TC/LP 5) <95715> **DOUBT** | | 1 | 25 |

– Trust me / Who? where? why? / International bright young thing / I'm burning / Right here right now / Real real real / Welcome back Victoria / Two and two / Stripped / Blissed. (re-iss. Mar94 cd/c;)

| Feb 91. | (c-s/7") (TC+/FOOD 28) **WHO? WHERE? WHY? (Crisis mix). / CARICATURE** | | 21 | |

(10"+=) (10FOOD 28) – ('A'-Foot mix) / Kill today.
(cd-s+=) (CDFOOD 28) – ('A'-Foot mix) / ('A'-lp version).
(12") (12FOOD 28) – ('A'extended) / ('A'-Foot mix) / ('A'-Crisis instrumental mix) / ('A'-Chaos mix).

| Mar 91. | (c-s) <07345> **RIGHT HERE, RIGHT NOW / MOVE ME** | | - | 2 |
| Jul 91. | (c-s/7") (TC+/FOOD 30) **RIGHT HERE, RIGHT NOW. / WELCOME BACK VICTORIA** | | 31 | - |

(12"+=/cd-s+=) (12/CD FOOD 30) – Info psycho / Broken bones.

| Aug 91. | (c-s) <07364> **REAL, REAL, REAL / MARYLAND** | | - | 4 |
| Jan 93. | (c-s/7") (TC+/PERV 1) **THE DEVIL YOU KNOW. / PHOENIX** | | 10 | |

(12"+=/cd-s+=) (12/CD PERV 1) – What to know.

| Jan 93. | (cd/c/lp) (FOOD CD/TC/LP 8) <80647> **PERVERSE** | | 6 | 59 |

– Zeroes and ones / The Devil you know / Get a good thing / From love to war /

Yellow brown / Magazine / The right decision / Your crusade / Don't believe it / Tongue tied / Spiral / Idiot stare.

| Mar 93. | (c-s/7") (TC+/PERV 2) **THE RIGHT DECISION. / STARTING FROM SCRATCH** | | 36 | |

(12"+=/cd-s+=) (12/CD PERV 2) – ('A'mixes).

| Jun 93. | (c-s) (TCFOOD 44) **ZEROES AND ONES. / MACHINE DRUG / ('A'mixes)** | | 30 | |

(cd-s) (CDFOOD 44) – ('A'side) / Real real real (rhythm 2) / International bright young thing / Right here, right now.
(12") (12FOOD) – ('A'side) / ('A'mixes).

			E.M.I.	S.B.K.
Jun 97.	(c-s) (TCEM 476) **THE NEXT BIG THING / TOGETHER**		49	

(cd-s+=) (CDEM 476) – Right here right now / Who what why.
(cd-s) (CDEMS 476) – ('A'side) / Idiot stare / Man on the moon / Far out in nowhere.

			Food	Food
Aug 97.	(7"tangerine) (FOOD 102) **CHEMICAL #1. / NATURAL STATE OF GRAY**			

(cd-s+=) (CDFOOD 102) – Zeroes and ones (Liam Howlett mix) / Change of season.
(cd-s) (CDFOODS 102) – ('A'mixes; Kris Needs / Optical / Soundscandal).

| Aug 97. | (cd/c/lp) (<FOOD CD/TC/LP 22>) **ALREADY** | | | |

– The next big thing / Run on empty / Look out tomorrow / Top of the world / Rails / Wishing it away / Chemical #1 / Motion / They're out here / For a moment / Addiction / Obsession and me / February.

JESUS LIZARD (dig out; Great Alt & Indie ...)

JESUS LOVES YOU (see under ⇒ BOY GEORGE)

JETHRO TULL

Formed: London, England ... late 1967 by Scots-born IAN ANDERSON and GLENN CORNICK, who had both been in Blackpool band, JOHN EVANS' SMASH for four years alongside school friends EVANS and JEFFREY HAMMOND-HAMMOND. IAN and GLENN brought in former McGREGORY'S ENGINE members MICK ABRAHAMS plus CLIVE BUNKER, adopting the 18th Century name of an English agriculturist/inventor, JETHRO TULL. It was often mistaken by the uninitiated, as the name of the lead singer, IAN ANDERSON. Early in 1968, through agents Terry Ellis & Chris Wright, 'M.G.M.' issued their debut single, 'SUNSHINE DAY', mistakenly credited as JETHRO TOE at the pressing plant (it has since changed hands for over £100 at record fairs). On the 29th of June '68, after a residency at the Marquee Club, they supported PINK FLOYD at a free rock concert in Hyde Park, London. Following another enthusiastically received concert at Sunbury's Jazz & Blues Festival in August, they signed to 'Island'. By the end of the year, their debut album, 'THIS WAS', had cracked the UK Top 10, even managing to break into the American Top 75. Early in '69, they hired TONY IOMMI (future BLACK SABBATH) and DAVID O'LIST (of The NICE), for a few gigs following the departure of ABRAHAMS. In May '69, with the addition of MARTIN BARRE, they secured a UK Top 3 placing with the classic 'LIVING IN THE PAST' single. This was quickly followed by the UK No.1 album, 'STAND UP', which also made the Top 20 in the States. They then signed to associate label, 'Chrysalis', scoring two more UK Top 10 singles in 'SWEET DREAM' and 'THE WITCHES PROMISE'. By this juncture, the band were moving away from their early blues-orientated sound into the murky waters of progressive rock, ANDERSON's songwriting voice becoming more vocal with each successive release. With his fevered, one- legged flute playing and laughably outlandish vagrant garb, ANDERSON gave the group its visual trademark; for many people he was *JETHRO TULL*. After a series of line-up changes and continued success in America, the band released 'AQUALUNG' (1971), a million selling concept album through which ANDERSON expressed his contempt for organised religion. This was nothing, however, compared to the contempt which ANDERSON himself would be subject to from a volatile music press whose patience was wearing thin. If the ambitious 'THICK AS A BRICK' (1972) received a less than enthusiastic response from the press, then 'PASSION PLAY's whimsical self-indulgence was met with a critical mauling. As is often the case, the public ignored the reviews and queued up in droves for a copy, especially in America. 'WAR CHILD' and 'MINSTREL IN THE GALLERY' heralded a return to more traditional song structures but by this time, the critics had it in for the band. 'TULL did little to improve the situation by releasing the execrable 'TOO OLD TO ROCK'N'ROLL, TOO YOUNG TO DIE' (1976). Cast into the ghetto of eternal unhipness with the onslaught of punk, JETHRO TULL carried on unhindered, their live shows attracting hordes of die-hard fans. While their recorded output took on a more folky bent with 'SONGS FROM THE WOOD' and 'HEAVY HORSES', the beast that was the 'TULL live phenomenon was beamed around the world by satellite from a show at New York's Madison Square Garden in 1978. ANDERSON began working on a solo album in 1980 with ex-members of ROXY MUSIC and FAIRPORT CONVENTION, the finished article, "A", eventually being released as an official JETHRO TULL album. While the record was greeted with enthusiasm from fans, the follow-up ANDERSON solo lp, 'WALK INTO THE LIGHT' (1983) and subsequent group project 'UNDER WRAPS' (1984) tested even the most ardent 'TULL devotees with their cod-electronica. After a few years break, the band released 'CREST OF A KNAVE' (1987), a harder rocking affair and a return to form of sorts. 'ROCK ISLAND' (1989) and 'CATFISH RISING' (1991) were disappointing in comparison while the live 1992 album, 'A LITTLE LIGHT MUSIC', saw the band in refreshing semi-acoustic mode. 1995 marked a fair solo effort by ANDERSON and a well received 'TULL album, 'ROOTS TO BRANCHES'. While the band's studio output continues to be inconsistent at best, the prospect of a JETHRO TULL live show still has old prog die-hards parting with their hard-earned cash. • **Songwriters:** ANDERSON lyrics / group compositions, except BOUREE (J.S.Bach) / JOHN BARLEYCORN (trad.) / CAT'S SQUIRREL (Cream). • **Trivia:** ANDERSON still controls his trout-farming business in Northern Scotland. In 1974, he produced STEELEYE SPAN's 'Now We Are Six' album.

Album rating: THIS WAS (*6) / STAND UP (*7) / BENEFIT (*6) / AQUALUNG (*8) / THICK AS A BRICK (*5) / LIVING IN THE PAST part compilation/live (*7) / A PASSION PLAY (*7) / WAR CHILD (*6) / MINSTREL IN THE GALLERY (*6) / M.U. – THE BEST OF JETHRO TULL compilation (*8) / TOO OLD TO ROCK'N'ROLL, TOO YOUNG TO DIE (*4) / SONGS FROM THE WOOD (*4) / REPEAT – THE BEST OF JETHRO TULL, VOL.II compilation (*6) / HEAVY HORSES (*6) / JETHRO TULL LIVE – BURSTING OUT (*5) / STORMWATCH (*4) / "A" (*4) / THE BROADSWORD AND THE BEAST (*4) / UNDER WRAPS (*3) / CREST OF A KNAVE (*6) / 20 YEARS OF JETHRO TULL boxed-set compilation (*8) / ROCK ISLAND (*4) / CATFISH RISING (*5) / A LITTLE LIGHT MUSIC (*3) / THE BEST OF JETHRO TULL: THE ANNIVERSARY COLLECTION compilation (*7) / NIGHTCAP rare material (*4) / ROOTS TO BRANCHES (*4) / J-TULL DOT COM (*3) / Ian Anderson: WALK INTO LIGHT (*3)

IAN ANDERSON (b.10 Aug'47, Edinburgh, Scotland) – vocals, flute / **GLENN CORNICK** (b.24 Apr'47, Barrow-in-Furness, England) – bass / **MICK ABRAHAMS** (b. 7 Apr'43, Luton, England) – guitar, vocals (ex-McGREGORY'S ENGINE) / **CLIVE BUNKER** (b.12 Dec'46) – drums (ex-McGREGORY'S ENGINE)

		M.G.M.	not iss.
Mar 68.	(7"; as JETHRO TOE) (MGM 1384) **SUNSHINE DAY. / AEROPLANE**	–	–

		Island	Reprise
Aug 68.	(7") (WIP 6043) **A SONG FOR JEFFREY. / ONE FOR JOHN GEE**		–
Oct 68.	(lp; mono/stereo) (ILP/+S 9805) <6336> **THIS WAS**	10	62 Feb69
	– My Sunday feeling / Some day the sun won't shine for you / Beggar's farm / Move on alone / Serenade to a cuckoo / Dharma for one / It's breaking me up / Cat's squirrel / A song for Jeffrey / Round. (re-iss. Jan74 lp/c; CHR/ZCHR 1041) (cd-iss. 1986; CCD 1041) (lp re-iss. Apr99; 499468-1)		
Dec 68.	(7") (WIP 6048) **LOVE STORY. / A CHRISTMAS SONG**	29	–
Mar 69.	(7") <0815> **LOVE STORY. / A SONG FOR JEFFREY**	–	

—— **MARTIN BARRIE** (b.17 Nov'46) – guitar repl. MICK ABRAHAMS who formed BLODWYN PIG

May 69.	(7") (WIP 6056) **LIVING IN THE PAST. / DRIVING SONG**	3	–
Jul 69.	(lp) (ILPS 9103) <6360> **STAND UP**	1	20 Oct69
	– A new day yesterday / Jeffrey goes to Leicester Square / Bouree / Back to the family / Look into the sun / Nothing is easy / Fat man / We used to know / Reasons for waiting / For a thousand mothers. (re-iss. Nov83 on 'Fame' lp/c; FA/TCFA 413086-1/-4) (cd-iss. Jan89; CCD 1042) (re-iss. Feb97 on 'E.M.I.'; LPCENT 8)		

		Chrysalis	Reprise
Oct 69.	(7") (WIP 6070) **SWEET DREAM. / 17**	9	
Oct 69.	(7") <0886> **SWEET DREAM. / REASONS FOR WAITING**	–	
Jan 70.	(7") (WIP 6077) <0899> **THE WITCH'S PROMISE. / TEACHER**	4	

—— augmented by **JOHN EVAN** (b.28 Mar'48) – keyboards (he later joined full-time)

Apr 70.	(lp) (ILPS 9123) <6400> **BENEFIT**	3	11
	– With you there to help me / Nothing to say / Alive and well and living in / Son / For Michael Collins, Jeffrey and me / To cry you a song / A time for everything / Inside / Play in time / Sossity; you're a woman. (re-iss. Jan74 lp/c; CHR/ZCHR 1043) (cd-iss. Jun87; CPCD 1043)		
May 70.	(7") (WIP 6081) **INSIDE. / ALIVE AND WELL AND LIVING IN**		–
Jul 70.	(7") <0927> **INSIDE. / A TIME FOR EVERYTHING**	–	

—— **JEFFREY HAMMOND-HAMMOND** (b.30 Jul'46) – bass repl. CORNICK who formed WILD TURKEY

Mar 71.	(lp) (ILPS 9145) <2035> **AQUALUNG**	4	7 Apr 71
	– Aqualung / Cross-eyed mary / Cheap day return / Mother goose / Wond'ring aloud / Up to me / My God / Hymn #43 / Slipstream / Locomotive breath / Wind up. (re-iss. Jan74 lp/c; CHR/ZCHR 1044) (cd-iss. 1988; CCD 933-2) (re-iss. cd Mar94; CD25CR 08) (cd re-iss. Jun96 +=; CD25CR 08) – (sessions):- Lick your fingers clean / Wind up (quad version) / (Ian Anderson interview) / Song for Jeffrey / Fat man / Bouree.		
Jul 71.	(7") <1024> **HYMN #43. / MOTHER GOOSE**	–	91

—— **ANDERSON, BARRE, HAMMOND-HAMMOND** and **EVAN** were joined by **BARRIEMORE BARLOW** (b.10 Sep'49) – drums (ex-JOHN EVAN'S SMASH) who repl. BUNKER who joined BLODWYN PIG

Sep 71.	(7"ep) (WIP 6106) **LIFE IS A LONG SONG / UP THE POOL. / DR. BOGENBROOM / FOR LATER / NURSIE**	11	–
Oct 71.	(7") <1054> **LOCOMOTIVE BREATH. / WIND**		–

		Chrysalis	Reprise
Mar 72.	(lp) (CHR 1003) <2071> **THICK AS A BRICK**	5	1 May72
	– Thick as a brick (side 1) / Thick as a brick (side 2). (re-iss. Jan74 lp/c; CHR/ZCHR 1003) (cd-iss. 1986; ACCD 1003) (cd-re-iss. Apr89 on 'Mobile Fidelity'; UDCD 510) (cd re-iss. as part of 25th Anniversary on 'E.M.I.' +=; CDCNTAV 5) – Thick as a brick (live at Madison Square Gardens 1978) / (interview).		

		Chrysalis	Chrysalis
Apr 72.	(7") <1153> **THICK AS A BRICK (edit £1). / HYMN #43**	–	
Jul 72.	(d-lp) (CJT 1) <2106> **LIVING IN THE PAST** (live / studio compilation)	8	3 Nov72
	– A song for Jeffrey / Love story / Christmas song / Teacher / Living in the past / Driving song / Bouree / Sweet dream / Singing all day / Witches promise / Teacher / Inside / Just trying to be / By kind permission of / Dharma for one / Wond'ring again / Locomotive breath / Life is a long song / Up the pool / Dr. Bogenbroom / For later / Nursie. (re-iss. Oct87; CCD 1035) (re-iss. Mar94 cd/c; ZCJTD 1)		
Oct 72.	(7") <2006> **LIVING IN THE PAST. / CHRISTMAS SONG**	–	11
May 73.	(7") <2012> **A PASSION PLAY (edit #8). / A PASSION PLAY (edit #9)**	–	80
Jul 73.	(lp) (<CHR/ZCHR 1040>) **A PASSION PLAY**	13	1
	– A passion play (part 1; including 'The story of the hare who lost his spectacles' part 2)- -/- (part 2) / A passion play (part 2). (cd-iss. Jan89; CCD 1040)		

Aug 73.	(7") <2017> **A PASSION PLAY (edit #6). / A PASSION PLAY (edit #10)**	–	
Oct 74.	(7") (CHS 2054) <2101> **BUNGLE IN THE JUNGLE. / BACK-DOOR ANGELS**		12
Oct 74.	(lp/c) (<CHR/ZCHR 1067>) **WAR CHILD**	14	2
	– Warchild / Queen and country / Ladies / Back-door angels / Sealion / Skating away on the thin ice of a new day / Bungle in the jungle / Only solitaire / The third hooray / Two fingers. (cd-iss. Apr99 on 'Mobile Fidelity'; UDCD 745)		
Jan 74.	(7") <2103> **SKATING AWAY ON THE THIN ICE OF A NEW DAY. / SEA LION**	–	–
Sep 75.	(lp/c) (<CHR/ZCHR 1082>) **MINSTREL IN THE GALLERY**	20	7
	– Minstrel in the gallery / Cold wind to Valhalla / Black satin dancer / Requiem / One white duck / 0x10 = Nothing at all / Baker St. Muse (including Pig-me and the whore – Nice little tune – Crash barrier waltzer – Mother England reverie) / Grace. (cd-iss. 1986; CCD 1082)		
Oct 75.	(7") (CHS 2075) <2106> **MINSTREL IN THE GALLERY. / SUMMER DAY SANDS**		79

—— **JOHN GLASCOCK** (b.1953) – bass (ex-CHICKEN SHACK, ex-TOE FAT) repl. HAMMOND-HAMMOND

Mar 76.	(7") (CHS 2086) **TOO OLD TO ROCK'N'ROLL, TOO YOUNG TO DIE. / RAINBOW BLUES**		–
Mar 76.	(lp/c) (<CHR/ZCHR 1111>) **TOO OLD TO ROCK'N'ROLL: TOO YOUNG TO DIE**	25	14 May76
	– Quizz kid / Crazed institution / Salamander / Taxi grab / From a dead beat to an old greaser / Bad-eyed and loveless / Big dipper / Too old to rock'n'roll: too young to die / Pied piper / The chequered flag (dead or alive). (cd-iss. 1986; CCD 1111)		
Apr 76.	(7") <2114> **TOO OLD TO ROCK'N'ROLL, TOO YOUNG TO DIE. / BAD- EYED AND LOVELESS**	–	

—— added **DAVID PALMER** – keyboards (He had been their past orchestrator)

Nov 76.	(7"ep) (CXP 2) **RING OUT, SOLSTICE BELLS / MARCH THE MAD SCIENTIST. / A CHRISTMAS SONG / PAN DANCE**	28	–
Jan 77.	(7") (CHS 2135) **THE WHISTLER. / STRIP CARTOON**	59	Apr77
Feb 77.	(lp/c) (<CHR/ZCHR 1132>) **SONGS FROM THE WOOD**	13	8
	– Songs from the wood / Jack-in-the-green / Cup of wonder / Hunting girl / Ring out, solstice bells / Velvet green / The whistler / Pibroch (cap in hand) / Fire at midnight. (cd-iss. 1986; ACCD 1132)		
Apr 78.	(7") (CHS 2214) **MOTHS. / LIFE IS A LONG SONG**		–
Apr 78.	(lp/c) (<CHR/ZCHR 1175>) **HEAVY HORSES**	20	19
	– ...And the mouse police never sleeps / Acres wild / No lullaby / Moths / Journeyman / Rover / One brown mouse / Heavy horses / Weathercock. (cd-iss. 1986; CCD 1175)		
Nov 78.	(7",7"white) (CHS 2260) **A STITCH IN TIME. / SWEET DREAM (live)**		–
Nov 78.	(d-lp/c) (CJT/ZCJT 4) <1201> **LIVE-BURSTING OUT**	17	21 Oct78
	– No lullaby / Sweet dream / Skating away on the thin ice of a new day / Jack in the green / One brown mouse / A new day yesterday / Flute solo improvisation – God rest ye merry gentlemen – Bouree / Songs from the wood / Thick as a brick / Hunting girl / Too old to rock'n'roll: too young to die / Conundrum / Cross-eyed Mary / Quatrain / Aqualung / Locomotive breath / The dambusters march.		
Sep 79.	(7") (CHS 2378) **NORTH SEA OIL. / ELEGY**		–
Sep 79.	(lp/c) (<CDL/ZCDL 1238>) **STORMWATCH**	27	22
	– North Sea oil / Orion / Home / Dark ages / Warm sporran / Something's on the move / Old ghosts / Dun Ringill / Flying Dutchman / Elegy. (cd-iss. Jan89; CCD 1238)		
Nov 79.	(7") <2387> **HOME. / WARM SPORRAN**	–	–
Nov 79.	(7"ep) (CHS 2394) **HOME / KING HENRY'S MADRIGAL (THEME FROM MAINSTREAM). / WARM SPORRAN / RING OUT SOLSTICE BELLS**		–

—— ANDERSON for what was supposed to be a solo album retained **BARRE** / plus new **DAVE PEGG** (b. 2 Nov'47, Birmingham, England) – bass (ex-FAIRPORT CONVENTION) repl. GLASCOCK who died. / **EDDIE JOBSON** (b.28 Apr'55, England) – keyboards (ex-ROXY MUSIC, ex-CURVED AIR, etc) repl. EVANS and PALMER who took up session work / **MARK CRANEY** (b. Los Angeles, Calif.) – drums repl. BARLOW who went solo.

Aug 80.	(lp/c) (<CDL/CDC 1301>) **"A"**	25	30 Sep 80
	– Crossfire / Fylingdale flyer / Working John, working Joe / Black Sunday / Protect and survive / Batteries not included / 4.W.D. (low ratio) / The Pine Marten's jig / And further on.		
Oct 80.	(7") (CHS 2468) **WORKING JOHN, WORKING JOE. / FYLINGDALE FLYER**		–

—— **PETER JOHN VITESSE** – keyboards repl. JOBSON who went solo / **GERRY CONWAY** – drums (ex-STEELEYE SPAN) repl. CRANEY

Apr 82.	(lp/c) (<CDL/CDC 1380>) **THE BROADSWORD AND THE BEAST**	27	19 May82
	– Beastie / Clasp / Fallen on hard times / Flying colours / Slow marching band / Broadsword / Pussy willow / Watching me watching you / Seal driver / Cheerio. (cd-iss. Apr83; CCD 1380)		
May 82.	(7") <2613> **PUSSY WILLOW. / FALLEN ON HARD TIMES**	–	–
May 82.	(7"/7"pic-d) (CHS/+P 2616) **BROADSWORD. / FALLEN ON HARD TIMES**		–

—— **DOANNE PERRY** – drums repl. CONWAY

Sep 84.	(lp/pic-lp/c/cd) (CDL/CDLP/ZCDL/CCD 1461) <1-/0-/4-/2-1461> **UNDER WRAPS**	18	76
	– Lap of luxury / Under wraps #1 / European legacy / Later that same evening / Saboteur / Radio free Moscow / Nobody's car / Heat / Under wraps #2 / Paparazzi / Apogee. (c+=/cd+=) – Automatic engineering / Astronomy / Tundra / General crossing.		
Sep 84.	(7") (TULL 1) **LAP OF LUXURY. / ASTRONOMY**	70	
	(d7"+=/12"+=) (TULL D/X 1) – Tundra / Automatic engineering.		
Jun 86.	(7") (TULL 2) **CORONIACH. / JACK FROST AND THE HOODED CROW**		
	(12"+=) (TULLX 2) – Living in the past / Elegy.		

—— ANDERSON, BARRE, PEGG and PERRY recruited new member **MARTIN ALLCOCK** – keyboards (ex-FAIRPORT CONVENTION) repl. VITESSE

Sep 87.	(lp/c/cd) (CDL/ZCDL/CCD 1590) <1-/4-/2-1590> **CREST OF A KNAVE**	19	32
	– Steel monkey / Farm on the freeway / Jump start / Said she was a dancer / Dogs		

in midwinter * / Budapest / Mountain men / The waking edge * / Raising steam. (cd+= *)

Oct 87. (7"/7"pic-d) (TULL /+P 3) **STEEL MONKEY. / DOWN AT THE END OF YOUR ROAD** ☐ ☐
(12"+=)(c-s+=) (TULLX/ZTULL 3) – Too many too / I'm your gun.

Dec 87. (7"/7"pic-d) (TULL /+P 4) **SAID SHE WAS A DANCER. / DOGS IN MIDWINTER** [55] ☐
(12"+=) (TULLX 4) – The waking edge.
(cd-s+=) (TULLCD 4) – Down at the end of your road / Too many too.

Aug 89. (lp/pic-lp/c/cd) (CHR/CHRP/ZCHR/CCD 1708) <1-/0-/4-/2-21708> **ROCK ISLAND** [18] [56]
– Kissing Willie / The rattlesnake trail / Ears of tin / Undressed to kill / Rock Island / Heavy water / Another Christmas song / The whalers dues / Big Riff and Mando / Strange avenues.

Aug 89. (c-s) **KISSING WILLIE. / EARS OF TIN** [-] ☐

Nov 89. (7") (TULL 5) **ANOTHER CHRISTMAS SONG. / SOLSTICE BELLS** ☐ ☐
(12"+=) (TULLX 5) – Jack Frost.
(12"+=/cd-s+=) (TULL EX/CD 5) – ('A'side) / Intro – A Christmas song (live) / Cheap day return – Mother goose / Outro – Locomotive breath (live).

——— **ANDY GIDDINGS** – keyboards (3) / **MATT PEGG** – bass (3) / etc. repl. ALLCOCK

Aug 91. (7"/c-s) (TULL /+XMC 6) **THIS IS NOT LOVE. / NIGHT IN THE WILDERNESS** ☐ ☐
(12"+=/cd-s+=) (TULL X/CD 6) – Jump start (live).

Sep 91. (cd/c/lp) (CCD/ZCHR/DCHR 1886) <2-/4-/1-1863> **CATFISH RISING** [27] [88]
– This is not love / Occasional demons / Rocks on the road / Thinking round corners / Still loving you tonight / Doctor to my disease / Like a tall thin girl / Sparrow on the schoolyard wall / Roll yer own / Gold-tipped boots, black jacket and tie. (free 12"ep) – WHEN JESUS CAME TO PLAY. / SLEEPING WITH THE DOG / WHITE INNOCENCE

——— **DAVID MATTACKS** – drums, percussion, keyboards repl. PERRY and guests

Mar 92. (12"pic-d) (TULLX 7) **ROCKS ON THE ROAD. / JACK-A-LYNN (demo) / AQUALUNG – LOCOMOTIVE BREATH (live)** [47] ☐
(c-s) (TULLMC 7) – ('A'side) / Bouree (live) / Mother goose – Jack-a-Lyn (live).
(2xbox-cd-s+=) (TULLCD 7) – Tall thin girl (live) / Fat man (live).

Sep 92. (cd/c/d-lp) (CCD/ZCHR/CHR 1954) <2-/4/-1-1954> **A LITTLE LIGHT MUSIC (live in Europe '92)** [34] ☐
– Someday the sun won't shine for you / Living in the past / Life is a long song / Rocks on the road / Under wraps / Nursie / Too old to rock and roll, too young to die / One white duck / A new day yesterday / John Barleycorn / Look into the sun / A Christmas song / From a dead beat to an old greaser / This is not love / Bouree / Pussy willow / Locomotive breath.

——— **PERRY** returned to repl. MATTACKS; bass playing was provided by **DAVE PEGG / STEVE BAILEY**

Sep 95. (cd/c/d-lp) (CCD/ZCHR/CHR 6109) <2-/4/-1-6109> **ROOTS TO BRANCHES** [20] ☐
– Roots to branches / Rare and precious chain / Out of the noise / This free will / Valley / Dangerous veils / Beside myself / Wounded old and treacherous / At last, forever / Stuck in the August rain / Another Harry's bar.

——— **ANDERSON, BARRE, GIDDINGS + PERRY** were joined by **JONATHAN NOYCE** – bass

		Papillon	unknown

Aug 99. (cd) (BTFLYCD 0001) **J-TULL DOT COM** [44] ☐
– Spiral / Dot com / Awol / Nothing @ all / Wicked windows / Hunt by numbers / Hot mango flush / El Nino / Black mamba / Mango surprise / Bends like a willow / Far Alaska / The dog-ear years / A gift of roses.

Nov 99. (cd-s) (BTFLYS 0001) **BENDS LIKE A WILLOW / BENDS LIKE A WILLOW (version) / IT ALL TRICKLES DOWN** ☐ [-]

– compilations, others, etc. –

on 'Chrysalis' unless mentioned otherwise

Jan 76. (7") (CHS 2081) **LIVING IN THE PAST. / REQUIEM** ☐ ☐

Jan 76. (lp/c) (<CHR/ZCHR 1078>) **M.U. – THE BEST OF JETHRO TULL** [44] [13]
– Teacher / Aqualung / Thick as a brick (edit #1) / Bungle in the jungle / Locomotive breath / Fat man / Living in the past / A passion play (#8) / Skating away on the thin ice of a new day / Rainbow blues / Nothing is easy. (cd-iss. Dec85; ACCD 1078)

Feb 76. (7") <2110> **LOCOMOTIVE BREATH. / FAT MAN** [-] [62]

Nov 77. (lp/c) (<CHR/ZCHR 1135>) **REPEAT – THE BEST OF JETHRO TULL VOL.2** [94]
– Minstrel in the gallery / Cross-eyed Mary / A new day yesterday / Bouree / Thick as a brick (edit #9) / War child / A passion play (edit #9) / To cry you a song / Too old to rock'n'roll, too young to die / Glory row. (cd-iss. Apr86; CCD 1135)

Dec 82. (d-c) (ZCDP 105) **M.U. / REPEAT** [-]

Oct 85. (lp/c/cd) (JTTV/ZJTTV/CCD 1515) **ORIGINAL MASTERS** [63] ☐

Aug 87. (7") Old Gold; (OG 9637) **LIVING IN THE PAST. / THE WITCHES' PROMISE** ☐ [-]

Jun 88. (5xlp-box/3xc-box/3xcd-box) (T/MC/CD BOX 1) <41653> **20 YEARS OF JETHRO TULL** [78] [97]
– THE RADIO ARCHIVES:- A song for Jeffrey / Love story * / Fat man / Bouree / Stormy Monday blues * / A new day yesterday * / Cold wind to Valhalla * / Minstrel in the gallery / Velvet green / Grace * / The clasp / Pibroch (pee-break) – Black satin dancer (instrumental) * / Fallen on hard times // THE RARE TRACKS:- Jack Frost and the hooded crow / I'm your gun / Down at the end of your road / Coronach * / Summerday sands * / Too many too / March the mad scientist / Pan dance / Strip cartoon / King Henry's madrigal / A stitch in time / 17 / One for John Gee / Aeroplane / Sunshine day // FLAWED GEMS:- Lick your fingers clean * / The Chateau Disaster Tapes: Scenario / Audition – No reheasal / Beltane / Crossword * / Saturation * / Jack-A-Lynn / Motoreyes * / Blues instrumental (untitled) / Rhythm in gold // THE OTHER SIDES OF TULL:- Part of the machine / Mayhem, maybe * / Overhang * / Kelpie / Living in these hard times / Under wraps II * / Only solitaire / Cheap day return / Wond'ring aloud * / Dun Ringill * / Salamander / Moths * / Nursie * / Life is a long song * / One white duck – 0x10 = Nothing at all // THE ESSENTIAL TULL:- Songs from the wood / Living in the past * / Teacher * / Aqualung * / Locomotive breath * / The witches promise * / Bungle in the jungle / Farm on the freeway / Thick as a brick / Sweet dream. (re-iss. Aug88 as d-lp/d-c/d-cd; tracks *; CHR/ZCHR/CCD 1655)

Jun 88. (pic-cd) (TULLPCD 1) **PART OF THE MACHINE / STORMY MONDAY BLUES (live) / LICK YOUR FINGERS CLEAN (live) / MINSTREL IN THE GALLERY (live) / FARM ON THE FREEWAY (live)** ☐ [-]

Jan 91. (cd/c/lp) Raw Fruit; (FRS CD/MC/LP 004) **LIVE AT HAMMERSMITH 1984 (live)** ☐ [-]

Apr 93. (4xcd-box) (CDCHR 60044) **25th ANNIVERSARY BOXED SET** ☐ ☐
– REMIXED (CLASSIC SONGS) / CARNEGIE HALL N.Y. (RECORDED LIVE NEW YORK CITY 1970) / THE BEACON'S BOTTOM (TAPES) / POT POURRI (LIVE ACROSS THE WORLD AND THROUGH THE YEARS)

May 93. (7") (CHS 3970) **LIVING IN THE PAST. / HARD LINER** [32] ☐
(12") (12CHS 3970) – ('A'side) / ('A'club) / ('A'dub ravey master) / ('A'dub N.Y. mix).
(d-cd-s) (23970-1) – Living in the (slightly more recent) past (live) / Silver river turning / Rosa on the factory floor / I don't want to be me / ('A'side) / Truck stop runner / Piece of cake / Man of principle.

May 93. (d-cd/d-c) (CDCHR/ZCHR 6001) **THE VERY BEST OF JETHRO TULL – THE ANNIVERSARY COLLECTION** ☐ ☐
– A song for Jeffrey / Beggar's farm / A Christmas song / A new day yesterday / Bouree / Nothing is easy / Living in the past / To cry you a song / Sweet dream / Cross-eyed Mary / Mother goose / Aqualung / Locomotive breath / Life is a long song / Thick as a brick (extract) / Skating away on the thin ice of a new day / Bungle in the jungle / Minstrel in the gallery / Too old to rock'n'roll / Songs from the wood / Jack in the green / The whistler / Heavy horses / Dun Ringill / Fylingdale flyer / Jack-a-Lynn / Pussy willow / Broadsword / Under wraps II / Steel monkey / Farm on the freeway / Jump start / Kissing Willie / This is not love.

Nov 93. (d-cd) (CDCHR 6057) **NIGHTCAP – THE UNRELEASED MASTERS 1973-1991** ☐ ☐
– CHATEAU D'ISASTER – First post / Animelee / Tiger Moon / Look at the animals / Law of the bungle / Law of the bungle part II / Left right / Solitaire / Critique oblique / Post last / Scenario / Audition / No rehearsal/ / UNRELEASED & RARE TRACKS – Paradise steakhouse / Sealion II / Piece of cake / Quartet / Silver river turning / Crew nights / The curse / Rosa on the factory floor / A small cigar / Man of principle / Commons brawl / No step / Drive on the young side of life / I don't want to be me / Broadford bazaar / Lights out / Truck stop runner / Hard liner.

Apr 95. (cd) Windsong; (WINCD 070) **IN CONCERT (live)** ☐ [-]

Feb 97. (cd) EMI Gold; (CDGOLD 1079) **THROUGH THE YEARS** ☐ [-]

Mar 97. (cd) Disky; (DC 87861-2) **THE JETHRO TULL COLLECTION** ☐ [-]

Apr 97. (3xcd-box) (CDOMB 021) **THE ORIGINALS** ☐ [-]
– (THIS WAS / STAND UP / BENEFIT)

IAN ANDERSON

solo album augmented by **PETER JOHN VITESSE** – synth, keyboards

		Chrysalis	Chrysalis

Nov 83. (7") (CHS 2746) **FLY BY NIGHT. / END GAME** ☐ [-]

Nov 83. (lp/c) <(CDL /ZCDL 1443)> **WALK INTO LIGHT** [78] [-]
– Fly by night / Made in England / Walk into light / Trains / End game / Black and white television / Toad in the hole / Looking for Eden / User-friendly / Different Germany. (cd-iss. Jun97 on 'Beat Goes On'; BGOCD 350)

Sep 98. (cd) (CDC 555262-2) **DIVINITIES (12 DANCES WITH GOD)** ☐ ☐
– In a stone circle / In sight of a minaret / In a black box / In the grip of stronger stuff / In material grace / In the moneylender's temple / At their father's knee / En Afrique / In the olive garden / In the pay of Spain / In times of India (Bombay valentine).

Joan JETT

Born: 22 Sep'60, Philadelphia, Pennsylvania, USA. Following a baptism by new-wave fire in all-girl act, The RUNAWAYS, JETT relocated to London, where she hooked up with STEVE JONES and PAUL COOK (both ex-SEX PISTOLS). The results were to eventually surface in 1979 on UK indie label 'Cherry Red' as 'AND NOW . . . THE RUNAWAYS'. Back in America, the singer came under the wing of veteran 60's producer/session man Kenny Laguna, who helped finance the independent US release of JETT's eponymous solo debut (issued by 'Ariola' in Europe) in 1980. Intense interest subsequently led to a deal with Neil Bogart's 'Boardwalk' operation, the record remixed and re-released the following year as 'BAD REPUTATION'. With backing by The BLACKHEARTS (RICKY BIRD, GARY RYAN and LEE CRYSTAL), the album was a heady hoedown of post-glitter raunch-pop, cruising on a hefty dose of punk energy and a healthy, two-fingered attitude to music industry convention. Culled from follow-up set, 'I LOVE ROCK'N'ROLL' (1981), the sledgehammer riffing and foot-stomping bravado of the anthemic title track saw JETT and her BLACKHEARTS scale the US charts and stay there for nigh-on two months; the single also made a significant impact in the UK, which JETT would nevertheless find difficult to sustain. Although the album itself narrowly missed the top spot Stateside, the harder hitting set only spawned one other major hit, a cover of Tommy James & The Shondells' 'CRIMSON AND CLOVER', Bogart's surprise death casting a shadow over proceedings. Moving to 'M.C.A.' for her third set, the originally titled 'ALBUM' (1983), the record witnessed JETT expanding her musical horizons somewhat, attempting a partially successful run-through of Sly Stone's 'EVERYDAY PEOPLE'. The spunky 'GLORIOUS RESULTS OF A MISSPENT YOUTH' (1984) was another strong set, although by this point, JETT's commercial muscle was flagging. Despite being three years in the making, 'GOOD MUSIC' (1987) did little to rectify matters, its diversions into rock-rap failing to mask a lack of inspiration. With an acting appearance alongside Michael J.Fox in 'Light Of Day' and a US Top 10 hit with 'I HATE MYSELF FOR LOVING YOU', JETT's fortunes took a turn for the better in 1988. With TOMMY PRICE and CASMIN SULTAN replacing CRYSTAL and RYAN respectively, the accompanying album, 'UP YOUR ALLEY' (1988), saw the group benefitting from the golden pen of Desmond Child. No such help was needed on 'THE HIT LIST' (1990), a solid covers set which took in everything from The

Sex Pistols ('PRETTY VACANT') to Creedence Clearwater Revival ('HAVE YOU EVER SEEN THE RAIN'). 1992's 'NOTORIOUS' again saw Child (along with Diane Warren) share writing duties, while JETT duetted with The REPLACEMENTS' PAUL WESTERBURG on the poignant 'BACKLASH'. While her raw power may only surface in fits and starts, JOAN JETT remains something of a cult figurehead for female anti-rockers, L7 and BABES IN TOYLAND contributing to the BLACKHEART's 'Warners' debut, 'YEAH, RIGHT' (1994; US title, 'PURE AND SIMPLE'). • Other covers: I CAN'T CONTROL MYSELF (Troggs) / BITS AND PIECES (Dave Clark Five) / I'M GONNA RUN AWAY FROM YOU (Tammi Lynn) / I LOVE ROCK'N'ROLL (Arrows) / SHOUT (Isley Brothers) / WOOLY BULLY (Sam The Sham & The Pharoahs) / TOSSIN' AND TURNIN' (Searchers) / DO YOU WANNA TOUCH ME + I LOVE YOU LOVE ME LOVE (Gary Glitter) / TULANE (Chuck Berry) / LITTLE DRUMMER BOY (Harry Simone Chorale) / LIGHT OF DAY (Bruce Springsteen) / FUN FUN FUN (Beach Boys). THE HIT ALBUM was full of covers:- DIRTY DEEDS (Ac-Dc) / LOVE HURTS (Everly Brothers) / PRETTY VACANT (Sex Pistols) / TUSH (ZZ Top) / ROADRUNNER (Jonathan Richman) / HAVE YOU EVER SEEN THE RAIN (Creedence Clearwater Revival) / LOVE ME TWO TIMES (Doors) / CELLULOID HEROES (Kinks) / TIME HAS COME TODAY (Chamber Brothers). • Trivia: In 1989, JOAN tried to sue Playboy magazine for publishing nude pics of a lookalike, although the case was allegedly dropped when JOAN failed to turn up in court.

Album rating: JOAN JETT (aka BAD REPUTATION) (*6) / I LOVE ROCK'N'ROLL (*7) / ALBUM (*6) / GLORIOUS RESULTS OF A MISSPENT YOUTH (*6) / GOOD MUSIC (*5) / UP YOUR ALLEY (*5) / THE HIT LIST (*5) / NOTORIOUS (*5) / FLASHBACK collection (*6) / PURE AND SIMPLE (*5)

JOAN JETT – vocals, rhythm guitar (ex-RUNAWAYS) / with **RICKY BIRD** – lead guitar repl. ERIC AMBLE / **GARY RYAN** – bass / **LEE CRYSTAL** – drums (later to become The BLACKHEARTS)

		Ariola	not iss.
Apr 80.	(7") (ARO 227) **MAKE BELIEVE. / CALL ME LIGHTNING**		-
Jun 80.	(lp) (ARL 5058) **JOAN JETT**		-

– (Do you wanna) Touch me (oh yeah) / Make believe / You don't know what you've got / You don't own me / Too bad on your birthday / Bad reputation / Shout / Let me go / Doin' all right with the boys / Jezebel / Don't abuse me / Wooly bully.

Jun 80.	(7") (ARO 235) **YOU DON'T KNOW WHAT YOU GOT. / DON'T ABUSE ME**		-
Aug 80.	(7") (ARO 242) **JEZEBEL. / BAD REPUTATION**		-

JOAN JETT & THE BLACKHEARTS

(same line-up)

		Epic	Boardwalk
Mar 81.	(lp/c) (EPC/40 25045) <37065> **BAD REPUTATION** (debut remixed)		51

– Bad reputation / Make believe / You don't know what you've got / You don't own me / Too bad on your birthday / Doing all right with the boys / Do you wanna touch me (oh yeah) / Let me go / Jezebel / Shout / Don't abuse me / Wooly bully.

Jan 82.	(7") <135> **I LOVE ROCK'N'ROLL. / YOU DON'T KNOW WHAT YOU GOT**	-	1
Mar 82.	(7"/7"pic-d) (EPCA/+11 2152) **I LOVE ROCK'N'ROLL. / LOVE IS PAIN**	4	-
Mar 82.	(lp/c) (EPC/40 85686) <33245> **I LOVE ROCK'N'ROLL**	25	2 Dec81

– I love rock'n'roll / (I'm gonna) Run away / Bits and pieces / Love is pain / Nag / Crimson and clover / Victim of circumstance / Bits and pieces / Be straight / You're too possessive / Little drummer boy. (pic-lp.1983; EPC11 85686) (cd-iss. Feb97 on 'Columbia'; 486509-2)

Jun 82.	(7"/7"pic-d) (EPCA/+11 2485) <144> **CRIMSON AND CLOVER. / OH WOE IS ME**	60	7 Apr82
Jul 82.	(7") <150> **DO YOU WANNA TOUCH ME (OH YEAH). / VICTIM OF CIRCUMSTANCE**	-	20
Aug 82.	(7") (EPCA 2674) **DO YOU WANNA TOUCH ME (OH YEAH). / JEZEBEL**		-
Oct 82.	(7") (EPCA 2880) **YOU DON'T KNOW WHAT YOU'VE GOT. / (I'M GONNA) RUN AWAY**		-
Nov 82.	(7") <5706> **YOU DON'T OWN ME. / JEZEBEL**	-	

		Epic	Blackheart-MCA
Jul 83.	(7") <52240> **FAKE FRIENDS. / NIGHTIME**	-	35
Jul 83.	(12"+=) <52256> – Coney Island whitefish.		
Jul 83.	(7") (EPCA 3615) **FAKE FRIENDS. / CONEY ISLAND WHITEFISH**		-
Jul 83.	(12"+=) (TA 3615) – Nightime.		
Jul 83.	(lp/c) (EPC/40 25414) <5437> **ALBUM**		20

– Fake friends / Handyman / Everyday people / A hundred feet away / Secret love / The French song / Tossin' and turnin' / Why can't we be happy / I love playin' with fire / Coney Island whitefish / Had enough. (c+=) – Star, star.

Aug 83.	(7") <52256> **FAKE FRIENDS. / HANDY MAN**	-	
Sep 83.	(7") (EPCA 3790) <52272> **EVERYDAY PEOPLE. / WHY CAN'T WE BE HAPPY**		37
May 84.	(7") (EPCA 4391) **I NEED SOMEONE. / TALKIN' 'BOUT MY BABY**		-
May 84.	(12"+=) (TA 4391) – The French song.		
Oct 84.	(7") (EPCA 4851) **I LOVE YOU LOVE ME LOVE. / LONG TIME**		-
Oct 84.	(12"+=) (TA 4851) – Bird dog.		
Sep 84.	(7") <52472> **I LOVE YOU LOVE ME LOVE. / TALKIN' 'BOUT MY BABY**		-
Jan 85.	(lp) (EPCA 25993) <5476> **GLORIOUS RESULTS OF A MISSPENT YOUTH**		67 Oct84

– Cherry bomb / I love you love me love / Frustrated / Hold me / Long time / 'Talkin' 'bout my baby / I need someone / Love like mine / New Orleans / Someday / Push and stomp / I got no answers.

(below 45 with others from film and soundtrack of same name)

		Polydor	Blackheart
Feb 87.	(7"; as The BARBUSTERS) <06692> **LIGHT OF DAY. / ROADRUNNER**	-	33
Jul 87.	(7") (POSP 877) <06336> **GOOD MUSIC. / FANTASY**		83 Oct86
Jul 87.	(12"+=) (POSPX 877) – Fun, fun, fun (with The BEACH BOYS).		
Sep 87.	(lp/c/cd) (833 078-1/-4/-2) <40544> **GOOD MUSIC**		Oct86

– Good music / This means war / Roadrunner / If ya want my luv / Light of day / Black leather / Outlaw / Just lust / You got me floatin' / Fun, fun, fun / Contact.

——— In Jan'88, they featured on 'B' side of BANGLES 45 from the film 'Less Than Zero'. The track SHE'S LOST YOU on 'Def Jam'.

——— retained **BIRD**, and recruited **TOMMY PRICE** – drums (ex-BILLY IDOL) / **CASMIN SULTAN** – bass (ex-TODD RUNDGREN / UTOPIA)

		London	Blackheart
Aug 88.	(7"sha-pic-d) (LONP 195) <07919> **I HATE MYSELF FOR LOVING YOU. / LOVE IS PAIN**	46	8 Jun88
Aug 88.	(12"+=) (LONX 195) – I can't control myself.		
Aug 88.	(cd-s++=) (LONCD 195) – ('A'live version).		
Sep 88.	(lp/c)(cd) (LON LP/C 67)(837 158-2) <44146> **UP YOUR ALLEY**		19 May88

– I hate myself for loving you / Ridin' with James Dean / Little liar / Tulane / I wanna be your dog / I still dream about you / You want in I want out / Just like in the movies / Desire / Back it up / Play that song again.

Oct 88.	(7") <08095> **LITTLE LIAR. / WHAT CAN I DO FOR YOU**	-	19

		Chrysalis	Blackheart
Jan 90.	(c-s,12") <73267> **DIRTY DEEDS. / LET IT BLEED**	-	36
Mar 90.	(7"/c-s) (CHS/+MC 3518) **DIRTY DEEDS (DONE DIRT CHEAP). / PRETTY VACANT**	69	-
Mar 90.	(12"+=/12"pic-d+=/cd-s+=) (CHS 12/P12/CD 3518) – ('A'extended).		
Apr 90.	(cd/c/lp) (CHR/ZCHR/CCD 1773) **THE HIT LIST**		36 Jan90

– Dirty deeds (done dirt cheap) / Love hurts / Pretty vacant / Celluloid heroes / Tush / Time has come today / Up from the skies / Have you ever seen the rain? / Love me two times / Roadrunner USA (1990 version).

Apr 90.	(c-s) <73314> **LOVE HURTS. / HANDYMAN**	-	
Jul 90.	(7") (CHS 3546) **LOVE HURTS. / UP FROM THE SKIES**	-	
Jul 90.	(12"+=/cd-s+=) (CHS 12/CD 3546) – Tush.		

		Silenz	Epic
Feb 92.	(c-s) <74067> **DON'T SURRENDER. / ('A'-Most Excellent version)**	-	
Apr 92.	(cd-s) **TREADIN' WATER / WAIT FOR ME / MISUNDERSTOOD**	-	
Apr 92.	(cd/c) (907080-2/-4) **NOTORIOUS**		

– Backlash / Ashes in the wind / The only good thing (you ever said was goodbye) / Lie to me / Don't surrender / Goodbye / Machismo / Treadin' water / I want you / Wait for me.

		Reprise	Reprise
Feb 94.	(7"/c-s) (W 0232/+C) **I LOVE ROCK'N'ROLL. / ACTIVITY GRRRL**	75	
Feb 94.	(cd-s+=) (W 0232CD) – Wayne's World theme.		

		Blackheart	Warners
Jun 94.	(cd/c) <45567> **YEAH, RIGHT** <US-title 'PURE AND SIMPLE'>		

– Go home / Eye to eye / Spinster / Torture / Rubber & glue / as I am / Activity grrrl / Insecure / Wonderin' / Consumed / You got a problem / Brighter day.

JEWEL

Born: JEWEL KILCHER, 23 May '74, Homer, Alaska, USA, daughter of a struggling farmer. She had an equally tough time as a waitress in San Diego, California for over two years, while residing in her car and tirelessly working her way through California's seedier nightspots. She was signed to 'Atlantic' in 1994, recording her debut set, 'PIECES OF YOU' at NEIL YOUNG's studio (another rock veteran, DYLAN is also apparently a fan). The album stiffed upon its 1995 release; however, a year later, after much airplay for the hit single, 'WHO WILL SAVE YOUR SOUL', sales of the re-issued debut began to pick up (it has since sold over five million copies hitting Top 5 in the process). Fortuitously, the currently buoyant American female singer/songwriter scene (i.e. SHERYL CROW, ALANIS MORISSETTE and JOAN OSBORNE), has given JEWEL a platform for her rootsy, intelligent folk-pop; of course, her stunning blonde looks haven't hindered her any. Her not inconsiderable charms have recently attracted the romantic attentions of actor, SEAN PENN (once the husband of MADONNA), while BILL CLINTON invited her to one his 1996 inaugural balls. Her album was still riding high in the US charts in 1997, although Britain has only recently begun to take note, the single 'YOU WERE MEANT FOR ME' hitting the Top 40 by the end of the year. • Trivia: In 1995, JEWEL played Dorothy in the TV concert production of 'The Wizard Of Oz'.

Album rating: PIECES OF YOU (*7) / SPIRIT (*5)

JEWEL – vocals, acoustic guitar

		Atlantic	Atlantic
May 96.	(c-s) <87151> **WHO WILL SAVE YOUR SOUL / NEAR YOU ALWAYS**	-	11
Jun 96.	(cd/c) (7567 82700-2/-4) <> **PIECES OF YOU**		4 May96

– Who will save your soul / Pieces of you / Little sister / Foolish games / Near you always / Painters / Morning song / Adrian / I'm sensitive / You were meant for me / Don't / Daddy / Angel standing by / Amen / Foolish games edit.

Feb 97.	(c-s) (A 8514C) **WHO WILL SAVE YOUR SOUL / PIECES OF YOU**		-
Feb 97.	(cd-s+=) (A 8514CD) – Emily.		

(re-iss. May97; same)

Nov 96.	(c-s) <87021> **YOU WERE MEANT FOR ME / FOOLISH GAMES**	-	2
Jul 97.	(c-s) (A 5463C) **YOU WERE MEANT FOR ME / COLD SONG**	52	-
Jul 97.	(cd-s+=) (A 5463CD) – Rocker girl.		

(re-iss. Nov97, hit UK No.32)

Jan 98. (c-s) *(A 0022C)* **FOOLISH GAMES / ANGEL NEEDS A RIDE** ☐ | -
(cd-s+=) *(A 0022CD)* – Everything breaks.
Nov 98. (c-s/cd-s) *(AT 0055 C/CD1) <radio play>* **HANDS /**
INNOCENCE MAINTAINED | 41 | 6
(cd-s) *(AT 0055CD2)* – ('A'side) / Who will save your soul (live) / You were meant for me (live).
Nov 98. (c-s) *(7567 82950-2/-4)>* **SPIRIT** | 54 | 3
– Deep water / What's simple is true / Hands / Kiss the flame / Down so long / Innocence maintained / Jupiter / Fat boy / Enter from the east / Barcelona / Life uncommon / Do you / Absence of fear.
Jun 99. (c-s) *(AT 0069C)* **DOWN SO LONG / DEEP WATER** | 38 | 59 Apr99
(cd-s) *(AT 0069CD)* – Emily.
Nov 99. (cd/c) *<83250>* **JOY: A HOLIDAY COLLECTION** | - | 32

JIM'S SUPER STEREOWORLD (see under ⇒ CARTER THE UNSTOPPABLE SEX MACHINE)

Billy JOEL

Born: WILLIAM MARTIN JOEL, 9 May'49, Hicksville, Long Island, New York, USA. In 1965, the classically trained JOEL played piano in his first group, The ECHOES, having been a welterweight boxing champ for local Long Island boys' club. In 1967, he joined The HASSLES who signed to 'United Artists' and released a couple of albums, after an initial SAM & DAVE cover version 45, 'YOU GOT ME HUMMIN'. In 1969, JOEL became a rock critic for 'Changes' art-magazine and formed his own hard-rock duo, ATTILA, with JON SMALL. They issued one 1970 album for 'Epic', before disbanding. JOEL then suffered a bout of depression and entered Meadowbrook mental hospital, with psychiatric problems. In 1971 he was back in circulation to sign a solo contract with Family Productions' Artie Ripp (allegedly known as 'Ripp-off' to his employees, due to his large percentage of artist royalties). JOEL's debut solo effort, 'COLD SPRING HARBOR' was soon issued but, due to a mixing fault, was pressed at the wrong speed!! Embarrassingly for JOEL, who had been well-received by live audiences, this version hit the shops without being corrected, and it made him sound slightly Chipmunk-ish (an 80's re-release rectified matters). Nevertheless, JOEL's piano playing was faultless and with the ballad, 'SHE'S GOT A WAY', he proved his songwriting calibre. He subsequently moved to Los Angeles, soon marrying the ex-wife of JON SMALL, Elizabeth Weber. Culled from JOEL's experiences of playing incognito in piano bars, the 'PIANO MAN' (1973) opus gave him a deserved break with 'Columbia', after his 'CAPTAIN JACK' track was played on FM radio. The following year, the album made the US Top 30, as did its title track. 'STREETLIFE SERENADE' (1974) carried on in much the same vein, JOEL at his strongest on ballad material like 'ROBERTA'. 'TURNSTILES' (1976) sounded more assured, 'NEW YORK STATE OF MIND' JOEL's most accomplished track of his career up to that point. This promise was realised with 'THE STRANGER' (1977), which reached No.2 in the US chart and spawned such enduring candlelight smoochers as 'JUST THE WAY YOU ARE' (written for Elizabeth) and 'SHE'S ALWAYS A WOMAN'. The hits were coming thick and fast, '52nd STREET' (1978) giving JOEL another No.1 album, while the rollicking piano pop/rock of 'MY LIFE' hit NO.3 in the American singles chart and furnished the singer with his biggest UK hit single to date. 'GLASS HOUSES' (1980) kept up the momentum, the retro pastiche of 'IT'S STILL ROCK'N'ROLL TO ME' giving JOEL his first No.1 single (US) while proving he could still be relied upon for cringe-inducing lyrics. With 'THE NYLON CURTAIN' (1982), however, JOEL turned his attention to more pressing concerns, addressing, SPRINGSTEEN style, such issues as Vietnam veterans ('GOODNIGHT SAIGON') and unemployment ('ALLENTOWN'). 'AN INNOCENT MAN' (1984), on the other hand, saw JOEL revisiting his musical roots. By far the biggest success of his career, the record was a highly listenable blend of doo-wop, soul and early rock'n'roll. It was also packed with hits; 'UPTOWN GIRL' (his first UK No.1), 'TELL HER ABOUT IT' and the title track all went Top 10 on both sides of the Atlantic, JOEL enjoying his greatest UK success to date. 'THE BRIDGE' (1986) carried on in a vaguely similar, if not so successful vein, while 'STORM FRONT' (1989) rose to the top of the US charts on the back of the 'WE DIDN'T START THE FIRE' single, an uncharacteristically ballsy rocker which set the tone for the rest of the album, a partially successful attempt at stadium bombast. Employing a new cast of seasoned musicians, JOEL recorded 'RIVER OF DREAMS' (1993), another big selling opus. While the doo-wop influenced title track went Top 5, the other singles failed to make any headway. Nevertheless, over almost three decades, JOEL has proved himself a consistent writer and performer, an elder statesman of pop/rock who pays little heed to constant press barbs. Songwriters: Covered: BACK IN THE USSR + I'LL CRY INSTEAD (Beatles) / THE TIMES THEY ARE A CHANGIN' + TO MAKE YOU FEEL MY LOVE (Bob Dylan) / LIGHT AS THE BREEZE (Leonard Cohen) / and a few more. • **Trivia:** Divorced from his wife (Elizabeth) in July '82, he soon married supermodel and star of his 'UPTOWN GIRL' promo video, Christine Brinkley. In 1989, he fired his manager ex-brother-in-law Frank Weber, after an audit of the accounts showed nearly $100 million missing. The following year, JOEL was awarded $2 million by the courts, and a countersuit by Weber for $30 million was thrown out.

Album rating: COLD SPRING HARBOR (*4) / PIANO MAN (*5) / STREETLIFE SERENADE (*5) / TURNSTILES (*6) / THE STRANGER (*8) / 52ND STREET (*7) / GLASS HOUSES (*6) / SONGS IN THE ATTIC (*6) / THE NYLON CURTAIN (*7) /

AN INNOCENT MAN (*6) / GREATEST HITS, VOLUME 1 & 2 compilation (*8) / THE BRIDGE (*5) / KOHU,EPT (LIVE IN LENINGRAD) (*4) / STORM FRONT (*5) / RIVER OF DREAMS (*6) / GREATEST HITS, VOLUME III compilation (*6)

The HASSLES

BILLY JOEL – piano / **JOHN DIZEK** – vocals / **RICHARD McKENNAR** – guitar / **HOWARD BLAUVELT** – bass / **JONATHAN SMALL** – drums

		U.A.	U.A.
1968.	(7") *<50215>* **YOU GOT ME HUMMIN'. / I'M THINKIN'**	☐	☐
1968.	(7") *<50258>* **EVERY STEP I TAKE (EVERY MOVE I MAKE). / I HEAR VOICES**	-	☐
——	Released 2 lp's 'THE HASSLES' and 'HOUR OF THE WOLF' in US.		
1968.	(7") *<50450>* **4 O' CLOCK IN THE MORNING. / LET ME BRING YOU SUNSHINE**	-	☐
1969.	(7") *<50315>* **NIGHT AFTER DAY. / COUNTRY BOY**	-	☐
1969.	(7") *<50586>* **GREAT BALLS OF FIRE. / TRAVELIN' BAND**	-	☐

ATTILA

—— formed by JOEL and SMALL

		not iss.	Epic
1970.	(lp) *<30030>* **ATTILA**	-	☐

– Wonder woman / California flash / Revenge is sweet / Amplifier fire: part 1 – Godzilla, part 2 – March of the Huns / Rollin' home / Tear this castle down / Holy Moses / Brain invasion. *(cd-iss. Apr93 on 'Sony Europe')*

BILLY JOEL

—— went solo adding many session people

		Philips	Family
May 72.	(7") *(6078 001) <0900>* **SHE'S GOT A WAY. / EVERYBODY LOVE YOU NOW**	☐	☐
Jun 72.	(lp) *(6269 150) <2700>* **COLD SPRING HARBOUR**	☐	☐ Nov71

– She's got a way / You can make me free / Everybody loves you now / Why Judy why / Falling of the rain / Turn around / You look so good to me / Tomorrow is today / Nocturne / Got to begin again. *(re-iss. re-mixed Jan84 on 'C.B.S.' lp/c; CBS/40 32400) – hit UK No.95 (cd-iss. Jan84; CD 26108) (re-iss. Sep91 on 'Pickwick' cd/c; 982637-2/-4)*

| Jan 73. | (7") *<0906>* **TOMORROW IS TODAY. / EVERYBODY LOVES YOU NOW** | - | ☐ |
| Apr 74. | (7") *(6078 018)* **THE BALLAD OF BILLY THE KID. / IF I ONLY HAD THE WORDS (TO TELL YOU)** | ☐ | - |

—— Stage band around this time were **DON EVANS** – guitar / **PAT McDONALD** – bass / **TOM WHITEHORSE** – steel guitar, banjo / **RHYS CLARK** – drums

		C.B.S.	Columbia
Jun 74.	(7") *<46055>* **WORSE COMES TO THE WORST. / SOMEWHERE ALONG THE LINE**	-	80
Aug 74.	(7") *<10015>* **TRAVELIN' PRAYER. / AIN'T NO CRIME**	-	77
Apr 75.	(lp/c) *(CBS/40 80719) <32544>* **PIANO MAN**	☐	27 Nov73

– Travelin' prayer / Piano man / Ain't no crime / You're my home / The ballad of Billy The Kid / Worse comes to the worst / Stop in Nevada / If I only had the words (to tell you) / Somewhere along the line / Captain Jack. *(re-iss. Mar81 lp/c; CBS/40 32002) – hit UK No.98 in Jun84 (cd-iss. Sep85; CD 80719) (cd re-iss. Apr89; CD 32002) (cd re-iss. Jul97 on 'Columbia'; 487938-2)*
(above should have been released May74 by 'Philips' – withdrawn)

Nov 74.	(7") *<10064>* **THE ENTERTAINER. / THE MEXICAN CONNECTION**	-	34
Apr 75.	(7") *(CBS 3183) <45963>* **PIANO MAN. / YOU'RE MY HOME**	☐	25 Feb74
Sep 75.	(7") *(CBS 3469)* **IF I ONLY HAD THE WORDS (TO TELL YOU). / STOP IN NEVADA**	☐	☐
Jul 75.	(lp/c) *(CBS/40 80766) <33146>* **STREETLIFE SERENADE**	☐	35 Nov74

– Streetlife serenader / Los Angelenos / The great suburban showdown / Root beer rag / Roberta / Last of the big time spenders / Weekend song / Souvenir / The Mexican connection. *(re-iss. Mar81 lp/c; CBS/40 32035) (cd-iss. Mar87; CD 80766) (cd re-iss. Feb97 on 'Columbia'; 484461-2)*

—— band now incl. **NIGEL OLSSON + DEE MURRAY** (both ex-ELTON JOHN)

| Jul 76. | (lp/c) *(CBS/40 81195) <33848>* **TURNSTILES** | ☐ | Jun76 |

– Say goodbye to Hollywood / Summer, Highland falls / All you wanna do is dance / New york state of mind / James / Prelude / Angry young man / I've loved these days / Miami 2017 (seen the lights go on Broadway). *(re-iss. Nov81 lp/c; CBS/40 32057) (cd-iss. Mar87; Cd 81195) (re-iss. Nov89 on 'Pickwick' lp/cd/cd; 902197-1/-4/-2) (cd re-iss. Feb97 on 'Columbia'; 474681-2)*

Jul 76.	(7") *<10412>* **SUMMER, HIGHLAND FALLS. / JAMES**	-	-
Oct 76.	(7") *<10562>* **I'VE LOVED THESE DAYS. / SAY GOODBYE TO HOLLYWOOD**	-	☐
Nov 76.	(7") *(CBS 4686)* **SAY GOODBYE TO HOLLYWOOD. / STOP IN NEVADA**	☐	☐
Sep 77.	(7") *<10624>* **MOVIN' OUT (ANTHONY'S SONG). / SHE'S ALWAYS A WOMAN**	☐	☐
Dec 77.	(lp/c) *(CBS/40 82311) <34987>* **THE STRANGER**	25	2 Oct77

– Movin' out (Anthony's song) / The stranger / Just the way you are / Scenes from an Italian restaurant / Vienna / Only the good die young / She's always a woman / Get it right the first time / Everybody has a dream. *(re-iss. May87 lp/c; 450914-1/-4) (cd-iss. Dec85; CD 82311) (cd re-iss. Jun89; 450914-2)*

Jan 78.	(7") *(CBS 5872) <10646>* **JUST THE WAY YOU ARE. / GET IT RIGHT THE FIRST TIME**	19	3 Nov77
Mar 78.	(7") *<10708>* **MOVIN' OUT (ANTHONY'S SONG). / EVERYBODY HAS A DREAM**	-	17
Apr 78.	(7") *(CBS 6266)* **SHE'S ALWAYS A WOMAN. / EVERYBODY HAS A DREAM**	-	-
May 78.	(7") *<10750>* **ONLY THE GOOD DIE YOUNG. / GET IT RIGHT THE FIRST TIME**	-	24
Jun 78.	(7") *(CBS 6412)* **MOVIN' OUT (ANTHONY'S SONG). / VIENNA**	35	-
Aug 78.	(7") *<10788>* **SHE'S ALWAYS A WOMAN. / VIENNA**	-	17

Nov 78. (lp/c) *(CBS/40 83181)* 35609> **52nd STREET** — | 10 | | 1 | Oct78
– Big shot / Honesty / My life / Zanzibar / Stiletto / Rosalind's eyes / Half a mile away / Until the night / 52nd Street. *(re-iss. Nov85 lp/c; CBS/40 32693) (cd-iss. Nov87; CD 83181) (cd re-iss. Feb95 on 'Columbia'; CK 64412)*

Nov 78. (7") *(CBS 6821)* <10853> **MY LIFE. / 52nd STREET** | 12 | | 3 |

Feb 79. (7") <10913> **BIG SHOT. / ROOT BEER BAG** | - | | 14 |

Mar 79. (7") *(CBS 7242)* **UNTIL THE NIGHT. / ROOT BEER RAG** | 50 | | - |

Jun 79. (7") *(CBS 7422)* <10959> **HONESTY. / THE MEXICAN CONNECTION** | | | 24 | Apr79

Feb 80. (7") *(CBS 11229)* **SOUVENIR. / ALL FOR LENYA** | - | | - |

Mar 80. (lp/c) *(CBS/40 86108)* <36384> **GLASS HOUSES** | 9 | | 1 |
– You may be right / Sometimes a fantasy / Don't ask me why / It's still rock'n'roll to me / All for Lenya / I don't want to be alone / Sleeping with the television on / C'Etait toi (you were the one) / Close to the borderline / Through the long night. *(cd-iss. Dec85; CD 86108) (re-iss. Nov86 lp/c; 450087-1/-4) (cd-iss. Mar91; 450087-2) (re-iss. May94 on 'Columbia' cd/c; 450067-2/-4)*

Mar 80. (7") *(CBS 8325)* **ALL FOR LEYNA. / CLOSE TO THE BORDERLINE** | 40 | | - |

Mar 80. (7") <11231> **YOU MAY BE RIGHT. / CLOSE TO THE BORDERLINE** | - | | 7 |

May 80. (7") *(CBS 8643)* **YOU MAY BE RIGHT. / THROUGH THE LONG NIGHT** | | | |

Jul 80. (7") *(CBS 8753)* <11276> **IT'S STILL ROCK'N'ROLL TO ME. / THROUGH THE LONG NIGHT** | 14 | | 1 | May80

Oct 80. (7") *(CBS 9031)* <11331> **DON'T ASK ME WHY. / C'ETAIT TOI (YOU WERE THE ONE)** | | | 19 | Aug80

Oct 80. (7") <11379> **SOMETIMES A FANTASY. / ALL FOR LEYNA** | - | | 36 |

Jan 81. (7") *(CBS 9419)* **SOMETIMES A FANTASY. / SLEEPING WITH THE TELEVISION ON** | | | - |

Sep 81. (7") *(CBS 1642)* <02518> **SAY GOODBYE TO HOLLYWOOD (live). / SUMMER, HIGHLAND FALLS (live)** | | | 17 |

Sep 81. (lp/c) *(CBS/40 85273)* <37461> **SONGS IN THE ATTIC (live)** | 57 | | 8 |
– Miami 2017 (seen the lights go out on Broadway) / Summer, Highland Falls / Streetlife serenade / Los Angelenos / She's got a way / Everybody loves you now / Say goodbye to Hollywood / Captain Jack / You're my home / The ballad of Billy The Kid / I've loved these days. *(re-iss. Nov83 lp/c; CBS/40 32364) (cd-iss. May87; CD 85273) (cd re-iss. Jun89)*

Nov 81. (7") *(A 1808)* **YOU'RE MY HOME (live). / THE BALLAD OF BILLY THE KID (live)** | - | | - |

Jan 82. (7") *(A 2002)* <02628> **SHE'S GOT A WAY (live). / THE BALLAD OF BILLY THE KID (live)** | | | 23 | Nov81

Sep 82. (7") *(A 2730)* <03244> **PRESSURE. / LAURA** | 27 | | 20 |

Sep 82. (lp/c) *(CBS/40 85959)* <38200> **THE NYLON CURTAIN** | 27 | | 7 |
– Allentown / Laura / Pressure / Goodnight Saigon / She's right on time / A room on your own / Surprises / Scandinavian skies / Pressure / Where's the orchestra. *(cd-iss. Jan83; CD 85959) (re-iss. Mar88 lp/c; 460186-1/-4)*

Nov 82. (7") *(A 2981)* <03413> **ALLENTOWN. / ELVIS PRESLEY BOULEVARD** | | | 17 |

Feb 83. (7") *(A 3029)* **GOODNIGHT SAIGON. / WHERE'S THE ORCHESTRA** | | | - |

Feb 83. (7") <03780> **GOODNIGHT SAIGON. / A ROOM OF OUR OWN** | | | 56 |

Aug 83. (7") *(A 3655)* <04012> **TELL HER ABOUT IT. / EASY MONEY** | | | 1 | Jul83

Sep 83. (lp/c) *(CBS/40 25554)* <38837> **AN INNOCENT MAN** | 2 | | 4 | Aug83
– Easy money / An innocent man / The longest time / This night / Tell her about it / Uptown girl / Careless talk / Christie Lee / Leave a tender moment alone / Keeping the faith. *(cd-iss. Aug84; CD 25554)*

Oct 83. (7") *(A 3775)* <04149> **UPTOWN GIRL / CARELESS TALK** | 1 | | 3 | Sep83
(12"+=) *(TA 3775)* – Just the way you are / It's still rock'n'roll to me.

Dec 83. (7") *(A 3655)* **TELL HER ABOUT IT. / EASY MONEY** | 4 | | - |
(12"+=) *(TA 3655)* – You got me hummin' (live).

Dec 83. (7") <04259> **AN INNOCENT MAN. / I'LL CRY INSTEAD** | - | | 10 |

Feb 84. (7") *(A 4142)* **AN INNOCENT MAN. / YOU'RE MY HOME (live)** | 8 | | - |
(12"+=) *(TA 4142)* – She's always a woman / Until the night.

Apr 84. (7") *(A 4280)* <0440> **THE LONGEST TIME. / CHRISTIE LEE** | 25 | | 14 | Mar84
(12"+=) *(TA 4280)* – Captain Jack (live) / The ballad of Billy the kid (live).

Jun 84. (7") *(A 4521)* **LEAVE A TENDER MOMENT ALONE. / GOODNIGHT SAIGON** | 29 | | - |
(12"+=) *(TA 4521)* – Movin' out (Anthony's song) / Big shot / You may be right.

Jul 84. (7") <04514> **LEAVE A TENDER MOMENT ALONE. / THIS NIGHT** | - | | 27 |

Nov 84. (7") *(A 4884)* **THIS NIGHT. / I'LL CRY INSTEAD (live)** | - | | - |

Jan 85. (7") <04681> **KEEPING THE FAITH. / SHE'S RIGHT ON TIME** | - | | 18 |

—— featured on the 'USA FOR AFRICA' single, 'WE ARE THE WORLD'.

Jun 85. (7") *(A 6378)* <05417> **YOU'RE ONLY HUMAN. / SURPRISES** | | | 9 |
(12"+=) *(TA 6378)* – Keeping the faith / Scenes from an Italian restaurant.

Oct 85. (7") *(A 6622)* <05657> **THE NIGHT IS STILL YOUNG. / SUMMER, HIGHLAND FALLS** | | | 34 |

Jul 86. (7") *(A 7247)* <06118> **MODERN WOMAN. / SLEEPING WITH THE TELEVISION ON** | | | 10 | Jun86
(d7"+=) *(DA 7247)* – Uptown girl / All for love.
(12"+=) *(TA 7247)* – The night is still young / You're only human.

Aug 86. (lp/c/cd) *(CBS/40/CD 86323)* <40402> **THE BRIDGE** | 38 | | 7 |
– Running on ice / This is the time / A matter of trust / Modern woman / Baby grand (w/ RAY CHARLES) / Big man on Mulberry Street / Temptation / Code of silence (w/ CYNDI LAUPER) / Getting closer. *(re-iss. Oct89 lp/c; 465 561-1/-4) (re-iss. Feb94 on 'Columbia' cd/c; 465561-2)*

Sep 86. (7") *(650057-7)* <06108> **A MATTER OF TRUST. / GETTING CLOSER** | 52 | | 10 | Aug86
(12"+=) *(650057-6)* – An innocent man / Tell her about it.

Nov 86. (7") <06526> **THIS IS THE TIME. / CODE OF SILENCE (with CYNDI LAUPER)** | - | | 18 |

Mar 87. (7"; BILLY JOEL featuring RAY CHARLES) <06994> **BABY GRAND. / BIG MAN ON MULBERRY STREET** | - | | 75 |

Nov 87. (d-lp/c/cd/d) *(460407-1/-4/-2)* <40996> **KOHUEPT – LIVE IN LENINGRAD (live)** | 92 | | 38 |

– Odoya / Angry young man / Honesty / Goodnight Saigon / Stiletto / Big man on Mulberry Street / Baby grand / An innocent man / Allentown / A matter of trust / Only the good die young / Sometimes a fantasy / Uptown girl / Big shot / Back in the U.S.S.R. / The times they are a-changin'. *(cd-iss. Oct90 on 'Columbia'; 467448-2)*

Nov 87. (7") *(651206-7)* <07626> **BACK IN THE U.S.S.R. (live). / BIG SHOT (live)** | | | |
(12"+=)(cd-s+=) *(651206-6)* *(CDEWF 1)* – A matter of trust (live) / The times they are a-changin' (live).

Feb 88. (7") <07664> **THE TIMES THEY ARE A-CHANGIN' (live). / BACK IN THE U.S.S.R. (live)** | - | | - |

—— new band **MINDY JOSTIN** – rhythm guitar, violin, harp / **DAVID BROWN** – guitar / **MARK RIVIERA** – sax / **LIBERTY DeVITO** – drums / **SCHUYLER DEALE** – bass / **JEFF JACOBS** – synthesizers / **CRYSTAL TALIEFERO** – vocals, percussion

Sep 89. (7"/c-s) *(JOEL/+M 1)* <73021> **WE DIDN'T START THE FIRE. / HOUSE OF BLUE LIGHT** | 7 | | 1 | Oct89
(12"+=/cd-s+=) *(JOEL T/C 1)* – Just the way you are.

Oct 89. (lp/c/cd) *(465658-1/-4/-2)* <44366> **STORM FRONT** | 5 | | 1 |
– That's not her style / We didn't start the fire / The downeaster "Alexa" / I go to extremes / Shameless / Storm front / Leningrad / State of Grace / When in Rome / And so it goes. *(cd re-iss. Mar96 on 'Columbia'; 4656583)*

Dec 89. (7"/c-s) *(JOEL/+M 3)* **LENINGRAD. / THE TIMES THEY ARE A-CHANGIN' (live)** | 53 | | - |
(cd-s+=) *(CDJOEL 3)* – Uptown girl (live) / Back in the USSR (live).
(3"cd-s+=) *(JOELC 3)* – Goodnight Saigon / Vienna / Scandinavian skies.

Mar 90. (7"/c-s) *(JOEL/+M 2)* <73091> **I GO TO EXTREMES. / WHEN IN ROME** | 70 | | 6 | Jan90
(12"+=/cd-s+=) *(JOEL T/C 2)* – Uptown girl / All for Leyna.
(7"ep+=) *(JOELEP 2)* – Prelude / Angry young man / Tell her about it / Leave a tender moment alone.

Apr 90. (c-s) <73333> **THE DOWNEASTER "ALEXA" / AND SO IT GOES** | - | | 57 |

May 90. (7"/c-s) *(JOEL/+M 4)* **THE DOWNEASTER "ALEXA". / AND SO IT GOES / STREETLIFE SERENADE** | - | | - |
(12"+=/cd-s+=) *(JOELT/CDJOEL 4)* – I've loved these days / An innocent man.
(pic-cd-s+=) *(JOELC 4)* – Say goodbye to Hollywood / Allentown / Only the good die young.

Jul 90. (c-s) <73602> **THAT'S NOT HER STYLE / AND SO IT GOES** | - | | 77 |

Oct 90. (7"ep/cd-ep) **THAT'S NOT HER STYLE / WE DIDN'T START THE FIRE / UNTIL THE NIGHT / JUST THE WAY YOU ARE** | - | | - |

Oct 90. (c-s) <73602> **AND SO IT GOES / THE DOWNEASTER ALEXA / SHAMELESS / STATES OF GRACE** | - | | 37 |

Jan 91. (c-s) **SHAMELESS / STORM FRONT (live)** | - | | |
(below from film 'Honeymoon In Las Vegas' on 'Epic records')

Aug 92. (7"/c-s) *(658343-7/-4)* <74422> **ALL SHOOK UP. / (b-side by Ricky Van Shelton)** | 27 | | 92 |
(cd-s+=) *(658343-2)* – (other artist).
other musicians; **DAN KORTCHMAR, TOMMY BYRNES, LESLIE WEST** – guitar / **T.H. STEVENS, LONNIE HILLER** – bass / **STEVE JORDAN, ZACHARY ALFORD, LIBERTY DeVITTO** – drums

Jul 93. (7"/c-s) *(659543-7/-4)* <77086> **THE RIVER OF DREAMS. / NO MAN'S LAND** | 3 | | 3 |
(cd-s+=) *(659543-2)* – The great wall of China.

Aug 93. (cd/c/lp) *(473872-2/-4/-1)* <53003> **RIVER OF DREAMS** | 3 | | 1 |
– No man's land / The great wall of China / Blonde over blue / A minor variation / Shades of grey / All about soul / Lullabye (goodnight, my angel) / The river of dreams / Two thousand years / Famous last words.

Oct 93. (7"/c-s) *(659736-7/-4)* <77254> **ALL ABOUT SOUL. / YOU PICKED A REAL BAD TIME** | 32 | | 29 |
(cd-s+=) *(659736-2)* – (2-'A'mixes).

Feb 94. (7"/c-s) *(659920-7/-4)* **NO MAN'S ISLAND. / SHADES OF GREY (live)** | 50 | | - |
(cd-s+=) *(659920-2)* – ('A'mix).

Mar 94. (c-s) <77363> **LULLABYE (GOODNIGHT MY ANGEL) / TWO THOUSAND YEARS** | - | | 77 |

Aug 97. (c-s,12",cd-s) <78641> **TO MAKE YOU FEEL MY LOVE /** | - | | 50 |

Oct 97. (cd/c) *(488236-2/-4)* <67347> **GREATEST HITS – VOLUME III (compilation)** | 23 | | 9 | Aug97
– Keeping the faith / An innocent man / A matter of trust / Baby grand / This is the time / Leningrad / We didn't start the fire / I go to extremes / And so it goes / Downeaster Alexa / Shameless / All about soul / Lullabye / River of dreams / To make you feel my love / Hey girl / Light as a breeze.

– compilations etc. –

on 'CBS' UK / 'Columbia' US unless mentioned otherwise

Oct 79. (3-lp-box) *(CBS 66352)* **3-LP BOX SET** | | | - |
– 'TURNTILES' / 'THE STRANGER' / '52nd STREET'

1980. (7") Columbia; **DOWN IN THE BOONDOCKS. / 21ST CENTURY MAN** | | | - |

Feb 83. (7"ep) Epic; *(EPCA 2619)* **GREATEST ORIGINAL HITS** | | | - |
– Just the way you are / Movin' out (Anthony's song) / My life / She's a woman. *(c-iss.Aug82)*

Jul 84. (7") *(A 4591)* **JUST THE WAY YOU ARE. / MY LIFE** | | | - |

Jul 85. (d-lp/c/cd) *(CBS/40/CD 88666)* **GREATEST HITS VOL.1 & VOL.2** | 7 | | 6 |
– Piano man / Say goodbye to Hollywood / New York state of mind / The stranger / Just the way you are / Movin' out (Anthony's song) / Only the good die young / She's always a woman / My life / Big shot / Honesty / You may be right / It's still rock and roll to me / Pressure / Allentown / Goodnight Saigon / Tell her about it / Uptown girl / The longest time / You're only human (second wind) / The night is still young. *(d-cd-iss. Sep92 on 'Columbia'; CD 88666)*

Feb 86. (7") *(A 6862)* **SHE'S ALWAYS A WOMAN. / JUST THE WAY YOU ARE** | 53 | | - |

Apr 86. (lp/c) Showcase; *(SHLP/SHTC 114)* **CALIFORNIA FLASH** | | | - |

Jul 87. (d-lp) *(BJ 241)* **THE STRANGER / AN INNOCENT MAN** | | | - |

1988. (d-c) *(4022143)* **PIANO MAN / STREETLIFE SERENADE** | | | - |

Aug 88. (3"cd-ep) <38K 07950> **IT'S STILL ROCK'N'ROLL TO ME. / JUST THE WAY YOU ARE** | - | | - |

Nov 91. (4xcd-box/4xc-box) *Columbia*; *(469174-2/-4)* **THE BILLY JOEL SOUVENIR – THE ULTIMATE COLLECTION INTERVIEW WITH BILLY JOEL** □ -
　 – (GREATEST HITS VOL.1 & 2 / STORM FRONT / LIVE AT THE YANKEE STADIUM plus 50 minute interview)
Jun 92. (c/cd) *Tring*; *(MC+/JHD 004)* **FURTHER THAN HEAVEN** □ -
Sep 92. (d-cd) *Columbia*; **THE BRIDGE / GLASS HOUSES** □ -
Mar 93. (d-cd) *Columbia*; *(471604-2)* **AN INNOCENT MAN / THE STRANGER** □ □
　 (re-iss. Feb95; 478478-2)
Oct 96. (3xcd-box) *Columbia*; *(485320-2)* **AN INNOCENT MAN / STORM FRONT / THE STRANGER** □ -
Jun 98. (3xcd-box) *(491274-2)* **THE GREATEST HITS COLLECTION VOLUMES I, II & III** 33 □

Elton JOHN

Born: REGINALD KENNETH DWIGHT, 25 Mar'47, Pinner, Middlesex, England. After learning piano at an early age, he attained a scholarship from The Royal Academy Of Music. In the early 60's, he joined BLUESOLOGY, and by 1965 had written his first 45, 'COME BACK BABY' for 'Fontana', the band subsequently touring in the UK as back-up to American acts (i.e. MAJOR LANCE, The BLUE BELLES with PATTI LaBELLE, etc). Late in 1966, the group were joined by five others including singer LONG JOHN BALDRY, who virtually took over the show, much to the dislike of the young REG DWIGHT. In 1967, he left BLUESOLOGY and auditioned for 'Liberty', but after failure found other writer BERNIE TAUPIN (b.22 May'50, Lincolnshire). They wrote LONG JOHN BALDRY's b-side, 'Lord You Made The Night Too Long', for his UK No.1 'Let The Heartaches Begin'. DWIGHT of course became ELTON JOHN, taking names from BLUESOLOGY members ELTON DEAN and LONG JOHN BALDRY. In 1968, ELTON and BERNIE joined the Dick James Music Publishing (later D.J.M.) stable, and earned around £10 a week each. With CALEB QUAYE (ex-BLUESOLOGY) on production, ELTON released debut solo single 'I'VE BEEN LOVING YOU TOO LONG' for 'Philips'. Early in '69, he gained needed airplay for 'LADY SAMANTHA', but when this failed, he tried to join KING CRIMSON, to no avail. The pair then wrote a number for the Eurovision Song Contest, 'I CAN'T GO ON LIVING WITHOUT YOU', which was heard but rejected by LULU for eventual winner, 'Boom Bang A Bang'. Early in 1969, ELTON signed to 'DJM', and flopped with both 45 'IT'S ME THAT YOU NEED' & lp 'EMPTY SKY'. To make ends meet, ELTON played on The HOLLIES 'He Ain't Heavy . . . ' session, and worked for budget labels 'Pickwick' & 'MFP', on some pop covers. In 1970 after more HOLLIES sessions, he released 'BORDER SONG', which, when picked up by 'Uni', broke into US Top 100. The accompanying eponymous album (the first of many to be produced by Gus Dudgeon) made the American Top 5 and the UK Top 20, ELTON finally setting out on the road to superstardom that would see him become one of the most unlikely pop icons of the 70's. With the liltingly effective 'YOUR SONG', the JOHN/TAUPIN writing partnership also stepped up a gear, the chemistry obvious from the beginning despite TAUPIN's often impenetrable lyrics. Later that year, ELTON made his US stage debut (along with guitarist CALEB QUAYE – yes, part of the same clan as FINLAY – and the rhythm section of NIGEL OLSSON and DEE MURRAY) at the Troubadour in L.A., giving the Americans a taste of the flamboyant showmanship which would become ever more OTT as the decade wore on and which subsequently resulted in the LIBERACE comparisons. A relatively successful attempt at retro Americana, 'TUMBLEWEED CONNECTION' (1970) was another big seller and included the rustic beauty of 'COUNTRY COMFORT', later covered in memorable style by ROD STEWART, although 'MADMAN ACROSS THE WATER' (1971) saw Paul Buckmaster's overbearing string arrangements come in for some critical flak. With DAVY JOHNSTONE replacing QUAYE, 'HONKY CHATEAU' (1972) was the first album to be credited to the ELTON JOHN GROUP; a more robust affair and his first No.1 (US), it saw ELTON begin to adopt the musical maverick approach which would characterise most of his 70's albums, spawning a massive hit in the soaring 'ROCKET MAN'. 'DON'T SHOOT ME I'M ONLY THE PIANO PLAYER' (1973) consolidated his commercial appeal, a transatlantic No.1 which saw him flirting gamely with bubblegum pop on 'CROCODILE ROCK' (his first No.1 single) and adult balladry on 'DANIEL'. The pinnacle of JOHN's early career, however, came with 'GOODBYE YELLOW BRICK ROAD' (1973) a massive selling double set which saw ELTON's chameleon-like talent embrace a dazzling, occasionally over-ambitious, array of styles, from the musclebound piano assault of 'SATURDAY'S ALRIGHT FOR FIGHTING' and the cloying bombast of 'BENNIE AND THE JETS' to his poignant Marilyn Monroe tribute, 'CANDLE IN THE WIND'. The same year, ELTON did the obligatory rock star thing and formed his own label, 'Rocket', KIKI DEE and NEIL SEDAKA being two of his more prominent signings. JOHN also working with JOHN LENNON the following year on his comeback single, 'Whatever Gets You Thru The Night'. 'CAPTAIN FANTASTIC AND THE BROWN DIRT COWBOY' (1975) was a concept affair documenting the development of the JOHN/TAUPIN partnership through the years, the soul baring 'SOMEONE SAVED MY LIFE TONIGHT' ranking among the pair's best. As well as making a cameo appearance in Ken Russell's screen version of The WHO's 'Tommy' (sporting one of the rather more erm, exotic models from his famed sunglasses collection), JOHN let go longstanding sidemen, MURRAY and OLSON, revamping his band prior to recording 'ROCK OF THE WESTIES' (1975), his last No.1 album for almost fifteen years. The latter half of

the decade saw JOHN retire from performing and, to a large extent, from recording; 1976's lengthy double-set, 'BLUE MOVES', marked the end of his partnership with TAUPIN, and JOHN subsequently busied himself with chairing his beloved Watford F.C. Though it spawned the Top 5 'SONG FOR GUY', 'A SINGLE MAN' (1978) was hardly a convincing return and the early 80's marked a creative nadir as ELTON fumbled his way through a series of confused albums and ill-advised musical experiments. Only a reunion with TAUPIN halted the slide on 1983's 'TOO LOW FOR ZERO' and its defiant hit single, 'I'M STILL STANDING'. 'BREAKING HEARTS' (1984) continued the renaissance with insidiously catchy 'PASSENGERS' and the cheesy but gorgeous 'SAD SONGS (SAY SO MUCH)', Top 10 hits both. Nevertheless, like many of his contemporaries, JOHN was now a card carrying member of the glossy, MOR brigade whose airbrushed, MTV sterility partly defined the 80's. But as his music became smoother, his personal life was in turmoil; an ill-fated marriage to Renate Blauer, well documented drug/alcohol problems and throat surgery all gave the gutter press hours of speculative fun. JOHN had the last laugh, however, when he successfully sued The Sun newspaper in October '88. Openly gay, JOHN increasingly devoted his time and money into AIDS care and research, founding the Elton John AIDS Foundation in 1992 and announcing that, from 'THE ONE' onwards, he'd donate all future royalties from singles sales. 1993 saw the release of the 'DUETS' album, featuring JOHN in tandem with everyone from TAMMY WYNETTE to LEONARD COHEN, while a suitably camp run through of 'DON'T GO BREAKING MY HEART' with RuPAUL hit the UK Top 10. The bland 'MADE IN ENGLAND' (1995) has been only the singer's second set of new material in the 90's so far, its embarrassingly awful title track incredibly/unsurprisingly hitting the UK Top 20. However, by far the most high profile of ELTON's more recent activites was his rendition of 'CANDLE IN THE WIND' at the funeral of Diana, Princess Of Wales, the single subsequently re-issued and a hysterical public pushing it to the top of the charts. • **Covered:** GET BACK + LUCY IN THE SKY WITH DIAMONDS + I SAW HER STANDING THERE (Beatles; on which ELTON did duet with JOHN LENNON) / PINBALL WIZARD (Who; from the film 'Tommy', in which he featured) / JOHNNY B. GOODE (Chuck Berry) / WHERE HAVE ALL THE GOOD TIMES GONE (Kinks) / I HEARD IT THROUGH THE GRAPEVINE (hit; Marvin Gaye) / I'M YOUR MAN (Leonard Cohen) / etc.

Album rating: EMPTY SKY (*4) / ELTON JOHN (*7) / TUMBLEWEED CONNECTION (*8) / "FRIENDS" soundtrack (*3) / 11-17-70 (*4) / MADMAN ACROSS THE WATER (*7) / HONKY CHATEAU (*8) / DON'T SHOOT ME I'M ONLY THE PIANO PLAYER (*8) / GOODBYE YELLOW BRICK ROAD (*9) / CARIBOU (*4) / GREATEST HITS compilation (*9) / CAPTAIN FANTASTIC AND THE BROWN DIRT COWBOY (*7) / ROCK OF THE WESTIES (*5) / HERE AND THERE (*4) / BLUE MOVES (*6) / GREATEST HITS, VOL.II compilation (*8) / A SINGLE MAN (*6) / VICTIM OF LOVE (*3) / 21 AT 33 (*5) / THE FOX (*4) / JUMP UP! (*5) / TOO LOW FOR ZERO (*6) / BREAKING HEARTS (*5) / ICE ON FIRE (*5) / LEATHER JACKETS (*5) / LIVE IN AUSTRALIA (*4) / GREATEST HITS, VOL.III, 1979-1987 compilation (*6) / REG STRIKES BACK (*5) / SLEEPING WITH THE PAST (*5) / THE VERY BEST OF ELTON JOHN compilation (*8) / THE ONE (*5) / DUETS (*4) / MADE IN ENGLAND (*6) / LOVE SONGS compilation (*6) / BIG PICTURE (5) / ELTON JOHN AND TIM RICE'S AIDA (*3)

BLUESOLOGY

REG DWIGHT – vocals, piano / **STUART BROWN** – guitar, vocals / **REX BISHOP** – bass / **MICK INKPEN** – drums

		Fontana	not iss.
Jul 65.	(7") *(TF 594)* **COME BACK BABY. / TIME'S GETTING TOUGHER THAN TOUGH**	□	-
Feb 66.	(7") *(TF 668)* **MISTER FRANTIC. / EVERYDAY (I HAVE THE BLUES)**	□	-

—— added **LONG JOHN BALDRY** – vocals / **CALEB QUAYE** – guitar / **ELTON DEAN** – sax / **PETE GAVIN, NEIL HUBBARD + MARK CHARIG** – wind

		Polydor	not iss.
Oct 67.	(7"; as STU BROWN & BLUESOLOGY) *(56195)* **SINCE I FOUND YOU BABY. / JUST A LITTLE BIT**	□	-

ELTON JOHN

(solo) – vocals, piano with session people, incl.**NIGEL OLSSON** (note most of BLUESOLOGY later joined SOFT MACHINE)

		Philips	Congress
Mar 68.	(7") *(BF 1643)* **I'VE BEEN LOVING YOU TOO LONG. / HERE'S TO THE NEXT TIME**	□	-
Jan 69.	(7") *(BF 1739)* **LADY SAMANTHA. / ALL ACROSS THE HEAVENS**	□	-
1969.	(7") *<6017>* **LADY SAMANTHA. / IT'S ME THAT YOU NEED**	-	□
1969.	(7") *<6022>* **BORDER SONG. / BAD SIDE OF THE MOON**	-	□

—— In 1969, ELTON was part of BREAD & BEER BAND, who issued 1 'Decca' single 'THE DICK BARTON THEME. / BREAKDOWN BLUES. (re-iss. 1972)

		D.J.M.	Uni
May 69.	(7") *(DJS 205)* **IT'S ME THAT YOU NEED. / JUST LIKE STRANGE RAIN**	□	□
Jun 69.	(lp; mono/stereo) *(DJMLP/DJLPS 403)* *<2130>* **EMPTY SKY**	□	□

– Empty sky / Valhalla / Western Ford gateway / Hymn 2000 / Lady what's tomorrow / Sails / The scaffold / Skyline pigeon / Gulliver – Hay chewed – Reprise. *<US re-iss. Jan75 on 'M.C.A.'; 2130>* – reached No.6 *(re-iss. May81 lp/c; DJM 2/-4 2086) (cd-iss. Oct86; DJMCD 13) (re-iss. May87 lp/c; PRICE/PRIMC 97) (cd re-iss. Jun87; 823017-2) <US cd-iss. Jun88; 31000>* (cd re-iss. May95 on 'Rocket';)

—— now with band **NIGEL OLSSON** (b.10 Feb'49, Merseyside) – drums / **DEE MURRAY** (b.DAVID MURRAY OATES, 3 Apr'46, Southgate, London) – bass / **CALEB QUAYE** – guitar (ex-BLUESOLOGY)

Mar 70. (7") (DJS 217) <55246> **BORDER SONG. / BAD SIDE OF THE MOON** [ ] [92] Jul70

Apr 70. (lp/c) (DJLPS 2/4 0406) <73090> **ELTON JOHN** [11] [4] Sep70
– Your song / I need you to turn to / Take me to the pilot / No shoestrings on Louise / First episode at Heinton / Sixty years on / Border song / Greatest discovery / The cage / The king must die. (re-iss. May81 lp/c; DJM 2/4 2087) (re-iss. Apr87 lp/c; PRICE/PRIMC 98) (cd-iss. Jun87; 827689-2) (cd re-iss. May95 on 'Rocket';)

Jun 70. (7") (DJS 222) **ROCK AND ROLL MADONNA. / GREY SEAL** [ ] [-]

Oct 70. (lp/c) (DJLPS 2/4 0410) <73096> **TUMBLEWEED CONNECTION** [6] [5] Jan71
– Ballad of well-known gun / Come down in time / Country comfort / Son of your father / My father's gun / Where to now St. Peter / Love song / Amoreena / Talking old soldiers / Burn down the mission. (re-iss. May81 lp/c; DJM 2/4 2088) (re-iss. Apr87 lp/c; PRICE/PRIMC 99) (cd-iss. Jun87; 829248-2) (cd re-iss. May95 on 'Rocket')

Nov 70. (7") <55265> **YOUR SONG. / TAKE ME TO THE PILOT** [-] [8]

Jan 71. (7") (DJS 233) **YOUR SONG. / INTO THE OLD MAN'S SHOES** [7] [-]

Apr 71. (7") (DJS 244) <55277> **FRIENDS. / HONEY ROLL** [34] [-] Mar 71

Apr 71. (lp/c) (DJLPS 2/4 0414) <93105> **17.11.70 (live)** [20] [11] May71
– Take me to the pilot / Honky tonk women / Sixty years on / Can I put you on / Bad side of the Moon / Burn down the mission: My baby left me – Get back. (re-iss. Mar78 on 'Hallmark' lp/c; SHM 942/HSC 314) (cd-iss. Sep95 on 'Rocket')

Nov 71. (lp/c) (DJH 2/4 0420) <93120> **MADMAN ACROSS THE WATER** [41] [8]
– Tiny dancer / Levon / Razor face / Madman across the water / Indian sunset / Holiday inn / Rotten Peaches / All the nasties / Goodbye. (re-iss. May81 lp/c; DJM 2/4 2089) (re-iss. Apr87 lp/c; PRICE/PRIMC 100) (cd-iss. Jun87; 825487-2) (cd re-iss. Aug95 on 'Rocket')

Dec 71. (7") <55314> **LEVON. / GOODBYE** [-] [24]

Feb 72. (7") <55318> **TINY DANCER. / RAZOR FACE** [-] [41]

—— **DAVEY JOHNSTONE** (b. 6 May'51, Edinburgh, Scotland) – guitar (ex-MAGNA CARTA) repl. QUAYE. Added **RAY COOPER** – percussion

Apr 72. (7"m) (DJX 501) **ROCKET MAN. / HOLIDAY INN / GOODBYE** [2] [-]

May 72. (7") <55328> **ROCKET MAN. / SUZIE (DREAMS)** [-] [6]

May 72. (lp/c) (DJLPH 2/4 0423) <93135> **HONKY CHATEAU** [2] [1] Jun72
– Honky cat / Mellow / I think I'm going to kill myself / Susie (dramas) / Rocket man / Salvation / Slave / Amy / Mona Lisas and mad hatters / Hercules. (re-iss. May81 lp/c; DJM 2/4 2090) (re-iss. Apr87 lp/c; PRICE/PRIMC 101) (cd-iss. Jun87; 829249-2) (cd re-iss. Aug95 on 'Rocket')

Aug 72. (7"m) (DJS 269) **HONKY CAT. / LADY SAMANTHA / IT'S ME THAT YOU NEED** [31] [-]

Aug 72. (7") <55343> **HONKY CAT. / SLAVE** [-] [8]
D.J.M. / M.C.A.

Oct 72. (7") (DJS 271) <40000> **CROCODILE ROCK. / ELDERBERRY WINE** [5] [1] Dec72

Jan 73. (7") (DJS 275) <40046> **DANIEL. / SKYLINE PIGEON** [4] [2] Apr73

Feb 73. (lp/c) (DJLPH 2/4 0427) <2100> **DON'T SHOOT ME I'M ONLY THE PIANO PLAYER** [1] [1]
– Daniel / Teacher I need you / Elderberry wine / Blues for my baby and me / Midnight creeper / Have mercy on the criminal / I'm going to be a teenage idol / Texan love song / Crocodile rock / High flying bird. (re-iss. May81 lp/c; DJM 2/4 2091) (re-iss. Apr87 lp/c; PRICE/PRIMC 105) (cd-iss. Jun87; 827690-2) (cd re-iss. May95 on 'Rocket')

Jun 73. (7"m) (DJX 502) <40105> **SATURDAY NIGHT'S ALRIGHT FOR FIGHTING. / JACK RABBIT / WHEN YOU'RE READY (WE'LL GO STEADY AGAIN)** [7] [12] Jul73

Sep 73. (7") (DJS 285) <40148> **GOODBYE YELLOW BRICK ROAD. / SCREW YOU** [6] [-]

Oct 73. (7") <40148> **GOODBYE YELLOW BRICK ROAD. / YOUNG MAN'S BLUES** [-] [2]

Oct 73. (d-lp-d-c) (DJE 2/4 9001) <10003> **GOODBYE YELLOW BRICK ROAD** [1] [1]
– Funeral for a friend / Love lies bleeding / Bennie and the jets / Candle in the wind / Goodbye yellow brick road / This song has no title / Grey seal / Jamaica jerk off / I've seen that movie too / Sweet painted lady / The ballad of Danny Bailey (1909-34) / Dirty little girl / All the girls love Alice / Your sister can't twist (but she can rock'n'roll) / Saturday night's alright for fighting / Roy Rogers / Social disease / Harmony. (re-iss. Nov87 lp/c; PRICE/PRIMC 13) (cd-iss. Nov87; DJMCD 2) (cd re-iss. May95 on 'Rocket')

Nov 73. (7") (DJS 290) <65018> **STEP INTO CHRISTMAS. / HO! HO! HO! WHO'D BE A TURKEY AT CHRISTMAS** [24] [-]

Feb 74. (7") <40198> **BENNY AND THE JETS. / HARMONY** [-] [1]

Feb 74. (7") (DJS 297) **CANDLE IN THE WIND. / BENNIE AND THE JETS** [11] [-]

May 74. (7") (DJS 302) <40259> **DON'T LET THE SUN GO DOWN ON ME. / SICK CITY** [16] [2] Jun74

Jun 74. (lp/c) (DJLH 2/4 0439) <2116> **CARIBOU** [1] [1]
– The bitch is back / Pinky / Grimsby / Dixie Lily / Solar prestige a gammon / You're so static / I've seen the saucers / Stinker / Don't let the sun go down on me / Ticking. (re-iss. May81 lp/c; DJM 2/4 2092) (re-iss. Nov87 lp/c; PRICE/PRIMC 106) (cd-iss. Nov87; DJMCD 6) (cd re-iss. May95 on 'Rocket')

Sep 74. (7") (DJS 322) <40297> **THE BITCH IS BACK. / COLD HIGHWAY** [15] [4]

Nov 74. (7") (DJS 340) <40344> **LUCY IN THE SKY WITH DIAMONDS. / ONE DAY AT A TIME** [10] [1]

Feb 75. (7"; ELTON JOHN BAND) (DJS 354) <40364> **PHILADELPHIA FREEDOM. / I SAW HER STANDING THERE (with JOHN LENNON)** [12] [1]

May 75. (lp/c) (DJX 1) <2142> **CAPTAIN FANTASTIC AND THE BROWN DIRT COWBOY** [2] [1]
– Captain Fantastic and the brown dirt cowboy / Tower of Babel / Bitter fingers / Tell me when the whistle blows / Someone saved my life tonight / (Gotta get a) Meal ticket / Better off dead / Writing / We fall in love sometimes / Curtains. (re-iss. pic-disc '78; DJLPX 1) (re-iss. May81 lp/c; DJM 2/4 2094) (re-iss. Nov87 lp/c; PRICE/PRIMC 108) (cd-iss. Nov87; 821746-2) (cd re-iss. Aug95 on 'Rocket')

Jun 75. (7") (DJS 385) <40421> **SOMEONE SAVED MY LIFE TONIGHT. / HOUSE OF CARDS** [22] [4]

—— ELTON now w/ others, after firing MURRAY and OLSSON (to BILLY JOEL)

Sep 75. (7") (DJS 610) <40461> **ISLAND GIRL. / SUGAR ON THE FLOOR** [14] [1]

Nov 75. (lp/c) (DJH 2/4 0464) <2163> **ROCK OF THE WESTIES** [5] [1]
– Medley: Yell help – Wednesday night – Ugly / Dan Dare (pilot of the future) / Island girl / Grow some funk of your own / I feel like a bullet (in the gun of Robert Ford) / Street kids / Hard luck story / Billy Bones and the white bird. (re-iss. May81 lp/c; DJM 2/4 2093) (re-iss. Nov87 lp/c; PRICE/PRIMC 107) (cd-iss. Nov87; DJMCD 9) (cd re-iss. Aug95 on 'Rocket')

Jan 76. (7") (DJS 629) <40505> **GROW SOME FUNK OF YOUR OWN. / I FEEL LIKE A BULLET (IN THE GUN OF ROBERT FORD)** [-] [14]

Mar 76. (7") (DJS 652) **PINBALL WIZARD. / HARMONY** [7] [-]

May 76. (lp/c) (DJH 2/4 0473) <2197> **HERE AND THERE (live)** [6] [4]
– Skyline pigeon / Border song / Honky cat / Love song / Crocodile rock / Funeral for a friend / Love lies bleeding / Rocket man / Bennie and the jets / Take me to the pilot. (re-iss. Sep78 as 'LONDON AND NEW YORK' on 'Hallmark' lp/c; SHM 942/HSC 333) (cd-iss. Sep95 on 'Rocket')

Rocket / M.C.A.

Jun 76. (7"; ELTON JOHN & KIKI DEE) (ROKN 512) <40585> **DON'T GO BREAKING MY HEART. / SNOW QUEEN** [1] [1]

Oct 76. (d-lp/d-c) (ROLL/TC2ROLL 12) <11004> **BLUE MOVES** [3] [3]
– Your starter for... / Tonight / One horse town / Chameleon / Boogie pilgrim / Cage the songbird / Crazy water / Shoulder holster / Sorry seems to be the hardest word / Out of the blue / Between seventeen and twenty / The wide-eyed and laughing / Someone's final song / Where's the shoorah / If there's a God in Heaven (what's he waiting for) / Idol / Theme from a non-existant TV series / Bite your lip (get up and dance!). (re-iss. Sep84 d-lp/d-c; PRID/+C 2) (cd-iss. Jun89; 822818-2)

Oct 76. (7") (ROKN 517) <40645> **SORRY SEEMS TO BE THE HARDEST WORD. / SHOULDER HOLSTER** [11] [6]

Feb 77. (7") <40677> **BITE YOUR LIP (GET UP AND DANCE!). / CHAMELEON** [-] [28]

Feb 77. (7") (ROKN 521) **CRAZY WATER. / CHAMELEON** [27] [-]

May 77. (7")(12") (RU 1) **BITE YOUR LIP (GET UP AND DANCE!). / CHICAGO** [28] [-]

Apr 78. (7") (ROKN 538) <40892> **EGO. / FLINTSTONE BOY** [34] [34]

Oct 78. (7") (XPRES 1) <40973> **PART-TIME LOVE. / I CRY AT NIGHT** [15] [22]

Oct 78. (lp/c) (TRAIN/SHUNT 1) <3027> **A SINGLE MAN** [8] [15]
– Shine on through / Return to Paradise / I don't care / Big dipper / Georgia / It ain't gonna be easy / Part-time love / Georgia / Shooting star / Madness / Reverie / Song for Guy. (re-iss. Jun83 lp/c; PRICE/PRIMC 24) (cd-iss. Jun83; 826805-2)

Dec 78. (7") <40993> **SONG FOR GUY. / LOVESICK** [4] [-]

May 79. (7") (XPRES 13) **ARE YOU READY FOR LOVE (part 1). / (part 2)** [42] [-]
(12"+=) (XPRES 13-12) – Three way love affair / Mama can't buy you love.

Jun 79. (12"m) <13921> **THE THOM BELL SESSIONS (recorded 1977)** [-] [51]
– Are you ready for love / Three way love affair / Mama can't buy you love.

Jun 79. (7") <41042> **MAMA CAN'T BUY YOU LOVE. / THREE WAY LOVE AFFAIR** [-] [9]

Sep 79. (7") (XPRES 21) <41126> **VICTIM OF LOVE. / STRANGERS** [-] [31]

Oct 79. (lp/c) (HISPD/REWND 125) M5104> **VICTIM OF LOVE** [41] [35]
– Johnny B. Goode / Warm love in a cold climate / Born bad / Thunder in the night / Spotlight / Street boogie / Born Bad / Victim of love. (re-iss. Jul84 lp/c; PRICE/PRIMC 70)

Dec 79. (7") <41159> **JOHNNY B. GOODE. / GEORGIA** [ ] [ ]

Dec 79. (7"/12") (XPRES 24/+12) **JOHNNY B. GOODE. / THUNDER IN THE NIGHT** [ ] [ ]

May 80. (7") (XPRES 32) <41236> **LITTLE JEANNIE. / CONQUER THE SUN** [33] [3]

May 80. (lp/c) (HISPD/REWND 126) <5121> **21 AT 33** [12] [13]
– Chasing the crown / Little Jeannie / Sartorial eloquence / Two rooms at the end of the world / White lady, white powder / Dear God / Never gonna fall in love again / Take me back / Give me the love. (re-iss. Jul84 lp/c; PRICE/PRIMC 71) (cd-iss. Jun89; 800055-2)

Aug 80. (7") (XPRES 41) <41293> **SARTORIAL ELOQUENCE. / WHITE MAN DANCER; CARTIER** [44] [39]

Nov 80. (7") (XPRESS 45) **DEAR GOD. / TACTICS** [-] [-]
(d7") (XPRESS 45 – ELTON 1) – Steal away child / Love so cold.

Rocket / Geffen

May 81. (7") (XPRES 54) <49722> **NOBODY WINS. / FOOLS IN FASHION** [42] [21]

May 81. (lp/c) (TRAIN/SHUNT 016) <2002> **THE FOX** [12] [21]
– Breaking down barriers / Heart in the right place / Just like Belgium / Nobody wins / Fascist faces / Carla etude / Fanfare / Chloe / Heels of the wind / Elton's song / The fox. (re-iss. Jul84 lp/c; PRICE/PRIMC 72) (cd-iss. Jun89; 800063-2)

Jul 81. (7") (XPRESS 59) **JUST LIKE BELGIUM. / CAN'T GET OVER LOSING YOU** [-] [-]

Jul 81. (7") <49788> **CHLOE. / TORTURED** [-] [34]

Mar 82. (7") (XPRES 71) <29954> **BLUE EYES. / HEY PAPA LEGBA** [8] [12] Jul82

Apr 82. (lp/c) (HISPD/REWND 127) <2013> **JUMP UP!** [13] [17]
– Dear John / Spiteful child / Ball and chain / Legal boys / I am your robot / Blue eyes / Empty garden /Princess / Where have all the good times gone? / All quiet on the western front. (cd-iss. 1983; 800037-2)

May 82. (7"/7"pic-d) (XPRES/XPPIC 77) <50049> **EMPTY GARDEN. / TAKE ME DOWN TO THE OCEAN** [51] [13] Mar82

Sep 82. (7") (XPRES 85) **PRINCESS. / THE RETREAT** [-] [-]

Nov 82. (7") (XPRES 88) **ALL QUIET ON THE WESTERN FRONT. / WHERE HAVE ALL THE GOOD TIMES GONE?** [-] [-]

Nov 82. (7") <29846> **BALL AND CHAIN. / WHERE HAVE ALL THE GOOD TIMES GONE?** [-] [-]

Apr 83. (7") (XPRES 91) **I GUESS THAT'S WHY THEY CALL IT THE BLUES. / LORD CHOC ICE GOES MENTAL** [5] [-]

May 83. (7") <29639> **I'M STILL STANDING. / LOVE SO COLD** [-] [12]

Jun 83. (lp/c)(cd) (HISPD/REWND 24)(811052-2) <4006> **TOO LOW FOR ZERO** [7] [25]
– Cold at Christmas / I'm still standing / Too low for zero / Religion / I guess that's

why they call it the blues / Crystal / Kiss the bride / Whipping boy / Saint / One more arrow. (cd re-mast.Jun98; 558475-2)

Jul 83. (7"/7"sha-pic-d)(12") (EJ S/PIC 1)(EJS 1-12) **I'M STILL STANDING. / EARN WHILE YOU LEARN** — 4 / -

Aug 83. (7") <29568> **KISS THE BRIDE. / LORD CHOC ICE GOES MENTAL** — - / 25

Oct 83. (7"/12") (EJS 2/+12) **KISS THE BRIDE. / DREAMBOAT** — 20 / -
(d7"+=) (EJS 2 – FREEJ 2) – Ego / Song for Guy.

Oct 83. (7") <29460> **I GUESS THAT'S WHY THEY CALL IT HTE BLUES. / THE RETREAT** — - / 4

Dec 83. (7") (EJS 3) **COLD AT CHRISTMAS. / CRYSTAL** — 33 / -
(12"+=) (EJS 3-12) – J'veux de la tendresse.
(d7"+=) (EJS 3-2) – Don't go breaking my heart / Snow queen.

May 84. (7"/7"sha-pic-d)(12") (PH/+PIC 7)(PH 7-12) <29292> **SAD SONGS (SAY SO MUCH). / SIMPLE MAN** — 7 / 5

Jun 84. (lp/c)(cd) (HISPD/REWND 25)(882088-2) <24031> **BREAKING HEARTS** — 2 / 20
– Restless / Slow down Georgie (she's poison) / Who wears these shoes? / Breaking hearts (ain't what it used to be) / Li'l fridgerator / Passengers / In neon / Burning bridges / Did he shoot her? / Sad songs (say so much).

Aug 84. (7"/12") (EJS 5/+12) **PASSENGERS (remix). / LONELY BOY** — 5 / -

Sep 84. (7") <29189> **WHO WEARS THESE SHOES? / LONELY EYES** — - / 16

Oct 84. (7") (EJS 6) **WHO WEARS THESE SHOES? / TORTURED** — 50 / -
(12"+=) (EJS 6-12) – I heard it through the grapevine.

Nov 84. (7") <29111> **IN NEON. / TACTICS** — - / 38

Feb 85. (7") (EJS 7) **BREAKING HEARTS (AIN'T WHAT IT USED TO BE). / IN NEON** — 59 / -

Jun 85. (7"; ELTON JOHN & MILLIE JACKSON) (EJS 8) <28956> **ACT OF WAR (part 1). / (part 2)** — 32 / -
(12"+=) (EJS 8-12) – (part 3) / (part 4).

Sep 85. (7") (EJS 9) **NIKITA. / THE MAN WHO NEVER DIED** — 3 / -
(12"+=)(d7"+=) (EJS 9-12)(EJSD 9) – Sorry seems to be the hardest word (live) / I'm still standing (live).

Oct 85. (7") <28873> **WRAP HER UP. / THE MAN WHO NEVER DIED** — - / -

Nov 85. (lp/c)(cd) (HISPD/REWND 26)(826213-2) <24077> **ICE ON FIRE** — 3 / 48
– Wrap her up / Satellite / Tell me what the papers say / Candy by the pound / Shoot down the Moon / This town / Cry to heaven / Soul glove / Nikita / Too young. (c+=/cd+=) – Act of war (with MILLIE JACKSON). (cd re-mast.Jun98; 558476-2)

Nov 85. (7"/7"sha-pic-d) (EJ SC/PIC 10) **WRAP HER UP. / RESTLESS (live with GEORGE MICHAEL)** — 12 / -
(ext.d12"+=) (EJS 10-12 – EJS 9-12) – Nikita / The man who never died / Sorry seems to be the hardest word (live) / I'm still standing (live).

Jan 86. (7") <28800> **NIKITA. / RESTLESS** — - / 7

Feb 86. (7") (EJS 11) **CRY TO HEAVEN. / CANDY BY THE POUND** — 47 / -
(12"+=) (EJS 11-12) – Rock'n'roll medley.
(d7"++=) (EJSD 11) – Your song.

Sep 86. (7") (EJS 12) <28578> **HEARTACHES ALL OVER THE WORLD. / HIGHLANDER** — 45 / 55
(12"+=) (EJS 12-12) – ('A'version).
(d7"+=) (EJSD 12) – Passengers / I'm still standing.

Nov 86. (lp/c)(cd) (EJLP/EJMC 1)(830487-2) <24114> **LEATHER JACKETS** — 24 / 91
– Leather jackets / Hoop of fire / Go it alone / Don't trust that woman / Gypsy heart / Slow rivers / Heartache all over the world / Angeline / Memory of love / Paris / I fall apart.

Nov 86. (7"pic-d/c-s; ELTON JOHN & CLIFF RICHARD) (EJS P/C 13) **SLOW RIVERS. / BILLY AND THE KIDS** — 44 / -
(12"+=) (EJS 13-12) – Lord of the flies.

Rocket / M.C.A.

Jun 87. (7") (EJS 14) **YOUR SONG (live). / DON'T LET THE SUN GO DOWN ON ME (live)** — - / -
(12"+=) (EJS 14-12) – I need you to turn to / The greatest discovery.

Sep 87. (d-lp/d-c/cd) (EJBX L/C/D 1) <8022> **LIVE IN AUSTRALIA (live)** — 43 / 24 Jul87
– Sixty years on / I need you to turn to / The greatest discovery / Tonight / Sorry seems to be the hardest word / The king must die / Take me to the pilot / Tiny dancer / Have mercy on the criminal / Madman across the water / Candle in the wind / Burn down the mission / Your song / Don't let the Sun go down on me. (cd re-mast.Jun98; 558477-2)

Dec 87. (7"/7"pic-d) (EJS/+P 15) <53196> **CANDLE IN THE WIND (live). / SORRY SEEMS TO BE THE HARDEST WORD (live)** — 5 / 6 Nov87
(12"+=)(cd-s+=) (EJS 15-12)(EJSCD 15) – Your song (live) / Don't let the sun go down on me (live).

Mar 88. (7") **TONIGHT. / TAKE ME TO THE PILOT** — - / -

May 88. (7"/7"pic-d) (EJS/+IP 16) <53345> **I DON'T WANT TO GO ON WITH YOU LIKE THAT. / ROPE AROUND A FOOL / (interview)** — 30 / 2 Jun88
(12"+=)(cd-s+=) (EJS 16-12)(EJSCD 16) – ('A'-Shep Pettibone mix).

Jun 88. (lp/c)(cd) (EJLP/EJMC 3)(834701-2) <6240> **REG STRIKES BACK** — 18 / 16
– Town of plenty / A word in Spanish / Mona Lisas and mad hatters (part 2) / I don't want to go on with you like that / Japanese hands / Goodbye Marlon Brando / The camera never lies / Heavy traffic / Poor cow / Since God invented girls. (cd re-mast.Jun98; 558478-2)

Sep 88. (7") (EJSLB 17) **TOWN OF PLENTY. / WHIPPING BOY** — 74 / -
(12"+=) (EJS 17-12) – My baby's a saint.
(cd-s++=) (EJSCD 17) – I guess that's why they call it the blues.

Nov 88. (7") (EJS 18) <53408> **A WORD IN SPANISH. / HEAVY TRAFFIC** — - / 19 Sep88
(12"+=) (EJS 18-12) – Live in Australia medley: Song for Guy – I guess that's why they call it the blues – Blue eyes.
(cd-s++=) (EJSCD 18) – Daniel.

—— In Apr'89, he was credited on 'THROUGH THE STORM' UK No.41 / No.16 single with ARETHA FRANKLIN.

Aug 89. (7"; +MC 19) <53692> **HEALING HANDS. / DANCING IN THE END ZONE** — 45 / 13
(12"+=)(cd-s+=) (EJS 19-12)(EJCD 19) – ('A'version).

Sep 89. (lp/c/cd) (838839-1/-4/-2) <6321> **SLEEPING WITH THE PAST** — 1 / 23
– Durban deep / Healing hands / Whispers / Club at the end of the street / Sleeping with the past / Stone's throw from hurtin' / Sacrifice / I never knew her name / Amazes me / Blue avenue.

Oct 89. (7"/c-s) (EJS/+MC 20) <53750> **SACRIFICE. / LOVE IS A CANNIBAL** — 55 / 18 Jan90
(12"+=)(cd-s+=) (EJS 20-12)(EJSCD 20) – Durban deep.

Apr 90. (7") <53818> **CLUB AT THEN END OF THE STREET. / SACRIFICE** — - / 28

Jun 90. (7"/c-s) (EJS/+MC 22) **SACRIFICE. / HEALING HANDS** — 1 / -
(12"+=)(cd-s+=) (EJS 22-12)(EJSCD 22) – Durban deep.

Aug 90. (7"/c-s) (EJS/+MC 23) **CLUB AT THE END OF THE STREET. / WHISPERS** — 47 / -
(12"+=) (EJS 23012) – I don't wanna go on with you like that.
(cd-s+=) (EJSCD 23) – Give peace a chance.

Oct 90. (7"/c-s) (EJS/+MC 24) <53953> **YOU GOTTA LOVE SOMEONE. / MEDICINE MAN** [UK-only] — 33 / 43 Nov90
(12"+=)(cd-s+=) (EJS 24-12)(EJSCD 24) – ('B'-Adamski version).

Nov 90. (7"/c-s) (EJS/+MC 25) **EASIER TO WALK AWAY. / SWEAR I HEARD THE NIGHT TALKING** — 63 / -
(12"+=)(cd-s+=) (EJS 25-12)(EJSCD 25) – Made for me.

—— DEE MURRAY died of a heart attack, after suffering from cancer

May 92. (7"/c-s) (EJS/+MC 28) <54423> **THE ONE. / SUIT OF WOLVES** — 10 / 9 Jun92
(cd-s+=) (EJSCD 28) – Fat boys and ugly girls.

Jun 92. (cd/c/lp) (512360-2/-4/-1) <10614> **THE ONE** — 2 / 8
– Simple life / The one / Sweat it out / Runaway train / Whitewash county / The North / When a woman doesn't want you / Emily / On dark street / Understanding women / The last song. (cd re-mast.Jun98; 558477-2)

Jul 92. (7"/c-s; ELTON JOHN & ERIC CLAPTON) (EJS/+MC 29) **RUNAWAY TRAIN. / UNDERSTANDING WOMEN** — 31 / -
(cd-s+=) (EJSCD 29) – Made for me.
(cd-s) (EJSCDX 29) – ('A'side) / Through the storm (with ARETHA FRANKLIN) / Don't let the sun go down on me (with GEORGE MICHAEL) / Slow rivers (with CLIFF).

Oct 92. (7"/c-s) (EJS/+MC 30) <54510> **THE LAST SONG. / THE MAN WHO NEVER DIED / SONG FOR GUY** — 21 / 23
(cd-s) (EJSCD 30) – ('A'side) / Are you ready / Three way love affair / Mama can't buy you love.

Feb 93. (c-s) <54581> **SIMPLE LIFE / THE NORTH** — - / 30

May 93. (7"/c-s) (EJS/+MC 31) **SIMPLE LIFE. / THE LAST SONG** — 44 / -
(cd-s+=) (EJSCD 31) – The north.

Nov 93. (7"/c-s; ELTON JOHN & KIKI DEE) (EJS/+MC 32) **TRUE LOVE. / THE SHOW MUST GO ON** — 2 / -
(cd-s+=) (EJSCD 32) – Runaway train.
(cd-s) (EJSCDX 32) – ('A'side) / Wrap her up / That's what friends are for / Act of war.

Nov 93. (c-s; ELTON JOHN & KIKI DEE) <54762> **TRUE LOVE / RUNAWAY TRAIN (with ERIC CLAPTON)** — - / 56

Nov 93. (cd/c/d-lp) (516478-2/-4/-1) <10926> **DUETS** (with other artists) — 5 / 25
– Teardrops (k.d.LANG) / When I think about love (I think about you) (P.M.DAWN) / The power (LITTLE RICHARD) / Shakey ground (DON HENLEY) / True love (KIKI DEE) / If you were me (CHRIS REA) / A woman's needs (TAMMY WYNETTE) / Don't let the Sun go down on me (GEORGE MICHAEL) / Old friend (NIK KERSHAW) / Go on and on (GLADYS KNIGHT) / Don't go breaking my heart (RuPAUL) / Ain't nothing like the real thing (MARCELLA DETROIT) / I'm your puppet (PAUL YOUNG) / Love letters (BONNIE RAITT) / Born to lose (LEONARD COHEN) / Duets for one (ELTON JOHN solo).

Feb 94. (7"/c-s; ELTON JOHN & RuPAUL) (EJS/+MC 33) <54813> **DON'T GO BREAKING MY HEART. / DONNER POUR DONNER** — 7 / 92
(cd-s+=) (EJCD 33) – A woman's needs.
(cd-s) (ERJMX 33) – ('A'side) / (5-'A'mixes).

—— In May 94, he & MARCELLA DETROIT (ex-SHAKESPEAR'S SISTER) hit UK No.24 with 'AIN'T NOTHIN' LIKE THE REAL THING'.

Jun 94. (7"/c-s) (EJS/+MC 34) <64543> **CAN YOU FEEL THE LOVE TONIGHT. / ('A'mix)** — 14 / 4 May94
(cd-s+=) (EJCD 34) – Hakuna Matata / Under the stars.
(above & below from the animated 'Hollywood' movie 'The Lion King')

Sep 94. (c-s) <64516> **CIRCLE OF LIFE / ('A'mix)** — 11 / 18 Aug94
(cd-s+=)/pic-cd-s+=) (EJS CD/CX 35) – I just can't wait to be king / This land.

—— with GUY BABYLON – keyboards/ BOB BIRCH – bass/ DAVEY JOHNSTONE – guitar, mandolin, banjo/ CHARLIE MORGAN – drums/ RAY COOPER – percusion

Feb 95. (c-s) (EJSMC 36) **BELIEVE / SORRY SEEMS TO BE THE HARDEST WORD (live)** — 15 / -
(cd-s+=) (EJCD 36) – Believe (live).
(cd-s) (EJCDX 36) – ('A'side) / The one / The last song.

Rocket / Rocket

Mar 95. (c-s) <856014> **BELIEVE / THE ONE (live)** — - / -

Mar 95. (cd/c/lp) (<526185-2/-4/-1>) **MADE IN ENGLAND** — 3 / 13
– Believe / Made in England / House / Cold / Pain / Belfast / Latitude / Please / Man / Lies / Blessed.

May 95. (c-s) (EJSMC 37) <852092> **MADE IN ENGLAND / DANIEL (live) / CAN YOU FEEL THE LOVE TONIGHT** — 18 / 52
(cd-s+=) (EJSCD 37) – Your song / Don't let the sun go down on me.
(cd-s) (EJCDX 37) – ('A'side) / Whatever gets you thru the night / Lucy in the sky with diamonds / I saw her standing there.

Oct 95. (c-s) (EJSMC 38) <852394> **BLESSED / LATITUDE** — - / 34
(cd-s) (EJSCD 38) – ('A'side) / Made in England (mixes).
(cd-s) (EJSDD 38) – ('A'side) / Honky cat (live) / Take me to the pilot (live) / The bitch is back (live).

Nov 95. (cd/c) (528788-2/-4) **LOVE SONGS** (compilation) — **7** / **24** Sep96
– Sacrifice / Candle in the wind / I guess that's why they call it the blues / Don't let the sun go down on me (with GEORGE MICHAEL) / Sorry seems to be the hardest word / Blue eyes / Daniel / Nikita / Your song / The one / Someone saved my life tonight / True love (with KIKI DEE) / Can you feel the love tonight / Circle of life / Blessed / Please / Song for Guy.

Jan 96. (c-s) (EJSMC 40) **PLEASE / LATITUDE** — **33** / –
(cd-s+=) (EJSCD 40) – Made in England (mixes).
(cd-s) (EJSCDX 40) – ('A'side) / Honky cat (live) / Take me to the pilot (live) / The bitch is back (live).

Oct 96. (c-s) <55222> **YOU CAN MAKE HISTORY (YOUNG AGAIN) / SONG FOR GUY** — – / **70**
Rocket Mercury

Dec 96. (c-s; by ELTON JOHN & LUCIANO PAVAROTTI) (LLHMC 1) **LIVE LIKE HORSES** / ('A'live finale) — **9** / –
(cd-s+=) (LLHCD 1) – ('A'solo studio) / I guess that's why they call it the blues.
(cd-s) (LLHDD 1) – ('A'side) / Step into Christmas / Blessed.

Sep 97. (c-s) (EJSMC 41) **SOMETHING ABOUT THE WAY YOU LOOK TONIGHT / I KNOW I'M IN LOVE**
(cd-s+=) (EJSCD 41) – No valentines ('A'extended).
(cd-s+=) (EJSCX 41) – You can make history (young again) / ('A'extended).
(above was withdrawn after the events below)

Sep 97. (c-s/cd-s) (PT MC/CD 1) **CANDLE IN THE WIND 1997 / SOMETHING ABOUT THE WAY YOU LOOK TONIGHT** — **1** / **1**
(cd-s+=) (568108-2) – You can make history (young again).
(above double 'A'side was a tribute to Princess Diana who recently died in a car crash)

Oct 97. (cd/c) <(536266-2/-4)> **THE BIG PICTURE** — **3** / **9**
– Long way from happiness / Live like horses / The end will come / I can bend / Love's got a lot to answer for / Something about the way you look tonight / If the river can bend / The big picture / Recover your soul / January / I can't steer my heart / Wicked dreams.

Feb 98. (c-s) (EJSMC 42) <568762> **RECOVER YOUR SOUL / I KNOW WHY I'M IN LOVE** — **16** / **55** Apr98
(cd-s+=) (EJSCD 42) – Big man in a little suit / ('A'mix).
(cd-s+=) (EJSCX 42) – No valentines.

Jun 98. (c-s) (EJSMC 43) **IF THE RIVER CAN BEND / BENNIE AND THE JETS** — **32**
(cd-s+=) (EJSCD 43) – Saturday night's alright for fighting / ('A'original).
(cd-s) (EJSDD 43) – ('A'side) / Don't let the sun go down on me (live) / I guess that's why they call it the blues (live) / Sorry seems to be the hardest word (live).

Feb 99. (c-s; ELTON JOHN & LeANN RIMES) (EJSMC 45) <566918> **WRITTEN IN THE STARS / (VARIOUS SNIPPETS)** — **10** / **29**
(cd-s+=) (EJSCD 45) – ('A'side) / ('A' alt mix) / Various snippets AIDA.
(cd-s) (EJSDD 45) – ('A'side) / ('A' alt mix) / Recover your soul.

—— next with "friends" STING, LENNY KRAVITZ, TINA TURNER, SHANIA TWAIN, the SPICE GIRLS, JAMES TAYLOR, JANET JACKSON, LeANN RIMES + HEATHER HEADLEY

Mar 99. (cd/c; ELTON JOHN & FRIENDS) <(524628-2/-4)> **ELTON JOHN AND TIM RICE'S AIDA** — **29** / **41**
– Another pyramid / Written in the stars / Easy as life / My strongest suit / I know the truth / Not me / Amneris' letter / A step too far / Like father like son / Elaborate lives / How I know you / The messenger / Gods love Nubia / Enchantment passing through / Orchestral finale.

– compilations, others, etc. –

on 'DJM' UK / 'MCA' in the US unless mentioned otherwise

Apr 71. (lp) Paramount; (SPFL 269) <6004> **FRIENDS** (soundtrack) — / **36**
Nov 74. (lp/c) (DJH 2/4 0442) <2128> **ELTON JOHN'S GREATEST HITS** (compilation) — **1** / **1**
– Your song / Daniel / Honky cat / Goodbye yellow brick road / Saturday night's alright for fighting / Rocket man / Candle in the wind / Don't let the Sun go down on me / Border song / Crocodile rock / The bitch is back / Lucy in the sky with diamonds / Sorry seems to be the hardest word / Don't go breaking my heart / Someone saved my life tonight / Philadelphia freedom / Island girl / Grow some funk of your own / Benny & the jets / Pinball wizard. (cd-iss. Oct84; DJMCD 3)

Sep 76. (7") (DJS 10705) **BENNIE AND THE JETS. / ROCK AND ROLL MADONNA** — **37** / –
May 77. (7"ep) (DJR 18001) **FOUR FROM FOUR EYES**
– Your song / Rocket man / Saturday night's alright for fighting / Whenever you're ready (we'll go steady again).

Sep 77. (lp/c) (DJH 2/4 0520) <3027> **GREATEST HITS VOL.2** — **6** / **21**
Sep 78. (12"ep) (DJT 15000) **FUNERAL FOR A FRIEND; LOVE LIES BLEEDING / CURTAINS / WE ALL FALL IN LOVE SOMETIMES** — / –
Sep 78. (12x7"box) (EJ 12) **THE ELTON JOHN SINGLES COLLECTION**
(also available separately as below)
Sep 78. (7") (DJS 10901) **LADY SAMANTHA. / SKYLINE PIGEON**
Sep 78. (7") (DJS 10902) **YOUR SONG. / BORDER SONG**
Sep 78. (7") (DJS 10903) **HONKY CAT. / SIXTY YEARS ON**
Sep 78. (7") (DJS 10904) **CROCODILE ROCK. / COUNTRY COMFORT**
Sep 78. (7") (DJS 10905) **ROCKET MAN. / DANIEL**
Sep 78. (7") (DJS 10906) **GOODBYE YELLOW BRICK ROAD. / SWEET PAINTED LADY**
Sep 78. (7") (DJS 10907) **DON'T LET THE SUN GO DOWN ON ME. / SOMEONE SAVED MY LIFE**
Sep 78. (7") (DJS 10908) **CANDLE IN THE WIND. / I FEEL LIKE A BULLET (** ...
Sep 78. (7") (DJS 10909) **THE BITCH IS BACK. / GROW SOME FUNK OF YOUR OWN**
Sep 78. (7") (DJS 10910) **ISLAND GIRL. / SATURDAY NIGHT'S ALRIGHT FOR FIGHTING**
Sep 78. (7") (DJS 10911) **PHILADELPHIA FREEDOM. / BENNIE AND THE JETS**
Sep 78. (7") (DJS 10912) **PINBALL WIZARD. / BENNIE AND THE JETS**

Feb 79. (d-lp/d-c) Pickwick; (PDA/PDC 047) **THE ELTON JOHN LIVE COLLECTION** — / –
– (live albums of Apr71 + May76) (re-iss. Nov88 as 'THE COLLECTION'; PWKS 551)
Aug 79. (5xlp-box) (DJV 2300) **ELTON JOHN**
(originally released in US contains 'EARLY YEARS', 'ELTON ROCKS', 'MOODS', 'SINGLES' & 'CLASSICS')
Oct 80. (lp/c) (DJM 2/4 2085) **LADY SAMANTHA** (rare 'B's) — **56**
Nov 80. (7") (DJS 10961) **HARMONY. / MONA LISA AND THE MAD HATTERS**
Mar 81. (7") (DJS 10965) **I SAW HER STANDING THERE. / WHATEVER GETS YOU THROUGH THE NIGHT / LUCY IN THE SKY WITH DIAMONDS** (with JOHN LENNON) — **30** / –
1988. (d-c) **ROCK OF THE WESTIES / ELTON JOHN'S GREATEST HITS**
1988. (d-c) **EMPTY SKY / GREATEST HITS VOL.2**
1988. (d-c) **CAPTAIN FANTASTIC AND THE BROWN DIRT COWBOY / ELTON JOHN**
1988. (d-c) **DON'T SHOOT ME I'M ONLY THE PIANO PLAYER / TUMBLEWEED CONNECTION**
1988. (d-c) **GREATEST HITS / ROCK OF THE WESTIES**
Note: All 'Rocket' releases were issued on 'MCA' in the US.
Apr 77. (7"mail-order) Rocket; (GOALD 1) **THE GOALDIGGER SONG. / (spoken)** — / –
Mar 81. (7") Rocket; (XPRESS 49) **DON'T GO BREAKING MY HEART. / SNOW QUEEN**
Oct 90. (cd/c/d-lp) Rocket; (846947-2/-4/-1) **THE VERY BEST OF ELTON JOHN** — **1** / –
– Your song / Rocket man / Crocodile rock / Daniel / Goodbye yellow brick road / Saturday night's alright for fighting / Candle in the wind / Don't let the Sun go down on me / Lucy in the sky with diamonds / Philadelphia freedom / Someone saved my life tonight / Don't go breaking my heart / Bennie and the jets / Sorry seems to be the hardest word / Song for Guy / Part time love / Blue eyes / I guess that's why they call it the blues / I'm still standing / Kiss the bride / Sad songs / Passengers / Nikita / Sacrifice / You gotta love someone. (cd+=/c+=) – Pinball wizard / The bitch is back / I don't wanna go on with you like that / Easier to walk away. (re-iss. Nov91 UK No.29)

Feb 91. (7"/c-s) **DON'T LET THE SUN GO DOWN ON ME. / SONG FOR GUY** — / –
(12"+=/cd-s+=) – Sorry seems to be the hardest word.
Nov 91. (cd-box/c-box) <10110> **TO BE CONTINUED ...** — – / **82**
Sep 87. (cd,c,lp) <24153> **ELTON JOHN'S GREATEST HITS, VOLUME III, 1979-1987** — – / **84**
Jan 78. (lp) St.Michael; (2094 0102) **CANDLE IN THE WIND**
Oct 80. (lp) K-Tel; (NE 1094) **THE VERY BEST OF ELTON JOHN** — **24** / –
Sep 81. (lp/c) Hallmark; (SHM/HSC 3088) **THE ALBUM**
Nov 82. (lp/c) T.V.; (TVA/TVC 3) **LOVE SONGS**
(re-iss. Feb84 on 'Rocket' lp/c/cd; 814 085-2)
Jun 83. (lp/c) Premier; (CBR/KCBR 1027) **THE NEW COLLECTION**
1984. (lp/c) Premier; (CBR/KCBR 1036) **THE NEW COLLECTION VOL.2**
1983. (d-c) Cambra; (CRT 003) **ELTON JOHN** (hits)
May 84. (d-c) Cambra; (CRT 130) **SEASONS ... THE EARLY LOVE SONGS**
Oct 84. (cd) (DJMCD 4) **THE SUPERIOR SOUND OF ...**
Feb 88. (7") Old Gold; (OG 9776) **NIKITA. / I'M STILL STANDING**
Jun 88. (7") Old Gold; (OG 9789) **DON'T GO BREAKING MY HEART. / I GOT THE MUSIC IN ME** (Kiki Dee)
Jun 88. (7") Old Gold; (OG 9791) **SONG FOR GUY. / BLUE EYES**
1988. (cd) Starr; (825 173-2) **BIGGEST**
below, a guest spot w/KIKI DEE.
Apr 81. (7") Ariola; (ARO 269) **LOVING YOU IS SWEETER THAN EVER. / 24 HOURS** — / –
May 87. (7") CBS; (650865-7/-6) / Epic; <07119> **FLAMES OF PARADISE. / CALL ON ME** — / **36**
above JENNIFER RUSH & ELTON JOHN single
Mar 94. (cd/c) Spectrum; (550213-2/-4) **ROCK & ROLL MADONNA** — / –
Feb 95. (cd-s) D.J.; **UNITED WE STAND / NEANDERTHAL MAN** — / –
(above credited to REG DWIGHT) (early recordings)
Apr 95. (cd) RPM; (RPM 142) **CHARTBUSTERS GOES POP** — / –

JOHN AND MARY (see under ⇒ **10,000 MANIACS**)

JOHNNY & THE SELF-ABUSERS (see under ⇒ **SIMPLE MINDS**)

JOHN'S CHILDREN (dig out; Great Alt & Indie ...)

Holly JOHNSON (see under ⇒ **FRANKIE GOES TO HOLLYWOOD**)

Linton Kwesi JOHNSON

Born: 1952, Chapelton, Jamaica, West Indies. Following his parents to England in 1963, he was introduced to the politics, history and literature that would inspire him to write poetry through membership of the Black Panthers, discovering whilst there the mighty 'Souls Of Black Folk' by W.E.B. DuBois. His first band, RASTA LOVE, formed in the early seventies, accompanied poetry with rasta drummers and was to form the foundation of his unique style of dub poetry. After studying Sociology at Goldsmith's College and becoming writer-in-residence for the London Borough of Lambeth in 1977, the Brixton based journal 'Race Today' published two collections of poetry in 1974/75;

'VOICES OF THE LIVING AND THE DEAD' and 'DREAD BEAT AN' BLOOD', the latter collection used as the title of his debut album on 'Virgin' in 1978. Featuring the musicianship of The DENNIS BOVELL DUB BAND, a partnership that was to continue throughout the 80's and 90's, it confronted the reality of living in a racist society, with songs like 'FIVE NIGHTS OF BLEEDING' and 'SONG OF BLOOD' graphically capturing the increasingly apocalyptic mood of disenfranchised Black London. In 1980, 'Race Today' published his third collection, 'INGLAN IS A BITCH', a track featured on his album of the same year, 'BASS CULTURE'. Two more albums followed on the 'Island' label, 'LKJ IN DUB', which mixed tracks off the previous two albums to great effect, especially the anti-sus oem, 'SONNY'S LETTAH', and 'MAKING HISTORY'. By 1981, JOHNSON had launched his own label, the logo for the label being the sharp-suited image first seen on the 'BASS CULTURE' LP sleeve. Two singles from the Jamaican poet Michael Smith, 'Mi Cyan Believe It' and 'Roots', were issued in the first year, with later releases by jazz trumpeter Skake Keane and writer Jean Binta Breeze to follow in the early 80's. Regularly touring with The DENNIS BOVELL DUB BAND and putting together a radio series about Jamaican popular music for Radio One, as well as reporting for Channel 4's The Bandung File, 'LKJ LIVE IN CONCERT WITH THE DUB BAND' was independently released in 1985. 'TINGS AN' TIMES' followed in 1991, and for the first time tackled issues outside of Britain in the song 'MI REVOLUTIONARY FRIEN', focusing on the dramatic changes taking place in Eastern Europe. The selected poems of LKJ were co-published in the same year by Bloodaxe Books and LKJ Music Publishers and in 1992, 'LKJ IN DUB: VOLUME TWO' was released, again combining the talents of BOVELL and JOHNSON. Now performing more frequently without a band, his most recent album, 'A CAPPELLA LIVE', reflects the emphasis on his poetry as a social conscience with a potent challenge to those in power.

Album rating: DREAD BEAT AN' BLOOD (*5; as Poet & The Roots) / FORCES OF VICTORY (*8) / BASS CULTURE (*7) / LKJ IN DUB (*6) / MAKING HISTORY (*7) / LINTON KWESI JOHNSON (*6) / IN CONCERT WITH THE DUB BAND (*5) / TINGS AN' TIMES (*5) / A CAPPALLA LIVE (*4)

POET & THE ROOTS

aka LINTON KWESI JOHNSON, plus DENNIS BOVELL of MATUMBI

	Virgin	not iss.
Dec 77. (12"ep) *(VS 190-12)* **DREAD BEAT AND BLOOD. / ALL WE DOIN' IS DEFENDING** / ('A'dub version)	☐	-

LINTON KWESI JOHNSON

solo poet/singer.

	Island	not iss.
Apr 79. (lp) *(ILPS 9566)* **FORCES OF VICTORY**	66	
– Want fi goh rave / It noh funny / Sonny's lettah (anti-sus poem) / Independant intavenshan / Fite dem back / Forces of viktry / Time come. *(re-iss. Oct86 lp/c; ILPM/ICM 9566) (re-iss. Sep91 on 'Reggae Refreshers' cd/c; RR CD/CT 32)*		
May 79. (7"/12") *(WIP/12XWIP 6494)* **WANT FI GOH RAVE. / REALITY POEM**	☐	-
Sep 79. (7"ep) *(WIP 6528)* **SONNY'S LETTAH (ANTI-SUS POEM). / IRON BAR DUB / TEK CHANCE / FUNNY DUB**	☐	-
Jan 80. (7") *(WIP 6554)* **DI BLACK PETTY BOSSHWAH. / STRAIGHT TO MADRAY'S HEAD**	☐	-
(12"+=) *(12WIP 6554)* – Action line / Action (dub).		
Apr 80. (lp) *(ILPS 9605)* **BASS CULTURE**	46	-
– Bass culture / Street 66 / Reggae fi Peach / Di black petty bosshwah / Inglan is a bitch / Loriane / Reggae sounds / Two sides of silence. *(re-iss. Jan91 on 'Reggae Refreshers' cd/c; RR CD/CT 26)*		
Nov 80. (lp) *(ILPS 9650)* **LKJ IN DUB**		-
– Victorious dub / Reality dub / Peach dub / Shocking dub / Iron bar dub / Bitch dub / Cultural dub / Brain smashing dub. *(re-iss. Sep91 on 'Reggae Refreshers' cd/c; RR CD.CT 34)*		
Feb 84. (lp) *(ILPS 9770)* **MAKING HISTORY**	73	-
– Di eagle an' di bear / Wat about di workin' class? / Di great insoreckshan / Making history / Reggae fi Radni / Reggae fi Dada / New craas massahkah.		

	Rough Trade Shanachie	
Oct 84. (d-lp) *(ROUGH 78)* **LINTON KWESI JOHNSON IN CONCERT (live with The DUB BAND)**	☐	☐ 1986
– Five nights of bleeding / Dread beat an' blood / Intro / All wi doin' is defendin' / It dread inna Inglan / Man free / Wnat fi goh rave / It noh funny / Forces of viktry / Independant intavenshan / Reggae fi Peach / Di black petty bosshwah / New craas Massahkah / Reality poem / Wat about di workin' claas / Di great insohreckshan / Making history. *(re-iss. May88 on 'Shanachie' d-lp/d-c/d-cd; SHAN/+C/CD 43034) (cd-iss. Apr95 on 'LKJ'; LKJCD 03)*		

	not iss.	Sterns
1980's. (7") **HISTORY REPEATS ITSELF**	-	-

	LKJ	not iss.
Jun 91. (cd/lp) *(LKJ CD/LP 001)* **TINGS AN' TIMES**		-
– Story / Sense outta nansense / Tings an' times / Mi revalueshangry fren / Di good life / Di anfinish revalueshan / Dubbing for life. *(re-iss. Nov95 cd/lp; LKJ CD/LP 013)*		
Apr 95. (cd/lp) *(LKJ CD/LP 009)* **LKJ IN DUB VOLUME 2**	☐	-
Oct 96. (cd) *(LKJCD 016)* **LKJ ACAPPELLA LIVE (live)**	☐	-

– compilations, etc. –

Jul 81. (lp) *Virgin; (VX 1002)* **DREAD BEAT 'N' BLOOD** (1978 material)	☐	-
– Dread beat 'n' blood / Five nights of bleeding / Down de road / Song of blood / It dread inna Inglan (for George Lindo) / Come wi goh dung deh / Man free (for Darcus Howe) / All wi doin' is defending. *(c-iss.1987; TCVX 1002) (cd-iss. 1988 on 'Heartbeat'; HBCD 01) (cd re-iss. Sep90 as POET & THE ROOTS on 'Frontline'; CDFL 9009)*		

May 85. (lp/c) *Island; (IRG/+C 6)* **REGGAE GREATS**	☐	-
(cd-iss. Apr88; CIDRG 6) (cd re-iss. 1989; IMCD 14) (c re-iss. 1990; ICM 2033)		

Mike JOHNSON (see under ⇒ DINOSAUR JR)

Robert JOHNSON

Born: 8 May, 1911, Hazlehurst (a small industrialised railway town in the deep South of) Mississippi, USA. The seminal blues and Delta slide hero spent the early part of his life in a migrant labour camp after a fleeting affair with a W.A.P. worker (Noah Johnson) had forced ROBERT's mother, Julia Dodds, to flee to Memphis. After moving back with her original husband, Charles Spencer, Dodds was incapable of raising young ROBERT due to the struggles of parenthood and his increasingly disturbing and arrogant behaviour. ROBERT and his mother subsequently moved to Robinsonville, a sleepy Northern cotton community 40 miles out of Memphis, where she married Willie Willis in 1916 and settled down to raise ROBERT properly. Throughout his teenage years ROBERT became fascinated with music and instruments: he experimented with his new-found Jews Harp before moving onto harmonica and then finally the guitar. His friend R.L. WINDUM occasionally accompanied him on Harp while RJ played the popular blues on his guitar, but this relationship was very short-lived due to ROBERT's subsequent attendance at the Indiana Creek School. In the early 20's he left school when his eye-sight frequently failed him during exams and important lectures. Heading nowhere, he acquired the help of WILLIE BROWN, a talented local musician who introduced ROBERT to a string of "Jook" houses (blues venues) throughout the decade, giving the talented bluesman a valid chance to broaden and advance his musical horizons. In 1929 and rumoured to be somewhat of a ladies man, 18-year old ROBERT married 16-year old Virginia Travis and they subsequently bought a farmhouse when she fell pregnant. Then tragedy struck the following April: Virginia and the baby died during childbirth. This catapulted ROBERT into extreme depression. The only way he felt he could cure his melancholia was to play raw edged Delta blues which displayed a degree of fiery passion, not heard since BLIND WILLIE JOHNSON's (no relation) 'DARK WAS THE NIGHT . . .'. It was said that he sat alone at night in the forest, engulfed in his own thoughts, strumming his guitar with an eerie, but beautiful prowess. Two months later he followed the advice of his mentor, WILLIE BROWN, and set off to Wisconsin to record for 'Paramount'. There he created his most vivid and stripped-down recordings with preacher-cum-bluesman SON HOUSE, a remarkable pioneer who altered ROBERT's perception on standard blues playing. After a short stint on the road, he returned back to his home town of Hazlehurst, where he met IKE ZINNERMAN, an eccentric gothic blues guitarist, who claimed that he had self taught himself the blues whilst sitting on gravestones in the local crematorium in the dead of night! ROBERT remarried in 1931 to Calletta Craft who was 10 years his senior, although he abandoned her after she had a nervous breakdown. He began playing the "Jook" houses in the early 30's and enjoyed acclaim from a huge group of people who packed out venues wherever he played. However, this attraction made ROBERT deranged and paranoid; he would never reveal the chords or notes to any of his songs and he could be seen frequently leaving the stage midway through a set because he claimed the audience were eyeing him too closely! He continued travelling and after a brief residency in Arkansas he was approached by Ernie Oertle, a talent scout for the deep south who took him to San Antonio to record, during which time he produced the awesome ~'TERRAPLANE BLUES'. A feast of slide and fast-handed guitar, with ROBERT's falsetto ramblings a highlight, the song became a huge success in America, providing this new-found blues hero with instant fortune and a mass following. Tours of dancehalls, camps and "Jook" houses followed, along with the arrival of no less than eleven single 78 rpm records: a total of 41 recordings. The tour path led ROBERT through Detroit, New York City, New Jersey, St. Louis, Canada, Windsor and back to the south. By this time he had grown fond of drinking and was said to be the "life of a party" when drunk. His final excursion came in the summer of 1938 when he stopped off in Greenwood County to play in a bar called Three Forks. According to sources, ROBERT had become infatuated with the owner's wife, which caused a bad atmosphere within the joint. He was handed an open bottle of whiskey by the proprietor which was immediately slapped out of his hand by a friend who told him: "Don't ever take a drink from an open bottle, you don't know what could be in it!". ROBERT took another bottle and less than an hour later he was struggling to sing on stage. Leaving halfway through his set, he was found outside vomiting violently. It was then evident that he had been poisoned by the jealous barman. He lay sick that night in bed, contracting pneumonia before he finally passed away three day later on August the 16th, 1938. Remembered as one of the great blues guitarists of his time, ROBERT JOHNSON's influence still remains to this day. Among BOB DYLAN, MUDDY WATERS, KEITH RICHARDS and ERIC CLAPTON, the inexplicable artist has never failed to wow audiences and musicians alike; his warped interpretation of blues guitar and his haunting vocals have provided a catalyst for many inspired guitarists and vocalists who could not shake the sound of ROBERT JOHNSON's exploding originality from their mind. KEITH RICHARDS wrote in the booklet which accompanied 'THE COMPLETE RECORDINGS OF ROBERT JOHNSON' (1991): "I have never heard anybody before or since use the form and bend so much to make it work for himself . . . he came out with such compelling themes . . . it was almost like listening to Bach, you know, you think you can handle the blues until you've heard ROBERT JOHNSON . . ."

Best CD compilations: THE BEST OF THE DELTA BLUES SINGERS (*9) / THE BEST OF THE DELTA BLUES SINGERS VOL.2 (*8) / THE COMPLETE RECORDINGS (*9)

ROBERT JOHNSON – vocals, acoustic guitar
original very limited & rare singles below had a first and second pressing and are worth over £2,500 each! – the 4th one over £6,000

		not iss.	Vocalion – Arc
Feb 37.	(78) <03416> – <7-03-56> **TERRAPLANE BLUES. / KINDHEARTED WOMAN BLUES**	-	
Mar 37.	(78) <03445> – <7-04-60> **32-20 BLUES. / LAST FAIR DEAL GONE DOWN** <re-iss. 1937 on 'Oriole'; 7-04-60>	-	
Apr 37.	(78) <03475> – <7-04-81> **I BELIEVE I'LL DUST MY BROOM. / DEAD SHRIMP BLUES** <re-iss. 1937 on 'Conqueror'; 8871>	-	
May 37.	(78) <03519> – <7-05-81> **CROSS ROAD BLUES. / RAMBLING ON MY MIND**	-	
Jun 37.	(78) <03563> – <7-07-57> **COME ON IN MY KITCHEN. / THEY'RE RED HOT**	-	
Jul 37.	(78) <03601> **SWEET HOME CHICAGO. / WALKIN' BLUES**	-	
Aug 37.	(78) <03623> – <7-09-56> **HELL HOUND ON MY TRAIL. / FROM FOUR UNTIL LATE**	-	
Sep 37.	(78) <03665> – <7-10-65> **MILKCOW'S CALF BLUES. / MALTED MILK** <re-iss. 1937 on 'Conqueror'; 8944>	-	
Nov 37.	(78) <03723> – <7-12-57> **STONES IN MY PASSWAY. / I'M A STEADY ROLLIN' MAN** <re-iss. 1937 on 'Conqueror'; 8973>	-	
Jan 38.	(78) <04002> **STOP BREAKIN' DOWN BLUES. / HONEYMOON BLUES**	-	
Feb 38.	(78) <04108> **ME AND THE DEVIL BLUES. / LITTLE QUEEN OF SPADES**	-	
May 38.	(78) <04630> **LOVE IN VAIN BLUES. / PREACHING BLUES**		

—— Tragically, on the 16th of August, 1938, JOHNSON was dead after being poisoned (see above).

– posthumous releases, etc. –

1962.	(lp) *Philips; (BBL 7539)* **ROBERT JOHNSON 1936-1937**		-
1966.	(lp) *C.B.S.; (BPG 62456) / Columbia; <CL 1654>* **KING OF THE DELTA BLUES SINGERS**		1961

– Cross road blues / Terraplane blues / Come on in my kitchen / Walkin' blues / Last fair deal gone down / 32-20 blues / Kind hearted woman blues / If I had possession over judgement day / Preaching blues / When you got a good friend / Rambling on my mind / Stones on my passway / Traveling riverside blues / Milkcow's calf blues / Me and the Devil blues / Hell hound on my trail. <cd-iss. Nov94; CK 52944> <cd re-iss. Sep96 on 'Columbia'; 484419) <cd re-iss. Jan99 on 'Sony Jazz;; 493006-2)

1967.	(lp) *Kokomo; (K 1000)* **ROBERT JOHNSON**		-
1960's.	(lp) *Smokestack; (SSLP 1)* **BLUES LEGEND 1936-1937**		-
1970.	(lp) *C.B.S.; (64102) / Columbia; <30034>* **KING OF THE DELTA BLUES SINGERS VOL.2**		1966

– Kind hearted woman blues / I believe I'll dust my broom / Sweet home Chicago / Rambling on my mind / Phonograph blues / They're red hot / Dead shrimp blues / Preaching blues / I'm steady rollin' man / From four till late / Little queen of spades / Malted milk / Drunken hearted man / Stop breakin' down blues / Honeymoon blues / Love in vain blues.

Jun 85.	(d-lp/d-c) *C.B.S.; (CBS/40 22190)* **KING OF THE DELTA BLUES VOL.1 & 2**		-
Nov 85.	(lp/c) *Deja Vu; (DVLP/DVMC 2050)* **THE COLLECTION**		-
Sep 89.	(lp/c/cd) *Aldabra; <(ALB 1001/+MC/CD)>* **DELTA BLUES NUMBER 1**		
Sep 89.	(lp/c/cd) *Aldabra; <(ALB 1002/+MC/CD)>* **DELTA BLUES NUMBER 2**		
Apr 90.	(lp/c/cd) *Aldabra; <(ALB 1003/+MC/CD)>* **DELTA BLUES – THE ALTERNATE TAKES**		
Nov 90.	(d-cd/d-c) *Columbia; <(467246-2)>* **THE COMPLETE RECORDINGS** (re-iss. May94 d-cd/d-c; CD/40 46222) (d-cd-iss. Sep99 on 'Definitive'; DRCD 11147)		
Apr 92.	(cd/c) *Charly; (CDBM/TCBM 13)* **DELTA BLUES LEGEND**		-
Aug 92.	(cd)(c) *Blues Encore; (CD 52019/BEMC 1519)* **TRAVELLING RIVERSIDE BLUES**		-
Dec 92.	(cd/c) *Deja Vu; (D2CD/D2MC 14)* **THE GOLD COLLECTION**		-
Mar 93.	(cd) *Charly; (CHCD 1049)* **THE LEGENDARY BLUES SINGER**		-
1993.	(cd) *Blues Collection; <BLVC 006>* **RED HOT BLUES**		-
Mar 95.	(cd) *Indigo; (IGOCD 2017)* **HELL HOUND ON MY TRAIL**		-
Apr 95.	(cd) *Deja Vu; (DVBC 905-2)* **ROBERT JOHNSON: COLLECTOR'S EDITION**		-
Jun 95.	(cd) *Nectar; (NTMCD 504)* **CROSS ROAD BLUES: THE BEST OF ROBERT JOHNSON** (re-iss. Feb98 on 'Reactive'; REMCD 504)		-
Jan 96.	(d-cd) *Deja Vu; (R2CD 4014)* **GOLD**		-
Feb 96.	(d-cd) *Fremeaux; (FA 251)* **THE BLUES (SAN ANTONIO / DALLAS)**		-
Oct 96.	(cd) *Music Memoria; (842027-2)* **ALL-TIME BLUES CLASSICS**		-
Oct 97.	(cd) *Legacy-Columbia; <(487844-2)>* **KING OF THE DELTA**		-
Nov 97.	(cd) *Eagle; (EABCD 067)* **THE MASTERS**		-
Apr 98.	(cd/c) *Hallmark; (30567-2/-4)* **LOVE IN VAIN**		-
May 98.	(cd) *Summit; (SUMCD 4194)* **I WENT DOWN TO THE CROSSROADS**		-
Jun 98.	(3xcd-box; with Various Artists) *Catfish; <(KATCD 107)>* **ROOTS AND BRANCHES . . .**		-
Nov 98.	(3xcd-box; with SON HOUSE & MUDDY WATERS) *Sony Jazz; (492740-2)* **KING OF THE DELTA BLUES**		-
Mar 99.	(3xcd-box; with MUDDY WATERS & RAY CHARLES) *Summit; (SDCDBX 3668)* **PREACHING THE BLUES**		-

---

Jun 99.	(cd) *A.B.M.; (ABMMCD 1047)* **THE LAST OF THE GREAT BLUES SINGERS**		
Aug 99.	(d-cd) *Snapper; (SMCD 234)* **THE BIRTH OF BLUES**		
Sep 99.	(cd) *Definitive; (DRCD 11142)* **THE COMPLETE ORIGINAL TAKES**		

JON & VANGELIS (see under ⇒ VANGELIS)

Grace JONES (dig out; 4th edition)

John Paul JONES (see under ⇒ LED ZEPPELIN)

Rickie Lee JONES

Born: 8 Nov'54, Chicago, Illinois, USA. A rebellious child, JONES and a friend ran away from home at the age of fifteen, stealing a car in the process; she was later expelled from a number of schools in Olympia, Washington, where she grew up. Relocating to L.A. in 1973, JONES took waitressing work while writing and performing in her spare time; with her beat-poet jazz influences and West Coast, piano-tinkling cool, JONES found a musical soulmate in TOM WAITS (she's allegedly the dame on the cover of WAITS' 'Blue Valentine' album), while the late, great LOWELL GEORGE (of LITTLE FEAT) recorded one of her songs, 'EASY MONEY', on his 1979 solo album. With such notable references, it was only a matter of time before she was signed up, 'Warners' releasing her eponymous debut set in summer '79. Eventually reaching the US Top 5 following the success of the classic 'CHUCK E.'S IN LOVE' single, the album established JONES as a unique talent within L.A.'s musical elite; her swinging boho narratives also divided opinion, there were few waverers. The more ambitious 'PIRATES' (1981) set failed to spawn any hits, although her cult appeal again saw the album making the US Top 5. 1983's 'GIRL AT HER VOLCANO' was a mini-set consisting largely of jazz covers, while 'THE MAGAZINE' (1984) found JONES veering too close to synth-centric electro-rock for comfort. Never the most prolific of artists, it would be a further five years before a fourth set appeared, the more accessible and grounded 'FLYING COWBOYS'. Produced by WALTER BECKER (STEELY DAN) and featuring contributions from Scots mood masters, The BLUE NILE, the album's release found JONES enjoying her most praiseworthy reviews in years. More ill-advised was 'POP POP' (1991), a confused collection of unlikely torch ballad cover versions, while 'TRAFFIC FROM PARADISE' (1993) saw her working with an array of star names including LYLE LOVETT and LEO KOTTKE.
• **Songwriters:** Co-wrote with PASCAL NABAT-MAYER in '89. She covered; WALK AWAY RENEE (Four Tops) / ANGEL WINGS (Tom Waits) / ON BROADWAY (Drifters) / DON'T LET THE SUN CATCH YOU CRYING (Gerry & The Pacemakers) / FRIDAY ON MY MIND (Easybeats) / etc.

Album rating: RICKIE LEE JONES (*8) / PIRATES (*6) / GIRL AT HER VOLCANO mini (*5) / THE MAGAZINE (*6) / FLYING COWBOYS (*6) / POP POP (*5) / TRAFFIC FROM PARADISE (*5) / NAKED SONGS – LIVE AND ACOUSTIC (*4) / GHOSTYHEAD (*5)

RICKIE LEE JONES – vocals, keyboards, guitar / with session people

		Warners	Warners
Jun 79.	(lp/c) *(K/K4 56628) <3296>* **RICKIE LEE JONES**	18	3 Apr79

– Chuck E.'s in love / On Saturday afternoons in 1963 / Night train / Young blood / Easy money / Last chance Texaco / Danny's all star joint / Coolsville / Weasel and the white boys cool / Company / After hours (twelve bars past goodnight). (cd-iss. 1989; K2 56628)

Jun 79.	(7") *(K 17390) <8825>* **CHUCK E.'S IN LOVE. / ON SATURDAY AFTERNOONS IN 1963**	18	4 Apr79
Aug 79.	(7") *(K 17445) <49018>* **YOUNG BLOOD. / COOLSVILLE**		40 Jul79
Oct 79.	(7") *<49100>* **DANNY'S ALL-STAR JOINT. / LAST CHANCE TEXACO**		
Nov 79.	(7") *(K 17477)* **DANNY'S ALL-STAR JOINT. / NIGHT TRAIN**	-	
Jan 80.	(7") *(K 17556)* **EASY MONEY. / COMPANY**	-	
Jul 81.	(lp/c) *(K/K4 56816) <3432>* **PIRATES**	37	5

– We belong together / Living it up / Skeletons / Woody and Dutch on the slow train to Peking / Pirates / Traces of the western slopes / Returns. (cd-iss. Jan86; K2 56816)

Aug 81.	(7") *<49816>* **A LUCKY GUY. / SKELETONS**	-	64
Sep 81.	(7") *(K 17851)* **WOODY AND DUTCH ON THE SLOW TRAIN TO PEKING. / SKELETONS**	-	
Oct 81.	(7") *<49871>* **WE BELONG TOGETHER. / THE RETURNS**		-
Jan 82.	(7") *<50046>* **PIRATES. / SKELETONS**	-	
Jun 83.	(10"m-lp/c) *(923805-1/-4) <23805>* **GIRL AT HER VOLCANO**	51	39

– Lush life / Walk away Renee / Hey, Bub / My funny valentine / Under the boardwalk / Rainbow sleeves / So long. (c+=) – Something cool / Letters from the 9th ward.

Aug 83.	(7") *(W 9559) <29559>* **UNDER THE BOARDWALK. / SO LONG**		
Oct 84.	(lp/c) *(925117-1/-4) <25117>* **THE MAGAZINE**	40	44

– (prelude to gravity) / Gravity / Juke box fury / It must be love / Magazine / The real end / Deep space / Runaround / Rorschachs – Theme for the Pope – The unsigned painting – The weird beast. (cd-iss. Mar86; 925117-2)

Sep 84.	(7") *<29191>* **THE REAL END. / WOODY AND DUTCH ON A SLOW TRAIN TO PEKING**	-	83
Oct 84.	(7"/12") *(W 9191/+T)* **THE REAL END. / MAGAZINE**	-	
Apr 85.	(7") *<29059>* **IT MUST BE LOVE. / MAGAZINE**	-	

		Geffen	Geffen
Sep 89.	(lp/c/cd) *(WX 309/+C)(924249-2) <24246>* **FLYING COWBOYS**	50	39

– The horses / Just my baby / Ghetto of my mind / Rodeo girl / Satellites / Ghost train / Flying cowboys / Don't let the sun catch you crying / Love is gonna bring us back alive / Away from the sky / Atlas' marker. *(cd re-iss. Nov91 & Sep97; GEFD 24246)*

Sep 89. (7") *(GEF 64)* **SATELLITES. / GHOST TRAIN**

☐ -

    (12"+=/cd-s+=) *(GEF 64 T/CD)* – Friday on my mind.

Aug 91. (cd/c/lp) *<(GED/GEF 24426)>* **POP POP**

☐ -

    – My one and only love / Spring can really hang you up the most / Hi-li hi-lo / Up from the skies / Second time around / Dat dere / I'll be seeing you / Bye bye blackbird / The ballad of the sad young men / I won't grow up / Love junkyard / Come back to me. *(re-iss. cd Oct95; GFLD 19293)*

—— with **JOHN LEFTWICH** – bass, cello, vocals / **LEO KOTTKE** – guitars, vocals / **SAL BERNARDI** – acoustic guitar, vocals / **JIM KELTNER** – drums / **BOBBY BRUCE** – violin / **BRAD DUTZ** – percussion / **DOUG LYONS** – French horn / + guest guitarists on 1 track each **DAVID HIDALGO, BRIAN SETZER, DEAN PARKS + DAVID BAERWALD**

Sep 93. (cd/c) *<(GED/GEC 24602)>* **TRAFFIC FROM PARADISE**

    – Pink flamingos / Alter boy / Stewart's coat / Beat angels / Tigers / Rebel rebel / Jolie Jolie / Running from mercy / A stranger's car / The albatross. *(cd re-iss. Sep97; GED 24602)*

	Reprise	Reprise

Oct 95. (cd/c) *<(9362 45950-2/-4)>* **NAKED SONGS – LIVE AND ACOUSTIC** (live)

    – The horses / Weasel and the white boy's cool / Altar boy / It must be love / Young blood / The last chance Texaco / Skeletons / Magazine / Loving it up / We belong together / Coolsville / Flying cowboys / Stewart's coat / Chuck E.'s in love / Autumn leaves.

	WEA	WEA

Sep 97. (c-s) *(W 0418C)* **FIREWALKER / ('A'mix)**

    (12"+=/cd-s+=) *(W 0418 T/CD)* – ('A'mixes).

Sep 97. (cd/c) *<(9362 46557-2/-4)>* **GHOSTYHEAD**

    – Little yellow town / Road kill / Matters / Firewalker / Howard / Ghostyhead / Sunny afternoon / Scary Chinese movie / Cloud of unknowing / Vessel of light.

Tom JONES

Born: THOMAS JONES WOODWARD, 7 Jun'40, Pontypridd, Wales. After a hard-bitten working class upbringing (his dad was a coal miner), the 16-year old JONES moved on from juvenile troublemaking to a marriage that would subsequently be kept separate from his public ladies man persona. Cutting his teeth as a part-time pub singer, he eventually formed his own combo under the pseudonymous moniker of TOMMY SCOTT & THE SENATORS. In 1963, he was spotted by fellow countryman, Gordon Mills, who, in turn, became both his manager and co-writer. By mid '64, he'd become TOM JONES (after the success of the British comedy movie of the same name) and having secured a deal with London label 'Decca', released a cover of Ronnie Love's 'CHILLS AND FEVER' as his debut in August '64. Although it was a flop, JONES made his name early the following year with the classic 'IT'S NOT UNUSUAL'. A chart topper in the UK, the single showcased JONES' powerful, versatile vocal prowess while his charismatic TV appearances wowed the ladies with a hip-swiveling stage style influenced by the likes of JERRY LEE LEWIS, SOLOMON BURKE and ELVIS "The Pelvis" PRESLEY. A fully-fledged Welsh "sex bomb", medallion man JONES became a regular fixture in both the UK and US charts with such timeless pop nuggets as 'WHAT'S NEW PUSSYCAT' (a Bacharach & David-penned title theme to the 1965 movie), 'GREEN, GREEN GRASS OF HOME' (a UK No.1 in '66), 'I'LL NEVER FALL IN LOVE AGAIN' (No.2 in Britain), 'I'M COMING HOME' (also a No.2) and his piece de resistance, 'DELILAH' (yet another to narrowly miss out on prime position, the song was taken into the Top 10 seven years on by ALEX HARVEY!). His golden period was extended into the early 70's with further full-scale hits in the shape of 'I (WHO HAVE NOTHING)', 'SHE'S A LADY', 'TILL' and 'THE YOUNG NEW MEXICAN PUPPETEER'. Yet as his flares grew wider, the hits became thinner on the ground with the advent of "glam-rock" and JONES decamped to the glitzy cabaret circuit of Las Vegas having earlier moved to California. Having achieved a certain degree of mid-80's success in the US country charts, JONES made his UK comeback in '87 with the aptly titled near chart-topper 'A BOY FROM NOWHERE'. This served as a springboard from which he went on to re-establish himself as a credible crooner with a collaboration with the ART OF NOISE on a hit cover of Prince's 'KISS'. JONES' critical rehabilitation continued well into the 90's when – after the success of singles, 'ALL YOU NEED IS LOVE' (for the Childline appeal) and 'IF I ONLY KNEW' (a No.11 hit in '94) – the cream of the latter day alt-pop scene (save for a few oldsters like VAN the man!) queued up to work with him on the massively successful 'RELOAD' (1999). Among the collaborations featured were Talking Heads' 'BURNING DOWN THE HOUSE' (with the CARDIGANS), Ray Charles' 'BABY, IT'S COLD OUTSIDE' (with CERYS from CATATONIA) and Randy Newman's 'MAMA TOLD ME NOT TO COME' (with other Welsh youngsters, STEREOPHONICS) alongside duets with ROBBIE WILLIAMS (whom he'd appeared with in 1998's Brit awards), DIVINE COMEDY, SPACE, JAMES DEAN BRADFIELD, MOUSSE T, HEATHER SMALL, PRETENDERS, PORTISHEAD, SIMPLY RED, NATALIE IMBRUGLIA, BARENAKED LADIES and ZUCCHERO. • **Songwriters:** Outside writers and covers (singles only and er, selective):- WITH THESE HANDS (Billy Eckstine) / PROMISE HER ANYTHING (Burt Bacharach) / THUNDERBALL (John Barry) / GREEN, GREEN GRASS OF HOME (Curly Putnam) / DETROIT CITY (Bobby Bare) / I'LL NEVER FALL IN LOVE AGAIN (Lonnie Donegan) / SIXTEEN TONS (Tennessee Ernie Ford) / DELILAH (Les Reed & Barry Mann) / WITHOUT LOVE (Clyde McPhatter) / I (WHO HAVE NOTHING) (Ben E.King) / PUPPET MAN (Neil Sedaka) / TILL (Angels) / A BOY FROM NOWHERE (Mike Leander) / MOVE CLOSER (Phyllis Nelson) / COULDN'T SAY GOODBYE (Diane Warren & Albert Hammond) /

CARRYING A TORCH (Van Morrison). He also interpreted many Italian language tunes, and covered more than 100 others on his lp's. • **Trivia:** In 1988, he appeared with other Welsh artists in the musical version of Dylan Thomas' 'Under Milk Wood'. A year later, Katherine Berkeley won a paternity suit against TOM and the court made him pay £200 a week for the child's maintenence. He is still married, much to the dismay of his largely female knicker-throwing fans.

Album rating (selective): CARRYING A TORCH (*5) / THE COMPLETE TOM JONES compilation (*7) / THE LEAD AND HOW TO SWING IT (*5) / RELOAD (*8)

TOM JONES – vocals with session people

		Decca	Parrot	
Aug 64.	(7") *(F 11966)* **CHILLS AND FEVER. / BREATHLESS**		-	
Jan 65.	(7") *(F 12062) <9737>* **IT'S NOT UNUSUAL. / TO WAIT FOR LOVE (IS TO WASTE YOUR LIFE AWAY)**	1	10	Mar65
Apr 65.	(7") *(F 12121)* **ONCE UPON A TIME. / I TELL THE SEA**	32		
May 65.	(lp) *(LK 4693)* **ALONG CAME JONES**	11		

    – Some other guy / I've got a heart / It takes a worried man / Spanish Harlem / Autumn leaves / Skye boat song / Memphis Tennessee / Watcha gonna do / I need your loving / If you need me / Endlessly / It's just a matter of time / When the world was beautiful.

Jun 65.	(7") *<9765>* **WHAT'S NEW PUSSYCAT? / ONCE UPON A TIME**	-	3	
Jun 65.	(7") *(F 12191)* **WITH THESE HANDS. / UNTRUE**	13	-	
Jun 65.	(lp) *<71004>* **IT'S NOT UNUSUAL**	-	54	
Aug 65.	(7") *<9787>* **WITH THESE HANDS. / SOME OTHER GUY**	-	27	
Aug 65.	(7") *(F 12203)* **WHAT'S NEW PUSSYCAT? / ROSE**	11	-	
Sep 65.	(lp) *<71006>* **WHAT'S NEW PUSSYCAT?**	-		

    (UK-iss.on cd Jun88 on 'London', 4 extra tracks)

Jan 66.	(7") *(F 12292) <9801>* **THUNDERBALL. / KEY TO MY HEART**	35	25	Nov65
Jan 66.	(lp; mono/stereo) *(LK/SKL 4743)* **A-TOM-IC JONES**			

    – Doctor Love / Face of a loser / It's been a long time coming / In a woman's eyes / More / I'll never let you go / The loser / To make a big man cry / Key to my heart / True love comes only once in a lifetime / You're so good to me / Where do you belong / These things don't forget / Stop breaking my heart. *(cd-iss. Nov88 on 'London'+=; 820556-2)* – Hide and seek / Not responsible / This and that / Promise her anything / Thunderball.

Feb 66.	(7") *<9809>* **PROMISE HER ANYTHING. / A LITTLE YOU**	-	74	
Feb 66.	(7") *(F 12349)* **STOP BREAKING MY HEART. / NEVER GIVE AWAY LOVE**	-		
May 66.	(7") *(F 12390)* **NOT RESPONSIBLE. / ONCE THERE WAS A TIME**	18	58	Jun66
Aug 66.	(7") *(F 12461)* **THIS AND THAT. / CITY GIRL**	44		
Sep 66.	(lp; mono/stereo) *(LK/SKL 4815)* **FROM THE HEART**	23		

    – You came a long way from St. Louis / Kansas City / Someday (you'll want me to want you) / If ever I would leave you / Georgia on my mind / A taste of honey / The nearness of you / My foolish heart / When I fall in love / Begin the beguine / Hello young lovers / It's magic / My prayer / That old black magic. *(cd-iss. Apr89 on 'London'+=; 820557-2)* – (4 extra).

Nov 66.	(7") *(F 12511)* **GREEN, GREEN GRASS OF HOME. / PROMISE HER ANYTHING**	1	-	
Dec 66.	(7") *<40009>* **GREEN, GREEN GRASS OF HOME. / IF I HAD YOU**	-	11	
Feb 67.	(7") *(F 22555)* **DETROIT CITY. / IF I HAD YOU**	8	-	
Mar 67.	(7") *<40012>* **DETROIT CITY. / TEN GUITARS**	-	27	
Mar 67.	(lp; mono/stereo) *(LK/SKL 4855) <71009>* **GREEN, GREEN GRASS OF HOME**	3	65	Feb67

    – Green, green grass of home / My mother's eyes / He'll have to go / Riders in the sky / Funny familiar forgotten feelings / Sixteen tons / Two brothers / Ring of fire / Field of yellow daisies / Wish I could say no / All I get from you is heartaches / Mohair Sam / Cool water / Detroit City. *(cd-iss. Sep88 on 'London'; 820182-2)*

Apr 67.	(7") *(F 12599)* **FUNNY FAMILIAR FORGOTTEN FEELINGS. / I'LL NEVER LET YOU GO**	7	49	May67
Jun 67.	(lp; mono/stereo) *(LK/SKL 4874) <71014>* **LIVE! AT THE TALK OF THE TOWN** (live) *<US-title TOM JONES LIVE!>*	6		Jul67

    – The star theme / Ain't that good news / Hello young lovers / I can't stop loving you / What's new pussycat? / Not responsible / I believe / My Yiddish momma / Shake / That lucky old Sun / Thunderball / Green, green grass of home / It's not unusual / Land of a 1000 dances. *<US re-iss. Mar69; same>* – hit No.13

Jul 67.	(7") *(F 12639)* **I'LL NEVER FALL IN LOVE AGAIN. / THINGS I WANNA DO**	2	-	
Aug 67.	(7") *<40016>* **SIXTEEN TONS. / THINGS I WANNA DO**	-	68	
Sep 67.	(7") *<40018>* **I'LL NEVER FALL IN LOVE AGAIN. / ONCE UPON A TIME**	-	49	

    <US re-iss. Jul69; same> – hit No.6

Nov 67.	(7") *(F 12693) <40024>* **I'M COMING HOME. / THE LONELY ONE**	2	57	Dec67
Dec 67.	(lp; mono/stereo) *(/LK/SKL 4909)* **13 SMASH HITS**	5		

    – Don't fight it / You keep me hangin' on / Hold on I'm coming / I was made to love her / Keep on running / Get ready / I'll never fall in love again / I know / I wake up crying / Funny how time slips away / Danny boy / It's a man's man's world / Yesterday. *(cd-iss. Jun88 on 'London'; 820524-2)*

Feb 68.	(7") *(F 12747) <40025>* **DELILAH. / SMILE AWAY YOUR BLUES**	2	15	Mar68
Jul 68.	(lp; mono/stereo) *(LK/SKL 4946)* **DELILAH** *<US-title 'TOM JONES FEVER ZONE'>*	1	14	Jun68

    – Delilah / You can't stop love / Only a fool breaks his own heart / Take me / My elusive dreams / Make this heart of mine smile again / Weeping Annaleah / Just out of reach (of my empty arms) / Why can't I cry / Lingering on / One day soon / Laura (what's he got that I ain't got). *(cd-iss. Sep88 on 'London'; 820486-2)*

Jul 68.	(7") *(F 12812) <40029>* **HELP YOURSELF. / DAY BY DAY**	5	35	Aug68
Nov 68.	(7") *(F 12854) <40035>* **A MINUTE OF YOUR TIME. / LOOKING OUT MY WINDOW**	14	48	Dec68
Nov 68.	(lp; mono/stereo) *(LK/SKL 4982) <71025>* **HELP YOURSELF**	4	5	Jan69

    – Help yourself / I can't break the news to myself / The bed / Isadora / Set me free / I get carried away / This house (the house song) / So afraid / If I promise / If you go away / My girl Maria / All I can say is goodbye / Ten guitars / What a party.

(cd-iss. Jan89 on 'London'+=; 820559-2) – Looking out my window / Can't stop loving you / Let there be love / Without love.

May 69. (7") *(F 12924) <40038>* **LOVE ME TONIGHT. / HIDE AND SEEK** — 9 — 13

Jun 69. (lp; mono/stereo) *(LK/SKL 5007) <71028>* **THIS IS TOM JONES** — 2 — 4
– Fly me to the moon / Little green apples / Wichita lineman / (Sittin' on) The dock of the bay / Dance of love / Hey Jude / Without you (non che lei) / That's all any man can say / That wonderful sound / Only once / I'm a fool to want you / Let it be me. *(cd-iss. Nov88 on 'London'; 820234-2)*

Nov 69. (lp; mono/stereo) *(LK/SKL 5032) <71031>* **LIVE IN LAS VEGAS – AT THE FLAMINGO (live)** <US-title 'TOM JONES LIVE IN LAS VEGAS'> — 3 — 3
– Turn on your love light / The bright lights and you girl / I can't stop loving you / Hard to handle / Delilah / Danny boy / (It looks like) I'll never fall in love again / Help yourself / Yesterday / Hey Jude / Love me tonight / It's not unusual / Twist and shout. *(cd-iss. Jun88 on 'London'; 820318-2)*

Dec 69. (7") *(F 12990) <40045>* **WITHOUT LOVE (THERE IS NOTHING). / THE MAN WHO KNOWS TOO MUCH** — 10 — 5

Apr 70. (7") *(F 13013) <40048>* **DAUGHTER OF DARKNESS. / TUPELO MISSISSIPPI FLASH** — 5 — 13

Apr 70. (lp; mono/stereo) *(LK/SKL 5045) <71037>* **TOM** — 4 — 6
– I can't turn you loose / Polk salad Annie / Proud Mary / Sugar, sugar / Venus / I thank you / Without love / You've lost that lovin' feeling / If I ruled the world / Can't stop loving you / Impossible dream / Let there be love.

Aug 70. (7") *(F 13061) <40051>* **I (WHO HAVE NOTHING). / STOP BREAKING MY HEART** — 16 — 14

Nov 70. (lp; mono/stereo) *(LK/SKL 5072) <71039>* **I, WHO HAVE NOTHING** — 10 — 23
– Daughter of darkness / I have dreamed / Love's been good to me / Lodi / Try a little tenderness / I (who have nothing) / What the world needs now is love / With one exception / To love somebody / Brother, can you spare a dime / See-saw.

Nov 70. (7") *<40056>* **CAN'T STOP LOVING YOU. / NEVER GIVE AWAY LOVE** — – — 25

Jan 71. (7") *(F 13113) <40058>* **SHE'S A LADY. / MY WAY** — 13 — 2

May 71. (lp) *(SKL 5089) <71046>* **TOM JONES SINGS SHE'S A LADY** — 9 — 17
– She's a lady / Do what you gotta do / In dreams / Nothing rhymed / 'Til I can't take it anymore / Resurrection shuffle / Puppet man / It's up to the woman / Eb tide / (I ain't no) One night only love maker / You're my world. *(re-iss. Nov77 on 'E.M.I.'; EMC 3205)*

May 71. (7") *(F 13183) <40062>* **PUPPET MAN. / EVERY MILE** — 49 — 26

Jun 71. (7") *<40064>* **RESURRECTION SHUFFLE. / PUPPET MAN** — – — 38

Oct 71. (7") *(F 13236)* **TILL. / THE SUN DIED** — 2 —

Oct 71. (7") *<40067>* **TILL. / ONE DAY SOON** — – — 41

Nov 71. (d-lp) *(DKL 1/1-1/2) <71049>* **TOM JONES LIVE AT CAESARS PALACE, LAS VEGAS (live)** — 27 — 43 Oct71
– I'll never fall in love again – Daughter of darkness – Love me tonight – It's not unusual – Hi-heel sneakers (hits medley) / Dance of love / Cabaret / Soul man / I (who have nothing) / Delilah / Bridge over troubled water / My way / God bless the children / Resurrection shuffle / She's a lady / Till / Rock'n'roll medley: Johnny B. Goode – Bony moronie – Long tall Sally. *(re-iss. Oct77 on 'M.F.P.'; 5035-1) (cd/c-iss.Oct91; CD/TC MFP 5931)*

Mar 72. (7") *(F 13298) 40070>* **THE YOUNG NEW MEXICAN PUPPETEER. / ALL THAT I NEED IS SOME TIME** — 6 — 80 Apr72

Jun 72. (lp) *(SKL 5132) <71055>* **CLOSE UP** — 17 — 64
– Witch queen of New Orleans / Tired of being alone / Woman, you took my life / Young New Mexican puppeteer / All I ever need is you / You've got a friend / Time to get it together / I won't be sorry to see Suzanne again / Kiss an angel good mornin'.

Mar 73. (7") *(F 13393) <40074>* **LETTER TO LUCILLE. / THANK THE LORD** — 31 — 60 May73

Jun 73. (lp) *(SKL 5162) <71060>* **THE BODY AND SOUL OF TOM JONES** — 31 — 60
– Runnin' bear / Ain't no sunshine when she's gone / (If loving you is wrong) I don't want to be right / Since I loved you last / Lean on me / Letter to Lucille / Today I started loving you again / I'll share my world with you / I still love you enough (to love you all over again) / Ballad of Billie Joe.

Jul 73. (7") *(F 13434)* **TODAY I STARTED LOVING YOU AGAIN. / I STILL LOVE YOU ENOUGH** — — —

Nov 73. (7") *(F 13471)* **GOLDEN DAYS. / GOODBYE, GOD BLESS YOU BABY** — — —

Feb 74. (7") *(F 13490)* **LA LA LA (JUST HAVING YOU HERE). / LOVE LOVE LOVE** — — —

Aug 74. (7") *(F 13550)* **SOMETHIN' 'BOUT YOU BABY I LIKE. / KEEP A-TALKING 'BOUT LOVE** — 36 — —

Nov 74. (lp) *(SKL 5197)* **SOMETHIN' 'BOUT YOU BABY I LIKE**
– Somethin' 'bout you baby I like / You make me smile / Till I get it right / Rainin' in my heart / It never hurts to be nice to somebody / Run Cleo run / Make believe world / Which way home / Sing for the good times / Right place, wrong time.

Nov 74. (7") *(F 13564)* **PLEDGING MY LOVE. / I'M FAR TOO GONE (TO TURN AWAY)** — — —

Apr 75. (7") *(F 13575)* **AIN'T NO LOVE. / WHEN THE BAND GOES HOME** — — —

Jul 75. (7") *(F 13590)* **I GOT YOUR NUMBER. / THE PAIN OF LOVE** — — —

Sep 75. (7") *(F 13598)* **MEMORIES DON'T LEAVE LIKE PEOPLE DO. / MY HELPING HAND** — — —

Oct 75. (lp) *(SKL 5214)* **MEMORIES DON'T LEAVE LIKE PEOPLE DO**
– Memories don't leave like people do / I got your number / Pain of love / Mr. Helping hand / City life / Lusty lady / We got love / Son of a fisherman / You inspire me / Us.

	E.M.I.	Epic

Jan 77. (7") *<50308>* **SAY YOU'LL STAY UNTIL TOMORROW. / LADY LAY** — – — 15

Jan 77. (7") *(EMI 2583)* **SAY YOU'LL STAY UNTIL TOMORROW. / NOTHING RHYMED** — 40 — –

Apr 77. (lp) *(EMC 3178) <34468>* **SAY YOU'LL STAY UNTIL TOMORROW** — – — 76 Feb77
– Say you'll stay until tomorrow / One man woman, one woman man / Anniversary

song / When it's just you and me / Papa / Take me tonight / At every end there's a beginning / Come to me / We had it all / Have you ever been lonely.

Jul 77. (7") *(EMI 2662)* **HAVE YOU EVER BEEN LONELY. / ONE MAN WOMAN, ONE WOMAN MAN** — — —

Feb 78. (7") *(EMI 2756)* **NO ONE GAVE ME LOVE. / THAT'S WHERE I BELONG** — — —

Feb 78. (lp) *(EMC 3221)* **WHAT A NIGHT** — — —
– What a night / We don't live here / No one gave me love / Day to day affair / If this is love / I wrote this song to send my love to you / That's where I belong / Easy to love / The heart / Ramblin' man.

	Lotus	not iss.

Sep 78. (lp/c) *<WH 5/6 001>* **I'M COMING HOME** — 12 — —
– (It looks like) I'll never fall in love again / To wait for love (is to waste your life away) / I can't stop loving you / Once there was a time / Untrue / Someday (you'll want me to want you) / To make a big man cry / (Won't you give him) One more chance / He'll have to go / Some other guy / Field of yellow daisies / I wake up crying / Autumn leaves / Funny familiar forgotten feelings. *(cd/c-iss.May93 on 'Spectrum'; 550020-2/-4)*

	Columbia	Columbia

Jul 79. (7") *(DB 9098)* **DO YOU TAKE THIS MAN. / IF I SING YOU A LOVE SONG** — — —

Sep 79. (lp/c) *(SCX/TC-SCX 6620)* **DO YOU TAKE THIS MAN** — — —
– Do you take this man / How deep is the ocean / Out of mercy / Baby as you turn away / Go easy lady / Love is in the air / You're so good / Going through the motions / Lady put the light out / If I sing you a love song / But if you'd ever leave me / Hey love it's a feeling.

Jun 80. (lp/c) *(SCX/TC-SCX 6628)* **RESCUE ME** — — —
– Rescue me / Never had a lady before / Somebody out there will / Dancing endlessly / Dark storm on the horizon / What becomes of the broken hearted? / Once you hit the road / Flashback / Don't cry for me Argentina.

	Polydor	Mercury

Oct 81. (lp/c) *(2480/3194 622) <4010>* **DARLIN'** — — — May81
– Darlin' / But I do / Lady lay down / No guarantee / What in the world's come over you? / One night / A daughter's question / I don't want to know you that well / Dime queen of Nevada / Things that matter most to me / Come home Rhondda boy. *<re-iss. Aug87 lp/c/cd; 818898-1/-4/-2>*

Nov 81. (7") *(POSP 371)* **COME HOME RHONDDA BOY. / WHAT IN THE WORLD'S COME OVER YOU?** — — —

Feb 82. (7") *(POSP 410)* **BUT I DO. / ONE NIGHT WITH YOU** — — —

Apr 83. (7") **TOUCH ME (I'LL BE YOUR FOOL ONCE MORE). /** — – —

Sep 83. (7") **IT'LL BE ME. /** — – —

Nov 83. (lp) **DON'T LET OUR DREAMS DIE YOUNG** — – —

Jan 84. (7") **I'VE BEEN RAINED ON TOO. /** — – —

May 84. (7") **THIS TIME. /** — – —

Nov 84. (lp) **LOVE IS ON THE RADIO** — – —

Dec 84. (7") **I'M AN OLD ROCK'N'ROLLER (DANCING TO A DIFFERENT BEAT). /** — – —

	RCA Camden	Mercury

Mar 85. (lp/c) *(CDS/CAM 2074)* **THE COUNTRY SIDE OF TOM JONES** — — –
– (his US-only releases from 1983-85)

1986. (lp) **TENDER LOVING CARE** — – —

1986. (7") **IT'S FOUR IN THE MORNING. /** — – —

	Epic	Epic

Apr 87. (7") *(OLE 1)* **A BOY FROM NOWHERE. / (excerpts from I'LL DRESS YOU IN MOURNING + DANCE WITH DEATH + TO BE A MATADOR)** — 2 —
(12"+=) (OLET 1) – (full B-side versions).

Apr 87. (lp/c/cd) *(VIVA/+MC/CD 1)* **MATADOR – THE MUSICAL LIFE OF EL CORDOBES** — 26 —
– Overture / There's no way out of here / To be a matador / I was born to be me / Only other people / Manolete! Belmonte! Joselito! / A boy from nowhere / Wake up Madrid / I'll take you out to dinner / This incredible journey / Don't be deceived / I'll dress you in mourning / Dance with death / A Panama hat.

Nov 87. (7"/7"s) *(OLE/+Q 4)* **I WAS BORN TO BE ME. / A PANAMA HAT** — — —
(12"+=) (OLET 4) – A boy from nowhere.

—— In Oct'88, JONES collaborated with The ART OF NOISE on a joint single, 'KISS', which hit UK No.5 & US No.31.

	Jive	Jive

Apr 89. (7") *(JIVE 203)* **MOVE CLOSER. / 'TIL THE END OF TIME** — 49 — —
(12"+=/cd-s+=) (JIVET 203) – ('A'instrumental).

Apr 89. (lp/c/cd) *(TOM TV/TC/CD 1)* **AT THIS MOMENT** — 34 —
– Kiss / Move closer / Who's gonna take you home tonight / I'm counting on you / 'Til the end of time / What you been missing / After the tears / I can't get no satisfaction / Touch my heart.

Sep 89. (7") *(JIVE 209)* **AT THIS MOMENT. / AFTER THE TEARS** — — —
(12") (JIVEX 209) – ('A'side) / Green, green grass of home (live) / It's not unusual (live).
(cd-s) (JIVECD 209) – ('A'side) / Help yourself (live) / I'll never fall in love again (live) / Delilah (live).

	Dover-Chrysalis	Chrysalis

Jan 91. (7") *(ROJ 10)* **COULDN'T SAY GOODBYE. / ZIP IT UP** — 51 — —
(12"+=/cd-s+=) (ROJ T/CD 10) – Kiss (Art Of Noise remix).

Mar 91. (7") *(ROJ 12)* **CARRYING A TORCH. / WALK TALL (VALLEY OF THE SHADOWS)** — — —
(12"+=/cd-s+=) (ROJ T/CD 12) –

Mar 91. (cd/c/lp) *(CCD/ZDD/ADD 20)* **CARRYING A TORCH** — 44 —
– Carrying a torch / Some peace of mind / I'm not feelin' it anymore / Do I ever cross your mind / Fool for rock'n'roll / Only in America / Couldn't say goodbye / Killer in the sheets / Give me a chance / Zip it up / It must be you / Old flame blue.

	Childline	not iss.

Jan 93. (c-s/cd-s) *(CHILD C/CD 93)* **ALL YOU NEED IS LOVE / ('A'mixes; with DAVE STEWART)** — 19 — –

	Z.T.T.	Interscope

Oct 94. (7"/c-s) *(ZANG 59/+C)* **IF I ONLY KNEW. / ('A'–Cold Stop)** — 11 — –
(12"+=/cd-s+=) (ZANG 59 T/CD) – ('A'–Fade out version).

Nov 94. (cd/c/lp) *(6544 92498-2/-4/-1)* <*IND 92498*> **THE LEAD AND HOW TO SWING IT** `55` `[ ]`
– If I only knew / A girl like you / I wanna get back with you / Situation / Something for your head / Fly away / Love is on our side / I don't think so / Life me up / Show me / I'm ready / Changes. (cd re-iss. Sep97 on 'Interscope'; IND 92498)

Mar 95. (7"/c-s) *(ZANG 64/+C)* **I WANNA GET BACK WITH YOU (featuring TORI AMOS). / IF I ONLY KNEW** `[ ]` `-`
(12"+=/cd-s+=) *(ZANG 64 T/CD)* – Situation / I don't think so.

`Gut` `unsure`

Sep 99. (c-s; TOM JONES & The CARDIGANS) *(CAGUT 026)* **BURNING DOWN THE HOUSE / (Delakota mix) / (Pepe Deluxe mix)** `7` `[ ]`
(cd-s+=) *(CDGUT 026)* – ('A'-DJ Scissorkicks instrumental).
(cd-s) *(CXGUT 026)* – ('A'live) / Unbelievable (live) / Come together (live).

Sep 99. (cd/c) *(GUT CD/MC 009)* **RELOAD** `1` `[ ]`
– Burning down the house (with the CARDIGANS) / Mama told me not to come (with STEREOPHONICS) / Are you gonna go my way (with ROBBIE WILLIAMS) / All mine (with the DIVINE COMEDY) / Sunny afternoon (with SPACE) / I'm left, you're right, she's gone (with JAMES DEAN BRADFIELD) / Sex bomb (with MOUSSE T.) / You need love like I do (with HEATHER SMALL) / Looking out of my window (with JAMES TAYLOR QUARTET) / Sometimes we cry (with VAN MORRISON) / Lust for life (with the PRETENDERS) / Little green bag (with BARENAKED LADIES) / Ain't that a lot of love (with SIMPLY RED) / She drives me crazy (with ZUCCHERO) / Never tear us apart (with NATALIE IMBRUGLIA) / Baby, it's cold outside (with CERYS from CATATONIA) / Motherless child (with PORTISHEAD). (cd+=) – Green green grass of home / (It looks like) I'll never fall in love again.

Dec 99. (c-s; TOM JONES & CERYS from CATATONIA) *(CAGUT 029)* **BABY, IT'S COLD OUTSIDE / (part 2)** `17` `[ ]`
(cd-s) *(CDGUT 029)* –
(cd-s) *(CXGUT 029)* –

– compilations, others, etc. –

Mar 65. (7"ep) *Decca; (DFE 8617)* **ON STAGE (live with The SQUIRES)** `[ ]` `-`
May 65. (7") *Columbia; (DB 7566) / Tower;* <*126*> **LITTLE LONELY ONE. / THAT'S WHAT WE'LL DO** `[ ]` `42`
Oct 65. (7") *Columbia; (DB 7733) / Tower;* **LONELY JOE. / I WAS A FOOL** `[ ]` `-`
Dec 65. (7"ep) *Columbia; (SEG 8464)* **TOM JONES** `[ ]` `-`
– Little lonely one / I was a fool / Lonely Joe / That's what we'll do.
Jan 67. (7"ep) *Decca; (DFE 8668)* **WHAT A PARTY** `[ ]` `-`
– What a party / Any day now / Promise her anything / It ain't gonna be that way.
Dec 73. (lp) *Decca; (SKL 5176) / Parrot;* <*71062*> **TOM JONES' GREATEST HITS** `15` `[ ]`
Mar 75. (d-lp/d-c) *Decca; (TJD 1-1/1-2)* **20 GREATEST HITS** `1` `-`
Dec 75. (lp) *Decca; (SPA 454)* **THE WORLD OF TOM JONES** `[ ]` `-`
Dec 76. (d-lp)(d-c) *Decca; (DKL7 1/2)(KDKC2 8061)* **TOM JONES SINGS 24 GREAT STANDARDS** `[ ]` `-`
Apr 79. (lp) *A&M; (GXM 9010)* **THE SUPER DISC OF TOM JONES** `[ ]` `-`
Aug 79. (lp/c) *Columbia; (SCX/TC-SCX 6613)* **TOM JONES SINGS THE HITS** `[ ]` `-`
Jan 80. (lp/c) *Music For Pleasure; (MFP/TC-MFP 50459)* **THE VERY BEST OF TOM JONES** `[ ]` `-`
Oct 80. (lp) *Decca; (TAB 2)* **THE GOLDEN HITS** `[ ]` `-`
(cd-iss. Mar87 on 'London'; 810192-2)
Nov 81. (7") *Recorded Delivery; (RDR 007)* **SONNY BOY. / WORDS I WOULD HAVE LOVED TO SAY** `[ ]` `-`
Mar 82. (lp/c) *Contour; (CN/+4 2053)* **IT'S NOT UNUSUAL** `[ ]` `-`
(cd-iss. 1989 on 'Pickwick'; PWKS 529)
Oct 82. (lp/c) *Contour; (CN/+4 2057)* **DELILAH** `[ ]` `-`
(cd-iss. Oct95 on 'Laserlight'; 12575)
May 83. (lp) *Decca; (TAB 67)* **GREEN, GREEN GRASS OF HOME – TOM JONES COUNTRY STYLE** `[ ]` `-`
Aug 83. (lp/c) *Contour; (CN/+4 2065)* **16 LOVE SONGS** `[ ]` `-`
(cd-iss. Jun87 on 'Chrysalis'; CPCD 1605)
Sep 83. (7") *Decca; (JONES 1)* **I'LL BE HERE WHERE MY HEART IS. / MY LAST GOODBYE** `[ ]` `-`
Sep 83. (lp) *Decca; (TOM 1)* **THE TOM JONES ALBUM** `[ ]` `-`
Sep 83. (7"ep/c-ep) *Scoop; (7SR/7SC 5004)* **6 TRACK HITS** `[ ]` `-`
– Daughter of darkness / My way / What becomes of the broken hearted / Raining in my heart / Till / Say you'll stay until tomorrow.
Oct 83. (7") *Old Gold; (OG 9337)* **GREEN, GREEN GRASS OF HOME. / IT'S NOT UNUSUAL** `[ ]` `-`
Oct 83. (7") *Old Gold; (OG 9352)* **DELILAH. / HELP YOURSELF** `[ ]` `-`
Nov 83. (lp/c) *Hallmark; (SHM/HSC 3128)* **SOMETHIN' 'BOUT YOU BABY I LIKE** `[ ]` `-`
Feb 86. (lp) *Decca; (TAB 91)* **THE SOUL OF TOM JONES** `[ ]` `-`
(cd/c-iss.Mar92 on 'Pickwick'; PWK S/MC 4101P)
Apr 86. (lp/c) *Arcade; (ADAH/+C 438)* **LOVE SONGS** `[ ]` `-`
May 87. (lp/c) *Contour; (CN/+4 2086)* **THE GREAT LOVE SONGS** `[ ]` `-`
(cd-iss. Jul90 on 'Pickwick'; PWKS 587)
May 87. (lp/c/cd) *Telstar; (STAR/STAC/TCD 2296)* **TOM JONES – THE GREATEST HITS** `16` `-`
May 87. (7") *London; (F 103)* **IT'S NOT UNUSUAL. / DELILAH** `17` `-`
(12"+=) *(FX 103)* – ('A'extended) / Land of a 1000 dances (live).
Jul 87. (lp/c)(cd) *Decca; (TOM/KTOM 2)(820544-2)* **IT'S NOT UNUSUAL – HIS GREATEST HITS** `[ ]` `-`
Aug 87. (7") *London; (F 104)* **WHAT'S NEW PUSSYCAT? / HARD TO HANDLE** `[ ]` `-`
Jan 88. (cd) *London; (820773-2)* **STOP BREAKING MY HEART** `[ ]` `-`
Jun 89. (lp/c/cd) *Stylus; (SMR/SMC/SMD 978)* **AFTER DARK** `46` `-`
Sep 90. (lp/c) *Pickwick; (PWKS/+C 4027P)* **A MINUTE OF YOUR TIME** `[ ]` `-`
Mar 92. (cd/c) *Music Club; (MCCD/MCTC 057)* **THE VOICE** `[ ]` `-`
(cd re-iss. Mar99; MCCD 382)
Jul 93. (d-cd) *London; (844096-2)* **VELVET & STEEL / GOLD** `[ ]` `-`

Jun 92. (cd/c/lp) *London; 844286-2/-4/-1)* **THE COMPLETE TOM JONES** `8` `[ ]`
– It's tot unusual / Delilah / Kiss / (It looks like) I'll never fall in love again / She's a lady / Green green grass of home / Love me tonight / Without love / Daughter of darkness / A boy from nowhere / What's new pussycat? / I'm coming home / Help yourself / I (who have nothing) / Move closer / Detroit city / Couldn't say goodbye / Till / Something 'bout you baby I like / The young New Mexican puppeteer.
Jun 92. (7"/c-s) *London; DELILAH. / KISS* `[ ]` `-`
(cd-s+=) –
Jun 92. (cd) *Tring; (MCJHD 033)* **IT'S NOT UNUSUAL** `[ ]` `-`
Apr 94. (cd) *Laserlight; (Cd 12331)* **HITS** `[ ]` `-`
May 94. (cd) *Disky; (WMCD 5693)* **SIMPLY THE BEST – SHE'S A LADY** `[ ]` `-`
Jul 94. (cd; shared w/ ENGELBERT HUMPERDINCK) *Disky; (DCD 5385)* **THE LOVE ALBUM** `[ ]` `-`
Mar 95. (cd) *Emperio; (EMPRCD 555)* **KISS** `[ ]` `-`
(re-iss. Nov96 on 'Tring'; QED 014)
Mar 95. (cd/c) *Castle; (CCS CD/MC 431)* **THE COLLECTION** `[ ]` `-`
Aug 95. (cd/c) *Spectrum; (551340-2/-4)* **IN NASHVILLE** `[ ]` `-`
Aug 95. (cd/c) *Spectrum; (551520-2/-4)* **TOM JONES COLLECTION** `[ ]` `-`
Jan 96. (cd) *Deram; (844552-2)* **THE LEGENDARY TOM JONES** `[ ]` `-`
Sep 96. (3xcd-box) *Disky; (SA 87250-2)* **TOUCH MY SOUL** `[ ]` `-`
Jul 97. (d-cd) *Pulse; (PDSCD 549)* **AT HIS BEST** `[ ]` `-`
Oct 97. (cd/c) *Pulse; (PLS CD/MC 239)* **GREAT SONGS OF OUR TIME** `[ ]` `-`
Nov 97. (4xcd-box) *Camden; (CDN 40014)* **THE ULTIMATE COLLECTION** `[ ]` `-`
Nov 97. (3xcd-box) *Charly; (CPCD 8323-2)* **SINGS THE ALL-TIME HITS** `[ ]` `-`
Jan 98. (cd) *Collection; (COL 077)* **THE COLLECTION** `[ ]` `-`
Feb 98. (cd) *Disky; (LS 86553-2)* **20 GREAT LOVE SONGS** `[ ]` `-`
Feb 98. (cd/c) *London; (844823-2/-4)* **THE VERY BEST OF TOM JONES** `[ ]` `-`
Mar 98. (cd) *Reactive; (REMCD 521)* **THE ULTIMATE PERFORMANCE** `[ ]` `-`
Mar 98. (5xcd-box) *Charly; (CDDIG 21)* **SONGBOOK** `[ ]` `-`
Apr 98. (d-cd) *Thirty-Two; (6041232035-2)* **GREATEST PERFORMANCES** `[ ]` `-`
Apr 98. (cd) *Repertoire; (REP 4694)* **I, WHO HAVE NOTHING / SHE'S A LADY** `[ ]` `-`
Apr 98. (cd) *Repertoire; (REP 4695)* **THE YOUNG NEW MEXICAN PUPPETEER / THE BODY AND SOUL OF TOM JONES** `[ ]` `-`
Jun 98. (cd/c) *Pulse; (PLS CD/MC 292)* **TOM JONES SINGS COUNTRY** `[ ]` `-`
Jun 98. (d-cd) *Camden; (CDN 1013)* **FEVER (live)** `[ ]` `-`
Aug 98. (3xcd-box) *Pulse; (PBXCD 316)* **THE SENSATIONAL TOM JONES** `[ ]` `-`
Aug 98. (3xcd-box) *Hallmark; (390662)* **60 TV CLASSICS (duets)** `[ ]` `-`
Aug 98. (cd) *Laserlight; (21138)* **THE SHOW, VANCOUVER 1981 (live)** `[ ]` `-`
Oct 98. (cd/c) *Hallmark; (30986-2/-4)* **HITS OF THE 60's (live)** `[ ]` `-`
Oct 98. (d-cd) *Double Gold; (DBG 53064)* **GREEN, GREEN GRASS OF HOME – THE LEGENDARY PERFORMANCES** `[ ]` `-`
Nov 98. (cd/c) *London; (844901-2/-4)* **THE ULTIMATE COLLECTION** `[ ]` `-`
Nov 98. (cd) *Lost Moment; (LMCD 057)* **THE TELEVISION SHOWS** `[ ]` `-`
Mar 99. (3xcd-box) *R.E.D.X.; (RBOX 31055)* **THE GREAT . . .** `[ ]` `-`
Mar 99. (d-cd) *Snapper; (SMDCD 201)* **COAST TO COAST (Love Classics)** `[ ]` `-`
Apr 99. (cd) *Hallmark; (31138-2)* **ROCK AND SOUL** `[ ]` `-`
May 99. (cd) *R.E.D.X.; (RX 1042)* **THE ESSENTIAL** `[ ]` `-`
Jun 99. (cd/c) *Hallmark; (31153-2/-4)* **DUETS** `[ ]` `-`
Jul 99. (cd/c) *Hallmark; (31156-2/-4)* **THE VOICE (different)** `[ ]` `-`
Jul 99. (cd/c) *Hallmark; (31173-2/-4)* **SEND IN THE CLOWNS** `[ ]` `-`
Jul 99. (d-cd) *Disky; (HR 85767-2)* **ORIGINAL GOLD** `[ ]` `-`
Aug 99. (d-cd) *Snapper; (SMDCD 202)* **COAST TO COAST (Classics)** `[ ]` `-`
Aug 99. (d-cd) *Castle Pie; (PIEDD 094)* **HOT AND LIVE** `[ ]` `-`
Oct 99. (cd/c) *Spectrum; (544173-2)* **FROM LAS VEGAS TO LONDON – THE BEST OF TOM JONES LIVE (live)** `[ ]` `-`
Oct 99. (cd/c) *Spectrum; (551520-2/-4)* **THE COLLECTION** `[ ]` `-`
Dec 99. (cd) *Castle Pie; (PIESD 192)* **THE HIT MIX** `[ ]` `-`

Janis JOPLIN

Born: 19 Jan'43, Port Arthur, Texas, USA. In the early 60's, she hitched to California and San Francisco, where she sang in The WALLER CREEK BOYS trio alongside future 13th FLOOR ELEVATORS member R.POWELL ST.JOHN. In 1963, she subsequently appeared opposite JORMA KAUKONEN (later JEFFERSON AIRPLANE) at local night spots. In 1966, after nearly giving up singing and her hippy drug-taking ways for a life of domesticity, she returned to Texas where she briefly rehearsed with The 13th FLOOR ELEVATORS. That same year, she again ventured to San Francisco, this time joining BIG BROTHER & THE HOLDING COMPANY. They released two albums, the second of which, 'CHEAP THRILLS', stayed at the top of the US charts for 8 weeks. When they temporarily folded late in '68, she went solo, although her alcohol and drug abuse was becoming increasingly pronounced. After three major concerts; London's Royal Albert Hall, Newport Festival and New Orleans Pop Festival, she unleashed her 1969 solo debut, 'I GOT DEM OL' KOSMIC BLUES AGAIN', which made the US Top 5. In May '70, she formed her new backing group, The FULL-TILT BOOGIE BAND, beginning work on an album in the Autumn of 1970. Before it was completed, however, on the 4th of October 1970, JANIS was found dead in her Hollywood hotel room. The coroner's verdict reported that her death was due to an accidental drug overdose. Early in 1971, her last recording, 'PEARL' was issued, topping the US charts for 9 weeks, also giving her a first taste of UK chart action. She again hit pole position in the States with a great version of

KRIS KRISTOFFERSON's 'ME AND BOBBY McGEE'. But for her death, she would probably have become the greatest female singer of all-time, her powerful 3-octave vocals having the capacity to transform the most run-of-the-mill tune into a tour de force. • **Songwriters:** She used many outside writers, including JERRY RAGAVOY, and covered; PIECE OF MY HEART (hit; Erma Franklin) / MAYBE (Chantells) / TO LOVE SOMEBODY (Bee Gees) / etc. • **Trivia:** In 1979, a film, 'The Rose', was released based on her life, featuring BETTE MIDLER in her role.

Album rating: I GOT DEM OL' KOSMIC BLUES AGAIN MAMA (*6) / PEARL (*7) / JOPLIN IN CONCERT posthumous (*5) / JANIS JOPLIN'S GREATEST HITS compilation (*8) / JANIS early stuff (*4) / FAREWELL SONG (*4) / 18 ESSENTIAL SONGS compilation (*8)

JANIS JOPLIN – vocals (ex-BIG BROTHER & THE HOLDING COMPANY) / **SAM ANDREW** – guitar (ex-BIG BROTHER & THE HOLDING COMPANY) / others in her KOZMIC BLUES BAND were **BRAD CAMPBELL** (aka KEITH CHERRY) – bass / **TERRY CLEMENTS** – saxophone / **RICHARD KERMODE** – organ repl. BILL KING (Feb69) / **LONNIE CASTILLE** – drums repl. ROY MARKOWITZ (Apr69) / **TERRY HENSLEY** – trumpet repl. MARCUS DOUBLEDAY (Apr69) / added **SNOOKY FLOWERS** – saxophone (Feb69)

—— (Jul69) **JOHN TILL** – guitar, vocals repl. SAM ANDREW / **MAURY BAKER** – drums repl. CASTILLE / **DAVE WOODWARD** – trumpet repl. GASCA who repl. HENSLEY

	C.B.S.	Columbia
Oct 69. (lp) *(CBS 63546)* <9913> **I GOT DEM OL' KOZMIC BLUES AGAIN MAMA!**		5

– Try (just a little bit harder) / Maybe / One good man / As good as you've been to this world / To love somebody / Kozmic blues / Little girl blue / Work me, Lord. *(re-iss. 1983 lp/c; CBS/40 32063) (cd-iss. 1988; CD 63546) (cd re-iss. Jan91;)*

	C.B.S.	Columbia
Nov 69. (7") <45023> **KOZMIC BLUES. / LITTLE GIRL BLUE**	-	41
Dec 69. (7"w-drawn) *(CBS 3683)* **TURTLE BLUES. / PIECE OF MY HEART**	-	-
Jan 70. (7") <45080> **TRY (JUST A LITTLE BIT HARDER). / ONE GOOD MAN**	-	-
Apr 70. (7") <45128> **MAYBE. / WORK ME, LORD**	-	

—— JANIS JOPLIN & THE FULL TILT BOOGIE BAND

retained **CAMPBELL** and **TILL** / added **RICHARD BELL** – piano / **KEN PEARSON** – organ / **CLARK PIERSON** – drums/ On the 4th Oct70, JANIS died of a drug overdose. She had just recorded below album

	C.B.S.	Columbia
Jan 71. (lp) *(CBS 64188)* <30322> **PEARL**	50	1

– Move over / Cry baby / A woman left lonely / Half Moon / Buried alive in the blues / My baby / Me and Bobby McGee / Mercedes Benz / Trust me / Get it while you can. *(re-iss. Jan84 lp/c; CBS/40 32064) (cd-iss. 1988; CD 64188) (cd re-iss. Jan91 & Jul95 on 'Columbia'; 480415-2)*

	C.B.S.	Columbia
Jan 71. (7") *(CBS 7019)* <45314> **ME AND BOBBY McGEE. / HALF MOON**		1
May 71. (7") *(CBS 7217)* <45379> **CRY BABY. / MERCEDES BENZ**		42
Sep 71. (7") <45433> **GET IT WHILE YOU CAN. / MOVE OVER**	-	78

– other posthumous JANIS JOPLIN releases –

on 'CBS' UK / 'Columbia' US unless mentioned otherwise

	C.B.S.	Columbia
Oct 71. (7"ep) *(CBS 9136)* **MOVE OVER / CRY BABY. / TRY (JUST A LITTLE BIT HARDER) / PIECE OF MY HEART**		
Jul 72. (d-lp) *(CBS 67241)* <31160> **JANIS JOPLIN IN CONCERT (live half with BIG BROTHER & THE HOLDING COMPANY / half with FULL TILT BOOGIE BAND)**	30	4 May72

– Down on me / Bye, bye baby / All is loneliness / Piece of my heart / Road block / Flower in the sun / Summertime / Ego rock / Half moon / Kozmic blues / Move over / Try (just a little bit harder) / Get it while you can / Ball and chain. *(re-iss. Sep87; 460128-1/4) (cd-iss. Aug93; 466838-2)*

	C.B.S.	Columbia
Jul 72. (7") *(CBS 8241)* <45630> **DOWN ON ME (live). / BYE, BYE BABY (live)**		91
Jul 73. (lp) *(CBS 65470)* <32168> **JANIS JOPLIN'S GREATEST HITS**		37

– Piece of my heart / Summertime / Try (just a little bit harder) / Cry baby / Me and Bobby McGee / Down on me / Get it while you can / Bye, bye baby / Move over / Ball and chain. *(re-iss. Sep82 & May90 lp/c; CBS/40 32190) (cd-iss. 1988; 831 726-2) (cd re-iss. Oct94 on 'Sony'; 476555-2)*

	C.B.S.	Columbia
May 75. (d-lp) *(CBS 88115)* <33345> **JANIS (soundtrack) (includes rare 1963-65 material)**		54
1975. (7") (13-33205) **ME AND BOBBY McGHEE. / GET IT WHILE YOU CAN**		-
Mar 76. (7") *(CBS 3960)* **PIECE OF MY HEART. / KOZMIC BLUES**		-
Jul 80. (d-lp) <*(CBS 88492)*> **ANTHOLOGY** *(d-cd-iss. Jun97 on 'Columbia'; 467 405-2)*		-
Feb 82. (lp) *(CBS 85354)* **FAREWELL SONG**		-
Nov 84. (d-c) **PEARL / CHEAP THRILLS**		-
Jun 86. (lp/c) *(CBS/40 54731)* **GOLDEN HIGHLIGHTS OF JANIS JOPLIN**		-
Dec 90. (3xcd-box) (467387-2) **CHEAP THRILLS / PEARL / I GOT DEM OL' KOZMIC BLUES AGAIN**		-
Sep 92. (d-cd) *Sony*; (4610202) **PEARL / I GOT DEM OL' KOZMIC BLUES AGAIN!**		-
Nov 92. (cd) *I.T.M.; (ITM 960001)* **MAGIC OF LOVE**		-
Sep 93. (cd) *I.T.M.; (ITM 960007)* **LIVE AT WOODSTOCK, 1969 (live)**		
Jan 94. (3xcd-box) *Legacy; (CD 48845-2)* **JANIS**		
Dec 94. (cd) *Columbia;* **THE BEST**		
Apr 95. (cd) *Legacy; (478515-2)* **18 ESSENTIAL SONGS**		
Aug 98. (cd) ; **THE ULTIMATE COLLECTION**	26	

JOSEF K / Paul HAIG (dig out; Great Alt & Indie . . .)

JOURNEY

Formed: San Francisco, California, USA . . . early 1973, originally as The GOLDEN GATE BRIDGE by NEAL SCHON, GEORGE TICKNER, ROSS VALORY and PRAIRIE PRINCE. Due to manager Walter Herbert auditioning through a radio station for the group name, they settled with JOURNEY. They made their live debut on the 31st of December 1973 in front of over 10,000 people at San Francisco's 'Wonderland' venue. Prior to the recording of their eponymous first album in 1975, (the group had secured a deal with 'Columbia'), another SANTANA veteran, GREGG ROLIE, was added, while English-born AYNSLEY DUNBAR replaced the TUBES-bound 'PRINCE. The debut, and subsequent releases, 'LOOK INTO THE FUTURE' (1976) and 'NEXT' (1977), focused on jazzy art-rock, although major changes were afoot by 1978's 'INFINITY'. With the addition of ex-ALIEN PROJECT vocalist, STEVE PERRY, the group were transformed from noodling jam-merchants into sleek AOR-pomp exponents set for American FM radio domination. Produced by Roy Thomas Baker (QUEEN), the album saw PERRY's strident, impressively dynamic vocals given free rein over a new improved pop-friendly format, gleaming synths and irresistible hooks now the order of the day. The record also gave JOURNEY a near brush with the Top 20, a feat they'd achieve with 'EVOLUTION' (1979). By this juncture, DUNBAR had departed for JEFFERSON STARSHIP, his replacement being STEVE SMITH on a set which provided JOURNEY with their biggest hit single to date (Top 20) in 'LOVIN', TOUCHIN', SQUEEZIN'. The following year's 'DEPARTURE' album performed even better, JOURNEY finally nearing their ultimate destination, i.e. the top of the US charts. Enhanced by the polished pop instincts of ex-BABYS' frontman JONATHAN CAIN (a replacement for ROLIE, who went solo, later forming The STORM with VALORY and SMITH), JOURNEY scored their first (and only) No.1 album with the massively successful 'ESCAPE' (1981). The record spawned an unprecedented three US Top 10 hits, namely 'WHO'S CRYING NOW', 'OPEN ARMS' and the swooning 'DON'T STOP BELIEVIN'. Despite almost universal critical derision from the more elitist factions of the music press, JOURNEY continued to capture the lucrative middle ground between pop and tasteful metal, even breaking into the previously impenetrable UK Top 10 with 'FRONTIERS' (1983). The same month, SCHON released his second solo collaboration with keyboard wizard, JAN HAMMER, 'HERE TO STAY', while PERRY subsequently launched his solo career to huge success with the melodramatic 'OH SHERRIE' single and 'STREET TALK' (1984) album. JOURNEY eventually regrouped in the mid-80's, the band now comprising the core trio of PERRY, SCHON and CAIN, augmented by RANDY JACKSON and LARRIE LONDIN. The resulting album, 'RAISED ON RADIO' (1986) proved to be JOURNEY's end, the group bowing out on a high point. Following an official split in early '87, CAIN (along with VALORY) joined MICHAEL BOLTON, while SCHON eventually hooked up with JOHN WAITE in BAD ENGLISH, before forming HARDLINE in '92 with ROLIE and SMITH. • **Trivia:** A couple of JOURNEY tracks, featured on the 1980 & 1981 film soundtracks of 'Caddyshack' & 'Heavy Metal'.

Album rating: JOURNEY (*3) / LOOK INTO THE FUTURE (*4) / NEXT (*3) / IN THE BEGINNING compilation (*4) / INFINITY (*6) / EVOLUTION (*5) / DEPARTURE (*4) / CAPTURED (*7) / ESCAPE (*8) / FRONTIERS (*6) / RAISED ON RADIO (*7) / THE BEST OF JOURNEY compilation (*8) / TIME 3 compilation (*7) / TRIAL BY FIRE (*4)

NEAL SCHON (b.27 Feb'54, San Mateo, Calif.) – lead guitar, vocals (ex-SANTANA) / **GREGG ROLIE** (b.17 Jun'47) – vocals, keyboards (ex-SANTANA) / **GEORGE TICKNER** – guitar, vocals / **ROSS VALORY** (b. 2 Feb'49) – bass, vocals (ex-STEVE MILLER BAND) / **AYNSLEY DUNBAR** (b.1946, Liverpool, England) – drums (ex-FRANK ZAPPA, ex-JOHN MAYALL, ex-JEFF BECK) repl. PRAIRIE PRINCE who joined The TUBES

	C.B.S.	Columbia
Apr 75. (lp/c) *(CBS/40 80724)* <33388> **JOURNEY**		

– Of a lifetime / In the morning day / Kohoutek / To play some music / Topaz / In my lonely feeling – Conversations / Mystery mountain. *(cd-iss. Oct93 on 'Sony Collectors'; 983313-2) (cd re-iss. Oct94 on 'Columbia'; 477854-2)*

	C.B.S.	Columbia
Jun 75. (7") <10137> **TO PLAY SOME MUSIC. / TOPAZ**	-	

—— (Apr'75) reverted to a quartet when TICKNER departed

	C.B.S.	Columbia
Jan 76. (lp/c) *(CBS/40 69203)* <33904> **LOOK INTO THE FUTURE**		100

– On a Saturday nite / It's all too much / Anyway / She makes me (feel alright) / You're on your own / Look into the future / Midnight dreamer / I'm gonna leave you. *(re-iss. Mar82; CBS 32102)*

	C.B.S.	Columbia
Mar 76. (7") <10324> **ON A SATURDAY NIGHT. / TO PLAY SOME MUSIC**	-	
Jul 76. (7") <10370> **SHE MAKES ME (FEEL ALRIGHT). / IT'S ALL TOO MUCH**	-	
Feb 77. (7") <10522> **SPACEMAN. / NICKEL AND DIME**	-	
Feb 77. (lp/c) *(CBS/40 81554)* <34311> **NEXT**		85

– Spaceman / People / I would find you / Here we are / Hustler / Next / Nickel & dime / Karma.

—— (Jun'77) added **ROBERT FLEISCHMAN** – lead vocals

—— (Oct77) **STEVE PERRY** (b.22 Jan'53, Hanford, Calif.) – lead vocals; repl. FLEISCHMAN

	C.B.S.	Columbia
Mar 78. (7") *(CBS 6238)* <10700> **WHEEL IN THE SKY. / CAN DO**		57
May 78. (lp/c) *(CBS/40 82244)* <34912> **INFINITY**	21	Feb78

– Lights / Feeling that way / Anytime / La do da / Patiently / Wheel in the sky / Somethin' to hide / Winds of March / Can do / Opened the door. *(cd-iss. 1988; CD 82244) (cd re-iss. Nov96 on 'Columbia'; 486665-2)*

	C.B.S.	Columbia
Jun 78. (7") <10757> **ANYTIME. / CAN DO**	-	83
Aug 78. (7") *(CBS 6392)* **LIGHTS. / OPEN THE DOOR**	-	-
Aug 78. (7") <10800> **LIGHTS. / SOMETHIN' TO HIDE**	-	68

—— (Nov'78) **STEVE SMITH** – drums repl. DUNBAR who joined JEFFERSON STARSHIP (above now alongside SCHON, ROLIE, PERRY and VALORY)

Apr 79. (lp/c) (CBS/40 83566) <35797> **EVOLUTION** `100` `20`
– Sweet and simple / Just the same way / Do you recall / City of angels / Lovin', touchin', squeezin' / Daydream / When you're alone (it ain't easy) / Lady luck / Too late / Lovin' you is easy / Majestic. (re-iss. Jul83 lp/c; CBS/40 32342) (cd-iss. Oct93 on 'Sony Collectors'; 982737-2) (cd re-iss. Nov96 on 'Columbia'; 486666-2)

Apr 79. (7") <10928> **JUST THE SAME WAY. / SOMETHIN' TO HIDE** `-` `58`

Sep 79. (7") (CBS 7890) <11036> **LOVIN', TOUCHIN', SQUEEZIN'. / DAYDREAM** `-` `16` Jul79

Dec 79. (7") <11143> **TOO LATE. / DO YOU RECALL** `-` `70`

Feb 80. (7") <11213> **ANY WAY YOU WANT IT. / WHEN YOU'RE ALONE (IT AIN'T EASY)** `-` `23`

Mar 80. (lp/c) (CBS/40 84101) <36339> **DEPARTURE** `8`
– Any way you want it / Walks like a lady / Someday soon / People and places / Precious time / Where were you / I'm cryin' / Line of fire / Departure / Good morning girl / Stay awhile / Homemade love. (re-iss. Feb86 lp/c; CBS/40 32714) (cd-iss. 1987; CD 84101) (cd re-iss. Nov96 on 'Columbia'; 486667-2)

May 80. (7"/12") (CBS/12 8558) **ANY WAY YOU WANT IT. / DO YOU RECALL** `-`

May 80. (7") <11275> **WALKS LIKE A LADY. / PEOPLE AND PLACES** `-`

Aug 80. (7") <11339> **GOOD MORNING GIRL. / STAY AWHILE** `-` `55`

Feb 81. (d-lp) (CBS 88525) <37016> **CAPTURED (live)** `9`
– Majestic / Where were you / Just the same way / Line of fire / Lights / Stay awhile / Too late / Dixie highway / Feeling that way / Anytime / Do you recall / Walks like a lady / La da da / Lovin', touchin', squeezin' / Wheel in the sky / Any way you want it / The party's over (hopelessly in love). (re-iss. Sep87 d-lp/d-c/cd; 451132-1/-4/-2) (cd re-iss. Jun89; CD 88525) (cd re-iss. Nov96 on 'Columbia'; 486661-2)

Mar 81. (7") (CBS 9578) <60505> **THE PARTY'S OVER (HOPELESSLY IN LOVE) (live). / WHEEL IN THE SKY (live)** `34` Feb81

—— (Apr'81) **JONATHAN CAIN** (b.26 Feb'50, Chicago, Illinois) – keyboards, guitar, vocals (ex-BABYS) repl. ROLIE who went solo, and later formed The STORM with VALORY and SMITH

Aug 81. (lp/c) (CBS/40 85138) <37408> **ESCAPE** `32` `1`
– Don't stop believin' / Stone in love / Who's crying now / Keep on runnin' / Still they ride / Escape / Lay it down / Dead or alive / Mother, father / Open arms. (cd-iss. May87; CD 85138) (cd re-iss. Feb88 lp/c; 460185-1/-4) (cd re-iss. Apr89; 460285-2) (cd re-iss. Nov96 on 'Columbia'; 486662-2)

Jul 81. (7") <02241> **WHO'S CRYING NOW. / MOTHER, FATHER** `4`

Aug 81. (7"/12") (A/TA 1467) **WHO'S CRYING NOW. / ESCAPE** `-`

Dec 81. (7"/12"/12"pic-d) (A/+13/11 1728) <02567> **DON'T STOP BELIEVIN'. / NATURAL THING** `62` `9` Oct81

Apr 82. (7") (A 2057) <02687> **OPEN ARMS. / LITTLE GIRL** `2` Jan82

May 82. (7") <02883> **STILL THEY RIDE. / RAZA DEL SOL** `-` `19`

Aug 82. (7") (A 2725) **WHO'S CRYING NOW. / DON'T STOP BELIEVIN'** `46` `-`
(12") (TA 2725) – ('A'side) / The Journey story (14 best snips).

Oct 82. (7") (A 2890) **STONE IN LOVE. / ONLY SOLUTIONS** `-` `-`

Feb 83. (lp/c) (CBS 25261) <38504> **FRONTIERS** `6` `2`
– Separate ways (worlds apart) / Send her my love / Chain reaction / After the fall / Faithfully / Edge of the blade / Troubled child / Back talk / Frontiers / Rubicon. (cd-iss. 1988; CD 25261) (cd re-iss. Nov96 on 'Columbia'; 486663-2)

Feb 83. (7"/12") (A/+13 3077) <03513> **SEPARATE WAYS (WORLDS APART). / FRONTIERS** `8`

Apr 83. (7") <03840> **FAITHFULLY. / FRONTIERS** `12`

Apr 83. (7") (A 3358) **FAITHFULLY. / EDGE OF THE BLADE** `-`

Jul 83. (7") <04004> **AFTER THE FALL. / OTHER SOLUTIONS** `-` `23`

Jul 83. (7") (A 3692) **AFTER THE FALL. / RUBICON** `-`
(12"+=) (TA 3692) – Any way you want me / Don't stop believin'.

Sep 83. (7") <04151> **SEND HER MY LOVE. / CHAIN REACTION** `-`

—— (the band take on some solo projects, see further below)

Feb 85. (7") (A 6058) <29090> **ONLY THE YOUNG. / (B-side by Sammy Hagar)** `-` `9` Jan85
(above songs from the film 'Vision Quest' on 'Geffen' records)

—— **PERRY, SCHON** and **CAIN** regrouped and added **RANDY JACKSON** – bass (ex-ZEBRA) / **LARRIE LONDIN** – drums

Apr 86. (7") (A 7095) <05869> **BE GOOD TO YOURSELF. / ONLY THE YOUNG** `9`
(12"+=) (TA 7095) – Any way you want it / Stone in love.
(d7"+=) (DA 7095) – After the fall / Rubicon.

May 86. (lp/c/cd) (CBS/40/CD 26902) <> **RAISED ON RADIO** `22` `4`
– Girl can't help it / Positive touch / Suzanne / Be good to yourself / Once you love somebody / Happy to give / Raised on radio / I'll be alright without you / It could have been you / The eyes of a woman / Why can't this night go on forever. (re-iss. Apr91 on 'Columbia' cd/c; 467992-2/-4) (cd re-iss. Nov96 on 'Columbia'; 486664-2)

Jul 86. (7") (A 7265) <06134> **SUZANNE. / ASK THE LONELY** `17` Jun86
(12"+=) (TA 7265) – Raised on radio.

—— (Aug'86) **MIKE BAIRD** – drums repl. LONDIN

Oct 86. (7") (650116-7) <06302> **GIRL CAN'T HELP IT. / IT COULD HAVE BEEN YOU** `17` Aug86

Dec 86. (7") <06301> **I'LL BE ALRIGHT WITHOUT YOU. / THE EYES OF A WOMAN** `14`

Apr 87. (7") <07043> **WHY CAN'T THIS NIGHT GO ON FOREVER. / POSITIVE TOUCH** `-` `60`

—— split early '87. CAIN and VALORY joined MICHAEL BOLTON. SCHON joined BAD ENGLISH in '89, then HARDLINE in '92 with ROLIE and SMITH.

NEAL SCHON / JAN HAMMER

collaboration with HAMMER – keyboards (solo)

		C.B.S.	Columbia

Nov 81. (lp/c) (CBS/40 85355) <37600> **UNTOLD PASSION** (instrumental) `Oct81`
– Wasting time / I'm talking to you / The ride / I'm down / Arc / It's alright / Hooked on love / On the beach / Untold passion.

Feb 83. (lp/c) (CBS/40 25229) <38428> **HERE TO STAY**
– No more lies / Don't stay away / (You think you're) So hot / Turnaround / Self

defence / Long time / Time again / Sticks and stones / Peace of mind / Covered by midnight.

Mar 83. (7") <03785> **NO MORE LIES. / SELF DEFENCE** `-` `-`

—— **NEAL SCHON** collaborated next (May'84) on album 'THROUGH THE FIRE' with **SAMMY HAGAR, KENNY AARONSON** & **MIKE SHRIEVE.**

STEVE PERRY

		C.B.S.	Columbia

May 84. (7") (A 4342) <04391> **OH SHERRIE. / DON'T TELL ME WHY YOU'RE LEAVING** `3` Mar84
(12"+=) (TA 4342) – I believe.

May 84. (lp/c) (CBS/40 25967) <39334> **STREET TALK** `12` Apr84
– Oh Sherrie / I believe / Go away / Foolish heart / It's only love / She's mine / You should be happy / Running alone / Captured by the moment / Strung out.

Jul 84. (7") (A 4638) <04496> **SHE'S MINE. / YOU SHOULD BE HAPPY** `21` Jun84

Sep 84. (7") <04598> **STRUNG OUT. / CAPTURED BY THE MOMENT** `-` `40`

Jan 85. (7") (A 6017) <04693> **FOOLISH HEART. / IT'S ONLY LOVE** `-` `18` Nov84

—— **STEVE PERRY** released solo recordings between 88-89. In Aug'94, 'Columbia' issued his album 'FOR THE LOVE OF STRANGE MEDICINE' (it hit UK No.64), the record included US hits, 'YOU BETTER WAIT' and 'MISSING YOU'.

The STORM

ROLIE – vocals, keyboards / **ROSS VALORY** – bass / **STEVE SMITH** – drums) with **KEVIN CHALFANT** – vocals (ex-707) / **JOSH RAMOS** – guitar (ex-LE MANS)

		East West	Interscope

Oct 91. (c-s) <98726> **I'VE GOT A LOT TO LEARN ABOUT LOVE / GIMME LOVE** `-` `26`

Nov 91. (cd/c/lp) <(7567 91741-2/-4/-1)> **THE STORM** `-`
– You got me waiting / I've got a lot to learn about love / In the raw / You're gonna miss me / Call me / Show me the way / I want you back / Still loving you / Touch and go / Gimme love / Take me away / Can't live without your love.

—— **RON WIKSO** – drums repl. SMITH

		not iss.	Bulletproof

Jan 96. (cd) **EYE OF THE STORM** `-`
– Don't give up / Waiting for the world to change / I want to be with the one / To have and to hold / Livin' it up / Love isn't easy / Fight for the right / Give me tonight / Sould of a man / What ya doing tonight / Come out of the rain / Long time coming.

HARDLINE

NEAL SCHON – lead guitar, vocals / **JOHNNY SCHON** – vocals / **JOEY GIOELLI** – guitar / **TODD JENSEN** – bass (ex-DAVID LEE ROTH) / **DEAN CASTRONOVO** – drums (ex-BAD ENGLISH)

		M.C.A.	M.C.A.

May 92. (cd) <(MCAD 10586)> **DOUBLE ECLIPSE** `-`
– Life's a bitch / Dr. love / Red car / Change of heart / Everything / Taking me down / Hot Cheri / Bad taste / Can't find my way / I'll be there / 31-91 / In the hands of time.

Jun 92. (c-s) <54548> **CAN'T FIND MY WAY / HOT CHERIE / TAKIN' ME DOWN / I'LL BE THERE** `-` `-`

JOURNEY

re-formed the quintet in 1996

		Columbia	Columbia

Oct 96. (cd/c) (4852644-2/-4) **TRIAL BY FIRE** `3`
– Message of love / One more / When you love a woman / If he should break your heart / Forever in blue / Castles burning / Don't be down on me baby / Still she cries / Colours of the spirit / When I think of you / Easy to fall / Can't tame the lion / It's just the rain / Trial by fire / Baby I'm leaving you.

Oct 96. (c-s) <78428> **WHEN YOU LOVE A WOMAN / MESSAGE OF LOVE / OPEN ARMS** `-` `12`

– compilations, others, etc. –

on 'CBS' UK / 'Columbia' US, unless mentioned otherwise

Sep 80. (d-lp) (CBS 22073) <36324> **IN THE BEGINNING** (from first 3 albums) `Jan80`

Dec 82. (c-ep) (40 2908) **CASSETTE EP** `-`
– Don't stop believin' / Who's crying now / Open arms / Lovin' touchin' squeezin'.

Aug 82. (7") <03133> **OPEN ARMS. / THE PARTY'S OVER** `-`

Aug 82. (7") <03134> **DON'T STOP BELIEVIN'. / WHO'S CRYING NOW** `-`

Feb 83. (d-c) (EPC-40 22150) **INFINITY / NEXT** `-`

Aug 87. (d-lp) (CBSJ 241) **FRONTIERS / ESCAPE** `-`

Nov 88. (lp/c/cd) (463149-1/-4/-2) <44493> **GREATEST HITS** `10`
– Only the young / Don't stop believin' / Wheel in the sky / Faithfully / I'll be alright with you / Any way you want it / Ask the lonely / Who's crying now / Separate ways (worlds apart) / Lights / Lovin', touchin', squeezin' / Open arms / Girl can't help it / Send her my love / Be good to yourself. (cd re-iss. Apr96 on 'Columbia'; 463149-2)

Jan 89. (7") (654541-7) **WHO'S CRYING NOW. / OPEN ARMS** `-`
(12"+=/cd-s+=) (654541-6/-2) – Suzanne / Don't stop believing.

—— (now on 'Columbia' unless mentioned otherwise)

Dec 92. (t-cd/t-c) (472810-2/-4) <48937> **TIME 3** `90`
(re-iss. Apr98; C3K 65159)

Jan 93. (c-s) <74842> **LIGHTS (live) / (6 album excerpts)** `-` `74`

Apr 98. (cd/c) (489703-2/-4) <69139> **GREATEST HITS LIVE (live)**

JOY DIVISION

Formed: Salford, Manchester, England . . . mid'77 initially as The STIFF KITTENS by IAN CURTIS, BERNARD ALBRECHT, PETER HOOK and STEPHEN MORRIS. By the time they were ready to take the stage for the first time, the group were going under the WARSAW moniker, finally settling on JOY DIVISION later that year. A term used by the Nazis for Jewish prostitutes, the band had taken the name from the book, 'House Of Dolls'; unsurprisingly, they ran into a little media trouble, the press subsequently speculating about their supposedly fascistic tendencies and unfairly branding them little Adolfs. Particularly controversial was the track, 'AT A LATER DATE', included on the 'Virgin' various artists punk sampler, 'Short Circuit: Live At The Electric Circus'. A vinyl debut proper came with the limited EP, 'AN IDEAL FOR LIVING', although it was through manager Rob Gretton and a subsequent deal with the emerging 'Factory' records that JOY DIVISION's career really got off the ground. Their first recordings for the label were a couple of tracks, 'GLASS' and 'DIGITAL', featured on a 'Factory' sampler (In mid-'79, a further two tracks, 'AUTO-SUGGESTION' and 'FROM SAFETY TO WHERE', surfaced on the 'Fast' records compilation EP, 'Earcom 2'), while their legendary Martin Hannett-produced debut album, 'UNKNOWN PLEASURES' was finally released later that summer. Groundbreaking in its bass-heavy, skeletal sound and evocation of urban alienation, isolation and despair, the record ensured CURTIS's position as a latter day messiah of existential angst; while his lyrics trawled the underbelly of the human psyche with disturbing clarity, his sub-JIM MORRISON ruminations were a blueprint for every pasty-faced goth pretender of the next decade. Tony Wilson's faith in the band was such that he contributed his life savings of over £8,000 towards the album's cost, the 'Factory' supremo's investment rewarded as the record topped the indie charts and JOY DIVISION became the foremost post-punk cult act. Yet even as the hypnotic rhythms of sublime new single, 'TRANSMISSION', hinted at an equally compelling new direction, CURTIS's robotic contortions and trance-like stage presence were giving way to epileptic fits as the singer struggled to cope with the increasing demands of live work. Tragically, on the 18th May, 1980, depressed with the break-up of his marriage and his worsening illness, CURTIS hanged himself. Ironically, JOY DIVISION scored their first chart hit a month later with the seminal 'LOVE WILL TEAR US APART'; the loss of such a fiercely individual talent was underlined as the track suggested a singer (and indeed, band) at the very apex of their creative potential. CURTIS had actually recorded a full album's worth of material before his death, released that summer as 'CLOSER'; even more lyrically unsettling, the record's bleak vision nevertheless pre-empted rock's dancefloor embrace on the synth-laced likes of 'ISOLATION', as well as forming the basis for NEW ORDER's experiments in cross-genre innovation. The latter act were formed later that year from JOY DIVISION's ashes, while further CURTIS-era material was posthumously released in late '81 as 'STILL'. The band remain one of the most revered and certainly one of the most influential outfits to emerge from the punk 'revolution', the best of NEW ORDER's work an indication as to what musical heights JOY DIVISION might have scaled had CURTIS prolonged the battle with his personal demons.

Album rating: UNKNOWN PLEASURES (*10) / CLOSER (*10) / STILL part compilation/live (*8) / SUBSTANCE compilation (*9) / PERMANENT: JOY DIVISION 1995 remixes (*6)

IAN CURTIS (b.15 Jul'56, Macclesfield, England) – vocals / **BERNARD ALBRECHT** (b. BERNARD DICKEN, 4 Jan'56) – guitar, vocals / **PETER HOOK** (b.13 Feb'56, Salford, Manchester) – bass / **STEPHEN MORRIS** (b.28 Oct'57, Macclesfield) – drums

		Enigma	not iss.
Jun 78.	(7"ep) *(PSS 139)* **AN IDEAL FOR LIVING**	☐	-

 – An ideal for living / Warsaw / Leaders of men / No love lost / Failures. *(re-iss. Jul78 on 'Anonymous' 12"ep; ANON 1)*

		Factory	not iss.
Aug 79.	(lp) *(FACT 10)* **UNKNOWN PLEASURES**	☐	-

 – Disorder / Day of the lords / Candidate / Insight / New dawn fades / She's lost control / Shadowplay / Wilderness / Interzone / I remember nothing. *(re-dist.Jul80, hit No.71) (re-iss. Jul82; same) (c-iss.Nov84; FACT 10C) (cd-iss. Apr86; FACD 10) (re-iss. Jul93 on 'Centredate-London' cd/c; 520016-2) <US-iss.1989 on 'Qwest' lp/c/cd; 1-/4-/2-25840>*

Oct 79.	(7") *(FAC 13)* **TRANSMISSION. / NOVELTY**	☐	-	

 (re-iss. Oct80 as 12"; FAC 13-12)

Mar 80.	(7") *(SS 33-002)* **ATMOSPHERE. / DEAD SOULS**	-	- France	

 (above single released on 'Sordide Sentimentale' & now worth lots)

Jun 80.	(7") *(FAC 23)* **LOVE WILL TEAR US APART. / THESE DAYS**	13	-	

 (re-iss. Oct80 as 12"+=; FAC 23-12) – ('A'version). (re-iss. Oct83; same); hit UK No.19)

Jul 80.	(lp) *(FACT 25)* **CLOSER**	6	-	

 – Heart and soul / 24 hours / The eternal / Decades / Atrocity exhibition / Isolation / Passover / Colony / Means to an end. *(c-iss.Jul82; FACT 25C) (cd-iss. Apr86; FACD 25) (re-iss. Jul93 on 'Centredate-London' cd/c; 520015-2) <US-iss.1989 on 'Qwest' lp/c/cd; 1-/4/-2-25841>*

⎯⎯ After another fit of depression, IAN CURTIS hanged himself 18th May 1980. The others became NEW ORDER

– compilations, others, etc. –

Sep 80.	(12") *Factory Benelux; (FACTUS 2)* **ATMOSPHERE. / SHE'S LOST CONTROL**	☐	-
Apr 81.	(free 7"flexi) *Factory; (FAC 28)* **KOMAKINO. / INCUBATION**	-	-
May 81.	(7"ep/12"ep; as WARSAW) *Enigma; (PSS 138)* **THE IDEAL BEGINNING**	☐	-

 – Inside the line / Gutz / At a later date.

Oct 81.	(d-lp) *Factory; (FACT 40)* **STILL (live & rare)**	5	-

 – Exercise one / Ice age / The sound of music / Glass / The only mistake / Walked in line / The kill / Something must break / Dead souls / Sister Ray / Ceremony / Shadowplay / Means to an end / Passover / New dawn fades / Transmission / Disorder / Isolation / Decades / Digital. *(c-iss.Dec86; FACT 40C) (cd-iss. Mar90; FACD 40) (re-iss. Jul93 on 'Centredate-London' cd/c; 520014-2/-4) <US-iss.1989 on 'Qwest' lp/c/cd; 26495>*

Nov 86.	(12"ep) *Strange Fruit; (SFPS 013)* **THE PEEL SESSIONS (31.1.79)**	☐	-

 – Exercise one / Insight / She's lost control / Transmission. *(re-iss. Jul88 cd-ep; SFPSCD 013)*

Sep 87.	(12"ep) *Strange Fruit; (SFPS 033)* **THE PEEL SESSIONS 2 (26.11.79)**	☐	-

 – Love will tear us apart / 24 hours / Colony / The sound of music. *(re-iss. Jul88 cd-ep; SFPSCD 033)*

1987.	(7"ep+book) *Stampa; (SCONIC 001)* **YOU'RE NO GOOD FOR ME / KOMAKINO / INCUBATION / INCUBATION (version)**	-	- Italy

Jun 88.	(7") *Factory; (FAC 213-7)* **ATMOSPHERE. / THE ONLY MISTAKE**	34	-

 (12"+=) *(FAC 213)* – The sound of music.
 (cd-s) *(FACD 213)* – ('A'side) / Love will tear us apart / Transmission.

Jul 88.	(lp/c/dat)(cd) *Factory; (FACT 250/+C/D)(FACD 250) / Qwest; <1-/4-/2-25747>* **SUBSTANCE** (The best of..)	7	-

 – She's lost control / Dead souls / Atmosphere / Love will tear us apart / Warsaw / Leaders of men / Digital / Transmission / Auto-suggestion. *(cd+=) – (7 extra tracks). (re-iss. Jul93 on 'Centredate-London' cd/c; 520 014-2/-4)*

Sep 90.	(cd/c) *Strange Fruit; (SFR CD/MC 111)* **COMPLETE PEEL SESSIONS**	☐	-

Jun 95.	(c-s) *London; (YOJC 1)* **LOVE WILL TEAR US APART (radio version)** *('A'-original version)*	19	-

 (12"+=/cd-s+=) *(YOJ T/CD 1)* – These days / Transmission.

Jun 95.	(cd/c/d-lp) *London; (828 624-2/-4/-1) / Warners; <45979>* **PERMANENT: JOY DIVISION 1995** (remixes)	16	- Aug95

 – Love will tear us apart / Transmission / She's lost control / Shadow play / Day of the lords / Isolation / Passover / Heart and soul / 24 hours / These days / Novelty / Dead souls / The only mistake / Something must break / Atmosphere / Love will tear us apart (Permanent mix).

Jan 98.	(4xcd-box) *London; (<828 968-2>)* **HEART AND SOUL** (all material)	70	-
Feb 98.	(cd+book) *Sonic Book; (SB 10)* **ALL THE LYRICS**	☐	-

JUDAS PRIEST

Formed: Birmingham, England . . . 1969 by KK DOWNING and IAN HILL. In 1971, they recruited singer ROB HALFORD and drummer JOHN HINCH. Three years later, with a few hundred gigs behind them, they brought in second guitarist GLENN TIPTON. Signed to 'Decca' off-shoot label 'Gull', they unleashed a debut album, 'ROCKA ROLLA', the same year. The record made little impact and after replacing HINCH with ALAN MOORE, the band surfaced again in '76 with the excellent 'SAD WINGS OF DESTINY'. Following a resoundingly triumphant appearance at that year's Reading Festival, they signed to 'C.B.S.' in early '77. They soon had a UK Top 30 album with the ROGER GLOVER (Deep Purple)-produced 'SIN AFTER SIN', another metal masterpiece which included an unlikely, but effective cover of Joan Baez's 'DIAMONDS AND RUST'. While the leather clad JUDAS PRIEST weren't exactly original in their steadfast adherence to the leaden riffing and helium overdose of heavy metal, they helped to shape the genre's increasing preoccupation with all things grim 'n' nasty. 'STAINED CLASS' (1978), another Top 30 UK album, preferred such lyrical delights as 'SAINTS IN HELL', 'SAVAGE' and 'BEYOND THE REALMS OF DEATH', plus a cover of SPOOKY TOOTH's 'BETTER BY YOU, BETTER THAN ME', the record later having serious repercussions for the band (see below). Coming at the height of the NWOBHM explosion, 'BRITISH STEEL' (1980), was the band's biggest critical and commercial success to date, the Top 20 success of the 'LIVING AFTER MIDNIGHT' and 'BREAKING THE LAW' singles showing the more accessible, hook-driven face of the band. This was to be one of the most fertile periods of the 'PRIEST's career with a trio of consistent Top 20 albums; 'POINT OF ENTRY' (1981), 'SCREAMING FOR VENGEANCE' (1982) and 'DEFENDERS OF THE FAITH' (1984) were all testosterone-saturated howlers, the kind of British metal that just doesn't exist anymore. The latter housed the PMRC-baiting 'EAT ME ALIVE', securing the band's postion as perceived deviant enemy of the nation's lank-haired youth alongside the equally wholesome W.A.S.P. Late in 1985, two of their fans shot themselves while listening to a track off the 'STAINED CLASS' album, prompting the boys' parents to sue both JUDAS PRIEST and their label, 'Columbia'. They alleged the record contained subliminal satanic messages hidden in the lyrics, thus forcing the boys to commit suicide. This fiasco finally got to court in July '90, the judge ruling against the dead boys' parents, although he did fine the label a 5-figure sum for withholding the master tapes!!? Despite the controversy, fans were less enamoured with 'TURBO' (1986), 'PRIEST's attempts at guitar synthesized innovation cutting no ice with the band's metal diehards. 'RAM IT DOWN' (1988) was a return to harder fare while the band underwent a critical rebirth of sorts with the thrash-y 'PAINKILLER' (1990), their status acknowledged as grandaddy's of heavy metal and a glaring influence on the likes of METALLICA and SLAYER. ROB HALFORD has since left the band after forming side-project, FIGHT, the group soon turning into a full-time affair. The 'PRIEST returned in 1997 with a new frontman, the cornily-monikered "RIPPER" OWENS lending his eardrum-rupturing shriek over the tuneless assault of the poorly-received comeback set, 'JUGULATOR'.
• **Songwriters:** TIPTON, HALFORD & DOWNING on most, except extra

covers; THE GREEN MANALISHI (Fleetwood Mac) / JOHNNY B. GOODE (Chuck Berry).

Album rating: ROCKA ROLLA (*2) / SAD WINGS OF DESTINY (*8) / SIN AFTER SIN (*7) / STAINED CLASS (*6; recommended only to those without access to a gun, a bazooka, a tank or any tactical nuclear weapon) / KILLING MACHINE (*6) / UNLEASHED IN THE EAST (*7) / BRITISH STEEL (*8) / POINT OF ENTRY (*4) / SCREAMING FOR VENGEANCE (*8) / DEFENDERS OF THE FAITH (*6) / TURBO (*5) / PRIEST . . . LIVE! (*6) / RAM IT DOWN (*6) / PAINKILLER (*8) / METAL WORKS compilation (*8) / JUGULATOR (*3)

ROB HALFORD (b.25 Aug'51) – vocals repl. ALAN ATKINS / **KK DOWNING** (b. KENNETH, 27 Oct'51, West Midlands) – guitars / **GLENN TIPTON** (b.25 Oct'48, West Midlands) – guitar, vocals / **IAN HILL** (b.20 Jan'52, West Midlands) – bass / **JOHN HINCH** – drums repl. JOHN ELLIS

		Gull	Janus
Aug 74.	(7") (GULS 6) **ROCKA ROLLA. / NEVER SATISFIED**		-
Sep 74.	(lp) (GULP 1005) **ROCKA ROLLA**		-

– One for the road / Rocka rolla / Winter / Deep freeze / Winter retreat / Cheater / Never satisfied / Run of the mill / Dying to meet you / Caviar and meths. (re-iss. Sep77; same) <US-iss.Oct82 on 'Visa'; 7001> (re-iss. Nov85 on 'Fame' lp/c; FA41 3137-2/-4) (cd-iss. Nov87 on 'Line'; LICD 900101) (cd-iss. Mar93 on 'Repertoire'; RR 4305)

—— **ALAN MOORE** – drums (who had been 1971 member) returned to repl. HINCH

| Mar 76. | (7") (GULS 31) **THE RIPPER. / ISLAND OF DOMINATION** | | - |
| Apr 76. | (lp) (GULP 1015) <7019> **SAD WINGS OF DESTINY** | | |

– Prelude / Tyrant / Genocide / Epitaph / Island of domination / Victim of changes / The ripper / Epitaph / Dreamer deceiver. (pic-lp.Sep77; PGULP 1015) (re-iss. 1984 on 'Line' white-lp; LILP 4.00112) (cd-iss. Nov87; LICD 9.00112) (re-iss. cd May95 on 'Repertoire';)

—— **SIMON PHILLIPS** – drums repl. MOORE

		C.B.S.	Columbia
Apr 77.	(7") (CBS 5222) **DIAMONDS AND RUST. / DISSIDENT AGGRESSOR**		-
Apr 77.	(lp/c) (CBS/40 82008) <34587> **SIN AFTER SIN**	23	

– Sinner / Diamonds and rust / Starbreaker / Last rose of summer / Let us prey / Call for the priest / Raw deal / Here come the tears / Dissident aggressor. (re-iss. Mar81; CBS 32005) (re-iss. cd.Nov93 on 'Sony Collectors'; 983286-2) (cd re-iss. Feb97 on 'Epic'; 474684-2)

—— **LES BINKS** – drums repl. PHILLIPS

| Jan 78. | (7") (CBS 6077) **BETTER BY YOU, BETTER BY ME. / INVADER** | | - |
| Feb 78. | (lp/c) (CBS/40 82430) <35296> **STAINED CLASS** | 27 | |

– Exciter / White heat, red hot / Better by you, better by me / Stained class / Invader / Saints in Hell / Savage / Beyond the realms of death / Heroes end. (re-iss. Nov81; CBS 32075) (re-iss. May91 on 'Columbia' cd/c; CD/40 32075)

| Sep 78. | (7") (CBS 6719) **EVENING STAR. / STARBREAKER** | | - |
| Nov 78. | (red-lp/c) (CBS/40 83135) <36179> **KILLING MACHINE** <US-title 'HELL BENT FOR LEATHER'> | 32 | |

– Delivering the goods / Rock forever / Evening star / Hell bent for leather / Take on the world / Burnin' up / Killing machine / Running wild / Before the dawn / Evil fantasies. (re-iss. red-lp.Sep82; CBS 32218)

Oct 78.	(7") (CBS 6794) **BEFORE THE DAWN. / ROCK FOREVER**		-
Jan 79.	(7") (CBS 6915) **TAKE ON THE WORLD. / STARBREAKER (live)**		14
	(12"+=) (CBS12 6915) – White heat red hot (live).		
Apr 79.	(7") (CBS 7312) **EVENING STAR. / BEYOND THE REALMS OF DEATH**	53	
	(12"clear+=) (CBS12 7312) – The green Manalishi.		
May 78.	(7") <11000> **ROCK FOREVER. / THE GREEN MANALISHI (WITH THE TWO-PRONGED CROWN)**		-
Sep 79.	(lp/c) (CBS/40 83852) <36179> **UNLEASHED IN THE EAST (live)**	10	70

– Exciter / Running wild / Sinner / The ripper / The green manalishi (with the two-pronged crown) / Diamonds and rust / Victim of changes / Genocide / Tyrant. (free 7"w.a.) ROCK FOREVER / HELL BENT FOR LEATHER. / BEYOND THE REALMS OF DEATH (cd-iss. 1988; CD 83852) (re-iss. May94 on 'Columbia' cd/c; 468604-2/-4)

| Dec 79. | (7") <11135> **DIAMONDS AND RUST (live). / STARBREAKER (live)** | - | - |

—— **DAVE HOLLAND** – drums repl. BINKS

Mar 80.	(7") (CBS 8379) **LIVING AFTER MIDNIGHT. / DELIVERING THE GOODS (live)**	12	-
	(12"+=) (CBS12 8379) – Evil fantasies (live).		
Apr 80.	(lp/c) (CBS/40 84160) <36443> **BRITISH STEEL**	4	34

– Rapid fire / Metal gods / Breaking the law / Grinder / United / You don't have to be old to be wise / Living after midnight / The rage / Steeler. (re-iss. Jan84 lp/c; CBS/40 32412) (cd-iss. 1988; CD 32412) (cd re-iss. Jun94 on 'Sony'; 982725-2)

May 80.	(7") <11308> **LIVING AFTER MIDNIGHT. / METAL GODS**	-	
May 80.	(7") (CBS 8644) **BREAKING THE LAW. / METAL GODS**	12	
Aug 80.	(7") (CBS 8897) <11396> **UNITED. / GRINDER**	26	-
Feb 81.	(7") (CBS 9520) **DON'T GO. / SOLAR ANGELS**	51	-
Feb 81.	(lp/c) (CBS/40 84834) <37052> **POINT OF ENTRY**	14	39

– Heading out to the highway / Don't go / Hot rockin' / Turning circles / Desert plains / Solar angels / You say yes / All the way / Troubleshooter / On the run.

Apr 81.	(7") (A 1153) **HOT ROCKIN' / BREAKING THE LAW (live)**	60	-
	(12") (A12 1153) – ('A'side) / Steeler / You don't have to be old to be wise.		
Apr 81.	(7") <02083> **HEADING OUT TO THE HIGHWAY. / ROCK FOREVER**	-	-
Jul 82.	(lp/c) (CBS/40 85941) <38160> **SCREAMING FOR VENGEANCE**	11	17

– The hellion / Electric eye / Riding on the wind / Bloodstone / (Take these) Chains / Pain and pleasure / Screaming for vengeance / You've got another thing comin' / Fever / Devil's child. (re-iss. Feb86 lp/c; CBS/40 32712)

Aug 82.	(7"/7"pic-d) (A/+11 2611) **YOU'VE GOT ANOTHER THING COMIN'. / EXCITER (live)**	66	-
Oct 82.	(7") <03168> **YOU'VE GOT ANOTHER THING COMIN'. / DIAMONDS AND RUST.**	-	67
Oct 82.	(7") (A 2822) **(TAKE THESE) CHAINS. / JUDAS PRIEST AUDIO FILE**	-	-

Jan 84.	(7") (A 4054) **FREEWHEEL BURNING. / BREAKING THE LAW**	42	-
	(12"+=) (TA 4054) – You've got another thing comin'.		
Jan 84.	(lp/c) (CBS/40 25713) <39219> **DEFENDERS OF THE FAITH**	19	18

– Freewheel burning / Jawbreaker / Rock hard ride free / The sentinel / Love bites / Eat me alive / Some heads are gonna roll / Night comes down / Heavy duty / Defenders of the faith. (cd-iss. Jul84; CD 25713)

Feb 84.	(7") <04371> **SOME HEADS ARE GONNA ROLL. / BREAKING THE LAW (live)**	-	-
Mar 84.	(7") (A 4298) **SOME HEADS ARE GONNA ROLL. / THE GREEN MANALISHI (WITH THE TWO-PRONGED CROWN)**	-	-
	(12"+=) (TA 4298) – Jawbreaker.		
Apr 86.	(7") <04436> **JAWBREAKER. / LOVE BITES**	-	-
Apr 86.	(lp/c/cd) (CBS/40/CD 26641) <40158> **TURBO**	33	17

– Turbo lover / Locked in / Private property / Parental guidance / Rock you all around the world / Out in the cold / Wild night, hot and crazy days / Hot for love / Reckless. (re-iss. Feb89 lp/c/cd; 463365-1/-4/-2)

Apr 86.	(7") <07048> **TURBO LOVER. / HOT FOR LOVE**	-	-
May 86.	(7") (A 7144) **LOCKED IN. / RECKLESS**	-	-
	(ext.12"+=) (QTA 7144) – Desert plains (live) / Free wheel burning (live).		
May 86.	(7") <05856> **LOCKED IN. / HOT FOR LOVE**	-	-
Aug 86.	(7") <06142> **TURBO LOVER. / RESTLESS**	-	-
Nov 86.	(7") <06281> **PARENTAL GUIDANCE. / ROCK YOU AROUND THE WORLD**	-	-
Jun 87.	(d-lp/d/c/cd) (450639-1/-4/-2) <40794> **PRIEST . . . LIVE! (live)**	47	38

– Out in the cold / Heading out to the highway / Metal gods / Breaking the law / Love bites / Some heads are gonna roll / The sentinel / Private property / Rock you all around the world / Electric eye / Turbo lover / Free wheel burning / Parental guidance / Living after midnight / You've got another thing comin'. (cd+=) – Shout – Oh yeah!

		Atlantic	Columbia
Apr 88.	(7") (A 9114) <89114> **JOHNNY B. GOODE. / ROCK YOU ALL AROUND THE WORLD (live)**	64	
	(12"+=) (AT 9114) – Turbo lover (live).		
	(3"cd-s++=) (A 9114CD) – Living after midnight (live).		
May 88.	(lp/c/cd) (461108-1/-4/-2) **RAM IT DOWN**	24	31

– Ram it down / Heavy metal / Love zone / Come and get it / Hard as iron / Blood red skies / I'm a rocker / Johnny B. Goode / Love you to death / Monsters of rock.

—— **SCOTT TRAVIS** – drums (ex-RACER-X) repl. HOLLAND

		C.B.S.	Columbia
Sep 90.	(7"/c-s) (656273-7/-4) **PAINKILLER. / UNITED**	74	
	(12"+=/cd-s+=) (656273-6/-2) – Better by you, better than me.		
Sep 90.	(cd/c/lp) (467290-2/-4/-1) <46891> **PAINKILLER**	24	26

– Painkiller / Hell patrol / All guns blazing / Leather rebel / Metal meltdown / Night crawler / Between the hammer and the anvil / A touch of evil / Battle hymn (instrumental) / One shot at glory.

		Columbia	Columbia
Mar 91.	(7"/7"sha-pic-d/c-s) (656589-7/-0/-4) **A TOUCH OF EVIL. / BETWEEN THE HAMMER AND THE ANVIL**	58	
	(12"+=/cd-s+=) (656589-6/-2) – You've got another thing comin' (live).		

—— In Oct'92, HALFORD left after already forming FIGHT in 1991, taking with him SCOTT TRAVIS.

Apr 93.	(7"/c-s) (659097-7/-4) **NIGHT CRAWLER (Edit) / BREAKING THE LAW**	63	
	(cd-s+=) (659097-2) – Living after midnight.		
Apr 93.	(d-cd/d-c/t-lp) (473050-2/-4/-1) <53932> **METAL WORKS '73-'93** (compilation)	37	

– The hellion / Electric eye / Victim of changes / Painkiller / Eat me alive / Devil's child / Dissident aggressor / Delivering the goods / Exciter / Breaking the law / Hell bent for leather / Blood red skies / Metal gods / Before the dawn / Turbo lover / Ram it down / Metal meltdown// Screaming for vengeance / You've got another thing comin' / Beyond the realms of death / Solar angels / Bloodstone / Desert plains / Wild nights, hot & crazy days / Heading out to the highway / Living after midnight / A touch of evil / The rage / Night comes down / Sinner / Freewheel burning / Night crawler.

—— **"RIPPER" OWENS** – vocals; completed the line-up

		S.P.V.	CMC Int
Nov 97.	(cd/c/lp) (SPV 085 1878-2/-4/-1) <86224> **JUGULATOR**		82

– Jugulator / Blood stained / Dead meat / Death row / Decapitate / Burn in hell / Brain dead / Abductors / Bullet train / Cathedral spires.

– compilations, etc. –

Feb 78.	(pic-lp/lp) Gull; (P+/GULP 1026) **THE BEST OF JUDAS PRIEST** (early work)		-
	(cd-iss. May87 +=; GUCD 1026) – (2 extra tracks).		
Aug 80.	(7") Gull; (GULS 71) **THE RIPPER. / VICTIMS OF CHANGE**		-
	(12"+=) (GUL 71-12) – Never satisfied.		
Jun 83.	(12"white) Gull; (GULS 76-12) **TYRANT. / ROCKA ROLLA / GENOCIDE**		-
Jan 83.	(c-ep) C.B.S.; (A40 3067) **CASSETTE EP**		-
	– Breaking the law / Living after midnight / Take on the world / United.		
Aug 83.	(d-c) C.B.S.; (22161) **SIN AFTER SIN / STAINED GLASS**		-
Sep 83.	(7"ep/c-ep) (7SR/ 5018) **6 TRACK HITS**		-
	– Sinner / Exciter / Hell bent for leather / The ripper / Hot rockin' / The green manalishi.		
Aug 86.	(pic-lp) Shanghai; (PGLP 1026) **JUDAS PRIEST**		-
Nov 87.	(cd) Line; (LICD 900414) **HERO HERO**	-	- German
	(re-iss. 1988 on 'Gull' c/lp; ZC+/GUD 2005-6) (cd re-iss. Jul95 on 'Connoisseur'; CSAPCD 119)		
Feb 89.	(7") Old Gold; (OG 9864) **LIVING AFTER MIDNIGHT. / BREAKING THE LAW**	-	-
May 89.	(lp/c/cd) Castle; (CCS LP/MC/CD 213) **THE COLLECTION**	-	-
	– (first two albums)		
Mar 93.	(3xcd-box) Columbia; (468328-2) **BRITISH STEEL / SCREAMING FOR VENGEANCE / STAINED GLASS**	-	-
Apr 97.	(cd) Columbia; (487242-2) **LIVING AFTER MIDNIGHT**	-	-

JUNGLE BROTHERS

Formed: Brooklyn, New York, USA . . . 1986 by MIKE G, AFRIKA BABY BAMBAATAA and SAMMY B. After initiating a rap collective the NATIVE TONGUES (alongside compatriots DE LA SOUL and QUEEN LATIFAH) and sending a demo to DJ RED ALERT (of WRKS-FM), they subsequently landed a deal with the independent 'Idlers' label. A debut single in 1987, 'JIMBROWSKI' became an immediate underground fave, although it was the B-side, 'I'LL HOUSE YOU', which made The JUNGLE BROTHERS famous. A key track in the short-lived hip-house crossover scene, it became a Top 30 UK hit when re-issued as their first effort for 'Gee Street' in 1988. Along with the likes of PM DAWN, A TRIBE CALLED QUEST and the aforementioned DE LA SOUL, The JUNGLE BROTHERS purveyed a mellow strain of hip-hop perfectly suited to the second summer of love generation. Following on from their acclaimed debut set, 'STRAIGHT OUT THE JUNGLE' (1988), the group signed to 'Warners' at the turn of the decade. 'DONE BY THE FORCES OF NATURE' made the UK Top 50 early in 1990 yet despite being a hit among the hip hop fraternity and critics, it never took off commercially in the States. The 'BROTHERS were bypassed throughout the 90's as their contemporaries left them behind and gangsta rap reared its ugly head. Nevertheless, they made the first of many comeback attempts in 1993 via the 'J.BEEZ WIT THE REMEDY' album which featured former JB's, BOOTSY COLLINS, GARY "Mudbone" COOPER and BERNIE WORRELL. Four years on and newly signed to 'Gee Street', the group released 'RAW DELUXE' (1997), another consummate collection of retro-flavoured beats that pleased the faithful but failed to win many new converts. It did, however, spawn a couple of minor UK hits in the shape of 'BRAIN' and 'JUNGLE BROTHER', while a summer '98 remixed re-issue of 'I'LL HOUSE YOU' saw the boys back in the UK Top 30. They scored another Top 30 entry later that year with 'BECAUSE I GOT IT LIKE THAT', making it a hat-trick in summer '99 with the title track from the accompanying 'V.I.P.' album. An experimental effort co-written and recorded with the help of The PROPELLERHEADS' ALEX GIFFORD, the record proved that The JUNGLE BROTHERS were no longer backwards at going forwards as the new millennium loomed.

Album rating: STRAIGHT OUT THE JUNGLE (*8) / DONE BY THE FORCES OF NATURE (*7) / J. BEEZ WITH THE REMEDY (*5) / RAW DELUXE (*5) / V.I.P. (*5)

MIKE G (b. MICHAEL SMALL, 13 May'69) – vocals / **AFRIKA BABY BAMBAATAA** (b. NATHANIEL HALL, 22 Jun'70) – vocals / **SAMMY B** (b. SAMUEL BURWELL, 9 Dec'67) – DJ / with posse of others on keyboards, etc

	Warlock	Idlers
Oct 87. (12") <WAR 014> **JIMBROWSKI. / I'LL HOUSE YOU**	-	

Jul 88. (lp) (WAR 2704) **STRAIGHT OUT THE JUNGLE**
– Straight out the jungle / What's going on / Black is black / Jimbrowski / I'm gonna do you / I'll house you / On the run / Behind the bush / Because I got it like that / Braggin' and boastin' / Sounds of the safari / Jimmy's bonus beat. (re-iss. Oct88 on 'Gee Street' lp/c; GEE A/C 001) (cd-iss. Jul91; GEECD 001) (re-iss. Jul98 cd/d-lp; GEE 100283-2/-1)

Aug 88. (7"/12") (WAR 022/+12) **GIRL I'LL HOUSE YOU. /** ('A'instrumental)

	Gee Street	Gee Street
Oct 88. (7") (GEE 003) **I'LL HOUSE YOU. /**	22	
(12"+=/cd-s+=) (GEE 12/CD 003) – ('A'acappella) / Straight out the jungle.		
Feb 89. (7") (GEE 015) **BLACK IS BLACK. / STRAIGHT OUT THE JUNGLE**	72	
(12"+=) (GEET 015) – Ultrablack / In time.		
Feb 90. (7") (GEE 28) **'CAUSE I GOT IT LIKE THAT. / DUB IT LIKE THAT**		
(12"+=) (GEET 28) – ('A'instrumental) / Jungle pella.		
(12") (GEER 28) – ('A'-Ultranation mix) / ('A'-Ultranation instrumental) / ('A'-Richie Rich mix) / The break.		

	Warners	Warners
Jan 90. (lp/c/cd) (WX 332/+C)(K 926 072-2) **DONE BY THE FORCES OF NATURE**	41	

– Doin' our own dang (do it to the JB's mix) / Beyond this world / Feelin' alright / Sunshine / What 'U' waitin' '4' / "U" make me sweat (jungle fever mix) / Acknowledge your own history / Belly dancin' Dina / Good newz comin' / Done by the forces of nature / Beeds on a string / Tribe vibes / J. Beez comin' through / Black woman / In dayz "2" come / Kool accordin' "2" a jungle brother. (cd remixed.Aug90; 7599 26364-2)

Mar 90. (7"/c-s) (W 9865/+C) **WHAT 'U' WAITIN' '4'. / J.BEEZ COMING THRU (remix)** `35`
(12"+=/cd-s+=) (W 9865 T/CD) – ('A'-C.Jungle, C.Jungle mix) / ('A'-orchestra mix).
(cd-s) (W 9865CDX) – ('A'-Ritchie Fernie mix) / ('A'-Tony Humphries remix) / ('A'-Connection house mix).

Jul 90. (7"/c-s) (W 9754/+C) **DOIN' OUR OWN DANG. / ('A'-do it to the JB's mix)** `33`
(12") (W 9754T) – ('A'side) / ('A'-Norman Cook remix) / ('A'-Richie Fernie remix).
(cd-s) (W 9754CD) – ('A'-4 mixes above).
(cd-s) (W 9754CDX) – ('A'version) / ('A'instrumental) / ('A'dub plate mix).

—— added **TORTURE** (b. COLIN BOBB, 18 Oct'74, Guyana) – vocals

Jun 93. (cd/c/lp) <(7599 26679-2/-4/-1)> **J.BEEZ WIT THE REMEDY**
– 40 below trooper / Book of rhyme pages / My Jimmy weighs a ton / Good de hype shit / Blah bludify / Spark a new flame / I'm in love with Indica / Simple as that / All I think about is you / Good lookin' out / JB's comin' through / Spittin' wicked randomness / For the headz at Company Z / Man made material.

Jul 93. (7"/c-s) (W 0178/+C) **40 BELOW TROOPER. / ('A'version)**
(12"+=/cd-s+=) (W 0178 T/CD) – ('A'-2 instrumental remixes).

	Inner City Dance	not iss.
Sep 94. (cd-s) (ICD 003) **ORIGINAL GANGSTER. /**		-

	Gee Street	Gee Street
May 97. (cd/c/lp) (GEE 100028-2/-4/-1) <27001> **RAW DELUXE**		

– Jungle brother / Changes / Black man on track / Toe to toe / Moving along / Gettin money / Where you wanna go / Brain / Handle my business / How ya want it we got it / Bring it on / Jungle brother.

Jul 97. (12"/cd-s) (GEE 500038-6/-3) **BRAIN /** `52`
(cd-s) (500038-8) –

Nov 97. (12"/cd-s) (GEE 500049-6/-3) **JUNGLE BROTHER /** `56`
(cd-s) (GEE 500049-8) –
(re-iss. Apr98; same) – hit UK No.18.

Jun 98. (12"/cd-s) (FX/FCD 338) **I'LL HOUSE YOU '98 (mixes; Hitmen radio / Anthony acid & DJ Skribble vocal club / original / Hitmen)** `26`
(above issued on 'Ffrr')

—— now without SAMMY B (BURWELL)

Nov 98. (c-s/cd-s) (GEE 500359-5/-3) **BECAUSE I GOT IT LIKE THAT (mixes)** `32`
(cd-s) (GEE 500460-3) – ('A'mixes).
(12") (GEE 500359-6) – ('A'mixes).

—— in Feb'99, they were credited on a JUNIOR DELGADO single, 'BUFFALO SOLDIER' and a B-side of a PROPELLERHEADS platter

—— added **ALEX GIFFORD** (of The PROPELLERHEADS)

Jun 99. (12"/cd-s) (GEE 500795-6/-3) **V.I.P. (mixes by WISEGUYS & URBAN TAKEOVER)** `33`
(cd-s) (GEE 500795-8) – ('A'side) / Down with the Jbeez (featuring BLACK EYED PEAS and SENSE live).

Oct 99. (12"/cd-s) (GEE 501015-6/-3) **GET DOWN (mixes)** `52`
(cd-s) (GEE 501015-8) – ('A'mixes).

Nov 99. (cd/c/d-lp) (GEE 100829-2/-4/-1) <32532> **V.I.P.** `2000`
– V.I.P. / I remember / Get down / Early morning / Down with the J.Beez / Brothers / Party goin' on / Sexy body / Playing for keeps / J.Beez rock the dancehall / Freakin' you / Strictly dedicated / Jungle brother (true blue).

JUSTIFIED ANCIENTS OF MU MU (see under ⇒ KLF)

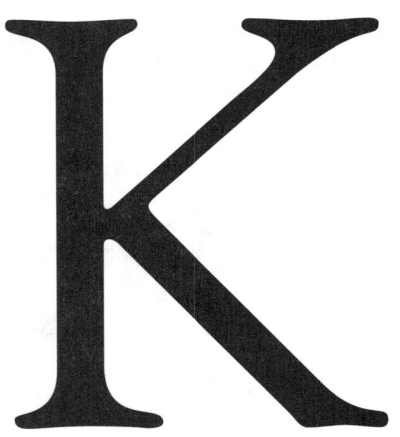

KALEIDOSCOPE US (dig out; Great Psychedelic . . .)

KALEIDOSCOPE UK (dig out; Great Psychedelic . . .)

KANSAS

Formed: Topeka, Kansas, USA . . . 1970 initially as WHITE CLOVER, by KERRY LIVGREN, DAVE HOPE and PHIL EHART. With the addition of classically trained ROBBY STEINHARDT, RICH WILLIAMS and frontman STEVE WALSH, the group adopted the KANSAS moniker during 1972. Two years of constant touring later, they signed to 'Kirshner' (the new label set up by industry guru, Don Kirshner) and hit the US Top 200 with their eponymous debut set. A windswept American answer to the British art-rock scene of the early 70's, KANSAS combined progressive, harmony laden muscle (somewhat akin to the likes of BOSTON or STYX) with ambitiously intricate 'suites'. Throughout the 70's, the band enjoyed increasing commercial success, the Jeff Glixman-produced 'LEFTOVERTURE' (1976) taking them into the US Top 5 for the first time on the back of the grandiose Top 10 smash, 'CARRY ON WAYWARD SON. For many fans, the subsequent triple-platinum 'POINT OF KNOW RETURN' (1977) marked the peak of the group's career, its string-laden pseudo-classical pretensions providing another Top 10 hit with 'DUST IN THE WIND'. KANSAS' more indulgent tendencies were glaringly evident on the rambling live set, 'TWO FOR THE SHOW' (1978), although as the 70's turned into the 80's, the group increasingly pursued a more accessible approach. Disillusioned with this direction, WALSH had already recorded a solo debut, 'SCHEMER-DREAMER' in 1980, eventually leaving the band following the 'AUDIO-VISIONS' (1980) set and forming a harder rocking outfit, STREETS. LIVGREN, meanwhile, had become a born-again Christian, the inspiration for his solo debut, 'SEEDS OF CHANGE' (1980). With JOHN ELEFANTE now in place as frontman, KANSAS cut a further couple of albums, 'VINYL CONFESSIONS' (1982) and 'DRASTIC MEASURES' (1983), before splitting in late '83. While LIVGREN and ELEFANTE both went on to successful careers in the Christian music field, EHART and WILLIAMS subsequently reformed KANSAS with former vocalist STEVE WALSH, fellow ex-STREETS man, BILLY GREER, and guitar maestro STEVE MORSE. Now signed to 'M.C.A.', the new improved KANSAS enjoyed middling chart success with 'POWER' (1986), an album which bore the stamp of WALSH's heavier work with STREETS. A follow-up set, 'IN THE SPIRIT OF THINGS' (1988), was a commercial failure, however, and the band found themselves without a record deal. Ploughing on, they re-introduced violin to their sound in 1991 courtesy of DAVID RAGSDALE, MORSE having left by the independently released concert set, 'LIVE AT THE WHISKY' (1993). A belated studio set, 'FREAKS OF NATURE' (1995) finally appeared in summer '95, KANSAS retaining a core fanbase despite their absence from the charts.

Album rating: KANSAS (*6) / SONG FOR AMERICA (*6) / MASQUE (*5) / LEFTOVERTURE (*7) / POINT OF KNOW RETURN (*6) / TWO FOR THE SHOW (*5) / MONOLITH (*6) / AUDIO-VISIONS (*6) / VINYL CONFESSIONS (*5) / DRASTIC MEASURES (*4) / THE BEST OF KANSAS compilation (*7) / POWER (*5) / IN THE SPIRIT OF THINGS (*5) / LIVE AT THE WHISKY (*2) / FREAKS OF NATURE (*3)

STEVE WALSH (b.1951, St. Joseph, Missouri) – vocals, keyboards, synthesizer / **KERRY LIVGREN** (b.18 Sep'49) – guitar, piano, synthesizer / **ROBBY STEINHARDT** (b.1951, Mississippi) – violin / **RICH WILLIAMS** (b.1951) – guitar / **DAVE HOPE** (b. 7 Oct'49) – bass / **PHIL EHART** (b.1951) – drums

		Kirshner	Kirshner
Nov 74.	(7") <4253> **CAN I TELL YOU. / THE PILGRIMAGE**	-	
Feb 75.	(7") <4256> **BRINGING IT ALL BACK. / LONELY WIND**	-	
Apr 75.	(lp) (KIR 80174) <32817> **KANSAS**		Jun74

– Can I tell you / Bringing it back / Lonely wind / Belexes / Journey from Mariabronn / The pilgrimage / Apercu / Death of Mother Nature suite. (cd-iss. Apr92 on 'Sony Collectors'; 982733-2) (cd re-iss. Feb97 on 'Epic'; 468883-2)

Apr 75.	(7") <4258> **SONG FOR AMERICA. / (part 2)**	-	

Aug 75.	(lp) (KIR 80740) <33385> **SONG FOR AMERICA**		57 Mar75

– Down the road / Song for America / Lamplight symphony / Lonely street / The Devil game / Incomudro – hymn to the Atman.

Feb 76.	(7") <4259> **IT TAKES A WOMAN'S LOVE (TO MAKE A MAN). / IT'S YOU**	-	
May 76.	(lp) (KIR 81180) <33806> **MASQUE**		70 Dec75

– It takes a woman's love (to make a man) / Two cents worth / Icarus – borne on wings of steel / All the world / Child of innocence / It's you / Mysteries and mayhem / The pinnacle.

Dec 76.	(lp) (KIR 81728) <34224> **LEFTOVERTURE**		5 Nov76

– Carry on wayward son / The wall / What's on my mind / Miracles out of nowhere / Opus insert / Questions of my childhood / Cheyenne anthem / Magnus opus: Father Padilla meets the gnat – Howling at the Moon – Man overboard – Industry on parade – Release the beavers – Gnat attack. (re-iss. Nov92 on 'Sony Collectors' cd/c; 982837-2/-4)

Dec 76.	(7") <4267> **CARRY ON WAYWARD SON. / QUESTIONS OF MY CHILDHOOD**	-	11
May 77.	(7") <4270> **WHAT'S ON MY MIND. / LONELY STREET**	-	
Nov 77.	(lp)<US-pic-lp> (KIR 82234) <34929> **POINT OF KNOW RETURN**		4 Oct77

– Point of know return / Paradox / The spider / Portrait (he knew) / Closet chronicles / Lightning's hand / Dust in the wind / Sparks of the tempest / Nobody's home / Hopelessly human. (cd-iss. Jul89 on 'C.B.S.'; CD 32361)

Dec 77.	(7") (S-KIR 5820) <4273> **POINT OF KNOW RETURN. / CLOSET CHRONICLES**		28 Oct77
Mar 78.	(7") (S-KIR 6205) <4274> **DUST IN THE WIND. / PARADOX**		6 Jan78
Jun 78.	(7") (S-KIR 4932) <4275> **CARRY ON WAYWARD SON. / QUESTIONS OF MY CHILDHOOD**	51	-
Jun 78.	(7") <4276> **PORTRAIT (HE KNEW). / LIGHTNING'S HAND**	-	64
Dec 78.	(d-lp) (KIR 88318) <PZ2 35560> **TWO FOR THE SHOW (live)**		32 Nov78

– Songs for America / Point of know return / Paradox / Icarus – borne on wings of steel / Portrait (he knew) / Carry on wayward son / Journey from Mariabronn / Dust in the wind / Lonely wind / Mysteries and mayhem / Lamplight symphony / The wall / Closet chronicles / Magnum opus: Father Padilla meets the gnat – Howling at the Moon – Man overboard – Industry on parade / Release the beavers – Gnat attack.

Jan 79.	(7") <4280> **LONELY WIND (live). / SONG FOR AMERICA (live)**	-	60
Jun 79.	(7") (S-KIR 7426) <4284> **PEOPLE OF THE SOUTH WIND. / STAY OUT OF TROUBLE**		23
Jul 79.	(lp) (KIR 83644) <36000> **MONOLITH**		10 May79

– On the other side / People of the south wind / Angels have fallen / How my soul cries out for you / A glimpse of home / Away from you / Stay out of trouble / Reason to be.

Sep 79.	(7") <4285> **REASON TO BE. / HOW MY SOUL CRIES OUT FOR YOU**	-	52
Sep 80.	(7") <4291> **HOLD ON. / DON'T OPEN YOUR EYES**	-	40
Oct 80.	(lp) (KIR 84500) <36588> **AUDIO-VISIONS**		26 Sep80

– Relentless / Anything for you / Hold on / Loner / Curtain of iron / Got to rock on / Don't open your eyes / No one together / No room for a stranger / Back door. (cd-iss. Mar96 on 'Epic'; 481161-2)

Dec 80.	(7") <4292> **GOT TO ROCK ON. / NO ROOM FOR A STRANGER**	-	76

—— **JOHN ELEFANTE** (b.1958, Levittown, N.Y.) – vocals, keyboards repl. WALSH who continued on recent solo work

Jul 82.	(7") (S-KIR 2408) <02903> **PLAY THE GAME TONIGHT. / PLAY ON**		17 May82
Jul 82.	(lp) (KIR 85714) <38002> **VINYL CONFESSIONS**		16 Jun82

– Play the game tonight / Right away / Fair exchange / Chasing shadows / Diamonds and pearls / Face it / Windows / Borderline / Play on / Crossfire. (cd-iss. Mar96 on 'Epic'; 481162-2)

Aug 82.	(7") <03084> **RIGHT AWAY. / WINDOWS**	-	73

—— now w/out STEINHARDT

		Epic	CBS Assoc.
Aug 83.	(7") <04057> **FIGHT FIRE WITH FIRE. / INCIDENT ON A BRIDGE**	-	58
Sep 83.	(lp) (EPC 25561) <38733> **DRASTIC MEASURES**		41

– Fight fire with fire / Everybody's my friend / Mainstream / Andi / Going through the motions / Get rich / Don't take your love away / End of the age / Incident on a bridge. (cd-iss. Mar96 on 'Epic'; 481163-2)

Sep 83.	(12"m) (TA 3696) **FIGHT FIRE WITH FIRE. / CARRY ON WAYWARD SON / DUST IN THE WIND**		-
Nov 83.	(7") **EVERYBODY'S MY FRIEND. / END OF THE AGE**	-	

—— Disbanded late 1983. Re-formed 1986 but without LIVGREN, HOPE & ELEFANTE. Past members EHART & WILLIAMS brought back STEVE WALSH. They recruited **STEVE MORSE** (b.28 Jul'54, Hamilton, Ohio) – guitar (ex-DIXIE DREGS) / **BILLY GREER** – bass (ex-STREETS)

		M.C.A.	M.C.A.
Dec 86.	(lp/c) (MCG/+C 6021) <5838> **POWER**		35 Nov86

– Silhouettes in disguise / Power / All I wanted / Secret service / We're not alone anymore / Musicatto / Taking in the view / Three pretenders / Tomb 19 / Can't cry anymore.

Jan 87.	(7"/12") (MCA/+S 1116) <52958> **ALL I WANTED. / WE'RE NOT ALONE ANYMORE**		19 Oct86
Feb 87.	(7") <53027> **POWER. / TOMB 19**	-	84
Apr 87.	(7") <53070> **CAN'T CRY ANYMORE. / THREE PRETENDERS**	-	
Oct 88.	(lp/c/cd) <(MCA/MCAC/DMCA 6254)> **IN THE SPIRIT OF THINGS**		

– Ghosts / One big sky / Inside of me / One man, one heart * / House on fire / Once in a lifetime * / Stand beside me / I counted on love * / The preacher / Rainmaker / T.O. Witcher * / Bells of Saint James. (cd+= *)

Nov 88.	(7") <53425> **STAND BESIDE ME. / HOUSE ON FIRE**	-	

—— In 1991, they added **DAVID RAGSDALE** – violin

—— **WALSH / LIVGREN / EHART / RAGSDALE**

	not iss.	Now & Then
Jul 93. (cd) **LIVE AT THE WHISKY** (live)	–	–
	Essential	Intersound

Jul 95. (cd/c) *(ESS CD/MC 299)* **FREAKS OF NATURE**
– I can fly / Desperate times / Hope once again / Black fathom four / Under the knife / Need / Freaks of nature / Cold grey morning / Peaceful and warm.

– compilations, others –

Sep 84. (lp/c) Epic; *(EPC/40 26065)* / CBS Assoc; *<39283>* **THE BEST OF KANSAS**
– Carry on wayward son / The point of know return / Fight fire / No one together / Play the game tonight / The wall. *(cd-iss. Nov85; CD 26065) (cd re-iss. Aug90; 461036-2)*

Jul 94. (d-cd) Legacy; *(CD 47364)* **THE KANSAS BOXED SET**

—— STEVE WALSH and KERRY LIVGREN both issued solo releases, although they were of the soft-rock/AOR variety.

Paul KANTNER & Grace SLICK (see under ⇒ JEFFERSON AIRPLANE)

Mick KARN (see under ⇒ JAPAN)

John KAY (see under ⇒ STEPPENWOLF)

KENICKIE (dig out; 4th edition or Great Alt & Indie . . .)

KERBDOG (dig out; Great Metal . . .)

K.G.B. (see under ⇒ ELECTRIC FLAG)

KHAN (see under ⇒ HILLAGE, Steve)

Johnny KIDD (& The PIRATES)

Born: FREDERICK HEATH, 23 Dec'39, Willesden, London, England. In 1956, together with ALAN CADDY, he formed skiffle combo, FREDDIE HEATH & THE NUTTERS, although they never made it onto vinyl. Early in 1959, after toying with calling himself CAPTAIN KIDD, the singer adopted the stage name of JOHNNY KIDD. Signing for 'H.M.V.', his debut single, 'PLEASE DON'T TOUCH' (written w/ manager Gus Robinson), hit the UK Top 30, attitude-laden rock'n'roll to match America's GENE VINCENT. KIDD borrowed his limp follow-up, 'IF YOU WERE THE ONLY GIRL IN THE WORLD', from the music hall tradition and unsurprisingly it bombed. In 1960, a new approach was needed, KIDD enlisting back-up band, The PIRATES (i.e. MICK GREEN – guitar, JOHNNY SPENCE – bass, FRANK FARLEY – drums) in an attempt to beef up his sound (they even dressed as pirates!). Now trading under the moniker of JOHNNY KIDD & THE PIRATES, they returned to the UK Top 30 with a rendition of Marv Johnson's 'YOU GOT WHAT IT TAKES'. With the classic 'SHAKIN' ALL OVER', however, the band introduced a dirty, reverb-heavy R&B sound which became a template for the more basic, riff-centric bands of the UK beat boom. Although the track topped the UK charts, their subsequent 45's failed to generate the same level of interest. Although these were still rockin', KIDD was another to be taken over by the aforementioned British Invasion (c. 1963/64). Still without an album to his name, KIDD formed his new PIRATES, who included DEEP PUPLE-bound NICK SIMPER. Tragically, on the 7th of October 1966, JOHNNY was killed after his tour van collided with a lorry on the M1. He was only 26 years of age and would have certainly enjoyed a renewed acquaintance with success following the advent of hard rock towards the end of the decade.
• **Songwriters:** Although not prolific, JOHNNY wrote/co-wrote some fine gems. Also covered; LINDA LU (Ray Sharpe) / THE BIRDS AND THE BEES (Jewel Atkins) / I CAN TELL (Bo Diddley) / A SHOT OF RHYTHM AND BLUES (Arthur Alexander) / MY BABE (Little Walter) / ALWAYS AND EVER (Latin-American standard) / WHOLE LOTTA WOMAN (Marvin Rainwater) / etc. • **Trivia:** NICK SIMPER, later an early member of DEEP PURPLE, was also injured in the crash.

Best CD compilation: THE COMPLETE JOHNNY KIDD (*8)

JOHNNY KIDD – vocals (solo with session people)

	H.M.V.	not iss.
May 59. (7") *(POP 615)* **PLEASE DON'T TOUCH. / GROWL**	25	–
Dec 59. (7") *(POP 674)* **IF YOU WERE THE ONLY GIRL IN THE WORLD. / FEELIN'**		–

JOHNNY KIDD & THE PIRATES

(still session men) His live line-up **ALAN CADDY** – guitar / **TONY DOHERTY** – rhythm guitar / **JOHNNY GORDON** – bass / **KEN McKAY** – drums / **MIKE WEST** and **TOM BROWN** – backing vocals

Feb 60. (7") *(POP 698)* **YOU GOT WHAT IT TAKES. / LONGIN' LIPS**	25	–

—— KIDD retained only **CADDY** (JOE MORETTI – lead guitar on below 1 only) with **BRIAN GREGG** – bass (ex-BEAT BOYS) / **CLEM CATTINI** – drums (ex-BEAT BOYS)

	H.M.V.	Capitol
Jun 60. (7") *(POP 753)* **SHAKIN' ALL OVER. / YES SIR, THAT'S MY BABY** *(re-iss. Feb76 on 'EMI')*	1	
Sep 60. (7") *(POP 790)* **RESTLESS. / MAGIC OF LOVE**	22	
Mar 61. (7") *(POP 853)* **LINDA LU. / LET'S TALK ABOUT US**	47	

—— KIDD now reverted to session men

| Sep 61. (7") *(POP 919)* **PLEASE DON'T BRING ME DOWN. / SO WHAT** | | |

—— KIDD completely changed his PIRATES line-up; **JOHNNY PATTO** – guitar / **JOHNNY SPENCE** – bass / **FRANK FARLEY** – drums (all ex-CUDDLY DUDLEY) repl. ALAN, BRIAN + CLEM who all joined COLIN HICKS' Band

| Jan 62. (7") *(POP 978)* **HURRY ON BACK TO LOVE. / I WANT THAT** | | |

—— **MICK GREEN** – guitar repl. PATTO

Nov 62. (7") *(POP 1088)* **A SHOT OF RHYTHM AND BLUES. / I CAN TELL**	48	
Jun 63. (7") *(POP 1173)* **I'LL NEVER GET OVER YOU. / THEN I GOT EVERYTHING**	4	Oct63
Nov 63. (7") *(POP 1228)* **HUNGRY FOR LOVE. / ECSTACY**	20	–
Apr 64. (7") *(POP 1269)* **ALWAYS AND EVER. / DR. FEELGOOD**	46	–

—— added **VIC COOPER** – organ

| Jun 64. (7") *(POP 1309)* **JEALOUS GIRL. / SHOP AROUND** | | – |

—— **JOHN WIEDER** – guitar (ex-TONY MEEHAN) repl. MICK to BILLY KRAMER

Oct 64. (7") *(POP 1353)* **WHOLE LOTTA WOMAN. / YOUR CHEATIN' HEART**		–
Feb 65. (7") *(POP 1397)* **THE BIRDS AND THE BEES. / DON'T MAKE THE SAME MISTAKE AS I DID**		–
May 65. (7") *(POP 1424)* **SHAKIN' ALL OVER '65. / I GOTTA TRAVEL ON**		–

—— KIDD, SPENCE, FARLEY and COOPER recruited **JON MORSHEAD** – guitar repl. WIEDER who later joined ERIC BURDON

| Apr 66. (7"; by JOHNNY KIDD) *(POP 1520)* **IT'S GOT TO BE YOU. / I HATE TO GET UP IN THE MORNING** | | – |

—— JOHNNY KIDD brought in completely new musicians **MICK STEWART** – guitar repl. MORSHEAD / **NICK SIMPER** – bass (ex-SIMON RAVEN CULT) repl. SPENCE / **ROGER TRUTH** – drums (ex-SIMON RAVEN CULT) repl. FARLEY / also **RAY SOAPER** – keyboards (left before recording below). First three that left became band The PIRATES.

—— JOHNNY KIDD was killed in a car crash on the 7th October '66. Below released posthumously

| Nov 66. (7") *(POP 1559)* **THE FOOL. / SEND FOR THAT GIRL** | | – |

—— without KIDD the new PIRATES continued until May67. SIMPER to DEEP PURPLE

– compilations, etc. –

on 'E.M.I.' unless mentioned otherwise

	H.M.V.	Capitol
1960. (7"ep) H.M.V.; *(7EG 8628)* **SHAKIN' ALL OVER** – Shakin' all over / Please don't touch / You got what it takes / Restless.		–
1964. (7"ep) H.M.V.; *(7EG 8834)* **JOHNNY KIDD AND THE PIRATES** – I'll never get over you / A shot of rhythm and blues / Hungry for love / Then I got everything.		–
1971. (lp) Regal Starline; *(SRS 5100)* **SHAKIN' ALL OVER**		–
Aug 77. (7") *(EMI 2667)* **I'LL NEVER GET OVER YOU. / PLEASE DON'T TOUCH**		–
Apr 78. (lp) EMI Nut; *(NUTM 12)* **THE BEST OF JOHNNY KIDD & THE PIRATES** – A shot of rhythm & blues / Shakin' all over / Longing lips / Restess / Growl / I want that / Linda Lu / You've got what it takes / Your cheatin' heart / I'll never get over you / Hungry for love / I can tell / Jealous girl / Shop around / Please don't touch / Always and ever. *(re-iss. Feb87 on 'E.M.I.' lp/c; EMS/TC-EMS 1120)*		
Jun 80. (7") H.M.V.; *(POP 2005)* **SHAKIN' ALL OVER. / A SHOT OF RHYTHM AND BLUES**		–
Oct 83. (7") Old Gold; *(OG 9366)* **SHAKIN' ALL OVER. / I'LL NEVER GET OVER YOU**		–
May 87. (lp) See For Miles; *(SEE 120)* **RARITIES** *(cd-iss. Oct89; SEECD 120) (re-iss. cd+c Aug93)*		–
Feb 90. (lp/cd) See For Miles; *(SEE/+CD 287)* **CLASSIC AND RARE** *(re-iss. Aug93)*		–
Aug 92. (d-cd/d-c) E.M.I.; *(CD/TC KIDD 11)* **THE COMPLETE JOHNNY KIDD & THE PIRATES**		–
Jul 95. (cd/c) E.M.I.; *(CD/TC SL 8256)* **THE VERY BEST OF JOHNNY KIDD & THE PIRATES**		–

KID LOCO

Born: JEAN-YVES PRIEUR, early 1960's, Orleans, Paris, France. A former punk/hip hop afficionado, he initiated his own label, 'Bondage', in the late 70's. Influenced by an array of musical backgrounds (i.e. mixer ANDREW WEATHERALL), PRIEUR recorded his solo masterpiece, 'A GRAND LOVE STORY', in 1997. Initially issued on the 'Yellow' imprint, the album (dedicated to wife, Rachida) was picked up by 'East West', who duly gave it a quick re-issue early in '98 while the not-so-crazy KID toured supporting STEREOLAB. The French had certainly found themselves a future star; although the album was only an underground success in Britain, relying on word of mouth, excellent reviews and the should-have-been hit singles, 'SHE'S MY LOVER (A SONG FOR R.)' and 'LOVE IS SWEET', the latter with KATRINA MITCHELL of The PASTELS on vocals. The rest of the set was an "out of this world" trip-hop trip, fusing elements of funky avant-jazz (the cool 'RELAXIN' WITH CHERRY' a must!), bluesy ambience and eerie psychedelia ('COSMIC TURNAROUND' the best example). We await the LOCO man's re re-birth of the Cool.

Album rating: "A GRAND LOVE STORY" (*9) / DJ KICKS various (*7)

JEAN-YVES PRIEUR – samples, etc. / with **JENDAH MANGA** – bass / **NACER ARAB** – cool guitar riff (track 2) / **KATRINA MITCHELL** – vocals (track 3)

		Yellow	Yellow
Jan 98.	(cd/lp) (YP 031 CD/LP) <3984 20805-2> **"A GRAND LOVE STORY"**	☐	☐ Nov97

– A grand love theme / Relaxin' with Cherry / Love me sweet / The bootleggers / Calling aventura king / Sister Curare / She's my lover (a song for R.) / She woolf daydreaming / Alone again so / Cosmic supernatural. (cd re-iss. Feb98 on 'East West'; same as US)

		East West	East West
Jan 98.	(12"ep) (YP 028) **SHE'S MY LOVER (A SONG FOR R.) / ('A'mix). / PEARLY GIRLY MAN / CUM ON**	☐	☐
Mar 98.	(12"/cd-s) (EW 153 T/CD1) **SHE'S MY LOVER / ('A'-A revolution sitting stoned in a field mix). / PEARLY GIRLY MAN / SHE'S MY LOVER (bang bang remix)** (cd-s) (EW 153CD2) – ('A'mixes).	☐	☐

		Yellow	not iss.
Aug 98.	(c-s/10"/12"/cd-s) (EW 172 C/TE/T/CD) **LOVE ME SWEET / CUM-ON. / ('A'mixes)**	☐	☐
Dec 98.	(12") (YP 052) **RELAXIN' WITH CHERRY. / ALONE AGAIN SO**	☐	-

		Studio K	not iss.
Aug 99.	(cd; featuring Various Artists) <(3984 26912-2)> **KID LOCO PRESENTS JESUS LIFE FOR CHILDREN UNDER 12**	☐	☐
Oct 99.	(cd/d-lp; with Various Artists) (K7 081 CD/LP) **DJ KICKS (mixed by KID LOCO)**	☐	-
Dec 99.	(12") (K 7081EP) **DJ KICKS EP**	☐	-

– (mixes; original / original edit / . . . And the beat goes on).

KID ROCK

Born: ROBERT RITCHIE, Romeo, Michigan, USA. This white rapper-cum-metalist debuted with the depthless 'GRITS SANDWICHES FOR BREAKFAST' (1990) before his stab at major label success via the even weaker 'THE POLYFUZE METHOD' (1993). The baseball clad, cigar smoking MC shot to notoriety in 1997 – one year after the release of the single 'EARLY MORNING STONED PIMP' – when a leading radio station in Motor City played his infamous 'YODELING IN THE VALLEY' track (from the debut album) and were subsequently fined for obscene broadcasting. KID ROCK signed to 'Atlantic' in 1997 and issued his third set 'DEVIL WITHOUT A CAUSE' the following year. Like the string of white suburban metal bands, ROCK relied heavily on bad language, songs about drugs (and "bitches") and endless references to the degenerate culture, which somehow made this album sound like a bit of a charlatan. The entertainer (who's now going down a storm with WWF mob!) spent much of his time prancing around on stage in a pair of horrible silver MC HAMMER-esque baggy trousers – with a dwarf and two lap dancers in tow – proving he could yet become a novelty act for juvenile teens after all.

Album rating: GRITS SANDWICHES FOR BREAKFAST (*4) / THE POLYFUZE METHOD (*3) / DEVIL WITHOUT A CAUSE (*6)

KID ROCK – rapper, bass, guitar / with various friends

		not iss.	Novus-Jive
Oct 90.	(c-s/12") <1349/+1> **YO-DA-LIN IN THE VALLEY**	-	☐
Nov 90.	(cd/c/lp) <1409-2/-4/-1> **GRITS SANDWICHES FOR BREAKFAST**	-	☐

– Yo-da-lin in the valley / Genuine article / Cramp ya style / New York's not my home / Super rhyme maker / With a one two / Wax the booty / Pimp of the nation / Abdul Jabar cut / Step in stride / Upside / Style of X pression / Trippin' over a rock.

		Continuum	Continuum
1992.	(c-s/12"/cd-s) <19255> **BACK FROM THE DEAD (extended). / ('A'-short) / ('A'-instrumental)**	-	☐
Aug 93.	(12"/cd-s) (12/CD CTUM 101) <12205> **U DON'T KNOW ME /**	-	☐ Feb93
Sep 93.	(cd/lp) (CD+/CTUM 2) <19205-2/-4> **THE POLYFUZE METHOD**	☐	☐

– Fred / Killin' brain cells / Prodigal son / Cramper / 3 sheets to the wind / Fuck U blind / Desperate (radio) / Back from the dead / My Oedipus complex / Balls in your mouth / Trippin' with Dick Vitale / TV dinner / Pancake breakfast / Blow me / In so deep / U don't know me.

Dec 93.	(m-cd/m-c) <15205> **FIRE IT UP**	-	☐

– I am the bullgod / My Oedipus complex / Country boy can survive / Balls in your mouth / Cramper / Rollin' on the island.

		not iss.	Top Dog
Jan 96.	(c-ep/cd-ep) <50001> **EARLY MORNIN' STONED PIMP**	-	☐

—— now backed by band, TWISTED BROWN TRUCKER:- **KENNY OLSON** – guitar / **STEFANIE EULINBERG** – drums / **TWEEDS KRACKER** – turntables / **JIMMY BONES** – keyboards / **JASON KRAUSE** – guitar / **MISTY LOVE + SHIRLEY HAYDEN** – backing vocals

		Lava – Atlantic	Lava – Atlantic
Jun 99.	(cd/c) <(7567 83119-2/-4)> **DEVIL WITHOUT A CAUSE**	☐	5 Aug98

– Bawitdaba / Cowboy / Devil without a cause / I am the bullgod / Roving gangster (rollin') / Wasting time / Welcome 2 the party (ode 2 the old skool) / I got one for ya / Somebody's gotta feel this / Fist of rage / Only God knows why / Fuck off (w/ EMINEM) / Where U at Rock (w/ EMINEM) / Black chick, white guy *w/ EMINEM). <clean version-iss.Oct98; 83152>

Oct 99.	(c-s/cd-s) (AT 0076 C/CD) <84520> **COWBOY / COWBOY (album version) / I AM THE BULLGOD (live)**	36	82

KILBURN & THE HIGH ROADS (see under ⇒ DURY, Ian)

KILLING JOKE

Formed: Notting Hill, London, England . . . 1979 by JAZ COLEMAN and PAUL FERGUSON, who subsequently added GEORDIE (K. WALKER) and YOUTH (MARTIN GLOVER). After borrowing money to finance a debut EP (contained three tracks including 'TURN TO RED'), the band were the subject of some interest to DJ John Peel who championed their alternative rock sound. This immediately led to KILLING JOKE signing a deal with 'Island', who virtually re-issued the aforementioned single/EP in abbreviated 7" form (A-side, 'NERVOUS SYSTEM'), adding a fourth track on the 12". While supporting the likes of JOY DIVISION and The RUTS, they released a follow-up double A-sided single, 'WARDANCE' / 'PSYCHE', resurrecting their own 'Malicious Damage' label in the process. The left-field 'E.G.' operation were quick to spot the group's potential, taking on both KILLING JOKE and their label. The first results of this partnership came in the form of 'REQUIEM', the single taken from their pioneering eponymous UK Top 40 album. Replacing the anger of punk with apocalyptic doom-mongering, KILLING JOKE were akin to a sonically disturbing, industrialised BLACK SABBATH. Now regarded as a catalytic classic in metal circles, the album also inspired many US hardcore acts, as well as such big guns as METALLICA, MINISTRY, SOUNDGARDEN and NIRVANA. By the release of follow-up set, 'WHAT'S THIS FOR' (1981), KILLING JOKE had taken their occult punk-like chants/anthems to extreme new dimensions. Nevertheless, they retained a strange accessiblity which saw the single, 'FOLLOW THE LEADERS' attaining a minor UK chart placing and incredibly, a hit on the American dancefloors! A third set, 'REVELATIONS' (1982), eased up a little on the intensity factor, although it peaked at No.12 having already spawned another hit single, 'EMPIRE SONG'. Convinced of imminent world destruction, the occult-fixated COLEMAN remained in Iceland after a tour, YOUTH initially returning home but later following his lead to the frozen north. He subsequently flew back to England, teaming up with FERGUSON and newfound friend, PAUL RAVEN to form BRILLIANT. However, both FERGUSON and RAVEN soon departed from YOUTH's group, taking off for Iceland in search of the missing COLEMAN. Eventually locating their frontman, all three returned to UK shores and re-entered the studio (GEORDIE also in tow) with a view to recording new KILLING JOKE material. The resulting album, 'FIRE DANCES' (1983), only managed to scrape into the Top 30, its lack of bite and experimentation possibly a hangover from their northern treks. The following year, KILLING JOKE released only two 45's, although one of them, 'EIGHTIES' (a minor hit), was showcased in all its eccentric glory on Channel 4's new pop show, 'The Tube'. Having overcome the mental obstacle of 1984 (and all of its apocalyptic implications), COLEMAN and Co. unleashed their most focused work to date in 'NIGHT TIME' (a near Top 10 album), the 'LOVE LIKE BLOOD' single preceding the set and breaking into the Top 20 in early '85. The latter half of the eighties weren't so kind, both critically and commercially, the albums, 'BRIGHTER THAN A THOUSAND SUNS' (1986) and 'OUTSIDE THE GATE' (1988), taking a more self-indulgent keyboard-orientated approach. Following major personnel upheavals, KILLING JOKE decided to take a brief sabbatical, COLEMAN finding time to release a collaborative album with ANNE DUDLEY (ex-ART OF NOISE), 'SONGS FROM THE VICTORIOUS CITY' (1990). The same year, COLEMAN, GEORDIE, RAVEN and newcomer MARTIN ATKINS, returned with the acclaimed 'EXTREMITIES, DIRT AND VARIOUS REPRESSED EMOTIONS' album. Having spent most of the early 90's globetrotting in various exotic locations, KILLING JOKE (now COLEMAN, GEORDIE and the returning YOUTH), were back with a vengeance on 1994's 'PANDEMONIUM'. Their biggest selling album to date, the record and the 'PANDEMONIUM' single from it, both making the Top 30 (the previous 'MILLENIUM' made Top 40), while also seeing an American release on the 'Zoo' label. Another, increasingly metallic/industrial set, 'DEMOCRACY' followed in 1996, although COLEMAN now spends the bulk of his time in New Zealand, where he is composer in residence for the country's Symphony Orchestra.

Album rating: KILLING JOKE (*9) / WHAT'S THIS FOR . . .! (*7) / REVELATIONS (*5) / HA! KILLING JOKE LIVE (*5) / FIRE DANCES (*7) / NIGHT TIME (*7) / BRIGHTER THAN A THOUSAND SUNS (*6) / OUTSIDE THE GATE (*6) / EXTREMITIES, DIRT AND VARIOUS REPRESSED EMOTIONS (*7) / LAUGH? I NEARLY BOUGHT ONE! compilation (*8) / PANDEMONIUM (*8) / DEMOCRACY (*6)

JAZ COLEMAN (b. JEREMY, 26 Feb'60, Cheltenham, England; raised Egypt) – vocals, keyboards / **GEORDIE** (b. K.WALKER, 18 Dec'58, Newcastle-upon-Tyne, England) – guitar, synthesizers / **YOUTH** (b. MARTIN GLOVER, 27 Dec'60, Africa) – bass, vocals (ex-RAGE) / **PAUL FERGUSON** (b.31 Mar'58, High Wycombe, England) – drums

		Malicious Damage	not iss.
Oct 79.	(10"ep) (MD 410) **ARE YOU RECEIVING ME. / TURN TO RED / NERVOUS SYSTEM**	☐	-

		Island	not iss.
Nov 79.	(7") (WIP 6550) **NERVOUS SYSTEM. / TURN TO RED** (12"+=) (12WIP 6550) – Almost red / Are you receiving me.	☐	-

		Malicious Damage	not iss.
Mar 80.	(7") (MD 540) **WARDANCE. / PSYCHE**	☐	-

	E.G. – Malicious Damage	Editions

Sep 80. (7") *(EGMD 1.00)* **REQUIEM. / CHANGE**
(12"+=) *(EGMX 1.00)* – Requiem 434 / Change (version).   [ ] -

Oct 80. (lp/c) *(EGMD/+C 545)* **KILLING JOKE**   **39** -
– Requiem / Wardance / Tomorrow's world / Bloodsport / The wait / Complications /
S.O. 36 / Primitive. *(re-iss. Jan87 lp/c/cd; EG LP/MC/CD 57)* <US cd-iss. 1987 on
'Caroline'; 1538>

May 81. (7") *(EGMDS 1.01)* **FOLLOW THE LEADERS. / TENSION**   **55** -
(10"+=) *(EGMDX 1.010)* – Follow the leaders – dub.

Jun 81. (lp/c) *(EGMD/+C 550)* <111> **WHAT'S THIS FOR . . .!**   **42** -
– The fall of Because / Tension / Unspeakable / Butcher / Follow the leaders /
Madness / Who told you how? / Exit. *(re-iss. Jan87 lp/c/cd; EG LP/MC/CD 58)* <US
cd-iss. 1987 on 'Caroline'; 1539>

	E.G.	Caroline

Mar 82. (7") *(EGO 4)* **EMPIRE SONG. / BRILLIANT**   **43** -

—— **GUY PRATT** – bass; repl. YOUTH who formed BRILLIANT

Apr 82. (lp/c) *(EGMD/+C 3)* **REVELATIONS**   **12** -
– The hum / Empire song / We have joy / Chop chop / The Pandys are coming /
Chapter III / Have a nice day / Land of milk and honey / Good samaritan / Dregs.
(re-iss. Jan87 lp/c/cd; EG LP/MC/CD 59) <US cd-iss. 1987 on 'Caroline'; 1540>

Jun 82. (7") *(EGO 7)* **CHOP CHOP. / GOOD SAMARITAN**   [ ] -

Oct 82. (7") *(EGO 10)* **BIRDS OF A FEATHER. / FLOCK THE B-SIDE**   **64** -
(12"+=) *(EGOX 10)* – Sun goes down.

Nov 82. (10"m-lp/m-c) *(EGMD T/C 4)* **HA – KILLING JOKE LIVE
(live)**   **66** -
– Psyche / Sun goes down / The Pandys are coming / Take take take / Unspeakable /
Wardance.

—— **PAUL RAVEN** – bass (ex-NEON HEARTS) repl. PRATT who joined ICEHOUSE

Jun 83. (7") *(EGO 11)* **LET'S ALL GO (TO THE FIRE DANCES). /
DOMINATOR (version)**   **51** -
(12"+=) *(EGOX 11)* – The fall of Because (live).

Jul 83. (lp/c) *(EGMD/+C 5)* **FIRE DANCES**   **29** -
– The gathering / Fun and games / Rejuvenation / Frenzy / Harlequin / Feast of
blaze / Song and dance / Dominator / Let's all go (to the fire dances) / Lust almighty.
(re-iss. Jan87 lp/c/cd; EG LP/MC/CD 60) <US cd-iss. 1987 on 'Caroline'; 1541>

Oct 83. (7") *(EGOD 14)* **ME OR YOU?. / WILFUL DAYS**   **57** -
(with free 7") *(KILL 1-2)* – ('A'side) / Feast of blaze.
(d12"++=) *(EGOXD 14)* – Let's all go (to the fire dances) / The fall of Because
(live) / Dominator (version).

Mar 84. (7") *(EGO 16)* **EIGHTIES. / EIGHTIES (Coming mix)**   **60** -
(12"+=) *(EGOX 16)* – ('A'-Serious dance mix).

Jun 84. (7") *(EGO 17)* **A NEW DAY. / DANCE DAY**   **56** -
(12"+=) *(EGOX 17)* – ('A'dub).

Jan 85. (7") *(EGO 20)* **LOVE LIKE BLOOD. / BLUE FEATHER**   **16** -
(12"+=) *(EGOY 20)* – ('A'-Gestalt mix).
(12"++=) *(EGOX 20)* – ('A'instrumental).

Feb 85. (lp/c) *(EGMD/+C 6)* <1531> **NIGHT TIME**   **11** -
– Night time / Darkness before dawn / Love like blood / Kings and queens / Tabazan /
Multitudes / Europe / Eighties. *(re-iss. Jan87 lp/c/cd; EG LP/MC/CD 61)*

Mar 85. (7") *(EGO 21)* **KINGS AND QUEENS. / THE MADDING
CROWD**   **58** -
(12"+=) *(EGOX 21)* – ('A'-Right Royal mix).
(12"+=) *(EGOY 21)* – ('A'-Knave mix).

Aug 86. (7") *(EGO 27)* **ADORATIONS. / EXILE**   **42** -
(d7"+=) *(EGOD 27)* – Ecstacy / ('A'instrumental).

	E.G.	Virgin

Oct 86. (7") *(EGO 30)* **SANITY. / GOODBYE TO THE VILLAGE**   **70** -
(free c-s with-7") *(above tracks)* – Wardance (remix).
(12"+=) *(EGOX 30)* – Victory.

Nov 86. (lp/c/cd) *(EG LP/MC/CD 66)* <90568-1/-4/-2> **BRIGHTER
THAN A THOUSAND SUNS**   **54** -
– Adorations / Sanity / Chessboards / Twilight of the mortal / Love of the masses /
A southern sky / Wintergardens / Rubicon. *(c+=/cd+=)* – Goodbye to the village /
Victory.

	E.G.	Caroline

Apr 88. (7") *(EGO 40)* **AMERICA. / JIHAD (Beyrouth edit)**   [ ] -
(12"+=) *(EGOX 40)* – ('A'extended).
(cd-s++=) *(EGOCD 40)* – Change (original 1980 mix).

Jun 88. (lp/c/cd) *(EG LP/MC/CD 73)* <1378> **OUTSIDE THE GATE**   **92** -
– America / My love of this land / Stay one jump ahead / Unto the ends of the
Earth / The calling / Obsession / Tiahuanaco / Outside the gate. *(cd+=)* – America
(extended) / Stay one jump ahead (extended).

Jul 88. (7") *(EGO 43)* **MY LOVE OF THIS LAND. / DARKNESS
BEFORE DAWN**   [ ] -
(12"+=) *(EGOX 43)* – Follow the leaders (dub) / Psyche.
(10"+=) *(EGOT 43)* – Follow the leaders (dub) / Sun goes down.

—— **JAZ + GEORDIE** brought in new members **MARTIN ATKINS** (b. 3 Aug'59, Coventry,
England) – drums (ex-PUBLIC IMAGE LTD.) repl. FERGUSON / **TAFF** – bass
repl. ANDY ROURKE (ex-SMITHS) who had repl. RAVEN. Early 1990, **JAZ
COLEMAN** teamed up with ANNE DUDLEY (see; ART OF NOISE)

—— **KILLING JOKE** reformed (COLEMAN, GEORDIE, ATKINS + RAVEN)

	Noise Int.	R.C.A.

Nov 90. (cd/c/lp) *(AGR 054-2/-4/-1)* <4828-2/-4> **EXTREMITIES, DIRT
AND VARIOUS REPRESSED EMOTIONS**   [ ] [ ]
– Money is not our god / Age of greed / Beautiful dead / Extremities / Inside the
termite mound / Intravenus / Solitude / North of the border / Slipstream / Kalijuga
struggle.

Jan 91. (12")/cd-s) *(AG 054-6/-3)* **MONEY IS NOT OUR GOD. /
NORTH OF THE BORDER**   [ ] -

	Invisible	Invisible

Jul 93. (d-lp) *(<INV 004>)* **THE COURTHOLD TALKS**   [ ] [ ]
– (spoken word with JAZ, GEORDIE & JAFF SCANTLEBURY on percussion)

—— **YOUTH** returned to repl. RAVEN

—— **GEOFF DUGMORE** – drums (ex-ART OF NOISE) repl. ATKINS (to PIGFACE, etc)

	Butterfly	Volcano-Zoo

Mar 94. (10"ep/cd-ep) *(BFL T/D 11)* **EXORCISM. / ('A'live) / ('A'-
German mix) / WHITEOUT (Ugly mix) / ANOTHER CULT
GOES DOWN (mix) / ('A'-Bictonic revenge mix)**   [ ] -

Apr 94. (7"clear/c-s) *(BFL/+C 12)* **MILLENIUM. / ('A'-Cybersank
remix)**   **34** -
(12"+=/cd-s+=) *(BFL T/D 12)* – ('A'-Drum Club remix) / ('A'Juno Reactor remix).

Jul 94. (12"/c-s/cd-s) *(BFL T/C/D 17)* <14178> **PANDEMONIUM. /
('A'mix)**   **28** Oct94
(cd-s) *(BFLD 17)* – ('A'side) / Requiem (Kris Weston & Greg Hunter remix).

Jul 94. (cd/c/d-lp) *(BFL CD/MC/LP 9)* <31085> **PANDEMONIUM**   **16** Aug94
– Pandemonium / Exorcism / Millenium / Communion / Black Moon / Labyrinth /
Jana / Whiteout / Pleasures of the flesh / Mathematics of chaos.

—— re-united originals JAZ COLEMAN / GEORDIE + YOUTH

Jan 95. (cd-ep) *(BFLDA 21)* **JANA (Youth remix) / JANA
(Dragonfly mix) / LOVE LIKE BLOOD (live) / WHITEOUT**   **54** -
(12"ep/cd-ep+=) *(BFL T/DB 21)* – Jana (live) / Wardance (live) / Exorcism (live) /
Kings and queens (live).

Mar 96. (cd-s) *(BFLDA 33)* <34262> **DEMOCRACY / DEMOCRACY
(Rooster mix by Carcass) / MASS**   **39** [ ]
(cd-s) *(BFLDB 33)* – ('A'-United Nations mix) / ('A'-Russian tundra mix) /
('A'-Hallucinogen mix).

Apr 96. (cd/c) *(BFL CD/MC 17)* <31127> **DEMOCRACY**   **71** [ ]
– Savage freedom / Democracy / Prozac people / Lanterns / Aeon / Pilgrimage /
Intellect / Medicine wheel / Absent friends / Another bloody election.

– compilations, etc. –

on 'Virgin' unless mentioned otherwise

Sep 92. (12"/c-s) *(VST/VSC 1432)* **CHANGE. / REQUIEM**   [ ] -
(cd-s) *(VSCDT 1432)* – ('A'spiral tribe mix). / ('B'trash Greg Hunter mix).
(cd-s) *(VSCDX 1432)* – ('A'-Youth mix). / ('B'-Youth mix).

Oct 92. (cd/c) *(CDV/TCV 2693)* / Caroline; <1596> **LAUGH? I NEARLY
BOUGHT ONE!**   [ ] [ ]
– Turn to red / Psyche / Requiem / Wardance / Follow the leaders / Unspeakable /
Butcher / Exit / The hum / Empire song / Chop-chop / The Sun goes down / Eighties /
Darkness before dawn / Love like blood / Wintergardens / Age of greed.

May 95. (cd) *(CDOVD 440)* / Caroline; <1884> **WILFUL DAYS** (remixes)   [ ] [ ]

Oct 95. (cd) Windsong; *(WINCD 068)* **BBC LIVE IN CONCERT** (live)   [ ] [ ]

Apr 98. (12") Dragonfly; <48> **LOVE LIKE BLOOD. / INTELLECT**   - -

Aug 98. (cd) Imprint; <114151> **WAR DANCE** (remix album)   - [ ]

Albert KING (dig out; 4th edition)

B.B. KING

Born: RILEY B. KING, 16 Sep'25, Indianola, Mississippi, USA, the cousin
of respected country bluesman, BUKKA WHITE. A self-taught guitarist
(earliest influences being jazz players CHARLIE CHRISTIAN and DJANGO
REINHARDT, although T-BONE WALKER would become his future idol),
KING initiated a blues style that became a cornerstone of rock music. The son
of a sharecropper, as a young man he picked cotton (through the depression)
for around 20 dollars a week; the chances of buying a $200-$300 guitar were
remote, not to mention the fact that his town didn't have any electricity!
KING performed with The ELKHORN SINGERS in his teens and moved to
Memphis in 1946 to look for work as a musician, linking up with SONNY
BOY WILLIAMSON and initially playing a residency at the 16th Avenue
Grill. Subsequently talent-spotted, he won his own, regular 10-minute spot
(The Sepia Swing Show) on a black music radio station, WDIA, and word of
his prowess spread; the station's PR man dubbed him 'The BEALE STREET
BLUES BOY' which was shortened to 'BLUES BOY' and eventually 'BB'.
Towards the end of 1949, KING signed to the 'Bullett' label and debuted with
'MISS MARTHA KING', while the following year, he inked a deal with the
'Kent/Modern/RPM' group of labels through their talent scout, IKE TURNER,
remaining there until 1962 (he also formed his own, short-lived 'Blue Boy'
label during the 50's). BB developed his own sound on his Gibson guitar,
LUCILLE (so named because of an incident after a gig in Twist, Arkansas
during which a fight – caused by a woman named Lucille – ended up with
the venue being evacuated). In February 1952, KING hit US number 1 for
fifteen weeks in the R&B charts with 'THREE O'CLOCK BLUES' (written
by LOWELL FULSON), while in November, 'YOU DIDN'T WANT ME',
repeated the feat. KING was to enjoy regular R&B chart success over the next
five years, including two more chart toppers, 'PLEASE LOVE ME' (1953)
and 'YOU UPSET ME BABY' (1954). The big man achieved his first national
chart success in 1957 via 'BE CAREFUL WITH A FOOL' and followed it
with 'I NEED YOU SO BAD' which also broke into the US Top 100. KING
subsequently left 'Kent' in 1962 for the larger 'A.B.C.' label, with whom
he was to record until their absorption into 'M.C.A.' in 1979. His first ABC
release was a version of Louis Jordan's 'HOW BLUE CAN YOU GET',
while in May '62, 'ROCK ME BABY' (written by ARTHUR 'BIG BOY'
CRUDUP and recorded for 'Kent' before his move) was his first recognised
pop hit, entering the US Top 40 and becoming the subject of countless
cover versions by UK R&B bands. 'LIVE AT THE REGAL' recorded at the
Regal Theatre, Chicago in 1960 and released in 1965, captured him at his
best playing songs that were to be mainstays of his set for years to come –
Memphis Slim's 'EVERYDAY I HAVE THE BLUES', 'HOW BLUE CAN
YOU GET' and 'IT'S MY OWN FAULT' (written by JOHN LEE HOOKER).
'LIVE IN COOK COUNTY JAIL' (1971) was in the same vein featuring
'WORRY WORRY', 'THREE O'CLOCK BLUES' and the unmistakeable
'THE THRILL IS GONE' (his only US Top 20 single). At the end of the

decade (after achieving his second US Top 40 hit with 'PAYING THE COST TO BE THE BOSS'), he left his long term manager, Lou Zito, after an argument over money, his accountant, Sidney Siedenberg, took over. On the 4th of April 1968 (the night that MARTIN LUTHER KING was assassinated) KING, BUDDY GUY and JIMI HENDRIX played an all-night blues session, passing the hat round to collect money for the Southern Leadership fund. The following year, after the release of albums, 'LUCILLE' and 'BLUES ON TOP OF BLUES', he made his first trip to Europe, appeared at numerous festivals including the Newport Jazz Festival and opened for The ROLLING STONES on their sixth US tour. KING's manager subsequently encouraged him to widen his fan base and steered him away from his traditional (although declining) black audience towards the middle class white kids involved in the R&B/blues revival. In December that year, his version of Roy Hawkins' 'THE THRILL IS GONE' gave him his biggest hit single so far, reaching the US Top 20, with the accompaning album, 'COMPLETELY WELL' achieving similar results. His next album, 'HUMMINGBIRD' and the jazzy Top 30 set, 'INDIANOLA MISSISSIPPI SEEDS' were both released at the turn of the decade, while 1971 brought him a Grammy for 'THE THRILL IS GONE'; a string of minor hits followed, both singles and albums. In August 1979, 'TAKE IT HOME', gave him his first UK album chart success (reaching No.60), although it struggled to achieve a similar position in the States. 'THERE MUST BE A BETTER WORLD SOMEWHERE' (1981), with music and lyrics by DR. JOHN and DOC POMUS, was one of his finest studio albums, cuts such as 'THE VICTIM' and the ironic 'LIFE AIN'T NOTHING BUT A PARTY' enduring highlights. In 1982, KING demonstrated what a thoroughly generous guy he was when he donated his entire record collection (20,000 discs including 7,000 rare blues 78's) to the Mississippi University Centre For The Study Of Southern Culture. His second Grammy came in February for 'THERE MUST BE A BETTER WORLD SOMEWHERE' and on September the 16th (his 57th birthday), he recorded 'BLUES N JAZZ' which won him another Grammy in 1984. He added yet another one to the trophy cabinet in 1986 with 'MY GUITAR SINGS THE BLUES', a track taken from his 50th album, 'SIX SILVER STRINGS'. In 1988, he surprisingly recorded a one-off track with U2, 'WHEN LOVE COMES TO TOWN' making the UK Top 10 for the first and only time in his chequered history. Meanwhile, KING continued with his charity work, performing at a concert for the National Coalition For The Homeless and a Dallas based group for the homeless, Common Ground (later performing at the Roy Orbison All Star Benefit Tribute and helping to raise $500,000 for homeless charities). In December 1989, he featured on the album, 'HAPPY ANNIVERSARY CHARLIE BROWN' which commemorated the 40th year of the Peanuts cartoon strip (he later continued his association with cartoon characters by playing guitar on 'BORN UNDER A BAD SIGN' for the 'SIMPSONS SINGS THE BLUES' album in 1990 and 'MONDAY MORNING BLUES' for 'AM I COOL, OR WHAT?', a homage to Garfield the cat in 1991). KING went into hospital in April 1990 because of problems relating to his diabetes, resulting in the cancellation of some concerts although he soon got back to his intensive recording and touring schedule (he averages 300 one-nighters a year – mainly to pay for his compulsive gambling habit). February 1991 brought him another Grammy, this time for 'LIVE AT SAN QUENTIN' (recorded 20 years earlier!) and in May that year he opened his own restaurant and night club (BB KING's MEMPHIS BLUES CLUB) on Beale Street, Memphis. This busy year year continued in October with the release of his best studio album in a decade, 'THERE IS ALWAYS ONE MORE TIME', highlights being 'I'M MOVIN' ON' and 'THE BLUES COME OVER ME'. In 1992, he received a Grammy for 'LIVE AT THE APOLLO', reached UK Top 60 with GARY MOORE on 'SINCE I MET YOU BABY' and in December performed at the Gainsville Drug Treatment Centre in Florida before 300 prison inmates including his daughter, PATTY, who was serving a 3-year term for trafficking. March 1993 saw him headline a benefit concert in Chattanooga, raising $90,000 for the Bessie Smith Hall (opened later in the year) and in September, 'BLUES SUMMIT' (recorded with ROBERT CRAY, ALBERT COLLINS, ETTA JAMES, JOHN LEE HOOKER, BUDDY GUY and IRMA THOMAS) breached the US Top 200. KING returns to his old neighbourhood each year and puts on a weekend of free concerts; a tireless ambassador for the blues, he succeeded in bringing the form into the mainstream and remains one of the most well-known artists in the genre's near hundred year history. • **Covered:** LOVE ME TENDER (hit; Elvis Presley) / ONE OF THOSE NIGHTS (Conway Twitty) / DON'T CHANGE ON ME (James Holiday & Edward Reeves) / LEGEND IN MY TIME (Don Gibson) / YOU'VE ALWAYS GOT THE BLUES + TIME IS A THIEF (Mickey Newbury) / NIGHTLIFE (Willie Nelson) / PLEASE SEND ME SOMEONE TO LOVE (Percy Mayfield) / YOU AND ME, ME AND YOU (Will Jennings) / YOU SHOOK ME (Willie Dixon) / PLAYIN' WITH MY FRIENDS (Robert Cray & T-Bone Walker) / YOU'RE THE BOSS (Lieber-Stoller) / etc. • **Trivia:** He gave his "Lucille" guitar a cameo role in the 1985 movie, 'INTO THE NIGHT' and two years later appeared in 'Amazon Women On The Moon'.

Album rating (selective): ROCK ME BABY (*7) / LIVE AT THE REGAL (*8) / BLUES IS KING (*7) / LUCILLE (*7) / LIVE AND WELL (*7) / COMPLETELY WELL (*6) / INDIANOLA MISSISSIPPI SEEDS (*7) / LIVE IN COOK COUNTY JAIL (*7) / B.B. KING IN LONDON (*6) / L.A. MIDNIGHT (*6) / GUESS WHO (*6) / THE BEST OF B.B. KING compilation (*7) / TO KNOW YOU IS TO LOVE YOU (*6) / FRIENDS (*6) / TOGETHER FOR THE FIRST TIME ... LIVE with Bobby Bland (*7) / LUCILLE TALK BACK (*6) / TOGETHER AGAIN ... LIVE with Bobby Bland (*6) / KING SIZE (*6) / MIDNIGHT BELIEVER (*6) / TAKE IT HOME (*6) / NOW APPEARING AT OLE MISS (*6) / THERE MUST BE A BETTER WORLD SOMEWHERE (*7) / BLUES 'N' JAZZ (*6) / BLUES SUMMIT

(*7) / HEART & SOUL: A COLLECTION OF BLUES BALLADS compilation (*6)

B.B. KING – vocals, guitar

			not iss.	Bullet
1949.	(78) <309>	**MISS MARTHA KING. / WHEN YOUR BABY PACKS UP AND GOES**	-	☐

Note: All release dates in the 50's & 60's are approximate guesses, through working out dates / years of session recordings relating to catalogue numbers.

			not iss.	R.P.M.
1949.	(78) <315>	**GOT THE BLUES. / TAKE A SWING WITH ME**	-	
Oct 50.	(78) <304>	**MISTREATED WOMAN. / B.B.'S BOOGIE**	-	☐
Jan 51.	(78) <311>	**THE OTHER NIGHT BLUES. / WALKIN' AND CRYIN'**	-	☐

B.B.KING & HIS ORCHESTRA

Mar 51.	(78) <318>	**MY BABY'S GONE. / DON'T YOU WANT A MAN LIKE ME**	-	☐
Jun 51.	(78) <323>	**SHE'S DYNAMITE. / B.B.'S BLUES**	-	☐
Sep 51.	(78) <330>	**SHE'S A MEAN WOMAN. / HARD WORKING WOMAN**	-	☐
Dec 51.	(78) <339>	**3 O'CLOCK BLUES. / THAT AIN'T THE WAY TO DO IT**	-	☐
Mar 52.	(78) <348>	**SHE DON'T MOVE ME NO MORE. / FINE LOOKING WOMAN**	-	☐
May 52.	(78) <355>	**MY OWN FAULT DARLIN'. / SHAKE IT UP AND GO**	-	☐
Jul 52.	(78) <360>	**SOME DAY SOME WHERE. / GOTTA FIND MY BABY**	-	☐
Sep 52.	(78) <363>	**YOU KNOW I LOVE YOU. / YOU DIDN'T WANT ME**	-	☐
Nov 52.	(78) <374>	**STORY FROM MY HEART AND SOUL. / BOOGIE WOOGIE WOMAN**	-	☐
Jan 53.	(78) <380>	**DON'T HAVE TO CRY (PAST DAY). / WOKE UP THIS MORNING (MY BABY WAS GONE)**	-	☐
Mar 53.	(78) <386>	**PLEASE LOVE ME. / HIGHWAY BOUND**	-	☐
May 53.	(78) <391>	**NEIGHBORHOOD AFFAIR. / PLEASE HURRY HOME**	-	☐
Jul 53.	(78) <395>	**WHY DID YOU LEAVE ME. / BLIND LOVE (WHO CAN YOUR GOOD MAN BE)**	-	☐
Sep 53.	(78) <403>	**PRAYING TO THE LORD. / PLEASE HELP ME**	-	☐

B.B. "BLUES BOY" KING & HIS ORCHESTRA

(same label)

Nov 53.	(78) <408>	**I LOVE YOU BABY. / THE WOMAN I LOVE**	-	☐
Jan 54.	(78) <411>	**EVERYTHING I DO IS WRONG. / DON'T YOU WANT A MAN LIKE ME**	-	☐
Feb 54.	(78) <412>	**WHEN MY HEART BEATS LIKE A HAMMER. / BYE! BYE! BABY**	-	☐
1954.	(78) <416>	**YOU UPSET ME BABY. / WHOLE LOT OF LOVIN'**	-	☐
1955.	(78) <421>	**EVERYDAY I HAVE THE BLUES. / SNEAKIN' AROUND**	-	
1955.	(78) <425>	**JUMP WITH YOU BABY. / LONELY AND BLUE**	-	☐
1955.	(78) <430>	**SHUT YOUR MOUTH. / I'M IN LOVE**	-	☐
1955.	(78) <435>	**WHAT CAN I DO (JUST SING THE BLUES). / TEN LONG YEARS (I HAD A WOMAN)**	-	☐
Feb 56.	(78) <450>	**I'M CRACKING UP OVER YOU. / RUBY LEE**	-	☐
Mar 56.	(78) <451>	**SIXTEEN TONS. / CRYING WON'T HELP YOU**	-	☐
May 56.	(78) <457>	**DID YOU EVER LOVE A WOMAN. / LET'S DO THE BOOGIE**	-	☐
Jun 56.	(78) <459>	**DARK IS THE NIGHT. / (part 2)**	-	☐
Sep 56.	(78) <468>	**SWEET LITTLE ANGEL. / BAD LUCK**	-	☐
Feb 57.	(78) <479>	**ON MY WORD OF HONOUR. / BIM BAM**	-	☐
Apr 57.	(78) <486>	**EARLY IN THE MORNING. / YOU DON'T KNOW**	-	☐
May 57.	(78) <490>	**HOW DO I LOVE YOU. / YOU CAN'T FOOL MY HEART**	-	☐
Jun 57.	(78) <492>	**I WANT TO GET MARRIED. / TROUBLES TROUBLES (TROUBLES)**	-	☐
Jul 57.	(78) <494>	**BE CAREFUL WITH A FOOL. / (I'M GONNA) QUIT MY BABY**	-	☐
Oct 57.	(78) <498>	**I NEED YOU SO BAD. / I WONDER**	-	95
Dec 57.	(78) <501>	**THE KEY TO MY KINGDOM. / MY HEART BELONGS TO YOU**	-	85

			not iss.	Kent/Crown
1958.	(lp) <5020>	**SINGING THE BLUES** (compilation)	-	☐

– 3 o'clock blues / You know I love you / Woke up this morning / Please love me / You upset me baby / Everyday I have the blues / Ten years long (I had a woman) / Did you ever love a woman / Crying won't help you / Sweet little angel / Bad luck.

1958.	(lp) <5063>	**THE BLUES** (compilation)	-	☐

– Boogie woogie woman / Don't have to cry (past day) / Don't you want a man like me / When my heart beats like a hammer / What can I do (just sing the blues) / Ruby Lee / Early in the morning / I want to get married / Troubles troubles / Why does everything happen to me.

Sep 58.	(7") <301>	**WHY DOES EVERYTHING HAPPEN TO ME. / YOU KNOW I GO FOR IT**	-	☐
Nov 58.	(7") <307>	**DON'T LOOK NOW, BUT I'VE GOT THE BLUES. / DAYS OF OLD**	-	☐
Feb 59.	(7"; by B.B.KING & THE VOCAL CHORDS) <315> **PLEASE ACCEPT MY LOVE. / YOU'VE BEEN AN ANGEL**			-	☐
1959.	(lp) <5115>	**WAILS**	-	☐

– Tomorrow is another day / We can't make it / I've got papers on you baby (do what I say) / Sweet thing / Treat me right (oh baby) / Time to say goodbye / I love you so / The woman I love / The fool (a fool too long) / Come by here.

B.B. KING

(same label)

Aug 59.	(7") <317> **I AM. / WHY WORRY**	-	
Sep 59.	(7") <319> **COME BY HERE. / THE FOOL (A FOOL TOO LONG)**	-	
Oct 59.	(7") <325> **A LONELY LOVER'S PLEA. / THE WOMAN I LOVE**	-	
Nov 59.	(7") <327> **EVERYDAY I HAVE THE BLUES. / TIME TO SAY GOODBYE**	-	

(above 'A'side featured members of The COUNT BASIE BAND)

Dec 59.	(7") <329> **MEAN OLE FRISCO. / SUGAR MAMA**	-	
Jan 60.	(7") <5> **SWEET SIXTEEN. / (part 2)**	-	

(above on 'Modern' records)

Feb 60. (lp) <568> **SWEET SIXTEEN** (compilation) — Sweet sixteen (parts 1 & 2) / Days old old / Be careful with a fool / (I'm gonna) Quit my baby / What can I do (just sing the blues) / Ten long years (I had a woman) / I was blind / Whole lotta lovin' / Someday baby.

Feb 60.	(7") <333> **(I'VE) GOT A RIGHT TO LOVE MY BABY. / MY OWN FAULT**	-	
Mar 60.	(7") <336> **CRYING WON'T HELP YOU. / PLEASE LOVE ME**	-	
Apr 60.	(7") <337> **BLIND LOVE (WHO CAN YOUR GOOD MAN BE). / YOU UPSET ME BABY**	-	
May 60.	(7") <338> **TEN LONG YEARS (I HAD A WOMAN). / EVERYDAY I HAVE THE BLUES**	-	
May 60.	(7") <339> **THREE O'CLOCK BLUES. / DID YOU EVER LOVE A WOMAN**	-	
Jun 60.	(7") <340> **YOU DONE LOST YOUR GOOD THING NOW. / SWEET LITTLE ANGEL**	-	

(above 4 singles were recorded between 1953-56)

Jul 60. (7") <346> **GOOD MAN GONE BAD. / PARTIN' TIME** -

Aug 60. (lp) <5167> **KING OF THE BLUES** — (I've) Got a right to love my baby / Good man gone bad / Partin' time / Long nights (the feeling they call the blues) / I'll survive / What a way to go / Feel like a million / If I lost you / You're on top / I'm king. (UK-iss.1976 on 'Music For Pleasure'; 50259)

Sep 60.	(7") <350> **YOU DONE LOST YOUR GOOD THING NOW. / WALKING DR.BILL**	-	
Oct 60.	(7") <351> **THINGS ARE NOT THE SAME. / FISHIN' AFTER ME (CATFISH BLUES)**	-	
Nov 60.	(7") <353> **GET OUT OF HERE. / BAD LUCK SOUL**	-	

Jan 61. (lp) <5188> **MY KIND OF BLUES** — You done lost your good thing now / Walking Dr. Bill / Fishin' after me (catfish blues) / Hold that train / Understand / Someday baby / Mr. Pawnbroker / Driving wheel / My own fault (baby) / Please set a date.

Feb 61.	(7") <358> **HOLD THAT TRAIN. / UNDERSTAND**	-	
Jun 61.	(7") <360> **PEACE OF MIND. / SOMEDAY BABY**	-	

Jul 61. (lp) <5230> **MORE B.B.KING** — My reward / Don't cry anymore / You're breaking my heart / Blues for me (groovin' twist) / Just like a woman (rockin' twist) / Bad case of love / Bad luck soul / Get out of here / Shut your mouth.

Oct 61. (7") <362> **BAD CASE OF LOVE. / YOU'RE BREAKING MY HEART** -

Nov 61. (lp) <5248> **TWIST WITH B.B.KING** (compilation recent & old) -

Feb 62. (lp) <5286> **EASY LISTENING BLUES** — Hully gully (twist) / Easy listening (blues) / Blues for me / Slow walk (slow burn) / Shoutin' the blues / Night long / Confessin' / Don't touch / Rambler / Walkin'.

Mar 62. (7") <372> **HULLY GULLY (TWIST). / GONNA MISS YOU AROUND HERE** -

1962. (lp) <7708> **BLUES FOR ME** — Got 'em bad / I can't explain / You're gonna miss me / Troubles don't last / Strange things / Down hearted / So many days / I need you baby / The wrong road / The letter / You never know / Sundown / You won't listen.

<above issued on 'United'>

		H.M.V.	ABC Paramount
Apr 62.	(7") <10316> **YOU ASK ME. / I'M GONNA SIT IN TILL YOU GIVE IN**	-	
Jun 62.	(7") <10334> **BLUES AT MIDNIGHT. / MY BABY'S COMIN' HOME**	-	
Sep 62.	(7") <10361> **SNEAKIN' AROUND. / CHAINS OF LOVE**	-	
Nov 62.	(7") <10367> **TOMORROW NIGHT. / A MOTHER'S LOVE**	-	

1963. (lp) <456> **MR. BLUES** — Young dreamers / By myself / Chains of love / A mother's love / Blues at midnight / Sneakin' around / On my word of honor / Tomorrow night / My baby's comin' home / Guess who / You ask me / I'm gonna sit in 'til you give in.

Mar 63.	(7") <10390> **GUESS WHO. / BY MYSELF**	-	
Jun 63.	(7") <10455> **YOUNG DREAMERS. / ON MY WORD OF HONOR**	-	
Oct 63.	(7") <10486> **HOW DO I LOVE YOU. / SLOWLY LOSING MY MIND**	-	
Feb 64.	(7") <10527> **HOW BLUE CAN YOU GET. / PLEASE ACCEPT MY LOVE**	-	97
May 64.	(7") <10552> **HELP THE POOR. / I WOULDN'T HAVE IT ANY OTHER WAY**	-	98
Jul 64.	(7") <10576> **THE HURT. / WHOLE LOTTA LOVIN'**	-	
Oct 64.	(7") <10599> **NEVER TRUST A WOMAN. / WORRYIN' BLUES**	-	90
Dec 64.	(7") <10616> **WORST THING IN MY LIFE. / PLEASE SEND ME SOMEONE TO LOVE**	-	
Feb 65.	(7") <10634> **IT'S MY OWN FAULT. / EVERYDAY I HAVE THE BLUES**	-	
Apr 65.	(7") <10675> **TIRED OF YOUR JIVE. / NIGHT OWL**	-	
Jun 65.	(7") <10724> **ALL OVER AGAIN. / THE THINGS YOU PUT ME THROUGH**	-	

Jul 65. (lp) (CLP 1870) <ABCD 509> **LIVE AT THE REGAL** (live in Chicago 1964) — Everyday (I have the blues) / Sweet little angel / It's my own fault / How blue

can you get / Please love me / You upset me baby / Worry, worry / Woke up this mornin' / You done lost you good thing / Help the poor. *<re-iss. Sep71; ABCS 724> (re-iss. Oct83 on 'Charly'; CH 86) (cd-iss. Dec94 on 'Beat Goes On'; BGOCD 235)*

Aug 65.	(7") <10754> **I'D RATHER DRINK MUDDY WATER. / GOIN' TO CHICAGO BLUES**	-	

Mar 66. (lp) (CLP 3514) <528> **CONFESSIN' THE BLUES** — See see rider / Do you call that a buddy / Wee baby blues / I'd rather drink muddy water / In the dark / Confessin' the blues / Goin' to Chicago blues / I'm gonna move to the outskirts of town / World of trouble / How long blues / Cherry red / Please send me someone to love.

Jun 66.	(7") <10766> **TORMENTED. / YOU'RE STILL A SQUARE**	-	
Dec 66.	(7") <10856> **DON'T ANSWER THE DOOR. / (part 2)**		72 Oct66

Jan 67. (lp) (CLP 3608) <704> **BLUES IS KING** — Waitin' on you / Gambler's blues / Tired of your jive / Night life / Buzz me / Don't answer the door / Blind love / I know what you're puttin' down / Baby get lost / Gonna keep on loving you. *(re-iss. Nov87 on 'See For Miles'; SEE 216) (cd-iss. Jul92; SEECD 216)*

		Stateside	Bluesway
1967.	(7") (POP 1580) <10889> **NIGHT LIFE. / WAITIN' ON YOU**		

Jul 67. (lp) (SSL 10238) <BLS 6011> **BLUES ON TOP OF BLUES** — Heartbreaker / Losing faith in you / Dance with me / That's wrong little mama / Having my say / I'm not wanted anymore / Worried dream / Paying the cost to be the boss / Until I found you / I'm gonna do what they do to me / Raining in my heart / Now that you've lost me. *(re-iss. 1989 on 'B.G.O.' lp/cd; BGO/+CD 69)*

1967.	(7") <61004> **THINK IT OVER. / MEET MY HAPPINESS**	-	
1967.	(7") (POP 1594) **I DON'T WANT YOU CUTTIN' YOUR HAIR. / THINK IT OVER**		-
1967.	(7") <61007> **WORRIED DREAM. / THAT'S WRONG LITTLE MAMA**	-	
1967.	(7") <61011> **HEARTBREAKER. / RAINING IN MY HEART**	-	
1968.	(7") <61012> **SWEET SIXTEEN. / (part 2)**	-	
May 68.	(7") (SS 2112) <61015> **PAYING THE COST TO BE THE BOSS. / HAVING MY SAY**		39 Feb68
Jun 68.	(7") <61018> **I'M GONNA DO WHAT THEY DO TO ME. / LOSING FAITH IN YOU**	-	74
Sep 68.	(7") <61019> **THE B.B. JONES. / YOU PUT IT ON ME**		98 / 82
Dec 68.	(7") <61021> **DANCE WITH ME. / PLEASE SEND ME SOMEONE TO LOVE**	-	

—— (below feat. musicians The MAXWELL DAVIS BAND

Jan 69. (lp) (SSL 10272) <6016> **LUCILLE** — Lucille / You move me so / Country girl / No money no luck / I need your love / Rainin' all the time / I'm with you / Stop putting the hurt on me / Watch yourself *(re-iss. 1977 on 'A.B.C.'; 712) (cd-iss. Feb89 on 'Beat Goes On' lp/cd; BGO/+CD 36)* [Oct68]

Feb 69. (7") (SS 2141) <61022> **DON'T WASTE MY TIME. / GET MYSELF SOMEBODY**

Mar 69. (lp) (SSL 10284) <6022> **THE ELECTRIC B.B.KING** (compilation) — Tired of your jive / Don't answer the door / B.B.Jones / All over again / Paying the cost to the boss / Think it over / I done got wise / Meet my happiness / Sweet sixteen / You put it on me / I don't want you cuttin' off your hair. *(re-iss. Jan89 on 'Beat Goes On' lp/cd; BGO/+CD 37)*

Apr 69.	(7") <61024> **WHY I SING THE BLUES. / FRIENDS**	-	61
Jun 69.	(7") <61026> **GET OFF MY BACK WOMAN. / I WANT YOU SO BAD**		74
Jun 69.	(lp) (SSL 10297) <6031> **LIVE AND WELL** (half live)		56

— Don't answer the door / Just a little love / My mood / Sweet little angel / Please accept my love / I want you so bad / Friends / Get off my back woman / Let's get down to business / Why I sing the blues. *<cd-iss. Jun88 on 'M.C.A.'; 31191> (cd-iss. Jul94 on 'Beat Goes On'; BGOCD 233)*

Sep 69. (7") (573161) <57-3161> **EVERYDAY I HAVE THE BLUES. / FIVE LONG YEARS**

—— (above iss.UK on 'Blue Horizon')

Oct 69.	(7") <61029> **JUST A LITTLE LOVE. / MY MOOD**	-	76
Feb 70.	(7") (SS 2161) <61032> **THE THRILL IS GONE. / YOU'RE MEAN**		15 Jan70
Feb 70.	(lp) (SSL 10299) <6037> **COMPLETELY WELL**		38 Dec69

— The thrill is gone / So excited / No good / You're losing me / What happened / Confessin' the blues / Key to my kingdom / Crying won't help you now / You're mean. *(cd-iss. Jul87 on 'M.C.A.'; CMCAD 31039)*

		Probe	A.B.C.
May 70.	(7") (SS 2169) <61035> **SO EXCITED. / CONFESSIN' THE BLUES**		54 Mar70
Aug 70.	(7") (SS 2176) <11268> **HUMMINGBIRD. / ASK ME NO QUESTIONS**		48 Jun 70
Oct 70.	(7") (PRO 516) <11280> **CHAINS AND THINGS. / KING'S SPECIAL**		45
Nov 70.	(lp) (SPBA 6255) <713> **INDIANOLA MISSISSIPPI SEEDS**	-	26 Oct70

— Nobody loves me but my mother / You're still my woman / Ask me no questions / Until I'm dead and cold / King's special / Ain't gonna worry my life anymore / Chains and things / Go underground / Hummingbird. *(re-iss. May88 on 'Castle' lp/c/cd; CLA LP/MC/CD 141) (cd re-iss. Apr95 on 'Beat Goes On'; BGOCD 237)*

Feb 71.	(7") <11268> **ASK ME NO QUESTIONS. / NOBODY LOVES ME BUT MY MOTHER**	-	40
Mar 71.	(7") (PRO 528) **ASK ME NO QUESTIONS. / HELP THE POOR / HUMMING BIRD**		-
Mar 71.	(lp) (SPB 1032) <723> **LIVE IN COOK COUNTY JAIL** (live)		25 Feb71

— Every day I have the blues / How blues can you get / Worry, worry, worry / 3 o'clock blues / Darlin' you know I love you / Sweet sixteen / The thrill is gone / Please accept my love. *(re-iss. Oct87 on 'M.C.A.'; IMCA 27005) <US cd-iss. Jun88 on 'M.C.A.'; 31080> (d-cd-iss. Jul96 on 'M.C.A.'; MCD 33007)*

Jun 71.	(7") <11302> **HELP THE POOR. / LUCILLE'S GRANNY**	-	90
Aug 71.	(7") <11310> **GHETTO WOMAN. / SEVEN MINUTES**	-	68

below feat. **RINGO STARR, DR.JOHN, ALEXIS KORNER + STEVE MARRIOTT**

Oct 71. (lp) (SB 1041) <730> **B.B. KING IN LONDON** | | 57 — Introduction / Every day I have the blues / Night life / Love the life I'm living / When it all comes down (I'll still be around) / I've got a right to give up livin' /

Encore. (re-iss. 1977 on 'A.B.C.'; ABC 5015) (re-iss. Oct88 on 'Beat Goes On' lp/cd; BGO/+CD 42)

Oct 71. (7") <11316> **AIN'T NOBODY HOME. / ALEXI'S BOOGIE**   –   **46**

Feb 72. (7") <11319> **SWEET SIXTEEN. / I'VE BEEN BLUE TOO LONG**   –   **93**

Feb 72. (lp) (SPB 1051) <743> **L.A. MIDNIGHT**   **53**
– I got some help I don't need help / The poor / Can't you hear me talking to you / Midnight / Sweet sixteen / I believe (I've been blue too long) / Lucille's granny.

May 72. (7") <11321> **I GOT SOME HELP I DON'T NEED IT. / LUCILLE'S GRANNY**   –   **92**

Aug 72. (7") <11330> **GUESS WHO. / BETTER LOVIN' MAN**   –   **62**

Aug 72. (lp) (SPB 1063) <759> **GUESS WHO**   **65**
– Summer in the city / Just can't please you / Any other way / You don't know nothin' about love / Found what I need / Neighborhood affair / It takes a young girl / Better lovin' man / Guess who / Shouldn't have left me / Five long years <re-iss. 1974 on 'A.B.C.'; 5021> (re-iss. May89 on 'Beat Goes On' lp/cd; BGO LP/CD 71)

Oct 72. (7") <11339> **FIVE LONG YEARS. / SUMMER IN THE CITY**   –

Nov 72. (7") (PRO 573) **SUMMER IN THE CITY. / FOUND WHAT I NEED**   –

Jul 73. (7") (PRO 603) <11373> **TO KNOW YOU IS TO LOVE YOU. / I CAN'T LEAVE**   **38**

Aug 73. (lp) (SPB 1083) <794> **TO KNOW YOU IS TO LOVE YOU**   **71**
– I like to live the love / Respect yourself / Who are you / Love / I can't leave / To know you is to love you / Thank you for loving the blues / Oh to me. (re-iss. Oct74 on 'A.B.C.'; 5083)

Jan 74. (7") (PRO 613) <11406> **I LIKE TO LIVE THE LOVE. / LOVE**   **28**
           A.B.C.   A.B.C.

Aug 74. (7") (ABC 4005) <11433> **WHO ARE YOU. / OH TO ME**   **78** Jun 74

Aug 74. (lp) (ABCL 5051) <825> **FRIENDS**
– Friends / I got them blues / Baby I'm yours / Up at 5 a.m. / Philadelphia / When everything else is gone / My song. (cd-iss. Sep91 on 'Beat Goes On'; BGOCD 125)

Oct 74. (7") (ABC 4017) <12029> **PHILADELPHIA. / UP AT 5 P.M.**   **64**

Nov 74. (d-lp; B.B. KING & BOBBY BLAND) Anchor; (ABCD 605) / Dunhill; <751096> **TOGETHER FOR THE FIRST TIME . . . LIVE** (live)   **43**
– Introduction / 3 o'clock in the morning / It's my own fault baby / Driftin' blues / That's the way love is / I'm sorry / I'll take care of you / Don't cry no more / Don't want a soul hangin' around / Medley / Everybody wants to know why I sing the blues / Goin' down slow / I like to live the love. (cd-iss. Jun94 on 'Beat Goes On'; BGOCD 161)

Jan 75. (7") <12053> **FRIENDS. / MY SONG**   –

Sep 75. (7") <12158> **HAVE FAITH. / WHEN I'M WRONG**   –

Oct 75. (lp) (5149) <898> **LUCILLE TALKS BACK**
– Lucille talks back (copulation) / Breaking up somebody's home / Reconsider baby / Don't make me pay for his mistakes / When I'm wrong / I know the price / Have faith / Everybody lies a little.

Jul 76. (lp; BOBBY BLAND & B.B. KING) Impulse; (IMPL 8027) <9317> **TOGETHER AGAIN . . . LIVE** (live)   **73**
– Let the good times roll / Strange things happen / Feel so bad / Mother-in-law blues / Mean old world / Everyday (I have the blues) / The thrill is gone / I ain't gonna be the first to cry. (re-iss. Jan90 on 'M.C.A.' lp/cd; MCA/+D 4160) (cd re-iss. Feb93 on 'Beat Goes On'; BGOCD 162)

1976. (7") Impulse; <31006> **LET THE GOOD TIMES ROLL. / STRANGE HINGS HAPPEN**   –

1976. (7") Impulse; <31009> **EVERYDAY (I HAVE THE BLUES). / THE THRILL IS GONE**   –

Feb 77. (lp) (95148) <977> **KINGSIZE**
– Confessin' the blues / Paying the cost to be the boss / Think it over / You move me so / Heartbreaker / I'm gonna do what they do to me / What happened / By myself / That's wrong little mama / How long, how long blues / I'm not wanted anymore / My baby's comin' home.

1977. (7") <12247> **I WONDER WHY. / SLOW AND EASY**   –

1977. (7") <12380> **LET ME MAKE YOU CRY A LITTLE LONGER. / NEVER MADE A MOVE TOO SOON**

Mar 78. (7") <12412> **I JUST CAN'T LEAVE YOUR LOVE ALONE. / ?**

Apr 78. (lp) (ABCL 5246) <1061> **MIDNIGHT BELIEVER**
– When it all comes down / Midnight believer / I just can't leave your love alone / Hold on (I feel our love is changing) / Never make a move too soon / A world full of strangers / Let me make you cry a little longer. (re-iss. Jun84 on 'M.C.A.' lp/c; MCL/+C 1802) (cd-iss. May90; DMCL 1802) (re-iss. Jan93 cd/c; MCL D/C 19170)

Jun 78. (7") (ABC 4236) **HOLD ON (I FEEL OUR LOVE IS CHANGING). / MIDNIGHT BELIEVER**
           M.C.A.   M.C.A.

Aug 79. (7") (MCA 515) <41062> **BETTER NOT LOOK DOWN. / HAPPY BIRTHDAY BLUES**

Aug 79. (lp) (MCF 3010) <3151> **TAKE IT HOME**   **60**
– Better not look down / Same old story / Happy birthday blues / I've always been lonely / Second hand woman / Tonight I'm gonna make you a star / The beginning of the end / A story everybody knows / Take it home. (re-iss. Feb84 lp/c; MCL/+C 1784)

Oct 79. (7") (MCA 535) **TAKE IT HOME. / SAME OLD STORY**

Apr 80. (d-lp) <2-8016> **NOW APPEARING AT OLE MISS** (live)
– B.B. King theme / Caledonia / Don't answer the door / You done lost your good thing now / I need love so bad / Nobody loves me but my mother / Hold on (I feel our love is changing) / I got some outside help (I don't really need) / Darlin' you know I love you / When I'm wrong / The thrill is gone / Never made a move too soon / Three o'clock in the morning / Rock me baby / Guess who / I just can't leave your love alone. (UK-iss.Feb86 d-lp/d-c; MCDL/+C 601)

May 80. (7") (MCA 588) **CALEDONIA (live). / ROCK ME BABY** (live)   –   –

Feb 81. (7") <51101> **THERE MUST BE A BETTER WORLD SOMEWHERE. / YOU'RE GOING WITH ME**   –

Feb 81. (lp) (ABC 3095) <5162> **THERE MUST BE A BETTER WORLD SOMEWHERE**
– Life ain't nothing but a party / Born again human / There must be a better world somewhere / More, more, more / You're going with me. (cd-iss. Sep91 on 'Beat Goes On'; BGOCD 124)

Apr 82. (7") (MCA 772) **LEGEND IN MY TIME. / LOVE ME TENDER**   –

Apr 82. (lp) (MCF 3139) <5307> **LOVE ME TENDER**   –

– One of these nights / Love me tender / Don't change on me / (I'd be) A legend in my time / You've always got the blues / Please send me someone to love / You and me, me and you / Since I met you baby / Time is a thief / A world I never made

Jun 82. (7") (MCA 788) <52057> **ONE OF THESE NIGHTS. / SINCE I MET YOU BABY**
augmented The CRUSADERS and The Royal Philharmonic Orchestra on the 'Street Life' single.

Sep 82. (7") <52125> **LOVE ME TENDER. / THE WORD I NEVER MADE**   –

Jul 83. (7") <52218> **INFLATION BLUES. / SELL MY MONKEY**   –

Jul 83. (lp) (MCF 3170) <5413> **BLUES 'N' JAZZ**   Jun83
– Inflation blues / Broken hearted / Sell my monkey / Heed my warning / Teardrops from my eyes / Rainbow riot / Darlin' you know I love you / I can't let you go. (re-iss. Oct87 lp/c; MCL/+C 1836)

Jul 85. (7") (MCA 947) <52530> **INTO THE NIGHT. / CENTURY CITY CHASE**
(12"+=) (MCAT 947) – Midnight believer.

Sep 85. (lp/c) (MCF/+C 3281) <5616> **SIX SILVER STRINGS**
– Strings / Big boss man / In the midnight hour / Into the night / My Lucille / Memory lane / My guitar sings the blues / Double trouble.

Sep 85. (7") <52574> **MY LUCILLE. / Keep It Light (by Thelma Houston)**   –

Nov 85. (7") <53675> **BIG BOSS MAN. / MY GUITAR SINGS THE BLUES**

Feb 86. (7") <52751> **SIX SILVER STRINGS. / MEMORY LANE**   –

Mar 87. (7") (MCA 1124) **STANDING ON THE EDGE OF LOVE. / DON'T TELL ME NOTHNG**   –
(12"+=) (MCAT 1124) – Let yourself in for it.

Sep 87. (7") (MCA 1196) **IN THE MIDNIGHT HOUR. / HEED MY WARNING**

Jan 89. (7") <53872> **GO ON. / LAY ANOTHER LOG ON THE FIRE**   –

Feb 89. (lp/c/cd) (MCG/MCGC/DMCG 6038) **KING OF THE BLUES 1989**
– (You've become a) Habit to me / Drowning in the sea of love / Can't get enough / Standing on the edge / Go on / Let's straighten it out / Change in your lovin' / Undercover man / Lay another log on the fire / Business with my baby tonight.

—— (Apr89), BB was credited on U2's UK Top10 hit 'WHEN LOVE COMES TO TOWN'.

Aug 89. (7") (MCA 1354) **AIN'T NOBODY HOME. / LAY ANOTHER LOG ON THE FIRE**   –
(cd-s+=/12"+=) (D+/MCAT 1354) – Standing on the edge.

Oct 91. (lp/c/cd) (MCA/+C/D 10295)**THERE IS ALWAYS ONE MORE TIME**
– I'm moving on / Back in L.A. / The blues come over me / Fool me once / The lowdown / Mean and evil / Something up my sleeve / Roll, roll, roll / There is always one more time.

Feb 92. (c-s) <54339> **THE BLUES COME OVER ME (wild & bluesy club mix) / ('A'-integrity mix)**   –   –

Jul 93. (cd/c) (MCD/MCC 10710) **BLUES SUMMIT**
– Playin' with my friends / Since I met you baby / I pity the fool / You shook me / Something you got / There's something on your mind / Call it stormy Monday / You're the boss / We're gonna make it / Medley: I gotta move out of this neighborhood – Nobody loves me but my mother / Little by little / Everybody had the blues.

Nov 93. (cd-s; by B.B.KING / PHILIP BENT & TONY REMY / DIANE SCHUUR) **MERRY CHRISTMAS BABY. /** (above on 'G.R.P.')

Nov 97. (cd) <(MCD 1172-2)> **DEUCES WILD** (compilation)   **86**
– If you love me / The thrill is gone / Rock me baby / Please send me someone to love / Baby I love you / Ain't nobody home / Pauly's birthday boogie / There must be a better world somewhere / Confessin' the blues / Hummingbird / etc

– compilations, others, etc. –

1959. (7") RPM; <451> **CRYING WON'T HELP YOU. / PLEASE LOVE ME**

1959. (7") RPM; **WOKE UP THIS MORNING (MY BABY WAS GONE). / BAD CASE OF LOVE**   –

1960. (7") Modern; <7> **EVERYDAY I HAVE THE BLUES. / TIME TO SAY GOODBYE**

1960. (7") RPM; <457> **DID YOU EVER LOVE A WOMAN. / 3 O'CLOCK BLUES**

1960. (7") Modern; **YOU UPSET ME BABY. / WHEN MY HEART BEATS LIKE A HAMMER**

1961. (7") Modern; <19> **TEN LONG YEARS (I HAD A WOMAN). / YOU KNOW I LOVE YOU**

1962. (7") Modern; **BLUES STAY AWAY. / EYESIGHT TO THE BLIND**

1962. (lp) Kent; <7733> **ROCK ME BABY**
– You know I love you / Bad case of love / You upset me baby / Rock me baby / Woke up this morning / 3 o'clock blues / When my heart beats like a hammer / Sweet sixteen / Ten long years / Sneakin' around / Every day I have the blues / Sweet little angel / Please love me. (re-iss. Jun64 on 'United')

1962. (lp) Kent; <7734> **LET ME LOVE YOU**
– You're gonna miss me / I'm gonna quit my baby / Come by here / Whole lotta lovin' / I've got a right to love my baby / I can't explain / Walking Dr. Bill / Hold that train / Let me love you / Driving wheel / Did you ever love a woman / Troubles don't last.

1963. (7") Kent; <373> **MASHED POTATO TIME. / 3 O'CLOCK STOMP**

1963. (7") Kent; <381> **MASHING TO POPEYE. / TELL ME BABY**

1963. (7") Kent; <383> **WHEN MY HEART BEATS LIKE A HAMMER. / GOING DOWN SLOW**

1963. (lp) Kent; <7771> **LIVE** (live)
(also iss.US on 'United')

Nov 63. (7") Kent; <386> **3 O'CLOCK BLUES. / YOUR LETTER**   –

Dec 63. (7") Kent; <387> **CHRISTMAS CELEBRATION. / EASY LISTENING (BLUES)**   –

(re-iss. Nov64, hit US special Christmas Top 20)

Jan 64.	(7") *Kent;* <388> **DOWN NOW. / WHOLE LOTTA LOVIN'**		-	
Feb 64.	(7") *Kent;* <390> **THE ROAD I TRAVEL. / MY REWARD**		-	
Mar 64.	(7") *Kent;* <391> **THE LETTER. / YOU NEVER KNOW**		-	
	(above iss.UK Apr65 on 'Sue')			
1964.	(lp) *Kent;* <617> **PURE SOUL**		-	
Apr 64.	(7"-B.B. KING with The CHARIOTEERS-) *Kent;* **PRECIOUS LORD. / ARMY OF THE LORD**			
May 64.	(7") *Kent;* <393> **ROCK ME BABY. / I CAN'T LOSE**			34
	(also iss.US on 'Modern')			
	Note all below released on 'Kent'.			
Jul 64.	(7") <396> **LET ME LOVE YOU. / YOU'RE GONNA MISS ME**		-	
Oct 64.	(7") <403> **BEAUTICIAN BLUES. / I CAN HEAR MY NAME**		-	82
Feb 65.	(7") <415> **THE WORST THING IN MY LIFE. / GOT 'EM BAD**		-	
Apr 64.	(7") <421> **PLEASE LOVE ME. / BABY LOOK AT YOU**		-	
Jun 65.	(7") <426> **BLUE SHADOWS. / AND LIKE THAT**		-	97
Aug 65.	(7") <429> **WHY DOES EVERYTHING HAPPEN TO ME. / JUST A DREAM**		-	
Nov 65.	(7") <435> **BROKEN PROMISE. / HAVE MERCY BABY**		-	
Mar 66.	(7") <441> **EYESIGHT TO THE BLIND. / JUST LIKE A WOMAN (ROCKIN' TWIST)**		-	
May 66.	(7") <445> **FIVE LONG YEARS. / LOVE HONOR AND BABY**		-	
Jun 66.	(7") <447> **AIN'T NOBODY'S BUSINESS. / I WONDER WHY**		-	
Aug 66.	(7") <450> **I STAY IN THE MOOD. / EARLY EVERY MORNING**		-	
Nov 66.	(7") <458> **BLUES STAY AWAY. / IT'S A MEAN WORLD**		-	
Dec 66.	(lp) <531> **THE JUNGLE**		-	
	– The jungle / Eyesight to the blind / Ain't nobody's business / Five long years / Blue shadows / Worst thing in my life / Blues stay away / Beautician blues / I stay in the mood / I can hear my name / Got 'em bad / It's a mean world.			
Mar 67.	(7") <462> **THE JUNGLE. / LONG GONE BABY**		-	94
1967.	(7") <470> **BAD BREAKS. / GROWING OLD**		-	
1967s.	(lp) <7750> **BOSS OF THE BLUES**		-	
1967.	(d-lp) <533> **FROM THE BEGINNING**		-	
1967.	(lp) <535> **UNDERGROUND BLUES**		-	
1968.	(lp) <539> **THE INCREDIBLE SOUL OF B.B.KING**		-	
	(UK-iss.Apr70 on 'Polydor')			
1968.	(7") <484> **WHY DOES EVERYTHING HAPPEN TO ME. / WORRY WORRY**		-	
1968.	(lp) <548> **TURN ON WITH B.B. KING**		-	
1968.	(lp) **GREATEST HITS VOL.1**		-	
Sep 68.	Blue Horizon; (57-3144) / *Kent;* (7") <492> **THE WOMAN I LOVE. / YOU PUT IT ON ME**		-	94
1969.	(lp) <561> **BETTER THAN EVER**		-	
1969.	(lp) <563> **DOING MY THING LORD**		-	
1969.	(lp) <565> **B.B. KING LIVE** (live)		-	
1969.	(lp) <568> **THE ORIGINAL SWEET SIXTEEN**		-	
1969.	(7") <510> **YOUR FOOL. / SHOUTING THE BLUES**		-	
1970.	(lp) <5815> **ON STAGE LIVE** (live)		-	
1970.	(lp) **THE SOUL OF B.B. KING**		-	
	(most of lp's above were also iss.on 'United', above only also on 'Custom' & 'Festival')			
Apr 71.	(7") <4542> **THAT EVIL CHILD. / HELP THE POOR**		-	97
1967.	(lp) *Crown Ember;* (EMB 3379) **R & B SOUL**			-
1968.	(lp) *Blue Horizon;* (763216) **THE B.B.KING STORY**			-
1969.	(lp) *Blue Horizon;* (763226) **THE B.B.KING STORY, CHAPTER TWO**			-
	(both above re-iss. US Jul88 on'Joker')			
1971.	(lp) *Blue Horizon;* (2431004) **TAKE A SWING WITH ME**			-
Sep 71.	(lp) *ABC;* (ABCD 509) **LIVE AT THE REGAL** live 1964)			78
Feb 73.	(lp/c) *ABC;* **THE BEST OF B.B.KING**			
	(re-iss. Oct74) (re-iss. Jan83 on 'Fame') (re-iss. +cd.1987 on 'Ace')			
1976.	(lp/c) *ABC;* **B.B.KING ANTHOLOGY**			
1977.	(lp/c) *ABC;* **CLASSICS REVISITED**			
1977.	(lp/c) *ABC;* **MR.BLUES**			
1973.	(lp) *Bluesway;* **BACK IN THE ALLEY**		-	
Nov 87.	(lp/c) *MCA;* (MCB/+C 8001) **INTRODUCING B.B.KING**			
	(cd-iss. Apr89)			
Sep 90.	(cd/c/lp) *M.C.A.;* (DMCG/MCGC/MCG 6103) **LIVE AT SAN QUENTIN** (live 1970)			
	(re-iss. cd+c Sep94)			
Nov 92.	(4xcd-box/4xc-box) *M.C.A.;* **KING OF THE BLUES**			
Aug 93.	(cd/c) *MCA;* (MCL D/C 19214) **KING OF THE BLUES 1989**			
1974.	(lp) *New World;* **B.B.KING VOLUME 1**			-
1974.	(lp) *New World;* **B.B.KING VOLUME 2**			-
May 81.	(7") *Ace;* (NS 69) **BIM BAM. / SHAKE HOLLER AND RUN**			-
Jan 85.	(c) *Ace;* (CHC 801) **THE BEST OF MEMPHIS MASTERS**			-
Aug 86.	(lp/c/cd) *Ace;* (C H/HC/DCH 187) **SPOTLIGHT ON LUCILLE**			-
Nov 86.	(d-lp/c) *Ace;* (CDX/TCDX 14) **COMPLETELY LIVE AND WELL**			-
	– (The 2 albums from 1969)			
Jan 87.	(lp/c/cd) *Ace;* (C H/HC/DCH 199) **THE BEST OF B.B.KING VOLUME 2**			
Apr 87.	(lp) *Ace;* (CHD 201) **ONE NIGHTER BLUES**			-
Aug 89.	(lp/cd) *Ace;* (CHD 271) **LUCILLE HAD A BABY**			-
Aug 91.	(cd/c) *Ace;* (CDFAB/FABC 004) **THE FABULOUS B.B.KING**			-
Jul 92.	(cd) *Ace;* (CDCHD 300) **MY SWEET LITTLE ANGEL**			-
Nov 85.	(lp/c) *Deja Vu;* **20 BLUES GREATS**			
	– Help the poor / Everyday I have the blues / Woke up this morning / Worry worry / Sweet little angel / How blue can you get / You upset me baby / It's my own fault / Please love me / She don't love me no more / Three o'clock blues / Fine looking woman / Blind love / You know I love you / Ten long years / Mistreated woman / Shake it up and go / Sweet sixteen / You done lost your good thing now / Outside help. *(cd-iss. Sep87)*			
Apr 93.	(cd) *Sixteen;* **THE GOLD COLLECTION**			-

Feb 86.	(lp/c) *Crown;* (GEM/+C 001) **AMBASSADOR OF THE BLUES**			
Jan 87.	(cd) *Kingdom Jazz;* **LIVE (w / PAT METHENY / DAVE BRUBECK / HEATH BROS.)**			
Aug 87.	(lp) *Blues Boy;* (BB 301) **THE RAREST B.B.KING**			-
Oct 89.	(lp/cd) *Blue Moon;* (BMLP/CDBM 076) **B.B.'S BOOGIE**			
	(cd-iss. Jan95 on 'Success')			
Jun 91.	(cd/c/lp) *G.R.P.;* (GR/+C/+D 9637) **LIVE AT THE APOLLO** (live)			
Mar 94.	(cd/c) *Nectar;* (NTR CD/C 013) **HOW BLUE CAN YOU GET**			
Aug 94.	(cd) *Connoisseur;* (CSAPCD 117) **GREATEST HITS 1951-1960**			
Nov 94.	(cd/c) *Pickwick;* (PWK S/MC 4211) **KING OF THE BLUES**			
Nov 94.	(cd) *Charly;* (CDCBL 752) **KANSAS CITY 1972** (live)			
Feb 95.	(cd) *Castle;* (CCSCD 412) **THE COLLECTION**			
Jul 95.	(cd) *MCA;* (MCD 33008) **LUCILLE / FRIENDS**			
Dec 95.	(cd) *Opal;* (OCD 101) **THE EARLY BLUES BOY YEARS VOLUME 1**			
Dec 95.	(cd) *Opal;* (OCD 102) **THE EARLY BLUES BOY YEARS VOLUME 2**			
Apr 99.	(cd/c) *Universal TV;* (547340-2/-4) **HIS DEFINITIVE GREATEST HITS**		24	

Ben E. KING

Born: BENJAMIN EARL NELSON, 23 Sep'38, Henderson, North Carolina, USA. Relocating to Harlem with his family in 1947, KING began singing in gospel choirs. He subsequently played with high school doo-wop group The FOUR B's before moving on to join his first full-time band, The FIVE CROWNS, in his late teens. Although they cut a series of unsuccessful records, The 'CROWNS eventually struck lucky in summer 1958 when DRIFTERS manager, George Treadwell, fired his entire band and recruited KING & Co as replacements. Teamed up with crack writers JERRY LEIBER and MIKE STOLLER, the new look DRIFTERS were rejuvenated by a string of US Top 20 hits including 'THERE GOES MY BABY', 'DANCE WITH ME', 'THIS MAGIC MOMENT', SAVE THE LAST DANCE FOR ME' and 'I COUNT THE TEARS'; KING's emotive balladeering was at the epicentre of the group's appeal, flanked by lush strings and lilting latin rhythms. In May 1960, however, a complaint about low wages contributed to their star vocalist departing for a solo career. The partnership with LEIBER & STOLLER endured (alongside writers DOC POMUS and MORT SHUMAN), the pair even using new apprentice PHIL SPECTOR to help them pen KING's first solo Top 10, 'SPANISH HARLEM', later that year. Yet the song that marked the definitive chapter in his career was penned by KING himself; a goose-bump hymn to the endurance of love amid impending catastrophe, 'STAND BY ME' was KING's masterpiece and a deserved US Top 5 in summer '61. Ironically enough, the track didn't make much headway in the UK chart (No.27!) until 1987 when it climbed to No.1 after being used in the film of the same name (a poignant tale of boyhood coming-of-age starring a young River Phoenix). Over the ensuing two years, the man had a further couple of major hits with 'DON'T PLAY THAT SONG (YOU LIED)' and 'I (WHO HAVE NOTHING)' although his success thereafter was largely confined to the R&B chart. The late 60's and early 70's proved a particularly tough time but a return to 'Atlantic' in 1975 found him back in the US Top 5 with 'SUPERNATURAL THING'. The accompanying Top 40 album, 'SUPERNATURAL' (1975), spawned a further minor hit with 'DO IT IN THE NAME OF LOVE' although that was to be his last chart action for over a decade. In mid '77, he teamed up with transplanted Scottish funksters The AVERAGE WHITE BAND for the 'BENNY & US' album, resulting in two R&B hits. Following 1981's 'STREET TOUGH' album, KING cut his losses and rejoined The DRIFTERS although he later briefly resurrected his solo career after the success of the aforementioned 'STAND BY ME' re-issue. • **Trivia:** KING gave a very brief cameo performance on the 1974 GENESIS album, 'The Lamb Lies Down on Broadway'; the soul legend was drafted in to sing two closing words, "On Broadway" in the style of the original DRIFTERS hit which ironically he hadn't originally performed!

Best CD compilation: STAND BY ME (THE ULTIMATE COLLECTION) (*7)

BEN E. KING – vocals with session players

			London	Atco
Oct 60.	(7") <6166> **SHOW ME THE WAY. / BRACE YOURSELF**		-	
Dec 60.	(7") (HLK 9258) <6185> **FIRST TASTE OF LOVE. / SPANISH HARLEM**		27	53 10
Jun 61.	(7") (HLK 9358) <6194> **STAND BY ME. / ON THE HORIZON**		27	4 *Apr61*
Sep 61.	(7") (HLK 9416) <6203> **AMOR. / SOUVENIR OF MEXICO**		38	18 *Jul61*
Nov 61.	(lp; mono/stereo) (HA-K 2395/SAH-K 6195) <33133> **SPANISH HARLEM**			57 *Jul61*
	– Amor / Sway / Come closer to me / Perfidia / Granada / Sweet and gentle / Quizas, quizas, quizas (Perhaps, perhaps, perhaps) / Frenesi / Souvenir of Mexico / Besame mucho / Love me, love me / Spanish Harlem. *(UK re-iss. Jun67 on 'Atlantic'; 590 001)* – hit No.30			
Nov 61.	(7") (HLK 9457) <6207> **HERE COMES THE NIGHT. / YOUNG BOY BLUES**			81 66 *Oct61*
Mar 62.	(7") (HLK 9517) <6215> **ECSTASY. / YES**			56 *Feb62*
May 62.	(7") (HLK 9544) <6222> **DON'T PLAY THAT SONG (YOU LIED). / THE HERMIT OF MISTY MOUNTAIN**			11 *Apr62*
Aug 62.	(7") (HLK 9586) <6231> **TOO BAD. / MY HEART CRIES FOR YOU**			88
Oct 62.	(lp) (HA-K 8012) <33142> **DON'T PLAY THAT SONG**			
	– Don't play that song (you lied) / Ecstasy / On the horizon / Show me the way /			

Here comes the night / First taste of love / Stand by me / Yes / Young boy blues / The hermit of misty mountain / I promise love / Brace yourself

Nov 62. (7") (HLK 9631) <6237> **I'M STANDING BY. / WALKING IN THE FOOTSTEPS OF A FOOL** — —

Jan 63. (7") <6246> **TELL DADDY. / AUF WIEDERSEHEN** —

Mar 63. (7") (HLK 9691) <6256> **HOW CAN I FORGET. / GLORIA, GLORIA** 85

Sep 63. (7") (HLK 9778) <6267> **I (WHO HAVE NOTHING). / THE BEGINNING OF TIME** 29 Jun63

Dec 63. (7") (HLK 9819) <6275> **I COULD HAVE DANCED ALL NIGHT. / GYPSY** 72 Oct63

Jan 64. (lp; mono/stereo) (HA-K/SH-K 8026) <333137> **SONGS FOR SOULFUL LOVERS** Oct63 — My heart cries for you / He will break your heart / Dream lover / Will you love me tomorrow / My foolish heart / Fever / Moon River / What a difference a day made / Because of you / at last / On the street where you live / It's all in the game.

Jan 64. (7") <6284> **WHAT NOW MY LOVE. / GROOVIN'** — —

Feb 64. (7") (HLK 9840) **AROUND THE CORNER. / GROOVIN'** —

Atlantic **Atco**

1964. (lp) (ATL 5016) <33165> **GREATEST HITS** (compilation) — Stand by me / Don't play that song (you lied) / Amor / Young boy blues / Goodnight my love / Spanish Harlem / How can I forget / It's all over / I (who have nothing) / Save the last dance for me / I Count the tears / This magic moment. (re-iss. 1973 on 'Atlantic') (re-iss. cd+c May93 on 'Prestige')

Mar 64. (7") <6288> **THAT'S WHEN IT HURTS. / AROUND THE CORNER** — 63

Jun 64. (7") <6303> **WHAT CAN A MAN DO. / SI SENOR**

Oct 64. (7") (AT 4007) <6315> **IT'S ALL OVER. / LET THE WATER RUN DOWN** 72 Sep64

Jan 65. (7") (AT 4018) <6328> **SEVEN LETTERS. / RIVER OF TEARS** 45 Dec64

Jan 65. (lp) <33174> **SEVEN LETTERS** — Seven letters / River of tears / I'm standing by / Jamaica / Down home / Si senor / It's all over / Let the water run down / This is my dream / It's no good for me / In the middle of the night / Don't drive me away. (UK-iss.1968; 588 125)

Apr 65. (7") (AT 4025) <6343> **THE RECORD (BABY I LOVE YOU). / THE WAY YOU SHAKE IT** 84

Jun 65. (7") <6357> **NOT NOW (I'LL TELL YOU WHEN). / SHE'S GONE AGAIN** —

Sep 65. (7") (AT 4043) <6371> **CRY NO MORE. / THERE'S NO PLACE TO HIDE**

Nov 65. (7") <6390> **GOODNIGHT MY LOVE, PLEASANT DREAMS. / I CAN'T BREAK THE NEWS TO MYSELF** — 91

Jan 66. (7") (AT 4065) **GOODNIGHT MY LOVE, PLEASANT DREAMS. / TELL DADDY** —

May 66. (7") (584 008) <6413> **SO MUCH LOVE. / DON'T DRIVE ME AWAY** 96

Oct 66. (7") (584 046) <6431> **I SWEAR BY THE STARS ABOVE. / GET IN A HURRY**

Jan 67. (7") (584 069) <6454> **WHAT IS SOUL? / THEY DON'T GIVE MEDALS TO YESTERDAY'S HEROES**

Feb 67. (lp) (587 072) **WHAT IS SOUL?** — — The record (baby I love you) / She's gone again / There's no place to hide / Cry no more / Goodnight my love / Katherine / I can't break the news to myself / I swear by stars above / Get in a hurry / They don't give medals to yesterday's heroes / Teeny weeny little bit / What is soul?

Apr 67. (7") (584 106) <6472> **TEARS, TEARS, TEARS. / MAN WITHOUT A DREAM** — 93

Jul 67. (7") <6493> **TEENY WEENIE LITTLE BIT. / KATHERINE**

Oct 67. (7") <6527> **SHE KNOWS WHAT TO DO FOR ME. / DON'T TAKE YOUR SWEET LOVE AWAY** —

Jan 68. (7"; as BEN E. KING & DEE DEE SHARPE) <6557> **WE GOT A THING GOING ON. / WHATCHA GONNA DO** —

Apr 68. (7") (584 184) <6571> **DON'T TAKE YOUR LOVE FROM ME. / FORGIVE THIS FOOL**

Aug 68. (7") (584 205) <6596> **IT'S AMAZING. / WHERE'S THE GIRL**

Feb 69. (7") (584 238) <6637> **TIL I CAN'T TAKE ANYMORE. / IT AIN'T FAIR**

May 69. (7") <6666> **WHEN YOU LOVE SOMEBODY. / HEY LITTLE ONE** —

Crewe **Maxwell**

1970. (7") (CRW 2) **GOODBYE MY OLD GIRL. / I CAN'T TAKE IT LIKE A MAN**

1970. (lp) (CRWS 203) <88001> **ROUGH EDGES** — She lets her hair down (early in the morning) / Little green apples / Wishing for tomorrow / If you've gotta make a fool of somebody / Come together / One man / In the midnight hour / Lay lady lay / Don't let me down / Tonight I'll be staying here with you.

C.B.S. **Mandala**

Feb 72. (7") (CBS 7785) <2512> **TAKE ME TO THE PILOT. / I GUESS IT'S GOODBYE**

Feb 72. (lp) (CBS 64570) <3007> **THE BEGINNING OF IT ALL** — Take me to the pilot / I guess it's goodbye / Travellin' woman / Love is / Into the mystic / White moon / Love is gonna get you / Beginning of it all / Only you and I know / All of your tomorrows / She does it right.

May 72. (7") <2513> **INTO THE MYSTIC. / WHITE MOON** —

Aug 72. (7") <2518> **SPREAD MYSELF AROUND. /** —

Atlantic **Atlantic**

Apr 75. (7") (K 10565) <3241> **SUPERNATURAL THING. / (part 2)** 5 Feb75

Apr 75. (lp/c) (K/K4 50118) <18132> **SUPERNATURAL** 39 — Supernatural thing (part 1 & 2) / You're lovin' ain't good enough / Drop my heart off (on your way to the door) / Do it in the name of love / Happiness is where you find it / Do you wanna do a thing / Imagination / What do you want me to do.

Jun 75. (7") (K 10618) **HAPPINESS IS WHERE YOU FIND IT. / DROP MY HEART OFF (ON YOUR WAY TO THE DOOR)** — —

Jul 75. (7") (K 10636) <3274> **DO IT IN THE NAME OF LOVE. / IMAGINATION** 60 May75

Jan 76. (7") (K 10708) <3308> **I HAD A LOVE. / WE GOT LOVE**

Apr 76. (lp/c) (K/K4 50264) <18169> **I HAD A LOVE** — I had a love / I betcha didn't know that / Smooth sailing / No danger ahead / Everybody plays the fool / Standing in the wings of heartache / We got love / Tower of strength / You're stepping on my heart.

May 76. (7") <3337> **I BETCHA DIDN'T KNOW THAT. / SMOOTH SAILING** —

Dec 76. (7") <3359> **SOMEBODY'S KNOCKING. / ONE MORE TIME** —

Apr 77. (7") <3402> **GOT IT UP FOR LOVE. / KEEPIN' IT TO MYSELF** —

—— (mid'77) KING teamed up with AVERAGE WHITE BAND on LP, 'BENNY & US'

Jan 79. (lp/c) (K/K4 50527) <19200> **LET ME LIVE IN YOUR LIFE** — Fifty years / Tippin' / Spoiled / Wonder woman / Let me live in your life / I see the light / Fly away (to my wonderland) / Dark storm on the horizon / Family jewels / Sweet rhapsody / Fifty years.

Feb 79. (7") <3494> **TIPPIN'. / I SEE THE LIGHT** —

Apr 79. (7") <3535> **SPOILED. / FLY AWAY TO MY WONDERLAND** —

Nov 79. (7") (K 11407) <3635> **MUSIC TRANCE. / AND THIS IS LOVE**

May 80. (lp/c) (K/K4 50713) <19269> **MUSIC TRANCE** — And this is love / Music trance / Touched by your love / You've only got one chance to be young / Hired gun / Work that body.

Jun 80. (7") (K 11495) **YOU'VE ONLY GOT ONE CHANCE TO BE YOUNG. / MUSIC TRANCE**

May 81. (lp/c) (K/K4 50787) <19300> **STREET TOUGH** — Street tough / Staying power / Souvenirs of love / Stay a while with me / Something to be loved / Made for each other / Why is the question / You made the difference to my life.

May 81. (7") <3808> **STREET TOUGH. / WHAT IS THE QUESTION** —

Oct 81. (7") <3839> **SOUVENIRS OF LOVE. / YOU MADE THE DIFFERENCE TO MY LIFE**

—— In 1982, he rejoined The DRIFTERS. By the late 80's, he had resurrected solo career after hitting No.1 w 'STAND BY ME'.

Bold Reprieve **not iss.**

May 87. (7"/12") (BRM 003/+T) **SPREAD MYSELF AROUND. / DO IT NOW** —

Syncopate **not iss.**

Jun 87. (7"/12") (SY/12SY 3) **DANCING IN THE NIGHT. / ('A'version)** —

Manhattan Manhattan

Jun 87. (7"/12") (MT/12MT 25) **SAVE THE LAST DANCE FOR ME. / WHEEL OF LOVE** 69

Nov 87. (7") (MT 33) **LOVER'S QUESTION. / BECAUSE OF LAST NIGHT** (12"+=) (12MT 33) – Stand by me (1987 version).

Nov 87. (cd/c/lp) <(CD/TC+/MT 1013)> **SAVE THE LAST DANCE FOR ME** Apr88 — Wheel of love / Save the last dance for me / Because of last night / Lover's question / Whatever this is (it ain't true love) / Halfway to Paradise / Let a man do it for you / I cry for you / Test of time / Two lovers.

—— semi-retired from the studio

– compilations, etc. –

on 'Atlantic' unless mentioned otherwise

1963. (7"ep) London; (REK 1361) **BEN E. KING** —

1963. (7"ep) London; (REK 1386) **I'M STANDING BY** —

1964. (7"ep) (AET 6004) **WHAT NOW MY LOVE** —

Mar 67. (7"; as BEN E. KING & THE DRIFTERS) (584 090) **SAVE THE LAST DANCE FOR ME. / STAND BY ME** —

Apr 67. (7") (584 106) **TEARS, TEARS, TEARS. / A MAN WITHOUT A DREAM** —

Feb 68. (7") (584 149) **SEVEN LETTERS. / GOODNIGHT MY LOVE** —

Jul 71. (7") (584 205) **IT'S AMAZING. / TEARS, TEARS, TEARS** —

Sep 71. (7"ep) **SAVE THE LAST DANCE FOR ME (with the DRIFTERS) / UNDER THE BOARDWALK (with the DRIFTERS). / SPANISH HARLEM / STAND BY ME** —

Jul 75. (lp) (K 50139) **THE BEN E. KING STORY** —

Apr 80. (7"ep) **WHAT IS SOUL? / STAND BY ME. / (two by PERCY SLEDGE)** —

Jul 81. (7") Old Gold; (OG 9101) **SPANISH HARLEM. / STAND BY ME** (re-iss. Mar90; same)

May 84. (lp) Edsel; (ED 131) **HERE COMES THE NIGHT** —

Oct 84. (c) Dynamic; (SD 33165) **GREATEST HITS** —

Jan 87. (7") (A 9361) <89361> **STAND BY ME. / Coasters: YAKETY YAK** 1 9 Sep86 (12"+=) (A 9361T) – Music trance.

Feb 87. (lp/c)(cd) (WX 90/+C)(780213-2) **STAND BY ME (THE ULTIMATE COLLECTION)** 14 — Stand by me / Save the last dance for me / I (who have nothing) / That's when it hurts / I could have danced all night / First taste of love / Dream lover / Moon river / Spanish Harlem / Amor / I count the tears / Don't play that song / This magic moment / Young boy blues / It's all in the game / Supernatural thing (pt.1). (above also featured DRIFTERS tracks)

Mar 87. (7"/12") Creole; (CR/+T 97) **SPANISH HARLEM. / FIRST TASTE OF LOVE** — —

Apr 87. (7") (YZ 118) **SPANISH HARLEM. / FIRST TASTE OF LOVE** (12"+=) (YZ 118T) – Medley: Spanish Harlem – Stand by me – Don't play that song.

May 88. (lp/c) Flashback; (3/6 4045) **STAND BY ME** — — (cd-iss. May89 on 'Object Ent.'; ONN 45)

1988. (cd) K-Tel; (ONCD 5118) **BEN E. KING & THE DRIFTERS** —

Jan 89. (cd; as BEN E. KING & THE DRIFTERS) MCS Look Back; (120 111) **GREATEST HITS** —

Jun 92. (c/cd) Ichiban; (ICH 1133 MC/CD) **WHAT'S IMPORTANT TO ME** — —

Oct 92. (cd) *Carlton; (SMS 058)* **SOUL KINGS VOL.3**	☐	-
Apr 93. (cd) *Prestige; (CDSGP 045)* **GREATEST HITS**	☐	-
Oct 93. (d-cd) *<8122 71215-2)>* **ANTHOLOGY**	☐	-
Nov 94. (cd) *B.A.M.; (KLMCD 033)* **PEARLS OF THE PAST**	☐	-
Jan 95. (cd/c; as BEN E. KING & THE DRIFTERS) *K-Tel; (ECD3/EMC2 044)* **BROTHERS IN SOUL**	☐	-
Jan 95. (cd) *The Collection; (COL 055)* **THE COLLECTION**	☐	-
Dec 95. (cd) *Javelin; (HADCD 180)* **THE LEGENDARY BEN E.KING**	☐	-
Sep 96. (cd) *Sequel; (RSACD 837)* **THE DEFINITIVE ANTHOLOGY VOL.1: CLASSICS FROM THE ATCO MASTERS – SPANISH HARLEM**	☐	
Sep 96. (cd) *Sequel; (RSACD 838)* **THE DEFINITIVE ANTHOLOGY VOL.2: CLASSICS FROM THE ATCO MASTERS – SINGS FOR SOULFUL LOVERS**	☐	
Sep 96. (cd) *Sequel; (RSACD 839)* **THE DEFINITIVE ANTHOLOGY VOL.3: CLASSICS FROM THE ATCO MASTERS – DON'T PLAY THAT SONG**	☐	
Nov 96. (cd) *Sequel; (RSACD 853)* **THE DEFINITIVE ANTHOLOGY VOL.4: CLASSICS FROM THE ATCO MASTERS – SEVEN LETTERS**	☐	
Nov 96. (cd) *Sequel; (RSACD 854)* **THE DEFINITIVE ANTHOLOGY VOL.5: CLASSICS FROM THE ATCO MASTERS – WHAT IS SOUL?**	☐	
Nov 96. (cd) *Sequel; (RSACD 855)* **THE DEFINITIVE ANTHOLOGY VOL.6: CLASSICS FROM THE ATCO MASTERS – SUPERNATURAL THING**	☐	
Nov 96. (cd) *Sequel; (RSACD 856)* **THE DEFINITIVE ANTHOLOGY VOL.7: CLASSICS FROM THE ATCO SERIES – BENNY & US**	☐	
May 97. (cd/c; as BEN E. KING & THE DRIFTERS) *A-Play; (10171-2/-4)* **THE HITS COLLECTION**	☐	-
May 98. (cd) *Rhino; <(8122 72970-2)>* **THE VERY BEST OF BEN E. KING**	☐	
Aug 98. (cd) *Collectables; (CCLCD 62102)* **SPANISH HARLEM / DON'T PLAY THAT SONG**	☐	-
May 99. (d-cd/d-c; as BEN E. KING & THE DRIFTERS) *Global TV; (RAD CD/MC 108)* **THE BEST OF . . .**	☐	

Carole KING

Born: CAROLE KLEIN, 9 Feb'40, Brooklyn, New York, USA. Taught to play piano and sing by her mother from an early age, CAROLE's first serious forays into songwriting were with PAUL SIMON in 1958. She then met lyricist (and future husband) GERRY GOFFIN at college, the pair subsequently forming one of the most prolific and successful writing partnerships the music business has ever seen. Setting up shop in New York's famed 'Brill Building' (working for AL NEVINS and DON KIRSHNER's 'Aldon Music'), the duo scored their first success in 1961 when 'WILL YOU STILL LOVE ME TOMORROW' (by the SHIRELLES) and 'TAKE GOOD CARE OF MY BABY' (by BOBBY VEE), both hit the US top spot. The following year, 'THE LOCOMOTION' (by LITTLE EVA), gave them their third No.1, a track they also arranged, conducted and produced for the young singer. The hits kept on coming and meanwhile, KIRSHNER had persuaded CAROLE to release her solo version of 'IT MIGHT AS WELL RAIN UNTIL SEPTEMBER', which subsequently went UK Top 3 and US Top 30. The hit was a one-off though, and KING wasn't to resume her recording career until the late 60's. A relatively lean spell ensued (during which CAROLE and GERRY were divorced, although they kept the writing partnership going) before STEVE LAWRENCE took a GOFFIN-KING number back to the top of the US charts, 'GO AWAY LITTLE GIRL' (also a hit for DONNY OSMOND). Nor were the duo fazed by the onset of psychedelia, scoring hits for the ANIMALS ('DON'T BRING ME DOWN'), THE MONKEES ('PLEASANT VALLEY SUNDAY', they also recorded 'TAKE A GIANT STEP') and The BYRDS (a brilliant version of 'GOIN' BACK', they also transformed 'WASN'T BORN TO FOLLOW' into a psych-country classic). At the height of the hippy scene in 1967, GOFFIN, KING and columnist, AL ARONOWITZ, founded their own label, 'Tomorrow', signing up flower power outfit, The MYDDLE CLASS. The project flopped, although the band's bass player, CHARLES LARKEY (ex-FUGS) would soon become KING's second husband. He and KING subsequently formed their own band, The CITY, with DANNY 'KOOTCH' KORTCHMAR (guitar, ex-FUGS) and JIM GORDON (drums). The outfit released one poor selling album, 'NOW THAT EVERYTHING'S BEEN SAID' (1969) on LOU ADLER's 'Ode' label, KING soon striking out on her own for a solo career. Encouraged to pen her own lyrics by fellow Laurel Canyon singer/songwriter JAMES TAYLOR (for whom CAROLE had played piano on his debut 'Apple' album, 'Sweet Baby James'), the first hesitant results came in the form of the 'WRITER' album in 1970, KING remaining with 'Ode' records. A breakthrough came with 'TAPESTRY' in 1971, a multi-million seller that became the biggest album in recording history up to that point. From the opening shimmy of 'I FEEL THE EARTH MOVE', to the melancholy reflection of 'SO FAR WAY' and 'HOME AGAIN', KING sounded more confident and self-possessed, her unpretentious vocal style and straight talking, confessional lyrics proving a winning combination. The record also benefitted from the midas touch of Lou Adler's production and the backing of 'The Section', the semi-legendary session team of KORTCHMAR, LELAND SKLAR (bass), RUSS KUNKEL (drums) and CRAIG DOERGE (keyboards), creating a highly commercial pop/rock/white soul fusion making up in melody what it lacked in earthiness. The album not only set the tone for the MOR dominated American music of the 70's, but initiated a slew of similar releases by songwriters desperate to get out

from behind a desk. Sales of 'TAPESTRY' were further boosted when JAMES TAYLOR had a US No.1 in the summer of '71 with a cover of 'YOU'VE GOT A FRIEND'. KING's follow-up albums, 'MUSIC' (1971), 'RHYMES AND REASONS' (1972), 'FANTASY' (1973) and 'WRAP AROUND JOY' (1974) all carried on in much the same vein, going gold and spawning such reliable AOR fare as 'SWEET SEASONS' (Top 10 in 1971) and 'JAZZMAN' (No.2 in 1974). The latter album employed the lyric-writing services of DAVID PALMER, later of STEELY DAN. None of the records, however, achieved the consistency of 'TAPESTRY', although they did cement KING's position as a fully paid-up superstar member of the L.A. elite. She eventually reunited with GOFFIN in 1976 for 'THOROUGHBRED' , her last album for 'Ode', subsequently signing for 'Capitol'. Her first release for the company, 'SIMPLE THINGS' (1977) saw her hooking up with backing band NAVARRO who numbered KING's future husband, RICK EVERS among their ranks. Tragedy struck the following year, however, when EVERS died of a drug overdose. It marked the beginning of a relatively barren period for KING, only her 'PEARLS – SONGS OF GOFFIN AND KING' (1980) album making any impact on the charts, and even that consisted of rehashed past glories. A brief move to 'Atlantic' and the return of KORTCHMAR and KUNKEL failed to resurrect her career and KING hasn't had a hit album or single since. She remains a respected figure within the business, however, and continues to tour and record, releasing material on her own 'King's X' label, finally receiving the dubious honour of being inducted into the Rock'n'roll Hall Of Fame in 1990.

Album rating: WRITER: CAROLE KING (*6) / TAPESTRY (*8) / MUSIC (*7) / RHYMES & REASONS (*6) / FANTASY (*7) / WRAP AROUND JOY (*7) / REALLY ROSIE (*6) / THOROUGHBRED (*6) / SIMPLE THINGS (*4) / HER GREATEST HITS compilation (*7) / WELCOME HOME (*4) / TOUCH THE SKY (*4) / PEARLS – SONGS OF GOFFIN AND KING (*5) / ONE TO ONE (*4) / SPEEDING TIME (*3) / CITY STREETS (*4) / IN CONCERT (*3) / COLOR OF YOUR DREAMS (*3) / A NATURAL WOMAN: THE ODE COLLECTION compilation (*8)

CAROLE KING – vocals, piano (with session people)

	not iss.	ABC-Paramount
Jan 59. (7") *<9921>* **GOIN' WILD. / THE RIGHT GIRL**	-	
Mar 59. (7") *<9986>* **BABY SITTIN'. / UNDER THE STARS**	-	
	not iss.	RCA Victor
May 59. (7") *<7560>* **QUEEN OF THE BEACH. / SHORT MORT**	-	
	not iss.	Alpine
Nov 59. (7") *<57>* **OH NEIL!. / A VERY SPECIAL BOY**	-	

—— She keeps on writing for others husband GERRY GOFFIN. After two and a half years she returned to solo work for . . .

	London	Dimension
Aug 62. (7") *(HLU 9591) <2000>* **IT MIGHT AS WELL RAIN UNTIL SEPTEMBER. / NOBODY'S PERFECT**	3	22

<first issued in US on 'Companion'; 2000> (re-iss. Sep72; HL 10391) (reached No.43 UK)

Nov 62. (7") *<1004>* **SCHOOL BELLS ARE RINGING. / I DIDN'T HAVE ANY**	-	-
Apr 63. (7") *<1009>* **HE'S A BAD BOY. / WE GROW UP TOGETHER**	-	94

—— Soon divorced her husband GERRY, although they still carried on writing.

	London	Tomorrow
Apr 66. (7") *(HL 10036) <7502>* **SOME OF YOUR LOVIN'. / ROAD TO NOWHERE**	☐	☐

The CITY

CAROLE KING with **CHARLES LARKEY** – bass (of FUGS) / **DANNY 'KOOTCH' KORTCHMAR** – guitar / **JIM GORDON** – drums

	A & M	Ode
Jan 69. (lp) *<244012>* **NOW THAT EVERYTHING'S BEEN SAID**	-	☐

– Snow queen / I wasn't born to follow / Now that everything's been said / Paradise alley / Man without a dream / Victim of circumstance / Why are you leaving / Lady / My sweet home / I don't believe it / That old sweet roll (hi-de-do) / All my time.

Feb 69. (7") *<113>* **PARADISE ALLEY. / SNOW QUEEN**	-	☐
May 69. (7") *<119>* **THAT OLD SWEET ROLL. / WHY ARE YOU LEAVING**	-	☐

CAROLE KING

—— solo, with session people

May 70. (lp) *(AMLS 996) <77006>* **WRITER: CAROLE KING**		☐

– Spaceship races / No easy way down / Child of mine / Goin' back / To love / What have you got to lose / Eventually / Raspberry jam / Can't you be real / I can't hear you no more / Sweet sweetheart / Up on the roof. *<re-prom.Apr71 hit US No.84>* *(re-iss. Feb79 on 'Epic'; EPC 82318)*

Mar 70. (7") **EVENTUALLY. / UP ON THE ROOF**	-	☐

—— now again with regulars LARKEY and KORTCHMAR plus **RUSS KUNKEL** – drums and guest **JAMES TAYLOR** – guitar, backing vocals (solo artist)

Nov 70. (lp/c) *(AMLS/CAM 2025) <77009>* **TAPESTRY**	4	1

– I feel the earth move / So far away / It's too late / Home again / Beautiful / Way over yonder / You've got a friend / Where you lead / Will you still love me tomorrow / Smackwater Jack / Tapestry / (You make me feel like) A natural woman. *(re-iss. 1977 on 'Epic'; EPC 82308) (re-iss. Aug84 on 'Epic' lp/c; EPC/40 32110) (cd-iss. May84 on 'Polydor'; 821 194-1) (cd re-iss. 1988 on 'C.B.S.'; CDCBS 82308) (cd re-iss. Jun89; CD 32110) (cd re-iss. Sep95 on 'Epic'; 480422-2)*

Apr 71. (7") *(AMS 849) <66015>* **IT'S TOO LATE. / I FEEL THE EARTH MOVE**	6	1
Jul 71. (7") *(AMS 867) <66019>* **SO FAR AWAY. / SMACKWATER JACK**		14
Dec 71. (lp/c) *(AMLH/CAM 67013) <77013>* **MUSIC**	18	1

– Brother, brother / Song of long ago / Brighter / Surely / Some kind of wonderful / It's going to take some time / Music / Sweet seasons / Carry your load / Growing away from me / Too much rain / Back to California. *(re-iss. Feb79 on 'Epic'; EPC 82319) (re-iss. 1983 on 'C.B.S.' lp/c; CBS/40 32066) (cd-iss. Jun91 on 'Pickwick'; 982595-2) (cd re-iss. Feb97 on 'Epic'; 484462-2)*

Jan 72. (7") *(AMS 887)* <66022> **SWEET SEASONS. / POCKET MONEY** | | 9 |

Mar 72. (7") **BROTHER, BROTHER. / IT'S GOING TO TAKE SOME TIME** | - | - |
| | Ode | Ode |

Oct 72. (7") <*(ODS 66031)*> **BEEN TO CANAAN. / BITTER WITH THE SWEET** | | 24 |

Nov 72. (lp/c) <77016> **RHYMES AND REASONS** | 40 | 2 | Oct72
— Come down easy / My my she cries / Peace in the valley / Feeling sad tonight / The first day in August / Bitter with the sweet / Goodbye don't mean I'm gone / Stand behind me / Gotta get through another day / I think I can hear you / Ferguson Road / Been to Canaan.

Jun 73. (7") <*(ODS 66035)*> **YOU LIGHT UP MY LIFE. / BELIEVE IN HUMANITY** | | 28 |
| | | 67 |

Jul 73. (lp/c) <77018> **FANTASY** | 6 | Jun73 |
— Fantasy beginning / You've been around too long / Being at war with each other / Directions / That's how things go down / Weekdays / Haywood / A quiet place to live / Welfare symphony / You light up my life / Corazon / Believe in humanity / Fantasy end. *(cd-iss. Oct93 on 'Sony Collectors'; 983307-2) (cd re-iss. Jul97 on 'Epic'; 487939-2)*

Oct 73. (7") <*ODS 66039*> **CORAZON. / THAT'S HOW THINGS GO DOWN** | - | 37 |

—— added guest TOM SCOTT – saxophone

Jul 74. (7") <*(ODS 66101)*> **JAZZMAN. / YOU GO YOUR WAY, I'LL GO MINE** | | 2 |

Oct 74. (lp/c) <77024> **WRAP AROUND JOY** | | 1 | Sep74
— Nightingale / Change in mind, change of heart / Jazzman / You go your way, I'll go mine / You're something new / We are all in this together / Wrap around joy / You gentle me / My lovin' eyes / Sweet Adonis / A night this side of dying / The best is yet to come. *(cd-iss. May92 on 'Thunderbolt'; CDTB 137)*

Jan 75. (7") <*(ODS 66106)*> **NIGHTINGALE. / YOU'RE SOMETHING NEW** | - | 9 |

Mar 75. (lp) <77027> **REALLY ROSIE** (children's TV) | - | 20 |
— Really Rosie / One was Johnny / Alligators all around / Pierre / Screaming and yelling / The ballad of chicken soup / Chicken soup and rice / Ave. P / My simple humble neighborhood / The awful truth / Such suffer / Really Rosie. *(cd-iss. Sep93 on 'Sony Collectors'; 983257-2)*

Jul 75. (7") <> **PIERRE. / CHICKEN SOUP WITH RICE** | - | |

Jan 76. (7") <*ODS 66119*> **ONLY LOVE IS REAL. / STILL HERE THINKING OF YOU** | | 37 |

Jan 76. (lp/c) <77034> **THOROUGHBRED** | | 3 |
— So many ways / Daughter of light / High out of time / Only love is real / There's a space between us / I'd like to know you better / We all have to be alone / Ambrosia / Still here thinking of you / It's gonna work out fine. *(re-iss. Jul84 on 'C.B.S.' lp/c; CBS/40 31841)*

Jul 76. (7") <*ODS 66123*> **HIGH OUT OF TIME. / I'D LIKE TO KNOW YOU BETTER** | | 76 | May76

—— She now worked with backing band NAVARRO, which included new 3rd husband **RICK EVERS** – guitar

| | Capitol | Capitol |

Jul 77. (7") *(CL 15934)* <4455> **HARD ROCK CAFE. / TO KNOW THAT I LOVE YOU** | | 30 |

Aug 77. (lp/c) *(EA-ST 11667)* **SIMPLE THINGS** | | 17 |
— Simple things / Hold on / In the name of love / Labyrinth / You're the one who knows / Hard rock cafe / Time alone / God only knows / To know that I love you / One.

Oct 77. (7") <4497> **HOLD ON. / SIMPLE THINGS** | - | - |
Nov 77. (7") *(CL 15949)* **LABYRINTH. / SIMPLE THINGS** | - | |
Apr 78. (lp/c) *(EA-ST 11785)* **WELCOME HOME** | - | |
— Main Street Saturday night / Sunbird / Venusian diamond / Changes / Morning sun / Disco tech / Ways of love / Ride the music / Everybody's got the spirit / Welcome home.

Apr 78. (7") <4593> **MAIN STREET SATURDAY NIGHT. / CHANGES** | - | - |
Aug 78. (7") <4649> **MORNING SUN. / SUNBIRD** | - | - |
Aug 78. (lp) *(CL 16009)* **DISCO TECH. / VENUSIAN DIAMOND** | - | - |

—— Her husband RICK died Mar78 of a drug overdose. She recorded next album with ex-JERRY JEFF WALKER's musicians.

Jul 79. (lp/c) <*(EA-ST 11953)*> **TOUCH THE SKY** | - | Jun79 |
— Time gone by / Move lightly / Dreamlike I wander / Walk with me / Good mountain people / You still want her / Passing of the days / Crazy / Eagle / Seeing red.

Aug 79. (7") *(CL 16093)* <4718> **MOVE LIGHTLY. / WHISKEY** | - | - |
Oct 79. (7") <4766> **TIME GONE BY. / DREAMLIKE I WANDER** | - | |

—— ex-husband **LARKEY** returned on bass and **CHRISTOPHER CROSS** – guitar

Jun 80. (lp/c) <*(EA-ST 12073)*> **PEARLS – SONGS OF GOFFIN AND KING** (new versions old songs) | | 44 |
— Dancin' with tears in my eyes / Locomotion / One fine day / Hey girl / Snow queen / Chains / Oh no not my baby / Hi de ho / Wasn't born to follow / Goin' back.

Jun 80. (7") *(CL 16152)* <4864> **ONE FINE DAY. / RULERS OF THE WORLD** | | 12 | May80

Aug 80. (7") <4911> **LOCOMOTION. / OH NO NOT MY BABY** | - | - |
Oct 80. (7") <4941> **CHAINS. / HEY GIRL** | - | - |

—— Now with new session people

| | Atlantic | Atlantic |

Mar 82. (lp/c) *(K/K4 50880)* <19344> **ONE TO ONE** | | |
— One to one / It's a war / Lookin' out for number one / Life without love / Golden man / Read between the lines / Love is like (a boomerang) / Goat Annie / Someone you never met before / Little prince.

Mar 82. (7") <4026> **ONE TO ONE. / GOAT ANNIE** | - | 45 |
Apr 82. (7") *(K 11725)* **READ BETWEEN THE LINES. / GOLDEN MAN** | - | - |
May 82. (7") <4062> **READ BETWEEN THE LINES. / LIFE WITHOUT LOVE** | - | - |
Jun 82. (7") *(K 11738)* **LITTLE PRINCE. / SOMEONE YOU NEVER MET BEFORE** | - | - |

—— **KUNKEL** and **KORTCHMAR** returned to line-up

Dec 83. (lp/c/cd) <*(780 118-1/-4)*> **SPEEDING TIME** | | |
— Computer eyes / Small voice / Crying in the rain / Sacred heart of stone / Speeding time / Standin' on the border line / So ready for love / Chalis Borealis / Dancing / Alabaster lady.

Dec 83. (7") <89756> **CRYING IN THE RAIN. / A SACRED HEART OF STONE** | - | - |
Feb 84. (7") <89694> **SPEEDING TIME. /** | - | - |
— In 1985, she and JOHN SEBASTIAN wrote songs for the "Care Bears" film
| | Capitol | Capitol |

Apr 89. (7") <44336> **CITY STREETS. / TIME HEALS ALL WOUNDS** | | - |
Apr 89. (7") *(CL 527)* **CITY STREETS. / I CAN'T STOP THINKING ABOUT YOU** | | - |
(12"+=/cd-s+=) *(12/CD CL 527)* – Time heals all wounds.

Apr 89. (cd/c/lp) *(CD/TC+/EST 2092)* <90885> **CITY STREETS** | | |
— City streets / Sweet life / Down to the darkness / Lovelight / I can't stop thinking about you / Legacy / Ain't that the way / Midnight flyer / Homeless heart / Someone who believes in you.
(above featured ERIC CLAPTON – guitar / MAX WEINBERG – drums)

Jul 89. (7") <44444> **SOMEONE WHO BELIEVES IN YOU. / CITY STREETS** | - | - |
| | Quality | Rhythm Safari |

Mar 93. (cd) <57197> **COLOR OF YOUR DREAMS** | | |
— Lay down my life / Hold out for love / Standing in the rain / Now and forever / Wishful thinking / Color of your dreams / Tears falling down on me / Friday's tie-dye nightmare / Just one thing / Do you feel love / It's never too late.

Mar 94. (cd/c) *(CKING CD/MC 01)* <53878> **IN CONCERT – THE GREATEST HITS LIVE** (live) | | |
— Hard Rock Cafe / Up on the roof / Smackwater Jack / So far away / Beautiful / A natural woman (you make me feel like) / Hold out for love / Will you love me tomorrow / Jazzman / It's too late / Chains / I feel the earth move / You've got a friend / The locomotion / You've got a friend.
above was recorded at LA's Amphitheater, with guest spots for CROSBY & NASH, plus SLASH of GUNS N' ROSES playing guitar on 'The Locomotion'.

– compilations etc. –

Note; All below releases on 'Epic' were issued on 'Ode' US.

May 78. (lp/c) Epic; *(EPC 86043)* / Ode; <34967> **HER GREATEST HITS** | | 47 | Mar78
— Jazzman / So far away / Sweet seasons / I feel the Earth move / Brother, brother / Only love is real / It's too late / Nightingale / Smackwater Jack / Been to Canaan / Corazon / Believe in humility. *(re-iss. Jul83 lp/c; EPC/40 32345) (cd-iss. Mar87 on 'C.B.S.'; CD 86043) (cd re-iss. Mar91; CD 32345)*

Jun 79. (7") Epic; *(EPC 7067)* **IT'S TOO LATE. / YOU'VE GOT A FRIEND** | - | - |

Oct 83. (7") Old Gold; *(OG 9355)* **IT MIGHT AS WELL RAIN UNTIL SEPTEMBER. / THE ROAD TO NOWHERE** | | - |

Jul 94. (cd) Connoisseur; *(VSOPCD 199)* **PEARLS / TIME GONE BY** | | - |

Oct 94. (d-cd/d-c) Legacy-Epic; *(E2K/E2T 48833)* **A NATURAL WOMAN – THE ODE COLLECTION 1968-1976** | | - |

Nov 96. (cd) Epic; *(485104-2)* **LIVE AT CARNEGIE HALL** (live) | | - |
Jun 97. (cd) Marginal; *(MAR 010)* **HITS AND RARITIES** | | - |

Freddie KING   (dig out; 4th edition)

KING BISCUIT TIME (see under ⇒ BETA BAND)

KING CRIMSON

Formed: Bournemouth, England . . . summer 1967 by ROBERT FRIPP, plus brothers MIKE and PETE GILES, who formed the soft-rock trio BRAIN, then GILES, GILES & FRIPP. After signing to 'Deram' early in '68 and adding couple, IAN McDONALD and JUDY DYBLE, they issued flop album, 'THE CHEERFUL INSANITY OF . . . ', in September of that year. With IAN now replacing PETE, the trio soon became KING CRIMSON, adding new vocalist GREG LAKE, who debuted at The Speakeasy in London on the 9th of April 1969. Three months later, they supported The ROLLING STONES at Hyde Park's free concert, a performance which attracted the attention of the 'Island' label. Subsequently signed up, they unleashed 'IN THE COURT OF THE CRIMSON KING' in October '69, a masterful debut album which made UK Top 5 and US Top 30. At this stage, the group were basically a prog-rock neo-classical outfit, their initial MOODY BLUES' mellotron-sound soon swapped for experimental, occasionally self-indulgent guitar-mastery of FRIPP. KING CRIMSON found themselves in turmoil when a couple of group members departed, leaving FRIPP and lyricist/road manager, PETE SINFIELD, to work things out. Eventually, with augmentation from session men and ex-members, they recorded the 1970 follow-up album, 'IN THE WAKE OF POSEIDON'. An aggregation of KING CRIMSON members had earlier performed the weird 'CAT FOOD' single on 'Top Of The Pops'; this release signalled a move towards avant-jazz territory, a sound they'd develop over the course of early 70's albums, 'LIZARD', 'ISLANDS' and 'LARKS' TONGUES IN ASPIC'. Throughout this turbulent period, FRIPP and Co. went through even more upheavals, although they still scored with astounding album successes ('STARLESS AND BIBLE BLACK' and 'RED' – both 1974) until they disbanded for the first time late in '74. FRIPP had already been a prolific session man for the likes of VAN DER GRAAF GENERATOR and (BRIAN) ENO, and together with the latter was co-credited on two experimental budget lp's, 'NO PUSSYFOOTIN' (1973) and 'EVENING STAR' (1975). He then moved to New York in 1977 and worked with PETER GABRIEL on his first three albums, at the same time lending his expertise to BOWIE's 'Heroes'. In 1979, FRIPP released his debut solo album,

'EXPOSURE', which featured many of his close friends handling vocals (GABRIEL, HAMILL, etc). The following year, his instrumental set, 'GOD SAVE THE QUEEN / UNDER HEAVY MANNERS' developed his patented brand of electro-experimentation, dubbed "Frippertronics", the record trailed by a short-lived project/band, The LEAGUE OF GENTLEMEN. In 1981, he reformed KING CRIMSON with BILL BRUFORD, ADRIAN BELEW and TONY LEVIN, recording a clutch of slightly more accessible albums, before FRIPP was again left contemplating a revived solo career. During the period, 1982-84, the guitarist collaborated on two albums, 'I ADVANCE MASKED' and 'BEWITCHED', with ANDY SUMMERS (POLICE guitarist). Like many of their contemporaries, KING CRIMSON reformed in 1994, issuing a series of studio and live sets. • **Trivia:** In the mid-80's, FRIPP married singer/actress, TOYAH WILLCOX, even collaborating on an album, 'THE LADY OR THE TIGER', in 1987.

Album rating: Giles, Giles & Fripp: THE CHEERFUL SANITY OF . . . (*5) / King Crimson: IN THE COURT OF THE CRIMSON KING (*9) / IN THE WAKE OF POSEIDON (*6) / LIZARD (*6) / ISLANDS (*7) / EARTHBOUND (*4) / LARKS' TONGUES IN ASPIC (*8) / STARLESS & BIBLE BLACK (*8) / RED (*8) / U.S.A. (*5) / A YOUNG PERSON'S GUIDE TO KING CRIMSON compilation (*8) / DISCIPLINE (*6) / BEAT (*6) / THREE OF A PERFECT PAIR (*5) / FRAME BY FRAME – THE ESSENTIAL KING CRIMSON compilation (*8) / VROOOM (*5) / THRAK (*5) / B'BOOM: OFFICIAL SOUNDTRACK – LIVE IN ARGENTINA (*5) / Robert Fripp: EXPOSURE (*7) / GOD SAVE THE QUEEN – UNDER HEAVY MANNERS (*7) / LET THE POWER FALL (FRIPPERTRONICS) (6) / LEAGUE OF GENTLEMEN (*5) / NETWORK collection (*6) / GOD SAVE THE KING (*5) / ROBERT FRIPP AND THE LEAGUE OF CRAFTY GUITARISTS!: LIVE (*5) / THE BRIDGE BETWEEN (*5) / 1995 SOUNDTRACKS, VOLUME 2 – LIVE IN CALIFORNIA (*5) / RADIOPHONICS: 1995 SOUNDSCAPES VOLUME 1 (*5) / INTERGALACTIC BOOGIE EXPRESS – LIVE IN EUROPE 1991 (*5) / THAT WHICH PASSES (*5)

GILES, GILES & FRIPP

PETE GILES – bass / **MICHAEL GILES** (b.1942)– drums / **ROBERT FRIPP** (b.16 May'46, Wimbourne, Dorset, England)– guitar, mellotron

	C.B.S.	not iss.
May 67. (7"; as BRAIN) (R 5595) **NIGHTMARES IN RED. / KICK THE DONKEY**	☐	–
	Deram	not iss.
Jun 68. (7") (DM 188) **ONE IN A MILLION. / NEWLY-WEDS**	☐	–

—— added **IAN McDONALD** (b.25 Jun'46, London) – keyboards / and guest **JUDY DYBLE** – vocals (ex-FAIRPORT CONVENTION) also featured as did KING CRIMSON lyricist **PETE SINFIELD**

Sep 68. (lp; mono/stereo) (DML/SML 1022) **THE CHEERFUL INSANITY OF GILES, GILES & FRIPP**
– The Saga of Rodney Toady / One in a million / Just George / Thursday morning / North meadow / Call tomorrow / Newly-weds / Digging my lawn / Suite No.1 / Little children / The crukster / How do you know / The sun is shining / Brudite eyes / Elephant song. (re-iss. 1970; SPA 423) (re-iss. Apr82 on 'Editions-EG'; EGED 16) (re-iss. Aug93 cd/c+=; 820 965-2/-4) – (extra versions).

—— IAN now on vocals (JUDY left to join TRADER HORNE)

Sep 68. (7") (DM 210) **THURSDAY MORNING. / ELEPHANT SONG**   ☐ –

KING CRIMSON

ROBERT, IAN + MIKE recruited **GREG LAKE** (b.10 Nov'48) – vocals, bass (ex-GODS)

	Island	Atlantic	
Oct 69. (7") (WIP 6071) <2703> **THE COURT OF THE CRIMSON KING (part 1). / (part 2)**	☐	80	Dec69
Oct 69. (lp) (ILPS 9111) <8245> **IN THE COURT OF THE CRIMSON KING**	5	28	Dec69

– 21st century schizoid man (including; Mirrors) / I talk to the wind / Epitaph (including; March for no reason – Tomorrow and tomorrow) / Moonchild (including; The dream – The illusion) / The court of the Crimson King (including; The return of the fire witch – The dance of the puppets). <US re-iss. 1970; SD 19155> (re-iss. Mar77 on 'Polydor' lp/(c); 2302 057)(3100 357) (cd-iss. May83 on 'Polydor'; 800 030-2) (re-iss. Jan87 & Nov91 on 'E.G.' lp/c/cd; EG LP/MC/CD 1)

—— **PETE GILES** – bass (ex-GILES, GILES & FRIPP) repl. IAN who with MIKE had formed McDONALD & GILES. IAN later formed FOREIGNER. MIKE appeared below. Added **KEITH TIPPET** – piano (other two were FRIPP & LAKE)

Mar 70. (7") (WIP 6080) **CAT FOOD. / GROON**   ☐ –

—— added **MEL COLLINS** – saxophone (ex-CIRCUS) / plus guest on 1 track **GORDON HASKELL** – vocals

May 70. (lp) (ILPS 9127) <8266> **IN THE WAKE OF POSEIDON**   4   31   Sep70
– Peace – a beginning / Pictures of a city (including; 42nd at Treadmill) / Cadence and cascade / In the wake of Poseidon (including; Libra's theme) / Peace – a theme / Cat food / The Devil's triangle: Merday morn – Hand of Sceiron – Garden of worm / Peace – an end. (re-iss. Mar77 on 'Polydor' lp/(c); 2302 058)(3100 358) (re-iss. Jan87 & Nov91 on 'E.G.' lp/c/cd; EG LP/MC/CD 2)

—— **GORDON HASKELL** (now full-time) repl. GREG who formed EMERSON, LAKE & PALMER (earlier). FRIPP had also retained **MEL COLLINS / ANDY McCULLOCH** – drums repl. MIKE

Dec 70. (lp) (ILPS 9141) <8278> **LIZARD**   30   ☐
– Cirkus (including; Entry of the chameleons) / Indoor games / Happy family / Lady of the dancing water / Lizard suite: Prince Rupert awakes – Bolero-The peacock's tale – The battle of glass tears; (a) Dawn song – (b) Last skirmish – (c) Prince Rupert's lament / Big top. (re-iss. Apr77 on 'Polydor' lp/(c); 2302 059)(3100 359) (re-iss. Jan87 & Nov91 on 'E.G.' lp/c/cd; EG LP/MC/CD 4)

—— **BOZ BURRELL** (b. RAYMOND, 1946, Lincoln, England) – vocals, bass repl. HASKELL who went solo / **IAN WALLACE** (b.29 Sep'46, Bury, England) – drums repl. McCULLOCH who joined GREENSLADE

Dec 71. (lp) (ILPS 9175) <7212> **ISLANDS**   30   76
– Formentera lady / The sailor's tale / Letters / (prelude) / Song of the gulls – Islands / Ladies of the road. (re-iss. Apr77 on 'Polydor' lp/(c); 2302 060)(3100 360) (re-iss. Jan87 on 'E.G.' lp/c/cd; EG LP/MC/CD 5)

—— FRIPP was sole survivor (lyricist **PETE SINFIELD** left early '72, to go into production for ROXY MUSIC's debut and be lyricist for Italians P.F.M.) / **JOHN WETTON** (b.12 Jul'49, Derby, England) – vocals, bass (ex-FAMILY) repl. BOZ who formed BAD COMPANY / **BILL BRUFORD** (b.17 May'48, London, England) – drums (ex-YES) repl. WALLACE who joined STREETWALKERS / **DAVID CROSS** (b.1948, Plymouth, England) – violin, flute repl. COLLINS who later joined CAMEL + sessions / added **JAMIE MUIR** – percussion and new lyricist **RICHARD PALMER-JAMES**

Mar 73. (lp) (ILPS 9230) <7263> **LARKS' TONGUES IN ASPIC**   20   61
– Larks' tongues in aspic (part one) / Book of Saturday / Exiles / Easy money / The talking drum / Larks' tongues in aspic (part two). (re-iss. Apr77 on 'Polydor' lp/(c); 2302 061)(3100 361) (re-iss. Jan87 & Nov91 on 'E.G.' lp/c/cd; EG LP/MC/CD 7)

—— Reverted to a quartet when JAMIE became a Tibetan monk

Feb 74. (7") (WIP 6189) <3016> **THE NIGHT WATCH. / THE GREAT DECEIVER**   ☐ ☐

Feb 74. (lp) (ILPS 9275) <7298> **STARLESS AND BIBLE BLACK**   28   64
– The great deceiver / Lament / We'll let you know / The night watch / Trio / The mincer / Starless and bible black / Trio / Fracture. (re-iss. Apr77 on 'Polydor' lp/(c); 2302 065)(3100 365) (re-iss. Jan87 & Nov91 on 'E.G.' lp/c/cd; EG LP/MC/CD 12)

—— now just basically a trio of FRIPP, WETTON and BRUFORD with old guests **MEL COLLINS, IAN McDONALD** and the departing **CROSS** augmenting on a track

Oct 74. (lp) (ILPS 9308) <18110> **RED**   45   66
– Red / Fallen angel / One more red nightmare / Providence / Starless. (re-iss. Apr77 on 'Polydor' lp/c; 2302 066)(3100 366) (re-iss. Jan87 & Nov91 on 'E.G.' lp/c/cd; EG LP/MC/CD 15)

—— Split just before last album. Next live album was recorded with DAVID CROSS

Apr 75. (lp) (ILPS 9316) <18136> **U.S.A. (live)**   ☐ ☐
– Larks' tongues in aspic (part II) / Lament / Exiles / Asbury park / Easy money / 21st century schizoid man. (re-iss. Dec79 on 'Polydor'; 2302 067) (re-iss. Jan87 on 'E.G.' lp/c/cd; EG LP/MC/CD 18)

—— JOHN WETTON joined BRIAN FERRY, then URIAH HEEP and later ASIA etc. As above BILL BRUFORD went solo and formed UK, after GONG stints.

ROBERT FRIPP

solo adding keyboards and a number of friends **PETER GABRIEL, PETER HAMILL & DARYL HALL** on vox, plus **PHIL COLLINS, BARRY ANDREWS, TONY LEVIN & MICHAEL NARADA WALDEN** – other instruments

	E.G.	E.G.-Polydor
Apr 79. (lp/c) (EG LP/MC 101) <6201> **EXPOSURE**	71	79

– (prelude) / You burn me up I'm a cigarette / Breathless / Disengage / North star / Chicago / NY3 / Mary / Exposure / Haaaden two / Urban landscape / I may not have had enough of me but I've had enough of you / (first inaugural address to the J.A.C.E. Sherborne House) / Water music I / Here comes the flood / Water music II / Postscript. (cd-iss. Jan87 & Apr89; EGCD 41)

Mar 80. (lp/c) (EG LP 105) <PL 6266> **GOD SAVE THE QUEEN / UNDER HEAVY MANNERS (instrumental)**   ☐ ☐
– Under heavy manners / The zero of the signified / Red two scorer / God save the Queen / 1983. (re-iss. Jan87 lp/c/cd; EG LP/MC/CD 45)

	E.G.-Editions	not iss.
Apr 81. (lp/c) (EGED/+C 10) **LET THE POWER FALL (FRIPPERTRONICS)**	☐	–

– 1984 / 1985 / 1986 / 1987 / 1988 / 1989. (cd-iss. Jan87; EEGCD 10)

LEAGUE OF GENTLEMEN

FRIPP retained **BARRY ANDREWS** adding **SARA LEE** – bass (ex-JANE AIRE) / **JOHNNY TOOBAD** – drums

	E.G.-Editions	Polydor
Dec 80. (7") (EGEND 1) **HEPTAPARAPARSHINOKH. / MARRIAGEMUZIC**	☐	–
Mar 81. (lp) (EGED 9) <16317> **LEAGUE OF GENTLEMEN (instrumental)**	☐	–

– Indiscreet / Inductive recurrance / Minor man / Heptaparaparshinokh / Dislocated / Pareto optimum 1 / Eye needles / Indiscreet II / Pareto optimum 2 / Cognitive dissonance / H.G. Wells / Trap / Ochre / Indiscreet III.

Mar 81. (7") (EGEND 2) **DISLOCATED. / 1984**   ☐ –

KING CRIMSON

FRIPP along with past member BRUFORD recruits newcomers **ADRIAN BELEW** (b. ROBERT STEVEN BELEW, 23 Dec'49, Covington, Kentucky) – guitar, vocals (ex-TOM TOM CLUB) / **TONY LEVIN** (b. 6 Jun'46, Boston, Mass.) – bass (ex-session man including PETER GABRIEL)

	E.G.	Warners
Sep 81. (lp/c) (EG LP/MC 49) <BSK 3629> **DISCIPLINE**	41	45

– Elephant talk / Frame by frame / Matte Kudasai / Indiscipline / Thelahun ginjeet / The sheltering sky / Discipline. (re-iss. Jan87 & Nov91 lp/c/cd; EG LP/MC/CD 49)

Nov 81. (7") (EGO 2) **MATTE KUDASAI. / ELEPHANT TALK**   ☐ ☐

Jun 82. (lp/c) (EG LP/MC 51) <23692-1> **BEAT**   39   52
– Neal and Jack and me / Heartbeat / Sartori in Tangier / Waiting man / Neurotica / Two hands / The howler / Requiem. (cd-iss. Apr84 on 'Polydor'; 821 194-2) (re-iss. Jan87 & Nov91 lp/c/cd; EG LP/MC/CD 51)

Jun 82. (7") (EGO 6) <29964> **HEARTBEAT. / REQUIEM (excerpt)**   ☐ ☐

Feb 84. (7") (EGO 15) <29309> **SLEEPLESS. / NUAGES**
(12") (EGOX 15) – ('A'side) / ('A'instrumental & dance mixes).

Mar 84. (lp/c/cd) (EG LP/MC/CD 55) <25071> **THREE OF A PERFECT PAIR**   30   58
– Three of a perfect pair / Model man / Sleepless / Man with an open heart / Nuages (that which passes, passes like clouds) / Industry / Dig me / No warning / Lark's tongues in aspic (part three). (re-iss. Jan87 & Nov91; same)

—— FRIPP disbanded KING CRIMSON project for a decade.

– compilations, others, etc. –

Jun 72. (lp) Help-Island; (HELP 6) **EARTHBOUND (live)**   ☐ –

– 21st century schizoid man / Peoria / The sailor's tale / Earthbound / Groon. *(re-iss. Oct77 on 'Polydor' lp)(c; 2343 092)(3192 385) (re-iss. Apr82 on 'EG')*

Feb 76. (d-lp) *Island; (ISLP 7)* **A YOUNG PERSON'S GUIDE TO KING CRIMSON** □　-
– Epitaph (including; (a) March for no reason – (b) Tomorrow and tomorrow / Cadence and cascade / Ladies of the road / I talk to the wind / Red / Starless / The night watch / Book of Saturday / Peace – a beginning / Cat food / Groon / Coda from Larks' tongues in aspic part 2 / Moonchild; (a) Mirrors – (b) The illusion / Trio / The court of the crimson king (including; (a) The return of the fire witch – (b) Dance of the puppets / 21st century schizoid man. *(re-iss. Mar77 on 'Polydor' d-lp/c; 2612 035)(3500 123) (cd-iss. 1986 on 'E.G.'; EGCD 22)*

Feb 76. (7") *Island; (WIP 6274)* **21st CENTURY SCHIZOID MAN. / EPITAPH** □　-

Dec 80. (d-lp) *Polydor;* **IN THE COURT OF THE CRIMSON KING / LARKS' TONGUES IN ASPIC** □　-

Dec 86. (cd/d-lp/d-c) *E.G.; (EG CD/MC/LP 68)* **THE COMPACT KING CRIMSON** □　-

Apr 87. (7"; by BRAIN) *Bam Caruso; (OPRA 63)* **NIGHTMARES IN RED. / (other artist)** □　-

Dec 89. (3xcd-box/3xc-box/3xlp-box) *E.G.; (EGBC/EGBM/EGBL 6)* **KING CRIMSON BOXED SET** □　-
– (IN THE COURT OF THE CRIMSON KING / LARKS' TONGUES IN ASPIC / DISCIPLINE)
(above 3 albums were packaged with other 'Island' artists)

1991. (cd-ep) *Virgin;* **THE ABBREVIATED KING CRIMSON – HEARTBEAT (medley)** □　-
– The King Crimson barber shop – 21st century schizoid man (abbreviated) – In the court of the crimson king (abbreviated) – Elephant talk (edit) – Matte Kudesai – Heartbeat (edit).

Dec 91. (4xcd-box) *Virgin; (KCBOX 1)* **FRAME BY FRAME: THE ESSENTIAL KING CRIMSON** □　-

Nov 92. (4xcd-box) *Virgin; (KCDIS 1)* **THE GREAT DECEIVER** □　-

Sep 93. (cd/c) *Virgin; (CDV/TCV 2721)* **SLEEPLESS: THE CONCISE KING CRIMSON** □　-
– 21st century schizoid man / Epitaph / In the court of the crimson king / Cat food / Ladies of the road / Starless (abridged) / Red / Fallen angel / Elephant talk / Frame by frame / Matte Kudasai / Heartbeat / Three of a perfect pair / Sleepless.

Dec 93. (3xcd-box) *Virgin;* **IN THE COURT OF THE CRIMSON KING / IN THE WAKE OF POSEIDON / LIZARD** □　-

Apr 97. (d-cd) *Discipline; (DGM 9607)* **EPITAPH (live in 1969)** □　-

ROBERT FRIPP / LEAGUE OF GENTLEMEN

	EG-Editions	E.G.

Jun 85. (lp/c) *(EGED/+C 9)* **GOD SAVE THE KING** □　□
– God save the King / Under heavy manners / Heptaparparshinokh / Inductive resonance / Cognitive dissonance / Dislocated / HG Wells / Eye needles / Trap. *(cd-iss. Jan87; EEGCD 9)*

Nov 86. (lp/c/cd) *(EGED/+C 43)* **ROBERT FRIPP AND THE LEAGUE OF CRAFTY GUITARISTS: LIVE! (live)** □　□
– Guitar craft theme 1: Invocation / Tight muscle party at Love Beach / The chords that bind / Guitar craft theme 3: Eye of the needle / All or nothing II / Guitar craft theme 2: Aspiration / All or nothing I / Circulation / A fearful symmetry / The new world / Crafty march. *(cd-iss. Jan87; EEGCD 43)*

—— Late 1988, FRIPP / FRIPP (TOYAH) toured augmented by **TREY GUNN** – stick bass / **PAUL BEAVIS** – percussion, drums

—— In mid'93, ROBERT FRIPP collaborated with ex-JAPAN singer DAVID SYLVIAN on near UK Top 20 album 'THE FIRST DAY'.

—— In Aug'94, FRIPP was part of FFWD alongside THOMAS FEHLYN, KRIS WESTON + Dr.ALEX PATTERSON of The ORB. In Sep'94, FRIPP again teamed up with DAVID SYLVIAN on album 'DAMAGE'.

KING CRIMSON

FRIPP / BRUFORD / BELEW / LEVIN / GUNN / MASTELOTTO

	Discipline	Virgin

Dec 94. (cd) *(DGM 0004)* **VROOOM** □　□
– Vrooom / Sex, sleep, eat, drink, dream / Cage / Thrak / When I say stop, continue / One time.

Apr 95. (cd/cd/c) *(KC CDX/CDY/MC 1) <40313>* **THRAK** 58　83
– Vrooom / Coda: Marine 475 / Dinosaur / Walking on air / B'boom / Thrak / Inner garden I / People / Radio I / One time / Radio II / Inner garden II / Sex, sleep, eat, drink, dream / Vrooom vrooom / Vrooom vrooom coda.

Aug 95. (d-cd) *(DGM 9503)* **B'BOOM: OFFICIAL SOUNDTRACK – LIVE IN ARGENTINA (live** □　-
– Vrooom / Frame by frame / Sex, sleep, eat, drink, dream / Red / One time / B'boom / Thrak / Improv – Two sticks / Elephant talk / Indiscipline // Vrooom vrooom / Matte Kudesai / The talking drum / Lark's tongues in aspic (part 2) / Heartbeat / Sleepless / People / B'boom / Thrak.

May 96. (cd) *(DGM 9604)* **THRAKATTAK** □　-

Sep 96. (cd) *(DGMVC 1)* **LIVE IN JAPAN 1995 (live)** □　-
– Frame by frame / Dinosaur / One time / Red / B'room / Thrak / Matte kudasai / Three of a perfect pair / Vroom vroom / Sex, sleep, eat, drink, dream / Elephant talk / Indiscipline / Talking drum / Larks' tongues in aspic part II / People / Walking on air.

ROBERT FRIPP

	Discipline	Virgin

Nov 94. (cd; ROBERT FRIPP STRING QUARTET) *(DGM 9303)* **THE BRIDGE BETWEEN** □　□

Feb 95. (cd) *(DGM 9402-2)* **1999 SOUNDSCAPES – LIVE IN ARGENTINA (live)** □　-
– 1999 (part one) / 2000 / 2001 / Interlude / 2002.

Oct 95. (cd) *(DGM 9502)* **INTERGALACTIC BOOGIE EXPRESS – LIVE IN EUROPE 1991 (live with The LEAGUE OF CRAFTY GUITARISTS)** □　-
– A Connecticut Yankee in the court of King Arthur / Rhythm of the universe /

Lark's hrak / Circulation 1 / Intergalactic boogie express / G force / Eye of the needle / Corrente / Driving force / Groove penetration / Flying home / Circulation II / Fireplace / Fragments of skylab / Asturias / Prelude circulation / Cheeseballs / Prelude in c minor / Wabash cannonball / Fractual Jazn / Ashesis. *(re-iss. Mar97; same)*

Mar 96. (cd) *(DGM 9505)* **RADIOPHONICS: 1995 SOUNDSCAPES VOL.1 (live in Argentina)** □　-
– Radiophonic I / Radiophonic II / Buenos Aires suite: I- Atmosphere, II- Elegy (for mothers and children), III- Streets, IV- Sky.

Sep 96. (cd) *(DGM 9506)* **A BLESSING OF TEARS: 1995 SOUNDSCAPES – VOLUME TWO (live in California)** □　-
– The cathedral of tears / First light / Midnight blue / Reflection 1 / Second light / A blessing of tears / Returning I / Returning II.

May 96. (cd; LEAGUE OF GENTLEMEN) *(DGM 9602)* **THRANG THRANG GOZINBULX** □　-

Sep 96. (cd) *(DGM 9507)* **THAT WHICH PASSES** □　-
– On acceptance / On the approach of doubt / Worm in Paradise / New worlds / On triumph / On awe / This too shall pass / Fear of light / Time to die.

Jun 97. (cd-ep) *(<DGM 9704>)* **PIE JESU EP** □　Sep97
– Pie Jesu / Midnight blue / Abandonment to divine providence / Sometimes God hides.

Apr 98. (cd) *(DGM 9608)* **GATES OF PARADISE** □　-
– Outer darkness: the outer darkness / Gates of Paradise: Abandonment to divine / Outer darkness: In fear of trembling / Gates of Paradise: Sometimes God hides.

– FRIPP compilations, etc. –

Jan 87. (10"m-lp/c) *E.G.; (EGM LP/MC 4)* **NETWORK** □　□
– North star / (i) Water music 1 – (ii) Here comes the flood / God save the king / Under heavy manners.

May 91. (cd; ROBERT FRIPP & LEAGUE OF CRAFTY GUITARISTS) *E.G.; (EEG 21022)* **SHOW OF HANDS** □　□

KINGDOM COME (dig out; Great Metal . . .)	□

KINGMAKER (dig out; Great Alt & Indie . . .)	□

KINGSMEN

Formed: Portland, Oregon, USDA . . . 1958 by schoolboys LYNN EASTON and JACK ELY, who soon enlisted MIKE MITCHELL, BOB NORDBY and DON GALLUCCI. In May '63, after tours supporting PAUL REVERE & THE RAIDERS, they gained studio time, recording the classic garage cover of RICHARD BERRY's 'LOUIE LOUIE'. This was soon given a release on 'Jerden', becoming a hit in Boston before it was re-issued on 'Wand'. Although banned in certain states, it soared to No.2 in the American charts, becoming a standard for many future rock/pop groups. At the time of its success, the group went through turmoil when EASTON took over both the leadership and vocals of the group (this led to his friend ELY departing). On American TV, EASTON was seen miming to ELY's raunchy vocals. They continued in the same vein covering many standards in their inimitable garage-punk style. • Covers: LOUIE LOUIE (Richard Berry) / MONEY (Barrett Strong) / LITTLE LATIN LUPE LU (Righteous Brothers) / KILLER JOE (Rocky Fellers) / etc.

Best CD compilation: THE BEST OF THE KINGSMEN (*7)

LYNN EASTON – saxophone, vocals / **JACK ELY** – vocals, guitar / **MIKE MITCHELL** – lead guitar / **BOB NORDBY** – bass / **DON GALLUCCI** – organ

	not iss.	Jalynne
1962. (7") <108> **DIG THIS. / LADY'S CHOICE**	-	-

	not iss.	Jerden
Jun 63. (7") <712> **LOUIE LOUIE. / HAUNTED CASTLE**	-	-

	Pye Inter	Wand
Jan 64. (7") *(7N 25231)* <143> **LOUIE LOUIE. / HAUNTED CASTLE**	26	2 Sep63

<US re-iss. May66; same>; hit No.97>

—— (Aug63) EASTON took over vox from ELY who moved to drums! just before he departed / **GARY ABBOTT** – drums repl. ELY. **NORM SUNDHOLM** – bass repl. NORDBY

Jan 64. (lp) *(NPL 28050)* <657> **LOUIE LOUIE: THE KINGSMEN IN PERSON (live Portland)**　20
– Louie Louie / The waiting / Mojo workout / Fever / Money / Bent scepter / Long tall Texan / You can't sit down / Twist & shout / J.A.J. / Night train / Mashed potatoes.

Mar 64. (7") <150> **MONEY. / BENT SCEPTER** -　16

—— **BARRY CURTIS** – organ repl. **DON DICK PETERSON** – drums repl. GARY

Jul 64. (7") *(7N 25262)* <157> **LITTLE LATIN LUPE LU. / DAVID'S MOOD**　46

Sep 64. (7") *(7N 25273)* <164> **DEATH OF AN ANGEL. / SEARCHING FOR LOVE**　42

Feb 65. (7") *(7N 25292)* <172> **THE JOLLY GREEN GIANT. / LONG GREEN**　4 Jan65

Feb 65. (lp) *(NPL 28054)* <659> **THE KINGSMEN, VOLUME II (live)**　15 Sep64
– Kingsmen introduction / Little Latin Lupe Lu / Long green / Do you love me / New Orleans / Walking the dog / David's mood / Something's got a hold on me / Come on baby, let the good times roll / Ooh poo pah doo / Great balls of fire / Linda Lou / Earth of an angel.

Feb 65. (lp) <662> **THE KINGSMEN, VOLUME 3 (live)** -　22
– The jolly green giant / Over you / That's cool, that's trash / Don't you just know it / I go crazy / La-do-dada / Long green / Mother-in-law / Shout / Searching for love / Tall cool one / Comin' home baby.

Jun 65. (7") *(NPL 25311)* <183> **THE CLIMB. / WAITING**　65 May65

Jul 65. (7") <189> **ANNIE FANNY. / GIVE HER LOVIN'** -　47

Aug 65. (7") *(NPL 25322)* **ANNIE FANNY. / SOMETHING'S GOT A HOLD ON ME** □　-

Feb 66. (7") <1107> **(YOU GOT) THE GAMMA GOOCHE. / IT'S ONLY THE DOG** -　-

Mar 66. (lp) *(NPL 28068)* <670> **THE KINGSMEN ON CAMPUS
(live)** | | **68** Oct65
– Annie Fanny / Rosalie / A hard day's night / I like it like that / Stand by me / Little green thing / The climb / Sticks and stones / Peter Gunn / Some times / Shotgun / Genevieve.

Jun 66. (7") *(7N 25370)* <1115> **KILLER JOE. / LITTLE GREEN THING** | | **77** Mar66

Jun 66. (7") **THE KRUNCH. / THE CLIMB** | | - |

Sep 66. (lp) *(NPL 28085)* <674> **THE KINGSMEN'S GREATEST HITS**
<US-title '15 GREAT HITS'> (compilation & new) | | **87** Aug66
– Killer Joe / Good lovin' / Jenny take a ride / Ooh poo pah doo / Fever / Quarter to three / Poison Ivy / Satisfaction / Twist and shout / Money / Searchin' / Hang on Sloopy / Do you love me / Shout / New Orleans.

Sep 66. (7") <1127> **LITTLE SALLY TEASE. / MY WIFE CAN'T COOK** | - | |

Nov 66. (7") <1137> **IF I NEEDED SOMEONE. / THE GRASS IS
GREEN**

Jan 67. (7") *(7N 25406)* <1147> **DAYTIME SHADOWS. / TROUBLE**
                                                              Wand   Wand

Jan 67. (lp) <*(WNS 6)*> **UP AND AWAY**
– Trouble / If I needed someone / Grass is green / Tosin' and turnin' / Under my thumb / Wild thing / (I have found) Another girl / Daytime shadows / Shake a tailfeather / Children's caretaker / Land of a thousand dances / Mustang Sally / Little Sally tease / Hushabye.

Mar 67. (7") <1154> **THE WOLF OF MANHATTAN. / CHILDREN'S
CARETAKER**

Jul 67. (7") <1157> **DON'T SAY NO. / ANOTHER GIRL (I HAVE
FOUND)**

———— In Jul'67, EASTON left group as they soon dissolved.

1968. (7") <1164> **BO DIDDLEY BACH. / JUST BEFORE THE
BREAK OF DAY**

1968. (7") <1174> **GET OUT OF MY LIFE WOMAN. / SINCE
YOU'VE BEEN GONE**

1968. (7") **I GUESS I WAS DREAMIN'. / ON LOVE**

———— split in Sep'68. Re-formed in 1972 with **FREDDIE DENNIS** – bass / **STEVE FRIEDSON** – keyboards (added to MIKE MITCHELL, DICK PETERSON + BARRY CURTIS)

– compilations, etc. –

on 'Pye International'; unless mentioned otherwise

1964. (7"ep) *(NEP 44023)* **THE KINGSMEN**

1965. (7"ep) *(NEP 44040)* **MOJO WORKOUT**

1966. (7"ep) *(NEP 44063)* **FEVER**

Apr 66. (7") *(7N 25366)* **LITTLE LATIN LUPE LU. / LOUIE LOUIE**

1969. (lp) *Marble Arch; (MAL 829)* **THE KINGSMEN'S GREATEST
HITS**

1971. (7") *Wand; (WN 14)* **LOUIE LOUIE. / IF I NEEDED SOMEONE**

1972. (lp) *Scepter; <18002>* **THE BEST OF THE KINGSMEN**
(re-iss. Jan86 on 'Rhino'; RNLP 126) (cd-iss. Sep91)

1980. (lp) *Piccadilly; <3329>* **A QUARTER TO THREE**

1980. (lp) *Piccadilly; <3330>* **YA YA**

1980. (lp) *Piccadilly; <3346>* **HOUSE PARTY**

1980. (lp) *Piccadilly; <3348>* **GREAT HITS**

Jul 81. (7") *Old Gold; (OG 9054)* **LOUIE LOUIE. / THE JOLLY GREEN
GIANT**

Jan 87. (lp) *Decal; (LIK 6)* **LOUIE LOUIE – GREATEST HITS**
– Louie Louie / Money (that's what I want) / The jolly green giant / Death of an angel / The climb / Get out of my life woman / Little Latin lupe lu / Killer Joe / Annie Fanny / Long green / Little Sally tease / Trouble / If I needed someone.

1989. (cd) *Rhino; <70745>* **THE BEST OF THE KINGSMEN**
– Louie, Louie / Money / Little latin lupe lu / Death of an angel / Jolly green giant / Climb / Rosalie / Haunted castle / Long green / That's cool, that's trash / J.A.J. / Genevieve / Annie Fanny / Little green thing / Killer Joe / Give her lovin' / Little Sally tease / Trouble.

Jan 96. (cd) *Instant; (CPCD 8160)* **LOUIE LOUIE**

KING'S X (dig out; Great Metal . . .)

KINKS

Formed: Muswell Hill, London, England . . . 1963 by brothers RAY and DAVE DAVIES, who recruited PETER QUAIFE from The RAVENS. With help from managers Robert Wace and Grenville Collins, they met Larry Page who gave them the name KINKS late '63. He also arranged demos, which were soon heard by American SHEL TALMY, securing them a deal with 'Pye' early '64. Two singles flopped, but the third, 'YOU REALLY GOT ME', stormed the top spot in the UK, soon breaking into US Top 10. With its scuzzy, propulsive guitar riff, the song is oft cited as one of the first real "heavy rock" records, although it's debatable whether RAY DAVIES would admit to inspiring a multitude of poodle-maned Van Halen soundalikes. A top-selling eponymous lp followed, as did a series of Top 10 sixties singles, including two more UK No.1's, 'TIRED OF WAITING FOR YOU' and 'SUNNY AFTERNOON'. As RAY's songwriting developed, the band moved to a quieter, more reflective sound, his camp, semi-detached vocals complementing the wry observations and quintessential Englishness of the lyrical themes. Come 1967, when every band worth their weight in spiked sugarcubes were looking towards the 'East', Davies looked no further than his proverbial back garden. 'SOMETHING ELSE', with its heartfelt eulogies to a mythical England past, still stands as the KINKS' greatest moment, the aching melancholy of 'WATERLOO SUNSET' its crowning glory. Davies' nostalgic bent continued on 1968's 'THE KINKS ARE THE VILLAGE GREEN PRESERVATION SOCIETY', an enchanting concept album that reached ever further into a faded history of rural simplicity. It also included the KINKS' sole dalliance with psychedelia, 'WICKED ANNABELLA', a Brothers Grimm-like fairytale-cum-nightmare fantasy. DAVIES' lyrical obsessions were given

centre stage once more on 'ARTHUR (OR THE DECLINE OF THE ROMAN EMPIRE)' (1969) wherein the rosy hue of the past was contrasted with the grey decline of modern day Britain. The mood lightened somewhat with 1970's surprise No.2 hit single, 'LOLA', a tongue in cheek tribute to a male cross-dresser and the standout track from the subsequent album, 'LOLA VERSUS POWERMAN AND THE MONEYGOROUND PART 1'. 1971's 'MUSWELL HILLBILLIES' echoed 'VILLAGE GREEN's collection of storybook vignettes although the band were beginning to lose their focus and the hits were about to dry up. 'SUPERSONIC ROCKETSHIP' went top 20 in 1972 but the follow-up, 'CELLULOID HEROES', failed to chart. Both songs were taken from the album, 'EVERYBODY'S IN SHOWBIZ', and were high points in an otherwise unremarkable affair. The remainder of the 70's saw the KINKS become bogged down in ill-advised concept albums and self-parody although while the band were virtually ignored in the UK, they still had a sizeable following in America, hitting the US Top 30 with the patchy 'SLEEPWALKER' album in 1977. With the release of the harder rocking 'LOW BUDGET' a couple of years later, the band were embraced fully by the US rock fraternity and hitched a lucrative ride on the stadium rock circuit as well as gaining a sizeable piece of chart action. While the early 80's albums, 'GIVE THE PEOPLE WHAT THEY WANT' and 'STATE OF CONFUSION' were competent albeit largely uninspired, the Americans lapped them up and the band even found themselves back in the UK Top 20 with the classic 'COME DANCING' single. Throughout the 80's the band once again descended into inconsistency and commercial wilderness, their live shows being the sole factor in keeping the KINKS' spirit intact. Fast forward to 1995 and BLUR were riding high on the 'Britpop' wave with their heavily KINKS-influenced 'Parklife' album. Overrated and trailing in the KINKS' shadows, the album's success nevertheless gave Blur mainman DAMON ALBORN the opportunity to express his admiration for his hero RAY DAVIES and perform a poignant TV duet with the great man on 'WATERLOO SUNSET'. The renewed interest also resulted in a TV documentary on the KINKS and a solo tour by Ray, not to mention autobiographies by both RAY and DAVE. • **Songwriters:** RAY DAVIES wrote all of work, except covers; LONG TALL SALLY (Ernie Johnson) / TOO MUCH MONKEY BUSINESS (Chuck Berry) / GOT LOVE IF YOU WANT IT (Slim Harpo) / MILK COW BLUES (Elvis Presley) / etc. • **Trivia:** RAY produced 1969 lp 'Turtle Soup' for The TURTLES. He was married on the 12th December '64 to Rasa Dicpetri, but later divorced her (see KINKS biography by Johnny Rogan). In 1981, he divorced his second wife Yvonne. (RAY had a relationship with CHRISSIE HYNDE of The PRETENDERS for three years). She gave him a daughter, Natalie, in February '83, although they separated when she started dating JIM KERR (of SIMPLE MINDS). In 1986, RAY appeared in the film musical, 'Absolute Beginners'.

Album rating: THE KINKS – YOU REALLY GOT ME (*6) / KINDA KINKS (*5) / KINKS-SIZE (*6) / THE KINK KONTROVERSY (*5) / KINKS KINKDOM (*5) / THE KINKS GREATEST HITS! compilation (*8) / FACE TO FACE (*8) / LIVE AT KELVIN HALL (*5) / SOMETHING ELSE BY THE KINKS (*7) / VILLAGE GREEN PRESERVATION SOCIETY (*8) / ARTHUR (OR THE DECLINE AND FALL OF THE BRITISH EMPIRE) (*8) / LOLA VERSUS POWERMAN AND THE MONEYGOROUND, PART ONE (*7) / PERCY soundtrack (*4) / MUSWELL HILLBILLIES (*7) / EVERYBODY'S IN SHOW-BIZ (*6) / THE GREAT LOST KINKS ALBUM early (*6) / PRESERVATION ACT I (*6) / PRESERVATION ACT II (*6) / SOAP OPERA (*4) / SCHOOLBOYS IN DISGRACE (*5) / SLEEPWALKER (*6) / MISFITS (*7) / LOW BUDGET (*6) / ONE FOR THE ROAD (*5) / GIVE THE PEOPLE WHAT THEY WANT (*6) / STATE OF CONFUSION (*6) / WORD OF MOUTH (*5) / THINK VISUAL (*4) / COME DANCING WITH THE KINKS – THE BEST OF . . . 1977-1986 compilation (*7) / THE ROAD (*4) / THE ULTIMATE COLLECTION compilation (*9) / UK JIVE (*4) / PHOBIA (*5) / TO THE BONE (*6)

RAY DAVIES (b.21 Jun'44) – vocals, guitar / **DAVE DAVIES** (b. 3 Feb'47) – guitar, vocals / **PETER QUAIFE** (b.31 Dec'43, Tavistock, Devon) – bass with session drummers
                                                                           Pye   Cameo

Mar 64. (7") *(7N 15611)* <308> **LONG TALL SALLY. / I TOOK MY
BABY HOME** | | Apr64
<US re-iss. Nov64; 345>
                                                                           Pye   Reprise

May 64. (7") *(7N 15636)* **YOU STILL WANT ME. / YOU DO
SOMETHING TO ME** | | - |
                                                                           Pye   Reprise

Aug 64. (7") *(7N 15673)* <0306> **YOU REALLY GOT ME. / IT'S
ALRIGHT** | **1** | **7** Sep64

———— **MICK AVORY** (b.15 Feb'44) – drums was now used although he joined 9 months previously

Oct 64. (lp) *(NPL 18096)* <6143> **THE KINKS** <US-title 'YOU
REALLY GOT ME'> | **3** | **29** Dec64
– Beautiful Delilah / So mystifying / Just can't go to sleep / Long tall Shorty / You really got me / Cadillac / Bald headed woman / Revenge / Too much monkey business / Revenge / I've been driving on Bald mountain / Stop your sobbing / Got love if you want it. *(re-iss. Jan67 on 'Golden Guinea'; GGL 0357) (re-iss. May80 as 'YOU REALLY GOT ME'; NSPL 18615) (re-iss. Oct87 on 'P.R.T.' lp/c/cd; PYL/PYM/PYC 6002) (cd re-iss. Dec89 on 'Castle'; CLACD 155)*

Oct 64. (7") *(7N 15714)* <0334> **ALL DAY AND ALL OF THE NIGHT. /
I GOTTA MOVE** | **2** | **7** Dec64
(re-iss. Oct84 on 'P.R.T.'; KIS 003) (re-iss. Jan88 on 'P.R.T.'; PYS 4)

Jan 65. (7") *(7N 15759)* <0347> **TIRED OF WAITING FOR YOU. /
COME ON NOW** | **1** | **6** Mar65

Mar 65. (lp) <6158> **KINKS-SIZE** | - | **13**
– Tired of waiting for you / Louie Louie / I've got that feeling / Revenge / I gotta move / Things are getting better / I gotta go now / I'm a lover not a fighter / Come on now / All day and all of the night.

Mar 65. (lp) *(NPL 18112)* <6173> **KINDA KINKS** | **3** | **60** Aug65
– Look for me baby / Got my feet on the ground / Nothin' in the world can stop me worryin' 'bout that girl / Naggin' woman / Wonder where my baby is tonight / Tired of waiting for you / Dancing in the street / Don't ever change / Come on now / So

long / You shouldn't be sad / Something better beginning. *(re-iss. Oct87 on 'P.R.T.' lp/c/cd; PYL/PYM/PYC 6003) (cd re-iss. Dec89 on 'Castle'; CLACD 156)*

Mar 65. (7") *(7N 15813) <0366>* **EVERYBODY'S GONNA BE HAPPY. / WHO'LL BE THE NEXT IN LINE** `11` `Apr65`
<above 45 flipped over in the States with B-side hitting No.34>

May 65. (7") *(7N 15854) <0379>* **SET ME FREE. / I NEED YOU** `9` `23` Jun65

Jul 65. (7") *(7N 15919) <0409>* **SEE MY FRIEND. / NEVER MET A GIRL LIKE YOU BEFORE** `10`

Nov 65. (7") *<0420>* **A WELL RESPECTED MAN. / MILK COW BLUES** `-` `13`

Nov 65. (7") *(7N 15981) <0454>* **TILL THE END OF THE DAY. / WHERE HAVE ALL THE GOOD TIMES GONE** `6` `50` Mar66

Nov 65. (lp) *(NPL 18131) <6197>* **THE KINK KONTROVERSY** `9` `95` Apr66
– Milk cow blues / Ring the bells / Gotta get the first plane home / When I see that girl of mine / Till the end of the day / The world keeps going round / I'm on the island / Where have all the good times gone / It's too late / What's in store for me / You can't win. *(re-iss. Oct87 on 'P.R.T.' lp/c/cd; PYL/PYM/PYC 6004) (cd re-iss. Dec89 on 'Castle'; CLACD 157)*

Dec 65. (lp) *<6184>* **KINKS KINKDOM** `-` `47`
– Well respected man / Such a shame / Wait 'til the summer comes along / Naggin' woman / Who'll be the next in line / Don't you fret / I need you / It's all right / Louie Louie.

Feb 66. (7") *(7N 17064) <0471>* **DEDICATED FOLLOWER OF FASHION. / SITTING ON MY SOFA** `4` `36` May66

—— **JOHN DALTON** – bass deputised on tour for QUAIFE while injured

Jun 66. (7") *(7N 17125) <0497>* **SUNNY AFTERNOON. / I'M NOT LIKE EVERYBODY ELSE** `1` `14` Aug66

Aug 66. (lp) *<6217>* **THE KINKS GREATEST HITS** (compilation) `-` `9`
– Dedicated follower of fashion / Tired of waiting for you / All day and all of the night / You really got me / Well respected man / Who'll be the next in line / Everybody's gonna be happy / Till the end of the day / Set me free / Something better beginning.

—— **JOHN DALTON** sessioned between 66-69, QUAIFE's photo on covers

Oct 66. (lp; mono/stereo) *(NPL/NSPL 18145) <6228>* **FACE TO FACE** `12` Feb67
– Party line / Rosy won't you please come home / Dandy / Too much on my mind / Session man / Rainy day in June / House in the country / Sunny afternoon / Holiday in Waikiki / Most exclusive residence for sale / Fancy / Little Miss Queen of Darkness / You're looking fine / I'll remember. *(re-iss. Oct87 on 'P.R.T.' lp/c/cd; PYL/PYM/PYC 6005) (cd re-iss. Dec89 on 'Castle'; CLACD 158)*

Nov 66. (7") *(7N 17125) <0540>* **DEAD END STREET. / BIG BLACK SMOKE** `5` `73` Jan67

May 67. (7") *(7N 17321)* **WATERLOO SUNSET. / ACT NICE AND GENTLE** `2` `-`

May 67. (lp; mono/stereo) *(NPL/NSPL 18191) <6260>* **LIVE AT KELVIN HALL (live in Glasgow)** *<US-title 'THE LIVE KINKS'>* Sep67
– Till the end of the day / I'm on an island / You really got me / All day and all of the night / A well respected man / You're looking fine / Sunny afternoon / Dandy / Come on now / Milk cow blues – Batman theme – Tired of waiting for you. *(re-iss. Oct87 on 'P.R.T.' lp/c/cd; PYL/PYM/PYC 6007) (cd re-iss. Dec89 on 'Castle'; CLACD 160)*

Jun 67. (7") *<0587>* **MR. PLEASANT. / HARRY RAG** `-` `80`

Sep 67. (7") *<0612>* **WATERLOO SUNSET. / TWO SISTERS** `-`

Oct 67. (lp; mono/stereo) *(NPL/NSPL 18193) <6279>* **SOMETHING ELSE BY THE KINKS** `35` Feb68
– David Watts / Death of a clown / Two sisters / No return / Harry Rag / Tin soldier man / Situation vacant / Love me till the sun shines / Lazy old sun / Afternoon tea / Funny face / End of the season / Waterloo sunset. *(re-iss. Oct87 on 'P.R.T.' lp/c/cd; PYL/PYM/PYC 6006) (cd re-iss. Dec89 on 'Castle'; CLACD 159)*

Oct 67. (7") *(7N 17400) <0647>* **AUTUMN ALMANAC. / MR. PLEASANT** `3`

Apr 68. (7") *(7N 17468) <0691>* **WONDERBOY. / POLLY** `37`

Jul 68. (7") *(7N 17573) <0762>* **DAYS. / SHE'S GOT EVERYTHING** `12`

Jul 68. (lp; mono/stereo) *(NPL/NSPL 18233) <6327>* **THE KINKS ARE THE VILLAGE GREEN PRESERVATION SOCIETY**
– Village green preservation society / Do you remember Walter / Picture book / Johnny Thunder / The last of the steam powered trains / Big sky / Sitting by the riverside / Animal farm / Village green / Starstruck / Phenomenal cat / All my friends were there / Wicked Annabella / Monica / People take pictures of each other. *(re-iss. Nov85 on 'Flashback-PRT'; FBLP 8091) (re-iss. Oct87 on 'P.R.T.' lp/c/cd; PYL/PYM/PYC 6008) (cd re-iss. Oct89 on 'Castle'; CLACD 161) (cd re-iss. Feb97 on 'Original Recordings'; ORRLP 005)*

Apr 69. (7") *(7N 17724) <0743>* **PLASTIC MAN. / KING KONG** `31`

Apr 69. (7") *<0806>* **STARSTRUCK. / PICTURE BOOK** `-`

—— **JOHN DALTON** (b.21 May'43) – bass officially repl. QUAIFE

Jun 69. (7") *<0847>* **WALTER. / VILLAGE GREEN PRESERVATION SOCIETY** `-`

Jun 69. (7"; b-side by KINKS featuring DAVE DAVIES) *<7N 17776>* **DRIVIN'. / MINDLESS CHILD OF MOTHERHOOD**

Sep 69. (7") *(7N 17812)* **SHANGRI-LA. / THIS MAN HE WEEPS TONIGHT**
(above initially had 'LAST OF THE STEAM-POWERED TRAINS' on B-side)

Oct 69. (lp) *(NSPL 18317) <6366>* **ARTHUR (OR THE DECLINE AND FALL OF THE BRITISH EMPIRE)**
– Victoria / Yes sir, no sir / Some mother's son / Brainwashed / Australia / Shangri-la / Mr. Churchill says / She bought a hat like Princess Marina / Young and innocent days / Nothing to say / Arthur. *(re-iss. Oct87 on 'P.R.T.' lp/c/cd; PYL/PYM/PYC 6009) (cd re-iss. Oct89 on 'Castle'; CLACD 162)*

Dec 69. (7") *(7N 17865)* **VICTORIA. / MR. CHURCHILL SAYS** `33` `-`

Jan 70. (7") *<0863>* **VICTORIA. / BRAINWASHED** `-` `62`

Jun 70. (7") *(7N 17961)* **LOLA. / BERKELEY MEWS** `2` `-`

Aug 70. (7") *<0930>* **LOLA. / MINDLESS CHILD OF MOTHERHOOD** `9`

Nov 70. (lp) *(NSPL 18359) <6423>* **LOLA VERSUS POWERMAN & THE MONEYGOROUND, PART ONE** `35`
– The contenders / Strangers / Denmark Street / Get back in line / Lola / Top of the pops / The moneygoround / This time tomorrow / A long way from home / Rats / Apeman / Powerman / Got to be free. *(re-iss. Oct87 on 'P.R.T.' lp/c/cd; PYL/PYM/PYC 6010) (cd re-iss. Oct89 on 'Castle'; CLACD 163)*

Nov 70. (7") *(7N 45016) <0979>* **APEMAN. / RATS** `5` `45` Jan71

Mar 71. (lp) *(NSPL 18365)* **(SOUNDTRACK FROM THE FILM) "PERCY"** `-`

– God's children / Lola / The way love used to be / Completely / Running round town / Moments / Animals in the zoo / Just friends / Helga / Willesden Green / God's children – end. *(re-iss. Oct87 on 'P.R.T.' lp/c/cd; PYL/PYM/PYC 6011) (cd re-iss. Oct89 on 'Castle'; CLACD 164)*

Apr 71. (7") *(7N 8001)* **GOD'S CHILDREN. / MOMENTS** `-`
(7"m+=) *(7NX 8001)* – The way love used to be / Dreams.

Apr 71. (7") *<1017>* **GOD'S CHILDREN. / THE WAY LOVE USED TO BE** `-`

—— added **JOHN GOSLING** – keyboards (he guested on 'LOLA' album), plus **LAURIE BROWN** – trumpet / **JOHN BEECHAM** – trombone / **ALAN HOLMES** – saxophone recruited from The MIKE COTTON SOUND. The three became full-time members '73, adding to **R. DAVIES, D. DAVIES, AVORY** and **DALTON**

	R.C.A.	R.C.A.

Nov 71. (lp) *(SF 8243) <LSP 4644>* **MUSWELL HILLBILLIES** `100`
– 20th century man / Acute schizophrenia paranoia blues / Holiday / Skin and bone / Alcohol / Complicated life / Here come the people in the grey / Have a cuppa tea / Holloway jail / Oklahoma U.S.A. / Uncle son / Muswell hillbilly.

Feb 72. (7") *<74-0620>* **20th CENTURY MAN. / SKIN AND BONE** `-`

May 72. (7") *(RCA 2211) <74-0807>* **SUPERSONIC ROCKET SHIP. / YOU DON'T KNOW MY NAME** `16`

Aug 72. (d-lp) *(DPS 2035) <6065>* **EVERYBODY'S IN SHOWBIZ** `70`
– Here comes yet another day / Maximum consumption / Unreal reality / Hot potatoes / Sitting in my hotel / You don't know my name / Supersonic rocket ship / Look a little on the sunny side / Celluloid heroes / Motorway / **EVERYBODY'S A STAR (live)** – Top of the pops / Brainwashed / Mr. Wonderful / Acute schizophrenia paranoia blues / Holiday / Muswell Hillbilly / Alcohol / Banana boat song / Skin and bone / Baby face / Lola.

Nov 72. (7") *(RCA 2299) <74-0852>* **CELLULOID HEROES. / HOT POTATOES** `-`

Jun 73. (7") *<74-0940>* **ONE OF THE SURVIVORS. / SCRAPHEAP CITY** `-`

Jun 73. (7") *(RCA 2387)* **SITTING IN THE MIDDAY SUN. / ONE OF THE SURVIVORS** `-`

Sep 73. (7") *(RCA 2418)* **SWEET LADY GENEVIEVE. / SITTING IN MY HOTEL** `-`

Sep 73. (7") *<5001>* **SWEET LADY GENEVIEVE. / SITTING IN THE MIDDAY SUN** `-`

Dec 73. (d-lp) *(SF 8392) <LPL 5002>* **PRESERVATION ACT I**
– Morning song / Daylight / Sweet lady Genevieve / There's a change in the weather / Where are they now / One of the survivors / Cricket / I am your man / Here comes Flash / Sitting in the midday Sun / Demolition.

—— next 45 only contained **RAY & DAVE DAVIES**, before full 5 + 3 again

Apr 74. (7") *(RCA 5015)* **MIRROR OF LOVE. / CRICKET** `-`

Jun 74. (7") *<0275>* **MONEY TALKS. / HERE COMES FLASH** `-`

Jun 74. (d-lp) *<LPL2 5040>* **PRESERVATION ACT II**
– (announcement) / Introduction to solution / When a solution comes / Money talks / (announcement) / Shepherds of the nation / Scum of the Earth / Secondhand car spiv / He's evil / Mirror of love / (announcement) / Nobody gives / Oh where oh where is love? / Flash's dream / Flash's confession / Nothing lasts forever / (announcement) / Artificial man / Scrapheap city / (announcement) / Salvation Road.

Jul 74. (7") *(RCA 5042) <APBO 10019>* **MIRROR OF LOVE. / HE'S EVIL** `-`

Oct 74. (7") *(RCA 2478)* **HOLIDAY ROMANCE. / SHEPHERDS OF THE NATION** `-`

Oct 74. (7") *<APBO 10121>* **PRESERVATION. / SALVATION** `-` `-`

Apr 75. (7") *<APBO 10251>* **ORDINARY PEOPLE. / STAR MAKER** `-`

Apr 75. (7") *(RCA 2546)* **DUCKS ON THE WALL. / RUSH HOUR BLUES** `-`

May 75. (lp) *(SF 8411) <LPI 5081>* **SOAP OPERA** `51`
– Everybody's a star (starmaker) / Ordinary people / Rush hour blues / Nine to five / When work is over / Have another drink / Underneath the neon sign / Holiday romance / You make it all worth while / Ducks on the wall / Face in the crowd / You can't stop the music. *(re-iss. Jul84)*

May 75. (7") *(RCA 2567)* **YOU CAN'T STOP THE MUSIC. / HAVE ANOTHER DRINK** `-`

Nov 75. (lp) *(RS 1028) <FLI 5102>* **SCHOOLBOYS IN DISGRACE** `45`
– Schooldays / Jack the idiot dunce / Education / The first time we fall in love / I'm in disgrace / Headmaster / The hard way / The last assembly / No more looking back / (finale).

Nov 75. (7") *<10551>* **THE HARD WAY. / I'M IN DISGRACE** `-`

Jan 76. (7"m) *(RCM 1)* **NO MORE LOOKING BACK. / JACK THE IDIOT DUNCE / THE HARD WAY** `-`

—— Now down to basic 5-piece after the 3 brass section members departed

	Arista	Arista

Feb 77. (lp/c) *(SP/TC ARTY 1002) <AL 4106>* **SLEEPWALKER** `21`
– Life on the road / Mr. Big man / Sleepwalker / Brother / Juke box music / Sleepless night / Stormy sky / Full moon / Life goes on.

Mar 77. (7") *(ARIST 97) <0240>* **SLEEPWALKER. / FULL MOON** `48`

Jun 77. (7") *(ARIST 114)* **JUKE BOX MUSIC. / SLEEPLESS NIGHT** `-`

Jun 77. (7") *<0247>* **JUKE BOX MUSIC. / LIFE GOES ON** `-`

—— **ANDY PYLE** – bass (ex-BLODWYN PIG, ex-SAVOY BROWN, etc) repl. DALTON

Dec 77. (7") *(ARIST 153) <0296>* **FATHER CHRISTMAS. / PRINCE OF THE PUNKS** `-`

May 78. (lp/c) *(SP/TC ART 1055) <AL 4167>* **MISFITS** `40`
– Misfits / Hay fever / Live life / Rock'n'roll fantasy / In a foreign land / Permanent waves / Black Messiah / Out of the wardrobe / Trust your heart / Get up.

May 78. (7") *(ARIST 189) <0342>* **ROCK'N'ROLL FANTASY. / ARTIFICIAL LIGHT** `30` Jul78

Jul 78. (7") *(ARIST 199)* **LIVE LIFE. / IN A FOREIGN LAND** `-`

Jul 78. (7") *<0372>* **LIVE LIFE. / BLACK MESSIAH** `-` `-`

Sep 78. (7") *(ARIST 210)* **BLACK MESSIAH. / MISFITS** `-`

—— **RAY DAVIES, DAVE DAVIES** and **MICK AVORY** recruited new members **GORDON EDWARDS** – keyboards (ex-PRETTY THINGS) repl. GOSLING (to NETWORK) / **JIM RODFORD** (b. 7 Jul'45, St. Albans, England) – bass (ex-ARGENT, ex-PHOENIX) repl. PYLE (to NETWORK)

Jan 79. (7"/12") *(ARIST/+12 240)* **(WISH I COULD FLY LIKE) SUPERMAN. / LOW BUDGET** `-`

───── **IAN GIBBON** – keyboards repl. EDWARDS

Apr 79. (7") *<0409>* **(WISH I COULD FLY LIKE) SUPERMAN. /**
PARTY LINE — | 41

Sep 79. (7") *(ARIST 300)* **MOVING PICTURES. / IN A SPACE** — | —

Sep 79. (lp/c) *(SP/TC ART 1099) <AB 4240>* **LOW BUDGET** — | 11 Jul79
– Attitude / Catch me now I'm falling / Pressure / National health / (I wish I could
fly like) Superman / Low budget / In a space / Little bit of emotion / Gallon of gas /
Misery / Moving pictures. *(cd-iss. Apr88; 251 146)*

Sep 79. (7") *<0448>* **GALLON OF GAS. / LOW BUDGET** — | —

Nov 79. (7") *<0458>* **CATCH ME NOW I'M FALLING. / LOW**
BUDGET — | —

Nov 79. (7") *(ARIST 321)* **PRESSURE. / NATIONAL HEALTH** — | —

Jul 80. (d-lp) *(DARTY 6) <8401>* **ONE FOR THE ROAD (live)** — | 14 Jun80
– The hard way / Catch me now I'm falling / Where have all the good times gone /
Lola / Pressure / All day and all of the night / 20th century man / Misfits / Prince
of the punks / Stop your sobbing / Low budget / Attitude / (Wish I could fly like)
Superman / National health / Till the end of the day / Celluloid heroes / You really
got me / Victoria / David Watts.

Jul 80. (7"ep) *(ARIST 360)* **WHERE HAVE ALL THE GOOD TIMES**
GONE (live) — | —
– Where have all the good times gone / Victoria / Attitude / David Watts.

Aug 80. (7") *<0541>* **LOLA (live). / CELLULOID HEROES (live)** — | 81

Oct 80. (7") *<0577>* **YOU REALLY GOT ME (live). / ATTITUDE**
(live) — | —

Jun 81. (lp/c) *(SP/TC ART 1171) <9567>* **GIVE THE PEOPLE WHAT**
THEY WANT — | 15
– Around the dial / Give the people what they want / Killer's eyes / Predictable /
Add it up / Destroyer / Yo-yo / Back to front / Art lover / A little bit of abuse / Better
things.

Jun 81. (7") *(ARIST 415)* **BETTER THINGS. / MASSIVE REDUCTIONS** 46 | —
(d7"+=) *(KINKS 1)* – Lola / David Watts.

Oct 81. (7",7"pic-d) *(ARIST 426)* **PREDICTABLE. / BACK TO FRONT** — | —

Oct 81. (7") *<0619>* **DESTROYER. / BACK TO FRONT** — | 85

Nov 81. (7") *<0649>* **BETTER THINGS. / YO-YO** — | 92

Jun 83. (lp/c) *(205/405 275) <8018>* **STATE OF CONFUSION** — | 12
– State of confusion / Definite maybe / Labour of love / Come dancing / Property /
Don't forget to dance / Young Conservatives / Heart of gold / Cliches of the world
(B movie) / Bernadette. *(cd-iss. 1988 on 'Ariola')*

Jul 83. (7"/12") *(ARIST/+12 502) <1054/9016>* **COME DANCING. /**
NOISE 12 | 6 May83

Aug 83. (7") *<9075>* **DON'T FORGET TO DANCE. / YOUNG**
CONSERVATIVES — | 29

Sep 83. (7",12") *(ARIST 524)* **DON'T FORGET TO DANCE. /**
BERNADETTE 58 | —

Mar 84. (7") *(ARIST 560)* **STATE OF CONFUSION. / HEART OF**
GOLD — | —
(12"+=) *(ARIST12 560)* – 20th century man (live) / Lola (live).

Jul 84. (7") *(ARIST 577)* **GOOD DAY. / TOO HOT** — |
(ext.12"+=) *(ARIST12 577)* – Don't forget to dance.

Nov 84. (lp/c) *(206/406 685) <8264>* **WORD OF MOUTH** — | 57
– Do it again / Word of mouth / Good day / Living on a thin line / Sold me out /
Massive reductions / Guilty / Too hot / Missing persons / Summer's gone / Going
solo. *(cd-iss. Jun88; 259 047)*

Apr 85. (7") *(ARIST 617) <9309>* **DO IT AGAIN. / GUILTY** — | 41 Dec84
(12"+=) *(ARIST12 617)* – Summer's gone.

Apr 85. (7") *<9334>* **SUMMER'S GONE. / GOING SOLO** — | —

Oct 86. (d-lp/c) *(302/502 778) <8428>* **COME DANCING WITH**
THE KINKS – THE BEST OF THE KINKS 1977-1986
(compilation) — | Jul86

───── Returned to original line-up of **RAY, DAVE + MICK**, plus sessioners. (RODFORD
and GIBBONS departed).

	London	M.C.A.

Nov 86. (7") *<52960>* **ROCK'N'ROLL CITIES. / WELCOME TO**
SLEAZY TOWN — | —

Nov 86. (lp/c)(cd) *(LON LP/C 27)(828 030-2) <5822>* **THINK VISUAL** — | 81
– Working at the factory / Lost and found / Repetition / Welcome to Sleazy Town /
The video shop / Rock'n'roll cities / How are you / Think visual / Natural gift /
Killing time / When you were a child.

Dec 86. (7") *(LON 119)* **HOW ARE YOU. / KILLING TIME** — | —
(12"+=) *(LONX 119)* – Welcome to Sleazy town.

Mar 87. (7") *(LON 132) <53015>* **LOST AND FOUND. / KILLING**
TIME — | —
(12"+=) *(LONX 132)* – (Ray Davies interview).

May 87. (7") *<53093>* **HOW ARE YOU. / WORKING AT THE**
FACTORY — | —

Feb 88. (7") *(LON 165)* **THE ROAD. / ART LOVER** — | —
(ext.12"+=) *(LONX 165)* – Come dancing.

May 88. (lp/c)(cd) *(LON LP/C 49)(828 078-2) <42107>* **THE ROAD**
(live / studio *) — | Feb88
– The road * / Destroyer / Apeman / Come dancing / Art lover / Cliches of the world
(B-movie) / Living on a thin line / Lost and found / It * / Around the dial / Give the
people what they want.

───── **BOB HENRIT** (b. 2 May'45)- drums repl. AVORY / added **MARK HALEY** –
keyboards, vocals

Sep 89. (7") *(LON 239)* **DOWN ALL THE DAYS (TILL 1992). / YOU**
REALLY GOT ME (live) — | —
(12"+=/cd-s+=) *(LON X/CD 239)* – Entertainment.

Oct 89. (lp/c/cd) *(828 165-1/-4/-2) <6337>* **UK JIVE** — | —
– Aggravation / How do I get close / UK jive / Now and then / What are we doing /
Entertainment / War is over / Down all the days (till 1992) / Loony balloon / Dear
Margaret. *(c+=/cd+=)* – Bright lights / Perfect strangers. *(re-iss. Apr91;)*

Feb 90. (7") *(LON 250)* **HOW DO I GET CLOSE. / DOWN ALL THE**
DAYS (TILL 1992) — | —
(12"+=/cd-s+=) *(LON X/CD 250)* – War is over.

Mar 90. 7") *<53699>* **HOW DO I GET CLOSE. / WAR IS OVER** — | —

	Columbia	Columbia

Mar 93. (cd/c) *(472489-2/-4)* **PHOBIA** — | —
– Opening / Wall of fire / Drift away / Still searching / Phobia / Only a dream /

Don't / Babies / Over the edge / Surviving / It's alright (don't think about it) / The
informer / Hatred (a duet) / Somebody stole my car / Close to the wire / Scattered.
(cd+=) – Did ya.

Jul 93. (cd-s) **SCATTERED. / HATRED (A DUET) / DAYS** — | —

Nov 93. (7") *(659922-7)* **ONLY A DREAM (Radio Version) /**
SOMEBODY STOLE MY CAR — | —
(cd-s+=) *(659922-2)* – Babies.

	Konk	not iss.

Oct 94. (cd/c/lp) *(KNK CD/MC/LP 1)* **TO THE BONE (live)** — | —
– All day and all of the nigt / Apeman / Tired of waiting for you / See my friend /
Death of a clown / Waterloo sunset / Muswell hillbillies / Better things / Don't forget
to dance / Autumn almanac / Sunny afternoon / Dedicated follower of fashion / You
really got me.

Oct 94. (cd-ep) *(KNKD 2)* **WATERLOO SUNSET E.P. (live)** — | —
– Waterloo sunset / You really got me / Elevator man / On the outside.

	When!	not iss.

Jan 97. (c-ep/cd-ep) *(WEN M/X 1016)* **DAYS EP** 35 | —
– Days / You really got me / Dead end street / Lola.

– compilations etc. –

on 'Pye' UK / 'Reprise' US, unless mentioned otherwise

Nov 64. (7"ep) *(NEP 24200)* **KINKSIZE SESSION** — | —
– I've gotta go now / I've got that feeling / Things are getting better / Louie Louie.

Jan 65. (7"ep) *(NEP 24203)* **KINKSIZE HITS** — | —
– You really got me / It's alright / All day and all of the night / I gotta move.

Sep 65. (7"ep) *(NEP 24221)* **KWYET KINKS** — | —
– Wait till the summer / Such a shame / A well respected man / Don't you fret.

Jun 66. (lp) *Marble Arch; (MAL 612)* **WELL RESPECTED KINKS** 5 | —

Jul 66. (7"ep) *(NEP 24258)* **DEDICATED KINKS** — | —
– Dedicated follower of fashion / Till the end of the day / See my friend / Set me
free.

Sep 67. (lp) *Marble Arch; (MAL 716)* **SUNNY AFTERNOON** 9 | —

Apr 68. (7"ep) *(NEP 24296)* **SOMETHING ELSE** — | —
– David Watts / Two sisters / Lazy old sun / Situation.

Feb 69. (lp) *Marble Arch; (MAL 1100)* **KINDA KINKS** — | —

Feb 70. (d-lp) *(NPL 18326)* **THE KINKS** — | —

Aug 71. (7"ep) *(PMM 100)* **YOU REALLY GOT ME. / WONDERBOY /**
SET ME FREE / LONG TALL SALLY — | —

Oct 71. (lp) *Golden Hour; (GH 501)* **THE GOLDEN HOUR OF THE**
KINKS 21 | —
(cd-iss. Apr89 on 'Castle'; GHCD 1)

Oct 71. (lp) *Hallmark; (HMA 201)* **LOLA** — | —

Apr 72. (lp) *<6454>* **THE KINK KRONICLES** — | 94

Feb 73. (lp) **THE GREAT LOST KINKS ALBUM** — | —

Jun 73. (lp) *(GH 558)* **THE GOLDEN HOUR OF THE KINKS VOL.2** — | —
(cd-iss. Apr91 on 'Knight'; KGHCD 148)

1973. (lp) *Hallmark; (HMA 244)* **THE KINKS** — | —

Nov 73. (4xlp-box) **ALL THE GOOD TIMES** — | —
– (THE KINKS double / ARTHUR / THE KINKS PART 1).

Dec 73. (7") *(7N 45313)* **WHERE HAVE ALL THE GOOD TIMES**
GONE. / LOLA — | —

Oct 74. (d-lp) *Golden Hour; (GHD 50)* **LOLA, PERCY AND THE**
POWERMAN COME FACE TO FACE WITH THE VILLAGE
GREEN PRESERVATION SOCIETY – SOMETHING ELSE! — | —

May 75. (7") *(7N 45482)* **SUNNY AFTERNOON/. SITTING ON MY**
SOFA — | —

Jun 76. (lp/c) *R.C.A.; (RS/+C 1059) <1743>* **CELLULOID HEROES –**
THE KINKS GREATEST — | —

May 77. (12"ep) *Big Deal; (BD 105)* **LOLA / SUNNY AFTERNOON. /**
WATERLOO SUNSET / DEDICATED FOLLOWER OF
FASHION — | —

Nov 77. (d-lp) *(FILD 001)* **THE KINKS FILE** — | —

Jul 78. (7") *(7N 46102)* **DEDICATED FOLLOWER OF FASHION. /**
WATERLOO SUNSET — | —
(re-iss. Mar82 on 'Old Gold'; OG 9140)

Oct 78. (d-lp) *Ronco-Pye; (RPL 2031)* **THE KINKS 20 GOLDEN**
GREATS 19 | —

Nov 78. (7"ep) **EP** — | —
– Long tall Sally / I took my baby home / You still want me / You do something to me.

Apr 79. (7") *Flashback; (FBS 1)* **YOU REALLY GOT ME. / ALL DAY**
AND ALL OF THE NIGHT — | —
(re-iss. Feb80 on 'Pye'; RK 1027) *(re-iss. Jun84 on 'Old Gold'; OG 9408)*

Jun 80. (7"ep) *Flashback; (FBEP 104)* **WATERLOO SUNSET / DAVID**
WATTS. / A WELL RESPECTED MAN / STOP YOUR
SOBBIN' — | —

Jul 80. (lp) *Pickwick; (PDA 072)* **THE KINKS COLLECTION** — | —

Oct 80. (d-lp) *P.R.T.; (SPOT 1009)* **SPOTLIGHT ON THE KINKS** — | —

Jun 82. (c) *P.R.T.; (ZCTON 102)* **100 MINUTES OF . . .** — | —

Oct 82. (d-lp) *P.R.T.; (SPOT 1029)* **SPOTLIGHT ON THE KINKS**
VOL.2 — | —

Feb 83. (7") *Flashback; (FBS 15)* **SUNNY AFTERNOON. / TIRED**
OF WAITING FOR YOU — | —

Apr 83. (lp) *P.R.T.; (DOW 4)* **SHAPE OF THINGS TO COME** — | —

Jul 83. (lp) *P.R.T.; (DOW 12)* **CANDY FROM MR. DANDY** — | —

Oct 83. (d-lp) *P.R.T.; (KINK 1)* **KINKS' GREATEST HITS – DEAD**
END STREET 96 | —

Oct 83. (7"/7"pic-d) *P.R.T.; (KD/KPD 1)* **YOU REALLY GOT ME. /**
MISTY WATER 47 | —
(12"pic-d+=) *(DKL 1)* – All day and all of the night.

Oct 84. (cd/c/lp) *P.R.T.; (CD/TC+/KINK 7251)* **THE KINKS GREATEST**
HITS — | —

Nov 84. (lp) *P.R.T.; (KINK 7252)* **KOLLECTABLES** — | —

Nov 84. (lp) *P.R.T.; (KINK 7253)* **KOVERS** — | —

Nov 84. (3xlp-box) *P.R.T.; (KINKX 7254)* **THE KINKS BOX SET** — | —

Nov 85. (d-lp/c) *Castle; (CCS LP/MC 113)* **THE COLLECTION** — | —
(cd-iss. 1988; CCS CD 113) *(cd re-iss. Jul92 on 'BMG-RCA';)*

Dec 85. (d-lp/c)(cd) *Starblend; (TRACK/+K 1)(CDTRACK 1)*
BACKTRACKIN' – THE DEFINITIVE COLLECTION — | —

Mar 86.	(7"pic-d) P.R.T.; (7P 355) **DEDICATED FOLLOWER OF FASHION. / AUTUMN ALMANAC** (re-iss. Mar88; PYS 7)	☐	-
Mar 86.	(7") Old Gold; (OG 9577) **SUNNY AFTERNOON. / TIRED OF WAITING FOR YOU** (re-iss. Jul87 on 7"pic-d 'P.R.T.'; PYS 2)	☐	-
Mar 86.	(7") Old Gold; (OG 9579) **LOLA. / APEMAN**	☐	-
Oct 87.	(lp/c/cd) P.R.T.; (PYL/PYM/PYC 4001) **HIT SINGLES**	☐	-
Oct 87.	(d-lp/d-c/d-cd) P.R.T.; (PYL/PYM/PYC 7001) **THE KINKS ARE WELL RESPECTED MEN**	☐	-
Nov 88.	(cd-ep) Old Gold; (OG 6102) **YOU REALLY GOT ME / ALL DAY AND ALL OF THE NIGHT / TIRED OF WAITING FOR YOU**	☐	-
Feb 89.	(cd-ep) Old Gold; (OG 6117) **WATERLOO SUNSET / SUNNY AFTERNOON / LOLA**	☐	-
Apr 89.	(c) Legacy; (C 901) **C90 COLLECTOR**	☐	-
May 89.	(lp/c)(cd) Pickwick; (SHM/HSC 3265)(PWKS 527) **THE BEST OF THE KINKS – 1964-66**	☐	-
Sep 89.	(lp/c/cd) Castle; (CTV LP/MC/CD 001) **THE ULTIMATE COLLECTION**	35	-
	– You really got me / All day and all of the night / Tired of waiting for you / Everybody's gonna be happy / Set me free / Till the end of the day / Dedicated follower of fashion / Sunny afternoon / Dead end street / Waterloo sunset / Autumn almanac / Wonder boy / Days / Plastic man / Victoria / Lola / Apeman / David Watts / Where have all the good times gone / Well respected man / I'm not like everybody else / End of the season / Death of a clown (DAVE DAVIES) / Suzannah's still alive (DAVE DAVIES).		
Jun 90.	(lp/c/cd) See For Miles; (SEE/+K/CD 295) **THE EP COLLECTION**	☐	-
1990.	(cd) Nightriding; (KNCD 10019) **THE KINKS**	☐	-
Jan 91.	(d-cd) Decal; (CDLIK 74) **THE SINGLES COLLECTION 1964-1970**	☐	-
Aug 91.	(d-c) Pickwick; (PWK S/MC 4075) **THE BEST OF THE KINKS 1966-67**	☐	-
Sep 91.	(d-cd) Rhino; **PRESERVATION (A PLAY IN TWO ACTS)**	☐	-
Nov 91.	(cd/c) Castle; (CCS CD/MC 300) **THE COMPLETE COLLECTION**	☐	-
Feb 92.	(cd/c) See For Miles; (SEE CD/K 329) **THE EP COLLECTION VOL.2**	☐	-
Apr 93.	(cd) Arista; (74321 13687-2) **THE BEST OF THE BALLADS**	☐	-
Sep 93.	(cd/c) Polygram TV; (516 465-2/-4) **THE DEFINITIVE COLLECTION – THE KINKS' GREATEST HITS** (re-iss. Mar97; same)	18	-
Dec 93.	(cd) Gold-Disky; (GOLD 205) **GOLD: GREATEST HITS**	☐	-
May 94.	(cd/c) B.R.Music; (BR CD/MC 15) **GREATEST HITS**	☐	-
May 94.	(cd/c) Prima; (PMM 0569-2/-4) **DANDY**	☐	-
Jul 94.	(cd) Spectrum; (550 722-2) **YOU REALLY GOT ME**	☐	-
Feb 95.	(cd) Essential; (ESBCD 288) **REMASTERED**	☐	-
Aug 95.	(cd) Spectrum; (550 723-2) **LOLA**	☐	-
Apr 97.	(cd/c) Polygram TV; (537554-2/-4) **THE VERY BEST OF THE KINKS**	42	-

DAVE DAVIES

		Pye	Reprise
Jul 67.	(7") (7N 17356) <0614> **DEATH OF A CLOWN. / LOVE ME TILL THE SUN SHINES**	3	☐ Aug67
Nov 67.	(7") (7N 17429) <0660> **SUSANNAH'S STILL ALIVE. / FUNNY FACE**	21	☐
Aug 68.	(7") (7N 17514) **LINCOLN COUNTY. / THERE IS NO LOVE WITHOUT LIFE**	☐	☐
Jan 69.	(7") (7N 17678) **HOLD MY HAND. / CREEPING JEAN**	☐	☐
		R.C.A.	R.C.A.
Sep 80.	(7") <PB 12089> **IMAGINATION'S REAL. / WILD MAN**	-	☐
Sep 80.	(lp/c) (PL/PK 13603) <AFL-1-3603; the US title> **DAVE DAVIES**		42 Jul80
	– Where do you come from / Doing the best for you / Move over / Visionary dreamer / Nothin' more to lose / Imagination real / In you I believe / See the beast / Run / The world is changing hands.		
Nov 80.	(7") <PB 12147> **DOING THE BEST FOR YOU. / NOTHING MORE TO LOSE**	-	☐
Dec 80.	(7") (PB 9620) **DOING THE BEST FOR YOU. / WILD MAN**	-	☐
Oct 81.	(lp/c) (RCA LP/K 6005) <AFL-1-4036> **GLAMOUR**		☐ Jul81
	– Is this the only way / Reveal yourself / World of our own / Two serious / Glamour / 7th channel / Body / Eastern eyes / Body.		
		Warners	Warners
Sep 83.	(lp/c) (92-3917-1/-4) <23917-1/-4> **CHOSEN PEOPLE**	☐	☐ Aug 83
	– Mean disposition / Love gets you / Take one more / True story / Danger zone / Tapes / Freedom lies / Fire burning / Cold winter / Matter of decision / Is it any wonder / Charity / Chosen people.		
Sep 83.	(7") <7-29509> **LOVE GETS YOU. / ONE NIGHT WITH YOU**	-	☐
Nov 83.	(7") <7-29425> **MEAN DISPOSITION. / COLD WINTER**	-	☐

– (DAVE DAVIES) compilations, etc. –

Apr 68.	(7"ep) Pye; (NEP 24289) **DAVE DAVIES HITS**	☐	☐
Aug 82.	(7") Old Gold; (OG 9128) **DEATH OF A CLOWN. / SUSANNAH'S STILL ALIVE**	☐	-
Feb 88.	(lp/c) P.R.T.; (PYL/PYK 6012) **DAVE DAVIES – THE ALBUM THAT NEVER WAS** – (1960's singles)	☐	-
Jul 92.	(cd) Mau Mau; (MAUDCD 617) **DAVE DAVIES / GLAMOUR**	☐	-

RAY DAVIES

—— In 1984, the lp 'RETURN TO WATERLOO' was withdrawn.
     (below from film 'Absolute Beginners')

		Virgin	Virgin
May 86.	(7"/12") (VS 865/+12) **QUIET LIFE. / VOICES IN THE DARK**	☐	☐

KIPPINGTON LODGE (see under ⇒ **BRINSLEY SCHWARZ**)

KISS

Formed: New York City, New York, USA ... late '71 by ex-WICKED LESTER members GENE SIMMONS and PAUL STANLEY, who recruited guitarist ACE FREHLEY and drummer PETER CRISS. After a year of touring in '73, they were signed to the new 'Casablanca' label, hitting the US Top 100 with an eponymous debut album in early '74. This, together with subsequent follow-up albums, 'HOTTER THAN HELL' (1974) and 'DRESSED TO KILL' (1975) set the greasepainted scene for what was to follow; low-rent glitter-metal so tacky it almost stuck to the speakers. Though these early albums sound like they were recorded on a cheap walkman in a sawmill, they contained some of KISS' finest groin-straining moments; 'STRUTTER', 'DEUCE' and 'ROCK AND ROLL ALL NITE' were anthemic shout-alongs for white college kids who could pretend to be rebellious for three minutes. But KISS undoubtedly built their reputation on a garish image and the sensory overkill of their live show, ALICE COOPER-style make-up and onstage schlock the order of the day. Accordingly, it was the double live album, 'ALIVE' (1975) that finally powered the band into the US Top 10 and the stadium major league. With 'DESTROYER' (produced by COOPER mentor, BOB EZRIN), the band refined their sound slightly, even recording a ballad, the PETER CRISS-penned/crooned teen heartbreaker, 'BETH' which furnished the band with their biggest ever hit single. This mid-70's career peak also saw a further three releases achieve platinum status, 'ROCK AND ROLL OVER' (1976), 'LOVE GUN' (1977) and 'ALIVE II'. KISS had struck a resounding chord in some back alley of the American consciousness and now boasted a merchandise line almost as long as SIMMONS' grotesque tongue, a perverted, proto-SPICE GIRLS marketing job from the dark side. And you couldn't get a much better marketing coup than releasing four solo albums simultaneously on the same day, which is exactly what KISS did (one by each member), probably because they knew they could get away with it. Unsurprisingly, most of the material was self-indulgent rubbish and, with the threat of punk never far away, the band began to falter. Although the 'DYNASTY' (1979) album went Top 10 and provided a massive hit with 'I WAS MADE FOR LOVIN' YOU', CRISS soon bowed out, the drum stool filled by session man ANTON FIG for the 'UNMASKED' (1980) album. A permanent replacement was found in ERIC CARR who made his debut on the ill-advised concept nonsense of 'THE ELDER' (1981), though the new musical direction was just too much for FREHLEY to take and he wisely departed the following year. His place was filled by VINNIE VINCENT, who played on the back-to-basics 'CREATURES OF THE NIGHT'. When this album failed to revive their commercial fortunes, the band did the unthinkable, removing their make-up for the 'LICK IT UP' album. Perhaps as a result of the public discovering they weren't blood sucking ghouls after all but (relatively) normal looking people, the album went Top 30. Ironically, the band had just started to re-establish themselves in Britain, where 'LICK IT UP' made the Top 10, no doubt giving them heart in their struggle back to world domination. KISS then went through more line-up changes, with VINCENT being replaced first by MARK ST. JOHN, then BOB KULICK. With the unashamedly commercial 'CRAZY CRAZY NIGHTS' single and 'CRAZY NIGHTS' (1987) album, the band enjoyed their biggest success since their 70's heyday, both releases reaching No.4 in the UK. After another reasonably successful album, 'HOT IN THE SHADE' (1989), tragedy struck the band in the early 90's when CARR died following heart problems and cancer. Shaken but unbowed the band carried on with ERIC SINGER on drums, going back to the hoary sound of old with the 'REVENGE' (1992) opus, an album that saw them showing the young bucks who had patented the moves. It had to happen of course; 1996 marked a money-spinning, full-blown reunion tour with the original line-up and re-applied warpaint, the perfect KISS-off to those who had written them off for dead. • **Songwriters:** Most by STANLEY or SIMMONS, with some ballads by CRISS. Covered; THEN (S)HE KISSED ME (Crystals) / GOD GAVE ROCK'N'ROLL TO YOU (Argent). MICHAEL BOLTON co-wrote with STANLEY their minor hit ballad 'FOREVER'. GENE SIMMONS solo covered; WHEN YOU WISH UPON A STAR (Judy Garland). • **Trivia:** In 1977, Marvel Comics started a KISS feature series in their monthly mag. In 1984, SIMMONS starred as a villain in the film 'Runaway' alongside Tom Selleck. Two years later 'The Bat-Winged Vampire' featured in films 'Never Too Young To Die', 'Trick Or Treat' & 'Wanted Dead Or Alive'. In 1994, a tribute album 'KISS MY ASS' was released by 'Mercury'. It featured star cover versions by LENNY KRAVITZ, GARTH BROOKS, ANTHRAX, GIN BLOSSOMS, TOAD THE WET SPROCKET, SHANDI's ADDICTION, DINOSAUR JR., EXTREME, LEMONHEADS, etc.

Album rating: KISS (*7) / HOTTER THAN HELL (*7) / DRESSED TO KILL (*7) / ALIVE! (*8) / DESTROYER (*8) / ROCK AND ROLL OVER (*6) / LOVE GUN (*6) / ALIVE II (*7) / DOUBLE PLATINUM compilation (*8) / DYNASTY (*6) / UNMASKED (*5) / (MUSIC FROM) THE ELDER (*4) / KILLERS compilation (*5) / CREATURES OF THE NIGHT (*6) / LICK IT UP (*6) / ANIMALIZE (*5) / ASYLUM (*6) / CRAZY NIGHTS (*5) / SMASHES, THRASHES AND HITS compilation (*7) / HOT IN THE SHADE (*6) / REVENGE (*6) / ALIVE III (*7) / MTV UNPLUGGED (*5) / CARNIVAL OF SOULS (*5)

GENE SIMMONS (b. GENE KLEIN, 25 Aug'49, Haifa, Israel) – vocals, bass / **PAUL STANLEY** (b. STANLEY EISEN, 20 Jan'52, Queens, N.Y.) – guitar, vocals / **ACE FREHLEY** (b. PAUL FREHLEY, 22 Apr'51, Bronx, N.Y.) – lead guitar, vocals / **PETER CRISS** (b. PETER CRISSCOULA, 27 Dec'47, Brooklyn, N.Y.) – drums, vocals

Casablanca Casablanca

Feb 74. (7") <0004> **NOTHIN' TO LOSE. / LOVE THEME FROM KISS**   [-] [-]
Feb 74. (lp) <9001> **KISS**   [-] [87]
– Strutter / Nothin' to lose / Fire house / Cold gin / Let me know / Kissin' time / Deuce / Love theme from Kiss / 100,000 years / Black diamond. *(UK-iss.Feb75; CBC 4003) (re-iss. May77 red-lp; CAL 2006) (re-iss. Feb82 lp/c; 6399/7199 057) (re-iss. Jul84 lp/c; PRICE/PRIMC 68) (cd-iss. Aug88; 824146-2)*
May 74. (7") <0011> **KISSIN' TIME. / NOTHIN' TO LOSE**   [-] [83]
Aug 74. (7") <0015> **STRUTTER. / 100,000 YEARS**   [-] [-]
Nov 74. (lp) <7006> **HOTTER THAN HELL**   [-] [100]
– Got to choose / Parasite / Goin' blind / Hotter than Hell / Let me go, rock'n'roll / All the way / Watchin' you / Mainline / Comin' home / Strange ways. *(UK-iss.May77 red-lp; CAL 2007) (re-iss. Feb82 lp/c; 6399/7199 058) (cd-iss. Aug88; 824147-2)*
Jan 75. (7") (CBX 503) **NOTHIN' TO LOSE. / LOVE THEME FROM KISS**   [ ] [-]
Mar 75. (7") <823> **LET ME GO ROCK'N'ROLL. / HOTTER THAN HELL**   [ ] [ ]
Aug 75. (lp) (CBC 4004) <7016> **DRESSED TO KILL**   [32] Mar75
– Room service / Two timer / Ladies in waiting / Getaway / Rock bottom / C'mon and love me / Anything for my baby / She / Love her all I can / Rock and roll all nite. *(re-iss. May77 red-lp; CAL 2008) (re-iss. Feb82 lp/c; 6399/7199 059) (cd-iss. Aug88; 824148-2)*
May 75. (7") <829> **ROCK AND ROLL ALL NITE. / GETAWAY**   [-] [68]
Jun 75. (7") (CBX 510) **ROCK AND ROLL ALL NITE. / ANYTHING FOR MY BABY**   [ ] [-]
Oct 75. (7") <841> **C'MON AND LOVE ME. / GETAWAY**   [ ] [-]
Nov 75. (7") <850> **ROCK AND ROLL ALL NITE (live). / ('A'studio mix)**   [-] [12]
Apr 76. (7") (CBX 516) <854> **SHOUT IT OUT LOUD. / SWEET PAIN**   [31] Mar76
May 76. (lp) (CBC 4008) <7025> **DESTROYER**   [22] [11] Mar76
– Detroit rock city / King of the night time world / God of thunder / Great expectations / Flaming youth / Sweet pain / Shout it out loud / Beth / Do you love me. *(re-iss. May77 red-lp; CAL 2009) (re-iss. Feb82 lp/c; 6399/7199 064) (cd-iss. Apr87; 824149-2)*
Jun 76. (7") <858> **FLAMING YOUTH. / GOD OF THUNDER**   [-] [74]
Jun 76. (d-lp) (CBC 4011+2) <7020> **ALIVE! (live)**   [49] [9] Oct75
– Deuce / Strutter / Got to choose / Hotter than Hell / Firehouse / Nothin' to lose / C'mon and love me / Parasite / She / Watchin' you / 100,000 years / Black diamond / Cold gin / Rock and roll all nite / Let me go, rock'n'roll. *(re-iss. May77 red-lp; CALD 5001) (re-iss. Feb82; 6640 064) (re-iss. Sep84 d-lp/d-c; PRID/+C 3) (cd-iss. Apr87; 822780-2)*
Aug 76. (7") <863> **BETH. / DETROIT ROCK CITY**   [-] [7]
Jul 76. (7") (CBX 519) **BETH. / GOD OF THUNDER**   [ ] [ ]
Feb 77. (red-lp) (CALH 2001) <NBLP 7037> **ROCK AND ROLL OVER**   [ ] [11] Nov76
– I want you / Take me / Calling Dr. Love / Ladies room / Baby driver / Love 'em and leave 'em / Mr. Speed / See you in your dreams / Hard luck woman / Makin' love. *(re-iss. Feb82 lp/c; 6399/7199 060) (cd-iss. Aug88; 824150-2)*
Dec 76. (7") <873> **HARD LUCK WOMAN. / MR. SPEED**   [-] [15]
Mar 77. (7") <880> **CALLING DR. LOVE. / TAKE ME**   [-] [16]
May 77. (7"m) (CAN 102) **HARD LUCK WOMAN. / CALLING DR. LOVE / BETH**   [ ] [ ]
Jun 77. (lp) (CALH 2017) <7057> **LOVE GUN**   [ ] [4]
– I stole your love / Christine sixteen / Got love for sale / Shock me / Tomorrow and tonight / Love gun / Hooligan / Almost human / Plaster caster / The she kised me. *(re-iss. Feb82 lp/c; 6399/7199 063) (re-iss. Jul84 lp/c; PRICE/PRIMC 69) (cd-iss. Aug88; 824151-2)*
Jul 77. (7") <889> **CHRISTINE SIXTEEN. / SHOCK ME**   [-] [25]
Aug 77. (7"m/12"m) (CAN/L 110) **THEN SHE KISSED ME. / HOOLIGAN / FLAMING YOUTH**   [ ] [-]
Sep 77. (7") <895> **LOVE GUN. / HOOLIGAN**   [-] [61]
Nov 77. (d-lp/d-c) (CALD/+C 5004) <7076> **KISS ALIVE II**   [60] [7]
– Detroit rock city / King of the night time world / Ladies room / Makin' love / Love gun / Calling Dr. Love / Christine sixteen / Shock me / Hard luck woman / Tomorrow and tonight / I stole your love / Beth / God of thunder / I want you / Shout it out loud / All American man / Rockin' in the U.S.A. / Larger than life / Rocket ride / Anyway you want it. *(re-iss. Feb82 d-lp/d-c; 6685 043/(7599 512) (cd-iss. May89; 822781-2)*
Jan 78. (7") <906> **SHOUT IT OUT LOUD (live). / NOTHIN' TO LOSE (live)**   [ ] [54]
Feb 78. (7") <915> **ROCKET RIDE. / TOMORROW AND TONIGHT**   [-] [39]
Mar 78. (7") (CAN 117) **ROCKET RIDE. / LOVE GUN (live)**   [ ] [ ]
(12"+=) (CANL 117) – Detroit rock city (live).
Jun 78. (7") (CAN 126) **ROCK AND ROLL ALL NITE. / C'MON AND LOVE ME**   [ ] [-]

—— Took time to do solo projects (all same label on below)

GENE SIMMONS

Sep 78. (lp/pic-lp) <NBLP/NBPIX 7120> **GENE SIMMONS**   [-] [22]
– Radioactive / Burning up with fever / See you tonite / Tunnel of love / True confessions / Living in sin / Always near you – Nowhere to hide / Man of 1000 faces / Mr. Make Believe / See you in your dreams / When you wish upon a star. *<re-iss. 1987 pic-lp; NBLPP 7120>*
Oct 78. (7") <NB 951> **RADIOACTIVE. / SEE YOU IN YOUR DREAMS**   [ ] [-]
Jan 79. (7",7"red) (CAN 134) **RADIOACTIVE. / WHEN YOU WISH UPON A STAR**   [41] [-]

ACE FREHLEY

Sep 78. (lp/pic-lp) <NBLP/NBPIX 7121> **ACE FREHLEY**   [-] [26]
– Rip it out / Speedin' back to my baby / Snow blind / Ozone / What's on your mind / New York groove / I'm in need of love / Wiped-out / Fractured mirror. *<re-iss. 1987 pic-lp; NBLPP 7121> (cd-iss. May88; 826916-2)*
Nov 78. (7"blue) (CAN 135) <NB 941> **NEW YORK GROOVE. / SNOW BLIND**   [ ] [13] Sep78

PETER CRISS

Sep 78. (lp/pic-lp) <NBLP/NBPIX 7122> **PETER CRISS**   [-] [43]
– I'm gonna love you / You matter to me / Tossin' and turnin' / Don't you let me down / That's the kind of sugar papa likes / Easy thing / Rock me, baby / Kiss the girl goodbye / Hooked on rock'n'roll / I can't stop the rain. *<re-iss. 1987 pic-lp; NBLPP 7122> (cd-iss. Nov91; 826917-2) (re-iss. Aug94 cd+red-lp+book on 'Megarock')*
Dec 78. (7") (NB 952) **DON'T YOU LET ME DOWN. / HOOKED ON ROCK AND ROLL**   [ ] [ ]
Feb 79. (7"green) (CAN 139) **YOU MATTER TO ME. / HOOKED ON ROCK AND ROLL**   [ ] [ ]

PAUL STANLEY

Sep 78. (lp/pic-lp) <NBLP/NBPIX 7123> **PAUL STANLEY**   [-] [40]
– Tonight you belong to me / Move on / Ain't quite right / Wouldn't you like to know / Take me away (together as one) / It's alright / Hold me, touch me (think of me when we're apart) / Love in chains / Goodbye. *(re-iss. 1987 pic-lp; NBLPP 7123) (cd-iss. Nov91; 826918-2)*
Feb 79. (7",7"purple) (CAN 140) **HOLD ME TOUCH ME. / GOODBYE**   [ ] [-]

KISS

—— returned to studio

Casablanca Casablanca

Jun 79. (7") (CAN 152) <983> **I WAS MADE FOR LOVIN' YOU. / HARD TIMES**   [50] [11] May79
(12") (CANL 152) – ('A'side) / Charisma.
Jun 79. (lp/c) (CALH/+C 2051) <7152> **DYNASTY**   [50] [9]
– I was made for lovin' you / 2,000 man / Sure know something / Dirty livin' / Charisma / Magic touch / Hard times / X-ray eyes / Save your love. *(re-iss. Oct83 lp/c; PRICD/PRIMC 42) <cd-iss. 1988; > (cd-iss. Aug88; 812770-2)*
Aug 79. (7") (CAN 163) <2205> **SURE KNOW SOMETHING. / DIRTY LIVIN'**   [ ] [47]
Feb 80. (7"m/12"m) (NB/+L 1001) **2000 MAN. / I WAS MADE FOR LOVIN' YOU / SURE KNOW SOMETHING**   [ ] [ ]

Mercury Casablanca

Jun 80. (7") <2282> **SHANDI. / SHE'S SO EUROPEAN**   [-] [47]
Jun 80. (7") (MER 19) **TALK TO ME. / SHE'S SO EUROPEAN**   [ ] [ ]
Jun 80. (7") (6302 032) <7225> **UNMASKED**   [48] [35]
– Is that you / Shandi / Talk to me / Naked city / What makes the world go 'round / Tomorrow / Two sides of the coin / She's so European / Easy as it seems / Torpedo girl / You're all that I want. *(cd-iss. May83; 800041-2)*
Aug 80. (7") (KISS 1) **WHAT MAKES THE WORLD GO 'ROUND. / NAKED CITY**   [ ] [ ]
Aug 80. (7") <2299> **TOMORROW. / NAKED CITY**   [-] [ ]

—— (May'80) **ERIC CARR** (b.12 Jul'50) – drums, producer repl. CRISS who went solo (early 80's pop albums; 'OUT OF CONTROL' / 'LET ME ROCK YOU')
Nov 81. (lp/c) (6302/7144 163) <7261> **MUSIC FROM 'THE ELDER'**   [51] [75]
– The oath / Fanfare / Just a boy / Dark light / Only you / Under the rose / A world without heroes / Mr. Blackwell / Escape from the island / Odyssey / I. *(cd-iss. Jun89; 825153-2)*
Nov 81. (7") <2343> **A WORLD WITHOUT HEROES. / DARK LIGHT**   [-] [56]
Jan 82. (7"/7"pic-d) (KISS/+P 2) **A WORLD WITHOUT HEROES. / MR. BLACKWELL**   [55] [-]

—— **VINNIE VINCENT** (b. VINCENT CUSANO) – guitar repl. BOB KULICK who had repl. FREHLEY (he formed FREHLEY'S COMET)

Casablanca Casablanca

Oct 82. (7") <2365> **DANGER. / I LOVE IT LOUD**   [ ] [ ]
Oct 82. (7") (KISS 3) **KILLER. / I LOVE IT LOUD**   [ ] [ ]
(12"+=) (KISS 3-12) – I was made for lovin' you.
Oct 82. (lp/c) (6302/7144 219) <7270> **CREATURES OF THE NIGHT**   [22] [45]
– Creatures of the night / Saint and sinner / Keep me comin' / Rock and roll Hell / Danger / I love it loud / I still love you / Killer / War machine. *(cd-iss. Aug88; 824154-2)*
Mar 83. (7") (KISS 4) **CREATURES OF THE NIGHT. / ROCK AND ROLL ALL NITE (live)**   [34] [-]
(12"+=) (KISS 4-12) – War machine.

Vertigo Mercury

Oct 83. (7") <814 671-7> **LICK IT UP. / DANCE ALL OVER YOUR FACE**   [66] [ ]
Oct 83. (7"/7"sha-pic-d) (KISS 5/+P) **LICK IT UP. / NOT FOR THE INNOCENT**   [34] [-]
(12"+=) (KISS 5-12) – I still love you.
Oct 83. (lp/c) (VERL/+C 9) <814 297> **LICK IT UP**   [7] [24]
– Exciter / Not for the innocent / Lick it up / Young and wasted / Gimme more / All Hell's breakin' loose / A million to one / Fits like a glove / Dance all over your face / And on the 8th day. *(cd-iss. Dec89 on 'Mercury'; 814297-2)*
Jan 84. (7") <818 216-2> **ALL HELL'S BREAKIN' LOOSE. / YOUNG AND WASTED**   [ ] [ ]

—— **MARK (NORTON) ST. JOHN** – guitar repl. VINCENT who formed VINNIE VINCENT'S INVASION
Sep 84. (7") (VER 12) <880 205-7> **HEAVEN'S ON FIRE. / LONELY IS THE HUNTER**   [43] [49]
(12"+=) (VERX 12) – All hell's breakin' loose.
Sep 84. (lp/c) (VERL/+C 18) <822 495> **ANIMALIZE**   [11] [19]
– I've had enough (into the fire) / Heaven's on fire / Burn bitch burn / Get all you can take / Lonely is the hunter / Under the gun / Thrills in the night / While the city sleeps / Murder in high-heels. *(cd-iss. Dec89 on 'Mercury'; 822 495-2)*
Nov 84. (7") <880 535-2> **THRILLS IN THE NIGHT. / BURN BITCH BURN**   [ ] [ ]

—— **BRUCE KULICK** – guitar repl. MARK who became ill
Oct 85. (lp/c) (VERH/+C 32) <826 099> **ASYLUM**   [12] [20]
– King of the mountain / Any way you slice it / Who wants to be lonely / Trial by fire / I'm alive / Love's a deadly weapon / Tears are falling / Secretly cruel / Radar for love / Uh! All night. *(cd-iss. May89 on 'Mercury'; 826 303-2)*
Oct 85. (7") <884 141-7> **TEARS ARE FALLING. / ANY WAY YOU SLICE IT**   [-] [51]

Oct 85. (7") *(KISS 6)* **TEARS ARE FALLING. / HEAVEN'S ON FIRE** (live) | 57 | - |
(12"+=) *(KISS 6-12)* – Any way you slice it.

Sep 87. (7"/7"s) *(KISS 7/+P)* <888 796-7> **CRAZY CRAZY NIGHTS. / NO, NO, NO** | 4 | 65 |
(12"+=) *(KISS 7-12)* – Lick it up / Uh! All night.
(12"pic-d+=) *(KISSP 7-12)* – Heaven's on fire / Tears are falling.

Oct 87. (lp/c) *(VERH/+C 49)* <832626> **CRAZY NIGHTS** | 4 | 18 |
– Crazy crazy nights / I'll fight Hell to hold you / Bang bang you / No, no, no / Hell or high water / My way / When your walls come down / Reason to live / Good girl gone bad / Turn on the night / Thief in the night. *(cd-iss. Feb91; 832 626-2)*

Dec 87. (7"/7"s) *(KISS/+P 8)* <870 022-7> **REASON TO LIVE. / THIEF IN THE NIGHT** | 33 | 64 |
(c-s+=) *(KISSMC 8)* – Who wants to be lonely.
(12"++=) *(KISS 8-12)* – Thrills in the night.
(12"pic-d++=) *(KISSP 8-12)* – Secretly cruel.
(cd-s+=) *(KISCD 8)* – Tears are falling / Crazy crazy nights.

Feb 88. (7"/7"s) *(KISS/+P 9)* <870 215-7> **TURN ON THE NIGHT. / HELL OR HIGH WATER** | 41 | |
(12"+=/12"pic-d+=) *(KISS/+P 9-12)* – King of the mountain / Any way you slice it.
(cd-s+=) *(KISCD 9)* – Heaven's on fire / I love it loud.

Oct 89. (7"/7"red/c-s) *(KIS S/R/MC 10)* <876 146-7> **HIDE YOUR HEART. / BETRAYED** | 59 | 66 |
(12"+=/cd-s+=) *(KIS SX/CD 10)* – Boomerang.
(10"pic-d) *(KISP 10-10)* – ('A'side) / Lick it up / Heaven's on fire.

Oct 89. (lp/c/cd) <(838 913-2/-4/-1)> **HOT IN THE SHADE** | 35 | 29 |
– Rise to it / Betrayed / Hide your heart / Prisoner of love / Read my body / Love's a slap in the face / Forever / Silver spoon / Cadillac dreams / King of hearts / The street giveth and the street taketh away / You love me to hate you / Somewhere between Heaven and Hell / Little Caesar / Boomerang.

Mar 90. (7"/7"s) *(KISS/+P 11)* <876 716-7> **FOREVER (remix). / THE STREET GIVETH AND THE STREET TAKETH AWAY** | 65 | 8 Feb90 |
(12"white+=) *(KISS 12-12)* – Deuce (demo) / Strutter (demo).
(12"/12"g-f) *(KIS SX/XG 11)* – ('A'side) / All American man / Shandi / The Oath.
(cd-s) *(KISCD 11)* – ('A'side) / Creatures of the night / Lick it up / Heaven's on fire.

Jun 90. (c-s) <875096> **RISE TO IT. / SILVER SPOON** | - | 81 |

—— In May'91, ERIC CARR underwent open heart surgery. He was admitted to hospital again but they found malignant cancer growth. He died on the 24th Nov'91. In Jan'92, KISS hit UK No.4 with 'GOD GAVE ROCK'N'ROLL TO YOU II' from the film 'Bill & Ted's Bogus Journey'. On the same single issued on 'Interscope' were tracks by 'KINGS X' & 'SLAUGHTER'.

—— **ERIC SINGER** – drums (ex-BADLANDS, ex-BLACK SABBATH) repl. CARR

May 92. (7"/c-s) *(KISS/KISMC 12)* **UNHOLY. / GOD GAVE ROCK'N'ROLL TO YOU II** | 26 | |
(12"+=/12"pic-d+=)(cd-s+=) *(KISS/+P 12-12)(KISCD 12)* – Partners in crime / Deva / Strutter (demos).

May 92. (cd/c/lp) <848 037-2/-4/-1> <48037> **REVENGE** | 10 | 6 |
– Unholy / Take it off / Tough love / Spit / God gave rock'n'roll to you II / Domino / Heart of chrome / Thou shalt not / Every time I look at you / Paralyzed / I just wanna / Carr jam 1981.

May 93. (cd/c) <(514 827-2/-4)> **KISS ALIVE III (live)** | 24 | 9 |
– Creatures of the night / Deuce / I just wanna / Unholy / Heaven's on fire / Watchin' you / Domino / I was made for lovin' you / I still love you / Rock'n'roll all nite / Lick it up (featuring BOBBY WOMACK) / Take it off / I love it loud / Detroit rock city / God gave rock'n'roll to you / Star spangled banner.

Mar 96. (cd/c/lp) <(528 950-2/-4/-1)> **MTV UNPLUGGED (live)** | 74 | 15 |
– Comin' home / Plaster caster / Goin' blind / Do you love me / Domino / Sure know something / A world without heroes / Rock bottom / See you tonight / I still love you / Every time I look at you / 2,000 man / Beth / Nothin' to lose / Rock and roll all nite.

Oct 97. (cd/c) <(536 323-2/-4)> **CARNIVAL OF SOULS** | | 27 |
– Hate / Rain / Master and slave / Childhood's end / I will be there / Jungle / In my head / It never goes away / Seduction of the innocent / I confess / In the mirror / I walk alone.

—— originals were back again **(SIMMONS, STANLEY, FREHLEY + CRISS)**

Sep 98. (cd/c) <(558992-2/-4)> **PSYCHO-CIRCUS** | 47 | 3 |
– Psycho-circus / Within / I pledge allegience (to the state of rock & roll) / Into the void / We are one / You wanted the best / Raise your glasses / I finally found my way / Dreamin' / Journey of 1,000 years.

– compilations etc. –

Aug 76. (t-lp) *Casablanca;* <7032> **THE ORIGINALS** (first 3 albums) | - | |

May 78. (d-lp) *Casablanca;* *(CALD 5005)* <7100 1-2> **DOUBLE PLATINUM** | | 24 |
(re-iss. Feb82; 6641 907) (re-iss. May85 d-lp/d-c; PRID/+C 8) cd-iss. Jun87; 824 148-2)

Jan 81. (lp) *Casablanca;* *(6302 060)* **THE BEST OF THE SOLO ALBUMS** | - | - |

Jun 82. (lp) *Casablanca;* *(CANL 1)* **KILLERS** | 42 | - |

Nov 88. (7") *Mercury;* <872 246-7> **LET'S PUT THE 'X'. / CALLING DR. LOVE** | - | 97 |

Nov 88. (lp/c/cd) *Vertigo / Mercury;* <(836 759-1/-4/-2)> **SMASHES, THRASHES AND HITS** | 62 | 21 |
– Let's put the X in sex / Crazy, crazy nights / (You make me) Rock hard / Love gun / Detroit rock city / I love it loud / Reason to live / Lick it up / Heavens on fire / Strutter / Beth / Tears are falling / I was made for lovin' you / Rock and roll all nite / Shout it out loud.

Oct 88. (5"vid-cd) *Vertigo;* *(080 232-2)* **CRAZY, CRAZY NIGHTS. / NO, NO, NO / WHEN YOUR WALLS COME DOWN / THIEF IN THE NIGHT** | | |

1989. (7") *Mercury;* <814 303-7> **BETH. / HARD LUCK WOMAN** | - | - |

1989. (7") *Mercury;* <814 304-7> **ROCK AND ROLL ALL NITE. / I WAS MADE FOR LOVIN' YOU** | - | - |

Sep 89. (5"vid-cd) *Vertigo;* *(080 044-2)* **LICK IT UP. / DANCE ALL OVER YOUR FACE / GIMME MORE / FITS LIKE A GLOVE** | | - |

Sep 89. (5"vid-cd) *Vertigo;* *(080 058-2)* **TEARS ARE FALLING. / ANY WAY YOU SLICE IT / WHO WANTS TO BE LONELY / SECRETLY CRUEL** | | - |

—— (all lp's were released as pic-lp's in Europe)

Jul 96. (cd/c) *Mercury;* <(532 741-2/-4)> **YOU WANTED THE BEST, YOU GOT THE BEST (live compilation)** | | 17 |

Jul 97. (cd/c) *Polygram TV;* <(536 159-2/-4)> **GREATEST HITS** | 58 | 77 Apr97 |

KLF

Formed: KOPYRIGHT LIBERATION FRONT. Based; London, England . . . 1986 by BILL DRUMMOND and JIM CAUTY. Raised in Clydebank, Scotland, DRUMMOND was already a seasoned music industry veteran when he teamed up with CAUTY, having helped to form the pivotal 'Zoo' label in the late 70's, initially home to such Merseyside legends as TEARDROP EXPLODES and ECHO & THE BUNNYMEN. DRUMMOND also worked as an A&R bod for 'WEA', signing up the band BRILLIANT with whom CAUTY played guitar. Eventually, the pair ditched their existing music industry responsibilities with the intention of subverting the notion of the 'pop star' and began working on their first project, JUSTIFIED ANCIENTS OF MU MU. Under that improbably titled moniker, the pair released their first album, '1987 – WHAT THE FUCK IS GOING ON' (1987), a question one might well have asked oneself in those dark, RICK ASTLEY-dominated days. The JAMMS answer was to desecrate the works of such revered musical greats as The BEATLES, LED ZEPPELIN and ABBA, the latter taking great offence to this and demanding that the band destroy the offending copies . . . all 500 of them. The JAMMS went on to bigger and better things with their dancefloor-friendly Dr. Who/GARY GLITTER pastiche, 'DOCTORIN' THE TARDIS' (released under The TIMELORDS moniker) at the height of the first house explosion in 1988. The record went to No.1, prompting the group to make their ninth official release a mock-guide book to the music industry, detailing how to make No.1 with the minimum of effort. Next was the pair's most famous incarnation as the KLF, DRUMMOND and CAUTY experimenting with house and ambient music to create a string of tracks that were massive club hits as well as Top 5 singles, at the turn of the decade. 'WHAT TIME IS LOVE?', 'LAST TRAIN TO TRANSCENTRAL' and '3 A.M. ETERNAL' were all collected on 'THE WHITE ROOM' (1991) album, the latter single even reaching the US Top 5 in 1990. The album went to No.3 in Britain, becoming a consistent seller until the band deleted it the following year. A fertile period for the KLF, the outfit also released the highly regarded ambient album, 'CHILL OUT' (1990), while CAUTY played a major part in the formation of The ORB. Taking the opportunity to resurrect the JAMMS, the duo released 'IT'S GRIM UP NORTH', a hilarious run through of dismal English towns, as well as roping in TAMMY WYNETTE for an improbable duet on 'JUSTIFIED AND ANCIENT (STAND BY THE JAMMS)'. While the single was a massive cross-Atlantic hit, the lines were becoming blurred as to who was taking the piss out of who. But the KLF had yet to play their trump card, and after a suitably overwrought version of 'WHAT TIME IS LOVE' went Top 5, they decided enough was enough and set out to sabotage the success they'd created. Invited to play at the annual Brit awards ceremony in 1992, the KLF proceeded to obliterate 'WHAT TIME IS LOVE' with the help of hardcore punk/thrash merchants 'EXTREME NOISE TERROR'. The numerous rumours about the duo mutilating a dead sheep on stage never materialised although they created enough of a furore to keep the press speculating for weeks. A couple of months later the duo announced that the KLF was officially no more, the back catalogue promptly deleted. CAUTY and DRUMMOND subsequently turned their guerilla tactics on the art world, and under the guise of the mysterious K Foundation, awarded Rachel Whiteread a £40,000 prize for the worst art piece of the year. The Foundation's shortlist for the prize was identical to that of the shortlist for the Turner prize, an annual award for the best piece of non-mainstream art which Whiteread had also scooped. The K Foundation further bemused a sceptical art world when they exhibited £1,000,000 in banknotes, profits from their hit making which they nailed to a board for a private viewing. CAUTY and DRUMMOND then made the most radical statement of their career and one of the most radical "art" statements in history when they literally torched the money in a farmhouse on a remote Scottish island, even filming the event for posterity. Roundly condemned as a highly irresponsible waste of cash that could have been donated to charity etc, etc, the questions that the duo raised were predictably ignored. More recently, CAUTY was allegedly cautioned by police after scaring cows with high freqency electronic sound waves (!), while the duo contributed a suitably bizarre track to the 1995 'HELP' Warchild charity album. The K Foundation also released a single, 'F**K THE MILLENNIUM', in late '97, asking people to phone in and cast their 'vote' on the matter. Towards the end of a tiring decade (for some of us!) CAUTY was unmasked as the man behind that novelty hit by the SOLID GOLD CHARTBUSTERS, '1-2-1'; I hate mobile phones even worse now.

Album rating: WHO KILLED THE JAMMS? (*6) / SHAG TIMES (*6) / WHAT TIME IS LOVE STORY (*6) / CHILL OUT (*7) / THE WHITE ROOM (*8)

JUSTIFIED ANCIENTS OF MU MU

(aka J.A.M.M.s) **KING BOY D** (aka BILL DRUMMOND) (b.29 Apr'53, Butterworth, South Africa) – synths (ex-BIG IN JAPAN, ex-LORI & THE CHAMELEONS) / **ROCKMAN ROCK** (aka JIM CAUTY) (b.1954) – guitar (ex-BRILLIANT, etc.)

	KLF Comm.	not iss.
May 87. (one-sided-12") *(JAMS 23)* **ALL YOU NEED IS LOVE** | | - |
(12"+=) *(JAMS 23T)* – Ivum naya / Rap, rhyme and scratch yourself.
(7") *(JAMS 23s)* – ('A'-Me Ru Con mix) / ('A'-Ibo version).

Jun 87. (lp; w-drawn) *(JAMS LP1)* **1987 (WHAT THE FUCK IS GOING ON?)** | - | - |

	KLF Comm.	TVT	

Sep 87. (one-sided-12") *(JAMS 24T)* **WHITNEY JOINS THE JAMS (120 bpm)** — | - | - Scots

Nov 87. (12") *(JAMS 25T)* **1987 – THE 45 EDITS**
– (excerpts from the unissued lp) | - | -

Dec 87. (12") *(JAMS 27)* **DOWN TOWN (A-side mix). / DOWN TOWN (B-side mix)**
(above also available as 2 one-sided-12"; same)
(7"/ext.12") *(JAMS 27 s/T)* – Down town (118 bpm) / Down town. | | -

Dec 87. (12"; as DISCO 2000) *(D 2000)* **I GOTTA CD. / I LOVE DISCO 2000** | | -

Feb 88. (lp) *(JAMS LP2)* **WHO KILLED THE JAMS?**
– The candy store / The candy man / Disaster fund collection / King boy's dream / The porpoise song / The Prestwich prophet's grin / Burn the bastards. *(w/ free KLF 1987 COMPLETIST LIST discography; KLF 001)* | | -

Mar 88. (export-12"ep) *(JAMS 26T)* **BURN THE BEAT EP**
– Burn the bastards / Burn the beat (I) / Prestwich prophet's grin (dance mix 90 bpm) / The porpoise song (dance mix 114 bpm). | - | -

Mar 88. (one-sided-12"grey) *(JAMS 28T)* **IT'S GRIM UP NORTH** | | -

K.L.F.

—— just a justified change of name

	KLF Comm.	TVT	

Mar 88. (7") *(KLF 002)* **BURN THE BEAT (II). / THE PORPOISE SONG**
(12") *(KLF 002T)* – ('A'side) / Burn the bastards. | | -

Apr 88. (12"; as DISCO 2000) *(D 2002)* **ONE LOVE NATION. / ('A'edit) / ('A'instrumental)** | | -

May 88. (7"/7"sha-pic-d; as TIMELORDS) *(KLF 003 s/P) <4025>* **DOCTORIN' THE TARDIS. / ('A'-minimal version)**
(12"+=) *(KLF 003T)* – ('A'club version).
(video-cd-s++=) *(KLFCD 003)* – ('A'-video mix).
(12"+=) *(KLF 003R)* – ('A'-with Gary Glitter). | 1 | 66 Nov88

Jan 89. (7"; as DISCO 2000) *(D 2003)* **UPTIGHT (EVERYTHING'S ALRIGHT (Banana 2000 mix). / MR. HOTTY LOVES YOU (edit)**
(12") *(D 2003)* – ('A'-discorama mix) / ('B'side). | | -

—— JIM CAUTY released eponymous album under **SPACE** banner mid-1990 on 'Space-Rough Trade'; *LP/CD 1.*

Jun 89. (12") *(KLF 004T)* **WHAT TIME IS LOVE? (trance). / ('A'mix 2)**
(12") *(KLF 004R)* – ('A'-primal remix) / ('A'-Techno slam) / ('A'-Trance mix). | | -

Sep 89. (12") *(KLF 005T)* **3 A.M. ETERNAL. / ('A'-Break for love mix) / ('A'-Pure trance mix)**
(remix.12") *(KLF 005R)* – ('A'original) / ('A'-Blue Danube Orbital mix) / ('A'-Moody Boy mix). | | -

Oct 89. (lp/cd) *(JAMS LP/CD 4)* **THE WHAT TIME IS LOVE STORY**
– What time is love? (original) / Relax your body / What time is love? (Italian) / Heartbeat / No limit (dance mix) / What time is love? (live at the Land of Oz). | |

Dec 89. (12"; not issued) *(KLF 008R)* **LAST TRAIN FROM TRANCENTRAL** | - | -

Mar 90. (cd/lp) *(JAMS CD/LP 5)* **CHILL OUT** | - | -

Jul 90. (7"/ext.12") *(KLF 010 s/PT)* **KYLIE SAID TO JASON. / KYLIE SAID TRANCE**
(cd-s+=) *(KLF 010CD)* – Madrugaral eternal. | | -

—— added **MAXINE HARVEY** – vocals

	KLF	Arista	

Aug 90. (7"/12"/c-s) *(KLF 004/+X/C)* **WHAT TIME IS LOVE (live at Trancentral). / ('A'-Techno gate mix)**
(12") *(KLF 004P)* – ('A'side) / ('A'-Wandafull mix).
(cd-s) *(KLF 004CD)* – ('A'radio) / ('A'side) / ('A'-Trance).
(remix.12") *(KLF 004Y)* – ('A'-Moody Boys vs. the KLF) / ('A'-Echo & The Bunnymen mix) / ('A'-Virtual reality mix). | 5 |

Jan 91. (7"/12"/c-s) *(KLF 005 R/X/C) <2230>* **3 A.M. ETERNAL (live at SSL). / ETERNAL (GUNS OF MU MU)**
(12"+=/cd-s+=) *(KLF 005 Y/CD)* – ('A'-Break for love mix). | 1 | 5 Jun91

Mar 91. (cd/c/lp) *(JAMS CD/MC/LP 6) <8657>* **THE WHITE ROOM**
– What time is love / Make it rain / 3 a.m. eternal (live at the S.S.L.) / Church of the KLF / Last train to Transcentral / Build a fire / The white room / No more tears / Justified and ancient. | 3 | 39 Jun91

Apr 91. (7"/12"/c-s) *(KLF 008/+X/C)* **LAST TRAIN TO TRANSCENTRAL. / THE IRON HORSE**
(12"+=) *(KLF 008T)* – Live from the Lost Continent.
(cd-s++=) *(KLF 008CD)* – ('A'-Pure trance version '89). | 2 |

Oct 91. (c-s,cd-s) *<2365>* **WHAT TIME IS LOVE? / BUILD A FIRE** | - | 57

Nov 91. (7"/12"/c-s; as JUSTIFIED ANCIENTS OF MU MU) *(JAMS 028/+T/C)* **IT'S GRIM UP NORTH. / (part 2)**
(cd-s+=) *(JAMS 028CD)* – Jerusalem on the Moors. | 10 |

Nov 91. (7"/c-s; as The KLF featuring THE FIRST LADY OF COUNTRY: TAMMY WYNETTE) *(KLF 099/+C) <12401>* **JUSTIFIED AND ANCIENT (STAND BY THE JAMS). / ('A'original version)**
(12"+=/cd-s+=) *(KLF 099 T/CD)* – Let them eat ice-cream / Make mine a 99 / All bound for Mu Mu land (with MAXINE). | 2 | 11 Jan92

Jan 92. (7"/c-s) **P.O. 3 A.M. ETERNAL / ('A'-Guns of MuMu mix)**
(12"+=/cd-s+=) – ('A'diff.versions). | |

Feb 92. (7"/c-s) *(KLFUSA 004/+C) <12366>* **AMERICA: WHAT TIME IS LOVE. / AMERICA NO MORE**
(12"+=/cd-s+=) *(KLFUSA 004 T/CD)* – (other 'A'mixes). | 4 |

—— both now used KLF as art movement, causing controversy with their large inner city billboards nearly gaining Turner prize. Late in 1993, they collaborated on EXTREME NOISE TERROR version of '3 A.M. ETERNAL'.

	Blast First	not iss.

Oct 97. (12"/cd-s; as 2K) *(BFFP 146 TK/CDK)* *****K THE MILLENNIUM (mixes)** | 28 | -

---

– compilations, etc. –

Jan 89. (d-lp/cd; as JUSTIFIED ANCIENTS OF MU MU) *KLF; (DLP/DCD 3)* **SHAG TIMES**
– All you need is love / Don't take five (take what you want) / Whitney joins the JAMS / Downtown / Candyman / Burn the bastards / Doctorin' the tardis / 114 BPM / 90 BPM / 118 BPM / 125 BPM / 120 BPM / 118 BPM / 120 BPM (all releases, from all aliases) | | -

Terry KNIGHT & THE PACK (see under ⇒ GRAND FUNK RAILROAD)

Mark KNOPFLER (see under ⇒ DIRE STRAITS)

Al KOOPER

Born: 5 Feb'44, Brooklyn, New York, USA. After leaving school at 15, he formed his first pro-band, The ROYAL TEENS, for whom he played guitar. They scored a minor US novelty hit with 'SHORT SHORTS', before he became a noted session man for first half of the 60's. He also set up a writing partnership with IRWIN LEVINE and BOBBY BRASS, penning hits for GARY LEWIS & THE PLAYBOYS ('This Diamond Ring'), GENE PITNEY ('I Must Be Seeing Things') and ROCKIN' BERRIES ('Water Is Over My Head'). In 1965, he was asked by producer TOM WILSON to sit in on a BOB DYLAN session, which led him to play organ accompaniment to MIKE BLOOMFIELD's guitar. Their electric sound was noteably highlighted on DYLAN's 'Like A Rolling Stone' from the classic 'Highway 61 Revisited' album. The following year, he stayed for 'Blonde On Blonde', while sessioning for other folk stars TOM RUSH plus PETER, PAUL & MARY. That year (1966) saw him join his first rock band, BLUES PROJECT, with whom he recorded three albums, 'LIVE AT THE CAFE AU GO GO', 'PROJECTIONS' and 'LIVE AT THE TOWN HALL'. His departure in 1967, was due to his formation of R&B brass-laden hitmakers, BLOOD, SWEAT & TEARS; however arguments over direction led him to depart after only one 1968 album, 'CHILD IS FATHER TO THE MAN'. His next project was inspired by MOBY GRAPE's 'Grape Jam' and he decided to do the same on a collaboration with MIKE BLOOMFIELD (ex-ELECTRIC FLAG) and STEVE STILLS (ex-BUFFALO SPRINGFIELD). The subsequent album, 'SUPER SESSION', was a massive hit in the States, resulting in label 'Columbia' asking AL and MIKE to do another. Early in 1969, their live in the studio, self-indulgent double-lp, 'THE LIVE ADVENTURES OF MIKE BLOOMFIELD & AL KOOPER' was complete and this also made US Top 20 lists. Later in the year, KOOPER released his solo debut 'I STAND ALONE' but this failed to emulate predecessors. During these releases, KOOPER had kept up his session work for the likes of JIMI HENDRIX EXPERIENCE ('Electric Ladyland' lp) and The ROLLING STONES ('Let It Bleed' lp). For the next decade KOOPER continued as a solo artist, although session and production work for LYNYRD SKYNYRD, NILS LOFGREN and The TUBES took up most of his time. In the early 70's, he re-united for concerts with past group BLUES PROJECT and set up own label 'Sounds Of The South'. The early 80's saw him complete a new album 'CHAMPIONSHIP WRESTLING', superseding his involvement in ad hoc outfit SWEET MAGNOLIA. In 1991, he came out of semi-retirement in Nashville to produce GREEN ON RED's 'Scapegoats'. Over the last three decades or so, KOOPER has become an accomplished blues musician although his singing voice was questioned by critics of the day. • **Songwriters:** Self-penned many with others. He covered some classics including; PARCHMAN FARM (Mose Allison) / 59th STREET BRIDGE SONG (Simon & Garfunkel) / DEAR MR. FANTASY (Traffic) / GREEN ONIONS (Booker T & The MG's) / BLUE MOON OF KENTUCKY (Bill Monroe) / BABY PLEASE DON'T GO (. . .Williams) / CHANGES (Phil Ochs) / PACK UP YOUR SORROWS (Richard Farina) / etc. • **Trivia:** In the 80's, he also produced EDDIE & THE HOT RODS ('Fish & Chips') / LEO SAYER ('Here') / DAVID ESSEX ('Be-Bop The Future') and an album for JOHNNY VAN ZANDT.

Album rating: (see ELECTRIC FLAG n' MIKE BLOOMFIELD for early stuff) / I STAND ALONE (*5) / YOU NEVER KNOW WHO YOUR FRIENDS ARE (*4) / KOOPER SESSION – WITH SHUGGIE OTIS (*4) / EASY DOES IT (*7) / NEW YORK CITY (YOU'RE A WOMAN) (*5) / A POSSIBLE PROJECTION OF THE FUTURE – CHILDHOOD'S END (*3) / NAKED SONGS (*4) / AL'S BIG DEAL (UNCLAIMED FREIGHT) compilation (*7) / ACT LIKE NOTHING'S WRONG (*4) / CHAMPIONSHIP WRESTLING (*3) / REKOOPERATION collection (*5) / SOUL OF A MAN: LIVE (*6) / YOU NEVER KNOW WHO (*4)

AL KOOPER – vocals, keyboards, guitar (with sessioners)

	Mercury	Verve Folkways	

Nov 65. (7"; as ALAN KOOPER) *(MF 885)* **PARCHMAN FARM. / YOU'RE THE LOVING END** | | - |

—— became a session man for BOB DYLAN, etc.

1967. (7") *<5026>* **CHANGES. / PACK UP YOUR SORROWS** | - | |

—— Joined The BLUES PROJECT then BLOOD, SWEAT & TEARS before returning solo. Also see under ELECTRIC FLAG (albums with MIKE BLOOMFIELD)

	C.B.S.	Columbia	

Mar 69. (lp) *(63596) <CS 9718>* **I STAND ALONE**
– Overture / I stand alone / Camille / One / Coloured rain / Soft landing on the Moon / I can love a woman / Blue Moon of Kentucky / Toe hold / Right now for you / Hey, Western Union man / Song and dance for the unborn, frightened child. | | 54 Feb69

Apr 69. (7") *(4011) <44748>* **YOU NEVER KNOW WHO YOUR FRIENDS ARE. / SOFT LANDING ON THE MOON** | | Dec68

Jul 69. (7") *(4160)* <44811> **HEY, WESTERN UNION MAN. / I STAND ALONE**

1969. (lp) *(63651)* <CS 9855> **YOU NEVER KNOW WHO YOUR FRIENDS ARE**　Oct69
– Magic in my socks / Lucille / Too busy thinking about my baby / First time around / Loretta (Union turnpike eulogy) / Blues part IV / You never know who your friends are / The great American marriage – Nothing / I don't know why I love you / Mourning glory story / Anna Lee (what can I do for you) / Never gonna let you down.

—— next with SHUGGIE OTIS – guitar / STU WOODS – bass / WELLS KELLY – drums

1970. (lp) *(63697)* <CS 9951> **KOOPER SESSION – WITH SHUGGIE OTIS**　Jan70
– Bury my body / Double or nothing / One room country shack / Lookin' for a home / The blues:- 12:15 Slow goonbash blues – Shuggie's old time dee-di-lee-di-leet-deet slide boogie – Shuggie's shuffle.

1970. (7") <45093> **BURY MY BODY. / ONE ROOM COUNTRY SHACK**　-

—— Reverted to numerous session people

1970. (d-lp) *(66252)* <G 30031> **EASY DOES IT**　Sep70
– Brand new day (main theme from 'The Landlord') / I got a woman / Country road / I bought you the shoes (you're walking away with it) / Easy does it / Buckskin boy / Love theme from 'The Landlord' / Sad, sad sunshine / Let the Duchess know / She gets me where I live / A rose and a baby Ruth / Baby please don't go / God sheds his grace on thee.

1970. (7") *(45148)* **GOD SHEDS HIS GRACE ON THEE. / SHE GETS ME WHERE I LIVE**　-

Mar 71. (7") *(5146)* <45179> **BRAND NEW DAY. / LOVE THEME FROM THE LANDLORD**

1971. (7") <45243> **I GOT A WOMAN. / EASY DOES IT**　-

—— a few of above tracks appeared on 1971 'United Artists' UK film soundtrack of 'THE LANDLORD' (UAS 29120), which also featured The STAPLE SINGERS and LORRAINE ELLISON.

Jul 71. (lp) *(64340)* <C 30506> **NEW YORK CITY (YOU'RE A WOMAN)**　Jun71
– New York City (you're a woman) / John The Baptist (Holy John) / Can you hear it now (500 miles) / The ballad of the hard rock kid / Going quietly mad / Medley: Oo wee baby, I love you- Love is a man's friend / Back on my feet / Come down in time / Dearest darling / Nightmare No.5 / The warning (someone's on the cross again).

Jul 71. (7") *(7376)* <45412> **JOHN THE BAPTIST. / BACK ON MY FEET**

1972. (7") <45566> **THE MONKEY TIME. / BENDED KNEES (PLEASE DON'T LEAVE ME NOW)**　-

Jul 72. (lp) *(64208)* <KC 31159> **A POSSIBLE PROJECTION OF THE FUTURE / CHILDHOOD'S END**　Apr72
– Bended knees (please don't leave me now) / Possible projection of the future / Childhood's end / The man in me / Please tell me why / Love trap / The monkey time / Let your love shine / Swept for you baby.

1972. (7") <45691> **SAM STONE. / BE REAL**　-

1973. (lp) *(65193)* <KC 31793> **NAKED SONGS**
– Be real / As the tears go passing by / Jolie / Blend baby / Been and gone / Sam Stone / Peacock lady / Touch the hem of his garment / Where were you when I needed you / Unrequited.

1973. (7") <45735> **JOLIE. / BE REAL**　-

1975. (d-lp) *(88093)* <KG 33169> **AL'S BIG DEAL (UNCLAIMED FREIGHT)** (compilation)
– I can't quit her / I love you more than you'll ever know / My days are numbered / Without her / So much love – Underture / Albert's shuffle / Season of the witch / If dogs run free / The 59th Street Bridge song (feelin' groovy) / The weight / Bury my body / Jolie / I stand alone / Brand new day / Sam Stone / New York City (you're a woman) / I got a woman.

	U.A.	U.A.

Dec 76. (7") <879> **HOLLYWOOD VAMPIRE. / THIS DIAMOND RING**　-

Jan 77. (lp) *(UAG 30020)* <LA 702-G> **ACT LIKE NOTHING'S WRONG**　Dec76
– Is we on the downbeat? / This diamond ring / She don't ever lose her groove / I forgot to be your lover / Missing you / Out of left field / (Please not) One more time / In my own sweet way / Turn my head towards home / A visit to the Rainbow bar & grill / Hollywood vampire.

	C.B.S.	Columbia

1982. (7"; with VALERIE CARTER) <38-03312> **TWO SIDES (TO EVERY SITUATION). / SNOWBLIND**　-

1982. (lp) <KC 38137> **CHAMPIONSHIP WRESTLING**　-
– I wish you would / Two sides / Wrestless with this / Lost control / I'd rather be an old man's sweetheart / The heart is a lonely hunter / Bandstand / Finders keepers / Snowblind.

—— returned to production work before . . .

	Limelight	Limelight

Jun 94. (cd) *(844 400-2)* **REKOOPERATION**
– Downtime / After the lights go down low / When the spell is broken / How am I ever gonna get over you / Sneakin' round the barnyard / Soul twist-ed / Looking for clues / Honky tonk / Clean up woman / Don't be cruel / Alvino Johnson's shuffle / Johnny B Goode / I wanna little girl.

—— next featured backing by The BLUES PROJECT, The REKOOPERATORS + BLOOD, SWEAT & TEARS

	Music Masters	Music Masters

Jan 97. (d-cd) <(MM 65113)> **SOUL OF A MAN: LIVE (live February 1994)**　1995
– Somethin' goin' on / Can't keep from cryin' sometimes / I stand alone medley: I stand alone – I can . . . . / Flute thing / Don't tell (repo man) / Two trains running / Heartbeat / Sleepwalk / Just one smile / I can't quit her / I wanna little girl / My days are numbered / I love you more than you'll ever know / Vocal into / / Downtime / Violets of dawn / Albert's shuffle / Closing medley: You can't always get what you want – Seasons of the witch.

George KOOYMANS (see under ⇒ GOLDEN EARRING)

KORN

Formed: Bakersfield / Huntington Beach, California, USA . . . 1993 out of CREEP, by JONATHAN DAVIS, J MUNKY SHAFFER, BRIAN 'HEAD' WELCH, FIELDY and DAVID. Signed to 'Epic' the following year, they unleashed to the public their eponymous US Top 75 debut. A barrage of aural psychosis, DAVIS' tortured performance more than lived up to the hype surrounding the record's release. Among its schizophrenic highs and lows were the disturbing but cathartic ten minute (+) emotional minefield, 'DADDY', which cried out from the core of DAVIS' very soul. Bizarrely, DAVIS turned his hand (and elbow) to the bagpipes on the nursery rhyme parody, 'SHOOTS AND LADDERS', a track that even GAVIN FRIDAY might have disowned in his VIRGIN PRUNES heyday! Consolidating this seminal meisterwork, KORN toured the world, resurfacing in 1996 with another primal scream of sinuous, bass-heavy angst-metal in the shape of 'LIFE IS PEACHY'. The album contained no less than three UK Top 30 hits, 'NO PLACE TO HIDE', 'A.D.I.D.A.S.' (which stands for "All Day I Dream About Sex"; nothing to do with the sports company) and 'GOOD GOD', the set also featuring covers of Oshea Jackson's 'WICKED' and War's 'LOWRIDER'. A US Top 3, the record also cracked the UK Top 40, due largely to the strong Kerrang! support only rivalled in 1997 by DAVIS's more attention-seeking contemporary, MARILYN MANSON. Two further chart-topping albums, 'FOLLOW THE LEADER' (1998) and the concept 'ISSUES' (1999), didn't sell quite so well in Britain, the grim storytelling of KORN's leader beginning to get short thrift from some of his gloomy disciples.

Album rating: KORN (*9) / LIFE IS PEACHY (*8) / FOLLOW THE LEADER (*5) / ISSUES (*6)

JONATHAN DAVIS – vocals, bagpipes / **J MUNKY SHAFFER** (b. JAMES) – guitar, vocals / **BRIAN 'HEAD' WELCH** – guitar, vocals / **FIELDY** – bass, vocals / **DAVID** – drums, vocals

		Epic	Immortal
Jul 95.	(cd/c) *(478080-2/-4)* <66633> **KORN**　– Blind / Ball tongue / Need to / Clown / Divine / Faget / Shoots and ladders / Predictable / Fake / Lies / Helmet in the bush / Daddy.		72 Nov94
Oct 95.	(10"ep) *(KORN 1)* **BLIND**		
Oct 96.	(7"white) *(663845-0)* **NO PLACE TO HIDE. / PROUD**　(cd-s+=) *(663845-2)* – Sean Olsen.　(cd-s) *(663845-5)* – ('A'side) / Shoots and ladders (Dust Brothers industrial mix) / Shoots and ladders (Dust Brothers hip-hop mix).	26	
Oct 96.	(cd/c/lp/cd-rom) *(485369-2/-4/-1/-6)* <67554> **LIFE IS PEACHY**　– Twist / Chi / Lost / Swallow / Porno creep / Good God / Mr. Rogers / K"£o%! / No place to hide / Wicked / A.D.I.D.A.S. / Lowrider / Ass itch / Kill you.	32	3
Feb 97.	(10"white-ep) *(664204-0)* **A.D.I.D.A.S. / CHI (live). / LOWRIDER – SHOOTS AND LADDERS (live)**　(cd-ep+=) *(664204-2)* – Ball tongue (live).　(cd-ep) *(664204-5)* – ('A'side) / Faget / Porno creep / Blind.	22	
Jun 97.	(cd-ep) *(664658-2)* **GOOD GOD / GOOD GOD (Mekon mix) / GOOD GOD (Dub Pistols mix) / WICKED (Tear The Roof Off mix)**　(cd-ep) *(664658-5)* – ('A'side) / A.D.I.D.A.S. (Synchro dub) / A.D.I.D.A.S. (Under Pressure mix) / A.D.I.D.A.S. (The Wet Dream mix).　(12"ep) *(664658-6)* – ('A'-Mekon mix) / ('A'-Dub Pistols mix) / A.D.I.D.A.S. (Synchro dub) / A.D.I.D.A.S. (Under Pressure mix).	25	
Aug 98.	(ltd-cd-s) *(666391-2)* **GOT THE LIFE / (12"mixes by DeeJay Punk-Roc and D.O.S.E.)**　(cd-s) *(666391-5)* – ('A'side) / I can remember / Good god (oomph! vs such a surge mix).	23	
Aug 98.	(cd/c/lp) *(491221-2/-4/-1)* <69001> **FOLLOW THE LEADER**　– It's on / Freak on a leash / Got the life / Dead bodies eveywhere / Children of the korn / B.B.K. / Pretty / All in the family / Reclaim my place / Justin / Seed / Cameltosis / My gift to you.	5	1
Apr 99.	(cd-s) *(667252-2)* **FREAK ON A LEASH / FREAK ON A LEASH (Dante Ross mix) / FREAK ON A LEASH (Josh A's beast on a leash mix)**　(cd-s) *(667252-5)* – ('A'-Freakin' bitch mix) / ('A'-Josh A's beast on a leash mix) / ('A'-Dante Ross mix).　(12") *(667252-6)* – ('A'mixes; above).	24	
Nov 99.	(cd/c/lp) *(496359-2/-4/-1)* <63710> **ISSUES**　– Dead / Falling away from me / Trash / 4U / Beg for me / Make me bad / It's gonna go away / Wake up / Am I going crazy / Hey daddy / Somebody someone / No way / Let's get the party started / I wish you could be me / Counting / Dirty.	37	1

Paul KOSSOFF (see under ⇒ FREE)

Leo KOTTKE

Born: 11 Sep'45, Athens, Georgia, USA. Subsequently raised in various locations around the States including Muskogee, Oklahoma, the young KOTTKE mastered the guitar at an early age despite a hearing impediment in one ear. Having dropped out of first the Navy (where he suffered further ear damage), then college, he developed his heavily folk/blues influenced style while hitch-hiking around the country. Eventually securing a residency at the Scholar coffee house in Minneapolis, KOTTKE cut his first album (the live set, 'TWELVE STRING BLUES') in 1968 under the auspices of the bar's owner. Following a one-off long player ('SIX AND TWELVE-STRING GUITAR') for JOHN FAHEY's 'Takoma' label, the acoustic maestro secured a deal with 'Capitol', via manager DENNY BRUCE (a former ZAPPA cohort). KOTTKE's major label debut, 'MUDLARK' (1971) was pored over by guitar enthusiasts and more discerning critics who excused his limited vocal ability, the beginnings of a cult following firmly in place. From 1972 to 1976, his label issued a series of albums which saw KOTTKE's unique style become increasingly popular, two 1974 sets, 'ICE WATER' and the instrumental 'DREAMS AND ALL THAT STUFF' making the US Top 75. This was achieved without any loss of artistic integrity, the guitarist headlining the Cambridge Folk Festival at the peak of his appeal in the mid 70's. After a final album for 'Capitol', 'CHEWING PINE' (which bubbled under the US Top 100), he signed to 'Chrysalis' where his sales took a bit of a dip. This was no reflection on the quality of his output however, KOTTKE's relatively prolific recording schedule continuing apace into the 80's and 90's. Amongst his best work was 1989's 'A SHOUT TOWARDS NOON' and 1994's 'PECULIAROSO', the latter featuring production by RICKIE LEE JONES and the session talents of VAN DYKE PARKS, LYLE LOVETT and MARGO TIMMINS. • Covered: JESUS MARIA (Carla Bley) / MID-AIR (Willard O. Peterson) / POOR BOY (Bukka White) / LITTLE MARTHA (Allman Brothers Band) / ARMS OF MARY (Sutherland Brothers) / etc.

Album rating: 12-STRING BLUES: LIVE AT THE SCHOLAR COFFEE HOUSE (*5) / LEO KOTTKE & HIS 6 & 12 STRING GUITAR (*5) / CIRCLE ROUND THE SUN (*5) / MUDLARK (*6) / GREENHOUSE (*7) / MY FEET ARE SMILING (*7) / ICE WATER (*7) / DREAMS AND ALL THAT STUFF (*5) / CHEWING PINE (*5) / LEO KOTTKE 1971-1976 – DID YOU HEAR ME? compilation (*6) / LEO KOTTKE (*7) / BURNT LIPS (*5) / GUITAR MUSIC (*7) / TIME STEP (*7) / A SHOUT TOWARD NOON (*7) / REGARDS FROM CHUCK PINK (*7) / MY FATHER'S FACE (*5) / THAT'S WHAT (*5) / GREAT BIG BOY: ESSENTIAL LEO KOTTKE compilation (*7) / PECULIAROSO (*7) / LIVE (*5) / STANDING IN MY SHOES (*6)

LEO KOTTKE – vocals, guitar

		not iss.	Oblivion
1969.	(lp) <S-1A> **12-STRING BLUES: LIVE AT THE SCHOLAR COFFEE HOUSE** (live) <re-iss. 1970 as 'CIRCLE ROUND THE SUN' on 'Symposium'; 2001>	-	

		not iss.	Takoma
1971.	(lp) <1024> **LEO KOTTKE & HIS 6 & 12 STRING GUITAR** – The driving of the year / Nail / The last of the Arkansas greyhounds / Ojo / Crow river waltz / The sailor's grave on the prairie / Vaseline machine gun / Jack Fig / Watermelon / Jesu, joy of a man's desiring / The fisherman / The Tennessee toad / Busted bicycle / The brain of the purple mountain / Coolidge rising. *(UK-iss.1979 on 'Sonet'; SNTF 629) <US re-iss. Apr84 lp/c; TKMLP/ZCTKM 6002> (cd-iss. May96 on 'Ace-Takoma'; CDTAK 1024)*		

—— added guests **LARRY TAYLOR + ROY ESTRADA + WAYNE MOSS** – bass / **JOHN HARRIS** – piano / **PAUL LAGOS + KEN BUTTREY** – drums / **KIM FOWLEY** – vocals

		Capitol	Capitol
Sep 71.	(lp) <E-ST 682> **MUDLARK** – Cripple Creek / Eight miles high / June bug / The ice miner / Bumblebee / Stealing / Monkey lust / Poor boy / Lullaby / Machine #2 / Hear the wind howl / Bach: Bourree / Room 8 / Standing in my shoes. *(re-iss. May91 on 'Beat Goes On' lp/cd; BGO LP/CD 101)*		Jun71

—— now with **STEVE GAMMELL + JOHN FAHEY** – guitar (next solo)

Mar 72.	(lp) <E-ST 11000> **GREENHOUSE** – Bean time / Tiny island / The song of the swamp / In Christ there is no east or west / Last steam engine train / From the cradle to the grave / Louise / The Spanish entomologist / Owls / You don't have to need me / Lost John. *(re-iss. Jun89 on 'Beat Goes On'; BGOLP 50) (cd-iss. Oct90; BGOCD 50)*		Feb72
Apr 73.	(lp) <E-ST 11164> **MY FEET ARE SMILING** (live) – Hear the wind howl / Busted bicycle / Easter / Louise / Blue dot / Stealing / Living in my country / June bug / Standing in my shoes / The fisherman / Bean time / Eggtooth / Medley:- Crow river waltz – Jesu, joy of man's desiring – Jack Fig. *(cd-iss. Mar92 on 'Beat Goes On'; BGOCD 134)*		Mar73

—— now with **BILL PETERSON** – bass / **BILL BARBER** – synthesizers / **BILL BERG** – percussion / **CAL HAND** – steel guitar

Feb 74.	(lp) <E-ST 11262> **ICE WATER** – Morning is the long way home / Pamela Brown / A good egg / Tilt billings and the student prince / All through the night / Short stories / You tell me why / You know I know you know / Born to be with you / A child should be a fish. *(cd-iss. Sep92 on 'Beat Goes On'; BGOCD 146)*		69 Jan74

—— added **JACK SMITH + HERB PILHOFER** – piano / **MIKE JOHNSON** – guitar

Jan 75.	(lp) <E-ST 11335> **DREAMS AND ALL THAT STUFF** – Mona Ray / When shrimps learn to whistle / Twilight property / Bill Cheatham / Vertical trees / Constant traveler / Why ask why? / Taking a sandwich to a feast / Hole in the day / Mona Roy. *(cd-iss. ec92 on 'Beat Goes On'; BGOCD 132)*		45 Nov74

—— now with **JOHNSON, CAL + HERB**

Dec 75.	(lp) <E-ST 11446> **CHEWING PINE** – Standing on the outside / Power failure / Venezuela, there you go / Don't you think / Regards from Chuck Pink / Monkey money / The Scarlatti rip-off / Wheels / Grim to the brim / Rebecca / Trombone / Can't quite put it into words. *(cd-iss. Mar93 on 'Beat Goes On'; BGOCD 148)*		Oct75

—— now retaining only the two BILL's

		Chrysalis	Chrysalis
Jan 77.	(lp/c) <(CHR/ZCHR 1106)> **LEO KOTTKE** – Buckaroo / The white ape / Hayseed suede / Rio Leo / The range / Airproofing / Maroon / Waltz / Death by reputation / Up tempo / Shadowland. *(cd-iss. Jan95 on 'Beat Goes On'; BGOCD 257)*		
Apr 77.	(7") (CHS 2123) **BUCKAROO. / THE RANGE**		
Jan 79.	(lp/c) <(CHR/ZCHR 1191)> **BURNT LIPS** – Endless sleep / Cool water / Frank forgets / Sonora's death row / The quiet man / Everybody lies / I called back / A low thud / Orange room / The credits: Out-takes from Terry's movie / Voluntary target / Burnt lips / Sand Street / The train and the gate: from Terry's movie. *(cd-iss. Jan95 on 'Beat Goes On'; BGOCD 259)*		Aug78

above solo but below with **JOHN HARRIS + BOBBY OGDIN** – piano / **MIKE LEECH** – bass / **KEN BUTTREY** – drums

Aug 79.	(lp/c) <(CHR/ZCHR 1234)> **BALANCE** – Tell Mary / I don't know why / Embryonic journey / Disguise / Whine / Losin'		

everything / Drowning Dolores / 1/2 acre of garlic / Learning the game. *(cd-iss. Aug95 on 'Beat Goes On'; BGOCD 263)*

Jul 80.	(lp/c) <(CHR/ZCHR 1284)> **LIVE IN EUROPE** (live) – The train and the gate / Open country joy (constant traveler): theme and adnesions / Airproofing / Tell Mary / Wheels / Up tempo / Palm Blvd. / Shadowland / Eggtooth. *(cd-iss. Aug95 on 'Beat Goes On'; BGOCD 265)*		
Apr 81.	(lp/c) <(CHR/ZCHR 1328)> **GUITAR MUSIC** – Part two / Available space / Side two suite: Some birds – Sounds like – Slang – My double – Three walls and bars – Some birds (reprise) / Perforated sleep / Strange / Little shoes / Jib's hat / Tumbling tumbleweeds / Agile N. / A song for the night of the hunter / All I have to do is dream / Sleepwalk. *(cd-iss. Jun95 on 'Beat Goes On'; BGOCD 261)*		

—— now with **ALBERT LEE** – guitar / **DAVID MINER** – bass / **DAVID KEMPER** – drums / **DENNIS KEELEY** – percussion / **EMMYLOU HARRIS + DON HEFFINGTON** – vocals

May 83.	(lp/c) <(CHR/ZCHR 1411)> **TIME STEP** – Running all night long / The bungle party / Rings / Mr.Fonebone / Julie's house / Memories are made of this / Saginaw, Michigan / I'll break out again tonight / Starving / Here comes that rainbow again. *(cd-iss. May95 on 'Beat Goes On'; BGOCD 255)*		

		Private Music	Private Music
May 88.	(lp/c/cd) (209/409/259. 641) <20252> **REGARDS FROM CHUCK PINK** – I yell at traffic / Foster's feet / Dan's tune / Skinflint / Pink Christmas / Short wave / Dog quiver / Busy signal / Theme from 'Doodles' / The late zone / Taxco steps / Ojo / Mary.		

—— now with guests **DAVID HIDALGO / JIM KELTNER / T-BONE BURNETT / MICHAEL BLAIR**

Jun 89.	(lp/c/cd) (209/409/259. 910) **MY FATHER'S FACE** – Times twelve / Everybody lies / B.J. / Why can't you fix my car / Theme from 'Rick And Bob Report' / My Aunt Francis / William Powell / Back in Buffalo / Mona Ray / Jack gets up / Doorbell.		
Nov 89.	(lp/c/cd) (209/409/259. 959) <20272> **A SHOUT TOWARDS NOON** – Little beaver / A shout toward noon / Little Martha / Easter again / Piece 17 / Three quarter north / Air proofing two / Echoing Gilewitz / A virtuoso is his own reward / Four four north / The ice field / First to go.		

—— now with **BILLY PETERSON** – bass, drums, piano, synthesizers / **BRUCE PAULSON** – trombones / **GORDY KNUDTSON** – percussion

1990.	(cd/c) (260/410 883) **THAT'S WHAT** – Little snoozer / Buzzby / What the arm said / Creature feature / Oddball / Czech bounce / Mid-air / The great one / "Husbandry" / Jesus Maria.		
Nov 91.	(cd/c) (261/411 820) **GREAT BIG BOY** – Running up the stairs / The other day (near Santa Cruz) / Great big boy / Driver / Pepe hush / Big mob on the hill / Ice cream / Nothin' works / Summer's growing old / I still miss someone.		
Apr 94.	(cd) (01005 82111-2) **PECULIAROSO** – Peg leg / Poor boy / Parade / Wonderland by night / World made to order / Room service (at the Tahiti motel) / Turning into Randolph Scott (humid child) / Porky and Pale / Arms of Mary / The room at the top of the stairs / Big situation / Twilight time.		
Mar 96.	(cd) <(01005 82132-2)> **LIVE** (live) – William Powell / Room at the top of the stairs / Airproofing / Jack gets up / Combat / Peg leg / Twilight time / Bean time / Roy Autry / Parade / I yell at traffic / Flattened brain / Little Martha / Oddball / Arms of Mary.		Oct95

– compilations, etc. –

1975.	(lp) Sonet; (SNTF 675) **LEO KOTTKE, PETER LANG & JOHN FAHEY** *(cd-iss. Jun96 on 'Ace-Takoma'; CDTAK 1040)*		-
Feb 77.	(lp) Capitol; <(E-ST 11576)> **LEO KOTTKE 1971-1976 – DID YOU HEAR ME?**		Nov75
Feb 79.	(d-lp/d-c) Capitol; (ESTSP/TCESTSP 21) **THE BEST OF LEO KOTTKE**		
Apr 87.	(cd) E.M.I.; (CDP 746 486-2) **THE BEST OF LEO KOTTKE** – Stealing / Last steam engine train / Cripple creek / Grim to the brim / Louise / Wheels / Poor boy / Morning is the long way home / The Spanish entemologist / Pamela Brown / Bean time / Busted bicycle / Lost John / Living in the country / Machine No.2. *(cd-iss. Jul95 on 'Beat Goes On'; BGOCD 277)*		

KRAFTWERK

Formed: Dusseldorf, Germany . . . 1969 as ORGANISATION by RALF HUTTER, FLORIAN SCHNEIDER-ESLEBEN and three others, namely BUTCH HAUF, FRED MONICKS and BASIL HAMMOND. After one CONRAD PLANK-produced album, 'TONE FLOAT', for 'R.C.A.' in 1970, the pair broke away to form KRAFTWERK (German for POWERPLANT), with KLAUS DINGER and THOMAS HOMANN. After one album for 'Philips', RALF & FLORIAN became KRAFTWERK, releasing the 1973 album (titled after their Christian names) for 'Vertigo' in the process. In 1974, they added KLAUS ROEDER & WOLFGANG FLUR, issuing their magnus-opus 'AUTOBAHN'. This UK & US Top 5 album contained a 22-minute title track, which, edited into 3 minutes, also became a hit. The next album, 'RADIO ACTIVITY' (which was also issued on their own 'Kling Klang' label in Germany), disappointed most and failed to secure a Top 50 placing. In 1978, they were back in the UK Top 10 at least, with an excellent return to form, 'THE MAN MACHINE'. In the early 80's, they enjoyed another hit album, 'COMPUTER WORLD', and a run of UK hit singles, one of which, 'THE MODEL' (from 1978 lp) made the top spot. A projected album by the name of 'TECHNOPOP', was pencilled in for release in 1983 and allegedly 'E.M.I.' were even supplied with artwork. The record never appeared, and of course, given KRAFTWERK's reclusive reticence, no explanation was offered. The same year, however, the band did release a one-off 12" single, 'TOUR DE FRANCE', no doubt inspired by HUTTER's preoccupation with cycling. It was to be another three years before the band released a full album, the disappointing 'ELECTRIC CAFE'. By this point the band were starting to tread water, an assumption that seemed to be confirmed when fans had to wait another five years for 'new' material. 'THE MIX', released in 1991, was actually an album of reworkings of old tracks, a bit of a hit and miss affair which failed to deliver any original pieces per se. Both BARTOS and FLUR had left the band before the album's release, allegedly sick of the laboriously slow and detailed recording process and the band's reclusive inertia. Despite a reputation for a disciplined working ethos, the band remain defiantly distant from the music industry. Their studio apparently possesses neither fax nor phone, they've no management and they've turned down all offers of remix work and collaborations. Whether they can remain on the cutting edge in such a vacuum remains to be seen and for the moment, their Guru-like status is based on past glories, sounds that continue to permeate almost all strands of pop culture, now more than ever. It's testament to their towering influence that despite releasing no new material for more than a decade, they recently headlined the Tribal Gathering dance festival. This robotic electronic rock act with minimalist synth-tunes, being at times (on stage!) twiddled by dummies, were more inspirational than their contemporaries TANGERINE DREAM. KRAFTWERK became a major influence for ULTRAVOX!, GARY NUMAN, DAVID BOWIE, 77, JEAN-MICHEL JARRE, SIMPLE MINDS, OMD, etc. Stop press: KRAFTWERK have just released a German-only (for now?) single, 'EXPO 2000' – the showroom dummies are back! • **Songwriters:** RALF & FLORIAN. • **Trivia:** They have been sampled by many, including AFRIKA BAMBAATAA on his single, 'Planet Rock'.

Album rating: Organisation: TONE FLOAT (*4) / Kraftwerk: KRAFTWERK (HIGHRAIL) (*4) / KRAFTWERK 2 (VAR) (*4) / RALF AND FLORIAN (*5) / AUTOBAHN (*8) / RADIOACTIVITY (*4) / TRANS-EUROPE EXPRESS (*8) / THE MAN MACHINE (*8) / COMPUTER WORLD (*7) / ELECTRIC CAFE (*4) / THE MIX remixes (*5)

ORGANISATION

RALF HUTTER (b.1946, Krefeld, Germany) – electric organ, strings / **FLORIAN SCHNEIDER-ESLEBEN** (b.1947, Dusseldorf)– flute, echo unit, strings / **BUTCH HAUF** – bass, percussion / **FRED MONICKS** – drums / **BASIL HAMMOND** – percussion, vocals

	R.C.A.	not iss.
Aug 70. (lp) (SF 8111) **TONE FLOAT** – Tone float / Milk float / Silver forest / Rhythm salad / Noitasinagro.		-

KRAFTWERK

HUTTER + SCHNEIDER with **KLAUS DINGER** – guitar, keyboards / **THOMAS HOMANN** – percussion

	Philips	not iss.
1971. (lp) (6305 058) **KRAFTWERK** – Ruckzuck / Stratowargius / Megaherz / Vom Himmel hoch.	-	- German

—— **HUTTER + SCHNEIDER** trimmed to a duo. (DINGER and HOMANN formed NEU!)

1972. (lp) (6305 117) **KRAFTWERK 2** – Klingklang / Atem / Strom / Spule 4 / Wellenlange / Harmonika.	-	- German

	Vertigo	Vertigo
Nov 72. (d-lp) (6641 077) **KRAFTWERK** (2 German lp's combined)		
Nov 73. (lp) (6360 616) **RALF & FLORIAN** – Elektrisches roulette (Electric roulette) / Tongebirge (Mountain of sound) / Kristallo (Crystals) / Heimatklange (The bells of home) / Tanzmusik (Dance music) / Ananas symphonie (Pineapple symphony). <US-iss.Sep75; 2006>		

—— added **KLAUS ROEDER** – violin, guitar / **WOLFGANG FLUR** – percussion

Nov 74. (lp/c) (6360/ 620) <2003> **AUTOBAHN** – Autobahn / Kometenmelodie 1 & 2 (Comet melody) / Mitternacht (Midnight) / Morgenspaziergang (Morning walk). (re-iss.Mar82 on 'E.M.I.' lp/c; EMC/TC-EMC 3405); hit 61 UK) (re-iss. Jun85 on 'Parlophone' lp/c; AUTO/TCAUTO 1) (cd-iss. Jun87 & Aug95 on 'E.M.I.'; CDP 746153-2)	4	5
Feb 75. (7") (6147 012) **AUTOBAHN. / KOMETENMELODIE**	11	-
Feb 75. (7") <203> **AUTOBAHN. / MORGENSPAZIERGANG**	-	25
Jul 75. (7") (6147 015) **KOMETENMELODIE 2. / KRISTALLO**		-
Jul 75. (7") <204> **KOMETENMELODIE 2. / MITTERNACHT**	-	

—— In Oct'75, **KARL BARTOS** – percussion repl. ROEDER

	Capitol	Capitol
Nov 75. (lp/c) (<EST/TC-EST 11457>) **RADIO-ACTIVITY** – Geiger counter / Radio-activity / Radioland / Airwaves / (intermission) / News / The voice of energy / Antenna / Radio stars / Uran / Transistor / Ohm sweet ohm. (re-iss.Jun84 on 'Fame' lp/c; FA 413103-1/-4) (re-iss. 1985 on 'E.M.I.' lp/c; EMS/TC-EMS 1256) (cd-iss. May87 on 'E.M.I.'; CDP 746474-2) (re-iss. Aug87 on 'E.M.I.' lp/c; ATAK/TCATAK 104) (re-iss. cd Apr95 on 'Cleopatra';) (re-iss. cd Apr95 on 'E.M.I.';)		
Feb 76. (7") (CL 15853) <4211> **RADIO-ACTIVITY. / ANTENNA**		
Apr 77. (lp/c) (<EST/TC-EST 11603>) **TRANS-EUROPE EXPRESS** – Europe endless / The hall of mirrors / Showroom dummies / Trans-Europe express / Metal on metal / Franz Schubert / Endless endless. (in Feb82, they hit UK No.49 Feb82) (re-iss. 1985 on 'E.M.I.' lp/c; FA 413151-1/-4) (cd-iss. May87 on 'E.M.I.'; CDP 746473-2) (re-iss. cd Apr94 on 'Cleopatra';)		
Apr 77. (7") (CL 15917) **TRANS-EUROPE EXPRESS. / EUROPE ENDLESS**		-
Aug 77. (7") (CLX 104) **SHOWROOM DUMMIES / EUROPE EXPRESS**		
May 78. (7") <4460> **TRANS-EUROPE EXPRESS. / FRANZ SCHUBERT**	-	67
May 78. (lp/c) (<EST/TC-EST 11728>) **THE MAN MACHINE** – The robots / Spacelab / Metropolis / The model / Neon lights / The man machine. (re-iss. Mar85 on 'Fame' lp/c; 413118-1/-4) (re-iss. Jul88 on 'Fame' cd/c/lp; CD/TC+/FA 3118) (re-iss. cd Apr94 on 'Cleopatra'; CLEO 5877CD) (re-iss. cd/c Apr95 on 'E.M.I.'; CD/TC EMS 1520) (cd re-iss. Jun97 on 'E.M.I.'; CDCNTAV 4)	9	
May 78. (7") (CL 15981) **THE ROBOTS (edit). / SPACELAB**		
Jun 78. (7") <4620> **NEON LIGHTS. / THE ROBOTS**	-	

Sep 78. (7"/12"luminous) (CL/12CL 15998) **NEON LIGHTS. / TRANS-EUROPE EXPRESS / THE MODEL**	53	
Nov 78. (12"m) (CL 16098) **SHOWROOM DUMMIES. / EUROPE ENDLESS / SPACELAB**		-

	E.M.I.	Warners
Apr 81. (7") (EMI 5175) <49723> **POCKET CALCULATOR. / DENTAKU** (12"+=) (12EMI 5175) – Numbers. (c-s) (TCEMI 5175) – ('A'extended) / ('A'side) / Numbers.	39	
May 81. (lp/c) (EMC/TC-EMC 3370) <3549> **COMPUTER WORLD** – Pocket calculator / Numbers / Computer-world / Computer love / Home computer / It's more fun to compute. (re-iss. Apr95 cd/c; CD/TC EMS 1547)	15	72
Jun 81. (7"/12") (EMI/12EMI 5207) **COMPUTER LOVE. / THE MODEL** (Dec81; flipped over, hit UK No.1) (re-iss. May84; G45 16)	36	-
Jun 81. (7") <49795> **COMPUTER LOVE. / NUMBERS**	-	-
Feb 82. (7") (EMI 5272) **SHOWROOM DUMMIES. / NUMBERS** (12"+=) (12EMI 5272) – Pocket calculator.	25	-

—— (In May'83, they had album 'TECHNO POP' cancelled)

Jul 83. (7") (EMI 5413) <29342> **TOUR DE FRANCE. / TOUR DE FRANCE (instrumental** (c-s+=/12"+=) (TC/12 EMI 5413) – ('A'version).	22	-
Aug 84. (7") (EMI 5413) **TOUR DE FRANCE (remix). / TOUR DE FRANCE** (12"+=) (12EMI 5413) – ('A'instrumental).	24	-
Oct 86. (7"/ext.12") (EMI/12EMI 5588) **MUSIQUE NON-STOP. / MUSIQUE NON STOP (version)**		
Nov 86. (lp/c)(cd) (EMD/TC-EMD 3370)(CDP 746416-2) <25525> **ELECTRIC CAFE** – Boom boom tschak / Techno pop / Musique non stop / The telephone call / Sex object / Techno pop / Electric cafe. (cd re-iss. Aug95; CDEMS 1546)	58	-
Feb 87. (7") (EMI 5602) <28441> **THE TELEPHONE CALL. / DER TELEFON ANRUF** (12"+=) (12EMI 5602) – House phone.		

—— **FRITZ HIJBERT** repl. WOLFGANG FLUR

May 91. (c-s/7") (TC+/EM 192) **THE ROBOTS (re-recorded). / ROBOTRONIK** (12"+=) (12EM 192) – ('A'album version). (cd-s+=) (CDEM 192) – Robotnik.	20	
Jun 91. (cd/c/d-lp) (CD/TC+/EM 1408) **THE MIX** ('91 remixes) – The robots / Computer love / Pocket calculator / Dentaku / Autobahn / Radioactivity / Trans-Europe express / Abzug / Metal on metal / Homecomputer / Musique non-stop. (cd re-iss. Aug95; CDEM 1408)	15	
Oct 91. (c-s/7") (TC+/EM 201) **RADIOACTIVITY (Francois Kevorkian remix). / ('A'-William Orbit mix)** (12"+=/cd-s+=) (12/CD EM 201) – ('A'extended).	43	

—— In Jul'91, BARTOS and FLUR formed their own project, ELEKTRIC

	Kling Klang	not iss.
Dec 99. (12"/cd-s) (EXPO 1/+CD) **EXPO 2000** (mixes)		-

– compilations, others, etc.

on 'Vertigo' unless mentioned otherwise

Oct 75. (lp) (6360 629) **EXCELLER 8**		-
Oct 80. (7") (CUT 108) **AUTOBAHN. / (b-side by BEGGAR'S OPERA)**		-
Apr 81. (lp) (6449 066) **ELEKTRO KINETIC**		-
May 81. (7") (VER 3) **KOMETENMELODIE 2. / VON HIMMEL HOCH**		-

—— <In the US compilation lp 'THE ROBOTS' on 'Capitol'; 9445>

Apr 94. (cd) Cleopatra; (CLEO 6843CD) **SHOWROOM DUMMIES** (re-iss. May97; same)		-
Apr 94. (cd) Cleopatra; (CLEO 5761-2) **THE MODEL (The Best Of Kraftwerk 1975-1978)**		-
Mar 97. (12") Discopromo; (D 762) **NUMBERS**		-
Mar 97. (12") Discopromo; (D 801) **TOUR DE FRANCE**		-
May 97. (d-cd) Cleopatra; (CLEO 9416-2) **THE CAPITOL YEARS**		-
Oct 99. (12"/cd-s) E.M.I.; (887421-0/-6) **TOUR DE FRANCE** (mixes)	61	-

Wayne KRAMER (see under ⇒ MC5)

Lenny KRAVITZ

Born: 26 May'64, New York City, New York, USA, son of a Russian Jew and black Bahamas-born actress. As a teenager, he moved with his family to Los Angeles, where he joined the local boys' choir and taught himself to play guitar and piano. In 1987, KRAVITZ formed his own one-man band, ROMEO BLUE, marrying girlfriend of two years, 'Cosby Show' actress Lisa Bonet. Over the course of the ensuing two years, he recorded demos which were soon heard by Henry Hirsch, who recommended them to 'Virgin'. In October '89, after many arguments with the record company over production techniques, etc., KRAVITZ finally released a debut album and single, 'LET LOVE RULE'. A back to basics operation of luddite proportions, the record slavishly imitated KRAVITZ's paisley heroes of yesteryear (HENDRIX, CURTIS MAYFIELD, DYLAN) in much the same fashion as The BLACK CROWES paid homage to The FACES and The ALLMAN BROTHERS. Yet, despite charges of plagiarism from critics, much like The 'CROWES debut, 'LET LOVE RULE' was consistently listenable. Unsurprisingly then, the album subsequently notched up sales of half a million copies in the US, eventually reaching Top 60 in the UK. In 1990, the title track became KRAVITZ's first Top 40 success in Britain, tempting MADONNA into requesting his writing skills (along with INGRID CHAVEZ) for her controversial 'Justify My Love' single. Quite a celebrity in his own right, KRAVITZ played up the part of Hollywood socialite to the max, immaculately decked out in nouveau-retro clobber (a la PRINCE) and de rigeur dreadlocks. Later that year, he also appeared in Liverpool at YOKO ONO's tribute to her late husband JOHN LENNON. 'MAMA SAID' (1991) was a more accomplished, soulful affair which fleshed out the sound with brass and strings, songs alternating between introspective mood pieces (he'd recently split with his wife) and gritty funk-rock. Early in '92, LENNY settled out of court over royalties owing to INGRID CHAVEZ from the MADONNA collaboration, although the whole thing seeming a bit of a sham bearing in mind that the main thrust of the song was highly reminiscent of PUBLIC ENEMY's 'Security Of The First World'. Nevertheless, KRAVITZ could well afford to pay, 'MAMA SAID' notching up considerable American and British sales, while the single, 'IT AIN'T OVER 'TIL IT'S OVER' was a US No.2. After writing a passable album for sexy French goddess, VANESSA PARADIS, KRAVITZ re-emerged in thundering rock-God mode (replete with red leather trousers, no less) for 'ARE YOU GONNA GO MY WAY', a HENDRIX-esque song that made the UK Top 5. The album of the same name was KRAVITZ's biggest success to date, scaling the album charts in Britain, although it was clear the singer was running out of fresh ideas (or at least fresh ways of presenting old ideas). 'CIRCUS' (1995) carried on in much the same vein, successful but stale. • Covered; COLD TURKEY + GIVE PEACE A CHANCE (John Lennon) / IF SIX WAS NINE (Jimi Hendrix) / DEUCE (Kiss) / AMERICAN WOMAN (Guess Who). • Trivia: SLASH of GUNS N' ROSES played guitar on 2 tracks from 'MAMA SAID'.

Album rating: MAMA SAID (*8) / LET LOVE RULE (*7) / ARE YOU GONNA GO MY WAY (*7) / CIRCUS (*5) / 5 (*5)

LENNY KRAVITZ – vocals, guitar, piano, bass, drums with on session / **HENRY HIRSCH** – keyboards / **KARL DENSON** – sax / + guests

		Virgin	Virgin
Oct 89.	(7"/7"w-poster) (VUS/+P 10) <99166> **LET LOVE RULE. / EMPTY HANDS** (12"+=/cd-s+=) (VUS T/CD 10) – Blues for Sister Someone / Flower child.		89
Nov 89.	(lp/c/cd) (VUSLP/VUSMC/CDVUS 10) <91290> **LET LOVE RULE**	56	61

– Sitting on top of the world / Let love rule / Freedom train / My precious love / I build this garden for us / Fear / Does anybody out there even care / Mr. Cab driver / Rosemary / Be. (c+=) – Blues for Sister Someone / Flower child. (cd++=) – Empty hands.

Jan 90.	(7"/c-s) (VUS/+C 17) **I BUILT THIS GARDEN FOR US. / FLOWER CHILD** (12"+=/cd-s+=) (VUS T/CD 17) – Fear.	81	-
May 90.	(7"/c-s) (VUS/+C 20) **MR. CAB DRIVER. / BLUES FOR SISTER SOMEONE (live) / DOES ANYBODY OUT THERE EVEN CARE (live)** (12"/cd-s) (VUS T/CD 20) – (first 2 tracks) / Rosemary (live). (10") (VUSA 20) – ('A'side / Rosemary (live) / Let love rule (live).	58	
Jul 90.	(7"/c-s) (VUS/+C 26) **LET LOVE RULE. / COLD TURKEY (live)** (12"+=) (VUSTG 26) – Flower child (live). (cd-s+=) (VUSCD 26) – My precious love (live). (10") (VUSA 26) – ('A'side) / If six was nine (live) / My precious love (live).	39	-
Mar 91.	(7"/c-s) (VUS/+C 34) **ALWAYS ON THE RUN. / ('A'instrumental)** (12"+=/12"box+=) (VUST/+X 34) – Light skin girl from London. (cd-s+==) (VUSCD 34) – Butterfly.	41	-
Apr 91.	(cd)(c/lp) (CDVUS 31)(VUS MC/LP 31) <91610> **MAMA SAID**	8	39

– Fields of joy / Always on the run / Stand by my woman / It ain't over 'til it's over / More than anything in this world / What goes around comes around / The difference is why / Stop draggin' around / Flowers for Zoe / Fields of joy (reprise) / All I ever wanted / When the morning turns to night / What the . . .. are we saying? / Butterfly.

May 91.	(7"/c-s) (VUS/+C 43) **IT AIN'T OVER 'TIL IT'S OVER. / THE DIFFERENCE IS WHY** (12"+=/cd-s+=) (VUST 43) – I'll be around. (12"pic-d) (VUSTY 43) – ('A'side) / (interview).	11	-
May 91.	(c-s) <98795> **IT AIN'T OVER 'TIL IT'S OVER / I'LL BE AROUND**	-	2
Sep 91.	(7"/c-s) (VUS/+C 45) **STAND BY MY WOMAN. / FLOWERS FOR ZOE** (12"+=) (VUST 45) – Stop dragging on (live). (cd-s+=) (VUSCD 45) – What the . . .. are we saying? (live) / Always on the run (live).	55	-
Oct 91.	(c-s) <98736> **STAND BY MY WOMAN / LIGHT SKIN GIRL FROM LONDON**	-	76
——	now with **CRAIG ROSS** – electric guitar (co-writes some music) / **TONY BRETT** – bass / **MICHAEL HUNTER** – flugel horn		
Feb 93.	(7"/c-s) (VUS/+C 65) **ARE YOU GONNA GO MY WAY. / MY LOVE** (cd-s) (VUSCD 65) – ('A'side) / Always on the run / It ain't over 'til it's over / Let love rule.	4	-
Mar 93.	(cd)(c/lp) (CDVUS 60)(VUS MC/LP 60) <86984> **ARE YOU GONNA GO MY WAY**	1	12

– Are you gonna go my way / Believe / Come on and love me / Heaven help / Just be a woman / Is there any love in your heart / Black girl / My love / Sugar / Sister / Eleutheria.

May 93.	(7"/c-s) (VUS/+C 72) <12662> **BELIEVE. / FOR THE FIRST TIME** (10"pic-d+=/cd-s+=) (VUS T/CD 72) – ('A'acoustic) / Sitar (acoustic).	30	60
Aug 93.	(7"/c-s) (VUS/+C 73) **HEAVEN HELP. / ELEUTHERIA** (cd-s+=) (VUSDG 73) – Ascension / Brother.	21	-
Nov 93.	(7"pic-d/12") (VUS P/T 76) **IS THERE ANY LOVE IN YOUR HEART. / ALWAYS ON THE RUN (live)** (cd-s+=) (VUSDG 76) – What goes around comes around (live) / Freedom train (live).	52	
Mar 94.	(c-s) <38412> **HEAVEN HELP / SPINNING AROUND OVER YOU**	-	80

Aug 95.	(c-s) (VUSC 93) **ROCK AND ROLL IS DEAD / ANOTHER LIFE** (10"+=/cd-s+=) (VUS AB/CD 93) – Confused / Is it me or is it you.	22	-
Sep 95.	(c-s) <38514> **ROCK AND ROLL IS DEAD / ARE YOU GONNA GO MY WAY (live)**	-	75
Sep 95.	(cd/c/lp) (CDVUS/VUSLP/MUSMC 86) <40696> **CIRCUS**	5	10

– Rock and roll is dead / Circus / Beyond the 7th sky / Tunnel vision / Can't get you off my mind / Magdalene / God is love / Thin ice / Don't go and put a bullet in your head / In my life today / The resurrection.

Dec 95.	(c-s) (VUSC 96) **CIRCUS / ('A'acoustic)** (10"+=/cd-s+=) (VUS A/CD 96) – Tunnel vision (live) / Are you gonna go my way (live).	54	
Feb 96.	(7"/c-s) (VUS A/C 100) <38535> **CAN'T GET YOU OFF MY MIND. / EMPTY HANDS** (cd-s+=) (VUSCD 100) – Stand by my woman.	54	62
Sep 96.	(10") (VUSA 107) **THE RESURRECTION (live). /** (cd-s+=) (VUSCD 107) –		-
May 98.	(c-s) (VUSC 130) **IF YOU CAN'T SAY NO / WITHOUT YOU** (12"+=/cd-s+=) (VUS T/CD 130) – ('A'-Zero & BT . . . mixes).	48	
May 98.	(cd/c) (CDVUS/VUSMC 140) <47758> **5**	18	28

– Live / Supersoulfighter / I belong to you / Black velveteen / If you can't say no / Thinking of you / Take time / Fly away / It's your life / Straight cold player / Little girl's eyes / You're my flavor / Can we find a reason? (cd re-iss. Jun99; CDVUSX 140)

Sep 98.	(c-s) (VUSC 138) **I BELONG TO YOU / IF YOU CAN'T SAY NO (Flunky in the attic mix)** (cd-s+=) (VUSCD 138) – If you can't say no (BT twilo dub).	75	
Feb 99.	(c-s/cd-s) (VUSC/+D 141) <radio cut> **FLY AWAY / FLY AWAY (live acoustic) / BELIEVE (live acoustic)**	1	12 Nov98
Jun 99.	(c-s) (VUSC 146) **BLACK VELVETEEN / LIVE / FLY AWAY** (cd-s) (VUSCD 146) – (first 2 tracks) / Supersoulfighter. (cd-s) (VUSCDX 146) – (first & third tracks) / Straight cold player. (re-iss. Dec99; same)		
Aug 99.	(c-s) (VUSC 153) <radio cut> **AMERICAN WOMAN / THINKING OF YOU (Nick Hexam's dancehall mix)** (cd-s+=) (VUSCD 153) – Straight cold player (live) / Fields of joy (live).		49 Jul99

Kris KRISTOFFERSON

Born: 22 Jun'36, Brownsville, Texas, USA. A PhD student who won a Rhodes scholarship to Oxford in 1958, KRISTOFFERSON was also a budding songwriter and after a brief spell in the army he relocated to Nashville where he continued writing while holding down various jobs (including a spell as a janitor at the Columbia studios). Having befriended country legend JOHNNY CASH, his first break came in 1969 when CASH handed KRISTOFFERSON's 'ME AND BOBBY McGHEE' to country maverick ROGER MILLER who in turn, took it into the country charts. CASH himself hit with KRIS's definitive 'SUNDAY MORNIN' COMIN' DOWN' later that year and the lanky, bearded songwriter secured a deal with the 'Monument' imprint. Titled simply 'KRISTOFFERSON' (1970), his debut album caught the attention of both rock and country critics as the fabled "outlaw" movement began to coalesce around CASH, WAYLON JENNINGS, WILLIE NELSON etc. 1971 proved a pivotal year as friend JANIS JOPLIN took 'ME AND BOBBY McGHEE' to No.1. (US). While SAMMI SMITH scored a US Top 10 hit with 'HELP ME MAKE IT THROUGH THE NIGHT' (a track that has since, like much of his material, become a country standard) at the same time, KRISTOFFERSON's second album, 'THE SILVER TONGUED DEVIL AND I' (1971) finally saw him racking up sales in his own right. Literate, laconic and liberal, he helped steer country music away from the middle of the road and on to a far more interesting path. While hardly the most gifted of singers, his laid-back style was perfect for the kind of freewheeling rebel image he liked to portray (he certainly wins top prize for references to getting stoned, hardly a typical Nashville topic) and, like his hero BOB DYLAN, KRIS's songs were ripe for interpretation. Branching out into acting in the early 70's, he made his film debut in Dennis Hopper's (another close friend) 'The Last Movie' before going on to star in cult classics, 'Cisco Pike' and 'Pat Garrett And Billy The Kid' (alongside James Coburn and BOB DYLAN, who penned the sublime soundtrack). Singer RITA COOLIDGE also appeared in the latter, KRISTOFFERSON marrying her the same year (1973). In the meantime – although his stock with the critics had gone down – he'd scored his first US No.1 with 'WHY ME', from 1972's 'JESUS WAS A CAPRICORN' album. As well as recording duets with his new wife, he continued cutting his own albums to diminishing critical returns, among them 'FULL MOON' (1973), 'BREAKAWAY' (1974), 'WHO'S TO BLESS AND WHO'S TO BLAME' (1975) and 'THIRD WORLD WARRIOR' (1976). KRISTOFFERSON's biggest success of the decade came with a remake of 'A Star Is Born' (1976), in which he co-starred with Barbra Streisand. The accompanying soundtrack (written and sung by the man himself) sold millions and spawned his last major hit of the decade, 'WATCH CLOSELY NOW'. While his recordings dried up in the 80's he continued to concentrate on acting, appearing in everything from 'Heaven's Gate' (1980) to John Sayles' 'Lone Star' (1986). The mid-80's also found him hooking up with veteran outlaw mates JOHNNY CASH, WAYLON JENNINGS and WILLIE NELSON for the acclaimed 'HIGHWAYMEN' (1985) album. The quartet went on to record a sequel, 'HIGHWAYMEN II' (1990) as well as 1995's 'ROAD GOES ON FOREVER'. KRISTOFFERSON himself did win back the critics to a certain extent in the 90's, recording comeback set, 'A MOMENT OF FOREVER' for Texas label, 'Justice', in 1995. The close of the millennium meanwhile, found KRISTOFFERSON in fine fettle with 'THE AUSTIN SESSIONS' (1999), featuring new versions of his many classic tunes.

Best CD compilation: THE VERY BEST OF KRIS KRISTOFFERSON (*7)

KRIS KRISTOFFERSON – vocals; with numerous session people

Monument Monument

Apr 70. (7") <1210> **SUNDAY MORNIN' COMIN' DOWN. / TO BEAT THE DEVIL** | - | |

May 70. (7") (MON 1050) **BLAME IT ON THE STONES. / HELP ME MAKE IT THRU' THE NIGHT** | | - |

Jun 70. (lp) <(SMO 5042)> **KRISTOFFERSON**
– Blame it on the stones / To beat the Devil / Me and Bobby McGee / The best of all possible worlds / Help me make it thru' the night / The law is for protection for the people / Casey's last ride / Just the other side of nowhere / Darby's castle / For the good times / Duvalier's dream / Sunday mornin' comin' down. <US re-iss. Sep71 as 'ME AND BOBBY McGEE'; 30817> – hit No.43 (re-iss. Oct71 as 'ME AND BOBBY McGEE'; MNT 64631)

Jun 71. (lp) (MNT 64636) <30679> **THE SILVER-TONGUED DEVIL AND I** | | 21 |
– The silver-tongued devil and I / Jody and the kid / Billy Dee / Good Christian soldier / Breakdown / Loving her was easier (than anything I'll ever do again) / The taker / When I love her / The pilgrim: chapter 33 / Epitaph. (re-iss. 1974; same)

Oct 71. (7") (MNT 7523) <8525> **LOVING HER WAS EASIER (THAN ANYTHING I'LL EVER DO AGAIN). / EPITAPH** | | 26 | Aug71

Dec 71. (7") <8531> **THE TAKER. / THE PILGRIM: CHAPTER 33** | - | |

Mar 72. (7") <8536> **JOSIE. / BORDER LORD** | | 63 |

Apr 72. (lp) (MNT 64963) <31302> **BORDER LORD** | | 41 | Mar72
– Josie / Burden of freedom / Stagger mountain tragedy / Border Lord / Somebody nobody knows / Little girl lost / Smokey put the sweet on me / When she's wrong / Gettin' by high and strange / Kiss the world goodbye.

1972. (7"m) (MNT 9154) **BREAKDOWN. / THE PILGRIM CHAPTER 33/ LOVING HER WAS EASIER** | | - |

Dec 72. (7") (MNT 65391) <31909> **JESUS WAS A CAPRICORN** | | 31 | Nov72
– Jesus was a Capricorn / Nobody wins / It sure was / Enough for you / Help me Lord / Jesse Younger / Give it time to be tender / Out of mind, out of sight / Sugar man / Why me.

Feb 73. (7") (MNT 1188) <8558> **JESUS WAS A CAPRICORN. / ENOUGH FOR YOU** | | 91 | Dec72

Feb 73. (7") <8564> **JESSE YOUNGER. / GIVE IT TIME TO BE TENDER** | | - |

May 73. (7") (MNT 1461) **IT SURE WAS. / NOBODY WINS** | | - |

—— in Sep73, 'A&M' issued his collaboration album 'FULL MOON' with new wife RITA COOLIDGE. It hit US No.26 and contained two US hit singles 'A SONG I'D LIKE TO SING' and 'LOVING ARMS'.

Oct 73. (7") (MNT 1482) <8571> **WHY ME. / HELP ME LORD** | | 16 | Mar73

Jun 74. (lp) (MNT 69074) <32914> **SPOOKY LADY'S SIDESHOW** | | 78 | May74
– Same old song / Broken freedom song / Shandy / Starspangled bummer / Lights of Magdala / I may smoke too much / One for the money / Late again / Stairway to the bottom / Rescue mission / Smile at me again / Rock and roll time.

Jun 74. (7") <8618> **LIGHTS OF MAGDALA / I MAY SMOKE TOO MUCH** | - | |

KRIS KRISTOFFERSON & RITA COOLIDGE

Dec 74. (lp) (MNT 80547) <33278> **BREAKAWAY**
– Lover please / We must have been out of our minds / Dakota / What'cha gonna do / The thing I might have been / Slow down / Rain / Sweet Susannah / I've got to have you / I'd rather be sorry / Crippled crow.

Jan 75. (7") (MNT 2871) <8630> **RAIN. / WHAT'CHA GONNA DO**

Mar 75. (7") <8636> **SLOW DOWN. / LOVER PLEASE** | - | |

May 75. (7") <8646> **SWEET SUSANNAH. / WE MUST HAVE BEEN OUT OF OUR MINDS** | - | |

KRIS KRISTOFFERSON

Nov 75. (lp) (MNT 69158) <33379> **WHO'S TO BLESS . . . AND WHO'S TO BLAME**
– The year 200 minus 25 / If it's all the same to you / Easy, come on / Stallion / Rocket to stardom / Stranger / Who's to bless . . . and who's to blame / Don't cuss the fiddle / Silver.

Nov 75. (7") <8658> **ROCKET TO STARDOM. / EASY, COME ON** | - | |

Feb 76. (7") <8679> **IF IT'S ALL THE SAME TO YOU. / THE YEAR 2000 MINUS 25** | - | |

Aug 76. (lp) (MNT 81496) <34254> **SURREAL THING**
– You show me yours / Killing time / The prisoner / Eddie the eunuch / It's never gonna be the same again / I got a life of my own / The stranger I love / The golden idol / Bad love story / If you don't like Hank Williams.

Aug 76. (7") <8707> **IT'S NEVER GONNA BE THE SAME AGAIN. / THE PRISONER** | - | |

—— Late in '76 the 'Columbia' soundtrack of the film re-make of 'A STAR IS BORN', which starred BARBRA STREISAND and KRIS. The No.1 album (also UK No.1 Apr'77; (CBS 86021), featured duets from both as well as 3 solo tracks from KRIS including 'C.B.S.' single below . . .

Jun 77. (7") (CBS 5336) <10525> **WATCH CLOSELY NOW. / CRIPPLED CROW** | | 52 | May77

Apr 78. (lp) (MNT 86056) <35310> **EASTER ISLAND** | | 86 | Mar78
– Risky bizness / How do you feel / Forever in your love / The sabre and the rose / Spooky lady's revenge / Easter Island / The bigger the fool / Lay me down / The fighter / Living legend.

Jun 78. (7") (MNT 6474) **LOVER PLEASE. / SLOW DOWN** | | - |

—— In 1978, 'A&M' released KRIS lp alongside RITA COOLIDGE; 'NATURAL ACT' <(AMLH 64690)>

Sep 79. (lp/c) (MNT/40 83793) <36135> **SHAKE HANDS WITH THE DEVIL**
– Shake hands with the Devil / Prove it to you one more time again / Whiskey whiskey / Lucky in love / Seadream / Killer barracuda / Come sundown / Michoacan / Once more with feeling / Fallen angel.

Mar 81. (lp/c) (MNT/40 84818) <36885> **TO THE BONE**
– Magdalene / Star-crossed / Blessing in disguise / The Devil to pay / Daddy's song / Snakebit / Nobody loves anybody anymore / Maybe you heard / The last time / I'll take any chance I can with you.

Jan 83. (d-lp/d-c; by KRIS KRISTOFFERSON, WILLIE NELSON, DOLLY PARTON & BRENDA LEE) (MNT/40 88611) <38389> **KRIS, WILLIE, DOLLY & BRENDA . . . THE WINNING HAND**
– You're gonna love yourself (in the morning) / Ping pong / You'll always have someone / Here comes that rainbow again / The bigger the fool, the harder the fall / Help me make it through the night / Happy happy birthday baby / You left me a long, long time ago / To make a long story short, she's gone / Someone loves you honey / Everything's beautiful (in it's own way) / Bring on the sunshine / Put it off until tomorrow / I never cared for you / Casey's last ride / King of a lonely castle / The little things / The bandits of Beverly Hills / What do you think about lovin' / Born to love me.

Jan 83. (7") <21000> **HERE COMES THAT RAINBOW AGAIN. /** | - | |

—— In Oct'84, 'Columbia' US <39531> released WILLIE NELSON and KRIS lp 'MUSIC FROM THE SONGWRITER' in which they co-starred together. On the same label, the same pair plus JOHNNY CASH and WAYLON JENNINGS, released lp 'THE HIGHWAYMAN' in August '85.

Mercury Mercury

Mar 87. (lp/c)(cd; as KRIS KRISTOFFERSON & THE BORDERLORDS) (MERH/+C 103)<(830460-2)> **REPOSSESSED**
– Mean old man / Shipwrecked in the eighties / They killed him / What about me / El Gavilan (the hawk) / El coyote / Anthem / The heart / This old road / Love is the way.

Jan 90. (cd/c/lp) <(834629-2/-4/-1)> **THIRD WORLD WARRIOR**
– The eagle and the bear / Third World warrior / Aquila del norte / The hero / Don't let the bastards (get you down) / Love of money / Third World war / Jesse Jackson / Mal sacate / Sandinista.

—— The HIGHWAYMEN released the set, 'THE ROAD GOES ON FOREVER' in Apr'95

Transatla. Justice

Apr 96. (cd) (TRACD 220) **A MOMENT OF FOREVER** | | | Aug95
– A moment of forever / Worth fighting for / Johnny Lobo / The promise / Shipwrecked in the eighties / Slouching towards the millennium / Between Heaven and here / Casey's last ride / Good love (shouldn't feel so bad) / A new game now / New mister me / Under the gun / Road warrior's lament / Sam's song (ask any working girl).

Warner Warner
ESP ESP

Oct 99. (cd) <(7567 83208-2)> **THE AUSTIN SESSIONS**
– Me and Bobby McGee / Sunday morning coming down / For the good times / The silver tongued devil and I / Help me make it through the night / Loving her was easier (than anything I'll ever do again) / To beat the Devil / Who's to bless and who's to blame / Why me? / Nobody wins / The pilgrim: chapter 33 / Please don't tell how the story ends.

– compilations, others, etc. –

1975. (7") Monument; (ZS 88920) **WHY ME. / JESUS WAS A CAPRICORN** | | - |

May 77. (lp) Monument; (82002) <34687> **SONGS OF KRISTOFFERSON** | | 45 |
(re-iss. Nov82 lp/c; MNT/40 32106)

1984. (lp/c) CBS-Embassy; (EMB/40 31839) **HELP ME MAKE IT THROUGH THE NIGHT**

1988. (lp/c/cd) Country Store; (CST/CSTK/CDCST 5) **KRIS KRISTOFFERSON**

Apr 90. (cd/c/d-lp) Connoisseur; (KKVSOP CD/MC/LP 141) **THE LEGENDARY YEARS** | | - |

Apr 98. (cd) Spectrum; (554009-2) **THE COUNTRY COLLECTION** | | - |

Jun 99. (cd/c) Columbia; (494188-2/-4) **THE VERY BEST OF KRIS KRISTOFFERSON**

KROKUS   (dig out; Great Metal . . .)

KRS-ONE

Born: LAURENCE KRISNA PARKER, 20 Aug'65, The Bronx, New York, USA. Leaving home in his teens, PARKER lived on the streets initially, self-educating himself in philosophy and metaphysics while perfecting his rhyming skills through verbal jousting with other would-be MC's in the Bronx homeless shelters where he often slept. It was in one of these shelters that he met social worker, SCOTT STERLING aka DJ SCOTT LaROCK, the pair hooking up and recording 'CRIMINAL MINDED' under the moniker BDP (BOOGIE DOWN PRODUCTIONS). Eventually released by 'B-Boy' records in 1987, this influential set of proto-gangsta rap showcased PARKER's hard hitting rapping style on tracks like the classic 'SOUTH BRONX', a stinging rebuke to vinyl claims that rap had originated in the Queens district of New York. Later that year, LaROCK was tragically gunned down after attempting to break up a street quarrel between two teenagers, PARKER bravely struggling on to make the acclaimed 'BY ALL MEANS NECESSARY' album. Released by 'Jive' in 1988, the record saw PARKER aka KRS-ONE (KNOWLEDGE RULES SUPREME OVER NEARLY EVERYONE) develop his trademark educational style, promoting self-awareness and self-knowledge on the likes of 'MY PHILOSOPHY'. Standing in stark contrast to the emerging gangsta movement, the record also took a staunch anti-violence stance, the track 'STOP THE VIOLENCE' subsequently adopted by the loose collective of rappers/pressure group which KRS-ONE organised as the Stop The Violence Movement. Musically, the album also stood apart, its clever use of reggae influences resulting in a tough but fresh sound which KRS-ONE would develop over subsequent releases like 'GHETTO MUSIC: THE BLUEPRINT OF HIP HOP' (1989) and 'EDUTAINMENT' (1990), the rapper increasingly putting the emphasis on his self-appointed role as humanist educator as the latter's title suggests. Having already established himself as a lecturer on the college circuit, KRS-ONE (or 'The Teacher' as he's known within hip hop circles) initiated the H.E.A.L. (Human Education Against Lies) project in 1991, a compilation with contributions from the likes of CHUCK D and QUEEN LATIFAH as well as rock/folk artists such as R.E.M. and BILLY BRAGG. With CHUCK D, KRS-ONE featured on KOOL MOE DEE's 1991 minor hit 'Rise 'n' shine'. KRS-ONE's final album under the BDP moniker, 'SEX AND VIOLENCE' (1992) was the most Jamaican-influenced release of his career, the rapper's reggae credentials secure through having worked with the likes of SLY & ROBBIE and SHABBA RANKS. The rapper's humanistic leanings were called into question the same year, however, when he attacked Prince Be of PM Dawn at a New York gig, allegedly in retaliation for comments made in a magazine article. Nevertheless, KRS-ONE continues to command respect from a wide cross-section of the hip hop community, his solo career continuing apace with such acclaimed releases as 'RETURN OF DA BOOM BAP' (1993), 'KRS ONE' (1995) and more recently 'I GOT NEXT' (1997). The latter album made the US Top 3, the rapper finally reaping substantial financial reward for his years of hip hop innovation and campaigning, the album containing his collaboration with drum 'n' bass guru, GOLDIE.

Album rating: Boogie Down Productions: CRIMINAL MINDED (*8) / BY ALL MEANS NECESSARY (*7) / GHETTO MUSIC: THE BLUEPRINT OF HIP HOP (*6) / EDUTAINMENT (*5) / LIVE HARDCORE WORLDWIDE (*4) / SEX AND VIOLENCE (*5) / KRS-One: RETURN OF DA BOOM RAP (*6) / KRS-ONE (*7) / I GOT NEXT (*6)

BOOGIE DOWN PRODUCTIONS

LAURENCE KRISNA PARKER (aka KRS-ONE) – rapper / **SCOTT STERLING** (aka DJ SCOTT LaROCK) – DJ

		B.Boy	B.Boy
Sep 87.	(12") <*BB 1400*> **POETRY. /**		
Sep 87.	(lp) <*BB 4787*> **CRIMINAL MINDED**		

– Poetry / South Bronx / 9mm goes bang / Word from our sponsor / Elementary / Dope beat / Remix for P is free / The bride is over / Super-hoe / Criminal minded.

—— on the 25th August, 1987 – while intervening a street argument – LaROCK was shot dead (he was only 24) / **PARKER** recruited his brother **KENNY PARKER + D-NICE** (DERRICK JONES) – DJ's

		Jive	Jive
May 88.	(7"/12"/12") (*JIVE/+T/X 170*) **MY PHILOSOPHY. / STOP THE VIOLENCE**	69	
Jun 88.	(lp/c/cd) (*HIP/HIPC/CHIP 63*) <*1097*> **BY ALL MEANS NECESSARY**	38	75 Apr88

– My philosophy / Ya slippin' / Stop the violence / Illegal business / Nervous / I'm still #1 / Part time suckers / Jimmy / T'cha – t'cha / Necessary.

Jul 88.	(12") (*JIVET 179*) **I'M STILL #1. / ESSAYS ON B.D.P. / JIMMY**		
Dec 88.	(7"/12") (*JIVE/+T 192*) **JACK OF SPADES. /**		
Jul 89.	(7"/c-s/12") (*JIVE/+C/T 210*) **WHY IS THAT? / HIP HOP RULES**		
Jul 89.	(lp/c/cd) (*HIP/HIPC/CHIP 80*) <*1187*> **GHETTO MUSIC: THE BLUEPRINT OF HIP HOP**	32	36

– Style you haven't done yet / The blueprint / Jah rulez / Who protects us from you? / Hip hop rules / Gimme dat, (woy) / World peace / Why is that? / Jack of spades / Breath control / You must learn / B~o! Bo! Bo~! / Ghetto music.

Jul 89.	(12") (*JIVE 1187-1*) **GHETTO MUSIC. / THE BLUEPRINT**		-
Feb 90.	(12") (*JIVET 241*) **YOU MUST LEARN. / JAH RULEZ / WORLD PEACE**		
Aug 90.	(cd/c/lp) (*HIP/HIPC/HIP 100*) <*1358*> **EDUTAINMENT**	52	32

– Black man in effect / Ya know the rules / Beef / House niggas / Love's gonna get'cha (material love) / 100 guns / Ya strugglin' / Breath control II / Edutainment / The homeless / The Kenny Parker show / Original lyrics / The racist / 7 dee jays / 30 cops or more.

Mar 91.	(cd/c/lp) <*1425*> **LIVE HARDCORE WORLDWIDE (live)**	-	

– KRS-One intro / Lick a shot / The eye opener / Jack of spades / My philosophy / Still #1 (freestyle) / Poetry / House nigga's / Criminal minded / Jimmy / The bridge is over / Ya know the rules / Kenny Parker intro / South Bronx / Reggae medley (incl. 9mm) / Super hoe / Up to date / Why is that? / Stop the violence / B~o! Bo! Bo! / Come to the teacher / Breath control / Self destruction.

Mar 92.	(cd/c/lp) (*CHIP/HIPC/HIP 120*) <*41470*> **SEX AND VIOLENCE**		42

– The original way / Duck down / Drug dealer / Like a throttle / Build and destroy / Ruff ruff (featuring FREDDIE FOXXX) / 13 and good / Poisonous products / Questions and answers / Say gal / We in there / Sex and violence / How not to get jerked / Who are the pimps? / The real holy place.

—— KRS-ONE disbanded this project to go solo (DERRICK done the same)

– compilations, etc. –

1988.	(lp; as DJ SCOTT LaROCK & KRS-ONE) *B.Boy;* <*(BBOY 2)*> **MEMORY OF A MAN & HIS MUSIC**		

KRS-ONE

LAURENCE "KRIS" PARKER – vocals, etc

Oct 93.	(cd/c/lp) (*CHIP/HIPC/HIP 142*) <*41517*> **RETURN OF DA BOOM BAP**		37

– Return of the boom bap / Slap them up / Black cop / I can't wake up / Mad crew / Outta here / "P" is still free / Mortal thought / Sound of da police / Brown skin woman / Higher level / KRS-One attacks / Uh oh / Stop frontin'. *(re-iss. May97; same)*

Jan 94.	(c-s) <*42192*> **SOUND OF DA POLICE (remix) / HIP HOP VS RAP / BLACK COP**	-	89
Sep 95.	(12"/cd-s) (*JIVE T/CD 384*) <*42319*> **MC'S ACT LIKE THEY DON'T KNOW.** / ('A'-Represent The Real Hip Hop (with **DAS EFX**)		57
Oct 95.	(cd/c/lp) (*CHIP/HIPC/HIP 165*) <*41570*> **KRS-ONE**		19

– Rappaz r n dainja / De automatic (with FAT JOE) / MC's act like they don't

know / Ah yeah / R.E.A.L.I.T.Y. / Free mumia (with CHANNEL live) / Hold / Wannabemceez (with MAD LION) / Represent the real hip hop (with DAS EFX) / Truth / Build ya skillz (with BUSTA RHYMES) / Out for fame / Squash all beef / Health wealth self.

May 96.	(c-s) (*JIVEC 396*) **RAPPAZ R N DAINJA /**	47	
	(12"+=/cd-s+=) (*JIVE T/CD 396*) – ('A'mixes).		
Jan 97.	(12"/cd-s) (*JIVE T/CD 418*) **WORD PERFECT (mixes). / THE MC / CAN'T STOP, WON'T STOP**	70	

—— guests now DJ MUGGS, REDMAN + RICH NICE

Apr 97.	(12"/cd-s) (*JIVE T/CD 411*) **STEP INTO A WORLD (RAPTURE'S DELIGHT). /**	24	70 Mar97
May 97.	(cd/c) <*41601*> **I GOT NEXT**	58	3

– 1st quarter – The commentary / / 2nd quarter – Free throws / MC / I got next – Nevva hadda gun / Heartbeat / Step into a world (rapper's delight) / Friend / H.I.P.H.O.P. / Halftime / 3rd quarter: The commentary / Klassicks / Blowe / Real hip-hop, pt.2 / Come to da party / Can't stop, won't stop / Over ya head / Just to prove a point / 4th quarter – Free throws / Untitled.

—— In Aug'97, KRS-ONE plus ICE CUBE, B REAL and SHAQUE O'NEILL collaborated on minor US hit single, 'Men Of Steel'.

Sep 97.	(12"/cd-s) (*JIVE T/CD 431*) **HEARTBEAT. / A FRIEND / STEP INTO A WORLD (Puff Daddy remix)**		

Victor KRUMMENACHER (see under ⇒ CAMPER VAN BEETHOVEN)

KUKL (see under ⇒ BJORK)

KULA SHAKER

Formed: Highgate, London, England . . . mid 90's out of mods The KAYS by CRISPIAN MILLS. They initially played down the fact his mother was the famous English actress Hayley Mills (daughter of Sir John Mills) and father being director, Roy Boulting. In the late 80's, CRISPIAN and ALONZA BEVIN set up a school group, The LOVELY LADS, later becoming The OBJECTS. In 1995, after jointly winning the 'In The City' new band competition and a Glastonbury appearance, KULA SHAKER signed to 'Columbia', through A&R man Ronnie Gurr. They debuted that Xmas with the limited edition single, 'TATTVA'. Their first single proper, 'GRATEFUL WHEN YOU'RE DEAD', was a tribute of sorts to the late, great JERRY GARCIA and earned them their first Top 40 hit. Their follow-up, a re-vamped version 'TATTVA', fared even better, making the Top 5. 'HEY DUDE', the next single, kept up the momentum, reaching No.2 following a blinding 'T In The Park' appearance in Scotland (they returned there in 1997 as headliners). CRISPIAN MILLS' songwriting was heavily influenced by a combination of classic 60's psychedelia and grandoise 70's rock, much in evidence on their debut album 'K' (1996). Relying on similar Eastern influences as 'TATTVA', 'GOVINDA' was another slice of elaborate, but cliched psychedelia, while 'HUSH' (1997) was workman-like in its similarity to the DEEP PURPLE version of the JOE SOUTH original. KULA SHAKER continued to musically spar with their tried and tested cod-mod/psychedelia, a Top 3 single in '98, 'SOUND OF DRUMS', testament to just that. The track was also included on their Bob Ezrin-produced sophomore set, 'PEASANTS, PIGS & ASTRONAUTS' (1999), a pretentious set of good-time cosmic rock'n'roll that gave ammunition to the gun-totting music journos all ready to shoot them down at any opportunity. Two further Top 20 singles, 'MYSTICAL MACHINE GUN' and 'SHOWER YOUR LOVE', marked the end for CRISPIAN and his chums as the band split that September; the frontman is expected to go solo any time. • **Covered:** BALLAD OF A THIN MAN (Bob Dylan).

Album rating: K (*7) / PEASANTS, PIGS & ASTRONAUTS (*5)

CRISPIAN MILLS (b.18 Jan'73) – vocals, guitars / **ALONZA BEVIN** (b.24 Oct'70) – bass, piano, tabla, vocals / **JAY DARLINGTON** (b. 3 May'69, Sidcup, England) – keyboards / **PAUL WINTERHART** (b.19 Sep'71) – drums

		Columbia	Columbia
Dec 95.	(ltd; 7"/cd-s) (*KULA 71/CD1*) **TATTVA (Lucky 13 mix)/ HOLLOW MAN (part II)**		-
Apr 96.	(c-s) (*KULAMC 2*) **GRATEFUL WHEN YOU'RE DEAD – JERRY WAS THERE. / ANOTHER LIFE**	35	-
	(cd-s+=) (*KULACD 2*) – Under the hammer.		
Jun 96.	(7") (*KULA 3*) **TATTVA. / TATTVA ON ST. GEORGE'S DAY / DANCE IN YOUR SHADOW**	4	-
	(cd-s) (*KULACD 3*) – (first & third tracks) / Moonshine / Tattva (lucky 13).		
	(cd-s) (*KULACD 3K*) – (second & third tracks) / Red balloon (Vishnu's eyes).		
Aug 96.	(7"/c-s) (*KULA/+MC 4*) **HEY DUDE. / TROUBLED MIND**	2	-
	(cd-s+=) (*KULACD 4*) – Grateful when you're dead (Mark Radcliffe session) / Into the deep (Mark Radcliffe session).		
	(cd-s) (*KULACD 4K*) – ('A'side) / Tattva / Drop in the sea / Crispian reading from the Mahabharata.		
Sep 96.	(cd/c/lp) (*SHAKER CD/MC/LP 1*) <*67822*> **K**	1	Oct96

– Hey dude / Knight on the town / Temple of the everlasting light / Govinda / Smart dogs / Magic theatre / Into the deep / Sleeping jiva / Tattva / Grateful when you're dead – Jerry was there / 303 / Start all over / Hollow man (parts 1 & 2). *(also ltd-cd; SHAKER CD1K)*

Nov 96.	(c-s) (*KULAMC 5*) **GOVINDA / GOKULA**	7	-
	(cd-s+=) (*KULACD 5*) – Hey dude (live) / Alonza Bevan's The Leek.		
	('A'-Hari & St.George mix-cd-s+=) (*KULACD 5K*) – ('A'-Monkey Mafia Pigsy's vision) / ('A'-Monkey Mafia Ten to ten version).		
	(7"mail-order+=) (*KULA 75*) – Temple of everlasting light.		
Feb 97.	(c-s) (*KULAMC 6*) **HUSH / RAAGY ONE (WAITING FOR TOMORROW)**	2	-

(cd-s+=) *(KULACD 6)* – Knight on the town (live) / Smart dogs (live).

(cd-s+=) *(KULACD 6K)* – Under the hammer (hold on to the magical key) / Govinda (live).

—— (all above cd-singles were re-iss. Jul98; *KULA 71-76CD*)

Jul 97.　(cd-ep) <*68514*> **SUMMER SUN EP**　　　｜-｜　｜　｜
– Govinda / Gokula / Dance in your shadow / Raagy one (waiting for tomorrow) / Moonshine / Troubled mind.

Apr 98.　(c-s) *(KULA 21MC)* **SOUND OF DRUMS / HURRY ON SUNDOWN (HARI OM SUNDOWN)**　　｜3｜　｜-｜
(cd-s+=) *(KULA 21CD)* – Reflections of love / Fairyland (featuring DON PECKER).

(cd-s+=) *(KULA 21CDX)* – The one that got away / Smile.

Feb 99.　(c-s) *(KULA 22MC)* **MYSTICAL MACHINE GUN / GUITAR MAN**　　　｜14｜　｜-｜
(cd-s+=) *(KULA 22CD)* – Prancing bride.

(cd-s) *(KULA 22CDX)* – ('A'side) / Avalanche / Holy river.

Mar 99.　(cd/c/lp) *(SHAKER 2 CD/MC/LP)* **PEASANTS, PIGS & ASTRONAUTS**　　｜9｜　｜　｜
– Great Hosannah / S.O.S. / Mystical machine gun / Radhe radhe / I'm still here / Shower your love / 108 battles / Sound of drums / Timeworn / Last farewell / Golden avatar / Namami nanda nandana.

May 99.　(c-s) *(KULA 23MC)* **SHOWER YOUR LOVE / GOODBYE TIN TERRIERS**　　　｜14｜　｜-｜
(cd-s+=) *(KULA 23CD)* – Sound of drums (live).

(cd-s) *(KULA 23CDX)* – ('A'side) / The dancing flea / Light of the day.

—— disbanded in September '99

KYUSS

Formed: Palm Springs, California, USA . . . 1991 by JOHN GARCIA, JOSH HOMME, SCOTT REEDER and ALFREDO HERNANDEZ. Initially playing bluesy punk, the group's rather lacklustre debut, 'WRETCH', was followed up by the blinding intensity of 'BLUES FOR THE RED SUN' (1992). Seemingly coming from out of nowhere, it had taken MASTERS OF REALITY retro guru CHRIS GOSS to develop the band's latent genius. A smouldering slab of frazzled flare-rock, the band had dragged garage-psych stoned and stumbling into the 90's, carving a new benchmark for would-be sonic archivists. Live, most commentators were in agreement that KYUSS were peerless, the group soon finding themsleves playing on the same bill as the likes of DANZIG and METALLICA. 'Elektra' were sufficiently impressed to offer the band a deal when their label went belly-up, KYUSS once again working with GOSS on the fuzzed-up bludgeon of 'WELCOME TO SKY VALLEY' (1994). Despite the critical raving, the group's label were unsure how to market their hippy-rock sound with the result that KYUSS' record sales were less than impressive. So it was then, that after a final masterpiece, 'AND THE CIRCUS LEAVES TOWN' (1995), the group decided to call it a day. The fact that KYUSS were obviously only beginning to reach their full potential was illustrated with the 'QUEENS OF THE STONE AGE' (1997) set. A combination of unreleased KYUSS material and a clutch of new, even more mind-altering tracks from HOMME's similarly titled new outfit (also numbering GOSS, VAN CONNER and VIC THE STICK), the album was a disorientatingly heavy testament (including a suitably trippy cover of Black Sabbath's 'INTO THE VOID') to one of the most criminally ignored bands of the 90's. Meanwhile, KYUSS' former frontman, GARCIA, was making his name with a new outfit, UNIDA.

Album rating: WRETCH (*7) / BLUES FOR THE RED SUN (*9) / WELCOME TO SKY VALLEY (*8) / . . .AND THE CIRCUS LEAVES TOWN (*8) / QUEENS OF THE STONE AGE (*8)

JOHN GARCIA – vocals / **JOSH HOMME** (b.1973) – guitar / **SCOTT REEDER** – bass; repl. NICK OLIVERI (b.1971) who joined DWARVES / **ALFREDO HERNANDEZ** (b.1966) – drums

	Dali-Chameleon	Dali-Chameleon
1991.　(cd) **WRETCH**	-	

– HWY 74 (beginning of what's about to happen) / Love has passed me by / Son of a bitch / Black widow / Katzenjammer / Deadly kiss / The law / Isolation / I'm not / Big bikes / Stage III.

Feb 93.　(cd/c) <*3705 61340-2/-4*> **BLUES FOR THE RED SUN**　　｜　｜　｜　｜
– Thumb / Green machine / Molten universe / 50 million years trip / (Downside up) / Thong song / Apothecaries' weight / Catepillar march / Freedom run / 800 / Writhe / Capsized. *(cd+=)* – Allen's wrench / Mondo generator / Yeah.

	Elektra	Warners

Jun 94.　(cd/c/lp) <*7559 61571-2/-4/-1*> **WELCOME TO SKY VALLEY**　　｜　｜　｜
– I / Gardenia / Asteroid / Supa scoopa and mighty scoop / II / 100 degrees / Space cadet / Demon cleaner / III / Odyssey / Conan troutman / N.O. / Whitewater.

Sep 94.　(7"blue) *(EKR 192)* **DEMON CLEANER. / FREEDOM RUN (live)**　　｜　｜　｜
(cd-s) *(EKR 192CD1)* – ('A'side) / Day one (to Dave & Chris) / El rodeo / Hurricane.

(cd-s) *(EKR 192CD2)* – ('A'side) / Gardenia (live) / Thumb (live) / Conan trout man (live).

Feb 95.　(cd-s) *(EKR 197CD)* **GARDENIA / U.N. SANDPIPER / CONAN TROUT MAN (live)**　　｜　｜　｜

Jun 95.　(cd/c) <*7559 61811-2/-4*> **. . .AND THE CIRCUS LEAVES TOWN**　　｜　｜　｜
– Hurricane / One inch man / Thee of boozeroony / Gloria Lewis / Phototropic / El rodeo / Jumbo blimp jumbo / Tango zizzle / Size queen / Catamarran / Spaceship landing.

—— split in 1995 leaving some recordings below. HOMME formed QUEENS OF THE STONE AGE, which was released by below label as KYUSS' epitaph album. He was joined by **VAN CONNER** – bass (SCREAMING TREES) / **CHRIS GOSS** (MASTER OF REALITY) / **VIC THE STICK** – drums

Jul 97.　(10") *(MR 015)* **INTO THE VOID. / FATSO FORGETSO**

	Man's Ruin	Man's Ruin

Dec 97.　(cd) <*(MR 063)*> **QUEENS OF THE STONE AGE**
– Into the void / Fatso forgotso / Fatso Forgotso phase II / If only everything / Born to hula / Spiders and vinegaroons.

QUEENS OF THE STONE AGE

—— **JOSH HOMME** – vocals, guitar / **NICK OLIVERI** – bass / **ALFREDO HERNANDEZ** – drums

	Man's Ruin	Man's Ruin

Sep 98.　(10"ep/cd-ep) *(MR 141/+CD)* **QUEENS OF THE STONE AGE / BEAVER EP**
– The bronze / These aren't the droids you're looking for / BEAVER: Absence without leave / Morocco.

	Roadrunner	Roadrunner

Oct 98.　(cd) <*(RR 8674-2)*> **QUEENS OF THE STONE AGE**
– Regular John / Avon / If only / Walkin' on the sidewalks / You would know / How to handle a rope / Mexicola / Hispanic impressions / You can't quit me baby / Give the mule what he wants / I was a teenage hand model.

—— added 4th live member **DAVE CATCHING** – guitar

—— HOMME was the mainman behind The DESERT SESSIONS, a group of musicians (from KYUSS, SOUNDGARDEN and EARTHLINGS) who released late in 1998, a 10"/cd, 'VOL III/IV' for 'Man's Ruin'.

LABRADFORD (dig out; Great Alt & Indie . . .)

L.A. GUNS (dig out; Great Alt & Indie . . .)

LAIBACH (dig out; Great Alt & Indie . . .)

LAIKA (dig out; Great Alt & Indie . . .)

Greg LAKE (see under ⇒ EMERSON, LAKE & PALMER)

LAMBCHOP

Formed: Nashville, Tennessee, USA . . . 1992 initially as POSTERCHILD by KURT WAGNER, the 90's country-lounge answer to 60's icons, CAT STEVENS and TIM HARDIN. His hesitant but heavy-lidded vocal monotone sat perfectly against the lethargic drowsiness of the country-jazz played by his large backing ensemble. Although they could hardly be termed rock, LAMBCHOP emerged from the flourishing alternative roots scene with an album on 'Merge' ('City Slang' UK) 'I HOPE YOU'RE SITTING DOWN' (1995). A post-modern cousin of CHET ATKINS (although at times at least twice removed!), the record revealed WAGNER's love of vintage string-laden production and his penchant for beer-soaked, meandering tales of ordinary madness. Early the following year, KURT and LAMBCHOP delivered another collection of near comatose country vignettes, 'HOW I QUIT SMOKING', this time around wrapped up in a classic 70's Nashville production sheen courtesy of arranger, John Mock. One of the record's highlights, 'THE MAN WHO LOVED BEER', was issued as the first LAMBCHOP single and has since been adopted as author, Martin C. Strong's theme tune. Joking aside, 1996 also saw the release of a third set, the critically acclaimed live/festival (1995) recorded 'HANK', relaxzzzed audiences no doubt giving WAGNER and Co the first ever horizontal standing ovation. A third studio album, meanwhile, sauntered onto the scene in 1997, the LAMBCHOP man surely being just a tad ironic in naming it 'THRILLER', although opening cuts, 'MY FACE YOUR ASS' and 'YOUR SUCKING FUNNY DAY', raised the pulse a little. Prolific as ever, WAGNER and his entourage (they had all worked on VIC CHESNUTT's 'The Salesman & Bernadette') returned in 1998 with possibly his/their best album to date, 'WHAT ANOTHER MAN SPILLS', featuring croonsome classic, 'THE SATURDAY OPTION', alongside a few covers by F.M. CORNOG (i.e. EAST RIVER PIPE) and one by Curtis Mayfield, 'GIVE ME YOUR LOVE'.

Album rating: I HOPE YOU'RE SITTING DOWN (*6) / HOW I QUIT SMOKING (*7) / HANK (*7) / THRILLER (*6) / WHAT ANOTHER MAN SPILLS (*7)

KURT WAGNER – vocals, guitar / **BILL KILLEBREW** – guitar / **MARC TROVILLION** – bass / **STEVE GOODHUE** – drums / **ALLEN LOWREY** – percussion / **JONATHAN MARX** – clarinet / **SCOTT CHASE** – washboard, maracas

	not iss.	Thump Audio
1992. (7"ep; as POSTERCHILD) <1> **AN OPEN FRESCA / A MOIST TOWELETTE / (other two by Crop Circle Hoax)**		
	City Slang	Merge
1992. (7") <MRG 048> **NINE. / MOODY FUCKER**	-	
1994. (5") <#1> **SCARED OUT OF MY SHOES. / (other track by Spent)**	-	
— <above issued for 'I-sore 5' club'> <below on 'Sunday Driver'>		
1994. (7") <02> **MY CLICHE. / LORETTA LUNG** (re-iss. 1999 on Spanish label 'Elefant'; ER 15913-69>	-	
Aug 94. (7") <MRG 066> **SOAKY IN THE POOPER. / TWO KITTENS DON'T MAKE A PUPPY**	-	
1994. (7") **IT'S IMPOSSIBLE. / (other track by NONPAREILS AND BARTLEBEES)** (above on 'Contrast International') <below on 'Bloodsucker'>	-	
1995. (7"ep) <19846> **I CAN HARDLY SPELL MY NAME / THE SCARY CAROLER. / (other tracks by CYOD)**	-	

— line-up **WAGNER, CHASE, MARX, TROUVILLION, LOWREY, KILLEBREW +**

GOODHUE added **PAUL NIEHAUS** – lap steel guitar, trombone, vocals / **JOHN DELWORTH** – organs / **DEANNA VARAGON** – vocals, alto sax, banjo, cello / **MIKE DOSTER** – bass (on 1)

Mar 95. (cd/d-lp) (efa 04953-2/-1) <MRG 70> **I HOPE YOU'RE SITTING DOWN / JACK'S TULIPS**		Sep94
— Begin / Betweemus / Soaky in the pooper / Because you are the very air he breathes / Under the same moon / I will drive slowly / Oh, what a disappointment / Hellmouth / Bon soir, bon soir / Hickey / Breathe deep / So I hear you're moving / Let's go bowling / What was he wearing? / Cowboy on the moon / The pack-up song.		
1995. (7") <7003-7> **YOUR LIFE AS A SEQUEL. / SMUCKERS**	-	
— <above on 'Mute America'>		
Jan 96. (cd/d-lp) (efa 04969-2/-1) <MRG 97> **HOW I QUIT SMOKING**		
— For which we are truly thankful / The man who loved beer / The militant / We never argue / Life's little tragedy / Suzieju / All smiles and mariachi / The scary caroler / Smuckers / The militant / Garf / Your life as a sequel / Theone / Again.		
Apr 96. (7"m)(cd-s) (efa 04974-45)(efa 04977-03) **THE MAN WHO LOVED BEER. / ALUMNI LAWN / BURLY & JOHNSON**		-
— added guest **HANK TILBURY** – banjo		
Jul 96. (m-cd/10"m-lp) (efa 04979-2/-1) <MRG 108> **HANK (live)**		
— I'm a stranger here / Blame it on the brunette / The tin chime / Randi / Doak's need / Poor bastard. (cd+=) – I sucked my boss's dick. below by VIC CHESNUTT, DAVE LOWERY, KURT WAGNER + PAUL NIEHAUS		
1996. (7") <25075> **A LOOSE CONFEDERATION OF SATURDAY CITY-STATES**	-	
— Plagarism / How can I face tomorrow.		
— added **PAUL BIRCH, MARKY NEVERS, ALEX MacMANUS + JOHN CATCHINGS ; to repl. STEVE + BILL**		
Jul 97. (7") <(MRG 124)> **CIGARETTIQUETTE. / MR. CRABBY** (above & below 45's released on 'Merge' only)		
Sep 97. (7") <(MRG 126)> **WHITEY. / PLAYBOY, THE SHIT**		
Sep 97. (cd/lp) (efa 04998-2/-1) <MRG 130> **THRILLER**		
— My face your ass / Your fucking sunny day / Hey, where's your girl / Crawl away / Gloria Leonard / Thriller / The old fat robin / Superstar in France.		
Nov 97. (cd-ep) (efa 0870-03) **YOUR SUCKING FUNNY DAY / THE PETRIFIED FLORIST / THE THEME FROM THE NEAL MILLER SHOW**		-
— added **DENNIS CRONIN, MIKE GRIFFITH, VIC CHESNUTT + TONY CROW**		
Sep 98. (cd/lp) (efa 08711-2/-1) <MRG 146> **WHAT ANOTHER MAN SPILLS**		
— Interrupted / The Saturday option / Shucks / Give me your love (love song) / Life #2 / Scamper / It's not alright / N.O. / I've been lonely for so long / Magnificent obsession / King of nothing never / The theme from the Neil Miller show.		
Nov 98. (ltd-12") <fu 003> **GIVE ME YOUR LOVE (LOVE SONG) – Doppenganger remix. / ('A'-album & Doppelganger instrumental)**	-	
— <above on City Slang's 'For Us' records, below on own label>		
Dec 98. (cd-s) <none> **CHRISTMAS TIME IS HERE / CHRISTMAS TIME IS HERE**	-	- radio
Apr 99. (ltd-7") <(ER 198)> **LA DISTANCIA DESCE ELLA HASTA ALLI (THE DISTANCE FROM HER TO THERE). / THE BOOK I HAVEN'T READ** (above issued on Spanish 'Elefant 6') (below on 'Third Gear')	-	
Nov 99. (7") (3G 23) **UP WITH PEOPLE. / Dump: Die For The Memory**		-

— Nov'99, KURT WAGNER was credited on an EP, 'Chester' with JOSH ROUSE

Ronnie LANE

Born: 1 Apr '46, Plaistow, London, England. Raised in Forest Gate, he began learning the guitar after leaving school, forming his first band The OUTCASTS with drummer KENNY JONES. Shortly after the group's demise, the pair hooked up with STEVE MARRIOTT and JIMMY WINSTON to form The SMALL FACES. The classic line-up fell into place (with IAN McLAGAN replacing WINSTON) soon after the band's first chart success and they went on to become one of the most successful UK acts of the mid-late 60's alongside fellow London mods The WHO. While LANE's laid-back songwriting was a key ingredient in The SMALL FACES' success it was also at odds with the tougher hard rock sound proposed by MARRIOTT. The inevitable split finally came in 1969 when the latter abruptly departed (and subsequently formed HUMBLE PIE) after a serious argument. Amid the wreckage, like the proverbial phoenix rising from the ashes, came The FACES, a sloppy but brilliant rock'n'roll act comprising LANE, McLAGAN, JONES, RON WOOD and eventually ROD STEWART as the swaggering frontman. Flawed genius, The FACES became infamous for their laddish lyrics, raucous live shows and general boozy shenannigans yet the massive success of STEWART's parallel solo career was eventually the band's undoing. LANE was unhappy with ROD the Mod's growing celebrity status eclipsing the band and the final straw came when STEWART made some disparaging press comments about the band's fourth album, 'OOH LA LA' (1973). Incensed, LANE walked out and retreated to the Welsh countryside with his new belle, Kate McKinnerney, immersing himself in the rural lifestyle to the extent that he enrolled in agricultural college(!). His musical vision was as strong as ever though and he formed the first version of SLIM CHANCE with BENNY GALLAGHER and GRAHAM LYLE. The group made their live debut on Guy Fawkes Night 1973 at Clapham Common under the canvas of Chipperfield's Circus. There, they previewed the soon-to-be hit single, 'HOW COME', which nearly made the UK Top 10 early the following year. Signed to 'G.M.', the label of ROD STEWART/FACES manager, Billy Gaff, RONNIE LANE'S SLIM CHANCE released their debut album, 'ANYONE FOR ANYMORE', in summer '74. A natural progression from LANE's mellow, freewheeling songwriting which had made the FACES albums so special ('RICHMOND', 'DEBRIS', 'YOU'RE SO RUDE' etc.), the record's good-time folkiness was a sign of things to come. To promote the album, LANE and Kate initiated the most ambitious project of his career, a wandering minstrel caravan-cum-circus named 'The Passing Show' complete with clowns, jugglers and even fire-eaters. While the show itself attracted some favourable reviews, a lack of proper planning and logistical problems meant it was an unmitigated financial disaster. Debt-ridden but hardly discouraged, LANE recruited a new cast of players (with a core of CHARLIE HART, BRIAN BELSHAM and STEVE SIMPSON) for a second (eponymous) album of rough'n'ready folk-rock originals and choice covers (CHUCK BERRY, The DILLARDS, FATS DOMINO, etc). Although he commanded a faithful core audience and critical admiration, LANE's solo records sold little and after a third and final album, 'ONE FOR THE ROAD' (1976), his resources had almost run dry. In desperate straits, LANE reluctantly agreed to join a SMALL FACES reunion; he lasted only one night. He then approached old mate PETE TOWNSHEND (of The WHO) about the prospect of a collaborative effort and the result was the critically acclaimed 'ROUGH MIX' (1977). With both friends and LANE himself acknowledging he was becoming increasingly physically debilitated, he was finally diagnosed with multiple sclerosis (the disease which had already killed his mother). Following 1980's one-off solo effort, 'SEE ME', his worsening condition made it increasingly difficult to record and perform. In 1983, largely through the efforts of producer GLYN JOHNS, former ROLLING STONE, IAN STEWART and ERIC CLAPTON, a benefit concert was organised featuring the likes of JIMMY PAGE, CLAPTON, STEVE WINWOOD and JEFF BECK. The million dollar profit was donated to British MS charity 'ARMS' and the concert's success prompted a similar event in the States. Although the American shows were equally successful, a drawn-out legal battle ensued over the management of the proceeds. Exhausted and in failing health, RONNIE moved to Austin, Texas where he married his third wife, Susan Gallegos and occasionally performed locally. 1990 saw his last touring work (Japan and the USA), LANE and his wife moving to the small Colorado hamlet of Trinidad in 1994 where he spent the last few years of his life. Sadly, on 4th June 1997, LANE succumbed to the disease that had plagued him for more than 20 years and had finally robbed British music of one of its most talented, affecting songwriters and performers. • **Covered:** SWEET VIRGINIA (Rolling Stones) / ROLL ON BABE (. . . Adams) / YOU NEVER CAN TELL (Chuck Berry) / WALK ON BY (. . . Hayes).

Album rating: ANYMORE FOR ANYMORE (*5) / RONNIE LANE'S SLIM CHANCE (*6) / ONE FOR THE ROAD (*6) / SEE ME (*4) / KUSCHTY RYE – THE SINGLES compilation (*6)

RONNIE LANE & SLIM CHANCE

RONNIE LANE – vocals, guitar (ex-SMALL FACES) / **BENNY GALLAGHER** – guitar, vocals / **GRAHAM LYLE** – mandolin, vocals / **KEVIN WESTLAKE** – guitar / **BILLY LIVSEY** – keyboards / **CHRISSIE STEWART** – bass / **JIMMY JEWELL** – saxophone / **BRUCE ROWLAND** – drums (ex-JOE COCKER, ex-TERRY REID)

	G.M.	G.M.
Nov 73. (7"m) (GMS 011) **HOW COME. / TELL EVERYONE / DONE THIS ONE BEFORE**	11	

—— **BIDDY WRIGHT** – bass; repl. STEWART (to JOE COCKER then FRANKIE MILLER)

Jun 74. (7") (GMS 024) **THE POACHER. / BYE AND BYE (GONNA SEE THE KING)**	36	-
Jul 74. (lp) (GML 1024) <1017> **ANYMORE FOR ANYMORE**		

– Careless love / Don't you cry for me / Bye and bye (gonna see the king) / Silk stockings / The poacher / Roll on babe / Tell everyone / Amelia Earhart's last flight / Anymore for anymore / Only a bird in a gilded cage / Chicken wired. (cd-iss. May92 & Jun96 on 'See For Miles'+=; SEECD 338) – How come / Done this one before. (cd re-iss. Jan98 on 'Burning Airlines'; PILOT 015)

Feb 75. (7") (GMS 033) **ANYMORE FOR ANYMORE. / ROLL ON BABE**		-

—— his live band – mid'74 to replace WRIGHT, GALLAGHER & LYLE (latter became duo) – were **ROBIN LUCAS + DREW McCULLOCH** – guitar / **STEVE BINGHAM** – bass / **KEN SLAVEN** – violin

—— later in the year for studio work **RONNIE LANE** brought in new lads **STEVE SIMPSON** – guitar / **BRIAN BELSHAW** – bass / **CHARLIE HART** – keyboards, violin / **RUAN O'LOCHLAINN** – saxophone, keyboards / **GLEN DE FLEUR** – drums

	Island	A&M
Feb 75. (7") (WIP 6216) **WHAT WENT DOWN. / LOVELY**		
Feb 75. (lp) (ILPS 9321) <3638> **RONNIE LANE'S SLIM CHANCE**		

– Little piece of nothing / Stone / Bottle of brandy / Street gang / Anniversary / I'm gonna sit right down and write myself a letter / I'm just a country boy / Ain't no lady / Blue Monday / Give me a penny / You never can tell / Tin and tambourine / Single saddle. (cd-iss. Apr96 on 'Edsel'; EDCD 463)

Apr 75. (7") (WIP 6229) **BROTHER CAN YOU SPARE A DIME. / AIN'T NO LADY**		-
Jan 76. (lp) (ILPS 9366) **ONE FOR THE ROAD** (live)		

– Don't try 'n' change my mind / 32nd Street / Snake / Burnin' summer / One for the road / Steppin' and reelin' / Harvest home / Nobody's listenin' / G'morning. (cd-iss. Feb96 on 'Edsel'; EDCD 464)

Jan 76. (7") (WIP 6258) **DON'T TRY 'N' CHANGE MY MIND. / WELL WELL HELLO**		-

—— RONNIE LANE had already disbanded SLIM CHANCE; he subsequently received credit on RON WOOD's (of the ROLLING STONES) 1976 soundtrack lp, 'MAHONEY'S LAST STAND'. The following year, the same happened w/ PETE TOWNSHEND (of The WHO) on the collaboration lp, 'ROUGH MIX'.

RONNIE LANE

—— went solo again

	Gem-RCA	not iss.
Jul 79. (7") (GEMS 12) **KUSCHTY RYE. / YOU'RE SO RIGHT**		-
Jan 80. (7") (GEMS 19) **ONE STEP TWO STEP. / LAD'S GOT MONEY**		-
Jul 80. (lp/c) (GEM LP/K 107) **SEE ME**		

– One step two step / Good ol' boys boogie / Lad's got money / She's leaving / Barcelona / Kuschty rye / Don't tell me now / You're so right / Only you / Winning with women / Way up yonder. (cd-iss. Jul96 on 'Edsel'; EDCD 492)

—— LANE retired from the music biz after developing multiple sclerosis. Sadly, RONNIE died on the 4th of June, 1997 after this long illness.

– compilations, others, etc. –

	G.M.-WEA	not iss.
Jan 77. (7"m) (GMS 9044) **HOW COME. / THE POACHER / TELL EVERYONE**		-
Oct 90. (cd/c/lp) Marquee; (MQC CD/MC/LP 002) **RONNIE LANE**		-
Jun 97. (d-cd; as RONNIE LANE with SLIM CHANCE) Burning Airlines; (PILOT 011) / WEA; <41385> **YOU NEVER CAN TELL**		
Sep 97. (cd) Burning Airlines; (PILOT 019) **KUSCHTY RYE – THE SINGLES**		-
Jul 98. (cd) Burning Airlines; (PILOT 036) **TIN AND TAMBOURINE**		-
Apr 99. (cd) Burning Airlines; (PILOT 020) **APRIL FOOL** (rarities and outtakes)		-
Apr 99. (4xcd-box) Burning Airlines; (HOWCOME 1) **THE PLONK BOX SET**		-

– (ANYMORE FOR ANYMORE / TIN AND TAMBOURINE / KUSCHTY RYE / LUCKY 7).

Mark LANEGAN (see under ⇒ SCREAMING TREES)

k.d. LANG

Born: KATHRYN DAWN LANG, 2 Nov'61, Consort, Alberta, Canada. A genuine cowgirl, LANG was raised in a remote rural town, developing her impressive voice from the age of 5 and picking up a guitar at age 10. Her infatuation with country, and more specifically with PATSY CLINE, began when LANG played a 'CLINE-type' character in a play at college. Hooking up with backing band The RECLINES, LANG toured her sensual, often campy, stage show around Canada, releasing a debut album, 'A TRULY WESTERN EXPERIENCE' (1984) on the Canadian independent label, 'Bumstead'. Her live reputation brought LANG to the attention of 'Sire' head, SEYMOUR STEIN, and with a revamped RECLINES: HAROLD BRADLEY (bass), JIMMY CAPPS (rhythm guitar), BUDDY HARMAN (drums), PETE WADE (guitar), HAL RUGG (stee guitar), HENRY STRZELECKI (bass), ROB HAJACOBS (fiddle), MARCUS 'PIG' ROBBINS (piano), TONY MIGLIORE (piano), BUDDY EMMONS (pedal steel) and BEN MINK (co-writer and violin), LANG set about recording her major label debut, 'ANGEL WITH A LARIAT' (1987). Produced by DAVE EDMUNDS, the record was tougher and more considered than the debut with LANG at her best on cover material, whether the effervescent swirl of Lynn Anderson's 'ROSE GARDEN' or the dark introspection of Eddie Miller & W.S. Stevenson's 'THREE CIGARETTES IN AN ASHTRAY'. Mooted as a bid to prove her credentials, 'SHADOWLAND' (1988) saw LANG in stone country mode, teaming up with Nashville production maestro, OWEN BRADLEY and even rounding up the likes of BRENDA LEE, KITTY WELLS and LORETTA LYNN for vocal contributions. Early the following year, she notched up further kudos by duetting with ROY ORBISON on his classic 'CRYING', released as the B-side to his hit, 'YOU GOT IT'. The performance subsequently netted the pair a Grammy award, LANG again working with ORBISON later that summer on 'BLUE BAYOU' (released as the B-side to his 'California Blue' single) as well as guesting on DION's 'Yo Frankie' album. LANG's third opus, 'ABSOLUTE TORCH AND TWANG' (1989) was more adventurous, consolidating her status as one of country music's most versatile and original performers. Whether poring over lovelorn laments like 'TRAIL OF BROKEN HEARTS' or tearing through Willie Nelson & Faron Young's 'THREE DAYS', LANG injected her music with a sass and style that the cobwebbed corners of Nashville hadn't glimpsed since EMMYLOU HARRIS emerged in the mid-70's. The record won LANG another Grammy, although as the 80's turned into the 90's, increasing column inches were dedicated to personal matters rather than praise for her music. While LANG had long been adopted as an icon by lesbians, the style press jumped on her quiffed, smouldering tomboy looks when she officially admitted her homosexuality in gay publication, 'The Advocate'. Surprisingly, this revelation didn't seem to affect sales of 'INGENUE' (1992), presumably because LANG's fanbase was now far wider than the conservative confines of country. Her most accessible release to date, the record found LANG inflecting her country with a subtle pop nous and silky sophistication, the album becoming a UK Top 30 hit while the gorgeously languid 'CONSTANT CRAVING' eventually made the Top 40. Following her appearance in the 1991 Percy Adlon film, 'Salmonberries', LANG continued her dalliance with the movie world by scoring the soundtrack to GUS VAN SANT's 'EVEN COWGIRLS GET THE BLUES' (1993). Her next album proper came with 'ALL YOU CAN EAT' (1995), a more playful affair that saw LANG more at ease with her sexuality (she was once press fodder for her association with tennis star, Martini Navratilova) and moving even further

from her country roots. Of recent times, the album 'DRAG' has kept the buying public in awe of her capability to turn basic tunes into joyful torch ballads.
• **Songwriters:** LANG collaborates with BEN MINK. Covered; CRAZY + I FALL TO PIECES (Patsy Cline) / LOCK, STOCK AND TEARDROPS (Roger Miller) / WESTERN STARS (Chris Isaak) / JOHNNY GET ANGRY (Carol Deene) / SO IN LOVE (Cole Porter) / FULL MOON FULL OF LOVE (Jeannie Smith & Leroy Preston) / BIG BIG LOVE (Wynn Stewart) / WHAT'S NEW PUSSYCAT? (Bacharach-David) / etc. The 'DRAG' album featured covers THEME FROM THE VALLEY OF THE DOLLS (Dory & Andre Previn) / HAIN'T IT FUNNY (Jane Siberry) / THE JOKER (Steve Miller) / MY LAST CIGARETTE (Boo Hewerdine).

Album rating: A TRULY WESTERN EXPERIENCE (*4) / ANGEL WITH A LARIAT (*6) / SHADOWLAND (*6) / ABSOLUTE TORCH AND TWANG (*6) / INGENUE (*8) / EVEN COWGIRLS GET THE BLUES (*4) / ALL YOU CAN EAT (*6) / DRAG (*6)

k.d. LANG – vocals, acoustic guitar with / **STEWART MacDOUGALL** – keyboards repl. MIKE CREBER + TED BOROWIECKI / **JOHN DYMOND** – bass repl. DENNIS MARCENKO + FARLEY SCOTT / **MICHEL POULIOT** – drums repl. DAVE BARNSON / **GORDIE MATTHEWS** – guitar (other early members **GARY KOLIGER** – slide guitar / **JAMIE KIDD** – organ)

			not iss.	Bumstead
1983.	(7"ltd.) *<none>* **DAMNED OLD DOG. / FRIDAY DANCE PROMENADE**		-	- Canada
Feb 84.	(lp) *<none>* **A TRULY WESTERN EXPERIENCE**		-	- Canada

– Bopatena / Pine and stew / Up to me / Tickled pink / Hanky Panky / There you go / Busy being blue / Stop, look and listen / Hooked on junk.

k.d. LANG & The RECLINES, with in 1986 **HAROLD BRADLEY** – bass / **JIMMY CAPPS** – rhythm guitar / **BUDDY HARMAN** – drums / **PETE WADE** – guitar / **HAL RUGG** – steel guitar / **HENRY STRZELECKI** – bass / **ROB HAJACOBS** – fiddle / **MARCUS 'Pig' ROBBINS** – piano / **TONY MIGLIORE** – piano / **BUDDY EMMONS** – steel / **BEN MINK** – violin

			Sire	Sire
Jan 87.	(7") *(W 8465) <28465>* **ROSE GARDEN. / HIGH TIME FOR A DETOUR**		☐	☐
Feb 87.	(lp/c) *(K 92544-1/-4)* **ANGEL WITH A LARIAT**			

– Turn me around / High time for detour / Diet of strange places / Got the bull by the horns / Watch your step polka / Tune into my wave / Rose garden / Angel with a lariat / Pay dirt / Three cigarettes in an ashtray.

| Apr 88. | (7") *(29919)* **I'M DOWN TO MY LAST CIGARETTE. / WESTERN STARS** | | - | |
| Apr 88. | (lp/c/cd) *(WX 171/+C/CD) <25724>* **SHADOWLAND** | | | 73 |

– Western stars / Lock, stock and teardrops / Sugar moon / I wish I didn't love you so / Once again around the dancefloor / Black coffee / Shadowland / Don't let the stars get in your eyes / Tears don't care who cries them / I'm down to my last cigarette / Too busy, being blue / Honky tonk angel's medley: In the evening (when the Sun goes down) – You nearly lose your mind – Blues stay away from me.

| Jun 88. | (7") *<27813>* **LOCK, STOCK AND TEARDROPS. / DON'T LET THE STARS GET IN YOUR EYES** | | - | |
| Jun 88. | (7") *(W 7841)* **SUGAR MOON. / HONKY TONK ANGELS MEDLEY** | | | |

(12"+=) *(W 7841T)* – I'm down to my last cigarette.
(below 'A'side featured in the soundtrack to 'Shag' film.

| Nov 88. | (7") *(W 7697)* **OUR DAY WILL COME. / THREE CIGARETTES IN AN ASHTRAY (live)** | | | |

(12"+=) *(W 7697T)* – Johnny get angry (live).

— Jan'89, she duetted on ROY ORBISON's 'Crying', a B-side to 'You Got It'. The same song featured on his B-side to Mar'89 single 'She's A Mystery To Me'. In Jul89, she again sang with the recently deceased ROY on 'Blue Bayou', which was a B-side to his 'California Blue'. The song had originally featured in the 1987 film 'Hiding Out'. In Jun'89, she guested on DION's album 'Yo Frankie'.

— Her band still included **MINK, POULIOT, DYMOND, MATTHEWS, CREBER** plus **GREG LEISZ** – steel guitar / **GRAHAM BOYLE** – perc. / **DAVID PILTCH** – fretless bass

| May 89. | (7") *<22932>* **WALLFLOWER WALTZ. / FULL MOON OF LOVE** | | - | ☐ |
| May 89. | (lp/c/cd) *(WX 259/+C/CD) <25877>* **ABSOLUTE TORCH AND TWANG** | | | 69 |

– Luck in my eyes / Three days / Trail of broken hearts / Big boned gal / Didn't I / Wallflower waltz / Full moon full of love / Pullin' back the reins / Big big love / It's me / Walkin' in and out of your arms / Nowhere to stand.

| Nov 89. | (7") *<22734>* **TRAIL OF BROKEN HEARTS. / THREE DAYS** | | - | ☐ |

— In Jul'90, she guested on WENDY & LISA's album 'Eroica'.

| Oct 90. | (7") *(W 9535)* **RIDIN' THE RAILS. / (track by Darlene Love)** | | | ☐ |

— (above single appeared on 'Warners' and the soundtrack to 'Dick Tracy') Late in 1991, she guested on JANE SIBERRY's song 'Calling All Angels'.

— She is now credited solo, but still retaining some or most of band.

| Mar 92. | (cd/c/lp) *<(7599 26840-2/-4/-1)>* **INGENUE** | | 3 | 18 |

– Save me / The mind of love (where is your head Kathryn) / Miss Chatelaine / Wash me clean / So it shall be / Still thrives this love / Season of hollow soul / Outside myself / Tears of love's recall / Constant craving.

| May 92. | (7"/c-s) *(W 0100/+C)* **CONSTANT CRAVING. / BAREFOOT** | | 52 | - |

(12"+=/cd-s+=) *(W 0100 T/CD)* – Season of hollow soul.

| Jul 92. | (c-s) *<18942>* **CONSTANT CRAVING / SEASON OF HOLLOW SOUL** | | - | 38 |

— CRYING was re-issued by 'Virgin' Aug'92 as 'A'side and hit UK No.13. 2 months later it again featured as a 'B'side. This time on his 'Heartbreak Radio'.

| Sep 92. | (7"/c-s) *(W 0135/+C)* **MISS CHATELAINE. / ('A'-St.Tropez edit)** | | | ☐ |

(cd-s+=) *(W 0135CD)* – Wash me clean / The mind of love.
(12"+=) *(W 0135TW)* – 2-'A'-St.Tropez mixes).

| Feb 93. | (7"/c-s) *(W 0157/+C)* **CONSTANT CRAVING. / MISS CHATELAINE** | | 15 | - |

(cd-s+=) *(W 0157CD)* – Wash me clean (live) / The mind of love (live).
(cd-s) *(W 0157CDX)* – ('A'side) / Big boned gal (live) / Outside myself (live).

| Apr 93. | (7"/c-s) *(W 0170/+C)* **THE MIND OF LOVE (WHERE IS YOUR HEAD KATHRYN?). / THE MIND OF LOVE (live)** | | 72 | ☐ |

(cd-s+=) *(W 0170CD1)* – Pullin' back the reins.
(cd-s) *(W 0170CD2)* – ('A'side) / Three cigarettes in a ashtray / Trail of broken hearts / Busy being blue.

| Jun 93. | (7"/c-s) *(W 0181/+C)* **MISS CHATELAINE. / ('A'mix)** | | 68 | ☐ |

(cd-s) *(W 0181CD)* – ('A'side) / ('A'-St.Tropez mix) / ('A'-Paris 92 mix).

| Nov 93. | (cd/c) *<(9362 45433-2/-4)>* **EVEN COWGIRLS GET THE BLUES (soundtrack)** | | 36 | 82 |

– Just keep me moving / Much finer place / Or was I / Hush sweet lover / Myth / Apogee / Virtual vortex / Lifted by love / Overture / Kundalini yoga waltz / In perfect dreams / Curious soul astray / Ride of Bonanza Jellybean / Don't be a lemming polka / Sweet little Cherokee / Cowgirl pride.

| Dec 93. | (7"/c-s) *(W 0227/+C)* **JUST KEEP ME MOVING. / IN PERFECT DREAMS** | | 59 | ☐ |

(12"/cd-s) *(W 0227 T/CD)* – ('A'side) / ('A'wild planet mixes) / ('A'moving mixes).

			Warners	Warners
Sep 95.	(c-s) *(W 0319C)* **IF I WERE YOU / WHAT'S NEW PUSSYCAT**		53	

(cd-s+=) *(W 0319CD)* – Get some.

| Oct 95. | (cd/c) *<(9362 46034-2/-4)>* **ALL YOU CAN EAT** | | 7 | 37 |

– If I were you / Maybe / You're ok / Sexuality / Get some / Acquiesce / This / World of love / Infinite and unforeseen / I want it all.

| May 96. | (c-s) *(W 0332C)* **YOU'RE OK** | | 44 | ☐ |

(12"+=/cd-s+=) *(W 0332 T/CD)* –

| Jul 97. | (cd/c) *<(9362 46623-2/-4)>* **DRAG** | | 19 | 29 |

– Don't smoke in bed / The air that I breathe / Smoke dreams / My last cigarette / The joker / Theme from the Valley Of The Dolls / Your smoke screen / My old addiction / Till the heart caves in / Smoke rings / Hain't it funny? / Love is like a cigarette.

Daniel LANOIS   (dig out; 4th edition)

LARD (see under ⇒ DEAD KENNEDYS)

LA'S

Formed: Liverpool, England . . . 1984 by songwriters MIKE BADGER (ex-KINDERGARTEN PAINTSET) and LEE MAVERS, along with drummer JOHN TIMSON; a limited V/A sampler 'A Secret Liverpool' exists of these times. When an inexperienced young bass player JOHN POWER joined the well-touted LA'S (alongside brief member PAUL HEMMINGS), things began to change. Friction also set-in between BADGER and MAVERS, the former bailing out and disappearing into the world of sculpture and painting (he had been a great fan of CAPTAIN BEEFHEART!). Signing to 'Go! Discs' early in 1987, the new LA'S (with MAVERS at the helm) released the charming retro-pop debut single, 'WAY OUT'. The record was well received but failed to chart and replacing TIMSON with CHRIS SHARROCK, the band followed up the single with the seminal BYRDS-like pop genius of 'THERE SHE GOES', all soaring melodies and youthful vigour. Incredibly, the single failed to chart, although it later reached the Top 20 when it was re-released in 1990 at the same time as the eponymous debut. Over the two year period it took to record the album, MAVERS' friend BARRY SUTTON replaced SHARROCK on the drum stool while JAMES JOYCE was recruited for the departing POWER (who went on to form the highly successful CAST). CAMMY, another guitarist, was also added. Part of the problem was the notoriously perfectionist MAVERS who obsessed over every tiny detail of the recording process in his search for an 'authentic' sound. 'Go! Discs' became increasingly worried about the escalating cost of the project and decided to go ahead and release the album against MAVERS' wishes. He retaliated by criticising the company in press interviews and dismissed the debut as a collection of demos. In reality, the album was a seamless collection of post-baggy guitar pop, drawing comparisons with the STONE ROSES and garnering almost universal acclaim. After a tour of America and Japan in 1991, the band went to ground and little has been heard from them since, save a brief, disastrous appearance supporting PAUL WELLER in 1994. While rumours continue to abound, the band remain one of the greatest modern day musical enigmas. BADGER finally emerged as a solo artist (he had worked for SPACE on the cover of 'Tin Planet') at the beginning of 1999, an album 'VOLUME' (on his SPACE mate TOMMY SCOTT's new 'Viper' imprint and produced by now LIGHTNING SEEDS man PAUL HEMMINGS) was the missing piece in The LA'S troubled rock'n'roll history. A subsequent tabloid grouch by the equally reclusive MAVERS on the worthiness of CAST frontman JOHN POWER was given short shrift – meanwhile SIXPENCE NONE THE RICHER (how well named) were high in the US charts with the LA'S classic, 'THERE SHE GOES'.

Album rating: THE LA'S (*8) / Mike Badger: VOLUME (*6)

LEE MAVERS (b. 2 Aug'62) – vocals, guitar / **JOHN TIMSON** – drums / added **JOHN POWER** (b.14 Sep'67) – bass

— (late '86) MIKE BADGER was repl. by **PAUL HEMMINGS** – guitar / **JOHN 'BOO' BYRNE** – guitar

			Go! Discs	London
Oct 87.	(7") *(GOLAS 1)* **WAY OUT. / ENDLESS**		☐	☐

(12"+=) *(GOLAS 1-12)* – Knock me down.
(12"++=) *(GOLAR 1-12)* – Liberty ship (demo) / Freedom song (demo).

— **CHRIS SHARROCK** – drums (ex-ICICLE WORKS) repl. TIMSON

| Nov 88. | (7") *(GOLAS 2)* **THERE SHE GOES. / COME IN, COME OUT** | | 59 | ☐ |

(12"+=)(cd-s+=) *(GOLAS 2-12)(LASCD 2)* – Who knows / Man I'm only human.
(7"ep+=) *(LASEP 2)* – Who knows / Way out (new version).

May 89. (7";w-drawn) *(GOLAS 3)* **TIMELESS MELODY. / CLEAN PROPHET** `-` `-`
(10"+=; w-drawn) *(LASEP 3)* – All by myself / There she goes.
(cd-s+=; w-drawn) *(LASCD 3)* – All by myself / Ride yer camel.

—— **NEIL MAVERS** (b. 8 Jul'71) – drums repl. SHARROCK / **JAMES JOYCE** (b.23 Sep'70) – bass repl. POWER who formed CAST / added **CAMMY** (b.PETER JAMES CAMELL, 30 Jun'67) – guitar (ex-MARSHMALLOW)

Sep 90. (7"-s) *(GOLAS/LASMC 4)* **TIMELESS MELODY. / CLEAN PROPHET** `57`
(12"purple+=)(cd-s+=) *(GOLAS 4-12)(LASCD 4)* – Knock me down / Over.

Oct 90. (7"-s) *(GOLAS/LASMC 5)* **THERE SHE GOES (new version). / FREEDOM SONG** `13` `-`
(12"+=)(cd-s+=) *(GOLAS 5-12)(LASCD 5)* – All by myself.

Feb 91. (7"-s) *(GOLAS/LASMC 6)* **FEELIN'. / DOLEDRUM** `43`
(12"+=)(cd-s+=)(7"ep+=) *(GOLAS 6-12)(LASCD 6)(GOLAB 6)* – I.O.U. (alt.version) / Liberty ship.

Oct 90. (cd/c/lp) *(<828 202-2/-4/-1>)* **THE LA'S** `30`
– Son of a gun / I can't sleep / Timeless melody / Liberty ship / There she goes / Doledrum / Feelin' / Way out / I.O.U. / Freedom song / Failure / Looking glass. *(cd re-iss. Sep99 on 'Polydor'; 828202-2)*

Jun 91. (c-s) *<869 370-4>* **THERE SHE GOES / ALL BY MYSELF** `-` `49`

—— had already disbanded just prior to above. In Apr'97 a various artists EP (taken from the movie, 'Fever Pitch', featured 'THERE SHE GOES' (issued on 'Blanco Yo Negro'; *NEG 104 C/T/CD)*

– compilations, etc. –

Sep 99. (cd-s) *Polydor; (561403-2)* **THERE SHE GOES / COME IN COME OUT / WHO KNOWS** `65`
Oct 99. (cd/lp) *Viper; (VIPER 2 CD/LP)* **BREAKLOOSE (LOST LA'S 1984-1986)**
– Breakloose (live) / Open your heart / Sweet 35 / Trees and plants / Red deer stalk / Dovecot dub / Walk / Get down over / What do you do / I did the painting / My girl sits like reindeer / Money in your talk / You blue / Moonlight.

LAST POETS

Formed: Harlem, New York, USA . . . 1968 by DAVID NELSON, GYLAN KAIN and CHUCK DAVIS (aka ABIODUN OYEWOLE). Coming together via an impromptu poetry performance at a Malcolm X birthday celebration in a Harlem park, the trio subsequently set up the East Wind cultural center/poetry workshop where they were joined by FELIPE LUCIANO. The collective's ranks were swelled by the addition – in quick succession – of JALAL MANSUR NURIDDIN, OMAR BIN HASSAN and ALAFIA PUDIM, taking the name The LAST POETS from a poem DAVIS had written after being inspired by the work of South African writer, K. William Kokafili. Although they'd set out to promote black unity, internal divisions soon led to a split with NELSON, KAIN and LUCIANO forming one group and OYEWOLE, NURRIDIN, BIN HASSAN and PUDIM forming another. Both camps soon got down to recording, OYEWOLE's bunch emerging with 1970's acclaimed 'THE LAST POETS' on 'Douglas' (the label owned by jazz man, Alan Douglas, who also produced the album), while NELSON and Co took a little longer on their debut long-player, 'RIGHT ON!' (1971). The former set boasted stark, uncompromising material – with the deliberate use of the derogatory term 'nigger' – intended to both rouse Afro-Americans from their torpor and act as a metaphorical call to arms. Recorded with minimal percussive accompaniment, the likes of 'NIGGERS ARE SCARED OF REVOLUTION' and 'WHEN THE REVOLUTION COMES' were heavily influential on the young GIL SCOTT-HERON who'd record in a similar style on his 1972 debut, 'Small Talk At 125th & Lennox' (125th Street, incidentally, being the location of the East Wind workshop). OYEWOLE & Co enjoyed the greatest success with 'THE LAST POETS' album even entering the US Top 30, largely by word of mouth sales. OYEWOLE, meanwhile subsequently found himself behind bars for armed robbery and was therefore absent from the recording of Spring 1971's equally militant follow-up set, 'THIS IS MADNESS'; the record's scathing criticisms of the Nixon administration allegedly landed them on an FBI counter-intelligence black list. At the same time the aforementioned 'RIGHT ON!' (billed as The ORIGINAL LAST POETS) was displaying similar sentiments, bubbling under the US Top 100 in tandem with their Muslim counterparts. HASSAN subsequently left for a religious sect (replaced by SULIAMAN EL-HADI) prior to 1972's 'CHASTISEMENT', a more musically dense affair utilising back-up singers. The following year saw the release of perhaps the best-loved LAST POETS-related album, 'HUSTLER'S CONVENTION'. A jive-talkin' concept affair based on the real life 1959 hustler's convention at Hamhock's Hall, the album was recorded by JALAL (who'd now taken over the reins of the 'POETS) under the alias LIGHTNIN' ROD and told the story of Sport and his buddy Spoon, two hustlers who eventually go straight after a series of misadventures. Superfunk musical backing was provided by KOOL & THE GANG, BILLY PRESTON and BROTHER GENE DINWIDDIE amongst others, the album going on to become a minor legend and influencing the styles of rap progenitors such as KOOL HERC and MELLE MEL. The free-jazz stylings of 1974's 'AT LAST' served as the next LAST POETS release, heralding a lay-off of three years before 'DELIGHTS OF THE GARDEN' (1977). Issued on 'Casablanca', the latter set featured the EL-HADI penned jazz-funk floorfiller, 'IT'S A TRIP' as well as JALAL's epic 'BEYONDER', both tracks backed by the drums of veteran BERNARD PURDIE. As rap and hip-hop revolutionised black music in the late 70's/early 80's, The LAST POETS were conspicuous by their absence from the recording front. They eventually re-emerged in 1984

on Bill Laswell's 'Celluloid' imprint with the album, 'OH MY PEOPLE', less frenetic than of old but still as committed as ever; P-funk man, BERNIE WORRELL guested on two tracks, the electro-influenced 'GET MOVIN' and 'HOLD FAST'. Another four years ensued before 'FREEDOM EXPRESS' (1988) while the early 90's saw JALAL working with London's premier acid-jazzers, GALLIANO. In 1995, there arose yet another situation whereby two groups released material as The LAST POETS; OYEWOLE and HASSAN re-emerged with the 'HOLY TERROR' album while JALAL and SULIAMAN released the 'SCATTERRAP' single. Despite the schism, The LAST POETS remain one of the most influential black music formations of the last thirty years, their militant stance echoed in the work of PUBLIC ENEMY while their records remain highly prized collectors items sampled by the likes of A TRIBE CALLED QUEST amongst others.

Album rating: THE LAST POETS (*8) / RIGHT ON!; by The Original Last Poets (*7) / THIS IS MADNESS (*6) / CHASTISEMENT (*6) / HUSTLER'S CONVENTION as Lightnin' Rod – aka Jalal (*8) / DELIGHTS OF THE GARDEN (*7) / OH, MY PEOPLE (*5) / FREEDOM EXPRESS (*4) / HOLY TERROR (*5) / THE BEST OF THE LAST POETS compilation (*8) / REAL RAP compilation (*8)

ABIODUN OYEWOLE (aka CHUCK DAVIS) – vocals / **GYLAN KAIN** – vocals / **DAVID NELSON** – vocals / **FELIPE LUCIANO** – vocals / **JALAL MANSUR NURIDDIN** – vocals / **OMAR BIN HASSAN** – vocals / **ALAFIA PUDIM** – vocals

—— the departing NELSON, LUCIANO and KAIN went on to release one album, 'RIGHT ON!' in Feb'71 for 'Juggernaut' *<8802>*

	Douglas	Douglas
Jun 70. (lp) *<3>* **THE LAST POETS** `-` `29`
– Run nigger / On the subway / Niggers are scared of revolution / Black thighs / Gashman / Wake up, niggers / New York, New York / Jones comin' down / Just because / Black wish / When the revolution comes / Two little boys / Surprises. *(cd-iss. Dec93 on 'Celluloid'; CELD 6101) (cd re-iss. Jun96 on 'Charly'; CPCD 8184)*

—— now without OYEWOLE who was imprisoned

—— added **NILAJA** – percussion
1972. (lp) *(DGL 69012) <30583>* **THIS IS MADNESS** `Mar71`
– True blues / Related to what / Black is / Time / Mean machine / White man's got a God complex / Opposites / Black people what y'all gon' do / O.D. / This is madness. *(cd-iss. Dec93 on 'Celluloid'; CELD 6105) (cd re-iss. Nov95 on 'Charly'; CPCD 8154)*

—— added **SULIAMAN EL-HADI** – drums / plus **OBABI, OMIYINKA + OMONIDE** – congas / **JOHN HART** – bass / **SAM HARKNESS** – sax

	not iss.	Blue Thumb
1972. (lp) *<BTS 39>* **CHASTISEMENT** `-` `-`
– Tribute to Obabi (Ogun) / Jazzoetry / Black soldier / E pluribus unum / Before the white man came / Hands off / Bird's word. *(cd-iss. Dec93 on 'Celluloid'; CELD 6209) (cd re-iss. Apr97 on 'Charly'; CPCD 822)*

—— In 1973, JALAL (under the moniker of LIGHTNIN' ROD) issued the album, 'HUSTLER'S CONVENTION'.

1974. (lp) **AT LAST** `-` `-`

—— (NILAJA left) JALAL + SULIAMAN added **BERNARD PURDIE** – drums / **ALEX BLAKE** – bass / **ABU MUSTAPHA** – vocals, percussion

	not iss.	Casablanca
1977. (lp) *<NBLP 7051>* **DELIGHTS OF THE GARDEN** `-` `-`
– It's a trip / Ho Chi Minh / Blessed are those who struggle / The pill / Delights of the garden / Beyonder: 1. Be – 2. Yond – 3. Er. *(cd-iss. Dec93 on 'Celluloid'; CELD 6136) (cd re-iss. Sep96 on 'Charly'; CPCD 8191)*

—— the pair were joined by **BERNIE WORRELL** – synthesizer / **BILL LASWELL** – percussion, electric drums / **AIYB DIENG** – percussion, drums / **JAMAL ABDUS SABUR** – bass / **KENYATTI ABDUR RAHMAN** – synthesizer / **PHILIP WILSON** – percussion

	Celluloid	Celluloid
Apr 85. (lp) *<(CELL 6108)>* **OH, MY PEOPLE** `-` `-`
– Get movin' / This is your life / What will you do / Oh, my people / Hold fast / Parting comany. *(cd-iss. Nov92 on 'Mau Mau'; MAUCD 627) (cd re-iss. Dec93 on 'Celluloid'; CELL 6108) (cd re-iss. Mar96 on 'Charly'; CPCD 8174)*
Jul 85. (12") *<CEL 703>* **GET MOVIN'. / MEAN MACHINE**

	Acid Jazz	Celluloid
Jan 89. (lp/cd) *(JAZID 8 LP/CD) <CELL 6172>* **FREEDOM EXPRESS** `Nov88`
– Tough enough / Woodshed walk / Freedom express / Geronimo / Un-holy alliance. *(cd re-iss. Dec93 on 'Celluloid'; CELD 6172) (cd re-iss. Jan97 on 'Movieplay Gold'; MPG 74040) (cd re-iss. Feb98 on 'Charly'; CPCD 8329)*

—— JALAL also issued three other solo releases, the 10" for 'On-U-Sound' 'MANKIND' (1993), 'ON THE ONE' (1996) and 'FRUITS OF RAP' (1997).

—— **JALAL + SULIAMAN** were the LAST POETS who released . . .

	Bond Age	not iss.
1995. (cd) **SCATTERRAP. / HOME** `-` `-` French

—— **OYEWOLE + HASSAN** reclaimed The LAST POETS moniker also (guests included BOOTSY COLLINS, GEORGE CLINTON + GRANDMASTER MELLE MEL)

	Black Arc– Rhino	Black Arc – Rhino
May 95. (cd) *<(RCD 10319)>* **HOLY TERROR**
– Invocation / Homesick / Black rage / Men-tality / Late rite / Talk show / Illusion of self / If only we knew / Funk / Phelhourinho. *(re-iss. Mar97; same)*
Jul 95. (12") *<(RA 121048)>* **BLACK & STRONG (HOMESICK). / (instrumental)**

– compilations, etc. –

Dec 93. (cd) *Celluloid; <(CELD 6208)>* **RETRO FIT**
Apr 95. (cd/c) *On The One; (SPOA 22/21)* **THE BEST OF THE PRIME TIME RHYME VOL.1**
Nov 95. (cd/lp) *On The One; (SPOA 32/31)* **THE BEST OF THE PRIME TIME RHYME**
Mar 97. (cd) *Charly; (CDNEW 105)* **THE BEST OF THE LAST POETS**

Sep 97. (cd) *Music Club; (MCCD 311)* **BEATS RHYME AND REVOLUTION**		□	-
Mar 99. (d-cd) *Snapper; (SMCD 183)* **REAL RAP**		□	-

Bill LASWELL

Born: 12 Feb'55, Salem, Illinois, USA. A guitarist turned bassman, LASWELL's early experience on the Detroit funk scene put him in good stead for a move to the more experimental climes of late 70's New York. Initially intended as a back-up vehicle for DAEVID ALLEN's (NEW YORK) GONG, MATERIAL served as LASWELL's first real band alongside MICHAEL BEINHORN, FRED MAHER (ex-RICHARD HELL), CLIFF CULTRERI and DON DAVIS. The quintet's debut outing in 1979, 'TEMPORARY MUSIC 1' (a 12" EP), represented a stark contrast to other late 70's stylings in that it fused jazz, punk, funk, No Wave and disco. MATERIAL returned in '81 with new guitarist RONNIE DRAYTON (who replaced CULTRERI and DAVIS), the new-look line-up making their long-awaited re-appearance with the single, 'BUSTIN' OUT', a collaboration with former LaBELLE chanteuse NONA HENDRYX. Over the course of the next six months, the quartet delivered two albums, the mini 'TEMPORARY MUSIC TWO' and 'MEMORY SERVES', the latter seeing the arrival of seasoned avant-rock man FRED FRITH. Having secured a deal with 'Elektra', LASWELL and Co had more time and a bigger budget for 1983's celebrated 'ONE DOWN', an experimental dance/fusion set that incredibly, introduced the talents of a young female guest singer going by the name of er . . . WHITNEY HOUSTON (where is she now we all ask!?). With LASWELL much in demand as a producer, session man and label boss (i.e. 'Celluloid'), MATERIAL was put on the back burner while the man also committed himself to some solo work. 'BASELINES' (1983) was finally released by 'Rough Trade' the following year, although LASWELL again sought out collaborators such as JOHN ZORN, The GOLDEN PALOMINOS and LAST EXIT (the latter a punishing free-jazz 4-piece featuring PETER BROTZMANN, SONNY SHARROCK and RONALD SHANNON JACKSON). After a further solo set, 'HEAR NO EVIL' (1988), he transplanted most of the album's backing musicians (including NICKY SKOPELITIS, L. SHANKAR and AIYB DIENG) into a new incarnation of MATERIAL. 1989's Arabic-influenced 'SEVEN SOULS' (his/their second set for cutting-edge imprint 'Venture') also featured SLY DUNBAR, who stuck around for 1991's 'THIRD POWER'. The first release on LASWELL's new 'Axiom' imprint, the record found him taking a backseat production/co-writing role for a cast of funk-orientated musos:- ROBBIE SHAKESPEARE, JEFF BOVA, BERNIE WORRELL, NICKY SKOPELITIS, The JUNGLE BROTHERS (BABY BAM and MIKE G), JALALUDDIN MANSUR NURUDDIN (of The Last Poets), SHABBA RANKS, GARY MUDBONE COOPER, BOOTSY COLLINS, HERBIE HANCOCK and AIYB DIENG; not forgetting horn section FRED WESLEY, MACEO PARKER and PEE WEE ELLIS. LASWELL, DUNBAR, COLLINS, WORRELL and poet/novelist WILLIAM BURROUGHS formed the basic line-up for the final MATERIAL studio effort, 'HALLUCINATION ENGINE' (1994), an ambient-influenced affair that signalled the way for BILL's future experiments/projects. In the meantime, LASWELL had expanded his musical CV with the hip-hop influenced PRAXIS and the more extreme JOHN ZORN-initiated PAINKILLER (who unleashed two sets for UK Grindcore/noise label 'Earache'!). The maverick dubstrumentalist had even travelled as far as Morocco, where he recorded two sets of indigenous music centered on the MASTER MUSICIANS OF JAJOUKA. The latter half of the 90's also saw LASWELL work under a plethora of different pseudonyms, the main ones being DEADLINE, DIVINATION and AXIOM FUNK. LASWELL's production work (often sessioning too) was virtually a who's who of 80's rock including HERBIE HANCOCK co-(Future Shock + Sound-System + Village Life + Perfect Machine) / NONA HENDRYX (Nona + The Art Of Defense) / LAURIE ANDERSON co-(Mister Heartbreak) / MICK JAGGER co-(She's The Boss) / LAST POETS (Oh My People) / SLY & ROBBIE (Language Barrier + Rhythm Killers) / YOKO ONO (Star Peace) / PUBLIC IMAGE LTD. co-(Album) / GINGER BAKER (Horses And Trees) / RYUICHI SAKAMOTO co-(Neo Geo) / IGGY POP (Instinct) / AFRIKA BAMBAATAA co-(The Light) / WHITE ZOMBIE (Make Them Die Slowly) / RAMONES co-(Brain Drain) / SWANS co-(Burning The World).

Album rating (selective): Material: TEMPORARY MUSIC 1 & 2 (*6) / MEMORY SERVES (*5) / ONE DOWN (*8) / THE THIRD POWER (*8) / Bill Laswell: BASELINES (*6) / HEAR NO EVIL (*7) / DIVINATION – LIGHTS IN EXTENSION (*6) / INVISIBLE DESIGN (*7) / IMAGINARY CUBA (*6)

BILL LASWELL – bass / **MICHAEL BEINHORN** – keyboards, synthesizers / **FRED MAHER** – drums (ex-RICHARD HELL) / **CLIFF CULTRERI** – guitar / **DON DAVIS** – alto sax

		Red	Red
Sep 79. (12"ep) *(REDEP 001)* <*ZU-EP 100*> **TEMPORARY MUSIC 1**		□	□
– O.A.O. / On sadism / White man / Process – Motion.			
—— w/out CULTRERI + DAVIS who were repl.by **RONNIE DRAYTON** – guitar			
1980. (7") <*RS 004*> **DISCOURSE. / SLOW MURDER**		-	□
Aug 81. (12"ep) <*(RS12 008)*> **TEMPORARY MUSIC TWO**		□	Apr81
– Reduction / Heritage / Secret life / Dark things.			
Oct 81. (lp) <*CEL 6576*> **TEMPORARY MUSIC**		-	□
(UK-imported Mar85; same as US/French)			

	Ze-Island	Celluloid
May 81. (7"; MATERIAL & NONA HENDRYX) *(WIP 6713)* <*CEL 6592*> **BUSTIN' OUT. / OVER AND OVER**	□	□
(12"+=) *(12WIP 6713)* – ('A'long version).		

1981. (12"ep) <*IPR 2052*> **IT'S A HOLIDAY. / THINGS FALL APART**	-	□
(above 'A'&'B' sides with NONA HENDRYX and CHRISTINA respectively)		

—— added **FRED FRITH** – guitar, violin, vibes / **SONNY SHARROCK** – guitar / **HENRY THREADGILL** – alto sax / **GEORGE LEWIS** – trombone / **OLU DARA** – trumpet / **CHARLES K. NOYES** – drums, percussion / **BILLY BANG** – violin

Oct 81. (lp) *(ILPS 9693)* <*CEL 529.812*> **MEMORY SERVES**	□	Feb82
– Memory serves / Disappearing / Upriver / Metal test / Conform to the rhythm / Unauthorized / Square dance / Silent land.		

—— now without MAHER who joined LOU REED

	Red	Ze
Mar 82. (7"/12") <*(RS/+12 011)*> **CIGURI. / DETACHED**	□	□

—— **LASWELL, BEINHORN, FRITH + DRAYTON + NICKY SKOPOLITES** – guitar / **DANIEL PONCE** – bongos / **YOGI HORTON + J.T.LEWIS** – drums / **NICKY MARRERO** – percussion / + guest **WHITNEY HOUSTON** (!)

Sep 82. (7") **I'M THE ONE. /**	-	-

	Elektra	Elektra
Mar 83. (lp) <*E 60206*> **ONE DOWN**	□	□
– Take a chance / I'm the one / Time out / Let me have it all / Come down / Holding on / Memories / Don't lose control.		

—— disbanded while all concentrated on solo and collaborative work including DEADLINE (with PHILIP JOHNSON), CURLEW and MASSACRE (with FRITH)

CURLEW

LASWELL with **GEORGE CARTWRIGHT** – saxes, flute / **TOM CORA** – cello / **NICKY SKOPELITIS** – guitar / **BILL BACON** – drums, percussion

	not iss.	Landslide
1984. (lp) <*LD 1004*> **CURLEW**	-	□
– Panther burn / The bear / Bitter thumbs / The victim / The hard wood / Sports / Bruno / But get it / Rudders / Binoculars / The ole miss exercise song. (UK-iss.Mar85; same as US)		

—— CURLEW continued without LASWELL (FRED FRITH then ANN RUPEL took his place); other sets:- 'NORTH AMERICA' (1985) and 'BEE' (1990)

BILL LASWELL

—— with **MICHAEL BEINHORN** – synthesizers, tapes / **FRED FRITH** – guitar, violin / **MARTIN BISI** – drums, percussion / **RALPH CARNEY** – sax / **RONALD SHANNON JACKSON + PHILIP WILSON** – drums / **DAVID MOSS** – vocals, steel drums / etc.

	Rough Trade	Celluloid
May 84. (lp) *(ROUGH 51)* **BASELINES**	□	1982
– Activate / Work song / Hindsight / Uprising / Barricade / Upright man / Moving target / Lowlands / Conservations. (cd-iss. Apr97 on 'Charly'; CPCD 8284)		
1984. (12") *(MEGA12 8332)* **WORK SONG.** /	□	

—— BILL then recorded in 1985 with JOHN ZORN + METLABLE SNAPS on two German albums 'Points Blank' & 'Metable Snaps'; (No Man's Land; NML 8604)

—— now w / **SKOPELITIS / SHANKAR / PONCE + AIYB DIENG + ZAKIR HUSSAIN** – percussion

	Venture	Venture
Mar 88. (lp/c/cd) *(VE/TCVE/CDVE 12)* **HEAR NO EVIL**	□	□
– Lost roads / Bullet hole memory / Illinois Central / Assassin / Stations of the cross / Kingdom come.		

MATERIAL

—— re-formed with **LASWELL / SKOPELITIS / DIENG / SLY DUNBAR** – drums / **JEFF BOVA** – keyboards / **SHANKAR + SIMON SHAHEEN** – violin / + guest vocalists

	Virgin	Virgin
Jul 89. (cd/c/lp) *(CD/TC+/V 2596)* **SEVEN SOULS**	□	□
– Ineffect / Seven souls / Soul killer / The western lands / Deliver / Equation / The end of words.		

—— LASWELL now just as producer/co-writer (see above biog)

	Axiom	Axiom
Jul 91. (cd/c/lp) <*(AX CD/CT/LPS 3005)*> **THE THIRD POWER**	□	□
– Reality / Playin' with fire / Cosmic slop / E-pluribus-unum / Drive-by / Power of soul (black chant) / Mellow mood / Glory.		
Jul 93. (12"/cd-s; with SHABBA RANKS) *(12AXM/CDAXM 2)* **REALITY.** / **(2-'A'mixes)**	□	□
Jul 93. (12"/cd-s) *(12AXM/AXMCD 1)* **MANTRA.** / **(2-'A'mixes)**	□	□

—— **SLY DUNBAR, BOOTSY COLLINS, BERNIE WORRELL, BILL LASWELL + WILLIAM BURROUGHS**

Feb 94. (cd/lp) *(518351-2/-1)* **HALLUCINATION ENGINE**	□	□
– Black light / Mantra / Ruins / Eternal drift / Words of advice / Cucumber slumber / Hidden garden: Naima.		

– (MATERIAL) compilations, etc. –

Jul 86. (d-lp) *Jungle; (FREUD 11)* **SECRET LIFE 1979-81**	□	-
(re-iss. Aug91 lp/cd; FREUD/+CD 011)		
Mar 94. (cd) *D.I.W.; (DIW 389)* **LIVE FROM SOUNDSCAPE** (live)	□	-

DEADLINE

BILL LASWELL – bass / with **PHILIP WILSON** – drums / **MANU DiBANGO** – saxophone / + guests PAUL BUTTERFIELD + JACO PASTORIUS + STEVE TURRE + ROBERT MUSSO

	Celluloid	not iss.
May 85. (7") *(CEL 704)* **MAKOSSA ROCK.** /	-	- French
Jun 85. (lp/c) *(CEL L/C 6111)* **DOWN BY LAW**	-	- French
– Afro beat / Boat peoples / Baliphone dub / Makossa rock / Gammatron / Doo rot. (cd-iss. Dec93; CELD 6111) (cd re-iss. Jun96 on 'Charly'; CPCD 8192)		

LASWELL with other bassmen, **BOOTSY COLLINS + JONAS HELLBORG** plus **BERNIE WORRELL + JENS JOHANSSEN** – keyboards / **NICKY SKOPELITIS** – guitar / **AIYB DIENG** – percussion

		not iss.	Day Eight

1992. (cd) <DEMCD 027> **DISSIDENT**
– Who's who / Black swans / World disorder / Refrain / Heart of darkness / Stone that speaks / Broken edge.

DIVINATION

LASWELL + JEFF BOVA, NICKY SKOPELITIS, ROBERT MUSSO, BUCKETHEAD + LIU SOLA

		Stoned Heights	Subharmonic

Oct 93. (cd) <SBM 7001> **AMBIENT DUB VOLUME 1**
– Divination one / Seven heavens / Erratta / Delta / Tian zhen / Agrippa / Godspeed / Ain soph sour.

—— JAH WOBBLE + MICK HARRIS repl. NICKY, BUCKETHEAD + LIU

Jan 94. (cd) <SBM 7003> **AMBIENT DUB VOLUME 2: DEAD SLOW**
– Dead slow / Baraka / Silent fields / Evil eye / Dream light / Journeys.
Jun 94. (SHCDD 001) **DIVINATION – LIGHT IN EXTENSION**
– (above tracks +) Na-jam-al-din / The last words of Hassan I Sabbath.

—— LASWELL now with ANTON FIER – drums / HAROUMI HOSONO + MICK HARRIS
1995. (d-cd) <SBM 7011> **AKASHA**
– Descent / Rain dream / Ascesis / Stir / Tangier space draft / Navigations / Illuminoid assassin.
Feb 96. (d-cd) <SBM 9803> **DISTILL**
– Green evil / Subharmonic invocation of the dark . . . . / Ether vibes / There / Zone / Blue filter / Interlink / Laswell, Bill.

AXIOM FUNK

LASWELL + BOOTSY COLLINS, BERNIE WORRELL, GEORGE CLINTON, MACEO PARKER, FRED WESLEY, SLY STONE, SLY & ROBBIE, NICKY SKOPELITIS, ROBERT MUSSO, ZIGGY MODELESTE, AIYB DIENG, BOBBY BYRD, HERBIE HANCOCK, ANTON FIER, GARY MUDDBONE COOPER + now deceased guitarist EDDIE HAZEL

		Axiom	Axiom

Nov 94. (d-cd/lp) <(524053-2/-1)> **AXIOM AMBIENT – LOST IN THE TRANSLATION**
– Eternal drift / Peace [cd-only] / Aum / Cosmic trigger [cd-only] / Dharmapala / Flash of panic [cd-only] / Holy mountain / Ruins [cd-only] / Eternal drift (techno mix) [lp-only] / Aum (drift mix) [lp-only].
Aug 95. (d-cd/d-c) <(524077-2/-4)> **FUNKCRONOMICON**   Jul95
– Order within the universe / Under the influence (Jes crew) / If 6 was 9 / Orbitron attack / Cosmic slop / Gree-base (Godzillatron cush) / Tell the world / Pray my soul / Hideous mutant freekz / Sax machine / Animal behavior / Trumpets and violins, violins / Telling time / Jungle free-bass / Blackout / Sacred to the pain.

—— In Oct'95, LASWELL was credited on MJ HARRIS cd 'SOMNIFIC FLUX' for 'Sentrax'.

BILL LASWELL

—— note: chronological sequence not adhered to at times (sorry)

		Sub Rosa	East Side Digital

Oct 96. (m-lp) (SR 109V) **OSCILLATIONS**
(re-iss. Sep97; QUANTUM 726)
Jul 97. (cd) (SR 114) <ESD 11> **CITY OF LIGHT**
– Nothing / Kala / Kashi / Above the Earth.
Oct 97. (cd/d-lp) <(SR 122 CD/V)> **OSCILLATIONS** (remixes featuring other artists)
Jun 98. (cd) (SR/+C 133) **OSCILLATIONS VOL.2: ADVANCED DRUM N BASS**
– Virus / Autopia / El hombre invisible / Red night.
Feb 99. (cd; as BILL LASWELL PROJECT) (SR 154) **HASHISHEEN**

		R.O.I.R.	R.O.I.R.

Jul 96. (cd) (RUSCD 821) <8225> **SACRED SYSTEM, CHAPTER ONE: BOOK OF ENTRANCE**
– Babylon ghost / Dread internal / Cyborg assault / Galactic zone / Sub terrain.
(re-iss. Feb99 as 'NAGUAL SITE' on 'Wicklow'; 09026 63263-2) (check this)

		Word Sound	Word Sound

1996. (cd; as BILL LASWELL, MICK HARRIS & ERALDO BERNOCCHI) **EQUATIONS OF ETERNITY**
– Collector / Eons geography / 5th element / Loa / Stream / Shadow sewer / Fifty gates / Descent / Slow bleed.
Jan 97. (cd; as BILL LASWELL, MICK HARRIS & ERALDO BERNOCCHI) <(WSCD 015)> **EQUATIONS OF ETERNITY, VOL.2: VEVE**   Aug98
– Baron Samedi / Magamat / Kurukulla / Luk krok / Set rising / Aether / Madre de agua / Yama / Maka.
1997. (cd) <WSCD 021> **SACRED SYSTEM, CHAPTER TWO**
– Thunupa / Anubis / Purana / Akapana.

		Douglas	Douglas

Jul 97. (cd) <(ADC 7)> **ASANA**
– Devabandha / Om namah shiva / Mantra.

		Triloka	Triloka

Jan 99. (cd/d-lp; as MATERIAL & WILLIAM BURROUGHS) <(3145 589021-2/-1)> **ROAD TO WESTERN ROADS**

		Felmay	Felmay

Jan 99. (cd; as BILL LASWELL, ERALDO BERNOCCHI & The TIBETAN MONKS) <(FY 8013CD)> **SOMMA I (HOOKED LIGHT RAYS)**

		Tzadik	Tzadik

Feb 99. (cd) <(TZA 7044)> **INVISIBLE DESIGN**
– Black aether / Commander Guevara / Oceans of borrowed money / Aisha / Night air & low frequency / White are spiral / Aghora.

		Wicklow	Wicklow

Oct 99. (cd) <(09026 63514-2)> **IMAGINARY CUBA**
– Habana transmission #1 – Avisale a la vecina / Para clave y guaguanco / Loungin' with F.E. / Chacon and Daniel / Dejala en la puntica / Habana transmission #2 – Cuban evolution / Los ibellis / Habana transmission #3 – Shango sound scan / Hombre lobo, no! hombre nuevo, si / Guerillero heroico / Shango / Pompa at the house / Madre no me pida in dub / Chaos in the heat / Drafting shadows – Leaving la Habana.

– others, etc. –

1996. (cd) Cleopatra; <8508> **DARK MASSIVE: AMBIENT COMPENDIUM**
– "Fractint" / Descent / Maps of impossible worlds / Angel tech / Aion / Monochrome existence / Open Uri / Distal sonority / Broken dream / "Fractint" / Tangier space draft / Black dawn / Evil eye / Ports of entry / Ancient evenings / Zurvan akarana / Asiyah dub / White lies.
Nov 96. (cd; by BILL LASWELL – PETE NAMLOOK) efa; <24> **PSYCHONAVIGATION VOL.2**
– Under Heaven / Blue shift / Fate of energy / Hell of the same / Infinium.
Nov 96. (cd; by BILL LASWELL – PETE NAMLOOK) efa; <28> **OUTLAND, VOL2**
– African virus part I-VI.
Jun 97. (cd) Movieplay Gold; (MPG 74043) **INTO THE OUTLANDS**
– Voice of thunder / Speed of light.
Jul 97. (cd) APC Tracks; (APC 003) **PHAT DUB VOL.1**
Jul 97. (cd) APC Tracks; (APC 004) **PHAT DUB VOL.2**
Aug 97. (cd/lp; BILL LASWELL meets STYLE SCOTT) (EFA 01221-2/-1) **DUB MELTDOWN**
– Crooklyn dub syndicate / Fourth column / Aeon / Emergency at the planet / Radioactive dub / Fallout / A greater source of power / Melting pot dub.
Jul 98. (cd; by BILL LASWELL – PETE NAMLOOK) efa; <20549> **OUTLAND, VOL.3**
– Definition of life / Question of containment / Keeper of the purple twilight / DSTC.
Jul 98. (12") Douglas; <17> **MOODY'S MOOD FOR LOVE**
Aug 98. (cd) Douglas; **JAZZONIA**
– Moody's mood for love / Little boy don't get scared / Swan blues / I'm gone / Blue / Cottontail / Angel eyes / Twisted / Fade.
Oct 98. (cd) Meta; <2> **DIVINATION: SACRIFICE**
– Reflection / Waterbass / Still / Airbass.
Jan 99. (cd; as BILL LASWELL – PETE NAMLOOK – KLAUS SCHULZE) efa; <4326> **DARK SIDE OF THE MOOG VII**
– Obscured by Klaus (6 versions).
Feb 99. (cd) A.P.C.; <15> **BONICHE DUB**
– Alger Alger dub / Amir Leghram dub / Mezelt ma jetch dub / Yakhalbi Khali l'Hal dub / Saadi rite Elbarrah dub / Je chanterai toujours la musique orientale / Touchia rem-el-maya.
Jun 99. (cd; as BILL LASWELL – PETE NAMLOOK) efa; <108> **PSYCHONAVIGATION 4**
– Arena / Samira / Entib 2060 / The good and bad.

LAUGHING CLOWNS / Ed KUEPPER

(dig out; Great Alt & Indie . . .)

Cyndi LAUPER

Born: CYNTHIA LAUPER, 22 Jun'53, New York City, New York, USA. Raised by her mother in the Italian district of Queens following her parents' divorce, she dropped out of high school before hitch-hiking across Canada. Her music career began with a position as lead singer of Long Island band, DOC WEST although she soon quit to join FLYER. Having never been professionally trained as a vocalist, she was on the brink of permanently damaging her voice and sought out tuition before forming BLUE ANGEL in 1979 alongside JOHN TURI. An earthy rock outfit that amassed a sizeable fanbase around the New York area, they briefly signed to 'Polydor' and released a solitary eponymous album before the whole project fell apart. Declaring herself bankrupt, LAUPER returned to playing clubs although a chance meeting with manager David Wolff in 1982 led to a long-term professional and personal partnership. The following year he secured her a solo deal with CBS subsidiary, 'Portrait', her classic debut single, 'GIRLS JUST WANT TO HAVE FUN', emerging to huge transatlantic success that Christmas. A joyously upbeat paean to female frivolity, the track made No.2 in both Britain and America while the video utilised the new medium of MTV to present LAUPER as a wide-eyed, tousle-haired rebel-child, her squeaky, Noo Yoik voice (though often tempted, she never took elocution lessons) only adding (or not, depending which way you look at it) to her eccentric charm. Her debut album, 'SHE'S SO UNUSUAL' followed hot on its heels although the UK release wasn't until January '84. A spirited collection of effervescent uptempo pop/rock and ballad material all executed in her uniquely extrovert style, it climbed into both the US & UK Top 20, eventually going on to sell in its millions following the success of four consecutive US Top 5 hits. Save 'GIRLS . . .', chief among these was 'TIME AFTER TIME', a tender love song with a slow-burning intensity that saw it top the US chart. Sophomore effort, 'TRUE COLORS' (1986) was almost as successful, a more sophisticated effort that spawned another No.1 single with the torch song title track, while a cover of Marvin Gaye's 'WHAT'S GOIN' ON' made the US Top 20. Despite being castigated by right wing religious groups for the supposed adult nature of the 'SHE BOP' single (from 1984), LAUPER converted to Christianity prior to the release of her third set, 'NIGHT TO REMEMBER' (1989). While it spawned the transatlantic Top 10 hit, 'I DROVE ALL NIGHT' (subsequently a posthumous hit for ROY ORBISON), the record came in for a critical pasting and only just made the Top 40 in her homeland (Top 10 in the UK).

A difficult period for the ageing rebel, both her personal and professional partnership with Wolff came to an end while a further venture into acting again bore little commercial fruit. 'HAT FULL OF STARS' (1993) was similarly unsuccessful despite representing her most mature and considered work to date with contributions from the likes of MARY-CHAPIN CARPENTER, old mates The HOOTERS and even New York club guru JUNIOR VASQUEZ. Now more successful in Britain than the States, she scored a UK Top 5 hit in 1994 with '(HEY NOW) GIRLS JUST WANT TO HAVE FUN', a reggae-fied remake of her old chestnut that spurred on sales of cheesily titled retrospective, '12 DEADLY CYNS . . . AND THEN SOME' (1994). With the help of co-writer and producer Jan Pulsford, she finally re-emerged with new material in the shape of 1997's 'SISTERS OF AVALON', again ignored by America but spawning a Top 30 hit in Britain with 'YOU DON'T KNOW'. • **Covers & outside writers:** GIRLS JUST WANT TO HAVE FUN (Robert Hazard) / ALL THROUGH THE NIGHT + STEADY (Jules Shear) / TRUE COLORS (Kelly-Steinberg) / WHEN YOU WERE MINE (Prince) / IKO IKO (hit; Dixie Cups) / CHANGE OF HEART (Essra Mohawk) / etc. • **Trivia:** Jazz legend, MILES DAVIS covered her US No.1 'TIME AFTER TIME'. In 1990, she guested on ROGER WATERS 'The Wall' concert in Berlin.

Album rating: BLUE ANGEL; by Blue Angel (*4) / SHE'S SO UNUSUAL (*7) / TRUE COLORS (*5) / A NIGHT TO REMEMBER (*4) / HAT FULL OF STARS (*4) / TWELVE DEADLY CYNS . . . AND THEN SOME compilation (*7) / SISTERS OF AVALON (*5)

BLUE ANGEL

were formed by **CYNDI LAUPER** – vocals / **JOHN TURI** – saxophone, keyboards / plus **ARTHUR NEILSON** – guitar / **LEE BROVITZ** – bass / **JOHN MORELLI** – drums

			Polydor	Polydor
Feb 81.	(lp) *(2391 486)* **BLUE ANGEL**			

– Maybe he'll know / I have a love / Fade / Anna Blue / Cut out / Can't blame me / Late / Take a chance. / Just the other day / I'm gonna be strong / Lorraine / Everybody's got an angel.

Jan 81.	(7") *(POSP 211)* **I'M GONNA BE STRONG. / ANNA BLUE**		
Apr 81.	(7") *(POSP 241)* **I HAVE A LOVE. / CAN'T BLAME ME**		

—— they had already split by the time of the above UK releases

CYNDI LAUPER

—— went solo; augmented at first by The HOOTERS

		Portrait	Portrait
Jan 84.	(7") *(A 3943)* <04120> **GIRLS JUST WANT TO HAVE FUN. / RIGHT TRACK WRONG TRAIN**	**2**	**2** Dec83
	(12"+=) *(TA 3943)* – Witness.		
	(US-12"+=) – Money changes everything.		
Feb 84.	(lp/c) *(PRT/40 25792)* <38930> **SHE'S SO UNUSUAL**	**16**	**4** Dec83

– Money changes everything / Girls just want to have fun / When you were mine / Time after time / She bop / All through the night / Witness / I'll kiss you / He's so unusual / Yeah yeah. *(cd-iss. 1988; CD 25792) (re-iss. Feb89 on 'Epic' lp/c/cd; 463362-1/-4/-2)*

Mar 84.	(7"/7"pic-d) *(A/WA 4290)* <04432> **TIME AFTER TIME. / I'LL KISS YOU**	**3**	**1** Apr84
	(12") *(TA 4290)* – ('A'side) / Girls just want to have fun (extended) / Fun with V. Knutz (instrumental).		
Aug 84.	(7"/7"pic-d/12") *(T/WA/TA 4620)* <04516> **SHE BOP. / WITNESS**	**46**	**3** Jul84
Nov 84.	(7"/12") *(A/TA 4849)* <04639> **ALL THROUGH THE NIGHT. / WITNESS**	**64**	**5** Sep84
Dec 84.	(7") <04737> **MONEY CHANGES EVERYTHING. / ('A'live)**	**–**	**27**
Feb 85.	(7") *(A 6009)* **MONEY CHANGES EVERYTHING. / HE'S SO UNUSUAL**		**–**
	(12"+=) *(TX 6009)* – Yeah yeah / Girls just want to have fun.		
	(12") *(TA 6009)* – ('A'live version) / Extra fun (live).		
Jun 85.	(7") *(PRT 6139)* <04918> **THE GOONIES 'R' GOOD ENOUGH. / WHAT A THRILL**		**10** May85
	(above from the film 'The Goonies')		
Aug 86.	(7") <06247> **TRUE COLORS. / HEADING FOR THE MOON**	**–**	**1**
Sep 86.	(7") *(650026-7)* **TRUE COLOURS. / MONEY CHANGES EVERYTHING**	**12**	**–**
	(12"+=) *(650026-0)* – Heading for the moon.		
Oct 86.	(lp/c/cd) *(PRT/TCPRT/CDPRT 26948)* <40313> **TRUE COLORS**	**25**	**4** Sep86

– Change of heart / Maybe he'll know / Boy blue / True colors / Calm inside the storm / What's going on / Iko Iko / The faraway nearby / 911 / One track mind. *(cd re-iss. Aug90; 462493-2)*

Nov 86.	(7") <06431> **CHANGE OF HEART. / WITNESS**	**–**	**3**
Dec 86.	(7") *(CYNDI 1)* **CHANGE OF HEART / WHAT A THRILL**	**67**	**–**
	(ext-12"+=) *(CYNDI 1T)* – Heartbeat.		
Mar 87.	(7"/7"pic-d) *(CYN/+P 1)* <06970> **WHAT'S GOING ON. / ONE TRACK MIND**	**57**	**12**
	(d7"+=) *(CYND 1)* – Change of heart / What a thrill.		
	(12") *(CYNT 1)* – ('A'extended) / ('A'instrumental) / ('A'club).		
Jul 87.	(7") *(CYN 2)* <07181> **BOY BLUE. / THE FARAWAY NEARBY**		**71** Jun87
	(12"+=) *(CYNT 2)* – Time after time.		

		Epic	Epic
Jul 88.	(7") *(CYN 3)* <07940> **HOLE IN MY HEART (ALL THE WAY TO CHINA). / BOY BLUE (live)**		**54** Jun88
	(12"+=/cd-s+=) *(CYN T/C 3)* – ('A'extended).		
May 89.	(7"/7"pic-d/c-s) *(CYN/+P/M 4)* <68759> **I DROVE ALL NIGHT. / MAYBE HE'LL KNOW**	**7**	**6** Apr89
	(12"+=) *(CYNT 4)* – Boy blue (live).		
	(cd-s++=) *(CYNC 4)* – Girls just want to have fun.		
	(cd-s+=) *(CYNCD 4)* – What's going on (club version) / Time after time.		
Jun 89.	(lp/c/cd) *(462499-1/-4/-2)* <44318> **A NIGHT TO REMEMBER**	**9**	**37** May89

– I drove all night / Primitive / My first night without you / Like a cat / Heading west /

A night to remember / Unconditional love / Insecurious / Dancing like a stranger / I don't want to be your friend / Kindred spirit.

Jul 89.	(7"/c-s) *(CYN/+M 5)* <68945> **MY FIRST NIGHT WITHOUT YOU. / UNABBREVIATED LOVE**	**53**	**62**
	(12"+=/cd-s+=) *(CYN T/C 5)* – True colours / All through the night.		
	(3"cd-s+=) *(655091-2)* – Iko Iko / When you were mine.		
Nov 89.	(7"/c-s) *(CYN/+M 6)* **HEADING WEST. / INSECURIOUS**	**68**	
	(12"+=/12"pic-d+=/cd-s+=) *(CYN T/TC/CD 6)* – She bop (live) / Money changes everything (live).		

—— In 1991, she starred in the film 'Off And Running'.

—— Below she was from the film 'Starmania' which changed title to 'Tycoon'.

May 92.	(7") *(657970-7)* **THE WORLD IS STONE. / LEARN TO LEAVE ALONE**	**15**	
	(cd-s+=) *(657970-2)* – Time after time.		
	(cd-s+=) *(657970-5)* – What's going on.		
Nov 93.	(c-s) *(659894-7)* **THAT'S WHAT I THINK / ('A'mix)**	**31**	
	(12"+=/cd-s+=) *(659879-6/-2)* – ('A'extra mixes – 3 dub).		
	(cd-s) *(659879-5)* – ('A'side) / I drove all night / True colours / Girls just want to have fun.		
Nov 93.	(cd/c/lp) *(473054-2/-4/-1)* <52878> **HAT FULL OF STARS**	**56**	Jun93

– That's what I think / Product of misery / Who let in the rain / Lies / Broken glass / Sally's pigeons / Feels like Christmas / Dear John / Like I used to / Someone like me / A part hate / Hat full of stars.

Jan 94.	(7"/c-s) *(659039-7/-4)* **WHO LET IN THE RAIN. / COLD**	**32**	
	(cd-s+=) *(659039-2)* – Like I used to.		
	(cd-s) *(659039-5)* – ('A'side) / Girls just want to have fun (remix) / That's what I think (deep mix) / Girls just want to have fun.		
Aug 94.	(cd/c) *(477363-2/-4)* <66100> **TWELVE DEADLY CYNS . . . AND THEN SOME** (compilation)	**2**	**81** Jul95

– I'm gonna be strong / Girls just want to have fun / Money changes everything / Time after time / She bop / All through the night / Change of heart / True colors / What's going on / I drove all night / The world is stone / Who let in the rain / That's what I think / Sally's pigeons / Hey now (girls just want to have fun) / Come on home.

Sep 94.	(c-s) *(660807-4)* **(HEY NOW) GIRLS JUST WANT TO HAVE FUN / ('A'mix)**	**4**	**–**
	(cd-s+=) *(660807-2)* – ('A'mixes).		
Jan 95.	(c-s) *(661196-4)* **I'M GONNA BE STRONG / A PART HATE**	**37**	
	(cd-s+=) *(661196-5)* – Product of misery.		
	(cd-s) *(661196-2)* – ('A'side) / Broken glass / Dear John.		
Jul 95.	(c-s) *(661424-4)* **COME ON HOME / HEY NOW (GIRLS JUST WANT TO HAVE FUN)**	**39**	**–**
	(cd-s+=) *(661424-2)* – ('A'-Junior's soundfactory version) / ('A'-Techno mix).		
	(c-s/cd-s) *(661425-4/-2)* – (6 different 'A'mixes; incl. Techno dub / Jungle box).		
Aug 95.	(c-s) <77967> **HEY NOW (GIRLS JUST WANT TO HAVE FUN) / WHO LET IN THE RAIN**	**–**	**87**

—— she now used a host of musicians including co-writer and producer **JAN PULSFORD**

Jan 97.	(c-s/cd-s) *(664184-4/-2)* **YOU DON'T KNOW / MOTHER**	**27**	
	(cd-s) *(664184-5)* – ('A'side) / Time after time / True colours / I drove all night.		
Feb 97.	(cd/c) *(485370-2/-4)* **SISTERS OF AVALON**	**59**	

– Sisters of Avalon / Ballad of Cleo & Joe / Fall into your dreams / You don't know / Love to hate / Hot gets a little cold / Unhook the stars / Searching / Say a prayer / Mother / Fearless / Brimstone and fire.

– compilations etc. –

Sep 86.	(c) *Portrait; (PRT 450129-4)* **THE 12" TAPE** (12"mixes)		**–**
	– Girls just want to have fun / Time after time / She bop / All through the night / Money changes everything.		
Sep 92.	(7"/c-s) *Epic; (658320-7/-4)* **GIRLS JUST WANT TO HAVE FUN. /**		**–**
	(cd-s+=) *(658320-2)* –		
	(cd-s+=) *(658320-5)* –		
Oct 94.	(3xcd-box) *Epic; (471622-2)* **A NIGHT TO REMEMBER / SHE'S SO UNUSUAL / TRUE COLOURS**		
	(re-iss. Nov97; 485322-2)		
Feb 95.	(d-cd) *Epic; (478483-2)* **SHE'S SO UNUSUAL / A NIGHT TO REMEMBER**		

LAW (see under ⇒ RODGERS, Paul)

LEADBELLY

Born: HUDSON WILLIAM LEDBETTER, 29th of January, 1889, Mooringsport, Los Angeles, USA. A blues legend in his own right, HUDDIE LEDBETTER displayed a unique musical talent at an early age and had ambition beyond range or scope. When he was 13, he had managed to learn to read and write (a very difficult thing to achieve for a black man at the start of the century) and had a substantial grasp on the ethics of guitar playing and performing. The teenager spent most of his nights wandering aimlessly through the red light districts and town squares on his home turf, attracting an audience with his own take-on of popular blues and spiritual music. After his marriage soured in the first decade of the 20th century, LEADBELLY changed his guitar format from 6-string to 12-string, a choice that bettered his career and enabled him to broaden his musical style. He re-worked a traditional song called 'IRENE', which became one of his most treasured songs, and impressed BLIND LEMON JEFFERSON so much that he decided to teach LEADBELLY slide guitar. However, success was not forthcoming, and due to his violent outbursts LEADBELLY constantly found himself on the wrong side of the law. In 1917, he was given a life sentence for murder and was sent to Texas

State prison, where, ironically, he wrote his best material. His songs became increasingly popular with the prison inmates and governors, and in 1925, the man performed for one particular Texas governor who subsequently pardoned the enigmatic guitarist. When he was released from prison, LEADBELLY tried his best to keep on a straight path by doing odd and regular jobs. He was arrested again in 1930 and sentenced to life imprisonment for attempted murder. In Louisiana prison he met John Lomax (a travelling researcher for the Library of Congress) who was gathering Americana and blues-related music with his son. Lomax was more than impressed with LEADBELLY's talents and managed to record material on his small portable studio in prison. In 1934, Lomax persuaded the Congress to free the bluesman, and with the aid of father and son, he became a minor hero in the white community. Lomax subsequently booked LEADBELLY for sessions at the "American record company", which brought coherence to his creations with smooth, clean and professionally recorded songs. However, LEADBELLY's relationship with Lomax was on the rocks due to manipulative and manufactured concerts where he was forced to dress up in a striped prison uniform; ultimately a gimmick to spread LEADBELLY's notoriety. Their partnership expired with LEADBELLY subsequently flitting to New York City in search of a more respectful audience – and that he found. Members of the Bohemian intelligentsia and folk/roots fans created a huge and almost cult following which attracted the attention of Moe Asch, manager of 'Folkway' records. It was here that perhaps the man's finest works were drawn: songs depicting the horrors of World War II were particularly ahead of their time. He continued to record for Asch and 'Capitol' records throughout the 40's although inevitably he fell ill and died on the 6th of December 1949. In his final encore at Texas University he promised the audience he would return, explaining his new doctor would help him make a speedy recovery. Sadly, this was untrue as LEADBELLY died a month later. Like many blues legends, fame came to LEADBELLY in death: The WEAVERS had a hit single with their rendition of 'GOODNIGHT IRENE' in 1951, while skiffle-king LONNIE DONEGAN also had a hit with 'ROCK ISLAND LINE' in 1957. Most memorably and most recent was when KURT COBAIN performed a poignant, gut-wrenching version of 'WHERE DID YOU SLEEP LAST NIGHT'. As always, the legend lives on . . .

Best CD compilation: THE VERY BEST OF LEADBELLY (*8)

LEADBELLY – vocals, acoustic guitar

		not iss.	Mus
1939.	(78) <223> FRANKIE AND ALBERT. / unknown	-	
1939.	(78) <224> FRANKIE AND ALBERT. / unknown	-	
1939.	(78) <225> FANNIN STREET. / unknown	-	
1939.	(78) <226> DE KALB BLUES. / THE BOLL WEEVIL	-	
1939.	(78) <227> THE GALLIS POLE. / THE BOURGEOIS BLUES	-	

		not iss.	Victory
1940.	(78) <27266> HAM AN' EGGS. / MIDNIGHT SPECIAL	-	
1940.	(78) <27267> GREY GOOSE. / STEW-BALL	-	
1940.	(78) <27268> ALABAMA BOUND. / PICK A BALE OF COTTON		
	(UK-iss.1955 on 'H.M.V.'; MH 190)		

		not iss.	Bluebird
1940.	(78) <B 8550> DON'T YOU LOVE YOUR DADDY NO MORE? / SAIL ON, LITTLE GIRL, SAIL ON	-	
1940.	(78) <B 8559> T.B. BLUES. / ALBERTA	-	
1940.	(78) <B 8570> WORRIED BLUES. / EASY RIDER	-	
1941.	(78) <B 8709> RED CROSS STORE BLUES. / ROBERTA	-	
1941.	(78) <B 8750> YOU CAN'T LOSE-A ME CHOLLY. / NEW YORK CITY	-	
1941.	(78) <B 8791> GOOD MORNING BLUES. / LEAVING BLUES	-	
1941.	(78) <B 8981> I'M ON MY LAST GO ROUND. /	-	

		not iss.	Asch
1941.	(78) <SC 26/27> HA HA THISAWAY. / LITTLE SALLY WALKER	-	
1941.	(78) <SC 32/34> REDBIRD. / CHRISTMAS SONG	-	
1941.	(78) <SC 79/80> SKIP TO MY LOU. / YOU CAN'T LOSE ME CHOLLY	-	
1942.	(78) <101> TAKE THIS HAMMER. / CORN BREAD ROUGH	-	
1942.	(78) <102> ROCK ISLAND LINE. / OL' RILEY	-	
1942.	(78) <103> OLD MAN. / HAUL AWAY, JOE	-	
1943.	(78) <343-1> HOW LONG BLUES. / GOOD MORNING BLUES	-	
	(UK-iss.1951 on 'Melodisc'; 1140)		
1943.	(78) <343-2> IRENE. / AIN'T YOU GLAD	-	
	(UK-iss.1951 on 'Melodisc'; 1151) – 'A'side 'GOODNIGHT IRENE'		
1943.	(78) <343-3> ON A MONDAY. / JOHN HENRY	-	
	(UK-iss.1951 on 'Melodisc'; 1187)		
1944.	(78) <561-1> MEETING AT THE BUILDING. / BRING ME A LIL' WATER SYLVIE	-	
1944.	(78) <561-2> PLAYING WITH YOUR POODLE. / FIDDLER'S DRAM	-	
1944.	(78) <561-3> BIG FAT WOMAN. / JOHN HARDY	-	

		not iss.	Musicraft
1944.	(78> <310> YELLOW GAL. / WHEN THE BOYS WERE ON THE WESTERN PLAIN	-	
1944.	(78) <311> ROBERTA. / JOHN HARDY	-	
1944.	(78) <312> IN NEW ORLEANS. / (BLACK GIRL) WHERE DID YOU SLEEP LAST NIGHT	-	
1944.	(78) <313> BILL BRADY. / PRETTY FLOWER IN MY BACKYARD	-	

		not iss.	Asch
1944.	(78) <331-1> LITTLE SALLY WALKER. / MO' YET	-	
1944.	(78) <331-2> HOW DO YOU KNOW. / SKIP TO MY LOU	-	
1944.	(78) <331-3> (WHAT ARE) LITTLE BOYS (MADE OF). / MOTHER'S BLUES	-	

		Capitol	not iss.
1945.	(78) <40038> SWEET MARY BLUES. / GRASSHOPPERS IN MY PILLOW	-	
1945.	(78) <40130> BACKWATER BLUES. / IRENE	-	
1945.	(78) <15628> ROCK ISLAND LINE. / Nappy Lamare: HIGH SOCIETY	-	
1945.	(78) <15629> EAGLE ROCK RAG. / Nappy Lamare: AT THE JAZZ BAND BALL	-	

		not iss.	Disc
1945.	(78) <6043> MIDNIGHT SPECIAL. / HAM AND EGGS	-	
1945.	(78) <6044> YELLOW GAL. / GRAY GOOSE	-	
1945.	(78) <6045> STEW BALL. / ALABAMY BOUND	-	

—— LEADBELLY continued to record until he died on the 6th of Dec'49

– compilations, others, etc. –

on 'Melodisc' unless mentioned otherwise

1950.	(78) Capitol; (CL 13282) EAGLE ROCK RAG. / BACKWATER BLUES	
1950.	(78) Tempo; (R 11) BECKY BEEM, SHE WAS A GAMBLIN' GAL. / PIG MEAT PAPA	
	(re-iss. 1955 on 'Jazz Collector'; L 124)	
1950.	(78) Tempo; (R 13) FOUR DAY WORRY BLUES. / NEW BLACK SNAKE MOAN	
	(re-iss. 1954 on 'Jazz Collector'; L 108)	
1950.	(78) Tempo; (R 16) DIGGIN' MY POTATOES. / DEFENSE BLUES	
1953.	(10"lp) Capitol; (LC 6597) LEADBELLY SINGS CLASSICS IN JAZZ	
1956.	(7"ep) (EPM7 63) HOW LONG BLUES	
1957.	(10"lp) (MLP 511) LEADBELLY MEMORIAL ALBUM VOL.1	
1957.	(10"lp) (MLP 512) LEADBELLY MEMORIAL ALBUM VOL.2	
1958.	(10"lp) (MLP 515) LEADBELLY MEMORIAL ALBUM VOL.3	
1958.	(7"ep) (EPM7 77) LEADBELLY	
1958.	(7"ep) (EPM7 82) SEE SEE RIDER	
1958.	(10"lp) (MLP 517) PLAYS PARTY SONGS	
1959.	(7"ep) (EPM7 87) PARTY PLAYS AND SONGS	
1959.	(lp) (MLP12 107) THE SAGA OF LEADBELLY	
1959.	(lp) (MLP12 113) LEADBELLY'S LAST SESSIONS VOLUME 2 PART 1	-
1959.	(lp) (MLP12 114) LEADBELLY'S LAST SESSIONS VOLUME 2 PART 2	-
1959.	(7"ep) R.C.A.; (RCX 146) ROCK ISLAND LINE	-
1960.	(lp) Folkways; <FC 7533> NEGRO FOLK SONGS FOR YOUNG PEOPLE	
1961.	(7"ep) Capitol; (EAP1 20111) LEADBELLY	
1961.	(7"ep; shared with BLIND LEMON JEFFERSON) Jazz Collector; (JEL 124) THE MALE BLUES VOLUME 8	
1962.	(lp) Folkways; <FA 2024> LEGACY VOL.3	
1962.	(lp) Folkways; <FA 2034> LEGACY VOL.4 – "EASY RIDER"	
1962.	(lp) Storyville; (SLP 124) A DEMON OF A MAN – BLUES ANTHOLOGY VOL.7	-
	(re-iss. 1969 as 'IN THE EVENING WHEN THE SUN GOES DOWN' on 'Storyville'; 616 003)	
1962.	(7"ep) Storyville; (SEP 337) LEADBELLY BLUES ANTHOLOGY	
1963.	(lp) Storyville; (SLP 139) LEADBELLY 2 – T.B. BLUES	
	(re-iss. 1969 as 'GOODNIGHT IRENE' on 'Storyville'; 616 004)	
1963.	(lp) Capitol; (T 1821) HIS GUITAR, HIS VOICE, HIS PIANO: HUDDIE LEDBETTER'S BEST	-
1963.	(7"ep) Capitol; (EAP1 1821) HUDDIE LEDBETTER'S BEST NO.1	
1963.	(7"ep) Capitol; (EAP4 1821) HUDDIE LEDBETTER'S BEST VOL.2	
1963.	(lp) RCA Victor; (RD 7567) GOOD MORNING BLUES	
1965.	(lp; stereo/mono) Verve; (S+/VLP 5002) / Folkways; <FTS 31019> TAKE THIS HAMMER	
1965.	(lp) Society; (SOC 994) LEADBELLY PLAYS AND SINGS	
1966.	(d-lp) Elektra; <(EKL 301-2)> THE LIBRARY OF CONGRESS RECORDINGS	
1967.	(lp; stereo/mono) Verve; (S+/VLP 5011) KEEP YOUR HANDS OFF HER	-
1967.	(t-lp) Folkways; <FA 2941> LAST SESSIONS VOL.1	-
1967.	(t-lp) Folkways; <FA 2942> LAST SESSIONS VOL.2	-
1968.	(d-lp) Xtra; (XTRAD 1017) THE LEADBELLY BOX SET	
1969.	(lp) Xtra; (XTRA 1046) / Folkways; <FTS 31006> LEADBELLY SINGS FOLK SONGS	1968
	(re-iss. Aug95 on 'Smithsonian Folkways' cd/c; SFW CD/MC 40010)	
1970.	(lp) C.B.S.; (64103) / Columbia; <C 30035> LEADBELLY	-
1971.	(lp) Xtra; (XTRA 1126) / Folkways; <FTS 31030> SHOUT ON	-
1972.	(lp) Ember; (CW 132) / Folkmusic; <FS 202> LEADBELLY	1969
1973.	(lp) Playboy; <PB 119> LEADBELLY	-
1976.	(lp) Folkways; <FTS 31046> MIDNIGHT SPECIAL	-
1978.	(lp) Capitol; <SM 1821> LEADBELLY BEST	-
Oct 86.	(lp/c) Deja Vu; (DVLP/DVMC 2072) THE COLLECTION: 20 BLUES GREATS	
Feb 87.	(lp/c) Spartan; (SMPC/SPMC 5001) LAST SESSIONS VOL.1	
Oct 87.	(lp) Blue Moon; (BMLP 1038) EARLY MORNING BLUES	
Jan 88.	(c) Demand Performance; (DPC 405) LEGENDARY LEADBELLY	
Apr 88.	(lp) Travellin' Man; (TM 810) LEADBELLY 1935	
Jun 88.	(lp) Bluetime; (BT 2011) GOOD MORNING BLUES	
	(cd-iss. Nov94 on 'Indigo'; IGOCD 2007) (cd re-iss. Oct95 on 'Topaz Jazz'; TPZ 1029)	
Feb 89.	(lp) Document; (DLP 544) LEADBELLY 1934-46	-

Jan 90. (cd/c/lp) *Bluebird; (ND/NK/NL 90321)* **ALABAMA BOUND**

Jun 90. (lp/cd) *Aldabra; (ALB 1004/+CD)* **CONVICT BLUES**

Nov 91. (cd/c) *Columbia; <(467893-2/-4)>* **KING OF THE TWELVE STRING GUITAR**

Feb 92. (cd) *Rounder; <(ROUCD 1044)>* **MIDNIGHT SPECIAL (LIBRARY OF CONGRESS RECORDINGS VOL.1)**

Feb 92. (cd) *Rounder; <(ROUCD 1045)>* **GWINE DIG A HOLE TO PUT THE DEVIL IN (LIBRARY OF CONGRESS RECORDINGS VOL.2)**

Mar 92. (cd) *Rounder; <(ROUCD 1046)>* **LET IT SHINE ON ME (LIBRARY OF CONGRESS RECORDINGS VOL.3)**

May 93. (cd) *Music Club; (MCCD/MCTC 106)* **THE VERY BEST OF LEADBELLY**
– Midnight special / Sylvie / Matchbox blues / You must have that pure religion, halleloo / Fannin' street / Green corn / Bourgeois blues / When I was a cowboy / Cow cow yicky yicky yea / CC rider / Rock island line / Governor o.k. Allen / De kalb blues / Leavin' blues / Roberta / Frankie and Albert / Alberta / Gray goose / Careless love / Goodnight Irene.

Nov 93. (cd) *Blues Encore; (CD 52028)* **IRENE GOODNIGHT**

Mar 94. (lp/c/cd) *Aldabra; (ALB 1007/+MC/CD)* **CONGRESS BLUES**

Apr 94. (cd) *Document; (DOCD 5226)* **COMPLETE RECORDED WORKS VOL.1: 1939-40**

Apr 94. (cd) *Document; (DOCD 5227)* **COMPLETE RECORDED WORKS VOL.2: 1940-43**

Apr 94. (cd) *Document; (DOCD 5228)* **COMPLETE RECORDED WORKS VOL.3: 1943-44**

Apr 94. (cd) *Rounder; <(ROUCD 1097)>* **THE TITANIC (LIBRARY OF CONGRESS RECORDINGS VOL.4)**

Apr 94. (cd) *Rounder; <(ROUCD 1098)>* **NOBODY KNOWS THE TROUBLE I'VE SEEN (LIBRARY OF CONGRESS RECORDINGS VOL.5)**

Apr 94. (cd) *Rounder; <(ROUCD 1099)>* **GO DOWN OLD HANNAH (LIBRARY OF CONGRESS RECORDINGS, VOL.6)**

Oct 94. (4xcd-set/4xc-box) *Smithsonian Folkways; <(SFW CD/MC 40068)>* **THE LAST SESSIONS**

Dec 94. (cd) *Document; (DOCD 5310)* **COMPLETE RECORDED WORKS VOL.4: 1944**

Dec 94. (cd) *Document; (DOCD 5311)* **COMPLETE RECORDED WORKS VOL.5: 1944-46**

Oct 95. (cd) *Aim; (COLLECT 4CD)* **THE LEGENDARY MASTERS SERIES**

Feb 96. (cd) *Tradition; (TCD 1006)* **GOODNIGHT IRENE**

Apr 96. (cd/c) *Smithsonian Folkways; (SFW CD/MC 40044)* **WHERE DID YOU SLEEP LAST NIGHT (THE LEADBELLY LEGACY VOL.1)**

May 96. (cd) *Tradition; (TCD 1018)* **IN THE SHADOWS OF THE GALLOW'S POLE**

Jun 96. (cd) *Document; (DOCD 5461)* **LEADBELLY & JOSH WHITE / PEETIE WHEATSTRAW 1924 – MID 1940's**

Sep 96. (cd) *Blue Moon; (CDBM 119)* **THE MASTERS**

Oct 96. (cd) *Music Memoria; (842032-2)* **ALL TIME BLUES CLASSICS**

Nov 96. (cd) *I.M.P.; (IMP 310)* **GOODNIGHT IRENE**

May 97. (cd) *Smithsonian Folkways; (SFWCD 40045)* **BOURGEOIS BLUES (THE LEADBELLY LEGACY VOL.2)**

Jun 97. (cd; shared with BLIND WILLIE McTELL) *Biograph; (BCD 144)* **MASTERS OF THE COUNTRY BLUES**

Sep 97. (cd) *Document; (DOCD 5568)* **COMPLETE RECORDED WORKS VOL.6: 1947**

Dec 97. (3xcd-box; shared with SONNY BOY WILLIAMSON & ROBERT JOHNSON) *Indigo; (IGOBCD 001)* **THE ESSENTIAL BLUES GREATS**

Feb 98. (cd) *Document; (DOCD 5591)* **REMAINING LIBRARY OF CONGRESS RECORDINGS VOL.1: 1934-1935**

Feb 98. (cd) *Document; (DOCD 5592)* **REMAINING LIBRARY OF CONGRESS RECORDINGS VOL.2: 1935**

Feb 98. (cd) *Document; (DOCD 5593)* **REMAINING LIBRARY OF CONGRESS RECORDINGS VOL.3: 1935**

Feb 98. (cd) *Document; (DOCD 5594)* **REMAINING LIBRARY OF CONGRESS RECORDINGS VOL.4: 1935-1938**

Feb 98. (cd) *Document; (DOCD 5595)* **REMAINING LIBRARY OF CONGRESS RECORDINGS VOL.5: 1938-1942**

Mar 98. (cd) *Beat Goes On; (BGOCD 403)* **HUDDIE LEDBETTER'S BEST**

Apr 98. (cd) *Smithsonian Folkways; (SFWCD 40105)* **SHOUT ON (THE LEADBELLY LEGACY VOL.3)**

Feb 99. (cd) *Members Edition; (UAE 30282)* **LEADBELLY**

Mar 99. (cd) *Smithsonian Folkways; (SFWCD 45047)* **LEADBELLY SINGS FOR CHILDREN**

May 99. (cd/c) *Platinum; (PLA TCD/C 290)* **MIDNIGHT SPECIAL**

May 99. (cd; shared with JOSHUA WHITE) *Document; (DOCD 1018)* **THE BLACK FOLK SINGERS**

Jun 99. (cd) *A.B.M.; (ABMMCD 1055)* **LEADBELLY VOL.1**

Jul 99. (cd) *Document; (DOCD 5640)* **THE COMPLETE RECORDED WORKS VOL.7: 1947-1949**

Oct 99. (cd) *Catfish; (KATCD 131)* **EASY RIDER**

Oct 99. (cd) *A.B.M.; (ABMMCD 1173)* **LEADBELLY VOL.2**

Nov 99. (d-cd) *Recall; (SMDCD 240)* **MY LAST GO ROUND**

LEAD INTO GOLD (see under ⇒ MINISTRY)

LEAGUE OF GENTLEMEN
(see under ⇒ KING CRIMSON)

LEAVES (dig out; Great Psychedelic . . .)

LED ZEPPELIN

Formed: London, England ... mid '68 out of The NEW YARDBIRDS, by guitar wizard JIMMY PAGE, session bassist JOHN PAUL JONES and frontman ROBERT PLANT. Another session musician, drummer JOHN BONHAM, completed the line-up, arriving in time for their live debut at Surrey University on the 15th October '68. Taking the group name from one of KEITH MOON's catchphrases, "going down like a lead zeppelin", the band came under the wing of PETER GRANT, one of the most notoriously shrewd managers in the history of rock and an integral part of the 'ZEPPELIN legend. Following some early dates in Scandinavia and the UK, GRANT secured a lucrative worldwide deal with 'Atlantic', the group subsequently touring America with fellow proto-metallers, VANILLA FUDGE. Universally saddled with the dubious honour of inventing heavy metal, the group nevertheless started out as a power-blues outfit, as evidenced on their blistering 1969 debut set, the eponymous 'LED ZEPPELIN'. From the beginning it was obvious 'ZEPPELIN had a musical chemistry more electric than any rock'n'roll band that had gone before; in spite of, or perhaps as a result of, the fact that BONHAM and JONES came from a soul background while PLANT and PAGE were coming from the heavy blues/R&B angle, the group had an almost superhuman grasp of dynamics. Whether negotiating the climactic blues of 'BABE I'M GONNA LEAVE YOU' or ripping out the power drill rhythms of 'COMMUNICATION BREAKDOWN', each musician wielded their instrument like a weapon, deadly accurate and timed to perfection. PLANT, meanwhile, had one of the most distinctive, orgasmic blues wails in rock, bringing it down to a rustic canter on the folkier numbers. These would come later, though, the sole folk song on the blues-dominated debut being the trad-based instrumental, 'BLACK MOUNTAIN SIDE'. The album's centrepiece was the tortured 'DAZED AND CONFUSED', PAGE's guitar trawling the depths of black despair, while PLANT put in one of his career best performances over a track which would become a mainstay of the LED ZEPPELIN live extravaganza. These were marathon events, with solos and improvisation aplenty, albeit in a more focussed way than the likes of the GRATEFUL DEAD. The shows were also concentrated, initially at least, in America, where GRANT was intent upon breaking the band. While the debut was a transatlantic Top 10 success, the follow-up, 'LED ZEPPELIN II' (1969), scaled both the UK and US charts later that year. Cited by many as the birthdate of British heavy metal, the sledgehammer, divebombing riff of 'WHOLE LOTTA LOVE' ushered in a new era for rock, blasting the competition out of the water. Recorded on the road, the album was graced with more than a little of the improvisatory tension of the live show; the grungy groove of 'MOBY DICK' panned out to a marathon display of BONHAM's rhythmic alchemy, while the middle part of 'WHOLE LOTTA LOVE' lingered in a kind of suspended animation as PAGE engendered all manner of bizarre effects and PLANT got himself all hot and bothered. 'THANK YOU' and 'RAMBLE ON' indicated the direction 'ZEPPELIN would follow on subsequent releases while 'LIVING LOVING MAID (SHE'S JUST A WOMAN)' and 'BRING IT ON HOME', were itchy, funky blues/metal barnstormers, the latter boasting one of the most effective intros and majestic, f***-off riffs in the 'ZEP pantheon. Prepared at 'Bron-Y-Aur' cottage in rural Wales, 'LED ZEPPELIN III' (1970) was something of a departure, at least in its equal billing for the gentler acoustic folk numbers such as 'THAT'S THE WAY' and 'TANGERINE'. Nevertheless, proceedings opened with the lumbering battlecry of 'IMMIGRANT SONG', while PAGE performed one of his most endearingly rocking solos midway through 'CELEBRATION DAY'. Though the album again topped the British and US charts (without the aid of any UK singles; LED ZEPPELIN famously never released any British singles, all part of GRANT's masterplan), critics were sceptical of the change in emphasis. They soon changed their tune with the arrival of the group's fourth effort, an untitled affair with four mystical runes adorning the cover. This immersion in myth and mysticism (PAGE had even purchased the notoriously haunted 'Boleskine Lodge' on the shores of Loch Ness, previously home to occult figurehead, Aleister Crowley) was reflected in the material contained within; the epic 'STAIRWAY TO HEAVEN' remains the most (in)famous LED ZEPPELIN song, its pseudo-hippie musings and acoustic strumming leading into one of the most revered guitar solos of all time. Basically, if you want to spank your plank, this is where you're supposed to start. 'MISTY MOUNTAIN HOP' was another hippie fantasy, while 'THE BATTLE OF EVERMORE' was a folk-rock epic blessed by the golden tonsils of SANDY DENNY. 'BLACK DOG' and 'ROCK AND ROLL' were funky, chunky riffathons, the album's heaviest track surprisingly placed at the end of side two, the wailing, harmonica-driven, rolling thunder of 'WHEN THE LEVEE BREAKS', arguably 'ZEPPELIN's most hauntingly effective update of the delta blues tradition. BONHAM's drumming didn't get get much better than this, his molten rhythms subsequently sampled by arch-rappers The BEASTIE BOYS on their massive landing debut album. At the other end of the spectrum, the sun-bleached warmth of 'GOING TO CALIFORNIA' was 'ZEPPELIN at their folky, laidback best, PLANT adopting a mellow, down-home drawl. And this was exactly what the group did, spending most of their time on the road and a fair portion of it in America. With British bands not exactly known for their good manners abroad, LED ZEPPELIN had the most infamous reputation by far. Chief suspects were BONHAM and road manager RICHARD COLE, their alleged appetite for groupies and general debauchery the stuff of rock'n'roll legend; any reader with an interest in such matters will no doubt find the gory details in any of the many books written on 'ZEPPELIN's antics. The embodiment of 70's excess, the band even leased their own jet, nicknamed 'The Starship', which reportedly turned into a 'flying brothel'. With LED ZEPPELIN having released their most successful album to date, one of the most successful albums ever, in fact, they were now riding high as probably the biggest group on the planet. They knew they could get away with anything they wanted and with 'HOUSES OF THE HOLY' (1973), they clearly fancied a bit of experimentation. The majority of critics remained unimpressed with their half-baked attempts at funk ('THE CRUNGE') and reggae ('D'YER MAKER'), 'ZEPPELIN sounding more at home on familiar ground, especially the evocative 'OVER THE HILLS AND FAR AWAY' and JONES' scathing 'NO QUARTER'. Regardless of what commentators might've thought, 'ZEPPELIN remained the crown kings of rock, the album predictably topping the charts and the group undertaking their biggest US tour to date. Subsequently activating their own record label, 'Swan Song', the group took artistic control into their own hands, releasing the ambitious double set, 'PHYSICAL GRAFFITI' in Spring '75. While the quality control was spread rather thin in places, there were some unforgettable moments, obviously the exultant 'KASHMIR', but also the affecting 'CUSTARD PIE', the booty-shaking 'TRAMPLED UNDERFOOT' and the obligatory blues odyssey, 'IN MY TIME OF DYING'. Although the group's popularity ensured massive sales, 'PRESENCE' (1976) saw major cracks appearing in the LED ZEPPELIN armoury; in a set which sounded merely slung together, only 'ACHILLES LAST STAND' put up a fight. The double live set, 'THE SONG REMAINS THE SAME' (1976), was also overblown, the album a soundtrack to a rockumentary/movie of the same name featuring live footage from '73 spliced with dodgy 'dream sequences'. Having recovered from a car crash in 1975, PLANT was dealt another blow when his young son, KARAC, died from a viral infection in the summer of '77. Amid much speculation that the group would finally call it a day, LED ZEPPELIN re-emerged in 1979 with 'IN THROUGH THE OUT DOOR', another patchy effort which nevertheless initiated a comeback tour. Following UK dates at Knebworth and a European jaunt, the group went into rehearsals for a full-scale US tour. It never happened. On the 25th of September 1980, BONHAM was found dead after another sizeable drinking session and the group officially split shortly before Christmas. A posthumous collection of outtakes, 'CODA', was issued in late '82, while more recently, the celebrated 'REMASTERS' (1990) set brought together the cream of 'ZEPPELIN's material on shiny, remastered compact disc. While PLANT went on to record solo material in the early 80's, the transatlantic Top 5, 'PICTURES AT ELEVEN' (1982) and the equally fine 'THE PRINCIPLE OF MOMENTS' (1983), PAGE recorded a sole soundtrack effort, 'DEATH WISH II' (1982). PAGE and PLANT finally got back together in 1984 via the mediocre HONEYDRIPPERS R&B/soul project along with JEFF BECK. Then came The FIRM, PLANT and PAGE hooking up with veteran BAD COMPANY frontman, PAUL RODGERS. Despite the expectation, both 'THE FIRM' (1985) and 'MEAN BUSINESS' (1986) were disappointing, suffering from turgid supergroup syndrome. Much more worthy of attention were PLANT's 'SHAKEN 'N' STIRRED' (1985), 'NOW AND ZEN' (1988) and 'MANIC NIRVANA' (1990), the singer maintaining his experimental spirit throughout, dabbling with everything from hip hop rhythms to metallic blues. Even better was 1993's 'FATE OF NATIONS', the likes of '29 PALMS' and a delicate cover of TIM HARDIN's 'IF I WERE A CARPENTER' seeing PLANT in wistfully reflective, folky mood. Save a one-off collaboration with his old mucker, ROY HARPER ('Whatver Happened To Jugula?' 1985), PAGE's only solo outing proper came with 1988's 'OUTRIDER', a competent, if hardly rivetting set of hard rocking blues (vocals courtesy of seasoned hands JOHN MILES and CHRIS FARLOWE). In 1993 however, PAGE teamed up with WHITESNAKE frontman DAVID COVERDALE to record the highly successful but rather derivative album, 'COVERDALE – PAGE'. While PLANT and PAGE teamed up once more in the mid-90's for a startling album of ethnically reworked 'ZEPPELIN classics (including four new tracks), 'NO QUARTER – UNLEDDED' (1994), the prospect of a LED ZEPPELIN reunion looks as improbable as ever and with the death of PETER GRANT (of a heart attack) on the 21st November 1995, another part of the 'ZEPPELIN legend was laid to rest. Still, fans could console themselves with the release of the acclaimed 'BBC SESSIONS' at Christmas '97, featuring a couple of electrifying performances from the earliest part of their career. Early the following year, PAGE & PLANT were back again with a complete set of new recordings on 'WALKING INTO CLARKSDALE' (1998), the material being of LED ZEPPELIN standard. JOHN PAUL JONES, meanwhile, was working on his solo project, although why the appropriately titled 'ZOOMA' (1999) was ever issued is beyond me; "What is and what should never have been" are words that spring to mind. • **Songwriters:** PAGE + PLANT wrote nearly all with some help from JONES and/or BONHAM. They also covered; I CAN'T QUIT YOU BABY (Otis Rush) / YOU SHOOK ME (Willie Dixon) / BRING IT ON HOME (Sonny Boy Williamson) / GALLOW'S POLE + HATS OFF TO HARPER (trad.) / etc. JIMMY PAGE covered; HUMMINGBIRD (B.B.King). The HONEYDRIPPERS;- SEA OF LOVE (Phil Phillips with the Twilights). ROBERT PLANT: LET'S HAVE A PARTY (Elvis Presley). • **Trivia:** In the early 70's, C.C.S. (aka. ALEXIS KORNER) had a Top 10 hit with 'WHOLE LOTTA LOVE' (later adopted for the Top Of The Pops theme). In 1985, with PHIL COLLINS on drums, LED ZEPPELIN played LIVE AID. JOHN BONHAM's drumming son, JASON, formed his own band, BONHAM in the late 80's. Around the same time, a kitsch mickey-take outfit DREAD ZEPPELIN, hit the music scene, playing reggae adaptations of the group's classics. In 1992, Australian 60's hitmaker and TV personality ROLF HARRIS destroyed 'STAIRWAY TO HEAVEN', hitting the charts in the process. It was even worse than 1985's FAR CORPORATION version, which also hit the UK Top 10. **Early work:**

As well as session work with many (THEM, etc.), JIMMY PAGE released a solo single in early '65 ('SHE JUST SATIFIES' / 'KEEP MOVIN') for 'Fontana' (TF 533) – it's now worth 250 quid! He had earlier played on 45's by NEIL CHRISTIAN & THE CRUSADERS, plus CARTER-LEWIS & THE SOUTHERNERS. JOHN PAUL JONES played in The TONY MEEHAN COMBO, before issuing a solo 45 in April '64 ('A FOGGY DAY IN VIETNAM' / 'BAJA'), for 'Pye' label. ROBERT PLANT had been part of LISTEN, who released one 45 in November '66; ('YOU'D BETTER RUN' / 'EVERYBODY'S GOTTA SAY'; 202456). He stayed with the label for two solo releases in March '67; ('OUR SONG' / 'LAUGHING, CRYING, LAUGHING') (202656), and July '67 ('LONG TIME COMING' / 'I'VE GOT A SECRET') (2858). He subsequently teamed up that year with BONHAM, to form Birmingham-based group, BAND OF JOY. All these rare singles now fetch upwards of 100 quid.

Album rating: LED ZEPPELIN (*9) / LED ZEPPELIN II (*10) / LED ZEPPELIN III (*9) / UNTITLED (LED ZEPPELIN IV) (*10) / HOUSES OF THE HOLY (*8) / PHYSICAL GRAFFITI (*10) / PRESENCE (*6) / THE SONG REMAINS THE SAME (*6) / IN THROUGH THE OUT DOOR (*6) / CODA (*5) / REMASTERS compilation (*10) / Robert Plant: PICTURES AT ELEVEN (*6) / PRINCIPLE OF MOMENTS (*7) / MANIC NIRVANA (*7) / FATE OF NATIONS (*7) / Jimmy Page: OUTRIDER (*6) / Page & Plant: UNLEDDED (*7) / WALKING INTO CLARKSDALE (*7) / John Paul Jones: ZOOMA (*3)

ROBERT PLANT (b.20 Aug'48, West Bromwich, England) – vocals (ex-LISTEN) / **JIMMY PAGE** (b. JAMES PATRICK PAGE, 9 Jan'44, Heston, England) – lead guitars (ex-YARDBIRDS) / **JOHN PAUL JONES** (b. JOHN BALDWIN, 3 Jun'46, Sidcup, Kent, England) – bass / **JOHN BONHAM** (b.31 May'48, Redditch, England) – drums

			Atlantic	Atlantic
Mar 69.	(lp) (588 171) <8216> **LED ZEPPELIN**		6	10 Feb69

– Good times bad times / Babe I'm gonna leave you / You shook me / Dazed and confused / Your time is gonna come / Black mountain side / Communication breakdown / I can't quit you baby / How many more times. (re-iss. Mar72 lp/c; K/K4 40031) (cd-iss. Jan87 & 1989 special; 240031) (re-iss. Jul94 & Aug97 cd/c; 7567 82632-2) (lp re-iss. Oct99 on 'Classic'; SD 19126)

Mar 69.	(7") <2613> **GOOD TIMES BAD TIMES. / COMMUNICATION BREAKDOWN**		–	80
Oct 69.	(lp) (588 198) <8236> **LED ZEPPELIN II**		1	1

– Whole lotta love / What is and what should never be / The lemon song / Thank you / Heartbreaker / Livin' lovin' maid (she's just a woman) / Ramble on / Moby Dick / Bring it on home. (re-iss. Mar72 lp/c; K/K4 40037) (cd-iss. Jan87 & 1989 special; 240037) (re-iss. Jul94 & Aug97 cd/c; 7567 82633-2)

Nov 69.	(7") <2690> **WHOLE LOTTA LOVE. / LIVING LOVING MAID (SHE'S JUST A WOMAN)**		–	4 65
Oct 70.	(lp) (2401 002) <7201> **LED ZEPPELIN III**		1	1

– Immigrant song / Friends / Celebration day / Since I've been loving you / Out on the tiles / Gallows pole / Tangerine / That's the way / Bron-y-aur stomp / Hats off to (Roy) Harper. (re-iss. Mar72 lp/c; K/K4 50002) (cd-iss. Jan87 & 1989 special; 250002) (cd-iss. Aug97; 7567 82678-2)

Nov 70.	(7") <2777> **IMMIGRANT SONG. / HEY HEY WHAT CAN I DO**		–	16
Nov 71.	(lp) (2401 012) <7208> **(UNTITLED – 4 SYMBOLS)**		1	2

– Black dog / Rock and roll / The battle of Evermore / Stairway to Heaven / Misty mountain hop / Four sticks / Going to California / When the levee breaks. (re-iss. Mar72 lp/c; K/K4 50008) (lilac-lp Nov78; K 50008) (cd-iss. Jul83; 250008) (cd-iss. Jan87 & 1989 special; 250008) (re-iss. Jul94 & Aug97 cd/c; 7567 82638-2/-4)

Dec 71.	(7") <2849> **BLACK DOG. / MISTY MOUNTAIN HOP**		–	15
Mar 72.	(7") <2865> **ROCK AND ROLL. / FOUR STICKS**		–	47
Apr 73.	(lp/c) (K/K4 50014) <7255> **HOUSES OF THE HOLY**		1	1

– The song remains the same / The rain song / Over the hills and far away / The crunge / Dancing days / D'yer mak'er / No quarter / The ocean. (cd-iss. Jan87; 250014) (re-iss. Jul94 & Aug97 cd/c; 7567 82639-2/-4)

Jun 73.	(7") <2970> **OVER THE HILLS AND FAR AWAY. / DANCING DAYS**		–	51
Oct 73.	(7") <2986> **D'YER MAK'ER. / THE CRUNGE**		–	20

			Swan Song	Swan Song
Mar 75.	(d-lp/d-c) (SSK/SK4 89400) <200> **PHYSICAL GRAFFITI**		1	1

– Custard pie / The rover / In my time of dying / Houses of the holy / Trampled underfoot / Kashmir / In the light / Bron-y-aur / Down by the seaside / Ten years gone / Night flight / The wanton song / Boogie with Stu / Black country woman / Sick again. (d-cd-iss. Jan87; 294800) (re-iss. Oct94 & Aug97 on 'Atlantic' cd/c; 7567 92442-2)

Mar 75.	(7") <70102> **TRAMPLED UNDERFOOT. / BLACK COUNTRY WOMAN**		–	38
Apr 76.	(lp/c) (SSK/SK4 59402) <8416> **PRESENCE**		1	1

– Achilles last stand / For your life / Royal Orleans / Nobody's fault but mine / Candy store rock / Hots on for nowhere / Tea for one. (cd-iss. Jun87; 259402) (re-iss. Oct94 & Aug97 on 'Atlantic' cd/c; 7567 92439-2/-4)

May 76.	(7") <70110> **CANDY STORE ROCK. / ROYAL ORLEANS**		–	
Oct 76.	(d-lp/d-c) (SSK/SK4 89402) <201> **The soundtrack from the film 'THE SONG REMAINS THE SAME' (live)**		1	2

– Rock and roll / Celebration day / The song remains the same / Rain song / Dazed and confused / No quarter / Stairway to Heaven / Moby Dick / Whole lotta love. (d-cd-iss. Feb87; 289402) (cd re-iss. Aug97 on 'Atlantic'; SK2 89402)

—— Above was also a film from concerts at Madison Square Gardens in 1973. It featured some dream sequences / fantasies of each member.

Aug 79.	(lp/c) (SSK/SK4 59410) <16002> **IN THROUGH THE OUT DOOR**		1	1

– In the evening / South bound Saurez / Fool in the rain / Hot dog / Carouselambra / All my love / I'm gonna crawl. (cd-iss. Jan87; 259410) (re-iss. Oct94 & Aug97 on 'Atlantic' cd/c: 7567 92443-2)

Dec 79.	(7") <71003> **FOOL IN THE RAIN. / HOT DOG**		–	21

—— Disbanded when JOHN BONHAM died after a drinking session 25 Sep'80.

—— JOHN PAUL JONES was already a top producer. In 1992, he contributed string arrangements to R.E.M.'s classic album 'Automatic For The People'. ROBERT PLANT went solo and teamed up with JIMMY PAGE in The HONEYDRIPPERS. PAGE also went solo and formed The FIRM.

—— In Aug 94; JOHN PAUL JONES turned up on an unusual collaboration (single 'Do You Take This Man') between himself and loud punk-opera diva DIAMANDA GALAS.

– compilations, others, etc. –

on 'Atlantic' unless mentioned otherwise

Nov 82. (lp/c) *Swan Song*; (A 0051/+4) <90051> **CODA** (demos from 68-79) .... 4 / 6 Dec82
– We're gonna groove / Poor Tom / I can't quit you baby / Walter's walk / Ozone baby / Darlene / Bonzo's Montreaux / Walter's walk / Wearing and tearing. *(cd-iss. Jul87; 790051) (cd re-iss. Aug97 on 'Atlantic'; 7567 92444-2)*

Oct 90. (4xcd/4xc/5xlp) (<7567 82144-2/-4/-1>) **LED ZEPPELIN: THE REMASTERS BOX** .... 48 / 18

Nov 90. (d-cd/d-c/t-lp) (ZEP/+C/CD 1) <82371> **REMASTERS** .... 10 / 47 Mar92
– Communication breakdown / Babe I'm gonna leave you / Good times bad times / Dazed and confused / Whole lotta love / Heartbreaker / Ramble on / Immigrant song / Celebration day / Since I've been loving you / Black dog / Rock and roll / The battle of Evermore / Misty mountain hop / Stairway to Heaven / The song remains the same / The rain song / D'yer mak'er / No quarter / Houses of the holy / Kashmir / Trampled underfoot / Nobody's fault but mine / Achilles last stand / All my love / In the evening. *(re-iss. cd Sep92; 7567 80415-2) (cd re-iss. Aug97 hit UK No.27; as last)*

Sep 93. (2xcd-box/2xc-box) (<7567 82477-2/-4>) **BOXED SET II** .... 56 / 87

Oct 93. (10xcd-box) (<7567 82526-2>) **REMASTERS 2** ....

Nov 96. (cd) *Tring*; (QED 107) **WHOLE LOTTA LOVE** (Bootleg Zep) .... -

Sep 97. (cd-s) (AT 0013CD) **WHOLE LOTTA LOVE / BABY COME ON HOME / TRAVELLING RIVERSIDE BLUES** 21

Nov 97. (d-cd/d-c) (<7567 83061-2/-4>) **BBC SESSIONS** .... 23 / 12
– You shook me / I can't quit you baby / Communication breakdown / Dazed and confused / The girl I love / What is and what should never be / Communication breakdown / Travelling riverside blues / Whole lotta love / Something else / Communication breakdown / I can't quit you baby / You shook me / How many more times / Immigrant song / Since I've been loving you / Black dog / Dazed and confused / Stairway to Heaven / Going to California / That's the way / Whole lotta love / Thank you.

Nov 99. (cd/c) (<7567 83268-2/-4>) **EARLY DAYS: THE BEST OF LED ZEPPELIN VOLUME ONE** 71

ROBERT PLANT

—— with **BOBBIE BLUNT** – guitar / **JEZZ WOODRUFFE** – keyboards / **PAUL MARTINEZ** – bass / **COZY POWELL** – drums / guest **PHIL COLLINS** – drums, percussion

Swan Song / Swan Song

Jul 82. (lp/c) (SSK/+4 59418) <8512> **PICTURES AT ELEVEN** .... 2 / 5
– Burning down one side / Moonlight in Samosa / Pledge pin / Slow dancer / Worse that Detroit / Fat lip / Like I've never been gone / Mystery title. *(cd-iss. 1984; SSK2 59418)*

Sep 82. (7") (SSK 19429) <99979> **BURNING DOWN ONE SIDE. / MOONLIGHT IN SAMOSA** .... 73 / 44
(12"+=) (SSK 19429T) – Far post.

Nov 82. (7") <99952> **PLEDGE PIN. / FAT LIP** .... - / 74

—— **RITCHIE HAYWARD** – drums (ex-LITTLE FEAT) repl. COZY / —— added **BOB MAYO** – keyboards, guitar

Es Paranza / Es Paranza

Jul 83. (lp/c) (790101-1/-4) <90101> **THE PRINCIPLE OF MOMENTS** .... 7 / 8
– Other arms / In the mood / Messin' with the Mekon / Wreckless love / Thru with the two-step / Horizontal departure / Stranger here . . .than over there / Big log. *(cd-iss. 1984; 790101-2)*

Jul 83. (7") (B 9848) **BIG LOG. / MESSIN' WITH THE MEKON** .... 11 / -
(12"+=) (B 9848T) – Stranger here . . . than over there.

Sep 83. (7") <99844> **BIG LOG. / FAR POST** .... - / 20

Nov 83. (7") <99820> **IN THE MOOD. / HORIZONTAL DEPARTURE** .... - / 39

Jan 84. (7") (B 6970) **IN THE MOOD. / PLEDGE PIN** (live) .... - / -
(12"+=) (B 6970T) – Horizontal departure.

May 85. (7") (B 9640) **PINK AND BLACK. / TROUBLE YOUR MONEY** .... - / -

May 85. (7") <99644> **LITTLE BY LITTLE. / TROUBLE YOUR MONEY** .... - / 36

May 85. (lp/c/cd) (790265-1/-4/-2) <90265> **SHAKEN 'N' STIRRED** .... 19 / 20
– Hip to hoo / Kallalou Kallalou / Too loud / Trouble your money / Pink and black / Little by little / Doo doo a do do / Easily led / Sixes and sevens.

Jul 85. (7") <99622> **TOO LOUD. / KALLALOU KALLALOU** .... - / -

Aug 85. (7") (B 9621) **LITTLE BY LITTLE** (remix). / **DOO DOO A DO DO** .... - / -
(ext.12"+=) (B 9621T) – Easily led (live).
(d7"++=) (B 9621F) – Rockin' at midnight (live).

—— now with **DOUG BOYLE** – guitars / **PHIL SCRAGG** – bass / **PHIL JOHNSTONE** – keyboards, co-writer / **JIMMY PAGE** – guitar / **CHRIS BLACKWELL** – drums, percussion / **MARIE PIERRE, TONI HALLIDAY + KIRSTY MacCOLL** – backing vocals

Jan 88. (7") (A 9373) <99373> **HEAVEN KNOWS. / WALKING TOWARDS PARADISE** .... 33 /
(ext.12"+=/ext.3"cd-s+=) (A 9373 T/CD) – Big log.
(ext.12"box+=) (A 9373TB) – ('A'-Astral mix).

Feb 88. (lp/c/cd) (WX 149/+C)(790863-2) <90863> **NOW AND ZEN** .... 10 / 6
– Heaven knows / Dance on my own / Tall cool one / The way I feel / Helen of Troy / Billy's revenge / Ship of fools / Why / White, clean and neat. *(cd+=)* – Walking towards Paradise.

Apr 88. (7") (A 9348) <99348> **TALL COOL ONE** (remix). / **WHITE, CLEAN AND NEAT** .... - / 25
(12"+=) (A 9348T) – ('A'extended).
(3"cd-s+++=) (A 9348CD) – Little by little.

Aug 88. (7") (A 9281) **SHIP OF FOOLS. / HELEN OF TROY** .... - / -
(12"+=/12"w-poster+=) (A 9281 T/TF) – Heaven Knows (live).
(3"cd-s+=/3"box-cd-s+=) (A 9281 CD/+B) – Dimples (live).

Aug 88. (7") <99333> **SHIP OF FOOLS. / BILLY'S REVENGE** .... - / 84

—— **PAT THORPE** – drums repl. BLACKWELL who became ill

—— now with **BLACKWELL, CHARLIE JONES, JOHNSTONE and BOYLE**

Mar 90. (lp/c/cd) (WX 229/+C/CD) <91336> **MANIC NIRVANA** .... 15 / 13

– Hurting kind (I've got my eyes on you) / Big love / S S S & Q / I cried / She said / Nirvana / The dye on the highway / Your ma said you cried in your sleep last night / Anniversary / Liars dance / Watching you.

Mar 90. (7") <98985> **HURTING KIND (I'VE GOT MY EYES ON YOU). / I CRIED** .... - / 46

Apr 90. (7") (A 8985) **HURTING KIND (I'VE GOT MY EYES ON YOU). / OOMPAH (WATERY BINT)** .... 45 / -
(12"+=) (A 8985T) – I cried / One love.
(cd-s+=) (A 8985CD) – Don't look back / One love.

Jun 90. (7"/c-s) (A 8945/+C) **YOUR MA SAID YOU CRIED IN YOUR SLEEP LAST NIGHT. / SHE SAID** ....
(12"/cd-s) (A 8945 T/CD) – ('A'side) / ('A'version) / One love.

—— with **KEVIN SCOTT MACMICHAEL** – guitar / **PHIL JOHNSTONE** – electric piano / **CHARLIE JONES** – bass / **MICHAEL LEE** – drums / **CHRIS HUGHES** – drums, co-producer / plus guests **FRANCIS DUNNERY, MAIRE BRENNAN, NIGEL KENNEDY + RICHARD THOMPSON**

Fontana / Es Paranza

Apr 93. (7") (FATE 1) **29 PALMS. / 21 YEARS** .... 21 /
(c-s+=) (FATEM 1) – Dark moon.
(cd-s++=) (FATEX 1) – Whole lotta love (you need love).

May 93. (cd/c/lp) (<514 867-2/-4/-1>) **FATE OF NATIONS** .... 6 / 34
– Calling to you / Down to the sea / Come into my life / I believe / 29 palms / Memory song (hello, hello) / If I were a carpenter / Colours of a shade / Promised land / The greatest gift / Great spirit / Network news.

Jun 93. (7"/c-s) (FATE/+M 2) **I BELIEVE. / GREAT SPIRIT** (acoustic mix) 64
(cd-s+=) (FATEX 2) – Hey Jayne.
(12"pic-d++=) (FATETP 2) – Whole lotta love (you need love).

Aug 93. (c-s) (FATEM 3) **CALLING TO YOU. / NAKED IF I WANT TO** ....
(12"+=/cd-s+=) (FATE/+X 3) – 8.05.

Dec 93. (c-s) (FATEM 2) **IF I WERE A CARPENTER / I BELIEVE** (live) 63
(cd-s+=) (FATED 4) – Going to California (live).
(cd-s+=) (FATEX 4) – ('A'side) / Ship of fools (live) / Tall cool one (live).

JIMMY PAGE

—— solo with **CHRIS FARLOWE** – vocals / **DAVE LAWSON + DAVID SINCLAIR WHITTAKER + GORDON EDWARDS** – piano / **DAVE PATON** – bass / **DAVE MATTACKS** – drums

Swan Song / Swan Song

Feb 82. (lp) (SSK 59415) <8511> **DEATH WISH II (Soundtrack)** .... 40 / 50 Mar82
– Who's to blame / The chase / City sirens / Jam sandwich / Of Carole's theme / The release / Hotel rats and photostats / Shadow in the city / Jill's theme / Prelude / Big band, sax and violence / Hypnotizing ways (oh mamma).

—— In 1985, PAGE collaborated with friend ROY HARPER on dual album 'WHATEVER HAPPENED TO JUGULA', which hit UK Top 50.

—— In 1987, he released soundtrack blue-lp 'LUCIFER RISING' for 'Boleskine House'; <BHR 666>

—— now guest vocals – **JOHN MILES, ROBERT PLANT, CHRIS FARLOWE JASON BONHAM** – drums / **DURBAN LEVERDE** – bass / **FELIX KRISH, TONY FRANKLIN, BARRYMORE BARLOW** – drums

Geffen / Geffen

Jun 88. (lp/c)(cd) (WX 155/+C)(924188-2) <24188> **OUTRIDER** .... 27 / 26
– Wasting my time / Wanna make love / Writes of winter / The only one / Liquid mercury / Hummingbird / Emerald eyes / Prison blues / Blues anthem (if I cannot have your love . . .). *(re-iss. Feb91 cd/c; GEFD/GEFC 24188)*

Jun 88. (7"w-drawn) (GEF 41) **WASTING MY TIME. / WRITES OF WINTER** .... -

– other recordings, etc –

Jan 82. (lp; JIMMY PAGE, SONNY BOY WILLIAMSON & BRIAN AUGER) *Charly*; (CR 30193) **JAM SESSION** (rec.1964) .... -
– Don't send me no flowers / I see a man downstairs / She was so dumb / The goat / Walking / Little girl, how old are you / It'a a bloody life / Getting out of town.
below featured on session; **JOHN PAUL JONES / ALBERT LEE / NICKY HOPKINS + CLEM CATTINI**

Sep 84. (lp/c/cd; by JIMMY PAGE & FRIENDS) *Thunderbolt*; (THBL/THBC/CDTB 007) **NO INTRODUCTION NECESSARY** ....
– Lovin' up a storm / Everything I do is wrong / Think it over / Boll Weevil song / Livin' lovin' wreck / One long kiss / Dixie friend / Down the line / Fabulous / Breathless / Rave on / Lonely weekends / Burn up. *(re-iss. cd May93;)*
below from early 70's featuring; **JOHN BONHAM, JEFF BECK, NOEL REDDING + NICKY HOPKINS** + actually a re-issue of LORD SUTCH AND HEAVY FRIENDS album.

May 85. (lp/c) *Thunderbolt*; (THB L/C 2002) **SMOKE AND FIRE** .... -
– Wailing sounds / 'Cause I love you / Flashing lights / Gutty guitar / Would you believe / Smoke and fire / Thumping beat / Union Jack car / One for you baby / L-O-N-D-O-N / Brightest lights / Baby come back. *(cd-iss. Aug86; CDTB 2002)*
below featured him in session with; **JET HARRIS & TONY MEEHAN / MICKIE MOST / DAVE BERRY / MICKEY FINN / The FIRST GEAR / solo / etc.**

Jan 90. (lp/cd) *Archive Int.*; <AIP/+CD 10041> **JAMES PATRICK PAGE SESSION MAN VOLUME 1** .... -

Jul 90. (lp/cd) *Archive Int.*; <AIP/+CD 10053> **JAMES PATRICK PAGE SESSION MAN VOLUME 2** .... -

Aug 92. (cd) *Sony*; <AK 52420> **JIMMY'S BACK PAGES: THE EARLY YEARS** .... -
In the US, 'EARLY WORKS ' was issued on 'Springboard' <SPB 4038>

HONEYDRIPPERS

ROBERT PLANT – vocals / **JIMMY PAGE** – guitar / **JEFF BECK** – guitar (solo artist) / **NILE RODGERS** – producer, etc.

		Es Paranza	Es Paranza
Oct 84.	(7") <99701> SEA OF LOVE. / I GET A THRILL		3
Nov 84.	(10"m-lp/c) (790220-2/-4) <90220> VOLUME 1	56	4 Oct84
	– I get a thrill / Sea of love / I got a woman / Young boy blues / Rockin' at midnight.		
	(cd-iss. Feb93; 7567 90220-2)		
Jan 85.	(7") (YZ 33) SEA OF LOVE. / ROCKIN' AT MIDNIGHT	56	-
Mar 85.	(7") <99686> ROCKIN' AT MIDNIGHT. / YOUNG BOY BLUES	-	25

THE FIRM

JIMMY PAGE – guitar / **PAUL RODGERS** – vocals (ex-FREE, ex-BAD COMPANY) / **TONY FRANKLIN** – bass, keys / **CHRIS SLADE** – drums (ex-MANFRED MANN'S EARTH BAND)

		Atlantic	Atlantic
Feb 85.	(lp/c/cd) (781 239-1/-4/-2) <81239> THE FIRM	15	17
	– Closer / Make or break / Someone to love / Together / Radioactive / You've lost that lovin' feeling / Money can't buy satisfaction / Satisfaction guaranteed / Midnight moonlight.		
Feb 85.	(7"/7"sha-pic-d) (A 9586/+P) <89586> RADIOACTIVE. / TOGETHER		28
	(12") (A 9586T) – ('A'-special mix) / City sirens (live) / Live in peace (live).		
	(12") (A 9586TE) – (all 4 above).		
Apr 85.	(7") <89561> SATISFACTION GUARENTEED. / CLOSER	-	73
Apr 86.	(lp/c)(cd) (WX 43/+C)(781628-2) <81628> MEAN BUSINESS	46	22 Feb86
	– Fortune hunter / Cadillac / All the King's horses / Live in peace / Tear down the walls / Dreaming / Free to live / Spirit of love.		
Apr 86.	(7") (A 9458) <89458> ALL THE KING'S HORSES. / FORTUNE HUNTER		61
Jun 86.	(7") <89421> LIVE IN PEACE. / FREE TO LIVE	-	

— In 1993, JIMMY collaborated with DAVID COVERDALE (of WHITESNAKE) to make one hit album 'COVERDALE • PAGE'.

JIMMY PAGE & ROBERT PLANT

— with **CHARLIE JONES** – bass, percussion / **PORL THOMPSON** – guitar, banjo / **MICHAEL LEE** – drums, percussion / **NAJMA AKHTAR** – vocals / **JOE SUTHERLAND** – mandolin, bodhran / **NIGEL EASTON** – hurdy gurdy / **ED SHEARMUR** – hammond organ & orchestral arrangements for (large) English + Egyptian Ensemble + London Metropolitan Orchestra

		Fontana	Atlantic
Nov 94.	(cd/c/d-lp) (526362-2/-4/-1) <82706-2/-4/-1> NO QUARTER – UNLEDDED	7	4
	– Nobody's fault but mine / Thank you / No quarter / Friends / Yallah / City don't cry / Since I've been loving you / The battle of Evermore / Wonderful one / Wah wah / That's the way / Gallows pole / Four sticks / Kashmir.		
Dec 94.	(7") (PP 2) GALLOWS POLE. / CITY DON'T CRY	35	-
	(pic-cd-s+=) (PPCD 2) – The rain song.		
	(pic-cd-s+=) (PPDD 2) – ('A'side) / Four sticks / What is and what should never be.		
Mar 95.	(cd-ep) <CD5 85591-2> WONDERFUL ONE (2 versions) / WHAT IS AND WHAT SHOULD NEVER BE / WHEN THE LEVEE BREAKS	-	-

— **PLANT & PAGE** were actually a 4-piece with other rhythm section & co-writers, **CHARLIE JONES** – bass / **MICHAEL LEE** – drums

		Mercury	Atlantic
Mar 98.	(7") (PP 3) MOST HIGH. / THE WINDOW	26	
	(cd-s+=) (PPCD 3) – Upon a golden horse.		
Apr 98.	(cd/c/lp) (558025-2/-4/-1) <83092> WALKING INTO CLARKSDALE	3	8
	– Shining in the light / When the world was young / Upon a golden horse / Blue train / Please read the letter / Most high / Heart in your hand / Walking into Clarksdale / Burning up / When I was a child / House of love / Sons of freedom.		
Jun 98.	(7") (MER 506) SHINING IN THE LIGHT. / MOST HIGH (guitar mix)		
	(cd-s+=) (MERDD 506) – How many more times (live).		
	(cd-s) (MERCD 506) – ('A'side) / Walking into Clarksdale (live) / No quarter (live).		

JOHN PAUL JONES

		Discipline	Discipline
Sep 99.	(cd) <(DGM 9909)> ZOOMA		
	– Zooma / Grind / Smile of your shadow / Bass'n'drums / B fingers / Snake eyes / Nosumi blues / Tidal.		

Alvin LEE (see under ⇒ TEN YEARS AFTER)

Arthur LEE (see under ⇒ LOVE)

LEFT BANKE (dig out; Great Psychedelic . . .)

LEFTFIELD

Formed: London, England . . . 1990 by ex-teacher of English NEIL BARNES and PAUL DALEY, formerly of Balearic housers A MAN CALLED ADAM. Barnes had previously released the 'Mississippi Burning'-sampling 'NOT FORGOTTEN' on dance indie 'Outer Rhythm' and when the single became an underground club hit, contractual problems ensued. Undeterred, the duo kept a high profile with remix work (including David Bowie and Inner City) before setting up the Hard Hands label and cutting two singles in 1992, 'RELEASE THE PRESSURE' and 'SONG OF LIFE', the latter a slow building progressive house epic which further enhanced their dancefloor reputation and nudged into the lower regions of the pop charts. But the song that really branded

LEFTFIELD into the musical consciousness of the nation was the pounding crossover hit, 'OPEN UP'. A collaboration with P.I.L.'s JOHN LYDON, his blood curdling wail of 'BURN HOLLYWOOD BURN' was scarier than Michael Bolton's mullet cut and was enough to have the video banned from ITV's Chart Show. Spookily enough, the song was released at the same time as a spate of Californian fires . . . The single was a corking tune into the bargain and climbed to No.13 in the charts. The debut album, 'LEFTISM' was greeted with critical plaudits galore upon its release in 1995, reaching No.3 in the U.K. and even being nominated for The Mercury Music Prize. An exhilarating cross-fertilisation of musical stylings, the album took pumping techno trance as its base ingredient, interspersing this with everything from cerebral sonic tapestries ('MELT') to dark, foreboding drum 'n' bass ('STORM 3000'). It contained all the aforementioned singles (save the earlier 'NOT FORGOTTEN') as well as a vocal-led collaboration with goth goddess Toni Halliday. LEFTFIELD enjoyed further chart success with tracks and remixes from the album and contributed material to both the 'Shallow Grave' and 'Trainspotting' film soundtracks. A nationwide tour and a series of legendary festival appearances in 1996 cemented their position as one of the key players in the new techno vanguard alongside UNDERWORLD, PRODIGY et al. 'PHAT PLANET' (from that Guinness ad with the white horses riding the waves) was LEFTFIELD's first musical/video venture for some time, the duo finally releasing (in September '99) the excellent bass-heavy track on the B-side of another CHRIS CUNNINGHAM-directed single/promo, 'AFRIKA SHOX' (with of course, the man BAMBAATAA). Around the same time, the duo finally unleashed their (chart-topping) second album proper, 'RHYTHM AND STEALTH', an enjoyable journey through four years of hard toil in the studio; had their contemporaries beaten them to the prizes though? • **Songwriters:** BARNES / DALEY / guests and some samples. • **Trivia:** Their label 'Hard Hands' run by manager LISA HORRAN, also included acts VINYL BLAIR, DELTA LADY, DEE PATTEN and SCOTT HARRIS.

Album rating: BACKLOG compilation (*6) / LEFTISM (*9) / RHYTHM AND STEALTH (*7)

NEIL BARNES – DJ, percussion, synthesizers / **PAUL DALEY** – samples (ex-A MAN CALLED ADAM)

		Outer Rhythm	not iss.
Mar 90.	(12") (FOOT 003) NOT FORGOTTEN. / PATELL'S ON THE CASE / ('A'version)		-
Feb 91.	(12") (FOOT 009) NOT FORGOTTEN (Hard Hands mix). / MORE THAN I KNOW		-
	(12") (FOOT 009R) – ('A'&'B'remixes).		

		Hard Hands	Medicine
Aug 92.	(12"ltd.; featuring EARL SIXTEEN) (HAND 001T) RELEASE THE PRESSURE (3 track vocal)		
	(12"ltd.) (HAND 001R) – Release the dubs (instrumental mixes). (re-iss. Mar99; same)		
Nov 92.	(12"ltd.) (HAND 002T) SONG OF LIFE / FANFARE OF LIFE / DUB OF LIFE	59	
	(12") (HAND 002R) – ('A'-3 Underworld mixes).		
	(cd-s) (HAND 002CD) – ('A'side) / Fanfare of life / Release the dub. (re-iss. Mar99; same)		
Dec 92.	(cd) (OUTERCD 001) BACKLOG (compilation of above material on 'Outer Rhythm')		-

below single with JOHN LYDON (of PUBLIC IMAGE LTD) on vocals

Nov 93.	(7"/c-s; as LEFTFIELD / LYDON) (HAND 009/+MC) <42232> OPEN UP (radio edit). / ('A'instrumental)	13	Feb94
	(12"+=)(cd) (HAND 009 T/CD) – ('A'vocal 12"mix) / ('A'-Dervish overdrive mix) / ('A'-Andrew Weatherall mix) / ('A'-Dust Brothers mix). (re-iss. Mar99; same)		
	(12") (HAND 9R) – ('A'remixes).		

		Hard Hands	Sony-Columbia
Jan 95.	(cd/c/d-lp) (HAND CD/MC/LP 002/+D) <67231-2/-4/-1> LEFTISM	3	
	– Release the pressure / Afro-left / Melt / Song of life / Original / Black flute / Space shanty / Inspection (check one) / Storm 3000 / Open up / 21st century poem. (iss.Apr95, 3x12"+=) (HANDLP 2T) – Half past dub. (cd w/ bonus disc) – Afro-left (Afro-ride) / Release the pressure (release one) / Original (live dub) / Filter fish / Afro-left (Afro-Central) / Release the pressure (release four).		

below single as featured TONI HALLIDAY (ex-CURVE) on vocals

Mar 95.	(c-ep/cd-ep; as LEFTFIELD & HALLIDAY) (HAND 018 MC/CD) ORIGINAL / ('A'-live mix) / ('A'jam mix) / FILTER FISH	18	-
	(12"ep) (HAND 018T) – ('A'-Drift version) – repl. ('A'live)		
Jul 95.	(12"ep/c-ep/cd-ep; LEFTFIELD featuring DJUM DJUM) (HAND 023 T/MC/CD) <78045> AFRO-LEFT EP	22	
	– Afro left / Afro ride / Afro sol / Afro central.		
Jan 96.	(c-s) (HAND 029MC) RELEASE THE PRESSURE (remix 96 vocal): RELEASE ONE / RELEASE TWO	13	
	(12"+=) (HAND 029T) – Release four.		
	(cd-s++=) (HAND 029CD) – Release three.		
Sep 99.	(12"/cd-s; as LEFTFIELD. BAMBAATAA) (HAND 057 T/CD1) AFRIKA SHOX. / PHAT PLANET (Dave Clarke mix) / AFRIKA SHOX (Jedis elastic bass mix)	7	
	(cd-s) (HAND 057CD2) – ('A'mixes; VX / etc).		
Sep 99.	(cd/c/d-lp) (HAND CD/MC/LP 004) RHYTHM AND STEALTH	1	
	– Dusted / Phat planet / Chant of a poor man / Double flash / El Cid / Afrika shox / Dub gussett / Swords / 6-8 war / Rhino's prayer.		
Nov 99.	(12"/cd-s; as LEFTFIELD w/ ROOTS MANUVA) (HAND 058 T/CD) DUSTED (mixes)	28	
	(cd-s) (HAND 058CD2) – ('A'mixes).		

LEMONHEADS

Formed: Boston, Massachusetts, USA . . . 1983 by EVAN DANDO. Raised by middle-class parents (they were divorced when he was 12), the singer was originally the band's drummer and in March '86 he was joined by one-time school-friend, jazz-bassist JESSE PORETZ. With BEN DEILY completing the line-up, this early incarnation of The LEMONHEADS released their debut EP, the amateurish indie squall of 'LAUGHING ALL THE WAY TO THE CLEANERS' on the recently formed Boston label, 'Taang!'. The band stayed with the label for their first three releases, belting out spirited melodic punk (drawing comparisons with DINOSAUR JR, HUSKER DU, REPLACEMENTS etc,) on 'HATE YOUR FRIENDS' (1987), 'CREATOR' (1988) and 'LICK' (1989), the latter the pick of the bunch with a beguiling cover of Suzanne Vega's 'LUKA'. 'Atlantic' records were sufficiently confident in the band's pop-grunge abilities to offer them a deal, the initial fruits of which, the well received 'LOVEY' (1990), saw DANDO take more of a leading role following the departure of DEILY. From this point on he steered the band in an increasingly mellow, country-flavoured direction (an area he'd already explored on his 1990 solo EP, 'FAVOURITE SPANISH DISHES') with a brilliant cover of Mike Nesmith's 'DIFFERENT DRUM', while 'LOVEY' featured a fairly faithful rendition of his hero Gram Parsons' 'BRASS BUTTONS'. Yet the ever unpredictable DANDO split the band up after the major label debut, eventually reforming with the help of girlfriend JULIANA HATFIELD and DAVE RYAN, the latter having played on 'LOVEY'. A spell in Australia seemed to have further mellowed the singer and the resultant album, 'IT'S A SHAME ABOUT RAY', was the most accessible LEMONHEADS release to date, heavy on harmonies and melody. Despite a favourable critical reception, the album lingered in the lower reaches of the album chart and it was only when 'Atlantic' issued the band's power pop cover of Simon & Garfunkel's 'MRS. ROBINSON', that The LEMONHEADS became a household name. Re-released to include the track, 'IT'S A SHAME ABOUT RAY' enjoyed a commercial comeback, eventually making it into the UK Top 40. Suddenly DANDO's long-haired, slacker-extraordinaire visage was staring out from every magazine cover from NME to The FACE, although this sudden thrust into the limelight seemed to drive DANDO further into drug abuse, a follow-up album, 'COME ON FEEL THE LEMONHEADS', eventually surfacing in late 1993. The record was another mellow beauty, powering into the UK Top 5 on the back of a successful Love Positions' cover, 'INTO YOUR ARMS', and even featuring contributions from legendary pedal steel player, SNEAKY PETE KLEINOW. Predictably, the Yanks just didn't get it, preferring the bluster of PEARL JAM instead. Lack of success in his home country sent DANDO spiralling further into drug use, although he had apparently cleaned up by the end of the year, undertaking a solo acoustic tour of the US. However, after a much criticised appearance at the 1995 Glastonbury festival, DANDO went to ground, spending much of his time in Australia strung out on heroin and LSD. A shorn, torn and frayed DANDO eventually surfaced in 1997 with 'CAR BUTTON CLOTH', the first LEMONHEADS album in four years, finding DANDO in reflective and world weary mood, the melancholy side of his songwriting more pronounced than ever. • **Songwriters:** DANDO, although DELLY or MADDOX were contributors early on. Covered; I AM A RABBIT (Proud Scum) / HEY JOE + AMAZING GRACE (trad.) / MOD LANG (Big Star) / STRANGE (Patsy Cline) / YOUR HOME IS WHERE YOU ARE HAPPY (C. MANSON / PLASTER CASTER (Kiss) / SKULLS (Misfits) / GONNA GET ALONG WITHOUT YA NOW (Hoagy Carmichael) / STEP BY STEP (New Kids On The Block) / FRANK MILLS (from 'Hair' musical) / KITCHEN (Hummingbirds) / MISS OTIS REGRETS (Cole Porter) / FADE TO BLACK (Metallica) / LIVE FOREVER (Oasis) / KEEP ON LOVING YOU (Reo Speedwagon) / TENDERFOOT (Tom Morgan / Adam Young) / GALVESTON (Jimmy Webb) / PIN YR HEART (Jacobites). Between 1994-1996, he co-wrote 'PURPLE PARALLELOGRAM' with Noel Gallagher (Oasis) + 'IF I COULD TALK I'D TELL YOU' with Eugene Kelly (Eugenius). • **Trivia:** DANDO and JOHN STROHM appeared on BLAKE BABIES lp, 'Slow Learners'.

Album rating: HATE YOUR FRIENDS (*4) / CREATOR (*4) / LICK (*7) / LOVEY (*5) / IT'S A SHAME ABOUT RAY (*8) / COME ON FEEL THE LEMONHEADS (*7) / CAR BUTTON CLOTH (*6) / THE BEST OF THE LEMONHEADS compilation (*8)

EVAN DANDO (b. 4 Mar'67) – vocals, guitar + some drums / **JESSE PERETZ** – bass / **BEN DEILY** – guitar, + some drums

		not iss.	ArmoryArms
Jul 86.	(7"ep) <1-2-Huh-Bag 1> **LAUGHING ALL THE WAY TO THE CLEANERS**	-	

– Glad I don't know / I like to / I am a rabbit / So I fucked up.

—— added **DOUG TRACHTON** – drums

		World Service	Taang!
May 88.	(lp)<US-lp some colrd> (SERVM 001) <T 15> **HATE YOUR FRIENDS**		Jun87

– I don't wanna / 394 / Nothing time / Second change / Sneakyville / Amazing Grace / Belt / Hate your friends / Don't tell yourself it's ok / Uhhh / Fed up / Rat velvet. (US-cd 1989; same +=) – Glad I don't know / I like to / I am a rabbit / So I fucked up / Ever / Sad girl / Buried alive / Gotta stop. (re-iss. cd Mar93 with the extra tracks)

—— **EVAN,** on bass, also joined BLAKE BABIES in 1988, alongside girlfriend JULIANA HATFIELD. **JOHN STROHM** – drums (ex-BLAKE BABIES) repl. DOUG.

Sep 88.	(lp)(c) (SERV 001) <T 23> **CREATOR**

– Burying ground / Sunday / Clang bang clang / Out / Your home is where you're happy / Falling / Die right now / Two weeks in another town / Plaster caster / Come

to my window / Take her down / Postcard / Live without. (US-cd 1989; same +=) – Luka (live) / Interview / Mallo cup. (re-iss. Sep92 on 'Taang!', with 6 extra live tracks included) (re-iss. cd Mar93 with all re-issued tracks + 2 acoustic)

—— **COREY LOOG BRENNAN**– guitar (ex-BULLET LAVOLTA) repl. JOHN STROHM

Apr 89.	(7"colrd) <T 31> **LUKA. / STRANGE / MAD**

(scheduled UK Nov89 unissued 12"/cd-s; SEVS 010/+CD) (UK-iss. 7"/12"/cd-s Apr93)

May 89.	(lp/cd) (SERV/+CD 007) <T 32> **LICK**

– Mallo cup / Glad I don't know / 7 powers / A circle of one / Cazzo di ferro / Anyway / Luka / Come back D.A. / I am a rabbit / Sad girl / Ever. (US-cd+=) – Strange / Mad. (re-iss. cd Mar93)

—— **MARK "BUDOLA"** – drums, toured until he checked out mid '89. (COREY also left to concentrate on his PhD.

		Roughneck	not iss.
Jun 90.	(7") (HYPE 3) **DIFFERENT DRUM. / PAINT**		-

(12"+=)(cd-s+=) (12 HYPE 3)(HYPE 3CD) – Ride with me. (re-iss. Feb91 12"ep/cd-ep; HYPE 3 T/CD)

		Atlantic	Atlantic
Jun 90.	(cd-ep) <786088-2> **FAVORITE SPANISH DISHES EP**	-	

– Different drum / Paint / Ride with me / Skulls / Step by step.

—— **DAVID RYAN** (b.20 Oct'64, Fort Wayne, Indiana) – drums repl. DEILY

Oct 91.	(cd/c/lp) <(7567 82137-2/-4/-2)> **LOVEY** Aug90

– Ballarat / Half the time / Year of the cat / Ride with me / Li'l seed / Stove / Come downstairs / Left for dead / Brass buttons / (The) Door. (re-iss. cd/c/lp Nov93)

—— In Sep'90, **DANDO** recruited **BEN DAUGHTY** – drums (ex-SQUIRREL BAIT) repl. RYAN / **BYRON HOAGLAND** – bass (ex-FANCY PANTS) repl. PERETZ.

Sep 91.	(7") (A 7709) **GONNA GET ALONG WITHOUT YA NOW. / HALF THE TIME** -

(12"ep+=) (TA 7709) – PATIENCE AND PRUDENCE EP: Stove (remix) / Step by step.

—— **DANDO, RYAN + JULIANA HATFIELD** (b. 2 Jul'67, Wiscasset) – bass, vocals (ex-BLAKE BABIES)

Jul 92.	(cd/c/lp) <(7567 82137-2/-4/-2)> **IT'S A SHAME ABOUT RAY** 69 68

– Rockin' stroll / Confetti / Rudderless / My drug buddy / The turnpike down / Bit part / Alison's starting to happen / Hannah and Gaby / Kitchen / Ceiling fan in my spoon / Frank Mills. (album hit UK No.33 Jan'93) (re-iss. Feb95)

Oct 92.	(7"/c-s) (A 7423/+C) **IT'S A SHAME ABOUT RAY. / SHAKEY GROUND** 70 -

(10"+=/cd-s+=) (A 7423 TE/CD) – Dawn can't decide / The turnpike down.

Nov 92.	(7"/c-s) (A 7401/+C) **MRS. ROBINSON. / BEING AROUND** 19 -

(10"+=/cd-s+=) (A 7401 TE/CD) – Divan / Into your arms.

—— 1993 line-up: **DANDO, RYAN, NIC DALTON** (b.14 Jun'64, Australia) although she did provide b.vox for 1993 releases. – bass HATFIELD formed own trio

Jan 93.	(7"/c-s) (A 7430/+C) **CONFETTI (remix). / MY DRUG BUDDY** 44 -

(10"+=/cd-s+=) (A 7430 TE/CD) – Ride with me (live) / Confetti (acoustic).

Mar 93.	(c-s) (A 5764C) **IT'S A SHAME ABOUT RAY / ALISON'S STARTING TO HAPPEN** 31 -

(cd-s+=) (A 5764CD) – Different drum (Evan acoustic) / Stove (Evan acoustic). (10"+=) (A 5764TE) – Different drum (acoustic) / Rockin' stroll (live). (cd-s) (A 5764CDX) – ('A'live) / Confetti / Mallo cup / Rudderless (all 4 live).

Oct 93.	(7"/c-s) (A 7302/+C) <87294> **INTO YOUR ARMS. / MISS OTIS REGRETS** 14 67

(10"+=/cd-s+=) (A 7302 TE/CD) – Little black egg / Learning the game.

Oct 93.	(cd/c/lp) <(7567 82537-2/-4/-1)> **COME ON FEEL THE LEMONHEADS** 5 56

– The great big no / Into your arms / It's about time / Down about it / Paid to smile / Big gay heart / Style / Rest assured / Dawn can't decide / I'll do it anyway / Rick James style / Being around / Favourite T / You can take it with you / The jello fund. (lp+=) – Miss Otis regrets.

Nov 93.	(7"/c-s) (A 7296/+C) **IT'S ABOUT TIME. / RICK JAMES ACOUSTIC STYLE** 57 -

(10"+=/cd-s+=) (A 7296 TE/CD) – Big gay heart (demo) / Down about it (acoustic). (above 'A'side was written about JULIANA. I'LL DO IT ANYWAY for BELINDA CARLISLE)

May 94.	(c-ep/10"ep/cd-ep) (A 7259 C/TE/CD) **BIG GAY HEART / DEEP BOTTOM COVE / HE'S ON THE BEACH / FAVORITE T (session)** 55 -

—— Offending lyrics to above 'A'side, were changed; with Stroke & Brick.

—— DALTON departed Sep '94

—— **PATRICK MURPHY** – drums (ex-DINOSAUR JR) repl.RYAN

—— other members with DANDO; **BILL GIBSON** – bass, guitar / **DINA WAXMAN** – bass / **KENNY LYON** – guitar / **RICH GILBERT** – pedal steel / **BRYCE GOGGIN** – vocals, keyboards / etc.

Sep 96.	(c-s) (A 5495C) **IF I COULD TALK I'D TELL YOU /** 39 -

(cd-s) (A 5495CD) – ('A'side) / How will I know (acoustic & electric version) / I don't want to go home / Seagulls aren't free. (cd-s) (A 5495CDX) – ('A'side) / It's all true (acoustic – no drums) / Sexual bryceulidge.

Oct 96.	(cd/c) <(7567 92726-2/-4)> **CAR BUTTON CLOTH** 28

– It's all true / If I could talk I'd tell you / Break me / Hospital / The outdoor type / Losing your mind / Something's missing / Knoxville girl / 6ix / C'mon daddy / One more time / Tenderfoot / Secular rockuledge.

Nov 96.	(c-s) (A 5635C) **IT'S ALL TRUE / LIVE FOREVER** 61 -

(10"+=/cd-s+=) (A 5635 TE/CD) – Fade to black / Keep on loving you.

Mar 97.	(c-s) (A 5620C) **THE OUTDOOR TYPE (remix) / PIN YR HEART**

(cd-s+=) (A 5620CD) – Losing your mind (live acoustic).

Aug 97.	(7") (AT 0012) **BALANCING ACTS. / GALVESTON**

– compilations, etc. –

1990.	(cd) Taang!; <T 15/T23> **CREATE YOUR FRIENDS** -

– (HATE YOUR FRIENDS / CREATOR / LAUGHING E.P.)

Aug 98.	(cd/c) Atlantic; <(7567 80851-2/-4)> **THE BEST OF THE LEMONHEADS**

– Confetti / Into the arms / Mrs. Robinson / Rudderless / It's a shame about Ray / The great big no / Ride with me (acoustic) / My drug buddy / Big gay heart / It's about time / The outdoor type / It's all true / If I could talk I'd tell you / Hospital / Rudy with a flashlight / Into your arms (acoustic) / Down about it (acoustic) / Being around / Rick James acoustic style.

LEMON INTERRUPT (see under ⇒ UNDERWORLD)

John LENNON

Born: JOHN WINSTON LENNON, 9 Oct'40, Liverpool, England. While still a member of The BEATLES (late 1968), he teamed up with his new girlfriend at the time, YOKO ONO, to record the controversial, 'UNFINISHED MUSIC NO.1: TWO VIRGINS'. The cover-shot displayed a full-frontal nude photo of the couple and the album was subsequently sold in brown paper wrapping to apparently save embarrassment to both the customers and the retailers! During Spring next year, its follow-up, 'UNFINISHED MUSIC NO.2: LIFE WITH THE LIONS', hit the shops and continued their anti-commercial, free-form direction, the songs mainly recorded on a small cassette player. Now divorced from his wife CYNTHIA, JOHN married YOKO on the 20th March '69, even changing by deed poll his middle name from WINSTON to ONO. After the LENNONs completed an 8-day peace protest by publicly lying/sitting in a hotel bed, they released The PLASTIC ONO BAND's debut hippy anthem, 'GIVE PEACE A CHANCE'. This gave JOHN his first non-BEATLES hit, rising into the UK Top 3 and US Top 20. Later that year, 'COLD TURKEY' (a drug withdrawal song), also gave him a Top 30 smash on both sides of the Atlantic. Late 1969, he unveiled two albums, one, an avant-garde collaboration with YOKO, 'THE WEDDING ALBUM', and the other a more standard commercial product from The PLASTIC ONO BAND, 'LIVE IN TORONTO 1969', a record which breached the US Top 10. They also scored with another UK/US Top 5 hit, 'INSTANT KARMA', which was produced by PHIL SPECTOR early in 1970. In May that year, The BEATLES officially split prior to the release of another No.1 album, 'Let It Be'. JOHN then concentrated wholly on his solo career, returning with the album, 'JOHN LENNON: PLASTIC ONO BAND'. This was followed by another Top 20 anthem, 'POWER TO THE PEOPLE'. On the 3rd of September '71, he went to New York to live with YOKO and a month later, his classic album, 'IMAGINE', topped the charts in both the US and the UK (its US-only released title track, hitting No.3). In 1971, he failed in a bid to have a Christmas hit in the States with 'HAPPY XMAS (WAR IS OVER)', although this reached the UK Top 5 a year later. During the next three years, during which he released three albums, he fought to stay in America after being ordered by immigration authorities to leave. During this period, in which he temporarily split from YOKO, he went through drinking bouts with his buddy HARRY NILSSON, the pair recording an album, 'PUSSY CATS', together. On the 9th of October '75, YOKO gave birth to their first child, SEAN. LENNON then went into retirement to look after the boy in their Manhattan apartment, leaving behind a charting greatest hits, 'SHAVED FISH'. He was soon to receive his green card, allowing him to permanently reside in the States. However, in 1980 he returned to the studio once again, David Geffen offering to release an album on his self-titled label. In November that year, 'DOUBLE FANTASY' was released, soon topping both US and UK album charts. There was also a return to the singles chart, when the appropriately titled '(JUST LIKE) STARTING OVER' made the Top 10. Tragically on the 8th of December 1980, JOHN was shot five times by a deranged fan, Mark Chapman, outside the LENNON's apartment block. He died shortly afterwards at Roosevelt hospital. Not surprisingly, his previous 45 climbed back up the charts and peaked at No.1, with a re-issue of 'IMAGINE' following it to the top early in 1981. His killer was sent to a mental institution for the rest of his life, and we can only ponder what the 40-year-old might have achieved in the 80's & 90's had he lived. He remains a much revered genius, an artist who attempted to alienate the pop industry with non-conventional music styles. He was also a peaceful man, whose outbursts and human faults seemed to be portrayed falsely by the media, especially in his BEATLES days. His love of YOKO was undoubtably a turning point, finding both himself and the world around him a happier place to live. Although some of his songs exploded into frenetic rock anthems of anti-war and anti-government sentiments, his music, in its many facets, showed a poetic beauty and untouched romance. • **Songwriters:** LENNON, except covers album 'ROCK'N'ROLL' which contained;- BE-BOP-A-LULA (Gene Vincent) / STAND BY ME (Ben E.King) / PEGGY SUE (Buddy Holly) / AIN'T THAT A SHAME (Fats Domino) / SWEET LITTLE SIXTEEN + YOU CAN'T CATCH ME (Chuck Berry) / BONY MORONIE (Larry Williams) / BRING IT HOME TO ME + SEND ME SOME LOVIN' (Sam Cooke) / JUST BECAUSE (Lloyd Price) / YA YA (Lee Dorsey) / RIP IT UP + SLIPPIN' AND SLIDIN' + READY TEDDY (Little Richard) / DO YOU WANT TO DANCE (Bobby Freeman). • **Trivia:** In 1967, JOHN acted in the movie, 'How I Won The War', also appearing in many zany films with The BEATLES. In 1975, he co-wrote 'Fame' with DAVID BOWIE, which topped the US charts. His son from his first marriage, JULIAN, has previously enjoyed chart action, while SEAN has also been more visible, appearing at benefits, etc.

Album rating: UNFINISHED MUSIC NO.1: TWO VIRGINS (*3) / UNFINISHED MUSIC NO.2: LIFE WITH THE LIONS (*3) / THE WEDDING ALBUM (*2) / THE PLASTIC ONO BAND – LIVE PEACE IN TORONTO 1969 (*5) / JOHN LENNON – PLASTIC ONO BAND (*8) / IMAGINE (*9) / SOMETIME IN NEW YORK CITY (*5) / MIND GAMES (*7) / WALLS AND BRIDGES (*6) / ROCK'N'ROLL (*5) / SHAVED FISH compilation (*8) / DOUBLE FANTASY (*7) / THE JOHN LENNON

COLLECTION compilation (*10) / MILK & HONEY posthumous (*4) / LIVE IN NEW YORK CITY early stuff (*4) / MENLOVE AVE. (*4) / LENNON LEGEND boxed-set (*9)

JOHN LENNON & YOKO ONO

JOHN LENNON – vocals, guitar, etc. / **YOKO ONO** (b.18 Feb'33, Tokyo, Japan) – wind, vocals

		Apple	Apple
Nov 68.	(lp; stereo/mono) (S+/APCOR 2) <5001> **UNFINISHED MUSIC NO.1: TWO VIRGINS** – Section 1, 2, 3, 4, 5, 6 / Side 2. (cd-iss. Jan93 on'Rock Classics';) (cd re-iss. Jun97 on 'Rykodisc'; RCD 10411)	☐	☐
		Zapple	Zapple
May 69.	(lp) (ZAPPLE 01) <3357> **UNFINISHED MUSIC NO.2: LIFE WITH THE LIONS** (1/2 live) – Cambridge 1969 / No bed for Beatle John / Baby's heartbeat / Two minutes silence / Radio play. (cd-iss. Jun97 on 'Rykodisc'; RCD 10412)	☐	☐

The PLASTIC ONO BAND

		Apple	Apple
Jul 69.	(7") (APPLE 13) <1809> **GIVE PEACE A CHANCE. / REMEMBER LOVE** (re-iss. Jan81, reached UK No.33)	2	14
Oct 69.	(7") (APPLES 1001) <1813> **COLD TURKEY. / DON'T WORRY KYOKO (MUMMY'S ONLY LOOKING FOR A HAND IN THE SNOW)**	14	30 Dec69
Dec 69.	(lp; as JOHN ONO LENNON & YOKO ONO LENNON) (SAPCOR 11) <3361> **WEDDING ALBUM** – John and Yoko / Amsterdam. (cd-iss. Jun97 on 'Rykodisc'; RCD 10413)		
———	JOHN and YOKO hired the following musicians **ERIC CLAPTON** – guitar (ex-YARDBIRDS, ex-CREAM, ex-BLUESBREAKERS) / **KLAUS VOORMAN** – bass (ex-MANFRED MANN) / **ALAN WHITE** – drums		
Dec 69.	(lp) (CORE 2001) <3362> **THE PLASTIC ONO BAND – LIVE PEACE IN TORONTO 1969** (live 13 Sep'69) – Blue Suede shoes / Money (that's what I want) / Dizzy Miss Lizzy / Yer blues / Cold turkey / Give peace a chance / Don't worry Kyoko / John John (let's hope for peace).	☐	10 Jan70
Feb 70.	(7"; LENNON / ONO WITH PLASTIC ONO BAND) (APPLES 1003) <1818> **INSTANT KARMA!. / Yoko Ono: WHO HAS SEEN THE WIND?**	5	3

JOHN LENNON & THE PLASTIC ONO BAND

———	The **LENNON's** retained only **KLAUS / RINGO STARR** – drums (ex-BEATLES) repl. WHITE who later joined YES		
Dec 70.	(lp) (SAPCOR 17) <3372> **JOHN LENNON: PLASTIC ONO BAND** – Mother / Hold on / I found out / Working class hero / Isolation / Remember / Love / Well well well / Look at me / God / My mummy's dead. (re-iss. Jul84 on 'Fame' lp/c; 41-3102-1/-4) (cd-iss. Apr88 on 'E.M.I.'; CDP 746770-2) (cd re-iss. Dec94 on 'Fame'; CDFA 3310)	11	6
Dec 70.	(7") <1827> **MOTHER. / WHY** (Yoko Ono)	-	43
———	next single also credited with **YOKO ONO**		
Mar 71.	(7") (R 5892) **POWER TO THE PEOPLE. / OPEN YOUR BOX**	7	-
Mar 71.	(7") <1830> **POWER TO THE PEOPLE. / Yoko Ono: TOUCH ME**	-	11
Oct 71.	(lp) (PAS 10004) <3379> **IMAGINE** – Imagine / Crippled inside / Jealous guy / It's so hard / I don't want to be a soldier / Give me some truth / Oh my love / How do you sleep? / How? / Oh Yoko!. (also on quad-lp Jun72; Q4PAS 10004) (cd-iss. May87 on 'Parlophone'; CDP 746641-2) (re-iss. Nov97; LPCENT 27)	1	1 Sep71
Oct 71.	(7") <1840> **IMAGINE. / IT'S SO HARD**	-	3
May 72.	(7") <1848> **WOMAN IS THE NIGGER OF THE WORLD. / Yoko Ono: SISTERS, OH SISTERS**	-	57
———	with **ELEPHANT'S MEMORY & FLUX / INVISIBLE STRINGS** and lots of guests including **FRANK ZAPPA, ERIC CLAPTON,** etc.		
Sep 72.	(d-lp; JOHN & YOKO / PLASTIC ONO BAND) (PCSP 7161) <3392> **SOMETIME IN NEW YORK CITY** (live) – Woman is the nigger of the world / Sisters o sisters / Attica state / Born in a prison / New York City / Sunday bloody Sunday / The luck of the Irish / John Sinclair / Angela / We're all water / (w/ CAST OF THOUSANDS); Cold turkey / Don't worry Kyoko / (w/ The MOTHERS); Jamrag / Scumbag / Au. (re-iss. Feb86 on 'Parlophone'; see LIVE IN NEW YORK CITY')	11	48
———	Next single credited as **JOHN & YOKO / PLASTIC ONO BAND** with The **HARLEM COMMUNITY CHOIR**		
Nov 72.	(7",7"green) (R 5970) **HAPPY XMAS (WAR IS OVER). / LISTEN THE SNOW IS FALLING** (re-iss. Dec74; same; hit No.48) (re-iss. Dec80; same); No.2) (re-iss. Dec81; same; No.28) (re-iss. Dec82; ; hit 56)	4	☐ Nov71

JOHN LENNON

Nov 73.	(7") (R 5994) <1868> **MIND GAMES. / MEAT CITY**	26	18
Nov 73.	(lp/c; JOHN LENNON & PLASTIC U.F.ONO BAND) (PCS/TC-PCS 7165) <3414> **MIND GAMES** – Mind games / Tight a $ / Aisumasen (I'm sorry) / One day (at a time) / Bring on the Lucie (Freeda people) / Nutopian international anthem / Intuition / Out of the blue / Only people / I know (I know) / You are here / Meat city. (re-iss. Oct80 on 'Music For Pleasure' lp/c; MFP/TCMFP 50509) (cd-iss. Aug87 & Sep91 on 'Parlophone'; CDP 746769-2)	13	9
Oct 74.	(7"; JOHN LENNON & THE PLASTIC ONO NUCLEAR BAND featuring ELTON JOHN) (R 5998) <1874> **WHATEVER GETS YOU THRU' THE NIGHT. / BEEF JERKY**	36	1 Sep74
Oct 74.	(lp/c) (PC/+TC 253) <3416> **WALLS AND BRIDGES**	6	1

– Going down on love / Whatever gets you thru the night / Old dirt road / What you got / Bless you / £9 dream / Surprise surprise (sweet bird of Paradise) / Steel and glass / Beef jerky / Nobody loves you (when you're down and out) / Ya-ya / Scared. *(re-iss. Jan85 on 'Parlophone' lp/c; ATAK/TC-ATAK 43) (cd-iss. Jul87; CDP 746768-2)*

Jan 75. (7") *(R 6003) <1878>* **£9 DREAM. / WHAT YOU GOT**	23	9
Feb 75. (lp/c) *(PCS/TC-PCS 7169) <3419>* **ROCK'N'ROLL**	6	6

– Be-bop-a-lula / Stand by me / Medley: Rip it up – Ready Teddy / You can't catch me / Ain't that a shame / Do you want to dance / Sweet little sixteen / Slippin' and slidin' / Peggy Sue / Medley: Bring it on home to me – Send me some lovin' / Ya ya / Just because. *(re-iss. Nov81 on 'Music For Pleasure' lp/c; MFP/TCMFP 50522) (cd-iss. Jul87 on 'Parlophone'; CDP 746 707-2) (re-iss. Feb97 on 'E.M.I.'; LPCENT 9)*

Apr 75. (7") *(R 6005) <1881>* **STAND BY ME. / MOVE OVER MS. L**	30	20 Mar75

(re-iss. Apr81; same)

Oct 75. (7") *(R 6009)* **IMAGINE. / WORKING CLASS HERO**	6	-

(re-iss. Dec80; same); hit No.1)

Nov 75. (lp/c) *(PCS 7173) <3421>* **SHAVED FISH** (compilation)	8	12

– Give peace a chance / Cold turkey / Instant karma / Power to the people / Mother / Woman is the nigger of the world / Imagine / Whatever gets you thru the night / Mind games / £9 dream / Happy Xmas (war is over) / Give peace a chance (reprise). *(cd-iss. May87 on 'E.M.I.'; CDP 746642-2)*

—— JOHN was also credited on a few singles by ELTON JOHN – Feb75 'I Saw Her Standing There' which was also realeased Mar81 with 2 other. In Jul71 a rare single 'GOD SAVE US'/'DO THE OZ' was released by him and Plastic Ono Band backing 'BILL ELLIOT AND THE ELASTIC OZ BAND'

JOHN LENNON & YOKO ONO

returned after a long break

	Geffen	Geffen
Oct 80. (7") *(K 79186) <49604>* **(JUST LIKE) STARTING OVER. / KISS KISS KISS** (Yoko Ono)	1	1
Nov 80. (lp/c) *(K/K4 99131) <2001>* **DOUBLE FANTASY**	1	1

– (Just like) Starting over / Every man has a woman who loves him (YOKO ONO) / Clean up time / Give me something (YOKO ONO) / I'm losing you / I'm moving on (YOKO ONO) / Beautiful boy (darling boy) / Watching the wheels / I'm your angel (YOKO ONO) / Dear Yoko / Beautiful boys (YOKO ONO) / Kiss kiss kiss (YOKO ONO) / Woman / Hard times are over (YOKO ONO). *(re-iss. Jan89 on 'Capitol' cd)(c/lp; CDP 791 425-2)(TC+/EST 2083)*

Jan 81. (7"/c-s) *(K/MK 79195) <49644>* **WOMAN. / Yoko Ono: BEAUTIFUL BOYS**	1	2
Mar 81. (7"/c-s) *(K/MK 79207) <49695>* **WATCHING THE WHEELS. / Yoko Ono: YES, I'M YOUR ANGEL**	30	10

—— His last two singles were released after his tragic murder 8th Dec'80

JOHN & YOKO

had recorded one more album prior to his death.

	Polydor	Polydor
Jan 84. (lp) *(<817 238-1>)* **A HEART PLAY: UNFINISHED DIALOGUE** (interview with Playboy)		
Jan 84. (7") *(POSP 700) <817254>* **NOBODY TOLD ME. / O SANITY**	6	5
Jan 84. (lp/pic-lp/c)(cd) *(POLH/+P/C 5)(<817160-2>)* **MILK AND HONEY**	3	11

– I'm stepping out / Sleepless night (YOKO ONO) / I don't wanna face it / Don't be scared (YOKO ONO) / Nobody told me (YOKO ONO) / Borrowed time / Your hands (YOKO ONO) / (Forgive me) My little flower princess / Let me count the ways (YOKO ONO) / Grow old with me / You're the one (YOKO ONO).

Mar 84. (7") *(POSP 701)* **BORROWED TIME. / YOUR HANDS** (Yoko Ono)	32	

(12"+=) (POSPX 701) – Never say goodbye.

Jul 84. (7") *(POSP 702) <821107>* **I'M STEPPING OUT. / SLEEPLESS NIGHT** (Yoko Ono)		55

(12"+=) (POSPX 702) – Loneliness.

Nov 84. (7") *(POSP 712)* **EVERY MAN HAS A WOMAN WHO LOVES HIM. / IT'S ALRIGHT**		

(above from various compilation 'B'-side by his son SEAN ONO LENNON)

– posthumous releases, etc. –

on 'Parlophone' UK /'Capitol' US, unless mentioned otherwise

Jun 81. (8xlp-box) *Apple; (JLB 8)* **JOHN LENNON (BOXED)**		

– (all lp's from LIVE PEACE – SHAVED FISH) *(4xcd-box-iss.Oct90; LENNON 1)*

Nov 82. *E.M.I.; (EMTV/TC-EMTV 37) / Geffen; <GHSP 2023>* **THE JOHN LENNON COLLECTION**	1	33

– (nearly as 'SHAVED FISH') *(re-iss. Jun85; same) (cd-iss. Oct89; CDEMTV 37) – (2 extra tracks).*

Nov 82. (7") *(R 6059)* **LOVE. / GIVE ME SOME TRUTH**	41	
Mar 84. (7") *EMI Gold; (G45 17)* **GIVE PEACE A CHANCE. / COLD TURKEY**		-
Nov 85. (7") *(R 6117)* **JEALOUS GUY / GOING DOWN ON LOVE**	65	

(12"+=) (12R 6117) – Oh Yoko!

Feb 86. (lp/c)(cd) *(PCS/TC-PCS 7301)(CDP 746 196-2) <12451>* **LIVE IN NEW YORK CITY** (live)	55	41
Nov 86. (lp/c/cd) *(PCS/TCPCS/CDPCS 7308) <12533>* **MENLOVE AVE.**		

(sessions 74-75)
– Here we go again / Rock'n'roll people / Angel baby / Since my baby left me / To know her is to love her / Steel and glass / Scared / Old dirt road / Nobody loves you (when you're down and out).

May 87. (7") *Antar;* **TWO MINUTES SILENCE. / TWO MINUTES SILENCE** (dub!)		
Aug 87. (cd) **LIVE JAM** (half of SOMETIME lp)		
Oct 88. (cd-d/cd-d-lp) *(CD/+TC/+P 722) <90803>* **IMAGINE: THE MOVIE** (Music from the Motion Picture; with some songs by The BEATLES)	64	31

– Real love / Twist and shout / Help! / In my life / Strawberry fields forever / A day in the life / Revolution / The ballad of John & Yoko / Julia / Don't let me down / Give peace a chance / How? / Imagine (rehearsal) / God / Mother / Stand by me / Jealous guy / Woman / Beautiful boy (darling boy) / (Just like) Starting over / Imagine.

Oct 88. (cd-s) *<44230>* **JEALOUS GUY**	-	80
Nov 88. (7"/7"pic-d) *(R/RP 6199)* **IMAGINE. / JEALOUS GUY**	45	-

(12"+=/12"pic-d+=) (12R/+P 6199) – Happy Xmas (war is over).
(cd-s+=) (CDR 6199) – Give peace a chance.

Oct 97. (cd/c) *(<8 21954-2/-4/-1>)* **LENNON LEGEND – THE VERY BEST OF JOHN LENNON**	4	65 Mar98

– Imagine / Instant karma / Mother / Jealous guy / Power to the people / Cold turkey / Love / Mind games / Whatever gets you thru the night / No.9 dream / Stand by me / (Just like) Starting over / Woman / Beautiful boy / Watching the wheels / Nobody told me / Borrowed time / Working class hero / Happy Xmas (war is over) / Give peace a chance.

Sep 98. (3xcd-box) *Dressed To Kill; (DTKBOX 92)* **IN MY LIFE**		-
Nov 98. (4xcd-box+book) *(<8 30614-2>)* **JOHN LENNON ANTHOLOGY** (alt.takes, live rarities and home recordings)	62	99

– ASCOT / NEW YORK CITY / THE LOST WEEKEND / DAKOTA)

Nov 98. (cd/c) *(497639-2/-4)* **WONSAPONATIME** (above highlights)		-
Dec 99. (c-s/cd-s) *(TCR/CDR 6534)* **IMAGINE / HAPPY XMAS (WAR IS OVER) / GIVE PEACE A CHANCE**	3	-

Julian LENNON

Born: JOHN CHARLES JULIAN LENNON, 8 Apr'63, Liverpool, England. Although not as successful as his father JOHN, JULIAN LENNON produced several acceptable albums and singles throughout the 80's and 90's that eerily evoked the ghost of his dad. The offspring from JOHN's first marriage with his wife Cynthia, JULIAN grew up in the estates of Liverpool whilst his father was out carving a career as one of the world's most adored rock'n'rollers. JULIAN was said to be the main inspiration for songs such as 'Lucy In The Sky With Diamonds' (themed around a psychedelic class painting!, aye right!) and the seminal break-up song 'Hey Jude'. The young LENNON developed a passion for music at an early age, and became very fond of playing the piano, as well as the guitar, drums and occasional vocals. Aged 10, he debuted on his father's 'Ya Ya' track from the 'Walls And Bridges' (1974) album, banging along reasonably tunefully on the drums side by side with JOHN's enlightened lyrics. After his dad's death and hoping to pursue a career in his own right, JULIAN signed with 'Atlantic' records. He enlisted the help of YOKO ONO for plans to release a lost LENNON song from the vaults, although he was unsuccessful when the contract fell through. However, he sprang back into action with his debut album 'VALOTTE' (1984), apparently named so after the French chateau it was recorded in. The set spawned four singles, two of which being the UK Top 10 hits 'VALOTTE' and 'TOO LATE FOR GOODBYES'. Despite his denial, JULIAN was, to many older fans, the reincarnation of his father: the similarities in looks were almost spooky, and JULIAN's style of singing and playing were identical. 'VALOTTE' earned JULIAN a nomination for 'Best New Artist' at the 'Grammy' awards at the end of '84, although success had ultimately got the better of JULIAN when his sophomore set, 'THE SECRET VALUE OF DAYDREAMING' (1986), failed through personal demons and lack of attention to detail. 'MR. JORDAN' (1989) became his third set, and his least successful as the new boy-wonder tried to veer away from his LENNON connections. In this he created a dark and brooding atmosphere similar to LOU REED and DAVID BOWIE's earlier works. 1991's 'HELP YOURSELF' was perhaps more promising, the touching ballad 'SALTWATER' entering the British Top 10 and giving him a healthy comeback of sorts. Apart from this newfound success, JULIAN made himself scarce for the next seven years, issuing bits and bobs and contributing to film soundtracks such as 1993's 'The Addams Family Values'. 'PHOTOGRAPHIC SMILE' was delivered in the Spring of 1998. An indie album by all means, its release was only intended for Europe and Japan, but due to popular demand, it followed its Stateside calling the following year. • **Songwriters:** Collaborates with others. Covered; MOTHER MARY (John Lennon) / RUBY TUESDAY (Rolling Stones). • **Trivia:** He and half-brother SEAN (YOKO's son) sang 'STAND BY ME' on stage at Beacon Theater, New York.

Album rating: VALOTTE (*5) / THE SECRET VALUE OF DAYDREAMING (*4) / MR. JORDAN (*4) / HELP YOURSELF (*4) / PHOTOGRAPH SMILE (*5)

JULIAN LENNON – vocals, guitar (with many session people)

	Charisma	Atlantic
Sep 84. (7"/12") *(JL 1/+12)* **TOO LATE FOR GOODBYES. / WELL I DON'T KNOW**	6	-
Oct 84. (7") *<89609>* **VALOTTE. / WELL I DON'T KNOW**	-	9
Oct 84. (lp/c/cd) *(JL LP/MC/CD 1) <80184>* **VALOTTE**	20	17

– Valotte / OK for you / On the phone / Space / Well I don't know / Too late for goodbyes / Lonely / Say you're wrong / Jesse / Let me be.
(re-iss. Apr90 on 'Virgin' lp/c; OVED/+C 286) (cd re-iss. Oct96 on 'Virgin-VIP'; CDVIP 162)

Dec 84. (7"/7"sha-pic-d) *(JL/+S 2)* **VALOTTE. / LET ME BE**	55	

(12"+=) (JL 2-12) – Bebop.

Dec 84. (7") *<89589>* **TOO LATE FOR GOODBYES. / LET ME BE**	-	5
Feb 85. (7") *(JL 3)* **SAY YOU'RE WRONG. / BEBOP**	75	-

(12"+=) (JL 3-12) – Too late for goodbyes.

Apr 85. (7") *<89567>* **SAY YOU'RE WRONG. / BIG MAMA**	-	21
Jul 85. (7") *<89529>* **JESSE. / BEBOP**	-	54
Nov 85. (7") *(EMI 5538)* **BECAUSE. / ('A'instrumental)**	40	

(above on 'E.M.I.' and from film of same name)

Apr 86. (7") *(CB 420/+12) <89437>* **STICK AROUND. / ALWAYS THINK TWICE**		32 Mar86
Apr 86. (lp/c) *(CHC/+MC 71) <81640>* **THE SECRET VALUE OF DAYDREAMING**	93	32

– Stick around / You get what you want / Let me tell you / I've seen your face / Coward till the end / This is my day / You didn't have to tell me / Everyday / Always think twice / I want your body. *(cd-iss. Jul87; CASCD 1171)*

May 86. (7") **WANT YOUR BODY. / EVERYDAY**
May 86. (7") *(CB 423)* **THIS IS MY DAY. / EVERYDAY** — Jul86
Jul 86. (7"/12") *(EMI/12EMI 5556)* **TIME WILL TEACH US ALL. /**
('A'instrumental)
(above also on 'E.M.I.')

	Virgin	Atlantic
Feb 89. (7") *(VS 1154)* <88925> **NOW YOU'RE IN HEAVEN. / THE SECOND TIME**	59	93 Apr89

(12"+=) *(VST 1154)* – ('A'-Orbit mix).
(3"cd-s++=) *(VSCD 1154)* – Too late for goodbyes.
Mar 89. (lp/c/cd) *(JL LP/MC/CD 3)* <81928> **MR. JORDAN** [87]
– Now you're in Heaven / I get up / Angilette / Make it up with you / The second time / You're the one / Mother Mary / Open your eyes / Sunday morning / I want you to know.
Jun 89. (7") *(VS 1182)* **YOU'RE THE ONE. / SUNDAY MORNING**
(12"+=/3"cd-s+=) *(VST/VSCD 1182)* – Stand by me.
Aug 91. (7"/c-s) *(VS/+C 1361)* **SALTWATER. / REBEL KING (live)** [6]
(12"+=) *(VST 1361)* – Creo awe voy a Llorar.
(cd-s++=) *(VSCD 1361)* – Mother Mary.
Sep 91. (cd/c/lp) *(CD/TC+/V 2668)* **HELP YOURSELF** [42]
– Rebel key / Saltwater / Get a life / Would you / Maybe I was wrong / Help yourself / Listen / Other side of town / New psysies rant / Take me home / Imaginary lines / Keep the people working.
Nov 91. (7"/c-s) *(VS/+C 1379)* **HELP YOURSELF. / TAKE ME HOME** [53]
(cd-s+=) *(VSCD 1379)* – Angilette.
(cd-s++=) *(VSCDX 1379)* – Saltwater (acoustic).
Apr 92. (7"/c-s) *(VS/+C 1398)* **GET A LIFE. / ('A'mix)** [56]
(cd-s+=) *(VSCD 1398)* – Saltwater / Ruby Tuesday.

—— JULIAN took a six-year sabbatical

	Music From Another Room	unknown
May 98. (cd-s) *(JULIAN 4CD)* **DAY AFTER DAY / DON'T LET ME DOWN**	66	

May 98. (cd/c) *(MFAR 44 CD/MC)* **PHOTOGRAPH SMILE**
– Day after day / Cold / I should have known / How many times / I don't wanna know / Crucified / Walls / Believe / Good to be lonely / Kiss beyond the catcher / And she cries / Photograph smile / Faithful / Way to your heart.
Aug 98. (cd-s) *(JULIAN 5CD)* **I DON'T WANNA KNOW / I NEED YOU**
(cd-s) *(JULIAN 5CDX)* – ('A' mix)

Sean LENNON

Born: SEAN ONO LENNON, 9 Oct'75, New York, USA, son of JOHN LENNON and YOKO ONO (in fact, he had the same birthday as his famous dad!). When his father was brutally shot dead by manic BEATLES fan, Mark Chapman, in December 1980, SEAN was was only five years old. After studying abroad from an early age (mainly in Geneva accompanied by his mother), the young SEAN plotted his own venture into music, his timing appropriate as his older step-brother, JULIAN, was failing to build upon the successes he'd notched up in the latter half of the 80's. Still only 22, SEAN, who had previously befriended punk rappers, The BEASTIE BOYS, found a home at their 'Grand Royal' imprint. Having acquired the necessary skills for a multi-instrumentalist and with the help of his girlfriend, YUKA HONDA (of CIBO MATTA – another person with musical talent aplenty), SEAN went into the studio. He eventually emerged in 1998 with 'INTO THE SUN', a delightful debut that shone through for most discerning critics not looking for – or comparing to – a new JOHN LENNON, its eclectic bubblegum experimentation blending free-jazz with great lyrical insight and delivery (missed since his father!). However, its sales were a little disappointing, although tracks like 'SPACESHIP', 'TWO FINE LOVERS' and 'HOME' will endure until a second set delivers him to deserved critical acclaim.

Album rating: INTO THE SUN (*6)

SEAN LENNON – vocals, guitars, bass, drums, keyboards, synthesizers, etc. / with **YUKA HONDA** – synthesizer, guitars, vibes, keyboards, producer, etc. (of CIBO MATTA) / + various guests

	Grand Royal	Grand Royal
Apr 98. (7") *(GR 058)* **HOME. / 5/8**		

May 98. (cd/lp) <(494551-2/-4)> **INTO THE SUN**
– Mystery juice / Into the sun / Home / Bathtub / One night / Spaceship / Photosynthesis / Queue / Two fine lovers / Part one of the cowboy trilogy / Wasted / Breeze / Sean's theme.
Feb 99. (7") *(CL 807)* **QUEUE. /** — -
(cd-s+=) *(CDCL 807)* –

Annie LENNOX (see under ⇒ EURYTHMICS)

Deke LEONARD (see under ⇒ MAN)

LEVELLERS

Formed: Brighton, England . . . early '88 by MARK CHADWICK, JEREMY CUNNINGHAM, CHARLIE HEATHER, JON SEVINK and ALAN MILES. Taking their name from the English political radicals of the 17th Century, The LEVELLERS were one of the most successful and consistent bands to emerge from the free festival/crusty scene, building up a loyal grassroots fanbase with their raggle-taggle blend of folk and punk. After Phil Nelson took over as manager the following year, he released a couple of raw EP's on

his own 'Hag' imprint, before the band signed to European label, 'Musidisc', and began work on a debut album with WATERBOYS producer, Phil Tennant. While 'WEAPON CALLED THE WORD' helped introduce their rootsy assault to a larger audience, the band subsequently broke from their contract and signed to 'China', while MILES was replaced by songwriter/guitarist, SIMON FRIEND. Another hectic UK tour followed and by Autumn '91, The LEVELLERS' popularity was such that the 'LEVELLING THE LAND' album made the Top 20 with only the support of minor hit single, 'ONE WAY'. With a more accessible anthemic rock/folk approach, the album took the band's defiantly pro-earth, pro-equality philosophy overground and into the mainstream, 'BATTLE OF THE BEANFIELD' commemorating the famous festival stand-off between hippies and police. In Spring '92, The LEVELLERS scored their biggest hit to date with the 'FIFTEEN YEARS' EP, almost making the Top 10, while they chose to end the year with a series of 'Freakshows' combining the likes of fellow agit-poppers, CHUMBAWAMBA with such established crusty pastimes as juggling and fire-eating. The following year's eponymous album missed the No.1 spot by a whisker, spawning a trio of Top 20 singles in 'BELARUSE', 'THIS GARDEN' and the lovely 'JULIE'; although The LEVELLERS were now rather unlikely but fully fledged pop stars, they also became embroiled in a war of words with the music press and fellow musicians. Not that this affected their popularity one iota, the band finally topping the UK charts with 'ZEITGEIST' (1995) as they found themselves surfing the new wave of enthusiasm for British music in general. Certainly one of the UK's more conscientious bands, The LEVELLERS are sadly part of a dying breed who still believe that music and politics are a feasible combination. • **Songwriters:** Group compositions except; THE DEVIL WENT DOWN TO GEORGIA (Charlie Daniels Band) / TWO HOURS (McDermott) / GERM FREE ADOLESCENCE (X-Ray Spex) / PRICE OF LOVE (Everly Brothers) / HANG ON TO YOUR EGO (Frank Black). • **Trivia:** The FENCE released one single in May '87 on 'Flag'; FROZEN WATER / EXIT.

Album rating: WEAPON CALLED THE WORD (*7) / LEVELLING THE LAND (*8) / THE LEVELLERS (*6) / ZEITGEIST (*5) / HEADLINES, WHITE LINES, BLACK TAR RIVERS – BEST LIVE (*6) / MOUTH TO MOUTH (*5) / ONE WAY OF LIFE (THE BEST OF . . .) compilation (*8)

MARK CHADWICK – vocals, guitar, banjo (ex-FENCE) / **JEREMY CUNNINGHAM** – bass, bazouki / **CHARLIE HEATHER** – drums / **JON SEVINK** – violin (ex-FENCE) / **ALAN MILES** – vocals, guitar, mandolin, harmonica

	Hag	not iss.
May 89. (12"ep) *(HAG 005)* **CARRY ME**		-

– Carry me / What's in the way / The lasy days of winter / England my home /
Oct 89. (12"ep) *(HAG 006)* **OUTSIDE INSIDE. / HARD FIGHT / I HAVE NO ANSWERS / BARREL OF A GUN** — -

	Musidisc	not iss.
Apr 90. (7") *(105 577)* **WORLD FREAK SHOW. / BARREL OF A GUN (acoustic)**		

(12"+=) *(108 936)* – What you know.
Apr 90. (cd/c/lp) *(10557-2/-4/-1)* **WEAPON CALLED THE WORD**
– World freak show / Carry me / Outside-inside / Together all the way / Barrel of a gun / Three friends / I have no answers / No change / Blind faith / The ballad of Robbie Jones / England my home / What you know.
Oct 90. (7") *(106897)* **TOGETHER ALL THE WAY. / THREE FRIENDS (re-mix) (Arfa mix short version)**
(12"+=) *(106896)* – Cardboard box city / Social insecurity.

—— **SIMON FRIEND** – guitars, vocals repl. ALAN.

	China	Elektra
Sep 91. (7"/c-s) *(WOK/+MC 2008)* **ONE WAY. / HARD FIGHT (acoustic) / THE LAST DAYS OF WINTER**	51	-

(12"+=/cd-s+=) *(WOK T/CD 2008)* – ('A'-Factory mix) / The Devil went down to Georgia.
Oct 91. (lp/c/cd) *(WOL/+MC/CD 1022)* <61325-1/-4/-2> **LEVELLING THE LAND** [14] — May92
– One way / The game / The boatman / The liberty song / Far from home / Sell out / Another man's cause / The road / The riverflow / Battle of the beanfield. (cd re-iss. Jul99; 4509 96100-2)
Nov 91. (7"/c-s) *(WOK/+MC 2010)* **FAR FROM HOME. / WORLD FREAK SHOW (live)** [71] — -
(12"+=/cd-s+=) *(WOK T/CD 2010)* – Outside inside (live) / The boatman (live) / Three friends (live).
May 92. (c-ep/12"pic-d-ep/12"ep/cd-ep) *(WOK MC/X/T/CD 2020)* **15 YEARS / DANCE BEFORE THE STORM. / RIVERFLOW (live) / PLASTIC JEEZUS** [11] — -
Jun 93. (c-s) *(WOKMC 2034)* **BELARUSE / SUBVERT (live at Trancentral) / BELARUSE RETURN** [12] — -
(12"+=/cd-s+=) *(WOK T/CD 2034)* – Is this art?
Sep 93. (lp/c/cd) *(WOL/+MC/CD 1034)* <61532> **THE LEVELLERS** [2] — -
– Warning / 100 years of solitude / The likes of you and I / Is this art? / Dirty Davey / This garden / Broken circles / Julie / The player / Belaruse. (cd re-iss. Jul99; 4509 95908-2)
Oct 93. (7"pic-d/c-s) *(WOK P/MC 2039)* **THIS GARDEN. / LIFE (acoustic)** [12] — -
(12"+=/cd-s+=) *(WOK T/CD 2039)* – ('A'-Marcus Dravs remix) / ('A'-Banco De Gaia remix).
May 94. (7"clear-ep/c-ep/10"pic-d-ep/cd-ep) *(WOK/+MC//CD 2042)* **THE JULIE EP** [17] — -
– Julie (new version) / English civil war / Warning (live) / 100 years of solitude / The lowlands of Holland.
Jul 95. (7"pic-d) *(WOKP 2059)* **HOPE ST. / LEAVE THIS TOWN** [12] — -
(7"pic-d) *(WOKPX 2059)* – ('A'side) / Miles away.
(cd-s++=/c-s++=) *(WOK CD/MC 2059)* – Busking on Hope Street.
Aug 95. (lp/c/cd) *(WOL/+MC/CD 1064)* <61887> **ZEITGEIST** [1] — -
– Hope St. / The fear / Exodus / Maid of the river / Saturday to Sunday / 4.am /

Forgotten ground / Fantasy / P.C. Keen / Just the one / Haven't made it / Leave this town / Men-an-tol. *(cd re-iss. Jul99; 0630 11597-2)*

Oct 95. (7"/c-s/cd-s) *(WOK/+MC/CD 2067)* **FANTASY. / SARA'S BEACH / SEARCHLIGHTS (extended)** | **16** | **-** |
(below featured JOE STRUMMER (ex-CLASH) on piano)

Dec 95. (7"/c-ep/cd-ep) *(WOK/+MC/CD 2076)* **JUST THE ONE / A PROMISE. / YOUR 'OUSE / DRINKING FOR ENGLAND** | **12** | **-** |

Jul 96. (7"ep/c-ep/cd-ep) *(WOK/+MC/CD 2082)* **EXODUS – LIVE (live)** | **24** | **-** |
– Exodus / Another man's cause / Leave this town / P.C. Keen.

Aug 96. (cd/c) *(WOL CDX/MC 1074)* **HEADLIGHTS, WHITE LINES, BLACK TAR RIVERS – BEST LIVE (live)** | **13** | **-** |
– Sell out / Hope St. / 15 years / Exodus / Carry me / The boatman / 3 friends / Men-an-tol / The road / One way / England my home / England my home / Battle of the beanfield / Liberty / The riverflow. *(cd re-iss. Jul99; 0630 15783-2)*

Aug 97. (c-s/cd-s) *(WOK MC/CD 2088)* **BEAUTIFUL DAY / BAR ROOM JURY / ALL YOUR DREAMS** | **13** | **-** |
(cd-s) *(WOKCDX 2088)* – ('A'side) / Germ free adolescence / Price of love / Hang on to your ego.

Aug 97. (lp/c/cd) *(WOL/+MC/CD 1084)* **MOUTH TO MOUTH** | **5** | **-** |
– Dog train / Beautiful day / Celebrate / Rain and snow / Far away / C.C.T.V. / Chemically free / Elation / Captains' courageous / Survivors / Sail away / Too real. *(cd re-iss. Jul99; 0630 19856-2)*

Oct 97. (c-ep/cd-ep) *(WOK MC/CD 2089)* **CELEBRATE / RAIN & SNOW (The White Mountain Yarn mix) / SEA OF PAIN / SURVIVORS** | **28** | **-** |
(cd-s) *(WOKCDX 2089)* – ('A'side) / Men-an-tol (live acoustic) / 4 + 20 / Ring of fire.

Dec 97. (12"ep/c-ep/cd-ep) *(WOK/+MC/CD 2090)* **DOG TRAIN / LAST DAYS OF WINTER. / CARRY ME / WHAT'S IN THE WAY** | **24** | **-** |

Mar 98. (12"ep/c-ep/cd-ep) *(WOK/+MC/CD 2091)* **TOO REAL (mixes; Steve Osborne / Morcheeba / Indian Rope Man / Lean Fiddler / Morcheeba instrumental / Bliss)** | **46** | **-** |

Oct 98. (7"/c-s) *(WOK/+MC 2096)* **BOZOS. / DON'T YOU GRIEVE** | **44** | **-** |
(cd-s) *(WOKCD 2096)* – Plastic factory.
(cd-s) *(WOKCDR 2096)* – ('A'side) / New York mining disaster 1941 / Supercharger (heavy metal mix).

Oct 98. (cd/c) *(052173-2/-4)* **ONE WAY OF LIFE (THE BEST OF . . .) (compilation)** | **15** | **-** |
– One way / What a beautiful day / Fifteen years / Shadow on the sun / Hope street / Belaruse / Celebrate / Too real (12"mix) / Bozos / This garden / Carry me / Fantasy / Julie / Dog train / Far from home / Just the one. *(ltd.d-cd+=)* – Far from home / Just the one / PC Keen / Sell out / Hope Street / 15 years / Men-an-to.

Jan 99. (c-s) *(WOKMC 2102)* **ONE WAY (new version). / ANGEL** | **33** | **-** |
(cd-s+=) *(WOKCD 2102)* – Windows.
(cd-s) *(WOKCDX 2102)* – ('A'side) / England my home / I have no answers.

– compilations, etc. –

Jan 92. (7") *Musidisc; (105 557)* **WORLD FREAK SHOW (remix). / WHAT YOU KNOW** | | **-** |
(12"+=/cd-s+=) *(10893 6/2)* – Barrel of a gun / What you know.

Mar 93. (lp/c/cd) *China; (WOL 1035/+MC/CD)* **SEE NOTHING, HEAR NOTHING, DO SOMETHING (early material)** | | **-** |

LEVON & THE HAWKS (see under ⇒ BAND)

Huey LEWIS & THE NEWS

Formed: Marin County, California, USA . . . 1979 as AMERICAN EXPRESS by ex-CLOVER cohorts, HUEY LEWIS and SEAN HOPPER together with session players (who all had previously backed VAN MORRISON) JOHNNY COLLA, CHRIS HAYES, MARIO CIPOLLINA and BILL GIBSON. Country-rockers CLOVER had issued a number of 45's and two albums ('UNAVAILABLE' and 'LOVE ON THE WIRE') for 'Vertigo' in the late 70's; HOPPER had also featured on ELVIS COSTELLO's 1977 debut album, 'My Aim Is True'. AMERICAN EXPRESS, meanwhile, changed their name upon signing to 'Chrysalis', an eponymous debut album, 'HUEY LEWIS AND THE NEWS' arriving in summer 1980. Despite a muted reaction, the group were to make their breakthrough two years on with a song they'd borrowed from CLOVER producer Robert 'Mutt' Lange. The track in question, 'DO YOU BELIEVE IN LOVE', made the US Top 10 and powered follow-up album, 'PICTURE THIS' (1982) into the US Top 20. With their mainstream rock credentials now at least partly established, the workaday, everyman appeal of LEWIS and Co saw them hitting paydirt with 1983's multi-million selling 'SPORT' album. The record topped the US chart and spawned three Top 10 hits, 'HEART AND SOUL', 'I WANT A NEW DRUG (CALLED LOVE)' and 'IF THIS IS IT', the band's inoffensive all-American humor and stultifying predictability making them mass market icons. While the latter track had just edged into the UK Top 40, HUEY LEWIS only became big news in Britain after scoring with the 'THE POWER OF LOVE', a track written for the soundtrack to Steven Spielberg's 'Back To The Future'. As well as becoming the band's first US No.1 in 1985, the single also narrowly missed the UK Top 10 and introduced British audiences to LEWIS' jocular rasp. While the subsequent 'FORE!' (1986) album made the UK Top 10, only the annoyingly bouncy 'STUCK WITH YOU' was a major British hit. It was a different story in the States where The NEWS were still a headline act, scooping two No.1 singles ('STUCK WITH YOU' and the BRUCE HORNSBY-penned 'JACOB'S LADDER') and a No.1 album ('FORE!') through '86-'87. While critics remained almost entirely unconvinced that it was actually 'HIP TO BE SQUARE', LEWIS carried on regardless, coming in for more press flak with the more adventurous 'SMALL WORLD' (1988)

set. Although the 'PERFECT WORLD' single went Top 3, no further major hits were forthcoming. HUEY LEWIS & THE NEWS entered the 90's with only middling success, the 'HARD AT PLAY' (1991) album just scraping the US Top 30. Even a new deal with 'Elektra' and a cliched album of rock'n'roll covers, 'FOUR CHORDS AND SEVERAL YEARS AGO' (1994) failed to curtail the commercial rot for a band who truly merit the term 'Dad Rock'. • **Songwriters:** LEWIS penned except many covers; BUZZ BUZZ BUZZ (Hollywood Flames) / HEART AND SOUL (hit; Exile) / HOPE YOU LOVE ME LIKE ME YOU SAY YOU LOVE ME (Wet Willie) / TATTOO (Phil Lynott) / SHAKE RATTLE AND ROLL (Bill Haley) / BLUE MONDAY (Fats Domino) / SEARCHING FOR MY LOVE (R.Moore) / (SHE'S) SOME KIND OF WONDERFUL (J.Ellison) / BUT IT'S ALRIGHT (J.Jackson-P.Tubbs) / IF YOU GOTTA MAKE A FOOL OF SOMEBODY (R.Clark) / MOTHER IN LAW (Allen Toussaint) / LITTLE BITTY PRETTY ONE (R.Byrd) / GOOD MORNING LITTLE SCHOOLGIRL (Lightnin' Hopkins) / STAGGER LEE (Lloyd Price) / SHE SHOT A HOLE IN MY SOUL (M.Gayden-C.Neese) / SURELY I LOVE YOU (M.Oliver-J.Bracken) / YOU LEFT THE WATER RUNNING (R.Hall-D.Penn-O.Franck) / YOUR CASH AIN'T NOTHIN' BUT TRASH (C.Calhoun) / FUNCTION AT THE JUNCTION (F.Long-E.Holland) / BETTER TO HAVE AND NOT NEED (Don Covay) / GOING DOWN SLOW (J.Olden) / etc. • **Trivia:** In the mid-80's, LEWIS sued and received an out of court settlement from RAY PARKER JR. who admitted to plagiarising HUEY's 'I WANT A NEW DRUG (CALLED LOVE)' on his hit 'Ghostbusters'.

Album rating: HUEY LEWIS & THE NEWS (*4) / PICTURE THIS (*6) / SPORTS (*6) / FORE! (*5) / SMALL WORLD (*4) / HARD AT PLAY (*4) / THE HEART OF ROCK'N'ROLL – THE BEST OF HUEY LEWIS & THE NEWS compilation (*6) / FOUR CHORDS AND SEVERAL YEARS AGO (*4) / TIME FLIES: THE BEST OF HUEY LEWIS & THE NEWS part compilation (*6)

HUEY LEWIS (b. HUGH ANTHONY CREGG III, 5 Jul'50, New York) – vocals, harmonica / **SEAN HOPPER** (b.31 Mar'53) – keyboards, vocals / **JOHNNY COLLA** (b. 2 Jul'52) – guitar, saxophone (ex-SLY STONE) / **CHRIS HAYES** (b.24 Nov'57) – guitar, vocals / **MARIO CIPOLLINA** (b.10 Nov'54) – bass (ex-RONNIE MONTROSE) / **BILL GIBSON** (b.13 Jul'51) – drums, percussion, vocals

		Mercury	Mercury
Apr 79. (7"; as AMERICAN EXPRESS) *(6007 212)(9198 168)* **EXODISCO. / KICKBACK**			

		Chrysalis	Chrysalis
Jul 80. (lp/c) *<(CHR/ZCHR 1292)>* **HUEY LEWIS AND THE NEWS**			

– Some of my lies are true / Sooner or later / Don't make me do it / Stop trying / Now here's you / I want you / Don't ever tell me that you love me / Hearts / Troubles in Paradise / Who cares / If you really love me you'll let me go. *(cd-iss. Apr87; CCD 1292)*

Feb 82. (lp/c) *<(CHR/ZCHR 1340)>* **PICTURE THIS** | | | **13** |
– Change of heart / Tell me a little lie / Giving it all up for love / Hope you love me like you say you do / Workin' for a livin' / Do you believe in love / Is it me / Whatever happened to true love / The only one / Buzz buzz buzz. *(cd-iss. Jun87; CCD 1340)*

Mar 82. (7") *<(CHS 2589)>* **DO YOU BELIEVE IN LOVE. / IS IT ME** | | **7** Jan82 |

May 82. (7") *<2604>* **HOPE YOU LOVE ME LIKE YOU SAY YOU DO. / WHATEVER HAPPENED TO TRUE LOVE** | **-** | **36** |

Jun 82. (7"ep/7"pic-d-ep) *(CHS/+P 2620)* **TATTOO** | | **-** |
– Giving it all up for love / Do you believe in love / Some of my lies are true.

Aug 82. (7") *<2630>* **WORKIN' FOR A LIVIN'. / ('A'live)** | **-** | **41** |

Sep 83. (lp/c) *<(CHR/ZCHR 1412)>* **SPORTS** | | **1** |
– The heart of rock'n'roll / Heart and soul / Bad is bad / I want a new drug (called love) / Walking on a thin line / Finally found a home / If this is it / You crack me up / Honky tonk blues. *(re-iss. Nov84 lp/cd*; ACCD 1412)* – hit UK No.23 in Sep85 *(cd re-iss. Apr89 on 'Mobile Fidelity'; UDCD 509) (cd re-iss. Mar94; CD25CD 20) (cd re-iss. Mar99 on 'E.M.I.'; CDP 321412-2)*

Nov 83. (7") *(CHS 2748) <42726>* **HEART AND SOUL. / YOU CRACK ME UP** | | **8** Sep83 |

Mar 84. (7") *(CHS 2776) <42766>* **I WANT A NEW DRUG (CALLED LOVE). / FINALLY FOUND A HOME** | | **6** Jan84 |
(12"+=) *(12CHS 2776)* – ('A'extended) / Heart and soul / Tattoo.

Apr 84. (7") *<42782>* **THE HEART OF ROCK'N'ROLL. / WORKIN' FOR A LIVIN' (live)** | **-** | **6** |

Jun 84. (7"/7"sha-pic-d) *(CHS/+P 2798)* **THE HEART OF ROCK'N'ROLL. / DO YOU BELIEVE IN LOVE** | | **-** |
(12"+=/12"pic-d+=) *(12/+CHSP 2798)* – I want a new drug (called love) / Heart and soul / Tattoo.

Sep 84. (7") *(CHS 2803) <42803>* **IF THIS IS IT. / CHANGE OF HEART** | **39** | **6** Jul84 |
(12"+=) *(12CHS 2803)* – I want a new drug (called love) / Heart and soul.
(d7"+=) *(CHSD 2803)* – Walking on a thin line (live) / Workin' for a livin' (live).

Oct 84. (7") *<42825>* **WALKING ON A THIN LINE. / THE ONLY ONE** | **-** | **18** |

Aug 85. (7")*<7"pic-d-US>* *(HUEY 1) <42876>* **THE POWER OF LOVE. / BAD IS BAD** | **11** | **1** Jun85 |
(12"+=/d7"+=) *(HUEY X/D 1)* – I want a new drug (called love) (live) / It's all right (live).

Nov 85. (7"ep/12"ep) *(HUEY/+X 2)* **HEART AND SOUL. / HOPE YOU LOVE ME LIKE YOU SAY YOU DO / THE HEART OF ROCK'N'ROLL / BUZZ BUZZ BUZZ (live)** | **61** | **-** |

Jan 86. (7"/7"pic-d) *(HUEY/+P 3)* **THE POWER OF LOVE. / DO YOU BELIEVE IN LOVE** | **9** | **-** |
(12"+=) *(HUEYX 3)* – Back in time.

Apr 86. (7") *(HUEY 4)* **THE HEART OF ROCK'N'ROLL. / HOPE YOU LOVE ME LIKE YOU SAY YOU DO** | **49** | **-** |
(d7"+=/ext-12"+=/12"pic-d+=) *(HUEY D/X/P 4)* – Bad is bad / Tattoo (giving it all up for love).

Aug 86. (7") *(HUEY 5) <43019>* **STUCK WITH YOU. / DON'T EVER TELL ME THAT YOU LOVE ME** | **12** | **1** Jul86 |
(12"+=) *(HUEYX 5)* – The heart of rock'n'roll (live) / Trouble in Paradise (live).

Sep 86. (lp/c/cd) (CDL/ZCDL/CCD 1534) <41534> **FORE!** [8] [1]
– Jacob's ladder / Stuck with you / Whole lotta lovin' / Doing it all for my baby / Simple as that / Hip to be square / I know what I like / I never walk alone / The power of love / Forest for the tree / Naturally / Simple as that. (re-iss. Dec92 on 'Fame' cd/c; CD/TC FA 3284) (re-iss. Jul94 cd/c; same as original) (cd re-iss. Sep98 on 'E.M.I.'; CCD 1534)

Nov 86. (7") (HUEY 6) <43065> **HIP TO BE SQUARE. / SOME OF MY LIES ARE TRUE** [41] [3] Oct86
(12"+=) (HUEYX 6) – ('A'version).

Jan 87. (7") <43097> **JACOB'S LADDER. / THE HEART OF ROCK & ROLL (live)** [-] [1]

Mar 87. (7") (HUEY 7) **SIMPLE AS THAT. / WALKING ON A THIN LINE** [47] [-]
(12"+=/cd-s+=) (HUEYX/CDE 7) – Do you believe in love / Bad is bad / Workin' for a living (live).
(d7"+=) (HUEYD 7) – The power of love / Do you believe in love.

Mar 87. (7") <43108> **I KNOW WHAT I LIKE. / FOREST FOR THE TREES** [-] [9]

Jul 87. (7") <43143> **DOING IT ALL FOR MY BABY. / NATURALLY** [-] [6]

Jul 87. (7") (HUEY 8) **DOIN' IT ALL (FOR MY BABY). / JACOB'S LADDER** [-] [-]
(12"+=) (HUEYX 8) – I know what I like.

Oct 87. (7") (HUEY 9) **BAD IS BAD. / GIVING IT ALL UP FOR LOVE** [-] [-]
(12"+=) (HUEYX 9) – Doing it all for my baby / Back in time.

Jul 88. (7") (HUEY 10) <43265> **PERFECT WORLD. / SLAMMIN'** [48] [3]
(12"+=/cd-s+=) (HUEYX/HUCD 10) – Workin' for a livin' (live).

Aug 88. (lp/c/cd) (CDL/ZCDL/CCD 1622) <41622> **SMALL WORLD** [12] [11]
– Small world (part 1) / Old Antone's / Perfect world / Bobo tempo / Small world (part 2) / Walking with the kid / World to me / Better be true / Give me the keys (and I'll drive you crazy) / Slammin'.

Sep 88. (7") (HUEY 11) <43306> **SMALL WORLD. / (part 2)** [-] [25]
(cd-s+=) (HUEYCD 11) – Trouble in paradise (live) / It's all right (live).

Nov 88. (7") (HUEY 12) **WORLD TO ME. / IT'S ALL RIGHT** [-] [-]
(12"+=/cd-s+=) (HUEY X/CD 12) - Naturally.

Jan 89. (7") <43335> **GIVE ME THE KEYS (AND I'LL DRIVE YOU CRAZY). / IT'S ALL RIGHT (live)** [-] [47]

Feb 89. (7") (HUEY 13) **WALKING WITH THE KID. / BAD IS BAD** [-] [-]
(12"+=/cd-s+=) (HUEY X/CD 13) – Back in time / I wanna new drug (called love).

	Chrysalis	E.M.I.
May 91. (cd/c/lp) (CCD/ZCHR/CHR 1847) <93355> **HARD AT PLAY**	39	27

– Build me up / It hit me like a hammer / Attitude / He don't know / Couple days off / That's not me / We should be making love / The best of me / Do you love me, or what? / Don't look back / Time ain't money. (re-iss. Mar94 cd/c;)

Jul 91. (7"/7"s/c-s) (HUEY/+LH/MC 14) <50364> **IT HIT ME LIKE A HAMMER. / DO YOU LOVE ME, OR WHAT?** [-] [21]
(12"+=/cd-s+=) (HUEY X/CD 14) – ('A'sax version).

Sep 91. (7"/c-s) (HUEY/+MC 15) <50346> **COUPLE DAYS OFF. / TIME AIN'T MONEY** [-] [11] Apr91
(12"+=) (HUEYX 15) – The heart of rock'n'roll.
(cd-s+++=) (HUEYCD 15) – ('A'version).

Nov 92. (cd/c/lp) (CD/TC+/CHR 1934) **THE HEART OF ROCK'N'ROLL: THE BEST OF HUEY LEWIS & THE NEWS** (compilation) [23] [-]
– Power of love / Hip to be square / Do you believe in love / If this is it / Some of my lies are true / Workin' for a livin' (live) / Bad is bad / I want a new drug / The heart of rock & roll / Heart and soul / Jacob's ladder / Stuck with you / Trouble in Paradise / Walking on a thin line / Perfect world / Small world (part one) / Back in time.

	Elektra	Elektra
May 94. (c-s) <64542> **(SHE'S) SOME KIND OF WONDERFUL / GOOD MORNING LITTLE SCHOOLGIRL**	-	44

May 94. (7"/c-s) (EKR 182/+C) **(SHE'S) SOME KIND OF WONDERFUL. / IT'S ALL RIGHT** [-] [-]
(cd-s+=/s-cd-s+=) (EKR 182CD/+X) – Good morning little schoolgirl / Going down slow.

May 94. (cd/c) <(7559 61500-2/-4)> **FOUR CHORDS AND SEVERAL YEARS AGO** [-] [55]
– Shake, rattle and roll / Blue Monday / Searching for my love / (She's) Some kind of wonderful / But it's alright / If you gotta make a fool of somebody / Mother in law / Little bitty pretty one / Good morning little schoolgirl / Stagger Lee / She shot a hole in my soul / Surely I love you / You left the water running / Your cash ain't nothin' but trash / Function at the junction / Better to have and not need / Going down slow.

Aug 94. (c-s) (EKR 188C) <64524> **BUT IT'S ALRIGHT / (SHE'S) SOME KIND OF WONDERFUL (live)** [-] [54]
(cd-s+=) (EKR 188CD) – Flip, flop & fly / ('A'live).

Mar 96. (cd-s) **ONCE UPON A TIME IN NEW YORK CITY /** [-] [-]

Oct 96. (cd-s) **100 YEARS FROM NOW** [-] [-]

Oct 96. (cd) <61977> **TIME FLIES . . . THE BEST OF HUEY LEWIS & THE NEWS** (compilation + 4 new songs)
– The heart of rock & roll / Heart and soul / Doing it all for my baby / Do you believe in love / Trouble in Paradise / Power of love / If this is it / Bad is bad / Workin' for a livin' / It's alright / Stuck with you / I want a new drug / 100 years from now / So little kindness / 'Til the day after / When the time has come.

– compilations, others, etc. –

Aug 95. (cd-s) Old Gold; (OG 6317) **POWER OF LOVE / I WANT A NEW DRUG** [-] [-]

Nov 95. (3xcd-box) Chrysalis; (CDOMB 010) **HUEY LEWIS & THE NEWS / PICTURE THIS / SPORTS** [-] [-]

Oct 97. (cd) EMI Gold; (821088-2) **THE GOLD COLLECTION** [-] [-]

Feb 98. (cd) Disky; <(DC 88282-2)> **THE ONLY ONE** [-] [-]

Sep 98. (cd) Beat Goes On; (BGOCD 417) **HUEY LEWIS & THE NEWS / PICTURE THIS** [-] [-]

Mar 99. (cd) Beat Goes On; (BGOCD 432) **SMALL WORLD / SPORTS** [-] [-]

Jul 99. (d-cd) Disky; <(HR 85776-2)> **ORIGINAL GOLD** [-] [-]

Jerry Lee LEWIS

Born: 29 Sep'35, Ferriday, Louisiana, USA. In 1949, his parents mortgaged their house to buy him a piano which the young JERRY mastered in two weeks! A few years later, after being expelled from a religious school that taught music, he married a preacher's daughter; he soon deserted her however, bigamously marrying another girl in true shotgun style. In 1956, LEWIS went to Memphis, Tennessee with his father and through perseverance, set up recording time in Sam Phillips' 'Sun' studios. The following year, after his debut, 'CRAZY ARMS', was banned from airplay, LEWIS secured a couple of appearances on the Steve Allen TV Show, the exposure leading to massive sales of his second single, 'WHOLE LOTTA SHAKIN' GOIN' ON'. Although LEWIS didn't actually write any of his material, his demented rock'n'roll performances (he even pummelled the piano with his feet!) earned him the rather unfortunate nickname, "The Killer". Later in '57, JERRY bigamously married again!, this time secretly to his 13 year-old second cousin, Myra Gale Brown. Perhaps inspired by his recent activities, LEWIS scored two enormous worldwide classics in the appropriately titled 'GREAT BALLS OF FIRE' and 'BREATHLESS'. Meanwhile, he divorced his second wife and brought the wrath of the religious establishment and moral majority when his questionable lifestyle was disclosed; LEWIS' UK arrival (in May '58) caused uproar and near tour cancellation after newspapers had a field day over his "minor" misdemeanours. Although JERRY LEE made a few more sporadic returns to the charts, his career had been severely dented by this late 50's hysteria. While Myra gave birth to his second son, Steve Allen, in February '59, LEWIS's intake of alcohol and pills was increasing every month. Tragedy struck in April '62, when his aforementioned son drowned in a swimming pool accident. Around a year and a half later, coinciding with LEWIS' signature for new imprint 'Smash', Myra produced another child, this time a daughter, Phoebe Allen. In the early 70's, Myra finally divorced him, claiming neglect, etc. It didn't stop him marrying a fourth time, although this time he did it legally in late '71. With his career enjoying something of a resurrection in 1973 (by which time he'd traded in his blue suede shoes for Stetson-styled country-pop), tragedy struck again when his son (his drummer on tour) JERRY LEE JR was killed in a motoring accident. In 1976, LEWIS was involved in two gun incidents, one when he accidently shot his bassman, NORMAN OWENS, the other occurring outside Graceland (Elvis Presley's home) hours after being charged with drunk driving. He signed to 'Elektra' in 1978, although a few albums and a serious stomach ulcer operation later, he sued the label. In 1982, his estranged fourth wife, Jaren Gunn Lewis (née Pate), drowned in a mysterious swimming pool incident just prior to their divorce settlement. The following year, coming up for his 50th birthday, the irrepressible LEWIS tied the knot yet again, this time to a 25 year-old, Shawn Michelle Stevens; just over two months later, she was to be found dead in their home. Although suspected of foul play, no case was brought and LEWIS, proving that he was a family man at heart, went on to marry his sixth wife, the 22 year-old, Kerrie McCarver, who, in early '87, gave birth to a son, Jerry Lee Lewis III. A few years later, his biopic film story appeared (Nick Tosches' celebrated biography, 'Hellfire', had previously hit the shelves in 1982) featuring re-recordings of his oldies, his part played by actor, Dennis Quaid. • **Songwriters:** Covers: CRAZY ARMS (Ray Price) / WHOLE LOTTA SHAKIN' GOIN' ON (D.Williams & Sunny Dave) / YOU WIN AGAIN + SETTIN' THE WOODS ON FIRE (Hank Willliams) / WHAT'D I SAY + HIT THE ROAD JACK (Ray Charles) / BREAK UP + I'LL MAKE IT ALL UP TO YOU (Charlie Rich) / SWEET LITTLE SIXTEEN + LITTLE QUEENIE (Chuck Berry) / GOOD GOLLY MISS MOLLY + LONG TALL SALLY (Little Richard) / ME AND BOBBY McGEE (Kris Kristofferson) / GREEN GREEN GRASS OF HOME (Curly Putnam) / CHANTILLY LACE (Big Bopper) / JACK DANIELS (Heads, Hands & Feet) / DRINKIN' WINE SPO . . . (Stick McGhee) / RITA MAE (Bob Dylan) etc. • **Trivia:** His sister, LINDA GAIL LEWIS, also issued solo recordings between 1965 and 74. Another unlikely cousin of JERRY LEE is the TV evangelist, Jimmy Swaggart!

Best CD compilation: ALL KILLER, NO FILLER: THE ANTHOLOGY (*8)

JERRY LEE LEWIS – vocals, piano + sessions

	London	Sun
Dec 56. (7") <259> **CRAZY ARMS. / END OF THE ROAD**	-	
Jul 57. (7",78) (HLS 8457) <267> **WHOLE LOTTA SHAKIN' GOIN' ON. / IT'LL BE ME**	8	3 Jun57
Nov 57. (7") <281> **GREAT BALLS OF FIRE. / YOU WIN AGAIN**	-	2 / 95
Dec 57. (7",78) (HLS 8529) **GREAT BALLS OF FIRE. / MEAN WOMAN BLUES**	1	-
Feb 58. (7",78) (HLS 8559) **YOU WIN AGAIN. / I'M FEELIN' SORRY**	-	-
Apr 58. (7",78) (HLS 8592) <288> **BREATHLESS. / DOWN THE LINE**	8	7 Feb58
Jun 58. (7") <301> **THE RETURN OF JERRY LEE. / LEWIS BOOGIE**	-	
Sep 58. (7",78) (HLS8700) <303> **BREAK-UP. / I'LL MAKE IT ALL UP TO YOU**		52 / 85 Aug58
Jan 59. (lp) (HAS 2138) <1230> **JERRY LEE LEWIS**		Dec57

– Don't be cruel / Goodnight Irene / Put me down / It all depends / Ubangi stomp / Crazy arms / Jambalaya / Fools like me / High school confidential / Where the saints go marching in Matchbox / It'll be me. (re-iss. May82 on 'Mercury' lp/c; 6463/7145 042) (cd-iss. Apr86 on 'Pickwick'; PCD 814)

Jan 59. (7",78) (HLS 8780) <296> **HIGH SCHOOL CONFIDENTIAL. / FOOLS LIKE ME** [12] [12] May58

Apr 59. (7",78) (HLS 8940) <317> **LOVIN' UP A STORM. / BIG BLON' BABY** — | 28 |

Sep 59. (7",78) (HLS 8941) <324> **LET'S TALK ABOUT US. / THE BALLAD OF BILLY JOE**

Nov 59. (7",78) (HLS 8993) <330> **LITTLE QUEENIE. / I COULD NEVER BE ASHAMED OF YOU**

Mar 60. (7") (HLS 9083) <312> **I'LL SAIL MY SHIP ALONE. / IT HURT ME SO** — | 93 | Dec 58

May 60. (7") (HLS 9131) <337> **BABY, BABY, BYE, BYE. / OLD BLACK JOE** — | 47 |

Oct 60. (7") (HLS 9202) <344> **JOHN HENRY. / HANG UP MY ROCK'N'ROLL SHOES**

Dec 60. (7") <352> **WHEN I GET PAID. / LOVE MADE A FOOL OF ME** — |

Apr 61. (7") (HLS 9335) <356> **WHAT'D I SAY. / LIVIN' LOVIN' WRECK** — | 10 | 30 |

1961. (lp) <1265> **JERRY LEE'S GREATEST** (part compilation) —

Sep 61. (7") (HLS 9414) <364> **IT WON'T HAPPEN WITH ME. / COLD COLD HEART**

Oct 61. (7") (HLS 9446) **AS LONG AS I LIVE. / WHEN I GET PAID** — |

Oct 61. (7") <367> **SAVE THE LAST DANCE FOR ME. / AS LONG AS I LIVE** — |

Dec 61. (7") <371> **MONEY. / BONNIE B** — |

Mar 62. (7") (HLS 9526) <374> **I'VE BEEN TWISTIN'. / RAMBLING ROSE** — |

May 62. (lp) (HAS 2440) **JERRY LEE LEWIS VOL.2** — | 14 |
– Money / As long as I live / Country music is here to stay / Frankie and Johnny / Home / Hello baby / Let's talk about us / What'd I say Breakup / Great balls of fire / Cold, cold heart / Hello Josephine. (cd-iss. Apr86 on 'Pickwick'; PCD 840)

Aug 62. (7") (HLS 9584) <379> **SWEET LITTLE SIXTEEN. / HOW'S MY EX TREATING YOU** — | 38 | 95 |

Feb 63. (7") (HLS 9688) <382> **GOOD GOLLY MISS MOLLY. / I CAN'T TRUST ME (IN YOUR ARMS ANYMORE)** — | 31 | Dec62 |

May 63. (7") (HLS 9722) <384> **TEENAGE LETTER. ("& LINDA GAIL LEWIS") / SEASONS OF MY HEART** — | Feb63 |
Philips   Smash

1963. (7") (AMT 1216) <1857> **HIT THE ROAD JACK. / PEN AND PAPER** — |

Mar 64. (7") (BF 1324) <1886> **I'M ON FIRE. / BREAD AND BUTTER MAN** — | 98 |

1964. (7") <1906> **SHE WAS MY BABY. / THE HOLE HE SAID HE'D DIG FOR ME** — | ' |

Oct 64. (7") (BF 1371) <1930> **HI HEAL SNEAKERS. / YOU WENT BACK ON YOUR WORD** — | 91 |

Dec 64. (7") **WHOLE LOTTA SHAKIN' GOIN' ON (live). / BREATHLESS (live)** — |

Feb 65. (7") **GREAT BALLS OF FIRE (live). / HIGH SCHOOL CONFIDENTIAL (live)**

Apr 65. (7") (BF 1407) <1969> **BABY HOLD ME CLOSE. / I BELIEVE IN YOU**

May 65. (lp) (SBL 7650) <67650> **THE GREATEST LIVE SHOW ON EARTH (live)** — | 71 | Dec64 |
– Jenny Jenny / Who will the next fool be / Memphis Tennessee / Hound dog / Mean woman blues / Hi-heel sneakers / No particular place to go / Together again / Long tall Sally / Whole lotta shakin' goin' on / Little Queenie (intro) / How's my ex treating you / Johnny B. Goode / Green, green grass of home / What'd I say (part 2) / You win again / I'll sail my ship alone / Cryin' time / Money / Roll over Beethoven.

Jul 65. (7") (BF 1425) **ROCKIN' PNEUMONIA AND THE BOOGIE WOOGIE FLU. / THIS MUST BE THE PLACE**

Jul 65. (lp) (SBL 7668) <67063> **THE RETURN OF ROCK** — | May65 |
– I believe in you / Maybeline / Flip, flop and fly / Roll over Beethoven / Baby, hold me close / Herman the hermit / Don't let go / You went back on your word / Corrine, Corrina / Sexy ways / Johnny B.Goode / Got you on my mind.

1965. (7") <2006> **GREEN GREEN GRASS OF HOME. ("& LINDA GAIL LEWIS") / BABY, YOU'VE GOT WHAT IT TAKES** — |

Jan 66. (lp) (SBL 7688) <67071> **COUNTRY SONGS FOR CITY FOLKS**
– Green green grass of home / Wolverton mountain Funny how time slips away North to Alaska / The wild side of life / Ray of fire / Detroit city / Crazy arms King of the road / Seasons of my heart.

1966. (7") <2027> **STICKS AND STONES. / WHAT A HECK OF A MESS** — |

May 66. (lp) (SBL 7706) <67079> **MEMPHIS BEAT**
– Memphis beat / Mathilda / Darlin' wine spo-dee-o-dee / Hallelujah, I love her so / She thinks I still care / Just because / Sticks and stones / Whenever you're ready / Lincoln limousine / Big boss man / Too young / The urge.

Oct 66. (7") (BF 1521) <2053> **MEMPHIS BEAT. / IF I HAD TO DO IT OVER**

Jan 67. (lp) (SBL 7746) <67086> **BY REQUEST – MORE GREATEST LIVE SHOW ON EARTH (live)**
– Introduction / Little Queenie / How's my ex treating you / Johnny B.Goode / Green green grass of home / What'd I say / You win again / I'll sail my ship alone / Crying time / Money / Roll over Beethoven.

Jul 67. (7") (BF 1594) <2103> **IT'S A HANG-UP BABY. / HOLDIN' ON**
Mercury   Smash

Mar 68. (7") (MF 1020) <2146> **ANOTHER TIME ANOTHER PLACE. / WALKING THE FLOOR OVER YOU** — | 97 |

Jul 68. (lp) (MCL 20117) <67097> **SOUL MY WAY**
– Turn on your love light / It's a hang-up baby / Dream baby (how long must I dream / Just dropped in Wedding bells / He took it like a man / Hey baby / Treat her right / Holdin' on Shotgun man I bet you're gonna like it.

Aug 68. (7") (MF 1045) <2164> **WHAT MADE MILWALKEE FAMOUS. / ALL THE GOOD IS GONE** — | 94 |

1968. (7") <2186> **SHE STILL COMES AROUND. / SLIPPIN' AROUND** — |

Jan 69. (lp) (SMWL 21011) <67104> **ANOTHER PLACE ANOTHER TIME** — | Jun68 |
– What made Milwaukee famous Play me a song I can cry to / On the back row /

Walking the floor over you All night long / I'm a lonesome fugitive Another place, another time / Break my mind / Before the next teardrop falls / All the good is gone / We live in two different worlds (w/ Linda)

Mar 69. (7") (MF 1088) <2202> **TO MAKE LOVE SWEETER FOR YOU. / LET'S TALK ABOUT US** — | Dec68 |

May 69. (lp) (SMCL 20147) <67112> **SHE STILL COMES AROUND (TO LOVE WHAT'S LEFT OF ME)** — | Feb69 |
– To make love sweeter for you / Let's talk about us / I can't get over you / Out of my mind / Today I started loving you again / She still comes around (to love what's lxeft of me) / Louisiana man / Release me / Listen, they're playing my song / There stands the glass / Echoes.

May 69. (7") (MF 1105) **LONG TALL SALLY. / JENNY JENNY** — |

1969. (7") <2220> **DON'T LET ME CROSSOVER. / WE LIVE IN TWO DIFFERENT WORLDS** — |

1969. (7"; JERRY LEE LEWIS & LINDA GAIL LEWIS) <2224> **ONE HAS MY NAME. / I CAN'T STOP LOVING YOU** — |

Feb 70. (lp; JERRY LEE LEWIS & LINDA GAIL LEWIS) (SMCL 20172) <67126> **TOGETHER** — | Nov69 |
– Milwaukee here I come / Jackson / Don't take it out on me / Cryin' time / Sweet thing / Secret places / Don't let me cross over / Gotta travel on / We live in two different worlds / Earth up above / Roll over Beethoven.

1970. (7") <2224> **SHE EVEN WOKE ME UP TO SAY GOODBYE. / ECHOES** — |

Jun 70. (lp) (6338 010) <67128> **SHE EVEN WOKE ME UP TO SAY GOODBYE** — | Feb70 |
– Once more with feeling / Working man blues / Waiting for a train / Brown eyed handsome man / My only claim to fame / Since I met you baby / She woke me up to say goodbye / Wine me up / When the grass grows over me / You went out of your way / Echoes.

Aug 70. (7") <2257> **ONCE MORE WITH FEELING. / YOU WENT OUT OF YOUR WAY** — |

Nov 70. (7") <73155> **I CAN'T HAVE A MERRY CHRISTMAS MARY (WITHOUT YOU). / IN LOVING MEMORIES** — |

1971. (7") <73099> **THERE MUST BE MORE TO LOVE THAN THIS. / HOME AWAY FROM HOME** — |

Jun 71. (lp) (6338 045) <61323> **THERE MUST BE MORE TO LOVE THAN THIS** — | Jan71 |
– There must be more to love than this / Bottles and barstools / Rueben James / I'd be talkin' / All the time / One more time / Sweet Georgia Brown / Woman, woman / I forget more than you'll ever know / Foolaid / Home away from home / Life's little ups and downs.

Jul 71. (7") <73192> **TOUCHING HOME. / WOMAN, WOMAN** — |

Jul 71. (lp) <61343> **TOUCHING HOME**

1971. (7") <73227> **WHEN HE WALKS ON YOU. / FOOLISH KIND OF MAN** — |

Feb 72. (lp) (6338 071) <61346> **WOULD YOU TAKE ANOTHER CHANCE ON ME?** — | Nov71 |

Jan 72. (7") (6052 117) <73248> **ME AND BOBBY McGEE. / WOULD YOU TAKE ANOTHER CHANCE ON ME** — | 40 |

Apr 72. (7") (6502 141) <73273> **CHANTILLY LACE. / THINK ABOUT IT DARLIN'** — | 33 | 43 |

Jun 72. (7") <73296> **TURN ON YOUR LOVELIGHT. / LONELY WEEKENDS** — | 95 |

Jun 72. (7") (6052 162) **TURN ON YOUR LOVELIGHT. / I'M WALKIN'** — |

1972. (7"; JERRY LEE LEWIS & LINDA GAIL LEWIS) <73328> **WHO'S GONNA PLAY THIS OLD PIANO. / NO HONKY TONKS IN HEAVEN**

Mar 73. (7") (6052 260) <73374> **DRINKIN' WINE SPO-DEE O'DEE. / ROCK & ROLL MEDLEY** — | 41 |

Apr 73. (d-lp) (6672 008) <803> **THE SESSION** — | 37 | Mar73 |
– Johnny B. Goode / Trouble in mind / Early morning rain / No headstone on my grave / Pledgin' my love / Memphis / Drinkin' wine spo-dee o'dee / Music to the man / Bad Moon rising / Sea cruise / Sixty minute man / Moving on down the line / What'd I say / Medley: Good golly Miss Molly – Long tall Sally – Jenny . . . – Tutti frutti – Whole lotta shakin' goin' on. (cd-iss. May85; 822751-2)
(above recorded with PETER FRAMPTON, ALBERT LEE, RORY GALLAGHER, ALVIN LEE)

1973. (7") <73361> **NO MORE HANGING ON. / THE MERCY OF A LETTER** — |

1973. (7") <73402> **NO HEADSTONE ON MY GRAVE. / JACK DANIELS (OLD No.7)** — |

Jul 73. (lp) (6338 148) <61278> **LIVE AT THE INTERNATIONAL, LAS VEGAS (live)** — | Oct70 |
– Mean woman blues / High school confidential / Money / Matchbox / What'd I say / What'd I say (pt.2) / Great balls of fire / Good golly Miss Molly / Lewis boogie / Your cheating heart / Hound dog / Long tall Sally / Whole lotta shakin' goin' on.

Sep 73. (7") (6052 378) **TAKING MY MUSIC TO THE MAN. / JACK DANIELS** — |

1973. (7") <73423> **SOMETIMES A MEMORY AIN'T ENOUGH. / I NEED TO PRAY** — |

1974. (7") <73462> **JUST A LITTLE BIT. / MEAT MAN** — |

Mar 74. (lp) (6338 452) <SRM-1 690> **SOUTHERN ROOTS**
– Meat man / When a man loves a woman / Hold on I'm coming / Just a little bit / Born to be a loser / The haunted house / Blueberry hill The revolutionary man / Big blue diamond / That Old Bourbon Street church.

1974. (7") <73491> **TELL TALE SIGNS. / COLD, COLD MORNING LIGHT** — |

1974. (7") <73518> **HE CAN'T FILL MY SHOES. / TOMORROW'S TAKING BABY AWAY** — |

1974. (7") <73661> **I CAN STILL HEAR THE MUSIC IN THE RESTROOM. / REMEMBER ME I'M THE ONE WHO LOVES YOU** — |

1975. (7") <73685> **BOOGIE WOOGIE COUNTRY MAN. / I'M STILL JEALOUS OF YOU**

1975. (7") <73729> **A DAMN GOOD COUNTRY SONG. / WHEN I TAKE MY VACATION IN HEAVEN** — |

Nov 75. (lp) (6338 602) **I'M A ROCKER** — |

1976. (7") <73763> **DON'T BOOGIE WOOGIE. / THAT KIND OF FOOL**

1976. (7") <73822> **LET'S PUT IT BACK TOGETHER AGAIN. / JERRY LEE'S ROCK'N' ROLL REVIVAL SHOW**

1976. (7") <73872> **THE CLOSEST THING TO YOU. / YOU BELONG TO ME**

1977. (7") <55011> **MIDDLE-AGE CRAZY. / GEORGIA ON MY MIND**

1978. (7") <55021> **COME ON IN. / WHO'S SORRY NOW**

1978. (7") <55028> **I'LL FIND IT WHERE I CAN. / DON'T LET THE STARS GET IN YOUR EYES**

Nov 78. (d-lp) (6641 869) **BACK TO BACK**

1979. (7") <76146> **I'M SO LONESOME I COULD CRY. / PICK ME UP ON THE WAY DOWN**

                             Elektra   Elektra

May 79. (7") <46030> **ROCKIN' MY LIFE AWAY. / I WISH I WAS EIGHTEEN AGAIN**

May 79. (7") (K 12351) **DON'T LET GO. / I WISH I WAS EIGHTEEN AGAIN**

Apr 79. (lp/c) (K/K4 52132) <184> **JERRY LEE LEWIS**
– Don't let go / Rita May / Every day I have to cry / I like it like that / Number one lovin' man / Rockin' my life away / Who will the next fool be (you've got) / Personality / I wish I was eighteen again / Rockin' little angel. (re-iss. Apr90 as 'ROCKIN' MY LIFE AWAY' on 'Tomato' lp/c/cd; 269661-1/-4/-2)

Aug 79. (7") (K 12374) **ROCKIN' MY LIFE AWAY. / RITA MAE**

1979. (7") <46067> **WHO WILL THE NEXT FOOL BE? / RITA MAE**

Nov 79. (7") (K 12399) **EVERYDAY I HAVE TO CRY. / WHO WILL THE NEXT FOOL BE?**

Feb 80. (7") (K 12432) <46642> **ROCKIN' JERRY LEE. / GOOD TIME CHARLIE'S GOT THE BLUES**

Apr 80. (7") <46591> **WHEN TWO WORLDS COLLIDE. / GOOD NEWS TRAVELS FAST**

Apr 80. (lp) (K 52113) <254> **WHEN TWO WORLDS COLLIDE**
– Rockin' Jerry Lee / Who will buy the wine / Love game / Alabama jubilee / Goodtime Charlie's got the blues / When two worlds collide / Good news travels fast / I only want a buddy not a sweetheart / Honky tonk stuff / Toot toot Tootsie.

1980. (7") <46642> **HONKY TONK STUFF. / ROCKIN' JERRY LEE**

Jan 81. (7") <47026> **FOLSAM PRISON BLUES. / OVER THE RAINBOW**

May 81. (lp) (K 52246) <291> **KILLER COUNTRY**
– Folsam prison blues / I'll do it all over again / Jukebox junkie / Too weak to fight / Late night lovin' man / Change places with me / Let me on / Thirty-nine and holding / Mama, this one's for you / Over the rainbow. (re-iss. Feb87; ED 250)

May 81. (7") <47095> **THIRTY-NINE AND HOLDING. / CHANGE PLACES WITH ME**

Aug 81. (7") <69962> **I'D DO IT ALL AGAIN. / WHO WILL BUY THE WINE**

—— On Apr'82, he was one of the stars alongside JOHNNY CASH & CARL PERKINS to feature on 'THE SURVIVORS' album, recorded in Germany 1981 for 'CBS-Columbia'.

                             M.C.A.   M.C.A.

Jan 83. (7") (MCA 808) <52151> **MY FINGERS DO THE TALKIN'. / FOREVER FORGIVING**

May 83. (lp) (MCF 3162) **MY FINGERS DO THE TALKING**
– My fingers do the talkin' / She sure makes leaving look easy / Why you been gone so long / She sings Amazing Grace / Better not look down / Honky tonk rock and roll piano man / Come as you were / Circumstantial evidence / Forever forgiving / Honky tonk Heaven.

May 83. (7") <52188> **CIRCUMSTANTIAL EVIDENCE. / COME AS YOU WERE**

Aug 83. (7") <52233> **SHE SINGS AMAZING GRACE. / WHY YOU BEEN GONE SO LONG**

Jun 84. (7") <52369> **I AM WHAT I AM. / THAT WAS THE WAY IT WAS THEN**

Jul 84. (lp) (MCL 1810) **I AM WHAT I AM**
– I am what I am / Only you (and you alone) / Get out your big roll daddy / Have I got a song for you / Careless hands / Candy kisses / I'm looking over a four leaf clover / Send me the pillow that you dream on / Honky tonk heart / That was the way it was then. (re-iss. May85 lp/c; MCL/+C 1810) (re-iss. Aug89 on 'Instant' cd/c/lp; CD/TC+/INS 5008)

                             not iss.   Sire

Jun 90. (7") <19809> **IT WAS THE WHISKEY TALKIN' (NOT ME). / ('A'-Rock'n'roll version)**

                             Warners Warners

Jun 95. (cd/c) <(7559 61795-2/-4)> **YOUNG BLOOD**
– House of blue lights / Young blood / Things / It was the whiskey talkin' (not me) / Goosebumps / Crown Victoria custom '51 / Restless heart / High school pressure / One of them old things / Poison love / Down the road apiece / Gotta travel on / Miss the Mississippi and you / I'll never get out of this world alive.

– compilations, others, etc. –

1958. (7"ep) Sun; **GREAT BALLS OF FIRE**
– Whole lotta shakin' goin' on / Mean woman blues / I'm feeling sorry / Turn around.

Nov 58. (7"ep) London; (RE-S 1140) **JERRY LEE LEWIS**

May 59. (7"ep) London; (RE-S 1186) **JERRY LEE LEWIS No.2**

May 59. (7"ep) London; (RE-S 1187) **JERRY LEE LEWIS No.3**

Nov 61. (7"ep) London; (RE-S 1296) **JERRY LEE LEWIS No.4**

Sep 62. (7"ep) London; (RES 1336) **JERRY LEE LEWIS No.5**

Mar 63. (7"ep) London; (RES 1351) **JERRY LEE LEWIS No.6**

Aug 63. (7"ep) London; (RES 1378) **FOUR MORE FROM JERRY LEE LEWIS**

Mar 64. (7") London; (HLS 9861) **LEWIS BOOGIE. / BONNIE B**

Jul 65. (7") London; (HLS 9980) **I KNOW WHAT IT MEANS. / CARRY ME BACK TO OLD VIRGINIA**

Nov 65. (lp) London; (HA-S 8251) **WHOLE LOTTA SHAKIN' GOIN'**
(re-iss. +c.Oct74) (re-iss. 10"lp.Jul82 on 'Charly') (re-iss. Jul86 on 'Sun')

Jun 67. (lp) London; (HAS 8323) **BREATHLESS**

1960. (7") Philips Int.; **IN THE MOOD. (as "The HAWK") / I GET THE BLUES WHEN IT RAINS**

Jun 64. (lp) Philips/ US= Smash; (SBL 7622) **GOLDEN HITS OF JERRY LEE LEWIS**
(re-iss. 1976 on 'Mercury')

Apr 65. (lp) Philips; (SBL 7646) **LIVE AT THE STAR CLUB, HAMBURG (live w / NASHVILLE TEENS)**
(re-iss. Feb80 on 'Mercury') (re-iss. Sep84)

Mar 67. (7"ep) Philips; (BE 12599) **COUNTRY STYLE**

Aug 87. (lp/c) Philips; (HO 3) **THE VERY BEST OF JERRY LEE LEWIS**

Oct 67. (7") Philips/ US= Smash; (BF 1615) **TURN ON YOUR LOVELIGHT. / SHOTGUN MAN**

May 68. (7") London/ US= Smash; (HLS 10193) **WHAT'D I SAY. / I'VE BEEN TWISTING**

Apr 68. (7") Mercury/ US= Smash; (MF 1110) **GREAT BALLS OF FIRE. / WHOLE LOTTA SHAKIN' GOIN' ON**

Sep 69. (lp) Mercury/ US= Smash; (20156 SMCL) **I'M ON FIRE**

Sep 69. (lp) Mercury/ US= Smash; (20157 SMCL) **COUNTRY MUSIC HALL OF FAME HITS VOL.1**   May 69

Sep 69. (lp) Mercury/ US= Smash; (20158 SMCL) **COUNTRY MUSIC HALL OF FAME HITS VOL.2**   May 69
(above re-iss. d-lp 'THE BEST OF . . . ' Apr81)

Sep 70. (lp/c) Mercury/ US= Smash; **THE BEST OF JERRY LEE LEWIS**

Jun 72. (lp) (6338088) **THE KILLER ROCKS ON**   Apr 72

Oct 74. (lp) Mercury; (6338496) **FAN CLUB CHOICE**

Feb 87. (cd) Mercury; (8302072) **THE 30th ANNIVERSARY**

Nov 89. (3xlp/c/cd) Mercury; **THE KILLER: THE MERCURY YEARS 1963-1968, VOL.1 / 1969-1972, VOL.2 / 1973-1977, VOL.3**

Oct 68. (lp) Fontana; **GOT YOU ON MY MIND**
Below releases on 'Sun International' until stated.

1969. (7") **INVITATION TO YOUR PARTY. / I COULD NEVER BE ASHAMED OF YOU**

1969. (7") **ONE MINUTE PAST ETERNITY. / FRANKIE AND JOHNNY**

1970. (7") **I CAN'T SEEM TO SAY GOODBYE. / GOODNIGHT IRENE**

1970. (7") **WAITING FOR A TRAIN. / BIG LEGGED WOMAN**

Oct 70. (7") **BREATHLESS. / GREAT BALLS OF FIRE**

Oct 70. (lp) (6467002) **ORIGINAL GOLDEN HITS VOL.1**   Sep 69

Jan 71. (lp) **ORIGINAL GOLDEN HITS VOL.2**   Sep 69

Mar 71. (lp) **A TASTE OF COUNTRY**

Aug 71. (lp) **ROCKIN' RHYTHM AND BLUES**

Sep 71. (7"m) **GREAT BALLS OF FIRE. / WHOLE LOTTA SHAKIN' GOIN' ON / HIGH SCHOOL CONFIDENTIAL**

Oct 71. (lp) **THE GOLDEN CREAM OF THE COUNTRY**

Oct 71. (lp) **JOHNNY CASH AND JERRY LEE LEWIS SING HANK WILLIAMS**

Nov 71. (lp) (6467019) **MONSTERS**

1971. (7") **LOVE ON BROADWAY. / MATCHBOX**

1972. (7") **YOUR LOVIN' WAYS. / I CAN'T TRUST ME (IN YOUR ARMS)**

Aug 72. (lp) (6467020) **OLD TYME COUNTRY MUSIC**

Nov 72. (lp) **SUNDAY DOWN SOUTH (w / JOHNNY CASH)**

1973. (7") **I CAN'T TRUST ME (IN YOUR ARMS). / GOOD ROCKIN' TONIGHT**

Apr 74. (d-lp) **ROCKIN' UP A STORM**
(re-iss. Feb87)

Jul 74. (lp) (6467029) **ROCKIN' AND FREE**

1978. (7") **AM I TO BE THE ONE. / MATCHBOX**

Jan 79. (lp) (SUNLP 1002) **DUETS**

1979. (7") Charly; (CYS 147) **HELLO JOSEPHINE. / COLD COLD HEART**

May 80. (lp) (SUN 1004) **TRIO PLUS (w / other 'Sun' artists)**

Jul 82. (10"lp) Charly; (CFM 514) **THE PUMPIN' PIANO CAT**
(re-iss. lp Jul86)

Jul 82. (10"lp) Charly; (CFM 517) **THE WILD ONE AT THE HIGH SCHOOL HOP**
(re-iss. lp Aug86)

1983. (7"ep) **THE FABULOUS JERRY LEE LEWIS VOL.1**

1983. (7"ep) **THE FABULOUS JERRY LEE LEWIS VOL.2**

Sep 89. (8xcd-box) (CDSUNBOX 1) **THE SUN YEARS**

Nov 89. (lp) (SUNLP 1051) **KILLER'S BIRTHDAY CAKE**

Nov 89. (lp) (SUNLP 1053) **KILLER'S RHYTHM & BLUES**

1973. (lp/c) Hallmark; **GREAT BALLS OF FIRE**
(re-iss. 10"lp.Jul82 & lp Aug86 on 'Charly', re-as d-lp+cd.Jul89) (cd re-iss. Dec89 on 'Pickwick')

Apr 75. (lp/c) Hallmark; **GOOD ROCKIN' TONIGHT**
(re-iss. Feb80 on 'Sun')

Mar 76. (d-lp/c) Hallmark; **THE JERRY LEE LEWIS COLLECTION**
Note; All below on UK 'Charly' until stated.

Oct 75. (lp) **JERRY LEE LEWIS AND HIS PUMPING PIANO**

Oct 75. (lp) Charly; (CR 30006) **RARE JERRY LEE LEWIS VOL.1**

Oct 75. (lp) Charly; (CR 30007) **RARE JERRY LEE LEWIS VOL.2**

Oct 76. (lp) Charly; (CR 30111) **THE ORIGINAL JERRY LEE LEWIS**

Dec 76. (7"ep) **LEWIS BOOGIE**

Mar 77. (lp) Charly; (CR 30121) **NUGGETS**

Apr 77. (7") **OLD BLACK JOE. / THE RETURN OF JERRY LEE**

Aug 77. (7") **IN THE MOOD. / GREAT BALLS OF FIRE**

Dec 77. (lp) Charly; (CR 30129) **NUGGETS VOL.2**

Aug 78. (7") **WHOLE LOTTA SHAKIN' GOIN' ON. / (other artist)**

Oct 78. (lp) **THE ESSENTIAL JERRY LEE LEWIS**

Dec 78. (7") **SAVE THE LAST DANCE FOR ME. / AM I TO BE THE ONE (by "JERRY LEE LEWIS & FRIEND")**

Dec 78.	(12") **BREATHLESS. / HIGH SCHOOL CONFIDENTIAL**	-
Feb 79.	(7") **MY GIRL JOSEPHINE. / WHAT'D I SAY**	-
Feb 81.	(lp) *Charly; (CRM 2008)* **JERRY LEE'S GREATEST**	-
Mar 86.	(cd) *Charly; (CDCHARLY 1)* **FERRIDAY FIREBALL**	-
Apr 87.	(cd) *Charly; (CDCHARLY 70)* **RARE AND ROCKIN'**	-
Mar 89.	(cd-ep) *Charly; (CDS 2)* **GREAT BALLS OF FIRE / HIGH SCHOOL CONFIDENTIAL / BREATHLESS / WHOLE LOTTA SHAKIN' GOIN' ON**	-
Feb 93.	(cd) *Charly; (CDCD 1016)* **GOOD ROCKIN' TONITE**	-
Mar 93.	(11xcd-box) *Sun;* **THE SUN YEARS**	-
Nov 78.	(d-lp) *Arcade;* **SHAKIN' JERRY LEE**	-
Jul 79.	(lp) *Hammer; (HMB 7002)* **JERRY LEE LEWIS**	-
Sep 79.	(7") *Hammer;* **LONG TALL SALLY. / BREATHLESS**	-
Jan 80.	(7"ep) *Bulldog;* **JERRY LEE LEWIS** – Bonnie B / Baby baby bye bye / Down the line / I'm feeling sorry.	-
Feb 80.	(c) *Bravo; (BRC 2504)* **GOOD GOLLY MISS MOLLY**	
Apr 81.	(7") *Old Gold; (OG 9110)* **GREAT BALLS OF FIRE. / WHOLE LOTTA SHAKIN' GOIN' ON**	-
Feb 89.	(12"m) *Old Gold;* **GREAT BALLS OF FIRE / WHOLE LOTTA SHAKIN' GOIN' ON. / WHAT'D I SAY (part 1 & 2)**	-
Sep 83.	(7"ep/c-ep) *Scoop; (7S R/C 5014)* **6 TRACK HITS**	-
Nov 84.	(c/lp) *Topline; (KTOP/TOP 105* **THE KILLER STRIKES**	-
Feb 85.	(lp/c) *Cambra; (CR/+T 100)* **JERRY LEE LEWIS**	-
Mar 86.	(d-lp/c) *Pickwick;* **THE JERRY LEE LEWIS COLLECTION**	-
Apr 88.	(cd) *Pickwick; (PWK 015)* **THE COUNTRY SOUND OF JERRY LEE LEWIS**	-
Jul 86.	(d-lp/c) *Castle; (CCS LP/MC 143)* **THE COLLECTION** (cd-iss. Dec90)	-
Apr 87.	(lp/c) *Starblend;* **AT THE COUNTRY STORE** (cd-iss. Mar89)	-
Nov 87.	(lp) *Zu Jazz; (Z 2003)* **KEEP YOUR HANDS OFF IT**	-
Oct 88.	(lp) *Zu Jazz; (Z 2004)* **DON'T DROP IT**	-
Apr 89.	(lp/c/cd) *Ocean; (OCN 2021W-L/-K/-D)* **THE CLASSIC JERRY LEE LEWIS**	-
May 89.	(cd) *Magnum Force; (CDMF 071)* **LIVE IN ITALY (live)**	-
Jul 89.	(cd/c/lp) *Polydor; (839516-2/-4/-1)* **GREAT BALLS OF FIRE: ORIGINAL MOTION PICTURE SOUNDTRACK**	62
Sep 89.	(7"/12") *Polydor; (PO/PZ 57)* **GREAT BALLS OF FIRE. / BREATHLESS**	-
Feb 90.	(cd/c/lp) *Instant; (CD/TC+/INS 5023)* **ROCKET**	-
Dec 90.	(lp/cd) *See For Miles; (SEE/+CD 307)* **THE EP COLLECTION**	-
Apr 91.	(cd) *Ace; (CDCH 326)* **LIVE AT THE VAPORS CLUB (live)**	-
Dec 91.	(cd) *Ace; (CDCH 332)* **HONKY TONK ROCK'N'ROLL PIANO MAN**	-
Apr 92.	(cd) *Ace; (CDCH 348)* **PRETTY MUCH COUNTRY**	-
Sep 91.	(cd) *Electrovert;* **THE KILLERS' PRIVATE STASH**	-
Feb 92.	(d-cd) *Tomato;* **THE COMPLETE PALAMINO SESSIONS**	-
Sep 92.	(cd) *Music Club; (MCCD 081)* **THE BEST OF JERRY LEE LEWIS** – Great balls of fire / Whole lotta shakin' goin' on / Drinkin' wine spo-dee-o-dee / Lewis boogie / Mean woan blues / You win again / Jailhouse rock / Lovin' up a storm / Pumpin' piano rock / High school confidential / Fools like me / Down the line / Breathless / Wild one / Milkshake mademoiselle / Pink pedal pushers / I could never be ashamed of you / In the mood / Let's talk about us / What'd I say.	-
Jun 93.	(d-cd) *Tomato; (2696742)* **THE COMPLETE PALOMINO CLUB RECORDINGS**	-
Aug 93.	(cd) *Tomato; (598006729)* **HEARTBREAKER**	-
Mar 94.	(cd/c) *Spectrum; (550180-2/-4)* **CHANTILLY LACE**	-
Mar 94.	(cd/c) *Charly; (CDCHARLY 185)* **GREAT BALLS OF FIRE**	-
May 94.	(cd) *Charly; (CDTT 5)* **TWO ON ONE (w / CARL PERKINS)**	-
Apr 94.	(cd) *See For Miles; (SEECD 397)* **THE EP COLLECTION ... PLUS: VOLUME 2**	-
Jul 94.	(cd/c) *Success;* **GREATEST HITS LIVE**	-
Jul 94.	(cd/c) *Success;* **GREAT BALLS OF FIRE**	-
Aug 94.	(cd) *Wisepack; (LECD 079)* **JERRY LEE LEWIS**	-
Dec 94.	(9xcd-box) *Bear Family; (BCD 15783)* **LOCUST YEARS & THE RETURN TO THE PROMISED LAND**	-
Feb 95.	(cd) *B.A.M.; (KLMCD 012)* **PEARLS OF THE PAST**	-
Apr 95.	(4xcd-box+book) *Charly; (CDDIG 8)* **SUN CLASSICS**	-
Apr 95.	(d-cd) *Wisepack; (LECD 610)* **THE ESSENTIAL COLLECTION**	-
May 95.	(cd/c) *Pickwick; (PWK S/MC 4255)* **KILLER HITS! – THE ORIGINAL CLASSICS**	-
Jul 95.	(cd) *Summit;* **HIGH SCHOOL CONFIDENTIAL**	-

Jaki LIEBEZEIT (see under ⇒ CAN)

Gordon LIGHTFOOT

Born: 17 Nov'38, Orillia, Ontario, Canada. At 19, having just spent 18 months at the Westlake School of Music in L.A., LIGHTFOOT returned to Canada equipped with composition and sight-reading skills. He moved to Toronto, 80 miles south east of his place of birth and sunk his way deep into the mid-60's folk-club scene attracting attention for his low, smooth voice and melodious blend of folk and country. He subsequently caught the attention of folkies IAN & SYLVIA (TYSON) who introduced his music to the American audiences with their recordings of 'FOR LOVIN' ME' and 'EARLY MORNING RAIN'. A number of American musicians began picking up on Lightfoot's songs including Grand Ole Opry ole timer MARTY ROBBINS who took 'RIBBON OF DARKNESS' to the top spot in the country charts in '65. PETER, PAUL & MARY, meanwhile, had success with 'FOR LOVIN' ME' two months earlier (No.30 in the Hot 100). GORDON duly signed to 'United Artists', showcasing his DYLAN aspirations with a debut cover of 'JUST LIKE TOM THUMB'S BLUES' taken from his debut LP, 'LIGHTFOOT' (1965). 'THE WAY I FEEL' (1967) included 'CANADIAN RAILROAD TRILOGY', the first of many songs he wrote harking back to the birth of his nation. Three

more albums followed before 1970's $1,000,000 label switch to 'Reprise', where he was paired up with producer LENNY WARONKER. LIGHTFOOT's first outing for the company, 'IF YOU COULD READ MY MIND' (1970), acquainted the man with singer songwriter RANDY NEWMAN (at his peak), JOHN SEBASTIAN and blues scholar RY COODER. Recorded in Nashville, 'SUMMER SIDE OF LIFE' (1972) was one of LIGHTFOOT's most melodic and beautiful albums but it wasn't until the million selling title track of 'SUNDOWN' (1974) that he scored his second major commercial success ('IF YOU COULD . . .' had already made Top 5). Yet another US Top 10 hit followed hot on its heels, 'CAREFREE HIGHWAY'. 'THE WRECK OF THE EDMUND FITZGERALD' from the 1976 album, 'SUMMERTIME DREAM' resurrected the traditional purpose of folk music by telling a story of an event of the times rather than from a history book. LIGHTFOOT had been a major figure in the folk scene from its mid 60's dawn to mid 70's dusk, and although he scored a minor US chart entry with 1982's 'SHADOWS' LP, the man faded into folk cultdom. Stop press:- Late in '98, GORDIE's 'IF YOU COULD READ MY MIND' was given the STARS on 54 (yes, 54!) treatment by 'Tommy Boy' hip hop acts ULTRA NATE, AMBER and JOCELYN ENRIQUEZ; it hit US No.52.

Album rating: LIGHTFOOT (*6) / THE WAY I FEEL (*7) / DID SHE MENTION MY NAME (*7) / BACK HERE ON EARTH (*5) / SUNDAY CONCERT (*6) / SIT DOWN YOUNG STRANGER (*7) / SUMMER SIDE OF LIFE (*5) / DON QUIXOTE (*5) / OLD DAN'S RECORDS (*4) / SUNDOWN (*7) / COLD ON THE SHOULDER (*4) / GORD'S GOLD compilation (*7) / SUMMERTIME DREAM (*6) / ENDLESS WIRE (*4) / DREAM STREET ROSE (*4) / SHADOWS (*4) / SALUTE (*5) / EAST OF MIDNIGHT (*5) / WAITING FOR YOU (*5) / A PAINTER PASSING THROUGH (*5)

GORDON LIGHTFOOT – vocals, acoustic guitar / with at first TWO TONES collaborator TERRY WHELAN

		Decca	Chateau
Oct 62.	(7"; as GORD LIGHFOOT) (F 11527) <142> **(REMEMBER ME) I'M THE ONE. / DAISY-DOO** *<re-iss. 1965 on 'ABC Paramount'; 10352>*		

		Fontana	Chateau
1963.	(7"; as GORDIE LIGHTFOOT) (267275 TF) <148> **NEGOTIATIONS. / IT'S TOO LATE, HE WINS** *<re-iss. 1965 on 'ABC Paramount'; 10373>*		
1963.	(7"; as GORDIE LIGHTFOOT) (TF 405) **THE DAY BEFORE YESTERDAY. / TAKE CARE OF YOURSELF**		
1964.	(7"; as GORDIE LIGHTFOOT) <152> **I'LL MEET YOU IN MICHOOAN. / IS MY BABY BLUE TONIGHT**	-	

—— now with **DAVID REA + BRUCE LANGHORNE** – guitar / **BILL LEE** – bass

		U.A.	U.A.
Oct 65.	(7") (UP 1109) <929> **JUST LIKE TOM THUMB'S BLUES. / RIBBON OF DARKNESS**		
Jan 66.	(lp) <UAS 6487> **LIGHTFOOT** – Rich man's spiritual / Long river / The way I feel / For lovin' me / The first time / Changes / Early morning rain / Steel rail blues / Sixteen miles / I'm not sayin' / Pride of man / Ribbon of darkness / Oh, Linda / Peaceful waters.	-	
1966.	(7") <50055> **FOR LOVIN' ME. / SPIN, SPIN**	-	

—— now with **RED SHEA** – guitar / **JOHN STOCKFISH** – bass

1967.	(lp) <UAS 6587> **THE WAY I FEEL** – Walls / If you got it / Softly / Crossroads / A minor ballad / Go-go round / Rosanna / Home from the forest / I'll be alright / Song for a winter's night / Canadian railroad trilogy / The way I feel. *(UK-iss.1971 on 'Sunset'; SLS 50231) (cd-iss. Dec95 on 'Beat Goes On'; BGOCD 296)*	-	
1967.	(7") <50114> **GO-GO ROUND. / I'LL BE ALRIGHT**	-	
1967.	(7") <50152> **THE WAY I FEEL. / PEACEFUL WATERS**	-	
Apr 68.	(7") (UP 2216) <50281> **BLACK DAY IN JULY. / PUSSY WILLOWS, CAT-TAILS**		
May 68.	(lp) (SULP 1199) <6649> **DID SHE MENTION MY NAME** – The last time I saw her / Black day in July / May I / Magnificent outpouring / Does your mother know / The mountain and Maryann / Pussy willows, cat-tails / I want to hear it from you / Something very special / Boss man / Did she mention my name.		
Mar 69.	(7") (UP 2272) **THE CIRCLE IS SMALL. / DOES YOUR MOTHER KNOW**		
Mar 69.	(7") <50447> **BITTER GREEN. / DOES YOUR MOTHER KNOW**	-	
May 69.	(7") (UP 35020) **BITTER GREEN. / MAY I**	-	-
Jun 69.	(lp) (SULP 1239) <6672> **BACK HERE ON EARTH** – Long way back home / Unsettled ways / Long thin dawn / Bitter green / The circle is small / Marie Christine / Cold hands from New York / Affair on 8th Avenue / Don't beat me down / The gypsy / If I could / Wherefore and why.		
Sep 69.	(7") (UP 35036) **EARLY MORNING RAIN. / THE GYPSY**		-
Feb 70.	(lp) (UAS 29040) <6714> **SUNDAY CONCERT (live at Massey Hall, Toronto)** – Canadian railroad trilogy / Pussy willows, cat-tails / Boss man / Softly / Ballad of Yarmouth Castle / Bitter green / Apology / Medley: Ribbon of darkness / I'm not sayin' / The lost children / In a windowpane / Peaceful waters / Oh, Linda. *(cd-iss. Mar93 on 'Bear Family'+=; BCD 15691)*		Nov69

—— **RICK HAYNES** – bass; repl. JOHN

		Reprise	Reprise
Nov 70.	(7") <0926> **ME AND BOBBY McGEE. / THE PONY MAN**	-	
Jan 71.	(lp) (K 44091) <6392> **SIT DOWN YOUNG STRANGER** – Minstrel of the dawn / Me and Bobby McGee / Approaching Lavender / Saturday clothes / Cobweb and dust / Poor little Alison / Sit down young stranger / Your love's return / The pony man. *(re-titled.Jun71 'IF YOU COULD READ MY MIND') (cd-iss. Feb93; 7599 27451-2)*		12 May70
May 71.	(7") (K 20974) <0974> **IF YOU COULD READ MY MIND. / POOR LITTLE ALISON**	30	5 Dec70
Jun 71.	(7") <1020> **TALKING IN YOUR SLEEP. / NOUS VIVONS ENSEMBLE**	-	64

—— now w /diff. session people.

Jun 71. (lp) *(K 44132) <2037>* **SUMMER SIDE OF LIFE** — [ ] | 38 | May71
– 10 degrees and getting colder / Miguel / Go my way / Summer side of life / Cotton Jenny / Talking in your sleep / Nous vivons ensemble / Same old loverman / Redwood Hill / Love and maple syrup / Cabaret.

Aug 71. (7") *<1035>* **SUMMER SIDE OF LIFE. / LOVE AND MAPLE SYRUP** — [-] | 98

—— the above 1970 personnel added **TERRY CLEMENTS** – guitar

Mar 72. (7") *<1088>* **BEAUTIFUL. / DON QUIXOTE** — [-] | 58

Apr 72. (lp) *(K 44166) <2056>* **DON QUIXOTE** — 44 | 42 | Mar72
– Don Quixote / Christian Island / Alberta bound / Looking at the rain / Ordinary man / brave mountaineers / Ode to big blue second cup of coffee / Beautiful / On Susan's floor / The patriot's dream.

May 72. (7") *(K 14176)* **BEAUTIFUL. / CHRISTIAN ISLAND** — [ ] | [-]

Nov 72. (7") *<1128>* **THE SAME OLD OBSESSION. / YOU ARE WHAT I AM** — [-] | [ ]

Nov 72. (lp) *(K 44219) <2116>* **OLD DAN'S RECORDS** — [ ] | 95
– Old Dan's records / Farewell to Annabelle / That same old obsession / Lazy mornin' / You are what I am / Can't depend on love / My pony won't go / It's worth believin' / Mother of a miner's child / Hi way songs.

Jan 73. (7") *(K 14251) <1145>* **CAN'T DEPEND ON LOVE. / IT'S WORTH BELIEVIN'** — [ ] | [ ]

—— brought back **JOHN STOCKFISH** – bass

May 74. (7") *(K 14327) <1194>* **SUNDOWN. / TOO LATE FOR PRAYIN'** — 33 | 1 | Apr74

Jun 74. (lp) *(K 44258) <2177>* **SUNDOWN** — 45 | 1 | Jan74
– Sundown / Somewhere U.S.A. / High and dry / Seven Island suite / Circle of steel / Is there anyone here / The watchman's gone / Carefree highway / The list / Too late for prayin'. *<US re-iss. 1980 on 'Mobile'> (cd-iss. Feb93; 7599 27211-2)*

Nov 74. (7") *(K 14370) <1309>* **CAREFREE HIGHWAY. / SEVEN ISLAND SUITE** — 10 | Aug74

Mar 75. (lp) *(K 54033) <2206>* **COLD ON THE SHOULDER** — 10 | Feb75
– Rainy day people / Bells of the evening / Rainbow trout / Cold on the shoulder / A tree to weak to stand / All the lovely ladies / Fine as can be / Now and then / Slide on over / Bend with the water / Soul is the rock / Cherokee band.

Apr 75. (7") *(K 14389) <1328>* **RAINY DAY PEOPLE. / CHEROKEE BAND** — [ ] | 26 | Mar75

—— live band now **RED SHEA + TERRY CLEMENTS** – guitar / **RICK HAYNES** – bass / **PEE WEE CHARLES** – steel guitar / **JIM GORDON** – (studio) drums

Dec 75. (d-lp) *(K 64033) <2237>* **GORD'S GOLD** (remixed compilation) — [ ] | 34 | Nov75
– I'm not sayin' – Ribbon of darkness / Song for a winter's night / Canadian railroad trilogy / Softly / For lovin' me – Did she mention my name / Affair on 8th Avenue / Steel rail blues / Wherefore and why / Bitter green / Early morning rain / Minstrel of the dawn / Sundown / Beautiful / Summer side of life / Rainy day people / Cotton Jenny / Don Quixote / Circle of steel / Old Dan's records / If you could read my mind / Cold on the shoulder / Carefree highway.

Aug 76. (lp/c) *(K/K4 54067) <2246>* **SUMMERTIME DREAM** — [ ] | 12 | Jun76
– The wreck of the Edmund Fitzgerald / Race among the ruins / I'm not supposed to care / I'd do it again / Never too close / Protocol / The house you live in / Summertime dream / Spanish moss / Too many clues in the room.

Nov 76. (7") *(K 14451) <1369>* **THE WRECK OF THE EDMUND FITZGERALD. / THE HOUSE YOU LIVE IN** — 40 | 2 | Aug76

Feb 77. (7") *<1380>* **RACE AMONG THE RUINS. / PROTOCOL** — [-] | 65
                                                Warners | Warners

Feb 78. (lp/c) *(K/K4 56444) <3149>* **ENDLESS WIRE** — [ ] | 22 | Jan78
– Endless wire / If there's a reason / Daylight Katy / The circle is small (I can see it in your eyes) / Sweet Guinevere / Hangdog hotel room / Dreamland / Songs of the minstrel / Sometime I don't mind / If children had wings.

Feb 78. (7") *<8518>* **THE CIRCLE IS SMALL (I CAN SEE IT IN YOUR EYES). / SWEET GUINEVERE** — [-] | 33

Jul 78. (7") *(K 17214) <8579>* **DAYLIGHT KATY. / HANGDOG HOTEL ROOM** — 41 | [ ]

Nov 78. (7") *<8644>* **DREAMLAND. / SONGS THE MINISTER SANG** — [-] | [ ]

Jun 80. (lp/c) *(K/K4 56802) <3426>* **DREAM STREET ROSE** — [ ] | 60 | Mar80
– Sea of tranquility / Ghosts of Cape Horn / Dream street Rose / On the high seas / Whisper my name / If you need me / Hey you / Make way for the lady / Mister rock of ages / Auctioneer.

Jun 80. (7") *(K 17637) <49230>* **DREAM STREET ROSE. / MAKE WAY FOR THE LADY** — [ ] | [ ]

Feb 82. (lp/c) *(K/K4 56970) <3633>* **SHADOWS** — [ ] | 87
– 14 karat gold / In my fashion / Shadows / Blackberry wine / Heaven help the Devil / Thank you for the promises / Baby step back / All I'm after / Triangle / I'll do anything / She's not the same.

May 82. (7") *(K 17945) <50012>* **BABY STEP BACK. / THANK YOU FOR THE PROMISES** — [ ] | 50 | Mar82

Sep 83. (lp/c) *<(9 23901-1/-4)>* **SALUTE** — [ ] | [ ] | Jul83
– Salute (a lot more livin' to do) / Gotta get away / Whispers of the north / Someone to believe in / Romance / Knotty pine / Biscuit city / Without you / Tattoo / Broken dreams.

Sep 86. (7") *<28553>* **STAY LOOSE. / MORNING GLORY** — [-] | [ ]

Oct 86. (lp/c) *<(K9 25482-1/-4)>* **EAST OF MIDNIGHT** — [ ] | [ ] | Aug86
– Stay loose / Morning glory / East of midnight / A lesson in love / Anything for love / Let it ride / Ecstasy made easy / You just gotta be / A passing ship / I'll tag along.

Nov 86. (7") *<28222>* **ECSTASY MADE EASY. / MORNING GLORY** — [-] | [ ]

—— LIGHTFOOT's band now incl. **TERRY CLEMENTS** – guitar / **RICK HAYNES** – bass / **MIKE HEFFERNAN** – keyboards / **BARRY KEANE** – drums

Nov 88. (d-lp/c/cd) *<(K9 25784-1/-4/-2)>* **GORD'S GOLD, VOLUME II** (remixed compilation) — [ ] | [ ]
– If it should please you / Endless wire / Hangdog hotel room / I'm not supposed to care / High and dry / The wreck of the Edmund Fitzgerald / The pony man / Race among the ruins / Christian Island / All the lovely ladies / Alberta bound / Cherokee band / Triangle / Shadows / Make way (for the lady) / Ghosts of Cape Horn / Baby step back / It's worth believin'.

                                           not iss. | Reprise

Apr 93. (cd) *<45208>* **WAITING FOR YOU** — [-] | [ ]
– Restless / Ring them bells / Fading away / Only love would know / Welcome to try / I'll prove my love / Waiting for you / Wild strawberries / I'd rather press on / Drink yer glasses empty.

May 98. (cd) *<46949>* **A PAINTER PASSING THROUGH** — [-] | [ ]
– Drifters / My little love / Ringneck loon / I used to be a country singer / Boathouse / Much to my surprise / A painter passing through / On Yonge Street / Red velvet / Uncle Toad said.

– compilations, etc. –

1966. (7") *Warners; <(WB 5621)>* **I'M NOT SAYIN'. / FOR LOVIN' ME** — [ ] | [ ]

1968. (7") *President; (PT 138)* **ADIOS ADIOS. / MY BABY IS BLUE TONIGHT** — [ ] | [ ]

Sep 69. (lp) *United Artists; <UAS 29012>* **EARLY LIGHTFOOT** — [-] | [ ]

Jul 71. (lp) *United Artists; <(UAS 5510)>* **CLASSIC LIGHTFOOT (THE BEST OF GORDON LIGHTFOOT, VOL.2)** — [ ] | Jun71

1972. (7"ep) *Reprise; (K 14210)* **IF YOU COULD READ MY MIND. / ME AND BOBBY McGEE. / SUMMER SIDE OF LIFE / TALKING IN YOUR SLEEP** — [ ] | [ ]

1974. (7"ep) *Reprise;* **IF YOU COULD READ MY MIND / CHRISTIAN ISLAND. / ODE TO BIG BLUE SECOND CUP OF COFFEE / ME AND BOBBY McGEE** — [ ] | [ ]

Jul 74. (d-lp) *United Artists; <LA 243>* **THE VERY BEST OF GORDON LIGHTFOOT VOL.I & II** — [ ] | [ ]

1975. (d-lp) *Reprise; (K 64022)* **TWO ORIGINALS OF . . .** — [ ] | [ ]
– (albums 'DON QUIXOTE' + 'SUMMER SIDE OF LIFE')

May 81. (lp/c) *Reprise; (K/K4 56915)* **THE BEST OF GORDON LIGHTFOOT** — [ ] | [ ]
– Early morning rain / The wreck of Edmund Fitzgerald / Carefree highway / Minstrel / Rainy day people / Sundown / Summer side of life / Cold on the shoulder / Endless wire / If you could read my mind / Canadian railroad trilogy / If there's a reason / Cotton Jenny / Song for the winters night / Daylight Katy / Old Dan's records / Me and Bobby McGee / The circle is small.

Nov 76. (lp) *Sunset; (SLS 50398)* **EARLY MORNING RAIN** — [ ] | [-]

Mar 86. (7") *Old Gold; (OG 9572)* **IF YOU COULD READ MY MIND. / SUNDOWN** — [ ] | [-]

Feb 92. (cd) *Bear Family; <(BCD 15576)>* **LIGHTFOOT! / THE WAY I FEEL** — [ ] | [-]

Apr 93. (cd) *Beat Goes On; (BGOCD 166)* **EARLY LIGHTFOOT / SUNDAY CONCERT** — [ ] | [-]

Apr 93. (cd) *Beat Goes On; (BGOCD 167)* **DID SHE MENTION MY NAME / BACK HERE ON EARTH** — [ ] | [-]

LIGHTNING SEEDS

Formed: by IAN BROUDIE, 4 Aug'58, Liverpool, England. This seasoned Scouser had previously been an integral part of BIG IN JAPAN (Autumn 77-78), before joining The SECRETS and then London-based band, ORIGINAL MIRRORS, in late '78. The latter outfit cut one eponymous album (c. early 1980) for 'Mercury', although BROUDIE left soon after to go into production work, chosen by ECHO & THE BUNNYMEN, The WAH!, The FALL and ICICLE WORKS, amongst the many to request his services. He subsequently helped form The CARE in 1983, with ex-WILD SWANS leader PAUL SIMPSON, although they disbanded after around a year and three singles; one of them, 'MY FLAMING SWORD', hit No.48 in the UK charts. After production work (mainly Merseyside bands), BROUDIE resurfaced in 1989, when he and a few session people formed The LIGHTNING SEEDS. The group signed to new indie label 'Ghetto', immediately scoring with surely one of the most fey, quintessentially indie-pop yet swoonsomely gorgeous singles ever, 'PURE'. This and its parent album, 'CLOUDCUCKOOLAND' (1990), surprised many by also making the US lists in '91 and BROUDIE garnered enough interest for 'Virgin' to sign him up for 1992's 'SENSE' album. Despite another batch of pristine, gilt-edged pop nuggets, the album hung around tentatively on the fringes of the album chart like a shy kid at the playground gates. Only 'THE LIFE OF RILEY' single managed to dent the Top 30. Perhaps as a response, 'JOLLIFICATION' (1994) was more blatantly commercial. The change was very subtle, but it was definitely there; in the way every track sounded like a muso rerun of 'PURE', in the way BROUDIE's little-boy-lost vocals now seemed to grate rather than soothe and in the way that the whole shebang continually teetered on the verge of self-parody. The resultant live shows, with their cack-handed rock approach, confirmed that BROUDIE was now writing for 20-something couples who had grown too old to go down the indie disco. The final nail in the coffin was the utterly nauseating England Euro '96 football theme, 'THREE LIONS', a track that sounded even more limp-wristed than NEW ORDER's World Cup effort two years previously. They think it's all over . . . it is now (we live in hope!?). The LIGHTNING SEEDS were back in the music game by 1999, although their comeback album of-sorts, 'TILT', did nothing to seriously shake up the indie-pop world.
• **Songwriters:** BROUDIE obviously, except SOMETHING IN THE AIR (Thunderclap Newman) / HANG ON TO A DREAM (Tim Hardin) / LUCIFER SAM (Pink Floyd) / HERE TODAY (Beach Boys) / ANOTHER GIRL, ANOTHER PLANET (Only Ones) / WHOLE WIDE WORLD (Wreckless Eric) / OUTDOOR MINER (Wire) / YOU SHOWED ME (Byrds; minor hit Turtles). LUCKY YOU + FEELING LAZY + MY BEST DAY were co-written & sung w/ TERRY HALL + IAN McNABB + ALISON MOYET respectively. The track OPEN GOALS sampled; LOOK KA PY PY (Meters).
• **Trivia:** The track 'PERSUASION' featured IAN McCULLOCH (ex-ECHO & THE BUNNYMEN). He has also produced NORTHSIDE, PRIMITIVES and TERRY HALL.

Album rating: CLOUDCUCKOOLAND (*7) / SENSE (*6) / JOLLIFICATION (*6) / PURE LIGHTNING SEEDS compilation (*7) / DIZZY HEIGHTS (*7) / TILT (*5)

IAN BROUDIE – vocals, keyboards, guitar / with **PETER COYLE** + **PAUL SIMPSON** (ex-LOTUS EATERS + WILD SWANS)

			Ghetto	M.C.A.	
Jun 89.	(7") *(GTG 004)* <53816> **PURE. / FOOLS**		16	31	Apr90

(12"+=) *(GTGT 004)* – God help them.
(cd-s++=) *(GTG 004CD)* – All I want.

Aug 89. (lp/c/cd) *(GHETT/+C/CD 3)* <MCA/+C/D 6404>
CLOUDCUCKOOLAND   50   46
– All I want / Bound in a nutshell / Pure / Sweet dreams / The nearly man / Joy / Love explosion / Don't let go / Control the flame / The price / Fools / Frenzy. *(c+=/cd+=)* – God help them. *(re-iss. cd May92; CDOVD 436)*

Oct 89. (7") *(GTG 6)* **JOY. / FRENZY**   ☐ ☐
(12"+=/cd-s+=) *(GTGT/CDGTG 6)* – Control The Flame.
(US cd-ep+=) – Hang on to a dream.

Apr 90. (7") *(GTG 9)* <24054> **ALL I WANT. / PERSUASION** ☐ ☐ Aug90
(12"+=/cd-s+=) *(GTGT/CDGTG 9)* – ('A'extended).

—— BROUDIE made appearance on WILD SWANS non-UK album 'SPACE FLOWER'.

		Virgin	M.C.A.	
Mar 92.	(7"/c-s) *(VS/VSC 1402)* <54195> **THE LIFE OF RILEY. /**			

SOMETHING IN THE AIR   28   98
(12"+=/cd-s+=) *(VST/VSCDG 1402)* – Marooned.
(US c-s) <54195> – ('A'side) / excerpts: Blowing bubbles – Sense – A cool place.

Apr 92. (cd/c/lp) *(CDV/TCV/V 2690)* <MCA D/C 10388> **SENSE**   53
– Sense / The life of Riley / Blowing bubbles / A cool place / Where flowers fade / A small slice of heaven / Tingle tangle / Happy / Marooned / Thinking up, looking down.

May 92. (7"/c-s) *(VS/VSC 1414)* <54431> **SENSE. / FLAMING SWORD**   31   ☐ Jun92
(12"+=/cd-s+=) *(VST/VSCDT 1414)* – The life of Riley (remix) / Hang on to a dream.

May 92. (c-s) <54425> **SENSE / TINGLE TANGLE**   –
(cd-s) <54431> – ('A'side) / The life of Riley / Flaming sword / Lucifer Sam.

—— BROUDIE added **SIMON ROGERS** – instruments, co-producer / **CLIVE LAYTON** – Hammond organ / **MARINA VAN RODY** – vocals (Why Why Why). The live band **BROUDIE** – vocals, guitar / with **ALI KANE** – keyboards / **MARTYN CAMPBELL** – bass / **CHRIS SHARROCK** – drums

		Epic	Trauma-Interscope
Aug 94.	(7"/c-s) *(660 628-8/-4)* <51002> **LUCKY YOU. / ('A'lunar**		

mix)   43
(12"/cd-s (660 628-6/-2) – ('A'hard luck mix) / ('A'lucky devil mix) / ('A'lunar cabaret mix).

—— Above was co-written w / **TERRY HALL**. They are now best known for contributing football theme to Match of the Day's 'Goal Of The Month'. ALISON MOYET wrote a track for the next album.

Sep 94. (cd/c/lp) *(477237-2/-4/-1)* <71008> **JOLLIFICATION**   12   ☐ Dec94
– Perfect / Lucky you / Open goals / Change / Why why why / Marvellous / Feeling lazy / My best day / Punch & Judy / Telling tales.

Jan 95. (7")(c-s) *(660 986-7/-4)* **CHANGE. / SAY YOU WILL**   13   –
(cd-s+=) *(660 986-5)* – Dust.
(cd-s) *(660 986-2)* – ('A'side) / The life of Riley (instrumental) / Lucky you (live).

Apr 95. (c-s) *(661 426-4)* **MARVELLOUS / LUCIFER SAM**   24   –
(cd-s+=) *(661 426-5)* – I met you.
(cd-s) *(661 426-2)* – ('A'side) / ('A'club mix) / ('A'dub mix) / All I want.

Jul 95. (c-s) *(662 179-4)* **PERFECT / HOWL**   18   –
(cd-s+=) *(662 179-2)* – ('A'acoustic) / Blowing bubbles (extended remix).
(cd-s) *(662 179-5)* – ('A'side) / Change (live) / Flaming sword (live).

Oct 95. (c-s) *(662 518-4)* **LUCKY YOU / LUCKY YOU (Lunar mix)**   15   –
(cd-s) *(662 518-2)* – ('A'side) / Life of Riley (live) / Pure (live) / Here today (live).
(cd-s) *(662 518-5)* – ('A'side) / Open your eyes / The likely lads.

Feb 96. (c-s) *(662 967-4)* **READY OR NOT / PUNCH AND JUDY (electric '96 version)**   20   –
(cd-s+=) *(662 967-5)* – Outdoor miner.
(cd-s) *(662 967-2)* – ('A'side) / Another girl, another planet / Whole wide world.

May 96. (7"/c-s; BADDIEL & SKINNER & The LIGHTNING SEEDS *(663 273-7/-4)* **THREE LIONS (The Official Song Of The England Football Team) / ('A'-Karaoke version)**   1   –
(cd-s+=) *(663 273-2)* – ('A'-Jules Rimet extended version).
(the '98 World Cup version returned to No.1 in Jun'98)

		Epic	Sony
Oct 96.	(c-s) *(663863-4)* **WHAT IF . . . / HERE TODAY (live)**	14	–

(cd-s) *(663863-2)* – ('A'side) / Never / The crunch / ('A'-Leuroj's slo'n'easy mix).
(cd-s) *(663863-5)* – ('A'side) / Lightning Seeds mix'n'match / ('A'-Leuroj's easy disco dub mix).

Nov 96. (cd/c) *(486640-2/-4)* <68054> **DIZZY HEIGHTS**   11
– Imaginary friends / You best your life / Waiting for today to happen / What if . . . / Sugar coated iceberg / Touch and go / Like you do / Wishaway / Fingers and thumbs / You showed me / Ready or not / Fishes on the line.

Jan 97. (c-s) *(664043-4)* **SUGAR COATED ICEBERG / THIS POWER**   12
(cd-s+=) *(664043-2)* – S.F. sorrow is born / Porpoise song.
(cd-s) *(664043-5)* – ('A'side) / Why why why / Telling tales.

Apr 97. (cd/c) *(664328-2)* **YOU SHOWED ME (mixes by Attica Blues / The Wiseguys & DJ Pulse)**   8
(c-s+=) *(664328-4)* – (Todd Terry mix).
(cd-s) *(664328-5)* – (Todd Terry mixes).

Nov 97. (cd/c) *(<489034-2/-4>)* **LIKE YOU DO . . . THE BEST OF** (compilation)   5
– What you say / Life of Riley / Lucky you / You showed me / Change / Waiting for today to happen ('97 mix) / Pure / Sugar coated iceberg / Ready or not / All I want / Perfect / What if? / Sense / Marvellous / Three lions.

		Epic	Alex
Nov 97.	(c-s) *(665367-4)* **WHAT YOU SAY / BE MY BABY**	41	Apr98

(cd-s+=) *(665367-2)* <6090> – Weirdaway / Blue.
(cd-s) *(665367-5)* <6050> – ('A'-Psyche Beach trip pts.1-3) / ('A'mixes by Ballistic Brothers & Wiseguys).

Nov 99. (c-s) *(668150-4)* **LIFE'S TOO SHORT / EVERYDAY AND EVERYNIGHT**   27   –
(cd-s+=) *(668150-2)* – ('A'-ATFC remix).
(cd-s) *(668150-5)* – ('A'mixes by; 3 Jays & Way Out West).

Nov 99. (cd/c) *(496263-2/-4)* **TILT**   46   ☐
– Life's too short / Sweeter soul sensation / If only / City bright lights / I wish I was in love / Happy satellite / Get it right / Cigarettes and lies / Crowd pleaser / Tales of the riverbank / Pussy foot / All the things.

– compilations, etc. –

on 'Virgin' unless otherwise mentioned

May 96. (cd/c/lp) *(CDV/TCV/V 2805)* **PURE LIGHTNING SEEDS**   27   –
May 96. (c-s) *(VSC 1586)* **LIFE OF RILEY / SOMETHING IN THE AIR**   ☐ ☐
(cd-s+=) *(VSCDT 1586)* – Marooned.
(cd-s) *(VSCDX 1586)* – ('A'side) / Control the flame / ('A'remix).

LILYS (dig out; Great Alt & Indie . . .)

LIMP BIZKIT

Formed: Jacksonville, Florida, USA . . . 1994 by FRED DURST, WES BORLAND, SAM RIVERS, JOHN OTTO and DJ LETHAL, the latter snatched from the recently defunct, HOUSE OF PAIN. Drawing inevitable comparisons to KORN and RAGE AGAINST THE MACHINE, the band thrusted their bass-chunky metal funk/rap into the melting pot of 90's rock with favourable results. Of a generally more sprightly disposition than the aforementioned bands, this goatee-bearded fly-shaded posse released their 'Interscope' debut, 'THREE DOLLAR BILL, Y'ALL$' in the summer of '97. Not content with BIZKIT's minor breakthrough, DURST also guested for COLD, SOULFLY and KORN on their early 1998 sets. With METHOD MAN from WU-TANG CLAN (on the track, 'N 2 GETHER NOW') and a celebrity feast of stars courtesy of KORN, STONE TEMPLE PILOTS and PRIMUS all on show, how could their follow-up album, 'SIGNIFICANT OTHER', fail. In fact, its MTV-friendly hardcore rap was all the rage with trendy young teenagers who helped it get all the way to No.1 on its first week of release. However, the more discerning Brit was not quite convinced (it only reached No.26).

Album rating: THREE DOLLAR BILL, Y'ALL$ (*7) / SIGNIFICANT OTHER (*4)

FRED DURST – vocals / **WES BORLAND** – guitar / **SAM RIVERS** – bass / **JOHN OTTO** – drums / **DJ LETHAL** (b. LEOR DiMANT, 18 Dec'72, Latvia) – turntables (ex-HOUSE OF PAIN)

		Interscope	Interscope
Jul 97.	(cd) <(IND 90124)> **THREE DOLLAR BILL, Y'ALL$**	☐	22

– Intro / Pollution / Counterfeit / Stuck / Nobody loves me / Sour / Stalemate / Clunk / Faith / Stinkfinger / Indigo flow / Leech / Everything.

Jul 99. (cd/c/d-lp) *(IND/INC/INT2 90335)* <490335> **SIGNIFICANT OTHER**   26   1
– Intro / Jusy like this / Nookie / Break stuff / Re-arranged / I'm broke / Nobody like you / Don't go off wondering / 9 teen 90 nine / N 2 gether now / Trust / No sex / Show me what you got / Lesson learned / Outro.

Jul 99. (-) <*radio cut*> **NOOKIE**   –   80

Nov 99. (c-s/cd-s; as LIMP BIZKIT featuring METHOD MAN)
<497183> **N 2 GETHER NOW**   –   78

Nov 99. (-) <*radio cut*> **RE-ARRANGED**   –   90

LINDISFARNE

Formed: Newcastle-upon-Tyne, England . . . 1969 as BRETHREN by SIMON COWE (guitar, mandolin), RAY JACKSON (guitar, mandolin, mouth harp), JEFF SANDLER (guitar), ROD CLEMENTS (bass, violin, vocals) and ROY LAIDLAW (drums) (The latter two had earlier been part of Newcastle band The DOWNTOWN FACTION). With singer/songwriter ALAN HULL (who released a solo credited single in 1969, 'WE CAN SWING TOGETHER' / 'OBADIAH'S GRAVE' for 'Transatlantic') soon replacing SANDLER, the band took a more mellow folk approach, adopting the name LINDISFARNE. Initially gaining some support on the college circuit, the band had soon secured a contract on Tony Stratton-Smith's 'Charisma' label. The 1970 debut, 'NICELY OUT OF TUNE', was a folky gem, featuring the atmospheric 'LADY ELEANOR' and introducing the band's impressive use of harmony. For the follow-up, 'FOG ON THE TYNE', the band hooked up with Nashville producer Bob Johnston. Released in late '71, the album scaled the UK charts the following year, aided by the Top 5 success of the exquisitely melodic 'MEET ME ON THE CORNER' single and a re-issued 'LADY ELEANOR'. The band retained JOHNSTON for the 'DINGLY DELL' (1972) album, although this time the pairing was a recipe for commercial and critical failure. In summer 1973, the band split; COWE, CLEMENTS and LAIDLAW going off to form JACK THE LAD while ALAN HULL released a solo effort, 'PIPEDREAM'. Later that year, HULL resurrected the band along with JACKSON, recruiting a new line-up of CHARLIE HARCOURT (guitar), KENNY CRADDOCK (keyboards), TOMMY DUFFY (bass) and PAUL NICHOLS (drums). After a couple of flop albums, 'ROLL ON RUBY' (1973) and 'HAPPY DAZE' (1974), the band once again called it a day, HULL releasing a solo follow-up, 1975's 'SQUIRE'. Three years later, the original line-up reformed, scoring a new deal with 'Mercury' and a Top 10 UK hit with the harmony-laden classic, 'RUN FOR HOME'. The cringe-ingly titled 'BACK AND FOURTH' album made the British Top 30, although subsequent releases foundered and the band were once again confined to the margins. Not content with churning out rock 'n' roll medley's, the band teamed up with top arsehole PAUL GASCOIGNE (Rangers and England footballer) in 1990 for a 'hilarious' run through of 'FOG ON THE TYNE'. While the single made No.2, it's doubtful if it won the band any new admirers outside their loyal Geordie fanbase. • **Songwriters:** HULL, JACKSON plus others contributed.

Album rating: NICELY OUT OF TUNE (*7) / FOG ON THE TYNE (*8) / DINGLY DELL (*6) / LINDISFARNE LIVE (*5) / ROLL ON RUBY (*4) / HAPPY DAZE (*5) / BACK AND FOURTH (*6) / MAGIC IN THE AIR (*4) / THE NEWS (*4) / SLEEPLESS NIGHTS (*4) / LINDISFARNETASTIC (*4) / LINDISFARNETASTIC VOLUME 2 (*3) / DANCE YOUR LIFE AWAY (*3) / THE BEST OF LINDISFARNE compilation (*7) / AMIGOS (*4) / CAUGHT IN THE ACT live collection (*7) / ELVIS LIVES ON THE MOON (*4) / ANOTHER FINE MESS (*4)

ALAN HULL (b.20 Feb'45) – vocals, guitar (ex-CHOSEN FEW, solo artist) / **RAY JACKSON** (b.12 Dec'48, Wallsend, England) – guitar, mandolin, mouth harp / **SIMON COWE** (b. 1 Apr'48, Tynemouth, England) – guitar, mandolin / **ROD CLEMENTS** (b.17 Nov'47, North Shields, England) – bass, violin, vocals / **ROY LAIDLAW** (b.28 May'48, North Shields) – drums

		Charisma	Elektra
Sep 70.	(7") (CB 137) **CLEAR WHITE LIGHT – PART 2. / KNACKERS YARD BLUES**	□	-
Nov 70.	(lp) (CAS 1025) **NICELY OUT OF TUNE**	□	-

– Lady Eleanor / Road to kingdom come / Winter song / Turn a deaf ear / Clear white light (part II) / We can swing together / Alan in the river with flowers / Down / The things I should have said / Jackhammer blues / Scarecrow song. (re-dist.Jan 72, hit No.8) (re-iss. Aug86 lp/c; CHC/+MC 31) (cd-iss. Aug88 on 'Virgin'; CASCD 1025) (+=) – Knackers yard blues / Nothing but the marvellous is beautiful.

Jan 71.	(7") (CB 153) **LADY ELEANOR. / NOTHING BUT THE MARVELLOUS IS BEAUTIFUL**	□	-

(re-iss. May72, hit UK No.3)

Sep 71.	(7") (CB 153) **LADY ELEANOR. / DOWN**	-	□

<re-iss. US; Aug72, hit No.82>

Oct 71.	(lp) (CAS 1050) **FOG ON THE TYNE**	1	

– Meet me on the corner / Alright on the night / Uncle Sam / Together forever / January song / Peter Brophy don't care / City song / Passing ghosts / Train in G major / Fog on the Tyne. (re-iss. Oct86 lp/c; CHC/+MC 52) (cd-iss. Aug88 + Feb91 on 'Virgin'; CASCD 1050) (+=) – Scotch mist / No time to lose.

Feb 72.	(7"m) (CB 173) **MEET ME ON THE CORNER. / SCOTCH MIST / NO TIME TO LOSE**	5	-
Mar 72.	(7") **MEET ME ON THE CORNER. / FOG ON THE TYNE**	5	-
Sep 72.	(7") (CB 191) **ALL FALL DOWN. / WE CAN SWING TOGETHER (live)**	34	
Sep 72.	(lp/c) (CAS 1057) **DINGLY DELL**	5	

– All fall down / Plankton's lament / Bring down the government / Poor old Ireland / Don't ask me / Oh, no not again / Dingle regatta / Wake up little sister / Go back / Court in the act / Mandolin king / Dingly dell. (cd-iss. Aug88 on 'Virgin'; CASCD 1057) (+=) – We can swing together (live).

Dec 72.	(7") (CB 199) **COURT IN THE ACT. / DON'T ASK ME**	□	-
Jul 73.	(lp/c) (CLASS 2) **LINDISFARNE LIVE (live)**	25	-

– No time to lose / Meet me on the corner / All right on the night / Train in G major / Fog on the Tyne / We can swing together / Jackhammer blues. (re-iss. Sep83 lp/c; CHC/+MC 7)

— COWE, CLEMENTS and LAIDLAW bailed out to form JACK THE LAD. Made 4 albums **JACK THE LAD** (1974) / **OLD STRAIGHT TRACK** (1974) / **ROUGH DIAMONDS** (1975) . The 4th **JACKPOT** (1976) on 'United Art' was without CLEMENTS, COWE or LAIDLAW.

ALAN HULL

		Charisma	Warners
Jun 73.	(7"m) (CB 208) **NUMBERS (TRAVELLING BAND). / DRINKING SONG / ONE OFF PAT**	□	-
Jul 73.	(lp/c) (CAS 1069) **PIPEDREAM**	29	

– Breakfast / Monkey game / Country gentleman's wife / Just another sad song / Numbers (travelling band) / For the bairns / Drinking song / Song for a windmill / United States of mind / I hate to see you cry / Blue murder. (re-iss. Mar83 lp/c; CHC/+MC 16) (cd-iss. Feb91 & Mar94 on 'Virgin'; CASCD 1069)

Sep 73.	(7") (CB 211) **JUST ANOTHER SAD SONG. / WAITING**	□	-

LINDISFARNE

re-formed Autumn 1973. Same label. **HULL & JACKSON** brought in **CHARLIE HARCOURT** – lead guitar / **KENNY CRADDOCK** – keyboards / **TOMMY DUFFY** – bass / **PAUL NICHOLS** – drums

Dec 73.	(lp/c) (CAS 1076) **ROLL ON RUBY**	□	□

– Taking care of business / North Country boy / Steppenwolf / Nobody loves you anymore / When the war is over / Moonshine / Lazy / Roll on river / Tow the line / Goodbye.

Mar 74.	(7") (CB 228) **TAKING CARE OF BUSINESS. / NORTH COUNTRY BOY**	□	□

		Warners	Asylum
Oct 74.	(lp/c) (K/K4 56070) **HAPPY DAZE**	□	□

– Tonight / In yer head / River / You put the laff on me / No need to tell me / I'm juiced / Up to lose / Dealer's choice / Nellie / The man down there / Gin and tonic all round / Tomorrow.

Jan 75.	(7") (K 16489) **TONIGHT. / NO NEED TO TELL ME**	□	□

— Disbanded again.

ALAN HULL

returned with own studio work.

		Warners	Warners
May 75.	(7") (K 16561) **DAN THE PLAN. / ONE MORE BOTTLE OF WINE**	□	□
May 75.	(lp/c) (K/K4 56121) **SQUIRE**	□	□

– Squire / Dan the plan / Picture a little girl / Nuthin' shakin' / One more bottle of wine / Golden oldies / I'm sorry squire / Waiting / Bad side of town / Mr.Inbetween.

Aug 75.	(7") (K 16599) **SQUIRE. / ONE MORE BOTTLE OF WINE**	□	□
Dec 75.	(7") (K 16643) **CRAZY WOMAN. / GOLDEN OLDIES**	□	□

LINDISFARNE

— the original 1970 line-up re-formed

		Mercury	Atco
May 78.	(7") (6007 177) **RUN FOR HOME. / STICK TOGETHER**	10	33 Sep 78
Jun 78.	(lp) (9109 609) **BACK AND FOURTH**	22	

– Juke box gypsy / Warm feeling / Woman / Only alone / Run for home / Kings X blues / Get wise / You and me / Marshall Riley's army / Angels at eleven / Make me want to stay. (re-iss. Dec83 lp/c; PRICE/PRIMC 54) (cd-iss. 1991; 848 226-2)

Sep 78.	(7") (6007 187) **JUKE BOX GYPSY. / WHEN IT GOES THE HARDEST**	56	-
Nov 78.	(7") (6007 195) **BRAND NEW DAY. / WINTER SONG**	□	-
Dec 78.	(7") **WARM FEELING. / WOMAN**	□	-
Dec 78.	(d-lp) (6641 877) **MAGIC IN THE AIR (live)**	□	-

– Lady Eleanor / Road to kingdom come / Turn a deaf ear / January song / Court in the act / Meet me on the corner / Bye bye birdie / Train in G-major / Scarecrow song / Dingly dell / Scotch mist / No time to lose / Winter song / Uncle Sam / Wake up little sister / All fall down / We can swing together / Fog on the Tyne / Clear white light.

Feb 79.	(7") (6007 205) **WARM FEELING. / CLEAR WHITE LIGHT (live)**	□	-
Aug 79.	(7") (NEWS 1) **EASY AND FREE. / WHEN FOREVER COMES ALONG**	□	-
Sep 79.	(lp)(c) (9109 626)(7231 439) **THE NEWS**	□	-

– Call of the wild / People say / 1983 / Log on your fire / Evening / Easy and free / Miracles / When Friday comes along / Dedicated hound / This has got to end / Good to be here.

Oct 79.	(7") (6007 241) **CALL OF THE WILD. / DEDICATED HOUND**	□	-

		Subterranean	not iss.
Jun 80.	(7") (SUB 1) **FRIDAY GIRL. / 1983**	□	-

		Hangover	not iss.
Nov 81.	(7") (HANG 9) **I MUST STOP GOING TO PARTIES. / SEE HOW THEY RUN**	□	-

		L.M.P.	not iss.
Jun 82.	(7") (LM 1) **SUNDERLAND BOYS. / CRUISING TO DISASTER**	□	-

		Fog	
Sep 82.	(7") (FOG 1) **NIGHTS. / DOG RUFF**	□	-
Oct 82.	(lp/c) (GET/ZCGET 1) **SLEEPLESS NIGHTS**	□	-

– Nights / Start again / Cruising to disaster / Same way down / Winning the game / About you / Underland boys / Love is a pain / Do what I want / Never miss the water / I must stop going to parties / Stormy weather. (cd-iss. May93 on 'Castle'; CLACD 382)

Jan 83.	(7") (FOG 2) **DO WHAT I WANT. / SAME WAY DOWN**	□	-
Sep 84.	(lp) (GET 2) **LINDISFARNTASTIC LIVE (live)**	□	-
Nov 84.	(lp/c) (GET/ZCGET 3) **LINDISFARNTASTIC VOL.2 (live)**	□	-
Jun 85.	(7") (FOG 3) **I REMEMBER THE LIGHTS (acappella version). / DAY OF THE JACKAL**	□	-
Dec 85.	(7"; at concerts) (FOG 4) **CHRISTMAS EP (live)**	□	-

– Warm feeling / Red square dance / Run for home / Nights (acappella version).

— **HULL + JACKSON** added **MARTY CRAGGS** – saxophone / + 4th member/producer **STEVE DAGGETT** – keyboards

		River City	not iss.
Sep 86.	(7"m) (LIND 1) **SHINE ON. / HEROES / DANCE YOUR LIFE AWAY (Gogo mix)**	□	-
Oct 86.	(lp/c) (LIND LP/C 1) **DANCE YOUR LIFE AWAY**	□	-

– Shine on / Love on the run / Heroes / All in the same boat / Dance your life away / Beautiful day / Broken doll / One hundred miles to Liverpool / Take your time / Song for a stranger. (cd-iss. 1988; LINCD 1) (re-iss. cd May93 on 'Castle'; CLACD 383)

Feb 87.	(7") (LIND 2) **LOVE ON THE RUN. / ONE HUNDRED MILES TO LIVERPOOL**	□	-

(w/ free 7") (LIND 2A) – Save our ales. / Save our ales (sub mix).

		Honeybee	not iss.
Dec 87.	(7"/ext.12") (HONEY 3/+12) **PARTY DOLL. / Medley; C'MON EVERYBODY – DO YOU WANNA DANCE – TWIST AND SHOUT – DO YOU LOVE ME**	□	-

		Virgin	not iss.
Nov 88.	(7") (LADY 1) **LADY ELEANOR '88. / MEET ME ON THE CORNER**	□	-

(12"+=) (LIND 1-12) – Lost in space.
(3"cd-s++=) (LADYCD 1) – Reason to be.

		Black Crow	not iss.
Nov 89.	(lp/cd) (CRO/+CD 224) **AMIGOS**	□	-

– One world / Everything changes / Working for the man / Roll on that day / You're the one / Wish you were here / Do it like this / Any way the wind blows / Strange affair / When the night comes down / Don't say goodnight / Another world. (re-iss. cd May93 on 'Castle'; CLACD 384)

— Below w/ Geordie England footballer GAZZA (aka PAUL GASCOIGNE)

		Best	not iss.
Nov 90.	(7"/7"pic-d/c-s; by GAZZA & LINDISFARNE) (ZB/ZA/ZK 44083) **FOG ON THE TYNE (REVISITED). / ('A'instrumental)**	2	-

(ext.12"+=/cd-s+=) (ZT/ZD 44083) – ('A'extended).

— now without JACKSON; repl. by **KENNY CRADDOCK** – multi

		Essential	not iss.
May 93.	(7"/12") (ESS/+T 2026) **DAY OF THE JACKAL. / DEMONS**	□	-

(cd-s+=) (ESSX 2026) – So lonely / ('A'extended).

Jun 93.	(cd/c) (ESS CD/MC 197) **ELVIS LIVES ON THE MOON**	□	-

– Day of the jackal / Soho Square / Old peculiar feeling / Mother Russia / Demons / Don't leave me tonight / Elvis lives on the Moon / Keeping the rage / Heaven waits / Spoken like a man / Think.

Sep 94.	(cd-s) (ESSX 2044) **WE CAN MAKE IT / WALK IN THE SEA (live)**	□	-
Sep 94.	(cd) (ESSCD 214) **ON TAP: A BARREL FULL OF HITS** (compilation)	□	-

– Run for home / Lady Eleanor / Meet me on the corner / We can make it / All fall down / Warm feeling / Winter song / Road to kingdom come / Fog on the tyne / Miracles / No time to lose / Running man / Elvis lives on the Moon / Juke box gypsy / Dance your life away / Evening / Roll on that day / Clear white light II.

—— line-up HULL / CLEMENTS / CRAGGS / LAIDLAW / + DAVE DENHOLM – guitars / **IAN THOMSON** – bass

		Grapevine	not iss.

Jul 96. (cd) *(GRACD 211)* **ANOTHER FINE MESS (live 2 July '95)** | | | – |
– Clear white light (part 2) / Squire / Lady Eleanor / Meet me on the corner / Evening / City song / One world / All fall down / Winter song / This heart of mine / We can make it / Road to kingdom come / Money / Run for home / Fog on the Tyne.

—— sadly, ALAN HULL died of a heart attack on 17th of November '95

– compilations, others –

on 'Charisma' unless mentioned otherwise

Date	Description	Chart	
1974.	(7") *(CB 232)* **FOG ON THE TYNE. / MANDOLIN KING**		–
Oct 75.	(lp) *(lp/c) (CAS 1108)* **FINEST HOUR** *(re-iss. Sep83; same)*	55	–
Nov 75.	(7") *(CB 266)* **LADY ELEANOR. / FOG ON THE TYNE**		–
Aug 77.	(lp/c) *Hallmark; (SHM/SHC 919)* **LADY ELEANOR**		–
May 81.	(7") *(CB 409)* **CLEAR WHITE LIGHT. / THE TRAVELLER**		–
May 81.	(lp/c) *(BG/+C 5)* **REPEAT PERFORMANCE: THE SINGLES ALBUM**		–
Jul 82.	(7") *Old Gold; (OG 9005)* **MEET ME ON THE CORNER. / LADY ELEANOR**		–
Mar 83.	(d-c) **FOG ON THE TYNE / NICELY OUT OF TUNE**		–
Oct 87.	(d-lp/d-c/d-cd) *Stylus; (SMR/SMC/SMD 738)* **C'MON EVERYBODY**		–
Nov 88.	(12"ep/cd-ep) *Strange Fruit; (SFPS/+CD 059)* **THE PEEL SESSION** (8.5.72)		–
– Mandolin king / Poor old Ireland / Lady Eleanor / Road to kingdom come.			
Sep 89.	(lp/c/cd) *VIP-Virgin; (VVIP/+C/D 103)* **THE BEST OF LINDISFARNE** *(re-iss. cd Dec93; CDVIP 103)*		–
Aug 92.	(cd) *Castle; (CCSCD 346)* **CAUGHT IN THE ACT**		–
– Moving house / Taxman / Lady Eleanor / Nights / Mr.Inbetween / Brand new day / Mystery play / Lover not a fighter / Day of the jackal / Stormy weather / I must stop going to parties / Marshall Riley's army / Warm feeling / Fog on the tyne / Run for home / Meet me on the corner / Clear white light.			
Nov 92.	(cd) *Virgin; (CDVM 9012)* **BURIED TREASURES VOLUME 1**		–
Nov 92.	(cd) *Virgin; (CDVM 9013)* **BURIED TREASURES VOLUME 2**		–
Jun 93.	(cd) *Code 90; (NINETY 5)* **LIVE – 1990 (live)**		–

ALAN HULL

		Rocket	not iss.
Apr 79.	(7") *(XPRES 12)* **I WISH YOU WELL. / LOVE IS THE ANSWER**		–
May 79.	(lp) *(TRAIN 6)* **PHANTOMS**		–

– Anywhere is everywhere / Corporation rock / Dancin' / I wish you well / Love is an alibi / Love is the answer / Madman and loonies / Make me want to stay / Somewhere out there / A walk in the sea.

Jul 79.	(7") *(XPRES 19)* **A WALK IN THE SEA. / CORPORATION ROCK**		–

		Black Crow	not iss.
Oct 83.	(7") *(CROS 2)* **MALVINAS MELODY. / ODE TO A TAXMAN**		
Nov 83.	(lp) *(CRO 206)* **ON THE OTHER SIDE**		
Jun 88.	(lp) *(CRO 219)* **ANOTHER LITTLE ADVENTURE**		

		Mooncrest	not iss.
Jul 94.	(cd) *(CRESTCD 017)* **BACK TO BASICS**		

– United states of mind / Poor old Ireland / All fall down / Lady Eleanor / Wintersong / Walk in the sea / Mother Russia / This heart of mine / Mister inbetween / January song / Breakfast / Day of the jackal / Oh no not again / Run for home / Fog on the Tyne.

LIT

Formed: Orange County, California, USA . . . 1990 by songwriting brothers, JEREMY and A. JAY POPOFF; the line-up being completed by KEVIN BALDES and ALLAN SHELLENBERGER. The band, who looked, but didn't sound like the "SINATRA" rat pack, took their influences primarily from COSTELLO and PRESLEY. An EP, 'FIVE SMOKIN' TRACKS FROM LIT' was released in 1996 and didn't really do much for the rap-metal/pop punk quartet, neither did the debut, 'TRIPPING THE LIGHT FANTASTIC', which bagged some excellent reviews. It wasn't until 1999 that LIT unleashed 'MY OWN WORST ENEMY', the single that predictably sent melodramatic US teens into hyper mode, proving to be just as successful on British shores too. The song was a darkly comic cartoon punk (can you feel the ghosts of early GREEN DAY) track about a white trash alcoholic's misadventures with his argument-happy girlfriend. The album that followed, 'A PLACE IN THE SUN' didn't even graze the US billboard charts and hardly reached boiling-point selling figures in Europe. This could possibly be blamed on the band's rivals, SUGAR RAY, who sounded familiarly similar.

Album rating: FIVE SMOKIN' TRACKS FROM LIT mini (*5) / TRIPPING THE LIGHT FANTASTIC (*6) / A PLACE IN THE SUN (*6)

A. JAY POPOFF – vocals / **JEREMY POPOFF** – guitar / **KEVIN BALDES** – bass / **ALLAN SHELLENBERGER** – drums

		not iss.	Malicious Vinyl
Dec 96.	(m-cd) *<MV 5001>* **FIVE SMOKIN' TRACKS FROM LIT**	–	
– Bitter / Fireman / No big thing / Beginning / Stain.			
Apr 97.	(cd) *<MV 5016>* **TRIPPING THE LIGHT FANTASTIC**	–	
– Beginning / My world / Fuel / No big thing / Habib / Explode / Bitter / Amount to nothing / Dozer / Fireman / Cadillac / I don't get it. | | | |

		R.C.A.	R.C.A.
Jun 99.	(7"/c-s) *(74321 61265-7/66999-4) <radio cut>* **MY OWN WORST ENEMY. / BITTER**	16	51 Apr99
	(cd-s) *(74321 66999-2)* – ('A'side) / Money / Lovely day.		
Jun 99.	(cd/c/lp) *(74321 67859-2/-4/-1) <07863 67775-2/-4>* **A PLACE IN THE SUN**	55	31 Feb99
– Four / My own worst enemy / Down / Miserable / No big thing / Zip-lock / Lovely day / Perfect one / Quicksand / Happy / The best is yet to come undone / A place in the sun.			
Sep 99.	(c-s) *(74321 70185-4)* **ZIP-LOCK / QUICKSAND**	60	
	(cd-s+=) *(74321 70185-2)* – ('A'album version).		

LITTLE ANGELS

Formed: Scarborough, England . . . May '87 by TOBY JEPSON and MARK PLUNKETT, who had cut their teeth in school band, ZEUS, in 1984. Just over a year later, they formed an embryonic MR. THRUD along with BRUCE JOHN DICKINSON, recruiting his brother JIMMY DICKINSON by the end of the year. Having been spotted by manager Kevin Nixon, they completed the line-up with DAVE HOPPER, appearing on Channel 4's 'Famous For 15 Minutes' on the 20th November '87 as The LITTLE ANGELS. They had already issued an EP on 'Powerstation', a label co-run by their manager, repackaging the material along with some new tracks later in the year as the mini-lp 'TOO POSH TO MOSH'. Securing a deal with 'Polydor', the group supported YNGWIE MALMSTEEN and CINDERELLA on British and US dates, before issuing a single, '90° IN THE SHADE'. A year later (late '89), with drummer MICHAEL LEE replacing HOPPER, they finally delivered a full-length album, 'DON'T PREY FOR ME', a promising if inconsistent set which won the band a solid core of UK fans. Following in the footsteps of classic 80's Brit-rock, the group's effervescent, musclebound sound took occasional sidesteps into American acoustic balladry. Their first taste of major chart action was provided early in 1990, when a track from the aforementioned album, 'KICKIN' UP DUST', hit the UK Top 50. Following a clutch of infectious hit singles, the group utilised songwriter JIM VALLANCE to arrive at a smoother, more overtly Americanised sound with the 'YOUNG GODS' album of early '91. This approach worked commercial wonders, spawning hit after hit with 'BONEYARD', 'PRODUCT OF THE WORKING CLASS', 'YOUNG GODS' and 'I AIN'T GONNA CRY'. Early in '93, with new drummer MARK RICHARDSON (who actually joined a year previously), they issued another set of equally charismatic hard bluesy-rock, which surprisingly entered the UK chart at pole position, although they still failed to break into the US market despite a support slot to VAN HALEN. They subsequently split, leaving behind a 1994 compilation, while the DICKINSONs moved on to become b.l.o.w., releasing a handful of albums in the mid 90's. • **Covers:** TIE YOUR MOTHER DOWN (Queen) / BROKEN WINGS OF AN ANGEL (Hugh Cornwall) / FORTUNATE SON (Creedence Clearwater Revival) / RADICAL YOUR LOVER (co-with; Dan Reed) / BABYLON'S BURNING (Ruts) / OH WELL (Fleetwood Mac) / FUNK 49 (James Gang) / TIRED OF WAITING FOR YOU (Kinks) / WON'T GET FOOLED AGAIN (Who) / JAILHOUSE ROCK (Elvis Presley) / THE MIGHTY QUINN (Bob Dylan) / – Feb '92 – German single cover; FIRST CUT IS THE DEEPEST (Cat Stevens).

Album rating: TOO POSH TO MOSH mini (*5) / DON'T PREY FOR ME (*5) / YOUNG GODS (*6) / JAM (*6) / LITTLE OF THE PAST compilation (*7)

TOBY JEPSON – vocals, acoustic guitar / **BRUCE JOHN DICKINSON** – guitars, banjo / **JIMMY DICKINSON** – keyboards, vocals / **MARK PLUNKETT** – bass, vocals / **DAVE HOPPER** – drums

		Song Management	not iss.
Jul 87.	(12"ep) *(LAN 001)* **THE '87 EP**		–
– Bad or just no good / Better than the rest / Burning me / Reach for me. | | | |

		Powerstation	not iss.
Nov 87.	(m-lp) *(AMP 14)* **TOO POSH TO MOSH**		–
– (1st EP tracks) / Too posh to mosh / No more whiskey / Down in the night. | | | |

—— **MICHAEL LEE** – drums, percussion (ex-HOLOSAIDE) repl. HOPPER

		Polydor	Polydor
Nov 88.	(7"/7"w-poster/7"pic-d) *(LTL/+D/XP)* **90 DEGREES IN THE SHADE. / ENGLAND ROCKS (live)**		
	(12"+=) *(LTLX 1)* – Big bad world.		
Feb 89.	(7") *(LTL 2)* **SHE'S A LITTLE ANGEL. / BETTER THAN THE REST**	74	
	(c-ep+=/12"+=/cd-ep+=) **THE BIG BAD EP** *(LTL EC/EP/CD 2)* – Don't waste my time / Sex in cars.		
Sep 89.	(7") *(LTL 3)* **DO YOU WANNA RIOT. / MOVE IN SLOW**		
	(12"+=/cd-s+=) *(LTL X/CD 3)* – Some kind of alien (live).		
	(10"++=) *(LTLXV 3)* – Snatch (edited highlights of below lp).		
Nov 89.	(lp/c/cd) *(841 254-1/-4/-2)* **DON'T PREY FOR ME**		
– Do you wanna riot / Kick hard / Big bad world / Kickin' up dust / Don't prey for me / Broken wings of an angel / Bitter and twisted / Promises / When I get out of here / No solution / She's a little angel. *(c+=)* – Pleasure pyre. *(cd+=)* – Radical your lover (version) / Broken wings of an angel (version). *(re-dist.Jun90)*			
Nov 89.	(7"/c-s) *(LTL/+CS 4)* **DON'T PREY FOR ME. / RADICAL YOUR LOVER**		
	(ext.12"+=) *(LTLX 4)* – What do you want.		
	(cd-s+=) *(LTLCD 4)* – ('A'extended Bob Clearmountain mix).		
	(12") *(LTLXP 4)* – ('A'live) / She's a little angel (live) / Pleasure pyre (live) / Tie your mother down (live).		
Feb 90.	(7"/7"box) *(LTL/+B 5)* **KICKIN' UP DUST. / ('A'live)**	46	
	(12"+=) *(LTLX 5)* – Big bad world (Nashville version).		
	(cd-s+=) *(LTLLCD 5)* – Pleasure pyre (live) / Kick hard (live).		

(12"pic-d) *(LTLXP 5)* – ('A'live) / Sex in cars (live) / When I get out of here (live) / Kick hard (live).

Apr 90. (7"/7"box/c-s) *(LTL/+B/CS 6)* **RADICAL YOUR LOVER. / DON'T LOVE YOU NO MORE** `34` ☐
(12"+=/12"pic-d-ep+=/cd-ep+=) **GET RADICAL EP** *(LTL X/XP/CD 6)* – ('A'-adult remix) / Promises (live).

Jul 90. (7"/c-s)(7"w-poster) *(LTL/+CS 7)(APLTL 7)* **SHE'S A LITTLE ANGEL. / DOWN ON MY KNEES** `21` ☐
(12"+=) *(LTLX 7)* – ('A'-Voodoo mix).
(club.12"+=) *(LTLXP 7)* – When I get out of here (live).
(7") *(LTLT 7)* – ('A'side) / Sex in cars (live).

Jan 91. (7"/c-s) *(LTL/+CS 8)* **BONEYARD. / FORTUNATE SON** `33` ☐
(12"+=) *(LTLX 8)* – Sweet love sedation.
(ext.12"box++=) *(LTLBX 8)* – ('A'-Bonecrusher mix).
(12"pic-d+=) *(LTLXP 8)* – Jump the gun / ('A'album mix).

Feb 91. (cd/c/lp) *(<847 486-2/-4/-1>)* **YOUNG GODS** `17` ☐
– Back door man / Boneyard / Young gods (stand up, stand up) / I ain't gonna cry / The wildside of life / Product of the working class / That's my kinda life / Juvenile offender / Love is a gun / Sweet love sedation / Smoke in my eyes / Natural born fighter / Feels like the world has come undone (featuring the angel's anthem). *(re-iss. cd Apr95; same)*

Mar 91. (7"/c-s) *(LTL/+CS 9)* **PRODUCT OF THE WORKING CLASS. / REVIVAL** `40` ☐
(12"+=) *(LTLX 9)* – Take it off.
(12"++=) *(LTLXG 9)* – ('A'-Hot sweat'n'groove mix).
(cd-s+=) *(LTLCD 9)* – ('A'-Hot sweat'n'groove mix) / Might like you better.

May 91. (7"/c-s) *(LTL/+CS 10)* **YOUNG GODS. / GO AS YOU PLEASE** `34` ☐
(12"+=) *(LTLX 10)* – Frantic.
(12"box+=/cd-s+=) *(LTL XB/CD 10)* – Bad imitation.

Jul 91. (7"/c-s) *(LTL/+CS 11)* **I AIN'T GONNA CRY. / BABYLON'S BURNING** `26` ☐
(12"+=) *(LTLX 11)* – Funk 49.
(12"++=/cd-s++=) *(LTL BX/CD 11)* – Oh well.

—— **MARK 'Rich' RICHARDSON** – drums repl. LEE

Nov 92. (7"/c-s) *(LTL/+CS 12)* **TOO MUCH TOO YOUNG. / THE FIRST CUT IS THE DEEPEST** `22` ☐
(12"+=/cd-s+=) *(LTL X/CD 12)* – 90 degrees in the shade / Young gods.

Jan 93. (7"/c-s) *(LTL/+CS 13)* **WOMANKIND. / SCHIZOPHRENIA BLUES** `12` ☐
(12"+=/cd-s+=) *(LTL X/CD 13)* –

Jan 93. (cd/c/lp) *(<517 642-2/-4/-1>)* **JAM** `1` ☐
– The way that I live / Too much too young / Splendid isolation / Soapbox / S.T.W. / Don't confuse sex with love / Womankind / Eyes wide open / The colour of love / I was not wrong / Sail away / Tired of waiting for you (so tired) / S.T.W. (reprise).
(w/ ltd.live cd+lp + extra tracks 1-side of c) (517 676-2/-1) **LIVE JAM** – She's a little angel / Product of the working class (grooved & jammed) / I ain't gonna cry / Boneyard 1993 (featuring Big Dave Kemp) / Don't prey for me (extended version) / Won't get fooled again. *(re-iss. cd Apr95; same)*

Apr 93. (7"/c-s) *(LTL/+CS 14)* **SOAPBOX (remix). / I GOT THE SHAKES** `33` ☐
(cd-s+=) *(LTLCD 14)* – Womankind (live) / Too much too young (live).
(cd-s) *(LTLCDX 14)* – ('A'side) / Young gods (live) / Jailhouse rock (live) / I ain't gonna cry (live).

Sep 93. (12"/c-s) *(LTL X/CS 15)* **SAIL AWAY. / I AIN'T GONNA CRY (live) / SOAPBOX (live)** `45` ☐
(cd-s) *(LTLCD 15)* – ('A'side) / The mighty Quinn / This ain't the way it's supposed to be.

Mar 94. (c-s) *(LTLCS 16)* **TEN MILES HIGH. / HARD TIMES** `18` ☐
(12"+=/cd-s+=) *(LTL X/CD 16)* – Overrated.
(cd-s) *(LTLDD 16)* – ('A'side) / Just one night (acoustic) / Too much too young (acoustic).

Apr 94. (cd/c/lp) *(<521 936-2/-4/-1>)* **LITTLE OF THE PAST** (compilation) `20` ☐
– She's a little angel / Too much too young / Radical your lover / Womankind / Boneyard / Kickin' up dust / I ain't gonna cry / Sail away / Young gods / 90 degrees in the shade / Product of the working class / Soapbox / The first cut is the deepest / Ten miles high / I wanna be loved by you / Don't pray for me.

—— now w/out JIMMY + BRUCE DICKINSON who formed b.l.o.w. (released a handful of albums on their own 'Cottage Industry' imprint).

– compilations, etc –

Jun 94. (cd/c/lp) *Essential; (ESM CD/MC/LP 398)* **TOO POSH TO MOSH, TOO GOOD TO LAST!** `18` `–`
– All roads lead to you / Forbidden fruit / I want love (with Doris) / Reach for me / Bad or just no good / Burning me / No more whiskey / Down in the night / Better than the rest / Too posh to mosh / Some kind of alien.

LITTLE FEAT

Formed: Los Angeles, California, USA . . . late 1969 out of The FACTORY, by ex-ZAPPA cohorts LOWELL GEORGE and ROY ESTRADA, plus BILL PAYNE and RICHIE HAYWARD, both recent members of cult act The FRATERNITY OF MAN. Having all previously played together in the aforementioned outfits, the formation of LITTLE FEAT was more of a natural progression, GEORGE bailing out of ZAPPA's band after playing on 'Hot Rats' and 'Weasels Ripped My Flesh'. Signed to 'Warners' on the strength of three demo tracks ('WILLIN', 'TRUCK STOP GIRL' and 'BRIDES OF JESUS'), the band began work on their eponymous debut with producer RUSS TITELMAN. Eventually surfacing in late 1970, 'LITTLE FEAT' announced the arrival of a major force in American music; the aforementioned 'WILLIN' was GEORGE's statement of intent, a much covered nugget that gave LITTLE FEAT more exposure than was ever afforded their overlooked debut. In its earliest incarnation, the song was a lean sliver of poor-boy country blues,

GEORGE on resolutely unadorned vocal form with RY COODER carving out shards of wiry slide guitar. Just as raggedly affecting was 'TRUCK STOP GIRL'; closer in spirit to traditional country heartbreak than anything GEORGE would subsequently write, the song was given a wonderfully sympathetic reading by CLARENCE WHITE the same year on The BYRDS self-titled, half live/half studio opus. The 'FORTY FOUR BLUES/HOW MANY MORE YEARS' medley called to mind the mutant blues of CAPTAIN BEEFHEART while 'SNAKES ON EVERYTHING' and 'STRAWBERRY FLATS' were by turns, swaggering and shambling R&B. Though the record was met with ecstatic reviews, LITTLE FEAT didn't appear to be high on 'Warners' list of priorities, a bottom of the bill slot on a BEEFHEART/RY COODER double header more or less the only exposure the band were afforded. Returning to the studio, they cut 'SAILIN' SHOES' (1972), an album that more successfully melted LITTLE FEAT's eclectic Americana into a rich, gumbo stew. 'WILLIN' had been lovingly refashioned into a work of resonant, almost transcendent beauty, embellished by wisps of pedal steel (courtesy of 'SNEAKY' PETE KLEINOW) and PAYNE's graceful piano. 'EASY TO SLIP' was as commercial as LITTLE FEAT got, and that was part of the problem, at least in terms of widespread commercial acceptance. There was a brilliantly gritty surrealism and warped humour to GEORGE's lyrics at odds with the prevailing Californian decadence of The EAGLES/DOOBIE BROTHERS axis and the hippie utopianism of CROSBY, STILLS and NASH. This skewed vision of modern America's seedy underbelly also touched the music, the likes of 'TRIPE FACE BOOGIE' and 'TEENAGE NERVOUS BREAKDOWN' highly original, blistering slabs of rock'n'roll while the title track was a subversive slice of gospel blues. 'SAILIN' SHOES' was also the first record to feature the gaudy, surrealist artwork of NEON PARK, a regular fixture for the remainder of the band's career. Although the record again sold poorly and ROY ESTRADA left for CAPTAIN BEEFHEART's MAGIC BAND, LITTLE FEAT regrouped with extra members KENNEY GRADNEY, SAM CLAYTON (both from DELANEY & BONNIE) and PAUL BARRERE, entering the studio in late '72 to begin work on 'DIXIE CHICKEN' (1973). The pinnacle of LITTLE FEAT's career, this release represented the band's most consistent and complete body of work. Rooted in the swamp funk of New Orleans, the album was a swaggering, intoxicating masterpiece. LOWELL had developed into a frighteningly good slide player, his soaring, smoking runs interlocking with PAYNE's piano and CLAYTON's percussion to create a vibe that many have since tried and failed to imitate. The title track, 'TWO TRAINS' and 'FAT MAN IN THE BATHTUB' were anthemic stuff, BONNIE BRAMLETT and LOWELL's close friend BONNIE RAIT providing suitably soulful backing vocals. Elsewhere, LOWELL navigated a cover of ALLEN TOUSSAINT's 'ON YOUR WAY DOWN' with trenchant ease, his gilt-edged gravel/molasses vocals oozing class. The PAYNE/BARRERE-penned 'WALKIN' ALL NIGHT', meanwhile, strutted like a catwalk model. Sensual, sexy and insidiously funky, it remains a mystery why 'Warners' failed to make any commercial headway with 'DIXIE CHICKEN'. Subsequent low sales led to tension in the ranks and the band briefly split up. In the interim, GEORGE worked on ROBERT PALMER's 'Sneakin' Sally Through The Alley' and BONNIE RAITT's 'Takin' My Time' amongst other session work while PAYNE toured with labelmates, The DOOBIE BROTHERS. By May '74, the band were back together, ensconced in their Maryland studio and working on a fourth album, 'FEATS DON'T FAIL ME NOW' (1974). While the record gave them belated success, it marked a turning point in LITTLE FEAT's musical evolution. The opening salvo of 'ROCK AND ROLL DOCTOR' and 'OH ATLANTA' were skintight R&B numbers, entertaining but hardly possessed of the trademark LITTLE FEAT genius. The VAN DYKE PARKS-produced 'SPANISH MOON' was more like it, slinky and sexy with a louche, after-midnight feel. Elsewhere on the album, there was a worrying move towards jazz fusion noodling, PAYNE and BARRERE muscling in on the songwriting as GEORGE took a backseat. This was partly due to his belief in band democracy and increasingly due to his immersion in more hedonistic pleasures rendering the ever more girthsome GEORGE unable to exert full control over the band's direction. Ironically, just as LOWELL began to retreat, Warner Brothers began to show some support, sending the band on a European package tour with The DOOBIE BROTHERS, MONTROSE, TOWER OF POWER etc., early in 1975. The London show became the stuff of legend, GEORGE and Co. receiving a rapturous reception that lasted well into the DOOBIE's set. 'THE LAST RECORD ALBUM' (1975) confirmed the worst, however, PAYNE/BARRERE collaborations dominating proceedings. While the likes of 'ALL THAT YOU DREAM' was charming, its jazz-pop sound strayed far from the path of LITTLE FEAT's original vision. Of GEORGE's contributions, 'LONG DISTANCE LOVE' saw him at his bittersweet best while 'DOWN BELOW THE BORDERLINE' and 'MERCENARY TERRITORY' showed his songwriting had lost none of its bite. 'TIME LOVES A HERO' (1977) continued the descent into WEATHER REPORT territory with the double concert set, 'WAITING FOR COLUMBUS' (1978) was met with mixed reviews, revealing little of the fire and spark that marked the numerous live bootlegs on the market. GEORGE had already released his solo album, 'THANKS, I'LL EAT IT HERE' (1979) by the time the band embarked on recording sessions for 'DOWN ON THE FARM' (1979). By the time the latter had been completed, LOWELL had left the band completely although a number of his compositions featured, notably the lovely 'KOKOMO'. Bloated and tired, LOWELL's heart finally packed in on him that summer (29th June) while promoting his album. Tragically cut down in his prime (aged just 34), GEORGE may have suffered a typical rock'n'roll death, but he was no ordinary musician; revered by everyone from MICK JAGGER to JIMMY PAGE, the man was a one-off, a troubled genius whose music had the rare power to move hearts, minds and feet and whose ultimate potential will sadly never be realised. LITTLE FEAT was subsequently reformed in the mid-80's by ESTRADA, PAYNE and HAYWARD together with past collaborator FRED TACKET and CRAIG FULLER (ex-PURE PRAIRIE LEAGUE). The new-look 'FEAT released a string of listenable, if ultimately forgettable albums in 'LET IT ROLL' (1988), 'SHAKE ME UP' (1991) and 'AIN'T HAD ENOUGH FUN' (1995), succeeding in keeping the name alive if not exactly adding to the legacy. • Covered: HOW MANY MORE YEARS (Howlin' Wolf) / ON YOUR WAY DOWN (Allen Toussaint) / etc. LOWELL solo:- EASY MONEY (Rickie Lee Jones) / + a few more.

Album rating: LITTLE FEAT (*6) / SAILIN' SHOES (*8) DIXIE CHICKEN (*9) / FEATS DON'T FAIL ME NOW (*8) / THE LAST RECORD ALBUM (*7) / TIME LOVES A HERO (*7) / WAITING FOR COLOMBUS (*6) / DOWN ON THE FARM (*5) / HOY-HOY collection (*7) / AS TIME GOES BY – THE BEST OF LITTLE FEAT compilation (*9) / LET IT ROLL (*5) / REPRESENTING THE MAMBO (*4) / SHAKE ME UP (*4) / AIN'T HAD ENOUGH FUN (*5) / LIVE FROM NEON PARK (*4) / Lowell George: THANKS, I'LL EAT IT HERE (*6)

LOWELL GEORGE (b.13 Apr'45) – vocals, guitar (ex-MOTHERS OF INVENTION/ZAPPA) / **ROY ESTRADA** (b. Santa Ana) – bass, vocals (ex-MOTHERS OF INVENTION/ZAPPA) / **BILL PAYNE** (b.12 Mar'49, Waco, Texas) – keyboards, vocals (ex-FRATERNITY OF MAN) / **RICHIE HAYWARD** – drums (ex-FRATERNITY OF MAN)

		Warners	Warners
May 70.	(7") <7431> **STRAWBERRY FLATS. / HAMBURGER MIDNIGHT**	-	
Nov 70.	(lp) (K 46072) <1890> **LITTLE FEAT**		

– Snakes on everything / Strawberry flats / Truck stop girl / Brides of Jesus / Willin' / Hamburger midnight; (a) Forty four blues, (b) How many more years / Crack in your door / I've been the one / Takin' my time / Crazy Captain Gunboat Willie. (cd-iss. Dec93; 7599 27189-2)

| May 72. | (7") <7553> **EASY TO SLIP. / CAT FEVER** | - | |
| May 72. | (lp) (K 46156) <2600> **SAILIN' SHOES** | | |

– Easy to slip / Cold cold cold / Trouble / Tripe face boogie / Willin' / Apolitical blues / Sailin' shoes / Teenage nervous breakdown / Got no shadows / Cat fever / Texas rose cafe. (cd-iss. 1988; K2 46156)

—— **KENNY GRADNEY** (b. New Orleans) – bass (ex-DELANEY AND BONNY) repl. ESTRADA who joined CAPTAIN BEEFHEART & HIS MAGIC BAND / added **PAUL BARRERE** (b. 3 Jul'48, Burbank, California) – guitar, vocals / **SAM CLAYTON** – congas / **BONNIE BRAMLETT** – guest vocals

| Nov 72. | (7") <7689> **DIXIE CHICKEN. / LAFAYETTE RAILROAD** | - | |
| Feb 73. | (lp) (K 46200) <2686> **DIXIE CHICKEN** | | |

– Dixie chicken / Two trains / Roll um easy / On your way down / Kiss it off / Fool yourself / Walkin' all night / Fat man in the bathtub / Juliette / Lafayette railroad. (cd-iss. Jul88; K2 46200)

—— Band split for 6 months (Oct '73-May '74). BILL joined DOOBIE BROTHERS and others, mainly LOWELL went into sessions. The sextet re-formed May74

Jul 74.	(7") <8054> **OH ATLANTA. / DOWN THE ROAD**	-	
Sep 74.	(7") <8091> **SPANISH MOON. / DOWN THE ROAD**	-	
Sep 74.	(lp) (K 56030) <2784> **FEATS DON'T FAIL ME NOW**		36

– Rock and roll doctor / Cold cold cold / Tripe face boogie / The fan / Oh Atlanta / Skin it back / Down the road / Spanish moon / Down the road / Feats don't fail me now. (cd-iss. Jan89; K2 56030)

| Feb 75. | (7") (K 16524) **DIXIE CHICKEN. / OH ATLANTA** | - | |
| Nov 75. | (lp/c) (K/K4 56156) <3015> **THE LAST RECORD ALBUM** | 36 | 36 |

– Romance dance / All that you dream / Long distance love / Day or night / One love / Down below the borderline / Somebody's leavin' / Mercenary territory. (cd-iss. Jul88; K2 56156)

Feb 76.	(7") (K 16689) **LONG DISTANCE LOVE. / ROMANCE DANCE**		Oct75
Feb 76.	(7") <8219> **ALL THAT YOU DREAM. / ONE LOVE**	-	
May 77.	(lp/c) (K/K4 56349) <3140> **TIME LOVES A HERO**	8	34

– Time loves a hero / Hi roller / New elhi freight train / Old folks boogie / Red streamliner / Keepin' up with the Joneses / Rocket in my pocket / Missin' you / Day at the dog races. (cd-iss. Jul88; K2 56349)

Jun 77.	(7") <8420> **TIME LOVES A HERO. / SAILIN' SHOES**	-	
Jul 77.	(7") (K 16694) **TIME LOVES A HERO. / ROCKET IN MY POCKET**		-
Mar 78.	(d-lp/d-c) (K/K4 66075) <3140> **WAITING FOR COLUMBUS (live)**	43	18

– Join the band / Fat man in the bathtub / All that you dream / Oh Atlanta / Old folks boogie / Time loves a hero / Day or night / Mercenary territory / Spanish moon / Dixie chicken / Tripe face boogie / Rocket in my pocket / Don't bogart that joint / Willin' / Apolitical blues / Sailin' shoes / Feats don't fail me now. (cd-iss. Dec93; 7599 2734-2)

| Jul 78. | (7") <8566> **WILLIN' (live). / OH ATLANTA (live)** | - | |
| Oct 79. | (lp/c) (K/K4 56667) <3345> **DOWN ON THE FARM** | 46 | 29 |

– Down on the farm / Six feet of snow / Perfect imperfection / Kokomo / Be one now / Straight from the heart / Front page news / Wake up dreaming / Feel the groove. (cd-iss. Jul88; K2 56667)

—— The had by this time split (Apr79). BARRERE and CLAYTON joined NICOLETTE LARSON. BARRERE went solo '83 and released 'ON MY OWN TWO FEET'. The others went into sessions.

– compilations, etc. –

on 'Warners' unless otherwise mentioned

| Oct 75. | (d-lp) (K 66038) **TWO ORIGINALS OF LITTLE FEAT** | | - |

– (LITTLE FEAT / DIXIE CHICKEN).

| Aug 81. | (d-lp/d-c) (K/K4 66100) <3538> **HOY-HOY!** (remixes of rare material) | 76 | 39 |

– Rocket in my pocket / Rock and roll doctor / Skin it back / Easy to slip / Red streamliner / Lonesome whistle / Front page news / The fan / Forty-four blues / Teenage nervous breakdown (live) / Framed / Strawberry flats / Gringo / Over the edge / Two trains / China white / All that you dream / Feats don't fail me now.

| Aug 81. | (7") <49801> **EASY TO SLIP. / FRONT PAGE NEWS** | - | |
| Oct 81. | (7") <49841> **GRINGO. / STRAWBERRY FLATS** | - | |

| Aug 86. | (lp/c)(cd) (WX 36/+C)(240 863-2) **THE BEST OF LITTLE FEAT – AS TIME GOES BY** | | - |

– Dixie chicken / Willin' / Rock and roll doctor / Trouble / Sailin' shoes / Spanish moon / Feats don't fail me now / All that you dream / Long distance love / Mercenary territory / Old folks boogie / Twenty million dollars.

LOWELL GEORGE

—— - solo (vocals, guitar) with **FRED TACKETT** – guitar / **EDDIE ZIP** – keyboards,vocals / **PETER WASNER** – keyboards / **JERRY JUMONVILLE** – saxophone / **LEE THORNBERG** – trumpet / **MAXINE DIXON** – b. vocals / **ARMANDO COMPION** – bass / **DON HEFFINGTON** – drums

		Warners	Warners
Apr 79.	(7") <8847> **WHAT DO YOU WANT THE GIRL TO DO. / 20 MILLION THINGS**	-	
Apr 79.	(lp/c) (K/K4 56487) <3194> **THANKS, I'LL EAT IT HERE**		71

– What do you want the girl to do / Honest man / Two trains / Can't stand the rain / Cheek to cheek / Easy money / 20 million things / Find a river / Himmler's ring. (cd-iss. Dec93; 7599 26755-2)

| Jul 79. | (7") (K 17379) **CHEEK TO CHEEK. / HONEST MAN** | | - |

—— Tragically LOWELL died 29th June '79 of a drug induced heart attack. He had gigged the night before. In 1983, PAUL BARRERE issued his debut album 'ON MY OWN TWO FEET' for 'Mirage'; 25-0093-1/-4)

LITTLE FEAT

—— re-formed 1988. (BARRERE, PAYNE, HAYWARD & FRED TACKETT) plus **CRAIG FULLER** – vocals (ex-PURE PRAIRIE LEAGUE) / **KENNY GRADNEY** – bass / **SAM CLAYTON** – percussion, vocals

		Warners	Warners
Jul 88.	(lp/c)(cd) (WX 192/+C)(925750-2) <25750> **LET IT ROLL**		36

– Hate to lose your lovin' / One clear moment / Cajun girl / Hangin' on to the good times / Listen to your heart / Let it roll / Long time till I get over you / Business as usual / Changin' luck / Voices on the wind.

Jul 88.	(7") <27728> **HATE TO LOSE YOUR LOVIN'. / CAJUN GIRL**		
Sep 88.	(7") <27684> **ONE CLEAR MOMENT. / CHANGIN' LUCK**		
Apr 90.	(cd/c/lp) <(7599 26163-2/-4/-1)> **REPRESENTING THE MAMBO**		45

– Texas twister / Daily grind / Representing the mambo / Woman in love / Rad gumbo / Teenage warrior / That's her, she's mine / Feelin's all gone / Those feet'll steer ya wrong sometimes / The ingenue / Silver screen.

		Polydor	Morgan Creek
Oct 91.	(cd/c/lp) (511310-2/-4/-1) <20005> **SHAKE ME UP**		

– Spider's blues (might need it sometime) / Shake me up / Things happen / Mojo haiku / Loved and lied to / Don't try so hard / Boom boy car / Fast & furious / Livin' on dreams / Clownin' / Down in flames.

—— **SHAUN MURPHY** – vocals; repl. FULLER

		Zoo	Zoo
Jun 95.	(cd/c/lp) <(72445 11097-2/-4/-1)> **AIN'T HAD ENOUGH FUN**		

– Drivin' blind / Blue jean blues / Cadillac hotel / Romance without finance / Big bang theory / Cajun rage / Heaven's where you find it / Borderline blues / All that you can stand / Rock & roll every night / Shakeytown / Ain't had enough fun / That's a pretty good love.

| Jun 96. | (d-cd) <11129> **LIVE FROM NEON PARK (live)** | | - |

– (introductions) / Two trains / Spanish moon – Skin it back / Rock & roll every night / Down on the farm / Willin' / Hate to lose / Can't be satisfied – They're red hot / Cadillac hotel / Changin' luck / You're taking up another man's place / Oh, Atlanta / Texas twister / Fat man in the bathtub / Representing the mambo / Long distance love / Rad gumbo / Dixie chicken / Feats don't fail me now / Sailin' shoes / Let it roll – High roller.

LITTLE RICHARD

Born: RICHARD WAYNE PENNIMAN, 5 Dec'35, Macon, Georgia, USA, raised in a large family by preacher parents who schooled him in the ways of gospel singing. Aged 16, the petite RICHARD was given the opportunity (through singer, BILLY WRIGHT) to record for 'RCA-Victor'. After four flop singles for the imprint, LITTLE RICHARD subsequently moved on to Don Robey's 'Peacock' label in 1953, where he sessioned for doo-wop group, The TEMPO-TOPPERS. After fronting The JOHNNY OTIS ORCHESTRA in 1955, the man signed a solo deal with 'Specialty'. His first single for the label, 'TUTTI FRUTTI', gave him his maiden entry into the US Top 20. Outrageously attired in flamboyant pink body-suits, this eccentric, clowning pioneer of rock'n'roll, was like nothing the white music establishment had ever encountered; in both his image and his hollering, tongue-in-cheek assault, the effeminate RICHARD borrowed nothing from his contemporaries. Over the course of the next few years, he flounced his way through a series of classic hits which would subsequently become standards:- 'LONG TALL SALLY', 'RIP IT UP', 'THE GIRL CAN'T HELP IT' (exposure from the rock'n'roll movie of the same name gave him yet another UK hit), 'LUCILLE', 'JENNY, JENNY', 'KEEP A KNOCKIN' and 'GOOD GOLLY, MISS MOLLY'. At the height of his fame, RICHARD was to publicly renounce his "evil" rock'n'roll music/lifestyle, reverting back to gospel and pledging his life to Jeeesus. In 1960, the now Rev. LITTLE RICHARD spent a couple of years under the production of QUINCY JONES, returning to rock'n'roll in 1964. Although he had a few minor hits, including 'BAMA LAMA BAMA LOO', his new material was overshadowed by British acts covering his earlier work. In the 70's, RICHARD released a few albums, while collaborating with the likes of CANNED HEAT and DELANEY & BONNIE, swinging back and forth between rock'n'roll and God, homosexuality and heterosexuality. By the mid 80's, the veteran showman was back in the limelight when he took up the offer to appear in the movie, 'Down And Out In Beverley Hills'. From then on in, LITTLE RICHARD has successfully kept his profile high via guest spots in TV series including 'Miami Vice', while also fraternising with top named celebrities such as ELTON JOHN, TANYA TUCKER and er, KERMIT THE FROG!

Best CD compilation: THE GEORGIA PEACH (*9)

LITTLE RICHARD – vocals, piano + sessions

	not iss.	RCA Victor
1952. (7") <4392> EVERY HOUR. / TAXI BLUES	-	
1952. (7") <4582> GET RICH QUICK. / THINKIN' 'BOUT MY MOTHER	-	
1952. (7") <4772> WHY DID YOU LEAVE. / AIN'T NOTHIN' HAPPENIN'	-	
1953. (7") <5025> I BROUGHT IT ALL ON MYSELF. / PLEASE HAVE MERCY ON ME	-	

The TEMPO-TOPPERS Featuring LITTLE RICHARD

	not iss.	Peacock
1953. (7") <1616> AIN'T THAT GOOD NEWS. / FOOL AT THE WHEEL	-	
1954. (7") <1628> ALWAYS. / RICE, RED BEANS & TURNIP GREENS	-	

—— On the same label, he joined The JOHNNY OTIS BAND in 1955. They released 2

	not iss.	Peacock
1955. (7") <1658> LITTLE RICHARD BOOGIE. / DIRECTLY FROM MY HEART TO YOU	-	
1955. (7") <1673> MAYBE I'M RIGHT. / I LOVE MY BABY	-	

LITTLE RICHARD

went solo again, backed by RED TYLER – saxophone / LEE ALLEN – saxophone / FRANK FIELDS – bass / ERNEST McLEAN & JUSTIN ADAMS – guitar / EARL PALMER – drums / plus pianists HUEY SMITH, EDWARD FRANK, LITTLE BOOKER & SALVADOR DOUCHETTE.

	London	Specialty
Dec 55. (7") <561> TUTTI FRUTTI. / I'M JUST A LONELY GUY	-	17
Mar 56. (7") <572> LONG TALL SALLY. / SLIPPIN' AND SLIDIN' (PEEPIN' AND HIDIN')	-	6 / 33
Jul 56. (7",78) (HLO 8336) <579> RIP IT UP. / READY TEDDY	30	17 / 44
1956. (7") <584> SHE'S GOT IT. / HEEBIE JEEBIES	-	
Jan 57. (7",78) (HLO 8366) LONG TALL SALLY. / TUTTI FRUTTI	3	- / 29
Feb 57. (7") <591> THE GIRL CAN'T HELP IT. / ALL AROUND THE WORLD	-	49
Feb 57. (7",78) (HLO 8382) SHE'S GOT IT. / THE GIRL CAN'T HELP IT	15	- / 9
Jun 57. (7",78) (HLO 8446) <598> LUCILLE. / SEND ME SOME LOVIN'	10	21 / 54 Mar57

Jul 57. (lp) (HA-O 2055) <2100> **HERE'S LITTLE RICHARD** — 13
– Tutti frutti / True fine mama / Ready Teddy / Baby / Slippin' and slidin' (peepin' and hidin') / Long tall Sally / Miss Ann / Oh why / Rip it up / Jenny, Jenny / She's got it / Can't believe you wanna leave. (re-iss. Feb85 on 'Ace'; CH 128) (cd-iss. Jun89; CDCHM 128)

	London	Specialty
Aug 57. (7",78) (HLO 8470) <606> JENNY, JENNY. / MISS ANN	11	14 / 56 Jun57
Nov 57. (7",78) (HLO 8509) <611> KEEP A KNOCKIN'. / CAN'T BELIEVE YOU WANNA LEAVE	21	8 Sep57
Feb 58. (7",78) (HLU 8560) <624> GOOD GOLLY MISS MOLLY. / HEY HEY HEY HEY	8	10
Jun 58. (7",78) (HLO 8647) <633> OOH! MY SOUL. / TRUE FINE MAMA	22	31 / 68
Dec 58. (7",78) (HLU 8770) <645> BABY FACE. / I'LL NEVER YOU GO	2	41 Sep58

Dec 58. (lp) (HA-U 2126) <2103> **LITTLE RICHARD 2**
– Keep a knocking / Send me some lovin' / I'll never let you go / All around the world / By the light of the silvery Moon / Good golly Miss Molly / Baby face / Hey hey hey hey / Ooh my soul / Lucille / The girl can't help it. (re-iss. Feb85 on 'Ace'; CH 131) (cd-iss. Jul89; CDCHM 131)

	London	Specialty
Jan 59. (7") <652> SHE KNOWS HOW TO ROCK. / EARLY ONE MORNING		
Mar 59. (7") <660> BY THE LIGHT OF THE SILVERY MOON. / WONDERING		
Mar 59. (7",78) (HLU 8831) BY THE LIGHT OF THE SILVERY MOON. / EARLY ONE MORNING	17	-
May 59. (7",78) (HLU 8868) <664> KANSAS CITY. / LONESOME AND BLUE	26	95

1959. (lp) (HA-U 2193) <2104> **THE FABULOUS LITTLE RICHARD**
– Shake a hand / Chicken little baby / All night long / Most I can offer / Lonesome and blue / Wonderin' / Whole lotta shakin' goin' on / She knows how to rock / Kansas City / Directly from my heart / Maybe I'm right / Early one morning / I'm just a lonely girl. (re-iss. Jul80 on 'Sonet'; SNTF 5027) (re-iss. Feb85 on 'Ace'; CH 133) (cd-iss. Aug89 & Sep91; CDCHM 133)

	London	Specialty
1959. (7") <670> SHAKE A HAND. / ALL NIGHT LONG	-	
1959. (7") <680> WHOLE LOTTA SHAKIN' GOIN' ON. / MAYBE I'M RIGHT	-	
Feb 60. (7",78) (HLU 9065) <681> BABY. / I GOT IT	-	Dec 59
1960. (7") <686> DIRECTLY FROM MY HEART. / THE MOST I CAN OFFER	-	

	not iss.	Coral
1960. (7") <62366> NEED HIM. / MILKY WHITE WAY	-	

	Mercury	Mercury
1961. (7") (AMT 1165) <71884> HE'S NOT JUST A SOLDIER. / JOY JOY JOY		
1962. (7") <71911> DO YOU CARE. / RIDE ON KING JESUS	-	
Sep 62. (7") (AMT 1189) <71965> HE GOT WHAT HE WANTED. / WHY DON'T YOU CHANGE YOUR WAYS	38	

	London	Woodman
Apr 63. (7") (HLK 9708) <2181> CRYING IN THE CHAPEL. / HOLE IN THE WALL		

(re-dist.US 1963 on 'Atlantic')

	London	Atlantic
Jul 63. (7") (HLK 9756) <2192> TRAVELLIN' SHOES. / IT IS NO SECRET		

1964. (lp) (LVA 9220) <757446> **COMING HOME**
– ust a closer walk with thee / Coming home / Search me Lord / I want Jesus to walk with me / Milky white way / Need him / Every time I feel the spirit / Does Jesus care / God is real / I'm trampin' / Jesus walked this lonesome valley / Precious Lord.

	London	Specialty
Apr 64. (7") <692> BAMA LAMA BAMA LOO. / ANNIE'S BACK	-	82
May 64. (7") (HL 9896) BAMA LAMA BAMA LOO. / KEEP A KNOCKIN'	20	-

	Stateside	Vee-Jay
Sep 64. (7") (SS 340) <612> WHOLE LOTTA SHAKIN' GOIN' ON. / GOODNIGHT IRENE		
1964. (7") (SON 5001) <699> POOR BOY PAUL. / WONDERIN'	-	

(UK-iss.1976 on 'Specialty')

	Stateside	20th Century
1964. (lp) (SL 10054) LITTLE RICHARD SINGS GOSPEL		

– Every time I feel the spirit / I'm trampin' / Milky white way / Does Jesus care / Coming home / I know the Lord / I've just come from the fountain / God is real / Troubles of the world / Certainly Lord / Tell God my troubles / Precious Lord. (re-iss. Jul82 on 'Bulldog')

	Mercury	Mercury
Jan 65. (7") (MF 841) PEACE IN THE VALLEY. / JOY JOY JOY		
Jan 65. (lp) (MCL 20036) IT'S REAL		

– It's real / Joy, joy, joy / Do you care / The captain calls for you / In times like these / Do Lord, remember me / Ride on King Jesus / (There'll be) Peace in the valley (for me) / He's not just a soldier / My desire / He's my star / It takes everything to serve the Lord.

	Fontana	Vee-Jay
Jan 65. (7") (H 519) <625> BLUEBERRY HILL. / CHERRY RED		
Feb 65. (lp) (TL 5235) <1107> LITTLE RICHARD IS BACK!		

– A whole lotta shakin' goin' on / Going home tomorrow / Money honey / Only you ./ Hound dog / Goodnight Irene / Lawdy Miss Clawdy / Groovy little Suzy / Short Fat Fanny / Cherry red / Memories are made of this / Blueberry hill. <re-iss Jul68 on 'Joy'; 100>

	Fontana	Vee-Jay
Oct 65. (7") (H 652) <698> I DON'T KNOW WHAT YOU'VE GOT BUT IT'S GOT ME. / (Part 2)		92

	Sue	Vee-Jay
Feb 66. (7") (SR 4001) <665> WITHOUT LOVE. / DANCE WHAT YOU WANNA		
Jul 66. (7") (WI 4015) <652> CROSS OVER. / IT AIN'T WHAT'CHA DO		

	Stateside	Modern
May 66. (7") (SS 508) <1018> HOLY MACKEREL. / BABY DON'T YOU WANT A MAN LIKE ME		
1966. (7") <1019> DO YOU FEEL IT. / (Part 2)	-	
1966. (7") <1022> DIRECTLY FROM THE HEART. / I'M BACK	-	
1966. (7") <1043> BABY WHAT YOU WANT ME TO DO. / (Part 2)		

<re-iss. Feb69 on 'Action'>

	not iss.	Kent
1966. (7") <4567> IN THE NAME. / DON'T YOU KNOW I	-	

	Columbia	Okeh
1966. (7") (DB 7974) <7251> POOR DOG (WHO CAN'T WAG HIS TAIL). / WELL		
1966. (7") (DB 8058) <7262> I NEED LOVE. / THE COMMANDMENTS OF LOVE		
Jan 67. (7") (DB 8116) <7271> GET DOWN WITH IT. / ROSEMARY		
Apr 67. (7") (DB 8263) <7271> HURRY SUNDOWN. / I DON'T WANT TO DISCUSS IT	-	

May 67. (lp) (6136) <14117> **THE EXPLOSIVE LITTLE RICHARD**
– I don't want to discuss it / Land of a 1000 dances / Commandments of love / Money / Poor dog / I need love / Never gonna let you go / Don't deceive me / Function at the junction / Well.

	Columbia	Okeh
1967. (7") <7278> DON'T DECEIVE ME (PLEASE DON'T GO). / NEVER GONNA LET YOU GO	-	
Jul 67. (7") (DB 8240) LITTLE BIT OF SOMETHING. / MONEY	-	
Aug 67. (lp) <14121> LITTLE RICHARD'S GREATEST HITS (live)	-	

<re-iss. Jul68 on 'Joy'; 100>

	Columbia	Okeh
1967. (7") <7325> LUCILLE. / WHOLE LOTTA SHAKIN' GOIN' ON	-	

	M.C.A.	Brunswick
Mar 68. (7") (MU 1006) <55362> TRY SOME OF MINE. / SHE'S TOGETHER		
1968. (7") <55377> TEAR MY CLOTHES. / STINGY JENNY	-	
1968. (7") <55386> SOUL TRAIN. / CAN I COUNT ON YOU	-	

	Reprise	Reprise
Jun 70. (7") (RS 20907) <0907> FREEDOM BLUES. / DEW DROP INN		47
Aug 70. (7") <0942> GREENWOOD MISSISSIPPI. / I SAW HER STANDING THERE	-	85
1970. (lp) <(RSLP 6406)> THE RILL THING		

– Freedom blues / Greenwood, Mississippi / Two-time loser / Dew Drop Inn / Somebody saw you / Spreadin' Natta, what's the matter / The rill thing / Lovesick blues / I saw her standing there.

1971. (7") <1005> **SHAKE A HAND. / SOMEBODY SAW YOU**

Nov 71. (lp) *(K 44156)* <6462> **THE KING OF ROCK AND ROLL**
– King of rock'n'roll / Joy to the world / Brown sugar / In the name / Dancing in the street / Midnight special / The way you do the things you do / Green power / I'm so lonesome I could die / Settin' the woods on fire / Born on the bayou. *(re-iss. Jul88 on 'Entertainers' lp/c; ENT LP/MC 13044) (cd-iss. same; ENTCD 264)*

Dec 71. (7") **SHAKE A HAND. / SOMEBODY SAW YOU**

Feb 72. (7") *(K 14150)* <1062> **MONEY RUNNER. / MONEY IS**

1972. (7") *(K 14915)* **MOCKINGBIRD SALLY. / ROCKIN' ROCKIN' BOOGIE**

1972. (lp) <2107> **THE SECOND COMING**
– Mockingbird Sally / It ain't what you do, it's the way that you do it / The saints / Nuki Suki / Rockin' rockin' boogie / Prophet of peace / Thomasine / Sanctified, satisfied toe-tapper.

—— (Around this time, he teamed up with CANNED HEAT on lp, 'ROCKIN' WITH THE KING')

	not iss.	Green Mountain
1973. (7") <413> **IN THE MIDDLE OF THE NIGHT. / WHERE WILL I FIND A PLACE TO SLEEP THIS EVENING**	-	

	Reprise	not iss.
1974. (7"ep) *(K 14343)* **ROCKIN' ROLLIN' BOOGIE / KING OF THE ROCK'N'ROLL / SAINTS / MOCKINGBIRD SALLY**		-

	not iss.	Atlantic
1976. (7") <7007> **CALL MY NAME. / STEAL MISS LIZA**		

	not iss.	Mainstream
1979. (lp) **GOD'S BEAUTIFUL CITY**	-	
1980. (7") <5572> **TRY TO HELP YOUR BROTHER. / (part 2)**		

—— Next from film 'Down And Out In Beverley Hills'

	M.C.A.	M.C.A.
Feb 86. (7") *(MCA 1049)* <52780> **GREAT GOSH A'MIGHTY (IT'S A MATTER OF TIME). / THE RIDE**		42
(12"+=) *(MCAT 1049)* – Down and out in Beverley Hills.		

	W.E.A.	Warners
Oct 86. (7"/12") *(YZ 89/+T)* **OPERATOR. / BIG HOUSE REUNION**		
Oct 86. (lp/c)(cd) *(WX 72/+C)(242018-2)* <42018> **LIFETIME FRIEND**		

– Great gosh a'mighty (it's a matter of time) / Operator / Somebody's comin' / Destruction / I found my way / The world can't do me / One ray of sunshine / Someone cares / Big house reunion.

Jan 87. (7") *(YZ 98)* **SOMEBODY'S COMIN'. / ONE RAY OF SUNSHINE**

	Atco	Atco
Nov 87. (7"pic-d/12"pic-d; LITTLE RICHARD & The BEACH BOYS) *(B 9392/+TP)* <99392> **HAPPY ENDING. / CALIFORNIA GIRLS**		

—— collaborated with PHILIP BAILEY (Earth, Wind & Fire) on the the single, 'TWINS', which was from the film of the same name

– compilations, others, etc. –

1962. (7") *Little Star;* **I'M IN LOVE AGAIN. / EVERYNIGHT ABOUT THIS TIME**

1963. (7") *Little Star;* **THE VALLEY OF TEARS. / FREEDOM RIDE**

1963. (lp) *Little Star;* **LITTLE RICHARD AND SISTER ROSETTA**

Aug 65. (lp) *Ember; (NR 5022)* **REALLY MOVING GOSPEL**

1974. (lp) *Ember; (EMB 3434)* **FRIENDS FROM THE BEGINNING (with JIMI HENDRIX)**

Mar 66. (lp) *Fontana/ US= Vee Jay; (TL 5314)* **LITTLE RICHARD'S GREATEST HITS**

May 68. (lp) *Fontana; (SFL 13010)* **KING OF THE GOSPEL SINGERS**

May 68. (7") *President; (PT 201)* **WHOLE LOTTA SHAKIN' GOIN' ON. / LAWDY MISS CLAWDY**

May 68. (7")*London; (HLU 10194)* **GOOD GOLLY MISS MOLLY. / LUCILLE**

1971. (lp) *Specialty;* **WELL ALL RIGHT** (rec.'59)

1973. (7") *Bell;* **GOOD GOLLY MISS MOLLY. / (pt.2)**

Oct 76. (lp) *Sonet; SNTF 5017)* **20 LITTLE RICHARD ORIGINAL HITS**
Note; Below issued on 'Sonet' UK/ 'Specialty' US, until stated.

1976. (7") **TUTTI FRUTTI. / KEEP A KNOCKIN'**

1976. (7") **GOOD GOLLY MISS MOLLY. / ALL AROUND THE WORLD**

1976. (7") *(SONE 1)* **LONG TALL SALLY. / HEEBIE GEEBIES**

1976. (7"ep) **I GOT IT / ROCK'N'ROLL IS HERE TO STAY. / KEEP A KNOCKIN' / BAMA LAMA BAMA LO**

Jun 80. (lp) *(SNTF 5027)* **HIS BIGGEST HITS**

Jun 77. (7"m) *Creole;* **GOOD GOLLY MISS MOLLY. / RIP IT UP / BY THE LIGHT OF THE SILVERY MOON**   **37**

Oct 77. (lp) *Creole; (CRLP 510)* **LITTLE RICHARD – NOW**

Sep 78. (7") *Creole; (CR 161)* **SEND ME SOME LOVIN' 1978. / KING SAX**

1979. (7"m) *Creole; (CR 140)* **GOOD GOLLY MISS MOLLY. / BABY FACE / THE GIRL CAN'T HELP IT**
(re-iss. Mar82 on 'Jukebox') (re-iss. Aug82)

Jul 77. (7") *Charly;* **LUCILLE. / GOOD GOLLY MISS MOLLY**

1980. (lp) *Charly; (CR 30190)* **GEORGIA PEACH**

??. (lp) *Charly; (CR 30009)* **DOLLARS, DOLLARS AND DOLLARS MORE**

1983. (lp) *Charly; (CR 30216)* **OOH! MY SOUL**

Aug 86. (c/lp) *Charly; (TC/+CR 30258)* **ROCK'N'ROLL RESURRECTION**
(cd-iss. Mar87)

Feb 93. (cd) *Charly; (CDCD 1014)* **THE WILDEST**

1981. (10"lp) *Ace-Chiswick; (CH 38)* **THE MODERN SIDES: LITTLE RICHARD**

Dec 86. (lp/c/cd) *Ace; (CH/CHC/CDCH 193)* **20 CLASSIC CUTS**
– Long tall Sally / Ready Teddy / The girl can't help it / Rip it up / Miss Ann / She's got it / Lucille / Keep a knockin' / Good golly Miss Molly / Send me some lovin' / Hey-hey-hey-hey / Slippin' and slidin' / Tutti frutti / Heeby jeebies / Baby face / Jenny Jenny / By the light of the silvery Moon / Ooh! my soul / True fine mama / Bama lama bama loo. (cd+c+=) – Can't believe you leave / I'll never let you go.

Apr 87. (7"m) *Ace;* **TUTTI FRUTTI / SHE'S GOT IT / I'LL NEVER LET YOU GO**

Oct 89. (lp-box/c-box/cd-box) *Ace; (ABOX LP/MC/CD 1)* **THE SPECIALTY SESSIONS**

Feb 80. (lp) *Bravo; (BRC 2510)* **LUCILLE**
(re-iss. +c.1984) (re-iss. 1988 on 'Lifetime')

Jul 82. (lp/c) *Bulldog; (BD L/C 1042)* **WHOLE LOTTA SHAKIN'**

Oct 82. (lp) *Edsel; (ED 114)* **GET DOWN WITH IT**

Aug 83. (lp/c) *Cambra; (CR/+T 102)* **LITTLE RICHARD**

Jul 84. (lp/c) *CBS/ US= Columbia; (32185/4032185)* **GREATEST HITS**
(cd-iss. 1988 on 'Pickwick')

Nov 84. (lp/c) *Topline; (TOP/KTOP 101)* **HE'S GOT IT**

May 87. (cd) *Topline; (TOPCD 517)* **RIP IT UP**

Jan 85. (7") *Old Gold; (OG 9492)* **GOOD GOLLY MISS MOLLY. / THE GIRL CAN'T HELP IT**

Jan 85. (7") *Old Gold; (OG 9493)* **TUTTI FRUTTI. / LONG TALL SALLY**

Jan 85. (7") *Old Gold; (OG 9494)* **LUCILLE. / BABY FACE**

Oct 86. (lp/c) *RCA; (N L/K 89965)* **ROCKIN' AND RAVIN' ("LITTLE RICHARD with BOTTS BROWN & HIS BLOCKBUSTERS")**

Jan 87. (lp/c) *Deja Vu; (DV LP/MC 2083)* **LITTLE RICHARD**

Feb 87. (lp/c) *Arena; (ARA/C 1002)* **16 ROCK AND ROLL CLASSICS**

Mar 87. (lp) *Sunjay; (SJLP 565)* **EARLY STUDIO OUTTAKES**

Apr 87. (cd) *Delta; (11071)* **TUTTI FRUTTI**

May 87. (cd) *Bescol; (CD 31)* **16 GREATEST HITS**

Sep 83. (lp) *Magnum Force; (MFM 018)* **THE REAL THING**

Nov 86. (lp) *Magnum Force; (MFLP 1035)* **OOH MA SOUL!**

Jun 87. (7"ep) *Magnum Force; (MFEP 012)* **I'M QUITTING SHOW BUSINESS**
– I've just come from the mountain / Search me Lord / Coming home / I'm quitting show business.

Oct 87. (lp) *Demand; (DEMAND 0025)* **THE GREAT LITTLE RICHARD**

Oct 87. (lp) *Subway; (55185)* **THE SESSIONS**

May 88. (lp/c) *Black Tulip; (28/48 013)* **20 GREATEST HITS: LITTLE RICHARD**

May 88. (cd-ep) *Rhino; (R 373014)* **LIL' BIT OF GOLD**
– Tutti frutti / Good Golly Miss Molly / Slippin' and slidin' / The girl can't help it.

1988. (lp) *Joker; (SM 3881)* **AT HIS WILDEST VOL.1**

1988. (lp) *Joker; (SM 3882)* **AT HIS WILDEST VOL.2**

1988. (lp) *Joker; (SM 3883)* **AT HIS WILDEST VOL.3**

1988. (lp/c) *GNP Crescendo; (GNP S/5 9033)* **BIG HITS**

Jul 88. (lp/c) *Entertainers; (ENT LP/MC 13044)* **KING OF ROCK'N'ROLL**

Dec 88. (lp/c) *Sierra; (FED B/C 5023)* **REPLAY ON LITTLE RICHARD**

Sep 86. (lp/c) *Castle; (SH LP/TC 150)* **LONG TALL SALLY**
(cd-iss. Dec87)

Jul 89. (lp/c/cd) *Castle; (CCS LP/MC/CD 227)* **THE COLLECTION**

Jul 89. (lp/c/cd) *Ocean; (OCN 2030W – L/-K/-D)* **LITTLE RICHARD**

Jul 89. (cd) *Bear Family; (BCD 15448)* **THE FORMATIVE YEARS 1951-1953**

Aug 89. (cd/c/lp) *Instant; (CD/TC INS 5014/INS 5014))* **SLIPIN', SLIDIN' & SHAKIN'**

Dec 91. (cd) *Quality; (QSCD 6002)* **WILD AND WONDERFUL**

Mar 93. (cd) *See For Miles; (SEECD 36)* **THE E.P. COLLECTION**

Jun 93. (cd) *Rhino; (RNCD 1007)* **NOW**

Feb 94. (cd/c) *Javelin; (HAD CD/MC 117)* **SPOTLIGHT ON LITTLE RICHARD**

Jul 94. (cd/c) *Success;* **GREATEST HITS**

Aug 94. (cd) *Dynamite;* **LITTLE RICHARD**

Feb 95. (cd) *B.A.M.; (KLMCD 004)* **PEARLS OF THE PAST**

Apr 95. (d-cd) *Wisepack; (LECD 609)* **THE ESSENTIAL COLLECTION**

Jun 95. (cd) *Collection;* **THE COLLECTION**

Jul 95. (cd) *Summit;* **THE BEST OF LITTLE RICHARD**

LITTLE VILLAGE (see under ⇒ LOWE, Nick)

LIVE

Formed: York, Pennsylvania, USA … early 90's by EDWARD KOWALCZYK, CHAD TAYLOR, PATRICK DAHLHEIMER and CHAD GRACEY. Coming up with a moniker that both displayed a complete lack of imagination and confused prospective fans, they nevertheless released a competent neo-grunge debut, 'MENTAL JEWELRY' (1991). Produced by JERRY HARRISON (ex-TALKING HEADS), the record (on MCA subsidiary, 'Radioactive') found a large US audience with its rather derivative hybrid of PEARL JAM and R.E.M. Three years in the making, 'THROWING COPPER' eventually scaled the US charts, largely due to a clutch of harder-edged tracks/singles such as, 'SELLING THE DRAMA' and the MTV fave, 'I ALONE'. These semi-classics also cracked the British charts, setting the scene for a show-stealing (LIVE!) slot at the 1995 Glastonbury Fest. A third album, 'SECRET SAMADHI' (1997), repeated the winning formula, although the more discerning fans considered the album overproduced. In October '99, LIVE were back to their near best, the fourth set 'THE DISTANCE TO HERE' winning back most of the fans. • **Covered:** LOVE MY WAY (Psychedelic Furs) / SUPERNATURAL (Vic Chesnutt).

Album rating: MENTAL JEWELRY (*6) / THROWING COPPER (*7) / SECRET SAMADHI (*5) / THE DISTANCE TO HERE (*6)

EDWARD KOWALCZYK – vocals, guitar / **CHAD TAYLOR** – guitar, vocals / **PATRICK DAHLHEIMER** – bass / **CHAD GRACEY** – drums, vocals

		Radioactive	Radioactive
Jan 92.	(7") <54387> **PAIN LIES ON THE RIVERSIDE. / HEAVEN WORE A SHIRT**	-	
Apr 92.	(lp/c/cd) <(RAR/+C/D 10346)> **MENTAL JEWELRY**		73 Jan92

– Pain lies on the riverside / Operation spirit (the tyranny of tradition) / The beauty of Gray / Brothers unaware / Tired of me / Mirror song / Waterboy / Take my anthem / You are the world / Good pain / Mother Earth is a vicious crowd / 10,000 years (peace is now).

| Apr 92. | (cd-ep) <54442> **OPERATION SPIRIT (THE TYRANNY OF TRADITION)** (live) / **THE BEAUTY OF GRAY** (live) / **GOOD PAIN / LIES ON THE RIVERSIDE** (live) | - | |
| Jun 92. | (7") (RAX 1) **OPERATION SPIRIT. / HEAVEN WORE A SHIRT** | | - |

(12"+=/cd-s+=) (RAX T/TD 1) – Negation / Good pain.

May 94.	(c-s) <54816> **SELLING THE DRAMA / LIGHTNING CRASHES**		43
Sep 94.	(c-s/cd-s) (RAX C/TD 11) **SELLING THE DRAMA. / ('A'acoustic) / WHITE DISCUSSION**		-
Oct 94.	(cd/c) <(RAD/RAC 10997)> **THROWING COPPER**	37	1 May94

– The dam at Otter Creek / Selling the drama / I alone / Iris / Lightning crashes / Top / All over you / Shit towne / T.B.D. / Stage / Waitress / Pillar of Davidson / White discussion. (cd hidden track +=) – Horse.

| Feb 95. | (7"clear/c-s) (RAX/+C 13) **I ALONE. / PAIN LIES ON THE RIVERSIDE** | 48 | - |

(cd-s+=) (RAXTD 13) – ('A'mix).

| Jun 95. | (c-s/cd-s) (RAX C/TD 17) **SELLING THE DRAMA / THE DAN AT OTTER CREEK** | 30 | - |

(cd-s+=) (RAXXD 17) – ('A'acoustic).

| Sep 95. | (c-s) (RAXC 20) **ALL OVER YOU / SHIT TOWNE** | 48 | - |

(cd-s+=) (RAXTD 20) – ('A'live at Glastonbury).
(cd-s) (RAXXD 20) – ('A'side) / Waitress (live) / Iris (live at Glastonbury).

| Jan 96. | (c-s/cd-s) (RAX C/TD 23) **LIGHTNING CRASHES / THE BEAUTY OF GRAY (bootleg) / TBD (acoustic)** | 33 | - |

(cd-s) (RAXXD 23) – ('A'side) / ('A'-live at Glastonbury) / White discussion (live at Glastonbury).

| Mar 97. | (7"silver) (RAX 28) **LAKINI'S JUICE. / SUPERNATURAL (remix)** | 29 | - |

(cd-s+=) (RAXXD 28) – White discussion (remix).
(cd-s) (RAD 49023) – ('A'side) / Pain lies on the riverside (remix) / Selling the drama (acoustic).

| Mar 97. | (cd/c/d-lp) <(RAD/RAC/RAR2 11590)> **SECRET SAMADHI** | 31 | 1 |

– Rattlesnake / Lakini's juice / Graze / Century / Ghost / Unsheathed / Insomnia and the hole in the universe / Turn my head / Heropsychodreamer / Freaks / Merica / Gas Hed goes west.

| Jun 97. | (7") (RAX 29) **FREAKS. / LOVE MY WAY** (live) | 60 | |

(cd-s+=) (RAXTD 29) – Freaks (Labor, Labor, Labor remix).
(cd-s) (RAXD 29) – ('A'side) / Lakini's juice (live) / Freaks (live).

| Oct 99. | (cd) (RAD 11966) <111966> **THE DISTANCE TO HERE** | 56 | 4 |

– The dolphin's cry / The distance / Sparkle / Run to the water / Sun / Voodoo lady / Where fishes go / Face and ghost (The children's song) / Feel the quiet river rage / Meltdown / They stood up for love / We walk in the dream / Dance with you.

| Nov 99. | (-) <radio cut> **THE DOLPHIN'S CRY** | - | 78 |

LIVING COLOUR

Formed: New York, USA . . . 1984 by English-born guitarist VERNON REID, who had studied performing arts at Manhattan community college. 1986 saw the arrival of COREY GLOVER (vocals) and WILL CALHOUN (drums), with MUZZ SKILLINGS (bass) completing the line-up the following year. After MICK JAGGER clocked the band at a CBGB's gig, he invited the outfit to play on his 'Primitive Cool' album. The 'STONES frontman also produced two demos for the group, helping to secure them a deal with 'Epic'. LIVING COLOUR's debut album, 'VIVID' (1988) attracted a lot of attention if only because the band were an all-black outfit playing hard rock, not so surprising, and in reality a very interesting prospect. Leaving most of their lunk-headed contemporaries at the starting post, LIVING COLOUR played rock with the invention of jazz and the spontaneity of funk. 'CULT OF PERSONALITY' was the album's highlight, a masterful blend of cutting political commentary and driving, spiralling riffs while 'GLAMOUR BOYS' was a playful piece of funk-pop vaguely reminiscent of PRINCE. But it was socially and politically aware material that formed the main thrust of the band's output, 'OPEN LETTER (TO A LANDLORD)' and 'WHICH WAY TO AMERICA' pointedly addressing the oppression of African-Americans to an eclectic, always soulful hard rock backing. The band became critical darlings, figureheads for the loose funk-rock movement that included The RED HOT CHILI PEPPERS and latterly FAITH NO MORE. They also won respect from many fellow musicians, REID contributing to KEITH RICHARDS' 'Talk Is Cheap' album, while the likes of LITTLE RICHARD, CARLOS SANTANA and MACEO PARKER all offered their services for LIVING COLOUR's follow-up effort, 'TIME'S UP' (1990). A wildly eclectic range of styles encompassed everything from hardcore thrash ('TYPE') to the PAUL SIMON ('GRACELAND'-era)-like 'SOLACE OF YOU', even spawning a UK Top 20 single with the meandering blues of 'LOVE REARS ITS UGLY HEAD'. Again the critics frothed although the album failed to match the commercial success of its predecessor. The 'BISCUITS' EP (1991) was a stop gap affair, hardly essential but worth hearing for inspired takes on JAMES BROWN's 'TALKIN' LOUD AND SAYING NOTHING' and HENDRIX's 'BURNING OF THE MIDNIGHT LAMP'. Shortly after the record's release, SKILLINGS departed, his replacement being ex-'Sugarhill' session man and TACKHEAD bassist DOUG WIMBISH. A third album, 'STAIN' (1993), a decidedly harder affair, failed to break any new

ground or spark any increase in sales, the band eventually splitting two years later when founder REID decided to pursue solo projects (i.e. the 1996 album, 'MISTAKEN IDENTITY'). • **Covers:** SHOULD I STAY OR SHOULD I GO (Clash) / FINAL SOLUTION (Pere Ubu) / MEMORIES CAN'T WAIT (Talking Heads) / BURNING OF THE MIDNIGHT LAMP (Jimi Hendrix) / TALKING LOUD AND SAYING NOTHING (James Brown) / LOVE AND HAPPINESS (Al Green) / SUNSHINE OF YOUR LOVE (Cream). • **Trivia:** COREY played a smart-assed soldier in the Vietnam film, 'Platoon'.

Album rating: VIVID (*7) / TIME'S UP (*7) / STAIN (*6) / PRIDE: THE GREATEST HITS compilation (*7) / Vernon Reid: MISTAKEN IDENTITY (*4)

COREY GLOVER (b. 6 Nov'64) – vocals / **VERNON REID** (b.22 Aug'58, London, England) – guitar / **MANUEL 'MUZZ' SKILLINGS** (b. 6 Jan'60, Queens, N.Y.) – bass / **WILLIAM CALHOUN** (b.22 Jul'64) – drums

		Epic	Epic
May 88.	(7"/7"sha-pic-d) (LCL/+P 1) **MIDDLE MAN. / DESPERATE PEOPLE**		

(12"+=/cd-s+=) (LCLT/CPLCL 1) – Funny vibe.

| May 88. | (lp/c/cd) (460 758-1/-4/-2) <44099> **VIVID** | | 6 |

– Cult of personality / I want to know / Middle man / Desperate people / Open letter (to a landlord) / Funny vibe / Memories can't wait / Broken hearts / Glamour boys / What's your favourite colour? / Which way to America?

| Jul 88. | (7"/7"-g-f)(7"pic-d) (LCL/+G 2)(CTLCL 2) **GLAMOUR BOYS. / WHICH WAY TO AMERICA?** | | |

(12"+=/cd-s+=) (LCLT/CDLCL 2) – Middle man / Rap track (conversation with LIVING COLOUR).

| Sep 88. | (7"/7"s) (LCL/+B 3) **CULT OF PERSONALITY. / OPEN LETTER (TO A LANDLORD)** | | |

(12"+=/cd-s+=) (LCLT/CDLCL 3) – Middle Man (live).

| Dec 88. | (7"/7"s) (LCL/+Q 4) **OPEN LETTER (TO A LANDLORD). / CULT OF PERSONALITY** (live) | | |

(12"+=/cd-s+=) (LCLT/CDLCL 4) – Talkin' 'bout a revolution (live).

| Feb 89. | (7") <68611> **CULT OF PERSONALITY. / FUNNY VIBE** | - | 13 |
| Apr 89. | (7") (LCL 5) **CULT OF PERSONALITY. / SHOULD I STAY OR SHOULD I GO** | | - |

(12"+=/cd-s+=) (LCLT/CDLCL 5) – What's your favourite colour.

| Jun 89. | (7") <68934> **OPEN LETTER (TO A LANDLORD). / TALKIN' 'BOUT A REVOLUTION** | - | 82 |
| Oct 89. | (7"/7"-g-f) (LCL/+G 6) <68548> **GLAMOUR BOYS (remix). / CULT OF PERSONALITY** (live) | | 31 Aug89 |

(12"+=) (LCLT 6) – Memories can't wait.
(pic-cd-s+=) (CDLCL 6) – I don't want to know.
(cd-s+=) (LCLC 6) – Middle man (live) / Open letter (to a landlord).

Oct 89.	(7") <73010> **FUNNY VIBE. / ('A'instrumental)**	-	
Aug 90.	(7") <73575> **TYPE. / SHOULD I STAY OR SHOULD I GO**	-	
Aug 90.	(7"/c-s) (LCL/+M 7) **TYPE. / FINAL SOLUTION**	75	

(12"+=/cd-s+=) (LCLGT/CDLCL 7) – Should I stay or should I go? / Middleman (live).

| Sep 90. | (cd/c/lp) (466 920-2/-4/-1) <46202> **TIME'S UP** | 20 | 13 |

– Time's up / History lesson / Pride / Love rears its ugly head / New Jack theme / Someone like you / Elvis is dead / Type / Information overload / Undercover of darkness / Olozy I / Fight the fight / Tag team partners / Solace of you / This is the life. (cd+=) – Final solution (live) / Middle man (live) / Love rears its ugly head (soul power mix).

| Jan 91. | (7"/7"sha-pic-d/c-s) (656 593-7/-0/-4) <73677> **LOVE REARS IT'S UGLY HEAD. / ('A'-Soul power mix)** | 12 | |

(12"+=) (656 593-6) – Type (remix).
(cd-s+=/pic-cd+=) (656 593-2/-5) – ('A'version) / Love and happiness.

| May 91. | (c-s,cd-s) <73800> **SOLACE OF YOU / SOMEONE LIKE YOU** | | - |
| May 91. | (7"/c-s) (656 908-7/-4) **SOLACE OF YOU. / NEW JACK THEME** | 33 | |

(12"+=) (656 908-8) – Elvis is dead (mix).
(cd-s+=) (656 908-9) – ('A'live) / Type (live) / Information overload (live) / Desperate people (live).

| Jul 91. | (7"/12"/cd-ep) **BURNING OF THE MIDNIGHT LAMP / MEMORIES CAN'T WAIT / TALKING LOUD AND SAYING NOTHING** | - | |
| Aug 91. | (m-cd) <47988> **BISCUITS** (live) | - | |

– Burning of the midnight lamp / Memories can't wait (live) / Talking loud and saying nothing / Desperate people (live) / Money talks / Love and happiness.

| Oct 91. | (7"/c-s) (657 535-7/-4) **THE CULT OF PERSONALITY. / LOVE REARS IT'S UGLY HEAD** (live) | 67 | - |

(12"+=) (657 535-6) – ('A'live) / Pride (live).
(cd-s+=) (657 535-2) – Talkin' loud and saying nothing / Burning of the midnight lamp.

—— MUZZ SKILLINGS departed Nov'91, and was replaced (Jun'92) by **DOUG WIMBUSH** (b.22 Sep'56, Hartford, Connecticut) – bass (ex-GEORGE CLINTON, ex-TACKHEAD)

| Feb 93. | (7") (658 976-7) **LEAVE IT ALONE. / 17 DAYS** | 34 | |

(12"pic-d+=/cd-s+=) (658 976-6/-2) – T.V. news / Hemp (extended).

| Feb 93. | (cd/c/lp) (472856-2/-4/-1) <52780> **STAIN** | 19 | 26 |

– Go away / Ignorance is bliss / Leave it alone / B1 / Mind your own business / Auslander / Never satisfied / Nothingness / Postman / W.T.F.F. / This little pig / Hemp / Wall / T.V. news / Love rears its ugly head (live).

| Apr 93. | (7"pic-d) (659 173-7) **AUSLANDER (remix). / AUSLANDER (Dublander mix)** | 53 | |

(12"colrd+=/pic-cd-s+=) (659 173-6/-2) – Auslander (Radio Days mix) / New Jack theme.

| May 93. | (7"colrd) (659 300-7) **NOTHINGLESS. / 17 DAYS** | | |

(cd-s+=) (659 300-2) – ('A'remix) / ('A'acoustic mix).

| Jan 94. | (c-ep) (660 780-4) **SUNSHINE OF YOUR LOVE / AUSLANDER (overload mix) / ('A'-Adrian Sherwood & S. McDonald mix)** | | |

(cd-ep) (660 780-2) – (first 2 tracks) / ('A'remix) / Love rears its ugly head (extended).

—— They disbanded early '95 after poor sales

Nov 95. (cd/c) *(481 021-2/-4)* **PRIDE – THE GREATEST HITS**
(compilation) □ □
– Pride / Release the pressure / Sacred ground / Visions / Love rears it's ugly head (soul power remix) / These are happy times / Memories can't wait / Cult of personality / Funny vibe / WTFF / Glamour boys / Open letter (to a landlord) / Solace of you / Nothingless / Type / Time's up / What's your favourite colour? (theme song).

VERNON REID

――― with various personnel

Jul 96. (cd/c) *<(483921-2/-4)>* **MISTAKEN IDENTITY** □ □
– C.P. time / Mistaken identity / You say he's just a psychic friend / Who are you (mutation 1) / Lightnin' / Projects / Uptown drifter / Saint Cobain / Important safety instructions (mutation 2) / What's my name / Signed ficticious / Call waiting to exhale (mutation 3) / My last nerve / Freshwater coconut / Mysterious power / Unborne embrace / Who invited you (mutation 4).

LL COOL J

Born: JAMES TODD SMITH, 16 Aug'69, Queens, New York, USA. Cocksure from the start, L.(ADIES) L.(OVE) COOL J(AMES) began making demos while still at school, one of these picked up by a young RICK RUBIN for his new 'Def Jam' label. Released in 1984, 'I NEED A BEAT' kickstarted not only the career of young JAMES but the 'Def Jam' empire, selling 100,000 copies and leading to L.L. prematurely abandoning his school career. Following up with the seminal B-Boy holler of 'I CAN'T LIVE WITHOUT MY RADIO', the rapper established himself as one of the key players in the new hip hop mafia alongside RUN D.M.C. and subsequently The BEASTIE BOYS. With RUBIN revving up L.L.'s solid arrangements via his trademark metal grind, 'RADIO' (1986) was the first in a string of groundbreaking 'Def Jam' albums, boasting such heavyweight knockouts as 'ROCK THE BELLS' alongside the first two singles. Live, L.L. could go twenty rounds with just about any other act on the scene, sleek with sweat from his gold-chained, bare-chested torso and stalking the stage like a panther. It came as something of a surprise, then, when L.L. played the sensitive, doomed romantic card with the rather limp ballad, 'I NEED LOVE' and although it broke him into both the UK Top 10 and the US Top 20, the track wasn't exactly representative of his street tough style. The accompanying album, 'BIGGER AND DEFFER' (1987) was also a bit of a disappointment, lacking the headstrong focus of the debut while the US Top 10 'WALKING WITH A PANTHER' (1989) alienated him from the more grassroots element of his fanbase with its overtly commercial sound, typified by the likes of 'I'M THAT TYPE OF GUY'. Its saving grace was the bizarre minimalism of 'GOIN' BACK TO CALI', a track featured on the 'Def Jam' soundtrack to cult film 'Less Than Zero' alongside metal acts like SLAYER and AEROSMITH. L.L.'s passport back to some kind of credibility came with the aid of veteran producer MARLEY MARL, the pair working together on the Grammy-winning 'MAMA SAID KNOCK YOU OUT' (1990), L.L.'s biggest selling and most consistently rounded release to date. In the early to mid 90's, COOL J again lost his way somewhat, taking vague aim at gangsta rap with '14 SHOTS TO THE DOME' (1993) and descending into self-parody and cliche with 'MR. SMITH' (1995). Ironically, it was via heavy metal, or rather heavy metal goons BEAVIS & BUTT-HEAD, that COOL J stormed his way back into the charts, collaborating with the gruesome twosome on a cover of CHAKA KHAN's 'AIN'T NOBODY' for the BEAVIS & BUTT-HEAD movie. The single was a UK No.1 in early '97, paving the way for L.L.'s re-invention as red-leather clad funk grinder on the brilliant 'PHENOMENON' single, another UK Top 10 later that year. Along with the likes of BUSTA RHYMES' scorching 'Put Your Hands Where My Eyes Can See', the track saw rap pared down to raw, minimalist funk, a visceral departure from the snooze-core, weed-obsessed hip hop of recent years. 'PHENOMENON' (1997) the album saw L.L. back in the US Top 10, back on form and working with some of the most respected artists in the game, including the aforementioned RHYMES, REDMAN and the WU TANG's METHOD MAN.

Album rating: RADIO (*7) / BIGGER AND DEFFER (*4) / WALKING WITH A PANTHER (*7) / MAMA SAID KNOCK YOU OUT (*8) / 14 SHOTS TO THE DOME (*5) / MR. SMITH (*6) / ALL WORLD: GREATEST HITS compilation (*8) / PHENOMENON (*5)

L.L. COOL J – vocals (with various back-up)

		Def Jam-CBS	Def Jam
Jan 86.	(7") *(A 6684)* **I CAN'T LIVE WITHOUT MY RADIO. / I CAN'T GIVE YOU MORE** (12"+=) – ('A'instrumental).	□	□
Feb 86.	(lp/c) *(DEF/40 26745) <40239>* **RADIO**	71	46 Jan86

– I can't live without my radio / You can't dance / Dear Yvette / I can give you more / Dangerous / Rock the bells / I need a beat / You'll rock / I want you. *(cd-iss. Jul95; 527352-2)*

Mar 86.	(7") *(A 7003)* **ROCK THE BELLS. / EL SHABAZZ** (12"+=) *(TA 7003)* – ('A'original mix). (d7"+=) *(DA 7003)* – I can't live without my radio / I can give you more.	□	□
Sep 86.	(7") *(650113-7)* **I CAN'T LIVE WITHOUT MY RADIO. / ROCK THE BELLS** (12"+=) *(650113-6)* – You'll rock / El shabazz.	□	□
Jun 87.	(7") *(650856-7) <07120>* **I'M BAD. / GET DOWN** (12"+=) *(650856-6)* – Dangerous. (7"pic-d) *(650856-8)* – ('A'side) / Rock the bells / I can't live without my radio.	71	84 May87
Jun 87.	(lp/c) *(450515-1/-4) <40793>* **BIGGER AND DEFFER**	54	3

– I'm bad / Get down / The Bristol hotel / The rhyme ain't done / 357 – Break it on down / Go cut creator go / Breakthrough / I need love / Ahh, let's get ill / The doo-wop / On the ill tip. *(cd-iss. 1991; 450515-2) (cd re-iss. Jul95; 527353-2)*

Aug 87.	(7") *(651101-7) <07350>* **I NEED LOVE. / MY RHYME AIN'T DONE** (12"+=) *(651101-6)* – ('A'mixes).	8	14 Jul87
Nov 87.	(7"/7"pic-d) *(LLCJ/+P 1)* **GO CUT CREATOR GO. / I NEED LOVE** (10"+=/12"+=/cd-s+=) *(LL CJQ/CJT/CD 1)* – The Bristol hotel / Kandy.	66	
Feb 88.	(7") *(LLCJ 2) <07679>* **GOIN' BACK TO CALI. / JACK THE RIPPER** (10"+=/12"+=) *(LLCJ Q/T 2)* – I can't live without my radio.	37	31
May 89.	(7"/c-s) *(LLCJ/+M 3) <68902>* **I'M THAT TYPE OF GUY. / IT GETS NO ROUGHER** (12"+=) *(LLCJT 3)* – Rock the bells. (cd-s+=) *(CDLLCJ 3)* – ('A'mixes).	43	15
Jun 89.	(lp/c/cd) *(465112-1/-4/-2) <45172>* **WALKING WITH A PANTHER**	43	6

– Droppin' em / Smokin' dopin' / Fast peg / Clap your hands / Nitro / You're my heart / I'm that type of guy / Why do you think they call it dope? / It gets no rougher / Big ole butt / One shot at love / 1-900 LL Cool J / Two different worlds / Jealous / Jingling baby / Def jam in the motherland. *(cd+=)* – Goin' back to Cali / Crime stories. *(c++=)* – Change your ways / Jack the ripper. *(cd re-iss. Jul95; 527355-2)*

| Sep 90. | (c-s) *<73457>* **THE BOOMIN' SYSTEM / ('A'-Underground mix)** | - | 48 |
| Oct 90. | (cd/c/lp) *(467315-2/-4/-1) <46888>* **MAMA SAID KNOCK YOU OUT** | 49 | 16 Sep90 |

– Boomin' system / Around the way girl / Eat 'em up L. Chill / Mr. Good bar / Murdergram (live at Rapmania) / Cheesy rat blues / Farmers boulevard (our anthem) / Mama said knock you out / Milky cereal / Jingling baby / To da break of dawn / 6 minutes of pleasure / Illegal search / Power of God. *(cd re-iss. Jul95; 523477-2)*

Nov 90.	(c-s) *<73609>* **AROUND THE WAY GIRL / ('A'remix)**	-	9
Nov 90.	(7") *(6564470-7)* **AROUND THE WAY GIRL. / MAMA SAID KNOCK YOU OUT** (12"+=/cd-s+=) *(6564470-6/-2)* – ('A'mixes). *(re-iss. Mar91; hit UK No.36)*	41	-
Apr 91.	(c-s) *<73706>* **MAMA SAID KNOCK YOU OUT / ('A'-Hot mix)**	-	17
Sep 91.	(c-s) *<73820>* **6 MINUTES OF PLEASURE / EAT EM UP L CHILL**	-	95
Mar 93.	(7") *(659169-7) <74811>* **HOW I'M COMIN'. / BUCKIN 'EM DOWN** (12"+=/cd-s+=) *(659169-6/-2)* – ('A'mixes).	37	57
Apr 93.	(cd/c/lp) *(473678-2/-4/-1) <53325>* **14 SHOTS TO THE DOME**	74	5

– How I'm comin' / Buckin' em down / Stand by your man / Little somethin' / Pink cookies in a plastic bag getting crushed by buildings / Straight from Queens / Funkadelic relic / All we got left is the beat / (NFA) No frontin' allowed / Back seat / Soul survivor / Ain't no stoppin' this / Diggy down / Crossroads. *(cd re-iss. Jan96; 523488-2)*

| Jun 93. | (c-s) *<74984>* **BACK SEAT (OF MY JEEP) / PINK COOKIES IN A PLASTIC BAG GETTING CRUSHED BY BUILDINGS** | - | 42 96 |
| Nov 95. | (cd/c) *(529724-2/-4) <529583>* **MR. SMITH** | | 20 |

– Make it hot / Hip hop / Hey lover (featuring BOYZ II MEN) / Doin' it / Life as / I shot ya / Mr. Smith / No aerplay / Loungin' / Hollis to Hollywood / God bless / Get the drop on 'em.

Jan 96.	(c-s; LL COOL J featuring BOYZ II MEN) *(DEFMC 14) <577494>* **HEY LOVER / ('A'instrumental)** (12"+=/cd-s+=) *(12DEF/DEFCD 14)* – ('A'mix. below featured guest vocals by LeSHAUN	17	3 Nov95
May 96.	(c-s) *(DEFMC 15) <576120>* **DOIN' IT / ('A'mix)** (12"+=/cd-s+=) *(12DEF/DEFCD 15)* – ('A'mixes).	15	9 Feb96
Sep 96.	(c-s) *(DEFMC 30) <575062>* **LOUNGIN' / SUMMER LUV** (12"+=/cd-s+=) *(12DEF/DEFCD 30)* – ('A'mixes).	7	3 Jun96
Nov 96.	(cd/c/d-lp) *<(534125-2/-4/-1)>* **ALL WORLD: GREATEST HITS** (compilation)	23	

– I can't live without my radio / Rock the bells / I'm bad / I need love / Goin' back to Cali / Jack the ripper / Jingling baby / Big ole butt / Boomin' system / Around the way girl / Mama said knock you out / Back seat / I need a beat / Doin' it / Loungin' (who do ya luv) / Hey lover (with BOYZ II MEN).

Dec 96.	(c-s) *<19410>* **AIN'T NOBODY / (track by Madd Head)**	-	46
Jan 97.	(c-s) *(GFSC 22195)* **AIN'T NOBODY / (track by Beavis & Butt-Head)** (12"+=/cd-s+=) *(GFST/+T 22195)* – ('A'mix). (above single on 'Geffen' & lifted from the animated movie 'Beavis & Butt-Head Do America')	1	-
Oct 97.	(cd/c/lp) *<(539186-2/-4/-1)>* **PHENOMENON**	37	7

– Phenomenon / Candy (with RALPH TRESVANT & RICKY BELL) / Starsky and Hutch (with BUSTA RHYMES) / Another dollar / Nobody can freak with you (with KEITH SWEAT & LeSHAUN) / Hot hot hot / 4,3,2,1 (with METHOD MAN, REDMAN, DMX, CANIBUS & MASTER P) / Wanna get paid (with LOST BOYZ) / Father / Don't be late don't come too soon (with TAMIA).

| Oct 97. | (c-s) *(568116-4)* **PHENOMENON / ('A'mix)** (12"/cd-s) *(568117-1/-2)* – ('A'mix) / Wanna get paid / Mama said knock you out. | 9 | 56 |
| Dec 97. | (cd-s; LL COOL J featuring METHOD MAN, REDMAN, DMX, CANIBUS & MASTER P) **4,3,2,1 /** | - | 75 |

– compilations, etc. –

| Mar 93. | (cd/c) *Def Jam; (473043-2/-4)* **12" TAPE** (versions) | □ | |

– Rock the bells / I need love / I can't live without my radio / Boomin' system / Around the way girl.

Richard LLOYD (see under ⇒ TELEVISION)

Los LOBOS

Formed: Los Angeles, California, USA ... 1974 by DAVID HIDALGO, LUIS PEREZ, CESAR ROSAS and CONRAD LOZANO, all members of L.A.'s Chicano community. Although they initially set out playing chart covers at local clubs, weddings etc., the group subsequently began exploring their musical roots in a traditional acoustic framework before going on to combine this approach with more popular American musical idioms. The 1978 debut set, 'JUST ANOTHER BAND FROM EAST L.A.', was a self-financed affair sold at gigs, the wider listening public not introduced to the LOS LOBOS sound until 1983 and the release of a mini-set, 'AND A TIME TO DANCE'. The first fruits of a new deal with 'Slash', the T-BONE BURNETT-produced set included a Grammy winning rendition of the traditional Mexican folk anthem, 'ANSELMA'. Moving into more adventurous territory with the acclaimed 'HOW WILL THE WOLF SURVIVE' (1984), LOS LOBOS proved themselves to be one of America's most authentically eclectic roots-rock purveyors. Inspired by the likes of RY COODER and FLACO JIMINEZ, the group moved effortlessly through Tex-Mex, country, norteno, R&B and rock without sacrificing their unique appeal. The record also saw LOS LOBOS make the US Top 50, its title track a minor hit in Britain. Although 'BY THE LIGHT OF THE MOON' (1987) featured arguably one of LOS LOBOS' finest ballads in 'RIVER OF FOOLS', the album was considered a disappointing follow-up by both fans and critics alike, its more politically aware mantle sitting uneasily on the shoulders of a band at their best on celebratory dance tunes. A cult attraction up to this point, LOS LOBOS became overnight pop stars via their contributions to the soundtrack for RICHIE VALENS biopic, 'LA BAMBA'; the strum 'n' shimmy of the title track was a massive transatlantic No.1 while the album itself (also featuring performances by the likes of MARSHALL CRENSHAW and BO DIDDLEY) topped the US charts. No doubt loathe to be bracketed as a rock'n'roll covers outfit, LOS LOBOS' next studio set, 'LA PISTOLA EL Y CORAZON' (1988) saw them returning squarely and convincingly to their Mexican roots (and chart oblivion). With this out of their system, the group resumed their innovative rock hybrid on 'THE NEIGHBOURHOOD' (1990), a solid set benefitting from the muscular backbeat of session veteran JIM KELTNER and featuring guest vocals from JOHN HIATT. Following a period of collaboration with The BAND on material for their comeback album, LOS LOBOS penned what many regard as their most accomplished and rewarding album, 'KIKO' (1992); by turns gutsy, instinctive, subtle and atmospheric, the record's shifting latin pop/rock/folk textures effectively transformed the band's experimentation into something with a completely separate and unique musical identity. LOS LOBOS filled in time until their next studio outing with a fine 1993 compilation set, 'JUST ANOTHER BAND ... THE BEST OF ...', also collaborating with LALO GUERRERO on low-key album, 'PAPA'S BREATH', in 1995. The following year, the band from East L.A. issued their first album for 'Warners', 'COLOSSAL HEAD', the record scoring their highest chart placing at No.81 US since the heady days of 'LA BAMBA'. • **Songwriters:** Group penned except; RIP IT UP (Little Richard) / CRYING, WAITING, HOPING (Buddy Holly) / and some trad. • **Trivia:** Country star, WAYLON JENNINGS, later covered 'HOW WILL THE WOLF SURVIVE'. HIDALGO and ROSAS featured on RY COODER's 1985 lp, 'Alamo Bay', with the former guesting on albums (King Of America) by ELVIS COSTELLO and (Gracelands) by PAUL SIMON, alongside other LL members.

Album rating: JUST ANOTHER BAND FROM EAST L.A. mini (*5) / ... AND A TIME TO DANCE mini (*6) / HOW WILL THE WOLF SURVIVE? (*8) / BY THE LIGHT OF THE MOON (*7) / LA BAMBA soundtrack (*5) / LA PISTOLA Y EL CORAZON (*6) / THE NEIGHBOURHOOD (*7) / KIKO (*7) / JUST ANOTHER BAND FROM E.L.A. – THE BEST OF compilation (*8) / COLOSSAL HEAD (*4)

DAVID HIDALGO (b. 6 Oct'54) – vocals, guitar, accordion / **CESAR ROSAS** (b.26 Sep'54) – vocals, guitar / **CONRAD LOZANO** (b.21 Mar'51) – bass, vocals, guitar / **LUIS PEREZ** (b.21 Mar'51) – drums, guitar

	not iss.	New Vista
1978. (m-lp) **JUST ANOTHER BAND FROM EAST L.A.**	-	

– Volver, volver / El cuchipe / La foria de la flores / Sabrami / Bella Maria de mi alma / What's going on / Wrong man these / Blue moods / New Zanda.

	Rough Trade	Slash
Jan 84. (m-lp) *(ROUGH 71)* <SLMP 1> **AND A TIME TO DANCE**		1983

– Let's say goodnight / Walking song / Anselma / Come on, let's go / How much can I do? / Why do you do / Ay te dejo en San Antonio. *(re-iss. Jan87 on 'Slash' lp/c; SLM P/C 17)*

—— added **STEVE BERLIN** (b.14 Sep'55, Philadelphia, Pennsylvania) – saxophone, soprano vocals (ex-BLASTERS)

	Slash-London	Slash-Warners
Nov 84. (lp/c) *(SLMP/SMMC 3)* <25177> **HOW WILL THE WOLF SURVIVE?**	77	47

– Don't worry baby / A matter of time / Corrida #1 / Our last night / The breakdown / I got loaded / Serenata Nortena / Evageline / I got to let you know / Lil' king of everything / Evangeline / Will the wolf survive?. *(re-iss. Jan87; same) (cd-iss. Apr89; 820184-2)*

Mar 85. (7"/12") *(LASH/+X 4)* <29093> **WILL THE WOLF SURVIVE? / DON'T WORRY BABY**	57	78

(10"+=) *(LASHT 4)* – ('A'live).

Jan 87. (lp/c/cd) *(SLA P/C 13)(828033-2)* <25523> **BY THE LIGHT OF THE MOON**	77	47

– One time one night / Shakin' shakin' shakes / Is this all there is? / Prenda del Alma / All I wanted to was dance / Set me free (Rosa Lee) / The hardest time / My boy's gone / River of fools / The mess we're in / Tears of God.

Feb 87. (7"m) *(LASH 10)* **SET ME FREE (ROSA LEE). / SHAKIN' SHAKIN' SHAKES / PREUDEABELALAMA**		-

(12"+=) *(LASHX 10)* – Will the wolf survive?

Mar 87. (7") <28464> **ONE TIME ONE NIGHT. / ALL I WANTED TO DO WAS DANCE**	-	

Apr 87. (7") *(LASH 11)* **ONE TIME ONE NIGHT. / RIVER OF FOOLS**		-

(12"+=) *(LASHX 11)* – Anselma / Don't worry baby.

Jul 87. (7"/c-s) *(LASH/LASCS 13)* <28336> **LA BAMBA. / CHARLENA**	1	1

(12"+=) *(LASHX 13)* – Rip it up.
(below album released on 'London'; Slash's UK paymaster

Aug 87. (lp/c)(cd) *(LON LP/C 36)(828058-2)* <25605> **LA BAMBA (soundtrack)**	24	1

– La Bamba / Come on, let's go / Ooh! my head / We belong together / Framed / Donna / Lonely teardrops (HOWARD HUNTSBERRY) / Crying, waiting, hoping (MARSHALL CRENSHAW) / Summertime blues (BRIAN SETZER) / Who do you love (BO DIDDLEY) / Charlena / Goodnight my love.

Sep 87. (7") *(LASH 14)* <28186> **COME ON, LET'S GO. / OOH! MY HEAD**	18	21

(10"+=/12"+=) *(LASH T/X 14)* – (track by MARSHALL CRENSHAW).

Nov 87. (7") *(LASH 16)* **DONNA. / FRAMED**		-

(12"+=)(10"+=) *(LASHX 16)(HL 8803)* – Goodnight my love.

Oct 88. (lp/c/cd) *(828 121-1/-4/-2)* <25790> **LA PISTOLA Y EL CORAZON**		

– La Guacamaya / Las amarillas / Si yo quisiera / (Sonajas) Mananitas Michoacanas / Estoy sentado aqui / El gusto / Que nadie sepa mi sufrir / El Canelo / La pistola y el corazon.

—— guests **JIM KELTNER** – drums / **JOHN HIATT** – vocals / **ALEX ACUNA** – percussion

Sep 90. (cd/c/lp) *(828 190-2/-4/-1)* <26131> **THE NEIGHBOURHOOD**		

– Down on the riverbed / Emily / I walk alone / Angel dance / Little John of God / Deep dark hole / Georgia slop / I can't understand / The giving tree / Take my hand / Jenny's got a pony / Be still / The neighbourhood.

May 92. (cd/c/lp) *(828 298-2/-4/-1)* <26786> **KIKO**		

– Dream in blue / Wake up Dolores / Angels with dirty faces / That train don't stop here / Kiko and the lavender Moon / Saint behind the glass / Reva's house / When the circus comes / Arizona skies / Short side of nothing / Two Janes / Wicked rain / Whiskey trail / Just a man / Peace / Rio de Tenampa.

Sep 93. (d-cd/d-c) *(828 400-2/-4)* <45367> **JUST ANOTHER BAND FROM EAST L.A. THE BEST OF LOS LOBOS** (compilation)		

– Volver, volver / El cuchipe / La feria de las flores / Saborami / Let's say goodnight / Anselma / Will the wolf survive? / A matter of time / I got to let you know / Don't worry baby / One time one night / Shakin' shakin' shakes / River of fools / Carabina 30-30 / Tears of God / Set me free (Rosa Lee) / Come on, let's go / La bamba / El gusto / Estoy sentado aqui / La pistola y el corazon / I wanna be like you (the monkey song) / Some day / Down on the riverbed / Be still / The neighbourhood / I can't understand / Angel dance / Bertha / Saint behind the glass / Angels with dirty faces / Wicked rain / Kiko and the lavender Moon / When the circus comes / Peace / Bella Maria de mi alma / What's going on / Wrong man theme / Blue moonlight / Politician / New Zandu.

—— Early in 1995, LOS LOBOS collaborated on an album, 'PAPA'S DREAM' with LALO GUERRERO on the label 'Music For Little People' (94256-2)

	WEA	Warners
Mar 96. (cd) *<(9362 46172-2)>* **COLOSSAL HEAD**		81

– Revolution / Everybody loves a train / Mas y mas / Maricela / Can't stop the rain / Little Japan / Life is good / Buddy Ebsen loves the night time / This bird's gonna fly / Colossal head / Manny's bones.

Nils LOFGREN

Born: 21 Jun'51, Chicago, USA. Raised in Maryland, Washington DC by Italian/Swedish parents, he formed PAUL DOWELL & THE DOLPHIN in 1969; two flop singles later he folded the outfit and formed the harder-edged GRIN. While building up their live reputation, LOFGREN sessioned for NEIL YOUNG & CRAZY HORSE on 'After The Goldrush', CRAZY HORSE also employing him the following year as a part-time writer and session man on their brilliant eponymous debut. Meanwhile, GRIN signed to 'Spindizzy' (distributed by 'Columbia') and issued their self-titled debut lp in late summer '71. The record only managed to scrape into the US Top 200, as did their follow-ups, '1 + 1' and 'ALL OUT' (the latter added NILS' younger brother TOM). In 1973, the group signed to 'A&M', although they subsequently split when NILS joined NEIL YOUNG & CRAZY HORSE for the sublime 'Tonight's The Night' (1975). As well as contributing haunting piano and vocals to the likes of 'Albuquerque' and 'Tired Eyes', LOFGREN cooked up some searing guitar licks on 'Speakin' Out' and the title track, his precocious talent confirmed with an eponymous 'A&M' solo debut. Released the same year as 'Tonight ...', the album found LOFGREN finally hitting his groove with an irrepressible verve and a rock-solid set of songs, from the brawny KEITH RICHARDS tribute, 'KEITH DON'T GO (ODE TO THE GLIMMER TWIN)' and the sensitive rendition of Carole King's 'GOIN' BACK' (also recorded by The BYRDS amongst others) to the infectious pop/rock of single, 'BACK IT UP'. Although the record failed to chart, LOFGREN enjoyed some belated chart success with the Al KOOPER-produced 'CRY TOUGH'. A more guitar-orientated affair, it made the UK Top 10 and the US Top 40, briefly elevating NILS to the level of recognition enjoyed by most of his peers. It wasn't to last though, the disappointing 'I CAME TO DANCE' (1977) failing to maintain the momentum, while the much improved 'NILS' (1979) sold even less despite the lyrical suss of guest, LOU REED. A new deal with 'Backstreet-M.C.A.' failed to turn things around and early 80's sets, 'NIGHT FADES AWAY' (1981) and 'WONDERLAND' (1983) made little impact. While 1983 had seen NILS again working with NEIL YOUNG (on the 'Trans' tour), LOFGREN initiated his marathon stint with BRUCE SPRINGSTEEN's E-STREET BAND the following year. Independently released in the UK, 'FLIP' (1985) was LOFGREN's final studio release of the decade, a frenetic set of high octane rockers which went down well with fans but again failed to cross over or break any new ground. The early 90's saw the singer/guitarist return with a new band (including ex-BAND man, LEVON HELM) and a couple of albums in the space of two years, an uncharacteristically prolific burst of creativity no doubt fuelled by his long years as a sideman. 1994 saw LOFGREN's first foray into soundtrack work for the movie 'Every Breath', while a further studio album, 'DAMAGED GOODS', and the obligatory unplugged set, 'ACOUSTIC LIVE', appeared in '95 and '97 respectively. The Mr. Nice of the rock establishment, LOFGREN remains one of the most respected, highly praised and in-demand guitarists around; the fact that his solo career never really took off only serves to fuel his cult status. • **Songwriters:** Self-penned except covers; FOR YOUR LOVE (Yardbirds) / ANYTIME AT ALL (Beatles) / IT'S ALL OVER NOW (Valentinos) / etc.

Album rating: NILS LOFGREN (*7) / BACK IT UP authorized bootleg (*6) / CRY TOUGH (*7) / I CAME TO DANCE (*5) / NIGHT AFTER NIGHT (*5) / NILS (*6) / NIGHT FADES AWAY (*4) / WONDERLAND (*6) / FLIP (*6) / CODE OF THE ROAD (*5) / THE BEST OF NILS LOFGREN – DON'T WALK . . . ROCK compilation (*7) / SILVER LINING (*4) / CROOKED LINE (*4) / EVERY BREATH (*4) / DAMAGED GOODS (*5) / ACOUSTIC LIVE (*5)

PAUL DOWELL & THE DOLPHIN

NILS LOFGREN – lead guitar, keyboards, / and **BOB GORDON** (b.1951, Oklahoma)– bass, vocals / unknown drummer

	not iss.	Sire
1968. (7") <4107> **THE LAST TIME I SAW YOU. / IT'S BETTER TO KNOW YOU**	-	

GRIN

(NILS + BOB)plus **BOB BERBERICH** (b.1949, Maryland)– drums (ex-REEKERS)

	C.B.S.	Spindizzy
Jul 71. (7") (CBS 5239) **WE ALL SUNG TOGETHER. / SEE WHAT A LOVE CAN DO**		Oct70
Aug 71. (lp) (CBS 64272) <30321> **GRIN**		Jun71

– Like rain / See what a love can do / Everybody's missin' the sun / 18 faced lover / Outlaw / We all sung together / If I were a song / Take you to the movies tonight / Direction / Pioneer Mary / Open wide / I had too much (Miss Dazi). (re-iss. 1975 on 'Spindizzy')

Sep 71. (7") (CBS 7405) <7405> **EVERYBODY'S MISSIN' THE SUN. / 18 FACED LOVER**		
Mar 72. (7") (CBS 7757) <4005> **WHITE LIES. / JUST TO HAVE YOU**	75	Jan72
Jun 72. (lp) (CBS 64652) <31038> **1 + 1**		Jan72

– White lies / Please don't hide / Slippery fingers / Moon tears / End unkind / Sometimes / Lost a number / Hi, hello home / Just a poem / Soft fun.

–––– added **TOM LOFGREN** – rhythm guitar

	Epic	Spindizzy
May 73. (lp) (EPC 65166) <31701> **ALL OUT**		Mar73

– That letter / Heavy Chevy / Don't be long / Love again / She ain't right / Love or else / Ain't love nice / Hard on fire / All out / Rusty gun. (cd-iss. Oct94; 477847-2)

	A&M	A&M
May 73. (7") (EPC 1463) **AIN'T LOVE NICE. / LOVE OR ELSE**		
Nov 73. (lp) <4415> **GONE CRAZY**	-	

– You're the weight / Boy and girl / What about me / One more time / True thrill / Beggar's day / Nightmare / Believe / Ain't for free. (UK-iss.Jan76; AMLH 64415)

Feb 74. (7") **YOU'RE THE WEIGHT. / BEGGAR'S DAY**		

–––– NILS joined NEIL YOUNG & CRAZY HORSE (Aug73-Mar74, on 'Tonight's The Night')

– (GRIN) compilations, others, etc. –

	C.B.S.	Columbia
Jun 76. (d-lp) (88024) **GRIN FEATURING NILS LOFGREN**		
– ('GRIN' & '1 + 1' albums)		
Jun 76. (7") (4339) **SOFT FUN. / SLIPPERY FINGERS**		
Oct 79. (lp) (31770) **THE BEST OF NILS LOFGREN AND GRIN**		

(re-iss. Feb86; 32717)

NILS LOFGREN

with **WORNELL JONES** – bass / **AYNSLEY DUNBAR** – drums

	A&M	A&M
Apr 75. (lp/c) (AMLH/CAM 64509) <4509> **NILS LOFGREN**		Mar75

– Be good tonight / Back it up / One more Saturday night / If I say it, it's so / I don't want to know / Keith don't go (ode to the Glimmer twin) / Can't buy a break / Duty / The sun hasn't set on this boy yet / Rock and roll crook / Two by two / Goin' back. (cd-iss. Apr97; 540 702-2)

Jun 75. (7") (AMS 7175) **BACK IT UP. / IF I SAY IT, IT'S SO**		
Nov 75. (7") (AMS 7197) **I DON'T WANT TO KNOW. / ONE MORE SATURDAY NIGHT**		
Jan 76. (ltd.lp) **BACK IT UP!! NILS LOFGREN LIVE – AN AUTHORIZED BOOTLEG** (live radio show)		

–––– added **TOM LOFGREN** – rhythm guitar, vocals (ex-GRIN)

Mar 76. (lp/c) (AMLH/CAM 64573) <4573> **CRY TOUGH**	8	32

– Cry tough / It's not a crime / Incidentally . . . it's over / For your love / Share a little / Mud in your eye / Can't get closer (WCGC) / You lit a fire / Jailbait. (re-iss. Jul83 on 'Fame' lp/c; FA/TCFA 3070) (cd-iss. Oct92; CDMID 122)

May 76. (7") (AMS 7229) **CRY TOUGH. / SHARE A LITTLE**		
Aug 76. (7") (AMS 7252) **IT'S NOT A CRIME. / SHARE A LITTLE**		

–––– **ANDY NEWMARK** – drums repl. ZACK

–––– added **PATRICK HENDERSON** – keyboards

Mar 77. (lp/c) (AMLH/CAM 64628) <4628> **I CAME TO DANCE**	30	36

– I came to dance / Rock me at home / Home is where your hurt is / Code of the road / Happy ending kids / Goin' south / To be a dreamer / Jealous gun / Happy.

May 77. (7") (AMS 7288) **I CAME TO DANCE. / CODE OF THE ROAD**		

–––– **DAVID PLATSHON** – drums repl. NEWMARK

Oct 77. (d-lp/d-c) (AMLH/CLM 64839) <3707> **NIGHT AFTER NIGHT (live)**	38	44

– Take you to the movies / Back it up / Keith don't go (ode to the Glimmer twin) / Like rain / Cry tough / It's not a crime / Goin' back / You're the weight / Beggars day / Moon tears / Code of the road / Rock and roll crook / Goin' south / Incidentally . . . it's over / I came to dance.

–––– now used mainly session people except TOM (on next only)

Jun 79. (lp/c) (AMLH/CAM 64756) <4756> **NILS**		54

– No mercy / I'll cry tomorrow / Baltimore / Shine silently / Steal away / Kool skool / A fool like me / I found her / You're so easy. (cd-iss. Jan97; 540 707-2)

Jul 79. (7") **NO MERCY. / KOOL SKOOL**	-	-
Jul 79. (7",7"colrd) (AMS 7455) **SHINE SILENTLY. / KOOL SKOOL**	-	-
Sep 79. (7") **SHINE SILENTLY. / BALTIMORE**	-	-
Oct 79. (7") (AMS 7486) **NO MERCY. / A FOOL LIKE ME**	-	-

	Backstreet-MCA	Backstreet
Sep 81. (lp/c) (MCF/+C 3121) <5251> **NIGHT FADES AWAY**	50	99

– Night fades away / I go to pieces / Empty heart / Don't touch me / Dirty money / Sailor boy / Anytime at all / Ancient history / Streets again / In motion. (re-iss. Feb84 on 'M.C.A.' lp/c; MCL/+C 1786)

Sep 81. (7") **NIGHT FADES AWAY. / ANCIENT HISTORY**	-	
Sep 81. (7"/12") (MCA/+T 749) **NIGHT FADES AWAY. / ANYTIME AT ALL**		-
Nov 81. (7") (MCA 757) **I GO TO PIECES. / ANCIENT HISTORY**		
Aug 83. (lp/c) (MCF/+C 3182) **WONDERLAND**		

– Across the tracks / Into the night / It's all over now / I wait for now / Daddy dream / Wonderland / Room without love / Confident girl / Lonesome ranger / Everybody wants / Deadline. (re-iss. Jun87 lp/c; MCL/+C 1851)

Oct 83. (7") (MCA 834) **ACROSS THE TRACKS. / DADDY DREAM**		

–––– Split his own band to join BRUCE SPRINGSTEEN & THE E-STREET SHUFFLE between 1984-1985. He returned to solo work, bringing back **NEWMARK + JONES** plus **TOMMY MANDELS + T. LAVITZ** – synthesizers

	Towerbell	Columbia
May 85. (7"/12") (TOW/+T 68) **SECRETS IN THE STREET. / FROM THE HEART**	53	

(d7"+=) (TOWG 68) – Message / Little bit of time.
(12"+=) (TOWRT 68) – ('A'extended).

Jun 85. (lp/c) (TOWLP/ZCTOW 11) <39982> **FLIP**	36	

– Flip ya flip / Secrets in the street / From the heart / Delivery night / King of the rock / Sweet midnight / New holes in old shoes / Dreams die hard / Big tears fall. (cd-iss. 1988; CDTOW 11) (re-iss. cd Dec92 on 'Castle'; CLACD 312)

Aug 85. (7"/ext.12") (TOW/+T 73) **FLIP YA FLIP. / NEW HOLES IN OLD SHOES**		-

(12"pic-d) (TOWTX 73) – ('A'extended) / Message (11 minute).

Aug 85. (7") **FLIP YA FLIP. / DELIVERY NIGHT**	-	
Nov 85. (7") (TOW 76) **DELIVERY NIGHT. / DREAMS DIE HARD**		

(12") (TOWT 76) – ('A'side) / Keith don't go (live).

–––– Live band = **JONES, TOM LOFGREN, STEWART SMITH, JOHNNY 'BEE' BADANJEK**

Mar 86. (d-lp/c) (TOWDLP/ZCTOWD 17) **CODE OF THE ROAD (live)**	86	

– Beggars day / Secrets in the street / Across the tracks / Delivery night / Cry tough / Dreams die hard / Believe / The sun hasn't set on this boy yet / Code of the road / Moon tears / Back it up / Like rain / Sweet midnight / No mercy / Anytime at all / New holes in old shoes / Keith don't go / Shine silently / I came to dance. (cd-iss. Dec92 on 'Castle'; CLACD 311)

Mar 86. (7") (TOW 86) **ANYTIME AT ALL (live). / NEW HOLES IN OLD SHOES (live)**		

–––– He decided to re-join BRUCE SPRINGSTEEN, mainly for stage work. Returned in '91 with main band **SCOTT THURSTON** – keyboards / **ANDY NEWMARK** – drums / **KEVIN McCORMICK** – bass, keyboards, percussion / + **LEVON HELM** – harmonica, vocals

	Essential	Rykodisc
May 91. (cd/c/lp) (ESS CD/MC/LP 145) <10170> **SILVER LINING**	61	Mar91

– Silver lining / Valentine / Walkin' nerve / Live each day / Sticks and stones / Trouble's back / Little bit of time / Bein' angry / Gun and run / Girl in motion. (cd re-iss. Apr96; same)

1991. (cd-s) **VALENTINE / ('A'-album version) / ('A'-original)**	-	
1991. (cd-s) **WALKIN' NERVE / KEITH DON'T GO**	-	
Jul 92. (cd/c/lp) (ESS CD/MC/LP 183) **CROOKED LINE**		

– A child could tell / Blue skies / Misery / You / Shot at you / Crooked line / Walk on me / Someday / New kind of freedom / Just a little / Drunken driver / I'll fight for you.

	Permanent	Permanent
Oct 94. (d-cd) <(PERMCD 28)> **EVERY BREATH (soundtrack)**		

(with free cd-s)
(above featured LOU GRAMM)

–––– next with **ANDY NEWMARK** – drums / **ROGER GREENAWALT** – bass, percussion, samples / **MICHAEL MATOUSEK** – production coordinator

	Essential	Rykodisc
Oct 95. (cd/c) (ESS CD/MC 337) **DAMAGED GOODS**		

– Damaged goods / Only five minutes / Alone / Trip to Mars / Here for you / Black books / Setting Sun / Life / Heavy hats / In the room / Nothin's fallin' / Don't be late for yesterday.

	Demon	Rykodisc
Aug 97. (cd) (FIENDCD 934) **ACOUSTIC LIVE (live)**		

– You / Sticks and stones / Some must dream / Little on up / Keith don't go / Wonderland / Big tears fall / Believe / Black books / To your heart / Man in the moon / I'll arise / Blue skies / Tears on ice / All out / Mud in your eye / No mercy.

– compilations, others, etc. –

on 'A&M' unless mentioned otherwise

Apr 82. (lp/c) (AMLH/CAM 68543) **A RHYTHM ROMANCE**	100	
Apr 82. (7") (AMS 8211) **SHINE SILENTLY. / KEITH DON'T GO (ODE TO THE GLIMMER TWIN)**		

Jun 85. (7") *(AM 262)* **SHINE SILENTLY. / I CAME TO DANCE** ☐ ☐
(12"+=) *(AMY 262)* – No mercy.

Jun 90. (cd/c/d-lp) *Connoisseur; (VSOP CD/MC/LP 152)* **THE BEST**
OF NILS LOFGREN – DON'T WALK . . . ROCK ☐ -
– Moon tears (live) / Back it up / Keith don't go (ode to the Glimmer twin) / The
sun hasn't set on this boy yet / Goin' back / Cry tough / Jailbait / Can't get closer
(WCGC) / Mud in your eye / I came to dance / To be a dreamer / No mercy / Steal
away / Baltimore / Shine silently / Secrets in the street / Flip ya flip / Delivery night /
Anytime at all (live).

Jun 94. (cd) *Windsong; (WHISCD 001)* **LIVE ON THE TEST** (live) ☐ -

May 95. (cd) *Spectrum; (5507502)* **SHINE SILENTLY** ☐ -

Jul 95. (cd) *Raven; (RVCD 44)* **SOFT FUN, TOUGH TEARS 1971-79** ☐ -

Mar 96. (d-cd) *(540 411-2)* **STEAL YOUR HEART AWAY (THE BEST**
OF NILS LOFGREN) ☐ -

Aug 97. (d-cd) *Snapper; (SMDCD 106)* **ACROSS THE TRACKS** ☐ -

LO-FIDELITY ALLSTARS

Formed: London, England . . . mid 90's by THE WREKKED TRAIN (aka
DAVE RANDALL), SHERIFF JOHN STONE (aka MATT), THE ALBINO
PRIEST (aka PHIL), THE SLAMMER (aka JOHNNY), A ONE MAN
CROWD CALLED GENTILEE (aka ANDY) and THE MANY TENTACLES
(aka MARTIN); DAVE and MATT were brought up in Sussex, while
JOHNNY and engineer MARTIN hail from Leeds. Having met while working
in Tower Records, PHIL and MATT found that they had similar tastes,
i.e. FUNKADELIC, BOOTSY COLLINS and late, great writer, CHARLES
BUKOWSKI. Signed to trendy Big Beat label, 'Skint', they debuted in 1997
with the 'KOOL ROC BASS' EP, the music press heralding them as leaders
of the new skool skunk-rock brigade that would also include The REGULAR
FRIES. As well as creating a bastard 90's fusion of HAPPY MONDAYS,
FLOWERED UP and trippy electro, these bands also shared a greasy haired,
dishevelled druggy image. Later the same year, they scored their first Top
50 entry with 'DISCO MACHINE GUN', followed by an even bigger
success (Top 30) with 'VISION INCISION', both lifted from their excellent
sampletastic Top 20 debut set, 'HOW TO OPERATE WITH A BLOWN
MIND' (1998); the record also featured a cover/collaboration of Pigeonhed's
'BATTLEFLAG', which became another hit single later in the year. By this
point, DAVE RANDALL had quit the show due to musical differences.

Album rating: HOW TO OPERATE WITH A BLOWN MIND (*8)

THE WREKKED TRAIN (aka DAVE RANDALL) – vocals / **THE ALBINO PRIEST** (aka
PHIL) – decks, samples / **A ONE MAN CROWD CALLED GENTILEE** (aka ANDY) –
bass / **THE SLAMMER** (aka JOHNNY) – drums / **SHERIFF JOHN STONE** (aka MATT) –
keyboards / plus **THE MANY TENTACLES** (aka MARTIN) – engineering, keyboards

	Skint	Sub Pop
Jun 97. (12"ep/cd-ep) *(skint 24/+cd)* **KOOL ROC BASS EP**	☐	-
(re-iss. Jun98; same) ('A' mixes) / One man's fear / Taking fear from behind.		
Sep 97. (12"ep/cd-ep) *(skint 30/+cd)* **DISCO MACHINE GUN EP**	50	-
– (mixes; radio / original / II) / Puppy Phat Number One.		
(withdrawn after 3 days due to a sample of The BREEDERS 'Cannonball')		
Apr 98. (12"ep/cd-ep) *(skint 33/+cd)* **VISION INCISION EP**	30	-
– (mixes; radio / 12 inch) / Midfield General shorter / Gringo's return.		
(12"ep) *(skint 33x)* – ('A'remixes).		
Apr 98. (cd/c/d-lp) *(brassic 8 cd/mc/lp) <69654>* **HOW TO OPERATE**		
WITH A BLOWN MIND	15	May98
– Warming up the brain farm / Kool roc bass / Kasparov's revenge / Blisters on my		
brain / How to operate with a blown mind / I used to fall in love / Battleflag (feat.		
Pigeonhed) / Lazer sheep dip funk / Will I get out of jail / Vision incision / Nightime		
story.		
Nov 98. (12"/cd-s; featuring PIGEONHED) *(SKINT 38/+CD) <41551>*		
BATTLEFLAG / PONY PRESSURE / BONUS BEATS	36	
(cd-s) *(SKINT 38XCD)* – ('A'edit) / ('A'-Space Raiders mix) / ('A'live).		

—— (Dec'98) DAVE RANDALL left the band

LONE JUSTICE (see under ⇒ McKEE, Maria)

LONE STAR (dig out; Great Alt & Indie . . .)

LONGPIGS

Formed: Sheffield, England . . . 1993 by mainman, CRISPIN HUNT,
RICHARD HAWLEY, SIMON STAFFORD and DEE BOYLE. The band's
career got off to a less than encouraging start when a car crash left CRISPIN in
a coma, their problems compounded when a deal with the UK arm of 'Elektra'
went awry; they were effectively prevented from recording and playing live
for two years, that is, until lawyer, John Stratham, bailed them out. With
an album's worth of previously recorded, GIL NORTON-produced material
in limbo, LONGPIGS eventually secured a new contract with 'Mother', re-
recording their debut and soon breaking into the UK Top 75 with their second
single, 'SHE SAID'. Finally released in the Spring of '96, 'THE SUN IS
OFTEN OUT' spawned a handful of classy hit singles ('FAR', 'ON & ON',
a re-issued 'SHE SAID' – Top 20 and 'LOST MYSELF') calling to mind
the heady swagger of SUEDE, AUTEURS and occasionally the dark majesty
of RADIOHEAD. Why it took three and a half years for a follow-up was
anybody's guess. A disastrous American tour which resulted in plenty of fights
between HUNT and DEE BOYLE (who had allegedly found God) might have
been to blame – the latter was unceremoniously ousted from the band early

in '99 while a single 'SWIM' failed to materialise. That "difficult" second
album, 'MOBILE HOME', finally hit the shops and the UK Top 40 in October
'99, The LONGPIGS were at long last getting back to work. However, just as
things took an upturn, the bitter BOYLE was reported to have stuck a glass
into HUNT's face after they bumped into each other at a PRETENDERS gig;
the frontman received six stitches.

Album rating: THE SUN IS OFTEN OUT (*7) / MOBILE HOME (*7)

CRISPIN HUNT – vocals, guitar / **RICHARD HAWLEY** – guitar, vocals / **SIMON STAFFORD**
– bass, piano / **DEE BOYLE** – drums, vocals (ex-CHAKK)

	Mother	Polygram
Mar 95. (7") *(MUM 63)* **HAPPY AGAIN. / SALLY DANCES**	☐	-
Jul 95. (7"/c-s) *(MUM/+C 66)* **SHE SAID. / TAKE IT ALL**	67	-
(cd-s+=) *(MUMCD 66)* – Devoted / Juicy.		
Oct 95. (7"red/c-s) *(MUM/+C 68)* **JESUS CHRIST. / SWEETNESS**	61	-
(cd-s+=) *(MUMCD 68)* – Vagina song / Whiteness.		
Feb 96. (7"/c-s) *(MUM/+C 71)* **FAR. / BLAH BLAH BLAH**	37	-
(cd-s+=) *(MUMCD 71)* – Amateur dramatics / Far (Sheffield version).		
Apr 96. (7"ep/c-ep/cd-ep) *(MUM/+C/CD 74) <569238>* **ON & ON /**		
YOUR FACE. / DOZEN WICKED WORDS / SLEEP	16	Jan97
May 96. (cd/c/lp) *(MUM CD/MC/LP 9602) <531542>* **THE SUN IS**		
OFTEN OUT	26	☐
– Lost myself / She said / Far / On and on / Happy again / All hype / Sally dances /		
Jesus Christ / Dozen wicked words / Elvis / Over our bodies.		
Jun 96. (7") *(MUM 77)* **SHE SAID. / FLARE IS METEOR**	16	-
(c-s+=/cd-s+=) *(MUM C/CD 77)* – Soap opera credo / Tendresse.		
(cd-s) *(MUMXD 77)* – ('A'side) / I lost myself / Far / On and on.		
Sep 96. (7"/c-s) *(MUM/+C 82)* **LOST MYSELF. / FLOSS**	22	-
(cd-s+=) *(MUMCD 82)* – Wonder drug / When you're alone.		
Mar 97. (7"/c-s/cd-s) *(MUM/+C/CD 90)* **SWIM**	☐	-
(above could well have been withdrawn)		
Sep 99. (7") *(MUM 113)* **BLUE SKIES. / HEADACHES**	21	-
(cd-s+=) *(MUMCD 113)* – Seventies just passing over.		
(cd-s) *(MUMXD 113)* – ('A'side) / I love you / On and on.		
Oct 99. (cd/c) *(MUM CD/C 9901)* **MOBILE HOME**	33	-
– The Frank sonata / Blue skies / Gangsters / Free toy / Baby blue / Dance baby		
dance / Miss believer / I lied I love you / Keep the light alight / Speech bubble / Dog		
is dead / Loud and clear / In the snow.		
Nov 99. (7") *(MUM 114)* **THE FRANK SONATA. / AS A GIRL**	57	-
(cd-s+=) *(MUMCD 114)* – New York.		
(cd-s) *(MUMXD 114)* – ('A'side) / ('A'-Echoboy remix) / ('A'-My Way remix).		

LONG RYDERS

Formed: Paisley, Los Angeles, California, USA . . . March '82, out of
The UNCLAIMED by SID GRIFFIN, BARRY SKANK, MATT ROBERTS
and STEVE WYNN. The latter soon formed his own band, The DREAM
SYNDICATE and was superseded by STEPHEN McCARTHY. This revised
line-up made an EP for 'Moxie', which included the tracks, 'Time to Time'
and 'Deposition Central'. As The LONG RYDERS (named so after the Walter
Hill film, 'The Long Riders'), they issued a debut album, '10-5-60' (a mini-
set), on their own 'Jem' label, a distinctive hybrid of jagged garage rock,
psychedelia and country. While the band were lumped in with their mates
under the catch-all term, "Paisley Underground", The LONG RYDERS always
wore their country influences more proudly. 'NATIVE SONS' (1984), their
debut for 'Zippo', marked the fruition of that experimentation, a finely hewn
tapestry of alternative country which featured GENE CLARK on the keening
'IVORY TOWER'. Heralded by the critics, the band signed to 'Island' in 1985
and recorded a further two albums, 'STATE OF OUR UNION' (1985) and
'TWO FISTED TALES' (1987). More overtly country and lyrically politically
pointed than their previous efforts, the latter proved to be the band's swansong
and they split the following year. SID GRIFFIN subsequently relocated to
London where he concentrated on his band The COAL PORTERS. The man
has also helped to keep the 'Cosmic American Music' flame burning by
penning a GRAM PARSONS biog and he continues to write for various music
mags. • **Songwriters:** GRIFFIN-McCARTHY compositions, except YOU'RE
GONNA MISS ME (13th Floor Elevators) / I SHALL BE RELEASED +
MASTERS OF WAR (Bob Dylan) / DIRTY OLD TOWN (Ewan MacColl) /
PRISONERS OF ROCK'N'ROLL (Neil Young) / ANARCHY IN THE
UK (Sex Pistols) / PUBLIC IMAGE (P.I.L. w/ STEVE MACK of THAT
PETROL EMOTION on vox). • **Trivia:** Will Birch produced them in 1985.
SID, STEPHEN + TOM featured on 'Zippo' lp THE LOST WEEKEND by
DANNY & DUSTY. They also guested on DREAM SYNDICATE album
'Medicine Show'.

Album rating: 10-5-60 (*6) / NATIVE SONS (*8) / STATE OF OUR UNION (*7) /
TWO-FISTED TALES (*5) / METALLIC B.O. early stuff (*4)

SID GRIFFIN (b.18 Sep'55, Louisville, Kentucky) – vocals, guitar / **STEPHEN McCARTHY**
(b.12 Feb'58, Richmond, Virginia) – steel guitar, vocals; repl. STEVE WYNN (to
DREAM SYNDICATE) / **DES BREWER** – bass; repl. BARRY SKANK / **MATT ROBERTS**
– drums

	not iss.	P.V.C.
1983. (m-lp) *<PVC 5906>* **10-5-60**	-	☐
– Join my gang / I don't care what's right, I don't care what's wrong / 105-60 / And		
she rides / Born to believe in you. *(UK-iss.1985 on 'P.V.C.'; PVC 50) (re-iss. Nov85*		
on 'Zippo'+=; ZANE 004) – The trip. *(cd-iss. Aug87 on 'Zippo'; CMCAD 31038)*		

—— **TOM STEVENS** (b.17 Sep'56, Elkhart, Indiana) – drums repl. DON McCALL who
had repl. DES BREWER

—— **GREG SOWDERS** (b.17 Mar'60, La Jolla, Calif.) – drums, repl. ROBERTS

Nov 84. (lp) (ZONG 004) <4606-1> **NATIVE SONS** [Zippo] [Frontier 1983]
– Final wild sun / Still by / Ivory tower / Run Dusty run / (Sweet) Metal revenge / Fair game / Tell it to the judge on Sunday / Too close to the light / Wreck of the 809 / Never get to meet the man / I had a dream. (cd-iss. Jan88; ZONGCD 003) – (w/ last m-lp tracks).

Apr 85. (7") (ZIPPO 45-2) **I HAD A DREAM. / TOO CLOSE TO THE LIGHT** (Buckskin mix)

Sep 85. (7") (IS 237) **LOOKING FOR LEWIS & CLARK. / CHILD BRIDE** [Island 59] [Island]
(d7"+=/10"+=) (ISD/10IS 237) – Southside of the story / If I were a bramble and you were a rose.

Oct 85. (lp/c) (ILPS/ICT 9802) <422842863-1> **STATE OF OUR UNION** [66]
– Looking for Lewis & Clark / Lights of downtown / WDIA / Mason-Dixon line / Here comes that train again / Years long ago / Good times tomorrow, hard times today / Two kinds of love / You just can't ride the boxcars anymore / Capturing the flag / State of my union. (cd-iss. Mar95 on 'Prima'+=) – If I were a bramble and you were a rose / Southside of the story / Child bride / Christmas in New Zealand.

Jun 87. (lp/c/cd) (ILPS/ICT/CID 9869) <422842864-1> **TWO FISTED TALES**
– Gunslinger man / I want you bad / A stitch in time / The light gets in the way / Prairie fire / Baby's in toyland / Long short story / Man of misery / Harriet Tubman's gonna carry me home / For the rest of my life / Spectacular fall. (cd re-iss. cd Mar96 on 'Prima'+=; SID 005) – Ring bells / Time keeps travelling / State of our union (live) / Baby we've all got to go down (live).

Jun 87. (7") (IS 330) **I WANT YOU BAD. / RING BELLS**
(12"+=) (12IS 330) – State of our union.

—— They split New Year '88. In Spring '90, GRIFFIN formed country-rock band The COAL PORTERS, who released first album 'REBELS WITHOUT APPLAUSE' in 1992. McCARTHY later appeared in GUTTERBALL with STEVE WYNN. GRIFFIN released a solo album in 1997.

– compilations, others, etc. –

Jan 91. (cd) Overground; (OVER 16CD) **METALLIC B.O.** (covers) [-]
– You're gonna miss me / Route 66 / Brand new headache / Prisoners of rock'n'roll / Dirty old town / Billy Jean / Circle round the sun / Six days on the road / Anarchy in the U.K. / Masters of war / Sandwich man / Blues theme / P.I.L. theme / I shall be released. (re-iss. Dec94; same)

May 94. (cd) Windsong; (WINCD 058) **BBC RADIO 1 LIVE IN CONCERT** (live) [-]

COAL PORTERS

GRIFFIN w / **ST.JOHN + McGARVEY**

Aug 92. (cd) <(RUB 17)> **REBELS WITHOUT APPLAUSE** [Rubber] [Rubber]
– Roll Columbia roll / I tell her all the time / The light that shines within / Rhythm and blues angel / Stealin' horses / Sittin' in an isle of palms (live). (UK+=) – Stuck on an island / John F. Kennedy blues (live) / March of the tap-dancing rats.

Sep 94. (cd) <(SID 002)> **THE LAND OF HOPE AND CROSBY** [Prima] [Prima]
– Imperial beach / Death like a valentine / She loved me / What am I doing? (in this thing called love) / How did we get this far? / You can see them there / Windy city / Playing dumb £1 / Everybody's fault but mine / What about tomorrow / All the colours of the world / The pipsqueaks theme.

Sep 95. (cd) <(SID 004)> **LOS LONDON**
– Me, here at the door / Crackin' at the seams / Chasing rainbows / A woman to love / Apple tree / It happened to me / Santa Mira / After it's broken / A Jacobite at heart / Someone's gonna love you too / Help me / Ain't no way I'll be your cowboy.

Mar 99. (cd) <(SID 010)> **THE GRAM PARSONS TRIBUTE CONCERT** (live)
– Luxury liner / Hickory wind / One hundred years from now / Drug store truck driving man / Sweet mental revenge / Sin city / Return of the grevious angel / Wheels / In my hour of darkness / Older guys / Hot burrito #2 / Six days on the road / Apple tree.

SID GRIFFIN

May 97. (cd) <(SID 007)> **LITTLE VICTORIES**
– When I'm out walking with you / Jimmy Reed / Good times tomorrow, hard times today / Rate of exchange / I wish I was a mountain / Distant trains / Sailors and soldiers / Man who invented the blues / Monk's moods / Flak jacket / Alma mater / Jerusalem road.

LOOP / MAIN (dig out; Great Alt & Indie . . .)

LOOPER (see under ⇒ BELLE & SEBASTIAN)

LOVE

Formed: Los Angeles, California, USA . . . early '65 originally as The GRASS ROOTS, by ARTHUR LEE and former BYRDS roadie BRYAN MacLEAN. The contrasting songwriters recruited JOHN ECHOLS, KEN FORSSI and DON CONKA (the latter being replaced by SNOOPY PFISTERER). When another band of the same name made the US charts, they became LOVE, soon signing to Jac Holzman's 'Elektra' records. In 1966, they released a snarling cover of Burt Bacharach's 'MY LITTLE RED BOOK', nearly breaking it into the US Top 50. With The LEAVES beating them to the US Top 40 on a cover of 'HEY JOE', LOVE opted instead for a British release, although it failed to chart. Soon after, an eponymous album hit the shops, a fairly competent folk-rock set that nevertheless contained the classics, 'SIGNED D.C.', 'CAN'T EXPLAIN' and the two singles. Around

the same time, the band scored their only Top 40 success with the galloping HENDRIX-like psych-out of '7 AND 7 IS'. Early in 1967, they followed up with the classic, 'DA CAPO' album, containing the ambitious 20-minute 'REVELATION' alongside such timeless jewels, 'ORANGE SKIES', 'SHE COMES IN COLORS', 'STEPHANIE KNOWS WHO', 'THE CASTLE' and the previous 45. Shacked-up in LEE's Hollywood mansion, the band eventually emerged with 'FOREVER CHANGES', often cited as one of the greatest albums of all-time. A psychedelic tour de force, it combined acoustic musings, Latin rhythms and the eerily surreal LEE-penned lyrics. Almost every track was flawless and it remains one of rock's great mysteries why the album's two singles, 'ALONE AGAIN OR' and 'ANDMOREAGAIN', failed to chart. Equally baffling was the fact that the album only made the highest position of No.154, while in Britain it hit the Top 30. The band recorded a further brilliant single, 'YOUR MIND AND WE BELONG TOGETHER', before LEE sacked the rest of the group "cause they couldn't cut it". He subsequently formed a "new" LOVE with JAY DONELLAN, JIM HOBSON, FRANK FAYAD, GEORGE SURANOVICH and some additional members. This line-up cut a fourth album, the disappointing 'FOUR SAIL', following it up with two others in the early 70's, 'OUT HERE' and 'FALSE START'. Eventually LEE was again left on his own, leading him to carve out a solo career, the album 'VINDICATOR' (1972) being released to a lukewarm reception. He re-created yet another LOVE in 1974, fans again bitterly disappointed with a commercial set that even unadvisedly touched on disco! After various other re-unions in the late 70's, LEE released a self-titled solo effort in 1981, before going AWOL again. In the early 90's, with renewed LOVE interest, LEE re-formed the group for a re-union album, 'ARTHUR LEE AND LOVE'. The current decade hasn't exactly been kind to this revered eccentric, LEE being diagnosed with Parkinson's Disease and, more recently, receiving a 12-year sentence for firearms offences. His former partner, born-again Christian MacLEAN (who had virtually retired in 1970, although he did pen songs for his half-sister MARIA McKEE and country-star PATTY LOVELESS) tragically died of a suspected heart attack on Christmas Day, 1998. • **Trivia:** In 1970, LEE was about to initiate a supergroup, BAND AID (not the charity) with STEVE WINWOOD and HENDRIX, but JIMI died on September '70. In 1973, he recorded an album, 'BLACK BEAUTY' for 'Buffalo' records. This was shelved, although illegal bootlegs did surface.

Album rating: LOVE (*6) / DA CAPO (*8) / FOREVER CHANGES (*10) / FOUR SAIL (*6) / OUT HERE (*4) / FALSE START (*4) / REEL TO REAL (*4) / LOVE LIVE (*4) / ARTHUR LEE AND LOVE (*4) / COMES IN COLOURS compilation (*8) / LOVE STORY 1966-1972 compilation (*8)

ARTHUR LEE (b. ARTHUR TAYLOR PORTER, 1945, Memphis, Tennessee) – vocals, guitar (ex-LAG'S, ex-AMERICAN FOUR) / **BRYAN MacLEAN** (b.1947) – guitar, vocals / **JOHN ECHOLS** (b.1945, Memphis) – lead guitar (ex-LAG'S) / **KEN FORSSI** (b.1943, Cleveland, Ohio) – bass (ex-SURFARIS) / **ALBAN 'SNOOPY' PFISTERER** (b.1947, Switzerland) – drums repl. DON CONKA

[London] [Elektra]
Mar 66. (7") <45603> **MY LITTLE RED BOOK. / A MESSAGE TO PRETTY** [-] [52]
Jun 66. (7") (HLZ 10053) **HEY JOE. / MY LITTLE RED BOOK** [-]
Sep 66. (7") (HLZ 10073) <45605> **7 AND 7 IS. / NO. FOURTEEN** [33 Aug66]
[Elektra] [Elektra]
Sep 66. (lp; mono/stereo) <(EKL/EKS 7-4001)> **LOVE** [57 Jul66]
– My little red book / A message to Pretty / Softly to me / Emotions / Gazing / Signed D.C. / Mushroom clouds / Can't explain / My flash on you / No matter what you do / You'll be following / Hey Joe / Coloured bells falling / And more. (re-iss. Jan72 lp/c; K/K4 42068) (re-iss. Feb87 on 'Edsel'; ED 218) (cd-iss. Feb93 & Dec93; 755974001-2)

—— added **MICHAEL STUART** – drums (ex-SONS OF ADAM) ('SNOOPY' now on keyboards) + **TJAY CANTRELLI** – saxophone

Dec 66. (7") (EKSN 45010) <45608> **SHE COMES IN COLOURS. / ORANGE SKIES**
Feb 67. (lp; mono/stereo) <(EKL/EKS 7-4005)> **DA CAPO** [80]
– Stephanie knows who / Orange skies / Que vida / 7 and 7 is / The castle / She comes in colors / Revelation. (re-iss. Jan72 lp/c; K/K4 42011) (cd-iss. 1989 on 'WEA'; 974005-2)

Mar 67. (7") <45613> **QUE VIDA (edit). / HEY JOE** [-]
Sep 67. (7") (EKSN 45016) **THE CASTLE. / SOFTLY TO ME** [-] [-]

—— Reverted to a quintet when 'SNOOPY' and TJAY left. (latter to DOMINIC TROIANO)

Jan 68. (7") <45629> **ALONE AGAIN OR (edit). / A HOUSE IS NOT A MOTEL** [-]
Jan 68. (7") (EKSN 45024) **ALONE AGAIN OR. / BUMMER IN THE SUMMER** [-]
(re-iss. Oct70; 2101-019)
Feb 68. (lp; mono/stereo) <(EKL/EKS 7-4013)> **FOREVER CHANGES** [24] [Jan68]
– Alone again or / A house is not a motel / Andmoreagain / The daily planet / Old man / The red telephone / Maybe the people would be the times or between Clark and Hilldale / Live and let live / Good honor man he sees everything like this / Bummer in the summer / You set the scene. (re-iss. Jan72 lp/c; K/K4 42015) (cd-iss. Jul88 on 'WEA'; 7559 60656-2)

Mar 68. (7") (EKSN 45024) **ANDMOREAGAIN. / THE DAILY PLANET** [-]
Sep 68. (7") (EKSN 45038) <45633> **YOUR MIND AND WE BELONG TOGETHER. / LAUGHING STOCK**

—— ARTHUR LEE dismissed others and recruited new people below **JAY DONELLAN** (LEWIS) – guitar / **JIM HOBSON** – keyboards / **FRANK FAYAD** – bass / **GEORGE SURANOVICH** – drums

—— augmented by **PAUL MARTIN** and **GARY ROWLES** – guitar plus **DRACKEN THEAKER** – keyboards (ex-CRAZY WORLD OF ARTHUR BROWN)

Nov 69. (lp) <(EKS 74049)> **FOUR SAIL** [Sep69]
– August / Your friend and mine – Neil's song / I'm with you / Good times / Singing cowboy / Dream / Robert Montgomery / Nothing / Talking in my sleep / Always see

your face. (re-iss. Jan72 lp/c; K/K4 42030) (re-iss. Nov87 on 'Thunderbolt'; THBL 047) (cd-iss. Jun88; CDBT 047)

		Harvest	Blue Thumb
Mar 70.	(7") (EKSN 45086) **I'M WITH YOU. / ROBERT MONTGOMERY**	☐	- ☐

May 70. (d-lp) (SHDW 3-4) <BTS 9000> **OUT HERE** 　[29] ☐Dec69
– I'll pray for you / Abalony / Signed D.C. / Listen to my song / I'm down / Stand out / Discharged / Doggone / I still wonder / Love is more than words or better late than never / Nice to be / Car lights on in the day time blues / Run to the top / Willow willow / Instra-mental / You are something / Gather round. (re-iss. Jul88 on 'Big Beat' lp; WIKA 69) (cd-iss. Jul90; CDWIKA 69)
May 70. (7") <BLU-7 106> **I'LL PRAY FOR YOU. / STAND OUT** 　- ☐ ☐
Nov 70. (7") (HAR 5030) <BLU-7 116> **KEEP ON SHINING. / THE EVERLASTING FIRST** 　☐ ☐

── **GARY ROWLES** now full time , repl. JAY
Jan 71. (lp) (SHVL 787) <BTS 8822> **FALSE START** 　☐ ☐Dec 70
– The everlasting first / Flying / Gimi a little break / Stand out / Keep on shining / Anytime / Slick Dick / Love is coming / Feel daddy feel good / Ride that vibration. (cd-iss. Jul92 on 'Beat Goes On'; BGOCD 127) (cd re-iss. Apr94 on 'One Way'; MCAD 22029)
Mar 71. (7") (HAR 5014) **STAND OUT. / DOGGONE** 　☐ - ☐

ARTHUR LEE

── a solo venture with BAND AID: **FAYAD** and new men **CHARLES KARP** – guitar / **CRAIG TARWATER** – guitar / **CLARENCE McDONALD** – keyboards / **DON PONCHA** – drums / + guest **DAVID HULL** – bass

		A&M	A&M

Aug 72. (lp) (AMLS 64356) <SP 4356> **VINDICATOR**
– Sad song / You can save up to 50% / Love jumped through my window / Find somebody / He said she said / Everytime I look up / Everybody's gotta live / He knows a lot of good women / You want change for your re-run / Hamburger breath stinkfinger / Ol' morgue mouth / Busted feet. (cd-iss. Apr97; 540697-2)
Aug 72. (7") <1361> **EVERYBODY'S GOT TO LIVE. / LOVE JUMPED THROUGH MY WINDOW** 　- ☐ ☐
Nov 72. (7") <1381> **SAD SONG. / YOU WANT TO CHANGE FOR YOUR RE-RUN** 　- ☐ ☐

LOVE

── ARTHUR LEE recruited **MELVIN WHITTINGTON** + **JOHN STERLING** – guitar / **SHERWOOD AKUNA** + **ROBERT ROZENO** – bass / **JOE BLOCKER** – drums

		R.S.O.	R.S.O.

Dec 74. (7") <SO 502> **TIME IS LIKE A RIVER. / WITH A LITTLE ENERGY** 　- ☐ ☐
Jan 75. (7") (2090 151) **TIME IS LIKE A RIVER. / YOU SAID YOU WOULD** 　☐ - ☐
Jan 75. (lp) (2394 145) <SO 4804> **REEL TO REAL**
– Time is like a river / Stop the music / Who are you? / Good old fashioned love / Which witch is which / With a little energy / Singing cowboy / Be thankful for what you got / You said you would / Busted feet / Everybody's gotta live.
Mar 75. (7") <SO 506> **YOU SAID YOU WOULD. / GOOD OLD FASHIONED DREAM** 　☐ - ☐

ARTHUR LEE

── solo again, using loads of session people

		Da Capo	not iss.

1977. (7"ep) (CAP 001) **I DO WONDER / JUST US. / DO YOU KNOW THE SECRET? / HAPPY YOU** 　☐ - ☐

		Beggars Banquet	Rhino

Jul 81. (lp) (BEGA 26) <RNLP 020> **ARTHUR LEE**
– One / I do wonder / Just us / Happy you / Do you know the secret / One and one / Seven and seven is / Mr. Lee / Bend down / Stay away from evil / Many rivers to cross.
── LOVE re-formed in Autumn '91, with **ARTHUR LEE, DON CONKA, SHUGGIE OTIS** – guitar / **MELLAN WHITTINGTON** – guitar / **SHERWOOD AKUNA** – bass

		New Rose	not iss.

May 92. (cd/lp) (ROSE CD/LP 288) **ARTHUR LEE AND LOVE** 　☐ - ☐
(re-iss. May94; 422214)
── ARTHUR was diagnosed with Parkinson's Disease in the early 90's (see biog above)

– LOVE compilations etc. –

on 'Elektra' unless mentioned otherwise
Aug 70. (7") <45700> **ALONE AGAIN OR. / GOOD TIMES** 　- ☐ [99]
Dec 70. (lp) (2469 009) <EKS 74049> **LOVE REVISITED** 　☐ ☐Aug70
(re-iss. Jan72 lp/c; K/K4 42091)
Feb 73. (lp/c) (K/K4 32002) **LOVE MASTERS** 　☐ - ☐
– My little red book / Signed D.C. / Hey Joe / 7 and 7 is / Stephanie knows who / Orange skies / Que vida / The castle / She comes in colours / Laughing stock / Your mind / And we belong together / Old man / The Daily Planet / A house is not a motel / Andmoreagain / Alone again or.
Jul 73. (7") (K 12113) **ALONE AGAIN OR. / ANDMOREAGAIN** 　☐ - ☐
(re-iss. Apr84; E 9740)
Sep 76. (7") (K 12231) **ALONE AGAIN OR. / THE CASTLE** 　☐ ☐
1980. (lp) Rhino; <RNLP 800> **THE BEST OF LOVE** 　- ☐
1981. (pic-lp) Rhino; <RNDF 251> **LOVE LIVE (live)** 　- ☐
1982. (lp) M.C.A.; <27025> **STUDIO / LIVE** 　- ☐
(UK cd-iss. Apr94 on 'One Way'; MCAD 22036)
1986. (lp) Rhino; <RNLP 70175> **GOLDEN ARCHIVE** 　- ☐
Jan 93. (cd) Raven; (RVCD 29) **COMES IN COLOURS** 　☐ - ☐
– My little red book / Can't explain / Message to pretty / Softly to me / Hey Joe / Signed D.C. / And more / 7 and 7 is / No.14 / Stephanie knows who / Orange skies /

Que vida / The castle / She comes in colors / Alone again or / Andmoreagain / Old man / A house is not a motel / Daily planet / Live and let live / Laughing stock / Your mind and we belong together / August / (Arthur Lee interview).

LOVE AND ROCKETS (see under ⇒ BAUHAUS)

LOVE / HATE (dig out; Great Metal . . .)

LOVERBOY (dig out; Great Alt & Indie . . .)

LOVE SCULPTURE (see under ⇒ EDMUNDS, DAVE)

LOVE SPIT LOVE (see under ⇒ PSYCHEDELIC FURS)

LOVIN' SPOONFUL

Formed: Greenwich Village, New York, USA ... early '65 by JOHN SEBASTIAN and ZAL YANOVSKY. They had been part of the N.Y. folk scene during '63-'64 and had played in bands The HALIFAX THREE and The MUGWUMPS, the latter featuring DENNY DOHERTY and CASS ELLIOT (future MAMAS & THE PAPAS). Via producer ERIK JACOBSEN, they secured a deal with the 'Kama Sutra' label, issuing debut 45, 'DO YOU BELIEVE IN MAGIC', which hit the US Top 10. A string of hits followed, including a 1966 US No.1, 'SUMMER IN THE CITY'. Its jaunty momentum was preceded by the meandering 'DAYDREAM', a No.2 on both sides of the Atlantic and the perfect soundtrack for "rolling a fat one" on a lazy midsummer's afternoon. Unfortunately for the band and especially YANOVSKY, the LOVIN' SPOONFUL had a renowned penchant for doing just that, amid other more serious narcotic dabblings. After a bust, he was allegedly sent packing by the rest of the band in 1967 for informing on his dealer. The next album, 'EVERYTHING PLAYING', lacked the effervescent sparkle of their previous material and stiffed big style. With nary a hit single in sight, the band struggled on with, ironically, YANOVSKY replacing the recently departed SEBASTIAN for a final lacklustre album. While the band's vaguely psychedelic pop was fine in 1966, by the following year's 'Summer of love' the 'SPOONFUL's happy go lucky ditties appeared a bit lukewarm in contrast to the cosmic soul searching of many other bands, especially their L.A. counterparts THE BYRDS and LOVE. Nevertheless, their jug-band pop/rock still has the power to put a smile on the glummest of faces and as well as the hits there were more than a few sweetly charming tracks like 'DARLIN' COMPANION' tucked away on their albums. SEBASTION was the only member to have any kind of solo success although the band regrouped fleetingly in 1980 for a guest appearance on Paul Simon's 'One Trick Pony'. • **Songwriters:** SEBASTIAN (with some traditional arrangements of 30's songs) until his departure when BUTLER was virtually going solo under LOVIN' SPOONFUL banner, although using pensmiths BONNER and GORDON. Covered; YOU BABY (Ronettes) / OTHER SIDE OF THIS LIFE (Fred Neil) / ALMOST GROWN (Chuck Berry) / SEARCHIN' (Coasters) / NEVER GOING BACK (John Stewart) / etc.

Album rating: DO YOU BELIEVE IN MAGIC (*7) / DAYDREAM (*6) / WHAT'S UP, TIGER LILY? soundtrack (*4) / HUMS OF THE LOVIN' SPOONFUL (*7) / THE BEST OF THE LOVIN' SPOONFUL compilation (*8) / YOU'RE A BIG BOY NOW (*5) / EVERYTHING PLAYING (*5) / REVELATION: REVOLUTION '69 (*3) / ANTHOLOGY compilation (*8)

JOHN SEBASTIAN (b.17 Mar'44, New York City, N.Y.) – vocals, guitar, harmonica, autoharp / **ZALMAN YANOVSKY** (b.19 Dec'44, Toronto, Canada) – guitar, vocals / **STEVE BOONE** (b.23 Sep'43, Camp Lejeune, New Connecticut) – bass, vocals / **JOE BUTLER** (b.16 Sep'43, Long Island, N.Y.) – drums, vocals

		Pye Inter	Kama Sutra
Oct 65.	(7") (7N 25327) <201> **DO YOU BELIEVE IN MAGIC. / ON THE ROAD AGAIN**	☐	[9] Jul65
Jan 66.	(7") (7N 25344) <205> **YOU DIDN'T HAVE TO BE SO NICE. / MY GAL**	☐	[10] Nov65
Mar 66.	(lp; mono/stereo) (NPL 28069) <KLP/+S 8050> **DO YOU BELIEVE IN MAGIC**	☐	[32] Nov65

– Do you believe in magic / Blues in the bottle / Sportin' life / My gal / You baby / Fishin' blues / Did you ever have to make up your mind / Wild about my lovin' / Other side of this life / Younger girl / On the road again / Night owl blues.
| Apr 66. | (7") (7N 25361) <208> **DAYDREAM. / NIGHT OWL BLUES** | [2] | [2] Feb66 |
| May 66. | (lp; mono/stereo) (NPL 28078) <KLP/+S 8051> **DAYDREAM** | [8] | [10] Mar66 |

– Daydream / There she is / It's not time now / Warm baby / Day blues / Let the boy rock and roll / Jug band music / Didn't want to have to do it / You didn't have to be so nice / Bald headed Lena / Butchie's tune / Big noise from Speonk. (re-iss. 1990 on 'Castle' lp/cd; CLA/+CD 194)
| May 66. | (7") <209> **DID YOU EVER HAVE TO MAKE UP YOUR MIND. / DIDN'T WANT TO HAVE TO DO IT** | - ☐ | [2] |

		Kama Sutra	Kama Sutra
Jul 66.	(7") <211> **SUMMER IN THE CITY. / BUTCHIE'S TUNE**	- ☐	[1]
Jul 66.	(7") (KAS 200) **SUMMER IN THE CITY. / BALD HEADED LENA**	[8]	- ☐
Sep 66.	(lp; mono/stereo) <KLP/+S 8053> **WHAT'S UP, TIGER LILY (Soundtrack)**	- ☐	☐

– (introduction to Flick) / POW / Gray prison blues / POW revisited / Unconscious minuet / Fishin' blues / Respoken / A cool million / Speakin' of spoken / Lookin' to spy / Phil's love theme / (end title).
Oct 66.	(7") <216> **RAIN ON THE ROOF. / POW**	- ☐	[10]
Oct 66.	(7") (KAS 201) **RAIN ON THE ROOF. / WARM BABY**	[8]	- ☐
Dec 66.	(lp; mono/stereo) (KLP 401) <KLP/+S 8054> **HUMS OF THE LOVIN' SPOONFUL**	☐	[14] Nov66

– Sittin' here lovin' you / Bes' friends / Voodoo in the basement / Darlin' companion / Henry Thomas / Full measure / Rain on the roof / Coconut grove / Nashville cats / 4 eyes / Summer in the city. *(re-iss. 1990 on 'Castle' lp/cd; CLA/+CD 195)*

Dec 66. (7") *(KAS 204) <219>* **NASHVILLE CATS. / FULL MEASURE** — `26` | `8` `87`

Feb 67. (7") *(KAS 207) <220>* **DARLING BE HOME SOON. / DARLIN' COMPANION** — `44` | `15`

Apr 67. (7") *<225>* **SIX O'CLOCK. / YOU'RE A BIG BOY NOW** — `-` | `18`

May 67. (lp; mono/stereo) *(KLP 402) <KLP/+S 8058>* **YOU'RE A BIG BOY NOW (Soundtrack)** — | Apr67
– You're a big boy now / Lonely (Amy's theme) / Wash her away / Kite chase / Try and be happy / Peep show percussion / Girl, beautiful girl / Darling be home soon / Dixieland big boy / Letter to Barbara / Barbara's theme / Miss Thing's thang / March / The finale.

May 67. (lp; mono/stereo) *(KLP 403) <KLP/+S 8056>* **THE BEST OF THE LOVIN' SPOONFUL (compilation)** — `3` Mar67
– Do you believe in magic / Did you ever have to make up your mind / Butchie's tune / Jug band music / Night owl blues / You didn't have to be so nice / Daydream / Blues in the bottle / Didn't want to have to do it / Wild about my lovin' / Younger girl / Summer in the city. *(re-iss. Mar69 on 'Marble Arch'; MAL 1115)*

May 67. (7") *(KAS 208)* **SIX O'CLOCK / THE FINALE** — `-`

Jul 67. (7") *<231>* **YOU'RE A BIG BOY NOW. / LONELY (AMY'S THEME)** — `-`

——— **JERRY YESTER** – guitar, vocals (ex-MODERN FOLK QUARTET) repl. YANOVSKY who was ostracized by rest, after reportedly being busted for drugs and incriminating others to avoid prosecution and deportation back to Canada.

Oct 67. (7") *(KAS 210) <239>* **SHE IS STILL A MYSTERY. / ONLY PRETTY, WHAT A PITY** — `27`

Nov 67. (7") *(KAS 211) <241>* **MONEY. / CLOSE YOUR EYES** — `48`

Mar 68. (lp) *(KLP 404) <KLPS 8061>* **EVERYTHING PLAYING** — | Jan68
– She is still a mystery / Priscilla millionaira / Boredom / Six o'clock / Forever / Darling be home soon / Younger generation / Money / Old folks / Only pretty, what a pity / Try a little bit / Close your eyes. *(cd-iss. Feb97 on 'Wooden Hill'; HILLCD 11)*

May 68. (lp; mono/stereo) *(KLP/+S 405) <KLPS 8064>* **THE BEST OF THE LOVIN' SPOONFUL VOL. 2 (compilation)** — | Mar68
– Money / She is still a mystery / Younger generation / Six o'clock / Darling be home soon / lovin' you / Boredom / Full measure / Nashville cats / Rain on the roof / Darlin' companion. *(re-iss. Mar69 on 'Marble Arch'; MAL 1116)*

——— Now a trio (BUTLER now vocals) after SEBASTIAN left to go solo.

Oct 68. (7") *(KAS 213) <250>* **NEVER GOING BACK. / FOREVER** — `-` | `73` Jul68

Oct 68. (7") *<251>* **(TIL I) RUN WITH YOU. / REVELATION** — `-`

Jan 69. (7") *<255>* **ME ABOUT YOU. / AMAZING AIR** — `-` | `91`

Jun 69. (lp; by The LOVIN' SPOONFUL featuring JOE BUTLER) *(620 009) <8073>* **REVELATION: REVOLUTION '69** — | Mar69
– Amazing air / Never going back / The prophet / Only yesterday / War games / (Til I) Run with you / Jug of wine / Revelation: revolution '69 / Me about you / Words.

——— BUTLER was virtually solo, with BONNER & GORDON the main songwriters.

——— In 1969, BUTLER packed in group name. 20 years later BUTLER, BOONE, JERRY YESTER and brother JIM YESTER re-formed for US concerts.

– compilations, etc. –

on 'Kama Sutra' unless mentioned

Jun 66. (7"ep) *(KEP 300)* **DID YOU EVER HAVE TO MAKE UP YOUR MIND** — `-`

Aug 66. (7"ep) *(KEP 301)* **JUG BAND MUSIC** — `-`

Oct 66. (7"ep) *(KEP 302)* **SUMMER IN THE CITY** — `-`

Feb 67. (7"ep) *(KEP 303)* **DAY BLUES** — `-`

Apr 67. (7"ep) *(KEP 304)* **NASHVILLE CATS** — `-`

Jun 67. (7"ep) *(KEP 305)* **LOVIN' YOU** — `-`

Oct 67. (7"ep) *(KEP 306)* **SOMETHING IN THE NIGHT** — `-`

Dec 68. (7") *(KAS 215)* **SUMMER IN THE CITY. / DAYDREAM** — `-`
(re-iss. Sep73; 2013 072) (re-iss. Jan83 on 'Flashback'; FBS 22) (re-iss. 1985 on 'WEA'; U 9023) (re-iss. Oct88 on 'Old Gold'; OG 9799)

Jun 70. (7") *(2013 009)* **DARLING BE HOME SOON. / NEVER GOING BACK** — `-`

Jun 71. (7"m) *(2013 023)* **SUMMER IN THE CITY. / DAYDREAM / DO YOU BELIEVE IN MAGIC?** — `-`

Dec 71. (lp) *(2361 002)* **ONCE UPON A TIME** — `-`

Jan 72. (lp) *(2361 003)* **JOHN SEBASTIAN SONGBOOK** — `-`

Oct 73. (d-lp) *(2683 034)* **GOLDEN SPOONFUL** — `-`
(re-iss. Aug74; KSMD 9001)

Aug 74. (lp) *(2683 042)* **MORE GOLDEN SPOONFUL** — `-`
(re-iss. Aug74; KSMD 9002)

1974. (lp/c) *Golden Hour; (GH 838)* **GOLDEN HOUR OF THE LOVIN' SPOONFUL'S GREATEST HITS** — `-`
(re-iss. 1990 on 'Knight' cd/c; KGH CD/MC 109)

Jul 75. (7") *(KSS 705)* **DAYDREAM. / YOU BABY** — `-`

May 76. (d-lp) *<2608>* **THE BEST OF THE LOVIN' SPOONFUL VOLS.1 & 2** — `-`

1977. (d-lp) *Pye; (FILD 009)* **THE FILE SERIES** — `-`

1977. (12"ep) *Buddah; (BD 118)* **SUMMER IN THE CITY / NASHVILLE CATS. / DAYDREAM / DO YOU BELIEVE IN MAGIC** — `-`

1978. (7") *Buddah; (BDS 474)* **SUMMER IN THE CITY. / NASHVILLE CATS** — `-`

Jun 80. (7"ep) *Pye Flashback; (FBEP 100)* **SUMMER SOUNDS** — `-`

1983. (lp) *Breakaway; (BWY 67)* **DISTANT ECHOES** — `-`

Apr 83. (10"lp/c) *P.R.T.; (DOW/ZCDOW 9)* **BEST IN THE WEST** — `-`

Apr 83. (7") *Old Gold; (OG 9291)* **DAYDREAM. / DO YOU BELIEVE IN MAGIC** — `-`

Mar 84. (7"ep/c-ep) *Scoop;* **6 TRACK HITS** — `-`

Jul 84. (7") *Old Gold; (OG 9415)* **SUMMER IN THE CITY. / (B-side by "Lemon Pipers")** — `-`

Jul 85. (lp/c) *Buddah; (252274-1/-4)* **GREATEST HITS** — `-`

1986. (lp) *Edsel; (ED 178)* **JUG BAND MUSIC** — `-`

1987. (c) *Design; (DSK 109)* **NASHVILLE CATS** — `-`

May 88. (lp/c/cd) *See For Miles; (SEE/+K/CD 229)* **THE EP COLLECTION** — `-`

1988. (d-lp/d-c/d-cd) *That's Original; (TFO LP/MC/CD 12)* **DO YOU BELIEVE IN MAGIC / EVERYTHING PLAYING** — `-`

Aug 88. (d-lp/c/cd) *Castle; (CCS LP/MC/CD 187)* **THE COLLECTION** — `-`
– Do you believe in magic / Did you ever have to make up your mind / Younger girl / Jug band music / Didn't want to have to do it / Daydream / You're a big boy now / Wash her away / Girl beautiful girl (Barbara's theme) / Bespoken / Darling be home soon / Lookin' to spy / You didn't have to be so nice / Sittin' here lovin' you / Darlin' companion / Rain on the roof / Coconut grove / Summer in the city / She is still a mystery / Boredom / Six o'clock / Younger generation / Till I run with you / Never going back.

1988. (cd-ep) *Special Edition; (CD3-11)* **THE LOVIN' SPOONFUL** — `-`

Sep 89. (lp/c/cd) *Mainline; (261530-1/-4/-2)* **20 GREATEST HITS** — `-`

1989. (lp) *Success; (2183)* **SUMMER IN THE CITY** — `-`
(cd-iss. 1990 on 'Movieplay'; MP 74003) (re-iss. Apr93 on 'Pulsar';) (re-iss. cd Jan95 on 'Spectrum'; 550 736-2)

1991. (cd) *Sequel; (NEXCD 176)* **THE LOVIN' SPOONFUL GO TO THE MOVIES** — `-`

Dec 93. (cd) *Disky;* **GOLD: GREATEST HITS** — `-`

Sep 95. (cd-s) *R.C.A.;* **SUMMER IN THE CITY /** — `-`

——— a various compilation WHAT'S SHAKIN' featured 4 songs was released Apr66 on 'Elektra'; EKS 4002>) *(re-iss. 1988 on 'Edsel'; ED 249)*

LOW

Formed: Duluth, Minnesota, USA ... late 1993 by Mormons ALAN SPARHAWK, his wife MIMI PARKER and third member, JOHN NICHOLS (replaced by ZAK SALLY after debut). Their early efforts, 'I COULD LIVE IN HOPE' (1994) and 'LONG DIVISION' (1995), were more or less ignored, although critics pricked up their ears for the low-key Lo-Fi/ambient classic, 'THE CURTAIN HITS THE CAST' (1996). LOW subsequently completed a few UK gigs to promote it during that summer and later cut a single for the legendary 'Sub Pop', 'VENUS'. The trio delivered a further two sets, namely 'SONGS FOR A DEAD PILOT' (1997) and 'ONE MORE REASON TO FORGET' (1998), described as "sad-core" in the music tabloids; it also featured 17-minute track, 'DO YOU KNOW HOW TO WALTZ?'. 1999 saw the return of the trio and the release of their 5th and best work to date, the bruised and ultra sensitive 'SECRET NAME' album. Recorded over a 7-day period with West Coast rock throwback and ex-BIG BLACK frontman STEVE ALBINI riding the faders, the band had hit a new creative peak with this warm and whispering alternative classic. Tracks such as 'SOON' and the harmonic 'MISSOURI' evoked blissful sensation and echoed tingling country heir to GRAM PARSONS. Others like 'TWO-STEP' and 'I REMEMBER' could easily be compared to a CARPENTERS ballad or something reminising GALAXIE 500. Meanwhile, ZAK SALLY moonlighted with another minimalist trio, ENEMYMINE (along with MIKE KUNKA of GODHEADSILO and DANNY SASAKI), recording an eponymous mini-set for Calvin Johnson's 'K' imprint. Towards the end of the millennium, LOW came up with 'THE CHRISTMAS EP', which featured four brand new tracks and cover of four traditional hymns that would peacefully send the children off to sleep by the fire come the festive season. • **Songwriters:** Group except SUNSHINE (Mitchell – Davis) / JACK SMITH (Supreme Dicks) / Transmission (Joy Division) / LONG LONG LONG (Beatles) / LITTLE DRUMMER BOY + BLUE CHRISTMAS + SILENT NIGHT + TAKING DOWN THE TREE.

Album rating: I COULD LIVE IN HOPE (*7) / LONG DIVISION (*8) / THE CURTAIN HITS THE CAST (*7) / SECRET NAME (*8)

ALAN SPARHAWK – vocals, guitar / **JOHN NICHOLS** – bass / **MIMI PARKER** – vocals, drums

	Quigley	Quigley
Aug 94. (cd) *<(QUIGD 5)>* **I COULD LIVE IN HOPE**		

– Words / Fear / Cut / Slide / Lazy / Lullaby / Sea / Down / Drag / Rope / Sunshine.

——— **ZAK SALLY** – bass; repl. NICHOLS

	Vernon Yard	Vernon Yard
1995. (cd) *<YARDCD 014>* **LONG DIVISION**	`-`	

– Violence / Below and above / Shame / Throw out the line / Swingin' / See-through / Turn / Caroline / Alone / Streetlight / Stay / Take. *(UK-iss.Feb97; same)*

	Hi-Rise	not iss.
Feb 96. (cd-ep) *(FLATSCD 24)* **TRANSMISSION EP**		

– Transmission / Bright / Cardine / Hands / Jack Smith / Untitled.

May 96. (cd-ep) *(YARD 022CD)* **FINALLY**
– Anon / Tomorrow one / Prisoner / Turning over.

Aug 96. (d-lp/cd) *(YARD/+CD 018)* **THE CURTAIN HITS THE CAST**
– Anon / The plan / Over the ocean / Mom says / Coat tails / Standby / Laugh / Lust / Stars gone out / Same / Do you know how to waltz / Dark. *(d-lp+=)* – Prisoner / Tomorrow one.

Nov 96. (7"/cd-s) *<(YARD 024/+CD)>* **OVER THE OCEAN. / CIOLENCE / BE THERE**

	Sub Pop	Sub Pop
Sep 97. (7") *<(SP 392)>* **VENUS. / BOYFRIEND**		

	Wurlitzer Jukebox	not iss.
Oct 97. (7") *(WJ 44)* **IF YOU WERE BORN TODAY (A SONG FOR LITTLE BABY JESUS). / BLUE CHRISTMAS**		

	Kranky	Kranky
Oct 97. (m-lp/m-cd) *<(KRANKY 021/+CD)>* **SONGS FOR A DEAD PILOT**		

– Will the night / Condescend / Born by the wires / Be there / Landlord / Hey Chicago.

	Tugboat	Kranky
May 98. (7") *(TUG 001)* **JOAN OF ARC. / LONG LONG LONG**	☐	☐
— (re-iss. Aug99 on 'Tugboat'; *same*)		
Jul 98. (cd) *(INR 1040CD)* **ONE MORE REASON TO FORGET**	☐	☐

– Be there / Venus / Condescend / Landlord / Over the ocean / Do you know how to waltz? / Shame / If you were born today (song for the little baby Jesus).
(above issued on 'Bluesanct Musak')

Feb 99. (7") *(TUGS 006)* **IMMUNE. / I REMEMBER**	☐	☐
Apr 99. (cd/d-lp) *(TUG CD/LP 007)* <*KRANKY 035*> **SECRET NAME**	☐	☐

– I remember / Starfire / 2-step / Weight for water / Don't understand / Soon / Immune / Lion – Lamb / Days of . . . / Will the night / Home.

Nov 99. (m-cd) <*(TUGCD 014)*> **CHRISTMAS**	☐

– Just like Christmas / Long way around the sea / Little drummer boy / If you were born today / Blue Christmas / Silent night / Taking down the tree / One special gift.
(above issued on 'Tugboat')

– compilations, etc. –

Jul 98. (cd) *Vernon Yard*; <*27*> **OWL** (LOW remixes by other artists)	-	☐

– Down / Annon (spore) / Over the ocean / Laugh / Anon (pollen) / Do you know how to waltz / Over the ocean / Words.

Nick LOWE

Born: 24 Mar '49, Woodchurch, Suffolk, England. In 1963, LOWE formed his first semi-serious musical enterprise, SOUND 4 PLUS 1, with schoolfriend, BRINSLEY SCHWARZ. This subsequently evolved into KIPPINGTON LODGE, a pseudo-psychedelic outfit which released a series of flop singles before re-launching in 1969 under the BRINSLEY SCHWARZ banner. Despite a disastrous beginning (see separate entry), the band became one of the leading lights of the 70's pub-rock scene and released a clutch of fine, rootsy albums before their eventual demise in 1975. As well as handling bass and vocal duties, LOWE had penned the bulk of the band's material, finally embarking on a solo career the following year. Although his first releases were a couple of pseudonymous, tongue-in-cheek singles (TARTAN HORDE – 'Bay City Rollers We Love You' / 'Rollers Theme' and DISCO BROTHERS – 'Let's Go To The Disco' / 'Everybody Dance'), LOWE was also making a name for himself as a producer (GRAHAM PARKER & THE RUMOUR, DR. FEELGOOD etc.) and in 1976 had a hand in setting up Jake Rivera's seminal 'Stiff' label. His debut single, 'SO IT GOES', was also Stiff's very first release, LOWE helping to shape both the operation's identity and the careers of its artists i.e. The DAMNED, IAN DURY, ELVIS COSTELLO amongst others. LOWE joined the latter in late '77 at Rivera's new venture, 'Radar', where he recorded the UK Top 10 single, 'I LOVE THE SOUND OF BREAKING GLASS', and Top 30 album, 'THE JESUS OF COOL' (1978). Released in America under the title, 'PURE POP FOR NOW PEOPLE', the album saw LOWE's writing take a distinctly more sardonic turn although his lyrical barbs were rarely as razor sharp as those of labelmate COSTELLO. He nevertheless proved himself to be witty, articulate and intelligent as well as a consummate musical chameleon capable of traversing rock'n'roll boundaries while injecting his songs with a rootsy authenticity. 1979's 'LABOUR OF LUST' spawned a second major hit single in 'CRUEL TO BE KIND', the song also making the American Top 20. From the summer of '77 onwards, LOWE had also been a member of DAVE EDMUNDS' band, ROCKPILE (EDMUNDS and other band members played on LOWE's solo material, the outfit graduating from live work to releasing an album, 'Seconds Of Pleasure', in 1980. Although the record was a minor success, the group folded shortly after and LOWE divided his time between production (working with The PRETENDERS, PAUL CARRACK, FABULOUS THUNDERBIRDS and JOHN HIATT amongst others) and solo work. The turn of the decade also saw him marrying CARLENE CARTER (daughter of JOHNNY CASH), a successful country singer in her own right who numbered among LOWE's production clients. Recorded with new backing band, The CHAPS (subsequently NOISE TO GO), 'NICK THE KNIFE' (1980) was his first album for 'Columbia' and his last to enjoy any kind of chart success. The 80's were a difficult period for LOWE; increasingly countrified sets such as 'THE ABOMINABLE SHOWMAN' (1983) and 'NICK LOWE & HIS COWBOY OUTFIT' (1984) were enjoyable enough if never threatening to break him into the mainstream. Towards the end of the decade, he sunk into depression and considered retiring from the music business before making a convincing return to form with 1990's 'PARTY OF ONE', an infectious, invigorating album which saw him reunited with EDMUNDS and featured the likes of JIM KELTNER and RY COODER. The latter two hooked up with LOWE and JOHN HIATT in a kind of critics' supergroup, LITTLE VILLAGE (the same formation that played on HIATT's 1987 album, 'Bring The Family'), releasing an eponymous, one-off album in 1992. A fairly average affair, the album nevertheless saw LOWE back in the UK Top 30 for the first time in more than a decade. Yet this success failed to have a knock-on effect in terms of his solo career, 'THE IMPOSSIBLE BIRD' (1994) failing to cross over to a wider audience despite widespread critical acclaim. It's typical of LOWE's career, the man remaining something of an unsung, backroom hero when at the very least, he deserves some kind of recognition for his contributions to popular music over a career spanning more than thirty years. • **Songwriters:** Self-penned except; PEACE, LOVE & UNDERSTANDING (Brinsley Schwarz) / HALFWAY TO PARADISE (Billy Fury) / ENDLESS SLEEP (Joey Reynolds) / I KNEW THE BRIDE (Dave Edmunds) / etc.

Album rating: JESUS OF COOL (aka PURE POP FOR NOW PEOPLE) (*8) / LABOUR OF LUST (*7) / NICK THE KNIFE (*6) / THE ABOMINABLE SHOWMAN

(*4) / NICK LOWE AND HIS COWBOY OUTFIT (*6) / THE ROSE OF ENGLAND (*6) / PINKER AND PROUDER THAN PREVIOUS (*5) / BASHER: THE BEST OF NICK LOWE compilation (*7) / PARTY OF ONE (*4) / THE WILDERNESS YEARS early stuff (*5) / THE IMPOSSIBLE BIRD (*6) / DIG MY MOOD (*6) / Little Village: LITTLE VILLAGE (*5)

NICK LOWE – vocals, bass, guitar (ex-BRINSLEY SCHWARZ) He was also a member of DAVE EDMUNDS' ROCKPILE group between Jul77-Feb81. His solo band included **EDMUNDS** – guitar and other ROCKPILE members **BILLY BREMNER** – guitar and **TERRY WILLIAMS** – drums (ex-MAN, etc.) used mainly on 2 albums below.

	Stiff	not iss.
Aug 76. (7") *(BUY 1)* **SO IT GOES. / HEART OF THE CITY**	☐	-
May 77. (7"ep) *(LAST 1)* **BOWI**	☐	-

– Born a woman / Shake that rat / Marie Provost / Endless sleep.

Oct 77. (7") *(BUY 21)* **HALFWAY TO PARADISE. / I DON'T WANT THE NIGHT TO END**	☐	-

	Radar	Columbia
Feb 78. (7") *(ADA 1)* **I LOVE THE SOUND OF BREAKING GLASS. / THEY CALLED IT ROCK**	7	-
Feb 78. (lp/c) *(RAD/RAC 1)* <*35329*> **THE JESUS OF COOL** <US-title 'PURE POP FOR NOW PEOPLE'>	22	-

– Music for money / I love the sound of breaking glass / Little Hitler / Shake & pop / Tonight / So it goes / No reason / 36 inches high / Marie Provost / Nutted by reality / Heart of the city. (re-iss. Oct88 on 'Demon' lp/c/cd; FIEND/+CASS/CD 131)

May 78. (7") *(ADA 12)* **LITTLE HITLER. / CRUEL TO BE KIND**	☐	-
Jul 78. (7") <*10734*> **HEART OF THE CITY. / SO IT GOES**	-	-
Sep 78. (7") <*10844*> **I LOVE THE SOUND OF BREAKING GLASS. / ENDLESS SLEEP**	-	☐
Nov 78. (7") *(ADA 26)* **AMERICAN SQUIRM. / Nick Lowe & His Sound: (WHAT'S SO FUNNY 'BOUT) PEACE, LOVE AND UNDERSTANDING**	☐	-
May 79. (7") *(ADA 34)* **CRACKING UP. / BASING STREET**	34	-
Jun 79. (lp/c) *(RAD/RAC 21)* <*36087*> **LABOUR OF LUST**	43	31

– Cruel to be kind / Cracking up / Big kick, plain scrap / Born fighter / You make me / Skin deep / Switchboard Susan / Grey ribbon / Without love / Dose of you / Love so fine. <US cd-iss. Jun88; CK 36087> (cd-iss. Apr90 on 'Demon'; FIENDCD 182)

Aug 79. (7") *(ADA 43)* <*11018*> **CRUEL TO BE KIND. / ENDLESS GREY RIBBON**	12	12 Jul79
Dec 79. (7") <*11131*> **SWITCHBOARD SUSAN. / BASING STREET**	-	☐

— After he split from ROCKPILE in Feb'81, LOWE formed his own band, **NICK LOWE & THE CHAPS**
(They became NOISE TO GO early '82) **MARTIN BELMONT** – guitar / **PAUL CARRACK** – keyboards / **BOBBY IRWIN** – drums

	F-Beat	Columbia
Feb 82. (7") *(XX 20)* **BURNING. / ZULU KISS**	☐	-
Feb 82. (lp/c) *(XX LP/MC 14)* <*37932*> **NICK THE KNIFE**	99	50

– Burning / Heart / Stick it where the sun don't shine / Queen of Sheba / My heart hurts / Couldn't love you (any more than I do) / Let me kiss ya / Too many teardrops / Ba doom / Raining raining / One's too many / Zulu kiss. (cd-iss. Apr90 on 'Demon'; FIENDCD 183)

Apr 82. (7") *(XX 23)* **MY HEART HURTS. / PET YOU AND HOLD YOU**	☐	-
(d7"+=) *(XX 23F – SAM 147)* – Cracking up / (What's so funny 'bout) Peace, love and understanding.		
Apr 82. (7") <*02813*> **MY HEART HURTS. / STICK IT WHERE THE SUN DON'T SHINE**	-	☐

— added **JAMES ELLER** – bass

Apr 83. (7") *(XX 31)* **RAGIN' EYES. / TANGUE-RAE**	☐	☐
(12"+=) *(XX 31T)* – Cool reaction.		
Jun 83. (lp/c) *(XX LP/MC 18)* **THE ABOMINABLE SHOWMAN**	☐	☐

– We want action / Ragin' eyes / Cool reaction / Time wounds all heels / Man of a fool / Tanque-Rae / Wish you were here / Chicken and feathers / Paid the price / Mess around with love / Saint beneath the paint / How do you talk to an angel. (cd-iss. Apr90 on 'Demon'; FIENDCD 184)

Jun 83. (7") <*03837*> **HOW DO YOU TALK TO AN ANGEL / I WISH YOU WERE HERE**	-	☐

NICK LOWE AND HIS COWBOY OUTFIT

— with **PAUL CARRACK, etc**

	F–Beat/ RCA	Columbia
May 84. (7") *(XX 340)* **HALF A BOY AND HALF A MAN. / AWESOME**	53	-
(12"+=) *(XX 34T)* – Cruel to be kind.		
May 84. (lp/c) *(ZL/ZK 79338)* <*39371*> **NICK LOWE & HIS COWBOY OUTFIT**	☐	☐

– Half a boy and half a man / You'll never get me up / (in one of those) / Maureen / God's gift to women / The Gee and the Rick and the three card trick / (Hey big mouth) Stand up and say that / Awesome / Breakaway / Love like a glove / Live fast, love hard, die young / L.A.F.S.

Aug 84. (7") *(XX 36)* **L.A.F.S. / (HEY BIG MOUTH) STAND UP AND SAY THAT**	☐	-
(12"+=) *(XX 36T)* – Baby it's you.		
Jul 85. (7") *(ZB 40303)* **I KNEW THE BRIDE (WHEN SHE USE TO ROCK AND ROLL). / DARLIN' ANGEL EYES**	☐	☐
(12"+=) *(ZT 40303)* – Seven nights to rock.		
Aug 85. (lp/c) *(ZL/ZK 70765)* <*39958*> **THE ROSE OF ENGLAND**	☐	☐

– Darlin' angel eyes / She don't love nobody / 7 nights to rock / Long walk back / The rose of England / Lucky dog * / I knew the bride (when she use to rock and roll) / Indoor fireworks / (Hope to God) I'm right / I can be the one you love / Everyone * / Bobo ska diddle daddle (re-iss. Dec88 on 'Demon' lp/c/cd; FIEND/+CASS/CD 73) – (omits tracks *)

Nov 85. (7") <*05570*> **I KNEW THE BRIDE (WHEN SHE USE TO ROCK AND ROLL). / LONG WALK BACK**	-	77

NICK LOWE

			Demon	Columbia
Jan 88.	(7") CRYING IN MY SLEEP. / LOVER'S JAMBOREE		-	
Feb 88.	(lp/c/cd) (FIEND/+CASS/CD 99) PINKER AND PROUDER **THAN PREVIOUS**			

– (You're my) Wildest dream / Crying in my sleep / Big hair / Love gets strange / I got the love / Black Lincoln Continental / Cry it out / Lover's jambouree / Geisha girl / Wishing well / Big big love.

—— now with DAVE EDMUNDS, PAUL CARRACK, JIM KELTNER / plus BILL KIRCHEN – electric guitar / AUSTIN DE LONE – piano, guitar / RY COODER – steel guitar

			Warners	Reprise
Apr 90.	(7") (W 9821) ALL MEN ARE LIARS. / GAI-GIN MAN			-

(12"+=/cd-s+=) (W 9821 T/CD) – I love the sound of breaking glass / Cruel to be kind.

Apr 90.	(cd)(lp/c) (<7599 26132-2>)(WX 337/+C) PARTY OF ONE			

– You got the look I like / (I want to build a) Jumbo ark / Gai-gin man / Who was that man? / What's shakin' on the hill / Shting-shtang / All men are liars / Rocky road / Refrigerator white / I don't know why you keep me on / Honeygun. (cd re-iss. Nov95 on 'Demon'; FIENDCD 767) – (extra tracks)

LITTLE VILLAGE

were another amalgamation of near superstars; NICK LOWE – vocals, bass / RY COODER – vocals, guitar / JOHN HIATT – vocals, guitar / JIM KELTNER – drums, percussion, guitar, composer

			Reprise	Reprise
Feb 92.	(cd)(lp/c) (<7599 26713-2>)(WX 462/+C) LITTLE VILLAGE		23	66

– Solar sex panel / The action / Inside job / Big love / Take another look / Do you want my job / Don't go away mad / Fool who knows / She runs hot / Don't think about her when you're trying to drive / Don't bug me when I'm working.

Mar 92.	(7"/c-s) SOLAR SEX PANEL. / DO WITH ME WHAT YOU **WANT TO DO**			

(12"+=/cd-s+=) – Haunted house.

May 92.	(7"/c-s) DON'T GO AWAY MAD. / BIG LOVE			

(12"+=/cd-s+=) – Do with me what you want to do.

NICK LOWE

			Demon	not iss.
Nov 94.	(cd-s) (NICKA 315) TRUE LOVE TRAVELS ON A GRAVEL **ROAD. / TWO SEATER / RAG DOLL / LAYING BLAME**			-
Nov 94.	(cd) (FIENDCD 757) THE IMPOSSIBLE BIRD			

– Soulful wind / The beast in me / True love travels on a gravel road / Trail of tears / Shelly my love / Where's my everything / 12-step program / Lover don't go / Drive-thru man / Withered on the vine / I live on a battlefield / 14 days / I'll be there.

Jan 98.	(cd) (FIENDCD 939) DIG MY MOOD			

– Faithless lover / Lonesome reverie / You inspire me / What lack of love has done / Time I took a holiday / Failed Christian / The man that I've become / Freezing / High on a hilltop / Lead me not / I must be getting over you / Cold grey light of dawn.

Jun 98.	(cd-ep) (VEXCD 17) YOU INSPIRE ME / SOULFUL WIN (live in Japan) / SHE DOESN'T LOVE NOBODY (live in Japan) / CRUEL TO BE KIND (live in Japan) / HALF A BOY AND HALF A MAN (live in Japan)			

– compilations etc. –

on 'Demon' unless mentioned otherwise

Sep 84.	(lp/c) (FIEND/+CASS 20) 16 ALL-TIME LOWES			-

– Born fighter / Marie Provost / American squirm / Skin deep / When I write the book / Little Hitler / Cruel to be kind / Heart of the city / Switchboard Susan / (I love the sound of) Breaking glass / Big kick plain scrap / Cracking up / Without love / Nutted by reality / So it goes / They called it rock. (cd-iss. 1986 as '20 ALL-TIME LOWES'; FIENDCD 20) – (4 extra tracks). (cd re-iss. Oct93 on 'Diablo'; DIAB 801)

Mar 86.	(lp/c/cd) (FIEND/+CASS/CD 59) NICK'S NACK			-
Aug 89.	(d-lp/c/cd) (FIEND/+CASS/CD 142) BASHER: THE BEST OF **NICK LOWE**			
Jun 91.	(cd) (FIENDCD 203) THE WILDERNESS YEARS			

– (rare material 1974-1977)

Jan 94.	(4xcd-box) (NICK 1) BOXED SET			-

– (JESUS OF COOL / ROSE OF ENGLAND / NICK LOWE AND HIS COWBOY OUTFIT / PINKER AND PROUDER THAN PREVIOUS)

L7

Formed: Los Angeles, California, USA ... 1986 by DONITA SPARKS (guitar/vocals) and SUZI GARDNER (guitar/vocals). Recruiting seasoned L.A. punk veteran JENNIFER FINCH on bass and drummer ANNE ANDERSON, the band signed for the small 'Epitaph' label. The feisty punk-metal noise of their 1988 eponymous debut attracted the attention of the now-famous 'Sub Pop' label the following year, DEE PLAKAS replacing ANDERSON and 'SMELL THE MAGIC' (1990) fuelling the band's growing cult reputation. 1990 also saw the girls touring with a relatively unknown NIRVANA, L7's infamous onstage antics almost causing as much of a stir as the headliners. The band were soon snapped up by 'Slash', hitting the UK Top 20 in 1992 with the pop-grunge of the 'PRETEND WE'RE DEAD' single. This was closely followed by the 'BRICKS ARE HEAVY' album, a hard hitting collision of girl power grunge and ultra hard line, often humorous, post-feminist lyrics. The band caused further uproar later that year when DONITA exposed her womanly charms on 'The Word', having already blessed that year's Reading Festival audience with a used tampon. Irreverent yet committed, L7 also formed 'Rock For Choice', a pro-abortion pressure group which won unprecedented support in the male-dominated environs of the music business. 'HUNGRY FOR STINK' (1994) was equally blistering, the frenetic

'FUEL MY FIRE' later covered by The PRODIGY on their landmark 'THE FAT OF THE LAND' album. • **Songwriters:** Group or SPARKS penned except THREE DAYS (Willie Nelson).

Album rating: L7 (*6) / SMELL THE MAGIC mini (*6) / BRICKS ARE HEAVY (*8) / HUNGRY FOR STINK (*6) / THE BEAUTY PROCESS: TRIPLE PLATINUM (*6) / SLAP-HAPPY (*6)

DONITA SPARKS (b. 8 Apr'63, Chicago, Illinois) – vocals, guitar / **SUZI GARDNER** (b. 1 Aug'60, Altus, Oklahoma) – guitar, vocals / **JENNIFER FINCH** (b. 5 Aug'66) – bass, vocals / **ANNE ANDERSON** (b.Chicago) – drums repl.by ROY KOUTSKY

			not iss.	Epitaph
Dec 88.	(lp/c/cd) <E 86401-1/-4/-2> L7		-	

– Bite the wax tadpole / Cat-o'-nine-tails / Metal stampede / Let's rock tonight / Uncle Bob / Snake handler / Runnin' from the law / Cool out / It's not you / I drink / Ms. 45. (UK-iss.Jun92; same)

—— **(DEMETRA) DEE PLAKAS** (b. 9 Nov'60, Chicago) – drums repl. ROY

			Glitterhouse	Sub Pop
Jan 90.	(7",7"green) <SP 58> SHOVE. / PACKIN' A ROD		-	

(UK-iss.Jan91 on 'Sub Pop'; EFA 08105)

Nov 90.	(12"ep,12"purple-ep) <(SP 79)> SMELL THE MAGIC			Aug90

– Shove / Til the wheels fall off / Fast'n'frightening / (Right on) Thru / Deathwish / Broomstick. (cd-ep Oct95+= ; SPCD 79) – Packin' a rod / Just like me / American society.

			Slash	Slash
Mar 92.	(7"red/c-s) (LASH/LACS 34) PRETEND WE'RE DEAD. / SHIT **LIST**		21	

(12"+=/cd-s+=) (LASHX/LASCD 34) – Lopsided head / Mr. Integrity.

Apr 92.	(cd/c/lp) (828 307-2/-4/-1) <26784> BRICKS ARE HEAVY		24	

– Wargasm / Scrap / Pretend we're dead / Diet pill / Everglade / Slide / One more thing / Mr. Integrity / Monster / Shit list / This ain't pleasure.

May 92.	(7"green) (LASH 36) EVERGLADE. / FREAK MAGNET		27	

(12"+=/cd-s+=) (LASHXP/LASHCD 36) – Scrap.

Sep 92.	(7"/c-s) (LASH/LACS 38) MONSTER. / USED TO LOVE HIM		33	

(12"+=/cd-s+=) (LASHX/LASCD 38) – Diet pill.

Nov 92.	(7"/c-s) (LASH/LACS 42) PRETEND WE'RE DEAD. / FAST **'N' FRIGHTENING (live)**		50	-

(cd-s+=) (LASCD 42) – (Right on) Thru / Shove / Shit list / Diet pill.

—— L7 appeared as CAMEL LIPS group in the film 'Serial Mom'.

Jun 94.	(7"colrd/12"colrd) (LASH/LASCS 48) ANDRES. / BOMB		34	

(cd-s+=) (LASCD 48) – (KRXT radio interview).

Jul 94.	(cd/c/lp) <(828 531-2/-4/-1)> HUNGRY FOR STINK		26	

– Andres / Baggage / Can I run / The bomb / Questioning my sanity / Riding with a movie star / Stuck here again / Fuel my fire / Freak magnet / She has eyes / Shirley / Talk box.

—— After recording 1996 album, FINCH left to form LYME. She was repl. by **GRETA BRINKMAN** who appeared on next album, before **GAIL GREENWOOD** (ex-BELLY) took over

Feb 97.	(cd/c) (828 868-2/-4) THE BEAUTY PROCESS: TRIPLE **PLATINUM**			

– Beauty process / Drama / Off the wagon / I need / Moonshine / Bitter wine / Masses are asses / Bad things / Must have more / Non existant Patricia / Me, myself and I / Lorenza, Giada, Alessandra / Guera.

			Bongload	Bongload
Aug 99.	(cd/lp) (BL 43 CD/V) SLAP-HAPPY PLATINUM			

– Crackpot baby / On my rockin' machine / Lackey / Human / Livin' large / Freeway / Stick to the plan / War with you / Long green / Little one / Freezer burn / Mantra down.

Lydia LUNCH (dig out; Great Alt & Indie ...)

LURKERS (dig out; Great Alt & Indie ...)

LUSCIOUS JACKSON (dig out; Great Alt & Indie ...)

LUSH

Formed: Camberwell, London, England ... October '88 by girls MIKI BERENYI (half-Japanese / half-Hungarian) and EMMA ANDERSON, plus lads STEVE RIPPON and CHRIS ACLAND. After supports slots to DARLING BUDS, etc, they signed to top independent label '4.a.d.' in 1989 (MERIEL BARHAM was also a member before she joined The PALE SAINTS). A 1989 debut EP, 'SCAR', introduced the band's delicate wash of sound, all hazy guitar effects and celestial harmonies; immediately hailed by the press as one of the front runners in the 'shoegazing' scene, the band even attracted the attentions of ROBIN GUTHRIE (of 'shoegazing' forebears, COCTEAU TWINS) who produced a follow-up, the 'MAD LOVE' EP. Along with MY BLOODY VALENTINE, RIDE etc., LUSH were now the toast of the UK indie scene, while also enjoying minor success in Europe and America. A further EP, 'BLACK SPRING', followed in Autumn '91 prior to the departure of RIPPON. With former NME employee, PHIL KING (ex-FELT, SERVANTS etc.) drafted in as a replacement, the band eventually completed work on a debut album, 'SPOOKY'. Issued to a mixed critical reaction in early '92, the record reached the UK Top 10 despite complaints about the suffocating GUTHRIE production. Nevertheless, the scene which had spawned LUSH was dying on its feet (still staring at its shoes, presumably) with the influx of American grunge and the group took time out to reconsider their approach. The resultant follow-up, 'SPLIT' (1994), was well received by fans but failed to break the band out of the indie margins. Finally, with the advent of Brit-pop, LUSH re-emerged with a more straightforward, spiky pop sound, the fey vocal affectations of old giving way to unashamed cockney wide-girl attitude on the 'LADYKILLERS' single while 'SINGLE GIRL' was as breezy as anything they'd ever recorded. An album, 'LOVELIFE', made the Top 10 later that summer and although older fans might've mourned the haunting textures of old, the simple approach suited them down to the ground. Yet this mini-revival in the band's fortunes was tragically marred later that year when the 30-year old CHRIS ACLAND took his own life. • **Songwriters:** MIKI and EMMA, except HEY HEY HELEN (Abba) / FALLIN' IN LOVE (Dennis Wilson) / OUTDOOR MINER (Wire) / LOVE AT FIRST SIGHT (Young Marble Giants) / I WANNA BE YOUR GIRLFRIEND (Rubinoos). • **Trivia:** In 1990, they all posed topless for an NME cover shot, although they were given the body paint treatment.

Album rating: SPOOKY (*8) / GALA (*7) / SPLIT (*6) / LOVELIFE (*8) / TOPOLINO compilation (*7)

MIKI BERENYI (b.18 Mar'67) – vocals, guitar / **EMMA ANDERSON** (b.10 Jun'67) – guitar, vocals / **STEVE RIPPON** – bass / **CHRIS ACLAND** (b. 7 Sep'66, Lancaster, England) – drums

		4 a.d.	Nesak
Oct 89.	(m-lp/m-c/m-cd) (JAD/+C 911/+CD) <911> **SCAR**		
	– Baby talk / Thoughtforms / Scarlet / Bitter / Second sight / Etheriel.		
Feb 90.	(12"ep/c-ep/cd-ep) (BAD/+C 0003/+CD) **MAD LOVE EP**	55	–
	– De luxe / Leaves me cold / Downer / Thoughtforms.		

		4 a.d.	4 a.d.-Reprise
Oct 90.	(7"/c-s) (AD/+C 0013) **SWEETNESS AND LIGHT. / BREEZE**	47	–
	(12"+=/cd-s+=) (BAD 0013/+CD) – Sunbathing.		
Dec 90.	(lp/c/cd) (CAD/+C 0017/+CD) <26463> **GALA**		
	– Sweetness and light / Sunbathing / Breeze / De luxe / Leaves me cold / Downer / Baby talk / Thoughtforms / Scarlet / Bitter / Second light / Etheriel / Hey hey Helen / Scarlet (alt.take).		
Sep 91.	(7"/c-s) (AD/+C 1016) <40231> **NOTHING NATURAL. / GOD'S GIFT**	43	–
	(12"ep+=/cd-ep+=) (BAD 1016/+CD) – 'BLACK SPRING EP' – Fallin' in love / Monochrome.		
Dec 91.	(12"ep/10"ep/c-ep)(cd-ep) (BAD/+D/C 2001)(BAD 2001CD) **FOR LOVE / STARLUST. / OUTDOOR MINER / ASTRONAUT**	35	–

—— Although on above + below recording RIPPON had left Oct'91.

Jan 92.	(lp/d-10"lp/c)(cd)(s-cd) (CAD/+D/C 2002)(CAD/+D 2002CD) <26798> **[SPOOKY]**	7	–
	– Stray / Nothing natural / Tiny smiles / Covert / Ocean / For love / Superblast! / Untogether / Fantasy / Take / Laura / Monochrome.		

—— RIPPON was replaced by **PHIL KING** (b.29 Apr'60) – bass (ex-SEE SEE RIDER, ex-APPLE BOUTIQUE, ex-FELT)

		4 a.d.	Warners
May 94.	(7") (AD 4008) **HYPOCRITE. / LOVE AT FIRST SIGHT**	52	–
	(12"+=/cd-s+=) (BAD 4008/+CD) – Cat's chorus / Undertow.		
May 94.	(7") (AD 4010) **DESIRE LINES. / WHITE WOOD**	60	–
	(12"+=)(cd-s+=) (BAD 4010/+CD) – Girl's world / Lovelife (suga bullit remix).		
Jun 94.	(lp/c/cd) (CAD/+C 4011/+CD) <45578> **SPLIT**	19	
	– Light from a dead star / Kiss chase / Blackout / Hypocrite / Lovelife / Desire lines / The invisible man / Undertow / Never-never / Lit up / Stardust / When I die.		
Jan 96.	(7"clear) (AD 6001) **SINGLE GIRL. / SWEETIE**	21	–
	(cd-s) (BAD 6001CD) – ('A'side) / Tinkerbell / Outside world / Cul de sac.		
	(cd-s) (BADD 6001CD) – ('A'side) / Pudding / Demystification / Shut up.		
Feb 96.	(7"green) (AD 6002) **LADYKILLERS. / I WANNA BE YOUR GIRLFRIEND**	22	–
	(cd-s) (BAD 6002CD) – ('A'side) / Matador / Ex / Dear me.		
	(cd-s) (BADD 6002CD) – ('A'side) / Heavenly / Carmen / Plums and oranges.		
Mar 96.	(clear-lp/c/cd) (CAD/+C 6004/+CD) <46170> **LOVELIFE**	8	–
	– Ladykillers / Heavenly nobodies / 500 / I've been here before / Papasan / Single girl / Ciao! / Tralala / Last night / Runaway / The childcatcher / Olympia.		

—— JARVIS COCKER (Pulp) featured vox with MIKI on the track 'Ciao!'.

Jul 96.	(7"red) (AD 6009) **500 (SHAKE BABY SHAKE). / I HAVE THE MOON**	21	–
	(cd-s+=) (BAD 6009CD) – Piledriver / Olympia (acoustic).		
	(cd-s) (BADD 6009CD) – ('A'side) / I'd like to walk around your mind / Kiss chase (acoustic) / Last night (hexadecimal dub mix).		

—— Sadly on the 17th of October '96, 30 year-old ACLAND committed suicide after returning from the States and splitting with his girlfriend. LUSH virtually gave up with the group after that. A dance group of the same name issued a single, 'GOLD', late '97 (nothing to do with the real LUSH). In 1998, EMMA teamed up with vocalist, LISA ONEIIL, to form SING-SING, debuting that year with a single, 'FEELS LIKE SUMMER'. It was released on the indie label, 'Bella Union' (with help of COCTEAU TWINS' ROBIN GUTHRIE and SIMON RAYMONDE), when EMMA couldn't find a new one after severing her association with '4 a.d.'.

– compilations, etc.

May 98.	(cd) 4 a.d.; <1102> **TOPOLINO**	–	–
	– 500 (shake baby shake) / I have the moon / Ex / I wanna be your girlfriend / Matador / Outside world / I'd like to walk around your mind / Carmen / Shut up / Cul de sac / Demystification.		

LUXURIA (see under ⇒ MAGAZINE)

John LYDON (see under ⇒ PUBLIC IMAGE LTD)

Phil LYNOTT (see under ⇒ THIN LIZZY)

LYNYRD SKYNYRD

Formed: Jacksonville, Florida, USA . . . 1966 initially as MY BACKYARD, by RONNIE VAN ZANT (vocals) who carefully hand picked a line-up of GARY ROSSINGTON (guitar), ALLEN COLLINS (guitar), BOB BURNS (drums) and LARRY JUNSTROM (bass) to realise his boyhood dream of creating an American equivalent to The ROLLING STONES. The band were blown away after witnessing an early incarnation of The ALLMAN BROTHERS, vowing to conquer the world with their own unique take on the roots music of the South. Continually brought to task for having long hair by gym teacher, Leonard Skinner, VAN ZANT and co. packed in school at the earliest opportunity, spending up to sixteen hours a day honing the sound of the band they'd eventually dub LYNYRD SKYNYRD after their schoolhouse nemesis (name slightly changed to protect themselves from enforced circuit training). At the time, the band's home town of Jacksonville boasted a thriving and eclectic music scene that saw the likes of future ALLMAN's DICKY BETTS and BERRY OAKLEY paying their dues, as well as a young TOM PETTY amongst a slew of others. SKYNYRD's first victory in their campaign to resurrect the glory of the South was winning a support slot to psychedelic one-hit wonders, STRAWBERRY ALARM CLOCK. By 1970, the band had almost notched up a mind boggling 1,000 gigs and the real touring hadn't even started. Record-wise, they had a limited issue single, 'NEED ALL MY FRIENDS', (released in 1968 by the local 'Shadetree' label) under their belts and in 1971, they issued a second single, 'I'VE BEEN YOUR FOOL', the cut taken from sessions the band had recorded at the famed Muscle Shoals studio in Sheffield, Alabama. Over the course of the sessions, the septet laid down early versions of the tracks that would later become their acclaimed debut, 'PRONOUNCED LEH-NERD SKIN-NERD' (1974), bassist LEON WILKINSON joining the band midway through the sessions, while future BLACKFOOT man, RICKY MEDLOCKE, contributed some drum and vocal parts. Manager ALAN WALDEN touted the demos around various companies to no avail, opportunity eventually knocking in the form of industry mover and shaker extraordinaire, AL KOOPER (ex-BLUES PROJECT), who was in the process of setting up the Atlanta-based 'Sounds Of The South' label with the backing of 'M.C.A.'. The purpose of this venture was to capitalise on the booming Southern music scene and in SKYNYRD, KOOPER knew he'd found a band to take Southern Rock to a new plateau. As Intense and driven as the band themselves, KOOPER constantly clashed with them during the recording of the debut which he had taken upon himself to produce. Nevertheless, KOOPER functioned like an extra member of the group, playing and singing on many of the tracks, his input pivotal in creating one of rock's great debut albums. A simmering gumbo stew that drew influences from the likes of The 'STONES, FREE and CREAM yet was also haunted by the spectre of raw country blues, the album's flagbearer and breathtaking finale was 'FREE BIRD', the song most people think of at the mention of SKYNYRD's name. From BILLY POWELL's piano-led intro (which, after writing, resulted in the former roadie being taken up as a full time member of the band), the song led into a gorgeously melancholy DUANE ALLMAN-style (whom the band would dedicate the song to after he was killed in a motorcycle crash) slide guitar part, eventually building up to a blistering triple guitar climax. The band achieved the latter by overdubbing an extra guitar part by COLLINS, authentically replicating the song live as LEON WILKINSON (who'd left prior to recording the album) later returned, allowing ED KING (who'd filled in as a bass player on the debut) to become a permanent member, switching to guitar and cementing the three-pronged attack of the classic 'SKYNYRD' line-up. Alongside 'FREE BIRD', the album contained some of the finest songs of the band's career in the mournful 'TUESDAY'S GONE', VAN ZANT's normally commanding voice sounding as forlorn as heroes MERLE HAGGARD and WAYLON JENNINGS. 'SIMPLE MAN' was another earthy ballad, RONNIE's lyrics as succinct and unpretentious as ever. 'THINGS GOIN' ON', meanwhile, was a biting criticism of underhand political dealings set to a rollicking honky tonk backing. KOOPER secured the band a support slot on The WHO's 1973 American tour, and immediately the band were thrown in at the deep end, playing to stadium-sized audiences. Incredibly, at almost every show, the band had won the normally fiercely partisan WHO crowd over by the end of their set and when 'SWEET HOME ALABAMA' (a rousing, tongue-in-cheek rebuke to NEIL YOUNG's 'Southern Man') made the US Top 10 the following year, the band were well on the way to becoming major league stars. 'SECOND HELPING' (1974) almost matched the power of the debut, the vicious sting of 'WORKIN' FOR M.C.A.' contrasting with the strum and slide of 'THE BALLAD OF CURTIS LOWE', a tribute to a black bluesman. And thus lay the contradiction with LYNYRD SKYNYRD; denounced as reactionary rednecks, their music was haunted by the music of black immigrants. As many commentators have noted, SKYNYRD didn't have any defined politics; VAN ZANT was fiercely proud of his upbringing, attempting in his own blunt way to speak out for a part of America that had been discredited after the civil war; charges of racism, however, were way off the mark. Similarly, an anti-firearms song, 'SATURDAY NIGHT SPECIAL', didn't exactly fit with the archetype of the rifle-toting redneck. The song formed the centrepiece of the band's third effort, 'NUTHIN' FANCY' (1975), a harder rockin' affair that nevertheless failed to break any new ground or capture the excitement of the band's live show. The album also marked the first of LYNYRD SKYNYRD's many casualties as BOB BURNS was replaced with ARTIMUS PYLE after freaking out on tour. The band had been on the road almost constantly from their inception and things began coming to a head, the trek that followed the release of 'NUTHIN' FANCY' coming to be dubbed the

'Torture Tour'. The tales of sex, drugs, violence and madness are legendary, VAN ZANT's infamous violent outbreaks particularly nauseating. While ED KING departed, the rest of the band soldiered on under the auspices of the notoriously unpredictable VAN ZANT, his dedication winning unfaltering loyalty despite his temper. KING's replacement was STEVE GAINES, brother of backing singer CASSIE. Though he was only featured on a handful of the tracks on the live 'ONE MORE FROM THE ROAD' (1976), his visceral playing re-energised a flagging 'SKYNYRD, helping to make 'STREET SURVIVORS' (1977) their best release since 'SECOND HELPING'. Inspired by the 'Outlaw' movement that saw country stars like WILLIE NELSON and TOMPALL GLASER moving away from the polished Nashville sound, 'STREET SURVIVORS' was more countrified than any previous release, right down to a cover of MERLE HAGGARD's 'HONKY TONK NIGHT TIME MAN'. It also includudded VAN ZANT's heartfelt anti-heroin track, 'THAT SMELL'. The song's lyrics and the album's cover art (featuring the band surrounded by flames) were to take on a chilling new resonance when, on October 20, en route to Baton Rouge, the aircraft carrying band and crew plummeted from the sky after both its engines failed. VAN ZANT was killed on impact, as were STEVE and CASSIE GAINES, and assistant road manager DEAN KILPATRICK. The remaining passengers were all seriously injured and the details of the crash were horrific, the effects of the tragedy still resonating to this day. The remaining members decided to disband LYNYRD SKYNYRD, even although 'STREET SURVIVORS' had become their biggest selling album ever, the remnants of 'SKYNYRD forming the ROSSINGTON-COLLINS BAND, who released two forgettable albums at the turn of the decade, COLLINS later forming his own band after the death of his wife KATHY. This wasn't the end to his strife; COLLINS was involved in a serious car accident in 1986 which killed his girlfriend and left him paralysed from the waist down (he died of pneumonia four years later). COLLINS wasn't the only one to suffer in the aftermath of the band's tragedy; suicide, drug addiction and even alleged child abuse dogged the survivors of the plane crash for years to come. In the late 80's, the remaining members regrouped for a memorial tour and subsequent live album, 'SOUTHERN BY THE GRACE OF GOD' (1988), RONNIE's brother, JOHNNY, fronting the band. Another reformation in 1991 resulted in the eponymous 'LYNYRD SKYNYRD 1991', a credible comeback that saw the return of ED KING. The band released a further three albums during the 90's, 'THE LAST REBEL' (1993), the unplugged 'ENDANGERED SPECIES' (1994) and 1997's 'TWENTY', the latter featuring BLACKFOOT man RICKEY MEDLOCKE, who'd played on sessions for the debut over a quarter of a century previously. None of these albums captured the intensity of the original line-up, however, and those looking for a comprehensive musical history lesson are pointed in the direction of the 1991 MCA boxed set. Alongside all the essential album cuts, the collection includes a spectral demo version of 'FREEBIRD' as well as unreleased gems like the impassioned 'HE'S ALIVE' and the spine-tingling 'ALL I CAN DO IS WRITE ABOUT IT', as revealing a song as to what drove the late VAN ZANT as the man ever penned. • **Songwriters:** Bulk by VAN ZANT + COLLINS or VAN ZANT + GAINES after '75. When they re-formed in '87, ROSSINGTON, KING and the new VAN ZANDT contributed all. Covered; SAME OLD BLUES + CALL ME THE BREEZE (J.J. Cale) / CROSSROADS (Robert Johnson) / NONE OF US ARE FREE (Mann-Weil-Russell) / etc.

Album rating: PRONOUNCED LEH-NERD SKIN-NERD (*8) / SECOND HELPING (*8) / NUTHIN' FANCY (*6) / GIMME BACK MY BULLETS (*6) / ONE MORE FROM THE ROAD (*8) / STREET SURVIVORS (*7) / SKYNYRD'S FIRST AND.. LAST posthumous (*6) / GOLD AND PLATINUM compilation (*9) / LEGEND rare live (*6) / SOUTHERN BY THE GRACE OF GOD: LYNYRD SKYNYRD TRIBUTE TOUR – 1987 (*5) / LYNYRD SKYNYRD 1991 (*5) / THE LAST REBEL (*5) / LYNYRD SKYNYRD boxed set (*9) / FREEBIRD – THE VERY BEST OF . . . compilation (*8) / ENDANGERED SPECIES (*4) / TWENTY (*4) / EDGE OF FOREVER (*5)

RONNIE VAN ZANT (b.15 Jan'48) – vocals / **GARY ROSSINGTON** (b. 4 Dec'51) – guitar / **ALLEN COLLINS** (b.19 Jul'52) – guitar / **GREG WALKER** (or) **LEON WILKESON** (b. 2 Apr'52) – bass / **RICKY MEDLOCKE** (or) **BOB BURNS** – drums

	not iss.	Shade Tree
1971. (7") **I'VE BEEN YOUR FOOL. / GOTTA GO**	-	☐

(UK-iss.Oct82 on 'M.C.A.'; 799)

—— **ED KING** – bass (ex-STRAWBERRY ALARM CLOCK) repl. LEON & GREG / added **BILLY POWELL** (b. 3 Jun'52) – piano (RICKY MEDLOCKE had now formed BLACKFOOT, after contributing vox + drums on 2 tracks 'White Dove' & 'The Seasons')

	M.C.A.	M.C.A.	
Nov 73. (7") <40158> **GIMME THREE STEPS. / MR. BANKER**	-	☐	
Jan 74. (lp/c) (MCG/+C 3502) <363> **PRONOUNCED LEH-NERD SKIN-NERD**	☐	27	Sep73

– I ain't the one / Tuesday's gone / Gimme three steps / Simple man / Things goin' on / Mississippi kid / Poison whiskey / Free bird. (re-iss. Jun84 lp/c; MCL/+C 1798) (cd-iss. Jul88; DMCL 1798) (cd re-iss. Nov91; MCLD 19072)

—— added returning **LEON WILKESON** – bass (ED KING now 3rd guitarist)

May 74. (7") (MCA 136) <40231> **DON'T ASK ME NO QUESTIONS. / TAKE YOUR TIME**	☐		Jan74
Oct 74. (lp/c) (MCF/+C 2547) <413> **SECOND HELPING**	☐	12	Apr74

– Sweet home Alabama / I need you / Don't ask me no questions / Workin' for MCA / The ballad of Curtis Loew / Swamp music / The needle and the spoon / Call me the breeze. (re-iss. 1983 lp/c; MCL/+C 1746) (re-iss. Oct87 on 'Fame' lp/c; FA/TC-FA 3194) (cd-iss. Aug89; DMCL 1746) (cd re-iss. Oct92; MCLD 19073)

Oct 74. (lp/c) (MCA 160) <40258> **SWEET HOME ALABAMA. / TAKE YOUR TIME**	☐	8	Jul74

Nov 74. (7") <40328> **FREE BIRD (edit). / DOWN SOUTH JUKIN'**	-	19	

—— (Dec74) **ARTIMUS PYLE** (b. 15 Jul'48, Spartanburg, South Carolina) – drums repl. BURNS

May 75. (lp/c) (MCF/+C 2700) <2137> **NUTHIN' FANCY**	43	9	Apr75

– Saturday night special / Cheatin' woman / Railroad song / I'm a country boy / On the hunt / Am I losin' / Made in the shade / Whiskey rock-a-roller. (re-iss. 1983 lp/c; MCL/+C 1760) (cd-iss. Aug87; CMCAD 31003) (cd re-iss. Nov94; MCLD 19074) (cd re-iss. Nov99; MCD 12024)

Jul 75. (7") (MCA 199) <40416> **SATURDAY NIGHT SPECIAL. / MADE IN THE SHADE**	☐	27	May75

—— Reverted to six-piece, when ED KING departed / added backing vocalists **CASSIE GAINES, LESLIE HAWKINS + JO JO BILLINGSLEY**

Feb 76. (7") (MCA 229) <40532> **DOUBLE TROUBLE. / ROLL GYPSY ROLL**	☐	80	
Mar 76. (lp/c) (MCF/+C 2744) <2170> **GIMME BACK MY BULLETS**	34	20	Feb76

– Gimme back my bullets / Every mother's son / Trust / (I got the) Same old blues / Double trouble / Roll gypsy roll / Searching / Cry for the bad man / All I can do is write about it. (re-iss. Feb82 lp/c; MCL/+C 1653) (cd-iss. Nov99; MCD 12023)

Jun 76. (7") <40565> **GIMME BACK MY BULLETS. / ALL I CAN DO IS WRITE ABOUT IT**	-		
Aug 76. (7"ep) (MCA 251) **FREE BIRD. / SWEET HOME ALABAMA / DOUBLE TROUBLE**	31	-	

(re-iss. Nov79, hit No.43) (re-iss. May82 hit No.21) (re-iss. Dec83 12" /12"pic-d; MCAT/+P 251)

—— added **STEVE GAINES** (b.14 Sep'49, Seneca, Missouri) – 3rd guitar (ex-SMOKEHOUSE)

Oct 76. (7") <40647> **TRAVELIN' MAN (live). / GIMME THREE STEPS (live)**	-	-	
Oct 76. (d-lp/d-c) (MCSP/+C 279) <6001> **ONE MORE FROM THE ROAD (live)**	17	9	Sep76

– Workin' for MCA / I ain't the one / Searching / Tuesday's gone / Saturday night special / Travelin' man / Whiskey rock-a-roller / Sweet home Alabama / Gimme three steps / Call me the breeze / T for Texas / The needle and spoon / Crossroads / Free bird. <US cd-iss. 1991 with edited applause> (d-cd-ss.Dec92; MCLDD 19139)

Nov 76. (7") <40665> **FREE BIRD (live). / SEARCHING (live)**	-	38	
Jan 77. (7") (MCA 275) **FREE BIRD (live edit). / GIMME THREE STEPS (live)**	☐	-	
Oct 77. (lp/c) (MCG/+C 3525) <3029> **STREET SURVIVORS**	13	5	

– What's your name / That smell / One more time / I know a little / You got that right / I never dreamed / Honky tonk night time man / Ain't no good life. (re-iss. Jul82 lp/c; MCL/+C 1694) (cd-iss. Oct94; MCLD 19248)

—— On 20th Oct'77, a few days after release of above album, the band's tour plane crashed. RONNIE VAN ZANT, STEVE & CASSIE GAINES plus roadie DEAN KILPATRICK were all killed. The remainder all suffered other injuries, but would recover. ARTIMUS went solo, the rest became ROSSINGTON-COLLINS BAND

Jan 78. (7") (MCA 342) <40819> **WHAT'S YOUR NAME. / I KNOW A LITTLE**	☐	13	Nov77
Mar 78. (7") <40888> **YOU GOT THAT RIGHT. / AIN'T NO GOOD LIFE**	-	69	

ROSSINGTON-COLLINS BAND

—— formed 1979 by **GARY & ALLEN** with **BILLY POWELL** – keyboards / **LEON WILKESON** – bass / **DALE KRANTZ** – vocals / **BARRY HAREWOOD** – guitars, slide / **DEREK HASS** – drums, percussion

	M.C.A.	M.C.A.
Jul 80. (lp/c) (MCG/+C 4011) <5130> **ANYTIME, ANYPLACE, ANYWHERE**	☐	13

– Prime time / Three times as bad / Don't misunderstand me / Misery loves company / One good man / Opportunity / Getaway / Winners and losers / Sometimes you can put it out. (re-iss. Jun87 lp/c; MCL/+C 1748) <US cd-iss. Jun88; 31220>

Aug 80. (7") (MCA 636) <41284> **DON'T MISUNDERSTAND ME. / WINNERS AND LOSERS**	☐	55
Oct 80. (7") <51023> **GETAWAY. / SOMETIMES YOU CAN PUT IT OUT**	-	
Oct 80. (7") (MCA 648) **ONE GOOD MAN. / MISERY LOVES COMPANY**	☐	-
Jun 81. (7") <51218> **GOTTA GET IT STRAIGHT. / DON'T STOP ME NOW**	-	
Oct 81. (lp/c) (MCF/+C 4018) <5207> **THIS IS THE WAY**	☐	24

– Gotta get it straight / Teshauna / Gonna miss it when it's gone / Pine box / Fancy ideas / Don't stop me now / Seems like every day / I'm free today / Next phone call / Means nothing to you.

Oct 81. (7") (MCA 752) **TESHAUNA. / GONNA MISS IT WHEN IT'S GONE**	☐	-

(12"+=) (MCAT 572) – Don't stop me now.

ROSSINGTON

—— with **GARY** & his wife **DALE** with **HASS** – drums / **JAY JOHNSON** – guitar / **TIM LINDSAY** – bass

	not iss.	Atlantic
Nov 86. (lp) **RETURNED TO THE SCENE OF THE CRIME**	-	-

– Turn it up / Honest hearts / God luck to you / Wounded again / Waiting in the shadows / Dangerous love / Can you forget about my love / Returned to the scene of the crime / Are you leaving me / Path less chosen.

Nov 86. (7") <89364> **TURN IT UP. / PATH LESS CHOSEN**	-	-

—— now with **TIM LINDSEY** – bass / **TIM SHARPTON** – keyboards / **RONNIE EADES** – sax / **MITCH RIGER** – drums

	M.C.A.	M.C.A.
Jul 88. (lp/c/cd; as The ROSSINGTON BAND) <42166> **LOVE YOUR MAN**	☐	☐

– Losin' control / Welcome me home / Call it love / Holdin' my own / Rock on / Love your man / Stay with me / Nowhere to run / Say it from the heart / I don't want to leave you.

ALLEN COLLINS BAND

—— with **COLLINS, HAREWOOD, POWELL, WILKESON, HESS,** plus **JIMMY DOUGHERTY** – vocals / **RANDALL HALL** – guitar

	not iss.	M.C.A.
1983. (lp) <*39000*> **HERE THERE AND BACK**	-	

– Just trouble / One known soldier / Hangin' judge / Time after time / This ride's on me / Ready to move / Chapter one / Commitments / Everything you need. *<US cd-iss. 1990's; MCAD 31324>*

—— After a spell in prison, POWELL joined Christian band VISION. Also in 1986, ALLEN COLLINS was involved in a car crash which killed his girlfriend, and paralized himself from the waist down. On the 23rd Jan'90 he died of pneumonia.

LYNYRD SKYNYRD

—— re-formed Autumn 1987 with **ROSSINGTON, POWELL, PYLE, WILKESON, KING** plus **DALE KRANTZ ROSSINGTON, RANDALL HALL + JOHNNY VAN ZANT** – vocals (ex-• 38 SPECIAL)

	M.C.A.	M.C.A.
Apr 88. (d-lp/d-c/cd) (*DCMDMCMDC/DMCMD 7004*) <*8027*> **SOUTHERN BY THE GRACE OF GOD (live)**		68

– Workin' for MCA / That smell / I know a little / Comin' home / You got that right / What's your name / Gimme back my bullets / Swamp music / Call me the breeze / Dixie – Sweet home Alabama / Free bird.

—— **LYNYRD SKYNYRD** re-formed again in 1991 with **ROSSINGTON, KING** and **HALL** – guitars / **JOHNNY VAN ZANT** – vocals / **POWELL** – keyboards / **WILKESON** – bass / **PYLE** – percussion, drums / **CUSTER** – drums, percussion

	Atlantic	Atlantic
Jun 91. (cd/c/lp) <(*7567 82258-2/-4/-1*)> **LYNYRD SKYNYRD 1991**		64

– Smokestack lightning / Keeping the faith / Southern women / Pure & simple / I've seen enough / Good thing / Money man / Backstreet crawler / It's a killer / Mama (afraid to say goodbye) / End of the road.

—— extended members **JERRY JONES** – bass, guitar / **DALE KRANTZ-ROSSINGTON** – backing vocals repl. ARTIMUS PYLE

Mar 93. (cd/c) <(*7567 82447-2/-4*)> **THE LAST REBEL**		64

– Good lovin's hard to find / One thing / Can't take that away / Best things in life / The last rebel / Outta Hell in my Dodge / Kiss your freedom goodbye / South of Heaven / Love don't always come easy / Born to run. *(re-iss. cd Feb95;)*

	not iss.	Capricorn
Aug 94. (cd/c) <*42028-2*> **ENDANGERED SPECIES**	-	

– Down south jukin' / Heartbreak hotel / Devil in the bottle / Things goin' on / Saturday night special / Sweet home Alabama / I ain't the one / Am I losin' / All I have is a song / Poison whiskey / Good luck, bad luck / The last rebel / Hillbilly blues.

	S.P.V.	S.P.V.
Jul 96. (d-cd) (*SPV 0874419-2*) **SOUTHERN KNIGHTS (live)**		

– Working for MCA / Ain't the one / Saturday night special / Down south jukin' / Double trouble / T for Texas / Devil in the bottle / That smell / Simple man / Whiskey rock and roller / What's your name / Gimme three steps / Sweet home Alabama / Free bird.

—— line-up now **ROSSINGTON, VAN ZANT, WILKESON, POWELL** plus **RICKEY MEDLOCKE** – guitars, vocals (ex-BLACKFOOT) / **HUGHIE THOMASSON** – guitars, vocals / **OWEN HALE** – drums, percussion

May 97. (cd) (*SPV 0854439-2*) **TWENTY**		97

– We ain't much different / Bring it on / Voodoo lake / Home is where the heart is / Travelin' man / Talked myself right into it / Never too late / O.R.R. / Blame it on a sad song / Berneice / None of us are free / How soon we forget.

	S.P.V.	CMC Int.
Aug 99. (cd) (*SPV 0852964-2*) <*86272*> **EDGE OF FOREVER**		96

– Workin' / Full moon night / Preacher man / Mean streets / Tomorrow's goodbye / Edge of forever / Gone fishin' / Through it all / Money back guarantee / G.W.T.G.G. / Rough around the edges / Fla.

– compilations, others, etc. –

All 'M.C.A.' unless otherwise stated.

Oct 78. (lp/c) (*MCG/+C 3529*) <*3047*> **SKYNYRD'S FIRST AND . . .LAST** (rec.1970-72)	50	15 Sep78

– Down south jukin' / Preacher's daughter / White dove / Was I right or wrong / Lend a helpin' hand / Wino / Comin' home / The seasons / Things goin' on. *(re-iss. Aug81 lp/c; MCL/+C 1627)*

Oct 78. (7") <*40957*> **DOWN SOUTH JUKIN'. / WINO**	-	
Oct 78. (7"ep) (*MCEP 101*) **DOWN SOUTH JUKIN' / THAT SMELL. / LEND A HELPIN' HAND / CALL ME THE BREEZE**		-
Jan 80. (d-lp/d-c) (*MCSP/+C 308*) <*11008*> **GOLD & PLATINUM**	49	12 Dec79

– Down south jukin' / Saturday night special / Gimme three steps / What's your name / You got that right / Gimme back my bullets / Sweet home Alabama / Free bird / That smell / On the hunt / I ain't the one / Whiskey rock-a-roller / Simple man / I know a little / Tuesday's gone / Comin' home. *(re-iss. Jul82 lp/c; MCDW/+C 456)*

Apr 82. (d-c) (*MCA2 107*) **PRONOUNCED LEH-NERD SKIN-NERD / SECOND HELPING**		-
Nov 82. (lp) <*5370*> **THE BEST OF THE REST**	-	
Jul 84. (7") Old Gold; (*OG 9421*) **FREE BIRD (edit). / SWEET HOME ALABAMA**		-

(re-iss. Aug95 on cd-s;)

Sep 86. (d-c) (*MCA2 111*) **NUTHIN' FANCY / GIVE ME BACK MY BULLETS**		-
Mar 87. (d-lp/c) Raw Power; (*RAW LP/TC 031*) **ANTHOLOGY**		-
Nov 87. (7") <*53206*> **WHEN YOU GOT GOOD FRIENDS. / TRUCK DRIVIN' MAN**	-	
Nov 87. (lp/c) (*MCF/+C*) **LEGEND** (rare live)		41 Oct87

– Georgia peaches / When you got good friends / Sweet little Missy / Four walls of Raiford / Simple man / Truck drivin' man / One in the sun / Mr. Banker / Take your time.

Jan 89. (7"/12") (*MCA/+T 1315*) **FREE BIRD. / SWEET HOME ALABAMA**		-
Apr 89. (lp/c/cd) (*MCG/MCGC/DMCG 6046*) **SKYNYRD'S INNYRDS**		

1990. (c-s) <*54306*> **FREE BIRD. / SWEET HOME ALABAMA**	-	
Feb 92. (3xcd-box) (*MCA3 10390*) **THE DEFINITIVE LYNYRD SKYNYRD COLLECTION**		
Mar 94. (cd/c) Nectar; (*NTR CD/C 015*) **FREEBIRD – THE VERY BEST**		

– Saturday night special / Whiskey rock & roller / Workin' for MCA / I ain't the one / Sweet home Alabama / Ballad of Curtis Loew / Tuesday's gone / Gimme 3 steps / The needle & the spoon / Free bird / Call me the breeze / What's your name / Swamp music / Gimme back my bullets / That smell / You got that right.

Sep 94. (cd) (*MCLD 19248*) **STREET SURVIVORS / SKYNYRD'S FIRST AND . . . LAST**		-
Sep 96. (cd) (*MCD 1147-2*) **FREEBIRD – THE MOVIE** (live at Knebworth 1976)		
Jun 97. (d-cd) Repertoire; (*RR 4637*) **OLD TIME GREATS**		
May 99. (cd/c) <*11941*> **THE MILLENNIUM COLLECTION: THE BEST OF LYNYRD SKYNYRD**	-	

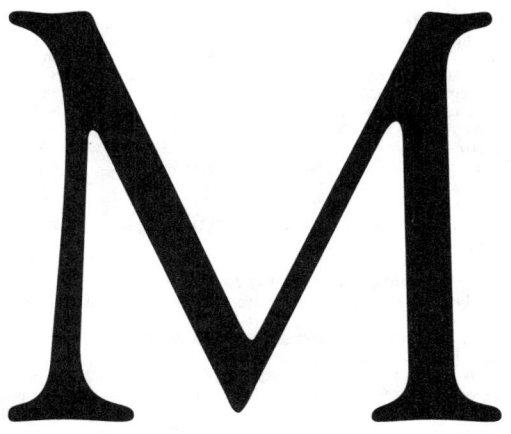

You're the one (with MAIRE BRENNAN) / Cracklin' Rosie / Bring down the lamp.

Dec 94. (c-s) *(ZANG 60C)* **THE SONG WITH NO NAME / NANCY WHISKEY** ☐ -
(12"+=/cd-s+=) *(ZANG 60 T/CD)* – Cracklin' Rosie.

Apr 95. (c-s; SHANE MacGOWAN & SINEAD O'CONNOR) *(ZANG 65C)* **HAUNTED. / THE SONG WITH NO NAME** 30 -
(cd-s+=) *(ZANG 65CD)* – Bring down the lamp / Cracklin' Rosie.

Jun 95. (c-s; SHANE MacGOWAN & MAIRE BRENNAN) *(ZANG 68C)* **YOU'RE THE ONE / AISLING** ☐ -
(cd-s) *(ZANG 68CD)* – Victoria.

Apr 96. (c-s; SHANE MacGOWAN) *(ZANG 79C)* **MY WAY / SONG WITH NO NAME** 29 -
(cd-s+=) *(ZANG 79CD)* – Aisling / My way (your way).

—— **LUCKY DOWLING** – bass; repl. BERNIE

—— added **KIERAN KIELY** – accordions, whistles, vocals + **JOHN MYERS** – fiddle, whistle, guitar

Oct 97. (cd-s) *(MACG 001CD)* **LONESOME HIGHWAY / A MAN CALLED HORSE / JOEY'S IN AMERICA** ☐ -

Oct 97. (cd/c) *(MACG 002 CD/C)* **THE CROCK OF GOLD** 59 -
– Paddy rolling stone / Rock'n'roll Paddy / Paddy public enemy No.1 / Back in County Hell / Lonesome highway / Come to the bower / Ceilidh cowboy / More pricks than kicks / Truck drivin' man / Joey's in America / B&I ferry / Mother mo chroi / Spanish lady / St. John of gods / Skipping rhymes / Maclennan / Wanderin' star.

Mar 98. (cd-s) *(MACG 003CD)* **ROCK'N'ROLL PADDY / SHE MOVES THROUGH THE FAIR** ☐ -

Shane MacGOWAN & THE POPES

Formed: King's Cross, London, England . . . early 1994 by ex-NIPPLE ERECTORS (1978), ex-NIPS (1978-'81) and ex-POGUES (1983-1991) frontman/legend, SHANE MacGOWAN (b.25 Dec '57, Kent, England), along with PAUL McGUINESS, BERNIE FRANCE, DANNY POPE and TOM McMANAMON. Following his messy departure from The POGUES in the early 90's, the Irish KEITH RICHARDS (though even RICHARDS' mythical debauchery would struggle to match MacGOWAN's self-destructiveness in terms of sheer dogged determination) threatened to form his own outfit, The POPES; sceptics who doubted the man could even form an opinion were at least partly silenced by MacGOWAN's late '92 duet with fellow maverick, NICK CAVE, on a brilliantly skewed cover of Louis Armstrong's 'WONDERFUL WORLD'. Two years on and much press rumination later, The POPES' debut single, 'THE CHURCH OF THE HOLY SPOOK', finally put an end to the speculation and announced that MacGOWAN's muse was as darkly fertile as ever. Released on 'Z.T.T.', the song's uptempo thrash recalled the unholy spirit of The POGUES' classic 'SICK BED OF CUCHULAINN', scraping into the UK Top 75. Follow-up single, 'THAT WOMAN'S GOT ME DRINKING' (excuses, excuses), made the Top 40, while Hollywood hearthrob, JOHNNY DEPP, played guitar on their debut Top Of The Pops appearance. The accompanying album, 'THE SNAKE', was the best album The POGUES never recorded in the last decade, finding MacGOWAN back at his cursing, doomed romantic best. Alongside the obligatory traditional songs ('THE RISING OF THE MOON' and 'NANCY WHISKEY'), the record featured an amusingly appropriate cover of Gerry Rafferty's 'HER FATHER DIDN'T LIKE ME ANYWAY', while 'HAUNTED' was a collaboration with SINEAD O'CONNOR which made the Top 30 when released as a single in Spring '95. CLANNAD's MAIRE BRENNAN also hooked up with MacGOWAN for 'YOU'RE THE ONE', underlining the depth of respect afforded the wayward genius, even among his more conventional peers. The live appearances which followed the record's release mightn't have matched the ferocious abandon of The POGUES in full flow but came damn near it, while MacGOWAN followed in SID VICIOUS' footsteps (the man's love of the SEX PISTOLS was recently revealed to the nation via a barely coherent admission on Jo Whiley's Channel 4 TV show) by recording a version of 'MY WAY' in gloriously two-fingered style. 1997 saw the release of a disappointing follow-up set, 'THE CROCK OF GOLD', a record that was at times easier on the ear but hardly threatened to set the pulse racing. • **Songwriters:** MacGOWAN except CRACKLIN' ROSIE (Neil Diamond) / THE RISING OF THE MOON + NANCY WHISKEY (trad). • **Trivia:** Their/his debut album also featured guest appearances from ex-POGUES; SPIDER and FINER, plus DUBLINERS musician/friend BARNEY McKENNA. 'VICTORIA' was written about his writer girlfriend at the time, VICTORIA CLARKE. MacGOWAN is still a reader & fan of writer JAMES JOYCE and Spanish poet LORCA.

Album rating: THE SNAKE (*8) / THE CROCK OF GOLD (*5)

SHANE McGOWAN – vocals (ex-POGUES, ex-NIPS) / **PAUL McGUINNESS** – guitar / **BERNIE FRANCE** – bass / **DANNY POPE** – drums / **TOM NcMANAMON** – banjo

		Z.T.T.	Warners
Sep 94.	(7"/c-s/cd-s) *(ZANG 57/+C/CD)* **THE CHURCH OF THE HOLY SPOOK. / RAKE AT THE GATES OF HELL**	74	-
	(cd-s+=) *(ZANG 57CDX)* – King of the bop / Nancy Whiskey.		
Oct 94.	(c-s) *(ZANG 56C)* **THAT WOMAN'S GOT ME DRINKING / HER FATHER DIDN'T LIKE ME ANYWAY**	34	-
	(12"+=/cd-s+=) *(ZANG 56 T/CD)* – Roddy McCorley / Minstrel boy.		
Oct 94.	(cd/c/lp) *(4509 98104-2/-4/-1)* <45821> **THE SNAKE**	37	☐ Jan95

– The church of the holy spook / That woman's got me drinking / The song with no name / Aisling / I'll be your handbag / Her father didn't like me anyway / A Mexican funeral in Paris / The snake with the eyes of Garnet / Donegal express / Victoria / The rising of the moon / Bring down the lamp. *(re-iss. Jun95 cd/c; 0630 10402-2/-4)* – Haunted (with SINEAD O'CONNOR) /

MACHINE HEAD

Formed: Oakland, California, USA . . . mid '92 by ex-VIOLENCE frontman ROBB FLYNN, LOGAN MADER, ADAM DUCE and CHRIS KONTOS. Dragging the flagging spirit of heavy metal kicking and screaming into the 90's, MACHINE HEAD roared into life with the universally acclaimed, COLIN RICHARDSON-produced debut album, 'BURN MY EYES' (1994). Rupturing eardrums with a bass-heavy bludgeon of mogadon guitars and a vocal style that alternated between CHRIS CORNELL (Soundgarden) and JAMES HETFIELD (Metallica), MACHINE HEAD became the ace in 'Roadrunner's (their label) pack, hitting the UK Top 30. Although they were signed to 'Interscope' in their native land, the group concentrated more on the British metal scene, especially after Kerrang! proclaimed them to be the best machine since ZAK DE LA ROCHA and Co (RATM). In 1995, one of the tracks from the album, 'OLD', was a surprise gatecrasher into the UK Top 50, the single backed by covers of POISON IDEA and CRO-MAGS material. With newcomer DAVE McCLAIN on the drumstool, their much-anticipated second set, 'THE MORE THINGS CHANGE . . .', was finally delivered early in 1997, the UK Top 20 album again proving that no frills, heavy-duty metal was still viable. Another round of ear-bashing was just what the doctor ordered, although not my doctor. Now without guitarist MADER (replaced by AHRUE LUSTER), MACHINE HEAD spurted out their third album, 'THE BURNING RED' (1999). The record entered the US Top 100 (their first to do so!) and the UK Top 20, although what the metal pundits from Kerrang! thought of their version of the Police's 'MESSAGE IN A BOTTLE', I dread to think. – take them away Sgt. STING.

Album rating: BURN MY EYES (*8) / THE MORE THINGS CHANGE . . . (*6) / THE BURNING RED (*4)

ROBB FLYNN – vocals, guitar (ex-VIOLENCE) / **LOGAN MADER** – guitar / **ADAM DUCE** – bass, vocals / **CHRIS KONTOS** – drums

		Roadrunner	Interscope
Aug 94.	(cd) *(RR 90169)* **BURN MY EYES**	25	☐

– Davidian / Old / A thousand lies / None but my own / The rage to overcome / Death church / A nation on fire / Blood for blood / I'm your god now / Real eyes, realize, real lies / Block. *(re-iss. May95 cd/c/lp; RR 9016-2/-4/-1)*

| Oct 94. | (12") **INFECTED. / PROTOPLAN** | ☐ | - |
| May 95. | (10"pic-d-ep) *(RR 23408)* **OLD / A NATION ON FIRE (demo) / REAL LIES – FUCK IT ALL (demo) / OLD (demo)** | 43 | ☐ |

(cd-ep) *(RR 23403)* – ('A'side) / Davidian (live) / Hard times (live) / Death church (demo).
(cd-s) *(RR 23405)* – ('A'side) / Death church (convent mix) / Old (eve of apocalypse mix) / The rage to overcome.

| Aug 95. | (10"pic-d) **DEATH CHURCH. / A NATION ON FIRE (demo)** | ☐ | ☐ |

(cd-s+=) – Fuck it all (demo) / Old (demo).
(cd-s) – ('A'side) / Old (mix) / The rage to overcome (demo).

—— **DAVE McCLAIN** – drums (ex-SACRED REICH) repl. KONTOS

| Mar 97. | (cd/c/lp) *(RR 8860-2/-4/-1)* <INT 846.371> **THE MORE THINGS CHANGE . . .** | 16 | ☐ |

– Ten ton hammer / Take my scars / Struck a nerve / Down to none / The frontlines / Spine / Bay of pigs / Violate / Blistering / Blood of the zodiac.

| Nov 97. | (cd-ep) *(RR 2257-3)* **TAKE MY SCARS / NEGATIVE CREEP / TAKE MY SCARS (live) / BLOOD FOR BLOOD (live)** | 73 | ☐ |

(cd-ep) *(RR 2257-5)* – (first 2 tracks) / Ten ton hammer (demo) / Struck a nerve (demo).

—— now without LOGAN MADER who was repl. by **AHRUE LUSTER**

| Aug 99. | (cd) <*(RR 8651-2)*> **THE BURNING RED** | 13 | 88 |

– Intro / Desire to fire / Nothing left / The blood the sweat the tears / Exhale the vile / Silver / From this day / Devil with king's card / Message in a bottle / I defy / Five / The burning red.

| Dec 99. | (cd-s) *(RR 2138-3)* **FROM THIS DAY / ALCOHOLOCAUST / HOUSE OF SUFFERING** | 74 | ☐ |

Billy MacKENZIE (see under ⇒ ASSOCIATES)

MADDER ROSE (dig out; Great Alt & Indie . . .)

MADNESS

Formed: Camden, London, England . . . early '79, out of Kentish Town ska outfit, The INVADERS. In its earliest incarnation MADNESS comprised MIKE BARSON (keyboards), LEE THOMPSON (saxophone, vocals) CHRIS FOREMAN (guitar), CHAS SMASH (horns, vocals, 'nutty' dancing), GRAHAM 'SUGGS' McPHERSON (vocals, equally 'nutty' dancing), MARK BEDFORD (bass) and DAN WOODGATE (drums). MADNESS were one of the leading lights of the ska revivalist '2-Tone' movement, the most exciting musical phenomenon since the advent of punk a few years earlier. Becoming friends with The SPECIAL AKA, MADNESS signed a one-off singles deal with JERRY DAMMERS' (the SPECIALS mainman) '2-Tone' label, releasing 'THE PRINCE' in August '79. An irrepressible dancefloor shuffle embellished with loose-limbed piano courtesy of BARSON, the track was a tribute to blue beat legend PRINCE BUSTER, whose song 'MADNESS' inspired the group's name and which they covered in their own inimitable style on the B-side. The track powered into the Top 20 and after a '2-Tone' tour with The SPECIALS and The SELECTER, MADNESS signed to 'Stiff', embarking upon an impressive run of chart domination. The follow-up single was 'ONE STEP BEYOND', its famous 'Hey you, don't watch that, watch this . . .' intro leading into a largely instrumental, sax-driven epic. The album of the same name reached No.2, confirming MADNESS had arrived. The group's "nutty boy" postures, madcap humour, cockney patois and unerringly catchy hooks won them a wide cross section of fans, from primary school kids and grannies to style-conscious teenagers, a far cry from their early audience of hardcore NF skinheads, most of whom they thankfully managed to shake off. As the band progressed from the likes of 'BAGGY TROUSERS' to the mordant social commentary of the '7' (1981) album, they moved away slightly from their ska roots, developing a highly original pop sound. After nine Top 10 hits, the band scored their first No.1 in 1982 with 'HOUSE OF FUN', a colourful coming of age yarn that contrasted with the increasing sense of melancholy that would come to mark their later work. Even earlier tracks like the brilliant 'BED AND BREAKFAST MAN' (from ONE STEP BEYOND) possessed a kind of bittersweet poignancy, as did the band's final single as a 7-piece, 'THE SUN AND THE RAIN'. MADNESS were still capable of a good old rave-up of course, as they illustrated with their previous effort, the celebratory calypso vibe of 'WINGS OF A DOVE', a No.2 hit in the summer of '83. With the departure of MIKE BARSON (one of the band's main writers), the band began to lose their trademark sound. Songs like 'MICHAEL CAINE' were interesting but not the MADNESS fans knew and loved, their declining popularity marked by increasingly lower chart positions. In 1984, the band formed their own label, 'Zarjazz', releasing work by FEARGAL SHARKEY as well as their own material which was, by this point, largely uninspired, coming to a juddering anti-climax with a cover of Scritti Politti's 'SWEETEST GIRL' and 'WELCOME TO THE GHOST TRAIN'. The band had already decided to split by the time of the latter's release in October '86, BEDFORD and WOODFORD subsequently joining VOICE OF THE BEEHIVE. In 1988, McPHERSON, THOMPSON, FOREMAN and SMASH re-froamed the band as THE MADNESS, an eponymous album not even breaching the Top 50. They had split for good by the end of the year, SUGGS going on to become a suitably "nutty" TV presenter as well as inflicting The FARM upon an unsuspecting music world at the turn of the decade. SMASH became an A&R man for 'Go! Discs', while THOMPSON and FOREMAN went back to ska basics with a new outfit, The NUTTY BOYS, releasing an album, 'CRUNCH!', in 1990. Back by popular demand, the original line-up reformed in 1992 for two sell-out shows in London's Finsbury Park where an army of 20-something's donned their pork pie hats and relived their days down the youth centre disco. The event was such a triumph that MADNESS repeated it in successive years. Not content with merely presenting Top Of The Pops now and again, SUGGS released a solo album, 'THE LONE RANGER', in 1995, subjecting innocent pop kids to an awful cod-reggae version of Simon & Garfunkel's 'CECILIA'. Maybe he's finally lost it. No, SUGGS was back to give us a second helping of his nutty pop songs, 'THE THREE PYRAMIDS CLUB' in 1998, followed a year later by a re-formed MADNESS set, 'WONDERFUL' (1999) – well, if you like that sort of thing. • **Songwriters:** Either McPHERSON-THOMPSON or BARSON or BEDFORD-FOREMAN. Covered; ONE STEP BEYOND (Cornell Campbell) / SWAN LAKE (Tchaikovski) / IT MUST BE LOVE (Labi Siffre) / THE HARDER THEY COME (Jimmy Cliff). SUGGS covered; I'M ONLY SLEEPING (Beatles). • **Trivia:** Early in 1982, SUGGS married singer and fellow 'Stiff' artist, BETTE BRIGHT.

Album rating: ONE STEP BEYOND (*8) / ABSOLUTELY (*6) / 7 (*6) / THE RISE AND FALL (*7) / COMPLETE MADNESS compilation (*9) / KEEP MOVING (*5) / MAD NOT MAD (*4) / UTTER MADNESS compilation (*6) / THE MADNESS (*6) / DIVINE MADNESS compilation (*9) / MADSTOCK (*5) / WONDERFUL (*5) / Suggs: THE LONE RANGER (*5) / THREE PYRAMIDS CLUB (*4)

GRAHAM 'SUGGS' McPHERSON (b.13 Jan'61, Hastings, England) – vocals / **MIKE BARSON** (b.21 May'58) – keyboards / **CHRIS 'CHRISSIE BOY' FOREMAN** (b. 8 Aug'58) – guitar / **LEE 'KIX' THOMPSON** (b. 5 Oct'57) – saxophone, vocals / **MARK 'BEDDERS' BEDFORD** (b.24 Aug'61) – bass / **DAN 'WOODY' WOODGATE** (b.19 Oct'60) – drums repl. JOHN HASLER / **CHAS SMASH** (b. CATHAL SMYTH, 14 Jan'59) – horns, vocals, dancer

	2-Tone-Chrysalis	not iss.
Aug 79. (7") (CHS TT3) **THE PRINCE. / MADNESS** (re-iss. Feb87 on 'Old Gold'; OG 9685)	16	–

	Stiff	Sire
Oct 79. (lp/c) (SEEZ/CSEEZ 17) <6085> **ONE STEP BEYOND . . .** – One step beyond / My girl / Night boat to Cairo / Believe me / Land of hope & glory / The prince / Tarzan's nuts / In the middle of the night / Bed and breakfast man / Razor blade alley / Swan Lake / Rockin' in Ab / Mummy's boy / Chipmunks are go. (re-iss. Aug88 on 'Virgin' lp/c; OVED/+C 133) (cd-iss. Apr90; CDOVED 133)	2	
Oct 79. (7") (BUY 56) **ONE STEP BEYOND. / MISTAKES** (12"+=) (BUYIT 56) – Nutty theme. (re-iss. Jun85 on 'Virgin' 7"; VS 780)	7	
Dec 79. (7") (BUY 62) **MY GIRL. / STEPPING INTO LINE** (12"+=) (BUYIT 62) – In the rain. (re-iss. Jun85 on 'Virgin' 7"; VS 781)	3	
Mar 80. (7"ep) (BUY 71) **WORK, REST & PLAY EP** – Night boat to Cairo / Deceives the eye / The young and the old / Don't quote me on that. (re-iss. Jun85 on 'Virgin' 7"ep; VS 782)	6	
Sep 80. (7") (BUY 84) **BAGGY TROUSERS. / THE BUSINESS** (re-iss. Jun85 on 'Virgin' 7"; VS 783)	3	
Sep 80. (lp/c) (SEEZ/CSEEZ 29) <6094> **ABSOLUTELY** – Baggy trousers / Embarrassment / E.R.N.I.E. / Close escape / Not home today / On the beat Pete / Solid gone / Take it or leave it / Shadow of fear / Disappear / Overdone / In the rain / You said / The return of the Los Palmas 7. (re-iss. Aug88 on 'Virgin' lp/c; OVED/+C 134) (cd-iss. Nov89; CDOVED 134)	2	
Nov 80. (7") (BUY 102) **EMBARRASSMENT. / CRYING SHAME**	4	
Jan 81. (7") (BUY 108) **THE RETURN OF THE LOS PALMAS 7. / THAT'S THE WAY TO DO IT** (12"+=) (BUYIT 108) – My girl (demo) / Swan Lake (live).	7	
Apr 81. (7"/c-s) (BUY/ZBUY 112) **GREY DAY. / MEMORIES**	4	–
Sep 81. (7") (BUY 126) **SHUT UP. / A TOWN WITH NO NAME** (12"+=) (BUYIT 126) – Never ask twice.	7	–
Oct 81. (lp/c) (SEEZ/CSEEZ 39) **7** – Cardiac arrest / Shut up / Sign of the times / Missing you / Mrs. Hutchinson / Tomorrow's dream / Opium eaters / Grey day / Pac-amac / Promises promises / Benny bullfrog / When dawn arrives / The opium eaters / Aeroplane. (re-iss. Aug88 on 'Virgin' lp/c; SEEZ/CSEEZ 135) (cd-iss. Nov89; CDOVED 135)	5	–

	Stiff	Geffen
Nov 81. (7"/12") (BUY/S'BUY 134) **IT MUST BE LOVE. / SHADOW ON THE HOUSE**	4	–
Feb 82. (7"/ext.12") (BUY/+IT 140) **CARDIAC ARREST. / IN THE CITY**	14	
Apr 82. (lp/c) (HITTV/ZHITV 1) **COMPLETE MADNESS** (compilation) – Embarrassment / Shut up / My girl / Baggy trousers / It must be love / The prince / Bed and breakfast man / Night boat to Cairo / One step beyond / House of fun / Cardiac arrest / Take it or leave it / Madness / The return of the Los Palmas 7 / In the city. (cd-iss. Jul 86 on 'Virgin'; HITCD 1)	1	–
May 82. (7"/7"pic-d) (BUY/P-BUY 140) **HOUSE OF FUN. / DON'T LOOK BACK** (re-iss. Jun85 on 'Virgin' 7"; VS 784)	1	
Jul 82. (7"/7"pic-d) (BUY/P-BUY 153) **DRIVING IN MY CAR. / ANIMAL FARM** (12"+=) (S'BUY 153) – Riding on my bike. (re-iss. Jun85 on 'Virgin' 7"; VS 785)	4	
Oct 82. (7"/7"pic-d) (BUY/P-BUY 163) **OUR HOUSE. / WALKING WITH MR WHEEZE** (12"+=) (BUYIT 163) – ('A'extended). (re-iss. Jun85 on 'Virgin' 7"; VS 786)	5	–
Nov 82. (lp/c) (SEEZ/CSEEZ 46) **PRESENTS THE RISE AND FALL** – Rise and fall / Tomorrow's (just another day) / Blue skinned beast / Primrose hill / Mr. Speaker (gets the word) / Sunday morning / Our house / Tiptoes / New Delhi / That face / Calling cards / Are you coming (with me) / Madness (is all in the mind). (re-iss. Aug88 on 'Virgin' lp/c; OVED/+C 190) (cd-iss. Nov89; CDOVED 190)	10	
Feb 83. (7"/7"pic-d) (BUY/P-BUY 169) **TOMORROW'S (JUST ANOTHER DAY). / MADNESS (IS ALL IN THE MIND)** (ext.12"+=) (BUYIT 169) – Blue beast / ('A'version with ELVIS COSTELLO). (re-iss. Jun85 on 'Virgin' 7"; VS 787)	8	
Mar 83. (lp) <4003> **MADNESS** – It must be love / Shut up / Rise and fall / Tomorrow's just another day / Primrose Hill / Madness (is all in the mind) / Grey day / House of fun / Blue skinned beast / Cardiac arrest / Night boat to Cairo / Shadow of fear.	–	41
May 83. (7"/12") <29668> **OUR HOUSE. / CARDIAC ARREST**	–	7
Aug 83. (7") <29562> **IT MUST BE LOVE. / CALLING CARDS**	–	33
Aug 83. (7"/7"pic-d) (BUY/P-BUY 181) **WINGS OF A DOVE. / BEHIND THE 8 BALL** ('A'-Blue train mix-12"+=) (BUYIT 181) – One's second thoughtlessness. (re-iss. Jun85 on 'Virgin' 7"; VS 788)	2	
Oct 83. (7"/7"pic-d) (BUY/P-BUY 192) **THE SUN AND THE RAIN. / FIREBALL XL5** (ext.12"+=) (BUYIT 192) – My girl (live). (re-iss. Jun85 on 'Virgin' 7"; VS 789)	5	
Jan 84. (7") <29350> **THE SUN AND THE RAIN. / TIME FOR TEA**	–	72

—— trimmed to a 6-piece, when BARSON went to stay in Holland with his Dutch wife.

	Stiff	Geffen
Jan 84. (7"/7"pic-d) (BUY/P-BUY 196) **MICHAEL CAINE. / IF YOU THINK THERE'S SOMETHING** (12"+=) (BUYIT 196) – ('A'extended). (re-iss. Jun85 on 'Virgin' 7"; VS 790)	11	
Feb 84. (lp/pic-lp/c) <4022> **KEEP MOVING** – Keep moving / Michael Caine / Turning blue / One better day / March of the gherkins / Waltz into mischief * / Brand new beat / Victoria Gardens. <US repl. w/> – Wings of a dove (a celebratory song) / The sun and the rain / Prospects / Samantha. (re-iss. Aug88 on 'Virgin' lp/c; OVED/+C 191) (cd-iss. Nov89; CDOVED 191)	6	
May 84. (7"/7"pic-d) (BUY/P-BUY 201) **ONE BETTER DAY. / GUNS** (12"+=) (BUYIT 201) – Victoria Gardens / Sarah. (re-iss. Jun85 on 'Virgin' 7"; VS 791)	17	

		Zarjazz	Virgin
Aug 85.	(7") *(JAZZ 5)* **YESTERDAY'S MEN. / ALL I KNEW**	18	

(ext.12") *(JAZZ 5-12)* – ('A'demo).
(7"square-pic-d/incl.free-7"+=) *(JAZZ D5)* – YESTERDAY'S MEN (harmonica mix) / IT MUST BE LOVE (live)

Oct 85.	(lp/c) *(JZ LP/MC 1)* **MAD NOT MAD**	16	

– I'll compete / Yesterday's men / Uncle Sam / White heat / Mad not mad / Sweetest girl / Burning the boats / Tears you can't hide / Time / Coldest day. *(cd-iss. Jul87; JZCD 1)*

Oct 85.	(7"/s7") *(JAZZ/+F 7)* **UNCLE SAM. / PLEASE DON'T GO**	21	

(7"pic-d+=) *(JAZZY 7)* – Inanity over Christmas.
(ext.12"+=) *(JAZZ 7-12)* – ('A'demo).

Jan 86.	(7"/one-sided-7"pic-d) *(JAZZ/+Y 8)* **SWEETEST GIRL. / JENNIE (A PORTRAIT OF)**	35	

(ext.12"+=) *(JAZZ 8-12)* – ('A'dub).
(d7"+=) *(JAZZ D8)* – Tears you can't hide / Call me.

―――― **BARSON** returned for swan-song

Oct 86.	(7"/7"square-pic-d) *(JAZZ/+S 9)* **(WAITING FOR) THE GHOST TRAIN. / MAYBE IN ANOTHER LIFE**	18	

(12"+=/12"w-booklet+=) *(JAZZ/+B 9-12)* – Seven year scratch.

Nov 86.	(lp/c/cd) *(JZ LP/MC/CD 2)* **UTTER MADNESS** (compilation)	29	

– Our house / Driving in my car / Michael Caine / Wings of a dove / Yesterday's men / Tomorrow's (just another day) / I'll compete / (Waiting for) The ghost train / Uncle Sam / The sun and the rain / Sweetest girl / One better day / Victoria Gardens. *(cd+=)* – Seven year scratch (hit megamix). *(re-iss. Apr90 on 'Virgin' lp/c; OVED/+C 287)*

―――― Had already split Sep'86. BEDDERS and WOODY joined VOICE OF THE BEEHIVE. They had recently backed female duo STRAWBERRY SWITCHBLADE.

THE MADNESS

―――― McPHERSON, THOMPSON, FOREMAN + SMYTH, re-formed Feb'88, with slight change of name (allowed to just prefix THE), bringing in some session people; **JERRY DAMMERS, STEVE NIEVE + BRUCE THOMAS**

		Virgin	Virgin
Mar 88.	(7") *(VS 1054)* **I PRONOUNCE YOU. / PATIENCE**	44	

(d7"+=/12"+=/cd-s+=) *(VS X/T/CD 1054)* – 4 BF / 11th hour.

May 88.	(lp/c/cd) *(V/TCV/CDV 2507)* **THE MADNESS**	65	

– Nail down the days / What's that / I pronounce you / Oh / In wonder / Song in red / Nightmare nightmare / Thunder and lightning / Beat the bride / Gabriel's horn. *(cd+=)* – 11th Hour / 4BF / Be Good Boy / Flashings.

May 88.	(7"/7"sha-pic-d) *(VS/+S 1078)* **WHAT'S THAT. / BE GOOD BOY.**		

(7"sha-pic-d) *(VSJ 1078)* – WHAT'S THAT. / FLASHINGS
(12"+=) *(VST 1078)* – Be good boy.

―――― Disbanded again in 1988. SUGGS became a TV presenter and the manager of The FARM, who he produced in 1985, and CHAS became A&R man for 'Go! Discs'. They were encouraged to re-unite for a one-off gig on 8 Aug'92 at Finsbury Park, after old hits re-charted (see further below).

MADNESS

(original line-up, see above)

		Go! Discs	London
Oct 92.	(cd/c/lp) *(828367-2/-4/-1)* **MADSTOCK** (live)	22	

– One step beyond / The Prince / Embarrassment / My girl / The Sun and the rain / Grey day / It must be love / Shut up / Driving in my car / Bed and breakfast man / Close escape / Wings of a dove / Our house / Night boat to Cairo / Madness / House of fun / Baggy trousers / The harder they come.

Nov 92.	(7"/c-s) *(GOD/+C 93)* **THE HARDER THEY COME (live). / TOMORROW'S JUST ANOTHER DAY (live) / TAKE IT OR LEAVE IT (live)**	44	

(cd-s+=) *(GODCD 93)* – Land of hope & glory.

STARVATION

MADNESS with other ska-groups (for charity)

		Zarjazz	not iss.
Feb 85.	(7") *(JAZZ 3)* **STARVATION. / TAM-TAM POUR L'ETHIOPIE**	33	-

(12"+=) *(JAZZ 3-12)* – Haunted / ('B'-part 2).

SUGGS

		WEA	Warners
Aug 95.	(c-s) *(YZ 975C)* **I'M ONLY SLEEPING / OFF ON HOLIDAY**	7	

(cd-s+=) *(YZ 975CD)* – Off on holiday (instrumental).
(cd-s+=) *(YZ 975CDX)* – Animal / When you came.

Oct 95.	(7"/c-s) *(WEA 019/+C)* **CAMDEN TOWN. / BEDAZZLED**	14	

(cd-s+=) *(WEA 019CD)* – ('A'-Chili pepper dub) / ('A'-Ragga in London mix).

Oct 95.	(cd/c) *(0630 12478-2/-4)* **THE LONE RANGER**	14	

– I'm only sleeping / Camden Town / Alcohol / 4 am / The tune / Cecilia / Haunted / Off on holiday / Green eyes / Fortune fish / She's gone.

Dec 95.	(7") *(WEA 031)* **THE TUNE. / ALRIGHT**	33	

(c-s+=/cd-s+=) *(WEA 031 C/CD)* – Sleigh ride.

Apr 96.	(c-s/cd-s) *(WEA 042 C/CD)* **CECILIA / I FEEL GOOD**	4	

(cd-s+=) *(WEA 052CDX)* – The tune.
above featured LOUCHIE LOU and MICHIE ONE, as did below

Sep 96.	(c-s/cd-s) *(WEA 065 C/CD1)* **NO MORE ALCOHOL / FORTUNE FISH**	24	

(cd-s+=) *(WEA 065CD2)* – ('A'mix).

May 97.	(c-s/cd-s; as SUGGS & CO. featuring CHELSEA TEAM) *(WEA 112 C/CD)* **BLUE DAY** ('A'–Road to Wembley mix)	22	-

(cd-s+=) *(WEA 112CD2)* – ('A'–Stamford Bridge mix) / ('A'–Strawberry Fields mix).

Aug 98.	(c-s) *(WEA 174C)* **I AM / SAME AGAIN**	38	-

(cd-s+=) *(WEA 174CD)* – It really would be nice.

Sep 98.	(cd/c) *(3984 23815-2/-4)* **THE THREE PYRAMIDS CLUB**		

– I am / So tired / Straight banana / Invisible man / Sing / Girl / The greatest show on earth / Our man / On drifting sand / The three pyramids club.

MADNESS

re-formed yet again

		Virgin	Virgin
Jul 99.	(c-s) *(VSC 1737)* **LOVESTRUCK. / WE ARE LOVE**	10	-

(cd-s+=) *(VSCDT 1737)* – ('A'-CD-Rom).
(12") *(VSLH 1737)* – ('A'side) / Round & round / Maddley (album medley).

Oct 99.	(cd-s) *(VSCDT 1740)* **JOHNNY THE HORSE / YOU'RE WONDERFUL (remix)**	44	

(c-s/cd-s) *(VSC/+DX 1740)* – ('A'side) / I was the one / Dreaming man.

Oct 99.	(cd/c) *(CDV/TCV 2889)* **WONDERFUL**	17	

– Lovestruck / Johnny the horse / Communicator / 4 a.m. / Wizard / Drip fed Fred / Going to the top / Elysium / Saturday night Sunday morning / If I didn't care / No money.

– compilations, etc. –

on 'Virgin' unless otherwise stated

Oct 86.	(12"ep) *Strange Fruit; (SFPS 007)* **THE PEEL SESSIONS (27.8.79)**		-

– The prince / Bed and breakfast man / Land of hope & glory / Stepping into line. *(c-ep.Jun87; SFPSC 007) (cd-ep.Jul88; SFPSCD 007)*

Nov 88.	(7") *Old Gold; (OG 9821)* **BAGGY TROUSERS. / EMBARRASSMENT**		
Nov 88.	(7") *Old Gold; (OG 9826)* **IT MUST BE LOVE. / MY GIRL**		
May 89.	(7") *(VS 1197)* **IT MUST BE LOVE. / THE RETURN OF THE LOS PALMAS 7**	6	-
Sep 90.	(lp/c/cd) *Pickwick;* **IT'S . . . MADNESS**		-

(re-iss. May94 on 'Virgin-VIP' cd/c; VVIP D/C 107)

Oct 90.	(3xcd-box) *(TPAKJ 8)* **ONE STEP BEYOND / ABSOLUTELY / THE RISE AND FALL**		-
1991.	(cd) *Pickwick; (cd)* **IT'S MADNESS . . . TOO**		-

(re-iss. Oct94 on 'Virgin-VIP' cd/c; VVIP D/C 115)

Jan 92.	(7"/c-s) *(VS/+C 1405)* **IT MUST BE LOVE. / BED AND BREAKFAST MAN**	6	-

(cd-s+=/pic-cd-s+=) *(VSCD T/P 1405)* – Airplane / Don't quote me on that.

Feb 92.	(cd/c/d-lp) *(CD/TC+/V 2692)* **DIVINE MADNESS**	1	

– The Prince / One step beyond / My girl / Night boat to Cairo / Baggy trousers / Embarrassment / The return of Los Palmas 7 / Grey day / Shut up / It must be love / Cardiac arrest / House of fun / Driving in my car / Our house / Tomorrow's just another day / Wings of a dove / The sun and the rain / Michael Caine / One better day / Yesterday's men / Uncle Sam / (Waiting for) The ghost train.

Apr 92.	(7"/c-s) *(VS/+C 1413)* **HOUSE OF FUN. / UN PASO ADELAINTE (ONE STEP BEYOND – Spanish version)**	40	

(12"+=/cd-s+=) *(VS T/CD 1413)* – Yesterday's men / Gabriel's horn (demo).

Aug 92.	(7"/c-s) *(VS/+C 1425)* **MY GIRL. / MADNESS**	27	

(cd-s) *(VSCD 1425)* – ('A'side) / E.R.N.I.E. / Embarrassment / Tomorrow's dream.
(cd-s) *(VSCDX 1425)* – ('A'side) / Precious one (live) / My girl (live) / Disappear (live).

Feb 93.	(7"/c-s) *(VS/+C 1447)* **NIGHT BOAT TO CAIRO. / ('A'mix)**	56	

(12"+=/cd-s+=) *(VS T/CD 1447)* – ('A'mixes).

Nov 93.	(3xcd-box) *(MADBOX 1)* **THE BUSINESS – THE DEFINITIVE SINGLES COLLECTION**		-

―――― In Oct'93, 'THE PRINCE' alongside other ska-revival bands on '2-TONE EP' hit UK No.30.

Jun 98.	(cd/c) *(CDV/TCV 2862)* **THE HEAVY HEAVY HITS**	19	

– Grey day / The sweetest girl / Michael Caine / Embarrassment / Night boat to Cairo / House of fun / Yesterday's men / It must be love / Driving in my car / (Waiting for the) Ghost train / Uncle Sam / Shut up / Cardiac arrest / Our house / My girl / The sun and the rain / Baggy trousers / Wings of a dove / Tomorrow's just another day / One better day / Return of the Los Palmas 7 / The prince / One step beyond.

Mar 99.	(cd) *Goldenvoice; (GVC 0440-2)* **UNIVERSAL MADNESS** (live)		-
Nov 99.	(6xcd-box) *(MADBOX 2)* **THE LOT**		-

MADONNA

Born: MADONNA LOUISE VERONICA CICCONE, 16th August '59, Rochester, Michigan, USA. After winning a scholarship to her local university (where she also learned ballet), the budding singer subsequently dropped out in the late 70's and headed for New York where she supported herself with waitressing and part-time model work (nude photos were later published in 1985 by top shelf mags, 'Penthouse' and 'Playboy'). To make ends meet (as they say), she also acted in a budget soft-porn flick, 'A Certain Sacrifice', later (1988) released on video without her consent; on first name terms with controversy from the beginning, MADONNA would nevertheless prove herself to be one of the 80's most deft media manipulators and arguably one of the most driven women in the history of the music business. Her first real experience of professional performance was as a touring dancer/backing singer for Hi-NRG legend, PATRICK HERNANDEZ (when will 'Born To Be Alive' ever get a re-release?!!!), although she soon returned to the Big Apple and began writing with ex-boyfriend, STEVE BRAY. Local DJ Mark Kamins was sufficiently impressed with the resulting material to help secure MADONNA a deal with 'Sire', the label releasing her debut single, 'EVERYBODY', late in '82. The track became a dancefloor favourite, as did US-only 12", 'BURNING UP', the singer subsequently hooking up with DJ 'Jellybean' Benitez to work on a whole album's worth of material. 'MADONNA' the album, hit the shelves in Autumn '83, its pilot single, 'HOLIDAY', finally making the jump from clubland to the charts (Top 20) a few months later. The track's unpretentious dance-pop and naive appeal served MADONNA well throughout this early period; the song

also hit the UK Top 20 and prompted the re-issue of second single, 'LUCKY STAR', while the teen-love poignancy of 'BORDERLINE' gave the singer her first US Top 10 early the following year. The album itself was well on its way to becoming a multi-million seller and, in late summer '84, MADONNA firmly imprinted herself on public consciousness with US No.1 (album and single), 'LIKE A VIRGIN' and its attendant video. Through a winning combination of coy sexuality, pouting girlishness, Nile Rodgers-enhanced rhythmic backing and pop savvy, MADONNA had invented herself as an icon for not only the 80's 'MATERIAL GIRL', but legions of gay men and hormonal adolescents. Accordingly, manager Freddie DeMann was quick to break the singer into a parallel acting career, helping her secure a minor part in the film 'Vision Quest' and a more high profile role alongside Rosanna Arquette in 'Desperately Seeking Susan'. While these didn't exactly present a case for Oscar nominations, their soundtracks did provide MADONNA with two further No.1 singles in 'CRAZY FOR YOU' and 'INTO THE GROOVE'. More transatlantic hits followed in 'DRESS YOU UP', 'ANGEL' and 'GAMBLER', although it was only with the 'TRUE BLUE' (1986) album and preceding No.1 singles, 'LIVE TO TELL' and 'PAPA DON'T PREACH', that MADDY began to win the grudging respect of the rock press and fully blossom as a powerful vocalist. The latter track, in particular, showed a quantum leap in songwriting ability, its controversial, teenage pregnancy subject matter seeing MADONNA finally spark debate for something other than her risque videos/stage show. Successive singles 'OPEN YOUR HEART' and the sultry 'LA ISLA BONITA' saw her top the charts yet again, while the album became her biggest selling to date. Summer '87 saw more movie action, her title track from the 'Who's That Girl' (in which she starred alongside Griffin Dunne) soundtrack scaling the charts on both sides of the Atlantic. Though the ensuing couple of years were a bit quieter on the recording front (save for a dodgy remix compilation, 'U CAN DANCE'), MADONNA's massive international superstar status and stormy marriage to actor Sean Penn (with whom she starred in 1986's 'Shanghai Surprise') ensured she was never far from the tabloid gossip columns. The more self-appointedly moralistic elements of the press had a field day with the video for 1989's 'LIKE A PRAYER', the sight of MADONNA making lewd advances to a black priest not going down (oops!) too well with the Vatican either. In the resulting furore, the pointy-bra'd one saw her sponsorship deal with 'Pepsi' go flat, although the intense interest guaranteed humungous sales of the accompanying album (also called 'LIKE A PRAYER'). Incidentally, the record was her most mature and fully realised piece of work to date, candidly exploring her favourite themes of religion and sex in a more frankly personal fashion than ever. The turn of the decade saw another feverish burst of activity with the release of two albums, 'I'M BREATHLESS' (as the sleeve states, 'Music Inspired By The Film Dick Tracy') and an impressive greatest hits set, wittily entitled 'THE IMMACULATE COLLECTION'. By far the most controversial offering of the year, however, was the 'JUSTIFY MY LOVE' single, its X-rated video (banned just about everywhere, it nevertheless enjoyed an airing on Channel 4's infamous ambassador of tack, 'The Word') and pre-orgasmic panting taking up almost as much column inches as the ensuing row over the writing credits (LENNY KRAVITZ and INGRID CHAVEZ at loggerheads). MADONNA took the increasingly overt sexuality angle to its ultimate conclusion with the simultaneous release of the 'EROTICA' (1992) album and 'Sex' book. The latter was MADONNA's first venture into publishing and possibly her last; the explicit soft-porn poses and woefully weak thematic thread saw the expensive (25 quid a throw, and you weren't even allowed to peruse the damn thing before you bought it!) panned by critics. Still, 1992 wasn't all bad as the singer signed a multi-million dollar agreement with 'Warners', giving added commercial oomph to her developing 'Maverick' label. Over the next five years, MADONNA was more often featured in the music press in connection with her business acumen (amongst others, she's secured the signature of ALANIS MORISSETTE) than her recorded output, 1994's 'BEDTIME STORIES' album offering up a limp R&B sound. Nevertheless, MADONNA's longtime blonde ambition was fulfilled in 1996 as she played the lead part of Eva Peron in the screen version of 'Evita', the singer finally winning unreserved critical plaudits from all quarters and even acquiring a fair degree of respectability among her moralising detractors.
• **Songwriters:** She collaborated on most material, the bulk with ex-boyfriend STEVE BRAY. Others & covers; PHYSICAL ATTRACTION (Reggie Lucas) / HOLIDAY (Jellybean Benitez) / LOVE DON'T LIVE HERE ANYMORE (Rose Royce; hit) / LIKE A VIRGIN (Tom Kelly & Billy Steinberg) / CRAZY FOR YOU (Jon Lind & John Bettis) / JUSTIFY MY LOVE (Lenny Kravitz & Ingrid Chavez) / FEVER (Peggy Lee) / LOVE SONG (co-w/ PRINCE) / BEDTIME STORY (Bjork) / GUILT BY ASSOCIATION with Joe Henry (Vic Chesnutt) / I WANT YOU (Marvin Gaye).
• **Album rating:** MADONNA (*6) / LIKE A VIRGIN (*6) / TRUE BLUE (*7) / YOU CAN DANCE remixes (*5) / LIKE A PRAYER (*8) / THE IMMACULATE COLLECTION compilation (*9) / I'M BREATHLESS soundtrack (*4) / EROTICA (*6) / BEDTIME STORIES (*7) / SOMETHING TO REMEMBER compilation (*7) / EVITA soundtrack (*5) / RAY OF LIGHT (*8)

MADONNA – vocals with session people, producers, etc.

		Sire	Sire
Dec 82.	(7"/12") (W 9899/+T) <29841> **EVERYBODY. / EVERYBODY (dub version)**		
May 83.	(7") <29609> **BURNING UP. / PHYSICAL ATTRACTION**	-	-
Oct 83.	(7") <29478> **HOLIDAY. / I KNOW IT**	-	16
Oct 83.	(7"/ext.12") (W 9522/+T) <29177> **LUCKY STAR. / I KNOW IT**		4 Aug84
	(12") (W 9522TV) – ('A'-U.S.remix) / I know it.		

	(re-prom.Mar84 hit UK No.14)		
Sep 83.	(lp/c) (923867-1/-4) <23867> **MADONNA** – Lucky star / Borderline / Burning up / I know it / Holiday / Think of me / Physical attraction / Everybody. (re-iss. Sep85 as 'THE FIRST ALBUM'; WX 22)	6	8 Aug83
Nov 83.	(7"/ext.12") (W 9405/+T) **HOLIDAY. / THINK OF ME** (re-prom.Jul85, hit UK-No.25; also 12"pic-d; W 9405P)	6	-
Mar 84.	(7") <29354> **BORDERLINE. / THINK OF ME**	-	10
May 84.	(7") (W 9260) **BORDERLINE. / PHYSICAL ATTRACTION** (d7"+=) (W 9260F) – Holiday / Think of me. (12") (W 9260T) – ('A'-U.S.remix) / ('A'dub remix) / ('B'side. (re-Prom.Jan86, hit UK No.2 – also 7"sha-pic-d; W 9260P)	56	-
Nov 84.	(7") (W 9210) <29210> **LIKE A VIRGIN. / STAY** (12") (W 9210T) <20239> – ('A' US dance remix) / ('B'side).	3	1
Nov 84.	(lp/c/(cd)) (WX 20/+C)(925157-2) <25157> **LIKE A VIRGIN** – Material girl / Angel / Like a virgin / Over and over / Love don't live here anymore / Dress you up / Shoo-be-doo / Stay / Pretender. (re-iss. Aug85 pic-lp/(cd+=; WX 20P)(925181-2) – Into the groove.	1	1
Feb 85.	(7") (W 9083) <29083> **MATERIAL GIRL. / PRETENDER** (12") (W 9083T) <20304> – ('A'-Jellybean dance mix) / ('B'side). (below single issued on 'Geffen' from the film 'Vision Quest')	3	2
Mar 85.	(7")(12") <29051><26325> **CRAZY FOR YOU. / (B-side by Berlin)**	-	1
Apr 85.	(7") <29008> **ANGEL. / (dance mix)** (12") <20335> – Angel (extended dance mix) / Into the groove.	-	5
Jun 85.	(7"/7"sha-pic-d) (A/WA 6323) **CRAZY FOR YOU. / (B-side by Sammy Hagar)** (below from the film 'Desperately Seeking Susan')	2	-
Jul 85.	(7"/7"sha-pic-d) (W 8934/+P) **INTO THE GROOVE. / SHOO-BE-DOO** (12"+=) (W 8934T) – Everybody.	1	-
Aug 85.	(7") <28919> **DRESS YOU UP. / SHOO-BEE-DOO** (12"+=) <20369> – ('A'-Casual instrumental mix).	-	5
Sep 85.	(7"/7"sha-pic-d) (W 8881/+P) **ANGEL. / BURNING UP** (12") (W 8881T) – ('A'-12"extended dance mix) / ('B'side. (below single issued on 'Geffen' from the film 'Vision Quest')	5	-
Oct 85.	(7"/7"+poster) (A/QA 6585) **GAMBLER. / (B-side by Black 'n' Blue)** (12") (TA 6585) – ('A'extended dance mix) / ('A'instrumental) / ('B'side).	4	-
Nov 85.	(7"/7"sha-pic-d) (W 8848/+P) **DRESS YOU UP. / I KNOW IT** (12"/12"+poster) (W 8848T/+F) – ('A'-instrumental).	5	-
Apr 86.	(7") (W 8717) <28717> **LIVE TO TELL. / ('A'instrumental)** (12"+=/12"+poster) (W 8717T/+W) <20461> – ('A'version).	2	1
Jun 86.	(7")(ext.12") <28660><20492> **PAPA DON'T PREACH. / PRETENDER**	-	1
Jun 86.	(7") (W 8636) **PAPA DON'T PREACH. / AIN'T NO BIG DEAL** (12"+=/12"+poster+=/12"pic-d+=) (W 8636T/+W/P) – ('A'extended).	1	-
Jul 86.	(lp/c)(cd) (WX 54/+C)(925442-2) <25442> **TRUE BLUE** – Papa don't preach / Open your heart / White heat / Live to tell / Where's the party / rue blue / La Isla Bonita / Jimmy Jimmy / Love makes the world go round.	1	1
Sep 86.	(7") (W 8550) **TRUE BLUE (remix). / HOLIDAY (lp version)** (12"/12"pic-d) (W 8550T/+P) – ('A'extended version version) / Holiday (full length).	1	-
Sep 86.	(7",7"blue) <28591> **TRUE BLUE. / AIN'T NO BIG DEAL** (12"+=) <20533> – ('A'Colour mix) / ('A'instrumental).	-	3
Dec 86.	(7") <28508> **OPEN YOUR HEART. / WHITE HEAT** (ext.12"+=) <20597> – ('A'extended).	-	1
Dec 86.	(7") (W 8480) **OPEN YOUR HEART. / LUCKY STAR** (ext.12"+=/ext.12"pic-d+=) (W 8480T/+P) – ('A'dub mix).	4	-
Mar 87.	(7") (W 8378) <28425> **LA ISLA BONITA (remix). / ('A'instrumental)** (12"/12"pic-d) (W 8378T/+P) <20633> – ('A'extended remix) / ('A'extended instrumental).	1	4
Jul 87.	(7"/ext.12"/ext.12"pic-d) (W 8341/+T/TP) <28341> **WHO'S THAT GIRL. / WHITE HEAT** (ext.12") (W 8341TX) <20692> – ('A'dub version). (above A-side from the film 'Who's That Girl') (the Various Artists Soundtrack hit UK 4 + US 7 in Aug'87)	1	1
Sep 87.	(7") (W 8224) <28224> **CAUSING A COMMOTION (Silver Screen mix). / JIMMY JIMMY** (12"+=/12"pic-d+=/c-s+=) (W 8224 T/TP/C) <20762> – ('A'-movie house mix).	4	2
Nov 87.	(lp/c)(cd) (WX 76/+C)(925535-2) <25535> **U CAN DANCE (remixes)** – Spotlight / Holiday / Everybody / Physical attraction / Over and over / Into the groove / Where's the party / Spotlight (dub) / Holiday (dub) / Into the groove (dub) / Over and over (dub). (re-iss. cd/c Feb95;)	5	14
Dec 87.	(7") (W 8115) **THE LOOK OF LOVE. / I KNOW IT** (12"+=/12"pic-d+=) (W 8115T/+P) – Love don't live here anymore.	9	-
Mar 89.	(7") (W 7539) <27539> **LIKE A PRAYER. / ACT OF CONTRITION** (ext.12"+=/ext.12"pic-d+=/c-s+=) (W 7539 T/TP/C) – ('A'club mix). (12") (W 7539TX) <21170> – ('A'-Churchapella mix) / ('A'side). (3"cd-s) (W 7539CD) – ('A'extended remix) / ('A'club mix).	1	1
Mar 89.	(lp/c)(cd) (WX 239/+C)(925844-2) <25844> **LIKE A PRAYER** – Like a prayer / Express yourself / Love song / Till death us do part / Promise to try / Cherish / Dear Jessie / Oh father / Keep it together / Spanish eyes / Act of contrition.	1	1
May 89.	(7"s/7"s/c-s) (W 2948 X/W/C) <22948> **EXPRESS YOURSELF. / THE LOOK OF LOVE** (c-s/cd-s/12"pic-d) (W 2948 CX/CD/TP) – ('A'side) / ('A'-Non-stop mix) / ('A'-Stop & go mix).	5	2
Aug 89.	(7"/c-s) (W 2883/+C) <22883> **CHERISH. / SUPERNATURAL** (12"pic-d+=/cd-s+=) (W 2883 TP/CD) – ('A'extended).	3	2
Nov 89.	(7"/7"pic-d/c-s) (W 2668/+P/C) **DEAR JESSIE. / TILL DEATH US DO PART** (12"+=/pic-cd-s+=) (W 2668 TW/CD/CDX) – Holiday (12"mix).	5	-
Nov 89.	(7"/c-s) <22723-7/-4> **OH FATHER. / PRAY FOR SPANISH EYES**	-	20
Jan 90.	(7"/c-s) <19986-7/-4> **KEEP IT TOGETHER. / (instrumental)**	-	8

Mar 90. (7"/7"pic-d/c-s) (*W 9851/+P/C*) **VOGUE. / KEEP IT TOGETHER**   [1]   [–]
(12"+=/cd-s+=) (*W 9851 TX/CD*) – ('A'-Strike-a-pose dub mix).
(12"pic-d+=) (*W 9851TW*) – ('A'Bette Davis dub).

Apr 90. (7"/c-s) <*19863-7/-4*> **VOGUE. / ('A'-Bette Davis dub)**   [–]   [1]
(12"+=/c-s+=/cd-s+=) <*21513-0/-4/-2*> – ('A'-Stike-a-pose dub).

May 90. (cd)(lp/c) <*7599 26209-2*>(*WX 351/+C*) **I'M BREATHLESS** (music inspired by the film 'Dick Tracy')   [2]   [2]
– He's a man / Sooner or later / Hanky panky / I'm going bananas / Cry baby / Something to remember / Back in business / More / What can you lose / Now I'm following you (pt.1 & 2) / Vogue.

Jul 90. (7"/c-s) (*W 9789/+C*) <*19789*> **HANKY PANKY. / MORE**   [2]   [10] Jun90
('A'-Bare Bottom mix;12"+=/12"pic-d+=/cd-s+=) (*W 9789 T/TP/CD*) <*21577*> – ('A'-Bare Bones mix).

Nov 90. (7"/c-s) (*W 9000/+C*) <*19485-7/-4*> **JUSTIFY MY LOVE. / EXPRESS YOURSELF**   [2]   [1]
(12"pic-d+=/cd-s+=) (*W 9000 TP/CD*) – ('A'-William Orbit mix).

Nov 90. (cd)(lp/c) <*7599 26440-2*>(*WX 370/+C*) **THE IMMACULATE COLLECTION** (compilation)   [1]   [5]
– Spotlight / Holiday / Everybody / Physical attraction / Over and over / Into the groove / Where's the party / Spotlight (dub) / Holiday (dub) / Into the groove (dub) / Over and over (dub).

Feb 91. (7"/7"sha-pic-d) (*W 0008/+P*) **CRAZY FOR YOU (remix). / KEEP IT TOGETHER**   [2]   [–]
(12"pic-d+=/c-s+=/cd-s+=) (*W 0008 TP/C/CD*) – Into the groove.

Feb 91. (c-s) <*19490-4*> **RESCUE ME (remix) / RESCUE ME (alternate mix)**   [–]   [9]

Apr 91. (7"/c-s) (*W 0024/+C*) **RESCUE ME (remix). / SPOTLIGHT (version)**   [3]   [–]
(cd-s+=) (*W 0024CD*) – ('A'-Titanic mix).

May 91. (7"/7"pic-d) (*W 0037/+P*) **HOLIDAY. / TRUE BLUE**   [5]   [–]
(cd-s+=/c-s+=) (*W 0037 CD/CT*) – Causin' a commotion / Who's that girl.
(12") (*W 0037T*) – ('A'side) / Where's the party / Everybody (remix).

—— Below from the film, 'A League Of Their Own'.

Jul 92. (7"/c-s) (*W 0122/+C*) <*18822*> **THIS USED TO BE MY PLAYGROUND. / (long version)**   [3]   [1]
(12"+=/cd-s+=) (*W 0122 T/CD*) – ('A'mixes).

	Maverick-Sire	Maverick-Sire

Oct 92. (7"/7"pic-d/c-s) (*W 0138/+P/C*) <*18782*> **EROTICA. / (instrumental)**   [3]   [3]
(12"+=/12"pic-d+=/cd-s+=) (*W 0138 T/TP/CD*) <*40585*> – ('A'mixes; William Orbit / Jeep beats / Underground club / Kenlou B-boy / etc).

Oct 92. (cd/c/lp) <*9362 45031-2/-4/-1*> **EROTICA**   [2]   [2]
– Erotica / Fever / Where life begins / Bye bye baby / Bad girl / Waiting / Deeper and deeper / Thief of hearts / Words / Rain / Why it's so hard / In this life / Did you do it / Secret garden.

Dec 92. (7"/c-s) (*W 0146/+C*) <*18639*> **DEEPER AND DEEPER. / ('A'instrumental)**   [6]   [13]
(12"pic-d+=/cd-s+=) (*W 0146 TP/CD*) <*40722*> – ('A'mixes; Shep's deep beats / David's deeper dub / David's klub mix / etc).

Feb 93. (c-s/cd-s) <*18650-4/-2*> **BAD GIRL / FEVER**   [–]   [36]
(c-s+=/cd-s+=) <*40793-4/-2*> – ('A'mixes; Murk Boys Deep South mix / Oscar G's dope mix / Shep's remedy mix / etc.)

Feb 93. (7"/c-s) (*W 0145/+C*) **BAD GIRL. / EROTICA (William Orbit mix)**   [10]   [–]
(12"pic-+=/cd-s+=) (*W 0145 TP/CD*) – ('A'mixes; see US above).

Mar 93. (7"pic-d/c-s) (*W 0168 P/C*) **FEVER. / ('A'remix)**   [6]   [–]
(12"pic-d+=/cd-s+=) (*W 0168 TP/CD*) – ('A'mixes).

Jul 93. (c-s/cd-s) <*18505-4/-2*> **RAIN / WAITING**   [–]   [14]
(12"+=/c-s+=) <*40988-0/-4/-2*> – Up down suite / ('A'album version).

Jul 93. (7"/c-s) (*W 0190/+C*) **RAIN. / OPEN YOUR HEART**   [7]   [–]
(12"pic-d+=/cd-s+=) (*W 0190 TP/CD*) – Up down suite (dub).

—— her backing; **DALLAS AUSTIN** – drums, keyboards, co-writer / **TOMMY MARTIN** – guitar / **ME'SHELL NDEGEOCELLO + COLIN WOLFE** – bass / **MARCUS DeVRIES** – prog. / **BABYFACE** – synth, drum prog / etc.

Mar 94. (7"/c-s) (*W 0240/+C*) <*18247*> **I'LL REMEMBER. / SECRET GARDEN**   [7]   [2]
(12"pic-d/cd-s) (*W 0240 TP/CD*) <*41355*> – ('A'-Orbit + Guerilla Beach mixes) / Why is it so hard? (live).

Sep 94. (c-s/cd-s) <*18035-4/-2*> **SECRET / (instrumental)**   [–]   [3]
(12"+=/cd-s+=) <*41772-0/-2*> – ('A'mixes; Junior Luscious various).

Sep 94. (7"pic-d/c-s) (*W 0268 P/C*) **SECRET. / LET YOUR GUARD DOWN (rough mix edit)**   [5]   [–]
(12"pic-d+=) (*W 0268TP*) – ('A'instrumental) / ('A'other version).
(cd-s) (*W 0268CD*) – ('A'side) / ('A'-Junior mixes).

Oct 94. (cd/c/lp) <*9362 45767-2/-4/-1*> **BEDTIME STORIES**   [2]   [3]
– Survival / Secret / I'd rather be your lover / Don't stop / Inside of me / Human nature / Forbidden love / Love tried to welcome me / Sanctuary / Bedtime story / Take a bow.

Dec 94. (7"pic-d/c-s) (*W 0278 T/C*) <*18000*> **TAKE A BOW. / ('A'-InDaSoul mix)**   [17]   [1]
(cd-s+=) (*W 0278CD*) <*41887*> – ('A'mixes; instrumental / Silky Soul).

—— Above single co-written w /BABYFACE as was 7th track. The singular title track was written by NELLEE HOOPER, BJORK & MARCUS DeVRIES. DAVE HALL co-wrote 5th, 6th & 8th track. Many samples included The ISLEYS (written) / AALIYAH / GAP BAND / GUTTERSNYPES / MAIN SOURCE / GRANT GREEN / HERBIE HANCOCK.

Feb 95. (c-s) (*W 0285C*) **BEDTIME STORY / ('A'-Junior's mix)**   [4]   [42] Apr95
(12"pic-d/cd-s) (*W 0285 TP/CD*) – ('A'side) / ('A'-Junior's wet dream mix) / ('A'-Junior's Dreamy drum dub) / ('A'-Orbital mix) / ('A'-Junior's sound factory mix).
(cd-s) (*W 0285CDX*) – ('A'-Junior's mix) / Secret (Allstar mix) / Secret (Some Bizarre mixes).

Apr 95. (c-s/cd-s) <*17924-4/-2*> **BEDTIME STORY / SURVIVAL**   [–]   [42]
(12"+=/cd-s+=) <*41895-0/-2*> – (see Junior mixes above).

Jul 95. (c-s/cd-s) <*17882-4/-2*> **HUMAN NATURE / SANCTUARY**   [–]   [46]
(12"/cd-s) <*41880-0/-2*> – ('A'mixes; I'm Not Your Bitch / Bottom Heavy dub / Love Is The nature / Runway Club / etc)

Aug 95. (c-s) (*W 0300C*) **HUMAN NATURE / ('A'-Chorus door slam mix)**   [8]   [–]
(cd-s+=) (*W 0300CD*) – ('A'club mix) / ('A'-Runway club mix) / I'm not your bitch.
(12"pic-d) (*W 0300TP*) – (all above except 'A'side).

Oct 95. (c-s) (*W 0324C*) <*17719*> **YOU'LL SEE / (instrumental)**   [5]   [6]
(cd-s+=) (*W 0324CD*) – Rain.
(cd-s) (*W 0324CDX*) – ('A'side) / Secret (Junior Luscious club mix) / Sooner or later / Bad girl.

Nov 95. (cd/c/lp) <*9362 46100-2/-4/-1*> **SOMETHING TO REMEMBER** (compilation)   [3]   [6]
– I want you / I'll remember (theme from "With Honors") / Take a bow / You'll see / Crazy for you / This used to be my playground / Live to tell / Love don't live here anymore (remix) / Something to remember / Forbidden love / One more chance / Rain / Oh father / I want you (orchestral).

Dec 95. (c-s) (*W 0326C*) **OH FATHER / LIVE TO TELL (live)**   [16]   [–]
(cd-s+=) – Why it's so hard (live).

Mar 96. (c-s) (*W 0337C*) **ONE MORE CHANCE / ('A'-Spanglish version)**   [11]   [–]
(cd-s+=) (*W 0337CD*) – You'll see (Spanish version).

Apr 96. (c-s/cd-s) <*17714-4/-2*> **LOVE DON'T LIVE HERE ANYMORE / ('A'-album version)**   [–]   [79]

Oct 96. (c-s/cd-s) (*W 0378 C/CD*) <*17495-4/-2*> **YOU MUST LOVE ME / RAINBOW HIGH**   [10]   [18]

Dec 96. (c-s/cd-s) (*W 0384 C/CD*) **DON'T CRY FOR ME ARGENTINA / SANTA EVITA**   [3]   [–]
(cd-s+=) (*W 0384CDX*) – Latin chant.

Feb 97. (c-s/cd-s) <*43809-4/-2*> **DON'T CRY FOR ME ARGENTINA / ('A'mixes; Spanlish / Miami dub & instrumental / etc).**   [–]
(above singles from the 'Warner Bros.' film 'EVITA', which she finally starred in. The various artists soundtrack hit UK No.7)

Mar 97. (c-s) (*W 0388C*) **ANOTHER SUITCASE IN ANOTHER HALL / DON'T CRY FOR ME ARGENTINA**   [7]   [–]
(cd-s+=) (*W 0388CDX*) – Waltz for Eva and Che.
(cd-s) (*W 0388CD*) – ('A'dance mix) / Hello and goodbye / You must love me.

Feb 98. (c-s/cd-s) (*W 0433C*) <*17244*> **FROZEN / SHANTI-ASHTANGI**   [1]   [2]
(12") (*W 0433T*) ('A'extended) / ('A'-Stereo Mc's mix) / ('A'-Meltdown mix).
(cd-s+=) (*W 0433T*) – ('A'-Widescreen mix).

Mar 98. (cd/c/lp) <*9362 46847-2/-4/-1*> **RAY OF LIGHT**   [1]   [2]
– Drowned world – Substitute for love / Swim / Ray of light / Candy perfume girl / Skin / Nothing really matters / Sky fits Heaven / Shanti – Ashtangi / Frozen / The power of good-bye / To have and not to hold / Little star / Mer girl.

Apr 98. (c-s) (*W 0444C*) <*17206*> **RAY OF LIGHT / HAS TO BE**   [2]   [5] Jun98
(12"+=/cd-s+=) (*W 0444 T/CD*) – ('A'mixes).
(cd-s) (*W 0444CD2*) – ('A'side) / ('A'-Sasha mix) / ('A'-Victor Calderone mix) / ('A'-William Orbit mix).

Aug 98. (c-s/cd-s) (*W 0453 C/CD2*) **DROWNED WORLD – SUBSTITUTE FOR LOVE / SKY FITS HEAVEN (Victor Calderone & Sasha remix)**   [10]   [–]
(cd-s) (*W 0453CD1*) – ('A'mixes by BT & Sasha).

Nov 98. (c-s/cd-s) (*W 0459 C/CD*) <*17160*> **THE POWER OF GOOD-BYE / LITTLE STAR**   [6]   [11] Oct98
(12") (*W 0459T*) – ('A'mixes) / Mer girl.

Mar 99. (c-s) (*W 471C*) <*17102*> **NOTHING REALLY MATTERS / TO HAVE AND NOT TO HOLD**   [7]   [93] Apr99
(cd-s) (*W 471CD1*) – ('A'mixes).
(cd-s) (*W 471CD2*) – ('A'mixes).
(12") (*W 471T*) – ('A'mixes).

Jun 99. (c-s) (*W 495C*) <*radio cut*> **BEAUTIFUL STRANGER / ('A'mix)**   [2]   [19]
(cd-s) (*W 495CD*) – ('A'mixes).
(cd-s) (*W 495T*) – ('A'mixes).

– compilations, exploitation releases, etc. –

on 'Replay' unless mentioned otherwise (many with OTTO WERNHERR)

Feb 87. (12") (*3006*) **WILD DANCING. / ('A'dance mix)**   [ ]   [–]
(*re-iss. cd-s Sep93 & Apr95*)

Apr 89. (12") (*3000*) **COSMIC CLUB (extended dance mix). / WE ARE THE GODS**   [ ]   [ ]
(*re-iss. cd-s Sep93*)

May 89. (12") (*3007*) **TIME TO DANCE (extended). / (instrumental) / (radio mix)**   [ ]   [ ]
(*cd-s-iss.Oct95; RRSCD 3007*)

Sep 89. (12") (*3008*) **ON THE STREET (edit). / (extended mix)**   [ ]   [ ]
(*cd-s-iss.Oct95; RRSCD 3008*)

May 90. (12") (*3009*) **OH MY!!! (edit). / ('A'disco mix)**   [ ]   [ ]

Aug 90. (cd/c) *Action Replay;* (*CDAR/ARLC 1005*) **THE BEST & THE REST OF MADONNA AND OTTO WERNKERR**   [ ]   [ ]

Sep 90. (12") (*3010*) **SHAKE (extended). / ('A'mix) / ('A'instrumental)**   [ ]   [ ]
(*cd-iss. Oct95; RRSCD 3010*)
now on 'Receiver' unless mentioned otherwise

1989. (cd/c/lp) (*CD/TC+/KNOB 1*) **IN THE BEGINNING**   [ ]   [ ]
(*cd re-iss. Oct98 on 'Gravity'; GTY 2001-2*) (*cd re-iss. Feb99; same as original*)

Oct 89. (lp/c/cd) (*RR LP/LC/CD 118*) **THE EARLY YEARS**   [ ]   [ ]

Jul 91. (cdlp) (*RR CD/LP 144*) **GIVE IT TO ME**   [ ]   [ ]

Apr 92. (7"/12"pic-d/pic-cd-s) **SHINE A LIGHT. / ON THE GROUND / LITTLE BOY**   [ ]   [ ]

Jul 93. (cd/c) (*CDAR/ARLC 1033*) **BEST OF THE REST VOLUME II**   [ ]   [ ]

MAD SEASON (see under ⇒ ALICE IN CHAINS)

MAGAZINE

Formed: Manchester, England . . . Spring 1977 by former BUZZCOCKS frontman HOWARD DEVOTO and guitarist JOHN McGEOGH, who recruited the rhythm section of BARRY ADAMSON and MARTIN JACKSON along with keyboard player, BOB DICKINSON. After six months of rehearsals, they played their debut gig on the final night of legendary Manchester punk club, The Electric Circus, subsequently signing to 'Virgin' on the strength of a demo. A classic debut single, 'SHOT BY BOTH SIDES' established MAGAZINE's post-punk credentials, its stark, uncompromising approach and lyrical despair paving the way for countless gaggles of miserable young men in trenchcoats. Although DICKINSON had left prior to recording the single, the band had recruited a replacement, DAVE FORMULA, in time for the debut album, 'REAL LIFE' (1978). Its icy keyboard textures and spiky sonic artistry announced the arrival of a unique talent although DEVOTO's hyper-intelligent wayward genius was nothing new for fans who'd admired the punk maverick since his BUZZCOCKS days. With major radio support from John Peel and a growing cult fanbase, the album made the UK Top 30, while JACKSON was replaced with JOHN DOYLE following the obligatory tour. A follow-up set, 'SECONDHAND DAYLIGHT' (1979), was even more liberal in its use of keyboards although MAGAZINE's leftfield approach could hardly be accused of straying into New Romantic territory (some of MAGAZINE did dip a toe into these waters when they guested for VISAGE). Although a further three singles (including the unsettling 'A SONG FROM UNDER THE FLOORBOARDS' and an unlikely cover of Sly Stone's 'THANK YOU') failed to chart, a third album, 'THE CORRECT USE OF SOAP' (1980), became their most successful to date. DEVOTO wasn't happy with the direction the band were headed, however, and the defection of McGEOGH to SIOUXSIE & THE BANSHEES led to a slow decline and a patchy final effort in 'MAGIC, MURDER AND THE WEATHER' (1981). By the time of the album's release, DEVOTO had already announced his departure, effectively ending MAGAZINE's limited shelf life. The singer went on to release a solo set, 'JERKY VERSIONS OF THE DREAM' before forming LUXURIA with NOKO. He subsequently quit the music business; BARRY ADAMSON has enjoyed greater recognition, initially with NICK CAVE & The BAD SEEDS and latterly with his acclaimed solo career. • **Songwriters:** DEVOTO penned all except; I LOVE YOU BIG DUMMY (Captain Beefheart). LUXURIA covered JEZEBEL (Marty Wilde).

Album rating: REAL LIFE (*9) / SECONDHAND DAYLIGHT (*6) / THE CORRECT USE OF SOAP (*8) / PLAY (*4) / MAGIC, MURDER AND THE WEATHER (*6) / AFTER THE FACT compilation (*8) / RAYS AND HAIL compilation (*8) / Howard Devoto: JERKY VERSIONS OF THE DREAM (*5) / Luxuria: THE UNANSWERABLE LUST (*5) / BEAST BOX (*4)

HOWARD DEVOTO – vocals (ex-BUZZCOCKS) / **JOHN McGEOGH** – guitar / **BARRY ADAMSON** – bass / **MARTIN JACKSON** – drums / **BOB DICKINSON** – keyboards (latter left before debut recording)

	Virgin	Int
Jan 78. (7") (VS 200) **SHOT BY BOTH SIDES. / MY MIND AIN'T SO OPEN**	41	-
Apr 78. (7") (VS 207) **TOUCH AND GO. / GOLDFINGER**	□	-

—— added **DAVE FORMULA** – keyboards

Jun 78. (lp/c) (V/TCV 2100) **REAL LIFE**
– Definitive gaze / My tulpa / Shot by both sides / Recoil / Burst / Motorcade / The great beautician in the sky / The light pours out of me / Parade. *(re-iss. Mar84; OVED 62) (cd-iss. Oct88; CDV 2100)* | 29 | □

—— **JOHN DOYLE** – drums repl. JACKSON (to CHAMELEONS, then SWING OUT SISTER)

| Nov 78. (7") (VS 237) **GIVE ME EVERYTHING. / I LOVE YOU, YOU BIG DUMMY** | □ | - |
| Feb 79. (7") (VS 251) **RHYTHM OF CRUELTY. / T.V. BABY** | □ | - |

Mar 79. (lp/c) (V/TCV 2121) **SECONDHAND DAYLIGHT** | 38 | □
– Feed the enemy / Rhythm of cruelty / Cut-out shapes / Talk to the body / I wanted your heart / The thin air / Back to nature / Believe that I understand / Permafrost. *(re-iss. 1987 lp/c; OVED/+C 84) (cd-iss. Oct88; CDV 2121)*

Feb 80. (7") (VS 321) **A SONG FROM UNDER THE FLOORBOARDS. / TWENTY YEARS AGO**	□	-
Mar 80. (7") (VS 328) **THANK YOU (FALETTINME BE MICE ELF AGIN). / THE BOOK**	□	-
Apr 80. (7") (VS 334) **UPSIDE DOWN. / THE LIGHT POURS OUT OF ME (live)**	□	-

May 80. (lp/c) (V/TCV 2156) <13144> **THE CORRECT USE OF SOAP** | 28 | □
– Because you're frightened / Model worker / I'm a party / You never knew me / Philadelphia / I want to burn again / Thank you (falettinme be mice elf agin) / Sweetheart contract / Stuck / A song from under the floorboards. *(re-iss. 1988 lp/c; OVED/+C 116) (cd-iss. Oct88; CDV 2156)*

Jul 80. (d7"/12"ep) (VS 368/+12) **SWEETHEART CONTRACT. / FEED THE ENEMY (live) // TWENTY YEARS AGO. / SHOT BY BOTH SIDES (live)** | 54 | -

—— **ROBIN SIMON** – guitar (ex-ULTRAVOX) repl. McGEOGH who joined SIOUXSIE . . . (above now alongside **DEVOTO, ADAMSON, FORMULA** and **DOYLE**)

	Virgin	I.R.S.
Nov 80. (lp/c) (V/TCV 2184) <70015> **PLAY (live at Melbourne Festival Hall)**	69	□

– Give me everything / A song from under the floorboards / Permafrost / The light pours out of me / Model worker / Parade / Thank you (falettinme be mice elf agin) / Because you're frightened / Twenty years ago / Definitive gaze. *(re-iss. 1988 lp/c; OVED/+C 117) (cd-iss. Oct88; CDV 2184)*

—— **BEN MANDELSON** – guitar (ex-AMAZORBLADES) repl. ROBIN.

| May 81. (7") (VS 412) **ABOUT THE WEATHER. / IN THE DARK** | □ | - |

(12"+=) (VS 412-12) – The operative.

Jun 81. (lp/c) (V/TCV 2200) <70020> **MAGIC, MURDER AND THE WEATHER** | 39 | □
– About the weather / So lucky / The honeymoon killers / Vigilante / Come alive / The great man's secrets / This poison / Naked eye / Suburban Rhonda / The garden. *(re-iss. 1988 lp/c; OVED/+C 141) (cd-iss. Oct88; CDV 2200)*

—— They split mid '81. DEVOTO went solo with help from FORMULA (see below). BEN MANDELSON joined The MEKONS, JOHN DOYLE later joined ARMOURY SHOW. BARRY ADAMSON joined PETE SHELLEY then later NICK CAVE & THE BAD SEEDS. FORMULA had also joined the group DESIGN FOR LIVING.

– compilations, etc. –

on 'Virgin' unless mentioned otherwise

| May 82. (lp/c) (VM/+C 1) **AFTER THE FACT** (best of) | □ | - |
| May 83. (12"ep) (VS 592-12) **SHOT BY BOTH SIDES** | □ | - |

– Shot by both sides / Goldfinger / Give me everything / A song from under the floorboards.

May 87. (cd) (COMCD 5) **RAYS AND HAIL 1978-81** (best of) | □ | -
– Shot by both sides / Definitive gaze / Motorcade / The light pours out of me / Feed the enemy / Rhythm of cruelty / Back to nature / Permafrost / Because you're frightened / You never knew me / A song from under the floorboards / I want to burn again / About the weather / Parade. *(re-iss. Jul93; CDVM 9020)*

| Jul 90. (cd) (CDOVD 312) **SCREE** (rarities 76-81) | □ | - |
| Aug 93. (cd) Windsong; (WINCD 040) **BBC RADIO 1 LIVE IN CONCERT** | □ | - |

HOWARD DEVOTO

—— went solo, with **DAVE FORMULA** – keyboards / **PAT AHORN** – drums / **ALAN ST. CLAIR** – guitar / **NEIL PYZER** – keyboards,synth / **MARTIN HEATH** – bass

	Virgin	I.R.S.
Jun 83. (7"/12") (VS 598/+12) **RAINY SEASON. / RAIN FOREST**	□	-

Aug 83. (lp/c) (V/TCV 2272) <SP 70036> **JERKY VERSIONS OF THE DREAM** | 57 | □
– Cold imagination / Topless / Rainy season / I admire you / Way out of shape / Some will pay (for what others pay to avoid) / Waiting for a train / Out of shape with me / Taking over Heaven / Seeing is believing. *(re-iss. Aug88; OVED 129) (cd-iss. Apr90; CDV 2272)*

Aug 83. (7"/12") (VS 642/+12) **COLD IMAGINATION. / OUT OF SHAPE WITH ME** | □ | -

—— PYZER and ST.CLAIR joined SPEAR OF DESTINY. HEATH and AHORN joined DAVE HOWARD SINGERS, DEVOTO guested for B.SZAJNER a French electronic wizard. He then took 4 years off before his new venture . . .

LUXURIA

DEVOTO with **NOKO** (b.Liverpool) – guitar, co-composer

	Beggars Banquet	Beggars Banquet
Jan 88. (7") (BEG 204) **REDNECK. / SHE'S YOUR LOVER NOW (pt.1)**	□	-

(12"+=) (BEG 204T) – She's your lover now (pt.2).

Feb 88. (lp/c)(cd) (BEGA/BEGC 90)(BEGA 90CD) <6990> **THE UNANSWERABLE LUST**
– Redneck / Flesh / Public highway / Pound / Lady 21 / Celebrity / Rubbish / Mile / Luxuria.

May 88. (7") (BEG 211) **PUBLIC HIGHWAY (Short cut) / SICKLY THUG AND I** | □ | -
(12"+=) (BEG 211T) – Luxuria (The wilderness mix).

Mar 90. (7"ep/12"ep/cd-ep) (BEG 233/+T/CD) **THE BEAST BOX IS DREAMING / BEAST BOX / USELESS LOVE**

Apr 90. (cd)(c/lp) (BEGA 106CD)(BEGC/BEGA 106) <2233-2/-4/-1> **BEAST BOX**
– The beast box is dreaming / Stupid blood / Against the past / Our curious leader / We keep on getting there / Ticket / Animal in the mirror / Dirty beating heart / Smoking mirror / I've been expecting you / Karezza / Beast box / Jezebel.

May 90. (7") **JEZEBEL. / SMOKING MIRROR (instrumental)** | □ | -
(12"+=) – Sickly thug and I.
(cd-s++=) – Luxuria (live).

—— after their split, NOKO went to ground for a while, re-emerging later in the 90's with hard techno act, APOLLO 440.

MAGICK (see under ⇒ BOND, Graham)

MAGMA (dig out; Great Psychedelic . . .)

MAGNAPOP (dig out; Great Alt & Indie . . .)

Taj MAHAL (dig out; 4th edition)

MAHAVISHNU ORCHESTRA
(see under ⇒ McLAUGHLIN, John)

MAHOGANY RUSH / Frank MARINO
(dig out; Great Metal . . .)

MAKAVELI (see under ⇒ 2PAC)

MAKE-UP (dig out; Great Alt & Indie . . .)

Yngwie MALMSTEEN (dig out; Great Metal . . .)

MAMAS AND THE PAPAS

Formed: St. Thomas, Virgin Islands, USA . . . 1964 as The NEW JOURNEYMAN by DENNY DOHERTY, and two JOURNEYMEN; JOHN PHILLIPS and MICHELLE GILLIAM. They soon brought in the larger-than-life CASS ELLIOT, relocating to California where they became The MAMAS & THE PAPAS (Mama being Hell's Angels slang for girlfriend). They were introduced to producer and owner of 'Dunhill' records Lou Adler, by 'Eve Of Destruction'-man, BARRY McGUIRE. He contracted them initially as backing singers for McGUIRE's 1965 album, 'Precious Time', which included PHILLIPS' 'CALIFORNIA DREAMIN'. The following year, this classic piece of harmony-orientated folk-pop became their debut 45, hitting the US Top 5. Their follow-up, 'MONDAY MONDAY', topped the charts (No.3 in the UK), succeeded by a string of hits, abruptly halted by the split of the group in '68. This was the result of the eventual marriage break-up of JOHN and MICHELLE, as well as drug busts and alleged record company rip-offs. All subsequently took off on solo ventures, often re-uniting for one-off concerts, etc. Tragically on the 29th of July '74, CASS ELLIOT died of a heart attack while choking on food. In 1982, the three remaining members re-grouped with a new singer, SPANKY McFARLANE (ex-SPANKY & HER GANG). MICHELLE had already begun an acting career, that has since seen her in US TV dramas such as 'Knot's Landing'. • **Songwriters:** PHILLIPS penned most. Covered; DANCING IN THE STREET (Martha & The Vandellas) / DEDICATED TO THE ONE I LOVE (Shireles) / DO YOU WANNA DANCE (Bobby Freeman) / I CALL YOUR NAME (Beatles) / etc. In 1967, PHILLIPS wrote No.1 smash, 'SAN FRANCISCO', for late 80's PAPA-to-be SCOTT McKENZIE. Twenty years later, JOHN co-wrote US No.1, 'Kokomo', with The BEACH BOYS. • **Trivia:** On the 31st October 1970, MICHELLE, now divorced from JOHN, married cult actor DENNIS HOPPER (but only for a week!).

Album rating: IF YOU CAN BELIEVE YOUR EYES AND EARS (*7) / THE MAMAS & THE PAPAS (*7) / THE MAMAS AND THE PAPAS DELIVER (*6) / FAREWELL TO THE FIRST GOLDEN ERA compilation (*7) / THE PAPAS & THE MAMAS (*6) / GOLDEN ERA, VOL.2 compilation (*6) / 16 OF THEIR GREATEST HITS compilation (*8) / PEOPLE LIKE US (*3) / CREEQUE ALLEY: HISTORY OF THE MAMAS & THE PAPAS compilation (*8) / Mama Cass: DREAM A LITTLE DREAM (*5) / BUBBLE GUM, LEMONADE & . . . SOMETHING FOR MAMA (*5) / MAMA'S BIG ONES compilation (*6)

JOHN PHILLIPS (b.30 Aug'35, Parris Island, South Carolina) – vocals / **CASS ELLIOT** (b. ELLEN NAOMI COHEN, 19 Sep'41, Baltimore, Maryland) – vocals / **MICHELLE GILLIAM** (b. HOLLY MICHELLE GILLIAM, 4 Jun'45, Long Beach, Calif.) – vocals (ex-JOURNEYMEN, with PHILLIPS) (ELLIOT ex-MUGWUMPS with DOHERTY) / **DENNY DOHERTY** (b.29 Nov'41, Halifax, Nova Scotia, Canada) – vocals

		R.C.A.	Dunhill	
Jan 66.	(7") (1503) <4020> **CALIFORNIA DREAMIN'. / SOMEBODY GROOVY**	23	4	Dec65
May 66.	(7") (1516) <4026> **MONDAY MONDAY. / GOT A FEELIN'**	3	1	Apr66
Jun 66.	(lp; mono/stereo) (RD 7803) <D/DS 50001> **IF YOU CAN BELIEVE YOUR EYES AND EARS**	3	1	Feb66
	– Do you wanna dance / Go where you wanna go / California dreamin' / Spanish harlem / Somebody groovy / Hey girl / You baby / In crowd / Monday, Monday / Straight shooter / Got a feelin' / I call your name. (cd-iss. 1990 on 'MCA';)			
Jul 66.	(7") (1533) <4031> **I SAW HER AGAIN. / EVEN IF I COULD**	11	5	Jun66

—— **JILL GIBSON** – vocals repl. MICHELLE for a while

Oct 66.	(7") (1551) <4050> **LOOK THRU MY WINDOW. / ONCE THERE WAS A TIME I THOUGHT**		24	

—— **MICHELLE** returned when she reconciled with husband JOHN

Jan 67.	(lp; mono/stereo) (RD/SF 7834) <D/DS 50010> **CASS JOHN MICHELLE DENNY**	24	4	Sep66
	– No salt on her tail / Trip, stumble and fall / Dancing bear / Words of love / My heart stood still / Dancing in the steet / I saw her again / Strange young girl / I can't wait / Even if I could / That kind of girl / Once was a time I thought.			
Jan 67.	(7") (1564) <4057> **WORDS OF LOVE. / DANCING IN THE STREET**	47	5	75
Mar 67.	(7") (1576) <4077> **DEDICATED TO THE ONE I LOVE. / FREE ADVICE**	2	2	Feb67
Apr 67.	(7") <4083> **CREEQUE ALLEY. / NO SALT IN HER TAIL**	-	5	
Jun 67.	(lp; mono/stereo) (RD/SF 7880) <D/DS 50014> **DELIVER**	4	2	Mar67
	– Dedicated to the one I love / My girl / Creeque alley / Sing for your supper / Twist and shout / Free advice / Look through any window / Boys and girls together / String man / Frustration / Did you ever want to cry / John's music box.			
Jul 67.	(7") (1613) **CREEQUE ALLEY. / DID YOU EVER WANT TO CRY**	9	-	
Sep 67.	(7") (1630) <4099> **12:30 (YOUNG GIRLS ARE COMING TO THE CANYON). / STRAIGHT SHOOTER**		20	Aug67
Dec 67.	(7") (1649) <4107> **GLAD TO BE UNHAPPY. / HEY GIRL**		26	Oct67
Dec 67.	(lp; mono/stereo) <D/DS 50025> **FAREWELL TO THE FIRST GOLDEN ERA** (compilation)		5	Oct67
	– Dedicated to the one I love / Go where you wanna go / Words of love / Look through any window / Dancing in the street / Monday Monday / Creeque alley / Got a feelin' / 12:30 (young girls are coming to the canyon) / I call your name / I saw her again last night / California dreamin'.			
Dec 67.	(7") <4113> **DANCING BEAR. / JOHN'S MUSIC BOX**		51	
Jun 68.	(7") (1710) <4125> **SAFE IN MY GARDEN. / TOO LATE**		53	May68
Sep 68.	(lp; mono/stereo) (RD/SF 7960) <DS 50031> **. . .PRESENTING THE PAPAS AND THE MAMAS**		15	May68
	– Dream a little dream of me / Gemini child / Ivy / Mansions / Meditation mama (transcendental woman travels) / Midnight voyage / Nothing's too good for my little			

girl / Rooms / Safe in my garden / The right somebody to love / Too late / Twelve thirty.

Sep 68.	(7") (1744) <4150> **FOR THE LOVE OF IVY. / STRANGE YOUNG GIRLS**		81	
Nov 68.	(7") <4171> **DO YOU WANNA DANCE. / MY GIRL**	-	76	

—— (Jul68) Disbanded, when JOHN and MICHELLE broke up. JOHN PHILLIPS later went solo, as did DENNY and MICHELLE.

MAMA CASS

had already gone solo.

		R.C.A.	Dunhill	
Aug 68.	(7") (1726) <4145> **DREAM A LITTLE DREAM OF ME (live). / MIDNIGHT VOYAGE**	11	12	Jul68
	(above also credited with The MAMAS AND THE PAPAS)			
		Stateside	Dunhill	
Nov 68.	(7") (SS 8002) 4166> **CALIFORNIA EARTHQUAKE. / TALKIN' TO YOUR TOOTHBRUSH**		67	Oct68
Dec 68.	(lp; stereo/mono) (S+/SL 5004) <DS 50040> **DREAM A LITTLE DREAM**		87	Oct68
	– Dream a little dream of me / California earthquake / The room nobody lives in / Talkin' to your toothbrush / Blues for breakfast / You know who I am / Rubber band / Long time loving you / Jane, the insane dog lady / What was I thinking of / Burn your hatred / Sweet believer.			
Feb 69.	(7") <4184> **MOVE IN A LITTLE BIT CLOSER. / ALL FOR ME**	-	58	
Mar 69.	(7") (SS 8014) **MOVE IN A LITTLE BIT CLOSER. / I CAN DREAM, CAN'T I**		-	
Jul 69.	(7") (SS 8021) <4195> **IT'S GETTING BETTER. / WHO'S TO BLAME**	8	30	May69
Nov 69.	(lp; stereo/mono) (S+/SL 5014) <DS 50055> **BUBBLEGUM, LEMONADE AND . . . SOMETHING FOR MAMA**		91	Jun69
	– Blow me a kiss / It's getting better / Easy come, easy go / I can dream, can't I / Welcome to the world / Lady Love / He's a runner / Move in a little closer, baby / When I just wear my smile / Who's to blame / Sour grapes. <US re-iss. Nov69 as 'MAKE YOUR OWN KIND OF MUSIC'; DS 50071> – Make your own kind of music.			

MAMA CASS ELLIOT

Nov 69.	(7") (SS 8031) <4114> **MAKE YOUR OWN KIND OF MUSIC. / LADY LOVE**		36	Oct69
Mar 70.	(7") (SS 8039) <4225> **NEW WORLD COMING. / BLOW ME A KISS**		42	Jan70
Mar 70.	(7") <4226> **SOMETHING TO MAKE YOU HAPPY. / NEXT TO YOU**	-		
Sep 70.	(7") (SS 8057) <4244> **A SONG THAT NEVER COMES. / I CAN DREAM, CAN'T I?**		99	Jul70
Nov 70.	(7") <4253> **DON'T LET THE GOOD TIMES PASS YOU BY. / A SONG THAT NEVER COMES**	-	-	
Mar 71.	(lp) (SPB 1020) <DS 50093> **MAMA'S BIG ONES** (compilation)	-	-	
	– Dream a little dream of me / Make your own kind of music / It's getting better / Easy come, easy go / Words of love / Move in a little closer, baby / Song that never comes / One way ticket / Ain't nobody else like you / Don't let the good life pass you by / The good times are coming / New world coming. (re-iss. Oct74 on 'A.B.C.'; ABCL 5017)			

—— Late 1970-early 1971, MAMA CASS teamed up with DAVE MASON on some releases.

MAMAS AND THE PAPAS

re-united.

		Probe	Dunhill	
Nov 71.	(lp) (SPB 1048) <DS 50106> **PEOPLE LIKE US**		84	Oct 71
	– Dream a little dream of me / Make your own kind of music / It's getting better / Easy come, easy go / Words of love / Move in a little closer, baby / Song that never comes / One way ticket / Ain't nobody else like you / Don't let the good life pass you by / The good times are coming / New world coming. (re-iss. Oct74 on 'A.B.C.'; ABCL 5017) (re-iss. Nov76 on 'Music For Pleasure'; 50299)			
Jan 72.	(7") <4301> **STEP OUT. / SHOOTING STAR**	-	81	
Feb 72.	(7") (PRO 552) **SHOOTING STAR. / NO DOUGH**	-	-	

—— Break-up, once again for final time. All try-out solo careers.

CASS ELLIOT

went solo again.

		R.C.A.	R.C.A.	
1972.	(7") (2179) <74-0644> **BABY I'M YOURS. / CHERRIES JUBILEE**			
Feb 72.	(lp) <(LSP 4619)> **CASS ELLIOT**			
	– Introduction – Dream a little dream of me / Extraordinary / I think a lot about you / Don't call me Mama anymore / My love / I'm coming to the best part of my life / The torchsong medley: I came here to sing a torchsong / I got a right to sing the blues – I've got it bad and that ain't good – Mean to me – Why was a born – I came here to sing a torchsong (reprise) / The night before / I like what I like / I'll be seeing you / Closing – I don't call me Mama anymore (reprise).			
1972.	(7") <74-0693> **THAT SONG. / WHEN IT DOESN'T WORK OUT**	-	-	
1972.	(7") <74-0764> **DISNEY GIRLS (1957). / BREAK ANOTHER HEART**	-	-	
1973.	(7") <74-0830> **DOES ANYBODY LOVE YOU. / THE ROAD IS NO PLACE FOR A LADY**	-	-	
1973.	(lp) (SF 8306) <LSP 4753> **THE ROAD IS NO PLACE FOR A LADY**			
1973.	(7") <74-0957> **LISTEN TO THE WORLD. / I THINK A LOT ABOUT YOU**	-	-	

Jul 74. (7") *(LPB 07521)* **IF YOU'RE GONNA BREAK ANOTHER HEART. / DON'T CALL ME MAMA ANYMORE** [ ] | -
Jul 74. (lp) *<(APL1-0303)>* **DON'T CALL ME MAMA ANYMORE**
– Introduction – Dream a little dream of me / Extraordinary / I think a lot about you / Don't call me Mama anymore / My love / I'm coming to the best part of my life / The torchsong medley: I came here to sing a torchsong – I got a right to sing the blues – I've got it bad and that ain't good – Mean to me – Why was I born – I came here to sing a torchsong (reprise) / The night before / I like what I like / I'll be seeing you / Closing – I don't call me Mama anymore (reprise).

—— On July '74, CASS ELLIOT died of a heart attack.

– (MAMAS & PAPAS) compilations, etc. –

below on 'Stateside' UK / 'Dunhill' US unless mentioned otherwise
1966. (7"ep) *<50006>* **IF YOU CAN BELIEVE YOUR EYES AND EARS** - | [ ]
Dec 68. (lp; stereo/mono) *(S+SL 5002)* *<DS 50038>* **GOLDEN ERA, VOL.2** [ ] | 53 Sep68
Feb 69. (7") *(SS 8009)* **YOU BABY. / MY GIRL** [ ] | -
Apr 69. (lp; stereo/mono) *(S+/SL 5007)* **HITS OF GOLD** 7 | [ ]
(re-iss. Oct74 on 'A.B.C.'; ABCL 5003) (re-iss. Aug81 on 'M.C.A.'; MCL 1614)
Sep 69. (lp) *<DS 50064>* **16 OF THEIR GREATEST HITS** - | 61
Sep 70. (7") *(SS 8058)* **GO WHERE YOU WANNA GO. / NO SALT ON HER TAIL** [ ] | -
below releases on 'Probe' UK/ 'Dunhill' US unless mentioned otherwise
Oct 70. (d-lp) *(SPB 1013-4)* *<DS 50073>* **A GATHERING OF FLOWERS** [ ] | [ ]
1971. (lp) *<DS 50100>* **MONTEREY INTERNATIONAL POP FESTIVAL** (live) [ ] | -
Jun 72. (7") *(GFF 102)* **CALIFORNIA DREAMIN'. / DEDICATED TO THE ONE I LOVE** [ ] | -
1972. (7"ep) *M.C.A.; <50106>* **PEOPLE LIKE US** - | [ ]
May 73. (lp) *(GTSP 200)* *<DS 50145>* **20 GOLDEN HITS** [ ] | Feb73
(re-iss. Oct74 on 'A.B.C.'; ABCL 5003) (re-iss. Oct80 on 'Music For Pleasure'; 50493) (re-iss. Mar82 on 'M.C.A.'; MCLD 613) (cd-iss. Dec92 on 'Music For Pleasure'; CDMFP 50493)
Sep 73. (7") *(GFF 124)* **MONDAY MONDAY. / CREEQUE ALLEY** [ ] | -
(re-iss. Sep76 on 'A.B.C.'; 4131)
Jan 74. (lp) *Music For Pleasure; (SPR 90025)* **MONDAY MONDAY** [ ] | -
Sep 74. (lp) *Music For Pleasure; (SPR 90050)* **CALIFORNIA DREAMING** [ ] | -
(re-iss. Apr79 on 'Marks & Spencer'; MO 101225)
1976. (lp) *M.C.A.; <30005>* **THE ABC COLLECTION: GREATEST HITS** - | [ ]
May 77. (lp) *Arcade; (ADEP 30)* **THE BEST OF THE MAMAS AND THE PAPAS** 6 | [ ]
Jun 80. (7"ep) *M.C.A.; (601)* **MONDAY MONDAY / CALIFORNIA DREAMIN'. / CREEQUE ALLEY / I SAW HER AGAIN** [ ] | -
Jul 82. (7") *Old Gold; (OG 9175)* **DEDICATED TO THE ONE I LOVE. / CREEQUE ALLEY** [ ] | -
Jul 82. (7") *Old Gold; (OG 9176)* **CALIFORNIA DREAMIN'. / MONDAY MONDAY** [ ] | -
Jul 85. (lp) *M.C.A.; (MCM 5001)* **GOLDEN GREATS** [ ] | -
(cd-iss. Dec88;)
Mar 88. (lp) *Platinum; (PLAT 302)* **THE VERY BEST OF THE MAMAS & THE PAPAS** [ ] | -
Jun 88. (d-lp/c/cd) *Connoisseur; (VSOP LP/MC/CD 119)* **ELLIOT, PHILLIPS, GILLIAM, DOHERTY** [ ] | -
Jun 88. (7"; MAMA CASS) *Old Gold; (OG 9796)* **IT'S GETTING BETTER. / DREAM A LITTLE DREAM OF ME** [ ] | -
Sep 88. (cd) *Pickwick; (PWKS 509)* **THE VERY BEST OF MAMAS & THE PAPAS** [ ] | -
Nov 88. (d-lp/c/cd) *Castle; (CCS LP/MC/CD 173)* **THE COLLECTION** [ ] | -
Jul 89. (cd) *Object;* **THE MAMAS & THE PAPAS** (live) [ ] | -
May 91. (d-cd) *M.C.A.; (MCAD2-10195)* **CREEQUE ALLEY: THE HISTORY OF THE MAMAS & PAPAS** [ ] | -
– Wild women / Winken', blinkin' and nod / I'll remember tonight / I don't wanna know / This precious time / (John Phillips dialogue) / California dreamin' / Go where you wanna go / Monday, Monday / You baby / Do you wanna dance / I call your name / Spanish harlem / Straight shooter / Got a feelin' / I saw her again last night / Look through my window / Words of love / Dancing in the street / (Mama Cass dialogue) / Once was a time I thought / No salt in her tail / Trip, stumble and fall / Dancing bear / Dedicated to the one I love / Creeque Alley / My girl / Twist and shout / I call your name / Twelve thirty (young girls are coming to the canyon) / Glad to be unhappy / For the love of Ivy / Safe in my garden / Midnight voyage / Dream a little dream of me / California earthquake / It's getting better / Mississippi / Watcha gonna do / (Mama Cass dialogue) / Step out / The achin' kind.
Jun 92. (cd/c) *See For Miles; (SEE CD/K 333)* **THE EP COLLECTION** [ ] | -
Nov 93. (d-cd) *Double Platinum; (DBP 102003)* **ALL TIME GREATEST HITS** [ ] | -
Jul 94. (cd/c) *Success;* **GREATEST HITS LIVE** (live) [ ] | -
Dec 94. (cd/c) *Polygram TV; (523 973-2/-4)* **CALIFORNIA DREAMING – THE VERY BEST OF THE MAMAS & THE PAPAS** 14 | -
(re-dist.Aug97; hit No.30)
Jul 97. (c-s/cd-s) *M.C.A.; (MCS C/TD 48058)* **CALIFORNIA DREAMIN' / DREAM A LITTLE DREAM FOR ME / MONDAY MONDAY / MAKE YOUR OWN KIND OF MUSIC** 9 | [ ]

—— JOHN PHILLIPS released a solo album 'THE WOLFKING OF L.A.' in 1970.

—— DENNY DOHERTY and MICHELLE PHILLIPS also released solo recordings around the mid 70's. MICHELLE appeared in the TV films 'Dillinger' & 'Valentino' 1977. Early in 1982, the remaining members plus SPANKY McFARLANE (ex-SPANKY & OUR GANG) re-formed The MAMAS & THE PAPAS, but only revived 60's circuit. MICHELLE had also been replaced by MacKENZIE PHILLIPS, daughter of JOHN.

MAN

Formed: Merthyr Tydfil, nr. Swansea, Wales . . . 1964 as The BYSTANDERS by MICKY JONES, CLIVE JOHN, RAY WILLIAMS and JEFFREY JONES. They released many 45's during a 4-year period, one of them, '98.6', hitting the Top 50 in early '67. The following year, they amalgamated with another Welsh group, The DREAM, locating singer/guitarist DEKE LEONARD. Signing to 'Pye' in 1969, MAN released their debut album, 'REVELATION', a conceptual affair which contained the European hit, 'EROTICA' (banned in the UK for its simulated orgasm sounds). Their subsequent effort, '2 OZS. OF PLASTIC WITH A HOLE IN THE MIDDLE', was another to embrace the West Coast sound of bands like QUICKSILVER MESSENGER SERVICE. Early in 1970, MARTIN ACE and TERRY WILLIAMS were drafted in to replace RAY and JEFFREY, the new line-up featuring on their eponymous third, rather self-indulgent set. Already established as a consummate live act, they released a fourth album, 'DO YOU LIKE IT HERE NOW, ARE YOU SETTLING IN?', which contained the acid-tinged classic, 'MANY ARE CALLED, BUT FEW GET UP'. The 1972 set (which didn't include the departed DEKE), 'BE GOOD TO YOURSELF AT LEAST ONCE A DAY', boasted yet another lengthy jewel, 'BANANAS'. They finally reached the Top 30 in 1973, with 'BACK TO THE FUTURE', before DEKE returned for an equally successful follow-up, 'RHINOS, WINOS AND LUNATICS'. During the first half of the 70's, MAN were continually dogged by personnel changes, the most recent member, MALCOLM MORLEY, leaving after the aforementioned album. The most astonishing of these personnel upheavals came with the addition of QUICKSILVER MESSENGER SERVICE figurehead/hero, JOHN CIPPOLINA. He stayed for only one album, the Top 30 live-set, 'MAXIMUM DARKNESS'. In 1976, they charted for the final time, with the disappointing, 'WELSH CONNECTION'. They split soon after, DEKE continuing a solo career (with MAN members) until he, MICKEY JONES, MARTIN ACE and JOHN WEATHER reformed the group in 1983. In 1995, they were still going strong, an album, 'CALL DOWN THE MOON', testament to their longevity. • **Songwriters:** Group penned from the 70's, except covers; CODINE (Buffy Sainte-Marie) / I'M GONNA LEAVE YOU (Quicksilver Messenger Service) / LET THE GOOD TIMES ROLL (Shirley & Lee) / etc. • **Trivia:** MAN also featured on the live Various Artists albums, 'GREASY TRUCKERS PARTY VOL.1' and 'CHRISTMAS AT THE PATTI', both on the 'United Artists' label (1972 + 1973).

Album rating: REVELATION (*6) / 2 ozs. OF PLASTIC WITH A HOLE IN THE MIDDLE (*6) / MAN (*5) / DO YOU LIKE IT HERE NOW, ARE YOU SETTLING IN? (*7) / LIVBE AT THE PADGET ROOMS, PENARTH (*5) / BE GOOD TO YOURSELF AT LEAST ONCE A DAY (*6) / BACK INTO THE FUTURE (*5) / RHINOS, WINOS AND LUNATICS (*6) / SLOW MOTION (*5) / MAXIMUM DARKNESS (*6) / THE WELSH CONNECTION (*4) / ALL'S WELL THAT ENDS WELL (*4) / FRIDAY THE 13th (*4) / THE TWANG DYNASTY (*4) / CALL DOWN THE MOON (*4) / PERFECT TIMING (THE U.A. YEARS 1970-75) compilation (*8)

THE BYSTANDERS

VIC OAKLEY – vocals / **MICKY JONES** – guitar, vocals / **CLIVE JOHN** – keyboards, vocals / **RAY 'TAFF' WILLIAMS** – bass (ex-EYES OF BLUE) / **JEFFREY JONES** – drums

			Pylot	not iss.
1965.	(7") *(WD 501)* **THAT'S THE END. / THIS TIME**		[ ]	-
			Piccadilly	not iss.
Jun 66.	(7") *(7N 35330)* **(YOU'RE GONNA) HURT YOURSELF. / HAVE I OFFENDED THE GIRL**		[ ]	-
Oct 66.	(7") *(7N 35351)* **MY LOVE – COME HOME. / IF YOU WALK AWAY**		[ ]	-
Dec 66.	(7") *(7N 35363)* **98.6. / STUBBORN KIND OF FELLOW**		45	-
May 67.	(7") *(7N 35382)* **ROYAL BLUE SUMMER SUNSHINE DAY. / MAKE UP YOUR MIND**		[ ]	-
			Pye	not iss.
Jul 67.	(7") *(7N 35399)* **PATTERN PEOPLE. / GREEN GRASS**		[ ]	-
Feb 68.	(7") *(7N 17476)* **WHEN JEZAMINE GOES. / CAVE OF CLEAR LIGHT**		[ ]	-
Apr 68.	(7") *(7N 17540)* **THIS WORLD IS MY WORLD. / PAINTING THE TIME**		[ ]	-

—— (disbanded 1968)

MAN

DEKE LEONARD – guitar, vocals (ex-The DREAM) / **MICKY JONES** – vocals, guitar / plus **CLIVE, RAY + JEFFREY**

		Pye	Philips
Jan 69.	(7") *(7N 17684)* **SUDDEN LIFE. / LOVE**	[ ]	-
Jan 69.	(lp) *(NSPL 18275)* **REVELATION** (US-title 'MANPOWER')	[ ]	-

– And in the beginning . . . / Sudden life / Empty room / Puella! Puella! (woman! woman!) / Love / Erotica / Blind man / And castles rise in children's eyes / Don't just stand there (come in out of the rain) / The missing pieces / The future hides its face. *(re-iss. Oct74 on 'See For Miles' lp/cd; SEE/+CD 274) (cd re-iss. Aug91 on 'Repertoire'; REP 4024WZ)*

		Dawn	Philips
Sep 69.	(lp) *(DNLS 3003)* **2 OZS OF PLASTIC WITH A HOLE IN THE MIDDLE**	[ ]	[ ]

– (prelude) – The storm / It is as it might be / Spunk box / My name is Jesus Smith / Parchment and candles / Brother Arnold's red and white striped tent. *(re-iss. Oct89 on 'See For Miles' lp/cd; SEE/+CD 273)*

—— **MARTIN ACE** – bass (ex-The DREAM) repl. RAY who joined The BIG SLEEP / **TERRY WILLIAMS** – drums (ex-The DREAM) repl. JEFFREY

		Liberty	U.A.

Oct 70. (lp) *(LBG 83464)* <9803> **MAN**
– Romain / Country girl / Would the Christians wait five minutes? the lions are having a draw / Daughter of the fireplace / The alchemist. *(re-iss. Feb76 as 'MAN 1970' on 'Sunset'; SLS 50380)*

Mar 71. (7") *(LBF 15448)* **DAUGHTER OF THE FIREPLACE. / COUNTRY GIRL**

		U.A.	U.A.

Nov 71. (lp) *(UAS 29236)* <1032> **DO YOU LIKE IT HERE NOW, ARE YOU SETTLING IN?**
– Angel easy / All good clean fun / We're only children / Many are called but few get up / Manillo / Love your life. *(re-iss. Aug80 on 'Liberty'; LBR 16-032)*

—— now a quartet when CLIVE joined PORWITH, PRITCHARD & THE NEUTRONS

Sep 72. (lp) *(USP 100)* **LIVE AT THE PADGET ROOMS, PENARTH (live)**
– Many are called, but few get up / Daughter of the fireplace / "H" / Samuel.

—— **MICKY + TERRY** + the returning **CLIVE** – guitar / recruited **PHIL RYAN** – keyboards (ex-EYES OF BLUE) repl. DEKE who went solo / **MICHAEL 'WILL' YOUATT** – bass (ex-ANCIENT GREASE) repl. MARTIN

Oct 72. (lp) *(UAG 29417)* <077> **BE GOOD TO YOURSELF AT LEAST ONCE A DAY**
– C'mon / Keep on crinting / Bananas / Life on the road. *(re-iss. May88 & Apr97 on 'Beat Goes On'; BGOLP 14) (cd-iss. Feb92; BGOCD 14)*

—— **ALAN 'TWEKE' LEWIS** – keyboards (ex-WILD TURKEY) repl. RYAN (in studio)

Sep 73. (d-lp) *(UAD 60053-4)* <170> **BACK INTO THE FUTURE** (half live / half studio)   `23`
– A night in dad's bag / Just for you / Back into the future / Don't go away / Ain't their fight / Never say nups to Nepalese / Sospan fack (featuring The Gwalia male choir) / C'mon / Jam up jelly tight. *(cd-iss. Dec93 on 'Beat Goes On'+=; BGOCD 211)* – Oh no, not again (spunk rock '73).

Sep 73. (7") <341> **DON'T GO AWAY. / BACK TO THE FUTURE**

—— **MICKY & TERRY** added the returning **DEKE LEONARD** – guitar, vocals / **MALCOLM MORLEY** – keyboards (ex-HELP YOURSELF) repl. WILL (to NEUTRONS) / **KEN WHALEY** – bass (ex-HELP YOURSELF, ex-BEES MAKE HONEY) repl. CLIVE and TWEKE

May 74. (lp) *(UAG 29631)* <247> **RHINOS, WINOS AND LUNATICS**   `24`
– Taking the easy way out again / The thunder and lightning kid / California silks and satins / Four day Louise / Intro / Kerosene / Scotch corner / Exit. *(cd-iss. Nov93 on 'Beat Goes On'; BGOCD 208)*

Jul 74. (7") *(UP 35703)* <505> **TAKING THE EASY WAY OUT AGAIN. / CALIFORNIA SILKS AND SATINS**

—— trimmed to a quartet when MALCOLM departed.

Oct 74. (7") *(UP 35739)* **DAY AND NIGHT. / HARD WAY TO LIVE (live)**

Nov 74. (lp) *(UAG 29675)* <345> **SLOW MOTION**
– Hard way to die / Grasshopper / Rock & roll you out / You don't like us / Bedtime bone / One more chance / Rainbow eyes / Day and night. *(cd-iss. Nov93 on 'Beat Goes On'; BGOCD 209)*

Nov 74. (7") <611> **DAY AND NIGHT. / RAINBOW EYES**

—— **MARTIN ACE** – bass returned to replace KEN who joined TYLA GANG. added American **JOHN CIPPOLINA** – guitar (ex-QUICKSILVER MESSENGER SERVICE)

Sep 75. (lp) *(UAG 29872)* **MAXIMUM DARKNESS (live)**   `25`
– Codine / 7171-551 / Babe I'm gonna leave you / Many are called, but few get up / Bananas. *(re-iss. Mar89 & Apr 97 on 'Beat Goes On'; BGOLP 43) (cd-iss. Feb92; BGOCD 43)*

—— **PHIL RYAN** – keyboards returned to replace CIPPOLINA / **JOHN McKENZIE** – bass (of GLOBAL VILLAGE TRUCKING CO.) repl. MARTIN ACE who joined The MOTORS

		M.C.A.	M.C.A.

Mar 76. (lp) *(MCF 2753)* <2190> **THE WELSH CONNECTION**   `40`
– The ride and the view / Out of your head / Love can find a way / The Welsh connection / Something is happening / Cartoon / Born with a future.

Mar 76. (7") *(MCA 236)* <40539> **OUT OF YOUR HEAD. / I'M A LOVE TAKER**

—— (disbanded Spring '76)

Nov 77. (lp) *(MCF 2815)* **ALL'S WELL THAT ENDS WELL (live farewell gigs)**
– Let the good times roll / The Welsh connection / The ride and the view / A hard way to live / Born with a future / Spunk Rock / Romain.

—— TERRY WILLIAMS continued in DAVE EDMUNDS' ROCKPILE, before joining The MOTORS and later DIRE STRAITS. PHIL RYAN joined PETE BROWN Band.

DEKE LEONARD

—— solo with ICEBERG at times with MAN members **MICKY JONES, MARTIN ACE, KEN WHALEY + TERRY WILLIAMS** / Others incl. **TOMMY RILEY** – drums, etc.

		U.A.	U.A.

Feb 73. (7") *(UP 35494)* **DIAMOND ROAD. / CIRCLES AND SQUARES**

Jul 73. (lp) *(UAG 29464)* **ICEBERG**
– Razor blade and rattlesnake / I just can't win / Lisa / Nothing is happening / Looking for a man / A hard way to live / Broken ovation / Jesse / Ten thousand takers / The ghost of Musket flat / Jesse / Crosby (second class citizen blues) / 7171 551. *(re-iss. Dec80 on 'Liberty'; LBR 1042) (cd-iss. Nov95 on 'Beat Goes On' with next album;)*

Sep 73. (7") *(UP 35556)* **A HARD WAY TO LIVE. / THE ACHING IS SO SWEET**

Oct 73. (7") **A HARD WAY TO LIVE. / JESSE (live)**

Mar 74. (lp) *(UAG 29544)* **KAMIKAZE**   `50`
– Cool summer rain / Jayhawk special / Sharpened claws / Taking the easy way out / The black gates of death / Stacia / Broken glass and limejuice / April the third / Louisiana hoedown / In search of Sarah and twenty-six horses / The Devil's gloves.

Apr 74. (7") *(UP 35668)* **LOUISIANA HOEDOWN. / SHE'S A CAR**

Feb 79. (7") *(UP 36488)* **MAP OF INDIA. / LADY IN THE BLUE TUXEDO**

Mar 81. (lp) *(UAG 30240)* **BEFORE YOUR VERY EYES**
– Someone is calling / Fools like me / Marlene / Oh / When am I coming back / Get off the line / Hiding in the darkness / Big hunk of love / I feel like a pill / The world exploded in my face / What am I gonna do when the money runs out / Bad luck.

Jun 81. (7") *(BP 400)* **BIG HUNK OF LOVE. / MARLENE**

MAN

—— reformed briefly 1983. **MICKY JONES, DEKE LEONARD, MARTIN ACE** plus **JOHN WEATHERS** – drums (ex-EYES OF BLUE, ex-GENTLE GIANT)

		Picasso	not iss.

Dec 83. (lp/c) *(PIK/+C 001)* **FRIDAY THE 13th (live Marquee, May '83)**
– C'mon / Talk about a morning / Kerosene / A hard way to die / Back into the future / The ride and the view / Romain. *(cd-iss. Aug93 on 'Great Expectations';)*

		Omox-ROR.	not iss.

1984. (7") **WHAT A NIGHT. / THE LAST BIRTHDAY PARTY**   –   – German

—— (1987 reformed again but only to do gigs) **TERRY WILLIAMS** – drums had returned to replace WEATHERS.

		Road Goes On Forever	not iss.

Feb 93. (cd/c) *(RGF CD/MC 1003)* **THE TWANG DYNASTY**
– A feather on the scales of justice / Mad on her / Jumpin' like a kangaroo / The chimes at midnight / Circumstances / The price / Women / The Chinese cut / Out of the darkness / Fast and dangerous / The wings of Mercury.

		Hypertension	not iss.

May 95. (cd) *(HYCD 200154)* **CALL DOWN THE MOON**
– Call down the Moon / If I were you / Dream away / Blackout / The man with x-ray eyes / Heaven and Hell / The girl is trouble / Drivin' around / Burn my workin' clothes.

– compilations, others, etc. –

Oct 73. (lp) *Pye; (GH 569)* **GOLDEN HOUR OF MAN**

Nov 76. (7"ep) *United Artists; (REM 408)* **BANANAS (part 1). / BANANAS (part 2)**

Nov 86. (lp) *Latymer; (DLATE 1)* **GREEN FLY**

Aug 90. (lp/cd; BYSTANDERS) *See For Miles; (SEE/+CD 301)* **BIRTH OF MAN**

Feb 91. (cd) *Worldwide;* **LIVE AT THE RAINBOW 1972 (live)**

Jun 91. (cd/c/lp) *E.M.I.; (CD/TC+/EMS 1403)* **PERFECT TIMING (THE U.A. YEARS: 1970-1975)**
(cd+=/c+=) – (3 extra tracks).

Mar 93. (cd) *Raw Fruit; (FRSCD 010)* **LIVE AT READING '83 (live)**

Oct 93. (cd; 1-side by DEKE LEONARD'S ICEBERG) *Windsong;* **BBC RADIO 1 LIVE IN CONCERT (live)**

Nov 93. (cd) *Great Expectations; (PIPCD 055)* **LIVE AT THE MARQUEE (live)**

Oct 95. (cd; DEKE LEONARD) *Beat Goes On; (BGOCD 288)* **ICEBERG / KAMIKAZE**

Apr 97. (cd) *Think Progressive; (EFA 035052)* **LIVE OFFICIAL BOOTLEG (live)**

MANIC STREET PREACHERS

Formed: Blackwood, Gwent, South Wales ... 1988 by JAMES DEAN BRADFIELD (vocals, guitar) and cousin SEAN MOORE (drums). With the addition of former school friends NICKY WIRE (bass) and RICHEY EDWARDS (rhythm guitar), the line-up was complete and the band set about recording their self-financed debut single, 'SUICIDE ALLEY'. The group began to attract attention with the release of the 'NEW ART RIOT' EP (1990), derivative but impassioned neo-punk which drew interest more for the band's defiant slurs on a range of targets (fellow musicians were shown no mercy) than its musical content. While the band looked the part (low rent glamour chic) and namechecked all the right people (RIMBAUD, The CLASH, etc.), their philosophy of kill your idols and then burn out, smacked of contrivance to say the least. When journalist STEVE LAMACQ said as much in an interview with EDWARDS in 1991, the guitarist proceeded to carve '4 REAL' into his arm with a razor, upping the ante in the band's already precarious relationship with the music press and causing furious debate between doubters and obsessive fans. The group proceeded to release a couple of raging singles on 'Heavenly', 'MOTOWN JUNK' and the stinging 'YOU LOVE US' (aimed at the press), before signing to 'Columbia' in 1991. After a couple of minor hits, 'STAY BEAUTIFUL' and 'LOVE'S SWEET EXILE', the MANICS cracked the Top 20 with a re-released 'YOU LOVE US', their much anticipated debut album, 'GENERATION TERRORISTS' following in February 1992. A sprawling double set, it kicked convincingly against the pricks, lashing out at such deserving targets as high street banks ('NAT WEST-BARCLAYS-MIDLAND-LLOYDS') and our beloved monarch ('REPEAT'). The band also proved they had a way with melody and songwriting in the soaring melancholy of 'MOTORCYCLE EMPTINESS'. Despite their original well intentioned claims to break up after the debut, the band rather predictably toured the album and began work on a new collection, 'GOLD AGAINST THE SOUL' (1993). Lacking the vicious kick of the debut, the record nevertheless contained some fine moments in the likes of 'LA TRISTESSE DURERA (SCREAM TO A SIGH)' and 'LIFE BECOMING A LANDSLIDE', reaching No.8 in the album charts. The MANIC STREET PREACHERS continued to court controversy with NICKY WIRE making his infamous comments about MICHAEL STIPE at the 1993 Reading Festival. The following year RICHEY EDWARDS' depression, self-mutilation and anorexia reached a head, the guitarist eventually admitted to a clinic for several weeks. His trauma was

detailed in the harrowing '4st 7lb' from their third album, 'The HOLY BIBLE' (1994), a dark night of the soul which centred on such grim topics as Nazi genocide. Then, on 1st February '95, with EDWARDS apparently recovered, he went AWOL from his London hotel. A fortnight later, his abandoned car was found at the Severn Bridge, and rumours of suicide abounded. Even after a protracted police search, there was no trace of the guitarist and at the time of writing, he is still missing. Numerous sightings have since been reported, most notably in Goa, India although the Police have continued to draw a blank. The remaining members eventually decided to carry on, contributing a poignant 'RAIN DROPS KEEP FALLING ON MY HEAD' to the 1995 Warchild charity album, 'HELP', and releasing their fourth album, 'EVERYTHING MUST GO' (1996). The group's most accomplished work to date, the record was preceded by their biggest hit single (No.2), the bitter 'A DESIGN FOR LIFE'. Embellished with soaring strings and lavish arrangements, the band scored with a succession of brilliant songs including 'AUSTRALIA' and the title track, compositions that were almost transcendant in their emotive power, the memory of EDWARDS never far away. It seemed that at last the MANIC STREET PREACHERS had lived up to their early boasts and in early 1997 their talent was recognised when 'EVERYTHING MUST GO' won the coveted Mercury Music Award. The top of the singles chart was the only place the MANICS hadn't been. This was remedied late summer '98 when 'IF YOU TOLERATE THIS YOUR CHILDREN WILL BE NEXT' made No.1, a taster from their massive selling parent album, 'THIS IS THE TRUTH TELL ME YOURS' (1998). Classic anthems such as 'THE EVERLASTING', 'YOU STOLE THE SUN FROM MY HEART', and 'TSUNAMI', also became top selling UK charts, although what was happening to their records in America?
• Covered: IT'S SO EASY (Guns N' Roses) / UNDER MY WHEELS (Alice Cooper) / SUICIDE IS PAINLESS (Theme from 'Mash') / CHARLES WINDSOR (McCarthy) / THE DROWNERS (Suede) / STAY WITH ME (Faces) / WROTE FOR LUCK (Happy Mondays) / RAINDROPS KEEP FALLING ON MY HEAD (Bacharach-David) / VELOCITY GIRL (Primal Scream) / TAKE THE SKINHEADS BOWLING (Camper Van Beethoven) / I CAN'T TAKE MY EYES OFF YOU (hit; Andy Williams) / TRAIN IN VAIN (Clash).
Album rating: GENERATION TERRORISTS (*8) / GOLD AGAINST THE SOUL (*9) / THE HOLY BIBLE (*9) / EVERYTHING MUST GO (*9) / THIS IS MY TRUTH TELL ME YOURS (*8)

JAMES DEAN BRADFIELD (b.21 Feb'69, Newport) – vocals, guitar / **RICHEY JAMES EDWARDS** (b.27 Dec'69) – rhythm guitar / **NICKY WIRE** (b. JONES, 20 Jan'69, Tredegar) – bass / **SEAN MOORE** (b.30 Jul'70, Pontypool) – drums

		S.B.S.	not iss.
Aug 89.	(7") (SBS 002) **SUICIDE ALLEY. / TENNESSEE (I FEEL SO LOW)**	☐	-

		Damaged Goods	not iss.
Jun 90.	(12"ep) (YUBB 4) **NEW ART RIOT** – New art riot / Stip it down / Last exit on yesterday / Teenage 20-20. (re-iss. Dec91, Jul93 + Sep96, 12"pink-ep/cd-ep; YUBB 4 P/CD)		-

		Heavenly	not iss.
Jan 91.	(12"ep/cd-ep) (HVN8 12/CD) **MOTOWN JUNK. / SORROW 16 / WE HER MAJESTY'S PRISONERS**	92	-
May 91.	(7") (HVN 10) **YOU LOVE US. / SPECTATORS OF SUICIDE** (12"+=/cd-s+=) (HVN 10 12/CD) – Starlover / Strip it down (live).	62	-

		Caff	not iss.
Jul 91.	(7") (CAFF 15) **FEMININE IS BEAUTIFUL: NEW ART RIOT. / REPEAT AFTER ME**		-

		Columbia	Columbia
Jul 91.	(7") (657337-7) **STAY BEAUTIFUL. / R.P. McMURPHY** (12"+=/12"w-poster/cd-s+=) (657337-6/-8/-2) – Soul contamination. (US-cd-ep+=) – Motown junk / Sorrow 16 / Star lover. (cd-ep re-iss. Sep97 on 'Epic' hit No.52; MANIC 1CD)	40	
Nov 91.	(7") (657582-7) **LOVE'S SWEET EXILE. / REPEAT** (12"+=/cd-s+=) (657582-6/-2) – Democracy coma. (12"ltd.++=) (657582-8) – Stay beautiful (live). (cd-ep re-iss. Sep97 on 'Epic' hit No.55; MANIC 2CD)	26	-
Jan 92.	(7"/c-s) (657724-7/-4) **YOU LOVE US. / A VISION OF DEAD DESIRE** (12"+=) (657724-6) – It's so easy (live). (cd-s+=) (657724-2) – We her majesty's prisoners. (cd-ep re-iss. Sep97 on 'Epic' hit No.49; MANIC 3CD)	16	-
Feb 92.	(pic-cd/cd/d-c/d-lp/pic-d-lp) (471060-0/-2/-4/-1/-9) <52474> **GENERATION TERRORISTS** – Slash 'n' burn / Nat West-Barclays-Midland-Lloyds / Born to end / Motorcycle emptiness / You love us / Love's sweet exile / Little baby nothing / Repeat (stars and stripes) / Tennessee / Another invented disease / Stay beautiful / So dead / Repeat (UK) / Spectators of suicide / Damn dog / Crucifix kiss / Methadone pretty / Condemned to rock'n'roll. (cd re-iss. Jan99; same)	13	
Mar 92.	(7"/c-s) (657873-7/-4) **SLASH 'N' BURN. / AIN'T GOING DOWN** (12"+=) (657873-6) – Motown junk. (cd-s++=/gold-cd-s++=) (657873-2/-0) – ('A'version). (cd-ep re-iss. Sep97 on 'Epic' hit No.54; MANIC 4CD)	20	-
Jun 92.	(7"/c-s) (658083-7/-4) **MOTORCYCLE EMPTINESS. / BORED OUT OF MY MIND** (12"pic-d+=) (658083-8) – Under my wheels. (cd-s++=/s-cd-s++=) (658083-2/-9) – Crucifix kiss (live). (cd-ep re-iss. Sep97 on 'Epic' hit No.41; MANIC 5CD)	17	-
Sep 92.	(7"/cd-s) (658382-7/-2) **THEME FROM M.A.S.H. (SUICIDE IS PAINLESS). / ('b'side by 'Fatima Mansions' – Everything I Do (I Do It For You)**	7	-
Nov 92.	(7") (658796-7) **LITTLE BABY NOTHING. / SUICIDE ALLEY** (12"+=/cd-s+=) (658796-6/-2) – Yankee drawl / Never want again. (cd-ep re-iss. Sep97 on 'Epic' hit No.50; MANIC 6CD)	29	-

Jun 93.	(c-s) (659337-4) **FROM DESPAIR TO WHERE. / HIBERNATION** (12"+=) (659337-6) – Spectators of suicide (Heavenly version). (cd-s+=) (659337-2) – Star lover (Heavenly version).	25	-
Jun 93.	(cd/c/lp/pic-lp) (474064-2/-4/-1/-9) <57386> **GOLD AGAINST THE SOUL** – Sleepflower / From despair to where / La tristesse durera (scream to a sigh) / Yourself / Life becoming a landslide / Drug drug druggy / Roses in the hospital / Nostalgic pushead / Symphony of tourette / Gold against the soul.	8	-
Jul 93.	(7"/c-s) (659477-7/-4) **LA TRISTESSE DURERA (SCREAM TO A SIGH). / PATRICK BATEMAN** (12"+=) (659477-6) – Repeat (live) / Tennessee. (cd-s+=) (659477-2) – What's my name (live) / Slash'n'burn (live).	22	-
Sep 93.	(7"/c-s) (659727-7/-4) **ROSES IN THE HOSPITAL. / US AGAINST YOU / DONKEY** (cd-s+=) (659727-2) – Wrote for luck. (12") (659727-6) – ('A'side) / (5-'A' mixes).	15	-

		Epic	Epic
Feb 94.	(c-s) (660070-4) **LIFE BECOMING A LANDSLIDE / COMFORT COMES** (12"+=) (660070-6) – Are mothers saints. (cd-s++=) (660070-2) – Charles Windsor.	36	-
Jun 94.	(7"/c-s) (660447-7/-4) **FASTER. / P.C.P.** (10"+=) (660447-0) – Sculpture of man. (cd-s++=) (660447-2) – New art riot (in E-minor).	16	-
Aug 94.	(10"/c-s) (660686-0/-4) **REVOL. / TOO COLD HERE** (cd-s+=) (660686-2) – You love us (original Heavenly version) / Love's sweet exile (live). (660686-5) – ('A'side) / (3 live at Glastonbury tracks).	22	-

—— RICHEY booked himself into a health clinic, after wasting himself down to 5 stone.

Aug 94.	(cd/c/pic-lp) (477421-2/-4/-0) <66967> **THE HOLY BIBLE** – Yes / Ifwhiteamericatoldthetruthforonedayit'sworldwouldfallapart / Of walking abortion / She is suffering / Archives of pain / Revol / 4st 7lb / Mausoleum / Faster / This is yesterday / Die in the summertime / The intense humming of evil / P.C.P.	6	-
Oct 94.	(10"/c-s) (660895-0/-4) **SHE IS SUFFERING. / LOVE TORN US UNDER (acoustic)** (cd-s+=) (660895-2) – The drowners / Stay with me (both live w/ BERNARD BUTLER). (cd-s+=) (660895-5) – ('A'side) / La tristesse durera (scream to a sigh) / Faster (Dust Brothers remixes).	25	-

—— RICHEY was now fully recuperated . . . but on 1st Feb '95, he went AWOL again after walking out of London's Embassy Hotel at 7 that morning. Two weeks later, his car was found abandoned and after police frog search the Severn, it was believed he might be dead. By the end of 1995, with RICHEY still missing, the group carried on as a trio.

—— Meanwhile, BRADFIELD produced the debut of NORTHERN UPROAR.

Apr 96.	(c-s) (663070-4) **A DESIGN FOR LIFE / BRIGHT EYES (live)** (cd-s) (663070-2) – ('A'side) / Mr Carbohydrate / Dead passive / Dead trees and traffic islands. (cd-s) (663070-5) – ('A'side) / ('A'-Howard Grey remix) / ('A'-Apollo 440 remix) / Faster (Chemical Brothers remix).	2	-
May 96.	(cd/c/lp) (483930-2/-4/-1) <67709> **EVERYTHING MUST GO** – Elvis impersonator: Blackpoool pier / A design for life / Kevin Carter / Enola – alone / Everything must go / Small black flowers that grow in the sky / The girl who wanted to be God / Removables / Australia / Interiors (song for Willem De Kooning) / Further away / No surface at all.	2	-
Jul 96.	(c-s) (663468-4) **EVERYTHING MUST GO / RAINDROPS KEEP FALLING ON MY HEAD (live)** (cd-s) (663468-2) – ('A'side) / Hanging on / Black garden / No-one knows what it's like to be me. (cd-s) (663468-5) – ('A'side) / ('A'-Stealth Sonic Orchestra remix) / ('A'-Chemical Brothers remix).	5	-
Sep 96.	(c-s) (663775-4) **KEVIN CARTER / EVERYTHING MUST GO (acoustic)** (cd-s) (663775-2) – ('A'side) / Horses under starlight / Sepia / First republic. (cd-s) (663775-5) – Kevin Carter busts loose (Jon Carter remix) / ('A'-Stealth Sonic Orchestra mixes).	9	-
Dec 96.	(c-s) (664044-4) **AUSTRALIA / A DESIGN FOR LIFE (live)** (cd-s) (664044-2) – ('A'side) / Velocity girl / Take the skinheads bowling / I can't take my eyes off you (acoustic). (cd-s) (664044-5) – ('A'side) / ('A'-Lionrock remix) / Motorcycle emptiness (Stealth Sonic Orchestra version).	7	-

		Epic	Imprint
Aug 98.	(c-s) (666345-4) **IF YOU TOLERATE THIS YOUR CHILDREN WILL BE NEXT / KEVIN CARTER (live)** (cd-s) (666345-2) – ('A'side) / Prologue to history / Montana Autumn '78. (cd-s) (666345-5) – ('A'side) / ('A'-Massive Attack remix) / ('A'-The Class Reunion Of The Sunset Marquis mix; aka David Holmes).	1	-
Sep 98.	(cd/c/lp) (491703-2/-4/-1) <111820> **THIS IS MY TRUTH TELL ME YOURS** – The everlasting / If you tolerate this your children will be next / You stole the sun from my heart / Ready for drowning / Tsunami / My little empire / I'm not working / You're tender and you're tired / Born a girl / Be natural / Black dog on my shoulder / Nobody loved you / S.Y.M.M.	1	-
Nov 98.	(c-s) (666686-4) **THE EVERLASTING / SMALL BLACK FLOWERS THAT GROW IN THE SUN (live at Nunex)** (cd-s) (666686-2) – ('A'side) / Blackholes for the young / Valley boy. (cd-s) (666686-5) – ('A'extended) / ('A'-Deadly Avenger's Psalm 315) / ('A'-Stealth Sonic Orchestra mix).	11	-
Mar 99.	(c-s) (666953-4) **YOU STOLE THE SUN FROM MY HEART / IF YOU TOLERATE THIS YOUR CHILDREN WILL BE NEXT (live)** (cd-s) (666953-2) – ('A'side) / Socialist serenade / Train in vain (live). (cd-s) (666953-5) – ('A'side) / ('A'mixes by David Holmes & Mogwai).	5	-
Jul 99.	(c-s) (667411-4) **TSUNAMI / MOTOWN JUNK (live)** (cd-s) (667411-2) – ('A'side) / Buildings for dead people / A design for life (video). (cd-s) (667411-5) – ('A'mixes by Cornelius & Stereolab).	11	-

Aimee MANN

Born: 9 Aug'60, Richmond, Virginia, USA. After moving to Boston to attend the Berklee School of Music, one of MANN's rather unlikely initial musical forays was working with AL JOURGENSEN / MINISTRY. This group, the YOUNG SNAKES (one 1982 EP exists) were around prior to her forming pop/rock outfit, 'TIL TUESDAY along with ROBERT HOLMES, JOEY PESCE and MICHAEL HAUSMANN. While many of the songs on the debut set, 'VOICES CARRY' (1985), sprang from MANN's break-up with former lover, HAUSMANN, the group's critically acclaimed third set, 'EVERYTHING'S DIFFERENT NOW' (1989), was largely inspired by MANN's relationship with co-writer, JULES SHEAR. In spite of, or perhaps because of this 'Rumours'-style emotional entanglement, the album was a compelling stepping stone to MANN's solo career and saw her developing into an accomplished and affecting songwriter. Yet the record sold poorly and the band dissolved amid record company hassles, MANN spending the next few years attempting to disentangle herself before embarking upon a solo career. She eventually emerged in Autumn '93 with a new deal ('Imago') and album, 'WHATEVER', her eclectic, BEATLES/PRETENDERS-like pop/rock drawing praise from such legendary songwriters as ELVIS COSTELLO, a personal friend and sometime collaborator. The record also provided her with her first major UK success, nudging into the Top 40, although just when it seemed as if MANN was finally beginning to establish herself as an artist in her own right, 'Imago' went bust. The ensuing hassles almost persuaded MANN to give it all up, 'Geffen' finally releasing a follow-up, 'I'M WITH STUPID', in 1995. With an array of guests including BERNARD BUTLER (who co-wrote 'SUGARCOATED'), JULIANA HATFIELD and the SQUEEZE songwriting axis of GLENN TILBROOK and CHRIS DIFFORD, the album was another critical success, its more acerbic lyrical bile no doubt a result of MANN's industry tribulations. • **Trivia:** In 1987, she guested on RUSH's hit single, 'Time Stand Still'.

Album rating: 'Til Tuesday: VOICES CARRY (*6) / WELCOME HOME (*5) / EVERYTHING'S DIFFERENT NOW (*4) / Aimee Mann: WHATEVER (*7) / I'M WITH STUPID (*6)

'TIL TUESDAY

AIMEE MANN – vocals, bass / **ROBERT HOLMES** (b.31 Mar'59, Hampton, England) – guitar, vocals / **JOEY PESCE** (b.14 Apr'62, Bronx, N.Y.) – synthesizers, piano, vocals / **MICHAEL HAUSMANN** (b.12 Jun'60, Philadelphia, Pennsylvania) – drums, percussion

			Epic	Epic
Apr 85.	(7") (EPCA 6120) <04795> **VOICES CARRY. / ARE YOU SERIOUS?**			8
Jun 85.	(lp/c) (EPC/40 26434) <39458> **VOICES CARRY**			19 Apr85
	– Love in a vacuum / Looking over my shoulder / I could get used to this / No more crying / Voices carry / Winning the war / You know the rest / Maybe Monday / Don't watch me bleed / Sleep. (cd-iss. 1988; CDEPC 26434)			
Aug 85.	(7") <04935> **LOOKING OVER MY SHOULDER. / DON'T WATCH ME BLEED**		-	61
Oct 85.	(7") **LOVE IN A VACUUM. / NO MORE CRYING**		-	
Jan 87.	(lp/c/cd) (EPC/40/EPCCD 57094) <40314> **WELCOME HOME**			49 Oct86
	– What about love / Coming up close / On Sunday / Will she just fall down / David denies / Lover's day / Have mercy / Sleeping and walking / Angels never call / No one is watching you now.			
Feb 87.	(7") (650125-7) <06289> **WHAT ABOUT LOVE. / WILL SHE JUST FALL DOWN**			26 Sep86
	(12"+=/ext.12"+=) (650125-6/-8) – Voices carry.			
Apr 87.	(7") <06571> **COMING UP CLOSE. / ANGELS NEVER CALL**		-	59

—— **MICHAEL MONTES** – keyboards / **JON BRION + CLAYTON SCOBEL** – guitar; repl. PESCE

Jan 89.	(7"/7"poster) (653064-7/-0) <08059> **(BELIEVED YOU WERE) LUCKY. / LIMITS TO LOVE**			95
	(12"+=/cd-s+=) (653064-6/-2) – Voices carry / What about love.			
Mar 89.	(lp/c/cd) (460737-1/-4/-2) <44041> **EVERYTHING'S DIFFERENT NOW**			Nov88
	– Everything's different now / R.I.P. in Heaven / Why must I / J for Jules / (Believed you were) Lucky / Limits to love / Long gone (buddy) / The other end (of the telescope) / Crash and burn / How can you give up.			
Jul 89.	(7") **R.I.P. IN HEAVEN. / HOW CAN YOU GIVE UP**		-	

—— disbanded after above album

AIMEE MANN

solo with **DAVE GREGORY** – guitar (of XTC)

			Imago	Imago
Aug 93.	(7"/c-s) (72787 25048-7/-4) **I SHOULD'VE KNOWN. / JIMMY HOFFA JOKES**		55	
	(cd-s+=) (72787 25048-2) – Jacob Marley's chains.			
Sep 93.	(cd/c/lp) <(72787 21017/-2/-4/-1)> **WHATEVER**		39	
	– I should've known / Fifty years after the fair / 4th of July / Could've been anyone / Put me on top / Stupid thing / Say anything / Jacob Marley's chain / Mr. Harris / I could hurt you now / I know there's a word / I've had it / Way back when. (cd re-iss. Jul96 on 'Geffen'; GFLD 19319)			
Nov 93.	(7"/c-s) (72787 25043-7/-4) **STUPID THING. / I'VE HAD IT**		47	-
	(cd-s) (72787 25043-2) – ('A'side) / Baby blue / Other end (of the telescope) (live) / Say anything (live).			
	(cd-s) (72787 25043-5) – ('A'side) / Put me on top (live) / Fourth of July (live) / I should've known (live).			

Nov 93.	(cd-s) <72787 25032-2> **I SHOULD'VE KNOWN / TAKE IT BACK**		-	
Feb 94.	(7"/c-s) (72787 25060-7/-4) **I SHOULD'VE KNOWN. / TRUTH ON MY SIDE (demo)**		45	-
	(cd-s+=) (72787 25060-2) – Fifty years after the fair (demo) / Put on some speed (demo).			
	(10") (72787 25060-0) – ('A'side) / 4th of July / Stupid thing / The other end (of the telescope).			

—— with **JON BRION** – guitars, drums, co-writer (some) / **JOHN SANDS** – drums / guests **BERNARD BUTLER** (co-writer SUGARCOATED) / **GLENN TILBROOK + CHRIS DIFFORD / JULIANA HATFIELD / MICHAEL PENN**

			Geffen	Imago
Jan 95.	(c-s) <25086> **THAT'S JUST WHAT YOU ARE / I SHOULD'VE KNOWN**		-	93
Nov 95.	(cd/c) <(GED/GEC 24951)> **I'M WITH STUPID**		51	82
	– Long shot / Choice in the matter / Sugarcoated / You could make a killing / Superball / Amateur / All over now / Par for the course / You're with stupid now / That's just what you are / Frankenstein / Ray / It's not safe.			
Apr 96.	(c-s) (GFSC 22133) **LONG SHOT / YOU'RE WITH STUPID NOW**			
	(cd-s+=) (GFSTD 22133) – Driving with one hand on the wheel.			

—— the album, 'BACHELOR NO.2' will be issued in early 2000, several AIMEE MANN tracks also surfaced on the soundtrack to 'Magnolia'.

Manfred MANN

Formed: London, England ... late '62, initially as The MANN-HUGG BLUES BAND, subsequently naming themselves MANFRED MANN after the band's keyboard player. MANN and HUGG then recruited DAVE RICHMOND, PAUL JONES and MIKE VICKERS, playing local gigs which secured them a deal with the 'H.M.V.' label. Early in 1964, after two flop singles, they had their first chart success, hitting the Top 5 with the harmonica-fuelled R&B classic, '5-4-3-2-1'. They continued to storm the charts throughout the 60's, reaching pole position three times with 'DOO WAH DIDDY DIDDY' (1964), 'PRETTY FLAMINGO' (1966) and 'THE MIGHTY QUINN' (1968). The last was fronted by MIKE D'ABO, who had replaced the solo bound PAUL JONES. In 1969, MANN and HUGG churned out commercial jingles for Michelen tyres and Ski yogurt before forming the heavier jazz-rock outfit, MANFRED MANN CHAPTER THREE. They delivered a couple of albums for 'Vertigo', soon reverting back to their original name in 1971. The following year, they re-emerged minus HUGG, with the more ambitious and progressive MANFRED MANN'S EARTH BAND. They struggled initially, although they created their own take on GUSTAV HOLST's "Jupiter suite" (from 'The Planets') in the form of 'JOYBRINGER' (a top 10 hit in 1973). A dry period of three years ensued, during which time they released three accessible rock albums, 'SOLAR FIRE', 'THE GOOD EARTH' and 'NIGHTINGALES AND BOMBERS'. The band saw a return to chart action with a cover of BRUCE SPRINGSTEEN's, 'BLINDED BY THE LIGHT', which also hit No.1 in America. Their albums fared a lot better from this point on, another SPRINGSTEEN re-hash, 'SPIRIT IN THE NIGHT', denting the US Top 40 in 1977. In the 80's (and 90's!), his EARTH BAND continued to tread the same ground, releasing a plethora of mediocre cover versions for the coffee-table set. One particular song, 'THE RUNNER', saw them sprinting back into the US Top 30 early in 1984. Over the course of the decade or so, MANFRED MANN delivered the odd pop-rock album, although it was in 1999 that he would return to some kind of press coverage, albeit over the sample/use of his song 'TRIBUTE' on MASSIVE ATTACK's 'Black Mark'; the Bristol posse settled out of court. • **Songwriters:** MANN-HUGG until latter's departure in '71. Covered; DOO WAH DIDDY DIDDY (Exciters) / SHA LA LA (Shirelles) / OH NO NOT MY BABY (Goffin-King) / SMOKESTACK LIGHTNING (Howlin' Wolf) / MY LITTLE RED BOOK (Bacharach-David) / WITH GOD ON OUR SIDE + IF YOU GOTTA GO, GO NOW + JUST LIKE A WOMAN + THE MIGHTY QUINN + PLEASE, MRS.HENRY + others (Bob Dylan) / SWEET PEA (Tommy Roe) / SO LONG DAD + LIVING WITHOUT YOU (Randy Newman) / MY NAME IS JACK (John Simon) / etc. His EARTH BAND covered FATHER OF DAY, FATHER OF NIGHT + YOU, ANGEL YOU + SHELTER FROM THE STORM (Bob Dylan) / SPIRIT IN THE NIGHT + BLINDED BY THE LIGHT + FOR YOU (Bruce Springsteen) / DON'T KILL IT CAROL (Mike Heron) / REDEMPTION SONG (Bob Marley) / DO ANYTHING YOU WANNA DO (Eddie & The Hot Rods) / GOING UNDERGROUND (Jam) / BANQUET (Joni Mitchell) / PLAY WITH FIRE (Rolling Stones) / NOTHING EVER HAPPENS (Del Amitri) / PLEASURE + PAIN (Chapman-Knight) / TUMBLING BALL (M. Spiro) / THE PRICE I PAY (Robert Cray) / LOSE THE TOUCH (C. Schumann) / THE COMPLETE HISTORY OF SEXUAL JEALOUSY (Momus) / 99 LBS (D Bryant) / etc. • **Trivia:** MIKE HUGG wrote 'SHAPES OF THINGS' in 1966 for fellow R&B hitmakers, The YARDBIRDS. MANFRED played Moog synthesizer on URIAH HEEP's 1971 album, 'Look At Yourself'. The 'GLORIFIED MAGNIFIED' track was used for the theme to Radio 1's 'Sound Of The 70's'.

Best CD compilation(s): AGES OF MANN (22 CLASSICS OF THE 60s) (*7) / 20 YEARS OF MANFRED MANN'S EARTH BAND (*6)

MANFRED MANN (b. MANFRED LUBOWITZ, 21 Oct'40, Johannesburg, South Africa) – keyboards / **PAUL JONES** (b.PAUL POND, 24 Feb'42, Portsmouth, England) – vocals, harmonica / **MIKE VICKERS** (b.18 Apr'41, Southampton, England) – guitar / **DAVE RICHMOND** – bass / **MIKE HUGG** (b.11 Aug'42, Andover, England) – drums

	H.M.V.	Prestige
Jul 63. (7") (POP 1189) **WHY SHOULD WE NOT. / BROTHER JACK**		-
Oct 63. (7") (POP 1225) **COCK-A-HOOP. / NOW YOU'RE NEEDING ME**		-

—— **TOM McGUINESS** (b. 2 Dec'41, Wimbledon, London, England) – bass (ex-ROOSTERS) repl. RICHMOND

	H.M.V.	Ascot
Jan 64. (7") (POP 1252) **5-4-3-2-1. / WITHOUT YOU**	5	☐ Mar64
Apr 64. (7") (POP 1282) <2151> **HUBBLE BUBBLE TOIL AND TROUBLE. / I'M YOUR KINGPIN**	11	
Jul 64. (7") (POP 1320) <2157> **DOO WAH DIDDY DIDDY. / WHAT YOU GONNA DO**	1	1 Aug64

(re-iss. Oct82; PMS 1003)

Sep 64. (lp) (CLP 1731) **THE FIVE FACES OF MANFRED MANN** [3] [-]
– Smokestack lightning / Don't ask me what I say / It's gonna work out fine / Sack of wool / What you gonna do / I'm your kingpin / Hoochie coochie / Down the road apiece / I've got my mojo working / Mr. Analles / Untie me / Bring it to Jerome / Without you / You've got to take it. *(cd-iss. Jun97 on 'E.M.I.'; DORIG 121)*

Oct 64. (7") (POP 1346) <2165> **SHA LA LA. / JOHN HARDY** [3] [12] Nov64

Nov 64. (lp) <16015> **THE MANFRED MANN ALBUM** [-] [35]
– Do wah diddy diddy / Sack o' woe / Don't ask me what I say / What you gonna do / Got my mojo working / I'm your hoochie coochie man / Smokestack lightning / It's gonna work out fine / Down the road apiece / Untie me / Bring it to Jerome / Without you.

Jan 65. (7") (POP 1381) <2170> **COME TOMORROW. / WHAT DID I DO WRONG** [4] [50] Feb65

Mar 65. (lp) <ALS 16018> **THE FIVE FACES OF MANFRED MANN** [-]
– Sha la la / Come tomorrow / She / Can't believe it / John Hardy / Did you have to do that / Watermelon man / I'm your kingpin / Hubble bubble (toil and trouble) / You've got to take it / Dashing away with the smoothing iron / Groovin'.

Apr 65. (7") (POP 1413) **OH NO NOT MY BABY. / WHAT AM I DOING WRONG** [11] [-]

Apr 65. (7") <2181> **POISON IVY. / I CAN'T BELIEVE WHAT YOU SAY** [-]

Jun 65. (7") <2184> **MY LITTLE RED BOOK. / WHAT AM I DOING WRONG** [-]
<re-iss. 1966; 2241>

Jul 65. (lp) <ALS 16201> **MY LITTLE RED BOOK OF WINNERS** [-]
– My little red book / Oh no, not my baby / What am I to do / One in the middle / You gave me somebody to love / You're for me / Poison Ivy / Without you / Brother Jack / Love like yours / I can't believe what you say / With God on your side.

Sep 65. (7") (POP 1466) **IF YOU GOTTA GO, GO NOW. / STAY AROUND** [2] [-]

Oct 65. (lp) (CLP 1911) <ALS 16024> **MANN MADE** [7]
– Since I don't have you / You're for me / Look away / L.S.D. / The abominable snowman / Watch your step / The way you do the things you do / Stormy Monday blues / Hi lili hi lo / I really do believe / Bear Hugg / You don't know me / I'll make it up to you. *(re-iss. Nov69 on 'Regal Starline'; SRS 5007)*

Oct 65. (7") <2194> **IF YOU GOTTA GO, GO NOW. / THE ONE IN THE MIDDLE** [-]

Jan 66. (7") <2210> **HI LILI, HI LO. / SHE NEEDS COMPANY** [-]

—— (PETE BURFORD and DAVID HYDE deputised for VICKERS on tour until) / **JACK BRUCE** (b.14 May'43, Lanarkshire, Scotland) – bass (ex-JOHN MAYALL, ex-GRAHAM BOND) repl. VICKERS / added **LYN DOBSON** – saxophone / **HENRY LOWTHER** – trumpet (McGUINESS now guitar)

	H.M.V.	U.A.
Apr 66. (7") (POP 1523) <50040> **PRETTY FLAMINGO. / YOU'RE STANDING BY**	1	29 Jun66

—— **MANN, HUGG** and **McGUINESS** added new members **MIKE D'ABO** (b. 1 Mar'44, Bethworth, England) – vocals (ex-BAND OF ANGELS) repl. JONES who went solo, etc. / **KLAUS VOORMAN** (b.29 Apr'42, Berlin, Germany) – bass repl. JACK BRUCE who formed CREAM.

Jun 66. (7") (POP 1541) **YOU GAVE ME SOMEBODY TO LOVE. / POISON IVY** [36] [-]

Sep 66. <50066> **DO YOU HAVE TO DO THAT. / WHEN WILL I BE LOVED** [-]

	Fontana	Mercury
Jul 66. (7") (TF 730) <72607> **JUST LIKE A WOMAN. / I WANNA BE RIGHT**	10	
Oct 66. (7") (TF 757) <72629> **SEMI-DETACHED SUBURBAN MR. JAMES. / MORNING AFTER THE PARTY**	2	
Oct 66. (lp; stereo/mono) (S+/TL 5377) **AS IS**	22	-

– Trouble and tea / A now and then thing / Each other's company / Box office draw / Dealer dealer / Morning after the party / Another kind of music / As long as I have lovin' / Autumn leaves / Superstitious guy / You're my girl / Just like a woman.

Dec 66. (lp) <6549> **PRETTY FLAMINGO** [-]
– Pretty flamingo / Let's go get stoned / Tired of trying / Bored with living / Scared of dying / I put a spell on you / It's getting late / You're standing by / Machines / Stay around / Tennessee waltz / Drive man / Do you have to do that.

Mar 67. (7") (TF 812) <72676> **HA! HA! SAID THE CLOWN. / FEELING SO GOOD** [4]

May 67. (7") (TF 828) **SWEET PEA. / ONE WAY** [36] [-]

Sep 67. (7") (TF 862) **SO LONG DAD. / FUNNIEST GIG** [-] [-]

Jan 68. (lp) (TL 5460) **UP THE JUNCTION (Soundtrack)** [-] [-]
– Up the junction (vocal) / Sing songs of love / Walking around up the junction (instrumental) / Love theme (instrumental) / Up the junction (vocal & instrumental) / Just for me / Love theme (instrumental) / Sheila's dance / Belgravia / Wailing horn / I need your love / Up the junction (vocal). *(re-iss. 1970; 6852 005)*

	Fontana	Mercury
Jan 68. (7") (TF 897) <72770> **MIGHTY QUINN. / BY REQUEST EDWIN GARVEY**	1	10

(re-iss. Jun82 on 'Old Gold'; OG 9252)

Mar 68. (lp) (SFL 13003) **WHAT A MANN (compilation)** [-] [-]
– Funniest gig / Sunny / Get away / With a girl like you / Sweet pea / Wild thing / The morning after the party / Feeling so good / One way / So long dad.

Mar 68. (7") (TF 908) **THEME – UP THE JUNCTION. / SLEEPY HOLLOW** [-] [-]

May 68. (lp) <61168> **MIGHTY QUINN** [-] [ ]
– Mighty Quinn / Ha! ha! said the clown / Every day another hair turns grey / It's so easy falling / Big Betty / Cubist town / Country dancing / Semi-detached suburban Mr. James / The vicar's daughter / Each and every day / No better, no worse.

Jun 68. (lp; stereo/mono) (S+/TL 5470) **MIGHTY GARVEY!** [ ]
– Happy families / No better, no worse / Each and every day / Country dancing / It's so easy falling / Happy families / Mighty Quinn / Big Betty / The vicar's daughter / Every day another hair turns grey / Cubist town / Ha! ha! said the clown / Harry the one-man band / Happy families.

Jun 68. (7") (TF 943) <72872> **MY NAME IS JACK. / THERE IS A MAN** [8]

Dec 68. (7") (TF 985) <72879> **FOX ON THE RUN. / TOO MANY PEOPLE** [5] [97]

May 69. (7") (TF 1013) <72921> **RAGAMUFFIN MAN. / A 'B' SIDE** [8]

—— split mid 69. TOM formed McGUINESS FLINT. D'ABO went solo, and VOORMAN joined JOHN LENNON's PLASTIC ONO BAND

MANFRED MANN'S CHAPTER III

MANFRED retained **MIKE HUGG** – vocals, electric piano. —— Recruited **BRIAN HUGG** – guitar / **STEVE YORK** – bass plus session singers, drummers and wind section

	Vertigo	Polydor
Nov 69. (lp) (VO 3) <4013> **MANFRED MANN CHAPTER THREE**		

– Travelling lady / Snakeskin garter / Konekuf / Sometimes / Devil woman / Time / One way glass / Mister you're a better man than I / Ain't it sad / A study in inaccuracy / Where am I going. *(cd-iss. Feb94 on 'Cohesion'; MFMCD 14)*

Mar 70. (7") <14026> **SNAKESKIN GARTER. / SOMETIMES** [-] [-]

—— on session **CHRIS SLADE** – drums (alongside others)

Sep 70. (7") <6059 012> **HAPPY BEING ME. / DEVIL WOMAN** [-] [-]

Oct 70. (lp) (6360 012) **MANFRED MANN CHAPTER III, VOL.2** [ ] [ ]
– Lady Ace / I ain't laughing / Poor sad Sue / Jump before you think / It's good to be alive / Happy being me / Virginia. *(cd-iss. Feb94 on 'Cohesion'; MFMCD 15)*

MANFRED MANN'S EARTH BAND

—— His new band now featured **CHRIS SLADE** – drums (now a full time member) / **MICK ROGERS** – vocals, guitar repl. MIKE HUGG / **COLIN PATTENDEN** – bass repl. STEVE YORK and BRIAN HUGG

	Philips	Polydor
Jun 71. (7"; as MANFRED MANN; w-drawn) <14074> **CALIFORNIA COASTLINE. / PART TIME**	-	
Jun 71. (7"; as MANFRED MANN) (6006 122) <14113> **LIVING WITHOUT YOU. / TRIBUTE**		69 Jan72
Sep 71. (7"; as MANFRED MANN) (6006 251) **MRS HENRY. / PRAYER**		

Feb 72. (lp) (6308 086) <5015> **MANFRED MANN'S EARTH BAND** [ ] [ ]
– California coastline / Captain Bobby Stout / Sloth / Living without you / Tribute / Mrs Henry / Jump sturdy / Prayer / Part time man / I'm up and leaving. *(re-iss. Apr77 & 1981 on 'Bronze' lp/cd; CLA LP/CD 150) (re-iss. Jan90 on 'Castle' lp/cd; BRON 252) (re-iss. Jan91 on 'Cohesion' lp/c/cd; COMME/+T/CD 6)*

Mar 72. (7") <14130> **PART TIME MAN. / I'M UP AND LEAVING** [-] [ ]

Sep 72. (lp) (6308 125) <5031> **GLORIFIED MAGNIFIED** [ ] [ ]
– Meat / Look around / One way glass / I'm gonna have you all / Down home / Our friend George / Ashes to the wind / It's all over now, baby blue / Glorified magnified. *(re-iss. Apr77 & 1981 on 'Bronze'; cd-iss. Dec93 on 'Cohesion'; MFMCD 11)*

Nov 72. (7") (6006 251) **MEAT. / GLORIFIED MAGNIFIED** [-] [ ]

Feb 73. (7") <14164> **IT'S ALL OVER NOW, BABY BLUE. / ASHES TO THE WIND** [-] [ ]

	Vertigo	Polydor
Apr 73. (7"; as EARTH BAND) (6059 078) **GET YOUR ROCKS OFF. / SADJOY**		

Jun 73. (lp) (6360 087) <5050> **MESSIN'** <US-title 'GET YOUR ROCKS OFF'> [ ] [ ]
– Buddah / Messin' / Cloudy eyes / Get your rocks off / Sadjoy / Black and blue / Mardi Gras day. *(re-iss. Apr77 & 1981 on 'Bronze'; BRON 261) (re-iss. Jan90 on 'Castle' lp/cd; CLA LP/CD 151) (re-iss. Jan91 on 'Cohesion' lp/c/cd; COMME/+T/CD 7)*

Jun 73. (7") <14173> **MARDI GRAS DAY. / SADJOY** [-] [ ]

Aug 73. (7") <14191> **GET YOUR ROCKS OFF. / ASHES TO THE WIND** [-] [ ]

Aug 73. (7") (6059 083) **JOYBRINGER. / CAN'T EAT MEAT** [9] [ ]

Sep 73. (7") <14205> **JOYBRINGER. / CLOUDY EYES** [-] [ ]

	Bronze	Polydor
Nov 73. (lp) (ILPS 9265) <6019> **SOLAR FIRE**		96

– Father of night, in the beginning / Pluto the dog / Solar fire / Saturn (Mercury) / Earth the circle (pts.1 & 2). *(re-iss. Apr77 & 1981; BRON 265) (re-iss. Nov87 on 'Legacy' lp/c/cd; LLP/LLK/LLCD 121) (re-iss. Jan91 on 'Cohesion' lp/c/cd; COMME/+T/CD 1)*

	Bronze	Warners
Mar 74. (7") **FATHER OF DAY, FATHER OF NIGHT. / SOLAR FIRE 2**		-
Oct 74. (7") (BRO 13) **BE NOT TOO HARD. / EARTH HYMN (part 2a)**		

Oct 74. (lp/c) (ILPS/ICT 9306) <BS 2826> **THE GOOD EARTH** [ ] [ ]
– Give me the good earth / Launching place / I'll be gone / Earth hymn (pts.1 & 2) / Sky high / Be not too hard. *(re-iss. Apr77 + 1981; BRON 306) (cd-iss. Dec93 on 'Cohesion'; MFMCD 12)*

Jul 75. (7") (BRO 18) <8152> **SPIRIT IN THE NIGHT. / AS ABOVE SO BELOW (part 2)** [ ] [ ]

Aug 75. (lp/c) (ILPS/ICT 9337) <BS 2877> **NIGHTINGALES AND BOMBERS** [ ] [ ]
– Spirit in the night / Countdown / Time is right / Crossfade / Visionary mountains / Nightingales and bombers / Fat Nelly / As above so below. *(re-iss. Apr77 + 1981; BRON 337) (re-iss. 1987 on 'Castle' lp/cd; CLA LP/CD 137) (re-iss. Jan91 on 'Cohesion' lp/c/cd; COMME/+T/CD 8)*

Feb 76. (7") <8176> **SPIRIT IN THE NIGHT. / AS ABOVE SO BELOW** [-] [97]

—— **CHRIS THOMPSON** – vocals repl. ROGERS who later formed AVIATOR / added **DAVE FLETT** – guitar

Aug 76. (7") *(BRO 29) <8252>* **BLINDED BY THE LIGHT. / STARBIRD No.2**

Aug 76. (lp/c) *(ILPS/ICT 9357) <BS 3055>* **THE ROARING SILENCE** | 6 | 1 |... | 10 | 10 |
 – Blinded by the light / Singing the dolphin through / Waiter, there's a yawn in my ear / The road to Babylon / This side of Paradise / Starbird / Questions. *(re-iss. Apr77 + 1981; BRON 357)* *(re-iss. Nov87 on 'Legacy' lp/c/cd; LLP/LLK/LLCD 122)* *(re-iss. Jan91 on 'Cohesion' lp/c/cd; COMME/+T/CD 2)*

Nov 76. (7") *(BRO 34)* **QUESTIONS. / WAITER, THERE'S A YAWN IN MY EAR No.2**

Dec 76. (7") *<8355>* **QUESTIONS. / SPIRIT IN THE NIGHT** | – |

—— **PAT KING** – bass (ex-SHANGHAI, etc.) repl. PATTENDEN (to TERRA NOVA)

Jun 77. (7") *<8355>* **SPIRIT IN THE NIGHT (remix). / ROAD TO BABYLON** | – | 40 |... | – |

Nov 77. (7") *(BRO 48)* **CALIFORNIA. / CHICAGO INSTITUTE**

Feb 78. (lp/c) *(BRON/+C 507) <BS 3157>* **WATCH** | 33 | 83 |
 – Circles / Drowning on dry land / Fish soup / California / Chicago institute / Davy's on the road again / Martha's madman / The mighty Quinn. *(re-iss. 1981; same)* *(re-iss. Nov87 on 'Legacy'; LLCD 123)* *(re-iss. Jan91 on 'Cohesion' lp/c/cd; COMME/+T/CD 3)*

Mar 78. (7") *(BRO 51)* **THE MIGHTY QUINN. / TINY** | | – |

Apr 78. (7") *(BRO 52) <8620>* **DAVY'S ON THE ROAD AGAIN. / BOUILLABAISE** | 6 | Sep78... | – |

Jul 78. (7") *(BRO 52)* **CALIFORNIA. / BOUILLABAISE** | – |

—— After a short split, MANN reformed band retaining **THOMPSON + KING / STEVE WALLER** – guitar (ex-GONZALES) repl. FLETT / **GEOFF BRITTON** – drums (ex-EAST OF EDEN, ex-WINGS, ex-ROUGH DIAMOND, ex-CHAMPION) repl. CHRIS SLADE who joined URIAH HEEP. He later joined The FIRM (see; LED ZEPPELIN)

Feb 79. (7") *(BRO 68)* **YOU ANGEL YOU. / OUT IN THE DISTANCE** | 54 | – |

Mar 79. (lp/c) *(BRON/+C 516) <3302>* **ANGEL STATION** | 30 |
 – Don't kill it Carol / You angel you / Hollywood town / Belle of the Earth / Platform end / Angels at my gate / Waiting for the rain / Resurrection. *(re-iss. Nov87 on 'Legacy' lp/c/cd; LLP/LLK/LLCD 124)* *(re-iss. Jan91 on 'Cohesion' lp/c/cd; COMME/+T/CD 4)*

May 79. (7") *<8850>* **YOU ANGEL YOU. / BELLE OF THE EARTH** | – | 58 |

Jun 79. (7"/7"pic-d) *(BRO/BPO 77)* **DON'T KILL IT CAROL. / BLINDED BY THE LIGHT** | 45 |

—— **JOHN LINGWOOD** – drums repl. BRITTON who became ill. / guests included **PETER MARSH, WILLY FINLAYSON.** (vocals – **CHRIS THOMPSON**)

Oct 80. (lp/c) *(BRON/+C 529) <BSK 3498>* **CHANCE** | 87 |
 – Lies (through the 80's) / On the run / For you / Adolescent dream / Fritz the blank / Stranded / This is your heart / No guarantee / Heart on the street. *(re-iss. 1987 on 'Castle' lp/cd; CLA LP/CD 133)* *(re-iss. Jan91 on 'Cohesion' lp/c/cd; COMME/+T/CD 9)*

Nov 80. (7") *(BRO 103) <49762>* **LIES (THROUGH THE 80'S). / ADOLESCENT DREAM** | Jun81 |

Jan 81. (7") *(BRO 113) <49678>* **FOR YOU. / A FOOL I AM**

—— **MATT IRVING** – bass (ex-DREAM POLICE, ex-BABYS, ex-LONGDANCER) repl. KING

Nov 81. (7") *(BRO 137)* **I (WHO HAVE NOTHING). / MAN IN JAM** | | – |
| | Bronze | Arista |

Feb 82. (7") *(BRO 141)* **EYES OF NOSTRADAMUS. / HOLIDAY'S END**
 (12"+=) *(BROX 141)* – Man in jam. | | – |

Jun 82. (7") *(BRO 150)* **REDEMPTION SONG (NO KWAZULU). / WARDREAM** | | – |

Nov 82. (7") *(BRO 157)* **TRIBAL STATISTICS. / WHERE DO THEY SEND THEM**

Jan 83. (lp/c) *(BRON/C 543) <8194>* **SOMEWHERE IN AFRIKA** | 87 | 40 | Mar84
 – Tribal statistics / Eyes of Nostradamus / Third world service / Demolition man / Brothers and sisters of Azania:- (a) Afrika suite – (b) Brothers and sisters of Afrika – (c) To ban Tustan – (d) Koze Kobenini (how long must we wait?) / Lalela / Redemption song (no Kwazulu) / Somewhere in Afrika. *(re-iss. Nov87 on 'Legacy' lp/c/cd; LLP/LLK/LLCD 125)* *(re-iss. Jan91 on 'Cohesion' lp/c/cd; COMME/+T/CD 1)*

Jan 83. (7") *(BRO 161)* **DEMOLITION MAN. / IT'S STILL THE SAME** | | – |

Feb 84. (7") *(BRO 177)* **DAVY'S ON THE ROAD AGAIN (live). / THE MIGHTY QUINN (live)**
 (12"+=) *(BROX 177)* – Don't kill it Carol (live). | | – |

Feb 84. (lp/c) *(BRON/+C 550)* **BUDAPEST (live)**
 – Spirits in the night / Demolition man / For you / Davy's on the road again / Lies (through the 80's) / Blinded by the light / Redemption song (no Kwazulu) / The mighty Quinn. *(cd-iss. 1988 on 'Ariola'; ACD 610163)* *(re-iss. Jan91 on 'Cohesion' lp/c/cd; COMME/+T/CD 10)*

—— **MICK RODGERS** – vocals, guitar returned to repl. WALLER (MANN, THOMPSON, LINGWOOD) also still in band. (IRVING left to join LORDS OF THE NEW CHURCH. He later joined PAUL YOUNG band).

Jan 84. (7") *(BRO 180)* **(THE) RUNNER. / NO TRANSKEI**
 (12"+=) *(BROX 180)* – Lies (through the 80's). | | – |

Jan 84. (7") *<9143>* **(THE) RUNNER. / WHERE DO THEY SEND THEM** | – | 22 |

Jun 84. (7") *<9203>* **REBEL. / FIGURES ON A PAGE** | – |
| | 10-Virgin | Virgin |

Mar 86. (7"/12") *(TEN 115/+12)* **DO ANYTHING YOU WANNA DO. / CROSSFIRE**

May 86. (7"/12") *(TEN/+T 121)* **GOING UNDERGROUND. / I SHALL BE RESCUED**

Jun 86. (lp/c/cd) *(XID/CXID/DIXCD 17)* **CRIMINAL TANGO**
 – Going underground / Who are the mystery kids / Banquet / Killer on the loose / Do anything you wanna do / Rescue / You got me through the heart / Hey bulldog / Crossfire.

—— **MAGGIE RYDER** – vocals repl. CHRIS THOMPSON who went solo (guests incl.**FRANK MEAD** – saxophone / **DENNY NEWMAN** – bass, vocals on 1)

Oct 87. (7"/12") *(TEN/+T 196)* **GERONIMO'S CADILLAC. / TWO FRIENDS**

Nov 87. (lp/c/cd) *(DIX/CDIX/DIXCD 69)* **MASQUE**
 – Joybringer (from 'Jupiter') / Billies orno bounce (including Billies bounce) / What you give is what you get (start) / Rivers run dry / Planets schmanets / Geronimo's

Cadillac / Sister Billies bounce (including Sister Sadie & Billies bounce) / Telegram to Monica / A couple of mates (from 'Mars' & 'Saturn') / Neptune *Icebringer) / The hymn (from 'Jupiter') / We're going wrong.

| | Kaz | Priority |

Aug 92. (cd) *(KAZCD 902) <57123>* **MANFRED MANN'S PLAIN MUSIC** | | |
 – Kiowa / Medicine song / Wounded Knee / Sikelele / Hunting bow / Salmon fishing / Laguna / Instrumedicine song / Sikelele II.

—— **MANFRED MANN** with **CHRIS THOMPSON + NOEL McCALLA** – vocals / **MICK ROGERS** – guitars / **STEVE KINCH** – bass / **CLIVE BUNKER + DAVID FARMER** – drums / + guests

| | Grapevine | not iss. |

Jun 96. (cd/c) *(GRA CD/MC 213)* **SOFT VENGEANCE** | | – |
 – SOFT: Pleasure and pain / Play with fire / Nothing ever happens / Shelter from the storm / Tumbling ball / The price I pay / Lose the touch / Adults only / Wherever love drops (part one) / (interval 10 seconds) / VENGEANCE: The complete history of sexual jealousy / 99 lbs / Miss you / Nature of the beast / Wherever love drops (part two).

– compilations, others, etc. –

Jul 77. (lp) *Vertigo; (9199 107)* **MANFRED MANN'S EARTH BAND 1971-73**

Oct 90. (7") *Cohesion;* **DAVY'S ON THE ROAD AGAIN. / BLINDED BY THE LIGHT** | | – |

Jan 91. (cd/c/lp) *Cohesion; (BOMME 1 CD/MC/LP)* **20 YEARS OF MANFRED MANN'S EARTH BAND 1971-1991** | | – |
 – Blinded by the light / California / Joybringer / Tribal statistics / Somewhere in Africa / Davy's on the road again / You angel you / The runner / Questions / The mighty Quinn / Angels at the gate / For you / Demolition man.

Nov 92. (10xlp-box/10xc-box/10xcd-box) *Cohesion; (COMME/+T/CD 6)* **MANFRED MANN'S EARTH BAND**
 – (albums from 1972-1986) *(free-12"+=)* –

– (MANFRED MANN) compilations etc. –

on 'H.M.V.' unless otherwise mentioned

Apr 64. (7"ep) *(7EG 8848)* **MANFRED MANN'S COCK-A-HOOP WITH 5-4-3-2-1** | | – |
 – Cock-a-hoop / 5-4-3-2-1 / Why should we not / Without you.

Dec 64. (7"ep) *(7EG 8876)* **GROOVIN' WITH MANFRED MANN** | | – |
 – Do wah diddy diddy / etc.

Jul 65. (7"ep) *(7EG 8908)* **ONE IN THE MIDDLE** | 6 |
 – With God on our side / Watermelon man / What am I to do / One in the middle.

Sep 65. (7"ep) *(7EG 8922)* **NO LIVING WITHOUT YOU** | | – |
 – Let's go get stoned / I put a spell on you / Tired of trying / (1).

Apr 66. (7"ep) *(7EG 8942)* **MACHINES** | | – |
 – She needs company / Machines / Tennessee waltz / When will I be loved.

Jun 66. (7"ep) *(7EG 8949)* **INSTRUMENTAL ASYLUM** | | – |

Sep 66. (lp) *(CLP 3559)* **MANN MADE HITS** | 11 |
 – Pretty flamingo / The one in the middle / Oh no not my baby / John Hardy / Spirit feel / Come tomorrow / Do wah diddy diddy / With God on our side / There's no living without your loving / Groovin' / I'm your kingpin / Sha la la / 5-4-3-2-1 / If you gotta go, go now.

Oct 66. (7"ep) *(7EG 8962)* **AS WAS** | | – |

Dec 66. (7"ep) *Fontana; (TE 17483)* **INSTRUMENTAL ASSASSINATION** | | – |
 – Wild thing / With a girl like you / Sunny / Get away.

Jan 67. (lp; mono/stereo) *(CLP/CSD 3594)* **SOUL OF MANN** (instrumentals) | 40 | – |
 – The abominable snowman / I got you babe / Bare Hugg / Spirit feel / Why should we not / L.S.D. / (I can't get no) Satisfaction / God rest ye merry gentlemen / My generation / Mr. Anello / Still I'm sad / Tengo tango / Brother Jack / Sack o' woe. *(re-iss. Jul85 on 'See For Miles'; SEE 82)*

Jan 67. (7") *Ascot;* **MY LITTLE RED BOOK. / I CAN'T BELIEVE WHAT YOU SAY** | – |

1971. (lp) *Music For Pleasure; (MFP 5269)* **THE GREATEST HITS OF MANFRED MANN**

Nov 71. (lp) *Philips; (6382 020)* **THIS IS . . . MANFRED MANN**

Jul 76. (lp) *Sonic; (SON 016)* **MANNERISMS**

Jul 77. (lp) *E.M.I.; (NUT 7)* **THE BEST OF MANFRED MANN**

Jul 77. (7"ep) *Philips; (6006 575)* **HA! HA! SAID THE CLOWN / MIGHTY QUINN. / SEMI-DETACHED SUBURBAN MR. JAMES / A 'B' SIDE**

Aug 77. (7"m) *E.M.I.; (EMI 2644)* **PRETTY FLAMINGO. / THE ONE IN THE MIDDLE / GOT MY MOJO WORKING**

Sep 79. (d-lp/c) *E.M.I.; (EMTV/TC-EMTV 19)* **SEMI-DETACHED SUBURBAN (20 GREAT HITS OF THE SIXTIES)** | 9 | – |
 – Do wah diddy diddy / 5-4-3-2-1 / Sha la la / Hubble bubble, toil and trouble / Hi lili hi lo / One in the middle / Got my mojo working / With God on our side / Come tomorrow / If you gotta go, go now / Pretty flamingo / Semi-detached suburban Mr. James / There's no living without your loving / Just like a woman / Oh no not my baby / Ha ha said the clown / My name is Jack / Fox on the run / Ragamuffin man / Mighty Quinn.

May 82. (lp/c) *E.M.I.; (CM/+K 105)* **THE R&B YEARS** *(re-iss. Nov86; same)* | | – |

Aug 83. (d-lp) *E.M.I.; (EDP 1546363)* **THE FIVE FACES OF MANFRED MANN / MANN MADE** | | – |

Oct 83. (7") *Old Gold; (OG 9376)* **PRETTY FLAMINGO. / 5-4-3-2-1** | | – |

May 84. (7") *E.M.I.; (G45 15)* **5-4-3-2-1. / PRETTY FLAMINGO** | | – |

Feb 86. (lp/c) *E.M.I.; (EMS/TC-EMS 1121)* **THE SINGLES ALBUM** *(cd-iss. Jul87 as 'THE SINGLES ALBUM PLUS'; CDP 746603-2)* | | – |

Apr 86. (lp/c/cd) *Fontana; (PRICE/PRIMC 66)* **HIT RECORDS 1966-69** | | – |

Apr 87. (7") *Old Gold; (OG 9697)* **PRETTY FLAMINGO. / COME TOMORROW** | | – |

Jun 89. (lp/c/cd) *E.M.I.; (SEE/+K/CD 252)* **THE EP COLLECTION** *(re-iss. cd Nov94; same)* | | – |

Jul 90. (cd/c/d-lp) *Castle; (CCS CD/MC/LP 245)* **THE COLLECTION** | | – |

Sep 92. (cd-ep) *Old Gold;* **PRETTY FLAMINGO / IF YOU GOTTA GO, GO NOW / COME TOMORROW** | | – |

Jan 93.	(cd/c/lp) *Polygram TV; (514362-2/-4/-1)* **AGES OF MANN (22 CLASSICS OF THE 60's)** *(re-iss. Sep95 cd/c; same)*	23	-
Jun 93.	(cd) *E.M.I.; (CDEMS 1500)* **THE BEST OF THE E.M.I. YEARS 1963-1965**		-
Dec 93.	(cd/c) *Music For Pleasure; (CD/TC MFP 5994)* **THE BEST OF MANFRED MANN 1964-1966**		-
Aug 94.	(cd/c) *Arcade; (ARC 31001-62/-74)* **THE VERY BEST OF MANFRED MANN'S EARTH BAND**	69	-
Jun 97.	(d-cd) *Chronicles; (534806-2)* **THE ASCENT OF MANN**		-

Marilyn MANSON

Formed: Fort Lauderdale, South Florida, USA ... early 90's by the once pneumonia-crippled MANSON (real name BRIAN WARNER), an ordained minister in the Church Of Satan (run by Anton LeVey), provoking the wrath of conservative America. MANSON had begun his infamous career as a music journalist, simultaneously forming MARILYN MANSON & THE SPOOKY KIDS and taking inspiration from schlock-meisters like ALICE COOPER, KISS and surprisingly, veteran UK goth throwbacks, ALIEN SEX FIEND. After interviewing TRENT REZNOR, he/they secured a support slot with Reznor's NINE INCH NAILS, ultimately resulting in a record deal with TRENT's 'Nothing' records. Although the ghoulish Edward Scissorhands lookalike MANSON dated porn-star TRACII LORDS, he caused uproar at a hometown show when he allegedly mouthed ROBIN FINCK's (NIN) "pink oboe". The piercingly contact-lensed MANSON, whose onstage regalia usually included surgical corset and stockings, completed his OTT persona by routinely mutilating himself with knives, light-bulbs and indeed anything that came to hand. Like ALICE COOPER before him, he overshadowed the rest of his band (who comprised DAISY BERKOWITZ, MADONNA WAYNE GACY, SARA LEE LUCAS and smackhead GIDGET GEIN – the latter was deposed by TWIGGY RAMIREZ). Typically subtle as the proverbial sledgehammer, the band member's names were stitched together from glamourous icons and serial killers! As for the music, MANSON's vinyl/cd freakshow began with 1994's sub-goth posturing of 'PORTRAIT OF AN AMERICAN FAMILY'. GINGER took over drum duties for their second set, a collection of remixes entitled 'SMELLS LIKE CHILDREN', which included gruesome versions of SWEET DREAMS (Eurythmics), I PUT A SPELL ON YOU (Screamin' Jay Hawkins) and ROCK'N'ROLL NIGGER (Patti Smith) – he had previously covered Gary Numan's 'DOWN IN THE PARK'. Later that year, MANSON and Co. finally launched a full-scale assault on the moral majority/minority (delete as appropriate) with the inflammatory 'ANTICHRIST SUPERSTAR', which crucified the Billboard chart at No.3. They finally drove a stake through England's conservative heart in 1997, when MANSON (currently the beau of MTV babe Julia Valet) wowed audiences at secret gigs around the country. By this point, they had also introduced new guitarist ZIM ZUM, who replaced DAISY for the UK Top 20 single, 'BEAUTIFUL PEOPLE', the unholy climax of MANSON's bizarre career to date. Whatever else he is, MANSON is a consummate showman, enticing ghoulish audiences with threats of onstage suicide, the ultimate in 90's entertainment, presumably ? (that's if the Christian extremists don't get 'im first). MANSON (BRIAN) re-invented himself and became a BOWIE-clone/freak "undressed" eunuchoid-fashion on the cover of the bands 1998 US chart-topping set, 'MECHANICAL ANIMALS', 'Aladdin INsane' you could say! The Manson who fell to Earth indeed, it looked like we'd have to wait even longer before his "Rock'n'roll Suicide". Earlier in the year, his first book, the autobiographical, 'The Long Hard Road Out Of Hell', was published and contained insights into how WARNER/MANSON's deranged brain evolved. With controversy never a light year away, the man's "evil-metal" music was even brought into question when two MARILYN MANSON-obsessed kamikaze teenagers gunned down thirteen people (12 students and a teacher – another 28 were injured) inside Columbine High School, near Denver. MANSON immediately cancelled the rest of the band's tour and sent his sympathies to the bereaved while answering Right-wing politicians who were intent on blaming MANSON and the world of Heavy Metal – they should ask themselves how easy it was for "easily-led" youngsters (and anyone with that constitution) to obtain firearms and does any other music genre such as Country or Pop get the same media furore when one of its klan goes haywire.

Album rating: PORTRAIT OF AN AMERICAN FAMILY (*6) / SMELLS LIKE CHILDREN (*6) / ANTICHRIST SUPERSTAR (*8) / MECHANICAL ANIMALS (*7) / THE LAST TOUR ON EARTH (*5)

REVEREND MARILYN MANSON (b. BRIAN WARNER, 1969, Canton, Ohio) – vocals / **MADONNA WAYNE GACY** (b. STEPHEN) – keyboards, organ, theremin, saxophone, samples / **DAISY BERKOWITZ** (b. SCOTT MITCHELL PUTESKY) – guitars / **TWIGGY RAMIREZ** – bass; repl. GIDGET GEIN (b.BRAD STEWART) / **SARA LEE LUCAS** (b. FREDDY STREITHORST) – drums

		Nothing-Interscope	Nothing-Interscope
Jun 94.	(cd-ep) <*INTDM 95902*> **GET YOUR GUNN / MISERY MACHINE / MOTHER INFERIOR GOT HER GUNN / REVELATION No.9**	-	
Dec 94.	(cd/c/d-lp) <*(IND 92344)*> **PORTRAIT OF AN AMERICAN FAMILY** – Prelude (the family trip) / Cake and sodomy / Lunchbox / Organ grinder / Cyclops / Dope hat / Get your gunn / Wrapped in plastic / Dogma / Sweet tooth / Snake eyes and sissies / My monkey / Misery machine. *(re-iss. cd Jul96 on 'Nothing-Interscope'; same) (lp re-iss. Sep99 on 'Simply Vinyl'; SVLP 121)*		

Feb 95.	(cd-ep) <*INTDM 95806*> **LUNCHBOX / NEXT MOTHERFUCKER (remix) / DOWN IN THE PARK / BROWN BAG (remix) / METAL (remix)**		-	
——	**GINGER FISH** – drums, repl. SARA LEE			
Aug 96.	(cd-ep) *(IND 95504)* **SWEET DREAMS (ARE MADE OF THIS) / DANCE OF THE DOPE HATS (remix) / DOWN IN THE PARK / LUNCHBOX (NEXT MOTHERF****R)**			
Aug 96.	(cd) <*(IND 92641)*> **SMELLS LIKE CHILDREN**		31	Oct95

– The hands of small children / Diary of a dope fiend / S****y chicken gang bang / Kiddie grinder (remix) / Sympathy for the parents / Sweet dreams (are made of this) / Everlasting c***sucker (remix) / F*** Frankie / I put a spell on you / May cause discoloration of the urine or feces / Scatos, guns and peanut butter / Dance of the dope hats (remix) / White trash (remixed by Tony F. Wiggins) / Dancing with the one-legged . . . / Rock'n'roll nigger. *(cd re-iss. Aug98; same)*

——	**ZIM ZUM** – guitar; repl. DAISY after below recording (he subsequently turned up with JACK OFF JILL in '98)		
Oct 96.	(cd/c) <*(IND 90006-2/-4)*> **ANTICHRIST SUPERSTAR**	73	3

– Irresponsible hate anthem / The beautiful people / Dried up, tied up and dead to the world / Tourniquet / Little horn / Cryptorchid / Deformography / Wormboy / Mister Superstar / Angel with the scabbed wings / Kinderfeld / Antichrist superstar / 1996 / Minute of decay / The reflecting God / Man that you fear.

Jun 97.	(cd-ep) *(IND 95541)* **THE BEAUTIFUL PEOPLE / THE HORRIBLE PEOPLE (Danny Sabre remix) / SWEET DREAMS (lp version) / CRYPTORCHID**	18	

(cd-ep) *(INDX 95541)* – ('A'side) / The not so beautiful people (Jim Thirlwell remix) / Snake eyes and sissies / Deformography.
(10"pic-d) *(INVP 95541)* – The horrible people (Danny Sabre remix) / The not so beautiful people (Jim Thirlwell remix).

Sep 97.	(10"pic-d) *(INVP 95552)* **TOURNIQUET. / TOURNIQUET (Prosthetic dance mix)**	28	

(cd-s+=) *(IND 95552)* – ('A'-Prosthetic dance mix edit).
(cd-s) *(INDX 95552)* – ('A'side) / Lunchbox / Next MF (remix).

Apr 98.	(m-cd) <*(IND 95017)*> **REMIX & REPENT**		Dec97

– The horrible people (remixed by Danny Saber) / Tourniquet (prosthetic dance mix) / Dried up, tied and dead to the world (live in Utica, NY) / Antichrist superstar (live in Hartford, CT) / Man that you fear (acoustic requiem for Antichrist Superstar).

——	**JOHNNIE 5** – guitar; repl. ZIM ZUM		
Sep 98.	(cd/c) <*(IND/INC 98273)*> **MECHANICAL ANIMALS**	8	1

– Great big white world / The dope show / Mechanical animals / Rock is dead / Disassociative / The speed of pain / Posthuman / I want to disappear / Don't like the drugs (like the drugs like me) / New model No.15 / User friendly / Fundamentally loathsome / The last day on earth / Coma white. *(ltd-cd-iss. Jun99; IND 90394)*

Nov 98.	(one-sided-10"pic-d) *(INVP 95610)* **THE DOPE SHOW**	12	

(cd-s+=) *(IND 95610)* – Sweet dreams (live) / Apple of Sodom (live).
(cd-s+=) *(INDX 95610)* – The beautiful people (live) / ('A'-CD-rom video).

——	now without the sacked ZIM ZUM; **JOHN LOWERY** was his replacement		
Jun 99.	(10"pic-d) *(W 486TE)* **ROCK IS DEAD. / I DON'T LIKE DRUGS (BUT THE DRUGS LIKE ME) (every day mix)**	23	

(cd-s) *(W 486CD)* – ('A'side) / Man that you fear (acoustic requiem for Antichrist Superstar) / Baxter (television radio edit).
(cd-s) *(W 486CDX)* – ('A'side) / I don't like the drugs (but the drugs like me) (absinthe makes the heart grow fonder mix) / Baxter (I can't see why album version) / ('A'-CD-ROM video).

Nov 99.	(d-cd) *(490524-2)* **THE LAST TOUR ON EARTH (live)**	61	

– Inauguration of the mechanical Christ / Reflecting God / Great big white world / Get your gunn / Sweet dreams / Hell outro / Rock is dead / Dope show / Lunchbox / I don't like the drugs (but the drugs like me) / Antichrist superstar / The beautiful people / The last day on Earth / Coma white / Get off my rocks / Coma white / Rose in a baby rose.

– others, etc. –

Dec 96.	(cd-ep) *Interscope; (INTDM 95806)* **LUNCHBOX**			
Dec 96.	(cd-ep) *Interscope; (INTDM 95902)* **GET YOUR GUN**			
Nov 97.	(cd+book) *UFO; (UFOCD 15BX)* **SMELLS LIKE WHITE TRASH**		-	
Jun 99.	(cd-book) *Hallmark; (8086)* **STAR PROFILE**		-	

MANSUN

Formed: Chester, England ... 1995 originally as MANSON, by songwriter PAUL DRAPER, DOMINIC CHAD, STOVE, THE HIB and MARK STENT. After one single under this moniker ('TAKE IT EASY CHICKEN'), they caused a minor rumpus with the legal team of notorious killer CHARLES MANSON. The band claimed their name was taken from a VERVE b-side, 'A MAN CALLED SUN', deliberately slightly altering it to avoid court action. With name change now complete, they issued their follow-up, 'SKIN UP PIN UP'. A month later with the help of A&R man, Keith Wozencroft, they were part of Parlophone's enviable roster. Their blend of melodic, alternative rock, was described as a 90's indie update of TEARS FOR FEARS. Two UK Top 40 hits appeared as the EP's, 'ONE' & 'TWO' in 1996, paving the way for further successes, 'STRIPPER VICAR' and 'WIDE OPEN SPACE'. The year 1997 began on a high note with a Top 10 hit, the charmingly titled 'SHE MAKES MY NOSE BLEED' and a No.1 album, 'ATTACK OF THE GREY LANTERN'. Ambitious in its stylistic diversity, it contained additional Top 20 hits, 'TAXLO$$' and 'CLOSED FOR BUSINESS'. In the summer of '98, MANSUN were back in the hit parade with two EP's, 'LEGACY' (their eighth in the series) and 'NINE' (leading in with 'BEING A GIRL'), both taken from their pseudo-concept follow-up album, 'SIX', which, spookily enough, reached the same number in the charts. • **Covers:** RAILINGS (Howard Devoto). Everyone Must Win was co-written with the ex-MAGAZINE frontman.

Album rating: ATTACK OF THE GREY LANTERN (*8) / SIX (*7)

PAUL DRAPER – vocals, guitars, piano, synthesizer / **DOMINIC CHAD** – lead guitar, piano, vocals, synthesizer / **STOVE KING** – bass / **THE HIB** – drums / **MARK 'SPIKE' STENT** – beatbox

		Regal	not iss.
Sep 95.	(7"; as MANSON) *(REG 2)* **TAKE IT EASY CHICKEN. /** ('A'version) *(above also issued on own 'Sci Fi Hi Fi' label; MANSON 1)*	☐	-
Nov 95.	(7"white) *(REG 3)* **SKIN UP PIN UP. / FLOURELLA** (cd-s+=) *(REG 3CD)* – Take it easy chicken.	☐	-

—— early '96, MARK suddenly departed

		Parlophone	Sony
Mar 96.	(cd-ep/c-ep/7"ep) *(CDRS/TCR/R 6430)* **MANSUN – ONE** – Egg shaped Fred / Ski jump nose / Lemonade secret drinker / Thief.	37	-
Jun 96.	(cd-ep/c-ep/7"ep) *(CD/TC+/R 6437)* **MANSUN – TWO** – Take it easy chicken / Drastic sturgeon / The greatest pain / Moronica.	32	-

—— lost another member when THE HIB quit

—— **ANDIE RATHBONE** – drums; repl. temp. JULIAN (ex-KINKY MACHINE)

Sep 96.	(7"clear) *(R 6447)* **STRIPPER VICAR. / NO ONE KNOWS US** (cd-ep+=) *(CDR 6447)* **THREE EP** – An open letter to the lyrical trainspotter / Things keep falling off buildings. (cd-ep) *(CDRS 6447)* **THREE EP** – ('A'side) / The edge / Duchess.	19	-
Nov 96.	(7"white) *(R 6453)* **WIDE OPEN SPACE. / REBEL WITHOUT A QUILT** (cd-s+=) *(CDR 6453)* **FOUR EP** – Vision impaired / Skin up pin up. (cd-s) *(CDRS 6453)* **FOUR EP** – ('A'side) / The gods of not very much / Moronica (acoustic) / Lemonade secret drinker (acoustic).	15	-
Feb 97.	(7"red) *(R 6458)* **SHE MAKES MY NOSE BLEED. / THE HOLY BLOOD AND THE HOLY GRAIL** (cd-s+=) *(CDRS 6458)* **FIVE EP** – Live open space / Drastic sturgeon (live). (cd-s) *(CDRS 6458)* **FIVE EP** – ('A'side) / The most to gain / Flourella / ('A'acoustic).	9	-
Feb 97.	(cd/c/d-lp) *(CD/TC+PCS 3787)* <67935> **ATTACK OF THE GREY LANTERN** – The Chad who loved me / Mansun's only love song / Taxloss / You, who do you hate? / Wide open space / Stripper vicar / Disgusting / She makes my nose bleed / Naked twister / Egg shaped Fred / Dark Mavis.	1	☐
May 97.	(cd-ep) *(CDR 6465)* **SIX EP** – Taxloss / Grey lantern / Taxloss (Lisa Marie Experience remix). (cd-ep) *(CDRS 6465)* – ('A'side) / The impending collapse od it all / Ski jump nose (live) / Wide open space (acoustic). (12"ep) *(12R 6465)* – ('A'mixes:- John '00' Fleming remix / album version / Slam remix / Gaudi remix).	15	-
Oct 97.	(7"clear) *(R 6482)* **CLOSED FOR BUSINESS. / EGG SHAPED FRED (acoustic)** (cd-s) *(CDR 6482)* **SEVEN EP** – ('A'side) / K.I.Double.S.I.N.G. / Everyone must win / The world's still open. (cd-s) *(CDRS 6482)* **SEVEN EP** – ('A'side) / Dark Mavis (acoustic) / Stripper vicar (live) / Taxloss (video for PC or Mac).	10	-
Jun 98.	(c-ep) *(TCR 6497)* <57396> **LEGACY EP (EIGHT EP)** – Legacy / Wide open space (the Perfecto remix) / The acoustic collapse of it all / Ski jump nose (acoustic). (cd-ep) *(CDR 6497)* – ('A'side) / Wide open space (the Perfecto remix) / GSOH / Face in the crowd. (cd-ep) *(CDRS 6497)* – ('A'side) / Can't afford to die / Spasm of identity / Check under the bed.	7	Aug98
Aug 98.	(c-ep) *(TCR 6503)* **NINE EP** – Being a girl (part 1) / Wide open space (Trouse Enthusiasts mix) / Mansun's only acoustic song. (cd-ep) *(CDR 6503)* – ('A'side) / Railings / Been here before. (cd-ep) *(CDRS 6503)* – ('A'side) / Hideout / Wide open space (Trouser Enthusiasts mix).	13	-
Sep 98.	(cd/c/d-lp) *(96723-2/-4/-1)* <69748> **SIX** – (Part one):- Six / Negative / Shotgun / Inverse Midas / Anti-everything / Fall out / Serotonin / Cancer / (interlude) / Witness to a murder (part two) / (Part two):- Television / Special – Blown it (delete as appropriate) / Legacy / Being a girl.	6	Apr99
Oct 98.	(7") *(R 6508)* **NEGATIVE. / MANSUN'S ONLY LIVE SONG** (cd-s) *(CDR 6508)* – ('A'side) / I deserve what I get / Take it easy chicken (live). (cd-s) *(CDRS 6508)* – ('A'side) / When the wind blows / King of beauty.	27	-
Feb 99.	(7") *(R 6511)* **SIX. / BEING A GIRL (parts 1 & 2) / LIVE TELEVISION** (cd-s) *(CDR 6511)* – ('A'side) / But the trains run on time / What's it like to be hated. (cd-s) *(CDRS 6511)* – ('A'side) / Church of the drive thru Elvis / But the trains run on time.	16	☐

MARCY PLAYGROUND

Formed: New York, USA ... mid 90's by JOHN WOZNIAK, a one-time painkiller addict who had relocated to the Big Apple from Minneapolis – his school was called MARCY Open School, thus its name. Recruiting DYLAN KEEFE and DAN RIESER, their demo was loved by 'E.M.I.', although when the label folded (in the States only), 'Capitol' took over the reins. The trio soon became a firm favourite around the college circuit with their debut single, 'SEX AND CANDY', a "nerdy", NIRVANA-tinged melodic rock tune taken from their commercially successful eponymous debut album in 1997.

Album rating: MARCY PLAYGROUND (*6)

JOHN WOZNIAK – vocals, guitar / **DYLAN KEEFE** – bass / **DAN RIESER** – drums

		E.M.I.	Capitol
Apr 98.	(c-s/7") *(TC+/EM 508)* <58695> **SEX AND CANDY. / MEMPHIS** (cd-s+=) *(CDEM 508)* – The angel of the forever sleep.	29	8 Mar98
Apr 98.	(cd/c) *(853568-2/-4)* <53569> **MARCY PLAYGROUND** – Poppies / Sex and candy / Ancient walls of flowers / Saint Joe on the	61	21 Feb97

school bus / Clock of elvenkind / Sherry Fraser / Gone crazy / Opium / One more suicide / Dog and his master / Shadow of Seattle / Vampires of New York.

MARILLION

Formed: Aylesbury, Buckinghamshire, England ... late '78 initially as SILMARILLION, by MICK POINTER and DOUG IRVINE. Taking their name from a J.R.R. Tolkien novel, they soon shortened it to MARILLION the following year. By this point, the all-instrumental outfit had added STEVE ROTHERY and BRIAN JELLIMAN, subsequently recruiting Scots vocalist, FISH (and DIZ MINNITT), after IRVINE departed late in 1980. By March '82, FISH (aka DEREK WILLIAM DICK), POINTER and ROTHERY, finally completed the line-up with Irishman MARK KELLY and PETE TREWAVAS. The band had now been gigging for almost four years and had built up a sizeable following, something that 'E.M.I.' had noticed before securing them a major deal. Soon after, the company issued 'MARKET SQUARE HEROES', the single denting the UK Top 60. Surprisingly, given their prog-rock pretensions, they were voted the best newcomer in the rock-centric (now defunct) Sounds magazine early in 1983. A second single, 'HE KNOWS, YOU KNOW', hit the Top 40, preceding the release of a debut album, 'SCRIPT FOR A JESTER'S TEAR'. Featuring one of their best-loved tracks, 'GARDEN PARTY' (also a UK Top 20 hit), the record reached the Top 10. With GENESIS pursuing a more commercial direction, MARILLION were perfectly poised to fill the gap in the market; a giant of a man, the enigmatic FISH updated PETER GABRIEL's early 70's vocal mannerisms over a keyboard-dominated backing. Like punk never happened, FISH and the lads took us back a decade, sporting ornate lyrical concepts masterminded by the hulking frontman. A harder-edged affair, the follow-up album, 'FUGAZI' strengthened the band's reputation among British rock fans looking for a genuine alternative to AOR-brushed material churning out of America. In the summer of '85, after a rather unnecessary live mini-set, 'REAL TO REEL', they wooed the mainstream with the wistful love song, 'KAYLEIGH', a near chart-topper and an integral part of the conceptual yet accessible 'MISPLACED CHILDHOOD' opus. A UK No.1, the album also featured another top selling ballad, 'LAVENDER' and transformed MARILLION into a stadium-filling live proposition (although America proved impenetrable, 'KAYLEIGH' only scraping into their Hot 100). By 1987's top selling 'CLUTCHING AT STRAWS', FISH was uncomfortable with his newfound pop star status, his drink/drug problems fuelling speculation of an imminent split. The rumours proved all too true, when, just prior to the release of a double live set, 'THE THIEVING MAGPIE', the big man bailed out. While he contemplated a solo career, MARILLION decided to carry on, having found a worthy replacement in STEVE HOGARTH. An unknown quantity to many (although he had fronted minor chart group The EUROPEANS), HOGARTH's fluid, unassuming style nevertheless won over the majority of MARILLION fans, taking the band into unknown territory with the album, 'SEASON'S END' (1989). A competent set, the album's sole weak point was the Top 30 single, 'HOOKS IN YOU'. In 1992, they tried in vain to carry off a cover of Rare Bird's 'SYMPATHY', although this still managed a Top 20 placing, as did a singles collection. MARILLION found it hard to recapture the momentum of their halycon days, that is, until 1994's brilliant return to their conceptual roots with the album, 'BRAVE'. This fusion of folky melodic-rock and quasi-ambient atmospherics was their first to hit the Top 10 for some time, although two albums ('AFRAID OF SUNLIGHT' and the live 'MADE AGAIN') down the line, they finally parted company with 'E.M.I.'. Now on 'Raw Power' (the rocker's retirement stable), MARILLION subsequently released their 1997 set, 'THIS STRANGE ENGINE', a more accessible outing than of late.

Album rating: SCRIPT FOR A JESTER'S TEAR (*8) / FUGAZI (*6) / REAL TO REEL (*5) / MISPLACED CHILDHOOD (*7) / CLUTCHING AT STRAWS (*6) / THE THIEVING MAGPIE (*5) / SEASON'S END (*5) / A SINGLES COLLECTION 1982-1992 compilation (*8) / HOLIDAYS IN EDEN (*6) / BRAVE (*7) / AFRAID OF SUNLIGHT (*5) / THIS STRANGE ENGINE (*6) / RADIATION (*5) / MARILLION.COM (*4)

FISH (b. DEREK WILLIAM DICK, 25 Apr'58, Dalkeith, Scotland) – vocals / **MARK KELLY** (b. 9 Apr'61, Dublin, Eire) – keyboards repl. BRIAN JELLIMAN / **MICK POINTER** (b.22 Jul'56) – drums / **STEVE ROTHERY** (b.25 Nov'59) – guitar / **PETE TREWAVAS** (b.15 Jan'59) – bass repl. DOUG IRVINE

		E.M.I.	Capitol
Oct 82.	(7") *(EMI 5351)* **MARKET SQUARE HEROES. / THREE BOATS DOWN FROM THE CANDY** (12"+=/12"pic-d+=) *(12EMI 5351/+P)* – Grendel. *(re-entered.Apr83; hit No.53)*	60	-
Jan 83.	(7") *(EMI 5362)* **HE KNOWS, YOU KNOW. / CHARTING THE SINGLE** (12"+=) *(12EMI 5362)* – ('A'extended).	35	-
Mar 83.	(lp/c) *(EMC/TC-EMC 3429)* <12269> **SCRIPT FOR A JESTER'S TEAR** – Script for a jester's tear / He knows, you know / The web / Garden party / Chelsea Monday / Forgotten sons. *(pic-lp.Jun84; EMCP 3429)* *(cd-iss. Feb87; CDP 746237-2)* *(re-iss. May90 on 'Fame' cd/c/lp; CD/TC+/FA 3235)* *(re-iss. Mar96 on 'EMI Gold' cd/c; CD/TC GOLD 1012)*	7	☐
Jun 83.	(7"/7"sha-pic-d) *(EMI/+P 5393)* **GARDEN PARTY. / MARGARET (live)** (ext.12"+=/ext.12"w-poster+=) *(12EMI/+P 5393)* – Charting the single (live).	16	-

—— **ANDY WARD** – drums (ex-CAMEL) replaced POINTER / **IAN MOSLEY** (b.16 Jun'53) – drums (ex-STEVE HACKETT, ex-CURVED AIR) repl. WARD

Jan 84.	(7") *(MARIL 1)* **PUNCH AND JUDY. / MARKET SQUARE HEROES (new version)**	29	-

No

(12"+=/12"pic-d+=) *(12MARIL/+P 1)* – Three boats down from the candy (new version).

Mar 84. (lp/pic-lp)(c) *(MRL/+P 1)(TC-MRL 1)* **FUGAZI** | 5 |
– Assassing / Punch and Judy / Jigsaw / Emerald lies / She chameleon / Incubus / Fugazi. *(re-iss. May88 on 'Fame' cd/c/lp; CD/TC+FA 3196) (cd re-iss. May94; CDEMS 1516)*

Apr 84. (7")(ext;12"+=/12"pic-d+=) *(MARIL 2)(12MARIL/+P 2)* **ASSASSING. / CINDERELLA SEARCH** | 22 | - |

Nov 84. (m-lp/c) *(JEST/TC-JEST 1)* **REAL TO REEL (live)** | 8 |
– Assassing / Incubus / Cinderella search / Forgotten sons / Garden party / Market square heroes. *(pic-lp.Jan85; EG 2603036) (re-iss. Nov85 on 'Fame' lp/c/cd+=; FA/TC-FA/CD-FA 3142)* – Emerald lies. *(cd re-iss. Oct87; CDM 752 021-2)*

May 85. (7"/7"pic-d) *(MARIL/+P 3)* **KAYLEIGH. / LADY NINJA** | 2 | - |
(ext.12"+=/ext.12"pic-d+=) *(12MARIL/+P 3)* – ('A'-alternative).

Jun 85. (lp/pic-lp)(c)(cd) *(MRL/+P 2)(TC-MRL 2)(CDP 746160-2)* <12431> **MISPLACED CHILDHOOD** | 1 | 47 |
– The pseudo silk kimono / Kayleigh / Lavender / Bitter suite – Heart of Lothian / Waterhole (expresso bongo) / Lords of the backstage / Blind curve / Childhood's end? / White feather. *(cd re-iss. May94; CDEMS 1518)*

Aug 85. (7") *(MARIL 4)* <5539> **LAVENDER. / FREAKS** | 5 |
(12"+=/12"pic-d+=) *(12MARIL/+P 4)* – ('A'remix).

Sep 85. (7") <5493> **KAYLEIGH. / HEART OF LOTHIAN** | - | 74 |

Nov 85. (7") *(MARIL 5)* **HEART OF LOTHIAN. / CHELSEA MONDAY (live)** | 29 | - |
(12"+=/12"pic-d+=) *(12MARIL/+P 5)* – ('A'extended).

—— Early 1986, FISH teamed up with TONY BANKS (GENESIS) on a single.

Dec 85. (7") <5561> **HEART OF LOTHIAN. / LADY NINJA** | - | - |

Mar 86. (m-lp) <15023> **BRIEF ENCOUNTER (3 live early '86)** | - | 67 |
– Freaks / Fugazi / Kayleigh / Lady Ninja / Script for a jester's tear.

May 87. (7") *(MARIL 6)* <44043> **INCOMMUNICADO. / GOING UNDER** | 6 |
(12"pic-d+=)(cd-s+=) *(12MARILP 6)(CDMARIL 6)* – ('A'alternate).

Jun 87. (lp/pic-lp)(c/cd) *(EMD/+P 1002)(TC/CD EMD 1002)* <12539> **CLUTCHING AT STRAWS** | 2 |
– Hotel hobbies / Warm wet circles / That time of the night (the short straw) / Going under * / Just for the record / White Russian / Incommunicado / Torch song / Slainte Mhath / Sugar mice / The last straw. *(cd+= *) (re-iss. 1989 cd/c/lp; CZ 214)(TC+/ATAK 135)*

Jul 87. (7"/7"pic-d) *(MARIL/+P 7)* <44060> **SUGAR MICE. / TUX ON** | 22 |
(12"+=/12"pic-d+=) *(12MARIL/+P 7)* – ('A'extended).

Oct 87. (7") *(MARIL 8)* **WARM WET CIRCLES. / WHITE RUSSIAN (live)** | 22 | - |
(12"+=/12"pic-d+=) *(12MARIL/+P 8)* – Incommunicado (live).
(cd-s++=) *(CDMARIL 8)* – Up on top of a rainbow.

Nov 88. (d-cd/c/d-lp) *(CD/TC+/MARL 1)* <C 191463> **THE THIEVING MAGPIE (live)** | 25 |
– (intro) / La gazza ladra / Slainte mhath / He knows, you know / Chelsea Monday / Freaks / Jigsaw / Punch and Judy / Sugar mice / Fugazi / Script for a jester's tear / Incommunicado / White Russian / Misplaced childhood part 1:- Pseudo silk kimono – Kayleigh – Lavender – Bitter suite – Heart of Lothian. *(d-cd+=)* – Misplaced childhood part 2:- Waterhole (expresso bongo) – Lords of the backstage – Blind curve – Childhood's end? – White feather.

Nov 88. (7"/7"sha-pic-d) *(MARIL/+P 9)* **FREAKS (live). / KAYLEIGH (live)** | 24 | - |
(12/CD MARIL 9) – Childhood's end (live) / White feather (live).

—— STEVE HOGARTH – vocals (ex-HOW WE LIVE, ex-EUROPEANS, ex-LAST CALL) finally repl. FISH. (He had left to go solo Sep'88).

Aug 89. (c-s/7") *(TC+/MARIL 10)* **HOOKS IN YOU. / AFTER ME** | 30 | - |
(12"+=/12"pic-d+=) *(12MARIL 10/+P)* – ('A'-meaty mix).
(cd-s+=) *(CDMARIL 10)* – ('A'-seven mix).

Sep 89. (cd/c/lp) *(CD/TC+/EMD 1011)* <C 192877> **SEASON'S END** | 7 |
– King of sunset town / Easter / The uninvited guest / Season's end / Holloway girl / Berlin / After me / Hooks in you / The space. *(c+=/cd+=)* – After me. *(pic-lp.Dec89; EMDPD 1011)*

Nov 89. (7"/7"sha-pic-d)(c-s) *(MARIL/+PD 11)(TC-MARIL 11)* **THE UNINVITED GUEST. / THE BELL IN THE SEA** | 53 | - |
(12"+=/12"pic-d+=)(cd-s+=) *(12MARIL/+P 11)(CDMARIL 11)* – ('A'extended).

Mar 90. (7"/7"pic-d)(c-s) *(MARIL/+P 12)(TC-MARIL 12)* **EASTER. / THE RELEASE** | 34 | - |
(12"+=/12"g-f+=)(cd-s+=) *(12MARIL/+G 12)(CDMARIL 12)* – ('A'extended) / The uninvited guest (live).

Jun 91. (c-s/7") *(TC+/MARIL 13)* **COVER MY EYES (PAIN AND HEAVEN). / HOW CAN IT HURT** | 34 | - |
(12"+=/cd-s+=) *(12/CD MARIL 13)* – The party.

Jul 91. (cd/c/lp) *(CD/TC+/EMD 1022)* **HOLIDAYS IN EDEN** | 7 |
– Splintered heart / Cover my eyes (pain and Heaven) / The party / No one can / Holidays in Eden / Dry land / Waiting to happen / This town / The rakes progress / 100 nights.

Jul 91. (7"/7"box)(c-s) *(MARIL/+S 14)(TC-MARIL 14)* **NO ONE CAN. / A COLLECTION** | 33 | - |
(cd-s+=) *(CDMARIL 14)* – Splintered heart (live).

Sep 91. (c-s/7") *(TC+/MARIL 15)* **DRY LAND. / HOLLOWAY GIRL / AFTER ME** | 34 | - |
(12"+=) *(12MARIL 15)* – Substitute.
(10"clear+=) *(10MARIL 15)* – Waiting to happen.
(cd-s+=) *(CDMARIL 15)* – Easter / Sugar mice.
(12"pic-d+=) *(12MARILP 15)* – King of sunset town.

May 92. (c-s/7") *(TC+/MARIL 16)* **SYMPATHY. / KAYLEIGH (live)** | 17 | - |
(cd-s+=) *(MARILS 16)* – I will walk on water.
(12"+=)(cd-s+=) *(12MARILPD/CDMARIL 16)* – Dry land (live).

Jun 92. (cd/c/d-lp) *(CD/TC+/EMD 1033)* **A SINGLES COLLECTION 1982-1992 (compilation)** | 27 |
– Cover my eyes (pain & Heaven) / Kayleigh / Easter / Warm wet circles / Uninvited guest / Assassing / Hooks in you / Garden party / No one can / Incommunicado / Dry land / Lavender / I will walk on water / Sympathy.

Jul 92. (c-s/7") *(TC+/MARIL 17)* **NO ONE CAN. / A COLLECTION** | 26 | - |
(cd-s+=) *(CDMARIL 17)* – Splintered heart.

Feb 94. (cd/c/d-lp) *(CD/TC+/EMD 1054)* **BRAVE** | 10 | - |

– Bridge / Living with the big lie / Runaway / Goodbye to all that (i) Wave (ii) Mad (iii) The opium den (iv) The slide (v) Standing in the swing / Hard as love / The hollow man / Alone again in the lap of luxury (i) Now wash your hands / Paper lies / Brave / The great escape (i) The last of you (ii) Fallin' from the Moon / Made again.

Mar 94. (c-s/7") *(TC+/EM 307)* **THE HOLLOW MAN. / BRAVE** | 30 | - |
(cd-s+=) *(CDEM 307)* – Marouatte jam.
(cd-s) *(CDEM 307)* – ('A'side) / The last of you – Falling from the Moon (the great escape) / Winter trees.

Apr 94. (c-s) *(TCEM 318)* **ALONE AGAIN IN THE LAP OF LUXURY / LIVING WITH THE BIG LIE (live)** | 53 | - |
(12"pic-d+=) *(12EMPD 318)* – The space (live).
(cd-s+=) *(CDEM 318)* – River (live) / Bridge (live).
(cd-s) *(CDEM 318)* – ('A'side) / Cover my eyes / Slainte Mhath / Uninvited guest (all live).

Jun 95. (c-s/cd-s) *(TC/CD MARIL 18)* **BEAUTIFUL / AFRAID OF SUNRISE / ICON** | 29 | - |
(cd-s) *(CDMARILS 18)* – ('A'side) / Live forever / Great escape (demo) / Hard as love (demo).

Jun 95. (cd/c/lp) *(CD/TC+/EMD 1079)* **AFRAID OF SUNLIGHT** | 16 |
– Gazpacho / Cannibal surf babe / Beautiful / Afraid of sunrise / Out of this world / Afraid of sunlight / Beyond you / King.

Mar 96. (d-cd/d-c) *(CD/TC EMD 1094)* **MADE AGAIN (live)** | 37 |
– Splintered heart / Easter / No one can / Waiting to happen / Cover my eyes / The space / Hooks in you / Beautiful / Kayleigh / Lavender / Afraid of sunlight / King // Brave (live in Paris):- Bridge / Living with the big life / Runaway / Goodbye to all that / Wave / Mad / The opium den / Slide / Standing in the swing / Hard as love / Hollow man / Alone again in the lap of luxury / Now wash your hands / Paper lies / Brave / The great escape / The last of you / Falling from the Moon / Made again.

Raw Power   not iss.

May 97. (cd/c/pic-lp) *(RAW CD/MC/DP 121)* **THIS STRANGE ENGINE** | 27 | - |
– Man of 100 faces / One fine day / Eighty days / Estonia / Memory of water / An accidental man / Hope for the future / This strange engine.

May 97. (cd-s) *(RAWX 1044)* **MAN OF 1000 FACES / BEAUTIFUL / MADE AGAIN / ('A'mix)** | - | - |

Oct 97. (cd-s) *(RAWX 1049)* **EIGHTY DAYS / THIS STRANGE ENGINE (extended – live) / BELL IN THE SEA (live)** | - | - |

Sep 98. (cd-s) *(RAWX 1051)* **THESE CHAINS / FAKE PLASTIC TREES (live) / MEMORY OF WATER (Big Beat mix)** | 35 |

Sep 98. (cd) *(RAWCD 126)* **RADIATION**
– Costa del Slough / Under the sun / Answering machine / Three minute boy / Now she'll never know / These chains / Born to run / Cathedral wall / Few words for the deaf.

Oct 99. (cd) *(RAWCD 144)* **MARILLION.COM** | 53 | - |
– Legacy / Deserve / Go / Rich / Enlightened / Built in bastard radar / Tumble down the years / Interior Lulu / House.

– compilations etc. –

on 'E.M.I.' unless mentioned otherwise

Jan 88. (cd)(lp) *(CZ 39)(EMS 1295)* **B SIDES THEMSELVES (rare flips)** | 64 | - |

Nov 95. (3xcd-box) *(CDOMB 015)* **THE ORIGINALS** | - |
– (SCRIPT FOR A JESTER'S TEAR / FUGAZI / MISPLACED CHILDHOOD). *(re-iss. Apr97; same)*

Oct 96. (cd) *EMI Gold; (CDGOLD 1058)* **THE COLLECTION** | - | - |

Feb 97. (d-cd) *(CDEMC 3761)* **THE BEST OF BOTH WORLDS** | - | - |

Apr 97. (d-pic-lp) *(EMCF 3761)* **THE BEST OF BOTH WORLDS 1982-88** | - | - |

Apr 97. (d-pic-pic) *(EMCH 3761)* **THE BEST OF BOTH WORLDS 1989-PRESENT** | - | - |

Jun 97. (d-cd) *(CDEM 1603)* **REAL TO REEL / BRIEF ENCOUNTER** | - | - |

MARION   (dig out; 4th edition or Great Alt & Indie . . .)

Bob MARLEY

Born: ROBERT NESTA MARLEY, 2 Feb'45, Rhoden Hall, St. Ann's, Jamaica, the son of an English sailor/captain and a Jamaican woman. By the early 60's, in common with most other Jamaicans (save older Calypso fans), he became influenced by ska and bluebeat, cutting his debut single, 'JUDGE NOT (UNLESS YOU JUDGE YOURSELF)' with the help of producer LESLIE KING. Another 7", 'ONE CUP OF COFFEE', followed early in '63, MARLEY subsequently forming vocal quintet, The WAILIN' WAILERS (shortened to The WAILERS after the first single the following year. The outfit consisted of MARLEY (vocals, later also guitar), PETER TOSH (vocals, later also guitar), BUNNY LIVINGSTONE (vocals, percussion), JUNIOR BRAITHWAITE (vocals) and BEVERLEY KELSO (vocals) with instrumental backing by The SOUL BROTHERS and subsequently The SKATELITES. Teaming up with legendary producer COXSONE DODD, their first single, 'SIMMER DOWN', was a massive hit in Jamaica, the outfit recording a further string of 45's for DODD's seminal 'Studio One' and 'Coxsone' labels. MARLEY's career was put on hold, however, when he married RITA and subsequently spent a year in America visiting his mother who had moved there in 1963. He returned to his homeland in 1967, setting up his own 'Wailin' Soul' label with JOHNNY NASH and duly re-uniting with The WAILERS. Although their releases during this period met with little success, the group immersed themselves in the Rastafari religion which would subsequently influence much of their later work. In 1969, the outfit began working with pivotal songwriter/producer, LEE 'SCRATCH' PERRY, and over the course of the ensuing three years, developed from a soul/ska/R&B vocal outfit to form one of the cornerstones of reggae. With the addition of ASTON BARRETT on bass and brother CARLTON on drums (the former rhythm section of PERRY's UPSETTERS), the newly expanded WAILERS cut a further series of 7" singles under the guiding hand of PERRY, including such enduring tracks as 'KAYA', 'TRENCHTOWN ROCK' and 'SMALL AXE', as well as a debut album, 'SOUL REBEL' (1970). By 1971, The WAILERS had formed their own label, 'Tuff Gong', and had begun producing their own material. The following year, after JOHNNY NASH had taken MARLEY's 'STIR IT UP' into the UK Top 20, The WAILERS signed to 'Island', CHRIS BLACKWELL having previously distributed their early releases in the UK. He provided financial muscle for the outfit to record their major label debut in Jamaica, their first release to be promoted and widely available outside their home country. 'CATCH A FIRE' (1973) was scorching, bass-heavy vibrations providing a platform for impassioned, challenging lyrics on the likes of 'CONCRETE JUNGLE' and '400 YEARS', while the superior WAILERS version of 'STIR IT UP' glowed with laid back positivity. 'BURNIN' (1973) followed soon after, an even fierier set of spiritually and politically motivated songs that featured 'GET UP, STAND UP', a call for individual liberty powered by a knotty, insistent rhythm, as well as the plea for justice, 'I SHOT THE SHERIFF', a US No.1 for ERIC CLAPTON in the summer of '74. By the end of the year, however, PETER TOSH and BUNNY LIVINGSTONE (later renaming himself BUNNY WAILER) had both departed for solo careers, MARLEY recruiting the The I-THREES (a female vocal trio consisting of JUDY MOWAT, MARCIA GRIFFITHS and his wife, RITA) as a replacement as well as bringing in extra backing musicians. Under the revised moniker, BOB MARLEY & THE WAILERS, the outfit toured extensively for the first time in Europe, America and Africa, subsequently releasing the exceptional 'NATTY DREAD' (1975). A landmark roots reggae album, the set featured a studio version of the subsequent live hit, 'NO WOMAN NO CRY', a sublime love song with the I-THREES providing celestial harmonies and MARLEY putting in one of the most moving vocal performances of his career. Elsewhere, 'THEM BELLY FULL (BUT WE HUNGRY)' and 'REVOLUTION' were as politically charged as ever while 'SO JAH SEH' and the title track were ardent professions of MARLEY's rastafarian beliefs. 'LIVE!' was issused later that year, documenting an electric WAILERS performance in London the previous year, while 'RASTAMAN VIBRATION' (1976) gave The WAILERS their biggest commercial success to date, reaching Top 20 in the UK and Top 10 in the US on the back of the 'ROOTS, ROCK, REGGAE' single's Stateside success. Though 'EXODUS' (1977) made the US Top 20, it was the last release to make any significant commercial impact in America, the group's most vociferous fans residing in the UK, Europe, Africa and of course, Jamaica, where MARLEY was revered as if he was royalty. In general a more relaxed set than its predecessor, other highlights from 'EXODUS' included the gentle 'WAITING IN VAIN' and the hooky pop-reggae of 'THREE LITTLE BIRDS'. 'KAYA' (1978) carried on in a similar vein with the spliffed-out 'EASY SKANKING', the mellow 'SATISFY MY SOUL' and the meditative 'TIME WILL TELL' (later covered by The BLACK CROWES). After another live release, 'BABYLON BY BUS' (1978), the group recorded 'SURVIVAL' (1979), probably the most overtly political release of their career with MARLEY addressing the plight of his African brethren on 'ZIMBABWE' and 'AFRICA UNITE'. 'UPRISING' (1980) was released the same year as MARLEY was diagnosed with cancer, lending a new poignancy to tracks like 'REDEMPTION SONG', a beautiful, stripped down piece of African folk and arguably the singer's most spiritually resonant work. It also proved to be his epitaph, the final WAILERS release before MARLEY's death on the 11th of May '81. Later that summer, a Sunsplash Reggae Festival was dedicated to MARLEY and was attended by over 20,000 fans as well as his children, The MELODY MAKERS. More tragedy was to follow in 1987 when Ex-Wailers, CARLTON BARRETT and PETER TOSH, were both murdered in separate incidents, reflecting the inherently violent nature of Jamaican culture (MARLEY himself had earlier survived an attempt on his life in 1976 when gunmen broke into his Kingston home, shooting and injuring him, his wife and manager Don Taylor). Further controversy followed when RITA was ousted by the remaining WAILERS amid calls for an investigation into the MARLEY estate. Nevertheless, the legend of BOB MARLEY remains untarnished, the singer still a hero to countless Rastafarians and ordinary music fans alike. The singer's massive popularity was further illustrated in 1992 when 'SONGS OF FREEDOM', a collection of newly discovered demos, made the UK Top 10, a single culled from the set, 'IRON ZION LION', reaching No.5; MARLEY's has been hitting the charts in one way or another ever since (i.e. with LAURYN HILL). Original WAILERS singer, JUNIOR BRAITHWAITE, was sadly gunned down (in his hometown of Kingston, Jamaica) by an unknown assailant on the 2nd of June, 1999.

Album rating (selective): CATCH A FIRE (*8) / BURNIN' (*8) / NATTY DREAD (*9) / LIVE! (*6) / RASTAMAN VIBRATION (*7) / EXODUS (*8) / KAYA (*8) / BABYLON BY BUS (*6) / SURVIVAL (*8) / UPRISING (*8) / CONFRONTATION posthumous (*6) / LEGEND compilation (*10) / SONGS OF FREEDOM boxed collection (*6) / NATURAL MYSTIC collection (*6)

ROBERT MARLEY

		Island	not iss.
Dec 62.	(7"); (WI 088) **JUDGE NOT (UNLESS YOU JUDGE YOURSELF). / DO YOU STILL LOVE ME?**	☐	⊡
1963.	(7"); (WI 128) **ONE CUP OF COFFEE. / (B-side by Ernest Ranglin)**	☐	⊡

The WAILERS

were formed by **MARLEY** (-vocals, +later guitar) plus **PETER TOSH** (b.WINSTON HUBERT MacINTOSH, 19 Oct'44, Westmoreland, Jamaica) – vocals, +later guitar / **BUNNY LIVINGSTONE** (b.NEVILLE O'RILEY LIVINGSTONE, 10 Apr'47, Kingston, Jamaica) – vocals, percussion / **JUNIOR BRAITHWAITE** – vocals / **BEVERLEY**

KELSO – vocals / plus occasionally **RITA MARLEY** (b. ALPHARITA CONSTANTIA ANDERSON) – backing vocals / Instruments by SOUL BROTHERS then SKATELITES

		Ska Beat	not iss.
Jan 65.	(7"; as WAILIN' WAILERS) (JB 186) **SIMMER DOWN. / I DON'T NEED YOUR LOVE**	☐	⊡
——	Released in Jamaica earlier, UK in batches		
		Island	not iss.
Mar 65.	(7"); (WI 188) **IT HURTS TO BE ALONE. / MR.TALKATIVE**	☐	⊡
Apr 65.	(7"); (WI 206) **PLAY BOY. / YOUR LOVE**	☐	⊡
——	added **CHERRY SMITH** – backing vocals		
May 65.	(7"); (WI 211) **HOOT NANNY ROLL. / DO YOU REMEMBER**	☐	⊡
	(above A-side was actually credited to PETER TOUCH, the B-side BOB MARLEY, although all featured MARLEY, TOSH and The WAILERS		
May 65.	(7"); (WI 212) **HOOLIGAN. / MAGA DOG**	☐	⊡
Jun 65.	(7"; as PETER TOSH & THE WAILERS) (WI 215) **SHAME AND SCANDAL. / THE JERK**	☐	⊡
Jun 65.	(7"); (WI 216) **DON'T EVER LEAVE ME. / DONNA**	☐	⊡
Dec 65.	(7"); (WI 254) **WHAT'S NEW PUSSYCAT. / WHERE WILL I FIND**	☐	⊡
Mar 66.	(7"); (WI 260) **JUMBIE JAMBOUREE. / (B-side by The Skatelites)**	☐	⊡
Apr 66.	(7"); (WI 268) **PUT IT ON (FEEL THE SPIRIT). / LOVE WON'T BE MINE**	☐	⊡
		Ska Beat	not iss.
Aug 65.	(7"); (JB 211) **LONESOME FEELINGS. / THERE SHE GOES**	☐	⊡
Oct 65.	(7"); (JB 226) **I MADE A MISTAKE. / (B-side by The SOUL BROTHERS)**	☐	⊡
	(above A-side was probably by The WAILIN' RUDEBOYS)		
1966.	(7"); (JB 228) **LOVE AND AFFECTION. / TEENAGER IN LOVE**	☐	⊡
1966.	(7"); (JB 230) **AND I LOVE HER. / DO IT RIGHT**	☐	⊡
1966.	(7"); (JB 249) **LONESOME TRACK. / SINNER MAN**	☐	⊡
——	(below might be without MARLEY)		
		Rio	not iss.
1966.	(7"); (R 116) **DANCING SHOES. / DON'T LOOK BACK**	☐	⊡
——	MARLEY left Feb'66, to marry RITA but soon returned. CHERRY also left. LIVINGSTONE was imprisoned in 1966.		
		Doctor Bird	not iss.
1966.	(7"); (DB 1013) **RUDE BOY. / (B-side by Roland Al & The Soul Brothers)**	☐	⊡
1966.	(7"); (DB 1021) **GOOD GOOD RUDIE. / (B-side by City Slickers)**	☐	⊡
Nov 66.	(7"); (DB 1039) **RASTA PUT IT ON. / (B-side by Roland Al & The Soul Brothers)**	☐	⊡
	(re-iss. Apr67 on 'Island')		
——	(below iss.Jamaica on 'Rocksteady')		
1967.	(7"); (DB 1091) **NICE TIME. / HYPOCRITE**	☐	⊡
——	(below 2 without MARLEY)		
		Island	not iss.
Nov 66.	(7"); (WI 3001) **HE WHO FEELS IT KNOWS IT. / SUNDAY MORNING**	☐	⊡
Dec 66.	(7"); (WI 3009) **LET HIM GO (RUDE BOY GOT BAIL). / SINNER MAN**	☐	⊡
Apr 67.	(7"); (WI 3035) **BABY I NEED YOU. / (B-side by Ken Boothe)**	☐	⊡
——	Now a trio of MARLEY, TOSH & BUNNY. (KELSO and BRAITHWAITE departed)		
Apr 67.	(7"); (WI 3043) **BEND DOWN LOW. / FREEDOM TOWN**	☐	⊡
Apr 67.	(7"; PETER TOSH & THE WAILERS) (WI 3042) **I AM THE TOUGHEST. / (B-side by Marcia Griffiths)**	☐	⊡
		Studio One	not iss.
1967.	(7"); (SO 2010) **I STAND PREDOMINANT. / (B-side by Norma Fraser)**	☐	⊡
		Trojan	not iss.
Oct 68.	(7"); (TR 617) **STIR IT UP. / THIS TRAIN**	☐	⊡
		Bamboo	not iss.
1970.	(7"); (BAM 55) **JAILHOUSE. / (B-side by John Holt)**	☐	⊡
		Escort	not iss.
1970.	(7"); (ERT 842) **RUN FOR COVER. / TO THE RESCUE**	☐	⊡

BOB MARLEY & THE WAILERS

——	added **ASTON BARRETT** (b.22 Nov'46, KIngston) – bass / **CARLTON BARRETT** (b.17 Dec'50, Kingston) – drums		
		Upsetter	Shelter
1970.	(7"); (US 340) **MY CUP. / SON OF THUNDER (by "LEE PERRY & THE WAILERS")**	☐	⊡
1970.	(7"; by The WAILERS) (US 342) **VERSION OF CUP. / (B-side by The Upsetters)**	☐	⊡
Dec 70.	(7"); (US 348) **DUPPY CONQUEROR. / (B-side by The Upsetters)**	☐	⊡
Jan 71.	(7"); (US 354) **MR. BROWN. / (B-side by The Upsetters)**	☐	⊡
Feb 71.	(7"); (US 356) **KAYA. / (version by The Upsetters)**	☐	⊡
Feb 71.	(7"); (US 357) **SMALL AXE. / ALL IN ONE**	☐	⊡
1971.	(7"; as The WAILERS) (US 351) **DREAMLAND. / (B-side by The Upsetters)**	☐	⊡
1971.	(7"); (US 372) **MORE AXE. / (B-side by The Upsetters)**	☐	⊡
1971.	(7"; as RAS DAWKINS & THE WAILERS) (US 368) **PICTURE ON THE WALL. / (B-side by The Upsetters)**	☐	⊡
		Trojan	not iss.
Sep 70.	(7"); (TR 7759) **SOUL SHAKEDOWN PARTY. / (B-side by The Beverley All-Stars)**	☐	⊡
Dec 70.	(lp); (TBL 126) **SOUL REBEL**	☐	⊡

– There she goes / Put it on / How many times / Mellow mood / Changes are / Hammer / Tell me / Touch me / Treat you right / Soul rebel. *(re-iss.Sep81 on 'New Cross'; NC 001) (c-iss.Jan82 on 'Sun'; CFK 1020) (re-iss.Jun84 on 'Blue Moon' lp/c; BMLP/BMC 1018) (re-iss.Oct86 on 'Receiver' lp/c; RRLP/RRLC 106) (cd-iss. Jan90; RRCD 106) (re-iss. Apr90 on 'Action Replay' cd/c; CDAR/ARLC 1013)*

				Jackpot	not iss.
1971.	(7") *(JP 730)* **MR. CHATTERBOX. / WALK THROUGH THE WORLD**			☐	-

				Punch	not iss.
1971.	(7") *(PH 69)* **MORE AXE. / (B-side by Dave Berber)**			☐	-
1971.	(7"; as The WAILERS) *(PH 77)* **DOWN PRESSER. / (B-side by Junior Byles)**			☐	-
1972.	(7") *(PH 101)* **SCREW FACE. / FACE MAN**			☐	-

				Bullet	not iss.
1971.	(7") *(BU 464)* **SOULTOWN. / LET THE SUN SHINE ON ME**			☐	-
1971.	(7") *(BU 493)* **LICK SAMBA. / SAMBA**			☐	-

				Summit	not iss.
1971.	(7") *(SUM 8526)* **STOP THE TRAIN. / CAUTION**			☐	-
1971.	(7") *(SUM 8530)* **FREEDOM TRAIN. /**			☐	-

				Green Door	Tuff Gong
1971.	(7") *(GD 4002)* **LIVELY UP YOURSELF. / (B-side by Tommy McCook)**			☐	-
Nov 71.	(7") *(GD 4005)* **TRENCHTOWN ROCK. / GROOVING KINGDOM**			☐	-
1972.	(7") *(GD 4025)* **GUAVA JELLY. / REDDER THAN RED**			☐	-

——— (below was 1968 demo)

				C.B.S.	not iss.
May 72.	(7") *(CBS 4902)* **REGGAE ON BROADWAY. / OH LORD I GOT TO GET THERE**			☐	-

				Trojan	not iss.
Sep 72.	(7") *(US 392)* **KEEP ON MOVING. / AFRICAN HERBSMAN**			☐	-
1972.	(lp) *(TRL 62)* **AFRICAN HERBSMAN**			☐	-

– Lively up yourself / Small axe / Duppy conqueror / African herbsman / Trenchtown rock / Keep on moving / Fussing and fighting / Stand alone / All in one / Don't rock the boat / Put it on / Sun is shining / Kaya / Riding high / 400 years / Brain washing. *(re-iss. Jul84 lp/c; TRLS/ZCTRL 62) (cd-iss. Jun88; CDTRL 62) (re-iss. Nov83 on 'Fame' lp/c; FA/TCFA 41-3082-1/-4) (cd re-iss. Mar94 on 'Trojan'; same)*

The WAILERS

				Blue Mountain	not iss.
Jan 73.	(7") *(1021)* **BABY WE'VE GOT A DATE (ROCK IT BABY). / STOP THAT TRAIN**			☐	-

				Island	Island
Apr 73.	(7") *<1211>* **STOP THAT TRAIN. / ROCK IT BABY**			-	-
Apr 73.	(lp/c) *(<ILPS/ICT 9241>)* **CATCH A FIRE**				

– Concrete jungle / Slave driver / 400 years / Stop that train / Baby we've got a date (rock it baby) / Stir it up / Kinky reggae / No more trouble / Midnight ravers. *(re-iss. Oct86 lp/c; ILPM/ICM 9241) (re-iss. Jun90 on 'Tuff Gong' cd/c; RRCd/RRCT 1)*

Jun 73.	(7") *(WIP 6164)* **CONCRETE JUNGLE. / REINCARNATION SOUL**			☐	☐
Jul 73.	(7") *<1215>* **CONCRETE JUNGLE. / NO MORE TROUBLE**				-
Sep 73.	(7") *(WIP 6167) <1218>* **GET UP, STAND UP. / SLAVE DRIVER**			☐	
Nov 73.	(lp/c) *(<ILPS/ICT 9256>)* **BURNIN'**				

– Get up, stand up / Hallelujah time / I shot the sheriff / Burnin' and lootin' / Put it on / Small axe / Pass it on / Duppy conqueror / One foundation / Rastaman chant. *(re-iss. Mar87; ILPM 9256) (re-iss. Jun90 on 'Tuff Gong' cd/c; RRCD/RRCT 2)*

Feb 74.	(7") *<005>* **I SHOT THE SHERIFF. / PUT IT ON**				

——— added **The I-THREES** (female backers **JUDY MOWAT, MARCIA GRIFFITHS**, and **RITA**). They replaced PETER TOSH and BUNNY WAILER who both went solo.

BOB MARLEY & THE WAILERS

——— **MARLEY, ASTON** and **BARRETT** added **EARL LINDO** – keyboards / **BERNARD HARVEY** – keyboards / **AL ANDERSON** – guitar.

May 75.	(lp/c) *(<ILPS/ICT 9281>)* **NATTY DREAD**			43	92

– Lively up yourself / No woman no cry / Them belly full (but we hungry) / Rebel music (3 o'clock road block) / So jah seh / Natty dread / Bend down low / Talkin' blues / Revolution. *(re-iss. May87 lp/c/cd; ILPM/ICM/CID 9281; re-iss. Jun90 on 'Tuff Gong' cd/c; RRCD/RRCT 3)*

Jun 75.	(7") *(WIP 6212)* **NATTY DREAD. / SO JAH SEH**			☐	☐
Jun 75.	(7") *<027>* **LIVELY UP YOURSELF. / SO JAH SEH**				-

——— **TYRONE DOWNIE** – keyboards repl. HARVEY / **ALVIN 'SHECO' PATTERSON** – percussion repl. LINDO / added **JULIAN 'JUNIOR' MURVIN** – guitar

Aug 75.	(7") *(WIP 6244) <037>* **NO WOMAN NO CRY (live). / KINKY REGGAE**			22	☐
Dec 75.	(lp/c) *(<ILPS/ICT 9376>)* **LIVE! (live)**			38	90

– Trenchtown rock / Burnin' and lootin' / Them belly full (but we hungry) / Lively up yourself / No woman no cry / I shot the sheriff / Get up, stand up. *(re-iss. Jul81 + Sep86 as 'LIVE AT THE LYCEUM' lp/c; ILPM/ICM 9376) (cd-iss. Jan87; CID 9376) (re-iss. Nov90 on 'Tuff Gong' cd/c; RRCD/RRCT 4)*

Jan 76.	(7") *(WIP 6265)* **JAH LIVE. / CONCRETE JUNGLE (live)**			☐	☐
Apr 76.	(7") *(WIP 6296)* **JOHNNY WAS (WOMAN HANG HER HEAD AND CRY). / CRY TO ME**			☐	☐
Apr 76.	(lp/c) *(<ILPS/ICT 9383>)* **RASTAMAN VIBRATION**			15	8

– Positive vibration / Roots, rock, reggae / Johnny was / Cry to me / Want more / Crazy baldhead / Who the cap fit / Night shift / War / Rat race. *(re-iss. Apr87 lp/c/cd; ILPM/ICM/CID 9383) (re-iss.Nov90 on 'Tuff Gong' cd/c; RRCD/RRCT 5)*

Jun 76.	(7") *(WIP 6309)* **ROOTS ROCK REGGAE. / STIR IT UP**			☐	-
Jun 76.	(7") *<061>* **ROOTS ROCK REGGAE. / CRY TO ME**			-	51
Nov 76.	(7") *<072>* **WHO THE CAP FIT. /**			-	☐
May 77.	(lp/c) *(<ILPS/ICT 9498>)* **EXODUS**			8	20 Jun77

– Natural mystic / So much things to say / Guiltiness / The heathen / Exodus / Jamming / Waiting in vain / Turn your lights down low / Three little birds / One

love – People get ready. *(re-iss. Mar87 lp/cd; ILPM/ICM/CID 9498) (re-iss. Nov90 on 'Tuff Gong' cd/c; RRCD/RRCT 6)*

Jun 77.	(7") *(WIP 6390) <089>* **EXODUS. / EXODUS (dub)**			14	☐
Aug 77.	(7") *(WIP 6402) <092>* **WAITING IN VAIN. / ROOTS**			27	☐
Dec 77.	(7") *(WIP 6410)* **JAMMING. / PUNKY REGGAE PARTY**			9	-

——— added the returning **EARL 'WIRE' LINDO** – keyboards

Feb 78.	(7") *(WIP 6420) <099>* **IS THIS LOVE. / CRISIS (version)**			9	☐
	(12"-iss.Jun81;)				
Mar 78.	(lp/c) *(<ILPS/ICT 9517>)* **KAYA**			4	50

– Easy shanking / Kaya / The sun is shining / Is this love / Satisfy my soul / She's gone / Misty morning / Crisis / Running away / Time will tell. *(re-iss. Feb87 lp/c/cd; ILPM/ICM/CID 9517) (re-iss. Nov90 on 'Tuff Gong' cd/c; RRCD/RRCT 7)*

May 78.	(7") *(WIP 6440)* **SATISFY MY SOUL. / SMILE JAMAICA**			21	-
Dec 78.	(d-lp/c) *(<ISLD/ICT 9542>)* **BABYLON BY BUS (live)**			40	☐

– Positive vibration / Punky reggae party / Exodus / Stir it up / Rat race / Concrete jungle / Kinky reggae / Lively up yourself / Rebel music (3 o'clock road block) / War / No more trouble / Is this love / The heathen / Jamming. *(cd-iss. Feb87; CIDD 11) (re-iss. Nov90 on 'Tuff Gong' cd/c; RRCD/RRCT 8)*

Jan 79.	(7"; w-drawn) *(WIP 6478)* **STIR IT UP (live). / RAT RACE (live)**			-	-

(12") *(WIP12 6478)* – ('A'side) / War (live) / No more trouble (live).

Jul 79.	(7") *<49080>* **WAKE UP AND LIVE. / (part 2)**			-	☐
Sep 79.	(7") *(WIP 6510)* **SO MUCH TROUBLE IN THE WORLD. / ('A'instrumental)**			56	-
Oct 79.	(lp/c) *(<ILPS/ICT 9542>)* **SURVIVAL**			20	70

– Wake up and live / Top rankin' / Ambush in the night / Babylon system / Survival / Ride Natty ride / One drop / So much trouble in the world / Zimbabwe / Africa unite. *(re-iss. Mar87 lp/c/cd; ILPM/ICM/CID 9542) (re-iss. Nov90 on 'Tuff Gong' cd/c; RRCD RRCT 9)*

Nov 79.	(7") *<49156>* **ONE DROP. / KAYA**			-	☐
Nov 79.	(7") *(WIP 6553)* **SURVIVAL. / WAKE UP AND LIVE**			-	☐
Mar 80.	(7") *(WIP 6597)* **ZIMBABWE. / SURVIVAL**			-	☐

(12") *(WIP12 6597)* – ('A'side) / Africa unite / Wake up and live.

May 80.	(7") *(WIP 6610)* **COULD YOU BE LOVED. / ONE DROP**			5	-
	(12"+=) *(12WIP 6610)* – Ride natty ride.				
May 80.	(7") *<49547>* **COULD YOU BE LOVED. / RIDE NATTY RIDE**			-	☐
Jun 80.	(lp/c) *(<ILPS/ICT 9596>)* **UPRISING**			6	45

– Coming in from the cold / Real situation / Bad card / We and them / Work / Zion train / Pimper's paradise / Could you be loved / Forever loving Jah / Redemption song. *(cd-iss. Feb87; CID 9596) (re-iss.Nov90 on 'Tuff Gong' cd/c; RRCD/RRCT 10)*

Aug 80.	(7") *(WIP 6641)* **THREE LITTLE BIRDS. / EVERY NEED GOT AN EGO FEED**			17	-
Oct 80.	(7"/12") *(WIP/12WIP 6653)* **REDEMPTION SONG. / ('A'-Band version)**				
Nov 80.	(7") *<49636>* **REDEMPTION SONG. / COMING IN FROM THE COLD**			-	☐

——— In Oct'80, BOB was diagnosed with lung cancer and died 11th May '81.

– compilations, etc. –

1974.	(7") *Trojan; (TRO 7911)* **SOUL SHAKEDOWN PARTY. / CAUTION**			☐	-
Jul 74.	(lp) *Trojan; (TRLS 89)* **RASTA REVOLUTION**			☐	-

(re-iss. 1981 + Jul84 lp/c; TRLS/ZCTRL 89) (cd-iss. Jun88; CDTRL 89) (re-iss. Jul85 on 'Fame' lp/c; FA/TCFA 41 3127) (cd re-iss. Mar94)

Aug 74.	(7") *Trojan; (TRO 7926)* **MR.BROWN. / ('A'version)**			☐	-
1976.	(7") *Trojan; (TRO 7979)* **MR.BROWN. / TRENCHTOWN ROCK**			☐	-
Jun 81.	(7") *Trojan; (TRO 9065)* **THANK YOU LORD. / WISDOM**			☐	-
Oct 83.	(7") *Trojan; (TRO 9074)* **SOUL SHAKEDOWN PARTY. / CAUTION**			☐	-

('A'-disco 12") *(TROT 9074)* – Keep on skanking.

Jan 84.	(lp/c) *Trojan; (TRSL/ZCTRL 221)* **IN THE BEGINNING**			☐	-

(cd-iss. Jun88; CDTRL 221) (cd-iss. Mar94 on 'Trojan')

Jun 88.	(d-lp/d-c/d-cd) *Trojan; (TRLD/ZCTRL/CDTRD 406)* **SOUL REVOLUTION 1 & 2**			☐	-

(re-iss. Mar94 on 'Trojan' d-cd/d-c;)

Jun 89.	(cd) *Trojan; (CDTRD 406)* **SOUL REVOLUTION / RHYTHM ALBUM**			☐	-
May 91.	(cd-box)(lp-box) *Trojan;* **IN MEMORIAM**			☐	-
Jul 77.	(lp/c) *Epic; (EPC/40 82066)* **BIRTH OF A LEGEND VOL.1 (featuring PETER TOSH)**			☐	-

(re-iss. Jun80 + Nov81) (cd-iss. Jun91 on 'Pickwick')

Sep 77.	(lp/c) *Embassy; (CBS/40 31584)* **EARLY MUSIC**			☐	-

(re-iss. Nov81 on 'C.B.S.')

Oct 79.	(lp) *Hammer; (HMR 9006)* **BOB MARLEY & THE WAILERS**			☐	-
Oct 79.	(lp) *Psycho; (PLP 6002)* **IN THE BEGINNING**			☐	-

(re-iss. Jul84, cd-iss. Jun88 on 'Trojan')

Mar 81.	(lp/c) *Hallmark; (SHM/HSC 3048)* **BOB MARLEY & THE WAILERS WITH PETER TOSH**			☐	-

(re-iss. 1981 on 'SS International')

1981.	(lp) *Accord; (SN 7211)* **JAMAICAN STORM**			☐	-
Sep 81.	(lp/c) *Warners; (K/K4 99183) / Cotillion; <5228>* **CHANCES ARE**			☐	-
Sep 81.	(7") *Warners; (K 79250)* **REGGAE ON BROADWAY. / GONNA GET YOU**			☐	-
Nov 81.	(7") *Cotillion;* **CHANCES ARE. /**				☐
Jun 81.	(12") *Island; (12WIP 6244) <49755>* **NO WOMAN NO CRY (live). / JAMMING**			8	☐
Mar 82.	(7") *Island; (WIP 6774)* **NATURAL MYSTIC. / CARRY ON BEYOND**			-	☐
1982.	(9xlp-box) *Island; (EMSP 100)* **BOB MARLEY – THE BOXED SET**			☐	-
1982.	(lp/c) *Island; (ISTDA 1)* **COUNTRYMAN** (Soundtrack with 8 MARLEY songs)			☐	-
Apr 83.	(7"/12") *(IS/12IS 108)* **BUFFALO SOLDIER. / BUFFALO (dub)**			4	☐
May 83.	(lp/c) *Island; (<ILPS/ICT 9760> <90085>* **CONFRONTATION**			5	55

– Chant down Babylon / Buffalo soldier / Jump Nyabinghi / Mix up, mix up / Give thanks and praises / Blackman redemption / Trenchtown / Stiff neked fools / I know /

Rastaman live up!. (re-iss. Mar87) (cd-iss. 1988 on 'Mango') (re-iss. cd+c Jun90 on 'Tuff Gong')

Apr 84. (7") Island; (IS 169) **ONE LOVE. / PEOPLE GET READY** [5] [ ]
(12"+=/12"pic-d+=) (12IS/+P 169) – Keep on moving / So much trouble.

May 84. (lp/c) Island; (BMW/+C 1) <90169> **LEGEND** [1] [54]
– Is this love / Jamming / No woman no cry / Stir it up / Get up, stand up / Satisfy my soul / I shot the sheriff / One love / People get ready / Buffalo soldier / Exodus / Redemption song / Could you be loved / Want more. (cd-iss. Aug85; CID 103) (cd re-iss. May90 on 'Tuff Gong' hit UK No.11, Mar92 No.18 / Jul92 No.25)

Jun 84. (7") Island; (IS 180) **WAITING IN VAIN. / BLACK MAN REDEMPTION** [31] [ ]
(12"+=) (12IS 180) – Marley mix-up.

Aug 84. (7") Island; **IS THIS LOVE. / BLACK MAN REDEPTION** [-] [ ]

Nov 84. (7"/7"pic-d) (IS/+P 210) **COULD YOU BE LOVED. / NO WOMAN NO CRY** [71] [ ]
(12"+=) (12IS 210) – Jamming / Coming in from the cold.

Apr 85. (lp) Island; (IRG 15) **REGGAE GREATS** [ ] [ ]

Jun 85. (12"/c-s/7") Island; (12IC/+/IS 236) **THREE LITTLE BIRDS. / ('A'dub version)** [ ] [ ]

Jun 86. (lp/c/cd) Island; (ILPS/ICT/CID 9843) <90169> **REBEL MUSIC** [54] [ ]
(re-iss. cd+c.Jun90 on 'Tuff Gong')

Oct 83. (d-c) C.B.S.; (CBS 32088) **BIRTH OF A LEGEND / EARLY MUSIC** [ ] [ ]

May 84. (lp/c)(pic-lp) Breakaway; (DELP/ZCELP 301)(PIXLP 1) **THE ESSENTIAL** [ ] [ ]

Jun 84. (d-lp/c) Happy Bird; (DB/MDB9 80072) **25 GREATEST HITS** [ ] [-]

Nov 84. (lp/c) Topline; (TOP/KTOP 104) **MELLOW MOOD** [ ] [-]
(cd-iss. Apr87; TOPCD 104)

Dec 84. (lp/c) Premier; (CBR/KCBR 1001) **ONE LOVE** [ ] [-]
(re-iss. Feb90 on 'Pickwick'; PWK 002)

Feb 87. Premier; (lp)(c) (CBR 1046) **LIVELY UP YOURSELF** [ ] [-]
(cd-iss. Jun93 on 'Prestige')

Feb 85. (lp/c) Sierra; (FEDB/CFEDB 5000) **REPLAY ON BOB MARLEY** [ ] [-]

Feb 85. (d-lp/d-c) Cambra; (CR/+T 5147) **ETERNAL** [ ] [-]

Aug 85. (12") Daddy Kool; (DK 12-101) **RAINBOW COUNTRY. / (B-side by Pablo & The Upsetters)** [ ] [-]

Jan 86. (12") Daddy Kool; (DK 12-102) **NATURAL MYSTIC. / ('A'version)** [ ] [-]

Apr 86. (lp/c) Showcase; (SHLP/SHTC 109) **PUT IT ON** [ ] [-]

Apr 86. (d-lp/c) Castle; (CCS LP/MC 123) **THE COLLECTION** [ ] [-]
(cd-iss. 1988; CCSCD 123)

Nov 86. (lp/c) Blue Moon; (BMLP/BMLC 1032) **ROOTS** [ ] [-]
(cd-iss. 1988; BMCD 1032)

Dec 88. (cd) Blue Moon; (CDBM 1052) **ROOTS VOL.2** (incl. 'ONE LOVE' album) [ ] [-]

Feb 87. (lp) Konnexion; (BITR 78802223) **THE LEE PERRY SESSIONS** [ ] [-]

May 88. (lp/c/cd) Streetlife; (266 225-1/-4/-2) **GREATEST HITS** [ ] [-]

Sep 88. (cd-ep) Pickwick; (PWK 072) **REACTION / I GOTTA KEEP ON MOVING / PUT IT ON** [ ] [-]

Feb 87. (lp/c) Arena; (ARA/+C 010) **THE CLASSIC YEARS** [ ] [-]

Nov 88. (cd-ep) Arena; (CDEP 3C) **CLASSIC** (w/ TOOTS & THE MAYTALS) [ ] [-]

Jul 87. (cd) Intertape; (500 004) **BOB MARLEY** [ ] [-]

May 88. (lp/c) Black Tulip; (28014) **20 GREATEST HITS** [ ] [-]

Jun 90. (lp/c/cd) Connoisseur; (CSAP/+MC/CD 107) **THE BEST OF BOB MARLEY (1968-72)** [ ] [-]

Mar 91. (cd/c/lp) Tuff Gong; (TGL CD/MC/LP 12) <848243> **TALKIN' BLUES** [ ] [-]
– (radio sessions 1973 + interviews 1975)

May 91. (c-s/7") Tuff Gong; (TC+/TGX 1) **ONE LOVE – PEOPLE GET READY. / SO MUCH TROUBLE IN THE WORLD** [42] [-]
(12"+=/cd-s+=) (12/CD TGX 1) – ('A'extended) / Keep on moving.

Sep 92. (c-s/7") Tuff Gong; (TC+/TGX 2) **IRON ZION LION ('74 track). / COULD YOU BE LOVED** [5] [ ]
(12"/cd-s) (12/CD TGX 2) – ('A'side) / Smile Jamaica / Three little birds.

Sep 92. (4xcd-box/4xc-box) Tuff Gong; (TGCBX/TGMBX 1) <512280> **SONGS OF FREEDOM** (discovered demos) [10] [86]
(re-iss. May93 as 8xlp-box; TGLBX 1)

Nov 92. (c-s/7") Tuff Gong; (TC+/TGX 3) **WHY SHOULD I. / ('A-Kindread Spirit mix)** [42] [-]
(cd-s+=) (CDTGX 3) – Exodus (rebel the remix)

Apr 91. (lp/c/cd) Rohit; (RRTG/+C/CD 7757) **ALL THE HITS** [ ] [-]

Aug 91. (cd) Entity; (UCD1/UMK9 9026) **SAGA** [ ] [-]

Sep 91. (cd/c) Music Collector; (MCCD/MCTC 033) **THE VERY BEST OF THE EARLY YEARS 1968-74** [ ] [-]

Jun 92. (cd) Tring; (TTMC 018) **LIVELY UP YOURSELF** [ ] [-]

Jun 92. (cd/c) Tring; (CDAA/MCAA 047) **AUDIO ARCHIVE** [ ] [-]

Aug 92. (cd/c/lp) Lagoon; (LG 2/4/1 1040) **BOB MARLEY & THE WAILERS** [ ] [-]

Nov 92. (d-cd/d-cd) Tring; (MC+/TFP 010) **THE BOB MARLEY COLLECTION** [ ] [-]

Nov 92. (cd) Laserlight; (15499) **THE BEST** [ ] [-]

Feb 93. (cd) Charly; (CDCD 1036) **TREAT HER RIGHT** [ ] [-]

Nov 93. (cd) Charly; (CPCD 8009) **THE LEE PERRY SESSIONS** [ ] [-]

Nov 93. (cd) Charly; (CPCD 8029) **RIDING HIGH** [ ] [-]

Mar 94. (cd) Charly; (CDCD 1152) **RAINBOW COUNTRY** [ ] [-]

Sep 93. (4xlp-box) Trojan; **THE EARLY YEARS 1969-1973** [ ] [-]

Sep 93. (d-cd) Laserlight; (24090) **BOB MARLEY** [ ] [-]

Feb 94. (lp; WAILERS) Studio One; (S 1001) **THE WAILING WAILERS** [ ] [-]

Mar 94. (cd/c) Trojan; (CDTAL/ZCTAL 400) **IN MEMORIAM** [ ] [-]

Jun 94. (cd) Sony; (982588-2) **THE BIRTH OF A LEGEND (with PETER TOSH)** [ ] [-]

Jul 94. (cd) Success; **KEEP ON MOVING** [ ] [-]

Jul 94. (cd) Success; **SOUL REBEL** [ ] [-]

Jul 94. (cd) Success; **DON'T ROCK MY BOAT** [ ] [-]

Jul 94. (cd) Success; **SOUL SHAKEDOWN PARTY** [ ] [-]

Jan 95. (cd) Reggae Best; (RB 3010) **SOUL CAPTIVE** [ ] [-]

Feb 95. (cd) More Music; **POWER** [ ] [-]

Feb 95. (cd) B.A.M.; (KLMCD 003) **PEARLS OF THE PAST** [ ] [-]

Feb 95. (cd) B.A.M.; (KLMCD 038) **PEARLS OF THE PAST VOLUME 2** [ ] [-]

May 95. (c-s) Tuff Gong; (TCTGX 4) **KEEP ON MOVING / PIMPER'S PARADISE** [17] [ ]
(12+=/cd-s+=) (12/CD TGX 4) – ('A'mixes).

May 95. (lp/c/cd) Tuff Gong; (BMW/+C/CD 2) <524103> **NATURAL MYSTIC** [5] [67]

May 95. (cd) Heartbeat; (CDHB 171) **SIMMER DOWN AT STUDIO ONE** [ ] [-]

May 95. (cd) Heartbeat; (CDHB 172) **THE WAILING WAILERS AT STUDIO ONE** [ ] [-]

Jul 95. (cd) A&A; (AACD 88) **LEGEND IN SAX** [ ] [-]

Aug 95. (cd) Sony Europe;) **GOLD COLLECTION** [ ] [-]

Dec 95. (d-c) Columbia; (467954-2/-4) **EARLY COLLECTION** [ ] [-]

Jun 96. (c-s) Tuff Gong; (ANACA 002) **WHAT GOES AROUND COMES AROUND** [42] [ ]
(12"+=/cd-s+=) (ANA12/ANACD 002) –

Mar 98. (7") Impact!; (RANDYS 1056) **SUGAR SUGAR. / DON'T ROCK MY BOAT** [ ] [-]

Aug 98. (cd; as BOB MARLEY VS FUNKSTAR DE LUXE) ; **THE SUN IS SHINING** [56] [ ]

Sep 99. (c-s/12"/cd-s; as BOB MARLEY VS FUNKSTAR DE LUXE) (006673 9/0/5 CLU) **THE SUN IS SHINING (mixes)** [3] [ ]

Nov 99. (c-s/cd-s; BOB MARLEY & LAURYN HILL) Ruffhouse; (668436-4/-2) **TURN YOUR LIGHTS DOWN LOW / (mixes)** [15] [ ]

Nov 99. (cd/lp) Tuff Gong; (<546404-2/-1>) **CHANT DOWN BABYLON** (remixed with modern artists) [ ] [79]

—— BOB's son ZIGGY MARLEY (real name DAVID) & The MELODY MAKERS (other sons & daughters; STEPHEN, CEDELLA and SHARON) signed to EMI USA in 1986 and released album 'KEY WORLD'. In 1988, with producers TOM TOM CLUB (TINA WEXMOUTH and CHRIS FRANTZ of TALKING HEADS), they signed to 'Virgin' and had US No.23 hit album 'CONSCIOUS PARTY'. A single from it 'TOMORROW PEOPLE' made no.39 there mid-'88. A year later, the album 'ONE BRIGHT DAY' gave them last US chart appearance, hitting No.26.

Steve MARRIOTT (see under ⇒ HUMBLE PIE)

Chris MARS (see under ⇒ REPLACEMENTS)

MARTHA & THE VANDELLAS

Formed: Detroit, Michigan, USA . . . 1960 as The DEL-PHIS by MARTHA REEVES together with high school pals ROSALIND ASHFORD and ANNETTE STERLING BEARD. Although the trio cut a one-off side for 'Chess' subsidiary, 'Check-Mate', while still at school, their big break came after REEVES landed herself a job as A&R secretary at 'Motown'. When singer MARY WELLS failed to show up for a MARVIN GAYE session, the trio were called in at short notice to back GAYE on two tracks, 'Stubborn Kind Of Fellow' and 'Hitch Hike'. They also recorded a track of their own, 'I'LL HAVE TO LET HIM GO', releasing it in September '62 under the moniker, MARTHA & THE VANDELLAS (after Detroit's Van Dyke street and REEVES' heroine, DELLA REESE). The single stiffed but a follow-up, 'COME AND GET THESE MEMORIES', made the US Top 30. Cue the entrance of 'Motown' songsmiths par excellence, Holland/Dozier/Holland who proceeded to cook up the searing 'HEAT WAVE' as the group's first Top 5 hit in late '63. One of the definitive singles in the 'Motown' pantheon and a key record in developing the label as a brand name, 'HEAT WAVE' worked up a delirious aural sweat with a killer combination of thundering brass, hollering handclaps and fervent call and response vocals. The winning formula was repeated in early '64 with the Top 10 'QUICKSAND', after which BEARD was replaced by ex-VELVELETTE, BETTY KELLY. Successive singles, 'LIVE WIRE' and the less frenetic 'IN MY LONELY ROOM' hovered on the edges of the Top 40 yet the group hit paydirt after taking on a song rejected by labelmate KIM WESTON. Penned by GAYE, Ivy Jo Hunter and REEVES' erstwhile boss, Mickey Stevenson, 'DANCING IN THE STREET' was subsequently moulded in the VANDELLAS style and shimmied its way to No.2 that Autumn. Possibly the premier dancefloor anthem of 60's soul, the track was dusted down two decades later by rock stalwarts DAVID BOWIE and MICK JAGGER who performed the song at Live Aid and duly sent it to the top of the UK chart. The headlong rush of 'NOWHERE TO RUN' found them back in the Top 10 in 1965 and over the ensuing three years they sporadically hit the Top 10 with 'I'M READY FOR LOVE' and 'JIMMY MACK'. Early 68's 'HONEY CHILE' was the first track released under the expanded moniker, MARTHA REEVES & THE VANDELLAS, apeing the fashion in which The SUPREMES had become DIANA ROSS & THE SUPREMES a year earlier. While REEVES may have won this token concession, hers was a constant battle with label boss, Berry Gordy over what she saw as preferential treatment for The SUPREMES and especially ROSS. Whatever, 'HONEY CHILE' was the last Holland/Dozier/Holland track prior to their departure from 'Motown' and the VANDELLAS' commercial fortunes became progressively bleaker as they made do with lesser material. The group's last major success came in early '71 with the near Top 10 hit, 'FORGET ME NOT' before they finally called it a day late the following year. By the time of the split, REEVES was the only original remaining member. Profoundly affected by her experiences at 'Motown', she was struggling with drug dependence and emotional problems, having already suffered her first breakdown in 1969 (ironically, re-issues of both 'DANCING IN THE STREET' and 'NOWHERE TO RUN' hit the Top 5 in the UK around the same time). She finally left the label after a final 1973 single, 'NO ONE THERE', signing to 'M.C.A.' as a solo artist and cutting a couple of critically praised but unsuccessful albums, 'POWER OF LOVE' (1974) and 'THE REST OF MY LIFE' (1976). Following a final album on 'Fantasy', 'WE MEET AGAIN' (1978), REEVES retreated from the music scene as her personal problems took priority. Along with ASHFORD and BEARD, she successfully sued 'Motown' for back royalties in 1989, occasionally reuniting with the pair for one-off shows. Her mid-90's autobiography revealed the full extent of her dissatisfaction with 'Motown', the revelations echoing the complaints of contemporaries groomed by the label during its golden era.

Best CD compilation: LIVE WIRE! THE SINGLES (1962-1972) (*7)

MARTHA REEVES (b.18 Jul'41) – lead vocals / **ROSALIND ASHFORD** (b. 2 Sep'43) – vocals / **ANNETTE STERLING** – vocals

	Oriole	Gordy
Sep 62. (7") (CBA 1814) <7011> **I'LL HAVE TO LET HIM GO. / MY BABY WON'T COME BACK**	–	–
Mar 63. (7") (CBA 1819) <7014> **COME AND GET THESE MEMORIES. / JEALOUS LOVER**	–	29

Jun 63. (lp; (PS 40052) <902> **COME AND GET THESE MEMORIES**
– Come and get these memories / Can't get used to losing you / Moments to remember / This is when I need you most / love like ours (don't come knocking every day) / Tears on my pillow / To think you would hurt me / Old love (let's try it again) / There he is (at my door) / I'll have to let him go / Give him up / Jealous lover / Old love (let's try it again).

	Stateside	Gordy
Oct 63. (7") (SS 228) <7022> **HEAT WAVE. / A LOVE LIKE OURS**	–	4 Aug63
Nov 63. (lp) <907> **HEAT WAVE**	–	

– Heat wave / The he kissed me / Hey there lonely boy / More / Dance shoes / If I had a hammer / Hell stranger / Just one look / Wait till my Bobby gets home / My boyfriend's back / Mockingbird / Quicksand. (UK-iss.Mar65 on 'Tamla Motown'; TML 11005) (re-iss. Oct81)

Jan 64. (7") (SS 250) <7025> **QUICKSAND. / DARLING I HUM YOUR SONG**		8 Nov63

BETTY KELLY (b.16 Sep'44) – vocals; repl. STERLING

Apr 64. (7") (SS 272) <7027> **LIVE WIRE. / OLD LOVE (LET'S TRY IT AGAIN)**		42 Feb64
Jun 64. (7") (SS 305) <7031> **IN MY LONELY ROOM. / A TEAR FOR THE GIRL**		44 Apr64
Oct 64. (7") (SS 345) <7033> **DANCING IN THE STREET. / THERE HE IS (AT MY DOOR)**	28	2 Aug64
Jan 65. (7") (SS 383) <7036> **WILD ONE. / DANCING SLOW**		34 Dec64

	Tamla Motown	Gordy
Mar 65. (7") (TMG 502) <7039> **NOWHERE TO RUN. / MOTORING**	26	8 Feb65
Aug 65. (7") (TMG 530) <7045> **YOU'VE BEEN IN LOVE TOO LONG. / LOVE (MAKES ME DO FOOLISH THINGS)**		36 70
Sep 65. (lp) (TML 11013) <915> **DANCE PARTY**		– Apr65

– Dancing in the street / Dancing slow / Wild one / Nowhere to run / Nobody'll care / There he is (at my door) / Mobile Lil the dancing witch / Dance party / Motoring / The jerk / Mickey's monkey / Hitch hike.

Feb 66. (7") (TMG 549) <7048> **MY BABY LOVES ME. / NEVER LEAVE YOUR BABY'S SIDE**		22 Jan66
May 66. (7") (TMG 567) <7053> **WHAT AM I GONNA DO WITHOUT YOUR LOVE?. / GO AHEAD AND LAUGH**		71
Jun 66. (lp; mono/stereo) (TML/STML 11040) <917> **GREATEST HITS** (compilation)		50

– My baby loves me / Come and get these memories / Heatwave / Dancing in the street / Quicksand / Live wire / You've been in love too long / In my lonely room / Love (makes me do foolish things) / A love like yours / Nowhere to run / Wild one. (re-iss. Mar82) (cd-iss. Aug88)

Nov 66. (7") (TMG 582) <7056> **I'M READY FOR LOVE. / HE DOESN'T LOVE HER ANYMORE**	29	9 Oct66

Jan 67. (lp; mono/stereo) (TML/STML 11051) <920> **WATCHOUT!**
– I'm ready for love / One way out / Jimmy Mack / Let this day be / Keep it up / Happiness is guaranteed / I'll follow you / No more tear stained make-up / Go ahead and laugh / What am I going to do without your love / Tell me I'll never be alone / He don't live here anymore.

Mar 67. (7") (TMG 599) <7058> **JIMMY MACK. / THIRD FINGER, LEFT HAND**	21	10 Feb67

(re-entered UK chart Aug70, again hit No.21) (re-iss. Mar80)

Aug 67. (7") (TMG 621) <7062> **LOVE BUG LEAVE MY HEART ALONE. / ONE WAY OUT**		25
Sep 67. (lp) <925> **MARTHA & THE VANDELLAS LIVE!** (live)	–	

– Introduction – I'm ready for love / Love bug leave my heart alone / For once in my life / Love is like a heatwave / Nowhere to run / My baby loves me / I found a love / Jimmy Mack / You've been in love too long / Love (makes me do foolish things) / Do right woman / Respect / Medley: Dancing in the street – I can't help myself (sugar pie, honey bunch) – Sweet soul music – Uptight (everything's alright).

MARTHA REEVES & THE VANDELLAS

Jan 68. (7") (TMG 636) <7067> **HONEY CHILE. / SHOW ME THE WAY**	30	11 Nov67

LOIS REEVES (MARTHA's younger sister) – vocals (ex-ORLONS) repl. BETTY

Apr 68. (7") (TMG 657) <7070> **I PROMISE TO WAIT, MY LOVE. / FORGET ME NOT**		62 / 93

May 68. (lp; mono/stereo) (TML/STML 11078) <926> **RIDIN' HIGH**
– I promise to wait my love / Honey chile / (There's) Always something there to remind me / Leave it in the hands of love / Love bug leave my heart alone / I'm in love (and I know it) / To sir, with love / Forget me not / (We've got) Honey love / I say a little prayer / Without you / Show me the way.

Aug 68. (7") (TMG 669) <7075> **I CAN'T DANCE TO THAT MUSIC YOU'RE PLAYIN'. / I TRIED**		42
Oct 68. (7") <7080> **SWEET DARLIN'. / WITHOUT YOU**	–	80
Jan 69. (7") (TMG 684) **DANCING IN THE STREET. / QUICKSAND**	4	
Mar 69. (7") (TMG 694) **NOWHERE TO RUN. / LIVE WIRE**	42	–
Apr 69. (7") <7085> **(WE'VE GOT) HONEY LOVE. / I'M IN LOVE AND I KNOW IT)**	–	56

Feb 70. (lp; mono/stereo) (TML/STML 11134) <944> **SUGAR N' SPICE**
– Taking my love (and leaving me) / Shoe leather expressway / You're the loser now / I'm a winner / What now my love / Soul appeal / Loneliness is a lonely feelin' / I love the man / It ain't like that // I can't get along without you / Heartless / I hope that you have better luck than I did.

Oct 70. (7") <7103> **I'VE GOTTA LET YOU GO. / YOU'RE THE LOVER NOW**	–	93

(1971) SANDRA TILLEY – vocals (ex-VELVELETTES) repl. ASHFORD

Jan 71. (7") (TMG 762) **FORGET ME NOT (remix). / I GOTTA LET YOU GO**	11	–
Oct 71. (7") (TMG 794) <7110> **BLESS YOU. / HOP I DON'T GET MY HEART BROKEN**	33	53
Feb 72. (7") <7113> **YOUR LOVE MAKES IT ALL WORTHWHILE. / IN AND OUT OF MY LIFE**		

Mar 72. (lp) (STML 11204) <958> **BLACK MAGIC**
– No one there / Your love makes it worthwhile / Something / Benjamin / Tear it on down / The best years of my life I've been givin' you / Bless you / I want you back / In and out of my life / Anyone who had a heart / Hope I don't get my heart broke.

May 72. (7") <7118> **I WANT YOU BACK. / TEAR IT ALL DOWN**		
Nov 72. (7") <7127> **BABY DON'T LEAVE ME. / I WON'T BE THE FOOL I'VE BEEN AGAIN**		

they again broke-up (Dec'72) after farewell concert. LOIS joined QUIET ELEGANCE

MARTHA REEVES

went solo after initially providing songs with JJ JOHNSON on the 1973 film soundtrack 'WILLIE DYNAMITE' for 'M.C.A'.

	Tamla Motown	Gordy
Feb 73. (7") (TMG 843) **NO ONE THERE. / THE BEST YEARS OF MY LIFE**		

	M.C.A.	M.C.A.
Mar 74. (7") (MCA 125) <40194> **POWER OF LOVE. / STAND BY ME**		76
Jul 74. (lp) <(MUPS 7427)> **POWER OF LOVE**		Feb74

– Wild night / You've got me for company / Fascimile / Ain't that peculiar / Dixie highway / Power of love / My man (you changed my tune) / Sweet misery / I've got to use my imagination / Storm in my soul / Many rivers to cross.

Jul 74. (7") (MCA 148) **WILD NIGHT. / MY MAN (YOU CHANGED MY TUNE)**		–
Jul 74. (7") <40274> **WILD NIGHT. / STAND BY ME**		
Oct 74. (7") <40329> **MY MAN (YOU CHANGED MY TUNE). / FACSIMILIE**		
May 75. (7") (MCA 190) **I'VE GOT TO USE MY IMAGINATION. / YOU'VE GOT ME FOR COMPANY**		

	Arista	Arista
Oct 76. (7") <0124> **LOVE BLIND. / THIS TIME I'LL BE SWEETER**		
Dec 76. (7") (ARIST 36) <0160> **YOUR LOVE KEEPS LIFTING ME HIGHER AND HIGHER. / NOW THAT WE FOUND LOVE**		
Dec 76. (lp) (SPARTY 1030) <AL 4105> **THE REST OF MY LIFE**		

– This time I'll be sweeter / Love blind / Second chance / Love strong enough to move mountains / (Your love keeps lifting me) Higher and higher / Now that we found love.

Feb 77. (7") <0211> **THE REST OF MY LIFE. / THANK YOU**	–	
May 77. (7") <0228> **YOU'VE LOST THAT LOVIN' FELIN'. / NOW THAT WE FOUND LOVE**	–	

on 1st July '78, MARTHA & THE VANDELLAS re-united for a Will Geer (actor) benefit gig; MARTHA will retire from music business after below

	Fantasy	Fantasy
Jul 78. (7") <825> **YOU'RE LIKE SUNSHINE. / LOVE DON'T COME NO STRONGER**		
Jul 78. (lp) <(FT 544)> **WE MEET AGAIN**		

– Free again / You're like sunshine / I feel like magic / One line from every love song / Love don't come no stronger / What are you doing the rest of your life / Dedicated to your woman / Special to me.

Nov 78. (7") <868> **DANCING IN THE STREETS (SKATING IN THE STREETS). / WHEN YOU CAME**	–	
Feb 79. (7") <887> **THAT'S WHAT I WANT. / REALLY LIKE YOUR RAP**	–	

– compilations, etc. –

on ~'Tamla Motown' until mentioned otherwise

1973. (lp) **GREATEST HITS VOL.2**		
Sep 76. (7") (TMG 1051) **DANCING IN THE STREET. / JIMMY MACK**		
Jun 77. (lp) **ANTHOLOGY**		

(re-iss. Sep82 lp/c; STMR/CSTMR 9017)

Jan 80. (7") (TMG 1176) **DANCING IN THE STREET. / HEAT WAVE**		

(re-iss. Oct81 & Jun83; TMG 1176)

Feb 83. (7") (TMG 983) **FORGET ME NOT. / I'M READY FOR LOVE**		–
May 83. (c-ep) (CTME 2028) **FLIP HITS**	–	

– Dancing in the street / Forget me not / Jimmy Mack / I'm ready for love.

Mar 87. (cd) (ZD 72447) **COMPACT COMMAND PERFORMANCES – 24 GREATEST HITS**		

– Come and get these memories / (Love is like a) Heat wave / A love like yours (don't come knocking everyday) / Quicksand / Live wire / In my lonely room / Dancing in the street / Wild one / Motoring / Nowhere to run / You've been in love too long / Love (makes me do foolish things) / My baby loves me / I'm ready for love / Jimmy Mack / Third finger left hand / Love bug / Leave my heart alone / Honey chile / I promise to wait my love / I can't dance to that music you're playin' / Sweet darlin' / (We've got) Honey love / I gotta let you go / Bless you. (re-iss. Nov92)

Mar 87. (7") Creole; (SR 99) **JIMMY MACK. / DANCING IN THE STREET**		–

(12"+=) (CRT 99) – Medley / My guy.

Apr 88. (7") (ZB 41921) **NOWHERE TO RUN. / FORGET ME NOT**		–

Jul 88.	(7") A&M; (AM 444) <3022> **NOWHERE TO RUN. / James Brown: I GOT YOU (I FEEL GOOD)**	52
Jan 92.	(c) (530040-4) **24 GREATEST HITS**	
Apr 92.	(12") Motor City; **ANGEL IN DISGUISE. /**	-
Jul 93.	(cd) Southbound; (CDSEWD 083) **WE MEET AGAIN / GOTTA KEEP MOVING**	
Jul 93.	(7"/c-s) **DANCING IN THE STREET. / I CAN'T DANCE TO THE MUSIC YOU'RE PLAYIN'**	-
	(cd-s+=) – My baby loves me / Motoring.	
Aug 93.	(cd/c) **DANCING IN THE STREETS – THE GREATEST HITS**	
Jul 94.	(cd/c) Success; **DANCING IN THE STREET**	-
Jul 96.	(cd) Spectrum; (552117-2) **MOTOWN EARLY CLASSICS**	-
Oct 96.	(cd/c) Hallmark; (30544-2/-4) **DANCING IN THE STREET**	-
Sep 97.	(cd) See For Miles; (SEECD 486) **MARTHA REEVES**	
Aug 98.	(cd) (530858-2) **THE ULTIMATE COLLECTION**	

John MARTYN

Born: 28 Jun'48, Glasgow, Scotland. Having learned guitar techniques from folk singer HAMISH IMLACH, MARTYN moved to London in 1967 after being the first white solo artist to secure a deal with Chris Blackwell's 'Island' label. His early albums, 'LONDON CONVERSATION' (1968) and 'THE TUMBLER' (1968) were competent folk sets, the latter revealing the first glimmers of MARTYN's nascent jazz/blues leanings, employing the services of respected flautist HAROLD McNAIR. Following MARTYN's marriage to Coventry girl, BEVERLEY KUTNER, the pair began recording together in 1969, releasing two albums, 'STORMBRINGER' and 'THE ROAD TO RUIN' the following year. The latter set was the first of many MARTYN albums to feature the double bass work of friend (and then PENTANGLE member) DANNY THOMPSON, the only musical collaborator who would become a fairly permanent fixture in the singer's career. Following the birth of the MARTYN's second child in 1971, JOHN resumed his solo career with 'BLESS THE WEATHER'. His most heavily jazz-influenced set to date, the record was a blueprint for much of MARTYN's subsequent work; here were the first signs of the singer's trademark lounge lizard slur (a defiantly unique hybrid of ERIC CLAPTON, LOWELL GEROGE and TOM WAITS) with which he'd dextrously negotiate the grey area where jazz, blues, folk and rock meet. With RICHARD THOMPSON on additional guitar (he also played on 'BLESS..') and a rhythm section courtesy of FAIRPORT CONVENTION (bassist DAVE PEGG and drummer DAVE MATTACKS), 'SOLID AIR' (1973) was the pivotal early MARTYN album. Pioneering use of acoustic guitar echo lent the album a uniquely haunting quality, the set featuring some of MARTYN's most affecting material. The title track was a drifting, twilight tribute to NICK DRAKE while among the more conventional, folk-ish numbers, 'OVER THE HILL' and lovely 'MAY YOU NEVER' (later covered by ERIC CLAPTON on his 'Slowhand' album) were soul stirring highlights. The album considerably widened his large cult following which numbered musicians like STEVE WINWOOD, a collaborator on the follow-up, 'INSIDE OUT' (1973). The record traced the same nebulous path as its predecessor, as did 'SUNDAY'S CHILD' (1975), the latter employing the services of the late PAUL KOSSOFF (ex-FREE and latterly BACKSTREET CRAWLER). In the two year gap prior to his next studio project, MARTYN released a limited (10,000) mail-order only (from his Sussex home) live album, the acclaimed 'LIVE AT LEEDS' (1975). The speed at which the pressing sold out indicated the extent of MARTYN's fanbase. Nevertheless, the singer was yet to make an overt attempt to turn his standing into commercial success; 'ONE WORLD' (1977) was as esoteric as ever. Extending his range of influences to include dub and oblique ambience, the record was another key release in MARTYN's career featuring both the gorgeous 'COULDN'T LOVE YOU MORE' and the sly, insidious skank of 'BIG MUFF', a collaboration with Jamaican legend LEE PERRY. The ensuing three years saw MARTYN split with wife BEVERLEY, this harrowing period providing much of the impetus for 1980's 'GRACE AND DANGER'. While the album was a relatively sombre affair, the emergence of PHIL COLLINS (here contributing percussion, vocals and production) signalled a move towards a more mainstream sound. Inevitably, then, his 1981 album, 'GLORIOUS FOOL' (a political assault on newly elected US president Ronald Reagan) made the UK Top 30, the follow-up, 'WELL KEPT SECRET' (1982) reaching No.20. Since then, however, he's failed to consolidate this brief flurry of chart action, conceivably because MARTYN's albums rarely include any glaring hit singles. Though the 80's were a fairly fallow period for MARTYN, he returned in fine style at the turn of the decade with 'THE APPRENTICE' (1990) and the sophisti-jazz of 'COOLTIDE' (1991). The latter set surfaced on 'Permanent' for whom he'd revisit a batch of old material on two studio sets and a live album over the course of the early-mid 90's. A surprise move to 'Go Discs!', resulted in his first Top 40 entry of the decade with 'AND' (1996). Upon the label's demise, MARTYN joined the new 'Independiente' stable (alongside TRAVIS!) and cut a low-key covers set, 'THE CHURCH WITH ONE BELL' (1998); he subsequently used the profits generated to help him procure the church pictured on the album sleeve(!). MARTYN's body of work remains unique, a rich seam of inspiration for the uninitiated; it's just a pity his talents aren't widely acknowledged.
• **Covered:** COCAINE BLUES (trad.) / I'D RATHER BE THE DEVIL (Skip James) / JOHNNY TOO BAD (Slickers) / TIGHT CONNECTION TO MY HEART (Bob Dylan) / NEVER LET ME GO (Joe Scott) / HE'S GOT ALL THE WHISKEY (Bobby Charles) / GOD'S SONG (Randy Newman) / HOW FORTUNATE THE MAN WITH NONE (Dead Can Dance; words Bertholt Brecht) / SMALL TOWN TALK (Bobby Charles & Rick Danko) / EXCUSE

ME MISTER (Ben Harper) / STRANGE FRUIT (Billie Holiday) / THE SKY IS CRYING (Elmore James) / GLORY BOX (Portishead) / FEEL SO BAD (S. Hopkins) / DEATH DON'T HAVE NO MERCY (Reverend Gary Davis).
• **Trivia:** He has also guested on albums by CLAIRE HAMMILL, BURNING SPEAR and BACK STREET CRAWLER, to mention but a few.
Album rating: BLESS THE WEATHER (*7) / SOLID AIR (*8) / SO FAR SO GOOD (*7) / ONE WORLD (*7) / COOL TIDE (*6).

JOHN MARTYN – vocals, acoustic guitar

		Island	Warners
Oct 67.	(lp) (ILP 952) **LONDON CONVERSATION**		-
	– Fairy tale lullaby / Sandy grey / London conversation / Ballad of an elder woman / Cocaine blues / Run honey run / Back to stay / Rolling home / Who's grown up now / Golden girl / This time / Don't think twice. (re-iss. Aug91 cd/c; IMCD 134)(ICM 2074)		
—	added **HAROLD McNAIR** – flute / **PAUL WHEELER** – guitar / **DAVE MOSES** – bass		
Dec 68.	(lp) (ILPS 9091) **THE TUMBLER**		-
	– Sing a song of summer / The river / Goin' down to Memphis / The gardeners / A day at the sea / Fishin' blues / Dusty / Hello train / Winding boy / Fly on home / Knuckledy crunch and slipp ledee slee song / Seven black roses. (cd-iss. Apr94; IMCD 173)		

JOHN & BEVERLEY MARTYN

(as BEVERLEY, she recorded solo 45's) **BEVERLEY** nee KUTNER – vocals, with + **LEVON HELM** – drums (The BAND) / **PAUL HARRIS** – piano / **HARVEY BROOKS** – bass / **BIUX MUNDI + HERBIE LOVELL** – drums

Jan 70.	(7") (WIP 6076) **JOHN THE BAPTIST. / THE OCEAN**		-
Feb 70.	(lp) (ILPS 9113) <1854> **STORMBRINGER**		
	– Go out and get it / Can't get the one I want / Stormbringer / Sweet honesty / Woodstock / John the baptist / The ocean / Traffic light lady / Tomorrow time / Would you believe me. (re-iss. Aug91 cd/c; IMCD 131)(ICM 9113)		
Apr 70.	(7") **GO OUT AND GET IT. / CAN'T GET THE ONE I WANT**	-	
—	with **DANNY THOMPSON** – bass (of PENTANGLE) / **WELLS KELLY** – drums, bass + **PAUL HARRIS**		
Nov 70.	(lp) (ILPS 9133) <1882> **THE ROAD TO RUIN**		
	– Primrose hill / Parcels / Auntie aviator / New day / Give us a ring / Sorry to be so long / Tree garden / Say what you can / The road to ruin. (cd-iss. Mar93; IMCD 165)		

JOHN MARTYN

went solo again, with **DANNY THOMPSON** – double bass / **RICHARD THOMPSON** – guitar (solo artist) / **TONY REEVES –** (of COLOSSEUM) / **IAN WHITEMAN** and **ROGER POWELL** (of MIGHTY BABY)

		Island	Island
Nov 71.	(lp) (ILPS 9167) <9311> **BLESS THE WEATHER**		
	– Go easy / Bless the weather / Sugar lump / Walk to the water / Just now / Head and heart / Let the good times come / Back down the river / Glistening Glyndebourne / Singing in the rain. (re-iss. Aug91 cd/c; IMCD 135)(ICM 9167)		
—	retained **DANNY, RICHARD** and brought in **JOHN 'RABBIT' BUNDRICK** – keyboards / **DAVE PEGG** – bass / **DAVE MATTACKS** – drums / and **SPEEDY** (NEEMOI ACQUAYE) – congas / (all of FAIRPORT CONVENTION).		
Nov 72.	(7") (WIP 6116) **MAY YOU NEVER. / JUST NOW**		
Feb 73.	(lp) (ILPS 9226) <9325> **SOLID AIR**		
	– Over the hill / Don't want to know / I'd rather be with the Devil / Go down easy / Dreams by the sea / May you never / The man in the station / Easy blues / Solid air. (re-iss. Nov86 lp/c; ILPM/ICM 9226) (cd-iss. Feb87; CID 9226)		
Mar 73.	(7") **MAY YOU NEVER. / DON'T WANT TO KNOW ABOUT EVIL**	-	
—	retained **DANNY,** and brought in **BOBBY KEYES** and **REMI KABAKA** plus **STEVE WINWOOD** and **CHRIS WOOD** (both of TRAFFIC)		
Oct 73.	(lp) (ILPS 9253) <9335> **INSIDE OUT**		
	– Fine lines / Eibhli ghail ghiuin ni chearbhaill / Ain't no saint / Outside in / The glory of love / Look in / Beverley / Make no mistake / Ways to cry / So much in love with you. (cd-iss. Apr94; IMCD 172)		
—	with **DANNY THOMPSON** / **JOHN STEVENS** – drums / **PAUL KOSSOFF** – guitar (ex-FREE) and guests **BEVERLEY MARTYN** – vocals		
Jan 75.	(lp) (ILPS 9296) <9396> **SUNDAY'S CHILD**		
	– One day without you / Lay it all down / Root love / My baby girl / Sunday's child / Spencer the rover / Clutches / The message / Satisfied mind / You can discover / Call me crazy. (cd-iss. Mar93; IMCD 163)		
Sep 75.	(lp; ltd-mail order) (ILPS 9343) **LIVE AT LEEDS** (live)	-	-
	– Outside in / Solid air / Make no mistake / Bless the weather / The man in the station / I'd rather be the Devil. (re-iss. Jun87 on 'Cacophony'; SKELP 001) (cd-iss. May92 on 'Awareness'; AWCD 1036) (re-iss. cd Jul95 on 'Hypertension'; HYCD 200114) (cd re-iss. Aug98 on 'Blueprint'; OW 107CD)		
Feb 77.	(7") (WIP 6385) **OVER THE HILL. / HEAD AND HEART**		-
Mar 77.	(lp) (ILPS 9484) <9484> **SO FAR SO GOOD** (compilation)		
	– May you never / Bless the weather / Head and heart / Over the hill / Spencer the rover / Glistening Glyndebourne / Solid air / One day without you / I'd rather be the Devil.		
—	with guests **STEVE WINWOOD** – keyboards / **MORRIS PERT** – percussion.		
Nov 77.	(lp/c) (ILPS/ZCI 9492) **ONE WORLD**	54	-
	– Couldn't love you more / Certain surprise / Dancing / Small hours / Dealer / One world / Smiling stranger / Big Muff. (re-iss. Sep86 lp/c/cd; ILPM/ICM/CID 9492)		
Jan 78.	(7") (WIP 6414) **DANCING. / DEALER** (version)		
—	with **PHIL COLLINS** – drums,vocals / **JOHN GIBLIN** – bass (both of BRAND X) / **TOMMY EYRE** – keyboards (GREASE BAND) / **DAVE LAWSON** – keyboards (ex-GREENSLADE).		
		Island	Atlantic
Oct 80.	(lp/c) (ILPS/ICT 9560) **GRACE AND DANGER**	54	
	– Some people are crazy / Grace and danger / Lookin' on / Johnny too bad / Sweet little mystery / Hurt in your heart / Baby please come home / Save some for me / Our love. (cd-iss. May87; CID 9560)		
Oct 80.	(7") (WIP 6495) **JOHNNY TOO BAD. / ('A'instrumental)**		

Mar 81. (7") *(WIP 6547)* **JOHNNY TOO BAD. /** ('A' version)
(12") *(IPR 2046)* – ('A'ext. dub version) / Big Muff (ext.mix). — | -

May 81. (7") *(WIP 6718)* **SWEET LITTLE MYSTERY. / JOHNNY TOO BAD** — | —

—— with **PHIL COLLINS** – drums, vocals, producer / **ALAN THOMSON** – bass / **MAX MIDDLETON** – keyboards / **DANNY CUMMINGS** – percussion / **DICK CUTHELL** – horns 2.

	WEA	Duke
Aug 81. (7") *(K 79243)* **PLEASE FALL IN LOVE WITH ME. / DON'T YOU GO**		
Sep 81. (lp/c) *(K/K4 99178)* **GLORIOUS FOOL**	25	

  – Couldn't love you more / Amsterdam / Hold on my heart / Perfect hustler / Hearts and keys / Glorious fool / Never say never / Oascanel (get back home) / Didn't do that / Please fall in love with me / Don't you go.

Feb 82. (7") **COULDN'T LOVE YOU MORE. /** — | —

—— with **DANNY** and **ALAN** plus **JEFFREY ALLEN** – drums / **JIM PRIME** – keyboards / **MEL COLLINS** – sax / **MARTIN DROVER** – trumpet / **LEE KOSMIN** and **STEVE LANGE** – harmony.

Aug 82. (lp/c) *(K/K4 99255)* **WELL KEPT SECRET** | 20 |
  – Could've been me / You might need a man / Hung up / Gun money / Never let me go / Love up / Changes her mind / Hiss on the tape / Back with a vengeance / Livin' alone.

Sep 82. (7") *(K 79336)* **HISS ON THE TAPE. / LIVIN' ALONE** — | —

Nov 82. (7") *(259987-7)* **GUN MONEY (US remix). / HISS ON THE TAPE (live)** — | —

—— touring line-up **ALAN THOMSON** – bass / **JEFFREY ALLEN** – drums / **DANNY CUMMINGS** – percussion / **RONNIE LEAHY** – keyboards

	Body Swerve	not iss.
Nov 83. (lp) *(JMLP 001)* **PHILENTHROPY (live)**		-

  – Sunday's child / Don't want to know / Johnny too bad / Make no mistake / Root love / Lookin' on / Hung up / Smiling stranger. (re-iss. Mar86 on 'Dojo' lp/c/cd; *DOJO LP/TC/CD 26*)

—— **MARTYN** retained **JIM** and **ALAN** plus **BARRY REYNOLDS** add. guitar / **JACK WALDMAN** – keyboards / **ROBIN RANKIN** – keyboards / **JAMES HOOKER** – keyboards / **STEVEN STANLEY** – linn drums / **ANDY LYDEN** – linn drums / **UZZIAH 'STICKY' THOMPSON** – percussion / **COLIN TULLY** – saxophone / harmony by **MORWENNE LAIDLAW, TERRY NELSON** and **LORNA BROOKS**

	Island	Island
Oct 84. (7") *(IS 209)* **OVER THE RAINBOW. / ROPE SOUL'D**		
Nov 84. (lp/c) *(ILPS/ICT 9779)* **SAPPHIRE**	57	

  – Sapphire / Over the rainbow / You know / Watching her eyes / Fisherman's dream / Acid rain / Mad dog days / Climb the walls / Coming in on time / Rope soul'd. (cd-iss. Mar93; *IMCD 164*)

—— with **ALAN THOMSON** – fretless bass / **DANNY CUMMINGS** – percussion / **COLIN TULLY and FOSTER PATTERSON** – keyboards, vocals.

Feb 86. (lp/c/cd) *(ILPS/ICT/CID 9807)* **PIECE BY PIECE** | 28 |
  – Nightline / Lonely love / Angeline / One step too far / Piece by piece / Serendipity / Who believes in angels / Love of mine / John Wayne. (cd+=) – Tight connection to my heart / Solid air / One world / May you never.

Feb 86. (7") *(IS 265)* **ANGELINE. / TIGHT CONNECTION TO MY HEART** — | —
(12"+=) *(12IS 265)* – May you never / Certain surprise / One day without you.
(cd-ep+=) *(CID 265)* – May you never / Solid air / Glistening Glyndebourne.

May 86. (7") *(IS 272)* **LONELY LOVE. / SWEET LITTLE MYSTERY (live)** — | —
(12"+=) *(12IS 272)* – Fisherman's dream (live).

—— **DAVID BALL** – bass repl. THOMPSON / added **ARRAN AHMUN** – drums + **JEFF CASTLE** – keyboards

Oct 87. (lp/c/cd) *(ILPS/ICT/CID 9884)* **FOUNDATIONS (live)** — | —
  – Mad dog days / Angeline / The apprentice / May you never / Deny this love / Send me one line / John Wayne / Johnny too bad / Over the rainbow. (re-iss. cd Apr94; *IMCD 180*)

	Permanent	not iss.
Mar 90. (cd/c/lp) *(PERM CD/MC/LP 1)* **THE APPRENTICE**		-

  – Live on love / Look at that gun / Send me one line / Hold me / The apprentice / The river / Income town / Deny this love / UPO / Patterns in the rain. (cd+=) – The moment. (cd re-iss. Apr98 on 'Indelible'; *INDELCD 1*)

Aug 90. (7") *(PERM S12)* **DENY THIS LOVE (remix). / THE APPRENTICE (live)** — | —
(cd-s+=) *(CDPERM 1)* – ('A'-lp version).

Nov 91. (cd/c/lp) *(PERM CD/MC/LP 4)* **COOLTIDE** — | —
  – Hole in the rain / Annie says / Jack the lad / Number nine / The cure / Same difference / Father Time / Call me / Cooltide.

Apr 92. (cd-s) *(CDPERM 3)* **JACK THE LAD / ?** — | —

Sep 92. (7") *(PERM 6)* **SWEET LITTLE MYSTERY. / HEAD AND HEART** — | —
(12"+=/cd-s+=) *(12/CD PERM 6)* – Never let me go.

Oct 92. (cd/c/lp) *(PERM CD/MC/LP 9)* **COULDN'T LOVE YOU MORE** | 65 |
  – Lonely love / Couldn't love you more / Sweet little mystery / Head & heart / Could've been me / One day without you / Over the hill / Fine lines / May you never / One world / Ways to cry / Angeline / Man in the station / Solid air / Never let me go.

Jan 93. (cd-s) **LONELY LOVE / ?** — | —

—— with on next album **SPENCER COZENS** or **CHRIS CAMERON** – keyboards / **GERRY CONWAY** or **WAYNE STEWART** – drums / **ALAN THOMSON** or **JOHN GIBLIN** – bass / **MILES BOULD** or **MARK WALKER** – percussion / **DAVE GILMOUR** or **ALAN DARBY** or **BILL RUPERT** – guitar / **ANDY SHEPHERD** or **GERRY UNDERWOOD** – sax / **FRED NELSON** – piano / **LEVON HELM** – guest / and of course **PHIL COLLINS** – b.vocals, etc.

Jul 93. (cd/c) *(PERM CD/MC 14)* **NO LITTLE BOY** (old songs re-worked) — | -
  – Solid air / Ways to cry / Could've been me / I don't wanna know / Just now / One day without you / Sweet little mystery / Pascanel / Sunday's child / Head and heart / Fine lines / Bless the weather / Man in the station / One world / Rock salt and nails / Hole in the rain.

Jul 95. (d-cd/d-c) *(PERM CD/MC 33)* **LIVE AT THE SHAW THEATRE (live)** — | -

—— with **PHIL COLLINS, JOHN GIBLIN + ALAN THOMPSON, JERRY UNDERWOOD, SPENCER COZENS**, etc

	Go! Discs	unknown
Aug 96. (cd/d) *(828 798-2/-4)* **AND.**	32	

  – Sunshine's better / Suzanne / The downward pull of human nature / All in your favour / A little strange / Who are they? / Step it up / Carmine / She's a lover.

—— now with **GIBLIN, COZENS / + ARRAN AHMUN** – drums, percussion

	Blueprint	not iss.
Dec 97. (cd-ep) *(BP 276CD)* **SNOOO . . . / SHE'S A LOVER / ALL IN YOUR FAVOUR / STEP IT UP / A LITTLE STRANGE**		-

	Independiente	unknown
Mar 98. (cd) *(ISOM 3CD)* **THE CHURCH WITH ONE BELL**	51	

  – He's got all the whiskey / God's song / How fortunate the man with none / Small town talk / Excuse me mister / Strange fruit / The sky is crying / Glory box / Feel so sad / Death don't have no mercy.

Jun 98. (cd-s) *(ISOM 14MS)* **EXCUSE ME MISTER / GOD'S SONG (live) / ROCK, SALT AND NAIL (live) / JOHN WAYNE (live)** — | -

– compilations, etc. –

on 'Island' unless otherwise mentioned

Oct 82. (lp/c) *(ILPS/ICT 9715)* **THE ELECTRIC JOHN MARTYN** (cd-iss. Apr88; *CID 9715*) | | |

May 92. (cd) *Windsong; (WINCD 012)* **BBC RADIO 1 LIVE IN CONCERT (live)** | | - |

Nov 92. (d-cd) *(ITSCD 2)* **SOLID AIR / ONE WORLD** | | - |

Jun 94. (d-cd) *(CRNCD 4)* **SWEET LITTLE MYSTERIES – THE ISLAND ANTHOLOGY** | | - |

Mar 98. (cd) *Artful; (ARTFULCD 13)* **THE REST OF THE BEST** | | - |

J. MASCIS (see under ⇒ **DINOSAUR JR**)

Dave MASON (dig out; 4th edition)

Nick MASON (see under ⇒ **PINK FLOYD**)

MASSIVE ATTACK

Formed: Bristol, England . . . 1987 by 3-D, MUSHROOM and DADDY G. Having founded their own label, 'Wild Bunch' (named after the loose Bristol collective of DJ's, producers and musicians of which MASSIVE ATTACK were an integral part) five years earlier, they were subsequently snapped up by Virgin subsidiary, 'Circa' in 1990 and with only their second single, 'UNFINISHED SYMPATHY' – released under the revised moniker of MASSIVE (to distance themselves from any affiliation with the UN Gulf War policy) – crashed into the Top 20. Featuring the velvet tones of SHARA NELSON and luxuriant string arrangements to die for, this hypnotically beautiful track is oft cited as one of the most perfect singles ever crafted. While not boasting anything quite as tantalising, the classic debut album, 'BLUE LINES', hit the the Top 20 in Spring '91, a darkly sensual, spliff-heavy cocktail of sampladelic dub, hip-hop, funk and soul that can quite possibly lay claim to be the Big Daddy of that much-maligned genre, trip-hop. Alongside the aforementioned NELSON, the record featured guest vocalists, TRICKY (soon to carve out his own career in paranoid beats) and dub reggae veteran, HORACE ANDY. NELSON subsequently departed for a solo career and all was quiet from the MASSIVE' camp until the Autumn of '94, when they re-surfaced with the NELLEE HOOPER (Soul II Soul)-produced 'PROTECTION' album. An even darker, slinkier creature, it featured an array of guest vocalists, most effectively employing TRACY THORN on the aching 'BETTER THINGS' and the title track; TRICKY, meanwhile, sounded almost catatonic on the spellbinding voodoo bass-psyche of 'KARMACOMA' while the exotic tones of NICOLETTE graced a couple of tracks. More cohesive soundwise, the record was characterised by a haunting dub-reggae feel and while it was perhaps pushing it a bit to revamp a Doors track ('LIGHT MY FIRE'), the claustrophobic brilliance of 'SPYING GLASS' (featuring HORACE ANDY in peerless form) more than made up for it. London dub producer, The MAD PROFESSOR, later gave it a bowel quaking, full-on dub reworking early in '95, the results surfacing as the mind scrambling 'NO PROTECTION'. Stunningly original and defiantly self-sufficient, MASSIVE ATTACK continue to shrug off any labels hopeful journos may pin on them (and woe betide anyone who mentions tr*p h*p), and while their perfectionism means lengthy periods between new material, fans have learned to be patient. In the summer of '97, the trio returned with their darkest, scariest track to date, 'RISINGSON', a solitary taster for the following year's long-awaited UK chart-topper, 'MEZZANINE'. Yet again cleaning up across the critical board, MASSIVE ATTACK had created a work many regarded as the pinnacle of their career, an unflinchingly bleak, downbeat and introspective record mired in paranoia, despair and apocalytic pre-millennium tension. Nevertheless, 3-D, MUSHROOM and DADDY-G explored more musical possibilities than most bands of their ilk put together, even hooking up with LIZ FRASER (of the COCTEAU TWINS) on the track, 'TEARDROPS', subsequently a Top 10 hit. 1999 started a little painfully for the trio when MANFRED MANN threatened a lawsuit against them for the use of his song 'Tribute' on their track 'BLACK MARK'; an out of court settlement was soon agreed on. However, that was the least of their problems, MUSHROOM opting to bail out in July that year; MASSIVE ATTACK's future is obviously in jeopardy. • **Songwriters:** Group except; BE THANKFUL FOR WHAT YOU'VE GOT (William DeVaughn) /

LIGHT MY FIRE (Doors) / MAN NEXT DOOR (John Holt) / EXCHANGE (Bob Hilliard & Mort Garson). Sampled JAMES BROWN, PIECES OF A DREAM, YOUNG HOLT TRIO. • **Trivia:** Remixed PETER GABRIEL, LES NEGRESSES VERTES.

Album rating: BLUE LINES (*9) / PROTECTION (*9) / NO PROTECTION (*8; Massive Attack Vs. The Mad Professor) / MEZZANINE (*9)

3-D (b. ROBERT DEL NAJA, 21 Jan'65, Brighton, England) – vocals / **MUSHROOM** (b. ANDREW VOWLES, 10 Nov'67) – keyboards / **DADDY-G** (b. GRANT MARSHALL, 18 Dec'59) – keyboards

			Warners	Warners
Jul 88.	(12") *(MASS 001)* **ANY LOVE.** / ('A'mix)			

—— w / **SHARA NELSON** – vocals / **NELLEE HOOPER** – programmer / arranger

		Wild Bunch- Circa	Virgin
Nov 90.	(7"/c-s) *(WBR S/C 1)* **DAYDREAMING.** / ('A'instrumental)		-
	(12"+=/cd-s+=) *(WBR T/X 1)* – Any love (2).		
	(12") *(WBR TX 1)* – ('A'-luv it mix) / ('A'-Brixton bass mix) / ('A'-luv it dub).		
Feb 91.	(7"/c-s; as MASSIVE) *(WBR S/C 2)* **UNFINISHED SYMPATHY.** / ('A'-Nellee Hooper mix)	13	-
	(12"/cd-s) *(WBR T/X 2)* – ('A'side) / ('A'-Paul Oakenfold mix) / ('A'-P.O. instrumental) / ('A'instrumental).		

—— Below also featured **HORACE ANDY** – vox

Apr 91.	(cd/c/2x1"lp) *(WBR CD/MC/LP 1)* <91685> **BLUE LINES**	13		Aug91

– Safe from harm / One love / Blue lines / Be thankful for what you've got / Five man army / Unfinished sympathy / Daydreaming / Lately / Hymn of the big wheel. *(re-iss. Sep96; same; hit UK 21)*

May 91.	(7"/c-s) *(WBR S/C 3)* <96332> **SAFE FROM HARM.** / ('A'version)	25	

(cd-s+=) – ('A'-Perfecto mix).
(12") *(WBRT 3)* – ('A'-Perfecto mix) / ('A'dub mix) / ('A'instrumental).

Feb 92.	(7"ep/c-ep/12"ep/cd-ep) *(WBR S/C/T/X 4)* **MASSIVE ATTACK**	27	-

– Hymn of the big wheel / Home of the whale / Be thankful / Any love.

—— now w / **TRACY THORN** (Everything But The Girl) / **NICOLETTE** / **TRICKY** + **HORACE ANDY** – vocals. **CRAIG ARMSTRONG** – piano / **CHESTER KAMEN** – guitar / **ROB MERRIL** – drums

Sep 94.	(cd/c/lp) *(WBR CD/MC/LP 2)* <39883> **PROTECTION**	4	

– Protection / Karmacoma / Three / Weather storm / Spying glass / Better things / Eurochild / Sly / Heat miser / Light my fire (live).

Oct 94.	(c-s/cd-s) *(WBR C/X 5)* <38465> **SLY** / ('A'mix by UNDERDOG) / ('A'-Mad Professor mix) / ('A'-Tim Simenon mix)	24		Nov94

(12"s+=/cd-s+=) *(WBR T/DX 5)* – (extra-'A'mix).

Jan 95.	(cd-s; by MASSIVE ATTACK with TRACY THORN) *(WBRDX 6)* <38471> **PROTECTION** / ('A'-J.Sw!ft mix) / **THREE** (Don T's house mix)	14		Feb95

(c-s/cd-s) *(WBR C/X 6)* – (1st 2 tracks) / ('A'-Radiation for the nation mix) / ('A'-Eno mix).
(12"+=) *(WBRT 6)* – ('A'-Mad Professor mix).

Feb 95.	(cd/c/lp; as MASSIVE ATTACK VS MAD PROFESSOR) *(WBR CD/MC/LP 3)* **NO PROTECTION**	10	-

– Radiation ruling the nation (Protection) / Bumper ball dub (Karmacoma) / Trinity dub (Three) / Cool monsoon (Weather storm) / Eternal feedback (Sly) / Moving dub (Better things) / I spy (Spying glass) / Backward sucking (Heat miser).

Mar 95.	(12"ep) *(WBRT 7)* **KARMACOMA.** / ('A'-Napoli trip mix) / ('A'-Unkle mix) / **BLACKSMITH** – **DAYDREAMING**	28		Jul95

(cd-ep+=) *(WBRX 7)* – ('A'-Portishead experience mix) / ('A'-Bumper ball mix).
(c-ep++=/cd-ep++=) *(WBR C/DX 7)* – ('A'-Portishead mix).

—— next album/releases saw the addition of vocalists **HORACE ANDY, ELIZABETH FRASER, SARA JAY, ROBERT DEL NAJA** + **GRANT MARSHALL** / guitars – **ANGELO BRUSCHINI** / bass – **JOHN HARRIS, BOB LOCKE** + **WINSTON** / drums – **ANDY GANGADEEN**

Jul 97.	(12"/cd-s) *(WBR T/X 8)* **RISINGSON.** / **SUPERPREDATORS**	11	
Apr 98.	(cd/c/lp) *(WBR CD/MC/LP 4)* <45599> **MEZZANINE**	1	60	May98

– Angel / Risingson / Teardrop / Inertia creeps / Exchange / Dissolved girl / Man next door / Black milk / Mezzanine / Group four / (Exchange).
(below single featured LIZ FRAZER on vocals)

Apr 98.	(c-s) *(WBRC 9)* **TEARDROP / EURO ZERO HERO**	10	

(12"+=/cd-s+=) *(WBR T/X 9)* – ('A'mixes).

Jul 98.	(c-s) *(WBRC 10)* **ANGEL / GROUP 4**	30	

(12"+=/cd-s+=) *(WBR T/X 10)* – ('A'mixes by Blur & the Mad Professor).

Oct 98.	(d12"ep/cd-ep) *(WBR TD/DDX 11)* **INERTIA CREEPS** (mixes:- Manic Street Preachers mix / State of Bengal mix / Alpha mix / Back she comes – Inertia mixed by Mad Professor / Reflection)	-	-	-non

—— now without MUSHROOM who left mid-'99

MASTERS OF REALITY (dig out; Great Metal . . .)

---

matchbox20

Formed: Florida, USA . . . 1993 by singer/songwriter and ROB THOMAS and his army of rock-heavy cohorts, BRIAN YALE and drummer PAUL DOUCETTE. The chieftain of these south-coast rock exhibitionists, THOMAS, formed the group after dropping out of high school at the age of seventeen and performing in a number of local outfits where he met YALE and DOUCETTE. Polishing off the line-up with rhythm guitarist ADAM GAYNOR and KYLE COOK (who were both previously employees of 'Criteria recording studios' in Miami), the band subsequently recruited COLLECTIVE SOUL producer Matt Serletic and recorded several demo tapes which soon fell into the hands of 'Lava' (an offshoot of 'Atlantic'). The band issued 'YOURSELF OR SOMEONE LIKE YOU' (1996), continuing their

tour to the farthest reaches of America after the album was slandered a lame PEARL JAM rip-off by critics. It's not difficult to see why the band received this reaction: from the outset, the album displays a neat array of complex guitar solos, meaningful lyrics and soulful EDDIE VEDDER meets JOE COCKER-style vocals. 'LONG DAY' became the first single to be taken from the album and, despite its failure to attract any constructive attention, was heavily played on rotation from major American radio stations and MTV alike, carving the way for matchbox20's second and more successful single. After its release in America, 'PUSH' also began its rounds on national radio and televison, steadily climbing up the alternative/rock charts until it reached the Top Ten in the summer of 1997. The 'YOURSELF OR . . .' album was catapulted into the Billboard Top 40 after it had gone gold due to the popularity of 'PUSH'. Before the beginning of 1998, the album had gone double-platinum, with three more hit singles ('REAL WORLD', 'BACK 2 GOOD' and '3 AM') in the bag and a momentous following in Australia and Canada. More recently and significantly was ROB THOMAS moonlighting on SANTANA's 'Smooth' single (a track taken from 1999 Grammy-hit album, 'Supernatural') which also became a gigantic MTV/FM-friendly success worldwide. Meanwhile, matchbox20, were already getting set to unleash their sophomore set scheduled for the year 2000.

Album rating: YOURSELF OR SOMEONE LIKE YOU (*5)

ROB THOMAS – vocals / **KYLE COOK** – lead guitar / **ADAM GAYNOR** – rhythm guitar / **BRIAN YALE** – bass / **PAUL DOUCETTE** – drums

		Lava – Atlantic	Lava – Atlantic
Mar 98.	(7"/c-s) *(AT 0021/+C)* **PUSH.** / **TIRED**	38	
	(cd-s+=) *(AT 0021CD)* – Busted (acoustic).		
Apr 98.	(cd/c) <(7567 92721-2/-4)> **YOURSELF OR SOMEONE LIKE YOU**	50	5	Feb97

– Real world / Long day / 3 a.m. / Push / Girl like that / Back 2 good / Damn / Argue / Kody / Busted / Shame / Hang.

Jun 98.	(7"/c-s) *(AT 0034/+C)* **3 A.M.** / **PUSH** (acoustic)	64	

(cd-s+=) *(AT 0034CD)* – Shame.

Oct 98.	(7"/c-s) *(EW 773/+C)* *<radio play>* **REAL WORLD.** / **LONG DAY** (live)		38

(cd-s+=) *(EW 773CD)* – 3 a.m. (live).

Dec 98.	(-) *<radio cut>* **BACK 2 GOOD**	-	24
Jun 99.	(cd-s) *(AY 0052CD)* **REAL WORLD** /		

MATCHING MOLE (see under ⇒ WYATT, Robert)

MATERIAL (see under ⇒ LASWELL, Bill)

Dave MATTHEWS BAND

Formed: Charlottesville, Virginia, USA . . . 1991/92 by South African born MATTHEWS. A New Yorker since a very early age, the singer moved back to Johannesburg with his mother following the death of his father. Back in America, DAVE gathered together a multi-racial bunch of eclectic musicians (CARTER BEAUFORD, LEROI MOORE and FULLARTON) to back him on his 1993 self-financed debut, 'REMEMBER TWO THINGS'. A live acoustic-based jazz-tinged rock set, it caught the attention of 'R.C.A.' who he signed to later that year. The band's debut for the label, 'UNDER THE TABLE AND DREAMING' (1995), slowly but steadily scaled the US Top 20, selling three million copies in the process. The following year, MATTHEWS and Co. delivered another set of well-crafted rock tunes on 'CRASH', a record which shot straight in to No.2 with relatively little press or TV exposure (certainly none in the UK, where he is still a non-entity to this day). Of late, even a concert album, 'LIVE AT RED ROCKS' (1997), managed a similar feat, although we tentatively await its UK release.

Album rating: REMEMBER TWO THINGS (*5) / UNDER THE TABLE AND DREAMING (*8) / CRASH (*7) / LIVE AT RED ROCKS 8-15-95 (*6) / BEFORE THESE CROWDED STREETS (*6) / LIVE AT LUTHER COLLEGE (*5) / LISTENER SUPPORTED (*4)

DAVE MATTHEWS (b.1967) – vocals, acoustic guitar / **CARTER BEAUFORD** – drums, percussion, vocals / **LEROI MOORE** – saxes, vocals / **BOYD TINSLEY** – violin, vocals / **STEFAN LESSARD** – bass; repl. bassist FULLARTON

		not iss.	Bama Rags
1993.	(cd) <001> **REMEMBER TWO THINGS** (live0	-	

– Ants marching / Tripping Billies / Recently / Satellite / One sweet world / Song that Jane likes / Minarets / Seek up / I'll back you up / Christmas song. *<re-iss. 1994 cd/c; 720-2/-4>* *(re-iss. 1997 on 'R.C.A.'; 67547>*

		R.C.A.	R.C.A.
Mar 95.	(cd/c) <(7863 66449-2/-4)> **UNDER THE TABLE AND DREAMING**		11	Jul94

– The best of what's around / What would you say / Satellite / Rhyme and reason / Typical situation / Dancing Nancies / Ants marching / Lover lay down / Jimi thing / Warehouse / Pay for what you get / No.34.

Jun 96.	(7") *(74321 39483-7)* **TOO MUCH.** / **JIMI THING** (acoustic)		-

(cd-s+=) *(74321 39483-2)* – Ants marching.

Jul 96.	(cd/c) <(7863 66904-2/-4)> **CRASH**		2	May96

– So much to say / Two step / Crash into me / Too much / No.34 / Say goodbye / Drive in, drive out / Let you down / Lie in our graves / Cry freedom / Tripping billies / Proudest monkeys.

Nov 97.	(d-cd/d-c) <67587> **LIVE AT RED ROCKS 8-15-95** (live)	-	2

– Seek up / Proudest monkey / Satellite / Two step / Best of what's around / Recently / Lie in our graves / Dancing nancies / Warehouse / Tripping billies / Drive in, drive out / Lover lay down / Rhyme and reason / #36 / Ants marching / Typical situation / All along the watchtower.

May 98.	(cd) <(07863 67660-2)> **BEFORE THESE CROWDED STREETS**		1

– Pantala naga pampa / Rapunzel / Last stop / Don't drink the water / Stay (wasting time) / Halloween / Stone / Crush / Dreaming tree / Pig / Spoon.

Jan 99. (cd; by DAVE MATTHEWS & TIM REYNOLDS)
    <67755> **LIVE AT LUTHER COLLEGE** (live)   [-]   [2]
– One sweet world / #41 / Tripping billies / Jimi thing / Satellite / Crash into me / The deed is done / Lover lay down / What would you say / Minarets / Cry freedom / Dancing nancies / Typical situation / Stream / Warehouse / Christmas song / Seek up / Say goodbye / Ants marching / Little thing / Halloween / Granny / Two step.

Feb 99. (-) <*radio cut*> **CRUSH**   [-]   [75]

Nov 99. (d-cd) <67898> **LISTENER SUPPORTED**   [-]
– Intro / Pantala naga pampa / Rapunzel / Rhyme & reason / Stone / #41 / Crash into me / Jimi thing / #36 / Warehouse / Too much / True reflections / Two step / Granny / Stay / #40 / Long black veil / Don't drink the water / All along the watchtower.

Eric MATTHEWS

Born: 12 Jan'69, Gresham, Portland, Oregon, USA. A one time student of the San Francisco Conservatory classical music college, MATTHEWS' first love was trumpet although his penchant for classic orchestral pop and his decision to take up the guitar eventually led him to the thriving alternative music scene in Boston, Massachusetts. There, he hooked up with SEBADOH's LOU BARLOW and BOB FAY, with whom he cut an obscure EP in 1993 under the name of BELT BUCKLE. Subsequently finding a musical foil in Australian ex-MOLES leader, RICHARD DAVIES, MATTHEWS found an outlet for his lush arranging/instrumental talent as one-half of the acclaimed duo, The CARDINAL. Although they only lasted one album – an eponymous 1994 effort – the publicity generated helped MATTHEWS secure a solo deal with Seattle label, 'Sub Pop'. Hardly a typical signing for the former bastion of grunge, MATTHEWS surpassed all expectations with his 1995 solo debut, 'IT'S HEAVY IN HERE', a darkly luxuriant sequence of exquisitely arranged and executed orchestral pop. Showcasing a breathy, wistful vocal style that frequently brought comparisons with NICK DRAKE, MATTHEWS showed himself to be a master pop craftsman, layering trumpets, chiming guitars and melancholy string flourishes in a manner reminiscent of past masters like BRIAN WILSON, VAN DYKE PARKS and the largely unsung ROBERT KIRBY (NICK DRAKE's string arranger on his first two albums). Despite boasting a more extensive array of guest musicians, follow-up set, 'THE LATENESS OF THE HOUR' (1997) lost little of the debut's focus or sense of continuity, consolidating MATTHEWS' position as grand master of modern baroque pop for the thinking indie fan. • **Covered:** A CERTAIN KIND (Soft Machine).

Album rating: IT'S HEAVY IN HERE (*8) / THE LATENESS OF THE HOUR (*7)

ERIC MATTHEWS – on usual instruments & vocals (also conducts orchestra & produces) musicians mostly **JASON FALKNER** – guitars, bass / **STEVE HANFORD** – drums

                                             Sub Pop   Sub Pop
Nov 95. (lp/c/cd) <*SP/+MC/CD 312*> **IT'S HEAVY IN HERE**
– Fanfare / Forging plastic pain / Soul nation select them / Faith to clay / Angels for crime / Fried out broken girl / Lust takes time / Hop and tickle / Three-cornered moon / Distant mother reality / Flight and lion / Poison will pass me / Sincere sensation / Fanfare (reprise).

Feb 96. (7") <*SP 319*> **FANFARE. / LIDS, NAILS, SCREWS**
(cd-s+=) <*SPCD 319*> – A certain kind / Distant mother reality (S H mix).

—— now with **JASON FALKNER** – guitar, bass, piano, drums / **WES MATTHEWS** – guitar, bass, piano / **GREGG WILLIAMS** – drums, percussion / **TONY LASH** – drums, percussion, piano / **SPOOKEY RUBEN** – bass / plus others **DON SCHWARTZ** – bass / **ANDREW SHAW** – sax / **STEVEN HANFORD** – drums / **STEVEN MATTHEWS** – acoustic guitar

Nov 97. (lp/cd) <*SP 404/+CD*> **THE LATENESS OF THE HOUR**
– Ideas that died that day / My morning parade / Pair of cherry / To clear the air / Yes, everyone / Everything so real / Becomes dark blue / The pleasant kind / Gilded cages / dopeyness / Since the wheel free / Festival fun / No gnashing teeth.

Iain MATTHEWS

Born: IAIN MATTHEW MacDONALD, 16 Jun'46, Lincolnshire, England. In 1966, he joined London-based surf outfit, PYRAMID, who released a one-off single ('SUMMER OF LAST YEAR') for 'Deram'. MATTHEWS' career really began, however, after he joined experimental folk-rockers FAIRPORT CONVENTION in late '67. After cutting his teeth on such highly regarded albums as 'WHAT WE DID ON OUR HOLIDAYS' and 'UNHALFBRICKING', time honoured "musical differences" led to MATTHEWS going his own way in 1969. Released on 'Uni' ('Decca' in the States), his first effort was originally planned as a solo release entitled 'SOUTHERN COMFORT' although he changed his mind at the last minute and released it as a group concept, MATTHEWS' SOUTHERN COMFORT. Augmented by FAIRPORT mates RICHARD THOMPSON and ASHLEY HUTCHINGS as well as pedal steel man, GORDON HUNTLEY (who'd also play on ROD STEWART's classic 'Never A Dull Moment' album), 1970's eponymous debut album was sufficiently well received (featuring such choice cuts as the sitar-enhanced 'THOUGHTS FOR A FRIEND' and 'WHAT WE SAY') to justify the formation of a permanent line-up and a further two albums. HUNTLEY, CARL BARNWELL, MARK GRIFFITHS, ANDY LEIGH and RAY DUFFY joined MATTHEWS for the 'SECOND SPRING' (1970) and 'LATER THAT SAME YEAR' (1970) albums, a golden period that also saw the group score a surprise UK No.1 with an ethereal, country-tinged version of Joni Mitchell's 'WOODSTOCK'. MSC ranked as one of Britain's first country-rock outfits (even if their writing did have a quintessentially English folk slant),

MATTHEWS' high, understated tenor not too dissimilar to The BYRDS' ROGER McGUINN. Even so, their critical embrace wasn't entirely shared by music buyers and that one-off hit remains an isolated epitaph. As restless as ever, MATTHEWS left the group in 1971, SOUTHERN COMFORT carrying on without him for a further three albums: 'FROG CITY', 'SOUTHERN COMFORT' and 'STIR DON'T SHAKE'. Newly signed to 'Vertigo', the singer hired a cast of session players for his first couple of bonafide solo releases, 'IF YOU SAW THRO' MY EYES' (1971) and 'TIGERS WILL SURVIVE' (1972), the latter featuring an a capella version of The Crystals' 'DA DOO RON RON'. Around this time he also recorded the contract-filling 'JOURNEY FROM GOSPEL OAK' album, which was subsequently issued on the 'Mooncrest' label in summer '74. Meanwhile, MATTHEWS had formed another group, PLAINSONG (signed to 'Elektra'), who released the acclaimed 'IN SEARCH OF AMELIA EARHART' (1972) and recorded the shelved 'PLAINSONG II' before disbanding. Solo once more, he teamed up with ex-NAZZ man, TOM MOONEY and former CRAZY HORSE brothers MICHEL and RICK CURTIS, for the MIKE NESMITH-produced 'VALLEY HI' (1973) album. Yet again the record was a critical hit without troubling the charts and despite MATTHEWS' breathtakingly prolific work rate, he remained a cult figure. Through various labels and personnel he kept recording throughout the 70's, scoring another unexpected hit (US Top 20) in 1978 with 'SHAKE IT'. The single's success was overshadowed by legal hassles, however, MATTHEWS and the 'Mushroom' label involved in a half-million dollar wrangle. At the dawn of the 80's, he relocated to Seattle, USA, where he hooked up with ex-PAVLOV'S DOG man, DAVID SURKAMP. As HI-FI, the pair cut an independently released EP and album before MATTHEWS again went solo. The singer then added A&R man to his long and varied CV, working for both 'Island' and 'Windham Hill' through the mid-80's (in 1988, he released 'WALKING A CHANGING LINE' for the latter label, a collection of JULES SHEAR songs). The 90's, meanwhile, found him re-forming PLAINSONG for the 1992 Cambridge Folk Festival, resulting in a one-off album, 'DARK SIDE OF THE ROOM' (1993). Now based in Austin, Texas, MATTHEWS remains a maverick talent, the man releasing a further solo set, 'THE DARK RIDE', in 1994 as well as working with local group, HAMILTON POOL. • **Songwriters:** Self-penned, except other covers; DO RIGHT WOMAN (Aretha Franklin) / BROWN EYED GIRL (Van Morrison) / TELL ME WHY (Neil Young) / GIVE ME AN INCH (Robert Palmer) / etc.

Album rating: Matthews' Southern Comfort: MATTHEWS' SOUTHERN COMFORT (*6) / SECOND SPRING (*5) / LATER THAT SAME YEAR (*4) / THE BEST OF MATTHEWS' SOUTHERN COMFORT later compilation (*6) / Iain Matthews: IF YOU SAW THRO' MY EYES (*7) / TIGERS WILL SURVIVE (*5) / JOURNEYS FROM GOSPEL OAK (*6) / IN SEARCH OF AMELIA EARHART (*7; by Plainsong) / VALLEY HI (*7) / SOME DAYS YOU EAT THE BEAR SOME DAYS THE BEAR EATS YOU (*5) / GO FOR BROKE (*3) / HIT AND RUN (*4) / STEALIN' HOME (*5) / SIAMESE FRIENDS (*4) / DISCREET REPEAT (*4) / SPOT OF INTERFERENCE (*5) / MOODS FOR MALLARDS (*4; by Hi-Fi) / SHOOK (*3) / WALKING A CHANGING LINE (*5) / PURE & CROOKED (*5) / SKELETON KEYS (*5) / THE DARK RIDE (*4) / RETURN TO ZERO (*3; with HAMILTON POOL) / GOD LOOKED DOWN (*4)

PYRAMID

                                  Deram   not iss.
Jan 67. (7") (*DM 111*) **SUMMER OF LAST YEAR. / SUMMER EVENING**   [ ]   [-]

—— After a period (Nov67-Jan69) in FAIRPORT CONVENTION, he formed . . .

MATTHEWS' SOUTHERN COMFORT

IAIN MATTHEWS – vocals, guitar / **GORDON HUNTLEY** – pedal steel guitar / plus **RICHARD THOMPSON, GERRY CONWAY, ASHLEY HUTCHINGS, SIMON NICOL, POLL PALMER, DOLLY COLLINS**, etc

                                  Uni   Decca
Nov 69. (7") (*UNS 513*) **COLORADO SPRINGS ETERNAL. / THE STRUGGLE**   [ ]   [-]
Jan 70. (lp) (<*UNLS 108*>) **MATTHEWS' SOUTHERN COMFORT**   [ ]   [-]
– Colorado springs eternal / A commercial proposition / The castle far / Please be my friend / What we say / Dream song / Fly pigeon fly / The watch / Sweet bread / Thoughts for a friend / I've lost you / Once upon a lifetime. (re-iss. 1974 on 'MCA'; MCF 2675) <US re-iss. 1974 on 'Decca'; 75191> (cd-iss. Dec93 as 'FIRST' on 'Line'; LCCD 901261)
May 70. (7") (*UNS 521*) **THE BALLAD OF OBRAY RAMSAY. / PARTING**   [ ]   [-]
Jul 70. (7") <*32664*> **COLORADO SPRINGS ETERNAL. / THE WATCH**   [-]   [ ]

—— **MATTHEWS + HUNTLEY** were joined by **CARL BARNWELL** – guitar, vocals / **MARK GRIFFITHS** – lead guitar / **ANDY LEIGH** – bass / **RAY DUFFY** – drums / etc

Jul 70. (lp) (<*UNLS 112*>) **SECOND SPRING**   [52]
– Ballad of Obray Ramsay / Moses in the sunshine / Jinkson Johnson / Tale of the trail / Blood red roses / Even as / D'Arch Farrow / Something in the way she moves / Southern comfort. (re-iss. 1974 on 'M.C.A.'; MCF 2677) <US re-iss. 1974 on 'Decca'; 75242> (cd-iss. Dec93 on 'Line'; LCCD 901265) (cd re-iss. Jun96 on 'Beat Goes On'; BGOCD 313)
Sep 70. (7") (*UNS 526*) **WOODSTOCK. / SCION**   [1]   [-]
                                  M.C.A.   Decca
Dec 70. (lp) (*MKPS 2015*) <*75264*> **LATER THAT SAME YEAR**   [72]
– To love / And me / Tell me why / Jonah / My lady / And when she smiles (she makes the sun shine) / Mare, take me home / Sylvie / The brand new Tennessee waltz / For Melanie / Road to Ronderlin. (re-iss. 1974; MCF 2686) (cd-iss. Dec93 on 'Line'; LCCD 901264)
Feb 71. (7") <*32774*> **WOODSTOCK. / THE BALLAD OF OBRAY RAMSAY**   [-]   [22]

Jul 71. (7") <32845> **MARE, TAKE ME HOME. / BRAND NEW TENNESSEE WALTZ** — | 96
Oct 71. (7") <32874> **TELL ME WHY. / TO LOVE** — | 98

IAIN MATTHEWS

— went solo away from SOUTHERN COMFORT, they released three more albums 1971-1972 on Harvest, Columbia; 'FROG CITY', 'SOUTHERN COMFORT' & 'STIR DON'T SHAKE'.

— meanwhile, MATTHEWS brought in session people **ANDY ROBERTS** – guitar / **TIM RENWICK** – guitar / **GERRY CONWAY** – drums

	Vertigo	Vertigo

Jan 71. (7") (6059 041) <101> **HEARTS. / IF YOU SAW THRO' MY EYES**
May 71. (7") (6059 048) <102> **DESERT INN. / RENO, NEVADA**
Jun 71. (lp) (6360 034) <VEL 1002> **IF YOU SAW THRO' MY EYES**
– Desert Inn / Hearts / Never ending / Reno, Nevada / Litle known / Hinge / Southern wind / It came without warning / You couldn't lose / Morgan the pirate / If you saw thro' my eyes. *(cd-iss w/next lp; iss. Mar 93)*
Jan 72. (7") (6006 197) **DA DOO RON RON (WHEN HE WALKED ME HOME). / NEVER AGAIN**
Feb 72. (lp) (6360 056) <VEL 1010> **TIGERS WILL SURVIVE** —
– Never again / Close the door lightly when you go / House unamerican blues activity dream / Morning song / The only dancer / Tigers will survive / Midnight on the water / Right before my eyes / Da doo ron ron (when he walked me home) / Hope you know / Please be my friend.
Mar 72. (7") <103> **DA DOO RON RON (WHEN HE WALKED ME HOME). / HOUSE OF UNAMERICAN BLUES** — | 96
Mar 72. (7") (6059 081) **DEVIL IN DISGUISE / IF YOU SAW THRO' MY EYES**
Jun 72. (7") <105> **TIGERS WILL SURVIVE. / HOPE YOU KNOW** —

— Recorded solo lp 'JOURNEY FROM GOSPEL OAK', which was later issued Aug74 on 'Mooncrest' (CREST 18) (re-iss. Dec79 on 'Boulevard'; BD 3009) (re-iss. Mar91 cd/c; CREST CD/MC 004). A single from this period was also issued Jun74 'MET HER ON A PLANE'. / 'KNOWING THE GAME' (MOON 27). Also on 'Mooncrest' label was Mar77 single 'BRIDE 1945'. / 'SING ME BACK HOME' (MOON 53)

PLAINSONG

MATTHEWS with **ROB RONGA** – bass, vocals / **ANDY ROBERTS** – guitar, vocals / **DAVE RICHARDS** – keyboards, vocals

	Elektra	Elektra

Sep 72. (lp) (K 42120) **IN SEARCH OF AMELIA EARHART**
– For the second time / Yo yo man / Louise / Call the tune / Diesel on my tail / Amelia Earhart's last flight / I'll fly away / True story of Amelia Earhart / Ever the guiding light / Side roads / Raider.
Nov 72. (7") <45821> **YO YO MAN. /** — |

— They disbanded after recording shelved lp 'PLAINSONG II' (K 42136). ANDY ROBERTS went solo and issued a few lp's.

IAIN MATTHEWS

(solo again, having moved to California, USA)(same label) with **TOM MOONEY** – drums (ex-NAZZ) / **MICHAEL CURTIS** – guitar / **RICK CURTIS** – guitar (both ex-CRAZY HORSE)

	Elektra	Elektra

Sep 73. (lp) (K 42144) <EKS 75061> **VALLEY HI**
– Keep on sailing / Old man at the mill / Shady lies / These days / Leaving alone / 7 Bridges Road / Save your sorrows / What are you waiting for / Propinquity / Blue blue day. *(cd-iss. Mar97; 7559 61169-2)*
Oct 73. (7") **THESE DAYS. / SAME OLD MAN** — |
Jan 74. (7") <45871> **7 BRIDGES ROAD. / YOU FELL THROUGH MY MIND** — |

— toured the States as IAIN MATTHEWS & ANOTHER FINE MESS with **TOMMY NUNES** – guitar / **BILLY GRAHAM** – bass / **JOHN WARE** – drums / **JOEL TEPP** – harmonica

Jun 74. (lp) (K 42160) <EKS 75078> **SOME DAYS YOU EAT THE BEAR, SOME DAYS THE BEAR EATS YOU**
– I don't want to talk about it / A wailing goodbye / Keep on sailing / Tried so hard / The poor ditching boy / Do I still figure in your life / Home / Biloxi / The fault. *(cd-iss. Mar97; 7559 61168-2)*
Jun 74. (7") (K 12150) <45892> **DIRTY WORK. / WAILING GOODBYE**
Jan 76. (7") (K 12197) **I DON'T WANT TO TALK ABOUT IT. / KEEP ON SAILING**

— now with **DON WHALEY** – bass, vocals / **TRIS IMBODEN** – drums / **JAY LACY** – guitar / **DAVID BRIGGS** + **STEVE WOOD** – keyboards

	C.B.S.	Columbia

May 76. (7") (CBS 4256) <10374> **BROWN-EYED GIRL. / STEAM BOAT**
May 76. (lp) (CBS 81316) **GO FOR BROKE**
– Darkness, darkness / I'll be gone / Brown-eyed girl / Rhythm of the west / Groovin' / Lonely hunter / Steam boat / A fool like you / Just one look / When the morning comes.
Aug 76. (7") **A FOOL LIKE YOU. / I'LL BE GONE** — |

— **CHARLIE HARWOOD** – keyboards, vocals repl. BRIGGS + WOOD / **STEVEN HOOKS** – sax repl. loads of sessioners

May 77. (lp) (CBS 81936) **HIT AND RUN**
– The frame / One day without you / Times / I will not fade away / Tigers will survive / Just one look / Help to guide me (I need your help) / Shuffle / Hit and run.
Jun 77. (7") <10553> **TIMES. / TIGERS WILL SURVIVE** — |

— now w / new band **PHIL PALMER** + **BRYN HAWORTH** – guitar / **PETE WINGFIELD** – keyboards / **RICK KEMP** – bass / **JIM RUSSELL** – drums

	Rockburgh	Mushroom

Oct 78. (7") (ROCS 206) **MAN IN THE STATION. / SLIP AWAY**
Dec 78. (lp) (ROC 106) <MRS 5012> **STEALIN' HOME** | 80 | Aug78

– Give me an inch / Don't hang up your dancing shoes / King of the night / Man in the station / Let there be blues / Carefully taught / Stealin' home / Shake it / Yank and Mary / Slip away / Sail my soul.
Nov 78. (7") <7039> **SHAKE IT. / STEALIN' HOME** — | 13
Nov 78. (7") (ROCS 207) **GIVE ME AN INCH. / STEALIN' HOME** — | —
Dec 78. (7") (ROCS 208) **KING OF THE NIGHT. / LET THERE BE BLUES**
Feb 79. (7") (ROCS 210) **SHAKE IT. / SAIL MY SOUL**
Mar 79. (7") <7040> **GIVE ME AN INCH. / LET THERE BE BLUES** — | 67
May 79. (7") **SLIP AWAY. / DON'T HANG UP YOUR DANCING SHOES** —

— retained **RUSSELL** and recruited **MARK GRIFFITHS** – bass, guitar, vocals / **ROB METZGER** – guitar / **MICK WEAVER** – keyboards / **CRAIG BUHLER** – sax

Sep 79. (lp)(c) (ROC 107)(ROCC 302) **SIAMESE FRIENDS**
– You don't see me / Survival / Heatwave / Home somewhere / Crying in the night / The baby she's on the street / Hearts on the line / Anna / Lies / Runaway.
Nov 79. (7") (ROCS 214) **HEATWAVE. / YOU DON'T SEE ME**
Jan 80. (7") (ROCS 218) **CRYING IN THE NIGHT. / LIVE**
Jan 80. (7") **ANNA. / YOU DON'T SEE ME** —

— **WYNDER K. FROG** – keyboards / **DAVE WINTOUR** – bass / **BOB HENRIT** – drums repl. WEAVER, BUHLER + RUSSELL

	Rockburgh	R.S.O.

Jun 80. (lp) (2383 582) <3092> **SPOT OF INTERFERENCE**
– I survived the 70's / She may call you up tonight / I can't fade away / The hurt / Driftwood from disaster / Why am I? / No time at all / For the lonely hunter / See me / Civilisation / What do I do?. *(re-iss. Jun86 on 'Sundown'; SDLP 034)*
Jun 80. (7") (2059 255) **SHE MAY CALL YOU UP TONIGHT. / SEE ME**

— **MATTHEWS** moved to Seattle, Washington, and teamed up with **DAVID SURKAMP** (ex-PAVLOV'S DOG) to form

HI-FI

with **BRUCE HAZEN** – guitar / **GARY SHELTON** – bass, vocals / **BOB BAILEY** – drums
Apr 82. Butt; (12")(c) (FUNEP 3) **DEMONSTRATION RECORD** | —
– Savage / Heart of mine / I can't fade away / 9 o' clock / Man in a station.
Jul 83. Shanghai; (lp) (HAI 102) **MOODS FOR MALLARDS**
– Walk away / Blue shirt / Holding out for rain / Throw a line / Knocking on your door / Desire / Time after time / Alcohol / When you were mine. *(UK-iss.Aug86)*

IAIN MATTHEWS

WYNDER K.FROG – keyboards / **DAVE WINTOUR** – bass / **BOB HENRIT** – drums repl. WEAVER, BUHLER + RUSSELL
1984. (lp) (625784) **SHOOK** — | — German
– Shorting out / Views (dance goes on) / Wild places / Indiscreet / Wish / Driver / Tomorrow falls on Saturday / Fear strikes out / Over under sideways down / Room service. *(cd-iss. 1989 on 'Line'; LICD 900014)*

— In 1986, he briefly re-united with FAIRPORT CONVENTION for some gigs.

— new band:- **MARK HALLMAN** – guitar, vocals / **VAN DYKE PARKS** – piano / **PATRICK O'HEARN** – guitar, synth / **RAY NEOPOLITAN** – bass / **ELIZA GILKYSON** – vocals

	Windham Hill	Windham Hill

Apr 88. (lp/c/cd) (37 1070-1/-4/-2) **WALKING A CHANGING LINE**
– Dream sequence / Standing still / Except for a tear / Following every finger / Alive alone / On squirrel hill / Shadows break / This fabrication / Lovers by rote / Only a motion / Why fight.

	GoldCastle	GoldCastle

1990. (cd)(c)(lp) **PURE AND CROOKED**
– Like dominoes / Mercy Show / A hardly innocent mind / New shirt / Bridge of Cherokee / Busby's babes / Rains of '62 / Say no more / Perfect timing / Out of my range / This town's no lady. *(cd re-iss. Jan95 on 'Watermelon'; WMCD 1029)*

	Taxim	Taxim

1991. (cd) <(TX 2001CD)> **NIGHTS IN MANHATTAN – LIVE (live)**

	not iss.	Mesa Blue

May 93. (cd) **THE SKELETON KEYS**
– Cover girl / Jumping off the roof / Compass and chart / God's empty chair / True location of the heart / Back of the bus / Croos to bear / Ties we break / Timing / Get it back / Every crushing blow / Living in reverse.

	Watermelon	Watermelon

Sep 94. (cd) (<WMCD 1025>) **THE DARK SIDE**
– I drove / Girl with the clouds in her eyes / Ballad of Gruene Hall / Tigers will survive (part II) / The breath of life / Save her love / For better or worse / Davey's stung / Morning glory / In London / This is it / Rooted to the spot.
below trio = MATTHEWS + MICHAEL FRACASSO + MARK HALLMAN

	Watermelon	Watermelon

Apr 95. (cd; as HAMILTON POOL) (<WMCD 1031>) **RETURN TO ZERO**
– Apple pie / Imperfect angel / Shadowbox / The one that got away / Taker / Jewel / Backstreet girl / Second hand love / Eye on the road / On the inside / London girl / Evening sun / Destiny is.
Sep 96. (cd) (<WMCD 1055>) **GOD LOOKED DOWN**
– The beat I walk / God looked down / Southern wind / You'll know lightning / Alone again blues / This train / Power of blue / Eye of the needle / King of the hill / Trigger man / So many eyes / If it's not one thing, it's another.

– compilations, others, etc. –

Oct 75. (lp) M.C.A.; (MCF 2574) **THE BEST OF MATTHEWS SOUTHERN COMFORT** | —
(re-iss. Feb82; MCL 1644)
Mar 80. (d-lp) Rockburgh; (ROCD 109) **DISCREET REPEAT** | —
(cd-iss. Jan89 on 'Line'; LICD 900560)
Mar 80. (7"m) Rockburgh; (ROCS 221) **DA DOO RON RON (WHEN HE WALKED ME HOME). / SHAKE IT / GIVE ME AN INCH**
Jul 82. (7") Old Gold; (OG 9168) **WOODSTOCK. / (b-side by; Barry McGuire)** | —

Mar 87.	(c/d-lp) See For Miles; (TC+/SEE 85) **MATTHEWS SOUTHERN COMFORT MEET SOUTHERN COMFORT**	☐	-
Jun 88.	(7") Old Gold; (OG 9795) **WOODSTOCK. / (b-side by; Three Dog Night)**	☐	-
Aug 89.	(7") M.C.A.; (257456-7) **WOODSTOCK. / (other artist)** (12"+=/cd-s+=) (257 454-0/-2) – (other artist).	☐	-
Mar 92.	(d-cd) Line; (LICD 921193) **STEALIN' HOME / SIAMESE FRIENDS**	☐	-
1992.	(cd; by PLAINSONG) Taxim; (TX 2002CD) **AND THAT'S THAT**	☐	-
Nov 92.	(cd; by PLAINSONG) Band Of Joy; (BOJCD 005) **ON AIR (ORIGINAL BBC RECORDINGS FROM 1972)**	☐	-
Dec 92.	(cd) Dirty Linen; (CDL 102) **ORPHANS & OUTCASTS**	☐	-
Jul 93.	(cd) Dirty Linen; (CDL 104) **ORPHANS & OUTCASTS VOL.2; 1981-1989**	☐	-
Nov 93.	(cd) Elektra; (7559 61457-2) **THE SOUL OF MANY PLACES (THE ELEKTRA YEARS 1972-74)**	☐	-
May 94.	(cd; by MATTHEWS SOUTHERN COMFORT) Band Of Joy; (BOJCD 007) **SCION**	☐	-

PLAINSONG

re-formed by **MATTHEWS + ANDY ROBERTS** for 1992 Cambridge Folk Festival

		Line	not iss.
Dec 92.	(cd) (LICD 901247) **DARK SIDE OF THE ROOM**	☐	-
Sep 94.	(cd) (LICD 901288) **VOICE ELECTRIC**	☐	-
	– Gravy train / Unreal dreams / Where the coyotes roam / Steal that beat / The rat and the snake / Gunga Din / Christoforo's eyes / The clearances / William's canon / It's not just stars that are full.		

MAX Q (see under ⇒ INXS)

Brian MAY (see under ⇒ QUEEN)

Phil MAY & The FALLEN ANGELS (see under ⇒ PRETTY THINGS)

John MAYALL

Born: 29 Nov'33, Macclesfield, Cheshire, England. A National Service veteran from the Korean war in 1951-1955, he became a graphic artist (studying at Manchester Art College and working in an art studio attached to a local advertising agency) and picked up a taste for boogie from his trombone playing father. MAYALL started to master piano styles from boogie-woogie 78s by CRIPPLE CLARENCE LOFTON, PINETOP SMITH and others, before going on to learn the basics of harmonica and guitar. Although he initiated his first band, JOHN MAYALL's POWERHOUSE FOUR, in Manchester, he subsequently went to London at ALEXIS KORNER's request to form the BLUES SYNDICATE; this became the first of many BLUESBREAKERS featuring JOHN McVIE on bass, BERNIE WATSON on guitar and PETER WARD on drums (the latter was replaced by MARTIN HART when the band went full-time and gained a residency at the Scene, Great Windmill Street, London). Renowned for being a bit eccentric (he spent some time living in a self constructed tree-house), MAYALL was a strict bandleader and maintained an almost religious belief in blues purism. His songs were excellent pastiches of his heroes' compositions, his voice being reminiscent of OTIS RUSH, BUDDY GUY and his ultimate idol, J.B. LENOIR. Signing a short term deal with 'Decca', he released his 1965 debut album, 'JOHN MAYALL PLAYS JOHN MAYALL', a badly recorded live set which nevertheless captured the initimate atmosphere of a sweaty R&B club. One of the record's tracks (which was duly released as a single), 'CRAWLING UP A HILL', showcased MAYALL's soft voice being over-run by a distorted harmonica and Hammond organ. The best BLUESBREAKERS line-ups were those that included ERIC CLAPTON, PETER GREEN and MICK TAYLOR, all of whom left the band with greatly enhanced reputations which enabled them to command vast amounts of money. CLAPTON joined in 1965, straight from The YARDBIRDS – bringing respectability to the band as fans flocked to see the guitar hero – and virtually dominated the classic UK Top 10 'BLUESBREAKERS' (1966) set. CLAPTON departed the following year to form CREAM and was replaced by PETER GREEN (he had earlier replaced him for a one-off 3-day period), who played on 'A HARD ROAD'. GREEN excelled on the instrumentals 'THE STUMBLE' (a Freddie King number) and his own 'THE SUPERNATURAL' as well as providing soulful vocals on the likes of 'YOU DON'T LOVE ME' and 'THE SAME WAY'. GREEN eventually left in 1967, his replacement being a shy but exceptionally talented young guitarist by the name of MICK TAYLOR. Remaining with MAYALL until 1969 – before taking BRIAN JONES' slot in The ROLLING STONES – TAYLOR's tenure lasted up to and including 'BLUES FROM LAUREL CANYON' (a transatlantic Top 60 success), a period which also produced the brassier sounding 'CRUSADE' in 1967. 'DIARY OF A BAND VOLUMES 1 & 2' both hit the UK Top 30 in 1968 and featured the band's live sound from the previous year, the excellent work of KEEF HARTLEY and MICK TAYLOR a must to hear. 1968 also produced 'BARE WIRES', a record leaning towards jazz and featuring JON HISEMAN on drums and an experienced brass section of HENRY LOWTHER, CHRIS MERCER and DICK HECKSTALL-SMITH. Understandably, MAYALL became tired of running his band as a finishing school for aspiring megastars and disbanded The BLUESBREAKERS, subsequently signing to 'Polydor' and forming an

acoustic band including guitarist JON MARK and saxophonist JOHNNY ALMOND. This formation recorded the live album, 'TURNING POINT' (his biggest seller, his only gold disc and a near UK Top 10) in 1969 at the Fillmore East, featuring his best known song, 'ROOM TO MOVE' (his finest harp solo) and 'THOUGHTS ABOUT ROXANNE'. MARK and ALMOND soon moved on (after 'EMPTY ROOMS', another UK Top 10'er which included MAYALL's only US chart single, 'DON'T WASTE MY TIME') to form their own group, MARK-ALMOND, while MAYALL moved to Los Angeles and formed his own record label, 'Crusade'. 'USA UNION' with a backing band of Americans, notably, HARVEY MANDEL, DON 'SUGARCANE' HARRIS and LARRY TAYLOR was another Top 50 success, although critics rounded on the insipid lyrics. Following the double set, 'BACK TO THE ROOTS', MAYALL's work-rate declined, his output over the next few years of poor quality. The struggling bluesman signed to 'ABC/Blue Thumb' in 1975, releasing 'NEW YEAR, NEW BAND, NEW COMPANY'; for the first time, MAYALL had employed a female vocalist, DEE McKIMMIE along with future FLEETWOOD MAC guitarist RICK VITO. The album was to be his last US chart entry for 15 years; a number of albums followed although their success was limited by inadequate exposure and MAYALL stopped recording, only playing the odd local gig near his home in California. MAYALL toured Europe in 1988 to small but enthusiastic audiences, signing to 'Island' Records and releasing a belated comeback album, 'CHICAGO LINE'. The man never regained his success of the 60's, although he's now recognised as the Father Of British Blues and is still nurturing the occasional rising blues star from his now reformed and ever-changing BLUESBREAKERS (WALTER TROUT being one of the most recent). The 90's were kinder to MAYALL, 1990's 'A SENSE OF PLACE' on 'Island' (which marked his return to the US charts) and the brilliant 'WAKE UP CALL' (1993) on 'Silvertone' (UK Top 75) – with guest appearances by ALBERT COLLINS, BUDDY GUY, MICK TAYLOR and MAVIS STAPLES – being his best albums in years. • **Songwriters:** Self-penned alongside covers; MY BABY IS SWEETER (Willie Dixon) / DOUBLE TROUBLE + ALL YOUR LOVE (Otis Rush) / BERNARD JENKINS (Eric Clapton) / WHAT'D I SAY (Ray Charles) / DOUBLE CROSSIN' TIME (w/ Clapton) / DUST MY BLUES (Elmore James) / THE SUPERNATURAL (Peter Green) / SO MANY ROADS (Paul) / LOOKING BACK (Johnny Guitar Watson) / ALL MY LIFE (Robinson) / RIDIN' ON THE L & N (Barley Hampton) / IT HURTS ME TOO (London) / OH, PRETTY WOMAN (Big Joe Williams) / MAN OF STONE (Eddie Kirkland) / NIGHT TRAIN / LUCILLE (Little Richard) / PARCHMAN FARM (Mose Allison) / STEPPIN' OUT (Charles Brackeen) / etc.

Album rating: JOHN MAYALL PLAYS JOHN MAYALL (*7) / BLUESBREAKERS WITH ERIC CLAPTON (*8) / A HARD ROAD (*7) / CRUSADE (*6) / THE BLUES ALONE (*6) / THE DIARY OF A BAND VOL.1 (*5) / THE DIARY OF A BAND VOL.2 (*5) / BARE WIRES (*8) / BLUES FROM LAUREL CANYON (*6) / THE TURNING POINT (*7) / EMPTY ROOMS (*7) / LOOKING BACK compilation (*7) / U.S.A. UNION (*5) / BACK TO THE ROOTS (*5) / MEMORIES (*5) / JAZZ BLUES FUSION (*5) / MOVING ON (*5) / TEN YEARS ARE GONE (*5) / THE LATEST EDITION (*4) / NEW YEAR, NEW BAND, NEW COMPANY (*4) / TIME EXPIRED, NOTICE TO APPEAR (*4) / A BANQUET OF BLUES (*4) / LOTS OF PEOPLE (*4) / A HARD CORE PACKAGE (*4) / BOTTOM LINE (*4) / NO MORE INTERVIEWS (*4) / ROAD SHOW BLUES (*4) / BEHIND THE IRON CURTAIN (*4) / CHICAGO LINE (*4) / A SENSE OF PLACE (*7) / LONDON BLUES compilation (*7) / ROOM TO MOVE compilation (*7) / WAKE UP CALL (*7) / SPINNING COIN (*4) / BLUES FOR THE LOST DAYS (*5)

BLUESBREAKERS

JOHN MAYALL – vocals, keyboards, harmonica, guitar(ex-BLUES SYNDICATE) / **BERNIE WATSON** – guitar repl. JOHN GILBEY who had repl. SAMMY PROSSER / **JOHN McVIE** (b.26 Nov'45) – bass repl. PETE BURFORD who had repl. RICKY BROWN / **MARTIN HART** – drums repl. PETER WARD who had repl. KEITH ROBERTSON (note previous drummers early 1963 =BRIAN MYALL after SAM STONE.)

JOHN MAYALL'S BLUESBREAKERS

		Decca	not iss.
Apr 64.	(7"; as JOHN MAYALL & BLUES BREAKERS) (F 11900) **CRAWLING UP A HILL. / MR. JAMES**	☐	-
——	MAYALL retained only McVIE, and recruited **ROGER DEAN** – guitar replaced WATSON **HUGHIE FLINT** – drums (ex-BLUES SYNDICATE) repl. HART		
Feb 65.	(7"; by JOHN MAYALL) (F 12120) **CROCODILE WALK. / BLUES CITY SHAKEDOWN**	☐	-
Mar 65.	(lp; by JOHN MAYALL) (LK 4680) **JOHN MAYALL PLAYS JOHN MAYALL (live at Klook's Kleek)**	☐	-
	– Crawling up a hill / I wanna teach you everything / When I'm gone / I need your love / The hoot owl / R&B time; Night train – Lucille / Crocodile walk / What's the matter with you / Doreen / Runaway / Heartache / Chicago line. (cd-iss. Jun88 on 'London'; 820 536-2)		
——	**ERIC CLAPTON** (b.30 Mar'45, Ripley, England) – guitar, vocals (ex-YARDBIRDS) repl. DEAN		
		Immediate	Immediate
Oct 65.	(7") (IM 012) <502> **I'M YOUR WITCHDOCTOR. / TELEPHONE BLUES** (re-iss. Sep67 by JOHN MAYALL and the BLUESBREAKERS with ERIC CLAPTON; IM 051)	☐	☐
——	(a month earlier CLAPTON departed to join The GONADS.) (he was repl. by ?) **JACK BRUCE** (b.14 May'43, Lanarkshire, Scotland) – bass (ex-GRAHAM BOND ORGANISATION) repl. McVIE		
——	MAYALL's band were now FLINT, McVIE and CLAPTON again. (BRUCE joined MANFRED MANN)		

		Decca	London

Jul 66. (lp; mono/stereo; by JOHN MAYALL WITH ERIC CLAPTON) *(LK 4804) <LL3/PS 492>* **BLUES BREAKERS WITH ERIC CLAPTON** — **6** — **—**
– All your love / Hideaway / Little girl / Another man / Double crossin' time / What'd I say / Key to love / Parchman farm / Have you heard / Ramblin' on my mind; (a) Steppin' out – (b) It ain't right. *(re-iss. 1969 mono/stereo; LK/SLK 4804) <US re-iss. 1985 on 'Mobile Fidelity'; MFSL 183> (cd-iss. Feb89; 800 086-2) (re-iss. Aug90 on 'Deram' cd/lp; 800 086-2/-1)*

Sep 66. (7"; A-side solo) *(F 12490) <20016>* **PARCHMAN FARM. / KEY TO LOVE**

Nov 66. (7") *<20024>* **ALL YOUR LOVE. / HIDEAWAY** — **—** **—**

—— (Jul66) **PETER GREEN** (b. PETER GREENBAUM, 29 Oct'46) – guitar(on above b-side) repl. CLAPTON who formed CREAM

—— (Sep66) **AYNSLEY DUNBAR** – drums (ex-MOJOS) repl. FLINT who later formed McGuinness Flint

Oct 66. (7"; as JOHN MAYALL'S BLUESBREAKERS & PETER GREEN) *(F 12506)* **LOOKING BACK. / SO MANY ROADS** — — **—**

Oct 66. (7") *(F 12545)* **SITTING IN THE RAIN. / OUT OF REACH** — — **—**

Feb 67. (lp; mono/stereo) *(LK/SKL 4853) <PS 502>* **A HARD ROAD** **10** — —
– A hard road / It's over / You don't love me / The stumble / Another kinda love / Hit the highway / Leaping Christine / Dust my blues / There's always work / The same way / The super natural / Top of the hill / Someday after a while (you'll be sorry) / Living alone.

Mar 67. (7"; as BLUESBREAKERS) *(F 12588)* **CURLY. / RUBBER DUCK**

Apr 67. (7"ep) *(DFE-R 8673)* **BLUESBREAKERS WITH PAUL BUTTERFIELD**

—— **MICK FLEETWOOD** (b.24 Jun'47, Redruth, England) – drums repl. MICKEY WALLER who had repl. DUNBAR (to JEFF BECK GROUP) (others still in band MAYALL, GREEN and McVIE)

Apr 67. (7") *(F 12621)* **DOUBLE TROUBLE. / IT HURTS ME TOO**

—— added **TERRY EDMONDS** – rhythm guitar, (for Jun67 only before he joined FERRIS WHEEL) / **MICK TAYLOR** (b.17 Jan'48, Welwyn Garden City, England) – guitar, vocals (ex-GODS) repl. PETER who formed FLEETWOOD MAC / **KEEF HARTLEY** (b. 8 Mar'44, Preston, England) – drums (ex-ARTWOODS) repl. MICK who formed FLEETWOOD MAC / added **CHRIS MERCER + RIP KANT** – saxophones

Sep 67. (lp; mono/stereo) *(LK/SKL 4890) <PS 529>* **CRUSADE** **8** — —
– Oh pretty woman / Stand back baby / My time after a while / Snowy wood / Man of stone / Tears in my eyes / The death of J.B. Lenoir / I can't quit you baby / Streamline / Me and my woman / Checkin' up on my baby.

—— **MAYALL** retained **TAYLOR, HARTLEY** and **MERCER**, bringing in **PAUL WILLIAMS** – bass (ex-ZOOT MONEY) repl. McVIE who also joined FLEETWOOD MAC / **DICK HECKSTALL-SMITH** (b.26 Sep'34, Ludlow, England) – saxophone (ex-GRAHAM BOND) repl. KANT / added **HENRY LOWTHER** – trumpet

Sep 67. (7") *(F 12684)* **SUSPICIONS (part 1). / SUSPICIONS (part 2)**

Sep 67. (7") *<20035>* **SUSPICIONS. / OH PRETTY WOMAN** — **—** **—**

—— **KEITH TILLMAN** – bass repl. WILLIAMS

Dec 67. (7"; solo) *(F 12732) <20037>* **JENNY. / PICTURES ON THE WALL**

Jan 68. (lp; mono/stereo) *(LK/SKL 4918) <PS 570>* **THE DIARY OF A BAND VOL.1** (live interviews & chat) **27** **93** Feb70
– Blood on the night / (chat; Edmonton cooks Ferry Inn) / I can't quit you baby / (Keef Hartley interview x2) / Anzio Annie / (John Mayall interview x2) / Snowy wood / The lesson / My own fault / God save the queen.

Jan 68. (lp; mono/stereo) *(LK/SKL 4919) <PS 589>* **THE DIARY OF A BAND VOL.2** (live interviews & chat) <US-title 'JOHN MAYALL LIVE IN EUROPE'> **28** — Apr71
– (Gimme some lovin') / The train / Crying shame / (chat; local boy makes good) / Help me / Blues in Bb / Soul of a short fat man.

Feb 68. (7") **BROKEN WINGS. / SONNY BOY BLUE** — **—** —

—— **TONY REEVES** – bass repl. ANDY FRASER (to FREE) who had repl. TILLMAN / **JON HISEMAN** (b.21 Jun'44) – drums (ex-GRAHAM BOND, ex-GEORGIE FAME) repl. HARTLEY (to solo)

Jun 68. (lp; mono/stereo) *(LK/SKL 4945) <PS 537>* **BARE WIRES** **3** **59** —
– Where did I belong / I start walking / Open up a new door / Fire / I know now / Look in the mirror / I'm a stranger / Hartley quits / No reply / Killing time / She's too young / Sandy. *(cd-iss. Jun88 on 'London'; 820 538-2)*

Jun 68. (7") *(F 12792)* **NO REPLY. / SHE'S TOO YOUNG**

—— **MAYALL** only retained **MICK TAYLOR / COLIN ALLEN** – drums (ex-ZOOT MONEY) repl. HISEMAN who formed COLOSSEUM / **STEVE THOMPSON** – bass repl. REEVES. (he & HECKSTALL-SMITH also formed above) (also note MERCER left going into sessions and LOWTHER who joined KEEF HARLEY BAND)

Nov 68. (7") *(F 12846)* **THE BEAR. / 2401**

Dec 68. (lp; mono/stereo) *(LK/SKL 4972) <PS 545>* **BLUES FROM LAUREL CANYON** **33** **68** —
– Vacation / Walking on sunset / Laurel Canyon home / 2401 / Ready to ride / Medicine man / Somebody's acting like a child / The bear / Miss James / First time alone / Long gone midnight / Fly tomorrow. *(cd-iss. Jan88 on 'London'; 820 539-2)*

Dec 68. (7") **WALKING ON SUNSET. / LIVING ALONE** — **—** —

JOHN MAYALL

(his new band played without a drummer) **DUSTER BENNETT** – guitar, vocals repl. TAYLOR who joined ROLLING STONES / **JON MARK** (b. Cornwall, England) – guitar / **JOHNNY ALMOND** (b.20 Jul'46, Enfield, England) – saxophone repl. ALLEN who joined STONE THE CROWS / (after below lp **ALEX DMOCHOWSKI** – bass repl. THOMPSON who joined STONE THE CROWS)

		Polydor	Polydor

Oct 69. (lp; mono/stereo) *(582/583 571) <PD 4004>* **THE TURNING POINT** (live 1969) **11** **32** Sep69
– The laws must change / Saw mill gulch road / I'm gonna fight for you J.B. / So hard to share / California / Thoughts about Roxanne / California / Room to move. *(re-iss. May82 lp)(c; 2485 222)(3201 294) (cd-iss. Aug87; 823 305) (cd re-iss. Aug92 on 'Beat Goes On'; BGOCD 145)*

Oct 69. (7") *(56544) <>* **DON'T WASTE MY TIME. / DON'T PICK A FLOWER** — **81**

Jan 70. (7") **ROOM TO MOVE. / SAW MILL GULCH ROAD** — —

—— **LARRY TAYLOR** – bass deputised for the ill THOMPSON. (DMOCHOWSKI tour)

Mar 70. (lp) *(583 580) <PD 4010>* **EMPTY ROOMS** **9** **33** —
– Don't waste my time / Plan your revolution / Don't pick a flower / Something new / People cling together / Waiting for the right time / Thinking of my woman / Counting the days / When I go / Many miles apart / To a princess / Lying in my bed.

May 70. (7") *(2066 021)* **THINKING OF MY WOMAN. / PLAN YOUR REVOLUTION** — **—**

—— **MAYALL's** completely new band of US musicians **HARVEY MANDEL** (b.11 Mar'45, Detroit, Michigan) – guitar (ex-CANNED HEAT) repl. MARK who formed MARK-ALMOND / **DON 'SUGARCANE' HARRIS** – vocals (ex-FRANK ZAPPA) repl. ALMOND (as above) / **LARRY TAYLOR** – bass finally repl. DMOCHOWSKI

Dec 70. (lp) *(2425 020) <PD 4022>* **U.S.A. UNION** **50** **22** Oct70
– Nature's disappearing / You must be crazy / Night flyer / Off the road / Possessive emotions / Where did my legs go / Took the car / Crying / My pretty girl / Deep blue sea.

Jan 71. (7") **NATURE'S DISAPPEARING. / MY PRETTY GIRL** — **—** —

—— Next reunified MAYALL with nearly all old BLUESBREAKERS + new US musicians

Jun 71. (d-lp) *(2657 005) <PD 3002>* **BACK TO THE ROOTS** **31** **52** Apr71
– Prisons on the road / My children / Accidental suicide / Groupie girl / Blue fox / Home again / Television eye / Marriage madness / Looking at tomorrow / Dream with me / Full speed ahead / Mr. Censor man / Force of nature / Boogie Albert / Goodbye December / Unanswered questions / Devil's tricks / Travelling.

—— MAYALL retained only **LARRY TAYLOR** and recruited **JERRY McGEE** – guitar (ex-VENTURES) to replace MANDEL (who formed own band) and HARRIS

Nov 71. (lp) *(2425 085) <PD 5012>* **MEMORIES** — — —
– Memories / Wish I knew a woman / Back from Korea / Home in a tree / Separate ways / The fighting line / Grandad / The city / Nobody cares / Play the harp.

Feb 72. (7") **NOBODY CARES. / PLAY THE HARP** — **—** —

—— **MAYALL** and **TAYLOR** brought in a drummer! – **RON SELICO** / plus **FREDDY ROBINSON** – guitar to repl. McGEE / added **BLUE MITCHELL** – trumpet / **CLIFFORD SOLOMON** – saxophone

May 72. (lp) *(2425 103) <PD 5027>* **JAZZ-BLUES FUSION** (live) — **64**
– Country road / Mess around / Good time boogie / Change your ways / Dry throat / Exercise in c-major for harmonica, bass and shufflers / Got to be this way.

—— **VICTOR GASKIN** – bass repl. LARRY / **KEEF HARTLEY** – drums returned to repl. RON

—— added on next **CHARLES OWEN** – flute / **FRED JACKSON + ERNIE WATTS** – saxophones

Jan 73. (lp) *(2391 047) <PD 5036>* **MOVING ON** — — Oct72
– (a brief introduction by Bill Cosby) / Worried mind / Keep our country green / Christmas 71 / Things go wrong / Do it / Moving on / Red sky / Reasons / High pressure living.

Jan 73. (7") **MOVING ON. / KEEP OUR COUNTRY GREEN** — — —

Nov 73. (d-lp) *(2683 036) <PD 3005>* **TEN YEARS ARE GONE** — — Sep73
– Ten years are gone / Driving till the break of day / Drifting / Better pass you by / California campground / Undecided / Good looking stranger / I still care / Don't hang me up / (introduction) / Sitting here thinking / Harmonica free form / Burning Sun / Dark of the night.

Nov 74. (7") **GASOLINE BLUES. / BRAND NEW BAND** — **—** —

Dec 74. (lp) *(2391 141) <PD 6030>* **THE LATEST EDITION** — — —
– Gasoline blues / Perfect peace / Going to take my time / Deep down feelings / Troubled times / The pusher man / One of the few / Love song / Little kitchen / A crazy game.

Feb 75. (7") **LET ME GIVE. / PASSING THROUGH** — **—** —

—— MAYALL brought back **LARRY TAYLOR** and **SUGERCANE HARRIS** plus new members **DEE McKINNIE** – vocals / **RICK VITO** – guitar / **JAY SPELL** – keyboards / **SOKO RICHARDSON** – drums

		A.B.C.	A.B.C.

Mar 75. (lp) *(ABCL 5115) <6019>* **NEW YEAR, NEW BAND, NEW COMPANY** — — —
– Sitting on the outside / Can't get home / Step in the sun / To match the wind / Sweet Scorpio / Driving on / Taxman blues / So much to do / My train time / Respectively yours.

Apr 75. (7") **STEP IN THE SUN. / AL GOLDSTEIN BLUES** — **—** —

—— **MAYALL** now totally solo.

Nov 75. (lp) *(ABCL 5142) <ABCD 926>* **TIME EXPIRED, NOTICE TO APPEAR** — — —
– Lil boogie in the afternoon / Mess of love / That love / The boy most likely to succeed / Who's next who's now / Hail to the man who lives alone / There will be a way / Just knowing you is a pleasure / A hard day's night / Oldtime blues. *(cd-iss. Apr94 on 'M.C.A.'; MCAD 22070)*

—— His following albums feature session musicians.

Apr 76. (lp) *(ABCL 5187) <ABCD 958>* **A BANQUET OF BLUES** — — —
– Sunshine / You can't put me down / I got somebody / Turn me loose / Seven days too long / Table top girl / Lady / Fantasyland. *(cd-iss. Apr94 on 'M.C.A.'; MCAD 22075)*

May 76. (7") *<12216>* **SUNSHINE. / TURN ME LOOSE** — **—** —

Apr 77. (lp) *(ABCL 5126) <ABCD 992>* **LOTS OF PEOPLE** (live) — — —
– (spoken introduction by Red Holloway) / Changes in the wind / Burning down / Play the harp / A helping hand / I got to get down with you / He's a travelling man / Separate ways / Room to move. *(cd-iss. Apr94 on 'M.C.A.'; MCAD 22073)*

—— now with **JAMES QUILL SMITH** – vocals, guitar / **STEVE THOMPSON** – bass / **SOKO RICHARDSON** – drums / and a brass section

Feb 78. (lp) *<ABCD 1039>* **A HARD CORE PACKAGE** — **—** —
– Rock and roll hobo / Do I please you / Disconnected line / An old sweet picture / The last time / Make up your mind / Arizona bound / Now and then / Goodnight dreams / Give me a chance. *(cd-iss. Apr94 on 'M.C.A.'; MCAD 22071)*

—— now with loads of session people.

		D.J.M.	D.J.M.

May 79. (lp) *(DJF 20556) <23>* **BOTTOM LINE** — — —
– Bottom line / Dreamboat / Desert flower / I'm gonna do it / Revival / Game of love / Celebration / Come with me.

Jul 79. (7") (DJS 10918) **BOTTOM LINE. / DREAMBOAT** ☐ ☐
Dec 79. (lp) (DJF 20564) <29> **NO MORE INTERVIEWS** ☐ ☐
    – Hard going up / A bigger slice of pie / Falling / Take me home tonight / Sweet honey bee / Stars in the night / Consideration / Gypsy lady / Wild new lover.

—— now with **SMITH, RICHARDSON + KEVIN McCORMICK** – bass / **MAGGIE PARKER** – vox

May 81. (lp) (DJF2/DJH4 0570) **ROAD SHOW BLUES** ☐ ☐
    – Why worry / Road show / Mama talk to your daughter / A big man / Lost and gone / Mexico City / John Lee boogie / Reaching for a mountain / Baby what you want me to do. (re-iss. Jun88 on 'Thunderbolt' lp/cd; THBL/CDTB 060)
Jun 81. (7") **JOHN LEE BOOGIE. / WHY WORRY. / MAMA TALK TO YOUR DAUGHTER** ☐ ☐

—— **MAYALL'S** new line-up featured **COCO MONTAYA + WALTER TROUT** – guitar / **BOBBY HAYNES** – bass / **JOE YUELE** – drums

	P.R.T.	GNP Crescendo
May 86. (lp/c) (NCP/ZCNCP 709) <GNP S/5 2184> **BEHIND THE IRON CURTAIN** (rec.1984)	☐	☐ 1985

    – Somebody's acting like a child / Rolling with the blues / The laws must change / Parchman farm / Have you heard / Fly tomorrow / Steppin' out. (cd-iss. Dec95 on 'GNP Crescendo';)

—— After couple of years out of the studio he returned Spring '87. with famous guests **MICK TAYLOR, JOHN McVIE**, etc.

	Charly	Entente
Dec 88. (cd) (CDCHARLY 202) **CHICAGO LINE**	☐	☐

    – Chicago line / Gimme one more day / One life to live / The last time / Dream about the blues / Fascination lover / Cold blooded woman / The dirty dozen / Tears came rollin' down / Life in the jungle.

—— **FREEBO** – bass repl. HAYNES + TROUT

	Island	Island
Apr 90. (cd) (CID/ICT/ILPS 9958) **A SENSE OF PLACE**	☐	☐

    – I want to go / Congo square / Send me down to Vicksburg / Without her / Sensitive kind / Jacksboro highway / Let's work together / I can't complain / Black cat moon / Sugarcane / All my life. (cd re-iss. Mar93; IMCD 167)

—— **RICK CORTES** – bass repl. FREEBO

—— guests; **MICK TAYLOR / BUDDY GUY + ALBERT COLLINS**

	Silvertone	Silvertone
Apr 93. (cd/c/lp) (ORE CD/C/LP 527) **WAKE UP CALL**	61	☐

    – Mail order mystics / Maydell / I could cry / Wake up call / Loaded dice / Undercover agent for the blues / Light the fuse / Anything I can say / Nature's disappearing / I'm a sucker for love / Not at home / Ain't that lovin' you baby.
1993. (cd-s) **WAKE UP CALL /** ☐ ☐

—— **BUDDY WHITTINGTON** – guitar repl. MONTOYA
Feb 95. (cd/c/lp) (ORE CD/C/LP 537) **SPINNING COIN** ☐ ☐
    – When the Devil starts crying / Spinning coin / Ain't no brakeman / Double life feelings / Run / What passes for love / Fan the flames / Voodoo music / Long story short / No big hurry / Remember this. (cd re-iss. Mar97; same)
Apr 97. (cd) (ORECD 547) **BLUES FOR THE LOST DAYS** ☐ ☐
    – Dead city / Stone cold deal / All those heroes / Blues for the lost days / Trenches / One in a million / How can you live like that / Some other day / I don't mind / It ain't safe / Sen-say-shun / You are for real.

– compilations, exploitation, etc. –

Aug 66. (7"ltd; by JOHN MAYALL and ERIC CLAPTON) Purdah; (45-3502) **LONELY HEARTS. / BERNARD JENKINS** ☐ ☐
Nov 67. (lp) Ace Of Clubs; (SCL 1245) / London; <PS 543> **THE BLUES ALONE** (nearly all instruments himself) 24
    – Brand new start / Please don't tell / Down the line / Sonny Boy blow / Marsha's mood / No more tears / Catch that train / Cancelling out / Harp man / Brown sugar / Broken wings / Don't kick me. (cd-iss. Jun88 on 'London'; 820 535-2)
Aug 69. (lp; mono/stereo) Decca; (LK/SKL 5010) / London; <562> **LOOKING BACK** 14 79
    – Mr. James / Blues city shakedown / They call it stormy Monday / So many roads / Looking back / Sitting in the rain / It hurts me too / Double trouble / Suspicions (part 2) / Jenny / Picture on the wall. (cd-iss. Jan89 on 'London'; 820 331-2)
Jan 70. (lp; stereo/mono) Decca; (S+/PA 47) **THE WORLD OF JOHN MAYALL** ☐ ☐
Apr 71. (lp) Decca; (SPA 138) **THE WORLD OF JOHN MAYALL VOL.2** ☐ ☐
Oct 71. (lp) Decca; (SKL 5086) / London; <PS 600-1> **THRU THE YEARS** ☐ ☐
    (cd-iss. Jan91 on 'Deram'; 844 028-2)
Oct 71. (lp) Polydor; (2483 016) **BEYOND THE TURNING POINT** ☐ ☐
Feb 73. (d-lp) London; <PS 618-9> **DOWN THE LINE** ☐ ☐
    – (60's demos & 'JOHN MAYALL PLAYS JOHN MAYALL' lp)
Apr 76. (lp) Polydor; (2482 272) **JOHN MAYALL** ☐ ☐
1978. (lp) Decca; (ROOTS 8) **BLUES ROOTS** ☐ ☐
Oct 78. (7") Decca; (F 13804) **CROCODILE WALK. / SITTING IN THE RAIN** ☐ ☐
Nov 80. (d-lp)(c) Polydor; (2664 436)(3578 483) **GREATEST HITS** ☐ ☐
Feb 82. (lp/c) M.C.A.; (MCL/+C 1643) **LAST OF THE BRITISH BLUES** ☐ ☐
    (cd-iss. Apr94; MCAD 22074)
Apr 83. (lp/c) Decca; (TAB/KTBC 66) **PRIMAL SOLOS** ☐ ☐
    (cd-iss. Nov88; 820 320-2)
Oct 83. (lp) Decca; (TAB 74) **THE JOHN MAYALL STORY VOL.1** ☐ ☐
Oct 83. (lp) Decca; (TAB 75) **THE JOHN MAYALL STORY VOL.2** ☐ ☐
Apr 84. (lp) I.M.S.; (2486 041) **ROOM TO MOVE** ☐ ☐
    (re-iss. cd Mar93;)
Aug 84. (d-c) Decca; (KMC2 5004) **STORMY MONDAY** ☐ ☐
    (cd-iss. Sep94 on 'Spectrum'; 550 717-2)
Apr 86. (d-lp/c/cd) Castle; (CCS LP/MC/CD 137) **THE COLLECTION** ☐ ☐
    – Key to love / Hideaway / Ramblin' on my mind / All your love / They call it stormy Monday / Hoochie coochie man / Crocodile walk (1st version) / Crawling up a hill / Marsha's mood / Sonny Boy blow / Looking back / A hard road / The supernatural / You don't love me / Leaping Christine / Suspicions (part 2) / Picture on the wall / The death of J.B. Lenoir / Sandy / The bear / Walking the sunset / Fly tomorrow.
Apr 86. (lp) Decal; (LIK 1) **SOME OF MY BEST FRIENDS ARE BLUES** ☐ ☐

Jun 88. (lp/c/cd) Knight; (KN LP/MC/CD 10010) **NIGHTRIDING** ☐ –
Feb 90. (cd) Charly; (CDCHARLY 212) **THE POWER OF THE BLUES** ☐ –
Jun 91. (cd/c) Elite; **WAITING FOR THE RIGHT TIME** ☐ –
Mar 92. (cd/c) Charly; (CD/TC BM 4) **LIFE IN THE JUNGLE** (rec.'84) ☐ –
Apr 93. (cd) Pulsar; **A BIG MAN** ☐ –
Jul 93. (cd) Deram; **LONDON BLUES 1964-1969** ☐ –
Sep 93. (cd/c) Aim; (AIM CD/C 1004) **RETURN OF THE BLUESBREAKERS** ☐ –
Apr 94. (cd) One Way; (OW 30008) **THE 1982 REUNION CONCERT** (live) ☐ –
Jul 94. (cd) Success; **WHY WORRY** ☐ –
Dec 95. (cd) Charly; (CDCD 1278) **JOHN LEE BOOGIE** ☐ –
May 97. (cd) Experience; (EXP 024) **JOHN MAYALL** ☐ –

Curtis MAYFIELD

Born: 3 Jun'42, Chicago, Illinois, USA. Immersed in music from an early age, MAYFIELD was a self-taught guitarist and lyricist, strongly influenced by the sounds of the Northern Jubilee Gospel Singers (a local group that included JERRY BUTLER). In 1957, BUTLER asked MAYFIELD to join a newly formed group, The ROOSTERS, who would soon evolve into The IMPRESSIONS under the management of Eddie Thomas. As a songwriter for the group, MAYFIELD had his first hit in '58 with 'FOR YOUR PRECIOUS LOVE', prior to BUTLER's departure. The IMPRESSIONS scored their first Top 20 hit in '60 with 'GYPSY WOMAN', MAYFIELD's prolific writing career taking off via a new contract with 'A.B.C.' records. During the 60's, he penned a wealth of hits, including 'WE'RE A WINNER', the lyrical content highlighting MAYFIELD's awareness of the civil rights movement and the increasing confidence and self-determination of the African-American community. The decade also saw the soul man writing for record labels such as Okeh and Veejay as well as Chicago based artists including GENE CHANDLER and MAJOR LANCE. This work inspired CURTIS to set up his own label, 'Curtom' (distributed through 'Buddah'), releasing material by a number of successful acts, among them DONNY HATHAWAY. Leaving The IMPRESSIONS to go solo in 1970, his critically acclaimed self-titled debut set was characterised by his trademark funky organic sounds blended with socially aware lyrics. This album was followed by 'ROOTS', a record which included the groove-laden, 'KEEP ON KEEPING ON'. The turning point from acclaimed artist to international stardom arrived in 1972 when MAYFIELD was asked to score and perform the soundtrack for the blaxploitation film, 'Superfly'. The movie was a massive hit, MAYFIELD's soundtrack complementing the film perfectly and producing hits in the form of the title track and 'FREDDIE'S DEAD'. Still regarded as one of contemporary black music's most momentous recordings, 'SUPERFLY' represented the pinnacle of MAYFIELD's solo career. Although the man released some above average albums in the 70's and continued to oversee the creative development of the 'Curtom' imprint (now distributed by 'Warners'), he didn't really come close to matching the soundtrack's power. Arguably his finest post-'Superfly' work, 'SHORT EYES' was another soundtrack, written for a movie in which MAYFIELD also had an acting role. The 80's saw MAYFIELD touring regularly and scoring intermittent hits, a reunion tour with The IMPRESSIONS seeing the return of his old sparring partner, BUTLER. The beginning of the 90's saw tragedy strike when in August 1990, MAYFIELD was hit by a lighting rig that had been dislodged by high winds during an open air concert in Brooklyn; he was paralysed from the neck down. The next few years saw MAYFIELD elected into the Rock And Roll Hall Of Fame and various lifetime achievement awards bestowed on him, so it was all the more remarkable when his comeback album, 'NEW WORLD ORDER', was released in '96. The recording process involved was time consuming, although the result was worth the wait, MAYFIELD achieving his best solo work since the early 70's. Tragically, it would be CURTIS' swansong as the great man died of (a long suffering) cancer on Boxing Day, 1999.

Album rating: CURTIS (*7) / CURTIS/LIVE! (*6) / ROOTS (*7) / SUPERFLY (*8) / BACK TO THE WORLD (*7) / CURTIS IN CHICAGO (*6) / SWEET EXORCIST (*6) / GOT TO FIND A WAY (*5) / THERE'S NO PLACE LIKE AMERICA TODAY (*6) / GIVE, GET, TAKE AND HAVE (*5) / NEVER SAY YOU CAN'T SURVIVE (*4) / SHORT EYES soundtrack (*4) / DO IT ALL NIGHT (*5) / HEARTBEAT (*6) / THE RIGHT COMBINATION with Linda Clifford (*4) / SOMETHING TO BELIEVE IN (*4) / LOVE IS THE PLACE (*5) / HONESTY (*7) / WE COME IN PEACE WITH A MESSAGE OF LOVE (*4) / LIVE IN EUROPE (*5) / TAKE IT TO THE STREET (*4) / A MAN LIKE CURTIS – THE BEST OF compilation (*8) / NEW WORLD ORDER (*6)

CURTIS MAYFIELD – vocals, guitar, keyboards + live band

	Buddah	Curtom
Nov 70. (7") (2011 055) <1955> **(DON'T WORRY) IF THERE'S A HELL BELOW WE'RE ALL GOING TO GO. / THE MAKINGS OF YOU**	☐	29
Feb 71. (lp) (2318 015) <8005> **CURTIS**	☐	19 Sep70

    – (Don't worry) If there's a Hell below we're all going to go / The other side of town / The makings of you / We the people who are darker than blue / Move on up / Miss Black America / Wild and free / Give it up. (re-iss. Oct74; BDLH 5005) (re-iss. Jun76 on 'Warners'; K 56252) (cd-iss. Nov93 on 'Movieplay Gold'; MPG 74026) (re-iss. Mar94 on 'Curtom' cd/c; CUR 2012 CD/MC)
May 71. (7") <1960> **GIVE IT UP. / BEAUTIFUL BROTHER OF MINE** – ☐
Jun 71. (7"m) (2011 080) **MOVE ON UP. / GIVE IT UP / BEAUTIFUL BROTHER OF MINE** 12 –
Aug 71. (d-lp) (2659 004) <8008> **CURTIS / LIVE! (live)** ☐ 21 May71
    – Mighty mighty (spade and Whitey) / I plan to stay a believer / We're a winner

(rap) / We've only just begun / Check out your mind / People get ready / Stare and stare / Gypsy woman / The makings of you / We the people who are darker than blue / (Don't worry) If there's a Hell below we're all going to go / Stone junkie. *(re-iss. Oct74; BDLP 2001) (re-iss. Jun76 on 'Warners'; K 66047) (d-cd-iss. Mar94 on 'Movieplay Gold'; MPG 74176) (d-cd-iss. Jun94 on 'Curtom'; CPCD 8038)*

Sep 71. (7") *<1963>* **MIGHTY MIGHTY (SPADE AND WHITEY) (live).** / | - | |

Nov 71. (7") *(2011 101)* **WE GOT TO HAVE PEACE. / PEOPLE GET READY** | | |

Dec 71. (7") *<1966>* **GET DOWN. / WE'RE A WINNER** | - | 69 |

Jan 72. (lp) *(2318 065) <8009>* **ROOTS** | | 40 | Oct71
– Get down / Keep on keeping on / Underground / We got to have peace / Beautiful brother of mine / Now you're gone / Love to keep you in my mind. *(re-iss. Oct74; BDLH 5006) (re-iss. Jun76 on 'Warners'; K 56249) (cd-iss. Nov93 on 'Movieplay Gold'; MPG 74027) (cd re-iss. Jun94 on 'Charly'; CPCD 8037)*

Feb 72. (7") *<1968>* **WE GOT TO HAVE PEACE. / WE'RE A WINNER** | | |

Apr 72. (7") *<1972>* **BEAUTIFUL BROTHER OF MINE. / LOVE TO KEEP YOU IN MY MIND** | | |

May 72. (7") *(2011 119)* **KEEP ON KEEPING ON. / STONE JUNKIE** | | |

Jun 72. (7") *<1974>* **MOVE ON UP. / UNDERGROUND** | | |

Sep 72. (7") *(2011 141) <1975>* **FREDDIE'S DEAD (theme from "Superfly"). / UNDERGROUND** | 4 | Aug72

Nov 72. (lp) *(2318 065) <8014>* **SUPERFLY (Soundtrack)** | 26 | 1 | Aug72
– Little child runnin' wild / Freddie's dead / Give me your love / No thing on me (cocaine song) / Superfly / Pusherman / Junkie chase / Eddie you should know / Think. *(re-iss. Nov74; BDLH 4018) (re-iss. Aug79 on R.S.O.') (re-iss. Jun88 on 'Curtom' cd/c/lp; CD/ZC+/CUR 2002) (cd re-iss. Jun94 on 'Charly'; CPCD 8039)*

Nov 72. (7") *<1978>* **SUPERFLY. / UNDERGROUND** | - | 8 |

Feb 73. (7") *(2011 156)* **SUPERFLY. / GIVE ME YOUR LOVE (LOVE SONG)** | | - |

Jul 73. (7") *<1987>* **FUTURE SHOCK. / THE OTHER SIDE OF TOWN** | | 39 |

Sep 73. (lp) *(2318 085) <8015>* **BACK TO THE WORLD** | | 16 | Jun73
– Back to the world / Future shock / Right on for the darkness / If I were only a child again / Can't say nothin' / Keep on trippin' / Future song (love of a good woman, love of a good man). *(re-iss. Oct74; BDLH 5008) (re-iss. Jun76 on 'Warners'; K 56251) (cd-iss. Nov93 on 'Movieplay Gold'; MPG 74029) (cd re-iss. Jun94 on 'Charly'; CPCD 8040)*

Oct 73. (7") *(2011 187)* **BACK TO THE WORLD. / THE OTHER SIDE OF TOWN** | | - |

Oct 73. (7") *<1991>* **IF I WERE ONLY A CHILD AGAIN. / THINK** | - | 71 |

Jan 74. (7") *<1993>* **CAN'T SAY NOTHIN'. / FUTURE SHOCK** | - | 88 |

Mar 74. (lp) *(2318 091) <8018>* **CURTIS IN CHICAGO (TV Soundtrack)** | | | Nov73
– Superfly / For your precious love / I'm so proud / Once in my life (IMPRESSIONS) / Preacher man (IMPRESSIONS) / Duke of Earl (GENE CHANDLER) / Love oh love (LEROY HUTSON) / Amen. *(re-iss. Oct74; BDLH 5009) (re-iss. Jun76 on 'Curtom'; K 56250) (cd-iss. Oct94 on 'Charly'; CPCD 8046)*

Aug 74. (lp) *(2318 099) <8601>* **SWEET EXORCIST** | | 39 | May74
– Ain't got time / Sweet exorcist / To be invisible / Power to the people / Kung Fu / Suffer / Make me believe in you. *(re-iss. Oct74; BDLH 5001) (re-iss. Aug76 on 'Curtom'; K 56284) (cd-iss. Oct94 on 'Charly'; CPCD 8047)*

Aug 74. (lp) *(BDS 402) <1999>* **KUNG FU. / RIGHT ON FOR THE DARKNESS** | | 40 | Jun74

Oct 74. (7") *<2005>* **SWEET EXORCIST. / SUFFER** | - | |

Jan 75. (lp) *(BDLP 4029) <8604>* **GOT TO FIND A WAY** | | 76 | Nov74
– Love me (right in the pocket) / So you don't love me / A prayer / Mother's son / Cannot find a way / Ain't no love lost. *(cd-iss. Oct94 on 'Charly'; CPCD 8048)*

Mar 75. (7") *(BDS 426) <2006>* **MOTHER'S SON. / LOVE ME RIGHT IN THE POCKET** | | |

Jun 75. (7") **STASH THAT BUTT, SUCKER. / ZANZIBAR** | - | |
(above single issued on 'Columbia')

—— His band from this period onwards **GARY THOMPSON** – guitar / **RICH TUFO** – keyboards / **LUCKY SCOTT** – bass / **QUINTON JOSEPH** – drums

Aug 75. (lp) *(BDLP 4033) <5001>* **THERE'S NO PLACE LIKE AMERICA TODAY** | | | Jun75
– Billy Jack / When seasons change / So in love / Jesus / Blue Monday people / Hard times / Love to the people. *(re-iss. Jan89 on 'Curtom' cd/c/lp; CD/ZC+/CUR 2003)*

Sep 75. (7") *<0105>* **SO IN LOVE. / HARD TIMES** | - | 67 |

Jul 76. (7") *<0118>* **ONLY YOU BABE. / LOVE TO THE PEOPLE** | | |

Jul 76. (lp) *(BDLP 4042) <5007>* **GIVE, GET, TAKE AND HAVE** | | | Jun76
– In your arms again / This love is sweet / P.S. I love you / Party night / Get a little bit (give, get, take and have) / Soul music / Only you babe / Mr. Welfare you. *(re-iss. Mar94 on 'Curtom' cd/c; CUR 2011 CD/MC) (cd re-iss. Jun94 on 'Charly'; CPCD 8070)*

Sep 76. (7") *<0122>* **PARTY NIGHT. / P.S. I LOVE YOU** | - | |

| | | Curtom | Curtom |

Mar 77. (7") *<0125>* **SHOW ME LOVE. / JUST WANT TO BE WITH YOU** | - | |

Mar 77. (lp) *(K 56352) <5013>* **NEVER SAY YOU CAN'T SURVIVE** | | |
– Show me love / Just want to be with you / When we're alone / Never say you can't survive / I'm gonna win your love / All night long / When you used to be mine / Sparkle. *(re-iss. Mar94 on 'Curtom' cd/c; CUR 2010 CD/MC) (cd-iss. Oct94 on 'Charly'; CPCD 8049)*

Nov 77. (7") *<0131>* **DO DO WAP IS STRONG IN HERE. / NEED SOMEONE TO LOVE** | - | |

Feb 78. (lp) *(K 56430) <5017>* **SHORT EYES (Soundtrack)** | | | Nov77
– Do do wap is strong in here / Back against the wall / Need someone to love / A heavy dupe / Short eyes / Break it down / Another fool in love / Father confessor. *(cd-iss. Jun96 on 'Charly'; CPCD 8183)*

Jul 78. (7") *<0135>* **YOU ARE, YOU ARE. / GET A LITTLE BIT (GIVE, GET, TAKE AND HAVE)** | - | |

Sep 78. (7") *<0141>* **DO IT ALL NIGHT. / PARTY PARTY** | - | |

Oct 78. (lp) *<5022>* **DO IT ALL NIGHT** | | - |
– Do it all night / No goodbyes / Party party / Keeps me loving you / In love, in love, in love / You are, you are. *(cd-iss. Oct94 on 'Charly'; CPCD 8050)*

Nov 78. (7") *<0142>* **IN LOVE, IN LOVE, IN LOVE. / KEEPS ME LOVING YOU** | - | |

| | | Atlantic | not iss. |

Dec 78. (12") *(LV 1)* **NO GOODBYES. / PARTY PARTY** | 65 | - |

—— With various session people

| | | R.S.O. | R.S.O. |

Mar 79. (7") *(RSO 28) <919>* **THIS YEAR. / ('A'instrumental)** | | |

Sep 79. (lp) *(RSS 4) <3053>* **HEARTBEAT** | | 42 | Aug79
– Tell me, tell me (how ya like to be loved) / What is my woman for? / Between you baby and me / Victory / Over the hump / You better stop / You're so good to me / Heartbeat. *(cd-iss. Jun94 on 'Charly'; CPCD 8071)*

Aug 79. (7"; by LINDA CLIFFORD & CURTIS MAYFIELD) *<RSO 43) <941>* **BETWEEN YOU BABY AND ME. / YOU'RE SO GOOD TO ME** | | |

Jun 80. (lp; by LINDA CLIFFORD & CURTIS MAYFIELD) *(2394 269) <3084>* **THE RIGHT COMBINATION** | | |
– Rock to your socks / The right combination / I'm so proud / Ain't no love lost / It's lovin' time / Love's sweet sensation / Between you baby and me. *(cd-iss. Jun94 on 'Charly'; CPCD 8072)*

1980. (7"; by LINDA CLIFFORD & CURTIS MAYFIELD) *<1029>* **LOVE'S SWEET SENSATION. / ('A'instrumental)** | - | |

1980. (7") *<1036>* **LOVE ME, LOVE ME NOW. / IT'S ALRIGHT** | - | |

Sep 80. (lp) *(2394 271) <3077>* **SOMETHING TO BELIEVE IN** | | | Jul80
– Something to believe in / Love me, love me now / Never let me go / Tripping out / People never give up / I'm so proud / Never stop loving me. *(re-iss. Oct89 on 'Curtom' lp/c/cd; CUR/+MC/CD 2005) (cd re-iss. Jun94 on 'Charly'; CPCD 8073) (cd re-iss. Oct94 on 'Curtom'; CUR 2005CD)*

Sep 80. (7") *<1046>* **TRIPPING OUT. / NEVER STOP LOVING** | | |

Oct 80. (7") *(RSO 68)* **IT'S ALRIGHT. / SUPERFLY** | | |

| | | Epic | Boardwalk |

1981. (lp) *<2601 6012>* **LOVE IS THE PLACE** | | German
– She don't let nobody (but me) / Toot an' toot an' toot / Baby doll / Love is the place / Just ease my mind / You mean everything to me / You get all my love / Come free your people.

1981. (7") *<122>* **SHE DON'T LET NOBODY (BUT ME). / YOU GET ALL MY LOVE** | - | |

1981. (7") *<132>* **COME FREE YOUR PEOPLE. / TOOT AN' TOOT** | - | |

Oct 82. (7") *<155>* **HEY BABY (GIVE IT ALL TO ME). / SUMMER HOT** | - | |

Mar 83. (lp/c) *(EPC/40 25317) <2601 6022>* **HONESTY** | | - | German
– Hey baby (give it all to me) / Still within your heart / Dirty laundry / Nobody but you / If you need me / What you gawn do? / Summer hot.

Mar 83. (7") *<169>* **DIRTY LAUNDRY. / NOBODY BUT YOU** | - | |

| | | not iss. | C.R.C. |

Sep 85. (lp) *<447>* **WE COME IN PEACE WITH A MESSAGE OF LOVE** | | - |
(UK-iss.Feb91 on 'Curtom' lp/c/cd; CRC 2001/+MC/CD)

| | | 98.6 | 98.6 |

Nov 86. (7"/12") *(CURT 1/+T)* **BABY IT'S YOU. / BREAKIN' IN THE STREETS** | | |

—— In mid'87 he was credited on BLOW MONKEYS single 'Celebrate The Day'.

| | | Capitol | Capitol |

1987. (lp; withdrawn) **LIVE IN LOS ANGELES (live)** | - | - |

| | | Ichiban | Ichiban |

Jun 88. (cd/c/lp) *(CD/ZC+/CUR 2901)* **LIVE IN EUROPE (live)** | | |
– (intro) / Freddie's dead / We gotta have peace / People get ready / Move on up / Back to the world / Gypsy woman / Pusher man / We've only just begun / When seasons change / (Don't worry) If there's a Hell below we're all going to go.

Jul 88. (7"/12") *(CUR/12CUR 101)* **MOVE ON UP (live). / LITTLE CHILD RUNNIN' WILD (live)** | | |

| | | Curtom | Arista |

May 89. (7"; w/ FISHBONE) **HE'S A FLY GUY. / ('A'instrumental)** | - | - |

May 89. (7") *(7CUR 102)* **I MO GIT U SUCKA. / HE'S A FLY GUY** | - | - |
(12"+=/cd-s+=) *(12/CD CUR 102)* – ('A'extended).

Feb 90. (7"/12") *(7/12 CUR 106)* **HOMELESS. / PEOPLE NEVER GIVE UP** | | |

Mar 90. (cd/c/lp) *(CD/ZC+/CUR 2008)* **TAKE IT TO THE STREET** | | |
– Homeless / Got to be real / Who was that lady / On and on / He's a fly guy / Don't push / I mo git u sucka. *(cd re-iss. Apr96 on 'Charly'; CPCD 8179)*

Jun 90. (7") *(7CUR 108)* **DO BE DOWN. / GOT TO BE REAL** | | |
(12"+=) *(12CUR 108)* – ('A'extended) / ('A'-radio version).

—— On the 13th August, 1990, while CURTIS prepared for a gig, a high wind brought down a lighting scaffold which struck him. This left him permanently paralysed from the neck downwards (his house subsequently burned down a month later!).

| | | Capitol | Capitol |

Sep 90. (7"; as CURTIS MAYFIELD & ICE-T) *(CL 586)* **SUPERFLY 1990. / ('A'mix)** | 48 | |
(12"+=/cd-s+=) *(12/CD CL 586)* – ('A'mixes).

—— CURTIS returned to the studio 1995/96 with session backing

| | | Warners | WEA Int. |

Jan 97. (cd/c) *<(9362 46348-2/-4)>* **NEW WORLD ORDER** | 44 | |
– New world order / Ms. Martha / Back to living again / No one knows about a good thing (you don't have to cry) / Just a little bit of love / We people who are darker than blue / I believe in you / Here but I'm gone / It was love that we needed / The got dang song / The girl I find stays on my mind / Let's not forget / Oh so beautiful.

—— on the 26th of December 1999, after suffering with cancer for a long time, CURTIS died in an Atlanta hospital

– compilations, others, etc. –

Nov 74. (lp) *Buddah; (BDLP 4015)* **MOVE ON UP – THE BEST OF CURTIS MAYFIELD** | | |

Nov 74. (7") *Buddah; (BDS 410)* **MOVE ON UP. / GIVE IT UP** | | |

Jan 83. (7") *Flashback; (FBS 23)* **MOVE ON UP. / (b-side by Melba Moore)** | | |

Feb 90. (cd/c) *Essential; (ESS CD/MC 003)* **PEOPLE GET READY (live At Ronnie Scott's)** | | |
(cd re-iss. 1993 on 'Castle'; CLACD 329)

Nov 90.	(d-lp/c/cd) *Curtom; (CUR 22902/+MC/CD)* **OF ALL TIME –** **THE CLASSIC COLLECTION**	☐	-
Nov 92.	(cd) *Music Collection; (MUSCD 007)* **A MAN LIKE CURTIS –** **THE BEST OF . . .**	☐	-

– Move on up / Superfly / (Don't worry) If there's a Hell below we're all gonna go / You are, you are / Give me your love / Never stop loving me / Tripping out / Soul music / This year / Ain't no love lost / Pusherman / Freddie's dead / Do do wop is strong in here / Hard times / In your arms again (shake it) / So in love.

Sep 93.	(cd) *Traditional Line; (TL 001333)* **HARD TIMES**	☐	-
Jan 94.	(cd) *Windsong; (WINDCD 052)* **BBC RADIO 1 LIVE IN** **CONCERT**	☐	-
May 94.	(cd/c) *Laserlight; (1/7 2364)* **CURTIS MAYFIELD**	☐	-
Jun 94.	(cd) *Charly; (CPCD 1211)* **POWER FOR THE PEOPLE**	☐	-
Aug 94.	(cd) *Charly; (CPCD 8043)* **GROOVE ON UP**	☐	-
Nov 94.	(cd) *Charly; (CPCD 8065)* **TRIPPING OUT**	☐	-
Feb 95.	(d-cd) *Charly; (CPCD 8034)* **GET DOWN TO THE FUNKY** **GROOVE**	☐	-
Mar 96.	(cd) *Sequel; (NEMCD 783)* **LOVE IS THE PLACE / HONESTY**	☐	-
Apr 96.	(cd) *Audiophile; (APH 102802)* **MOVE ON UP**	☐	-
Apr 96.	(cd) *Castle; (CCSCD 806)* **THE VERY BEST OF CURTIS** **MAYFIELD**	☐	-

—— CURTIS also collaborated on other Film Soundtracks, 'CLAUDINE' in Aug74 with GLADYS KNIGHT & THE PIPS, 'LET'S DO IT AGAIN' in Sep76 with STAPLE SINGERS and 'SPARKLE' Oct76 with ARETHA FRANKLIN. There were also a few tribute cd's about the shops in the mid-90's.

MAZZY STAR

Formed: Santa Monica, Los Angeles, California, USA . . . by Paisley Underground veteran, DAVID ROBACK and the young HOPE SANDOVAL. She had met him around six years previous after a friend, KENDRA SMITH (erstwhile member of RAINY DAY alongside ROBACK), had introduced the pair. SANDOVAL initially joined ROBACK's band, OPAL, a short-lived affair which came to a premature end after a tour in '87. The couple were reunited at the beginning of '89 as MAZZY STAR, a darkly languid, soft-VELVETS style project which fused haunting folk/country and dreamy psychedelia to mesmerising effect. The resulting album, 'SHE HANGS BRIGHTLY' (1990), surprised many in the rock world, although it was their 1993 set, 'SO TONIGHT THAT I MIGHT SEE' which cracked the US Top 50. An even more soporific set of stoned acoustic rock, the album even spawned a near Top 40 hit with the gorgeously melancholy 'FADE INTO YOU'. Fans had to wait another three long years before their next fix, 'AMONG MY SWAN' delighting the faithful if not exactly taking any risks. • Covers: BLUE FLOWER (Slapp Happy) / I'M GONNA BAKE MY BISCUIT (McCoy) / I'M SAILIN' (Lawler) / FIVE STRING SERENADE (. . . Lee) / GIVE YOU MY LOVIN' . RAINY DAY covered I'LL KEEP IT WITH MINE (Bob Dylan) / SLOOP JOHN B. (Beach Boys) / I'LL BE YOUR MIRROR (Velvet Underground). • Trivia: HOPE SANDOVAL guested on The JESUS & MARY CHAIN's 1994 single, 'SOMETIMES ALWAYS'.

Album rating: SHE HANGS BRIGHTLY (*6) / SO TONIGHT THAT I MIGHT SEE (*8) / AMONG MY SWAN (*6) / Rainy Day: RAINY DAY (*6) / Opal: HAPPY NIGHTMARE BABY (*7) / EARLY RECORDINGS compilation (*6)

RAINY DAY

DAVID ROBACK – guitar, vocals, piano, bass (ex-RAIN PARADE) / **WILL GLENN** – violin, cello (of RAIN PARADE) / **MICHAEL QUERICO** – vocals, bass, guitar (of THREE O'CLOCK) / **MATT PIUCCI** – guitar (of RAIN PARADE) / **KENDRA SMITH** – bass, vocals + **KARL PRECODA** – guitar + **DENNIS DUCK** – drums (3 of DREAM SYNDICATE) / **ETHAN JAMES** – keyboards / + **SUSANNA HOFFS** + **VICKI PETERSON** – backing vocals (of BANGLES)

		Rough Trade	Llama
Apr 84.	(lp) *(ROUGH 70)* <*E-1024*> **RAINY DAY**	☐	-

– I'll keep it with mine / John Riley / Flying on the ground is wrong / Sloop John B. / Holocaust / On the way home / I'll be your mirror / Rainy day, dream away.

Jun 84.	(7") *(RT 140)* **I'LL KEEP IT WITH MINE. / HOLOCAUST**	☐	-

OPAL

DAVID ROBACK / + KENDRA SMITH – bass

		One Big Guitar	not iss.
1986.	(12"ep) *(OBG 002T)* **NORTHERN LINE. / EMPTY BOTTLES /** **SOUL GIVER**	☐	-

—— split but left compilation below . . .

		not iss.	S.S.T.
Sep 87.	(lp/c/cd) <*SST+C/CD 103*> **HAPPY NIGHTMARE BABY**	-	☐

– Rocket machine / Magick power / Revelation / A falling star / She's a diamond / Supernova / Siamese trap / Happy nightmare baby / Soul giver.

—— when KENDRA left ROBACK, he introduced friend **HOPE SANDOVAL** – vocals, guitar (ex-GOING HOME); disbanded sometime in '88

		Rough Trade	not iss.
Nov 89.	(cd/c/lp) *(CD/C+/ROUGH 128)* **EARLY RECORDINGS**	☐	-

– Empty box blues / She's a diamond / My only friend / Empty bottles / Grains of sand / Brigit on Sunday / Northern line / Strange delight / Fell from the sun / Harriet Brown / Lullabye / All souls. *(cd+=)* – Hear the wind blow.

MAZZY STAR

MAZZY STAR

—— **ROBACK + HOPE SANDOVAL** – vocals (ex-GOING HOME)

		Rough Trade	Capitol
Apr 90.	(cd/c/lp) *(CD/TC+/R 158)* <*C2/C4 96508*> **SHE HANGS** **BRIGHTLY**	☐	Feb91

– Halah / Blue flower / Ride it on / She hangs brightly / I'm sailin' / Give you my lovin' / Taste of blood / Ghost highway / Free / Before I sleep. *(re-iss. May93 + Sep94 on 'Capitol' cd/c; CD/TC EST 2196)*

		Capitol	Capitol
Oct 93.	(cd/c/lp) *(CD/TC+/EST 2206)* <*98253*> **SO TONIGHT THAT** **I MIGHT SEE**	68	36

– Fade into you / Bells ring / Mary of silence / Five string serenade / Blue light / She's my baby / Unreflected / Wasted / Into dust / So tonight that I might see. *(re-iss. Jun94; same)*

Aug 94.	(c-s) <*58286*> **FADE INTO YOU / HALAH**	-	44
	(cd-s) <*58121*> – ('A'side) / I'm gonna take my biscuit / Under my car / Bells ring.		
Aug 94.	(cd-s) *(CDCL 720)* **FADE INTO YOU / BLUE FLOWER /** **I'M GONNA BAKE MY BISCUIT**	48	-

(10") *(10CL 720)* – ('A'side) / Five string serenade / Under my car / Bells ring (acoustic).

—— The track 'TELL ME NOW' featured in the film 'Batman Forever' and the was on B-side of U2's 'Hold Me, Kiss Me, Kill Me!'.

Oct 96.	(7"/cd-s) *(CL/CDCLS 781)* **FLOWERS IN DECEMBER. / TELL** **YOUR HONEY / HAIR AND SKIN**	40	-

(cd-s) *(CDCL 781)* – ('A'side) / Ride it on (live) / Had a thought.

Nov 96.	(cd/c) *(CD/TC+/EST 2288)* <*27224*> **AMONG MY SWAN**	57	68 Oct96

– Disappear / Flowers in December / Rhymes of an hour / Cry cry / Take everything / Still cold / All your sisters / I've been let down / Roseblood / Happy / Umbilical / Look on down from the bridge.

David McALMONT

(dig out; 4th edition or Great Alt & Indie . . .)

McAULEY-SCHENKER GROUP
(see under ⇒ SCHENKER, Michael)

Paul McCARTNEY

Born: JAMES PAUL McCARTNEY, 18 Jun'42, Liverpool, England. An integral part of The BEATLES throughout the 60's, he and JOHN LENNON were easily the greatest contemporary writing partnership of the 20th Century. The band officially split on 11 April 1970, prior to issuing their final album, 'LET IT BE', (there was also a docu-film of the same name, detailing the last days of the fab four). Released three weeks previous was McCARTNEY's first solo outing, the eponymous 'McCARTNEY', which included backing from new wife, LINDA (whom he married on the 12th of March '69). By virtue of its relative acoustic simplicity (PAUL played every instrument himself), the record remains one of the better releases from a time when self indulgence and wildly ambitious concepts were the order of the day. Though berated by critics at the time, the album contained one of PAUL's finer efforts in 'MAYBE I'M AMAZED', going on to top the American charts but being held off the UK No.1 by SIMON & GARFUNKEL's 'Bridge Over Troubled Water'. The following year, McCARTNEY scored a cross-Atlantic Top 5 with his debut solo single, 'ANOTHER DAY', and then took the unusual step of co-crediting his wife LINDA (though she did actually contribute keyboards, backing vocals and percussion) on the subsequent album, 'RAM' (1971). Sales wise, the album reversed the chart positions of its predecessor, spawning the whimsical US-only No.1 single, 'UNCLE ALBERT – ADMIRAL HALSEY'.'RAM' had also featured the drumming talents of DENNY SEIWELL who, together with ex-MOODY BLUES man, DENNY LAINE (guitar, vocals), would form one half of McCARTNEY's new group, WINGS, later that year. With the husband and wife duo of PAUL and LINDA completing the line-up, McCARTNEY hit an unprecedented critical low with WINGS' vaguely reggae-ish debut effort, 'WILDLIFE'. Unfazed, McCARTNEY took his band out on a low key college tour, beefing up the sound with the addition of HENRY McCULLOUGH (who had previously worked with JOE COCKER) on guitar and backing vocals. The next WINGS' release was the controversial (and surprisingly successful given its political sentiments) 'GIVE IRELAND BACK TO THE IRISH'. Annoyed at a radio ban, WINGS then put music to nursery rhyme with 'MARY HAD A LITTLE LAMB', a rather excessive anti-censorship statement that made the UK Top 10 but lost the band valuable credibility. The McCARTNEY's then underwent a series of drug busts and another pedantic BBC ban with their next hit, 'HI HI HI'. In Spring '73, PAUL McCARTNEY & WINGS topped the US charts with the single, 'MY LOVE', and another under par album, 'RED ROSE SPEEDWAY'. Following later that summer was the much more impressive 'LIVE AND LET DIE', a much covered McCARTNEY-penned theme song for the James Bond film of the same name. With the departure of SEIWELL and McCULLOUGH immediately prior to recording the fourth album, WINGS were reduced to a core of The McCARTNEY's and LAINE, one that endured for the remainder of the band's career. Going it alone, the trio surprisingly came up with the most successful album of their career, 'BAND ON THE RUN' (1973). Where before, McCARTNEY's compositions had been perfectly formed but lacking in substance, he silenced his critics with impassioned pop/rock of the highest calibre, notably on 'JET' and the title track. The album went on to sell over 6 million copies during its two year-plus stay in both the UK & US charts, PAUL finally proving his post-BEATLES mettle. The subsequent addition of JIMMY McCULLOCH and GEOFF BRITTON saw the band expanded to a 5-piece again, BRITTON only playing on one single, 'JUNIOR'S FARM'. His replacement was JOE ENGLISH, the new line-up recording the mediocre quasi-concept album, 'VENUS AND MARS' (1975). The album topped the American and British charts all the same, although the single 'LETTING GO' didn't even make the Top 40, a pattern that would continue into the late 70's and beyond. 'WINGS AT THE SPEED OF SOUND' (1976) gets points deducted for McCARTNEY's well intentioned but annoying insistence that each band member get a lead vocal although 'SILLY LOVE SONGS' and 'LET 'EM IN' were finely honed hit singles. The triple live set, 'WINGS OVER AMERICA' (1977), was impressive if overly long proof of the band's well deserved live reputation, showcasing McCARTNEY's vocal and multi-instrumentalist talents to often dazzling effect. In early 1977, the band were reduced to a trio once more with the departure of McCULLOCH and ENGLISH for The SMALL FACES and SEA LEVEL respectively. Incredibly, WINGS bounced back with their biggest single to date, the windswept sentimental indulgence that was 'MULL OF KINTYRE'. Blissfully oblivious to punk, McCARTNEY even employed a warts and all Scottish pipe band to give the song that 'authentic' Caledonian appeal. It obviously worked; the record stood proudly at the top of the UK charts for nine weeks, becoming the biggest selling UK single ever. Incredibly, given the yanks' taste for anything remotely celtic, the single's B-side was promoted in the States, consequently stalling in the lower regions of the chart. WINGS had more US success via the single, 'WITH A LITTLE LUCK', a No.1 from the otherwise forgettable 'LONDON TOWN' (1978). The addition of LAURENCRE JUBER and STEVE HOLLY failed to prevent another critical pasting with 'BACK TO THE EGG' (1979). By the time WINGS had officially been laid to rest, PAUL had already released the Yuletide cutesiness of the 'WONDERFUL CHRISTMASTIME' single as well as the 'McCARTNEY II' (1980) album, a stripped down affair that heralded a new phase in his career. From the international chart topping 'EBONY AND IVORY' (a duet with STEVIE WONDER) onwards, the first half of the new decade saw McCARTNEY collaborating with the cream of the MOR elite. The results were sometimes intriguing, often downright dull. 'TUG OF WAR' (1982) and 'PIPES OF PEACE' (1983) kept the singer's profile high, the latter featuring 'SAY SAY SAY', a duet with buddy, MICHAEL JACKSON. While fans voted with their feet, critics were not so generous, although they saved their most vicious scorn for 'GIVE MY REGARDS TO BROAD STREET' (1984), McCARTNEY's own feature film and accompanying soundtrack. While 'NO MORE LONELY NIGHTS' was an affecting, if slight, ballad, the bulk of the project consisted of pointless BEATLES rehashes. It was two years before McCARTNEY surfaced again, although 'PRESS TO PLAY' (1986) failed to rectify matters. After finding a writing partner in ELVIS COSTELLO, McCARTNEY recorded his most committed and consistent work for more than a decade with 'FLOWERS IN THE DIRT' (1989). Recruiting a fairly permanent backing band: PAUL WICKENS (keyboards), CHRIS WHITTEN (drums), ROBBIE McINTOSH (guitar) and HAMISH STUART (guitar, bass), McCARTNEY set off on another world tour, documented on the fine 'TRIPPING THE LIVE FANTASTIC' (1990). An obligatory MTV unplugged set was released the following year, while an ambitious foray into classical music, 'LIVERPOOL ORATORIO' (1991) saw McCARTNEY working with the likes of CARL DAVIS and DAME KIRI TEKANEWA. His next album proper, 'OFF THE GROUND' (1993), failed to get that far, his solo career subsequently put on ice as he hooked up with his old chums, GEORGE HARRISON and RINGO STARR, to make the 'ANTHOLOGY' series of albums and videos tracing the history of The BEATLES. With his profile at its highest since the WINGS days, PAUL released 'FLAMING PIE' (1997), a work that even surpassed 'FLOWERS IN THE DIRT' and finally saw him live up to his reputation as one the greatest songwriters popular music has ever known. However, tragedy was to strike the McCARTNEY's, when wife LINDA lost her battle against breast cancer on the 17th of April 1998 (PAUL was beside her to the end); a tribute album for her work, 'Wild Prairie' was issued that November while PAUL was inducted as a solo artist into the Rock And Roll Hall Of Fame – "about fucking time!" was fashion designer daughter STELLA's T-shirted opinion of the matter. On the music front, MACCA was back with a bluesy rock'n'roll covers set, 'RUN DEVIL RUN' (1999), although underneath all the showbiz glitz of a comeback tour, PAUL was still hurting inside. • **Songwriters:** 99% by PAUL, except some with group. Covered; MONY MONY (Tommy James & The Shandells) / GO NOW (Moody Blues) / RUDOLPH THE RED-NOSED REINDEER (Christmas trad.) / KANSAS CITY (Wilbert Harrison) / MATCHBOX (Carl Perkins) / TWENTY FLIGHT ROCK (Eddie Cochran) / LAWDY MISS CLAWDY + IT'S NOW OR NEVER + BLUE MOON OF KENTUCKY (Elvis Presley) / BE-BOP-A-LULA (Gene Vincent) / BACK ON MY FEET (co-with Elvis Costello) / HI-HEEL SNEAKERS (Tommy Tucker) / GIVE PEACE A CHANCE (John Lennon) / AIN'T THAT A SHAME (Fats Domino) / etc., and many past BEATLES songs live. • **Trivia:** The 'BAND ON THE RUN' album sleeve featured the group being caught escaping alongside celebrities; Michael Parkinson, Kenny Lynch, James Coburn, Clement Freud, Christopher Lee & John Conteh.

Album rating: McCARTNEY (*6) / RAM (*6) / WILD LIFE (*4) / RED ROSE SPEEDWAY (*5) / BAND ON THE RUN (*9) / VENUS AND MARS (*6) / WINGS AT THE SPEED OF SOUND (*4) / WINGS OVER AMERICA (*6) / LONDON TOWN (*5) / WINGS GREATEST compilation (*7) / BACK TO THE EGG (*5) / McCARTNEY II (*5) / TUG OF WAR (*5) / PIPES OF PEACE (*4) / GIVE MY REGARDS TO BROAD STREET (*3) / PRESS TO PLAY (*4) / ALL THE BEST! compilation (*8) / FLOWERS IN THE DIRT (*6) / TRIPPING THE LIVE FANTASTIC (*4) / UNPLUGGED (THE OFFICIAL BOOTLEG) (*6) / CHOBA B CCCP – THE RUSSIAN ALBUM (*4) / OFF

THE GROUND (*4) / PAUL IS LIVE! (*4) / FLAMING PIE (*6) / RUN DEVIL RUN (*5)

PAUL McCARTNEY – vocals, bass, guitar, keyboards, drums (ex-BEATLES) with **LINDA McCARTNEY** (b. LINDA EASTMAN, 24 Sep'42, Scarsdale, New York, USA) – backing vocals

			Apple	Apple
Apr 70.	(lp/c) (PCS/TC-PCS 7102) <3363> **McCARTNEY**		2	1

– The lovely Linda / That would be something / Valentine day / Every night / Hot as sun / Glasses / Junk / Man we was lonely / Momma miss America / Teddy boy / Singalong junk / Maybe I'm amazed / Kreen-Akrove. (re-iss. May84 on 'Fame' lp/c; FA41 3100-1/-4) (cd-iss. Apr87; CDP 746 611-2) (re-iss. Apr90 lp/c; ATAK/TC-ATAK 152) (re-iss. Jun93 cd/c;)

			Apple	Apple
Feb 71.	(7") (R 5889) <1829> **ANOTHER DAY. / OH WOMAN OH WHY**		2	5

—— **PAUL** – vocals, guitar, bass / **LINDA** – keyboards, backing vocals, percussion / added **DENNY SEIWELL** – drums, vocals (plus various session people)

May 71.	(lp/c; PAUL & LINDA McCARTNEY) (PAS/TC-PAS 10003) <3375> **RAM**		1	2

– Too many people / Three legs / Ram on / Dear boy / Uncle Albert – Admiral Halsey / Smile away / Heart of the country / Monkberry moon delight / Eat at home / Long-haired lady / Ram on / The back seat of my car. (re-iss. on 'Parlophone'; CDP 746 612-2) (re-iss. Jan88; ATAK/TC-ATAK 12) (re-iss. Jun93 cd/c;)

Aug 71.	(7"; PAUL & LINDA McCARTNEY) (R 5914) **THE BACK SEAT OF MY CAR. / HEART OF THE COUNTRY**		39	–
Aug 71.	(7"; PAUL & LINDA McCARTNEY) <1837> **UNCLE ALBERT – ADMIRAL HALSEY. / TOO MANY PEOPLE**		–	1

WINGS

—— was the group the above trio formed; adding **DENNY LAINE** – guitar, vocals (ex-MOODY BLUES, ex-UGLYS, ex-BALLS, etc.)

Dec 71.	(lp/c) (PCS/TC-PCS 7142) <3386> **WILD LIFE**		8	10

– Mumbo / Bip bop / Love is strange / Wild life / Some people never know / I am your singer / Tomorrow / Dear friend. (re-iss. Apr84 on 'Fame' lp/c; FA/TCFA 3101) (cd-iss. Oct87 +=; CDFA 3101) – Mary had a little lamb / Little woman love / Oh woman, oh why. (re-iss. Jun93 cd/c;)

—— added **HENRY McCULLOCH** – guitar, vocals (ex-JOE COCKER, etc.)

Feb 72.	(7") (R 5936) <1847> **GIVE IRELAND BACK TO THE IRISH. / ('A'version)**		16	21 Mar72
May 72.	(7") (R 5949) <1851> **MARY HAD A LITTLE LAMB. / LITTLE WOMAN LOVE**		9	28 Jun72
Dec 72.	(7") (R 5973) <1857> **C MOON. / HI HI HI** (above flipped over in the States)		5	10

PAUL McCARTNEY AND WINGS

Mar 73.	(7") (R 5985) <1861> **MY LOVE. / THE MESS (live)**		9	1 Apr73
May 73.	(lp/c) (TC+/PCTC 251) <3409> **RED ROSE SPEEDWAY**		5	1

– Big barn bed / My love / Get on the right thing / One more kiss / Little lamb dragonfly / Single pigeon / When the night / Hold me tight – Lazy dynamite – Hands of love – Power cut / Loup (1st Indian on the Moon). (re-iss. Jan85 on 'Parlophone' lp/c; ATAK/TC-ATAK 16) (re-iss. Oct87 on 'Fame' lp/c/cd+=; FA/TCFA/CDFA 3193) (re-iss. Jun93) – The mess (live) / I lie around / Country dreamer.

Jun 73.	(7"; as WINGS) (R 5987) <1863> **LIVE AND LET DIE. / I LIE AROUND**		9	2 Jul73

—— **PAUL, LINDA + DENNY LAINER. (McCULLOCH went solo, SEIWELL to sessions)**

Oct 73.	(7") (R 5993) <1869> **HELEN WHEELS. / COUNTRY DREAMER**		12	10 Nov 73
Dec 73.	(lp/c) (PAS/TC-PAS 10007) <3415> **BAND ON THE RUN**		1	1

– Band on the run / Jet / Bluebird / Mrs. Vanderbilt / Let me roll it / Mamunia / No words / Picasso's last words (drink to me) / Nineteen hundred and eighty-five. <US pic-lp; > (re-iss. Jan85 on 'Parlophone' lp/c; ATAK/TC-ATAK 19) (cd-iss. Feb85 +=; CDP 746055-2) – Helen wheels. (re-iss. Jun93 cd/c;) (special 25th anniversary edition Mar99 d-cd/d-lp; 499176-2/-1/-) – (extra versions). (hit No.69)

Feb 74.	(7") (R 5996) <1871> **JET. / LET ME ROLL IT**		7	7
Apr 74.	(7") <1873> **BAND ON THE RUN. / 1985**		–	1
Jun 74.	(7") (R 5997) **BAND ON THE RUN. / ZOO GANG**		3	–

—— added **JIMMY McCULLOCH** (b. 4 Jun'53) – guitar, vocals (ex-THUNDERCLAP NEWMAN, ex-STONE THE CROWS) + **GEOFF BRITTON** – drums (ex-EAST OF EDEN)

Nov 74.	(7") (R 5999) <1875> **JUNIOR'S FARM. / SALLY G**		16	3 / 17

WINGS

—— **JOE ENGLISH** (b. Rochester, New York) – drums (ex-JAM FACTORY) repl. BRITTON who joined CHAMPION

			Capitol	Capitol
May 75.	(7") (R 6006) <4091> **LISTEN TO WHAT THE MAN SAID. / LOVE IN SONG**		6	1
Jun 75.	(lp/c) (PCTC/TC-PCTC 254) <11419> **VENUS AND MARS**		1	1

– Venus and Mars rock show / Love in song / You gave me the answer / Magneto and Titanium man / Letting go / Venus and Mars (reprise) / Spirits of ancient Egypt / Medicine jar / Call me back again / Listen to what the man said / Treat her gently – lonely old people / Crossroads theme. (re-iss. Jan85 on 'Parlophone' lp/c; ATAK/TC-ATAK 14) (cd-iss. Nov88 cd+=/c/lp; CD/TC+/FA 3213) – Zoogang / My carnival / Lunch box – odd socks. (re-iss. Jun93 cd/c;)

			E.M.I.	Capitol
Sep 75.	(7") (R 6008) <4145> **LETTING GO. / YOU GAVE ME THE ANSWER**		41	39
Nov 75.	(7") (R 6010) <4175> **VENUS AND MARS ROCK SHOW. / MAGNETO AND TITANIUM MAN**			12
Apr 76.	(lp/c) (PAS/TC-PAS 10010) <11525> **WINGS AT THE SPEED OF SOUND**		2	1

– Let 'em in / The note you never wrote / She's my baby / Beware my love / Wino junko / Silly love songs / Cook of the house / Time to hide / Must do something about it / San Ferry Anne / Warm and beautiful. *(re-iss. Jan85 lp/c; ATAK/TCATAC 13) (cd-iss. Jul89 on 'Parlophone'; CDPAS 10010) (re-iss. Oct89 on 'Fame' cd/c/lp; re-iss. Jun93 cd/c;)*

May 76. (7") *(R 6014)* <4256> **SILLY LOVE SONGS. / COOK OF THE HOUSE** — | 2 | 1 Apr76

Jul 76. (7") *(R 6015)* <4293> **LET 'EM IN. / BEWARE MY LOVE** | 2 | 3

Jan 77. (t-lp/d-c) *(PCSP/TC-PCSP 720)* <11593> **WINGS OVER AMERICA (live)** | 8 | 1 Dec76
— Venus and Mars rock show / Jet / Let me roll it / Spirits of ancient Egypt / Medicine jar / Maybe I'm amazed / Call me back again / Lady Madonna / The long and winding road / Live and let die / Picasso's last words (drink to me) / Richard Cory / Bluebird / I've just seen a face / Yesterday / You gave me the answer / Magnet and Titanium man / Go now / My love / Listen to what the man said / Let 'em in / Time to hide / Silly love songs / Beware my love / Letting go / Band on the run / Hi hi hi / Soily. *(d-cd-iss. May87; CDS 746715-2) (re-iss. 1989 d-lp/d-c; ATAK/TC-ATAK 17)*

Feb 77. (7") *(R 6017)* <4385> **MAYBE I'M AMAZED (live). / SOILY (live)** | 28 | 10

—— cut to trio of **PAUL, LINDA** and **DENNY** when JIMMY joined SMALL FACES, and JOE joined SEA LEVEL (ex-ALLMANS).

| | Capitol | Capitol |

Nov 77. (7",7"blue) *(R 6018)* <4504> **MULL OF KINTYRE. / GIRLS SCHOOL** | 1 | 33
(above flipped over in the States)

—— added **STEVE HOLLY** – drums (on session but joined f/t Jul'78)

| | Parlophone | Capitol |

Mar 78. (7") *(R 6019)* <4559> **WITH A LITTLE LUCK. / CUFF LINK: BACKWARDS TRAVELLER** | 5 | 1

Apr 78. (lp/c) *(PAS/TC-PAS 10012)* <11777> **LONDON TOWN** | 4 | 2
— London town / Cafe on the Left Bank / I'm carrying / Backwards traveller – Cuff link / Children children / Girlfriend / I've had enough / With a little luck / Famous groupies / Deliver your children / Name and address / Don't let it bring you down / Morse Moose and the Grey Goose. *(re-iss. Jan85 lp/c; ATAK/TCATAK 18) (re-iss. Aug89 on 'Fame' cd/c/lp; CD/TC+/FA 3223) (re-iss. Jun93 cd/c;)*

Jun 78. (7") *(R 6020)* <4594> **I'VE HAD ENOUGH. / DELIVER YOUR CHILDREN** | 42 | 25

Aug 78. (7") *(R 6021)* <4625> **LONDON TOWN. / I'M CARRYING** | 60 | 39

Nov 78. (lp/c) *(PCTC/TC-PCTC 256)* <11905> **WINGS GREATEST** (compilation) | 5 | 29
— Another day / Silly love songs / Live and let die / Junior's farm / With a little luck / Band on the run / Uncle Albert – Admiral Halsey / Hi hi hi / Let 'em in / My love / Mull of Kintyre. *(re-iss. Jan85 lp/c; ATAK/TCATAK 15) (cd-iss. 1989; CDP 746056-2) (re-iss. Aug93 cd/c;)*

—— added **LAURENCE JUBER** – guitar, vocals

| | Parlophone | Columbia |

Mar 79. (7"/ext.12") *(R/12R 6023)* <10939> **GOODNIGHT TONIGHT. / DAYTIME NIGHTIME SUFFERING** | 5 | 5

Jun 79. (7") *(R 6026)* **OLD SIAM, SIR. / SPIN IT ON** | 35 | –

Jun 79. (7") <11020> **GETTING CLOSER. / SPIN IT ON** | – | 20

Jun 79. (lp/c) *(PCTC/TC-PCTC 257)* <36057> **BACK TO THE EGG** | 6 | 8
— Reception / Getting closer / We're open tonight / Spin it on / Again and again and again / Old Siam, sir / Arrow through me / Rockestra theme / To you / After the ball – Million miles / Winter rose – Love awake / The broadcast / So glad to see you here / Baby's request. *(cd-iss. Jul89; CDPCTC 257) (re-iss. Aug93 cd/c;)* <US pic-lp promo, became worth $1,000; PCTCP 257>

Aug 79. (7") *(R 6027)* **GETTING CLOSER. / BABY'S REQUEST** | 60 | –

Sep 79. (7") <11070> **ARROW THROUGH ME. / OLD SIAM, SIR** | – | 29

PAUL McCARTNEY

—— went solo, augmented by **LINDA** plus session people

| | Parlophone | Columbia |

Nov 79. (7") *(R 6029)* <11162> **WONDERFUL CHRISTMASTIME. / RUDOLPH THE RED-NOSED REINDEER** | 6 |
<US re-iss. Nov83; same>

Apr 80. (7") *(R 6035)* <11263> **COMING UP. / COMING UP (live) / LUNCH BOX – ODD SOX** | 2 | 1

May 80. (lp/c) *(PCTC/TCPCTC 258)* <36511> **McCARTNEY II** | 1 | 3
— Coming up / Temporary secretary / On the way / Waterfalls / Nobody knows / Front parlour / Summer's day song / Frozen Jap / Bogey music / Darkroom / One of these days. *(re-iss. Sep87 on 'Fame' cd+=/c/lp; CD/TC+/FA 3191)* — Secret friend / Check my machine. *(re-iss. Aug93 cd/c;)*

Jun 80. (7") *(R 6037)* <11335> **WATERFALLS. / CHECK MY MACHINE** | 9 |

Sep 80. (12") *(12R 6039)* **TEMPORARY SECRETARY. / SECRET FRIEND** | | –

Apr 82. (7"; PAUL McCARTNEY & STEVIE WONDER) *(R 6054)* <02860> **EBONY AND IVORY. / RAINCLOUDS** | 1 | 1
(12"+=) *(12R 6054)* – ('A'solo version).

Apr 82. (lp/c) *(PCTC/TC-PCTC 259)* <37462> **TUG OF WAR** | 1 | 1
— Tug of war / Take it away / Somebody who cares / What's that you're doing? / Here today / Ballroom dancing / The pound is sinking / Wanderlust / Get it / Be what you see / Dress me up as a robber / Ebony and ivory. *(cd-iss. Jan85; CDP 746 057-2) (re-iss. Nov88 on 'Fame' cd/c/lp; CD/TC+/FA 3210) (re-iss. Aug93 cd/c;)*

Jun 82. (12"m) *(R 6056)* <03018> **TAKE IT AWAY. / I'LL GIVE YOU A RING / DRESS ME UP AS A ROBBER** | 15 | 10

Sep 82. (7") *(R 6057)* <03235> **TUG OF WAR. / GET IT** | 53 | 53

—— (In Oct'82, duetted w/ MICHAEL JACKSON on 'THE GIRL IS MINE' Top 10)

Oct 83. (7"; by PAUL McCARTNEY & MICHAEL JACKSON) *(R 6062)* <04168> **SAY SAY SAY. / ODE TO KOALA BEAR** | 2 | 1
(12"+=) *(12R 6062)* – ('A'instrumental).

Nov 83. (lp/c) *(PCTC/TCPCTC 1)* <39149> **PIPES OF PEACE** | 4 | 15
— Pipes of peace / Say say say / The other me / Keep under cover / So bad / The man / Sweetest little show / Average person / Hey hey / Tug of peace / Through our love. *(cd-iss. Jan84; CDP 746 018-2) (re-iss. Aug93 cd/c;)*

Dec 83. (7") *(R 6064)* <04296> **PIPES OF PEACE. / SO BAD** | 1 | 23 B-side

Sep 84. (7") *(R 6080)* <04581> **NO MORE LONELY NIGHTS. / ('A' extended)** | 2 | 6
(12"+=/12"pic-d+=) *(12R/+P 6080)* – Silly love songs.

Oct 84. (d-lp/c)(cd) *(PCTC/TCPCTC 2)(CDP 746043-2)* <39613> **GIVE MY REGARDS TO BROAD STREET – ORIGINAL SOUND TRACK** | 1 | 21
— No more lonely nights (ballad) / Good day sunshine / Corridor music / Yesterday / Here, there and everywhere / Wanderlust / Ballroom dancing / Silly love songs (reprise) / Not such a bad boy / No values / No more lonely nights (reprise) / For no one / Eleanor Rigby – Eleanor's dream / The long and winding road / No more lonely nights (play out version). *(re-iss. Aug93 cd/c;)*

Nov 84. (7"/7"sha-pic-d; by PAUL McCARTNEY & THE FROG CHORUS) *(R/+P 6086)* **WE ALL STAND TOGETHER. / ('A'-Humming version)** | 3 | –
(re-iss. Dec85, reached No.34)

| | Parlophone | Capitol |

Nov 85. (7"/7"sha-pic-d) *(R/+P 6118)* <5537> **SPIES LIKE US. / MY CARNIVAL** | 16 | 7
(12"+=/12"pic-d+=) *(12R/+P 6118)* – ('A'-party mix).

Jul 86. (7") *(R 6133)* <5597> **PRESS. / IT'S NOT TRUE** | 25 | 21
(12"+=) *(12R 6133)* – Hanglide. / ('A' dub).
(10"++=) *(10R 6133)* – ('A'version).

Sep 86. (cd/c/lp) *(CD/TC+/PCSD 103)* <12475> **PRESS TO PLAY** | 8 | 30
— Stranglehold / Good times coming – Feel the sun / Talk more talk / Footprints / Only love remains / Press / Pretty little head / Move over busker / Angry / However absurd. *(cd+=)* – Write away / It's not true / Tough on a tightrope. *(re-iss. Aug93 cd/c;)*

Oct 86. (7") *(R 6145)* **PRETTY LITTLE HEAD. / WRITE AWAY** | |
(12"+=/c-s+=) *(12R/TCR 6145)* – Angry.

Nov 86. (7") <5636> **STRANGLEHOLD. / ANGRY (remix)** | – | 81

Dec 86. (7"/12") *(R/12R 6148)* <5672> **ONLY LOVE REMAINS. / TOUGH ON A TIGHTROPE** | 34 |
(7" w-free 7") *(R 6018)* – Mull of Kintyre / Girls school.

Nov 87. (7") *(R 6170)* **ONCE UPON A LONG AGO. / BACK ON MY FEET** | 10 | –
(12"+=) *(12R 6170)* – Midnight special / Don't get around much anymore.
(12"+=) *(12RX 6170)* – Lawdy Miss Clawdy / Kansas City.
(cd-s+=) *(CDR 6170)* – Don't get around much anymore / Kansas City.

Nov 87. (cd/c/lp) *(CD/TC+/PMTV 1)* <48287> **ALL THE BEST!** (compilation) | 2 | 62
— Coming up / Ebony and ivory (w/ STEVIE WONDER) / Listen to what the man said / No more lonely nights / Silly love songs / Let 'em in / C Moon / Pipes of peace / Live and let die / Another day / Maybe I'm amazed / Goodnight tonight / Once upon a long time ago / Say say say / With a little luck / My love / We all stand together / Mull of Kintyre / Jet / Band on the run. <US slightly different tracks>

—— now with **LINDA / WIX** (PAUL WICKENS) – keyboards / **CHRIS WHITTEN** – drums / **ROBBIE McINTOSH** – guitar / **HAMISH STUART** – guitar, bass (ex-AVERAGE WHITE BAND)

May 89. (7") *(R 6213)* <44367> **MY BRAVE FACE. / FLYING TO MY HOME** | 18 | 25
(12"+=/c-s+=/cd-s+=) *(12R/TCR/CDR 6213)* – I'm gonna be a wheel someday / Ain't that a shame.

Jun 89. (cd/c/lp) *(CD/TC+/PCSD 106)* <91653> **FLOWERS IN THE DIRT** | 1 | 21
— My brave face / Rough ride / You want her too / Distractions / We got married / Put it there / Figure of eight / This one / Don't be careless love / That day is done / How many people / Motor of love. *(cd+=)* – Ou est le soleil. *(re-iss. Nov89 as 'FLOWERS ... WORLD TOUR PACK' cd/lp; CD+/PCSDX 106) (w/free 7")* – PARTY PARTY (free 3"cd-s.w/cd version) *(re-iss. Aug93 cd/c;)*

Jul 89. (c-s/7") *(TC+/R 6223)* <44438> **THIS ONE. / THE FIRST STONE** | 18 | 94
(12"+=/cd-s+=) *(12R/CDR 6223)* – I wanna cry / I'm in love again.

Nov 89. (c-s/7") *(TC+/R 6235)* <44489> **FIGURE OF EIGHT. / OU EST LE SOLEIL?** | 42 | 92
(12"+=) *(12R 6235)* – ('B'dub mix).
(3"cd-s+=) *(CD3R 6235)* – Rough ride.
(12") *(12RX 6235)* – ('A'side) / This one (club mix).
(cd-s) *(CDR 6235)* – ('A'side) / Long and winding road / Loveliest thing.

Feb 90. (c-s/7") *(TC+/R 6246)* **PUT IT THERE. / MAMA'S LITTLE GIRL** | 32 | –
(12"+=/cd-s+=) *(12R/CDR 6246)* – Same time next year.

Oct 90. (c-s/7") *(TC+/R 6271)* **BIRTHDAY (live). / GOOD DAY SUNSHINE (live)** | 29 | –
(12"+=/cd-s+=) *(12R/CDR 6271)* – P.S. I love you (live) / Let 'em in (live).

Nov 90. (d-cd-d-c/t-lp) *(CD/TC/PCST 7346)* <94778> **TRIPPING THE LIVE FANTASTIC (live)** | 17 | 26
— Figure of eight / Jet / Rough ride / Got to get you into my life / Band on the run / Birthday / Ebony and ivory / we got married / Inner city madness / Maybe I'm amazed / The long and winding road / Cracking up / Fool on the hill / Sgt. Pepper's lonely hearts club band / Can't buy me love / Matchbox / Put it there / Together / Things we said today / Eleanor Rigby / This one / My brave face / I saw her standing there / Back in the USSR / Twenty flight rock / Coming up / Sally / Let it be / Ain't that a shame / Live and let die / If I were not upon the stage / Hey Jude / Yesterday / Get back / Golden slumbers – Carry that weight – The end / Don't let the Sun catch you crying.

Dec 90. (c-s/7") *(TC+/R 6278)* **ALL MY TRIALS (live). / C MOON (live)** | 35 | –
(12"+=) *(12R 6278)* – Mull of Kintyre / Put it there.
(cd-s+=) *(CDR 6278)* – Live medley:- Strawberry fields forever / Help / Give peace a chance.

—— **BLAIR CUNNINGHAM** – drums (ex-LLOYD COLE) repl. WHITTEN

Jun 91. (cd/c/lp) *(CD/TC+/PCSD 116)* <96413> **UNPLUGGED – THE OFFICIAL BOOTLEG** | 7 | 14
— Be-bop-a-lula / I lost my little girl / Here there and everywhere / Blue Moon of Kentucky / We can work it out / San Francisco Bay blues / I've just seen a face / Every night / She's a woman / Hi-heel sneakers / And I love her / That would be something / Blackbird / Ain't no sunshine / Good rockin' tonight / Singing the blues / Junk. *(re-iss. Aug91 as 'CHOBA B CCCP' cd/c/lp; CD/TC+/PCSD 117)* – hit UK No.63 *(re-iss. Sep94)*

Jan 93. (c-s/7") *(TC+/R 6330)* <44904> **HOPE OF DELIVERANCE. / LONG LEATHER COAT** | 18 | 83

(12"/cd-s) (12R/CDR 6330) – ('A'side) / Big boys bickering / Deliverance (dub) / Kicked around no more.

Feb 93. (cd/c/lp) (CD/TC+/PCSD 125) <80362> **OFF THE GROUND** 5 17
– Off the ground / Looking for changes / Hope of deliverance / Mistress and maid / I owe it all to you / Biker like an icon / Peace in the neighbourhood / Golden Earth girl / The lovers that never were / Get out of my way / Winedark open sea / C'mon people.

Feb 93. (c-s/7") (TC+/R 6338) **C'MON PEOPLE. / I CAN'T IMAGINE** 41 –
(cd-s+=) (CDR 6338) – Down to the river / Keep coming back to love.

Nov 93. (cd/c/lp) (CD/TC+/PCSD 147) <27704> **PAUL IS LIVE! (live)** 34 78
– Drive my car / Let me roll it / Looking for changes / Peace in the neighbourhood / All my loving / Robbie's bit / Good rocking tonight / We can work it out / Hope of deliverance / Michelle / Biker like an icon / Here there and everywhere / My love / Magical mystery tour / C'mon people / Lady Madonna / Paperback writer / Penny Lane / Live and let die / Kansas City / Welcome to Soundcheck / Hotel in Benidorm / I wanna be your man / A fine day.

–––– In 1995, PAUL had his biggest hit in a long time (No.19), when he was part of The SMOKIN' MOJO FILTERS ('Come Together') alongside PAUL WELLER and NOEL GALLAGHER (Oasis).

May 97. (7"pic-d) (RP 6462) **YOUNG BOY. / LOOKING FOR YOU** 19 [ ]
(cd-s+=) (CDR 6462) – Oobu Joobu medley (part 1).
(cd-s) (CDR 6462) – ('A'side) / Broomstick / Oobu Joobu medley (part 2).

May 97. (cd/c/lp) (CD/TC+/PCSD 171) **FLAMING PIE** 2 2
– Song we were singing / The world tonight / If you wanna / Somedays / Young boy / Calico skies / Heaven on a Sunday / Used to be bad / Souvenir / Little willow / Really love you / Beautiful night / Great day.

Jul 97. (7"pic-d) (RP 6472) **THE WORLD TONIGHT. / USED TO BE BAD** 23 64 May97
(cd-s+=) (CDRS 6472) – Oobu joobu (part 3).
(cd-s) (CDR 6472) – Oobu joobu (part 1).

Dec 97. (c-s/7") (TC+/R 6489) **BEAUTIFUL NIGHT. / LOVE COME TUMBLING DOWN** 25 [ ]
(cd-s+=) (CDRS 6489) – Oobu joobu (part 6).
(cd-s) (CDR 6489) – ('A'side) / Oobu joobu (part 6) / Same love.

Oct 99. (cd/c/lp) (<5 22351-2/-4/-1>) **RUN DEVIL RUN** 12 27
– Blue jean bop / She said yeah / All shook up / Run Devil run / No other baby / Lonesome town / Try not to cry / Movie mag / Brown eyed handsome man / What it is / Coquette / I got stung / Honey hush / Shake a hand / Party. (8x7"box-iss.Nov99; 523229-1)

Oct 99. (7") (R 6527) **NO OTHER BABY. / BROWN EYED HANDSOME MAN** 42 [ ]
(cd-s+=) (CDRS 6527) – Fabulous.
(cd-s) (CDR 6527) – (all three tracks in mono).

– compilations, etc. –

Feb 81. (lp) E.M.I.; (CHAT 1) / Columbia; <36987> **McCARTNEY INTERVIEW** 34 [ ]

– under an alias (various connections) –

–––– PAUL's brother MIKE McGEAR with a sibling collaboration
Oct 74. (7"; COUNTRY HAMS) E.M.I.; (EMI 2220) **WALKING IN THE PARK WITH ELOISE. / BRIDGE OVER THE RIVER SUITE** [ ] [ ]

–––– PAUL under a new moniker
Apr 77. (7"; as PERCY 'THRILLS' THRILLINGTON) E.M.I.; (EMI 2594) **UNCLE ALBERT, ADMIRAL HALSEY. / EAST AT HOME** [ ] [ ]
(also album, 'THRILLINGTON' lp/c; EMC/TC-EMC 3175)

–––– next by LINDA McCARTNEY's band
Aug 79. (7"/7"yellow; by SUZY & THE RED STRIPES) A&M; (AMS/+P 7461) / Epic; <50403> **SEASIDE WOMAN. / B SIDE TO SEASIDE** 59 Jun77
(re-iss. Jul80, 7"/7"pic-d; AMS/+P 7548) (re-iss. 1986 on 'E,M,I,' 7"12"; EMI/12EMI 5572)

–––– PAUL had also guested on numerous singles and albums. DENNY LAINE has also had solo career, although with no commercial success.

Dave McCOMB (see under ⇒ **TRIFFIDS**)

Ian McCULLOCH (see under ⇒ **ECHO & THE BUNNYMEN**)

Country Joe McDONALD (& THE FISH)

Born: 1 Jan'42, Washington, D.C., USA. In the early 60's, McDONALD joined the navy, although he left after his service period was over. In 1964, he augmented fellow troubadour, BLAIR HARDIMAN, on his very rare 'GOODBYE BLUES' album, forming COUNTRY JOE & THE FISH the following year. The band cut a few EP's for the local 'Rag Baby' magazine, and, through its editor Ed Denson, they signed a recording contract with folk label, 'Vanguard'. In the summer of '67, after a much heralded Monterey Pop Festival outing, their debut album, 'ELECTRIC MUSIC FOR THE MIND AND BODY', breached the US Top 40. McDONALD was the quintessential urban folk-country star, whose satirical politico-drugs and anti-war themes induced many to identify with his anarchic outfit during the 60's. In 1968, they released a second set, 'I-FEEL-LIKE-I'M-FIXIN'-TO-DIE', which featured his ode to his ex-girlfriend, JANIS JOPLIN and the anti-nuke anthem, 'THE

BOMB SONG'. The band issued a third album, 'TOGETHER', although this was their last to secure a major chart placing. Other albums followed, some solo, although in 1970, he was convicted and fined $500 for obscenity, inciting anti-social crowd behaviour after chanting 'Gimme a F.*.*.*.'. This 'Fish Cheer' had been an audience participation ritual since the mid-60's. In the 70's, he took the country element in his music to its natural conclusion, with a string of rootsy albums. • Trivia: In 1971, he joined actors JANE FONDA and DONALD SUTHERLAND, in a 'Free The Army' revue. In 1976, he campaigned to 'SAVE THE WHALES', even writing a single with that title.

Album rating: COUNTRY JOE AND BLAIR HARDMAN (*4) / ELECTRIC MUSIC FOR THE MIND AND BODY (*4) / I FEEL LIKE I'M FIXIN' TO DIE (*6) / TOGETHER (*5) / HERE WE ARE AGAIN (*4) / COUNTRY JOE & THE FISH – GREATEST HITS compilation (*6) / THINKING OF WOODY solo (*5) / C.J. FISH (*4) / TONIGHT I'M SINGING JUST FOR YOU solo (*5) / HOLD ON IT'S COMING (*4) solo / WAR, WAR, WAR solo (*4) / INCREDIBLE! LIVE! solo (*4) / THE LIFE AND TIMES OF COUNTRY JOE & THE FISH FROM HAIGHT-ASHBURY TO WOODSTOCK compilation (*6) / PARIS SESSIONS solo (*4) / COUNTRY JOE solo (*5) / PARADISE WITH AN OCEAN VIEW solo (*4) / LOVE IS A FIRE solo (*4) / REUNION (*4) / ROCK'N'ROLL MUSIC FROM PLANET EARTH solo (*4) / LEISURE SUITE solo (*4) / ON MY OWN solo (*4) / INTO THE FRAY (*4) / CHILDS PLAY (*4) / PEACE ON EARTH solo (*4) / VIETNAM EXPERIENCE solo (*4) / SUPERSTITIOUS BLUES solo (*4) / CARRY ON solo (*4) / THE COLLECTED COUNTRY JOE & THE FISH compilation (*7)

COUNTRY JOE & THE FISH

JOE McDONALD – vocals, guitar / **BARRY 'THE FISH' MELTON** (b.1947, Brooklyn, New York) – guitar, vocals / **CARL SHRAGER** – washboard / **BILL STEEL** – bass / **MIKE BEARDSLEE** – harp, vocals

			not iss.	Rag Baby
Oct 65.	(7"ep) <1001> **COUNTRY JOE & THE FISH**		–	[ ]

– I-feel-like-I'm-fixin'-to-die rag / Superbird. / PETER KRUG: Fire in the city / Johnny's gone to war.

McDONALD + MELTON introduced **BRUCE BARTHOL** (b.1947, Berkeley, Calif.) – bass / **DAVID COHEN** (b.1942, Brooklyn, N.Y.) – electric guitar / **CHICKEN HIRSCH** (b.1940, Calif.) – drums / **PAUL ARMSTRONG** – harp / **JOHN FRANCIS GUNNING** – drums

Jun 66. (7"ep) <1002> **RAG BABY** [ ] [ ]
– Bass strings / Section 43 / (Thing called) Love.

MARK RYAN repl. BRUCE

		Fontana	Vanguard
Jul 67.	(7") <35052> **NOT SO SWEET MARTHA LORRAINE. / THE MASKED MARAUDER**	–	95
Oct 67.	(lp; stereo/mono) (S+/TFL 6081) <VSD 79244> **ELECTRIC MUSIC FOR THE MIND AND BODY**		39 Apr67

– Flying high / Not so sweet Martha Lorraine / Death sound blues / Porpoise mouth / Section 43 / Superbird / Sad and lonely times / Love / Bass strings / The masked marauder / Grace. (re-iss. Mar69 & Feb72 on 'Vanguard'; SVRL 19026) (re-iss. Mar89 on 'Start' lp/c/cd; VM5/TC6/CD6 301) (cd re-iss. Oct95; VMD 79244)

Nov 67. (7") (TF 882) **NOT SO SWEET MARTHA LORRAINE. / LOVE** – –
Nov 67. (7") <35059> **JANIS. / JANIS (instrumental)** – –
Jan 68. (7") <35061> **WHO AM I? / THURSDAY** – –
Mar 68. (lp; stereo/mono) (S+/TFL 6086) <VSD 79266> **I-FEEL-LIKE-I'M-FIXIN'-TO-DIE** 67 Nov67
– (the fish cheer) / I-feel-like-I'm-fixin'-to-die rag / Who am I / Pat's song / Rock coast blues / Magoo / Janis / Thought dream / Thursday / Eastern jam / Colors for Susan. (re-iss. Mar69 & Feb72 on 'Vanguard'; SVRL 19029) (re-iss. Jul89 on 'Start' lp/c/cd; VM LP5/TC6/CD7 306) (cd re-iss. Oct95; VMD 79266)

		Vanguard	Vanguard
Jul 68.	(7") <35068> **ROCK AND SOUL MUSIC. / (part 2)**	–	23 Jul68
Nov 68.	(lp) (SVRL 19006) <VSD 79277> **TOGETHER**		[ ]

– Rock and soul music / Susan / Mojo navigator / Bright suburban Mr. & Mrs. Clean machine / Good guys – bad guys cheer / The streets of your town / The fish moan / The Harlem song / Waltzing in the moonlight / Away bounce my bubbles / Cetacean / An untitled protest. (cd re-iss. Oct95; VMD 79277)

JOE + BARRY recruited new members **MARK KAPNER** – keyboards to replace COHEN (He joined BLUES PROJECT). **PETER ALBIN** – bass (ex-BIG BROTHER & THE HOLDING COMPANY) / **DAVID GETZ** – drums (ex-BIG BROTHER & THE HOLDING COMPANY) repl. others.

Jun 69. (7") <35090> **HERE I GO AGAIN. / BABY YOU'RE DRIVING ME CRAZY** – [ ]
Sep 69. (lp) (STVL 19048) <VSD 79299> **HERE WE ARE AGAIN** [ ] Jun69
– Here I go again / Donovan's reef / It's nice to have love / Baby, you're driving me crazy / Crystal blues / For no reason / I'll survive / Maria / My girl / Doctor of electricity.

Oct 69. (7") (VA 3) **HERE I GO AGAIN. / IT'S SO NICE TO HAVE LOVE** [ ] –

DOUG METZNER – bass repl. ALBIN / GREG DEWEY – drums (ex-MAD RIVER) repl. GETZ who went solo.

Jun 70. (7") <35112> **I FEEL LIKE I'M FIXIN' TO DIE RAG. / JANIS** – [ ]
Jun 70. (7") (6076 250) **I FEEL LIKE I'M FIXIN' TO DIE RAG. / MARIA** [ ] –
Oct 70. (lp) (6359 002) <VSD 6555> **C.J. FISH** [ ] Apr70
– Sing sing sing / She's a bird / Mara / Hang on / The baby song / Hey Bobby / Silver and gold / Rocking 'round the world / The love machine / The return of sweet Lorraine / Hand of man. (re-iss. Feb72; same)

They split Autumn 1970

COUNTRY JOE McDONALD

had solo releases between 69-71. with **HAROLD BRADLEY** – guitar, bass / **RAY EDENTON** – guitar / **GRADY MARTIN** – guitar / **NORMAN PUTMAN** – bass / **BUDDY HARMON** – drums / **HARGUS 'PIG' ROBBINS** – percussion

			Vanguard	Vanguard

Apr 70. (lp; stereo/mono) *(S+/VRL 19057)* <VSD 6546> **THINKING OF WOODY GUTHRIE** ☐ ☐ Dec69
– Pastures of plenty / Talkin' dust bowl / Blowing down that old dusty road / So long it's been good to know yuh / Tom Joad / The sinking of Rueben James / Roll on Columbia / Pretty Boy Floyd / When the curfew blows / This land is your land. *(re-iss. Feb72;) (re-iss. Sep89 on 'Start' cd/c; CDVMD/MCCV 6546)*

Jan 71. (lp) *(6359 004)* <VSD 6557> **TONIGHT I'M SINGING JUST FOR YOU** ☐ ☐ Mar70
– Ring of fire / Tennessee stud / Heartaches by the number / Tiger by the tail / Crazy arms / You've done me wrong / All of me belongs to you / Oklahoma hills / Tonight I'm singing just for you / Friend, lover, woman, wife / Six days on the road. *(re-iss. Feb72;)*

──── solo releases now post-FISH, were augmented by some UK session men

Jan 71. (7") *<35133>* **HOLD ON IT'S COMING. / PLAYING WITH FIRE** ☐ ☐ –

Sep 71. (lp) <(VSD 79314)> **HOLD ON IT'S COMING** ☐ ☐ Apr71
– Hold on it's coming / Air Algiers / Only love is worth this pain / Playing with fire / Travelling / Joe's blues / Mr. Big pig / Balancing on the edge of time / Jamila / Hold on it's coming No.2.

Sep 71. (7") *(6076 252)* **HOLD ON IT'S COMING. / (take 2)** ☐ –

──── with **ANNA RIZZO** – vocals / **GREG DEEY** – drums / **NACKO DEWEY** – harp / **JOHN REWIND** – guitar / **VIC SMITH** – bass

1971. (7"ep) *>1003>* **COUNTRY JOE McDONALD & GROOTNA** – ☐
– Kiss my ass / Tricky Dicky / Free some day.
(above was issued in the States on his 'Rag Baby' label.)

Jan 72. (lp) <(VSD 79315)> **WAR WAR WAR** ☐ ☐ Aug71
– The call / Forward / Young fellow, my lad / The man from Aphabaska / The munition maker / The twins / Jean Desprez / War widow / The march of the dead.

1972. (7") *<35150>* **HANG ON. / HAND OF MAN** ☐ ☐

Jul 72. (lp) <(VSD 79316)> **INCREDIBLE! LIVE! COUNTRY JOE!** ☐ ☐ Feb72
– Entertainment is my business / Sweet Marie / Kiss my ass / Living in the future in a plastic dome / Walk in Santiago / Tricky Dicky / You know what I mean / Fly so high / Deep down in our hearts / Free some day / I'm on the road again.

COUNTRY JOE

formed his ALL-STAR BAND with **PETER ALBIN** – bass / **DAVID GETZ** – drums / **TUCKI BAILEY** – saxophone / **DOROTHY MOSCOWITZ** – vocals, piano (ex-UNITED STATES OF AMERICA) / **PHIL MARSH** – guitar repl. **BARRY MELTON** / **ANNA RIZZO** – drums repl. SALLY HENDERSON – vocals / **SEBASTIAN NICHOLSON** – congas repl. **SUSAN LYDON** – vocals

			Vanguard	Vanguard

Apr 73. (7") *<35161>* **FANTASY. / I SEE A ROCKET** – –

Aug 73. (lp) <(VSD 79328)> **PARIS SESSIONS** ☐ ☐
– Fantasy / Movieola / I'm so tired / Moving / I don't know why / Zombies in a house of madness / Sexist pig / Colorado Town / Coulene Anne / St. Tropez.

Oct 73. (7") *(VAN 1006)* **FANTASY. / HOLD ON IT'S COMING** ☐ –

──── **GINNY WHITTAKER** – drums, repl. GETZ, BAILEY, MARSH + NICHOLSON

──── (Feb'74) **COUNTRY JOE** toured as duo with **BARRY MELTON**. Still solo below.

Nov 74. (7") *<35181>* **DR. HIP. / SATISFACTORY** ☐ ☐

Apr 75. (lp) <(VSD 79348)> **COUNTRY JOE** ☐ ☐ Dec74
– Dr. Hip / Old Joe Corey / Making money in Chile / You messed over me / Memories / Chile / Pleasin' / Jesse James / Satisfactory / It's finally over.

Apr 75. (7") *<35184>* **JESSE JAMES. / CHILE** ☐ ☐

COUNTRY JOE McDONALD

also augmented by ENERGY CRISIS (below) **PHIL MARSH** – guitar / **BRUCE BARTHOL** – bass / **JOHN BLAKELEY** – guitar / **PETER MILIO** – drums / **TED ASHFORD** – keyboards

			Fantasy	Fantasy

Oct 75. (lp) *(FTA 3002)* <9495> **PARADISE WITH AN OCEAN VIEW** ☐ ☐
– Tear down the walls / Holy roller / Lost my connection / The limit / Save the whales / Oh! Jamaica / Lonely on the road / Tricks / Breakfast for two.

Jan 76. (7") *(FTC 123)* <758> **BREAKFAST FOR TWO. / LOST MY CONNECTION** ☐ 92 Nov75

Apr 76. (7") *(FTC 130)* <765> **SAVE THE WHALES. / OH! JAMAICA** ☐ ☐

Aug 76. (lp) *(FTA 3005)* <9511> **LOVE IS A FIRE** ☐ ☐
– It won't burn / You're the song / In love naturally / Oh no / Baby baby / True love at last / Who's gonna fry your eggs / Colortone / I need you (this and that) / Love is a fire.

Oct 76. (7") <780> **I NEED YOU. / LOVE IS A FIRE** – ☐

Oct 76. (7") *(FT 135)* **IN LOVE NATURALLY. / WHO'S GONNA FRY YOUR EGGS** ☐ –

──── next solo albums used BARRY MELTON and session people.

Apr 77. (lp) *(FT 529)* <9525> **GOODBYE BLUES** ☐ ☐
– Copiapo / Thought dreams / Goodbye blues / Let's go ridin' in the car / Blood on the ice / Primitive people / TV blues / Dark clouds / Little blue whale / Wilderness trail.

Oct 77. (7") *(FT 143)* **LA DI DA. / RING OF FIRE** ☐ –

May 78. (lp) *(FT 539)* <9544> **ROCK'N'ROLL MUSIC FROM PLANET EARTH** ☐ ☐ Feb78
– Coyote / Bring back the sixties man / Sunshine through my window / Rock & roll again / Dark ship / Y.O.U. / Southern cross / Space patrol / U.F.O. / Get it together.

Mar 78. (7") *(FTC 154)* <814> **COYOTE. / SOUTHERN CROSS** ☐ ☐

Jul 78. (7") <822> **SUNSHINE THROUGH MY WINDOW. / BRING BACK THE 60'S MAN** ☐ –

──── (Sep78) **COUNTRY JOE** reformed THE FISH, with **BARRY MELTON** – guitar, vocals / **PETER ALBIN** – bass / **BOB FLURIE** – guitar / **HAROLD ACEVES** – drums

──── continued solo work.

Dec 79. (lp) *(FT 565)* <9586> **LEISURE SUITE** ☐ ☐
– Private parts / Take this time out / Doo-wop-oh / Hard work no play / La di da / Sure cure for the blues / Reaching for the stars. *(cd-iss. late'90 on 'Rag Baby'; RBCD900317)*

Dec 79. (7") **TAKE THIS TIME OUT. / PRIVATE PARTS** – ☐

			Rag Baby	Rag Baby

Aug 81. (lp) *(RAG 1012)* <147 406> **ON MY OWN** (totally solo) ☐ ☐
– Standing at the crossroads / Calamity Jane / Give some love, get some back / C-O-U-N-T-R-Y / The Halloween tree / Slide trombone blues / Your last few records just didn't make it / Power plant blues / A Vietnam veteran still alive / Yankee doodle / Darlin' Dan.

──── now with ever-changing personnel.

Jun 82. (d-lp) *(RAG 2001)* **INTO THE FRAY** (live) – ☐
– Kiss my ass / Quiet days in Clichy / Sexist pig / Here I go again / Breakfast for two / Love is a fire / Picks and lasers / Coyote / Hold on it's coming / Entertainment is my business / Holy roller / Not so sweet Martha Lorraine / Janis / Get it all together / A Vietnam veteran still alive / Breakfast for two / Fixin'-to-die-rag / Save the whales / Ring of fire. *(UK-iss.Feb89; same) (cd-iss. late'90; RBCD 900603)*

Oct 83. (lp) *<RAG 1018>* **CHILDS PLAY** ☐ ☐
– Not in a Chinese restaurant / Power plant blues / Picks and lasers / Ice pack / One more good year of good times / Vietnam never again / America my home / Star Yeck: Voyage of the good ship Undersize / Mi Corazon. *(UK-iss.same; same)*

			Line	not iss.

Feb 85. (lp) *(RB 9.00068)* **PEACE ON EARTH** – – German
– Live in peace / Sunshine / Let it rain / You can get it if you really want / War hero / Feeling better / The girl next door / Darlin' man (the rocket man) / Pledging my love / Garden of Eden / Space lovin' / Peace on Earth. *(cd-iss. Feb89 & Oct94 on 'Rag Baby'; RBCD 9.00068)*

1986. (d-lp) *(LI 9.00418)* **VIETNAM EXPERIENCE** – – German
– I-feel-like-I'm-fixin'-to-die rag / Foreign policy blues / Agent Orange song / The girl next door (combat nurse) / Kiss my arse / Secret agent / Vietnam veteran still alive / Vietnam never again / Mourning blues / Welcome home / Vietnam requiem – part 1:- The beginning, part 2:- The end. *(cd-iss. Jun89; LICD 9.00418)*

──── returned to the recording studio in 1990

			Rykodisc	Rykodisc

Jan 91. (cd) *(RBCD 90094-2)* <10201> **SUPERSTITIOUS BLUES** ☐ ☐
– Standing at the crossroads / Eunicita / Superstitious blues / Tranquility / Starship ride / Cocaine (rock) / Blues for breakfast / Clara Barton / Blues for Michael.

			Line	Rykodisc

Jan 95. (cd) *(90130-2)* **CARRY ON** ☐ ☐
– Picks and lasers / Lady with the lamp / Joe's blues / Hold on to each other / Stolen heart blues / Trilogy / Going home / Carry on / My last song.

– compilations, etc. (with the FISH *) –

Mar 70. (lp) *Vanguard; (SVRL 19058)* <VSD 6545> **COUNTRY JOE & THE FISH / GREATEST HITS** ☐ 74 Dec69

Nov 73. (d-lp) *Vanguard; (VSD 27-28)* **THE LIFE AND TIMES OF COUNTRY JOE AND THE FISH FROM HAIGHT – ASHBURY TO WOODSTOCK** ☐ ☐ Oct71

Jul 76. (d-lp) *Vanguard; (VSD 85-86)* **THE ESSENTIAL COUNTRY JOE McDONALD** ☐ ☐

Mar 77. (lp/c) *Golden Hour-Pye; (GH/ZCGH 865)* **THE GOLDEN HOUR OF COUNTRY JOE McDONALD** ☐ ☐

Jun 76. (lp) *Fantasy; <9530>* **REUNION** (live '67-'69 line-up) – –

Jun 81. (lp) *Rag Baby; <AMR 3309>* **THE EARLY YEARS** – –
– (tracks as below)

Jul 81. (lp) *Rag Baby; (RAG 1000)* **COLLECTOR'S ITEMS – THE FIRST THREE EP'S** ☐ ☐
(re-iss. Mar87 on 'New World'; NEW 87) (re-iss. Apr87 on 'Decal'; LIK 8) (cd-iss. 1992 on 'Sequel';)

Aug 83. (lp) *Animus; (FEEL 1)* **ANIMAL TRACKS** ☐ ☐

Sep 83. (7") *Animus; (TOUCH 1)* **BLOOD ON THE ICE. / (no b-side)** ☐ –

──── (also appeared on Various Artists compilations WOODSTOCK, QUIET DAY IN CLICHY, CELEBRATION – BIG SUE FESTIVAL (live), A TRIBUTE TO WOODY GUTHRIE, ZACHARIAH (Soundtrack).

Jun 91. (cd) *Pickwick; (VCD 111)* **COLLECTED COUNTRY JOE & THE FISH** ☐ –
– Superbird / Bass strings / Section 43 / Flying high / Not so sweet Martha Lorraine / Death sound blues / Porpoise mouth / Sad and lonely times / The fish cheer – I-feel-like-I'm-fixin'-to-die rag / Rock coast blues / Janis / Eastern jam / Good guys – bad guys cheer / Rock and roll music / An unlimited protest / Here I go again / Maria, my own / Crystal blues / Rockin' round the world.

Jul 92. (cd) *Big Beat; (CDWIK 108)* **CLASSICS** ☐ ☐

Aug 96. (cd) *Volt; (VCD 139)* **LIVE AT THE FILLMORE WEST 1969** ☐ –

John McENTIRE (see under ⇒ TORTOISE)

MC5

Formed: Detroit, Michigan, USA . . . 1965 by ROB TYNER, FED 'SONIC' SMITH and WAYNE KRAMER. After two limited single releases, MC5 (MOTOR CITY FIVE) signed a contract with 'Elektra' in mid '68, helped by counter-cultural activist and DJ, John Sinclair. In addition to becoming the band's manager, he heavily influenced both their political extremism and warped takes on free jazz improvisation. Reflecting the harsher geographical and economic climate of Detroit, the band espoused revolution and struggle as opposed to the love and peace ethos of the sun-kissed Californian flower children. The riotous proto-punk of their legendary, acid-fuelled live show was captured on the controversial debut, 'KICK OUT THE JAMS'. Recorded in late October '68, it eventually hit the shops in May '69 and while the original uncensored pressings contained the line "Kick Out The Jams, Motherfuckers!", the offending word was later supplanted with the milder "Brothers And Sisters". Unfortunately, this wasn't enough to prevent some record stores from refusing to stock the lp, and after the band explicitly aired their views on one of the aforementioned dealers in a local newspaper, they were duly given the boot by Elektra. Nevertheless, the album reached No.30 in America and although it sounds a bit dated to modern ears, it was way radical for the time, remaining an inspiration to each new generation of noiseniks. After a split with Sinclair, the band signed with 'Atlantic' and began to move away from the overtly subversive nature of their earlier material to a more straightahead rock approach, evidenced on their Jon Landau-produced follow-up album, 'BACK IN THE U.S.A.'. Wired rock'n'roll of an impeccable degree, the record didn't fare well in the laid-back, doped-up climate of the early 70's. An ambitious third album in 1971, 'HIGH TIME', featuring horns and even Salvation Army musicians, still failed to cut any commercial ice and the band split in 1972. KRAMER subsequently spent five years in jail for cocaine dealing before embarking on a low key solo career while former manager, Sinclair, was sentenced to ten years in the early 70's for a minor dope charge, serving only two after appeal. Tragically, ROB TYNER died from a heart attack in 1991 aged only 46. Pioneers in the true sense of the word, the MC5 together with the STOOGES were the first real punk bands, the originators who were never bettered. **Songwriters:** Group compositions, except; I CAN ONLY GIVE YOU EVERYTHING (Them) / TUTTI FRUTTI (Little Richard).

Album rating: KICK OUT THE JAMS (*9) / BACK IN THE USA (*7) / HIGH TIME (*5) / BABES IN ARMS collection (*5) / LOOKING AT YOU collection (*4)

ROB TYNER (b. ROBERT DERMINER, 12 Dec'44) – vocals, harmonica / **WAYNE KRAMER** (b.30 Apr'48) – guitar, vocals, keyboards / **FRED 'SONIC' SMITH** (b. West Virginia) – guitar / **MICHAEL DAVIS** – bass / **DENNIS THOMPSON** – drums

		not iss.	A.M.G.
1966.	(7") <AMG 1001> **I CAN ONLY GIVE YOU EVERYTHING. / I JUST DON'T KNOW** *(above credited to MOTOR CITY FIVE)*	-	□

		not iss.	A2.
Mar 68.	(7") <A2 333> **LOOKING AT YOU. / BORDERLINE**	-	□

—— added 6th member **Brother J.C.CRAWFORD** – rapper / narrative

		Elektra	Elektra
May 69.	(7") (EKSN 45056) <EK 45648> **KICK OUT THE JAMS. / MOTOR CITY IS BURNING**	□	82 Mar 69
May 69.	(lp) (mono/stereo; EKL/EKS 74042) **KICK OUT THE JAMS**	□	30 Mar 69

– Ramblin' rose / Kick out the jams / Come together / Rocket reducer No.62 (rama lama fa fa) / Borderline / Motor city is burning / I want you right now / Starship. (re-iss. May77.) (re-iss. +cd.Nov91) (re-iss. cd+c Mar93 on 'Pickwick') (re-iss. cd/c Sep95 on 'Warners')

		Atlantic	Atlantic
Aug 69.	(7") (EKSN 45067) **RAMBLIN' ROSE. / BORDERLINE**	□	-
Oct 70.	(7") <2678> **TONIGHT. / LOOKING AT YOU**	-	□
Nov 70.	(lp) (2400 016) <SD 8247> **BACK IN THE U.S.A.**	□	Feb 70

– Tutti frutti / Tonight / Teenage list / Looking at you / Let me try / High school / Call me animal / The American ruse / Shakin' Street / The human being lawnmower / Back in the U.S.A. (re-iss. Feb77.) (cd-iss. May93 on 'Rhino-Atlantic')

1970.	(7") <2724> **SHAKIN' STREET. / THE AMERICAN RUSE**	-	□
Oct 71.	(lp) (2400 123) <SD 8285> **HIGH TIME**	□	□

– Sister Anne / Baby won't ya / Miss X / Gotta keep movin' / Future – Now / Poison / Over nnd over / Skunk (sonically speaking). (cd-iss. May93 on 'Rhino-Atlantic')

—— (split early '72 when DAVIS departed) THOMPSON, SMITH and DAVIS formed short-lived ASCENSION. FRED SMITH married PATTI SMITH and later formed SONIC'S RENDEZVOUS BAND. TYNER was credited on HOT RODS single, late '77. (see ⇒ EDDIE & THE HOT RODS.

– compilations, etc. –

1969.	(7") A.M.G.; <AMG 1001> **I CAN ONLY GIVE YOU EVERYTHING. / ONE OF THE GUYS**	-	□
Jul 83.	(c) R.O.I.R.; <A 122> **BABES IN ARMS** *(re-iss. Apr90 & Dec92 on 'Danceteria' lp/cd; DAN LP/CD 031)*	-	□
May 94.	(cd) Receiver; (RRCD 185) **BLACK TO COMM**	□	□
Oct 94.	(10"lp/cd) Alive; (ALIVE 005/+CD) **POWER TRIP**	□	□
Nov 94.	(cd) Receiver; (RRCD 193) **LOOKING AT YOU**	□	□
Feb 95.	(10"lp/cd) Alive; (NER/+CD 2001) **THE AMERICAN RUSE**	□	□
Mar 95.	(10"lp) Alive; (ALIVE 008) **ICE PICK SLIM** *(cd-iss. Feb97; ALIVECD 8)*	□	□
Sep 95.	(10"ep/cd) Alive; (ALIVE 0010/+CD) **FRIDAY, THE 13TH**	□	□
Dec 96.	(cd) Dressed To Kill; (DTKLP 002) **THUNDER EXPRESS – ONE DAY IN THE STUDIO**	□	□
Mar 97.	(lp) Alive; (NER 3008) **TEENAGE LUST**	□	□

WAYNE KRAMER

—— went solo after spending 5 years in prison for cocaine dealing.

		Stiff-Chiswick	not iss.
Oct 77.	(7") (DEA-SUK 1) **RAMBLIN' ROSE. / GET SOME**	-	-

		Radar	not iss.
Jul 79.	(7") (ADA 41) **THE HARDER THEY COME. / EAST SIDE GIRL**	□	-

		not iss.	Pure&Easy
1983.	(7") <PE 017> **NEGATIVE GIRLS. / STREET WARFARE**	-	□

—— GANG WAR formed in 1980 with **JOHNNY THUNDERS** – vocals

		Zodiac	not iss.
1987.	(7"ep; WAYNE KRAMER'S GANG WAR) (800) **GANG WAR (live at Max's May 1980)**	□	-
May 90.	(lp) (LP 1001) **GANG WAR** (live/studio)	□	□

—— WAYNE had joined the DEVIANTS in 1984 for their album HUMAN GARBAGE.

		Curio	Progressive
1987.	(7"; as WAYNE KRAMER'S DEATH TONGUE) **SPIKE HEELS EP**	-	-

—— (WAYNE played late 80's with DAS DAMEN and G.G. ALLIN)

Nov 91.	(d-cd/d-lp) (ITEM 2 CD/LP) <PRO 023> **DEATH TONGUE**	□	□

– Take your clothes off / Sike heels / Spend the rent / Negative girls / Death tongue / Leather skull / The scars never show / McArthur Park / Fun in the final days / Who shot you Dutch.

—— In Sep'91, ROB TYNER was found dead after suffering heart attack. He was 46.

—— with on first **KEITH MORRIS, BRETT REED, MATT FREEMAN, DALE CROVER, JOSH FREESE, BRETT GUREWITZ, CHRIS BAGAROZZI,** etc

		Epitaph	Epitaph
Jan 95.	(cd/c/lp) <(E 86447-2/-4/-1)> **THE HARD STUFF**	□	□

– Crack in the universe / Junkie romance / Bad seed / Poison / Realm of the pirate kings / Incident on Stock Island / Pillar of fire / Hope for sale / Edge of the switchblade / Sharkskin suit.

Feb 96.	(cd/lp) <(86458-2/-1)> **DANGEROUS MADNESS**	□	□

– Dangerous madness / Back to DEtroit / Wild America / Something broken in the promised land / Take exit '97 / God's worst nightmare / The boy's got that look in their eyes / Dead man's vest / It's never enough / Rats of illusion / Dead movie stars.

May 97.	(cd) <(6488-2)> **CITIZEN WAYNE**	□	□

– Stranger in the house / Back when dogs could talk / Revolution in apt.29 / Down on the ground / Shining Mr. Lincoln's shoes / Dope for democracy / No easy way out / You don't know my name / Count time / Snatched defeat / Doing the work / Farewell to whiskey.

—— MC5 were about to reform with KRAMER, DAVIS + THOMSON

—— next with rhythm **DOUGLAS LUNN + RIC PARNELL**

Nov 98.	(cd/lp) <(86539)> **LLMF** (Live Like A Motherfucker)	□	□

– Bad seed / Stranger in the house / It's never enough / Something broken in the promised land / Take your clothes off / Down on the ground / Junkie romance / Poison / Count time / No easy way out / Crack in the universe / So long, Hank / Kick out the jams / Bomb day in Paris.

– others, etc. –

Nov 96.	(cd; by WAYNE KRAMER – DENIZ TEK – SCOTT MORGAN) Alive; <(ALIVE 25)> **DODGE MAIN**	□	□

– City slang / 1.94 / Citizen of time / Future – Now / Fire comin' / 100 fools / The harder they come / Over and over / Better than that / I got a right.

Roger McGUINN (see under ⇒ BYRDS)

Maria McKEE

Born: 17 Aug'64, Los Angeles, California, USA. The stepsister of BRYAN MACLEAN (of legendary L.A. band, LOVE, and whom she had previously sung with as a duo), McKEE had more than a little to live up to when she formed country-rock outfit, LONE JUSTICE, in 1984. With RYAN HEDGECOCK (guitar), TONY GILKYSON (guitar), MARVIN ETZIONI (bass) and DON HEFFINGTON (drums) completing the line-up, the band soon secured a deal with 'Geffen'. An eponymous debut received rave reviews upon its Summer '85 release, the record featuring a number of songs co-penned with TOM PETTY while also drawing praise from luminaries like BOB DYLAN and U2, the latter inviting LONE JUSTICE onto their 'Joshua Tree' tour. McKEE's profile was further heightened when FEARGAL SHARKEY (ex-UNDERTONES) took one her songs, 'A GOOD HEART' to No.1 in the UK later that year. In 1986, she recruited an entire new line-up for the 'SHELTER' album, the second and final LONE JUSTICE release. When McKEE split for a solo career the following year, she took two of the new members, guitarists SHANE FONTAYNE and BRUCE BRODY, both of whom played on her acclaimed eponymous solo debut. Released in 1989, the album gave McKEE free rein with her doomed-romantic songwriting and diaphragm-rupturing vocal talent, the likes of 'I'VE FORGOTTEN WHAT IT WAS IN YOU (THAT PUT THE NEED IN ME)' and 'NOBODY'S CHILD' (co-written with ROBBIE ROBERTSON) reminding the Nashville pretenders what the term 'country' really meant. Despite the lack of any real success in America, McKEE scored a UK No.1 the following summer with 'SHOW ME HEAVEN', a fairly atypical number penned by the singer for the 'Days Of Thunder' film soundtrack. Another one-off venture came in the unlikely form of UK club hit, 'SWEETEST CHILD', a track recorded with the help of ubiquitous ex-KILLING JOKE man, YOUTH. She eventually began work on a follow-up album in 1992, teaming up with BLACK CROWES producer, GEORGE DRAKOULIAS. Ex-LONE JUSTICE members MARVIN ETZIONI and DON HEFFINGTON returned to the fold while the sessions also featured JAYHAWKS men MARK OLSEN and GARY LOURIS. Consequently, 'YOU GOTTA SIN TO GET SAVED' (1993) was tougher in a rootsy kind of way, McKEE surpassing herself on the gospel-rock of the title track and the bittersweet 'I CAN'T MAKE IT ALONE'. The following year, the tortured lament of 'IF LOVE WAS A RED DRESS (HANG ME IN RAGS)' saw McKEE featured on the ultra-hip 'Pulp Fiction' soundtrack, her female NICK CAVE-style voodoo country one of the record's highlights. On 'LIFE IS SWEET' (1996), however, McKEE comes over all post-modern, with decidedly mixed results. • **Covered:** SWEET JANE (Velvet Underground) / HAS HE GOT A FRIEND FOR ME (Richard Thompson) / WICHITA LINEMAN (Jim Webb).

Album rating: Lone Justice: LONE JUSTICE (*7) / SHELTER (*5) / Maria McKee: MARIA McKEE (*6) / YOU GOTTA SIN TO GET SAVED (*7) / LIFE IS SWEET (*6)

LONE JUSTICE

MARIA McKEE – vocals / **RYAN HEDGECOCK** (b.27 Feb'61) – guitar / **TONY GILKYSON** – guitar / **MARVIN ETZIONI** (b.18 Apr'56, New York City, N.Y.) – bass / **DON HEFFINGTON** (b.20 Dec'50) – drums

		Geffen	Geffen
Apr 85.	(7") (A 6218) <29023> **WAYS TO BE WICKED. / CACTUS ROSE**	□	71

(12"+=) (TX 6218) – You are the light.

Jun 85. (lp) *(GEF 26288)* <24060> **LONE JUSTICE**   `49` `56` Apr85
– East of Eden / After the flood / Ways to be wicked / Don't toss us away / Working late / Sweet, sweet baby (I'm falling) / Pass it on / Wait 'til we get home / Soap, soup and salvation / You are the light. *(re-iss. Apr86 lp/c; GEF/40 32784) (re-iss. Mar91 lp/c/cd; GEF/+C/D 24060) (re-iss. Apr92 cd/c; GFL D/C 19058)*

Aug 85. (7") *(A 6426)* **SWEET, SWEET BABY (I'M FALLING). / PASS IT ON**   ☐ `-`
(12"+=) *(TA 6426)* – Go 'way little boy.

Aug 85. (7") <28965> **SWEET, SWEET BABY (I'M FALLING). / DON'T TOSS US AWAY**   `-` `73`

──── **MARIA McKEE** brought in entire new band, **SHANE FONTAYNE** – guitar (ex-STEVE FORBERT) who repl. HEDGECOCK / **BRUCE BRODY** (b.11 Dec'50) – guitar (ex-PATTI SMITH) who repl. GILYKSON / **GREG SUTTON** – bass who repl. ETZIONI / **RUDY RICHMAN** – drums who repl. HEFFINGTON

Oct 86. (7") *(GEF 16)* **SHELTER. / CAN'T LOOK BACK**   ☐ `-`
(12"+=) *(GEF 16T)* – Belfry.

Nov 86. (lp/c/cd) *(WX 73/+C)(924122-2)* <24122> **SHELTER**   `84` ☐
– I found love / Shelter / Reflected (on my side) / Beacon / Wheels / Belfry / Dreams come true (stand up and take it) / The gift / Inspiration / Dixie storms. *(re-iss. Mar91 lp/c/cd; GEF/+C/D 24122) (re-iss. Apr92 cd/c; GFL D/C 19059)*

Dec 86. (7") <28520> **SHELTER. / BELFRY**   `-` `49`

Feb 87. (7") *(GEF 18)* **I FOUND LOVE. / IF YOU DON'T LIKE THE RAIN**   ☐ `45`
(12"+=/12"pic-d+=) *(GEF 18 T/P)* – ('A'extended).
(d7"+=) *(GEF 18F)* – Sweet Jane (live) / Don't toss us away (live).

──── split after above. Past members – ETZIONI solo; released two albums for 'Restless' between 1992 and 1993; 'THE MANDOLIN MAN' and 'BONE'. HEDGECOCK solo in 1992; 'ECHO PARK' for 'Yellow Moon' UK.

MARIA McKEE

──── went solo, taking with her **FONTAYNE + BRODY** plus session people

Jun 89. (lp/c)(cd) *(WX 270/+C)(924229-2)* <24229> **MARIA McKEE**   `49` ☐
– I've forgotten what it was in you (that put the need in me) / To miss someone / Am I the only one (who's ever felt this way?) / Nobody's child / Panic beach / Can't pull the wool (over the little lamb's eyes) / More than a heart can hold / This property is condemned / Breathe / Has he got a friend for me? / Drinkin' in my Sunday dress. *(re-iss. Mar91 lp/c/cd; GEF/+C/D 24229) (re-iss. Mar93 cd/c; GFL D/C 19200)*

Aug 90. (7") *(656 303-7)* **SHOW ME HEAVEN. / (track by Hans Zimmer)**   `1` ☐
(12"+=/cd-s+=) *(656 303-6/-2)* – (track by Apollo Smile).
(above from the film, 'Days Of Thunder' on 'Epic')

Nov 90. (7"/c-s) <22800> **TO MISS SOMEONE. / PANIC BEACH**   ☐ ☐
(12"+=/cd-s+=) – Drinkin' in my Sunday dress.

Jan 91. (7"/c-s) *(GFS/+C 1)* **BREATHE. / PANIC BEACH**   `59` ☐
(12"+=/cd-s+=) *(GFST/+D 1)* – Drinkin' in my Sunday dress.

Jul 92. (7"/c-s) *(GFS/+C 23)* **SWEETEST CHILD. / ('A'acappella remix)**   `45` ☐
(12"+=/cd-s+=) *(GFST/+D 23)* – ('A'-Trans tribal ritual stomp mix).

──── FONTAYNE joined BRUCE SPRINGSTEEN in 1992. The JAYHAWKS' MARK OLSON and GARY LOURIS appeared on below album.

May 93. (c-s) *(GFSC 39)* **I'M GONNA SOOTHE YOU. / WHY WASN'T I MORE GRATEFUL (WHEN LIFE WAS SWEET)**   `35` ☐
(cd-s+=) *(GFSTD 39)* – This thing (don't lead to Heaven).
(cd-s) *(GFSXD 39)* – ('A'side) / If love was a red dress (hang me in rags) / Show me Heaven (acoustic demo).

Jun 93. (cd/c/lp) <(GED/GEC/GEF 24508)> **YOU GOTTA SIN TO GET SAVED**   `26` ☐
– I'm gonna soothe you / My lonely sad eyes / My girlhood among the outlaws / One only / I forgive you / I can't make it alone / Precious time / The way young lovers do / Why wasn't I more grateful (when life was sweet) / You gotta sin to be saved. *(cd re-iss. Oct95; GFLD 19290)*

Aug 93. (c-s) *(GFSC 53)* **I CAN'T MAKE IT ALONE. / MY GIRLHOOD AMONG THE OUTLAWS**   `74` `-`
(cd-s+=) *(GFSTD 53)* – I'm gonna soothe you / Wichita lineman (both acoustic).
(cd-s+=) *(GFSXD 53)* – I wish I was your mother.

Feb 96. (cd/c) <(GED/GEC 24819)> **LIFE IS SWEET**   ☐ ☐
– Searlover / This perfect dress / Absolutely barking stars / I'm not listening / Everybody / Smarter / What else you wanna know / I'm awake / Human carried / Life is sweet / Afterlife.

Apr 96. (cd-s/cd-s) *(GFS C/TD 22134)* **THIS PERFECT DRESS / MAGDALEINE**   ☐ ☐
(cd-s+=) *(GFSXD 22134)* – Amnesia blues (sandpaper clues).

– compilation, etc. –

Dec 93. (cd; LONE JUSTICE) Windsong; *(WINCD 048)* **BBC RADIO 1 LIVE IN CONCERT (live)**   ☐ `-`

Sarah McLACHLAN

Born: 28 Jan'68, Halifax, Nova Scotia, Canada. Professionally schooled in singing, guitar and piano as a child, McLACHLAN's first taste of the music business came with local band, OCTOBER GAME. After initially turning down a deal from 'Nettwerk' due to her art school studies, she later signed to the Canadian label as a solo artist and cut a 1988 debut album, 'TOUCH'. 'Arista' were sufficiently impressed to offer her a long term contract, re-issuing the record in 1989. A sophomore set, 'SOLACE' (1991), showcased a flowering songwriting talent within her trademark rootsy framework, the singer's Celtic heritage echoed in every chord. McLACHLAN would be profoundly influenced by a subsequent trip to Asia where she worked on a Canadian documentary about poverty and exploitation, her experiences at least partly inspiring 1994's 'FUMBLING TOWARDS ECSTASY'. Generally regarded as her finest album, this immaculately produced record found her

exploring more ambitious musical textures while putting in a compelling vocal performance. The club-influenced 'POSSESSION' single even scraped into the US Top 100 although she couldn't quite garner the same crossover audience enjoyed by her expanding bunch of female contemporaries. Nevertheless, McLACHLAN was instrumental in organising the 1997 'Lilith Fair' tour, an all-female affair featuring the likes of NATALIE MERCHANT. Later that year, her fourth set, 'SURFACING', surpassed all expectations by slowly rising into the US Top 3. It even broke her in Britain, albeit a year later when single 'ADIA' made the Top 20. • **Covered:** OL' 55 (Tom Waits) / SOLISBURY HILL (Peter Gabriel) / BLUE (Joni Mitchell) / etc

Album rating: TOUCH (*5) / SOLACE (*6) / FUMBLING TOWARDS ECSTASY (*7) / SURFACING (*7) / MIRRORBALL (*6)

SARAH McLACHLAN – vocals, guitar, piano; with session people

			Nettwerk	Nettwerk

Jan 89. (lp/cd) *(NET/+CD 007)* <8594> **TOUCH**
– Out of the shadows / Vox / Strange world / Trust / Touch / Steaming / Sad clown / Uphill battle / Ben's song. *(re-iss. Aug89 on 'Arista' lp/c/cd+=; 209/409/259 872)* – Vox (extended).

1990. (7"/12") <9804-5> **VOX. / TOUCH**   `-` ☐

			Arista	Arista

Feb 92. (c-s) *<12390>* **INTO THE FIRE /**   `-` ☐

Mar 92. (cd/c/lp) *(261/411/211 955)* <18631> **SOLACE**   `-` ☐
– Drawn to the rhythm / Into the fire / The path of thorns (terms) / I will not forget you / Lost / Back door man / Shelter / Black / Home / Mercy / Wear your love like heaven.

Apr 94. (c-s) *<12662>* **POSSESSION / BLACK (live)**   `-` `73`

Sep 94. (c-s) *<12690>* **GOOD ENOUGH / BLUE**   `-` `77`

Oct 94. (cd/c) *(74321 19032-2/-4)* <18725> **FUMBLING TOWARDS ECSTASY**   ☐ `50`
– Possession / Wait / Plenty / Good enough / Mary / Elsewhere / Circle / Ice / Hold on / Ice cream / Fear / Fumbling towards ecstasy.

Apr 95. (cd+cd-rom) *<18784>* **THE FREEDOM SESSIONS**   `-` `78`

Feb 96. (c-s) *(74321 33979-4)* *<12893>* **I WILL REMEMBER YOU / ICE CREAM**   `65` Oct95
(12"/cd-s) *(74321 33979-1/-2)* – ('A'side) / Good enough / Hold on / Possession.

Aug 97. (c-s,cd-s) *<13395>* **BUILDING A MYSTERY /**   `-` `13`

Oct 97. (cd/c) *<(18970-2/-4)>* **SURFACING**   ☐ `2` Jul97
– Building a mystery / I love you / Sweet surrender / Adia / Do what you have to do / Witness / Angel / Black & white / Full of grace / Last dance. *(re-prom.Oct98 hit UK No.47; same) (lp-iss.Oct99 on 'Rock The House'; RTH 18970)*

Feb 98. (c-s,cd-s) *<13453>* **SWEET SURRENDER /**   `-` `28`

Sep 98. (c-s) *(74321 61390-4)* <13497> **ADIA / ANGEL**   `18` `3`
(cd-s+=) *(74321 61390-2)* – Possession.   `56` May98

Nov 98. (-) <radio cut> **ANGEL**   `-` `4`

May 99. (-) <radio cut> **I WILL REMEMBER YOU (live)**   `-` `14`

Sep 99. (cd) *<19049>* **MIRRORBALL (live: greatest hits)**   `-` `3`
– Building a mystery / Hold on / Good enough / I will remember you / Adia / I love you / Do what you have to do / Path of thorns / Fear / Posession / Sweet surrender / Ice cream / Fumbling towards ecstasy / Angel.

– compilations, etc. –

Jan 93. (cd) Nettwerk; *(W 26313)* **SARAH McLACHLAN LIVE (live)**   ☐ ☐

Sep 97. (cd) Nettwerk; *(30105)* **RARITIES B-SIDES AND OTHERS**   ☐ ☐

John McLAUGHLIN / MAHAVISHNU ORCHESTRA

Born: 4 Jan'42, Yorkshire, England. Although he learned piano and violin at an early age, it was the guitar which vied for his attention as a teenager. His first professional music business experience came in the mid-60's when he spent time in both the GRAHAM BOND ORGANISATION and the BRIAN AUGER TRINITY. His debut solo outing, 'EXTRAPOLATION' (1969), was evidence of McLAUGHLIN's increasing immersion in jazz, the virtuoso having been recruited by none other than the legendary MILES DAVIS. During his stint with the celebrated trumpeter, JOHN played on two of his most groundbreaking albums, 'In A Silent Way' and 'Bitches Brew'. During this prolific time for McLAUGHLIN at the turn of the decade, he also featured in TONY WILLIAMS' jazz-rock outfit, LIFETIME, who released two highly influential albums, 'Emergency' and 'Turn It Over'. This group featured JACK BRUCE, with whom he'd previously collaborated (alongside JON HISEMAN and DICK HECKSTALL-SMITH) on the 'THINGS WE LIKE' set in '69. By this point, McLAUGHLIN, who was now a practising vegetarian and convert to Sri Chimnoy, was taking his music in a more meditative Eastern-influenced direction. Another prolific period ensued during which he released three albums in quick succession, one of them, 'MY GOAL'S BEYOND' (1973), was issued under the banner of MAHAVISHNU JOHN McLAUGHLIN – the adopted name given him by his newfound guru. In turn, McLAUGHLIN was inspired to form The MAHAVISHNU ORCHESTRA, an exceptionally talented group of musicians who boasted the likes of BILLY COBHAM and JAN HAMMER. An American Top 100 entry, 'THE INNER MOUNTING FLAME' (1972), quickly established the group as one of the world's leading jazz-rock fusionists, while follow-up set, 'BIRDS OF FIRE', broke them through commercially. After a live set, 'LIVE – BETWEEN NOTHINGNESS AND ETERNITY' and a collaborative album with CARLOS SANTANA, McLAUGHLIN dissolved the original line-up and recruited a more string-orientated cast of musicians including JEAN-LUC PONTY. Two albums (the occasionally brilliant 'VISIONS OF THE EMERALD BEYOND' and

'INNER WORLDS') later, McLAUGHLIN abandoned the project completely, opting for a more overtly spiritual direction with Indian classical outfit, SHAKTI. Towards the end of the decade, the erstwhile fusion pioneer returned to electric guitar with the ONE TRUTH BAND before following a twin fusion/classical direction throughout the following two decades as a solo artist.
• **Songwriters:** McLAUGHLIN compositions except BLUES IN GREEN (Miles Davis) / PASHA'S LOVE (Gurtu – band member 1990) / THE WIND CRIES MARY (Jimi Hendrix) / etc.

Album rating: EXTRAPOLATION (*5) / DEVOTION (*5) / INNER MOUNTING FLAME (*6; as Mahavishnu Orchestra with John McLaughlin) / MY GOAL'S BEYOND (*4; as Mahavishnu John McLaughlin) / Mahavishnu Orchestra: BIRDS OF FIRE (*7) / BETWEEN NOTHINGNESS AND ETERNITY (*6) / APOCALYPSE (*5) / VISIONS OF THE EMERALD BEYOND (*5) / INNER WORLDS (*4) / Shakti with John McLaughlin: SHAKTI WITH JOHN McLAUGHLIN (*4) / A HANDFUL OF BEAUTY (*4) / NATURAL ELEMENTS (*4) / John McLaughlin: ELECTRIC GUITARIST (*5) / ELECTRIC DREAMS (*4; with the One Truth Band) / FRIDAY NIGHT IN SAN FRANCISCO (*5; with Al Di Meola & Paco De Lucia) / BELO HORIZONTE (*4) / PASSION, GRACE & FIRE (*4; with Al Di Meola & Paco Lucia) / MAHAVISHNU (*4) / ADVENTURES IN RADIOLAND (*4) / LIVE AT THE ROYAL FESTIVAL HALL (*4) / AFTER THE RAIN (*4)

JOHN McLAUGHLIN

solo with **JOHN SURMAN** – saxophone / **BRIAN ODGERS** – bass / **TONY OXLEY** – drums

		Marmalade	Polydor
1969.	(lp) (608 007) **EXTRAPOLATION**		Oct 72

– Extrapolation / It's funny / Argen's bag / Pete the poet / This is for us to share / Spectrum / Binky's beam / Really you know / Two for two / Peace piece. (re-iss. 1974 on 'Polydor'; 2343 012) (re-iss. 1977 on 'Polydor'; 2310 018) (cd-iss. Oct90 on 'Polydor'; 841 498-2)

—— He was then credited on album 'THINGS WE LIKE' with JACK BRUCE, JON HISEMAN & DICK HECKSTAL-SMITH. McLAUGHLIN then went to America to join (TONY WILLIAM'S) LIFETIME, playing on 2 lp's 'EMERGENCY' + 'TURN IT OVER'. Around the same time MILES DAVIS gave him work on his 'IN A SILENT WAY' and 'BITCHES BREW'. Returned to solo work once more. —— Augmented by **BUDDY MILES** – drums / **JERRY GOODMAN** – violin (ex-FLOCK) / **BILLY RICH** – bass / **LARRY YOUNG** (aka KHALID YASIN) – keyboards

		Douglas	Columbia
Jan 71.	(lp) (DGL 65075) **DEVOTION**		1972

– Devotion / Dragon song / Marbles / Siren / Don't let the dragon eat your mother / Purpose of when. <US cd-iss. Dec93 on 'Celluloid'; CELD 5010> (cd re-iss. Jan97 on 'Charly'; CPCD 8232)

—— **BILLY COBHAM** (b.16 May'44, Panama) – drums, percussion (ex-MILES DAVIS) repl. BUDDY MILES

1971.   (lp; as MAHAVISHNU JOHN McLAUGHLIN) (DGL 69014) **MY GOAL'S BEYOND**
– Peace one / Peace two / Goodbye pork-pie hat / Something spiritual / Hearts and flowers / Philip Lane / Waltz for Bill Evans / Follow your heart / Song for my mother / Blue is green. (re-iss. Mar82 on 'Elektra Musician'; K 52364) (cd-iss. May92 on 'Rykodisc'; RCD 10051)

—— next featured **JOHN SURMAN / KARL BERGER / STU MARTIN + DAVE HOLLAND**

		Dawn	not iss.
Mar 71.	(lp) (DNLS 3018) **WHERE FORTUNES SMILES**	-	

– Glancing backwards (for Junior) / Earth bound hearts / Where fortune smiles / New place, old place / Hope. (cd-iss. Jul93 on 'Beat Goes On'; BGOCD 191)

MAHAVISHNU ORCHESTRA

John McLAUGHLIN with **COBHAM + GOODMAN** and adding **RICK LAIRD** (b. 5 Feb'41, Dublin, Ireland) – bass / **JAN HAMMER** (b.17 Apr'48, Prague, Czech) – keyboards

		C.B.S.	Columbia
Jan 72.	(lp/c) (CBS/40 64717) **THE INNER MOUNTING FLAME**		89

– Meeting of the Spirits / Dawn / The noonward race / A lotus on Irish streams / Vital transformation / You know you know / The dance of Maya / Awakening. <US cd-iss. 1989; CD 31067>

| Feb 73. | (lp/c) (CBS/40 65321) **BIRDS OF FIRE** | 20 | 15 |

– Birds of fire / Miles beyond (Miles Davis) / Celestial terrestrial commuters / Sapphire bullets of pure love / Thousand Island park / Hope / One word / Sanctuary / Open country joy / Resolution. (quad-lp 1974; CQ 31996) (re-iss. Nov83 lp/c/cd; CBS/40/CD 32280) (re-iss. cd Jun89; CD 65321) (re-iss. Jan92 on 'Columbia-Legacy'; 468 224-2)

| May 73. | (7") **OPEN COUNTRY BOY. / CELESTIAL COMMUTERS** | - | |

—— Mid'73, released collaboration Top 20 album 'LOVE DEVOTION SURRENDER' with CARLOS SANTANA. (see: SANTANA ⇒)

| Jan 74. | (lp/c) (CBS/40 69046) **LIVE – BETWEEN NOTHINGNESS & ETERNITY** (live) | | 41 Dec 73 |

– Trilogy / The sunlit path – La mere de la mer – Tomorrow's story not the same / Sister Andrea / Dream. (cd-iss. 1988 on 'Beat Goes On' lp/cd; BGO LP/CD 31) (cd re-iss. Dec91 on 'Columbia-Legacy'; 468 225-2)

—— (Jan74) McLAUGHLIN disbanded group, COBHAM went solo as did JAN HAMMER. Recruited new people **JEAN LUC-PONTY** – electric violin (ex-Solo, ex-ZAPPA) / **MICHAEL NARADA WALDEN** – drums / **GAYLE MORAN** – keyboards, vocals / **RALPHE ARMSTRONG** – bass / **STEVE FRANKOVITCH** – brass / **BOB KNAPP** – reeds / plus **PHILIP HIRSCHI** – cello / **MARSHA WESTBROOK** – viola / **CAROL SHIRE** – violin / **STEVE KINDLER** – violin also credited The LONDON SYMPHONY ORCHESTRA conducted by MICHAEL TILSON-THOMAS

| Jun 74. | (lp/c) (CBS/40 69076) **APOCALYPSE** | | 43 May 74 |

– Power of love / Vision of a naked sword / Smile of the beyond / Wings of Karma / Hymn to him. <US cd-iss. Dec90 on 'Columbia-Legacy'; 467 092-2>

| Jan 75. | (lp/c) (CBS/40 69109) **VISIONS OF THE EMERALD BEYOND** | | 68 |

– Eternity's breath (part 1 & 2) / Lila's dance / Can't stand your funk / Pastoral / Faith / Cosmic strut / If I could see / Be happy / Earth ship / Pegasus / Opus 1 / On the way home to Earth. <US cd-iss. Jun91 on 'Columbia-Legacy'; 467 904-2>

| Feb 75. | (7") (CBS 3007) <10134> **CAN'T STAND YOUR FUNK. / ETERNITY'S BREATH** (part 1) | | |

—— Retained **WALDEN, PONTY, ARMSTRONG**. New **STU GOLDBERG** – keyboards

| Feb 76. | (lp/c; as MAHAVISHNU ORCHESTRA / JOHN McLAUGHLIN) (CBS/40 69216) **INNER WORLDS** | | |

– All in the family / Miles out / In my life / Gita / Morning calls / The way of the pilgrim / River of my heart / Planetary citizen / Louis feet / Inner worlds (parts 1 & 2). (cd-iss. Nov94 on 'Columbia-Legacy'; 476 905-2)

SHAKTI

SHAKTI:- LEVI SHANKAR – violin / **JOHN McLAUGHLIN** – guitar / **TH VINYAKRAM** – percussion, vocals / **ZAKIR HUSSAIN** – percussion

		C.B.S.	Columbia
Jun 76.	(lp) (CBS 81388) **SHAKTI** (live)		

– Joy / Lotus feet / What need have I for this? – What need have I for that? / I am dancing at the feet of my Lord / All bliss – All bliss. (cd-iss. 1990 on 'Columbia'; 46868)

| Mar 77. | (lp) (CBS 81664) **A HANDFUL OF BEAUTY** | | |

– La danse du bonheur / Lady L / India / Kriti / Isis / Two sisters.

| Dec 77. | (lp) (CBS 82329) **NATURAL ELEMENTS** | | |

– Mind ecology / Face to face / Come on baby dance with me / The daffodil and the eagle / Happiness is being together / Bridge of sighs / Get down and strut / Peace of mind.

– SHAKTI compilations –

| Jun 91. | (cd) Sony; (467 905-2) **SHAKTI WITH JOHN McLAUGHLIN** | | |
| Jan 95. | (cd) Koch Int.; (MRCD 1010) **THE BEST OF SHAKTI** | | - |

JOHN McLAUGHLIN

went solo again, using past band members, etc.

| May 78. | (lp/c) (CBS/40 82702) **ELECTRIC GUITARIST** | | |

– New York on my mind / Friendship / Every tear from your eye / Do you hear the voices that you left behind / Are you the one? are you the one? / Phenomenon: Compulsion / My foolish heart. (cd-iss. Jan92 on 'Columbia-Legacy'; 467 093-2)

—— Next with ONE TRUTH BAND, who were **SHANKER** – violin / **ANTHONY ALLEN SMITH** – drums / **STU GOLDBERG** – keyboards

| May 79. | (lp/c; JOHN McLAUGHLIN / ONE TRUTH BAND) (CBS/40 83256) **ELECTRIC DREAMS, ELECTRIC SIGHS** | | Apr 79 |

– Guardian angels / Miles Davis / Electric dreams, electric sighs / Desire and the comforter / Love and understanding / Singing Earth / The dark prince / The unknown dissident. (cd-iss. 1993 on 'Columbia-Legacy'; 476 905-2)

| Jun 81. | (lp; by JOHN McLAUGHLIN with PACO DE LUCIA & AL DI MEOLA) (CBS 84962) **FRIDAY NIGHT IN SAN FRANCISCO: LIVE** (live) | 97 | May 81 |

– Mediterranean sundance – Rio Ancho / Short tales of the Black Forest / Frevo resgado / Fantasia suite / Guardian angels. (cd-iss. 1988 on 'Philips'; 800 047-2) (re-iss. cd 1990 on 'Columbia'; 467 010-2)

		WEA	Warners
Jan 82.	(lp) (K/K4 99185) **BELO HORIZONTE**		Dec 81

– Belo horizonte / La baleine / Very early / One melody / Stardust on your sleeve / Waltz for Katia / Zamfir / Manita's d'aro (for Paco De Lucia).

| 1982. | (lp) (K 99254) **MUSIC SPOKEN HERE** | | - |

– Aspan / Blues for L.W. / The translators / Honky-tonk Heaven / Viene Clare Ando / David / Negative ions / Briese de coeur / Loro.

		Mercury	Columbia
Jun 83.	(lp; by DiMEOLA, McLAUGHLIN, DE LUCIA) (MERL 24) **PASSION, GRACE & FIRE**		

– Aspen / Orient blue / Chiquito / Sichia / David / Passion, grace & fire. (re-iss. 1990 on 'Philips'; 811 334-1)

—— with **MITCHELL FORMAN** – keyboards / **BILL EVANS** – saxophone / **JONAS HELLBORG** – bass / **DANNY GOTTLIEB** – drums

		WEA	WEA
Jan 85.	(lp/c; as MAHAVISHNU) (251 351-1/-4) **MAHAVISHNU**		

– Radio activity / Nostalgia / Nightriders / East side west side / Clarendon hills / Jazz / The unbeliever / Pacific express / When blue turns gold.

		Polygram	Intercord
Jul 87.	(lp/c/cd; as JOHN McLAUGHLIN AND MAHAVISHNU) (SOS/+MC/CD 2020) **ADVENTURES IN RADIOLAND**		

– The wait / Just ideas / Jozy / Half man, half cookie / Florianapolis / Gotta dance / The wall will fall / Reincarnation / Mitch match / 20th century limited. (re-iss. cd 1990's on 'Verve'; 519 397-2)

—— with **KAI ECKHARDT** – bass / **TRILOK GURTU** – percussion

		J.M.T.	J.M.T.
Apr 90.	(cd/c/lp; by JOHN McLAUGHLIN TRIO) (834 436-2/-4/-1) **LIVE AT THE ROYAL FESTIVAL HALL** (live)		

– Blue in green / Medley: Just ideas – Jozy / Florianapolis / Pasha's love / Mother tongues. (c+=/cd+=) – Blues for L.W.

—— with **LONDON SYMPHONY ORCHESTRA & MICHAEL TILSON THOMAS / KATIA LABEQUE** – piano

		C.B.S.	Columbia
1990.	(lp/cd; JOHN McLAUGHLIN with The LSO & KATIA LABEQUE) (MK/+CD 45578) **MEDITERRANEAN GUITAR CONCERTO**		

– (I)- Rhythmic / (II)- Slow & sad / (III)- Animato / Briese de coeur / Montana / Two sisters / Until such time / Zakir.

		Verve	Verve
1991.	(cd; by JOHN McLAUGHLIN TRIO) (837 260-2) **QUE ALEGRIA**		

—— with **JOEY DeFRANCESCO** – organ + **DENNIS CHAMBERS** – drums

| Feb 94. | (cd) (519 861-2) **TIME REMEMBERED: JOHN McLAUGHLIN PLAYS BILL EVANS** | | |
| May 94. | (cd; by The FREE SPIRITS featuring JOHN McLAUGHLIN) (521 870-2) **TOKYO LIVE** (live) | | |

—— **ELVIN JONES** – drums repl. CHAMBERS

| Jun 95. | (cd) (527 467-2) **AFTER THE RAIN** | | |

– Take the Coltrane / My favorite things / Sing me softly of the blues / Encuentros / Naima / Tones for Elvin Jones / Crescent / Afro blue / After the rain.

Feb 96. (cd) *(528 828-2)* **THE PROMISE**   ☐ ☐
– Django / Thelonius Melodius / Amy and Joseph / No return / El ciego / Jazz jungle / The wish / English jam / Tokyo decadence / Shin Jin Rui / The peacocks.

– compilations, others, etc. –

Oct 75. (d-lp) *Polydor; (2675 091)* **IN RETROSPECT**   ☐ -

Jun 80. (lp/c) *C.B.S.; (CBS/40 84232)* **THE BEST OF THE MAHAVISHNU ORCHESTRA**   ☐ -
(cd-iss. Jan92 on 'Columbia-Legacy'; 468 226-2)

Jan 81. (lp/c) *C.B.S.; (CBS/40 84455)* **THE BEST OF JOHN McLAUGHLIN**   ☐ -
– A love supreme / New York on my mind / The dark prince / La danse du bonheur / Friendship / Face to face / The unknown dissident / Lotus feet.

1989. (cd) *Verve; (516 114-2)* **COMPACT JAZZ: JOHN McLAUGHLIN**   ☐ -

Apr 91. (cd/c/lp) *Columbia; (467010-2/-4/-1)* **JOHN McLAUGHLIN – GREATEST HITS**   - ☐

Oct 91. (cd) *Castle; (CCSCD 305)* **JOHN McLAUGHLIN & THE MAHAVISHNU ORCHESTRA: THE COLLECTION**   ☐ -

---

Don McLEAN

Born: 2 Oct'45, New Rochelle, New York, USA. Having been a club singer from 1963, he acquired a residency at Lena's bar in 1968, and was dubbed 'The Hudson River Troubadour'. The following year, he was invited to join PETE SEEGER on his expedition tour of the Hudson river. This 6-week journey involved over 25 concerts at various riverside destinations, and made people aware of the river's industrial pollution. In 1970, McLEAN's efforts were finally rewarded, when 'Mediarts' released his debut lp, 'TAPESTRY'. Although the album failed to chart, PERRY COMO scored with a cover of one of the tracks, 'AND I LOVE YOU SO', while McLEAN's soft, pastel-shaded style presumably inspired the songwriting team of Norman Gimbel and Charles Fox to pen the haunting 'Killing Me Softly' (a massive hit for ROBERTA FLACK and later The FUGEES) in his honour. Later that year, McLEAN's enduring BUDDY HOLLY tribute, 'AMERICAN PIE', almost provided him with a transatlantic No.1 while the album of the same name achieved similar success and spawned a UK No.1 hit in 'VINCENT', a tribute to another of McLEAN's heroes, painter, Vincent Van Gogh. These two huge chart hits became something of an albatross round the singer's neck, McLEAN spending the rest of the decade attempting to distance himself from the success. 'DON McLEAN' (1973) and 'HOMELESS BROTHER' (1974) continued his socially aware balladeering, although his profile remained low for much of the 70's. A new deal with 'E.M.I.' ('Millennium' in the States) brought a brief period of chart action at the turn of the decade when he again topped the UK singles lists with a version of Roy Orbison's 'CRYING'. Since, then, however, McLEAN has moved increasingly into C&W and easy listening territory, his last recording to date being 1989's 'FOR THE MEMORIES'. • **Covered:** EVERYDAY (Buddy Holly) / CRYING IN THE CHAPEL (Elvis Presley) / MULE SKINNER BLUES (Fendermen) / SUNSHINE LIFE FOR ME (George Harrison) / FOOLS PARADISE (Linsley – Petty – LeGlaire) / GOING FOR THE GOLD (C.Bowder – J.W. Ryles) / MOUNTAINS OF MOURNE (P. French – H. Collinson) / SINCE I DON'T HAVE YOU (Skyliners) / LOVE HURTS (Everly Brothers) / etc. Albums 'PLAYIN' FAVOURITES', 'LOVE TRACKS' & 'FOR THE MEMORIES VOLUMES 1 & 2' were collections of other people's material.

Album rating: TAPESTRY (*5) / AMERICAN PIE (*8) / DON McLEAN (*6) / PLAYIN' FAVORITES (*4) / HOMELESS BROTHER (*5) / SOLO (*4) / PRIME TIME (*4) / CHAIN LIGHTNING (*5) / BELIEVERS (*4) / DOMINION (*3) / DON McLEAN'S GREATEST HITS – THEN AND NOW compilation (*6) / THE VERY BEST OF DON McLEAN compilation (*7) / FOR THE MEMORIES (*6) / HEADROOM (*3) / RIVER OF LOVE (*4)

DON McLEAN – vocals, guitar (with session people)

	not iss.	Mediarts
Feb 71. (7") *<108>* **CASTLES IN THE AIR. / AND I LOVE YOU SO**	-	☐
Feb 71. (lp) *<none>* **TAPESTRY**	-	☐

– Castles in the air / General store / Magdalene lane / Tapestry / Respectable / Orphans of wealth / Three flights up / And I love you so / Bad girl / Circus song / No reason for your dreams. *<US re-dist.Feb72 on 'United Artists'; 5522> (UK-iss.Jun72 on 'United Artists'; UAS 29350)* – hit No.16. *(re-iss. Sep84 on 'Fame'; FA41 3107-1) (cd-iss. Jul94 on 'Beat Goes On'; BGOCD 232)*

	U.A.	U.A.
Sep 71. (7") *<50796>* **AND I LOVE YOU SO. / CASTLES IN THE AIR**	-	☐
Nov 71. (7";w-drawn) *(UP 35323) <50856>* **AMERICAN PIE. / EMPTY CHAIRS**	-	☐
Jan 72. (7") *(UP 35325) <50856>* **AMERICAN PIE (part 1). / (part 2)**	2	1 Nov71

(re-iss. Jan84 + Sep86)

Feb 72. (lp) *(UAS 29285) <5535>* **AMERICAN PIE**	3	1 Nov71

– American pie (parts 1 & 2) / Till tomorrow / Vincent / Crossroads / Winterwood / Empty chairs / Everybody loves me, baby / Sister Fatima / The grave / Babylon. *(re-iss. May81 on 'Greenlight'; GO 2004) (re-iss. May82 on 'Fame' lp/c; FA/TC-FA 3023) (cd-iss. May88; CDFA 3023)*

Apr 72. (7") *(UP 35359) <50887>* **VINCENT. / CASTLES IN THE AIR**	1	12 Mar72
Jan 73. (7") *(UP 35481) <51100>* **DREIDEL. / BRONCO BILL'S LAMENT**	☐	21 Dec72
Jan 73. (lp/c) *(UAS 29299) <5651>* **DON McLEAN**	☐	23 Dec72

– If we try / Narcisissma / Dreidel / Bronco Bill's lament / Birthday song / The pride parade / The more you pay / Falling through time / On the Amazon / Oh my what a shame. *(cd-iss. Mar95 on 'Beat Goes On'; BGOCD 246)*

Mar 73. (7") *(UP 35519)* **EVERYDAY. / THE MORE YOU PAY (THE MORE IT'S WORTH)**	38	-

Mar 73. (7") *<206>* **IF WE TRY. / THE MORE YOU PAY (THE MORE IT'S WORTH)**	-	58
Oct 73. (7"m) *(UP 35607)* **MOUNTAINS O' MOURNE. / MEDLEY (BILL CHEETHAM – OLD JOE CLARK)**	☐	☐
Nov 73. (lp/c) *(UAG/UAC 29528) <LA 161>* **PLAYIN' FAVOURITES**	42	☐

– Sittin' on top of the world / Living with the blues / Mountains O'mourne / Fool's paradise / Love o love / Medley:- (Bill Cheetham – Old Joe Clark) / Ancient history / Over the mountains / Lovesick blues / New mule skinner blues / Happy trails. *(re-iss. 1989 on 'Beat Goes On'; BGO 21) (cd-iss. Jun95; BGOCD 21)*

Mar 74. (7") *(UP 35661)* **FOOL'S PARADISE. / HAPPY TRAILS**	☐	-
Jun 74. (7") *<541>* **NEW MULE SKINNER BLUES. / SITTIN' ON TOP OF THE WORLD**	☐	☐
Nov 74. (lp/c) *(UAG/UAC 29646) <315>* **HOMELESS BROTHER**	☐	☐

– Winter has me in its grip / La la love you / Homeless brother / Sunshine life for me (sail away Raymond) / The legend of Andrew McCrew / Wonderful baby / We have lived / Great big man / Tangled (like a spider in her hair) / Crying in the chapel / Did you know. *(cd-iss. Nov94 on 'Beat Goes On'; BGOCD 247)*

Apr 75. (7") *<579>* **HOMELESS BROTHER. / LA LA LOVE YOU**	☐	☐
Jun 75. (7") *<614>* **WONDERFUL BABY. / BIRTHDAY SONG**	-	93
Jun 75. (7") *(UP 35764)* **WONDERFUL BABY. / HOMELESS BROTHER**	☐	☐
Sep 76. (d-lp) *(UAD 60139) <LA 652>* **SOLO (live)**	☐	☐

– Magdalene lane / Masters of war / Wonderful baby / Where were you bany / Empty chairs / Geordie's lost his penker / Babylon / And I love you so / MacTavish is dead / New mule skinner blues / Great big man / Bronco Bill's lament / Happy trails / Circus song / Birthday song / On the Amazon / American pie / Over the waterfall / Arkansas traveller / Homeless brother / Three flights up / Lovesick blues / Winter has me in its grip / The legend of Andrew McCrew / Dreidel / Vincent / Till tomorrow. *(d-cd-iss. Nov95 on 'Beat Goes On'; BGOCD 300)*

	EMI Int.	Arista
Sep 77. (7") <> **PRIME TIME. / THE STATUE**	-	☐
Nov 77. (lp) *(INS 3011) <4149>* **PRIME TIME**	☐	Jun77

– Prime time / The statue / Jump / Redwing / The wrong thing to do / The pattern is broken / When love begins / Colour TV blues / Building my body / Down the road / Sally Ann / When one good thing goes bad / South of the border (down Mexico way).

Nov 77. (7") **PRIME TIME. / REDWING**	☐	-
Jan 78. (7") *(INT 549)* **WHEN LOVE BEGINS. / COLOUR TV BLUES**	☐	☐

	EMI Int.	Millennium
Feb 79. (7") *(INT 575)* **IT DOESN'T MATTER ANYMORE. / IF WE TRY**	☐	☐
Mar 79. (lp) *(INS 3025) <7756>* **CHAIN LIGHTNING**	☐	☐

– Words and music / Crying / It's just the sun / Lotta lovin' / Your cheating heart / Wonderful night / It doesn't matter anymore / Since I don't have you / Genesis (in the beginning) / It's a beautiful life. *(UK re-dist.May80, hit No. 19) <US re-iss. Feb81, hit No.28>*

Apr 79. (7") *(INT 588)* **WORDS AND MUSIC. / YOUR CHEATING HEART**	☐	-

	E.M.I.	Millennium
Mar 80. (7") *(EMI 5051) <11799>* **CRYING. / GENESIS (IN THE BEGINNING)**	1	5 Jan81
Jul 80. (7") *(EMI 5094)* **SINCE I DON'T HAVE YOU. / IT'S A BEAUTIFUL LIFE**	☐	☐
Apr 81. (7") *<1804>* **SINCE I DON'T HAVE YOU. / YOUR CHEATING HEART**	-	23
Jul 81. (7") *<11809>* **IT'S JUST THE SUN. / WORDS AND MUSIC**	-	83
Jan 82. (7") *(EMI 5258) <11819>* **CASTLES IN THE AIR. / CRAZY EYES**	47	36 Oct81
Jan 82. (lp/c) *(EMC/TC-EMC 3396) <7762>* **BELIEVERS**	☐	Nov81

– Castles in the air / Love hurts / Jerusalem / Crazy eyes / Love letters / Sea cruise / I tune the world out / Isn't it strange / Left for dead on the road of love / Believers / Sea man.

Nov 82. (7") **JERUSALEM. / LEFT FOR DEAD ON THE ROAD OF LOVE**	☐	-
Nov 82. (7") *(EMI 5356)* **THE VERY THOUGHT OF YOU. / LEFT FOR DEAD ON THE ROAD OF LOVE**	☐	☐
Feb 83. (d-lp/d-c) *(DOM/TC-DOM 82)* **DOMINION (live)**	☐	☐

– It's just the sun / Building my body / Wonderful baby / The very thought of you / Fool's paradise / You're so square (baby I don't care) / You have lived / Prime time / American pie / Left for dead on the road of love / Believers / Sea man / It's a beautiful life / Chain lightning / Crazy eyes / La la love you / Dream lover / Crying / Vincent.

Apr 87. (7") **HE'S GOT YOU. /**	☐	-
Apr 87. (cd) *(CDP 746586-2)* **DON McLEAN'S GREATEST HITS – THEN AND NOW** (part compilation)	☐	☐

– He's got you / American pie / To have and to hold / Castles in the air / But she loves me / Superman's ghost / Vincent / And I love you so / Crying / Don't burn the bridge.

	Capitol	Capitol
Dec 87. (7") *<44098>* **YOU CAN'T BLAME THE TRAIN. / PERFECT LOVE**	☐	☐
Jun 88. (7") *<44186>* **LOVE IN THE HEART. / EVERY DAY'S A MIRACLE**	☐	☐
Sep 88. (7") *<44258>* **IT'S NOT YOUR FAULT. / EVENTUALLY**	☐	☐
Nov 89. (lp/c/cd) *(1711330)* **FOR THE MEMORIES**	☐	☐

– Don't / Crazy / Travelin' man / You don't know me / Sittin' in the balcony / Wonderful world / I can't help it / Maybe baby / White sports coat / If I only had a match / But beautiful / Over the weekend / Someone to watch over me / Somebody loves me / Count your blessings / It had to be you / Not a moment too soon / Change partners / Nobody knows you when you're down and out / Stardust.

	Curb	Curb
Oct 91. (cd) *(469170-2) <77427>* **HEADROOM**	☐	☐

– Headroom / Fashion victim / 1967 / Infinity / One in a row / You who love the truth / Lady in waiting / Have you seen me / Siamese twins (joined at the heart) / Brand new world.

Nov 95. (cd) *(CURCD 19) <77791>* **THE RIVER OF LOVE**	☐	Oct95

– The river of love / You're my little darlin' / If I hadn't met you / Better still / You got a way about you, baby / Angry words / This little girl (daddy-o) / Planet noise / From a beautiful star / Little cowboy / My love was true.

– compilations, others, etc. –

on 'United Artists' unless mentioned otherwise

1974. (7") **VINCENT. / DREIDEL**
Jun 78. (7") **AND I LOVE YOU SO. / VINCENT**
Aug 80. (lp/c) (UAG/UAC 30314) **THE VERY BEST OF DON McLEAN** `4` `-`
Sep 88. (lp/c) Music For Pleasure; (MFP/TC-MFP 5836) **LOVE TRACKS**
Oct 89. (cd/c/lp) E.M.I.; (CD/TC+/EMS 1346) **AND I LOVE YOU SO**
1990. (cd/c/lp) Goldcastle; **GREATEST HITS LIVE!** (live 1980)
Nov 91. (cd/c) Manhattan; (CD/TC MTL 1065) **THE BEST OF DON McLEAN**
– American pie / Castles in the air (1981 version) / Dreidel / Winterwood / Everyday / Sister Fatima / Empty chairs / The birthday song / Wonderful baby / La la I love you / Vincent / Crossroads / And I love you so / Fool's Paradise / If we try / Mountains of Mourne / The grave / Respectable / Going for the gold / Crying. (cd+=) – Bronco Bill's lament / Oh my what a shame / If we try / Babylon / Love in my heart.

Aug 91. (c-s/7") Liberty; **AMERICAN PIE. / VINCENT** `-`
(cd-s+=) – Castles in the air.
Nov 94. (cd) BR Music; (BX 417-2) **CRYING** `-`

G.W. McLENNAN (see under ⇒ GO-BETWEENS)

Ian McNABB

Born: ROBERT IAN McNABB, 3 Nov'60, Liverpool, England. After a spell with CITY LIGHTS, then SUNSET BOULEVARD, he formed The ICICLE WORKS in 1979 with CHRIS LAYHE and CHRIS SHARROCK. A cassingle appeared on 'Probe' in 1981, followed a year later by their vinyl debut 'NIRVANA', the single surfacing on manager Tony Barwood's 'Troll Kitchen' label. After their classy 45, 'BIRDS FLY' won over numerous indie legions, they moved upstairs in 1983 to 'Beggars Banquet' and immediately made an impact in the Top 20 with 'LOVE IS A WONDERFUL COLOUR'. A re-issue of 'BIRDS FLY (WHISPER TO A SCREAM)', didn't fare as well, although it surprisingly broke them into the US Top 40. Their eponymous debut album also cracked the American market having already gone Top 30 in the UK. Still sounding SCOTT WALKER-ish at this early stage, McNABB (complete with attached microphone gadget) was a compelling frontman for this college circuit power-rock trio. Follow-up set, 'THE SMALL PRICE OF A BICYCLE' (1985), featured a number of good reasons ('SEVEN HORSES' and 'ALL THE DAUGHTERS' for starters) why they deserved promotion from Rock's second division, while 'IF YOU WANT TO DEFEAT YOUR ENEMY SING HIS SONG' (1987) finally gave them a UK Top 30 album. The following year, 'BLIND' also scraped into the Top 40, although this was their final effort for the label, having signed to 'Epic'. Major label status did them no favours, the disappointing 'PERMANENT DAMAGE' seeing a slide in their popularity and leading to them being dropped. McNABB was virtually left in the cold, that is until 'Way Cool' released his debut solo single, 'GREAT DREAMS OF HEAVEN' in 1991. This was closely followed by another independently released 45, McNABB's deserved break coming the following year when ANDREW LAUDER signed him to his 'This Way Up' label. Early in 1993, McNABB was back in the album charts, 'TRUTH & BEAUTY' nearly making the UK Top 50. He subsequently realised one of his longheld musical dreams when he secured the services of the legendary CRAZY HORSE, initially for live work before going into the studio to record a whole album together. The resulting 'HEAD LIKE A ROCK' (1994), was short-listed for a Mercury Music Award, his critical rehabilitation now complete. In 1996, McNABB released his third solo set, 'MERSEYBEAST', his second consecutive Top 30 achievement and a worthy addition to his increasingly impressive back catalogue. • **Songwriters:** Mostly McNABB compositions for ICICLE WORKS except; SEA SONG (Robert Wyatt) / NATURE'S WAY (Spirit) / COLD TURKEY (John Lennon) / INTO THE MYSTIC (Van Morrison) / YOU AIN'T SEEN NOTHIN' YET (Bachman-Turner Overdrive) / SHOULD I STAY OR SHOULD I GO (Clash) / ROCK'N'ROLL (Led Zeppelin) / PRIVATE REVOLUTION (World Party) / ROADHOUSE BLUES (Doors) / TRIAD – CHESTNUT MARE (Byrds) / MR SOUL + FOR WHAT IT'S WORTH (Buffalo Springfield). McNABB covered UNKNOWN LEGEND + THE NEEDLE AND THE DAMAGE DONE (Neil Young) / CAROLINE NO (Brian Wilson). • **Trivia:** In Aug'85, an ICICLE WORKS off-shoot MELTING POT, were supposed to have had a single 'IT MAKES NO DIFFERENCE' issued.

Album rating: Icicle Works: THE ICICLE WORKS (*6) / THE SMALL PRICE OF A BICYCLE (*7) / IF YOU WANT TO DEFEAT YOUR ENEMY SING HIS SONG (*6) / BLIND (*5) / PERMANENT DAMAGE (*5) / THE BEST OF THE ICICLE WORKS compilation (*8) / Ian McNabb: TRUTH & BEAUTY (*6) / HEAD LIKE A ROCK (*8) / MERSEYBEAST (*6)

ICICLE WORKS

IAN McNABB – vocals, guitar, keyboards / **CHRIS LAYHE** – bass, keyboards, vocals / **CHRIS SHARROCK** – drums, percussion

	Probe	not iss.
Mar 81. (c-ep) (private) **ASCENDING**		-

	Troll Kitchen	not iss.
Oct 82. (7"m) (WORKS 001) **NIRVANA. / LOVE HUNT / SIROCCO**		-

	Situation2	not iss.
Jun 83. (7") (SIT 22) **BIRDS FLY (WHISPER TO A SCREAM). / REVERIE GIRL**		-
(12"+=) (SIT 22T) – Gunboys.		

	Beggars Banquet	Arista
Oct 83. (7"/7"pic-d) (BEG 99/+P) **LOVE IS A WONDERFUL COLOUR. / WATERLINE**	`15`	
(ext.12"+=/ext.12"pic-d+=) (BEG 99 T/TP) – In the dance the Shamen led.		
(d7"++=) (BEG 99 + ICE 1) – The Devil on horseback.		
Mar 84. (7") (BEG 108) **BIRDS FLY (WHISPER TO A SCREAM). / IN THE CAULDRON OF LOVE**	`53`	-
(12"+=) (BEG 108T) – Ragweed campaign / Scarecrow.		
(12"+=) (BEG 108TD) – ('A'-Frantic mix).		
Mar 84. (lp/c) (BEGA/BEGC 50) <8202> **THE ICICLE WORKS**	`24`	`40`
– Chop the tree / Love is a wonderful colour / Reaping the rich harvest / As the dragonfly flies / Lover's day / In the cauldron of love / Out of season / A factory in the desert / Birds fly (whisper to a scream) / Nirvana. (cd-iss. Jul86; BEGA 50CD) (re-iss. Jul88 lp/c/cd; BBL/+C 50/+CD)		
Mar 84. (7") <9155> **BIRDS FLY (WHISPER TO A SCREAM). / IN THE DANCE THE SHAMEN LED**	-	`37`
Sep 84. (7") (BEG 119) **HOLLOW HORSE. / THE ATHEIST**		-
(12"+=) (BEG 119T) – Nirvana (live).		
(12"+=) (BEG 119TR) – ('A'remix).		
May 85. (7") (BEG 133) **ALL THE DAUGHTERS (OF HER FATHER'S HOUSE). / A POCKETFUL OF NOTHING**		-
(12"+=) (BEG 133T) – Mr. Soul.		
Jul 85. (7") (BEG 142) **SEVEN HORSES. / SLINGSHOT**		-
(d7"+=) (BEG 142D) – Beggars legacy / Goin' back.		
(12") (BEG 142T) – ('A'-American) / ('B'side) / Beggars legacy.		
Sep 85. (lp/c) (BEGA/BEGC 61) **THE SMALL PRICE OF A BICYCLE**	`55`	-
– Hollow horse / Perambulator / Seven horses / Rapids / Windfall / Assumed sundown / Saint's sojourn / All the daughter's (of her father's horse) / Book of reason / Conscience of kings. (re-iss. Jan89 lp/c/cd; BBL/+C 61/+CD)		
Oct 85. (7") (BEG 151) **WHEN IT ALL COMES DOWN. / (LET'S GO) DOWN TO THE RIVER**		-
('A'unabridged-12"+=) (BEG 151T) – Cold turkey.		
Feb 86. (m-lp/c) (BEGA/BEGC 71) **SEVEN SINGLES DEEP** (compilation)	`52`	-
– Hollow horse / Love is a wonderful colour / Birds fly (whisper to a scream) / All the daughters (of her father's house) / When it all comes down / Seven horses / Rapids. (c+=) – I never saw my hometown 'til I went around the world / (Let's go) Down to the river / Slingshot / The atheist / Into the mystic / A pocketful of nothing / Goin' back. (re-iss. Sep88 lp/c/cd; BBL/+C 71/+CD) (cd+=) – Perambulator / Lover's day / Out of season / Saints sojourn / Nirvana / Conscience of kings.		

	Beggars Banquet	Beggars Banquet
Jun 86. (7") (BEG 160) **UNDERSTANDING JANE. / I NEVER SAW MY HOMETOWN 'TIL I WENT AROUND THE WORLD**	`52`	-
(12"+=) (BEG 160T) – Into the mystic.		
(d7"+=) (BEG 160 + ICE 3) – Hollow horse (live) / You ain't seen nothin' yet (live).		
(c-s+=) (BEG 160C) – Seven horses (live) / Perambulator (live) / Rapids (live).		
Sep 86. (7") (BEG 172) **WHO DO YOU WANT FOR YOUR LOVE. / UNDERSTANDING JANE (live)**	`54`	-
(w/ free c-s+=) (BEG 172F) – John Geoffrey Muir shopkeeper / Impossibly three lovers.		
(12"+=) (BEG 172T) – Should I stay or should I go (live) / Roadhouse blues (live).		
Dec 86. Situation2; (12"ep) (SIT 45T) **UP HERE IN THE NORTH OF ENGLAND. / SEA SONG (Ian McNabb) / NATURE'S WAY / IT MAKES NO DIFFERENCE / WAYLAID (Chris Layhe)**		-
Jan 87. (7") (BEG 181) **EVANGELINE. / EVERYBODY LOVES TO PLAY THE FOOL**	`53`	-
(12"+=) (BEG 181T) – Waiting in the wings / ('A'demo).		
(c-s+=) (BEG 181C) – It makes no difference / Nature's way / Sea song.		
Mar 87. (lp/c)(cd) (BEGA/BEGC 78)(BEGA 78CD) <6447> **IF YOU WANT TO DEFEAT YOUR ENEMY SING HIS SONG**	`28`	
– Hope springs eternal / Travelling chest / Sweet Thursday / Up here in the north of England / Who do you want for your love / When you were mine / Evangeline / Truck driver's lament / Understanding Jane / Walking with a mountain. (c+=) – Everybody loves to play the fool / Don't let it rain on my parade. (cd++=) – I never saw my hometown 'til went around the world / Into the mystic. (re-iss. Feb90 lp/c/cd; BBL/+C 78/+CD)		
Nov 87. (7"/s7") (BEG 203/+S) **HIGH TIME. / BROKEN HEARTED FOOL**		-
(12"+=) (BEG 203T) – Travelling chest (live) / Private revolution (live).		
Feb 88. (7") (BEG 208) **THE KISS OFF. / SURE THING**		-
(12"ep/c-ep+=/cd-ep+=) (BEG IW/+C/CD) – THE NUMB EP – High time (acoustic) / Whipping boy.		
Apr 88. (7") (BEG 220) **LITTLE GIRL LOST. / TIN CAN**	`59`	-
(12"+=/pic-cd-s+=) (BEG 215 T/CD) – Hot profit gospel / One time.		
May 88. (lp/c)(cd) (IWA/IWC 2)(IWA 2CD) <8424> **BLIND**	`40`	
– (intro) Shit creek / Little girl lost / Starry blue-eyed wonder / One true love / Blind / Two two three / What do you want me to do? / Stood before Saint Peter / The kiss off / Here comes trouble / Walk a while with me.		
Jun 88. (7") (BEG 220) **HERE COMES TROUBLE. / STARRY BLUE-EYED WONDER**		-
(12"+=)(12"box) (BEG 220T)(IW 3) – Rock'n'roll (live) / For what it's worth (medley live).		

—— **ZAK STARKEY** (b.13 Sep'65, London, England, son of RINGO) – drums repl. LAYHE SHARROCK who joined WILD SWANS + The LA'S / added **DAVE GREEN** – keyboards / **ROY CORKHILL** – bass (both ex-BLACK)

—— (1989) **IAN and ROY** brought in **DAVE BALDWIN** – keyboards / **MARK REVELL** – guitar, vocals / **PAUL BURGESS** – drums

	Epic	Work-Epic
Mar 90. (7") (WORKS 100) **MOTORCYCLE RIDER. / TURN ANY CORNER**	`73`	
(12"+=/12"etched+=) (WORKS T/E 100) – People change.		
(cd-s++=) (WORKS C100) – Victoria's ghost.		
(12") (WORKS Q100) – ('A'side) / Let's get loaded / Red lightning.		

May 90. (cd/c/lp) *(466 800-2/-4/-1)* **PERMANENT DAMAGE** ☐ ☐ -
– I still want you / Motorcycle rider / Melanie still hurts / Hope street rag / I think I'm gonna be OK / Baby don't burn / What she did to my mind / One good eye / Permanent damage / Woman on my mind / Looks like rain / Dumb angel.

May 90. (7") *(WORKS 101)* **MELANIE STILL HURTS. / WHEN THE CRYING'S DONE** ☐ ☐ -
(12"+=) *(WORKS T101)* – Mickey's blue.
(7"ep++=/cd-ep++=) *(WORKS Q/C 101)* – I dreamt I was a beautiful woman.

Jul 90. (7"/c-s) *(WORKS/+M 102)* **I STILL WANT YOU. / I WANT THAT GIRL** ☐ ☐ -
(12"+=) *(WORKST 102)* – It's gonna rain forever.
(10"++=/cd-ep++=) *(WORKS Q/C 102)* – Sweet disposition.

—— McNABB joined the WILD SWANS briefly before going solo.

– compilations, etc. –

Nov 88. (12"ep) *Nighttracks; (SFNT 015)* **THE EVENING SHOW SESSIONS** (14.11.82) ☐ ☐ -
– Birds fly (whisper to a scream) / Lover's day / Love hunt / As the dragonfly flies.

Jan 90. (7") *Old Gold; (OG 9918)* **LOVE IS A WONDERFUL COLOUR. / BIRDS FLY (WHISPER TO A SCREAM)** ☐ ☐ -

Aug 92. (cd)(c) *Beggars Banquet; (BEGA 124CD)(BEGC 124)* **THE BEST OF THE ICICLE WORKS** 60 -
– Hollow horse (long version) / Love is a wonderful colour / Birds fly (whisper to a scream) / Understanding Jane ('92 version) / Shit creek / High time (acoustic) / Who do you want for your love? / Evangeline / Little girl lost / When it all comes down ('92 version) / Starry blue eyed wonder / Out of season / The kiss off / Up here in the North of England / Firepower / Blind. *(ltd. w/ free cd 'BEST KEPT SECRET'; BEGA 124CD2) (re-iss. cd Sep95; BBL 124CD)*

Aug 92. (7") *Beggars Banquet; (BEG 262)* **UNDERSTANDING JANE '92. / LITTLE GIRL LOST** ☐ ☐ -
(12"+=) *(BEG 262T)* – When it all comes down '92 / Firepower.
(cd-s+=) *(BEG 262CD)* – Solid ground / Like weather.

Mar 94. (cd) *Windsong; (<WINCD 053>)* **BBC RADIO 1 LIVE IN CONCERT** (live) ☐ ☐ -

Jul 97. (cd) *Dutch East India; <8004>* **THE PEEL SESSIONS** - ☐

IAN McNABB

                    Way Cool   not iss.

Jun 91. (12"ep/cd-ep) *(WAYCOOL 14 T/CD)* **GREAT DREAMS OF HEAVEN / THAT'S WHY I BELIEVE. / MAKE LOVE TO YOU / POWER OF SONG** ☐ ☐ -
                    Fat Cat   not iss.

Oct 91. (12"ep/cd-ep) *(FC 001/+CD)* **THESE ARE THE DAYS. / TRAMS IN AMSTERDAM / GREAT DREAMS OF HEAVEN (acoustic)** ☐ ☐ -
                    This Way Up   not iss.

Jan 93. (7") *(WAY 211)* **IF LOVE WAS LIKE GUITARS. / TRAMS IN AMSTERDAM** 67 -
(cd-s+=) *(WAY 233)* – Great dreams of Heaven.

Jan 93. (cd/c/d-lp) *(514 378-2/-4/-1)* **TRUTH AND BEAUTY** 51 -
– (I go) My own way / These are the days / Great dreams of Heaven / Truth and beauty / I'm game / If love was like guitars / Story of my life / That's why I believe / Trip with me / Make love to you / Presence of the one. *(re-iss. cd/c Apr95; same)*

Mar 93. (7"/c-s) *(WAY 811/844)* **GREAT DREAMS OF HEAVEN. / UNKNOWN LEGEND** ☐ ☐ -
(12"+=/cd-s+=) *(WAY 822/833)* – I'm game / Caroline no.

Jun 93. (7") *(WAY 1211)* **I'M GAME. / A PIRATE LOOKS AT FORTY** ☐ ☐ -
(cd-s) *(WAY 1233)* – ('A'side) / What's it all about / ('A'version).

Sep 93. (7"/c-s/cd-s) *(WAY 1611/1644/1655)* **(I GO) MY OWN WAY / PLAY THE HAND THEY DEAL YOU** ☐ ☐ -
(10"+=/cd-s+=) *(WAY 1688/1633)* – If my daddy could see me now / For you, angel.

—— with **RALPH MOLINA + BILLY TALBOT** (of NEIL YOUNG's CRAZY HORSE) + **MIKE 'TONE' HAMILTON** (of SMITHEREENS)

Jun 94. (7"/c-s) *(WAY 3111/3144)* **YOU MUST BE PREPARED TO DREAM. / THAT'S WHY THE DARKNESS EXISTS** 54 -
(12"/cd-s) *(WAY 3122/3133)* – ('A'side) / Sometimes I think about you / Woo yer.
(cd-s) *(WAY 3199)* – ('A'side) / ('A'radio) / Love is a wonderful colour / When it all comes down (both acoustic).

Jul 94. (cd/c) *(522 298-2/-4)* **HEAD LIKE A ROCK** 29 -
– Fire inside my soul / You must be prepared to dream / Child inside a father / Still got the fever / Potency / Go into the light / As a life goes by / Sad strange solitary Catholic mystic / This time is forever / May you always.

Aug 94. (c-s) *(WAY 3644)* **GO INTO THE LIGHT / TIME YOU WERE IN LOVE** ☐ ☐ -
(cd-s+=) *(WAY 3633)* – For you, angel.
(12") *(WAY 3622)* – ('A'side) / ('A'-Celestial dub mix) / For you, angel.
(cd-s) *(WAY 3699)* – ('A'side) / I stood before St.Peter / Rock / ('A'-Celestial dub mix).

Apr 96. (7"/c-s) *(WAY 5011/5044)* **DON'T PUT YOUR SPELL ON ME. / DON'T PATRONISE ME** ☐ ☐ -
(cd-s+=) *(WAY 5033)* – What she did to my mind.

May 96. (cd/c/d-lp) *(524 215-2/-4/-1)* **MERSEYBEAST** 30 -
– Merseybeast / Affirmation / Beautiful old mystery / Love's young dream / Camaraderie / Don't put your spell on me / Heydays / Little bit of magic / You stone my soul / Too close to the sun / They settled for less than they wanted / I'm a genius / Available light / Merseybeast (reprise). *(some cd's w/ free cd 'NORTH WEST COAST'; 524 240-2)*

Jun 96. (7") *(WAY 5211)* **MERSEYBEAST. / UP HERE IN THE NORTH OF ENGLAND (demo Jan 86)** 74 -
(cd-s+=) *(WAY 5233)* – Permanent damage (demo Sept 88) / Merseybeast (demo March 95).
(cd-s) *(WAY 5266)* – ('A'side) / Pretty boys with big guitars / The slider / Snaked.

Tony McPHEE (see under ⇒ GROUNDHOGS)

MC REN (see under ⇒ N.W.A.)

MD.45 (see under ⇒ MEGADETH)

MEAT LOAF

Born: MARVIN LEE ADAY, 27 Sep'48, Dallas, Texas, USA, his nickname given to him after he trod on the toes of his school master. In 1966 he moved to Los Angeles and formed psychedelic-rock outfit POPCORN BLIZZARD, who opened for The WHO, AMBOY DUKES and The STOOGES, before disbanding in early 1969. That year, MEAT LOAF successfully auditioned for the 'Hair' musical, where he met female soul singer STONEY. In 1970, they made a self-titled lp together for 'Rare Earth', although he soon rejoined the 'Hair' tour in Cleveland, the behemoth subsequently taking the role of Buddha in the musical 'Rainbow'. A year and a half later, he starred in JIM STEINMAN's Broadway musical 'More Than You Deserve', a partnership that was to flower, both creatively and commercially, as the decade wore on. The following year, MEAT LOAF acted/sang in Richard O'Brien's Broadway musical 'The ROCKY HORROR PICTURE SHOW', which was soon made into a film with MEAT LOAF taking the part of EDDIE. He and STEINMAN went on to tour with the comedy show 'National Lampoon', MEAT LOAF playing the part of a priest in the 'Rockabye Hamlet' sketch. Keeping his finger in the rock'n'roll pie, he contributed vocals to TED NUGENT's 1976 set, 'Free For All'. Early the following year, the big man got together again in New York with STEINMAN, starting work on the 'NEVERLAND' project. They signed to 'R.C.A.', although the partnership changed stables (to 'Epic'-affiliated label 'Cleveland International') after it was clear the label didn't want to work with producer TODD RUNDGREN. Late in 1977, they finally unleashed the finished article as 'BAT OUT OF HELL', and with heavy tours, the record eventually made the US Top 20 (also hitting the UK Top 10). A bombastic rock opera, the album shook up the punk/new wave dominated music scene, its heavyweight, anthemic choruses and vein-bursting vocal histrionics reclaiming the territory that "rock" had lost in the past few years. It crossed over to such an extent that it became part of nearly everyone's record collection, selling millions in the process and residing in the charts for over eight years. Songs such as 'YOU TOOK THE WORDS RIGHT OUT OF MY MOUTH', 'TWO OUT OF THREE AIN'T BAD', 'PARADISE BY THE DASHBOARD LIGHT' and the epic title track, took rock'n'roll to melodramatic new heights, its crescendos gripping and lulling the listener into submission. Sweating like a builder's arse crack, MEAT LOAF strained and contorted his way through each song with a theatrical passion as yet unwitnessed in rock. However, it wasn't without a price, the hairy one subsequently suffering throat and alcohol problems over the course of the next few years as the pressures of fame took their toll. Nevertheless, he starred in the film 'Roadie' (1980), alongside DEBBIE HARRY and her group BLONDIE. Impatient with MEAT LOAF's problems, STEINMAN released the 'BAD FOR GOOD' (May '81) album under his own name, although this was intended for MEAT. The long-awaited MEAT LOAF follow-up, 'DEAD RINGER FOR LOVE' was finally issued four months later, and although it hit the top of the charts, it only managed to scrape into the US Top 50. Having used ELLEN FOLEY as a vocal foil on his last meisterwork, MEAT LOAF employed the powerful tonsils of CHER on the title track (also a hit single). With STEINMAN out of the picture, MEAT LOAF concentrated his activities in Britain, where he soon became a widely known celebrity, losing a few stone in the process. While mid 80's albums like 'MIDNIGHT AT THE LOST AND FOUND' (1983), 'BAD ATTITUDE' (1984) and 'BLIND BEFORE I STOP' (1986) did little to improve his critical standing, fans still came out in their droves for live appearances. Inevitably perhaps, MEAT LOAF and STEINMAN eventually got back together, 'Virgin' (having just lost MIKE OLDFIELD's massive selling 'Tubular Bells II' to 'Warners') being the lucky backer of a million-selling 1993 sequel, funnily enough called 'BAT OUT OF HELL II – BACK INTO HELL'. This provided the once 20-stone rocker with a return to transatlantic chart domination, the accompanying single 'I'D DO ANYTHING FOR YOU (BUT I WON'T DO THAT)'. This rejuvenated the singer's flagging career, a British beef ban unable to prevent MEAT LOAF (and new writer DIANE WARREN) once again making the UK Top 3 with the 'WELCOME TO THE NEIGHBOURHOOD' album in 1995. • **Songwriters:** MEATLOAF co-wrote w/ PAUL CHRISTIE + others in 1983. P. JACOBS + S. DURKEE took the bulk of the load in 1984. Covered; MARTHA (Tom Waits) / OH WHAT A BEAUTIFUL MORNING (Rogers-Hammerstein) / WHERE ANGELS SING (Davis) / WHATEVER HAPPENED TO SATURDAY NIGHT (Richard O'Brien) / COME TOGETHER + LET IT BE (Beatles).

Album rating: BAT OUT OF HELL (*10) / DEAD RINGER (*6) / MIDNIGHT AT THE LOST AND FOUND (*5) / HITS OUT OF HELL compilation (*7) / BAD ATTITUDE (*6) / MEAT LOAF LIVE AT WEMBLEY (*5) / BLIND BEFORE I STOP (*5) / BAT OUT OF HELL II: BACK INTO HELL (*6) / WELCOME TO THE NEIGHBOURHOOD (*4) / THE VERY BEST OF MEAT LOAF compilation (*7)

STONEY AND MEATLOAF

STONEY – vocals,(who later joined BOB SEGER).

		Rare Earth	Rare Earth
Apr 71.	(7") <5027-F> **WHAT YOU SEE IS WHAT YOU GET. / LADY OF MINE**	-	71
Jun 71.	(7") <5033-F> **IT TAKES ALL KINDS OF PEOPLE. / THE WAY YOU DO THE THINGS YOU DO**	-	
Oct 71.	(7") (RES 103) **WHAT YOU SEE IS WHAT YOU GET. / THE WAY YOU DO THE THINGS YOU DO** (re-iss. Mar79 on 'Prodigal'; PROD 10)	-	
Oct 72.	(lp) <SRE 3005> <R 528-1> **STONEY AND MEATLOAF**		Oct71

– Jimmy Bell / She waits by the window / It takes all kind of people / Stone heart / Who is the leader of the people / What you see is what you get / Kiss me again / Sunshine (where's Heaven) / Jessica White / Lady be mine / Everything under the sun. <(re-iss. Oct78/Mar79 as 'MEATLOAF (FEATURING STONEYAND MEATLOAF)' on 'Prodigal'; P7 10029> (PDL 2010) (re-iss. Oct81 c; CPDL 2010) (re-iss. 1986 as 'MEAT LOAF' on 'Motown'; ZL 72217)

——— Returned to feature in the musical 'Hair' (plus see above biography).

MEAT LOAF

		not iss.	R.S.O.
1974.	(7") <RS 407> **MORE THAN YOU DESERVE. / PRESENCE OF THE LORD**	-	
		Ode	Ode
Oct 75.	(7"w-drawn) (ODS 66304) **CLAP YOUR HANDS AND STAMP YOUR FEET. / STAND BY ME** (above was recorded in 1973)		

——— **MEAT LOAF** – vocals / **JIM STEINMAN** – composer, keyboards, percussion / **TODD RUNDGREN** – multi- / **ROY BITTAN** – piano, keyboards / **MAX WEINBERG** – drums / **KASIM SULTAN** – bass / **ROGER POWELL** – synth. / **ELLEN FOLEY + RORY DODD** – back.vox

		Epic	Epic
Jan 78.	(lp/c)(pic-lp) (EPC/40 82419)(EPC11 82419) <34974> **BAT OUT OF HELL**	9	14 Oct77

– You took the words right out of my mouth (hot summer night) / Heaven can wait / All revved up with no place to go / Two out of three ain't bad / Bat out of hell / For crying out loud / Paradise by the dashboard light: (I)- Paradise, (II)- Let me sleep on it, (II)- Praying for the end of time. (cd-iss. 1983; EPCCDEPC 82419) (re-iss. pic-cd Dec90; 467732-2) (re-iss. Jul91 lp/c+=; EPC/40 82419) – Dread ringer for love. (hit UK No.14, re-entered Jan92, peaked again at No.24-Jul92, returned to hit UK No.19 Autumn 1993) (cd re-iss. Jul95; 480411-2) (lp re-iss. Jun99 on 'Simply Vinyl'; SVLP 86)

Mar 78.	(7") (SEPC 5980) <50467> **YOU TOOK THE WORDS RIGHT OUT OF MY MOUTH. / FOR CRYING OUT LOUD**	33	Jan78
Jul 78.	(7") (SEPC 6281) <50513> **TWO OUT OF THREE AIN'T BAD. / FOR CRYING OUT LOUD**	32	11 Mar78
Aug 78.	(7") <50588> **PARADISE BY THE DASHBOARD LIGHT. / "BAT" OVERTURE**	-	39
Sep 78.	(7") (SEPC 6797) **PARADISE BY THE DASHBOARD LIGHT. / ALL REVVED UP WITH NO PLACE TO GO**		
Nov 78.	(7") <50634> **YOU TOOK THE WORDS RIGHT OUT OF MY MOUTH. / PARADISE BY THE DASHBOARD LIGHT**	-	39
Jan 79.	(7"/ext.12"red) (SEPC/+12 7018) **BAT OUT OF HELL. / HEAVEN CAN WAIT** (re-iss. Apr81)	15	

——— MEAT LOAF now brought in many session people, including **CHER** on title track.

Sep 81.	(lp/c)(pic-lp) (EPC/40 83645)(EPC11 83645) <36007> **DEAD RINGER**	1	45

– Peel out / I'm gonna love her for both of us / More than you deserve / I'll kill you if you don't come back / Read 'em and weep / Nocturnal pleasure / Dead ringer for love / Everything is permitted. (re-iss. Nov85 lp/c; EPC 32692) (cd-iss. Nov87; EPCCD 83645)

Sep 81.	(7") (EPCA 1580) <02490> **I'M GONNA LOVE HER FOR BOTH OF US. / EVERYTHING IS PERMITTED**	62	84
Nov 81.	(7"/7"pic-d) (EPCA/+11 1697) **DEAD RINGER FOR LOVE. / MORE THAN YOU DESERVE** (re-iss. Aug88)	5	-
Mar 82.	(7") (EPCA 2012) **READ 'EM AND WEEP. / EVERYTHING IS PERMITTED** (12"+=) (EPCA 12-2012) – (interview with MEAT LOAF).		-
Apr 82.	(7") <02607> **READ 'EM AND WEEP. / PEEL OUT**	-	-
1982.	(12"ep-clear) (EPCA 12-2251) **MEAT LOAF IN EUROPE '82 (live)**		

– Two out of three ain't bad / You took the words right out of my mouth / I'm gonna love her for both of us / Dead ringer for love.

May 83.	(lp/c) (EPC 25243)(450360-4) **MIDNIGHT AT THE LOST AND FOUND**	7	

– Razor's edge / Midnight at the lost and found / Wolf at your door / Keep driving / The promised land / You never can be too sure about the girl / Priscilla / Don't you look at me like that / If you really want to / Fallen angel. (re-iss. Jan87 lp/c/cd; EPC 450360-1/-4/-2)

May 83.	(7") (A 3357) **IF YOU REALLY WANT TO. / KEEP DRIVING** (12"+=/12"pic-d+=) (TA/WA 3357) – Lost love.	59	-
Jul 83.	(7"/7"pic-d) (A/WA 3511) **RAZOR'S EDGE. / YOU NEVER CAN BE TOO SURE ABOUT THE GIRL** (12"+=) (TA 3511) – Don't look at me like that.		-
Sep 83.	(7"/7"pic-d) (A/WA 3748) **MIDNIGHT AT THE LOST AND FOUND. / FALLEN ANGEL** (d7"+=/12"+=) (DA/TA 3748) – Bat out of hell (live) / Dead ringer for love (live).	17	-
Jan 84.	(7") (A 4080) <04028> **RAZOR'S EDGE (remix). / PARADISE BY THE DASHBOARD LIGHT** (12"+=) (TA 4080) – Read 'em and weep.	41	

		Arista	R.C.A.
Sep 84.	(7"/7"sha-pic-d) (ARIS T/DP 585) **MODERN GIRL. / TAKE A NUMBER** (d7"/12")(12"pic-d) (ARIST 585/+D)(ARIPD12 585) – ('A'-Freeway mix) / ('B'extended).	17	-
Nov 84.	(lp)(c)(cd) (206619)(406610)(610187) <5451> **BAD ATTITUDE**	8	74 May85

– Bad attitude / Modern girl / Nowhere fast / Surf's up / Piece of the action / Jumpin' the gun / Cheatin' in your dreams / Don't leave your mark on me / Sailor to a siren. (re-iss. May86 on 'Fame' lp/c; FA41/TCFA 3150) (cd re-iss. Jun88 & Feb94; 259049)

Nov 84.	(7"/7"s/7"g-f/7"sha-pic-d) (ARI ST/PU/SG/SD 600) **NOWHERE FAST. / CLAP YOUR HANDS** (ext.12"+=) (ARIST12 600) – Stand by me.	67	-
Mar 85.	(12") <14050> **MODERN GIRL. / ('A'long version)**	-	-
Mar 85.	(7"/7"sha-pic-d) (ARIS T/D 603) **PIECE OF THE ACTION. / SAILOR TO A SIREN** (d7"+=) (ARIST 603 + FS603) – Bat out of hell (live) / Modern Girl (US remix). (ext.12"+=) (ARIST12 603) – Bad attitude. (ext.d12"++=) (ARIST12 603 + FS12 603) – (see d7"above FS603).	47	
May 85.	(7") <14101> **(GIVE ME THE FUTURE WITH A) MODERN GIRL. / SAILOR TO A SIREN**	-	-
Aug 85.	(7") <14149> **SURF'S UP. / JUMPIN' THE GUN** (12") <14141> – ('A'extended) / ('A'side) / Bad attitude.	-	-
Aug 86.	(7"/7"sha-pic-d/7"white-sha-pic-d/12"/12"pic-d; by MEAT LOAF and JOHN PARR) (ARIST 666/+P/XP) **ROCK'N'ROLL MERCENARIES. / REVOLUTIONS PER MINUTE**	31	-
Sep 86.	(lp/c/cd) (207/407/257 741) **BLIND BEFORE I STOP**	28	

– Execution day / Rock'n'roll mercenaries / Getting away with murder / One more kiss / Night of the soft parade / Blind before I stop / Burning down / Standing on the outside / Masculine / Man and a woman / Special girl / Rock'n'roll hero. (re-iss. cd Feb94; 259741)

Nov 86.	(7"/7"sha-pic-d)(10") (ARIST 683/+P)(ARIST10 683) <89340> **GETTING AWAY WITH MURDER. / ROCK'N'ROLL HERO** (12") (ARIST12 683) – ('A'-Scot free mix)/ ('B'extended).		-
Feb 87.	(7"/12") (RIS/+T 3) **BLIND BEFORE I STOP. / EXECUTION DAY** (12"+=) (RIST 3R) – Dead ringer for love (live) / Paradise by the dashboard light (live).		-
Mar 87.	(7") <89303> **ROCK'N'ROLL MERCENARY. / EXECUTION DAY**		-
Apr 87.	(7") (RIS 14) **SPECIAL GIRL. / ONE MORE KISS** (12"+=/cd-s+=) (RIS T/CD 14) – Dead ringer for love (live) / Paradise by the dashboard light (live).		-
Oct 87.	(7"/ext.12") (RIS/+T 41) **BAT OUT OF HELL (live). / MAN AND A WOMAN**		-
Nov 87.	(lp/c/cd) (208/408/258 599) **LIVE AT WEMBLEY (live)**	60	-

– Blind before I stop / Rock & roll mercenaries / Took the words / Midnight at the lost and found / Modern girl / Paradise by the dashboard light / Two out of three ain't bad / Bat out of Hell. (free 12"ep/cd+=) – Masculine / Rock'n'roll medley: Johnny B. Goode – Slow down – Jailhouse rock – Blue suede shoes.

——— now with **MRS LOUD** – female vocal / **ROY BITTAN & BILL PAYNE** – piano / **TIM PIERCE & EDDIE MARTINEZ** – guitar / **KENNY ARONOFF & RICK MAROTTA & BRIAN MEAGHER & JIMMY BRALOWER** – drums / **STEVE BUSLOWE** – bass / **PAT THRALL** – guitar solo / **LENNY PICKETT** – sax / **JEFF BOVA** – synth. & prog. / **etc.**

		Virgin	M.C.A.
Sep 93.	(cd/c/lp) (CDV/TCV/V 2710) <10699> **BAT OUT OF HELL II: BACK INTO HELL**	1	1

– I'd do anything for love (but I won't do that) / Life is a lemon and I want my money back / Rock and roll dreams come through / It just won't quit / Out of the frying pan (and into the fire) / Objects in the rear view mirror may appear closer than they are / Wasted youth / Everything louder than everything else / Good girls go to heaven (bad girls go everywhere) / Back into Hell / Lost boys and golden girls. (ltd.pic-lp Dec93; VP 2710) (re-iss. Nov95; same)

Sep 93.	(c-s) <54626> **I'D DO ANYTHING FOR LOVE (BUT I WON'T DO THAT) / ('A'edit)**	-	1
Oct 93.	(7"/c-s) (VS/+C 1443) <54626> **I'D DO ANYTHING FOR LOVE (BUT I WON'T DO THAT). / BACK INTO HELL** (cd-s+=) (VSCDT 1443) – Everything louder than everything else (live NYC). (cd-s) (VSCDG 1443) – ('A'side) / You took the words right out of my mouth (live NYC) / Bat out of hell (live NYC).	1	-
Jan 94.	(c-s) <54757> **ROCK AND ROLL DREAMS COME THROUGH / I'D DO ANYTHING FOR LOVE (BUT I WON'T DO THAT) (live)**	-	13
Feb 94.	(7"pic-d/c-s) (VSP/VSC 1479) **ROCK AND ROLL DREAMS COME THROUGH. / WASTED YOUTH** (cd-s+=) (VSCDT 1479) – I'd do anything for love (but I won't do that) (live NYC). (cd-s+=) (VSCDG 1479) – Heaven can wait (live) / Paradise by the dashboard light (live).	11	-
Apr 94.	(7"/c-s) (VS/+C 1492) <54848> **OBJECTS IN THE REAR VIEW MIRROR MAY APPEAR CLOSER THAN THEY ARE. / TWO OUT OF THREE AIN'T BAD (live)** (cd-s) (VSCDT 1492) – ('A'side) / Rock and roll dreams come through (live) / All revved up (live).	26	38
Oct 95.	(c-s) (VSC 1563) <55134> **I'D LIE FOR YOU (AND THAT'S THE TRUTH). / I'D DO ANYTHING FOR LOVE (BUT I WON'T DO THAT)** (cd-s+=) (VSCDG 1563) – Whatever happened to Saturday night. (cd-s) (VSCDT 1563) – ('A'-Fountain Head mix) / Oh, what a beautiful mornin' / Runnin' for the red light (I gotta life).	2	13
Oct 95.	(cd/c/d-lp) (CD/TC+/V 2799) <11341> **WELCOME TO THE NEIGHBOURHOOD**	3	17 Nov95

– When the rubber meets the road / I'd lie for you (and that's the truth) / Original sin / 45 seconds of ecstacy / Runnin' for the red light (I gotta life) / Fiesta de las Almas Perdidas / Left in the dark / Not a dry eye in the house / Amnesty is granted / If this is the last kiss (let's make it last all night) / Martha / Where angels sing.

Jan 96.	(c-s) (VSC 1567) <55174> **NOT A DRY EYE IN THE HOUSE / I'D LIE TO YOU (AND THAT'S THE TRUTH)** (cd-s+=) (VSCDT 1567) – Where the rubber meats the road (live). (cd-s) (VSCDX 1567) – ('A'side) / Come together / Let it be.	7	82

Apr 96. (c-s) *(VSC 1582)* **RUNNIN' FOR THE RED LIGHT (I GOTTA LIFE) / LIFE IS A LEMON AND I WANT MY MONEY BACK (live) / AMNESTY IS GRANTED**   `21` `[ ]`
(cd-s+=) *(VSCDX 1582)* – Dead ringer for love.
(12"pic-d) *(VSTP 1582)* – ('A'side) / Dead ringer for love (live) / All revved up (live) / Midnight at the lost and found (live).

Nov 98. (cd/c) *(CDV/TCV 2868)* **THE VERY BEST OF MEAT LOAF** (compilation)   `14` `[ ]`
– Home by now / No matter what / Life is a lemon and I want my money back / You took the words right out of my mouth (hot summer night) / Two out of three ain't bad / Modern girl / Rock'n'roll dreams come through / Is nothing sacred / Paradise by the dashboard lights / Heaven can wait / I'd do anything for love (but I won't do that) / A kiss is a terrible thing to waste / I'd lie for you (and that's the truth) / Not a dry eye in the house / Nocturnal pleasure / Dead ringer for love / Midnight at the lost and found / Objects in the rear view mirror may appear closer than they are / Bat out of Hell.

Apr 99. (c-s/cd-s; by MEAT LOAF featuring PATTI RUSSO) *(VSC/+DT 1734)* **IS NOTHING SACRED / NO MATTER WHAT / DEAD RINGER FOR LOVE (live)**   `15` `[ ]`
(cd-s) *(VSCDX 1734)* – ('A'side) / What you see is what you get (live) / Out of the frying pan (and into the fire) (live).

– compilations, others, etc. –

on 'Epic' records (unless stated)

Aug 82. (c-ep) *(EPCA40 2621)* **GREATEST ORIGINAL HITS EP**   `[ ]` `-`
– Bat out of Hell / Read 'em and weep / Dead ringer for love / I'm gonna love her for both of us. *(7"ep-iss.Mar83; EPCA 2621)*

Jan 85. (lp/c/cd) *(EPC/40/EPCCD 26156)* **HITS OUT OF HELL**   `2` `[ ]`
– Bat out of Hell / Read 'em and weep / Midnight at the lost and found / Two out of three ain't bad / Dead ringer for love / Modern girl / I'm gonna love her for both of us / You took the words right out of my mouth (hot summer night) / Razor's edge / Paradise by the dashboard light. *(re-iss.Mar89 lp/c; 450447-1/-4) (re-iss. cd Mar91 & Jul99; EPC 450447-2)*

Sep 86. (c-ep) *(450131-4)* **MEAT LOAF**   `[ ]` `-`
– Bat out of Hell / Dead ringer for love / Read 'em and weep / If you really want to / Razor's edge.

Aug 87. (d-lp) *(EPCML 241)* **BAT OUT OF HELL / HITS OUT OF HELL**   `[ ]` `-`

Jan 88. (7") Old Gold; *(OG 9751)* **BAT OUT OF HELL. / DEAD RINGER FOR LOVE**   `[ ]` `-`

Feb 89. (7") Old Gold; *(OG 9865)* **YOU TOOK THE WORDS RIGHT OUT OF MY MOUTH. / MIDNIGHT AT THE LOST AND FOUND**   `[ ]` `-`

Nov 89. (lp/c/cd) Arista; *(210/410/260 363)* **PRIME CUTS**   `[ ]` `-`

Nov 89. (lp/c/cd; with tracks by BONNIE TYLER) Telstar; *(STAR/STAC/TCD 2361)* **HEAVEN AND HELL**   `[ ]` `-`
(re-iss. cd-c.May93 & Dec95 on 'Columbia')

Jun 91. (7"/c-s) *(656982-7/-4)* **DEAD RINGER FOR LOVE. / HEAVEN CAN WAIT**   `53` `[ ]`
(12"+=/cd-s+=) *(656982-6/-2)* – Bat out of Hell.

Jun 92. (7"/c-s) *(657491-7/-4)* **TWO OUT OF THREE AIN'T BAD. / MIDNIGHT AT THE LOST AND FOUND**   `69` `[ ]`
(12"+=/cd-s+=) *(657491-6/-2)* – I'm gonna love her for both of us.

Jul 92. (c-s) M.C.A.; *(<54557>)* **PARADISE BY THE DASHBOARD LIGHT. /**   `-` `[ ]`
(above from the 'Leap Of Faith' soundtrack starring Steve Martin)

Oct 92. (cd/c) Pickwick; *(PWK CD/S 4121)* **ROCK'N'ROLL HERO**   `[ ]` `-`
(re-iss. May94; same)

Feb 93. (cd) *(CDX 82419)* **BAT OUT OF HELL – REVAMPED**   `[ ]` `-`

Feb 93. (d-cd) *(CDX 82419D)* **DEAD RINGER / BAT OUT OF HELL**   `[ ]` `-`

Apr 93. (d-cd) *(474032-2)* **DEAD RINGER / MIDNIGHT AT THE LOST AND FOUND**   `[ ]` `-`
(re-iss. Feb95; 478486-2)

Sep 93. (cd/c) Ariola; *(74321 1528-2/-4)* **THE COLLECTION**   `[ ]` `-`

Dec 93. (12"pic-d-ep/c-ep/pic-cd-ep) *(660006-6/-4/-2)* **BAT OUT OF HELL / READ 'EM AND WEEP. / OUT OF THE FRYING PAN (AND INTO THE FIRE) / ROCK AND ROLL DREAMS COME THROUGH** (Jim Steinman)   `8` `[ ]`

Oct 94. (cd; with BONNIE TYLER) **THE BEST**   `[ ]` `[ ]`

Oct 94. (cd/c/lp) Pure Music; *(PM CD/MC/LP 7002)* **ALIVE IN HELL (live)**   `33` `-`
– (tracks on 'LIVE AT WEMBLEY' album) + (studio tracks;-) Piece of the action / Bad attitude / Surf's up.

Apr 95. (cd) Arista; *(74321 25957-2)* **BLIND BEFORE I STOP / BAD ATTITUDE**   `[ ]` `-`

Jun 96. (cd/c) Camden; *(74321 39336-2/-4)* **ROCK'N'ROLL HERO**   `[ ]` `-`

(1989) and continuing critical praise led to a deal with 'London'. Their major label debut, 'FORBIDDEN PLACES' (1991) was accomplished but lacked the high-noon intensity of their earlier work. After a step-up from KURT COBAIN (see below), the raw 'NO JOKE' (1995) album at last saw The MEAT PUPPETS reaping some financial rewards, sales of the album going on to break the half million mark. • **Songwriters:** Most by CURT, some with CRIS or DERRICK. Covered TUMBLIN' TUMBLEWEEDS (Bob Nolan) / EL PASO CITY (Marty Robbins) / GOODNIGHT IRENE (Leadbelly). • **Trivia:** On 18 Nov'93, CURT & CRIS guested with NIRVANA's on an unplugged MTV spot. The tracks they performed were 'PLATEAU', 'OH ME' and 'LAKE OF FIRE'.

Album rating: MEAT PUPPETS mini (*5) / MEAT PUPPETS II (*7) / UP ON THE SUN (*8) / OUT MY WAY mini (*6) / MIRAGE (*8) / HEUVOS (*6) / MONSTERS (*7) / NO STRINGS ATTACHED compilation (*6) / FORBIDDEN PLACES (*6) / TOO HIGH TO DIE (*7) / NO JOKE! (*6)

CURT KIRKWOOD (b.10 Jan'59, Amarillo, Texas) – guitar, vocals / **CRIS KIRKWOOD** (b.22 Oct'60, Amarillo) – vocals, bass, rhythm guitar / **DERRICK BOSTROM** (b.23 Jun'60, Phoenix) – drums

	not iss.	World Inv.

Sep 81. (7"ep) **IN A CAR / BIG HOUSE. / DOLFIN FIELD / OUT IN THE GARDINER / FOREIGN LAWNS**   `-` `[ ]`
(cd-ep iss.Nov88 on 'S.S.T.'; SST 044CD)

	S.S.T.	S.S.T.

Jan 82. (m-lp) *<SST 009>* **MEAT PUPPETS**   `[ ]` `[ ]`
– Reward / Love offering / Blue green god / Walking boss / Melons rising / Saturday morning / Our friends / Tumblin' tumbleweeds / Milo, Sorghum and maize / Meat puppets / Playing dead / Litterbox / Electromud / The goldmine. *(re-iss. May93 lp/c/cd; SST 009/+C/CD)*

Apr 84. (lp) *<SST 019>* **MEAT PUPPETS II**   `[ ]` `1983`
– Split myself in two / Magic toy missing / Lost plateau / Aurora Borealis / We are here / Climbing / New gods / Oh, me / Lake on fire / I'm a mindless idiot / The whistling song. *(re-iss. May93 lp/c/cd; SST 019/+C/CD)*

Apr 85. (lp) *<SST 039>* **UP ON THE SUN**   `[ ]` `[ ]`
– Up on the sun / Maiden's milk / Away / Animal kingdom / Hot pink / Swimming ground / Bucket head / Too real / Enchanted pork fist / Seal whales / Two rivers / Creator. *(cd-iss. Sep87; SST 039CD) (re-iss. May93 cd/c; SST 039 CD/C)*

Aug 86. (m-lp) *<(SST 049)>* **OUT MY WAY**   `[ ]` `[ ]`
– She's hot / Out my way / Other kinds of love / Not swimming ground / Mountain line / Good golly Miss Molly. *(cd-iss. Sep87; SST 049CD) (re-iss. May93 cd/c; SST 049 CD/C)*

Apr 87. (lp/cd) *<(SST 100/+CD)>* **MIRAGE**   `[ ]` `[ ]`
– Mirage / Quit it / Confusion fog / The wind and the rain / Mighty zero / Get on down / Leaves / I am a machine / Beauty / A hundred miles / Love your children forever / Liquified: Mighty zero – I am a machine – Liquified – Rubberneckin'. *(re-iss. May93 cd/c; SST 100 CD/C)*

Oct 87. (lp/cd) *<(SST 150/+CD)>* **HEUVOS**   `[ ]` `[ ]`
– Paradise / Look at the rain / Bad love / Sexy music / Crazy / Fruit / Automatic mojo / Dry rain / I can't be counted on at all. *(re-iss. May93 cd/c; SST 150 CD/C)*

Oct 87. (12") *<(PSST 150)>* **I CAN'T BE COUNTED ON AT ALL. / PARADISE**   `[ ]` `[ ]`

Oct 89. (lp/cd) *<(SST 253/+CD)>* **MONSTERS**   `[ ]` `[ ]`
– Attacked by monsters / Light / Meltdown / In love / The void / Touchdown king / Party till the world obeys / Flight of the fire weasel / Strings on your heart / Like being alive.

Nov 90. (d-lp/cd) *<(SST 265/+CD)>* **NO STRINGS ATTACHED** (compilation)   `[ ]` `[ ]`
– Big house / In a car / Tumblin' tumbleweeds / Reward / The whistling song / New gods / Lost / Lake of fire / Split myself in two / Up on the Sun / Swimming ground / Maiden's milk / Bucket head / Out my way / Confusion fog / I am a machine / Quit it / Beauty / Look at the rain / I can't be counted on at all / Automatic mojo / Meltdown / Like being alive / Attacked by monsters.

	London	London

Nov 91. (cd/c/lp) *<(828254-2/-4/-1)>* **FORBIDDEN PLACES**   `[ ]` `[ ]`
– Sam / Nail it down / This day / Open wide / Another Moon / That's how it goes / Whirlpool / Popskull / No longer gone / Forbidden places / Six gallon pie.

Mar 94. (cd/c/lp) *<(828484-2/-4/-1)>* **TOO HIGH TO DIE**   `[ ]` `62`
– Violet eyes / Never to be found / We don't exist / Severed goddess head / Flaming heart / Shine / Backwater / Roof with a hole / Station / Things / Why / Evil love / Comin' down / Lake of fire.

Jul 94. (cd-ep) *<857553>* **BACKWATER / OPEN WIDE / ANIMAL / UP ON THE SUN / WHITE SPORT COAT**   `-` `47`

Dec 94. (10"ep) *<1109>* **RAW MEAT EP**   `[ ]` `[ ]`
– We don't exist / Up on the sun / El Paso city / White sport coat / Goodnight Irene.

Oct 95. (cd/c) *<(828665-2/-4)>* **NO JOKE!**   `[ ]` `[ ]`
– Scum / Nothing / Head / Taste of the sun / Vampires / Predator / Poison arrow / Eyeball / For free / Cobbler / Inflamable / Sweet ammonia / Chemical garden.

MEDICINE HEAD	(dig out; Great Psychedelic . . .)

MEGA CITY FOUR	
(dig out; 4th edition or Great Alt & Indie . . .)	

MEAT PUPPETS

Formed: Tempe, Phoenix, Arizona, USA . . . 1980 by brothers CURT and CRIS KIRKWOOD. They were soon snapped up by rising US indie label 'SST' in 1981, after a debut on their own label. Their first recording for the company, 'MEAT PUPPETS 1' (1982), was a demanding blast of howling noise and twisted country that barely hinted at the compelling sound they'd invent with the follow-up 'MEAT PUPPETS II' (1983). A hybrid of mystical GRATEFUL DEAD-like psychedelia that short-fused hardcore punk rock and the country-boy slur of CRIS, the record was the blueprint for most of their subsequent output. 'UP ON THE SUN' (1985) was slightly more polished and saw the band garner snowballing critical acclaim. By the release of 'MIRAGE' (1987), the band had fully realised their desert-rock vision with a collection of weather beaten, psychedelic country classics; tracks like 'BEAUTY' and 'CONFUSION FOG' rank among the MEAT PUPPETS' best. Yet the record failed to sell and the band returned to a rawer, ZZ TOP-influenced sound on 'HUEVOS'. This album, together with the more mainstream 'MONSTERS'

MEGADETH

Formed: San Francisco, California, USA . . . 1983 by ex-METALLICA guitarist/vocalist, DAVE MUSTAINE, alongside DAVE ELLEFSON (bass), CHRIS POLAND (guitar) and GAR SAMUELSON (drums). MUSTAINE soon secured the band a deal with the small 'Combat' label, who released MEGADETH's breakneck debut album, 'KILLING IS MY BUSINESS . . . AND BUSINESS IS GOOD' (1985). Taking the aural assault of METALLICA as a template, MUSTAINE and Co. had carved out an even more intense, speed-driven variation on heavy metal, but unlike many of their similarly speed-obsessed peers, MEGADETH had the instrumental prowess to pull it off. Signing to 'Capitol', the band followed up with 'PEACE SELLS . . . BUT WHO'S BUYING?' (1986), after which MUSTAINE sacked both POLAND and SAMUELSON. Replacing them with JEFF YOUNG and CHUCK BEHLER respectively, the band returned in February '88 with a fierce cover of the SEX PISTOLS' 'ANARCHY IN THE U.K.' , complete with original 'PISTOLS' guitarist, STEVE JONES. 'SO FAR . . . SO GOOD . . . SO WHAT!' followed in March, the pinnacle of their career thus far and one of the finest metal albums of that year. Lyrically, MUSTAINE was as reliably pessimistic as ever, 'IN MY DARKEST HOUR' seeing the frontman wracked with bitterness and frustrated rage. Which possibly accounts for his headlong descent into substance abuse following the album's success, MUSTAINE again firing his musicians and not surfacing again until the cover of ALICE COOPER's 'NO MORE MR. NICE GUY' in late '89, his first Top 20 hit. Going on MUSTAINE's track record, there had never been a MR. NICE GUY, although new recruits MARTY FRIEDMAN (guitar) and NICK MENZA (drums) have been with the band now for an unprecedented eight years and MUSTAINE obviously had it together enough to record the critically acclaimed 'RUST IN PEACE' (1990). 'HOLY WARS . . . THE PUNISHMENT DUE' was the first single from the album, an uncannily prescient piece of writing in light of the Gulf War, the record made even more eerie by dint of its wailing Arab-esque embellishments. The whole set was more mature, both musically and lyrically, FRIEDMAN ripping out solos at furious speed, note for perfect note while MUSTAINE tackled subjects from alien cover-ups ('HANGER 18', another Top 30 hit) to the threat of nuclear weapons ('RUST IN PEACE . . .POLARIS'). 'COUNTDOWN TO EXTINCTION' (1992) featured equally topical lyrical themes, mainly dealing with the danger to the earth's environment. Musically, the band had inevitably slowed the pace down somewhat; allowing more consideration for melody and structure, MEGADETH scored their biggest success to date, the album reaching No.2 in America, No.5 in Britain. 'SKIN O' MY TEETH' recounted MUSTAINE's brushes with death; rather than banging on about saving the planet, perhaps MUSTAINE should have dealt with his own affairs first as rumours began to surface about drug problems marring sessions for the 'YOUTHANASIA' (1994) album. Nevertheless, by the time of the album's release, MUSTAINE had apparently finally cleaned up and on the strength of the record, no one could really argue. It was another masterful effort, a transatlantic Top 10 that signalled MUSTAINE was hot on the heels of his old muckers METALLICA. After an odds'n'sods collection in '95, the band returned a few years later with 'CRYPTIC WRITINGS', a disappointing affair that should've served as MEGADETH's epitaph. However, they stood their ground for another cocktail of pitbull metal in the shape of 9th set, 'RISK' (1999); another transatlantic Top 30 entry. Thanks.

Album rating: KILLING IS MY BUSINESS . . . AND BUSINESS IS GOOD (*6) / PEACE SELLS . . . BUT WHO'S BUYING? (*8) / SO FAR . . . SO GOOD . . . SO WHAT? (*7) / RUST IN PEACE (*7) / COUNTDOWN TO EXTINCTION (*7) / YOUTHANASIA (*6) / HIDDEN TREASURES (*5) / CRYPTIC WRITINGS (*4) / RISK (*3)

DAVE MUSTAINE (b.13 Sep'61, La Mesa, Calif.) – vocals, lead guitar (ex-METALLICA) / **CHRIS POLAND** – guitar / **DAVE ELLEFSON** (b.12 Nov'64, Minnesota) – bass / **GAR SAMUELSON** – drums

	Music For Nations	Combat
Jun 85. (lp) *(MFN 46)* <970546> **KILLING IS MY BUSINESS . . . AND BUSINESS IS GOOD**		

– Last rites – Loved to death / Killing in my business . . .and business is good / The skull beneath the skin / These boots / Rattlehead / Chosen ones / Looking down the cross / Mechanix. *(cd-iss. Aug87; CDMFN 46) (pic-lp May88; MFN 46P) (cd re-iss. Nov99 on 'Century Media'; 66034-2)*

—— POLAND was replaced by MIKE ALBERT (ex-KING CRIMSON) briefly until his return

	Capitol	Capitol
Nov 86. (lp/pic-lp)(c) *(EST/+P 2022)(TCEST 2022)* <12526> **PEACE SELLS . . . BUT WHO'S BUYING?**		76

– Wake up dead / The conjuring / Peace sells / Devils island / Good mourning – Black Friday / Bad omen / I ain't superstitious / My last words. *(cd-iss. Sep88; CDP 746148-2) (re-iss. Jul94 cd/c; CDEST 2022)*

Nov 87. (7"/7"pic-d) *(CL/+P 476)* **WAKE UP DEAD. / BLACK FRIDAY (live)**	65	

(12"+=,12"w/7"pic-d) *(12CL 476)* – Devil's island (live).

—— **CHUCK BEHLER** – drums replaced SAMUELSON / **JEFF YOUNG**– guitar repl. JAY REYNOLDS who had briefly repl. POLAND

Feb 88. (7"/7"pic-d) *(CL/+P 480)* **ANARCHY IN THE U.K. / LIAR**	45	

(12"+=) *(12CL 480)* – 502.

Mar 88. (lp/pic-lp)(c/cd) *(EST/+P 2053)(CD/TC EST 2053)* <48148> **SO FAR . . . SO GOOD . . . SO WHAT!**	18	28 Jan88

– Into the lungs of Hell / Set the world afire / Anarchy in the U.K. / Mary Jane / 502 / In my darkest hour / Liar / Hook in mouth.

May 88. (7"/7"pic-d) *(CL/+P 489)* **MARY JANE. / HOOK IN MOUTH**	46	

(12"+=) *(12CL 489)* – My last words.

—— Late '88, YOUNG joined BROKEN SILENCE and BEHLER joined BLACK & WHITE

Nov 89. (7"/7"pic-d)(c-s) *(SBK/+PD 4)(TCSBK 4)* **NO MORE MR. NICE GUY. / DEAD ON: Different Breed**	13	

(12"+=/cd-s+=) *(12/CD SBK 4)* – DANGEROUS TOYS: Demon bell (the ballad of Horace Pinker).
(above single released on 'S.B.K.')

—— (Mar90) **MUSTAINE + ELLEFSON** bring in new members **MARTY FRIEDMAN** (b. 8 Dec'62, Washington, D.C.) – guitar (ex-CACOPHONY) / **NICK MENZA** (b.23 Jul'64, Germany) – drums

Sep 90. (c-s/7") *(TC+/CLP 588)* **HOLY WARS . . . THE PUNISHMENT DUE. / LUCRETIA**	24	

(12"+=/cd-s+=) *(12/CD CLP 588)* – Information.
(12"pic-d) *(12LP 588)* – ('A'side) / (13-minute interview).

Oct 90. (cd/c)(lp/pic-lp) *(CD/TC EST 2132)(EST/+P 2132)* <91935> **RUST IN PEACE**	8	23

– Holy wars . . . the punishment due / Hangar 18 / Take no prisoners / Five magics / Poison was the cure / Lucretia / Tornado of souls / Dawn patrol / Rust in peace . . . Polaris. *(re-iss. Sep94 cd/c; same)*

Mar 91. (7"/7"sha-pic-d) *(CL/+PD 604)* **HANGAR 18. / THE CONJURING**	26	

(cd-s+=) *(12/CD CLG 604)* – ('A'live) / Hook in mouth (live).

Jun 92. (7") *(CLS 662)* **SYMPHONY OF DESTRUCTION. / PEACE SELLS**	15	-

(12"clear+=/cd-s+=) *(12CLS/CDCL 662)* – Go to Hell / Breakpoint.
(7"pic-d) *(CLPD 662)* – ('A'side) / *In my darkest hour (live).*

Jul 92. (cd/c/lp) *(CD/TC+/ESTU 2175)* <98531> **COUNTDOWN TO EXTINCTION**	5	2

– Skin o' my teeth / Symphony of destruction / Architecture of aggression / Foreclosure of a dream / Sweating bullets / This was my life / Countdown to extinction / High speed dirt / Psychotron / Captive honour / Ashes in your mouth.

Oct 92. (c-s) <44886> **SYMPHONY OF DESTRUCTION / SKIN O' MY TEETH**	-	71

Oct 92. (7"/7"pic-d)(c-s) *(CL/+P 669)(TCCL 669)* **SKIN O' MY TEETH. / HOLY WARS . . . THE PUNISHMENT DUE (General Norman Schwarzkopf)**	13	

(cd-s+=) *(CDCL 669)* – ('A'version) / Lucretia.
(10"+=) *(10CL 669)* – High speed drill / (Dave Mustaine interview).

May 93. (c-s/7") *(TC+/CL 692)* **SWEATING BULLETS. / ASHES IN YOUR MOUTH (live)**	26	

(12"/cd-s) *(12/CD CL 692)* – ('A'side) / Countdown to extinction (live '92) / Symphony of destruction (gristle mix) / Symphony of destruction (live).

Oct 94. (cd/c/blue-lp) *(CD/TC+/EST 2244)* <29004> **YOUTHANASIA**	6	4

– Reckoning day / Train of consequences / Addicted to chaos / A tout le monde / Elysian fields / The killing road / Blood of heroes / Family tree / Youthanasia / I thought I knew it all / Black curtains / Victory.

Dec 94. (7"clear) *(CL 730)* **TRAIN OF CONSEQUENCES. / CROWN OF WORMS**	22	

(cd-s+=) *(CDCL 730)* – Peace sells . . . but who's buying? (live) / Anarchy in the UK (live).
(laser-etched 12") *(12CL 730)* – ('A'side) / Holy wars . . . the punishment due (live) / Peace sells . . . but who's buying? (live) / Anarchy in the U.K. (live).

Aug 95. (d-cd) *(CDESTS 2244)* <33670> **HIDDEN TREASURES**	28	90

– No more Mr. Nice guy / Breakpoint / Go to Hell / Angry again / 99 ways to die / Paranoid / Diadems / Problems.

Jul 97. (cd/c/lp) *(CD/TC+/EST 2297)* **CRYPTIC WRITINGS**	38	10

– Trust / Almost honest / Use the man / Mastermind / The disintegrators / I'll get even / Sin / A secret place / Have cool, will travel / She-wolf / Vortex / FFF.

Sep 99. (cd) *(499130-2)* <99134> **RISK**	29	16

– Insomnia / Prince of darkness / Enter the arena / Crush 'em / Breadline / Doctor is calling / I'll be there / Wanderlust / Ecstasy / Seven / Time (the beginning) / Time (the end).

– compilations, etc. –

Mar 97. (3xcd-box) *E.M.I.; (CDOMB 019)* **THE ORIGINALS**
– (PEACE SELLS . . . BUT WHO'S BUYING / SO FAR . . . SO GOOD . . . SO WHAT / RUST IN PEACE).

MD.45

DAVE MUSTAINE – guitar / **LEE VING** – vocals (ex-FEAR) / **KELLY LEMIEUX** – bass / **JAMES DE GRASSO** – drums

	Capitol	Capitol
Jul 96. (cd/c) *(CD/TC EST 2286)* **THE CRAVING**		

– Hell's motel / Day the music died / Fight hate / Designer behavior / Cartoon (segue) / The creed / My town / Voices / Nothing is something / Circus (segue) / Hearts will bleed / No pain / Roadman / Alley cat (segue).

Dieter MEIER (see under ⇒ YELLO)

MEKONS (dig out; Great Alt & Indie . . .)

Melle MEL (see under ⇒ GRANDMASTER FLASH)

MELANIE

Born: MELANIE SAFKA, 3 Feb'47, Astoria, Long Island, New York, USA, of Ukrainian-Italian parentage. In 1966, while auditioning for a bit part in a play, she accidentally walked into a music publisher's office where she was asked to sing and play her guitar. Fortunately, they liked her and invited her back, the company in question being none other than 'Columbia' records. The budding singer/songwriter was assigned to producer, PETER SCHEKERYK, who was to become her husband and the father of her three children. After two flop singles, MELANIE signed to 'Buddah' late in 1968 and her first album, 'BORN TO BE', revealed her to be a child-like and coy vocalist inspired by LOTTE LENYA and EDITH PIAF. When this hit the shops in May '69, she was invited to play the 'Woodstock' festival later that year. In 1970, the folk-oriented SEEKERS had a US hit with one of her better known tracks, 'WHAT HAVE THEY DONE TO MY SONG, MA?', while she herself made the UK Top 10 with the melancholy 'RUBY TUESDAY' (from the pen of JAGGER-RICHARDS). Both songs were gleaned from the accompanying Top 5 album, 'CANDLES IN THE RAIN', this golden period seeing the release of three further successful albums, the last of which, 'GATHER ME', featured an

American US No.1 (UK No.4), 'BRAND NEW KEY'. The aforementioned album appeared on her newly formed 'Neighborhood' label, an imprint she had initiated with her husband. Despite this venture, MELANIE's commercial clout dwindled as the 70's wore on. As her record sales fell away, so her label eventually went belly-up in the mid-70's. Help was at hand from 'Atlantic', however, who picked her up for 1979's 'PHOTOGRAPH'. While she couldn't quite manage to regain her former star status, MELANIE's cult following allowed her to go on releasing albums throughout the 80's, mainly on independent labels. Her only release of the 90's was 'SILENCE IS KING' (1995). • **Covered**: JIGSAW PUZZLE + WILD HORSES (Rolling Stones) / MR. TAMBOURINE MAN + SIGN ON THE WINDOW + LAY LADY LAY (Bob Dylan) / CAROLINA ON MY MIND (James Taylor) / LOVER'S CROSS (Jim Croce) / PRETTY BOY FLOYD (Woody Guthrie) / I THINK IT'S GOING TO RAIN TODAY (Randy Newman) / WILL YOU LOVE ME TOMORROW (Goffin-King) / CHORDS OF FAME (Phil Ochs) / MY FATHER (Judy Collins) / YOU CAN'T HURRY LOVE (Supremes) / etc. • **Trivia**: Her Neighborhood label also signed folky outfit, MIKE HERON'S REPUTATION (ex-INCREDIBLE STRING BAND) in 1973.

Album rating: BORN TO BE (*4) / AFFECTIONATELY MELANIE (*4) / CANDLES IN THE RAIN (*7) / LEFTOVER WINE (*5) / THE GOOD BOOK (*6) / GATHER ME (*7) / GARDEN IN THE CITY (*4) / STONEGROUND WORDS (*4) / MELANIE AT CARNEGIE HALL (*4) / MADRUGADA (*4) / AS I SEE IT NOW (*4) / SUNSET AND OTHER BEGINNINGS (*4) / PHOTOGRAPH (*4) / PHONOGENIC – NOT JUST A PRETTY FACE (*5) / ARABESQUE (*4) / SEVENTH WAVE (*4) / AM I REAL OR WHAT (*4) / COWABONGA – NEVER TURN YOUR BACK ON A WAVE (*4) / THE BEST OF MELANIE compilation (*7) / SILENCE IS KING (*4) / OLD BITCH WARRIOR (*4)

MELANIE – vocals, acoustic guitar

			not iss.	Columbia
1967.	(7") <44349> **BEAUTIFUL PEOPLE. / GOD'S ONLY DAUGHTER**		-	
1968.	(7") <45524> **GARDEN IN THE CITY. / (WHY) DIDN'T MY MOTHER TELL ME?**		-	

			Buddah	Buddah
Dec 68.	(7") (201 027) **MR. TAMBOURINE MAN. / CHRISTOPHER ROBIN**			
Feb 69.	(7") (201 028) <113> **BOBO'S PARTY. / I'M BACK IN TOWN**			
May 69.	(lp) (203 019) <BDLH 5002> **BORN TO BE**			Jan69

– In the hour / I'm back in town / Bobo's party / Mr. Tambourine man / Momma momma / I really loved Harold / Animal crackers / Christopher Robin (is saying his prayer) / Close to it all / Merry Christmas. <re-pack Nov69 as 'MY FIRST ALBUM'; BDS 5074> (re-iss. Aug74; BDLH 5002) (cd-iss. Jul92 on 'C5'; C5CD 582)

Sep 69.	(7") <135> **BEAUTIFUL PEOPLE. / ANY GUY**		-	
Sep 69.	(7") (201 063) **BEAUTIFUL PEOPLE. / UPTOWN DOWN**		-	
Dec 69.	(lp) (203 028) <BDLP 4016> **AFFECTIONATELY MELANIE**			Nov69

– I'm back in town / Tuning my guitar / Soul sister Annie / Any guy / Uptown down again / Beautiful people / Johnny boy / Baby guitar / Deep down low / For my father / Take me home. (re-iss. Aug74; BDLP 4016) (cd-iss. Nov93 on 'Sequel';)

Feb 70.	(7") <161> **TAKE ME HOME.**		-	
Apr 70.	(7") (2011 013) <167> **LAY DOWN (CANDLES IN THE RAIN). / ANIMAL CRACKERS**			
Aug 70.	(7") (2011 038) **RUBY TUESDAY. / WHAT HAVE THEY DONE TO MY SONG MA?**	9		

(above 45 was flipped over Jan71 with B-side reaching No.39 in UK)

Sep 70.	(lp) (2318 009) <BDLP 5003> **CANDLES IN THE RAIN**	5	17	May70

– The good guys / Lovin' baby girl / Ruby Tuesday / Leftover wine / Lay down (candles in the rain) / Carolina in my mind / Citiest people / What have they done to my song ma. (re-iss. UK-Aug74 diff.order tracks +=) (BDLH 2003) – Alexander Beetle. (cd-iss. Jan88 on 'Rock Machine';) (re-iss. Jul91 on 'Razor';)

Nov 70.	(7") (2011 039) <186> **PEACE WILL COME (ACCORDING TO PLAN). / CLOSE TO IT ALL**			Aug70
Nov 70.	(7") <202> **RUBY TUESDAY. / MERRY CHRISTMAS**	-	52	

───── with **RONALD FRAGIPANE** – keyboards / etc, & onwards with sessioners

Nov 70.	(lp) (2318 011) <BDLH 5004> **LEFTOVER WINE (live Carnegie Hall)**	22	33	Sep70

– Close to it all / Uptown and down / Momma momma / The saddest thing / Beautiful people / Animal crackers / I don't eat animals / Happy birthday / Tuning my guitar / Psychotherapy / Leftover wine / Peace will come (according to plan). (re-iss. Aug74; BDLH 5004)

Feb 71.	(7") (2011 064) **STOP! I DON'T WANNA HEAR IT ANYMORE. / BEAUTIFUL PEOPLE**		-	
Feb 71.	(7") <224> **THE GOOD BOOK. / WE DON'T KNOW WHERE WE'RE GOING**		-	
May 71.	(lp) (2322 001) <5006> **THE GOOD BOOK**	9	80	Feb71

– The good book / Babe rainbow / Sign on the window / The saddest thing / Nickel song / Isn't it a pity / My father / Chords of fame / You can go fishin' / Birthday of the sun / The prize / Babe rainbow. (cd-iss. Mar93 on 'C5'; C5CD 597)

May 71.	(7") (2011 071) **THE NICKEL SONG. / THE GOOD BOOK**		-	
Aug 71.	(lp) (2318 034) **ALL THE RIGHT NOISES (Soundtrack)**			Dec70

– (basically orchestrated versions of her earlier work)

			Buddah	N'bourhood
Nov 71.	(7") (2011 105) <4201> **BRAND NEW KEY. / SOME SAY (I GOT DEVIL)**	4	1	Oct71
Dec 71.	(lp) (2322 002) <47001> **GATHER ME**	14	15	Nov71

– Little bit of me / Some day I'll be a farmer / Ring around the Moon / Steppin' / Brand new key / Ring around the Moon / shine the living light (chant) – Ring the living light – Shine the living light (chant reprise) / Railroad / Kansas / Some say (I got Devil) / Center of the circle / What wondrous love / Baby day / Tell me why. (re-iss. Aug74; BDLP 4022) (cd-iss. Oct92 on 'C5'; C5CD 597)

Mar 72.	(7") (2011 115) <4202> **RING THE LIVING BELL. / RAILROAD**		31	Jan72
Jul 72.	(7") <4204> **SOMEDAY I'LL BE A FARMER. / STEPPIN'**		-	

			N'bourhood	N'bourhood
Jul 72.	(7") (2011 136) **SOMEDAY I'LL BE A FARMER. / LAY LADY LAY**		-	
Oct 72.	(7") <4207> **TOGETHER ALONE. / CENTER OF THE CIRCLE**	-	86	
Oct 72.	(7") (NBH 1) **TOGETHER ALONE. / SUMMER WEAVING**		-	
Nov 72.	(lp) (NHTC 251) <47005> **STONEGROUND WORDS**		70	

– Together alone / Between the road signs / Summer weaving / My rainbow race / Do you believe / I am not a poet (night song) / Stoneground words / Song of the south (based on a theme from song of the north, adapted from the original) / Maybe I was (a golf ball) / Here I am. (re-iss. Jan75 on 'Anchor'; ABCL 5077)

Jan 73.	(7") (NBH 5) <4209> **DO YOU BELIEVE?. / STONEGROUND WORDS**			
Feb 73.	(7") (NBH 6) <4210> **BITTER BAD / DO YOU BELIEVE?**		36	
Jun 73.	(7") (NBH 8) <4212> **SEEDS. / SOME SAY (I GOT DEVIL)**			
Jul 73.	(d-lp) (NHLP 301) <49001> **AT CARNEGIE HALL (live)**			May73

– Baby guitar / Lay your hands / Across the six strings / Pretty Boy Floyd / Someday I'll be a farmer / Baby rainbow / It's me again / Any guy / Brand new key / Some day / Bitter sad / Psycho therapy / Together alone / Beautiful people / Hearing the news / Seasons to change / Peace will come (according to plan) / My rainbow race / Poet / Ring the living bell – Shine the living light / The actress.

Nov 73.	(7") (NBH 9) <4213> **WILL YOU LOVE ME TOMORROW?. / HERE I AM**	37	82	
Mar 74.	(7") (NBH 10) <4214> **LOVE TO LOSE AGAIN. / PINE AND FEATHER**			
May 74.	(7") (NBH 11) <4215> **LOVER'S CROSS. / HOLDING OUT**			
May 74.	(lp) (NH 3003) <48001> **MADRUGADA**			

– Love to lose again / Lover's cross / Pretty Boy Floyd / Wild horses / Think it's going to rain today / Maybe not for a lifetime / Holding out / I am being guided / The actress / Pine and feather. (re-iss. Jan75 on 'Anchor'; ABCL 5085)

Jan 75.	(7") <10000> **YOU'RE NOT A BAD GHOST, JUST AN OLD SONG. / EYES OF A MAN**	-		
Feb 75.	(7") (SNBH 2994) **YOU'RE NOT A BAD GHOST, JUST AN OLD SONG. / MONOGAUELA RIVER**	-		
Feb 75.	(lp) (SNBH 80636) <3000> **AS I SEE IT NOW**			

– Yankee man / You're not a bad ghost / Just an old song / Record machine / Eyes of man / Stars up there / Don't think twice, it's alright / Sweet misery / Monongahela River / Yes sir, that's my baby / Autumn lady / Chart song / As I see it now.

Apr 75.	(7") (SNBH 3250) **YES SIR, THAT'S MY BABY. / RECORD MACHINE**		-	
Jun 75.	(7") <10001> **SWEET MISERY. / RECORD MACHINE**	-		
Sep 75.	(7") (SNBH 3640) **YOU CAN'T HURRY LOVE – MAMA SAID. / THE SUN AND THE MOON**			
Oct 75.	(lp) (NBH 69168) <3001> **SUNSET AND OTHER BEGINNINGS**			

– Perceive it / Almost like being in love / Loving my children / You can't hurry love – Mama said / People are just getting ready / Ol' man river / I got my mojo working / Where's the band / Dream seller (meet me on the corner) / What do I keep / Sandman / The Sun and the Moon / Afraid of the dark.

			not iss.	Atlantic
Nov 75.	(7") (SNBH 3789) **ALMOST LIKE BEING IN LOVE. / BEAUTIFUL PEOPLE (live)**	-		
1976.	(lp) <18190> **PHOTOGRAPH**		-	

– Cyclone / If I needed you / The letter / Groundhog day / Nickel song / Photograph / I'm so blue / Secret of the darkness (I believe) / Save me / Raindance / Friends & co.

			R.C.A.	Midsong
Jan 77.	(7") <3380> **CYCLONE. / IF I NEEDED YOU**			

			R.C.A.	Tomato
Sep 78.	(7") <40858> **I'D RATHER LEAVE WHILE I'M IN LOVE. / RECORD PEOPLE**		-	
Sep 78.	(lp) (XL 13056) <3033> **PHONOGENIC – NOT JUST A PRETTY FACE**		-	

– Knock on wood / Bon apetite / Spanky / Runnin' after love / We can work it out / I'd rather leave while I'm in love / Let it be me / Yankee man / Record people / California dreamin'.

			R.C.A.	Tomato
Nov 78.	(7") <40903> **KNOCK ON WOOD. / RECORD PEOPLE**		-	
Aug 79.	(7") <10007> **RUNNIN' AFTER LOVE. / HOLDIN' OUT**		-	
Aug 79.	(d-lp) (XL 03073) <9003> **BALLROOM STREETS (live)**		-	

– Runnin' after love / Holdin' out / Cyclone / Beautiful sadness / Do you believe? / Nickel song / Any guy / What have they done to my song, ma? / I believe / Poet / Save me / Together alone / Ruby Tuesday / Buckle down / Miranda / Brand new key / Groundhog day / Friends and company.

			R.C.A.	R.C.A.
Apr 82.	(7") <1> **DETROIT OR BUFFALO. / IMAGINARY HEROES**	-	-	
Apr 82.	(7") (RCA 253) **DETROIT OR BUFFALO. / ROADBURN**	-		
Aug 82.	(lp) (RCALP 3078) **ARABESQUE**	-		

– Detroit or Buffalo / It don't matter now / Anyway that you want me / Roadburn / Fooling yourself / Too late / Standing on the other side / Love you to loathe me / When you're dead and gone / Imaginary heroes / Chances.

			N'bourhood	N'bourhood
Aug 82.	(7") <110> **DETROIT OR BUFFALO. / WHEN YOU'RE DEAD AND GONE**	-	-	
Sep 83.	(7"/7"pic-d) (NB/+P 1) **EVERY BREATH OF THE WAY. / LOVERS LULLABY**	70		

(12"+=) (NBT 1) – Put a hat on your head.

Nov 83.	(lp) (NBL 100) **SEVENTH WAVE**			

– Every breath of the way / Apathy / Dance to the music / Lovers lullaby / If you go your way / Son of a rotten gambler / Lonesome eyes / The nickel song / Refrain from music, music, music / Lovin' the boy next door / Lay down Sally / Didn't you ever love somebody / What do I keep.

			not iss.	Amherst
Nov 83.	(7") (NB 2) **DIDN'T YOU EVER LOVE SOMEBODY. / DANCE TO THE MUSIC**	-		
1985.	(7") <300> **WHO'S BEEN SLEEPING IN MY BED. / MAYBE I'M LONELY**	-		
1985.	(lp) **AM I REAL OR WHAT**	-		

– Who's been sleeping in my bed / Maybe I'm lonely / Private parts / Cut the cord / Am I real to you / Crack seeks the edge / Abuse / Every breath of the way / Some buddy love.

	Food For Thought	Relativity
Mar 89. (7") *(YUM 117)* **RUBY TUESDAY ('89 version). / SHOW YOU** (12"+=/cd-s+=) *(12/CD YUM 117)* – Rock'n'roll heart.	□	-
Apr 89. (c/lp) *(T+/GRUB 12)* **COWABONGA – NEVER TURN YOUR BACK ON A WAVE** – Ruby Tuesday / Racing heart / Show you / To be a star / What have they done to the rain / On a lamb from a cow / Another lie / Window pain / Lovin' / Prematurely gay / Chosen few / The boy next door.	□	

	Hypertens	not iss.
Feb 95. (cd) *(HYCD 200130)* **SILENCE IS KING** – Estate sale / Silence is king / I will get over / In my rock'n'roll heart / A hard rain's a-gonna fall / Gone with the wind / Detroit or Buffalo / Fallen angel / Wear it like a flag / Undertow / Some day I'll be an old record.	□	-

	R.C.A.	R.C.A.
Feb 96. (cd) *<(74321 29357-2)>* **OLD BITCH WARRIOR** – Rock in the road / No time to smell flowers / Something warm / Old bitch warrior / These nights / You don't know me / I don't know what love is / Beautiful people / Any time at all / Freedom knows my name / Summer of love / Ballerina / I will survive / Candles in the rain / Ruby Tuesday / Look what they've done to my song, ma.	□	-

– compilations, etc. –

on 'Buddah' unless otherwise mentioned

Oct 71. (7"m) *(2011 093)* **ALEXANDER BEETLE. / CHRISTOPHER ROBIN. / ANIMAL CRACKERS**	□	-
Nov 71. (7") *<268>* **THE NICKEL SONG. / WHAT HAVE THEY DONE TO MY SONG, MA**	-	35
Mar 72. (lp) *(2318)* *<5095>* **GARDEN IN THE CITY** – Garden in the city / Love in my mind / We don't where we're going / Lay lady lay / Jigsaw puzzle / Don't you wait by the water / Stop I don't want to hear it anymore / Somebody loves me / People in the front row. *(re-iss.Aug74; BDLP 4017)*	19	Dec71
Sep 72. (d-lp) *(2659 013)* **THE FOUR SIDES OF MELANIE** – Somebody loves me / Beautiful people / In the hour / I really loved Harold / Johnny boy / Any guy / I'm back in town / What have they done to my song, ma / Lay down / Peace will come (according to plan) / Good book / The nickel song / Babe rainbow / Mr.Tambourine man / Carolina on my mind / Ruby Tuesday / Sign in the window / Lay lady lay / Christopher Robin / Animal crackers / I don't eat animals / Psychotherapy / Leftover wine. *(re-iss.Aug74; BDLP 2002)*	23	Mar72
Oct 72. (7") **JOHNNY BOY. / I'M BACK IN TOWN**	-	
Apr 73. (7") *(2011 166)* **THE NICKEL SONG. / CLOSE TO IT ALL**		
May 73. (lp) *(2318 080)* **THE VERY BEST OF MELANIE** *(re-iss.Aug74; BDLP 4001)*		
Oct 73. (7"flexi) *Lyntone; (2673-4)* **A GIFT FROM HONEY** – I am not a poet / Song of the south / Brand new key (live) / Seeds.		
Dec 73. (lp) *(2318 090)* **PLEASE LOVE ME**		
Apr 75. (lp) *A.B.C.; (ABCL 5124)* **FROM THE BEGINNING**		
1976. (lp) *(BDLP 5705)* **BEST OF MELANIE** *(re-iss.Jul85; 2522 121)*	□	
Feb 77. (lp) *Golden Hour-Pye; (GH 861)* **GOLDEN HOUR OF MELANIE**	□	-
Jun 77. (12"ep) *Buddah-Pye; (BD 104)* **LAY DOWN. / BRAND NEW KEY. / RUBY TUESDAY. / WHAT HAVE THEY DONE TO MY SONG, MA?**	□	-
Oct 82. (d-lp) *P.R.T.; (SPOT 1020)* **SPOTLIGHT ON . . .**	□	-
Jan 83. (7") *Flashback-Pye; (FBS 26)* **BRAND NEW KEY. / RUBY TUESDAY**	□	-
Jun 88. (d-lp/c/cd) *Castle; (CCS LP/C/CD 195)* **THE COLLECTION**	□	-
Jul 88. (lp/c) *Knight; (11007)* **EASY RIDING**	□	-
Dec 88. (lp/c/cd) *BR Music; (BR LP/MC/CD 23)* **VERY BEST OF MELANIE**	□	-
May 89. (cd) *Laserlight; (15120)* **MELANIE**	□	-
Oct 89. (lp/c/cd) *Mainline; (262 554-1/-4/-2)* **20 GREATEST HITS**	□	-
Mar 91. (cd/c) *Music Club; (MC CD/TC 011)* **THE BEST OF MELANIE** – Ruby Tuesday / Brand new key / Animal crackers / Mr.Tambourine man / Baby day / Beautiful people / Save the night / Lay down (candles in the rain) / Close to it all / What have they done to my song ma / Lay lady lay / Some day I'll be a farmer / Good book / Peace will come according to my plan / Gardens in the city / Nickel song / Pebbles in the sand / Tell me why.	□	-
Mar 91. (cd/c) *O.N.O.; (ONN 83 CD/MC)* **CAROLINA ON MY MIND**	□	-
Jul 92. (cd) *Sequel; (NEXCD 205)* **THE BEST OF THE REST OF MELANIE: THE BUDDAH YEARS**	□	-
May 93. (cd) *Royal Collection; (RC 83104)* **LOOK WHAT THEY'VE DONE**	□	-
Aug 93. (cd/c) *Marble Arch; (MAT CD/MC 276)* **THE BEST OF MELANIE**	□	-
Dec 93. (cd) *Gold; (GOLD 203)* **GOLD: GREATEST HITS**	□	-
Feb 94. (d-cd) *Hypertension; (HYCD 200136)* **SILVER ANNIVERSARY**	□	-
Apr 94. (cd) *Disky; (DISK 4505)* **HIT SINGLE COLLECTABLES**	□	-
May 94. (cd/c) *Prima; (PMM 0571 2/4)* **RUBY TUESDAY**	□	-
Nov 96. (d-cd) *Laserlight; (24337)* **HER GREATEST HITS LIVE & NEW (FROM WOODSTOCK TO THE WORLD)**	□	-

John (Cougar) MELLENCAMP

Born: 7 Oct'51, Seymour, Indiana, USA. After graduating from high school, where he played in two bands, CREPE SOUL (!) and SNAKEPIT BANANA BARN, the young MELLENCAMP left home in 1970 and moved to Valonia where he married his pregnant girlfriend, Priscilla. Although he formed glam-rock outfit, TRASH (alongside LARRY CRANE) in the early 70's, it would be another three years before MELLENCAMP made any serious inroads into the music business. By this point, he'd graduated from university, separated from his wife and child and secured a deal with 'M.C.A.' as well as management company 'Mainman' (home to DAVID BOWIE), after sending a demo to the latter's Tony DeFries. Released in 1976, his debut album, 'CHESTNUT STREET INCIDENT', was credited (reportedly unbeknownst

to MELLENCAMP) to JOHN COUGAR, as DeFries had christened him. Not that many people noticed anyway, poor sales of both his debut and the follow-up, 'THE KID INSIDE' (1977) seeing him part company with the label and sign to 'Riva', an imprint run by ROD STEWART's manager, Billy Gaff, and indeed the recording home of the leopard-print trousered legend himself. At this stage, MELLENCAMP's recycled rock'n'roll struggled to even match the negligible quality of STEWART's airbrushed fodder and both the UK-only 'A BIOGRAPHY' (1978) and 'JOHN COUGAR' (1979) failed to come up with anything resembling originality although the latter set nevertheless spawned a minor US hit in 'I NEED A LOVER'. The appallingly titled, STEVE CROPPER-produced 'NOTHIN' MATTERS, & WHAT IF IT DID' (1981) continued in the same empty, rock-posturing vein although for the first time it saw MELLENCAMP in the (US) Top 40. Finally managing to combine hard-bitten authenticity with epic anthem-rock a la TOM PETTY, MELLENCAMP scored a surprise US No.1 with the MTV favourite, 'JACK & DIANE'. The accompanying album, 'AMERICAN FOOL' (1982) also topped the chart and almost spawned a further two No.1's in 'HURTS SO GOOD' and 'HAND TO HOLD ON TO'. Now commanding a bit of commercial leverage, the singer ensured that 'UH-HUH!' (1984) was issued under the JOHN COUGAR MELLENCAMP moniker, his newfound confidence evident on a set which consolidated the earlier success and convincingly announced the arrival of a major league contender. Placing MELLENCAMP's small-town ideology into the context of the American farming crisis, 'SCARECROW' (1985) was a work of seemingly heartfelt conviction with cast-iron rockouts to match; the record spawned five hit singles (including the Top 10 triple whammy of 'LONELY OL' NIGHT', 'SMALL TOWN' and 'R.O.C.K. IN THE U.S.A.'), its impact lent extra weight via MELLENCAMP's role in organising Farm Aid (alongside NEIL YOUNG and WILLIE NELSON). Expanding his troupe of backing musicians to include the likes of LISA GERMANO (here playing violin), the proletarian rocker embraced a more folky approach on 'THE LONESOME JUBILEE' (1987). Painting a bleak picture of contemporary life for the average down-at-heel American, the record included some of MELLENCAMP's most memorable songs, not least the bitter 'PAPER IN FIRE'. The latter track made the Top 10, as did the album itself and for the first time, MELLENCAMP began making an impact in Britain where the record almost went Top 30. Perversely enough, the singer's most introspective album to date, 'BIG DADDY' (1989) – he had recently become a grandad – was his most successful UK release; utilising a distinctively more subdued musical approach, the rootsy, melancholy backing echoed the more intensely personal lyrical fare. The late 80'/early 90's proved a difficult time for the artist as he re-evaluated his musical direction (meantime starring in the film, 'Falling From Grace'), suffered nervous exhaustion and saw his keyboard player, JOHN CASCELLA, meet an untimely death aged only 35. MELLENCAMP himself would come face to face with his own mortality in 1994 when his touring plans were abandoned following a heart attack. Ironically, that year's album, 'DANCE NAKED', was his finest of the decade so far, following on from the return to harder territory of 'WHATEVER WE WANTED' (1991) and 'HUMAN WHEELS' (1993). It also spawned the rather unlikely (US) Top 3 duet with ME'SHELL NDEGECELLO on a cover of Van Morrison's 'WILD NIGHT'. While he's never quite lived up to the 'new SPRINGSTEEN' tag which greeted his 70's arrival, MELLENCAMP has earned his place as a pillar of trad US rock by dint of sheer hard graft, honesty and not a little talent. • **Songwriters:** Penned most himself, with collaborations mainly stemming from CRANE. Covered; KICKS (Paul Revere & The Raiders) / JAILHOUSE ROCK (Elvis Presley) / OH PRETTY WOMAN (Roy Orbison) / DO YOU BELIEVE IN MAGIC (Lovin' Spoonful) / UNDER THE BOARDWALK (Drifters) / etc. • **Trivia:** Due to his height, he produced under the alias of The LITTLE BASTARD. His work in this field has included; MITCH RYDER (Never Kick A Sleeping Dog) / BLASTERS (Hard Line).

Album rating: CHESTNUT STREET INCIDENT (*3) / THE KID INSIDE (*4) / A BIOGRAPHY (*4) / JOHN COUGAR (*5) / NOTHIN' MATTERS AND WHAT IF IT DID (*5) / AMERICAN FOOL (*6) / UH-HUH (*6) / SCARECROW (*7) / THE LONESOME JUBILEE (*7) / BIG DADDY (*8) / WHENEVER WE WANTED (*7) / HUMAN WHEELS (*6) / DANCE NAKED (*6) / MR. HAPPY GO LUCKY (*5) / JOHN MELLENCAMP (*5) / THE BEST THAT I COULD DO compilation (*7) / ROUGH HARVEST compilation (*6)

JOHNNY COUGAR

- vocals, guitar

	not iss.	M.C.A.
1976. (lp) **CHESTNUT STREET INCIDENT** – American dream / Oh pretty woman / Jailhouse rock / Dream killin' town / Supergirl / Chestnut street revisited / Good girls / Do you believe in magic / Twentieth century fox / Sad lady. *(UK-rel.Oct84 on 'MainMan'; MML 602) (re-iss. Apr86 on 'Castle' lp/c/cd; CLA LP/MC/CD 113) (cd re-iss. Feb98 on 'Snapper'; SMMCD 513)*	-	

—— his band **TIGER FORCE** were **LARRY CRANE** – guitars / **TOM WINCE** – keyboards / **DAVID PARMAN** – bass, guitar, violin, percussion / **TERENCE SALSA** – drums, percussion / **WAYNE HALL** – saxophone, flute, percussion

1977. (lp) **THE KID INSIDE** – Kid inside / Take what you want / Cheap shot / Side-walks and street lights / R.Gang / American son / Gearhead / Young genocides / Too young to live / Survive. *(UK-iss.May86 on 'Castle'; CLALP 112) (cd-iss. Nov86; CLACD 112) (cd re-iss. Feb98 on 'Snapper'; SMMCD 510)*	-	-

	not iss.	Gulcher
1977. (7"ep) **U.S. MALE** – 2000 a.d. / Lou-ser / Hot man / Kicks.	-	□

			Riva	Riva
Mar 78.	(7") *(RIVA 14)* **I NEED A LOVER. / BORN RECKLESS**		☐	–

(re-iss. Nov79 as JOHN COUGAR; same)

Mar 78. (lp/c) *(RV LP/4 6)* **A BIOGRAPHY** ☐ –
– Born reckless / Factory / Night slumming / Taxi dancer / I need a lover / Alley of the angels / High "C" Cherie / Where the side walk ends / Let them run your lives / Goodnight.

Jun 78. (7") *(RIVA 16)* **FACTORY. / ALLEY OF THE ANGELS** ☐ –

JOHN COUGAR

		Riva	Riva
Jun 79.	(7",7"pic-d) *(RIVA 20)* **MIAMI. / DO YOU THINK THAT'S FAIR**	☐	–

Jul 79. (lp/c) *(RV LP/4 9)* <7401> **JOHN COUGAR** ☐ 64
– A little night dancin' / Small Paradise / Great mid-west / Miami / Take home pay / Sugar Marie / Welcome to Chinatown / Pray for me / Do you think that's fair / Taxi dancer. *(re-iss. Jun88 on 'Mercury'; PRICE 119) (cd-iss. Jan86; 814 995-2)*

Sep 79. (7") <202> **I NEED A LOVER. / WELCOME TO CHINATOWN** – 28
Oct 79. (7") *(RIVA 21)* **TAXI DANCER. / SMALL PARADISE** – –
Feb 80. (7") <203> **SMALL PARADISE. / SUGAR MARIE** – 87
Apr 80. (7") <204> **PRAY FOR ME. / A LITTLE NIGHT DANCIN'** – –
Sep 80. (7") *(RIVA 25)* <RIVA 205> **THIS TIME. / DON'T UNDERSTAND ME** 27
Jan 81. (7") <207> **AIN'T EVEN DONE WITH THE NIGHT. / MAKE ME FEEL** – 17
Feb 81. (lp/c) *(RV LP/4 10)* <7403> **NOTHIN' MATTERS AND WHAT IF IT DID** 37 Sep80
– Hot night in a cold town / Ain't even done with the night / Don't understand me / This time / Make me feel / T.o M.G. (wherever she may be) / Tonight / Wild angel / Cheap shot. *(cd-iss. Jan86; 814 994-2.)*

Feb 81. (7") *(RIVA 30)* **HOT NIGHT IN A COLD TOWN. / TONIGHT** – –
May 81. (7") *(RIVA 31)* **AIN'T EVEN DONE WITH THE NIGHT. / TO M.G. WHEREVER SHE MAY BE** – –

—— his live band consisted of **LARRY CRANE** – guitar, vocals / **MIKE WANCHIC** – guitar, vocals / **TOBY MYERS** – bass, vocals / **KENNY ARONOFF** – drums, vocals

May 82. (7") *(RIVA 36)* **HURTS SO GOOD. / CLOSE ENOUGH** ☐ 2 Apr 82
Jul 82. (7") <210> **JACK & DIANE. / CAN YOU TAKE IT** – 1
Nov 82. (lp/c) *(RV LP/4 16)* <7501> **AMERICAN FOOL** 37 1 May82
– Hurts so good / Jack & Diane / Hand to hold on to / Danger list / Can you take it / Thundering hearts / China girl / Close enough / Weakest moments. *(re-iss. Sep85 on 'Mercury' lp/c; PRICE/PRIMC 85) (cd-iss. Jan85; RVCD 7501) (re-iss. cd 1988; 814 993-2)*

Sep 82. (7") *(RIVA 37)* **JACK & DIANE. / DANGER LIST** 25 –
(12"+=) *(RIVA 37T)* – Need a lover.
Nov 82. (7") <211> **HAND TO HOLD ON TO. / SMALL PARADISE** – 3
Jan 83. (7",7"pic-d/12") *(RIVA 38/+T)* **HAND TO HOLD ON TO. / HURTS SO GOOD** ☐ –

JOHN COUGAR MELLENCAMP

Nov 83. (7"/12") *(JCM 1/+12)* <214> **CRUMBLIN' DOWN. / GOLDEN GATES** ☐ 9 Oct 83
Dec 83. (7") <215> **PINK HOUSES. / SERIOUS BUSINESS** – 8
Feb 84. (lp/c) *(RIVL/+C 1)* <7504> **UH-HUH** 92 9 Oct83
– Crumblin' down / Pink houses / Authority song / Warmer place to sleep / Jackie O / Play guitar / Serious business / Lovin' mother fo ya / Golden Gates. *(cd-iss. Oct84; 814 485-2)*

Feb 84. (7") *(JCM 2)* **AUTHORITY SONG. / HURTS SO GOOD** ☐ –
(12"+=) *(JCM 212)* – Thundering hearts.
Mar 84. (7") <216> **AUTHORITY SONG. / PINK HOUSES (acoustic)** – 15
Jun 84. (7") *(JCM 3)* **PINK HOUSES. / WARMER PLACE TO SLEEP** ☐ –

—— added **JOHN CASCELLA** – keyboards plus others on session

Oct 85. (7") *(JCM 4)* <880 984-7> **LONELY OL' NIGHT. / JACK & DIANE** ☐ 6 Aug 85
(12"+=) *(JCMX 4)* – Rumbleseat.
Nov 85. (lp/c)(cd) *(RIVH/+C 2)* <(824865-2)> **SCARECROW** ☐ 2 Sep85
– Rain on the scarecrow / Grandma's theme / Small town / Minutes to memories / Lonely ol' night / The face of the nation / Justice and independence / Between a laugh and a tear / Rumbleseat / Close enough / R.O.C.K. in the U.S.A. *(c+=)(cd+=)* – The kind of fella I am.

Jan 86. (7"/12") *(JCM/+X 5)* <884 202-7> **SMALL TOWN. / SMALL TOWN (acoustic)** 53 6 Oct 85
(d7"+=) *(JCMDP 5)* – Hurts so good / The kind of fella I am.
(d12"+=) *(JCMXD 5)* – Pink houses / Small town (acoustic).
Apr 86. (7") *(JCM 6)* <884 455-7> **R.O.C.K. IN THE U.S.A. / UNDER THE BOARDWALK** 67 2 Jan 86
Apr 86. (7") <884 635-7> **RAIN ON THE SCARECROW. / PRETTY BALLERINA** – 21
Jun 86. (7") <884 856-7> **RUMBLESEAT. / COLD SWEAT** – 28
Nov 86. (7") *(JCM 7)* (as "CONSPIRACY OF HOPE"): **PINK HOUSES. / (Howard Jones: No One Is To Blame)** ☐ –
(12"+=) *(JCMX 7)* – Pink houses (acoustic).

—— added **LISA GERMANO** – violin / **PAT PETERSON** – backing vocals, percussion

		Mercury	Mercury
Sep 87.	(7") *(JCM 8)* <888 763-7> **PAPER IN FIRE. / NEVER TOO OLD**	☐	9 Aug 87

(12"+=) *(JCMX 8)* – Cold sweat.
Sep 87. (lp/c)(cd) *(MERH/+C 109)* <(832465-2)> **THE LONESOME JUBILEE** 31 6
– Paper in fire / Down and out in paradise / Check it out / Real life / Cherry bomb / We are the people / Empty hands / Hard times for an honest man / Hot dogs and hamburgers / Rooty toot toot.

Nov 87. (7") *(JCM 9)* <888 934-7> **CHERRY BOMB. / SHAMA LAMA DING DONG** ☐ 8 Oct87
(12"+=) *(JCMX 9)* – Under the boardwalk.
(cd-s+++=) *(JCMCD 9)* – Pretty ballerina (live).

Feb 88. (7") *(JCM 10)* <870 126-7> **CHECK IT OUT. / WE ARE THE PEOPLE** ☐ 14
(12"+=) *(JCMX 10)* – Shama lama ding dong / Pretty ballerina.
(cd-s+=) *(JCMCD 10)* – Pink houses (acoustic) / Check it out (live).
Jul 88. (7") *(JCM 11)* <870 327-7> **ROOTY TOOT TOOT. / CHECK IT OUT (live)** ☐ 61 May 88
(12"+=) *(JCMX 11)* – Pretty ballerina / Like home (acoustic).
(cd-s+=) *(JCMCD 11)* – Never too old / Cold sweat.
Apr 89. (7") *(EKR 90)* **RAVE ON. / (Beach Boys: Kokomo)** ☐ ☐
(12") *(EKRT 90)* – ('A'side) / (Fabulous Thunderbirds: Powerful Stuff) / (Starship: Wild Again).
(above single from the film 'Cocktail' on 'Elektra' label)

—— added **CRYSTAL TALIEFERO** – backing vocals, percussion

May 89. (lp/c/cd) <(838220-1/-4/-2)> **BIG DADDY** 25 7
– Big daddy of them all / To live / Martha say / Theo and weird Henry / Jackie Brown / Pop singer / Void in my heart / Mansions in Heaven / Sometimes a great notion / Country gentlemen / J.M.'s question. *(cd+=)* – Let it all hang out.

Jun 89. (7") *(JCM 12)* <874 012-7> **POP SINGER. / J.M.'S QUESTION** ☐ 15 Apr 89
(12"+=) *(JCM 1212)* – Like a rolling stone (live).
(cd-s++=) *(JCMCD 12)* – Check it out (live).
Jul 89. (7") <874 644-7> **JACKIE BROWN. / JACKIE BROWN (acoustic)** – 48

JOHN MELLENCAMP

Sep 91. (7") *(MER 354)* <867890-7> **GET A LEG UP. / WHENEVER WE WANTED** ☐ 14
(c-s+=/12"+=/cd-s+=) *(MER MC/X/CD 354)* – Seventh son.
Oct 91. (cd/c/lp) <(510151-2/-4/-1)> **WHENEVER WE WANTED** 39 17
– Love and happiness / Now more than ever / I ain't ever satisfied / Get a leg up / Crazy ones / Last chance / They're so tough / Melting pot / Whenever we wanted / Again tonight. *(re-iss. cd Apr95)*

Jan 92. (7"/c-s) *(MER/+MC 362)* **LOVE AND HAPPINESS. / ('A'-L.A. rock dance mix)** ☐ –
(12") *(MERX 362)* – ('B'mix) / ('A'-Jezzard mix) / ('A'-dub).
(cd-s+=) *(MERCD 362)* – (all mixes + 'A'side above).
Feb 92. (c-s) <866414-7> **AGAIN TONIGHT / GET A LEG UP (live)** – 36
Apr 92. (7") *(MER 368)* **NOW MORE THAN EVER. / JACK AND DIANE (live)** ☐ –
(cd-s+=) *(MERCD 368)* – Check it out (live) / Martha say (live).
(c-s) *(MERMC 368)* – ('A'side) / Lonely ol' night.
(cd-s) *(MERCB 368)* – (above 2) / Small town / Pink houses.

—— Mid-'92, MELLENCAMP suffered nervous exhaustion and cancelled gigs when his bassist MYERS severed a big toe in a boating accident. 14th Nov '92 also saw his keyboard player JOHN CASCELLA die. He was only 35, but still played on half of next album. He was replaced by **MALCOLM BURN** – organ, guitar, harmonica, synth.

—— **DAVID GRISSOM** – guitars, mandolin, bass repl. CRANE

Sep 93. (cd/c) <(518088-2/-4)> **HUMAN WHEELS** 37 7
– When Jesus left Birmingham / Junior / Human wheels / Beige to beige / Case 795 (the family) / Suzanne and the jewels / Sweet evening breeze / What if I came knocking / French shoes / To the river. *(cd re-iss. Sep97; same)*

Oct 93. (c-s) <862702-7> **HUMAN WHEELS / ('A'edit)** – 48

—— now w / **WANCHIC, MYERS, ARONOFF, ME'SHELL NDEGECELLO** (bass, vocals), **GERMANO, PETERSON + ANDY YORK** – guitar

Jun 94. (cd/c) <(522428-2/-4)> **DANCE NAKED** ☐ 13
– Dance naked / Brothers / When Margaret comes to town / Wild night / L.U.V. / Another sunny day 12 / 25 / Too much to think about / The big jack / The breakout. *(cd re-iss. Sep97; same)*

Jun 94. (c-s) <858738> **WILD NIGHT / BROTHERS (live)** – 3
Aug 94. (7"yellow/c-s) *(MER/+MC 409)* **WILD NIGHT. / HURTS SO GOOD** 34 –
(cd-s) *(MERCD 409)* – ('A'side) / Jack and Diane / Pink houses / R.O.C.K. in the U.S.A. (a salute to the 60's).
(cd-s) *(MERCX)* – ('A'side) / Dance naked (live) / When Jesus left Birmingham / Small town (acoustic).
Nov 94. (c-s) <856346> **DANCE NAKED / R.O.C.K. IN THE U.S.A.** – 41
<with free live c-s> – Human wheels / Pink houses.
Aug 96. (c-s) <578398> **KEY WEST INTERMEZZO (I SAW YOU FIRST) / LIKE A ROLLING STONE** ☐ 14
Sep 96. (cd-ep) *(MERCD 474)* **KEY WEST INTERMEZZO (I SAW YOU FIRST) / WILD NIGHT (live) / WHAT IF I CAME KNOCKING (live) / SMALL TOWN (live acoustic)** ☐ –
(cd-ep) *(MERCX 474)* – ('A'side) / Cold sweat (live) / Check it out (live) / Like a rolling stone (live).
Oct 96. (cd/c) <(532896-2/-4)> **MR. HAPPY GO LUCKY** ☐ 9 Sep96
– Overture / Jerry / Key west intermezzo (I saw you first) / Just another day / This may not be the end of the world / Emotional love / Mr. Bellows / The full catastrophe / Circling around the Moon / Large world turning / Jackamo road / Life is hard.

Feb 97. (cd-s) **JUST ANOTHER DAY /** – 46
Nov 97. (c-s,cd-s) **THE BEST THAT I CAN DO /** – 33

	Columbia	Columbia
Feb 99. (cd/c) *(491652-2/-4)* <69602> **JOHN MELLENCAMP**	41	Oct98

– Fruit trader / Your life is now / Positively crazy / I'm not running anymore / Where the world began / It all comes true / Eden is burning / Chance meeting at the Tarantula / Miss Missy / Break me off some / Summer of love / Days of farewell.

– compilations, etc. –

Mar 86. (lp/c/cd; JOHN COUGAR) Castle; *(CCS LP/MC/CD 124)* **THE COLLECTION** (early) ☐ –
Jan 98. (cd/c) Mercury; *(536738-2/-4)* **THE BEST THAT I COULD DO (1978-1988)** 25 33
– Jack and Diane / R.O.C.K. in the U.S.A. / Hurts so good / I need a lover / Ain't even done with the night / Crumblin' down / Pink houses / Authority song / Lonely ol' night / Small town / Paper in fire / Cherry bomb / Check it out / Without expression.

Aug 99. (cd) *Mercury*; <(558355-2)> **ROUGH HARVEST** ☐ 99
– Love and happiness / In my time of dying / Between a laugh and a tear / Human wheels / Rain on the scarecrow / Farewell Angelina / Key West intermezzo (I saw you first) / Jackie Brown / When Jesus left Birmingham / Full catastrophe of life / Minutes to memories / Under the boardwalk / Wild night.

MELVINS (dig out; Great Alt & Indie . . .)

MEMBERS (dig out; Great Alt & Indie . . .)

ME ME ME (see under ⇒ ELASTICA)

MENSWE@R (dig out; 4th edition or Great Alt & Indie . . .)

MEN THEY COULDN'T HANG

(dig out; 4th edition or Great Alt & Indie . . .)

Natalie MERCHANT

Born: 26 Oct'63, Jamestown, New York, USA. Focal point with the 10,000 MANIACS since 1981, she embarked on a solo career in 1993. Spending over a year in the studio, she returned in fine style with her debut album, 'TIGERLILY' (1995), an emotive and eclectic collection of songs that stayed high in the American charts for some time. Three singles were lifted from it, 'CARNIVAL', 'WONDER' and 'JEALOUSY', all stirring up enough support for Top 30 placings; the latter's B-side featured a cover of The Rolling Stones' 'SYMPATHY FOR THE DEVIL'. • **Other covers:** SPACE ODITTY (David Bowie) / AFTER THE GOLD RUSH (Neil Young) / THE GULF OF ARABY (Katell Keineg).

Album rating: TIGERLILY (*6) / OPHELIA (*6) / LIVE IN CONCERT (*6)

NATALIE MERCHANT – vocals / with **JENNIFER TURNER** – guitars, vocals / **BARRY MAGUIRE** – bass, guitar / **PETER YANOWITZ** – drums, percussion

		Elektra	Elektra
Jun 95. (cd/c) <(7559 61745-2/-4)> **TIGERLILY**		39	13

– San Andreas fault / Wonder / Beloved wife / River / Carnival / I may know the word / The letter / Cowboy romance / Jealousy / Where I go / Seven years.

Jul 95. (c-s) *(EKR 203C)* <64413> **CARNIVAL / I MAY KNOW THE WORD** ☐ 10
(cd-s+=) *(EKR 203CD)* – ('A'edit).

Nov 95. (c-s) <64376> **WONDER / BABY I LOVE YOU** - 20

Apr 96. (c-s/cd-s) *(EKR 217 C/CD1)* **WONDER / TAKE A LOOK (live) / THE WORK SONG (live)** ☐ -
(cd-s) *(EKR 217CD2)* – ('A'side) / Sympathy for the Devil (live) / All I want (live medley).

May 96. (c-s) <64301> **JEALOUSY / SYMPATHY FOR THE DEVIL (live)** - 23

Jun 98. (cd/c) <(7559 62196-2/-4)> **OPHELIA** 52 8 May98
– Ophelia / Life is sweet / Kind & generous / Frozen Charlotte / My skin / Break your heart / King of May / Thick as thieves / Effigy / The living / When they ring the golden bells / Ophelia (reprise).

Nov 98. (cd-s) *(E 3831CD)* **KIND & GENEROUS / FROZEN CHARLOTTE / WONDER** ☐ ☐

May 99. (cd-s) *(E 3786CD)* **BREAK YOUR HEART / BREAK YOUR HEART / CARNIVAL** ☐ -

Nov 99. (cd/c) <(7559 62479-2/-4) <62444> **LIVE IN CONCERT (New York City – June 13, 1999)** ☐ 82
– Wonder / San Andreas fault / Beloved wife / Space oddity / Carnival / Dust bowl / After the gold rush / Gun shy / The gulf of Araby / Ophelia / Seven years.

Freddie MERCURY (see under ⇒ QUEEN)

MERCURY REV

Formed: Buffalo, New York, USA . . . 1988 by JONATHAN DONAHUE, DAVID BAKER, GRASSHOPPER (aka SEAN MACKIOWIAK), DAVE FRIDMANN, JIMY CHAMBERS and SUZANNE THORPE, who claimed they had all met while attending a psychiatric hospital. Admittedly, their sound, which came about by playing their own soundtrack to nature TV programmes! ('VERY SLEEPY RIVERS' indeed) was certainly deliciously deranged enough for this explanation of their secret history. Just over two years of rehearsals passed (DONAHUE, co-producer FRIDMANN and GRASSHOPPER were part-time members of FLAMING LIPS and utilised some spare studio time), before they finally surfaced with the mini-lp, 'YERSELF IS STEAM' (1991). Perhaps the most immaculate marriage of searing noise and crystalline pop ever committed to vinyl, this freaky guitar-angst rock classic mixed up psychedelia, noise, film dialogue and exhilarating experimentation in a way only previously matched by The FLAMING LIPS; other indie influences were also apparent (i.e. BIRTHDAY PARTY, STUMP, VERY THINGS and MY BLOODY VALENTINE). The inspired opening salvo of 'CHASING A BEE', 'SYRINGE MOUTH' and 'CONEY ISLAND CYCLONE', alone was enough to give the album a resounding thumbs-up by the British press and record buying public alike. Later that year, the 'CAR WASH HAIR' EP/track (recorded with DEAN WAREHAM of GALAXIE 500), further convinced commentators of MERCURY REV's volatile genius although squabbling and widely publicised, wildly unpredictable live shows led to break-up rumours. These were subsequently quashed when the band

were snapped up by 'Beggars Banquet', a follow-up album, 'BOCES' (1993), carrying on in the established schizophrenic mould but too often straying into wanton self-indulgence at the expense of conventional tunes. However, it did satisfy some punters by becoming their first record to hit the UK Top 50. The following year, the band's infamous in-fighting reach a head as the proverbial time-honoured musical differences led to the wayward BAKER pursuing a noisier career of his own as SHADY. Although a solitary MERCURY REV single, 'EVERLASTING ARM', appeared in summer '94 (featuring ALAN VEGA of SUICIDE), it would be another long year before the release of 'SEE YOU ON THE OTHER SIDE' (1995), although by this time the first chapter of MERCURY REV's maverick career had already drawn to a close. While critics marvelled over the album's more accessible but wonderfully eclectic pop-jazz experiments, DONAHUE and GRASSHOPPER were in the process of completing a debut album, 'PARALYZED MIND OF THE ARCHANGEL VOID' (1995) for their revamped side-project, HARMONY ROCKETS. A few years later, the pair resurrected the MERCURY REV moniker with a complete new cast (namely ADAM SNYDER, JUSTIN RUSSO, JASON RUSSO and JEFF MERCEL), although the subsequent return of THORPE, FRIDMANN and CHAMBERS (SNYDER was retained) resulted in a more fully-fledged reformation. V.I.P. HARMONY ROCKETS guests, LEVON HELM and GARTH HUDSON of The BAND, were also brought on board for the album no one thought was possible, 'DESERTER'S SONGS' (1998). Issued on Richard Branson's new imprint, 'V2' ('Epic' in the States), the record was widely hailed as THE album of the year as MERCURY REV enjoyed one of the critical rebirths of the decade. Older and wiser, the band (or THE BAND, take your pick!) had possibly stumbled upon what GRAM PARSONS really meant when he dreamt of his "cosmic American music", a wistful (in a far-out sort of way) melange of quixotic pop, spacey orchestration and lullaby romanticism quite possibly unlike anything you've ever heard. If long-time fans were hoping to hear the anarchic spark of old they were in for a drastic shock, tracks such as 'TONITE IT SHOWS', 'OPUS 40', 'DELTA SUN BOTTLENECK BLUES' and 'ENDLESSLY', meandering to a more mature muse, the latter even incorporating their own heavy-lidded interpretation of traditional carol, 'Silent Night'. A couple of months previous to the album's release, GRASSHOPPER & His GOLDEN CRICKETS (including flautist, SUZANNE THORPE) had taken their own, off-beat journey into the psychedelic musical galaxy with the album, 'THE ORBIT OF ETERNAL GRACE'. • **Covered:** IF YOU WANT ME TO STAY (Sly Stone) / SHHH – PEACEFUL (Miles Davis) / DEADMAN (Alan Vega) / RAINDROPS KEEP FALLING ON MY HEAD (Bacharach & David) / HE WAS A FRIEND OF MINE (Bob Dylan) / SILVER STREET (Nikki Sudden) / MOTION PICTURES (Neil Young) / The HARMONY ROCKETS covered I'VE GOT A GOLDEN TICKET (from 'Charlie & The Chocolate Factory') / L'APOCALYPSE DES ANIMAUX (Vangelis) / etc..

Album rating: YERSELF IS STEAM (*8) / BOCES (*6) / SEE YOU ON THE OTHER SIDE (*8) / DESERTER'S SONGS (*9) / Harmony Rockets: PARALYZED MIND OF THE ARCHANGEL VOID (*6) / Grasshopper & The Golden Crickets: THE ORBIT OF ETERNAL GRACE (*7)

DAVID BAKER – vocals / **JONATHAN DONAHUE** – vocals, guitar (ex-FLAMING LIPS) / **SEAN 'Grasshopper' MACKIOWIAK** – guitar / **DAVID FRIDMANN** – bass / **JIMY CHAMBERS** – drums / **SUZANNE THORPE** – woodwind

		Mint Films	Mint Films
Feb 91. (cd/c/blue-lp) <*(MINT CD/C/LP 4)>* **YERSELF IS STEAM**			

– (Rocket): Chasing a bee / Syringe mouth / Coney Island cyclone / Blue and black / Sweet oddysee of a cancer cell t' th' center of yer heart / (Harmony): Frittering / Continuous trucks and thunder under a mother's smile / Very sleepy rivers. (re-iss. Nov92 on 'Beggars Banquet' as d-cd+=/d-c+=/d-lp+=; BBQ CD/MC/LP 125) **LEGO MY EGO** – If you want me to stay / Shhh – Peaceful – Very sleepy rivers / Frittering / Coney Island cyclone / Car wash hair / Syringe mouth / Blood on the moon / Chasing a girl (mmm . . . it's out there / I better let my pants back on / My mom is coming over. <US cd re-iss. Nov92 on 'Columbia'; 53030> (re-iss. Feb99; same)

		Rough Trade	not iss.
Nov 91. (12"ep/cd-ep) <*(MINT 5 T/CD)>* **CAR WASH HAIR (The Bee's Chasing me) full pull / CHASING A BEE (demo) / CONEY ISLAND CYCLONE (demo)**			

		Beggars Banquet	Columbia
Apr 92. (7") *(45REV 6)* **IF YOU WANT ME TO STAY. / THE LEFT-HANDED RAYGUN OF PAUL SHARITS (RETIREMENT JUST LIKE THAT)**			-
Nov 92. (12"/cd-s) *(BBQ 1/+CD)* <74717> **CHASING A BEE. / CONEY ISLAND CYCLONE**		☐	☐
Mar 93. (10"/cd-s) *(BBQ 5 T/CD)* <74907> **THE HUM IS COMING FROM HER. / SO THERE (with ROBERT CREELY)**		☐	☐ Apr93
May 93. (7") *(BBQ 14)* **SOMETHING FOR JOEY. / THREE SPIDER'S EGGS (live)**		☐	-

(12"+=) *(BBQ 14/+T)* – Suzanne peels out.
(cd-s++=) *(BBQ 14CD)* – Noise. (re-iss. Jul93)

Jun 93. (cd/c/lp) *(BBQ CD/MC/LP 140)* <53217> **BOCES**		43	☐

– Meth of a rockette's kick / Trickle down / Bronx cheer / Boys peel out / Downs are feminine balloons / Something for Joey / Snorry mouth / Hi-speed boats / Continuous drunks and blunders / Girlfren.

Jul 93. (cd-ep) <*CSK 5532>* **SOMETHING FOR JOEY / SO THERE / BOYS PEEL OUT / VERY SLEEPY RIVERS / (Ron Jeremy interview)** - ☐

Feb 94. (cd-ep) <*77112>* **BRONX CHEER / THERE'S SPIDER EGGS IN BUBBLA YHUM / SUZANNE PEELS OUT**		-	☐

— now without BAKER who re-surfaced as SHADY, releasing towards the end of '94, a solo album, 'WORLD' (for 'Beggars Banquet' UK, 'Atlantic' US), which included members of SWERVEDRIVER, ROLLERSKATE SKINNY, Th' FAITH

HEALERS, SHARKBOY and BOO RADLEYS. A single, 'NARCOTIC CANDY' was taken from it with a subsequent single, 'PEARLS', coming out a year later.

Jun 94. (12"white/cd-s) *(BBQ 37 T/CD)* **EVERLASTING ARM. / DEADMAN** ☐ ☐ –

May 95. (cd/c/lp)(pic-lp) *(BBQ CD/MC/LP 176)(BBQ 176P) <64362>* ☐ ☐ Sep95 **SEE YOU ON THE OTHER SIDE**
– Empire state (Sun House in excelsis) / Young man's stride / Sudden ray of hope / Everlasting arm / Racing the tide / Close encounters of the 3rd grade / A kiss from an old flame (a trip to the Moon) / Peaceful night.

— split late '94, as DONAHUE and GRASSHOPPER were already moonlighting as the HARMONY ROCKETS. The former and MERCURY REV collaborated on The CHEMICAL BROTHERS 'Dig Your Own Hole' track, 'Private Psychedelic Reel'.

HARMONY ROCKETS

— **DONAHUE + GRASSHOPPER** plus **LEVON HELMS + GARTH HUDSON** (The BAND) (they also guested on MERCURY REV's comeback album) / **ZOOT ROLLO HORN** (ex-CAPTAIN BEEFHEART)

		Rockville	Rockville
		Big Cat	Big Cat

Jun 93. (7") *(ROCK 6113-7)* **SKELETON MAN. /** ☐ ☐

Oct 95. (lp/cd) *<(ABB 90/+CD)>* **PARALYZED MIND OF THE ARCHANGEL VOID** ☐ ☐ Sep98
– Paralyzed mind of the archangel void.

		Big Cat	No.6

Oct 97. (cd-s) *(ABB 151SCD) <45>* **GOLDEN TICKET EP** ☐ ☐ Nov98
– I've got a golden ticket / L'apocalypse des animaux / Tale scendeva l'etternale adore / I've got a golden ticket.

MERCURY REV

— **JONATHAN + GRASSHOPPER** reformed the band in the summer of '97 with **ADAM SNYDER** – keyboards / **JUSTIN RUSSO** – keyboards / **JASON RUSSO** – bass / **JEFF MERCEL** – drums

— by 1998, **SNYDER** was the only person that **JONATHAN + GRASSHOPPER** retained, bringing back **DAVE FRIDMANN, SUZANNE THORPE + JIMY CHAMBERS**

		V2	Epic

Oct 98. (cd/lp) *(VVR 100277-2/1-1) <27027>* **DESERTER'S SONGS** 27 Sep98
– Holes / Tonite it shows / Endlessly / I collect coins / Opus 40 / Hudson line / The happy end (the drunk room) / Goddess on a hiway / The funny bird / Pick up if you're there / Delta sun bottleneck stomp. *(also on special cd; VVR 100379-2)*

Nov 98. (7") *(VVR 500332-7)* **GODDESS ON A HIWAY. / RAGTAG** 51 ☐
(cd-s+=) *(VVR 5000332-3)* – I only have eyes for you.

Jan 99. (12") *(VVR 500541-6)* **DELTA SUN BOTTLENECK STOMP. /** 26
('A'-Chemical Brothers mix) / ENDLESSLY (instrumental)
(cd-s) *(VVR 500541-3)* – (first two tracks) / Vampire blues (live).
(cd-s) *(VVR 500616-3)* – ('A'side) / Holes (live) / Isolation (live).

May 99. (7") *(VVR 500696-7)* **OPUS 40. / MOTION PICTURES (live)** 31 ☐
(cd-s) *(VVR 500697-3)* – ('A'side) / He was a friend of mine (live) / Raindrops keep falling on my head (live).
(cd-s) *(VVR 500696-3)* – ('A'side) / He was a friend of mine (live) / Tonite is shows (live).

Aug 99. (7") *(VVR 500849-7)* **GODDESS ON A HIWAY. / CAROLINE SAYS** 26 ☐
(cd-s) *(VVR 500849-3)* – ('A'side) / I don't wanna be a soldier / Car wash hair (live).
(cd-s) *(VVR 500849-8)* – ('A'side) / I dreamt / Very sleepy rivers (live).

GRASSHOPPER AND THE GOLDEN CRICKETS

with **SUZANNE THORPE** – flute, co-producer (of MERCURY REV) + others

		Beggars Banquet	Beggars Banquet

Jul 98. (7") *(BBQ 325)* **SILVER BALLOONS. / SOLAR POWERED HORNET BEYOND THE SHADOWS OF OVERLOOK MOUNTAIN** ☐ ☐ –
(cd-s+=) *(BBQ 325CD)* – ('A'mix).

Aug 98. (cd/lp) *(BBQ CD/LP 201) <80201>* **THE ORBIT OF ETERNAL GRACE**
– Silver balloons / The ballad of the one-eyed angelfish / O-ring (baby talk) / Nickel in a lemon / The orbit of eternal grace / September's fool / Univac bug track / Smpte for the Devil / N.Y. avenue playground / Sketches of Saturn (love in space) / Midnight express / N.Y. avenue playground (reprise).

METALHEADZ (see under ⇒ GOLDIE)

METALLICA

Formed: Norvale, California, USA … 1981 by LARS ULRICH (this Danish-born drummer had previously filled the stool on a UK tour by DIAMOND HEAD, whose songs METALLICA would later cover) and JAMES HETFIELD (guitar vocals; ex-OBSESSION). Recruiting LLOYD GRAND on guitar, the band recorded their first demo, 'NO LIFE TILL LEATHER' and a one-off 7" single, 'LET IT LOOSE'. In early '82, LLOYD was replaced by future MEGADETH mainman DAVE MUSTAINE, while RON McGOVNEY was brought in on bass. After a brief period of relative stability, MUSTAINE was fired for drunkenness early the following year, being replaced by former EXODUS guitarist KIRK HAMMETT. By this point CLIFF BURTON (ex-TRAUMA) had joined on bass following the departure of McGOVNEY. This was the classic early METALLICA line-up that played on the first three albums, redefining the boundaries of metal

and touring constantly until the tragic death of BURTON in 1986. Moving to New Jersey in early '83, the band signed to John Zazula's 'Megaforce' label and unleashed their high octane debut, 'KILL 'EM ALL' (licensed to 'Music For Nations' for UK release). While it certainly wasn't without cliche, both lyrically and musically, there was a vibrancy in the speed and loudness of their sonic attack that drew on hardcore and punk, particularly in 'SEEK AND DESTROY', a track that would come to be a staple of the band's live set. The record also featured, horror of horrors, a track that consisted entirely of a bass solo! But METALLICA weren't trying to resurrect the indulgence of the 70's, their follow-up opus, 'RIDE THE LIGHTNING' (1984), confirming METALLICA's status as one of the most inventive, promising bands in the metal canon. The group had welded a keening sense of melody to their visceral thrash, alternating between grinding, bass heavy, mid-tempo uber-riffing (the title track and 'FOR WHOM THE BELL TOLLS') and all out pummelling ('FIGHT FIRE WITH FIRE' and 'TRAPPED UNDER ICE'). They even came close to ballad territory with the bleakly beautiful 'FADE TO BLACK', arguably one of the best tracks the band have ever penned. Then came 'MASTER OF PUPPETS' (1986), a masterful collection that rightfully saw METALLICA hailed as one of, if not the, foremost metal act in the world, at the heavier end of the spectrum at least. Opening with the relentless fury of 'BATTERY', followed by the epic, breathtaking dynamics of the title track, the album was almost flawless from start to finish, again using the combination of all-out thrashers alternated with bowel-quaking grinders ('THE THING THAT SHOULD NOT BE', 'WELCOME HOME (SANITARIUM)') to maximum effect. The album went Top 30 in the States without the help of a hit single or even radio play, eventually achieving platinum status. The band subsequently toured with metal godfather, OZZY OSBOURNE, playing to rapturous crowds wherever they went. Disaster struck, however, when the band's tour bus crashed on 27th September '86, BURTON losing his life in the accident. METALLICA decided to carry on, replacing BURTON with JASON NEWSTED (ex-FLOTSAM & JETSAM) and fulfilling their touring commitments. The following summer, the band released an EP of covers, '$5.98 EP – GARAGE DAYS REVISITED', a hotch potch of inspired reworkings from the likes of DIAMOND HEAD, BUDGIE and The MISFITS. The record made both the UK and US Top 30, the US edition containing an extra former KILLING JOKE track (see below). Their next album proper, ' …AND JUSTICE FOR ALL' (1988), was marred by overly ambitious structures and complex arrangements as well as a poor production, subduing the trademark gut intensity. Nevertheless, there were moments of brilliance, most notably with 'ONE', a distressing first person narrative of a soldier kept alive on a life support machine. The song almost made the UK Top 10, winning the band a Grammy the following year for Best Metal Performance. With the eponymous transatlantic No.1, 'METALLICA' (1991), the band entered the major league alongside the likes of U2 and R.E.M. as one of the biggest rock bands in the world. The aptly named Bob Rock had given the record a cleaner, 'big rock' sound that complemented the more melodic and accessible material contained within. Not that METALLICA had gone limp on the Beavis & Butt-head element of their fanbase, 'ENTER SANDMAN' was as crunchingly heavy as ever, yet the single possessed a sufficiently strong melodic hook to see it go Top 5 in the UK. With 'NOTHING ELSE MATTERS', METALLICA really had penned a WISHBONE ASH-esque ballad, replete with strings (!) which saw the band notch up another Top 10 UK hit. After undertaking the biggest tour heavy rock has ever seen (obliterating co-headliners GUNS N' ROSES in the process), the band came back with another work of mature rock majesty, 'LOAD' (1996). From morbid metal to LYNYRD SKYNYRD-style rootsy acoustics, METALLICA once more developed and expanded their sonic palate, gaining widespread acclaim. The album went on to sell almost ten million copies, the band headlining the American Lollapolooza tour to promote it, again blowing most of the other acts away. Not exactly the most prolific of bands, METALLICA surpassed themselves by releasing a successor to 'LOAD' the following year, entitled, appropriately enough, 'RE-LOAD'. While other heavy rock acts flounder under the weight of 90's expectations, METALLICA continue to innovate and energise a tired genre, even, God forbid, cutting their hair(!) in line with their new standing as the post-modern kings of metal. In the Spring of '99, HETFIELD, ULRICH and Co were planning an orchestrated performance with composer MICHAEL KAMEN at the helm of the San Francisco Symphony Orchestra, a 'best of' live album, 'S&M' hitting the bemused public later in the year. • **Songwriters:** ULRICH-HETFIELD, bar other covers on record; BLITZKRIEG (Blitzkrieg) / CRASH COURSE IN BRAIN SURGERY + BREADFAN (Budgie) / AM I EVIL? + THE PRINCE + HELPLESS + IT'S ELECTRIC (Diamond Head) / LAST CARESS – GREEN HELL + DIE DIE MY DARLING (Misfits) / KILLING TIME (Sweet Savage) / THE SMALL HOURS (Holocaust) / THE WAIT (Killing Joke) / STONE COLD CRAZY (Queen) / SO WHAT (Anti-Nowhere League) / SABBRA CADABRA (Black Sabbath) / Medley: EVIL – CURSE OF THE PHARAOHS – SATAN'S FALL – A CORPSE WITHOUT SOUL – INTO THE COVEN (Mercyful Fate) / LOVERMAN (Nick Cave) / WHISKEY IN THE JAR (Thin Lizzy) / TURN THE PAGE (Bob Seger & The Silver Bullet Band) / TUESDAY'S GONE (Lynyrd Skynyrd) / OVERKILL + STONE DEAD FOREVER + DAMAGE CASE + TOO LATE, TOO LATE (Motorhead) / FREE SPEECH FOR THE DUMB + THE MORE I SEE (Discharge) / ASTRONOMY (Blue Oster Cult).

Album rating: KILL 'EM ALL (*7) / RIDE THE LIGHTNING (*8) / MASTER OF PUPPETS (*9) / … AND JUSTICE FOR ALL (*7) / METALLICA (*10) / LOAD (*8) / RE-LOAD (*6) / GARAGE INC. (*5) / S&M (*5)

JAMES HETFIELD (b. 3 Aug'63, Los Angeles) – vocals, rhythm guitar (ex-OBSESSION, etc) / **LARS ULRICH** (b.16 Dec'63, Gentoss, Copenhagen, Denmark) – drums / with **LLOYD GRAND** – guitar

		not iss.	Bootleg
Dec 81.	(7") **LET IT LOOSE. / KILLING TIME**	–	–

—— (Jan'82) **DAVE MUSTAINE** (b.13 Sep'63, La Mesa, Calif.) – lead guitar, co-writer / **RON McGOVNEY** – bass repl. GRAND (JEF WARNER also played guitar in 1982)

—— (early '83) **KIRK HAMMETT** (b.18 Nov'62, San Francisco) – lead guitar (ex-EXODUS) repl. MUSTAINE who was fired due to drunkeness. He was soon to form rivals MEGADETH.

—— **CLIFF BURTON** (b.10 Feb'62) – bass (ex-TRAUMA) replaced McGOVNEY

		Music For Nations	Megaforce
Jul 83.	(lp) (MFN 7) <MRI-069> **KILL 'EM ALL**		

– Hit the lights / The four horsemen / Motorbreath / Jump in the fire / (Anesthesia) Pulling teeth / Whiplash / Phantom Lord / No remorse / Seek and destroy / Metal militia. <US re-iss. Mar86; same> (pic-lp.Aug86; MFN 7P) (cd-iss. Apr87; CDMFN 7) <US re-iss. Feb88 on 'Elektra'+=; 60766> – Am I evil? / Blitzkreig. (re-iss. Nov89 on 'Vertigo' lp/c/cd; 838 142-1/-4/-2)

Jan 84.	(12",12"red) (12KUT 105) <MRS 04> **JUMP IN THE FIRE /**		

[us-only] WHIPLASH (special neckbrace mix). / SEEK AND DESTROY (live) / PHANTOM LORD (re-iss. Mar86, 7"sha-pic-d; PKUT 105)

Jul 84.	(lp/c) (MFN/TMFN 27) <769> **RIDE THE LIGHTNING**	87	100

– Fight fire with fire / Ride the lightning / For whom the bell tolls / Fade to black / Trapped under ice / Escape / Creeping death / The call of Ktulu. (re-iss. Sep86 cd/pic-lp; CDMFN 27/CDMFN 27P) <US re-iss. Oct84 on 'Elektra'; 60396> (re-iss. Nov89 on 'Vertigo' lp/c/cd; 838410-1/-4/-2)

		Music For Nations	Elektra
Nov 84.	(12"pic-d/12") (P+/12KUT 112) **CREEPING DEATH. / AM I EVIL. / BLITZKRIEG**		

(re-iss. Jan87 12"gold/12"blue; GV/CV 12KUT 112)

Mar 86.	(lp/pic-d-lp)(c/cd) (MFN 60/+P)(T/CD MFN 60) <9-60439-1> **MASTER OF PUPPETS**	41	29

– Battery / Master of puppets / The thing that should not be / Welcome home (sanitarium) / Disposable heroes / Leper messiah / Orion / Damage, Inc. (re-iss. Dec87 d-lp; MFN 60DM) (re-iss. May89 on 'Vertigo' lp/c/cd; 838 141-1/-4/-2)

—— **JASON NEWSTEAD** (b. 4 Mar'63, Battle Creek, Missouri) – bass (ex-FLOTSAM AND JETSAM) repl. CLIFF who was killed in tour bus crash 27 Sep'86 Sweden.

		Vertigo	Elektra
Aug 87.	(12"ep) (METAL 1-12) <60757> **$5.98 EP – GARAGE DAYS RE-REVISITED**	27	28

– Helpless / Crash course in brain surgery / The small hours / Last caress – Green hell. <US+=> – The Wait. (cd-iss. May90 on 'Metal'; 888 788-1/-4/-2)

Sep 88.	(7") <69357> **EYE OF THE BEHOLDER. / BREADFAN**	–	
Sep 88.	(12"ep/cd-ep) (METAL 2-12/CD2) **HARVESTER OF SORROW. / BREADFAN. / THE PRINCE**	20	
Oct 88.	(d-lp)(c)(cd) (VERH/+C 61)(836 062-2) <60812> **. . .AND JUSTICE FOR ALL**	4	6 Sep88

– Blackened / . . .And justice for all / Eye of the beholder / One / The shortest straw / Harvester of sorrow / The frayed ends of sanity / To live is to die / Dyers eve.

Feb 89.	(7") <69329> **ONE. / THE PRINCE**	–	35

(3"cd-s+=) – Eye of the beholder.

Mar 89.	(7")(10"pic-d) (MET 5)(METPD 5-10) **ONE. / SEEK AND DESTROY (live)**	13	

(12")(cd-s) (MET 5-12)(METCD 5) – ('A'demo) / For whom the bell tolls (live) / Welcome home (sanitarium) (live). (12"g-f+=) (METG 5-12) – Creeping death (live).

Jul 91.	(7"pic-d) (METAL 7) <64857> **ENTER SANDMAN. / STONE COLD CRAZY**	5	16

(12"+=/12"box+=)(cd-s+=) (METAL/BX 7-12)(METCD 7) – Holier than thou.

Aug 91.	(cd/c/d-lp) (510022-2/-4/-1) <61113> **METALLICA**	1	1

– Enter sandman / Sad but true / Holier than thou / The unforgiven / Wherever I may roam / Don't tread on me / Through the never / Nothing else matters / Of wolf and man / The god that failed / My friend of misery / The struggle within.

Nov 91.	(7"/7"pic-d) (METAL/METAP 8) <64814> **THE UNFORGIVEN. / KILLING TIME**	15	35

(12"+=)(cd-s+=) (METAL 8-12)(METCD 8) – ('A'demo) / So what.

Apr 92.	(7"/7"pic-d) (META L/P 10) <64770> **NOTHING ELSE MATTERS. / ENTER SANDMAN (live)**	6	34 Mar92

(12"+=)(cd-s+=) (METAL 10-12)(METCD 10) – Harvester of sorrow (live) / ('A'demo). (live-cd-s+=) (METCL 10) – Stone cold crazy (live) / Sad but true (live).

—— On tour only **JOHN MARSHALL** (of **METAL CHURCH**) repl. injured (burnt) HETFIELD

Oct 92.	(7"/7"pic-d) (METAL/METAP 9) <64741> **WHEREVER I MAY ROAM. / FADE TO BLACK (live)**	25	82 Jul92

(pic-cd-s+=) (METCD 9) – ('A'demo). (cd-s) (METCB 9) – ('A'side) / Last caress – Am I evil? – Battery (live medley). (12"+=) (METAL 9-12) – ('A'demo).

Oct 92.	(c-s) <64696> **SAD BUT TRUE / SO WHAT?**	–	98
Feb 93.	(7") (METAL 11) <64696> **SAD BUT TRUE. / NOTHING ELSE MATTERS**	20	–

(12"+=,12"pic-d+=)(cd-s+=) (METAL 11-12)(METCD 11) – Creeping death (live) / ('A'demo). (pic-cd-s) (METCH 11) – ('A'side) / ('B'live) / ('A'live).

Dec 93.	(d-cd/d/d-c) (518 726-2/-4) <61594> **LIVE SHIT: BINGE & PURGE (live)**	54	26

– Enter sandman / Creeping death / Harvester of sorrow / Welcome home (sanitarium) / Sad but true / Of wolf and man / Guitar doodle / The unforgiven / And justice for all / Solos (bass/guitar) / Through the never / From whom the bell tolls / Fade to black / Master of puppets / Seek & destroy / Whiplash / Nothing else matters / Wherever I may roam / Am I evil? / Last caress / One / Battery. (d-c+=) – The four horsemen / Motorbreath / Stone cold crazy. (also issued 3 videos + book, etc 'METALLICAN')

May 96.	(10"red-ep) (METAL 12) **UNTIL IT SLEEPS. / 2x4 (live) / UNTIL IT SLEPS (Moby remix)**	18	–

(cd-s) (METCD 12) – ('A'-Herman Melville mix) / 2x4 (live) / F.O.B.D. (aka; Until It Sleeps – demo). (cd-s) (METCX 12) – (first & third tracks) / Kill – Ride (medley; Ride the lightning – No remorse – Hit the lights – The four horsemen – Phantom Lord – Fight fire with fire).

May 96.	(c-s) <64276> **UNTIL IT SLEEPS / OVERKILL**	–	10
Jun 96.	(cd/c/d-lp) (532 618-2/-4/-1) <61923> **LOAD**	1	1

– Ain't my bitch / 2 x 4 / The house Jack built / Until it sleeps / King Nothing / Hero of the day / Bleeding me / Cure / Poor twisted me / Wasting my hate / Mama said / Thorn within / Ronnie / The outlaw torn.

Sep 96.	(12"ep) (METAL 13) **HERO OF THE DAY / MOULDY (aka HERO OF THE DAY – early demo version). / HERO OF THE DAY (outta b sides mix) / OVERKILL**	17	–

(cd-ep) (METCD 13) – ('A'side) / Overkill / Damage case / Hero of the day (outta b sides mix). (cd-ep) (METCX 13) – ('A'side) / Stone dead forever / Too late too late / Mouldy (aka 'Hero Of The Day' – early demo version). (cd-ep) (METCY 13) – ('A'side) / Overkill / Damage case / Stone dead forever / Too late too late. (because of length of above, it also hit 47 in UK album charts)

Oct 96.	(c-s) <64248> **HERO OF THE DAY / KILL – RIDE (medley)**	–	60
Nov 96.	(7"pic-d) (METAL 14) **MAMA SAID. / AIN'T MY BITCH (live)**	19	

(cd-s) (METCD 14) – ('A'side) / King Nothing (live) / Whiplash (live) / ('A'edit). (cd-s) (METCX 14) – ('A'side) / So what (live) / Creeping death (live) / ('A'-early demo).

Feb 97.	(cd-s) (METCD 15) **KING NOTHING /**	–	90
Nov 97.	(7") (METAL 15) <64126> **THE MEMORY REMAINS. / FOR WHOM THE BELL TOLLS (Haven't Heard It Yet mix)**	13	28

(cd-s) (METCD 15) – ('A'side) / Fuel for memory / Memory (demo). (cd-s) (METDD 15) – ('A'side) / The outlaw torn (Unencumbered By Manufacturing Restrictions version) / King Nothing (Tepid mix).

—— MARIANNE FAITHFULL supplied backing vocals on above single

Nov 97.	(cd/c/d-lp) (536409-2/-4/-1) <62126> **RELOAD**	4	1

– Fuel / The memory remains / The Devil's dance / Unforgiven II / Better than you / Carpe diem baby / Prince Charming / Bad seed / Where the wild things are / Slither / Low man's lyric / Attitude / Fixxer.

Feb 98.	(cd-ep) (METCD 17) <64114> **THE UNFORGIVEN II / HELPLESS (live) / The four horsemen (live) / Of wolf and man (live)**	15	59 Mar98

(cd-ep) (METDD 17) – ('A'side) / The thing that should not be (live) / The memory remains (live) / King nothing (live). (cd-ep) (METCX 17) – ('A'side) / No remorse (live) / Am I evil? (live) / The unforgiven II (demo).

Jun 98.	(cd-ep) (METCD 16) **FUEL / SAD BUT TRUE (live) / NOTHING ELSE MATTERS (live)**	31	

(cd-ep) (METDD 16) – ('A'side) / Wherever I roam (live) / One (live). (cd-ep) (METED 16) – ('A'side) / Until it sleeps (live) / ('A'live) / ('A'demo).

Nov 98.	(d-cd/d-c/d-lp) (538351-2/-4/-1) <62323> **GARAGE INC. (the covers)**	29	2

– Free speech for the dumb / It's electric / Sabba cadabra / Turn the page / Die die my darling / Loverman / Mercyful Fate medley:- Evil – Curse of the pharaohs – Satan's fall – A corpse without soul – Into the coven / Astronomy / Whiskey in the jar / Tuesday's gone / The more I see / Helpless / The small hours / The wait / Crash course in brain surgery / Last caress – Green hell / Am I evil? / Blitzkrieg / Breadfan / The prince / Stone cold crazy / So what? / Killing time / Overkill / Damage case / Stone dead forever / Too late, too late.

Nov 98.	(cd-s) (566591-2) **TURN THE PAGE / STONE COLD CRAZY (live) / THE WAIT (live) / BLEEDING ME (live)**		
Feb 99.	(cd-s) (566855-2) **WHISKEY IN THE JAR / BLITZKREIG (live) / THE PRINCE (live)**	29	

(cd-s) (566857-2) – ('A'side) / The small hours (live) / Killing time (live). (cd-s) (566859-2) – ('A'side) / Last caress – Green hell (live) / Whiskey in the jar (live).

Jun 99.	(cd-ep) (METCD 20) **DIE DIE MY DARLING / SABBRA CADABRA (live) / MERCYFUL FATE MEDLEY (live)**		
Nov 99.	(d-cd/d-c) (546797-2/-4) <62463> **S&M (with the San Francisco Symphony Orchestra)**	33	2

– Ecstasy of gold / Call of the Ktulu / Master of puppets / Of wolf and man / The thing that should not be / Fuel / Memory remains / No leaf clover / Hero of the day / Devil's dance / Bleeding me / Nothing else matters / Until it sleeps / For whom the bell tolls / Human / Wherever I may roam / Outlaw torn / Sad but true / One / Enter sandman / Battery.

– compilations, others, etc. –

Aug 87.	(7"ep/7"pic-ep) Megaforce; <MRS 04/+P> **WHIPLASH EP**		
Feb 90.	(cd/c) Vertigo; (642 219-2/-4) **METALLICA**		

– (JUMP IN THE FIRE + CREEPING DEATH singles).

May 90.	(6x12"box) Vertigo; (875 487-1) **THE GOOD, THE BAD & THE LIVE – THE 6 1/2 YEARS ANNIVERSARY COLLECTION**	56	–
Apr 98.	(cd) Ranch Life; (CRANCH 1) **BAY AREA THRASHERS**		

(also pic-lp on 'Collectors Picture Disc Series'; CPD 014)

METERS (see under ⇒ **NEVILLE BROTHERS**)

METHOD MAN (see under ⇒ **WU-TANG CLAN**)

George MICHAEL

Born: GEORGIOS KYRIACOS PANAYIOTOU, 25 Jun'63, Finchley, Middlesex, England. After meeting and befriending ANDREW RIDGELEY (b.26 Jan'63, Windlesham, Surrey, England) at Bushey Meads comprehensive school, the pair left in 1979 to form ska band, The EXECUTIVE, with DAVID

AUSTIN, ANDREW LEAVER and RIDGELEY's brother, PAUL. A couple of years later, the Adonis-like MICHAEL and the chiselled RIDGELEY broke away to form their own teen-dream duo, WHAM!, subsequently signing to Mark Dean's new 'Innervision' label. Disposable and contrived as they may have been, 'WHAM RAP (ENJOY WHAT YOU DO)' was as subversive as any po-faced post-punk outfit with its lyrical subtext of no work and all play, while 'YOUNG GUNS (GO FOR IT)' was in the same vein as The Special's 'TOO MUCH TOO YOUNG' (thematically, not musically!). With hit after hit of bouncy, sun-kissed lads-on-the-pull glam-pop, WHAM! certainly brightened up the dour early 80's scene, their debut album, 'FANTASTIC' (1983), topping the UK charts. MICHAEL made his first inroads to America, meanwhile, when 'WAKE ME UP BEFORE YOU GO-GO' gave WHAM! a transatlantic No.1 in summer '84. Having finally broken free from 'Innervision' after a protracted legal battle, WHAM! were now signed to 'Epic', MICHAEL simultaneously making the first tentative steps towards a solo career via the moody 'CARELESS WHISPER', another UK/US No.1. With the breathless heartbreak of 'FREEDOM', WHAM! approached pop genius, going out on a high with a further couple of stellar No.1's ('I'M YOUR MAN' and 'THE EDGE OF HEAVEN'), a tour of China (!) and a knicker-wetting farewell concert at Wembley Stadium. The band split around the same time as MICHAEL scored his second No.1 solo hit with 'A DIFFERENT CORNER', and by now it was abundantly clear which one of the duo was destined for greater things. Having previously sung 'Don't Let The Sun Go Down On Me' at Live Aid with ELTON JOHN, MICHAEL teamed up with soul belter, ARETHA FRANKLIN in early '87 for a rendition of 'I KNEW YOU WERE WAITING (FOR ME)', another No.1 hit. His solo debut proper came later that summer with the deliberately controversial 'I WANT YOUR SEX', a semi-successful attempt at PRINCE-like raunch-funk which hardly warranted its BBC ban. Much more effective was the boot-tapping strum'n'roll of 'FAITH', MICHAEL desperate to prove his newly acquired 'adult' cred with the obligatory designer stubble, biker jacket, 501's and shades. The accompanying album of the same name was a transatlantic million seller, going down particularly well in the States where its streamlined pop/rock found a massive audience; out of an incredible four further hit singles, two ('ONE MORE TRY' and 'MONKEY') topped the US charts. MICHAEL's subsequent retreat from the glare of the media spotlight and a more introspective, soul baring follow-up in 'LISTEN WITHOUT PREJUDICE VOL.1' (1990) led to the GEORGE MICHAEL hit machine faltering somewhat; though it again made the No.1 spot, the record only spawned two major hits in 'PRAYING FOR TIME' and the mercifully more upbeat 'FREEDOM '90'. Freedom from the machinations of the music industry, is MICHAEL's grievances leading him into a marathon court battle with 'Sony'; the singer complained that the company had done little to promote his new direction, still wanting to present him as a sex symbol against his wishes. His restraint of trade action against the corporation was eventually thrown out of court in summer '94 when the judge upheld MICHAEL's multi-million pound contract, the singer duly vowing never to record for the company again. The whole sorry debacle was eventually resolved in summer '95 when 'Sony' released MICHAEL from his contract with a number of attached conditions (share of profits from future works etc.), 'Virgin' ('Dreamworks' in the States) signing the superstar in a multi-million pound deal. His absence from the charts certainly hadn't affected his popularity and his first single in almost four years, the delicate 'JESUS TO A CHILD', made the UK No.1 in early '96. A funkier follow-up, 'FASTLOVE', also topped the charts as did his comeback album, 'OLDER' (1996). Older and no doubt wiser, MICHAEL was nevertheless still seemingly troubled by the moody angst which had characterised 'LISTEN . . .', although this time around there was less navel contemplation and more melodic sophistication. Although he may have joined the ranks of the ultra-tasteful MOR brigade alongside ELTON JOHN, ERIC CLAPTON etc., MICHAEL continues to command a wide cross section of fans, not least the WHAM! teenyboppers who grew up with his music. However, tabloids were having a field day on the 7th of April, 1998, after GEORGE was arrested for lewd behavoir in a Beverly Hills park toilet; the undercover policeman we assume was not 'taking the Michael'. It was not a shock to most people that GEORGE was indeed gay, having admittedly never been intimate with a woman for over ten years. He was subsequently fined nearly $1000 and ordered to deliver meals to AIDS sufferers as part of an 80-hour community service order; the American TV cameras were of course there to interview GEORGE – he also appeared on the David Letterman show. The police officer in question, Marcello Rodriguez, was none too happy when GEORGE's next video for his single, 'OUTSIDE', allegedly depicted mock scenes of the arrest; the man would later sue. Meanwhile, a 'greatest hits' package, 'LADIES AND GENTLEMEN' (1998), was a success all over the world, although what the fans made of MICHAEL's end of the millennium covers album, 'SONGS FROM THE LAST CENTURY' (1999), is anyone's guess.

Album rating: Wham!: FANTASTIC (*5) / MAKE IT BIG (*5) / THE FINAL (*4) / George Michael: FAITH (*8) / LISTEN WITHOUT PREJUDICE VOL.1 (*7) / OLDER (*6) / LADIES AND GENTLEMEN – THE BEST OF GEORGE MICHAEL compilation (*8) / SONGS FROM THE LAST CENTURY (*5)

WHAM!

GEORGE MICHAEL – vocals, bass / **ANDREW RIDGELEY** – guitar, keyboards

			Innervision	Columbia
Jun 82.	(7") *(IVLA 2442)* <> **WHAM RAP! (ENJOY WHAT YOU DO). / WHAM RAP! (unsocial mix)** (12"+=) *(IVLA13 2442)* – ('A'-Special US mix).			Feb83

(re-act.Jan83, hit UK No.8)

		Epic	Columbia
Sep 82.	(7"/12") *(INVA/+13 2766)* **YOUNG GUNS (GO FOR IT). / GOING FOR IT**	3	–
May 83.	(7"/7"pic-d) *(INVA/INVWA 3143)* <03932> **BAD BOYS. / ('A'instrumental)**	2	60 Aug83
Jul 83.	(lp/c; US – as WHAM UK) *(INV/40 25328)* <038911> **FANTASTIC** – Bad boys / A ray of sunshine / Love machine / Wham rap (enjoy what you do) / Club Tropicana / Nothing looks the same in the light / Come on / Young guns (go for it). *(cd-iss. Jan84; CD 25328)* *(re-iss. Mar88 on 'Epic' lp/c; 450090-1/-4)* *(re-iss. +=)* – (extra tracks).	1	83
Jul 83.	(7"/7"pic-d) *(INVA/INVWA 3613)* **CLUB TROPICANA. / BLUE (ARMED WITH LOVE)** (12"+=) *(INVA13 3613)* – ('A'instrumental).	4	–
Nov 83.	(7") *(A 3586)* **CLUB FANTASTIC MEGAMIX. / A RAY OF SUNSHINE (instrumental)** (12"+=) *(INVA13 3586)* – Come on / Love machine.	15	–

		Epic	Columbia
May 84.	(7") *(A 4440)* <04552> **WAKE ME UP BEFORE YOU GO-GO. / ('A'instrumental)** (12"+=) *(TA 4440)* – A ray of sunshine.	1	1 Sep84

––––– <in the US still credited to **WHAM featuring GEORGE MICHAEL**>

		Epic	Columbia
Jul 84.	(7"/7"sha-pic-d/12"; by GEORGE MICHAEL) *(A/WA/TA 4603)* <04691> **CARELESS WHISPER. / ('A'instrumental)**	1	1 Dec84
Oct 84.	(7"/7"sha-pic-d) *(A/QA 4743)* **FREEDOM. / (instrumental)** (12"+=) *(TA 4743)* – ('A'extended).	1	–
Nov 84.	(lp/c/cd) *(EPC/40/CD 86311)* <39595> **MAKE IT BIG** – Wake me up before you go-go / Everything she wants / Heartbeat / Like a baby / Freedom / If you were there / Credit card baby / Careless whisper. *(re-iss. Oct89 lp/c; 465576-1/-4)* <US pic-lp; >	1	1
Dec 84.	(7"/12") *(WHAM/+T 1)* **LAST CHRISTMAS. / EVERYTHING SHE WANTS**	2	–
Feb 85.	(7") <04840> **EVERYTHING SHE WANTS. / LIKE A BABY**	–	1
Jul 85.	(7") <05409> **FREEDOM. / HEARTBEAT**	–	3

––––– (In Jun'85, he dueted with ELTON JOHN for LIVE AID on his single 'DON'T LET THE SUN GO DOWN ON ME'). Also from same source Nov85, 'WRAP HER UP' again w / ELTON JOHN was issued as 45 and hit UK No.12, US No.20.

		Epic	Columbia
Nov 85.	(7") *(A 6716)* <05721> **I'M YOUR MAN. / DO IT RIGHT (instrumental)** (12"+=/12"pic-d+=) *(TA/WTA 6716)* – ('A'acapella version).	1	20
Dec 85.	(7") (re-issue) **LAST CHRISTMAS. / BLUE (ARMED WITH LOVE) (live)** (12"+=) (re-issue) – Everything she wants.	6	–
Mar 86.	(7"/12"; by GEORGE MICHAEL) *(A/TA 7033)* <05888> **A DIFFERENT CORNER. / ('A'instrumental)**	1	7
Jun 86.	(7") *(FIN 1)* **THE EDGE OF HEAVEN. / WHERE DID YOUR HEART GO?** (d7"+=/12"+=) *(FIN/+T 1)* – Battlestations / Wham rap '86.	1	–
Jun 86.	(7") <06182> **THE EDGE OF HEAVEN. / BLUE (live in China)** (12"+=) <40285> – Where did your heart go? / Battlestations / Wham rap '86 / A different corner.	–	10
Oct 86.	(7") <06294> **WHERE DID YOUR HEART GO?. / WHAM RAP '86**	–	50

––––– (WHAM! by this time had already split)

		Epic	Columbia
Oct 86.	(d-lp/c/cd) *(EPC/40/CD 88681)* **THE FINAL** – Wham! rap (enjoy what you do) / Young guns (go for it!) / Bad boys / Club Tropicana / Wake me up before you go-go / Careless whisper / Last Christmas (pudding mix) / Everything she wants (remix) / I'm your man / A different corner / Battlestations / Where did your heart go? / The edge of Heaven. *(also iss.on 2 gold-lp's)* *(re-hit UK No.27 in Jun99)*	1	–

– compilations, etc. –

on 'Epic' unless mentioned otherwise

		Epic	Columbia
Sep 86.	(c-ep) *(EPC 450 125-4)* **THE 12" TAPE** – Wham rap / Careless whisper / Freedom / Everything she wants / I'm your man.	–	–
Dec 86.	(7") *(650 269-7)* **LAST CHRISTMAS. / WHERE DID YOUR HEART GO** (12"+=) *(650 269-6)* – ('A'&'B'extended).	–	–
Dec 86.	(lp) *(WHAM 2)* **WHAM! BOXED SET**	–	–
Nov 97.	(cd/c) **THE BEST OF WHAM!**	4	–

GEORGE MICHAEL

		Epic	Columbia
Jan 87.	(7"/12"; by ARETHA FRANKLIN & GEORGE MICHAEL) *(DUET/+T 2)* <9559> **I KNEW YOU WERE WAITING (FOR ME). / (instrumental)** (above jointly issued on 'Arista':- ARETHA's label)	1	3

––––– GEORGE went solo, as did his WHAM! partner, ANDREW RIDGELEY

		Epic	Columbia
Jun 87.	(7") *(LUST 1)* <07164> **I WANT YOUR SEX. / (instrumental)** (c-s+=/12"+=/12"pic-d+=)(cd-s+=) *(LUST C/T/QT 1)(CDLUST 1)* – Rhythm 1 – Lust / Rhythm 2 – Brass in love / Rhythm 3 – A last request.	3	2
Oct 87.	(7") *(EMU 3)* <07623> **FAITH. / HAND TO MOUTH** (c-s+=/12"+=/12"pic-d+=) *(EMU C/T/P 3)* – ('A'instrumental). (cd-s+=) *(CDEMU 3)* – Hard day (mix).	2	1
Nov 87.	(lp/c/cd/pic-cd) *(460000-1/-4/-2/-9)* <40867> **FAITH** – Faith / Father figure / I want your sex (part 1 & 2) / One more try / Hard day / Hand to mouth / Look at your hands / Monkey / Kissing a fool. *(re-iss. Sep90, hit UK 40)*	1	1
Dec 87.	(7"/7"sha-pic-d) *(EMU/+P 4)* **FATHER FIGURE. / LOVE'S IN NEED OF LOVE TODAY** (12"+=/cd-s+=) *(EMUT/CDEMU 4)* – ('A'instrumental).	11	–
Jan 88.	(7") <07682> **FATHER FIGURE. / ('A'instrumental)**	–	1
Apr 88.	(7"/7"s/12"/pic-cd-s) *(EMU/EMUB/EMYT/CDEMU 5)* <07773> **ONE MORE TRY. / LOOK AT YOUR HANDS**	8	1

Jul 88. (7") *(EMU 6) <07941>* **MONKEY. / MONKEY (acappella)** | 13 | 1 |
(12"+=/cd-s+=) *(EMUT/CDEMU 6)* – ('A'extended versions).
Nov 88. (7") *(EMU 7) <08050>* **KISSING A FOOL. / (instrumental)** | 18 | 5 | Oct88
(12"+=/cd-s+=) *(EMUT/CDEMU 7)* – Rhythm 3 – A last request.
Aug 90. (7"-c-s) *(GEO/+M 1) <73512>* **PRAYING FOR TIME. / IF YOU WERE MY WOMAN** | 6 | 1 |
(12"+=/cd-s+=) *(GEOT/CDGEO 1)* – Waiting (reprise).
Aug 90. (cd/c/lp) *(467 295-2/-4/-1) <46898>* **LISTEN WITHOUT PREJUDICE VOL.1** | 1 | 2 |
– Praying for time / Freedom '90 / They won't go when I go / Something to save / Cowboys and angels / Waiting for that day / Mother's pride / Head the pain / Soul free / Waiting (reprise).
Oct 90. (7"/c-s/12") *(GEO/+M/T 2)* **WAITING FOR THAT DAY. / FANTASY** | 23 | – |
(cd-s+=/pic-cd-d+=) *(GEOC/CDGEO 2)* – Kissing a fool / Father figure.
Oct 90. (c-s) *<73559>* **FREEDOM / FANTASY** | – | 8 |
Dec 90. (7"/c-s) *(GEO/+M 3)* **FREEDOM '90. / FREEDOM (mix)** | 28 | – |
(12"+=/cd-s+=) *(GEO T/C 3)* – Mother's pride.
Jan 91. (c-s) *<73663>* **MOTHER'S PRIDE. / WAITING FOR THAT DAY** | – | 46 |
| | | 27 |
Feb 91. (7"/c-s/12"/cd-s) *(656 647-7/-4/-6/-2)* **HEAL THE PAIN. / SOUL FREE** | 31 | – |
(cd-s+=) *(656 647-5)* – Hand to mouth.
Mar 91. (7"/c-s/12"/cd-s) *(656 774-7/-4/-6/-2)* **COWBOYS AND ANGELS. / SOMETHING TO SAVE** | 45 | – |
Nov 91. (7"-c-s; GEORGE MICHAEL & ELTON JOHN) *(657 646-7/-4) <74086>* **DON'T LET THE SUN GO DOWN ON ME. / I BELIEVE (WHEN I FALL IN LOVE IT WILL BE FOREVER)** | 1 | 1 |
(12"+=) *(657 646-6)* – Last Christmas.
(cd-s+=) *(657 646-2)* – If you were my woman / Fantasy.
Jun 92. (7"-c-s/ext-12"/ext.cd-s) *(658 058-7/-4/-6/-2) <74353>* **TOO FUNKY. / CRAZYMAN DANCE** | 4 | 10 |

—— In Nov'92, GEORGE took 'Sony' to court for around $50m. In April '93, he teamed up with QUEEN on UK No.1 + US No.46 'FIVE LIVE EP'.

| | | Virgin | Dreamworks |
Jan 96. (c-s/cd-s) *(VSC/+DG 1571) <59000>* **JESUS TO A CHILD / ONE MORE TRY (live gospel version)** | 1 | 7 |
(cd-s+=) *(VSCDX 1571)* – Older (instrumental).
Apr 96. (12"/c-s) *(VST/VSC 1579) <59001>* **FASTLOVE / I'M YOUR MAN** | 1 | 8 |
(cd-s+=) *(VSCD 1579)* – Fastlove (part II).
May 96. (cd/c/lp) *(CD/TC+/V 2802) <50000>* **OLDER** | 1 | 6 |
– Jesus to a child / Fastlove / Older / Spinning the wheel / It doesn't really matter / The strangest thing / To be forgiven / Move on / Star people / You have been loved / Free. *(cd-iss. Dec97 as 'OLDER AND UPPER' +=; CDVX 2802)* – Fastlove (part II) / Spinning the wheel / The strangest thing / You know what I want to do / Safe.
Aug 96. (7"/c-s) *(VSLH/VSC 1595)* **SPINNING THE WHEEL. / ('A'mix)** | 2 | – |
(cd-s+=) *(VSCDG 1595)* – You know that I want to / Safe.
(cd-s) *(VSCDX 1595)* – ('A'-Forthright mix) / Fastlove (Forthright edit) / ('A'-Jon Douglas mix).
Jan 97. (7"ep/c-ep/cd-ep) *(VS LH/C/CDG 1626)* **OLDER / I CAN'T MAKE YOU LOVE ME. / DESAFINADO / THE STRANGEST THING (live)** | 3 | – |
(cd-ep) *(VSCDE 1626)* – ('A'mixes).
May 97. (c-s/12"/cd-s) *(VSC/VSLH/VSCDG 1641)* **STAR PEOPLE '97. / EVERYTHING SHE WANTS** | 2 | – |
(cd-s) *(VSCDX 1641)* – ('A'mixes).

—— In Jun'97, GEORGE was credited on the UK Top 10 single 'Waltz Away Dreaming' by TOBY BOURKE.

Sep 97. (c-s/cd-s) *(VSC/VSDG 1663)* **YOU HAVE BEEN LOVED / THE STRANGEST THING '97 / FATHER FIGURE** | 2 | – |
(cd-s+=) *(VSCDX 1663)* – Praying for time.

| | | Epic | Epic |
Oct 98. (c-s/cd-s) *(666562-4/-2)* **OUTSIDE / FANTASY (1998 remix)** | 2 | |
(cd-s) *(666562-5)* – ('A'mixes).
Nov 98. (cd/c) *(491705-2/-4) <69635>* **LADIES AND GENTLEMEN – THE BEST OF GEORGE MICHAEL** (compilation) | 1 | 24 |
– Jesus to a child / Father figure / Careless whisper / Don't let the sun go down on me / You have been loved / Kissing a fool / I can't make you love me / Heal the pain / A moment with you / Desafinado / Cowboys and angels / Praying for time / One more time / A different corner / Waltz away dreaming / Outside / As / Fastlove / Too funky / Freedom 90 / Star people 97 / Killer – Papa was a rollin' stone / I want your sex / Strangest thing 97 / Fantasy / Spinning the wheel / Waiting for the day / I knew you were waiting (for me) / Faith. *(c+=)* – Hard day / Somebody to love.
Mar 99. (c-s; by GEORGE MICHAEL & MARY J BLIGE) *(667012-4)* **AS / A DIFFERENT CORNER** | 4 | |
(cd-s) *(667012-2)* – ('A'mixes).
(cd-s) *(667012-5)* – ('A'mixes).
Dec 99. (cd/c) *(CD TC/VX 2920)* **SONGS FROM THE LAST CENTURY** | 2 | |
– Brother can you spare a dime / Roxanne / You've changed / My baby just cares for me / The first time I ever saw your face / Miss Sarajevo / I remember you / Secret love / Wild is the wind / Where or when.

MIDNIGHT OIL

Formed: Sydney, Australia ... 1976 by JAMES MOGINIE, ROB HIRST, ANDREW JAMES and MARTIN ROTSEY, who had played together for a number of years as The FARM (no, not that one!), before recruiting law student, PETER GARRETT, as a formidably articulate frontman and changing their name. Defiantly self-sufficient and alternative from the start, the band not only secured their own tour bookings but set up their own label, 'Powderworks', through which they released their first three albums. 'MIDNIGHT OIL' (1978) introduced their gritty, politicised pop/rock, the band already building up a fearsome live reputation through constant gigging (including many benefits)

and scoring the first of many domestic successes with the following year's 'HEAD INJURIES'. While MOGINIE and HIRST were initially the chief songwriters, GARRETT's influence became increasingly pronounced as the group signed to a major label, 'C.B.S.', and enjoyed their first worldwide release with '10,9,8,7,6,5,4,3,2,1' (1983). With a fuller, more animated sound and caustic anti-establishment lyrics, the record made Britain and America aware that there was actually a more intelligent, non-sexist but equally hard hitting Australian alternative to AC/DC. The mid-80's saw no let-up in the band's activities as 'RED SAILS IN THE SUNSET' (1985) met with widespread critical acclaim, the band stepping up their political commitment (especially with regard to the problems of the aborigines) as GARRETT was very nearly elected to the Australian parliament as a representative of the Nuclear Disarmament Party. Replacing JAMES with PETER GIFFORD, the group finally crossed over commercially in the international marketplace with the anthemic plea, 'BEDS ARE BURNING'. The accompanying album, 'DIESEL AND DUST' (1988) made the UK Top 20, narrowly missing a similar position in America, while its Australian sales broke new records; generally considered to be the best set of their career, the album's high-octane agit-pop was one of the most exciting marriages of politics and music since the heyday of The CLASH. 'BLUE SKY MINING' (1990) was even more scathingly political, the title track centering on the victims of the blue asbestos cancer which killed thousands of immigrant workers in Western Australia. A further series of albums in the 90's demonstrated that these hardy campaigners were far from being a spent force, their laudable commitment something more than a few lesser bands might learn from.

Album rating: MIDNIGHT OIL (*4) / HEAD INJURIES (*5) / PLACE WITHOUT A POSTCARD (*5) / 10,9,8,7,6,5,4,3,2,1 (*6) / RED SAILS IN THE SUNSET (*7) / DIESEL AND DUST (*7) / BLUE SKY MINING (*7) / SCREAM IN BLUE – LIVE (*5) / EARTH AND SUN AND MOON (*6) / BREATHE (*5) / 20,000 WATTS R.S.L. – THE COLLECTION (*7)

PETER GARRETT – vocals / **JAMES MOGINIE** – guitar, keyboards / **MARTIN POTSEY** – guitar / **DWAYNE 'Bones' HILLMAN** (b.New Zealand) – bass, vocals (ex-SWINGERS) / **ROB HIRST** – drums, vocals

| | | | Powderworks not iss. |
1978. (lp) **MIDNIGHT OIL** | – | – | Austra
– Powderworks / Head over heels / Dust / Used and abused / Surfing with a spoon / Run with you / Nothing lost . . . nothing gained. *(UK-iss.Feb94 on 'Columbia' cd/c; 450902-2/-4)*
1979. (7") **RUN BY NIGHT. /** | – | – | Austra

—— **ANDREW JAMES** – bass, vocals repl. HILLMAN
1979. (lp) *(MLF 322)* **HEAD INJURIES** | – | – | Austra
– Cold cold change / Section 5 (bus to Bondi) / Naked flame / Bad on the borderline / Koal spirit / No reaction / Stand in line / Profiteers / Is it now? *(UK-iss.Apr91 on 'Columbia' cd/c; 450903-2/-4)*
Nov 80. (12"ep) **BIRD NOISES** | – | – | Aust
– No time for games / Knife's edge / Wedding cake Island / I'm the cure.
1981. (lp) **PLACE WITHOUT A POSTCARD** | – | – | Aust
– Don't wanna be the one / Brave faces / Armistice day / Someone else to blame / Basement flat / Written in the heart / Burnie / Quinella holiday / Loves on sale / If Ned Kelly was king / Lucky country. *(UK-iss.Apr91 on 'Columbia' lp/c/cd; 460897-1/-4/-2)*

| | | C.B.S. | Columbia |
May 83. (7") *(A 3343)* **U.S. FORCES. / OUTSIDE WORLD** | | – |
(12"+=) *(TA 3343)* – Some kids / Knife edge.
Jun 83. (lp/c) *(CBS/40 25314) <38996>* **10,9,8,7,6,5,4,3,2,1** | | |
– Outside world / Only the strong / Short memory / Read about it / Scream in blue / U.S. Forces / The power and the passion / Maralinga / Tin legs and tin mines / Somebody's trying to tell me something. *(cd-iss. Jun88 on 'Collector's Choice'; CK 38996)* *(re-iss. Mar93 on 'Columbia' cd/c; 462488-2/-4)*
Jul 83. (7"/12") *(A/TA 3176)* **THE POWER AND THE PASSION. / GLITCH BABY GLITCH** | | |
Sep 83. (7") **TIN LEGS AND TIN MINES. / THE POWER AND THE PASSION** | – | |
Feb 84. (7") **OUTSIDE WORLD. / READ ABOUT IT** | – | |
Jul 85. (7") *(A 6383)* **BEST OF BOTH WORLDS. / KOSCRUSKO** | – | |
(12"+=) *(TA 6383)* – The power and the passion.
Jul 85. (lp/c) *(CBS/40 26355) <39987>* **RED SAILS IN THE SUNSET** | | |
– When the generals talk / Best of both worlds / Sleep / Minutes to midnight / Jimmy Sharman's boxers / Bakerman / Who can stand in the way / Kosciusko / Helps me helps you / Harrisburg / Bells and horns in the back of beyond / Shipyards of New Zealand. *(cd-iss. Jun88 on 'Collector's Choice'; CK 39987)* *(re-iss. Apr91 lp/c/cd; 463083-1/-4/-2)*
Sep 85. (7") *(A 6583)* **WHEN THE GENERALS TALK. / WHO CAN STAND IN THE WAY** | | |

—— **PETER GIFFORD** – bass repl. ANDREW JAMES
Mar 88. (7") *<07433>* **BEDS ARE BURNING. / BULLROARER** | – | 17 |
Mar 88. (7") *(OIL 1)* **BEDS ARE BURNING. / GUN BARREL HIGHWAY** | 48 | – |
(12"+=/cd-s+=) *(OILT/CDOIL 1)* – Hercules.
Apr 88. (lp/c/cd) *(465653-1/-4/-2) <40967>* **DIESEL AND DUST** | 19 | 21 | Feb88
– Beds are burning / Put down that weapon / Dreamworld / Whoah / Arctic world / Warakurna / The dead heart / Whoah / Bullroarer / Sell my soul / Sometimes.
Jun 88. (7"/c-s) *(OIL/+C 2) <07964>* **THE DEAD HEART. / KOSCIUSKO** | 68 | 53 |
(12"+=/cd-s+=) *(OILT/CDOIL 2)* – ('A'extended) / Beds are burning (Tamarama mix).
Nov 88. (7") **PROGRESS. / DREAMWORLD** | – | – |
(cd-s+=) – Species Deseases – Hercules / Blossom and blood / Pictures.
Feb 89. (7") *(OIL 3)* **BEDS ARE BURNING. / THE POWER AND THE PASSION** | 6 | – |
(12"+=/cd-s+=) *(OILT/CDOIL 3)* – Hercules.
Jun 89. (7"/c-s) *(OIL/+C 4)* **THE DEAD HEART. / WHOAH** | 62 | – |
(12"+=/cd-s+=) *(OILT 4)* – Progress.
(7"ep+=) *(OILEP 4)* – Blossom and blood / Pictures.

—— **DWAYNE 'Bones' HILLMAN** (b. New Zealand) – bass repl. GIFFORD

Feb 90. (7"/c-s) *(OIL/+C 5) <73250>* **BLUE SKY MINE. / WEDDING CAKE ISLAND** — `66` `47`
  (12"+=/cd-s+=) *(OILT/CDOIL 5)* – Beds are burning.

Mar 90. (cd/c/lp) *(465653-2/-4/-1) <45398>* **BLUE SKY MINING** `28` `20`
  – Blue sky mine / Stars of Warburton / Forgotten years / Bedlam bridge / Mountains of Burma / King of the mountain / River runs red / Shakers and movers / One country / Antarctica. *(re-iss. cd+c Sep93 on 'Columbia')*

May 90. (7"/c-s) *(OIL/+C 6)* **FORGOTTEN YEARS. / YOU MAY NOT BE RELEASED**
  (12"+=/cd-s+=) *(OILT/CDOIL 6)* – Shakers and movers / Don't wanna be the one.

May 92. (7"/c-s) **SOMETIMES (live '89). / USED AND ABUSED (live)**
  (cd-s+=) – Written in my heart (live).
  (cd-s) – ('A'side) / No reaction (live) / Wharf rat.

Jun 92. (cd/c/lp) *(4171453-2/-4/-1) <52731>* **SCREAM IN BLUE (live '82-'90)**
  – Scream in blue / Read about it / Dreamworld / Brave faces / Only the strong / Stars of Warburton / Progress / Beds are burning / Sell my soul / Sometimes / Hercules / Powderworks.

Mar 93. (12"/cd-s) *(659 049-6/-2)* **TRUGANINI. / BEDS ARE BURNING / READ ABOUT IT / STARS OF WARBURTON** `29`

Apr 93. (cd/c/lp) *(473605-2/-4/-1) <53793>* **EARTH AND SUN AND MOON** `27` `49`
  – Feeding frenzy / My country / Renaissance man / Earth and sun and moon / Trugnanini / Bushfire / Drums of Heaven / Outbreak of love / In the valley / Tell me the truth / Now or never land.

May 93. (c-s/cd-s) *(659 370-6/-2)* **MY COUNTRY (radio Version). / GLITCH BABY GLITCH** `66`

Nov 93. (7") *(659 849-7)* **IN THE VALLEY. / SHIPS OF FREEDOM / MY COUNTRY (live)** `60`
  (12"+=/cd-s+=) *(659 849-6/-2)* – Blue sky mine (live).

Oct 96. (cd-s) *(663736-2)* **UNDERWATER / GRAVELRASH / I SEE YOU / SMASH THE WOBBLE BOARD / KINGDOM OF FLAUNT** `-`

Oct 96. (cd/c) *(485402-9/-3) <67882>* **BREATHE**
  – Underwater / Surf's up tonight / Common ground / Time to heal / Sins of omission / One too many / Times / Star of hope / In the rain / Bring on the change / Home / E-beat / Barest degree / Gravelrash.

Nov 98. (cd/c) *(489971-2/-4) <69682>* **REDNECK WONDERLAND**
  – Redneck wonderland / Concrete / Cemetry in my mind / Comfortable place on the couch / Safety chain blues / Return to sender / Blot / Great gibber plain / Seeing is believing / White skin black heart / What goes on / Drop in the ocean.

– compilations, etc. –

on 'Columbia' unless stated otherwise

Dec 90. (3xcd-box) *(467392-2)* **RED SAILS IN THE SUNSET / PLACE WITHOUT A POSTCARD / 10,9,8,7,6,5,4,3,2,1** `-`

Jun 93. (cd) *(474040-2)* **DIESEL AND DUST / 10,9,8,7,6,5,4,3,2,1** `-`

Jul 93. (cd) *(450902-2)* **MIDNIGHT OIL / RED SAILS IN THE SUNSET** `-`

Oct 94. (3xcd-box) *(477520-2)* **DIESEL AND DUST / HEAD INJURIES / MIDNIGHT OIL** `-`

Nov 97. (cd/c) *(488 866-2/-4) <68848>* **20,000 WATT R.S.L.**
  – What goes on / The power and the passion / Dreamworld / White skin black heart / Kosciuszko / Dead heart / Blue sky mine / U.S. forces / Beds are burning / One country / Truganini / King of the mountain / Hercules / Surf's up tonight / Back on the borderline / Don't wanna be the one / Forgotten years.

MIGHTY LEMON DROPS (dig out; Great Alt & Indie . . .)

MIGHTY MIGHTY BOSSTONES

Formed: Boston, Massachusetts, USA … 1985 as an 8-piece SPECIALS/MADNESS type ska-rock led by "cool" singer, DICKY BARRETT, an ex user of that nose-numbing powder, cocaine. The line-up was completed by NATE ALBERT, JOE GITTLEMAN, JOE SIROIS, TIM BURTON, DENNIS BROCKENBOROUGH, KEVIN LENEAR and dancer BEN CARR. The forefathers of the currently popular so-called US ska scene, they debuted in 1990 with the 'DEVILS NIGHT OUT' album. However, it would take three years before some kind of commercial breakthrough as 'DON'T KNOW HOW TO PARTY' cracked the US Top 200. The 1994 follow-up, 'QUESTION THE ANSWERS', sold a little better as the group set up their own 'Big Rig' label soon after. Following in the wake of NO DOUBT and RANCID's Stateside success, The MIGHTY MIGHTY BOSSTONES powered their way into the US Top 30 with 1997's 'LET'S FACE IT'. Released a year later in the UK (where Kerrang! had surprisingly given them column inches) and with the help of a Top 20 hit, 'THE IMPRESSION THAT I GET', it even made the British Top 40. • **Covers:** SWEET EMOTION (Aerosmith) / AIN'T TALKIN' 'BOUT LOVE (Van Halen) / ENTER SANDMAN (Metallica) / SIMMER DOWN (Bob Marley) / THINK AGAIN (Minor Threat) / etc.

Album rating: DEVILS NIGHT OUT (*6) / MORE NOISE AND OTHER DISTURBANCES (*5) / DON'T KNOW HOW TO PARTY (*4) / QUESTION THE ANSWERS (*6) / SKA-CORE, THE DEVIL AND MORE mini (*5) / LET'S FACE IT (*6) / LIVE FROM THE MIDDLE EAST (*3)

DICKY BARRETT – vocals / **NATE ALBERT** (b.1971) – guitar / **JOE GITTLEMAN** (b.1968) – bass / **JOE SIROIS** (b.1971) – drums / **KEVIN LENEAR** (b.1970) – saxophone / **TIM BURTON** (b.1964) – saxophone / **DENNIS BROCKENBOROUGH** (b.1970) – trombone / **BEN CARR** (b.1968) – dancer

---

Nov 90. (cd) *(EM 9358-1)* **DEVILS NIGHT OUT** — Emergo / Emergo
  – Devils night out / Howwhywuz, howwhyyam / Drunks and children / Hope I never lose my wallet / Haji / The bartender's song / Patricia / The cave / Do something crazy / A little bit ugly. *(lp-iss.Mar93 on 'Roadrunner'; RR 9358-1) (lp re-iss. Dec96 on 'Taang'; TAANG 044LP) (re-iss. May98 10"d-lp+=/cd; TAANG 044 D/CD)* – WHERE'D YOU GO EP. *(cd re-iss. May98 on 'Roadrunner'; RR 9358-2)*

Jan 92. (7"ep/cd-ep) *<(TAANG 048/+CD)>* **WHERE'D YOU GO? EP** — Taang / Taang
  – Where'd you go? / Sweet emotion / Enter sandman / Do something crazy / Ain't talkin' 'bout love.

Jun 92. (lp/cd) *<(TAANG 060/+CD)>* **MORE NOISE AND OTHER DISTURBANCES**
  – Awfully quiet / Where'd you go? / Dr. D / It can't hurt / What's at stake / Cowboy coffee / I'll drink to that / Guns and the young / He's back / Bad in plaid / They came to Boston. *(re-iss. May98; same)*

Jan 93. (7") **HARDWARE & LUMBER. / SWIRL** — not iss. / Dink-Mercury

Mar 93. (m-cd) *(514 551-2)* **SKA CORE THE DEVIL** `-`
  – Someday I suppose / Think again / Lights out / Police beat / Simmer down / Drugs and kittens / I'll drink to that. *(UK-iss.Jan96 & Jun98 on 'Mercury'; same)*

May 93. (cd) *(514 836-2)* **DON'T KNOW HOW TO PARTY** `-`
  – Almost anything goes / Last dead mouse / Someday I suppose / Don't know how to party / Illegal left / Holy smoke / Issachar / Our only weapon / Man without / Seven thirty seven – Shoe glue / Tin soldiers / What was was over. *(UK-iss.Jun98; same)*

Oct 94. (cd) *(522 845-2)* **QUESTION THE ANSWERS** `-`
  – Bronzing the garbage / Hell of a hat / Pictures to prove it / Dollar and a dream / We should talk / Toxic toast / 365 days / Dogs and chaplains / Jump through the hoops / Kinder words / Sad silence / Stand-off. *(UK-iss.Jun98 on 'Mercury'; same)*

May 97. (lp) *(RIG 00050-1) <534 472-2>* **LET'S FACE IT** `27`
  – Noise brigade / The rascal king / Royal oil / The impression that I get / Let's face it / That bug bit me / Another drinkin' song / Numbered days / Break so easily / Nevermind me / Desensitized / 1-2-8. *(cd-iss. May98 on 'Mercury'; 534 472-2)* – hit UK No.40

Mar 97. (7") *(RIG 00050-2)* **THE IMPRESSION THAT I GET. / IS IT** — Big Rig-Mercury / Big Rig-Mercury

Apr 98. (c-ep/cd-ep) *(574 843-4/-2)* **THE IMPRESSION THAT I GET / DESENSITIZED / IS IT / STORM HIT** `12`
  (cd-ep) *(568 815-2)* –

Jun 98. (c-s) *(566 108-4)* **THE RASCAL KING / A SAD SILENCE** `63`
  (cd-s+=) *(566 111-2)* – Stand-off.
  (cd-s) *(566 109-2)* – ('A'side) / At it again / Hell of a hat.

Nov 98. (cd) *<(558 900-2)>* **LIVE FROM THE MIDDLE EAST (live in Cambridge, Boston)** — Sep98
  – 1-2-8 / Do somethin' crazy / He's back / Devil's night out / Kinder words / Noise brigade / The rascal king / Hell of a hat / Holy smoke / Hope I never lose my wallet / I'll drink to that / Royal oil / Cowboy coffee / Doves and civilians / Let's face it / Howwhywuz, howwhyam / Dr. D / Where'd you go? / Seven thirty seven – Shoe clue / The impression that I get / Someday I suppose / Lights out.

MIKE + THE MECHANICS (see under ⇒ GENESIS)

Frankie MILLER

Born: 1950, Glasgow, Scotland. After serving his musical apprenticeship in a series of pub outfits during the late 60's, MILLER relocated to London in mid '71. Newly installed in the capital, he formed JUDE alongside guitar maestro ROBIN TROWER and a rhythm section of JIM DEWAR and CLIVE BUNKER. The project proved short-lived, however, as TROWER went solo early the following year, taking DEWAR with him. Teaming up with ex-members of the underrated BRINSLEY SCHWARZ (i.e. NICK LOWE, BOB ANDREWS, BILLY RANKIN and BRINSLEY SCHWARZ himself), MILLER proceeded to cut a debut solo album, 'ONCE IN A BLUE MOON' (1973) for 'Chrysalis'. The record failed to chart and the footloose singer-songwriter upped sticks for New Orleans where he hooked up with semi-legendary Crescent City soul guru, Allen Toussaint for the 'HIGHLIFE' (1974) album. Despite furnishing classic hits for Betty Wright ('SHOORAH SHOORAH') and Three Dog Night ('PLAY SOMETHING SWEET'), the album provided scant commercial pickings for MILLER himself. Returning to the UK, he amassed a band consisting of HENRY McCULLOCH, MICK WEAVER, CHRISSIE STEWART and STU PERRY, cutting a third album, 'THE ROCK' (1975). Again sales were disappointing and it was 1977 before MILLER scored a rare Top 30 hit with 'BE GOOD TO YOURSELF', the lead track on that year's 'FULL HOUSE' album. Released under the moniker FRANKIE MILLER'S FULL HOUSE, the record was recorded with a new band that lasted barely a year before MILLER again went solo. Augmented by such talents as PAUL CARRACK, 1978's 'DOUBLE TROUBLE' was another fine set of gravel-throated blues-rock that failed to notch up respectable sales. Retaining CARRACK and utilising a cast of session men, MILLER was finally rewarded for his efforts when the foot-tappin' parched-blues balladry of 'DARLIN' made the UK Top 10. Incredibly, the accompanying album 'FALLING IN LOVE … PERFECT FIT' (1979) still failed to chart, as did 1980's 'EASY MONEY' set, the latter representing his last release for 'Mercury'. Eventually picked up by 'Capitol', MILLER recorded 'STANDING ON THE EDGE' (1982) before cutting 'DANCING IN THE RAIN' (1986) for 'Vertigo' with a band that included such distinguished veterans as BRIAN ROBERTSON and SIMON KIRKE. Having already begun an acting career in 1979 with Peter McDougall's TV play, 'Just A Boy's Game' (for which he also penned/sang the theme tune, 'Playin' The Game'), MILLER increasingly concentrated his energies on thespian matters as the 80's wore on.

Despite a brief moment of fame in the early 90's when Tennent's Lager used 'Caledonia' in a TV ad, MILLER's career has of late been severely curtailed by serious illness after he suffered a brain aneurysm on the 25th August, 1994. One of Scottish music's great unsung voices, MILLER remains almost universally respected among rock's elder statesmen and we here at The Great Rock Discography think a reassessment of the man's career is long overdue. • **Note:** There was also a FRANKIE MILLER from the States, who had albums on 'Starday'.

Album rating: ONCE IN A BLUE MOON (*6) / HIGH LIFE (*6) / THE ROCK (*6) / FULL HOUSE (*6) / DOUBLE TROUBLE (*6) / FALLING IN LOVE ... PERFECT FIT (*5) / EASY MONEY (*5) / STANDING ON THE EDGE (*5) / DANCING IN THE RAIN (*4) / THE VERY BEST OF FRANKIE MILLER compilation (*7)

FRANKIE MILLER – vocals (ex-JUDE) with ex-members of BRINSLEY SCHWARZ (aka NICK LOWE – bass / **BOB ANDREWS** – keyboards / **BRINSLEY SCHWARZ** – guitar / **BILLY RANKIN** – drums)

Chrysalis Chrysalis

Jan 73. (lp) (<CHR 1036>) **ONCE IN A BLUE MOON**
– You don't need to laugh (to be happy) / I can't change it / Candlelight sonata in f major / Ann Eliza Jane / It's all over / In no resistance / After all (I live my life) / Just like Tom Thumb's blues / Mail box / I'm ready. (cd-iss. Oct98 on 'Repertoire'; REP 4725)

—— brought in a number of session men to replace last band

Jan 74. (lp) (<CHR 1052>) **HIGH LIFE**
– High life / Play something sweet (brickyard blues) / Trouble / A fool / Little angel / With you in mind / The devil gun / I'll take a melody / Just a song / Shoorah shoorah / I'm falling in love again. (cd-iss. Mar94; CD25CR 04) (cd re-iss. Oct98 on 'Repertoire'; REP 4724)

FRANKIE MILLER BAND

—— with **HENRY McCULLOCH** – guitar / **MICK WEAVER** – keyboards / **CHRISSIE STEWART** – bass / **STU PERRY** – drums

Sep 75. (7") (CHS 2074) **A FOOL IN LOVE. / I KNOW WHY THE SUN DON'T SHINE**
Sep 75. (lp) (<CHR 1088>) **THE ROCK**
– A fool in love / The heartbreak / The rock / I know why the Sun don't shine / Hand on the lever / Ain't got no money / All my love to you / I'm old enough / Bridgeton / Drunken nights in the city. (cd-iss. Oct98 on 'Repertoire'; REP 4726)
Jul 76. (7") (CHS 2095) **THE ROCK. / THE HEARTBREAK**
Oct 76. (7") (CHS 2103) **LOVING YOU IS SWEETER THAN EVER. / I'M OLD ENOUGH**
May 77. (7") (CHS 2147) **BE GOOD TO YOURSELF. /**   27

FRANKIE MILLER'S FULL HOUSE

—— with **RAY MINHINNIT** – guitar / **JAMES HALL** – keyboards / **CHARLIE HARRISON** – bass / **GRAHAM DEACON** – drums

Jun 77. (lp/c) (<CHR/ZCHR 1128>) **FULL HOUSE**
– Be good to yourself / The doodle song / Jealous guy / Searching / Love letters / Take good care of yourself / Down the Honky Tonk / The love of mine / Let the candlelight shine / (I'll never) Live in vain. (cd-iss. Feb99 on 'Repertoire'; REP 4728)
Jun 77. (7") <CHS 2145> **THE DOODLE SONG. / (I'LL NEVER) LIVE IN VAIN**   -   71
Aug 77. (7") (CHS 2166) **LOVE LETTERS. / LET THE CANDLELIGHT SHINE**
Nov 77. (7"ep) (CHS 2184) **ALVERIC'S ELFLAND JOURNEY EP**
– Jealous guy / A fool in love / Brickyard blues / Sail away.

—— went solo again, augmented by **PAUL CARRACK** – keyboards / **RAY RUSSELL** – guitar / **MARTIN DROVER** – trumpet / **CHRIS MERCER** – saxophone / **B.J. WILSON** – drums

Apr 78. (lp) (<CHR 1174>) **DOUBLE TROUBLE**
– Have you seen me lately Joan / Double heart trouble / The train / You'll be in my mind / Good time love / Love waves / (I can't) Breakaway / Stubborn kind of fellow / Love is all around / Goodnight sweetheart. (cd-iss. Feb99 on 'Repertoire'; REP 4727)
Jun 78. (7"colrd) (CHS 2221) **STUBBORN KIND OF FELLOW. / GOOD TIME LOVE**

FRANKIE MILLER

—— FRANKIE only retained **CARRACK**, and brought in **CHRIS HALL** – keyboards / **TIM RENWICK** + **STEVE SIMPSON** + **TERRY BRITTON** – guitar / **RON ASPERY** – horns / **TEX COMER** + **DAVE WINTOUR** – bass / **CHRIS SLADE** + **FRAN BYRNE** – drums

Oct 78. (7") (CHS 2255) **DARLIN'. / DRUNKEN NIGHTS IN THE CITY**   6
Jan 79. (7") (CHS 2276) **WHEN I'M AWAY FROM YOU. / AIN'T GOT NO MONEY**   42
Jan 79. (lp) (CHR 1220) **FALLING IN LOVE ... PERFECT FIT**
– When I'm away from you / Is this love / If I can love somebody / Darlin' / And it's your love / A woman to love / Falling in love with you / Everytime a teardrop falls / Pappa don't know / Good to see you. (cd-iss. Feb99 on 'Repertoire'; REP 4729)
Apr 79. (7") (CHS 2299) **GOOD TO SEE YOU. / COLD AND RAINY NIGHT**

—— his backing band were now **REGGIE YOUNG** + **BOBBY THOMPSON** – guitar / **JOE OSBOURNE** – bass / **LARRY LONDIN** – drums

Jun 80. (7") (CHS 2436) **SO YOUNG, SO YOUNG. / TEARS**
Jul 80. (lp) (<CHR 1268>) **EASY MONEY**
– Easy money / The woman in you / Why don't you spend the night / So young so young / Forget about me / Heartbreak radio / Cheap ...thrills / No chance / Gimme love / Tears. (cd-iss. Jun99 on 'Repertoire'; REP 4731)
Jul 80. (7") (CHS CHS 2448) **WHY DON'T YOU SPEND THE NIGHT. / HEARTBREAK RADIO**

—— now with **BARRY BECKETT** – keyboards, producer / **DAVID HOOD** – bass / **ROGER HAWKINS** – drums / **CHRIS SPEDDING** – guitar

Capitol Capitol

Jun 82. (7") (CL 253) <5131> **TO DREAM THE DREAM. / DON'T STOP**   62
Jun 82. (lp/c) (<EST/TC-EST 12206>) **STANDING ON THE EDGE**
– Danger danger / Standing on the edge / Zap zap / To dream the dream / Don't stop / Angels with dirty faces / Firin' line / Jealousy / It's all coming down tonight / On my way.
Aug 82. (7") (CL 259) **ANGELS WITH DIRTY FACES. / JEALOUSY**
Sep 82. (7") **DANGER DANGER. / ON MY WAY**   -

—— brought in **BRIAN ROBERTSON** – lead guitar / **CHRISSIE STEWART** – bass / **SIMON KIRKE** – drums (ex-BAD COMPANY)

Vertigo not iss.

Mar 86. (7") (VER 25) **I'D LIE TO YOU FOR LOVE. / DANCING IN THE RAIN**
(12"+=) (VERX 25) – Do it till we drop.
Apr 86. (lp/c)(cd) (VERH/+C 34)(826647-2) **DANCING IN THE RAIN**
– I'd lie to you for love / Do it till we drop / That's how long my love is / How many tears can you hide / Dancing in the rain / Shakey ground / The boys and girls are doing it / Game of love / Gladly go blind / You're a puzzle I can't put down.

—— FRANKIE concentrated more on acting in the mid 80's

M.C.S. not iss.

Mar 92. (7"/c-s/cd-s) (MCS 2001/+C/CD) **CALEDONIA. / I'LL NEVER BE THAT YOUNG AGAIN**   45

—— In the past year (from August 1994) FRANKIE has suffered serious ill health due to a brain aneurysm

– compilations, etc. –

Feb 87. (7") Old Gold; (OG 9688) **DARLIN'. / BE GOOD TO YOURSELF**
Mar 94. (cd/c) Chrysalis; (CD/TC 1981) **THE VERY BEST OF FRANKIE MILLER**
– Darlin' When I'm away from you / Be good to yourself / I can't change it / High life / Brickyard blues / A fool in love / Have you seen me lately Joan / Love letters / Caledonia / Stubborn kind of fellow / Devil gun / Hard on the levee / Tears / I'm ready / Shoo-rah shoo-rah / Double heart trouble / So young, so young.
Apr 94. (cd) Windsong; (WINDCD 54) **BBC RADIO 1 LIVE IN CONCERT (live)**
Mar 96. (cd) Disky; (DC 86432-2) **LOVE LETTERS**

Steve MILLER

Born: 5 Oct'43, Milwaukee, Wisconsin, USA; raised in Dallas, Texas. After forming school band, The MARKSMAN COMBO, with BOZ SCAGGS, he later played for bluesman JIMMY REED at a 1957 gig. In the early 60's, he and SCAGGS joined The ARDELLS, who, along with BEN SIDRAN, became The FABULOUS NIGHT TRAIN. In 1964, after a brief spell in Denmark, he moved to Chicago, where he sessioned for MUDDY WATERS, HOWLIN' WOLF and PAUL BUTTERFIELD. The following year, he partnered BARRY GOLDBERG in the group, The WORLD WAR III BAND, who issued a one-off 45, 'THE MOTHER SONG' (Epic 9865) as The GOLDBERG-MILLER BAND. Late in '66, he moved to San Francisco and formed The MILLER BAND with JAMES 'Curly' COOKE, LONNIE TURNER and TIM DAVIS, later adding JIM PETERMAN, and replacing COOKE with SCAGGS. After a June appearance at The Monterey Pop Festival, they signed to 'Capitol', recording three songs for the 'Revolution' film soundtrack, which eventually hit the shops late in '69. Their debut album, 'CHILDREN OF THE FUTURE', was issued in the Spring of '68, making all of No.134 in the US charts. Its mild success was overshadowed by the follow-up, 'SAILOR', which introduced his trademark 'GANGSTER OF LOVE' motif. The album gave them their first of many entries into the US Top 30, although with each successive release, they moved further away from the neo-psychedelic experimentation which had characterised their earlier releases. In 1973, after a lean couple of years, they hit US No.1 with 'THE JOKER', a song that lyrically revived his "Gangster Of Love". Although it was regarded as a classic in the UK, it still failed to chart (that is, until 1990, when it topped the charts after being given fresh exposure on a Levi jeans TV ad). The single was the title track of the album, which became his biggest selling album to date, hitting US No.2 and staying in the chart for nine months. After a prolonged break, MILLER returned with his most accessible and commercial album to date, 1976's 'FLY LIKE AN EAGLE'. The record showcased a more straightforward approach with finely crafted songs and strong hooks, spawning a slew of hit singles that even reached the UK Top 20. Its title track was a return to the laid-back psychedelia MILLER had flirted with back in the 60's (more recently it was a hit for SEAL). The next effort, 'BOOK OF DREAMS', was almost as big; No.2 stateside and No.12 in Britain. Following another hiatus, the band released 'CIRCLE OF LOVE' (1981), a collection of radio-friendly rockers that stuck more or less to MILLER's proven formula. The title track of the band's 1982 album, 'ABRACADABRA' was a worldwide smash, its quirky jack-in-the-box feel making it a quintessential 80's record, although the album sounded somewhat laboured. After a live album and a disappointing couple of studio sets, MILLER went solo in 1988, going back to his roots on 'BORN 2 B BLUE' and releasing a further solo album in 1993, 'WIDE RIVER'. • **Songwriters:** MILLER and BEN SIDRAN compositions, except covers on 87 & 88 albums. • **Trivia:** On '69 song 'MY DARK HOUR', PAUL McCARTNEY played bass under pseudonym MARK RAMON.

Album rating: CHILDREN OF THE FUTURE (*7) / SAILOR (*7) / BRAVE NEW WORLD (*7) / YOUR SAVING GRACE (*6) / NUMBER FIVE (*6) / LIVING IN THE U.S.A. (*7) / ROCK LOVE (*3) / RECALL THE BEGINNING ... (*5) / ANTHOLOGY:

THE BEST OF STEVE MILLER BAND 1968-1973 compilation (*8) / THE JOKER (*6) / FLY LIKE AN EAGLE (*8) / BOOK OF DREAMS (*6) / GREATEST HITS 1974-1978 compilation (*7) / CIRCLE OF LOVE (*6) / ABRACADABRA (*6) / STEVE MILLER BAND – LIVE! (*4) / ITALIAN X-RAYS (*4) / LIVING IN THE 21st CENTURY (*4) / BORN 2B BLUE (*5) / WIDE RIVER (*4)

STEVE MILLER BAND

STEVE MILLER – vocals, guitar / **LONNIE TURNER** (b.24 Feb'47, Berkeley, Calif.) – bass, vocals / **BOZ SCAGGS** (b. 8 Jun'44, Ohio) – guitar / **JIM PETERMAN** – organ, vocals / **TIM DAVIS** – drums

Apr 68. (7") *(CL 15539)* <2156> **SITTIN' IN CIRCLES. / ROLL WITH IT**

Sep 68. (lp; stereo/mono) *(S+T 2920)* <718> **CHILDREN OF THE FUTURE** — Apr68
– Children of the future / Pushed me to it / You've got the power / In my first mind / The beauty of time is that it's snowing / Baby's callin' me home / Steppin' stone / Roll with it / Junior saw it happen / Fanny Mae / Key to the highway. <re-iss. 1980; SN 16262> (cd-iss. Apr97 on 'E.M.I.'; REPLAYCD 19)

Oct 68. (7") *(CL 15564)* <2287> **LIVING IN THE U.S.A. / QUICKSILVER GIRL** — 94

Jan 69. (lp; stereo/mono) *(S+T 2984)* <719> **SAILOR** — 24 Oct68
– Song for our ancestors / Dear Mary / My friend / Living in the U.S.A. / Quicksilver girls / Lucky man / Gangster of love / You're so fine / Overdrive / Dime-a-dance romance. <re-iss. Nov83 on 'Fame' lp/c; FA41/TCFA 3085-1/4> (re-iss. Apr91 cd/c/lp; CD/TC+/FA 3254) (cd re-iss. Apr97 on 'E.M.I.'; REPLAYCD 17)

Jan 69. (7") <2447> **DEAR MARY. / SITTIN' IN CIRCLES** –

—— Trimmed to a trio of **MILLER, TURNER** and **DAVIS** with session men. (PETERMAN left just after SCAGGS who went solo) **BEN SIDRAN** – keyboards (joined briefly)

(Mar69) **NICKY HOPKINS** – keyboards (ex-JEFF BECK GROUP) repl. SIDRAN

Sep 69. (lp) <(E-ST 184)> **BRAVE NEW WORLD** — 22 Jun69
– Brave new world / Space cowboy / Got love 'cause you need it / It's a midnight dream / Can't you hear daddy's heartbeat / Celebration song / Seasons / Kow kow calculator / My dark hour. (re-iss. Feb84 on 'E.M.I.'; IC 038 80117) (cd-iss. Apr97 on 'E.M.I.'; REPLAYCD 20)

Jul 69. (7") *(CL 15604)* <2520> **MY DARK HOUR. / SONG FOR OUR ANCESTORS**

Nov 69. (7") *(CL 15618)* <2638> **LITTLE GIRL. / DON'T LET NOBODY TURN YOU AROUND**

Mar 70. (lp) <(E-ST 331)> **YOUR SAVING GRACE** — 38 Nov69
– Little girl / Just a passin' fancy in a midnite dream / Don't let nobody turn you around / Baby's house / Motherless children / The last wombat in Mecca / Feel so glad / Your saving grace. (cd-iss. May91 on 'E.M.I.'; CZ 434) (cd re-iss. Apr97 on 'E.M.I.'; REPLAYCD 21)

—— **BOBBY WINKLEMAN** – bass, vocals repl. TURNER and HOPKINS who joined QUICKSILVER MESSENGER SERVICE

Nov 70. (lp) <(EA-ST 436)> **NUMBER 5** — 23 Jul70
– Good morning / I love you / Going to the country / Hot chili / Tokin's / Going to Mexico / Steve Miller's midnight tango / Industrial military complex hex / Jackson-Kent blues / Never kill another man. (cd-iss. Apr97 on 'E.M.I.'; REPLAYCD 18)

Sep 70. (7") *(CL 15665)* <2878> **GOING TO THE COUNTRY. / NEVER KILL ANOTHER MAN** — 69 Aug70

Dec 70. (7") <2945> **GOING TO MEXICO. / STEVE MILLER'S MIDNIGHT TANGO** –

—— **STEVE MILLER** recruited entire new band **ROSS VALORY** – bass, vocals repl. WINKLEMAN / **JACK KING** – drums, vocals repl. DAVIS who went solo

Sep 71. (7") <3228> **ROCK LOVE. / LET ME SERVE YOU**

Nov 71. (lp) <(EA-ST 748)> **ROCK LOVE** — Oct71
– The gangster is back / Blues without blame / Love shock / Let me serve you / Rock love / Harbor lights / Deliverance.

—— **GERALD JOHNSON** – bass, vocals repl. VALORY who later joined JOURNEY / added **DICKY THOMPSON** – keyboards / **ROGER ALAN CLARK** – 2nd drummer

May 72. (lp) <(EST 11022)> **RECALL THE BEGINNING . . . A JOURNEY FROM EDEN** — Mar72
– Welcome / Enter Maurice / High on you mama / Heal your heart / The sun is going down / Somebody somewhere help me / Love's riddle / Fandango / Nothing lasts / Journey from Eden. (re-iss. Feb84 on 'E.M.I.'; IC 062 81099)

May 72. (7") <3344> **FANDANGO. / LOVE'S RIDDLE** –

—— (Mar72) **JOHN KING** – drums repl. JACK and ROGER / **LONNIE TURNER** – bass, vocals returned to repl. JOHNSON who joined BOZ SCAGGS

Oct 73. (7") *(CL 15765)* <3732> **THE JOKER. / SOMETHING TO BELIEVE IN** — 1

Oct 73. (lp) <(EST 11235)> **THE JOKER** — 2
– Sugar babe / Mary Lou / Loving cup / Shu ba da du ma ma / Your cash ain't nothin' but trash / The joker / Lovin' cup / Come on into my kitchen / Evil / Something to believe in. (re-iss. Oct80; same) (re-iss. Jan83 on 'E.M.I.'; IC 062 81514) (re-iss. Oct90 on 'Fame' cd/c/lp; CD/TC+/FA 3250)

Feb 74. (7") <3837> **YOUR CASH AIN'T NOTHIN' BUT TRASH. / EVIL** – 51

—— (May74) **STEVE MILLER** retired for a while, when THOMPSON and KING departed.

—— (Jul75) **MILLER** retained **TURNER** and recruited for Knebworth festival **LES DUDEK** – guitar, vocals / **DOUG CLIFFORD** – drums (ex-CREEDENCE CLEARWATER REVIVAL)

—— (1976) **GARY MALLABER** (b.11 Oct'46, Buffalo, N.Y.) – drums repl. CLIFFORD and DUDEK

	Mercury	Capitol
May 76. (7") *(6078 800)* <4260> **TAKE THE MONEY AND RUN. / SWEET MARIE**		11 Apr76
May 76. (lp)(c) *(9286 177)(7100 925)* <11497> **FLY LIKE AN EAGLE**	11	3

– (Space intro) / Fly like an eagle / Wild mountain honey / Serenade / Dance, dance, dance / Mercury blues / Take the money and run / Rock'n'me / You send me / Blue odyssey / Sweet Marie / The window. (re-iss. Nov84 lp/c; PRICE/PRIMC 75) (re-iss. Jun92 on 'Arcade' cd/c; ARC 94710-2/4)

Aug 76. (7") <4323> **ROCK'N'ME. / LIVING IN THE U.S.A.** — 1

Aug 76. (7") *(6078 802)* **FLY LIKE AN EAGLE. / MERCURY BLUES**

Oct 76. (7") *(6078 804)* **ROCK'N'ME. / THE WINDOW** — 11 –

Dec 76. (7") <4372> **FLY LIKE AN EAGLE. / LOVIN' CUP** — – 2

Jan 77. (7") *(6078 808)* **SERENADE. / DANCE, DANCE, DANCE** — –

—— (Oct76) added **DAVID DENNY** – guitar, vocals (ex-TERRY & THE PIRATES) / **BYRON ALLRED** – keyboards / **NORTON BUFFALO** – harmonica, vocals

Apr 77. (7") *(6078 811)* <4424> **JET AIRLINER. / BABES IN THE WOOD** — 8

May 77. (lp)(c) *(9286 455)(7299 393)* <11630> **BOOK OF DREAMS** — 12 2
– Threshold / Jet airliner / Winter time / Swingtown / True fine love / Wish upon a star / Jungle love / Electro lux imbroglio / Sacrifice / The stake / My own space / Babes in the wood. (re-iss. Jan85 lp/c; PRICE/PRIMC 78) (re-iss. Jun92 on 'Arcade' cd/c; ARC 94730-2/4)

Sep 77. (7") *(6078 812)* <4466> **JUNGLE LOVE. / WISH UPON A STAR** — 23 Jul77

Jan 78. (7") *(6078 813)* <4496> **SWINGTOWN. / WINTER TIME** — 17 Oct77

—— trimmed to a quintet of **MILLER, MALLABER, ALLRED, DOUGLAS** and **BUFFALO**

Oct 81. (lp/c) *(6302/7144 061)* <ST 12121> **CIRCLE OF LOVE** — 26
– Heart like a wheel / Get on home / Baby wanna dance / Circle of love / Macho city. (re-iss. Jun92 on 'Arcade' cd/c; ARC 94730-2/4)

Oct 81. (7") <5068> **HEART LIKE A WHEEL. / TRUE FINE LOVE** — – 24

Nov 81. (7"m) *(STEVE 1)* **HEART LIKE A WHEEL. / JET AIRLINER / THRESHOLD** — –

Jan 82. (7") <5086> **CIRCLE OF LOVE. / (part 2)** — – 55

Feb 82. (7") *(STEVE 2)* **MACHO CITY. / FLY LIKE AN EAGLE** —

—— **KENNY LEWIS** – guitar / **JOHN MASSARO** – guitar both repl. DOUGLAS

May 82. (7") *(STEVE 3)* **ABRACADABRA. / GIVE IT UP** — – 1

Jun 82. (7") *(STEVE 3)* **ABRACADABRA. / NEVER SAY NO** — 2 –
(re-iss. Oct84;)

Jun 82. (lp/c) *(6302/7144 204)* <ST 12216> **ABRACADABRA** — 10 3
– Keeps me wondering why / Abracadabra / Something special / Give it up / Never say no / Things I told you / Young girl's heart / Goodbye love / Cool magic / While I'm waiting. (cd-iss. Jan83; 800090-2) (re-iss. Jun92 on 'Arcade' cd/c; ARC 94740-2/4)

Aug 82. (7") *(STEVE 4)* **KEEPS ME WONDERING WHY. / GET ON HOME** — 52
(12"+=) *(STEVE 4-12)* – Abracadabra.

Oct 82. (7") *(STEVE 5)* **GIVE IT UP. / ROCK'N'ME** — –

Oct 82. (7") <5162> **COOL MAGIC. / YOUNG GIRL'S HEART** — – 57

Dec 82. (7") <5194> **GIVE IT UP. / HEART LIKE A WHEEL** — – 60

Mar 83. (7") <5223> **LIVING IN THE U.S.A. (live). / BUFFALO SERENADE** — –

Apr 83. (lp/c)(cd) *(MERL/+C 18)(811020-2)* <12263> **THE STEVE MILLER BAND LIVE! (live)** — 79
– Gangster of love / Rock'n'me / Living in the U.S.A. / Fly like an eagle / Jungle love / The joker / Mercury blues / Take the money and run / Abracadabra / Jet airliner. (cd+=) – Buffalo serenade.

Apr 83. (7") *(STEVE 6)* **TAKE THE MONEY AND RUN (live). / THE JOKER (live)** — –
(12"+=) *(STEVE 6-12)* – Buffalo serenade (live).

—— Now without MASSARO

Oct 84. (7") *(STEVE 7)* <5407> **SHANGRI-LA. / CIRCLE OF LOVE** — 57
(12"+=) *(STEVE 7-12)* – Abracadabra.

Nov 84. (lp/c)(cd) *(MERL/+C 50)(822823-2)* <12339> **ITALIAN X-RAYS** —
– Radio 1 / Italian x-rays / Daybreak / Shangri-la / Who do you love / Harmony of the spheres 1 / Radio 2 / Bongo bongo / Out of the night / Golden opportunity / The Hollywood dream / One in a million / Harmony of the spheres 2. (re-iss. Jun92 on 'Arcade' cd/c; ARC 94750-2/4)

Jan 85. (7") *(STEVE 8)* <5442> **BONGO BONGO. / GET ON HOME** — 84

Mar 85. (7") <5476> **ITALIAN X-RAYS. / WHO DO YOU LOVE** —

—— **MILLER** with **MALLABER** and **BUFFALO** bring back **LES DUDEK** – guitar

	Capitol	Capitol
Jan 87. (lp/c)(cd) *(EST/TC-EST 2027)(CDP 746326-2)* **LIVING IN THE 20TH CENTURY**		65 Nov86

– Nobody but you baby / I want to make the world turn around / Slinky / Living in the 20th century / Maelstrom / I wanna be loved / My babe / Big boss man / Caress me baby / Ain't that lovin' you baby / Behind the barn.

Mar 87. (7"/12") *(CL/12CL 444)* <5646> **I WANT TO MAKE THE WORLD TURN AROUND. / SLINKY** — 97 Nov86

Apr 87. (7") <5671> **NOBODY BUT YOU BABY. / MAELSTROM** — –

Jun 87. (7") <5704> **I WANNA BE LOVED. / (part 2)** — –

STEVE MILLER

solo with **BEN SIDRAN** – keyboards / **BILLY PATERSON** – bass / **GORDY KNUDTSON** – drums

Sep 88. (7") *(CL 506)* **YA YA. / FILTHY McNASTY**
(12"+=) *(12CL 506)* – ('A'remix by Steve Weiss).

Sep 88. (cd/c/lp) *(CD/TC+/EST 2072)* <48303> **BORN 2B BLUE**
– Zip-a-dee-doo-dah / Ya ya / God bless the child / Filthy McNasty / Born to be blue / Mary Ann / Just a little bit / When Sunny gets blue / Willow weep for me / Red top.

	Polydor	Sailor
Jul 93. (cd/c) *(519441-2/-4)* **WIDE RIVER**		85

– Wide river / Midnight train / Blue eyes / Lost in your eyes / Perfect world / Horse and rider / Circle of fire / Conversation / Cry cry cyr / Stranger blues / Walks like a lady / All your love (I miss loving).

Jul 93. (c-s/cd-s) <85919-4/-2> **WIDE RIVER / STRANGER BLUES** — 64

– compilations, etc. –

on 'Capitol' unless mentioned otherwise

Feb 72. (7"ep) *(33RPM 7)* **MY DARK HOUR. / SONG FOR OUR ANCESTORS / THE GANGSTER IS BACK** — –

Mar 73. (d-lp) *(ESTSP 12)* <11114> **ANTHOLOGY** — 56 Nov72

1973. (d-lp) *(STBB 717)* **CHILDREN OF THE FUTURE / LIVING IN THE U.S.A.**

Jun 74. (7") *(CL 15786)* <3884> **LIVING IN THE U.S.A. / KOW KOW CALCULATOR** — 49 May74

Oct 75. (lp) *(VMP 1008)* **THE LEGEND**

Mar 77. (lp) *(EST 24058)* **THE BEST OF THE STEVE MILLER BAND 1968-73**   ☐ ☐
– Living in the U.S.A. / I love you / Don't let nobody turn you around / Seasons / Shu ba da du ma ma ma / Kow kow calculator / The joker / Going to the country / My dark hour / Your saving grace / Celebration song / Space cowboy. *(re-iss. May82 on 'Fame' lp/c; FA/TC-FA 3030)* *(re-iss. Aug86 on 'E.M.I.' lp/c; ATAK/TCATAK 86)* *(re-iss. Sep90; EST 2133)* (hit UK No.34)(cd+=) – (4 extra).

Oct 78. (7") *(6078 815)* **THE JOKER. / THE STAKE**   ☐ ☐

Nov 78. (lp)(c) *(9199 916)(7299 883)* <11822> **GREATEST HITS 1974-78**   ☐ 18
(cd-iss. Jan83; 800 058-2) *(re-iss. Aug85 on 'Mercury' lp/c; PRICE/PRIMC 86)*

Jan 83. (7") *(CL 258)* **THE JOKER. / MY DARK HOUR. / LIVING IN THE U.S.A.**   ☐ -

May 87. Mercury; (lp/c)(cd) *(MERH/+C 105)(830978-2)* **GREATEST HITS – A DECADE OF AMERICAN MUSIC (1976-1986)**   ☐

Aug 90. (7"/c-s) *(CL/TCCL 583)* **THE JOKER. / DON'T LET NOBODY TURN YOU AROUND**   1
(12"+=) *(12CL 583)* – Shu ba da du ma ma ma.
(cd-s+=) *(CDCL 583)* – Living in the U.S.A.

Oct 91. Arcade; (7"/cd-s) *(AR 91621-7/-2)* **SPACE INTRO. / FLY LIKE AN EAGLE**   ☐ -

Sep 98. (cd/c) Polygram TV; *(559240-2/-4)* **GREATEST HITS**   58 -

---

MILLTOWN BROTHERS (dig out; Great Alt & indie . . .)

Zodiac MINDWARP (dig out; Great Metal . . .)

MINISTRY

Formed: Chicago, Illinois, USA . . . 1981 by ex-SPECIAL EFFECT member AL JOURGENSEN. The latter bunch included FRANKIE NARDIELLO (who'd replaced TOM HOFFMAN), MARTY SORENSON and HARRY RUSHAKOFF, this synth-pop aggregation releasing a couple of 7" singles and a soundtrack album at the turn of the decade. Continuing in this vein, JOURGENSEN co-formed the 'Wax Trax' label and issued a debut MINISTRY 12" in 1982, 'COLD LIFE'. A further string of limp electro singles and a debut album, 'WITH SYMPATHY' (1983; European title 'WORK FOR LOVE') followed, before JOURGENSEN adopted a decidedly harder electronic sound on 'TWITCH' (1986). Around the same time, the MINISTRY mainman initiated a number of offshoot projects, the most high profile being The REVOLTING COCKS, who included in the ranks RICHARD 23, LUC VAN ACKER (the former later replaced by CHRIS CONELLY of FINI TRIBE). JOURGENSEN was said to have described this bunch as "Disco For Psychopaths", the 12", 'NO DEVOTION' and the long-player, 'BIG SEXY LAND' were aural proof. Another single, 'YOU OFTEN FORGET' (1987) was equally controversial, having already annoyed the PMRC (Parental Music Resource Center) with their overtly blasphemous debut. A live album, 'GODDAMNED SON OF A BITCH' was The REVOLTING COCKS next release in 1988, drummer BILL RIEFLIN now a steady part of both JOURGENSEN's groups. Meanwhile, MINISTRY had recruited bassist PAUL BARKER (and brother ROLAND BARKER), the outfit consolidated their harsher industrial approach with the viscious 1989 set, 'LAND OF RAPE AND HONEY'. To end the decade, MINISTRY unleashed yet another uncompromisingly bleak set of industrial grinding, 'THE MIND IS A TERRIBLE THING TO TASTE', while four months later, The REVOLTING COCKS offered some light relief with a decidedly unsympathetic version of Olivia Newton John's '(LET'S GET) PHYSICAL'. This was lifted from parent album, 'BEERS, STEERS AND QUEERS', the title track a brilliant must-hear send-up of backwoods American perversion. The REVOLTING COCKS gained even more notoriety when a proposed tour (which was to include onstage strippers and livestock) was the subject of an outraged House Of Commons discussion. Having briefly collaborated with JELLO BIAFRA (ex-DEAD KENNEDYS) on a project entitled LARD, JOURGENSEN released a one-off single under the 1000 HOMO DJ's banner, the main track being a cover of Black Sabbath's 'SUPERNAUT'. With the addition of guitarist MIKE SCACCIA and the unhinged guest vocals of GIBBY HAYNES (Butthole Surfers), MINISTRY recorded arguably their finest moment to date, 'JESUS BUILT MY HOTROD'. This was closely followed by MINISTRY's breakthrough Top 40 (on both sides of the Atlantic!) album, 'PSALM 69: THE WAY TO SUCCEED AND THE WAY TO SUCK EGGS', a highly regarded set which saw the group veering towards sonic metal. A Top 50 single, 'N.W.O.' followed a successful near headlining slot on the Lollapalooza 1992 tour, PAUL BARKER also moonlighting in yet another MINISTRY offshoot, LEAD INTO GOLD (releasing the 'AGE OF REASON' a follow-up to 1990's mini-cd 'CHICKS & SPEED'). A year later, The REVOLTING COCKS returned with their inimitably twisted brand of black humour, a version of Rod Stewart's 'DO YA THINK I'M SEXY' one of the highlights of their 1993 album, 'LINGER FICKEN' GOOD'. The two main MINISTRY men, AL JOURGENSEN and PAUL BARKER, replaced the departing RIEFLIN with RAY WASHAM and moved the operation to Texas (JOURGENSEN set up a country label). Late in 1995, after AL escaped a drugs bust, MINISTRY ventured even further into metal territory with the 'FILTH PIG' opus, a collection that contained a murderous version of Bob Dylan's 'LAY LADY LAY'. In 1999, AL, PAUL and the MINISTRY were growling once again at the music industry, 'DARK SIDE OF THE SPOON' (redneck punk, et AL); however the album failed to make its commercial impact – sadly, the release was around the same time as guitarist WILLIAM TUCKER committed suicide by slashing his throat.

Album rating: WORK FOR LOVE (aka WITH SYMPATHY) (*5) / TWITCH (*5) / LAND OF RAPE AND HONEY (*7) / THE MIND IS A TERRIBLE THING TO TASTE (*6) / IN CASE YOU DIDN'T FEEL LIKE SHOWING UP (*4) / PSALM 69: HOW TO SUCCEED AND HOW TO SUCK EGGS (*8) / FILTH PIG (*6) / DARK SIDE OF THE SPOON (*8) / Revolting Cocks: BIG SEXY LAND (*6) / YOU GODDAMNED SON OF A BITCH (*5) / BEERS, STEERS & QUEERS (*7) / LINGER FICKEN' GOOD . . . AND OTHER BARNYARD ODDITIES (*6)

SPECIAL EFFECT

AL JOURGENSEN (b. 9 Oct'58, Havana, Cuba) – guitar / **FRANKIE NARDIELLO** – vocals; repl. TOM HOFFMAN / **MARTY SORENSON** – bass / **HARRY RUSHAKOFF** – drums

		not iss.	Special Effect
1979.	(7"ep) <2955> **MOOD MUSIC EP** – I know a girl / Vertigo feeling / Innocense / Dress me dolls.	-	☐
1980.	(lp; soundtrack) <008028> **TOO MUCH SOFT LIVING**	-	☐

—— also flexidisc from 'Praxis' magazine; HEADACHE. / NUCLEAR GLOOM

		not iss.	Thermidor
Oct 81.	(7") <T 5> **EMPTY HANDED. / THE HEAT**	-	☐

MINISTRY

AL JOURGENSEN – guitar, keyboards, synthesizers, vocals / **LAMONT WELTON** – bass / **STEVO** – drums

		Situation 2	Wax Trax
Mar 82.	(12"m) *(SIT 17T)* <110072X> **COLD LIFE. / I'M FALLING / COLD LIFE (dub) / PRIMENTAL**	☐	☐

—— AL used musicians on next lp; **SHAY JONES** – vocals / **WALTER TURBETT** – guitar / **JOHN DAVIS** – keyboards / **ROBERT ROBERTS** – keyboards / **STEPHEN GEORGE** – drums / **MARTIN SORENSEN** – bass

		Arista	Arista
Feb 83.	(7"/12") *(ARIST/+12 510)* **WORK FOR LOVE. / FOR LOVE (instrumental)**	☐	-
Apr 83.	(7"/12") <9021> **REVENGE (YOU DID IT AGAIN). / SHE'S GOT A CAUSE**	-	☐
Jun 83.	(7") *(ARIST 533)* <9068> **I WANTED TO TELL HER. / A WALK IN THE PARK** (12"+=) *(ARIST12 533)* <9102> – ('A'-Tongue Tied mix).	☐	☐
Sep 83.	(lp/c) *(205/405 306)* <6608> **WORK FOR LOVE** <US title 'WITH SYMPATHY'> – Work for love / Do the Etawa / I wanted to tell her / Say you're sorry / Here we go / Effigy / Revenge / She's got a cause / Should have known better. *(cd-iss. 1989 as 'WITH SYMPATHY'+=; ARCD 8016)* *(cd-iss. Mar93 +=; 255 306)* – What He Say.	☐	96 Jun83
Nov 83.	(7") *(ARIST 549)* **REVENGE (YOU DID IT AGAIN). / EFFIGY** (12"+=) *(ARIST12 549)* – Work for love.	☐	-

—— now basically AL solo

		Wax Trax	Wax Trax
Oct 85.	(12") *(WAXUK 009)* **NATURE OF LOVE. / ('A'-Cruelty mix)**	☐	-

		Sire	Sire
Apr 86.	(lp/c) *(925309-1/-4)* <25309> **TWITCH** – Just like you / We believe / All day remix / The angel / Over the shoulder / My possession / Where you at now? / Crash and burn / Twitch (version II). *(cd+=)* – Over the shoulder (mix) / Isle Of Man.	☐	☐

—— added partner **PAUL BARKER** (b. 8 Feb'50, Palo Alto, Calif.) – bass, programming (ex-FRONT 242) + **WILLIAM RIEFLIN** (b.30 Sep'60, Seattle, Washington) – drums / **ROLAND BARKER** (b.30 Jun'57, Mountainview, Calif.) – keyboards

Jan 89.	(lp/c/cd) *(925799-1/-4/-2)* <25799> **THE LAND OF RAPE AND HONEY** – Stigmata / The missing / Deity / Golden dawn / Destruction / The land of rape and honey / You know what you are / Flashback / Abortive. *(cd+=)* – Hizbollah / I prefer. *(cd re-iss. Dec92; 7599 25799-2)*	☐	☐ Nov88
Feb 90.	(cd/c/lp) <(7599 26004-2/-4/-1)> **THE MIND IS A TERRIBLE THING TO TASTE** – Thieves / Burning inside / Never believe / Cannibal song / Breathe / So what / Test / Faith collapsing / Dream song. *(cd re-iss. Dec92)*	☐	☐ Dec89
Sep 90.	(cd/lp) <(7599 26266-2/-1)> **IN CASE YOU DIDN'T FEEL LIKE SHOWING UP (live)** – The missing / deity / So what / Burning inside / Seed / Stigmata. *(UK cd-iss. Dec92 on 'WEA'; same)*	-	-

—— next with guest **GIBBY HAYNES** (of BUTTHOLE SURFERS)

—— added **MIKE SCACCIA** (b.14 Jun'65, Babylon, N.Y.) – guitar

Apr 92.	(7") *(W 0096)* **JESUS BUILT MY HOTROD. / TV SONG** (12"+=/cd-s+=) *(W 0096 T/C)* – ('A'-Red line-white line version).	☐	☐
Jul 92.	(cd/c/10"lp) <(7599 26727-2/-4/-1)> **PSALM 69: HOW TO SUCCEED AND HOW TO SUCK EGGS** – N.W.O. / Just one fix / TV II / hero / Jesus built my hot rod / Scarecrow / Psalm 69 / Corrosion / Grace.	33	27
Jul 92.	(10") *(W 0125)* **N.W.O. / F***ED (non lp version)** (cd-s+=) *(W 0125CD)* – ('A'extended dance mix).	49	☐

—— JOURGENSEN + PAUL BARKER + SCACCIA recruited **RAY WASHAM** – drums (of JESUS LIZARD) / **DUANE BUFORD** – keyboards / **LOUIS SVITEK** – guitar (ex-MINDFUNK)

		W.E.A.	Warners
Dec 95.	(c-s) *(W 0328C)* **THE FALL / RELOAD** (cd-s+=) *(W 0328CD)* – TV III.	53	☐
Jan 96.	(cd/c/lp) <(92538 45838-2/-4/-1)> **FILTHPIG** – Reload / Filth pig / Crumbs / Useless / Lava / Dead guy / The face / Brick windows / Gane show / Lay lady lay / Reload (edit).	43	19
Feb 96.	(c-s) *(W 0338C)* **LAY LADY LAY / LAY LADY LAY (album version)** (cd-s+=) *(W 0338CD)* – Paisley / Scarecrow (live).	☐	☐

—— line-up JOURGENSEN, BARKER, RAY WASHUM + LOUIS SVITEK

Jun 99.	(cd/c) <(9362 47311-2/-4)> **DARK SIDE OF THE SPOON**	☐	92

– Supermanbiac soul / Whip or the chain / Bad blood / Eureka pie / Step / Nursing home / Kaif / Vex ans siolence / 10-10.

──── now without guitarist E. WILLIAM TUCKER who committed suicide by slashing his throat (after taking pills) on the 14th May, 1999 (aged 38)

– compilation, others, etc. –

1985.	(lp) *Hot Trax; (WAXC 35)* **12" INCH SINGLES 1981-1984**	-	

REVOLTING COCKS

AL's studio outfit, with FRONT 242 members; LUC and RICHARD 23. The latter was soon replaced CHRIS CONNELLY of FINI TRIBE.

		Wax Trax	Wax Trax
Feb 86.	(12"m) *(WAXUK 011)* **NO DEVOTION. / ATTACK SHIPS / ON FIRE**		
Nov 86.	(lp)(cd) *(WAXUK 017)(WAX 017CD)* **BIG SEXY LAND**		

– 38 / We shall cleanse the world / Attack ships on fire / Big sexy land / Union carbide (West Virginia version) / T.V. mind / No devotion / Union carbide (Bhopal version). *(re-iss. Mar92 on 'Devotion' cd/c/lp; CD/T+/DVN 6)*

Feb 87.	(12") *(WAXUK 022)* **YOU OFTEN FORGET. / ('A'version)**
	AL now with **BARKER, VAN ACKER, RIEFLIN + CONNELLY** – vocals
Jun 88.	(d-lp/cd) *(WAX UK/CD 22)* **LIVE! – YOU GODDAMNED SON OF A BITCH** (live + 2 studio)

– You Goddamned son of a bitch / Cattle grind / We shall cleanse the world / 38 / In the neck / You often forget / TV mind / Union carbide / Attack ships on fire / No devotion. *(re-iss. May92 on 'Devotion' cd/c/lp; CD/T+/DVN 8)*

Mar 89.	(12") <*WAX 042*> **STAINLESS STEEL PROVIDERS. / AT THE TOP**
	──── AL + PHIL were also part of JELLO BIAFRA's (Dead Kennedys) group LARD.
May 90.	(cd/c/lp) *(WAX 063 CD/MC/LP)* **BEERS, STEERS + QUEERS**

– Beers, steers + queers / (Let's get) Physical / In the neck / Get down / Stainless steel providers / Can't sit still / Something wonderful / Razor's edge. *(cd+=)* – (Let's talk) Physical. *(re-iss. Feb92 on 'Devotion' cd/c/lp; CD/T+/DVN 4)*

May 90.	(cd-s) *(WAX 086CD)* **(LET'S GET) PHYSICAL. / (LET'S TALK) PHYSICAL**
	──── now without RIEFLIN (on below only TRENT REZNOR of NINE INCH NAILS)

Apr 91.	(12"ep/cd-ep; 1000 HOMO DJ'S) <*WAX 032*> **SUPERNAUT / HEY ASSHOLE / APATHY / BETTER WAYS**			1987
		Devotion	Devotion

Sep 93.	(12"ep/cd-ep) *(12/CD DVN 111)* **DA YA THINK I'M SEXY? / SERGIO GUITAR / WRONG** (sexy mix)	61	
Sep 93.	(cd/c/d-lp) *(CD/T+/DVN 22)* **LINGER FICKEN' GOOD . . . AND OTHER BARNYARD ODDITIES**	39	

– Gila copter / Creep / Mr.Lucky / Crackin' up / Sergio / Da ya think I'm sexy? / The rockabye / Butcher flower's woman / Dirt / Linger ficken' good.

Jun 94.	(12"/cd-s) *(12/CD DVN 112)* **CRACKIN' UP. / ('A'-Amylnitrate mix) / GUACOPTER** (version 2)		-

PTP

AL, PAUL + WILL (SCORPIO + ALIEN DOG STAR + FRENCHIE L'AMOUR)

		Wax Trax	Wax Trax
1989.	(12) *(WAX 9073)* **RUBBER GLOVE SEDUCTION. / MY FAVOURITE THINGS**		

ACID HORSE

GALLOPIN' SCORPIO SADDLEBUTT + TENNESSEE KING BIFF + HAROLD SANDOZ + ALIEN DOG STAR

1989.	(12") *(WAX 9081)* **NO NAME NO SLOGAN. / ('A'-produced by CABARET VOLTAIRE)**

LEAD INTO GOLD

PAUL BARKER with AL JOURGENSEN + WILD BILL RIEFLIN

		not iss.	SPV
1990.	(m-cd) <*SPV 91942*> **CHICKS & SPEED**		

– Faster than light / The stripper / Beauty / Idiot / Blackened heart / Hatred.

──── added STUART BANG ZECHMAN – guitar

		Wax Trax	Wax Trax
Aug 90.	(lp/cd) <*(WAX 116/+CD)*> **AGE OF REASON**		

– Age of reason / Unreason / Snake oil / A giant on Earth / Faster than light / Lunatic – Genius / Sweet thirteen / Fell from Heaven. *(re-iss. Mar92 on 'Devotion' cd/c/lp; CD/T+/DVN 7)*

MINOR THREAT (see under ⇒ FUGAZI)

MINUTEMEN (dig out; Great Alt & Indie . . .)

MIRACLES

Formed: Detroit, Michigan, USA . . . 1957 as The MATADORS by 15-year old WILLIAM 'SMOKEY' ROBINSON together with school friends RONNIE WHITE, BOBBY ROGERS and his sister CLAUDETTE (whom SMOKEY married in late '59), PETE MOORE and MARVIN TARPLIN. Following a debut single, 'I LOVE YOU SO', on the 'Fury' label in 1958, the ROBINSON-penned 'GOT A JOB' (a response to The SILHOUETTES recent No.1 hit, 'Get A Job') caused a local stir, sold respectably and prompted BERRY GORDY Jnr. (whom the group had met a year earlier when auditioning for JACKIE WILSON's manager) to initiate the fledgling 'Motown'. The MATADORS' fourth single, 'BAD GIRL', was released on 'Chess' while GORDY distributed it locally and its minor chart success persuaded the budding mogul to expand his enterprise. In early '61, the newly renamed

MIRACLES furnished 'Tamla/Motown' with the first of countless massive hits, 'SHOP AROUND' (US No.2). Again the track had been penned by ROBINSON and he went on to write for many of the label's artists, providing them with many of their biggest hits. For his troubles he was made company vice-president, becoming GORDY's right-hand man during his lifelong tenure at the label (he even named his kids BERRY and TAMLA!). A towering talent – he was famously named 'America's greatest living poet' by none other than BOB DYLAN – with a creamy falsetto vocal and a headful of lovestruck metaphors, he led The MIRACLES on a chart crusade throughout the 60's. While he could throw down footstomping R&B (a la 'MICKEY'S MONKEY' and 'GOING TO A GO-GO' – US Top 10 and 20 respectively) with the best of them, his forte was the tortured ballad and they don't come much more deliciously painful than 'THE TRACKS OF MY TEARS', a US Top 20 hit in summer '65 hot on the heels of 'OOH BABY BABY'. While the chart positions never really reflected the greatness of these songs, the sheer volume of Top 40 hits (well in excess of 20) at least partly made up for it. Ironically, SMOKEY's works became bigger hits in the hands of other 'Motown' artists, MARY WELLS taking 'MY GUY' to the top of the charts in 1964. His most favoured act upon which to lavish his writing/production skills, however, were The TEMPTATIONS, who hit No.1 with 'MY GIRL' while MARVIN GAYE and The MARVELETTES also scored with SMOKEY material. Prior to The MIRACLES' biggest hit to date, 'I SECOND THAT EMOTION' (No.4 in late '67 and one of the few tracks to make the UK Top 30), ROBINSON's pivotal role was recognised by prefixing the group's name with his own. Success was patchier in the late 60's/early 70's as artists like STEVIE WONDER and MARVIN GAYE pushed for more creative control and The TEMPTATIONS went psychedelic under the aegis of Norman Whitfield. Nevertheless, SMOKEY ROBINSON & THE MIRACLES hit paydirt one last time in 1970 with the pop perfection of 'TEARS OF A CLOWN', a transatlantic No.1. Aged 30, SMOKEY left for a solo career in 1972 and WILLIAM GRIFFIN was brought in as a replacement. While never recreating the magic of the SMOKEY years, the MIRACLES continued fairly successfully right up until the mid-70's when they scored a massive transatlantic hit with 'LOVE MACHINE (part 1)'. A move to 'Columbia' proved less successful and following a final, eponymous album in 1978, they disbanded.

Best CD compilation: THE GREATEST HITS (*8)

SMOKEY ROBINSON (b. WILLIAM, 19 Feb'40) – lead vocals / **RONNIE WHITE** (b. 5 Apr'39) – vocals / **BOBBY ROGERS** (b.19 Feb'40) – vocals / **CLAUDETTE ROGERS** (b.1942) – vocals / **PETE MOORE** (b.19 Nov'39) – vocals / **MARVIN TARPLIN** – guitar, musical director

		not iss.	Fury
1958.	(7") <*1001*> **I LOVE YOU SO. / YOUR LOVE (IS ALL I NEED)**	-	
		not iss.	End
1958.	(7") <*1016*> **GOT A JOB. / MY MAMA DONE TOLD ME**	-	
1959.	(7") <*1084*> **I CRY. / MONEY**	-	
		not iss.	Chess
Sep 59.	(7") <*1734*> **BAD GIRL. / I LOVE YOU BABY**	-	93
Jan 60.	(7") <*1768*> **I NEED A CHANGE. / ALL I WANT**	-	
		London	Tamla
Mar 60.	(7"; by RON & BILL) **DON'T SAY BYE BYE. / IT** <*originally issued 1958 on 'Argo'*>		
Jun 60.	(7") <*74028*> **WAY OVER THERE. / DEPEND ON ME**	-	
Feb 61.	(7") *(HL 9276)* <*54034*> **SHOP AROUND. / WHO'S LOVIN' YOU**		2 Dec60
Feb 61.	(lp) *(PS 40044)* <*220*> **HI, WE'RE THE MIRACLES**		

– Who's lovin' you / Depend on me / Heart like mine / Shop around / Won't you take me back / 'Cause I love you / Your love / After all / Way over there / Money / Don't leave me. *(UK-iss Jul 63 on 'Oriole')*

Apr 61.	(7") *(HL 9366)* <*54036*> **AIN'T IT BABY. / THE ONLY ONE I LOVE**		49 Mar61
Jul 61.	(7") <*54044*> **MIGHTY GOOD LOVIN'. / BROKEN HEARTED**	-	51
Oct 61.	(7") <*54048*> **EVERYBODY'S GOTTA PAY SOME DUES. / I CAN'T BELIEVE**	-	52
Nov 61.	(lp) <*223*> **COOKIN' WITH THE MIRACLES**	-	

– Embraceable you / Everybody's gotta pay some dues / Mama / You never miss a good thing / That's the way I feel / Ain't it baby / Determination / Broken hearted / Only one I love / I can't believe.

		Fontana	Tamla
Mar 62.	(7") *(H 384)* <*54053*> **WHAT'S SO GOOD ABOUT GOODBYE. / I'VE BEEN SO GOOD TO YOU**		35 Dec61
May 62.	(7") <*54059*> **I'LL TRY SOMETHING NEW. / YOU NEVER MISS A GOOD THING**	-	39
Jun 62.	(lp) <*230*> **I'LL TRY SOMETHING NEW**	-	

– I'll try something new / Speak low / What's so good about goodbye / I've got you under my skin / On the street where you live / Love that can never be / If your mother only knew / I've been good to you / He don't care about me / This I swear, I promise.

Sep 62.	(7") <*54069*> **WAY OVER THERE. / IF YOUR MOTHER ONLY KNEW**	-	94
Dec 62.	(lp) <*236*> **CHRISTMAS WITH THE MIRACLES** (festive)	-	
		Oriole	Tamla
Jan 63.	(7") *(CBA 1794)* <*54073*> **YOU'VE REALLY GOT A HOLD ON ME. / HAPPY LANDING**		8 Nov62
Mar 63.	(7") <*54058*> **A LOVE SHE CAN COUNT ON. / I CAN TAKE A HINT**	-	31
Sep 63.	(7") *(CBA 1863)* <*54083*> **MICKEY'S MONKEY. / WHATEVER MAKES YOU HAPPY**		8 Jul63
Oct 63.	(lp; mono/stereo) *(TML/STML 10055)* <*241*> **THE MIRACLES ON STAGE** (live)		

– Mighty good lovin' / A love she can count on / Happy landing / I've been good to you / What's so good about goodbye / You've really got a hold on me / Way over there.

	Stateside	Tamla	

Dec 63. (lp) <245> **DOIN' MICKEY'S MONKEY**   —   ☐
– Mickey's monkey / Dance what you wanna / The Wah-Watusi / The twist / Dancin' holiday / Land of a 1000 dances / I gotta dance to keep from crying / The monkey time / The groovey thing / Twist and shout / Do you love me.

Feb 64. (7") (SS 263) <54089> **I GOTTA DANCE TO KEEP FROM CRYING. / SUCH IS LOVE, SUCH IS LIFE**   ☐   35 Nov63

Apr 64. (7") (SS 282) <54092> **(YOU CAN'T LET THE BOY OVERPOWER) THE MAN IN YOU. / HEARTBREAK ROAD**   ☐   59 Jan64

Aug 64. (7") (SS 324) <54098> **I LIKE IT LIKE THAT. / YOU'RE SO FINE AND SWEET**   ☐   27 Jun64

Nov 64. (lp) (SL 10099) <238> **THE FABULOUS MIRACLES**   ☐   Jun63
– The man in you / Such is love, such is life / I can take a hint / Heartbreak Road / Your love / He don't care about me / Speak low / I've been good to you / If your mother only knew / Won't you take me back / A love that can never be / On the street where you live.

Nov 64. (7") (SS 353) <54102> **THAT'S WHAT LOVE IS MADE OF. / WOULD I LOVE YOU**   ☐   35 Sep64

Jan 65. (7") (SS 377) <54109> **COME ON DO THE JERK. / BABY DON'T YOU GO**   ☐   50 Nov64

	Tamla Motown	Tamla	

Mar 65. (7") (TMG 503) <54113> **OOH BABY BABY. / ALL THAT'S GOOD**   ☐   16

Apr 65. (lp) (TML 11003) **I LIKE IT LIKE THAT**   ☐   Oct64

Jul 65. (7") (TMG 522) <54118> **THE TRACKS OF MY TEARS. / A FORK IN THE ROAD**   ☐   16 Jun65

Nov 65. (7") (TMG 540) <54123> **MY GIRL HAS GONE. / SINCE YOU WON MY HEART**   ☐   14 Sep65

Feb 66. (7") (TMG 547) <54127> **GOING TO A GO-GO. / CHOOSEY BEGGAR**   44   11 Dec65

Feb 66. (lp) (TML 11024) <267> **GOING TO A GO-GO**   ☐   8 Nov65
– The tracks of my tears / Going to a go-go / Ooh baby baby / My girl has gone / In case you need love / Choosey beggar / Since you won my heart / From head to toe / All that's good / My baby changes like the weather / Let me have some / A fork in the road.

Jul 66. (d-lp) (STML 11031) <254> **GREATEST HITS FROM THE BEGINNING** (compilation)   ☐   21 Apr65
– Get a job / I cry / Mama done told me / (I need some) Money / Bad girl / I love your baby / I need a change / All I want is you / (You can) Depend on me / Who's loving you / That's what love is made of / Mickey's monkey / I gotta dance to keep from crying / You've really got a hold on me / I like it like that / A love she can count on / Shop around / Way over there / I've been good to you / Would I love you / I'll try something new / What's so good about goodbye.

Jul 66. (7") (TMG 569) <54134> **WHOLE LOT OF SHAKIN' IN MY HEART (SINCE I MET YOU). / OH BE MY LOVE**   ☐   46 May66

Dec 66. (7") (TMG 584) <54140> **(COME ROUND HERE) I'M THE ONE YOU NEED. / SAVE ME**   45   17 Oct66

Feb 67. (lp; mono/stereo) (TML/STML 11044) **AWAY WE A GO-GO**   ☐   41 Dec66
– Whole lot of shakin' in my heart (since I met you) / You don't have to say you love me / Save me / (Come 'round here) I'm the one you need / Oh be my love / etc.

SMOKEY ROBINSON & THE MIRACLES

Feb 67. (7") <54145> **THE LOVE I SAW IN YOU WAS JUST A MIRAGE. / COME SPY WITH ME**   —   20

Mar 67. (7") (TMG 598) **THE LOVE I SAW IN YOU WAS JUST A MIRAGE. / SWEPT FOR YOU BABY**   ☐   —

Jun 67. (7") (TMG 614) <54152> **MORE LOVE. / SWEPT FOR YOU BABY**   —   23

Jul 67. (7") (TMG 614) **MORE LOVE. / COME SPY WITH ME**   ☐   —

Nov 67. (7") (TMG 631) <54159> **I SECOND THAT EMOTION. / YOU MUST BE LOVE**   27   4 Oct67

Feb 68. (lp; mono/stereo) (TML/STML 11067) <276> **MAKE IT HAPPEN**   28 Oct67
– Soulful shack / Love I saw in you was just a mirage / My love for you / I'm on the outside looking in / Don't think it's me / My love is your love (forever) / More love / After you put back the pieces / It's a good feeling / You must be love / Dancing's alright / Tears of a clown. <US re-iss. Dec70 as 'TEARS OF A CLOWN'; 276>

Mar 68. (7") (TMG 648) <54162> **IF YOU CAN WANT. / WHEN THE WORDS FROM YOUR HEART GET CAUGHT UP IN YOUR THROAT**   50   11 Feb68

Jun 68. (lp; mono/stereo) (TML/STML 11233) <280> **GREATEST HITS, VOL.2** (compilation)   7 Feb68
– Going to a go go / The tracks of my tears / I second that emotion / Ooo baby baby / My girl has gone / Come on do the jerk / Whole lot of shakin' in my heart (since I met you) / The love I saw in you was just a mirage / (Come 'round here) I'm the one you need / More love / Choosey beggar / Save me. (re-iss. Jul73)

Jun 68. (7") (TMG 661) <54167> **YESTER LOVE. / MUCH BETTER OFF**   31 May68

Oct 68. (7") (TMG 673) <54172> **SPECIAL OCCASION. / GIVE HER UP**   26 Aug68

Jan 69. (lp; mono/stereo) (TML/STML 11089) <290> **SPECIAL OCCASION**   42 Oct68
– Yester love / If you can wait / Special occasion / Everybody needs love / Just losing you / Give her up / I heard it through the grapevine / Yesterday / Your mother's only daughter / Much better off / You only build me up to tear me down.

Feb 69. (7") (TMG 687) <54178> **BABY, BABY DON'T CRY. / YOUR MOTHER'S ONLY DAUGHTER**   8 Jan69

Apr 69. (7") (TMG 696) **THE TRACKS OF MY TEARS. / COME ON DO THE JERK**   9   —

May 69. (lp; mono/stereo) (TML/STML 11107) <289> **LIVE!** (live)   71 Feb69
– Once in a lifetime / You and the night and the music / I second that emotion / The tracks of my tears / Poinciana / Up, up and away / Theme from 'Valley of the Dolls' / Yester love / Walk on by / Yesterday / If you can wait / Mickey's monkey / Ooh baby baby / Going to a go-go.

Jul 69. (7") <54183> **DOGGONE RIGHT. / HERE I GO AGAIN**   —   33
37

Jul 69. (7") <54184> **ABRAHAM, MARTIN AND JOHN. / MUCH BETTER OFF**   —   33

Dec 69. (7") <54189> **POINT IT OUT. / DARLING DEAR**   —   37
100

Feb 70. (lp; mono/stereo) (TML/STML 11129) <295> **TIME OUT FOR SMOKEY ROBINSON AND THE MIRACLES**   25 Aug69

Feb 70. (7") <54194> **WHO'S GONNA TAKE THE BLAME. / I GOTTA THING FOR YOU**   —

Jul 70. (lp) (STML 11151) <297> **FOUR IN BLUE**   78 Dec69
– You send me (with your good lovin') / Dreams, dreams / Tomorrow is another day / Hey Jude / California soul / A legend in his own time / You've lost that lovin' feelin' / We can make it if we can / When nobody cares / Don't say you love me / Wish I knew / My world is empty without you.

May 70. (lp) <301> **WHAT LOVE HAS JOINED TOGETHER**   —   97
– What love has joined together / My cherie amour / If this world were mine / You've made me so very happy / This guy's in love with you / And I love her.

Jul 70. (7") (TMG 745) **THE TEARS OF A CLOWN. / YOU MUST BE LOVE**   1   —

Oct 70. (7") <54199> **THE TEARS OF A CLOWN. / PROMISE ME**   —   1

Oct 70. (lp) (STML 11172) <306> **A POCKETFUL OF MIRACLES**   —   46
56

Jan 71. (7") (TMG 761) **(COME ROUND HERE) I'M THE ONE YOU NEED. / WE CAN MAKE IT, WE CAN**   13   —

Feb 71. (lp) (STML 11172) **SMOKEY ROBINSON & THE MIRACLES**   ☐

May 71. (7") (TMG 774) <54205> **I DON'T BLAME YOU AT ALL. / THAT GIRL**   11   18 Mar71

Jun 71. (7") <54206> **CRAZY 'BOUT THE LA LA LA. / OH BABY BABY I LOVE YOU**   —   56

Sep 71. (lp) <312> **ONE DOZEN ROSES**   —   92

Nov 71. (7") <54211> **SATISFACTION. / FLOWER GIRL**   —   49

Apr 72. (7") (TMG 811) **CRAZY 'BOUT THE LA LA LA. / MY GIRL HAS GONE**   —

Jun 72. (7") <54220> **WE'VE COME TOO FAR TO END IT NOW. / WHEN SUNDOWN COMES**   —   46

Jul 72. (lp) <318> **FLYING HIGH TOGETHER**   —   46
– I can't stand to see you cry / Love story / We've come too far to end it now / Flying high together / With you love came / It will be alright / Oh girl / You ain't livin' you're lovin' / We had a love so strong / Got to be there / Betcha by golly wow.

Dec 72. (7") <54225> **I CAN'T STAND TO SEE YOU CRY. / WITH YOUR LOVE CAME**   —   45

—— In Jul'72, SMOKEY ROBINSON had already left to concentrate on his solo career while The MIRACLES also continued on 'Tamla' until 1978

The MIRACLES

—— replaced him with **WILLIAM GRIFFIN** – vocals

	Tamla Motown	Tamla	

Jul 73. (7") <54237> **DON'T LET IT END ('TIL YOU LET IT BEGIN). / WIGS AND LASHES**   —   56

Oct 73. (lp) (STMA 8010) <325> **RENAISSANCE**   ☐   May73
– What is a heart good for / If you're ever in the neighbourhood / I wanna be with you / Wigs and lashes / Don't let it end (til you let it begin) / I love you secretly / I don't need no reason / Nowhere to go / I didn't realise the show was over.

Mar 74. (7") (TMG 891) **DON'T LET IT END (TIL YOU LET IT BEGIN). / I WANNA BE WITH YOU**   —

Aug 74. (7") <54248> **DO IT BABY. / I WANNA BE WITH YOU**   13

Aug 74. (7") (TMG 914) **DO IT BABY. / WIGS AND LASHES**   ☐

Dec 74. (lp) (STML 11276) <334> **DO IT BABY**   41 Sep74
– Do it baby / Up again / Where are you going to my love / What is a heart good for / You are love / Give me just another day / We feel the same / Calling out your name / A foolish thing to say / Can't get ready for losing you.

Dec 74. (7") <54256> **DON'T CHA LOVE IT. / UP AGAIN**   —   78

Feb 75. (7") (TMG 940) **WHERE ARE YOU GOING TO MY LOVE. / UP AGAIN**   ☐

Sep 75. (7") <54259> **YOU ARE LOVE. / GEMINI**   —

Nov 75. (7") (TMG 1015) <54262> **LOVE MACHINE (part 1). / LOVE MACHINE (part 2)**   3   1 Oct75

Nov 75. (lp) (STML 12010) <339> **CITY OF ANGELS**   33 Oct75
– Overture / City of angels / Free press / Ain't nobody straight in L.A. / Night life / Love machine / My name is Michael / Poor Charlotte / Waldo Roderick / Dehammersmith / Smog.

Feb 76. (7") <54268> **NIGHT LIFE. / SMOG**   —

Feb 76. (7") (TMG 1023) **NIGHT LIFE. / THE MIRACLE WORKERS: OVERTURE**   ☐   —

Apr 76. (lp) (STML 12020) <336> **LOVE MACHINE** <US-title 'DON'T CHA LOVE IT'>   96 Jan75
– Love machine / Don't cha love it / Keep on keepin' on (doin' what you do) / Sweet sweet lovin' / Got me goin' (again) / You are love / Gemini / Take it all / Broken-hearted girl, broken-hearted boy / A little piece of Heaven / Gonna tell the world (wedding song).

Oct 76. (lp) (STML 12038) <344> **THE POWER OF MUSIC**   ☐
– The power of music / Love to make love / Can I pretend / Let the children play (overture) / gossip / Let the children play / Street of love / You need a miracle.

	C.B.S.	Columbia	

Jan 77. (7") (CBS 4936) <10464> **SPY FOR BROTHERHOOD. / THE BIRD MUST FLY AWAY**   ☐   ☐

Feb 77. (lp) (CBS 881696) <34910> **LOVE CRAZY**   ☐   ☐
– Love crazy – introductory / Love crazy – overture / Too young / Spy for brotherhood / A better way to live / Women (make the world go round) / The bird must fly away / I can touch the sky.

Jun 77. (7") (CBS 10517) <10517> **WOMEN (MAKE THE WORLD GO ROUND). / I CAN TOUCH THE SKY**   ☐   ☐

Jul 78. (lp) <34910> **MIRACLES**   ☐
– I can't stand it / Love doctor / The magic of your eyes (Laura's eyes) / Freeway / Hot dance / Mean machine / Sad rain / Reach for the sky.

Jul 78. (7") <10706> **MEAN MACHINE. / THE MAGIC OF YOUR EYES (LAURA'S EYES)**   —   ☐

—— disbanded around 1978

649

– compilations, etc. –

on 'Tamla Motown' until mentioned otherwise

Apr 73.	(d-lp) (STMA 8008) <320> **1957-1972 (live)**		**75** Dec72
Apr 73.	(7"m) (TMG 853) **GOING TO A GO-GO. / WHOLE LOT OF SHAKIN' IN MY HEART (SINCE I MET YOU) / YESTER LOVE**		-
Sep 73.	(lp) Music For Pleasure; **I HEARD IT THROUGH THE GRAPEVINE**		-
Mar 74.	(t-lp) <793> **SMOKEY ROBINSON & THE MIRACLES' ANTHOLOGY**		**97** Feb74
	(re-iss. +c.Sep82, cd-iss. Jun87 & Apr89)		
Sep 76.	(7") (TMG 1048) **THE TEARS OF A CLOWN. / THE TRACKS OF MY TEARS**	**34**	-
Jan 79.	(lp) Music For Pleasure; (MFP 50422) **THE TEARS OF A CLOWN**		-
Sep 80.	(7") (TMG 957) **(COME ROUND HERE) I'M THE ONE YOU NEED. / I SECOND THAT EMOTION**		-
May 83.	(c-ep) (CTME 2028) **SMOKEY ROBINSON & THE MIRACLES**		-
	– The tears of a clown / (Come round here) I'm the one you need / The tracks of my tears / Don't blame you at all.		
Jun 83.	(7") (TMG 1048) **THE TEARS OF A CLOWN. / THE TRACKS OF MY TEARS**		-
Oct 86.	(cd) (ZD 72458) **GOING TO A GO-GO / THE TEARS OF A CLOWN**		
May 87.	(7") (ZB 41373) **THE TRACKS OF MY TEARS. / I SECOND THAT EMOTION**		
	(12"+=) (ZT 41373) – Going to a go-go / Shop around.		
Oct 87.	(cd) (ZD 72419) **COMPACT COMMAND PERFORMANCES (18 GREATEST HITS)**		
	– Shop around / You've really got a hold on me / I'll try something new / You can depend on me / Mickey's monkey / Tracks of my tears / Going to a go-go / I second that emotion / If you can wait / Baby, baby don't cry / Doggone right / Tears of a clown / I don't blame you at all / Baby come close / Baby that's backatcha / Quiet storm / Cruisin' / Being with you (last 3 SMOKEY ROBINSON solo).		
Aug 89.	(cd) (ZD 72510) **COMPACT COMMAND PERFORMANCES VOL.2**		
Nov 92.	(cd/c/lp) (530121-2/-4/-1) **THE GREATEST HITS**		
May 93.	(cd/c) Spectrum; (550073-2/-4) **TEARS OF A CLOWN**		-
Jun 93.	(cd/c) WEA; (8122 71181-2/-4) **WHATEVER MAKES YOU HAPPY: MORE BEST OF SMOKEY ROBINSON & THE MIRACLES 1961-1971**		
Nov 94.	(cd/c) Spectrum; (550405-2/-4) **CHRISTMAS WITH THE MIRACLES**		
Jul 96.	(cd) Spectrum; (552125-2) **MOTOWN EARLY CLASSICS**		-
Aug 98.	(cd) (530857-2) **THE ULTIMATE COLLECTION**		

MISFITS (dig out; Great Alt & Indie . . .)

MISSION

Formed: Leeds, England . . . late 1985 by ex-SISTERS OF MERCY members WAYNE HUSSEY and CRAIG ADAMS. After falling out with the aforementioned band's singer ANDREW ELDRITCH, the pair recruited SIMON HINKLER (ex-ARTERY) and MICK BROWN (ex-RED LORRY YELLOW LORRY), forming a new band originally under The SISTERHOOD moniker. Calculated to annoy their former colleague, ELDRITCH retaliated by releasing a single under a similar name, HUSSEY and Co. subsequently switching to The MISSION. In Spring '86, the band signed to indie label, 'Chapter 22', releasing the enjoyably amateurish goth theatrics of the 'SERPENT'S KISS' single a couple of months later. Another single, 'GARDEN OF DELIGHT', appeared that summer before the band were snapped up by 'Mercury'. The debut album, 'GOD'S OWN MEDICINE', appeared towards the end of the year, almost making the UK Top 10. Given a bit of a rough ride by critics for its often overbearing goth pompousness, the record was nevertheless a fairly accomplished set of adult rock, a bit like what U2 might have sounded like had they been born in Leeds and developed a penchant for wearing pointy shoes and smearing their faces with flour. The grandiose 'WASTELAND' made No.11 when it was released as a single early the following year, staking The MISSION's claim as the new Goth messiahs and no doubt making ELDRITCH sick to his stomach. But much as they liked to be serious fellows on record, they liked to party hard behind the scenes, CRAIG ADAMS coming a cropper on a particularly gruelling US tour and briefly leaving the band. His temporary replacement was PETE TURNER who filled in for the remainder of the tour and also played at The MISSION's triumphant Reading Festival headlining appearance later that summer. With ADAMS back in the fold, the band began work on a new album with LED ZEPPELIN bassist JOHN PAUL JONES on production chores. The less than impressive result was 'CHILDREN' (1988), a No.2 hit despite its critical lashing. Preceded by the delicate 'BUTTERFLY ON A WHEEL', the 'CARVED IN SAND' album was eventually released to expectant fans in early 1990. More elegantly refined than their normal heavy handed approach, the set remains their most listenable effort, if not their most successful. The band resumed heavy touring following the album's release, HINKLER subsequently storming out on the American jaunt. His replacement for the remainder of the tour was another ex-RED LORRY YELLOW LORRY man, DAVID WOLFENDEN, the band eventually recruiting guitarist ETCH (PAUL ETCHELLS, ex-GHOST DANCE) as a semi-permanent fixture later that year. Following the ambitious 'MASQUE' (1992) set (which featured the violin playing of FAIRPORT CONVENTION's RIC SAUNDERS), MARK THWAITE (ex-SPEAR OF DESTINY) and RIK

CARTER (ex-PENDRAGON) were brought in after the departure of ADAMS. Two further albums appeared on the band's own label, 'Equator', following the end of their tenure with 'Mercury', none making any substantial commercial headway. • **Songwriters:** HUSSEY penned, except LIKE A HURRICANE (Neil Young) / DANCING BAREFOOT (Patti Smith) / SHELTER FROM THE STORM (Bob Dylan) / OVER THE HILLS AND FAR AWAY (Led Zeppelin) / LOVE (John Lennon) / ATOMIC (Blondie). • **Trivia:** In 1991, HUSSEY was ushered off James Whale's late night TV show for being drunk and abusive to its ever-polite presenter!!

Album rating: GOD'S OWN MEDICINE (*7) / CHILDREN (*6) / CARVED IN SAND (*5) / GRAINS OF SAND out-takes (*5) / MASQUE (*5) / SUM AND SUBSTANCE compilation (*7) / NEVERLAND (*4)

WAYNE HUSSEY (b.26 May'59, Bristol, England) – vocals, guitar (ex-SISTERS OF MERCY, ex-DEAD OR ALIVE, ex-HAMBI & THE DANCE, ex-WALKIE TALKIES) / **CRAIG ADAMS** – bass (ex-SISTERS OF MERCY, ex-EXPELAIRES) / **SIMON HINKLER** – guitar (ex-ARTERY) / **MICK BROWN** – drums (ex-RED LORRY YELLOW LORRY)

			Chapter 22	not iss.
May 86.	(7") (CHAP 6-7) **SERPENT'S KISS. / WAKE (R.S.V.)**		**70**	-
	(12"+=) (CHAP 6) – Naked and savage.			
Jul 86.	(7") (CHAP 7) **GARDEN OF DELIGHT. / LIKE A HURICANE**		**50**	-
	(12"+=) (12CHAP 7) – Over the hills and far away / The crystal ocean.			
	(12"+=) (L12CHAP 7) – Dancing barefoot / The crystal ocean.			
			Mercury	Mercury
Oct 86.	(7") (MYSG 1) **STAY WITH ME. / BLOOD BROTHER**		**30**	
	(12"+=) (MYSGX 1) – Islands in a stream.			
Nov 86.	(lp/c)(cd) (MERH/+C 102)(<830603-2>) **GODS OWN MEDICINE**		**14**	
	– Wasteland / Bridges burning / Garden of delight (hereafter) / Stay with me / Blood brother * / Let sleeping dogs lie / Sacrilege / Dance on glass / And the dance goes on / Severina / Love me to death / Island in a stream *. (c+=/cd+= *)			
Jan 87.	(7") (MYTH 2) **WASTELAND. / SHELTER FROM THE STORM**		**11**	
	(12"+=) (MYTHX 2-1) – Dancing barefoot (live).			
	('A'-Anniversary mix.12"+=) (MYTHX 2-2) – 1969 (live) / Wake (live).			
	(d7") (MYTHB 2) – 1969 (live) / Serpent's kiss (live).			
Mar 87.	(7"/7"s) (MYTH/+P 3) **SEVERINA. / TOMORROW NEVER KNOWS**		**25**	
	(12"+=) (MYTHL 3) – Wishing well.			

– **PETE TURNER** – bass; took over on tour while ADAMS recovered from illness

– **CRAIG ADAMS** was soon back after a 4 month lay-off.

Jan 88.	(7") (MYTH 4) **TOWER OF STRENGTH. / FABIENNE**		**12**	
	(ext.12"+=) (MYTHX 4) – Dream on / Breathe (instrumental).			
	(ext.cd-s+=) (MTHCD 4) – Dream on / Breathe (vocal).			
Mar 88.	(lp/c)(cd) (MISH/+C 2)(<834263-2>) **CHILDREN**		**2**	
	– Beyond the pale / A wing and a prayer / Fabienne * / Heaven on Earth / Tower of strength / Kingdom come / Breathe / Child's play / Shamera kye / Black mountain mist / Dream on * / Heat / Hymn (for America). (c+=/cd+= *)			
Jul 88.	(7") (MYTH 6) **BEYOND THE PALE. / TADEUSZ (1912-1988)**		**32**	
	('A'-Armageddon mix.12"+=) (MYTHX 6) – Love me to death / For ever more.			
	('A'-Armageddon mix.cd-s+=) (MTHCD 6-2) – Tower of strength (Bombay edit).			
Nov 88.	(7") (MYTH 7) **KINGDOM COME. / CHILD'S PLAY (live)**			
	(12"+=) (MYTHX 7) – The crystal ocean.			
	(cd-s++=) (MTHCD 7) – Garden of delight (live).			

– (all formats on above single withdrawn)

Jan 90.	(7"/c-s) (MYTH/MTHMC 8) **BUTTERFLY ON A WHEEL. / THE GRIP OF DISEASE**		**12**	
	(12"+=/cd-s+=/box-cd-s+=)(10"+=) (MYTHX/MTHCD/MYCDB 8)(MYTH 8-10) – ('A'-Magni-octopus) / Kingdom come (forever and again).			
Feb 90.	(cd/c/lp) (<842251-2/-4/-1>) **CARVED IN SAND**		**7**	
	– Amelia / Into the blue / Butterfly on a wheel / Sea of love / Deliverance / Grapes of wrath / Belief / Paradise (will shine like the Moon) / Hungry as the hunter / Lovely.			
Mar 90.	(7"/c-s) (MYTH/MTHMC 9) **DELIVERANCE. / MR. PLEASANT**		**27**	
	(12"+=/cd-s+=/pic-cd-s+=)(10"+=) (MYTHX/MTHCD/MYCDB 9)(MYTH 9-10) – Heaven sends us.			
May 90.	(7"/c-s) (MYTH/MTHMC 10) **INTO THE BLUE. / BIRD OF PARADISE**		**32**	
	(12"+=/cd-s+=) (MYTHX/MTHCD 10) – Divided we fall.			

– **DAVID WOLFENDEN** – guitar (ex-RED LORRY YELLOW LORRY) repl. HINKLER.

– (Oct'90) added **ETCH** – guitar (ex-GHOST DANCE)

Oct 90.	(cd/c/lp) (846937-2/-4/-1) **GRAINS OF SAND** (out-takes)		**28**	
	– Hands across the ocean / The grip of disease / Divided we fall / Mercenary / Mr.Pleasant / Kingdom come (forever and again) / Heaven sends you / Sweet smile of a mystery / Love / Bird of passage. (c+=/cd+=) – Tower of strength (Casbah mix) / Butterfly on a wheel (Troubadour mix).			
Nov 90.	(7"/c-s) (MYTH/MTHMC 11) **HANDS ACROSS THE OCEAN. / AMELIA / LOVE**		**28**	-
	(12"+=) (MYTHX 11) – Amelia (live) / Tower of strength (mix) / Mercenary.			
	(cd-s+=) (MTHCD 11) – Amelia (live) / Stay with me / Mercenary.			
			Vertigo	Mercury
Apr 92.	(7"/c-s) (MYTH/MTHMC 12) **NEVER AGAIN. / BEAUTIFUL CHAOS**		**34**	-
	(12"+=/cd-s+=) (MYTHX/MTHCD 12) – ('A'-F1 mix) / ('A'-Zero G mix).			
Jun 92.	(cd/c/lp) <(512121-2/-4/-1)> **MASQUE**		**23**	
	– Never again / Shades of green (part II) / Even you may shine / Trail of scarlet / Spider and the fly / She conjures me wings / Sticks and stones / Like a child again / Who will love me tomorrow? / You make me breathe / From one Jesus to another / Until there's another sunrise. (re-is.cd.c Aug94; same)			
Jun 92.	(7"/c-s) (MYTH/MTHMC 13) **LIKE A CHILD AGAIN (remix). / ALL TANGLED UP IN YOU**		**30**	-
	(12"+=/cd-s+=) (MYTHX/MTHCD 13) – ('A'-Mark Saunders remix) / Hush a bye baby (child again) (Joe Gibbs remix).			

Oct 92. (7"/c-s) *(MYTH/MTHMC 14)* **SHADES OF GREEN. / YOU MAKE ME BREATHE** — `49` `-`
(cd-s) *(MTHCD 14)* – ('A'side) / Sticks and stones / Trail of scarlet / Spider and the fly.
(etched-12"+=) *(MYTHX 14)* – ('A'mix).

—— (Nov'92) **MARK THWAITE** – guitar (ex-SPEAR OF DESTINY) repl. HINKLER + ADAMS. Note:- **RIC SAUNDERS** – violin (of FAIRPORT CONVENTION) on last lp

Jan 94. (7") *(MYTH 15)* **TOWER OF STRENGTH (Youth remix). / WASTELAND** — `33` `-`
(12"+=) *(MYTHX 15)* – Serpent's kiss.
(cd-s) *(MYTCD 15)* – ('A'mixes) / ('A'-East India Cairo mix) / Deliverance.

Feb 94. (cd/c/d-lp) *<518447-2/-4/-1>* **SUM AND SUBSTANCE** (compilation) — `49`
– Never again / Hands across the ocean / Shades of green / Like a child again / Into the blue / Deliverance / Tower of strength / Butterfly on a wheel / Kingdom come / Beyond the pale / Severina / Stay with me / Wasteland / Garden of delight / Like a hurricane / Serpent's kiss / Sour puss / Afterglow.

Mar 94. (7") *(MYTH 16)* **AFTERGLOW. / SOUR-PUSS** — `53`
(cd-s+=) *(MYTCD 16)* – Cold as ice / Valentine.

	Equator	not iss.
Oct 94. (7"ep/cd-ep) *(HOOK S/CD 001)* **MISSION 1 EP**	☐	`-`
– Raising Cain / Sway / Neverland.		
Jan 95. (7"ep/cd-ep) *(HOOK S/CD 002)* **MISSION 2 EP**	`73`	`-`

– Swoon / Where / Wasting away.
(cd-ep+=) *(HOOKCDR 002)* – ('A'-Resurrection mix).

Feb 95. (cd/c/lp) *(SMEE CD/MC/LP 001)* **NEVERLAND** — `58` `-`
– Raising Cain / Sway / Lose myself / Swoon / Afterglow (reprise) / Stars don't shine without you / Celebration / Cry like a baby / Heaven knows / Swim with the dolphins / Neverland / Daddy's going to Heaven now.

Jun 96. (cd/c/lp) *(SMEE CD/MC/LP 002)* **BLUE** — `73` `-`
– Coming home / Get back to you / Drown in blue / damaged / More than this / That tears shall drown the wind / Black & blue / Bang bang / Cannibal / Dying room / Evermore & again.

– compilations, others, etc. –

Jun 87. (lp/c) *Mercury; (MISH/+C 1) <832527-1/-4>* **THE FIRST CHAPTER** — `35` `May88`
(cd-iss. May88; 832527-2)

Jul 94. (cd/lp) *Nighttracks; (CDNT/LPNT 005)* **SALAD DAZE** — ☐ `-`

Aug 95. (d-cd) *Mercury; (528805-2)* **CHILDREN / CARVED IN SAND** — ☐ `-`

MISSION OF BURMA (dig out; Great Alt & Indie . . .)

Joni MITCHELL

Born: ROBERTA JOAN ANDERSON, 7 Nov'43, Fort MacLeod, Alberta, Canada. In 1964, she performed at the Mariposa Folk Festival in Ontario, and married CHUCK MITCHELL in June '65, although after they relocated to Detroit the following year, they divorced. She retained the surname and moved to New York, where her songs were gradually recorded by others, mainly JUDY COLLINS ('BOTH SIDES NOW' & 'MICHAEL FROM MOUNTAINS') and TOM RUSH ('THE CIRCLE GAME'). Her self-titled DAVID CROSBY-produced debut lp came out in Summer of '68 and managed to only scrape into US Top 200. In August 1969 on the advice of David Geffen, she pulled out of WOODSTOCK free festival, and instead wrote the classic song of that name. It was later a US hit for CROSBY, STILLS, NASH & YOUNG, and also a UK No.1 for MATTHEWS' SOUTHERN COMFORT. Her second lp, 'CLOUDS', broke through into US Top 40 after her non-appearance, another classic album of the late 60's. Her third outing, 'LADIES OF THE CANYON' contained the aforementioned hippie mysticism of 'WOODSTOCK' as well as the surprise UK hit 'BIG YELLOW TAXI', making MITCHELL a household name in Britain when the album went to No.8. The romanticism had all but vanished by 'BLUE', one of the starkest, most soul searching records of the singer/songwriter era. The autobiographical intensity of the record is borne out by the fact that MITCHELL allegedly allowed no one but the engineer into the studio during recording. Not quite so intense but arguably more introspective was her 1972 album, 'FOR THE ROSES', a more experimental edge creeping into the arrangements and the first signs of MITCHELL's increasing preoccupation with jazz stylings. A combination of glittering melody and a light jazz sheen created one of her most listenable and commercially successful albums, 1974's 'COURT AND SPARK'. The assured sophistication of MITCHELL's blossoming talent was also evident in her live work, 'MILES OF AISLES', matching 'COURT AND SPARK's No.2 position on the US chart. Her next two albums, 'THE HISSING OF SUMMER LAWNS' and 'HEJIRA' marked a significant move away from the relative simplicity of her earlier work into more sophisticated sonic textures, underscored by jazz and world-inflected rhythms while her lyrical musings followed suit, away from personal confession towards pointed observation and cultural commentary. Alienated from the rock community which had nurtured her and amid scathing reviews, she moved ever further into obscure jazz fusion throughout the latter half of the 70's with the double album 'DON JUAN'S RECKLESS DAUGHTER' (1977) and ultimately, her collaboration with jazz legend CHARLES MINGUS, released in 1979 and simply titled, 'MINGUS'. Come the 80's, MITCHELL seemed to lose her focus. 'WILD THINGS RUN FAST', saw her treading water although 1985's THOMAS DOLBY-produced 'DOG EAT DOG' was an impassioned attack on the rampant materialism and hypocrisy of the 80's, singling out such worthy targets as the TV evangelists of the religious right. The insipid banality of 'CHALK MARK IN A RAINSTORM' (1988) is best passed over while

1991's 'NIGHT RIDE HOME' saw a return to form of sorts, combining the jazz textures and lyrical expansiveness of her earlier work. Around this time, MITCHELL exhibited some of her paintings in London and Edinburgh to critical acclaim while her most recent album to date, 'TURBULENT INDIGO' was a mature, accomplished set taking on such controversial issues as domestic violence. Like her old sparring partner NEIL YOUNG, MITCHELL remains one of the few survivors of the hippy era to avoid falling in terminal self-parody, admirably still challenging herself and her fans with each successive release. • **Songwriters:** All self-penned except; TWISTED (Annie Ross) / WHY DO FOOLS FALL IN LOVE (Frankie Lymon) / BABY I DON'T CARE (hit; Elvis Presley) / SLOUCHING TOWARDS BETHLEHEM (poem; W.B.Yeats).

Album rating: JONI MITCHELL (*7) / CLOUDS (*7) / LADIES OF THE CANYON (*9) / BLUE (*9) / FOR THE ROSES (*7) / COURT AND SPARK (*9) / MILES OF AISLES (*6) / THE HISSING OF SUMMER LAWNS (*7) / HEJIRA (*9) / DON JUAN'S RECKLESS DAUGHTER (*5) / MINGUS (*6) / SHADOWS AND LIGHT (*6) / WILD THINGS RUN FAST (*6) / DOG EAT DOG (*5) / CHALK MARK IN A RAINSTORM (*7) / NIGHT RIDE HOME (*5) / TURBULENT INDIGO (*6) / JONI MITCHELL HITS compilation (*8) / TAMING THE TIGER (*5)

JONI MITCHELL – vocals, acoustic guitar, piano with **STEPHEN STILLS** – bass / etc (on first)

	Reprise	Reprise
Jun 68. (lp) *(RSLP 6293) <6293>* **JONI MITCHELL**	☐	`Mar68`

– I CAME TO THE CITY:- I had a king / Michael from the mountains / Night in the city / Marcie / Nathan la Freneer / OUT OF THE CITY AND DOWN TO THE SEASIDE:- Sisotowbell Lane / The dawntreader / The pirate of penance / Song to a seagull / Cactus tree. *(cd-iss. Jan88; K2 44051)*

Jul 68. (7") *(RS 20694)* **NIGHT IN THE CITY. / I HAD A KING** — ☐ `-`

Aug 69. (7") *(23402)* **CHELSEA MORNING. / BOTH SIDES NOW** — ☐ `-`
<US-iss.Jun72; 1154>

Oct 69. (lp) *(RSLP 6341) <6341>* **CLOUDS** — ☐ `31` `May69`
– Tin angel / Chelsea morning / I don't know where I stand / That song about the Midway / Roses blue / The gallery / I think I understand / Songs to ageing children come / The fiddle and the drum / Both sides now. *(cd-iss. Jan88; K2 44070)*

—— next guests **MILT HOLLAND** – percussion / **TERESSA ADAMS** – cello / **JIM HORN** – baritone sax / **PAUL HORN** – clarinet, flute

May 70. (lp) *(RSLP 6376) <6376>* **LADIES OF THE CANYON** — `8` `27` `Apr70`
– Morning Morgantown / For free / Conversation / Ladies of the canyon / Willy / The arrangement / Rainy night house / The priest / Blue boy / Big yellow taxi / Woodstock / The circle game. *(cd-iss. Jul88; K2 44085)*

Jun 70. (7") *(RS 20906) <0906>* **BIG YELLOW TAXI. / WOODSTOCK** — `11` `67`

—— with **STILLS + JAMES TAYLOR** – guitar / **SNEAKY PETE KLEINOW** – steel guitar / **RUSS KUNKEL** – drums

Jul 71. (lp) *(K 44128) <2038>* **BLUE** — `3` `15` `Jun71`
– All I want / My old man / Little green / Carey / Blue / California / This flight tonight / River / A case of you / The last time I saw Richard. *(cd-iss. Jan87; K2 44128)*

Aug 71. (7") *<1029>* **CAREY. / THIS FLIGHT TONIGHT** — `-` `93`
Aug 71. (7") *(K 14099)* **CAREY. / MY OLD MAN** — `-` ☐
Apr 72. (7") *(K 14130) <1049>* **CALIFORNIA. / A CASE OF YOU** — `-` `Oct71`
Jul 72. (7") *<1155>* **CAREY. / BIG YELLOW TAXI** — `-` ☐

—— Her band now **STILLS + NASH** (her recent boyfriend) + **KUNKEL / WILTON FELDER / JAMES BURTON** – guitar / **TOM SCOTT** – wind

	Asylum	Asylum
Nov 72. (7") *(AYM 511) <11010>* **YOU TURN ME ON, I'M A RADIO. / URGE FOR GOING**	☐	`25`
Dec 72. (lp) *(SYLA 8753) <5057>* **FOR THE ROSES**	`11`	`Nov72`

– Banquet / Cold blue steel and sweet fire / Barangrill / Lesson in survival / Let the wind carry me / For the roses / See you sometime / Electricity / You turn me on, I'm a radio / Blonde in the bleachers / Woman of heart and mind / Judgement of the Moon and stars (Ludwig's tune). *(cd-iss. Dec87; K2 53007)*

Mar 73. (7") *(AYM 515)* **COLD BLUE STEEL AND SWEET FIRE. / BLONDE IN THE BLEACHERS** — ☐ `-`

—— Retained **TOM SCOTT's L.A. EXPRESS** with new boyfriend **JOHN GUERIN** – drums / **WILTON FELDER** – bass / **LARRY CARLTON** – guitar / **CHUCK FINDLEY** – trumpet / **JOE SAMPLE** – keyboards / **ROBBIE ROBERTSON** – guitar

Jan 74. (7") *(AYM 524) <11029>* **RAISED ON ROBBERY. / COURT AND SPARK** — ☐ `65` `Dec73`
Mar 74. (lp) *(SYLA 8756) <7E 1001>* **COURT AND SPARK** — `14` `2` `Feb74`
– Court and spark / Help me / Free man in Paris / People's parties / The same situation / Car on a hill / Down to you / Just like this train / People's parties / Raised on robbery / Trouble child. *(re-iss. Jun76 lp/c; K/K4 53002) (cd-iss. May83; 253002-2)*

Mar 74. (7") *<11034>* **HELP ME. / JUST LIKE THIS TRAIN** — `-` `7`
Jul 74. (7") *<11041>* **FREE MAN IN PARIS. / PEOPLE'S PARTIES** — `-` `22`
Oct 74. (7") *(AYM 533)* **FREE MAN IN PARIS. / CAR ON A HILL** — `-` `-`
Jan 75. (7") *(AYM 537) <45221>* **BIG YELLOW TAXI (live). / RAINY NIGHT HOUSE (live)** — ☐ `24` `Dec74`
Jan 75. (d-lp) *(SYSP 902) <202>* **MILES OF AISLES** — `34` `2` `Nov74`
– You turn me on, I'm a radio / Big yellow taxi / Rainy night house / Woodstock / Cactus tree / Cold blue steel and sweet fire / Woman of heart and mind / A case of you / The circle game / People's parties / All I want / Real good for free / Both sides now / Carey / The last time I saw Richard / Jericho / Love or money. *(re-iss. Jun76 d-lp/d-c; K/K4 63001) (cd-iss. 1989; K2 63001)* – (omits some dialogue).
(above also with **TOM SCOTT & THE L.A. EXPRESS;- SCOTT / GUERIN** plus **ROBBEN FORD** – guitar / **LARRY NASH** – piano / **MAX BENNETT** – bass

Nov 75. (lp/c) *(K/K4 53018) <7E 1051>* **THE HISSING OF SUMMER LAWNS** — `14` `4`
– In France they kiss on Main Street / The jungle line / Edith and the kingpin / Don't interrupt the sorrow / Shades of Scarlett conquering The hissing of summer lawns / The boho dance / Harry's house – Centerpiece / Sweet bird / Shadows and light. *(cd-iss. Nov87; K2 53018)*

Mar 76. (7") *(K 13035) <45296>* **IN FRANCE THEY KISS ON MAIN STREET. / BOHO DANCE** — ☐ `66` `Feb76`
Nov 76. (lp/c) *(K/K4 53053) <7E 1087>* **HEJIRA** — `11` `13`
– Coyote / Amelia / Furry sings the blues / A strange boy / Hejira / Song for Sharon / Black crow / Blue motel room / Refuge of the roads. *(cd-iss. Oct87; 253053-2)*

Feb 77. (7") *(K 13072)* <45377> **COYOTE. / BLUE MOTEL ROOM** □ □

—— now with **JACO PASTORIUS** – bass / **GLENN FREY** – vocals / **WAYNE SHORTER** – sax / **J.D.SOUTHER + CHAKA KHAN** – both backing vocals

Dec 77. (d-lp/d-c) *(K/K4 63003)* <101> **DON JUAN'S RECKLESS DAUGHTER** [20] [25]
– Overture – Cotton Avenue / Talk to me / Jericho / Paprika plains / Otis and Marlena / The tenth world / Dreamland / Don Juan's reckless daughter / Off night backstreet / The silky veils of Ardor. *(cd-iss. 1988; K2 63003)*

Feb 78. (7") *(K 13110)* **OFF NIGHT BACKSTREET. / JERICHO** [-] [-]
Feb 78. (7") <45467> **JERICHO. / DREAMLAND** [-] [-]

—— now with **JACO PASTORIUS** – bass / **WAYNE SHORTER** – sax / **HERBIE HANCOCK** – keyboards / **PETER ERSKINE** – drums / **DON ALIAS + EMIL RICHARDS** – percussion

Jun 79. (7") *(K 13154)* <46506> **THE DRY CLEANER FROM DES MOINES. / GOD MUST BE A BOOGIE MAN** [-] [-]

Jul 79. (lp/c) *(K/K4 53091)* <505> **MINGUS** [24] [17] Jun79
– Happy birthday 1975 (rap) / God must be a boogie man / Funeral (rap) / A chair in the sky / The wolf that lives in Lindsey / I's a muggin' (rap) / Sweet sucker dance / Coin in the pocket (rap) / The dry cleaner from Des Moines / Lucky (rap) / Goodbye pork pie hat. *(cd-iss. 1988; K2 53091)*

—— now with **PAT METHENY** – lead guitar / **JACO PASTORUS** – bass / **LYLE MAYS** – keyboards / **DON ALIAS** – drums / **MICHAEL BRECKER** – saxophone

Sep 80. (d-lp/d-c) *(K/K4 62030)* <704> **SHADOWS AND LIGHT (live)** [63] [38]
– (introduction) / In France they kiss on Main Street / Edith and the kingpin / Coyote / Goodbye pork pie hat / The dry cleaner from Des Moines / Amelia / Pat's solo / Hejira / Black crow / Dreamland / Free man in Paris / (band introduction) / Furry sings the blues / Why do fools fall in love? / Shadows and light / God must be a boogie man / Woodstock.

Oct 80. (7") *(K 12478)* <47038> **WHY DO FOOLS FALL IN LOVE? (live). / BLACK CROW (live)** □ □

—— **LARRY KLEIN** – bass (she married him Nov'82) / **LARRY WILLIAMS** – keyboards / **LARRY CARLTON / JOHN GUERIN / VICTOR FELDMAN** / etc.

                                             Geffen   Geffen

Nov 82. (7") *(GEF 2950)* <29849> **(YOU'RE SO SQUARE) BABY, I DON'T CARE. / LOVE** □ [47]

Nov 82. (lp/c) *(GEF/40 25102)* <GHS 2019> **WILD THINGS RUN FAST** [32] [25]
– Chinese cafe – Unchained melody / Wild things run fast / Ladies man / Moon at the window / Solid love / Be cool / (You're so square) Baby, I don't care / You dream flat tyres / Man to man / Underneath the streetlight / Love. *(cd-iss. Jul88; GEFD 02019) (re-iss. Jul92 cd/c; GFLD/GFLC 19129)*

Feb 83. (7") <29757> **BE COOL. / UNDERNEATH THE STREETLIGHT** [-] [-]
Feb 83. (7") *(GEF 3122)* **CHINESE CAFE. / LADIES MAN** [-] [-]
(d7"+=) *(DA 3122)* – (interview).

Nov 85. (7") *(A 6740)* <28840> **GOOD FRIENDS. / SMOKIN' (EMPTY TRY ANOTHER)** □ [85]

—— Above feat. guest duet **MICHAEL McDONALD**

—— now with co-producer **THOMAS DOLBY** – synthesizers / etc.

Nov 85. (lp/c) *(GEF/GEC 26455)* <24074> **DOG EAT DOG** [57] [63]
– Good friends / Fiction / Three great stimulants / Tax free / Smokin' (empty, try another) / Dog eat dog / Shiny toys / Ethiopia / Impossible dreamer / Lucky girl. *(cd-iss. May86; K 924074-2) (re-iss. Oct87 lp/c; K 924074-1/-4) (re-iss. Mar93 cd/c; GFLD/GFLC 19198)*

Apr 86. (7"/12") *(A/TA 7124)* **SHINY TOYS. / THREE GREAT STIMULANTS** □ □

—— guests **THOMAS DOLBY, TOM PETTY, WILLIE NELSON, DON HENLEY, WENDY & LISA, BILLY IDOL, PETER GABRIEL,** etc. **KLEIN** co-produced, as was next

Mar 88. (lp/c)(cd) *(WX 141/+C)(924172-2)* <24172> **CHALK MARK IN A RAIN STORM** [26] [45]
– My secret place / Number one / Lakota / The tea leaf prophecy / Dancing clown / The beat of black wings / Snakes and ladders / The recurring dream / The bird that whistles. *(re-iss. Jan91 lp/cd; GEF/+C/D 24172) (re-iss. Mar93 cd/c; GFLD/GFLC 19199)*

Apr 88. (7") <27887> **MY SECRET PLACE. / LAKOTA** [-] [-]
May 88. (7") *(GEF 37)* **MY SECRET PLACE. / NUMBER ONE** □ □
(12"+=/3"cd-s+=) *(GEF 37 T/CD)* – Chinese eyes – Unchained melody / Good friends.

—— ('A' featured **PETER GABRIEL**)

—— retained **KLEIN** with band **VINNIE COLAIUTA** – drums / **ALEX ACUNA** – percussion / **WAYNE SHORTER** – saxophone / **BILL DILLON + MICHAEL LANDAU** – guitars

Mar 91. (lp/c/cd) <(GEF/+C/D 24302)> **NIGHT RIDE HOME** [25] [41]
– Night ride home / Passion play (when all the slaves are free) / Cherokee Louise / The windfall (everything for nothing) / Slouching towards Bethlehem / Come in from the cold / Nothing can be done / The only joy in town / Ray's dad's cadillac / Two grey rooms.

Jul 91. (7") **COME IN FROM THE COLD. / RAY'S DAD'S CADILLAC** □ □
(cd-s+=/pic-cd-s+=) – ('A'extended.

                                             Reprise   Reprise

Oct 94. (cd/c) <(9362 45786-2/-4)> **TURBULENT INDIGO** [53] [47]
– Sunny Sunday / Sex kills / The Magdalene laundries / Turbulent indigo / How do you stop / Last chance lost / Not to blame / Borderline / Yvette in English / The sire of sorrow (Job's sad song).

Nov 94. (c-s/cd-s) *(W 0273 C/CD)* **HOW DO YOU STOP / THE SIRE OF SORROW / MOON AT THE WINDOW** □ □

Sep 98. (cd/c) <(9362 46451-2/-4)> **TAMING THE TIGER** [57] [75]
– Harlem in Havana / Man from Mars / Love puts on a new face / Lead balloon / No apologies / Taming the tiger / Crazy cries of love / Stay in touch / Facelift / Here's to you / Taming bones.

– compilations, others, etc. –

May 74. (7"ep) *Reprise; (K 14345)* **CAREY / BOTH SIDES NOW. / BIG YELLOW TAXI / WOODSTOCK** □ [-]
Oct 82. (d-c) *Reprise; (K4 64046)* **CLOUDS / BLUE** □ [-]
Jul 76. (7") *Asylum; (K 13048)* **YOU TURN ME ON, I'M A RADIO. / FREE MAN IN PARIS** □ [-]
Nov 83. (d-c) *Asylum;* **FOR THE ROSES / COURT AND SPARK** □ [-]

Oct 96. (cd/c) *Reprise; <(9362 46326-2/-4)>* **HITS** □ □
– Urge for going / Chelsea morning / Big yellow taxi / Woodstock / The circle game / Carey / California / You turn me on I'm a radio / Raised on robbery / Help me / Free man in Paris / River / Chinese cafe – Unchained melody / Come in from the cold / Both sides, now.

Oct 96. (cd/c) *Reprise; <(9362 46358-2/-4)>* **MISSES** □ □
May 97. (cd) *Experience; (EXP 025)* **JONI MITCHELL** [-] [-]
Jun 97. (cd) *Metro; (OTR 1100027)* **GHOSTS** [-] [-]

MOBY

Born: RICHARD MELVILLE HALL, 11 Sep '65, New York City, New York, USA. After being raised by his middle-class mother in Darien, Connecticut, he joined hardcore outfit The VATICAN COMMANDOES, which led to him having a brief stint in the similar, FLIPPER. He didn't record anything with the band and moved back to New York to become a DJ, making hardcore techno/dance records under the guise of BRAINSTORM and UHF3, etc. He subsequently became a mixer for The PET SHOP BOYS, ERASURE and MICHAEL JACKSON, before and during his return into solo work in the early 90's. His UK debut, 'GO', hit the Top 10 in October '91, having just breached the charts 3 months earlier. Sampling the 'Twin Peaks' theme, the song was a compelling piece of techno-pop that remains a dancefloor favourite. Little was subsequently heard of him barring a few US imports, although this led to UK semi-indie, 'Mute', taking him on board in mid '93. First up was his near Top 20 single, 'I FEEL IT', beginning a series of hits, albeit sporadic. Early in 1995, his album 'EVERYTHING IS WRONG' had critics lavishing praise on the man for his combination of acid-dance and ambience. 'ANIMAL RIGHTS', the 1996 follow-up added a new dimension; heavy industrial punk-metal which gave him a new found Kerrang! audience. Towards the tail-end of '97, the shaven-headed Christian vegan released the James Bond Theme to 'TOMORROW NEVER DIES', and although it rocketed into the UK Top 10, the accompanying soundtracks album, 'I LIKE TO SCORE', failed to gain the same chart momentum. Eager to once more turn up his amps to number 11, MOBY this time took elements of Southern Blues (courtesy of BESSIE JONES' 'Sometimes') and threw it into his punk/dance melting pot for next single, 'HONEY'. Although it deserved a better chart placing than No.33, it did pave the way for a series of diverse releases kicking off with CANNED HEAT-esque 'RUN ON' (aka 'Run On For A Long Time' by BILL LANDFORD), a taster from his fourth 'Mute' album, 'PLAY' (1999). Opening with the aforementioned 'HONEY', the second track 'FIND MY BABY' took a similar trek back in time (via a sample of the BOY BLUE's 'Joe Lee's Rock') while further UK hit singles, 'BODYROCK' and 'WHY DOES MY HEART FEEL SO BAD', rattled and graced the dancefloors respectively.
• **Songwriters:** Himself, and a few with singer, MIMI GOESE:- 'Into The Blue' + 'When It's Cold I'd Like To Die'. Other singers on 1995 album; ROZZ MOREHEAD / MYIM ROSE / NICOLE ZARAY / KOOKIE BANTON / SAUNDRA WILLIAMS. Samples BADALAMENTI's 'Twin Peaks' on 'GO'. Covered NEW DAWN FADES (Joy Division) / THAT'S WHEN I REACH FOR MY REVOLVER (Mission Of Burma). • **Trivia:** In 1992, he remixed JAM & SPOON's club smash 'Stella', which had sampled his 'GO'. He also provided vox for RECOIL's 1992 album , 'Bloodline'. MOBY remixed The B-52's, ESKIMOS AND EGYPT, LFO, FORTRAN 5, ORBITAL, ENO, PET SHOP BOYS + The OTHER TWO.

Album rating: MOBY (*6) / AMBIENT (*5) / THE STORY SO FAR (*6) / EVERYTHING IS WRONG (*9) / ANIMAL RIGHTS (*8) / I LIKE TO SCORE (*7) / PLAY (*9)

MOBY – vocals, keyboards, etc.

                                           Outer   Rhythm   Instinct

Jul 91. (12") *(FOOT 15)* <237> **GO (analog mix). / ('A'-Night time mix) / ('A'-Soundtrack mix)** [46] □ Jan92
(12") *(FOOT 15R)* – ('A'side) / ('A'-video aux w/ LYNCH & BADALAMENTI) / ('A'-Rain forest mix).
(cd-s) *(FOOT 15CD)* – ('A'side) / ('A'-Low spirit mix) / ('A'-Woodtick mix). *(re-iss. Oct91, hit No.10; same)*

1992. (12"/cd-s) <240> **DROP A BEAT (mixes)** [-] [-]
1992. (m-cd/m-c) <241> **MOBY** [-] [-]
– Drop a beat / Everything / Yeah / Electricity / Next is the E / Mercy. *<cd re-iss. 1995 on 'Elektra' +=; 61838>* – Go / Help me to believe / Have you seen my baby / Ah ah / Slight return / Stream.

1992. (12"/cd-s) <247> **NEXT IS THE E (mixes)** [-] [-]
Jan 93. (cd) <253> **AMBIENT** [-] [-]
– My beautiful blue sky / Heaven / Tongues / J Breas / Myopia / House of blue leaves / Bad days / Piano & string / Sound / Dog / 80 / Lean on me. *(UK-iss.Oct93 on 'Equator Arctic' cd/c/lp; ATLAS CD/MC/LP 002) (re-iss. Nov98 on 'Pinnacle'; PLRCD 015)*

                                           Equator   Instinct

Jun 93. (c-s) *(AXISMC 001)* **I FEEL IT. / THOUSAND** [38] □
(12"/cd-s) *(AXIS T/CD 001)* – (3-'A'mixes).
(12") *(AXISM 001)* – ('A'remixes).

Aug 93. (cd/c/lp) *(ATLAS CD/MC/LP 001)* **THE STORY SO FAR** □ [-]
– Ah ah / I feel it / Everything / Help me to believe / Go (woodtick mix) / Yeah / Drop a beat (the new version) / Thousand / Slight return / Go (sublimal mix unedited version) / Stream. *(cd+=)* – Mercy. *(cd re-iss. Nov98 on 'Pinnacle'; PLRCD 014)*

                                           Mute   Elektra

Sep 93. (c-s) *(CMUTE 158)* <61568> **MOVE (YOU MAKE ME FEEL SO GOOD). / ('A'-disco threat mix)** [21] □
(12"/cd-s) *(12/CD MUTE 158)* – ('A'side) / ('A'-Subversion) / ('A'-xtra mix) / ('A'-MK-Blades mix).
(cd-s) *(LCDMUTE 158)* – ('A'side) / All that I need is to be loved / Unloved

symphony / Rainfalls and the sky shudders.
(12") (L12MUTE 158) – (last track repl. by)- Morning dove.

May 94. (c-s) (CMUTE 161) **HYMN – THIS IS MY DREAM (extended) / ALL THAT I NEED IS TO BE LOVED (H.O.S. mix)** `31`
(cd-s+=) (CDMUTE 161) – ('A'-European edit) / ('A'-Laurent Garnier mix).
(12") (12MUTE 161) – ('A'extended) / ('A'-Laurent Garnier mix) / ('A'-Upriver mix)/ ('A'-Dirty hypo mix).
(cd-s) (LCDMUTE 161) – Hymn (alternate quiet version 33 mins).

Oct 94. (c-s) (CMUTE 173) <66180> **FEELING SO REAL. / NEW DAWN FADES** `30`
(cd-s+=) (CDMUTE 173) – ('A'-Unashamed ecstatic piano mix) / ('A'-Old skool mix).
(cd-s) (LCDMUTE 173) – ('A'-Westbam remix) / ('A'-Ray Keith remix) / ('A'dub mix) / Everytime you touch me (remix parts).
(12") (12MUTE 173) – ('A'side) / (4-versions from cd's above).

Feb 95. (c-s/7"dinked) (C+/MUTE 176/+D) <66154> **EVERYTIME YOU TOUCH ME / THE BLUE LIGHT OF THE UNDERWATER SUN** `28`
(cd-s+=) (CDMUTE 176) – ('A'-Beatmasters mix) / ('A'-competition winner; Jude Sebastian mix) / ('A'Freestyle mix).
(cd-s+++) (LCDMUTE 176) – ('A'-Uplifting mix).
(12") (12MUTE 176) – ('A'-Sound Factory mix) / ('A'-SF dub) / ('A'-Follow me mix) / ('A'-Tribal mix).

Mar 95. (cd/c/d-lp) (CD/C+/Stumm 130) <61701> **EVERYTHING IS WRONG** `21`
– Hymn / Feeling so real / All that I need is to be loved / Let's go free / Everytime you touch me / Bring back my happiness / What love? / First cool hive / Into the blue / Anthem / Everything is wrong / God moving over the face of the waters / When it's cold I'd like to die. (cd/c w/free cd/c) (XLCD/XLC+/Stumm 130) – Underwater (parts 1-5).

Jun 95. (c-s) (CMUTE 179) **INTO THE BLUE / ('A'-Shining mix)** `34`
(cd-s+=) (LCDMUTE 179) – ('A'-Summer night mix) / ('A'-Beastmasters mix).
(12"/cd) (12/CD MUTE 179) – ('A'-Beastmasters mix) / ('A'-Jnr Vasquez mix) / ('A'-Phil Kelsey mix) / ('A'-Jon Spencer Blues mix).

Jan 96. (cd/c) (XLStumm 130) **EVERYTHING IS WRONG – MIXED AND REMIXED** `25`

—— The track 'GOD MOVING OVER THE FACE OF THE WATERS' was used for the Rover 400 TV commercial. Toyota had earlier sampled his 'GO'.

Aug 96. (12") (12MUTE 184) **THAT'S WHEN I REACH FOR MY REVOLVER. / ('A'-Rollo & Si Star Bliss mix)** `50`
(cd-s) (CDMUTE 184) – ('A'side) / Lovesick / Displaced / Sway.
(cd-s) (LCDMUTE 184) – ('A'side) / Every one of my problems / God moving over the face of the waters (dark mix).

Oct 96. (cd/c/d-lp) (CD/C+/Stumm 150) <62031> **ANIMAL RIGHTS** `38`
– Now I let it go / Come on baby / Someone to love / Heavy flow / You / My love will never die / Soft / Say it's all mine / That's when I reach for my revolver / Face it / Living / Love song for my mom. (cd w/ free cd) **LITTLE IDIOT** (LCDStumm 150) – Degenerate / Dead city / Walnut / Old / A season in Hell / Love song for my mom / The blue terror of lawns / Dead sun / Reject.

Nov 96. (12"ep) (12MUTE 200) **COME ON BABY / LOVE HOLE / WHIP IT / GO / ALL THAT I NEED TO BE IS LOVED / HYMN**
(cd-ep) (CDMUTE 200) – ('A'-Eskimos And Egypt mix) / ('A'-Crystal method mix) / ('A'-Eskimos And Egypt extended).

Jul 97. (7") <SP 377> **THAT'S WHEN I REACH FOR MY REVOLVER. /** `-` `_`

—— <above issued on 'Sub Pop'>

Nov 97. (c-s/12"/cd-s) (C/12/CD MUTE 210) <040> **JAMES BOND THEME: TOMORROW NEVER DIES** `8`
– (mixes:- extended dance / Grooverider's Jeep remix / Da Bomb remix / CJ Bolland remix / Dub Pistols remix / CJ Bolland – Dubble-oh Heaven remix).
(12") (XL12MUTE 210) – ('A'mixes; re-version / Grooverider / Danny Tenaglia dub).

Nov 97. (cd/c/lp) (CD/C+/Stumm 168) <62094> **I LIKE TO SCORE**
– Novio / James Bond theme / Go / Ah ah / I like to score / Oil / New dawn fades / God moving over the face of the waters / First cool hive / Nash / Love theme / Grace.

Aug 98. (cd-s) (CDMUTE 218) <2186> **HONEY / HONEY (Mario Caldato Jnr. mix) / MICRONESIA / MEMORY GOSPEL** `33`
(cd-s) (LCDMUTE 218) – ('A'-Rollo & Sister Bliss blunt edit) / ('A'-Moby's 118 mix) / ('A'-Westbam & Hardy mix) / ('A'-Aphrodite & Micky Finn mix).
(12") (12MUTE 218) – ('A'-Rollo & Sister Bliss mix) / ('A'-Sharam Jey's sweet honey mix) / ('A'-Moby's low side mix).

Apr 99. (cd-s) (CDMUTE 221) **RUN ON (mixes) / SPIRIT** `33`
(cd-s) (LCDMUTE 221) – ('A'side) / Running / Sunday / Down slow.
(12") (12MUTE 221) – ('A'mixes).

May 99. (cd/c/d-lp) (CD/C+/STUMM 172) <27049> **PLAY** `33`
– Honey / Find my baby / Porcelain / Why does my heart feel so bad? / South side / Rushing / Bodyrock / Natural blues / Machete / 7 / Run on / Down slow / If things were perfect / Everloving / Inside / Guitar flute & string / The sky is broken / My weakness.
(above album will hit No.1 early in 2000)

Jul 99. (cd-s) (CDMUTE 225) **BODYROCK / SUNSPOT / ARP** `38`
(12"/cd-s) (12/LCD MUTE 225) – ('A'-Olav Basoski da hot funk mix) / ('A'-Da freak funk mix) / ('A'-B&H Bodyrock mix) / ('A'-Dani Konig mix).

Oct 99. (cd-s) (LCDMUTE 230) **WHY DOES MY HEART FEEL SO BAD / FLYING FOXES / PRINCESS** `16`
(12"/cd-s) (12/CD MUTE 230) – ('A'mixes by ATB, FERRY CORSTEN, SHARP BOYS + SUBSONIC LEGACY).

– compilations, specials, etc –

Nov 93. (12") Mute; (12NEMY 2) **ALL THAT I NEED IS TO BE LOVED. / (3 other 'A'mixes)** `_` `-`

Sep 94. (c-s) Mute; (CNOCAR 1) **GO (woodtick mix) / ('A'-Low spirit mix)** `_` `-`
(12"+=) (12NOCAR 1) – ('A'-Voodoo chile mix).

(12"+=) (12LNOCAR 1) – ('A'-Appathoski mix) / ('A'-Amphemetix mix).
(cd-s+=) (CDNOCAR 1) – ('A'-Delirium mix).

Mar 95. (10"ltd.) Soapbar; (SBR 15) **FEELING SO REAL (mixes)** `_` `-`
Nov 98. (cd) Pinnacle; (PLRCD 016) **EARLY UNDERGROUND** `_` `-`
Nov 98. (d-cd) Pinnacle; (PLRCD 017) **RARE (collected B-sides)** `_` `-`

MOBY GRAPE

Formed: San Francisco, California, USA . . . September '66 by manager/self-styled scenester MATTHEW KATZ (who'd previously worked with JEFFERSON AIRPLANE) and ex-'AIRPLANE drummer turned guitarist SKIP SPENCE. Unknowns PETER LEWIS, BOB MOSELEY, JERRY MILLER and DON STEVENSON were drafted in and the fledgling GRAPES apparently took their name from a (pathetic) joke doing the rounds at the time: 'What's purple and lives at the bottom of the sea?' (who said the Americans don't have a sense of humour?!) KATZ himself wasn't exactly a laugh a minute, allegedly harassing the band into signing an outrageous contract that gave him complete control over the personnel in the band as well as the name MOBY GRAPE. After signing to 'Columbia', the band released their self-titled debut just as the "summer of love" was fermenting in June 1967. The album showcased the distinctive guitar triumvirate of SPENCE, LEWIS and MILLER, a sound that enhanced the fertile songwriting and close-knit harmonies. So confident were the record company in the band's profit-making potential, they released five singles simultaneously. All the tracks could've been hits in their own right, but this foolhardy gesture was seen as a blatant attempt to hype the band, the result being a severe dent in their credibility and a lowly No.88 chart placing for the classic 'OMAHA'. The other four singles stiffed without trace. It didn't help matters when three of the band were caught with under-age girls on the night of the album launch. Nevertheless, the album reached the US Top 30 and the band's psychedelic mesh of country, rock, folk and blues made them favourites on the Bay Area scene. The sessions for the unfortunately-titled follow-up, 'WOW', were beset with problems, not least SKIP SPENCE running amok with an axe and being carted off to hospital in a straitjacket. Unsurprisingly, the record was a patchy affair bolstered with gimmicks like the 'GRAPE JAM' disc, given away free with the album. With SPENCE out of the picture, the band released another two albums that mined a rootsier seam, 'MOBY GRAPE '69' and 'TRULY FINE CITIZEN', although the absence of SPENCE's incendiary genius was glaringly apparent. The band called it a day in 1969 only to reform in 1971, a process that'd be repeated over the following decade amid ever shifting line-ups. Due to the dodginess of their aforementioned management contract, KATZ retained the MOBY GRAPE name and set up his own version of the band in the early 70's, all very confusing, and although some decent stuff was produced, none of the various incarnations met with any commercial success. SKIP SPENCE, meanwhile, released a one-off solo album of sublime psychedelic country in 1969, 'OAR', before fading into obscurity. All in all, yet another case of what might've been, had not drugs, bad luck and even worse deals not prematurely snuffed out their talent. Sadly, years of living on the streets of Santa Cruz (while attending the local Dominican hospital) took its toll on SKIP SPENCE, when he died of lung cancer on the 16th of April 1999, leaving behind four children; like MOSLEY, he was diagnosed a schizophrenic. • **Songwriters:** Individually penned, either SPENCE, MOSLEY, MILLER & STEVENSON or LEWIS. • **Trivia:** Watch out for a track on the original 'WOW' lp, which spins at 78 rpm (impossible to play on most modern turntables).

Album rating: MOBY GRAPE (*8) / WOW (*6) / MOBY GRAPE '69 (*6) / TRULY FINE CITIZEN (*5) / 20 GRANITE CREEK (*6) / LIVE GRAPE (*5) / MOBY GRAPE '84 (*5) / VINTAGE: THE VERY BEST OF MOBY GRAPE compilation (*8) / Alexander Skip Spence: OAR (*8)

SKIP SPENCE (b. ALEXANDER, 18 Apr'46, Windsor, Ontario, Canada) – vocals, guitar (ex-JEFFERSON AIRPLANE) / **PETER LEWIS** (b.15 Jul'45, Los Angeles, Calif.) – guitar, vocals (ex-CORNELLS) / **JERRY MILLER** (b.10 Jul'43, Tacoma, Washington) – guitar, vocals (ex-FRANTICS) / **BOB MOSELEY** (b. 4 Dec'42, Paradise Valley, Calif.) – bass (ex-MISFITS) / **DON STEVENSON** (b.15 Oct'42, Seattle, Washington) – drums (ex-FRANTICS) repl. KENT DUNBAR

		C.B.S.	Columbia
Jun 67. (7") <44170> **CHANGES. / FALL ON YOU**		`-`	`_`
Jun 67. (7") <44171> **SITTING BY THE WINDOW. / INDIFFERENCE**		`-`	`_`
Jun 67. (7") <44172> **8:05. / MISTER BLUES**		`-`	`_`
Jun 67. (7") (CBS 2953) <44173> **OMAHA. / HEY GRANDMA**			`88`
Jun 67. (7") <44174> **COME IN THE MORNIG. / HEY GRANDMA** (above 5 singles released similtaneously)		`-`	`_`
Jun 67. (lp; stereo/mono) (S+/BPG 63090) <9498/2698> **MOBY GRAPE**			`24`

– Hey grandma / Mr. Blues / Fall on you / 8:05 / Come in the morning / Omaha / Naked, if I want to / Someday / Ain't no use / Sitting by the window / Changes / Lazy me / Indifference. (re-iss. Sep84 on 'Edsel'; ED 137) (cd-iss. Apr89; EDCD 137)

Jul 68. (lp) (63271) <9613> **WOW** `20` Apr68
– The place and the time / Murder in my heart for the judge / Bitter wind / Can't be so bad / Just like Gene Autry; a foxtrot [plays at 78 rpm] / He / Motorcycle Irene / Three-four / Funky-tunk / Rose colored eyes / Miller's blues / Naked, if I want to. <US +free live-lp> **GRAPE JAM** <CXS 3> – Never / Boysenberry jam / Black currant jam / Marmalade / The lake.
above featured AL KOOPER & MIKE BLOOMFIELD.

Jul 68. (7") <44567> **CAN'T BE SO BAD. / BITTER WIND**		`-`	`_`
Jul 68. (7") (CBS 3555) **CAN'T BE SO BAD. / MURDER IN MY HEART FOR THE JUDGE**		`-`	`_`

—— SPENCE became a serious drug addict, and left, going into a mental hospital for six months. He went solo later in 1969, releasing OAR album (see further below). He is now under residential-care at his home in San Jose, California.

Feb 69. (lp) (63430) <9696> **MOBY GRAPE '69**
– Ooh mama ooh / Ain't that a shame / I am not willing / It's a beautiful day today / Hoochie / Trucking man / If you can't learn from my mistakes / Captain Nemo / What's to choose / Going nowhere / Seeing. *(re-iss. Aug76; same)*

Feb 69. (7") <44789> **TRUCKING MAN. / IF YOU CAN'T LEARN FROM MY MISTAKES**

Feb 69. (7") (CBS 3945) **TRUCKING MAN. / OOH MAMA OOH**

Jun 69. (7") <44885> **OOH MAMA OOH. / IT'S SO BEAUTIFUL TODAY**

—— session man **BOB MOORE** – bass repl. MOSLEY who joined the US marines. He issued a self-titled album for 'Reprise' in 1972.

Sep 69. (lp) (63698) <9912> **TRULY FINE CITIZEN**
– Changes, circles spinning / Looper / Truly fine citizen / Beautiful is beautiful / Love song / Right before my eyes / Open up your heart / Now I know high / Treat me bad / Tongue-tied / Love song (part 2).

—— MOBY GRAPE had already split Spring 1969. For nearly 2 years, MILLER and STEVENSON joined The RHYTHM DUKES. Original quintet re-formed with newcomer **GORDON STEVENS** – viola, mandolin

	Reprise	Reprise
Sep 71. (7") <1040> **GYPSY WEDDING. / APOCAYPSE**	-	
Nov 71. (7") <1055> **GOIN' DOWN TO TEXAS. / ABOUT TIME**	-	

Jan 72. (lp) (K 44152) <6460> **20 GRANITE CREEK**   Sep71
– Gypsy wedding / I'm the kind of man that baby you can trust / About time / Goin' down to Texas / Road to the Sun / Apocalypse / Chinese song / Roadhouse blues / Ode to the man at the end of the bar / Wild oats moan / Horse out in the rain. *(re-iss. May86 on 'Edsel' lp/c; ED/CED 176)*

Jul 72. (7"; as BOB MOSLEY & MOBY GRAPE) <1096> **GONE FISHING. / GYPSY WEDDING**

—— In the early 70's, their manager Matthew Katz had put together a fake **MOBY GRAPE** with **FRANK RECARD** – vocals, guitar / **TOMMY SPURLOCK** – guitar / **DANNY TIMMS** – keyboards / **BOB NEWKIRK** – drums. BOB MOSLEY had gone solo Mar'72 releasing eponymous album on 'Warner Bros.'. The real MOBY GRAPE re-formed late 1973-Spring'75 with **LEWIS, MILLER, MOSLEY**, plus **JEFF BLACKBURN** – guitar & **JOHN CRAVIOTTA** – drums. With no new record deal, they broke again and **LEWIS, MILLER, CRAVIOTTA** and **MICHAEL BEAN** – guitar (ex-H.P. LOVECRAFT) formed **FINE WINE**. They issued one eponymous album in Germany mid'75. With NEIL YOUNG; MOSLEY, CRAVIOTTA and BLACKBURN formed the shortly defunct DUCKS (mid'77).

—— **MOBY GRAPE** re-formed again, this time with **SKIP SPENCE** returning with **MILLER + LEWIS**, plus newboys **CORNELIUS BUMPUS** – keyboards / **CHRISTIAN POWELL** – bass / **JOHN OXENDINE** – drums.

	not iss.	Escape
Apr 78. (lp) <JAM 95018> **LIVE GRAPE (live)**	-	

– The last horizon / Here I sit / Honk tonk / Cuttin' in / Must be goin' now dear / Your rider / Up in the air / Set me down easy / Love you so much / You got everything I need. *(UK-iss.Jun87 on 'Line'; 400 335)*

—— Finally let go around the late 70's, although some releases surfaced.

	not iss.	San Fran Sound
1984. (lp) <4830> **MOBY GRAPE '84**	-	

– Silver wheels / Better days / Hard road to follow / Sitting and watching / City lights / Queen of the crow / Lost horizon / I didn't lie to you / Suzzam / Too old to boogie / Think it over / American dream / Reprise.

1989. (lp; as MOSLEY GRAPE) **LIVE AT INDIGO RANCH (live)** -

—— They re-formed mid 1990 as The MELVILLES, then The LEGENDARY GRAPE; released eponymous cassette in 1991 on 'Herman'. Line-up:- MILLER, LEWIS, MOSLEY, STEVENSON + DAN ABERTNATHY – guitar + KIRT TUTTLE – drums. In 1993, JERRY MILLER issued cassette 'NOW I SEE' for 'Herman'.

– compilations, others, etc. –

on 'CBS / Columbia' unless mentioned otherwise
Jun 74. (lp) (64743) <31098> **GREAT GRAPE**
Jun 76. (lp) (53371) **THE BEST OF MOBY GRAPE** - - Europe
Feb 86. (lp) Edsel; (ED 171) **MURDER IN MY HEART** (2nd-4th lp's)
– Murder in my heart for the judge / He / Can't be so bad / Motorcycle Irene / Three-four / Rose coloured eyes / Bitter wind / I am not willing / It's a beautiful day today / If you can't learn from my mistakes / What's to choose / Seeing / Changes, circles spinning / Right before my eyes.

Nov 93. (d-cd) Legacy; (CD 53041) **VINTAGE: THE VERY BEST OF MOBY GRAPE**
(re-iss. Jun96 on 'Columbia'; 483958-2)

ALEXANDER SKIP SPENCE

—— solo (all instruments)

	not iss.	Columbia
Oct 69. (lp) <CS 9831> **OAR**	-	-

– Little hands / Cripple creek / Diana / Margaret – Tiger rug / Weighted down (the prison song) / War in peace / Broken heart / All come to meet her / Book of Moses / Dixie peach promenade / Lawrence of Euphoria / Grey / Afro. *(UK-iss.Sep88 on 'Edsel'; ED 282)* (cd-iss. Feb91; EDCD 282)

MOCK TURTLES (dig out; Great Alt & Indie . . .)

MODERN LOVERS (see under ⇒ RICHMAN, Jonathan)

MOGWAI

Formed: Glasgow, Scotland . . . 1995 by DOMINIC AITCHISON, STUART LESLIE BRAITHWAITE and MARTIN BULLOCH. In the Spring of '96, the band debuted with 'TUNER' / 'LOWER', a precursor to the band's double whammy NME Singles Of The Week, 'SUMMER' and 'NEW PATHS TO

HELICON'. Early in 1997, they signed to the suffocatingly hip Glasgow-based 'Chemikal Underground' (home of BIS and friends, ARAB STRAP), the first outing being 'THE 4 SATIN EP'. A fine collection of their early singles was released a month later in June, although another label was responsible. That summer, the new 5-piece MOGWAI (complete with JOHN CUMMINGS and former TEENAGE FANCLUB member, BRENDON O'HARE) alternately bludgeoned/charmed the NME tent at Scotland's premier festival 'T In The Park' with their striking hybrid of SONIC YOUTH, METALLICA and pre-'Blue Monday' NEW ORDER! The feverishly anticipated "proper" debut album, 'MOGWAI YOUNG TEAM' was released late '97 to rave reviews, also scraping into the Top 75. Stunningly dynamic, the record shifted seamlessly from tranquil, bleakly beautiful soundscapes to brain scrambling white noise and sledgehammer riffing. Prime examples were 'LIKE HEROD', 'WITH PORTFOLIO' and 'MOGWAI FEAR SATAN', while 'TRACY' was a near 10-minute collage of drifting, childlike charm segueing into a taped phone conversation. Another track, 'R U STILL IN 2 IT', featured the mumbling vocal talents of ARAB STRAP's AIDAN MOFFAT. Prior to the album's release, O'HARE was summarily dismissed, apparently for yapping his way through an ARAB STRAP gig (tsk, tsk!). 1998 was indeed a busy year for the "young team", five releases hitting the shops between March and August and nearly all making the Top 75. The first of these, ' . . . ... DO THE ROCK BOOGALOO' was a split affair with fellow noisemongers MAGOO, the title not an EP but the "un"-covering of two classic BLACK SABBATH tracks, MOGWAI having a laugh with 'SWEET LEAF'. 'FEAR SATAN' was then chosen for the remix treatment (MY BLOODY VALENTINE's the highlight), while a full album, 'KICKING A DEAD PIG: MOGWAI SONGS REMIXED', was all their best tunes reworked by others including ARAB STRAP, KID LOCO and ALEC EMPIRE. 'Chemikal Underground' put their two-pennith in by issuing the 'NO EDUCATION = NO FUTURE (FUCK THE CURFEW)' ep, while 'TEN RAPID' was an early singles collection. The following March (with newcomer pianist BARRY BURNS now a fully-fledged member) 'COME ON DIE YOUNG' was the gangland war cry they chose as the title of their more sedate second album proper. A hard album indeed, in the sense that it took time to "get into" (probably due to the slight omission of their characteristic sonic crescendos), it unearthed a softer, more delicate style which was rewarded with a Top 30 entry. Opening with 'PUNK ROCK' (complete with IGGY POP archive interview as voiceover), the Slo-Fi 'CODY' and the sludgedelic 'HELP BOTH WAYS, the album proved the young MOGWAI were top of the class; 'EX-COWBOY' and the emotional MORRICONE-inspired finale 'PUNK ROCK / PUFF DADDY / ANtICHRISt' were also noteworthy. Towards the end of '99, they delivered a self-titled e.p., attributing 'STANLEY KUBRICK' as the lead track. The year 2000 could indeed see MOGWAI as the saviours of "Rock" music . . . here's hoping. • **Covered:** HONEY (Spacemen 3).

Album rating: MOGWAI YOUNG TEAM (*9) / KICKING A DEAD PIG: MOGWAI SONGS REMIXED (*7) / TEN RAPID compilation (*8) / COME ON DIE YOUNG (*8)

pLasmatroN (b. STUART BRAITHWAITE) – guitar, vocals / **DEMONIC** (b. DOMINIC AITCHISON) – bass / **bionic** (b. MARTIN BULLOCH) – drums

	Rock Action	not iss.
Feb 96. (ltd-7") (RAR 001) **TUNER. / LOWER**		-
	Che	not iss.
May 96. (ltd-7"green) (che 61) **ANGELS VERSUS ALIENS. / (other side by DWEEB)**		-
	Love Train	not iss.
Sep 96. (ltd-7"; "CAMDEN CRAWL II") (PUBE 011) **A PLACE FOR PARKS. / (other artists)**		-
Oct 96. (ltd-7"; "TEN DAY WEEKEND") (PUBE 012) **I AM NOT BATMAN. / (other artists)**		-
Nov 96. (ltd-7") (PUBE 014) **SUMMER. / ITHICA 27 o 9**		-
	Wurlitzer Jukebox	not iss.
Jan 97. (ltd-7") (WJ 22) **NEW PATHS TO HELICON**		-

– Helicon 1 / Helicon 2.

—— added **Cpt. Meat** (aka JOHN CUMMINGS) – guitar

	F&J/13th Note	not iss.
Mar 97. (ltd-7"; "CLUB BEATROOT part four") (SHAG 13.05) **STEREO DEE (live). / (other side by Ph FAMILY)**		-
	Chemikal Underground	Jetset
May 97. (12"ep/cd-ep) (chem 015/+cd) <TWA 14CD> **4 SATIN EP**		

– Superheroes of BMX / Now you're taken / Stereo Dee. <US++> – Guardians of space. *(re-iss. Apr99; same)*

—— added **+the relic+** (aka BRENDAN O'HARE – piano (of-MACROCOSMICA, ex-TEENAGE FANCLUB, ex-TELSTAR PONIES)

Oct 97. (cd/d-lp) (chem 018 cd/lp) <7> **MOGWAI YOUNG TEAM** **75**
– Yes! I am a long way from home / Like Herod / Radar maker / Tracy / Summer (Priority version) / With portfolio / R u still in 2 it / A cheery wave from stranded youngsters / Mogwai fear Satan. *(re-iss. Apr99; same)*

—— now without O'HARE, who was sacked (see above)

Mar 98. (7"; split w/ MAGOO) (NING 47CD) **` . ... DO THE ROCK BOOGALOO** **60** -
– Black Sabbath (by MAGOO) / Sweet leaf.
(above issued on 'Fierce Panda', below 2 for 'eye q' / US 'Jetset')

Apr 98. (cd-ep) (eyeuk 032cd) **FEAR SATAN remixes** **57**
– Mogwai remix / U-ziq remix / Surgeon remix / My Bloody Valentine remix. *(re-iss. Apr99; same)*

May 98. (cd/d-lp) (eyeuk cd/lp) <TWA 13 CD/LP> **KICKING A DEAD PIG: MOGWAI SONGS REMIXED** Jun98
– Like Herod (Hood remix) / Helicon 2 (Max Tundra remix) / Summer (Klute's

weird winter remix) / Gwai on 45 (Arab Strap remix) / A cheery wave from stranded youngsters (Third Eye Foundation tet offensive remix) / Like Herod (Alec Empire's face the future remix) / Mogwai fear Satan (Surgeon remix) / R U still in to it? (DJ Q remix) / Tracy (Kid Loco's playing with the young team remix) / Mogwai fear Satan (Mogwai remix). *(re-iss. Apr99; same)*

Jun 98. (12"ep/cd-ep) *(chem 026/+cd)* <111230> **NO EDUCATION = NO FUTURE (FUCK THE CURFEW) e.p.**   `68` `[ ]`
– Xmas steps / Rollerball / Small children in the background. *(re-iss. Apr99; same)*

—— added **BARRY BURNS** – piano, flute, guitar

Mar 99. (d-lp/cd) *(chem 033/+cd)* **COME ON DIE YOUNG**   `29` `[ ]`
– Punk rock: / Cody / Helps both ways / Year 2000 non-compliant cardia / Kappa / Waltz for Aidan / May nothing but happiness come through your door / Oh! how the dogs stack up / Ex-cowboy / Chocky / Christmas steps / Punk rock – Puff Daddy – ANtICHRISt.

Oct 99. (12"ep/cd-ep) *(chem 036/+cd)* **MOGWAI e.p.**   `[ - ]`
– Stanley Kubrick / Christmas song / Burn girl prom-queen / Rage: man.

– compilations, etc. –

Aug 98. (cd) *Rock Action; (rock act 05cd) / Jetset; <TWA 05LP>* **TEN RAPID (collected recordings 1996-1997)**   `[ ]` `Aug97`
– Summer / Helicon 2 / Angels versus aliens / I am not Batman / Tuner / Ithica 27 o 9 / A place for parks / Helicon 1 / End.

MOIST (dig out; Great Metal . . .)

MOLLY HATCHET (dig out; Great Metal . . .)

MONACO (see under ⇒ NEW ORDER)

MONKEES

Formed: Los Angeles, California, USA . . . 1965, the brainchild of Hollywood TV producers, BOB RAFELSON and BERT SCHNEIDER. The pair had wanted to make a sit-com based around The BEATLES' film, 'A Hard Day's Night' and in September of that year, they ran a wanted ad for four boys aged between 17 and 21. Out of over four hundred applicants, they picked the lucky DAVY JONES, MICKEY DOLENZ, MIKE NESMITH & PETER TORK, signing them to the 'Colpix' label. All had fairly notable previous experience (see below), and were duly sent for acting/grooming lessons early in '66. Following difficulties on the songwriting front, BOB & BERT brought in pensmiths TOMMY BOYCE and BOBBY HART (on appointment from 'Screen Gems' top man, Don Kirshner), who also became the group's producers. Other writers were brought in, namely NEIL DIAMOND, GERRY GOFFIN & CAROLE KING, NEIL SEDAKA plus BARRY MANN & CYNTHIA WEIL. On the 12th of September 1966, "The MONKEES" TV show premiered on NBC, and although not an overnight success, became a teenage favourite. A month later, their debut 45, 'LAST TRAIN TO CLARKSVILLE', was released, showcasing their BEACH BOYS-style harmonies and soon climbing to US No.1. Their follow-up, 'I'M A BELIEVER' (penned by NEIL DIAMOND), also hit the top, and with their show now on BBC TV, it repeated the feat in Britain. Another DIAMOND composition, 'A LITTLE BIT ME, A LITTLE BIT YOU', made both Top 3's in March '67 (two of their albums also having amassed cross-Atlantic success). The aforementioned 45's virtually turned the group into an overnight pop phenomenon, their boyish good looks and "zany" antics endearing their bubblegum psychedelia to the nation's teenyboppers (although their music has surprisingly stood the test of time, giving them cult status). For the remainder of the 60's (with NESMITH increasingly dominating the songwriting), they carried on with further TV series (one featuring ZAPPA, another with TIM BUCKLEY) and some major hits. Their show was axed towards the end of the decade, by which time they had gone into the movies, making the box-office disaster, 'HEAD', with writers BOB RAFELSON and JACK NICHOLSON (yes that one!). • **Covered:** DAYDREAM BELIEVER (John Sebastian) / D.W. WASHBURN (Leiber-Stoller) / etc. • **Trivia:** In 1967, their 'RANDY SCOUSE GIT' (taken from the character Alf Garnett in British sit-com 'Til Death Us Do Part') was banned by the BBC, and later given the 'ALTERNATIVE TITLE' motif.

Best CD compilation: HERE THEY COME – THE GREATEST HITS OF . . . (*8)

DAVY JONES (b.30 Dec'46, Manchester, England) – vocals, rhythm guitar (ex-apprentice jockey, actor UK TV 'Coronation Street' & 'Z Cars' / solo artist) / **MICKEY DOLENZ** (b. GEORGE MICHAEL DOLENZ JR., 8 Mar'45, Tarzana, Calif.) – drums, vocals (child actor 'Circus Boy' as Corky, 'Peyton Place', etc.) / **MIKE NESMITH** (b. ROBERT MICHAEL NESMITH, 30 Dec'42, Houston, Texas) – guitar, vocals (ex-folk solo act as MICHAEL BLESSING on 'Colpix' label) / **PETER TORK** (b. PETER THORKELSON, 13 Feb'44, Washington, D.C.) – bass, vocals (ex-AU GO GO SINGERS with RICHIE FURAY / recommended by STEPHEN STILLS)

Session men on discs were; JAMES BURTON, GLEN CAMPBELL, LEON RUSSELL, HAL BLAINE + DAVID GATES.

                      RCA Victor Colgems

Oct 66. (7") *(RCA 1547)* <1001> **LAST TRAIN TO CLARKSVILLE. / TAKE A GIANT STEP**   `[ ]` `1` `Sep66`
(late Jan'67; – debut single hit UK No.23)

Dec 66. (7") *(RCA 1560)* <1002> **I'M A BELIEVER. / I'M NOT YOUR STEPPING STONE**   `1` `1` / `20`

Jan 67. (lp; mono/stereo) *(RD/SF 7844)* <101> **THE MONKEES**   `1` `1` `Oct66`
– Theme from The Monkees / Saturday's child / I wanna be free / Tomorrow's gonna be another day / Papa Gene's blues / Take a giant step / Last train to Clarksville /

This just doesn't seem to be my day / Let's dance on / I'll be true to you / Sweet young thing / Gonna buy me a dog. *<re-iss. Aug86 on 'Rhino' hit No.92; 70140> (cd-iss. Apr88 on 'Arista'; 258773) (cd-iss. Dec94 on 'Warners'; 4509 97655-2)*

Mar 67. (7") *(RCA 1580)* <1004> **A LITTLE BIT ME, A LITTLE BIT YOU. / THE GIRL I KNEW SOMEWHERE**   `3` `2` / `39`

Apr 67. (lp; mono/stereo) *(RD/SF 7868)* <102> **MORE OF THE MONKEES**   `1` `1` `Feb67`
– When love comes knockin' (at your door) / She / Mary, Mary / Hold on girl / Your Auntie Grizelda / (I'm not you) Steppin' stone / Look out (here comes tomorrow) / The kind of girl I could love / The day we fell in love / Sometime in the morning / Laugh / I'm a believer. *<re-iss. Aug86 on 'Rhino' hit No.96; 70142> (cd-iss. Jun88 on 'Arista'; 259052) (cd-iss. Dec94 on 'Warners'; 4509 97658-2)*

Jun 67. (7") *(RCA 1604)* **ALTERNATIVE TITLE. / FORGET THAT GIRL**   `2` `-`
(above was to have been called 'RANDY SCOUSE GIT')

Jul 67. (lp; mono/stereo) *(RD/SF 7868)* <103> **HEADQUARTERS**   `2` `1` `Jun67`
– You told me / I'll spend my life with you / Forget that girl / Band 6 / You just may be the one / Shades of grey / I can't get her off my mind / For Pete's sake / Mr. Webster / Sunny girlfriend / Zilch / No time / Early morning blues and greens / Randy Scouse git. *<re-iss. Aug86 on 'Rhino'; 70143> (cd-iss. Feb95 on 'Warners'; 4509 97662-2)*

Jul 67. (7") *(RCA 1620)* 1007> **PLEASANT VALLEY SUNDAY. / WORDS**   `11` `3` / `11`

Nov 67. (7") *(RCA 1645)* <1012> **DAYDREAM BELIEVER. / GOING DOWN**   `5` `1`

Jan 68. (lp; mono/stereo) *(RD/SF 7912)* <104> **PISCES, AQUARIUS, CAPRICORN AND JONES LTD.**   `5` `1` `Nov67`
– Salesman / She hangs out / The door into summer / Love is only sleeping / Cuddly toy / Words / Hard to believe / What am I doing hangin' round? / Peter Percival Patterson's pet pig Porky / Pleasant Valley Sunday / Daily nightly / Don't call on me / Star collector. *<re-iss. Aug86 on 'Rhino'; 70141> (cd-iss. Feb95 on 'Warners'; 4509 97663-2)*

Mar 68. (7") *(RCA 1673)* <1019> **VALLERI. / TAPIOCA TUNDRA**   `12` `3` / `34`

May 68. (lp; mono/stereo) *(RD/SF 7948)* <109> **THE BIRDS, THE BEES & THE MONKEES**   `[ ]` `3`
– Dream world / Auntie's municipal court / We were made for each other / Tapioca tundra / Daydream believer / Writing wrongs / I'll be back on my feet / The poster / P.O. Box 9847 / Magnolia Simms / Valleri / Zor and Zam. *<re-iss. Aug86 on 'Rhino'; 70144> (cd-iss. Dec94 on 'Warners'; 4509 97665-2)*

Jun 68. (7") *(RCA 1706)* <1023> **D.W. WASHBURN. / IT'S NICE TO BE WITH YOU**   `17` `19` / `51`

Sep 68. (7") <1031> **THE PORPOISE SONG. / AS WE GO ALONG**   `[ - ]` `62`

—— now down to trio when TORK departed. (he still appeared on below s/track)

Mar 69. (7") *(RCA 1802)* <5000> **TEARDROP CITY. / A MAN WITHOUT A DREAM**   `46` `56` `Feb69`

May 69. (lp; mono/stereo) *(RD/SF 8016)* <113> **INSTANT REPLAY**   `[ ]` `32` `Feb69`
– Through the looking glass / Don't listen to Linda / I won't be the same without her / Me without you / Just a game / Don't wait for me / You and I / While I cry / Teardrop city / The girl I left behind me / Man without a dream / Shorty Blackwell. *<re-iss. Oct86 on 'Rhino'; 70147> (cd-iss. Feb95 on 'Warners'; 4509 97661-2)*

Jun 69. (7") *(RCA 1824)* <5004> **SOMEDAY MAN. / LISTEN TO THE BAND**   `47` `81` / `63`

Aug 69. (7") *(RCA 1862)* **DADDY'S SONG. / THE PORPOISE SONG**   `[ ]` `[ ]`

Sep 69. (lp; mono/stereo) *(RD/SF 8051)* <5008> **HEAD (Soundtrack)**   `[ ]` `45` `Dec68`
– Opening ceremony / The porpoise song / Ditty Diego-war chant / Circle sky / Supplicio / Can you dig it / Gravy / Superstitious / As we go along / Dandruff / Daddy's song / Poll / Long title: Do I have to do this all over again / Swami-plus strings. *<re-iss. Oct86 on 'Rhino'; 70146> (cd-iss. Dec94 on 'Warners'; 4509 97659-2)*

Sep 69. (7") *(RCA 1887)* <5005> **GOOD CLEAN FUN. / MOMMY AND DADDY**   `[ ]` `82`

Oct 69. (lp) <117> **THE MONKEES PRESENT . . .**   `[ - ]` `100`
– Little girl / Good clean fun / If I knew / Bye bye baby bye bye / Never tell a woman yes / Looking for the good times / Ladies Aid Society / Listen to the band / French song / Mommy and daddy / Oklahoma backroom dancer / Pillow time. *<re-iss. Nov86 on 'Rhino'; 70147> (cd-iss. Dec94 on 'Warners'; 4509 97660-2)*

—— now down to **JONES + DOLENZ** duo when NESMITH left to go solo.

Jun 70. (7") *(RCA 1958)* <5011> **OH MY MY. / LOVE YOU BETTER**   `[ ]` `98`

1970. (lp) <119> **CHANGES**
– Oh my my / Ticket on a ferry ride / You're so good to me / It's got to be love / Acapulco sun / 99 pounds / Tell me love / Do you feel it too / I love you better / All alone in the dark / Midnight train / I never thought it peculiar. *<re-iss. Aug86 on 'Rhino'; 70148> (cd-iss. Dec94 on 'Warners'; 4509 97657-2)*

MONKEES

—— re-formed with **DOLENZ, JONES + TORK** and session people.

                      Arista   Arista

Oct 86. (7"pic-d-4/7") *(ARIST 1/2/3/4+/673)* <9505> **THAT WAS THEN, THIS IS NOW. / THEME FROM THE MONKEES**   `68` `20` `Jul86`
(12"+=) *(ARIST 12-673)* – Pleasant valley Sunday / Last train to Clarksville.

Oct 86. (lp/c/cd) *(207/407/257 874)* <8432> **THEN & NOW . . . THE BEST OF THE MONKEES** (w/ 3 new)   `[ ]` `21` `Jul86`
– Then and now / Tripwire / Theme from The Monkees / Last train to Clarksville / Take a giant step / I'm a believer / I'm not your stepping stone / A little bit me, a little you / Anytime, anyplace, anywhere / That was then, this is now / The girl I knew somewhere / Pleasant valley Sunday / What am I doing hangin' 'round / Daydream believer / Valeri / Kicks.

Oct 86. (7") <9532> **DAYDREAM BELIEVER. / RANDY SCOUSE GIT**   `[ - ]` `79`

                      Rhino   Rhino

Aug 87. (7") <74408> **HEART AND SOUL. / M.G.B.G.T.**   `[ - ]` `87`

Aug 87. (lp/c/cd) <(RN IN/IC/CD 70706)> **POOL IT!**   `[ ]` `72`
– Heart and soul / (I'd go the) Whole wide world / Long way home / Secret heart / Gettin' in / (I'll) Love you forever / Every step of the way / Don't bring me down /

Midnight / She's movin' in with Rico / Since you went away / Counting on you. *(cd-iss. Nov95;)*

Nov 87. (7") **EVERY STEP OF THE WAY. / I LOVE YOU FOREVER**   - ☐

—— the original four re-formed in 1996

		Artful	Artful

Jan 97. (cd/c) *(ARTFUL CD/MC 6) <72542>* **JUSTUS**
– Circle sky / Never enough / Oh what a night / You and I / Unlucky stars / Admiral Mike / Dyin' of a broken heart / Regional girl / Run away from life / I believe you / It's my life / If 't not too late.

– compilations, etc. –

Date	Entry	UK	US
Jun 69.	(lp) *Colgems; <115>* **GREATEST HITS**	-	89
1971.	(lp) *Colgems; <329>* **GOLDEN HITS**	-	
1972.	(lp) *Colgems; <1001>* **BARREL FULL OF MONKEES**	-	
1973.	(d-lp) *Laurie House; <8009>* **THE MONKEES**	-	
1974.	(lp) *Bell; <6081>* **RE-FOCUS**	-	
May 74.	(7") *Bell; (BLL 1354)* **MONKEES THEME. / I'M A BELIEVER** *(re-iss. Mar90 on 'Old Gold'; OG 9123)*		-
Sep 74.	(c) *Sounds Superb; (SPR 80032)* **THE MONKEES**		
1974.	(c) *Bell; (TCBEL 148)* **25 HITS**		
Aug 76.	(lp) *Arista; <4089>* **THE MONKEES' GREATEST HITS**	-	58
Feb 80.	(7"ep) *Arista; (ARIST 326)* **THE MONKEES**	33	

– Daydream believer / Last train to Clarksville / I'm a believer / A little bit me, a little bit you.

| Jun 81. | (7"ep) *Arista; (ARIST 402)* **THE MONKEES VOL.2** | | |

– I'm not your stepping stone / Pleasant valley Sunday / Alternative title (Randy Scouse git) / What am I doing.

Jun 81.	(d-lp/d-c) *Arista; (DARTY/TCDAR 12)* **THE MONKEES**	99	
Jun 81.	(lp/c) *Music For Pleasure; (MFP/TCMFP 50499)* **THE BEST OF THE MONKEES**		-
Aug 82.	(7"ep) *Arista; (ARIST 487)* **I'M A BELIEVER**		

– I'm a believer / Don't listen to Linda / Last train to Clarksville / Theme from 'The Monkees'.

Jul 82.	(7") *Old Gold; (OG 9117)* **DAYDREAM BELIEVER. / LAST TRAIN TO CLARKSVILLE**		
Oct 82.	(lp/c) *Ronco; (RTL /4CRTL 2085)* **20 GOLDEN GREATS**		-
Jun 84.	(7"ep/c-ep) *Scoop; (7SR /7SC 5035)* **6 TRACK HITS**		-

– I'm a believer / Valleri / Alternative title (Randy Scouse git) / Somebody man / A little bit you, a little bit me / Pleasant valley Sunday.

Jul 84.	(lp) *Rhino; <RNLP 113>* **MONKEE FLIPS**	-	
1984.	(lp/pic-lp) *Rhino;* **MONKEE BUSINESS**	-	
Nov 84.	(lp/c) *Platinum; (PLAT/PLAC 05)* **THE MONKEES' GREATEST HITS** *(cd-iss. 1988; PLATCD 05)*		-
Oct 87.	(lp/c/cd) *Rhino; (RN LP/C/CD 70139)* **LIVE 1967 (live)**	-	
Oct 87.	(lp/c) *Rhino; (RN LP/C 70150)* **MISSING LINKS (rare)**	-	
Jun 88.	(7") *Old Gold; (OG 9117)* **DAYDREAM BELIEVER. / LAST TRAIN TO CLARKSVILLE**		
Mar 89.	(7"ep/3"cd-ep) *Arista; (112/662 157)* **THE MONKEES**	62	

– Daydream believer / A little bit me, a little bit you / Theme from The Monkees.

| Apr 89. | (7"ep/3"cd-ep) *Arista; (112/662 158)* **THE MONKEES VOL.2** | | |

– Last train to Clarksville / I'm a believer / Pleasant valley Sunday.

| Apr 89. | (lp/c/cd) *K-Tel; (NE1/CD2/NCD3 432)* **HEY HEY IT'S THE MONKEES – GREATEST HITS** | 12 | |

– Theme from The Monkees / Pleasant valley Sunday / The girl I knew somewhere / D.W. Washburn / Last train to Clarksville / A little bit me, a little bit you / teardrop city / Some day man / What am I doing hangin' 'round / Daydream believer / I'm not your stepping stone / Alternative title (randy scouse git) / Words / I'm a believer / Listen to the band / Valeri / Tapioca tundra / That was then, this is now.

| Apr 94. | (cd/c) *Movieplay Gold; (MPV/+4 5544)* **GREATEST HITS** | | |
| Mar 97. | (cd/c) *Telstar; (954835218-2/-4)* **HERE THEY COME: THE GREATEST HITS OF THE MONKEES** | 15 | - |

MONKS OF DOOM (see under ⇒ **CAMPER VAN BEETHOVEN**)

MONOCHROME SET (dig out; Great Alt & Indie . . .)

MONSTER MAGNET

Formed: New Jersey, USA . . . 1989 by porn-fixated DAVE WYNDORF (vocalist/guitarist) along with JOHN McBAIN (guitar), JOE CALANDRA (bass) and JOHN KLEINMAN (drums). Signing to European indie label 'Glitterhouse' ('Primo Scree' in the States), MONSTER MAGNET released their eponymous debut in 1991, drawing favourable reviews from the inkies and metal press alike. Akin to a heavier THEE HYPNOTICS, the band were evidently classic psych-rock fetishists with HAWKWIND as an obvious reference point as well as the mogadon riffing of IRON BUTTERFLY etc. Arguably 'grunge' in the true sense of the word; sludgy, filthy, mind-numbingly heavy and bloody scary, 'SPINE OF GOD' (1992) was a tour de force of 'like, heavy, man' drug-rock featuring the legendary album sleeve boast, 'It's a satanic drug thing . . . you wouldn't understand', erm.. right. God knows exactly what kind of drugs these guys were on (DAVE had been apparently selling and taking the stuff since he was 14!) but it sure as hell wasn't 'E'. After a tour supporting SOUNDGARDEN, the band replaced the departing McBAIN with ED MUNDELL, signing with 'A&M' and releasing their major label debut, 'SUPERJUDGE' (1993). Even more of a headbang than 'SPINE..', this was perhaps the heaviest psychedelia ever laid down on vinyl, the likes of 'CYCLOPS REVOLUTION' and 'ELEPHANT BELL' practically redefining the term, while a cover of HAWKWIND's 'BRAINSTORM' was reliably bowel-quaking. 'DOPES TO INFINITY' (1995) carried on in much the same bludgeoning fashion,

advising mere mortals who're happy with a pint down the pub (as opposed to munching handfuls of nasty hallucinogens) to 'LOOK TO YOUR ORB FOR THE WARNING', eh? With guitarist PHIL CAIVANO now on board, MONSTER MAGNET's musical spaceship took off once more. Fourth album, 'POWERTRIP' (1998), was exactly that with numbers such as the title track and 'SPACE LORD' greasing up the UK Top 50 early the following year. • **Covered:** KICK OUT THE JAMS (MC5).

Album rating: SPINE OF GOD (*8) / SUPERJUDGE (*8) / DOPES TO INFINITY (*7) / POWERTRIP (*6)

DAVE WYNDORF – vocals, guitar / **JOHN McBAIN** – guitar / **JOE CALANDRA** – bass / **JOHN KLEINMAN** – drums

		Glitterhouse	PrimoScree
Nov 90.	(12"ep/cd-ep) *(EFA 08123-90)* **MONSTER MAGNET**	-	German

– Snake dance / Tractor / Nod scene / Freak shop USA / Lizard Johnny. *(UK cd-iss. May99 on 'Global Warming'; GRCD 123)*

| Oct 91. | (m-cd) *(GRCD 158) <CAROL 1471>* **TAB** | | |

– Tab / 25 / Longhair / Lord 13. *(re-iss. May99; as US) (re-iss.May99; as UK)*

| Jun 92. | (cd/c/lp) *(GR 017-2/-4/-1) <EFA 08172-08>* **SPINE OF GOD** | | Dec91 |

– Pill shovel / Medicine / Nod scene / Black mastermind / Zodiac lung / Spine of God / Snake dance / Sin's a good man's brother / Ozium. *(cd re-iss. Mar99 on 'Caroline'; CAROL 1718) (cd re-iss. May99; as original)*

| May 93. | (12"/cd-s) *(GR/+CD 204)* **EVIL. / ELEPHANT BELL / SPINE OF GOD (live)** | | |

—— **ED MUNDEL** – lead guitar; repl. McBAIN

		A&M	A&M
Apr 93.	(cd/c/red-lp) *(540 079-2/-4/-1) <31454-0079-2/-4/-1>* **SUPERJUDGE**		

– Cyclops revolution / Twin earth / Superjudge / Cage around the sun / Elephant bell / Dinosaur vacume / Evil (is going on) / Stadium / Face down / Brainstorm / Black balloon.

May 93.	(7") *(580 280-7)* **TWIN EARTH. / NOD SCENE (live)**	67	
	(12"+=/cd-s+=) *(580 281-1/-2)* – Medicine (live).		
Mar 95.	(7"sha-pic-d) **NEGASONIC TEENAGE WARHEAD. / BLOW 'EM OFF**	49	
	(cd-s+=) – Murder (live) / Superjudge live).		
	(cd-s) – ('A'side) / Eclipse this / Third alternative / Look into your orb for a warning.		
Mar 95.	(cd/d-lp) *(540 315-2/-1)* **DOPES TO INFINITY**	51	

– Dopes to infinity / Megasonic teenage warhead / Look to your orb for the warning / All friends and kingdom come / Ego, the living planet / Blow 'em off / Third alternative / I control, I fly / King of Mars / Dead Christmas / Theme from "Masterburner" / Vertigo. *(d-lp+=)* – Forbidden planet.

Apr 95.	(7"pic-d) *(581 032-7)* **DOPES TO INFINITY. / I'M FIVE YEARS AHEAD OF MY TIME**	58	-
	(cd-s+=) *(581 033-2)* – Looking to the orb for a warning.		
	(cd-s+=) *(581 032-2)* – Dinosaur vacume / Theme from "Masterburner".		

—— added 5th member, **PHIL CAIVANO** – guitar

| Jun 98. | (cd) *<(540 908-2)>* **POWERTRIP** | 65 | 97 |

– Crop circle / Powertrip / Space Lord / Temple of your dreams / Bummer / Baby Gotterdamerung / 19 witches / 3rd eye landslide / See you in Hell / Tractor / Atomic clock / Goliath and the vampires / Your lies become you. *(re-iss. Feb99; same) (special d-cd May99; 490377-2)*

Jan 99.	(one-sided-7") *(582822-7)* **POWERTRIP**	39	-
	(cd-s+=) *(582823-2)* – Dead Christmas / ('A'-CD-Rom enhanced).		
	(cd-s) *(582825-2)* – ('A'side) / Twin Earth / Negasonic teenage warhead (enhanced).		
Feb 99.	(7"pic-d) *(563274-7)* **SPACE LORD. / THE GAME**	45	
	(cd-s) *(563275-2)* – ('A'side) / Big God / ('A'-CD-Rom).		
	(cd-s) *(563277-2)* – ('A'side) / Kick out the jams / Powertrip.		

MONTROSE (dig out; 4th edition or Great Metal . . .)

MOODY BLUES

Formed: Birmingham, England . . . May '64 by DENNY LAINE (who had just dissolved his DIPLOMATS band), MIKE PINDER, RAY THOMAS, CLINT WARWICK and GRAEME EDGE. They hooked up with manager, Tony Secunda, who subsequently secured them a deal with 'Decca' records. Their debut 45, 'LOSE YOUR MONEY', bombed, but by early '65 they were at the top spot with the BESSIE BANKS cover, 'GO NOW'. They tried desperately to emulate its success, and although they scored a few minor chart hits, they disbanded in October '66. The band quickly re-united a month later, after finding JUSTIN HAYWARD and JOHN LODGE to replace DENNY LAINE and recent member ROD CLARKE. Late in the summer of '67, they switched to the more adventurous 'Deram', immediately hitting with the concept album, 'DAYS OF FUTURE PASSED'. It broke from their mid-60's R&B/pop sound, to a more ambitious hybrid of rock and orchestral pop. A haunting piece from it, 'NIGHTS IN WHITE SATIN', became a massive seller and an all-time classic in the process. After a rare concert at London's Queen Elizabeth Hall, they issued a follow-up concept album, 'IN SEARCH OF THE LOST CHORD'. Another massive seller, it was succeeded by their first No.1 album, 'ON THE THRESHOLD OF A DREAM', in 1969. Later that year they founded their own label, 'Threshold', continuing the winning formula on a further clutch of early 70's albums, in addition to some finely crafted 45's, including 'QUESTION', 'ISN'T LIFE STRANGE' and 'I'M JUST A SINGER (IN A ROCK AND ROLL BAND)'. In the mid-70's, The MOODY BLUES was put on ice while they ventured into side projects. All had a relative degree of success, most notably the BLUE JAYS (aka HAYWARD & LODGE) who had a more mainstream sounding pop hit, 'BLUE GUITAR' (1975 & produced by 10cc). With new Swiss-born keyboard wizard PATRICK MORAZ on board

(fresh from a spell with YES), they released the comeback album, 'OCTAVE', in 1978, the record subsequently returning them to platinum status. Although early 80's album, 'LONG DISTANCE VOYAGER', went Top 10 on both sides of the Atlantic (No.1 in the US), creatively, the band were becoming stale.
• **Songwriters:** LAINE wrote most of material, until LODGE or HAYWARD took over late '66. Also covered; I DON'T WANT TO GO ON WITHOUT YOU (Drifters) / IT AIN'T NECESSARILY SO (Gershwin) / TIME IS ON MY SIDE (Rolling Stones) / BYE BYE BIRD (Sonny Boy Williamson) / etc.
Album rating: THE MAGNIFICENT MOODIES (*5) / DAYS OF FUTURE PASSED (*8) / IN SEARCH OF THE LOST CHORD (*7) / ON THE THRESHOLD OF A DREAM (*8) / TO OUR CHILDREN'S CHILDREN'S CHILDREN (*6) / A QUESTION OF BALANCE (*6) / EVERY GOOD BOY DESERVES FAVOUR (*7) / SEVENTH SOJOURN (*6) / THIS IS THE MOODY BLUES compilation (*8) / CAUGHT LIVE + 5 (*5) / OCTAVE (*5) / LONG DISTANCE VOYAGER (*7) / THE PRESENT (*5) / VOICES IN THE SKY – THE BEST OF THE MOODY BLUES compilation (*8) / THE OTHER SIDE OF LIFE (*6) / SUR LA MER (*4) / GREATEST HITS compilation (*7) / KEYS OF THE KINGDOM (*4) / A NIGHT AT RED ROCKS WITH THE COLORADO SYMPHONY ORCHESTRA (*4) / TIME TRAVELLER boxed-set (*8) / STRANGE TIMES (*4) / Justin Hayward & John Lodge: BLUE JAYS (*6)

DENNY LAINE (b. BRIAN HINES, 29 Oct'44, Jersey, England) – vocals, guitar (ex-DIPLOMATS) / **MIKE PINDER** (b.12 Dec'41) – keyboards, vocals (ex-CREWCATS) / **RAY THOMAS** (b.29 Dec'42, Stourport-on-Severn, England) – flute, vocals, harmonica / **CLINT WARWICK** (b. CLINTON ECCLES, 25 Jun'39) – bass, vocals / **GRAHAM EDGE** (b.30 Mar'42, Rochester, England) – drums (ex-GERRY LEVENE AND THE AVENGERS)

	Decca	London
Aug 64. (7"; as MOODYBLUES) (F 11971) **STEAL YOUR HEART AWAY. / LOSE YOUR MONEY (BUT DON'T LOSE YOUR MIND)**		–
Nov 64. (7") (F 12022) **GO NOW! / IT'S EASY CHILD**	1	–
Feb 65. (7") (F 12095) **I DON'T WANT TO GO ON WITHOUT YOU. / TIME IS ON MY SIDE**	33	
Feb 65. (7") <9726> **GO NOW! / LOSE YOUR MONEY (BUT DON'T LOSE YOUR MIND)**	–	10
May 65. (7") (F 12166) <9764> **FROM THE BOTTOM OF MY HEART (I LOVE YOU). / AND MY BABY'S GONE**	22	93

Jul 65. (lp) (LK 4711) <LP 428> **THE MAGNIFICENT MOODIES** <US-title 'GO NOW! – THE MOODY BLUES'>
– I'll go crazy / Something you got / Go now! / Can't nobody love you / I don't mind / I've got a dream / Let me go / Stop! / Thank you baby / It ain't necessarily so / True story / Bye bye bird. (cd-iss. Nov88 & Jan93 on 'Decca'; 820 758-2) (re-iss. Mar93 on 'Repertoire' +=;)– Steal your heart away / Lose your money (but don't lose your mind) / It's easy child / I don't want to go on without you (come back) / Time is on my side / From the bottom of my heart (I love you) / And my baby's gone.

	Decca	London
Oct 65. (7") (F 12266) **EVERYDAY. / YOU DON'T (ALL THE TIME)**	44	
Mar 66. (7") <9810> **STOP! / BYE BYE BIRD**	–	98

—— (Jul66) **ROD CLARKE** – bass repl. WARWICK

	Decca	London
Oct 66. (7") (F 12498) **BOULEVARD DE LA MADELAINE. / THIS IS MY HOUSE (BUT NOBODY CALLS)**		

—— (Nov'66) **JUSTIN HAYWARD** (b.14 Oct'46, Swindon, England) – vocals, guitar (ex-WILDE THREE, ex-solo artist) repl. DENNY who went solo (and later to WINGS) / **JOHN LODGE** (b.20 Jul'45) – bass, vocals (ex-EL RIOT & THE REBELS) repl. CLARKE

	Decca	London
Jan 67. (7"; w-drawn after a day) (F 12543) **LIFE'S NOT LIFE. / HE CAN WIN**	–	–
May 67. (7") (F 12607) **FLY ME HIGH. / REALLY HAVEN'T GOT THE TIME**		

	Deram	Deram
Aug 67. (7") (F 12670) **LOVE AND BEAUTY. / LEAVE THIS MAN ALONE**		
Nov 67. (7") (DM 161) <85023> **NIGHTS IN WHITE SATIN. / CITIES**	19	–

<re-iss. Jul72; same>; hit No.2> (re-iss. Nov72; same); hit No.9) (re-iss. Mar76; same) (re-iss. Oct79; same); hit No.14) (re-iss. Oct83 & Jun88 on 'Old Gold'; OG 9349)

	Deram	Deram
Nov 67. (lp; mono/stereo) (DML/SML 707) <18012> **DAYS OF FUTURE PASSED**	27	3 Apr68

– The day begins / Dawn:- Dawn is a feeling / The morning:- Another morning / Lunch break:- Peak hour / The afternoon:- Forever afternoon (Tuesday) / Time to get away / Evening:- The sunset / Twilight time / The night:- Nights in white satin. <US re-iss. Sep72 hit No.3> (cd-iss. 1983 on 'Threshold'; 800 082-2) (re-iss. Nov84 lp/c; DOA/KDOAC 6) (re-iss. Apr91 cd/c/lp; 820006-2/-4/-1)

	Deram	Deram
Jul 68. (7") <85028> **TUESDAY AFTERNOON (FOREVER AFTERNOON). / ANOTHER MORNING**	–	24
Jul 68. (7") (DM 196) **VOICES IN THE SKY. / DR. LIVINGSTONE, I PRESUME**	23	–
Jul 68. (lp; mono/stereo) (DML/SML 711) <18017> **IN SEARCH OF THE LOST CHORD**	5	23 Sep68

– Departure / Ride my see-saw / Dr. Livingstone, I presume / House of four doors (part 1) / Legend of a mind / House of four doors (part 2) / Voices in the sky / The best way to travel / Visions of paradise / The actor / The word / Om. (re-iss. Nov84 lp/c; DOA/KDOAC 7) (cd-iss. Aug86 & Apr91 on 'London'; 820 168-2)

	Deram	Deram
Oct 68. (7") <85033> **RIDE MY SEE-SAW. / VOICES IN THE SKY**	–	61
Nov 68. (7") (DM 213) **RIDE MY SEE-SAW. / A SIMPLE GAME**	42	–
Apr 69. (7") (DM 247) <85044> **NEVER COMES THE DAY. / SO DEEP WITHIN YOU**		91
Apr 69. (lp; mono/stereo) (DML/SML 1035) <18025> **ON THE THRESHOLD OF A DREAM**	1	20 May69

– In the beginning / Lovely to see you / Dear diary / Send me no wine / To share our love / So deep within you / Never comes the day / Lazy day / Are you sitting comfortably / The dream / Have you heard (part 1) / The voyage / Have you heard (part 2). (cd-iss. Aug86 on 'London'; 820 170-2)

	Threshold	Threshold
Oct 69. (7") (TH 1) **WATCHING AND WAITING. / OUT AND IN**		–

	Threshold	Threshold
Nov 69. (lp; mono/stereo) (<THM/THS 1>) **TO OUR CHILDREN'S CHILDREN'S CHILDREN**	2	14 Jan70

– Higher and higher / Eyes of a child (part 1) / Floating / Eyes of a child (part 2) / I never thought I'd live to be a hundred / Beyond / Out and in / Gypsy / Eternity road / Candle of life / Sun is still shining / I never thought I'd live to be a million / Watching and waiting / The balance. (cd-iss. Aug86 on 'London'; 820 364-2)

	Threshold	Threshold
Apr 70. (7") (TH 4) <67004> **QUESTION. / CANDLE OF LIFE**	2	21

(re-iss. Oct83 on 'Old Gold'; OG 9348)

	Threshold	Threshold
Aug 70. (lp) (<TH 3>) **A QUESTION OF BALANCE**	1	3 Sep70

– Question / How is it (we are here) / And the tide rushes in / Don't you feel small / Tortoise and the hare / It's up to you / Minstrel's song / Dawning is the day / Melancholy man / The balance. (re-iss. Aug86 & Jul92 on 'London'; 820 211-2)

	Threshold	Threshold
Jul 71. (lp) (<TH 5>) **EVERY GOOD BOY DESERVES FAVOUR**	1	2 Aug71

– Procession / The story in your eyes / Our guessing game / Emily's song / After you came / One more time to live / Nice to be here / You can never go home / My song. (cd-iss. Aug86 & Apr91 on 'London'; 820 160-2)

	Threshold	Threshold
Aug 71. (7") <67006> **THE STORY IN YOUR EYES. / MELANCHOLY MAN**	–	23
Apr 72. (7") (TH 9) <67009> **ISN'T LIFE STRANGE. / AFTER YOU CAME**	13	29
Nov 72. (lp) (<TH 7>) **SEVENTH SOJOURN**	5	1

– Lost in a lost world / New horizons / For my lady / Isn't life strange / You and me / The land of make-believe / When you're a free man / I'm just a singer (in a rock'n'roll band). (cd-iss. Sep86 on 'London'; 820 159-2)

	Threshold	Threshold
Jan 73. (7") (TH 13) <67012> **I'M JUST A SINGER (IN A ROCK'N'ROLL BAND). / FOR MY LADY**	36	12

—— Split early '73 but only for a 5 year trial period, releasing own solos released (2) compilations while they split

	Threshold	Threshold
Nov 74. (d-lp) (MB 1-2) <2-12-13> **THIS IS THE MOODY BLUES**	14	11

– Question / The actor / The word / Eyes of a child / Dear diary / Legend of a mind / In the beginning / Lovely to see you / Never comes the day / Isn't life strange / The dream / Have you heard / Voyage / Ride my see-saw / Tuesday afternoon / And the tide rushes in / New horizons / Simple game / Watching and waiting / I'm just a singer (in a rock'n'roll band) / For my lady / Story in your eyes / Melancholy man / Nights in white satin. (d-cd-iss. Aug89; 820 007-2)

	Decca	London
Apr 77. (d-lp) (MB 3-4) <690-1> **CAUGHT LIVE + 5** (live '69 +1 studio side)		26 Jun77

– Gypsy / The sunset / Dr. Livingstone, I presume / Never comes the day / Peak hour / Tuesday afternoon / Are you sitting comfortably / Have you heard (part 1) / The voyage / Have you heard (part 2) / Nights in white satin / Legend of a mind / Ride my see-saw / Gimme a little somethin' / Please think about it / Long summer days / King and Queen / What am I doing here.

—— re-formed mid 1978; **(HAYWARD, LODGE, EDGE, PINDER and THOMAS)**

	Decca	London
Jun 78. (lp/blue-lp/c) (TX/+S/C 129) <PS 708> **OCTAVE**	6	13

– Steppin' in a slide zone / Under moonshine / Had to fall in love / I'll be level with you / Driftwood / Top rank suite / I'm your man / Survival / One step into the light / The day we meet again. (cd-iss. Oct86 & Jan93; 820 329-2)

	Decca	London
Jul 78. (7") (F 13790) <270> **STEPPIN' IN A SLIDE ZONE. / I'LL BE LEVEL WITH YOU**		39
Oct 78. (7") (F 13809) <273> **DRIFTWOOD. / I'M YOUR MAN**		59

—— **PATRICK MORAZ** (b.24 Jun'48, Morges, Switzerland) – keyboards (ex-YES, solo artist, ex-REFUGEE) repl. PINDER

	Threshold	Threshold
May 81. (lp/c) (TXS 139) <TRL-1 2901> **LONG DISTANCE VOYAGER**	7	1 Jun81

– The voice / Talking out of turn / Gemini dream / In my world / Meanwhile / 22,000 days / Nervous / Painted smile / Reflective smile / Veteran cosmic rocker. (cd-iss. Oct86; 820 105-2)

	Threshold	Threshold
Jun 81. (7") (TH 27) <601> **GEMINI DREAM. / PAINTED SMILE**		12
Jul 81. (7") (TH 33) <602> **THE VOICE. / 22,000 DAYS**		15
Nov 81. (7"/7"pic-d) (TH/+PD 29) <603> **TALKING OUT OF TURN. / VETERAN COSMIC ROCKER**		65
Aug 83. (7") (TH 30) **BLUE WORLD. / GOING NOWHERE**	35	–
Sep 83. (lp/c)(cd) (TXS/+C 140)(810119-2) <2902> **THE PRESENT**	15	26

– Blue world / Meet me halfway / Sitting at the wheel / Going nowhere / Hole in the world / Under my feet / It's cold outside of your heart / Running water / I am / Sorry. (cd re-iss. Apr91 on 'London'; same)

	Threshold	Threshold
Sep 83. (7") <604> **SITTING AT THE WHEEL. / GOING NOWHERE**	–	27
Oct 83. (7") (TH 31) **SITTING AT THE WHEEL. / SORRY**	–	–
	(12"+=) (THX 31) – Gemini dream.		
Nov 83. (7") <605> **BLUE WORLD. / SORRY**	–	62
Feb 84. (7") <606> **UNDER MY FEET. / RUNNING WATER**		

	Polydor	Polydor
Mar 86. (7"/12") (POSP/+X 787) <883906> **YOUR WILDEST DREAMS. / TALKIN' TALKIN'**		9 Apr86
May 86. (lp/c)(cd) (POLD/+C 5190)(829179-2) <829179> **OTHER SIDE OF LIFE**	24	9

– Your wildest dreams / Talkin' talkin' / Rock'n'roll over you / I just don't care / Running out of love / The other side of life / The spirit / Slings and arrows / It may be a fire. (cd re-iss. Feb97; same)

	Polydor	Polydor
Aug 86. (7") (POSP 830) <885201> **THE OTHER SIDE OF LIFE. / NIGHTS IN WHITE SATIN** (live)		58

(12"+=) (POSPX 830) – The spirit. <US; b-side>

	Polydor	Polydor
May 88. (7") (POSP 921) <887600> **I KNOW YOU'RE OUT THERE SOMEWHERE. / MIRACLE**	52	30

(12"+=) (POSPX 921) – ('A'extended).
(cd-s+=) (POCD 921) – Rock'n'roll over you (live).

	Polydor	Polydor
Jun 88. (lp/c)(cd) (POLH/+C 43)(<835756-2>) **SUR LA MER**	21	38

– I know you're out there somewhere / Want to be with you / River of endless love / No more lies / Here comes the weekend / Vintage wine / Breaking point / Miracle / Love is on the run / Deep. (cd re-iss. Feb97; same)

	Polydor	Polydor
Dec 88. (7") (PO 27) **NO MORE LIES. / RIVER OF ENDLESS LOVE**		

(12"+=) (PZ 27) – The other side of life.

	Polydor	Polydor
Jun 91. (7"/c-s) **SAY IT WITH LOVE. / LEAN ON ME (TONIGHT)**		

(12"+=/cd-s+=) – Highway.

Aug 91. (cd/c/lp) (<849433-2/-4/-1>) **KEYS OF THE KINGDOM** | 54 | 94 |
– Say it with love / Bless the wings (that bring you back) / Is this Heaven? / Say what you mean (pt.1 & 2) / Lean on me (tonight) / Hope and pray / Shadows on the wall / Celtic sonant / Magic / Never blame the rainbows for the rain. *(cd+=/c+=)* – Once is enough. *(re-iss. Jan93; same)*

Mar 93. (cd/c) (517977-2/-4) **A NIGHT AT RED ROCKS (live)** | | |
– Overture / Late lament / Tuesday afternoon (forever afternoon) / For my lady / Lean on me (tonight) / I know you're out there somewhere / The voice / Your wildest dreams / Isn't life strange / The other side of life / I'm just a singer (in a rock and roll band) / Nights in white satin / Question / Ride my see-saw. *(cd re-iss. Fen97; 517977-2)*

	Universal	Universal
Sep 99. (cd) (<1 53265-2>) **STRANGE TIMES** | | 93 |
– English sunset / Haunted / Sooner or later (walkin' on air) / Wherever you are / Foolish love / Love don't come easy / All that is real is you / Strange times / Words you say / My little lovely / Forever now / One / Swallow / Nothing changes.

– compilations, etc. –

May 65. (7"ep) *Decca; (DFE 8622)* **THE MOODY BLUES** | | - |
– Go now / Lose your money (but don't lose your mind) / Steal your heart away / I don't want to go on without you.

Nov 84. (7") *Threshold; (TH 33)* **THE VOICE. / GEMINI DREAM** | | - |
(12"+=) *(TH/+X 33)* – Nights in white satin.

Nov 84. (lp/c)(cd) *Threshold; (SKL/KSKC 5341)* <820155> **VOICES IN THE SKY – THE BEST OF THE MOODY BLUES** | | Mar85 |
– Ride my see-saw / Talking out of turn / Driftwood / Never comes the day / I'm just a singer (in a rock and roll band) / Gemini dream / The voice / After you came / Question / Veteran cosmic rocker / Isn't life strange / Nights in white satin. *(cd re-iss. Apr91)*

Oct 79. (lp/c) *K-Tel; (NE/+C 1051)* **OUT OF THIS WORLD** | 15 | - |

Sep 83. (lp/c) *A.K.A.* **GO NOW** | | - |

Sep 85. (7") *Old Gold; (OG 9509)* **GO NOW. / I DON'T WANT TO GO ON WITHOUT YOU** | | - |

Sep 85. (d-lp/c) *Castle; (CCS LP/MC/CD 105)* **THE MOODY BLUES COLLECTION** | | - |

Sep 87. (cd) *London; (820 517-2)* **PRELUDE** | | - |

Nov 89. (lp/c/cd) *Polydor; (<840 659-1/-4/-2>)* **GREATEST HITS** | 71 | - |
(re-iss. Feb97; same)

Sep 90. (cd/c/lp) *Pickwick; (PWK S/MC/LP 4022P)* **BLUE** | | - |

Sep 93. (cd/c) *Laserlight; (CD1/MC7 2209)* **GO NOW** | | - |

Sep 94. (5xcd-box) *Polydor; (516436-2)* **TIME TRAVELLER** | | - |
(re-iss. Feb97; 535223-2)

Sep 96. (cd/c) *Polygram TV; (535 800-2/-4)* **THE VERY BEST OF** | 13 | - |

Jun 97. (cd) *O.T.R.; (OTR 1100025)* **IN WORDS AND MUSIC** | | - |

—— solo work, etc. they released during 5 year trial split

Keith MOON (see under ⇒ WHO)

Gary MOORE

Born: 4 Apr'52, Belfast, N.Ireland. In the late 60's, he joined psychedelic outfit, GRANNY'S INTENTIONS, a band that included NOEL BRIDGEMAN on drums. While they later went on to record the 'HONEST INJUN' album for 'Deram', GARY and NOEL formed SKID ROW with bassist BRENDAN SHIELDS. Relocating to London in 1970, the band signed to 'C.B.S.', releasing two albums of progressive blues rock, 'SKID' (1970) and '34 HOURS' (1971) before MOORE left to form his own outfit (during this time he'd also undertaken some live work with DR. STRANGELY STRANGE, as well as guesting on their 1970 album, 'HEAVY PETTIN'). With a line-up of JAN SCHELHAAS (keyboards, ex-NATIONAL HEAD BAND), JOHN CURTIS (bass), PEARCE KELLY (drums) and session man PHILIP DONNELLY on guitar, The GARY MOORE BAND cut one album in 1973, 'GRINDING STONE'. The group never actually got round to making a follow-up as MOORE joined THIN LIZZY (PHIL LYNOTT had been a brief member of SKID ROW in its earliest incarnation) for three months as a replacement for the departed ERIC BELL. MOORE was eventually succeeded by SCOTT GORHAM and BRIAN ROBERTSON, the guitarist joining COLOSSEUM II and recording three albums with the group, 'STRANGE NEW FLESH' (1976), 'ELECTRIC SAVAGE' (1977) and 'WARDANCE' (1977). In addition to his rapidly improving guitar playing, MOORE sang lead vocals on some tracks, the material significantly heavier than the band's earlier incarnation as a progressive jazz rock outfit. Leaving COLOSSEUM in 1977, MOORE filled in for an injured BRIAN ROBERTSON on THIN LIZZY's American tour, eventually going full time with the band in the summer of 1978. At the same time MOORE resumed his solo career with the help of friends DON AIREY (keyboards; of COLOSSEUM II), JOHN MOLE (bass), SIMON PHILIPS (drums), plus PHIL LYNOTT and BRIAN DOWNEY of THIN LIZZY. Together they recorded an album, 'BACK ON THE STREETS' (1979) and two singles, one of which was the classic 'PARISIENNE WALKWAYS'. Featuring LYNOTT on vocals, the track was an epic piece of emotive axe work, MOORE's undulating soloing among the best work of his career. A Top 10 hit upon its original release in 1979, the track remains the guitarist's most played and most purchased record. Although MOORE remained a member of THIN LIZZY long enough to feature on their seminal UK Top 3 album, 'BLACK ROSE (A ROCK LEGEND)' in 1979, he left the band midway through an American tour, eventually setting up his own outfit, G-FORCE, in 1980. After a solitary eponymous album the same year, the group came to nothing, MOORE joining the GREG LAKE BAND for a couple of years. At the same time he also worked on a solo career, recruiting CHARLIE HUHN (vocals, ex-JACK LANCASTER), TOMMY EYRE (keyboards, ex-GREG

LAKE BAND), NEIL MURRAY (bass, ex-WHITESNAKE) and IAN PAICE (drums, ex-WHITESNAKE, ex-DEEP PURPLE, ex-PAICE, ex-ASHTON & LORD, phew!!). The first album, 'CORRIDORS OF POWER' (1982) made the UK Top 30, although it failed to spawn any hit singles. For 1984's 'VICTIMS OF THE FUTURE', MOORE recruited a whole new band again, numbering NEIL CARTER (keyboards, guitar, ex-UFO, ex-WILD HORSES), BOBBY CHOUINARD (drums, although PAICE contributed to the next two albums) and CRAIG GRUBER (bass, ex-BILLY SQIER, although MURRAY appeared on the album). The set almost made the Top 10, while the melancholy ballad-ish 'EMPTY ROOMS' was a minor hit single. Replacing GRUBER first with BOB DAISLEY and then GLENN HUGHES (ex-DEEP PURPLE) while PAUL THOMPSON (ex-ROXY MUSIC) and TED McKENNA (ex-SAHB) took over on drums, MOORE once again hooked up with PHIL LYNOTT for the blistering 'OUT IN THE FIELDS', a No. 5 hit in 1985. Later that summer, a re-issued 'EMPTY ROOMS' went to No.23, while the album, 'RUN FOR COVER' almost made the Top 10. At last MOORE seemed to be on a bit of a roll, hooking up with Irish folk legends, The CHIEFTAINS for 'OVER THE HILLS AND FAR AWAY', another Top 20 hit. 'WILD FRONTIER' (1987) was released early the following Spring and saw MOORE looking back to his Irish roots for inspiration, the cover art depicting a bleak Celtic landscape. On the title track, MOORE tackled the equally bleak Irish political landscape, his wailing riffs echoing his feelings of frustration. With COZY POWELL on drums, 'AFTER THE WAR' (1989) continued in a similar vein, again exploring the Irish question in songs like 'BLOOD OF EMERALDS'. Throughout the 90's, harder-edged rock took a back seat for more blues-orientated material, MOORE releasing the acclaimed 'STILL GOT THE BLUES' in 1990. Subsequent albums 'AFTER HOURS', 'BLUES ALIVE', 'BLUES FOR GREENY' (a tribute to PETER GREEN) and the most recent 'DARK DAYS IN PARADISE' followed a similar direction. • Covered: DON'T LET ME BE MISUNDERSTOOD (hit; Animals) / SHAPES OF THINGS (Yardbirds) / FRIDAY ON MY MIND (Easybeats) / DON'T YOU TO ME (Hudson Whittaker) / THE BLUES IS ALRIGHT (Milton Campbell) / KEY TO LOVE (John Mayall) / JUMPIN' AT SHADOWS (Duster Bennett) / etc. • Trivia: MOORE also sessioned on 1975's 'Peter & The Wolf', and ANDREW LLOYD WEBBER's 1978 lp 'Variations'. In 1980, he was heard on ROD ARGENT's 'Moving Home' & COZY POWELL's 'Over The Top'.

Album rating: GRINDING STONE (*4) / BACK ON THE STREETS (*6) / G-FORCE with G-Force (*5) / CORRIDORS OF POWER (*6) / VICTIMS OF THE FUTURE (*6) / WE WANT MOORE (*6) / RUN FOR COVER (*6) / WILD FRONTIER (*6) / AFTER THE WAR (*6) / STILL GOT THE BLUES (*8) / AFTER HOURS (*7) / BLUES ALIVE (*7) / BLUES FOR GREENY (*7) / BALLADS AND BLUES 1982-1994 compilation (*8) / DARK DAYS IN PARADISE (*4) / OUT IN THE FIELDS – THE VERY BEST OF GARY MOORE compilation (*8)

GARY MOORE BAND

GARY MOORE – guitar, vocals (ex-SKID ROW) with **JAN SCHELHAAS** – keyboards (ex-NATIONAL HEAD BAND) / **JOHN CURTIS** – bass / **PEARCE KELLY** – drums / plus session man **PHILIP DONNELLY** – guitar

	C.B.S.	Peters
1973. (lp) *(CBS 65527)* <9004> **GRINDING STONE** | | |
– Grinding stone / Time to heal / Sail across the mountain / The energy dance / Spirit / Boogie my way back home. *(re-iss. Nov85 lp/c; CBS/40 32699)* *(re-iss. Oct90 cd/c/lp; 467449-2/-4/-1)*

—— In 1974 GARY joined THIN LIZZY ⇒ for 3 mths. May75 he joined COLOSSEUM II before returning to THIN LIZZY p/t for 5 mths early'77 and f/t Aug'78.

GARY MOORE

also started a new solo career at this time with friends **DON AIREY** – keyboards (of COLOSSEUM) / **JOHN MOLE** – bass / **SIMON PHILLIPS** – drums / plus THIN LIZZY'S – **PHIL LYNOTT** and **BRIAN DOWNEY**

	M.C.A.	Jet
Dec 78. (7") *(MCA 386)* **BACK ON THE STREETS. / TRACK NINE** | | |
Jan 79. (lp) *(MCF 2853)* <JZ 36187> **BACK ON THE STREETS** | 70 | |
– Back on the streets / Don't believe a word / Fanatical fascists / Flight of the snow moose / Hurricane / Song for Donna / What would you rather bee or wasp / Parisienne walkways. *(re-iss. Aug81 lp/c; MCL/MCLC 1622)* *(re-iss. Apr92 cd/c; MCL D/C 19011)*
Apr 79. (7") *(MCA 419)* <5061> **PARISIENNE WALKWAYS. / FANATICAL FASCISTS** | 8 | |
(above single featured PHIL LYNOTT – vocals (of THIN LIZZY))
Oct 79. (7") *(MCA 534)* **SPANISH GUITAR. / SPANISH GUITAR (instrumental)** | | - |
Oct 79. (7") <5066> **BACK ON THE STREETS. / SONG FOR DONNA** | - | - |

G-FORCE

GARY MOORE – guitar, vocals / **TONY NEWTON** – vocals / **WILLIE DEE** – keyboards, bass, vocals / **MARK NAUSEEF** – drums, percussion (ex-THIN LIZZY, ex-ELF, ex-IAN GILLAN BAND)

	Jet	Jet
Jun 80. (7") *(JET 183)* **HOT GOSSIP. / BECAUSE OF YOUR LOVE** | | |
Jun 80. (lp/pic-lp) *(JET/+PD 229)* **G-FORCE** | | |
– You / White knuckles – Rockin' & rollin' / She's got you / I look at you / Because of your love / You kissed me sweetly / Hot gossip / The woman's in love / Dancin'. *(re-iss. Feb91 on 'Castle' cd/c/lp; CLA CD/MC/LP 212)*
Aug 80. (7") *(JET 194)* **YOU. / TRUST YOUR LOVIN'** | | |
Nov 80. (7") *(JET 7005)* **WHITE KNUCKLES – ROCKIN' & ROLLIN'. / I LOOK AT YOU** | | |

—— In '81 and '83 he was part of the GREG LAKE BAND. Although he did continue his solo career

GARY MOORE

with **CHARLIE HUHN** – vocals (ex-JACK LANCASTER) / **TOMMY EYRE** – keyboards (ex-GREG LAKE BAND) / **NEIL MURRAY** – bass (ex-WHITESNAKE) / **IAN PAICE** – drums (ex-WHITESNAKE, ex-DEEP PURPLE, ex-PAICE, ex-ASHTON & LORD)

	Jet	not iss.
Oct 81. (12"ep; as GARY MOORE & FRIENDS) (JET12 016) **NUCLEAR ATTACK. / DON'T LET ME BE MISUNDERSTOOD / RUN TO YOUR MAMA**		–

	Virgin	Mirage
Sep 82. (7"/7"pic-d) (VS/+Y 528) <99896> **ALWAYS GONNA LOVE YOU. / COLD HEARTED**		Feb83
Oct 82. (lp/c) (V/TCV 2245) <90077> **CORRIDORS OF POWER**	30	Apr83

– Don't take me for a loser / Always gonna love you / Wishing well / Gonna' break my heart again / Falling in love with you / End of the world / Rockin' every night / Cold hearted / I can't wait until tomorrow. (free live 7"ep) (VDJ 34) – PARISIENNE WALKWAYS. / ROCKIN' EVERY NIGHT / BACK ON THE STREETS (re-iss. Jun85 lp/c; OVED/+C 210) (cd-iss. Jul85; CDV 2245)

—— **JOHN SLOMAN** – vocals, keyboards repl. HUHN / **DON AIREY** – keyboards (see above) (ex-OZZY OSBOURNE) repl. EYRE

Feb 83. (7"/7"pic-d) (VS/+Y 564) <99856> **FALLING IN LOVE WITH YOU. / ('A'instrumental)**		May83
(12"+=) (VST 564) – Wishing well.		

—— GARY MOORE recruited new personnel after SLOMAN departed / **NEIL CARTER** – keyboards, guitar (ex-UFO, ex-WILD HORSES) repl. AIREY / **BOBBY CHOUINARD** – drums 1/2 repl. PAICE (he appeared on most of next 2 lp's) / on tour Mar 84 **CRAIG GRUBER** – bass (ex-BILLY SQUIER) 1/2 replaced MURRAY (he appeared on lp) (note that all: MURRAY, AIREY and PAICE rejoined past bands WHITESNAKE, OZZY OSBOURNE and DEEP PURPLE respectively)

	10-Virgin	Mirage
Jan 84. (7"/7"sha-pic-d) (TEN/+S 13) **HOLD ON TO LOVE. / DEVIL IN HER HEART**	65	–
(12"+=) (TEN 13-12) – Law of the jungle.		
Feb 84. (lp/c/cd) (DIX/+C/CD 2) <90154> **VICTIMS OF THE FUTURE**	12	May84

– Victims of the future / Teenage idol / Shapes of things / Empty rooms / Murder in the skies / All I want / Hold on to love / Law of the jungle. (re-iss. Jun88 on 'Virgin' lp/c; OVED/+C 206)

Mar 84. (7"/7"sha-pic-d) (TEN/+S 19) **SHAPES OF THINGS. / BLINDER**		–
(12"+=) (TEN 19-12) – (an interview with Alan Freeman).		
Aug 84. (7") (TEN 25) **EMPTY ROOMS. / NUCLEAR ATTACK (live)**	51	–
(12"+=) (TEN 25-12) – ('A'extended).		
Aug 84. (7") **EMPTY ROOMS. / MURDER IN THE SKIES**	–	–
Oct 84. (lp-d/c-d/cd-d) (GMDL/CGMDL/GMDLD 1) **WE WANT MOORE (live)**	32	–

– Murder in the skies / Shapes of things / Victims of the future / Cold hearted / End of the world / Back on the streets / So far away / Empty rooms / Don't take me for a loser / Rockin' and rollin'.

—— **GLENN HUGHES** – bass (ex-DEEP PURPLE) repl. BOB DAISLEY who repl. GRUBER / **PAUL THOMPSON** (ex-ROXY MUSIC) and **TED McKENNA** (ex-SAHB) took over drums

May 85. (7"/7"sha-pic-d; GARY MOORE & PHIL LYNOTT) (TEN/+S 49) **OUT IN THE FIELDS. / MILITARY MAN**	5	–
(12"+=) (TEN 49-12) – Still in love with you.		
(d7"+=) (TEND 49) – Stop messin' around (live).		
Jul 85. (7") (TEN 58) **EMPTY ROOMS. / OUT OF MY SYSTEM**	23	–
(12"+=) (TEN 58-12) – Parisienne walkways (live) / Empty rooms (summer '85).		
(d7"+=) (TEND 58) – Parisienne walkways (live) / Murder in the skies (live).		
Sep 85. (lp/c) (DIX/CDIX 16) <90482> **RUN FOR COVER**	12	Feb86

– Run for cover / Reach for the sky / Military man / Empty rooms / Out in the fields / Nothing to lose / Once in a lifetime / All messed up / Listen to your heartbeat. (cd-iss. Feb86 +=; DIXCD 16) – Out of my system. (pic-lp-iss.1986; DIXP 16) (re-iss. 1989 on 'Virgin' lp/c; OVED/+C 274)

—— GARY now used members of The CHIEFTAINS. Retained **CARTER + DAISLEY**

Dec 86. (7"/7"sha-pic-d) (TEN/+S 134) **OVER THE HILLS AND FAR AWAY. / CRYING IN THE SHADOWS**	20	–
(d7"+=) (TEND 134) – All messed up (live) / Out in the fields (live).		
(12"+=) (TENT 134) – All messed up (live) / ('A'version).		
Feb 87. (7") (TEN 159) **WILD FRONTIER. / RUN FOR COVER (live)**	35	–
(12"+=) (TENT 159) – ('A'live) / ('A'extended).		
(d7"+=) (TEND 159) – Murder in the skies (live) / Wild frontier (live).		
(cd-s+=) (KERRY 159) – Over the hills and far away / Empty rooms / Out in the fields / Shapes of things.		
Mar 87. (lp/c/cd) (DIX/CDIX/DIXCD 56) <90588> **WILD FRONTIER**	8	May87

– Over the hills and far away / Wild frontier / Take a little time / The loner / Friday on my mind / Strangers in the darkness / Thunder rising / Johnny boy. (cd+=) – Crying in the shadows / Over the hills and far away (12"version) / Wild frontier (12"version) (re-iss. Sep87. WILD FRONTIER (SPECIAL EDITION); DIXG 56) (incl.extra 12"ep) (pic-cd-iss. Jan89; DIXPCD 56) (re-iss. Apr90 on 'Virgin' lp/c; OVED/+C 285)

Apr 87. (7"/7"pic-d) (TEN/+P 164) **FRIDAY ON MY MIND. / REACH FOR THE SKY (live)**	26	–
(12"+=) (TENT 164) – ('A'version).		
(cd-s+=) (KERRY 164) – Parisienne walkways (live) / ('A'-Kool rap version).		
Aug 87. (7"/ext.7"s) (TEN/+C 178) **THE LONER. / JOHNNY BOY**	53	–
(12"+=) (TENT 178) – ('A'live).		
Nov 87. (7") (TEN 190) **TAKE A LITTLE TIME. / OUT IN THE FIELDS**	75	–
(d7"+=) (TEND 190) – All messed up (live) / Thunder rising (live).		

—— brought back **COZY POWELL** – drums

	Virgin	Virgin
Jan 89. (7"/7"g-f/7"pic-d) (GMS/+G/Y 1) **AFTER THE WAR. / THIS THING CALLED LOVE**	37	
(12"+=) (GMST 1) – Over the hills and far away.		
(3"cd-s+=) (GMSCD 1) – Emerald / Thunder rising.		
Jan 89. (cd/c/lp) (CD/TC/+V 2575) <91066> **AFTER THE WAR**	23	Mar89

– After the war / Speak for yourself / Livin' on dreams / Led clones / Running from the storm / This thing called love / Ready for love / Blood of emeralds. (c+=/cd+=)

—— Dunlace (pt.1 & 2) / The messiah will come. (re-iss. Sep90 lp/c; OVED/+C 335)

Mar 89. (7") (GMS 2) **READY FOR LOVE. / WILD FRONTIER**	56	–
(12"+=/12"g-f+=/cd-s+=) (GMS T/TG/CD 2) – The loner (live).		
(3"cd-s+=) (GMSCDX 2) – Military man (live).		
Apr 89. (7") <99211> **SPEAK FOR YOURSELF. / LED CLONES**	–	–

—— **CHRIS SLADE** – drums (ex-MANFRED MANN'S EARTH BAND, ex-FIRM) repl. COZY POWELL

Oct 89. (7") (VS 1219) **LIVIN' ON DREAMS. / THE MESSIAH WILL COME AGAIN**	–	–
(12"+=) (VST 1219) – ('A'extended).		

—— His band were now **DON AIREY** – keyboards / **BOB DAISLEY + ANDY PYLE** – bass / **GRAHAM WALKER + BRIAN DOWNEY** – drums / **FRANK MEAD** – tenor sax / **NICK PAYN** – sax

Mar 90. (7"/c-s) (VS/+C 1233) **OH PRETTY WOMAN. / KING OF BLUES**	48	
(12"+=/12"s+=/cd-s+=) (VS T/TP/CDT 1233) – The stumble.		
Mar 90. (cd/c/lp) (CD/TC/+V 2612) <91369> **STILL GOT THE BLUES**	13	83 Jun90

– Moving on / Oh pretty woman / Walking by myself / Still got the blues / Texas strut / Too tired / King of the blues / As the years go passing by / Midnight blues / That kind of woman / All your love / Stop messin' around.

May 90. (7"/c-s) (VS/+C 1267) <98854> **STILL GOT THE BLUES (FOR YOU). / LET ME WITH THE BLUES**	31	97 Jan91
(12"+=) (VST 1267) – ('A'extended) / The sky is crying.		
(cd-s+=) (VSCDT 1267) – Further on up the road / The sky is crying.		
(cd-s+=) (VSCDX 1267) – Mean cruel woman.		
Aug 90. (7") (VS 1281) **WALKING BY MYSELF. / ALL YOUR LOVE**	48	
(12"+=) (VST 1281) – ('A'live).		
(cd-s++=) (VSCDT 1281) – Still got the blues (live).		
Dec 90. (7"; GARY MOORE featuring ALBERT COLLINS) (VS/+C 1306) **TOO TIRED. / TEXAS STRUT**	71	–
(12"+=/cd-s+=) (VS T/CDT 1306) – ('A'live).		
(cd-s) (VSCDX 1306) – ('A'side) / All your love (live) / The stumble.		

—— He featured on TRAVELING WILBURYS single 'She's My Baby'.

—— **WILL LEE + JOHNNY B.GAYDON** – bass repl. PYLE / **ANTON FIG** – drums repl. DOWNEY / **TOMMY EYRE** – keyboards repl. AIREY / added on horns **MARTIN DROVER, NICK PENTELOW, ANDREW LOVE + WAYNE JACKSON RICHARD MORGAN** – oboe / backing vocals – **CAROLE KENYON + LINDA TAYLOR**

Feb 92. (7"/c-s; GARY MOORE & THE MIDNIGHT BLUES BAND) (VS/+C 1393) **COLD DAY IN HELL. / ALL TIME LOW**	24	
(cd-s+=) (VSCDT 1393) – Stormy Monday (live) / Woke up this morning.		
Mar 92. (cd/c/lp) (CD/TC/+V 2684) <91825> **AFTER HOURS**	4	

– Cold day in Hell / Don't lie to me (I get evil) / Story of the blues / Since I met you baby / Separate ways / Only fool in town / Key to love / Jumpin' at shadows / The blues is alright / The hurt inside / Nothing's the same.

May 92. (7"/c-s) (VS/+C 1412) **STORY OF THE BLUES. / MOVIN' ON DOWN THE ROAD**	40	
(cd-s+=) (VSCDT 1412) – King of the blues.		
(cd-s+=) (VSCDG 1412) – Midnight blues (live).		
Jul 92. (7"/c-s; GARY MOORE & B.B. KING) (VS/+C 1423) **SINCE I MET YOU BABY. / THE HURT INSIDE**	59	
(cd-s+=) (VSCDT 1423) – Moving on (live) / Texas strut (live).		
(cd-s+=) (VSCDX 1423) – Don't start me talking / Once in a blue mood (instrumental).		
Oct 92. (7"/c-s) (VS/+C 1437) **SEPARATE WAYS. / ONLY FOOL IN TOWN**	59	
(cd-s+=) (VSCDT 1437) – You don't love me (live) / The stumble (live).		
(cd-s+=) (VSCDX 1437) – Further on up the road (live with ALBERT COLLINS) / Caledonia (live with ALBERT COLLINS).		
Apr 93. (7"/c-s) (VS/+C 1456) **PARISIENNE WALKWAYS (live '93). / STILL GOT THE BLUES**	32	
(cd-s+=) (VSCDT 1456) – Since I met you baby (live with B.B. KING) / Key to love.		
(cd-s+=) (VSCDX 1456) – Stop messin' around / You don't love me.		

	Pointblank	Virgin
May 93. (cd/c/d-lp; as GARY MOORE & THE MIDNIGHT BLUES BAND) (CD/TC+/V 2716) **BLUES ALIVE**	8	

– Cold day in Hell / Walking by myself / Oh pretty woman / Separate ways / Too tired / Still got the blues / Since I met you baby / The sky is crying / Further on up the road / King of the blues / Parisienne walkways / Jumpin' at shadows.

—— In Jun '94, MOORE teamed up with JACK BRUCE + GINGER BAKER (ex-CREAM, and both solo artists) to form BBM. They had UK Top10 album 'AROUND THE NEXT DREAM' for 'Virgin' records.

	Virgin	Virgin
Nov 94. (cd/c/lp) (CD/TC+/V 2768) **BALLADS AND BLUES 1982-1994** (compilation)	33	

– Always gonna love you / Still got the blues / Empty rooms / Parisienne walkways / One day / Separate ways / Story of the blues / Crying in the shadows / With love (remember) / Midnight blues / Falling in love with you / Jumpin' at shadows / Blues for Narada / Johnny boy.

below a tribute to PETER GREEN (ex-Fleetwood Mac) guitarist

—— musicians:- **TOMMY EYRE** – keyboards / **ANDY PYLE** – bass / **GRAHAM WALKER** – drums / **NICK PENTELOW + NICK PAYN** – brass

May 95. (cd/c/lp) (CD/TC+/V 2784) **BLUES FOR GREENY**	14	
– If you be my baby / Long grey mare / Merry go round / I loved another woman / Need your love so bad / The same way / The supernatural / Driftin' / Showbiz blues / Love that burns. (cd+=) – Looking for somebody.		
Jun 95. (7"ep/c-ep/cd-ep) (VS/+C/CD 1546) **NEED YOUR LOVE SO BAD / THE SAME WAY (acoustic). / THE WORLD KEEPS ON TURNIN' (acoustic) / STOP MESSIN' AROUND (acoustic)**	48	

—— with **GUY PRATT** – bass / **GARY HUSBAND** – drums / **MAGNUS FIENNES + PAUL NICHOLAS** – keyboards

May 97. (c-s) *(VSC 1632)* **ONE GOOD REASON / BEAST OF BURDEN** ☐ –
(cd-s+=) *(VSCDT 1632)* – Burning in our hearts / There must be a way.

May 97. (cd/c) *(CDV/TCV 2826)* **DARK DAYS IN PARADISE** ☐ 43
– One good reason / Cold wind blows / I have found my love in you / One fine day /
Like angels / What are we here for? / Always there for you / Afraid of tomorrow /
Where did we go wrong? / Business as usual.

Jun 97. (c-s) *(VSC 1640)* **I HAVE FOUND MY LOVE IN YOU / MY**
FOOLISH PRIDE ☐ –
(cd-s+=) *(VSCDT 1640)* – All the way from Africa.

Nov 97. (c-s) *(VSC 1674)* **ALWAYS THERE FOR YOU / RHYTHM**
OF OUR LIVES ☐ –
(cd-s+=) *(VSCDT 1674)* – ('A'mixes).

Oct 98. (cd/c) *(CDV/TCV 2871)* **OUT IN THE FIELDS – THE VERY**
BEST OF GARY MOORE (compilation) ☐ 54
– After the war / Run for cover / Still in love with you / Parisienne walkways / Out
in the fields / Empty rooms / The loner / Shapes of things / Still got the blues /
Ready for love / Military man / Wild frontier / Wishing well / Friday on my mind /
Cold day in Hell / Over the hills and far away. (d-cd+=; *CDVX 2871*) – Emerald /
All messed up (live) / Livin' on dreams (remix) / Military man (live) / Thunder
rising (live) / Devil in her heart / Blinder / Reach for the sky (live) / Over the hills
and far away (live) / Stop messin' around (live).

– compilations, etc. –

Jun 84. (lp/c) *Jet; (JET LP/CA 241)* **DIRTY FINGERS** ☐ –
(cd-iss. Nov86; *JETCD 007*) (re-iss. Apr87 on 'Castle' lp/c/cd; *CLA LP/MC/CD 131*)

Jun 84. (7") *Jet; (7043)* **DON'T LET ME BE MISUNDERSTOOD. /**
SHE'S GOT YOU (live) ☐ –

Oct 85. (lp) *Raw Power; (RAWLP 006)* **WHITE KNUCKLES** ☐ –
(re-iss. Apr86 c/cd; *RAW TC/CD 006*)

Jun 86. (lp/c/cd) *10-Virgin; (XID/CXID/XIDCD 1)* **ROCKIN' EVERY**
NIGHT (live in Japan) ☐ 99
(re-iss. cd.Jun88; *ZIDCD 1*) (cd re-iss. Aug97 on 'Disky'; *VI 88238-2*)

Sep 86. (d-lp/d-c) *Raw Power; (RAW LP/TC 033)* **ANTHOLOGY** ☐ –

Jun 87. (lp/c/cd) *Raw Power; (RAW LP/TC/CD 034)* **LIVE AT THE**
MARQUEE (live) ☐ –
(re-iss. Feb91 on 'Castle' cd/c/lp; *CLA CD/MC/LP 211*)

Nov 87. (lp/c) *M.C.A.; (MCL/+C 1864)* **PARISIENNE WALKWAYS** ☐ –
(cd-iss. May90; *DMCL 1864*) (re-iss. Oct92 cd/c; *MCL D/C 19076*)

Mar 88. (d-lp/c/d-cd) *That's Original; (TFO LP/MC/CD 2)* **G-FORCE /**
LIVE AT THE MARQUEE ☐ –

1988. (cd-ep) *Special Edition; (CD3-4)* **GARY MOORE E.P.** ☐ –
– Don't let me be misunderstood / Parisienne walkways (live) / White knuckles –
Rockin' & rollin'.

Jun 90. (cd/c) *Nightriding; (KN CD/MC 10014)* **GOLDEN DECADE OF**
GARY MOORE ☐ –

Sep 90. (cd/c/lp) *by SKID ROW) Essential; (ESS CD/MC/LP 025)*
GARY MOORE, BRUSH SHIELDS, NOEL BRIDGEMAN ☐ –

Oct 90. (cd/c/d-lp) *Castle; (CCS CD/MC/LP 273)* **THE COLLECTION** ☐ –
– Nuclear attack / White knuckles – Rockin' & rollin' / Grinding stone / Spirit / Run
to your mama / Don't let me be misunderstood / Bad news / I look at you / She's got
you / Back on the streets (live) / Hiroshima / Parisienne walkways (live) / Dancin' /
Really gonna rock tonight / Dirty fingers.

Nov 91. (cd-box) *Virgin; (TPAK 18)* **CD BOX SET** ☐ –
– (AFTER THE WAR / RUN FOR COVER / WILD FRONTIER)

Feb 92. (cd-box) *Castle; (CLABX 904)* **CD BOX SET** ☐ –

Sep 94. (cd/c) *Spectrum; (550 738-2/-4)* **WALKWAYS** ☐ –

May 97. (d-cd) *Snapper; (SMDCD 123)* **LOOKING AT YOU** ☐ –

Thurston MOORE (see under ⇒ SONIC YOUTH)

MOOSE (dig out; Great Alt & Indie . . .)

MORCHEEBA

Formed: London, England . . . mid 90's by the GODFREY brothers, PAUL
and ROSS, who subsequently recruited female singer, SKYE EDWARDS.
Launched into musical orbit at roughly the same time as fellow trip-hoppers
PORTISHEAD, TRICKY et al., MORCHEEBA offered a London-centric
take on what was still essentially a Bristol-based phenomenon. With a bit
of Southern-fried slide guitar thrown in for good measure, MORCHEEBA's
paranoid beat collages were even compared to LYNYRD SKYNYRD at one
point! Before you start dusting down your old copy of 'Freebird', however,
be assured that this bunch dealt in a musical hybrid throughly 90's in make-
up. Blessed with the satin-silk vocals of SKYE, the debut 'IndoChina' album,
'WHO CAN YOU TRUST?' (1996) enjoyed lavish praise among even the
most bpm-hardened journos. Liable to lull the listener into a soporific sense of
insecurity with its deceptively laid back grooves, MORCHEEBA's edgy trip-
hop sound reflected the urban unease of its native environment. Yet this bunch
retain a certain warmth and accessibility missing in their contemporaries, an
obvious fondness for folk, blues and vintage hammond grooves occasionally
melting the glacial veneer of icy coolness. Autumn '96 saw the band's
first Top 40 success with a re-released 'TRIGGER HIPPIE', a series of
festival appearances and a growing fanbase seeing follow-up album, 'BIG
CALM' make the UK Top 20. Another consummate collection of sculptured
soundscapes infused with a healthy helping of pastoral strumming, the album
garnered universal praise and was high on the year-end lists of many critics
and music fans alike.

Album rating: WHO CAN YOU TRUST? (*7) / BIG CALM (*8)

SKYE EDWARDS – vocals / **PAUL GODFREY** – programming, scratching, live drums,
lyrics / **ROSS GODFREY** – guitars, sitar, keyboards, synthesizer, bass / plus **PETE NORRIS**
– synthesizer programming

Feb 96. (c-s) *(WOKMC 2081)* **TRIGGER HIPPIE / KILLER HIPPIE** China ☐ not iss. –
(12"+=/cd-s+=) *(WOK T/CD 2081)* – ('A' & 'B' mixes)

Apr 96. (12"/cd-s) *(INDO 44 T/CD)* **NEVER AN EASY WAY** (mixes) Indochina ☐ Discovery –

Apr 96. (cd/c/lp) *(ZEN 009 CD/MC/LP) <77050>* **WHO CAN YOU**
TRUST? ☐ Sep96
– Moog Island / Trigger hippie / Post houmous / Tape loop / Never an easy way /
Howling / Small town / Enjoy the wait / Col / Who can you trust? / Almost done /
End theme. (re-dist.Apr97 hit No.70) (cd re-iss. Nov97 / US=Dec98 on 'Sire'+=
'BEATS AND B-SIDES'; *ZEN 009CDX)<31049>* – Killer hippie / On the Rhodes
again / Tape loop / Dungeness / Baby sitar / Ray payola / Shoulder holster / Post
houmous.

Jul 96. (c-s/cd-s) *(INDO 45 MC/CD)* **TAPE LOOP (shortcheeba**
mix) / TAPE LOOP (Diabolical Brothers mix) / MADE
ISLAND (live) / **ON THE RHODES AGAIN** ☐ 42 –

Oct 96. (c-s/cd-s) *(INDO 52 MC/CD)* **TRIGGER HIPPIE / TRIGGER**
HIPPIE (mix) / THE SEA ☐ 40 –
(cd-s) *(INDO 52CDR)* – ('A'remixes).

Feb 97. (c-s) *(INDO 54MC) <35001>* **THE MUSIC THAT WE HEAR** Indochina China-Sire
(MOOG ISLAND) / (Arthur Baker mix) ☐ 47 Dec97
(cd-s+=) *(INDO 54CD)* – ('A'-Omni Trio mix).
(cd-s) *(IDO 54CDR)* – ('A'remixes).

Sep 97. (c-s/cd-s) *(IDO 64 MC/CD)* **SHOULDER HOLSTER / ('A'-**
Diabolical Brothers mix) / ('A'instrumental) / Payola
(Curly Wurly mix) ☐ 53 –
(cd-s+=) *(IDO 64CDX)* – ('A'side) / ('A'-DJ Swamp mix) / ('A'-Rolling Boulder mix) /
('A'-Nation Of Teflon Souls mix) / ('A'-Low Pressure mix).

Feb 98. (cd-s) *(IDO 66CD)* **THE SEA / BIG CALM** ☐ –

Mar 98. (cd/c/lp) *(ZEN 017 CD/MC/LP) <31020>* **BIG CALM** ☐ 18
– The sea / Shoulder holster / Part of the process / Blindfold / Let me see / Bullet
proof / Over and over / Friction / Diggin' a watery grave / Fear and love / Big calm.

Mar 98. (ltd;12"ep/pic-cd-ep) *(IDO 70 T/CD)* **BLINDFOLD / THE**
SEA / THREE ORANGE WHIPS ☐ 56 Indochina WEA

Jun 98. (c-s) *(IDO 76C) <42387>* **LET ME SEE / LET ME SEE (Magnus**
Fiennes mix) / DON'T LET IT GET YOU DOWN ☐ 46 Nov98
(cd-s+=) *(IDO 76CD)* – ('A'-Talvin Singh mix).
(cd-s) *(IDO 76CDX)* – (first & third mixes) / ('A'mix by Reflections Eternal, Circa
1963 & QD 111) / Trigger hippie (live CD-Rom).

Aug 98. (c-s) *(WOKMC 2097)* **PART OF THE PROCESS / THE** China Indochina
DYSLEXIC PORN STAR WHO FUNKED IN HER SPACE ☐ 38
(12"+=/cd-s+=) *(WOK T/CD 2097)* – ('A'-The Americruiser Morfeedback mix).

Dec 98. (c-s) *(WOKMC 2102) <2101>* **SUMMERTIME /**
('A'–Rhapsody) ☐ –
(cd-s+=) *(WOKCD 2102)* – (same)

Alanis MORISSETTE

Born: 1 Jun'74, Ottawa, Canada, to a French-Canadian father and Hungarian
mother, both schoolteachers. She began writing songs at age ten and
subsequently became a regular on the American cable show, 'You Can't Do
That On Television'. Her debut, self-financed single 'FATE STAY WITH ME'
(on 'Lamor'), was released around the same time and by the age of sixteen,
the budding singer/songwriter had cut two disco/pop albums ('ALANIS' and
'NOW IS THE TIME'). MORISSETTE then left her native Canada for the lure
of Los Angeles, subsequently hawking her demo unsuccessfully around almost
every major record company. Salvation came in the form of MADONNA who
recognised her talent, signing ALANIS to her own 'Maverick' label. 'JAGGED
LITTLE PILL' (1995) was duly released to major critical acclaim, climbing to
No.1 in America and scooping four Grammys and a Brit Award the following
year. Confrontational and uncompromising as well as evocative and emotional,
MORISSETTE's singing demanded attention, her pent-up adolescent angst
finding an outlet in the likes of 'PERFECT', 'YOU OUGHTA KNOW' and
'ONE HAND IN MY POCKET', the latter two both fairly successful UK
singles. Musically, the album was largely straightahead guitar rock, solid, if
not exactly hard-edged, with ALANIS playing guitar while backed up by
BENMONT TENCH (organ, ex-TOM PETTY), LANCE MORRISON (bass)
and MATT LAUG (drums). Touting a decidedly more earthy strain of 'girl
power' than the SPICE GIRLS, it remains to be seen whether MORISSETTE
can keep the momentum going and achieve a similar career trajectory to
contemporaries like SHERYL CROW. • **Songwriters:** Writes all music with
GLEN BALLARD, who also plays guitar and keyboards. • **Trivia:** Guests on
her debut included FLEA (Red Hot Chilis) and DAVE NAVARRO (ex-Jane's
Addiction).

Album rating: JAGGED LITTLE PILL (*9) / SUPPOSED FORMER INFATUATION
JUNKIE (*6) / MTV UNPLUGGED (*5)

ALANIS MORISSETTE – vocals / with **BENMONT TENCH** organ (ex-TOM PETTY) / **LANCE**
MORRISON – bass / **MATT LAUG** – drums

Maverick Maverick

Jun 95. (cd/c/lp) *<(9362-45901-2/-4/-1)>* **JAGGED LITTLE PILL** 1 1
– All I really want / You oughta know / Perfect / Hand in my pocket / Right through
you / Forgiven / You learn / Head over feet / Mary Jane / Ironic / Not the doctor /
Wake up. (cd+=) – Your house.

Jul 95. (c-s) *(W 0307C)* **YOU OUGHTA KNOW (clean version) /**
PERFECT (version) ☐ 22 –
(cd-s+=) *(W 0307CD)* – ('A'-Jimmy The Saint blend) / Wake up.

Oct 95. (c-s) *(W 0312C)* **HAND IN MY POCKET / HEAD OVER**
FEET (live acoustic) ☐ 26 –
(cd-s+=) *(W 0312 CD1)* – Not the doctor (live acoustic).
(cd-s) *(W 0312 CD2)* – ('A'side) / Right through you (live acoustic) / Forgiven (live
acoustic).

Feb 96. (c-s) *(W 0334C)* **YOU LEARN / YOUR HOUSE (live)** | 24 | | - |
(cd-s+=) *(W 0334CD)* – Wake up (modern rock live) / Hand in my pocket (version).

Mar 96. (c-s) *<17698>* **IRONIC / FORGIVEN (live) / NOT THE DOCTOR (live)** | - | | 4 |

Apr 96. (c-s) *(W 0343C)* **IRONIC / YOU OUGHTA KNOW (live acoustic)** | 11 | | - |
(cd-s+=) *(W 0343CD)* – Mary Jane (live) / All I really want (live).

Jul 96. (c-s) *<17644>* **YOU LEARN / YOU OUGHTA KNOW (live)** | - | | 6 |

Jul 96. (c-s) *(W 0355C)* **HEAD OVER FEET / HAND IN MY POCKET (live)** | 7 | | - |
(cd-s+=) *(W 0355CD)* – You learn (live) / Right through you (live).

Nov 96. (c-s) *(W 0382C)* **ALL I REALLY WANT / IRONIC (live from Sydney)** | 59 | | - |
(cd-s+=) *(W 0382CD)* – Hand in my pocket (live from Brisbane).

—— now with **BENMONT** (again) + **NICK LASHLEY** + **JOEL SHEARER** – guitar / **CHRIS CHANEY** – bass / **GARY NOVAK** – drums

Oct 98. (c-s) *(W 0458C)* *<radio play>* **THANK U / UNINVITED (demo)** | 5 | | 17 |
(cd-s+=) *(W 0458CD)* – Pollyanna flower.

Nov 98. (cd/c/lp) *<(9362 47094-2/-4/-1)>* **SUPPOSED FORMER INFATUATION JUNKIE** | 3 | | 1 |
– Front row / Baba / Thank U / Are you still mad / Sympathetic character / That I would be good / Couch / Can't not / UR / I was hoping / One / Would not come / Unsent / So pure / Joining you / Heart of the house / Your congratulations.

Jan 99. (-) *<radio cut>* **UNSENT** | - | | 58 |

Mar 99. (c-s) *(W 472C)* **JOINING YOU / YOUR HOUSE (live)** | 28 | | - |
(cd-s+=) *(W 472CD2)* – London (live).
(cd-s+=) *(W 472CD1)* – These are the thoughts (live).

Jul 99. (c-s) *(W 492C)* **SO PURE / I WAS HOPING (acoustic modern rock live)** | 38 | | - |
(cd-s+=) *(W 492CD1)* – ('A'-Pure ecstasy mix).
(cd-s+=) *(W 492CD2)* – Would not come (live).

Nov 99. (cd/c) *<(9362 47589-2/-4)>* **MTV UNPLUGGED (live)** | 59 | | 63 |
– Uninvited / Ironic / You oughta know / You learn / These are the thoughts / Princess familiar / That I would be good / King of pain / Joining you / No pressure over cappuccino / Head over feet / I was hoping.

Dec 99. (c-s/cd-s) *(W 509 C/CD)* **THAT I WOULD BE GOOD (MTV unplugged live) / WOULD NOT COME (reverb live) / FORGIVE (reverb live) / I WAS HOPING (99X live)** | | | |
(above might be delayed until Jan'2000)

MORPHINE

Formed: Boston, Massachusetts, USA . . . 1990 out of TREAT HER RIGHT by MARK SANDMAN and DANA COLLEY, who subsequently added drummer JEROME DUPREE. Certainly not your average Boston indie band, MORPHINE employed a musical set-up that defied standard rock convention; while SANDMAN offered up subtle, often treated vocals and a pioneering two-string bass played like a bottleneck guitar, COLLEY contributed breathless baritone/tenor sax over DUPREE's spare, jazzy backbeat. The trio quickly made their mark with an independently released US-only debut album, 'GOOD' (1992), the record drawing across the board praise from America's alternative media network and resulting in a long term deal with 'Rykodisc'. The label subsequently gave it a new lease of life as well as releasing the set in Britain where MORPHINE were also fast rising cult stars. Although new drummer BILLY CONWAY was soon to replace DUPREE, the musical chemistry was even stronger than ever on 1993's follow-up, 'CURE FOR PAIN', another inspired set of avant blues/jazz. Two years on, MORPHINE had the critics intoxicated yet again with 'YES' (1995), a more spontaneous album that swung between low-key introspection and upfront affirmation. One of the few alt-rock acts to be honoured with a 'DreamWorks' contract (US-only), SANDMAN and Co finally eased their way into chart territory (Top 75) via their fourth album, 'LIKE SWIMMING' (1997). Just as MORPHINE looked to be on the verge of something big, tragedy struck on the 3rd of July 1999, when frontman SANDMAN had a fatal heart attack while onstage in Italy.

Album rating: GOOD (*7) / CURE FOR PAIN (*6) / YES (*8) / LIKE SWIMMING (*8) / B-SIDES AND OTHERWISE compilation (*7)

MARK SANDMAN (b. 1952) – vocals, 2-string bass (ex-TREAT HER RIGHT) / **DANA COLLEY** – saxophones / **JEROME DUPREE** – drums

	not iss.	Accurate-Distortion

Jan 92. (cd) **GOOD** | - | | - |
– Good / Saddest song / Have a lucky day / You speak my language / You look like rain / Do not go quietly unto your grave / Lisa / Only one / Test tube baby / Shoot'm down / Other side / I know you (pts.1 & 2). *<(cd re-iss. Sep92=US/Jul93=UK & Apr97 on 'Rykodisc'; RCD 10263)>*

	Rykodisc	Rykodisc

—— **BILLY CONWAY** – drums (ex-TREAT HER RIGHT) repl. JEROME

Jan 94. (cd/c) *<(RCD/RACS 10262)>* **CURE FOR PAIN** | | | Sep93 |
– Dawna / Buena / I'm free now / All wrong / Candy / Head with wings / In spite of me / Thursday / Cure for pain / Mary, won't you call my name / Let's take a trip together / Sheila / Miles Davis' funeral. *<(cd re-iss. Apr97; same)>*

Jan 94. (cd-s) *<RCD 51033>* **CURE FOR PAIN /** | - | | |

Mar 94. (cd-ep) *<(RCD 51035)>* **BUENA / SHAME / MORPHINE PROFILE – INTERVIEW** | | | |

Mar 94. (7") *<(RA7 1036)>* **THURSDAY. / MARY WON'T YOU CALL MY NAME? (live)** | | | |
(cd-s+=) *<(RCD5 1036)>* – You look like rain.

Mar 95. (7") *<(RA7 1046)>* **SUPERSEX. / I KNOW YOU** | | | |
(cd-s+=) *<(RCD5 1046)>* – All wrong.

Apr 95. (cd/c/lp) *<(RCD/RAC/RALP 10320)>* **YES** | | | |
– Honey white / Scratch / Radar / Whisper / Yes / All your way / Supersex / I had my chance / Jury / Sharks / Free love / Gone for good. *<(cd re-iss. Apr97; same)>*

Jun 95. (7"clear) *<(RA7 1047)>* **HONEY WHITE. / BIRTHDAY CAKE** | | | |
(cd-s+=) *<(RCD5 1047)>* – Lucky day / Sunday afternoon weightlessness.

	Rykodisc	DreamWorks

Mar 97. (cd/c) *(RCD/RAC 10362)* *<50009>* **LIKE SWIMMING** | | 67 | |
– Lilah / Potion / I know you (part 3) / Early to bed / Wishing well / Like swimming / Murder for my money / French lines with pepper / Empty box / Eleven o'clock / Hanging on a curtain / Swing it low.

May 97. (cd-s) *(RCD5 1057)* **MURDER FOR MY MONEY / KEROUAC** | | | |

– compilations, etc. –

Sep 97. (cd) *Rykodisc; <(RCD 10387)>* **B SIDES AND OTHERWISE** | | | |
– Have a lucky day / All wrong (live) / I know you (live) / Bo's veranda / Mile high / Shame / Down love's tributaries / Kerouac / Pulled over the car / Sunday afternoon weightlessness / Virgin bride / Mail / My brain.

Ennio MORRICONE

Born: 11 Oct'28, Rome, Italy. A graduate of Rome's Conservatory Of Santa Cecilia, MORRICONE initially worked in radio before he began scoring films in the early 60's. Although he'd already worked with other directors on various Italian westerns, it would be his subsequent partnership with "Spaghetti Western" king, Sergio Leone, which would both revolutionise the concept of the film soundtrack and transform him into a cult figure. While Leone's unshaven, existential gunslingers aimed point blank at the heart of the great Western myth, MORRICONE conjured up the striking soundtracks to their invariably short lives and the unforgiving, sun-parched terrain they roamed in. Masterfully arranging seemingly incongruous instrumentation into a dazzling, seamless whole, MORRICONE employed everything from rattlesnake castanets and heartbreaking mariachi horns to thundering church organ, ghostly harmonica, jews harp and grunting native indian-style chants. Add to this his basic recipe of sweeping orchestration and echo-soaked, DUANE EDDY-style guitar twang and you had a musical vista unparalleled in the history of film. What's more, the likes of 'A FISTFUL OF DOLLARS', 'FOR A FEW DOLLARS MORE' and the sublime 'ONCE UPON A TIME IN THE WEST' don't even need the visual accompaniment. As contemporary sounding today as they undoubtedly were back then, these records have such hauntingly potent imagery locked in their collective grooves you need only don a set of headphones and close your eyes. This fertile period also produced the theme MORRICONE is most readily identified with even today, 'THE GOOD, THE BAD AND THE UGLY' (1968). Originally released as 'IL BUONO, IL BRUTTO, IL CATTIVO' in 1966, the theme was subsequently covered by HUGO MONTENEGRO who took it to the top of the UK chart (US No.2) and was duly inspired to record a whole album's worth of classic MORRICONE material. The Italian's incredibly prolific output (even the man himself doesn't know how many films he's worked on though it's rumoured to be in excess of 500!) continued throughout the 70's as he moved away from Westerns and worked with the cream of the world's directors. In 1972, he composed the theme to a film version of Mikhail Bulgakov's brilliant satirical novel, 'The Master And Margarita' (by Yugoslav director, Aleksander Petrovic) while 1977 saw him scoring 'Exorcist' follow-up, 'THE HERETIC'. Yet serious mainstream recognition didn't arrive until 1981 when the BBC dug up an obscure single from three years previous, 'CHI MAI'. Used as the theme tune to their 'Life & Times Of David Lloyd George' period drama, the track was a surprise No.2 UK hit. Starring Robert De Niro in a lead role, 'ONCE UPON A TIME IN AMERICA' (1984) was another massive soundtrack success for MORRICONE, while he subsequently went on to win an Oscar for 'THE MISSION' (1986) which utilised Native Indian melodies to haunting effect. In addition to these high profile projects, he spent the 80's and 90's working on all manner of obscure and not so obscure films, many of them in his native Italy. A seismic influence on modern music, the spectre of MORRICONE can be heard in the work of artists as diverse as NICK CAVE, GALLON DRUNK, PORTISHEAD, TINDERSTICKS and JOHN ZORN. For committed fans and new initiates alike, the problem is that the bulk of the man's work is out of print, although a large chunk of previously unavailable Italian-only material hit the shops in the late 80's & early 90's. While 'B.M.G.' have recently repackaged his classic trio of 60's Spaghetti Westerns on one double-CD set, there are rumours of a boxed set in progress from the same people so watch this space.

Album rating (selective): A FISTFUL OF DOLLARS (*8) / FOR A FEW DOLLARS MORE (*7) / THE GOOD, THE BAD AND THE UGLY (*8) / ONCE UPON A TIME IN THE WEST (*9) / BURN (*7) / EXORCIST II: THE HERETIC (*6) / ONCE UPON A TIME IN AMERICA (*6) / THE MISSION (*8) / THE UNTOUCHABLES (*6) / RAMPAGE (*6) / CASUALTIES OF WAR (*7) / CINEMA PARADISO (*6) / DISCLOSURE (*5) / WOLF (*7) / FILM MUSIC BY ENNIO MORRICONE compilation (*7)

ENNIO MORRICONE – composer / credited with ORCHESTRA

	RCA Victor	RCA Victor

Jun 67. (lp; mono/stereo) *(RD/SF 7875)* *<1135>* **A FISTFUL OF DOLLARS** (soundtrack) | | | |
– Titoli / Almost dead / Square dance / The chase / The result / Without pity / Theme from a fistful of dollars / "A Fistful Of Dollars" suite.

1967. (7") *(RCA 1596)* **A FISTFUL OF DOLLARS. / THE MAN WITH NO NAME** | | | |

1967. (lp) **FOR A FEW DOLLARS MORE** (soundtrack) | - | | - | Italian
– La resa dei conti / Osservatori osservati / Il vizio di uccidere / Il colpo / Addio

colonnello / Per qualche dollaro in piu / Poker d'assi / Carillion. (UK-iss.1970 w/ 'A FISTFUL OF DOLLARS' on 'RCA Camden'; CDS 1052) (c-iss.May74; CAM 411)

1967. (7") (RCA 1634) **FOR A FEW DOLLARS MORE. / LA RESI DEI CONTI**

	U.A.	U.A.
	☐	☐

Oct 68. (lp; stereo/mono) (S+/ULP 1197) <5172> **THE GOOD, THE BAD AND THE UGLY** (soundtrack)

	☐	4	Feb68

– The good, the bad and the ugly – main title (Il buono, il brutto, il cattivo)/ The sundown (Il tramonto) / The strong (Il forte) / The desert (Il deserto) / The carriage of the spirits (La carrozza dei fantasmi) / Marcia (Marcetta) / The story of a soldier (La storia de un soldato) / Marcia without hope (Marcetta senza speranza) / The death of a soldier (Morte de un soldato) / The ecstasy of gold (L'estasi dell'oro) / The trio – main title (Il triello). (re-iss.May85 on 'E.G.' lp/c; EG 260582-1/-4) (<cd-iss. Sep88 on 'EMI Manhattan'; CDP7 48408-2>) (cd re-iss. Jul93 on 'Silva Screen'; 46408-2)

—— New York-born composer HUGO MONTENEGRO also went US Top 10 with a collection of the above three soundtracks – the man also took the title track to No.2 (Feb'68) & No.1 (Sep'68) in the US & UK respectively. Around the same time, HUGO also scored with another Clint Eastwood-starring movie, 'Hang 'Em High'.

1969. (7") (UP 35004) **PROFESSIONAL GUN. / PACO**

	R.C.A.	not iss.

1969. (lp) **ONCE UPON A TIME IN THE WEST** (soundtrack)

	☐	☐	Italian

– Once upon a time in the west / As a judgement / Farewell to Cheyenne / The transgression / The first tavern / The second tavern / Once upon a time in the west (reprise) / Man with a harmonica / A dimly lit room / Bad orchestra / The man / Jill's America / Death rattle / Finale. (UK-iss.Jul78 lp/c; PL/PK 31387) (re-iss. Oct83 lp/c; NL 70032) (cd – iss.Jun88; ND 71704) (cd re-iss. Feb90 on 'Silva Screen'; 4736.2)

1969. (7") (RCA 1892) **ONCE UPON A TIME IN THE WEST. / FINALE**
(re-iss. Oct79; PB 6197)

	Stateside	not iss.
	☐	-

1970. (lp) (SSL 10307) **THE SICILIAN CLAN** (soundtrack)

	C.B.S.	Columbia

1970. (70067) **LOVE CIRCLE**

	not iss.	U.A.

1970. (lp) <LA 303> **BURN** (soundtrack)
– Abolicao / Jose Dolores / Queimada seconda / Preparazione / Verso il futuro / Jose' E Dolores / Osanna / Queimada prima / Studi per un finale / Titoli di testa / L'estasi Dell'oro / Il Triello / Titoli / Titoli / Titoli di testa / Resa / Titoli finiali. <cd-iss. Nov96 as 'QUEIMADA (BURN)' on 'Varese Sarabande'; VCDS 7020>

Jan 72. (lp; with JOAN BAEZ) (SF 8211) **SACCO AND VANZETTI**

	R.C.A.	not iss.
	☐	-

– Hope for freedom / The ballad of Sacco and Vanzetti (introduction – part 1) / In prison / The ballad of Sacco and Vanzetti (part 2) / Sacco and his son / The ballad of Sacco and Vanzetti (part 3) / Freedom from hope / Sentenced to death / Electric chair / Here's to you. (re-iss. Jan89 on 'Silva Screen'; NL 70231) <US cd-iss. 1990's on 'Omega'; OCD 3015>

1973. (lp) (SPFL 275) **THE RED TENT**

	Paramount	Paramount

– Love theme / Do dreams go on / Death at the pole / Love like the snow / Message from Rome / They're alive / Farewell / Others, who will follow us. (re-iss. Jan89 on 'Silva Screen'; 255064-1) (cd-iss. Aug94 on 'Legend'; LEGENDCD 15)

1976. (lp/c) (NL/NK 43738) **1900** (soundtrack)

	R.C.A.	R.C.A.

Feb 77. (lp) (NSPH 28503) **MOSES** (original soundtrack)

	Pye	Pye
	43	-

Jun 77. (lp) <3068> **EXORCIST II: THE HERETIC** (soundtrack)

	not iss.	Warners

– Regan's theme / Pazuzu / Interrupted melody / Rite of magic / Little Afro – Flemish mass / Great bird of the sky / Magic and ecstasy / Seduction and magic / Regan's theme / Dark revelation / Night flight / Interrupted melody / Exorcism.

Mar 78. (7") (PVT 148) **CHI MAI. / COME MADDALENA**

	Private Stock	Private Stock

(re-iss. Apr81 as BBC theme from the TV series 'The Life And Times Of David Lloyd George'; RESL 92) – hit No.2

Jun 78. (7") (7N 46092) **WORLD CUP ARGENTINA. / WORLD CUP MARCH '78**

	Pye	not iss.
	☐	-

Sep 82. (lp) (MCF 3148) **THE THING** (soundtrack)

	M.C.A.	M.C.A.

– Humanity (part 1) / Shape / Contamination / Bestiality / Solitude / Eternity / Wait / Humanity (part 2) / Sterilization / Despair. (re-iss. Oct85; MCA 6111) (cd/c-iss.Aug91 on 'Varese Sarabande'; VDS/VCS 5278)

Mar 84. (7") (RBUS 88) **SAHARA. / (instrumental)**

	Red Bus	not iss.
	☐	-

Nov 84. (lp)(c)(cd) (MERH 45)(PRIMC 121)(<822334-2>) **ONCE UPON A TIME IN AMERICA** (soundtrack)

	Mercury	Mercury

– Once upon a time in America / Poverty / Deborah's theme / Childhood memories / Amapola / Friends / Prohibition dirge / Cockeye's song / Amapola – part 2 / Childhood poverty / Photographic memories / Friends / Friendship and love / Speakeasy / Deborah's theme – Amapola. <cd re-iss. Oct95 on 'Musicrama'; 4003>

Oct 86. (lp/c/cd; with the London Philharmonic Orchestra) (V/TCV/CDV 2402) <90567> **THE MISSION** (soundtrack)

	Virgin	
	73	Feb87

– On earth as it is in Heaven / Falls / Gabriel's oboe / Ava Maria Guarani / Brothers / Carlotta / Vita nostra / Climb / Remorse / Penance / The mission / River / Gabriel's oboe / Te deum guarani / Refusal / Asuncion / Alone / Guarani / The sword / Miserere.

Oct 86. (7") (VS 909) **ON EARTH AS IT IS IN HEAVEN. / (part 2)**
(12"+=) (VS 909-12) – Gabriel's oboe.

	☐	-

Oct 87. (lp/c/cd) (<39 3909-1/-4/-2>) **THE UNTOUCHABLES** (soundtrack)

	A&M	A&M

– The untouchables / Al Capone / Waiting at the border / Death theme / On the rooftops / Victorious / The man with the matches / The strength of the righteous / Ness and his family / False alarm / The untouchables / Four friends / Machine gun lullaby.

May 88. (lp/c/cd) (<K9 60782-1/-4/-2>) **FRANTIC** (soundtrack)

	Elektra	Elektra

– I'm gonna lose you (by SIMPLY RED) / Frantic / On the roofs of Paris / One flugel horn / Six short interludes / Nocturne for Michel / In the garage / Paris project / Sadly nostalgic. (cd re-iss. Oct93 on 'WEA'; 7559 60782-2)

Jun 88. (lp/c/cd) (V/TCV/CDV 2491) <42685> **RAMPAGE** (soundtrack)

	Virgin	Fastlane

– Rampage / Son / Findings / Over to the jury / Run, run, run / Since childhood / Magma / Gruesome discovery / Carillion / District attorney / Mother / Recollections.

Dec 88. (lp/c/cd) (V/TCV/CDV 2539) **A TIME OF DESTINY** (soundtrack)
(re-iss. Jan89 on 'Silva Screen' lp/c/cd; 790938-1/-4/-2)

Jan 89. (cd) (BL/BK/BD 71559) **SECRET OF THE SAHARA** (1987 soundtrack)

	R.C.A.	not iss.
	☐	-

– Secret of the Sahara / Red ghosts / Sholomon / Mountain / Kerim / Hawk / Golden door / Myth and the adventure / Anthea and the desert / Farewell Orso / Death od Tamameth / Saharan dram / Miriam and Philip / Second dedication / First dedication. (<cd re-iss. Jun96; 74321 34226-2>)

Sep 89. (lp/c/cd) (V/TCV/CDV 2602) **THE ENDLESS GAMES** (soundtrack)

	Virgin	not iss.
	☐	-

– The endless games / Alec's journey / The game goes on / Summer solitude / Caroline's song / From Russia / The love game / Anif / Silvia's game / Just a game / Chess game.

Jan 90. (cd/c/cd) (466016-2/-4/-1) <CK/SCT 45359> **CASUALTIES OF WAR** (1989 soundtrack)

	C.B.S.	Columbia
	☐	Feb90

Jun 90. (cd/c) (CDSBL/SBLC 12598) **NUOVO CINEMA PARADISO** (1988 soundtrack)

	S.B.L.	not iss.

(re-iss. Jul93 on 'D.R.G.' cd/c; DRG CD/MC 12598)

Jun 91. (cd/c/lp) (CD/TC+/VMM 3) **HAMLET** (1990 soundtrack)

	Virgin	Virgin

– Hamlet (version 1) / The king is dead / Ophelia (version 1) / What a piece of work is man / The prayer / The ghost / The play / The banquet / Dance for the queen / Ophelia (version 2) / Hamlet's madness / Hamlet (version 2) / Simulated madness / The closet / Second madness / To be or not to be / Solid flesh / The vaults. (cd re-iss. Jan94 on 'Silva Screen'; 91600-2)

Jul 91. (cd/c) (MCA D/C 10019) **STATE OF GRACE** (1990 soundtrack)

	M.C.A.	M.C.A.

Dec 91. (cd/c) (VSD/VSC 5326) **CROSSING THE LINE** ('THE BIG MAN' soundtrack)

	Varese Sarabande	not iss.
	☐	-

– Running in the park / Main titles / Beth says "no" / Road training 1 / Road training 3 / Rain in Gobi Desert / Journey to fight / Round four / Road training 2 / The wasteland / Round one / Round two / Round six / "There's blood on that money" / Danny runs home / End titles.

Mar 92. (cd/c) (469371-2/-4) **BUGSY** (1991 soundtrack)

	Epic	Epic

Nov 92. (cd) (ACCD 1025) <EK 52750> **CITY OF JOY** (soundtrack)

	☐	Apr92

– City of joy / Family of the poor / One night, by chance / Crack down / Hope / In the labyrinth / Family of the poor / Surgeon in despair / One night, by chance / For a daughter's dowry / Godfather of the bustee / Monsoon / Calcutta / Bustee day / Birth / The worm turns / Labyrinth / To Calcutta / Family of the poor / To Roland.

Sep 93. (cd/c) (474285-2/-4) **IN THE LINE OF FIRE** (soundtrack)

	Columbia	Sony

Aug 94. (cd/c) (476601-2/-4) <64231-2/-4> **WOLF** (soundtrack)
– Wolf and love / Barn / Dream and the deer / Moon / Laura goes to join Wolf / Laura and Wolf united / First transition / Howl and the city / Animals and encounters / Laura transformed / Wolf / Second transition / Will's final goodbye / Chase / Confirmed doubts / Talisman / Third transition / Shock for Laura / Laura and Will / Laura.

Feb 95. (cd) (CDVMM 16) <40162> **DISCLOSURE** (soundtrack)

	Virgin	Virgin
	☐	Jan95

– Serene family / Unusual approach / With energy and decision / Virtual reality / Preparation and victory / Disclosure / Sad family / Unemployed / Sex and computers / Computers and work / Sex and power / First passacaglia / Second passacaglia / Third passacaglia / Sex, power and computers.

1997. (cd) **LOLITA** (soundtrack)

	B.M.G.	B.M.G.

Nov 98. (cd) (<09026 63253-2>) **BULWORTH** (soundtrack)

	RCA Victor	RCA Victor
	☐	Jun98

– Suite one: Bulworth (part 1) / Suite two: Bulworth (part 2).

– belated soundtracks, etc. –

		Silva Screen	Silva Screen
Jan 89.	(lp) Silva Screen; (SP 8013) **MENAGE ALL'ITALIANA** (1965)	☐	-
Jan 89.	(lp) Silva Screen; (SP 8016) **EL GRECO** (1966 soundtrack)	☐	-
Jan 89.	(lp) Silva Screen; (SP 8018) **SVEGLIATI E UCCIDI** (1966; 'Hawks And Sparrows')	☐	-
Jan 89.	(lp) Silva Screen; (SP 8020) **COME IMPARAI AD AMARE LE DONNE** (1966)	☐	-
Jan 89.	(lp) Silva Screen; (SP 8021) **AD OGNI COSTO** (1967; 'Grand Slam')	☐	-
Jan 89.	(lp) Silva Screen; (SP 8022) **L'AVVENTURA** (1959; 'The Rover')	☐	-
Jan 89.	(lp) Interior Music; (IM 004) **FACCIA A FACCIA** (1967; 'Face To Face')	☐	-
Jan 89.	(lp/c) M.C.A.; (MCA/+C 25103) **GUNS FOR SAN SEBASTIAN** (1968)	☐	-
Jan 89.	(lp) Cerebus; (CBUS 101) **MY NAME IS NOBODY**	☐	-
Jan 89.	(lp) Cerebus; (CBUS 102) **LA CAGE AUX FOLLES** (1978 soundtrack)	☐	-
Jan 89.	(lp) Cerebus; (CBUS 103) **THE CHOSEN / HOLOCAUST 2000** (1978)	☐	-
Jan 89.	(lp) Cerebus; (CBUS 106) **TEPEPA** (1969)	☐	-
Jan 89.	(lp) Cerebus; (CBUS 108) **THE BIRD WITH THE CRYSTAL PLUMAGE** (soundtrack)	☐	-

Jan 89. (lp) *Cerebus; (CBUS 111)* **SONNY AND JED / THE CANNIBALS**

Jan 89. (lp) *Cerebus; (CBUS 112)* **L'ASSOLUTO NATURALE** (1969)

Jan 89. (lp) *Cerebus; (CBUS 115)* **IL PRATO / LITTLE NUNS**

Jan 89. (lp) *Silva Screen; (803036)* **INVESTIGATION OF A CITIZEN ABOVE SUSPICION**
(re-iss. Jan93 on 'Cinevox'; CDCIA 5086)

Jan 89. (lp) *Varese Sarabande; (STV 81131)* **BLOODLINE** (1979)

Jan 89. (lp) *Varese Sarabande; (STV 81147)* **THE ISLAND** (1980)

Jan 89. (lp) *Silva Screen; (803026)* **LE PROFESSIONNEL** (1981 soundtrack)

Jan 89. (lp) *Cerebus; (CBUS 118)* **WHEN MAN IS THE PREY** (soundtrack)

Jan 89. (lp) *Cerebus; (CBUS 119)* **A TIME TO DIE** (1983 soundtrack)

Jan 89. (lp) *Cerebus; (CBUS 120)* **THE SCARLET AND THE BLACK** (1983 soundtrack)

Jan 89. (lp) *Varese Sarabande; (STV 81211)* **SAHARA** (1983 soundtrack)
(cd re-iss. Mar93 on 'Intrada'; MAF 7074D)

Jan 89. (lp/c) *Varese Sarabande; (STV/CTV 81248)* **RED SONJA** (1985 soundtrack)

Jan 92. (cd) *Alhambra; (A 8916)* **OCCHIO ALLA PENNA** (1981)

Feb 92. (cd) *Alhambra; (A 8919)* **REVOLVER** (1973)

Feb 92. (cd) *Alhambra; (A 8922)* **MACHINE GUN McCAIN**

Feb 92. (cd) *Alhambra; (A 8924)* **WITHOUT APPARENT MOTIVE**

Feb 92. (cd) *Alhambra; (A 8928)* **LA CALIFFA** (1970)
<US-iss.Feb99 on import w/extra tracks; 7305>

Mar 92. (cd) *Prometheus; (<PCD 115>)* **COSI' COME SEI** (1978; 'Stay As You Are') — Jul95

Mar 92. (cd) *Prometheus; (<PCD 116>)* **LA DAME AUX CAMELIAS** (soundtrack; 'Lady Of The Camelias') — Jul95

Apr 92. (cd) *Prometheus; (<PCD 119>)* **LA DONNA DELLA DOMENCIA / LA MOGLIE PIU BELLA** (?; 'Sunday Woman' & ? '?') — Jul95

Jul 92. (cd) *Milano Dischi; (OST 122)* **LA CLASSE OPERAIA VA IN PARADISO**

Jan 93. (cd) *Milano Dischi; (OST 101)* **THE ACHILLE LAURO AFFAIR** (soundtrack; 'Voyage Of Terror')

Jan 93. (cd) *Milano Dischi; (OST 109)* **SHIPHUNTERS** (soundtrack)

Jan 93. (d-cd) *Milano Dischi; (OST 113)* **MOSES THE LAWGIVER**

Jan 93. (cd) *Prometheus; (PCD 107)* **HUNDRA** (1982)

Jan 93. (cd) *Prometheus; (<PCD 108>)* **BUTTERFLY** (1981) — Jul95

Jul 93. (cd) *Legend; (LEGENDCD 1)* **ORCA – KILLER WHALE** (1977)

Nov 93. (cd) *Cam; (COS 1)* **STANNO TUTTI BENE** (1990; 'Everybody's Fine') — Italian

Nov 93. (cd) *Cam; (COS 3)* **MIO CARO DOTTOR GRASLER** (1990; 'Dear Dr. Grasler') — Italian

Nov 93. (cd; w/ GIUSEPPE TORNATORE & TULLIO) *Cam; (COS 6)* **LA DOMINICA SPECIALMENTE** (1991) — Italian

Nov 93. (cd) *Cam; (CSE 48)* **SUN SPOTS / EAT IT** (1969) / MACCHIE SOLARI) —

Nov 93. (cd) *Cam; (CSE 50)* **PROFESSIONE FIGLIO** (1980; 'Venetian Lies')

Nov 93. (cd) *Cam; (CSE 51)* **GRAZIE ZIA** (1968; 'Thank You Aunt') — Italian

Nov 93. (cd) *Cam; (CSE 52)* **COMANDAMENTI PER GANGST** (soundtrack; 'Commandment For Gangster') — Italian

Nov 93. (cd) *Cam; (CSE 53)* **ESCALATION** (1968) — Italian

Nov 93. (cd) *Cam; (CSE 55)* **I CANNIBALI** (1969; 'Cannibals' — Italian

Nov 93. (cd) *Cam; (CSE 57)* **INCONTRO** (soundtrack; 'Meeting') — Italian

Nov 93. (cd) *Cam; (CSE 58)* **MANI SPORACE** (soundtrack) 'Dirty Hands') — Italian

Nov 93. (cd) *Cam; (CSE 59)* **LEREDITA FERRAMONTI** (soundtrack; 'Inheritance') — Italian

Nov 93. (cd) *Cam; (CSE 66)* **SAI COSA FACEVA STALIN ALLE DONNE** (soundtrack; 'Stalin's Women') — Italian

Nov 93. (cd) *Cam; (CSE 99)* **IL BANDITO DAGLI OCCHI AZZURRI** (1980; 'The Blue Eyed Bandit') — Italian

Nov 93. (cd) *Cam; (CSE 101)* **QUANDSO LAMORE E SENSUALITA** (soundtrack; 'When Love Is Lust')

1994. (cd) *Chameleon; (2259)* **L'EREDITA'FERRAMONTI / LIBERA AMORE MIO** (1976 & 1975) — Italian

1994. (cd) *Chameleon; (2263)* **L'IMMORALITA'** (1978) — Italian

1994. (cd) *Chameleon; (2265)* **IL PRATO** (1979; 'The Meadow') — Italian

1994. (cd) *Chameleon; (7060)* **UNA VITA VENDUTA** (1976) — Italian

1994. (cd) *P.N.T.; <101>* **IL GATTO A NOVE CODE** (1971)

Aug 94. (cd) *Tristar; (80952)* **LA SCORTA** (1993) — Italian

1994. (cd) *Cam; (COS 14)* **IL LUNGO SILENZIO** (1993; 'The Long Silence') — Italian

1994. (cd) *Cam; (COS 15)* **JONA CHE VISSE NELLA BALENA** (1993; 'Jonah And The Whale') — Italian

Jan 95. (cd) *Preamble; (PRCD 107)* **PIAZZA DI SPAGNA** (1991)

Apr 96. (cd) *Silva Screen; (HW 620562)* **THE STARMAKER**

Apr 96. (cd) *Varese Sarabande; (VCDS 7018)* **IL MERCENARIO** (1968)

Apr 96. (cd) *Preamble; (PRCD 116)* **LA DONNA INVISIBLE** (1969)

1996. (cd) *D.R.G.; <DRGCD 32916>* **DRAMMI GOTICI** (GOTHIC DRAMAS)

1997. (cd) *Intermezzo Media; <136>* **PRIMA DELLA RIVOLUZIONE**

Jul 98. (cd) *Intermezzo Media; <309>* **IL DESERTO DEI TARTARI** (1976; 'Desert Of The Tartars')

Nov 98. (cd) *Intermezzo Media; <314>* **IMPUTAZIONE DI OMICIDIO PER UNO STUDENTE** ('Murder Charge For A Student')

Mar 99. (cd) *Intermezzo Media; <312>* **VITE STROZZATE** (1996)

1999. (cd) *B.M.G.; <9392>* **AD OGNI COSTO**

Sep 99. (cd) *D.R.G.; <DRGCD 32916>* **PHANTOM OF THE OPERA** (1998; 'Il Fantasma Dell'opera')

Sep 99. (cd) *D.R.G.; <DRG 12621>* **THE STENDHAL SYNDROME** (1996; 'La Sindrome Di Stendhal')

Sep 99. (cd) *D.R.G.; <DRG 12622>* **THE FOURTH KING** (1997; 'Il Quarto Re')

Dec 99. (cd) *Intermezzo Media; <319>* **IL GIORNO PRIMA** ('Control')

– compilations, etc. –

Sep 71. (lp) *Sunset; (SLS 50248)* **WESTERN THEMES – ITALIAN STYLE**
– (cuts from the soundtracks of 'THE GOOD, THE BAD AND THE UGLY', 'DEATH RIDES A HORSE', 'NAVAJO JOE' & 'THE BIG GUNDOWN')

Nov 80. (lp/c) *RCA Int.; (INT S/K 5059)* **FILM HITS**
– Once upon a time in the west / For a few dollars more / Moses theme (main title) / Bye bye colonel / A fistful of dollars / A gun for Ringo / The ballad of Sacco and Vanzetti / Here's to you / The vice of killing / Paying off scores / The adventurer / What have you done to Solange / Violent night / Mertello. (re-iss. Sep84 lp/c; NL/NK 70091)

Apr 81. (lp) *E.M.I.; (THIS 33)* **THIS IS ENNIO MORRICONE** 23

Apr 81. (lp/c) *B.B.C.; (REH/ZCR 414)* **CHI MAI** 29
– Chi Mai / Lontano / A fistful of dynamite / Poem of a woman / The secret / Come Maddelena / Once upon a time in the west / Good luck Jack / Here's to you / My name is nobody

Jun 81. (7") *B.B.C.; (RESL 93)* **ONCE UPON A TIME IN THE WEST. / THE SECRET**

May 84. (7") *Old Gold; (OG 9413)* **CHI MAI. / Who Pays The Ferryman** (by Yannis Markopoulos)

Jul 84. (lp) *R.C.A,; (CL 31559)* **MASTERPIECES**

Oct 84. (lp) *R.C.A.; (PD 70324)* **BEST OF ENNIO MORRICONE**
– For a few dollars more / A fistful of dynamite / My name is nobody / A fistful of dollars / Sacco and Vanzetti / Moses theme / Metello / God with us / Once upon a time in the west / 1900 / Death rides a horse / Life's tough, isn't it? / Ciribiribin / Scetate.

Jan 88. (d-cd-d-c/d-lp) *Virgin; (CD/TC+/VD 2516)* **FILM MUSIC BY ENNIO MORRICONE**
– The good, the bad and the ugly / The Sicilian clan / Chi Mai / The man with the harmonica / La Califfa / Gabriel's oboe / A fistful of dynamite / Once upon a time in the west (main theme) / Cockey's song / The mission (remix) / Come Maddelena / Falls / My name os nobody / Le vent, le cri / Deborah's theme. (re-iss. Sep93 on 'Virgin-VIP' cd/c; CD/TC VIP 123)

Aug 88. (lp/c/cd) *Venture; (VE/TCVE/CDVE 24)* **CHAMBER MUSIC**
– Sestetto / Musica per 11 violini / 3 studi / Ricercare per pianoforte / 4 pezzi per chitarra / Suoni per dino / Distanze.

Jan 89. (cd) *Silva Screen; (T 8710)* **LIVE IN CONCERT** (live)

Jan 89. (lp) *Silva Screen; (I-MGM 009)* **MUSIC FROM THREE SERGIO CORBUCCI WESTERNS**
– ('Hellbenders', 'Companeros' & 'C'Entriamo Noi Con La Revolutione')

Jan 90. (cd) *R.C.A.; (039126)* **FOR A FEW DOLLARS MORE / A FISTFUL OF DOLLARS**

Jan 92. (cd) *R.C.A.; (ND 74021)* **THE GOOD, THE BAD AND THE UGLY / A FISTFUL OF DOLLARS / FOR A FEW DOLLARS MORE**

Mar 92. (cd) *Milano Dischi; (OST 111)* **EL GRECO / GIORDANO BRUNO**

Sep 92. (cd/c) *Music Club; (MCCD/MCTC 056)* **THE VERY BEST OF ENNIO MORRICONE**

Jan 93. (cd/c) *Edel; (EDL 2549-2/-4)* **OCTOPUS / ALLE ORIGINI DELLA MAFIA** (? & 1976; 'All About The Mafia')

Jan 93. (cd) *Milano Dischi; (OST 103)* **ALLONSANFAN / METELLO** (1974 & 1970)

Jan 93. (cd) *Milano Dischi; (OST 107)* **DEATH RIDES A HORSE / A PISTOL FOR RINGO**

Jan 93. (cd) *Milano Dischi; (OST 118)* **L'UMANOIDE / NIGHTMARE CASTLE** (1979; 'The Humanoid' & ?)

Jan 93. (cd) *Milano Dischi; (OST 120)* **L'AVVENTURA / OCEANO** (1959 & 1971)

Jan 93. (cd/c) *Cinevox; (AK/AT 47705)* **GUNS FOR SAN SEBASTIAN / HANG 'EM HIGH** (1970 & 1968)

Jan 93. (cd) *Cinevox; (CDCIA 5087)* **FATTI DI GENTE PERBENE / DIVINA CREATURA** (1974; 'The Bird With The Crystal Plume' & 1975 'Divine Creature')

Aug 93. (c) *Epic; (473802-4)* **HIS GREATEST THEMES: MOVIE SOUND** (cd-iss. Nov95 on 'Accord'; 76>

Nov 93. (cd) *P.M.F.; (90.696-2)* **ENNIO MORRICONE**

Jul 94. (cd) *Silva Screen; (CDCR 17)* **SEPOLTA VIVA / THE ANTICHRIST**

Jan 95. (cd) *Preamble; (PRCD 106)* **D'AMORE SI MUORE / LE DUE STAGIONI DELLA VITA**

May 95. (cd) *R.C.A.; (<74321 26495-2>)* **SPAGHETTI WESTERN**
– (from the films 'A Gun For Ringo', 'At Times Life Is Very Hard, Isn't That Fate?', 'Guns For The McGregor's', 'Gunfight And Red Sands', 'Bullets Don't Argue', 'Seven Women For The McGregor's', 'Death Rides A Horse', 'We'll Be Back, Isn't That Fate' and 'The Return Of Ringo').

May 95. (cd) *Silva Screen; (MASKMK 701)* **FACCIA A FACCIA** ('Face To Face') / **LA RESA DEI CONTI** ('The Big Gundown')

May 95. (cd) *Milano Dischi; (OST 127)* **CITTA VIOLENTA / SVEGLIATI E UCCIDI**

Jul 95. (d-cd) *D.R.G.; (<DRGCD 32907>)* **AN ENNIO MORRICONE WESTERN QUINTET**
– ('A Fistful Of Dynamite', 'My Name Is Nobody', 'A Fist Goes West', 'Blood And Guns' and 'Campaneros')

Sep 95. (d-cd) *D.R.G.; (DRGCD 32908)* **AN ENNIO MORRICONE ANTHOLOGY** (film scores)

Sep 95. (cd) *D.R.G.; (DRGCD 32911)* **AN ENNIO MOORICONE DARLO ARGENTO**
– (THE BIRD WITH THE CRYSTAL PLUMAGE / FOUR FLIES ON GREY VELVET / CAT O'NINE TAILS).

Sep 95. (cd) *R.C.A,; <98732>* **ACTION THRILLERS**

Oct 95. (cd) *D.R.G.; (DRGCD 32913)* **WITH LOVE**

Nov 95. (cd) *Cameo; (CD 3509)* **THE MUSIC OF ENNIO MORRICONE**

Dec 95. (cd) *Replay; <4063>* **AN HOUR WITH ENNIO MORRICONE**

Feb 96. (cd) *R.C.A.; (74321 31551-2)* **TIME OF ADVENTURE**	☐	☐
Feb 96. (cd) *R.C.A.; (74321 31552-2)* **TV FILM MUSIC**	☐	☐
Apr 96. (cd) *Milano Dischi; (OST 130)* **THE MUSIC FROM THE FILMS OF PIER PAOLO PASOLINI** – (UCCELLACCI / LE STREGNE / TEOREMA)	☐	-
Apr 96. (cd) *Preamble; (PRCD 117)* **LE FOTO PROHIBITE DI UNA SIGNORA PERBENE / IL SEGRETO**	☐	-
Apr 96. (cd) *Preamble; (PRCD 121)* **BLUEBEARD / LA MONACA DI MONZA**	☐	-
Apr 96. (cd) *Preamble; (PRCD 122)* **GIORNATA NERA PER L'ARIETE / LI OCCHI FREDDI DELLA PAURA**	☐	-
Apr 96. (cd) *Silva Screen; (DE 76)* **FIVE MAN ARMY / THE LINK**	☐	-
Oct 96. (cd) *Legend; (LEGENDCD 26)* **LA VIOLENZA: QUINTO POERA** ('Sicilian Checkmate') **/ UNA BRAVA STAGIONE** ('A Brief Season')	☐	-
Dec 96. (d-cd) *D.R.G.; (DRGCD 32920)* **MAIN TITLES 1965-1996**	☐	-
May 99. (lp) *Studio Uno; (STN 1007LP)* **CLUB MORRICONE**	☐	-

Van MORRISON

Born: GEORGE IVAN MORRISON, 31 Aug'45, Belfast, N.Ireland. Reared on such eclectic musical fare as HANK WILLIAMS, JIMMIE RODGERS, LEADBELLY and DUKE ELLINGTON, the young VAN began his professional musical apprenticeship on the Irish showband circuit, mastering guitar, piano and saxophone and laying the fertile seed-bed of vocal improvisation and innovation that would come to distinguish his career. A rough and tumble tour of Germany with The MONARCHS was followed by spells in The MANHATTAN SHOWBAND, The GOLDEN EAGLES and finally, The GAMBLERS, who, in turn, evolved into THEM, the brooding R&B bovver boys with whom MORRISON first stamped his gutteral howl on a nation's musical consciousness. Along with The ANIMALS, The PRETTY THINGS and The ROLLING STONES, THEM formed an integral part of the mid-60's British R&B boom from whence came rock music as we now know and love (or loathe, as the case may be) it today. Though the band only released two official albums, 'THEM' (1965) and 'THEM AGAIN' (1966), their place in legend was assured as the garage leer of 'GLORIA' came to be one of the most covered songs in rock history. One of the few constants in their ramshackle approach and ever changing line-up was MORRISON; his dour, threatening demeanour and erratically electric live performances coupled with a precocious gift for songwriting indicated a star in the ascendant. When THEM finally disintegrated, VAN took up an invitation from BERT BERNS (composer of THEM's hit, 'HERE COMES THE NIGHT' – he had also produced the band) to lay down some tracks in New York for his fledgling 'Bang' label. The resulting sessions produced eight finished songs, among them the youthful exuberance of 'BROWN EYED GIRL' and the harrowing, churning claustrophobia of 'T.B. SHEETS', polar opposites between which MORRISON began to develop his songcraft. The former song edged its way into the US Top 10 during the summer of love in 1967, the label subsequently releasing all the tracks as an album, 'BLOWIN' YOUR MIND', in September (without the consent, and much to the annoyance, of MORRISON himself). Nevertheless, the singer entered the studio once again later that year to record another series of tracks, including early versions of 'BESIDE YOU' and 'MADAME GEORGE' (later appearing in their full glory on 'ASTRAL WEEKS'), some surfacing on the hopefully titled 1970 cash-in, 'The BEST OF VAN MORRISON', while the remainder were eventually unearthed on 1974's 'T.B. SHEETS'. Following the sudden death of BERNS in December '67, VAN moved north to Cambridge, Massachusetts, where he was eventually spotted and signed to a management deal with New York's 'Inherit Productions'. A contract was subsequently secured with 'Warners' and the cream of the Big Apple's jazz musicians were rounded up to back VAN on his solo debut proper, 'ASTRAL WEEKS'. As hotly debated, analysed, shrouded in myth and generally deified as any recording in the history of music, the enigmatic, ethereal allure of the album remains ultimately impenetrable. Recorded, quintessentially MORRISON-style, in two spontaneous four-hour sessions, the record transcended any notion of "rock" per se, nor could it be bracketed under jazz. A darkly intoxicating stream of inspired musical consciousness, 'ASTRAL WEEKS' traded in conventional verse/chorus song structures for freeform explorations and fragments, languidly vivid imagery floating in and out of focus. From the yearning warmth and acoustic strum of the title track and 'SWEET THING' to the harpsichord tapestry of 'CYPRUS AVENUE' and the epic, dizzying 'MADAME GEORGE', MORRISON set out the blueprint for much of his later work, an eternal quest for spiritual enlightenment that both embraced and transcended hope and despair, contentment and restlessness. Fittingly, then, this music is timeless, the only indication of its 1968 birthdate the supple potency of VAN's young voice. An instrument in its own right, MORRISON's vocal faculty is arguably among the most powerful, seductive and ultimately healing to have emerged in the last thirty or so years, capable of everything from a primal grunt a la JAMES BROWN, to a child-like, awestruck breathlessness. An album that has grown in stature with each passing year, 'ASTRAL WEEKS' was met with mixed reviews upon its original release, and it initially sold relatively poorly. Undeterred, VAN moved to Woodstock with his new wife, Janet Planet (yep, she was a fully paid up hippy), where he penned most of the material for a follow-up album, 'MOONDANCE'. Released in early 1970, the record was a more solidly constructed affair, MORRISON reining in his more abstract tendencies into tighter, shorter, brassy bursts. Much of the album reflected VAN's love of soul and R&B, punchy horn flourishes replacing the meandering acoustics of 'ASTRAL WEEKS'.

The soporific 'AND IT STONED ME' and the classic 'INTO THE MYSTIC' were closest in spirit to the debut, the latter track condensing the albums theme of the redemptive power of love. By this point, the critics were catching on to the stocky Irishman's genius, lauding the album and heralding MORRISON as one of the rock world's most talented visionaries. He was also arguably one of the few white musicians to interpret black music forms in such a way as to retain the spontaneity and richness while creating something completely original. In saying that, it could be argued that 'VAN MORRISON, HIS BAND AND THE STREET CHOIR' (1970) relied too heavily on a straight soul/R&B formula, lacking any real depth as a result. 'DOMINO' was the standout track, a driving, hedonistic slice of white R&B that gave VAN his biggest (US) hit to date. The album's inside cover showed a scene of communal domesticity, an apparent contentedness (only rarely glimpsed since) that continued with 'TUPELO HONEY' (1971), a country-tinged collection celebrating love and romance. The lush balladeering of the title track saw VAN putting in one of the sweetest vocal performances of his career thus far, most of the songs finding the singer in laid-back, family man mode. Entertaining as the album was, 'ST. DOMINIC'S PREVIEW' (1972) was far more compelling. Tellingly, by the time VAN came to record the album, his relationship with Janet was on the rocks. While the disc opened with the life-affirming soul shout of 'JACKIE WILSON SAID', the epic 'LISTEN TO THE LION' formed the album's centrepiece, a musical and spiritual marathon that set out VAN's agenda of personal quest more explicitly than ever before. The title track was equally inspiring while the almost gospel-like 'REDWOOD TREE' was manna for the soul, healing harmonies of hope and forgiveness. The billowing, hypnotic ambience of the album closed the album in suitably enigmatic style, and bizarrely enough, recalled the PINK FLOYD of 'Wish You Were Here' (though don't let that put you off!). 'ST. DOMINIC'S PREVIEW' came at a time when VAN was regaining his confidence on stage after a period of relative withdrawal from live performance. To catalogue the ever shifting personnel of MORRISON's various bands would probably warrant a book in its own right although the general concensus is that the man reached a zenith of sorts with his CALEDONIA SOUL ORCHESTRA. Recorded for posterity on the double live album, 'IT'S TOO LATE TO STOP NOW' (1974), MORRISON's summer '73 shows are the stuff of legend. One of the classic live albums, MORRISON takes his songs to places they were probably never designed for, stretching, remoulding and re-inventing them in his inimitable R&B preacher/spiritual warrior fashion. The result is rarely less than breathtaking. Ironically enough, 'HARD NOSE THE HIGHWAY' (1973), MORRISON's studio effort of the time, lacked the intensity of the live work although 'THE GREAT DECEPTION' is probably VAN's angriest song, berating the showbusiness falsity that he's always made a point of distancing himself from. The remainder of the 70's were MORRISON's wilderness years as he seemingly struggled to focus on any kind of musical direction, taking time out to explore his spiritual journey on a personal level. 'VEEDON FLEECE' (1974), apparently inspired by a return to his native Ireland after years in exile, presaged this more intense period of searching. Arguably closest in spirit to VAN's cosmic debut than anything else he's since released, the record shared 'ASTRAL WEEKS' otherworldly sense of drifting in and out of consciousness, set against a backdrop of Ireland's rich heritage. The Celtic folk influence was most prominent on 'STREETS OF ARKLOW', haunting Irish pipes conjuring up images of brooding, silent faces peering from rain lashed doorways. The album remains a pivotal release, signalling the more overtly Celtic and spiritual direction MORRISON's music would take in the 80's and after completing this milestone, the Irishman didn't surface again until 1977 with the poorly received 'PERIOD OF TRANSITION'. 'WAVELENGTH' (1978) saw VAN back on track, although 'INTO THE MUSIC' (1979) was really the beginning of a new phase in his career. Joyously religious but never dogmatic, the album found MORRISON flirting with Christianity; 'FULL FORCE GALE' was a revelation, a rock of strength and deep-seated conviction. A rich seam of hope and inspiration runs through the whole album, culminating in 'AND THE HEALING HAS BEGUN'. From here on in, MORRISON's albums were increasingly concerned with religious redemption, Celtic mysteries and ultimately the healing power of music (or navel-gazing nonsense, if you erred towards cynicism) . 'COMMON ONE' (1980) divided the critics with its esoteric New Age slant, while other early 80's efforts like 'BEAUTIFUL VISION' (1982) and 'INARTICULATE SPEECH OF THE HEART' (1983) introduced a kind of airbrushed, synthesizer sound that didn't sit particularly well with MORRISON's organic voice and approach. 'NO GURU, NO METHOD, NO TEACHER' (1986) was a convincing return to form, 'ONE IRISH ROVER' a taster for his other great work of the decade, 'IRISH HEARTBEAT' (1988), the triumphant collaboration with Irish traditionalists, The CHIEFTAINS. The record found MORRISON in boisterous form, the resulting tour inspiring some of the most positive reactions since his seminal live shows of the 70's. The devotional 'POETIC CHAMPIONS COMPOSE' (1987) was sandwiched between these two, another work of nomadic spiritual searching, MORRISON singing his pain on the haunting 'SOMETIMES I FEEL LIKE A MOTHERLESS CHILD'. Incredibly, VAN's first Top 20 UK solo hit came with 'WHENEVER GOD SHINES HIS LIGHT', a duet with CLIFF RICHARD the following year. The success of the single helped to boost VAN's commercial clout, the mellow 'AVALON SUNSET' (1989) opus reaching No.13 while subsequent albums, 'ENLIGHTENMENT' (1990) and the heavily gospel-orientated 'HYMNS TO THE SILENCE' (1991) both reached the UK Top 5. The latter's title could be used to describe the music that has made up a large part of MORRISON career, songs of love and devotion unique in rock'n'roll. While more recent releases like 'TOO LONG

IN EXILE' (1993) and 'DAYS LIKE THIS' (1995) have lacked just such inspiration, VAN's live work was again re-energised and the live 'A NIGHT IN SAN FRANCISCO' (1994) was roundly praised, one of the record's many highlights an electric run-through of 'GLORIA' with old jamming mate, JOHN LEE HOOKER. VAN had also taken to playing with jazz maestro, GEORGIE FAME, a breezy live set recorded at Ronnie Scott's in Soho, released as 'HOW LONG HAS THIS BEEN GOING ON' (1996). 'THE HEALING GAME' in 1997 saw the man return to Top 10 territory and a subsequent tour with BOB DYLAN helped maintain his profile; a 'Basement Tapes'-type of double CD set 'THE PHILOSOPHER'S STONE' (1998) saw a slight connection still, while VAN recorded a cover of 'MULESKINNER BLUES' on DYLAN's new imprint, 'Egyptian'. VAN's final album of the 90's, 'BACK ON TOP' was his first for Virgin offshoot 'Pointblank', the transatlantic Top 30 long-player even supplying his first Top 40 single in years, 'PRECIOUS TIME'. A grumpy curmudgeon to some, a Celtic visionary to others, VAN MORRISON remains as much of an enigma as his best work. • **Songwriters:** Self-penned except covers; CALEDONIA (Fleecie Moore) / HELP ME (Sonny Boy Williamson) / BRING IT HOME TO ME (Sam Cooke) / SANTA FE (co-written w / Jackie DeShannon) / LONELY AVENUE (Doc Pomus) / GOOD MORNING LITTLE SCHOOLGIRL (Sonny Boy Williamson) / THE LONESOME ROAD (N.Shikret – G.Austin) / MOODY'S MOOD FOR LOVE (James Moody) / I'LL TAKE CARE OF YOU (Brook Benton) / BEFORE THE WORLD WAS MADE (W.B.Yeats / music; Kenny Craddock) / YOU DON'T KNOW ME (hit; Ray Charles) / I'LL NEVER BE FREE (Benjamin-Weiss) / THAT OLD BLACK MAGIC (hit; Sammy Davis Jnr).

Album rating: BLOWIN' YOUR MIND (*5) / ASTRAL WEEKS (*10) / MOONDANCE (*9) / HIS BAND AND THE STREET CHOIR (*6) / TUPELO HONEY (*8) / SAINT DOMINC'S PREVIEW (*9) / HARD NOSE THE HIGHWAY (*7) / IT'S TOO LATE TO STOP NOW (*9) / VEEDON FLEECE (*9) / A PERIOD OF TRANSITION (*5) / WAVELENGTH (*7) / INTO THE MUSIC (*8) / COMMON ONE (*6) / BEAUTIFUL VISION (*6) / INARTICULATE SPEECH OF THE HEART (*6) / LIVE AT THE GRAND OPERA HOUSE, BELFAST (*7) / A SENSE OF WONDER (*6) / NO GURU, NO METHOD, NO TEACHER (*7) / POETIC CHAMPIONS COMPOSE (*7) / IRISH HEARTBEAT with the Chieftains (*8) / AVALON SUNSET (*7) / THE BEST OF VAN MORRISON compilation (*9) / ENLIGHTENMENT (*7) / HYMNS TO THE SILENCE (*7) / THE BEST OF VAN MORRISON, VOLUME TWO compilation (*6) / TOO LONG IN EXILE (*6) / A NIGHT IN SAN FRANCISCO (*7) / DAYS LIKE THIS (*6) / HOW LONG HAS THIS BEEN GOING ON with Georgie Fame & Friends (*4) / THE HEALING GAME (*6) / THE PHILOSOPHER'S STONE (THE UNRELEASED TAPES VOL.1) collection (*6) / BACK ON TOP (*6)

VAN MORRISON – vocals, guitar, saxophone (ex-THEM) with loads of session persons.

	London	Bang
Jun 67. (7") *(HLZ 10150)* <*545*> **BROWN EYED GIRL. / GOODBYE BABY (BABY GOODBYE)**		10

(re-iss. Mar71 on 'President'; PT 328) (re-iss. Apr74; HLM 10453)

Sep 67. (7") <*552*> **RO RO ROSEY. / CHICK-A-BOOM**		-
Nov 67. (7") <*585*> **SPANISH ROSE / MIDNIGHT ROSE**		-
Feb 68. (lp; mono/stereo) *(HA-Z 8346)* <*BLP/+S 218*> **BLOWIN' YOUR MIND**		Sep67

– Brown eyed girl / He ain't give you none / T.B. sheets / Spanish rose / Goodbye baby (baby goodbye) / Ro Ro Rosey / Who drove the red sports car? / Midnight special. *(cd-iss. Jul95 on 'Epic';) (re-iss. Nov98 on 'Simply Vinyl'; SVLP 49)*

now with **LARRY FALLON** – conductor, arranger / **JAY BERLINER** – guitar / **RICHARD DAVIS** – bass / **CONNIE KAY** – drums / **JOHN PAYNE** – flute, soprano sax / **WARREN SMITH JR** – percussion, vibraphone

	Warners	Warners
Sep 69. (lp) (<*WS 1768*>) **ASTRAL WEEKS**		Nov68

– In the beginning: Astral weeks / Beside you / Sweet thing / Cypress avenue / Afterwards: Young lovers do / Madame George / Ballerina / Slim slow rider. *(re-iss. Aug 71; K 46024) (cd-iss. May87; K 246024)*

now with **JOHN PLATANIA** – guitar / **JEFF LABES** – keys / **JACK SHROER** – sax / **GARY MALLABER** – drums / **JOHN KLINGBERG** – bass

Mar 70. (lp) (<*WS 1835*>) **MOONDANCE**	32	29

– And it stoned me / Moondance / Crazy love / Into the mystic / Caravan / Come running / These dreams of you / Brand new day / Everyone / Glad tidings. *(re-iss. Aug71; K 46040) (cd-iss. Jan86; K 246040)*

May 70. (7") *(WB <*7383*>)* **COME RUNNING. / CRAZY LOVE**	39	Apr70
Dec 70. (lp) (<*WS 1884*>) **HIS BAND AND THE STREET CHOIR**	32	Nov70

– Domino / Crazy face / I've been working / Call me up in Dreamland / I'll be your lover, too / Blue money / Virgo clowns / Gypsy queen / Sweet Janine / If I ever needed someone / Street choir. *(re-iss. Aug71; K 46066) (cd-iss. Feb93;)*

Dec 70. (7") *(WB <*7434*>)* **DOMINO. / SWEET JANINE**		9 Oct70

(re-iss. Jul71; K 16044)

Feb 71. (7") <*7462*> **BLUE MONEY. / SWEET THING**	-	23
Apr 71. (7") <*7488*> **CALL ME UP IN DREAMLAND. / STREET CHOIR**	-	95

now with **MALLABER, SHROER + BILL CHURCH** – bass / **RONNIE MONTROSE** – guitar / **RICK SCHLOSSER** – drums + **CONNIE KAY** – drums

Sep 71. (7") <*7518*> **WILD NIGHT. / WHEN THAT EVENING SUN GOES DOWN**	-	28
Nov 71. (lp) *(K 46114)* <*WS 1950*> **TUPELO HONEY**		27 Oct 71

– Wild night / (Straight to your heart) Like a cannonball / Old old Woodstock / Starting a new life / You're my woman / Tupelo honey / I wonna roo you / When that evening sun goes down / Moonshine whiskey. *(re-iss. Aug89 & Feb94 on 'Polydor' lp/c/cd; 839161-1/-4/-2)*

Dec 71. (7") <*7543*> **TUPELO HONEY. / STARTING A NEW LIFE**	-	47
Mar 72. (7") <*7573*> **(STRAIGHT TO YOUR HEART) LIKE A CANNONBALL / OLD OLD WOODSTOCK**	-	-

LEROY VINNEGAR – bass repl. CHURCH (who later joined MONTROSE) / **ROY ELLIOT** – guitar + **MARK NAFTALIN** – piano repl. SCHOSSLER + MALLABER

Jul 72. (7") *(K 16210)* <*7616*> **JACKIE WILSON SAID (I'M IN HEAVEN WHEN YOU SMILE). / YOU'VE GOT THE POWER**		61

Aug 72. (lp) *(K 46172)* <*WS 2633*> **SAINT DOMINIC'S PREVIEW**		15

– Jackie Wilson said (I'm in Heaven when you smile) / Gypsy / I will be there / Listen to the lion / Saint Dominic's preview / Redwood tree / Almost Independance day. *(re-iss. Aug89 on 'Polydor' lp/c/cd; 839162-1/-4/-2) (cd-iss. Apr95;)*

Oct 72. (7") *(7638)* **REDWOOD TREE. / SAINT DOMINIC'S PREVIEW**	-	98
Jan 73. (7") <*7665*> **GYPSY. / SAINT DOMINIC'S PREVIEW**	-	-

RONNIE now formed MONTROSE went through various session personnel: **DAVID HAYES** – bass and most of new band.

Jul 73. (7") *(K 16299)* <*7706*> **WARM LOVE. / I WILL BE THERE**		Jun73
Jul 73. (lp) *(K 46242)* <*WS 2712*> **HARD NOSE THE HIGHWAY**	22	27

– Snow in San Anselmo / Warm love / Hard nose the highway / Wild children / The great deception / Green / Autumn song / Purple heather. *(re-iss. Aug89 on 'Polydor' lp/c/cd; 839163-1/-4/-2) (cd-iss. Apr95;)*

Sep 73. (7") <*7744*> **GREEN. / WILD CHILDREN**	-	-
Feb 74. (7") <*7797*> **AIN'T NOTHING YOU CAN DO. / WILD CHILDREN**	-	-
Feb 74. (d-lp) *(K 86007)* <*WS 2760*> **IT'S TOO LATE TO STOP NOW (live)**		53

– Ain't nothing you can do / Warm love / Into the mystic / These dreams of you / I believe to my soul / I've been working / Help me / Wild children / Domino / I just wanna make love to you / Bring it on home to me / Saint Dominic's preview / Take your hand out of my pocket / Listen to the lion / Here comes the night / Gloria / Caravan / Cypress Avenue. *(re-iss. Aug89 on 'Polydor' d-lp/d-c/d-cd; 839166-1/-4/-2) (cd-iss. Apr95;)*

May 74. (7") *(K 16392)* **CALDONIA (WHAT MAKES YOUR BIG HEAD HARD?). / WHAT'S UP, CRAZY PUP**		-
Oct 74. (lp/c) *(K/K4 56068)* <*WS 2805*> **VEEDON FLEECE**	41	53

– Streets of Arklow / Country fair / Cul de sac / Linden Arden stole the highlights / Fair play / Bulbs / You don't pull no punches but you don't push the river / Comfort you / Come here my love / Who was that masked man. *(re-iss. Aug89 on 'Polydor' lp/c/cd; 839164-1/-4/-2) (cd-iss. Apr95;)*

Jul 74. (7") <*8029*> **BULBS. / CUL DE SAC**	-	-
Nov 74. (7") *(K 16486)* **BULBS. / WHO WAS THAT MASKED MAN**	-	-

below featured **DR. JOHN** – piano

Mar 77. (lp/c) *(K/K4 56322)* <*2987*> **A PERIOD OF TRANSITION**	23	43

– You gotta make it through the world / It fills you up / The eternal Kansas City / Joyous sound / Flamingoes fly / Heavy connection / Cold wind in August. *(re-iss. +cd.Aug89 on 'Polydor')*

Apr 77. (7") *(K 16939)* **THE ETERNAL KANSAS CITY. / JOYOUS SOUND**		-
Jul 77. (7") *(K 16986)* **JOYOUS SOUND. / MECHANICAL BLISS**		
Oct 77. (7") **COLD WIND IN AUGUST. / MOONDANCE**		

PETER VAN HOOKE – drums / **HERBIE ARMSTRONG** – guitar etc

Oct 78. (lp/c) *(K/K4 56526)* <*3212*> **WAVELENGTH**	27	28

– Kingdom hall / Checkin' it out / Natalia / Venice U.S.A. / Lifetimes / Wavelength / Santa Fe / Beautiful obsession / Hungry for your love / Take it where you find it. *(re-iss. Aug89 & Feb94 on 'Polydor' lp/c/cd; 839169-1/-4/-2) (re-iss. Apr98 on 'Polydor';)*

Oct 78. (7") *(K 17254)* **WAVELENGTH. / CHECKIN' IT OUT**		42
Feb 79. (7") *(K 17322)* **NATALIA. / LIFETIMES**		-
Apr 79. (7") **CHECKIN' IT OUT. /**		-

now with **HOOKE, ARMSTRONG, HAYES / + MARK JORDAN** – keyboards / **MARK ISHAM** – trumpet / **PEE WEE ELLIS** – saxophone

	Mercury	Warners
Aug 79. (lp/c) *(9102/? 852)* <*3390*> **INTO THE MUSIC**	21	43

– Bright side of the road / Full force gale / Stepping out queen / Troubadours / Rolling hills / You make me feel so free / Angeliou / And the healing has begun / It's all in the game / You know what they're writing about. *(re-iss. May83 lp/c; PRICE/PRIMC 2) (re-iss. Aug89 & Feb94 on 'Polydor' lp/c/cd; 839603-1/-4/-2) (re-iss. Apr98 on 'Polydor'; 537540-2)*

Sep 79. (7") *(6001 121)* **BRIGHT SIDE OF THE ROAD. / ROLLING HILLS**	63	
Dec 79. (7") **FULL FORCE GALE. / YOU MAKE ME FEEL SO FREE**	-	

JOHN ALLAIR – keyboards + **MICK COX** – guitar repl. JORDAN + MARCUS

Sep 80. (lp/c) *(6302/7144 021)* <*3462*> **COMMON ONE**	53	73

– Haunts of ancient peace / Summertime in England / Satisfied / Wild honey / Spirit / When heart is open. *(re-iss. May83 lp/c; PRICE/PRIMC 1) (cd-iss. 1986; 800 043-2) (re-iss. Aug89 & Apr95 on 'Polydor' lp/c/cd; 839600-1/-4/-2) (cd re-iss. Apr98; 537541-2)*

added **TOM DONLINGER** – drums

Feb 82. (lp/c) *(6302/7144 122)* <*3652*> **BEAUTIFUL VISION**	31	44

– Celtic Ray / Northern muse (solid sound) / Dweller on the threshold / Beautiful vision / She gives me religion / Cleaning windows / Vanlose stairway / Aryan mist / Scandinavia / Across the bridge where angels dwell / Scandinavia. *(re-iss. Mar85 lp/c; PRICE/PRIMC 82) (re-iss. Aug89 & Feb94 on 'Polydor' lp/c/cd; 839601-1/-4/-2) (re-iss. Apr98 on 'Polydor'; 537542-2)*

Mar 82. (7") **CLEANING WINDOWS. / SCANDINAVIA**	-	
Mar 82. (7") *(MER 99)* **CLEANING WINDOWS. / IT'S ALL IN THE GAME**	-	
Jun 82. (7") *(MER 110)* **DWELLER ON THE THRESHOLD. / SCANDINAVIA**	-	

CHRIS MICHIE – guitar repl. COX

Feb 83. (7") *(MER 132)* **CRY FOR HOME. / SUMMERTIME IN ENGLAND (live)**		

(12"+=) (MERX 132) – All saints day.

Mar 83. (lp/c) *(MERL/+C 16)* <*23802*> **INARTICULATE SPEECH OF THE HEART**	14	

– Higher than the world / Connswater / River of time / Celtic swing / Rave on, John Donne / Inarticulate speech of the heart No.1 / Irish heartbeat / The street only knew your name / Cry for home / Inarticulate speech of the heart No.2 / September night. *(re-iss. Oct86 lp/c; PRICE/PRIMC 93) (cd-iss. May86; 811 140-2) (re-iss. Aug89 & Feb94 on 'Polydor'; 839604-1/-4/-2) (re-iss. Apr98 on 'Polydor'; 537543-2)*

May 83. (7") *(MER 141)* **CELTIC SWING. / MR. THOMAS**		

(12"+=) (MERX 132) – Rave on, John Donne.

Feb 84. (lp/c) *(MERL/+C 36)* **LIVE AT THE GRAND OPERA HOUSE, BELFAST (live)**	47	-

– (intro) / Into the music / Inarticulate seech of the heart / Dweller on the threshold / It's all in the game – You know what they're writing about / She gives me religion / Haunts of ancient peace / Full force gale / Beautiful vision / Vanlose stairway / Rave on, John Donne – Rave on (part 2) / Northern muse (solid ground) / Cleaning windows. *(cd-iss. 1986; 818336-2) (re-iss. Aug89 on 'Polydor' lp/c/cd; 839602-1/-4/-2) (cd re-iss. Apr98 on 'Polydor'; 537544-2)*

Mar 84. (7") *(MER 159)* **DWELLER ON THE THRESHOLD (live). / NORTHERN MUSE (SOLID GROUND)** ☐ ☐

Mercury   Mercury

Nov 84. (7"/12") *(MER/+X 178)* **A SENSE OF WONDER. / HAUNTS OF ANCIENT PEACE (live)** ☐ ☐

Feb 85. (lp/c)(cd) *(MERH/+C 54)(<822 895-2>)* **A SENSE OF WONDER** [25] [61]
– Tore down a La Rimbaud / Ancient of days / Evening meditation / The master's eyes / What would I do / A sense of wonder / Boffyflow and Spike / If you only knew / Let the slave / A new kind of man. *(re-iss. May90 & Apr95 on 'Polydor' cd/c/lp; 843116-2/-4/-1) (cd re-iss. Apr98; 537545-2)*

Jun 86. (7") *(MER 223)* **IVORY TOWER. / NEW KIND OF MAN** ☐ ☐
(12"+=) *(MERX 223)* – A sense of wonder / Cleaning windows.

Jul 86. (lp/c)(cd) *(MERH/+C 94)(<830077-2>)* **NO GURU, NO METHOD, NO TEACHER** [27] [70]
– Got to go back / Oh the warm feeling / Foreign window / Town called Paradise / In the garden / Tir na nog / Here comes the night / Thanks for the information / One Irish rover / Ivory tower. *(re-iss. Sep91 & Feb94 on 'Polydor'; 849619-2/-4/-1) (re-iss. Apr98 on 'Polydor'; 537546-2)*

Aug 86. (7") *(MER 231)* **GOT TO GO BACK. / IN THE GARDEN** ☐ ☐

——— note: HOOKE + ISHAM left early '84 / **ELLIS + DONLINGER** in '85 / now new band

Sep 87. (lp/c)(cd) *(MERH/+C 110)(<832585-2>)* **POETIC CHAMPIONS COMPOSE** [26] [90]
– Spanish steps / The mystery / Queen of the slipstream / I forgot that love existed / Sometimes I feel like a motherless child / Celtic excavation / Someone like you / Alan Watts blues / Give me my rapture / Did ye get healed? / Allow me. *(cd re-iss. 1992 on 'Polydor'; 517217-2)*

Sep 87. (7") *(MER 254)* **DID YE GET HEALED?. / ALLOW ME** ☐ ☐

Apr 88. (7") *(MER 261)* **QUEEN OF THE SLIPSTREAM. / SPANISH STEPS** ☐ ☐

Jun 88. (lp/c)(cd; VAN MORRISON & THE CHIEFTAINS) *(MERH/+C 124)(<834496-2>)* **IRISH HEARTBEAT** [18]
– Star of the County Down / Irish heartbeat / Ta mo chleamhnas deanta / Raglan road / She moved through the fair / I'll tell me ma / Carrickfergus / Celtic Ray / My lagan love / Marie's wedding. *(cd re-iss. Apr98 on 'Polydor'; 537548-2)*

Jun 88. (7") *(MER 262)* **I'LL TELL ME MA. / TA MO CHLEAMHNAS DEANTA** ☐ ☐
(12"+=/cd-s+=) *(MER X/CD 262)* – Carrickfergus.

Polydor   Polydor

May 89. (lp/c/cd) *(<839262-1/-4/-2>)* **AVALON SUNSET** [13] [91]
– Whenever God shines his light / Contacting my angel / I'd love to write another love song / Have I told you lately (that I love you) / Coney Island / I'm tired Joey boy / When will I ever learn to live in God / Orangefield / Daring night / These are the days.

Jun 89. (7"/c-s) *(VAN S/CS 1)* **HAVE I TOLD YOU LATELY (THAT I LOVE YOU). / CONTACTING MY ANGEL** [74]
(12"+=) *(VANX 1)* – Listen to the lion.
(cd-s+=) *(VANCD 1)* – Irish heartbeat.

Nov 89. (7"/c-s; by VAN MORRISON & CLIFF RICHARD) *(VAN S/CS 2)* **WHENEVER GOD SHINES HIS LIGHT. / I'D LOVE TO WRITE ANOTHER LOVE SONG** [20]
(12"+=) *(VANX 2)* – Cry for home.
(cd-s++=) *(VANCD 2)* – ('A'-lp version).

Dec 89. (7") *(VANS 3)* **ORANGEFIELD. / THESE ARE THE DAYS** ☐ ☐
(12"+=) *(VANX 3)* – And the healing has begun.
(cd-s++=) *(VANCD 3)* – Coney Island.

Feb 90. (7"/c-s) *(VAN S/CS 4)* **CONEY ISLAND. / HAVE I TOLD YOU LATELY THAT I LOVE YOU** ☐ ☐
(12"+=) *(VANX 4)* – A sense of wonder.
(cd-s++=) *(VANCD 4)* – Spirit.

Mar 90. (cd/c/lp) *(<841970-2/-4/-1>)* **THE BEST OF VAN MORRISON** (compilation) [4] [41] May90
– Bright side of the road / Gloria (THEM) / Moondance / Baby please don't go (THEM) / Have I told you lately / Brown eyed girl / Sweet thing / Warm love / Wonderful remark / Jackie Wilson said (I'm in Heaven when you smile) / Full force gale / And it stoned me / Here comes the night (THEM) / Domino / Did ye get healed / Wild night / Cleaning windows / Whenever God shines his light (w / CLIFF RICHARD). *(c+cd.iss.has extra tracks) (cd re-iss. Apr98; 537459-2)*

Jul 90. (7"/c-s) *(VANS/+C 5)* **GLORIA (by Them). / RAVE ON, JOHN DONNE** ☐ ☐
(12"+=) *(VANX 5)* – Vanlose stairway.
(cd-s++=) *(VANCD 5)* – Bright side of the road.

Sep 90. (7"/c-s) *(VAN S/CS 6)* **REAL REAL GONE. / START ALL OVER AGAIN** ☐ ☐
(12"+=/cd-s+=) *(VAN X/CD 6)* – Cleaning windows.

Oct 90. (cd/c/lp) *(<847 100-2/-4/-1>)* **ENLIGHTENMENT** [5] [62]
– Real real gone / Enlightenment / So quiet in here / Avalon of the heart / See me through / Youth of 1,000 summers / In the days before rock'n'roll / Start all over again / She's a baby / Memories. *(lp re-iss. Aug99 on 'Simply Vinyl'; SVLP 109)*

Nov 90. (7"/c-s) *(VAN S/CS 7)* **IN THE DAYS BEFORE ROCK'N'ROLL. / I'D LOVE TO WRITE ANOTHER LOVE SONG** ☐ ☐
(12"+=/cd-s+=) *(VAN X/CD 7)* – Coney Island.

Jan 91. (7") *(VANS 8)* **ENLIGHTENMENT. / AVALON OF THE HEART** ☐ ☐
(12"+=/cd-s+=) *(VAN X/CD 8)* – Jackie Wilson said.

——— (VAN is credited w/ TOM JONES on his Mar91 single 'CARRYING A TORCH')

May 91. (7"/c-s; by VAN MORRISON & THE CHIEFTAINS) *(VAN S/CS 9)* **I CAN'T STOP LOVING YOU. / ALL SAINTS DAY** ☐ ☐
(12"+=/cd-s+=) *(VAN X/CD 9)* – Carrying a torch.

Aug 91. (7"/c-s) *(VAN S/CS 10)* **WHY MUST I ALWAYS EXPLAIN?. / SO COMPLICATED** ☐ ☐
(12"+=/cd-s+=) *(VAN X/CD 10)* – Enlightenment.

Sep 91. (d-cd/d-c/d-lp) *(<849 026-2/-4/-1>)* **HYMNS TO THE SILENCE** [5] [99]
– Professional jealousy / I'm not feeling it anymore / Ordinary life / Some peace

of mind / So complicated / I can't stop loving you / Why must I always explain? / Village idiot / See me through part II (just a closer walk with thee) / Take me back / By his Grace / All Saints day / Hymns to the silence / On Hyndford Street / Be thou my vision / Carrying a torch / Green mansions / Pagan streams / Quality Street / It must be you / I need your kind of loving.

Feb 93. (cd/c/lp) *(<517 760-2/-4/-1>)* **THE BEST OF VAN MORRISON VOLUME 2** (compilation) [31] ☐
– Real real gone / When will I ever learn to live in God / Sometimes I feel like a motherless child / In the garden / A sense of wonder / I'll tell me ma / Coney Island / Enlightenment / Rave on John Donne – Rave on part two live / Don't look back / It's all over now, baby blue / One Irish Rover / The mystery / Hymns to the silence / Evening meditation.

May 93. (7"/c-s; by VAN MORRISON & JOHN LEE HOOKER) *(VAN S/CS 11)* **GLORIA. / IT MUST BE YOU (live)** [31] ☐
(cd-s+=) *(VANCD 11)* – And the healing has begun (live) / See me through (live).
(cd-s) *(VANDR 11)* – ('A'side) / Whenever God shines his light (live) / It fills you up (live) / The star of County Down (live).

Jun 93. (cd/c/lp) *(<519 219-2/-4/-1>)* **TOO LONG IN EXILE** [4] [29]
– Too long in exile / Big time operators / Lonely avenue / Ball & chain / In the forest / Till we get the healing done / Gloria / Good morning little schoolgirl / Wasted years / The lonesome road / Moody's mood for love / Close enough for jazz / Before the world was made / I'll take care of you – Instrumental – Tell me what you want.

Apr 94. (d-cd/d-c) *(<521 290-2/-4>)* **A NIGHT IN SAN FRANCISCO (live)** [8]
– Did ya get healed? / It's all in the game / Make it real one more time / I've been working / I forgot that love existed / Vanlose stairway / Trans-Euro train / Fool for you / You make me feel so real / See me through / Soldier of fortune / Thankyoufalettinmebemiseldagain / Ain't that lovin' you baby / Stormy Monday / Have you ever loved a woman / No rollin' blues / Help me / Good morning little schoolgirl / Tupelo honey / Moondance / My funny valentine / Jumpin' with Symphony Sid / It fills you up / I'll take care of you / It's a man's man's man's world / Lonely avenue / 4 o'clock in the morning / So quiet in here / That's where it's at / In the garden / You send me / Allegheny / Have I told you lately that I love you / Shakin' all over / Gloria.

Jun 95. (cd-s) *(VANCD 12)* **DAYS LIKE THIS / YO** [65] ☐
(7"+=/c-s+=/cd-s+=) *(VAN/+CS/CDX 12)* – I don't want to go on without you / That old black magic.

Jun 95. (cd/c/lp) *(<527 307-2/-4/-1>)* **DAYS LIKE THIS** [5] [33]
– Perfect fit / Russian roulette / Rain check / You don't know me / No religion / Underlying depression / Songwriter / Days like this / I'll never be free / Melancholia / Ancient highway / In the afternoon.

Sep 95. (c-s) *(577 014-4)* **PERFECT FIT / RAINCHECK** [−]
(cd-s+=) *(577 015-2)* – Cleaning windows.

Nov 95. (cd-s) *(577 488-4)* **NO RELIGION / HAVE I TOLD YOU LATELY** [54]
(cd-s+=) *(577 489-2)* – Whenever God shines his light / Gloria.
(cd-s) *(577 579-2)* – ('A'side) / Days like this / Raincheck.
below credited as VAN MORRISON with GEORGIE FAME & FRIENDS

Oct 95. (cd/c/lp) *(<529 136-2/-4/-1>)* **HOW LONG HAS THIS BEEN GOING ON (live 3 May'95 at Ronnie Scott's)** [55] Jan96
– I will be there / The new symphony Sid / Early in the morning / Who can I turn to? / Sack o'woe / Moondance / Centerpiece / How long has this been going on? / Your mind is on vacation / All saint's day / Blues in the night / Don't worry about a thing / That's life / Heathrow shuffle.

Feb 96. (c-s) *(576 204-4)* **THAT'S LIFE / MOONDANCE (live)** [−]
(cd-s+=) *(576 205-2)* – That's life (live).
(above two releases on 'Verve', as was a credit on the 1996 GEORGIE FAME with BEN SIDRAN, VAN MORRISON and MOSE ALLISON set 'SONGS OF MOSE ALLISON')

Feb 97. (c-s) *(573 390-4)* **THE HEALING GAME / FULL FORCE GALE '96** [46] [−]
(cd-s+=) *(573 391-2)* – Look what the good people done / Celtic Spring.
(cd-s) *(573 393-2)* – ('A'side) / Have I told you lately / Whenever God shines his light (with CLIFF RICHARD) / Gloria (with JOHN LEE HOOKER).

Mar 97. (cd/c/lp) *(<537 101-2/-4/-1>)* **THE HEALING GAME** [10] [32]
– Rough God goes riding / Fire in the belly / This weight / Waiting game / Piper at the gates of dawn / Burning ground / It once was my life / Sometimes we cry / If you love me / The healing game.

Apr 97. (c-s) *(573 933-4)* **ROUGH GOD GOES RIDING / THE HEALING GAME (alt. version)** ☐ ☐
(cd-s+=) *(573 933-2)* – At the end of the day.

Jun 98. (d-cd/d-c) *(<531 789-2/-4>)* **THE PHILOSOPHER'S STONE (THE UNRELEASED TAPES – VOLUME ONE)** [20] [87]
– Really don't know / Ordinary people / Wonderful remark / Not supposed to break down / Laughing in the wind / Madame Joy / Contemplation rose / Don't worry about tomorrow / Try for sleep / Lover's prayer / Drumshanbo hustle / Twilight zone / Foggy mountain top / Naked in the jungle / There there child // The street only knew your name / John Henry / Western plain / Joyous sound / I have finally come to realise / Flamingoes fly / Stepping out queen part 2 / Bright side of the road / Street theory / Real real gone / Showbusiness / For Mr. Thomas / Crazy Jane on God / Song of being a child / High spirits. *(re-iss. Jul99; same)*

Pointblank   Pointblack

Feb 99. (cd-s) *(POBD 14)* **PRECIOUS TIME / JACKIE WILSON SAID (I'M IN HEAVEN WHEN YOU SMILE) (live) / CALL ME UP IN DREAMLAND (live)** [36] [−]
(cd-s) *(POBDX 14)* – ('A'side) / Naked in the jungle (live) / Give me a kiss (live).

Mar 99. (cd/c) *(VPB CD/TC 50)* *<47148>* **BACK ON TOP** [11] [28]
– Goin' down Geneva / The philosopher's stone / In the midnight / Back on top / When the leaves come falling down / High summer / Reminds me of you / New biography / Precious time / Golden Autumn day.

May 99. (cd-s) *(POBD 15)* **BACK ON TOP / JOHN BROWN'S BODY / I'M READY** [69] [−]
(cd-s) *(POBDX 15)* – ('A'side) / Tell me / Sax instrumental No.1.

Aug 99. (cd-s) *(POBD 16)* **THE PHILOSOPHER'S STONE / THESE DREAMS OF YOU / RAINCHECK** ☐ [−]

– compilations, others, etc. –

May 71. (lp) *President; (PTLS 1045) / Bang; <BLPS 222>* **THE BEST OF VAN MORRISON** ☐ ☐ 1970
(nearly a re-issue of debut '67 lp)

Mar 74. (lp) *London; (HSM 5008) / Bang; <BLPS 400>* **T.B. SHEETS** (a near re-issue of debut 1967 lp) ☐ ☐ Jan74
(cd-iss. May91 on 'Columbia'; 467827-2)

Sep 77. (lp) *Bang; (6467 625)* **THIS IS WHERE I CAME IN** ☐ ☐ -
(nearly a re-issue of debut '67 lp)

Oct 75. (d-lp) *Warners; (K 86009)* **TWO ORIGINALS OF VAN MORRISON** ☐ ☐ -
– (VAN MORRISON, HIS BAND AND STREET CHOIR / TUPELO HONEY)

Oct 77. (7") *Warners; <8450>* **MOONDANCE. / COLD WIND IN AUGUST** - 92

Oct 82. (d-c) *Warners; (K 466116)* **MOONDANCE / . . .HIS BAND AND STREET CHOIR** ☐ -

Jan 92. (c) *Moles; (MRILC 012)* **CUCHULAINN** (spoken word) ☐ -

Mar 92. (d-cd/c) *Columbia; (468309-2/-4)* **BANG MASTERS** ☐ -

Jan 93. (cd) *Movieplay Gold; (74012)* **THE LOST TAPES VOLUME 1** ☐ -

Jan 93. (cd) *Movieplay Gold; (74013)* **THE LOST TAPES VOLUME 2** ☐ -

May 94. (cd) *Charly; (CDP 8035-2)* **PAYIN' DUES (The Best Of The 1965 Studio Recordings)** ☐ -

Apr 96. (cd) *Audiophile; (APH 102805)* **BROWN EYED GIRL** ☐ -

Mar 97. (t-lp) *Get Back; (GET 501)* **NEW YORK SESSIONS 1967** ☐ -

Mar 98. (cd) *Squire; (GUV 1)* **BROWN EYED GIRL** ☐ -

Apr 98. (d-cd) *Multimedia; (7956 766664-2)* **BROWN EYED BEGINNINGS** ☐ -

Nov 98. (d-cd) *Double Classics; (DC 31014)* **BROWN EYED GIRL** ☐ -

MORRISSEY

Born: STEPHEN PATRICK MORRISSEY, 22 May'59, Manchester, England. After his bust-up with SMITHS guitarist JOHNNY MARR in August '87, MORRISSEY, one of rock music's most intellectually incisive wordsmiths, hastily embarked upon a relatively successful solo career. Remaining with 'E.M.I.', his debut effort, 'VIVA HATE', was subsequently released on the re-activated 'H.M.V.' imprint in Spring '88. With the music co-written by his new producer, STEPHEN STREET, and a backing band that numbered VINI REILLY (guitar, keyboards; ex-DURUTTI COLUMN) and ANDREW PARESI (drums), the album was a strong start, reaching No.2 in the UK charts on the back of the catchy 'SUEDEHEAD' single (incredibly, the singer's first ever Top 5 hit single). Another stand-out track was the lavish melancholy of 'EVERYDAY IS LIKE SUNDAY', arguably his best solo track to date and a song which gave him another Top 10 hit later that summer. Though the album received a relatively warm critical reception, it was, as ever, not without controversy. 'BENGALI IN PLATFORMS' was an ambiguous address to immigrants which he later unsuccessfully attempted to play down while 'MARGARET ON THE GUILLOTINE' was self explanatory, no doubt meeting with a little more empathy. Recruiting a new band composed of NEIL TAYLOR (guitar) and ex-SMITHS', CRAIG GANNON, ANDY ROURKE and MIKE JOYCE, MORRISSEY returned the following year with another couple of fine singles, the playfully coy 'LAST OF THE INTERNATIONAL PLAYBOYS' and 'INTERESTING DRUG', both records going Top 10. The line-up didn't last, however, and he brought in a completely new cast for his next single 'OUIJA BOARD, OUIJA BOARD', a song that suffered scathing reviews in the music press and barely made the Top 20. The following year, a projected album was scrapped although its title, 'BONA DRAG', was retained for an impressive career resume that appeared in late 1990. The collection also contained some new material, notably the grim 'NOVEMBER SPAWNED A MONSTER' and the contentious narrative, 'PICCADILLY PALARE', both released as singles. With a fresh backing group that included ex-MADNESS bassist BEDDERS and MORRISSEY's new writing partner, MARK E. NEVIN (ex-FAIRGROUND ATTRACTION), the singer cut the 'KILL UNCLE' opus. Released in 1991 to mixed reviews, the album failed to deliver on the promise of the earlier singles, although MORRISSEY subsequently recruited a rockabilly backing band: ALAIN WHYTE (guitar), GARY DAY (bass), BOZ BOORER (guitar, ex-POLECATS) and SPENCER COBRIN (drums), touring the album around the world, his first live appearances since the prime of The SMITHS. The tour was largely a success and, enlivened and inspired, MORRISSEY cut the 'YOUR ARSENAL' (1992) set. Produced by MICK RONSON and co-penned with WHYTE, the album took the watered down glam-rock of 'KILL UNCLE' and kickstarted it with some raw rockabilly, resulting in MORRISSEY's highest chart placing for years (No.4). Though the record failed to spawn any major hits, it contained such thoughtful material as 'I KNOW IT'S GONNA HAPPEN SOMEDAY' and 'YOU'RE THE ONE FOR ME, FATTY', the former subsequently covered by DAVID BOWIE, another of MORRISSEY's idols. The same year, MORRISSEY hit the headlines with his scathing criticism of Johnny Rogan, author of the SMITHS biography, 'Morrissey & Marr: The Severed Alliance'. It wasn't the last time the 'Oscar Wilde of Rock' would be in the news, MORRISSEY subsequently losing a well publicised court battle with MIKE JOYCE over unpaid SMITHS royalties. More controversy surrounded the singer following his disastrous appearance at the 1993 'Madstock' concert in London's Finsbury Park. Supporting headliners MADNESS, MORRISSEY was given an extremely hostile reception after coming out draped in a Union Jack, further fuelling debate over the perceived ambiguity of his motivations. Following all this strife, 'VAUXHALL AND I' (1994) resurrected MORRISSEY's career, a sympathetic production by STEVE LILLYWHITE setting the scene for his most considered and consistent album to date. The record was also MORRISSEY's first No.1, a critically acclaimed opus that was marked by more emotionally-charged lyrics, laying off the trademark caustic barbs. Moving to 'R.C.A.', MORRISSEY released 'SOUTHPAW GRAMMAR'

almost a year later, a bizarre album that focussed on the singer's apparent boxing fixation. Unsurprisingly, the record met with bewilderment from critics, though it consolidated his position as one of rock's few genuine mavericks. In 1997, MORRISSEY once again shifted stables, this time to 'Island' who got their chance to showcase the bard on some new work, 'MALADJUSTED'.
• Covered: THAT'S ENTERTAINMENT (Jam) / SKIN STORM (Bradford).
• Trivia: In the late 80's, MORRISSEY made a cameo appearance in Channel 4's 'Brookside' off-shoot, 'South'.

Album rating: VIVA HATE (*9) / BONA DRAG collection (*7) / KILL UNCLE (*8) / YOUR ARSENAL (*8) / BEETHOVEN WAS DEAF (*5) / VAUXHALL AND I (*9) / WORLD OF MORRISSEY part compilation (*7) / SOUTHPAW GRAMMAR (*6) / MALADJUSTED (86) / SUEDEHEAD (THE BEST OF . . .) compilation (*7)

MORRISSEY – vocals; with **STEPHEN STREET** – guitar, bass, producer, co-writer / **ANDREW PARESI** – drums / **VINI REILLY** – guitar, keyboards (of DURUTTI COLUMN)

		H.M.V.	Sire
Feb 88. (7") (POP 1618) **SUEDEHEAD. / I KNOW VERY WELL HOW I GOT MY NAME**		5	☐

(12"+=) (12POP 1618) – Hairdresser on fire.
(c-s+=/cd-s++=) (TC/CD POP 1618) – Oh well, I'll never learn.

Mar 88. (cd/c/lp) (CD/TC+/CDS 3787) <25699> **VIVA HATE**   2   48
– Alsatian cousin / Little man, what now? / Everyday is like Sunday / Bengali in platforms / Angel, angel, down we go together / Late night, Maudlin Street / Suedehead / Break up the family / The ordinary boys / I don't mind if you forget me / Dial-a-cliche / Margaret on the guillotine. (re-iss. Mar94 on 'Parlophone' cd/c; same) (cd re-iss. Mar97 on 'E.M.I.'+=; CDCNTAV 2) – Let the right one slip in / Pashernate love / At amber / Disappointed (live) / Girl least likely to / I'd love to / Michael's bones / I've changed my plea to guilty.

Jun 88. (7") (POP 1619) **EVERYDAY IS LIKE SUNDAY. / DISAPPOINTED**   9   ☐
(12"+=) (12POP 1619) – Sister I'm a poet.
(c-s+=/cd-s++=) (TC/CD+/POP 1619) – Will never marry.

—— **MORRISSEY** only retained **STREET**. He brought in **NEIL TAYLOR** – guitar and re-united with (ex-SMITHS):- **CRAIG GANNON, ANDY ROURKE + MIKE JOYCE**

Feb 89. (7") (POP 1620) **THE LAST OF THE FAMOUS INTERNATIONAL PLAYBOYS. / LUCKY LIPS**   6   ☐
(12"+=/cd-s+=) (12/CD POP 1620) – Michael's bones.

Apr 89. (7"/etched-12") **INTERESTING DRUG. / SUCH A LITTLE THING MAKES SUCH A BIG DIFFERENCE**   9   ☐
(c-s+=/12"+=/cd-s+=) (TC/12/CD POP 1621) – Sweet and tender hooligan (live).

—— He brought in complete new line-up:- **KEVIN ARMSTRONG** – guitar / **MATTHEW SELIGMAN** – bass / **STEVE HOPKINS** – drums and returning **ANDREW PARESI** – keyboards

Nov 89. (7") (POP 1622) **OUIJA BOARD, OUIJA BOARD. / YES, I AM BLIND**   18   ☐
(c-s+=/12"+=/cd-s+=) (TC/12/CD POP 1622) – East west.

—— **ANDY ROURKE** returned to repl. SELIGMAN + HOPKINS / added guest **MARY MARGARET O'HARA** – vocals (up & coming solo artist)

Apr 90. (c-s/7") (TC+/POP 1623) **NOVEMBER SPAWNED A MONSTER. / HE KNOWS I'D LOVE TO SEE HIM**   12   ☐
(12"+=/cd-s+=) (12/CD POP 1623) – The girl least likely to.

Oct 90. (c-s/7") (TC+/POP 1624) **PICCADILLY PALARE. / GET OFF THE STAGE**   18   ☐
(12"+=/cd-s+=) (12/CD POP 1624) – At amber.

Oct 90. (cd/c/lp) (CD/TC+/CSD 3788) <26221> **BONA DRAG**   9   59
– Piccadilly palare / Interesting drug / November spawned a monster / Will never marry / Such a little thing makes such a big difference / The last of the famous international playboys / Ouija board, ouija board / Hairdresser on fire / Everyday is like Sunday / He knows I'd love to see him / Yes, I am blind / Lucky lisp / Suedehead / Disappointed. (re-iss. Mar94 on 'Parlophone' cd/c; same)

—— He now retained **ANDREW PARESI**. Newcomers were **BEDDERS** – bass (ex-MADNESS) / **MARK E.NEVIN** – guitars, co-composer (ex-FAIRGROUND ATTRACTION) plus **STEVE HEART + SEAMUS BEAGHAN** – keyboards / **NAWAZISH ALI KHAN** – violin

Feb 91. (c-s/7") (TC+/POP 1625) **OUR FRANK. / JOURNALISTS WHO LIE**   26   ☐
(12"+=/cd-s+=) (12/CD POP 1625) – Tony the pony.

Feb 91. (cd/c/lp) (CD/TC+/CSD 3789) <26514> **KILL UNCLE**   8   52 Mar91
– Our Frank / Asian rut / Sing your life / Mute witness / King Leer / Found found found / Driving your girlfriend home / The harsh truth of the camera eye / (I'm) The end of the family line / There's a place in Hell for me and my friends.

—— His tour band Spring '91; **ALAIN WHYTE** – guitar / **GARY DAY** – bass / **BOZ BOORER** – guitar (ex-POLECATS) / **SPENCER COBRIN** – drums

Apr 91. (c-s/7") (TC+/POP 1626) **SING YOUR LIFE. / THAT'S ENTERTAINMENT**   33   ☐
(12"+=/cd-s+=) (12/CD POP 1626) – The loop.

Jul 91. (c-s/7") (TC+/POP 1627) **PREGNANT FOR THE LAST TIME. / SKIN STORM**   25   ☐
(12"+=/cd-s+=) (12/CD POP 1627) – Cosmic dancer (live) / Disappointed (live).

Oct 91. (c-s/7") (TC+/POP 1628) **MY LOVE LIFE. / I'VE CHANGED MY PLEA TO GUILTY**   29   ☐
(12"+=/cd-s+=) (12/CD POP 1628) – There's a place in Hell for me and my friends.

late 91. (cd-ep) **MORRISSEY AT KROQ** (live)   -   ☐
– There's a place in Hell for my friends / My love life / Sing your life.

May 92. (c-s/7") (TC+/POP 1629) **WE HATE IT WHEN OUR FRIENDS BECOME SUCCESSFUL. / SUEDEHEAD**   17   ☐
(12"+=) (12POP 1629) – Pregnant for the last time.
(cd-s+=) (CDPOP 1629) – I've changed my plea to guilty.

Jul 92. (c-s/7") (TC+/POP 1630) **YOU'RE THE ONE FOR ME, FATTY. / PASHERNATE LOVE**   19   ☐
(12"+=/cd-s+=) (12/CD POP 1630) – There speaks a true friend.

Jul 92. (cd/c/lp) (CD/TC+/CSD 3790) <26994> **YOUR ARSENAL**   4   21
– You're gonna need someone on your side / Glamorous glue / We'll let you know / The National Front disco / Certain people I know / We hate it when our friends become successful / You're the one for me, Fatty / Seasick, yet still docked / I know it's gonna happen someday / Tomorrow.

Dec 92. (c-s/7") *(TC+/POP 1631)* **CERTAIN PEOPLE I KNOW. /**
JACK THE RIPPER | 35 |
(12"+=/cd-s+=) *(12/CD POP 1631)* – You've had her.

Parlophone   E.M.I.

May 93. (cd/c/lp) *(CD/TC+/CSD 3791)* <89061> **BEETHOVEN WAS**
DEAF (live) | 13 |
– You're the one for me, Fatty / Certain people I know / National Front disco /
November spawned a monster / Seasick, yet still docked / The loop / Sister I'm a
poet / Jack the ripper / Such a little thing makes such a big difference / I know it's
gonna happen someday / We'll let you know / Suedehead / He knows I'd love to
see him / You're gonna need someone on your side / Glamorous glue / We hate it
when our friends become successful. *(re-iss. Sep94 on 'Parlophone' cd/c; same)*

—— **BOZ BOORER + ALAIN WHYTE** – guitars / **JONNY BRIDGEWOOD** – bass /
WOODIE TAYLOR – drums

Parlophone   Sire

Mar 94. (c-s/7") *(TCR/R 6372)* <18207> **THE MORE YOU IGNORE**
ME, THE CLOSER I GET. / USED TO BE A SWEET BOY | 8 | | 46 |
(12"+=/cd-s+=) *(12R/CDR 6372)* – I'd love to.
Mar 94. (cd/c/lp) *(CD/TC+/PCSD 148)* <45451> **VAUXHALL AND I** | 1 | | 18 |
– Now my heart is full / Spring-heeled Jim / Billy Budd / Hold on to your friends /
The more you ignore me, the closer I get / Why don't you find out for yourself / I
am hated for loving / Lifeguard sleeping, girl drowning / Used to be a sweet boy /
The lazy sunbathers / Speedway.
Jun 94. (c-s/7") *(TCR/R 6383)* **HOLD ON TO YOUR FRIENDS. /**
MOONRIVER | 47 |
(12"/cd-s) *(12R/CDR 6383)* – (extended versions).
Aug 94. (c-s/7"; by MORRISSEY and SIOUXSIE) *(TCR/R 6365)*
INTERLUDE. / ('A'extended) | 25 |
(12"+=/cd-s+=) *(12R/CDR 6365)* – ('A'mix).
Jan 95. (c-s/7") *(TC+/R 6400)* **BOXERS. / HAVE-A-GO MERCHANT** | 23 |
(12"+=/cd-s+=) *(12/CD R 6400)* – Whatever happens, I love you.
Feb 95. (cd/c/lp) *(CD/TC+/PCSD 163)* <45879> **WORLD OF**
MORRISSEY (part compilation) | 15 |
– Whatever happens, I love you / Billy Budd / Jack the ripper (live) / Have-a-go
merchant / The loop / Sister I'm a poet (live) / You're the one for me, Fatty (live) /
Boxers / Moon river (extended) / My love life / Certain people I know / The last of
the famous international playboys / We'll let you know / Spring-heeled Jim.

—— **SPENCER JAMES COBRIN** – drums repl. WOODIE

RCA Victor RCA Victor

Aug 95. (7"/c-s) *(74321 29980-7/-4)* **DAGENHAM DAVE. / NOBODY**
LOVES US | 26 |
(cd-s+=) *(74321 29980-2)* – You must please remember.
Aug 95. (cd/c/lp) *(74321 29953-2/-4/-1)* <45939> **SOUTHPAW**
GRAMMAR | 4 | | 66 |
– The teachers are afraid of the pupils / Reader meet author / The boy racer / The
operation / Dagenham Dave / Do your best and don't worry / Best friend on the
payroll / Southpaw.
Nov 95. (7") *(74321 33294-7)* **THE BOY RACER. / LONDON (live)** | 36 |
(cd-s+=) *(74321 33295-2)* – Billy Budd (live).
(cd-s) *(74321 33294-2)* – ('A'side) / Spring heeled Jim (live) / Why don't you find
out for yourself (live).

Parlophone   Capitol

Dec 95. (c-s/7") *(TC+/R 6243)* **SUNNY. / BLACK-EYED SUSAN** | 42 |
(cd-s+=) *(CDR 6243)* – A swallow on my neck.

Island   Polygram

Jul 97. (c-s/7") *(C+/IS 667)* **ALMA MATTERS. / I CAN HAVE BOTH** | 16 |
(12"+=/cd-s+=) *(12IS/CID 667)* – Heir apparent.
Aug 97. (cd/c/lp) *(CID/ICT/ILPS 8059)* <536036> **MALADJUSTED** | 8 | | 61 |
– Maladjusted / Alma matters / Ambitious outsiders / Trouble loves me / Papa Jack /
Ammunition / Wide to receive / Roy's keen / He cried / Satan rejected my soul.
Oct 97. (c-s/7") *(C+/IS 671)* **ROY'S KEEN. / LOST** | 42 |
(12"+=/cd-s+=) *(12IS/CID 671)* – The edges are no longer parallel.
Dec 97. (c-s/7") *(C+/IS 686)* **SATAN REJECTED MY SOUL. / NOW**
I AM I WAS | 39 |
(cd-s+=/12"+=) *(CID/12IS 686)* – This is not your country.

– compilations, etc. –

Sep 97. (cd/c/lp) E.M.I.; *(<CD/TC+/EMC 3771>)* **SUEDEHEAD (THE**
BEST OF MORRISSEY) | 26 |
– Suedehead / Interesting drug / Boxers / Last of the famous international playboys /
Sunny / Tomorrow / Interlude / Everyday is like Sunday / Hold on to your friends /
My love life / Our Frank / Piccadilly palare / Ouija board, ouija board / You're the
one for me, fatty / We hate it when our friends become successful / Pregnant for
the last time / November spawned a monster / The more you ignore me, the closer
I get / That's entertainment. *(special edition; CDEMCX 3771)*

MOTHER LOVE BONE (see under ⇒ **PEARL JAM**)

MOTHER'S FINEST (dig out; Great Metal . . .)

MOTHERS (OF INVENTION)
(see under ⇒ **ZAPPA, Frank**)

MOTLEY CRUE

Formed: Los Angeles, California, USA . . . early 1981 by NIKKI SIXX (bass,
ex-LONDON) who recruited VINCE NEIL (vocals, ex-ROCK CANDY),
TOMMY LEE (drums) and finally MICK MARS (guitar). In 1981, they
issued their debut album, 'TOO FAST FOR LOVE', on their own US label,
'Leathur'. From its 'STICKY FINGERS'-esque, crotch-shot cover to the low-
rent sleaze-rock contained within, the album announced MOTLEY CRUE's
status as wannabe metal successors to the likes of AEROSMITH and The NEW

YORK DOLLS. There were certainly worse reference points to have, and the
record was an amateurish, minor classic, the title track and 'PIECE OF YOUR
ACTION' pouting highlights. After being signed to 'Elektra', the record was
re-issued the following year while the band began work on a follow-up with
producer Tom Werman. 'SHOUT AT THE DEVIL' (1983) added cod-satanic
imagery to their glam fixation while beefing up the guitars. But VENOM
this band were not and songs like 'GOD BLESS THE CHILDREN OF THE
BEAST' were downright ridiculous. If catchy pop-metal like 'TOO YOUNG
TO FALL IN LOVE' was the work of the devil, then God certainly had nothing
to fear. Nevertheless, after a nationwide tour supporting KISS, the album hit
the US Top 20 and things were looking up for the band. However on the
8th of December '84, VINCE NEIL was involved in a serious car accident;
NICK 'RAZZLE' DINGLEY (drummer with HANOI ROCKS) was killed in
the crash while two others were injured. NEIL was subsequently ordered to
pay $2.5 million compensation and sentenced to 20 days in jail, after being
convicted of vehicle manslaughter. The tragedy overshadowed much of the
'THEATRE OF PAIN' (1985) album, a record that went on to sell more than
two million copies after its cover of Brownsville Station's 'SMOKIN' IN THE
BOYS ROOM' was a Top 20 hit. The album also boasted the surprisingly
poignant power ballad, 'HOME SWEET HOME', an MTV favourite later
that year. 'GIRLS, GIRLS, GIRLS' (1987) was a marked improvement; the
lyrics cementing The 'CRUE's reputation as the 'bad' boys of metal, the
music confident and cocksure. Tracks like 'WILD SIDE', showed a newfound
adventurousness, the first signs that the band were capable of promotion from
the metal second division. Early in 1988, MATTHEW TRIPPE sued the CRUE
for royalties, alleging he masqueraded and wrote songs as NIKKI SIXX, while
he recovered from a 1983 car crash. This was later proved to be false, although
there is still much speculation on how SIXX's face was bloated on some mug
pics. Having survived a near-death experience after a heroin o.d., SIXX and
the newly cleaned up 'CRUE delivered another album, 'DR. FEELGOOD',
which duly topped the US charts (while hitting Top 5 in the UK). It was to be
NEIL's parting shot, the singer ousted in the early 90's following media overkill
on his war of words with AXL ROSE. While he released a solo album in '93,
the group recruited a new frontman, JOHN CORABI, although the subsequent
album, 'MOTLEY CRUE' found few takers. NEIL and the group had patched
up their differences by 1997, the album, 'GENERATION SWINE' giving
them a return to the US Top 5. • **Covered:** HELTER SKELTER (Beatles) /
JAILHOUSE ROCK (Leiber-Stoller). • **Trivia:** Late 1985, TOMMY LEE
married actress Heather Lockear, although did not last. He is now the spouse
of Baywatch actress PAMELA ANDERSON, although in the mid-90's press
speculation was rife about an impending split. Around the same time, she gave
birth to their first child, although the domestic bliss was short-lived; at the time
of writing the couple are heading for a divorce while TOMMY faces a lengthy
jail sentence for wife-beating. In Dec '87, MICK married one-time PRINCE
girlfriend VANITY (star of 'Purple Rain'). In May '90, NIKKI was hitched to
former Playboy centre-fold Brandi Brandt.

Album rating: TOO FAST FOR LOVE (*5) / SHOUT AT THE DEVIL (*6) / THEATRE
OF PAIN (*5) / GIRLS, GIRLS, GIRLS (*7) / DR. FEELGOOD (*5) / DECADE
OF DECADENCE compilation (*7) / MOTLEY CRUE (*5) / GENERATION SWINE
(*5) / THE BEST OF MOTLEY CRUE compilation (*6) / Vince Neil: EXPOSED (*4) /
CARVED IN STONE (*3)

VINCE NEIL (b. VINCENT NEIL WHARTON, 8 Feb'61, Hollywood, Calif.) – vocals (ex-
ROCK CANDY) / **NIKKI SIXX** (b. FRANK FERRANNO, 11 Dec'58, San Jose, Calif.)
– bass (ex-LONDON) / **MICK MARS** (b. BOB DEAL, 3 Apr'56, Huntington, Indiana)
– guitar / **TOMMY LEE** (b. THOMAS LE BASS, 3 Oct'62, Athens, Greece) – drums
(ex-SUITE 19)

not iss.   Leathur

1981. (lp) **TOO FAST FOR LOVE** | - |
– Live wire / Public enemy No.1 / Take me to the top / Merry-go-round / Piece
of your action / Starry eyes / Come on and dance / Too fast for love / On with
the show. *(UK-iss.Oct82 as 'MOTLEY CRUE' on 'Elektra' lp/c; K/K4 52425)* <US
re-iss. Nov83 on 'Elektra'; 60174> *(cd-iss. Feb93 on 'Elektra'; 7559 60174-2)*
1982. (7"gig freebie) **TOAST OF THE TOWN. / STICK TO YOUR**
GUNS | - |

Elektra   Elektra

Sep 83. (lp/c) *(960 289-1/-4)* <60289> **SHOUT AT THE DEVIL** | | 17 |
– In the beginning / Shout at the devil / Looks that kill / Bastard / Knock 'em dead,
kid / Danger / Too young to fall in love / Helter skelter / Red hot / Ten seconds 'til
love / God bless the children of the beast. *(cd-iss. Jan89; 960 289-2)*
Jul 84. (7") *(E 9756)* <69756> **LOOKS THAT KILL. / PIECE OF**
YOUR ACTION | | 54 |Jan84
(12"+=) *(E 9756T)* – Live wire.
Oct 84. (7"/12") *(E 9732/+T)* <69732> **TOO YOUNG TO FALL IN**
LOVE. / TAKE ME TO THE TOP | | 90 |Jun84
Jul 85. (lp/c) *(EKT 8/+C)* <60418> **THEATRE OF PAIN** | 36 | | 6 |
– City boy blues / Smokin' in the boys' room / Louder than Hell / Keep your eye
on the money / Home sweet home / Tonight (we need a lover) / Use it or lose it /
Save our souls / Raise your hands to rock / Fight for your rights. *(cd-iss. Jul86; 960
418-2)*
Aug 85. (7"/7"sha-pic-d/12") *(EKR 16/+P/T)* <69625> **SMOKIN' IN**
THE BOYS' ROOM. / USE IT OR LOSE IT | 71 | | 16 |Jul85
<US-12"> – ('A'side) / Helter skelter / Piece of your action / Live wire.
Oct 85. (7") <69591> **HOME SWEET HOME. / RED HOT** | - | | 89 |
Jan 86. (7"/7"sha-pic-d) *(EKR 33/+P)* **SMOKIN' IN THE BOYS'**
ROOM. / HOME SWEET HOME | 51 | | - |
(12"+=) *(EKR 33T)* – Shout at the Devil.
Jun 87. (lp/c)(cd) *(EKT 39/+C)(960 725-2)* <60725> **GIRLS, GIRLS,**
GIRLS | 14 | | 2 |
– The wild side / Girls, girls, girls / Dancing on glass / Bad bad boogie / Nona /
Five years dead / All in the name of . . . / Sumthin' for nuthin' / You're all I need /
Jailhouse rock (live).

Jul 87. (7"/7"w-poster) (EKR 59/+P) <69465> **GIRLS, GIRLS, GIRLS. / SUMTHIN' FOR NUTHIN'**   `26`   `12` May87
(12"+=/12"pic-d+=) (EKR 59T) – Smokin' in the boys' room.

Sep 87. (7") <69449> **THE WILD SIDE. / FIVE YEARS DEAD**   `-`

Nov 87. (7") <69429> **YOU'RE ALL I NEED. / ALL IN THE NAME OF ROCK**   `-`   `83`

Jan 88. (7") (EKR 65) **YOU'RE ALL I NEED. / WILD SIDE**   `23`
(12"+=/12"pic-d+=/12"boxed+=) (EKR 65 T/+P/B) – Home sweet home / Looks that kill.

Jul 88. (m-lp/m-cd) <25XD 1052> **HOME SWEET HOME** (RAW TRACKS)   `-`
– Live wire / Piece of your action / Too young to fall in love / Knock 'em dead, kid / Home sweet home.

Sep 89. (lp/c)(cd) (EKT 59/+C)(960 829-2) <60829> **DR. FEELGOOD**   `4`   `1`
– Same ol' situation (S.O.S.) / Slice of your pie / Rattlesnake shake / Kickstart my heart / Without you / Don't go away mad (just go away) / She goes down / Sticky sweet / Time for a change / T.N.T. (Terror 'n' Tinseltown) / Dr. Feelgood.

Oct 89. (7"/7"sha-pic-d/c-s) (EKR 97/+P/C) <69271> **DR. FEELGOOD. / STICKY SWEET**   `50`   `6` Aug89
(ext.12"+=/ext.3"cd-s+=) (EKR 97 T/CD) – All in the name of rock.

Nov 89. (c-s) <69248> **KICKSTART MY HEART. / SHE GOES DOWN**   `-`   `27`

Feb 90. (c-s) <64985> **WITHOUT YOU. / SLICE OF YOUR LIFE**   `-`   `8`

Apr 90. (7"/7"pic-d/c-s) (EKR 109/+P/C) **WITHOUT YOU. / LIVE WIRE**   `39`   `-`
(12"+=/cd-s+=) (EKR 109 T/CD) – Girls, girls, girls / All in the name of rock.

May 90. (c-s) <64962> **DON'T GO AWAY MAD (JUST GO AWAY). / RATTLESNAKE SHAKE**   `-`   `19`

Aug 90. (c-s) <64942> **SAME OL' SITUATION (S.O.S.). / WILD SIDE**   `-`   `78`

Nov 90. (m-cd) <WPCP 3462> **RAW TRACKS II**   `-`

Aug 91. (7"/c-s) (EKR 133/+C) <64848> **PRIMAL SCREAM. / DANCING ON GLASS**   `32`   `63`
(12"+=/cd-s+=) (EKR 133 T/CD) – Red hot (live) / Dr. Feelgood (live).

Oct 91. (cd)(lp/c) <7559 61204-2)>(EKT 95/+C)> **DECADE OF DECADENCE** (compilation)   `20`   `2`
– Live wire / Piece of your action / Shout at the Devil / Looks that kill / Home sweet home / Smokin' in the boys' room / Girls, girls, girls / Wild side / Dr. Feelgood / Kickstart my heart / Teaser / Rock'n'roll junkie / Primal scream / Angela / Anarchy in the UK.

Dec 91. (7") (EKR 136) <64818> **HOME SWEET HOME '91. / YOU'RE ALL I NEED**   `37`   `37` Nov91
(12"+=/12"pic-d+=/cd-s+=) (EKR 136 T/TP/CD) – Without you / ('A'original mix).

—— Had already split temporarily Apr'91 to do own projects. The group parted company with VINCE NEIL, who went solo early 1992.

—— brought in **JOHN CORABI** (b.26 Apr'59, Philadelphia, Pennsylvania) – vocals (ex-SCREAM)

Feb 94. (7"yellow) (EKR 180) **HOOLIGAN'S HOLIDAY. / HYPNOTIZED (demo)**   `36`
(12"+=/cd-s+=/cd-s+=) (EKR 180 T/CD/CDX) – ('A'-Brown nose edit) / ('A'-album version a.k.a. – The Dregs of Society – featuring – The Slime City Sinners & The Canadian Connection) / Hypnotized (demo).

Mar 94. (cd/cd-lp) <(7559 61534-2/-4/-1)> **MOTLEY CRUE**   `17`   `7`
– Power to the music / Uncle Jack / Hooligan's holiday / Misunderstood / Loveshine / Poison apples / Hammered / 'Til death us do part / Welcome to the numb / Smoke the sky / Droppin' like flies / Drift away.

May 94. (7"w-drawn) (EKR 183) **MISUNDERSTOOD. /**   `-`   `-`

—— **VINCE NEIL** returned to repl. CORABI

Jun 97. (cd/c) <(7559 61901-2/-4)> **GENERATION SWINE**   `4`
– Find myself / Afraid / Flush / Generation swine / Confessions / Beauty / Glitter / Anybody out there / Let us prey / Rocketship / Rat like me / Shout at the Devil '97 / Brandon.

Jul 97. (cd-s) (E 3936CD1) **AFRAID / AFRAID (Swine mix) / LUST FOR LIFE / WELCOME TO THE PLANET BOOM**   `58`
(cd-s) (E 3936CD2) – ('A'side) / Generation swine / Father / Bittersweet.
(cd-s) (E 3936CD3) – ('A'-alternative rave mix) / Shout at the Devil '97 / All in the name of . . . (live) / Girls, girls, girls (live).

         Virgin   Motley

Nov 98. (cd) (CDVIR 77) <78002> **THE BEST OF MOTLEY CRUE**   `20`
<US-title 'GREATEST HITS'> (compilation & 2 new)
– Bitter pill / Enslaved / Girls, girls, girls / Kickstart my heart / Wild side / Glitter (remix) / Dr. Feelgood / Same ol' situation / Home sweet home / Afraid / Don't go away mad (just go away) / Without you / Smokin' in the boys room / Primal scream / Too fast for love / Looks that kill / Shout at the Devil '97.

VINCE NEIL

—— Self-penned collaborations with either STEVE STEVENS + PHIL SOUSSAN or JACK BLADES + TOMMY SHAW except BLONDES HAVE MORE FUN (Rod Stewart) / I WANNA BE SEDATED (Ramones).

VINCE NEIL – vocals, guitar with friends **STEVE STEVENS** – lead guitar, bass / **VIK FOXX** – drums, percussion / **ROBBIE BUCHANAN** keyboards / **ROBBIE CRANE** – bass / **DAVE MARSHALL** – rhythm guitar / **TOMMY FUNDERBURKE, TIMOTHY B. SCHMIDT, DONNA McDANIEL & CHRISTINA NICHOLS** – backing vocals

         Hollywood Hollywood

Sep 92. (7"/c-s) (HWD 123/+C) **YOU'RE INVITED (BUT YOU'RE FRIEND CAN'T COME). / Luxury Cruiser (by T-RIDE)**   `63`
(12"+=/cd-s+=) (HWD 123 T/CD) – Get the hell out of here (by STEVE VAI).

         Warners   Warners

May 93. (cd/c) <(9362 45260-2/-4)> **EXPOSED**   `44`   `13`
– Look in her eyes / Sister of pain / Can't have your cake / Fine, fine wine / The edge / Can't change me / Set me free / Living is a luxury / You're invited (but your friend can't come) / Gettin' hard / Forever (featuring BOBBY WOMACK).

May 93. (7") **SISTER OF PAIN. / BLONDES (HAVE MORE FUN)**
(cd-s+=) – I wanna be sedated.

Sep 95. (cd/c) <(9362 45877-2/-4)> **CARVED IN STONE**
– Breakin' in the gun / Black promises / The crawl / One way / Skylar's song / Writing on the wall / Make U feel / The rift / One less mouth to feed / Find a dream.

MOTORHEAD

Formed: London, England . . . Jun '75 by LEMMY (aka IAN KILMISTER; vocals, bass) who decided to form his own band when, after a five year stint with hyperspace hippies HAWKWIND, he was finally given the boot. His sharp exit came after he was briefly detained in Canada on drugs charges; a notorious speed freak, his penchant for amphetamines was directly translated into MOTORHEAD's music, a synapse-crunching racket that somehow lent itself to a tune or two (the title of the band's first single, 'WHITE LINE FEVER', said it all really). Following his departure from HAWKWIND, LEMMY toyed with the name BASTARD, before opting for the MOTORHEAD moniker, the title of the last song he'd penned for his previous band. He subsequently hooked up with LARRY WALLIS (guitar, vocals) of the PINK FAIRIES and LUCAS FOX (drums), although by early '76 these two had been replaced with 'FAST' EDDIE CLARKE and PHIL 'PHILTHY ANIMAL' TAYLOR respectively. The initial line-up had recorded a relatively laid back outing, 'ON PAROLE' for 'United Artists' in 1975, although this was shelved until 1979 when the label cashed in on the band's success. The aforementioned 'WHITE LINE FEVER' single was also held back, 'Stiff' only releasing it once MOTORHEAD's commercial credentials had been established. It was the 'Chiswick' label who finally had the balls to release something, the eponymous 'MOTORHEAD' album in 1977. It was the first opus from the definitive MOTORHEAD line-up, a combination that would become one of the most infamous in the history of heavy metal and create some of the most enduring material in the band's career. Yet while MOTORHEAD were the epitome of headbanging metal, their maniacal energy also attracted hardcore punks in the same way IRON MAIDEN's early performances had a foot in both camps. Over a series of shit kicking albums, 'OVERKILL' (1979), 'BOMBER' (1979) and 'ACE OF SPADES' (1980), MOTORHEAD became a legend, laying the foundations of thrash with testosterone saturated anthems like 'NO CLASS', 'OVERKILL' and 'BOMBER'. This last album was the landmark MOTORHEAD release, its title track the ultimate outlaw anthem and a Top 20 hit to boot. The record went to No.4, illustrating how quickly the band had risen through the metal ranks. While CLARKE and TAYLOR provided the musical fuel, LEMMY was undoubtedly the beast's engine, his dirty, propulsive bass driving MOTORHEAD ever onwards like the aural equivalent of road rage. And crucially, like all genuine badass outlaws, LEMMY was 'orrible!, yet he still got the chicks, and he had style. In bucketloads. Decked out in his white cowboy boots, bullet belt and mutton chop sideburns, he stood centre stage, rooted to the spot, head stretched up to the mike (maybe LIAM GALLAGHER clocked a few shows) like he was summoning up the God of Thunder (possibly). LEMMY didn't sing in the conventional sense, or even in the heavy metal sense, rather he rasped like a piece of industrial strength sandpaper scraped across a blackboard. He also had more charisma than most of the preening queens that passed as frontmen, his sharp wit and biting sense of humour making him quite a celebrity in his own right and ensuring that his band never fell into parody. MOTORHEAD gained further press attention when they hooked up with rock chicks, GIRLSCHOOL, for the 'ST. VALENTINE'S DAY MASSACRE' EP, released, appropriately enough, in February '81. Credited to HEADGIRL (guffaw, guffaw), the assembled n'er do wells ran through a suitably leering version of Johnny Kidd's 'PLEASE DON'T TOUCH'. Their blistering live set was finally laid down on vinyl in the form of 'NO SLEEP 'TIL HAMMERSMITH' (1981), the band's first (and only) No.1 album and deservedly so. Surely the tightest rock band on the planet at that point, MOTORHEAD ran through a hair whipping frenzy of favourites, from 'STAY CLEAN' and '(WE ARE) THE ROAD CREW' to 'IRON HORSE', LEMMY's tribute to Hell's Angel leader, Tramp. This line-up recorded a further album, the slightly disappointing 'IRON FIST' (1982), before CLARKE left to from his own outfit, FASTWAY. His replacement was BRIAN ROBERTSON (ex-THIN LIZZY, ex-WILD HORSES) who played on only one album, 1983's 'ANOTHER PERFECT DAY'. His more subtle style didn't sit well with the trademark MOTORHEAD cacophony and he soon departed for the more appropriate FRANKIE MILLER BAND, PHIL CAMPBELL and MICHAEL BURSTON (aka WURZEL) replacing him. TAYLOR also departed, PETE GILL (ex-Saxon) being recruited to fill the drum stool and complete the new look four piece MOTORHEAD. The new band made their debut on 'NO REMORSE' (1984), a compilation that collected MOTORHEAD's meanest tracks and showcased four new ones, among them the uber-grind of 'KILLED BY DEATH', possibly LEMMY and Co.'s finest hour. The band almost made the Top 20 once again with the BILL LASWELL-produced 'ORGASMATRON' (1986), LEMMY sounding almost inhuman on the brilliant title track; part android, part wild beast. TAYLOR returned to the fold the following year for the 'ROCK 'N' ROLL' album, its 'EAT THE RICH' track used on the 'Comic Strip' film of the same name, in which LEMMY made his acting debut. Another live album followed, 'NO SLEEP AT ALL' (1988), although it failed to make the same commercial impact as its predecessor. Following a move to L.A. (it had to come sooner or later), the band were back in the charts and back on form with '1916' (1991), its title track an unprecedented show of emotion from LEMMY as he narrated the tale of a young soldier lost in battle. The wart-ridden one also indulged his war fixation on the title track to 'MARCH OR DIE' (1992), while the three most recent releases, 'BASTARDS' (1993), 'SACRIFICE' (1995) and 'PROTECT THE INNOCENT' (1997) have seen MOTORHEAD content to cruise rather than let rip. Still, as long as LEMMY dons his bass and rides into onstage battle, there'll be a willing bunch of masochists ready to have their ears bled dry by some of the loudest, filthiest rock'n'roll on the face of the earth. • Covers:

LOUIE LOUIE (hit; Kingsmen) / TRAIN KEPT A-ROLLIN' (Johnny Burnette Trio) / PLEASE DON'T TOUCH (Johnny Kidd) / (I'M YOUR) HOOCHIE COOCHIE MAN (Willie Dixon) / CAT SCRATCH FEVER (Ted Nugent).

Album rating: MOTORHEAD (*5) / OVERKILL (*8) / BOMBER (*6) / ACE OF SPADES (*8) / NO SLEEP 'TIL HAMMERSMITH (*9) / IRON FIST (*5) / ANOTHER PERFECT DAY (*5) / NO REMORSE (*7) / ORGASMATRON (*6) / ROCK'N'ROLL (*5) / NO SLEEP AT ALL (*6) / 1916 (*7) / MARCH OR DIE (*5) / SACRIFICE (*5) / PROTECT THE INNOCENT (*6) / EVERYTHING LOUDER THAN EVERYONE ELSE (*6)

LEMMY (b. IAN KILMISTER, 24 Dec'45, Stoke-On-Trent, England) – vocals, bass (ex-HAWKWIND, ex-OPAL BUTTERFLY, ex-SAM GOPAL'S DREAM, ROCKIN' VICKERS) / **PHIL 'ANIMAL' TAYLOR** (b.21 Sep'54, Chesterfield, England) – drums / **FAST EDDIE CLARKE** – guitar, vocals (ex-BLUE GOOSE, ex-CURTIS KNIGHT & ZEUS) (below withdrawn)

		Stiff	not iss.
Dec 76.	(7") (BUY 9) **LEAVING HERE. / WHITE LINE FEVER**	-	-
	(withdrawn but iss.Dec78 in 'Stiff' box set Nos.1-10)		

		Chiswick	not iss.
Jun 77.	(7",12") (S 13) **MOTORHEAD. / CITY KIDS**		-
	(re-iss. Sep79 on 'Big Beat' 7"colrd/7"pic-d; NS/+P 13)		
Aug 77.	(lp) (WLK 2) **MOTORHEAD**	43	-

– Motorhead / Vibrator / Lost Johnny / Iron horse – Born to lose / White line fever / Keepers on the road / The watcher / Born to lose / Train kept a-rollin'. (re-iss. white-lp 1978; CWK 3008) (re-iss. Sep81 red-lp,clear-lp; WIK 2) (cd-iss. Jun88 & Feb 91 on 'Big Beat'; CDWIK 2)

		Bronze	not iss.
Sep 78.	(7") BRO 60) **LOUIE LOUIE. / TEAR YA DOWN**	68	-
Feb 79.	(7"/12") (BRO/12BRO 67) **OVERKILL. / TOO LATE, TOO LATE**	39	-
Mar 79.	(lp,green-lp) (BRON 515) **OVERKILL**	24	-

– Overkill / Stay clean / Pay your price / I'll be your sister / No class / Damage case / Tear ya down / Metropolis / Limb for limb. (cd-iss. Jul87 on 'Legacy'; LLMCD 3011) (re-iss. Jul90 on 'Fame' cd/c/lp; CD/TC+/FA 3236) (re-iss. Feb91 on 'Castle' cd/c/lp; CLA CD/MC/LP 178) (re-iss. Aug96 on 'Essential'; ESMCD 310)

Jun 79.	(7") (BRO 78) **NO CLASS. / LIKE A NIGHTMARE**	61	-
Oct 79.	(lp,blue-lp) (BRON 523) **BOMBER**	12	-

– Dead men tell no tales / Lawman / Sweet revenge / Sharpshooter / Poison / Stone dead forever / All the aces / Step down / Talking head / Bomber. (cd-iss. Jul87 on 'Legacy'; LLMCD 3012) (re-iss. Apr91 on 'Castle' cd/c/lp; CLA CD/MC/LP 227) (re-iss. Aug96 on 'Essential'; ESMCD 311)

Nov 79.	(7",7"blue) (BRO 85) **BOMBER. / OVER THE TOP**	34	-
Apr 80.	(7"ep/12"ep) (BRO/12BRO 92) **THE GOLDEN YEARS (live)**	8	-

– Leaving here / Stone dead forever / Dead men don't tell tales / Too late, too late.

		Bronze	Mercury
Oct 80.	(7"/12") (BRO/+X 106) **ACE OF SPADES. / DIRTY LOVE**	15	
Oct 80.	(lp/gold-lp) (BRON/+G 531) <4011> **ACE OF SPADES**	4	

– Ace of spades / Love me like a reptile / Shoot you in the back / Live to win / Fast and loose / (We are) The road crew / Fire, fire / Jailbait / Dance / Bite the bullet / The chase is better than the catch / The hammer. (cd-iss. Aug87 on 'Legacy'; LLMCD 3013) (re-iss. cd Aug96 on 'Essential'; ESMCD 312)

Feb 81.	(7"ep/10"ep; as HEADGIRL) (BRO/+X 116) **ST.VALENTINE'S DAY MASSACRE**	5	-

– Please don't touch (by MOTORHEAD & GIRLSCHOOL) / Emergency (by MOTORHEAD) / Bomber (GIRLSCHOOL).

Jun 81.	(lp/gold-lp/c) (BRON/+G/+C 535) **NO SLEEP 'TIL HAMMERSMITH (live)**	1	-

– Ace of spades / Stay clean / Metropolis / The hammer / Iron horse / No class / Overkill / (We are) The road crew / Capricorn / Bomber / Motorhead. (cd-iss. Aug87 on 'Legacy'; LLMCD 3014) (re-iss. Feb90 on 'Castle' cd/c/lp; CLA CD/MC/LP 179) (re-iss. cd Aug96 on 'Essential'; ESMCD 313)

Jul 81.	(7"/7"pic-d) (BRO/+P 124) **MOTORHEAD (live). / OVER THE TOP (live)**	6	

below, one-off (MOTORHEAD and The NOLANS)

Oct 81.	(7"; as YOUNG AND MOODY BAND) (BRO 130) **DON'T DO THAT. / HOW CAN I HELP YOU TONIGHT**	63	-
Mar 82.	(7",7"red,7"blue) (BRO 146) **IRON FIST. / REMEMBER ME, I'M GONE**	29	-
Apr 82.	(lp/c) (BRNA/+C 539) <4042> **IRON FIST**	6	

– Iron fist / Heart of stone / I'm the doctor / Go to Hell / Loser / Sex and outrage / America / Shut it down / Speedfreak / (Don't let 'em) Grind ya down / (Don't need) Religion / Bang to rights. (re-iss. Mar87 on 'Castle' lp/c/cd; CLA LP/MC/CD 123) (cd re-iss. Aug96 on 'Essential'; ESMCD 372)

Sep 82.	(7"m; by LEMMY & WENDY) (BRO 151) **STAND BY YOUR MAN. / NO CLASS (Plasmatics) / MASTERPLAN (Motorhead)**		-

BRIAN ROBERTSON (b. 2 Feb'56, Clarkston, Scotland) – guitar, vocals (ex-THIN LIZZY, ex-WILD HORSES) repl. CLARKE who formed FASTWAY

May 83.	(7") (BRO 165) **I GOT MINE. / TURN YOU AROUND AGAIN**	46	
	(12"+=) (BROX 165) – Tales of glory.		
May 83.	(lp/c) (BRON/+C 546) <811365> **ANOTHER PERFECT DAY**	20	

– Back at the funny farm / Shine / Dancing on your grave / Rock it / One track mind / Another perfect day / Marching off to war / I got mine / Tales of glory / Die you bastard. (re-iss. cd on 'Castle' cd/c/lp; CLA CD/MC/LP 225) (re-iss. cd Sep96 on 'Essential'; ESMCD 438)

Jul 83.	(7") (BRO 167) **SHINE. / HOOCHIE COOCHIE MAN (live)**	59	-
	(12"+=) (BROX 167) – (Don't need) Religion.		

LEMMY with **PHIL CAMPBELL** (b. 7 May'61, Pontypridd, Wales) – guitar / **WURZEL** (b. MICHAEL BURSTON, 23 Oct'49, Cheltenham, England) – guitar both replace ROBERTSON who joined FRANKIE MILLER BAND / **PETE GILL** (b.9 Jun'51, Sheffield, England) – drums (ex-SAXON) repl. TAYLOR

Aug 84.	(7"/7"sha-pic-d) (BRO/+P 185) **KILLED BY DEATH. / UNDER THE KNIFE**	51	
	(12"+=) (BROX 185) – Under the knife (version).		
Sep 84.	(d-lp) (PRO MOTOR 1) **NO REMORSE** (compilation)	14	

– Ace of spades / Motorhead / Jailbait / Stay clean / Killed by death / Bomber / Iron fist / Shine / Dancing on your grave / Metropolis / Snaggletooth / Overkill /

Please don't touch / Stone dead forever / Like a nightmare / Emergency / Steal your face / Louie Louie / No class / Iron horse / (We are) The road crew / Leaving here / Locomotive. (re-iss. 1988 on 'Castle' d-lp/c/cd+=; CLA LP/MC/CD 121) – Too late, too late. (re-iss. cd Aug96 on 'Essential'; ESDCD 371) (cd re-iss. Jul97; ESMCD 557)

		G.W.R.	GWR-Profile
Jun 86.	(7") (GWR 2) **DEAF FOREVER. / ON THE ROAD (live)**	67	-
	(12"+=) (GWT 2) – Steal your face (live).		
Aug 86.	(lp/c/cd) (GW LP/TC/CD 1) <1223> **ORGASMATRON**	21	Nov86

– Deaf forever / Nothing up my sleeve / Ain't my crime / Claw / Mean machine / Built for speed / Riding with the driver / Doctor Rock / Orgasmatron. (pic-lp.Aug89; GWPD 1) (re-iss. cd Mar92; CLACD 283)

PHIL CAMPBELL – drums returned to repl. GILL

Aug 87.	(7") (GW LP/MC/CD 14) <1240> **ROCK'N'ROLL**	43	Oct87

– Rock'n'roll / Eat the rich / Blackheart / Stone deaf in the USA / The wolf / Traitor / Dogs / All for you / Boogeyman.

Nov 87.	(7") (GWR 6) **EAT THE RICH. / CRADLE TO GRAVE**		
	(12"+=) (GWR 6) – Power.		
	(above from the soundtrack of the film 'Eat The Rich')		
Oct 88.	(lp/c/cd) (GW LP/MC/CD 31) **NO SLEEP AT ALL (live)**	79	

– Dr. Rock / Stay clean / Traitor / Metropolis / Dogs / Ace of spades / Eat the rich / Built for speed / Deaf forever / Just cos you got the power / Killed by death / Overkill. (cd+=) – (3 extra). (re-iss. cd Mar92 on 'Castle' cd/c; CLA CD/MC 285)

		Epic	W.T.G.
Jan 91.	(7"/7"sha-pic-d/c-s) (656578-7/-0/-4) **THE ONE TO SING THE BLUES. / DEAD MAN'S HAND**	45	
	(12"+=/cd-s+=) (656578-6/-2) – Eagle rock / Shut you down.		
Jan 91.	(cd/c/lp/pic-lp) (467481-2/-4/-1) <46858> **1916**	24	Mar91

– The one to sing the blues / I'm so bad (baby I don't care) / No voices in the sky / Going to Brazil / Nightmare – The dreamtime / Love me forever / Angel city / Make my day / Ramones / Shut you down / 1916.

TAYLOR returned but was soon repl. by **MIKEY DEE** (b.31 Oct'63, Olundby, Sweden) – drums

Aug 92.	(cd/c/lp) (471723-2/-4/-1) **MARCH OR DIE**	60	

– Stand / Cat scratch fever / Bad religion / Jack the ripper / I ain't no nice guy / Hellraiser / Asylum choir / Too good to be true / You better run / Name in vain / March or die.

Nov 92.	(12"ep/cd-ep) (658809-6/-2) **'92 TOUR (live)**	63	

– Hellraiser / You better run / Going to Brazil / Ramones.

Above 1st track co-written w / OZZY OSBOURNE

		ZYX	not iss.
Nov 93.	(cd/lp) (20263-2/-1) **BASTARDS**	-	- German

– On your feet or on your knees / Burner / Death or glory / I am the sword / Born to raise hell / Don't let daddy kiss me / Bad woman / Liar / Lost in the ozone / I'm your man / We bring the shake / Devils.

		Arista	Arista
Nov 94.	(7"/c-s; by MOTORHEAD with ICE-T & WHITFIELD CRANE) (74321 23915-7/-4) **BORN TO RAISE HELL. / ('A'mix)**	49	
	(12"+=/cd-s+=) (74321 23915-1/-2) – ('A'mix).		

		S.P.V.	CMC Int
Apr 95.	(cd/c/lp) (SPV 085-7694-2/-4/-1) **SACRIFICE**		

– Sacrifice / Sex & death / Over your shoulder / War for war / Order – Fade to black / Dog-face boy / All gone to hell / Make 'em blind / Don't waste your time / In another time / Out of the sun.

Oct 96.	(cd/c) (SPV 085-1830-2/-4) **OVERNIGHT SENSATION**		

– Civil war / Crazy like a fox / I don't believe a word / Eat the gun / Overnight sensation / Love can't buy you money / Broken / Them not me / Murder show / Shake the world / Listen to your heart.

Mar 99.	(d-cd) (SPV 087-2114-2) <86268> **EVERYTHING LOUDER THAN EVERYONE ELSE (live)**		

– Iron fist / Stay clean / On your feet or on your knees / Over your shoulder / Civil war / Burner / Metropolis / Nothing up my sleeves / I'm so bad, baby I don't care / Chase I better than the catch / Take the blame / No class / Overnight sensation / Sacrifice / Born to raise hell / Lost in the ozone / One to sing the blues / Capricorn / Love for sale / Orgasmatron / Going to Brazil / Killed by death / Bomber / Ace of spades / Overkill.

– compilations, etc. –

Oct 79.	(lp) Liberty; (LBR 1004) **ON PAROLE**	65	-

– Motorhead / On parole / Vibrator / Iron horse – Born to lose / City kids / Fools / The watcher / Leaving here / Lost Johnny. (was to be have been released Dec75) (re-iss. May82 on 'Fame' lp/c; FA/TC-FA 3009) (cd-iss. Oct90; CD-FA 3251) (cd remastered Feb97 on 'EMI Gold'; CDGO 2070)

Nov 80.	(7"ep,7"blue-ep,7"pink-ep,7"orange-ep/12"ep,12"blue-ep,12"pink-ep,12"orange-ep) Big Beat! (NS/SWT 61) **BEER DRINKERS EP**	43	-

– Beer drinkers & hell raisers / On parole / Instro / I'm your witch doctor.

Mar 83.	(lp/c) Big Beat; (NED/+C 2) **WHAT'S WORDS WORTH (live at the Roundhouse 18/2/78)**	71	-

– The watcher / Iron horse – Born to lose / On parole (in A) / White line fever / Keep us on the road / Leaving here / I'm your witchdoctor / The train kept a-rollin' / City kids. (re-iss. Jan90; WIKM 49)

Aug 82.	(d-c) Bronze; (3574 138) **OVERKILL / BOMBER**		-
Nov 84.	(lp/c) Astan; <2/4 0041> **RECORDED LIVE (live)**	-	-
Apr 86.	(lp/c) Raw Power; (RAW LP/MC 011) **ANTHOLOGY**		
	(cd-iss. Dec86; RAWCD 011)		
Apr 86.	(lp/c) Dojo; (DOJO LP/TC 18) **BORN TO LOSE**		
1986.	(cd) Legacy; (LLMCD 3004) **ANTHOLOGY VOL.1**		
Apr 88.	(lp/cd) That's Original; (TFO LP/CD 8) **OVERKILL / ANOTHER PERFECT DAY**		
1988.	(3"cd-ep) Special Edition; (CD3-10) **ACE OF SPADES / BOMBER / MOTORHEAD / OVERKILL**		
Nov 89.	(lp/cd) Receiver; (RR LP/CD 120) **BLITZKRIEG ON BIRMINGHAM LIVE '77 (live)**		
Jan 90.	(cd/lp) Receiver; (RR CD/LP 123) **DIRTY LOVE**		
Apr 90.	(cd/d-lp) Castle; (CCS CD/LP 237) **WELCOME TO THE BEAR TRAP**		

Apr 90. (cd/c/d-lp) *That's Original; (TFO CD/MC/LP 024)* **BOMBER / ACE OF SPADES** [ ] [-]

Apr 90. (cd/c/lp) *G.W.R.; (GW CD/MC/LP 101)* **THE BIRTHDAY PARTY (live '85)** [ ] [-]
(cd+=) – (3 extra tracks). *(also on 'Roadrunner'; RR 9376-1)*

Jun 90. (cd/c/lp) *Receiver; (RR CD/MC/LP 130)* **LOCK UP YOUR DAUGHTERS (live 1977)** [ ] [-]

Jul 90. (cd) *Marble Arch; (cd)* **GRIND YA DOWN** [ ] [-]
(re-iss. Jul94 on 'Success';)

Jul 90. (cd/c) *Action Replay; (ARLC/CDAR 1014)* **THE BEST OF THE REST OF MOTORHEAD** [ ] [-]
(re-iss. Jul93 cd/c; CDAR/ARLC 1032)

Nov 90. (cd/c/lp) *Knight; (NEX CD/MC/LP 136)* **FROM THE VAULTS** [ ] [-]

Jul 91. (3xcd-box/3xlp-box) *Essential; (ESB CD/LP 146)* **MELTDOWN** [ ] [-]

Feb 92. (3xcd-box) *Castle; (CLABX 901)* **3 ORIGINALS** [ ] [-]
– (NO REMORSE / ACE OF SPADES / NO SLEEP 'TIL HAMMERSMITH)

Feb 92. (cd/c/lp) *Receiver; (RR CD/LP 005)* **LIVE JAILBAIT (live)** [ ] [-]

Sep 92. (cd/c/lp) *Roadrunner; (RR 9125-2/-4/-1)* **THE BEST OF MOTORHEAD** [ ] [-]

Apr 93. (c/cd) *Tring; (MC+/JHD 081)* **LIVE (live)** [ ] [-]

Jun 93. (4xcd-box) *Receiver; (RRZCD 501)* **MOTORHEAD BOX SET** [ ] [-]

Aug 93. (c-s/12"/cd-s) *W.G.A.F.; (MC/12/CD WGAF 101)* **ACE OF SPADES (THE C.C.N.remix).** *('A'mixes)* [23] [-]

Nov 93. (cd/c/lp) *Castle TV; (CTV CD/MC/LP 125)* **ALL THE ACES** [ ] [-]

Mar 94. (cd/c/lp) *Roadrunner; (RR 9009-2/-4/-1)* **LIVE AT BRIXTON ACADEMY (live)** [ ] [-]

Aug 94. (cd) *Spectrum; (550 724-2)* **ACES HIGH** [ ] [-]

Sep 94. (cd) *Cleopatra; (CLEO 94132)* **IRON FIST AND THE HORDES FROM HELL** [ ] [-]

May 95. (cd) *Spectrum; ()* **ULTIMATE METAL** [ ] [-]

Jul 95. (2xcd-box) *Griffin; (GCD 2192)* **FISTFUL OF ACES / THE BEST OF MOTORHEAD** [ ] [-]

Oct 95. (cd) *Elite; (ELITE 019CD)* **HEADBANGERS** [ ] [-]

Apr 96. (cd/c) *Hallmark; (30369-2/-4)* **MOTORHEAD – LIVE** [ ] [-]

Nov 96. (cd) *Emperio; (EMPRCD 692)* **LIVE** [ ] [-]

Nov 96. (cd) *Steamhammer; (CD 0857694-2)* **WE'RE MOTORHEAD AND WE'RE GONNA KICK YOUR ASS** [ ] [-]

Feb 97. (cd) *Receiver; (RRCD 238)* **STONE DEAD FOREVER** [ ] [-]

May 97. (d-cd) *(Snapper; (SMDCD 127)* **TAKE NO PRISONERS** [ ] [-]

Jul 97. (cd) *Going For A Song; (GFS 073)* **MOTORHEAD** [ ] [-]

Aug 97. (4xcd-box) *(ESBCD 562)* **PROTECT THE INNOCENT** [ ] [-]

MOTT THE HOOPLE

Formed: Hereford, England ... Jun '69 by OVEREND WATTS, DALE GRIFFIN, VERDEN ALLEN and MICK RALPHS, who were part of The SHAKEDOWN SOUND with singer STAN TIPPINS. With new manager and producer Guy Stevens placing an ad in a music paper, the group found a replacement frontman in IAN HUNTER (he had once guested on a 45 by CHARLIE WOLFE). Naming themselves MOTT THE HOOPLE (after a novel by Willard Manus), they signed to Chris Blackwell's burgeoning 'Island' label. Their eponymous debut gained a minor chart placing, the record introducing HUNTER's bluesy DYLAN-esque delivery over a tentative set of earthy rock'n'roll. Although three more lacklustre albums were completed in quick succession, the group split in 1972 after the last of them, 'BRAIN CAPERS' failed to match its predecessors' Top 50 status. Fortunately for them, a young DAVID BOWIE was re-establishing himself in the songwriting stakes, the ascending glamster offering the band a lifeline in the form of 'ALL THE YOUNG DUDES'. Securing a new contract with 'C.B.S.', MOTT THE HOOPLE roared into the UK Top 3 with a new lease of life, although VERDEN had departed soon after the recording of the similarly-titled hit parent album. Using the glam-rock craze as their launch pad, the band straddled the widening gap between the teen-pop market and the college circuit. A trio of Top 20 hits in 1973, 'HONALOOCHIE BOOGIE', 'ALL THE WAY FROM MEMPHIS' and 'ROLL AWAY THE STONE' proved that the group were no overnight sensations, although the last of these had been recorded without RALPHS who joined BAD COMPANY. Together with VERDEN's deputy MICK BOLTON, he was replaced by ARIEL BENDER and MORGAN FISHER, two veterans of the British music scene. Releasing 'THE HOOPLE' album as a follow-up to 1973's 'MOTT', the band once again hit the UK and US charts, although the critical tide was turning against glam and everyone connected with it (i.e. SWEET, SLADE, GLITTER, QUATRO, etc). With BENDER (aka LUTHER GROSVENOR) opting to join heavyweights WIDOWMAKER, the band (with ex-BOWIE sidekick, MICK RONSON, now taking on guitar duties) also opted for a harder-edged direction after a single, 'SATURDAY GIGS', failed to scrape into the Top 40. Suffering from exhaustion, HUNTER was eager to follow a less high-profile solo career, RONSON also taking the same route, the pair, in addition touring together as The HUNTER-RONSON BAND. The remainder (OVEREND, DALE and MORGAN) re-grouped in 1975 as MOTT, enlisting the services of new frontman NIGEL BENJAMIN and guitarist RAY MAJORS for a new album, 'DRIVE ON'. Another uninspiring set, 'SHOUTING AND POINTING' was to appear in 1976, the band soon giving up amid general lack of interest, although they did resurface as the more overtly hard-rockin' BRITISH LIONS. • **Songwriters:** HUNTER or others wrote most except; YOU REALLY GOT ME (Kinks) / LAUGH AT ME (Sonny Bono) / CROSSROADS (Sir Douglas Quintet) / KEEP A KNOCKIN' (Little Richard) / WHOLE LOTTA SHAKIN' GOIN' ON (Jerry Lee Lewis) / LAY DOWN (Melanie) / COME ON BABY, LET'S GO DOWNTOWN (Crazy Horse) / YOUR OWN BACKYARD (Dion) / etc.

Album rating: MOTT THE HOOPLE (*6) / MAD SHADOWS (*5) / WILD LIFE (*4) / BRAIN CAPERS (*6) / ALL THE YOUNG DUDES (*7) / MOTT (*8) / THE HOOPLE (*7) / LIVE (*4) / DRIVE ON (*3) / SHOUTING AND POINTING (*2) THE BALLAD OF MOTT THE HOOPLE – A RETROSPECTIVE compilation (*8)

IAN HUNTER (b. 3 Jun'46, Shrewsbury, England) – vocals, guitar, piano / **MICK RALPHS** (b.31 May'44) – guitar, vocals / **VERDEN ALLEN** (b.26 May'44) – organ / **OVEREND WATTS** (b.13 May'49, Birmingham, England) – bass, vocals / **DALE 'BUFFIN' GRIFFIN** (b.24 Oct'48, Hereford) – drums, vocals

	Island	Atlantic
Oct 69. (7") *(WIP 6072)* **ROCK AND ROLL QUEEN. / ROAD TO BIRMINGHAM**		
Nov 69. (lp) *(ILPS 9108)* <8258> **MOTT THE HOOPLE**	66	-

– You really got me / At the crossroads / Laugh at me / Backsliding fearlessly / Rock and roll queen / Rabbit foot and Toby time / Half Moon Bay / Wrath and wroll.

Jan 70. (7") **ROCK AND ROLL QUEEN. / BACKSLIDING FEARLESSLY**	-	
Sep 70. (lp) *(ILPS 9119)* <8272> **MAD SHADOWS**	48	

– Thunderbuck ram / No wheels to ride / You are one of us / Walkin' with a mountain / I can feel / Threads of iron / When my mind's gone.

Feb 71. (lp) *(ILPS 9144)* <8284> **WILDLIFE**	44	

– Whisky woman / Angel of 8th avenue / Wrong side of the river / Waterloo / Lay down / It must be love / Original mixed-up lad / Home is where I want to be / Keep a knockin'.

Sep 71. (lp) *(ILPS 9178)* <8304> **BRAIN CAPERS** [ ] [ ]
– Death maybe your Santa Claus / Darkness darkness / Your own backyard / Journey / Sweet Angeline / Wheel of the quivering meat conception / Second love / Moon upstairs.

Oct 71. (7") *(WIP 6105)* **MIDNIGHT LADY. / THE DEBT** [ ] [ ]

Dec 71. (7") *(WIP 6112)* **DOWNTOWN. / HOME IS WHERE I WANT TO BE** [ ] [ ]

	C.B.S.	Columbia
Jul 72. (7") *(8271)* <45673> **ALL THE YOUNG DUDES. / ONE OF THE BOYS**	3	37
Sep 72. (lp/c) *(CBS/40 65184)* <31750> **ALL THE YOUNG DUDES**	21	89 Nov72

– Sweet Jane / Momma's little jewel / All the young dudes / Sucker / Jerkin' crocus / One of the boys / Soft ground / Ready for love – After lights / Sea diver.

Jan 73. (7") <45754> **ONE OF THE BOYS. / SUCKER**		96
Mar 73. (7") <45784> **SWEET JANE. / JERKIN' CROCUS**		-

—— **MICK BOLTON** – keyboards filled in for departing VERDEN who went solo

May 73. (7") *(1530)* <45882> **HONALOOCHIE BOOGIE. / ROSE**	12	
Jul 73. (lp/c) *(CBS/40 69038)* <32425> **MOTT**	7	35 Aug73

– All the way from Memphis / Whizz kid / Hymn for the dudes / Honaloochie boogie / Violence / Drivin' sister / Ballad of Mott The Hoople (March 26, 1972 – Zurich) / I'm a Cadillac – El Camino Dolo Roso / I wish I was your mother. *(cd-iss. 1988 on 'Castle'; CLACD 138X) (cd-iss. Mar95 on 'Rewind';)*

Aug 73. (7") **ALL THE WAY FROM MEMPHIS. / BALLAD OF MOTT THE HOOPLE (MARCH 26, 1972 – ZURICH)**	10	-
Sep 73. (7") <45920> **ALL THE WAY FROM MEMPHIS. / I WISH I WAS YOUR MOTHER**	-	-

—— **ARIEL BENDER** (b. LUTHER GROSVENOR, 23 Dec'49, Evesham, England) – guitar (ex-SPOOKY TOOTH) replaced RALPHS who joined BAD COMPANY / **MORGAN FISHER** – keyboards (ex-LOVE AFFAIR) repl. BOLTON (above 2 with HUNTER, WATTS and GRIFFIN.)

Nov 73. (7") *(1895)* **ROLL AWAY THE STONE. / WHERE DO YOU ALL COME FROM**	8	-
Mar 74. (7") *(2177)* <46035> **THE GOLDEN AGE OF ROCK'N'ROLL. / REST IN PEACE**	16	96 May74
Mar 74. (lp/c) *(CBS/40 69062)* <32871> **THE HOOPLE**	11	28 Apr74

– The golden age of rock'n'roll / Marionette / Alice / Crash Street kidds / Born late '58 / Trudi's song / Pearl 'n' Roy (England) / Through the looking glass / Roll away the stone.

Apr 74. (7") <46076> **ROLL AWAY THE STONE. / THROUGH THE LOOKING GLASS**	-	-
Jun 74. (7") *(2439)* **FOXY FOXY. / TRUDI'S SONG**	33	-

—— **BLUE WEAVER** – organ on tour (ex-AMEN CORNER)

Nov 74. (lp/c) *(CBS/40 69093)* <33282> **LIVE** (live; Broadway – Nov73 / Hammersmith – May74)	32	23

– All the way from Memphis / Sucker / Rest in peace / All the young dudes / Walkin' with a mountain / Sweet Angeline / Rose / Medley:- (a) Jerkin' crocus – (b) One of the boys – (c) Rock'n'roll queen – (d) Get back – (e) Whole lotta shakin' – (f) Violence.

—— **MICK RONSON** – guitar, vocals (Solo artist, ex-DAVID BOWIE; SPIDERS FROM MARS) repl. ARIEL who formed WIDOWMAKER

Oct 74. (7") *(2754)* **SATURDAY GIGS. / MEDLEY; JERKIN' CROCUS – SUCKER** (live)	41	-
Dec 74. (7") <10091> **ALL THE YOUNG DUDES** (live). / **ROSE**	-	-

—— Split Dec'74. HUNTER and RONSON formed duo and went solo.

MOTT

(OVEREND, DALE and **MORGAN**) were joined by **NIGEL BENJAMIN** – vocals (ex-ROYCE) / **RAY MAJORS** – guitar (ex-HACKENSHACK)

	C.B.S.	Columbia
Aug 75. (7") *(3528)* **MONTE CARLO. / SHOUT IT ALL OUT**		
Sep 75. (lp/c) *(CBS/40 69154)* <33705> **DRIVE ON**	45	

– By tonight / Monte Carlo / She does it / I'll tell you something / Stiff upper lip / Love now / Apologies / The great white wall / Here we are / It takes one to know one / I can show you how it is.

Oct 75. (7") *(3741)* **BY TONIGHT. / I CAN SHOW YOU HOW IT IS** [ ] [ ]

Feb 76. (7") *(4055)* **IT TAKES ONE TO KNOW ONE. / I'LL TELL YOU SOMETHING** [ ] [ ]

Jun 76. (lp/c) *(CBS/40 81289)* <34236> **SHOUTING AND POINTING** [ ] [ ]
– Shouting and pointing / Collision course / Storm / Career (no such thing as rock'n'roll) / Hold on, you're crazy / See you again / Too short arms (I don't care) / Broadside outcasts / Good times.

– compilations, etc. –

Oct 72.	(lp) *Island; (ILPS 9215) / Atlantic; <7297>* **ROCK'N'ROLL QUEEN**		Jul74
Feb 76.	(7") *C.B.S.; (3963)* **ALL THE YOUNG DUDES. / ROLL AWAY THE STONE** *(re-iss. Apr83 on 'Old Gold'; OG 9312)*		-
Mar 76.	(lp/c) *C.B.S.; (CBS/40 81225) <34368>* **GREATEST HITS** – All the way from Memphis / Honaloochie boogie / Hymn for the dudes / Born late '58 / All the young dudes / Roll away the stone / Ballad of Mott The Hoople / Golden age of rock'n'roll / Foxy lady / Saturday gigs. *(re-iss. Jun81 lp/c; CBS/40 32007) (cd-iss. Apr89; CD 32007)*		
Mar 81.	(lp) *Island; (IRSP 8)* **TWO MILES FROM HEAVEN**		-
Mar 81.	(lp/c) *Hallmark; (SHM 3055)* **ALL THE WAY FROM MEMPHIS**		-
Jul 84.	(7") *C.B.S.; (A 4581)* **ALL THE YOUNG DUDES. / HONALOOCHIE BOOGIE**		-
1988.	(cd) *Castle; (CCSCD 174)* **THE COLLECTION**		-
Jun 90.	(cd) *Island; (IMCD 87)* **WALKING WITH A MOUNTAIN (BEST OF 1969-1972)** – Rock and roll queen / At the crossroads / Thunderbuck ram / Whiskey woman / Waterflow / The Moon upstairs / Second love / The road to Birmingham / Black scorpio (mama's little jewel) / You really got me / Walking with a mountain / No wheels to ride / Keep a knockin' / Midnight lady / Death may be your Santa Claus / Darkness darkness / Growing man blues / Black hills.		
Jun 92.	(7"/c-s) *Columbia; (658177-7/-4)* **ALL THE YOUNG DUDES. / ONCE BITTEN TWICE SHY (by Ian Hunter)** *(cd-s+=) (658177-2)* – Roll Away The Stone.		
Dec 92.	(cd) *Edsel; (EDCD 361)* **MOOT THE HOOPLE / MAD SHADOWS**		-
Jun 93.	(cd) *See For Miles; (SEECD 7)* **MOTT THE HOOPLE FEATURING STEVE HYAMS**		-
Nov 93.	(d-cd) *Legacy; (CD 46973)* **THE BALLAD OF MOTT THE HOOPLE – A RETROSPECTIVE** *(re-iss. Jun96 on 'Coulmbia'; 474420-2)*		-
Jun 96.	(cd-s) *Old Gold; (126236380-2)* **ALL THE YOUNG DUDES / ONE OF THE BOYS**		-
Jul 96.	(cd) *Windsong; (WINCD 064)* **THE ORIGINAL MIXED UP KIDS – THE BBC SESSIONS 1970-71**		-
——	In Feb80, MOTT THE HOOPLE tracks were included on double album 'SHADES OF IAN HUNTER – THE BALLAD OF IAN HUNTER & MOTT THE HOOPLE' on 'CBS'; (88476)		

BRITISH LIONS

MOTT + **JOHN FIDDLER** – vocals (ex-MEDICINE HEAD) repl. NIGEL who joined ENGLISH ASSASSINS

		Vertigo	R.S.O.
Feb 78.	(7") *(6059 192)* **ONE MORE CHANCE TO RUN. / BOOSTER**		
Feb 78.	(lp) *(9120 019) <3032>* **BRITISH LIONS** – One more chance to run / Wild in the streets / Break this fool / International heroes / Fork talking man / My life in your hands / Big drift away / Booster / Eat the rich.		83 Apr78
Apr 78.	(7") *(6059 201)* **INTERNATIONAL HEROES. / EAT THE RICH**	-	
Jul 78.	(7") *<898>* **WILD IN THE STREETS. / BOOSTER**	-	87

		Cherry Red	not iss.
May 80.	(lp) *(ARED 7)* **TROUBLE WITH WOMEN** – Trouble with women / Any port in a storm / Lady don't fall backwards / High noon / Lay down your love / Waves of love / Electric chair / Won't you give him up.		-

—— When they split MORGAN FISHER went solo releasing single 'GENEVE'. GRIFFIN and WATTS went into production incl. HANOI ROCKS.

Bob MOULD (see under ⇒ HUSKER DU)

MOUNTAIN

Formed: The Bronx, New York, USA . . . 1969 by FELIX PAPPALARDI and guitarist LESLIE WEST. A veteran producer, PAPPALARDI had worked with the likes of LOVIN' SPOONFUL, JOAN BAEZ, The YOUNGBLOODS etc., as well as helping CREAM to achieve their groundbreaking power trio crunch. He first came into contact with the girthsome WEST after being landed with the job of producing some salesworthy product by Long Island popsters The VAGRANTS. In the event he failed and the band split; impressed by WEST's guitar skills, however, the natural next move was for the pair to hook up, PAPPALARDI producing WEST's first solo set, 'MOUNTAIN' (1969). The record's encouraging reception duly persuaded the duo to make MOUNTAIN a full-time concern, PAPPALARDI playing bass alongside drummer NORMAN D. SMART and new recruit, keyboard player STEVE KNIGHT. This was the line-up which no doubt caused more than a few bad trips at 'Woodstock' in August '69, the group blasting the hippies with their warp-factor blues/sludge-metal on only their fourth ever gig. The 'MOUNTAIN CLIMBING!' (1970) set was unleashed the following Spring, the rousing 'MISSISSIPPI QUEEN' single pushing the album into the US Top 20. 'NANTUCKET SLEIGHRIDE' (1971) was another sizable Stateside success, its dense title track later used as the theme tune for ITV's long running 'World In Action' series. A third set, 'FLOWERS OF EVIL' (1972) didn't fare so well, the rather predictable organ-dominated riff overkill beginning to grate. A concert set, then, 'MOUNTAIN LIVE – THE ROAD GOES EVER ON' (1972), was just what the doctor didn't order, especially one where 'NANTUCKET SLEIGHRIDE' was spun out over a sanity-defying two sides-plus of vinyl; the solo goes on forever, anyone?. Wisely perhaps, PAPPALARDI opted to resume production work and the first incarnation of MOUNTAIN was no more. Along with CORKY LAING, who had replaced SMART in the drum stool, WEST engaged the

services of ex-CREAM bassist, JACK BRUCE to form WEST, BRUCE & LAING. The trio secured a deal with 'Columbia', achieving moderate success with the album 'WHY DON'CHA' (1972) and releasing a second set through MOUNTAIN's label, 'Windfall'. By the time a posthumous live album was issued in 1974, WEST had already rejoined PAPPALARDI in a revamped MOUNTAIN, the pair bringing in ALLEN SCHWARZBERG and ROBERT MANN. Worryingly, their first release was a live album, 'TWIN PEAKS' (1974), and a subsequent studio set, 'AVALANCHE' (1974) was met with a muted response. MOUNTAIN faded from view once more, PAPPALARDI recording two solo albums for 'A&M', 'FELIX PAPPALARDI AND CREATION' (1976) and 'DON'T WORRY MUM?' (1979), before retiring to Japan. WEST, meanwhile, released two solo sets for 'R.C.A.', the self-deprecatingly titled 'THE GREAT FATSBY' (1975) and 'THE LESLIE WEST BAND' (1976). Another MOUNTAIN reformation was probably inevitable, however, and it came in 1981, the project later overshadowed by the death of PAPPALARDI, shot dead on 17th April '83 by his wife, Gail Collins. Ex-RAINBOW and URIAH HEEP man, MARK CLARKE was eventually hired as a replacement and the group cut a disappointing album for 'Scotti Brothers', 'GO FOR YOUR LIFE' (1985). MOUNTAIN were finally buried and WEST once again hooked up with JACK BRUCE for 'THEME' (1988) and 'ALLIGATOR' (1989), the legend given something of a dusting down via the release of 1995's 'Sony' retrospective, 'OVER THE TOP'. • **Songwriters:** WEST-PAPPALARDI penned except; THIS WHEEL'S ON FIRE (Bob Dylan) / ROLL OVER BEETHOVEN (Chuck Berry) / WHOLE LOTTA SHAKIN' GOIN' ON (Jerry Lee Lewis). LESLIE WEST solo covered; RED HOUSE (Jimi Hendrix) / SPOONFUL (Cream) / THE STEALER (Free) / I PUT A SPELL ON YOU (Screaming Jay Hawkins) / HALL OF THE MOUNTAIN KING (Grieg) / DREAM LOVER (Bobby Darin) / THEME FROM EXODUS (Gold) / SEA OF FIRE (Cintron). • **Trivia:** On their live double album 'TWIN PEAKS', they used 1 album and a bit for track 'NANTUCKET SLEIGHRIDE'.

Album rating: LESLIE WEST – MOUNTAIN (*6) / MOUNTAIN CLIMBING! (*7) / NANTUCKET SLEIGHRIDE (*6) / FLOWERS OF EVIL (*6) / THE ROAD GOES ON FOREVER – MOUNTAIN LIVE (*4) / THE BEST OF MOUNTAIN (FEATURING LESLIE WEST & FELIX PAPPALARDI) compilation (*8) / AVALANCHE (*5) / TWIN PEAKS (*4) / GO FOR YOUR LIFE (*4) / OVER THE TOP part compilation (*7) / West, Bruce & Laing: WHY DONTCHA (*5) / WHATEVER TURNS YOU ON (*4) / LIVE 'N' KICKIN' (*4) / Leslie West: THE GREAT FATSBY (*4) / THE LESLIE WEST BAND (*3) / THEME (*3) / ALLIGATOR (*4)

LESLIE WEST

(b. LESLIE WEINSTEIN, 22 Oct'45, Queens, N.Y.) – vocals, lead guitar (ex-VAGRANTS) / with **FELIX PAPPALARDI** (b.1939) – bass, keyboards / **NORMAN LANDSBERG** – keyboards / **NORMAN D.SMART** (b. Boston) – drums

		Bell	Windfall
Sep 69.	(lp) *<4500>* **MOUNTAIN** – Blood of the sun / Long red / Better watch out / Blind man / Baby I'm down / Dreams of milk & honey / Storyteller man / This wheel's on fire / Look to the wind / Southbound train / Because you are my friend.	-	72
Oct 69.	(7") *(BLL 1078) <530>* **DREAMS OF MILK AND HONEY. / THIS WHEEL'S ON FIRE**		
Jan 70.	(7") *<531>* **BLOOD OF THE SUN. / LONG RED**	-	

MOUNTAIN

named after last album. **STEVE KNIGHT** – keyboards (ex-DEVIL'S ANVIL) repl. LANDSBERG (This line-up appeared at 'Woodstock' festival)

—— **CORKY LAING** (b.26 Jan'48, Montreal, Canada) – drums repl. SMART

Mar 70.	(lp) *(SBLL 133) <4501>* **MOUNTAIN CLIMBING!** – Mississippi queen / Theme for an imaginary western / Never in my life / Silver paper / For Yasgur's farm / To my friend / The laird / Sittin' on a rainbow / Boys in the band. *(re-iss. Aug91 on 'Beat Goes On' cd/c; BGO CD/MC 112) (cd re-iss. Mar95 on 'Columbia'; 472180-2)*		17
May 70.	(7") *(BLL 1112) <532>* **MISSISSIPPI QUEEN. / THE LAIRD**		21 Mar70
Jun 70.	(7") *<533>* **FOR YASGUR'S FARM. / TO MY FRIEND**	-	
Oct 70.	(7") *(BLL 1125)* **SITTIN' ON A RAINBOW. / TO MY FRIEND**	-	

		Island	Windfall
May 71.	(lp) *(ILPS 9148) <5500>* **NANTUCKET SLEIGHRIDE** – Don't look around / Taunta (Sammy's tune) / Nantucket sleighride / You can't get away / Tired angels / The animal trainer and the toad / My lady / Travellin' in the dark / The great train robbery. *(cd-iss. Jun89 on 'Beat Goes On'; BGOCD 32)*	43	16 Jan71
Mar 71.	(7") *<534>* **THE ANIMAL TRAINER AND THE TOAD. / TIRED ANGELS**	-	76
Jul 71.	(7") *<535>* **TRAVELIN' IN THE DARK. / SILVER PAPER**	-	
Jan 72.	(lp) *(ILPS 9179) <5501>* **FLOWERS OF EVIL** – Flowers of evil / King's chorale / One last cold kiss / Crossroader / Pride and passion / (Dream sequence: Guitar solo) / Roll over Beethoven / Dreams of milk and honey – Variations – Swan theme / Mississippi queen. *(re-iss. Dec91 on 'Beat Goes On' cd/c; BGO CD/MC 113)*		35 Dec71
Feb 72.	(7") *(WIP 6119) <536>* **ROLL OVER BEETHOVEN. / CROSSROADER**		
Jun 72.	(lp) *(ILPS 9199) <5502>* **MOUNTAIN LIVE – THE ROAD GOES EVER ON (live)** – Long red / Waiting to take you away / Crossroader / Nantucket sleighride. *(re-iss. Dec91 on 'Beat Goes On' cd/c/lp; BGO CD/MC/LP 111)*	21	63 May71
Jul 72.	(7") *<537>* **WAITING TO TAKE YOU AWAY. / NANTUCKET SLEIGHRIDE (live excerpt)**	-	-

		Island	C.B.S.
Feb 73.	(lp) *(ILPS 9236) <32079>* **THE BEST OF MOUNTAIN (FEATURING LESLIE WEST & FELIX PAPPALARDI)** (compilation) – Never in my life / Taunta (Sammy's tune) / Nantucket sleighride / Roll over		72

Beethoven / For Yasgur's farm / The animal trainer and the toad / Mississippi queen / King's chorale / Boys in the band / Don't look around / Theme for an imaginary western / Crossroader. *(cd-iss. Apr89 on 'Beat Goes On'; BGOCD 33) (cd re-iss. Dec92 on 'Columbia'; 466335-2)*

—— Disbanded mid 1972

WEST, BRUCE & LAING

were formed by ex-MOUNTAIN men and **JACK BRUCE** – vocals, bass (ex-CREAM, etc)

				C.B.S.	Columbia		

Nov 72. (lp) *(CBS 65314) <31929>* **WHY DONTCHA** — `26` Oct72
 – Why dontcha / Out in the fields / The doctor / Turn me over / Third degree / Shake ma thing (Rollin' Jack) / While you sleep / Pleasure / Love is worth the blues / Pollution woman. *(re-iss. Aug85 on 'R.S.O.';) (cd-iss. Apr93 on 'Sony Europe')*

Dec 72. (7") *<45751>* **SHAKE MA THING (ROLLIN' JACK). / THE DOCTOR** —

Mar 73. (7") *<45829>* **WHY DONTCHA. / MISSISSIPPI QUEEN** —

				R.S.O.	Windfall		

Jul 73. (7") *(2090 113)* **DIRTY SHOES. / BACKFIRE**

Jul 73. (lp) *(2394 107) <32216>* **WHATEVER TURNS YOU ON**
 – Backfire / Token / Sifting sand / November song / Rock and roll machine / Scotch krotch / Slow blues / Dirty shoes / Like a plate. *(cd-iss. Apr93 on 'Sony Europe')*

May 74. (lp) *(2394 128) <32899>* **LIVE 'N' KICKIN' (live)**
 – Play with fire / The doctor / Politician / Powerhouse sod. *(cd-iss. Apr93 on 'Sony Europe')*

MOUNTAIN

had already re-formed late in 1973 with **WEST + PAPPALARDI** bringing in **ALLEN SCHWARZBERG** – drums / **ROBERT MANN** – keyboards

				C.B.S.	Columbia		

Feb 74. (d-lp) *<32818>* **TWIN PEAKS** (live in Japan '73) —
 – Never in my life / Theme for an imaginary western / Blood of the sun / Guitar solo / Nantucket sleigh ride / Nantucket sleigh ride (conclusion) / Crossroader / Mississippi queen / Silver paper / Roll over Beethoven. *(UK-iss.Nov77; CBS 88095)*

—— **DAVID PERRY** – rhythm guitar repl. ALLEN + ROBERT (FELIX now + keyboards)

				Epic	Epic		

Nov 74. (lp) *(CBS 80492) <33088>* **AVALANCHE**
 – Whole lotta shakin' goin' on / Sister justice / Alisan / Swamp boy / Satisfaction / Thumbsucker / You better believe it / I love to see you fly / Back where I belong / Last of the sunshine days. *(re-iss. Feb88 on 'Castle' lp/cd; CLA LP/CD 136X)*

—— Split again late in '74. FELIX PAPPALARDI signed to 'A&M' and released 2 albums **FELIX PAPPALARDI AND CREATION** (1976) and **DON'T WORRY MUM?** (1979). He retired to Japan, and later (17 Apr'83) was dead, shot by his wife GAIL COLLINS.

LESLIE WEST

went solo with band **CORKY LAING** – drums / **DON KRETMMAR** – bass / **FRANK VICARI** – horns / **etc.**

				R.C.A.	Phantom		

Feb 75. (7") *<10301>* **DON'T BURN UP. / E.S.P.** —

Mar 75. (lp) *(RS 1009) <0954>* **THE GREAT FATSBY**
 – Don't burn me / House of the rising sun / High roller / I'm gonna love you thru the night / E.S.P. / Honky tonk women / If I still had you / Doctor Love / If I were a carpenter / Little bit of love.

Feb 76. (7") *<10424>* **MONEY – DEAR PRUDENCE. / GET IT UP – SETTING SUN**

Mar 76. (lp) *(1258) <701>* **THE LESLIE WEST BAND**
 – Money (watcha gonna do) / Dear Prudence / Get it up (no bass – whatsoever) / Singapore sling / By the river / The twister / Setting sun / Sea of heartache / We'll find a way / We gotta get out of this place.

May 76. (7") *<10522>* **WE GOTTA GET OUT OF THIS PLACE. / BY THE RIVER** —

—— LESLIE WEST retired for a while, until . . .

MOUNTAIN

re-formed in 1981. (**WEST, PAPPALARDI, LAING** and 2 others). In 1984, after death of PAPPALARDI. added **MARK CLARKE** – bass, keyboards (ex-URIAH HEEP, ex-RAINBOW, etc)

				not iss.	Scotti Brothers		

Apr 85. (lp) *(40006)* **GO FOR YOUR LIFE** —
 – Hard times / Spark / She loves her rock (and she loves it hard) / Bardot damage / Shimmy on the footlights / I love young girls / Makin' it in your car / Babe in the woods / Little bit of insanity.

LESLIE WEST

brought in **JACK BRUCE** – vocals, bass / **JOE FRANCO** – drums (ex-TWISTED SISTER)

				not iss.	Passport		

Apr 88. (lp/cd) *<PB 606-1/-2>* **THEME** —
 – Talk dirty / Motherlode / Theme for an imaginary western / I'm crying / Red house / Love is forever / I ate it / Spoonful / Love me tender.

—— In Apr '89, he appeared on Various Artists live cd,c,d-lp,video 'NIGHT OF THE GUITAR' on his next label.

				I.R.S.	I.R.S.		

Oct 89. (cd) *<(EIRSACD 1017)>* **ALLIGATOR**
 – Sea of fire / Waiting for the F change / Whiskey / Alligator / I put a spell on you / All of me / The stealer / Medley: Hall of the mountain king – Theme from Exodus / Dream lover.

				not iss.	BluesBureau		

1994. (cd) **DODGIN' THE DIRT** —

MOUNTAIN

—— re-formed with **WEST, LAING + CLARKE**

				Viceroy	not iss.		

1996. (cd) *(34 766-423)* **MAN'S WORLD** — — German
 – In your face / Thunder / Man's world / So fine / Hotel happiness / I'm sorry / I look (power mix) / Is that okay? / Crest of a slump / You'll never be alone / I look (hit mix).

– compilations, etc. –

Jun 95. (d-cd) *Columbia; (483898-2)* **OVER THE TOP**

Mar 96. (cd; LESLIE WEST & MOUNTAIN) *Raven; (RVCD 49)* **BLOOD OF THE SUN**

MOVE

Formed: Birmingham, England . . . early 1966 by ROY WOOD, CARL WAYNE, TREVOR BURTON, ACE KEFFORD and BEV BEVAN. By that summer, they had found manager Tony Secunda, who helped them sign to 'Deram'. Early the next year, their debut 45, 'NIGHT OF FEAR' (based on the 1812 Overture), had crashed into the UK Top 3. After another Top 5 hit, their third single, 'FLOWERS IN THE RAIN' (the first record to be played on the newly launched BBC Radio 1), was another to make the Top 3 in October '67 on the recently formed 'Regal Zonophone' label. Their fourth successive Top 5 hit arrived in early '68 with 'FIRE BRIGADE', quickly followed by the Top 20 self-titled album. The aforementioned singles were, for the most part, classy bubblegum psychedelia penned by the multi-talented WOOD. After a surprise flop, they scored their first No.1 early in '69 with the single, 'BLACKBERRY WAY'. They never emulated this, WOOD becoming increasingly involved with his new project, The ELECTRIC LIGHT ORCHESTRA, in 1970. He subsequently departed, JEFF LYNNE taking over the leadership, while he ended The MOVE on a high-note in mid-'72 with the Top 10 hit, 'CALIFORNIA MAN'. Remaining at 'Harvest' records, WOOD formed the 50's pastiche rock'n'roll/glam outfit, WIZZARD (the band making their live debut at Wembley's Rock'n'roll festival in June '72). They hit the Top 10 with their first 45, 'BALL PARK INCIDENT', following it with two chart toppers, 'SEE MY BABY JIVE' and 'ANGEL FINGERS'. Around the same time (mid-'73), WOOD discarded his WIZZARD attire (tartan troosers, multi-coloured robe, topped with face-paint and a multi-coloured hair-do), entering the album charts with his solo (in every sense of the word), 'BOULDERS' album. He continued to work on both projects simultaneously, scoring many Top 20 chart hits. Following his signing to the 'Jet' label in 1975, the hits (bar a few minor ones) duly dried up. • **Covered;** LOVELY RITA + POLYTHENE PAM (Beatles). • **Trivia:** ROY also produced and wrote for DARTS, etc.

Best CD compilation(s): GREAT MOVE! THE BEST OF THE MOVE (*8) / THROUGH THE YEARS – THE BEST OF ROY WOOD (*7)

ROY WOOD (b. ULYSSES ADRIAN WOOD, 8 Nov'46) – guitar, vocals (ex-MIKE SHERIDAN & NIGHTRIDERS, ex-GERRY LEVENE & THE AVENGERS) / **TREVOR BURTON** (b. 9 Mar'44) – guitar, vox (ex-DANNY KING & THE MAYFAIR SET) / **CARL WAYNE** (b.18 Aug'44) – vocals (ex-CARL WAYNE & THE VIKINGS) / **CHRIS "ACE" KEFFORD** (b.10 Dec'46) – bass, vox (ex-CARL WAYNE & THE VIKINGS) / **BEV BEVAN** (b.24 Nov'44) – drums (ex-CARL WAYNE & THE VIKINGS, ex-DENNY LAINE & THE DIPLOMATS)

				Deram	Deram		

Dec 66. (7") *(DM 109) <7504>* **NIGHT OF FEAR. / DISTURBANCE** `2`

Apr 67. (7") *(DM 117) <7506>* **I CAN HEAR THE GRASS GROW. / WAVE THE FLAG, STOP THE TRAIN** `5`

				Regal Zonophone	A&M		

Sep 67. (7") *(RZ 3001)* **FLOWERS IN THE RAIN. / (HERE WE GO ROUND) THE LEMON TREE** `2`

Feb 68. (7") *(RZ 3005)* **FIRE BRIGADE. / WALK UPON THE WATER** `3`

Mar 68. (lp; stereo/mono) *(S+/LRZ 1002)* **THE MOVE** `15` —
 – Yellow rainbow / Kilroy was here / (Here we go round) The lemon tree / Weekend / Walk upon the water / Flowers in the rain / Useless information / Zing went the strings of my heart / The girl outside / Fire brigade / Mist on a Monday morning / Cherry blossom clinic. *(cd-iss. Nov92 on 'Repertoire' +=;) – (8 bonus tracks).*

—— quartet, (**BURTON** – bass, vocals) when KEFFORD formed ACE KEFFORD STAND

Jul 68. (7") *(RZ 3012)* **WILD TIGER WOMAN. / OMNIBUS** —

Sep 68. (7"ep) *(TRZ 2001)* **SOMETHING ELSE FROM THE MOVE** —
 – Stephanie knows who / So you want to be a rock 'n' roll star / Something else / It'll be me / Sunshine help me.

Sep 68. (7") *<966>* **SOMETHING. / YELLOW RAINBOW** —

—— added **RICHARD TANDY** – hapsicord, keyboards (of The UGLYS)

Jan 69. (7") *(RZ 3015) <1020>* **BLACKBERRY WAY. / SOMETHING** `1`

—— **RICK PRICE** (b.10 Jun'44) – bass (ex-SIGHT'N'SOUND) repl. BURTON + TANDY whom became part of The UGLYS

Aug 69. (7") *(RZ 3021) <1119>* **CURLY. / THIS TIME TOMORROW** `12`

Feb 70. (lp) *(SLRZ 1012) <SP 4259>* **SHAZAM**
 – Hello Susie / Beautiful daughter / Cherry blossom clinic revisted / Fields of people / Don't make my baby blue / The last thing on my mind. *(re-iss. 1982 on 'Cube';) (cd-iss. Mar93 on 'Repertoire' +=;) – Stephanie knows who / So you want to be a rock'n'roll star / Something else / It'll be me / Sunshine help me.*

—— now trio of **WOOD, PRICE** and **BEVAN**. (WAYNE became cabaret singer)

Mar 70. (7") *(RZ 3026) <1197>* **BRONTOSAURUS. / LIGHTNING NEVER STRIKES TWICE** `7`

—— added **JEFF LYNNE** (b.30 Dec'47) – vocals, guitar, keys (ex-IDLE RACE)

	Fly	Capitol
Sep 70. (7") (BUG 2) **WHEN ALICE COMES BACK TO THE FARM. / WHAT?**	☐	☐
Oct 70. (lp) (HIFLY 1) <ST 658> **LOOKING ON** – Looking on / Turkish tram conductor blues / What? / When Alice comes back to the farm / Open up said the world at the door / Brontosaurus / Feel too good. (cd-iss. Mar93 on 'Repertoire'+=;) – Blackberry way / Something / Curly / This time tomorrow / Lightning never strikes twice.	☐	☐

	Harvest	Capitol
May 71. (7"; unissued) (HAR 5036) **ELLA JAMES. / NO TIME**	–	–
Jun 71. (7") (HAR 5038) <3126> **TONIGHT. / DON'T MESS ME UP**	11	☐
Jul 71. (lp) (SHSP 4013) <ST 811> **MESSAGE FROM THE COUNTRY** – Message from the country / Ella James / No time / Don't mess me up / Until your moma's gone / It wasn't my idea to dance / The minister / Ben Crawley Steel Company / The words of Aaron / My Marge. (cd-iss. Jul94 on 'Beat Goes On'; BGOCD 238)	☐	☐

	Harvest	U.A.
Oct 71. (7") (HAR 5043) <50876> **CHINATOWN. / DOWN ON THE BAY**	23	☐

—— (Aug71) Now a trio when RICK PRICE left to go solo. The other three (WOOD, LYNNE and BEVAN) continued with The MOVE although they formed ELECTRIC LIGHT ORCHESTRA. The MOVE made one more single below before ROY WOOD also undertook solo career and formed WIZZARD.

May 72. (7"m) (HAR 5050) <50928> **CALIFORNIA MAN. / DO YA / ELLA JAMES**	7	☐

– compilations, etc. –

Mar 71. (lp) Fly; (TON 3) **THE BEST OF THE MOVE**	☐	–
Apr 72. (7"ep) MagniFly; (ECHO 104) **FIRE BRIGADE / I CAN HEAR THE GRASS GROW. / FLOWERS IN THE RAIN / NIGHT OF FEAR**	☐	–
Feb 73. (7") United Artists; <202> **TONIGHT. / MY MARGE**	–	
Feb 73. (lp) United Artists; <UAS 5666> **SPLIT ENDS**	–	
May 74. (lp) A&M; <SP 3625> **THE BEST OF THE MOVE**	–	
Jun 74. (7") A&M; **WILD TIGER WOMAN. / ZING WENT THE STRINGS OF MY HEART**	–	
Jul 74. (lp) Music For Pleasure; (MFP 50158) **ROY WOOD AND THE MOVE**	☐	☐
Sep 74. (7") Harvest; (HAR 5086) / United Artists; <50928> **DO YA. / NO TIME**	☐	93 Oct72
Oct 74. (lp) Harvest; (SHSP 4035) **CALIFORNIA MAN**	☐	–
Mar 78. (d-lp) Cube; (TOOFA 5-6) **SHAZAM / THE MOVE**	☐	–
May 78. (lp) Hallmark; (SHM 952) **THE GREATEST HITS VOL.1**	☐	–
Sep 79. (lp) Harvest; (SHSM 2029) **THE MOVE SHINES ON**	☐	–
Oct 81. (d-lp/d-c) Platinum; (PLAT/+C 1001) **THE PLATINUM COLLECTION**	☐	–
Jul 82. (7") Old Gold; (OG 9227) **NIGHT OF FEAR. / I CAN HEAR THE GRASS GROW**	☐	–
Aug 82. (7") Dakota; (BAK 6) **BLACKBERRY WAY. / I CAN HEAR THE GRASS GROW**	☐	–
Aug 82. (7") Dakota; (BAK 7) **NIGHT OF FEAR. / FIRE BRIGADE**	☐	–
Aug 82. (7") Dakota; (BAK 8) **FLOWERS IN THE RAIN. / BRONTOSAURUS**	☐	–
Nov 84. (d-lp/c) Sierra; (FEDD/CFEDD 1005) **OFF THE RECORD WITH THE MOVE**	☐	–
Apr 86. (d-lp/c/cd) Castle; (CCS LP/MC/CD 135) **THE COLLECTION**	☐	–
Sep 86. (12"ep) Archive; (TOF 111) **ARCHIVE 4** – I can hear the grass grow / Flowers in the rain / Fire brigade / Blackberry way.	☐	–
Jul 88. (lp/c) Knight; (KN LP/MC 10011) **NIGHTRIDING**	☐	–
Mar 90. (7") Old Gold; (OG 9226) **FLOWERS IN THE RAIN. / FIRE BRIGADE**	☐	–
Mar 91. (cd/c) Music Club; (MC CD/TC 009) **THE BEST OF THE MOVE**	☐	–
Nov 92. (cd) Dojo; (EARLD 7) **THE EARLY YEARS**	☐	–
Oct 94. (cd) Disky; **THE MOVE**	☐	–
Mar 95. (cd) Band Of Joy; (BOJCD 011) **BBC SESSIONS**	☐	–

ROY WOOD

in two bands (MOVE and ELO) had also gone solo. ROY played mostly every instrument himself.

	Harvest	U.A.
Feb 72. (7") (HAR 5058) **WHEN GRAN'MA PLAYS THE BANJO. / WAKE UP**	☐	☐

—— ROY WOOD solo (although he continued with his new band WIZZARD, see below)

Jun 73. (lp) (SHVL 803) <VALA 168> **BOULDERS** – Songs of praise / Wake up / Rock down low / Nancy sing me a song / Dear Elaine / a) All the way over the hill, b) Irish loafer (and his hen) / Miss Clarke and the computer / When gran'ma plays the banjo / Rock medley: a) Rockin' shoes, b) She's too good for me, c) Locomotive. (re-iss. Oct77/ RI 2021) (cd-iss. Mar94 on 'Beat Goes On'; BGOCD 219)	15	☐
Sep 73. (7") (HAR 5074) **DEAR ELAINE. / SONGS OF PRAISE**	18	☐
Nov 73. (7") (HAR 5078) **FOREVER. / MUSIC TO COMMIT SUICIDE BY**	8	☐
Jun 74. (7") (HAR 5083) **GOING DOWN THE ROAD. / THE PREMIUM BOND THEME**	13	☐

	Jet	U.A.
May 75. (7") (JET 754) **OH WHAT A SHAME. / BENGAL JIM**	13	☐
Nov 75. (7") (JET 761) **LOOK THRU' THE EYES OF A FOOL. / STRIDER**	☐	☐
Dec 75. (lp) (JETLP 12) <LA 575> **MUSTARD** – Mustard / Any old time will do / The rain came down on everything / You sure got		

it now / Why does such a pretty girl sing those sad songs / The song / Look thru' the eyes of a fool / Interlude / Get on down home / Rock'n'roll winter. (re-iss. as 'THE WIZZARD – ROY WOOD')

Mar 76. (7"; as ROY WOOD'S WIZZARD) (JET 768) **INDIANA RAINBOW. / THE THING IS THIS (THIS IS THE THING)**	☐	–
May 76. (7") (JET 785) **ANY OLD TIME WILL DO. / THE RAIN CAME DOWN ON EVERYTHING**	☐	–
May 76. (7") **ANY OLD TIME WILL DO. / WHY DOES SUCH A PRETTY GIRL SING THOSE SAD SONGS**	–	–

—— In Oct77, ROY WOOD made a duo single with ANNIE HASLAM of RENAISSANCE 'I NEVER BELIEVED IN LOVE. / INSIDE MY LIFE'. (from HASLAM's lp 'ANNIE IN WONDERLAND')

WIZZARD

(were formed August 1972 by **ROY WOOD** with **RICK PRICE**, plus other ex-MONGREL musicians) **CHARLIE GRIMA** – drums and **KEITH SMART** – drums also **HUGH McDOWELL** – cello and **BILL HUNT** – keyboards (both ex-ELO) and **NICK PENTELOW** – saxophone and **MICK BURNEY** – saxophone (ex-DALTONS)

	Harvest	U.A.
Nov 72. (7") (HAR 5062) **BALL PARK INCIDENT. / THE CARLSBERG SPECIAL**	6	☐
Apr 73. (7") (HAR 5070) **SEE MY BABY JIVE. / BEND OVER BEETHOVEN**	1	☐
Apr 73. (lp) (SHSP 4025) <LA 042> **WIZZARD BREW** – You can dance the rock & roll / Meet me at the jailhouse / Jolly cup of tea / Buffalo station – Get down to Memphis / Gotta crush / Wear a fast gun.	29	☐
Aug 73. (7") (HAR 5076) **ANGEL FINGERS. / YOU GOT THE JUMP ON ME**	1	☐

—— (Sep73) trimmed slightly when McDOWELL returned to ELECTRIC LIGHT ORCH. (Nov73) **BOB BRADY** – keyboards (ex-APPLEJACKS) repl. HUNT

Nov 73. (7") (HAR 5173) **I WISH IT COULD BE CHRISTMAS EVERY DAY. / ROB ROY'S NIGHTMARE**	4	☐

	Warners	U.A.
Apr 74. (7") (K 16357) **ROCK'N'ROLL WINTER. / DREAM OF UNWIN**	6	☐
Aug 74. (7") (K 16434) **THIS IS THE STORY OF MY LOVE (BABY). / MIXTURE**	34	☐
Aug 74. (lp) (K 56029) <LA 219> **INTRODUCING EDDY AND THE FALCONS** – (intro) / Eddy's rock / Brand new '88' / You got me runnin' / I dun lotsa cryin' over you / This is the story of my love / Everyday I wonder / Crazy jeans / Come back Karen / We're gonna rock & roll tonight.	19	☐
Oct 74. (7") (K 16466) **YOU'VE GOT ME RUNNIN'. / IT'S JUST MY IMAGINATION**	☐	☐
Dec 74. (7") (K 16497) **ARE YOU READY TO ROCK. / MARATHON MAN**	8	☐

—— (Feb75) **WOOD** was just left with **PRICE** and **BURNEY**, and sessioners. (BRADY joined FAIRPORT CONVENTION) (SMART joined ROCKIN' BERRIES)

	Jet	not iss.
Oct 75. (7") (JET 758) **RATTLESNAKE ROLL. / CAN'T HELP MY FEELINGS**	☐	–

ROY WOOD'S WIZZO BAND

(**ROY** only retained stalwart **RICK PRICE** now on pedal steel) also **GRAHAM GALLERY** – bass / **DAVE DONOVAN** – drums / **PAUL ROBBINS** – keyboards / **BILLY PAUL** – alto sax / **BOB WILSON** – trombone

	Warners	Warners
Aug 77. (7") (WB 16961) **THE STROLL. / JUBILEE**	☐	☐
Sep 77. (lp) (K 56388) <3065> **SUPERACTIVE WIZZO** – Life is wonderful / Waitin' at the door / Another wrong night / Sneakin' / Giant footsteps (jubilees) / Earthrise.	☐	☐

ROY WOOD

Feb 78. (7") (K 17094) **DANCIN' AT THE RAINBOW'S END. / WAITING AT THE DOOR**	☐	–
Nov 78. (7") (K 17248) **KEEP YOUR HANDS ON THE WHEEL. / JUBILEE**	☐	–
May 79. (7"/7"pic-d) (K/KP 17459) **(WE'RE) ON THE ROAD AGAIN. / SAXMANIACS**	☐	–
Aug 79. (lp) (BSK 3247) **ON THE ROAD AGAIN** – (We're) On the road again / Wings over the sea / Keep your hands on the wheel / Colourful lady / Road rocket / Backtown sinner / Jimmy lad / Dancin' at the rainbow's end / Another night / Way beyond the rain.	☐	–

ROY WOOD'S HELICOPTERS

with **MIKE DEACON** (ex-DARTS) / + members of RENAISSANCE & MAGNUM

	Cheapskate	not iss.
Nov 80. (7") (CHEAP 6) **GIVIN' YOUR HEART AWAY. / ROCK CITY**	☐	–

	E.M.I.	not iss.
Mar 81. (7") (EMI 5156) **GREEN GLASS WINDOWS. / DRIVING SONG**	☐	–

—— (released album in Jun81 'THE MANCUNIAN WAY' with 'Roy Perry'? on Deroy)

ROY WOOD

Jun 81. (7") (EMI 5203) **DOWN TO ZERO. / OLYMPIC FLYER**	☐	–
Jan 82. (7") (EMI 5261) **IT'S NOT EASY. / MOONRISER**	☐	–

	Cheapskate	not iss.
Dec 82. (7") (CHEAP 12) **SING OUT THE OLD. / WATCH THIS SPACE**	☐	–

		Legacy	not iss.
May 85.	(7"/12") *(LGY/+T 24)* **UNDERFIRE. / ON TOP OF THE WORLD**	☐	-
Nov 85.	(7"/12") *(LGY/+T 32)* **SING OUT THE OLD . . . BRING IN THE NEW.** / ('A'instrumental)	☐	-
Oct 86.	(7") *(LGY 53)* **RAINING IN THE CITY.** / ('A'instrumental)	☐	-
Feb 87.	(lp/c) *(LLP/LLK 106)* **STARTING UP**	☐	-

– Red cars are after me / Raining in the city / Under fire / Turn your body to the light / Hot cars / Starting up / Keep it steady / On top of the world / Ships in the night. *(cd-iss. May93 on 'Castle'; CLACD 387)*

—— WOOD had earlier (late '86) featured on DOCTOR & THE MEDICS Top 50 version of ABBA's 'Waterloo'.

		Woody	not iss.
Dec 95.	(c-s/cd-s; as The ROY WOOD BIG BAND) *(WOODY 001 CD/MC)* **I WISH IT WOULD BE CHRISTMAS EVERYDAY /**	☐	-

– (ROY WOOD) compilations, etc. –

Oct 74.	(lp; WIZZARD) *Harvest; (SHSP 4034)* **SEE MY BABY JIVE**		☐
Apr 76.	(d-lp) *Harvest; (SHDW 408)* **THE ROY WOOD STORY** (solo unless stated)		☐

– Ball park incident (WIZZARD) / Until you moma's gone / Dear Elaine / Ella James (MOVE) / First movement (ELECTRIC LIGHT ORCHESTRA) / California man (MOVE) / Whisper in the night / Chinatown (MOVE) / You can dance your rock'n'roll / Forever / Angel fingers (WIZZARD) / Look at me now (ELECTRIC LIGHT ORCHESTRA) / Tonight (MOVE) / See me baby jive (WIZZARD). *(re-iss. 1979 as 'YOU CAN DANCE THE ROCK'N'ROLL (THE ROY WOOD YEARS 1971-73)' lp/c; SHSM/TC-SHSM 2030)* *(re-iss. Jul89; CZ 177)* – Wake up / It wasn't my idea to dance / Nancy, sing me a song / Songs of praise.

Jul 82.	(lp) *Speed; (SPEED 1000)* **THE SINGLES** (all his bands' work)	37	-

– See my baby jive / Are you ready to rock / Oh what a shame / Fire brigade / Forever / I can hear the grass grow / O.T.T. / Blackberry way / Angel fingers / We're on the road again / Flowers in the rain / Green grass windows / Keep your hands on the wheel / Rock & roll winter / This is the story of my love (baby).

Nov 82.	(7") *Speed; (SPEED 5)* **O.T.T. / Mstery Song (Wizzo Band: CALIFORNIA MAN live)**	☐	-
Nov 84.	(7"; WIZZARD) *Harvest; (HAR 5173)* **I WISH IT COULD BE CHRISTMAS EVERY DAY. / SEE MY BABY JIVE**	☐	-
	(12"+=) *(12HAR 5173)* – Forever.		
Apr 85.	(lp/c) *Music For Pleasure; (MFP 41-5697-1/-4)* **THE BEST OF ROY WOOD (1970-1974)**	☐	-
Jul 87.	(7") *Jet; (JET7 048)* **ONE-TWO-THREE. / OH WHAT A SHAME**	☐	-
	(12"+=) *(JET12 048)* – ('A'extended).		
1988.	(cd-ep) *Counterpoint; (CDEP 12)* **ARE YOU READY TO ROCK / ROCK'N'ROLL WINTER.** / (2 by SLADE)	☐	-
Feb 90.	(cd/c) *Action Replay; (CDAR/ARLC 1009)* **THE BEST AND THE REST OF ROY WOOD & WIZZARD** *(re-iss. May91; same)*	☐	-
Oct 92.	(cd-ep; WIZZARD) *Old Gold; (...)* **SEE MY BABY JIVE / ANGEL FINGERS / BALL PARK INCIDENT** *(re-iss. Nov95 on 'Carlton'; 126236334-2)*	☐	-
Sep 93.	(cd/c) *Connoisseur; (VSOP CD/MC 189)* **THE ROY WOOD SINGLES**	☐	-
	– (Night Of Fear; MOVE – Oh What A Shame; ROY WOOD).		
May 94.	(cd/c) *BR Music; (BR CD/MC 50)* **THE DEFINITIVE ROY WOOD**	☐	-
Jul 95.	(cd/c) *Emporio; (EMPR CD/MC 573)* **16 GREATS OF ROY WOOD & WIZZARD)**	☐	-

MOVING SIDEWALKS (see under ⇒ ZZ TOP)

Alison MOYET

Born: GENEVIEVE ALISON MOYET, 18 Jun'61, Basildon, Essex, England. Nicknamed ALF by her French father, the singer's first forays into the music business came with Southend R&B outfits, The VICARS and The SCREAMING ABDABS. Early in 1982, she was invited by ex-DEPECHE MODE mainman, VINCE CLARKE, to join him in synth-pop duo, YAZOO (YAZ in the US). Over the course of the ensuing 18 months, the pair were a regular feature in the UK Top 20 with classic singles such as 'DON'T GO'. Their partnership was relatively brief however and after only two albums, both CLARKE and MOYET went their separate ways; CLARKE initially to The ASSEMBLY and later ERASURE, MOYET to a fairly successful if patchy solo career. Signing a solo contract with 'CBS-Columbia' around the same time as marrying long-time boyfriend Malcolm Lee and setting up home in Hertfordshire, MOYET got off to a good start with a summer '84 Top 10 hit, 'LOVE RESURRECTION'. A big woman with an even bigger vocal range, MOYET used her No.1 debut album, 'ALF' (1984) as a platform for her rich, earthy blues-soaked voice. The quality of the songs didn't always match the quality of the singer; when they did – as on the likes of 'ALL CRIED OUT' (another Top 10 hit) – MOYET was a diva to reckon with. Her smoky, sultry style definitely owed something of a debt to the golden era of jazz and with a graceful ease, MOYET applied her tonsils to Billie Holiday's 'THAT OLE DEVIL CALLED LOVE', narrowly missing the number one slot in Spring '85. Aiming straight for the coffee table pop-rock market, Top 10 hits 'IS THIS LOVE' and 'WEAK IN THE PRESENCE OF BEAUTY' were radically different, dividing critics but bolstering sales of another near No.1 album, 'RAINDANCING' (1987). More true to form was a cover of vintage standard, 'LOVE LETTERS', a Top 5 hit (not included on the album) later in the year. Taking time out in the latter half of the 80's, MOYET finally returned

in Spring '91 with the 'HOODOO' album, a stylistically diverse record that found her finally making the space to exercise her voice to the max. Critics marvelled but the public weren't so supportive, the album almost breaking the Top 10 but failing to produce any hit singles. She did make it back into the Top 20 with 1994's 'WHISPERING YOUR NAME' single although the accompanying album, 'ESSEX' made little headway. More successful was 1995's No.1 retrospective, 'SINGLES', gathering together for the the first time the cream of both her YAZOO and solo careers. • **Songwriters:** TONY SWAIN and STEVE JOLLEY wrote, produced and played on her debut album. She also covered; INVISIBLE (Lamont-Dozier) / LOVE LETTERS (Ketty Lester) / ROCK AND ROLL (Led Zeppelin). • **Trivia:** Female comedy duo FRENCH & SAUNDERS featured on the video of 'LOVE LETTERS'.

Album rating: ALF (*7) / RAINDANCING (*5) / HOODOO (*5) / ESSEX (*4) / SINGLES compilation (*7)

ALISON MOYET – vocals with session people

		C.B.S.	Columbia	
Jun 84.	(7") *(A 4497) <05411>* **LOVE RESURRECTION. / BABY I DO**	10	82	Jul85
	(12") *(TA 4497)* – ('A'-Love injected mix).			
Sep 84.	(7"/ext-12") *(A/TA 4757)* **ALL CRIED OUT. / STEAL ME BLIND**	8		
Nov 84.	(lp/c) *(CBS/40 26229) <39956>* **ALF**	1	45	Mar85
	– Love resurrection / Honey for the bees / For you only / Invisible / Steal me blind / All cried out / Money mile / Twisting the knife / Where hides sleep. *(cd-iss. Feb85; CD 26229)* *(re-iss. Sep96 on 'Columbia' cd/c; 483836-2/-4)*			
Nov 84.	(7"/remix-12") *(A/TA 4930) <04781>* **INVISIBLE. / HITCH HIKE (with The DARTS)**	21	31	Feb85
	(d7"+=) *(DA 4930)* – Love resurrection / Baby I do.			
Mar 85.	(7") *(A 6044)* **THAT OLE DEVIL CALLED LOVE. / DON'T BURN DOWN THE BRIDGES**	2		
	(12"+=) *(TA 6044)* – ('A'-Jazz version).			
	(d7"+=) *(DA 6044)* – ('A'live) / Twisting the knife (live).			
Aug 85.	(7") **MONEY MILE. / FOR YOU ONLY**	-		
Nov 86.	(7") *(MOYET 1)* **IS THIS LOVE? / BLOW WIND BLOW**	3		
	(12"+=) *(MOYETX 1)* – ('A'-L.A. mix).			
	(12") *(MOYETX1)* – ('A'side) / For you only (Europa mix).			
Mar 87.	(7") *(MOYETT 2)* **WEAK IN THE PRESENCE OF BEAUTY. / TO WORK ON YOU**	6		
	(ext-12"+=) *(MOYETX 2)* – Take my imagination to bed.			
	(d7"+=) *(MOYETD 2)* – Is this love / Blow wind blow.			
Apr 87.	(lp/c/cd) *(450152-1/-4/-2) <40653>* **RAINDANCING**	2	94	Jun87
	– Weak in the presence of beauty / Ordinary girl / You got me wrong / Without you / Sleep like breathing / Is this love? / Blow wind blow / Glorious love / When I say no (no giveaway) / Stay. *(re-iss. Mar90; same)*			
May 87.	(7") *(MOYET 3)* **ORDINARY GIRL. / PALM OF YOUR HAND (CLOAK AND DAGGER)**	43		
	(12"+=) *(MOYETT 3)* – ('A'-dance remix).			
Sep 87.	(7") *(MOYET 4)* **SLEEP LIKE BREATHING. / LOVE RESURRECTION (live)**			
	(12"+=) *(MOYETT 4)* – Ne me quitte pas (live).			
Nov 87.	(7") *(MOYET 5)* **LOVE LETTERS. / THIS HOUSE**	4		
	(12"+=) *(MOYETT 5)* – ('A'extended).			
	(cd-s++=) *(MOYETC 5)* – Ne me quitte pas (live).			

		Columbia	Columbia
Mar 91.	(7"/c-s) *(656757-7/-4)* **IT WON'T BE LONG. / MY RIGHT A.R.M.**	50	☐
	(12"+=/cd-s+=) *(656757-6/-2)* – Take of me.		
Apr 91.	(cd/c/lp) *(468272-2/-4/-1)* **HOODOO**	11	☐
	– Footsteps / It won't be long / This house / Rise / Wishing you were here / (Meeting with my) Main man / Hoodoo / Back where I belong / My right A.R.M. / Never too late / Find me.		
May 91.	(7"/c-s) *(656939-7/-4)* **WISHING YOU WERE HERE. / BACK WHERE I BELONG**	72	☐
	(12"+=/cd-s+=/pic-cd-s+=) *(656939-6/-2/-5)* – ('B'mixes).		
Oct 91.	(7"/c-s) *(657515-7/-4)* **THIS HOUSE. / COME BACK HOME**	40	☐
	(cd-s+=) *(657515-2)* – Love letters / That ole Devil called love.		
Oct 93.	(7"/c-s) *(659596-7/-4)* **FALLING. / ODE TO A BOY**	44	☐
	(cd-s+=) *(659596-2)* – ('A'mix).		
Feb 94.	(c-s) *(660162-4)* **WHISPERING YOUR NAME / F.O.S.**	18	☐
	(12") *(660162-6)* – ('A'extended mixes) / ('A'-Vince Clarke mix).		
	(cd-s) *(660162-2)* – ('A'side) / Rise / Wishing you were here / Rock and roll (all live).		
	(12"/cd-s) *(660162-5/-0)* – (*'A'side) / Hoodoo / Back where I belong.		
Mar 94.	(cd/c/lp) *(475955-2/-4/-1) <57448>* **ESSEX**	24	☐
	– Falling / Whispering your name / Getting into something / Dorothy / So am I / And I know / Ode to boy / Satellite / Another living day / Boys own / Take of me / Ode to boy II / Whispering your name (single mix).		
May 94.	(c-s) *(660356-4)* **GETTING INTO SOMETHING** / ('A'mix)	51	-
	(12"+=/cd-s+=) *(660356-6/-2)* – Never too late.		
	(cd-s++=) *(660356-5)* – Ne me quitte pas.		
Oct 94.	(c-s) *(660795-4)* **ODE TO BOY / LIFE IN A HOLE**	59	-
	(cd-s) *(660795-2)* – (2-'A'mixes) / Sunderland Glynn.		
	(12") *(660795-6)* – (5-'A'mixes).		
May 95.	(cd/c) *(480663-2/-4)* **SINGLES** (compilation)	1	☐
	– The first time ever I saw your face / Only you (YAZOO) / Nobody's diary (YAZOO) / Situation (YAZOO) / Love resurrection / All cried out / Invisible / That ole Devil called love / Is this love? / Weak in the presence of beauty / Ordinary girl / Love letters / It won't be long / Wishing you were here / This house / Falling / Whispering your name / Getting into somthing / Ode to boy II / Solid wood. *(d-cd-iss. Apr96 w/ 'LIVE'+=; 480663-9)* – Getting into something / Chain of fools / Love letters / All cried out / Dorothy / Ode to boy / Is this love? / Nobody's diary / Whispering your name / There are worse things I could do.		
Jun 95.	(c-s) *(662117-4)* **THE FIRST TIME EVER I SAW YOUR FACE / BLUE**	☐	-
	(cd-s+=) *(662117-2)* – Ode to boy / First time (are you sure?)		
	(cd-s+=) *(662117-5)* –		

Aug 95. (c-s) *(662326-4)* **SOLID WOOD / BLUE / ODE TO BOY** 〔44〕 〔-〕
(cd-s+=) *(662326-2)* – There are worse things I could do.
(cd-s+=) *(662326-5)* – Whispering your name / The first time ever I saw your face.

– compilations, etc. –

1988.　　(d-cd) *C.B.S.; (CDAM 241)* **ALF / RAINDANCING** 〔 〕 〔-〕

M PEOPLE

Formed: Manchester, England . . . 1990 by MIKE PICKERING, HEATHER SMALL and ex-ORANGE JUICE man, PAUL HEARD. A veteran of the UK club scene, PICKERING had been instrumental in the development of British house music and the rise of Manchester's Hacienda. As an A&R man for 'Factory' (he had also been a member of QUANDO QUANGO), he was responsible for the signing of the HAPPY MONDAYS while his DJ'ing credentials landed him a prime position at hip dance label, 'DeConstruction'. As well as signing acts, PICKERING initially cut tracks under the T-COY moniker before putting together M PEOPLE. Aiming to maintain a strong band profile in the faceless world of dance and develop into a longer-term albums act, the trio debuted with the forgettable 'COLOUR MY LIFE' in Spring '91. More enticing was 'HOW CAN I LOVE YOU MORE', a track that showcased SMALL's earthy, almost androgynous vocal prowess. It was also one of the better moments on debut album, 'NORTHERN SOUL' (1992), a largely uninspired affair let down by formulaic clubland songwriting. Yet 1993's 'ONE NIGHT IN HEAVEN' was a massive step forward, marrying intelligent dance-pop arrangements with a keening melody and SMALL's lung-busting soul power. The Mercury Music Prize-winning 'ELEGANT SLUMMING' (1993) confirmed it was no fluke, finely crafted songs like 'RENAISSANCE' and 'MOVING ON UP' transplanting the spirit of house music into glossy, coffee-table pop art. It's just a shame they lost that spirit with 'BIZARRE FRUIT' (1994), an album mired in insipid MOR balladry like 'SEARCH FOR THE HERO' (subsequently used on a TV car ad). Devoid of any of dance music's danger or excitement, M PEOPLE's increasingly sterile sound nevertheless found a lucrative market; new 4th member SHOVELL having now been added. So much so that their label were moved to release 'BIZARRE FRUIT II' the following year, a remix set with their pointless hit cover of The Small Faces' 'ITCHYCOO PARK' tagged on for good measure. Further albums, 'FRESCO' (1997) and a compilation set the following year consolidated the trio's position as predictable AOD (Adult Orientated Dance) mainstays. • **Songwriters:** PICKERING-HEARD and covers; SOMEDAY (Marshall Jefferson) / DON'T LOOK ANY FURTHER (hit. Dennis Edwards) / WHAT A FOOL BELIEVES (Doobie Brothers).

Album rating: NORTHERN SOUL (*5) / ELEGANT SLUMMING (*7) / BIZARRE FRUIT (*5) / FRESCO (*5) / THE BEST OF M PEOPLE compilation (*7)

HEATHER SMALL (b.20 Jan'65, London, England) – vocals (ex-HOT! HOUSE) / **MIKE PICKERING** (b.21 Feb'54) – programming (ex-QUANDO QUANGO) / **PAUL HEARD** (b. 5 Oct'60, London) – programming (ex-ORANGE JUICE, ex-WORKING WEEK) / with **JULIET ROBERTS, CARROL THOMPSON, BEVERLY SKEET, NU COLOURS, PAUL 'TUBBS' WILLIAMS** – backing vocals / **MARK BELL** – vocals / **SNAKE DAVIS** – sax, flute / **RODDY LORIMER** – trumpet / **CHRIS KIBBLE + ALISTER GAVIN** – piano / **GARETH TASKER** – bass / **ANDY GANGADEEN** – drums / **JIM WILLIAMS + GIOVANNI PARRICELLI** – guitar / **ROBIN JONES** – additional percussion

	R.C.A.	R.C.A.
May 91. (7"/c-s) *(PB/PK 44439)* **COLOUR MY LIFE (Oakenfold mix).** / **('A'-Osborne mix)** | 〔 〕 | 〔-〕
(12"+=/cd-s+=) *(PT/PD 44440)* – ('A'-Cuba mix). | |
Oct 91. (7"/c-s) *(PB/PK 44855)* **HOW CAN I LOVE YOU MORE. / HOLY LOVE** | 〔29〕 |
(cd-s+=) *(PD 44856)* – ('A'-club & acapella mixes). | |
(12") *(PT 44856)* – (above mixes). | |
Feb 92. (7"/c-s) *(PB/PK 45241)* **COLOUR MY LIFE. / SEXUAL FREEDOM** | 〔35〕 |
(12"+=/cd-s+=) *(PT/PD 45242)* – ('A'-part 2) / Landscape of love. | |
Mar 92. (cd/c/lp) *(PD/PK/PL 75157)* **NORTHERN SOUL** | 〔53〕 |
– Colour my life / How can I love you more / Inner city cruise / It's your world / Sexual freedom / Kiss it better / Tumbling down / Landscape of love / Life / Someday. *(c+=)* – Platini. *(cd++=)* – Inner city dub / Colour my life (original mix) / Kiss it better (guitar mix). *(re-iss. Nov92 on 'DeConstruction' cd/c; 74321 11777-2/-4)*

Apr 92. (7"/c-s; M PEOPLE with HEATHER SMALL) *(PB/PK 45369)* **SOMEDAY. / PLATINI** | 〔38〕 |
(12"+=/cd-s+=) *(PL/PD 45370)* – ('A'-part 2.

	Deconstr.	Epic
Oct 92. (7"/c-s) *(74321 11633-7/-4)* **EXCITED. / ('A'dub)** | 〔29〕 |
(12"+=/cd-s+=) *(74321 11633-1/-2)* – ('A'-Master mix) / ('A'Judge Jules dub). | |
Jan 93. (7"/c-s) *(74321 13023-7/-4)* **HOW CAN I LOVE YOU MORE. / ('A'-Sasha's ambient dub)** | 〔8〕 |
(12"+=/cd-s+=) *(74321 13023-1/-2)* – ('A'-Sasha's extended) / ('A'-Rollo's mix). | |
Jun 93. (7"/c-s) *(74321 15185-7/-4)* **ONE NIGHT IN HEAVEN. / ('A'-Hi-Gloss dub)** | 〔6〕 |
(12"+=/cd-s+=) *(74321 15185-1/-2)* – ('A'-Harri's dub & vocal). | |
Sep 93. (7"/c-s) *(74321 16616-7/-4)* <37392> **MOVING ON UP. / ('A'-dub)** | 〔2〕 | 〔34〕 Apr94
(12"+=/cd-s+=) *(74321 16616-1/-2)* – ('A'-Roger S gospel mixes). | |
Oct 93. (cd/c) *(74321 16678-2/-4/-1)* **ELEGANT SLUMMING** | 〔2〕 |
– One night in Heaven / Moving on up / Renaissance / You just have to be there / Love is in my soul / Don't look any further / Natural thing / Little packet / La vida loca / Melody of life. *(re-iss. Jun96; same)*
Nov 93. (7"/c-s) *(74321 17711-7/-4)* **DON'T LOOK ANY FURTHER. / LA VIDA LOCA** | 〔9〕 |
(12"+=/cd-s+=) *(74321 17711-1/-2)* – ('A'-Strip to the bone mix) / ('A'-Danny D mix). | |

Mar 94. (7"/c-s) *(74321 19413-7/-4)* **RENAISSANCE. / ('A'mix)** 〔5〕 〔 〕
(12") *(74321 19413-6)* – ('A'mixes; master / Roger S uplifting club / John Digweed's full on / MacSilva).
(cd-s++=) *(74321 19413-2)* – ('A'mixes above).
(above single used on the student TV docu-series 'The Living Soap')
Sep 94. (c-s/12"/cd-s) *(74321 23188-4/-1/-2)* **ELEGANTLY AMERICAN: ONE NIGHT IN HEAVEN (remixes). / MOVING ON UP (remixes)** 〔31〕 〔-〕
Nov 94. (7"/c-s) *(74321 24547-7/-4)* **SIGHT FOR SORE EYES. / SUGARTOWN** 〔6〕 〔 〕
(12"+=/cd-s+=) *(74321 24547-1/-2)* – ('A'mixes; master / Hed boys post-op).
Nov 94. (cd/c/lp) *(74321 24081-2/-4/-1)* **BIZARRE FRUIT** 〔4〕
– Sight for sore eyes / Search for the hero / Open your heart / Love rendezvous / Precious pearl / Sugar town / Walk away / Drive time / Padlock / . . .And finally. *(re-iss. & re-mixed Nov95 with 'BIZARRE FRUIT II'; 74321 32817-2/-4) (cd re-iss. Aug98; 74321 57755-2/-4)*
Jan 95. (12") *(74321 26153-1)* **OPEN YOUR HEART (mixes; master / Check Yer Head / Fire Island / Roach Motel)** 〔9〕
(cd-s+=) *(74321 26153-2)* – ('A'-Armand's Indian beat-down mix).
(cd-s) *(74321 26153-5)* – ('A'radio) / ('A'-Brothers In Rhythm mix) / Sight for sore eyes (E-Smoove mix).

——　the trio added **SHOVELL** (b. ANDREW LOVELL, 11 Feb'69, Jamaica) – keyboards

Jun 95. (12") *(74321 28796-1)* **SEARCH FOR THE HERO (mixes; Smith & Mighty searchin' / Smith & Mighty dub / Blacksmith's mellow flava / mastermix)** 〔9〕
(cd-s) *(74321 28796-1/-2)* – ('A'mixes; radio / Smith & Mighty plus Blacksmith mixes) / live).
Oct 95. (c-s/cd-s) *(74321 31928-4/-2)* **LOVE RENDEZVOUS / ('A'mixes)** 〔32〕
(cd-s) *(74321 31929-2)* – ('A'mixes)
(12") *(74321 31928-2)* – ('A'mixes).
Nov 95. (c-s) *(74321 33073-4)* **ITCHYCOO PARK / ('A'mix)** 〔11〕
(12"+=/cd-s+=) *(74321 33073-1/-2)* – ('A'mixes).
Sep 97. (c-s) *(74321 52300-4)* **JUST FOR YOU / ('A'mix)** 〔8〕
(12"+=/cd-s+=) *(74321 52300-1/-2)* – ('A'mixes).
Oct 97. (cd/c) *(74321 52490-23/-47/-16)* **FRESCO** 〔2〕
– Just for you / Fantasy island / Never mind love / Last night 10,000 / Smile / Red flower sunset / Angel St. / Lonely / Rhythm and blues / Believe it / Bohemia / Avalon.
Nov 97. (c-s) *(74321 54293-4)* **FANTASY ISLAND / ('A'mix)** 〔33〕
(12"+=/cd-s+=) *(74321 54293-1/-2)* – ('A'mixes).
Mar 98. (c-s) *(74321 56418-4)* **ANGEL ST. / SEARCH FOR THE HERO** 〔8〕
(cd-s+=) *(74321 56418-2)* – Sight for sore eyes (live) / One night in Heaven.
(cd-s) *(74321 56419-2)* – ('A'mixes).
Oct 98. (c-s/cd-s) *(74321 62173-4/-2)* **TESTIFY / ANGEL ST. (live) / LAST NIGHT 10,000 (live)** 〔12〕
(cd-s) *(74321 62174-2)* – ('A'-D*Influence mix) / ('A'-Rae & Christian remix) / ('A'-Big String remix).
Nov 98. (cd/c) *(<74321 61387-2/-4>)* **THE BEST OF M PEOPLE** (compilation) 〔2〕
– Testify / Search for a hero / Moving on up / Angel St. / One night in Heaven / Itchycoo park / Sight for sore eyes / Just for you / Colour my life / How can I love you more / Dreaming / Open your heart / Don't look any further / Someday / Renaisance / Fantasy island / What a fool believes. *(also d-cd; 74321 62728-2)*
Feb 99. (c-s/cd-s) *(74321 64535-4/-2)* **DREAMING / BABY DON'T CHANGE YOUR MIND (live) / THE BEST OF M PEOPLE MEGAMIX** 〔13〕
(cd-s) *(74321 64536-2)* – ('A'side) / ('A'-Morales 103.5 mix) / ('A'-Jimmy Gomez vocal remix).

> **MR. BIG** (dig out; Great Metal . . .)

> **MR. BUNGLE** (see under ⇒ FAITH NO MORE)

> **M.S.G.** (see under ⇒ SCHENKER GROUP, Michael)

MUDHONEY

Formed: Seattle, Washington, USA . . . 1988 by MARK ARM (vocals, guitar), STEVE TURNER (guitar), MATT LUKIN (bass) and DAN PETERS (drums). A band boasting impeccable credentials, ARM and TURNER had both graduated from the seminal GREEN RIVER (and The THROWN UPS), while LUKIN had previously been a member of Seattle noisemongers, The MELVINS. With as much a claim to the 'Godfathers of Grunge' crown as labelmates NIRVANA, MUDHONEY released the definitive 'Sub Pop' single in 1988 with 'TOUCH ME I'M SICK'. Arguably one of the few tracks to ever match the primal howl of The STOOGES, the single was a revelation, a cathartically dumb three chord bludgeon with ARM shrieking over the top like a man who was, erm, very sick indeed. A mini-album followed shortly after, the wonderfully titled 'SUPERFUZZ BIGMUFF' (rather disappointingly named after STEVE TURNER's favourite effects pedals, apparently). Visceral, dirty, fuzz-drenched rock'n'roll, this was one of the seminal records of the 80's and the blueprint for "grunge", a term that would later become bastardised to represent a glut of snooze-worthy, sub-metal toss. There was also a deep, underlying sense of unease and melancholy to these songs (especially 'NO ONE HAS' and 'NEED') that gave MUDHONEY an edge over most of their contemporaries, a subsequent cover of SONIC YOUTH'S 'HALLOWEEN' (released as a split single with SONIC YOUTH covering 'TOUCH ME..') sounding positively evil. Given all this, then, the debut album proper, 'MUDHONEY', was regarded as something of a disappointment when it was finally released in late '89. Nevertheless, 'THIS GIFT' and 'HERE COMES SICKNESS' were worth the price of admission alone. By summer

'91, MUDHONEY had modified their sound somewhat, releasing the 'LET IT SLIDE' EP as a taster for the forthcoming 'EVERY GOOD BOY DESERVES FUDGE' album (a UK Top 40 hit). The intensity of the EP harked back to 'SUPERFUZZ..', this time with more of a retro garage-punk feel on the blistering 'PAPERBACK LIFE' and 'OUNCE OF DECEPTION'. The album continued in this direction, adding funky (in the loosest sense of the term) hammond organ and harmonica to the mutant guitar buzz. Hell, they even came close to a pop song with 'GOOD ENOUGH'. Following a financial dispute with 'Sub Pop', MUDHONEY followed NIRVANA into the big league, signing with 'Reprise' and releasing the lacklustre 'PIECE OF CAKE' (1992). Having sold their souls to the corporate 'devil', it seemed MUDHONEY had had the life sucked out of them, the rough edges smoothed into a major production gloss. The mini-album, 'FIVE DOLLAR BOB'S MOCK COOTER STEW' (1993) was an improvement but it took Seattle legend, Jack Endino to summon forth the raw spontaneity of old on 'MY BROTHER THE COW' (1995), a return to form of sorts, notably on 'INTO YOUR SCHTIK' and 'GENERATION SPOKESMODEL'. MUDHONEY subsequently took a few years hiatus in which ARM went on tour with his side-project, BLOODLOSS, while TURNER continued with his label, 'Super-Electro' (MUDHONEY were allowed dual output for the imprint) and PETERS guested for solo MIKE JOHNSON (DINOSAUR JR). In the Autumn of '98, the quartet were back once again, although the album, 'TOMORROW HIT TODAY', disappointed most of their hardcore fanbase. • **Covers:** HATE THE POLICE (Dicks) / EVOLUTION (Spacemen 3) / OVER THE TOP (Motorhead) / PUMP IT UP (Elvis Costello) / TONIGHT I THINK I'M GONNA GO DOWNTOWN (Jimmie Dale Gilmore) / BUCKSKIN STALLION BLUES (Townes Van Zandt). MARK ARM solo:- MASTERS OF WAR (Bob Dylan).

Album rating: SUPERFUZZ BIGMUFF mini (*7) / MUDHONEY (*6) / BOILED BEEF & ROTTING TEETH (*6) / EVERY GOOD BOY DESERVES FUDGE (*7) / PIECE OF CAKE (*5) / MY BROTHER THE COW (*5) / TOMORROW HIT TODAY (*5)

MARK ARM (b.21 Feb'62, California) – vocals, guitar (ex-GREEN RIVER, ex-THROWN UPS) / **STEVE TURNER** (b.28 Mar'65, Houston, Texas) – guitar (ex-GREEN RIVER, ex-THROWN UPS) / **MATT LUKIN** (b.16 Aug'64, Aberdeen, Washington) – bass (ex-MELVINS) / **DAN PETERS** (b.18 Aug'67) – drums

	Glitterhouse	Sub Pop
Aug 88. (7",7"brown) <SP 18> **TOUCH ME I'M SICK. / SWEET YOUNG THING AIN'T SWEET NO MORE**	-	
Oct 88. (12"ep) (GR 0034) <SP 21> **SUPERFUZZ BIGMUFF** – No one has / If I think / In 'n' out of grace / Need / Chain that door / Mudride.		
Jan 89. (7",7"clear) <SP 26> ('A'side by 'Sonic Youth'). / **TOUCH ME I'M SICK**	-	
Jun 89. (7",7"white) (GR 060) <SP 33> **YOU GOT IT (KEEP IT OUTTA MY FACE). / BURN IT CLEAN / NEED (demo)** (re-iss. May93; same)		
Oct 89. (7",7"purple,12") (GR 0070) <SP 44AA> **THIS GIFT. / BABY HELP ME FORGET / REVOLUTION** (re-iss. May93; same)		
Oct 89 (lp/c/cd) (GR 0069) <SP 44/+A/B> **MUDHONEY** – This gift / Flat out f***ed / Get into yours / You got it / Magnolia caboose babyshit / Come to mind / Here comes sickness / Running loaded / The further I go / By her own hand / When tomorrow hits / Dead love.		
Jun 90. (7",7"pink) (GR 0102) <SP 63> **YOU'RE GONE. / THORN / YOU MAKE ME DIE** (re-iss. May93; same)	60	

	Sub Pop	Sub Pop
Jul 91. (7",12"grey) (SP 15154) <SP 95> **LET IT SLIDE. / OUNCE OF DECEPTION / CHECKOUT TIME** (cd-s+=) (SP 95B) – Paperback life / The money will roll right in.	60	
Aug 91. (lp/c/cd) <SP 160/+A/B> **EVERY GOOD BOY DESERVES FUDGE** – Generation genocide / Let it slide / Good enough / Something so clear / Thorn / Into the drink / Broken hands / Who you drivin' now / Move out / Shoot the Moon / Fuzzgun '91 / Poking around / Don't fade IV / Check out time.	34	

— MARK + STEVE took up time in MONKEYWRENCH, and DAN joined SCREAMING TREES, after below album.

	Warners	Reprise
Oct 92. (7"/c-s) (W 0137/+C) **SUCK YOU DRY. / DECEPTION PASS** (12"+=/cd-s+=) (W 0137 T/CD) – Underride / Over the top.	65	-
Oct 92. (cd/c) <(4509 90073-2/-4)> **PIECE OF CAKE** – No end in sight / Make it now / Suck you dry / Blinding sun / Thirteenth floor opening / Youth body expression explosion / I'm spun / Take me there / Living wreck / Let me let you down / Ritzville / Acetone.	39	
Jan 93. (cd-s) <40741> **BLIDING SUN /**	-	
Oct 93. (m-cd/m-c/m-lp) <(9362 45439-2/-4/-)> **FIVE DOLLAR BOB'S MOCK COOTER STEW** – In the blood / No song III / Between you & me kid / Six two one / Make it now again / Deception pass / Underide.		

— In Mar'94, MUDHONEY released a collab with JIMMIE DALE GILMOUR; 7"yellow/cd-ep 'BUCKSKIN STALLION BLUES' for 'Sub Pop' (SP 124/305/+CD) Also a single, 'PUMP IT UP, was released by 'Fox' in April '94

	Reprise	Reprise
Mar 95. (cd/c/lp) <(9362 45840-2/-4/-1)> **MY BROTHER THE COW** – Judgement, rage, retribution and thyme / Generation spokesmodel / What moves the heart? / Today, is a good day / Into yer schtik / In my finest suit / F.D.K. (Fearless Doctor KIllers) / Orange ball-pen hammer / Crankcase blues / Execution style / Dissolve / 1995.	70	
Apr 95. (7") **INTO YOUR SCHTIK. / YOU GIVE ME THE CREEPS** (above single on 'Super Electro')		
May 95. (7"colrd/c-s) (W 0292/+C) **GENERATION SPOKESMODEL. / NOT GOING DOWN THAT ROAD AGAIN** (cd-s+=) (W 0292CD) – What moves the heart live) / Judgement, rage, retribution and thyme (live).		

	Amphetam. Reptile	Amphetam. Reptile
Aug 95. (7") **GOAT CHEESE. /** (above on 'Amphetamine Reptile' and below on 'Super Electro')		
May 98. (ltd-7") (SE 716) **NIGHT OF THE HUNTED. / BRAND NEW FACE**		
Sep 98. (cd) <(9362 47054-2)> **TOMORROW HIT TODAY** – A thousand forms of mind / I have to laugh / Oblivion / Try to be kind / Poisoned water / Real low vibe / This is the life / Night of the hunted / Move with the wind / Ghost / I will fight no more forever / Beneath the valley of the underdog.		

– compilations, etc. –

	Sub Pop	Sub Pop
Nov 89. (cd-ep) Tupelo; (TUPCD 009) / Sub Pop; <SP 62> **BOILED BEEF AND ROTTING TEETH**		

THE FREEWHEELIN' MARK ARM

	Sub Pop	Sub Pop
Feb 91. (7",7"red,7"green) <(SP 87)> **MASTERS OF WAR. / MY LIFE WITH RICKETS**		Dec90

THROWN UPS

STEVE TURNER + MARK ARM + two others

	not iss.	Amphetam. Reptile
1987. (7") <Scale 5> **FLECH. /**	-	
1987. (7") <Scale 7> **SMILING PANTIES. /**	-	
1987. (7") <Scale 9> **EAT MY DUMP. /**	-	
1990. (3x7"box) <Scale 26> **MELANCHOLY GIRLHOLE** (3 singles boxed)	-	
Jan 97. (cd) <AR 55> **SEVEN YEARS GOLDEN** (compilation) – Your band sucks / She's fat / Eat my dump / Flubber mate / Bucking retards / Dude pump / The person in my bowel (is sad) / Fleshy web pit / Elephant crack / My cock is the coin / Hairy crater man / Sparse tits / Smiling panties / Be correct / Melancholy girlhole / Stock boy, superhero / Flech / Lard Butt / Sloppy pud love / Hot lunch / Ladies love me / Scabby like my love / My love is simple / R ladies R bitches / Patty has a problem / Slick lip / Thorp, Thorp.	-	

MONKEYWRENCH

— **MARK + STEVE** plus **TOM PRICE, TIM KERR + MARTIN BLAND**

	Sub Pop	Sub Pop
1992. (cd) <(SP 129CD)> **CLEAN AS A BROKE-DICK DOG** – I call my body home / Angelhead / Cold cold world / Codine / From you / Doubled over again / Great down here / Look back / Bottle up & go / The story as I was told / Notes & chords mean nothing to me / Stop this world / I'm blown.		

MUNGO JERRY

Formed: London, England ... 1969 out of GOOD EARTH and The MUNGOES, by RAY DORSET, COLIN EARL, PAUL KING and MIKE COLE. Newly signed to the 'Dawn' label, the band put in a superb performance at the Hollywood festival in Newcastle May '70 thus ensuring the massive success of their No.1 debut 45, 'IN THE SUMMERTIME'. Marrying DORSET's distinctive laid-back vocals to a chugging skiffle/jugband rhythm, the song's infectious good-time vibe duly saw it score a Top 3 placing in the States (their only US hit) while global sales eventually ran into millions. An eponymous debut album followed hot on its heels straight into the UK Top 20 although it'd be early '71 before the release of a second single, 'BABY JUMP'. Again the afro-coiffed DORSET and crew topped the chart although they couldn't quite match GERRY & THE PACEMAKERS' record of three novice consecutive hits; a third single, 'LADY ROSE', only managed the Top 5, probably due to its B-side, 'HAVE A WHIFF ON ME', being banned by the BBC. By this point their musical approach had more in common with an early 70's glam-rock scene that numbered the likes of SWEET, GARY GLITTER and T.REX. By late '71 and the Top 20 success of 'YOU DON'T HAVE TO BE IN THE ARMY TO FIGHT IN THE WAR', the original line-up (bar DORSET) had been completely replaced by JOHN GODFREY, JOHN POPE and TIM REEVES, the latter two making their debut on Spring 1972's Top 30 EP, 'OPEN UP'. 1972 also saw the release of DORSET's one and only solo set, 'COLD BLUE EXCURSION' while another sizeable hit (Top 3) arrived in summer '73 in the shape of 'ALRIGHT, ALRIGHT, ALRIGHT'. Lifted from the similarly titled album, 'LONGLEGGED WOMAN DRESSED IN BLACK' marked MUNGO JERRY's last chart placing in Spring '74. A subsequent move to 'Polydor' failed to resurrect their chart fortunes, nor did a change of billing to RAY DORSET & MUNGO JERRY. Nevertheless, DORSET surprised many by penning and producing KELLY MARIE's 1980 Hi-NRG/disco nugget, 'FEELS LIKE I'M IN LOVE', a huge No.1 hit. Unfortunately, he couldn't translate this success to a further two 80's comeback singles, 'SUNSHINE REGGAE' (as MUNGO JERRY & HORIZON) and a re-done (for a hard-hitting TV anti-drink driving campaign) 'IN THE SUMMERTIME' (as MUNGO JERRY & THE BROTHERS GRIMM).

Best CD compilation: ALL THE HITS PLUS MORE (*7)

RAY DORSET (b.21 Mar'46, Ashford, Kent, England) – vocals, guitar, washboard / **COLIN EARL** (b. 6 May'42, Hampton Court, England) – piano, vocals / **PAUL KING** (b. 9 Jan'48, Dagenham, England) – guitar, banjo / **MIKE COLE** – drums

	Dawn	Janus
May 70. (7"m) (DNX 2502) **IN THE SUMMERTIME. / MIGHTY MAN / DUST PNEUMONIA BLUES**	1	-
Jun 70. (7") <125> **IN THE SUMMERTIME. / MIGHTY MAN**	-	3
Jul 70. (lp) (DNLS 3008) <7000> **MUNGO JERRY**	13	64 Aug70

– Baby let's play house / Johnny B. Badde / San Francisco Bay blues / Sad eyed Joe / Maggie / Peace in the country / See me my friend / Mother *!*!*! boogie / Tramp / Daddie's brew.

Nov 70. (7") **JOHNNY B. BADDE. / SEE ME MY FRIEND**   –

Jan 71. (7"ep) (DNX 2505) **BABY JUMP / THE MAN BEHIND THE PIANO. / LIVE FROM HOLLYWOOD: MAGGIE – MIDNIGHT SPECIAL – MIGHTY MAN**   1

—— **JOHN GODFREY** – bass, vocals, keyboards; repl. COLE

	Dawn	Bell

Apr 71. (lp) (DNLS 3020) <3027> **ELECTRONICALLY TESTED** <US title 'MEMOIRS OF A STOCKBROKER'>   14
– She rowed / I just wanna make love to you / In the summertime / Somebody stole my wife / Baby jump / Follow me down / Memoirs of a stockbroker / You better leave that whisky alone / Coming back to you. (cd-iss. Aug91 on 'Repertoire'; REP 4179)

May 71. (7"ep) (DNX 2510) **LADY ROSE / SHE ROWED. / MILK COW BLUES / LITTLE LOUIS**   5   –

	Dawn	Pye

Sep 71. (7"ep) (DNX 2513) **YOU DON'T HAVE TO BE IN THE ARMY TO FIGHT IN THE WAR / THE SUN IS SHINING. / O'REILLY / WE SHALL BE FREE**   13   –

Oct 71. (lp) (DNLS 3028) **YOU DON'T HAVE TO BE IN THE ARMY**
– You don't have to be in the army to fight in the war / Ella Speed / Pigeon stew / Take me back / Give me love / Hey Rosalyn / Northcote Arms / There's a man going round taking names / Simple things / Keep your hands off her / On a Sunday / That old dust storm.

Jan 72. (7"; by RAY DORSET) (DNS 1018) **COLD BLUE EXCURSION. / I NEED IT**   –   –

Jan 72. (lp; by RAY DORSET) (DNLS 3033) **COLD BLUE EXCURSION**
– Got to be free / Cold blue excursion / With me / Have pity on me / Time is now / Livin' ain't easy / Help your friends / I need it / Because I want you / Nightime / Maybe that's the way / Always on my mind. (cd-iss. Jul95 on 'Beat Goes On'; BGOCD 282)

—— **JOHN POPE** – keyboards; repl. COLIN who formed KING-EARL BOOGIE BAND / **TIM REEVES** – drums; repl. PAUL who also joined above

Apr 72. (7"ep) (DNX 2514) **OPEN UP / GOING BACK HOME. / I DON'T WANNA GO BACK TO SCHOOL / NO GIRL REACTION**   21   –

Jul 72. (7"ep) (DNX 2515) **MY GIRL AND ME / 46 AND ON. / IT'S A GOODIE BOOGIE WOOGIE / SUMMER'S GONE**   –   –

Aug 72. (lp) (DNLS 3041) **BOOT POWER**
– Open up / She's gone / Lookin' for my girl / See you again / The demon / My girl and me / Sweet Mary Jane / Lady Rose / Dusty road / Brand new car / 46 and on.

Jun 73. (7") (DNS 1037) **ALRIGHT, ALRIGHT, ALRIGHT. / LITTLE MISS HIPSHAKE**   3

Nov 73. (lp) (DNLS 3045) **MUNGO JERRY'S GREATEST HITS** (compilation)   –   –

	Dawn	Bell

Oct 73. (7") (DNS 1051) **WILD LOVE. / GLAD I'M A ROCKER**   32

Mar 74. (7") (DNS 1061) **LONG LEGGED WOMAN DRESSED IN BLACK. / GONNA BOP TILL I DROP**   13

Sep 74. (lp) (DNLS 3501) **LONG LEGGED WOMAN**
– Long legged woman dressed in black / Glad I'm a rocker / Gonna bop 'til I drop / Wild love / O'Reilly / The sun is shining / Summer's gone / Don't stop / Going back home / No girl reaction / Little Miss Hipshake / Milk cow blues / I don't wanna go back to school / Alright, alright, alright.

Nov 74. (7"ep) (DNS 1092) **ALL DRESSED UP / SHAKE TILL I BREAK. / TOO FAST TO LIVE / BURNIN' UP**   –

	Polydor	not iss.

Jul 75. (7") (2058 603) **CAN'T GET OVER LOVING YOU. / LET'S GO**   –   –

Nov 75. (7") (2058 654) **HELLO NADINE. / BOTTLE OF BEER**   –   –

Feb 76. (lp) (2383 364) **IMPALA SAGA**   –   –
– Hello Nadine / Never mind I've still got my rock'n'roll / Ain't too bad / Too fast / It's a secret / Impala saga / Bottle of beer / Get down on your baby / Hit me / Quiet man / Never mind I've still got my rock'n'roll (reprise).

Jul 76. (7") (2058 759) **DON'T LET GO. / GIVE ME BOP**   –   –

Apr 77. (7") (2058 868) **HEAVY FOOT STOMP. / THAT'S MY BABY**   –   –

May 77. (lp) (2383 435) **LOVIN' IN THE ALLEYS, FIGHTIN' IN THE STREETS**   –   –
– All that a woman should be / I could never start lovin' you / Lovin' in the alleys, fightin' in the streets / The grease / Dragster queen / Heavy foot stomp / Gone to Malaya / Can't keep it down / Lovin' in the morning / Just can't say goodbye.

Jul 77. (7"m) (2230 103) **ALL THAT A WOMAN SHOULD BE. / DRAGSTER QUEEN / GET DOWN ON YOUR BABY**   –   –

Nov 77. (7") (2058 947) **WE'RE O.K. / LET'S MAKE IT**   –   –

RAY DORSET & MUNGO JERRY

DORSET now with **COLIN EARL** returning alongside **CHRIS WARNES** – bass / **PETE SULLIVAN** – drums

Jul 79. (7") (2059 127) **DANCIN' IN THE STREET. / ROCKIN' ON THE ROAD**   –   –

Dec 79. (lp) (2383 485) **RAY DORSET & MUNGO JERRY**   –   –

	Satellite	not iss.

Dec 79. (7"promo; by RAY DORSET) (RAY 100) **FORGOTTEN LAND. / NEW WAY OF LIFE**   –

Feb 80. (7"; as MUNGO JERRY) (SATS 1001) **WHAT'S HER NAME. / WHY D'YOU LIE TO ME**   –

	Scratch	not iss.

Aug 80. (7"ep; as MUNGO JERRY) (HS 406) **MUNGO'S SUMMER FUN PACKAGE EP**
– Summertime holiday / Hooray it's party time / Night on the town / Really had a good time.

	Stage Coach	not iss.

Oct 81. (7") (TR 101) **KNOCKIN' ON HEAVEN'S DOOR. / HAZEL EYES**   –   –

	Mach 1	not iss.

Jun 83. (7"; by RAY DORSET & THE TARTS) (MAGIC 008) **THERE GOES MY HEART AGAIN. / THINKING OF YOU**

	Orbit	not iss.

Jun 84. (7"; as MUNGO JERRY & HORIZON) (TRIP 4) **SUNSHINE REGGAE. / NIGHTLIFE**

	Pier 7	not iss.

Mar 87. (7"; by RAY DORSET & THE FABULOUS LATICS) (KS 1152) **COME ON YOU LATICS. / (WE'RE GONNA) BLAZE AWAY**

	Illegal	not iss.

Aug 87. (7"/12"; as MUNGO JERRY & BROTHERS GRIMM) (MUNG/+T 1) **IN THE SUMMERTIME. / GET A JOB**

	Prestige	not iss.

Aug 90. (cd/c; as MUNGO JERRY) (CDPC/ZPREC 5011) **SNAKEBITE**
– Snakebite / All I wanna do / Remember me / Sugar in the bowl / Rock'n'roll rock'n'roll / Heartbreak Avenue / Pick a bale o' cotton / Red leather an' chrome / Jesse James / Right on.

	RP Media	not iss.

Nov 97. (cd-s; as MUNGO JERRY & THE MUNGO MAGS) (MJCDS 002) **TOON ARMY STOMP / LADY ROSE**

	Saraja	not iss.

May 99. (c-s/cd-s; as MUNGO JERRY & TOON TRAVELERS) (TOON MC/CD 001) **SUPPORT THE TOON. / BLAYDON RACES (THE NEWCASTLE F.A. CUP SONG)**   57   –

– compilations, etc. –

Nov 74. (lp) Golden Hour-Pye; (GH 586) **THE GOLDEN HOUR PRESENTS MUNGO JERRY'S GREATEST HITS** (cd-iss. Apr89 on 'P.R.T.'; GHCD 4)

May 75. (7") Dawn; (DNS 1113) **IN THE SUMMERTIME. / SHE ROWED**

Sep 77. (12"ep; as RAY DORSET & MUNGO JERRY) Polydor; (2230 103) **MUNGO BOX EP**
– In the summertime / Mighty man / Lady Rose / Baby jump.

Nov 77. (d-lp/c) Pye; (FILE/ZCFLD 003) **THE MUNGO JERRY FILE**

Apr 79. (7") Flashback-Pye; (FBS 7) **IN THE SUMMERTIME. / BABY JUMP**

Jul 82. (7") Old Gold; (OG 9139) **BABY JUMP. / ALRIGHT, ALRIGHT, ALRIGHT**

Nov 82. (c) P.R.T.; (ZCTON 123) **100 MINUTES OF MUNGO JERRY**

Jul 83. (7") Old Gold; (OG 9292) **IN THE SUMMERTIME. / LONG LEGGED WOMAN DRESSED IN BLACK**

Nov 84. (lp/c) Astan; (2/4 0001) **GREATEST HITS**

Nov 84. (lp/c) Astan; (2/4 0002) **SIX-A-SIDE**

Apr 85. (c) Autograph; (ASK 796) **SOUL PARTY**

Oct 85. (lp/c) Flashback-Pye; (FBLP/ZCFBL 8075) **IN THE SUMMERTIME**
(cd-iss. Aug91 on 'Repertoire'; REP 4177WZ)

Mar 86. (c) P.R.T.; (C-90) **MUNGO JERRY**

Oct 87. (lp/c/cd) P.R.T.; (PYC/PYM/PYL 6027) **TOO FAST TO LIVE AND TOO YOUNG TO DIE**

1988. (lp) Vogue; (VG 509057) **GREATEST HITS . . . LADY ROSE, ALRIGHT, ALRIGHT, ALRIGHT**   –   – import

Jul 89. (cd-s) Old Gold; (OG 6139) **IN THE SUMMERTIME. / LONG LEGGED WOMAN DRESSED IN BLACK / BABY JUMP**

May 90. (cd/c/lp) Prestige; (CDPT/ZPRST/PRST 002) **ALL THE HITS PLUS MORE**
(re-iss. Jun92; same)

Jun 90. (cd/c) Knight; (KGH CD/MC 116) **GOLDEN HOUR OF MUNGO JERRY**

Jul 90. (cd/c) Laserlight; (15142)(79016) **MUNGO JERRY**

Nov 90. (cd-ep) B.B.C.; **IN THE SUMMERTIME (Dance Rave Medley 1990):- Lady Rose – Alright, alright, alright – Hello Nadine – In the summertime**

Mar 91. (cd/c) Music Collection; (ORO/ORT 135) **IN THE SUMMERTIME**

Jun 91. (cd/c) Woodford Music; (WM CD5/MC4 593) **IN THE SUMMERTIME**

Aug 91. (7"/c-s) Topline; **IN THE SUMMERTIME /**

Dec 91. (cd) Dojo; (EARLD 3) **THE EARLY YEARS**

Mar 92. (cd) Dojo; (EARLD 3) **GREATEST HITS**
– Maggie / Sad eyed Joe / Peace in the country / In the summertime / Midnight special (live) / Might man / Baby jump / The man behind the piano / Somebody stole my wife / Have a whiff on me / Lady Rose / You don't have to be in the army to fight in the war / Open up / Going back home / Alright alright alright / Wild love / Long legged woman dressed in black.

May 94. (cd/c) Prima; (PMM 0573-2/-4) **THE YEARS OF MUNGO JERRY**   –   –

Jul 94. (cd/c) Success; **GREATEST HITS VOLUME 1**

Jul 94. (cd/c) Success; **GREATEST HITS VOLUME 2**

Jan 95. (cd/c) Spectrum; (550749-2/-4) **SUMMERTIME**

Aug 95. (cd) Columbia; (4776449) **THE BEST OF MUNGO JERRY**
– Lana / It's a secret / Hello Nadine / Let's get started / Forgotten land / Drum song / In the summertime / Lady Rose / Somebody stole my wife / Alright, alright, alright / Long legged woman dressed in black / Sugar mama / That's my baby / Angel mama / I'm gonna bop till I drop / Rockin' on the road / Baby jump / You don't have to be in the army to fight in the war / Open up / Wild love / In the summertime ('95 mix).
(re-iss. May98; same)

Jan 96. (cd) Beat Goes On; (BGOCD 286) **MUNGO JERRY / ELECTRONICALLY TESTED**   –   –

Jan 96. (d-cd) Beat Goes On; (BGOCD 292) **YOU DON'T HAVE TO BE IN THE ARMY / BOOT POWER**   –   –

Jan 97. (cd) Summit; (SUMCD 4090) **THE VERY OF MUNGO JERRY**

May 97. (cd) Music Club; (MCCD 292) **THE BEST OF MUNGO JERRY – ALRIGHT, ALRIGHT, ALRIGHT**

May 97. (cd/c) A-Play; (10062-2/-4) **THE VERY BEST OF MUNGO JERRY**   –   –

Jun 98. (cd) *Carlton Select; (SELCD 526)* **IN THE SUMMERTIME** ☐ ☐ -
Sep 99. (d-cd) *Essential; (ESACD 777)* **BABY JUMP (THE DAWN ANTHOLOGY)** ☐ ☐ -

Peter MURPHY (see under ⇒ BAUHAUS)

MUSE

Formed: Teignmouth, Devon, England . . . 1997 by MATTHEW BELLAMY, CHRIS WOLSTENHOLME and drummer DOMINIC HOWARD. After playing dingey pubs and damp basements, the 3-piece from the south arose when they debuted at the 'In The City' A&R field day in 1998. HOWARD's THOM YORKE-esque vox impressed record peddlers so much that they took the group to America to showcase them for MADONNA's record label 'Maverik' – home to The DEFTONES, ALANIS MORISSETTE and, erm, WANK. The 20-something indie kids released a John Leckie (knob-twiddler for RADIOHEAD, STONE ROSES and somebody called JOHN LENNON) produced an EP entitled 'MUSE' at the beginning of 1999, which was only pressed on 999 copies (it can nowadays fetch up to £30). The EP sounded like many earlier RADIOHEAD efforts, with a little MY BLOODY VALENTINE twist thrown in for good measure. MUSE proceeded with the 'MUSCLE MUSEUM' EP (1999) and two singles 'UNO' and 'CAVE' before unveiling their debut set 'SHOWBIZ' in late '99. The album boasted nothing special (bar say, the track 'SUNBURN'), except that it may have contained some of the most melodramatic tracks since OASIS's 'WHAT'S THE STORY . . .'. It unleashed a new brand of genre that had the same ideology as Brit Pop: MOR – where have I heard this before? – rock. • **Note:** The MUSE who released the CD in '97 entitled 'Innocent Voices' were not the same band.

Album rating: SHOWBIZ (*7)

MATTHEW BELLAMY – vocals, guitar / **CHRIS WOLSTENHOLME** – bass / **DOMINIC HOWARD** – drums

	Dangerous	not iss.
May 98. (cd-ep) *(DREXCDEP 103)* **MUSE EP**	☐	-
– Overdue / Cave / Coma / Escape.		
Jan 99. (cd-ep) *(DREXCDEP 104)* **MUSCLE MUSEUM EP**	☐	-
– Muscle museum / Sober / Uno / Unintented / Instant messenger / Muscle museum #2.		

	Mushroom	Maverick
Jun 99. (7"clear) *(MUSH 50S)* **UNO. / AGITATED**	73	-
(cd-s) *(MUSH 50CDS)* – ('A'side) / Jimmy Kane / Forced in.		
Sep 99. (7"clear) *(MUSH 58S)* **CAVE / CAVE (instrumental remix)**	52	
(cd-s+=) *(MUSH 58CDS)* – Twin.		
(cd-s) *(MUSH 58CDX)* – ('A'side) / Host / Coma.		
Oct 99. (cd/c/lp) *(MUSH 59 CD/MC/LP)* **SHOWBIZ**	69	☐
– Sunburn / Muscle museum / Filip / Cave / Showbiz / Unintended / Uno / Sober / Escape / Overdue / Hate this and I'll love you.		
Nov 99. (7") *(MUSH 66S)* **MUSCLE MUSEUM. / ('A'live acoustic)**	43	☐
(cd-s+=) *(MUSH 66CDS)* – Do we need this?		
(cd-s) *(MUSH 66CDSX)* – ('A'extended) / Pink ego box / Con-science.		

MUSIC MACHINE (dig out; Great Psychedelic . . .)

MY BLOODY VALENTINE

Formed: Dublin, Ireland . . . 1984 by KEVIN SHIELDS and COLM O'CIOSOIG. Later the same year, the pair travelled to Germany where they hooked up with DAVE CONWAY and TINA to record a mini-lp, 'THIS IS YOUR BLOODY VALENTINE', for the small 'Tycoon' records. This was issued the following year although only 50 copies seem to have emerged (now very rare!). They subsequently moved to London, DEBBIE GOODGE replacing TINA for the recording of the 'GEEK!' EP on 'Fever'. After more 45's for 'Kaleidoscope' then 'Lazy' (home of The PRIMITIVES), the band really began to move away from their early twanging, IGGY POP-style sound following a move to 'Creation' in 1988 (masterminded by SLAUGHTER JOE FOSTER, ex-TV PERSONALITIES). With co-"vocalist", BILINDA BUTCHER now also on board, SHIELDS and Co. finally made the breakthrough in 1990 when the 'GLIDER' EP nearly went Top 40 in the UK, hot on the heels of the acclaimed 'ISN'T ANYTHING' (1988) album. The full extent of their pioneering guitar manipulation – responsible for a whole scene of "shoegazing" musical admirers, stand up RIDE, MOOSE, LUSH etc., etc. – was revealed as MBV released their most challenging and inventive track to date in 'TO HERE KNOWS WHEN' (from the Top 30 'TREMOLO' EP). Creating a whole new concept and language of sound, the song either enveloped the listener in blissful noise or just seemed out of bloody tune, there was no middle ground. 'LOVELESS' (1991), MBV's long awaited and much heralded follow-up, was a revelation. Its hypnotic, undulating noisescapes sounded not-of-this-earth and 'Creation' were saddled with an astronomical studio bill to match, almost going bankrupt as a result. They subsequently signed to 'Island' records, and nine (!!!) years on, fans are still awaiting some new product. Although MY BLOODY VALENTINE have arguably been the most influential indie band of the last decade and few doubt their potential to return with a masterpiece, their reclusive silence makes the late Stanley Kubrick appear prolific. Nevertheless, SHIELDS has surfaced occasionally as a remixer, notably for the single release of PRIMAL SCREAM's 'Stuka' and many more. • **Songwriters:** SHIELDS writes most of material, with words

after 1987 by BILINDA. Covered MAP REF 41 (Wire). • **Trivia:** A track, 'SUGAR', was given away free with 'The Catalogue' magazine of February '89.

Album rating: THIS IS YOUR BLOODY VALENTINE (*5) / ISN'T ANYTHING (*8) / ECSTASY AND WINE compilation (*7) / LOVELESS (*9)

KEVIN SHIELDS (b.21 May'63, Queens, New York) – guitar, vocals, occasional bass / **DAVE CONWAY** – vocals / **COLM CUSACK** (b. COLM MICHAEL O'CIOSOIG, 31 Oct'64) – drums / **TINA** – keyboards

	Tycoon	not iss.
1985. (m-lp) *(ST 7501)* **THIS IS YOUR BLOODY VALENTINE**	-	- German
– Forever and again / Homelovin' guy / Don't cramp my style / Tiger in my tank / The love gang / Inferno / The last supper.		

—— **DEBBIE GOOGE** (b.24 Oct'62, Somerset, England) – bass; repl. TINA

	Fever	not iss.
Apr 86. (12"ep) *(FEV 5)* **GEEK!**		-
– No place to go / Moonlight / Love machine / The sandman never sleeps.		
Jun 86. (7") *(FEV 5X)* **NO PLACE TO GO. / MOONLIGHT**		-

	Kaleidoscope Sound	not iss.
Oct 86. (12"ep) *(KS 101)* **THE NEW RECORD BY MY BLOODY VALENTINE**	☐	-
– Lovelee sweet darlene / By the danger in your eyes / On another rainy Sunday / We're so beautiful.		

	Lazy	not iss.
Feb 87. (7") *(LAZY 04)* **SUNNY SUNDAE SMILE. / PAINT A RAINBOW**	☐	-
(12"+=) *(LAZY 04T)* – Kiss the eclipse / Sylvie's head.		

—— **BILINDA BUTCHER** (b.16 Sep'61, London, England) – vocals, guitar; repl. CONWAY

Nov 87. (m-lp) *(LAZY 08)* **ECSTASY**	☐	-
– (Please) Lose yourself in me / The things I miss / I don't need you / Clair / (You're) Safe in your sleep / She loves you no less / Strawberry wine / Lovelee sweet darlene.		
Nov 87. (12"m) *(LAZY 07)* **STRAWBERRY WINE. / NEVER SAY GOODBYE / CAN I TOUCH YOU**	☐	-

	Creation	Relativity
Jul 88. (7") *(CRE 055)* **YOU MADE ME REALISE. / SLOW**	☐	-
(12"+=) *(CRE 055T)* – Thorn / Cigarette in your bed / Drive it all over me. *(re-iss. Mar90 as cd-ep; CRECD 55)*		
Oct 88. (7") *(CRE 061)* **FEED ME WITH YOUR KISSES. / EMPTINESS INSIDE**	☐	-
(12"+=) *(CRE 061T)* – I believe / I need no trust. *(re-iss. Mar90 as cd-ep; CRECD 61)*		
Nov 88. (lp/cd)(c) *(CRELP 040/+CD)(C-CRELP 040) <1006>* **ISN'T ANYTHING**	☐	☐
– Soft as snow (but warm inside) / Lose my breath / Cupid come / (When you wake) You're still in a dream / No more sorry / All I need / Feed me with your kiss / Sue is fine / Several girls galore / You never should / Nothing much to lose / I can see it (but I can't feel it). *(free 7"w/ lp)* – INSTRUMENTAL. / INSTRUMENTAL *<US cd re-iss. 1993 on 'Warners'; 45231>*		

	Creation	Sire
Apr 90. (7"ep/12"ep)(cd-ep) *(CRE 73/+T)(CRESCD 73) <26313>* **GLIDER**	41	☐
– Soon / Glider / Don't ask why / Off your face.		
Feb 91. (7"ep/12"ep)(cd-ep) *(CRE 085/+T)(CRESCD 085) <40024>* **TREMOLO**	29	☐ Apr91
– To here knows when / Swallow / Honey power / Moon song.		
Nov 91. (cd/lp)(c) *(CRE CD/LP 060)(C-CRELP 060) <26759>* **LOVELESS**	24	☐
– Only shallow / Loomer / Touched / To here knows when / When you sleep / I only said / Come in alone / Sometimes / Blown a wish / What you want / Soon.		

—— During there long hiatus, KEVIN SHIELDS contributed (1996) to an album 'Beyond The Pale' by EXPERIMENTAL AUDIO RESEARCH. It also featured SONIC BOOM (ex-SPACEMEN 3), KEVIN MARTIN (of GOD) & EDDIE PREVOST (of AMM). Meanwhile, DEBBIE GOOGE teamed up with KATHERINE GIFFORD and MAX CORRADI to form SNOWPONY.

– compilations, others, etc. –

Feb 89. (lp/cd) *Lazy; (LAZY 12/+CD)* **ECSTASY AND WINE**	☐	-
– Strawberry wine / Never say goodbye / Can I touch you / She loves you no less / The things I miss / I don't need you / Safe in your sleep / Clair / You've got nothing / Lose yourself in me.		

MY LIFE STORY (dig out; Great Alt & Indie . . .)

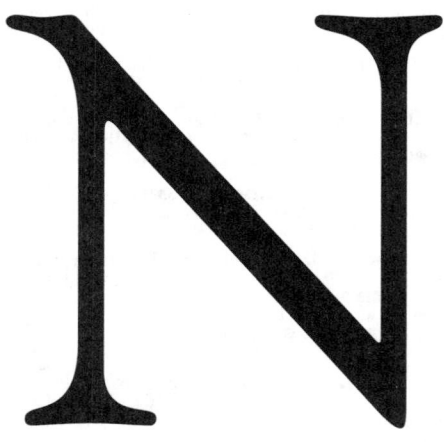

NAILBOMB (see under ⇒ SEPULTURA)

NAKED CITY (see under ⇒ ZORN, John)

NAPALM DEATH

Formed: Ipswich, England ... 1982 by "vocalist" LEE DORRIAN and guitarist BILL STEER. Building up a small but fiercely loyal grassroots following by constant gigging, 'DEATH finally made in onto vinyl with 'SCUM' in 1987. Released on the band's own 'Earache' label, the record was a proverbial tale of two halves with NICK BULLEN (bass, vocals), JUSTIN BROADRICK (guitar) and MICK HARRIS (drums) producing side one, while side two was the work of STEER, DORRIAN and JIM WHITELY. Needless to say, both sides were cranium-shreddingly extreme, pioneering white-hot blasts of a thrash/death-metal/punk hybrid which was duly christened "grindcore". Taking punk's short, sharp shock technique to its ultimate conclusion, many of the tracks were under a minute in length. John Peel's favourite, meanwhile, 'YOU SUFFER', lasted less than a second! The influential and ever eclectic PEEL would subsequently invite the band to record a session that year, acknowledging the group's sonic innovation while large sections of the metal press mocked them. The vocals, particularly, came in for a lot of stick; almost wholly unintelligible sub-human growling is how they might be best described although it's a style that has since been ripped off wholesale by legions of death-metal bands. And while the "singing" may have been incomprehensible to anyone missing a lyric sheet, the growling actually belied a radical political and social agenda, not exactly a priority of your average metal band. By the release of the 54-track (a single lp!) 'ENSLAVEMENT TO OBLITERATION' (1988), if anything more extreme than the debut, SHANE EMBURY had replaced WHITELY on bass. Further line-up changes ensued the following year when DORRIAN and STEER both quit to form their own outfits, CATHEDRAL and CARCASS respectively. Replacements were found in vocalist MARK 'Barney' GREENWAY and Mexican guitarist JESSE PINTADO, the group subsequently heading out on the infamous 'Grindcrusher' European tour. With another American guitarist, MITCH HARRIS, recruited to bolster the group's sound, NAPALM DEATH recorded 'HARMONY CORRUPTION'. Released in late 1990, the opus betrayed a more conventional death/thrash metal sound with longer songs. Prior to the release of the 'UTOPIA BANISHED' (1992) album, MICK HARRIS departed for scary ambient outfit, SCORN, his seat on the drum stool filled by DANNY HERARRA. More heavy touring followed, playing to NAPALM DEATH fans in the most unlikely, furthest flung corners of the globe. A 1993 cover of the Dead Kennedys' 'NAZI PUNKS FUCK OFF' proved the band hadn't left their roots behind completely and with the acclaimed 'FEAR, EMPTINESS, DESPAIR' (1994), the band finally managed to incorporate their uncompromising vision into a consistent, coherent set of songs. The album was their most successful to date, winning them a support from the music press which was consolidated with subsequent releases 'GREED KILLING' (a mini album; 1995) and 'DIATRIBES' (1996). In addition to their boundary-busting music, NAPALM DEATH have also helped cultivate the more extreme end of the music spectrum via their groundbreaking 'Earache' label, home to such uneasy listening experiences as GODFLESH, MISERY LOVES CO. etc.
• **Trivia:** NAPALM DEATH recorded the shortest track ever released (the 1 second) 'YOU SUFFER', for a free 7", given away with an 'Earache' sampler, 'Grindcrusher'. SHANE EMBURY exchanged death threats with another teeth-grinding outfit SORE THROAT (mainly band member RICH MILITIA).

Album rating: SCUM (*5) / FROM ENSLAVEMENT TO OBLITERATION (*6) / HARMONY CORRUPTION (*5) / UTOPIA BANISHED (*6) / DEATH BY MANIPULATION compilation (*7) / FEAR, EMPTINESS, DESPAIR (*4) / GREED KILLING mini (*4) / DIATRIBES (*4) / INSIDE THE TORN APART (*5) / BOOTLEGGED IN JAPAN (*3) / WORDS FROM THE EXIT WOUND (*4)

LEE DORRIAN – vocals (also runs own label 'Rise Above') / **BILL STEER** – guitar (also of CARCASS) / **SHANE EMBURY** – bass (also drummer of UNSEEN TERROR) / **MICK**

HARRIS – drums (also vocals of EXTREME NOISE TERROR) repl. FRANK HEALEY (other early drummer JUS of HEAD OF DAVID)

			Earache	not iss.
Jul 87.	(lp) (MOSH 003) **SCUM**		☐	-

– Multinational corporations / Instinct of survival / The kill / Scum / Caught . . . .in a dream / Polluted minds / Sacrificed / Siege of power / Control / Born on your knees / Human garbage / You suffer / Life? / Prison without walls / Point of no return / Negative approach / Success? / Deceiver / C.S. / Parasites / Pseudo youth / Divine death / As the machine rolls on / Common enemy / Moral crusade / Stigmatized / M.A.D. / Dragnet. (c-iss.May89; MOSH 003/+MC) (re-iss. cd Sep94; MOSH 003/+CD)

Nov 88.	(lp/c/cd) (MOSH 008/+MC/CD) **FROM ENSLAVEMENT TO OBLITERATION**		☐	-

– Evolved as one / It's a man's world / Lueid fairytale / Private death / Impressions / Unchallenged hate / Uncertainty blurs the vision / Cock rock alienation / Retreat to nowhere / Think for a minute / Display to me . . . / From enslavement to obliteration / Blind to the truth / Social sterility / Emotional suffocation / Practise what you preach / Inconceivable / Worlds apart / Obstinate direction / Mentally murdered / Sometimes / Make way. (pic-lp iss.Jul90; MOSH 008P) (re-iss. cd Sep94; same)

Aug 89.	(7") (7MOSH 014) **MENTALLY MURDERED. / CAUSE AND EFFECT**		☐	-

(12"+=) (MOSH 014T) – Rise above / Missing link – Mentally murdered / Walls of confinement / Cause and effect – No manual effort.

—— (Aug'89) **MARK 'Barney' GREENWAY** – vocals (ex-BENEDICTION) repl. LEE (LEE was to join CATHEDRAL, another 'Earache' band) **MITCH HARRIS** (b.Las Vegas, USA) + **JESSE PINTADO** (b.Mexico) – guitars repl. BILL who went full-time with CARCASS

Aug 90.	(7") (7MOSH 024) **SUFFER THE CHILDREN. / SIEGE OF POWER**		☐	-

(12"+=) (MOSHT 24) – Harmony corruption.

Sep 90.	(lp/c/cd) (MOSH 019/+MC/CD) **HARMONY CORRUPTION**	67	☐	-

– Vision conquest / If the truth be known / Inner incineration / Malicious intent / Unfit Earth / Circle of hypocrisy / Suffer the children / The chains that bind us / Mind snare / Extremity retained. (some w/free 12") (re-iss. cd Sep94; same)

May 91.	(7") (7MOSH 046) **MASS APPEAL MADNESS. / PRIDE ASSASSIN**		☐	-

(12"+=/cd-s+=) (MOSH 046 T/CD) – Unchallenged hate / Social sterility.

—— MICK HARRIS was arrested for jewel shop robbery & he left to join SCORN. He was soon replaced by **DANNY HERARRA** – drums

May 92.	(lp/c/cd) (MOSH 053/+MC/CD) **UTOPIA BANISHED**	58	☐	-

– Discordance / I abstain / Dementia access / Christening of the world / The world keeps turning / Idiosyncratic / Aryanisms / Cause and effect (pt.II) / Juidicial slime / Distorting the medium / Got time to kill / Upward and uninterested / Exile / Awake (to a life of misery) / Contemptious. (free 4 track 7"ep) (re-iss. cd Sep94; same)

Jun 92.	(12"ep/cd-ep) (MOSH 065 T/CD) **THE WORLD KEEPS TURNING EP**		☐	-

– The world keeps turning / A means to an end / Insanity excursion.

Jul 93.	(7"ep/cd-ep/+CD) (MOSH 092/+CD) **NAZI PUNKS FUCK OFF. / ARYANISMS / ('A'version) / CONTEMPTUOUS (xtreem mix)**		☐	-

May 94.	(lp/c/cd) (MOSH 109/+MC/CD) **FEAR, EMPTINESS, DESPAIR**		☐	-

– Twist the knife (slowly) / Hung / Remain nameless / Plague rages / More than meets the eye / Primed time / State of mind / Armageddon X7 / Retching on the dirt / Fasting on deception / Throwaway.

Nov 95.	(10"m-lp/m-c/m-cd) (MOSH 146/+MC/CD) **GREED KILLING**		☐	-

– Greed killing / My own worst enemy / Self betrayal / Finer truths, white lies / Antibody / All links severed / Plague rages (live).

Jan 96.	(10"d-lp/c/cd) (MOSH 141/+MC/CD) **DIATRIBES**	73	☐	-

– Greed killing / Glimpse into genocide / Ripe for the breaking / Cursed to crawl / Cold forgiveness / My own worst enemy / Just rewards / Dogma / Take the strain / Corrosive elements / Placate, sedate, eradicate / Diatribes / Take the strain.

—— In Nov'96, BARNEY was dismissed and was replaced by vocalist **PHIL VANE** (ex-EXTREME NOISE TERROR). This was brief when **BARNEY** returned

Jan 97.	(cd-ep) (MOSH 168CD) **IN TONGUES WE SPEAK EP**		☐	-

– Food chains / Upward and uninterested / (2 others by COALESCE).

Jun 97.	(d-lp/c/cd) (MOSH 171/+MC/CD) **INSIDE THE TORN APART**		☐	-

– Breed to breathe / Birth in regress / Section / Reflect on conflict / Down in the zero / Inside the torn apart / If systems persist / Prelude / Indispose / Purist realist / Low point / Lifeless alarm / Time will come / Bled dry / Ripe for the breaking.

Nov 97.	(cd-rom;ep) (MOSH 185CD) **BREED TO BREATHE / ALL INTENSIVE PURPOSES / STRANGER NOW / BLED DRY / TIME WILL COME / SUFFER THE CHILDREN (by; Fatality)**		☐	-

Jun 98.	(cd) (MOSH 209CD) **BOOTLEGGED IN JAPAN (live 5th August, 1997)**		☐	-

– Antibody / My own worst enemy / More than meets the eye / Hung / Greed killing / Suffer the children / Mass appeal madness / Cursed to crawl / Glimpse into genocide / I abstain / Lucid fairytale / Plague rages / Cold forgiveness / Control / Diatribes / Life / Siege of power / If the truth be known / Unchallenged hate / Nazi punks fuck off / From enslavement to obliteration / Kill / Scum / Ripe for the breaking.

Oct 98.	(cd) (MOSH 212CD) **WORDS FROM THE EXIT WOUND**		☐	-

– The infiltraitor / Repression out of uniform / Next of kin to chaos / Trio – Degradable / Affixed by disconcern / Cleanse impure / Devouring depraved / Ulterior exterior / None the wiser? / Clutching at barbs / Incendiary incoming / Throw down a rope / Sceptic in perspective.

– compilations, others, etc. –

May 88.	(12"ep) Strange Fruit; (SFPS 049) **THE PEEL SESSIONS (13.9.87)**		☐	-

– The kill / Prison without walls / Dead part one / Deceiver / Lucid fairytale / In extremis / Blind to the trash / Negative approach / Common enemy / Obstinate direction / Life? / You suffer (Part 2). (re-iss. May89 c-ep/cd-ep; SFPDS MC/CD 049)

Dec 89.	(cd/c) Strange Fruit; (SFP MCD/MC 201) **THE PEEL SESSIONS (13.9.87 & 8.3.88)**		☐	-

– (above tracks) / Multi-national corporations / Instinct of survival / Stigatised / Parasites / Moral crusade / Worlds apart / M.A.D. / Divine death / C 9 / Control / Walls / Raging in Hell / Conform or die / S.O.B.

Feb 92.	(lp/cd) Earache; (MOSH 051/+CD) **DEATH BY MANIPULATION**		☐	-

(free cd-ep) (re-iss. Oct92 & Sep94; same)

NAS

Born: NASIR ESCOBAR, 1973, Long Island, New York, USA. Raised by a jazz-performing father, he cut his rapping teeth at the age of ten, developing his lyrical skills in local hip-hop posse, The DEVASTIN' SEVEN. By the end of the 80's, having made attempts at TV work, he was introduced to MAIN SOURCE producer, LARGE PROFESSOR, for whom he made a demo tape. NAS subsequently featured on their debut album, 'Breaking Atoms', making a noted guest appearance on the track 'Live At The BBQ'. With his personal life in crisis (i.e. death of friend and shooting of his brother), NAS's recording career was put on hold for a few years in the early 90's. That is, until he contributed a track, 'HALF TIME' for the 'Zebra Head' movie in 1992/3, 'Columbia' subsequently impressed enough to give the precocious young rapper a sizeable deal. Guided by some of New York's most respected producers (including Q-TIP – A Tribe Called Quest, PREMIER – Gang Starr and PETE ROCK), he crafted 1994's acclaimed 'ILLMATIC' album. Two years on, NAS smashed into the US chart at No.1 with his follow-up, 'IT WAS WRITTEN', which spawned the hit singles, 'IF I RULED THE WORLD' and the crossover Eurythmics-inspired 'STREET DREAMS'. In the Autumn of '97, he collaborated with FOXY BROWN, AZ & NATURE, releasing the chart-topping 'THE FIRM – THE ALBUM', although for American ears only (so far that is). Two sets of differing quality were released before the century was out, the hard-hitting and absorbing 'I AM . . .' (1999) and the disappointing, 'NAStradamus' (1999).

Album rating: ILLMATIC (*6) / IT WAS WRITTEN (*7) / I AM . . . (*8) / NAStradamus (*5)

NAS – rapping, etc (with various producers, etc)

			Columbia	Columbia	
Apr 94.	(cd/c/lp) (475959-2/-4/-1) <57684> **ILLMATIC**			12	

– The genesis / N.Y. state of mind / Life's a bitch / The world is yours / Halftime / Memory lane (sittin' in da park) / One love / One time 4 your mind / Represent / It ain't hard to tell.

May 94.	(c-s) (660470-4) <77385> **IT AIN'T HARD TO TELL /** ('A'instrumental)	64	91	Mar94

(12"+=) (660470-6) – (2 other mixes).
(cd-s++=) (660470-2) – ('A'mixes).

Jul 96.	(c-s) (663402-4) <78327> **IF I RULED THE WORLD (IMAGINE THAT) /** ('A'instrumental)	12	53	Jun96

(12"/cd-s) (663402-6/-2) – ('A'mixes).

Jul 96.	(cd/c/lp) (484196-2/-4/-1) <67015> **IT WAS WRITTEN**	38	1	

– Intro / Message / Street dreams / I gave you power / Watch dem niggas / Take it in blood / Nas is coming / Affirmative action / Set up / Black girl lost / Suspect / Shootouts / Live nigga rap / If I ruled the world (imagine that).

Jan 97.	(c-s/12"/cd-s) (664130-4/-6/-2) <78409> **STREET DREAMS. / AFFIRMATIVE ACTION**	12	22	Nov96
Mar 99.	(c-s/cd-s) <79113> **NAS IS LIKE**	–	86	
Apr 99.	(cd/c/lp) (489419-2/-4/-1) <68773> **I AM . . .**	31	1	

– Hate me now / Afterlife / You won't see me tonight / Undying love / Nas is like / NY state of mind / Big things / Money is my bitch / Favour for a favour / Life is what you make it / Project window / We will survive.

May 99.	(c-s; NAS featuring PUFF DADDY) (667256-4) <79070> **HATE ME NOW /** ('A'mix)	14	62	Apr99

(cd-s) (667256-2) – ('A'mixes).
(cd-s) (667256-5) – ('A'mixes).

—— NAS featured on MISSY "MISDEMEANOR" ELLIOTT's hit single, 'Hot Boyz'

Nov 99.	(cd/c/lp) (495312-2/-4/-1) <63930> **NAStradamus**		7	

– Prediction / Life we choose / NAStradamus / Angels intro / Some of us have angels / Project windows / Naheim / Big girl / Hydro drops / Shoot 'em up / Last words / Hustler's and killers / Science / God love us / Quiet niggas / Come get me / Count down to 2000 / New world / You owe me / Outcome.

Dec 99.	(c-s/cd-s) <79299> **NAStradamus**	–	92	

Graham NASH (see under ⇒ CROSBY, STILLS, NASH & YOUNG)

NAZARETH

Formed: Dunfermline, Scotland . . . 1969 out of the ashes of The SHADETTES by DAN McCAFFERTY, PETE AGNEW and DARREL SWEET. With the addition of MANNY CHARLTON, the group turned pro and relocated to London, gaining a record contract with 'Pegasus' in the process. Already armed with a loyal homegrown support, the band released two earthy hard-rock albums for the label between late '71 and mid '72 before moving to 'Mooncrest'. This was the band's turning point, NAZARETH hitting immediately with a Top 10 smash, 'BROKEN DOWN ANGEL'. An obvious focal point for the Caledonian rockers was the mean-looking McCAFFERTY, his whisky-throated wail coming to define the band's sound. Their acclaimed third album, 'RAZAMANAZ' followed soon after, narrowly missing the UK Top 10 but nevertheless spawning another top selling rock classic, 'BAD, BAD BOY'. With ROGER GLOVER (ex-DEEP PURPLE) at the production desk, NAZARETH re-invented Joni Mitchell's classic, 'THIS FLIGHT TONIGHT', the band virtually claiming it as their own with a re-working startling in its stratospheric melodic power. The accompanying, appropriately-named 'LOUD 'N' PROUD' album (also released in '73!), followed the established formula by combining excellent cover versions with original material, thus its Top 10 placing. However, by the following year, only their fifth album, 'RAMPANT' had achieved any degree of success. America finally took NAZARETH to their hearts with the release of the much covered Boudleaux Bryant ballad, 'LOVE

HURTS', the single making the US Top 10 in 1975 (JIM CAPALDI of Traffic had pipped them to the post in Britain). McCAFFERTY returned to the UK charts that year in fine fettle with yet another classy cover, Tomorrow's 'MY WHITE BICYCLE'. The frontman even found time to complete and release a full album's worth of covers, the big man and the band suffering a backlash from some of their more hardcore fans. Switching labels to 'Mountain' (home of The SENSATIONAL ALEX HARVEY BAND) late in 1975, the band suffered a dip in profile, although having signed to 'A&M' in America (in the heyday) they consolidated their earlier Stateside success. The ALEX HARVEY connection took another twist with the addition of the latter's clown-faced sidekick ZAL CLEMINSON on guitar. This helped to pull back some of NAZARETH's flagging support, the following JEFF 'Skunk' BAXTER (ex-DOOBIES)-produced set, 'MALICE IN WONDERLAND' hitting Top 30 in America. ZAL departed soon after, his surprising replacement being the American JOHN LOCKE, who in turn (after an album, 'THE FOOL CIRCLE' 1981) was superseded by Glaswegian BILLY RANKIN. For the remainder of the 80's, NAZARETH churned out a plethora of reasonable albums, the band still retaining a North American fanbase while gaining a foothold in many parts of Europe. Founder member MANNY CHARLTON subsequently departed at the turn of the decade, RANKIN returning for their best album for ten years, 'NO JIVE' (1991). Surprisingly, after nearly 30 years in the business, NAZARETH are still plugging away, their most recent effort being 1997's 'MOVE ME'. A host of modern day hard-rockers such as AXL ROSE, MICHAEL MONROE, etc, claim to have been influenced by both McCAFFERTY and his three wise rockers, GUNS N' ROSES even covering 'HAIR OF THE DOG'. • **Songwriters:** Group penned, except SHAPES OF THINGS (Yardbirds) / DOWN HOME GIRL (Leiber-Stoller) / I WANT TO DO EVERYTHING FOR YOU (Joe Tex) / TEENAGE NERVOUS BREAKDOWN (Little Feat) / THE BALLAD OF HOLLIS BROWN (Bob Dylan) / YOU'RE THE VIOLIN (Golden Earring) / WILD HONEY (Beach Boys) / SO YOU WANT TO BE A ROCK'N'ROLL STAR (Byrds) / I DON'T WANT TO GO ON WITHOUT YOU (Berns/Wexler). DAN McCAFFERTY solo covered OUT OF TIME (Rolling Stones) / WHATCHA GONNA DO ABOUT IT (Small Faces) / etc.

Album rating: NAZARETH (*6) / EXERCISES (*6) / RAZAMANAZ (*7) / LOUD 'N' PROUD (*6) / RAMPANT (*6) / HAIR OF THE DOG (*7) / CLOSE ENOUGH FOR ROCK'N'ROLL (*5) / PLAY 'N' THE GAME (*4) / GREATEST HITS compilation (*8) / EXPECT NO MERCY (*5) / NO MEAN CITY (*5) / MALICE IN WONDERLAND (*5) / THE FOOL CIRCLE (*4) / 'SNAZ (*4) / 2XS (*4) / SOUND ELIXIR (*4) / THE CATCH (*4) / CINEMA (*4) / SNAKES AND LADDERS (*4) / THE SINGLES COLLECTION compilation (*8) / NO JIVE (*5) / MOVE ME (*4)

DAN McCAFFERTY – vocals / **MANNY CHARLTON** – guitar, vocals / **PETE AGNEW** (b.14 Sep'48) – bass / **DARRELL SWEET** – drums, percussion

		Pegasus	Warners	
Nov 71.	(lp) (PEG 10) <BS 2615> **NAZARETH**			Feb73

– Witchdoctor woman / Dear John / Empty arms, empty heart / If I had a dream / Red light lady / Fat man / Country girl / Morning dew / King is dead. (re-iss. Apr74 on 'Mooncrest'; CREST 10) (re-iss. Nov 75 & Apr80 on 'Mountain' lp/c; TOPC/TTOPC 5001) (cd-iss. May92 on 'Castle'; CLACD 286)

Jan 72.	(7") (PGS 2) **DEAR JOHN. / FRIENDS**			
Jul 72.	(7") (PGS 4) **MORNING DEW. / SPINNING TOP**			
Jul 72.	(7") <7599> **MORNING DEW. / DEAR JOHN**	–		
Jul 72.	(lp) (PEG 14) <BS 2639> **EXERCISES**			Nov72

– I will not be led / Cat's eye, apple pie / In my time / Woke up this morning / Called her name / Fool about you / Love now you're gone / Madelaine / Sad song / 1692 (Glen Coe massacre). (re-iss. Apr74 on 'Mooncrest'; CREST 14) (re-iss. Nov75 & Apr80 on 'Mountain' lp/c; TOPS/TTOPS 103) (re-iss. May85 on 'Sahara'; SAH 121) (cd-iss. Feb91 on 'Castle'; CLACD 220)

Sep 72.	(7") (PGS 5) **IF YOU SEE MY BABY. / HARD LIVING**			
		Mooncrest	A&M	
Apr 73.	(7") (MOON 1) **BROKEN DOWN ANGEL. / WITCHDOCTOR WOMAN**	9	–	
May 73.	(lp/c) (CREST 1) <SP 4396> **RAZAMANAZ**	11		

– Razamanaz / Alcatraz / Vigilante man / Woke up this morning / Night woman / Bad, bad boy / Sold my soul / Too bad, too sad / Broken down angel. (re-iss. Nov75 & Apr80 on 'Mountain' lp/c; TOPS/TTOPS 104) (re-iss. Oct82 on 'NEMS' lp/c; NEL/NEC 6023) (re-iss. Dec89 on 'Castle' lp/cd; CLA LP/CD 173) (cd re-iss. Sep96 on 'Essential'; ESMCD 370)

Jul 73.	(7"m) (MOON 9) **BAD, BAD BOY. / HARD LIVING / SPINNING TOP**	10	–	
Sep 73.	(7") <1453> **BROKEN DOWN ANGEL. / HARD LIVING**	–		
Oct 73.	(7") (MOON 14) **THIS FLIGHT TONIGHT. / CALLED HER NAME**	11		
Nov 73.	(lp/c) (CREST 4) <3609> **LOUD 'N' PROUD**	10		

– Go down fighting / Not faking it / Turn on your receiver / Teenage nervous breakdown / Freewheeler / This flight tonight / Child in the sun / The ballad of Hollis Brown. (re-iss. Nov75 & Apr80 on 'Mountain' lp/c; TOPS/TTOPS 105) (re-iss. Dec89 on 'Castle' lp/cd; CLA LP/CD 174) (cd re-iss. Oct96 on 'Essential'; ESMCD 379)

Nov 73.	(7") <1469> **BAD, BAD BOY. / RAZAMANAZ**	–		
Feb 74.	(7") <1511> **THIS FLIGHT TONIGHT. / GO DOWN FIGHTING**	–		
Mar 74.	(7") (MOON 22) **SHANGHAI'D IN SHANGHAI. / LOVE, NOW YOU'RE GONE**	41		
May 74.	(lp/c) (CREST 15) <3641> **RAMPANT**	13		

– Silver dollar forger (parts 1 & 2) / Glad when you're gone / Loved and lost / Shanghai'd in Shanghai / Jet lag / Light my way / Sunshine / a) Shapes of things – b) Space safari. (re-iss. Nov75 & Apr80 on 'Mountain' lp/c; TOPS/TTOPS 106) (cd-iss. Sep92 on 'Castle'; CLACD 242) (cd re-iss. May97 on 'Essential'; ESMCD 551)

Jul 74.	(7") <1548> **SUNSHINE. / THIS FLIGHT TONIGHT**	–		
Nov 74.	(7") (MOON 37) <1671> **LOVE HURTS. / DOWN**		8	Nov75
Mar 75.	(7") (MOON 44) **HAIR OF THE DOG. / TOO BAD, TOO SAD**		–	

Apr 75. (lp/c) *(CREST 27)* <4511> **HAIR OF THE DOG** | | `17`
– Hair of the dog / Miss Misery / Guilty * / Changin' times / Beggars day / Rose in the heather / Whisky drinkin' woman / Please don't Judas me. *(In the US, track* repl. by 'Love hurts') (re-iss. Nov75 & Apr80 on 'Mountain' lp/c; TOPS/TTOPS 107) (re-iss. Oct82 on 'NEMS' lp/c; NEL/NEC 6024) (re-iss. May85 on 'Sahara'; SAH 124) (cd-iss. Feb92 on 'Castle'; CLACD 241) (cd re-iss. May97 on 'Essential'; ESMCD 550)*

May 75. (7") <1671> **HAIR OF THE DOG. / LOVE HURTS**

May 75. (7") *(MOON 47)* **MY WHITE BICYCLE. / MISS MISERY** | `14`
(re-iss. 1979 on 'Mountain'; NAZ 10)

	Mountain	A&M
Oct 75. (7") *(TOP 3)* **HOLY ROLLER. / RAILROAD BOY** | `36` | `-`

Nov 75. (lp/c) *(TOPS/TTOPS 108)* <9020> **GREATEST HITS** (compilation) | `54` |
– Razamanaz / Holy roller / Shanghai'd in Shanghai / Love hurts / Turn on your receiver / Bad bad boy / This flight tonight / Broken down angel / Hair of the dog / Sunshine / My white bicycle / Woke up this morning. *(re-iss. Oct82 on 'NEMS' lp/c; NEL/NEC 6022) (re-iss. Apr89 on 'Castle' lp/c/cd; CLA LP/MC/CD 149)*

Feb 76. (7") *(TOP 8)* <1819> **CARRY OUT FEELINGS. / LIFT THE LID** | |

Mar 76. (lp/c) *(TOPS/TTOPS 109)* <4562> **CLOSE ENOUGH FOR ROCK'N'ROLL** | | `24`
– Telegram (part 1:- On your way / part 2:- So you want to be a rock'n'roll star / part 3:- Sound check / part 4:- Here we are again) / Vicki / Homesick again / Vancouver shakedown / Born under the wrong sign / Loretta / Carry out feelings / Lift the lid / You're the violin. *(re-iss. May85 on 'Sahara'; SAH 126) (re-iss. Jun90 on 'Castle' lp/c/cd; CLA LP/MC/CD 182)*

Jun 76. (7") *(TOP 14)* **YOU'RE THE VIOLIN. / LORETTA** | | `-`

Sep 76. (7") <1854> **LIFT THE LID. / LORETTA** | | `-`

Nov 76. (7") *(TOP 21)* **I DON'T WANT TO GO ON WITHOUT YOU. / GOOD LOVE** | | `-`

Nov 76. (lp/c) *(TOPS/TTOPS 113)* <4610> **PLAY 'N' THE GAME** | | `75`
– Somebody to roll / Down home girl / Flying / Waiting for the man / Born to love / I want to (do everything for you) / I don't want to go on without you / Wild honey / L.A. girls. *(re-iss. May85 on 'Sahara; SAH 131) (cd-iss. Feb91 on 'Castle'; CLACD 219)*

Dec 76. (7") <18??> **I WANT TO (DO EVERYTHING FOR YOU). / BLACK CATS** | `-` |

Jan 77. (7") *(TOP 22)* **SOMEBODY TO ROLL. / VANCOUVER SHAKEDOWN** | `-` |

Feb 77. (7") <1895> **I DON'T WANT TO GO ON WITHOUT YOU. / I WANT TO DO (EVERYTHING FOR YOU)** | `-` |

Apr 77. (7") <1936> **SOMEBODY TO ROLL. / THIS FLIGHT TONIGHT** | `-` |

Jun 77. (lp) <4643> **HOT TRACKS** (compilation) | `-` |

Sep 77. (7"ep) *(NAZ 1)* **HOT TRACKS** (compilation) | `15` | `-`
– Love hurts / This flight tonight / Broken down angel / Hair of the dog. *(re-iss. Jul80; HOT 1) (re-iss. Jan83 on 7"pic-ep on 'NEMS'; NEP 2)*

Nov 77. (lp/c) *(TOPS/TTOPS 115)* <4666> **EXPECT NO MERCY** | | `82`
– Expect no mercy / Gone dead train / Shot me down / Revenge is sweet / Gimme what's mine / Kentucky fried blues / New York broken toy / Busted / A place in your heart / All the king's horses. *(re-iss. May85 on 'Sahara'; SAH 123) (re-iss. Jun90 on 'Castle' cd/lp; CLA CD/LP 187) (re-iss. cd Sep93 on 'Elite'; ELITE 022CD)*

Jan 78. (7"m) *(NAZ 2)* **GONE DEAD TRAIN. / GREENS / DESOLATION ROAD** | `49` | `-`

Apr 78. (7") *(TOP 37)* **A PLACE IN YOUR HEART. / KENTUCKY FRIED BLUES** | `70` |

Apr 78. (7") <2009> **SHOT ME DOWN. / KENTUCKY FRIED BLUES** | | `-`

Jul 78. (7") <2029> **GONE DEAD TRAIN. / KENTUCKY FRIED BLUES** | `-` |

—— added **ZAL CLEMINSON** (b. 4 May'49, Glasgow, Scotland) – guitar, synth. (ex-SENSATIONAL ALEX HARVEY BAND)

Jan 79. (7") *(NAZ 3)* <2116> **MAY THE SUNSHINE. / EXPECT NO MERCY** | `22` |

Jan 79. (lp/c) *(TOPS/TTOPS 123)* <4741> **NO MEAN CITY** | `34` | `88`
– Just to get into it / May the sun shine / Simple solution (parts 1 & 2) / Star / Claim to fame / Whatever you want babe / What's in it for me / No mean city (parts 1 & 2). *(re-iss. May85 on 'Sahara'; SAH 120) (re-iss. May91 on 'Castle' lp/c/cd; CLA LP/MC/CD 213)*

Apr 79. (7",7"purple) *(NAZ 4)* <2130> **WHATEVER YOU WANT BABE. / TELEGRAM (PARTS 1, 2 & 3)** | |

Jul 79. (7") <2158> **STAR. / EXPECT NO MERCY** | `-` |

Jul 79. (7") *(TOP 45)* **STAR. / BORN TO LOVE** | `54` |

Jan 80. (7") *(TOP 50)* <2219> **HOLIDAY. / SHIP OF DREAMS** | | `87`

Jan 80. (lp/c) *(TOPS/TTOPS 126)* <4799> **MALICE IN WONDERLAND** | | `41`
– Holiday / Showdown at the border / Talkin' to one of the boys / Heart's grown cold / Fast cars / Big boy / Talkin' 'bout love / Fallen angel / Ship of dreams / Turning a new leaf. *(re-iss. Sep90 on 'Castle' cd/lp; CLA CD/LP 181)*

Apr 80. (7") <2231> **SHIP OF DREAMS. / HEARTS GROWN COLD** | `-` | `-`

	NEMS	A&M
Dec 80. (d7") *(BSD 1)* **NAZARETH LIVE** (live) | `-` | `-`
– Hearts grown cold / Talkin' to one of the boys / Razamanaz / Hair of the dog.

—— added **JOHN LOCKE** (b.25 Sep'43, Los Angeles, Calif.) – keyboards (ex-SPIRIT)

Feb 81. (lp/c) *(NEL/NEC 6019)* <4844> **THE FOOL CIRCLE** | `60` | `70`
– Dressed to kill / Another year / Moonlight eyes / Pop the Silo / Let me be your leader / We are the people / Every young man's dream / Little part of you / Cocaine (live) / Victoria. *(re-iss. Feb91 on 'Castle' cd/lp; CLA CD/LP 214)*

Mar 81. (7") *(NES 301)* <2324> **DRESSED TO KILL. / POP THE SILO** | |

—— **BILLY RANKIN** – guitar repl. ZAL who joined TANDOORI CASSETTE

Sep 81. (d-lp/c) *(NELD/NELC 102)* <6703> **'SNAZ** (live) | `78` | `83`
– Telegram (part 1:- On your way – part 2:- So you want to be a rock'n'roll star – part 3:- Sound check) / Razamanaz / I want to do everything for you / This flight tonight / Beggars day / Every young man's dream / Heart's grown cold / Java blues / Cocaine / Big boy / Holiday / Dressed to kill / Hair of the dog / Expect no mercy / Shape of things / Let me be your leader / Love hurts / Tush / Juicy Lucy / Morning dew. *(re-iss. Jan87 on 'Castle' lp/c/cd; CLA LP/MC/CD 130) (cd re-iss. May97 on 'Essential'; ESMCD 531)*

Sep 81. (7") *(NES 302)* <2378> **MORNING DEW (live). / JUICY LUCY (live)** | |

Dec 81. (7") <2389> **HAIR OF THE DOG (live). / HOLIDAY (live)** | `-` |

Jul 82. (7") *(NIS 101)* <2421> **LOVE LEADS TO MADNESS. / TAKE THE RAP** | |

Aug 82. (7") <2444> **DREAM ON. / TAKE THE RAP** | `-` |

Jan 83. (7") *(NIS 102)* **GAMES. / YOU LOVE ANOTHER** | `-` |

Feb 83. (lp/c) *(NIN 001)* <4901> **2XS** | | `Jun82`
– Love leads to madness / Boys in the band / You love another / Gatecrash / Games / Back to the trenches / Dream on / Lonely in the night / Preservation / Take the rap / Mexico. *(cd-iss. Feb91 on 'Castle'; CLACD 217)*

Jun 83. (7") *(NIS 103)* **DREAM ON. / JUICY LUCY** | `-` |

	Vertigo	Capitol
Jun 83. (lp) *(812396-1)* **SOUND ELIXIR** | `-` | `German`
– All nite radio / Milk and honey / Whippin' boy / Rain on the window / Backroom boys / Why don't you read the book / I ran / Rags to riches / Local still / Where are you now. *(re-iss. Jul85 on 'Sahara'; SAH 130) (cd-iss. Feb91 on 'Castle'; CLACD 218)*

Jul 83. (7") *(812 544-7)* **WHERE ARE YOU NOW. / ON THE RUN** | `-` | `German`

Sep 84. (lp/c) *(VERL/+C 20)* **THE CATCH** | `-` |
– Party down / Ruby Tuesday / Last exit Brooklyn / Moondance / Love of freedom / This month's Messiah / You don't believe in us / Sweetheart tree / Road to nowhere.

Sep 84. (7") *(VER 13)* **RUBY TUESDAY. / SWEETHEART TREE** | `-` |
(12"+=) *(VERX 13)* – This month's messiah / Do you think about it.

Oct 84. (7"/12") *(880 085-1/-Q)* **PARTY DOWN. / DO YOU THINK ABOUT IT** | `-` | `German`

1986. (lp/cd) *(830 300-1/-2)* **CINEMA** | `-` | `Europe`
– Cinema / Juliet / Just another heartache / Other side of you / Hit the fan / One from the heart / Salty salty / White boy / A veterans song / Telegram / This flight tonight.

1986. (7") *(884 982-7)* **CINEMA. / THIS FLIGHT TONIGHT (live)** | `-` | `Europe`
(12"+=) *(884 981-1)* – Telegram (live).

1989. (lp/cd) *(838 426-1/-2)* **SNAKES 'N' LADDERS** | `-` | `Europe`
– We are animals / Lady luck / Hang on to a dream / Piece of my heart / Trouble / The key / Back to school / Girls / Donna – Get off that crack / See you, see you / Helpless. *(UK cd-iss. May97 on 'Essential'; ESMCD 501)*

1989. (cd-s) *(874 733-2)* **PIECE OF MY HEART / LADY LUCK / SEE YOU SEE ME** | `-` |

1989. (7") *(876 448-7)* **WINNER ON THE NIGHT. / TROUBLE** | `-` | `German`
(12"+=/cd-s+=) *(876 448-1/-2)* – Woke up this morning (live) / Bad, bad boy (live).

—— **BILLY RANKIN** – guitar now totally repl. CHARLTON

	Mausoleum	Griffin
Nov 91. (cd/c/lp) *(3670010.2/.4/.1)* **NO JIVE** | | `1993`
– Hire and fire / Do you wanna play house / Right between the eyes / Every time it rains / Keeping our love alive / Thinkin' man's nightmare / Cover your heart / Lap of luxury / a.The Rowan tree (traditional) – b.Tell me that you love me / Cry wolf. *(cd+=)* – This flight tonight.

Jan 92. (7") *(3670010.7)* **EVERY TIME IT RAINS / THIS FLIGHT TONIGHT 1991** | | `-`
(12"+=/cd-s+=) *(3670010.0/.3)* – Lap of Luxury.

Mar 92. (cd-ep) *(903005.3)* **TELL ME THAT YOU LOVE ME / RIGHT BETWEEN THE EYES / ROWAN TREE – TELL ME THAT YOU LOVE ME (extended)**

	Essential	Rykodisc
May 97. (cd) *(ESMCD 503)* **MOVE ME** | | `1995`
– Let me be your dog / Can't shake these shakes / Crack me up / Move me / Steamroller / Stand by your beds / Rip it up / Demon alcohol / You had it comin' / Bring it on home to mama / Burning down.

– compilations, others, etc. –

Jun 85. (d-lp) *Sahara; (SAH 137)* **20 GREATEST HITS** | | `-`

Jun 88. (d-lp/c/cd) *That's Original; (TFO LP/TC/CD 13)* **RAMPANT / HAIR OF THE DOG** | |

Jul 88. (7") *Old Gold; (OG 9801)* **LOVE HURTS. / BAD BAD BOY** | |

Jul 88. (7") *Old Gold; (OG 9803)* **THIS FLIGHT TONIGHT. / BROKEN DOWN ANGEL** | |

Dec 88. (lp/c/cd) *Raw Power; (RAW LP/TC/CD 039)* **ANTHOLOGY** | |

Jan 89. (cd-ep) *Special Edition; (CD3-17)* **THIS FLIGHT TONIGHT / BROKEN DOWN ANGEL / LOVE HURTS / BAD, BAD BOY** | |

Jun 89. (cd) *Milestones; (MSSCD 102)* **MILESTONES** | |

1990. (cd) *Ariola Express; (295969)* **BROKEN DOWN ANGEL** | |

Jan 91. (lp/c/cd/d-lp) *Castle; (CLA CD/MC/LP 280)* **THE SINGLES COLLECTION** | |
– Broken down angel / Bad, bad boy / This flight tonight / Shanghai'd in Shanghai / Love hurts / Hair of the dog / My white bicycle / Holy roller / Carry out feelings / You're the violin / Somebody to roll / I don't want to go on without you / Gone dead train / A place in your heart / May the Sun shine / Star / Dressed to kill / Morning dew / Games / Love will lead to madness.

Oct 91. (3xcd-box) *Essential; (ESBCD 967)* **ANTHOLOGY** | | `-`

Nov 91. (cd) *Windsong; (WINDCD 005)* **BBC RADIO 1 LIVE IN CONCERT** | |

Dec 91. (cd) *Dojo; (EARLCD 2)* **THE EARLY YEARS** | |

Mar 92. (3xcd-box) *Castle; (CLABX 908)* **SNAZ / RAZAMANAZ / EXPECT NO MERCY** | |

Apr 93. (cd) *Sequel; (NEMCD 639)* **FROM THE VAULTS** | |

Jun 93. (cd/c) *Optima; (OPTM CD/C 009)* **ALIVE AND KICKING** | |

Jun 94. (cd) *BR Music; (BRCD 1392)* **GREATEST HITS** | |

Mar 96. (cd) *Disky; (CR 86711-2)* **CHAMPIONS OF ROCK** | |

Oct 96. (cd) *Essential; (ESMCD 369)* **GREATEST HITS** | |

NAZZ (see under ⇒ RUNDGREN, Todd)

NEARLY GOD (see under ⇒ TRICKY)

NED'S ATOMIC DUSTBIN

(dig out; 4th edition or Great Alt & Indie . . .)

NEGATIVLAND (dig out; Great Alt & Indie . . .)

Fred NEIL

Born: 1937, St. Petersburg, Florida, USA. Gravitating to New York in the late 50's, NEIL not only wrote for other artists (his most famous credit being 'CANDY MAN', the B-side of ROY ORBISON's 1961 hit, 'CRYING') but actually recorded a series of obscure solo tracks for various labels. At the same time he was also making a name for himself on the Greenwich Village folk scene as one of the most inventive, mesmeric and enigmatic singer/songwriters of the era. Captivating audiences with an oak-matured voice pitched right at the bottom end and lying somewhere between JOHNNY CASH and DAN PENN, NEIL's acolytes included the likes of JOHN SEBASTIAN and DAVID CROSBY, future folk-rockers both who regarded NEIL as their mentor. By 1964, he was working in tandem with VINCE MARTIN and the pair recorded a one-off album for 'Elektra', 'TEAR DOWN THE WALLS' (1965). Guests included a pre-LOVIN' SPOONFUL JOHN SEBASTIAN and future MOUNTAIN man, FELIX PAPPALARDI (incongruous as that may seem) on a set which paved the way for NEIL's solo debut proper, 'BLEECKER & MacDOUGAL' (1966). Featuring the oft-covered 'OTHER SIDE OF LIFE', the record was a bluesy affair which predated his flight into fully electrified folk-rock at 'Capitol'. 'FRED NEIL' (1967) was the man's definitive statement, an eddying stream of hazy, heavy-lidded folk/rock/blues A&R'd by L.A. whizzkid, Nik Venet and rooted in the unique, jazz-influenced style NEIL had developed. Leading off with the sublime 'THE DOLPHINS' (later the subject of an equally exquisite cover by TIM BUCKLEY), a haunting, bittersweet and almost otherworldly meditation on love gone wrong, the album also featured his ubiquitous escapist masterpiece, 'EVERYBODY'S TALKIN' alongside live staples 'THAT'S THE BAG I'M IN' and 'BA-DE-DA'. The fact that the former two tracks, especially 'EVERYBODY'S TALKIN' (HARRY NILSSON's 'Midnight Cowboy' version is just one of many), found greater fame with other artists sums up NEIL's career; content to guide, influence and lay down blueprints for fame-hungry young bucks, NEIL himself wanted no part in the fame game and subsequently withdrew completely from the music scene. Before he did, he released a further couple of albums for 'Capitol', the drawn-out studio jamming of 'SESSIONS' (1968) and 'THE OTHER SIDE OF THIS LIFE' (1971), a hotch potch of live cuts and unused studio tracks featuring an interesting GRAM PARSONS-enhanced cover of William Bell's 'YOU DON'T MISS YOUR WATER' (PARSONS also cut the track with The BYRDS on 1968's 'Sweetheart Of The Rodeo' album). The speed and effectiveness of NEIL's subsequent retreat from the music business was unequalled in the industry's history, the man's reclusiveness so complete that despite his contribution to modern music (NEIL's spirit permeates the work of TIM BUCKLEY and TIM HARDIN especially) he remains all but forgotten and unknown even among many 60's buffs, record collectors and musicians. While some of his recordings are occasionally re-issued in the States, nothing has been available in the UK since a 'VERY BEST OF..' in '86. Wait a minute . . . stop press . . . I've just come across the 'MANY SIDES OF', a double-CD which has everything. There . . . everything solved . . . and about bloody time too.

Album rating: TEAR DOWN THE WALLS with Vince Martin (*5) / BLEECKER & MacDOUGAL (*7) / FRED NEIL (*7) / SESSIONS (*4) / THE OTHER SIDE OF THIS LIFE (*5) / THE VERY BEST OF FRED NEIL compilation (*7) / THE MANY SIDES OF FRED NEIL compilation (*8)

FRED NEIL – vocals, guitar

		not iss.	F.M.
1964.	(lp; with Various Artists) <309> **HOOTENANNY LIVE AT THE BITTER END** (live)	-	
1964.	(lp; with Various Artists) <319> **WORLD OF FOLK MUSIC**	-	

		not iss.	Elektra
Mar 65.	(lp; by FRED NEIL & VINCE MARTIN) <EKS 7246> **TEAR DOWN THE WALLS**	-	

– I know you rider / Red flowers / Tear down the walls / Weary blues / Toy balloon / Baby / Morning dew / I'm a drifter / Linin' track / I got 'em / Wild child in a world of trouble / Dade County jail lonesome valley.

Mar 65.	(7"; by FRED NEIL & VINCE MARTIN) <EKSN 45009> **TEAR DOWN THE WALLS. / I KNOW YOU RIDER**	-	

—— next featured **PETE CHILDS** – guitar / **JOHN SEBASTIAN** – harmonica / **FELIX PAPPALARDI + DOUGLAS HATFIELD** – bass

Feb 66.	(lp) <EKS 7293> **BLEECKER AND MacDOUGAL**	-	

– Bleecker & MacDougal / Blues on the ceiling / Sweet mama / Little bit of rain / Country boy / Other side to this life / Mississippi train / Travelin' shoes / The water is wide / Yonder comes the blues / Candy man / Handful of gimme / Gone again. (UK-iss.1969; same as US) <re-iss. 1970 as 'LITTLE BIT OF RAIN'; EKS 74073> <US cd-iss. 1999 on 'WEA Int'; 2693>

		Capitol	Capitol
Jan 67.	(7") <5786> **BADI-DA. / THE DOLPHINS**	-	
Feb 67.	(lp) <ST 2665> **FRED NEIL**	-	

– The dolphins / I've got a secret / That's the bag I'm in / Badi-da / Faretheewell (Fred's tune) / Everybody's talkin' / Everything happens / Sweet cocaine / Green rocky road / Cynicrust-petefredjohn raga. <re-iss. 1969 as 'EVERYBODY'S TALKIN'; SM 294> (UK-iss.of re-iss. Jan94 on 'Creation Rev-Ola'; C-REV 21CD)

Sep 67.	(7") <2047> **I'VE GOT A SECRET. / THE DOLPHINS**	-	
Jan 68.	(7") <2091> **FELICITY. / PLEASE SEND ME SOMEONE TO LOVE**	-	
Feb 68.	(lp) <ST 2862> **SESSIONS**	-	

– Felicity / Please send me someone to love / Merry go round / Look over yonder / Fools are a long time coming / Looks like rain / Roll on Rosie.

Jul 68.	(7") <2256> **EVERYBODY'S TALKIN'. / THAT'S THE BAG I'M IN**		
Oct 69.	(7") (CL 15616) <2604> **EVERYBODY'S TALKIN'. / BADI-DA**	-	
1971.	(lp) <(E-ST 657)> **THE OTHER SIDE OF THIS LIFE** (live)	-	

– Other side of this life / Roll on Rosie / The dolphins / That's the bag I'm in / Sweet cocaine / Everybody's talkin' / Come back baby / Badi-da / Prettiest train / Ya don't miss your water / Felicity.

—— FRED had already retired from the music world in the late 60's

– compilations, others, etc. –

1968.	(7") (EKSN 45036) **CANDY MAN. / THE WATER IS WIDE**		-
Nov 86.	(lp) See For Miles; (SEE 77) **THE VERY BEST OF FRED NEIL**		-

– That's the bag I'm in / Badi-da / Faretheewell (Fred's tune) / Merry go round / Felicity / Everybody's talkin' / Everything happens / Sweet cocaine / Green rocky road / Cynicrustpetefredjohn raga / Please send me someone to love / Fools are a long time coming / The dolphins / I've got a secret (didn't we shake sugaree).

Mar 99.	(d-cd) Collector's; <(WSCCM 0070-2)> **THE MANY SIDES OF FRED NEIL**		

– The dolphins / I've got a secret (didn't we shake sugaree) / That's the bag I'm in / Badi-da / Faretheewell (Fred's tune) / Everybody's talkin' / Everything happens / Sweet cocaine / Green rocky road / Cynicrustpetefredjohn raga / Felicity / Please send me someone to love / Merry go round / Look over yonder / Fools are a long time coming / Looks like rain / Roll on Rosie / Other side of this life / Roll on Rosie (long) / The dolphins / That's the bag I'm in / Sweet cocaine / Everybody's talkin' / Come back baby / Badi-da / Prettiest train / You don't miss your water / Felicity / Long black veil / Bottom of the glass / Sweet mama / Trouble in mind / December's dream / Ride stormy weather / How long blues – Drown in tears / Other side of this life.

Vince NEIL (see under ⇒ MOTLEY CRUE)

NEKTAR (dig out; Great Psychedelic . . .)

Bill NELSON

Born: 18 Dec'48, Wakefield, Yorkshire, England. In the late 60's, after a job as a government officer, he joined local groups, GLOBAL VILLAGE TRUCKING COMPANY and GENTLE REVOLUTION. NELSON subsequently released an obscure and limited solo album, 'NORTHERN DREAM', on his own label in 1971, the record soon finding its way to Radio 1 DJ, John Peel, who gave it night-time airplay. That year, the singer/guitarist formed BE-BOP DELUXE alongside IAN PARKIN, ROBERT BRYAN, NICHOLAS CHATTERTON-DEW and RICHARD BROWN and after one single, they signed to 'Harvest'. Their first album, 'AXE VICTIM' (1974), showcased the talent of the gifted NELSON, a dextrous multi-instrumentalist whose talent for quirky glam/prog-rock won him an immediate cult following. The record's release was swiftly followed by a tour supporting COCKNEY REBEL, a group they were constantly compared with in the music press. In August '74, NELSON split the band up, subsequently re-forming the group with unhappy ex-REBELS, MILTON REAME-JAMES and PAUL AVRON JEFFRYS. The revamped line-up debuted on the well-received set, 'FUTURAMA' (1975), consolidating their critical standing early the next year with a UK Top 30 hit single, 'SHIPS IN THE NIGHT' (taken from follow-up album, 'SUNBURST FINISH'). BE-BOP DELUXE enjoyed a couple of years in the big league until NELSON decided to concentrate on another project, RED NOISE. After a promising 1979 album, 'SOUND ON SOUND', the man went solo, subsequently hitting the Top 10 with an adventurous, experimental double-set, 'QUIT DREAMING AND GET ON THE BEAM' (1981). Throughout the 80's and 90's, NELSON released a plethora of albums, mostly for his own obscure 'Cocteau' label. Having also worked with The SKIDS, The ASSOCIATES, YELLOW MAGIC ORCHESTRA and DAVID SYLVIAN, on collaborative efforts and production work, he subsequently released his best work for some time in 1996, 'AFTER THE SATELLITE SINGS'. • **Trivia:** His younger brother IAN (of RED NOISE), also had a minor hit with FIAT LUX.

Album rating: NORTHERN DREAM (*4) / Be-Bop Deluxe: AXE VICTIM (*5) / FUTURAMA (*4) / SUNBURST FINISH (*7) / MODERN MUSIC (*6) / LIVE IN THE AIR AGE (*5) / DRASTIC PLASTIC (*5) / RAIDING THE DIVINE ARCHIVES compilation (*8) / Bill Nelson: SOUND ON SOUND with Red Noise (*7) / QUIT DREAMING AND GET ON THE BEAM (*9) / DAS KABINETT (THE CABINET OF DR. CAGLIARI) (*4) / LA BELLE ET LA BETE (THE BEAUTY AND THE BEAST) (*4) / THE LOVE THAT WHIRLS (*6) / CHIMERA (*7) / SAVAGE GESTURE FOR CHARMS SAKE (*6) / GETTING THE HOLY GHOST ACROSS (*6) / CHAMBER OF DREAMS (*5) / SUMMER OF GOD'S PIANO (*5) / MAP OF DREAMS (*5) / CHANCE ENCOUNTERS IN THE GARDEN OF LIGHT (*5) / OPTIMISM (*5) / PAVILLIONS OF THE HEART AND SOUL (*6) / CATALOGUE OF OBSESSIONS (*6) / DUPLEX: THE BEST OF BILL NELSON compilation (*7) / LUMINOUS (*6) / BLUE MOONS AND LAUGHING GUITARS (*6) / CRIMSWORTH (FLOWERS, STONES, FOUNTAINS AND FLAMES) (*5) / CULTUREMIX (*6) / PRACTICALLY WIRED (*5) / AFTER THE SATELLITE SINGS (*7)

BILL NELSON – vocals, lead guitar

		Smile	not iss.
1971	(lp) (LAF 2182) **NORTHERN DREAM**		-

– Photograph (a beginning) / Everyone's hero / House of sand / End of the seasons / Rejoice / Love's a way / Northern dreamer (1957) / Bloo blooz / Sad fellings / See it through / Smiles / Chymepeace (an ending). (re-iss. Feb81, Mar82 & Aug86 on 'Butt'; BUTT 002) (cd-iss. Mar96 on 'Blueprint'; SM 777CD)

BE-BOP DELUXE

were formed by **BILL NELSON** plus **IAN PARKIN** – rhythm guitar / **ROBERT BRYAN** – bass / **NICHOLAS CHATTERTON-DEW** – drums / **RICHARD BROWN** – keyboards

	Smile	not iss.
Jan 73. (7") *(LAFS 001)* **TEENAGE ARCHANGEL. / JETS AT DAWN**		–

—— became trio, when BROWN departed.

	Harvest	Harvest
May 74. (7") *(HAR 5081)* **JET SILVER (AND THE DOLLS OF VENUS). / THIRD FLOOR HEAVEN**		

Jun 74. (lp) *(SHVL 813)* <*SM 11689*> **AXE VICTIM**
– Axe victim / Love is swift arrows / Jet Silver (and the dolls of Venus) / Third floor Heaven / Night creatures / Rocket cathedrals / Adventures in a Yorkshire landscape / Jets at dawn / No trains to Heaven / Darkness (l'immoralise). *(cd-iss. Feb91; CZ 327)* – (3 extra).

—— Aug74, **NELSON** recruited entire new line-up **MILTON REAME-JAMES** – keyboards (ex-COCKNEY REBEL) repl. IAN / **PAUL AVRON JEFFRYS** – bass (ex-COCKNEY REBEL) repl. ROBERT / **SIMON FOX** – drums (ex-HACKENSHACK) repl. NICHOLAS

—— (late 1974) **BILL** and **SIMON** were joined by **CHARLIE TUMAHAI** (b. New Zealand) – bass who repl. MILTON & PAUL

Feb 75. (7"; w-drawn) *(HAR 5091)* **BETWEEN THE WORLDS. / LIGHTS**	–	–

May 75. (lp) *(SHSP 4045)* <*ST 11432*> **FUTURAMA**
– Stage whispers / Love with the madman / Maid in Heaven / Sister seagull / Sound track / Music in Dreamland / Jean Cocteau / Between the worlds / Swan song. *(cd-iss. Feb91; CZ 328)* (cd re-iss. Apr97 on 'E.M.I.'; REPLAYCD 27)

Jun 75. (7") *(HAR 5098)* **MAID IN HEAVEN. / LIGHTS**		–
Jul 75. (7") <*4151*> **MAID IN HEAVEN. / SISTER SEAGULL**	–	

—— added **ANDREW CLARKE** – keyboards

Jan 76. (7") *(HAR 5104)* <*4244*> **SHIPS IN THE NIGHT. / CRYING TO THE SKY**	23	

Jan 76. (lp/c) *(SHSP/TC-SHSP 4053)* <*St 11478*> **SUNBURST FINISH**
– Fair exchange / Heavenly homes / Ships in the night / Crying to the sky / Sleep that burns / Beauty secrets / Life in the air age / Like an old blues / Crystal gazing / Blazing apostles. *(re-iss. Mar82 on 'Fame' lp/c; FA/TC-FA 3004) (re-iss. Jun86 on 'Revolver' lp/c; REV LP/MC 71) (cd-iss. Feb91 +=; CZ 329)* – Shine / Speed of the wind / Blue as a jewel.

Jan 76. (lp/c) *(SHSP/TC-SHSP 4053)* <*St 11478*>	17	96

Aug 76. (7") *(HAR 5110)* **KISS OF THE LIGHT. / Funky Phaser Unearthly Merchandise: SHINE**		–

Sep 76. (lp/c) *(SHSP/TC-SHSP 4058)* <*ST 11575*> **MODERN MUSIC**
– Orphans of Babylon / Twilight capers / Kiss of the light / The bird charmer's destiny / The gold at the end of my rainbow / Bring back the spark / Modern music / Dancing in the moonlight / Honeymoon on Mars / Lost in the neon world / Dance of the Uncle Sam humanoids / Modern music / Forbidden lovers / Down on Terminal street / Make the music magic. *(cd-iss. Feb91; CZ 330)* – (3 extra). *(cd re-iss. Apr97 on 'E.M.I.'; REPLAYCD 28)*

Sep 76. (lp/c)	12	88

Jul 77. (white-lp) *(SHVL 816)* <*11666*> **LIVE IN THE AIR AGE (live)**
– Life in the air age / Ships in the night / Piece of mine / Fair exchange / Mill street junction / Adventures in a Yorkshire landscape / Blazing apostles. *(free-7"ep)* **SHINE. / SISTER SEAGULL / MAID IN HEAVEN** *(cd-iss. Feb91; CZ 331)* – (3 extra ep tracks).

Jul 77. (white-lp)	10	65

Sep 77. (7") *(HAR 5135)* **JAPAN. / FUTURIST MANIFESTO**		–
Feb 78. (7") *(HAR 5147)* <*4571*> **PANIC IN THE WORLD. / BLUE AS A JEWEL**		

Feb 78. (lp/c) *(SHSP/TC-SHSP 4091)* <*ST 11750*> **DRASTIC PLASTIC**
– Electrical language / New precision / New mysteries / Surreal estate / Love in flames / Panic in the world / Dangerous stranger / Superenigmatix (lethal appliances for the home) / Islands of the dead / Visions of endless hopes / Possession / Islands of the dead. *(cd-iss. Feb91; CZ 332)* – (3 extra tracks). *(cd re-iss. Apr97 on 'E.M.I.'; REPLAYCD 29)*

Feb 78. (lp/c)	22	95

May 78. (7") *(HAR 5158)* **ELECTRICAL LANGUAGE. / SURREAL ESTATE**		–

—— Disbanded Spring 1978. TUMAHAI joined The DUKES, SIMON joined JACK GREEN. CLARKE joined NICO's band.

– compilations, others, etc. –

on 'Harvest' unless mentioned otherwise

Oct 76. (7"ep) *(HAR 5117)* **HOT VALVES**	36	

– Maid in Heaven / Blazing apostles / Jet Silver and the dolls of Venus / Bring back the spark.

Nov 78. (d-lp) *(SHDW 410)* **THE BEST OF AND THE REST OF BE-BOP DELUXE**
(cd-iss. May90; 794 158-2)

May 81. (lp/c) *(SHSM/TC-SHSM 2034)* **THE SINGLES A's & B's**
(cd-iss. Feb92 on 'See For Miles'; SEECD 336)

Aug 83. (7"m) *Cocteau; (COQ 7)* **PANIC IN THE WORLD. / MAID IN HEAVEN / ELECTRICAL LANGUAGE**
(re-iss. Jul85 as 12"m; COQT 7)

Sep 83. (d-lp) *(EDP 154 6793)* **AXE VICTIM / FUTURAMA**

May 84. (7") *EMI Gold; (G45 21)* **SHIPS IN THE NIGHT. / MAID IN HEAVEN**

Aug 86. (lp) *Dojo; (DOJOLP 42)* **BOP TO THE RED NOISE**

Mar 87. (lp/c) *(EMS/TC-EMS 1130)* **RAIDING THE DIVINE ARCHIVES**
– Jet silver (and the dolls of Venus) / Adventures in a Yorkshire landscape / Maid in Heaven / Ships in the night / Life in the air age / Kiss of light / Sister seagull / Modern music / Japan / Panic in the world / Bring back the spark / Forbidden lovers / Electrical language. *(re-iss. Apr90 on 'E.M.I.'+=; CDP 794 158-2)* – Fair exchange / Sleep that burns / Between the worlds / Music in Dreamland.

Sep 94. (cd) *Windsong; (WINCD 065)* **RADIOLAND – BBC RADIO 1 LIVE IN CONCERT (live)**

BILL NELSON'S RED NOISE

BILL NELSON with **ANDREW CLARKE** – keyboards / **RICK FORD** – drums / brother **IAN NELSON** – saxophone / **STEVE PEER** – drums

	Harvest	Harvest
Feb 79. (7"red) *(HAR 5176)* **FURNITURE MUSIC. / WONDERTOYS THAT LAST FOREVER / ACQUITTED BY MIRRORS**	59	
Feb 79. (lp/c) *(SHSP/TC-SHSP 4095)* **SOUND ON SOUND**	33	

– Don't touch me, I'm electric / For young moderns / Stop – go – stop / Furniture music / Radar in my heart / Stay young / Out of touch / A better home in the phantom zone / Substitute flesh / The atom age / Art – Empire – Industry / Revolt into style. *(re-iss. Nov85 on 'Cocteau' lp/c; JC/CJC 14)*

Apr 79. (7"blue) *(HAR 5183)* **REVOLT INTO STYLE. / OUT OF TOUCH**	69	

BILL NELSON

solo, with **TOM KELLICHAN** – drums / with sessioners

	Cocteau	not iss.
Jun 80. (7"ep) *(COQ 1)* **DO YOU DREAM IN COLOUR?**	52	–

– Do you dream in colour? / Ideal homes / Instantly yours / Atom Man loves Radium Girl.

	Crepescule	not iss.
Mar 81. (7") **ROOMS WITH BRITTLE VIEWS. / DADA GUITARS**	–	– Belgium

	Mercury	Mercury
Mar 81. (7") *(WILL 1)* **BANAL. / MR. MAGNETISN HIMSELF**		

(12"+=) *(WILL 1-12)* – Turn to fiction.

May 81. (lp/c) *(6359 055)(7557 010)* **QUIT DREAMIMG AND GET ON THE BEAM**
– Banal / Living in my limousine / Vertical games / Disposable / False alarms / Decline and fall / Life runs out like sand / A kind of loving / Do you dream in colour? / U.H.F. / Youth of nation on fire / Quit dreaming and get on the beam. *(w/ free-lp)* **SOUNDING THE RITUAL ECHO** – Annunciation / The ritual echo / Sleep / Near east / Emak bakia / My intricate image / Endless orchids / The heat in the room / Another willingly opened window / Vanishing parades / Glass fish (for the final aquarium) / Cubical domes / Ashes of roses / The shadow garden (opium). *(iss.on own.Jun85 on 'Cocteau'; JCS 12) (cd-iss. on own.Sep89; JCCD 12) (cd-iss. Jul86 on 'Cocteau'+=; JCCD 15)* – White sound.

May 81. (lp/c)	7	

Jun 81. (7") *(BILL 2)* **YOUTH OF NATION ON FIRE. / BE MY DYNAMO**	73	

(d7"+=) *(WILL 22)* – Rooms with brittle views / All my wives were iron.

Sep 81. (7") *(WILL 3)* **LIVING IN MY LIMOUSINE. / BIRDS OF TIME**		

(12"+=) *(WILL 3-12)* – Love in the abstract / White sound.

Apr 82. (7") *(WILL 4)* **EROS ARRIVING. / HAUNTING IN MY HEAD**		–

(d7"+=) *(WILL 44)* – Flesh / He and sleep were brothers.

Jun 82. (d-lp/d-c) *(WHIRL/CURL 3)* **THE LOVE THAT WHIRLS**	28	

– Empire of the senses / Hope for the heartbeat / Waiting for the voices / Private view / Eros arriving / Bride of Christ in Autumn / When your dream of perfect beauty comes true / Flaming desire / Portrait of Jan with flowers / Crystal escalator in the palace of God department store / Echo in her eyes / October man. *(re-iss. Jul86 on 'Cocteau', cd+=)* – Flesh / He and sleep were brothers.

Jul 82. (7"/12") *(WILL 5/+12)* **FLAMING DESIRE. / THE PASSION**		
May 83. (lp/c) *(MERB/+C 19)* **CHIMERA**	30	

– The real adventure / Acceleration / Every day feels like another new drug / Tender is the night / Glow world / Another day, another ray of hope. *(cd-iss. Sep87 on 'Cocteau', re-iss. Apr89)*

	Cocteau	Portrait
Aug 83. (7"m) *(COQ 10)* **TOUCH AND GLOW. / DANCING IN THE WILD / LOVE WITHOUT FEAR**		
Dec 83. (m-lp) *(JCM 3)* **SAVAGE GESTURES FOR CHARMS SAKE**		

– The man in the exine suit / Watching my dream boat go down in flames / The meat room / Another happy thought (carved forever in your cortex) / Portrait of Jan with Moon and stars. *(re-iss. Feb85)*

Aug 84. (7") *(COQ 15)* **ACCELERATION. / HARD FACTS FROM THE FICTION DEPARTMENT**		

(12"pic-d+=) *(COQT 15)* – ('A'short) / ('A'long).

Oct 84. (lp) <*BFR 39270*> **VISTAMIX**	–	

– The real adventure / Flaming desire / Acceleration / Empire of the senses / Everyday feels like another new drug / Do you dream in color? / A kind of loving / Tender is the night / Glow world / Another day, another ray of hope.

	Portrait	Portrait
Mar 86. (7"/12") *(A/TA 6928)* **WILDEST DREAMS. / SELF IMPERSONATION**		
Apr 86. (lp/c) *(PRT/40 26602)* <*R 40146*> **GETTING THE HOLY GHOST ACROSS** <US-title 'ON A BLUE WING'>	91	

– Suvasini / Contemplation / Theology / Wildest dreams / Lost in your mystery / Rise like a fountain / Age of reason / Hidden flame / Because of you / Living for the spangled moment / Word for word / Illusions of you / Heart and soul / Finks and stooges of the spirit. *(cd-iss. 1988 on 'C.B.S.'; CDCBS 26602)*

	Cocteau	Enigma
Jun 86. (lp) *(JC 7)* **CHAMBER OF DREAMS**		

– The blazing memory of innuendo / Into the luminous future / Dip in the swimming pool / Reactor / Tomorrowland (the threshold of 1947) / Listening to lizards / Endless torsion / My sublime perversion / Eros in Autumn / Sleeplessness / The latest skyline / Train of thought / Packs and fountains clouds and trees / Golden bough / Forever Orpheus / In arcadia / Sentimental / Autumn fires / Wild blue yonder. *(cd-iss. Aug89; JCCD 7)*

Oct 86. (lp/c) *(JC/TCJC 6)* **SUMMER OF GOD'S PIANO**		–

– Antennae two / N.B.C.97293 / The sleep of Hollywood / The celestial bridegroom / Under the red arch / Orient pearl / Sacrament / Falling blossoms / The difficulty of being / Zanoni / The Chinese nightingale / Soon September (another enchantment) / Rural shires / Perfido incanto / The lost years / The charm of transit / Night thoughts (twilight radio) / Wysteria / Swing / Snowfall / Real of dusk / Over ocean. *(cd-iss. Aug89; JCCD 6)*

Jan 87. (lp/c/cd) *(JC/TCJC/JCCD 19)* **MAP OF DREAMS**		–

– Legions of the endless night / Spinning creatures / At the gates of the singing garden / Heavenly message No.1, 2 & 3 / Fellini's picnic / Dark angel / Infernal regions / Dance of the fragrant woman / The alchemy of ecstasy / Aphrodite adorned / The wheel of fortune and the hand of fate / Forked tongues, mixed blessings / Another tricky mission for the celestial pilot / Water of life (transfiguration).

May 87. (12"; by SCALA: BILL NELSON & DARYL RUNSWICK) *(COQT 21)* **SECRET CEREMONY (theme from 'BROND'). / WIPING A TEAR FROM THE ALL SEEING EYE** [ ] -

Nov 87. (d-lp/c/cd) *(JEAN/+TC/CD 20)* **CHANCE ENCOUNTERS IN THE GARDEN OF LIGHT** [ ] -
– My dark demon / The dove consumed (the serpent slumbers) / Calling Heaven, calling Heaven overs / Path of return / Theurgia / Staircase to no place / Evocation of a radiant childhood / The kingdom of consequence / Divine raptures of a radiant childhood / Bright star (moonlight over the ocean blue) / A bird of the air shall earn the voice / Clothed in light amongst the stars / Hastening the chariot of my hearts desire / Transcendant conversation / West deep / The spirit cannot fail / Pilots of kite / Phantom gardens / The angel of hearth and home / Villefranche interior / Night tides / First memory / Azure extention / Radiant spires / Evening peal / Thremodia / Short drink for a certain fountain / Body of light / At the centre / Self-initiation / The word that became flesh / The hermetic garden / Revolving globes / The four square citadel / Orient of Memphis / Little daughters of light / Angel at the western window.

Sep 88. (lp/c/cd; as BILL NELSON ORCHESTRA ARCANA) *(JC/+TC/CD 21)* **OPTIMISM** [ ] -
– Exactly the way you want it / Why be lonely / Everyday is a better day / The receiver and the fountain pen / Welcome home Mr. Kane / This is true / Greeting a new day / The breath in my father's saxophone / Our lady of apparations / The whole city between us / Deva dance / Always looking forward to tomorrow / Profiles, hearts, stars / Alchemia.

Dec 88. (7") *(COQ 22)* **LIFE IN YOUR HANDS. / DO YOU DREAM IN COLOUR** [ ] -
(12"+=/cd-s+=) *(COQ T/CD 22)* – Get out of that hole / Drean demon.

Aug 89. (lp/cd) *(JC/+CD 8)* **PAVILLIONS OF THE HEART AND SOUL** [ ] -
– Gift of the August tide / Loving tongues / Blue nude / In the realms of bells / Your nebulous smile / The glance of a glittering stranger / Another kiss for your slender neck / The warmth of women's eyes / Seduction (ritual with roses) / Dreamed entrances / Four pieces for imaginary strings:- Herself with her shadow – The exquisite corpse – Ardent hands – Her laughing torso / Migrating angels / Les amoureaux / Meshes of the afternoon / Mountains of the heart / Willow silk / Tender encounters (states of grace) / Melancholia / The eternal female.

Aug 89. (lp/cd) *(JC/+CD 9)* **CATALOGUE OF OBSESSIONS** [ ] -
– Sex party six / Tune in Tokyo / Promise of perfume / View from a balcony / Test of affection / Birds in two hemispheres / Wider windows for the walls / The boy pilots of Bangkok / Talk technique / Glass breakfast / Edge of tears / Erotikon.

Sep 90. (cd/c) *(JCCD/TCJC 24)* **CHIMES AND RINGS** [ ] -
– Lady you're a strange girl / Kiss goodbye / Call of the wild / Lost to me / Dangerous lady / Working man / Giving it all away / Ice and fire / Wonder where we go / Dreams of yesterday / Sell my soul / Back to dreams / I wait for you / Walk away from Paradise / Playing Jesus to her Judas / Something's going on / The miracle belongs to you.

Sep 90. (cd/c) *(JCCD/TCJC 25)* **NUDITY** [ ] -
– Feels like up to me / Prize of years / Still waiting / Lover boy at heart / The wonder of it all / Devil in me / A little more time / What's it all about / Thunder on the wing / Shake it up / Love to win / Running / If love were gold / I want you / Kiss it off / Angel like you / Crying all night / Only love can tell.

Sep 90. (cd/c) *(JCCD/TCJC 26)* **HEARTBREAKLAND** [ ] -
– You know how to hurt / Broken / You make me cry / Mess around / Why? / Insanity / Confused / Heartbreakland / Lucky star / Heartbreak thru' the telephone / One day at a time / Tip the wink / Shadow haunting me / Raining / Love's immortal shining angel.

Sep 90. (cd/c) *(JCCD/TCJC 27)* **DETAILS** [ ] -
– Maybe it's the future / Wondering / Wasted lives / The best of you / Stay with me / Love and a bucket full of holes / Prisoner of love / Don't wait / Man on fire / Visionary / The world to me / Strong enough / Everything permitted / Aeroplane wings / One for you / Let it all pass you by.

	Imaginary	not iss.
Apr 91. (lp/cd) *(ILLUSION/+CD 24)* **LUMINOUS**	[ ]	-
	Venture	Virgin

Aug 92. (cd/c) *(CD/TC VE 912)* **BLUE MOONS AND LAUGHING GUITARS** [ ] -
– Ancient guitars / Girl from another planet / Spinnin' around / Shaker / God man slain / The dead we wake with upstairs drum / New moon rising / The glory days / Wishes / Angel in my system / Wings and everything / Boat to forever / The invisible man and the unforgettable girl / So it goes / Fires in the sky / Dream ships set sail.

	All Saints	not iss.
Mar 95. (cd) *(ASCD 022)* **PRACTICALLY WIRED**	[ ]	-

– Roses and rocketships / Spinning planet / Thousand fountain island / Piano 45 / Pink buddha blues / Kid with cowboy tie / Royal ghosts / Her presence in flowers / Big noise in Twangtown / Tiny little thing / Wild blue cycle / Every moment infinite / Friends from Heaven / Eternal for Eniko.

	Resurgence	not iss.
Feb 95. (cd) *(RES 104CD)* **CRIMSWORTH (FLOWERS STONES FOUNTAINS AND FLAMES)**	[ ]	-

– (part 1) / (part 2). *(re-iss. Oct96 & Apr97; same)*

Nov 95. (cd; CULTUREMIX & BILL NELSON) *(RES 113CD)* **CULTUREMIX** [ ] -
– Luna park / Radio head / Housewives on drugs / Dancematic / Four postcards home / Zebra / Exile / Tangram / Cave paintings. *(re-iss. Apr97; same)*

Oct 96. (cd) *(RES 114CD)* **AFTER THE SATELLITE SINGS** [ ] -
– Deeply dazed / Tomorrow yesterday / Flipside / Streamliner / Memory babe / Skull baby cluster / Zoom sequence / Rocket to Damascus / Beautiful nudes / Old goat / Squirm / Wow it's scootercar sexkitten / Phantom sedan / Ordinary idiots / V-ghost / Blink agog. *(re-iss. Apr97; same)*

	Populuxe	not iss.
Apr 97. (cd) *(POPU 003CD)* **ELECTRICITY MADE US ANGELS**	[ ]	-
Apr 97. (cd) *(POPU 004CD)* **BUDDHA HEAD**	[ ]	-

– My philosophy / Killing my desires / Buddha head / Way / Big river / Karma kisses / We will rise / Signs and signals / Lotus in the stream / Enlightenment / Eternally / Duality / Perfect world / Heart has its reasons / Sun will rise / Big illumination / Life as we know it.

Jun 97. (cd) *(POPU 005CD)* **DEEP DREAM DECODER** [ ] -
– Things to come / God bless me / Rise (above these things) / Snowing outside / It's all true / Head full of lights and a hat full of haloes / Girls I've loved / Amazing things / Deep dream decoder / Disolve / Year 44 (the birthday song) / Wing and a prayer / Dreamnoise and angel / Tired eyes / Golden girl / Spark.

– compilations, specials, others –

—— on 'Cocteau' unless mentioned otherwise

Nov 81. (lp) *(JC 2)* **DAS KABINET (OF DR. CAGLIARI)** [ ] -
– The asylum / Waltz / The fairground / Doctor Cagliari / Cesare the somnabulist / Murder / The funeral / The somnabulist and the children / The children / Cagliari disciplines Cesare / Cagliari opens the cabinet / Jane discovers Cesare / The attempted murder of Jane / The dream dance of Jane and the somnabulist / Escape over the rooftops / The unmasking / The shot / The cabinet closes. *(cd-iss. Jan85; JCCD 40)*

Jun 82. (lp) *(WHIRL 2)* **LA BELLE ET LA BETE (THE BEAUTY AND THE BEAST)** [ ] -
– Overture / The family / Sisters and Sedan chairs / In the forest of storms / The castle / The gates / The corridor / The great hall / Dreams (the merchant sleeps) / The rose and the beast / Magnificent (the white horse) / Beauty enters the castle / The door / The mirror / Candelabra and the gargoyles / Beauty and the beast / Transition No.1, 2 – The gift / The garden / Transitions No.3, 4 – The tragedy / Transitions No.5 – The enchanted glove / Tears as diamonds (the gift reverses) / The beast in solitude / Return of the magnificent / Transition No.6-The journey / The pavillion of Diana / Transformation No.1 & 2 / The final . . . *(above 2 albums re-iss. Jun85; JCCD 4)*

Nov 82. (5x7"box) *(JEAN 1)* **PERMANENT FLAME** [ ] -
Jan 85. (4xlp-box) *(JEAN 2)* **TRIAL BY INTAMACY** [ ] -
– (DAS KABINET / BEAUTY & THE BEAST / CHAMBER OF DREAMS / SUMMER OF GOD'S PIANO)

Feb 85. (cd) *(JCCD 10)* **THE TWO-FOLD ASPECT OF EVERYTHING** [ ] -
(d-lp-iss.Sep89; JC 10)

Nov 86. (lp/c; as ORCHESTRA ARCANA) *(JC/TCJC 18)* **ACONOGRAPHY** [ ] -

Sep 87. (d-cd) *(JCCD 17)* **CHIMERA / SAVAGE GESTURES FOR CHARMS SAKE** [ ] -

Aug 89. (lp/cd) *(JC/+CD 9)* **CATALOGUE OF OBSESSIONS** [ ] -

Sep 89. (cd/c/d-lp) *(CD/TC+/JCD 22)* **DUPLEX: THE BEST OF BILL NELSON** [ ] -
– Flaming desire / Acceleration (remix) / hope for the heartbeat (remix) / Here and now / Life in your hands / Glow world / The blazing memory of the innuendo / The angel at the western window / The man in the Rexine suit / Right then left / Half asleep in the hall of mirrors / Opening / Metaphysical jerks / Loving tongues / Radiant spires / Do you dream in clour / Living in my limousine (remix) / October man / Private view / Contemplation / Another day, another ray of hope / Another tricky mission / Portrait of Jan with flowers / Wiping a tear from the all-seeing eye / Secret ceremony (theme from 'Brond') / Broadcast news (from 'Right To Reply') / Loosening up with lady luck / The garden / Burning the groove of Satyre / Set me a seal upon thine heart.

Dec 89. (4xcd-box) *(JEANCD 89)* **DEMONSTRATIONS OF AFFECTION** [ ] -
Sep 90. (cd; mail order) *(JCCD 23)* **SIMPLEX** [-] -
Aug 92. (3xcd-box) *Magpie; (MAGPIE 3)* **QUIT DREAMING AND GET ON THE BEAM / CHIMERA – SAVAGE GESTURES / THE LOVE THAT WHIRLS** [ ] -

Dec 95. (4xcd-box) *Resurgence; (RES 111CD)* **BOX SET** [ ] -
(re-iss. Oct96; same)

Michael NESMITH

Born: ROBERT MICHAEL NESMITH, 30 Dec'43, Houston, Texas, USA. Raised in Farmers Branch near Dallas, NESMITH was a keen music fan although it wasn't until he left the airforce at the age of 20 that he began learning the guitar. Already a blues and soul buff, he subsequently became fascinated by folk music and after completing some session work for legendary Memphis soul label, 'Stax/Volt', he relocated to L.A. where he tried to make a name for himself on the burgeoning folk circuit. Although he performed as a duo with friend JOHN LONDON, he actually released a series of solo singles (some as MICHAEL BLESSING) prior to his successful audition for THE MONKEES in 1965. Proving himself to be more than just a pretty face, NESMITH steered the band away from prefabricated pop towards authentic creative expression and by his 1969 departure had already seen his freewheeling 'DIFFERENT DRUM' reach the US Top 20 courtesy of LINDA RONSTADT. He'd also released his debut solo album, 'THE WICHITA TRAIN WHISTLE SINGS' (1968), a bizarre set of instrumental (NESMITH-penned) MONKEES re-workings. At the suggestion of drummer JOHNNY WARE, NESMITH instigated THE FIRST NATIONAL BAND, a country-rock outfit featuring WARE, NESMITH, accomplished pedal steel player RED RHODES and NESMITH's old sparring partner JOHN LONDON. After two weeks of rehearsals, the band cut their debut album, 'MAGNETIC SOUTH' (1970), for 'RCA Victor'. According to NESMITH's own sleevenotes, his primary influences were HANK WILLIAMS, JERRY LEE LEWIS and JIMMIE RODGERS and there were certainly echoes of all those legends within the grooves. Never the strongest or most distinctive of vocalists, NESMITH often makes up for it with his inventive songwriting and arrangements. Among the highlights were the rollicking yodel spree of 'MAMA NANTUCKET', the trippy 'HOLLYWOOD' and the Top 30 US hit, 'JOANNE'. He even managed to marry country and Latin on 'TENGO AMORE', a standout from sophomore effort, 'LOOSE SALUTE' (1970) alongside the classic 'SILVER MOON' and a cover of Patsy Cline's 'I FALL TO PIECES'. If the albums weren't always consistent, NESMITH & Co. were at least a year or two ahead of the country-rock goldrush yet that was quite possibly the problem; largely ignored by the media, NESMITH carried on regardless, recruiting new members and releasing third album, 'NEVADA FIGHTER' (1971) to another muted press reaction. Around the same time, the ambitious ex-MONKEE talked of his plans to document the history of C&W music over a nine-volume series and although it was later shelved,

NESMITH would carry on with other equally grand plans. In the meantime, he formed the SECOND NATIONAL BAND (with RHODES as the only remaining original) for fourth set, 'TANTAMOUNT TO TREASON' (1972) before going completely solo and calling his fifth set – with typically dry humour – 'AND THE HITS JUST KEEP ON COMIN' (1972). The latter was a spartan near-acoustic affair which nevetheless retained RHODES and is considered by many afficionados as NESMITH's most affecting work. The high standard was maintained for his final 'R.C.A.' effort, 'PRETTY MUCH YOUR STANDARD RANCH STASH' (1973), an album that featured arguably his finest composition, 'SOME OF SHELLY'S BLUES'. The track had previously been a hit for The NITTY GRITTY DIRT BAND and its semi-acoustic rootsiness wouldn't have been out of place on one of ROD STEWART's classic early 70's efforts. Leaving country behind, NESMITH formed his 'Pacific Arts' film/music/video company in 1975 and initiated the first of many ambitious projects with concept album, 'THE PRISON' (1975). Next up was 'FROM A RADIO ENGINE TO A PHOTON WING' (1977), from which NESMITH released the single, 'RIO' and took it into the UK Top 30 with the help of one of the first ever promo videos. He took the idea further with the conceptual 'ELEPHANT PARTS', netting himself the first ever video Grammy in 1981. NESMITH also pioneered the idea of video programming, initiating the 'POPCLIPS' TV show which 'Warners' subsequently bought over and developed into MTV. NESMITH continued to work in video and film throughout the 80's, producing cult movie classic, 'Repo Man' amongst others. 1992 saw the release of his first solo album since the 70's, 'TROPICAL CAMPFIRES' while the mid-90's finally saw a bonafide MONKEES reunion for the recording of 'JUSTUS' (1996).

Album rating: WICHITA TRAIN WHISTLE SONGS (*5) / MAGNETIC SOUTH (*7) / LOOSE SALUTE (*5) / NEVADA FIGHTER (*5) / TANTAMOUNT TO TREASON (*5) / AND THE HITS JUST KEEP ON COMIN' (*6) / PRETTY MUCH YOUR STANDARD RANCH STASH (*6) / THE PRISON (*4) / THE BEST OF MICHAEL NESMITH compilation (*6) / COMPILATION compilation (*6) / FROM A RADIO ENGINE TO A PHOTON WING (*5) / LIVE AT THE PALAIS (*4) / INFINITE RIDER ON THE BIG DOGMA (*5) / THE NEWER STUFF compilation (*5) / THE OLDER STUFF compilation (*7) / TROPICAL CAMPFIRES (*6) / THE GARDEN (*4) / LIVE AT THE BRITT FESTIVAL (*5)

MICHAEL NESMITH – vocals, guitar

	not iss.	Omnibus
1963. (7"; by MIKE, JOHN & BILL) <239> **HOW CAN YOU KISS ME. / JUST A LITTLE LOVE**	-	☐

	not iss.	Edan
Sep 65. (7") <1001> **JUST A LITTLE LOVE. / CURSON TERRACE**	-	☐

	not iss.	Colpix
Oct 65. (7"; as MICHAEL BLESSING) <CP 787> **THE NEW RECRUIT. / A JOURNEY WITH MICHAEL BLESSING**	-	☐
Jan 66. (7"; as MICHAEL BLESSING) <CP 792> **UNTIL IT'S TIME FOR YOU TO GO. / WHAT SEEMS TO BE THE TROUBLE, OFFICER?**	-	☐

—— MICHAEL joined The MONKEES in 1966 but continued on solo sojourn

—— with the **WICHITA TRAIN WHISTLE** band:- JAMES BURTON – guitar / RED RHODES – steel guitar / CHUCK BERGHOFFER – bass / HAL BLAINE + SHORTY ROGERS – drums / (numerous session people)

	Dot	Dot
Jul 68. (7") <45-17152> **DON'T CRY NOW. / TAPIOCA TUNDRA**	-	☐
Oct 68. (lp) (DLP 516) <DLP 25861> **THE WICHITA TRAIN WHISTLE SONGS**	☐	☐ Jul68

– Nine time blues / Carlisle Wheeling / Tapioca tundra / Don't call on me / Don't cry now / While I cried / Papa Gene's blues / You just may be the one / Sweet young thing / You told me. <re-iss. Jun78 on 'Pacific Arts'; PAC 7-113>

MICHAEL NESMITH & THE FIRST NATIONAL BAND

—— with **RHODES + JOHN LONDON** – bass / **JOHN WARE** – drums + **EARL P. BALL** – piano

	R.C.A.	R.C.A.
Jun 70. (7") <47-9853> **LITTLE RED RIDER. / ROSE CITY CHIMES**	-	-
Aug 70. (7") <74-0368> **JOANNE. / ONE ROSE**	-	21
Sep 70. (7") (RCA 2001) **JOANNE. / THE CRIPPLED LION**	-	-
Sep 70. (lp) (SF 8136) <LSP 4371> **MAGNETIC SOUTH**	☐	☐ Jul70

– Calico girlfriend / Nine time blue / Little red rider / The crippled lion / Joanne / First National rag / Mama Nantucket / The keys to the car / Hollywood / One rose / Beyond the blue horizon. (cd/c-iss.Mar91 on 'Awareness'; AWCD/AWT 1023)

—— **GLEN D. HARDIN** – piano; repl. BALL

Dec 70. (lp) <LSP 4415> **LOOSE SALUTE**	-	☐

– Silver moon / I fall to pieces / Thanx for the ride / Dedicated friend / Conversations / Tengo amor / Listen to the band / Bye, bye, bye / Lady of the valley / Hello lady. (cd/c-iss.Mar91 on 'Awareness'; AWCD/AWT 1024)

Feb 71. (7") (RCA 2692) <74-0399> **SILVER MOON. / LADY OF THE VALLEY**	☐	42 Nov70

—— added **JOE OSBOURN + MAX BENNETT** – bass / **MICHAEL COHEN** – keyboards / **AL CASEY & JAMES BURTON** – guitar / **RON TUTT** – drums

Jun 71. (7") (RCA 2086) <74-0453> **NEVADA FIGHTER. / HERE I AM**	☐	70 Apr71
Jun 71. (7") <74-0540> **I'VE JUST BEGUN TO CARE (PROPINQUITY). / ONLY BOUND**	-	☐
Sep 71. (lp) (SF 8209) <LSP 4497> **NEVADA FIGHTER**	-	☐ May71

– Grand Ennui / I've just begun to care (Propinquity) / Here I am / Only bound / Nevada fighter / Texas morning / Tumbling tumbleweeds / I looked away / Rainmaker / Rene. (cd/c-iss.Mar91 on 'Awareness'; AWCD/AWT 1025)

MICHAEL NESMITH & THE SECOND NATIONAL BAND

—— with **RHODES / COHEN + JOHNNY MEEKS** – bass / **JACK PANELLI** – drums

Jan 72. (7") <74-0629> **MAMA ROCKER. / LAZY LADY**	-	☐
Aug 72. (lp) (SF 8276) <LSP 4563> **TANTAMOUNT TO TREASON VOLUME ONE**	☐	☐ Jan72

– Mama rocker / Lazy lady / You are my one / In the afternoon / Highway 99 with melange / Wax minute / Bonaparte's retreat / Talking to the wall / She thinks I still care. (cd-iss. Sep91 on 'Awareness'; AWCD 1026)

MICHAEL NESMITH & THE COUNTRYSIDE BAND

—— with **RED RHODES** (and others)

Aug 72. (7") <74-0804> **ROLL WITH THE FLOW. / KEEP ON**	☐	☐
Aug 72. (lp) <LSP 4695> **AND THE HITS JUST KEEP ON COMIN'**	☐	☐

– Tomorrow and me / The upside of good-bye / Lady love / Listening / Two different roads / The candidate / Different drum / Harmony constant / Keep on / Roll with the flow. (UK-iss.Jan77 on 'Island'; ILPS 9439) <US re-iss. 1978 on 'Pacific Arts'; PAC 7-116> (cd-iss. Sep91 on 'Awareness'; AWCD 1027) <(cd re-iss. Aug95 on 'Rio'; RIOD 2014)>

—— **NESMITH** added **JAY LACY + Dr. ROBERT WARFORD** – guitar / **DAVID BARRY** – piano / **BILLY GRAHAM** – bass, fiddle / **DENNY LANE** – drums, percussion

Oct 73. (lp) <APL 1-0164> **PRETTY MUCH YOUR STANDARD RANCH STASH**	-	☐

– Continuing / Some of Shelly's blues / Release / Winonah / Born to love you / The black porch and a fruit jar full of iced tea: The F.F.V.- Uncle Pen / Prairie lullaby. (UK-iss.Jan77 on 'Island'; ILPS 9440) <US re-iss. 1978 on 'Pacific Arts'; PAC 7-117> (cd-iss. Sep91 on 'Awareness'; AWCD 1028) <(cd re-iss. Jan95 on 'Rio'; RIO 2007)>

MICHAEL NESMITH

—— with various session people

	Island	Pacific Arts
Mar 75. (lp)<box-lp+book> (ILPS 9428) <PAC 101> **THE PRISON**	☐	☐

– (opening theme) / Life, the unsuspecting captive / Dance between the raindrops / Elusive ragings / Waking mystery / Hear me calling / Narie's theme / Closing theme (Lampost). (cd/c-iss.Dec90 on 'Awareness'; AWT 1020)

Mar 77. (7") (WIP 6373) <IP 084> **RIO. / LIFE, THE UNSUSPECTING CAPTIVE**	28	☐

(re-iss. Apr89 on 'Awareness'; AWP 014)

Mar 77. (lp) (ILPS 9486) <PAC 7-107> **FROM A RADIO ENGINE TO A PHOTON WING**	☐	☐

– Rio / Casablanca moonlight / More than we imagine / Navajo trail / We are awake / Wisdom has it's way / Love's first kiss / The other room. (cd-iss. Mar92 on 'Awareness'; AWCD 1029) <(cd re-iss. Jan95 on 'Rio'; RIO 2008)>

Jul 77. (7") (WIP 6398) **NAVAJO TRAIL. / LOVE'S FIRST KISS**	☐	-

—— now with **AL PERKINS** – guitar / **JAMES TRUMBO** – keyboards / **DAVID MacKAY** – bass / **JOHN WARE** – drums

Jun 78. (7") <PAC 45-101> **ROLL WITH THE FLOW (live). / I'VE JUST BEGUN TO CARE (PROPINQUITY)**	☐	☐
Aug 78. (lp) <PAC PAC 7-118> **LIVE AT THE PALAIS (live)**	☐	☐

– Grand Ennui / Calico girlfriend / I've just begun to care (Propinquity) / Joanne / Roll with the flow / Some of Shelly's blues / Silver moon / Nadine is it you.

—— **JOHN HOBBS** – keyboards / **PAUL LEIM** – drums / **LENNY CASTRO** – percussion / **TOM SAVIANO** – sax / **JOE CHEMAY** – vocals; repl. TRUMBO + WARE

Jun 79. (7") <PAC 45-106> **MAGIC. / DANCE**	☐	☐
Jul 79. (lp) <PAC 7-130> **INFINITE RIDER ON THE BIG DOGMA**	☐	☐

– Dance (dance & have a good time) / Magic (the night is magic) / Tonite (the television song) / Flying (silks & satins) / Carioca (blue carioca) / Cruisin' (Lucy and Ramona and Sunset Sam) / Factions (the daughter of rock'n'roll) / Light (the eclectic light) / Horserace (Beauty and the Magnum Force) / Capsule (hello people a hundred years from now). (cd-iss. Mar92 on 'Awareness'; AWCD 1032) <(cd re-iss. Jan95 on 'Rio'; RIO 2006)>

Aug 79. (7") <PAC 45-108> **CRUISIN'. / HORSERACE**	☐	☐

—— retired from recording for the whole of the 80's

Oct 92. (cd/c) <PAA D/C 5000> **TROPICAL CAMPFIRES**	☐	☐

– Yellow butterfly / Laugh kills lonesome / Moon over the Rio Grande / One / Juliana / Brazil (aquarela do brasil) / In the still of the night / Rising in love / Begin the beguine / I am not that / For the island / Twilight on the trail. (UK cd-iss. Jan95 on 'Rio'; RIO 2003)

	Rio	Rio
Aug 95. (cd) <(RIOD 2001)> **THE GARDEN**	☐	☐ 1994

– Garden's glow / Ficus carica / The city / Hills of time / Flowers dancing / Wisteria / Life becoming.

	Cooking Vinyl	not iss.
Sep 99. (d-cd) (COOKCD 129) **LIVE AT THE BRITT FESTIVAL (live)**	☐	-

– Two different roads / Papa Gene's blues / Propinquity / Some of Shelly's blues / Joanne / Tomorrow and me / Upside of goodbye / Harmony constant / Silver moon / 5 second concerts / Yellow butterfly / Moon over the Rio Grand / Juliana / Laugh kills lonesome / I am not that / Rising in love / Rio / Different drum / I am not that (reprise).

– compilations, etc. –

Aug 76. (lp) R.C.A.; (RS 1064) **THE BEST OF MICHAEL NESMITH**	☐	☐

– Silver moon / Different drum / Harmony constant / Two different roads / Mama Nantucket / Conversations / Joanne / Bonaparte's retreat / Some of Shelly's blues / Rainmaker / Listen to the band / Grand Ennui / I've just begun to care / Nevada fighter.

Sep 76. (7") Island; (IEP 4) **MICHAEL NESMITH & THE FIRST NATIONAL BAND**	☐	☐

– I fall to pieces / Silver moon / Some of Shelly's blues / Joanne.

Feb 77. (lp) Pacific Arts; <PAC 7-106> **COMPILATION**	-	☐

– Some of Shelly's blues / I fall to pieces / Born to love you / Different drum /

Harmony constant / Prairie lullaby / Joanne / Propinquity / Silver Moon / I looked away / Continuing / Roll with the flow.

Apr 89.	(lp/c/cd) *Awareness;* (*AWL /AWT/AWCD 1014*) / Rhino; <R1/R4/R2 70168> **THE NEWER STUFF** (rarities)	☐ ☐
Mar 92.	(cd) *Awareness;* (*AWCD 1032*) / Rhino; <R2/R4 70763> **THE OLDER STUFF: THE BEST OF MICHAEL NESMITH (1970-1973)**	☐ ☐
Sep 93.	(d-cd) *Pacific Arts;* <PAAD 5006> **COMPLETE** (the First/Second National Band albums)	- -
Sep 97.	(cd) *RCA-Camden;* (74321 52377-2) **LISTEN TO THE BAND**	☐ -
Mar 98.	(cd) *Eagle;* (*EABCD 105*) **THE MASTERS**	☐ -
Apr 99.	(cd) *Camden-RCA;* (74321 66044-2) **LOOSE SALUTE / MAGNETIC SOUTH**	☐ -

NEU!

Formed: Dusseldorf, Germany ...Autumn 1971 by breakaway KRAFTWERK members KLAUS DINGER and THOMAS HOMANN. The latter was soon deposed by MICHAEL ROTHER who appeared on their eponymous 1972 debut. Live gigs were augmented by EBERHARD KRAKNENN, who had also guested for KRAFTWERK. After only three acclaimed underground albums, they split in the mid-70's when ROTHER went solo. Encompassing repetitive trance-rock and avant-garde improvisation, they mined similar territory to early KRAFTWERK, AMON DUUL II or HAWKWIND (DAVE BROCK was a great fan). Along with the likes of CAN and FAUST, the band are held in high esteem by Krautrock connoisseurs. • **Songwriters:** ROTHER-DINGER. • **Trivia:** Produced by CONNY PLANK except 2nd lp.

Album rating: NEU! (*8) / NEU II (*8) / NEU '75 (*9) / BLACK FOREST GATEAU compilation (*9)

MICHAEL ROTHER – guitar, bass, keyboards, synths, percussion / **KLAUS DINGER** – guitar, vocals, drums, keyboards (ex-KRAFTWERK)

		U.A.	Billingsgate
1972.	(lp) (*UAS 29396*) <1001> **NEU!**		
	– Hallo Gallo / Sonderangebot / Weissensee / Jahresuebersicht / Im glueck / Negativland / Lieber honig. *(re-iss. May80 as 'HALLO GALLO' on 'Brain' Germany; 0040 145) (cd-iss. Jan98 on 'Germanofon'; 941025)*		
Jan 73.	(7") (*UP 35485*) **SUPER. / NEUSCHNEE**	☐	-
1973.	(lp) (*UAS 29500*) **NEU II**	☐	-
	– Fur immer / Spitzenqualitat / Gedenkminute / Lila engel / Neuschnee / Super 16 / Neuschnee / Cassetto / Super 78 / Hallo exentrico / Super. *(cd-iss. Jan98 on 'Germanofon'; 941026)*		
——	ROTHER joined HARMONIA, with CLUSTER members MOEBIUS + ROEDELIUS. They made two albums 'MUSIK VON HARMONIA' *(Brain; 1044)* & 'HARMONIA DELUXE' *(Brain 1073)*, before he returned to NEU!		
——	added **HANS LAMPE + THOMAS DINGER** – drums (ex-KRAFTWERK)		
Jun 75.	(7") (*UP 35874*) **ISI. / AFTER EIGHT**	☐	-
1975.	(lp) (*UAS 29782*) **NEU '75**	☐	-
	– Isi / Seeland / Leb' wohl / Hero / E-Musik / After eight. *(cd-iss. May98 on Germanofon'; 941030)*		
——	split after above; the DINGER's + LAMPE formed LA DUSSELDORF while ROTHER subsequently released a plethora of albums		

– compilations, others, etc. –

Nov 82.	(lp) *Cherry Red;* (*BRED 27*) **BLACK FOREST GATEAU**	☐	-
	– Hallo Gallo / Isi / E-Musik / Negativland / Seeland / Leb' wohl / After eight.		
Dec 96.	(cd) *Captain Trip;* (*CTCD 020*) **NEU! 4** (rec.mid-80's)	☐	-
Dec 96.	(cd) *Captain Trip;* (*CTCD 045*) **1972 LIVE!** (live)	☐	-
Jun 97.	(cd) *Captain Trip;* (*CTCD 051*) **LA NEU DUSSELDORF**	☐	-
Feb 98.	(cd) *Captain Trip;* (*CTCD 086*) **LA NEU ZEELAND LIVE 1997**	☐	-
Apr 98.	(cd) *Captain Trip;* (*CTCD 087*) **REMBRANDT**	☐	-
Jun 98.	(cd) *Captain Trip;* (*CTCD 098*) **DIE WITH DIGNITY**	☐	-
Jun 98.	(d-cd) *Captain Trip;* (*CTCD 100-101*) **CHA CHA 2000** (live in Tokyo)	☐	-

NEUTRAL MILK HOTEL (dig out; Great Alt & Indie . . .)

NEVILLE BROTHERS

Formed: New Orleans, USA ... mid-60's as The NEVILLE SOUNDS by ART and younger brother AARON, the former initiating the family's musical dynasty in 1955 when, as a member of seven-piece R&B outfit, The HAWKETTS, he recorded the seminal 'MARDIS GRAS GUMBO'. Adopted as an anthem for the annual New Orleans rave-up, the single's enduring popularity means that it still gets re-issued annually by the 'Chess' label. The late 50's saw ART augmenting his band work with a string of solo singles for 'Speciality' including 'ZING ZING' and 'CHA DOOKY-DOO' (both re-issued in 1976 as a double A-side), AARON taking his place (CHARLES NEVILLE also joined briefly) when he joined the US Navy in 1958. The HAWKETTS continued to record for 'Minit', while AARON scored his first solo hit at the turn of the decade with a cover of Sam Cooke's 'OVER YOU'. Blessed with one of the most affecting tenor quivers in the history of the crescent city, he finally hit the charts (narrowly missing the US No.1 spot) in 1966 with definitive soul classic, 'TELL IT LIKE IT IS'. By this point, ART had returned from his naval duties, hooking up with AARON, younger brother CYRIL, JOSEPH ZIGGY MODELISTE, GEORGE PORTER JR. and LEO NOCENTELLI to form The NEVILLE SOUNDS.

New Orleans production guru, ALLEN TOUSSAINT, subsequently took on ART, MODELISTE, PORTER and NOCENTELLI as his session band, the outfit eventually going under the METERS moniker; AARON and CYRIL, meanwhile, formed SOUL MACHINE, while the former continued to record for various labels with little success. Funking up recordings by the likes of DR. JOHN ('In The Right Place' and 'Desitively Bonaroo') and ROBERT PALMER ('Sneaking Sally Through The Alley') as well as LaBELLE and PAUL McCARTNEY, The METERS reputation as lean'n'spicy R&B sessioners was matched only by Memphis' MG's. They also recorded in their own right, releasing a string of dance instrumental singles (scoring minor US charts hits in 1969 with 'SOPHISTICATED CISSY' and 'CISSY STRUT') for the 'Josie' label before signing to 'Reprise' in 1972. Albums such as 'REJUVENATION' (1974) and 'FIRE ON THE BAYOU' (1975) mixed up visceral 70's funk with down-home New Orleans rhythms to create some of the most compelling dancefloor hits of the era, not least the brilliant 'JUST KISSED MY BABY'. The latter album saw the addition of CYRIL NEVILLE, while AARON and CHARLES joined up for 'TRICK BAG' (1976); all back together again, albeit briefly, the brothers hooked up with relatives GEORGE and AMOS LANDRY (members of a Mardi Gras Indian tribe, the WILD TCHOUPITOULAS) for a one-off set of carnival-crazy funk on 'Island', taking its title from the name of the tribe. The METERS released one further album later that summer, 'NEW DIRECTIONS', before metamorphosing into harmony vocal group, The NEVILLE BROTHERS, all the family save CHARLES featuring on their lukewarm eponymous debut set. Despite its shortcomings, the album (released on 'Capitol') caught the attentions of BETTE MIDLER who encouraged her label, 'A&M', to sign them at the turn of the decade. With all four reunited once more, they cut the vastly improved 'FIYO ON THE BAYOU' (1981), a move back to their New Orleans roots with some revamped blasts from the past. Despite fervent critical acclaim, the record failed to sell, and again the brothers found themsleves minus a record deal. An independently released home turf-recorded live set, 'NEVILLE-IZATION' (1984), demonstrated that the brothers' fearsome live reputation was more than justified, an electrifying set drawing on the cream of their career. As the 80's wore on it seemed The NEVILLE BROTHERS' commercial career was in terminal decline, the slide eventually stalled with the Daniel Lanois-produced 'YELLOW MOON' (1989). A haunting collection of inspired covers and new material, the record managed to reconcile the brothers' sound with a modern sensibility, even flirting with rap on the pro-civil rights track, 'SISTER ROSA'. Following the set's minor chart success, AARON scored one of his biggest commercial successes for years via his LINDA RONSTADT duet, 'DON'T KNOW MUCH'. The single's popularity rekindled interest in the eminently talented AARON, his subsequent solo set (co-produced by RONSTADT), 'WARM YOUR HEART' (1991), spawning another US Top 10 hit in 'EVERYBODY PLAYS THE FOOL'. The NEVILLE BROTHERS, meanwhile, had released the similarly impressive DAVE STEWART-produced 'BROTHER'S KEEPER' (1990), although they couldn't sustain the momentum with 'FAMILY GROOVE' (1992). The 90's have seen only one further release by the siblings, 1996's 'MITAKUYE OYASIN OYASIN', and while AARON tested his fans' patience with 'AARON NEVILLE'S SOULFUL CHRISTMAS' (1993), he was forgiven with the excellent 'TATTOOED HEART' (1995). • **Songwriters:** Each contributed, collaborating with other writers including more brothers IVAN and GAYNEILLE. Also HAWK WOLINSKI was added in 1992 alongside DARYL JOHNSON. Other recent collective contributors PHIL ROY, BOB THEILE and BILLY VALENTINE. Covered; BIRD ON A WIRE (Leonard Cohen) / WITH GOD ON OUR SIDE + THE BALLAD OF HOLLIS BROWN (Bob Dylan) / FLY LIKE AN EAGLE (Steve Miller Band) / IN THE STILL OF THE NIGHT (Cole Porter) / IT FEELS LIKE RAIN (John Hiatt) / LOUISIANA 1927 (Randy Newman) / DON'T GO PLEASE STAY (Bacharach-Milliard) / WITH YOU IN MIND + THAT'S THE WAY SHE LOVES (Allen Toussaint) / CLOSE YOUR EYES (. . .Willis) / AVE MARIA (Mozart) / LOVE THE ONE YOU'RE WITH (Stephen Stills) / YOU CAN'T ALWAYS GET WHAT YOU WANT (Rolling Stones) / LET MY PEOPLE GO + AMAZING GRACE (trad) / ONE LOVE – PEOPLE GET READY (Bob Marley). Aaron also covered: YOU NEVER CAN TELL (Chuck Berry) / SONG OF BERNADETTE + AIN'T NO CURE FOR LOVE (Leonard Cohen) / BETCHA BY GOLLY WOW (Stylistics). • **Trivia:** AARON's son IVAN NEVILLE, had a US Top 30 hit in 1988 with 'NOT JUST ANOTHER GIRL'.

Album rating: Aaron Neville: LIKE IT 'TIS (*6) / Meters: THE METERS (*5) / LOOK: KA PY PY (*7) / STRUTTIN' (*7) / CABBAGE ALLEY (*5) / REJUVENATION (*5) / FIRE ON THE BAYOU (*5) / TRICK BAG (*5) / THE WILD TCHOUPITOULAS as the Wild Tchoupitoulas (*6) / NEW DIRECTIONS (*4) / compilation FUNKIFY YOUR LIFE (*8) / Neville Brothers: THE NEVILLE BROTHERS (*5) / FIYO ON THE BAYO (*7) / NEVILLE-IZATION exploitation (*5) / TREACHEROUS: A HISTORY OF THE NEVILLE BROTHERS 1955-1985 compilation (*8) / YELLOW MOON (*7) / BROTHER'S KEEPER (*6) / TREACHEROUS TOO: A HISTORY OF THE NEVILLE BROTHERS VOL.2 (1955-1987) compilation (*6) / WARM YOUR HEART (*5; by Aaron Neville) / FAMILY GROOVE (*5) / LIVE ON PLANET EARTH (*6) / MITAKUYE OYASIN OYASIN – ALL MY RELATIONS (*5) / THE VERY BEST OF THE NEVILLE BROTHERS compilation (*8)

The HAWKETTS

(7-piece New Orleans band with **ART NEVILLE** (b.17 Dec'37) – vocals / **GEORGE DAVIS** – / etc.

1955.	(7") **MARDI GRAS MAMBO.** / <re-iss. annually by 'Chess' US>	-	☐

—— ART still performed with them, and released solo singles for 'Speciality' in 1957; ZING ZING + CHA DOOKY-DOO. Both re-issued 1976 as double 'A'side. A year later, ART joined the US Navy and was replaced by brother **AARON** (b.24 Jan'41) – vocals. He also issued duo 45 with ALLEN TOUSSAINT

AARON NEVILLE

			Minit	Minit
Jun 60.	(7") <612>	**OVER YOU. / EVERY DAY**	-	
Dec 60.	(7") <618>	**GET OUT OF MY LIFE. / SHOW ME THE WAY**	-	
Mar 61.	(7") <624>	**DON'T CRY. / REALITY**	-	
Aug 61.	(7") <631>	**I FOUND ANOTHER LOVE. / LET'S LIVE**	-	
Feb 62.	(7") <639>	**HOW MANY TIMES. / I'M WAITIN' AT THE STATION**	-	
Aug 62.	(7") <650>	**SWEET LITTLE MAMA. / HUMDINGER**	-	
Jan 63.	(7") <657>	**WRONG NUMBER. / HOW COULD I HELP BUT LOVE YOU**	-	

—— Early 1962, ART re-joined The HAWKETTS, releasing solo single, 'ALL THESE THINGS'. To end the year, they became The NEVILLE SOUNDS, who were an 8-piece band with ART, AARON & CYRIL (b.10 Oct'48), plus MODELISTE & PORTER. AARON

			Stateside	Par-Lo
Dec 66.	(7") (SS 584) <101>	**TELL IT LIKE IT IS. / WHY WORRY** (re-iss. Sep69 on 'B&C'; CB 107) (re-iss. Aug74 on 'Contempo'; CS 9009) (re-iss. 1976 on 'Island'; WIP 6332)	2	Nov66
Mar 67.	(7") <103>	**SHE TOOK YOU FOR A RIDE. / SPACE MAN**	-	92

			Liberty	Minit
May 67.	(lp) (LBY 3089) <24007>	**HERE 'TIS** – Over you / Get out of my life / I found another love / Don't cry / Sweet little mama / I'm waitin' at the station / How many times / Let's live / Everyday / Reality / Wrong number (I'm sorry, goodbye) / How dould I help but love you. (cd-iss. Jul91 on 'Music Club')		

			not iss.	Bell
Nov 68.	(7") <746>	**WHERE IS MY BABY. / YOU CAN GIVE, BUT YOU CAn"T TAKE**	-	
Jun 69.	(7") <781>	**YOU DON'T LOVE ME ANYMORE. / SPEAK TO ME**	-	

—— The NEVILLE SOUNDS break-up with AARON + CYRIL forming SOUL MACHINE.

The METERS

—— were founded by ex-NEVILLE SOUNDS people **ART NEVILLE** – keyboards, vocals / **JOSEPH ZIGGY MODELISTE** – drums, vocals / **GEORGE PORTER JR.** – bass, vocals / **LEO NOCENTELLI** – guitar, vocals

			Stateside	Josie
Feb 69.	(7") (SS 2140) <1001>	**SOPHISTICATED CISSY. / SEHORNS FARM**		34
Apr 69.	(7") <1005>	**CISSY STRUT. / HERE COMES THE METER MAN**	-	23
Jun 69.	(lp) (JOS 4010)	**THE METERS** (instrumental) – Sophisticated Cissy / Ease back / Cardova / Sehorns farm / 6v6 LA / Stormy / Cissy strut / Art / Ann / Here comes the meter man / Live wire / Simple song.	-	
Jul 69.	(7") <1008>	**EASE BACK. / ANN**	-	61

			Direction	Josie
Oct 69.	(7") <1013>	**LOOK-KA PY PY. / DRY SPELL**		
Jan 70.	(7") (58-4751) <1015>	**LOOK-KA PY PY. / THIS IS MY LAST AFFAIR**	-	56
Jan 70.	(lp) (JOS 4011)	**LOOK-KA PY PY** (instrumental) – Dry spell / Look-ka Py Py / Oh, Calcutta! / Rigor mortis / Yeah, you're right / This is my last affair / Thinking / Pungee / The mob / 9 'til 5 / Little old money maker / Funky miracle.	-	
Apr 70.	(7") <1018>	**CHICKEN STRUT. / HEY! LAST MINUTE**	-	50
Jun 70.	(lp) (JOS 4012)	**STRUTTIN'** – Chicken strut / Liver splash / Wichita lineman / Joog / Go for yourself / Same old thing / Hand clapping song / Darlin' darlin' / Tippi-toes / Britches / Britches / Hey! last minute / Ride your pony.		
Jun 70.	(7") <1021>	**HAND CLAPPING SONG. / JOOG**	-	89
Sep 70.	(7") <1024>	**A MESSAGE FROM THE METERS. / ZONY MASH**		
Feb 71.	(7") <1026>	**GROOVY LADY. / STRETCH YOUR RUBBER BAND**	-	
Apr 71.	(7") <1029>	**I NEED MORE TIME. / DOODLE OOP**	-	
Jul 71.	(7") <1031>	**SASSY LADY. / GOOD OLD FUNKY MUSIC**	-	

			Reprise	Reprise
1972.	(lp) (K 44242) <MS 2076>	**CABBAGE ALLEY** – You've got to change (You've got to reform) / Stay away / Birds / Flower song / Soul island / Do the dirt / Smiling / Lonesome and unwanted people / Gettin' funkier all the time / Cabbage alley.		
1972.	(7") <1086>	**DO THE DIRT. / SMILING**	-	
1972.	(7") <1106>	**CABBAGE ALLEY. / THE FLOWER SONG**	-	
1973.	(7") <1135>	**CHUG CHUG CHUG-A-LUG. / (part 2)**	-	

—— The METERS did session work for DR. JOHN and ROBERT PALMER

Jun 74.	(7") <1307>	**AFRICA. / HEY ROCK-A-WAY**	-	
Aug 74.	(7") <1314>	**PEOPLE SAY. / LOVING YOU IS ON MY MIND**	-	
Sep 74.	(7") (K 14367)	**PEOPLE SAY. / AFRICA**	-	
Oct 74.	(lp) (K 54027) <MS 2200>	**REJUVENATION** – People say / Love is for me / Just kissed my baby / What'cha say / Jungle man / Hey rocky a-way / It ain't no use Loving you is on my mind / Africa.	-	

—— added **CYRIL NEVILLE** – percussion, vocals (ex-SOUL MACHINE)

Jul 75.	(7") <1338>	**THEY ALL ASKED FOR YOU. / RUNNING FAST**	-	
Aug 75.	(lp) (K 54044) <MS 2228>	**FIRE ON THE BAYOU** – Out in the country / Fire in the bayou / Love slip upon ya / Talkin' about New Orleans / They all asked for you / Can you do without / Liar / You're a friend of mine / Middle of the road / Running fast / Mardi Gras mambo.		
Nov 75.	(7") (K 14405)	**FIRE ON THE BAYOU. / THEY ALL ASKED FOR YOU**		

—— added **AARON + CHARLES NEVILLE** (b.1939) – vocals

Sep 76.	(7") <1357>	**DISCO IS THE THING TODAY. / MISTER MOON**	-	
Sep 76.	(lp) <MS 2252>	**TRICK BAG** – Disco is the thing today / Find your self / All these things / I want to be loved by you / Suite for 20 G / The world is a little bit under the weather / Trick bag / Mister Moon / Chug-a-lug / Hang 'em high / Honky tonk women.		
Nov 76.	(7") <1372>	**TRICK BAG. / FIND YOURSELF**	-	

WILD TCHOUPITOULAS

aka The METERS

			Island	Island
Feb 77.	(7")	**MEET DE BOYS ON THE BATTLEFRONT. / BIG CHIEF GOT A GOLDEN CROWN**		
Apr 77.	(lp) <(ILPS 9360)>	**THE WILD TCHOUPITOULAS** – Brother John / Meet de boys on de battlefront / Here dey come / Hey pocky-a-way / Indian red / Big chief got a golden crown / Hey mama, hey hey. (re-iss. Apr88 lp/c/cd; ILPS/ICT/CID 9360) (re-iss. Feb90 cd)(c; IMCD 89)(ICM 2067)		
May 77.	(7") <071>	**BROTHER JOHN. / HERE DEY COME**		

AARON NEVILLE

			not iss.	Polydor
May 77.	(7") <14426>	**GREATEST LOVE. / PERFORMANCE**	-	

METERS

			Reprise	Warners
Jun 77.	(lp) (K 56378) <MS 3042>	**NEW DIRECTIONS** – No more okey doke / I'm gone / Be my lady / My name up in lights / Funkify your life / Stop that train / we got the kind of love / Give it all you can.		
Sep 77.	(7") <8434>	**BE MY LADY. / NO MORE OKEY DOKE**	-	78

The NEVILLE BROTHERS

(with all brothers except CHARLES)

			Capitol	Capitol
Oct 78.	(7") <4688>	**SPEED OF LIGHT. / IF IT TAKES ALL NIGHT**	-	
Mar 79.	(lp/c) <(EST/TC-EST 11865)>	**THE NEVILLE BROTHERS** – Dancing Jones / Washable ink / All nights all right / Audience for my pain / Break away / If it takes all night / Viclux carre rouge / Arianne / Speed of light.	-	Mar78

—— 4 brothers again (**AARON, ART, CYRIL + CHARLES**)

			not iss.	A&M
Aug 81.	(lp) <4866>	**FIYO ON THE BAYOU** – Hey pocky way / Sweet honey dripper / Fire on the bayou / The ten commandments of love / Sitting in limbo / Brother John / Iko Iko / Mona Lisa / Run Joe. (UK-iss.Jul86 on 'Demon' lp/c; FIEND/+CASS 65) (cd-iss. 1987; FIENDCD 65) (re-iss. Mar93 cd/c;)	-	
Sep 81.	(7") <2358>	**WHY ME? / BROHER JOHN – IKO IKO**	-	
Nov 81.	(7") <2388>	**SWEET HONEY DRIPPER. / BROTHER JOHN – IKO IKO**	-	
Jan 82.	(7")	**FIRE ON THE BAYOU. / MONA LISA**	-	
Jun 84.	(lp/c) (FIEND/+CASS 31) <BT 1031/+C>	**NEVILLE-IZATION** (live '82 New Orleans) – Fever / Woman's gotta have it / Mojo Hannah / Tell it like it is / Why you wanna hurt my heart? / Fear, hate, envy, jealousy / Caravan / Big chief / Africa. (cd-iss. Nov86; FIENDCD 31) (above issued on 'Demon' UK / 'Black Top' US)		

—— Late in 1988, AARON teamed up with WAS (NOT WAS) and BONNIE RAITT on 'A&M' single, 'BABY MINE'.

Mar 89.	(lp/c/cd) <(AMA/AMC/CDA 5240)>	**YELLOW MOON** – My blood / Yellow Moon / Fire and brimstone / A change is gonna come / Sister Rosa / With God on our side / Wake up / Voodoo / The ballad of Hollis Brown / Will the circle be unbroken / Healing chant / Wild Injuns. (re-iss. cd May95)		66
Apr 89.	(7"/12") (USA/+T 656)	**A CHANGE IS GONNA COME. / SISTER ROSA**		
Jun 89.	(7") (USA 657)	**YELLOW MOON. / WITH GOD ON OUR SIDE** (12"+=/cd-s+=) (USA T/CD 657) – Healing chant.		
Jul 89.	(7") <1277>	**VOODOO. / SISTER ROSA**	-	
Oct 89.	(7") <1410>	**SISTER ROSA. / ('A'-long version)**	-	
Nov 89.	(7") (AM 545)	**WITH GOD ON OUR SIDE. / VOODOO** (12"+=/cd-s+=) (AMY/CDEE 545) – Healing chant.	47	
Nov 89.	(7") <1434>	**YELLOW MOON. / HEALING CHANCE**	-	
Jan 90.	(7") (AM 548)	**A CHANGE IS GONNA COME. / WAKE UP** (live) (12"+=/cd-s+=) (AMY/CDEE 548) – Sister Rosa (live).		

—— Late 1989 & early 1990, AARON duetted on 2 hit singles; 'DON'T KNOW MUCH' and 'ALL MY LIFE', with LINDA RONSTADT. Below 'A'side from film of same name.

—— with band **WILLIE GREEN** – drums / **TONY HALL** – bass / **ERIC STRUTHERS** – guitar

Jun 90.	(7") (AM 568) <1499>	**BIRD ON A WIRE. / BLACK DIAMOND PEARL** (12"+=/cd-s+=) (AMY/CDEE 568) – ('A'version).	72	
Aug 90.	(cd/c/lp) (395312-2/-4/-1) <5312>	**BROTHER'S KEEPER** – Brother blood / Brother Jake / Steer me right / Fearless / Sons and daughters / Fallin' rain / Jah love / River of life / Witness / My brother's keeper / Sons and daughters (reprise) / Mystery train / Bird on a wire.	35	60
Aug 90.	(7")	**RIVER OF LIFE. / TELL IT LIKE IT IS (live)** (12"+=/cd-s+=) – Sister Rosa.		

Oct 90. (7") **FEARLESS. / SHAKE YOUR TAMBOURINE (live)**
(12"+=/cd-s+=) – A change is gonna come (live).

The METERS

—— re-formed in 1990, ART NEVILLE, NOCENTELLI + PORTER + **RUSSELL BATISTE** – drums; repl. MODELISTE

	Special Delivery	Rhino

May 92. (c/cd) (SPDC/+D 1041) **THE METERS JAM**

—— **BRIAN STOLTZ** – guitar repl. NOCENTELLI (before folding again)

– compilations, etc. –

1974. (lp) Island; (ILPS 9250) **CISSY STRUT**
Jan 76. (lp) Reprise; (K 54076) / Virgo; <SV 12002> **THE BEST OF THE METERS**
May 79. (lp) Pye; (PKL 5578) **GOOD OLD FUNKY MUSIC**
(re-iss. Oct90 on 'Special Delivery' lp/c/cd; PSD/+C/CD 1039) (cd-iss. Jan95 on 'Rounder'; ROUCD 2104)
Jul 80. (7"ep) Charly; (CTD 113) **LOOK-KA PY PY. / TIPPI-TOES / CISSY STRUT**
Nov 80. (lp) Charly; (CRB 1009) **SECOND LINE STRUT**
Apr 86. (lp) Charly; (CRB 1112) **HERE COME THE METERMEN**
Feb 87. (lp) Charly; (CRB 1009) **STRUTTIN'** (diff.)
Mar 91. (cd) Charly; (CDNEV 2) **FUNKY MIRACLE**
Sep 92. (cd) Sequel; (NEXCD 220) **UPTOWN RULERS: LIVE ON THE QUEEN MARY 1975 (live)**
Nov 92. (cd) Instant; **THE ORIGINAL FUNKMASTERS**
– Sophisticated Cissy / Funky miracle / Look-ka Py Py / Till 5 / Ease back / Ride your pony / Stormy / Dry spell / Cissy strut / Tippi-toes / Chicken strut / I need more time / Live wire / Hand clapping song / Message from the Metermen. (re-iss. Sep96 on 'Charly'; CPCD 8229)
Jun 94. (cd) Charly; (CPCD 8044) **FUNDAMENTALLY FUNKY**
Nov 94. (cd) Charly; (CPCD 8066) **CRESCENT CITY GROOVE MERCHANTS**
Aug 95. (cd; with The JB Horns) Lakeside; (LAKE 2026) **SECOND HELPING**
1995. (d-cd) Rhino; **FUNKIFY YOUR LIFE: THE METERS ANTHOLOGY**

NEVILLE BROTHERS

	A&M	A&M

Sep 92. (cd/c) (397180-2/-4) <5384> **FAMILY GROOVE**
– Fly like an eagle / One more day / I can see it in your eyes / Day to day thing / Line of fire / Take me to heart / Maori chant / It takes more / Family groove / True love / On the other side of Paradise / Let my people go / Saxafunk / Good song.
Oct 92. (7"/c-s) **FLY LIKE AN EAGLE. / ('A'instrumental)**
(cd-s+=) – ('A'-3 dub mixes) / ('A'other mix).
(12"++=) – (1 extra dub mix).
Apr 94. (cd/c) (540225-2/-4) <0225> **LIVE ON PLANET EARTH (live)**
– Shake your tambourine / Voodoo / Dealer / Junk man / Brother Jake / Sister Rosa / Yellow Moon / Her African eyes / Sands of time / Congo Square / Love the one you're with / You can't always get what you want / Let my people go / Get up stand up / Amazing Grace / One love – People get ready. (re-iss. cd May95; same)

—— In Jun 94, he duetted with TRICIA YEARWOOD on 'MCA' single, 'I FALL TO PIECES'.
May 96. (cd/c) (540512-2/-4) <0512> **MITAKUYE OYASIN OYASIN**
– Love spoken here / Sound / Holy spirit / Soul to soul / Whatever you do / Saved by the grace of your love / You're gonna make your momma cry / Fire on the mountain / Ain't no sunshine / Orisha dance / Sacred ground.

AARON NEVILLE

Jun 91. (7"/c-s) **EVERYBODY PLAYS THE FOOL. / ANGELA BOUND**
(12"+=/cd-s+=) – ('A'-Lovin' Eyes mix) / Hard times come around no more.
Jul 91. (c-s,cd-s) <1563> **EVERYBODY PLAYS THE FOOL / HOUSE ON A HILL** | – | **8** |
Jul 91. (cd/c/lp) (397148-2/-4/-1) <5354> **WARM YOUR HEART** | – | **44** |
– Louisiana 1927 / Everybody plays the fool / It feels like rain / Somewhere, somebody / Don't go, please stay / With you in mind / That's the way she looks / Angela bound / Close your eyes / La vie dansette / Warm your heart / I bid you goodnight / Ave Maria.
Aug 91. (7"/c-s) **SOMEWHERE SOMEBODY. / BROTHER JAKE**
(12"+=/cd-s+=) – Yellow moon.
Jan 92. (7") **LOUISIANA 1927. / HOUSE ON A HILL**
(12"+=/cd-s+=) – A change is gonna come (live).
May 93. (c-s,cd-s) <0240> **DON'T TAKE AWAY MY HEAVEN / THE ROADIE SONG** | – | **56** |
Aug 93. (cd/c) (540100-2/-4) <0086> **THE GRAND TOUR** | – | **37** |
– Don't take away my Heaven / I owe you one / Don't fall apart on me tonight / My brother, my brother / Betcha by golly wow / Song of Bernadette / You never can tell / The bells / These foolish things / The roadie song / Ain't no way / The grand tour / The Lord's prayer / Ronnie-O.
Sep 93. (c-s) <0312> **THE GRAND TOUR / THE ROADIE SONG** | – | **90** |
Nov 93. (cd) (540127-2) <0127> **AARON NEVILLE'S SOULFUL CHRISTMAS** (festive) | | **53** |
Apr 95. (cd/c) (540349-2/-4) <0349> **TATTOOED HEART** | | **64** |
– Can't stop my heart from loving you (the rain song) / Show some emotion / Everyday of my life / Down into muddy water / Some days are made for rain / Try (a little harder) / Beautiful night / My precious star / Why should I fall in love / Use me / For the good times / In your eyes / Little thing called life / Crying in the chapel.
Jun 95. (c-s,cd-s) <1038> **CAN'T STOP MY HEART FROM LOVING YOU (THE RAIN SONG) / IN YOUR EYES** | – | **99** |

– (NEVILLE BROTHERS) comps, others. –

Feb 86. (d-lp/c) Rhino; <(RNFP/RNFC 71494)> **TREACHEROUS: A HISTORY OF THE NEVILLE BROTHERS 1955-1985** | | Apr87 |

Apr 86. (lp; AARON NEVILLE) Demon; (VEX 6) **ORCHID IN THE STORM**
(cd-iss. May95 on 'Rhino'; 8122 70956-2)
Sep 86. (lp/c; AARON NEVILLE) Stateside; (SSL/TCSSL 6011) **HUMDINGER**
Nov 86. (lp; ART NEVILLE) Ace; (CHD 188) **MARDI GRAS ROCK'N'ROLL**
(cd-iss. Oct90; CDCHD 188)
Feb 87. (lp/c; ART NEVILLE) Charly; (CRB/TCCRB 1111) **MAKE ME STRONG**
(cd-iss. Feb87; CDCRB 1111)
Apr 87. (cd) E.M.I.; (CDP 746754-2) <17249> **UPTOWN** (special release with various star guests)
(re-iss. May91 on 'Fame' cd/c/lp; CD/TC+/FA 3255)
Jun 88. (lp) Demon; (FIEND 121) **LIVE AT TIPITINA'S VOL.II (live)**
(re-iss. Aug90 on 'Essential' cd/c/lp; ESS CD/MC/LP 130) (cd re-iss. Jun94 on 'Castle'; CLACD 347)
Sep 88. (lp; ART NEVILLE) Charly; (CRB 1177) **ROCK'N'ROLL HOOTENANNY**
Aug 89. (cd)(c/lp; AARON NEVILLE) Charly; (CDCHARLY 162)(TC+/CRB 1217) **SHOW ME THE WAY**
Apr 90. (d-cd/d-c) Charly; (CD/TC NEV 1) **LEGACY (A HISTORY OF THE NEVILLES)**
1990. (cd; AARON NEVILLE) Curb; **GREATEST HITS**
1991. (cd; AARON NEVILLE) Rounder; **MY GREATEST GIFT**
Jul 91. (cd) Rhino; **TREACHEROUS TOO!**
Sep 91. (cd; ART NEVILLE, EDDIE BO, CHARLES BROWN & WILLIE TEE) Rounder; <(ROUCD 2087)> **KEYS TO THE CRESCENT**
Jan 93. (cd; ART NEVILLE) Ace; (CDCHD 434) **HIS SPECIALITY RECORDINGS: 1956-1958**
Nov 93. (cd; AARON NEVILLE) Charly; (CPCD 8016) **HERCULES**
May 94. (cd) Traditional Line; (TL 1328) **LIVE AT TIPITINA'S (live)**
Nov 95. (cd) One Way; **THE NEVILLE BROTHERS**

NEW FAST AUTOMATIC DAFFODILS
(dig out; Great Alt & Indie . . .)

Randy NEWMAN

Born: RANDOLPH NEWMAN, 28 Nov'44, New Orleans, Louisiana, USA, although (at the age of 10) he moved with his Jewish family to Los Angeles. His uncle, Alfred Newman, had written over 200 scores for 20th Century Fox films, including 'Wuthering Heights'. In 1961, RANDY issued a one-off 45, 'GOLDEN GRIDIRON BOY' for 'Dot', which was produced by singer PAT BOONE. After its flop, he became a staff-writer for 'Liberty' records, writing hits for VIC DANA, GENE McDANIELS, CILLA BLACK!, GENE PITNEY, etc in the mid-60's. In 1967, ALAN PRICE started borrowing his songs, and he scored a hit with 'SIMON SMITH AND HIS AMAZING DANCING BEAR'. That year, NEWMAN became staff arranger/producer for 'Warners', working with the likes of VAN DYKE PARKS, The BEAU BRUMMELS and HARPER'S BIZARRE. In 1968, he finally issued his eponymous debut for Warners subsidiary 'Reprise'; two years later, another solo artist, NILSSON, was to release a whole album of his songs as 'NILSSON SINGS NEWMAN'. In April 1970, NEWMAN issued his second album, '12 SONGS', which included 'MAMA TOLD ME NOT TO COME', a record that went on to become a US chart topper for THREE DOG NIGHT. A much improved affair, NEWMAN finally began to formulate his unique style against a backdrop of classy slide guitar (provided by RY COODER), the arrangements more economical; the brilliant 'MY OLD KENTUCKY HOME' (covered by COODER in fine style on his debut album) was a darkly comic tale of everyday family dysfunction, while the warped tragedy of 'SUZANNE' was NEWMAN at his subversive best. 1972's 'SAIL AWAY' was another early classic, its lavish title track finding NEWMAN in one of his most convincing character roles to date, that of a slave trader in Africa. By this point, the man's slyly ironic sense of humour and idiosyncratic musical orchestrations were garnering considerable critical acclaim and a cult following, if not exactly endearing him to folks who took his work a bit too literally. A case in point was his 1974 quasi-concept set weaving together a cast of characters from the American South, his adoption of a racist perspective for 'REDNECKS', for example, baiting liberals while simultaneously mocking the attitudes of the song. In 'LOUISIANA 1927', meanwhile, NEWMAN showed how affecting his writing could really be when he wasn't satirising. The album marked his first foray into the US Top 40, while 'LITTLE CRIMINALS' (1977), his poorest set to date, ironically made the Top 10 on the strength of the near-No.1 hit, 'SHORT PEOPLE'. Possibly the most controversial of NEWMAN's stabs at twisted humour, its blunt send-up of bigots was understandably misinterpreted by some; perhaps the end didn't justify the means in this case. 'BORN AGAIN' (1979) brought further criticism that NEWMAN was crossing the fine line between satire and self-satisfied condescension, his collaboration with members of the EAGLES marking a move towards a more typical L.A. sound. The 'City Of Angels' formed part of the inspiration for the semi-conceptual 'TROUBLE IN PARADISE' (1983), NEWMAN deconstructing the facade around the world's more exotic cities against a slick schmooze-rock backdrop. During the mid-80's, he concentrated on film work with a score for 'The Natural' (1984) and contributions to the 'Three Amigos' (1987), NEWMAN also co-writing the script for the latter as well as making a cameo appearance; his previous film credits included contributions to cult classic, 'Performance' (1970) and a score for 'Ragtime' (1982), while the 90's saw him scoring a further two major productions, 'Parenthood' and 'Awakenings'. His only other studio set proper to date was 1988's 'LAND OF DREAMS', a patchy affair which nevertheless found NEWMAN in unprecedented autobiographical form on 'DIXIE FLYER' and 'NEW ORLEANS WINS THE WAR', both tracks alone worth the price of admission. For the first half of the 90's, NEWMAN worked feverishly on his very own rock opera project, 'RANDY NEWMAN'S FAUST' (1995). An ambitious update of the German literary classic with the L.A. old guard (DON HENLEY, JAMES TAYLOR, LINDA RONSTADT etc.) in starring roles, the semi-successful results appeared on 'A&M' in 1995, while a Broadway performance has yet to come to fruition.

Album rating: RANDY NEWMAN (*7) / 12 SONGS (*8) / RANDY NEWMAN – LIVE (*6) / SAIL AWAY (*8) / GOOD OLD BOYS (*8) / LITTLE CRIMINALS (*6) / BORN AGAIN (*6) / RAGTIME soundtrack (*4) / TROUBLE IN PARADISE (*5) / THE NATURAL soundtrack (*4) / LONELY AT THE TOP – THE BEST OF RANDY NEWMAN compilation (*8) / LAND OF DREAMS (*6) / PARENTHOOD soundtrack (*4) / AWAKENINGS soundtrack (*4) / THE PAPER soundtrack (*4) / RANDY NEWMAN'S FAUST (*5)

RANDY NEWMAN – vocals, piano

		not iss.	Dot
1962.	(7") **GOLDEN GRIDIRON BOY. / COUNTRY BOY**	-	

—— RANDY became semi-successful songwriter for other established acts. He eventually embarked on a long awaited solo career, after a US instrumental 1966 lp 'THE RANDY NEWMAN ORCHESTRA PLAYS MUSIC FROM THE HIT TELEVISION SERIES 'PEYTON PLACE' for 'Epic'. In 1968, he used over 30-piece orchestra.

		Reprise	Reprise
May 68.	(7") <0692> **BEEHIVE STATE. / I THINK IT'S GOING TO RAIN TODAY**	-	
Jun 68.	(lp) <(RSLP 6286)> **RANDY NEWMAN CREATES SOMETHING NEW UNDER THE SUN**		

– Love story / Bet no one ever hurt this bad / Living without you / So long dad / I think he's hiding / Linda / Laughing boy / Cowboy / The beehive state / I think it's going to rain today / Davy the fat boy. *(cd-iss. May95 on 'Warners'; 7599 26705-2)*

Jul 68.	(7") (RS 20692) **LOVE STORY. / I THINK IT'S GOING TO RAIN TODAY**		-
Nov 68.	(7") <0771> **I THINK HE'S HIDING. / LAST NIGHT I HAD A DREAM**	-	

—— his guests included **RY COODER** – slide guitar / **RON ELLIOTT** – guitar / **GENE PARSONS** – drums / **CLARENCE WHITE** – guitar / **AL McKIBBON** – bass / etc.

Apr 70.	(lp) <6459> **12 SONGS**		

– Have you seen my baby / Let's burn the cornfield / Mama told me not to come / Suzanne / Lover's prayer / Lucinda / Underneath the Harlem moon / Yellow man / Old Kentucky home / Rosemary / If you need oil / Uncle Bob's midnight oil. *(re-iss. Nov71; K 44084) (cd-iss. Sep89; 927449-2)*

May 70.	(7") <0917> **HAVE YOU SEEN MY BABY. / HOLD ON**	-	

(below from the soundtrack of the film 'Performance')

Nov 70.	(7") (RS 20945) <0945> **GONE DEAD TRAIN. / HARRY FLOWERS**		

—— **RANDY** – just vocals and piano only.

Nov 71.	(lp) (K 44151) <6459> **RANDY NEWMAN LIVE (live)**		Sep71

– Mama told me not to come / Tickle me / I'll be home / So long dad / Living without you / Last night I had a dream / I think it's going to rain today / Lover's prayer / Maybe I'm doing it wrong / Yellow man / Old Kentucky home / Davy the fat boy / Lonely at the top. *(cd-iss. May95 on 'Warners'; 7599 26706-2)*

Mar 72.	(7") (K 14155) **LONELY AT THE TOP (live). / MY OLD KENTUCKY HOME (live)**		

—— Reverted to solo / orchestra plus past and new session people. From then after he continued to employ famous musicians and singers.

Jul 72.	(lp) (K 44185) <2064> **SAIL AWAY**		Jun72

– Political science / Burn on / Memo to my son / Dayton, Ohio – 1903 / You can leave your hat on / God's song (that's why I love mankind) / Sail away / Lonely at the top / He gives us all his love / Last night I had a dream / Simon Smith and his amazing dancing bear / Old man. *(cd-iss. Sep89; 927203-2)*

Jul 72.	(7") (K 14190) <1102> **SAIL AWAY. / POLITICAL SCIENCE**		
Sep 72.	(7") <1123> **MEMO TO MY SON. / YOU CAN LEAVE YOUR HAT ON**		-
Sep 74.	(7") <1324> **NAKED MAN. / GUILTY**		-
Oct 74.	(lp/c) (K/K4 54022) <2193> **GOOD OLD BOYS**		36

– Rednecks / Birmingham / Marie / Mr. President (have pity on the working man) / Guilty / Louisiana 1927 / Every man a king / Kingfish / Naked man / Wedding in Cherokee County / Back on my feet again / Rollin'. *(cd-iss. Sep89; 927214-2)*

Nov 75.	(7") <1387> **LOUISIANA 1927. / MARIE**		

		Warners	Warners
Sep 77.	(lp/c) (K/K4 56404) <3079> **LITTLE CRIMINALS**		9

– Short people / You can't fool the fat man / Little criminals / Texas girl at the funeral of her father / Jolly coppers on parade / In Germany before the war / Sigmund Freud's impersonation of Albert Einstein in America / Baltimore / I'll be home / Rider in the rain / Kathleen / Old man on the farm. *(cd-iss. Jan88; K2 56349)*

Oct 77.	(7") (K 17034) <8492> **SHORT PEOPLE. / OLD MAN ON THE FARM**		2
Jun 78.	(7") (K 17205) **RIDER IN THE RAIN. / LITTLE CRIMINALS**		
Aug 78.	(7") <8550> **BALTIMORE. / YOU CAN'T FOOL THE FATMAN**	-	
Oct 78.	(7") <8630> **RIDER IN THE RAIN. / SIGMUND FREUD'S IMPERSONATION OF ALBERT EINSTEIN IN AMERICA**	-	
Aug 79.	(7") (K 17477) **THE STORY OF A ROCK AND ROLL BAND. / PRETTY BOY**		-
Sep 79.	(lp/c) (K/K4 56663) <3346> **BORN AGAIN**		41 Aug79

– It's money that I love / The story of a rock and roll band / Mr. Sheep / Pretty boy / They just got married / Ghosts / Spies / The girls in my life (part 1) / Half a man / William Brown / Pants. *(cd-iss. Feb93; 7599 25917-2)*

Nov 79.	(7") (K 17489) <49088> **IT'S MONEY THAT I LOVE. / GHOSTS**		Sep79
Nov 79.	(7") <49149> **THE STORY OF A ROCK AND ROLL BAND. / HALF A MAN**	-	

Feb 80.	(7") <49223> **SPIES. / POLITICAL SCIENCE**	-	
Feb 82.	(lp/c) (K/K4 52342) <5E 565> **RAGTIME (Soundtrack)**		

– Main title / Newsreel / I could love a million girls / Train ride / Tateh's picture book / Lower East Side / Delmonico polka / Coalhouse and Sarah / Waltz for Evelyn / One more hour / Sarah's responsibility / Change your way / Clef club No.1 / Atlantic City / Clef club No.2 / arah's funeral / Denouncement: Morgan Library takeover – Rhinelander Waldo / Coalhouse's prayer / Ragtime. *(re-iss. Jan89 on 'Screen')* (above soundtrack released on 'Elektra')

Jan 83.	(lp/c) (923755-1-/4) <23755> **TROUBLE IN PARADISE**		64

– I love L.A. / Christmas in Capetown / The blues / Same girl / The Mikey's / My life is good / Miami / Real emotional girl / Take me back / There's a party at my house / I'm different / Song for the dead. *(re-iss. Mar89 on 'Edsel'; ED 305) (cd-iss. Nov93)*

Jan 83.	(7"; RANDY NEWMAN & PAUL SIMON) (W 9803) <29803> **THE BLUES. / SAME GIRL**		51

(12") (W 9803T) – ('A'side) / Simon Smith and the amazing dancing bear / Short people / Mama told me not to come.

Apr 83.	(7") (W 9687) <29687> **I LOVE L.A. / SONG FOR THE DEAD**		
Oct 84.	(7") <29241> **THE NATURAL. / THE FINAL GAME – TAKE ME TO THE BALLROOM**	-	
Oct 84.	(lp/c) (925116-1/-/4) <25116> **THE NATURAL (Soundtrack)**		

– The natural / Prologue 1915-1923 / The whammer strike out / The old farm 1939 / The Majors: the mind is a strange thing / Knock the cover off the ball / Memo / Wrigley field / Iris and Roy / Winning / A father makes a difference / Penthouse party / The end title / The final game – Take me to the ballroom.

Sep 88.	(lp/c)(cd) (WX 212/+C)(925773-2) <25773> **LAND OF DREAMS**		80

– Dixie flyer / New Orleans wins the war / Four eyes / Falling in love / Something special / Bad news from home / Roll with the punches / Masterman and Baby J. / Follow the flag / It's money that matters / I want you to hurt like I do.

Oct 88.	(7") (W 7709) <27709> **IT'S MONEY THAT MATTERS. / ROLL WITH THE PUNCHES**		60

(12"+=/3"cd-s+=) (W 7709 T/CD) – Short people.

Feb 89.	(7") (W 7578) <27586> **FALLING IN LOVE. / BAD NEWS FROM HOME**		

(12"+=/3"cd-s+=) (W 7578 T/CD) – Miami. (above 'A'side from film of the same name)

Sep 89.	(7") <22798> **I'D LOVE TO SEE YOU SMILE. / END TITLE (I LOVE TO SEE YOU SMILE)**	-	
Jun 90.	(cd/c/lp) (925001-2/-4/-1) <25001> **PARENTHOOD (Soundtrack)**		Sep89

– Introduction – I love to see you smile / Kevin's graduation / Helen and Julie / Kevin's party (cowboy Gil) / Gary's in trouble / Father and son / Drag race / Todd and Julie / Kevin comes through / Karen and Gil (montage) / End title (I love to see you smile).

Mar 91.	(cd/c) <(7599 26466-2/-4)> **AWAKENINGS (Soundtrack)**		

– Leonard / Dr. Sayer / Lucy / Catch / Rilke's panther / L dopa / Awakenings / Outside / Escape attempt / Ward five / Dexter's tune / The reality of miracles / End title.

May 94.	(cd) <(9362 45616)> **THE PAPER (Soundtrack)**		

– Opening – Clocks / Henry goes to work / The sun / Bernie calls Deanne / Busting the guys / Marty and Henry / The newsroom 7.00 p.m. / More clocks / Henry leaves with McDougal / Bernie finds Deanne / Bernie / Stop the presses / Henry's fired / Marty / Marty's in trouble / To the hospital / Little Polenta is born / A new day 7.00 a.m. / Make up your mind.

—— now with guests **BONNIE RAITT / DON HENLEY / RY COODER / JAMES TAYLOR / LINDA RONSTADT / ELTON JOHN**

Sep 95.	(cd/c) <(9362 45672-2/-4)> **RANDY NEWMAN'S FAUST**		

– Glory train / Can't keep a good man down / How great our Lord / Best little girl / Northern boy / Bless the children of the world / Gainesville / Relax, enjoy yourself / Life has been good to me / Little island / The man / My hero / I gotta be your man / Feels like home / Bleeding all over the place / Sandman's coming / Happy ending.

– compilations, etc. –

May 84.	(lp/c) WEA; (WX 101/+C) **LONELY AT THE TOP – THE BEST OF RANDY NEWMAN**		

– Love story / Living without you / I think it's going to rain today / Mama told me not to come / Sail away / Simon Smith and his amazing dancing bear / Political science / God's song (that's why I love mankind) / Rednecks / Birmingham / Louisiana 1927 / Marie / Baltimore / Jolly coppers on parade / Rider in the rain / Short people / I love L.A. / Lonely at the top. *(cd-iss. Jul87 +=; 241126-2)* – My life is good / In Germany before the war / Christmas in Capetown / My old Kentucky home. *(re-iss. cd/c Nov93)*

—— (the 1987 movie 'THREE AMIGOS' also including several NEWMAN songs)

NEW MODEL ARMY

Formed: Bradford, England . . . 1980 by SLADE THE LEVELLER (aka JUSTIN SULLIVAN) alongside STUART MORROW and ROBB HEATON, taking their name from Oliver Cromwell's forces in the 17th century English civil war. Following a one-off release, 'BITTERSWEET', on the small 'Quiet' label, the band moved on to the larger independent operation, 'Abstract'. By the release of a debut mini-set, 'VENGEANCE' (1984), the group had attracted a notoriously partisan, clog-footed following, their uncompromising anti-Thatcherite stance and crusty-punk musical assault endearing them to those actively dropping out of the prevailing 80's ethos. Songs such as 'NO MAN'S LAND', 'SPIRIT OF THE FALKLANDS' and the raging title track laid out their political agenda in bruising style, NEW MODEL ARMY's growing popularity subsequently leading to a deal with 'E.M.I.'. The irony of signing with a multi-national corporation wasn't wasted on the band's more scathing critics, although the fact that their music was now more widely available than ever before was no doubt justification enough for such a move; a major label debut single, 'NO REST' / 'HEROIN' (the latter's subject matter resulting in an IBA ban), made the UK Top 30, while a full-length follow-up album, 'NO

REST FOR THE WICKED' (1985), almost made the Top 20. In light of this chart success, a ban from performing in America – reputedly on the grounds of poor artistic quality – looked all the more untenable. With JASON 'MOOSE' HARRIS replacing MORROW, the band continued to kick against the pricks throughout the latter half of the 80's on such grimly defiant albums as 'THE GHOST OF CAIN' and 'THUNDER AND CONSOLATION' (1989). In line with the new age travelling movement's increasing concern with environmental matters and the rise of bands like The LEVELLER's, NEW MODEL ARMY gradually moved away from jackboot punk towards a more traditional folky approach, the tellingly titled 'THE LOVE OF HOPELESS CAUSES' (1993) marking the first fruits of a new deal with 'Epic'. Never strangers to controversy, there was a minor storm over the attendant 'HERE COMES THE WAR' single, its enclosed instructions on how to construct a nuclear device typical of NEW MODEL ARMY's militantly subversive approach.
• **Songwriters:** All written by SULLIVAN / HEATON. • **Trivia:** SULLIVAN and HEATON played back-up to the former's girlfriend poet JOOLZ on many stage shows.

Album rating: VENGEANCE (*7) / NO REST FOR THE WICKED (*6) / THE GHOST OF CAIN (*5) / THUNDER AND CONSOLATION (*6) / IMPURITY (*6) / RAW MELODY MEN (*5) / HISTORY THE SINGLES compilation (*7) / THE LOVE OF HOPELESS CAUSES (*5) / STRANGE BROTHERHOOD (*4)

SLADE THE LEVELLER (b. JUSTIN SULLIVAN, 1956) – vocals, guitar / **STUART MORROW** – bass / **ROBB HEATON** (b.1962) -drums

May 83. (7"m) *(QS 002)* **BITTERSWEET. / BETCHA / TENSION** | Quiet | not iss. |
(w/free flexi-7") – FASHION / CAUSE.

Nov 83. (7") *(ABS 0020)* **GREAT EXPECTATIONS. / WAITING** | Abstract | not iss. |
(re-iss. Feb90 – 7"blue; ABS 090)

Apr 84. (m-lp) *(ABT 006)* **VENGEANCE** | 73 | - |
– Christian militia / Notice me / Smalltown England / A liberal education / Vengeance / Sex (the black angel) / Running / Spirit of the Falklands. *(c-iss.Nov85; ABTC 006) (cd-iss. Jun87 +=; ABT 006CD)* – Great expectations / Waiting / The price / 1984 / No man's land. *(blue-lp iss.Nov87 with 6xlp-box-set of 'Abstract' label records: 'SIX DISQUES BLEU')*

Oct 84. (7") *(ABS 0028)* **THE PRICE. / 1984** | | - |
(12"+=) (12ABS 0028) – No man's land / Notice me / Great expectations.

Apr 85. (c-s/7") *(TC+/NMA 1)* **NO REST. / HEROIN** | E.M.I. 28 | Capitol |
(d12"+=) (12NMA 1 – PSLP 387) – Vengeance (live) / The price (live) / No greater love (live).

May 85. (lp/c) *(EJ 240335-1/-4) <12453>* **NO REST FOR THE WICKED** | 22 | |
– Frightened / Ambition / Grandmother's footsteps / Better than them / My country / No greater love / No rest / Young, gifted & skint / Drag it down / Shot 18 / The attack. *(re-iss. May88 on 'Fame' lp/c; FA/TC-FA 3198) (cd-iss. Jul89; CDFA 3198)*

Jun 85. (d7") *(NMA 2)* **BETTER THAN THEM. / NO SENSE // ADRENELIN. / TRUST** | 49 | - |
(7"ep)(12"ep) (NMAD – NMA 22)(12NMA 2) – THE ACOUSTIC EP

———— **JASON 'MOOSE' HARRIS** repl. MORROW

Nov 85. (7") *(NMA 3)* **BRAVE NEW WORLD. / R.I.P.** | 57 | - |
(12"+=) (12NMA 3) – Brave new world 2.
(d12"+=) (12NMA 3 – PSLP 395) – Young, gifted & skint (live) / Sex (the black angel) (live)

Sep 86. (lp/c) *(EMC/TC-EMC 3516)* **THE GHOST OF CAIN** | 45 | |
– The hunt / Lights go out / 51st state / All of this / Poison street / Western dream / Love songs / Heroes / Ballad / Master race. *(cd-iss. Jul89; CDP 746695-2) (re-iss. Jul90 on 'Fame' cd/c/lp; CD/TC+/FA 3237)*

Oct 86. (7") *(NMA 4)* **51st STATE. / TEN COMMANDMENTS** | 71 | |
(d12"+=) (NMA 4 – PSLP 348) – A liberal education (live) / No rest (live) / No man's land (live).

Feb 87. (7",7"red) *(NMA 5)* **POISON STREET. / COURAGE** | 64 | - |
(12"+=) (12NMA 5) – ('A'extended version).
(d12"+=) (12NMA 5 – PSLP 1002) – All of this (live) / My country (live).

Jun 87. (7"ep/12"ep) *(NMA/12NMA 6)* **WHITE COATS / THE CHARGE. / CHINESE WHISPERS / MY COUNTRY** | 50 | - |

Dec 87. (m-lp/m-c) *<CLP/C4P 46928>* **SEVEN SONGS** | - | |
– My country (live) / Waiting / 51st state / The hunt (live) / White coats / The charge / Chinese whispers.

Jan 89. (7"/7"g-f) *(NMA/+G 7)* **STUPID QUESTIONS. / NOTHING TOUCHES** | 31 | - |
(12") (12NMA 7) – ('A'extended) / Betcha (live).
(cd-s++=) (CDNMA 7) – 51st state.

Feb 89. (cd/c/lp) *(CD/TC+/EMC 3552)* **THUNDER AND CONSOLATION** | 20 | |
– I love the world / Stupid questions / 225 / Inheritance / Green and grey / Ballad of Bodmin Hill / Family / Family life / Vagabonds / Archway towers. *(re-iss. Aug91 on 'Fame', cd+=/c/lp; CD/TC+/FA 3257)*– The charge / Chinese whispers / Nothing changes / White coats.

Feb 89. (7"/7"g-f/7"pic-d) *(NMA/+G/P 8)* **VAGABONDS. / DEAD EYE** | 37 | - |
(12"+=) (12NMA 8) – ('A'extended) / White coats (live).
(cd-s++=) (CDNMA 8) – Lights go out (extended).

Jun 89. (7"/7"pic-d) *(NMA/+P 9)* **GREEN AND GREY. / THE CHARGE (live)** | 37 | - |
(12") (12NMA 9) – ('A'side) / Family life (live) / 125 mph (live).
(cd-s+=) (CDNMA 9) – Green and grey (live).

———— **NELSON** – bass (ex-HIDING PLACE) repl. JASON

Aug 90. (7") *(NMA 10)* **GET ME OUT. / PRISON** | 34 | - |
(10"+=) (10NMA 10) – ('A'extended) / Waiting (live).
(12"+=) (12NMA 10) – ('A'extended) / White coats (live).
(cd-s+=) (CDNMA 10) – White coats (live) / Waiting (live).

Sep 90. (cd/c/lp) *(CD/TC+/EMC 3581)* **IMPURITY** | 23 | |
– Get me out / Space / Innocence / Purity / Whirlwind / Lust for power / Bury the hatchet / 11 years / Lurkstop / Before I get old / Vanity. *(cd+=)* – Marrakesh. *(re-iss. Oct92 & Jul98 on 'Fame' cd/c; CD/TC FA 3273)*

Oct 90. (c-s/7") *(TC+/NMA 11)* **PURITY (IS A LIE). / CURSE** | 61 | - |
(12"+=/cd-s+=) (12/CD NMA 12) – ('A'extended) / Vengeance (live).

May 91. (c-s/7") *(TC+/NMA 13)* **SPACE (live). / FAMILY LIFE** | 39 | - |
(12") (12NMA 13) – ('A'side) / No rest (live) / Stupid questions (live).
(cd-s) (CDNMA 13) – ('A'side) / 225 (live) / Ambition (live).
(10") (10NMA 13) – ('A'side) / Bury the hatchet (live) / Stupid questions (live).

Jun 91. (cd/c/lp) *(CD/TC+/EMC 3595)* **RAW MELODY MEN (live)** | 43 | - |
– Whirlwind / The charge / Space / Purity / White coats / Vagabonds / Get me out / Lib. fol / Better than them / Innocence / Love songs / Innhstaap / Archway towers / Smalltown England / Green & grey / The world. *(re-iss. Jun93 on 'Fame' cd/c; CD/TC FA 3296)*

Apr 92. (cd/c/lp) *(CD/TC+/EMC 3622)* **HISTORY THE SINGLES 1985-91 (compilation)** | | |
– No rest / Better than them / Brave new world / 51st state / Poison street / White coats / Stupid questions / Vagabonds / Green and grey / Get me out / Purity / Space (live). *(incl.free 12")*– Far Better Thing / Higher Wall / Adrenalin (version) Luurstaap (acoustic). *(cd+=/c+=)* – (2 extra tracks *)

———— Jun'92, JUSTIN was nearly killed when he was electrocuted on stage.

Jan 93. (7") *(658 935-7)* **HERE COMES THE WAR. / MODERN TIMES** | Epic 25 | Epic - |
(12"+=/cd-s+=) (658 935-6/-2) – Ghost of your father.

Mar 93. (cd/c/lp) *(473 356-2/-4/-1)* **THE LOVE OF HOPELESS CAUSES** | 22 | |
– Here comes the war / Fate / Living in the rose / White light / Believe it / Understand U / My people / These words / Afternoon song / Bad old world.

Jul 93. (12"ep/cd-ep) *(659 244-6/-2)* **THE BALLADS EP** | 51 | - |
– Living in a rose / Drummy B / Marry the sea / Sleepwalking.

———— split around 1994, although they arrived back four years later. Line-up: **SULLIVAN, HEATON, NELSON** plus **DAVE BLOMBERG** – guitar, keyboards, vocals / **DEAN WHITE** – keyboards, clarinet / plus a string & brass section

Apr 98. (cd/c) *(EAG CD/MC 021)* **STRANGE BROTHERHOOD** | Eagle 72 | not iss. - |
– Wonderful way to go / Whites of their eyes / Aimless desire / Over the wire / Queen of my heart / Gigabyte wars / Killing / No pain / Headlights / Big blue / Long goodbye / Lullaby.

Apr 98. (c-s) *(EAGCS 021)* **WONDERFUL WAY TO GO / REFUGEE** | | - |
(cd-s+=) (EAGXA 021) – South west / ('A'-radio edit).
(cd-s) (EAGXS 021) – ('A'side) / F?NY / BD7 / Ballad of Bodmin Pill.

– compilations, others, etc. –

on 'Abstract' unless mentioned otherwise

Apr 88. (m-lp/cd) *(ABT 017/+CD)* **RADIO SESSIONS (1983-1984 rare)** | | - |

Dec 93. (cd) Windsong; *(WINCD 051)* **BBC RADIO 1 LIVE IN CONCERT (live)** | | - |

Sep 94. (cd) E.M.I.; *(CDEMC 3688)* **B SIDES AND ABANDONED TRACKS** | | - |

Oct 94. (12"ep/cd-ep) **VENGEANCE 1994. / ('A'-Zion Train mix) / ('A'-The Headman mix) / ('A'-Pressure Of Speech mix)** | | - |

Jun 95. (d-cd) *(NMA 001CD)* **VENGEANCE / RADIO SESSIONS** | | - |

Apr 99. (cd) EMI Catalogue; *(499678-2)* **ALL OF THIS: THE "LIVE" RARITIES (live)** | | - |
– Vengeance / Young gifted and skint / A liberal education / No rest / No mans land / My country / All of this / Waiting / 57th state / The hunt / 125 mph / 225 / Ambition / Betcha.

NEW ORDER

Formed: Manchester, England ... mid 1980, from the fragments of JOY DIVISION following the death of frontman IAN CURTIS on the 18th of May 1980. The remaining JOY DIVISION members, vocalist/guitarist BERNARD ALBRECHT (now SUMNER), bassist PETER HOOK and drummer STEPHEN MORRIS remained with 'Factory' records, subsequently adopting the NEW ORDER moniker at the suggestion of manager Rob Gretton. With SUMNER taking over vocal duties, the group gigged around Manchester, eventually releasing a debut single, 'CEREMONY' in 1981. This broke the Top 40, as did the Martin Hannett-produced follow-up, 'PROCESSION' / 'EVERYTHING'S GONE GREEN' although in reality, these releases weren't much of a departure from the rumbling, melodic bass sound of old, critics unimpressed with SUMNER's weak vocals. With their debut album, 'MOVEMENT' (1981), however, NEW ORDER were beginning to crystallise their own unique sound, new recruit GILLIAN GILBERT embellishing the music with cutting keyboard swathes. A subtle dance feel was also edging its way in and with the release of 'TEMPTATION' the following year, NEW ORDER had begun experimenting openly with sequencing technology. The single married the raw cut 'n' thrust of alternative rock to danceable rhythms, echoing hip-hop's similar experimentation with European electronica (see AFRIKA BAMBAATAA's seminal KRAFTWERK-sampling 'Planet Rock') and creating sonic waves that rippled through the eclectic musical free-for-all of the 90's. Fittingly then, NEW ORDER's tour de force, 'BLUE MONDAY' was produced by cult US hip-hop producer, Arthur Baker. The best selling 12 inch single in the history of rock, the record was dominated by compelling, almost militaristic dancefloor beats behind SUMNER's moodily introspective, melancholy vocal musings and HOOK's insidious bass melody. A true crossover single, the record appealed to indie fans, B-boys and club posers alike, cementing NEW ORDER's reputation as one of the UK's most street-cred acts. The accompanying album (an inferior demo version of 'BLUE MONDAY', '5-8-6' was included at the expense of the original single), 'POWER, CORRUPTION AND LIES' (1983) made the Top 5, confirming NEW ORDER's commitment to electronic experimentation via a hypnotic, slightly hazy set. A further Arthur Baker-produced 12 inch

single followed, 'CONFUSION', the New Yorker also collaborating on the 1984 follow-up, 'THIEVES LIKE US'. But it wasn't until the acclaimed 'LOW LIFE' the following year that NEW ORDER successfully integrated the various strands which made up their inimitable sound. Previewed by the affecting 'PERFECT KISS' single and arguably the most consistently listenable NEW ORDER long player, the record convincingly welded driving, bass-heavy rock onto dance rhythms as well as featuring some interesting stylistic diversions. 'BROTHERHOOD' (1986) was a harder-edged affair, enjoyable enough and boasting the brilliant 'BIZARRE LOVE TRIANGLE', although hardly breaking new ground. 'TRUE FAITH' was another landmark NEW ORDER single; co-written and produced by STEPHEN HAGUE (who'd worked wonders on the PET SHOP BOYS' early material), the single was a hauntingly infectious piece of dance-pop, possibly the most commercial material NEW ORDER had ever released. Following the release of the best selling compilation, 'SUBSTANCE (1980-1987)' later that summer, the band went to ground, finally resurfacing in 1989 with 'TECHNIQUE' and quashing rumours of an imminent split. Heavily influenced by the house explosion of the late 80's and partly recorded on the Balearic Island of Ibiza, the album fully indulged the band's dancier leanings with a verve and passion that's missing from much of their later work. Deservedly, the album rode into the No.1 spot on the back of the club zeitgeist, a scene NEW ORDER had a major hand in creating. The single, 'FINE TIME', almost made the Top 10, an uncharacteristically humorous ditty featuring parodic mock-medallion man, BARRY WHITE-esque vocal rumblings. The following year, NEW ORDER were back at No.1 with their World Cup theme tune, 'WORLD IN MOTION'. Nationalist prejudice aside, this song seemed to set the trend for the nauseous, 'Enger-land' limp-wristed crap that the LIGHTNING SEEDS would update six years later for the European championships. Maybe NEW ORDER felt the same way, as the various members soon drifted away to their respective side projects; HOOK to the muscular REVENGE (subsequently stiffing with the 'ONE TRUE PASSION' album), GILBERT and MORRIS to The OTHER TWO (1993's 'THE OTHER TWO AND YOU' album getting lost in the ether when 'Factory' went belly-up) and SUMNER hooking up with JOHNNY MARR (ex-SMITHS) and occasionally NEIL TENNANT (PET SHOP BOYS) to form ELECTRONIC. By far the most successful NEW ORDER-offshoot, the group scored three Top 20 hit singles, including the pop wistfulness of 'GETTING AWAY WITH IT'. They also narrowly missed No.1 with their 1991 eponymous album, their akin to a breezier NEW ORDER, fusing house and indie-pop with wry, intelligent lyrics. With 'Factory' going bust following HAPPY MONDAYS' bank-breaking 'SUNSHINE AND LOVE' debacle, a belated NEW ORDER follow-up, 'REPUBLIC' (1993), was subsequently released on 'London' records. A strangely muted collection, the record nevertheless spawned a succession of Top 30 singles including the aptly named Top 5 hit, 'REGRET'. Rumours of tensions within the group persisted and after a final appearance at the 1993 Reading Festival, the various members soon went off to do their own thing once more. ELECTRONIC charted with another set, 'RAISE THE PRESSURE' in 1996 and HOOK came up with the highly-NEW ORDER-esque MONACO project the following year.
• **Songwriters:** All group compositions except; TURN THE HEATER ON (Keith Hudson). • **Trivia:** In 1987, they contributed some tracks to the movie, 'Salvation'.

Album rating: MOVEMENT (*8) / POWER, CORRUPTION AND LIES (*9) / LOW-LIFE (*8) / BROTHERHOOD (*8) / SUBSTANCE 1980-1987 compilation (*10) / TECHNIQUE (*9) / REPUBLIC (*6) / ? (THE BEST OF) compilation (*9) / THE REST OF NEW ORDER compilation (*7) / Electronic: ELECTRONIC (*8) / RAISE THE PRESSURE (*6) / TWISTED TENDERNESS (*6) / Revenge: ONE TRUE PASSION (*5) / Monaco: MUSIC FOR PLEASURE (*6) / Other Two: THE OTHER TWO AND YOU (*5) / SUPER HIGHWAYS (*5)

BERNARD SUMNER (b. BERNARD DICKEN, 4 Jan'56) – vocals, guitar / **PETER HOOK** (b.13 Feb'56) – bass / **STEPHEN MORRIS** (b.28 Oct'57, Macclesfield, England) – drums

			Factory	Streiwise
Mar 81.	(7"/ext.12") *(FAC 33/+T)* **CEREMONY. / IN A LONELY PLACE** *(re-iss. Jul81 re-recorded; FAC 33-12)*		34	-

—— added **GILLIAN GILBERT** (b.27 Jan'61) – keyboards, synth.

Sep 81.	(7") *(FAC 53)* **PROCESSION. / EVERYTHING'S GONE GREEN**		38	-
Nov 81.	(lp) *(FACT 50)* **MOVEMENT** – Dreams never end / Truth / Senses / Chosen time / I.C.B. / The him / Doubts even here / Denial. *(re-iss. Nov86 c)(cd; FACT 50C)(FACD 50) (re-iss. Jul93 on 'Centredate' cd/c;)*		30	-
Dec 81.	Factory Benelux; (12"m) *(FBN 8)* **EVERYTHING'S GONE GREEN (extended). / MESH / CRIES AND WHISPERS** *(re-iss. cd-ep Jul90; FBN 8CD)*		-	- Belg.
May 82.	(7"/ext.12") *(FAC 63/+T)* **TEMPTATION. / HURT**		29	-
Nov 82.	Factory Benelux; (m-lp) *(FACTUS 8)* **NEW ORDER 1981-82** (compilation)		-	- Belg.
Mar 83.	(12") *(FAC 73)* **BLUE MONDAY. / THE BEACH**		9	-
May 83.	(lp)(c) *(FACT 75)(FACTUS 12C) <25308>* **POWER, CORRUPTION AND LIES** – Your silent face / Ultraviolence / Ecstasy / Leave me alone / Age of consent / We all stand / The village / 5-8-6. *(re-iss. Nov86 c)(cd; FACT 75C)(FAC 75CD)* – Blue Monday / The beach. *(re-iss. Jul93 on 'Centredate' cd/c;)*		4	
Aug 83.	(12"ep) *(FAC 93)* **CONFUSION. / CONFUSED BEATS / CONFUSION (instrumental & Rough mixes)**		12	
Apr 84.	(12") *(FAC 103)* **THIEVES LIKE US. / LONESOME TONIGHT**		18	
May 84.	Factory Benelux; (12") *(FBN 22)* **MURDER. / THIEVES LIKE US (instrumental)**		-	- Belg.

			Factory	Qwest
May 85.	(7") *(FAC 123)* **THE PERFECT KISS. / THE KISS OF DEATH** (12"+=) *(FAC 123-12)* – Perfect pit.		46	-
Jun 85.	(7") **THE PERFECT KISS. / PERFECT PIT**		-	-
May 85.	(lp/c)(cd) *(FACT 100/+C)(FACD 100) <25289>* **LOW-LIFE** – Sooner than you think / Sub-culture / Face up / Love vigilantes / Elegia / The perfect kiss / This time of the night / Sunrise. *(c+=)* – The perfect kiss / The kiss of death / Perfect pit. *(re-iss. Jul93 on 'Centredate' cd/c;)*		7	94
Nov 85.	(7"/ext.12") *(FAC 133/+T)* **SUB-CULTURE. / DUB-CULTURE**		63	-
Mar 86.	(7") *(FAC 143)* **SHELLSHOCK. / THIEVES LIKE US (instrumental)** (12") *(FAC 143T)* – ('A'extended) / Shellshock (dub).		28	
Sep 86.	(ext.12"/7") *(FAC 153/+7)* **STATE OF THE NATION. / SHAME OF THE NATION**		30	-
Oct 86.	(lp/c/s-lp)(cd) *(FACT 150/+C/SP)(FACD 150) <25511>* **BROTHERHOOD** – Paradise / Weirdo / As it was when it was / Broken promise / Way of life / Bizarre love triangle / All day long / Angel dust / Every little counts. *(cd+=)* – State of the nation. *(re-iss. Jul93 on 'Centredate' cd/c;)*		9	
Nov 86.	(ext.12"/7") *(FAC 163/+7)* **BIZARRE LOVE TRIANGLE. / BIZARRE DUB TRIANGLE**		56	-
Mar 87.	(7") **BIZARRE LOVE TRIANGLE. / EVERY LITTLE COUNTS**		-	-
Jul 87.	(ext-12"/7") *(FAC 183/+7) <28271>* **TRUE FAITH. / 1963** (remix-12"+=) *(FAC 183R)* – ('A'extended).		4	32 Oct87
Aug 87.	(d-lp/d-c)(d-cd) *(FACT 200/+C)(FACD 200) <25621>* **SUBSTANCE (1980-1987)** (compilation) – Ceremony / Everthing's gone green / Temptation / Blue Monday / Confusion / Thieves like us / Perfect kiss / Subculture / Shellsock / State of the nation / Bizarre love triangle / True faith. *(d-c+=)* – Procession / Mesh / Hurt / In a lonely place / The beach / Confused / Murder / Lonesome tonight / Kiss of death / Shame of the nation / 1963. *(cd++=)* – Cries and whispers / Dub culture / Shellcock / Bizarre dub triangle. *(re-iss. Jul93 on 'Centredate' cd/c;)*; *hit UK No.32) (d-cd re-iss. Jun98; 520008-2)*		3	36
Dec 87.	(ext.12"/7") *(FAC 193/+7)* **TOUCHED BY THE HAND OF GOD. / TOUCHED BY THE HAND OF DUB** (cd-s) *(FACD 193)* – ('A'extended) / Confusion (dub '87) / Temptation (original).		20	-
Mar 88.	(7") **TOUCHED BY THE HAND OF GOD. / BLUE MONDAY 1988**		-	-
Dec 88.	(7") *(FAC 223-7)* **FINE TIME. / DON'T DO IT** (12"+=) *(FAC 223)* – Fine line. (cd-s+=) *(FACCD 223)* – ('A'-Silk mix) / ('A'-Messed around mix).		11	
Jan 89.	(cd)(lp/c/dat) *(FACD 275)(FACT 275/+C/D) <25845>* **TECHNIQUE** – Fine time / All the way / Love less / Round & round / Guilty partner / Run / Mr. Disco / Vanishing point / Dream attack. *(re-iss. Jul93 on 'Centredate' cd/c;)*		1	32
Mar 89.	(ext.12"/7") *(FAC 263/+7) <27524>* **ROUND & ROUND. / BEST AND MARSH** (ext.& club-12"+=) *(FAC 263R)* – ('A'-Detroit mix). (cd-s+=) *(FACD 263)* – Vanishing point (instrumental 'Making Out' mix) / ('A'-12"mix). (3"cd-s) *(FACD 263R)* – ('A'-Detroit) / ('A'-12") / ('A'-club).		21	64
Sep 89.	(7") *(FAC 273-7)* **RUN 2. / MTO** (12"+=) *(FAC 273)* – ('A'extended) / ('B'-Minus mix).		49	-
May 90.	(12"/7"/c-s; as ENGLAND / NEW ORDER) *(FAC 293/+7/C)* **WORLD IN MOTION . . . . / THE B SIDE** (cd-s+=) *(FACD 293)* – No alla violenza / ('A'-Subbuteo mix). (12") *(FAC 293R)* – ('A'-Subbuteo mix) / ('A'-Subbuteo dub) / No alla violenza mix / ('A'-Carabinieri mix).		1	-

—— Around the late 80's/early 90's, all members splintered to do own projects

			Centredate	Qwest
Apr 93.	(7"/c-s) *(NUO/+C 1) <18586>* **REGRET. / ('A'mix)** (cd-s+=) *(NUOCD 1)* – ('A'-Fire Island mix) / ('A'-Junior's dub mix). (12") *(NUOX 1)* – ('A'-Fire Island mix) / ('A'-Junior's dub mix) / (2-'A' Sabres mixes)		4	28
May 93.	(cd/c/lp) *(828413-2/-4/-1) <45250>* **REPUBLIC** – Regret / World / Ruined in a day / Spooky / Everyone everywhere / Young offender / Liar / Chemical / Times change / Special / Avalanche.		1	11
Jun 93.	(7"/c-s) *(NUO/+C 2)* **RUINED IN A DAY. / VICIOUS CIRCLE (mix)** (cd-s+=) *(NUOCD 2)* – ('A'mixes). (cd-s) *(NUOCDX 2)* – ('A'mixes). (12") *(NUOX 2)* – ('A'side) / World (the price of dub mix).		22	-
Aug 93.	(c-s) *(NUOC 3) <18432>* **WORLD (THE PRICE OF LOVE) / ('A'mixes)** (12"+=/cd-s+=) *(NUOX/NUOCD 3)* – ('A'-Perfecto + sexy club mixes). (cd-s) *(NUOCDX 3)* – ('A'-Brothers in rhythm mix) / ('A'dubstramental mix) / ('A'-Pharmacy dub).		13	-
Sep 93.	(c-s,cd-s) *<18432>* **WORLD (THE PRICE OF LOVE) / RUINED IN A DAY**		-	92
Dec 93.	(c-s/12"/cd-s) *(NUO MC/X/CD 4)* **SPOOKY. / (3 'A' mixes-magimix-minimix-moulimix)** (cd-s) *(NUCDP 4)* – ('A'-Out of order mix) / ('A'-Stadium mix) / ('A'-In Heaven mix) / ('A'-Boo-dub mix) / ('A'-Stadium instrumental).		22	
Nov 94.	(7"/c-s) *(NUO/+MC 5)* **TRUE FAITH '94. / ('A'-Perfecto mix)** (12"+=) *(NUOX 5)* – ('A'-sexy disco dub mix) / ('A'-TWA Gim Up North mix). (cd-s++=) *(NUOCD 5)* – ('A'radio mix).		9	
Nov 94.	(cd/c/d-lp) *(828 580-2/-4/-1) <45794>* **? (THE BEST OF)** (compilation) – True faith '94 / Bizarre love triangle '94 / 1963 / Regret / Fine time / The perfect kiss / Shellsock / Thieves like us / Vanishing point / Run (2) / Round and round '94 / World (price of love) / Ruined in a day / Touched by the hand of God / Blue Monday '88 / World in motion.		4	78
Jan 95.	(c-s) *(NUOMC 6)* **NINETEEN63 (Arthur Baker remix) / ('A'-'94 album version) / ('A'-Lionrock full throttle mix) / ('A'-Joe T Venelli remix)** (12") *(NUOX 6)* – ('A'-Lionrock & Joe T mixes / True faith (Eschreamer mix)/ ('A'-Eschreamer dub). (cd-s) *(NUOCD 6)* – ('A'-Arthur Baker remix) / Let's go/ Spooky (Nightstripper mix)/ True faith '87 (Shep Pettibone mix).		21	

Jul 95. (c-s) *(NUOMC 7)* **BLUE MONDAY '95** / **('A'-original)** | 17 | - |
(12"+=/cd-s+=) *(NUO X/CD 7)* – ('A'-Hardfloor mix) / ('A'-Jam & Spoon mix).

Jul 95. (cd-ep) *<20546>* **BIZARRE LOVE TRIANGLE (2 mixes)** /
STATE OF THE NATION (2 mixes) | - | 98 |

Aug 95. (cd/c) *(828 661-2/-4)* **THE REST OF NEW ORDER** (remixes,
etc) | 5 | |

– compilations, etc. –

Sep 86. (12"ep) *Strange Fruit; (SFPS 001)* **PEEL SESSIONS** (1.6.82.) | 54 | - |
– Turn the heater on / We all stand / 586 / Too late. *(re-iss. Jul87 c-ep; SFPSC 001)
(re-iss. Mar88 cd-ep; SFPSCD 001)*

Oct 87. (12"ep) *Strange Fruit; (SFPS 039)* **PEEL SESSIONS** (26.1.81.) | | - |
– Truth / Senses / I.C.B. / Dreams never end. *(re-iss. May88 cd-ep; SFPSCD 039)*

Mar 88. (7"/12") *Factory; (FAC 73-7/R)* / *Qwest; <27979>* **BLUE**
MONDAY 1988. / **BEACH BUGGY** | 3 | 68 |
(cd-s+=) *(FACD 73)* – ('A'original).

Sep 90. (m-cd/m-c/m-lp) *Strange Fruit; (SFR CD/C/LP 110)* **PEEL**
SESSIONS (2 ep's combined) | | - |

Feb 92. (cd/c/lp) *Windsong; (WIN CD/MC/LP 011)* **BBC RADIO 1 LIVE**
IN CONCERT (live June '87) | 33 | - |
– Touched by the hand of God / Temptation / True faith / Your silent face / Every
second counts / Bizarre love triangle / Perfect kiss / Age of consent / Sister Ray.

Sep 97. (12") *Touch; (502780314769)* **TOUCH TONE 7.1** | | - |

—— In Mar'89, issued two 5"cd-videos of TRUE FAITH + BLUE MONDAY '88.

ELECTRONIC

BERNARD SUMNER – vocals, guitar / **JOHNNY MARR** – guitar (ex-SMITHS) + both
programmers. also with **NEIL TENNANT** – vocals (of PET SHOP BOYS)

	Factory	Warners

Dec 89. (7"/c-s) *(FAC 257-7/-C) <19880>* **GETTING AWAY WITH**
IT. / **LUCKY BAG** | 12 | 38 |
(12"+=/cd-s+=) *(FAC 257)* – ('A'extended).
(12"+=) *(FAC 257)* – ('A'extra mixes).

—— added further guests **CHRIS LOWE, DONALD JOHNSON, DAVID PALMER, DENISE
JOHNSON, HELEN POWELL + ANDREW ROBINSON** (on same track)

Apr 91. (7"/c-s) *(FAC 287-7/-C)* **GET THE MESSAGE.** / **FREE WILL** | 8 | |
(cd-s+=) *(FACD 287)* – ('A'-DNA groove mix).
(12"+=) *(FAC-12 287)* – ('A' 2 other mixes).

May 91. (cd)(lp/c) *(FACD 290/FACT 290/+C) <26387>* **ELECTRONIC** | 2 | |
– Idiot country / Reality / Tighten up / The patience of a saint / Gangster / Soviet /
Get the message / Try all you want / Some distant memory / Feel every beat. *(re-iss.
Feb94 on 'Parlophone' cd/c; CD/TC PRG 1012)*

Sep 91. (7"/c-s) *(FAC 328-7/-C)* **FEEL EVERY BEAT.** / **LEAN TO THE**
INSIDE | 39 | |
(12"+=) *(FAC-12 328)* – ('A'dub version).
(cd-s+=) *(FACD 328)* – Second to none / ('A' DNA mix)

—— next with NEIL TENNANT again

	Parlophone	Warners

Jun 92. (c-s/7") *(TC+/R 6311)* **DISAPPOINTED.** / **IDIOT COUNTRY**
TWO | 6 | |
(12"+=/cd-s+=) *(12R/CDR 6311)* – ('A'-808 State mix) / ('B'-Ultimatum mix).

Jun 96. (c-s/7") *(TC+/R 6436)* **FORBIDDEN CITY.** / **IMITATION OF**
LIFE | 14 | |
(cd-s+=) *(CDR 6436)* – A new religion.

Jul 96. (cd/c) *(CD/TC+/PCS 7382) <45955>* **RAISE THE PRESSURE** | 8 | |
– Forbidden city / For you / Dark angel / One day / Until the end of time / Second
nature / If you've got love / Out of my league / Interlude / Freefall / Visit me / How
long / Time can tell.

Sep 96. (c-s) *(TCR 6445)* **FOR YOU** / **ALL THAT I NEED** | 16 | |
(cd-s+=) *(CDR 6445)* – I feel alright.
(cd-s) *(CDRS 6445)* – ('A'side) / Free will (12"mix) / Disappointed / Get the
message (DNA mix).

Feb 97. (c-s) *(TCR 6455)* **SECOND NATURE** / **TURNING POINT** | 35 | |
(cd-s+=) *(CDRS 6455)* – Feel every beat (12"remix).
(cd-s) *(CDR 6455)* – ('A'side) / ('A'-Plastik mix) / ('A'-Trance Atlantic dub) /
('A'-Sweet remix).

Apr 99. (12") *(12R 6514)* **VIVID.** / **PRODIGAL SON** (mixes; Two
Lone Swordsmen & Harvey's) | 17 | |
(cd-s) *(CDR 6514)* – ('A'side) / Radiation / Prodigal son (inch mix).
(cd-s) *(CDRS 6514)* – ('A'side) / Haze (alternative mix) / Prodigal son (Harvey's a
star in your mind mix).

Apr 99. (cd/c) *(498345-2/-4)* **TWISTED TENDERNESS** | 9 | |
– Make it happen / Haze / Vivid / Vivid / Breakdown / Can't find my way home /
Twisted tenderness / Like no other / Late at night / Prodigal son / When she's gone /
Flicker.

Jul 99. (12") *(12R 6519)* **LATE AT NIGHT.** / **MAKE IT HAPPEN** /
MAKE IT HAPPEN (Darren Price mix) | | - |
(cd-s) *(CDR 6519)* – ('A'side) / King for a day / Come down now (Cevin Fisher
mix).
(cd-s) *(CDRS 6519)* – ('A'side) / Warning sign / Make it happen (Darren Price mix).

REVENGE

PETER HOOK – bass / with **DAVE HICKS** – words, vocals / **C. JONES**

	Factory	Capitol

Nov 89. (7") *(FAC 247-7)* **REASONS.** / **JESUS I LOVE YOU** | | |
(12"+=) *(FAC 247)* – Love you 2.
(cd-s+=) *(FACD 247)* – ('B'version) / Bleach boy.

May 90. (7"/c-s) *(FAC 267-7/-C)* **PINEAPPLE FACE.** / **14K** | | |
(12"+=) *(FAC 267)* – ('A'-Revenge version).
(cd-s+=) *(FACD 267)* – ('A'-Last Lunge version).

Jun 90. (cd)(lp/c) *(FACD 230)(FAC 230/+C) <94053>* **ONE TRUE**
PASSION | | |
– Pineapple face / Big bang / Lose the chrome / Slave / Bleachman / Surf Nazi / Fag
hag / It's quiet.

Sep 90. (7") **(I'M NOT YOUR) SLAVE.** / **AMSTERDAM** | | |
(12"+=)(cd-s+=) – ('A' II version) / Slave.

—— DAVE HICKS departed Apr'91, replaced by **POTTSY**

Dec 91. (12"ep/cd-ep) *<98479>* **GUN WORLD PORN** | | Feb92 |
– Deadbeat (remix) / Cloud nine / State of shock / Little pig.

MONACO

PETER HOOK – bass (now departed from NEW ORDER) / **DAVID POTTS** – guitar, vocals

	Polydor	A&M

Mar 97. (7"/c-s) *(573 190-7/-4)* **WHAT DO YOU WANT FROM ME?** /
BICYCLE THIEF | 11 | - |
(cd-s+=) *(573 191-2)* – Ultra.

May 97. (c-s) *(571 054-4)* **SWEET LIPS** / **SHATTERED** | 18 | - |
(cd-s+=) *(571 055-2)* – ('A'-Tony De Vit mix) / ('A'-arley & Heller mix).
(cd-s) *(571 057-1/-2)* – ('A'side) / ('A'-Farley & Heller mix) / ('A'-Joey Negro mix).

Jun 97. (cd/c/lp) *(<537 242-2/-4/-1>)* **MUSIC FOR PLEASURE** | 11 | |
– What do you want from me? / Shine / Sweet lips / Buzz gum / Blue / Junk / Billy
Bones / Happy Jack / Tender / Sedona.

Sep 97. (7"/c-s) *(571 418-7/-4)* **SHINE (SOMEONE WHO NEEDS**
ME). / **COMIN' AROUND AGAIN** | | |
(cd-s+=) *(571 418-2)* – Tender / ('A' instrumental).

The OTHER TWO

STEPHEN + GILLIAN

	Parlophone	Warners

Oct 91. (7"/c-s) *(FAC 329-7/-C)* **TASTY FISH (Pascal mix).** / **('A'mix)** | 41 | - |
(12"+=/cd-s+=) *(FAC/+D 329)* – ('A'-Almond slice mix).

	London	London

Oct 93. (7"/c-s) *(TWO/+CD 1)* **SELFISH.** / **SELFISH (that pop mix)** | 46 | - |
(12"+=/cd-s+=) *(TWO X/CD 1)* – ('A'-East Village vocal mix) / ('A'-Waterfront
mix).

Nov 93. (cd/c/lp) *(<520028-2/-4/-1>)* **THE OTHER TWO AND YOU** | | - |
– Tasty fish / The greatest thing / Selfish / Movin' on / Ninth configuration / Feel
this love / Spirit level / Night voice / Innocence. *(cd+=)* – Love it.

Feb 99. (c-s/cd-s) *(TWO CS/CD 2)* **YOU CAN FLY** | | |
(cd-s) *(TWCDP 2)* – ('A'mixes).

Mar 99. (cd/c) *(566018-2/-4)* **SUPER HIGHWAYS** | | - |
– You can fly / Super highways / The river / One last kiss / Voytek / Unwanted /
New horizons / Cold feet / The grave / Hello / Ripple / Weird woman.

NEW POWER GENERATION (see under ⇒ PRINCE)

NEW RADICALS

Formed: Los Angeles, California, USA . . . 1997 by GREGG ALEXANDER,
who was originally an inhabitant of Grosse Point in Detroit, Michigan. He
received his first electric guitar at the tender age of twelve and began
composing songs while frequently listening to Soul and R&B. Graduating from
high school, ALEXANDER went on extensive travels before moving to L.A.
to set up The NEW RADICALS. They almost immediately signed to 'M.C.A.'
and began cutting the 'RADICALS debut release, 'MAYBE YOU'VE BEEN
BRAINWASHED TOO', which hit the shops late '98. The title suggested
a discomfort with the growing trend of "fake" artists that ALEXANDER
witnessed popping up everywhere in the American music scene. This angst
was heightened to the extreme when ALEXANDER (sporting his trade mark
fishing hat, worn over the eyes) lyrically commented in the band's Top 5 hit
single, 'YOU ONLY GET WHAT YOU GIVE':- ~"Beck, Courtney Love and
Marilyn Manson . . . go back to your mansions . . . we'll come around and kick
your ass in". To this, MANSON replied humorously:- ~"I'm not upset that he
said he was gonna kick my ass, I'm pissed off that he mentioned me in the
same line as Courtney Love!". The single proverbially set the music industry
buzzing with its 80's jangling keyboards and infectious chorus that brought
back memories of a young TODD RUNDGREN. Through lack of enthusiasm,
ALEXANDER abandoned the short-lived NEW RADICALS for a production
career, proving critics correct when they said that the group were only a "one
hit wonder". But, by God – what a one hit!

Album rating: MAYBE YOU'VE BEEN BRAINWASHED TOO (*6)

GREGG ALEXANDER – vocals, guitars / with many on session

	M.C.A.	M.C.A.

Mar 99. (c-s) *(MCSC 48111)* **YOU GET WHAT YOU GIVE** / **MAYBE**
YOU'VE BEEN BRAINWASHED TOO | 5 | 36 Nov98 |
(cd-s+=) *(MCSTD 48111)* – To think I thought.

Apr 99. (cd/c) *(MCD/MCC 11858)* **MAYBE YOU'VE BEEN**
BRAINWASHED TOO | 10 | 41 Nov98 |
– Mother we just can't get enough / You get what you give / I hope I didn't give
away the . . . . / I don't wanna die anymore / Jehovah made this whole joint for you /
Someday we'll know / Maybe you've been brainwashed too / In need of a miracle /
Gotta stay high / Technicolour lover / Flowers / Crying like a church on Monday.

Sep 99. (c-s) *(MCSC 40217)* **SOMEDAY WE'LL KNOW** / **DECENCY**
THE LEAGUE | 48 | |
(cd-s+=) *(MCSTD 40217)* – Technicolour lover.

NEW RIDERS OF THE PURPLE SAGE

Formed: San Francisco, California, USA ... 1969 when The GRATEFUL DEAD's JERRY GARCIA formed a loose country-rock outfit with guitarists/vocalists JOHN 'Marmaduke' DAWSON (ex-NEW DELHI RIVER BAND) and DAVID NELSON. The group were augmented by fellow 'DEAD' stalwarts PHIL LESH and MICKEY HART, although the latter two had been replaced by DAVE TORBERT (ex-NEW DELHI RIVER BAND) and SPENCER DRYDEN (ex-JEFFERSON AIRPLANE) respectively by the time the group secured a deal with 'Columbia' in 1971. Initially a 'DEAD' side project, opening for the infamous psychedelic rockers on their 1970 tours, the group soon became a sizable live draw in its own right. The 'RIDERS' eponymous debut made the American Top 40, a competent set of hippie-country reminiscent of The GRATEFUL DEAD's peerless 'American Beauty'. GARCIA bowed out soon after, the 'DEAD' road monster taking up too much of his time. A new pedal steel player was found in BUDDY CAGE, the group introducing a driving country-rock sound reminiscent of a more commercial FLYING BURRITO BROTHERS, whose 'DIM LIGHTS, THICK SMOKE (AND LOUD, LOUD MUSIC)' they covered on their follow-up album, 'POWERGLIDE' (1972). The group's followers were cut from the same hippy, tribal cloth as those of The GRATEFUL DEAD and, like that act, the band's live shows were more of an event than a concert. The flipside of this was that the 'RIDERS' record sales never reflected their popularity. 'THE ADVENTURES OF PANAMA RED' (1973) was the band's most commercially successful record, the early to mid-70's being their golden era. Ex-BYRD, SKIP BATTIN replaced TORBERT for a handful of albums before himself being succeeded by STEVE LOWE, an ex-member of fellow country rocker RICK NELSON'S STONE CANYON BAND. The late 70's albums appeared on 'M.C.A.', the band subsequently dropped at the turn of the decade and splitting after the poorly received 'FEELIN' ALRIGHT' (1981). While DAWSON later resurrected the band with new members, NELSON hooked up once more with JERRY GARCIA in his ACOUSTIC BAND, before forming his own outfit in the mid-90's. • **Songwriters:** DAWSON penned most on their debut, but all group shared duties on follow up. Covered; HELLO MARY LOU (Ricky Nelson) / WILLIE AND THE HAND JIVE (Johnny Otis) / LONESOME L.A.COWBOY (Peter Rowan) / KICK IN THE HEAD (Robert Hunter) / etc. • **Trivia:** ROBERT HUNTER of the 'DEAD, also initially wrote the band's lyrics.

Album rating: NEW RIDERS OF THE PURPLE SAGE (*7) / POWERGLIDE (*6) / GYPSY COWBOY (*4) / THE ADVENTURES OF PANAMA RED (*5) / HOME, HOME ON THE ROAD (*4) / BRUJO (*4) / OH, WHAT A MIGHTY TIME (*4) / NEW RIDERS (*4) / THE BEST OF ... compilation (*6) / WHO ARE THOSE GUYS (*3) / MARIN COUNTY LINE (*2) / FEELIN' ALRIGHT (*2) / KEEP ON KEEPIN' ON (*3) / WASTED TASTERS 1971-1975 compilation (*7)

JOHN 'Marmaduke' DAWSON (b.1945, San Francisco) – acoustic guitar, vocals (ex-NEW DELHI RIVER BAND) / **DAVID NELSON** (b. San Francisco) – vocals, guitars, mandolin / **DAVE TORBERT** – bass, acoustic guitar, vocals (ex-NEW DELHI RIVER BAND) repl. PHIL LESH (of GRATEFUL DEAD) / with **SPENCER DRYDEN** (b. 7 Apr'43, New York City, N.Y.) – drums, percussion (ex-JEFFERSON AIRPLANE) repl. MICKEY HART (of GRATEFUL DEAD) except 2 tracks / **JERRY GARCIA** (b. 1 Aug'42, San Francisco) – guitars, banjo (of GRATEFUL DEAD) / **COMMANDER CODY** – piano (2)

C.B.S.   Columbia

Oct 71. (lp) (CBS 64557) <30888> **THE NEW RIDERS OF THE PURPLE SAGE** ☐ 39 Sep71
– I don't know you / Whatcha gonna do / Portland woman / Henry / Dirty business / Glendale train / Garden of Eden / All I ever wanted / Last lonely eagle / Louisiana lady. (re-iss. Feb88 on 'Edsel'; ED 265) (cd-iss. Jul88; EDCD 265)
Oct 71. (7") <45469> **LOUISIANA LADY. / LAST LONELY LADY** - ☐
Jan 72. (7") <45526> **I DON'T KNOW YOU. / GARDEN OF EDEN** - ☐
—— Basic 4-piece (DAWSON, NELSON, TORBERT and **DRYDEN** – now full-time) / added **BUDDY CAGE** (b. Toronto, Canada) – pedal steel guitar
Jun 72. (lp) (CBS 64843) <31284> **POWERGLIDE** ☐ 33 May72
– Dim lights, thick smoke (and loud, loud music) / Rainbow / California day / Sweet lovin' one / Lochinvar / I don't need no doctor / Contract / Runnin' back to you / Hello Mary Lou / Duncan and Brody / Willie and the hand jive.
Jun 72. (7") <45607> **I DON'T NEED NO DOCTOR. / RUNNIN' BACK TO YOU** - 81
Dec 72. (7") (CBS 8035) **I DON'T NEED NO DOCTOR. / CALIFORNIA DAY** ☐ -
Dec 72. (7") <45682> **DIM LIGHTS, THICK SMOKE (AND LOUD, LOUD MUSIC). / RAINBOW** ☐ -
Dec 72. (lp) (CBS 65008) <31930> **GYPSY COWBOY** ☐ 85
– Gypsy cowboy / Whiskey / Groupie / Sutter's mill / Death and destruction / Linda / On my way back home / Superman / She's no angel / Long black veil / Sailin'.
Feb 73. (7") <45763> **GROUPIE. / SHE'S NO ANGEL** - ☐
Oct 73. (lp) (CBS 65687) <32450> **THE ADVENTURES OF PANAMA RED** ☐ 55
– Panamas red / It's alright with me / Lonesome L.A. cowboy / Important exportin' man / One too many stories / Kick in the head / You should have seen me running / L.A. lady / Thank the day / Cement, clay and glass. (re-iss. Feb89 on 'Beat Goes On'; BGOLP 26) (cd-iss. Aug92; BGOCD 26)
Feb 74. (7") <45976> **PANAMA RED. / CEMENT, CLAY AND GLASS** - ☐
Jun 74. (lp) (CBS 80060) <32870> **HOME, HOME ON THE ROAD (live)** ☐ 68 Apr74
– Hi, hello, how are you / She's no angel / Groupie / Sunday Susie / Kick in the head / Truck drivin' man / Hello Mary Lou / Sutter's mill.
—— **SKIP BATTIN** (b. 2 Feb'34, Gallipolis, Ohio) – bass (ex-BYRDS, ex-Solo artist) repl. TORBERT to KINGFISH
Nov 74. (7") <19967> **YOU ANGEL YOU. / PARSON BROWN** - ☐

Jan 75. (lp) (CBS 80405) <33145> **BRUJO** ☐ 68 Oct74
– Old man Noll / Ashes of love / You angel you / Instant armadillo blues / Workingman's woman / On the Amazon / Big wheels / Singing cowboy / Crooked judge / Parson Brown / Neon rose.
Dec 75. (lp) (CBS 69182) <33688> **OH, WHAT A MIGHTY TIME** ☐ Nov75
– Mighty time / I heard you been layin' my old lady / Strangers on a train / Up against the wall Redneck / Take a letter to Maria / Little old lady / On top of old Smokey / Over and over / La bamba / Going round the Horn / Farewell Angelina.

M.C.A.   M.C.A.

May 76. (7") **FIFTEEN DAYS UNDER THE HOOD. / DON'T PUT HER DOWN** ☐ ☐
Jul 76. (lp) (MCF 2758) <2196> **NEW RIDERS** ☐ Jun76
– Fifteen days under the hood / Annie May / You never can tell / Hard to handle / Dead flowers / Don't put her down / The honky tonkin' (I guess I done me some) / She's looking better after every beer / Can't get over you / The swimming song. (cd-iss. Apr94; MCAD 22108)
Aug 76. (7") (MCA 248) <40591> **DEAD FLOWERS. / SHE'S LOOKING BETTER AFTER EVERY BEER** ☐ ☐
—— **STEPHEN LOVE** (b. Indiana) – bass (ex-RICK NELSON's STONE CANYON BAND) repl. BATTIN who joined FLYING BURRITO BROTHERS
Feb 77. (7") <40715> **JUST ANOTHER NIGHT IN RENO. / HOME GROWN** ☐ ☐
Apr 77. (lp) (MCF 2793) <2248> **WHO ARE THOSE GUYS** ☐ ☐
– I can heal you / High rollers / Peggy Sue / Just another night in Reno / It never hurts to be nice to somebody / Love has strange ways / Hold on it's coming / By and by / When I need you / Home grown / Red hot woman and ice cold beer. (cd-iss. Apr94; MCAD 22109)
May 77. (7") (MCA 299) **LOVE HAS STRANGE WAYS. / RED HOT WOMAN AND ICE COOL BEER** ☐ ☐
Feb 78. (lp) (MCF 2830) <2307> **MARIN COUNTY LINE** ☐ ☐
– Jasper / Twenty good men / Echoes / Take a red / Knights and queens / A good woman likes to drink with the boys / Turkeys in a straw / Green eyes a flashing / Little Miss Bad / Echoes / Till I met you / Oh what a night / Llywelyn. (cd-iss. Apr94; MCAD 22107)
—— **ALLEN KEMP** – guitar, vocals / **PATRICK SHANAHAN** – drums / **MICHAEL WHITE** – bass repl. DRYDEN + LOVE

not iss.   A&M

Feb 81. (lp) <SP 4818> **FEELIN' ALRIGHT** - ☐
– Night for making love / No other love / The way she dances / Tell me / Fly right / Crazy little girl / Full moon at midnite / Pakalolo man / Daydreamin' girl / Saralyn.
Apr 81. (7") <2327> **NIGHT FOR MAKING LOVE. / FLY RIGHT** - ☐
Jul 81. (7") <2352> **FULL MOON AT MIDNIGHT. / NO OTHER LOVE** - ☐
—— added **RUSTY GAUTHIER** – guitar, etc

not iss.   M.U.

1982. (lp) <MU 31109> **KEEP ON KEEPIN' ON** - ☐
– Keep on keepin' on / Now I call it love / It's o.k. to cry / Bounty hunter / Barbaric splendor / Senorita / Night of the living lonely / Rancher's daughter / Big Ed / Friend of the Devil.
—— **DAWSON + NELSON** with
—— **GARY VOGENSEN** – vocals, guitar repl. KEMP

not iss.   Relix

1986. (lp; as NEW RIDERS) <2024> **BEFORE TIME BEGAN** - ☐
– Henry / All I ever wanted / Last lonely eagle / Cecilia / Garden of Eden / Superman / Deh Rominap / Handful of brains / I'm through with the fish, Harve / Och tamale / Handful of brains (part 2) / Where discipline comes in.
1992. (cd) <2050> **MIDNIGHT MOONLIGHT** - ☐
– Midnight moonlight / Sutter's mill / Charlie's garden / All I remember / Louisiana lady / Ballad of the deportees / Taking it hard / Glendale train / Change in the weather / Diesel on my tail / Lonesome L.A. cowboy.
—— **EVAN MORGAN** – guitar; repl. VOGENSEN
—— In 1994, NELSON, DAWSON + CAGE re-formed
Sep 94. (cd) <2065> **LIVE IN JAPAN (live)** - ☐
– Henry / Dire wolf / Rainbow / Early in the morning / Keep on keepin' on / Ripple / I don't know you / Friend of the Devil / Portland woman.

– compilations, etc. –

Dec 76. (lp) C.B.S.; (81742) / Columbia; <34367> **THE BEST OF NEW RIDERS OF THE PURPLE SAGE** ☐ ☐
1988. (lp) Relix; <RRCD 2025> **VINTAGE** - ☐
May 94. (cd) Raven; (RVCD 36) **WASTED TASTERS 1971-1975** ☐ ☐
– Hebry / Glendale train / Louisiana lady / I don't know you / Last lonely eagle / I don't need no doctor / Contract / Rainbow / Sweet lovin' one / Dim light thick smoke / She's no angel / Sutter's mill / Sailin' / Panama Red / Lonesome L.A. cowboy / Kick in the head / Teardrops in my eyes / Hello Mary Lou / Dead flowers / You angel you / Singing cowboy / I heard you been layin' my old lady / Farewell Angelina.

NEW YORK DOLLS

Formed: New York City, New York, USA ... late '71 by JOHNNY THUNDERS, DAVID JOHANSEN, BILLY MURCIA, ARTHUR KANE and RICK RIVETS. In March the following year, RIVETS left to form The BRATS, being swiftly replaced by SYLVAIN SYLVAIN. After a promising start as support act on a FACES British tour, the 'DOLLS' first casualty was MURCIA who died on the 6th of November '72 after drowning in his own bath (not, as widely believed, from a drug overdose). With JERRY NOLAN as a replacement, they signed to 'Mercury' in March '73 and promptly began work on an eponymous debut album with TODD RUNDGREN producing. Released in the summer of that year, 'THE NEW YORK DOLLS' was a proto-punk revelation, a way cool schlock of visceral rock'n'roll which combined the more essential moments of MC5, The PRETTY THINGS, PINK FAIRIES and The SHANGRI-LAS. The ROLLING STONES were another obvious reference point, JOHANSEN a dead-ringer for MICK JAGGER in terms of both vocal style and mascara'd looks. Inevitably, then, THUNDERS was the glam-punk KEITH RICHARDS, Glitter Twins to the JAGGERS/RICHARDS Glimmer coupling. The 'DOLLS' trashy transvestite attire also borrowed heavily from the 'STONES (circa '66 'Have You Seen Your Mother . . .'), although being American they'd obviously taken it to almost cartoon-esque proportions. The likes of 'PERSONALITY CRISIS', 'TRASH' and 'JET BOY' were seminal squalls of guitar abuse, making up in attitude what they lacked in musical ability. Although the record had the critics salivating, commercial success wasn't forthcoming and, unhappy with the record's production, the band opted for SHANGRI-LA's producer, GEORGE MORTON to work on 'TOO MUCH TOO SOON' (1974). Though the album had its moments, again the band had been paired with the wrong producer and the music press were emphatically unimpressed. The lukewarm reviews heightened inter-band tension and the 'DOLLS demise was swift and inevitable. Early the following year, Londoner MALCOLM McLAREN made a last-ditch attempt to save the band, revamping their image to no avail. THUNDERS was the first to leave, departing in 1975 to form The HEARTBREAKERS, while JOHANSEN and SYLVAIN subsequently sacked KANE before finally calling it a day the following Christmas. While THUNDERS went on to most acclaim with his HEARTBREAKERS (dying from an overdose on 23rd April '91), JOHANSEN recorded a number of solo albums, 'DAVID JOHANSEN' (1978), 'IN STYLE' (1979) and 'HERE COMES THE NIGHT' (1981) as well as releasing a 1988 set under the pseudonym of BUSTER POINDEXTER. NOLAN also met an untimely death, almost a year on from THUNDERS (14th January, 1992), suffering a fatal stroke while undergoing treatment for meningitis and pneumonia. A pivotal reference point for not only punk, but the US sleaze/glam metal movement of the mid-80's (FASTER PUSSYCAT, L.A. GUNS, GUNS N' ROSES, et al), The NEW YORK DOLLS influence remains hugely disproportionate to their relatively slim legacy. • **Songwriters:** JOHANSEN with THUNDERS or SYLVAIN. Covered PILLS (Bo Diddley) / DON'T START ME TALKIN' (Sonny Boy Williamson) / SHOWDOWN (Archie Bell) / SOMETHIN' ELSE (Eddie Cochran) / etc. • **Trivia:** Two songs 'PERSONALITY CRISIS' & 'WHO ARE THE MYSTERY GIRLS', appeared on the 1977 Various Artists compilation 'NEW WAVE'. JOHANSEN's filmography: 'Married To The Mob', 'Scrooged' and 'The Fisher King'.

Album rating: NEW YORK DOLLS (*8) / TOO MUCH TOO SOON (*7) / LIPSTICK KILLERS exploitation (*5) / ROCK & ROLL compilation (*7)

DAVID JOHANSEN (b. 9 Jan'50, Staten Island, N.Y.) – vocals / **JOHNNY THUNDERS** (b. JOHN GENZALE, 15 Jul'54) – guitar, vocals / **SYLVAIN SYLVAIN** (b. SIL MIZRAHI) – guitar, vocals repl. RICK RIVETS / **ARTHUR KANE** (b. 3 Feb'51) – bass / **JERRY NOLAN** (b. 7 May'51) – drums repl. BILLY MURCIA who died.

			Mercury	Mercury
Jul 73.	(7") <73414> **TRASH. / PERSONALITY CRISIS**		-	
Aug 73.	(lp) (6338 270) <SRM 675> **NEW YORK DOLLS**			Jul73
	– Personality crisis / Looking for a kiss / Vietnamese baby / Lonely planet boy / Frankenstein / Trash / Bad girl / Subway train / Pills / Private world / Jet boy. <US re-iss. 1984; same>			
Nov 73.	(7") (6052 402) **JET BOY. / VIETNAMESE BABY**			
Jul 74.	(lp) (6338 498) <SRM 1001> **TOO MUCH TOO SOON**			May74
	– Babylon / Stranded in the jungle / Who are the mystery girls? / (There's gonna be a) Showdown / It's too late / Puss 'n' boots / Chatterbox / Bad detective / Don't start me talkin' / Human being. <US re-iss. 1984; same>			
Jul 74.	(7") (6052 615) <73478> **STRANDED IN THE JUNGLE. / WHO ARE THE MYSTERY GIRLS?**			
Sep 74.	(7") <73615> **(THERE'S GONNA BE A) SHOWDOWN. / PUSS 'N' BOOTS**		-	
			not iss.	Trash
1974.	(fan club-7"ep) <TR 001> **LOOKING FOR A KISS (live). / WHO ARE THE MYSTERY GIRLS? (live) / SOMETHIN' ELSE (live)**		-	

—— **PETER JORDAN** – bass (the roadie filled in on stage when KANE was drunk)

—— Disbanded mid-1975, after **BOBBY BLAIN** – keyboards repl. CHRIS ROBINSON who had repl. THUNDERS (he formed The HEARTBREAKERS with NOLAN). **TOMMY MACHINE** (was last drummer). The NEW YORK DOLLS reformed again with JOHANSEN and SYLVIAN but only toured until late '76. SYLVIAN later formed The CRIMINALS. DAVID JOHANSEN went solo in 1978.

– compilations, others, etc. –

Jun 77.	(7"m) Mercury; (6160 008) **JET BOY. / BABYLON / WHO ARE THE MYSTERY GIRLS?**			-
Jul 77.	(d-lp) Mercury; (6641 631) **NEW YORK DOLLS / TOO MUCH TOO SOON** (re-iss. Apr86; PRID 12)			-
Nov 81.	(c) R.O.I.R.; <A 104> **LIPSTICK KILLERS – MERCER ST. SESSIONS** (re-iss. May90 on 'Danceteria' cd/lp; DAN CD/LP 038) (re-iss. cd Feb95 & Jun97 on 'ROIR Europe'; 885615027-2)		-	
Sep 82.	(12"ep) Kamera; (ERA 13-12) **PERSONALITY CRISIS / LOOKING FOR A KISS. / SUBWAY TRAIN / BAD GIRL** (re-iss. Jul90 on 'See For Miles' cd-ep; SEACD 3)			-
Sep 84.	(red-m-lp) Fan Club; (FC 007) **RED PATENT LEATHER (rec. 75)** – Girls / Downtown / Private love / Personality crisis / Pills / Something else / Daddy rollin' stone / Dizzy Miss Lizzy. (cd-iss. Oct88; FC 007CD) (UK cd-iss. Feb93 on 'Receiver'+=; RRCD 173) (cd re-iss. Apr97 on 'Last Call'; 42241-2)		-	France
Oct 84.	(7"white) Fan Club; (NYD 1) **PILLS (live). / DOWN, DOWN, DOWN TOWN (live)**		-	France
1985.	(lp) Mercury; <8260 941> **NIGHT OF THE LIVING DOLLS**		-	

Feb 86.	(7",12"pic-d,12"red) Antler; (DOLLS 1) **PERSONALITY CRISIS. / SUBWAY TRAIN**			-
Feb 86.	(7",12"pic-d,12"blue) Antler; (DOLLS 2) **LOOKING FOR A KISS. / BAD GIRL**			-
1986.	(lp; one-side by SEX PISTOLS) Receiver; (RRLP 102) **AFTER THE STORM**			-
Oct 94.	(cd) Mercury; (522 129-2) **ROCK'N'ROLL**			-

NICE

Formed: London, England . . . Oct'67 by ex-GARY FARR & THE T-BONES members, KEITH EMERSON and LEE JACKSON, who, along with DAVID O'LIST and BRIAN DAVIDSON, had backed-up British black soul singer, P.P.ARNOLD. Being part of Andrew Loog Oldham's 'Immediate' label, they moved in a different musical direction with their first 45, 'THOUGHTS OF EMERLIST DAVJACK'. This flopped, as did the similarly titled 1968 debut album containing their show-stopper, 'RONDO'. That summer, they surprised many when their rendition of Leonard Bernstein's 'AMERICA' (from 'West Side Story'), nearly hit the UK Top 20. It was banned in the States, however, where offence was taken to their promotional poster featuring the recently deceased Martin Luther King, Bobby and John F.Kennedy. During a subsequent performance at The Royal Albert Hall, NICE burned an American flag, riling Bernstein enough to prevent the 45 being issued in the States. Although their follow-up album, 'ARS LONGA VITA BREVIS' (1968) failed, subsequent efforts, 'THE NICE' (1969) and 'FIVE BRIDGES SUITE' (1970) both went Top 5. Pioneers of orchestral rock, NICE deconstructed classical music, arranging new interpretations around the keyboard-stabbing showman, KEITH EMERSON. This esteemed ivory-tinkler subsequently went on to even greater success with EMERSON, LAKE & PALMER. • **Songwriters:** Group compositions, using first letters of forenames (aka 'EMERLIST DAVJACK' until O'LIST left in 1968). Covered; AMERICA (Sondheim / Bernstein) / INTERMEZZO FROM KARELIA SUITE (Sibelius) / HANG ON TO A DREAM (Tim Hardin) / SHE BELONGS TO ME + MY BACK PAGES + COUNTRY PIE (Bob Dylan) / and other classical re-inditions.

Album rating: THE THOUGHTS OF EMERLIST DAVJACK (*7) / ARS LONGA VITA BREVIS (*6) / THE NICE (*6) / FIVE BRIDGES SUITE (*7) / ELEGY (*4) / THE NICE COLLECTION compilation (*8)

KEITH EMERSON (b. 2 Nov'44, Todmorden, England) – keyboards / **DAVID O'LIST** – guitar, vocals / **BRIAN DAVIDSON** (b.25 May'42, Leicester, England) – drums / **LEE JACKSON** (b. 8 Jan'43, Newcastle-upon-Tyne, England) – vocals, bass

			Immediate	Immediate
Nov 67.	(7") (IM 059) **THE THOUGHTS OF EMERLIST DAVJACK. / AZRIAL (ANGEL OF DEATH)**			
Dec 67.	(lp; mono/stereo) (IMLP/IMSP 016) <52004> **THE THOUGHTS OF EMERLIST DAVJACK** – Flower king of flies / The thoughts of Emerlist Davjack / Bonnie K. / Rondo / War and peace / Tantalising Maggie / Dawn / The cry of Eugene / Angel of death / America: 1A (adapted from 'West Side Story') – 1B second amendment / The diamond hard apples of the Moon. (re-iss. Jul68; same) (re-iss. 1978 on 'Charly'; CR 3000021) (cd-iss. 1988 on 'Line'; IMCD 900228) (cd re-iss. Feb94 on 'Charly'; CDIMM 010)			
Jun 68.	(7") (IM 068) **AMERICA (2nd Amendment). / THE DIAMOND HARD APPLES OF THE MOON** (re-iss. Dec82; same)	21		

—— now a trio, when O'LIST departed, later joining ROXY MUSIC

Dec 68.	(lp) (IMSP 020) <52020> **ARS LONGA VITA BREVIS** – Daddy, where did I come from? / Little Arabella / Happy Freuds / Intermezzo from Karelia / Don Edito el Gruva / Ars longa vita brevis – Prelude: 1st movement – Wakening ; 2nd movement – Realisation ; 3rd movement – Acceptance – Brandenburger ; 4th movement – Denial / Coda – Extention to the big note. (re-iss. Dec86 on 'Castle' lp/c/cd; CLA LP/MC/CD 120)			
Dec 68.	(7") (IM 072) **BRANDENBURGER. / HAPPY FREUDS**			-
Jul 69.	(7") **SHE BELONGS TO ME. / ('A'version)**			-
Aug 69.	(lp) (IMSP 026) <52022> **THE NICE** – Azrael revisited / Hang on to a dream / Diary of an empty day / For example / Rondo 69 / She belongs to me. (cd-iss. 1990's on 'Repertoire';)	3		
			Charisma	Mercury
Jun 70.	(lp) (CAS 1014) <SR 61295> **FIVE BRIDGES SUITE** – The five bridges suite:- Fantasia, 1st bridge – 2nd bridge – Choral, 3rd bridge – High level fugue, 4th bridge – Finale, 5th bridge / Intermezzo Karelia suite:- Pathetique, 'Symphony No.6. 3rd movement' / Country pie / Bach: Brandenburg concerto No.6 / One of those people. (cd-iss. Feb91; CASCD 1014)	2		
Jul 70.	(7") (CB 132) <73114> **COUNTRY PIE. / ONE OF THOSE PEOPLE**			

—— Disbanded mid 1970. KEITH formed EMERSON, LAKE & PALMER. LEE and BRIAN later surfaced as REFUGEE and made one eponymous album in 1974 for 'Charisma', which featured future YES man, PATRICK MORAZ.

– compilations, others, etc. –

Apr 71.	(lp) Charisma; (CAS 1030) / Mercury; <SR 61324> **ELEGY (live)** – Hang on to a dream / My back pages / 3rd movement – Pathetique / America (from 'West Side Story'). (re-iss. Sep83 lp/c; CHC/+MC 1) (cd-iss. Feb91 & Jun93 +=; CASCD 1030) – Diamonds blue apples of the Moon / Dawn / Tantalising Maggie / The cry of Eugene / Daddy, where did I come from? / Aziral.	5		
Feb 72.	(d-lp) Mercury; <SRM2 6500> **KEITH EMERSON WITH THE NICE** (4th + 5th albums) (cd-iss. UK 1988; 830 457-2)		-	
Mar 72.	(7"; as KEITH EMERSON & THE NICE) Mercury; <73272> **COUNTRY PIE – BRANDENBERG No.6. / FINALE – 5th BRIDGE**		-	

1972. (lp) *Charisma; (CS 1)* **AUTUMN 67 SPRING 68**	☐	–
Mar 76. (lp) *Immediate; (IML 1003)* **AMOENI REDIVI**	☐	–
Jan 78. (lp) *Immediate; (IML 2003)* **THE NICE GREATEST HITS**	☐	–
Mar 83. (lp) *Charisma; (CASMC 163)* **FIVE BRIDGES SUITE / AUTUMN 67 AND SPRING 68**	☐	–
Nov 85. (d-lp/c/cd) *Castle; (CCS LP/MC/CD 106)* **THE NICE COLLECTION**	☐	–

– America 1A (adapted from 'West Side Story') – 1B Second amendment / Happy Freuds / The cry of Eugene / The thoughts of Emerlist Davjack / Rondo / Daddy, where did I come from? / Little Arabella / Intermezzo from Karelia / Hang on to a dream / The diamond hard apples of the Moon / Angel of death / Ars longa vita brevis – Prelude:- 1st movement – Wakening, 2nd movement – Realisation, 3rd movement – Acceptance, Brandenburger, 4th movement – Denial / Coda – Extention to the big note. *(re-iss. cd Apr94; same)*

Aug 87. (lp/c) *Seal; (SLP/SC 002)* **THE 20th ANNIVERSARY OF THE NICE**	☐	–

(re-iss. Apr88 on 'Bite Back' lp/c/cd; BTE L/C/CD 2)

Dec 93. (cd) *Immediate; (CSL 6032)* **THE BEST OF THE NICE – AMERICA**	☐	–
Mar 94. (cd) *Laserlight; (CD 12334)* **AMERICA**	☐	–
Nov 95. (3xcd-box) *Charly; (CDIMMBOX 2)* **THE IMMEDIATE YEARS**	☐	–
Jul 96. (cd) *Receiver; (RRCD 224)* **AMERICA – THE BBC SESSIONS**	☐	–

Stevie NICKS

Born: STEPHANIE NICKS, 26 May '48, Phoenix, Arizona, USA. Raised in California, she made up one half of early 70's Bay Area duo, BUCKINGHAM NICKS, alongside guitarist and he of bouffant hair, LINDSEY BUCKINGHAM. The pair released one self-titled album in 1973 before BUCKINGHAM was invited to join the strife-torn FLEETWOOD MAC as a replacement for BOB WELCH. He accepted the offer with one proviso, that NICKS was also to be taken on board. 'MAC agreed, one of the shrewdest decisions they'd make in their long and chequered career. The youthful pair added a bit of much needed Californian style and sass to the band, as well as some sharp songwriting; the self-titled 'Fleetwood Mac' (1975) duly reaching the top of the US charts while its follow-up, 'Rumours' (1977) became one of the biggest selling albums of all time. NICKS was a key element of the band's allure, her huskily intoxicating vocals and sexually magnetic presence fuelling countless teen fantasies. While it goes without saying that at one time, she was arguably the sexiest woman on the planet, NICKS also penned some of FLEETWOOD MAC's most enduring songs including 'Rhiannon' (in which she fashioned the enigmatic temptress persona that would form the basis of her career), 'Gold Dust Woman' and the beautiful 'Sara'. Parallel to her 'MAC work, NICKS has also carved out a fairly successful solo career, debutting in 1981 on the TOM PETTY duet, 'STOP DRAGGIN' MY HEART AROUND'. The single made the US Top 3 while her debut album, 'BELLA DONNA', made the US No.1 spot, showcasing an AOR sound not unlike FLEETWOOD MAC, although lacking that band's songwriting consistency. NICKS continued to hit the charts with varying degrees of success throughout the mid-80's with material from 'THE WILD HEART' (1983) and 'ROCK A LITTLE' (1985). A gap of four years ensued before the release of 'THE OTHER SIDE OF THE MIRROR' (1989), a less satisfying collection that nevertheless contained one of NICKS' most affecting solo works, the soaring 'ROOMS ON FIRE'. In the five year period that followed, NICKS had to make do with the 'TIMESPACE' (1991) best of, no new material surfacing until 'STREET ANGEL' in 1994. In the interim, NICKS had left FLEETWOOD MAC to concentrate solely on her own work, maybe a wise move considering the poor commerical showing of her last album. While NICKS' material may sometimes let her down, her dreamy voice rarely fails to send a shiver up the spine (or a stirring in M.C. STRONG's loin!). • **Songwriters:** Writes herself except; covers MAYBE LOVE (Nowells-Stewart) / JUST LIKE A WOMAN (Bob Dylan) / DOCKLANDS (Trevor Horn- Betsy Cook).

Album rating: BELLA DONNA (*7) / THE WILD HEART (*6) / ROCK A LITTLE (*5) / THE OTHER SIDE OF THE MIRROR (*6) / TIMESPACE – THE BEST OF compilation (*7) / STREET ANGEL (*4)

	W.E.A.	Modern
Jul 81. (7"; by STEVIE NICKS with TOM PETTY & THE HEARTBREAKERS) *(K 79231) <7336>* **STOP DRAGGIN' MY HEART AROUND. / KIND OF WOMAN**	50	3
Jul 81. (lp/c) *(K/K4 99169) <139>* **BELLA DONNA**	11	1

– The highwayman / Stop draggin' my heart around / Bella donna / Edge of 17 / Kind of woman / Leather and lace / Outside the rain / After the glitter fades / Think about it / How still my heart. *(cd-iss. Jan84; K2 99169) (re-iss. Aug89 & Mar91 on 'EMI' lp/c/cd; EMC/TCEMC/CDEMC 3562)*

Sep 81. (7"; by STEVIE NICKS with DON HENLEY) *<7341>* **LEATHER AND LACE (w/DON HENLEY). / BELLA DONNA**	–	6
Oct 81. (7") *(K 79265)* **LEATHER AND LACE. / OUTSIDE THE RAIN**	–	–
Feb 82. (7") *<7401>* **EDGE OF SEVENTEEN (JUST LIKE THE WHITE WINGED DOVE). / ('A'live)**	–	11
May 82. (7") *(K 79264)* **EDGE OF SEVENTEEN. / OUTSIDE THE RAIN**	–	–
Jun 82. (7") *<7405>* **AFTER THE GLITTER FADES. / THINK ABOUT IT**	–	32
Jun 83. (7") *(U 9870) <99863>* **STAND BACK. / GARBO**	–	5

(12"+=) *(U 9870T)* – Wild heart.

Jun 83. (lp/c) *(250071-1/-4) <90048>* **THE WILD HEART**	28	5

– If anyone falls / Gate and garden / Enchanted / Sable on blond / Nightbird / Stand back / I will run to you / The wild heart / Nothing ever changes / Beauty and the beast. *(cd-iss. Jan84; 250071-2) (re-iss. Oct89 on 'EMI' lp/c/cd; EMC/TCEMC/CDEMC 3563)*

Aug 83. (7") *<99832>* **IF ANYONE FALLS. / WILD HEART**	–	14
Oct 83. (7") *(X 9590)* **IF ANYONE FALLS. / GATE AND GARDEN**	–	–
Dec 83. (7"; by STEVIE NICKS with SANDY STEWART) *<99799>* **NIGHTBIRD. / GATE AND GARDEN**	–	33

	Parlophone	Modern
Jan 84. (7") *(U 9690)* **NIGHTBIRD. / NOTHING EVER CHANGES**	☐	–
Dec 85. (lp/c)(cd) *(PCS/TCPCS 7300)(CDP 746201-2) <90479>* **ROCK A LITTLE**	30	12

– Sister honey / I can't wait / Rock a little / Imperial hotel / I sing for the things / Some become strangers / The nightmare / Has anyone ever written anything for you / If I were you / No spoken word / Talk to me.

Dec 85. (7"/12") *(R/12R 6110)* **I CAN'T WAIT. / ROCK A LITTLE**	54	–

—— returned the compliment to TOM PETTY, when providing vocals on their US hit version of 'NEEDLES AND PINS'.

Feb 86. (7") *<99565>* **I CAN'T WAIT. / THE NIGHTMARE**	–	16
Mar 86. (7") *(R 6124) <99582>* **TALK TO ME . / ONE MORE BIG TIME ROCK'N'ROLL STAR**	68	4 Nov85

(12"+=) *(12R 6124)* – Imperial hotel.

	E.M.I.	Modern
Aug 86. (7") *<99532>* **HAS ANYONE EVER WRITTEN ANYTHING FOR YOU. / IMPERIAL HOTEL**	–	60
Aug 86. (7") *(EMI 5574)* **HAS ANYONE EVER WRITTEN ANYTHING FOR YOU. / I CAN'T WAIT**		

(12"+=) *(12EMI 5574)* – No spoken word.

Apr 89. (7"/c-s) *(EM/TCEM 90) <99216>* **ROOMS ON FIRE. / ALICE**	16	16

(12"+=/12"w-poster+=)(3"cd-s+=) *(12EM/+P 90)(CDEM 90)* – Has anyone ever written anything for you.

Jun 89. (7"; STEVIE NICKS with BRUCE HORNSBY) **TWO KINDS OF LOVE. / REAL TEARS**	–	–
Jun 89. (lp/c/cd) *(EMD/TCEMD/CDEMD 1008) <91245>* **THE OTHER SIDE OF THE MIRROR**	3	10

– Rooms on fire / Long way to go / Two kinds of love / Oh my love / Ghosts / Whole lotta trouble / Fire burning / Cry wolf / Alice / Juliet / Doing the best I can (escape from Berlin) / I still miss someone. *(re-iss. Mar94 cd/c;)*

Jul 89. (7") *(EM 97)* **LONG WAY TO GO. / REAL TEARS**	60	

(12"+=/12"g-f+=) *(12EM/+G 97)* – ('A'remix).
(c-s+=/3"cd-s+=) *(TC/CD EM 97)* – No spoken word.

Oct 89. (7") **WHOLE LOTTA TROUBLE. / GHOSTS**	–	–
Oct 89. (7") *(EM 114)* **WHOLE LOTTA TROUBLE. / EDGE OF SEVENTEEN**	62	–

(12"+=/12"w-poster+=) *(12EM/+P 114)* – Beauty & the beast (live).
(c-s+=/cd-s+=) *(TC/CD EM 114)* – Rooms on fire.

Aug 91. (7"/7"s/c-s) *(EM/EMP/TCEM 203)* **SOMETIMES IT'S A BITCH. / DESERT ANGEL**	40	56

(12"+=/cd-s+=) *(12/CD EM 203)* – Battle of the dragons.

Aug 91. (cd)(c/lp) *(CDP 797623-2)(TC+/EMD 1024) <91711>* **TIMESPACE – THE BEST OF STEVIE NICKS** (compilation)	15	30

– Sometimes it's a bitch / Stop draggin' my heart / Whole lotta trouble / Talk to me / Stand back / Beauty and the beast / If anyone falls / Rooms on fire / Love's a hard game to play / Edge of seventeen / Leather and lace / I can't wait / Has anyone ever written anything for you. *(cd+=)* – Desert angel.

Nov 91. (7"/c-s) *(EM/TCEM 214)* **I CAN'T WAIT (remix). / EDGE OF SEVENTEEN (live)**	47	–

(cd-s+=) *(CDEM 214)* – ('A'version) / Sleeping angel.
(12") *(12EM 214)* – ('A'side) / ('A'dub version) / Sleeping angel.

—— with **MICHAEL CAMPBELL** (co-writer) + **BERNIE LEADON** + **ANDY FAIRWEATHER LOW** + **WADDY WACHTEL** – guitars / **PETER MICHAEL** – percussion / **PAT DONALDSON** – bass / **BENMONT TENCH** – hammond organ / **ROY BITTAN** – piano / **KENNY ARONOFF** – drums

May 94. (cd/c) *(CD/TC EMC 3671) <92246>* **STREET ANGEL**	16	45

– Blue denim / Gretta / Street angel / Docklands / Listen to the rain / Destiny / Unconditional love / Love is like a river / Rose garden / Maybe love will change your mind / Just like a woman / Kick it / Jane.

Jun 94. (c-s) *(TCEM 328) <98270>* **MAYBE LOVE WILL CHANGE YOUR MIND / INSPIRATION**	42	57

(cd-s+=) *(CDEM 328)* – Has anyone ever written anything for you.
(cd-s) *(CDEMS 328)* – ('A'side) / Thousand days / I can't wait / Stand back.

– compilations, etc. –

May 98. (4xcd-box) *Modern-Atlantic; <80393>* **THE ENCHANTED WORKS OF STEVIE NICKS**	–	85

NICO

Born: CHRISTA PAFFGEN, 16 Oct '38, Cologne, Germany. Her father died in a concentration camp, and, as a girl, she travelled throughout Europe with her mother. Developing a fondness for opera, she learned to play classical piano and harmonium. In 1959, while vacationing in Italy, she was introduced by new friends to film director Federico Fellini and following a bit-part in 'La Dolce Vita', she became a top model, appearing in Vogue magazine. In the early 60's, while working in films, she became the girlfriend of French actor Alain Delon. She later give birth to his son, having already borne a daughter to actor/dancer Eric Emerson. In 1963, she fell in love with up-and-coming folk-star BOB DYLAN, who wrote a song for her, 'I'LL KEEP IT WITH MINE'. In 1965, at his suggestion, she moved to London and signed for Andrew Loog Oldham's new label, 'Immediate'. A single, 'I'M NOT SAYING' (written by GORDON LIGHTFOOT) was issued, although the record subsequently flopped, even after an appearance on 'Ready Steady Go'. She then moved to New York, where she met pop-artist ANDY WARHOL. He asked her to feature in an avant-garde film, 'Chelsea Girl', also asking her to join LOU REED, JOHN CALE, MO TUCKER, etc. in his managerial group, The VELVET UNDERGROUND. Together they made one glorious late 1966 album, 'THE VELVET UNDERGROUND AND NICO', NICO leaving soon after for a return to solo work. Decribed as 'The Edith Piaf of the Blank Generation', she was an avant-garde, moody songstress who was anti-pop music in every sense. After a liaison with BRIAN JONES of The

ROLLING STONES, she became the opposite number of teenager and new penmith JACKSON BROWNE who wrote songs for her debut 1968 album, 'CHELSEA GIRL' (notably 'THESE DAYS'). Regarded as an artistic triumph, she nevertheless disagreed with producer Tom Wilson's string arrangements. Subsequently moving to Los Angeles, she started writing material for her follow-up 'Elektra' album, 'THE MARBLE INDEX'. She travelled constantly between America and Europe, starring in another underground film, 'La Cicatrice Interieupe' for Philippe Garrel. In 1971, she cut the JOHN CALE-produced 'DESERTSHORE', the track 'Le Petit Chevalier' featuring her son. Fleeing New York for France after she was involved in a bottle fight with a female Black Panther member, she later appeared at The Rainbow, London on 1st of June '74 alongside JOHN CALE, ENO and KEVIN AYERS. A track, 'THE END', was recorded, and 'Island' records promptly signed her for an album of the same name, with ENO and PHIL MANZANERA at the production helm. That year, she also contributed vocals to KEVIN AYERS' album, 'Confessions Of Dr. Dream', although she subsequently retired from music to live between Berlin, Los Angeles and Spain. In 1981, she made a comeback album, appropriately titled 'DRAMA OF EXILE', but after poor audience response on a SIOUXSIE & THE BANSHEES support slot, she again went AWOL, shacking up in Manchester, England with her live-in-boyfriend / poet JOHN COOPER CLARKE. After another dismissed vinyl return in 1985, she again retired, only to re-appear at a 1987 ANDY WARHOL tribute. Tragically on 18 Jul'88, on a holiday in Ibiza with CLARKE, she fell off her bike and died of a brain haemorrhage. • **Songwriters:** As said, and other covers; THE END (Doors) / DEUTSCHLAND UBER ALLES (German national anthem) / HEROES (David Bowie) / etc. Plus there are obviously a number of VELVET UNDERGROUND re-inditions littered about. • **Trivia:** In 1974, she joined LOU REED and JOHN CALE for a French filmed VELVET UNDERGROUND reunion.

Album rating: CHELSEA GIRL (*8) / THE MARBLE INDEX (*7) / DESERTSHORE (*7) / THE END (*5) / DRAMA OF EXILE (*4) / CAMERA OBSCURA (*4) / THE BLUE ANGEL collection (*6) / BEHIND THE IRON CURTAIN (*4) / LIVE IN TOKYO (*5) / posthumous:- HANGING GARDENS (*6) / HEROINE (*4) / ICON (*5)

NICO – vocals (plus session people)

	Immediate	not iss.
Aug 65. (7") *IM 003)* **I'M NOT SAYIN'. / THE LAST MILE**	☐	-

(re-iss. May82; IMS 003)
(above 'B'side featured JIMMY PAGE as guitarist/writer)

—— In 1966 she teamed up with The VELVET UNDERGROUND on their eponymous lp. Breaking from them the following year, she returned to solo work, augmented by JOHN CALE + LOU REED. Her beau JACKSON BROWNE at the time also became her main songwriter.

	not iss.	Verve
Feb 68. (lp) *<2353 025>* **CHELSEA GIRL**	-	☐

– The fairest of the seasons / These days / Little sister / Winter song / It was a pleasure then / Chelsea girls / I'll keep it with mine / Somewhere there's a father / Wrap your troubles in dreams / Eulogy to Lenny Bruce. *(UK-iss.Sep71 on 'MGM Select'; 2353 025) (re-iss. 1974 on 'Polydor'; same) (cd-iss. May88 & Apr94; 835 209-2)*

—— Retained JOHN CALE as producer, etc.

	Elektra	Elektra
Jul 69. (lp) *<(EKL 4029)>* **THE MARBLE INDEX**	☐	☐

– Prelude / Lawns of dawns / No one is there / Ari's song / Facing the wind / Julius Caesar (memento Hodie) / Frozen warnings / Evening of light. *(cd-iss. Apr91 on 'WEA'+=; 7559 61096-2)* – Roses in the snow / Nibelungen.

	Reprise	Reprise
Jan 71. (lp) *<(RSLP 6424)>* **DESERTSHORE**	☐	☐

– Janitor of lunacy / Falconer / My only child / Le petit chevalier / Abschied / Afraid / Mutterlein / All that is my own. *(re-iss. 1974; K 44102) (cd-iss. Apr91 on 'WEA'; 7599 25870-2)*

—— She retained **CALE** and brought in **ENO** – synthesizer / **PHIL MANZANERA** – guitar / **STERLING MORRISON** – guitar

	Island	not iss.
Oct 74. (lp) *(ILPS 9311)* **THE END**	☐	-

– It has not taken long / Secret side / You forgot to answer / Innocent and vain / Valley of the kings / We've got the gold / The end / Das lied der Deutschen. *(cd-iss. Apr94; IMCD 174)*

—— now with **ANDY CLARKE** – keyboards / **MUHAMMED HADI** – guitar / **DAVEY PAYNE** – sax / **STEVE CORDONA** – drums / **PHILIPPE QUILICHINI** – bass

	Aura	not iss.
Jul 81. (lp) *(AUL 715)* **DRAMA OF EXILE**	☐	-

– Genghis Khan / Purple lips / One more chance / Henry Hudson / I'm waiting for the man / Sixty forty / The sphinx / Orly flight / Heroes. *(cdiss.Mar88 on 'Line'; LILP 400106) (cd re-iss. Jul92 on 'Great Expectations'; PIPCD 037) (cd re-iss. Aug96 on 'See For Miles'; SEECD 449)*

	Flicknife	not iss.
Sep 81. (7") *(FLS 206)* **VEGAS. / SAETA**	☐	-

	Half	not iss.
Jul 82. (7") *(1/2 1)* **PROCESSION. / ALL TOMORROW'S PARTIES**	☐	-

(12"+=) (1/2 1-12) – Secret side (live) / Femme fatale (live).

	Aura	not iss.
Jun 83. (7") *(AUS 137)* **HEROES. / ONE MORE CHANCE**	☐	-

—— with **JAMES YOUNG** – keyboards / **GRAHAM DIDS** – percussion

	Beggars Banquet	not iss.
Jun 85. (7"/12"; as NICO & THE FACTION) **MY FUNNY VALENTINE. / MY HEART IS EMPTY**	☐	-
Jun 85. (lp/c/cd; as NICO & THE FACTION) *(BEG A/C/CD 63)* **CAMERA OBSCURA**	☐	-

– Camera obscura / Tananore / Win a few / My funny valentine / Das lied von einsamen Madchen / Fearfully in danger / My heart is empty / Into the arena / Konig. *(re-iss. Jan89 on 'Beggars Banquet-Lowdown' lp/c)(cd; BBL/+C 63)(BBL 63CD)*

—— added **ERIC RANDOM** – percussion, etc / **TOBY TOMAN** – drums

	Dojo	not iss.
Apr 86. (d-lp/c/cd) *(DOJO LP/TC/CD 27)* **BEHIND THE IRON CURTAIN** (live 1985)	☐	-

– All saints night from a Polish motorway / One more chance / Frozen warnings / The song of the lonely girl / Win a few / Konig / Purple lips / All tomorrow's parties / Fearfully in danger / The end / My funny valentine / 60-40 / Tananoori / Janitor of lunacy / My heart is empty / Femme fatale.

| 1987. (lp) *(DOJOLP 50)* **LIVE IN TOKYO, JAPAN** (live) | ☐ | - |

– My heart is empty / Purple lips / Tananore / Janitor of lunacy / You forgot to answer / 60-40 / My funny valentine / Sad lied von einsannen madchens / All tomorrow's parties / Femme fatale / The end. *(cd-iss. 1988 & Jun95; DOJOCD 50)*

—— NICO died 18th Jul'88 (see info above).

– compilations, others, etc. –

| 1983. (c) *R.O.I.R.; <A 117>* **DO OR DIE** | - | - |

(cd-iss. May93; RE 117CD)

| Sep 85. (lp/c/cd) *Aura; (AU L/C/CD 731)* **THE BLUE ANGEL** (best of) | ☐ | - |

– Femme fatale / All tomorrow's parties / I'll keep it with mine / Chelsea girls / Janitor of lunacy / Heroes / One more chance / Sixty forty / Waiting for the man / The end.

Oct 85. (7") *Aura; (AUS 147)* **I'M WAITING FOR THE MAN. / PURPLE LIPS** (live)	☐	-
Feb 87. (12"ep) *Archive 4; (TOF 110)* **LIVE** (live)	☐	-
Mar 87. (pic-lp) *V.U.; (NICO 1)* **LIVE IN DENMARK** (live)	☐	-
May 88. (c) *Half; (1/2 CASS 2)* **EN PERSONNE EN EUROPE**	☐	-
Nov 88. (12"ep/cd-ep) *Strange Fruit; (SFPS/+CD 064)* **THE PEEL SESSIONS** (2/2/71)		☐

– Secret side / No one is there / Janitor of lunacy / Frozen warnings.

Jun 89. (lp/cd) *Performance; (PERF 385/+CD)* **LIVE HEROES** (live)	☐	-
Nov 90. (cd/c/lp) *Emergo; (EM 9349-2/-4/-1)* **HANGING GARDENS**	☐	-
Jul 92. (cd) *Great Expectations; (PIPCD 039)* **CHELSEA GIRL LIVE** (live)	☐	-

(re-iss. Jun94 on 'Cleopatra'; CLEO 61062) (cd re-iss. Nov96 on 'See For Miles'; SEECD 461)

Sep 94. (cd) *Anagram; (CDMGRAM 85)* **HEROINE**	☐	-
Sep 96. (cd) *Cherry Red; (VICD 008)* **JANITOR OF LUNACY**	☐	-
Sep 96. (cd) *S.P.V.; (SPV 0849620-2)* **NICO'S LAST CONCERT (FATA MORGANA – DESERTSOUNDS IN THE PLANETARIUM)** (live)	☐	-

---

NIGHT RANGER (dig out; Great Metal . . .)

NILSSON

Born: HARRY EDWARD NELSON, 15 Jun'41, Brooklyn, New York, USA. Subsequently raised in California, he started a career as a supervisor at the Security First National Bank in Van Nuys. By day he was developing his songwriting and piano playing talents, eventually placing three of his tracks with PHIL SPECTOR (who duly recorded two with The RONETTES and one with the MODERN FOLK QUARTET). After a couple of early singles on the 'Tower' label, the budding singer/songwriter secured a contract with 'R.C.A.'. In the process of recording his debut album, 'PANDEMONIUM SHADOW SHOW' (1968), NILSSON's 'CUDDLY TOY' was covered by fellow 'R.C.A.' act, the MONKEES, finally persuading him to leave his job at the bank and concentrate on music full-time. There was a distinct BEATLES-esque feel to much of the debut, not merely down to a faithful cover of 'SHE'S LEAVING HOME' but in the orchestrated pop of 'WITHOUT HER' and 'IT'S BEEN SO LONG', NILSSON's rich voice and immaculate phrasing belying the fact he was American. Not much of a surprise then, that LENNON, McCARTNEY and Co. raved over the record, soon becoming good friends with the singer. The album also gained considerable praise from the critics, although NILSSON would have to wait until the summer of '69 before he gained any widespread commercial recognition. This came with his definitve reading of Fred Neil's 'EVERYBODY'S TALKIN', the wistful country-folk number used as the theme tune for the acclaimed 'Midnight Cowboy' movie and becoming a mainstay of the US Top 10 in 1969. The success of the single spurred on sales of 'ARIEL BALLET' (1968), while also creating interest for NILSSON's third album, 'HARRY' (1969). The same year, NILSSON's 'ONE' (from the debut) became a million seller for American rockers, THREE DOG NIGHT. Bizarrely enough, despite all this success, NILSSON never performed in front of a paying audience, while TV appearances were rare. The early 70's saw the singer record a critically acclaimed but poor selling album of RANDY NEWMAN covers, 'NILSSON SINGS NEWMAN' (1970) while the following year he wrote, narrated and sang the soundtrack for children's fantasy film, 'THE POINT' (1971). NILSSON really made his breakthrough in early '72 with a hauntingly intense version of PETE HAM/TOM EVANS' (of BADFINGER) 'WITHOUT YOU', the song latterly assuming an added poignancy following the suicides of both its writers. The accompanying album, 'NILSSON SCHMILSSON' (1972) subsequently went platinum, again showing the singer's penchant for diverse stylistic territory. 'SON OF SCHMILSSON' (1972) was a generally inferior version of its predecessor while 'A LITTLE TOUCH OF SCHMILSSON IN THE NIGHT' (1973) was a semi-successful attempt at pre-war schmaltz. NILSSON subsequently took another radical stylistic shift with 'PUSSY CATS' (1974), a darkly intense album of classic pop/rock covers recorded with, and produced by, drinking buddy JOHN LENNON. Recorded during the former BEATLES' 'lost' period (when he split from YOKO), the opus was a proverbial dark night of the soul for both artists. Following a further series of inconsistent albums throughout the late 70's including 'NILSSON . . . THAT'S THE WAY IT IS' (1976) and 'KNNILLSSON' (1977), the singer virtually retired from the music business in the early 80's, raising a family and setting up an L.A.-based film distribution company. In the early 90's, NILSSON threw himself afresh into recording and writing following a heart attack. Tragically, he suffered a fatal attack on the 15th of January '94, just days after completing a new long player. The following year, the music business paid tribute with the album, 'FOR THE LOVE OF HARRY: EVERYBODY SINGS NILSSON', featuring contributions from the likes of BRIAN WILSON and RANDY NEWMAN. • Covered: YOU CAN'T DO THAT + MOTHER NATURE'S SON (Beatles) / RIVER DEEP, MOUNTAIN HIGH (Phil Spector) to name but a few. NILSSON's songs that have been hits for others:- ONE (Three Dog Night) / THE STORY OF ROCK AND ROLL (Turtles) / THE PUPPY SONG (David Cassidy) / etc. • Trivia: Early in 1969, he wrote first film score, 'Skidoo', and even had a bit part as a security guard. In 1974, he provided the score and starred alongside RINGO STARR for the film, 'Son Of Dracula'.

Album rating: PANDEMONIUM SHADOW SHOW (*6) / ARIEL BALLET (*6) / HARRY (*6) / NILSSON SINGS NEWMAN (*7) / THE POINT (*6) / NILSSON SCHMILSSON (*8) / SON SCHMILSSON (*6) / A LITTLE TOUCH OF SCHMILSSON IN THE NIGHT (*5) / SON OF DRACULA (*4) / PUSSY CATS (*6) / DUIT ON MON DEI (*4) / SANDMAN (*4) / . . .THAT'S THE WAY IT IS (*4) / KNNILLSSONN (*4) / GREATEST HITS compilation (*7) / FLASH HARRY (*4) / ALL THE BEST compilation (*7) / PERSONAL BEST: THE HARRY NILSSON ANTHOLOGY (*8)

NILSSON – vocals, piano with session people and orchestra

			not iss.	Spindle Top
1963.	(7"; as JOHNNY NILES) <1929> **DONNA I UNDERSTAND. / WIG JOB** <re-iss. 1963 on 'Mercury'; 72132>		-	-

			not iss.	Crusader
1964.	(7"; as BO-PETE) <103> **BAA BAA BLACKSHEEP.** / (part 2)		-	-

			not iss.	Try
1964.	(7"; as BO-PETE) <TRY 501> **DO YOU WANNA (HAVE SOME FUN). / GROOVY LITTLE SUZIE**		-	-

			not iss.	Foto-Fi
1964.	(7"; by FOTO-FI FOUR) <107> **STAND UP AND HOLLER (THE BEATLES ARRIVE IN AMERICA). / ISMAEL**		-	-

			not iss.	Tower
1964.	(7") <103> **I'M GONNA LOSE MY MIND. / 16 TONS**		-	
1965.	(7") <136> **YOU CAN'T TAKE YOUR LOVE AWAY FROM ME. / BORN IN GRENADA**		-	
1966.	(7") <244> **GROWING UP. / SHE'S YOURS**		-	
1966.	(lp) <ST 5095> **SPOTLIGHT ON NILSSON** <re-iss. 1967; ST 5165>		-	

			R.C.A.	R.C.A.
Jun 67.	(7") (47-9206) **WITHOUT HER. / FRECKLES**		-	-
Sep 67.	(7") (RCA 1632) <47-9298> **YOU CAN'T DO THAT. / TEN LITTLE INDIANS**			
Dec 67.	(7") <47-9383> **RIVER DEEP, MOUNTAIN HIGH. / SHE BANGS HYMNS OUT OF TUNE**		-	
Mar 68.	(lp) (RD/SF 7928) <LSP 3874> **PANDEMONIUM SHADOW SHOW** – Ten little indians / 1941 / Cuddly toy / She sang hymns out of tune / You can't do that / Sleep late, my lady friend / She's leaving home / There will never be / Without her / Freckles / It's been so long / River deep, mountain high.			
Mar 68.	(7") (RCA 1675) <47-9462> **ONE. / SISTER MARIE**			
Aug 68.	(lp) (RD/SF 7973) <LSP 3956> **AERIAL BALLET** – Good old desk / Don't leave me / Mr. Richland's favorite song / Little cowboy / Together / Everybody's talkin' / I said goodbye to me / Mr. Tinker / One / The wailing of the willow / Bath.			
Apr 69.	(lp) (SF 8010) **SKIDOO (soundtrack)**		-	-

—— (Below 'A'side was now used in the film 'Midnight Cowboy')

Aug 69.	(7") (RCA 1707) <47-9544> **EVERYBODY'S TALKIN'. / DON'T LEAVE ME**			
Sep 69.	(lp) (SF 8046) <4197> **HARRY** – The puppy song / Nobody cares about the railroads anymore / Open your window / Mother nature's son / Fairfax rag / City life / Mournin' glory story / Marchin' down Broadway / I guess the Lord must be in New York City / Rainmaker / Mr. Bojangles / Simon Smith & his amazing dancing bear.			6 Aug69
Sep 69.	(7") <9675> **RAINMAKER. / I WILL TAKE YOU THERE**		-	-
Oct 69.	(7") (RCA 1864) **MAYBE. / THE PUPPY SONG**		-	-
Oct 69.	(7") (RCA 1913) <74-0261> **I GUESS THE LORD MUST BE IN NEW YORK CITY. / GOOD OLD DESK**			34 Nov69
Feb 70.	(7") (RCA 1935) <74-0310> **I'LL BE HOME. / WAITING**			
Mar 70.	(lp) (SF 8166) <LSP 4289> **NILSSON SINGS NEWMAN** – Vine Street / Love story (you and me) / Yellow man / Caroline / Cowboy / The beehive state / I'll be home / Living without you / Dayton Ohio, 1903 / So long, dad. (re-iss. Sep77; PL 42304) (cd-iss. Feb89; ND 90305)			
May 70.	(7") (RCA 1987) <74-0362> **DOWN TO THE VALLEY. / BUY MY ALBUM**			
Apr 71.	(lp) (SF 8166) <LSP 4417> **THE POINT!** (animated TV film soundtrack) – Everything's got 'em / The town (narration) / Me and my arrow / The game (narration) / Poli high / The trial and banishment (narration) / Think about your troubles / Thursday (why I did not go to work today) / Blanket for a sail / Down to the valley / The pointed man (narration) / P.O.V. waltz / The clearing in the woods (narration) / Are you sleeping? / Oblio's return (narration). (re-iss. Aug91 on 'Edsel' lp+=/cd+=; ED/+CD 340) – (extended versions).	46	25 Mar71
Mar 71.	(7") <74-0443> **ME AND MY ARROW. / ARE YOU SLEEPING?**	-	34
Jun 71.	(7") <74-0524> **WITHOUT HER. / GOOD OLD DESK**	-	-

Jan 72.	(7") (RCA 2165) <74-0604> **WITHOUT YOU. / GOTTA GET UP** (re-iss. Feb79 on 'RCA Gold')	1	1 Dec71
Jan 72.	(lp) (SF 8242) <LSP 4515> **NILSSON SCHMILSSON** – Gotta get up / Driving along / Early in the morning / Moonbeam / Down / Without you / Coconut / Let the good times roll / Jump into the fire / I'll never leave you. (re-iss. Apr80; INTS 5002) (re-iss. Nov84 lp/c/cd; NL/NK/ND 83464) (re-iss. Sep86 on 'Fame' lp/c; FA/TCFA 3166) (cd re-iss. Oct87; ND 83464)	4	3 Nov71
Mar 72.	(7") <74-0673> **JUMP INTO THE FIRE. / MOONBEAM**	-	27
May 72.	(7") (RCA 2214) **COCONUT. / MOONBEAM**	42	-
Jun 72.	(7") <74-0718> **COCONUT. / DOWN**	-	8
Jul 72.	(lp) (SF 8297) <LSP 4717> **SON SCHMILSSON** – Take 54 / Remember (Christmas) / Joy / Turn on your radio / You're breakin' my heart / Spaceman / The lottery song / At my front door / Ambush / I'd rather be dead / The most beautiful girl in the world.	41	12
Oct 72.	(7") (RCA 2266) <74-0788> **SPACEMAN. / YOU'RE BREAKIN' MY HEART**		23 Sep72
Dec 72.	(7") (RCA 2300) <74-0855> **REMEMBER (CHRISTMAS). / THE LOTTERY SONG** <re-iss. Nov75; PB 10130>		53
Jul 73.	(lp) (SF 8371) <APL-1 0097> **A LITTLE TOUCH OF SCHMILSSON IN THE NIGHT** – Lazy Moon / For me and my gal / It had to be you / Always / Makin' whoopee / You made me love you (I didn't want to do it) / Lullaby in ragtime / I wonder who's kissing her now / What'll I do / Nevertheless (I'm in love with you) / This is all I ask / As time goes by. (cd-iss. Aug91; ND 90582)	20	46
Jul 73.	(7") (RCA 2395) **AS TIME GOES BY. / MAKIN' WHOOPEE!**		
Aug 73.	(7") <APBO 0039> **AS TIME GOES BY. / LULLABY IN RAGTIME**	-	86
Apr 74.	(7") <APBO 0238> <APBO 0246> **DAYBREAK. / DOWN**	-	39
May 74.	(lp) <(APL-1 0220)> **SON OF DRACULA (Soundtrack)** – It is he who will be King / Daybreak / At my front door / Count Down meets Merlin and Amber / Moonbeam / Perhaps this is all a dream / Remember (Christmas) / Intro: Without you / The Count's vulnerability / Down / Frankenstein, Merlin and the operation / Jump into the fire / The abdication of Count Down / The end (moonbeam). (above was jointly issued on 'Rapple' & is a part compilation)		
Sep 74.	(7") (RCA 2459) <PB 10001> **MANY RIVERS TO CROSS. / DON'T FORGET ME**		60
Sep 74.	(lp) <(APL-1 0570)> **PUSSY CATS** – Many rivers to cross / Subterranean homesick blues / Don't forget me / All my life / Old forgotten soldier / Save the last dance for me / Mucho Mungo – Mt. Elga / Loop de loop / Black sails / Rock around the clock. (cd-iss. Jan92 on 'Edsel'; EDCD 337)		
Nov 74.	(7") <PB 10078> **MUCHO MUNGO – MT. ELGA. / SUBTERRANEAN HOMESICK BLUES**	-	
Jan 75.	(7") (RCA 2504) **SAVE THE LAST DANCE FOR ME. / ALL MY LIFE**		-
Feb 76.	(7") <PB 10139> **DON'T FORGET ME. / LOOP DE LOOP**		
Mar 75.	(lp) (RS 1008) <APL-1 0817> **DUIT EN MON DEI** – It's a jungle out there / Down by the sea / Kojak Columbo / Easier for me / Turn out the light / Salmon falls / Puget sound / What's your sign / Home / Good for God.		
Jun 75.	(7") (RCA 2565) <PB 10183> **KOJAK COLOMBO. / TURN OUT THE LIGHT**		
Sep 75.	(lp) (RS 1015) <APL-1 1031> **SANDMAN** – I'll take a tango / Something true / Pretty soon there'll be nothing left for everybody / The ivy covered walls / Here's why I did not go to work today / How to write a song / The flying saucer song / Will she miss me / Jesus Christ you're tall.		
Jan 76.	(7") (RCA 2649) **SOMETHING TRUE. / PRETTY SOON THERE'LL BE NOTHING**		-
May 76.	(7") (RCA 2687) <10634> **SAIL AWAY. / MOONSHINE BANDIT**		
Jul 76.	(lp) (RS 1062) <1119> **NILSSON . . . THAT'S THE WAY IT IS** – That is all / Just one look – Baby I'm yours / Moonshine bandit / I need you / A thousand miles away / Sail away / She sits down on me / Daylight has caught me / Zombie jambouree (back to back) / That is all (reprise).		
Aug 76.	(7"; as LYNDA LAWRENCE & NILSSON) <10759> **THAT IS ALL. / JUST ONE LOOK – BABY I'M YOURS**	-	-
Jan 77.	(7") <11059> **WHO DONE IT. / PERFECT DAY**	-	-
Mar 77.	(7") (PB 9048) **MOONSHINE BANDIT. / SHE SITS DOWN ON ME**		
Jun 77.	(7") <11144> **ALL I THINK ABOUT IS YOU. / I NEVER THOUGHT I'D GET THIS LONELY**	-	-
Jun 77.	(7") (PB 9104) **ALL I THINK ABOUT IS YOU. / OLD BONES**	43	-
Jul 77.	(lp/c) (PL/PK 12276) <2276> **KNNILLSSONN** – All I think about is you / I never thought I'd get this lonely / Who done it / Lean on me / Goin' down / Old bones / Sweet surrender / Blanket for a sail / Laughin' man / Perfect day.		
Nov 77.	(7") <11193> **AIN'T IT KINDA WONDERFUL. / I'M BRINGING A RED RED ROSE**		
Nov 77.	(7") (PB 9177) **LEAN ON ME. / WILL SHE MISS ME**		-

HARRY NILSSON

			Mercury	not iss.
Sep 80.	(7") (MER 40) **I DON'T NEED YOU. / IT'S SO EASY**		-
Sep 80.	(lp) (6302 022) **FLASH HARRY** – Harry / Cheek to cheek / Best move / Old dirt road / I don't need you / Rain / I've got it / It's so easy / How long can disco go on / Bright side of life.		
Nov 80.	(7") (MER 44) **RAIN. / BRIGHT SIDE OF LIFE**		-

			Polydor	not iss.
Aug 84.	(7") (POSP 703) **LONELINESS. / SILVER HORSE**		

			R.C.A.	not iss.
Dec 88.	(lp/c) (PL/PK 90251) **A TOUCH MORE SCHMILSSON IN THE NIGHT**		-

—— He virtually retired from the music business and was still a gun-control advocate after the death of his friend, JOHN LENNON. NILSSON died of a heart attack on the 15th January '94 at his home Agoura Hills, California.

– compilations, etc. –

on 'RCA' unless mentioned otherwise

1969.	(7") *Tower; <518>* **GOOD TIME. / GROWING UP**	–	
Feb 73.	(lp) *(SF 8326) <4543>* **AERIAL PANDEMONIUM BALLET**		Jun71
Sep 76.	(7"m) *(RCA 2733)* **WITHOUT YOU. / EVERYBODY'S TALKIN' / KOJAK, COLOMBO**	22	–
Jan 77.	(7") *<11318>* **ME AND MY ARROW. / SPACEMAN**		–
Jan 77.	(7") *PB 9000)* **ME AND MY ARROW. / THURSDAY**		–
Oct 77.	(lp) *D.J.M.; (22075)* **EARLY TYMES**		–
Jun 78.	(lp/c) *(PL/PK 42728) <2798>* **GREATEST HITS** *(re-iss. Nov82; INTS 5233) (cd-iss. Jan84; PD 89081)*		–
Oct 79.	(lp) *K-Tel; (NE 1050)* **HARRY AND . . .**		–
Jul 81.	(7") *(RCA GOLD 9630)* **WITHOUT YOU. / EVERYBODY'S TALKIN'** *(re-iss. Oct86 on 'Old Gold'; OG 9630)*		–
Sep 81.	(lp/c) *(RCA LP/K 3029)* **NILSSON'S GREATEST MUSIC**		–
Feb 82.	(c) *Orchid; (ORC 005)* **ALL FOR YOUR LOVE**		–
Apr 88.	(cd) *RCA Diamond;* **NILSSON**		–
Oct 90.	(cd) *(ND 90502)* **WITHOUT HER – WITHOUT YOU: THE VERY BEST OF NILSSON VOL.1**		–
Jun 92.	(cd) *(ND 90652)* **LULLABY IN RAGTIME: THE VERY BEST OF NILSSON**		–
Oct 92.	(cd-ep) *Old Gold;* **WITHOUT YOU / EVERYBODY'S TALKIN' / COCONUT**		–
Sep 93.	(cd/c) *Music Club; (MCCD/MCMC 129)* **ALL THE BEST** – Without you / Everybody's talkin' / Mother nature's son / It's been so long / Good old desk / Without her / Mournin' glory story / Mr. Richland's favourite song / Mr.Bojangles / She's leaving home / Lulaby in ragtime / Makin' whoopee! / Cuddly toy / River deep, mountain high / Little cowboy / As time goes by.		–
Feb 94.	(7"/c-s) *(74321 19309-7/-4)* **WITHOUT YOU. / EVERYBODY'S TALKIN'** *(cd-s+=) (74321 19309-2) –* Over the rainbow.	47	
1994.	(d-cd) *<66354-2>* **PERSONAL BEST: THE HARRY NILSSON ANTHOLOGY**	–	–
Oct 94.	(cd) *(74321 22315-2)* **THE BEST OF NILSSON**		–
Oct 95.	(cd) *R.P.M.; (RETRO 804)* **NILSSON '62 – THE DEBUT SESSIONS**		–

NINE INCH NAILS

Formed: San Francisco, California, USA . . . 1989 by classically trained pianist, TRENT REZNOR. He turned his attention to the darker textures of 'PRETTY HATE MACHINE' in the late 80's following a stint working in a recording studio. A solo effort – the album was written and played wholly by REZNOR – its despair and bitter self-pity were set against walls of churning synths and industrial rhythms, the compelling 'HEAD LIKE A HOLE' subsequently becoming a minor hit thanks to heavy MTV rotation. Around the same time, REZNOR recruited a band and struck out on that year's Lollapolooza trek, previewing a harder hitting, guitar influenced sound. Although the debut album was equal parts DEPECHE MODE/MINISTRY, REZNOR's follow-up, the mini-album, 'BROKEN' (1992), followed the metal/industrial fusion of the live shows. REZNOR seemed more tormented than ever on the likes of 'HELP ME I AM IN HELL', an explicitly masochistic video for the 'HAPPINESS IN SLAVERY' single courting not inconsiderable controversy. A punishing album of remixes, 'FIXED' followed a couple of months later, featuring such good-time party favourites as 'FIST FUCK' and 'SCREAMING SLAVE'. Clearly, REZNOR was rather discontented with his lot, his scary reputation heightened when it was revealed that he'd rented the L.A. pad where Charles Manson and Family had murdered Sharon Tate and her friends back in 1969. While REZNOR was allegedly unaware of this spook factor when he rented the property, it nevertheless gave 'THE DOWNWARD SPIRAL' (1994) a grim new resonance (the album was recorded in said abode). The consummation of everything REZNOR had been working towards, the record was a masterful alternative metal/industrial landmark, exploring the depths of human despair and depravity in its multifarious forms. REZNOR's tormented musings obviously struck a chord with the American populace, the album making No.2 in the US charts while NIN were given a rapturous reception at that year's Woodstock anniversary festival. Another album of remixes, 'FURTHER DOWN THE SPIRAL', appeared the following year, while REZNOR set up his own 'Nothing' label, nurturing such famous talent as the equally scary MARILYN MANSON. It had been five long years since the emergence of any new NINE INCH NAILS material (apart from TRENT producing the soundtrack to Oliver Stone's movie, 'Natural Born Killers'), however REZNOR and his nihilistic NIN completed their comeback set, 'THE FRAGILE' (1999). Packed with over twenty apocalyptic tracks it hit the top of the US charts (scraped Top 10 in the UK), doom, gloom and then boom, it was all here for America's forgotten youth of today. • **Songwriters:** 'The Terminator' REZNOR penned except PHYSICAL YOU'RE SO (Adam Ant). • **Trivia:** REZNOR appeared in the 1987 film 'LIGHT OF DAY'.

Album rating: PRETTY HATE MACHINE (*7) / BROKEN (*7) / THE DOWNWARD SPIRAL (*8) / THE FRAGILE (*6)

TRENT REZNOR (b.17 May'65, Mercer, Pennsylvania, USA) – vocals, guitar, keyboards, bass, drums, programming / **JAMES WOOLEY** – keyboards / **RICHARD** – guitar / **CHRIS VRENNA** – drums

		Island	Nothing-TVT
Nov 90.	(12"ep/cd-ep) *(12IS/CID 482)* **DOWN IN IT (skin). / TERRIBLE LIE (mix) / DOWN IN IT (shred – demo)**		
Sep 91.	(7"/10") *(IS/10ISP 484)* **HEAD LIKE A HOLE. / ('A'-Copper mix)**	45	

	(12"+=/cd-s+=) *(12IS/CID 484)* – ('A'-Opal mix).		
Sep 91.	(cd/c/lp) *(CID/ICT/ILPS 9973) <2610>* **PRETTY HATE MACHINE** – Head like a hole / Terrible lie / Down in it / Sanctified / Something I can never have / Kinda I want to / Sin / That's what I get / The only time / Ringfinger.	67	75 Nov90
Nov 91.	(c-s/7") *(C+/IS 508)* **SIN. / GET DOWN MAKE LOVE** *(10"+=/cd-s+=) (10IS/CID 508) –* Sin (dub).	35	
Sep 92.	(m-cd/m-c/m-lp) *(IMCD/ICM/ILPM 8004) <92246>* **BROKEN** – Pinion / Wish / Last / Help me I am in Hell / Happiness is slavery / Gave up. *(free 7"+/cd+=) –* Physical (you're so) / Suck.	18	7
Nov 92.	(m-cd/m-c/m-lp) *(IMCD/ICM/ILPM 8005)* **FIXED** (remixes) – Gave up / Wish / Happiness is slavery / Throw this away / Fist fuck / Screaming slave.		–

—— Below was controversially recorded at the house of the Charles Manson murders (some produced by /with FLOOD). Guests on 1 track each were **ADRIAN BELEW + DANNY LOHNER** – guitar / **CHRIS VRENNA + STEPHEN PERKINS + ANDY KUBISZEWSKI +** – drums (live:- **VRENNA, LOHNER, WOOLLEY + ROBIN FINCK**)

Mar 94.	(cd/c/d-lp) *(CID/ICT/ILPSD 8012) <92346>* **THE DOWNWARD SPIRAL** – Mr. Self destruct / Piggy / Heresy / March of the pigs / Closer / Ruiner / The becoming / I do not want this / Big man with a gun / A warm place / Eraser / Reptile / The downward spiral / Hurt.	9	2
Mar 94.	(cd-ep) *<95938>* **MARCH OF THE PIGS / REPTILLIAN / ALL THE PIGS, ALL LINED UP / A VIOLET FLUID / UNDERNEATH THE SKIN**	–	59
Mar 94.	(etched-7") *(IS 592)* **MARCH OF THE PIGS. / A VIOLENT FLUID** *(9"+=) (9IS 592) –* All the pigs, all lined up / Underneath the skin. *(cd-s) (CID 592) –* ('A'side) / Underneath the skin / Reptillian. *(cd-s+=) (CIDX 592) –* All the pigs, all lined up / Big man with a gun.	45	–
Jun 94.	(12"ep/cd-ep) *(12IS/CID 596)* **CLOSER / CLOSER TO GOD / MARCH OF THE FUCKHEADS / HERESY (BLIND) / MEMORABILIA** *(12"ep/cd-ep) (12ISX/CIDX 596) –* ('A'side) – (deviation) – (further away) / ('A'original) / ('A'-Precursor) / ('A'-Internal).	25	–
Jun 94.	(c-s) *<98263>* **CLOSER / MARCH OF THE PIGS (live)**	–	41
Jun 95.	(cd/c) *(IMCD/IMA 8041) <95811>* **FURTHER DOWN THE SPIRAL** (remixes) – Piggy (nothing can stop me) / The art of destruction (part one) / Self destruction (part three) / Heresy (version) / The downward spiral (the bottom) / Hurt / At the heart of it all / Ruiner (version) / Eraser (denial: realization) / Self destruction: final.		23
Sep 97.	(cd-ep) *(IND 95542)* **THE PERFECT DRUG (mixes; original / Meat Beat Manifesto / Plug / Nine Inch Nails / Spacetime Continuum / The Orb)** *(above from the movie 'Lost Highway' on the 'Interscope' imprint)*	43	46
Aug 99.	(c-s/cd-s) *<97026>* **THE DAY THE WORLD WENT AWAY**	–	17
Sep 99.	(d-cd/d-c/t-lp) *(CIDD/ICT/ILPST 8091) <490473>* **THE FRAGILE** – Somewhat damaged / The day the world went away / Frail / Wretched / We're in this together / The fragile / Just like you imagined / Even deeper / Pilgrimage / No you don't / La mer / Great below / Way out i through / Into the void / Where is everybody / Mark has been made / Please / Starfuckers Inc. / Complication / I'm looking forward to joining you finally / Pilgrimage / Big come down / Underneath it all.	10	1
Nov 99.	(cd-s) *(497140-2)* **WE'RE IN THIS TOGETHER / THE DAY THE WORLD WENT AWAY (quiet version) / THE DAY THE WORLD WENT AWAY (Porter Ricks mix)** *(cd-s) (497141-2) –* ('A'side) / 10 miles high / The new flesh. *(cd-s) (497183-2) –* ('A'side) / Complication / The perfect drug.	39	

NIPPLE ERECTORS / NIPS (see under ⇒ POGUES)

NIRVANA UK (dig out; 4th edition or Great Psychedelic . . .)

NIRVANA

Formed: Aberdeen, Washington, USA . . . 1987 by singer/songwriter/guitarist KURT COBAIN and bassist KRIST NOVOSELIC. Recruiting drummer CHAD CHANNING, they soon became a talking point and pivotal band in nearby Seattle where the likes of SOUNDARDEN and MUDHONEY were major players in the emerging grunge scene. Whereas those bands dealt in raw garage punk/metal, NIRVANA immediately stood out from the pack by dint of the subtle pop melodies which COBAIN craftily incorporated into his songs. They also fast gained a reputation for their ferocious live shows which drew comparisons with early WHO, if only for their sheer nihilistic energy, invariably ending in trashed equipment. Signing, of course, with the hub of the Seattle scene, 'Sub Pop', NIRVANA released their debut single, 'LOVE BUZZ' in October 1988, the album, 'BLEACH', following a year later. One of the seminal 'Sub Pop' releases alongside, MUDHONEY's 'SUPERFUZZ BIGMUFF' and TAD's 'GOD'S BALLS', this was a darkly brooding, often savagely angry collection, driven by bass and fuzz and interspersed with pockets of melody. The likes of 'SCHOOL' and the throbbing 'NEGATIVE CREEP' saw COBAIN lapse into his trademark howl, an enraged, blood curdling shriek, almost primal in its intensity. Conversely, 'ABOUT A GIRL' was an achingly melodic semi-acoustic shuffle, as steeped in hurt as the rest of the album but more resigned than angry. New guitarist JASON EVERMAN had contributed to the record's sonic bludgeon as well as paying for recording costs, although he soon parted ways (he went on to play with the much hyped MINDFUNK) with COBAIN and NOVOSELIC over the ever reliable, 'musical differences'. 'BLEACH' was heartily received by the indie/metal press, NIRVANA embarking on a heavy round of touring, first in the States, then Europe. Following the departure of CHANNING, MUDHONEY's DAN PETERS joined briefly and was involved with the 'SLIVER' single, a brilliantly chunk of pop-noise which further enhanced NIRVANA's underground kudos and raised expectations for a follow-up album to fever pitch. 'NEVERMIND' (1991) let down no-one, except possibly the anally-retentive sad-kids who accused the band of selling out to a major label ('Geffen'). Released immediately after a blinding set at England's Reading festival (where NIRVANA, who probably drew the most frenetic crowd reaction of the day, had to make do with a paltry afternoon slot; the following year they'd be headlining), and with appetites whetted via import copies of 'SMELLS LIKE TEEN SPIRIT', the record was met with an ecstatic press reaction. While the album brought the grunge phenomenon into the mainstream, NIRVANA had already moved on to a blistering power pop/punk sound, best evidenced in the sardonic fury of the aforementioned 'SMELLS . . .'. Here was an anthem for the blank generation, for all the people who'd given up before even starting; COBAIN had condensed the collective frustration/despair/apathy into an incendiary slice of pop genius not witnessed since The SEX PISTOLS' heyday. 'COME AS YOU ARE' was another piece of semi-acoustic bruised beauty while 'TERRITORIAL PISSINGS' was as extreme as the record went, a rabid blast of hardcore punk introduced with a sarcastic send-up pilfered from The YOUNGBLOOD's 60's love 'n' peace classic, 'GET TOGETHER'. Most of the other tracks lay somewhere in between, COBAIN never letting up the intensity level for a minute, whether on the deceptively breezy 'IN BLOOM' or the stinging 'BREED'. For a three piece (the drum seat had now been filled by DAVE GROHL, ex-SCREAM), the group made one hell of a racket, but it was a racket which was never less than 100% focused, the GROHL/NOVOSELIC rhythmic powerhouse underpinning every track with diamond-edged precision. It's fair to say that 'NEVERMIND' literally changed the face of music, American indie bands coming to dominate the scene until the arrival of OASIS in the mid-90's. COBAIN was heralded as the spokesman of a generation, although it was a role he was both unwilling and unable to cope with. As the inevitable, punishing round of touring ensued, the singer's health began to suffer once more; never the healthiest of people, COBAIN suffered from a chronic stomach complaint as well as narcolepsy, a condition which causes the sufferer to sleep for excessive periods of time. What's more, he was concerned that the irony of his lyrics was lost on his growing legions of fans (which now included the macho 'jocks' whom COBAIN so despised) who now doted on his every word. Amid all this confusion, COBAIN was married to HOLE's COURTNEY LOVE on the 24th February '92, the couple almost losing custody of their newborn child, Frances, later that summer following revelations of drug abuse. The end of the year saw the release of a compilation of rare material, 'INCESTICIDE', including two storming VASELINES' (obscure but brilliant Scottish punk-popsters) covers, 'MOLLY'S LIPS' and 'SON OF A GUN'. Rumours of COBAIN's heroin abuse were rife, however, and the singer overdosed twice the following year. 'IN UTERO' (1993) reflected the turmoil, an uncompromising wall of noise (courtesy of STEVE ALBINI) characterising most of the album. The melodies were still there, you just had to dig deeper in the sludge to find them. Despite 'Geffen's misgivings, the record was a transatlantic No.1, its success engendering another round of live work. After a final American show in January, the group set off for Europe, taking a break at the beginning of March. COBAIN remained in Rome, where, on the 4th March, LOVE found him unconscious in their hotel room, the result of an attempted tranquilizer overdose. Although COBAIN eventually recovered, the tour was abandoned and the couple returned to their Seattle home. Though it didn't come as a complete surprise, the music world was stunned nonetheless when, on the 8th April, news broke that COBAIN had finally killed himself, blowing his own head off with a shotgun. The most widely mourned rock'n'roll death since JOHN LENNON, COBAIN's suicide even sparked off a series of 'copycat' incidents in America by obsessive fans. Posthumously released later that year, the acoustic 'UNPLUGGED IN NEW YORK' (1994) live set was heavy going, a tragic poignancy underpinning the spare beauty of tracks like 'DUMB' and 'PENNYROYAL TEA' (from 'IN UTERO') while the heart-rendingly resigned 'ALL APOLOGIES' sounds like COBAIN's final goodbye to a world that he could no longer bear to be a part of. Eventually picking up the pieces, GROHL formed The FOO FIGHTERS, turning his hand to guitar playing/songwriting and recruiting ex-GERM, PAT SMEAR. After time spent campaigning for his native, war torn Yugoslavia, NOVOSELIC returned with his own band, SWEET 75, a collaboration with diminutive Venezuelan lesbian folk-singer, YVA LAS VEGAS. They finally released one unstartling eponymous set in 1997, which just might be their only outing. • **Songwriters:** COBAIN wrote late 80's songs. In the 90's, the group were credited with COBAIN lyrics. Covers; LOVE BUZZ (Shocking Blue) / HERE SHE COMES NOW (Velvet Underground) / DO YOU LOVE ME? (Kiss) / TURNAROUND (Devo) / JESUS WANTS ME FOR A SUNBEAM (Vaselines) / D7 (Wipers) / THE MAN WHO SOLD THE WORLD (David Bowie) / WHERE DID YOU SLEEP LAST NIGHT (Leadbelly).

Album rating: BLEACH (*8) / NEVERMIND (*10) / INCESTICIDE collection (*7) / IN UTERO (*10) / UNPLUGGED IN NEW YORK (*9) / FROM THE MUDDY BANKS OF THE WISHKAH (*8) / Sweet 75: SWEET 75 (*4)

KURT COBAIN (b.20 Feb'67, Hoquaim, Washington) – vocals, guitar / **CHRIS NOVOSELIC** (b.16 May'65) – bass / **CHAD CHANNING** (b.31 Jan'67, Santa Rosa, Calif.) – drums

	Tupelo	Sub Pop
Oct 88. (7") <SP 23> **LOVE BUZZ. / BIG CHEESE**	-	-

——— Early '89, added **JASON EVERMAN** – guitar Also guest drummer on 2 tracks **DALE CROVER**

Aug 89. (lp,white or green-lp/cd) (TUP LP/CD 6) <SP 34> **BLEACH**   ☐   ☐ Jun89
– Blew / Floyd the barber / About a girl / School / Paper cuts / Negative creep / Scoff / Swap meet / Mr.Moustache / Sifting / Big cheese. (cd+=) – Love buzz /

Downer. <US re-iss. Dec91 hit 89> (re-iss. Feb92 on 'Geffen'; GEFD 24433) (hit UK No.33) (c+=) – Big cheese. (re-iss. Oct95 on 'Geffen' cd/c; GFLD/GFLC 19291)

Dec 89. (12"ep/cd-ep) (TUP EP8/CD8) **BLEW / LOVE BUZZ. / BEEN A SON / STAIN**   ☐   -

——— **DAN PETERS** – drums (of MUDHONEY) repl. CHANNING (Apr90)

Jan 91. (7",7"green) (TUP 25) **SLIVER. / DIVE**   ☐   ☐ Sep 90
(12"+=) (TUP EP25) – About a girl (live). (US-iss.7"blue; SP 72)
(cd-s++=) (TUP CD25) – Spank thru (live).

Feb 91. (7",7"green) <SP 97> **MOLLY'S LIPS. / ('Candy' by FLUID)**   -   ☐
                  not iss.   Communion

Mar 91. (7"colrd) <Communion 25> **HERE SHE COMES NOW. / ('Venus In Furs' by MELVINS)**   -   ☐

——— (Apr'91 trio) **DAVE GROHL** (b.14 Jan'69, Warren, Ohio) – drums, vocals (ex-SCREAM) repl. PETERS and EVERMAN, who joined MIND FUNK

	Geffen	Geffen
Sep 91. (lp/c/cd) <(DGC/+C/D 24425)> **NEVERMIND**	7	1

– Smells like teen spirit / In bloom / Come as you are / Breed / Lithium / Polly / Territorial pissings / Drain you / Lounge act / Stay away / On a plain / Something in the way. (cd+=) – Endless nameless.

Oct 91. (c-s/cd-s) <19050> **SMELLS LIKE TEEN SPIRIT / EVEN IN HIS YOUTH**   -   6

Nov 91. (7"/c-s) (DGC/+C 5) **SMELLS LIKE TEEN SPIRIT. / DRAIN YOU**   7   -
(12"pic-d+=) (DGCTP 5) – Aneurysm.
(cd-s++=) (DGCCD 5) – Even in his youth.
(12") (DGCT 5) – ('A'side) / Even in his youth / Aneurysm.

Mar 92. (c-s/cd-s) <19120> **COME AS YOU ARE. / DRAIN YOU (live)**   -   32

Mar 92. (7"/c-s) (DGC/+C 7) **COME AS YOU ARE. / ENDLESS NAMELESS**   9   -
(12"+=/12"pic-d+=) (DGCT/+P 7) – School (live).
(cd-s++=) (DGCTD 7) – Drain you (live).

Jul 92. (7"/c-s) (DGCS/+C 9) **LITHIUM. / CURMUDGEON**   11   -
(12"pic-d+=) (DGCTP 9) – Been a son (live).
(cd-s++=) (DGCSD 9) – D7 (Peel session).

Jul 92. (c-s,cd-s) <19134> **LITHIUM / BEEN A SON (live)**   -   64

Nov 92. (7"/c-s) (GFS/+C 34) **IN BLOOM. / POLLY**   28   -
(12"pic-d+=/cd-s+=) (GFST P/D 34) – Sliver (live).

Dec 92. (cd/c/lp) <(GED/GEC/GEF 24504)> **INCESTICIDE** (rare material)   14   39
– Dive / Sliver / Stain / Been a son / Turnaround / Molly's lips / Son of a gun / (New wave) Polly / Beeswax / Downer / Mexican seafood / Hairspray queen / Aero zeppelin / Big long now / Aneurysm.

——— In Feb'93, NIRVANA's 'OH, THE GUILT' appeared on double'A'side with JESUS LIZARD's 'Puss'. Issued on 'Touch & Go' 7"blue/cd-s; (TG 83/+CD). It had UK No.12, and crashed out of the Top 60 the following week!.

——— GOODBYE MR MACKENZIE's BIG JOHN played guitar for them in mid'93.

——— In Aug'93, KURT COBAIN and WILLIAM S.BURROUGHS narrated 'The Priest, They Call Him By' on 10"lp/cd 'Tim Kerr'; (92 10/CD 044)

Aug 93. (7"/c-s) (GFS/+C 54) **HEART-SHAPED BOX. / MARIGOLD**   5   -
(12"+=/cd-s+=) (GFST/+D 54) – Milk it.

Sep 93. (cd/c/lp)<clear-lp> <(GED/GEC/GEF 24536)> <DGC 24607> **IN UTERO**   1   1
– Serve the servants / Scentless apprentice / Heart-shaped box / Rape me / Frances Farmer will have her revenge on Seattle / Dumb / Very ape / Milk it / Penny royal tea / Radio friendly unit shifter / Tourette's / All apologies. (cd+=) – Gallons of rubbing alcohol flow through the strip.

Dec 93. (7"/c-s) (GFS/+C 66) **ALL APOLOGIES. / RAPE ME**   32   -
(12"+=/cd-s+=) (GFST/+D 66) – MV.

——— On the 4th March '94, KURT overdosed while on holiday in Italy and went into a coma. A month later, on the 8th April he committed suicide, by shooting himself through the mouth. He was only 27, and this was certainly the biggest rock star death since JOHN LENNON. For more details see HOLE and the COURTNEY LOVE story.

below album featured **LORI GOLDSTON** – cello + **MEAT PUPPETS'** Curt & Cris **Kirkwood** on 3rd, 4th & 5th last songs.

Nov 94. (cd/c/white-lp) <(GED/GEC/GEF 24727)> **UNPLUGGED IN NEW YORK** (live acoustic)   1   1
– About a girl / Come as you are / Jesus doesn't want me for a sunbeam / Dumb / The man who sold the world / Pennyroyal tea / Polly / On a plain / Something in the way / Plateau / Oh me / Lake of fire / All apologies / Where did you sleep last night.

——— GROHL (now vox, guitar) formed The FOO FIGHTERS with ex-GERMS guitarist PAT SMEAR. Meanwhile NOVOSELIC formed the trio SWEET 75.

– compilations, etc. –

on 'Geffen' unless mentioned otherwise
Jul 95. (d-cd) <(GES 00001)> **BLEACH / INCESTICIDE**   ☐   ☐
Nov 95. (6xcd-s-box) <(GED 24901)> **6 CD SINGLE BOXED SET**   ☐   ☐
Oct 96. (cd/c/lp) <(GED/GEC/GEF 25105)> **FROM THE MUDDY BANKS OF THE WISHKAH** (live)   4   1
– Intro / School / Drain you / Aneurysm / Smells like teen spirit / Been a son / Lithium / Sliver / Spank thru / Scentless apprentice / Heart-shaped box / Milk it / Negative creep / Polly / Breed / Tourette's / Blew.

SWEET 75

KRIST NOVOSELIC – guitar (ex-NIRVANA) / **YVA LAS VEGAS** – vocals, bass / **ADAM WADE** – drums

	Geffen	Geffen
Aug 97. (cd/c) <(GED/GEC 25140)> **SWEET 75**	☐	☐

– Fetch / Lay me down / Bite my hand / Red dress / La vida / Six years / Take another stab / Poor Kitty / Ode to Dolly / Dogs / Cantos de Pilon / Nothing / Japan trees / Oral health.

NO DOUBT

Formed: Orange County, California, USA . . . 1987 by JOHN SPENCE, TOM DUMONT, TONY KANAL and ADRIAN YOUNG (SPENCE rocking the band by committing suicide the following year). Having gone to ground for a while, they returned in the early 90's with new blonde-bombshell frontwoman, GWEN STEFANI. Her brother, ERIC STEFANI, was also a member at this stage, although he eventually departed, having landed a job working on 'The Simpsons' TV cartoon series. After two albums for 'Trauma', an eponymous debut and 'BEACON STREET COLLECTION' they were licensed to 'Interscope' in 1995. The following year, NO DOUBT finally cracked the American market with 'TRAGIC KINGDOM', a slow starter which eventually topped the charts. Produced by MATTHEW WILDER, the record was an 80's-esque amalgam of soft-metallic ska-pop/rock, fusing elements of The POLICE and MADNESS hand in hand with tasty MADONNA lookalike, GWEN STEFANI's cutesie-pie vocal pouting. The album boasted the MTV friendly hit singles, 'JUST A GIRL' and the massive selling ballad, 'DON'T SPEAK', which boosted long term UK sales of the album in 1997. Heavy-metal mag Kerrang, also inconceivably took gorgeous GWEN to their leather-clad hearts (lending new weight to accusations of cock-rock inclinations). • **Songwriters:** STEFANI w/ TOM or TONY or ERIC (perm any three). • **Trivia:** GWEN was known to "hang out" with Scottish born GARBAGE singer SHIRLEY MANSON.

Album rating: NO DOUBT (*5) / THE BEACON STREET COLLECTION (*6) / TRAGIC KINGDOM (*7)

GWEN STEFANI – vocals / **TOM DUMONT** – guitar / **TONY KANAL** – bass / **ADRIAN YOUNG** – drums / **ERIC STEFANI** – piano, keyboards

			Interscope	Interscope
1992.	(cd) *<IND 92109>* **NO DOUBT**		-	☐

– BND / Let's get back / Ache / Get on the ball / Move on / Sad for me / Doormat / Big city train / Trapped in a box / Sometimes / Sinking / A little something refreshing / Paulina / Brand new day. *(UK-iss.Jul96; same)*

| Feb 95. | (cd) *<BS 03>* **THE BEACON STREET COLLECTION** (out-takes) | | - | ☐ |

– Open the gate / Total hate 95 / Stricken / Greener pastures / By the way / Snakes / That's just me / Squeal / Doghouse / Blue in the face. *(UK-is.Apr97; same)*
(above album on 'Beacon Street')

—— now without ERIC (see above)

| Jun 96. | (cd/c) *(IND/INC 90003) <92580>* **TRAGIC KINGDOM** | | ☐ | 1 Feb96 |

– Spiderwebs / Excuse me Mr. / Just a girl / Happy now? / Different people / Hey you / The climb / Sixteen / Sunday morning / Don't speak / You can do it / World go 'round / End it on this / Tragic kingdom. *(re-dist.Jan97 hit UK No.3)*

| Jun 96. | (c-s) *(INC 80034) <98116>* **JUST A GIRL / DIFFERENT PEOPLE** | | ☐ | 23 Dec95 |

(cd-s+=) *(IND 80034)* – Open the gate.
(re-iss. Oct96, hit UK 38)

| Feb 97. | (7"pic-d/c-s/cd-s) *(INSP/INC/IND 95515)* **DON'T SPEAK / DON'T SPEAK (alternate) / HEY YOU (acoustic) / GREENER PASTURES** | | 1 | - |

| Jun 97. | (c-s) *(INC 95539)* **JUST A GIRL / HEY YOU (live) / OB-LA-DI OB-LA-DA (live)** | | 3 | - |

(cd-s+=) *(INDX 95539)* – Different people.
(cd-s+=) *(IND 95539)* – ('A'side) / Open the gate / ('A'live) / End it on this (live).

| Sep 97. | (c-s) *(INC 95551)* **SPIDERWEBS / DJ'S (live)** | | 16 | - |

(cd-s+=) *(IND 95551)* – Let's get back / Excuse me sir (cd-rom version).
(cd-s+=) *(INDX 95551)* – ('A'side) / The climb (live) / Doghouse / Spiderwebs (cd-rom version).

| Dec 97. | (c-s) *(INC 95566)* **SUNDAY MORNING / SUNDAY MORNING (live)** | | 50 | - |

(cd-s+=) *(IND 95566)* – Oi to the world / By the way (live).
(cd-s+=) *(INDX 95566)* – (virtually the same tracks).

			Higher Ground	Higher Ground
May 99.	(7") *(HIGHS 22S)* **NEW. / NEW (New and approved remix)**		30	☐

(c-s) *(HIGHS 22)* – ('A'side) / (~'A'-New Doubt club mix).
(cd-s+=) *(HIGHS 22T)* – (all three above).

– compilations, etc. –

| Jul 99. | (cd-book) *Hallmark; (8081)* **STAR PROFILE** | | ☐ | - |

NORTHERN UPROAR (dig out; Great Alt & Indie . . .)

NORTHSIDE (dig out; Great Alt & Indie . . .)

NOTORIOUS B.I.G.

Born: CHRISTOPHER WALLACE, 21 May'72, Brooklyn, New York, USA. Under the moniker BIGGY SMALLS, WALLACE's talent as an NYC rapper caught the attention of east coast hip hop guru/owner of 'Bad Boy' records, Sean 'Puffy' Combs, who in turn brought the rising star to greater prominence through guest spots on records by the likes of MARY J. BLIGE. SMALLS' own recording debut (as NOTORIOUS B.I.G.), the US Top 30 single, 'JUICY', found him marking out his own territory at the slicker R&B/swing end of the gangsta rap spectrum. Arrested many times for robbery, assault and weapon offences, he at least knew what he was singing about, tackling the usual subjects of 'bitches', guns and money on the accompanying album, 'READY TO DIE' (1994). A string of Top 10 hits followed, inlcuding a collaboration with METHOD MAN and even a joint effort with west coast star TUPAC

SHAKUR, soon to become a sworn enemy. What had started out as a simmering east/west rivalry between 'Bad boy' and L.A. label, 'Death Row', turned into a bitter feud with 2PAC and SMALLS at its epicentre. Amid defiant threats exchanged both in the press and on vinyl, things spiralled out of control as 2PAC was gunned down by unknown assailants in Las Vegas on the 13th of September '96. The B.I.G. man's follow-up album, 'LIFE AFTER DEATH', dealt with the violence head on; the sense of fatalism running through many of the tracks was only compounded by the needless murder of BIGGIE himself, also gunned down (drive-by shooting in L.A.) on the 9th March 1997, only days before the album's release. Though the perpetrator of the crime remains unknown (a Crips gang member was said to be prime suspect), the incident only served to fan the flames of the dispute even higher. Every cynic knows that death sells; the massive transatlantic publicity surrounding this particular death ensured that the posthumously released record sold multi-millions. Two singles, 'HYPNOTIZE' and 'MO MONEY MO PROBLEMS', both topped the US charts, as did the tribute single, 'I'LL BE MISSING YOU', a joint effort of Puffy and SMALLS' wife, Faith Evans. In little moe than six months, an already ailing rap scene had lost two of its most talented figureheads, a worrying sign of the genre's increasing inability to distinguish the boundary between art and reality.

Album rating: READY TO DIE (*8) / LIFE AFTER DEATH (*7) / BORN AGAIN (*6)

NOTORIOUS B.I.G. – vocals

			Arista	Arista
Oct 94.	(c-s) *(74321 24010-4) <7-9004>* **JUICY / UNBELIEVABLE**		72	27

(12"+=/cd-s+=) *(74321 24010-1/-2)* – (2-'A'mixes).

| Oct 94. | (cd/c) *<(78612 73000-2/-4)>* **READY TO DIE** | | ☐ | 15 |

– Intro / Things done changed / Gimme the loot / Machine gun funk / Warning / Ready to die / One more chance / F*** me (interlude) / The what / Juicy / Everyday struggle / Me and my bitch / Big poppa / Respect / Friend of mine / Unbelievable / Suicidal thoughts. *(cd re-iss. May97; same)*

| Mar 95. | (12"/cd-s) *(74321 26341-1/-2) <7-9015>* **BIG POPPA. / WHO SHOT YA? / WARNING / BIG POPPA (mix)** | | 63 | 6 |

—— In Apr'95, the man featured on the TOTAL single, 'Can't You See'.

| Jun 95. | (12",cd-s; The NOTORIOUS B.I.G. and METHOD MAN) *<7-9031>* **ONE MORE CHANCE – STAY WITH ME / THE WHAT** | | - | 2 |

—— In Jan'97, The NOTORIOUS B.I.G. collaborated with 2PAC, RADIO, DRAMACYDAL & STRETCH on Top 100 US single, 'RUNNIN'.

| Mar 97. | (d-cd/c/q-lp) *<(78612 73011-2/-4/-1)>* **LIFE AFTER DEATH** | | 23 | 1 |

– Life after death / Somebody's gotta die / Hypnotize / Mad rapper / Kick in the door / Lovin' you tonight / Last day / Dice / I love the dough / What's beef / B.I.G. / I'm coming out (more money) / Niggaz bleed / Story to tell / Notorious thugs / Interlude / Missing you / Another man / Cali (interlude) / Goin' back to Cali / 10 crack commandments / Playa later / Interlude / Nasty boy / Interlude / Sky's the limit / The world is filled / Interlude / My downfall / Long kiss goodnight / You're nobody. *(best bits re-iss. Nov97 cd/c; 78612 73019-22/-46) (re-iss. Feb98; same)*

—— B.I.G. was shot dead on the 9th March, 1997.

| Apr 97. | (c-s) *(74321 46641-4)* **HYPNOTIZE / ('A'mix)** | | 10 | 1 |

(12"+=/cd-s+=) *(74321 46641-1/-2)* – ('A'mixes).

| Jul 97. | (c-s) *(74321 49249-4) <79100>* **MO MONEY MO PROBLEMS / ('A'mix)** | | 6 | 1 |

(12"+=/cd-s+=) *(74321 49249-1/-2)* – ('A'mixes).
(above credited in the States with PUFF DADDY & MASE)

| Feb 98. | (c-s; NOTORIOUS B.I.G. featuring 112) *(74321 56199-4) <79131>* **SKY'S THE LIMIT / GOIN' BACK TO CALI** | | 35 | 37 Nov97 |

(12"+=/cd-s+=) *(74321 56199-1/-2)* – Kick in the door.

—— In Mar'98, the B.I.G. man featured with BUSTA RHYMES on PUFF DADDY & THE FAMILY's Top 20 (US) hit, 'Victory'.

| Nov 99. | (-; as The NOTORIOUS B.I.G. featuring PUFF DADDY & LIL' KIM) *<album cut>* **NOTORIOUS B.I.G.** | | - | 82 |

| Dec 99. | (cd/c/d-lp) *(74321 71718-2/-4/-1) <73023>* **BORN AGAIN** | | 70 | 1 |

– Born again (w/ LIL' KIM & PUFF DADDY) / Dead wrong (w/ EMINEM) / Hope you niggas sleep (w/ HOT BOYS & BIG TIMER) / Dangerous MC's (w/ MARK CURRY, SNOOP DOGG & BUSTA RHYMES) / Biggie (w/ JUNIOR MAFIA) / Niggas / Big booty hoes (w/ TOO SHORT) / Would you lie for me (w/ TOO SHORT) / Come on (w/ SADAT) / Rap phenomenom (w/ REDMAN & METHOD MAN) / Let me get down (w/ G-DEP, CRAIG MACK & MISSY ELLIOT) / Tonight (w/ MOBB DEPP & JOE HOOKER) / If I should die before I wake (w/ BLACK ROB, ICE CUBE & BEANIE SIGAL) / Who shot ya / Can I get witcha (w/ LIL' CREASE) / I really want to show you (w/ K-CI, JOJO, NAS & MS WALLACE).

NOTTING HILLBILLIES (see under ⇒ DIRE STRAITS)

Heather NOVA (dig out; Great Alt & Indie . . .)

NOVA MOB (see under ⇒ HUSKER DU)

Ted NUGENT

Born: 13 Dec'48, Detroit, Michigan, USA. After earlier moving to Chicago, he formed garage/psych-rock band, The AMBOY DUKES in 1966. They soon signed to 'Mainstream' US, releasing a debut single, 'BABY PLEASE DON'T GO' (a Big Joe Williams number, more famously covered by THEM), in 1967. Their eponymous 1968 debut album broke into the US Top 200, and by the summer, the classic psychedelic single, 'JOURNEY TO THE CENTER OF THE MIND', was in the US Top 20. Ironically enough, NUGENT was a vehement non-drug taker, sacking anyone in the band who dabbled with even the softest narcotics (TED preferred hunting animals instead, his love of blood sports was well-publicised). Although The AMBOY DUKES toured constantly in the States for the next couple of years, the band only managed minor chart placings. In 1971, they evolved into TED NUGENT & THE AMBOY DUKES, snapped up by FRANK ZAPPA's 'Discreet' label and subsequently unleashing two albums in the mid-70's before dissolving. In 1975, NUGENT secured a solo deal with 'Epic', shooting up the US Top 30 with an eponymous Tom Werman-produced debut in early '76. By this point, NUGENT had come a long way from his 60's roots, adopting a bare-chested stone-age axe-grinding image (a good few years before MANOWAR). His next album in 1976, 'FREE FOR ALL' (which featured MEAT LOAF) ventured further and was the first to earn him a Top 40 placing in the UK. Abrasive as ever, TED "The Deer Hunter" NUGENT took a break from boasting about his conquests (musical, animal or otherwise . . .) to record his third heavy-metal onslaught, 'CAT SCRATCH FEVER', another acclaimed album which featured such pussy-tickling gems as 'WANG DANG SWEET POONTANG' and the glorious title track. NUGE (who had recently demonstrated his affection for a fan by enscribing his name with a bowie knife on their arm!), reached his 70's climax with the ripping 1978 concert set, 'DOUBLE LIVE GONZO', and although he released two more sturdy studio albums that decade, 'WEEKEND WARRIORS' and 'STATE OF SHOCK', he would never quite attain such testosterone-fuelled heights again. After two middling early 80's albums (one of them being the live 'INTENSITIES IN 10 CITIES'), TED signed to 'Atlantic', delivering a rather poor, directionless affair thoughtfully titled, 'NUGENT' (1982). Taking a few years to recover, the loinclothed one returned in good old feminist-baiting style with 'PENETRATOR' (1984) and 'LITTLE MISS DANGEROUS' (1986), NUGENT rather unconvincingly claiming that the title track of the latter could cure the emerging AIDS virus. Even more unbelievable was the news that NUGE was forming a new AOR-orientated supergroup, The DAMN YANKEES alongside TOMMY SHAW (Styx), JACK BLADES (Night Ranger) and MICHAEL CARTELLONE (er, drums). This was all too horribly confirmed in 1990 with the release of their eponymous debut, the Top 20 album boasting a US Top 3 smash, 'HIGH ENOUGH'. This quartet released another set in 1992, 'DON'T TREAD', although the only thing The DAMN YANKEES were treading was water. Thankfully NUGE abandoned this project and returned to his familiar bloodthirsty neck of the woods with the 1995 solo album, 'SPIRIT OF THE WILD'. • Trivia: In 1973, while working on a new record deal, he featured alongside other stars MIKE PINERA (Iron Butterfly), WAYNE KRAMER (MC5) and FRANK MARINO (Mahogany Rush), on the 'battle of the guitarists' stage shows. • Note: There was another group of the same name in the UK called The AMBOY DUKES, who released several singles on 'Polydor', around the mid-60's to '68.

Album rating: JOURNEYS & MIGRATIONS (*7) / TED NUGENT (*7) / FREE FOR ALL (*6) / CAT SCRATCH FEVER (*6) / DOUBLE LIVE GONZO! (*7) / WEEKEND WARRIORS (*5) / STATE OF SHOCK (*5) / SCREAM DREAM (*5) / INTENSITIES IN 10 CITIES (*6) / GREAT GONZOS! THE BEST OF TED NUGENT compilation (*6) / NUGENT (*2) / PENETRATOR (*5) / LITTLE MISS DANGEROUS (*4) / IF YOU CAN'T LICK 'EM, LICK 'EM (*4) / SPIRIT OF THE WILD (*4)

AMBOY DUKES

TED NUGENT – guitar, vox / plus **JOHN DRAKE** – vocals / **STEVE FARMER** – rhythm guitar / **BILL WHITE** – bass / **RICK LOBER** – keyboards / **DAVID PALMER** – drums

			Fontana	Mainstream
1967.	(7") <676> **BABY PLEASE DON'T GO. / PSALMS OF AFTERMATH**		-	
1967.	(7") (TF 971) **LET'S GO GET STONED. / IT'S NOT TRUE**		-	
1968.	(lp; stereo/mono) (S+/TL 5468) <6104> **THE AMBOY DUKES**			Jan68

– Baby please don't go / I feel free / Young love / Psalms of aftermath / Colors / Let's go get stoned / Down on Philips escalator / The lovely lady / Night time / It's not true / Gimme love. (cd-iss. Dec92 on 'Repertoire'+=;) – J.B. special.

RUSTY DAY – vocals repl. DRAKE + FARMER / **ANDY SOLOMAN** – keyboards repl. LOBER / **GREG ARAMA** – bass repl. WHITE

In the UK, they were now called The AMERICAN AMBOY DUKES

			London	Mainstream
Jul 68.	(7") <684> **JOURNEY TO THE CENTER OF THE MIND. / MISSISSIPPI MURDERER**		-	16
Oct 68.	(7") <693> **SCOTTISH TEA. / YOU TALK SUNSHINE, I BREATHE FIRE**		-	
Feb 69.	(lp; stereo/mono) (SH-T/HA-T 8378) <6112> **JOURNEY TO THE CENTER OF THE MIND**			74 Aug68

– Mississippi murderer / Surrender to your kings / Flight of the Byrd / Scottish tea / Dr. Slingshot / Journey to the center of the mind / Ivory castles / Why is a carrot more orange than an orange? / Missionary Mary / Death is life / Saint Philips friend / I'll prove I'm right / (Conclusion). (cd-iss. Dec92 on 'Repertoire'+=; MDCD 0911) – You talk sunshine, I breathe fire.

1969.	(7") <700> **PRODIGAL MAN. / GOOD NATURED EMMA**		-	
1969.	(lp; stereo/mono) (SH-T/HA-T 8392) <6118> **MIGRATION**		-	

– Migration / Prodigal man / For his namesake / I'm not a juvenile delinquent / Good natured Emma / Inside the outside / Shades of green and grey / Curb your elephant / Loaded for bear. (cd-iss. Dec92 on 'Repertoire'+=;) – Sobbin' in my mug of bear.

1969.	(7") <704> **FOR HIS NAMESAKE. / LOADED FOR BEAR**		-	
1969.	(7") <711> **MIGRATION. / FLIGHT OF THE BIRDS**		-	
1969.	(lp) <6125> **THE BEST OF THE ORIGINAL AMBOY DUKES** (compilation)		-	-

			Polydor	Polydor
Mar 70.	(lp) <4012> **MARRIAGE ON THE ROCKS – ROCK BOTTOM**		-	

– Marriage:- (a) Part 1 – Man / (b) Part 2 – Woman / (c) Part 3 – Music / Breast-fed 'gator (bait) / Get yer guns / Non-conformist wilderbeast man / Today's lesson / Children of the woods / Brain games of the yesteryear / The inexhaustable quest for the cosmic garbage (part 1 & 2) / (excerpt from Bartok).

NUGENT brought in new members **BOB GRANGE** – bass / **KJ KNIGHT** – drums retaining also **ANDY SOLOMAN** (RUSTY DAY joined CACTUS)

TED NUGENT & THE AMBOY DUKES

			Discreet	Discreet
Mar 71.	(lp) <4035> **SURVIVAL OF THE FITTEST** (live)		-	

– Survival of the fittest / Rattle my snake / Mr. Jones' hanging party / Papa's will / Slidin' on / Prodigal man. (UK-iss.1974 on 'Polydor'; 2675 141)

——— Disbanded in the early 70's, but re-formed with others **BOB GRANGE** – bass / **ANDY JEZOWSKI** – vocals / **GABRIEL MAGNO** – keyboards / **VIC MASTRIANNI** – drums

			Discreet	Discreet
Jun 74.	(lp) (K 59203) <2181> **CALL OF THE WILD**			

– Call of the wild / Sweet revenge / Pony express / Ain't it the truth / Renegade / Rot gut / Below the belt / Cannon balls. (re-iss. Oct89 on 'Edsel' lp/cd; ED/+CD 278)

Jun 74.	(7") (K 19200) **SWEET REVENGE. / AIN'T IT THE TRUTH**			

——— **Rev.ATROCIOUS THEODOLIUS** – guitar, vocals repl. MAGNO

1975.	(lp) (K 59203) <2203> **TOOTH FANG & CLAW**			

– Lady luck / Living in the woods / Hibernation / Free flight / Maybelline / The great wjite buffalo / Sasha / No holds barred. (re-iss. Oct89 on 'Edsel'; lp/cd; ED/+CD 295)

——— TED finally gave up AMBOY DUKES in 1975.

– compilations, etc. –

Apr 73.	(d-lp) Mainstream; <MRL 801> **JOURNEYS & MIGRATIONS**		-	
	<re-iss. Apr75 on 'Polydor'; 2801> (UK-iss.Feb83 on 'Audio Fidelity'; MRD 5008)			
Jun 77.	(lp) Polydor; <2664 344> **MARRIAGE ON THE ROCKS – ROCK BOTTOM / SURVIVAL OF THE FITTEST (AMBOY DUKES)**			
1977.	(d-lp) Warners; (K 69202) **TWO ORIGINALS OF . . . (AMBOY DUKES)**			-
	– (CALL OF THE WILD & TOOTH, FANG & CLAW) albums			
1991.	(cd/c) Thunderbolt; (CDTB/THBC 097) **ON THE EDGE** (early AMBOY DUKES material)			-
May 91.	(cd/c) Thunderbolt; (CDTB/THBC 120) **OVER THE TOP** (early AMBOY DUKES material)			-

TED NUGENT

(solo) with **ROB GRANGE** – bass / **DEREK St.HOLMES** – vocals, guitar (ex-SCOTT) / **CLIFF DAVIS** – drums / plus guests

			Epic	Epic
Nov 75.	(7") <50172> **MOTORCITY MADNESS. / WHERE HAVE YOU BEEN ALL MY LIFE**		-	
Mar 76.	(lp/c) (EPC/40 33692) <81196> **TED NUGENT**		56	28 Nov75

– Stranglehold / Stormtroopin' / Hey baby / Just what the doctor ordered / Snakeskin cowboys / Motor city madhouse / Where have you been all my life / You make me feel right at home / Queen of the forest.

Jun 76.	(7") (EPC 3900) <50197> **HEY BABY. / STORMTROOPIN'**			72 Mar76
Oct 76.	(lp/c) (EPC/40 81397) <34121> **FREE-FOR-ALL**		33	24 Sep76

– Free for all / Dog eat dog / Writing on the wall / Turn it up / Together / Street rats / Hammer down / Light my way / Love you so much I told a lie. (re-iss. Jan84; EPC 34121)

Nov 76.	(7") <50301> **DOG EAT DOG. / LIGHT MY WAY**		-	91
Nov 76.	(7") (EPC 4796) **DOG EAT DOG. / LOVE YOU SO MUCH I TOLD A LIE**		-	
Jan 77.	(7") <50363> **FREE-FOR-ALL. / STREET RAGS**		-	
Jun 77.	(lp/c) (EPC/40 82010) <34700> **CAT SCRATCH FEVER**		28	17

– Cat scratch fever / Wang dang sweet poontang / Death by misadventure / Live it up / Home bound / Workin' hard, playin' hard / Sweet Sally / A thousand knives / Fist fightin' son of a gun / Out of control. (cd-iss. Jun89; CD 32252) (cd re-iss. Aug93 on 'Columbia'; 468024-2)

Jul 77.	(7") <50425> **CAT SCRATCH FEVER. / WANG DANG SWEET POONTANG**		-	
Jul 77.	(7") (EPC 5482) **CAT SCRATCH FEVER. / A THOUSAND NIGHTS**			-
Feb 78.	(7") (EPC 5945) <50493> **HOME BOUND. / DEATH BY MISADVENTURE**			70
Feb 78.	(d-lp) (EPC 88282) <35069> **DOUBLE LIVE GONZO!** (live)		47	13

– Just what the doctor ordered / Yank me, crank me / Gonzo / Baby please don't go / Great white buffalo / Hibernation / Stormtroopin' / Stranglehold / Wang dang sweet poontang / Cat scratch fever / Motor city madhouse.

Mar 78.	(7") <50533> **YANK ME, CRANK ME (live). / CAT SCRATCH FEVER (live)**		-	58

——— **CHARLIE HUHN** – vocals, vocals repl. St. HOLMES (to St. PARADISE, etc) **DAVID HULL** – bass repl. BOB GRANGE (also to St. PARADISE, who released one eponymous album for 'Warners' in '79)

Nov 78.	(lp/c) (EPC/40 83036) <35551> **WEEKEND WARRIORS**			24

– Need you bad / One woman / I got the feelin' / Tight spots / Venom soup / Smokescreen / Weekend warriors / Cruisin' / Good friends and a bottle of wine / Name your poison.

Dec 78.	(7") <50648> **NEED YOU BAD. / I GOT THE FEELIN'**		-	84

——— **WALTER MONAHAN** – bass repl. HULL

Jun 79.	(lp/c)<US-pic-lp> (EPC/40 86092) <36000> **STATE OF SHOCK**			18 May79

– Paralyzed / Take it or leave it / Alone / It doesn't matter / State of shock / I want to tell you / It doesn't matter / Satisfied / Bite down hard / Snake charmer / Saddle sore. (cd-iss. Aug93 on 'Columbia'; 471456-2)

Jun 79.	(7") <50713> **I WANT TO TELL YOU. / BITE DOWN HARD**		-	
Jul 79.	(7"m) (EPC 7723) **I WANT TO TELL YOU. / PARALYSED / CAT SCRATCH FEVER**		-	
May 80.	(7"/12") (EPC/12 8640) **FLESH AND BLOOD. / MOTOR CITY MADHOUSE**		-	-
Jun 80.	(lp/c) (EPC/40 86111) <36404> **SCREAM DREAM**		37	13 May80

– Wango tango / Scream dream / Hard as nails / I gotta move / Violent love / Flesh and blood / Spit it out / Come and get it / Terminus El Dorada / Don't cry, I'll be back before you know it baby. (cd-iss. Aug93 on 'Columbia'; 471458-2)

Jul 80.	(7") <50907> **WANGO TANGO. / SCREAM DREAM**		-	86
Feb 81.	(7") <01046> **LAND OF A THOUSAND DANCES. / THE TNT OVERTURE**		-	-
Apr 81.	(lp/c) (EPC/40 84917) <37084> **(INTENSITIES) IN 10 CITIES**		75	51

– Put up or shut up / Spontaneous combustion / My love is like a tire iron / Jailbait / I am a predator / Heads will roll / The flying lip lock / Land of a thousand dances / The TNT overture / I take no prisoners.

Dec 81. (lp/c) (EPC/40 85408) <37667> **GREAT GONZOS! THE BEST OF TED NUGENT** (compilation)
– Cat scratch fever / Just what the doctor ordered / Free-for-all / Dog eat dog / Motor city madness / Paralysed / Stranglehold / Baby please don't go / Wango tango / Wang dang sweet poontang. (cd-iss. Feb97 on 'Columbia'; 471216-2)

––– **DEREK ST. HOLMES** – vocals returned from WHITFORD / ST. HOLMES to repl. HUHN / **DAVE KISWINEY** – bass repl. MONAGHAN / **CARMINE APPICE** – drums (ex-VANILLA FUDGE, ex-CACTUS, etc.) repl. DAVIS

	Atlantic	Atlantic

Aug 82. (lp/c) (K/K4 50898) <19365> **NUGENT**　　　□　　　[51] Jul82
– No, no, no / Bound and gagged / Habitual offender / Fightin' words / Good and ready / Ebony / Don't push me / Can't stop me now / We're gonna rock tonight / Tailgunner.

Sep 82. (7") <89998> **BOUND AND GAGGED. / HABITUAL OFFENDER**　　　–　　　□

Nov 82. (7") <89978> **NO, NO, NO. / HABITUAL OFFENDER**　　　–　　　□

––– **NUGENT** recruited entire new band again! **BRIAN HOWE** – vocals / **ALAN ST. JOHN** – keyboards / **DOUG LABAHN** – bass / **BOBBY CHOUINARD** – drums

Feb 84. (lp/c) (780 125-1/-4) <80125> **PENETRATOR**　　　□　　　[56]
– Tied up in love / (Where do you) Draw the line / Knockin' at your door / Don't you want my love / Go down fighting / Thunder thighs / No man's land / Blame it on the night / Lean mean R&R machine / Take me home.

Feb 84. (7") (A 9705) <89705> **TIED UP IN LOVE. / LEAN MEAN R&R MACHINE**　　　□　　　□

Apr 84. (7") <89681> **(WHERE DO YOU) DRAW THE LINE. / LEAN MEAN R&R MACHINE**　　　–　　　□

––– Took time out to appear in 'Miami Vice' US TV programme. He also played on charity single 'Stars' by aggregation 'HEAR'N AID' circa Spring 1986.

––– **DAVE AMATO** – guitar, vocals repl. HOWE who joined BAD COMPANY / **RICKY PHILIPS** – bass (ex-BABYS) repl. LABAHN

Nov 86. (lp/c/cd) (K 252388-1/-4/-2) <81632> **LITTLE MISS DANGEROUS**　　　□　　　[76] Mar86
– High heels in motion / Strangers / Little Miss Dangerous / Savage dancer / Crazy ladies / When your body talks / My little red book / Take me away / Angry young man / Painkiller.

Apr 86. (7") <89442> **HIGH HEELS IN MOTION. / ANGRY YOUNG MAN**　　　–　　　□

Jul 86. (7") <89436> **LITTLE MISS DANGEROUS. / ANGRY YOUNG MAN**　　　–　　　□

––– **NUGENT** re-recruited **DEREK ST.HOLMES** – vocals, guitar / **DAVE KISWINEY** – bass / plus new drummer / **PAT MARCHINO**

Feb 88. (lp/c/cd) (K 255385-1/-4/-2) <81812> **IF YOU CAN'T LICK 'EM . . . LICK 'EM**　　　□　　　□
– Can't live with 'em / She drives me crazy / If you can't lick 'em . . . lick 'em / Skintight / Funlover / Spread your wings / The harder they come (the harder I get) / Separate the men from the boys, please / Bite the hand / That's the story of love.

DAMN YANKEES

TED NUGENT – guitar, vocals / **TOMMY SHAW** (b.11 Sep'53, Montgomery, Alabama) – vocals (ex-STYX) / **JACK BLADES** (b.24 Apr'54, Palm Beach, Calif.) – bass (ex-NIGHT RANGER) / **MICHAEL CARTELLONE** (b. 7 Jun'62, Cleveland, Ohio) – drums, non-s/writer

	Warners	Warners

Apr 90. (cd/c/lp) <(7599 26159-2/-4/-1)> **DAMN YANKEES**　　[26]　　[13] Mar90
– Coming of age / Bad reputation / Runaway / High enough / Damn Yankees / Come again / Mystified / Rock city / Tell me how you want it / Piledriver.

Apr 90. (c-s,cd-s) <19838> **COMING OF AGE. / TELL ME HOW YOU WANT IT**　　　–　　　[60]

Jan 91. (7"/c-s) (W 0006/+C) <19595> **HIGH ENOUGH. / PILEDRIVER**　　　□　　　[3] Oct90
(12"+=/cd-s+=) (W 0006 T/CD) – Bonestripper.

Apr 91. (c-s,cd-s) <19408> **COME AGAIN. / ('A'radio version)**　　　–　　　[50]

Aug 92. (cd/c) <(9362 45025-2/-4)> **DON'T TREAD**　　　□　　　[22]
– Don't tread on me / Fifteen minutes of fame / Where you goin' now / Dirty dog / Mister please / Silence is broken / Firefly / Someone to believe / This side of Hell / Double coyote / Uprising. (re-iss. cd Feb95; same)

Jan 93. (7"/c-s) <18728> **WHERE YOU GOIN' NOW. / THIS SIDE OF HELL**　　　□　　　[20] Sep92
(12"+=/cd-s+=) – ('A'version).

Apr 93. (c-s) <18612> **SILENCE IS BROKEN / DOUBLE COYOTE**　　　–　　　[62]
(12"+=/cd-s+=) – High enough (live) / ('A'live version).

––– **STEVE SMITH** – drums (ex-JOURNEY) repl. NUGENT, although the band became SHAW BLADES, releasing one 'Warners' album, 'HALLICINATION' (9362 45835-2/-4).

Ted NUGENT

––– returned w/ **DAVE AMATO** – guitar / **CHUCK WRIGHT** – bass / **PAT TORPEY** – drums / + co-writers ST. HOLMES + LUTZ

	Atlantic	Atlantic

Dec 95. (cd/c) <(7567 82611)> **SPIRIT OF THE WILD**　　　□　　　[86] May95
– Thighraceous / Wrong side back / I shoot back / Toot, fang & claw / Lovejacker / Fred bear / Primitive man / Hot or cold / Kiss my ass / Heart & soul / Spirit of the wild / Just do it like this.

– compilations, others, etc. –

Feb 83. (d-c) Epic; **TED NUGENT / FREE FOR ALL**　　　□　　　–

Sep 86. (d-lp/d-c) Raw Power; (RAW LP/TC 026) **ANTHOLOGY**　　　□　　　–
(re-iss. Feb91 on 'Castle' cd/c; CCS CD/MC 282)

Jun 93. (cd) Sony; **THE VERY BEST OF TED NUGENT**　　　□　　　□

May 94. (d-cd/d-c) Epic-Legacy; (CD/40 47039) **OUT OF CONTROL**　　　□　　　□

May 97. (cd) Columbia; (471216-2) **LIVE AT HAMMERSMITH ODEON**　　　□　　　□

Gary NUMAN

Born: GARY WEBB, 8 Mar'58, Hammersmith, London, England. Inspired by 70's glam icons such as BOLAN and BOWIE as well as synthmeisters like KRAFTWERK, NUMAN formed punk outfit, MEAN STREET in 1977, subsequently appearing on the Various Artists compilation, 'Live At The Vortex'. To end the year, he set up TUBEWAY ARMY, basically his solo project although he was accompanied on live work by PAUL GARDINER and his uncle, GERALD LIDYARD. The debut vinyl outing, 'THAT'S TOO BAD', was issued by indie punk label, 'Beggars Banquet' in early '78. An eponymous debut album passed virtually unnoticed, although things changed dramatically in June '79, when they/he had a first No.1 with the monotonic synth-noir of 'ARE FRIENDS ELECTRIC', spurred on by a compelling appearance on UK's 'Top Of The Pops'. Its parent album, 'REPLICAS', also shot to the top the same month. A busy year for NUMAN, in addition to collaborating with ROBERT PALMER, of all people (he was initially part of offshoot outfit, DRAMATIS), he found time to record a second No.1 album, 'THE PLEASURE PRINCIPLE'. This collection was previewed with the hypnotic, sweeping electronica of the 'CARS' single, by far his most well known track and one that enjoyed a rejuvenation in 1996 after it was used in a British TV advert. NUMAN scored yet another No.1 album with 'TELEKON' (1980) the following year, his futuristic synth-based pop/rock gracing the upper reaches of the singles chart in the form of 'WE ARE GLASS' and 'I DIE: YOU DIE'. By this point, however, NUMAN was well on his way to becoming perhaps one of most visible targets of critical derision in the whole of the music industry, his neo-futurist posturing, dalek vocals, pretentious lyrics and worst of all, his vocal support of Margaret Thatcher raising the not inconsiderable ire of the music press. Nevertheless, NUMAN had a fiercely loyal grassroots following of clone-like fans (second only to NUMAN himself as figures of fun among rock circles) who ensured most of his subsequent output made the Top 50 at least. Despite the presence of such luminaries as MICK KARN (JAPAN), ROGER TAYLOR (QUEEN) and erm, NASH THE SLASH (solo artist from Canada, apparently), 'DANCE' (1981) was a decidedly ungroovy set of steely electronica and his last to achieve mainstream success. NUMAN released two further, increasingly pompous albums, 'I, ASSASSIN' (1982) and 'WARRIORS' (1983) before forming his own label, 'Numa', in 1984 to issue his own product along with material by his brother JOHN's outfit, HOHOKAM. 80's albums like 'THE FURY' (1985), 'STRANGE CHARM' (1986), 'METAL RHYTHM' (1988) and 'AUTOMATIC' (1989) continued to appeal mainly to hardcore fans although 'OUTLAND' (1991) managed to nudge into the Top 40. However, since the awful 'MACHINE AND SOUL' (1992), NUMAN has fallen further into cult status, his releases failing to even break the Top 100. • **Songwriters:** Wrote own material, with inspiration from psi-fi writers (i.e. WILLIAM S. BURROUGHS). Covered 1999 + U GOT THE LOOK (Prince). • **Trivia:** In the early 80's, he took up flying planes and bought his own aircrafts (mainly warplanes).

Album rating: Tubeway Army: TUBEWAY ARMY (*4) / REPLICAS (*7) / Gary Numan: THE PLEASURE PRINCIPLE (*7) / TELEKON (*6) / LIVING ORNAMENTS 1979 (*4) / LIVING ORNAMENTS 1980 (*4) / DANCE (*4) / I, ASSASSIN (*5) / WARRIORS (*4) / BERSERKER (*4) / WHITE NOISE (*4) / THE FURY (*4) / STRANGE CHARM (*3) / EXHIBITION compilation (*7) / METAL RHYTHM (*4) / AUTOMATIC (*3; as Sharpe & Numan) / THE SKIN MECHANIC (*4) / OUTLAND (*4) / MACHINE AND SOUL (*4) / THE BEST OF . . . compilation (*7) / DREAM CORROSION (*4) / DARL LIGHT (*4) / DARK LIGHT (*4) / HUMAN (*4) / EXILE (*3)

TUBEWAY ARMY

GARY NUMAN – vocals, guitar, synthesizer, keyboards (ex-MEAN STREET) / **PAUL 'Scarlett' GARDINER** – bass / **GERALD 'Rael' LIDYARD** – drums

	Beggars Banquet	Atco

Feb 78. (7") (BEG 5) **THAT'S TOO BAD. / OH! DIDN'T I SAY**　　　□　　　–

––– **BARRY BENN** – drums repl. BOB SIMMONDS who had repl. LIDYARD / added **SEAN BURKE** – guitar

Jul 78. (7"m) (BEG 8) **BOMBERS. / O.D. RECEIVER. / BLUE EYES**　　　□　　　–

Aug 78. (lp,blue-lp) (BEGA 4) **TUBEWAY ARMY**　　　□　　　–
– Listen to the sirens / My shadow in vain / The life machine / Friends / Something's in the house / Every day I die / Steal and you / My love is a liquid / Are you real / The dream police / Jo the waiter / Zero bass. (re-iss. Aug79 lp/c; BEGA/BEGC 4); hit No.14) (re-iss. May83 on 'Fame' lp/c; FA/TC-FA 3060) (re-iss. Jul88 lp/c; BBL/+C 4)

––– **JESS LIDYARD** – drums returned to replace BARRY and SEAN

Mar 79. (7") (BEG 17) **DOWN IN THE PARK. / DO YOU NEED THE SERVICE?**　　　□　　　–
(12"+=) (BEG 17T) – I nearly married a human 2.

May 79. (7"/7"pic-d) <US-7"/c-s> (BEG 18/+P) **ARE 'FRIENDS' ELECTRIC?. / WE ARE SO FRAGILE?**　　　[1]　　　□

Jun 79. (lp/c) <credited as GARY NUMAN & TUBEWAY ARMY> (BEGA/BEGC 7) <117> **REPLICAS**　　　[1]
– Me I disconnect from you / Are 'friends' electric? / The machman / Praying to the aliens / Down in the park / You are in my vision / Replicas / It must have been years / When the machines rock / I nearly married a human. (re-iss. +cd.Sep88) (re-iss. cd/c Apr95 on 'Music Club')

GARY NUMAN

––– solo retaining **PAUL GARDINER** – bass / **CEDRIC SHARPLEY** – drums / **CHRIS PAYNE** – synth, viola / **BILLY CURRIE** – keyboards

Aug 79. (7") (BEG 23) **CARS. / ASYLUM**　　　[1]　　　–

Sep 79. (lp/c) (BEGA/BEGC 10) <38120> **THE PLEASURE PRINCIPLE**　　　[1]　　　[16] Jan80
– Airplane / Metal / Complex / Films / M.E. / Tracks / Observer / Conversation / Cars / Engineers. (re-iss. Sep88 lp/c; BBL/+C 10)

Nov 79. (7") *(BEG 29)* **COMPLEX. / BOMBERS (live)** [6]
(12"+=) *(BEG 29T)* – Me I disconnect from you (live).

Jan 80. (7") *<7211>* **CARS. / METAL** [-] [9]

——— **DENNIS HAINES** – keyboards repl. CURRIE who returned to ULTRAVOX and VISAGE; added **RUSSELL BELL** – guitar (on tour) .

May 80. (7") *(BEG 35)* **WE ARE GLASS. / TROIS GYMNPEDIES (1st MOVEMENT)** [5]

Aug 80. (7") *(BEG 46)* **I DIE: YOU DIE. / DOWN IN THE PARK (piano version)** [6]

Sep 80. (lp/c) *(BEGA/BEGC 19)* *<32103>* **TELEKON** [1] [64]
– This wreckage / The aircrash bureau / Telekon / Remind me to smile / Sleep by windows / I'm an agent / I dream of wires / Remember I was a vapour / Please push no more / The joy circuit. *(free-7"w/ lp)* – REMEMBER I WAS A VAPOUR. / ON BROADWAY *(re-iss. Jul88 lp/c; BBL/+C 19)*

Sep 80. (7") **I DIE: YOU DIE. / SLEEP BY WINDOWS** [-]

Dec 80. (7") **REMIND ME TO SMILE. /** [-]

Dec 80. (7") *(BEG 50)* **THIS WRECKAGE. / PHOTOGRAPH** [20]

Apr 81. (d-lp/c) *(BOX/C 1)* **LIVING ORNAMENTS 1979-1980 (live)** [2] [-]

Apr 81. (lp) *(BEGA 24)* **LIVING ORNAMENTS 1979 (live)** [47] [-]
– Airplane / Cars / We are so fragile? / Films / Something's in the house / My shadow in vain / Conversation / The dream police / Metal.

Apr 81. (lp) *(BEGA 25)* **LIVING ORNAMENTS 1980 (live)** [39] [-]
– This wreckage / I die: you die / M.E. / Everyday I die / Down in the park / Remind me to smile / The joy circuit / Tracks / Are 'friends' electric? / We are glass.

——— GARY now recruited famous stars to replace BELL, SHARPLEY, HAINES and PAYNE. They became DRAMATIS. Jul'81 he guested on PAUL GARDINER single 'STORMTROOPER IN DRAG' *(BEG 61/+T)*, which hit UK No.49. Next with stars **MICK KARN** – bass (of JAPAN) / **ROGER TAYLOR** – drums (of QUEEN) + **NASH THE SLASH** – violin (Canadian solo artist)

Aug 81. (7") *(BEG 62)* **SHE'S GOT CLAWS. / I SING RAIN** [6]
(12"+=) *(BEG 62T)* – Exhibition.

Sep 81. (lp/c) *(BEGA/BEGC 28)* *<38-143>* **DANCE** [3]
– Slowcar to China / Night talk / A subway called you / Cry the clock said / She's got claws / Crash / Boys like me / Stories / My brother's time / You are you are / Moral. *(re-iss. Jan89 lp/c; BBL/+C 28)*

Nov 81. (7"; by GARY NUMAN and DRAMATIS) *(BEG 68)* **LOVE NEEDS NO DISGUISE. / TAKE ME HOME** [33]
(12"+=) *(BEG 68T)* – Face to face.

——— GARY NUMAN now used session people.

Feb 82. (7") *(BEG 70)* **MUSIC FOR CHAMELEONS. / NOISE NOISE** [19]
(ext.12"+=) *(BEG 70T)* – Bridge? what bridge.

Jun 82. (7") *(BEG 77)* **WE TAKE MYSTERY (TO BED). / THE IMAGE IS** [9]
(ext.12"+=) *(BEG 77T)* – ('A'early version).

Aug 82. (7") *(BEG 81)* **WHITE BOYS AND HEROES. / WAR GAMES** [20]
(ext.12"+=) *(BEG 81T)* – Glitter and ash.

Sep 82. (lp/c) *(BEGA/BEGC 40)* *<900141>* **I, ASSASSIN** [8]
– White boys and heroes / War songs / A dream of Siam / Music for chameleons / This is my house / I, assassin / The 1930's rust / We take mystery (to bed). *(re-iss. Jan89 lp/c; BBL/+C 40)*

Aug 83. (7"/7"sha-pic-d) *(BEG 95/+P)* **WARRIORS. / MY CAR SLIDES (1)** [20]
(ext.12"+=) *(BEG 95T)* – My car slides (2).

Sep 83. (lp/c) *(BEGA/BEGC 47)* **WARRIORS** [12] [-]
– Warriors / I am render / The iceman comes / This prison moon / My centurion / Sister surprise / The tick tock man / Love is like clock law / The rhythm of the evening. *(re-iss. Jan89 lp/c; BBL/+C 47)*

Oct 83. (7") *(BEG 101)* **SISTER SUPRISE. / POETRY AND POWER** [32]
(ext.12"+=) *(BEG 101T)* – Letters.

Numa   Warners

Oct 84. (7"/7"sha-pic-d) *(NU/+P 4)* **BERSERKER. / EMPTY BED, EMPTY HEART** [32]
(12"+=) *(NUM 4)* – ('A'extended).

Nov 84. (lp/c) *(NUMA/+C 1001)* **BERSERKER** [45]
– Berserker / This is new love / The secret / My dying machine / Cold warning / Pump it up / The God film / A child with the ghost / The hunter. *(c+=)* – (6 extra tracks). *(cd-iss. Dec95; NUMACD 1001)*

Dec 84. (7") *(NU 6)* **MY DYING MACHINE. / HERE I AM** [66]
(ext.12"+=) *(NUM 6)* – She cries.

——— next 45 with BILL SHARPE of SHAKATAK; and on 'Polydor' album 'Famous People'.

Feb 85. (7"/7"pic-d; by SHARPE & NUMAN) *(POSP/+P 722)* **CHANGE YOUR MIND. / REMIX, REMAKE, REMODEL** [17]
(ext.12"pic-d+=) *(POSPX 722)* – Fools in a world of fire.

Apr 85. (d-lp/c) *(NUMA D/C 1002)* **WHITE NOISE (live)** [29] [-]
– (intro) / Berserker / Metal / Me, I disconnect from you / Remind me to smile / Sister surprise / Music for chameleons / The iceman comes / Cold warning / Down in the park / This prison moon / I die; you die / My dying machine / We take mystery (to bed) / We are glass / This is new love / My shadow in vain / Are 'friends' electric?. *(d-cd-iss. May93; NUMACD 1002)*

May 85. (7"ep/12"ep,12"blue-ep,12"white-ep) *(NU/+M 7)* **THE LIVE EP (live)** [27]
– Are 'friends' electric? / Berserker / Cars / We are glass.

Jul 85. (7"/7"pic-d) *(NU/+P 9)* **YOUR FASCINATION. / WE NEED IT** [46]
(ext.12"+=/ext.12"pic-d+=) *(NUM/+P 9)* – Anthem.

Sep 85. (7") *(NU 11)* **CALL OUT THE DOGS. / THIS SHIP COMES APART** [49]
(ext.12"+=) *(NUM 11)* – No shelter.

Sep 85. (lp/pic-lp/c) *(NUMA/+P/K 1003)* **THE FURY** [24]
– Call out the dogs / This disease / Your fascination / Miracles / The pleasure skin / Creatures / Tricks / God only knows / Creatures / I still remember. *(c+)* – (all tracks extended). *(cd-iss. 1986; CDNUMA 1003) (re-iss. cd Nov96; NUMACDX 1003)*

Nov 85. (7",7"red,7"white/ext-12",ext-12"red,ext-12"white) *(NU/+M 13)* **MIRACLES. / THE FEAR** [49]

Apr 86. (7"/7"pic-d/ext-12"/ext-12"pic-d) *(NU/+P/M/MP 16)* **THIS IS LOVE. / SURVIVAL** [28]
(all w/ free 7"flexi)
(d12"+=) *(NUMX 16)* – Call out the dogs (extended) / No shelter / This ship comes apart.

Jun 86. (7"/7"sha-pic-d/ext-12"/picture-12"pic-d/club-10") *(NU/+P/M/MP/DJ 17)* **I CAN'T STOP. / FACES** [27]
(all w/ free 7"flexi)

Sep 86. (7"/7"pic-d/ext-12"/ext-12"pic-d; as SHARPE & NUMAN) *(NU/+P/M/MP 19)* **NEW THING FROM LONDON TOWN. / TIME TO DIE** [52]

Oct 86. (lp/c)(cd) *(NUMA/+C 1005)(CDNUMA 1005)* **STRANGE CHARM** [59]
– My breathing / Unknown and hostile / The sleep room / New thing from London Town / I can't stop / Strange charm / The need / This is love. *(re-iss. cd Nov96; NUMACD 1005)*

Nov 86. (7"/7"pic-d/ext-12"/ext-12"pic-d) *(NU/+P/M/MP 21)* **I STILL REMEMBER. / PUPPETS** [74] [-]

——— Early in 1987, he teamed up with RADIO HEART (see further below)

Polydor   Warners

Jan 88. (7",7"white,7"blue,7"clear/7"pic-d/ext-12"/ext-12"pic-d; as SHARPE & NUMAN) *(POSP/+P/X/PX 894)* **NO MORE LIES. / VOICES** [34]
(cd-s+=) *(POCD 894)* – ('A'extended) / Change your mind.

I.R.S.   I.R.S.

Sep 88. (7"/7"w-poster) *(ILS/+P 1003)* **NEW ANGER. / I DON'T BELIEVE** [46]
(12"+=/12"g-f+=) *(ILST/ILSG 1003)* – Children.
(cd-s+=) *(ILSCD 1003)* – Creatures (live) / I can't stop (live).

Oct 88. (lp/c/cd) *(ILP/+C/CD 035)* *<IRS/+D 82005>* **METAL RHYTHM** [48]
– Respect / Don't call my name / New anger / America / Hunger / Voix / Young heart / Cold metal rhythm / This is emotion. *(pic-lp iss.Mar89; ILPX 035)*

Nov 88. (7"/7"pic-d) *(ILS/+PD 1004)* **AMERICA (remix). / RESPECT (live)** [49]
(12"+=) *(ILST 1004)* – New anger (live).
(cd-s++=) *(ILSCD 1004)* – Call out the dogs (live).

——— again with **ROGER ODELL** – drums / **TESSA MILES + LINDA TAYLOR** – backing vocals

SHARPE & NUMAN

Polydor   M.C.A.

May 89. (7"/7"pic-d) *(PO/+PD 43)* **I'M ON AUTOMATIC. / LOVE LIKE A GHOST** [44]
(ext.12"+=/ext.12"pic-d+=) *(PZ/+PD 43)* – Voices ('89 remix).
(7"w-poster) *(POPB 43)* – ('A'side) / No more lies (new version).
(cd-s+=) *(POCD 43)* – (all 4 above).

Jun 89. (lp/c/cd) *(839520-1/-4/-2)* **AUTOMATIC** [59]
– Change your mind / Turn off the world / No more lies / Breathe in emotion / Some new game / I'm on automatic / Rip it up / Welcome to love / Voices / Nightlife. *(cd+=)* – No more lies (12"version) / I'm on automatic (12"version).

GARY NUMAN

——— solo with **RUSSELL BELL** – guitar / **CHRIS PAYNE** – keyboards, violin / **ADE ORANGE** – keyboards / **CEDRIC SHARPLY** – drums / **JOHN WEBB** – saxophone / **ANDY COUGHLAN** – bass / **VAL CHALMERS + EMMA CHALMER** – backing vocals

I.R.S.   I.R.S.

Oct 89. (lp/cd) *(EIRSA/+CD 1019)* **THE SKIN MECHANIC (live Sep88)** [55]
– Survival / Respect / Call out the dogs / Cars / Hunger / Down in the park / New anger / Creatures / Are 'friends' electric / Young heart / We are glass / I die: you die.

Mar 91. (7",7"red/c-s) *(NUMAN 1/+C)* **HEART. / SHAME** [43]
(12") – ('A'side) / Icehouse.
(cd-s) – ('A'side) / Tread careful.
(12") – ('A'side) / Are 'friends' electric?.

Mar 91. (lp/c/cd) *(EIRSA/+MC/CD 1039)* **OUTLAND** [39]
– Confession / My world storm / Interval 1 / From Russia infected / Interval 2 / They whisper you / Dark Sunday / Heart / Devotion / Outland / Interval 3 / 1999 / Dream killer.

Numa   Numa

Sep 91. (7"/c-s) *(NUD/NUC 22)* **EMOTION. / IN A GLASSHOUSE**
(12"+=) *(NUM 22)* – Hanoi.
(cd-s++=) *(NUCD 22)* – ('A'-different mix).

Mar 92. (7"/c-s) *(NU/+C 23)* **THE SKIN GAME. / DARK MOUNTAIN** [68]
(12"+=/cd-s+=) *(NUM/NUCD 23)* – U got the look / ('A'-digi mix).

Jul 92. (7") *(NU 24)* **MACHINE + SOUL. / ('A'-promo mix)** [72]
(cd-s+=) *(NUCD1 24)* – Cry baby / Wonder eye.
(cd-s+=) *(NUCD2 24)* – 1999 / The hauntings.
(12"+=) *(NUM1 24)* – Your fascination (live) / Outland (live) / Respect (live).
(12") *(NUM2 24)* – ('A'side) / Soul protection (live) / Confession (live) / From Russia infected (live).

Jul 92. (lp/c/cd) *(NUMA/+C/CD 1009)* **MACHINE + SOUL** [42]
– Machine + soul / Generator / Poison / I wonder / Emotion / Cry / U got the look / Love isolation. *(ext.cd re-iss. Sep93)*

——— Apr 94; He guested for GENERATOR on their version of 'ARE FRIENDS' ELECTRIC'.

——— NUMAN & DADAGANG; Apr 94 12"/cd-s LIKE A REFUGEE (I WON'T CRY) on 'Record Label', re-iss. Aug 94 as GARY NUMAN & FRIENDS

Aug 94. (12"ep/cd-ep) *(NU M/CD 25)* **DREAM CORROSION** [-]

Aug 94. (t-lp/d-c/d-cd) *(NUMA/+C/CD 1010)* **DREAM CORROSION (live)** [-]
– Mission / Machine and soul / Outland / Me, I disconnect from you / We are so fragile / Respect / Shame / Films / Dream killer / Down in the park / My world storm / Machman / Generator / Noise, noise / Cars / Voix / You are in my vision / It must have been years / That's too bad / Remind me to smile / I'm an agent / Are 'friends' electric / My breathing / I don't believe / Bombers / Jo the waiter / We are glass.

Oct 94. (12"ep/cd-ep) *(NU M/CD 26)* **A QUESTION OF FAITH** [-]

Mar 95. (cd/c/lp) *(NUMA/+C/CD 1011)* **SACRIFICE**

Mar 95. (12"/12"pic-d/cd-s/pic-cd-s) *(NU/+MP/CD/CDP 27)* **ABSOLUTION. / MAGIC (trick mix) / MAGIC (extended)** [-]

Jun 95. (12"ep/cd-ep) (NUM/+CD 28) **DARK LIGHT LIVE E.P. (live)** ☐ –
– Bleed / Everyday I die / The dream police / Listen to the sirens.

Jul 95. (d-cd/d-c) (NUMA CD/C 1012) **DARK LIGHT (live)** ☐ –
– Pray / A question of faith / I dream of wires / Noise noise / Listen to the sirens / Everyday I die / Desire / Friens / Scar / Magic / Praying to the aliens / Replicas I / Mean street / Stormtrooper in drag / Dead liner / Bleed / The dream police / I die, you die / The hunter / Remind me to smile / Are friends "electric"? / Do you need the service? / Love and napalm / Jo the waiter / I'm an agent.

Nov 95. (d-c/d-cd; with MICHAEL R. SMITH) (NUMA C/CD 1013)
HUMAN ☐ –
– Navigators / Bombay / We fold space / Cry in the dark / Manic / Empire / Little lost soul / Visitor / Magician / Undercover / Halloween / Embryo / Elm Street / Harmonos / Big alten / Blind faith / New life / Fairy tales / Disease / Tidal wave / Alone and afraid / Sahara / Cold / Do you wonder / Betrayal / Suspicion / Unborn / Lethal injection / Frantic / Mother / Black heart / Thunder road / Law and order / Needles / Climax / Inferno.

Feb 96. (cd) (WHENCD 006) **TECHNO ARMY**

	When!	not iss.
	☐	–

	Eagle	not iss.
Oct 97. (cd/c) (EAG CD/MC 008) **EXILE** | 48 | – |
– Dominion day / Prophecy / Dead heaven / Dark / Innocence bleeding / The angel wars / Absolution / An alien cure / Exile.

Apr 98. (c-s) (EAGCS 008) **DOMINION DAY / ANGEL WARS (extended)** ☐ –
(cd-s) (EAGXS 008) – ('A'side) / Voix (20th anniversary) / Dead heaven (extended) / Cars (live).
(cd-s) (EAGXA 008) – ('A'side) / Metal (20th anniversary) / Down in the park (20th anniversary) / Dominion day (live).

– compilations, etc. –

on 'Beggars Banquet' unless otherwise mentioned / * = TUBEWAY ARMY

Aug 79. (d7"*) (BACK 2) **THAT'S TOO BAD. / OH! I DIDN'T SAY/ / BOMBERS. / O.D. RECEIVER / BLUE EYES** ☐ –

Apr 81. (c-s*) WEA; (SPC 4) **ARE 'FRIENDS' ELECTRIC? / WE ARE SO FRAGILE? / DOWN IN THE PARK** ☐ –

Nov 82. (lp/c) TV-Virgin; (TVA/TVC 7) **NEW MAN NUMAN – THE BEST OF GARY NUMAN** | 45 | – |

Apr 83. (12"ep,12"yellow-ep*) (BEG 92E) **TUBEWAY ARMY '78 VOL.1** ☐ –
– That's too bad (alternate mix) / Oh! didn't I say / Bombers / O.D. receiver / Blue eyes / Do you need the service.

Sep 84. (lp/pic-lp*) (BEGA 55/+P) **THE PLAN** | 29 | – |
(re-iss. Jul88 lp/c; BBL/+C 55)

Dec 84. (12"ep,12"red-ep*) (BEG 123E) **TUBEWAY ARMY '78-'79 VOL.2** ☐ –
– Fade out / 1930 / The crazies / Only a downstate / We have a technical.

Dec 84. (12"ep,12"blue-ep*) (BEG 124E) **TUBEWAY ARMY '78-'79 VOL.3** ☐ –
– The Monday troup / Crime of assikon / The life machine / A game called Echo / Random / Oceans.

Aug 87. (12"ep/c-ep;*) Strange Fruit; (SFPS/+C 032) **THE PEEL SESSIONS** ☐ –
– Me I disconnect from you / Down in the park / I nearly married a human.

Aug 87. (7"/7"pic-d) (BEG 199/+P) **CARS (E-REG MODEL). / ARE FRIENDS ELECTRIC?** | 16 | ☐ |
(c-s+=/ext-12"+=) (BEG 199 C/T) – We are glass / I die: you die.
(ext-12"+=) – (BEG 199TR) – ('A'-Motorway mix).

Sep 87. (d-lp/d-cd) (BEGA 88/+CD)(BEGC 88) **EXHIBITION** | 43 | – |
– Me, I disconnect from you / That's too bad / My love is a liquid / Music for chameleons / We are glass / Bombers / Sister Surprise / Are 'friends' electric / I dream of wires / Complex / Noise noise / Warriors / Everyday I die / You're such a mystery to bed / I'm an agent / My centurion / Metal / You are in my vision / I die: you die / She's got claws / This wreckage / My shadow in vain / Down in the park / The iceman comes. (d-cd+=) – (11 tracks)

Dec 87. (cd) (BEGA 4CD) **REPLICAS / THE PLAN** ☐ –
(re-iss. d-cd Dec93; BEGA 152CD)

Dec 87. (cd) (BEGA 7CD) **TUBEWAY ARMY / DANCE** ☐ –
(re-iss. d-cd Dec93; BEGA 151CD)

Dec 87. (cd) (BEGA 10CD) **THE PLEASURE PRINCIPLE / WARRIORS** ☐ –
(re-iss. d-cd Dec93; BEGA 153CD)

Dec 87. (cd) (BEGA 19CD) **TELEKON / I, ASSASSIN** ☐ –
(re-iss. d-cd Dec93; BEGA 154CD)
(above series of cd's, omitted some tracks on each)

Oct 89. (d-lp/cd) Castle; (CCS LP/CD 229) **THE GARY NUMAN COLLECTION** ☐ –

Dec 89. (m-lp/cd) Strange Fruit; (SFPMA/+CD 202) **DOUBLE PEEL SESSIONS** ☐ –

1990. (pic-cd-ep) **THE SELECTION** ☐ –
– Cars ('E' reg.model) / Down in the park / I die: you die / Are 'friends' electric? / We are glass / Music for chameleons.

1990. (7") Old Gold; (OG 9917) **ARE FRIENDS ELECTRIC?. / I DID YOU** ☐ –

1990. (7") Old Gold; (OG 9919) **CARS. / WE ARE GLASS** ☐ –

Mar 92. (lp/c/cd) Numa; (NUMA/+C/CD 1008) **ISOLATE** ☐ –

Oct 92. (d-cd) Numa; (NUMACD 1007) **GHOST** ☐ –

Oct 92. (cd/lp) Receiver; (RR CD/LP 170) **THE OTHER SIDE OF GARY NUMAN** ☐ –

Dec 92. (cd) Connoisseur; (CSAPCD 113) **DOCUMENT SERIES PRESENTS . . .** ☐ –

Aug 93. (7"/c-s) (BEG 264/+C) **CARS. / ('A'mix)** | 53 | ☐ |
(12"sha-pic-d+=/cd-s+=) (BEG 264 L/CD) – Cars ('93 sprint mix) / Cars (Top Gear mix).

Sep 93. (cd)(c) (BEGA 150CD)(BEGC 150) **THE BEST OF GARY NUMAN 1978-1983** | 70 | – |

Jul 94. (cd) Receiver; (RRCD 186) **HERE I AM** ☐ –

Mar 95. (cd/c) Polygram TV; (531 149-2/-4) **GREATEST HITS** ☐ –

Mar 96. (7"/c-s/cd-s) Premier; (PRM/+MC/CD 1) **CARS (premier mix) / ARE FRIENDS ELECTRIC (live) / DOWN IN THE PARK (live)** | 17 | ☐ |

Mar 96. (cd/c) Premier; **THE PREMIER HITS** (compilation) | 21 | – |

Jul 96. (3xcd) Receiver; (RRXCD 505) **THE STORY SO FAR** ☐ –

Sep 96. (cd/c) Emporio; (EMPR CD/MC 666) **THE BEST OF GARY NUMAN** ☐ –

Oct 97. (12") Random; (RANDOM 2.1) **METAL (remixes). / DANS LE PARC** ☐ –

Nov 97. (12"green) Random; (RANDOM 2.2) **I DIE YOU DIE (Greenhaus mix) / CARS (Mike Dearborn mix) / CARS (Dave Clarke mix)** ☐ –

Jan 98. (12"blue) Random; (RANDOM 2.3) **WARRIORS (Dave Angel mix). / ARE 'FRIENDS' ELECTRIC (Liberator DJ's mix) / REMEMBER I WAS VAPOUR (Steve Stoll mix)** ☐ –

Feb 98. (12") Random; (RANDOM 2.4) **WE ARE GLASS (Claude Young mix) / FILMS (Alex Hazzard remix) / THE ICEMAN COMES (Peter Lazonby mix)** ☐ –

—— GARY has also contributed to other DRAMATIS recordings as well as joining RADIO HEART for one eponymous set

N.W.A.

Formed: NIGGAZ WITH ATTITUDE, Compton, L.A., California, USA . . . mid-80's by EAZY-E (aka ERIC WRIGHT and son of 70's soulman/funk guru, CHARLES WRIGHT) who set up his own label, 'Ruthless Records', in 1985. Allegedly founded with illegal profits, the label was a pivotal player in the burgeoning West Coast rap scene along with 24-hour hip hop radio station, KDAY. Hooking up with WORLD CLASS WRECKING CRU members, DR. DRE (aka ANDRE YOUNG) and DJ YELLA (ANTOINE CARRABY) as well as ex-STEREO CREW rapper, ICE CUBE, EAZY-E formed the core of what would become NWA. Along with the likes of ARABIAN PRINCE and The DOC, this loose affiliation recorded a promising debut set, 'NWA AND THE POSSE' (1987). EAZY-E's brutally frank 'BOYZ 'N' THE HOOD' was a sobering taster of what was to come. With MC REN (aka LORENZO PATTERSON) on board, a more compact posse of DRE, YELLA, CUBE and EAZY crafted the epochal 'STRAIGHT OUTTA COMPTON' (1989). Opening with an ominous 'You are now about to witness the strength of street knowledge . . .', the record slammed into the savage bass crunch of the title track, expletives rattled off like bullets from the proverbial AK. Next up was the infamous 'F*** THA POLICE', the boys leering their way through a defiant two-fingured salute to L.A.'s finest. The F.B.I. were sufficiently worried about the track to send the group a written warning, although they should've been more concerned with 'GANGSTA GANGSTA', a track which engendered a generation of violent, crime-obsessed albums and 'Gangsta' artists. While the rest of the set failed to maintain the vicious intensity of the opening three tracks, the damage had been done; violence-obsessed mysogynists or documenters of social realism?, the debate is still raging a decade on. While the record was initially issued as a low-key domestic release, word soon got round and a distribution deal was signed with 'Priority' records, the album going on to notch up sales of 750,000 before NWA had even toured. Like PUBLIC ENEMY before them, it was obvious that a fair portion of their audience were middle class white kids out for some vicarious thrills, a theory compounded when N.W.A.'s follow-up, 'EFIL4ZAGGIN' (1991) scaled the US charts. By this point, however, the posse were in dissaray; ICE CUBE had left after falling out with manager JERRY HELLER over royalty payments while DRE left soon after the record's release, accusing HELLER of turning EAZY-E against him. This in-fighting was set against a backdrop of UK obscenity charges aimed at 'EFIL..', copies of the album seized by British customs officials. Among the tracks which raised the authorities' ire were such inimitable ditties as 'TO KILL A HOOKER' and 'FINDUM, FUCKUM and FLEE'; although the group eventually won the case, the mindless nihilism of the bulk of the album indicated that NWA had crossed the line between commentary and hilarious, often dangerous self-parody. Which is a pity, as DRE turned in another fine production. No surprise then, that as NWA imploded, DRE's solo output towered over the likes of REN's 'KIZZ MY BLACK AZZ' (1992) and EAZY's 'REAL MUTHAPHUCKIN' G's' (1994), the latter an acerbic response to DRE's G-funk innovations. With 'THE CHRONIC' (1993), DRE traded in the ever popular JAMES BROWN for the more laid back GEORGE CLINTON, pioneering the use of FUNKADELIC/PARLIAMENT samples amid a haze of marijuana references. The record was released on his new 'Death Row' records, a joint project (you could say) with 'Interscope' and itself the subject of much recent controversy following the murder of rapper TUPAC SHAKUR and the much touted feud between the rival rap factions of east and west. While DRE's debut went triple platinum, influencing the likes of SNOOP DOGGY DOGG and his half-brother, WARREN G, the rapper was charged with battery (assault) in September '94 and sentenced to 8 months in prison. In March '95, EAZY-E succumbed to AIDS, his death finally seeing a reconciliation between DRE and ICE CUBE, the latter having gone on to even greater success. Yes, NWA sent shockwaves both through the rap scene and the white authorities and yes, 'STRAIGHT OUTTA COMPTON' remains one of the most visceral listening experiences of the 80's, but given the current bloodstained state of hip hop, the advent of 'gangsta' seems less and less like a bold step forward and more like a self-destructive blind alley. DR. DRE's album, '2001' (actually issued at the tail end of '99) was another commercial success, rumours now abound of a NWA reformation. • **Trivia:** Album 'EFIL4ZAGGIN' is actually NIGGAZ4LIFE spelt backwards (as seen on sleeve).

Album rating: N.W.A. AND THE POSSE (*6) / STRAIGHT OUTTA COMPTON (*9) / 100 MILES AND RUNNIN' mini (*6) / EFIL4ZAGGIN (*5) / GREATEST HITS compilation (*7) / Dr Dre: THE CHRONIC (*7) / 1ST ROUND KNOCKOUT (*6) / DR. DRE – 2001 (*6) / Eazy-E: EAZY-DUZ-IT (*7) / 5150 HOME 4 THA SICK mini (*4) / IT'S ON (DR. DRE 187UM) KILLA mini (*5) / ETERNAL E compilation (*7) / STR8 OFF THA STREETZ OF MUTHAPHUKKIN COMPTON (*5) / MC Ren: KISS MY BLACK AZZ (*5) / SHOCK OF THE HOUR (*4) / THE VILLAIN IN BLACK (*4) / RUTHLESS FOR LIFE (*4) / THE N.W.A. LEGACY VOLUME 1 1988-1998 compilation (*7)

ICE CUBE (b. O'SHEA JACKSON, 15 Jun'69) – vocals (ex-C.I.A.) / **DR DRE** (b. ANDRE YOUNG, 18 Feb'65) – producer (also of WORLD CLASS WRECKIN' CREW) / **EAZY-E** (b. ERIC WRIGHT, 7 Sep'73) – vocals / **M.C. REN** (b. LORENZO PATTERSON, 16 Jun'??) – vocals / **DJ YELLA** (b. ANTOINE CARRABY, 11 Dec'??) – turntables

		not iss.	Macola
1987.	(lp; Various Artists) **N.W.A. AND THE POSSE** (UK-iss.Oct89 on 'Rams Horn'; RHR 5134)	-	☐

		4th & Broad	Ruthless
Aug 89.	(7"/c-s) (BRW/BRCA 144) **EXPRESS YOURSELF. / STRAIGHT OUTTA COMPTON** (ext;12"+=/cd-s+=) (12BRW/BRCD 144) – ('A'-Bonus beats) / A bitch iz a bitch. (re-iss. May90; same) – hit UK No.26	50	☐
Aug 89.	(lp/c/cd) (BR LP/CA/CD 534) <SL/4XL/CDL 57102> **STRAIGHT OUTTA COMPTON** – Straight outta Compton / Fu** the police / Gangsta gangsta / If it ain't ruff / Parental discretion iz advised / 8 ball (remix) / Something like that / Express yourself / Compton's in the house (remix) / I ain't tha 1 / Dopeman (remix) / Quiet on the set / Something to dance to.	41	37
Aug 90.	(7"/c-s) (BRW/BRCA 191) **GANGSTA, GANGSTA / IF IT AIN'T RUFF** (12"+=/cd-s+=) (12BRW/BRCD 191) – Dopeman (remix).	70	☐

—— now without ICE CUBE who was now solo

Oct 90.	(7"/c-s) (BRW/BRCA 200) <7224> **100 MILES AND RUNNIN'. / REAL NIGGAZ** (12"+=/cd-s+=) (12BRW/BRCD 200) – ('A'side) / Just don't bite it / Sa prize (pt.2) / Kamurshoi.	38	27 Aug90
Apr 91.	(12"/cd-s) **F*** THE POLICE. / ('A'mixes)** (above written for RODNEY KING, the black motorist beat up by police. The court case instigated the race riots all around America.	-	☐
Jun 91.	(cd/c/lp) (BR CD/CA/LP 552) <57126> **EFIL4ZAGGIN** – Prelude / Real niggaz don't die / Real niggaz 4 life / Protest / Appetite for destruction / Don't drink that wine / Alwayz into somethin' / Message to B.A. / Real niggaz / To kill a hooker / One less bitch / Findum, f***um and flee / Automobile / She swallowed it / I'd rather f*** you / Approach to danger / 1-900-2 Compton / The dayz of wayback.	25	1
Nov 91.	(7"/c-s) (BRW/BRCA 238) **ALWAYZ INTO SOMETHIN'. / EXPRESS YOURSELF** (12"+=/cd-s+=) (12BRW/BRCD 238) – Something 2 dance 2.	60	☐

—— disbanded and all went solo

– compilations, etc. –

| Aug 96. | (cd/c) Priority; (CDPTY 126) / Ruthless; <50561> **GREATEST HITS** – Live intro (1989) / Arrested / angsta gangsta / F*** tha police / Compton's in the house (live) / Break out / Straight outa Compton (extended mix) / If it ain't ruff / Real niggaz / I ain't tha 1 / Alwayz into something / Don't drink that wine / Just don't bite it / Cash money / Express yourself (remix) / 100 miles & runnin' / A bitch iz a bitch / Real niggaz don't die. | 56 | 48 Jul96 |
| Mar 99. | (d-cd/d-c; Various Artists) Priority; <51111> **THE N.W.A. LEGACY 1988-1998** | - | 77 |

EAZY-E

		4th & Broad	Ruthless
Sep 89.	(lp/c/cd) (BR LP/CA/CD 535) <57100> **EAZY-DUZ-IT** – (Prelude) Still talkin' / Nobody move / 2 Hard muthas (featuring MC REN) / Boyz-n-the-hood (remix) / Eazy-duz-it / We want Eazy / Eazy-er said than dunn / Radio / No more ?'s / Imma break it down / Eazy – Chapter 8, verse 10. (re-iss. Jun91 on 'Island' lp/c/cd; ILPM/ICM 2070/(IMCD 124)	☐	41 Dec88
Jan 93.	(m-cd) <53815> **5150 HOME FOR THA SICK** – Neighbourhood sniper / Niggaz my height don't fight / Merry mutha***** Xmas / Only if you want it.	-	70
Oct 93.	(m-cd) <5503> **IT'S ON (DR.DRE) 187 UM KILLA** – Any last werdz / Real muthaphuckin G's / Still a nigga / Exxtra special thankz / Boyz-n-the-hood / Gimme that nutt / It's on.	☐	5
Jan 94.	(c-s,cd-s) <5508> **REAL MUTHAPHUCKIN' G'S / ANY LAST WERDZ**	-	42

—— Early in 1995, EAZY-E featured on BONE THUGS N HARMONY's hit single, 'Foe Tha Love Of'.

—— EAZY-E died of AIDS on the 26th March 1995 after only being diagnosed HIV a month earlier.

| Dec 95. | (c-s) (662 816-4) <5532> **JUST TAH LET U KNOW / THE MUTHAPHU**IN' REAL** (12"+=/cd-s+=) (662 816-6/-2) – ('A'-Ruthless "G" mix) / ('A'-Ba-da-ba-do acappella mix). (above issued on 'Epic') | 30 | 45 |
| Jan 96. | (cd/c) (CDPTY/PTYMC/PTYLP 122) <50544> **ETERNAL E** (compilation) – Automobile / Eazy-duz-it / Boyz-in-the-hood / Eazy-er said than dunn / Neighbourhood sniper / Radio / We want Eazy / Only if you want it / Nobody move / I'd rather funk you / 8 ball / Eazy street / Niggaz my height don't fight / No more ?'s. | ☐ | 84 Dec95 |

		Ruthless	Ruthless
Feb 96.	(cd/c) (483 576-2/-4) <5504> **STR8 OFF THA STREETZ OF MUTHAPH**IN – E.W. COMPTON** – Just tah let u know / Lickin' smokin' phuckin' / What would you do / Sorry Louie / Nutz on ya chin / Ole school shit / Slippin on a 4 / My baby'z mama / Muthaphuckin' real / Hit the hoods / Gangsta beat 4 tha street / Eternal E / Creep n crawl.	66	3

MC REN

		Ruthless	Ruthless
Jul 92.	(cd,c) <53802> **KIZZ MY BLACK AZZ** – Check it out y'all / Behind the scenes / Hound dogz / Kiss my black azz / Right up my alley / Final frontier.	-	12
Nov 93.	(cd,c) <5505> **SHOCK OF THE HOUR** – Fuck what ya hear / All bullshit aside / Attack on Babylon / Shock of the hour / Still the same nigga / You wanna fuck her / Same ol' shit / Mr. Fuck up / One false move / Mayday on the front line / 11.55 / Do you believe.	-	22
Nov 93.	(c-s,12") <5510> **SAME OL' SHIT. / (radio version)**	-	90

—— Above sampled; LET'S GET IT ON (Marvin Gaye) / I GOT A GOOD THING (James Brown) / LAD DI DA DI (Doug E.Fresh).

Apr 96.	(cd/c) (483900-2/-4) <5544> **THE VILLAIN IN BLACK** – Bitch made nigga killa / Bring it on / Mad scientist / Mind blown / Still the same nigga / Muhammed speaks / Live from Compton 'Saturday night' / It's like that / Keep it real / Great elephant.	☐	31
Apr 98.	(cd-s) **RUTHLESS FOR LIFE (mixes; LP / clean radio / instrumental)** (12"+=) – ('A'-A cappella).	-	-
Jun 98.	(cd/c) <69313> **RUTHLESS FOR LIFE** – Ruthless for life / Who in the f*** / N***a called Ren / Comin' after you / Voyage to Compton / Must be high / So whatcha want / Shot caller / All the same / Who got that street s*** / Pimpin' is free / CPT all day.	-	100

DR. DRE

		Interscope	Death Row
May 92.	(cd-s) <74547> **DEEP COVER / (instrumental)** (above from the film of the same name on 'Epic')	-	-
Feb 93.	(cd/c) (7567 92233-2/-4) <57128> **THE CHRONIC** – The chronic / Fuck wit Dre day (and everybody's celebrating) / Let me ride / The day the niggaz took over / Nuthin' but a "G" thang / Dreeez nuuuts / Bitches ain't shit / Lil' ghetto boy / A nigga witta gun / Rat-tat-tat-tat / The $20 sack pyramid / Lyrical gangbang / High powered / The doctor's office / Stranded on death row / The roach (the chronic outro).	☐	3
Mar 93.	(c-s) <53819> **NUTHIN' BUT A "G" THANG. / ('A'mix)** (club-12"+=)(cd-s+=) – ('A'-freestyle mix).	☐	2 Jan93
May 93.	(7"/c-s) <53827> **DRE DAY. / ('A'-flavour mix)** (cd-s+=) – ('A'extended club) / ('A'-UK Flavour mix) / ('A'instrumental) / ('A'again). (12") – (A+B) (above 2) / Puffin' on blunts and drinkin' tanqueray.	☐	8
Aug 93.	(c-s,cd-s,12") <53839> **LET ME RIDE / ('A'mixes)**	-	34
Jan 94.	(c-s) (A 8328C) **NUTHIN' BUT A G THANG (club) / ('A'mix)** (12") (A 8328T) - ('A'-version) / Let me ride (extended club mix). (cd-s) (A 8328CD) – (their club mixes).	31	-
Aug 94.	(7"/c-s) (A 8292/+C) **DRE DAY. / ('A'-UK radio mix)** (12"+=) (A 8292T) – (4-'A'-Puffin' on blunts and drinkin' tanqueray mixes). (cd-s+=) (A 8292CD) – ('A'-radio remix) / ('A'instrumental) / ('A'-2 other mixes).	59	-

—— In Sep'94, DR.DRE was convicted of battery (assault) and imprisoned for 8 months, although it seems likely he'll be out a lot sooner.

		Interscope	Hitman
Oct 94.	(cd,c) <51170> **CONCRETE ROOTS – ANTHOLOGY** (compilation of various artists)	☐	43

—— DR.DRE & ICE CUBE; below from the film 'Murder Was The Case'.

Mar 95.	(7"/c-s) (A 8197/+C) **NATURAL BORN KILLAZ / THA DOGG POUND: What Would U Do?** (cd-s+=) (A 8197CD) – (2 'A'versions).	45	
May 95.	(c-s) (PTYSC 103) <53188> **KEEP THEIR HEADS RINGIN'. / TAKE A HIT (mix)** (12"+=/cd-s+=) (PTY ST/CD 103) – (other mixes). above from the film 'Friday' on the label 'Priority')	25	10 Mar95
Jun 98.	(c-s; DR. DRE & LL COOL J) (INC 95594) **ZOOM /** (12"+=/cd-s) (INT/IND 95594) –	15	
Nov 99.	(cd/d-lp) <(490486-2/-1)> **DR. DRE 2001** – Lolo (w/ XZIBIT & TRAY-D) / Watcher / Fuck you (w/ THE DUDE & SNOOP DOGG) / Still D.R.E. (w/ SNOOP DOGG) / Big ego's (w/ HITTMAN) / Xplosive (w/ HITTMAN) / What's the difference (w/ EMINEM & XZIBIT) / Bar one (w/ TRACY NELSON, MS ROQ & EDDIE GRIFFIN) / Light speed (w/ EMINEM) / Next episode (w/ SNOOP DOGG) / Let's get high (w/ HITTMAN, KURUPT & MS ROQ) / Bitch niggaz (w/ SNOOP DOGG, HITTMAN & SIX-TWO) / Car bomb (w/ MEL-MAN & SHARI HENRY) / Education (w/ HITTMAN & MS ROQ) / Murderlink (w/ HITTMAN & MS ROQ) / Some L.A. niggaz (w/ DEFARI, XZIBIT, KNOCKTURNAL, TIMEBOMB, KING T, MC REN & KOKANE) / Pause 4 promo (w/ JAKE STEED) / Housewife (w/ KURUPT & HITTMAN) / Acrite (w/ HITTMAN) / Bang bang (w/ KNOCKTURNAL & HITTMAN) / The message (w/ MARY J. BLIGE & REIL).	48	2
Nov 99.	(c-s/cd-s; as DR. DRE featuring SNOOP DOGG) <497192> **STILL D.R.E.**	-	93

– compilations, etc. –

| Jun 96. | (cd,c) Triple X; <51226> **1ST ROUND KNOCKOUT** (compilation) – Bridgette (D.O.C.) / It's not over (ROSE ROYCE) / Nicety / Sex is on / Turn off the lights / Nickel slick nigga / Juice / Funky flute / The fly / Deep cover / He's bionic. | - | 52 |

—— In Oct'96, he featured on hit single by BLACKSTREET; 'No Diggity'.

—— In Dec'96, DR. DRE PRESENTS . . . THE AFTERMATH was the name of a Various Artists album for Interscope' <(IND/INC 90044)>

Laura NYRO

Born: LAURA NIGRO, 18 Oct'47, Bronx, New York, USA, of Italian/Jewish parentage. The daughter of a jazz trumpeter, NYRO began songwriting at an early age, later attending Manhattan's High School of Music and Art (where she underwent a bad LSD trip). An aversion to hallucinogenics was not the only thing separating NYRO from the burgeoning hippie movement, the crowd at 1967's Monterey Festival booing her soul revue-style performance. Only her second ever experience in front a live audience, this unfortunate incident resulted in prolonged stage fright during the early part of her career. Nevertheless, the singer/songwriter's debut album, 'MORE THAN A NEW DISCOVERY' (1966), while doing little to trouble the charts, contained a wealth of material which would later be successfully interpreted by other artists; close harmony popsters, FIFTH DIMENSION, took 'WEDDING BELL BLUES' to No.1 (US) in 1969, while BLOOD, SWEAT & TEARS almost managed a similar feat with 'AND WHEN I DIE' and BARBRA STREISAND carried 'STONEY END' into the UK Top 30 in 1970. Among the cream of NYRO's work, these tracks managed to marry her wayward poetic flights of confessional fancy with killer hooks and a melodic verve in a way which she'd find hard to sustain over the course of her career. In the meantime, a young David Geffen was impressed enough to offer NYRO his services as manager, the future record mogul soon securing her a deal with 'Columbia'. The resulting follow-up set, 'ELI AND THE THIRTEENTH CONFESSION' (1968), found NYRO honing her unique take on white soul/gospel/R&B, the singer's lamenting/rapturous testimonials delivered with characteristically idiosyncratic phrasing atop unconventional arrangements and time changes. Despite her quirky style, there was enough hit potential in the material to provide yet more chart success for FIFTH DIMENSION ('STONED SOUL PICNIC' and 'SWEET BLINDNESS'), while THREE DOG NIGHT went Top 10 with a cover of 'ELI'S COMING'. NYRO herself eventually enjoyed a bit of belated chart action with 1970's 'NEW YORK TENDABERRY', an even more oblique set of unadorned piano/vocal expressionism. 'CHRISTMAS AND THE BEADS OF SWEAT' carried on in a similar vein later that year, while 'GONNA TAKE A MIRACLE' (1972) stands as perhaps NYRO's most enjoyable outing, a Gamble/Huff-produced tribute to the pop/soul sounds of the 60's which saw the singer hooking up with LaBELLE and covering such standards as 'JIMMY MACK' and 'NOWHERE TO RUN'. Taking time out to get married and enjoy a period of domestic simplicity, NYRO returned in 1976 with 'SMILE', the record meeting with largely favourable reviews but achieving only minor chart success. She seemed to have lost her momentum and subsequent albums such as 'NESTED' (1978) met with diminishing critical and commercial returns. Over the ensuing decade, the singer released only one further album, 'MOTHER'S SPIRITUAL' (1984), NYRO further embracing an eco-conscious, Earth-Mother philosophy as she entered middle age. Despite her low-profile approach, sporadic live performances are not unknown and a rare concert set, 'LIVE AT THE BOTTOM LINE', appeared in 1989. Modern day female singer/songwriter, SHAWN COLVIN, acknowledged the debt her generation owe to NYRO's innovations when she teamed up with the cult singer on a one-off US-only single, 'LET IT BE ME', in 1990. NYRO, meanwhile, proved that she is still actually capable of producing the goods when she feels like it, 1994's 'WALK THE DOG AND LIGHT THE LIGHT' garnering a fair amount of critical acclaim. Just don't hold your breath for a follow-up . . .

Album rating: MORE THAN A NEW DISCOVERY (*6) / ELI AND THE THIRTEENTH CONFESSION (*8) / NEW YORK TENDABERRY (*7) / CHRISTMAS AND THE BEADS OF SWEAT (*6) / GONNA TAKE A MIRACLE (*6) / SMILE (*6) / SEASON OF LIGHTS . . . LAURA NYRO IN CONCERT (*5) / NESTED (*4) / IMPRESSIONS compilation (*6) / MOTHER'S SPIRITUAL (*4) / LIVE AT THE BOTTOM LINE (*4) / WALK THE DOG AND LIGHT THE LIGHT (*5) / STONED SOUL PICNIC: THE BEST OF LAURA NYRO compilation (*7)

LAURA NYRO – vocals, piano

		Verve	Verve Folkways
1966.	(lp) <FTS 3020> **MORE THAN A NEW DISCOVERY**	-	
	– Wedding bells blues / Goodbye Joe / Billy's blues / And when I die / Stoney end / Lazy Susan / Hands off the man / Buy and sell / He's a runner / Blowin' away / I never meant to hurt you / California shoeshine boys. (UK-iss.1969 as 'THE FIRST SONGS'; SVLP 6022) <same for US; re-iss. Jan73 on 'Columbia'; CBS 31410> – hit No.97.		
Oct 66.	(7") (VS 1502) <5024> **WEDDING BELL BLUES. / STONEY END**		
May 67.	(7") <5038> **GOODBYE JOE. / BILLY'S BLUES**	-	
Dec 67.	(7") <5051> **AND WHEN I DIE. / FLIM FLAM MAN**	-	

		C.B.S.	Columbia
Jul 68.	(7") (CBS 3604) <44531> **ELI'S COMIN'. / SWEET BLINDNESS**		
Aug 68.	(lp) (CBS 63346) <9626> **ELI AND THE THIRTEENTH CONFESSION**		
	– Luckie / Lu / Sweet blindness / Poverty train / Lonely women / Eli's comin' / Timer / Stoned good picnic / Emmie / Woman's blues / Once it was alright now (farmer Joe) / December's boudoir / The confession. (re-iss. 1974) (cd-iss. Mar97 on 'Columbia'; 487240-2)		
Oct 68.	(7") <44592> **SAVE THE COUNTRY. / TIMER**	-	
Jan 69.	(7") <44786> **ONCE IT WAS ALRIGHT NOW (FARMER JOE). / LU**	-	
Feb 69.	(7") (CBS 4031) **ONCE IT WAS ALRIGHT NOW (FARMER JOE). / WOMAN'S BLUES**		-
Jan 70.	(7") (CBS 4719) <45041> **TIME AND LOVE. / THE MAN WHO SENDS ME HOME**		
Jan 70.	(lp) (CBS 63510) <9737> **NEW YORK TENDABERRY**		32 Oct69
	– You don't love me when I cry / Captain for dark mornings / Tom cat good by / Mercy on Broadway / Save the country / Gibson Street / Time and love / The man who sends me home / Sweet lovin' baby / Captain Saint Lucifer / New york tendaberry. (re-iss. 1974)		
Mar 70.	(7") <45089> **SAVE THE COUNTRY. / NEW YORK TENDABERRY**	-	

—— now with session people

Oct 70.	(7") (CBS 5218) <45230> **UP ON THE ROOF. / CAPTAIN SAINT LUCIFER**		92
Dec 70.	(lp) (CBS 64157) <30259> **CHRISTMAS AND THE BEADS OF SWEAT**		
	– Brown earth / When I was a freeport and you were the main drag / Blackpatch / Been on a train / Upon the roof / Upstairs by a Chinese lamp / Map to the treasure / Beads of sweat / Christmas in my soul. (re-iss. 1974)		
Feb 71.	(7") (CBS 7028) <45298> **WHEN I WAS A FREEPORT AND YOU WERE THE MAIN DRAG. / BEEN ON A TRAIN**		

below was augmented by singing outfit, LaBELLE

Feb 72.	(lp) (CBS 64770) <30987> **GONNA TAKE A MIRACLE**		46 Dec71
	– I met him on a Sunday / The bells / Monkey time – Dancing in the street / Desiree / You've really got a hold on me / Spanish harlem / Jimmy Mack / Wind / Nowhere to run / It's gonna take a miracle. (re-iss. Feb89 on 'Beat Goes On'; BGOLP 27) (cd-iss. Nov91; BGOCD 27)		
Feb 72.	(7") <45537> **IT'S GONNA TAKE A MIRACLE. / DESIREE**		

—— LAURA retired for 4 years after getting married.

Mar 76.	(lp) (CBS 81171) <33912> **SMILE**		60
	– Sexy mama / Children of the junks / Money / I am the blues / Stormy love / The cat-song / Midnite blue / Smile.		
Aug 77.	(lp) (CBS 82183) <34786> **SEASON OF LIGHTS . . . LAURA NYRO IN CONCERT (live)**		Jun77
	– The confession / And when I die / Upstairs by a Chinese lamp / Sweet blindness / Captain Saint Lucifer / Money / The cat-song / When I was a freeport and you were the main drag / Timer / Emmie.		
Aug 78.	(lp) (CBS 82917) <35449> **NESTED**		
	– Mr. Blue (the song of communications) / Rhythm and blues / My innocence / Crazy love / The nest / American dreamer / Spring blown / Sweet sky / Light pops principle / Child in a universe.		
Mar 84.	(lp) <39215> **MOTHER'S SPIRITUAL**	-	
	– To a child / The right to vote / A wilderness / Melody in the sky / Late for love / A free thinker / Man in the Moon / Talk on a green tree / Trees of the ages / The brighter song / Roadnotes / Sophia / Mother's spiritual / Refrain. (UK-iss.Oct90 on 'Line'; CLCD 9.00924)		

—— She virtually retired from the music business around the mid-80's.

		Cypress	Cypress
Oct 89.	(lp/cd) (YL/YD 0128) **LIVE AT THE BOTTOM LINE (live)**		
	– Medley:- The confession – Hi heel sneakers / Roll of the ocean / Companion / Wild world / Medley:- My innocence – Sophia / To a child / And when I die / Park song / Broken rainbow / Women of the one world / Emmie / Wedding bell blues / The Japanese restaurant song / Stoned soul picnic / Medley:- La la means I love you – Trees of the ages – Up on the roof.		

—— In Nov'90, NYRO was credited on SHAWN COLVIN's single, 'LET IT BE ME' / 'CHRISTMAS SONG; CHESTNUTS ROASTING ON AN OPEN FIRE' on 'Columbia'.

		Sony	Sony
Jan 94.	(cd/c) (474296-2/-4) **WALK THE DOG AND LIGHT THE LIGHT**		
	– Oh yeah, oh yeah (the heebie jeebies) / A woman of the world / The descent of Luna Rose / Art of love / Like a flame (the animal rights song) / Louise's church / Broken rainbow / Walk the dog and light the light (song of the road) / To a child / I'm so proud / Dedicated to the one I love.		

– compilations, etc. –

on 'Verve Folkways' unless mentioned otherwise

1969.	(7") <5095> **STONEY END. / FLIM FLAM MAN**	-	
1969.	(7") <5104> **AND WHEN I DIE. / I NEVER MEANT TO HURT YOU**	-	
1969.	(7") <5112> **GOODBYE JOE. / I NEVER MEANT TO HURT YOU**	-	
1971.	(lp) C.B.S.; (CBS 64400) **HER SONGBOOK**	-	
Feb 73.	(7") C.B.S.; (1352) **WEDDING BELL BLUES. / HANDS OFF THE MAN (FLIM FLAM MAN)**		-
1975.	(7") C.B.S.; (13-33159) **ELI'S COMING. / SAVE THE COUNTRY**		-
Dec 80.	(lp) CBS-Embassy; (31864) **IMPRESSIONS**		
Jul 91.	(cd/c) Elite; (ELITE 015 CD/MC) **CLASSICS** (re-iss. Sep93; same)		
Feb 97.	(d-cd) Legacy; (485109-2) <4880> **STONED SOUL PICNIC: THE BEST OF LAURA NYRO**		
	– Wedding bell blues / Blowing away / Billy's blues / Stoney end / And when I die / Lu / Eli's coming / Stone soul picnic / Timer / Emmie / Confession / Captain Saint Lucifer / Gibsome Street / New York tendaberry / Save the country / Upstairs by a Chinese lamp / Beads of sweat / When I was a freeort and you were the main drag / I met him on a Sunday / Bells / Smile / Sweet blindness / Money / Mr. Blue / Wilderness / Mother's spiritual / Woman of the world / Louise's church / Broken rainbow / To a child / Lite a big flame (the animal rights song) / And when I die / Save the country.		

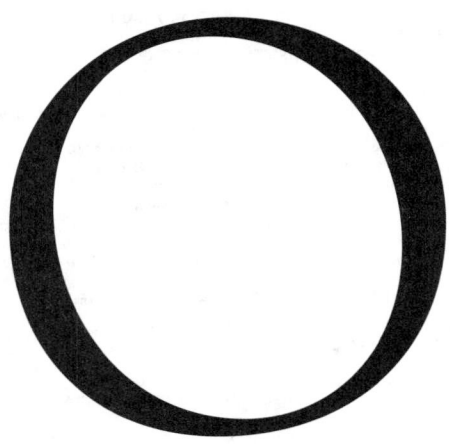

OASIS

Formed: Manchester, England ... summer 1992, by frontman LIAM GALLAGHER, rhythm guitarist PAUL 'BONEHEAD' ARTHURS, bassist PAUL McGUIGAN and drummer TONY McCARROLL. Initially called RAIN, they were soon joined by LIAM's older brother NOEL who had worked as a roadie for The INSPIRAL CARPETS. He was also a budding songwriter/guitarist with a concrete self-belief and after a year of rehearsals and occasional local gigs, they were signed by Creation's ALAN McGEE, after the eagle-eared Scotsman clocked them at a Glasgow gig in mid-1993. With a groundswell of interest not witnessed since the heady early days of The STONE ROSES, OASIS secured a near UK Top 30 placing with 'SUPERSONIC', a sneering, leering anthem with lyrics that SHAUN RYDER would've been proud to call his own. Later that summer the band released the follow-up, 'SHAKER MAKER', a rather tame effort in comparison which appeared to be modelled on the NEW SEEKERS' chestnut, 'I'd Like To Teach The World To Sing'. Nevertheless, what the single lacked in originality, it made up for in controversy and the stage was set for OASIS' first Top 10 hit, the classic 'LIVE FOREVER'. A life-affirming rush celebrating the strength of the human spirit, the song was lauded as single of the year, closely followed by the epochal debut album, 'DEFINITELY MAYBE' (1994). There were no maybes about it, this album defined an era in the same way that The SEX PISTOLS (an obvious influence) focused the frustrations of a generation with 'Never Mind The Bollocks', it's just a pity that the dubious 'Britpop' era spawned an interminable glut of production line indie chancers. The record opens on the same wave of freefall exhilaration as say, 'Exile On Main Street', (The ROLLING STONES were another oft cited influence), 'ROCK'N'ROLL STAR' with a palpable sense of what it actually means to want fame that badly. The feeling that this was "for real, man", never lets up until the last track fades, a visceral, exhaustive listen and one of the most consistent debut albums ever released. Another highlight from the album, the T.REX-esque nihilism of 'CIGARETTES AND ALCOHOL' was the next single, peaking at No.7 in late '94. Basically, OASIS were like all your favourite bands rolled into one, a kind of potted history of rock, NOEL having a unique talent for constructing classic songs that seemed somehow familiar yet annoyingly difficult to pin down. On top of this, LIAM was a natural, his piercing stare and cooly motionless stage presence coupled with his inimitably lethargic sneer a vital component of OASIS' rock'n'roll juggernaut. That Christmas the band narrowly missed No.1 with the string-laden, overtly BEATLES-esque 'WHATEVER', a poppier effort that hinted at the band's future direction. By this point, OASIS were a headline act, the scramble for tickets that accompanied any announcement of a gig becoming all too familiar over the next few years. As would the brothers' press profile, their loudmouth self-aggrandising and embarrassingly public fisticuffs becoming a regular feature of OASIS' increasingly cartoonish image. The first casualty of the well documented in-fighting was McCARROLL, his place in the drum seat subsequently filled by ALAN WHITE. The boasting was backed up by consistently strong material, however, and in the Spring of '95, OASIS deservedly scored their first No.1 with the soaring, yearning 'SOME MIGHT SAY'. The band's single releases had always been good value for money, the B-sides usually better than most indie bands' half-arsed lead tracks. This release was no exception, containing the affecting 'TALK TONIGHT' (NOEL on vocals) and the brilliant melodic noise of 'ACQUIESCE', arguably one of the group's finest tracks. Thus the stage was set for the media-created battle with the recently revitalised BLUR, both bands releasing a single simultaneously that August. In the event, despite the verbal jousting, BLUR took the top spot with 'Country House', OASIS forced to bite their tongue and, erm, 'ROLL WITH IT' at No.2. The Mancs had the last laugh, however, when their follow-up album '(WHAT'S THE STORY) MORNING GLORY' (1995) proceeded to sell multi-millions, catapulting OASIS into the musical stratosphere alongside U2 etc., something unheard of for a group who started out as, basically, another guitar band from Manchester. While the album lacked the serrated edge and amphetamine rush of the debut, the songwriting was once again faultless, tracks like 'WONDERWALL' (almost a Christmas No.1), 'DON'T LOOK BACK IN ANGER', and 'CHAMPAGNE SUPERNOVA' reflecting a newfound maturity and a more coffee-table friendly pop-rock sound. The rapid ascent of the GALLAGHER's continued the following year, with awards galore and a significant dent into the US market. The latter wasn't achieved without some cost to the band, however, as LIAM and NOEL had their most serious and most widely reported fracas to date, LIAM flying home midway through a US tour amid rumours that the band had split. It was merely a case of another day, another fight however, and the band went on to break British concert attendance records with two sell-out shows at Knebworth in August ('96). Early the following year, NOEL was the featured vocalist on The CHEMICAL BROTHERS' chart-topper, 'Setting Sun', effective psychedelia and right on. Return single in '97, 'D'YOU KNOW WHAT I MEAN?' hit No.1 and was reputed to have amassed UK sales of 162,000 copies on its first day of release (19th July). Shortly afterwards, their third album 'BE HERE NOW' was finally in the shops, the hype and media attention the record (and the brothers) received paying off big-time with a massive selling chart topper (No.2 in America). Probably its finest four minutes, 'STAND BY ME', surprisingly failed to make No.1, the album was also marked as a disappointment by some and was considered underwhelming to say the least. The posturing and epic feel of '(WHAT'S THE STORY) . . .' were still there but the record sounded like a parody of OASIS, if that's not a contradiction in terms. While the album broke records with its first day sales figures, it has hardly achieved the same momentum as its predecessor and if NOEL doesn't come up with material a tad more inspiring next time then its doubtful if OASIS can fully realise their long-held aim to be "best band in the world"; stop-gap collection of B-sides and rarities, 'THE MASTERPLAN' (1998), did little for any obsessed fan who already owned all the singles. In May '99, former drummer TONY McCARROLL won an out of court settlement of half a million £'s (£18m for unpaid royalties was the figure he originally wanted). The old band took time out for the rest of the 90's (BONEHEAD and GUIGSY also bailed out), although the GALLAGHER brothers were never far away from controversy and the tabloids; the year 2000 might just see OASIS fade away after the release of one final album. • **Songwriters:** NOEL, except I AM THE WALRUS (Beatles) / CUM ON FEEL THE NOIZE (Slade) / STREET FIGHTING MAN (Rolling Stones) / FEELIN' LONELY by NOEL (Small Faces). • **Trivia:** NOEL wrote 'SLIDE AWAY' on a Les Gibson guitar, which he bought from friend JOHNNY MARR (ex-Smiths) and which was once the property of PETE TOWNSHEND (The Who). After a long on-off relationship, LIAM married PATSY KENSIT (singer/actress and former estranged wife of Simple Minds voxman, JIM KERR) in 1997.

Album rating: DEFINITELY MAYBE (*10) / (WHAT'S THE STORY) MORNING GLORY? (*10) / BE HERE NOW (*7) / THE MASTERPLAN compilation (*7)

LIAM GALLAGHER (b.21 Sep'72) – vocals / **NOEL GALLAGHER** (b.29 May'67) – guitar / **PAUL 'BONEHEAD' ARTHURS** (b.23 Jun'65) – guitar / **PAUL McGUIGAN** (b.19 May'71) – guitar / **TONY McCARROLL** – drums

	Creation	Epic
Apr 94. (7") (CRE 176) <55332> **SUPERSONIC. / TAKE ME AWAY**	31	Jul94
(12"+=) (CRE 176T) – I will believe (live).		
(cd-s++=) (CRECD 176) – Columbia (demo).		
(re-iss. Nov96 c-s repl.7" as so below; same); hit No.47)		
Jun 94. (7"/c-s) (CRE/+CS 182) **SHAKERMAKER. / D'YER WANNA BE A SPACEMAN?**	11	–
(12"+=) (CRE 182T) – Alive (demo).		
(cd-s++=) (CRECD 182) – Bring it on down (live).		
(re-iss. Nov96; same); hit No.48)		
Aug 94. (7"/c-s) (CRE/+CD 185) **LIVE FOREVER. / UP IN THE SKY (acoustic)**	10	–
(12"+=) (CRE 185T) – Cloudburst.		
(cd-s++=) (CRECD 185) – Supersonic (live).		
(re-iss. Nov96; same); hit No.42)		
Aug 94. (cd/c/d-lp) (CRE CD/MC/LP 169) <66431> **DEFINITELY MAYBE**	1	58 Jan95
– Rock'n'roll star / Shakermaker / Live forever / Up in the sky / Columbia / Supersonic / Bring it down / Digsy's dinner / Cigarettes and alcohol / Slide away / Married with children. (d-lp+=) – Sad song. (re-iss. Nov96 as ' . . .SINGLES BOX – SILVER' cd/5xcd-s-box; CREDM 001/002); hit No.23)		
Oct 94. (7"/c-s) (CRE/+CS 190) **CIGARETTES AND ALCOHOL. / I AM THE WALRUS (live)**	7	–
(12"+=) (CRE 190T) – Fade away.		
(cd-s++=) (CRECD 190) – Listen up.		
(re-iss. Nov96; same); hit No.38)		
Dec 94. (7"/c-s) (CRE/+CS 195) **WHATEVER. / (IT'S GOOD) TO BE FREE**	3	–
(12"+=) (CRE 195T) – Slide away.		
(cd-s++=) (CRECD 195) – Half the world away.		
(re-iss. Nov96; same); hit No.34)		

—— After a punch-up McCARROLL left and was replaced by drummer **ALAN WHITE** (b.26 May'72, London) (ex-IDHA) and brother of STEVE WHITE (long-time sticksman with PAUL WELLER)

Apr 95. (7"/c-s) (CRE/+CS 204) **SOME MIGHT SAY. / TALK TONIGHT**	1	–
(12"+=) (CRE 204T) – Acquiesce.		
(cd-s++=) (CRECD 204) – Headshrinker.		
(re-iss. Nov96; same); hit No.40)		

—— their first 5 singles re-entered UK Top 60 in Jun'95

Aug 95. (7"/c-s) (CRE/+CS 212) **ROLL WITH IT. / IT'S BETTER, PEOPLE**	2	–
(12"+=) (CRE 212T) – Rockin' chair.		
(cd-s+=) (CRECD 212) – Live forever (live).		
(re-iss. Nov96; same)hit No.55)		

Oct 95. (cd/c/d-lp) *(CRE CD/MC/LP 189)* <67351> **(WHAT'S THE STORY) MORNING GLORY?** | 1 | 4 |
– Hello / Roll with it / Wonderwall / Don't look back in anger / Hey now! / Some might say / Cast no shadow / She's electric / Morning glory / Champagne supernova. *(d-lp+=)* – Bonehead's bank holiday. *(re-iss. Nov96 as '...SINGLES BOX – GOLD' cd/5xcd-s-box; CREMG 001/002); hit No.24)*

Oct 95. (7"/c-s) *(CRE/+CS 215)* **WONDERWALL / ROUND ARE WAY** | 2 | - |
(12"+=) (CRE 215T) – The swamp song.
(cd-s+=) (CRECD 215) – The masterplan.
(re-iss. Nov96; same); hit No.36)

Jan 96. (c-s,cd-s) <78216> **WONDERWALL / ROUND ARE WAY / TALK TONIGHT** | - | 8 |

—— NOEL also part of one-off supergroup The SMOKIN' MOJO FILTERS alongside PAUL WELLER and PAUL McCARTNEY. They had Top 20 hit with 'COME TOGETHER'.

Feb 96. (7"/c-s) *(CRE/+CS 221)* <78356> **DON'T LOOK BACK IN ANGER. / STEP OUT** | 1 | - |
(12"+=) (CRE 221T) – Underneath the sky.
(cd-s+=) (CRECD 221) – Cum on feel the noize.
(re-iss. Nov96; same); hit No.53)

Jul 96. (c-s,cd-s) <78356> **DON'T LOOK BACK IN ANGER / CUM ON FEEL THE NOIZE** | - | 55 |

—— NOEL met up with great pensmith and fan! BURT BACHARACH who wanted to do a collaboration. He also refused to accept his Ivor Novello award for best songwriter of the year, after he was told it would be shared with rivals BLUR. In Aug'96, NOEL objected to The SMURFS releasing 'WONDERWALL' on their album.

Jul 97. (7"/c-s) *(CRE/+CS 256)* **D'YOU KNOW WHAT I MEAN? / STAY YOUNG** | 1 | - |
(12"+=) (CRE 256T) – Angel child (demo).
(cd-s++=) (CRESCD 256) – Heroes.

Aug 97. (cd/c/lp) *(CRECD/CCRE/CRELP 219)* <68530> **BE HERE NOW** | 1 | 2 |
– D'you know what I mean? / My big mouth / Magic pie / Stand by me / I hope I think I know / Girl in the dirty shirt / Fade in-out / Don't go away / Be here now / All around the world / It's gettin' better (man) / All around the world (reprise).

Sep 97. (7"/c-s) *(CRE/+CS 278)* **STAND BY ME. / (I GOT) THE FEVER** | 2 | - |
(12"+=) (CRE 278T) – My sister lover.
(cd-s++=) (CRESCD 278) – Going nowhere.

Jan 98. (7"/c-s) *(CRE/+CS 282)* **ALL AROUND THE WORLD. / THE FAME** | 1 | - |
(12"+=) (CRE 282T) – Flashbox.
(cd-s++=) (CRESCD 282) – Street fighting man.

Nov 98. (cd/d-lp)(c) *(CRE CD/LP 241)(C-CRE 241)* <69647> **THE MASTERPLAN** (compilation) | 2 | 51 |
– Acquiesce / Underneath the sky / Talk tonight / Going nowhere / Fade away / The swamp song / I am the walrus / Listen up / Rockin' chair / Half the world away / (It's good) To be free / Stay young / Headshrinker / The masterplan.

—— now without BONEHEAD who left after supplying his part to the forthcoming album (GUIGSY also bailed out, his replacement being **ANDY BELL** (ex-HURRICANE #1, ex-RIDE)

—— In Oct'99, LIAM GALLAGHER was credited with STEVE CRADDOCK (of OCEAN COLOUR SCENE) on the UK Top 10 (JAM) tribute double-A side single, 'CARNATION' (flipped with BUFFALO TOM and 'Going Underground')

OCEAN COLOUR SCENE

Formed: Moseley, Birmingham, England . . .mid-'89 out of The FANATICS, by SIMON FOWLER, DAMON MINCHELLA and OSCAR HARRISON, who released a one-off '45 for the 'Chapter 22' label before recruiting BOYS' guitarist STEVE CRADOCK. In the summer of 1990, OCS found manager JOHN MOSTYN, who signed them to his new '!Phffft' stable. A debut track, 'SWAY', helped secure a joint venture with 'Phonogram' for a follow-up, 'YESTERDAY TODAY'. The latter track breached the Top 50 in March '91, and, just when it seemed as if a breakthrough was imminent, '!Phffft' was sold during the recording of their JIMMY MILLER-produced debut album. Now on 'Fontana', the momentum was lost as they re-recorded the whole project, a 1992 re-issue of 'SWAY' and the follow-up, 'GIVING IT ALL AWAY' sinking without trace. In April, the aforementioned eponymous album finally surfaced, although it brought criticism for its over-cooked production. After another 45, 'DO YOURSELF A FAVOUR' bombed, the group subsequently found themselves without a recording contract and up to their necks in debt. Aided by lawyer, Michael Thomas, they were successful in persuading Fontana's DAVE BATES to waive the million £'s they were still owing. OCS returned with a support slot to their newfound mate, PAUL WELLER, CRADOCK and FOWLER guested on his Autumn '93 classic 'Wildwood' album; CRADOCK subsequently became an integral part of WELLER's band over the course of the next year. Meanwhile in the summer of '94, OCEAN COLOUR SCENE supported OASIS and completed a 'Fontana' tour of the States supporting HOUSE OF LOVE and The CATHERINE WHEEL. A year later, all group members played for WELLER at some point, with CRADOCK and MINCHELLA guesting on his No.1 album, 'Stanley Road'. 1995 also saw the band recording their long-awaited follow-up album, having earlier signed to 'M.C.A.'. Early in '96 (with WELLER on organ), they scored their first of many Top 20 hits with 'THE RIVERBOAT SONG' (later chosen for Chris Evans' TFI Friday Show theme song). Dropping the indie-dance trappings of old, OCS adopted a heavier, funkier, white-soul/mod sound and a retro image to boot, dominating the charts in the wake of WELLER's massively successful return to a rootsier sound. 'YOU'VE GOT IT BAD' fared even better, followed by a BRENDAN LYNCH-produced album, 'MOSELEY SHOALS' (name of

their own studio), which hit the UK Top 3. The record inevitably featured WELLER on a few other tracks and the man augmented the group on their 'Later With Jools Holland' spot. Two further Top 10 smashes, 'THE DAY WE CAUGHT THE TRAIN' (their classiest so far) and 'THE CIRCLE' were culled from the album, an odds'n'sods collection, 'B-SIDES, SEASIDES & FREERIDES' keeping their profile high prior to the release of new material. A couple of Top 5 hits, 'HUNDRED MILE HIGH CITY' and 'TRAVELLERS TUNE', preceded an Autumn '97 album, 'MARCHIN' ALREADY', a lesser work which nevertheless reached the top of the UK charts. An easy target for the critics, only time will tell whether OCS's retro-lite and almost wholly teenage audience can stay the course. 'ONE FROM THE MODERN' (1999), was the next Top 5 album on the retro production line, OCS defiantly standing by their Mod roots while opener and lead single, 'PROFITS IN PEACE', showed they were a caring type of band. 'SO LOW' was the next single. Enough said.
• **Songwriters:** FOWLER lyrics / group music; except DO YOURSELF A FAVOUR (Stevie Wonder & Syreeta) / DAYTRIPPER (Beatles) / etc.
Album rating: OCEAN COLOUR SCENE (*6) / MOSELEY SHOALS (*8) / B-SIDES, SEASIDES & FREERIDES collection (*5) / MARCHIN' ALREADY (*6) / ONE FROM THE MODERN (*5)

FANATICS

SIMON FOWLER – vocals, acoustic guitar, harmonica / **DAMON MINCHELLA** – bass / **PAUL WILKES** – guitar / **OSCAR HARRISON** – drums, piano, vocals (ex- ECHO BASE) who repl. CAROLINE BULLOCK

		Chapter 22	not iss.
Mar 89. (12"ep) *(12CHAP 38)* **SUBURBAN LOVE SONGS** | | □ | - |
– Suburban love songs / 1.2.3.4. / My brother Sarah / Tight rope.

OCEAN COLOUR SCENE

STEVE CRADOCK – guitars, piano, vocals (ex-BOYS; late 80's mods) repl. WILKES

		!Phffft	not iss.
Sep 90. (7") *(FIT 001)* **SWAY. / TALK ON** | | □ | - |
(ext-12"+=/ext-cd-s+=) (FITX/FITCD 001) – One of these days.
Mar 91. (7") *(FIT 002)* **YESTERDAY TODAY. / ANOTHER GIRL'S NAME / FLY ME** | 49 | □ |
(12"+=/cd-s+=) (FITX/FITCD 002) – No one says.

		Fontana	not iss.
Feb 92. (7") *(OCSS 1)* **SWAY. / MY BROTHER SARAH** | | □ | - |
(12"+=/cd-s+=) (OCS 112/CD1) – Mona Lisa eyes / Bellechoux.
Apr 92. (7") *(OCSS 2)* **GIVING IT ALL AWAY. / THIRD SHADE OF GREEN** | | □ | - |
(12"+=/cd-s+=) (OCS 212/CD2) – Flowers / Don't play.
Apr 92. (cd/c/lp) *(<512269-2/-4/-1>)* **OCEAN COLOUR SCENE** | | □ | □ Sep92 |
– Talk on / How about you / Giving it all away / Justine / Do yourself a favour / Third shade of green / Sway / Penny pinching rainy Heaven days / One of these days / Is she coming home / Blue deaf ocean / Reprise. *(re-iss. Sep96, hit UK 54)*
May 92. (7") *(OCSS 3)* **DO YOURSELF A FAVOUR. / THE SEVENTH FLOOR** | | □ | - |
(12"+=/cd-s+=) (OCS 312/CD3) – Patsy in green / Suspended motion.

		M.C.A.	M.C.A.
Feb 96. (7"/c-s) *(MCS/+C 40021)* **THE RIVERBOAT SONG. / SO SAD** | 15 | - |
(cd-s+=) (MCSTD 40021) – Charlie Brown says.
Apr 96. (c-s) *(MCSTD 40036)* <55217> **YOU'VE GOT IT BAD / I WANNA STAY ALIVE WITH YOU** | 7 | □ Jul96 |
(cd-s+=) (MCSTD 40036) – Robin Hood / Huckleberry Grove.
(cd-s) (MCSXD 40036) – ('A'demo) / Here in my heart / Men of such opinion / Beautiful losers.
Apr 96. (cd/c/d-lp) *(<MCD/MCC/MCA 60008>)* **MOSELEY SHOALS** | 2 | - |
– The riverboat song / The day we caught the train / The circle / Lining your pockets / Fleeting mind / Forty past midnight / One for the road / It's my shadow / Policeman and pirates / Downstream / You've got it bad / Get away.
Jun 96. (c-s) *(MCSC 40046)* **THE DAY WE CAUGHT THE TRAIN / THE CLOCK STRUCK 15 HOURS AGO** | 4 | - |
(cd-s+=) (MCSTD 40046) – I need a love song / Chicken bones and stones.
(cd-s) (MCSXD 40046) – ('A'acoustic) / Travellers tune / Justine.
Sep 96. (c-s) *(MCSC 40077)* **THE CIRCLE / MRS JONES** | 6 | - |
(cd-s+=) (MCSTD 40077) – Cool cool water / Top of the world.
(cd-s) (MCSXD 40077) – ('A'acoustic) / Chelsea walk / Alibis / Daytripper (live).
Mar 97. (cd/c/d-lp) *(<MCD/MCC/MCA 60034>)* **B SIDES • SEASIDES & FREERIDES** (compilation) | 4 | - |
– Huckleberry grove / The day we caught the train (acoustic) / Mrs Jones / Top of the world / Here in my heart / I wanna stay alive with you / Robin Hood / Chelsea walk / Outside of a circle / The clock struck 15 hours ago / Alibis / Chicken bones and stones / Cool cool water / Charlie Brown says / Day tripper / Beautiful losers.
Jun 97. (7"/c-s) *(MCS/+C 40133)* **HUNDRED MILE HIGH CITY. / THE FACE SMILES BACK EASILY** | 4 | - |
(cd-s+=) (MCSTD 40133) – Falling to the floor / Hello Monday.
Aug 97. (7"/c-s) *(MCS/+C 40144)* <Alex 6055> **TRAVELLERS TUNE / SONG FOR THE FRONT ROW** | 5 | □ Apr98 |
(cd-s+=) (MCSTD 40144) – On the way home / All God's children need travelling shoes.
Sep 97. (cd/c/d-lp) *(<MCD/MCC/MCA 60048>)* **MARCHIN' ALREADY** | 1 | - |
– Hundred mile high city / Better day / Travellers tune / Big star / Debris road / Besides yourself / Get blown away / Tele he's not talking / Foxy's folk faced / All up / Spark and Cindy / Half a dream away / It's a beautiful thing. *(<also enhanced-cd; MCD 60053>)*
Nov 97. (7"/c-s) *(MCS/+C 40151)* **BETTER DAY. / THE BEST BET ON CHINASKI** | 9 | - |
(cd-s+=) (MCSTD 40151) – On and on.
Feb 98. (7"/c-s) *(MCS/+C 40157)* **IT'S A BEAUTIFUL THING. / MARINERS WAY** | 12 | □ |
(cd-s+=) (MCSTD 40157) – Going nowhere for a while / Expensive chair.
(above featured singer, P.P. ARNOLD)

		Island	Polygram
Aug 99.	(c-s/7") *(C+/IS 757)* **PROFIT IN PEACE. / IF YOU GET YOUR WAY**	13	
	(cd-s+=) *(CID 757)* – Flood tide rising.		
Sep 99.	(cd/c/d-lp) *(CID/ICT/ILPS 8090)* **ONE FROM THE MODERN**	4	

– Profit in peace / So low / I am the news / No one at all / Families / Step by step / July / Jane she got excavated / Emily Chambers / Soul driver / The waves / I won't get grazed.

—— In Oct'99, STEVE CRADDOCK was credited with LIAM GALLAGHER (of OASIS) on UK Top 10 (JAM) tribute double-A single, 'CARNATION' (flipped with 'Going Underground' by BUFFALO TOM)

Nov 99.	(c-s/7"/cd-s) *(CIS/IS/CID 759)* **SO LOW. / HOPING YOU'RE MAKING IT TOO**	34	

(cd-s+=) *(CIDX 759)* – Soul driver / Jane she got excavated.

Phil OCHS

Born: 19 Dec'40, El Paso, Texas, USA. OCHS was raised by Scottish/Polish parents, his family finally settling in Perrysburg, Ohio where he was brought up. Having spent time following his family tradition in the military, OCHS subsequently studied journalism at the local state university. Together with his room-mate JIM GLOVER, (through whom he became more aware of economics and socialist politics), he formed country-folk duo, The SUNDOWNERS. The group's lifespan was brief, OCHS subsequently heading for the emerging folk scene in New York's Greenwich Village. Throwing himself headlong into radical politics, OCHS was soon making waves following his solo debut on 15th March '63 supporting JOHN HAMMOND. He soon built up a grassroots following, playing many benefit gigs as well as the prestigious Newport Folk Festival. In 1964, he was signed to 'Elektra' by owner Jac Holzman, making his vinyl debut early the following year with acoustic folk set 'ALL THE NEWS THAT'S FIT TO SING'. A strident set of protest songs, OCHS proved himself an intelligent, witty and inspiring voice of dissent on such topical issues as the Cuban crisis and the spiralling Vietnam war, the record making the US Top 100 despite a TV ban. Later that summer, fellow folkie, JOAN BAEZ, took his more reflective 'THERE BUT FOR FORTUNE' into the UK Top 10, although such success would prove consistently elusive for OCHS himself. The title track of his next album, 'I AIN'T MARCHING ANYMORE' (1965) became an anthem for the 60's anti-war movement, although by 'PHIL OCHS IN CONCERT' (1966), the singer/songwriter was beginning to move away from direct political comment with tracks like the gentle 'CHANGES' and the aforementioned 'THERE BUT FOR FORTUNE'. Also including the mordant humour of 'LOVE ME, I'M A LIBERAL', the record went on to become one of OCHS' biggest sellers. However, with rival BOB DYLAN spearheading the newly electrified folk-rock explosion along with The BYRDS, OCHS decided to pursue a more ambitious direction. Relocating to L.A., the singer secured a new deal with 'A&M' through the help of brother/manager, MICHAEL, releasing 'PLEASURES OF THE HARBOR' in 1968. Something of a departure to say the least, the album saw OCHS' songs dressed up in sweeping orchestral arrangements. An eclectic collection, OCHS seemed to be lacking a musical focus, 'CROSS MY HEART' and 'FLOWER LADY' among the poppiest releases of his career while the title track and the epic 'CRUCIFIXION' were intensely introspective. There was also a nod to the satire of old with the jaunty 'OUTSIDE A SMALL CIRCLE OF FRIENDS'. While the album succeeded in raising the ire of the more traditional folkies, OCHS soldiered bravely on with 'TAPE FROM CALIFORNIA' (1968) a more consistent set combining the political and the personal. Among the highlights were 'WHITE BOOTS MARCHING IN A YELLOW LAND' (another Vietnam comment) and the seven minute plus 'JOE HILL', a compelling tale of a courageous but ultimately doomed union man. The same description could easily apply to OCHS himself. Severely troubled by the assassination of Bobby Kennedy and the ensuing riots at the 1968 democratic convention, OCHS became increasingly disillusioned. 'REHEARSALS FOR RETIREMENT' (1969) didn't make for easy listening, an angry, embittered record but all the more powerful for it. The sentiments of 'I KILL THEREFORE I AM' remain every bit as vital today as they were then while 'ANOTHER AGE' was almost pleading in tone. Like most of his 'A&M' releases, the record failed to take off and OCHS dreamed up the ill-advised idea of creating a persona which combined the rock'n'roll showmanship of ELVIS and the political fire of CHE GUEVARA. Nevertheless, the self-deprecatingly titled 'PHIL OCHS GREATEST HITS' (1970) remains arguably his most affecting release. Produced by Hollywood maverick, VAN DYKE PARKS, the record consisted of rollicking country-rock and more elaborate, PARKS-esque creations. The Spector-like, folk/gospel hybrid of 'ONE WAY TICKET HOME' was breathtaking, likewise the poignant, piano-led ballad, 'JIM DEAN OF INDIANA'. As for reclaiming his audience, however, the record was a non-starter. Touring the album, OCHS wore a gold lame suit onstage in keeping with his new concept. The audience remained unimpressed however, booing the BUDDY HOLLY medleys which OCHS had bizarrely brought into his stage show. A live document of one particularly confrontational show was later released in 1975 as 'GUNFIGHT AT CARNEGIE HALL'. OCHS subsequently went into semi-retirement, losing his self-belief as an artist although he did travel to South America, playing a benefit gig in aid of the (then) recently overthrown Chilean leader. He also travelled to Africa where, in addition to cutting a couple of singles, 'NIKO MCHUMBA NGOBE' and 'BWATUE' (pre-empting PAUL SIMON by more than a decade) he was mysteriously

attacked. His vocal chords were seriously damaged in the incident and this plunged OCHS further into depression and bouts of alcoholism. Finally, on the 9th of April, 1976, the singer hanged himself at his sister's home, tragically ending a career that had begun so buoyantly and full of hope. Music and politics, politics and life, were obviously inseparable to OCHS and his struggle for truth, for social justice was among the most courageous of the era.

Album rating: ALL THE NEWS THAT'S FIT TO SING (*7) / I AIN'T MARCHING ANYMORE (*7) / PHIL OCHS IN CONCERT (*7) / PLEASURES OF THE HARBOR (*7) / TAPE FROM CALIFORNIA (*6) / REHEARSALS FOR RETIREMENT (*6) / PHIL OCHS GREATEST HITS fresh recordings (*6) / GUNFIGHT AT CARNEGIE HALL (*5) / CHORDS OF FAME compilation (*7) / A TOAST TO THOSE WHO ARE GONE collection (*5)

PHIL OCHS – vocals, acoustic guitar / with **DANNY KALE** – acoustic guitar

		Elektra	Elektra
Mar 65.	(lp) *(EKL 269)* <7269> **ALL THE NEWS THAT'S FIT TO SING**		Nov64

– One more parade / The thresher / Talking Vietnam / Lou Marsh / Power and the glory / Celia / The bells / Automation song / Ballad of William Worthy / Knock on the door / Talking Cuban crisis / Bound for glory / Too many martyrs / What's that I hear. *(re-iss. Oct87 on 'Edsel'; ED 247)* *(re-iss. May89 on 'Carthage' lp/c; CG LP/C 4427)* *(cd-iss. May94 on 'Hannibal'+=; HNCD 4427)* – Bullets of Mexico.

Aug 65.	(lp) *(EKL 287)* <7287> **I AIN'T MARCHING ANYMORE**		May65

– I ain't marching anymore / In the heat of the summer / Draft dodger rag / That's what I want to hear / That was the president / Iron lady / The highway man / Links on the chain / Hills of West Virginia / The men behind the guns / Talking Birmingham jam / Ballad of the carpenter / Days of decision / Here's to the state of Mississippi. *(re-iss. May89 on 'Carthage' lp/c; CG LP/C 4422)* *(cd-iss. May94 on 'Hannibal'; HNCD 4422)*

Dec 65.	(7") *(EKSN 45002)* **I AIN'T MARCHING ANYMORE. / THAT WAS THE PRESIDENT**		
May 66.	(lp) *(EKL 310)* <7310> **PHIL OCHS IN CONCERT** (live)		Feb66

– I'm going to say it now / Bracero / Ringing of revolution / Is there anybody here? / Canons of Christianity / There but for fortune / Cops of the world / Santo Domingo / Changes / Love me, I'm a Liberal / When I'm gone.

		A&M	A&M
Nov 67.	(7") **CROSS MY HEART. / FLOWER LADY**	-	
Jan 68.	(lp; mono/stereo) *(AML/+S 913)* <4133> **PLEASURES OF THE HARBOR**		Oct67

– Cross my heart / Flower lady / Outside of a small circle of friends / I've had her / Miranda / The party / Pleasures of the harbor / The crucifixion.

Jan 68.	(7") *(AMS 716)* **OUTSIDE A SMALL CIRCLE OF FRIENDS. / MIRANDA**		
Jul 69.	(7") **THE WAR IS OVER. / THE HARDER THEY FALL**	-	
Oct 68.	(lp) *(AMLS 919)* <4148> **TAPE FROM CALIFORNIA**		Jul68

– Tape from California / White boots marching in a yellow land / Half a century high / Joe Hill / The war is over / The harder they fall / When in Rome / Floods of Florence.

May 69.	(lp) *(AMLS 934)* <4181> **REHEARSALS FOR RETIREMENT**		

– Pretty smart on my part / The doll house / I kill therefore I am / William Butler Yeats visits Lincoln Park and escapes unscathed / My life / The scorpion, departs but never returns / The world began in Eden and ended in Los Angeles / Doesn't Lenny live here anymore / Another age / Rehearsals for retirement.

Mar 70.	(lp) *(AMLS 973)* <4253> **PHIL OCHS GREATEST HITS** (not a compilation)		

– One way ticket home / Jim Dean of Indiana / My kingdom for a car / Boy in Ohio / Gas station women / Chords of fame / Ten cents a coup / Bach, Beethoven, Mozart and me / Basket in the pool / No more songs. *(re-iss. Jun86 on 'Edsel'; ED 201)* *(cd-iss. Jul90; EDCD 201)*

Mar 70.	(7") **ONE WAY TICKET HOME. / MY KINGDOM FOR A CAR**	-	

—— PHIL semi-retired after recording Apr'70 live album 'GUNFIGHT AT CARNEGIE HALL'. It was only issued in Canada 1975.

Sep 72.	(7") **KANSAS CITY BOMBER. / GAS STATION WOMEN**	-	
Feb 74.	(7") **HERE'S TO THE STATE OF RICHARD NIXON. / POWER & THE GLORY**	-	
1974.	(7") **BWATUE. / NIKO MCHUMBA NGOMBE**	-	Kenya
1975.	(lp) <9010> **GUNFIGHT AT CARNEGIE HALL** (live)		

– Mona Lisa / I ain't marchin' anymore / Oakie from Meskogee / Chords of fame / Buddy Holly medley:- Not fade away – I'm gonna love you too – Think it over – Oh boy – Everyday – It's so easy – Not fade away / Pleasures of the harbor / Tape from California / Elvis medley:- My baby left me – I'm ready – Heartbreak hotel – All shook up – Are you lonesome tonight – My baby left me (encore) / A fool such as I.

—— While visiting friend/singer/protester Victor Jaro in Chile, he was robbed and suffered throat damage which prevented him from singing. After bouts of heavy drinking and schizophrenia, he hanged himself on 9th Apr'76.

– compilations, others, etc. –

1976.	(lp) *Folkways*; <5320> **SINGS FOR BROADSIDES**	-	
1976.	(lp) *Folkways*; <5321> **BROADSIDE MAGAZINE INTERVIEWS**	-	
Jan 77.	(d-lp) *A&M*; *(AMLM 64599)* <4599> **CHORDS OF FAME**	-	1974

– I ain't marchin' anymore / No more parades / Draft dodger rag / Here's to the state of Richard Nixon / The bells / Bound of glory / Too many martyrs / There but for fortune / I'm going to say it now / Santo Domingo / Changes / Is there anybody here? / Love me, I'm a Liberal / When I'm gone / Outside of a small circle of friends / Pleasures of the harbor / Tape from California / Chords of fame / Crucifixion / War is over / Jim Dean of Indiana / The power and the glory / Flower lady / No more songs.

1980.	(lp) *Folkways*; <5362> **THE BROADSIDE TAPES**	-	

(UK-iss.Mar95 on 'Smithsonian Folkways' cd/c; SFW CD/MC 40008)

Mar 88.	(lp) *Edsel*; *(ED 242)* / *Rhino*; **A TOAST TO THOSE WHO ARE GONE** (lost tapes)		1986

– Do what I have to do / Ballad of Billie Sol / Coloured town / A.M.A. song / William Moore / Paul Crump / Going down to Mississippi / I'll be there / Ballad of Oxford / No Christmas in Kentucky / A toast to those who are gone / I'm tired / City boy / Song of my returning. *(cd-iss. 1995 on 'Diablo'; DIAB 813)*

May 89. (d-lp/c/cd) *Elektra; (K 960832-1/-4/-2)* **THERE BUT FOR FORTUNE** (some live 1965-66)
Mar 91. (cd) *Rhino;* **THERE AND NOW: LIVE IN VANCOUVER 1968** (live)
Jun 97. (d-cd) *A&M; (540 728-2)* **THE LAST AMERICAN TROUBADOUR**

Hazel O'CONNOR (dig out; Great Alt & Indie . . .)

Sinead O'CONNOR

Born: 8 Dec'66, Glenageary, Ireland. Raised in Dublin, her parents divorced when she was 8, and she was later sent to a Dominican nun-run centre for girls with behavioural problems. In 1985, after attending Dublin's College of Music, she joined local band TON TON MACOUTE, where she met boyfriend and future manager, FACHTNA O'CEALLAIGH. In 1986, he arranged for her to guest on U2's The EDGE's soundtrack album, 'Captive'. She was soon spotted by Nigel Grainge and Chris Hill of 'Ensign' records, who signed her up later that year. In April the following year, she guested for stablemates WORLD PARTY (aka KARL WALLINGER) on album 'Private Revolution'. Finally at the end of '87, she issued her debut solo 45, 'TROY', while early the following year, SINEAD scored her first Top 20 hit with 'MANDINKA', reactivating sales of the previously debut album, 'THE LION AND THE COBRA'. The record presented O'CONNOR as a shaven-headed, angel-faced nightingale in wolf's clothing, her soul-wrenching vocals capable of conveying the rawest of emotions from visceral rage to heartfelt compassion. Self-produced, the record also revealed the Irish maverick to be adept at flitting between contrasting musical styles with surprising ease, from the hypnotic pop of the aforementioned 'MANDINKA' to the suggestive rhythmic pulse of 'I WANT YOUR (HANDS ON ME)'. But while she proved to be a fiercely independent, original pop star, O'CONNOR applied the same passion to fanning the flames of controversy, the first furore of many coming when she allegedly defended the IRA. At this point, O'CONNOR was perhaps more famous for her outspokeness than her music, although that changed with the massive worldwide (also transatlantic No.1) success of 'NOTHING COMPARES 2 U' in early 1990. A cover of an obscure PRINCE song with arrangements by NELLEE HOOPER, the track's languid atmospherics provided a perfect platform for O'CONNOR's tear-soaked vocals. The song catapulted her into the superstar bracket and the accompanying album, 'I DO NOT WANT WHAT I HAVEN'T GOT' (1990), sold by the million. Recorded amid the break-up of her first marriage, the album was a largely downbeat affair with the angry intensity of old strangely muted. O'CONNOR the fiesty firebrand was back with a vengeance in 1992, however, the singer infamously ripping up a photo of Pope John Paul II on American TV show, 'Saturday Night Live'. Hardly endearing her to the country's Catholic population, this incident, combined with her earlier refusal to play a show which began with a rendition of the American national anthem, undoubtedly contributed to the strength of the anti-SINEAD feelings running high at the Madison Square Garden BOB DYLAN tribute in October that year. Booed off stage, a tearful O'CONNOR was led away by KRIS KRISTOFFERSON in what must've been one of the most harrowing moments of her career. The attendant press overkill all but obscured the fact she actually had a new album on the shelves, a covers set of vintage torch ballads entitled 'AM I NOT YOUR GIRL'. While the record made the UK Top 10, it unsurprisingly failed to perform quite so well in the States. 1993 brought trauma of a more personal nature; O'CONNOR's allegations of abuse by her mother resulted in a family feud with her father and brother and a subsequent breakdown and suicide attempt. Facing her demons head-on, the singer recorded some of her most nakedly uncompromising material to date for 'UNIVERSAL MOTHER' (1994), the often bleak starkness of the lyrics contrasting with the warmth of the tranquil arrangements and melodies. Although critically acclaimed, the album failed to match the sales of her previous efforts and her subsequent refusal to give interviews led to a drop in profile over the ensuing few years. The first fruits of her new deal with 'Columbia', even the defiant 'THIS IS A REBEL SONG' failed to charge up the enthusiasm of the record buying public in late '97. While many may point out that O'CONNOR is her own worst enemy, there's no denying the potential of her talents and it'd be a tragedy if this survivor were to be confined to the musical margins. • **The covers:** YOU DO SOMETHING TO ME + MY HEART BELONGS TO DADDY (Cole Porter) / SOMEONE TO WATCH OVER ME (Ira Gershwin) / DAMN YOUR EYES (Etta James) / SECRET LOVE (Doris Day) / ALL APOLOGIES (Nirvana). Her 1992 album was filled with covers originally sung by; WHY DONT YOU DO RIGHT? (Julie London; J.McCoy) / BEWITCHED, BOTHERED AND BEWILDERED (Ella Fitzgerald; L.Hart & R.Rodgers) / SECRET LOVE + BLACK COFFEE (Sarah Vaughan; F.Webster & S.Burke) / SUCCESS HAS MADE A FAILURE OF OUR HOME (Loretta Lynn; J.Mullins) / DON'T CRY FOR ME ARGENTINA (Elaine Page; Tim Rice & Andrew Lloyd Webber) / I WANT TO BE LOVED BY YOU (Marilyn Monroe; H.Stothart, H.Ruby & B.Kalmar) / GLOOMY SUNDAY (Billie Holiday; L.Javor, R.Seress & Lewis) / LOVE LETTERS (Alison Moyet; E.Heyman & V.Young) / HOW INSENSITIVE (Astrud Gilberto; V.de Morales, A.C.Jobim & Gimbel) / SCARLET RIBBONS (her mum & dad; J.Segal & E.Danzig). She co-writes w/COULTER or REYNOLDS and sample merchant TIM SIMENON for return 1994 album. Other covers; YOU MAKE ME FEEL SO REAL (Van Morrison).
Album rating: THE LION AND THE COBRA (*7) / I DO NOT WANT WHAT I HAVEN'T GOT (*9) / AM I NOT YOUR GIRL? (*5) / UNIVERSAL

MOTHER (*6) / SO FAR . . . THE BEST OF SINEAD O'CONNOR compilation (*8)

SINEAD O'CONNOR – vocals (ex-TON TON MACOUTE) / with **ENYA + MARCO PIRRONI**

	Ensign	Chrysalis
Oct 87. (7"/12") *(ENY/+X 610)* **TROY. / STILL LISTENING**		
Nov 87. (lp/c)(cd) *(CHEN/ZCHEN 7)(CCD 1612) <41612>* **THE LION AND THE COBRA**	27	36

– Jackie / Mandinka / Jerusalem / Just like U said it would B / Never get old / Troy / I want your (hands on me) / Drink before the war / Just call me Joe. *(re-dist.Jan90 hit UK No.37; same)*

| Dec 87. (7") *(ENY 611)* **MANDINKA. / DRINK BEFORE THE WAR** | 17 | |

(ext.12"+=) *(ENYX 611)* – ('A'dub mix).
(cd-s++=) *(ENYCD 611)* – Still listening.
(12"+=) *(ENYXR 611)* – ('A'-Jake's remix).

Apr 88. (7"; by SINEAD O'CONNOR with MC LYTE) *(ENY 613)*
I WANT YOUR (HANDS ON ME). / JUST CALL ME JOE
(12"+=/cd-s+=) *(ENY X/CD 613)* – ('A'dance) / ('A'-Street mix).
(12"+=) *(ENYXR 613)* – ('A'-Knee-trembler mix) / ('A'-Hickey on the neck mix).

Oct 88. (7") *(ENY 618)* **JUMP IN THE RIVER. / NEVER GET OLD** (live)
(12"+=/cd-s+=) *(ENY X/CD 618)* – ('A'duet with KAREN FINLAY).

—— Early 1989, she appeared on THE THE's album 'Mind Bomb', singing on 'Kingdom Of Rain'.

	Ensign	Ensign
Jan 90. (7"/7"box) *(ENY/+B 630) <23488>* **NOTHING COMPARES 2 U. / JUMP IN THE RIVER**	1	1 Mar90

(12"+=/cd-s+=) *(ENY X/CD 630)* – Jump in the river (instrumental).

| Mar 90. (cd)(c/lp) *(CCD 1759)(Z+/CHEN 14)* **I DO NOT WANT WHAT I HAVEN'T GOT** | 1 | 1 |

– Feel so different / I an stretched on your grave / Three babies / The Emperor's new clothes / Black boys in mopeds / Nothing compares 2 U / Jump in the river / You cause as much sorrow / The last day of our acquaintance / I do not want what I haven't got. *(re-iss. cd Mar94;)*

| Jul 90. (7"/7"box) *(ENY/+B 633) <23528>* **THE EMPEROR'S NEW CLOTHES. / WHAT DO YOU WANT** | 31 | 60 Jun90 |

(c-s+=) *(ENYMC 633)* – I am stretched on your grave.
(12"/cd-s) *(ENY X/CD 633)* – ('A'-Hank Shocklee remix) / I am stretched on your grave (Apple Brightness mix) / ('A'-Night until morning dub mix).

| Oct 90. (7") *(ENY 635)* **THREE BABIES. / TROY** (live) | 42 | |

(c-s+=/12"+=/cd-s+=) *(ENY MC/X/CD 635)* – Damn your eyes / The value of ignorance.

| May 91. (7") *(ENY 646)* **MY SPECIAL CHILD. / NOTHING COMPARES 2 U** (live) | 42 | |

(12"+=/cd-s+=) *(ENY X/CD 646)* – ('A'instrumental) / The Emperor's new clothes (live).
(12"+=)(c-s+=)(cd-s+=) – Standing on your grave.

| Dec 91. (7"/cd-s) *(ENY/+CD 652)* **SILENT NIGHT. / IRISH WAYS & IRISH LAWS** (live) | 60 | - |

—— Early in 1991, she was the first ever person to refuse her Grammy for alternative 1990 album. She protested about anti-legalizing Irish abortion on TV and press. After earlier ripping a photo of Pope John Paul II on US Saturday Night Live, she was booed off-stage (Oct92) at a Bob Dylan tribute concert at Madison Square Garden. Due to crowd noise which drowned out backing band, she eventually sang unaccompanied a Bob Marley! song 'War'. She announced that month she was to retire, although thankfully she retracted press statements by late '92.

—— now with **CHRIS PARKER** – drums / **DAVID FINCK** – bass / **RICHARD TEE** – piano / **IRA SIEGAL** – guitar / **DAVE LEBOLT** – synthesizer / plus a host of saxists, flautists, violinists, trumpeters & backing singers

| Sep 92. (7"/c-s) *(ENY/+MC 656)* **SUCCESS HAS MADE A FAILURE OF OUR HOME. / YOU DO SOMETHING TO ME** | 18 | |

(cd-s++=) *(ENYCD 656)* – I want to be loved by you.
(cd-s) *(ENYSCD 656)* – ('A'side) / Someone to watch over me / My heart belongs to daddy.

| Sep 92. (cd)(c/lp) *(CCD 1952)(Z+/CHEN 1952) <21952>* **AM I NOT YOUR GIRL?** | 6 | 27 |

– Why don't you do right? / Bewitched, bothered and bewildered / Secret love / Black coffee / Success has made a failure of our lives / Don't cry for me Argentina / I want to be loved by you / Gloomy Sunday / Love letters / How insensitive / Scarlet ribbons / Don't cry for me Argentina (instrumental).

—— In Oct'92, she collaborated on MARXMAN single 'Ship Ahoy'.

| Dec 92. (7"/c-s) *(ENY/+MC 657)* **DON'T CRY FOR ME ARGENTINA. / AVE MARIA** | 53 | |

(cd-s++=) *(CDENY 657)* – Scarlet ribbons.
(cd-s) *(CDENYS 657)* – ('A'side) / Love letters / Scarlet ribbons.

—— In Jun'93, she was credited on WILLIE NELSON single 'Don't Give Up'.

| Feb 94. (c-s/7") *(C+/IS 588)* **YOU MADE ME THE THIEF OF YOUR HEART. / THE FATHER AND HIS WIFE THE SPIRIT** | 42 | |

(12"+=/cd-s+=) *(12IS/CID 588)* – ('A'mixes).
(above single from film 'In The Name Of The Father'; on 'Island')

—— now with **JOHN REYNOLDS** – drums / **PHIL COULTER** – piano / **DAVE CLAYTON** – keyboards / **MARCO PIRRONI + VAN GILLIANO** – guitar / **TIM SIMENON** etc.

| Sep 94. (cd/c/lp) *(CD/TC+/CHEN 34)* **UNIVERSAL MOTHER** | 19 | 37 |

– Fire on Babylon / John I love you / My darling child / Am I human? / Red football / All apologies / A perfect Indian / Scorn not his simplicity / All babies / In this heart / Tiny grief song / Famine / Thank you for hearing me.

| Nov 94. (12"/c-s/cd-s) *(12/TC/CD ENY 662)* **THANK YOU FOR HEARING ME. / FIRE ON BABYLON** (remix) | 13 | |

(cd-s) *(CDENYS 662)* – ('A'side) / I believe in you / Streets of London / House of the rising sun.

—— In Apr'95, she duetted with SHANE MacGOWAN on his 'HAUNTED' hit.

| Aug 95. (c-s/cd-s) *(TC/CD ENY 663)* **FAMINE (extended) / FAMINE / ALL APOLOGIES** | 51 | |

(12") *(12ENY 663)* – ('A'extended) / Fire on Babylon (M Beat remix).

May 97. (c-ep/12"ep/cd-ep) *(TC/12/CD CHS 5051)* **GOSPEL OAK EP**

	Chrysalis	Chrysalis
	28	

– This is to mother you / I am enough for myself / Petit poulet / 4 my love.

Nov 97. (cd/c) *(821581-2/-4)* **SO FAR . . . THE BEST OF SINEAD**
O'CONNOR (compilation)

	28	

– Herpone / Mandinka / Jackie / Troy / Nothing compares 2 U / I am stretched on
your grave / Emperor's new clothes / Last day of our acquaintance / Success has
made a failure of our home / Thank you for hearing me / Fire on Babylon / John I
love you / Perfect Indian / You made me the thief of your heart / Empire / This is a
rebel song.

Nov 97. (c-s) *(665 299-4)* **THIS IS A REBEL SONG / REDEMPTION**
SONG

	Columbia	Columbia
	60	

(cd-s+=) *(665 299-2)* – Fire on Babylon.
(cd-s) *(665 299-5)* – ('A'side) / Thank you for hearing me / Last day of our
acquaintance.

OFFSPRING

Formed: Orange County, California, USA ... 1984 out of MANIC
SUBSIDAL and CLOWNS OF DEATH, by main songwriter DEXTER
HOLLAND and GREG KRIESEL. With the addition of JAMES LILJA
and KEVIN 'NOODLES' WASSERMAN they adopted THE OFFSPRING
moniker, releasing a debut 45, 'I'LL BE WAITING' on the self-financed
'Black' label. With RON WELTY subsequently replacing LILJA, the band
began working on demo material, eventually going into the studio with
Thom Wilson. The results eventually surfaced in the form of the eponymous
'OFFSPRING' (1989), issued on the 'Nitro' label. An ambitious and
experimental fusion of exotic hardcore, its schizoid ramblings not endearing
the band to many outside the scene. The next few years were tough for the band
as they struggled to find a steady record deal, even tougher for NOODLES
who was stabbed at a benefit concert. They eventually found a sympathetic ear
in the form of BRAD GUREWITZ (ex-BAD RELIGION) and his burgeoning
'Epitaph' operation, releasing a much improved follow-up album, 'IGNITION'
in 1992. However, it wasn't until 1994 and their follow-up, 'SMASH', that
OFFSPRING pogo'd into the US charts. Hard on the heels of GREEN DAY's
phenomenal worldwide success, the 4-piece found a very successful niche in
the larger than life, lads-together ska-core punk rock complete with dayglo
choruses and brutally addictive hooklines. The album went on to sell over a
million copies in the States and finally gained deserved recognition in Britain,
especially after the 'SELF ESTEEM' track became a Top 40 smash early
'95! Over the course of the ensuing two years, OFFSPRING almost became
part of 'Columbia's roster, although in the end a follow-up, 'INXAY ON
THE HOMBRE' appeared on 'Epitaph' in 1997. Building on the winning
formula of its predecessor, the album scored another transatlantic Top 20. The
dreadlocked DEXTER subsequently teamed up with JELLO BIAFRA (ex-
DEAD KENNEDYS) to play some charity gigs under the banner of F.S.U.
in aid of the homeless, human rights, etc. Album No.5 'AMERICANA' was
delivered late in '98, nobody in their right minds prophecising it would
unearth a UK chart-topper in the shape of fun novelty 45, 'PRETTY FLY
(FOR A WHITE GUY)'. More of the same was to follow, British hits, 'THE
KIDS AREN'T ALRIGHT' and 'SHE'S GOT ISSUES', boosting sales of an
otherwise flagging album – a pretty fly move, indeed! • **Covered:** HEY JOE
(hit; Jimi Hendrix) / SMASH IT UP (Damned) / KILLBOY POWERHEAD
(Didjits).

Album rating: THE OFFSPRING (*4) / IGNITION (*6) / SMASH (*7) / IXNAY ON
THE HOMBRE (*5) / AMERICANA (*5)

DEXTER HOLLAND (b. BRYAN HOLLAND, 1966) – vocals, guitar / **NOODLES** (b.
KEVIN WASSERMAN, 4 Feb'63, L.A.) – guitar / **GREG KRIESEL** (b.20 Jan'65, Glendale,
Calif.) – bass / **JAMES LILJA** – drums

	not iss.	Black
1986. (7") **I'LL BE WAITING. /** | - | |

—— **RON WELTY** (b. 1 Feb'71) – drums (ex-FQX) repl. LILJA

	not iss.	Nitro
1989. (lp) *<86460-1>* **THE OFFSPRING** | - | |

– Jennifer lost the war / Elders / Out on patrol / Crossroads / Demons / Beheaded /
Tehran / A thousand days / Black ball / I'll be waiting / Kill the president.
(UK-iss.Nov95 on 'Epitaph' cd/c; E 86460-2/-4)

	not iss.	Plastic Head
1991. (7") *<NEM 38>* **BAGHDAD. /** | - | |

	Epitaph	Epitaph
Oct 92. (cd/c/lp) *<(E 86424-2/-4/-1)>* **IGNITION** | | |

– Session / We are one / Kick him when he's down / Take it like a man / Get it
right / Dirty magic / Hypodermic / Burn it up / No hero / L.A.P.D. / Nothing from
something / Forever and a day.

Sep 94. (cd/c/lp) *<(E 86432-2/-4/-1)>* **SMASH**

	21	4 Apr94

– Time to relax / Nitro (youth energy) / Bad habit / Gotta get away / Genocide /
Something to believe in / Come out and play / Self esteem / It'll be a long time /
Killboy powerhead / What happened to you / So alone / Not the one / Smash.

Sep 94. (12"/cd-s) *(EPUK/+CD 001)* **COME OUT AND PLAY. /**
SESSION / ('A'acoustic)

		-

Oct 94. (7") *<IGN 3H>* *<65572>* **COME OUT AND PLAY. / COME**
OUT AND PLAY
(above on 'Ignition'/<'Phantom'> (below ltd. on 'Flying')

Dec 94. (10"ep) *(GOD 008)* **COME OUT AND PLAY EP**

		-

Feb 95. (c-s/12"/cd-s) *(MC/12/CD HOLE 001)* **SELF ESTEEM. /**
JENNIFER LOST THE WAR / BURN IT UP

	37	-

Aug 95. (7"/c-s/cd-s) *(WOOS 2/+CS/CDS)* **GOTTA GET AWAY. /**
SMASH

	43	-

(above single on 'Out Of Step' UK)

—— In the Spring of '96, they were fighting Epitaph and boss BRETT GUREWITZ for
the right to sign with another label 'Columbia' in the US-only.

Jan 97. (7"m/cd-s) *(6495-7/-2)* **ALL I WANT. / WAY DOWN THE**
LINE

	31	-

(cd-s+=) *(6491-2)* – Smash it up.

Feb 97. (cd/lp) *(6487-2/-1)* *<67810>* **IXNAY ON THE HOMBRE**

	17	9

– Disclaimer / Meaning of life / Mota / Me and my old lady / Cool to hate / Leave
it behind / Gone away / I choose / Intermission / All I want / Way down the line /
Don't pick it up / Amazed / Change the world.

Apr 97. (7"/cd-s) *(6504-7/-2)* **GONE AWAY. / D.U.I.**

	42	-

(cd-s+=) *(6498-2)* – Cool to hate / Hey Joe.

Nov 98. (cd/c) *(491656-2/-4)* *<69661>* **AMERICANA**

	Columbia	Columbia
	10	2

– Welcome / Have you ever / Staring at the sun / Pretty fly (for a white guy) / The
kids aren't alright / Feelings / She's got issues / Walla walla / End of the line / No
brakes / Why don't you get a job? / Americana / Pay the man. *(pic-lp-iss.May99;
491656-0)*

Jan 99. (7"/c-s/cd-s) *(666880-7/-4/-2)* *<41579>* **PRETTY FLY (FOR A**
WHITE GUY). / ('A'-The Geek mix) / NO BRAKES

	1	53 Nov98

Apr 99. (c-s/cd-s) *(667354-4/-2)* *<radio cut>* **WHY DON'T YOU GET**
A JOB? / BEHEADED / WHY DON'T YOU GET A JOB?
(remix by Baka Boyz)

	2	74 Mar99

(cd-s) *(667354-5)* – ('A'remixes).

Aug 99. (c-s) *(667763-4)* **THE KIDS AREN'T ALRIGHT / PRETTY FLY**
(FOR A WHITE GUY) (live)

	11	

(cd-s+=) *(667763-2)* – Why don't you get a job? (live).
(cd-s) *(667763-5)* – ('A'side) / Walla walla (live) / Pretty fly (for a white guy)
(video).

Nov 99. (c-s) *(668377-4)* **SHE'S GOT ISSUES / PRETTY FLY (Baka**
Boyz Low Rider mix)

	41	

(cd-s+=) *(668377-2)* – ('A'side) / Kids aren't alright (Wise Guys mix) / Kids aren't
alright (Wise Guys instrumental).
(cd-s) *(667377-5)* – ('A'side) / All I want (live in Vegas) / Kids aren't alright
(CD-Rom video).

Mary Margaret O'HARA

Born: Toronto, Canada. One of the most enigmatic female singer/songwriters
to have emerged over the last fifteen years, O'HARA's slim but revered body
of work has been something of a well kept secret in a genre that appears to
throw up a new starlet every other week. A graduate of Ontario art college,
she began her musical career in a soul-pop outfit called DOLLARS before
going on to join SONGSHIP, a band which soon changed name to the equally
bad GO DEO CHORUS. During her time with the band, she penned much of
the material which would later surface as her solo album; heard by 'Virgin'
in their GDC demo form, the songs were strong enough to persuade the label
to sign O'HARA as a solo artist. Despite teething problems – XTC's ANDY
PARTRIDGE allegedly stood down from production duties after only a day –
and interminable delays, the sessions were eventually mixed and co-produced
by noted guitarist, MICHAEL BROOKS and released in 1988 as 'MISS
AMERICA'. Forging her own improvisatory vocal style against a musical
canvas which alternated between vintage country, jazz and even mutoid funk
(on the tortured 'NOT BE ALRIGHT'), O'HARA was the toast of the more
discerning critic. While possessing a distinct ringing soprano, O'HARA's
singing occasionally brought to mind an artier STEVIE NICKS (especially on
'WHEN YOU KNOW YOU'RE HAPPY') or perhaps NATALIE MERCHANT
although few female singers have explored the fevered speaking-in-tongues
territory previously mapped out by the likes of VAN MORRISON. At its
most compulsive on 'BODY'S IN TROUBLE', 'MISS AMERICA' is a record
guaranteed to keep you second guessing. Come to that, many fans have been
second guessing whether MARY will ever get round to releasing a follow-up.
While the songstress parted company with 'Virgin' after the record buying Joe
Public failed to get the point, she went on to work with a variety of musicians
(i.e. MORRISSEY, THIS MORTAL COIL etc.) as well as appearing in a
number of low-key movies. Her most recent musical outing was a contribution
('FLORIDA') to the mid-90's VIC CHESNUTT tribute album, 'Sweet Relief
II'. • **Note:** Not to be confused with Irish singer/harpist, MARY O'HARA.

Album rating: MISS AMERICA (*7)

MARY MARGARET O'HARA – vocals, acoustic guitar / with **RUSTY McCARTHY** – guitar /
HENDRIK RIIK + DAVID PITCH – bass / **MICHAEL SLOSKI** – drums / **MICHAEL BROOK** –
guitar, co-producer / **DON ROOKE** – lap steel guitar / **HUGH MARSH** – violin / etc

	Virgin	Virgin
Oct 88. (cd/c/lp) *(CD/TC/V 2559)* **MISS AMERICA** | | |

– To cry about / Year in song / Body's in trouble / Dear darling / Anew day / When
you known why you're happy / My friends have / Help me lift you up / Keeping
you in mind / Not alright / You will be loved again. *(re-iss. Apr92 lp/c; OVED/+C
424)*

Feb 89. (7") *(MMOS 1)* **BODY'S IN TROUBLE. / THE YEAR IN**
SONG
(3"cd-s+=) *(MMOCD 1)* – To cry about (live) / When you know why you're happy
(live).

Nov 89. (7") *(VS 1225)* **A NEW DAY (remix). / TO CRY ABOUT**
(live)
(12"+=/cd-s+=) *(VS T/CD 1225)* – When you known why you're happy.

Dec 91. (cd-ep) **THE CHRISTMAS EP**
– Blue Christmas / Silent night / What are you doing New Year's Eve? / Christmas
evermore.

—— retired from her brief solo career

Mike OLDFIELD

Born: 15 May'53, Reading, England. He started playing guitar at the age of seven, and by 1968, had formed SALLYANGIE with sister SALLY. They signed to folk-orientated label, 'Transatlantic', who issued the lp, 'CHILDREN OF THE SUN'. After releasing a single, 'TWO SHIPS'. / 'COLOURS OF THE WORLD', in September '69, they split their partnership to concentrate on other projects. Following a spell in the short-lived BAREFOOT, MIKE became the bassist for KEVIN AYERS' band, The WHOLE WORLD, in March 1970, subsequently appearing on two albums, 'SHOOTING AT THE MOON' and 'WHATEVERSHEBRINGSWESING', between 1971 and 1972. Around this time, MIKE started work on his own solo project, gaining financial support in 1972 from Richard Branson's newly formed 'Virgin' label (the same year, he also contributed session work for EDGAR BROUGHTON BAND and DAVID BEDFORD). 'TUBULAR BELLS' finally saw the light of day in May '73, immediately garnering critical acclaim from the music press. A near-50-minute concept piece, overdubbed many times by multi-instrumentalist, MIKE, it went into the Top 3 a year later. Aided by a surprise US Top 10 single (an album excerpt) used in the horror movie, 'The Exorcist', 'TUBULAR BELLS' repeated the feat Stateside. In September '74, his follow-up, 'HERGEST RIDGE', was completed, going straight in at No.1. Critically lambasted by some commentators as "Son of Tubular Bells", it only managed to hit No.87 in America, OLDFIELD coming in for further flak as an orchestral Tubular Bells (conducted by DAVID BEDFORD) was panned by the rock press. The period between 1975 and 1978 saw him branch into African and folk-type origins on the albums, 'OMMADAWN' and 'INCANTATIONS', although at the same time, he embarrassed his rock following by releasing mainly festive hit 45's. Nevertheless, his contribution to the 70's, in terms of both the classical and rock fields, was arguably only matched by PINK FLOYD. The early 80's brought OLDFIELD a succession of more mainstream pop/rock albums, culminating with 1983's Top 10 'CRISES' album, which spawned his biggest ever hit single, 'MOONLIGHT SHADOW' (it featured the celestial vocal chords of MAGGIE REILLY, a member of his band and new co-writing team). Surprisingly, his next single, 'SHADOW ON THE WALL', bombed, although it did succeed in raising the profile of ex-FAMILY frontman, ROGER CHAPMAN. OLDFIELD continued to achieve reasonable chart success throughout the remainder of the decade, even scoring the soundtrack to classic Vietnam movie, 'THE KILLING FIELDS'. Although he never quite regained the ground he had broken with his debut, he nevertheless returned in 1992 with a belated "follow-up" in the form of the almost identical, but still appealing, 'TUBULAR BELLS II'. This seemed to breathe more life into OLDFIELD's flagging career, his most recent work (1996) taking on the "space-race" theme with 'VOYAGER'. • **Covered:** SAILOR'S HORNPIPE (trad.) / IN DULCE JUBILO (R.L. Pearsall) / WILLIAM TELL OVERTURE (Korsokov) / BLUE PETER (BBC copyright) / ARRIVAL (Abba) / WONDERFUL LAND (Shadows) / ETUDE (Francisco Tarrega). • **Trivia:** In the mid-70's, MIKE also had time to session on albums by Virgin artists; DAVID BEDFORD (Star's End) / ROBERT WYATT (Rock Bottom) / TOM NEWMAN (Fine Old Tom). MIKE's sister, SALLY, also went on to have a UK Top 20 hit with, 'MIRRORS' (late '78).

Album rating: TUBULAR BELLS (*10) / HERGEST RIDGE (*7) / THE ORCHESTRAL TUBULAR BELLS (*6) / OMMADAWN (*8) / INCANTATIONS (*8) / EXPOSED (*4) / PLATINUM (*4) / QE2 (*4) / FIVE MILES OUT (*6) / CRISES (*6) / DISCOVERY (*4) / THE KILLING FIELDS soundtrack (*6) / THE COMPLETE MIKE OLDFIELD compilation (*7) / ISLANDS (*4) / EARTH MOVING (*4) / HEAVEN'S OPEN (*4) / TUBULAR BELLS II (*6) / ELEMENTS: THE BEST OF MIKE OLDFIELD compilation (*7) / THE SONGS OF DISTANT EARTH (*4) / VOYAGER (*4) / XXV: THE BEST OF MIKE OLDFIELD compilation (*6) / TUBULAR BELLS III (*5) / GUITARS (*4) / THE MILLENNIUM BELL (*3)

MIKE OLDFIELD – guitar, bass, multi / except **TOM NEWMAN** – guitar / **JON FIELD** – flute / **STAN BROUGHTON** – drums / **LINDSAY COOPER** – wind; plus master of ceremonies, **VIVIAN STANSHALL** (ex-BONZO DOG BAND)

	Virgin	Virgin
May 73. (lp/c) *(T/TCV 2001)* <105> **TUBULAR BELLS**	1	3 Nov73

– Tubular bells (side 1) / Tubular bells (side 2). *(hit top Oct74; iss.quad-lp.Jul74; QV 2001) (pic-lp Dec78; VP 2001) (cd-iss. Jun83; CDV 2001; hit UK No.28) (re-iss. Feb97 on 'E.M.I.'; LPCENT 18) (cd re-mast.May98; CDVX 2001)*

Feb 74. (7") <55100> **TUBULAR BELLS (edit).** / **TUBULAR BELLS (excerpt)**	-	7
Jun 74. (7") *(VS 101)* **MIKE OLDFIELD'S SINGLE (theme from Tubular Bells).** / **FROGGY WENT A-COURTIN'**	31	-

—— now with **TERRY OLDFIELD** – wind / etc.

Sep 74. (lp/c) *(V/TCV 2013)* <109> **HERGEST RIDGE**	1	87

– Hergest ridge (side 1) / Hergest ridge (side 2). *(re-iss. Apr86 lp/c; OVED/+C 163) (cd-iss. Apr86; CDV 2013)*

Jan 75. (lp/c) *(V/TCV 2026)* **THE ORCHESTRAL TUBULAR BELLS (WITH THE ROYAL PHILHARMONIC ORCHESTRA)** (live & conducted by DAVID BEDFORD with guitar by OLDFIELD)	17	-

– The orchestral Tubular Bells part 1 / The orchestral Tubular Bells part 2. *(cd-iss. Jul87; CDV 2026) (re-iss. Sep89 on 'VIP-Virgin' lp/c/cd; VVIP/+C/D 101)*

Feb 75. (7") *(VS 112)* **DON ALFONSO.** / **IN DULCE JUBILO**	-	-

—— back-up were **JUBULA** (African musicians) / **PIERRE MOERLEN** (of GONG) / backing vocals by sister **SALLY OLDFIELD** + **CLODAGH SIMMONDS**

Nov 75. (lp/c) *(V/TCV 2043)* <33913> **OMMADAWN**	4	-

– Ommadawn (side 1) / Ommadawn (side 2). *(quad-lp Feb76; QV 2043) (cd-iss. 1986; CDV 2043) (cd re-iss. Apr97 on 'Virgin-VIP'; CDVIP 185)*

Nov 75. (7") *(VS 131)* **IN DULCI JUBILO.** / **ON HORSEBACK**	4	-
Nov 75. (7") <9508> **OMMADAWN (excerpt).** / **ON HORSEBACK**	-	-

Oct 76. (7") *(VS 163)* **PORTSMOUTH.** / **SPEAK (THO' YOU ONLY SAY FAREWELL)**	3	-
Nov 76. (7") <9510> **PORTSMOUTH.** / **ALGIERS**	-	-
Feb 77. (7") *(VS 167)* **THE WILLIAM TELL OVERTURE.** / **ALGIERS**	-	-
Dec 77. (7") *(VS 198)* **THE CUCKOO SONG.** / **PIPE TUNE**	-	-

—— added from last album; (see most musicians from following live album)

Nov 78. (d-lp/d-c) *(VDT/TCVDT 101)* **INCANTATIONS**	14	

– Incantations (part 1) / Incantations (part 2) / Incantations (part 3) / Incantations (part 4). *(cd-iss. Feb87; CDVD 101; omits last of 4 minutes side 3) (re-iss. Apr92 cd/c; OVED CD/C 417)*

Apr 79. (7") *(VS 245)* **GUILTY.** / **INCANTATIONS (excerpt)**	22	-

(12"blue) *(VS 245-12)* – ('A'side) / Guilty (live).

—— MIKE with **PIERRE MOERLEN** – drums, percussion / **RINGO McDONOUGH** – bodhran / **MIKE FRYE, BENOIT MOERLEN, DAVID BEDFORD** (also string arrangements) / **NICO RAMSDEN** – guitar / **PHIL BEER** – guitar, vocals / **PEKKA POHJOLA** – bass / **RAY GAY, RALPH IZEN, SIMO SALMINEN, COLIN MOORE** – trumpets / **SEBASTIAN BELL, CHRIS NICHOLLS** – flutes / **PETE LEMER, TIM CROSS** – keyboards / **MADDY PRIOR** – vocals / **JONATHAN KAHAN, DICK STUDT, BEN CRUFT, JANE PRYCE, LIZ EDWARDS, NICOLA HURTON** – violins / **VANESSA PARK, DAVID BUCKNALL, JESSICA FORD, NIGEL WARREN-GREEN** – cellos / **NICK WORTERS, JOE KIRBY** – bass / **DON McVAY, PAULINE MACK, DANNY DAGGERS, MELINDA DAGGERS, LIZ BUTLER, ROSS COHEN** – vocals, plus 11 piece choir.

Aug 79. (d-lp/d-c) *(VD/TCVD 2511)* **EXPOSED (live)**	16	-

– Incantations (parts 1 and 2) / Incantations (parts 3 and 4) / Tubular bells (part 1) / Tubular bells (part 2) / Guilty. *(d-cd-iss. Jul86; CDVD 2511)*

—— trimmed backing group down.

Nov 79. (7") *(VS 317)* **BLUE PETER.** / **WOODHENGE**	19	-
Dec 79. (lp/c) *(V/TCV 2141)* **PLATINUM**	24	-

– Platinum:- Airborne – Platinum – Charleston North star – Platinum finale / Woodhenge / Sally / Punkadiddle / I got rhythm. *(cd-iss. 1986; CDV 2141) (re-iss. 1989 lp/c; OVED/C 233)*

—— next featured **PHIL COLLINS** – drums

	Virgin	Epic
Sep 80. (7") *(VS 374)* **ARRIVAL.** / **POLKA**		
Oct 80. (lp/c) *(V/TCV 2181)* <FE 37358> **QE2**	27	

– Taurus I / Sheba / Conflict / Arrival / Wonderful land / Mirage / QE2 / Celt / Molly. *(cd-iss. 1986; CDV 2181) (re-iss. 1989 lp/c; OVED/+C 235)*

Nov 80. (7") *(VS 387)* **SHEBA.** / **WONDERFUL LAND**		
Dec 80. (d-lp/d-c) **AIRBORNE**		

– (see PLATINUM tracks, except 'Guilty' repl. – / / Tubular bells live part 1 / Incantations (segue of 20+ mins. studio and live recordings)

—— MIKE brought in **MAGGIE REILLY** – vocals (ex-CADO BELLE) / **TIM CROSS** – keyboards / **MORRIS PERT** – percussion, drums (ex-BRAND X) / **RICK FENN** – bass, guitar / **PIERRE MOERLEN** – drums, percussion returned to repl. MIKE FRYE / added **TIM RENWICK** – bass, guitar

Mar 82. (7"/7"pic-d) *(VS/+Y 464)* **FIVE MILES OUT.** / **LIVE PUNKADIDDLE**	43	
Mar 82. (lp/c) *(V/TCV 2222)* <FE 37983> **FIVE MILES OUT**	7	

– Taurus II / Family man / Orabidoo / Mount Teidi / Five miles out. *(cd-iss. 1983; CDV 2222) (re-iss. Apr90 lp/c; OVED/+C 293) (re-iss. Oct94 on 'Virgin-VIP' cd/c;)*

	Virgin	Virgin
Jun 82. (7"/7"pic-d) *(VS/+Y 489)* <02877> **FAMILY MAN.** / **MOUNT TEIDI**	45	
Sep 82. (7"/7"pic-d) *(VS/+Y 541)* **MISTAKE.** / **WALDBERG (THE PEAK)**		-

—— MIKE retained REILLY + MOERLEN. New members were **SIMON PHILLIPS** – drums / **PHIL SPALDING** – bass / **GRAEME PLEETH** – keyboards / **SIMON HOUSE** – violin

May 83. (7"/7"pic-d)(12") *(VS/+Y 586)(VS 586-12)* **MOONLIGHT SHADOW.** / **RITE OF MAN**	4	
May 83. (cd/c/lp) *(CD/TC/V 2262)* **CRISES**	6	

– Crises / Moonlight shadow / In high places / Foreign affair / Taurus III / Shadow on the wall. *(re-iss. Mar91 cd/c; OVED CD/C 351) (re-iss. May94 on 'Virgin-VIP' cd/c; CD/TC VIP 118)*

(below vocals by ROGER CHAPMAN, ex-FAMILY)

Sep 83. (7"/ext.12") *(VS 625/+12)* **SHADOW ON THE WALL.** / **TAURUS III**		
Jan 84. (7"/ext.12") *(VS 648/+12)* **CRIME OF PASSION.** / **JUNGLE GARDENIA**	61	

—— retained REILLY, PHILLIPS + SPALDING – adding guitar / plus **BARRY PALMER** – vocals / **MICKEY SIMMONDS** – keyboards / **HAROLD ZUSCHRADER** – synth.

Jun 84. (7") *(VS 686)* **TO FRANCE.** / **IN THE POOL**	48	

(ext.12"+=) *(VS 686-12)* – Bones.

Jul 84. (cd/c/lp) *(CD/TC/V 2308)* **DISCOVERY**	15	-

– To France / Poison arrows / Crystal gazing / Tricks of the light / Discovery / Talk about your life / Saved by a bell / The lake. *(re-iss. Apr92 cd/c; OVED CD/C 421)*

Sep 84. (7") *(VS 707)* **TRICKS OF THE LIGHT.** / **APEMAN**		
	(12"+=) *(VS 707-12)* – ('A'instrumental).	
Nov 84. (7"/ext.12") *(VS 731/+12)* **ETUDE.** / **EVACUATION**		
Dec 84. (cd/c/lp) *(CD/TC/V 2328)* **THE KILLING FIELDS (Soundtrack)**	97	

– Pran's theme / Requiem for a city / Evacuation / Pran's theme 2 / Capture / Execution / Bad news / Pran's departure / Worksite / The year zero / Blood sucking / The year zero 2 / Pran's escape – The killing fields / The trek / The boy's burial – Pran sees the red cross / Good news / Etude. *(re-iss. Jun88 lp/c; OVED/+C 183)*

—— **ANITA HEGERLAND** + **ALED JONES** – vocals repl. REILLY

Nov 85. (7") *(VS 836)* **PICTURES IN THE DARK.** / **LEGEND**	50	
	(ext.12") *(VS 836-12)* – The trap.	
Apr 86. (7"/7"sha-pic-d)(ext.12") *(VS/+S 863)(VS 863-12)* **SHINE.** / **THE PATH**		
May 87. (7") *(VS 955)* **IN HIGH PLACES.** / **POISON ARROWS**		-

(12"+=) *(VS 955-12)* – Jungle Gardenia.

—— vocalists – **JON ANDERSON** / **KEVIN AYERS** / **BONNIE TYLER**

Sep 87. (7") *(VS 990)* **ISLANDS.** / **THE WIND CHIMES (part one)**		

(c-s+=/ext.12"+=)(cd-s+=) *(VS/+C 990-12)(CDEP 6)* – When the night's on fire.

Oct 87. (cd/c/lp) (CD/TC+/V 2466) <90645> **ISLANDS** [29] [ ]
– The wind chimes (parts 1 & 2) / Islands / Flying start / North point / Magic touch / The time has come. (cd+=) – When the night's on fire. (re-iss. Apr92 cd/c; OVED CD/C 418)

Nov 87. (7") (VS 1013) **THE TIME HAS COME. / (final extract from) THE WIND CHIMES** [ ] [ ]
(12"+=) – ('A'original mix).

Nov 87. (7") **MAGIC TOUCH. / THE WIND CHIMES (part 1)** [-] [ ]

Feb 88. (7"/12") (VS 1047/+12) **FLYING START. / THE WIND CHIMES (part 2)** [ ] [ ]

Jul 89. (7") (VS 1189) **EARTHMOVING. / BRIDGE TO PARADISE** [ ] [ ]
(12"+=/cd-s+=) (VS T/CD 1189) – ('A'disco mix).

Jul 89. (cd/c/lp) (CD/TC+/V 2610) **EARTHMOVING** [30] [ ]
– Holy / Hostage / Far country / Innocent / Runaway son / See the light / Earthmoving / Blue night / Nothing but – Bridge to Paradise. (re-iss. Apr92 cd/c; OVED CD/C 420) (cd re-iss. Apr97 on 'Virgin-VIP'; CDVIP 169)

Oct 89. (7") (VS 1214) **INNOCENT. / EARTHMOVING (club mix)** [ ] [ ]
(12"+=/cd-s+=) (VS T/CD 1214) – ('A'extended).

Jun 90. (cd/c/lp) (CD/TC+/V 2640) **AMAROK** [49] [-]
– Amarok (part 1) / Amarok (part 2). (re-iss. Apr92 cd/c; OVED CD/C 422)

——— with **SIMON PHILLIPS** – drums / **DAVE LEVY** – bass / **MICKEY SIMMONDS** – keyboards / **ANDY LONGHURST** – keyboards / **COURTNEY PINE** – sax

Jan 91. (7"/12"/cd-s; as MICHAEL OLDFIELD) **HEAVEN'S OPEN. / EXCERPT FROM AMAROK** [ ] [-]

Feb 91. (cd/c/lp; as MICHAEL OLDFIELD) (CD/TC+/V 2653) **HEAVEN'S OPEN** [ ] [-]
– Make make / No dream / Mr. Shame / Gimme back / Heaven's open / Music from the balcony. (re-iss. Apr92 cd/c; OVED CD/C 422)

——— solo playing most instruments, except some guests & a bagpipe band.

	W.E.A.	Reprise
Sep 92. (cd)(lp/c) (4509 90618-2)(WX 2002/+C) **TUBULAR BELLS II**	[1]	[ ]

– Sentinel / Dark star / Clear light / Blue saloon / Sunjammer / Red dawn / The bell / Weightless / The great pain / Sunset door / Tattoo / Altered state / Maya gold / Moonshine.

Sep 92. (7"/c-s/cd-s) (YZ 698/+C/CD) **SENTINEL (SINGLE RESTRUCTION). / EARLY STAGES** [10] [ ]

Dec 92. (7"/c-s) (YZ 708/+C) **TATTOO. / SILENT NIGHT / SENTINEL (live)** [33] [ ]
(cd-ep+=) (YZ 708CD) – Live At Edinburgh Castle:- Moonshine / Reprise / Maya gold.

Apr 93. (7"/c-s) (YZ 737/+C) **THE BELL. / SENTINEL** [50] [ ]
(cd-s+=) (YZ 737CD) – ('A'-3 mixes).
(cd-s) (YZ 737??) – (5-'A'mixes).

Nov 94. (cd/c) (4509 98581-2/-4) **THE SONGS OF DISTANT EARTH** [24] [ ]
– In the beginning / Let there be light / Supernova / Magellan / First landing / Oceania / Only time will tell / Prayer for the Earth / Lament for Atlantis / The chamber / Hibernaculum / Tubular world / The shining ones / Crystal clear / The sunken forest / Ascension / A new beginning. (re-iss. Oct95; same)

Dec 94. (c-s) (YZ 871C) **HIBERNACULUM / MOONSHINE** [47] [ ]
(cd-s+=) (YZ 871CDX) – Solution hoedown / Jungle.
(cd-s) (YZ 871CD) – ('A'side) / The spectral army / The song of the boat men.

Aug 95. (c-s) (YZ 880C) **LET THERE BE LIGHT (Indian Lake mix) / LET THERE BE LIGHT (BT's entropic dub)** [51] [ ]
(12") (YZ 880T) – ('A'-BT's pure luminescence remix) / ('A'-Hardfloor mix) / ('A'club mix).
(cd-s) (YZ 880CD) – (above club mix) repl.by – ('A'-Ultraviolet mix).

Sep 96. (cd/c) (0630 15896-2/-4) **VOYAGER** [12] [ ]
– The song of the sun / Celtic rain / The hero / Women of Ireland / The voyager / She moves through the fair / Dark island / Wild goose flaps its wings / Flowers of the forest / Mont St Michel.

Mar 97. (c-s) (WEA 093C) **WOMEN OF IRELAND / ('A'mix)** [ ] [ ]
(12"+=/cd-s+=) (WEA 093 T/CD) – Mike's reel.
(re-iss. Nov97 hit No.70; same)

Nov 97. (cd/c) (3984 21218-2/-4) **XXV (THE BEST OF MIKE OLDFIELD)** [ ] [ ]
(compilation)
– Tubular bells / Hergest ridge / Ommadawn / Incantation / Moonlight shadow / Portsmouth / The killing fields / Sentinel (Tubular bells II) / The bell / Let there be light / Only time will tell / The voyager / Women of Ireland.

Aug 98. (cd/c) (3984 24349-2/-4) **TUBULAR BELLS III** [4] [ ]
– The source of secrets / The watchful eye / Jewel in the crown / Outcast / Serpent dream / The inner child / Man in the rain / The top of the morning / Moonwatch / Secrets / Far above the clouds.

Oct 98. (c-s) (WEA 194C) **MAN IN THE RAIN / THE INNER CHILD (live)** [ ] [-]
(cd-s+=) (WEA 194CD) – Serpent's dream (live).

Apr 99. (12"/cd-s) (WEA 206 T/CD1) **FAR ABOVE THE CLOUDS / (mixes)** [53] [ ]
(cd-s) (WEA 206CD2) – ('A'mixes).

May 99. (cd) (3984 27401-2) **GUITARS** [40] [ ]
– Muse / Cochise / Embers / Summit day / Out of sight / B blues / Four winds / Enigmatism / Out of mind / From the ashes.

Nov 99. (cd/c) (<8573 80885-2/-4>) **THE MILLENNIUM BELL** [ ] [ ]
– Peace on Earth / Pacha mama / Santa Maria / Sunlight shining through cloud / Doge's palace / Lake Constance / Mastermind / Broad sunlit uplands / Liberation / Amber light / The millennium bell.

– compilations, etc. –

——— on 'Virgin' unless otherwise mentioned

Nov 76. (4xlp-box) (VBOX 1) **BOXED** [22] [-]
– (TUBULAR BELLS / HERGEST RIDGE / OMMADAWN / + COLLABORATIONS (singles, etc.) (re-iss. 1985 4xlp/4xc; VBOX/TCVX 1) (4xcd-box Jul87; CDBOX 1)

Dec 78. (7"ep/12"ep) (VS/+T 238) **TAKE 4** [72] [-]
– Portsmouth / In dulce jubilo / Wrekorder wrondo / Sailor's hornpipe.

Oct 85. (cd/c/d-lp) (CD/C+/MOC 1) **THE COMPLETE MIKE OLDFIELD** [36] [-]
– Arrival / In dulce jubilo / Portsmouth / Jungle gardenia / Guilty / Blue Peter / Waldberg (the peak) / Etude / Wonderful land / Moonlight shadow / Family man / Mistake / Five miles out / Crime of passion / To France / Shadow on the wall / Excerpt from Tubular Bells / Sheba / Mirage / Platinum / Mount Tiede / Excerpt

from Ommadawn / Excerpt from Hergest Ridge / Excerpt from Incantations / Excerpt from Killing Fields.

Jun 88. (3"cd-ep) (CDT 7) **MOONLIGHT SHADOW (extended) / RITE OF MAN / TO FRANCE / JUNGLE GARDENIA** [ ] [-]

Jun 88. (cd-video) (080446-1) **THE WIND CHIMES (Soundtrack 1986)** [ ] [-]

Nov 90. (3xcd-box) (TPAK 15) **COLLECTORS' EDITION** [ ] [ ]
– (THE ORCHESTRAL TUBULAR BELLS / OMMADAWN / HERGEST RIDGE)

Nov 90. (3xcd-box) (TPAK 16) **COLLECTORS' EDITION** [ ] [ ]
– (QE2 / PLATINUM / FIVE MILES OUT)

Dec 90. (7"/c-s) **ETUDE. / GAKKAEN** [ ] [ ]
(12"+=/cd-s+=) – ('A'extended) (with "ONO GAGUKU KAI").

——— (The above 'A'side was now used on TV ad for 'Nurofen'.)

Sep 93. (cd/c/d-lp) (VT CD/MC/LP 18) **ELEMENTS: THE BEST OF MIKE OLDFIELD** [5] [ ]
– Tubular bells – opening theme / Family man / Moonlight shadow / Heaven's open / Five miles out / To France / Foreign affair / In dulce jubilo / Shadow on the wall / Islands / Etude / Sentinel / Ommadawn – excerpt / Incantations part four – excerpt / Amarok – excerpt / Portsmouth.

Sep 93. (4xcd-box) (CDBOX 2) **ELEMENTS – MIKE OLDFIELD 1973-1991** [ ] [ ]
– (all TUBULAR BELLS & other album excerpts, plus singles 1991)

Oct 93. (c-s) (VSC 1477) **MOONLIGHT SHADOW / MOONLIGHT SHADOW (extended version)** [52] [ ]
(cd-s+=) (VSCDT 1477) – In The Pool (Instrumental) / Bones (Instrumental).

Nov 93. (c-ep/cd-ep) **THE MIKE OLDFIELD CHRISTMAS EP** [ ] [ ]
– In dulci jubilo / Portsmouth / etc.

Mar 99. (3xcd-box) Disky; (HR 85458-2) **MIKE OLDFIELD VOL.1** [ ] [ ]

Mar 99. (3xcd-box) Disky; (HR 85459-2) **MIKE OLDFIELD VOL.2** [ ] [ ]

Will OLDHAM

Born: Louisville, Kentucky, USA. OLDHAM was raised by a large family (later his brothers would join him in THE PALACE BROTHERS) and began his dark, revered career as an actor in John Sayles' 1987 mining vehicle 'Matewan'. After a few more made-for-TV- movies, and a role in another bleedin' mining film, the repressed hillbilly for the 90's (at times compared to BECK!) photographed the front cover for SLINT's ~'Spiderland', and for his troubles was awarded the assistance of McMAHAN and WALFORD on his debut album 'THERE IS NO ONE WHAT WILL TAKE CARE OF YOU' (1993). A deep crooner by nature, OLDHAM, eased his way (however unsteady he sounds on guitar), into insular tales of death, sex and er . . . death in a small town community. Several country/gospel/folk albums appeared around 1992/3; the return to basics, 'PALACE' (1994) and 'VIVA LAST BLUES' (1995), showed a marked improvement in song structure and production value. Having drifted between 'Drag City' in the US and 'Domino' in the UK, PALACE made one last attempt at sounding sadder and deeper than LEONARD COHEN ('ARISE THEREFORE'), before OLDHAM persevered under his own name, releasing the, at times, unlistenable 'JOYA' (1997) and the rarities collection 'LOST BLUES AND OTHER SONGS' (also '97). Perhaps his most remarkable contribution to the music scene, 'I SEE A DARKNESS' (1999), was issued under the alias BONNIE 'PRINCE' BILLY, and saw OLDHAM take comic twists and turns throughout the set (sending his image up on an alarming scale). The album, recorded in a nondescript house, played like a beautiful ode to the Greek tragedy, whilst managing to substain a 'live' feel throughout. 'DEATH TO EVERYONE', possibly the finest track, was so bleak and sombre that it could quite literally make one roll around the ground with laughter by its sheer piss-take alone; maybe OLDHAM does do jokes after all?!

Album rating: Palace: THERE IS NO-ONE THAT WILL TAKE CARE OF YOU (*7) / PALACE – DAYS IN THE WAKE (*6) / VIVA LAST BLUES (*7) / ARISE THEREFORE (*7) / LOST BLUES AND OTHER SONGS collection (*8) / Will Oldham: JOYA (*6) / Bonnie 'Prince' Billy: I SEE A DARKNESS (*8)

PALACE BROTHERS

WILL OLDHAM – vocals, guitar / with **BRIAN McMAHAN** – guitar (of SQUIRREL BAIT and SLINT) / **BRITT WALFORD** – drums (of SLINT)

	Big Cat	Drag City
May 93. (7") (ABB 51S) **OHIO RIVER BOAT SONG. / DRINKING WOMAN**	[ ]	[ ] 1992
Jun 93. (lp/cd) (ABB/+CD 050) <DC 34> **THERE IS NO-ONE WHAT WILL TAKE CARE OF YOU**	[ ]	[ ]

– Idle hands are the Devil's playthings / Long before / I tried to stay healthy for you / The cellar song / Pulpit / There is no-one what will take care of you / O Lord are you in need / Merida / King me / I had a good mother and father / Riding / O Paul. (UK-lp re-iss. Jun97; DC 34)

——— now OLDHAM completely solo

	Domino	Drag City
Jun 94. (cd-ep) (RUG 21CD) **COME IN / HORSES / STABLE WILL / TRUDY DIES**	[ ]	[ ]
Sep 94. (cd/c/lp) (WIG CD/MC/LP 14) <DC 50> **PALACE** <aka 'DAYS IN THE WAKE'>	[ ]	[ ] Aug94

– You will miss me when I burn / Pushkin / Come a little dog / I send my love to you / Meaulnes / No more workhouse blues / All is grace / Whither thou goest / (Thou without) Partner / I am a cinemagrapher.

| Jan 95. (m-cd/m-lp; as PALACE SONGS) (WIG CD/LP 18) <DC 57> **HOPE** | [ ] | [ ] |

——— with **PAUL OLDHAM** – guitar / **HAYDEN + JOHN STITH** – bass / **GORDON TOWNSEND** – drums

| Jul 95. (12"ep/cd-ep; as PALACE SONGS) (RUG 35 T/CD) <DC 71> **MOUNTAIN EP** | [ ] | [ ] Aug95 |

– Mountain / Gulf shores / (End of) Traveling / West Palm Beach.

—— now with **BRYAN RICH** – guitar / **LIAM HAYES** – organ / **JASON LOWENSTEIN** – bass

Aug 95. (cd/c/lp; as PALACE MUSIC) *(WIG CD/MC/LP 21)* <DC 65> **VIVA LAST BLUES**
– More brothers rides / Viva ultra / Brute choir / Mountain low / Tonight's decision (and thereafter) / Work hard – play hard / New partner / Cat's blues / We all, us three, will ride / Old Jerusalem.

—— now simply as PALACE; with **NED OLDHAM** – bass / **DAVID GRUBBS** – piano / **MAYA TONE** – percussion, drums

Apr 96. (cd/c/lp) *(WIG CD/MC/LP 24)* <DC 88> **ARISE THEREFORE**
– Stablemate / Sucker's evening / Arise therefore / You have cum / Kid of Harith / Sun highlights / the lack in each / No gold digger / Disorder / Group of women / Give me children / Weaker soldier. *(also on ltd-cd; RUG 46CD)*

	Drag City	Drag City
Dec 96. (7") <*(DC 91)*> **LITTLE BLUE EYES.** /	☐	☐

WILL OLDHAM

—— now under his own moniker

	Domino	Drag City
Mar 97. (7") <*(DC 118)*> **PATIENCE.** /	☐	☐

Nov 97. (cd/lp) *(WIG CD/LP 39)* <DC 107> **JOYA**
– O let it be / Antagonism / New gypsy / Under what was oppression / Gator / Open your heart / Be still and know God (don't be shy) / Apocalypse, no! / I am still what I meant to be / Golden bode boy / Idea and deed.

	Palace	Acuarela
Oct 97. (cd-ep) *(WILL 1CD)* <AFF 002> **WESTERN MUSIC**	☐	Mar98

	Drag City	Drag City
Jun 98. (12"/cd-s) <*(DC 100/+CD)*> **BLACK/RICH MUSIC**	☐	☐

– Do what you will do / Do what you will do / Risen Lord / Allowance / Allowance / Black/rich tune / Black/rich / Do what you will do.

Jun 98. (cd-s) <*(DC 107X)*> **LITTLE JOYA: PROLOGUE / JOYA / EXIT MUSIC FOR A DICK**   ☐ ☐

BONNIE 'PRINCE' BILLY

with **BOB ARELLANO, COLIN GAGON, PAUL OLDHAM + PETER TOWNSEND**

	Domino	Palace
Nov 98. (cd-ep) *(RUG 81CD)* **BLUE LOTUS FEET**	☐	–

– One with the birds / Southside of the world / When die song / I am the sky / Blue lotus feet / Pole star / Door of my heart.

Jan 99. (cd/lp) *(WIG CD/LP 59)* <PR 22> **I SEE A DARKNESS**   ☐ ☐
– A minor place / Nomadic revery (all around) / I see a darkness / Another day full of dread / Death to everyone / Knockturne / Madeleine- Mary / Song for the new breed / Today I was an evil one / Black / Raining in darling.

	Palace	Palace
Jun 99. (7) <*(PR 20)*> **ONE WITH THE BIRDS.** /	☐	☐

– compilations, etc. –

Apr 97. (cd/d-lp; as PALACE MUSIC) *(WIG CD/LP 33)* <DC 110>
LOST BLUES AND OTHER SONGS
– Ohio river boat song / Riding / Valentine's day / Trudy dies / Come in / Little blue eyes / Horses / Stable will / Untitled / O how I enjoy the light / Marriage / West Palm Beach / Gulf shores / (End of) Travelling / Lost blues.

Oct 97. (7") *Skingraft; (GR 26)* **SIDES 5-6.** /

Dec 97. (lp/cd; as PALACE BROTHERS) *Drag City; (DC 50/+CD)*
DAYS IN THE WAKE   ☐ ☐

OL' DIRTY BASTARD (see under ⇒ WU-TANG CLAN)

OLIVIA TREMOR CONTROL   (dig out; Great Alt & Indie . . .)

OMD (see under ⇒ ORCHESTRAL MANOEUVRES IN THE DARK)

ONLY ONES

(dig out; 4th edition or Great Alt & Indie . . .)

Yoko ONO   (dig out; 4th edition & Great Psychedelic . . .)

OPAL (see under ⇒ MAZZY STAR)

OPERATION IVY (see under ⇒ RANCID)

'O'RANG (see under ⇒ TALK TALK)

ORANGE JUICE (see under ⇒ COLLINS, Edwyn)

ORB

Formed: South London, England . . . 1989 by remix supremo and ex-KILLING JOKE roadie Dr. ALEX PATERSON. Working as an A&R bod for ambient label EG (home to he likes of BRIAN ENO), PATERSON began recording similar ambient sounds in his spare time. He hooked up with the KLF's JIMMY CAUTY in 1988 and recorded an EP, 'KISS', using samples from NEW YORK's Kiss FM. The duo traded under the ORB moniker (which

PATTERSON had taken from the WOODY ALLEN sci-fi film 'Sleepers') and released the record the following year on the 'WAU!Mr Modo' label, a joint venture between PATTERSON and ex-KILLING JOKE bassist YOUTH. Around this time the multi-talented PATTERSON was doing a spot of DJ'ing in the chill-out room of PAUL OAKENFOLD's Land of Oz club, where, in a well documented incident, he met STEVE HILLAGE (ex-GONG). The two struck up an immediate friendship (HILLAGE no doubt impressed by the fact that PATTERSON had been spinning one of his old tracks at the time) and a series of mutual collaborations ensued. Meanwhile, the ORB carved out a place in the cobwebbed corners of music history by making what was arguably the first ever ambient dance track, entitled, pause for breath, 'A HUGE EVER GROWING PULSATING BRAIN THAT RULES FROM THE CENTRE OF THE ULTRAWORLD'. The psychedelic/progressive rock influence was glaringly obvious, not only in the overblown title but in the slowly shifting rhythms and tripped-out dub effects. The ORB's heavy use of samples continued, this time running into trouble with MINNIE RIPPERTON's 'LOVING YOU'. Come 1990, the band found themselves in the enviable position of being in-demand remixers and amid their growing reputation released another single, the celestial 'LITTLE FLUFFY CLOUDS'. This time penned by PATTERSON/YOUTH, the single saw the ORB run into sample trauma again, with RICKIE LEE JONES reportedly none too happy that her, frankly, out-of-it sounding tones were used on the single. During the sessions for the single, PATTERSON met a young engineer, THRASH, who would go on to become a fully fledged ORB member in late '91 as a replacement for the recently departed CAUTY. The much anticipated debut album, 'ADVENTURES BEYOND THE ULTRAWORLD', released in April '91 on 'Big Life', was a sprawling double set of blissed-out almost-beats and shimmering ambience. It was also a catalyst for the burgeoning ambient scene that would spawn the likes of MIXMASTER MORRIS and the APHEX TWIN, the music spilling out of chill-out rooms across the country into fully paid-up ambient club nights. In June '92, the ORB stormed into the top 10 with the 'BLUE ROOM' single. At a record breaking 39 minutes long, it wasn't exactly radio-friendly although the band 'performed' it on Top Of The Pops, sitting nonchalantly playing chess and the act's cult popularity saw the subsequent album, 'UFORB', go straight in at No.1. Following a dispute with YOUTH, PATTERSON signed with 'Island', fighting a protracted battle for the ORB name which he eventually won. His first release for the label was a live album, imaginatively titled 'LIVE '93', and culled from the legendary ORB stage show at various locations around the globe. A collaboration with German techno exponent THOMAS FEHLMAN resulted in the harder sounding 'POMMEFRITZ' album which included such wonderfully titled tracks as 'MORE GILLS, LESS FISHCAKES'. Another two albums, 'ORBUS TERRARUM' (1995) and 'ORBLIVION' (1997) ploughed similarly obscure furrows and divided critical opinion, although both hit top 20. Along with the likes of PRIMAL SCREAM, the ORB helped define an era, bringing overt psychedelia back into the pop charts and updating the genre for the 90's. • **Songwriters:** Most by WESTON and PATERSON. • **Trivia:** The ORB have remixed many including 'Mute' label stars; DEPECHE MODE / ERASURE & WIRE. In 1992, they caused upset in the Asian community by using their religious chants.

Album rating: ADVENTURES BEYOND THE ULTRAWORLD (*9) / U.F.ORB (*9) / LIVE 1993 (*6) / POMMEFRITZ (*6) / ORBUS TERRARUM (*5) / ORBLIVION (*7) / U.F.OFF – THE BEST OF THE ORB compilation (*7) / F.F.W.D.: F.F.W.D. collaboration (*6)

ALEX PATERSON – synth, keyboards / with **JIM CAUTY**

	Wau! Mr Modo	not iss.
May 89. (ltd.12"ep; as ROCKMAN ROCK & LX DEE) *(MWS 010T)* **KISS EP**	☐	–

– Kiss your love / Suck my kiss mix / The roof is on fire / Ambiorix mix.

Oct 89. (12"ep) *(MWS 017T)* **A HUGE EVER GROWING PULSATING BRAIN THAT RULES FROM THE CENTRE OF THE ULTRAWORLD: LOVIN' YOU (Orbital mix). / ('A'bucket and spade mix) / WHY IS 6 SCARED OF 7?**

	Big Life	Mercury
Jun 90. (12"ep) *(BLR 270T)* **(above with new vocals)**	☐	–

(cd-ep) *(BLR 270CD)* – (above) / Loving you (ambient house).

Jul 90. (12"ep/cd-ep) *(BLR 27 T/CD)* **(above remixed)** / **('A'-9 a.m. radio mix)** / **('A'-Aubrey mix I)**   ☐ –

Nov 90. (7") *(BLR 33)* **LITTLE FLUFFY CLOUDS.** / **('A'-Ambient mix Mk.1)**   ☐ –
(dance mix-12"ep+=/cd-ep+=) *(BLR 33 T/CD)* – Into the fourth dimension (Essenes beyond control).
(12"ep) *(BLR 33R)* – ('A'side) / ('A'-drum & vox version) / Into the fourth dimension.

—— In Nov90, they collaborated on STEVE HILLAGE's SYSTEM 7 release 'Sunburst'.

—— CAUTY was replaced by **STEVE HILLAGE** – guitar (ex-Solo artist, ex-GONG) / **MIQUETTE GIRAUDY** (ex-GONG) / **ANDY FALCONER**

Apr 91. (d-cd/d-c/d-lp) *(BLR CD/MC/LP 5)* <511034> **ADVENTURES BEYOND THE ULTRAWORLD**   29   Nov91
– Little fluffy clouds / Earth (Gaia) / Supernova at the end of the universe / Back side of the Moon / Spanish castles in space / Perpetual dawn / Into the fourth dimension / Outlands / Star 6 & 7 8 9 / A huge ever growing pulsating brain that rules from the centre of the Ultraworld.

Jun 91. (7"/c-s) *(BLR 46/+C)* **PERPETUAL DAWN (SOLAR YOUTH).** / **STAR 6&789 (phase II)**   61   –
(cd-ep+=) *(BLR 46CD)* – Perpetual dawn: Solar flare.
(12"ep+=) *(BLRT 46)* – (above version) / ('B'side) / ('A'-Ultrabass 1 mix).
(12"ep) *(BLR 46R)* – ORB IN DUB: Towers of dub (ambient mix) / Perpetual dawn (ultrabass II). *(re-iss. Jan94; same)* – (hit No.18)

—— In Nov91, SYSTEM 7 issued another release on '10-Virgin'; 'Miracle'.

Dec 91. (cd/c/lp) *(BLR CD/MC/LP 14) / Caroline; <CAROL 1717>* **THE AUBREY MIXES: THE ULTRAWORLD EXCURSIONS** (deleted after 1 day) `44` ☐
– Little fluffy clouds / (Pal Joey mix) / Black side of the moon (Steve Hillage remix) / Spanish castles in Spain (Youth remix) / Outlands (Ready made remix) / A huge ever growing pulsating brain (Jim Caldy & Dr. Alex Patterson remix).

—— **PATERSON** now with **THRASH (KRISTIAN WESTON)** – guitars, synthesizers, samplers, percussion, plus guests **YOUTH, STUART McMILLAN, GUY PRATT, JAH WOBBLE, STEVE HILLAGE, MIQUETTE GIRAUDY, THOMAS FEHLMANN, GREG HUNTER, ORDE MEIKLE, TOM GREEN, MARNEY PAX.**

Jun 92. (12"ep) *(BLRT 75)* **THE BLUE ROOM (part 1). / (part 2)** `8` `-`
(cd-ep) *(BLRDA 75)* – The blue room (40 minute version).
(cd-ep) *(BLRDB 75)* – The blue room (radio 7) / The blue room (excerpt 605) / Towers of dub (Mad Professor mix).

Jul 92. (d-cd/d-c/t-lp) *(BLR CD/MC/LP 18) <513749>* **UF ORB** `1` ☐
– O.O.B.E. / U.F. Orb / Blue room / Towers of dub / Close encounters / Majestic / Sticky end. *(free live lp at some shops 'Soundtrack To The Film: ADVENTURES BEYOND THE ULTRAWORLD: PATTERNS & TEXTURES') (re-iss. Apr96 on 'Island; (cd)(c) IMCD 219)(ICM 8033)*

Oct 92. (c-s) **ASSASSIN (the oasis of rhythm mix)** `12` ☐
(12"ep+=/cd-ep+=) *(BLR T/DA 81)* – U.F. ORB (Bandulu remix).
(cd-ep) *(BLRDB 81)* – ('A'-radio 7 mix) / ('A'-another live version) / ('A'-Chocolate hills of Bohol mix).

Nov 93. (c-ep/12"ep/cd-ep) *(BLR C/T/D 98)* **LITTLE FLUFFY CLOUDS. / ('A'mixes)** `10` `-`
Island Island

Nov 93. (d-cd/d-c/q-lp) *(CIDD/ICTT/ILPSQ 8022) <535004>* **LIVE 93 (live)** `23` ☐
– Plateau / The valley / Oobe / Little fluffy clouds / Star 6, 7, 8 & 9 / Towers of dub / Spanish castles in space / The blue room / Perpetual dawn / Assassin / Outlands / A huge ever pulsating brain that rules from the centre of the ultraworld. *(d-cd-iss. Mar97; IMCD 245)*

Jun 94. (cd/c/lp) *(ORB CD/MC/LP 1) <535007>* **POMMEFRITZ** `6` ☐
– Pommefritz / More gills less fishcakes / We're paste to be grill you / Banger'n'chips / Allers ist schoen / His immortal logness.

—— now w /out KRIS WESTON, who was repl. (after 1995 recording by) **ANDY HUGHES**

Mar 95. (cd/c/d-lp) *(CID/CIDX/ICT/ILPSD 8037) <524099>* **ORBUS TERRARUM** `20` ☐ Apr95
– Valley / Plateau / Oxbow lakes / Montagne d'or (der gute berg) / White river junction / Occidental / Slug dub.

May 95. (c-s) *(CIS 609)* **OXBOW LAKES. / ('A'-Everglades mix)** `38` `-`
(12"+=) *(12IS/CID 609)* – ('A'-Sabres No.1 mix).
(12") *(12ISX 609)* – ('A'-Carl Craig psychic pals family wealth plan mix) / ('A'-Evensong string arrangement mix).
(cd-s) *(CIDX 609)* – (all 5 mixes above).

—— In Jul'96, the label 'Deviant' released various artists compilation of their mixes 'AUNTIE AUBREY'S EXCURSIONS BEYOND THE CALL OF DUTY'.

—— line-up **LX PATERSON / ANDY HUGHES / THOMAS FEHLMANN**

Jan 97. (12"/cd-s) *(12IS/CID 652) <854907>* **TOXYGENE. / DELTA Mk.II** `4` ☐
(cd-s) *(CIDX 652)* – ('A'side) / Rose tinted.

Feb 97. (cd/c/lp) *(CID/ICT/ILPSD 8055) <524347>* **ORBLIVION** `19` ☐
– Delta mk II / Ubiquity / Asylum / Bedouin / Molten love / Pi / S.A.L.T. / Toxygene / Log of deadwood / Secrets / Passing of time / 72.

May 97. (12"/cd-s) *(12IS/CID 657)* **ASYLUM. / ('A'-Blood Sugar's mix 1) / ('A'-Andrea Parker's Bezirkskrankenhams mix)** `20` ☐
(cd-s) *(CIDX 657)* –

Oct 98. (cd/d-lp) *(CID/ILPSD 8078)* **U.F.OFF – THE BEST OF** (compilation) `38` ☐
– A huge ever growing pulsating brain rule from the centre of the world / Little fluffy clouds / Perpetual dawn / Blue room / Assassin / Pomme Fritz / Toxygene / Outlands / DJ Asylum / Mickey Mars / Towers of dub (part 1) / Oxbow lakes. *(d-cd+=; CIDD 8078)* – (other mixes).

Nov 98. (d12"ep) *(12ISD 729)* **LITTLE FLUFFY CLOUDS (mixes:- Danny Tenaglia's downtempo groove / Danny Tenaglia's detour mix / Adam Freeland Tsunami one mix / Cumulo nimbus mix / One True Parker mix)** `-` `-` -non

– compilations, others, etc. –

Nov 91. (cd/c/lp) *Strange Fruit; (SFR CD/MC/LP 118)* **THE PEEL SESSIONS**
– A huge ever growing brain that rules from the centre of the ultraworld. *(re-iss. Apr96; same)*

APOLLO XI

DR. ALEX PATERSON + guest **BEN WATKINS** (of SUNSONIC)
Wau! Mr Modo not iss.

Feb 91. (12"/cd-s) *(APOLLO 11/+CD)* **PEACE (IN THE MIDDLE EAST) / ('A'-Sea Of Tranquility mix). / ('A'radio) / ('A'-Is This Really The Orb mix?)** ☐ `-`

F.F.W.D.

aka **ROBERT FRIPP** – guitar / **THOMAS FEHLMANN** – electronics / **KRIS WESTON** – electronics / **DR. ALEX PATERSON**
Intermodo not iss.

Aug 94. (cd/c/d-lp) *(INTA 001 CD/TC/LP)* **F.F.W.D.** `48` `-`
– Hidden / Lucky saddle / Drone / Hempire / Collosus / What time is clock / Can of bliss / Elauses / Meteor storm / Buckwheat and grits / Klangtest / Suess wie eine nuss.

Roy ORBISON

Born: 23 Apr'36, Vernon, Texas, USA. After stints with local hillbilly groups The WINK WESTERNERS and The TEEN KINGS, he cut a solo single for the 'Jewel' label in 1955 before successfully auditioning for Sam Phillips' 'Sun' records. Written by two college friends, WADE MOORE and DICK PENNER, 'OOBY DOOBY' gave him his first Top 60 hit in 1956. Subsequent 50's rockabilly/pop singles for 'Sun' and 'R.C.A.' all failed, and after moving to Nashville with his wife, ORBISON focused his attentions on songwriting. 'CLAUDETTE' (written for his wife), was placed in the capable hands of The EVERLY BROTHERS who took the uptempo song into the US Top 30 (another, 'DISTANT DRUMS', was a massive hit for JIM REEVES, reaching No.1 after his untimely death in '66). In 1959, his solo career was re-activated when 'Monument' took the reins, ORBISON embracing a more ballad-esque approach which highlighted his lyrical genius, dramatic falsetto voice and trademark tearful crescendos. It was an approach which was to make the country boy a bonafide star; the following year, 'ONLY THE LONELY' was first of many million sellers throughout the early to mid sixties period. Classic after classic saw ROY O become a regular chart fixture, the likes of 'RUNNING SCARED', 'CRYING', 'DREAM BABY', 'IN DREAMS', 'BLUE BAYOU', 'IT'S OVER' and 'OH PRETTY WOMAN' transcending the era while his contemporaries sounded somewhat dated. His ubiquitous dark glasses were initially worn in 1963 after his regular spectacles were misplaced on a plane. In November '64, at the height of his success, ORBISON divorced Claudette due to her infidelity. Reconciled, they remarried in August '65, although tragedy struck ten months later when she was killed as her motorcycle hit a truck. Later that year, ROY O began a short-lived acting career, although his initial movie experience, 'The Fastest Guitar Alive', did poorly at the box-office. Nevertheless his solo career was still flourishing, especially in the UK, where his more countrified material was going down reasonably well. However, another tragedy befell him on the 14th September '68; while on tour, ORBISON's house caught fire, killing his two oldest sons, Roy Jr. and Tony. Understandably, perhaps, he subsequently semi-retired in 1970 to Bielefeld, Germany with his remaining son and new German-born wife, Barbara Wellhonen; together they reared another son, Roy Kelton. ORBISON's recording career went through a minor comeback (i.e. a cameo in the 1980 film, 'Roadie', with Emmylou Harris duetting 'You've Lost That Lovin' Feelin') before he sued Wesley Rose (head of 'Monument') for $50m in backdated royalties. In 1987, his career finally got back on track as he signed to 'Virgin' and began making new inroads into world popularity. The following year, he joined the TRAVELING WILBURYS, alongside other superstars, BOB DYLAN, GEORGE HARRISON, JEFF LYNNE and TOM PETTY. Their 'VOLUME 1' album became a US Top 3 and UK Top 20 later in the year, although tragically ROY O was to die of a heart attack on the 6th of December. The legend had just completed a tremendous comeback album, 'MYSTERY GIRL', which posthumously peaked in the British and American Top 5 (would've anyway!). One of the record's highlights, 'YOU GOT IT', gave the man his first entry into the US Top 10 for nearly 25 years. His 1987 concert, 'A BLACK AND WHITE NIGHT', featured guest appearances by the cream of the roots-rock aristocracy including k.d. LANG (on a duet of 'CRYING' which became a UK Top 10 hit), BRUCE SPRINGSTEEN, TOM WAITS, BONNIE RAITT, JACKSON BROWNE and ELVIS COSTELLO among others . . . • **Songwriters:** A brilliant poet of our time, ROY wrote most of the songs himself, at times collaborating in the 60's with JOE MELSON (1960-1963 + 1967) and BILL DEES (1964-66). His final material in the late 80's, was co-written w / JEFF LYNNE & TOM PETTY. Covered CANDY MAN (Fred Neil) / MEAN WOMAN BLUES (Elvis Presley) / LET THE GOOD TIMES ROLL (Shirley & Lee) / THE COMEDIANS (Elvis Costello) / SHE'S A MYSTERY TO ME (U2) / I DROVE ALL NIGHT (Cyndi Lauper) / AFTER THE LOVE HAS GONE (Earth, Wind & Fire). His songs, 'BLUE BAYOU' and 'CRYING', were huge hits for LINDA RONSTADT and DON McLEAN respectively.

Best CD compilation: THE VERY BEST OF ROY ORBISON (*9)

ROY ORBISON – vocals with early **BOB MOORE** – bass / **BILLY PAT ELLIS** – drums

		not iss.	Je-Wel
Jan 56.	(7",78; by TEEN KINGS) *<101>* **OOBY DOOBY. / TRYING TO GET TO YOU**	`-`	☐
		Sun	Sun
May 56.	(7",78; ROY ORBISON & The TEEN KINGS) *<242>* **OOBY DOOBY. / GO! GO! GO!**	`-`	`59`
Sep 56.	(7",78; ROY ORBISON & The TEEN KINGS) *<251>* **ROCK HOUSE. / YOU'RE MY BABY** (UK-iss.1964 on 'Ember'; EMBS 197)	`-`	☐
Nov 56.	(7",78; ROY ORBISON & The ROSES) *<265>* **SWEET AND EASY TO LOVE. / DEVIL DOLL**	`-`	☐
Dec 57.	(7",78) *<284>* **CHICKEN HEARTED. / I LIKE LOVE**	`-`	☐
May 58.	(7",78) *<353>* **SWEET AND EASY TO LOVE. / DEVIL DOLL**	`-`	☐
		not iss.	RCA Victor
Sep 58.	(7",78) *<7381>* **SWEET AND INNOCENT. / SEEMS TO ME**	`-`	☐
Dec 58.	(7",78) *<7447>* **ALMOST 18. / JOLIE**	`-`	☐
		London	Monument
Jul 59.	(7",78) *<409>* **PAPER BOY. / WITH THE BUG**	`-`	☐
Dec 59.	(7",78) *<412>* **UPTOWN. / PRETTY ONE**	`-`	`72`
Jun 60.	(7",78) *(HLU 9149) <421>* **ONLY THE LONELY. / HERE COMES THAT SONG AGAIN**	`1`	`2` May60
Oct 60.	(7") *(HLU 9207) <425>* **BLUE ANGEL. / TODAY'S TEARDROPS**	`11`	`9` Sep60

1961. (lp) *(HA-U 2342)* <14002> **LONELY AND BLUE**   [ ]   [ ] Dec60
– Only the lonely / Bye bye love / Cry / Blue avanue / I can't stop loving you / Come back to me (my love) / Blue angel / Raindrops / (I'd be) A legend in my time / I'm hurtin' / Twenty-tow days / I'll say it's my fault. *(UK re-dist.May63, hit No.15)*

Mar 61. (7") *(HLU 9307)* <433> **I'M HURTIN'. / I CAN'T STOP LOVING YOU**   [ ]   [27] Dec60

May 61. (7") *(HLU 9342)* <438> **RUNNING SCARED. / LOVE HURTS**   [9]   [1] Apr61
(re-iss. 1975 on 'Monument')

Sep 61. (7") *(HLU 9405)* <447> **CRYING. / CANDY MAN**   [25]   [2] / [25] Aug61

(re-iss. 1975 on 'Monument')

Feb 62. (7") *(HLU 9511)* <456> **DREAM BABY. / THE ACTRESS**   [2]   [4]

May 62. (lp) *(HA-U 2437)* <4007> **CRYING**   [ ]   [21] Apr62
– Crying / The great pretender / Love hurts / She wears my ring / Wedding day / Summersong / Dance / Lana / Loneliness / Let's make a memory / Nite life / Running scared. *(UK re-dist.Jun63, hit No.17)*

Jun 62. (7") *(HLU 9561)* <461> **THE CROWD. / MAMA**   [40]   [26]

Aug 62. (lp) <4009> **ROY ORBISON'S GREATEST HITS** (compilation)   [-]   [14]
– The crowd / Love star / Crying / Evergreen / Running scared / Mama / Candy man / Only the lonely / Dream baby / Blue angel / Uptown / I'm hurtin'. *(UK-iss.Sep67; 5007)* – hit No.40

Oct 62. (7") *(HLU 9607)* <467> **WORKIN' FOR THE MAN. / LEAH**   [50]   [33] / [25]

(re-iss. 1975 on 'Monument')

Feb 63. (7") *(HLU 9676)* <806> **IN DREAMS. / SHAHDOROBA**   [6]   [7]

May 63. (7") *(HLU 9727)* <815> **FALLING. / DISTANT DRUMS**   [9]   [22]

Sep 63. (7") *(HLU 9777)* <824> **BLUE BAYOU. / MEAN WOMAN BLUES**   [3]   [29] / [5]

(re-iss. 1975 on 'Monument')

Nov 63. (lp) *(HA-U/SH-U 8180)* <18003> **IN DREAMS**   [6]   [35] Aug 63
– In dreams / Lonely wine / Shahdaroba / No one will ever know / Sunset / House without windows / Dream / Blue bayou / (They call you) Gigolette / All I have to do is dream / Beautiful dreamer / My prayer.

Dec 63. (7") <830> **PRETTY PAPER. / BEAUTIFUL DREAMER**   [-]   [15]
(UK-iss.1975 on 'Monument')

Feb 64. (7") *(HLU 9845)* **BORNE ON THE WIND. / WHAT'D I SAY**   [15]   [-]

Apr 64. (7") *(HLU 9882)* <837> **IT'S OVER. / INDIAN WEDDING**   [1]   [9]

Aug 64. (7") *(HLU 9919)* <851> **OH PRETTY WOMAN. / YO TE AMO MARIA**   [1]   [1]

—— (above featured/credited The CANDYMEN)

Sep 64. (lp) <18024> **MORE OF ROY ORBISON'S GREATEST HITS** (compilation)   [-]   [19]
(UK-iss.1968; SMO 5014)

Nov 64. (7") <HLU 9930> **PRETTY PAPER. / SUMMER SONG**   [6]   [-]

Nov 64. (lp) *(HA-U 8207)* **OH PRETTY WOMAN** (compilation)   [4]   [-]
– Oh pretty woman / It's over / Falling / Indian wedding / Borne on the wind / Distant drums / The crowd / Yo te amo / Maria / Candy man / Mama.

Feb 65. (7") *(HLU 9951)* <873> **GOODNIGHT. / ONLY WITH YOU**   [14]   [21]

Jul 65. (7") *(HLU 9978)* <891> **(SAY) YOU'RE MY GIRL. / SLEEPY HOLLOW**   [23]   [39]
London   M.G.M.

Aug 65. (7") *(HLU 9986)* <13386> **RIDE AWAY. / WONDERIN'**   [34]   [25]

Sep 65. (lp) *(HA-U/SH-U 8252)* <4308> **THERE IS ONLY ONE ROY ORBISON**   [10]   [55]
– Ride away / You fool you / Two of a kind / This is your song / I'm in a blue, blue mood / If you can't say something nice / Claudette / Afraid to sleep / Sugar and honey / Summer love / Big as I can dream / Wondering.

Oct 65. (7") *(HLU 10000)* <13410> **CRAWLIN' BACK. / IF YOU CAN'T SAY SOMETHING NICE**   [19]   [46]

Jan 66. (7") *(HLU 10015)* <13446> **BREAKIN' UP IS BREAKIN' MY HEART. / WAIT**   [22]   [31]

Feb 66. (lp) *(HA-U/SH-U 8279)* <4322> **THE ORBISON WAY**   [11]   [ ]
– Crawling back / It ain't no big thing / Time changed everything / This is my land / The loner / Maybe / Breakin' up is breakin' my heart / Go away / A new star / Never / It wasn't very long ago / Why hurt the one who loves you.

Mar 66. (7") *(HLU 10034)* <13498> **TWINKLE TOES. / WHERE IS TOMORROW**   [29]   [39]

Jun 66. (7") *(HLU 10051)* **LANA. / HOUSE WITHOUT WINDOWS**   [15]   [-]
(above 45 an older 'Monument' recording)

Jul 66. (7") *(HLU 10067)* <13549> **TOO SOON TO KNOW. / YOU'LL NEVER BE SIXTEEN AGAIN**   [-]   [68]

Aug 66. (7") *(HLU 10067)* **TOO SOON TO KNOW. / YOU'LL NEVER BE SIXTEEN AGAIN**   [3]   [ ]

Sep 66. (lp) *(HA-U/SH-U 8279)* <4379> **THE CLASSIC ROY ORBISON**   [12]   [ ]
– You'll never be sixteen again / Pantomine / Twinkle toes / Losing you / City life / Wait / Growing up / Where is tomorrow / I'll never get over you / Going back to Gloria / Never love again / Just another name for rock'n'roll. *(re-iss. +c+cd.Apr89 on 'Ocean'UK / 'Rhino'US)*

Nov 66. (7") *(HLU 10096)* **THERE WON'T BE MANY COMING HOME. / GOING BACK TO GLORIA**   [18]   [-]

Dec 66. (7") <13634> **COMMUNICATION BREAKDOWN. / GOING BACK TO GLORIA**   [-]   [60]

Feb 67. (7") *(HLU 10113)* <13685> **SO GOOD. / MEMORIES**   [32]   [ ]

1967. (lp) *(HA-U 8318)* <4424> **SINGS DON GIBSON**
– A legend in my time / I'm hurtin' / The same street / Far far away / Big hearted me / Sweet dreams / Oh, such a stranger / Blue blue day / What about me / Give myself a party / Too soon to know / Lonesome number one.

Aug 67. (7") *(HLU 10143)* <13764> **CRY SOFTLY, LONELY ONE. / PISTOLERO**   [ ]   [52]

Sep 67. (lp) *(HA-U/SH-U 8357)* <4514> **CRY SOFTLY, LONELY ONE**
– She / Communication breakdown / Cry softly, lonely one / Girl like me / It takes one to know one / That's a no-no / Just let me make believe / Here comes the rain baby / Memories / Time to cry / Only alive / Just one time.

Oct 67. (7") *(HLU 10159)* <13817> **SHE. / HERE COMES THAT SONG AGAIN**   [ ]   [ ]

Jan 68. (7") *(HLU 10176)* <13889> **BORN TO BE LOVED BY YOU. / SHY AWAY**   [ ]   [ ]

Jan 68. (lp) *(HA-U/SH-U 8358)* **FASTEST GUITAR ALIVE (1966 Soundtrack)**   [ ]   [-]
– Whirlwind / Medicine man / River / The fastest guitar alive / Rollin' on / Pistolero / Good time party / Heading south / Best friend / There won't be many coming home.

Jul 68. (7") *(HLU 10206)* <13950> **WALK ON. / FLOWERS**   [39]   [ ]

Sep 68. (7") *(HLU 10222)* <13991> **HEARTACHE. / SUGARMAN**   [44]   [ ]

1969. (lp) <4559> **GREAT SONGS**   [-]

Apr 69. (7") *(HLU 10261)* <14039> **MY FRIEND. / SOUTHBOUND JERICO PATHWAY**   [35]   [ ]

May 69. (lp) <4636> **MANY MOODS**   [-]
– Truly, truly, true / Unchained melody / I recommend her / More / Heartache / Amy / Good morning, dear / What now my love / Walk on / Yesterday's child / Try to remember.

Aug 69. (7") *(HLU 109285)* <14079> **PENNY ARCADE. / TENNESSEE OWNS MY SOUL**   [27]   [-]

1969. (lp) <4683> **HANK WILLIAMS – THE ROY ORBISON WAY**
– Kaw-liga / Jambalaya (on the bayou) / (Last night) I heard you crying in your sleep / You win again / Your cheatin' heart / Cold, cold heart / A mansion on the hill / I can't help it (if I'm still in love with you) / There'll be no teardrops tonight / I'm so lonesome I could cry.

Nov 69. (7") *(HLU 10294)* **BREAK MY MIND. / HOW DO YOU START OVER**   [ ]   [-]

Nov 69. (lp) *(HA-U/SH-U 8406)* **THE BIG 'O'**   [ ]   [-]
– Break my mind / Help me Rhonda / Money / Only you / Down the line / When I stop dreaming / Living touch / Land of 1000 dances / Scarlet ribbons / She won't head her love out / Casting spell / Penny arcade. *(UK iss.Oct75 & 1982 on 'Charly')* *(re-iss. +cd.May89 on 'Pickwick')* *(cd-iss. Feb93)*

—— (above credited The ART MOVEMENT)

1970. (7") <14105> **SHE CHEATS ON ME. / HOW DO YOU START OVER**   [-]   [ ]

Apr 70. (7") *(HLU 10310)* <14121> **SO YOUNG. / IF I HAD A WOMAN LIKE YOU**   [ ]   [ ]

Aug 71. (7") *(HLU 10339)* <14293> **(LOVE ME LIKE YOU DID IT) LAST NIGHT. / CLOSE AGAIN**   [ ]   [ ]

Feb 72. (7") *(HLU 10358)* <14358> **GOD LOVE YOU. / CHANGES**   [ ]   [ ]

1972. (7") <14413> **REMEMBER THE GOOD. / HARLEM WOMAN (or) IF ONLY FOR A WHILE**   [ ]   [ ]

Sep 72. (7") *(HLU 10358)* <14441> **MEMPHIS TENNESSEE. / I CAN READ BETWEEN THE LINES**   [ ]   [ ]

1973. (lp) *(SH-U 8445)* <4867> **MEMPHIS**
– Memphis, Tennessee / Why a woman cries / Run baby run (back into my arms) / Take care of your woman / I'm a man on Susie's mind / I can't stop loving you / Run the engines up high / It ain't no big thing / I fought the law / The three bells / Danny boy.

1973. (7") <14552> **BLUE RAIN (COMING DOWN). / SOONER OR LATER**   [-]   [ ]

1973. (7") <14626> **I WANNA LIVE. / YOU LAY EASY ON MY MIND**   [-]   [-]

1974. (lp) <4934> **MILESTONES**
   Mercury   Mercury

Sep 74. (7") *(6167014)* 73610> **SWEET MAMA BLUE. / HEARTACHE**   [ ]   [ ]

Apr 75. (7") *(6167067)* <73652> **HUNG UP ON YOU. / SPANISH NIGHTS**   [ ]   [ ]

1975. (7") <73705> **IT'S LONELY. / STILL**   [ ]   [-]

1976. (lp) <SRMI 1045> **I'M STILL IN LOVE WITH YOU**   [ ]   [-]
– Pledging my love / Rainbow love / Heartache / Still / Circle / All I need is time / Spanish nights / It's lonely / Crying time / Hung up on you / Sweet mama blue. *(cd-iss. Aug89)*
   Monument   Monument

May 76. (7") *(MNT 4247)* <8690> **BELINDA. / NO CHAIN AT ALL**   [ ]   [ ]

Nov 76. (7") *(MNT 4797)* <200> **(I'M A) SOUTHERN MAN. / BORN TO LOVE ME**   [ ]   [ ]

Feb 77. (lp) *(81809)* <7600> **REGENERATION**
– (I'm a) Southern man / N chain at all / Old love song / Can't wait / Born to love me / Blues in my mind / Something they can't take away / Under suspicion / I don't really want you / Belinda.

Apr 77. (7") *(MNT 5151)* <215> **DRIFTING AWAY. / UNDER SUSPICION**   [ ]   [ ]

—— In 1978, he underwent major heart surgery, but steadily recovered.
   Asylum   Asylum

May 79. (7") *(K 13153)* <46048> **EASY WAY OUT. / TEARS**   [ ]   [ ]

Jul 79. (lp/c) *(K/K4 53092)* <6E 198> **LAMINAR FLOW**
– Easy way out / Love is a cold wind / Lay it down / I care / We're into something good / Movin' / Poor baby / Warm spot hot / Tears / Friday night / Hound dog man. *(cd-iss. Feb93)*

Sep 79. (7") <46541> **LAY IT DOWN. / POOR BABY**   [ ]   [ ]

Nov 79. (7") *(K 12391)* **LAY IT DOWN. / WARM SPOT HOT**   [-]   [-]

—— (below duet with **EMMYLOU HARRIS** from the film 'Roadie')
   Warners   Warners

Jun 80. (7") <49262> **THAT LOVING YOU FEELING AGAIN. / (b-by Craig Hindley)**   [-]   [55]

Apr 81. (7") *(K 18432)* **UNTIL THE NIGHT IS OVER. / LONG WAY BACK TO LOVE**   [ ]   [-]
   ZTT-Island   Island

Aug 85. (7") *(ZTAS 9)* **WILD HEARTS (TIME). / WILD HEARTS (VOICELESS)**   [ ]   [ ]
(d7"+=) – *(DZTAS 9)* – Ooby dooby (revive) / Crying (live).
(12"+=) – *(12ZTAS 9)* – Ooby dooby / Wild hearts (and time again).
   Virgin   Virgin

Jun 87. (7") *(ROY 1)* <99434> **IN DREAMS. / LEAH**   [ ]   [ ]

Jul 87. (d-lp/c/cd) *(VGD/+C/CD 3524)* <90604> **IN DREAMS: THE GREATEST HITS**   [86]   [95] Jan 89
– (new versions of old songs) Only the lonely / Leah / In dreams / Uptown / It's over / Crying / Dream baby / Blue angel / Working for the man / Candy man / Running scared / Falling / I'm hurtin' / Claudette / Oh pretty woman / Mean woman blues / Ooby dooby / Lana / Blue bayou.

—— In the fall of 1988, he teamed up with DYLAN, PETTY, HARRISON and LYNNE to form The TRAVELING WILBURYS. Tragedy struck on the 7th Dec'88, when he died of a heart attack. He had coincidentally just released comeback solo album.

Dec 88. (7") *(VS 1166)* <99245> **YOU GOT IT. / THE ONLY ONE** [3] [9]
(12"+=/3"cd-s+=) *(VS T/CD 1166)* – Crying (with k.d. LANG).

Jan 89. (cd/c/lp) *(CD/TC+/V 2576)* <91058> **MYSTERY GIRL** [2] [5]
– You got it / In the real world / (All I can do is) Dream you / A love so beautiful / California blue / She's a mystery to me / The comedians / The only one / Windsurfer / Careless heart.

Feb 89. (7") *(VS 1173)* **SHE'S A MYSTERY TO ME. / CRYING** [27]
(12"+=/cd-s+=) *(VS T/CD 1173)* – Dream baby (live).

Feb 89. (7") <99227> **SHE'S A MYSTERY TO ME. / DREAM BABY** [-]

Jul 89. (7") *(VS 1193)* <99202> **CALIFORNIA BLUE. / BLUE BAYOU (live with k.d.LANG)**
(12"+=) *(VST 1193)* – Leah (live).
(3"cd-s++=) *(VSCD 1193)* – In dreams (live).

Nov 89. (cd/c/lp) *(CD/TC+/V 2601)* <91295> **ROY ORBISON AND FRIENDS – A BLACK AND WHITE NIGHT (live Sep'87)** [51]
– Oh pretty woman / Only the lonely / In dreams / Dream baby (how long must I dream) / Leah / Move on down the line / Crying / Mean woman blues / Running scared / Blue bayou / Candy man / Uptown / Ooby dooby / The comedians / (All I can do is) Dream is you / It's over. *(re-iss. c+cd.Aug91)*

Nov 89. (7") *(VS 1224)* <99159> **OH PRETTY WOMAN ('87 version). / CLAUDETTE**
(12"+=/cd-s+=) *(VS T/CD 1224)* – ('A'-lp version).

– compilations, etc. –

Sep 57. (7"ep) *London; (REU RES 1089)* **HILLBILLY ROCK** [-]
Dec 60. (7"ep) *London; (REU 1274)* **ONLY THE LONELY** [-]
1961. (lp) *Sun; <1260>* **ROY ORBISON AT THE ROCKHOUSE** [-]
(re-iss. Feb81 on 'Charly'; CRM 2007)
Mar 63. (7"ep) *London; (REU 1354)* **ROY ORBISON** [-]
Jun 63. (7"ep) *London; (REU 1373)* **IN DREAMS** [-]
Aug 64. (7"ep) *London; (REU 1435)* **IT'S OVER** [-]
Dec 64. (7"ep) *London; (REU 1437)* **OH PRETTY WOMAN** [-]
Feb 65. (7"ep) *London; (REU 1439)* **ROY ORBISON'S STAGE SHOW HITS** [-]
Jun 65. (7"ep) *London; (REU 1440)* **LOVE HURTS** [-]
– Love hurts / All I have to do is dream / I can't stop loving you / The crowd.
1970. (lp) *London/ US= Sun;* **THE ORIGINAL SOUNDS OF ...** [-]
1972. (lp) *London/ US= Sun; (SHU 8435)* **ROY ORBISON SINGS** [-]
Jul 76. (d-lp) *London; (FOS U15/16)* **FOCUS ON ROY ORBISON** [-]
Jan 90. (lp/c/cd) *Sun; (SUNLP 1050)* **ROY ORBISON** [-]
Jul 64. (lp) *Ember; (NR 5013)* **THE EXCITING SOUNDS OF ROY ORBISON** [17] [-]
Jul 64. (7") *Ember; (EMBS 197)* **YOU'RE MY BABY. / ROCK HOUSE** [-]
Sep 64. (7") *Ember; (EMBS 200)* **THIS KIND OF LOVE. / I NEVER KNEW** [-]
1964. (7"ep) *Ember; (EP 4546)* **SWEET AND EASY TO LOVE** [-]
1964. (7"ep) *Ember; (EP 4563)* **TRYIN' TO GET TO YOU** [-]
Mar 65. (7") *Ember; (EMBS 209)* **SWEET AND EASY TO LOVE. / YOU'RE GONNA CRY** [-]
1965. (7"ep) *Ember; (EP 4570)* **DEVIL DOLL** [-]
1964. (lp) *Allegro; (ALL 778)* **ROY ORBISON SINGS** [-]
Oct 64. (lp) *Monument; (LMO/SMO 513)* **EARLY ORBISON** [-]
Oct 65. (7") *Monument; <906>* **LET THE GOOD TIMES ROLL. / DISTANT DRUMS** [-] [81]
Dec 65. (lp) *Monument; (SMO 5004)* **ORBISONGS** [-]
(UK-iss.Jul67, hit No.40) (cd-iss. Dec95)
Sep 66. *Monument; <6622>* **THE VERY BEST OF ROY ORBISON** [94]
1967. (lp) *Monument; (LMO/SMO 5007)* **ROY ORBISON'S GREATEST HITS** [-]
(re-iss. 1972)
1969. (lp) *Monument; (LMO/SMO 5014)* **MORE OF ROY ORBISON'S GREATEST HITS** [-]
1972. (7") *Monument;* **DREAM BABY. / BLUE ANGEL** [-]
Jan 73. (d-lp) *Monument; (MNT 67290)* **ALL-TIME GREATEST HITS** [39]
(cd-iss. Jan89) (re-iss. +cd.Dec88 on 'Skyline')
1975. (lp/c) *Monument; (69147)* **THE MONUMENTAL ROY ORBISON**
1975. (7") *Monument; (ZS 88906)* **ONLY THE LONELY. / UPTOWN**
1975. (7") *Monument; (ZS 88907)* **I'M HURTIN'. / DREAM BABY (HOW LONG MUST I DREAM)**
1975. (7") *Monument; (ZS 88908)* **THE CROWD. / IN DREAMS**
Jul 75. (7") *Monument; (ZS 88910)* **IT'S OVER. / OH PRETTY WOMAN**
Nov 75. (lp) *Monument; (69188)* **THE MONUMENTAL ROY ORBISON VOL.2** [-]
Mar 76. (7") *Monument; (MNT 3965)* **ONLY THE LONELY. / IT'S OVER**
Jan 78. (7") *Monument; (LR 8210)* **ONLY THE LONELY. / DREAM BABY**
Jul 81. (lp/c) *Monument-CBS; (MNT/40 10026)* **GOLDEN DAYS** [63]
(cd-iss. Jun92)
May 89. (lp/c/cd) *Monument; (463419-1/-4/-2)* **BEST LOVED STANDARDS**
(re-iss. +cd.Dec92)
May 89. (lp/c/cd) *Monument; (463418-1/-4/-2)* **RARE ORBISON**
May 89. (lp/c/cd) *Monument; (463417-1/-4/-2)* **OUR LOVE SONG**
Nov 93. (cd) *Monument; (4749562)* **LONELY AND BLUE / CRYING**
Nov 93. (cd) *Monument; (4749572)* **IN DREAMS / ORBISONGS**
Jul 67. (7") *MGM; <13756>* **CRAWLIN' BACK. / RIDE AWAY** [-]
Jul 67. (7") *MGM; <13757>* **BREAKIN' UP IS BREAKIN' MY HEART. / TOO SOON TO KNOW** [-]
Jul 67. (7") *MGM; <13758>* **TWINKLE TOES. / WHERE IS TOMORROW** [-]
Jul 67. (7") *MGM; <13759>* **SWEET DREAMS. / GOING BACK TO GLORIA** [-]
Jul 67. (7") *MGM; <13760>* **YOU'LL NEVER BE SIXTEEN AGAIN. / THERE WON'T BE MANY COMING HOME** [-] [-]

1974. (lp) *Hallmark; (NR 5013)* **THE EXCITING ROY ORBISON** [-]
Nov 75. (lp) *Arcade; (ADEP 19)* **THE BEST OF ROY ORBISON** [1] [-]
Dec 76. (7"ep) *Charly; (CEP 111)* **ROY ORBISON: OOBY DOOBY** [-]
Sep 78. (7") *Charly; (CYS 1043)* **OOBY DOOBY. / CURTIS LEE** [-]
Sep 84. (d-lp) *Charly; (CDX 4)* **THE SUN YEARS 1956-1958: THE DEFINITIVE COLLECTION** [-]
(cd-iss. Apr89 on 'Bear Family')
Oct 86. (cd) *Charly; (CD CHARLY 27)* **GO GO GO** [-]
Aug 83. (lp/c) *Decca; (TAB/KTB 72)* **THE BIG O COUNTRY** [-]
Sep 86. (d-lp/c) **THE ROY ORBISON COLLECTION** [-]
(cd-iss. Jul91 on 'Pickwick')
Jan 88. (lp) *Point; (SP 243)* **DANCIN' WITH ROY ORBISON** [-]
Jan 88. (lp) *Point; (SP 250)* **DREAMIN' WITH ROY ORBISON** [-]
Sep 82. (7"ep) *Bear Family;* **ALMOST EIGHTEEN / JOLIE / SWEET AND INNOCENT / THE BUG / PAPER BOY / SEEMS TO ME** [-] [-] Germ
Jul 87. (cd) *Bear Family; (BCD 15407)* **THE RCA SESSIONS: ROY ORBISON & SONNY JAMES** [-]
May 88. (7") *Zu-Jazz;* **PROBLEM CHILD. / ?** [-]
May 88. (lp) *Zu-Jazz; (Z 2006)* **PROBLEM CHILD** [-]
Oct 88. (lp/c/cd) *Telstar; (STA R/C 2330/TCD 2330)* **THE LEGENDARY ROY ORBISON** [1] [-]
– It's over / Only the lonely / Goodnight / Lana / The crowd / All I have to do is dream / Dream baby / Mean woman blues / Oh pretty woman / Love hurts / My prayer / Falling / Blue angel / In dreams / Blue bayou / The great pretender / Pretty paper.
Jan 89. (d-lp/c/cd) *Rhino;* **FOR THE LONELY; ROY ORBISON ANTHOLOGY, 1956-1965** [-]
Oct 90. (cd/c/lp) *Rhino;* **BALLADS – 22 CLASSIC LOVE SONGS** [38]
Feb 89. (c) *Venus; (VENUMC 6)* **THE MAGIC OF ROY ORBISON** [-]
May 89. (c,cd) *Pickwick; (HSC 3266/PWK 111)* **THE LEGEND** [-]
May 90. (cd/c/lp) *Pickwick; (PWKS 576/HSC/SHM 3303)* **THE HITS 1** [-]
May 90. (cd/c/lp) *Pickwick; (PWKS 582/HSC/SHM 3305)* **THE HITS 2** [-]
Jul 91. (cd) *Pickwick;* **ROY ORBISON VOL.2** [-]
Feb 89. (7") *Old Gold; (OG 9870)* **ONLY THE LONELY. / BLUE ANGEL** [-]
Feb 89. (7") *Old Gold; (OG 9872)* **RUNNING SCARED. / CRYING** [-]
Feb 89. (7") *Old Gold; (OG 9881)* **OH PRETTY WOMAN. / MEAN WOMAN BLUES** [-]
Feb 89. (7") *Old Gold; (OG 9883)* **IN DREAMS. / FALLING** [-]
Feb 89. (7") *Old Gold; (OG 9885)* **DREAM BABY. / PRETTY PAPER** [-]
Feb 89. (7") *Old Gold; (OG 9879)* **IT'S OVER. / BLUE BAYOU** [-]
Feb 89. (7") *Old Gold; (OG 9888)* **THE CROWD. / LANA** [-]
May 89. (d-lp/cd) *Polydor; (839234-1/-2)* **THE SINGLES COLLECTION 1965-1973** [-]
Sep 89. (cd/c/lp) *Instant; (CD/TC INS 510/INS 510)* **THE EARLY YEARS** [-]
Dec 89. (lp) *Raven;* **COMMUNICATION BREAKDOWN** [-]
(cd-iss. Feb91)
Jul 90. (cd-box/c-box/lp-box) *Knight; (ROY CD/MC/LP 47002)* **GOLDEN DECADE BOXED SET (1960-1970)** [-]
Jun 92. (7"/c-s) *M.C.A.; (MCS/+MC 1652)* <54287> **I DROVE ALL NIGHT. / FOREVER FRIENDS (with SHEENA EASTON)** [7]
(cd-s+=) *(MCSCD 1652)* – Trickster:- Line of fire.
Aug 92. (7"/c-s; ROY ORBISON & k.d. LANG) *Virgin America; (VUS/+CS 63)* **CRYING. / FALLING** [13]
(cd-s+=) *(CDVUS 63)* – Oh pretty woman / She's a mystery to me.
(cd-s+=) *(CDXVUS 63)* – Only the lonely / It's over.
Oct 92. (7"/c-s) *Virgin America; (VUS/+CS 68)* **HEARTBREAK RADIO. / CRYING (with k.d. LANG)** [36]
(cd-s) *(CDVUS 68)* – ('A'side) / In dreams / You got it / Dream baby.
(cd-s) *(CDVUSX 68)* – ('A'side) / Blue angel / Claudette / Lana.
Nov 92. (lp/c/cd) *Virgin; (VUSLP/VUSMC/CDVUS 58)* **KING OF HEARTS** (1988 recordings) [23]
– You're the one / Heartbreak radio / We'll take the night / Crying (with k.d.LANG) / After the love has gone / Love in time / I drove all night / Wild hearts run out of time / Coming home / Careless heart (original demo).
Nov 93. (7"/c-s) *Virgin America; (VUS/+CS 79)* **I DROVE ALL NIGHT. / CRYING** [47]
(cd-s+=) *(CDVUS 79)* – Oh pretty woman / After the love has gone.
Jun 93. (3xcd-box) *Sequel; (NXTCD 246)* **THE GOLDEN DECADE 1960-1969** [-]
Apr 93. (cd/c) *Ariola;* **ROY ORBISON / RAY PETERSON** [-]
May 94. (cd/c) *Laserlight; (1/7 2330)* **ROY ORBISON** [-]
Aug 94. (cd) *Legends In Music;* **ROY ORBISON** [-]
Oct 94. (3xcd-box) *Pickwick; (BOXD 23)* **THE HITS** [-]
Oct 94. (cd) *Monument;* **THE BEST** [-]
Mar 95. (cd) *Collection; (COL 027)* **THE COLLECTION** [-]
Sep 95. (cd) *Spectrum;* **CLASS OF '55 – MEMPHIS ROCK'N'ROLL HOMECOMING (with JOHNNY CASH/ JERRY LEE LEWIS/ CARL PERKINS)** [-]
Nov 95. (3xcd-box) *The Collection;* **ROY ORBISON** [-]
Nov 96. (cd/c) *Virgin; (CDV/TCV 2804)* **THE VERY BEST OF ROY ORBISON** [18]

ORBITAL

Formed: Seven Oaks, London, England . . . late 80's by brothers PHIL and PAUL HARTNOLL. United by a shared love of electro and punk, they were inspired by the outdoor party scene of '89 and named themselves after the infamous circular motorway which ravers used in delirious pursuit of their next E'd up shindig. A home produced 4-track demo, 'CHIME', brought the band almost instant fame and remains one of their best loved songs. Originally released on the small 'Oh-Zone' label, the track was given a full release in March 1990 on 'London' offshoot 'Ffrr', its subtly euphoric charms elevating 'CHIME' into the top 20 and the brothers onto a memorable 'Top Of The Pops' appearance where they sported defiant 'No Poll Tax' t-shirts. Although dance culture has since become increasingly politicised as a result of heavy handed legislation, it was unusual at the time for a techno act to be so passionately anti-establishment, an ethos the HARTNOLL brothers had carried over from their punk days and which would become a recurring theme throughout their career. Meanwhile, ORBITAL followed their debut with a trio of largely instrumental, synth-driven singles, the highlight being the pounding white noise of the BUTTHOLE SURFERS-sampling 'SATAN'. The track reached No.31 upon its release in August '91 although a subsequent live version stormed into the top 5 in early '99. Their untitled debut album, released in September of the same year, showcased cerebral electronic soundscapes which nevertheless retained a melancholy, organic warmth while their live shows moved feet and minds en masse. Alongside events like the Shamen's Synergy, which attempted to mix the spectacle of rock 'n' roll with the communal energy of house, ORBITAL were pivotal in pioneering dance music in the live environment. Rather than reproducing the songs live on stage, they improvised, restructuring tracks which had been pre-set into sequencers. This spontaneity was enhanced by an innovative light-show utilising state of the art technology, a heady combination that saw ORBITAL headline the Glastonbury festival two years running during the mid-90's. They were no less effective in the studio and their second untitled album was a finely tuned extension of the debut, encompassing such exotica as a sample from an Australian pedestrian crossing (!) With their third long player, 1994's cynically titled 'SNIVILISATION', the music took on an uneasy paranoia, seething with a bitter undercurrent that railed against the state of humanity in general, as well as issues closer to home such as the much hated Criminal Justice Bill. The record also introduced elements of drum 'n' bass, a dalliance that continued with their 'IN SIDES' album. Preceded by the near-half hour strangeness of 'THE BOX' single, the record marked the pinnacle of ORBITAL's sonic explorations, a luminous trip to the final frontiers of electronica. In spite of their experimentalism, a loyal following ensures that the duo are never short of chart success, the 'IN SIDES' album reaching No.5, while 1997 saw ORBITAL go top 3 in the singles chart twice (first with the aforementioned live version of 'SATAN' and then with their celebrated remake of 'THE SAINT'). After a slight delay, ORBITAL were back in circulation with a fifth set, 'THE MIDDLE OF NOWHERE' (1999), a happier affair that was premiered by hit single 'STYLE', the album also saw POOKA singers NATASHA JONES and SHARON LEWIS collaborate on the track, 'OTONO'. • **Songwriters:** The duo, except cover of THE SAINT (E. Astley) and noted samples; O EUCHARI (performed by Emily Van Evera). • **Trivia:** Vox on tracks 'SAD BUT TRUE' & 'ARE WE HERE?' by ALISON GOLDFRAPP.

Album rating: UNTITLED (ORBITAL 1) (*7) / UNTITLED (ORBITAL II) (*7) / SNIVILIZATION (*8) / IN SIDES (*9) / THE MIDDLE OF NOWHERE (*8)

PHIL HARTNOLL – keyboards / **PAUL HARTNOLL** – keyboards

		Oh-Zone	not iss.
Jan 90.	(12"ep) *(ZONE 001)* **CHIME. / DEEPER (full version)**	☐	-

		Ffrr-London	Ffrr-London
Mar 90.	(7"/c-s) *(F/+CS 135)* **CHIME. / DEEPER**	☐	-
	(cd-ep+=) *(FCD 135)* – ('A'version).		
	(12"ep) *(FX 135)* – ('A'-JZM remix) / ('A'-Bacardi mix).		
Jul 90.	(7"ep) *(F 145)* **OMEN. / 2 DEEP / OPEN MIND**	☐	-
	(cd-ep) *(FCD 145)* – (1st & 3rd track) / ('A'edit)		
	(12"ep) *(FX 145)* – Omen: The chariot / The tower / Wheel of fortune / The fool.		
	(12"ep) *(FXR 145)* – ('A'remixes).		
Jan 91.	(7") *(F 149)* **SATAN. / BELFAST**	31	-
	(12"ep+=/cd-ep+=) *(FX/FCD 149)* – L.C.1. *(cd-ep re-iss. Aug95 on 'Internal'; LIECD 25)*		
	(12"ep) *(FXR 149)* – ('A'-rhyme & reason mix) / L.C.2 (outer limits mix) / Chime.		
Aug 91.	(12") *(FX)* **MIDNIGHT. / CHOICE**	☐	-
	(12"ep) *(FX)* – Midnight (Sasha mix) / Choice (Orbital & Eye & I mix).		
	(cd-ep+=) *(FCD)* – Analogue test Feb'90. *(re-iss. Aug95 on 'Internal'; LIECD 26)*		
Sep 91.	(cd/c/lp) *(828248-2/-4/-1) <351001>* **UNTITLED (ORBITAL 1)**	71	-
	– The moebius / Speed freak / Oolaa / Desert storm / Fahrenheit 303 / Steel cube idolatry / High rise / Chime (live) / Midnight (live) / Belfast / Macrohead. *(cd w-out last track, repl. by)* – I think it's disgusting. *(c+=)* – Untitled. *(re-iss. Apr96 & Apr97 on 'Internal' cd/c; TRU CD/MC 9)* *(re-iss. Apr99 on 'London' cd/c; 828248-2/-4)*		
Feb 92.	(12"ep) *(FX 181)* **MUTATIONS (I): OOLAA (Joey Beltram remix) / OOLAA (Meat Beat Manifesto mix) / CHIME (Joey Beltram). / SPEED FREAK (Moby mix)**	24	-
	(12"ep) *(FX 181)* – MUTATIONS (II): Chime (Ray Keith mix) / Chime (Crime remix) / Steel cube idolatory / Farenheit 303.		
	(cd-ep) *(FCD 181)* – Oolaa (Joey Beltram mix) / Chime (Ray Keith mix) / Speed freak / Fahrenheit 303.		

		Internal	Ffrr-London
Sep 92.	(12"ep/cd-ep) *(LIARX/LIECD 1)* **RADICCIO EP**	37	-
	– Halycon / The naked and the dead.		
	(cd-ep) *(LIECD 2)* – The naked and the dead / Sunday.		
	(cd-ep re-iss. Aug95; LIECD 27)		
Apr 93.	(12"ep/c-ep) *(LIARX/LIEMC 7)* **LUSH 3-1. / LUSH 3-2 / LUSH 3-3 (Underworld mix)**	☐	-
	(12"ep) *(LIAXR 7)* – LUSH 3-4 (Psychick Warriors Ov Gaia) / LUSH 3-5 (CJ Bollard).		
	(cd-ep) *(LIECD 7)* – (all 5 tracks).		
Jun 93.	(cd/c/lp) *(TRU CD/MC/LP 2) <351026>* **UNTITLED (ORBITAL II)**	28	-
	– Time becomes / Planet of the shapes / Lush 3-1 / Lush 3-2 / Impact (the Earth is burning) / Remind / Walk now . . . / Monday / Halycon + on + on / Input out. *(re-iss. Aug95; same)* *(re-iss. Apr99 on 'London' cd/c; 828386-2/-4)*		
Mar 94.	(cd-ep/12"ep) *(LIECD/LIARX 12)* **THE JOHN PEEL SESSIONS EP**	☐	-
	– Lush (Euro-tunnel disaster '94) / Walk about / Semi detached / Attached.		
	(cd-ep) **DIVERSIONS EP** *(LIEDC 12)* – Impact USA / Lush 3 (Euro-Tunnel disaster		

'94) / Walkabout / Lush 3-5 (CJ Bolland) / Lush 3-4 (Warrior drift) / Lush 3-4 (Underworld).

Aug 94.	(cd/c/d-lp) *(TRU CD/MC/LP 5) <124027>* **SNIVILIZATION**	4	☐
	– Forever / I wish I had duck feet / Sad but true / Crash and carry / Science friction / Philosophy by numbers / Kein trink wasser / Quality seconds / Are we here? / Attached. *(re-iss. Aug95 & Apr97; same)* *(re-iss. Apr99 on 'London' cd/c; 828536-2/-4)*		
Sep 94.	(12"ep/c-ep) *(LIARX/LIEMC 15)* **ARE WE HERE? EP**	33	-
	– Are we here?: Who are they? – Do they here? – They did it (mix).		
	(cd-ep+=/s-cd-ep+=) *(LIE CD/DC 15)* – Are we here?: What was that? – Criminal Justice bill? – Industry standard?.		
——	In May'95, they issued 'Belfast'/'Wasted (vocal mix)' on special cd-s which hit UK No.53. THERAPY? was on flip side with 'Innocent X'.		
Aug 95.	(d7"ep/12"ep/cd-ep/s-cd-ep) *(LIE/LIARX/LIECD/LIEDP 23)* **UNTITLED EP**	☐	-
	– Times fly (slow) / Sad but new / Times fly (fast) / The tranquilizer. (above was not eligible for UK chart position due to it's length)		
Apr 96.	(12"/cd-s) *(LIARX/LIECD 30)* **THE BOX. / THE BOX**	11	-
	(cd-s+=) *(LICDP 30)* – (2 extra mixes).		
Apr 96.	(cd/cd/c/3x12"lp) *(TRU DC/CD/MC/LP 10) <124087>* **IN SIDES**	5	☐
	– The girl with the sun in her head / P.E.T.R.O.L. / The box / Dwr budr / Adnan's / Out there somewhere? *(cd re-iss. Apr97 on 'Dutch East India'; 124129CD)* *(cd re-iss. Apr99 on 'London'; 828881-2)*		
Jan 97.	(cd-s) *(LIECD 37) <850990>* **SATAN (live at New York) / OUT THERE SOMEWHERE (live at New York)**	3	Sep97
	(cd-s) *(LICDP 37)* – ('A'-live at Chelmsford) / Lush 3 (live at Boston) / The girl with the sun in her head (live at Boston).		
	(cd-s) *(LICDD 37)* – ('A'-Industry standard edit) / Chime (live at Chelmsford) / Impact (live at Chelmsford).		
——	(due to length of above it also hit No.48 in the UK album charts)		

		FFRR-London	FFRR-London
Apr 97.	(c-s/12"/cd-s) *(FCS/FX/FCD 296)* **THE SAINT / THE SINNER**	3	☐
	(cd-s+=) *(FCDP 296)* – Belfast (live) / Petrol (live).		
Aug 97.	(cd/c/lp) *(828939-2/-4)* **EVENT HORIZON (soundtrack)**	☐	☐
Mar 99.	(12") *(FX 358)* **STYLE. / OLD STYLE / BIG PIPE STYLE / NEW STYLE**	13	☐
	(cd-s) *(FCD 358)* – (first 2 tracks) / Mock Tudor.		
	(cd-s) *(FCDP 358)* – (Old style [repl. by]) An fhomhair.		
Apr 99.	(cd/c/d-lp) *(556076-2/-4/-1) <31065>* **THE MIDDLE OF NOWHERE**	4	☐
	– Way out – > / Spare parts express / Know where to run / I don't know you people / Otono / Nothing left 1 / Nothing left 2 / Style.		
Jul 99.	(12") *(FX 365)* **NOTHING LEFT. / MUCH ADO ABOUT**	32	-
	(cd-s+=) *(FCD 365)* – ('A'mixes).		
	(cd-s+=) *(FCDP 365)* – ('A'mixes).		

ORCHESTRAL MANOEUVRES IN THE DARK

Formed: West Kirby, Liverpool, England . . . Autumn 1978, initially as The ID, by ANDREW McCLUSKEY and PAUL HUMPHREYS. After a one-off indie single, the coldly pulsing 'ELECTRICITY', for 'Factory', they signed to 'Virgin' subsidary label, 'Dindisc'. Early in 1980, the group hit the UK Top 75 with 'RED FRAME – WHITE LIGHT', paving the way for an eponymous Top 30 parent album. Later that summer, they scored further chart successes with 'MESSAGES' and 'ENOLA GAY' (the name of the plane which dropped the Hiroshima bomb), the latter an infectiously melancholy swirl of electronica which belied its horrific subject matter. The song was also the highlight of the 'ORGANISATION' (1980) album, wherein the drum machines of previous recordings had been replaced with a live drummer, MALCOLM HOLMES. Heavily influenced by KRAFTWERK, OMD's cerebral electro-pop became progressively warmer and more commercial as the decade wore on. Beginning with the soporific lilt of 'SOUVENIR', McCLUSKEY and HUMPHREYS embarked upon the most successful period of their career, releasing a string of Top 5 hits and well-received albums, namely 'ARCHITECTURE & MORALITY' (1981), 'DAZZLE SHIPS' (1983), 'JUNK CULTURE' (1984) and 'CRUSH' (1985). O.M.D. were a constant feature in the singles chart through the early to mid 80's, like a more pretentious, less claustrophobic cousin to DEPECHE MODE, their biggest hit of the era being the breezy 'LOCOMOTION' (mercifully, not a cover of the LITTLE EVA number!), complete with horn stabs courtesy of the WEIR BROTHERS (NEIL & GRAHAM) who later joined the group as a permanent fixture. With the 'CRUSH' album, OMD enjoyed a brief flurry of Stateside success via the twee romanticism of the 'SO IN LOVE' and 'SECRET' singles, although by the release of the patchy 'PACIFIC AGE' (1986) the following year, the writing partnership of McCLUSKEY and HUMPHREYS was beginnning to falter. The latter eventually departed in 1989 to form The LISTENING POOL, while McCLUSKEY carried on with OMD as a solo project, resurfacing in early '91 with the annoying 'SAILING ON THE SEVEN SEAS', a Top 3 hit. The subsequent album, 'SUGAR TAX' (1991) also made the Top 3 although the revamped OMD was clearly an entirely different beast, airbrushed pop lacking the mystery and romance of the early material. A further album, 'LIBERATOR', carried on in a similar vein. • **Songwriters:** All material written by McCLUSKEY & HUMPHREYS, until the latter's exit. Covered; I'M WAITING FOR THE MAN (Velvet Underground) / NEON LIGHTS (Kraftwerk). • **Trivia:** An ID track 'JULIA'S SONG', appeared on an 'Open Eye' indie compilation album, 'Street To Street' in 1978.

Album rating: ORCHESTRAL MANOEUVRES IN THE DARK (*7) /

ORGANISATION (*6) / ARCHITECTURE & MORALITY (*7) / DAZZLE SHIPS (*5) / JUNK CULTURE (*6) / CRUSH (*6) / THE PACIFIC AGE (*4) / IN THE DARK – THE BEST OF OMD compilation (*8) / SUGAR TAX (*5) / LIBERATOR (*5) / UNIVERSAL (*5) / THE OMD SINGLES compilation (*7)

ANDREW McCLUSKEY (b.24 Jun'59, Wirral, England) – vocals, bass, synthesizers (ex-DALEK I) / **PAUL HUMPHRIES** (b.27 Feb'60, London, England) – keyboards, synths. (ex-The ID) with backing from computer 'Winston'.

	Factory	not iss.
May 79. (7") (FAC 6) **ELECTRICITY. / ALMOST**		-

	Dindisc	not iss.
Sep 79. (7") (DIN 2) **ELECTRICITY (re-recorded). / ALMOST**		
Feb 80. (7"/12") (DIN 6/+12) **RED FRAME – WHITE LIGHT. / I BETRAY MY FRIENDS**	67	-

—— guests **DAVID FAIRBURN** – guitar / **MALCOLM HOLMES** – drums / **MARTIN COOPER** – sax

Feb 80. (2x12"lp/c) (DID/+C 2) **ORCHESTRAL MANOEUVRES IN THE DARK**	27	

– Bunker soldiers / Almost / Mystereality / Electricity / The Messerschmit twins / Messages / Julia's song / Red frame – white light / Dancing / Pretending to see the future. (re-iss.Aug84 on 'Virgin' lp/c; OVED/+C 96) (cd-iss. Jul87; DIDCD 2)

May 80. (7") (DIN 15) **MESSAGES. / TAKING SIDES AGAIN**	13	

(ext-10") (DIN 15-10) – Waiting for the man.

—— added **DAVID HUGHES** – keyboards (ex-DALEK I LOVE YOU, ex-SECRETS) and now f/t member **MALCOLM HOLMES** – drums (ex-CLIVE LANGER & THE BOXES, ex-ID)

Sep 80. (7"/ext.12") (DIN 22/+12) **ENOLA GAY. / ANNEX**	8	-
Oct 80. (lp/c) (DID/+C 6) **ORGANISATION**	6	-

– Enola Gay / 2nd thought / VCL XI / Motion and heart / Statues / The misunderstanding / The more I see you / Promise / Stanlow. (free 7"ep) – INTRODUCING RADIOS / PROGRESS. / DISTANCE FADES BETWEEN US / WHEN I WAS SIX (re-iss. Aug88 on 'Virgin' lp/c; OVED/+C 147) (cd-iss. Jul87; DIDCD 6)

—— **MALCOLM COOPER** – saxophone, keyboards (ex-DALEK I LOVE YOU) repl. HUGHES

	Dindisc	Epic
Aug 81. (7"/ext.10") (DIN 24/+10) **SOUVENIR. / MOTION AND HEART (Amazon version) / SACRED HEART**	3	-
Oct 81. (7"/ext.12") (DIN 36/+12) **JOAN OF ARC. / THE ROMANCE OF THE TELESCOPE (unfinished version)**	5	-
Nov 81. (lp/c) (DID/+C 12) <37721> **ARCHITECTURE & MORALITY**	3	-

– New stone age / She's leaving / Souvenir / Sealand / Joan Of Arc / Joan Of Arc (Maid of Orleans) / Architecture and morality / Georgia / The beginning and the end. (cd-iss. 1988 on 'Virgin' lp/c; OVED/+C 276) (re-iss. Apr90; DIDCD 12) (cd re-iss. Jan95; CDIDX 12)

Jan 82. (7") (DIN 40) **MAID OF ORLEANS (THE WALTZ JOAN OF ARC). / NAVIGATION**	4	

(12"+=) (DIN 40-12) – Of all the things we've made. (3"cd-s Jun88; CDT 27)

	Virgin	Epic-Virgin
Jan 82. (7") **SOUVENIR. / NEW STONE AGE**	-	
Feb 83. (7"/7"pic-d)(12") (VS/+Y 527)<VS 527-12> **GENETIC ENGINEERING. / 4-NEU**	20	-
Mar 83. (lp/c) (V/TCV 2261) <38543> **DAZZLE SHIPS**	5	

– Radio Prague / Genetic engineering / ABC auto-industry / Telegraph / This is Helena / International / Dazzle ships / The romance of the telescope / Silent running / Radio waves / Time zones / Of all the things we've made. (cd-iss. 1985; CDV 2261) (re-iss. 1987 lp/c; OVED/+C 106) (cd re-iss. Apr97 on 'Virgin-VIP'; CDVIP 170)

Apr 83. (7"/7"pic-d)(12") (VS/+Y 580)(VS 580-12) **TELEGRAPH. / 66 AND FADING**	42	-
May 83. (7") **TELEGRAPH. / THIS IS HELENA**	-	

	Virgin	A&M
Apr 84. (7"/7"sha-pic-d) (VS/+Y 660) **LOCOMOTION. / HER BODY IN MY SOUL**	5	Nov84

(ext.12") (VS 660-12) – The avenue. (3"cd-s-iss.Jun88; CDT 12)

May 84. (lp/c) (V/TCV 2310) <5027> **JUNK CULTURE**	9	Nov84

– Junk culture / Tesla girls / Locomotion / Apollo / Never turn away / Love and violence / Hard day / All wrapped up / White trash / Talking loud and clear. (cd-iss. 1986; CDV 2310) (re-iss. Mar90 lp/c; OVED/+C 215) (cd re-iss. Aug98 on 'Virgin-VIP'; CDVIP 215)

Jun 84. (7"/7"pic-d)(12") (VS/+Y 685)(VS 685-12) **TALKING LOUD AND CLEAR. / JULIA'S SONG**	11	
Aug 84. (7") (VS 705) **TESLA GIRLS. / TELEGRAPH (live)**	21	

(12"+=)(c-s+=) (VS 705-12)(TVS 705) – Garden city.

Oct 84. (7"/7"pic-d) (VS/+Y 727) **NEVER TURN AWAY. / WRAP-UP**	70	

(ext.12") (VS 727-12) – Waiting for the man (live).

May 85. (7") (VS 766) **SO IN LOVE. / CONCRETE HANDS**	27	26 Aug85

(ext;12")(ext.12"pic-d) (VS 766-13)(VSY 766-14) – Maria Gallante.
(d7"++=) (VS 766) – White trash (live).

Jun 85. (lp)(c) (V/TCV 2349) <5077> **CRUSH**	13	38 Jul85

– So in love / Secret / Bloc bloc bloc / Women III / Crush / 88 seconds in Greensboro / The native daughters of the west / La femme accident / Hold you / The lights are going out. (cd-iss. Jan86; CDV 2349) (cd re-iss. Oct96 on 'Virgin-VIP'; CDVIP 155)

Jul 85. (7") (VS 796) **SECRET. / DRIFT**	34	-

(ext-d12"+=) (VS 796-12) – Red frame – white light / I betray my friends.

Oct 85. (7"/7"sha-pic-d) (VS/+S 811) **LA FEMME ACCIDENT. / FIREGUN**	42	

(ext.d12"+=) (VSD 811-12) – Locomotion (live) / Enola Gay (live).

Nov 85. (7") <2794> **SECRET. / FIREGUN**	-	63
Feb 86. (7") <2811> **IF YOU LEAVE. / LA FEMME ACCIDENT**	-	4
Apr 86. (7") (VS 843) **IF YOU LEAVE. / 88 SECONDS IN GREENSBORO**	48	

(12") (VS 843-12) – ('A'extended) / Locomotion (live).

—— added The **WEIR BROTHERS** (NEIL & GRAHAM) (had guested on earlier songs)

Aug 86. (7"/7"pic-d) (VS/+Y 888) <2872> **(FOREVER) LIVE AND DIE. / THIS TOWN**	11	19

(12"+=) (VS 888-13) – ('A'extended).

Sep 86. (cd/c/lp) (CD/TC+/V 2398) <5144> **THE PACIFIC AGE**	15	47 Oct86

– Stay (the black rose and the universal wheel) / (Forever) Live and die / The Pacific age / The dead girls / Shame / Southern / Flame of hope / Goddess of love / We love you / Watch us fall.

Nov 86. (7") (VS 911) **WE LOVE YOU. / WE LOVE YOU (dub)**	54	

(12"+=) (VS 911-12) – ('A'extended).
(d7"+=) (VSD 911) – If you leave / 88 seconds on Greensboro.
(free c-s w7"+=) (VSC 911) – Souvenir / Electricity / Enola Gay / Joan of Arc.

Apr 87. (7") (VS 938) **SHAME (re-recorded). / GODDESS OF LOVE**	52	

(12"+=) (VS 938-12) – ('B're-recorded version).
(cd-s+=) (MIKE 938-12) – (Forever) Live and die / Messages.

Jan 88. (7") (VSG 987) <3002> **DREAMING. / SATELLITE**	50	16 Feb88

(ext.12"pic-d) (VS 987-12) – Gravity never failed.
(cd-s++=/3"cd-s++=) (VDCD/+X 987) – Dreaming.
(re-dist.Jun88, hit Uk No.60)
(10") (VS 987-10) – ('A'side) / ('A'William Orbit mix) / Messages / Secret.

Feb 88. (pic-cd/cd/c/lp) (CDP/CD/TC+/OMD 1) <5186> **IN THE DARK – THE BEST OF O.M.D.** (compilation)	2	46

– Electricity / Messages / Enola Gay / Souvenir / Joan of Arc / Maid of Orleans (Joan Of Arc waltz) / Talking loud and clear / Tesla girls / Locomotion / So in love / Secret / If you leave / (Forever) Live and die / Dreaming. (cd+=) – Telegraph / We love you (12"version) / La femme accident (12"version) / Genetic engineering. (re-iss. Sep94; same)

OMD

—— **ANDY McCLUSKEY** now sole survivor after others left 1989. HUMPHREYS formed The LISTENING POOL in the early 90's. / added **STUART BOYLE** – guitar / **NIGEL IPINSON** – keyboards / **PHIL COXON** – keyboards / **ABE JUCKS** – drums

	Virgin	Virgin
Mar 91. (7"/c-s) (VS/+C 1310) **SAILING ON THE SEVEN SEAS. / BURNING**	3	

(12") (VS 1310-12) – ('A'extended) / Floating on the seven seas.
(cd-s) (VSCDX 1310) – ('A'extended) / Dancing on the seven seas / Big town.
(cd-s) (VSCD 1310) – ('A'side) / Floating on the seven seas / Dancing on the seaven seas (Larrabee mix) / Sugartax.

May 91. (cd/c/lp) (CD/TC+/V 2648) <91715> **SUGAR TAX**	3	

– Sailing on the seven seas / Pandora's box / Then you turn away / Speed of light / Was it something I said / Big town / Call my name / Apollo XI / Walking on air / Walk tall / Neon lights / All that glitters.

Jun 91. (7"/c-s) (VS/+C 1331) **PANDORA'S BOX. / ALL SHE WANTS IS EVERYTHING**	7	

(cd-s+=) (VSCD 1331) – ('A'-Constant pressure mix) / ('A'-Diesel fingers mix).
(12") (VS 1331-12) – (2-'A'mixes).
(cd-s) (VSCDX 1331) – (3-'A'mixes).

Sep 91. (7"/c-s) (VS/+C 1368) **THEN YOU TURN AWAY. / SUGAR TAX**	50	

(cd-s+=) (VSCD 1368) – Area / ('A'-Inforce repeat mix).
(cd-s) (VSCDG 1368) – ('A'side) / ('A'-Repeat mix) / Sailing on the seven seas / Vox humana.

Nov 91. (7"/c-s) (VS/+C 1380) **CALL MY NAME. / WALK TALL**	50	

(12") (VS 1380-12) – ('A'side) / Brides of Frankenstein.
(cd-s++=) (VSCD 1380) – ('A'side) / ('A'version) / Brides . . . (dub).

May 93. (7"/c-s) (VS/+C 1444) **STAND ABOVE ME. / CAN I BELIEVE YOU**	21	

(cd-s+=) (VSCDG 1444) – ('A'-Transcendental mix) / ('A'-Hynofunk mix).
(12") (VS 1444-12) – ('A'side) / ('A'-Transcendental mix) / ('A'-10 minute version).

Jun 93. (cd/c/lp) (CD/TC+/V 2715) <88225> **LIBERATOR**	14	

– Stand above me / Everyday / King of stone / Dollar girl / Dream of me (based on Love's theme) / Sunday morning / Agnus Dei / Love and hate you / Heaven is / Best years of our lives / Christine / Only tears. (cd re-iss. Aug98 on 'VIP-Virgin'; CDVIP 217)

Jul 93. (7"/c-s) (VS/+C 1461) **DREAM OF ME (BASED ON LOVE'S THEME). / ('A'mix)**	24	

(cd-s+=) (VSCDT 1461) – Strange sensations / The place you fear the most.
(cd-s) (VSCDX 1461) – ('A'side) / Enola Gay / Dreaming / Call my name.

Sep 93. (7"/c-s) (VS/+C 1471) **EVERYDAY. / ELECTRICITY (live)**	59	

(cd-s+=) (VSCDT 1471) – Walk tall (live) / Locomotion (live).

—— **STUART KERSHAW** – drums; repl. JUCKS

Aug 96. (c-s/cd-s) (VSC/+DT 1599) **WALKING ON THE MILKY WAY / MATTHEW STREET / NEW DARK AGE**	17	-

(cd-s) (VSCDG 1599) – ('A'side) / Joan of Arc (live) / Maid of Orleans (live) / Walking on air (live).

Sep 96. (cd/c) (CDV/TCV 2807) **UNIVERSAL**	24	-

– Universal / Walking on the Milky Way / The Moon & the Sun / The Black Sea / Very close to far away / The gospel of St Jude / That was then / Too late / The boy from the chemist is here to see you / If you're still in love with me / New head / Victory waltz.

Oct 96. (c-s) (VSC 1606) **UNIVERSAL / HEAVEN IS**	55	-

(cd-s+=) (VSCDT 1606) – Messages (live).
(cd-s) (VSCDG 1606) – ('A'side) / King of stone (live) / Talking loud & clear (live) / ('A'-abum version).

Sep 98. (cd-s) (VSCDT 1694) **THE OMD REMIXES: ENOLA GAY (OMD vs SASH!) / ELECTRICITY (Micronauts mix) / SOUVENIR (Moby mix)**	35	-

(12") (VST 1694) – (first mix) / Souvenir (hard house) / Souvenir (7am version).
(12") (VSTX 1694) – (first two mixes) / Apollo XI (Northern electric soul remix).

Sep 98. (cd/c) (CDV/TCV 2859) <46520> **THE OMD SINGLES** (compilation)	16	Nov98

– Electricity / Messages / Enola Gay / Souvenir / Joan of Arc / Maid of Orleans / Tesla girls / Locomotion / Talking loud and clear / So in love / If you leave / (Forever) Live and die / Dreaming / Sailing the seven seas / Pandora's box / Call my name / Dream of me (based on love's theme).

– compilations, etc. –

May 84. (lp) Epic; **ORCHESTRAL MANOEUVRES IN THE DARK**	-	

– (compilation of first 2 albums)

Feb 89. (12") *Old Gold; (OG 4099)* **ENOLA GAY. / ELECTRICITY** ☐ –
Mar 89. (12") *Old Gold; (OG 4109)* **SOUVENIR (extended). /**
TALKING LOUD AND CLEAR (extended) ☐ –
Feb 89. (12") *Virgin; (SP12 285)* **BRIDES OF FRANKENSTEIN (OMD**
megaremixes: LOCOMOTION / SO IN LOVE / SECRET /
IF YOU LEAVE / WE LOVE YOU) ☐ ☐
Nov 90. (3xpic-cd-box) *Virgin; (TPAK 7)* **CD BOXED SET** ☐ –
– (first 3 albums)

ORGANISATION (see under ⇒ KRAFTWERK)

ORGY

Formed: Los Angeles, California, USA . . . 1997 by JAY GORDON, RYAN SHUCK, AMIR DERAKH, PAIGE HALEY and BOBBY HEWITT. ORGY became the first group to sign for KORN's 'Elementree' imprint, the latter's mainman, JONATHAN DAVIS, guesting on the track, 'REVIVAL' from their debut album, 'CANDYASS' (1998). In fact, guitarist RYAN had played alongside the aforementioned singer in the band, SEX ART, co-writing 'BLIND', a track which made it onto KORN's debut album. Although their initial inception was KORN-inspired, ORGY were in fact tarty, alternative pop-metal, like DURAN DURAN sharing a bed with MINISTRY. In 1999, ORGY lifted their version of New Order's 'BLUE MONDAY' from the set and nearly had a minor hit. • **Trivia:** Singer, JAY, produced COAL CHAMBER's dark debut in '98.

Album rating: CANDYASS (*6)

JAY GORDON – vocals / **RYAN SHUCK** – guitar / **AMIR DERAKH** – guitar, synthesizer / **PAIGE HALEY** – bass / **BOBBY HEWITT** – drums

		Elementree/Reprise	Elementree/Reprise
Apr 99.	(cd) <(9362 46923-2)> **CANDYASS**	☐	32 Sep98
	– Social enemies / Stitches / Dissention / Platinum / Fetisha / Fiend / Blue Monday / Gender / All the same / Pantomime / Revival / Dizzy.		
Jun 99.	(c-s/12"/cd-s) *(W 484 C/T/CD)* <F-111 44555> **BLUE MONDAY.** ('A'-Club 69 mix) / ('A'-Top40-single mix)	☐	56 Dec98

Jim O'ROURKE

Born: 1969, Chicago, Illinois, USA. Tinkering with guitars at the age of six, O'ROURKE's subsequent career was hard to pinpoint as the soloist was so prolific in his future music. At university, the unique songwriter had composed enough material for a good few albums, collaborating with improvisational guitarist DEREK BAILEY on 'REMOVE THE NEED', 'TAMPER' and 'TERMINAL PHARMACY'. Whilst O'ROURKE contemplated a solo career, he also engaged in an ongoing experiment with rock troupe GASTR DEL SOL and worked as co-producer and co-writer for the German experimentalists FAUST (while maintaining a strong bond with post-angular rockers, TORTOISE). The man released the brilliant 'BAD TIMING' (on 'Drag City') which followed up 1997's quasi-acoustic 'HAPPY DAYS'. Springing back in early '99, he issued the "already-a" masterpiece 'EUREKA', a startling album that awoke new fans to JIM's ever existing genius. From the epic 7 minute plus opener, 'WOMEN OF THE WORLD' (a re-working of IVOR CUTLER'S comic opus, done O'ROURKE style of course!) through to the haunting piano and lap steel ballad 'GHOST SHIP IN A STORM', the bizarre artwork of a manchild holding a rabbit into his groin (!) didn't stop the word-of-mouth popularity surrounding the new SPIRIT-meets-FLOYD/NYMAN/TORTOISE long player. • **Note:** A different JIM O'ROURKE released a few lp's ('Ar Hoelion Wyth' and 'Y Bont') between 1984 and '88.

Album rating: REMOVE THE NEED (*5) / TAMPER (*5) / TERMINAL PHARMACY (*6) / HAPPY DAYS (*5) / BAD TIMING (*7) / EUREKA (*8)

JIM O'ROURKE – vocals, guitar, etc

		Staalplaat	not iss.
1992.	(d-cd) *(STCD 048)* **DISENGAGE** (UK-iss.Feb96; same)	–	– German

—— joined ex-SQUIRREL BAIT member DAVID GRUBBS in the duo, GASTR DEL SOL

		not iss.	Metamkine
1993.	(cd-ep) *(009)* **RULES OF REDUCTION**	–	–

		not iss.	Complacency
1993.	(cd-ep; JIM O'ROURKE / EDDIE PREVOST) *(9302)* **THIRD STRAIGHT DAY MADE PUBLIC** – Reason for eyelids / Two's company / Mean fiddle / On a slow mend.	–	☐

		Extreme	not iss.
Nov 93.	(cd) *(9)* **TAMPER**	–	– German
Sep 94.	(cd) *(18)* **REMOVE THE NEED**	–	– German

—— In 1994, O'ROURKE collaborated with HENRY KAISER on the CD album, 'TOMORROW KNOWS WHERE YOU LIVE' for 'Victo'; *VICTOCD 014*

		not iss.	Tzadik
1996.	(cd-ep) <7011> **TERMINAL PHARMACY / CEDE**	–	☐

		Revenant	Revenant
Feb 97.	(cd) <REV 101> **HAPPY DAYS** – Happy days. (UK-iss.Nov97; same)	–	☐

—— now with **JOHN McENTIRE** – drums / **JEB BISHOP** – trombone / **THYMME JONES** – trumpet

	Drag City	Drag City
Aug 97.	(lp/cd) <(DC 120/+CD)> **BAD TIMING** – There's hell in hello, but more in . . . . / 94 the long way / Bad timing / Happy trails.	☐	☐

	Some	not iss.
Mar 98.	(10"ep) *(SOME 08)* **PLEASE NOTE OUR FAILURE**	☐	–

—— now with **KEN CHAMPION** – piano / **JEB BISHOP** – trombone / **GLENN KOTCHKE** – drums / **DARIN GRAY** – bass / **JOAN MORRONE** – french horn / **ROB MAZUREK** – cornet / etc

	Domino	Drag City
Mar 99.	(cd/lp) *(WIG CD/LP 62)* <DC 162> **EUREKA** – Prelude to 110 or 220 – Women of the world / Ghost ship in a storm / Movie on the way down / Through the night softly / Please patronize our sponsors / Something big / Eureka / Happy holidays.	☐	–
Jul 99.	(cd; JIM O'ROURKE & GUNTER MULLER) *(4EARSCD 514)* **SLOW MOTION** (above issued on 'For 4 Ears')	☐	–
Nov 99.	(12"/cd-ep) *(RUG 103 T/CD)* **HALFWAY TO A THREEWAY / THE WORKPLACE. / NO SPORT, MARTIAL ART / FUZZY SUN**	☐	☐

Beth ORTON

Born: Dec'70, Norwich, England. A one-time Buddhist nun (after her mother died of cancer), she was discovered in 1991/2 by WILLIAM ORBIT who saw her performing in a play. Her collaborative work with ORBIT ('Superpinkymandy') was subsequently heard by The CHEMICAL BROTHERS and RED SNAPPER, the former act employing her downbeat but poignant vocals on the 1995 'Exit Planet Dust' album track, 'Alive Alone'. The following year, she found herself on the books of 'Heavenly' records, delivering her debut album, 'TRAILER PARK' soon after. An affecting blend of fragile folk and subtle lo-fi trip-hop rhythms, it won praise from such diverse camps as Folk Roots magazine and Mixmag (it was even nominated for the 1997 Mercury Music Prize). The same year (1997), BETH's four singles scored successively higher chart placings, the re-released 'SHE CRIES YOUR NAME', revealing the melancholy depths of her NICK DRAKE/SANDY DENNY-esque muse. The lanky ORTON (she's 6 feet tall) ended the year on a high note, collaborating with her long-time hero, TERRY CALLIER on the Top 40 EP 'BEST BIT'. The princess of bedsitter music served up a second helping of rich, thought-provoking tunes in the shape of 1999's 'CENTRAL RESERVATION'. A deserved UK Top 20 success (with guest appearances from BEN WATT, BEN HARPER, DAVE ROBACK and DR. JOHN), BETH also made some headway in the States where she had befriended BECK (to namecheck but a few). Songs such as 'STOLEN CAR', the title track (both Top 40 hits) and 'STARS ALL SEEM TO WEEP' were emotionally and lyrically attuned like paintings set on the deepest canvas taking every colour imaginable from palettes of silver. • **Songwriters:** Most with rhythm section FRIEND and BARNES, except SHE CRIES YOUR NAME; she co-wrote this with WILLIAM ORBIT. Covered IT'S NOT THE SPOTLIGHT (Bobby Bland; c.) / I WISH I NEVER SAW THE SUNSHINE (Spector – Greenwich – Barry) / DOLPHINS (Fred Neil).

Album rating: TRAILER PARK (*8) / CENTRAL RESERVATION (*8)

BETH ORTON – vocals; with **TED BARNES** – guitar (of JUNCTIONS) / **ALI FRIEND** – double bass (of RED SNAPPER) / **WILL BLANCHARD** – drums (of SANDALS) / guest **DAVID BOULTER** – harmonium / + string section

		Heavenly	Dedicated
Jul 96.	(7"one-sided) *(HVN 056)* **I WISH I NEVER SAW THE SUNSHINE**	☐	–
Sep 96.	(10"ep/cd-ep) *(HVN 60 10/CD)* **SHE CRIES YOUR NAME / TANGENT. / SAFETY / IT'S NOT THE SPOTLIGHT**	☐	–
Oct 96.	(cd/c/lp) *(HVNLP 17 CD/MC/LP)* <44007> **TRAILER PARK** – She cries your name / Tangent / Don't need a reason / Live as you dream / Sugar boy / Touch me with your love / Whenever / How far / Someone's daughter / I wish I never saw the sunshine / Galaxy of emptiness.	68	☐
Jan 97.	(10"ep/cd-ep) *(HVN 64 10/CD)* **TOUCH ME WITH YOUR LOVE. / PEDESTAL / GALAXY OF EMPTINESS**	60	–
Mar 97.	(c-ep/10"ep/cd-ep) *(HVN 65 CS/10/CD)* **SOMEONE'S DAUGHTER. / I WISH I NEVER SAW THE SUNSHINE / IT'S THIS I AM I FIND**	49	–
Jun 97.	(c-s) *(HVN 68CS)* **SHE CRIES YOUR NAME (1997 version) / IT'S NOT THE SPOTLIGHT** (10"+=/cd-s+=) *(HVN 68-10/CD)* – Bullet / Best bit.	40	–

		Heavenly	Heavenly
Dec 97.	(c-ep; BETH ORTON featuring TERRY CALLIER) *(<HVN 72CS>)* **BEST BIT EP** – Best bit / Skimming stone / Dolphins. (12"ep+=/cd-ep+=) *(<HVN 72 12/CD>)* – Lean on me.	36	☐

—— next with guitarist **BEN HARPER**

Mar 99.	(c-s) *(HVN 89CS)* **STOLEN CAR / PRECIOUS MAYBE** (cd-s+=) *(HVN 89CD)* – I love how you love me. (cd-s) *(HVN 89CD2)* – ('A'side) / Stars all seem to weep (shed version) / Touch me with your love (live).	34	☐
Mar 99.	(d-lp/c/cd) *(HVNLP 22/+MC/CD)* <19038> **CENTRAL RESERVATION** – Stolen car / Sweet decline / Couldn't cause me harm / So much more / Pass in time / Central reservation / Stars all seem to weep / Love like laughter / Blood red river / Devil song / Feel to believe / Central reservation.	17	☐
Sep 99.	(12"/cd-s) *(HVN 92 12/CD1)* **CENTRAL RESERVATION. / CENTRAL RESERVATION (Spiritual Life – Ibadan remix) / CENTRAL RESERVATION (William Orbit remix)** (cd-s) *(HVN 92CD2)* –	37	☐

Joan OSBORNE

Born: 1962, Anchorage, Kentucky, USA. Having dropped out of Louisville College in 1988, she subsequently relocated to New York where she sang in blues clubs, a varied repertoire including her celebrated version of BILLIE HOLIDAY's 'God Bless The Child'. Recorded with her new band, a live set surfaced on the 'Womanly Hips' imprint, a label initiated by her manager of the time, PAUL RISELLI. HOOTERS guitarist, ROB HYMAN, subsequently witnessed a live performance and tipped off producer, RICH CHERTOFF (previous credits include CYNDI LAUPER), who worked for 'Polygram'. This led to a major label deal and, in 1995, she appeared on Mercury off-shoot, 'Blue Gorilla' with the classy 'ONE OF US' single. A characteristically off-beat hypothesis centering on God's proletarian potential, the record was an impressive showcase for OSBORNE's gritty yet evocatively sensuous vocals and was even nominated for a Grammy early in '96. The track was also a taster for her critically acclaimed debut album, 'RELISH', which achieved similar success in the American charts around the same time. Coming on like a down-home version of PJ HARVEY fused with TORI AMOS, OSBORNE was equally effective whether covering the likes of Bob Dylan ('MAN IN THE LONG BLACK COAT') and Sonny Boy Williamson ('HELP ME') or huskily negotiating such smoking original material as 'RIGHT HAND MAN' and 'PENSACOLA', the usual subject material of religion, sex etc., shot through with an off-kilter perspective. OSBORNE's homegrown success was repeated on British shores in early '96, although in the last two years her position has been constantly challenged by a string of young pretenders. • **Songwriters:** She co-writes with her group and ex-HOOTERS guitarist ERIC BAZILIAN, who solely penned 'ONE OF US'. Samples CAPTAIN BEEFHEART (on Right Hand Man) and T.REX.

Album rating: RELISH (*7) / EARLY RECORDINGS collection (*5)

JOAN OSBORNE – vocals / **ERIC BAZILIAN** – guitar / **MARK EGAN** – bass / **ROB HYMAN** – organ, synth / **ANDY KRAVITZ** – drums (of CYPRESS HILL, URGE OVERKILL)

		Blue Gorilla	Blue Gorilla
Feb 96.	(c-s) (JOAMC 1) <852368> **ONE OF US** / ('A'edit)	6	4 Nov95
	(cd-s) (JOACD 1) – ('A'side) / Dracula Moon / Crazy baby (live).		
Mar 96.	(cd/c) (<526699-4/-2)> **RELISH**	5	9 Oct95
	– St. Teresa / Man in the long black coat / Right hand man / Pensacola / Dracula Moon / One of us / Ladder / Spider web / Let's just get naked / Help me / Crazy baby / Lumina.		
May 96.	(c-s) (JOAMC 3) **ST. TERESA / LUMINA**	33	Apr96
	(cd-s+=) (JOACD 3) – Spider web / ('A'edit).		
	(cd-s) (JOADD 3) – ('A'side) / Help me / One of us / ('A'edit).		
Jul 96.	(c-s) (JOAMC 4) **RIGHT HAND MAN (international edit) / LUMINA**		
	(cd-s+=) (JOACD 4) – Spider web (live) / St. Teresa (live).		
	(cd-s) (JOADD 4) – ('A'side) / One of us (live) / Help me / ('A'version).		
	(above was to have been issued in Mar'96; JOA CD/DD 2)		
Nov 96.	(cd/c) (534235-2/-4) **EARLY RECORDINGS** (rare material)		
	– Flyaway / Dreamin' about the day / His eyes are a blue million miles / Fingerprints / 4 camels / What you gonna do / Match burn twice / Billie listens / Wild world / Son of a preacher man / Get up Jack.		

Ozzy OSBOURNE

Born: JOHN MICHAEL OSBOURNE, 3 Dec'48, Aston, Birmingham, England. After eleven years as frontman for BLACK SABBATH, OSBOURNE was given his marching orders, forming his own BLIZZARD OF OZZ in 1980 alongside LEE KERSLAKE (drums, ex-URIAH HEEP), BOB DAISLEY (bass, ex-RAINBOW, ex-CHICKEN SHACK), DON AVERY (keyboards) and guitar wizard, RANDY RHOADS (ex-QUIET RIOT). Signing to Don Arden's 'Jet' label, OZZY and the band released their self-titled debut in 1980, hitting the UK Top 10 and narrowly missing the US Top 20. Hailed as OZZY's best work since 'SABBATH's heyday, the unholy alliance of RHOADS's music and OSBOURNE's lyrics (which, if anything, looked even more to the 'dark side' than the 'SABBATH material) produced such wonderfully grim fare as 'CRAZY TRAIN', 'SUICIDE SOLUTION' (later the subject of much JUDAS PRIEST-style courtroom controversy) and the epic 'MR. CROWLEY', inspiring multitudes of schoolkids to raise their pinkie and forefinger in cod-satanic salutation. The record went double platinum in the States, as did the follow-up, 'DIARY OF A MADMAN' (1981) (credited to OZZY solo), a cross-Atlantic Top 20 hit. Proving once and for all that the music industry is peopled by hard-bitten control freaks, OZZY proceeded to chomp on a live dove at a record company meeting later that year. Another infamous incident occurred only a few months later when the singer gnashed the head off a bat thrown onstage by a fan at a concert in Des Moines, cementing his reputation as heavy metal monster extrordinaire and public enemy No.1. 1982 proved to be an eventful year for 'the Oz', tragedy striking when his close friend and right hand man, RHODES, died in a plane crash in March. Consolation and a modicum of much needed stability came with his subsequent marriage to Don Arden's daughter, Sharon, on the 4th of July '82, the brave lass subsequently becoming his manager. BRAD GILLIS replaced RHODES for the live album of BLACK SABBATH covers, 'TALK OF THE DEVIL' (1982), before JAKE E. LEE was brought in as a more permanent fixture prior to 'BARK AT THE MOON' (1983). The rhythm section had also undergone numerous personnel changes with a final line-up of TOMMY ALDRIDGE (drums, ex-BLACK OAK ARKANSAS,etc.) and BOB DAISLEY. Another double platinum smash, the release of the record saw OZZY undertaking a

mammoth US tour during which he unwittingly relieved himself on a wall of the Alamo monument in San Antonio, consequently being charged and banned from playing there. OZZY had always been a hard drinker and drug user, Sharon finally forcing him to attend the first of many unsuccessful sessions at the Betty Ford Clinic in 1984. His albums continued to sell consistently, particularly in America, despite constant line-up changes. 1988 saw the arrival of guitarist ZAKK WILDE, heralded as a true successor to the revered RHODES. The late 80's also saw OSBOURNE retiring to his Buckinghamshire mansion with Sharon and his three kids, eventually kicking the booze and re-emerging in 1991 after being cleared of causing the death of three fans. In three separate, well-documented cases, parents claimed OZZY's 'SUICIDE SOLUTION' had driven their children to kill themselves. 'NO MORE TEARS' (1991) was a triumphant comeback, OSBOURNE claiming the album would be his last and subsequently embarking on a farewell tour. The last two shows of the jaunt were opened by a ROB HALFORD (of JUDAS PRIEST)-fronted BLACK SABBATH, RONNIE JAMES DIO refusing to perform. Talks of a 'SABBATH reunion came to nothing although OZZY couldn't resist another tour and eventually an album, 'OZZMOSIS' (1995). The record made the Top 5 in America where he's still regarded as something of a Metal Godfather; maybe it's the Brummie accent. OZZY then stunned the metal world by rejoining BLACK SABBATH for concerts and a reunion album in 1998. • **Songwriters:** OZZY lyrics, RHOADS music. OZZY later collaborated with BOB DAISLEY. • **Trivia:** In 1987, he played a bible-punching preacher in the film 'Trick Or Treat'.

Album rating: OZZY OSBOURNE'S BLIZZARD OF OZZ (*7) / DIARY OF A MADMAN (*6) / TALK OF THE DEVIL (*6) / BARK AT THE MOON (*5) / THE ULTIMATE SIN (*5) / TRIBUTE (*8) / NO REST FOR THE WICKED (*5) / JUST SAY OZZY (*5) / NO MORE TEARS (*7) / LIVE & LOUD (*6) / OZZMOSIS (*6) / THE OZZMAN COMETH – THE BEST OF . . . (*8)

OZZY OSBOURNE'S BLIZZARD OF OZZ

OZZY OSBOURNE – vocals (ex-BLACK SABBATH) / **RANDY RHOADS** – guitar (ex-QUIET RIOT) / **LEE KERSLAKE** – drums (ex-URIAH HEEP) / **BOB DAISLEY** – bass (ex-RAINBOW, ex-CHICKEN SHACK) / **DON AVERY** – keyboards

		Jet	Jet-CBS
Sep 80.	(7") (JET 197) **CRAZY TRAIN. / YOU LOOKING AT ME LOOKING AT YOU**	49	-
Sep 80.	(lp/c) (JET LP/CA 234) <36812> **OZZY OSBOURNE'S BLIZZARD OF OZZ**	7	21 Mar81
	– I don't know / Crazy train / Goodbye to romance / Dee / Mr. Crowley / No bone movies / Revelation (Mother Earth) / Steal away (the night). (re-iss. Nov87 on 'Epic' lp/c; 450453-1/-4) (cd-iss. Nov87 on 'Jet'; CDJET 234) (re-iss. cd Nov95 on 'Epic'; 481674-2)		
Nov 80.	(7") (JET 7-003) <37640> **MR. CROWLEY (live). / YOU SAID IT ALL (live)**	46	Apr82
	(12"+=/12"pic-d+=) (JET/+P 12-003) – Suicide solution (live).		
Apr 81.	(7") <02079> **CRAZY TRAIN. / STEAL AWAY (THE NIGHT)**	-	

OZZY OSBOURNE

(same line-up, except AVERY)

		Epic	Epic
Oct 81.	(lp/c) (JET LP/CA 237) <37492> **DIARY OF A MADMAN**	14	16
	– Over the mountain / Flying high again / You can't kill rock and roll / Believer / Little dolls / Tonight / S.A.T.O. / Diary of a madman. (cd-iss. May87; CDJET 237) (re-iss. Apr91 on 'Epic' cd/c; 463086-2/-4) (re-iss. cd Nov95 on 'Epic'; 481677-2)		
Nov 81.	(7"/12") (JET 7/12 017) **OVER THE MOUNTAIN. / I DON'T KNOW**		-
Nov 81.	(7") <02582> **FLYING HIGH AGAIN. / I DON'T KNOW**	-	-
Feb 82.	(7") <02707> **LITTLE DOLLS. / TONIGHT**	-	

—— (Nov'81) **RUDY SARZO** – bass (ex-QUIET RIOT) repl. DAISLEY (to URIAH HEEP) **TOMMY ALDRIDGE** – drums (ex-BLACK OAK ARKANSAS, etc) repl. KERSLAKE

—— (Apr'82) **BRAD GILLIS** – guitar (of NIGHT RANGER) repl. RANDY RHOADS who was killed in a light aeroplane crash on 19th Mar'82.

Nov 82.	(d-lp/d-c) (JET DP/CD 401) <38350> **TALK OF THE DEVIL** (live at Ritz Club, NY) <US-title 'SPEAK OF THE DEVIL'>	21	14
	– Symptom of the universe / Snowblind / Black sabbath / Fairies wear boots / War pigs / The wizard / N.I.B. / Sweet leaf / Never say die / Sabbath bloody sabbath / Iron man – Children of the grave / Paranoid. (re-iss. Sep87 on 'Epic' d-lp/d-c; 451124-1/-4) (cd-iss. Jun89; 451124-2) – (omits dialogue). (re-iss. cd/d-lp complete.Jul91 on 'Castle'; CCS CD/LP 296) (re-iss. cd Nov95 as 'SPEAK OF THE DEVIL' on 'Epic'; 481679-2)		
Dec 82.	(7"/7"pic-d) (JET/+P 7-030) **SYMPTOM OF THE UNIVERSE (live). / N.I.B.** (live)		-
	(12"+=) (JET 12-030) – Children of the grave (live).		
Feb 83.	(7") <03302> **IRON MAN (live). / PARANOID (live)**	-	

—— (Dec'82) **JAKE E. LEE** (b.JAKEY LOU WILLIAMS, San Diego, California, USA) – guitar (ex-RATT) repl. GILLIS who returned to NIGHT RANGER / **DON COSTA** – bass repl. PETE WAY (ex-UFO) who had deputised for the departing RUDY SARZO who had returned to QUIET RIOT. (He later joined WHITESNAKE)

—— **OZZY, JAKE E + TOMMY** re-recruited **BOB DAISLEY** to repl. COSTA

		Epic	CBS Assoc.
Nov 83.	(7"/12",12"silver/12"pic-d) (A/TA/WA 3915) **BARK AT THE MOON. / ONE UP ON THE B-SIDE**	21	
Dec 83.	(7") <04318> **BARK AT THE MOON. / SPIDERS**	-	-
Dec 83.	(lp/c) (EPC/40 25739) <38987> **BARK AT THE MOON**	24	19
	– Rock'n'roll rebel / Bark at the Moon / You're no different / Now you see it (now you don't) / Forever / So tired / Waiting for darkness / Spiders. (re-iss. Apr86 lp/c; EPC/40 32780) (cd-iss. Oct88; CD 32780) (re-iss. cd Nov95; 481678-2)		
Mar 84.	(7") (A 4260) <04383> **SO TIRED. / FOREVER (live)**		
	(12"+=/d7"+=) (TA/DA 4260) – Waiting for darkness / Paranoid (live).		

—— ALDRIDGE was briefly replaced (Mar-May84) on tour by CARMINE APPICE.

May 84. (7") *(A 4452)* **SO TIRED. / BARK AT THE MOON (live)** `20` `☐`
(12"+=,12"gold+=) *(WA 4452)* – Waiting for darkness / Suicide solution (live) / Paranoid (live).

—— **PHIL SOUSSAN** – bass repl. DAISLEY / **RANDY CASTILLO** – drums (ex-LITA FORD BAND) repl. ALDRIDGE
Jan 86. (7"/7"w-poster/12") *(A/QA/TA 6859)* **SHOT IN THE DARK. / ROCK'N'ROLL REBEL** `20` `-`
Feb 86. (lp/c) *(EPC/40 26404)* <40026> **THE ULTIMATE SIN** `8` `6`
– Lightning strikes / Killer of giants / Thank God for the bomb / Never / Shot in the dark / The ultimate sin / Secret loser / Never know why / Fool like you. *(cd-iss. Jul86; CD 26404)* (pic-lp Aug86; EPC 11-26404) (re-iss. Feb89 on 'C.B.S.' lp/c/cd; 462496-1/-4/-2) (re-iss. Nov95; 481680-2)
Mar 86. (7") <05810> **SHOT IN THE DARK. / YOU SAID IT ALL** `-` `68`
Jul 86. (7"/12") *(A/TA 7311)* **THE ULTIMATE SIN. / LIGHTNING STRIKES** `72` `-`
1988. (7") <08463> **SHOT IN THE DARK. / CRAZY TRAIN**

—— (Aug'88) **ZAKK WILDE** (b.ZACH ADAMS, 14 Jan'66) – guitar repl. JAKE who formed BADLANDS. / **DAISLEY** returned to repl. SOUSSAN (to BILLY IDOL) / added **JOHN SINCLAIR** – keyboards
Oct 88. (lp/c/cd) *(46258-1/-4/-2)* <44245> **NO REST FOR THE WICKED** `23` `13`
– Miracle man / Devil's daughter / Crazy babies / Breaking all the rules / Bloodbath in Paradise / Fire in the sky / Tattooed dancer / The demon alcohol. *(cd+=)* – Hero. *(re-iss. Jun94 & Nov95; cd/c; 481681-2)*
Oct 88. (7"/7"sha-pic-d) *(653063-0/-9)* **MIRACLE MAN. / CRAZY BABIES** `☐` `-`
(12"+=/12"w-poster/cd-s+=) *(653063-6/-8/-2)* – The liar.
Dec 88. (7") <08516> **MIRACLE MAN. / MAN YOU SAID IT ALL** `-` `☐`
Feb 89. (7") <68534> **CRAZY BABIES. / THE DEMON ALCOHOL** `-` `☐`

—— Earlier in the year OZZY had accompanied LITA FORD on 45 'CLOSE MY EYES FOREVER'. In Apr'89, it was to reach UK/US Top50.
—— **TERRY 'GEEZER' BUTLER** – bass was used for tour work late 1988.
Feb 90. (cd/c/lp) *(465940-1/-4/-2)* <45451> **JUST SAY OZZY (live)** `69` `58`
– Miracle man / Bloodbath in Paradise / Shot in the dark / Tattooed dancer / Sweet leaf / War pigs. *(re-iss. cd Nov95; 481517-2)*

—— In the late 80's, OZZY retired to his Buckinghamshire mansion with his manager/wife Sharon Arden and 3 kids. He had also kicked his alcohol addiction. Returned 1991 after being cleared of causing death of fan. See last studio line-up. Augmented also by **MICHAEL INEZ** – bass, inspiration repl. BUTLER

	Epic	Epic Assoc
Sep 91. (7") *(657440-7)* <73973> **NO MORE TEARS. / S.I.N.** `32` `71`
(c-s+=/12"+=/12"pic-d+=/cd-s+=) *(657440-8/-6/-?/-2)* – Party with the animals.
Oct 91. (cd/c/lp) *(467859-2/-4/-1)* <46795> **NO MORE TEARS** `17` `7`
– Mr. Tinkertrain / I don't want to change the world / Mama I'm coming home / Desire / No more tears / S.I.N. / Hellraiser / Time after time / Zombie stomp / A.V.H. / Road to nowhere. *(re-iss. cd Nov95; 481675-2)*
Nov 91. (7") *(657617-7)* <74093> **MAMA I'M COMING HOME. / DON'T BLAME ME** `46` `28` Feb92
(12"+=) *(657617-8)* – I don't know / Crazy train.
(cd-s+=) *(657617-9)* – (Ozzy on the Steve Wright show)
(12"+=) *(657617-6)* – Time after time / Goodbye to romance.
<US-cd-ep+=> <74265> – Party with the animals.
Jun 93. (d-cd) *(473798-2)* <46795> **LIVE & LOUD (live)** `☐` `22`
– Intro / Paranoid / I don't want to change the world / Desire / Mr. Crowley / I don't know / Road to nowhere / Flying high again / Guitar solo / Suicide solution / Goodbye to romance / Shot in the dark / No more tears / Miracle man / Drum solo / War pigs / Bark at the Moon / Mama, I'm coming home / Crazy train / Black sabbath / Changes. *(re-iss. Nov95; 481676-2)*
Jun 93. (12"/cd-s) *(659340-6/-2)* **CHANGES (live). / CHANGES / NO MORE TEARS / DESIRE** `☐` `☐`

—— next featured **MIKE INEZ** – bass (of ALICE IN CHAINS)
Oct 95. (cd/c/lp) *(481022-2/-4/-1)* <67091> **OZZMOSIS** `22` `4`
– Perry Mason / I just want you / Ghost behind my eyes / Thunder underground / See you on the other side / Tomorrow / Denial / My little man / My Jekyll doesn't hide / Old LA tonight.
Nov 95. (7"pic-d) *(662639-7)* **PERRY MASON. / LIVING WITH THE ENEMY** `23` `☐`
(cd-s+=) *(662639-2)* – The whole world's falling down.
(cd-s) *(662639-5)* – ('A'side) / No more tears / I don't want to change the world / Flying high again.

—— **ROBERT TRUJILLO** – bass (ex-SUICIDAL TENDENCIES) – bass repl. INEZ
Aug 96. (12") *(663570-6)* **I JUST WANT YOU. / AIMEE / VOODOO DANCER** `43` `☐`
(cd-s) *(663570-2)* – ('A'side) / Aimee / Mama, I'm coming home.
(cd-s) *(663570-5)* – ('A'side) / Voodoo dancer / Iron man (with THERAPY?).

– compilations, others, etc. –

on 'Epic' UK / 'CBS Assoc.' unless otherwise stated
May 87. (d-lp/c/cd) *(450475-1/-4/-2)* <40714> **TRIBUTE (live 1981 with RANDY RHOADS)** `13` `6`
– I don't know / Crazy train / Revelation (Mother Earth) / Believer / Mr. Crowley / Flying high again / No bone movies / Steal away (the night) / Suicide solution / Iron man – Children of the grave / Goodbye to romance / Paranoid / Dee *[not on cd]*. *(re-iss. Apr93 cd/c;)* (re-iss. cd Nov95; 481516-2)
Jun 87. (7"/12") *(650943-7/-6)* <07168> **CRAZY TRAIN (live 1981). / CRAZY TRAIN (live 1981)** `☐` `☐`
Jul 88. (12"ep/cd-ep) *(652 875-6/-2)* **BACK TO OZZ** `76` `-`
– The ultimate sin / Bark at the Moon / Mr. Crowley / Diary of a madman.
Aug 90. (cd) *Priority;* <57129> **TEN COMMANDMENTS** (rare) `-` `☐`
Mar 93. (d-cd) *(465211-2)* **BARK AT THE MOON / BLIZZARD OF OZZ** `☐` `☐`
Nov 97. (cd/c) *(487260-2/-4)* **THE OZZMAN COMETH – THE BEST OF** `68` `13`
– Black sabbath / War pigs / Goodbye to romance (live) / Crazy train (live) / Mr. Crowley (live) / Over the mountain (live) / Paranoid (live) / Bark at the moon / Shot in the dark / Crazy babies / No more tears / Mama, I'm coming home (live) / I just want you / I don't want to change the world / Back on earth. *(cd+=)* – Fairies wear boots / Beyond the wall of sleep.

OTHER ONES (see under ⇒ GRATEFUL DEAD)

OTHER TWO (see under ⇒ NEW ORDER)

OZRIC TENTACLES / EAT STATIC
(dig out; 4th edition or Great Alt & Indie)

P (see under ⇒ BUTTHOLE SURFERS)

Jimmy PAGE (see under ⇒ LED ZEPPELIN)

PAIN KILLER (see under ⇒ ZORN, John)

PALACE (see under ⇒ OLDHAM, Will)

PALE FOUNTAINS (see under ⇒ SHACK)

PALE SAINTS (dig out; Great Alt & Indie . . .)

Robert PALMER

Born: ALAN ROBERT PALMER, 19 Jan'49, Batley, Yorkshire, England. From the age of 3, PALMER lived with his family in Malta (his father being in the services), moving to London in 1969 after having his first musical experience in semi-pro group, MANDRAKE PADDLE STEAMER. Replacing the solo bound JESS RODEN, PALMER joined the ALAN BROWN SET, singing on the 'Deram' 45, 'GYPSY GIRL', later that year. The following year, he hooked up with jazz-rockers DADA, who boasted vocalist ELKIE BROOKS on their eponymous 'Atco' debut long player. Come 1971, the act had evolved into VINEGAR JOE, although after three poor selling albums for 'Island' (VINEGAR JOE / ROCK'N'ROLL GYPSIES / SIX-STAR GENERAL), they eventually split in March '74. After nearly replacing LOWELL GEORGE in LITTLE FEAT, PALMER was retained by 'Island' on a solo basis. His debut release, The LITTLE FEAT and METERS-enhanced 'SNEAKIN' SALLY THROUGH THE ALLEY' (1974), stiffed in the UK, although US sales almost resulted in a Top 100 placing. As well as a seamless cover of LITTLE FEAT's 'SAILIN' SHOES', the album's highlight was the ALLEN TOUSSAINT-penned title track although many of the collection's songs suffered from a characterlessness that coloured much of PALMER's subsequent output. The following year, he relocated to New York with his wife, subsequently flirting with reggae on his follow-up album, 'PRESSURE DROP'. Following a support slot on a LITTLE FEAT tour, the singer again relocated, this time to Nassau, Bahamas to consummate his love affair with the music of the Carribbean. The culmination of this period in PALMER's career was 1978's 'DOUBLE FUN', wherein the singer sauntered through a mellow, sun-bleached cover of ANDY FRASER's (ex-FREE) 'EVERY KINDA PEOPLE', subsequently PALMER's first US Top 20 hit. 'SECRETS' (1979) was a radical stylistic departure, anchored on balls-out rock and furnishing PALMER with a second Top 20 hit in MOON MARTIN's 'BAD CASE OF LOVING YOU (DOCTOR, DOCTOR)'. The immaculately attired crooner gained a deserved commercial leap in the early 80's when his polished-oak vocals combining surprisingly well with GARY NUMAN's synth-pop noodlings on the likes of 'JOHNNY AND MARY'. In 1982, the very ROD (STEWART)-ish 'SOME GUYS HAVE ALL THE LUCK' single gave PALMER some belated UK Top 20 success, the singer enjoying further British exposure three years later when he became frontman for the DURAN DURAN/CHIC offshoot, The POWER STATION. An often predictably derivative affair, they were also blatantly commercial, scoring with the likes of 'SOME LIKE IT HOT' and a cover of MARC BOLAN's 'GET IT ON'. Soon back on the solo trail, PALMER carried on in a hard rock style for his biggest album to date, 'RIPTIDE' (1985), a record which featured the Transatlantic Top 5 (US No.1) smash, 'ADDICTED TO LOVE'. An antiseptically raunchy piece of poppy-cock-rock, the single was accompanied by a semi-ironic video featuring PALMER surrounded by a troupe of blonde bombshells rocking in formation. Now an accomplished worldwide artist, PALMER emigrated to Lugano, Switzerland prior to releasing 'HEAVY NOVA' (1988). Another big seller, PALMER showed off his mastery of diverse styles, taking in everything from suave balladeering ('SHE MAKES MY DAY') to Swiss

yodelling ('CHANGE HIS WAYS') as well as scoring another massive US hit with the cliched rock of 'SIMPLY IRRESISTIBLE'. A surprisingly endearing collaboration with UB40 on BOB DYLAN's 'I'LL BE YOUR BABY TONIGHT' powered the 'DON'T EXPLAIN' (1990) album into the UK Top 10 while 'RIDIN' HIGH' (1992) was a passable tribute to the Tin Pan Alley era. Though possessed of smoothly soulful, impressively adaptable vocal chords and an often faultless choice in material, PALMER's work invariably suffers from a lack of cohesion. That said, you can't go wrong with his greatest hits' set, 1989's 'ADDICTIONS VOl.1'. • **Songwriters:** PALMER penned, except FROM A WHISPER TO A SCREAM (Allen Toussaint) / PRESSURE DROP (Lee Perry) / YOU REALLY GOT ME (Kinks) / JEALOUS + THE SILVER GUN (Alan Powell) / YOU ARE IN MY SYSTEM (System) / CAN WE STILL BE FRIENDS (Todd Rundgren) / SOME GUYS HAVE ALL THE LUCK (Persuaders) / I DIDN'T MEAN TO TURN YOU ON (hit; Cherrelle) / EARLY IN THE MORNING (Gap Band) / I'LL BE YOUR BABY TONIGHT (Bob Dylan) / MERCY MERCY ME (THE ECOLOGY) – I WANT YOU (Marvin Gaye) / WITCHCRAFT (hit; Frank Sinatra) / GIRL U WANT (Devo) / RESPECT YOURSELF (Staple Singers) / etc. • **Trivia:** PALMER produced many artists including The COMSAT ANGELS, DESMOND DEKKER and PETER BAUMANN.

Album rating: SNEAKIN' SALLY THROUGH THE ALLEY (*6) / PRESSURE DROP (*5) / SOME PEOPLE CAN DO WHAT THEY LIKE (*5) / DOUBLE FUN (*5) / SECRETS (*5) / CLUES (*5) / MAYBE IT'S LIVE (*4) / PRIDE (*4) / RIPTIDE (*7) / HEAVY NOVA (*5) / ADDICTIONS VOL.1 compilation (*7) / DON'T EXPLAIN (*4) / RIDIN' HIGH (*3) / ADDICTIONS 2 compilation (*5) / HONEY (*5) / THE VERY BEST OF ROBERT PALMER compilation (*8)

ROBERT PALMER – vocals with various session people

			Island	Island
Sep 74.	(lp) (<ILPS 9294>) **SNEAKIN' SALLY THROUGH THE ALLEY**		☐	☐ May75
	– Sailing shoes / Hey Julia / Sneakin' Sally through the alley / Through it all there's you / Get outside / Blackmail / How much fun / From a whisper to a scream / Through it all there's you. *(re-iss. Jan87 lp/c/cd; ILPM/ICM/CID 9294) (cd-iss. Aug89; IMCD 20)*			
Nov 74.	(7") <006> **SNEAKIN' SALLY THROUGH THE ALLEY. / EPIDEMIC**		☐	☐
Oct 75.	(7") (WIP 6250) <042> (WIP 6250) **WHICH OF US IS THE FOOL. / GET OUTSIDE**		-	☐
Feb 76.	(7") (WIP 6272) <049> **GIMME AN INCH. / PRESSURE DROP**		☐	☐
Mar 76.	(lp/c) (<ILPS/ICT 9372>) **PRESSURE DROP**		☐	☐ Nov75
	– Give me an inch / Work to make it work / Back in my arms / Riverboat / Pressure drop / Here with you tonight / Trouble / Fine time / Which of us is the fool. *(re-iss. Jan87 lp/c/cd; ILPM/ICM/CID 9372) (cd-iss. Aug89; IMCD 24)*			
Oct 76.	(7") (WIP 6345) **MAN SMART, WOMAN SMARTER. / FROM A WHISPER TO A SCREAM**		☐	-
Oct 76.	(lp/c) (<ILPS/ICT 9420>) **SOME PEOPLE CAN DO WHAT THEY LIKE**		46	68
	– One lost look / Keep in touch / Man smart, woman smarter / Spanish moon / Have mercy / Gotta get a grip on you (part II) / What can you bring me / Hard head / Off the bone / Some people can do what they like. *(cd-iss. Nov89; IMCD 69)*			
Oct 76.	(7") <075> **MAN SMART, WOMAN SMARTER. / KEEP IN TOUCH**		-	63
Mar 77.	(7") <081> **SOME PEOPLE CAN DO WHAT THEY LIKE. / ONE LOST LOOK**		-	☐
Jan 78.	(lp/c) (<ILPS 9476>) **DOUBLE FUN**		☐	45 Mar78
	– Every kinda people / Best of both worlds / Come over / Where can it go / Night people / Love can run faster / You overwhelm me / You really got me / You're gonna get what's coming. *(re-iss. Jan87 lp/c/cd; ILPM/ICM/CID 9476) (cd-iss. Aug89; IMCD 23)*			
Mar 78.	(7") <100> **EVERY KINDA PEOPLE. / HOW MUCH FUN**		-	16
Mar 78.	(7") (WIP 6425) **EVERY KINDA PEOPLE. / KEEP IN TOUCH**		53	-
May 78.	(7") <105> **COME OVER. / YOU OVERWHELM ME**		-	☐
Jun 78.	(7") (WIP 6445) **BEST OF BOTH WORLDS. / ('A'dub version)**		☐	☐
	(12"+=) (WIP12 6445) – Pressure drop.			
May 79.	(7") (WIP 6481) <49016> **BAD CASE OF LOVIN' YOU (DOCTOR, DOCTOR). / LOVE CAN RUN FASTER**		61	14 Jul79
Jun 79.	(lp/c) (<ILPS/ICT 9544>) **SECRETS**		54	19 Jul79
	– Bad case of loving you (doctor, doctor) / Too good to be true / Can we still be friends / In walks love again / Mean old world / Love stop / Jealous / Under suspicion / Woman you're wonderful / What's it take / Remember to remember. *(re-iss. Jan87 lp/c/cd; ILPM/ICM/CID 9544) (cd-iss. Aug89; IMCD 26)*			
Jul 78.	(7") <8697> **YOU'RE GONNA GET WHAT'S COMING. / WHERE CAN IT GO**		-	-
Aug 79.	(7") (WIP 6515) **JEALOUS. / WOMAN YOU'RE WONDERFUL**		☐	☐
Sep 79.	(7") <49094> **JEALOUS. / IN WALKS LOVE AGAIN**		-	☐
Nov 79.	(7") (WIP 6549) **CAN WE STILL BE FRIENDS. / BACK IN MY ARMS**		☐	☐
Dec 79.	(7") <49137> **CAN WE STILL BE FRIENDS. / REMEMBER TO REMEMBER**		-	52
Aug 80.	(7") <49554> **JOHNNY AND MARY. / STYLE KILLS**		-	☐
Aug 80.	(7") (WIP 6638) **JOHNNY AND MARY. / WHAT'S IT TAKE**		44	-
	(12"+=) (WIP12 6638) – Remember to remember.			
Aug 80.	(lp/c) (<ILPS/ICT 9595>) **CLUES**		31	59 Oct80
	– Looking for clues / Sulky girl / Johnny and Mary / What do you care / I dream of wires / Woke up laughing / Not a second time / Found you now. *(re-iss. Jan87 lp/c/cd; ILPM/ICM/CID 9595) (cd-iss. Jan89; IMCD 21)*			
Oct 80.	(7") <49620> **LOOKING FOR CLUES. / WOKE UP LAUGHING**		-	☐
Nov 80.	(7") (WIP 6651) **LOOKING FOR CLUES. / IN WALKS LOVE AGAIN**		33	-
	(12") (WIP12 6651) – ('A'side) / Good care of you / Style kills.			
Jun 81.	(7") (WIP 6678) **NOT A SECOND TIME. / WOKE UP LAUGHING**		☐	-

Jan 82. (7"pic-d) *(WIP 6754)* <50042> **SOME GUYS HAVE ALL THE LUCK. / TOO GOOD TO BE TRUE**   `16`   ☐
(12"pic-d) *(WIP12 6754)* – ('A'side) / Style kills / Si Chatouillieux / What do you care.

Mar 82. (lp/c) *(<ILPS/ICT 9665>)* **MAYBE IT'S LIVE (live)** `32` ☐ May82
– Sneakin' Sally through the alley / What's it take / Best of both worlds / Every kinda people / Bad case of loving you (doctor, doctor) / Style kills / Si Chatouillieaux / Maybe it's you / What do you care. *(re-iss. Apr91 c; ICM 9665) (re-iss. May98 on 'Spectrum' cd/c; 550068-2/-4)*

Nov 82. (7"pic-d) *(WIP 6833)* **PRIDE. / PRIDE (instrumental)** ☐ – ☐
(12") *(WIP 6833)* – ('A'side) / Parade of the obliterators.

Mar 83. (7"/12")*(IS/12IS 104)* <99866> **YOU ARE IN MY SYSTEM. / DEADLINE** `53` `78` Jun83
`37`

Apr 83. (lp/c) *(ILPS/ICT 9720)* <90065> **PRIDE**
– Pride / Deadline / Want you more / Dance for me / You are in my system / It's not difficult / Say you will / You can have it (take my heart) / What you waiting for / The silver gun. *(re-iss. Jan87 lp/c/cd; ILPM/ICM/CID 9720) (cd-iss. Jun89; IMCD 22)*

Jun 83. (7"pic-d) *(IS 121)* **YOU CAN HAVE IT (TAKE MY HEART). / THE SILVER GUN**   `66`   – ☐

—— From early '85, PALMER became lead singer of DURAN DURAN off-shoot band The POWER STATION. Their eponymous lp, hit both UK + US Top 20's, and spawned a few hits 'SOME LIKE IT HOT', 'GET IT ON' & 'COMMUNICATION'. (see DURAN DURAN ⇒)

Oct 85. (7") *(IS 242)* <99597> **DISCIPLINE OF LOVE. / DANCE FOR ME** ☐ `82`
(12"+=) *(12IS 242)* – Woke up laughing.

Nov 85. (lp/c/cd) *(ILPS/ICT/CID 9801)* <90471> **RIPTIDE** `5` `8`
– Riptide / Hyperactive / Addicted to love / Trick bag / Get it through your heart / I didn't mean to turn you on / Flesh wound / Discipline of love / Riptide (reprise). *(cd-iss. 1988; CID 130) (re-iss. Apr91 lp/c; ILPM/ICM 9801)*

Dec 85. (7") *(IS 256)* **RIPTIDE. / BACK IN MY ARMS** ☐ –
(12") *(12IS 256)* – ('A'side) / No not much (live) / Trick bag (live)
(d7"++=) *(ISD 256)* – (12"tracks) / Johnny and Mary.

Feb 86. (7") <99570> **ADDICTED TO LOVE. / LET'S FALL IN LOVE TONIGHT**   –   `1`

Apr 86. (7"/12") *(IS/12IS 270)* **ADDICTED TO LOVE. / REMEMBER TO REMEMBER** `5` –
(7"sha-pic-d) *(ISP 270)* – ('A'side) / More.

May 86. (7") <99545> **HYPERACTIVE. / WOKE UP LAUGHING** – `33`

Jun 86. (7"/12")*(IS/12IS 283)* <99537> **I DIDN'T MEAN TO TURN YOU ON. / GET IT THROUGH YOUR HEART** `9` `2` Aug86
(d7"+=) *(ISD 283)* – You are in my system / Johnny and Mary.

Oct 86. (7") *(IS 242)* **DISCIPLINE OF LOVE. / DANCE FOR ME** `68` –
(12"+=) *(12IS 242)* – Riptide (medley).
(d12"+=) *(12ISX 242)* – Remember to remember / Addicted to love.

Mar 88. (7") *(IS 352)* <99377> **SWEET LIES. / WANT YOU MORE** ☐ `94`
(12"+=) *(12IS 352)* – Riptide.
(cd-s++=) *(CID 352)* – ('A'extended).

               E.M.I.   **Manhattan**

Jun 88. (7"/7"pic-d) *(EM/+P 61)* <50133> **SIMPLY IRRESISTIBLE. / NOVA** `44` `2`
(12"+=/cd-s+=) *(12/CD EM 61)* – ('A'extended) / ('A'instrumental).

Jun 88. (cd/c/lp) *(CD/TC+/EMD 1007)* <48057> **HEAVY NOVA** `17` `13`
– Simply irresistible / More than ever / Change his ways / Disturbing behaviour / Early in the morning / It could happen to you / She makes my day / It could happen to you / Tell me I'm not dreaming / Between us / Casting a spell. *(re-iss. Mar94 cd/c; CD/TC EMD 1007)*

Oct 88. (7") *(EM 65)* **SHE MAKES MY DAY. / DISTURBING BEHAVIOUR** `6` –
(12"+=/cd-s+=) *(12/CD EM 65)* – Simply irresistible (extended).

Oct 88. (7") <50157> **EARLY IN THE MORNING. / DISTURBING BEHAVIOR** – `19`

May 89. (7"/7"pic-d) *(EM/+PD 85)* **CHANGE HIS WAYS. / MORE THAN EVER** `28` ☐
(12") *(12EM 85)* – (2 different mixes).
(cd-s++=) *(CDEM 85)* – She makes my day.

Jun 89. (7") <50206> **TELL ME I'M NOT DREAMING (2 versions) / MORE THAN EVER** – `60`

Aug 89. (c-s/7") *(TC+/EM 99)* **IT COULD HAPPEN TO YOU. / CHANGE HIS WAYS** `71` ☐
(12"+=) *(12EM 99)* – Early in the morning (get up mix).
(cd-s++=) *(CDEM 99)* – Casting a spell.

               E.M.I.   **E.M.I.**

Oct 90. (c-s/7"; ROBERT PALMER & UB40) *(TC+/EM 167)* **I'LL BE YOUR BABY TONIGHT. / DEEP END** `6` ☐
(12"+=/cd-s+=) *(12/CD EM 167)* – ('A'version).

Nov 90. (cd/cd/d-lp) *(CD/TC+/EMD 1018)* <93935> **DON'T EXPLAIN** `9` `88`
– Your mother should have told you / Light-years / You can't get enough of a good thing / Dreams to remember / You're amazing / Mess around / Happiness / History / I'll be your baby tonight / Housework / Mercy mercy me – I want you / Don't explain / Aeroplane / People will say we're in love / Not a word / Top 40 / You're so desirable / You're my thrill.

Nov 90. (c-s,cd-s) <50338> **YOU'RE AMAZING / SO EMBOLDENED** – `28`

Dec 90. (c-s/7") *(TC+/EM 173)* <50344> **MERCY MERCY ME (THE ECOLOGY) – I WANT YOU. / OH YEAH** `9` `16` Feb91
(12"+=/cd-s+=) *(12/CD EM 173)* – (2-'A'&'B'versions).

Apr 91. (c-s/7") *(TC+/EM)* **HAPPINESS. / ALL SHOOK UP** ☐ ☐
(12"+=/cd-s+=) *(12/CD EM)* – ('A'extended).

Jun 91. (c-s/7") *(TC+/EM 193)* **DREAMS TO REMEMBER. / MESS AROUND** `68` ☐
(12"+=) *(12EM 193)* – Happiness.
(cd-s+=) *(CDEM 193)* – Mercy mercy me (the ecology) – I want you.

Oct 92. (c-s/7") *(TC+/EM 251)* **WITCHCRAFT. / CHANCE** `50` ☐
(cd-s) *(CDEM 251)* – ('A'side) / She makes my day / Mercy mercy me – I want you.

Oct 92. (cd/cd/d-lp) *(CD/MC+/EMD 1038)* <98923> **RIDIN' HIGH** `32` ☐
– Love me or leave me / (Love is) The tender trap / You're my thrill / Want you more / Baby it's cold outside / Aeroplane / Witchcraft / What a little moonlight can

do / Don't explain / Chance / Goody goody / Do nothin' till you hear from me / Honeysuckle rose / No not much / Ridin' high / Hard head.
(above featured many 40's + 50's covers)

Jul 94. (c-s/7") *(TC+/EM 331)* **GIRL U WANT. / NO FUSS** `57` ☐
(cd-s+=) *(CDEMS 331)* – ('A'mixes).

Aug 94. (c-s/7") *(TC+/EM 343)* **KNOW BY NOW. / MERCY MERCY ME – I WANT YOU** `25` ☐
(cd-s+=) *(CDEM 343)* – Simply irresistable.
(cd-s) *(CDEMS 343)* – ('A'side) / ('A'mixes) / In the stars / She makes my day.

Sep 94. (cd/c/lp) *(CD/TC+/EMD 1069)* **HONEY** `25` ☐
– Honey A / Honey B / You're mine / Know by now / Nobody but you / Love takes time / Honeymoon / You blow me away / Close to the edge / Closer to the edge / Girl u want / Wham bam boogie / Big trouble / Dreams come true.

Dec 94. (c-s/7") *(TC+/EM 350)* **YOU BLOW ME AWAY. / SIMPLY IRRESISTABLE** `38` ☐
(cd-s) *(CDEM 350)* – ('A'side) / No control / ('A'mix) / Know by now.
(cd-s) *(CDEMS 350)* – ('A'side) / ('A'mixes) / Change his ways.

Sep 95. (c-s) *(TCEM 399)* **RESPECT YOURSELF / YOU BLOW ME AWAY** `45` ☐
(cd-s+=) *(CDEM 399)* – Girl u want / Race to the end of the set medley:- Bad case of loving you (doctor, doctor) – Simply irrisistible – Some guys have all the luck – I didn't mean to turn you on – Looking for clues – Addicted to love – You are in my system – Know by now – Some like it hot – I want you – Every kinda people.
(cd-s) *(CDEMS 399)* – ('A'side) / Get it on (45 mix) / Some like it hot (7"mix) / Respect yourself (FX mix).

Oct 95. (cd/c) *(CD/TC EMD 1088)* **THE VERY BEST OF ROBERT PALMER** (compilation) `4` ☐
– Addicted to love / Bad case of loving you (doctor, doctor) / Simply irresistable / Get it on (POWER STATION) / Some guys have all the luck / I didn't mean to turn you on / Looking for clues / You are in my system / Some like it hot (POWER STATION) / Respect yourself / I'll be your baby tonight (w/ UB40) / Johnny & Mary / She makes my day / Know by now / Every kinda people / Mercy mercy me – I want you (medley).

– compilations, etc. –

on 'Island' unless mentioned otherwise

Jul 87. (lp/c) C5; *(C5/+K 501)* **THE EARLY YEARS** ☐ –
– (above featured before solo work with The ALAN BOWN SET)

Nov 89. (7") *(IS 438)* **BAD CASE OF LOVING YOU (DOCTOR, DOCTOR). / SWEET LIES** ☐ ☐
(12"+=/cd-s+=) *(12IS/CID 438)* – What's it take.

Nov 89. (lp/c/cd) *(ILPS/ICT/CID 9944)* <91318> **ADDICTIONS VOL.1** `7` `79`
– Bad case of loving you (doctor, doctor) / Pride / Addicted to love / Sweet lies / Woke up laughing / Looking for clues / Some guys have all the luck / Some like it hot (POWER STATION) / What's it take? / Every kinda people / Johnny & Mary / Simply irresistable / Style kills.

Feb 92. (c-s/cd-s/7") *(CIS/CID/IS 498)* **EVERY KINDA PEOPLE. / ('A'radio mix)** `43` –

Mar 92. (cd/c) *(CID/ICT TV 4)* **ADDICTIONS VOL.2** `12` ☐
– Remember to remember / Sneakin' Sally through the alley / Maybe it's you / You are in my system / I didn't mean to turn you on / Can we still be friends / Man smart, woman smarter / Too good to be true / Every kinda people / She makes my day / Best of both worlds / Give me an inch / You're gonna get what's coming / I dream of wires / The silver gun.

Jun 92. (c-s/cd-s/7") *(CIS/CID/IS)* **YOU ARE IN MY SYSTEM. / YOU'RE GONNA GET WHAT'S COMING / TOO GOOD TO BE TRUE**

Nov 95. (d-cd) *(ISDCD 2)* **ADDICTIONS VOL.1 & 2** ☐ –

PANTERA

Formed: Texas, USA . . .1981 by TERRY GLAZE, 'DIAMOND' DARRELL, VINCE ABBOTT and REX ROCKER, taking their name from the Spanish word for panther. Initially a vaguely glam-influenced hard-rock band in the packet-bulging tradition of KISS and AEROSMITH, PANTERA began their career with 'METAL MAGIC' (1983), issued on their own homegrown 'Metal Magic' label. The album was fairly well-received Stateside and saw the band gain a firm foothold on the lower rungs of the hair-rock ladder. With subsequent releases like 'PROJECTS IN THE JUNGLE' (1984) and 'I AM THE NIGHT' (1985), however, the group began to adopt a more muscular approach, consolidated with the arrival of PHIL ANSELMO (as a replacement for GLAZE) on 1988's 'POWER METAL'. With a growing reputation and the help of a recommendation from JUDAS PRIEST's ROB HALFORD, the band secured a major label deal with 'Atco'. The resulting album, 'COWBOYS FROM HELL' (1990) was a dramatic turnaround, gone was the 80's metal garb and cheesy choruses; check shirts, tattoos and a brutally uncompromising thrash-based groove had forcibly taken their place. Clearly, something had made these boys angry and 'A VULGAR DISPLAY OF POWER' (1992) was arguably the most articulate and succinct fix of metallic aggression to be had that year; the likes of 'F**KING HOSTILE' said it all. The record also gave PANTERA their first taste of chart success, the 'WALK' single making the UK Top 40. So it was, then, that the stage was set for PANTERA to both consolidate their position as one of the most unrelentingly intense groups in the nu-metal hierarchy and smash into the UK album chart at pole position with 'FAR BEYOND DRIVEN' (1994). Incredibly their seventh album, the group were now virtually unrecognisable from their rather tame origins, the record's grim vignettes (select 'I'M BROKEN' and 'THROES OF REJECTION' for that ultimate feel-bad factor) were accompanied by a suitably severe Black Sabbath cover, 'PLANET CARAVAN'. The set also saw PANTERA climb to the uppermost regions of the American charts, their services sought out for a contribution to 'The Crow' soundtrack (a cover of Poison Idea's 'THE BADGE'). Silent for most of 1995 (bar ANSELMO who moonlighted with DOWN; sole album, 'NOLA'), PANTERA returned with a vengeance the following year, releasing 'THE GREAT SOUTHERN TRENDKILLERS' (1996). Easing back a little on the speed pedal, the group achieved an even more savagely focused intensity, ANSELMO raging from the depths of his tortured soul. It may have lent his lyrics and delivery a stark harshness, but surviving on the very precipice of existence eventually caught up with ANSELMO when, later that summer (13th July), the singer narrowly escaped death from a heroin overdose, later admitting to being dead for five minutes. Shaken but hardly beaten, PANTERA returned the following year with a well-overdue concert set, 'OFFICIAL LIVE – 101 PROOF', proving that there are still few to match the sheer, unadulterated heaviness of their impact.

Album rating: METAL MAGIC (*5) / PROJECTS IN THE JUNGLE (*5) / I AM THE NIGHT (*5) / POWER METAL (*4) / COWBOYS FROM HELL (*6) / A VULGAR DISPLAY OF POWER (*6) / FAR BEYOND DRIVEN (*7) / THE GREAT SOUTHERN TRENDKILLERS (*6) / OFFICIAL LIVE 101 PROOF (*6) / Down: NOLA (*5)

TERRY GLAZE – vocals, guitar / **DARRELL ABBOTT** (b.20 Aug'66, Dallas, Texas) – guitar / **REX ROCKER** (b.REX BROWN, 27 Jul'64, Graham, Texas) – bass / **VINCENT PAUL ABBOTT** (b.11 Mar'64, Dallas) – drums

		not iss.	Metal Magic
1983.	(lp) <MMR 1983> **METAL MAGIC**	-	

– Ride my rocket / I'll be alright / Tell me if you want it / Latest lover / Biggest part of me / Metal magic / Widowmaker / Nothin' on (but the radio) / Sad lover / Rock out!.

—— GLAZE became TERRENCE LEE, DARRELL prefixed the word DIMEBAG and VINCE was now VINNIE PAUL

| 1984. | (lp) <MMR 1984> **PROJECTS IN THE JUNGLE** | - | |

– All over tonite / Out for blood / Blue lite turnin' red / Like fire / In over my head / Projects in the jungle / Heavy metal rules! / Only a heartbeat away / Killers / Takin' my life.

| 1985. | (lp) <MMR 1985> **I AM THE NIGHT** | - | |

– Hot and heavy / I am the night / Onward we rock! / D.S.G.S.T.S.T.S.M. / Daughters of the queen / Down below / Come-on eyes / Right on the edge / Valhalla / Forever tonight.

—— **PHILIP ANSELMO** (b.30 Jun'68, New Orleans, Louisiana) – vocals repl. TERRY

| May 88. | (lp) <MMR 1988> **POWER METAL** | - | |

– Rock the world / Power metal / We'll meet again / Over and out / Proud to be loud / Down below / Death trap / Hard ride / Burnnn! / P*S*T*88.

		Atco	Atco
Jul 90.	(cd/c/lp) <(7567 91372-2/-4/-1)> **COWBOYS FROM HELL**		

– Cowboys from Hell / Primal concrete sledge / Psycho holiday / Heresy / Cemetery gates / Domination / Shattered / Clash with reality / Medicine man / Message in blood / The sleep / The art of shredding.

		64	44
Feb 92.	(cd/c/lp) <(7567 91758-2/-4/-1)> **A VULGAR DISPLAY OF POWER**	64	44

– Mouth for war / A new level / Walk / F**king hostile / This love / Rise / No good (attack the radical) / Live in a hole / Regular people (conceit) / By demons be driven / Hollow.

| Sep 92. | (7"/c-s) (A 5845/+C) **MOUTH FOR WAR. / RISE** | 73 | |

(cd-s+=) (A 5845CD) – Cowboys from Hell / Heresy.
(12") (A 5845T) – ('A'side) / ('A'-superloud mix) / Domination / Primal concrete sledge.

| Feb 93. | (12"m) (B 6076T) **WALK. / COWBOYS FROM HELL / PSYCHO HOLIDAY (live)** | 34 | |

(cd-ep) (B 6076CD) – ('A'side) / Fucking hostile / By demons be driven.
(cd-ep) (B 6076CDX) – ('A'side) / No good (attack the radical) / A new level / Walk (extended remixes by Jim 'Foetus' Thirlwell).

		East West	Atco
Mar 94.	(12"/cd-s) (B 5932 T/CD1) **I'M BROKEN. / SLAUGHTERED**	19	

(cd-s+=) (B 5932CD2) – Domination (live) / Primal concrete sledge.
(cd-s) (B 5932CD3) – ('A'side) / Cowboys from Hell (live) / Psycho holiday (live).
(12") (B 5932X) – ('A'side) / Walk (cervical edit) / Fuckin' hostile.

| Mar 94. | (cd/c/lp) <(7567 92302-2/-4/-1)> **FAR BEYOND DRIVEN** | 3 | 1 |

– Strength beyond strength / Becoming / 5 minutes alone / I'm broken / Good friends and a bottle of pills / Hard lines, sunken cheeks / Slaughtered / 25 years / Shedding skin / Use my third arm / Throes of rejection / Planet Caravan.

| May 94. | (7"white) (A 8293) **5 MINUTES ALONE. / THE BADGE** | | |
| Oct 94. | (7") (A 5836) **PLANET CARAVAN. / 5 MINUTES ALONE** | 26 | |

(12") (A 5836T) – ('A'side) / Cowboys from Hell / Heresay.
(cd-s) (A 5836Cd1) – ('A'side) / The badge / New level / Becoming.
(cd-s) (A 5836CD2) – ('A'side) / Domination / Hollow.

| May 96. | (cd/c/lp) <(7559 61908-2/-4/-1)> **THE GREAT SOUTHERN TRENDKILLERS** | 17 | 4 |

– Drag the waters / War nerve / It can't destroy my body / 13 steps to nowhere / Sandblasted skin / Underground in America / Suicide note (part 1) / Suicide note (part 2).

—— On 13th Jul'96, ANSELMO luckily survived a heroin overdose in which he admitted to being dead for five minutes.

| Aug 97. | (cd/c/lp) <(7559 62068-2/-4/-1)> **OFFICIAL LIVE – 101 PROOF (live)** | 54 | 15 |

– New level / Walk / Becoming / 5 minutes alone / Sandblasted skin / Suicide note (part 2) / War nerve / This love / Dom – Hollow / Strength beyond strength / I'm broken / Cowboys from Hell / Cemetery gates / Fuckin' hostile / Where you come from / I can't hide.

DOWN

PHIL ANSELMO – vocals / **PEPPER KEENAN** – guitar / **KIRK WINDSTEIN** – guitar / **TODD STRANGE** – bass / **JIMMY BOWER** – drums

		East West	East West
Sep 95.	(cd/c/lp) <(7559 61830-2/-4/-1)> **NOLA**	68	57

– Pray for the locust / Stone the crow / Bury me in smoke / Eyes of the south / Pillars of eternity / Underneath everything / Swan song / Temptation's wings / Jail / Lifer / Rehab / Losing all / Hail the leaf.

PARADISE LOST

Formed: Halifax, England ... April '88 by NICK HOLMES, GREGOR McINTOSH, AARON AEDY, STEPHEN EDMONDSON and MATT ARCHER, taking their name from the famous Milton poem. Initially playing death metal combining the grindcore element of the UK scene and the more extreme US sound with a vaguely gothic element, PARADISE LOST made their debut on 'Peaceville' in 1990 with the 'IN DUB' single and 'LOST PARADISE' album. Eschewing the gore-obsessed lyrics of their contemporaries, PARADISE LOST instead opted for a more existential take on the misery of life in keeping with their literary influences. A follow-up, 'GOTHIC' (1991), saw the band moving away from the death-metal genre, slowing things down and abandoning the requisite death grunt as well as adding keyboards (unheard of for a death-metal band!) and female vocals. Subsequently signing with 'Music For Nations', the group further embraced this direction with 'SHADES OF GOD' (1992) and 'ICON' (1993), the latter set especially, seeing them amass long overdue critical acclaim and a swelling crossover fanbase. By the release of the UK Top 20 set, 'DRACONIAN TIMES' (1995), PARADISE LOST had fashioned a compelling sound lying somewhere between METALLICA and The SISTERS OF MERCY with hints of latter-day DEPECHE MODE. Drawing praise from such esteemed admirers as the aforementioned METALLICA and Brazilian maestros SEPULTURA, the group went from strength to strength, the excellent, string-enhanced 'ONE SECOND' (1997) set further underlining their credentials as the foremost purveyors of atmospheric, misery-wallowing, gothic metal. • **Songwriters:** McINTOSH-HOLMES except DEATH WALKS BEHIND YOU (Atomic Rooster) / WALK AWAY (Sisters Of Mercy). • **Trivia:** In Mar'96, NICK HOLMES finished his 1,500 mile leukaemia charity motorcycle ride in Australia, travelling from Ayers Rock to Alice Springs and on to Darwin, raising 4,000 quid in the process.

Album rating: LOST PARADISE (*6) / GOTHIC (*7) / SHADES OF GOD (*6) / ICON (*7) / DRACONIAN TIMES (*8) / ONE SECOND (*8) / HOST (*6)

NICK HOLMES – vocals / **GREGOR MacINTOSH** – lead guitar / **AARON AEDY** – rhythm guitar / **STEPHEN EDMONDSON** – bass / **MATT ARCHER** – drums, percussion

		Peaceville	Rough Trade
Apr 90.	(lp/cd) (VILE 17/+CD) **LOST PARADISE**		-

– Intro / Deadly inner sense / Paradise lost / Our saviour / Rotting misery / Frozen illusion / Breeding fear / Lost Paradise. (cd+=) – Internal torment II. (re-iss. cd Apr95; CDVILE 17)

| Apr 90. | (12") (VILE 19T) **IN DUB** | | - |

– Rotting misery (doom dub) / Breeding fear (demolition dub).

| Apr 91. | (cd/lp) (CD+/VILE 26) **GOTHIC** | | |

– Gothic / Dead emotion / Shattered / Rapture / Eternal / Falling forever / Angel tears / Silent / The painless / Desolate.

| Jan 92. | (cd-ep) (CDVILE 41) **GOTHIC EP** | | - |

– Gothic / IN DUB (tracks) / The painless (mix). (re-iss. Jul94; same)

		Music For Nations	Music For Nations
Jun 92.	(cd/c/lp) (CD/T+/MFN 135) **SHADES OF GOD**		

– Mortals watch the day / Crying for eternity / Embraced / Daylight torn / Pity the sadness / No forgiveness / Your hand in mine / The word made flesh. (cd+=) – As I die.

| Oct 92. | (12"ep/cd-ep) (12/CD KUT 150) **AS I DIE / RAPE OF VIRTUE.** / DEATH WALKS BEHIND YOU / ETERNAL (live) | | |
| Sep 93. | (cd/c/d-lp) (CD/T+/MFN 152) **ICON** | | |

– Embers fire / Remembrance / Forging sympathy / Joys of the emptiness / Dying freedom / Widow / Colossal rains / Weeping words / Poison / True belief / Shallow seasons / Christendom / Deus misereatur.

| Feb 94. | (12"ep/cd-ep) (12/CD KUT 157) **SEALS THE SENSE** | | - |

– Embers fire / Sweetness / True belief / Your hand in mine (live).

—— **LEE MORRIS** – drums (ex-MARSHALL LAW) repl. ARCHER

| May 95. | (c-ep/12"ep/cd-ep) (T/12/CD KUT 165) **LAST TIME / I WALK AWAY. / LAID TO WASTE / MASTER OF MISRULE** | 60 | |
| Jun 95. | (cd/c/lp)(pic-lp) (CD/T+/MFN 184)(MFNP 184) **DRACONIAN TIMES** | 16 | |

– Enchantment / Hallowed land / The last time / Forever failure / Once solemn / Shadowkings / Elusive cure / Yearn for change / Shades of God / Hands of reason / I see your face / Jaded. (cd w/ltd cd+=) – Embers fire (live) / Daylight torn (live) / True belief (live) / Pity the sadness (live) / As I die (live) / Weeping words (demo) / The last time (demo) / I walk away / Laid to waste / Master of misrule / Forever failure (video edit).

| Oct 95. | (c-ep/12"ep/cd-ep) (T/12/CD KUT 169) **FOREVER FAILURE. / ANOTHER DESIRE / FEAR** | 66 | |
| Jun 97. | (12"ep) (12KUT 174) **SAY JUST WORDS / HOW SOON IS NOW? / SAY JUST WORDS (album mix) / CRUEL ONE** | 53 | |

(cd-ep) (CDKUT 174) – Soul courageous. [repl.2nd track]
(cd-ep) (CDXKUT 174) – Albino flogged black. [repl.4th track]

| Jul 97. | (cd/c/lp) (CD/T+/MFN 222) **ONE SECOND** | 31 | |

– One second / Say just words / Lydia / Mercy / Soul courageous / Another day / The sufferer / This cold life / Blood of another / Disappear / Sane / Take me down.

| Jul 98. | (c-s) (TKUT 177) **ONE SECOND / ONE SECOND (remix)** | | - |

(cd-s+=) (CDKUT 177) – The hour / Slave.
(cd-s) (CDXKUT 177) – ('A'side) / Mercy (live) / This cold life (live).

		Chrysalis	Chrysalis
Jun 99.	(cd) (520567-2) **HOST**	61	

– So much is lost / Nothing sacred / In all honesty / Harbour / Ordinary days / It's too late / Permanent solution / Behind the grey / Wreck / Made the same / Deep / Year of summer / Host.

– compilations, etc. –

on 'Music For Nations' unless mentioned otherwise

Apr 96.	(d-cd) (CDMFN 202) **SHADES OF GOD / ICON**		-
Oct 97.	(5xcd-ep-box) (CDMFNB 236) **THE SINGLES COLLECTION**		-
Aug 98.	(cd) (CDMFN 243) **REFLECTION**		

PARAMOUNTS (see under ⇒ PROCOL HARUM)

John PARISH & POLLY JEAN HARVEY (see under ⇒ HARVEY, PJ)

Graham PARKER

Born: 18 Nov'50, East London, England. Already something of a veteran (having played on the continent as well as fronting a succession of London outfits) when he placed an ad in Melody Maker for a backing band, singer/songwriter PARKER's emergence at the fag end of the pub-rock scene in the mid-70's was fortuitous in that he secured the services of The RUMOUR, a group formed from the remains of such scene stalwarts as BRINSLEY SCHWARZ and DUCKS DELUXE. With assistance from future 'Stiff' mainman, Dave Robinson (the brains behind The RUMOUR), he cut a demo tape and sent it to 'Phonogram', the label sufficiently impressed to sign him to their subsidiary label, 'Vertigo'. Featuring a line-up of PARKER, MARTIN BELMONT, BRINSLEY SCHWARZ, BOB ANDREWS, ANDREW BODNAR and STEVE GOULDING, the NICK LOWE-produced debut album, 'HOWLIN' WIND' (1976), remains one of the most enduring releases of PARKER's career. Mentioned in the same breath as classic American writers such as DYLAN and SPRINGSTEEN, his hungry, articulate approach had critics foaming at the mouth; while the sweaty fervour of tracks such as 'SOUL SHOES' and 'HEY LORD, DON'T ASK ME QUESTIONS' effectively demonstrated the combo's hard-nosed R&B approach, the gritty melancholy of 'BETWEEN YOU AND ME' left a deeper impression. A second set, 'HEAT TREATMENT', followed later that year, the fierce momentum holding out if not resonating with quite the same conviction. The record's minor chart success preceded a Top 30 hit with the 'PINK PARKER' EP in 1977 (featuring a cover of The Trammps' 'HOLD BACK THE NIGHT') and a Top 20 placing for the third album, 'STICK IT TO ME' (1977). While PARKER was now riding into the charts on the coattails of the punk/new wave explosion, critics laid into what they regarded as a poorly conceived rush job with constant comparisons to the emerging ELVIS COSTELLO not helping any. Unhappy with what he allegedly regarded as record company incompetence, PARKER reportedly cut the inferior live set, 'THE PARKERILLA' (1978) as a means of ending his tenure with 'Mercury'. Subsequently signing with 'Arista' in the States, the angry young man vented his pent-up frustration with the acclaimed 'SQUEEZING OUT SPARKS' (1979). An electrifying set more than living up to PARKER's early promise and widely held as his peak achievement, the album's simmering discontent was best sampled on the likes of 'LOCAL GIRLS' and 'DON'T GET EXCITED', while 'PASSION IS NO ORDINARY WORD' was testament to the man's cast-iron conviction. As well as making the Top 20 in Britain, the record broke PARKER, to a certain degree, in the States, where he was hailed by critics as one of the greatest songwriters of his generation. Yet he failed to build on all this, 'THE UP ESCALATOR' (1980) too often substituting lean invention for flabby formula; despite an all-time best chart placing in the UK, the album marked the beginning of a critical and commercial slump as well as the end of PARKER's musical partnership with his longtime backing band. 'ANOTHER GREY AREA' (1982) used an array of session players (including NICKY HOPKINS), carrying on in much the same vein as its predecessor with only the occasional inspired track to redeem it. Throughout the remainder of the 80's PARKER concentrated on the American market where he enjoyed minor success on a number of labels, enjoying something of a mini critical revival with 'THE MONA LISA'S SISTER' (1988) and 'HUMAN SOUL' (1989), which harnessed some of the wiry energy of old. While 'STRUCK BY LIGHTNING' (1991) and 'BURNING QUESTIONS' (1992) saw PARKER's new family man credentials take top billing, there was still enough firebrand R&B spark to keep longtime fans on their toes. Seemingly mellowing further with each passing year, 1995's '12 HAUNTED EPISODES' was a kind of PARKER equivalent to STING's 'Ten Summoner's Tales'. Much more rocking was the following year's concert set, 'LIVE FROM NEW YORK' (1996), the singer revamping the cream of his back catalogue with new backing crew, The EPISODES-Discog!!! • **Songwriters:** PARKER penned, except covers CUPID + A CHANGE IS GONNA COME (Sam Cooke) / SUBSTITUTE (Who) / IN BLOOM (Nirvana) / etc. • **Trivia:** In 1980, PARKER had book 'The Great Trouser Mystery' published.

Album rating: HOWLIN' WIND (*8) / HEAT TREATMENT (*7) / STICK TO ME (*6) / THE PARKERILLA (*3) / SQUEEZING OUT SPARKS (*8) / THE UP ESCALATOR (*6) / ANOTHER GREY AREA (*6) / THE REAL MACAW (*6) / STEADY NERVES (*4) / MONA LISA'S SISTER (*6) / HUMAN SOUL (*5) / LIVE! ALONE IN AMERICA (*5) / STRUCK BY LIGHTNING (*6) / BURNING QUESTIONS (*5) / THE BEST OF GRAHAM PARKER compilation (*8) / LIVE ALONE! DISCOVERING JAPAN (*5) / 12 HAUNTED EPISODES (*5) / LIVE FROM NEW YORK, NY (*4) / ACID BUBBLEGUM (*5)

GRAHAM PARKER & THE RUMOUR

GRAHAM PARKER – vocals, guitar / **MARTIN BELMONT** – guitar (ex-DUCKS DELUXE) / **BRINSLEY SCHWARZ** – guitar (ex-BRINSLEY SCHWARZ) / **BOB ANDREWS** – keys, sax, guitar (ex-BRINSLEY SCHWARZ) / **ANDREW BODNAR** – bass / **STEVE GOULDING** – drums (both ex-BONTEMPS ROULEE)

			Vertigo	Mercury
Mar 76.	(7") *(6059 135)* **SILLY THING. / I'M GONNA USE IT NOW**		☐	–

Apr 76.	(lp) *(6360 129)* <SRM-1 1095> **HOWLIN' WIND**		☐	☐

– White honey / Nothin's gonna pull us apart / Silly thing / Gypsy blood / Between you and me / Back to schooldays / Soul shoes / Lady doctor / You've got to be kidding / Howlin' wind / Not if it pleases me / Hey Lord, don't ask me questions. *(free live 7"+=)* – KANSAS CITY. / SILLY THING *(re-iss. Apr89 on 'Beat Goes On'; BGO 48)* *(cd-iss. May90 on 'Polydor'; 826273-2)*

Jul 76.	(7") *(6059 147)* **SOUL SHOES. / WILD HONEY**		☐	–
Sep 76.	(7") <73834> **SOUL SHOES. / YOU'VE GOT TO BE KIDDING**			–
Oct 76.	(7") *(6059 158)* **HOTEL CHAMBERMAID. / DON'T ASK ME QUESTIONS**		☐	–
Oct 76.	(lp) *(6360 137)* <SRM-1 1117> **HEAT TREATMENT**		52	–

– Heat treatment / That's what they all say / Turned up too late / Black honey / Hotel chambermaid / Pourin' it all out / Back door love / Something you're goin' thru / Help me shake it / Fool's gold. *(re-iss. May89 on 'Beat Goes On'; BGO 45)* *(cd-iss. May90 on 'Polydor'; 826274-2)*

Dec 76.	(7") <73876> **HEAT TREATMENT. / BACK DOOR LOVE**		☐	–
Jan 77.	(7") *(6059 161)* **POURIN' IT ALL OUT. / HELP ME SHAKE IT**		☐	–
Feb 77.	(7") <73970> **STICK TO ME. / HEAT IN HARLEM**		☐	–
Mar 77.	(7"pink-ep) *(PARK 001)* <74000> **THE PINK PARKER**		24	58

– Hold back the night / (Let me get) Sweet on you / White honey / Soul shoes.

Oct 77.	(lp) *(9102 017)* <SRM-1 3706> **STICK TO ME**		19	☐

– Stick to me / I'm gonna tear your playhouse down / Problem child / Soul on ice / Clear head / The New York shuffle / Watch the Moon come down / Thunder and rain / The heat in Harlem / The raid. *(cd-iss. May90 on 'Polydor'; 824808-2)*

Nov 77.	(7") *(6059 185)* **THE NEW YORK SHUFFLE. / BLEEP**		☐	–
Apr 78.	(7") *(PARK 2)* **HEY LORD, DON'T ASK ME QUESTIONS (live). / FOOL'S GOLD**		32	☐
May 78.	(d-lp) *(6641 797)* <SRM 2100> **THE PARKERILLA (live)**		14	☐

– Lady doctor / Fool's gold / I'm gonna tear your playhouse down / Hey Lord, don't ask me questions / Silly thing / The heat in Harlem / Gypsy blood / Back to schooldays / Heat treatment / Watch the Moon come down / The New York shuffle / Soul shoes / Hey Lord, don't ask me questions (studio 45 rpm). *(cd-iss. Jan94; 842263-2)*

GRAHAM PARKER

—— solo but still augmented by The RUMOUR

			Vertigo	Arista
Feb 79.	(7") *(6059 219)* **PROTECTION. / I WANT YOU BACK (live)**		☐	–
Mar 79.	(lp) *(9102 030)* <4223> **SQUEEZING OUT SPARKS**		18	40

– Discovering Japan / Local girls / Nobody hurts you / You can't be too strong / Passion is no ordinary word / Saturday nite is dead / Love gets you twisted / Protection / Waiting for the UFO's / Don't get excited.

Mar 79.	(7") <0439> **I WANT YOU BACK (ALIVE). / MERCURY POISONING**		☐	☐
May 79.	(7") *(6059 226)* **DISCOVERING JAPAN. / LOCAL GIRLS**		☐	–

GRAHAM PARKER & THE RUMOUR

			Stiff	Arista
Apr 80.	(7") *(BUY 72)* **STUPEFACTION. / WOMEN IN CHARGE**		☐	–
Apr 80.	(lp/c) *(SEEZ/CSEEZ 23)* <9517> **THE UP ESCALATOR**		11	40

– Up / No holding back / Devil's sidewalk / Stupefaction / Love without greed / Jolie Jolie / Endless night / Paralyzed / Manoeuvres / Empty lives / Beating of another heart. *(c+=)* – Women in charge. *(re-iss. Jun90 on 'Demon' lp/cd; FIEND/+CD 121)* *(cd re-iss. Jun96 on 'Razor & Tie'; RE 1980)*

Jun 80.	(7") *(BUY 82)* **LOVE WITHOUT GREED. / MERCURY POISONING**		☐	–

GRAHAM PARKER

—— solo, without The RUMOUR. PARKER now used **NICKY HOPKINS** – piano / **GEORGE SMALL** – keyboards / **HUGH McCRACKEN** – guitars, harmonica / **DAVID BROWN** – guitars / **DOUG STEGMEYER** – bass / **MICHAEL BRAUN** – drums / **KURT McKETTRICK** – sax, flute / **JIM CLOUSE** – sax / **PAUL PRESTINO** – banjo / **JACK DOUGLAS** – percussion / +backing vocalists

			R.C.A.	Arista
Feb 82.	(7") *(PARK 100)* <0652> **TEMPORARY BEAUTY. / NO MORE EXCUSES**		50	☐
Mar 82.	(lp/c) *(RCA LP/K 6029)* <9589> **ANOTHER GREY AREA**		40	51

– Temporary beauty / Another grey area / No more excuses / Dark side of the bright lights / Can't waste a minute / Big fat zero / You hit the spot / It's all worth nothing alone / Crying for attention / Thankless task / Fear not. *(re-iss. Jul91 on 'Great Expectations' lp/c/cd; PIP LP/MC/CD 026)*

Jul 82.	(7") *(RCA 243)* <0687> **NO MORE EXCUSES. / YOU HIT THE SPOT**		☐	☐

(12"+=) *(RCAT 243)* – Another grey area.

—— now with **SMALL** + **KEVIN JENKINS** – bass / **GILSON LAVIS** – drums (ex-SQUEEZE)

Jul 83.	(7"/12") *(RCA/+T 346)* **LIFE GETS BETTER. / ANNIVERSARY**		☐	59
Sep 83.	(lp/c) *(RCA LP/K 6086)* <8023> **THE REAL MACAW**		☐	☐

– You can't take love for granted / Glass jaw / Just like a man / assive resistance / Sounds like chains / Life gets better / A miracle a minute / Beyond a joke / Last couple on the dance floor / Anniversary / (Too late) The smart bomb. *(re-iss. Jul91 on 'Great Expectations' lp/c/cd; PIP LP/MC/CD 027)*

Sep 83.	(7") <9065> **LIFE GETS BETTER. / BEYOND A JOKE**		–	94
Oct 83.	(7") *(RCA 361)* **YOU CAN'T TAKE LOVE FOR GRANTED. / GLASS JAW**		☐	☐

GRAHAM PARKER & THE SHOT

—— with **SMALL, JENKINS + SCHWARTZ** plus **MICHAEL BRAUN** – drums repl. LAVIS

			Elektra	Elektra
Apr 85.	(7"/12") *(EKR/+T 6)* **BREAK THEM DOWN. / EVERYONE'S HAND IS ON THE SWITCH**		☐	–

(d7"+=) *(EKR 6 – SAM 239)* – Bricks and mortar / Too much to think.

Apr 85. (lp/c)(cd) *(EKT 4/+C)(960388-2)* <60388> **STEADY NERVES** ☐ 57
- Break them down / Mighty rivers / Lunatic fringe / Wake up (next to you) / When you do that to me / The weekend's too short / Take everything / Black Lincoln Continental / Canned laughter / Everyone's hand is on the switch / Locked into green. (cd+=) – Too much time to think.

Apr 85. (7") <69654> **WAKE UP (NEXT TO YOU). / BRICKS AND MORTAR** - 39

Jun 85. (7") *(EKR 13)* **WAKE UP (NEXT TO YOU). / CANNED LAUGHTER** ☐ -
(12"+=) *(EKRT 13)* – Locked into green.

GRAHAM PARKER

—— solo, with backers **BRINSLEY / ANDREW BODNAR** – bass / **JAMES HALLAWELL** – keyboards / **TERRY WILLIAMS** – drums

		Demon	R.C.A.

1988. (7") <8639> **(GET STARTED) START A FIRE. / ORDINARY GIRL** - -

Jul 88. (7") **I'M JUST YOUR MAN. / I DON'T KNOW** - -

Jul 88. (lp/c/cd) *(FIEND/+CASS/CD 122)* <8316> **THE MONA LISA'S SISTER** 77 May88
- Don't let it break you down / Under the mask of happiness / Back in time / I'm just your man / OK Hieronymous / Get started, start a fire / The girl isn't ready / Blue highways / Success / I don't know / Cupid.

Nov 88. (7") **CUPID. / BLUE HIGHWAYS** ☐ -

Apr 89. (lp/c/cd) *(FIEND/+CASS/CD 141)* **LIVE! ALONE IN AMERICA (live)** ☐ -
- White honey / Watch the moon come down / Black honey / Protection / Soul corruption / Gypsy blood / Back to schooldays / Durban poison / The 3 Martini lunch / Back in time / Hotel chambermaid / Don't let it break you down / You can't be too strong / A change is gonna come.

—— retained **SCHWARZ, BODNAR, HALLIWELL. PETE THOMAS** – drums repl. TERRY Also intrcl.**STEVE NIEVE** – synth. / **BEIZEL SICKS** – percussion / **SONIA JONES MORGAN + CARMEN DAYE** – backing vox / **MOLLY DUNCAN** – tenor sax / **J. NEIL SIDWELL** – trombone / **MARTIN DROVER** – trumpet

Oct 89. (lp/c/cd) *(FIEND/+CASS/CD 163)* <9876> **HUMAN SOUL** Feb90
- Little Miss understanding / My love's strong / Dancing for money / Call me your doctor / Big man on paper / Soultime / Everything goes / Sugar gives you energy / Daddy's a postman / Green monkeys / I was wrong / You got the world (rightwhere you want it) / Slash and burn.

		Demon	B.M.G.

Feb 91. (d-lp/c/cd) *(FIEND/+CASS/CD 201)* <3013> **STRUCK BY LIGHTNING** ☐ ☐
- She wants so many things / They murdered the clown / Strong winds / The kid with the butterfly net / And it shook me / That's where she ends up / A brand new book / Weeping statues / Wrapping paper / Ten girls ago / I'm into something good / Over the border (to America) / The Sun is gonna shine again / Guardian angels / Children and dogs / When I was king / Museum piece / Museum of stupidity.

		Demon	Capitol

Jul 92. (lp/c/cd) *(FIEND/+C/CD 721)* **BURNING QUESTIONS** ☐ ☐
- Release me / Too many knots to untangle / Just like Joe Meek's blues / Love is a burning question / Platinum blonde / Long stem rose / Short memories / Here it comes again / Mr.Tender / Just like Herm & Hesse / Yesterdays cloud / Oasis / Worthy of your love / Substitute.

Aug 92. (cd-ep) **BURNING QUESTIONS / RELEASE ME / PLATINUM BLONDE / SHORT MEMORIES** ☐ -

Aug 93. (lp/c/cd) *(FIEND/+CASS/CD 735)* **LIVE ALONE! DISCOVERING JAPAN (live)** ☐ -
- That's what they all say / Platinum blonde / Mercury poisoning / Sweet 16 / No woman no cry / Lunatic fringe / Long stem rose / Discovering Japan / Hey Lord, don't ask me questions / Watch the Moon come down (revisited) / Just like Herman Hesse / Too many knots to untabgle / Chopsticks / Short memories.

		Demon	DakotaArts

Dec 94. (cd-ep) *(GPCD 3)* **GRAHAM PARKER'S CHRISTMAS CRACKER** ☐ -
- Christmas is for mugs / New Year's revolution / Soul Christmas / (demo versions).

		Grapevine	Razor & Tie

Apr 95. (cd/c/lp) *(GRA CD/MC/LP 204)* **12 HAUNTED EPISODES** ☐ ☐
- Partner for life / Pollinate / Force of nature / Disney's America / Haunted episodes / Next phase / Honest work / Cruel stage / See yourself / Loverman / Fly / First day of Spring.

—— line-up:- **PARKER / + MITCH MARGOLD** – keyboards / **KENNY AARONSON** – bass, steel guitar / **DENNIS McDERMOTT** – drums

Aug 96. (cd; as GP + THE EPISODES) <7000> **LIVE FROM NEW YORK, NY (live)** - ☐
- Big man on paper / Fool's gold / Force of nature / Haunted episodes / Fly / Here it comes again / Crawlin' from the wreckage / Partner for life / Disney's America / Stick to me / See yourself / Over the border / Love gets you twisted / Wake up (next to you) / Get started, start a fire / Protection / In bloom.

		When!	Razor & Tie

Mar 97. (cd) *(WENCD 015)* **ACID BUBBLEGUM** ☐ ☐
- Turn it into hate / Sharpening axes / Get over it and move on / Bubblegum cancer / Impenetrable / She never let me down / Obsessed with Aretha / Beancounter / Girl at the end of the pier / Baggage / Milk train / Character assassination / They got it wrong as usual. (re-iss.Jul97 on 'Essential'; ESSCD 583)

– compilations, etc. –

May 80. (lp) *Vertigo; (9102 042)* **THE BEST OF GRAHAM PARKER & THE RUMOUR** ☐
- Soul shoes / Heat reatment / Howling wind / Hold back the night / Back to schooldays / You can't be too strong / Kansas City / Stick to me / The New York shuffle / Local girls / White honey / Hotel chambermaid / Between you and me / Hey Lord, don't ask me questions. (re-iss. May82 lp/c; VERB/+C 001)

May 84. (lp/c) *Philips; (PRICE/PRIMC 62)* **IT DON'T MEAN A THING IF IT AIN'T GOT THAT SWING** ☐ -

1991. (4xcd-box) *Demon; (GRAHAM 1)* **GRAHAM PARKER** ☐ ☐

—— (MONA LISA'S SISTER / HUMAN SOUL / LIVE ALONE IN AMERICA / THE UP ESCALATOR)

Sep 93. (cd/c) *Vertigo; (512149-2/-4)* **THE BEST OF GRAHAM PARKER** ☐ ☐
- Silly thing / I'm gonna use it now / Between you and me / Back to schooldays / White honey / You can't hurry love / Pourin' it all out / That's what they all say / Hotel chambermaid / Fool's gold / Watch the Moon come down / I'm gonna tear your playhouse down / Thunder and rain / Hold back the night / New York shuffle / Soul shoes / Hey Lord, don't ask me questions / I want you back / Discovering Japan / Local girls / You can't be too strong / Mercury poisoning.

Jun 94. (cd) *Windsong; (WHISCD 002)* **LIVE ON THE TEST (live)** ☐ -

Aug 95. (d-cd) *Vertigo; (528603-2)* **HOWLING WIND / HEAT TREATMENT** ☐ -

May 96. (cd) *Nectar; (NTMCD 518)* **EPISODES** ☐ -

Jun 96. (cd) *Windsong; (WINCD 083)* **BBC LIVE IN CONCERT (live)** ☐ -

Oct 96. (d-cd) *Vertigo; (534100-2)* **VERTIGO** ☐ -

Feb 97. (3xcd-box) *Demon; (FBOOK 15)* **NO HOLDING BACK** ☐ -

May 97. (cd) *R.C.A.; (74321 48728-2)* **TEMPORARY BEAUTY** ☐ ☐

—— In the US, 1976 a ltd 1,000 bootleg lp 'LIVE AT MARBLE ARCH' was issued. The **RUMOUR** also branched out with own releases includung several 45s and albums MAX (Jul 77, Vertigo) / FROGS, SPROUTS, CLOGS & KRAUTS (Apr 79, Stiff) / PURITY OF PRESENCE (Jul 80, Stiff).

Van Dyke PARKS

Born: 3 Jan'41, Hattiesburg, Mississippi, USA. In his early teens, PARKS moved to Hollywood, California, where he studied classical piano. He also made inroads into acting, starring alongside Grace Kelly in the film, 'The Swan'. With the onset of the folk boom in the early 60's, PARKS played the coffee-house circuit along with his brother Carson, eventually securing a deal with 'M.G.M.' (initially to score soundtracks for Walt Disney~!). A debut single, 'NUMBER NINE' was issued in early '66, a second, 'COME TO THE SUNSHINE' following a year later. Neither releases made much of an impact, although PARKS was making more of a name for himself with his writing, production and session work. His 'HIGH COIN' track became something of a folk chestnut, subsequently covered by everyone from BOBBY VEE to The WEST COAST POP ART EXPERIMENTAL BAND, while PARKS himself guested on records by The BYRDS and PAUL REVERE & THE RAIDERS. But the VAN DYKE PARKS myth really started to crystallise following his collaborations with BRIAN WILSON (BEACH BOYS) on the aborted 'SMILE' project. WILSON was fascinated by PARKS' incisive intellect and general enigmatic allure, while PARKS was in awe of WILSON's formidable talent and musical vision. With PARKS penning the lyrics, this bizarre pairing came up with such BEACH BOYS' classics as 'Heroes And Villains' and the epic 'Cabinessence'. The other BEACH BOYS were none too happy with the partnership, however, and PARKS pulled out of the project prior to its disintegration. VAN's solo debut, famously four years in the making, was released around the same time (1968) on 'Warners'. Entitled 'SONG CYCLE', the record was a concept affair in the spirit of 'SMILE' centering on PARKS' relationship with Hollywood and baffling critics with its impenetrably dense lyrics and avant garde, orchestrated arrangements while earning PARKS the questionable honour of creating the first 'art-rock' record. He subsequently went on to play session piano for, and produce other 'Warners' acts including RY COODER, LITTLE FEAT, ARLO GUTHRIE, TIM BUCKLEY, JUDY COLLINS and PHIL OCHS. A follow-up solo release eventually appeared in 1972, 'DISCOVER AMERICA', revealing PARKS' infatuation with Caribbean music and even featuring a calypso reworking of 'STARS AND STRIPES FOREVER'. 'THE CLANG OF THE YANKEE REAPER' (1975) was PARKS' most accessible release to date but still it sold poorly and he remained a cult phenomenon. Disillusioned with the Hollywood scene, it was almost a decade before PARKS returned with 'JUMP' (1984). Another concept project, the album was based on the Southern stories of the fictional Uncle Remus (originally written by Joel Chandler Harris) with an orchestrated, muzak backing. While 'TOKYO ROSE' (1989) focused on relations between America and Japan, PARKS hooked up with BRIAN WILSON once more in 1995 for the acclaimed 'ORANGE CRATE ART' (mostly written by PARKS bar a few covers of work by MICHAEL HAZLEWOOD and GEORGE GERSWIN). • **Trivia:** In 1979, PARKS contributed to the Robert Altman film, 'Popeye'.

Album rating: SONG CYCLE (*6) / DISCOVER AMERICA (*6) / THE CLANG OF THE YANKEE REAPER (*5) / JUMP! (*6) / TOKYO ROSE (*5) / FISHERMAN & HIS WIFE (*5) / IDIOSYNCRATIC PATH: THE BEST OF . . . compilation (*7) / ORANGE CRATE ART with Brian Wilson (*5)

VAN DYKE PARKS – vocals, piano with session people

		M.G.M.	M.G.M.

Mar 66. (7") *(MGM 1301)* <13441> **NUMBER NINE. / DO WHAT YOU WANTA** ☐ ☐

1967. (7") <13570> **COME TO THE SUNSHINE. / FARTHER ALONG** - ☐

		Warners	Warners

1968. (lp) <(WS 1727)> **SONG CYCLE** ☐ ☐
- Vine street / Palm desert / Widow's talk / The all golden / Van Dyke Parks / Public domain / Donovan's colours / The attic / Laurel Canyon Blvd. / By the people / Pot porri. (re-iss.Nov86 on 'Edsel'; ED 207) (cd-iss. Jul88 & Sep93; EDCD 207)

—— PARKS became session pianist and producer for many including RY COODER, LITTLE FEAT, ARLO GUTHRIE, TIM BUCKLEY, JUDY COLLINS, PHIL OCHS, etc.

Nov 70. (7") <7409> **ON THE ROLLING SEA WHEN JESUS SPEAKS TO ME. / EAGLE & ME** - ☐

Jul 72. (7") <7609> **ODE TO TOBAGO. / OCCAPELLA** - ☐

Aug 72. (lp) (K 46166) <2589> **DISCOVER AMERICA**
– Jack Palance / Introduction / Bing Crosby / Steelband music / The four Mills brothers / Be careful / John Jones / FDR in Trinidad / Sweet Trinidad / Occapella / Sailin' shoes / Riverboat / Ode to Tobago / Your own comes first / G-man Hoover / Stars & stripes forever. (re-iss. Nov86 on 'Edsel'; ED 210) (cd-iss. Aug88; EDCD 210) (cd re-iss. Jan96; 7599 26185-2)

Oct 72. (7") <7632> **RIVERBOAT. / JOHN JONES**

Dec 75. (lp) (K 56161) <BS 2878> **THE CLANG OF THE YANKEE REAPER**
– Clang of the yankee reaper / City on the hill / Pass that stage / Another dream / You're a real sweetheart / Love is the answer / Iron man / Tribute to space / Soul train / Cannon in D. (re-iss. Nov86 on 'Edsel'; Ed 213) (cd-iss. Aug88; EDCD 213) (cd re-iss. Jan96; 7599 26185-2)

Feb 84. (lp) (923829-1) <23829> **JUMP**
– Jump / Opportunity for two / Come along / I ain't goin' home / Many a mile to go / Taps / An invitation to say / Mona / After the ball / Look away / Homing grove. (cd-iss. Jan96; 7599 23829-2)

Aug 89. (lp/c/cd) (925968-1/-4/-2) <25968> **TOKYO ROSE**
– America / Tokyo Rose / Yankee go home / Cowboy / Manzanar / Calypso / White chrysanthmun / Trade war / Out of love / One home run. (cd re-iss. Jan96; 7599 25968-2)

Jul 91. (cd/c) <714> **FISHERMAN + HIS WIFE**
(above issued on 'Windham Hill')

Nov 95. (cd/c; BRIAN WILSON and VAN DYKE PARKS) <(9362 45427-2/-4)> **ORANGE CRATE ART**
– Orange crate art / Sail away / My hobo heart / Wings of a dove / Palm tree and moon / Summer in Monterey / San Francisco / Hold back time / My Jeanine / Movies is magic / This town goes down at sunset / Lullaby.

– compilations, etc. –

Mar 94. (cd) Diablo; (DIAB 807) **IDIOSYNCRATIC PATH: THE BEST OF VAN DYKE PARKS**
– Donovan's colours / John Jones / Pass that stage / Ode to Tobago / The attic / Clang of the yankee reaper / The four Mills brothers / You're a real sweetheart / Sailin' shoes / Vine Street / Palm desert / Tribute to Spree / Iron man / Sweet Trinidad / Be careful / Bing Crosby / Steelband music / Your own comes first / Stars and stripes forever. (re-iss. Nov95; same)

PARLIAMENT (see under ⇒ CLINTON, George)

Alan PARSONS PROJECT

Formed: London, England ... 1975 by the man who engineered The BEATLES' 'Abbey Road' and PINK FLOYD's 'Dark Side Of The Moon'. While working at Abbey Road studios with the likes of STEVE HARLEY & COCKNEY REBEL and PILOT, he formed a working partnership/group with manager and lyricist, ERIC WOOLFSON. Intended as a one-off, the Edgar Allan-Poe 'TALES OF MYSTERY AND IMAGINATION' was released on 'Charisma' in 1976, the concept piece surprising critics and even hitting the US Top 40. The following year, PARSONS and Co signed a new contract with 'Arista', issuing the more conventionally accessible US Top 10 set, 'I ROBOT' (based on science fiction writer, Isaac Asimov's book of the same name). The group/project continued to maintain US Top 30 status over the course of the late 70's/early 80's with albums such as 'PYRAMID' (1978), 'EVE' (1979), 'THE TURN OF A FRIENDLY CARD' (1980), 'EYE IN THE SKY' (1982) and 'AMMONIA AVENUE' (1984). These records spawned several major hit singles featuring an array of vocal talent including COLIN BLUNSTONE, CHRIS RAINBOW, LENNY ZAKATEK and DAVID TOWNSHEND. Later in the 80's, PARSONS employed the services of DAVID PATON on the 1985 project, 'VULTURE CULTURE' and JOHN MILES and GARY BROOKER on 'STEREOTOMY' in '86. However, the pop/rock appeal of PARSONS and his troupe of studio-bound sidemen waned after the relative commercial failure of 'GAUDI' (an album based on the works of Spanish architect, Antonio Gaudi). This seemed to be a major setback for PARSONS, who remained absent from the music scene for the ensuing six years, belatedly returning with a solo set, 'TRY ANYTHING ONCE', in 1993.

Album rating: TALES OF MYSTERY AND IMAGINATION (*7) / I ROBOT (*6) / PYRAMID (*5) / EVE (*5) / THE TURN OF A FRIENDLY CARD (*6) / EYE IN THE SKY (*6) / THE BEST OF THE ALAN PARSONS PROJECT compilation (*6) / AMMONIA AVENUE (*6) / VULTURE CULTURE (*4) / STEREOTOMY (*4) / GAUDI (*4) / THE BEST OF THE ALAN PARSONS PROJECT VOL.2 compilation (*6) / THE INSTRUMENTAL WORKS collection (*4) / TRY ANYTHING ONCE (*4) / THE DEFINITIVE COLLECTION compilation (*6)

ALAN PARSONS (b.1949) – guitar, keyboards, vocals, producer, engineer with **ERIC WOOLFSON** – keyboards, vocals / **IAN BAIRNSON** – guitars (ex-PILOT) / **DAVID PATON** – bass, vocals, guitar / **STUART TOSH** – drums

	Charisma	20th Century
Jun 76. (lp) (CDS/+MC 4003) <508> **TALES OF MYSTERY AND IMAGINATION**	56	38 May76
– A dream within a dream / The raven / The tell-tale heart / The cask of Amontillado / (The system of) Doctor Tarr and Professor Feather / The fall of the House of Usher: Prelude – Arrival – Intermezzo – Pavane / Fall / To one in Paradise.		
Jul 76. (7") (CB 293) <2297> **(THE SYSTEM OF) DOCTOR TARR AND PROFESSOR FEATHER. / A DREAM WITHIN A DREAM**		37
Sep 76. (7") <2308> **THE RAVEN. / PRELUDE TO THE FALL OF THE HOUSE OF USHER**	-	80
Oct 76. (7") (CB 298) **TO ONE IN PARADISE. / THE CASK OF AMONTILLADO**		-

—— added **DUNCAN MACKAY** – keyboards

	Arista	Arista
Jun 77. (lp/c) (SPARTY/TCARTY 1012) <7002> **I ROBOT**	30	9
– I robot / I wouldn't want to be like you / Some other time / Breakdown / Don't let it show / The voice / Nucleus / Day after day / Total eclipse / Genesis Ch.1 V.32. (re-iss. Mar89 lp/c/cd; 209/409/259 651)		
Aug 77. (7") (ARIST 134) <0260> **I WOULDN'T WANT TO BE LIKE YOU. / NUCLEUS**		36
(above featured **LENNY ZAKATEK** – vocals) / (below **DAVID TOWNSHEND** – vocals)		
Dec 77. (7") <0288> **DON'T LET IT SHOW. / I ROBOT**	-	92
Feb 78. (7") (ARIST 158) **I ROBOT. / SOME OTHER TIME**	-	-
Feb 78. (7") <0310> **BREAKDOWN. / DAY AFTER DAY**		-

—— added **STUART ELLIOTT** – drums (ex-10cc) repl. TOSH

May 78. (lp/c) (SPART/TCART 1054) <4180> **PYRAMID**	49	26
– Voyager / What goes up / The eagle will rise again / One more river / Can't take it with you / In the lap of the gods / Pyramania / Hyper-gamma-spaces / Shadow of a lonely man. (re-iss. Apr88 lp/c/cd; 209/409/259 983)		
Jun 78. (7") (ARIST 195) **PYRAMANIA. / IN THE LAP OF THE GODS**		
Sep 78. (7") <0352> **WHAT GOES UP. / IN THE LAP OF THE GODS**	-	87
Aug 79. (lp/c) (SPARTY/TCARTY 1100) <9504> **EVE**	74	13
– Lucifer / You lie down with dogs / I'd rather be a man / You won't be there / Winding me up / Damned if I do / Don't hold back / Secret garden / If I could change your mind. (re-iss. Jul83 on 'Fame' lp/c; FA/TCFA 3071) (re-iss. May88 lp/c/cd; 208/408/258 981)		
Aug 79. (7") (ARIST 294) **LUCIFER. / I'D RATHER BE A MAN**		-
(12") (ARIST12 294) – ('A'side) / Damned if I do / Secret garden.		
(below featured **ZAKATEK – vocals** (also on Jan81, Dec83 singles)		
Nov 79. (7") (ARIST 312) <0454> **DAMNED IF I DO. / IF I COULD CHANGE YOUR MIND**		27 Sep79
Jan 80. (7") <0491> **SECRET GARDEN. / YOU WON'T BE THERE**	-	-
Mar 80. (7") <0502> **LUCIFER. / YOU LIE DOWN WITH DOGS**		-

—— now w/out MACKAY

Nov 80. (lp/c) (DL/TC ART 1) <9518> **THE TURN OF A FRIENDLY CARD**	38	13
– May be a price to pay / Games people play / Time / I don't wanna go home / The gold bug / The turn of a friendly card: (part 1 – Snake eyes – The ace of swords; part 2 – Nothing left to lose). (re-iss. May88 lp/c/cd; 208/408/258 982)		
Nov 80. (7") (ARIST 374) **THE TURN OF A FRIENDLY CARD. / MAY BE A PRICE TO PAY**		-
Jan 81. (7") (ARIST 386) <0573> **GAMES PEOPLE PLAY. / THE ACE OF SWORDS**		16 Nov80
Aug 81. (7") (ARIST 423) <0598> **TIME. / THE GOLD BUG**		15 Apr81
Oct 81. (7") <0635> **SNAKE EYES. / I DON'T WANNA GO HOME**	-	67
(above featured **CHRIS RAINBOW** – vocals) (also on May85 single)		
May 82. (lp/c) (204/404 666) <9599> **EYE IN THE SKY**	28	7
– Sirius / Eye in the sky / Children of the moon / Gemini / Silence and I / You're gonna get your finger burned / Psychobabble / Mammagamma / Step by step / Old and wise. (re-iss. May87 lp/c/cd; 208/408/258 718)		
May 82. (7") (ARIST 470) <0696> **EYE IN THE SKY. / GEMINI**		3
(below featured **COLIN BLUNSTONE** – vocals (ex-ZOMBIES) (below **ELMER GANTRY**)		
Nov 82. (7") <1029> **PSYCHOBABBLE. / CHILDREN OF THE MOON**	-	57
Dec 82. (7") (ARIST 494) **OLD AND WISE. / CHILDREN OF THE MOON**	74	-
Feb 83. (7") <1048> **OLD AND WISE. / YOU'RE GONNA GET YOUR FINGERS BURNED**	-	-
Oct 83. (lp/c) (APP/TCAPP 1) <8193> **THE BEST OF THE ALAN PARSONS PROJECT** (compilation)	99	53
– I wouldn't want to be like you / Eye in the sky / Games people play / Time / Pyramania / You don't believe / Lucifer / Psychobabble / Damned if I do / Don't let it show / Can't take it with you / Old and wise. (cd-iss. Feb87; 601050) (cd re-iss. Aug95; 610052)		
Feb 84. (7") <9108> **YOU DON'T BELIEVE. / LUCIFER**		54
Feb 84. (lp/c/cd) (206/406/256 100) <8204> **AMMONIA AVENUE**	24	15
– Prime time / Let me go home / One good reason / Since the last goodbye / Don't answer me / Dancing on a high wire / You don't believe / Pipeline / Ammonia Avenue. (re-iss. May88 lp/c/cd; 208/408/258 885)		
Feb 84. (7"/7"sha-pic-d) (ARIS T/D 553) **DON'T ANSWER ME. / YOU DON'T BELIEVE**	58	-
(12"+=) (ARIST12 553) – Games people play / Old and wise.		
Feb 84. (7",12") <9160> **DON'T ANSWER ME. / DON'T LET IT SHOW**		15
Jun 84. (7") (ARIST 572) <9208> **PRIME TIME. / THE GOLD BUG**	-	34 May84
(12"+=) (ARIST12 572) – Pipeline (instrumental) / Sirius (instrumental).		
(below featured **DAVID PATON** – vocals)		
Jan 85. (7") (ARIST 588) <9282> **LET'S TALK ABOUT ME. / HAWKEYE**		56
(12+=) (ARIST12 588) – Pipeline.		
Feb 85. (lp/c/cd) (206/406/256 577) <8263> **VULTURE CULTURE**	40	46
– Let's talk about me / Separate lives / Days are numbered (the traveller) / Sooner or later / Vulture culture / Hawkeye / Somebody out there / The same old sun. (re-iss. May88 lp/c/cd; 208/408/258 884)		
Apr 85. (7") <9349> **DAYS ARE NUMBERED (THE TRAVELLER). / SOMEBODY OUT THERE**	-	71

—— next featured vocalists **JOHN MILES, CHRIS RAINBOW, GARY BROOKER**

Jan 86. (lp/c/cd) (207/407/257 463) <8384> **STEREOTOMY**		43
– Stereotomy / Beaujolais / Urbania / Limelight / In the real world / Where's the walrus? / Light of the world / Chinese whispers / Stereotomy two. (re-iss. Jun88 lp/c/cd; 209/259/409 050)		
Mar 86. (7"/12") (ARIST/+12 654) <9443> **STEREOTOMY. / URBANIA (instrumental)**		82 Feb86

—— added **LAURIE COTTLE** – bass / **RICHARD COTTLE** – saxophone, synthesizers / **GEOFF BARRADALE** – vocals (with usual vocalists) repl. BROOKER

Jan 87. (7") <9576><9548> **STANDING ON HIGHER GROUND. / INSIDE LOOKING OUT**	-	-
Jan 87. (lp/c/cd) (208/408/258 084) <8448> **GAUDI**	66	57
– La Sagrada familia / Too late / Closer to Heaven / Standing on higher ground /		

Money talks / Inside looking out / Paseo de gracia (instrumental). *(re-iss. Feb90 cd/c/lp; 260/410/260 171)*

Jan 88. (lp/c/cd) *(208/408/258 634)* **LIMELIGHT: THE BEST OF THE ALAN PARSONS PROJECT VOL.2** (compilation)
 – Limelight / Same old sun / Ammonia avenue / Mammagamma / Since the last goodbye / I robot / Prime time / Hawkeye / Return of the friendly card / Silence and I. *(cd re-iss. Oct95)*

ALAN PARSONS

Oct 93. (cd/c/lp) *(74321 16730-2/-4/-1)* <18741> **TRY ANYTHING ONCE**
 – The three of me / Turn it up / Wine from the water / Breakaway / Jigue / Mr. Time / Siren song / Back against the wall / Re-jigue / Oh life (there must be more). *(cd+c+=)* – I'm talking to you / Dreamscape.

– compilations, etc. –

Nov 87. (cd) *London; (832820-2)* **TALES OF MYSTERY AND IMAGINATION**
 – (remixed debut with new synth/guitar touches + narration by ORSON WELLS)
Nov 88. (lp/c/cd) *R.C.A.; (209/409/259 237)* **THE INSTRUMENTAL WORKS**
 – Pipeline / Where's the walrus? / I robot / Mammagamma / Hawkeye / Voyager / Paseo de Gracia / Urbania / The gold bug / Genesis Ch.1 V.32.
Dec 90. (cd-box/c-box) *Arista; (ND/NK 74374)* **ALAN PARSONS BOX SET**
Nov 91. (cd/c) *Connoisseur; (VSOP CD/MC 170)* **ANTHOLOGY**
Mar 95. (cd) <5086> **LIVE: THE BEST OF THE ALAN PARSONS PROJECT**
Sep 95. (d-cd) *R.C.A.; (74321 29208-2)* **BACK 2 BACK**
Jan 96. (cd) *RCA Victor; (09026 68229-2)* **THE VERY BEST OF THE ALAN PARSONS PROJECT**

Gram PARSONS

Born: CECIL INGRAM CONNOR, 5 Nov'46, Winter Haven, Florida, USA. Through a privileged but traumatic childhood in Waycross, Georgia, during which his father, Coon Dog, committed suicide and his mother died of alcohol-related illness (on the day he graduated from high school), GRAM diverted himself with music; although his first love was country, the traditional preserve of white Southerners, GRAM was inspired to get up on stage after witnessing the hip-swivelling suave of ELVIS PRESLEY. Developing his talents in high-school covers outfits such as The PACERS and The LEGENDS, he was also sidelining with solo gigs and, through manager, Buddy Freeman, secured an appearance on a Greenville, South Carolina, TV Station. This in turn led to GRAM forming The SHILOS (having previously sang as a duo with KENT LAVOIE – aka hitmaker, LOBO), a fairly staid folk outfit who recorded a session for a Greenville campus radio station (released in 1979 on 'Sundown' as 'GRAM PARSONS – THE EARLY YEARS 1963-65') and with whom PARSONS penned his most fully realised song to date, 'ZAH'S BLUES'. Inevitably, the band fell by the wayside following GRAM's enrolment at Harvard in 1965; bypassing classes for the lure of the local music scene, he barely lasted six months, hooking up with local musicians, IAN DUNLOP, JOHN NUESE and MICKEY GAUVIN to form The LIKE and pioneering a synthesis of R&B, rock'n'roll and country which would would inform the remainder of PARSON's relatively short career. Around this time, GRAM spoke of having a deal with 'R.C.A.' and although it's widely believed he never recorded for the label, two tracks, 'CAN'T TAKE IT ANYMORE' and 'REMEMBER', have recently been unearthed (thanks to eagle-eyed archives man, Ron Maharg) from the label's vaults. The former a BYRDS-esque jangle calling to mind 'Chimes Of Freedom' and the latter a version of 'NOVEMBER NIGHTS' (a staple of The LIKE's live set never recorded under its original title but subsequently covered by actor Peter Fonda), these tracks may well have been recorded at the same time as the legendary lost Brandon De Wilde session, which GRAM & Co. are rumoured to have played on (the actor was a close confidante of the band and a regular at their new communal home in The Bronx, New York); through the continuing efforts of GP obsessive and all-round top man, Keith Munro, the songs might just be given an official release – subject to legal complexities – in the near future through 'B.M.G.'. Whatever, they're certainly more representative of the direction PARSONS was headed than the lame film theme, 'THE RUSSIANS ARE COMING', which served as a debut single in Spring '67. By this point trading under The INTERNATIONAL SUBMARINE BAND moniker, GRAM & Co. were encouraged by the experimentation of renegade country artists like BUCK OWENS and the hard-driving B-side, 'TRUCK DRIVING MAN' was a truer taste of what was to come. After another flop single for 'Columbia', 'SUM UP BROKE', the group relocated to L.A., where the West Coast scene was sending out cultural shockwaves around the world. Hobnobbing with the likes of the aforementioned Peter Fonda, the group blagged a cameo role in hippy flick, 'The Trip', for which they also recorded a track, 'LAZY DAYS' (it belatedly turned up on the second FLYING BURRITO BROTHERS album). As country wasn't yet hip with the L.A. set, the song was rejected and the band ended up lip-synching to music by the more suitably psychedelic ELECTRIC FLAG. Bearing out such iniquities with their heads held high, the group eventually secured a contract with L.A. producer LEE HAZLEWOOD's 'L.H.I.' records. But the INTERNATIONAL SUBMARINE BAND that signed up wasn't the same beast that had moved to California only a matter of months earlier. DUNLOP and GAUVIN, tired of waiting around and eager to move in a more R&B/rock direction, hooked up with BARRY TASHIAN and BILLY BRIGGS for the first, short-lived incarnation of The FLYING BURRITO BROTHERS.

PARSONS and NUESE, meanwhile, pursued their idea of a pure country sound; JON CORNEAL, BOB BUCHANAN (co-writer of PARSONS' classic 'HICKORY WIND') and CHRIS ETHRIDGE all played on the resulting album, 'SAFE AT HOME' (1968) alongside Nashville veteran, EARL 'LES' BALL and pedal steel player, J.D. MANESS. While half the album was out and out country (including covers of Johnny Cash's 'I STILL MISS SOMEONE' and Merle Haggard's 'SOMEBODY ELSE YOU'VE KNOWN'), PARSONS was already in the process of creating something fresh and exciting with his original material; the little-boy-lost charm of 'BLUE EYES' was irresistible while the chugging 'LUXURY LINER' became something of a country-rock standard covered by EMMYLOU HARRIS amongst others, the whole record characterised by GRAM's quavering, frail but emotional depth-charge singing. Retrospectively hailed as the first ever country-rock album, it was nevertheless ignored at the time and to all intents and purposes, The BYRDS' 'Sweetheart Of The Rodeo' (1968) was the record which really introduced the concept to a wider public and more significantly, the rock and country establishments. With sales of 'SAFE AT HOME' barely registering, GRAM wasn't slow in taking up an invitation to join the band (The BYRDS), and, along with CHRIS HILLMAN, formed the main thrust of their move away from folk-rock to stone country. An album consisting almost wholly of cover versions, 'Sweetheart..'s only two originals were penned by PARSONS, the poignant 'ONE HUNDRED YEARS FROM NOW' and the aforementioned autumnal beauty of 'HICKORY WIND'. Ironically, GRAM's distinctive vocals were erased (in favour of ROGER McGUINN) on all but the latter track prior to release, the controversial reason given that PARSONS was still contracted to HAZLEWOOD (note-the original versions were belatedly released as part of The BYRDS' 1990 'C.B.S.' box set). Despite shaking up the Grand Ole Opry, drawing critical acclaim and setting in motion a return to roots music that would reverbate well into the 70's, GRAM, in what was already becoming a familiar career pattern, was quickly tiring of life as a BYRD. Following a messy departure on the eve of a South African tour (newfound buddies The ROLLING STONES were instrumental in persuading GRAM that such a venture was really like, not a hip thing to do, man), PARSONS flew back to L.A. and mused upon his fabled vision of a "Cosmic American Music". HILLMAN soon joined him and along with pedal steel maestro, SNEAKY PETE KLEINOW and old cohorts CORNEAL and ETHRIDGE, realised that vision and then some, with The FLYING BURRITO BROTHERS. Taking the name from the brief project put together by DUNLOP, GAUVIN etc, the group blended country, soul, R&B and rock into a seamless strand of Americana that to this day has never been bettered. Yet after only two albums (see The FLYING BURRITO BROTHERS section for the full lowdown on the band's trailblazing, hellraising heyday), PARSONS again bailed out, spending more and more time with KEITH RICHARDS; PARSONS' influence on The 'STONES was obvious, from the reworked hoedown of 'Honky Tonk Woman' ('Country Honk') to the stoned backwoods bliss of their finest album, 'Exile On Main Street'. Although he was never credited, GRAM is rumoured to be floating around somewhere in the murk of the latter masterpiece, certainly spending enough time at RICHARDS' French villa/makeshift recording studio to lend the claims some weight. With his career in limbo, PARSONS eventually returned to L.A. in 1972 and began recording his first fully fledged solo album; unable to secure the production services of his hero, MERLE HAGGARD, GRAM did the next best thing and hired the man's recording engineer, Hugh Davies, leaving the lion's share of the knob-twiddling to another English friend, RIK GRECH (erstwhile FAMILY member and part of the short-lived BLIND FAITH). Employing ELVIS stalwarts such as JAMES BURTON and GLEN D. HARDIN, GRAM assembled a crack band with the angel-voiced EMMYLOU HARRIS at its epicentre; a struggling folk singer when PARSONS met her, HARRIS was the musical other half that he'd been searching for all his life and vice versa. PARSONS schooled her in the ways of cosmic country and her crystal pure soprano ringing against GRAM's flawed but impassioned holler remains one of the most sublime sounds ever laid down on vinyl. Grand claims perhaps, but the pairing's magic transformed well-worn standards like 'STREETS OF BALTIMORE' and 'WE'LL SWEEP OUT THE ASHES IN THE MORNING' into bittersweet soul food, highlights – along with the fragile 'A SONG FOR YOU' – of 'G.P.' (1973). Again the critics frothed (at least the ones who could recognise the talent, others were more sceptical of what PARSONS was trying to achieve) and again the public remained indifferent. Undeterred, GRAM, EMMYLOU and manager, Eddie Tickner, took advantage of Warner's (GRAM was now signed to 'Reprise') enthusiasm for a bonafide tour and set about forming a road band, The FALLEN ANGELS. Despite managing only eight shows in an incident-packed month which saw GRAM falling further into drug oblivion, the tour was by all accounts a freewheeling success if not exactly an effective promotional tool; fans still in their nappies when GRAM's ragged country roadshow came to town can get at least some idea of what the fuss was about via a live set recorded for broadcast over a Long Island, NY radio station; 'LIVE 1973 (live with The FALLEN ANGELS)' (1994). Back in L.A., his personal life continuing to unravel with each passing month, GRAM got it together one last time and, as he eagerly told his friends upon its completion, finally made the album he'd been hearing in his head for years. Although a hotch-potch of old and new, borrowed and blue, the songs on 'GRIEVOUS ANGEL' (1974) resonate as deeply as any in the history of country, or rock for that matter. GRAM's voice had taken on a new lease of life, his duets with HARRIS, 'HEARTS ON FIRE' and 'LOVE HURTS' blessed with the kind of spiritual intensity normally found in gospel music. Similarly, the PARSONS/HARRIS pairing transformed 'HICKORY WIND' from a wistful country ballad into a transcendant country ballad (despite its cheesy mock-live setting), while 'RETURN OF THE GRIEVOUS ANGEL' combined a Beat-cowboy narrative with soaring harmonies and a swooning chorus to mesmerising effect. If 'BRASS BUTTONS' and '$1000 WEDDING' were GRAM at his most intimately confessional, then closing track, 'IN MY HOUR OF DARKNESS', read like both a prayer of hope and an uncanny portent of GRAM's own death. Within a matter of weeks, road manager/professional nanny/best friend, Phil Kaufman, was driving out to the Joshua Tree monument, Arizona desert in a ramshackle hearse, GRAM's lifeless body in the back. GRAM PARSONS died on the 19th of September '73, officially from a drugs overdose although suspicion still surrounds the events that took place in the Joshua Tree Inn that night, where the singer was taking a break with friends prior to a scheduled tour. True to the pact they'd made (at the funeral of revered country picker, CLARENCE WHITE), Kaufman burned GRAM's body in the desert heat, a fitting end perhaps, for an artist who'd blazed his way through the musical consciousness like a comet. 'GRIEVOUS ANGEL' was finally issued posthumously in early '74, although seemingly (at least initially) not even GRAM's death could spark interest in his music. While EMMYLOU HARRIS went on to an impressive and successful career of her own, belatedly popularising some of GRAM's songs, the GRAM PARSONS legend has since taken on such mythical proportions that there's even an annual event held at Joshua Tree each year. Yet while the myth threatens to obscure the actual music, a cursory glance around the country/alt-country scene of today is proof enough that GRAM's vision has endured. STOP PRESS: The Brandon De Wilde tapes mentioned above have apparently just been discovered, although their exact content remains unclear at present. You heard it here first.

Album rating: International Submarine Band: SAFE AT HOME (*5) / Gram Parsons: G.P. (*8) / GREVIOUS ANGEL (*8) / posthumous:- SLEEPLESS NIGHTS (*5) / GRAM PARSONS & THE FALLEN ANGELS (*6) / WARM EVENINGS, PALE MORNINGS, BOTTLED BLUES (*6) / COSMIC AMERICAN MUSIC demos (*4)

GRAM PARSONS – vocals, guitar / with **EMMYLOU HARRIS** – vocals / **JAMES BURTON** – guitar / **GLEN D.HARDIN** – piano / **RIK GRECH** – bass / etc.

			Reprise	Reprise
Jan 73.	(7") <1139> **SHE. / THAT'S ALL IT TOOK**		-	
Mar 73.	(lp) (K 44228) <MS 2123> **G.P.**			

– Still feeling blue / We'll sweep out the ashes in the morning / A song for you / Streets of Baltimore / She / That's all it took / The new soft shoe / Kiss the children / Cry one more time / How much I've lied / Big mouth blues.

Mar 73.	(7") (K 14245) **THE NEW SOFT SHOE. / SHE**			-
Jan 74.	(lp) (K 54018) <MS 2171> **GREVIOUS ANGEL**			

– Return of the grevious angel / Hearts on fire / I can't dance / Brass buttons / $1000 wedding / Medley live from Northern Quebec:- (a) Cash on the barrelhead – (b) Hickory wind / Love hurts / Ooh Las Vegas / In my hour of darkness.

Jan 74.	(7") <1192> **LOVE HURTS. / IN MY HOUR OF DARKNESS**		-	

―― GRAM died on the 19th September '73 after recording 90% of above album.

– compilations, etc. –

May 76.	(lp; GRAM PARSONS with The FLYING BURRITO BROTHERS) A&M; (AMLH 64578) <4578> **SLEEPLESS NIGHTS**		
Mar 79.	(lp) Shiloh; <SLP 4088> **GRAM PARSONS** (with The INTERNATIONAL SUBMARINE BAND)	-	
May 79.	(lp) Shiloh; <SRS 8702> **GRAM PARSONS – THE EARLY YEARS 1963-65**	-	
	(UK-iss.May84 on 'Sundown'; SDLP 1010)		
Dec 81.	(7") Warners; <50013> **THE RETURN OF THE GREVIOUS ANGEL (alt.take). / HEARTS ON FIRE**		
Jun 82.	(lp) Warners; (K 57008) <WS 5321> **GRAM PARSONS**		
Feb 83.	(7"ep; GRAM PARSONS with EMMYLOU HARRIS & The FALLEN ANGELS) Sundown; <GPEP 104> **THE BIG FINISH**	-	
1983.	(7") Sierra; <GP 105> **LOVE HURTS (live). / THE NEW SOFT SHOE (live)**	-	
Nov 83.	(lp; GRAM PARSONS with The FALLEN ANGELS & EMMYLOU HARRIS) Sundown; (SDLP 003) / Sierra; <GP 1973> **LIVE 1973 (live)**		Apr82
	(cd-iss. Jun94; CDSD 003)		
May 84.	(lp/c) Sundown; (SD LP/C 008) **MELODIES**		-
Nov 89.	(cd) Warners; (7599 26108-2) **G.P. / GREVIOUS ANGEL**		
	(re-iss. Nov93; same)		
Aug 92.	(lp) Raven; **WARM EVENINGS, PALE MORNINGS, BOTTLED BLUES**		-
Jun 95.	(cd) Sundown; (CDSD 077) **COSMIC AMERICAN MUSIC**		-

INTERNATIONAL SUBMARINE BAND

PARSONS / + **IAN DUNLOP** – bass, sax / **MICKEY GAUVIN** – drums / **JOHN NUESE** – guitar

			not iss.	Ascot
1967.	(7") <2218> **THE RUSSIANS ARE COMING. / TRUCK DRIVING MAN**		-	-
			not iss.	Columbia
1967.	(7") <43935> **SUM UP BROKE. / ONE DAY WEEK**		-	
			not iss.	L.H.I.
1967.	(7") <LHI 1205> **LUXURY LINER. / BLUE EYES**		-	
Apr 68.	(lp) <LHIS 12001> **SAFE AT HOME**		-	

– Blue eyes / I must be somebody else you've known / A satisfied mind / Polson Prison blues / That's all right / Miller's cave / I still someone / Luxury liner / Strong boy / Do you know how it feels to be lonesome. (re-iss. 1985 on 'Statik'; STATLP 26) <re-iss. 1985 on 'Rhino'; RNLP 069> (cd-iss. Feb91 on 'Sundown'; CDSD 071)

1968.	(7") <LHI 1217> **MILLER'S CAVE. / SOMEBODY ELSE YOU'VE KNOWN**	-	

Andy PARTRIDGE (see under ⇒ XTC)

PASSENGERS (see under ⇒ U2)

PASTELS (dig out; Great Alt & Indie . . .)

PAVEMENT

Formed: Stockton, California, USA . . . 1989 by frontman STEPHEN MALKMUS and longtime friend/guitarist, SCOTT KANNBERG. They were soon joined by drummer GARY YOUNG (although this was initially a loose arrangement), the band recording their early US-only EP's at YOUNG's home studio, the first of which, 1989's 'SLAY TRACKS', was released on the self-financed 'Treble Kicker' label. A further two EP's, 'DEMOLITION PLOT J-7' and 'SUMMER BABE', together with a mini-lp, 'PERFECT SOUND FOREVER', were subsequently issued on the US indie, 'Drag City' over the course of the ensuing two years. The lo-fi, shambling charm of the likes of 'SUMMER BABE' eventually secured the band a UK deal with 'Big Cat' records, PAVEMENT consistently hitting the charts in Britain throughout their career. The debut album, 'SLANTED AND ENCHANTED' was finally released amid much anticipation in early 1992, its covertly melodic, avant-indie drawing inevitable but favourable comparisons with The PIXIES, The VELVET UNDERGROUND and even KING CRIMSON! Masterfully combining chaotic dischord and shards of crystalline harmony, the record's most compelling moments lay in the lazy melancholia of 'TRIGGER CUT' or 'ZURICH IS STAINED'. MALKMUS' brilliantly cryptic lyrics and offhand phrasing together with the twisted beauty of their music saw the band consistently dubbed as an American FALL. No bad thing, and besides, the band were carving out their own niche on the live circuit, by now augmented with extra sticksman, BOB NASTANOVICH and bassist MARK IBOLD, wildman YOUNG's infamous onstage antics an added attraction. The debut reached the lower reaches of the UK chart while a compilation of the early EP's, 'WESTING (BY MUSKET & SEXTANT)' (1993) made the Top 30. Prior to the release of the follow-up proper, 'CROOKED RAIN CROOKED RAIN' (1994), the band parted company on less than amicable terms with YOUNG, his replacement being STEVE WEST. This folk-ish record marked the band's most enticingly melodic affair to date, the keening 'CUT YOUR HAIR' single almost making the Top 40, the record itself reaching No.15 and cementing PAVEMENT's position as the crown kings of lo-fi. Although PAVEMENT failed to breach the Billboard chart, they built up a loyal following on the US underground scene on the back of constant touring, the defiantly experimental and diverse 'WOWEE ZOWEE!' (1995) proving that the band were making no concessions to radio programmers. There were still perfect PAVEMENT moments of stark beauty, as on the single, 'FATHER TO A SISTER OF THOUGHT'. While the album may have put off those after the immediate pop fix of 'CROOKED . . .', PAVEMENT's next release, the meditative 'BRIGHTEN THE CORNERS' (1997) took a different tack again. It was clear that MALKMUS' songwriting was fast maturing, his work taking on a new depth and resonance that eschewed the stylistic grab-bag of old for a more straightforwardly direct approach. Feted by the likes of BLUR, who had previously pooh-pooh'd the American scene, PAVEMENT remain one of music's most resolutely individual bands. In 1999 and with drummer GARY YOUNG back into the fray, the band scored their first Top 30 single, 'CARROT ROPE', one of highlights on their Top 20 album, 'TERROR TWILIGHT'. Unfortunately, they bowed out towards the end of the decade. • **Covered:** THE CLASSICAL (Fall) / THE KILLING MOON (Echo & The Bunnymen). • **Trivia:** MALKMUS produced early 90's album 'Eyes Wide Smile' for FAITH OVER REASON. BOB and STEVEN played on SILVER JEW's (David Berman) album 'Starlite Walter'.

Album rating: PERFECT SOUND FOREVER mini (*5) / SLANTED AND ENCHANTED (*7) / WESTING (BY MUSKET & SEXTANT) compilation (*8) / CROOKED RAIN CROOKED RAIN (*7) / WOWEE ZOWEE (*8) / BRIGHTEN THE CORNERS (*7) / TERROR TWILIGHT (*8)

STEVEN MALKMUS (b. Santa Monica, California) – vocals, guitar / **SCOTT "SPIRAL STAIRS" KANNBERG** – guitar, vocals

			not iss.	Treble Kicker
1989.	(7"ep) <TK 001> **SLAY TRACKS 1933-1969**		-	

– You're killing me / Box elder / Maybe maybe / She believes / Price yeah!.

―― added **GARY YOUNG** (b.1953, Stockton) – drums

			not iss.	Drag City
1990.	(7"ep) <DC 2> **DEMOLITION PLOT J-7**		-	

– Forklift / Spizzle trunk / Recorder grot / Internal K-dart / Perfect depth / Recorder grot (rally).

―― (Aug90) added **BOB NASTANOVICH** – drums

1991.	(10"m-lp) <DC 4> **PERFECT SOUND FOREVER**		-

– Heckler spray / From now on / Angel carver blues – Mellow jazz docent / Drive by fader / Debris slide / Home / Krell vid-user.

―― (mid '91) added **MARK IBOLD** (b. New York) – bass (ex-DUSTDEVILS)

Jan 92.	(7"ep) <DC 9> **SUMMER BABE (Winter version) / MERCY: THE LAUNDROMAT. / BAPTISS BLACKTICK / MY FIRST MINE / MY RADIO**	-	
		Big Cat	Matador
Mar 92.	(lp/c/cd) (ABB 034/+C/CD) <OLE 038-2> **SLANTED AND ENCHANTED**	72	

– Summer babe (winter version) / Trigger cut – Wounded – Kite at: 17 / No life singed her / In a mouth of a desert / Conduit for sale / Chesleys little wrists / Loretta's scars / Here / Two states / Perfume-V / Fame throwa / Jackals, false grails – The lonesome era / Our singer / Zurich is stained.

Jul 92. (7"/12"/cd-s) *(ABB 35 S/T/SCD)* <OLE 042> **TRIGGER CUT. / SUE ME JACK / SO STARK (YOU'RE A SKYSCRAPER)**

Nov 92. (12"ep/12"pic-d-ep/cd-ep) *(ABB 38 T/P/SCD)* <OLE 044> **WATERY, DOMESTIC EP** `58`
– Texas never whispers / Frontwards / Feed 'em to the (Linden) lions / Shoot the singer (1 sick verse).

Mar 93. (lp/c/cd) *(ABB 40/+C/CD)* <Drag City; DC 14> **WESTING (BY MUSKET & SEXTANT)** (first 4 US singles material) `30`
(cd/lp re-iss. Sep98/Jan99 on 'Drag City'; same as US)

—— **STEVE WEST** (b. Richmond, Virginia) – drums. repl. GARY YOUNG – solo (single; 'PLANET MAN' 94)

Jan 94. (7"/12"/cd-s) *(ABB 55 S/T/CD)* <OLE 082> **CUT YOUR HAIR. / CAMERA / STARE** `52`

Feb 94. (lp/c/cd) *(ABB 56/+C/CD)* <OLE 079> **CROOKED RAIN CROOKED RAIN** `15`
– Silence kit / Elevate me later / Stop breathin / Cut your hair / Newark wilder / Unfair / Gold sound Z / 5-4 = unity / Range life / Heaven is a truck / Hit the plane down / Fillmore jive. *(s-lp w/free 7"; OLE 087)* – HAUNT YOU DOWN. / JAM KIDS

Jul 94. (7") *(ABB 70S)* **GOLD SOUNDZ. / KNEELING BUS** `-`
(12"+=/cd-s+=) *(ABB 70 T/SCD)* – Strings of Nashville / The exit theory.

—— line-up: STEPHEN MALKMUS / MARK IBOLD / ROBERT NASTANOVICH / STEVE WEST / SPIRAL STAIRS + FATAH RUARK

Jan 95. (7") *(ABB 77S)* **RANGE LIFE. / COOLIN' BY SOUND** `-`
(12"+=/cd-s+=) *(ABB 77 T/SCD)* – Raft.

Mar 95. (7"/12") *(ABB 86 S/T)* <OLE 134> **RATTLED BY THE RUSH. / FALSE SKORPION / EASILY FOOLED**
(cd-s+=) *(ABB 86SCD)* – Brink of the clouds.

Apr 95. (3-sided d-lp/c/cd) *(ABB 84/+C/CD)* <OLE 130> **WOWEE ZOWEE!** `18`
– We dance / Rattled by the rush / Black out / Brinx job / Grounded / Serpentine pad / Motion suggests / Father to a sister of thought / Extradition / Best friends arm / Grave architecture / At & t / Flux = rad / Fight this generation / Kennel district / Pueblo / Half a canyon / Western homes.

Jun 95. (7"ep/12"ep/cd-ep) *(ABB 91 S/T/SCD)* <OLE 169> **FATHER TO A SISTER OF THOUGHT. / KRIS KRAFT / MUSSLE ROCK (IS A HORSE IN TRANSITION)**

Aug 95. (7") <3G-08> **DANCING WITH THE ELDERS. / (other artist)** `-`

—— <above released on 'Third Gear'>

Jan 96. (cd-ep) *(ABB 110SCD)* <OLE 188CD> **PACIFIC TRIM EP:- GIVE IT A DAY / GANGSTERS & PRANKSTERS / SAGANAW**
(7"ep+=) *(ABB 110S)* <OLE 188> – I love Perth.

—— now without FATAH

		Domino	Capitol
Jan 97.	(7") *(RUG 51)* **STEREO. / BIRDS IN THE MAJIC INDUSTRY**	`48`	`-`

(cd-s) *(RUG 51CD)* – ('A'side) / Westie can drum / Winner of the . . .

Feb 97. (cd/c/lp) *(WIG CD/MC/LP 31)* <55226> **BRIGHTEN THE CORNERS** `27` `70`
– Stereo / Shady lane / Transport is arranged / Date with IKEA / Old to begin / Type slowly / Embassy row / Blue Hawaiian / We are underused / Passat dream / Starlings of the slipstream / Infinite spark.

		Domino	Matador
Apr 97.	(7") *(RUG 53)* <OLE 266> **SHADY LANE (KROSSFADER). / UNSEEN POWER OF THE PICKET FENCE**	`40`	Jun97

(cd-s) *(RUG 53CD)* – ('A'side) / Slowly typed / Cherry area.
(cd-s) *(RUG 53CDX)* – ('A'side) / Wanna mess you around / No tan lines.

—— drummer GARY YOUNG returned

May 99. (7") *(RUG 90)* **CARROT ROPE. / AND THEN** `27`
(cd-s) *(RUG 90CD1)* – ('A'side) / Harness your hopes / Roll with the wind.
(cd-s) *(RUG 90CD2)* – ('A'side) / Porpoise and the hand grenade / Rooftop rambler.

Jun 99. (cd/c/lp) *(WIG CD/MC/LP 66)* <OLE 260> **TERROR TWILIGHT** `19` `95`
– Spit on a stranger / Folk jam / You are a light / Cream of gold / Major leagues / Platform blues / Ann don't cry / Billie / Speak, see, remember / The hexx / Carrot rope.

Sep 99. (cd-s) *(RUG 96CD1)* **MAJOR LEAGUES / YOUR TIME TO CHANGE / STUB YOUR TOE / THE CLASSICAL**
(cd-s) *(RUG 96CD2)* – ('A'side) The killing moon / ('A'demo) / Decouvert de soleil.
(d7"set) *(RUG 96)* – (all above).

PAVLOV'S DOG (dig out; 4th edition or Great Metal . . .)

PEARL JAM

Formed: Seattle, Washington, USA . . . 1991 by JEFF AMENT and STONE GOSSARD, who, together with MARK ARM, STEVE TURNER and ALEX VINCENT had previously played in pivotal Seattle band, GREEN RIVER (ARM and TURNER went on to form the noisier, and some still argue, superior MUDHONEY). Widely held to be the first ever "Grunge" act, GREEN RIVER's distortion-heavy mash-up of punk and metal is best sampled on the 'DRY AS A BONE' EP (1987), one of the first releases on the seminal 'Sub Pop' label. Following the band's demise, GOSSARD, AMENT and BRUCE FAIRWEATHER (who had replaced TURNER in GREEN RIVER) recruited vocalist ANDREW WOOD (ex-MALFUNKSHUN) and drummer GARY GILMOUR to form the short lived MOTHER LOVE BONE. After an EP and a cult debut album, 'APPLE' (1990), WOOD overdosed on heroin (March '90), effectively bringing the band to an untimely end. However, it was within these 70's influenced grooves that AMENT and GOSSARD laid the musical foundations for what would later become PEARL JAM. The group evolved from a tribute project for the dead WOOD put together by SOUNDGARDEN

frontman, CHRIS CORNELL. Also featuring GOSSARD, AMENT, guitarist MIKE McCREADY, and SOUNDGARDEN sticksman MATT CAMERON, this loose aggregation released 'TEMPLE OF THE DOG' in 1991, a critically acclaimed opus that laid further groundwork for PEARL JAM's sound. With vocalist EDDIE VEDDER and drummer DAVE KRUSEN (subsequently superseded by DAVE ABBRUZZESE) replacing the SOUNDGARDEN boys, the outfit gradually evolved into PEARL JAM, the band still something of a cult act when their 'Epic' debut was released in America at the tail end of '91. 'TEN' eventually reached No.2 in the US chart and a hefty media buzz ensured a steady flow of UK imports, the record making the British Top 20 upon its Feb '92 release. With VEDDER penning the lyrics and GOSSARD and AMENT writing the music, 'TEN' was a powerfully assured debut, transforming the grunge monster into a sleekly melodic rock beast. VEDDER's soulful bellow was a key factor, the singer wringing emotion from every note of the anthemic 'ALIVE' and the affecting 'JEREMY'. Granted, comparisons to LED ZEPPELIN were a little unfair, but the band's lumbering sound seemed the antithesis of the cathartic rush with which NIRVANA had revolutionised a stale music scene and KURT COBAIN was spot on with his infamous criticisms, despite cries of sour grapes. While their intentions may have been honourable, PEARL JAM ushered in a tidal wave of dull as dishwater, sub-metal masquerading as grunge, most of it, funnily enough, released on major labels. Nevertheless, the kids loved it, especially the American ones, and the band embarked on a punishing touring schedule, finding time to make a cameo appearance as Matt Dillon's band in 'Singles', the Cameron Crowe film based on the Seattle music scene. As well as standing in for JIM MORRISON when The DOORS were eventually inducted into the Rock 'n' Roll Hall Of Fame, VEDDER performed a heart stopping version of BOB DYLAN's 'Masters Of War' (playing mandolin) at the veteran's annniversary concert in 1993. The same year also saw the release of a PEARL JAM follow-up, 'VS', the band's fiercely loyal fanbase propelling the album straight in at No.1 in the US charts. A more ragingly visceral affair, 'GO' gave VEDDER something to get his teeth into while the more reflective 'DAUGHTER' proved how affecting the band (and particularly VEDDER) could be when they dropped the derivative hard rock assault. Along with their mate NEIL YOUNG, PEARL JAM seemingly have an abiding love of vinyl, releasing 'VITALOGY' (1994) initially on record only, something which didn't prevent the band scaling the US chart once again. While not exactly vital, as the title might suggest, the record saw PEARL JAM going back to basics and injecting their behemoth-rock with a bit of stripped down energy. The following year saw PEARL JAM backing NEIL YOUNG on the so-so 'MIRROR BALL' (1995) album, the fruition of their musical partnership that had begun some years previous. In 1995, each member (except ABBRUZZESE), took time to carry out other projects, although the following year they returned to full force with 'NO CODE', an album that showed a lighter, acoustic side. • **Songwriters:** VEDDER wrote lyrics / GOSSARD and AMENT the songs except F***IN' UP (Neil Young). GREEN RIVER covered AIN'T NOTHIN' TO DO (Dead Boys) / QUEEN BITCH (David Bowie). • **Trivia:** Backed actor MATT DILLON's band CITIZEN DICK in the 1992 film 'Singles'. VEDDER co-wrote and sang on 2 tracks; 'THE LONG ROAD' + 'THE FACE OF LOVE' on the 1996 movie 'Dead Man Walking'.

Album rating: Green River: REHAB DOLL – DRY AS A BONE (*7) / Mother Love Bone: STARDOG CHAMPION collection (*8) / Pearl Jam: TEN (*10) / VS (*8) / VITALOGY (*7) / NO CODE (*8) / YIELD (*7) / LIVE ON TWO LEGS (*6)

GREEN RIVER

MARK ARM (b.21 Feb'62, California) – vocals / **STEVE TURNER** (b.28 Mar'65, Houston, Texas) – guitar / **STONE GOSSARD** (b.20 Jul'66) – guitar / **JEFF AMENT** (b.10 Mar'63, Big Sandy, Montana) – bass / **ALEX VINCENT** – drums

		not iss.	Homestead
Sep 85.	(12"ep) <HMS 031> **COME ON DOWN**	`-`	

– New god / Swallow my pride / Ride of your life / Corner of my eye / Tunnel of love. *(cd-ep-iss.May94; same)*

—— **BRUCE FAIRWEATHER** – guitar repl. TURNER who later joined MUDHONEY

		not iss.	I.P.C.
Nov 86.	(7"green) <ICP 01> **TOGETHER WE'LL NEVER. / AIN'T NOTHIN' TO DO**	`-`	

		Glitterhouse	Sub Pop
Jun 87.	(12"ep) <SP 11> **DRY AS A BONE**	`-`	

– Unwind / Baby takes / This town / PCC / Ozzie. *(UK-iss.Mar91 on 'Tupelo'; TUPLP 17)* *(cd-iss. May94; same)*

Feb 89. (12"ep) *(GR 0031)* <SP 15> **REHAB DOLL** `May88`
– Searchin' / Ain't nothin' to do / Forever means / Rehab girl / Swallow my pride / Together we'll never / Smilin' and dyin' / Porkfist / Take a dive / One more stitch. (c-ep+=) <SP 15A> – Queen bitch. *(US re-iss. c+cd-lp Jul88 as 'DRY AS A BONE' / 'REHAB DOLL')*

—— MARK ARM formed MUDHONEY

MOTHER LOVE BONE

formed by **AMENT, GOSSARD + FAIRWEATHER** plus **ANDREW WOOD** (b.1966) – vocals (ex-MALFUNKSHUN) / **GARY GILMOUR** – drums

		Polydor	Stardog
Mar 89.	(m-lp) <839011-2> **SHINE**	`-`	

– Thru fade away / Midshaker meltdown / Halfass monkey boy / Medley:- Chloe dancer / Lady Godiva blues.

Jul 90. (cd/c/lp) <(843191-2/-4/-1)> **APPLE** `Mar90`
– This is Shangri-la / Stardog champion / Holy roller / Bone China / Come bite the apple / Stargazer / Heartshine / Captain hi-top / Man of golden words / Mr.Danny boy / Capricorn sister / Crown of thorns. *(above 2 re-iss. cd as 'STAR DOG CHAMPION' Sep92 on 'Polydor'; 514177-2 / <314512 884-2>) (hit US No.77)*

—— ANDREW WOOD died on the 19th March '90 after a heroin overdose. AMENT and GOSSARD paid tribute to him by joining with SOUNDGARDEN ⇒ members in off-shoot outfit TEMPLE OF THE DOG. After this project was finished . . . PEARL JAM were formed

PEARL JAM

AMENT + GOSSARD with **EDDIE VEDDER** (b.23 Dec'66, Evanson, Illinois) – vocals / **MIKE McCREADY** (b. 5 Apr'65) – lead guitar / **DAVE ABBRUZZESE** (b.17 May'??) – drums repl. DAVE KRUZON

		Epic	Epic
Feb 92.	(cd/c/lp/pic-lp) (468884-2/-4/-1/-0) <47857> **TEN**	18	2 Dec91
	– Once / Even flow / Alive / Why go / Black / Jeremy / Oceans / Porch / Garden / Deep / Release. (re-dist.Dec92 yellow-cd+=/m-d; 468884-5/-3) – Alive (live) / Wash / Dirty Frank.		
Feb 92.	(7"white/c-s) (657572-7/-4) **ALIVE. / WASH**	16	
	(12"+=/cd-c-s+=) (657572-6/-5) – Once.		
Apr 92.	(7"/c-s) (657857-7/-4) **EVEN FLOW (remix). / OCEANS**	27	
	(12"white+=/cd-pic-s+=) (657857-8/-2) – Dirty Frank.		
Sep 92.	(7"white/c-s) (658258-7/-4) **JEREMY. / ALIVE (live)**	15	
	(12"pic-d+=) (658258-6) – Footsteps (live).		
	(pic-cd-s+=) (658258-4) – Yellow Ledbetter.		
Oct 93.	(cd/c/lp) (474549-2/-4/-1) <53136> **VS**	2	1
	– Go / Animal / Daughter / Glorified G / Dissident / W.M.A. / Blood / Rearviewmirror / Rats / Elderly woman behind the counter in a small town / Leash / Indifference.		
Oct 93.	(12"ep/cd-ep) (659795-6/-2) **GO. / ALONE / ELDERLY WOMAN BEHIND THE COUNTER IN A SMALL TOWN (acoustic)**		
	(free c-s+=) (659795-4) – Animal (live).		
Dec 93.	(7"red/c-s) (660020-7/-4) **DAUGHTER. / BLOOD (live)**	18	
	(12"+=/cd-s+=) (660020-6/-2) – Yellow ledbetter (live).		
May 94.	(7"/c-s) (660441-7/-4) **DISSIDENT. / REARVIEWMIRROR (live)**	14	
	(cd-s+=) (660441-2) – Release / Even flow (versions).		
	(cd-s) (660441-5) – ('A'side) / Deep / Even flow / Why go (versions).		

—— ABBRUZZESE departed and was repl. after below album by **JACK IRONS** (ex-RED HOT CHILI PEPPERS)

Nov 94.	(7"/c-s/cd-s) (661036-7/-4/-2) <77771> **SPIN THE BLACK CIRCLE. / TREMOR CHRIST**	10	58
			18
Dec 94.	(cd/c/d-lp) (477861-2/-4/-1) <66900> **VITALOGY**	6	1
	– Last exit / Spin the black circle / Not for you / Tremor Christ / Nothingman / Whipping / Pry, to / Corduroy / Bugs / Satan's bed / Better man / Aye davanita / Immortality / Stupid mop.		

—— McCREADY now also moonlighted for MAD SEASON (see under ALICE IN CHAINS) – lead singer being LAYNE STALEY. Meanwhile, STONE GOSSARD set up own record label 'Loosegroove' and signed MALFUNKSHUN, DEVILHEAD, WEAPON OF CHOICE, BRAD and PROSE AND CONCEPTS.

Feb 95.	(7"colrd/c-s/cd-s) (661203-7/-4/-2) **NOT FOR YOU. / OUT OF MY MIND (live)**	34	-
Dec 95.	(7"/cd-s) (662716-7/-2) <78199> **MERKINBALL**	25	7
	– I got I.D. / Long road.		
	(above both recorded w/ NEIL YOUNG)		

—— Group had already featured on NEIL YOUNG's album 'MIRRORBALL'. GOSSARD featured on THERMIDOR's 1996 album 'Monkey On Rico'.

—— mid-96; JEFF AMENT featured for minor supergroup THREE FISH

Aug 96.	(7"/c-s/cd-s) (663539-7/-4/-2) <78389> **WHO YOU ARE. / HABIT**	18	31
Sep 96.	(cd/c/d-lp) (484448-2/-4/-1) <67500> **NO CODE**	3	1
	– Sometimes / Habit / Who you are / In my tree / Smile / Hail hail / I'm open / Red mosquito / Lukin / Mankind / Black & red & yellow / Allnight.		
Jan 98.	(7"/c-s) (665394-7/-4) <78797> **GIVEN TO FLY. / PILATE**	12	21
	(cd-s+=) (665394-2) – Leatherman.		
Feb 98.	(cd/c/d-lp) (489365-2/-4/-1) <68164> **YIELD**	7	2
	– Brain of J. / Faithfull / No way / Given to fly / Wishlist / Pilate / Do the evolution / • / MFC / Low light / In hiding / Push me, pull me / All those yesterdays.		
May 98.	(7"/c-s) (665790-7/-4) <78896> **WISHLIST. / U**	30	47
	(cd-s+=) (665790-2) – Brain of J. (live).		
Nov 98.	(cd/c/d-lp) (489859-2/-4/-1) <69752> **LIVE ON TWO LEGS (live)**	68	15
	– Corduroy / Given to fly / Hail hail / Daughter / Elderly woman behind the counter in a small town / Untitled / MFC / Go / Off he goes / Even flow / Red mosquito / Nothingman / Do the evolution / Better man / Black / F*ckin' up.		
Aug 99.	(7"red/cd-s) (667479-7/-2) <79197> **LAST KISS. / SOLDIER OF LOVE**	42	2 May99

– others, etc. –

Jul 95.	(cd-ep) Epic; <77935> **JEREMY / YELLOW LEDBETTER / FOOTSTEPS**	-	79
Jan 96.	(cd-ep) Epic; <77938> **DAUGHTER / YELLOW LEDBETTER (live) / BLOOD (live)**	-	97

THREE FISH

JEFF AMENT – vocals, bass / **ROBBI ROBB** – vocals, guitar (of TRIBE AFTER TRIBE) / **RICHARD STUVERUD** – (of FASTBACKS)

		Epic	Epic
Jun 96.	(cd/c/d-lp) (484118-2/-4/-1) **THREE FISH**		
	– Solitude / Song for a dead girl / Silence at the bottom / Intellgent fish / Zagreb / All messed up / Here in the darkness / Hall of intelligent fish / Strangers in my head / Lovely meander / Elusive ones / Build / Stupid fish / A secret place / Laced. (d-lp+=) – If miles were alive / Can I come along / Easy way.		
Sep 96.	(cd-s) **LACED / CAN I COME ALONG? / IF MILES WERE ALIVE...**		

Jun 99.	(cd/c) **QUIET TABLE**	-	
	– Shiva and the astronaut / Tremor void / Myth of Abdou / Once in a day / All these things / Timeless / Hummingbird / My only foe / Transporting / Found a widow / Resonate / Chantreuse.		

PENETRATION	(dig out; Great Alt & Indie . . .)

PENTANGLE

Formed: London, England . . . early '67, the original members forming the basis for the band's first three albums, arguably their only truly essential works. Comprising the pure, jazz orientated vocals of JACQUI McSHEE with the immense talents of BERT JANSCH and JOHN RENBOURN on guitars and an innovative rhythm section of DANNY THOMPSON and TERRY COX on bass and drums respectively, PENTANGLE heralded the emergence of a fusion built around jazz and folk. Formed after RENBOURN and JANSCH had already had success with the sublime 'BERT AND JOHN' album, McSHEE joining after already having worked with RENBOURN on his first solo set, 'ANOTHER MONDAY'. The former ALEXIS KORNER rhythm section completed the band for 68's 'THE PENTANGLE', a brilliant and eclectic debut album produced by Shel Talmy and featuring folk standard, 'BRUNTON TOWN' as well as a blissful rendition of the Staple Singers' 'HEAR MY CALL'. The move into other genres continued on the next album, 69's 'SWEET CHILD', McSHEE's vocals shining on the enchanting 'SO EARLY IN THE SPRING' and the bluesy 'I'VE GOT A FEELING', while two Charles Mingus covers, 'GOODBYE PORK PIE HAT' and 'HAITIAN FLIGHT SONG' demonstrating the talents of COX and THOMPSON. 'BASKET OF LIGHT', released the following year, became a commercial hit, making the Top 5 in Britain and featuring 'LIGHT FLIGHT', which became a minor success in the singles chart and subsequently the theme tune to 60's TV series, 'Take Three Girls'. The overriding feature of this trilogy was the musicians' ability to complement each other in equal measure. After 'BASKET OF LIGHT', the material became progressively weaker as the band became less unified, while this in turn led to a break up in '73. While JANSCH and RENBOURN pursued their solo careers, the original line-up continued its interplay with McSHEE fronting the JOHN RENBOURN BAND between '74-'81. THOMPSON, meanwhile, worked with both JOHN MARTYN and NICK DRAKE, most notably on the former's 'Solid Air', and COX, after a stint as a session musician, backed French crooner, CHARLES AZNAVOUR. The original line-up re-formed in '82 for touring purposes as well as the reasonable long-player, 'OPEN THE DOOR', although commitments outwith the band meant that RENBOURN had been replaced by MIKE PIGGOTT. Although they released a few albums in the 80's and 90's, PENTANGLE never quite captured the spellbinding fusion sound of yesteryear. • **Songwriters:** JANSCH, RENBOURN and McSHEE, who also arranged traditional tunes. Amongst several covers, JANSCH did a fine version of HEARTBREAK HOTEL (hit; Elvis Presley).

Album rating: THE PENTANGLE (*6) / SWEET CHILD (*6) / BASKET OF LIGHT (*8) / CRUEL SISTER (*5) / SOLOMON'S SEAL (*5) / OPEN THE DOOR (*5) / IN THE ROUND (*5) / THE ESSENTIAL PENTANGLE VOL.1 & 2 compilations (*7's) / SO EARLY IN THE SPRING (*5) / ONE MORE ROAD (*5) / THINK OF TOMORROW (*4) / Bert Jansch: BERT JANSCH (*8) / IT DON'T BOTHER ME (*6) / JACK ORION (*8) / BERT & JOHN with John Renbourn (*6) / NICOLA (*6) / BIRTHDAY BLUES (*6) / ROSEMARY LANE (*5) / MOONSHINE (*5) / L.A. TURNAROUND (*5) / SANTA BARBARA HONEYMOON (*5) / A RARE CONUNDRUM (*5) / AVOCET (*5) / 13 DOWN (*5) / HEARTBREAK (*5) / FROM THE OUTSIDE (*5) / LEATHER LAUDERETTE with Rod Clements (*5) / SKETCHES (*5) / THE ORNAMENT TREE (*5) / THE GARDENER: THE ESSENTIAL BERT JANSCH 1965-1971 compilation (*7) / WHEN THE CIRCUS COMES TO TOWN (*6)

BERT JANSCH (b. 3 Nov'43, Glasgow, Scotland) – acoustic guitar, vocals / **JOHN RENBOURN** (b. 8 Aug'44, London, England) – guitars, sitar, vocals (ex-Solo artist) / **JACQUI McSHEE** (b.25 Dec'43) – vocals / **DANNY THOMPSON** (b. Apr'39, Devon, England) – double bass (ex-ALEXIS KORNER'S BLUES INC.) / **TERRY COX** (b. Buckinghamshire, England) – drums, percussion, glockenspiel, vocals (ex-ALEXIS KORNER'S BLUES INC.)

		Transatla.	Reprise
May 68.	(7") (BIG 109) **TRAVELIN' SONG. / MIRAGE**	21	-
Jun 68.	(lp) (TRA 162) <6315> **THE PENTANGLE**	21	
	– Let no man steal your thyme / Bells / Hear my call / Pentangling / Mirage / Way behind the Sun / Burton Town / Waltz. (cd-iss. 1988 on 'Transatlantic'/'Line'; 9.00549)		
Dec 68.	(7") **LET NO MAN STEAL YOUR THYME. / WAY BEHIND THE SUN**	-	
Dec 68.	(d-lp) (TRA 178) <6334> **SWEET CHILD (half live / half studio)**		
	– Market song / No more my Lord / Turn your money green / Haitian fight song / A woman like you / Goodbye pork pie hat / Three dances / Brentzal gay / La rotta / The Earl of Salisbury / Watch the stars / So early in the Spring / No exit / The time has come / Burton town / Sweet child / I loved a lass / Three part thing / Sovay / In time / In your mind / I've got a feeling / The trees they do grow high / Moon dog / Hole in my coal. (cd-iss. 1988 on 'Transatlantic'/'Line'; TACD 9.00552) – (omits 3)		
May 69.	(7") (BIG 124) **ONCE I HAD A SWEETHEART. / I SAW AN ANGEL**	46	
		5	
Oct 69.	(lp) (TRA 205) <6372> **BASKET OF LIGHT**		
	– Light flight / Once I had a sweetheart / Springtime promises / Lyke-Wake dirge / Train song / Hunting song / Sally go round the roses / The cuckoo / House carpenter. (cd-iss. Jul87 on 'Transatlantic'/'Line'; TACD 9.00555) (cd re-iss. 1989 on 'Transatlantic'/'Demon'; TRANDEMCD 7) (cd re-iss. Jun96 on 'Essential'; ESMCD 406)		
Feb 70.	(7") (BIG 128) **LIGHT FLIGHT. / COLD MOUNTAIN**	43	-

Nov 70. (lp) *(TRA 228)* <6430> **CRUEL SISTER** | 51 |
– Cruel sister / A maid that's deep in love / When I was in my prime / Lord Franklin / Jack Orion. *(re-iss. Mar77 on 'Xtra'; XTRA 1172) (cd-iss. 1988 on 'Transatlantic'/'Line';* TACD 44.055)

Nov 71. (lp) *(TRA 240)* <6463> **REFLECTION**
– Wedding dress / Omie wise / Will the circle be unbroken / When I get home / Rain and snow / Helping hand / So clear / Reflection. *(cd-iss. 1988 on 'Transatlantic'/'Line';)*

Reprise   Reprise

Sep 72. (lp) *(K 44197)* <2100> **SOLOMON'S SEAL**
– Sally free and easy / Cherry tree carol / The snows / High Germany / People on the highway / Willy O'Winsbury / No love is sorrow / Jump baby jump / Lady of Carlisle.

—— Disbanded Mar'73. THOMPSON and COX returned to session work. THOMPSON also went solo and joined JOHN MARTYN's group, to mention just one. JANSCH and RENBOURN continued to work on solo albums, with the latter being augmented by McSHEE.

– compilations, etc. –

on 'Transatlantic' unless mentioned otherwise

Jul 72. (lp) *(TRANSAM 23)* **HISTORY BOOK**
Aug 73. (lp) *(TRANSAM 29)* **PENTANGLING**
(re-iss. Aug 77 on 'Hallmark') (re-iss. May81)
1973. (7"m) *(BIG 567)* **LIGHT FLIGHT. / MARKET SONG / THE TIME HAS COME**
1975. (d-lp) *(89503/4)* **THE PENTANGLE COLLECTION**
(Europe only, re-iss. Apr88 on 'Castle' lp/c/cd; CCS/+MC/CD 184)
Jul 78. (lp) *(MTRA 2013)* **ANTHOLOGY**
Mar 82. (d-lp) *Cambra; (CR 054)* **AT THEIR BEST**
(c-iss.1985 on 'Autograph';)
Jul 87. (lp/cd) *(TRA LP/CD 602)* **THE ESSENTIAL PENTANGLE VOL.1**
– Once I had a sweetheart / Hear my call / Hole in the coal / Omie Wise / Waltz / The trees they do grow / Sweet child / A woman like you / Reflection / Will the circle be unbroken / Watch the stars / Helping hand / Goodbye pork pie hat / When I was in my prime.
Sep 87. (lp/cd) *(TRA LP/CD 606)* **THE ESSENTIAL PENTANGLE VOL.2**
– Pentangling / Bruton Town / Shake shake mama / Let no man steal your thyme / Soho / The cruel sister / Bells / Wedding dress / I've got a feeling / Three part thing / Rain and snow / Way behind the Sun / When I get home / The time has come.
Jul 90. (cd) *Shanachie; (79066)* **A MIND THAT'S DEEP DEEP IN LOVE**
Aug 92. (cd) *Shanachie; (79078)* **EARLY CLASSICS**
Apr 94. (c/cd) *Castle; (CCS/+CD 184)* **THE COLLECTION**
Jan 95. (cd/c) *Ariola Express; (2/4 95942)* **IN YOUR MIND**
Sep 95. (cd) *Band Of Joy; (cd) (BOJCD 013)* **LIVE AT THE BBC**

BERT JANSCH

Transatla.   Vanguard

1965. (lp) *(TRA 125)* **BERT JANSCH**
– Strolling down the highway / Smokey river / Oh how your love is strong / I have no time / Finches / Rambling's going to be the death of me / Veronica / Needle of death / Do you hear me now? / Running from home / Courting blues / Casbah / Dreams of love / Angie. *(re-iss. 1980 + Jan88; TRS 117) (re-iss. Jun88 on 'Transatlantic'/'Demon'; TRANDEM 1)*
Dec 65. (lp) *(TRA 132)* **IT DON'T BOTHER ME**
– Oh my babe / Ring-a-ding bird / Tinker's blues / Anti apartheid / The wheel / A man I'd rather be / My lover / It don't bother me / Harvest your thoughts of love / Lucky thirteen / As the day grows longer now / So long (been on the road so long) / Want my daddy now / 900 miles. *(re-iss. Jul76 as 'EARLY BERT' on 'Xtra'; XTRA 1163) (cd-iss. Oct93 on 'Transatlantic'/'Demon'+=; TDEMCD 16)* – The times has come / Soho / In this game / Dissatisfied blues.
1966. (lp) *(TRA 143)* **JACK ORION**
– The waggoner's lad / The first time ever I saw your face / Jack Orion / The gardener / Nottamun town / Henry Martin / Blackwaterside / Pretty Polly. *(re-iss. Jul76 as 'EARLY BERT VOL. 2' on 'Xtra'; XTRA 1164)*
1966. (lp; BERT JANSCH & JOHN RENBOURN) *(TRA 144)*
BERT AND JOHN
– Eastwind / Piano time / Goodbye pork pie hat / Soho / Tie tocative / Orlando / Red favourite / No exit / Along the way / The time has come / Stepping stones / After the dance.
1966. (7"ep) *(TRA EP 145)* **NEEDLE OF DEATH**
– Running from home / Tinker's blues / Needle of death / The wheel.

Transatla.   Reprise

Jun 67. (7") *(BIG 102)* **LIFE DEPENDS ON LOVE. / A LITTLE SWEET SUNSHINE**
Jul 67. (lp) *(TRA 157)* **NICOLA**
– Go your way my love / Woe is love my dear / Nicola / Come back baby / A little sweet sunshine / Love is teasing / Rabbit run / Life depends on love / Weeping willow blues / Box of love / Wish my baby was here / If the world isn't there. *(re-iss. Jul76 as 'EARLY BERT VOL. 3' on 'Xtra'+=; XTRA 1165)* – Come sing me a happy song to prove we can all get along the lumpy, bumpy road.
Dec 68. (lp) *(TRA 179)* <6343> **BIRTHDAY BLUES**
– Come and sing me a happy song / To prove / The bright new year / Tree song / Poison / Miss Heather / Rosemary Sewell / I've got a woman / A woman like you / I'm lonely / Promised land / Birthday blues / Wishing well blues.
Jun 71. (lp) *(TRA 235)* <6455> **ROSEMARY LANE**
– Tell me what is true love / Rosemary Lane / M'lady Nancy / A dream, a dream, a dream / Alman / Wayward child / Nobody's bar / Reynardine / Silly women / Peregrinations / Sylvie / Sarabanda / Bird song. *(re-iss. Jan77 as 'EARLY BERT VOL. 4' on 'Xtra'; XTRA 1170) (cd-iss. Sep94 on 'Transatlantic'/'Line'; TACD 9.007840)*

Reprise   Reprise

Feb 73. (lp) *(K 14234)* <2129> **MOONSHINE**
– Yarrow / Brought with the rain / January man / Night time blues / Moonshine / First time ever I saw your face / Rambleaway / Twa corbies / Oh my father. *(cd-iss. Sep95 on 'Jansch'; BJ 001CD)*

Mar 73. (7") *(K 14234)* **OH MY FATHER. / THE FIRST TIME EVER I SAW YOUR FACE**

Charisma   Kicking Mule

Sep 74. (lp) *(CAS 1090)* **L.A. TURNAROUND**
– Fresh as a sweet Sunday morning / Chambertin / One for Jo / Travelling man / Open up the Watergate (let the sunshine in) / Stone monkey / Of love and lullaby / Needle of death / Lady nothing / There comes a time / Cluck old hen / The blacksmith.
Oct 74. (7") *(CB 240)* **IN THE BLEAK MIDWINTER / ONE FOR JO**
Oct 75. (lp) *(CAS 1107)* **SANTA BARBARA HONEYMOON**
– Love a new / Mary and Joseph / Be my friend / Baby blue / Dance lady dance / You are my sunshine / Lost and gone / Blues run the game / Built another band / When the teardrops fell / Dynamite / Buckrabbit.
Nov 75. (7") *(CB 267)* **DANCE LADY DANCE. / BUILD ANOTHER BAND**
May 77. (lp) *(CAS 1127)* <202> **A RARE CONUNDRUM**
– Daybreak / One to a hundred / Pretty Saro / Doctor, doctor / 3 a.m. / The Curragh of Kildare / Instrumentally Irish / St.Flacre / If you see my love / Looking for a home / Poor mouth / Cat and mouse / Three chord trick / Lost love.

—— In 1978 he appeared on CONUNDRUM & RICHARD HARVEY single, 'Black Birds of Brittany'.

Feb 79. (lp) *(CLASS 6)* **AVOCET**
– Avocet / Bittern / Kingfisher / Kittiwake / Lapwing / Osprey.

Sonet   KIcking Mule

Apr 80. (7") *(SCK 44)* **TIME AND TIME. / UNA LINEA DI DOLCEZZA**
Jul 80. (lp) *by BERT JANSCH & CONUNDRUM) (SNTF 162)* <309> **13 DOWN**
– Una linea di dolcezza / Let me sing / Down river / Nightfall / If I had a lover / Time and time / In my mind / Sovay / Where did my life go / Single Nose / Ask your daddy / Sweet mother Earth / Bridge.

Logo   Kicking Mule

Feb 82. (lp) *(GOL 1035)* **HEARTBREAK**
– Is it real? / Up to the stars / Give me the time / If I were a carpenter / Wild mountain thyme / Heartbreak hotel / Sit down beside me / No rhyme nor reason / Blackwater side / And not a word was said. *(re-iss. May89 on 'Hannibal'; HNBL 1312) (cd-iss. Jul93; HNCD 1312)*

Mausoleum   not iss.

Feb 82. (7") *(GO 409)* **HEARTBREAK HOTEL. / UP TO THE STARS**
Sep 85. (lp) *(KOMA 788006)* **FROM THE OUTSIDE**
– Sweet rose in the garden / Black bird in the morning / Read all about it / Change the song / Shout / From the outside / If you're thinking 'bout me / Silver raindrops / Why me? / Get out of my life / Time is an old friend / From the inside. *(cd-iss. Aug93 on 'Hypertension' +=; HYCD 200128)* – River running / High emotion / From the inside.

Black Crow   not iss.

Mar 88. (lp/c/cd; BERT JANSCH & ROD CLEMENTS) *(CRO 218)* **LEATHER LAUNDERETTE**
– Strolling down the highway / Sweet Rose / Brafferton / Ain't no more cane / Why me? / Sundown station / Knight's move / Brownsville / Bogie's bonny belle / Leather launderette / Been on the road so long.

—— his backers now **PETER KIRTLEY** – guitar, b.vocals, percussion / **DANNY THOMPSON** – double bass, percussion, chimes / **STEVE BAKER** – blues harp / **STEFAN WULFF** – percussion / **FRANK WULFF** – percussion, alto-flute, etc.

Temple   Hypertension

Nov 90. (cd/c/lp) *(COMD2/CTP/TP 035)* **SKETCHES**
– Ring-a-ding bird / One for Jo / Poison / The old routine / Needle of death / Oh my father / Running, running from home / Afterwards / Can't hide love / Moonshine / A woman like you / A windy day. *(cd+=)* – As the day grows longer now.

Run River   not iss.

Nov 90. (lp/c/cd) *(RRA/+MC/CD 0012)* **THE ORNAMENT TREE**

Cooking Vinyl   not iss.

Sep 95. (cd) *(COOKCD 092)* **WHEN THE CIRCUS COMES TO TOWN**
– Walk quietly by / Open road / Back home / No-one around / Step back / When the circus comes to town / Summer heat / Just a dream / The lady doctor from Ashington / Stealing the night away / Honey don't you understand / Born with the blues / Morning brings peace of mind / Living in the shadows.

– his compilations, etc. –

on 'Transatlantic' unless mentioned otherwise

1966. (lp) *Vanguard; (VSD 97212)* **LUCKY THIRTEEN**
1969. (lp) *Vanguard; <VMD 6506>* **STEPPING STONES**
Nov 69. (lp) *(TRANSAM 10)* **THE BERT JANSCH SAMPLER**
Dec 72. (lp) *(TRANSAM 27)* **BOX OF LOVE – THE BERT JANSCH SAMPLER VOL. 2**
– Oh how your love is strong / In this game / The gardener / Soho / I am lonely / Renegrinations / Casbah / Dissatisfied blues / As the day grows longer now / Box of love / Birthday blues / Nobody's bar.
Mar 78. (lp) *(MTRA 2007)* **ANTHOLOGY**
Jul 87. (cd) *(TRA 604/TRACD 604)* **THE ESSENTIAL COLLECTION VOL.1**
Sep 87. (cd) *(TRA 607/TRACD 607)* **THE ESSENTIAL COLLECTION VOL.2**
Jul 93. (cd) *(TDEMCD 16)* **BERT JANSCH / JACK ORION**
Dec 93. (cd) *(TDEMCD 17)* **NICOLA / BIRTHDAY BLUES**
1980. (lp) *(lp) (TRA 333)* **THE BEST OF BERT JANSCH**
Jul 92. (cd) *Transatlantic-Demon; (TDEMCD 9)* **THE GARDENER: THE ESSENTIAL BERT JANSCH 1965-1971**
– The gardener / Alice's wonderland / Running from home / Tinker's blues / It don't bother me / The waggoner's lad / The first ever I saw your face / Go your way my love / My lover / Woe is love my dear / Black waterside / Rabbit run / A woman like you (studio) / Market song / A woman like you (live) / Wishing well / Rosemary Lane / Peregrinations / Poison / Miss Heather Rosemary Sewell / Reynardine / Bird song / When I get home / I am lonely.
Jul 93. (cd) *Virgin; (CDVM 9024)* **THREE CHORD TRICK** (74-79 material)
Sep 93. (cd) *Windsong; (WINCD 039)* **BBC RADIO 1 LIVE IN CONCERT** (live 1980-82 with CONUNDRUM)
Aug 96. (cd) *Jansch; (BJ 002CD)* **LIVE AT 12 BAR**

PENTANGLE

—— re-formed in the early 80's; **MIKE PIGGOTT** – guitar; repl. RENBOURN

	Spindrift	Varrick

Jul 85. (lp) (SPIN 111) <VR 017> **OPEN THE DOOR**
– Open the door / Dragonfly / Mother Earth / Child of the winter / The dolphin / Lost love / Sad lady / Taste of love / Yarrow / Street song.

1985. (7") **DRAGON FLY. / THE DOLPHIN**

—— **NIGEL PORTMAN SMITH** (b. 7 Feb'50, Sheffield, England) – bass, keyboards, accordian, vocals repl. DANNY

Feb 86. (7") (SURF 107) **PLAY THE GAME. / SATURDAY MOVIE**

1986. (d-lp) (SPIN 120) **IN THE ROUND** 1988
– Play the game / Open sea / She moved through the fair / Set me free / When the night is over come to me baby / Sunday morning blues / Chase that devil away / The Saturday movie / Suilagrar / Circle the Moon / Let me be. (re-iss. Apr90 on 'Episode' d-lp/c/cd; TA LP/MC/CD 2001)

1986. (7") (SURF 121) **SET ME FREE. / COME TO ME BABY**

	Shanachie	Shanachie

1989. (lp/c) (SHAN/+C 79066) **A MAID THAT'S DEEP IN LOVE**

—— **ROD CLEMENTS** – guitar, mandolin / **GERRY CONWAY** (b.11 Sep'47, Norfolk, England) – drums, percussion repl. PIGGOTT + COX

	Plane	GreenLinnet

Aug 89. (lp) (PLANE 88648) **SO EARLY IN THE SPRING** 1990
– New nothynge / The fish in the well / Pavan d'Aragon / Variations on my Lady Carey's dompe / Circle dance / The nine maidens: Clarsach – The nine maidens – The fiddler. (re-iss. Jun96 on 'Park' cd/c; PRK CD/MC 35)

—— **PETER KIRTLEY** (b.26 Sep'45, Hebburn-on-Tyne, England) – vocals, guitars repl. CLEMENTS

	Permanent	Green Linnet

Oct 91. (cd/c/lp) (PERM CD/MC/LP 3) **THINK OF TOMORROW**
– O'er the lonely mountain / Baby now it's over / Share a dream / he storyteller / Meat on the bone / Ever yes ever no / Straight ahead / The toss of golden hair / The lark in the clear air / The bonny boy / Colour my paintbook. (re-iss. Sep93 on 'Hypertension'; HY 200112LP) (cd re-iss. Mar95; HY 200112CD)

Aug 92. (cd/c/lp) (PERM CD/MC/LP 10) **25TH YEAR ANNIVERSARY**

May 93. (cd/c) (PERM CD/MC 11) **ONE MORE ROAD**
– Travelling solo / Oxford City / Endless sky / The lily of the west / One more road / High Germany / Hey, hey soldier / Willy of Winsbury / Somali / Manuel / Are you going to Scarborough fair.

—— (also some obvious trad. covers)

	Tandem	not iss.

Mar 94. (cd) (TDEM 12) **PEOPLE ON THE HIGHWAY**

	Hypertension	not iss.

Jun 95. (cd) (HYCD 20015-2) **LIVE 1994** (live)

PERE UBU

Formed: Cleveland, Ohio, USA ... September '75 out of ROCKET FROM THE TOMBS, by DAVID THOMAS (aka CROCUS BEHEMOTH; his alter-ego) and PETER LAUGHNER. Along with CHARLIE WEINER (guitar), GLEN 'THUNDERHAND' HACH (guitar) and TOM 'FOOLERY' CLEMENTS (drums), they became residents at THOMAS's workplace, the Viking Saloon; he was apparently a bouncer! A revamped RFTT saw THOMAS and LAUGHNER being joined by CRAIG BELL (bass), GENE 'CHEETAH CHROME' O'CONNOR (guitar) and 'JOHNNY BLIZ' MADANSKY, and it was this line-up who recorded sessions for WMMS radio stations, later to surface as a posthumous 1990 cd, 'LIFE STINKS'. A few embryonic UBU tracks, 'FINAL SOLUTION' and '30 SECONDS OVER TOKYO', plus covers of 'SATISFACTION' (Rolling Stones) and 'SEARCH AND DESTROY' (Stooges), featured on these rare master tapes. Even 'SONIC REDUCER' was hijacked by The DEAD BOYS bound, CHEETAH and BLITZ, the pair being united with STIV BATORS, who replaced THOMAS before the ROCKETS split. Meanwhile, PERE UBU (THOMAS and LAUGHNER) recruited other musicians; TIM WRIGHT, ALLEN RAVENSTINE, TOM HERMAN plus SCOTT KRAUSS, and took their name from a play by French writer, Alfred Jarry. The large-framed THOMAS formed his own 'Hearthan' label, issuing a classic debut, '30 SECONDS OVER TOKYO', which led to gigs at (New York's) Max's Kansas City in early '76. Another gem, 'FINAL SOLUTION', was unleashed soon after, although LAUGHNER departed (at this stage the line-up numbered THOMAS, RAVENSTINE, HERMAN, KRAUSE and newcomer, TONY MAIMONE) prior to the release of their third and fourth rare 45's, 'STREET WAVES' and 'THE MODERN DANCE'. The latter subsequently became the name of their debut album which gained a release early in 1978 on the obscure US 'Blank' label (a few months later it surfaced in the UK on 'Mercury'). The sound was clearly a break from the "New Wave", echoing as it did a revival of the avant-garde (CAPTAIN BEEFHEART and ENO-era ROXY MUSIC). On the strength of this masterwork, they signed to the major 'Chrysalis' label and, six months later, wowed the music world with another abstract beauty, 'DUB HOUSING' (1978). After the disappointing 'NEW PICNIC TIME' (1979), however, they were unceremoniously dropped by their label, the band's wayward eccentricity floating right over the average pop picker's head. PERE UBU (who had replaced HERMAN with veteran, MAYO THOMPSON – formerly of RED CRAYOLA) subsequently found a home with UK indie, 'Rough Trade', although they split after two poorly-received studio sets, 'THE ART OF WALKING' (1980) and 'SONG OF THE BAILING MAN' (1982), the latter boasting the drumming talents of ANTON FIER. Over the course

of the next five years, having released a debut album, 'THE SOUND OF THE SAND' early in '82, THOMAS embarked on an equally weird and anti-commercial solo career with albums, the live 'WINTER COMES HOME' (1983), 'VARIATIONS ON A THEME' (1983), 'MORE PLACES FOREVER' (1985), 'MONSTER WALKS THE WINTER LAKE' (1986) and 'BLAME THE MESSENGER' (1987). PERE UBU released a belated comeback album, 'THE TENEMENT YEARS', in 1988, a record which gathered together old UBU men, THOMAS, RAVENSTINE, MAIMONE and KRAUSE, while retaining CHRIS CUTLER and JIM JONES (previously part of THOMAS' solo band). For the 1989 set, 'CLOUDLAND', the group sought out former CAPTAIN BEEFHEART employee, ERIC DREW FELDMAN, who remained for a further two albums, 'WORLDS IN COLLISION' (1991) and 'STORY OF MY LIFE' (1993). Subsequently signing to 'Cooking Vinyl' (also now the rest home of BILLY BRAGG and The WEDDING PRESENT), PERE UBU cut one final effort, 'RAY GUN SUITCASE' (1995), before THOMAS once again opted for solo pastures with 'EREWHON' (1996). • **Songwriters:** All group compositions, except MIRROR MAN (Captain Beefheart) / DOWN BY THE RIVER (Neil Young). THOMAS collaborated with others on solo work and covered SLOOP JOHN B. (Beach Boys).

Album rating: THE MODERN DANCE (*9) / DUB HOUSING (*7) / NEW PICNIC TIME (*7) / THE ART OF WALKING (*6) / 390 DEGREES OF SIMULATED STEREO (*4) / SONG OF THE BAILING MAN (*5) / TERMINAL TOWER: AN ARCHIVAL COLLECTION compilation (*9) / THE TENEMENT YEAR (*6) / ONE MAN DRIVES WHILE THE OTHER MAN SCREAMS early live (*5) / CLOUDLAND (*6) / WORLDS IN COLLISION (*6) / STORY OF MY LIFE (*6) / RAYGUN SUITCASE (*7) / PENNSYLVANIA (*6) / David Thomas: THE SOUND OF THE SAND ... (*6) / WINTER COMES HOME (*5) / VARIATIONS ON A THEME (*6) / MORE PLACES FOREVER (*5) / MONSTER WALKS THE WINTER LAKE (*4) / BLAME THE MESSENGER (*5)

DAVID THOMAS (b.14 Jun'53) – vocals / **PETER LAUGHNER** (b.1953) – guitar / **TIM WRIGHT** – bass, guitar / **TOM HERMAN** (b.19 Apr'49) – guitar, bass / **SCOTT KRAUSE** (b.19 Nov'50) – drums / **ALLEN RAVENSTINE** (b. 9 May'50) – synthesizer

	not iss.	Hearthan

Dec 75. (7"ltd) <HR 101> **30 SECONDS OVER TOKYO. / HEART OF DARKNESS**

—— **DAVE TAYLOR** – synthesizer repl. RAVENSTINE

Mar 76. (7"ltd) <HR 102> **FINAL SOLUTION. / CLOUD 149**

—— **ALLEN RAVENSTINE** – synthesizer returned to repl. TAYLOR / **ALAN GREENBLATT** – guitar repl. LAUGHNER who formed FRICTION (he died of drug & alcohol abuse 22nd June '77)

—— **TONY MAIMONE** (b.27 Sep'52) – bass, piano repl. WRIGHT who joined DNA. (GREENBLATT left also) (were now a quintet with **THOMAS, HERMAN, KRAUSE, MAIMONE + RAVENSTINE**)

Nov 76. (7"ltd) <HR 103> **STREET WAVES. / MY DARK AGES**

Aug 77. (7"ltd) <HR 104> **THE MODERN DANCE. / HEAVEN**

	Mercury	Blank

Apr 78. (lp) (9100 052) <001> **THE MODERN DANCE** Jan78
– Non-alignment pact / The modern dance / Laughing / Street waves / Chinese radiation / Life stinks / Real world / Over my head / Sentimental journey / Humor me. (re-iss. Jan81 on 'Rough Trade'; ROUGH 22) (re-iss. Feb88 on 'Fontana' lp/cd; SF LP/CD 3)

	Radar	not iss.

Apr 78. (12"ep) (RDAR 1) **DATAPANIK IN THE YEAR ZERO (remixes compilation)**
– Heart of darkness / 30 seconds over Tokyo / Cloud 149 / Untitled / Heaven.

	Chrysalis	Rough Trade

Nov 78. (lp) (CHR 1207) <ROUGHUS 14> **DUB HOUSING**
– Navy / On the surface / Dub housing / Cagliari's mirror / Thriller / I will wait / Drinking wine Spodyody / Ubu dance party / Blow daddy-o / Codex. (cd-iss. Mar89 on 'Rough Trade'; ROUGHCD 6002)

Sep 79. (lp) (CHR 1248) <ROUGHUS 20> **NEW PICNIC TIME**
– One less worry / Make hay / Goodbye / The voice of the sand / Jehovah's kingdom comes / Have shoes will walk / 49 guitars and 1 girl / A small dark cloud / Small was fast / All the dogs are barking. (cd-iss. Mar89 on 'Rough Trade'; ROUGHCD 6003)

Oct 79. (7"m) (CHS 2372) **THE FABULOUS SEQUEL (HAVE SHOES WILL WALK). / HUMOR ME (live). / THE BOOK IS ON THE TABLE**

—— **MAYO THOMPSON** (b.26 Feb'44) – guitar, vocals (ex-RED CRAYOLA) repl. HERMAN who went solo

	Rough Trade	not iss.

Jun 80. (7") (RT 049) **FINAL SOLUTION. / MY DARK AGES**

Sep 80. (lp) (ROUGH 14) **THE ART OF WALKING**
– Go / Rhapsody in pink / Arabia * / Miles * / Misery goats / Loop / Rounder / Birdies / Lost in art / Horses / Crush this horn. (re-iss. 1981; same) – Arabian nights / Tribute to Miles; repl. *) (cd-iss. Apr89 tracks as re-issue; ROUGHCD 14)

Feb 81. (7") (RT 066) **NOT HAPPY. / LONESOME COWBOY DAVE**

May 81. (lp) (ROUGH 23) **390° OF SIMULATED STEREO – UBU LIVE: VOLUME 1** (live 76-79)
– Can't believe it / Over my head / Sentimental journey / 30 seconds over Tokyo / Humor me / Real world / My dark ages / Street waves / Laughing / Non-alignment pact / Heart of darkness / The modern dance. (cd-iss. Apr89; ROUGHCD 23)

—— added **ANTON FIER** (b.20 Jun'56) – drums, percussion (ex-FEELIES) / guest **EDDIE THORNTON** – trumpet

Jun 82. (lp) (ROUGH 33) **SONG OF THE BAILING MAN**
– The long walk home / Use of a dog / Petrified / Stormy weather / West Side story / Thoughts that go by steam / Big Ed's used farms / A day such as this / The vulgar boatman bird / My hat / Horns are a dilemma. (cd-iss. Apr89; ROUGHCD 33)

—— split mid 1982. MAYO returned to RED CRAYOLA (which also incl. most UBU's). KRAUSE + WRIGHT formed HOME & GARDEN, who released one album for 'Dead Man's Curve', 'HISTORY & GEOGRAPHY' (1986)

DAVID THOMAS & THE PEDESTRIANS

	Rough Trade	Recommended

Dec 81. (12"ep; by DAVID THOMAS) *(TRADE 5-12)* **VOCAL PERFORMANCES** ☐ –

—— included **THOMPSON, KRAUSE, FIER & RAVENSTINE** plus **CHRIS CUTLER** (b. 4 Jan'47) – drums / **JOHN GREAVES** – bass (both ex-HENRY COW) / **PHILIP MOXHAM** – multi (ex-YOUNG MARBLE GIANTS) / **RICHARD THOMPSON** – guitar

Jan 82. (lp) *(ROUGH 30)* **THE SOUND OF THE SAND AND OTHER SONGS OF THE PEDESTRIANS** ☐ ☐
– The birds are good ideas / Yiki Tiki / The crickets in the flats / Sound of the sand / The new atom mine / Big dreams / Happy to see you / Crush this horn – part 2 / Confuse did / Sloop John B. / Man's best friend.

Oct 82. (7") **PETRIFIED. / ?** ☐ ☐

—— w/ **CHRIS CUTLER** & **LINDSAY COOPER** – bassoon (ex-MIKE OLDFIELD)

Feb 83. (lp; DAVID THOMAS & HIS LEGS) *(DTLP)* **WINTER COMES HOME** (live Munich, 1982) ☐ ☐
– A day such as this / Winter comes home / West side story / Sunset / Stormy weather / Poetic license / Rhapsody in pink / Dinosaurs like me / Petrified / Bones in action / Contrasted views of the archaeopteryx.

—— added **RICHARD THOMPSON** etc. (CUTLER, COOPER)

Dec 83. (lp) *(ROUGH 60)* **VARIATIONS ON A THEME** ☐ ☐
– A day at the Botanical Gardens / Pedestrians walk / Bird town / The egg and I / Who is it / Song of hoe / Hurry back / The ram / Semaphore.

—— **TONY MAIMONE** – bass repl. GREAVES who joined The FLYING LIZARDS

	Rough Trade	Twin/Tone

May 85. (lp) *(ROUGH 80)* *<TTR 8551>* **MORE PLACES FOREVER** ☐ ☐
– Through the magnifying glass / Enthusiastic / Big breezy day / About true friends / Whale head king / Song of the bailing man / The farmer's wife / New broom.

DAVID THOMAS & THE WOODEN BIRDS

(**DAVID** retained **MAIMONE** and **CUTLER**) brought in **RAVENSTINE** again. (**DAVID HILD** – accordion of LOS LOBOS guested)

Apr 86. (lp/cd) *(ROUGH 90)* *<TTR/+CD 8667>* **MONSTER WALKS THE WINTER LAKE** ☐ ☐
– My theory of similtanious similtude – Red tin bus / What happened to me / Monster walks the winter lake / Bicycle / Coffee train / My town / Monster Magge king of the seas / Monster thinks about the good days / What happened to us.

—— **JIM JONES** (b.12 Mar'50) – guitar was added

Mar 87. (lp) *(ROUGH 120)* *<TTR 87105>* **BLAME THE MESSENGER** ☐ ☐
– The long rain / My town / King Knut / A fact about trains / When love is uneven / Storm breaks / Having time / Velikovsky / The two-step.

PERE UBU

(**THOMAS, RAVENSTINE, MAIMONE, CUTLER, JONES** and **KRAUSE**)

	Fontana	Enigma

Mar 88. (lp/c)(cd) *(SF LP/MC 5)(834 537-2)* *<73343>* **THE TENEMENT YEAR** ☐ ☐
– Something's gotta give / George had a hat / Talk to me / Busman's honeymoon / Say goodbye / Universal vibration / Miss you / Dream the Moon / Rhythm kind / The hollow Earth / We have the technology.

Jul 88. (7") *(UBU 1)* **WE HAVE THE TECHNOLOGY. / THE B-SIDE** ☐ ☐
(12"+=/cd-s+=) *(UBU 1-12/CD1)* – The postman drove a caddy / ('A'-different mix).

—— **ERIC DREW FELDMAN** (b.16 Apr'55) – drums (ex-CAPTAIN BEEFHEART) repl. RAVENSTINE + CUTLER

	Fontana	not iss.

Mar 89. (7") *(UBU 2)* **WAITING FOR MARY (WHAT ARE WE DOING HERE?). / WINE DARK SPARKS** ☐ ☐
(12"+=/cd-s+=) *(UBU 2-12/CD2)* – Flat.

May 89. (lp/c/cd) *(838 237-1/-4/-2)* **CLOUDLAND** ☐ ☐
– Breath / Bus called happiness / Race the sun / Waiting for Mary / Cry / Flat * / Ice cream truck / Lost nation road / Monday night / Pushin' / The wire * / The waltz. (cd+= *)

Jun 89. (7") *(UBU 3)* **LOVE LOVE LOVE. / FEDORA SATELLITE** ☐ ☐
(cd-s+=) *(UBUCD 3)* – Say goodbye.
(12") *(UBU 3-12)* – ('A'-cajun house mix) / ('A'132 bpm mix) / ('A'side).

Oct 89. (7") *(UBU 4)* **BREATH. / BANG THE DRUM** ☐ ☐
(12"+=) *(UBU 4-12)* – Over my head (live) / Universal initiation (live).
(cd-s+=) *(UBUCD 4)* – Humor me (live).

Mar 91. (7") *(UBU 5)* **I HEAR THEY SMOKE THE BARBEQUE. / INVISIBLE MAN** ☐ ☐
(12"+=/cd-s+=) *(UBU 5-12/CD5)* – Around the fire.

May 91. (cd/c/lp) *(848 564-2/-4/-1)* **WORLDS IN COLLISION** ☐ ☐
– Oh Catherine / I hear they smoke the barbeque / Turpentine / Goodnight Irene / Mirror man / Cry cry / World's in collision / Life of Riley / Over the Moon / Don't look back / Playback / Nobody knows / Winter in the Netherlands.

May 91. (7") *(UBU 6)* **OH CATHERINE. / LIKE A ROLLING STONE** ☐ ☐
(12"+=/cd-s+=) *(UBU 6-12/CD6)* – Down by the river.

	Fontana	Imago

Jan 93. (cd/c) *(514159-2/-4)* *<21024>* **STORY OF MY LIFE** ☐ ☐
– Wasted / Come home / Louisiana train wreck / Fedora satellite II / Heartbreak garage / Postcard / Kathleen / Honey Moon / Sleep walk / The story of my life / Last will and testament.

—— **THOMAS / KRAUSS / JONES / TEMPLE / YELLIN**

	Cooking Vinyl	Tim/Kerr

Aug 95. (cd) *(COOKCD 089)* *<TK 100>* **RAY GUN SUITCASE** ☐ ☐
– Folly of youth / Electricity / Beach Boys / Turquoise fins / Vacuum in my head / Memphis / Three things / Horse / Don't worry / Ray gun suitcase / Surfer girl / Red sky / Montana / My friend is a stooge for the media priests / Down by the river II.

Oct 95. (cd-ep) *(FRYCD 043)* *<TK 111-2>* **FOLLY OF YOUTH / BALL 'N' CHAIN (jam) / DOWN BY THE RIVER II (demo) / MEMPHIS (demo)** ☐ ☐ Feb96

—— **THOMAS** with **TOM HERMAN** + **JIM JONES** newcomer + **ROBERT WHEELER** – synthesizer / **MICHELE TEMPLE** – bass

	Tim/Kerr	Tim/Kerr

Mar 98. (cd) *<(TK 155)>* **PENNSYLVANIA** ☐ ☐
– Woolie bullie / Highwaterville / Sad txt / Urban lifestyle / Drive / Indiangiver / Monday morning / Perfume / Silent spring / Mr. Wheeler / Muddy waters / Slow / Fly's eye / Duke's Saharan ambitions / Wheelhouse.

May 98. (cd-ep) *<TK 830121>* **BEACH BOYS / DOWN BY THE RIVER / LOUISIANA TRAIN WRECK / MONTANA** ☐ ☐

– compilations, others, etc. –

Nov 85. (lp/cd) *Rough Trade; (ROUGH 83) / Twin/Tone; <TTR/+CD 8561>* **TERMINAL TOWER: AN ARCHIVAL COLLECTION** ☐ ☐
– (early 'Hearthan' sides + rare)

Mar 89. (cd) *Rough Trade; (ROUGHCD 93)* **ONE MAN DRIVES WHILE THE OTHER MAN SCREAMS - LIVE VOL.2: PERE UBU ON TOUR** ☐ ☐

Nov 95. (4x7"box) *Cooking Vinyl; (FRY 045) / Tim/Kerr; <TK 107>* **THE HEARTHAN SINGLES** ☐ ☐

Nov 95. (d-cd) *Movieplay Gold; (MPG 74178)* **MODERN DANCE / TERMINAL TOWER** ☐ ☐

Sep 96. (5xcd-box) *Cooking Vinyl; (COOKCD 098) / Geffen; <24969>* **DATAPANIK IN THE YEAR ZERO** ☐ ☐
– (first 5 albums + 1 free rarities album)

DAVID THOMAS

—— with **ANDY DIAGRAM** – trumpet (ex-PALE FOUNTAINS) / **PAUL HAMANN** – upright bass / **JIM JONES** – backing vocals

	Cooking Vinyl	Tim/Kerr

Sep 96. (cd; DAVID THOMAS & TWO PALE BOYS) *(COOKCD 105)* *<TK 145>* **EREWHON** ☐ ☐
– Obsession / Planet of fools / Nowheresville / Fire / Lantern / Morbid sky / Weird cornfields / Kathlen / Highway 61 revisited.

Jun 97. (5xcd-box) *(HR 110)* **MONSTER** (compilation of all his solo work) ☐ ☐

Carl PERKINS

Born: CARL LEE PERKINGS, 9 Apr'32, Ridgely, Tennessee, USA. In the early 50's, CARL and his brothers JAY and CLAYTON formed their own honky tonk outfit The PERKINS BROTHERS; the G in their surname had been inexplicably dropped. After relocating to Jackson, Memphis with his wife and inspiration Valda Crider, he struck up a deal with Sam Phillips' legendary 'Sun' label (also home of ELVIS PRESLEY, ROY ORBISON, JOHNNY CASH and JERRY LEE LEWIS). Phillips initially marketed him as a hillbilly/C&W artist on the small subsidiary 'Flip', CARL's siblings (along with newcomer W.S. 'Fluke' HOLLAND) continuing to back him on his debut solo single, early 1955's 'MOVIE MAGG'. With the subsequent defection of ELVIS to 'R.C.A.', PERKINS was groomed as Sun's "Great White Hope", perfecting his trademark combination of black rhythm and white melody early the following year with third single, 'BLUE SUEDE SHOES'. The song narrowly missed the US No.1 spot (it hit No.10 in Britain), and became a future classic although ELVIS subsequently popularised it while PERKINS lay in hospital recovering from a serious car crash; his brothers also had a lucky escape although JAY (who suffered a broken neck) was to die a few years later. Unable to capitalise on his success, CARL found it hard to re-establish his name after his absence. Four more minor Hot 100 placings (the last two for 'Columbia' between '58-'59) was all PERKINS could manage although it was no reflection on his abundant talent. Disillusioned, he succumbed to alcoholism as his career slid into decline. Nevertheless, stars like The BEATLES and JOHNNY CASH (also now a fellow devout Christian!) ensured the PERKINS name would not be forgotten; the Fab Four covered his songs while the latter giant of Country took him on as guest guitarist/featured solo singer. The stuff of classic C&W lyrics indeed, CARL's rollercoaster life took another bitter twist in 1974 when, after signing a new deal with 'Mercury', he had to cope with both the suicide of his brother CLAYTON and the death of his father. A few years later, he put his musical partnership with CASH on hold and subsequently toured in his own right with his sons as backing. Although his records never reached the heady commercial heights of yore, PERKINS joined up with old~ 'Sun' pals CASH and LEWIS (later ORBISON too) in '85 to instigate the aptly-monikered 'SURVIVORS'. Having spent the rest of the 80's and most of the 90's taking er . . . 'One Day At A Time', CARL was to sadly die after a paralysing stroke on the 19th of January, 1998; but for bad timing and even worse luck, CARL would have made it as a major league star in his own right although his contribution to popular music was recognised in 1987 when he was inducted into the Rock'n'Roll Hall Of Fame.

Best CD compilation: THE BEST OF CARL PERKINS on 'Columbia'(*6)

CARL PERKINS – vocals, electric guitar / with brothers **JAY** – acoustic guitar / **CLAYTON** – bass / **W.S. 'FLUKE' HOLLAND** – drums

	not iss.	Flip
	London	Sun

Jan 55. (7") *<501>* **MOVIE MAGG. / TURN AROUND** – ☐

Jul 55. (7") *<224>* **GONE, GONE, GONE. / LET THE JUKEBOX KEEP ON PLAYING** – ☐

Apr 56. (7") *(HLU 8271)* *<234>* **BLUE SUEDE SHOES. / HONEY DON'T** 10 2 Feb56

Apr 56. (7") *<235>* **SURE TO FAIL. / TENNESSEE** – ☐

Jun 56.	(7") <243> **BOPPIN' THE BLUES. / ALL MAMA'S CHILDREN**	-	70	
Nov 56.	(7") <249> **DIXIE FRIED. / I'M SORRY, I'M NOT SORRY**	-		
Apr 57.	(7") (HLS 8408) <261> **YOUR TRUE LOVE. / MATCHBOX**		67	Feb 57
May 57.	(7") <274> **THAT'S ALL RIGHT. / FOREVER YOURS**	-		
Dec 57.	(7") (HLS 8527) **GLAD ALL OVER. / FOREVER YOURS**		-	
Dec 57.	(7") <287> **GLAD ALL OVER. / LEND ME YOUR COMB**	-		
Apr 58.	(7") (HLS 8608) **THAT'S ALL RIGHT. / LEND ME YOUR COMB**		-	
1958.	(lp) <LP 1225> **CARL PERKINS** (US-title 'CARL PERKINS' DANCE ALBUM – TEENBEAT')	-		

– Blue suede shoes / Movie Magg / Sure to fall / Gone gone gone / Honey don't / Only you / All mama's children / Tennessee / Wrong yo-yo / Everybody's trying to be my baby / Matchbox / Your true love / Boppin' the blues. (UK-iss.Nov59 on 'London') (UK-iss.'THE DANCE ALBUM' Jul81 on 'Charly', cd-iss. Apr87 on 'Topline')

		Philips	Columbia	
Apr 58.	(7") <41131> **PINK PEDAL PUSHERS. / JIVE AFTER JIVE**	-	91	
Aug 58.	(7") <41207> **LEVI JACKET. / POP, LET ME HAVE THE CAR**	-		

—— In Oct'58, brother JAY died of cancer, after a car accident 2 years prev.

Feb 59.	(7") <41269> **Y-O-U. / THIS LIFE I LEAD**	-		
May 59.	(7") <41379> **POINTED TOE SHOES. / HIGHWAY OF LOVE**	-	93	
Jan 60.	(7") (PB 983) <41447> **ONE TICKET TO LONELINESS. / I DON'T SEE ME IN YOUR ARMS ANYMORE**			Oct 59
1960.	(7") <41651> **L-O-V-E-V-I-L-L-E. / TOO MUCH FOR A MAN TO UNDERSTAND**	-		
1960.	(7") <41825> **HONEY, 'CAUSE I LOVE YOU. / JUST FOR YOU**	-		
Sep 61.	(7") <42061> **ANYWAY THE WIND BLOWS. / THE UNHAPPY GIRLS**	-		Jul 61
1961.	(7") <42405> **HOLLYWOOD CITY. / THE FOOL I USED TO BE**	-		
1962.	(7") <42514> **HAMBONE. / TWISTER SISTER**	-		
1962.	(7") <42753> **FORGET ME NEXT TIME AROUND. / I JUST CAN'T GET BACK FROM THERE**	-		

—— Next 45, featured The NASHVILE TEENS.

		Brunswick	Decca
1963.	(7") <31548> **HELP ME FIND MY BABY. / FOR A LITTLE WHILE**	-	
1963.	(7") <31591> **AFTER SUNDOWN. / I WOULDN'T HAVE YOU**	-	
Apr 64.	(7") (05905) **HELP ME FIND MY BABY. / I WOULDN'T HAVE YOU**		-
Jun 64.	(7") (5909) **BIG BAD BLUES. / LONELY HEART**		-
Nov 64.	(7") (5923) <31709> **THE MONKEY SHINE. / LET MY BABY BE**		-
1964.	(7") <31786> **MAMA OF MY SONG. / ONE OF THESE DAYS**	-	

—— CARL became live guitarist for friend and country singer JOHNNY CASH, as well as continuing solo, signing for . . .

		Realm	not iss.
1966.	(lp) (52305) **WHOLE LOTTA CARL PERKINS**		-

– Whole lotta shakin' goin' on / Tutti frutti / Shake, rattle and roll / Sittin' on top of the world / Ready Teddy / Long tall Sally / That's all right / Where the Rio Rosa flows / Good rockin' tonight / I got a woman / Hey, good lookin' / Jenny, Jenny.

		Stateside	Dollie
Mar 67.	(7") (SS 599) <505> **A COUNTRY BOY'S DREAM. / IF I COULD COME BACK**		
1967.	(7") <508> **SHINE, SHINE, SHINE. / ALMOST LOVE**	-	
1967.	(7") <512> **WITHOUT YOU. / YOU CAN TAKE THE BOY OUT OF THE COUNTRY**	-	
1968.	(7") <514> **MY OLD HOMETOWN. / BACK TO TENNESSEE**	-	

		Spark	Dollie
May 68.	(7") (SRL 1009) <516> **LAKE COUNTY COTTON COUNTRY. / IT'S YOU**		

		London	Dollie
Sep 68.	(lp) (HAP/SHP 8366) <DLP 4001> **COUNTRY BOY'S DREAMS**		

– Country boy's dreams / If I could come back / Sweet misery / Stateside / Detroit City / Unmitigated gall / Shine, shine, shine / Dream on little dreamer / You can take the boy out of the door / The star of the show / Home (that's where the heart is) / Poor boy blues. (cd-iss. May92 with extra tracks)

		C.B.S.	Columbia	
Feb 69.	(7") (CBS 3932) <44723> **RESTLESS. / 1143**			1968
1969.	(7") <44883> **FOR YOUR LOVE. / FOUR LETTER WORD**	-		
1969.	(7") <44993> **SOUL BEAT. / C.C.RIDER (YOU'RE SO BAD)**	-		
1969.	(lp) <CS 9931> **ON TOP**	-		

– Superfool / I'm gonna set my foot down / A lion in the jungle / Baby, what you want me to do / Soul beat / Riverboat Annie / Champaign, Illinois / Power of my soul / Brown-eyed handsome man / C.C.rider (UK-iss.1972 as 'BROWN-EYED HANDSOME MAN')

—— Next with country rock revival band N.B.R.Q.; STEVE FERGUSON – guitar / JODY St.NICHOLAS – bass / TOM STANLEY – drums / DON ADAMS – trombone / FRANK GADLER

Mar 70.	(lp) (CBS 63826) <CS 9981> **BOPPIN' THE BLUES**		

– Blue suede shoes / I'm sorry, I'm not sorry / Let the juke box keep on playing / All mama's children / Honey don't / Dixie fried / Boppin' the blues / Your true love / That's alright / Matchbox / Lend me your comb / Gone, gone, gone. (re-iss. Nov84 on 'Topline')

May 70.	(7")(4991) <45107> **ALL MAMA'S CHILDREN. / STEP ASIDE**		
1970.	(7") <45132> **STATE OF CONFUSION. / MY SON MY SUN**	-	
1970.	(7") <45253> **JUST AS LONG. / WHAT EVERY BOY OUGHT TO KNOW**	-	
1971.	(7") <45347> **ME WITHOUT YOU. / RED HEADED WOMAN**	-	
1971.	(7") <45466> **COTTON TOP. / ABOUT ALL I CAN GIVE YOU IS LOVE**	-	
1971.	(7") <45582> **HIGH ON LOVE. / TAKE ME BACK TO MEMPHIS**	-	

		Mercury	Mercury
1971.	(7") <45694> **SOMEDAY. / THE TRIP**	-	
1974.	(7") <73393> **HELP ME DREAM. / YOU TORE MY HEAVEN ALL TO HELL**	-	
Mar 74.	(lp/c) (6338 475) <SRM-1-691> **MY KIND OF COUNTRY**	-	

– (Let's get) Dixiefried / You tore my Heaven to hell / Love sweet love / One more loser going home / Just as long / Goin' to Memphis / Never look back / Honky tonk song / Lord, I sinned again last night / Help me dream / Ruby, don't take your love to town.

1974.	(7") <73425> **(LET'S GET) DIXIE FRIED. / ONE MORE LOSER GOIN' HOME**	-	
1974.	(7") <73489> **RUBY (DON'T TAKE YOUR LOVE TO TOWN). / SING MY SONG**	-	

—— In Dec'74, his brother CLAYTON, takes his own life.

1975.	(7") <73653> **YOU'LL ALWAYS BE A LADY TO ME. / LOW CLASS**	-	
Oct 77.	(7") (ELV 15) <73690> **THE EP EXPRESS. / BIG BAD BLUES**	-	

—— (above was a tribute to the recently departed ELVIS PRESLEY)

—— toured with sons GREG – bass / STAN – drums, plus LEE McALPIN – piano / DAVID SEA – saxophone

		not iss.	Suede
1976.	(lp) <NR 6778> **CARL PERKINS SHOW (live)**	-	

		not iss.	Musichill
1970's.	(7") <MMI 1007> **BORN TO BOOGIE. / TAKE ME BACK**	-	

		Jet	Jet
Mar 78.	(7"m) (UP 36365) <5054> **BLUE SUEDE SHOES. / THAT'S ALL RIGHT / ROCK ON AROUND THE WORLD**	-	
Mar 78.	(lp/c) (JETLP 208/) <KZ 56704> **OL' BLUE SUEDES IS BACK**	38	

– Rock around the clock / That's alright mama / Kaw-liga / Tutti frutti / I'm in love again / Blue suede shoes / Be-bop-a-lula / Maybellene / Whole lotta shakin' goin' on / Hang up my rock'n'roll shoes / Shake, rattle and roll / Rock around the world.

Aug 78.	(7") (117) **MUSTANG WINE. / THE WHOLE WORLD MISSES YOU**		
Nov 80.	(7"ep) (JET 182) **TWENTY-FIVE**		

– Lovesick blues / Turn around / Miss misunderstood / Blue suede shoes.

—— Next album 'THE SURVIVORS' in May '82 was shared with JOHNNY CASH and JERRY LEE LEWIS and issued on 'CBS'.

—— The previous year, CARL guested on album 'Tug Of War' w/ PAUL McCartney. In 1985, he appeared in the John Landis film 'Into The Night'. Later that year, a British TV special 'BLUE SUEDE SHOES' is recorded with many rock celebrities incl. GEORGE HARRISON, RINGO STARR, ERIC CLAPTON, DAVE EDMUNDS, etc.

		M.C.A.	M.C.A.
Mar 86.	(lp/c) (MCF/+C 3315) <MCA 39035> **CARL PERKINS**		

– Matchbox / If I had a' known / Green green grass of home / Texas woman / Signs / Blue sued shoes / Honey don't / I'm walking / Matchbox / Susie Q / Memphis / Maybellene / Slippin' and slidin' / Be-bop-a-lula / Roll over Beethoven / Hound dog / Whole lotta shakin' goin' on / Lucille / Jailhouse rock / All shook up / That's alright mama / Bird dog / Rock Island line.

		Universal	Universal
Jun 89.	(lp/c/cd) (UVL 76001) <UVLC 76001> **BORN TO ROCK** (with the JORDANAIRES)		

– Born to rock / Charlene / The rain / Might wash your love away / Hambone / A lifetime last night / Cotton top / Baby, please answer the phone / Till I couldn't stand no more / Don't let go / Love makes dreams come true.

– (UK) compilations, others, etc. –

May 68.	(7") London; (HLS 10192) **BLUE SUEDE SHOES. / MATCHBOX**		

(re-iss. Jul76 & Feb78 on 'Charly')

May 68.	(lp) C.B.S.; (CBS 63309) **KING OF ROCK**		
Aug 69.	(lp) C.B.S.; (CBS 63676) **CARL PERKINS' GREATEST HITS**		

(re-iss. Jul77 on 'CBS-Embassy')

May 77.	(lp) Embassy; (31454) **LONG TALL SALLY**		-
Oct 70.	(lp) Sun; (6467 004) **ORIGINAL GOLDEN HITS**		-
Oct 70.	(lp) Sun; (6094 002) **BLUE SUEDE SHOES. / ONLY YOU**		-
Feb 71.	(lp) Sun; (6467 009) **BLUE SUEDE SHOES**		-
Jan 82.	(3xlp-box) Sun; (BOX 101) **THE SUN YEARS**		-

(cd-box iss.Feb90)

Aug 88.	(lp) Sun; (SUN 1014) **BLUE SUEDE SHOES**		-
Aug 88.	(lp) Sun; (SUN 1046) **PUT YOUR CAT CLOTHES ON**		-
Dec 76.	(7"ep) Charly; (CEP 106) **BOPPIN' THE BLUES**		-

– Boppin' the blues / Dixie fried / Sure to fall / Movie Magg.

Feb 78.	(lp) Charly; (CR 30003) **THE ROCKIN' GUITARMAN**		-

(re-iss. 1982) (re-iss. Sep83 on 'Magnum F.')(cd-iss. Feb93)

Mar 78.	(lp) Charly; (CR 30110) **THE ORIGINAL CARL PERKINS**		-
Jul 78.	(7"ep) Charly; (CEP 120) **PUT YOU CAT CLOTHES ON**		-

– Put your cat clothes on / Right string but the wrong yo-yo / Tennessee / Honey don't.

1978.	(7") Charly; (CYS 1014) **BLUE SUEDE SHOES. / MATCHBOX**		-
Sep 78.	(lp) Charly; (CR 30152) **SUN SOUNDS SPECIAL**		-
Jan 82.	(10"lp) Charly; (CFM 511) **HEP CATS SESSION ("& SONNY BURGESS")**		-
Mar 86.	(cd) Charly; (CD CHARLY 2) **DIXIE FRIED**		-
Feb 89.	(cd-ep) Charly; (CDS 9) **BLUE SUEDE SHOES / BOPPIN' THE BLUES / HONEY DON'T / EVERYBODY'S TRYING TO BE MY BABY**		-
Jan 90.	(cd-box) Charly; (CDSUNBOX 2) **THE CARL PERKINS CD BOX SET**		-
Apr 77.	(7"m) MCA; (MCA285) **THE MONKEY SHINE. / AFTER SUNDOWN / BIG BAD BLUES**		-
Aug 83.	(d-lp) Cambra; (CR 101) **CARL PERKINS**		-
Nov 83.	(lp) Bulldog; (BDL 2034) **20 GOLDEN PIECES OF CARL PERKINS**		-
Apr 84.	(lp/c) Allegience; (ALEB/ZCALB 2308) **THE HEART AND SOUL OF CARL PERKINS**		-

Sep 84. (lp) *Boplicity;* **INTRODUCING CARL PERKINS**		-
Nov 84. (lp) *Astan;* (20090) **DISCIPLE IN BLUE SUEDE SHOES**		-
Nov 84. (lp) *Astan;* (20092) **SWEETER THAN CANDY**		-
Nov 84. (lp/c) *Warwick;* (WW 5139/45139) **THE CARL PERKINS' ROCK'N'ROLL PARTY**		-
Sep 85. (lp) *Cultue;* (CP 2003) **TURN AROUND**		-
Nov 85. (d-lp/d-c) *Network;* (NETV/+C 1002) **ROCKIN' THE HOUSE DOWN**		-
Feb 86. (lp) *Magnum Force;* (MFLP 1042) **GOIN' BACK TO MEMPHIS**		-
1986. (7"ep) *Magnum Force;* (MFEP 013) **ROCK AND ROLL & COUNTRY SOUL**		-
– Didn't the 50's rock / Country soul / I don't like what I'm seeing in you.		
Oct 86. (d-lp) *Magnum Force;* (MFLP 2039) **THE MAN & THE LEGEND** (cd-iss. May95)		-
Jan 93. (cd) *Magnum Force;* (CDMF 084) **FRIENDS, FAMILY & LEGENDS**		-
Oct 87. (lp) *Demand;* (DEMAND 0015) **MR.COUNTRY ROCK**		-
1987. (7") *Old Gold;* (OG 9737) **BLUE SUEDE SHOES. / THAT'S ALL RIGHT**		-
May 88. (cd-ep) *Rhino;* (R 373015) **LIL' BIT OF GOLD**		-
– Blue suede shoes / Honey don't / Everybody's trying to be my baby / Matchbox.		
1988. (lp/c/cd) *Country Store* (CST/+K 53/CDCST 53) **CARL PERKINS**		-
1988. (lp/c) *Joker;* (SM/MC 3995) **EVERY ROAD**	-	-
1988. (lp) *Joker;* (SM 3996) **GOIN' BACK TO MEMPHIS VOL.2**	-	-
1988. (d-c) *Ditto;* (DTO 10089) **CARL PERKINS**	-	-
Apr 89. (lp) *Rounder;* (SS 27) **HONKY TONK GAL**	-	
Jun 89. (lp/c/cd) *Ocean;* (OCN 2036W – L/-K/-D) **THE CLASSIC CARL PERKINS**		-
Feb 90. (cd/c/lp) *Instant;* (CD/TC INS 5019/INS 5019) **TENNESSEE BOP**		-
Nov 86. (cd) *Bear Family;* (BCD 15246) **UP THROUGH THE YEARS 1954-1957**		-
Apr 90. (5xlp-box) *Bear Family;* BCD 15494) **THE CLASSIC CARL PERKINS**		-
May 90. (cd/c) *Pickwick;* (PWK /+MC 4037) **THE LEGENDARY CARL PERKINS**		-
– Born to boogie / I can feel it / Don't get off gettin' it on / Take me back / Redneck / The hurt put on by you / Sweeter than candy / Boppin' the blues / We did it in '54 / Mama / Standing in the need of love / What am I living for / '21 / Country soul / Georgia courtroom / I didn't want to fall in love again. *(re-iss. Jun91)*		
Apr 93. (cd) *Sony;* **RESTLESS**		-
Nov 93. (cd) *Fat Boy;* **ROCK'N'ROLL GREATS**		-
May 94. (cd/c) *Charly;* (CDTT 5) **TWO ON ONE** (w / JERRY LEE LEWIS)		-
Jul 94. (cd/c) *Success;* **THIS OLD HOUSE**		-
Nov 94. (cd/c) *Music Club;* (MC CD/TC 191) **THE SUN SESSIONS**		-
Feb 95. (cd) *Marble Arch;* (MATCD 324) **THE BEST OF CARL PERKINS**		-
Apr 95. (cd/c) *Muskateer;* (MU 5/4 062) **HOUND DOG**		-
May 95. (cd/c) *Pickwick;* **KING OF ROCKABILLY**		-
Jul 95. (cd) *Charly;* (CDCD 1252) **THE ROCKBILLY KING**		-
Jul 95. (cd) *Charly;* (CPCD 8102) **BOPPIN' BLUE SUEDE SHOES**		-
Jul 95. (cd) *Summit;* **BLUE SUEDE SHOES**		-

Brendan PERRY (see under ⇒ DEAD CAN DANCE)

Joe PERRY PROJECT (see under ⇒ AEROSMITH)

Lee PERRY

Born: RAINFORD HUGH PERRY, 20 Mar'36, Kendal, Parish of Hanover, Jamaica; although by some accounts he was born in St. Mary's, a different parish, in 1939. After leaving school in 1954 and briefly working as a bulldozer driver, he moved from the countryside to the capital, Kingston, in 1957, attracted by the soundsystems of DUKE REID. Rejected by REID because of the "look in PERRY's eye", he turned to the "downbeat" system of now legendary producer, "SIR COXONE" DODD, who employed him to move equipment, select records and fight off rival soundsystem spies. Working with PERRY was ex-boxer and first Jamaican ska star, PRINCE BUSTER, whose success with the FOWLKES BROTHERS' 'Oh Carolina' encouraged COXONE to start up his own label and recording studio, 'Studio One'. PERRY acted as a right hand man throughout this embryonic time, learning the ropes and making a name for himself in ska circles. After Jamaica gained independence in '62, ska became encouraged as a homebred musical form and PERRY's career took off. The following year, along with organist JACKIE MILTON, he co-produced backing tracks for COXONE, as well as having sole control over DELROY WILSON's 'Spit In The Sky' and TOOTS & THE MAYTALS' 'Six And Seven Books'. By this point, relations between PERRY and COXONE were strained and after recording more than a dozen tracks (including his first collaboration with The WAILERS, who sang back-up on his song, 'MAN TO MAN' and his first hit, 'CHICKEN SCRATCH', from which he was to take his most famous nickname), he acrimoniously split from the label in '66. After recording his first attack on 'Coxone', 'RUN FOR COVER', Joe Gibbs signed up PERRY to run his 'Amalgamated' label with almost immediate results; in '67 he produced The PIONEER's groundbreaking 'Longshot' and his own tune, 'I AM THE UPSETTER' (a warning to COXONE and a term that was to become his second nickname) as well as 'KIMBLE', an ode to David Jansen's 'The Fugitive'. After falling out with Gibbs in '68, PERRY retaliated by releasing 'PEOPLE FUNNY BOY' which combined the melody of 'Longshot' and the sounds of a crying baby, just to emphasize his discontent. Selling 60,000 copies in Jamaica, the record helped to popularise the new 'reggae' beat, inspired, according to PERRY, by hearing the congregation of a 'Pocomania' revivalist

church in full flow. PERRY's fame was to mushroom with the initiation of 'Upsetter Records' in '68 (originally with the help of Clive Chin and Errol Thompson), the man enjoyed instrumental hits with the studio's house band, The UPSETTERS aka GLADDY'S ALL STARS. PERRY's big break came in October '69 when 'RETURN OF DJANGO', an UPSETTER instrumental of FATS DOMINO's 'Sick And Tired' appeared in a British TV advertisement, capturing the No.5 spot on the charts and creating a UK fanbase of young white skinheads. Following this success, PERRY began to work exclusively with The WAILERS (featuring a young BOB MARLEY) in late '69; such classics as 'Mr Brown', 'Small Axe', 'My Cup', 'Try Me' and 'Duppy Conqueror' were recorded with PERRY a leading influence. A pivotal factor in the shaping of The WAILER's sound was PERRY's suggestion that MARLEY tighten up his voice and the band concentrate more on organ riffs (rather than the popular combination of horns and falsetto backing) while providing a more solid foundation of thunderous bass and drums for MARLEY's leads. These collaborations between SCRATCH and MARLEY remain some of the finest work PERRY ever produced and the following two years saw a plethora of now legendary and popularised songs including 'Kaya', 'Natural Mystic', PETER TOSH's '400 Years' and 'Beat Down Babylon' by JUNIOR BYLES. PERRY's relationship with MARLEY was never a smooth one and the honeymoon period of '69/'70 ended when The WAILERS took the BARRETT brothers from PERRY's original studio band and signed to 'Island' in '73. The early 70's also saw PERRY, in collaboration with OSBOURNE 'KING TUBBY' RUDDOCK, create a new sound by slowing down the beat and pioneering the new 'dub' style, in effect creating the concept of the 're-mix' in the process. He also cut the first hip-hop 'scratch' record with CHARLIE ACE, 'COW THIEF SKANK', rapping over the track that cuts between the beats of two different songs. In '74, the legendary 'Black Ark' studio was founded, having immediate success with 'Curly Locks' by JUNIOR BYLES and selling 100,000 copies worldwide. In the same year, PERRY worked on the dub masterpiece, 'BLACKBOARD JUNGLE', featuring one mix by PERRY and another by KING TUBBY, in opposing speakers. PERRY's production techniques at Black Ark are mythical; he used eccentric methods and basic equipment to make a four track sound like an eight track by dumping several cuts onto one and then repeating the process, whilst blowing marijuana smoke on the mastertapes as they rolled by and occasionally burying them in the garden after wiping them clean with his t-shirt(!). The magical aura that the studio acquired attracted the attentions of Chris Blackwell, who signed PERRY as a producer/writer for 'Island' in 1975. Over the course of the ensuing four years, the classic tracks became the studio's staple output; the death of Haile Selassie in August '75 led to the cutting of 'Jah Lives' by MARLEY, and in '76, 'Island' began to release a string of reverb-drenched, PERRY-produced classics, MAX ROMEO's 'War Inna Babylon', JAH LION's 'Columbia Colly', The UPSETTER's 'Super Ape', JUNIOR MURVIN's 'Police And Thieves' and CULTURE's anti-violence anthem, 'Two Sevens Clash', all reflecting the growing political tensions rife in Jamaica. As PERRY put the finishing touches to The CONGOES' 'Heart Of The Congoes' album at the end of '77, the international fame that he was now acquiring meant that a growing number of white rockers were beating at his door, such as PAUL WELLER, ROBERT PALMER, PAUL (and LINDA) McCARTNEY and The CLASH, who took their name from CULTURE's song and covered the aforementioned 'Police And Thieves'. As his reputation grew, so did his hours of production, fuelled by ganja, rum and dragon stout. Inevitably, the relationship with 'Island' deteriorated when they rejected three of his productions in a row, 'Heart Of The Congoes', PERRY's own debut vocal album, 'ROAST FISH, COLLIE WEED and CORN BREAD', and the jazzy 'RETURN OF THE SUPER APE'. Soon after, PERRY was fleeced by Dreadlock promoters who hustled him into funding a proposed Broadway musical about reggae, and PERRY turned his back on dreads, banning them from the premises. The beginning of '79, saw PERRY's final productions at Black Ark, including LINDA McCARTNEY and LEROY SIBBLE's 'GARDEN OF LIFE'. Soon after, his wife and business adviser, PAULINE, left, and PERRY set fire to his studio in an attempt to burn all the bridges of the past behind him. This episode led to ever increasing eccentric behaviour, people arriving at the defunct studio to find PERRY worshipping bananas, eating money and baptising visitors with a garden hose! It took the arrival of HANK TARGOWSKI from BLACK STAR LINER distributors to convince PERRY to clean up the master tapes, however, his mood swings continued. Now calling himself, PIPECOCK JACKXON in an apparent homage to MICHAEL JACKSON, he recorded albums of little musical significance. After working with the aforementioned man in '81, the early 80's saw PERRY working with The LITTLE TERRORISTS, a decidedly dodgy outfit from all accounts, and The MAJESTICS, whilst finding time to record two below par lp's, the latter one, 'HISTORY, MYSTERY AND PROPHECY' for 'Island' records. It was to be his last output for the label after accusing CHRIS BLACKWELL of sabotaging his album by not releasing it in the UK, as well as being responsible for the death of BOB MARLEY and infamously calling BLACKWELL "a vampire" on the '85 cut, 'JUDGEMENT INNA BABYLON' after he 'witnessed" him "drinking the blood of a chicken". After releasing 'ARMAGEDDON TIME' in '86, the mid-eighties saw PERRY working with ADRIAN SHERWOOD and his house band, The DUB SYNDICATE, to great effect on the album, 'TIME BOOM X DE DEVIL DEAD', hailed as his finest output since the heady days of the Black Ark, and many of the tracks from this session still remain unreleased in PERRY's private vaults. This partnership continued to produce the goods on the commercially successful 90's album, 'FROM THE SECRET LABORATORY', released on 'Island' despite PERRY's insistence that he would not work with the label

again. The early 90's also saw the release by 'Heartbeat' of 'THE UPSETTER AND THE BEAT', recorded in the late 80's with his old mentor COXSONE DODD and released after a legal tangle between the two. Now residing in Switzerland, PERRY's international reputation has been boosted by a wave of interest in the completist Island anthology set, 'ARKOLOGY', with new fans delving into the mass of recording material available through recent re-issues and compilations. Influential throughout the entire history of Jamaican popular music, PERRY has been and continues to be an inspirational phenomenon.
• **Trivia:** In 1980, PERRY cast a spell over MAGGIE THATCHER, prophesising that "the mirror God will chop off her head and kill the seven demons in her. As soon as this interview published, it happen".

Best CD compilation: ARKOLOGY boxed-set (*8)

LEE PERRY – vocals, etc

			R&B	not iss.
1963.	(7") *(JB 102)* **PRINCE IN THE BLACK. / DON'T COPY**		-	Jama
1963.	(7") *(JB 104)* **PRINCE AND DUKE. / OLD FOR NEW**		-	Jama
1963.	(7") *(JB 106)* **MAD HEAD. / MAN AND WIFE**		-	Jama
1964.	(7") *(JB 135)* **ROYALTY. / CAN'T BE WRONG**		-	Jama

		Port-O-Jam	not iss.
1964.	(7") *(PJ 4003)* **BAD MINDED PEOPLE. /** (other side by TOMMY McCOOK & HIS GROUP)	-	- Jama
1964.	(7") *(PJ 4010)* **CHATTY CHATTY WOMAN. /** (other side by TOMMY McCOOK & HIS GROUP)	-	- Jama

		Island	not iss.
1965.	(7") *(WI 210)* **PLEASE DON'T GO. / BYE, ST. JOHNNY** (with The SOULETTES)	☐	-
1965.	(7"; as UPSETTERS) *(WI 223)* **COUNTRY GIRL. / STRANGE COUNTRY** (above actually recorded by OSSIE & The UPSETTERS)	☐	-

		Rio	not iss.
1965.	(7"; by The UPSETTERS) *(R 70)* **WALK DOWN THE ISLE. / SO BAD**	☐	-

		Ska Beat	not iss.
1965.	(7") *(JB 201)* **ROAST DUCK. / HAND TO HAND, MAN TO MAN**	☐	-
1965.	(7") *(JB 203)* **TRAIL AND CROSSES. / JON TOM**	☐	-
1965.	(7") *(JB 212)* **WISHES OF THE WICKED. / HOLD DOWN**	☐	-
1965.	(7") *(JB 215)* **OPEN UP. /** (other track by ROLAND ALPHONSO)	☐	-
1966.	(7") *(JB 251)* **THE WOODMAN. / GIVE ME JUSTICE**	☐	-

		Island	not iss.
1966.	(7"; as KING PERRY) *(WI 292)* **DOCTOR DICK. /** (other side by The SOUL BROTHERS)	☐	-
1966.	(7"; as KING PERRY & The SOULETTES) *(WI 298)* **RUB AND SQUEEZE. /** (other side by SOUL BROTHERS)	☐	-

		Doctor Bird	not iss.
1966.	(7"; by OSSIE & The UPSETTERS) *(DB 1018)* **TURN ME ON. / TRUE LOVE**	☐	-
——	(on album me thinks that there's no PERRY connection, ?)		
1966.	(7"; by The UPSETTERS) *(DB 1034)* **WILDCAT. / I LOVE YOU SO**	☐	-
1967.	(7") *(DB 1073)* **RUN FOR COVER. / SOMETHING YOU'VE GOT** (as LEE 'KING' PERRY & The SENSATIONS)	☐	-
1967.	(7") *(DB 1098)* **WHOP WHOP MAN. / WIND-UP DOLL** (with The DYNAMITES)	☐	-
1968.	(7"; by The DEFENDERS – aka LEE PERRY & The SENSATIONS) *(DB 1104)* **SET THEM FREE. / DON'T BLAME THE CHILDREN**	☐	-
1968.	(7") *(DB 1146)* **PEOPLE FUNNY BOY. /** (other side by BURT WALTERS)	☐	-

		Amalgamated	not iss.
1968.	(7") *(AMG 808)* **THE UPSETTER. / THANK YOU BABY**	☐	-

UPSETTERS

—— **LEE PERRY +**

		Trojan	not iss.
1968.	(7"; by LEE 'SCRATCH' PERRY) *(TR 644)* **UNCLE DESMOND. / BRONCO**		-

		Duke	not iss.
1969.	(7") *(DU 11)* **EIGHT FOR EIGHT. / STAND BY ME** (by The INSPIRATIONS)		-

		Camel	not iss.
1969.	(7") *(CA 13)* **TASTE OF KILLING. / MY MOB**		-

		Punch	not iss.
1969.	(7") *(PH 18)* **RETURN OF THE UGLY. / I'VE CAUGHT YOU**	☐	-
1969.	(7") *(PH 19)* **DRY ACID. /** (other side by The REGGAE BOYS)	☐	-
1969.	(7") *(PH 21)* **CLINT EASTWOOD. / LENNOX MOOD**	☐	-

		Upsetter	not iss.
1969.	(7") *(US 300)* **EIGHT FOR EIGHT. / YOU KNOW WHAT I MEAN**	☐	-
Sep 69.	(7") *(US 301)* **RETURN OF DJANGO. / DOLLAR IN THE TEETH**	5	-
Sep 69.	(7") *(US 303)* **TEN TO TWELVE. /** Lee Perry: **PEOPLE FUNNY FI TRUE**	☐	-
Oct 69.	(7") *(US 307)* **NIGHT DOCTOR. /** (other track by The TERMITES)	☐	-
Oct 69.	(7") *(US 309)* **KIDDYO. / ENDLESSLY** (above actually by The SILVERTONES)	☐	-
Vov 69.	(7") *(US 310)* **A DANGEROUS MAN FROM M.I.5. /** (other track by The WEST INDIANS)	☐	-

Nov 69.	(7") *(US 313)* **LIVE INJECTION. /** (other track by The BLEECHERS)	☐	-
Dec 69.	(7") *(US 315)* **COLD SWEAT. / POUND GET A BLOW**	☐	-
Jan 70.	(7") *(US 317)* **VAMPIRE. /** (other track by The BLEECHERS)	☐	-
1970.	(7") *(US 318)* **SOULFUL I. /** (other track by MILTON HENRY)	☐	-
1970.	(7") *(US 321)* **DRUGS AND POISON. / STRANGER ON THE SHORE**	☐	-
1970.	(7"; by LEE 'SCRATCH' PERRY) *(US 324)* **YAKETY YAK. / TACKIO**	☐	-
1970.	(7"; by LEE 'SCRATCH' PERRY) *(US 325)* **KILL THE ALL. / SOUL WALK**	☐	-
1970.	(7") *(US 326)* **BRONCO. / ONE MORE**	☐	-
1970.	(7") *(US 332)* **NA NA HEY HEY. / PICK FOLK KINKYEST**	☐	-
1970.	(7") *(US 333)* **GRANNY SHOW. /** (version)	☐	-
1970.	(7") *(US 334)* **FIRE FIRE. / JUMPER**	☐	-
1970.	(7") *(US 335)* **THE PILLOW. / GROOVING**	☐	-
1970.	(7") *(US 336)* **SELF CONTROL**	☐	-
1970.	(7") *(US 338)* **FRESH UP. / TOOTHACHES**	☐	-
1970.	(7") *(US 342)* **DREAMLAND. /** (other track by BOB MARLEY)	☐	-
1970.	(7") *(US 343)* **SIPREANO. / FERRY BOAT**	☐	-
1970.	(7") *(US 346)* **BIGGER JOKE. / RETURN OF THE VAMPIRE**	☐	-
1970.	(7") *(US 352)* **HEART AND SOUL. / ZIG ZAG**	☐	-

		Spinning Wheel	not iss.
1970.	(7") *(SW 100)* **HAUNTED HOUSE. / DOUBLE WHEEL**	☐	-
1970.	(7") *(SW 101)* **THE MISER. /** (other track by CHUCK JUNIOR)	☐	-
1970.	(7") *(SW 102)* **THE CHOKIN' KIND. /** (other track by CHUCK JUNIOR)	☐	-
1970.	(7") *(SW 103)* **LAND OF KINKS. /** (other track by O'NEIL HALL)	☐	-

		Trojan	not iss.
1970.	(7") *(TR 7748)* **FAMILY MAN. / MELLOW MOOD**	☐	-
1970.	(7") *(TR 7749)* **CAPO. / MAMA LOOK**	☐	-

		Punch	not iss.
1970.	(7") *(PH 27)* **THE RESULT. / FEEL THE SPIRIT**	☐	-

		Bullet	not iss.
1971.	(7"; as LEE PERRY & The UPSETTERS) *(BU 461)* **ALL COMBINE. /** (part 2)	☐	-

		Upsetter	not iss.
1971.	(7"; by The UPSETTERS & KING TEDDY) *(US 353)* **ILLUSION. / BIG JOHN WAYNE**	☐	-
1971.	(7") *(US 361)* **CAPASETIC. / ALL AFRICANS** (above 'A' was actually by LORD COMIC, 'B' by LITTLE ROY)	☐	-
1971.	(7") *(US 365)* **EARTHQUAKE. /** (other side by JUNIOR BYLES)	☐	-
1971.	(7") *(US 370)* **DARK MOON. /** (other track by DAVID ISAACS)	☐	-
1972.	(7"; by LEE 'SCRATCH' PERRY) *(US 385)* **FRENCH CONNECTION. /** (The UPSETTERS version)	☐	-
1972.	(7"; LEE PERRY & DENNIS ALCAPONE) *(US 389)* **BACK BITER. /** (The UPSETTERS version)	☐	-
1972.	(7") *(US 393)* **CRUMMY PEOPLE. /** (other track by BIG YOUTH)	☐	-
1972.	(7") *(US 394)* **WATER PUMP. /** (part 2)	☐	-
1972.	(7") *(US 396)* **PUSS SEA HOLE. /** (other track by WINSTON GROOVY)	☐	-
1973.	(7"; LEE PERRY solo) *(US 397)* **JUNGLE LION. / FREAKOUT SKANK**	☐	-
1973.	(7"; LEE PERRY & CHARLIE ACE) *(US 398)* **COW THE SKANK. / SEVEN AND THREE QUARTERS SKANK**	☐	-

		Bread	not iss.
1973.	(7"; LEE PERRY solo) *(BR 1111)* **STATION UNDERGROUND. /** (other track by CARLTON & SHOES)	☐	-

		Downtown	not iss.
1973.	(7") *(DT 499)* **BLACK IPA. / IPA SKANK**	☐	-
1973.	(7") *(DT 506)* **SUNSHINE SHOWDOWN. / SUNSHINE VERSION**	☐	-
1973.	(7"; LEE PERRY solo) *(DT 513)* **BUCKY SKANK. / MID EAST ROCK**	☐	-

		Count Shelly	not iss.
1974.	(7") *(CS 502)* **SAN-SAN. /** (other track by OSBOURNE GRAHAM)	☐	-

		Dip	not iss.
1974.	(7") *(DL 5031)* **ENTER THE DRAGON. /** (other track by JOY WHITE)	☐	-
1974.	(7") *(DL 5032)* **REBELS TRAIN. / REBELS DUB**	☐	-
1974.	(7"; LEE PERRY & The SILVERTONES) *(DL 5037)* **DUB A PUM PUM. /** (version)	☐	-
1974.	(7") *(DL 5054)* **CANE RIVER ROCK. / RIVERSIDE ROCK**	☐	-
1974.	(7"; LEE PERRY & JUNIOR BYLES) *(DL 5060)* **DREADER LOCKS. / MILITANT ROCK**	☐	-
1974.	(7") *(DL 5073)* **KEY CARD. / DOMINO GAME**	☐	-

– (UPSETTERS) albums –

(on below label unless mentioned otherwise)

		Trojan	not iss.
1969.	(lp) *Pama Special; (PSP 1014)* **CLINT EASTWOOD**	☐	-
1969.	(lp) *(TTL 13)* **THE UPSETTER** (cd-iss. Apr96; CDTTL 13)	☐	-
1969.	(lp) *(TRL 19)* **THE RETURN OF DJANGO** (cd-iss. Apr96; CDTRL 19)	☐	-
1970.	(lp) *(TTL 28)* **SCRATCH THE UPSETTER AGAIN** (cd-iss. Apr95; CDTRL 352)	☐	-

1970.	(lp) *(TBL 119)* **THE GOOD, THE BAD AND THE UPSETTERS**	☐	–
	(cd-iss. Aug93 on 'Lagoon'; LG 21083)		
1970.	(lp) *(TBL 125)* **EASTWOD RIDES AGAIN**	☐	–
	(cd-iss. May96; CDTBL 125)		
1970.	(lp) *Pama; (SECO 24)* **THE MANY MOODS OF THE UPSETTERS**	☐	–
1971.	(lp; LEE PERRY & Various Artists) *(TBL 166)* **AFRICA BLOOD**	☐	–
	(re-iss. Jul80; same) (cd-iss. Jun96; CDTBL 166)		
1971.	(lp; UPSETTERS & Various) *(TBL 167)* **BATTLE AXE**	☐	–
	(cd-iss. Sep96; CDTBL 167)		
1974.	(lp) *(TRLS 70)* **DOUBLE SEVEN**	☐	–
	(cd-iss. Jul96; CDTRL 70)		

LEE 'SCRATCH' PERRY & THE UPSETTERS

—— aka **EARL SMITH** – guitar / **BORIS GARDENER** – bass / **MICKEY + BENBOW** – drums / **E. STIRLING** – keyboards / etc

		Island	Island
Jul 76.	(lp) *(ILPS 9417)* **SUPER APE**	☐	–
	– Zion's blood / Croaking lizard / Black vest / Underground / Curly dub / Dread lion / Three in one / Patience / Dub along / Super ape. *(re-iss. Sep90 on 'Reggae Refreshers' cd/c; RRCD/RRCT 13)*		
Aug 76.	(7") *(WIP 6326)* **ROAST FISH & CORN BREAD. / CORN FISH DUB**	☐	–
Aug 76.	(7") *(WIP 6328)* **THREE IN ONE. / CURLY DUB**	☐	–
Nov 76.	(7") *(WIP 6370)* **DREADLOCKS IN MOONLIGHT. / CUT THROAT**	☐	–
1979.	(lp) **SCRATCH ON THE WIRE**	☐	–
	(cd-iss. Apr95 on 'Trojan'; CDTRL 348)		

LEE 'SCRATCH' PERRY

		Cactus	not iss.
1979.	(lp) *(CTLP 112)* **REVOLUTION DUB**	☐	–
	(re-iss. Nov90 on 'Greensleeves'; TSLP 9006) (cd-iss. Dec92 on 'Rhino'; RNCD 2120)		

		Black Ark	not iss.
1979.	(lp) *(TSLP 9001)* **CLOAK AND DAGGER**	☐	–
	– Cloak and dagger / Sharp razor / Hail stone / Musical transplant / Liquid serenade / Side gate / Iron claw / Rude walking / Bad walking / Cave man skank / Pee Wee special. *(re-iss. May89; same)*		

		Seven Leaves	not iss.
Oct 82.	(lp) *(SLLP 1)* **HEART OF THE ARK**	☐	–
	– I've never had it so good / What's the use / Don't be afraid / Forward with love / Rasta fari / 4 & 20 dreadlocks / Nuh fe run down / Ellaine. *(cd-iss. Jul94; SLCD 1)*		
1983.	(lp) *(SLLP 2)* **MEGATON DUB**	☐	
	– Dem no know dub / Conscious man dub / Such is dub / Corn picker dub / Freedom dub / Megaton dub / Dreader dub / School girl dub. *(cd-iss. Sep94; SLCD 2)*		
Sep 84.	(lp) *(SLLP 5)* **MEGATON DUB 2**	☐	
	(cd-iss. Sep94; SLCD 5)		

LEE 'SCRATCH' PERRY & THE UPSETTERS

		Trojan	Trojan
Dec 85.	(7") *(TRO 9080)* **MERRY XMAS HAPPY NEW YEAR / RETURN OF DJANGO**	☐	–
	(12"+=) *(TROT 9080)* – All things are possible / Happy birthday.		
May 86.	(lp/c) *(TRLS/ZCTRL 227)* **MILLIONAIRE LIQUIDATOR** <US title 'BATTLE OF ARMAGIDEON'>	☐	–
	– Introducing myself / Drum song / Grooving / All things are possible / Show me that river / I am a madman / The joker / Happy birthday / Sexy lady / Time marches on. *(cd-iss. Oct88; CDTRL 227)*		
Sep 86.	(7") *(TRO 9082)* **ALL THINGS ARE POSSIBLE. / SEXY LADY**	☐	–
Dec 86.	(7"ep/12"ep) *(TRO/+T 9095)* **MERRY CHRISTMAS, HAPPY NEW YEAR**	☐	–
	– Merry Christmas (the dub mix) / I am a madman / Mad man dub wise.		

		On-U-Sound	not iss.
May 87.	(lp/c) *(ONULP 43/+C)* **TIME BOOM Z DE DEVIL DEAD**	☐	–
	– S.D.I. / Blinkers / The jungle / De Devil dead / Music and science lovers / Kiss the champion / Allergic to lies / Time conquer. *(re-iss. Oct87 on 'Syncopate' lp/c; SYLP/TCSYLP 6000) (cd-iss. Oct87; CDP 748442-2)*		

		Syncopate	not iss.
Sep 87.	(7"/10"; as LEE PERRY & The DUB SYNDICATE) *(SY/10SY 6)* **THE JUNGLE (radio plate). / THE JUNGLE (rhythm mix)**	☐	–
	(12"+=) *(12SY 6)* – Music and science.		

		Bullwackies	not iss.
Oct 88.	(lp) *(WACKIES 2740)* **SATAN KICKED THE BUCKET**	☐	–

		Heartbeat	Rounder
May 89.	(lp/c/cd) *(HB/+C/CD 53)* **CHICKEN SCRATCH**	☐	–
	– Please don't go / Chicken scratch / Feel like jumping / Solid as a rock / By Saint Peter / Tackoo / Roast duck / Man to man / Gruma / Jane Ann & the pumpkin / Just keep it up / Puss in bag.		

		Mango	Mango
Jan 90.	(7") *(MNG 737)* **THE GROOVE. / PARTY TIME**	☐	–
	(12"+=) *(12MNG 737)* – ('A'mixes).		
Jun 90.	(lp) *(MLPS 1035)* **FROM THE SECRET LABORATORY**	☐	–
	– Secret laboratory / Inspector Gadget / Groove / Vibrate one / African hitchhiker / You tonight I was dead / Too much money / Push push / African headcharge in the Hackney Empire / Party time / Seven devils dead. *(cd-iss. Aug97 on 'Reggae Refreshers'; RRCD 55)*		

		Heartbeat	Network
Sep 91.	(lp/cd) *(ZS/+CD 110)* <*NET LP/CD 018*> **LORD GOD MUSICK**	☐	Jul91
May 92.	(cd) *(CDHB 59)* **THE UPSETTER & THE BEAT**	☐	–
Nov 92.	(cd/c) *(HB CD/C 76)* **SOUNDZS FROM THE HOT LINE**	☐	–

		Rhino	Rhino
May 93.	(cd) *(RNCD 2007)* **HOLD OF DEATH**	☐	–
May 94.	(cd) *(RNCD 2057)* **GUITAR BOOGIE DUB**	☐	–
Apr 96.	(cd) *(RNCD 2137)* **REGGAE EMPEROR**	7-	
Sep 96.	(cd; LEE 'SCRATCH' PERRY & THE SCIENTIST) (<*RN 7005*>) **AT THE BLACKHEART STUDIO**		

		Black Art	not iss.
Jul 97.	(7"; UPSETTERS) *(ART 1)* **ENTER THE DRAGON. / BLACK BELT JONES**	☐	–
Jul 97.	(7"; LEE PERRY & JAH LLOYD) *(ART 2)* **WHITE BELLY RAT. / JUDAS DE WHITE BELLY RAT**	☐	–

– others, etc. –

1983.	(7") *Old Gold; (OG 9272)* **RETURN OF DJANGO. / Elizabethan Reggae**	☐	–
Feb 84.	(lp) *Pama; (PTLP 1028)* **THE BEST OF LEE PERRY & THE UPSETTERS VOL.2**	☐	–
Mar 84.	(lp) *Black Ark; (BALP 4001)* **BLACK ARK VOL.2**	☐	–
Jul 85.	(d-lp; UPSETTERS & Various) *Trojan; (PERRY 1)* **THE UPSETTER BOX SET**	☐	–
Aug 85.	(lp/c) *Heartbeat; (HB/+C 06)* **MYSTIC MIRACLE STAR**	☐	–
1985.	(lp/c) *Island; (IRG 13)* **REGGAE GREATS**	☐	–
	(re-iss. Sep90 on 'Reggae Refreshers' cd/c; RRCD/RRCT 10)		
Feb 86.	(lp/c) *Trojan; (TRLS/ZCTRL 195)* **THE UPSETTER COLLECTION**	☐	–
	(cd-iss. May89; CDTRL 195)		
Jul 87.	(lp/c/cd; LEE 'SCRATCH' PERRY & THE UPSETTERS) *Heartbeat; (HB/+C/CD 37)* **SOME OF THE BEAT**	☐	–
Feb 88.	(lp/c/cd; LEE PERRY & FRIENDS) *Trojan; (TRLS/ZCTRL/CDTRL 254)* **GIVE ME POWER**	☐	–
Jun 88.	(d-cd; LEE 'SCRATCH' PERRY & FRIENDS) *Trojan; (CDPRY 1)* **THE UPSETTER COMPACT DISC**	☐	–
1988.	(lp/c) *RAS; (LPCT/+C 0114)* **SCRATCH AND COMPANY**	☐	–
1988.	(lp/c; UPSETTERS) *RAS; (LPCT/+C 0115)* **BLACKBOARD JUNGLE DUB**	☐	–
1988.	(cd) *Clocktower; (LTCD 1415)* **SCRATCH ATTACK**	☐	–
Nov 88.	(cd-ep; by TONY TRIBE & The UPSETTERS) *Classic Tracks; (CDEP 4C)* **TONY TRIBE & THE UPSETTERS**	☐	–
Feb 89.	(lp/c; LEE 'SCRATCH' PERRY & THE UPSETTERS) *Clock Tower; (LPIR/+C 0000)* **ROAST FISH COLLIE WEED & CORN BREAD**	☐	–
Apr 89.	(lp/c) *Clock Tower; (LPIR/+C 0001)* **RETURN OF THE SUPER APE**	☐	
Apr 89.	(d-lp/cd; LEE 'SCRATCH' PERRY & FRIENDS) *Trojan; (PERRY/CDPRY 2)* **OPEN THE GATE: SHOCKS OF MIGHTY 1969-1974**	☐	–
Apr 89.	(c) *Trojan; (PERRYC 3)* **LEE PERRY**	☐	–
May 89.	(12") *Arkwell; (ARK 03)* **MASTER OF THE UNIVERSE. /**	☐	–
Jul 89.	(lp; LEE PERRY & The DUB SYNDICATE) *Anachron; (AAS 9003)* **MAGNETIC MIRROR MASTER MIX**	☐	–
Oct 89.	(lp) *Angella; (ANG 009)* **LEE PERRY MEETS MAD PROFESSOR IN DUB 2**	☐	–
Oct 89.	(lp; LEE 'SCRATCH' PERRY & THE MAD PROFESSOR) *Ariwa Sounds; (ARILP 054)* **MYSTIC WARRIOR**	☐	–
Oct 89.	(lp; LEE 'SCRATCH' PERRY & THE MAD PROFESSOR) *Ariwa Sounds; (ARILP 055)* **MYSTIC WARRIOR (DUB)**	☐	–
Jan 90.	(cd/lp) *Attack; (CDAT/ATLP 108)* **PUBLIC JESTERING 1974-76**	☐	–
Jan 90.	(cd/lp) *Trojan; (CDPRY/PERRY 3)* **BUILD THE ARK**	☐	–
Feb 90.	(lp; LEE PERRY & KING TUBBY) *Original Music; (OMLP 15)* **SENSI DUB VOLUME 2**	☐	–
Feb 90.	(lp) *Anachron; (AAS 9004)* **TURN AND FIRE**	☐	–
Jul 90.	(cd/lp) *La; (LACD/LALP 007)* **BLOOD VAPOUR**	☐	–
Jan 91.	(cd) *Angella; (ANGCD 8-9)* **LEE PERRY MEETS MAD PROFESSOR IN DUB 1 & 2**	☐	–
May 91.	(cd/c/lp) *Trojan; (CDTRL/ZCTRL/TRLS 297)* **OUT OF MANY – THE UPSETTER**	☐	–
Jun 92.	(cd) *Creole; (REG 105)* **CHAPTER ONE**	☐	–
	(re-iss. Feb93 on 'Lagoon'; LG 21068)		
Jun 92.	(cd) *Creole; (REG 108)* **LEE PERRY & KING TUBBY**	☐	–
Jun 92.	(cd) *Creole; (REG 109)* **CHAPTER TWO**	☐	–
	(re-iss. Feb93 on 'Lagoon'; LG 21069)		
Jun 92.	(cd) *Creole; (REG 113)* **LEE PERRY & KING TUBBY VOL.2**	☐	–
Sep 92.	(cd/lp) *Danceteria; (DAN CD/LP 066)* **LEE 'SCRATCH' PERRY MEETS BULLWACKIE IN SATAN'S DUB**	☐	–
	(re-iss. Nov94 on 'R.O.I.R.'; RE 178CD)		
Jul 93.	(cd; LEE 'SCRATCH' PERRY & THE UPSETTERS) *Lagoon; (LG 21025)* **MEETS MAFIA & FLUXY IN JAMAICA**	☐	–
Aug 93.	(cd/lp; LEE 'SCRATCH' PERRY & EARL SIXTEEN) *(SL CD/LP 8)* **PHOENIX OF PEACE**	☐	–
Sep 93.	(cd/lp) *Seven Leaves; (SLCD/TOLP 6)* **EXCALIBURMAN**	☐	–
Dec 93.	(cd) *Rhino; (RNCD 2027)* **MEET AT KING TUBBY'S**	☐	–
Mar 94.	(cd) *Red Honey; (ORCHCD 1)* **ORIGINAL BLACK BOARD JUNGLE**	☐	–
Apr 94.	(cd) *Runn; (RN 0029CD)* **FROM THE HEART OF THE CONGO**	☐	–
May 94.	(cd) *Trojan; (CDTRL 339)* **PEOPLE FUNNY BOY**	☐	–
May 94.	(cd) *Reggae Best; (RB 3001)* **HEAVY MANNERS**	☐	–
Jun 94.	(cd) *V.P.; (VPRL 1358)* **SMOKIN**	☐	–
Nov 94.	(lp) *Black Ark; (BLP 403)* **PRESENTS BLACK ARK MIGHTY DUB**	☐	–
Apr 95.	(cd; LEE 'SCRATCH' PERRY & KING TUBBY) *Lagoon; (LG 21107)* **DUB CONFRONTATION VOL.2**	☐	–
Jun 95.	(cd; LEE 'SCRATCH' PERRY & The UPSETTERS) *Justic League; (JLCD 5000)* **KUNG FU MEETS THE DRAGON**	☐	–
Jun 95.	(cd/lp; LEE 'SCRATCH' PERRY & THE MAD PROFESSOR) *Ariwa; (ARI CD/LP 114)* **BLACK ARK EXPERRYMENTS**	☐	–

Sep 95. (cd; Various Artists) *Nectar; (NTMCD 511)* **LARKS FROM THE ARK** ☐ -

Oct 95. (cd/lp; LEE 'SCRATCH' PERRY & THE MAD PROFESSOR) *Ariwa; (ARI CD/LP 115)* **EXPERRYMENTS AT THE GRASS ROOTS OF DUB** ☐ -

Oct 95. (cd) *Reggae Best; (cd) (RB 3015)* **GLORY DUB** ☐ -

Nov 95. (cd/lp; UPSETTERS) *Sprint; (SFCD 5)* **IN DUB AROUND THE WORLD** ☐ -

Mar 96. (cd; LEE 'SCRATCH' PERRY & THE UPSETTERS) *Original Music; (OMCD 11)* **REMINAH DUB** ☐ -

May 96. (cd) *Blue Silver; (CB 6007)* **INTRODUCING LEE PERRY** ☐ -

Jun 96. (cd) *Graylan; (GRCD 008)* **MEET SCIENTIST AT BLACK ART STUDIO** ☐ -

Sep 96. (cd/lp) *Ariwa; (ARI CD/LP 131)* **DUB TAKE THE VOODOO OUT OF REGGAE** ☐ -

Jun 97. (cd) *Hit Squad; (HS 2CD)* **THE GREAT KING OF DUB** ☐ -

Jul 97. (3xcd-box) *Island; (CRNCD 6)* **ARKOLOGY** ☐ 49

Jul 97. (cd/lp) *Upsetter; (UP CD/LP 002)* **THE BEST OF LEE 'SCRATCH' PERRY** ☐ -

Jul 97. (cd) *ROIR; (RUSCD 8232)* **TECHNOMAJICAL** ☐ -

Linda PERRY (see under ⇒ 4 NON BLONDES)

Mike PETERS (see under ⇒ ALARM)

PET SHOP BOYS

Formed: London, England ... August '81 by assistant editor of Smash Hits, NEIL TENNANT, together with architecture student CHRIS LOWE (ex-DUST). After two years spent plugging away at demos, they met disco producer Bobby 'O' Orlando, subsequently working together on the debut 1984 'Epic' single, 'WEST END GIRLS'. After the track flopped in Britain (it was a French & Belgian hit), they signed with manager Tom Watkins, who secured them a deal with 'Parlophone' early in 1985. Their first effort for the label, the sardonic 80's critique of 'OPPORTUNITIES (LET'S MAKE LOTS OF MONEY)' failed to make an impact, a Stephen Hague produced re-make of 'WEST END GIRLS' finally giving them a major breakthrough early the following year, hitting No.1 in many countries including Britain and the States. The debut album, 'PLEASE' (1986) was a Transatlantic Top 10 success, a classy collection of intelligent synth-pop, infectious melodies and wryly observant lyrics becoming the campy duo's trademark. 'OPPORTUNITIES' was hastily re-released in clanking, mechanically remixed form, almost making the Top 10, while a further single from the album, 'SUBURBIA', made No.8. Visually, the band were akin to a more stylish SPARKS or ERASURE, sharing the latter's sizeable gay following, while ironically also being idolised by thuggish football 'casuals' for their immaculate taste in designer wear. The 'BOYS' even penned a song about the Italian strain of the expensively kitted out thug, 'PANINARO', featured on their mini remix album, 'DISCO' (1986). 'IT'S A SIN' gave the act their second No.1 later that summer while the duo teamed up with 60's songstress DUSTY SPRINGFIELD for 'WHAT HAVE I DONE TO DESERVE THIS', a Transatlantic No.2 hit. The fact that the Americans had taken so keenly to The PET SHOP BOYS was odd, given that nation's notorious inability to appreciate irony; it's arguably a testament to the group's finely honed melodic mastery and perfectionist production that they broke the US market where other quintessentially English pop bands have consistently failed. 'ACTUALLY' (1987) was another successful slice of sophisticated pop nous, containing the aforementioned two singles as well as the poignant 'RENT' and two further No.1 singles in 'HEART' and a flamboyant synth/strings remake of Elvis' 'ALWAYS ON MY MIND'. The group further indulged their penchant for remix albums with 'INTROSPECTIVE' (1988), which included a version of the track they'd produced for EIGHTH WONDER (featuring a pre-LIAM Patsy Kensit), 'I'M NOT SCARED'. The following year saw The PET SHOP BOYS working with such diverse artists as LIZA MINNELLI (who subsequently hit the charts with their melodramatic, collaborative cover of Stephen Sondheim's 'LOSING MY MIND') and ELECTRONIC, while the next group project, 'BEHAVIOUR' (1990), was uncharacteristically introspective, spawning a solitary hit single, the wistful 'BEING BORING'. Only the PET SHOP BOYS could get away with splicing U2's 'Where The Streets Have No Name' and FRANKIE VALLI's 'Can't Take My Eyes Off You', a masterstroke of tongue-in-cheek pop genius that reached No.4 in Spring '91. It would be another two years before 'VERY', a consummate distillation of the PET SHOP BOYS' unique grasp of pure pop, previewed by their celebratory cover of The Village People's 'GO WEST'. A limited edition dance CD, 'RELENTLESS', was included with initial copies of 'VERY', The PET SHOP BOYS proving they were hip to a music style they had helped to create. TENNANT and LOWE have maintained a fairly low profile of late, releasing a second volume of 'DISCO' remixes in 1994 and a B-sides collection in '95, 'ALTERNATIVE'. 'BILINGUAL' (1996) boasted the usual spread of UK hit singles, although The PET SHOP BOYS were getting old hat while wearing many of them in the process. Nearing the end of the millennium (aarrgghh!), credible pop music was now big fashion again, it was just that TENNANT and LOWE were losing themselves in the mire of mediocrity; the 1999 album 'NIGHTLIFE' (which featured the appallingly camp 'NEW YORK CITY BOY') the proof that they were losing the place.

Album rating: PLEASE (*6) / DISCO remixes (*5) / ACTUALLY (*7) / INTROSPECTIVE mixes (*5) / BEHAVIOUR (*7) / DISCOGRAPHY – THE

COMPLETE SINGLES COLLECTION compilation (*8) / VERY (*7) / DISCO 2 remixes (*5) / ALTERNATIVE collection (*5) / BILINGUAL (*6) / NIGHTLIFE (*6)

NEIL TENNANT (b.10 Jul '54, Gosforth, Northumberland, England) – vocals / **CHRIS LOWE** (b. 4 Oct '59, Blackpool, England) – keyboards, synthesizers

	Epic	Bobcat 12"
Apr 84. (7"/ext.12") *<A/TA 4292>* **WEST END GIRLS. / PET SHOP BOYS**	☐	☐

	Parlophone	EMI America
Jun 85. (7") *(R 6097) <8321>* **OPPORTUNITIES (LET'S MAKE LOTS OF MONEY). / IN THE NIGHT**	☐	☐ Mar86

(12") *(12R 6097)* – ('A'dance mix) / ('B'extended).
(12") *(12RA 6097)* – ('A' Latin version) / ('B'dub for money).

Nov 85. (7") *(R 6115) <8307>* **WEST END GIRLS. / A MAN COULD GET ARRESTED** [1] [1] Jan 86
(10") *(10R 6115)* – ('A'remixed) / ('B'extended).
(12"+=) *(12R 6115)* – ('A'dance mix).
(12") *(12EA 6115)* – ('A'-Shep Pettibone mix) / ('A'dub mix) / ('B'extended).

Mar 86. (7") *(R 6116) <8338>* **LOVE COMES QUICKLY. / THAT'S MY IMPRESSION** [19] [62] Aug 86
(10"/12") *(10R/12R 6116)* – ('A'dance mix) / ('B'disco mix).

Mar 86. (lp/c)(cd) *(PSB/TCPSB 1)(CDP 7-46271-2) <17193>* **PLEASE** [3] [7]
– Two divide by zero / West end girls / Opportunities (let's make lots of money) / Love comes quickly / Suburbia / Tonight is forever / Violence / I want a lover / Later tonight / Why don't we live together / Opportunities (reprise).

May 86. (7") *(R 6129) <8330>* **OPPORTUNITIES (LET'S MAKE LOTS OF MONEY) (remix). / WAS THAT WHAT IT WAS** [11] [10]
(12") *(12R 6129)* – ('A'&'B'-Shep Pettibone mastermixes) / Opportunities (original dance mix) / Opportunities (reprise Shep Pettibone mix).

Sep 86. (7") *(R 6140) <8355>* **SUBURBIA. / PANINARO** [8] [70] Nov 86
('A'-Full horror mix-12") *(12R 6140)* – Jack the lad.
(c-s++=) *(TR 6140)* – Love comes quickly (Shep Pettibone remix).
(c-s) *(TCR 6140)* – ('A'-J.Mendelsohn remixed).
(d7"+=) *(RD 6140)* – Suburbia pt.2.

Nov 86. (lp/c)(cd) *(PRG/TCPRG 1001)(CDP 7-46450-2) <17246>* **DISCO** (The 12"mixes) [15] [95]
– In the night / Suburbia / Opportunities / Paninaro / Love comes quickly / West end girls.

Jun 87. (7") *(R 6158) <43027>* **IT'S A SIN. / YOU KNOW WHERE YOU WENT WRONG** [1] [9] Aug 87
(12"+=/c-s+=/cd-s+=) *(12R/TCR/CDR 6158)* – ('A'disco mix).
(12") *(12RX 6158)* – ('A'-Ian Levene remix) / ('B'-rough mix).

Aug 87. (7"; PET SHOP BOYS & DUSTY SPRINGFIELD) *(R 6163) <50107>* **WHAT HAVE I DONE TO DESERVE THIS? / A NEW LIFE** [2] [2] Dec 87
(ext;12"+=/c-s+=/cd-s+=) *(12R/TCR/CDR 6163)* – ('A'disco mix).

Sep 87. (cd/c/lp) *(CD/TC+/PCSD 104) <46972>* **ACTUALLY** [2] [25]
– One more chance / What have I done to deserve this? / Shopping / Rent / Hit music / It couldn't happen here / It's a sin / I want to wake up / Heart / King's Cross. (re-iss. May88; PCSDX 104) (w/free US 12" or cd-s) – Always on my mind.

Oct 87. (7") *(R 6168)* **RENT. / I WANT A DOG** [8]
(ext;12"+=/c-s+=/cd-s+=) *(12R/TCR/CDR 6168)* – Rent (dub).

Nov 87. (7") *(R 6171) <50123>* **ALWAYS ON MY MIND. / DO I HAVE TO?** [1] [4] Mar 88
(12"+=/c-s+=/cd-s+=) *(12R/TCR/CDR 6171)* – ('A'extended dance).
('A'-Phil Harding remix-12") *(12RX 6171)* – ('A'dub).

Mar 88. (7") *(R 6177)* **HEART. / I GET EXCITED (YOU GET EXCITED TOO)** [1]
('A'disco mix-12"+=/c-s+=/cd-s+=) *(12R/TCR/CDR 6177)* – ('A'dance mix).
('A'-J.Mendelsohn mix-12") *(12RX 6177)* – ('A'dub).

Jun 88. (12"/cd-s) **ACTUALLY. / ALWAYS ON MY MIND** [-]

Sep 88. (7"/7"s) *(R/RS 6190) <50161>* **DOMINO DANCING. / DON JUAN** [7] [18]
(disco;12"+=/c-s+=/cd-s+=) *(12R/TCR/CDR 6190)* – ('A'alternative mix).
(demo-12"+=) *(12RX 6190)* – ('A'remix).

Oct 88. (cd/c/lp) *(CD/TC+/PCS 7325) <90868>* **INTROSPECTIVE** (12"mixes) [2] [34]
– Left to my own devices / I want a dog / Domino dancing / I'm not scared / Always on my mind – In my house / It's alright. (re-iss. Mar89, 3x12"; PCSX 7325) (re-iss. Mar94)

Nov 88. (7"/7"s) *(R/RS 6198) <50171>* **LEFT TO MY OWN DEVICES. / THE SOUND OF THE ATOM SPLITTING** [4] [84] Jan 89
(12"+=/c-s+=/cd-s+=) *(12R/TCR/CDR 6198)* – ('A'disco mixes).

Jun 89. (7"/c-s/ext.12"/ext.cd-s) *(R/TCR/12R/CDR 6220)* **IT'S ALRIGHT. / ONE OF THE CROWD / YOUR FUNNY UNCLE** [5] [ ]
(10") *(10R 6220)* – ('A'alternative mix) / ('A'extended dance).
(12") *(12RX 6220)* – ('A'-Tyree mix) / ('A'-Sterling Void mix).

—— NEIL and CHRIS had guested late '89-91 for BERNARD SUMNER & JOHNNY MARR on their ELECTRONIC project. (see ⇒ NEW ORDER)

—— On tour augmented by **COURTNEY PINE / PETE GLEADALAS / DANNY CUMMINGS**

—— next featured **JOHNNY MARR** – guitar

Sep 90. (c-s/7") *(TC+/R 6269) <50329>* **SO HARD. / IT MUST BE OBVIOUS** [4] [62]
(12"+=) *(12R 6269)* – ('A'dub mix).
(cd-s++=) *(CDR 6269)* – ('A'dance mix).

Oct 90. (cd/c/lp) *(CD/TC+/PCSD 113) <94310>* **BEHAVIOUR** [2] [45]
– Being boring / This must be the place I waited years to leave / To face the truth / How can you expect to be taken seriously? / Only the wind / My October symphony / So hard / Nervously / The end of the world / Jealousy.

Nov 90. (c-s/7") *(TC+/R 6275)* **BEING BORING. / WE ALL FEEL BETTER IN THE DARK** [20]
(12"+=/cd-s+=) *(12R/CDR 6275)* – ('A'&'B'extended mixes).

Feb 91. (c-s,cd-s) *<50343>* **HOW CAN YOU EXPECT TO BE TAKEN SERIOUSLY? / WHAT HAVE I DONE TO DESERVE THIS?** [-] [93]

Mar 91. (c-s/7") *(TC+/R 6285)* **WHERE THE STREETS HAVE NO NAME (I CAN'T TAKE MY EYES OFF YOU). / HOW CAN YOU EXPECT TO BE TAKEN SERIOUSLY? (remix)** [4] [-]

(ext;12"+=/cd-s+=) *(12R/CDR 6285)* – But she's not your girlfriend.
(12"+=) *(12RX 6285)* – ('B'classical).

May 91. (c-s,cd-s) *<50351>* **WHERE THE STREETS HAVE NO NAME (I CAN'T TAKE MY EYES OFF YOU) / BET SHE'S NOT YOUR GIRLFRIEND** | – | 72 |

May 91. (c-s/7") *(TC+/R 6283)* **JEALOUSY. / LOSING MY MIND** | 12 | – |
(12"+=/cd-s+=) *(12R/CDR 6283)* – ('A'&'B'extended).
(cd-s+=) *(CDRS 6283)* – This must be the place / Waited for the years to leave (extended) / So hard (eclipsed mix).

Oct 91. (c-s/7") *(TC+/R 6301)* **DJ CULTURE. / MUSIC FOR BOYS** | 13 | – |
(12"+=/cd-s+=) *(12R/CDR 6301)* – ('A'-II version).

Nov 91. (cd/c/lp) *(CD/TC+/PMTV 3) <97097>* **DISCOGRAPHY – THE COMPLETE SINGLES COLLECTION** (compilation) | 3 | |
– West End girls / Love comes quickly / Opportunities (let's make lots of money) / Suburbia / It's a sin / What have I done to deserve this? / Rent / Always on my mind / Heart / Domino dancing / Left to my own devices / It's alright / So hard / Being boring / Where the streets have no name (can't take my eyes off you)/ Jealousy / DJ culture / Was it worth it?

Dec 91. (c-s/7") *(TC+/R 6306)* **WAS IT WORTH IT? / MISERABLISM** | 24 | |
(12"+=/cd-s+=) *(12R/CDR 6306)* – ('A'remixes).

Jun 93. (c-s/7") *(TC+/R 6348)* **CAN YOU FORGIVE HER? / HEY, HEADMASTER** | 7 | |
(12"+=/cd-s+=) *(12R/CDR 6348)* – ('A'-Rollo remix) / ('A'-Rollo dub).
(cd-s) *(CDRS 6348)* – ('A'remix) / I want to wake up (Johnny Marr remix) / What keeps mankind alive? / ('A' MK dub).

Sep 93. (c-s/7") *(TC+/R 6356)* **GO WEST. / SHAMELESS** | 2 | |
(12"+=/cd-s+=) *(12R/CDR 6356)* – ('A'mixes; movements).

Oct 93. (cd/c/lp) *(CD/TC+/PCSD 143) <89721>* **VERY** | 1 | 20 |
– Can you forgive her? / I wouldn't normally do this kind of thing / Liberation / A different point of view / Dreaming of the Queen / Yesterday, when I was mad / The theatre / One and one make five / To speak is a sin / Young offender / One in a million / Go west. *(free-cd) (CDPSDX 143)* **VERY RELENTLESS** – My head is spinning / Forever is love / KDX 125 / We came from outer space / The man who has everything / One thing leads to another.

Dec 93. (c-s/7") *(TC+/R 6370)* **I WOULDN'T NORMALLY DO THIS KIND OF THING. / TOO MANY PEOPLE** | 13 | |
(cd-s+=) *(CDR 6370)* – Violence (Hacienda mix) / West End girls (Sasha mix).
(cd-s) *(CDRS 6370)* – ('A'side) / ('A'mixes).

—— re-issued all 14 singles from 1987-1992 on cd-ep's Nov93.

Apr 94. (c-s/7") *(TC+/R 6377)* **LIBERATION. / DECADENCE** | 14 | |
(cd-s+=) *(CDR 6377)* – ('A'-E Smoove mix).
(cd-s/d12") *(CDRS/12RD 6377)* – ('A'-Murk mix) / ('B'unplugged mix) / Young offender (jam & spoon mix).

—— Below a second Comic Relief charity single, featuring vox from the TV series of that name; JENNIFER 'Edina' SAUNDERS and JOANNA 'Patsy' LUMLEY.

May 94. (c-s/7"; as ABSOLUTELY FABULOUS) *(TC+/R 6382)* **ABSOLUTELY FABULOUS. / ('A'mix)** | 6 | – |
(cd-s+=) *(CDR 6382)* – ('A'mixes).

Sep 94. (c-s) *(TCR 6386)* **YESTERDAY, WHEN I WAS MAD. / EUROBOY** | 13 | |
(cd-s) *(CDR 6386)* – ('A'side) / If love were all / Can you forgive her? (swing version) / ('A'-Jam & Spoon mix).
(cd-s) *(CDRS 6386)* – ('A'-Coconut 1 remix) / ('A'-Junior Vasquez dub & RAF zone mix) / Some speculation.
(12") *(12R 6386)* – ('A'-Jam & Spoon mix) / ('A'-Junior Vasquez dub & RAF zone mix).

Sep 94. (cd/c/lp) *(CD/TC+/PCSD 159) <28105>* **DISCO 2** (remixes) | 6 | 75 |

Jul 95. (c-s) *(TCR 6414)* **PANINARO '95 / IN THE NIGHT** | 15 | |
(cd-s+=) *(CDR 6414)* – Girls and boys (live in Rio).
(12") *(12R 6414)* – ('A'-Tracy's mix) / ('A'-Sharon's Sexy Boyz dub) / ('A'-Tin Tin Out mix) / ('A'extended).
(12") *(12RS 6414)* – ('A'-Angel Morales deep dance mix) / ('A'-Girls Boys in dub mix) / ('A'-Hot'n'spicy dub mix).

Aug 95. (d-cd/d-c/t-lp) *(CD/TC+/PCSD 166) <34023>* **ALTERNATIVE** (B-sides) | 2 | |
– In the night / A man could get arrested / That's my impression / Was that what it was? / Paninaro / Jack the lad / You know where you went wrong / A new life / I want a dog / Do I have to? / I get excited (you get excited too) / Don Juan / The sound of the atom splitting / One of the crowd / Your funny uncle / / It must be obvious / We all feel better in the dark / Bet she's not your girlfriend / Losing my mind / Music for boys / Miserablism / Hey, headmaster / What keeps mankind alive? / Shameless / Too many people / Violence (Hacienda version) / Decadence / If love were all / Euroboy / Some speculation.

Apr 96. (c-s) *(TCR 6431)* **BEFORE / THE TRUCK-DRIVER AND HIS MATE** | 7 | |
(cd-s+=) *(CDR 6431)* – Hit and miss / In the night 1995 ('New Clothes Show').
(cd-s/3x12") *(12R/CDRS 6431)* – ('A'remixes by; Love To Infinity / Joey Negro / Danny Tenaglia).

—— TENNANT now back with ELECTRONIC on hit single 'FORBIDDEN CITY'.

Aug 96. (c-s/12"pic-d) *(TCR/12RD 6443)* **SE A VIDA E (THAT'S THE WAY LIFE IS) / BETRAYED** | 8 | |
(cd-s+=) *(CDR 6443)* – How I learned to hate rock'n'roll.
(cd-s) *(CDRS 6443)* – (mixes by; Mark Picchiotti / Deep Dish / Pink Noise).

Sep 96. (cd/c) *(CD/TC PCSD 113)* **BILINGUAL** | 4 | 39 |
– Discoteca / Single / Metamorphosis / Electricity / Se a vida e (that's the way life is) / It always comes as a surprise / A red letter day / Up against it / The survivors / Before / To step aside / Saturday night forever.

Nov 96. (c-s) *(TCR 6452)* **SINGLE – BILINGUAL / DISCOTECA** | 14 | |
(cd-s+=) *(CDR 6452)* – Confidential (demo) / ('A'mix).
(cd-s+=) *(CDRS 6452)* – ('A'mix) / The calm before the storm.

Mar 97. (12") *(12R 6460)* **A RED LETTER DAY / THE BOY WHO COULDN'T KEEP HIS CLOTHES ON** | 9 | |
(cd-s+=) *(CDR 6460)* – Delusions of grandeur.
(cd-s) *(CDRS 6460)* – ('A'mixes).

Jun 97. (c-s) *(TCR 6470)* **SOMEWHERE / THE VIEW FROM YOUR BALCONY** | 9 | |
(cd-s+=) *(CDR 6470)* – To step aside (Ralphi's old school dub) / ('A'-Forthright vocal mix).

(cd-s) *(CDRS 6470)* – ('A'-orchestral) / Disco potential / ('A'-Trouser Enthusiasts mix) / ('A'-Forthright dub).

Jul 99. (c-s/cd-s) *(TCR/CDRS 6523)* **I DON'T KNOW WHAT YOU WANT BUT I CAN'T GIVE IT ANYMORE / SILVER AGE / SCREAMING** | 15 | |
(cd-s) *(CDR 6523)* – ('A'-David Morales mix) / ('A'-Thee Maddkatt 80 Coutship Witness mix) / Je t'aime . . . moi non plus.

Oct 99. (c-s/cd-s) *(TCR/CDRS 6525)* **NEW YORK CITY BOY / THE GHOST OF MYSELF / NEW YORK CITY (almighty definite mix)** | 14 | |
(cd-s) *(CDR 6525)* – ('A'side) / Casting a shadow / ('A'-Superchumbo's uptown mix).

Oct 99. (cd/c/lp) *(521847-2/-4/-1) <31086>* **NIGHTLIFE** | 7 | 84 | Nov99 |
– For your own good / Closer to Heaven / I don't know what you want but I can't give it any more / Happiness is an option / You only tell me you love me when you're drunk / Vampires / Radiophonic / The only one / Boy strange / In denial / New York city boy / Footsteps.

Tom PETTY

Born: 20 Oct'52, Gainesville, Florida, USA. In 1968, he formed school band The SUNDOWNERS, who later became The EPICS. By 1971, this outfit had evolved into MUDCRUTCH which also comprised guitarists MIKE CAMPBELL, TOMMY LEADON (brother of EAGLES man BERNIE) and drummer RANDALL MARSH. Their demo tape eventually came to the attention of Denny Cordell (co-owner of 'Shelter' records with LEON RUSSELL), who was suitably impressed enough to sign the band in 1975. They released a solitary single, 'DEPOT STREET', an album's worth of material lurking in the vaults due to the band's subsequent demise. PETTY was retained by Shelter and in 1976 he instigated The HEARTBREAKERS together with CAMPBELL, keyboardist BENMONT TENCH, bassist RON BLAIR and drummer STAN LYNCH. Later that year, the band released the eponymous 'TOM PETTY & THE HEARTBREAKERS', a raw statement on the future of roots rock'n'roll (The BYRDS, BOB DYLAN and ROLLING STONES are the most frequently cited influences) which initially flopped in the States. Perversely, the album was relatively successful in the UK and Europe, PETTY and Co. capitalising on the interest with a European tour that eventually wound its way back to the US during the summer of '77. They had already hit the UK Top 40 with two classic singles, 'ANYTHING THAT'S ROCK'N'ROLL' and 'AMERICAN GIRL' and in May '78, their first US Top 40 hit, 'BREAKDOWN', was used on the movie, 'FM'. At last there was a Stateside buzz surrounding the band and two months later their second album, 'YOU'RE GONNA GET IT', hit both the US & UK Top 40. Despite the ensuing critical and commercial success, PETTY filed for bankruptcy the following year, owing more than half a million dollars after Shelter was sold to 'ABC' and then 'MCA', the latter company duly suing him for breach of contract. Fortunately, the warring parties came to an agreement when 'MCA' decided to put his band on their Danny Bramson-run 'Backstreet' label. The late 1979 major label debut, 'DAMN THE TORPEDOES', sold only moderately in the UK, although it smashed into the US Top 3, sales of the album boosted by harder rocking tracks like 'REFUGEE' and 'DON'T DO ME LIKE THAT'. By this point PETTY was a major league star and he could afford to challenge his record company yet again, this time over the cover price of his forthcoming album, 'HARD PROMISES' (1981), which PETTY deemed too expensive. His persistence eventually won out and the album reached No.5 in the US, subsequently going platinum. The early 80's also saw PETTY hooking up with the delectable STEVIE NICKS on the 'STOP DRAGGIN' MY HEART AROUND' single (a US No.3) and producing DEL SHANNON's 'Drop Down And Get Me', with backing from The HEARTBREAKERS. Co-produced by PETTY, together with Jimmy Iovine and EURYTHMICS guitarist Dave Stewart, the acclaimed 'SOUTHERN ACCENTS' (1985) marked a newfound maturity, both lyrically and musically, the brooding 'DON'T COME AROUND HERE NO MORE' furnishing PETTY with his biggest UK hit single to date. Following a prolonged bout of touring and a further studio album, 'LET ME UP (I'VE HAD ENOUGH)', PETTY found himself in the company of rock's oldster hierarchy alongside BOB DYLAN, GEORGE HARRISON, JEFF LYNNE and ROY ORBISON in The TRAVELLING WILBURYS (who subsequently released two albums, rather confusingly titled 'TRAVELLING WILBURYS VOLUME 1' (1988) and 'TRAVELLING WILBURYS VOLUME 3' (1990). Around this time, PETTY also released his highly successful debut solo album, 'FULL MOON FEVER' (1989), with backing from a collection of HEARTBREAKERS and WILBURYS. One of his most overtly commercial outings, the record spawned the soaring 'FREE FALLIN' (a US Top 10) and contained what could be PETTY's signature tune, the defiant 'I WON'T BACK DOWN'. The album seemed to have breathed fresh life into PETTY's musical partnership with the HEARTBREAKERS and they teamed up once more for 1991's 'INTO THE GREAT WIDE OPEN', another highly melodic opus previewed by the impassioned 'LEARNING TO FLY' single. A follow-up PETTY solo set, 'WILDFLOWERS' (1994), was his first release for 'Warners', the singer having been back in the spotlight again after allegedly keeping the deal secret fom 'MCA'. Much like NEIL YOUNG, PETTY remains a stubborn maverick, refusing to play record company games and staying true to his muse. • **Covered:** SO YOU WANT TO BE A ROCK'N'ROLL STAR (Byrds) / NEEDLES AND PINS (Searchers) / FEEL A WHOLE LOT BETTER (Byrds) / SOMETHING IN THE AIR (Thunderclap Newman).

Album rating: TOM PETTY & THE HEARTBREAKERS (*6) / YOU'RE GONNA

GET IT (*7) / DAMN THE TORPEDOES (*8) / HARD PROMISES (*6) / LONG AFTER DARK (*5) / SOUTHERN ACCENTS (*6) / PACK UP THE PLANTATION – LIVE! (*4) / LET ME UP (I'VE HAD ENOUGH) (*5) / FULL MOON FEVER (*7) / INTO THE GREAT WIDE OPEN (*6) / GREATEST HITS compilation (*9) / WILDFLOWERS (*7) / SHE'S THE ONE (*5) / ECHO (*5)

TOM PETTY AND THE HEARTBREAKERS

TOM PETTY – vocals, guitar (ex-MUDCRUTCH) / **MIKE CAMPBELL** (b. 1 Feb'54, Panama City, Florida) – guitar (ex-MUDCRUTCH) / **BELMONT TENCH** (b. 7 Sep'54, Gainesville) – keyboards (ex-MUDCRUTCH) / **RON BLAIR** (b.16 Sep'52, Macon, Georgia) – bass / **STAN LYNCH** (b.21 May'55, Gainsville) – drums

		Island	Shelter
Jan 77.	(7") *<62006>* **BREAKDOWN. / THE WILD ONE, FOREVER**	-	
Feb 77.	(7") *(WIP 6377)* **AMERICAN GIRL. / THE WILD ONE, FOREVER**		-
May 77.	(lp/c) *(ILPS/ICT 5014) <52006>* **TOM PETTY AND THE HEARTBREAKERS**	24	55

– Rockin' around (with you) / Breakdown / Hometown blues / The wild one, forever / Anything that's rock'n'roll / Strangered in the night / Fooled again (I don't like it) / Mystery man / Luna / American girl. *(cd-iss. Jul87 on 'M.C.A.'; MCAD 37143) (re-iss. Nov90 cd/c; DMCL/MCLC 1715) (re-iss. 1991 cd/c; MCAD/MCA 10135) (re-iss. Apr92 cd/c; MCLD/MCLC 19012)*

May 77.	(7") *(WIP 6377)* **AMERICAN GIRL. / FOOLED AGAIN (I DON'T LIKE IT)**	-	
Jun 77.	(7"/12") *(WIP/+12 6369)* **ANYTHING THAT'S ROCK'N'ROLL. / FOOLED AGAIN (I DON'T LIKE IT)**	36	
Jul 77.	(7"/12") *(WIP/+12 6403)* **AMERICAN GIRL. / LUNA**	40	-
Oct 77.	(7") *<62008>* **BREAKDOWN. / FOOL AGAIN (I DON'T LIKE IT)**	-	40
May 78.	(lp/c) *(ISA/ISC 5017) <52029>* **YOU'RE GONNA GET IT**	34	23

– When the time comes / You're gonna get it / Hurt / Magnolia / Too much ain't enough / I need to know / Listen to her heart / No second thoughts / Restless / Baby's a rock'n'roller. *(cd-iss. Jun88 on 'M.C.A.'; MCAD 31171) (re-iss. Apr92 cd/c; MCLD/MCLC 19013)*

Jun 78.	(7"/12") *(WIP/+12 6426) <62010>* **I NEED TO KNOW. / NO SECOND THOUGHTS**		41
Sep 78.	(7"/12") *(WIP/+12 6455) <62011>* **LISTEN TO HER HEART. / I DON'T KNOW WHAT TO SAY TO YOU**		59

		M.C.A.	Backstreet
Nov 79.	(lp/c) *(MCF/+C 3044) <5105>* **DAMN THE TORPEDOES**	57	2

– Refugee / Here comes my girl / Even the losers / Century city / Don't do me like that / Shadows of a doubt (a complex kind) / What are you doin' in my life? / Louisiana rain / You tell me. *(re-iss. 1985; DMCA 108) (cd re-iss. Oct87; MCAD 5105) (cd re-iss. Jul88; DMCL 1872) (re-iss. Apr92 cd/c; MCLD/MCLC 19014)*

Nov 79.	(7") *(MCA 539) <41227>* **HERE COMES MY GIRL. / DON'T BRING ME DOWN**		59 Apr80
	(12"+=) *(MCAT 539)* – Casa Dega.		
Feb 80.	(7"/7"pic-d) *(MCA/+P 559) <41169>* **REFUGEE. / IT'S RAINING AGAIN**		15 Jan80
Jul 80.	(7") *(MCA 596) <41138>* **DON'T DO ME LIKE THAT. / CENTURY CITY**		10 Nov79
	(d7"+=) *(MCAD 596)* – Somethin' else / Stories we can tell.		

― **DONALD DUNN** – bass; repl. RON BLAIR

Apr 81.	(7") *(MCA 699) <51100>* **THE WAITING. / NIGHTWATCHMAN**		19
May 81.	(lp/c) *(MCF/+C 3098) <5160>* **HARD PROMISES**	32	5

– The waiting / A woman in love (it's not me) / Nightwatchman / Something big / King's road / Letting you go / A thing about you / Insider / The criminal kind / You can still change your mind. *(cd-iss. May86; CMCAD 31006) (cd re-iss. 1988; DIDX 344) (re-iss. Oct91 cd/c; MCLD/MCLC 19077)*

Jul 81.	(7") *(MCA 730) <51136>* **A WOMAN IN LOVE (IT'S NOT ME). / GATOR ON THE LAWN**		79

― PETTY and his band then were credited with backing STEVIE NICKS of FLEETWOOD MAC on a single 'Stop Draggin' My Heart Around' Aug81 hit US No.3.

Jul 82.	(7") *(MCA 788) <41169>* **REFUGEE. / THE INSIDER ("with STEVIE NICKS")**		

― **HOWARD EPSTEIN** (b.21 Jul'55) – bass repl. DUNN

Nov 82.	(7") *(MCA 801) <52144>* **YOU GOT LUCKY. / BETWEEN TWO WORLDS**		20
Nov 82.	(lp/c) *(MCF/+C 3155) <5360>* **LONG AFTER DARK**	45	9

– A one story town / You got lucky / Deliver me / Change of heart / Finding out / We stand a chance / Straight into darkness / The same old you / Between two worlds / A wasted life. *(re-iss. May86; MCAD 5360) (cd re-iss. Oct87; CMCAD 31027) (re-iss. Oct90 cd/c; DMCL/MCLC 1818) (re-iss. Jun92 cd/c; MCLD/MCLC 19078)*

Dec 82.	(7") *(MCA 805)* **STRAIGHT INTO DARKNESS. / HEARTBREAKERS BEACH PARTY**		-
Apr 83.	(7") *(MCA 814) <52181>* **CHANGE OF HEART. / HEARTBREAKERS BEACH PARTY**		21 Feb83
Apr 85.	(7"/12") *(MCA/+T 926) <52496>* **DON'T COME AROUND HERE NO MORE. / TRAILER**	50	13 Mar85
Apr 85.	(lp/c) *(MCF/+C 3260) <5486>* **SOUTHERN ACCENTS**	23	7

– Rebels / It ain't nothin' to me / Don't come around here no more / Southern accents / Make it better (forget about me) / Spike / Dogs on the run / Mary's new car / The best of everything. *(cd-iss. 1986; MCAD 5486) (cd re-iss. Jan90; DMCL 1896) (re-iss. Nov90 cd/c; MCLD/MCLC 19079)*

Jun 85.	(7") *(MCA 983) <52605>* **MAKE IT BETTER (FORGET ABOUT ME). / CRACKING UP**		54
	(12") *(MCAT 983)* – ('A'side) / ('A'instrumental).		
Aug 85.	(7") *<52658>* **REBELS. / SOUTHERN ACCENTS (live)**	-	74
Jan 86.	(d-lp/d-c) *(MCMD/+C 7001) <8021>* **PACK UP THE PLANTATION (live)**		22 Dec85

– So you want to be a rock'n'roll star / Needles and pins / The waiting / Breakdown / American girl / It ain't nothin' to me / Insider / Rockin' around (with you) / Refugee / I need to know * / Southern accents / Rebels / Don't bring me down / You got lucky * / Shout / The stories we can tell. *(cd-iss. Oct87; MCAD 8021) – (omits *) (re-iss. Nov91 cd/c; MCLD/MCLC 19142)*

Jan 86.	(7") *<52772>* **NEEDLES AND PINS (live). / SPIKE (live)**	-	37

Feb 86.	(7") *(MCA 1028)* **SO WANT TO BE A ROCK'N'ROLL STAR (live). / AMERICAN GIRL (live)**		-
	(12"+=) *(MCAT 1028)* – Spike (live).		
Aug 86.	(7"/12"; BOB DYLAN & THE HEARTBREAKERS) *(MCA/+T 1076)* **BAND OF THE HAND. / THEME FROM 'JOE'S DEATH'**		
Apr 87.	(7") *(MCA 1148) <53065>* **JAMMIN' ME. / LET ME UP (I'VE HAD ENOUGH)**		18
	(12"+=) *(MCAT 1148)* – Make that connection.		
Apr 87.	(lp/c/cd) *(MCG/MCGC/DMCG 6014) <5836>* **LET ME UP (I'VE HAD ENOUGH)**	59	20

– Jammin' me / Runaway trains / The damage you've done / It'll all work out / My life – Your world / Think about me / A self made man / Ain't love strange / How many more days / Let me up (I've had enough). *(cd re-iss. Aug90; DMCL 1905) (re-iss. Nov92 cd/c; MCLD/MCLC 19141)*

Sep 87.	(7") *(MCA 1190) <53153>* **ALL MIXED UP. / LET ME UP (I'VE HAD ENOUGH)**		
	(12"+=) *(MCAT 1190)* – Little bit of soul.		
Nov 87.	(7"; w-drawn) **THINK ABOUT ME. / MY LIFE – YOUR WORLD**		
	(12"+=) – The damage you've done.		

In 1988, before he went solo, TOM PETTY teamed up with BOB DYLAN, GEORGE HARRISON, JEFF LYNNE and ROY ORBISON in The TRAVELING WILBURYS

TOM PETTY

― solo with **JEFF LYNNE** – guitar, bass keyboards, vocals, co-writer / **MIKE CAMPBELL** – guitar, bass mandolin, keyboards, co-writer / **PHIL JONES** – drums, percussion / +guests **GEORGE HARRISON, ROY ORBISON, BENMONT TENCH, JIM KELTNER, HOWIE EPSTIEN, KELSEY CAMPBELL.**

		M.C.A.	M.C.A.
Apr 89.	(7") *(MCA 1334) <53369>* **I WON'T BACK DOWN. / THE APARTMENT SONG**	28	12
	(12"+=/cd-s+=) *(MCAT/DMCAX 1334)* – Don't treat me like a stranger.		
Jun 89.	(lp/c/cd) *(MCG/MCG/DMCG 6034) <6253>* **FULL MOON FEVER**	8	3 May89

– Free fallin' / I won't back down / Love is a long road / A face in the crowd / Runnin' down a dream / Feel a whole lot better / Yer so bad / Depending on you / The apartment song / Alright for now / A mind with a heart of it's own / Zombie zoo. *(cd re-iss. Dec98 on 'Mobile Fidelity'; UDCD 735)*

Aug 89.	(7"/c-s) *(MCA/+C 1359) <53682>* **RUNNIN' DOWN A DREAM. / ALRIGHT FOR NOW**	55	23 Jul89
	(12"+=/cd-s+=) *(MCAT/DMCAX 1359)* – Down the line.		
Nov 89.	(7") *<53748>* **FREE FALLIN'. / DOWN THE LINE**	-	7
Nov 89.	(7") *(MCA 1381)* **FREE FALLIN'. / LOVE IS A LONG ROAD**	64	-
	(12"+=/cd-s+=) *(MCAT/DMCAX 1381)* – ('A'live version).		
Feb 90.	(c-s,cd-s) *<53781>* **A FACE IN THE CROWD. / A MIND WITH A HEART OF ITS OWN**	-	46

TOM PETTY AND THE HEARTBREAKERS

― (originals reformed)

		M.C.A.	M.C.A.
Jun 91.	(7"/c-s) *(MCS/+CS 1555) <54124>* **LEARNING TO FLY. / TOO GOOD TO BE TRUE**	46	28
	(12"+=/cd-s+=) *(MCST/+D 1555)* – Baby's a rock'n'roller / I need to know.		
Jul 91.	(lp/c/cd) *<(MCA/+C/D 10317)>* **INTO THE GREAT WIDE OPEN**	3	13

– Learning to fly / Into the great wide open / Two gunslingers / The dark of the Sun / All or nothin' / All the wrong reasons / Too good to be true / Out in the cold / You and I will meet again / Makin' some noise / Built to last.

Aug 91.	(7"/c-s) *<54131>* **INTO THE GREAT WIDE OPEN. / MAKIN' SOME NOISE**		92 Oct91
	(cd-s+=) – Strangered in the night / Listen to her heart.		
Jan 92.	(7"/c-s) **KING'S HIGHWAY. / I WON'T BACK DOWN**		
	(cd-s+=) – Into the great wide open / Learning to fly.		
Mar 92.	(7"/c-s) *(MCS/+CS 1616)* **TOO GOOD TO BE TRUE. / THE DARK SIDE OF THE SUN**	34	
	(cd-s+=) *(MCSTD 1616)* – Hurt / Don't come around here no more.		
	(cd-s+=) *(MCSXD 1616)* – Psychotic reaction / I'm tired / Lonely.		
Oct 93.	(7"/c-s) *(MCS/+CS 1945)* **SOMETHING IN THE AIR. / THE WAITING**	53	-
	(cd-s+=) *(MCSTD 1945)* – American girl.		
Nov 93.	(cd/c/lp) *(MCD/MCC/MCA 10964) <10813>* **GREATEST HITS** (compilation)	10	8

– American girl / Breakdown / Anything that's rock'n'roll / Listen to her heart / I need to know / Refugee / Don't do me like that / Even the losers / Here comes my girl / The waiting / You got lucky / Don't come around here no more / I won't back down / Runnin' down a dream / Free fallin' / Learning to fly / Into the great wide open / Mary Jane's last dance / Something in the air.

Dec 93.	(c-s,cd-s) *<54732>* **MARY JANE'S LAST DANCE / THE WAITING**	-	14
Feb 94.	(c-s) *(MCSCS 1966)* **MARY JANE'S LAST DANCE / KING'S HIGHWAY (live)**	52	-
	(cd-s+=) *(MCSTD 1966)* – Make that connection (live) / Take out some insurance (live).		
	(cd-s) *(MCSXD 1966)* – ('A'side) / Casa dega / Gator on the lawn / Down the line.		

TOM PETTY

― with backing from HEARTBREAKERS, plus **STEVE FERRONE** – drums (ex-AVERAGE WHITE BAND, etc) repl. LYNCH

		Warners	Warners
Oct 94.	(c-s) *(W 0272C)* **YOU DON'T KNOW HOW IT FEELS / HOUSE IN THE WOODS**		-
	(cd-s+=) *(W 0272CD)* – Girl on L.S.D.		

Nov 94. (c-s,cd-s) <18030> **YOU DON'T KNOW HOW IT FEELS /
GIRL ON L.S.D.** | - | 13 |

Nov 94. (cd/c/lp) <(9362 45792-2/-4/-1)> **WILDFLOWERS** | 36 | 8 |
– Wildflowers / You don't know how it feels / Time to move on / You wreck me /
It's good to be king / Only a broken heart / Honey bee / Don't fade on me hard on
me / Cabin down below / To find a friend / A higher place / House in the woods /
Crawling back to you / Wake up time.

Feb 95. (c-s) (W 0283C) **YOU WRECK ME / CABIN DOWN BELOW
(acoustic)** | | - |
(cd-s+=) (W 0283CD) – Only a broken heart.

Apr 95. (c-s,cd-s) <17925> **IT'S GOOD TO BE KING / CABIN
DOWN BELOW (acoustic)** | - | 68 |

TOM PETTY AND THE HEARTBREAKERS

Aug 96. (cd/c) <(9362 46285-2/-4)> **SHE'S THE ONE (original
soundtrack)** | 37 | 15 |
– Walls (circus) / Grew up fast / Zero from outer space / Climb that hill / Change
the locks / Angel dream (No.4) / Hope you never / Asshole / Supernatural radio /
California / Hope on board / Walls (No.3) / Angel dream (No.2) / Hung up and
overdue / Airport.

Sep 96. (c-s,cd-s) <17593> **WALLS / WALLS (No.3 version)** | - | 69 |
Mar 97. (c-s) (W 0371C) **WALLS (CIRCUS) / HUNG UP AND
OVERDUE** | - | - |
(cd-s+=) (W 0371CD) – Walls (No.3 version).

—— now a quartet
Apr 99. (cd/c) <(9362 47294-2/-4)> **ECHO** | 43 | 10 |
– Room at the top / Swingin' / Counting on you / Free girl now / Lonesome sundown /
Accused of love / Echo / Won't last long / Billy the kid / I don't wanna fight / This
one's for me / No more / About to give out / Rhino skin / One more day, one more
night.

– compilations, others, etc. –
on 'M.C.A.' unless mentioned otherwise
Sep 84. (d-c) (MCA2 105) **DAMN THE TORPEDOES. / HARD
PROMISES** | | - |
Apr 86. (12"ep) (MCAT 1047) **REFUGEE / DON'T DO ME LIKE
THAT. / HERE COMES MY GIRL / THE WAITING** | | - |
Nov 95. (6xcd-box) (MCAD 611375) **PLAYBACK** | | |

Liz PHAIR

Born: 17 Apr'67, New Haven, Connecticut, USA. Chicago based, USA. After
graduating in Art History, PHAIR concentrated full-time on her songwriting
and, with the help of friend/COME guitarist, CHRIS BROKAW, secured a
contract with indie label, 'Matador' early in 1992. Hooking up
with musicians BRAD WOOD, CASEY RICE and LEROY BACH, PHAIR
translated her song sketches into a marathon double album, 'EXILE ON
GUYVILLE', its title a typically PHAIR-esque play on the classic 'STONES'
album. An engagingly eclectic, often brazenly confessional affair, PHAIR had
fashioned a folk-grunge mini-classic, fusing wry life-in-America / hard-hitting
sexual lyrics with beautiful country harmonies in a similar vein to MAZZY
STAR or THROWING MUSES. Critics loved it and in addition to the gushing
reviews, PHAIR became the first woman since JONI MITCHELL (in 1974)
to win the prestigious 'Village Voice' annual award. The sonic femme-thrust
of 'SUPERNOVA' previewed follow-up, 'WHIP-SMART' (1994), a record
that surprisingly received a less than enthusiastic response in comparison to
its predecessor. While the album may have lacked a little of the debut's
wayward charm, the songs were more focused and PHAIR's muse was as
fertile, and occasionally as candid as ever (even if her much talked about
stage-fright might've belied the bolshy, sexually liberated persona her music
projected). While 1995 saw the release of a stop-gap odds'n'sods collection,
'JUVENILIA' (1995), it would be another three years before another studio set,
'WHITECHOCOLATESPACEEGG' (1998). Reaching the Top 40 in America,
the album was once again the toast of the Rolling Stone readers, although her
Lo-Fi ramblings sounded a tad similar to BELLY or even SLEATER-KINNEY
for the more discerning Brits.

Album rating: EXILE IN GUYVILLE (*7) / WHIP-SMART (*8) / JUVENILIA
compilation (*4) / WHITECHOCOLATESPACEEGG (*6)

LIZ PHAIR – vocals, guitar / **BRAD WOOD** – drums, percussion / **CASEY RICE** – guitar /
LEROY BACH – bass

	Minty Fresh	not iss.
Aug 93. (7") (MF 4) **CANARY. / CARNIVORE**		-
	Matador	Matador
Aug 93. (cd/c/lp) <(OLE 051-2/-4/-1)> **EXILE IN GUYVILLE**		Jun93

– 6'1" / Help me Mary / Glory / Dance of the seven veils / Never said / Soap star
Joe / Explain it to me / Canary / Mesmerizing / Fuck and run / Girls! girls! girls! /
Divorce song / Shatter / Flower / Johnny Sunshine / Gunshy / Stratford-On-Guy /
Strange loop.

Sep 94. (7") <(OLE 103-7)> <98206> **SUPERNOVA. / COMBO PLATTER**		78	Jul94
	Atlantic	Atlantic
Sep 94. (cd/c/lp) <(7567 92429-2/-4/-1)><OLE 107> **WHIP-SMART**		27

– Chopsticks / Supernova / Support system / X-ray man / Shane / Nashville / Go
west / Cince de Mayo / Dogs of L.A. / Whip-smart / Jealousy / Crater lake / Alice
Springs / May queen.

Oct 94. (7"/c-s) (A 8224/+C) **SUPERNOVA. / X-RAY MAN** (remix) | | - |
(12"+=/cd-s+=) (A 8224 T/CD) – ('A'-clean version).

| | Matador – Capitol | Matador – Capitol |
| Aug 98. (cd/c/lp) <(OLE 191 – 7243 8 53554-2/-4/-1> **WHITECHOCOLATESPACEEGG** | | 35 |

– White chocolate space egg / Big tall man / Perfect world / Johnny Feelgood /
Polyester bride / Love is nothing / Baby got going / Uncle Alvarez / Only son / Go on
ahead / Headache / Ride / What makes you happy / Fantasize / Shitloads of money /
Girls' room.

– compilations, etc. –
Aug 95. (d7"ep/cd-ep) Matador; <(OLE 129-7/-2)> **JUVENILIA** | | |
– Jealousy / Turning Japanese / Animal girl / California / South Dakota / Batmobile /
Dead shark / Easy.

PHISH

Formed: Burlington, Vermont, USA . . . 1983 by TREY ANASTASIO, JON
FISHMAN and GORDON while they were students at the local university.
Following the addition of PAGE McCONNELL, the band began touring in
earnest, playing gigs across the States and in the process building up a
grassroots fanbase and a reputation gained largely by word of mouth. Not
since the heady days of the 70's have a band become so huge by dint of
sheer hard graft and a resolutely "authentic" sound, proving that even in
these days of 99p single giveaways, record company marketing muscle isn't
everything. An archetypal 'Great American Band', PHISH have undoubtedly
tapped into the same constituency of MOR-friendly, liberal/hippy Americans
who once followed (and probably still do) the GRATEFUL DEAD and now
dig HOOTIE & THE BLOWFISH. It is for exactly this reason that despite
being honoured with the obligatory Ben & Jerry's ice cream flavour in the
States, PHISH will probably only ever attract a minority audience in Britain.
Still, BLIND MELON proved at least a one-hit wonder was possible and with
their first two independently released albums, 'JUNTA' (1988) and 'LAWN
BOY' (1990), PHISH explored elements of blues, jazz, funk and rock in a
similarly improvisational spirit to The SPIN DOCTORS , BLUES TRAVELER
etc. In fact, PHISH actually toured with these bands under the banner of
HORDE (Horizon Of Rock Developing Everywhere)(!?), some sharp-witted
Stateside critic memorably dubbing this lot the "Living Dead" in honour of
their interminable jam sessions. Packing out venues in almost every State,
it was only a matter of time before the band were picked up by a major,
'Elektra' winning out and releasing 1992's 'A PICTURE OF NECTAR' set.
'RIFT' (1993) was PHISH's first major chart entry, the band reining in their
more wayward musical tendencies and even securing radio play for a couple
of tracks from 1994's (HOIST)' album. In the true spirit of JERRY GARCIA
& Co, 1995 saw PHISH releasing that most reviled of rock artefacts, a double
live album. The mellow, ALLMANS-esque 'FREE' incredibly remains the
band's only bonafide single release, one of the stand-out tracks from 1997's
'BILLY BREATHES' album, a US Top 10 and their most successful to date.
Now something of an American institution, PHISH seem to have effortlessly
navigated the shark-infested waters of the US music business without
compromising their original vision, 'SLIP STITCH AND PASS' (1997) and
'THE STORY OF THE GHOST' (1998) finding them swimming as freely as
ever.

Album rating: JUNTA (*6) / LAWN BOY (*6) / A PICTURE OF NECTAR (*6) / RIFT
(*6) / (HOIST) (*6) / A LIVE ONE (*7) / STASH compilation (*7) / BILLY BREATHES
(*8) / SLIP STITCH AND PASS (*7) / THE STORY OF THE GHOST (*7)

TREY ANASTASIO – vocals, guitar / **JON FISHMAN** – drums, vocals / **MIKE GORDON** –
bass, vocals / **PAGE McCONNELL** – keyboards, vocals

	not iss.	own label
1988. (lp) **JUNTA**		-

– Fee / You enjoy myself / Esther / Golgi apparatus / Foam / Dinner and a movie /
Divided sky / David Bowie / Fluffhead / Fluff's travels / Contact. <US d-cd-iss.
Dec97 on 'Elektra'+=; 61413-2> – Union federal / Sanity / Icculus.

| | Absolute A-Go-Go | Absolute A-Go-Go |
| Sep 90. (lp/c/cd) <(AGO 1992/+MC/CD)> **LAWN BOY** | | |

– Squirming coil / Reba / My sweet one / Split open and melt / Oh kee pa ceremony /
Bathtub gin / Run like an antelope / Lawn boy / Bouncing around the room. <(cd
re-iss. Jun97 on 'Elektra'; 7559 61273-2)>

| | Elektra | Elektra |
| May 92. (cd/c) <(7559 61274-2/-4)> **A PICTURE OF NECTAR** | | |

– Llama / Eliza / Cavern / Poor heart / Stash / Manteca / Guelah papyrus / Magilla /
Landlady / Glide / Tweezer / The mango song / Chalk dust torture / Faht / Catapult /
Tweezer (reprise). (cd re-iss. Jun97; same)

Feb 93. (cd/c) <7559 61433-2> **RIFT** | - | 51 |
– All things reconsidered / It's ice / Silent in the morning / Sparkle / Horn, Weigh /
The wedge / Mound / My friend, my friend / Rift / Maze / Lengthwise / The horse /
Fast enough for you. (UK cd-iss Jun97; same)

Mar 94. (cd/c) <7559 61628-2/-4> **(HOIST)** | - | 34 |
– Julius / Down with disease / If I could / Riker's mailbox / Axill (part 2) / Lifeboy /
Sample in a jar / Wolfman's brother / Scent of a mule / Dog faced boy / Demand.
(UK cd-iss. Jun97; same)

Jul 95. (d-cd) <7559 61772-2> **A LIVE ONE** (live) | - | 18 |
– Bouncing around the room / Harry Hood / Chalk dust torture / You enjoy myself /
Tweezer / Wilson / Stash / Squirming coil / Slave to the traffic light / Simple /
Montana / Gumbo.

Jul 96. (cd) <7559 61933-2)> **STASH** (compilation) | | |
– Stash / Scent of a mule / Maze / Bouncing around the moon / Gumbo / Sample in
a jar / Split open and melt / Fast enough for you / Down with disease / You enjoy
myself / If I could.

Feb 97. (cd/c) <7559 61971-2/-4)> **BILLY BREATHES** | 7 | Oct96
– Free / Character zero / Waste / Taste / Cars trucks buses / Talk / Theme from the
bottom / Train song / Bliss / Billy breathes / Swept away / Steep / Prince Caspian.

Mar 97. (c-s) (A 4205C) **FREE / STRANGE DESIGN** | | |
(cd-s+=) (A 4205CD) – Theme from the bottom.

Oct 97. (cd/c) <(7559 62121-2/-4)> **SLIP STITCH AND PASS** | | 17 |
– Cities / Wolfman's brother / Jesus just left Chicago / Weigh / Mike's song / Lawn
boy / Weekapaug groove / Hello my baby / Taste.

Nov 98. (cd) <(7559 62297-2)> **THE STORY OF THE GHOST** [ ] [8]
– The ghost / Birds of a feather / Meat / Guyute / Fikus / Shafty / Limb by limb / Frankie says / Brian and Robert / Water in the sky / Roggae / Wading in the velvet sea / Moma dance / End of session.

PHOTEK (dig out; 4th edition)

PHOTOS (dig out; Great Alt & Indie . . .)

Wilson PICKETT

Born: 18 Mar '41, Prattville, Alabama, USA. Moving to Detroit with his family when still in his teens, PICKETT initially honed his vocal chops in a gospel act before joining The FALCONS. Comprising MACK RICE and EDDIE FLOYD amongst others, this R&B act were already famous for their US Top 20 hit, 'YOU'RE SO FINE'; with PICKETT on vocals, they scraped a further Top 75 in summer '62 with 'I FOUND A LOVE'. The singer subsequently went solo and after a one-off single on the 'Cub' label, signed to LLOYD PRICE's 'Double L' imprint. There, he scored a trio of respectable PRICE-penned R&B hits which also made their way into the lower regions of the pop chart, yet it took a deal with soul giant 'Atlantic' to see the 'wicked' PICKETT really earn his famous nickname. Although his first two singles for the company were unequivocal flops, producer JERRY WEXLER duly directed him to the 'Stax' studios in Memphis where he hooked up with house band BOOKER T & THE MG's. In summer '65, he emerged with 'IN THE MIDNIGHT HOUR' (written with ace MG's guitarist STEVE CROPPER), netting him his first major US chart hit (UK Top 20 a few months later). As well as unleashing his super-stud nails'n'whisky growl, this sweaty, shuffling, groin-grinding classic also assured PICKETT a place in soul history. The man's feral, dancefloor-rooted style was based on some of the MG's tightest ever playing, engendering a series of vital US (and to a lesser extent, UK) hits: '634-5789 (SOULSVILLE, U.S.A.)', 'LAND OF 1000 DANCES', 'MUSTANG SALLY', 'FUNKY BROADWAY' etc. In 1968, PICKETT found a kindred spirit in BOBBY WOMACK whose 'I'M A MIDNIGHT MOVER' he took into the Top 30 and who would continue to be a source of inspiration for him. He also worked with DUANE ALLMAN on an unlikely cover of The Beatles' 'HEY JUDE' (the album of the same name even saw him running through Steppenwolf's 'BORN TO BE WILD'!), one of the PICKETT's biggest UK hits (Top 20). An even more unlikely cover of The Archies' 'SUGAR SUGAR' suggested that he was running out of ideas; a temporary solution came in the form of rising Philly production prodigies, GAMBLE & HUFF, with whom he recorded 1970's 'WILSON PICKETT IN PHILADELPHIA' album. The record's 'ENGINE No.9' hit the Top 20 as did further early 70's G&H productions, 'DON'T KNOCK MY LOVE' and 'DON'T LET THE GREEN GRASS FOOL YOU'. These efforts marked his last stand as a major-league artist and amid the usual succession of label changes and personal problems (infamous for his volatile off-stage temperament and heavy drinking bouts, he was arrested on 21st November '74 for threatening behaviour with a gun), PICKETT made a living on the supper club cabaret circuit. He did, however, hit the charts one more time (in '87) with the obligatory remix of 'IN THE MIDNIGHT HOUR'. The 90's, meanwhile, saw him give up recording completely; the man's alcohol problem brought tragedy in 1993 when he was found guilty of knocking down and killing a pensioner while drink driving, receiving a one year jail sentence. PICKETT returned to the recording front in 1999 with the tellingly titled 'IT'S HARDER NOW'. • Covered: LAND OF A 1000 DANCES (c. Chris Kenner) / MUSTANG SALLY (Mack Rice; of The Falcons) / EVERYBODY NEEDS SOMEBODY TO LOVE (Solomon Burke) / FUNKY BROADWAY (Dyke & The Blazers) / STAG-O-LEE (Lloyd Price) / HEY JOE (Jimi Hendrix) / YOU KEEP ME HANGIN' ON (Supremes) / FIRE AND WATER (Free) / MAMA TOLD ME NOT TO COME (Randy Newman) / etc.

Best CD compilation: A MAN AND A HALF: THE BEST OF . . . (*8)

WILSON PICKETT – vocals (with session people)

			not iss.	Lupine	
1962.	(7") <003> **ANNA. / YOU'RE ON MY MIND**		[-]	[ ]	
			not iss.	Cub	
1963.	(7") <9113> **MY HEART BELONGS TO YOU. / LET ME BE YOUR BOY**		[-]	[ ]	
	<re-iss. 1963 on 'Correctone'; 501>				
			Liberty	Double L	
May 63.	(7") <713> **IF YOU NEED ME. / BABY CALL ON ME**		[-]	[64]	
Aug 63.	(7") (LIB 10115) <717> **IT'S TOO LATE. / I'M GONNA LOVE YOU**			[49] Jul63	
Oct 63.	(7") <724> **I'M DOWN TO MY LAST HEARTBREAK. / I CAN'T STOP**		[-]	[95]	
			Atlantic	Atlantic	
1964.	(7") <2233> **I'M GONNA CRY. / FOR BETTER OR WORSE**		[-]	[ ]	
1964.	(7") <2271> **COME HOME BABY. / TAKE A LITTLE LOVE**		[-]	[ ]	
Sep 65.	(7") (AT 4036) <2289> **IN THE MIDNIGHT HOUR. / I'M NOT TIRED**		[12]	[21] Jul65	
Nov 65.	(7") (AT 4052) <2306> **DON'T FIGHT IT. / IT'S ALL OVER**		[29]	[53]	
Dec 65.	(lp) (ATL 5037) <SD 8114> **IN THE MIDNIGHT HOUR**			[ ] Oct65	

– In the midnight hour / Teardrops will fall / Take a little love / For better or worse / I found a love / That;s a man's way / I'm gonna cry / Don't fight it / Take this love I've got / Come home baby / I'm not tired / Let's kiss and make up. (cd-iss Aug93 on 'Rhino'; 8122 71275-2)

Feb 66.	(7") (AT 4072) <2320> **634-5789 (SOULSVILLE, U.S.A.). / THAT'S A MAN'S WAY**	[36]	[13] Jan66

Jun 66.	(7") (584 023) <2334> **NINETY-NINE AND A HALF (WON'T DO). / DANGER ZONE**	[ ]	[53] May66
Aug 66.	(7") (584 039) <2348> **LAND OF A 1000 DANCES. / YOU'RE SO FINE**	[22]	[6] Jul66
Sep 66.	(lp) (587/588 029) <SD 8129> **THE EXCITING WILSON PICKETT**	[21]	Aug66

– Land of 100 dances / Something you got / 634-5789 / Barefootin' / Mercy, mercy / You're so fine / In the midnight hour / 99 and a half (won't do) / Danger zone / I'm drifting / It's all over / She's so good to me. (re-iss. Jun88 / (cd-iss. Aug93 on 'Rhino')

Nov 66.	(7") (584 066) <2365> **MUSTANG SALLY. / THREE TIME LOSER**	[28]	[23]
Feb 67.	(7") (584 101) <2381> **EVERYBODY NEEDS SOMEBODY TO LOVE. / NOTHING YOU CAN DO**	[ ]	[29]
Feb 67.	(lp; mono/stereo) (587/588 057) <SD 8138> **THE WICKED PICKETT**		[42] Jan67

– Mustang Sally / New Orleans / Sunny / Everybody needs somebody to love / Ooh poo pah doo / She ain't gonna do right / Knock on wood / Time is on my side / Up tight good woman / You left the water running / Three time loser / Nothing you can do.

Mar 67.	(7") <2394> **I FOUND A LOVE (pt.1). / (pt.2)**	[-]	[32]
May 67.	(7") (584 107) **NEW ORLEANS. / SOUL DANCE NUMBER THREE**	[ ]	[-]
May 67.	(7") <2412> **SOUL DANCE NUMBER THREE. / YOU CAN'T STAND ALONE**	[-]	[55] / [70]
Aug 67.	(lp; mono/stereo) (587/588 057) <SD 8145> **THE SOUND OF WILSON PICKETT**		[54]

– Soul dance number three / Funky Broadway / I need a lot of loving every day / I found a love (part 1) / I found a love (part 2) / You can't stand alone / Mojo mamma / I found the one / Something within me / I'm sorry about that / Love is a beautiful thing.

Sep 67.	(7") (584 130) <2430> **FUNKY BROADWAY. / I'M SORRY ABOUT THAT**	[43]	[8] Aug67
Oct 67.	(lp; mono/stereo) (587/588 092) <SD 8151> **THE BEST OF WILSON PICKETT** (compilation)		[35]

– In the midnight hour / I found a love / 634-5789 / If you need me / Mustang Sally / Don't fight it / Everybody needs somebody to love / It's too late / Ninety-nine and a half (won't do) / Funky Broadway / Soul dance number three / Land of 1000 dances. (re-iss. Apr82 lp/c; 780170-1/-4) (cd-iss. Jul87; 781737-2) (cd re-iss. Aug93; 7567 81737-2)

Oct 67.	(7") (584 142) <2448> **STAGGER-LEE. / I'M IN LOVE**	[ ]	[22] / [45]
Feb 68.	(7") <2484> **JEALOUS LOVE. / I'VE COME A LONG WAY**	[-]	[50]
Mar 68.	(7") (584 173) **THAT KIND OF LOVE. / I'VE COME A LONG WAY**	[ ]	[-]
Apr 68.	(lp; mono/stereo) (587/588 107) <SD 8175> **I'M IN LOVE**		[70] Feb68

– Jealous love / Stagger lee / That kind of love / I'm in love / Hello sunshine / Don't cry no more / We've got to have love / Bring it on home to me / She's looking good / I've come a long way. (cd-iss. Jan96; 7567 80375-2)

May 68.	(7") (584 183) <2504> **SHE'S LOOKIN' GOOD. / WE'VE GOT TO HAVE LOVE**	[ ]	[15] Apr68
Aug 68.	(7") (584 203) <2528> **I'M A MIDNIGHT MOVER. / DEBORAH**	[38]	[24] Jun68
Sep 68.	(lp; mono/stereo) (587/588 111) <SD 8183> **THE MIDNIGHT MOVER**		[91] Jul68

– I'm a midnight mover / It's a groove / Remember, I been good to you / I'm gonna cry / Deborah / I found a true love / Down by the sea / Trust me / Let's get an understanding / For better or worse.

Nov 68.	(7") (584 221) <2558> **I FOUND A TRUE LOVE. / FOR BETTER OR WORSE**	[ ]	[42] Sep68
Nov 68.	(7") <2575> **A MAN AND A HALF. / PEOPLE MAKE THE WORLD (WHAT IT IS)**	[-]	[42]
Dec 68.	(7") (584 236) **HEY JUDE. / NIGHT OWL**	[16]	[-]
Jan 69.	(7") <2591> **HEY JUDE. / SEARCH YOUR HEART**	[ ]	[23] / [97]
Feb 69.	(lp) (588 170) <SD 8215> **HEY JUDE**		[ ]

– Save me / Hey Jude / Back in your arms / Toe hold / Night owl / My own style of loving / A man and a half / Sit down and talk this over / Search your heart / Born to be wild / People make the world (what it is). (cd-iss. Jan96; 7567 80375-2)

Mar 69.	(7") (584 261) <2611> **MINI SKIRT MINNIE. / BACK IN YOUR ARMS**	[ ]	[50]
Apr 69.	(lp) (2465 002) <SD 8250> **RIGHT ON**		[ ]

– Groovy little woman / Funky way / Sugar sugar / Sweet inspiration / This old town / You keep me hangin' on / Lord pity us all / It's still good / Woman likes to hear that / She said yes / Hey Joe / Steal away.

May 69.	(7") <2631> **BORN TO BE WILD. / TOE HOLD**	[-]	[64]
Jul 69.	(7") <2648> **HEY JOE. / NIGHT OWL**	[-]	[59]
Jan 70.	(7") (584 313) <2682> **YOU KEEP ME HANGIN' ON. / NOW YOU SEE ME, NOW YOU DON'T**	[ ]	[92] Nov69
May 70.	(7") (2091 005) <2722> **SUGAR SUGAR. / COLE, COOKE AND REDDING**	[ ]	[25] / [91]
Jul 70.	(7") (584 281) **HEY JOE. / BORN TO BE WILD**	[ ]	[ ]
Aug 70.	(7") <2753> **SHE SAID YES. / IT'S STILL GOOD**	[-]	[68]
Oct 70.	(7") (2091 032) <2765> **ENGINE No.9. / INTERNATIONAL PLAYBOY**	[ ]	[14]
Mar 71.	(7") <2781> **DON'T LET THE GRASS FOOL YOU. / AIN'T NO DOUBT ABOUT IT**	[-]	[ ]
Apr 71.	(7") (2091 086) **FIRE AND WATER. / DON'T LET THE GREEN GRASS FOOL YOU**	[ ]	[-]
Apr 71.	(lp) (2400 026) <SD 8270> **ENGINE No.9** <US title 'WILSON PICKETT IN PHILADELPHIA'>		[64] Sep70

– Run Joey run / Help the needy / Come right here / Bumble bee (sting me) / Don't let the green grass fool you / Get me back on time, engine number 9 (part 1) / Get me back on time, engine number 9 (part 2) / Days go by / International playboy / Ain't no doubt about it. (cd-iss. Jan96; 8122 72219-2)

Jun 71.	(lp) (K 20078) <8290> **THE BEST OF WILSON PICKETT, VOL.II** (compilation)	[73] May71

– Don't let the green grass fool you / Sugar sugar / Get me back on time, engine No.9 / I'm a midnight mover / A man and a half / Born to be wild / She's lookin' good / I'm in love / Hey Joe / Cole, Cooke & Redding / Hey Jude / You keep me hangin' on / I found a true love.

Oct 71. (7") *(2091 153)* <2824> **CALL MY NAME, I'LL BE THERE. / WOMAN LET ME BE DOWN HOME**		**52** Aug71
Dec 71. (7") <2852> **FIRE AND WATER. / PLEDGING MY LOVE**	-	**24**
Jan 72. (lp) *(K 40319)* <8300> **DON'T KNOCK MY LOVE**		Dec71

– Fire and water / (Your love has brought me) A mighty long way / Covering the same old ground / Don't knock my love (part 1) / Don't knock my love (part 2) / Call my name, I'll be there / Hot love / Not enough love to satisfy / You can't judge a book by its cover / Pledging my love / Mama told me not to come / Woman let me be down home.

Feb 72. (7") *(2091 124)* <2797> **DON'T KNOCK MY LOVE. / (part 2)**		**13** Apr71
Apr 72. (7") *(K 10166)* **DON'T LET THE GREEN GRASS FOOL YOU. / COVERING THE SAME OLD GROUND**		**17** Jan71
Jun 72. (7") *(K 10181)* <2878> **FUNK FACTORY. / ONE STEP AWAY**		**58** May72
Oct 72. (7") <2909> **MAMA TOLD ME NOT TO COME. / COVERING THE SAME OLD GROUND**	-	**99**

	R.C.A.	R.C.A.
1973. (7") <2961> **INTERNATIONAL PLAYBOY. / COME RIGHT HERE**		-
Mar 73. (7") *74 0898* **MR. MAGIC MAN. / I SHO' LOVE YOU**		**98**
Mar 73. (lp) *(SF 8390)* <0312> **MIZ LENA'S BOY** <US title 'MR. MAGIC MAN'>		

– Take a closer look at the woman you're with / Memphis, Tennessee / Soft spoul boogie woogie / Help me make it through the night / Never my love / You lay'd it on me / Is your love life better / Two women and a wife / Why don't you make up your mind / Take the pollution out your throat.

Nov 73. (7") *(RCA 2430)* <0049> **TAKE A CLOSER LOOK AT THE WOMAN YOU'RE WITH. / TWO WOMEN AND A WIFE**		**90** Sep73
Feb 74. (7") <*(APB 0174)*> **SOFT SOUL BOOGIE WOOGIE. / TAKE THE POLLUTION OUT OF YOUR THROAT**		
May 74. (lp) *(SF 8344)* <4858> **TONIGHT I'M MY BIGGEST AUDIENCE**		

– Mr. Magic man / Only I can sing this love / Love is beautiful / I sure love you / Baby man / Sin was the blame / What it is / If you need me / I can't slip my true love away / I keep walking straight ahead.

Aug 74. (7") *(RCA 2450)* <0309> **TAKE YOUR PLEASURE WHERE YOU FIND IT. / WHAT GOOD IS A LIE**		
Sep 74. (lp) *<APL1 0495>* **PICKETT IN THE POCKET**	-	

– Iron it out / Isn't that so / Take a look / I was too nice / Don't pass me by / What good is a lie / Young boy blues / Take your pleasure where you find it / You're the one.

Nov 74. (7") <10067> **I WAS TOO NICE. / ISN'T THAT SO**	-	
Dec 74. (d-lp) *<APL2 0669>* **LIVE IN JAPAN** (live)	-	

– T.S.O.P. (The Sound Of Philadelphia) / Proud Mary / People make the world / Sugar sugar / Don't let the green grass fool you / I'm in love / In the midnight hour / Fire and water / I found a love / Never my love / Glory hallelujah / Mustang Sally / Land of a 1000 dances / Soft soul boogie / Mr.Magic man / Don't knock my love / Goodnight my love.

Jul 75. (lp) *(SF 8439)* *<APL1 0856>* **JOIN ME AND LET'S BE FREE**		

– Join me and let's be free / Let's make love right / I've got a good friend / Smokin' in the United Nations / Gone / Good things / Higher consciousness / Bailin' hay on a rainy day / Mighty mouth.

	D.J.M.	Wicked
Nov 76. (7") <8101> **HOW WILL I EVER KNOW. / THE BEST PART OF A MAN**	-	
Nov 76. (lp) *(DJSL 064)* <26064> **PEACE BREAKER**	-	

	Atlantic	Big Tree
Feb 77. (7") <8107> **LOVE WILL KEEP US TOGETHER. / IT'S GONNA BE GOOD**	-	
Aug 78. (7") *<16121>* **WHO TURNED YOU ON. / DANCE YOU DOWN**		
Aug 78. (lp) *(K 50528)* <76011> **A FUNKY SITUATION**		

– Dance with me / She's so tight / The night we called a day / Dance you down / Hold on to your hiney / Groovin' / Lay me like you hate me / Funky situation / Time to let the sunshine on me / Who turned you on.

	EMI America	EMI America
Dec 78. (7") *<16129>* **GROOVIN'. / TIME TO LET THE SUNSHINE ON ME**	-	
Nov 79. (7") <8027> **I WANT YOU. / LOVE OF MY LIFE**	-	
Nov 79. (lp) *(AML 3007)* *<17019>* **I WANT YOU**	-	

– I want you / Love of my life / Shameless / Live with me / Groove city / Superstar / Granny.

Dec 79. (7"/12") *(EA/+12 104)* **GROOVE CITY. / YOU ARE THE LOVE OF MY LIFE**	-	-
Jan 80. (7") <8034> **LIVE WITH ME. / GRANNY**	-	
Apr 80. (7") *(EA 107)* **SHAMELESS. / SUPERSTAR**	-	
Feb 81. (7") *(EA 120)* <8070> **DON'T UNDERESTIMATE THE POWER OF LOVE. / AIN'T GONNA GIVE YOU ANY MORE**	-	-

(12"+=) *(EA12 120)* – I want you.

Mar 81. (lp) *(AML 3016)* *<17043>* **THE RIGHT TRACK**		

– Back on the right track / If you can't beat 'em join 'em / Help me be without / I ain't gonna give you no more / Maybe this time / Don't underestimate the power of love / It's you.

	not iss.	Erva
May 81. (7") <8082> **BACK ON THE RIGHT TRACK. / IT'S YOU**	-	

	not iss.	Precision
1985. (7") *<318>* **LOVE DAGGER. / TIME TO LET THE SUNSHINE ON ME**	-	

	Motown	Motown
1986. (7") *<703>* **MUSTANG SALLY (THE BOSS IS BACK). / ('A'instrumental)**	-	
Jun 87. (7") *<1898>* **DON'T TURN AWAY. / CAN'T STOP NOW**	-	
Sep 87. (7") *<1916>* **IN THE MIDNIGHT HOUR (remix). / JUST LET HER KNOW**	-	
Oct 87. (7") *(ZB 41583)* **IN THE MIDNIGHT HOUR (remix). / ('A'original)**	**62**	-

(12"+=) *(ZT 41584)* – ('A'dub version).

Oct 87. (lp/c/cd) *(ZL/ZK/ZD 72615)* **AMERICAN SOUL MAN**		

– A thing called love / When your heart speaks / Love never let me down / A man of value / (I wanna) Make love to you / In the midnight hour / Don't turn away / Just let her know / Can't stop now. *(re-iss. Mar94 on 'Spectrum' cd/c; 550178-2/-4)*

Dec 87. (7") *<1938>* **LOVE NEVER LET ME DOWN. / JUST LET HER KNOW**	-	-

<re-iss. 1988 on 'M.C.A.'; 53407>

	New York	Catawba
Feb 88. (7"/12"; by WILSON PICKETT & JACKIE MOORE) *(NY/+T 101)* <100> **SECONDS. / SECONDS (instrumental)**	not iss.	Montage
1988. (7"; by WILSON PICKETT & JACKIE MOORE) <1218> **PRECIOUS, PRECIOUS. /**	-	-

—— In October '93, PICKETT was given a 1-year jail sentence after being found guilty of drunk driving and killing a pensioner.

– compilations, etc. –

on 'Atlantic' unless mentioned otherwise

Jun 67. (7") London; *(HLU 10146)* **BILLY THE KID. / I DON'T WANT NO PART TIME LOVE**		-
1967. (lp) Wand; <672> **GREAT HITS** (cd-iss. May93)	-	-
Feb 68. (7") *(584 150)* **IN THE MIDNIGHT HOUR. / DANGER ZONE**	-	-
1972. (7"m) *(K 10269)* **EVERYBODY NEEDS SOMEBODY TO LOVE. / DON'T FIGHT IT / FIRE AND WATER**	-	-
Feb 73. (lp) *(K 60038)* **WILSON PICKETT'S GREATEST HITS**		-
Nov 73. (7") President; *(PT 322)* **I CAN'T STOP. / DOWN TO MY LAST HEARTBREAK**		-
1974. (lp) Joy; *<JOYS 181>* **IF YOU NEED ME**		-
1974. (7"m) *(K 10389)* **IN THE MIDNIGHT HOUR. / LAND OF 1000 DANCES / FUNKY BROADWAY**		-
Jul 78. (lp) *(MID 26001)* **STAR COLLECTION**		-
Apr 80. (7"ep) *(ATM 7)* **LAND OF A 1000 DANCES / IN THE MIDNIGHT HOUR. / (2 tracks by SAM & DAVE)**		-
Jan 85. (7") Old Gold; *(OG 9497)* **IN THE MIDNIGHT HOUR. / 634-5789**		-
Apr 91. (cd/c) Knight; *(KNCD/KNMC 12062)* **THE HEART AND SOUL OF WILSON PICKETT**		-
Jun 93. (cd) <*(8122 71212-2)*> **THE VERY BEST OF WILSON PICKETT**		-
Jul 93. (d-cd) Rhino-Atlantic; <*(8122 70287-2)*> **A MAN AND A HALF: THE BEST OF WILSON PICKETT**		Apr92

– I found a love (the FALCONS) / Let me be your boy / If you need me / It's too late / I'm gonna cry (cry baby) / Come home baby / In the midnight hour / Don't fight it / I'm not tired / That's a man's way / 634-5789 (Soulsville U.S.A.) / Ninety-nine and a half (won't do) / Land of 1000 dances / Mustang Sally / Three-time loser / Everybody needs somebody to love / Soul dance number three / You can't stand alone / Funky Broadway / I'm in love / Stagger Lee / Jealous love / I've come a long way / In the midnight hour (live & burnin') / I'm a midnight mover / I found a true love / She's looking good / Hey Jude / Mini-skirt Minnie / Toe hold / Hey Joe / You keep me hangin' on / She said yes / Cole, Cooke & Redding / Sugar sugar / Get me back on time engine number 9 / Don't knock my love (part 1) / Call my name, I'll be there / Fire and water / (Your love has brought me) A mighty long way / Funk factory / Funky Broadway. *(re-iss. Aug93; same)*

Jul 92. (cd/c) Castle; *(CCS CD/MC 338)* **THE COLLECTION**		-

– Hey Jude / You keep me hangin' on / Born to be wild / Sunny / Sugar sugar / Time is on my side / In the midnight hour / Knock on wood / Barefootin' / Fire and water / Stagger Lee / Hey Joe / Mama told me not to come / Land of a 1,000 dances.

Jul 96. (cd) Javelin; *(CWNCD 2018)* **IF YOU NEED ME MORE**		

(re-iss. Jul98 on 'Prestige'; CDSGP 0392)

Jun 98. (cd) Camden; *(74321 58814-2)* **TAKE YOUR PLEASURE WHERE YOU FIND IT (THE BEST OF THE R.C.A. YEARS)**	-	-

---

PIGBAG (dig out; Great Alt & Indie . . .)

PiL (see under ⇒ PUBLIC IMAGE LTD.)

PINK FAIRIES (dig out; 4th edition & Great Metal . . .)

PINK FLOYD

Formed: London, England . . . 1965 initially as The ABDABS by ROGER WATERS, RICHARD WRIGHT and NICK MASON, (with others; CLIVE METCALFE – bass, KEITH NOBLE and JULIETTE GALE on vocals). The last three were dismissed, when the band enlisted SYD BARRETT and adopted the moniker PINK FLOYD (the name taken from bluesmen PINK ANDERSON and FLOYD COUNCIL). In March '66, they secured a residency at the Marquee Club, where their Sunday afternoon gigs were described as "spontaneous underground". Having played the UFO club late in 1966, they were subsequently signed to EMI's 'Columbia' records by their new management team of Peter Jenner and Andrew King. PINK FLOYD's March '67 debut outing, 'ARNOLD LAYNE' (about a transvestite washing-line thief), surprisingly escaped a BBC ban. One of the first missives from the psychedelic underground to reach the Top 20, it was characterised by SYD's whimsically affected vocals. On the 29th of April, they were top of the bill at Alexandria Palace's 14-hour Technicolour Dream, one of the psychedelic era's most infamous events. Their follow-up, 'SEE EMILY PLAY' (originally titled 'GAMES FOR MAY'), hit the Top 10, preceding their classic debut album, 'THE PIPER AT THE GATES OF DAWN' (a pioneering work in the sense that it contained no singles). The collection dominated by BARRETT's eccentric songwriting, it featured the cosmic 'ASTRONOMY DOMINE' alongside the acid-fuelled space-rock of 'INTERSTELLAR OVERDRIVE'. These were contrasted with idiosyncratic ramblings like 'BIKE', 'MATILDA MOTHER' and 'SCARECROW'. Their third 45, 'APPLES AND ORANGES', suprisingly flopped late in 1967, BARRETT's mental condition deteriorating rapidly due to his excessive use of LSD. He increasingly missed shows and studio sessions, PINK FLOYD bringing in DAVE GILMOUR (an old school-friend of SYD's) to compensate. In the April '68, BARRETT was asked to leave the group, retreating to a life of reclusiveness in his mother's Cambridge home. It was widely speculated that PINK FLOYD would be creatively bankrupt without SYD, especially after a further single, 'IT WOULD BE SO NICE', flopped. However, WATERS and WRIGHT took up the reins on the bulk of the songwriting duties, the band soon unleashing their second, more percussive effort, 'A SAUCERFUL OF SECRETS'. Released to ecstatic reviews, the album repeated the debut's success. The tracks, 'SET THE CONTROLS FOR THE HEART OF THE SUN', 'LET THERE BE MORE LIGHT' and SYD's harrowing farewell, 'JUGBAND BLUES' being the undisputed highlights. On the 29th of June, they played their first free concert at London's Hyde Park, alongside JETHRO TULL and ROY HARPER. They finished the year with another flop single, 'POINT ME AT THE SKY', their last in the UK for 11 years. They now concentrated on albums, releasing the under par soundtrack to the Barbet Schroeder- directed 'MORE'. It was basically an instrumental set, 'CIRRUS MINOR' being the standout track of the Top 10 album. Later in '69, they moved to EMI's new 'Harvest' label, issuing the part live, part solo, double album, 'UMMA GUMMA'. Each member contributed a piece of individually credited material, the best being WATERS' bizarre creation, 'SEVERAL SPECIES OF SMALL FURRY ANIMALS GATHERED TOGETHER IN A CAVE AND GROOVING WITH A PICT'. The live disc combined the cream of their sprawling stage improvisations, 'CAREFUL WITH THAT AXE, EUGENE' making its first album appearance. In the autumn of 1970, they released their fifth album, 'ATOM HEART MOTHER' (their first No.1), a record consisting of one patchy, experimental, side of more conventionally structured songs, while the other was a side-long collage with RON GEESIN playing on the title track. The trumpeter was to collaborate with ROGER WATERS the same year, on a soundtrack for the Roy Battersby documentary film, 'THE BODY'. On the 15th of May '71, PINK FLOYD played at the Crystal Palace Garden Party, introducing a new piece of music, 'RETURN TO THE SUN OF NOTHING', which, in six months time, became 'ECHOES'. This composition subsequently took up a whole side of their Top 3 album, 'MEDDLE', which also featured 'ONE OF THESE DAYS', 'A PILLOW OF WINDS' and 'FEARLESS' (the latter notable for its sample of the Anfield Kop). The following year, their most recent recordings were used on another Schroeder film, 'La Vallee', the album being released as 'OBSCURED BY CLOUDS', and although disappointing many die hard FLOYD fans, it cracked the Top 50 in the States. The same year, the group premiered their own music film, 'LIVE AT POMPEII', in Edinburgh. In March 1973, after its spectacular January showing at the Planetarium, the masterpiece, 'DARK SIDE OF THE MOON', was unveiled. A meticulous concept set which the band had worked on for over a year, it dealt with such taboo themes as lunacy, depression and death. These subjects were dealt with on such compelling tracks as 'US AND THEM', 'BREATHE', 'TIME' and the Top 20 US hit 'MONEY'. Scaling both the UK and US charts, the album went on to amass sales of over 10 million, incredibly residing in the chart for nearly 300 consecutive weeks. It has subsequently become regarded by many as the greatest album of all time, breathing new life into stereo headphones. They returned to London's Earl's Court for a spectacular laser show, featuring the albums' all-girl backing singers, The BLACKBERRIES. In 1974, they did a benefit gig, raising £10,000 for their recently disabled friend, ROBERT WYATT (NICK MASON also producing his 'Rock Bottom' album). In the summer of '75, their majestic Knebworth Festival performance previewed another best selling album and subsequent chart-topper, 'WISH YOU WERE HERE'. The record featured some of PINK FLOYD's most enduring songs including the space-jazz ode to SYD BARRETT, 'SHINE ON YOU CRAZY DIAMOND', the oppressive futurism of 'WELCOME TO THE MACHINE', the ROY HARPER-sung 'HAVE A CIGAR' and the wistful melancholy of the title track. It was rounded off by a reprised version of 'SHINE ON', the recording sessions blessed with a rare visit by the song's subject, SYD. Late in 1976, they let loose their 40-foot inflatable pig after a promotional session for their forthcoming 'ANIMALS' album sleeve shot. The Civil Aviation Authority was alerted to warn pilots of the danger, but it was never found. However, the Top 3 album was sighted in shops early the following year. While MASON had produced albums for The DAMNED ('Music For Pleasure') and STEVE HILLAGE ('Green'), GILMOUR and WRIGHT released their own solo albums in 1978, 'DAVID GILMOUR' and 'WET DREAM' respectively. FLOYD returned in late 1979 with a new ROGER WATERS-penned concept double, 'THE WALL', which spawned a decidly unfestive Christmas chart topper in the lugubrious 'ANOTHER BRICK IN THE WALL (PART II)'. This was another unrelentingly cynical concept piece, centering on the life of PINK, a disillusioned pop star. The next few years were spent making it into a film, directed by Alan Parker and issued in 1982 (BOB GELDOF played the main character). By the time of its release, WRIGHT had already left the band after quarrelling with WATERS. In Spring 1983, they/WATERS issued a comeback album of sorts, 'THE FINAL CUT', which again hit UK No.1. However, it was found overbearingly depressing, derided by critics as a poor "son of The Wall". The year ended with WATERS recording a solo album, 'THE PROS AND CONS OF HITCH HIKING', subsequently fighting GILMOUR and MASON in court for the use of the PINK FLOYD name. In 1984, GILMOUR

released his second solo album, 'ABOUT FACE', followed a year later by a NICK MASON / RICK FENN set, 'PROFILES'. With WATERS finally leaving in 1986, WRIGHT returned a year later to boost their ever-impressive live shows (which helped them win the court battle with WATERS). PINK FLOYD returned with an extended GILMOUR-led line-up in 1987 on the Top 3 album, 'A MOMENTARY LAPSE OF REASON', which produced a couple of minor hit singles, 'ON THE TURNING AWAY' and 'ONE SLIP'. A live double album, 'THE DELICATE SOUND OF THUNDER' (which, ironically enough, sounded more PINK FLOYD than ever before). A seven year studio hiatus was broken in 1994 with the release of chart-topper 'THE DIVISION BELL', regarded by long-time fans as a return to form. • Trivia: MASON also made a 30-minute autobiographical film, 'Life Could Be A Dream' with his other outlet, racing driving, the main feature. In 1995, GILMOUR featured on JOHN 'RABBIT' BUNDRICK's ambient album, 'Dream Jungle'.

Album rating: THE PIPER AT THE GATES OF DAWN (*9) / A SAUCERFUL OF SECRETS (*8) / MORE soundtrack (*4) / UMMA GUMMA (*7) / ATOM HEART MOTHER (*7) / RELICS collection (*7) / MEDDLE (*8) / OBSCURED BY CLOUDS (*5) / THE DARK SIDE OF THE MOON (*10) / WISH YOU WERE HERE (*10) / ANIMALS (*8) / THE WALL (*8) / A COLLECTION OF GREAT DANCE SONGS collection (*4) / THE FINAL CUT (*6) / WORKS collection (*5) / A MOMENTARY LAPSE OF REASON (*5) / THE DELICATE SOUND OF THUNDER (*7) / THE DIVISION BELL (*6) / PULSE (*4) / David Gilmour: DAVID GILMOUR (*5) / ABOUT FACE (*5) / Richard Wight: WET DREAM (*4) / Nick Mason: FICTITIOUS SPORTS (*4) / PROFILES with Rick Fenn (*4)

SYD BARRETT (b. ROGER KEITH BARRETT, 6 Jan'46) – vocals, guitar / **RICHARD WRIGHT** (b.28 Jul'45, London) – keyboards / **ROGER WATERS** (b. GEORGE WATERS, 9 Sep'44, Surrey, England) – bass, vocals, percussion / **NICK MASON** (b.27 Jan'45, Birmingham, England) – drums, percussion

	Columbia	Tower
Mar 67. (7") *(DB 8156)* <333> **ARNOLD LAYNE. / CANDY AND THE CURRANT BUN**	20	
Jun 67. (7") *(DB 8214)* <356> **SEE EMILY PLAY. / SCARECROW**	6	
Aug 67. (lp; mono/stereo) *(SX/SCX 6157)* **THE PIPER AT THE GATES OF DAWN**	6	-

– Astronomy domine / Lucifer Sam / Matilda mother / Flaming / Pow R. Toc H. / Take up thy stethoscope and walk / Interstellar overdrive / The gnome / Chapter 24 / Scarecrow / Bike. *(re-iss. May83 on 'Fame' lp/c; FA/TCFA 3065) (cd-iss. Feb87; CDP 746384-2) (re-iss. Oct94 on 'E.M.I.' cd/c; CD/TC EMD 1073) (re-iss. Aug97 on 'E.M.I.' cd/lp hit UK No.44; CD+/EMD 1110)*

Nov 67. (lp) <5093> **PINK FLOYD** (nearly as above)	-	-
Nov 67. (7") *(DB 8310)* **APPLES AND ORANGES. / PAINTBOX**	-	-
Jan 68. (7") <378> **FLAMING. / THE GNOME**		-

—— added **DAVID GILMOUR** (b. 6 Mar'44, Cambridge, England) – guitar who soon repl. BARRETT who later went solo.

Apr 68. (7") *(DB 8401)* <426> **IT WOULD BE SO NICE. / JULIA DREAM**	-	
Jun 68. (lp; mono/stereo) *(SX/SCX 6258)* **A SAUCERFUL OF SECRETS**	9	

– Let there be more light / Remember a day / Set the controls for the heart of the sun / Corporal Clegg / A saucerful of secrets / See saw / Jugband blues. *(re-iss. Aug86 on 'Fame' lp/c; FA/TCFA 3163) (cd-iss. Feb87; CDP 746383-2) (re-iss. Jul94 on 'E.M.I.' cd/c; CD/TC EMD 1063)*

Jul 68. (7") <440> **LET THERE BE MORE LIGHT. / REMEMBER A DAY**		-
Dec 68. (7") *(DB 8511)* **POINT ME AT THE SKY. / CAREFUL WITH THAT AXE, EUGENE**	-	-
Jul 69. (lp/c) *(SCX/TCSCX 6346)* **MORE (soundtrack)**	9	-

– Cirrus minor / The Nile song / Crying song / Up the Khyber / Green is the colour / Cymbaline / Party sequence / Main theme / Ibiza bar / More blues / Quicksilver / A Spanish piece / Dramatic theme. *(cd-iss. Apr87; CDP 746386-2) (re-iss. Sep95 on 'E.M.I.' cd/c; CD/TC EMD 1084)*

	Harvest	Harvest
Nov 69. (d-lp)(d-c) *(SHDW 1-2)(TC2SHWD 4501)* <388> **UMMA GUMMA** (live */ others solo)	5	74

– Astronomy domine * / Careful with that axe, Eugene * / Set the control for the heart of the sun * / A saucerful of secrets * / RICHARD WRIGHT:- Sysyphus (parts 1-4) / ROGER WATERS:- Grantchester Meadows / Several species of small furry animals gathered together in a cave and grooving with a pict / DAVID GILMOUR: – The narrow way (parts 1-3) / NICK MASON:- The Grand Vizier's garden party – part 1; Entrance – part 2; Entertainment / part 3; Exit. *(d-cd-iss. Mar87; CDS 746404-2) (re-iss. Oct94 on 'E.M.I.' d-cd/d-c; CD/TC EMD 1074)*

Oct 70. (lp/c) *(SHVL/TCSHVL 781)* <382> **ATOM HEART MOTHER**	1	55

– Atom heart mother; (a) Father's shout – (b) Breast milky – (c) Mother fore – (d) Funky dung – (e) Mind your throats please – (f) Remergence / If / Summer '68 / Fat old Sun / Alan's psychedlic breakfast / Rise and shine / Sunny side up / Morning glory. *(cd-iss. Mar87; CDP 746381-2) (re-iss. Oct94 on 'E.M.I.' cd/c; CD/TC EMD 1072)*
(above featured **RON GEESIN** – horns, co-writer)

Nov 71. (lp/c) *(SHVL/TCSHVL 795)* <832> **MEDDLE**	3	70

– One of these days / A pillow of winds / Fearless (interpolating 'You'll never walk alone') / San Tropez / Seamus / Echoes. *(re-iss. Nov83 on 'Fame' lp/c; ATAK/TCATAK 35) (cd-iss. Aug84; CDP 746034-2) (re-iss. cd Apr89 on 'Mobile Fidelity'; UDCD 518) (re-iss. Aug94 on 'E.M.I.' cd/c; CD/TC EMD 1061)*

Dec 71. (7") <3240> **ONE OF THESE DAYS. / FEARLESS**	-	-
Jun 72. (lp/c) *(SHVL/TCSHVL 4020)* <11078> **OBSCURED BY CLOUDS**	6	46

– Obscured by clouds / When you're in / Burning bridges / The gold it's in the . . . / Wots . . . uh the deal / Mudmen / Childhood's end / Free four / Stay / Absolute curtains. *(cd-iss. Apr87; CDP 746385-2) (re-iss. Sep95 on 'E.M.I.' cd/c; CD/TC EMD 1083)*

Jul 72. (7") <3391> **FREE FOUR. / STAY**	-	
Mar 73. (lp/c) *(SHVL/TCSHVL 804)* <11163> **THE DARK SIDE OF THE MOON**	2	1

– Speak to me / Breathe / On the run / Time / The great gig in the sky / Money / Us and them / Any colour you like / Brain damage / Eclipse. *(cd-iss. Aug84; CDP 746001-2) (re-iss. cd.Mar93; same); hit UK No.4) (re-iss. Jul94 on 'E.M.I.' cd/c; CD/TC EMD 1064) (re-iss. Feb97 on 'E.M.I.'; LPCENT 11)*

May 73. (7") <3609> **MONEY. / ANY COLOUR YOU LIKE**	-	13

	Harvest	Columbia
Oct 73. (7") <3832> **US AND THEM. / TIME**	-	

Sep 75. (lp/c) *(SHVL/TCSHVL 814)* <33453> **WISH YOU WERE HERE** [1] [1]
– Shine on you crazy diamond (parts 1-5) / Welcome to the machine / Have a cigar / Wish you were here / Shine on you crazy diamond (parts 6-9). *(cd-iss. Aug84; CDP 746035-2) (re-iss. Jul94 on 'E.M.I.' cd/c; CD/TC EMD 1062)*

Oct 75. (7") <10248> **HAVE A CIGAR. / SHINE ON YOU CRAZY DIAMOND (excerpt)** [-] [ ]

Jan 77. (lp/quad-lp/c) *(SHVL/Q4SHVL/TCSHVL 815)* <34474> **ANIMALS** [2] [3] Feb77
– Pigs on the wing (part 1) / Dogs / Pigs (three different ones) / Sheep / Pigs on the wing (part 2). *(cd-iss. Jul86; CDP 746128-2) (re-iss. Jul94 on 'E.M.I.' cd/c; CD/TC EMD 1060)*

Nov 79. (7") *(HAR 5194)* <11187> **ANOTHER BRICK IN THE WALL (PART 2). / ONE OF MY TURNS** [1] [1] Jan80

Dec 79. (d-lp/d-c) *(SHWD/TC2SHWD 411)* <36183> **THE WALL** [3] [1]
– In the flesh / The thin ice / The happiest days of our lives / Another brick in the wall (part 2) / Mother / Goodbye blue sky / Empty spaces / Young lust / One of my turns / Don't leave me now / Another brick in the wall (part 3) / Goodbye cruel world / Hey you / Is there anybody out there? / Nobody home / Vera / Comfortably numb / The show must go on / Run like hell / Waiting for the worms / Stop / The trial / Outside the wall. *(d-cd-iss. Sep84; CDS 746036-2) (re-iss. UK & US Jul90;) (re-iss. Oct94 on 'E.M.I.' cd/c; CD/TC EMD 1071)*

Apr 80. (7") <11265> **RUN LIKE HELL. / DON'T LEAVE ME NOW** [-] [53]
Jun 80. (7") <11311> **COMFORTABLY NUMB. / HEY YOU** [-] [ ]
Jun 82. (7") <03118> **ONE OF MY TURNS. / ANOTHER BRICK IN THE WALL (part 2)** [-] [ ]
Jul 82. (d-lp) **SOUNDTRACK FROM THE FILM 'THE WALL'**
– (tracks from above + new singles)
Aug 82. (7") *(HAR 5222)* <01342> **WHEN THE TIGERS BROKE FREE. / BRING THE BOYS BACK HOME** [39] [ ]

—— Now just main trio WATERS, GILMOUR, MASON.(WRIGHT left to form ZEE) guests on lp were **ANDY BROWN** – organ, **RAY COOPER** – perc., **MICHAEL KAMEN** – piano, **RALPH RAVENSCROFT** – saxophone.

Mar 83. (lp/c) *(SHPF/TCSHPF 1983)* <38243> **THE FINAL CUT** [1] [6]
– The post war dream / Your possible pasts / One of the few / The hero's return / The gunners dream / Paranoid eyes / Get your filthy hands off my desert / The Fletcher memorial home / Southampton dock / The final cut / Not now John / Two suns in the sunset. *(cd-iss. Jul86; CDP 746129-2) (re-iss. Oct94 on 'E.M.I.' cd/c; CD/TC EMD 1070)*

May 83. (7") *(HAR 5224)* <03905> **NOT NOW JOHN. / THE HERO'S RETURN (pts.1 & 2)** [30] [ ]
(12"+=) *(12HAR 5224)* – ('A'version).

—— **MASON** and **GILMOUR** recruited new members below to replace WATERS who went solo. **TIM RENWICK** – guitar (ex-SUTHERLAND BROTHERS & QUIVER, ex-TV SMITH) / **GUY PRATT** – bass (ex-KILLING JOKE, ex-ICEHOUSE) / **SCOTT PAGE** – saxophone / **RICK WRIGHT** – keyboards also returned p/t.

	E.M.I.	Columbia

Sep 87. (lp/c/cd) *(EMD/TCEMD/CDEMD 1003)* <40599> **A MOMENTARY LAPSE OF REASON** [3] [3]
– Signs of life / Learning to fly / The dogs of war / One slip / On the turning away / Yet another movie / Round and around / A new machine (part 1) / Terminal frost / A new machine (part 2) / Sorrow.

Sep 87. (12"pink-ep) *(EMP 26)* <07363> **LEARNING TO FLY (edit) / ONE SLIP (edit). / TERMINAL FROST (lp version)** [ ] [70]
(cd-ep+=) *(CDEM 26)* – Terminal frost (DYOL version).

Dec 87. (7"/7"pink) *(EM/+P 34)* <07660> **ON THE TURNING AWAY. / RUN LIKE HELL (live)** [55] [ ]
(12"+=/cd-s+=) *(12/CD EM 34)* – ('A'live).

Jun 88. (7"/7"pink) *(EM/+G 52)* **ONE SLIP. / TERMINAL FROST** [50] [ ]
(12"+=/12"w-poster+=)(cd-s+=) *(12EM/+P 52)(CDEM 52)* – Dogs of war (live).

Nov 88. (d-lp/d-c/d-cd) *(EQ/TCEQ/CDEQ 5009)* <44484> **THE DELICATE SOUND OF THUNDER (live)** [11] [11]
– Shine on you crazy diamond / Learning to fly / Yet another movie / Round and around / Sorrow / The dogs of war / On the turning away / One of these days / Time / Wish you were here / Us and them * / Money / Another brick in the wall (part 2) / Comfortably numb / Run like hell. *(d-cd+= *)*

—— with **GILMOUR, MASON + WRIGHT** plus **GUY PRATT / TIM RENWICK / BOB EZRIN** – keyboards, percussion / **DICK PARRY** – tenor sax / **GARY WALLIS** – percussion / **JON CARIN** – programming + add.keyboards / + backing vocalists

Apr 94. (cd/c/lp) *(CD/TC+/EMD 1055)* <64200> **THE DIVISION BELL** [1] [1]
– Cluster one / What do you want from me / Poles apart / Marooned / A great day for freedom / Wearing the inside out / Take it back / Coming back to life / Keep talking / Lost for words / High hopes.

May 94. (c-s/7"colrd) *(TC+/EMS 309)* <77493> **TAKE IT BACK. / ASTRONOMY DOMINE (live)** [23] [73]
(cd-s+=) *(CDEMS 309)* – ('A'mix).

Oct 94. (c-s/7") *(TC+/EMS 342)* **HIGH HOPES. / KEEP TALKING** [26] [ ]
(12"+=/cd-s+=) *(12/CD EMS 342)* – One of these days.

Jun 95. (d-cd/d-c/q-lp)(video) *(CD/TC+EMD 1078/MVD 4914363)* <67065> **PULSE (live)** [1] [1]
– Shine on you crazy diamond / Astronomy domine / What do you want from me / Learning to fly / Keep talking / Coming back to life / Hey you / A great day for freedom / Sorrow / High hopes / Another brick in the wall (part 2) / One of these days *[not on cd]* / Speak to me / Breathe / On the run / Time / The great gig in the sky / Money / Us and them / Any colour you like / Brain damage / Eclipse / Wish you were here / Comfortably numb / Run like hell.

– compilations, etc. –

May 71. (lp) *(Starline; SRS 5071)* / *Harvest;* <759> **RELICS** [32] [ ]
– Arnold Layne / Interstellar overdrive / See Emily play / Remember a day / Paintbox / Julia dream / Careful with that axe, Eugene / Cirrus minor / The Nile song / Biding my time / Bike. *(re-iss. Oct78 on 'Music For Pleasure' lp/c; MFP/TCMFP 50397)*

Jan 74. (d-lp)(d-c) *Harvest;* *(SHDW 403)(TC2EXE 1013)* <11257> **A NICE PAIR** [21] [36] Dec73
– (THE PIPER AT THE GATES OF DAWN / A SAUCERFUL OF SECRETS)

Dec 79. (11xlp-box) *Harvest;* *(PF 11)* **THE FIRST XI (67-77)**

Nov 81. (lp/c) *Harvest;* *(SHVL/TCSHVL 822)* <37680> **A COLLECTION OF GREAT DANCE SONGS** (remixes) [37] [31]

– One of these days / Money / Another brick in the wall (part 2) / Wish you were here / Shine on you crazy diamond / Sheep. *(re-iss. 1985 on 'Fame' lp/c; ATAK/TCATAK 31) (cd-iss. Nov88; CDP 790732-2)*

Nov 81. (7"w-drawn) *Harvest;* *(HAR 5217)* **MONEY. / LET THERE BE MORE LIGHT** [-] [-]

Jun 83. (lp) *Capitol;* <12276> **WORKS (68-73)** [-] [68]

Nov 91. (12"/cd-s) *See For Miles;* *(SEA/+CD 4)* **TONITE LET'S ALL MAKE LOVE IN LONDON** [ ] [ ]

Nov 92. (9xcd-box) *E.M.I.;* *(PFBOX 1)* **SHINE ON** [ ] [ ]
– (A SAUCERFUL OF SECRETS – MOMENTARY LAPSE . . . + rare singles)

Nov 93. (cd) *See For Miles; (SFM 2)* **TONITE LET'S ALL MAKE LOVE IN LONDON . . . PLUS** [ ] [ ]
– Interstellar overdrive / Nick's boogie / (interviews with David Hockney & Lee Marvin).

Nov 95. (cd) *See For Miles; (SFMCD 3)* **LONDON '66-'67** [ ] [-]
– Interstellar overdrive / Nick's boogie.

DAVID GILMOUR

solo with **MICK WEAVER** – keyboards / **RICK WILLIS** – bass / **JOHN WILLIE WILSON** – drums

	Harvest	Columbia

Jun 78. (lp/c) *(SHVL/TCSHVL 817)* <35388> **DAVID GILMOUR** [17] [29]
– Mihalis / There's no way out of it / Cry from the street / So far away / Short and sweet / Raise my rent / No way / Deafinitely / I can't breathe anymore. *(re-iss. 1983 on 'Fame' lp/c; FA/TCFA 4130791)*

Jun 78. (7") *(HAR 5167)* <10803> **THERE'S NO WAY OUT OF IT. / DEAFINATELY** [ ] [ ]

—— Now with various sessioners incl.STEVE WINWOOD, JEFF PORCARO & JON LORD

Feb 84. (7"/ext.12") *(HAR/12HAR 5226)* <04378> **BLUE LIGHT. / CRUISE** [ ] [62]

Mar 84. (lp/c)(cd) *(SHSP 24-0079-1/-4)(CDP 746031-2)* <39296> **ABOUT FACE** [21] [32]
– Until we sleep / Murder / Love on the air / Blue light / Out of the blue / All lovers are deranged / You know I'm right / Cruise / Let's get metaphysical / Near the end. *(re-iss. Mar87 on 'Fame' lp/c; FA/TCFA 3171)*

May 84. (7"/7"pic-d) *(HAR/+P 5229)* **LOVE ON THE AIR. / LET'S GET METAPHYSICAL** [ ] [ ]

RICHARD WRIGHT

solo with **SNOWY WHITE** – guitar / **MEL COLLINS** – saxophone / **LARRY STEELE** – bass / **REG ISADORE** – drums

	Harvest	Columbia

Sep 78. (lp/c) *(SHVL/TCSHVL 818)* **WET DREAM** [ ] [ ]
– Medterranean c / Against the odds / Cat cruise / Summer elegy / Waves / Holiday / Mad Yannis dance / Drop in from the top / Pink's song / Funky deux.

—— In 1984, he formed ZEE duo, and returned to FLOYD later in the 80's.

with **DAVE HARRIS** – guitar, vocals, keyboards, synth (ex-FASHION)

Apr 84. (7"/ext.12"; by ZEE) *(HAR/12HAR 5227)* **CONFUSION. / EYES OF A GYPSY** [ ] [ ]

Apr 84. (lp/c; by ZEE) *(SHSP 240101/-1/-4)* **IDENTITY** [ ] [ ]
– Confusion / Voices / Private person / Strange rhythm / Cuts like a diamond / By touching / How do you do it / Seems we are dreaming.

	E.M.I.	Columbia

Oct 96. (cd/c) *(CD/TC+/EMD 1098)* **BROKEN CHINA** [61] [ ]
– Breaking water / Night of a thousand furry toys / Hidden fear / Runaway / Underground / Satellite / Woman of custom / Interlude / Black cloud / Far from the harbour wall / Drowning / Reaching for the rail / Blue room in Venice / Sweet July / Along the shoreline / Breakthrough.

NICK MASON

solo with **CARLA BLEY** and **ROBERT WYATT**

	Harvest	Columbia

May 81. (lp/c) *(SHSP/TCSHSP 4116)* <37307> **FICTITIOUS SPORTS** [ ] [ ]
– Can't get my motor to start / I was wrong / Siam / Hot river / Boo to you too / Do ya / Wervin' / I'm a mineralist.

Aug 85. (lp; by NICK MASON & RICK FENN) *(MAF 1)* <40142> **PROFILES** [ ] [ ]
– Malta / Lie for a lie / Rhoda / Profiles (part 1 & 2) / Israel / And the address / Mumbo jumbo / Zip code / Black ice / At the end of the day / Profiles (part 3).

Sep 85. (7"; by NICK MASON & RICK FENN) *(HAR 5238)* **LIE FOR A LIE. / AND THE ADDRESS** [ ] [ ]
(12"+=) *(12HAR 5238)* – Mumbo jumbo.

PIXIES

Formed: Boston, Massachusetts, USA . . . 1986 by L.A. born frontman and self-confessed UFO freak, BLACK FRANCIS (real name, deep breath . . . CHARLES MICHAEL KITRIDGE THOMPSON IV) along with guitarist JOEY SANTIAGO. Famously placing a newspaper ad requesting musicians with a penchant for PETER, PAUL AND MARY and HUSKER DU, the only taker was KIM DEAL who subsequently brought in drummer DAVID LOVERING. Originally trading under the moniker PIXIES IN PANOPLY, the band soon trimmed this down to the punchier PIXIES and began kicking up a storm on the Boston music scene with their spiky, angular noise-pop (that's two thirds noise, one third pop) and wilfully cryptic lyrics. Along with fellow Bostonians THROWING MUSES, the band were signed to '4 a.d.' by a suitably impressed Ivo Watts-Russell, the label releasing The PIXIES' debut 'COME ON PILGRIM' in late '87. Stunningly different, the record galvanised the early PIXIES sound, a bizarre hybrid of manic, strangulated vocals (often sung in Spanish), searing melodic noise and schizophrenic, neo-latin rhythms.

The album drew an early core of believers but it wasn't until the release of 'SURFER ROSA' (1988) that the band were hailed as the saviours of indie rock. Taking the formula of the debut to its brain splintering conclusion, the likes of 'BONE MACHINE', the incendiary 'SOMETHING AGAINST YOU' and careering 'BROKEN FACE' were utterly compelling in their blistering intensity. The sheer unhinged abandon with which BLACK FRANCIS threw himself into these songs has to be heard to be believed. You begin to fear that the man really has lost it when he asks 'WHERE IS MY MIND' in his inimitable melancholy howl. DEAL was equally affecting on the gorgeous 'GIGANTIC', the track building from a metaphorical whisper to a scream. Truly essential, 'SURFER ROSA' remains one of the most pivotal alternative rock records of the last ten years. Following their first headline UK tour, the band hooked up with producer Gil Norton for the 'DOOLITTLE' (1989) album. Previewed by the haunting 'MONKEY GONE TO HEAVEN', the record showcased a cleaner, more pop-friendly sound, most notably on (then) upcoming single, 'HERE COMES YOUR MAN'. Swoonfully poptastic, this song was guaranteed to have even the most miserable SMITHS fan grinning ear to ear, putting the toss that passes for modern 'indie-pop' to eternal shame. The demented 'DEBASER' was another highlight, becoming a dependable fixture at indie discos for oh, aeons. As well as a mammoth world tour, DEAL found time for her side project, The BREEDERS. A collaboration with the delectable TANYA DONELLY (ex-THROWING MUSES), the pair released the acclaimed 'POD' album in 1990. Later that year came 'BOSSANOVA', another breathtaking collection that had the music press in rapture. Lyrically, BLACK was in his element, losing himself in science fiction fantasy while the band raged and charmed in equal measure. The album reached No.3 in the UK charts and The PIXIES could apparently do no wrong, consolidating their position as one of the biggest American acts in Europe. Yet the critics turned on them with the release of 'TROMPE LE MONDE' (1991), in keeping with the times a decidedly grungier affair. Accusations of "Heavy Metal" were way off the mark. In reality, the record was still chokka with stellar tunes, you just had to dig deeper to find them. 'PLANET OF SOUND', 'SPACE (I BELIEVE IN)' and 'MOTORWAY TO ROSWELL' were all quintessential PIXIES, FRANCIS as endearingly fascinated as ever with the mysteries of the universe. Sadly, the singer was soon to turn his obsession into a solo venture, The PIXIES gone almost as quickly as they had arrived, leaving behind a brief but rich sonic legacy. With FRANCIS changing his name to the rather dull FRANK BLACK, he went on to release a moderately successful eponymous solo debut in 1993 and a wryly titled follow-up, 'TEENAGER OF THE YEAR' (1994), DEAL going on to make a further album with The BREEDERS. Inevitably, none of these projects approached the deranged genius of The PIXIES (Rock will never see their like again). The frontman continued to surface periodically and three albums, 'THE CULT OF RAY' (1996), 'FRANK BLACK AND THE CATHOLICS' (1998) and 'PISTOLLERO' (1999), have all met with diminishing fanbase response. • **Songwriters:** BLACK FRANCIS penned except; WINTERLONG + I'VE BEEN WAITING FOR YOU (Neil Young) / EVIL HEARTED YOU (Yardbirds) / HEAD ON (Jesus & Mary Chain) / CECILIA ANN (Surftones) / BORN IN CHICAGO (Paul Butterfield's Blues Band) / I CAN'T FORGET (Leonard Cohen). FRANK BLACK solo:- JUST A LITTLE (Beau Brummels) / RE-MAKE, RE-MODEL (Roxy Music) / HANG ON TO YOUR EGO (Beach Boys).

Album rating: COME ON PILGRIM mini (*7) / SURFER ROSA (*10) / DOOLITTLE (*9) / BOSSANOVA (*8) / TROMPE LE MONDE (*7) / DEATH TO THE PIXIES compilation (*8) / Frank Black: FRANK BLACK (*8) / TEENAGER OF THE YEAR (*8) / THE CULT OF RAY (*5) / FRANK BLACK & THE CATHOLICS (*5) / PISTOLLERO (*5)

BLACK FRANCIS (b. CHARLES MICHAEL KITRIDGE THOMPSON IV, 1965, Long Beach, Calif.) – vocals, guitar / **JOEY SANTIAGO** (b.10 Jun'65, Manila, Philippines) – lead guitar / **KIM DEAL** (Mrs.JOHN MURPHY) (b.10 Jun'61, Dayton, Ohio) – bass, vocals / **DAVE LOVERING** (b. 6 Dec'61) – drums

		4.a.d.	Elektra
Oct 87.	(m-lp) *(MAD 709)* <61296> **COME ON PILGRIM**		

– Caribou / Vamos / Islade encounter / Ed is dead / The holiday song / Nimrod's son / I've been tried / Levitate me.

Mar 88.	(lp/c)(cd) *(CAD/+C 803)(CAD 803CD)* <61295> **SURFER ROSA**		

– Bone machine / Break my body / Something against you / Broken face / Gigantic / River Euphrates / Where is my mind? / Cactus / Tony's theme / Oh my golly! / Vamos / I'm amazed / Brick is red. *(cd+=)* – COME ON PILGRIM (m-lp)

Aug 88.	(12"ep/cd-ep) *(BAD 805/+CD)* **GIGANTIC. / RIVER EUPHRATES. / VAMOS. / IN HEAVEN (LADY IN THE RADIATOR SONG)**		-

Mar 89.	(7") *(AD 904)* **MONKEY GONE TO HEAVEN. / MANTA RAY**	60	

(12"+=/cd-s+=) *(BAD 904/+CD)* – Weird at my school / Dancing the manta ray.

Apr 89.	(lp/c)(cd) *(CAD/+C 905)(CAD 905CD)* <60856> **DOOLITTLE**	8	98

– Debaser / Tame / Wave of mutilation / I bleed / There goes my gun / Here comes your man / Dead / Monkey gone to Heaven / La la love you / Mr. Grieves / Crackity Jones / #13 baby / Silver / Hey / Gouge away.

Jun 89.	(7") *(AD 909)* <66694> **HERE COMES YOUR MAN. / INTO THE WHITE**	54	

(12"+=/cd-s+=) *(BAD 909/+CD)* – Wave of mutilation (UK surf) / Bailey's walk.

——— KIM DEAL was also part of amalgamation The BREEDERS

Jul 90.	(7"/c-s) *(AD/+C 0009)* <66616> **VELOURIA. / I'VE BEEN WAITING FOR YOU**	28	

(12"+=/cd-s+=) *(BAD 0009/+CD)* – Make believe / The thing.

Aug 90.	(cd)(lp/c) *(CAD 0010CD)(CAD/+C 0010)* <60963> **BOSSANOVA**	3	70

– Cecilia Ann / Rock music / Velouria / Allison / Is she weird / Ana / All over the world / Dig for fire / Down to the wall / The happening / Blown away / Hang wire / Stormy weather / Havalina.

Oct 90.	(7"/c-s) *(AD/+C 0014)* <66596> **DIG FOR FIRE. / VELVETY (instrumental)**	62	

(12"+=/cd-s+=) *(BAD 0014/+CD)* – Winterlong / Santo.

May 91.	(7") *(AD 1008)* **PLANET OF SOUND. / BUILD HIGH**	27	

(c-s+=)(12"+=/cd-s+=) *(BADC 1008)(BAD 1008/+CD)* – Evil hearted you / Theme from Narc.

Sep 91.	(cd)(lp/c) *(CAD 1014CD)(CAD/+C 1014)* <61118> **TROMPE LE MONDE**	7	92

– Trompe de Monde / Planet of sound / Alec Eiffel / The sad punk / Head on / U-mass / Palace of the brine / Letter to Memphis / Bird dream Of the Olympus mons / Space (I believe in) / Subbacultcha / Distance equals rate times time / Lovely day / Motorway to Roswell / The Navajo know.

Nov 91.	(12"ep) **ALEC EIFFEL / MOTORWAY TO ROSWELL. / PLANET OF SOUND (live) / TAME (live)**		-

Feb 92.	(12"ep) <66444> **ALEC EIFFEL / LETTER TO MEMPHIS (instrumental). / BUILD LIFE / EVIL HEARTED YOU**	-	

——— Disbanded late in '92, with BLACK FRANCIS going solo as FRANK BLACK.

– compilations, etc. –

on '4 a.d.' / 'Elektra' unless otherwise mentioned

Sep 97.	(7") *(AD 7010)* **DEBASER (demo). / #13 BABY**	23	

(cd-s) *(BAD 7010CD)* – ('A'studio) / Bone machine / Gigantic / Isla de Encanta.
(cd-s) *(BADD 7010CD)* – ('A'live) / Holiday song (live) / Cactus (live) / Nimrod's son (live).

Oct 97.	(d-cd/d-c) *(DAD/+C 7011)* / <62118> **DEATH TO THE PIXIES**	28	

– Cecilia Ann / Planet of sound / Tame / Here comes your man / Debaser / Wave of mutilation / Dig for fire / Caribou / Holiday song / Nimrod's son / U mass / Bone machine / Gigantic / Where is my mind / Velouria / Gouge away / Monkey gone to Heaven / Debaser / Rock music / Isla De Encanta / Hangfire / Dead / Into the white / Monkey gone to Heaven / Gouge away / Gouge away / Here comes your man / Alidon / Hey / Gigantic / Crackity Jones / Something against you / Tame / Wave of mutilation / Where is my mind / Ed is dead / Vamos / Tony's theme. *(de-luxe version hit No.20 q-lp/d-cd; DADD 7011/+CD)*

Jul 98.	(cd) *(GAD 8013)* <62185> **PIXIES AT THE BBC (live)**	45	

– Wild honey pie / There goes my gun / Dead / Subbacultcha / Manta Ray / Is she weird? / Ana / Down to the well / Wave of mutilation / Letter to Memphis / Levitate me / Caribou / Monkey gone to Heaven / Hey / In Heaven (lady in the radiator song).

FRANK BLACK

——— with **ERIC DREW FELDMAN** – bass, keyboards, synthetics (ex-CAPTAIN BEEFHEART) / **NICK VINCENT** – drums, percussion / + extra guitars **SANTIAGO, MORRIS TEPPER + DAVID SARDY**

		4 a.d.	Elektra
Mar 93.	(lp/cd)(c) *(CAD 3004/+CD)(CADC 3004)* <61467> **FRANK BLACK**	9	

– Los Angeles / I heard Ramona sing / Hang on to your ego / Fu Manchu / Places named after numbers / Czar / Old black dawning / Ten percenter / Brackish boy / Two spaces / Tossed (instrumental version) / Parry the wind high, low / Adda Lee / Every time I go around here / Don't ya rile 'em. *(cd re-iss. Jul98; GAD 3004CD)*

Apr 93.	(7") *(AD 3005)* <8782-2> **HANG ON TO YOUR EGO. / THE BALLAD OF JOHNNY HORTON**		

(cd-s+=) *(BAD 3005CD)* – Surf epic.

——— same trio augmented by SANTIAGO, TEPPER + LYLE WORKMAN – guitar

May 94.	(7") *(AD 4007)* **HEADACHE. / ('A'mix)**	53	-

(10"/cd-s) *(BADD 4007/+CD)* – ('A'side) / Men in black / At the end of the world / Oddball.
(cd-s) *(BAD 4007CD)* – ('A'side) / Hate me / This is where I belong / Amnesia.

May 94.	(d-lp/cd)(c) *(DAD 4009/+CD)(DADC 4009)* <61618> **TEENAGER OF THE YEAR**	21	

– Whatever happened to Pong? / Thalassocracy / (I want to live on an) Abstract plain / Calistan / The vanishing spies / Speedy Marie / Headache / Sir Rockaby / Freedom rock / Two reelers / Fiddle riddle / Ole Mulholland / Fazer eyes / I could stay here forever / The hostess with the mostest / Superabound / Big red / Space is gonna do me good / White noise maker / Pure denizen of the citizens band / Bad, wicked world / Pie in the sky. *(re-iss. Jul98; GAD 4009CD)*

——— FRANK BLACK had earlier in the year teamed up with ex-SEX PISTOL; GLEN MATLOCK to form tribute band FRANK BLACK & THE STAX PISTOLS

		Noise Annoys	not iss.
Dec 95.	(cd/d-lp) *(ANAN CD/V 7)* **THE BLACK SESSIONS (live in Paris)**		-

(re-iss. Oct97; same)

——— now w/ **LYLE WORKMAN** – lead guitar / **DAVID McCAFFREY** – bass / **SCOTT BOUTIER** – drums

		Epic	Warners
Dec 95.	(ltd-7") *(662 671-7)* **THE MARXIST. / BETTER THINGS**		-
Jan 96.	(7") *(662 786-7)* **MEN IN BLACK. / JUST A LITTLE**	37	-

(cd-s+=) *(662 786-2)* – Re-make, re-model.
(cd-s) *(662 786-5)* – ('A'side) / You never heard of me / Pray a little faster / Announcement.

Jan 96.	(cd/c/lp) *(481 647-2/-4/-1)* <43070> **THE CULT OF RAY**	39	

– The Marxist / Men in black / Punk rock city / You ain't me / Jesus was right / I don't want to hurt you (every single time) / Mosh, don't pass the guy / Kicked in the taco / Creature crawling / Adventure and the resolution / Dance war / The cult of Ray / Last stand of Shazeb Andleeb.

Jul 96.	(7") *(663 463-7)* **I DON'T WANT TO HURT YOU (EVERY SINGLE TIME). / YOU AIN'T ME (live)**	63	-

(cd-s+=) *(663 463-2)* – The Marxist / Better things.
(cd-s) *(663 463-5)* – ('A'live) / Men in black (live) / Village of the sun (live) / The last stand of Shazeb Andleeb (live).

FRANK BLACK AND THE CATHOLICS

		Play It Again Sam	SpinArt

Apr 98. (7"ep/cd-ep) *(BIAS 347 7/CD)* **ALL MY GHOSTS / LIVING ON SOUL / HUMBOULDT COUNTY MASSACRE / CHANGING OF THE GUARDS**   □   –

May 98. (cd/c/lp) *(BIAS 370 CD/MC/LP)* <SPART 67> **FRANK BLACK AND THE CATHOLICS**   61
– All my ghosts / Back to Rome / Do you feel bad about it / Dog gone / I gotta move / I need peace / King and Queen of Siam / Six sixty six / Solid gold / Steak 'n' sabre / Suffering / Man who was too loud. *(ltd-cd+=; BIAS 370CDX)* – All my ghosts / Living on soul / Humboldt county massacre / Changing of the guards.

Mar 99. (cd) *(CDBIAS 390CD)* <SPART 70> **PISTOLLERO**
– Bad harmony / I switched you / Western star / Tiny heart / You're such a wire / I loved your brain / Smoke up / Billy Radcliffe / So hard to make things out / Eighty five weeks / I think I'm starting to lose it / I want to rock and roll / Skeleton man / So bay. *(lp-iss.Nov99 on 'SpinArt'; SPART 70)*

– compilations, etc. –

Jul 95. (12"ep/cd-ep) *Strange Fruit; (SFPS/+CD 091)* **PEEL SESSION**   □   –
– Handyman / The man who was too loud / The Jacques Tati / Sister Isabel.

Nov 97. (cd-ep; with TEENAGE FANCLUB) *Strange Fruit; (SFRSCD 042)* **THE JOHN PEEL SESSION**   □   –

PIZZAMAN (see under ⇒ COOK, Norman)

PLACEBO

Formed: South London, England . . . October '94 by the cosmopolitan pair of BRIAN MOLKO and STEFAN OLSDAL, who had attended the same school in Luxembourg. They met up again in a London tube having spent time in the States and Sweden respectively. Early the following year, they recruited Swedish drummer, ROBERT SCHULTZBERG, the trio subsequently becoming joint winners of the 'In The City' Battle Of The Bands competition. Late in '95, PLACEBO shared a one-off single, 'BRUISE PRISTINE', with the band, SOUP, on 'Fierce Panda' records. After only a handful of gigs, they signed for 'Deceptive' (home of ELASTICA), leading to tours with ASH, BUSH and WHALE. A solitary single later ('COME HOME'), MOLKO and Co., hit the proverbial jackpot with a deal with Virgin/Hut subsidiary, 'Elevator'. The openly bisexual, cross-dressing MOLKO, drew comparisons with 70's glam idols like BOLAN and BOWIE, the music, however, traded in the glitter for a darker listening experience. Taking the fast lane out of the post-grunge pile-up, they fused elements of avant-garde rock and cerebral metal, MOLKO's paint-stripping shrill drawing comparisons with Rush's GEDDY LEE and DAVID SURKAMP of the more obscure Pavlov's Dog. Their eponymous debut album was released in mid-'96 to a fawning music press, metal-mag Kerrang's strong support helping the record dent the UK Top 40. Hit singles 'TEENAGE ANGST' and the Top 5 'NANCY BOY', helped regenerate sales of a collection which many hailed as one of the year's best. In addition to the more incendiary tracks, the album also contained such hauntingly reflective songs as 'LADY OF THE FLOWERS' and 'HANG ON TO YOUR IQ'. PLACEBO – with STEVE HEWITT replacing SCHULTZBERG – were back with a bang (so to speak!) in the Autumn of '98, two blistering UK Top 5 singles in quick succession, 'PURE MORNING' and 'YOU DON'T CARE ABOUT US', premiering their equally superb sophomore set, 'WITHOUT YOU I'M NOTHING'. 'EVERY YOU EVERY ME' and collaborative title track with MOLKO's idol BOWIE kept the band in high profile the following year. • **Songwriters:** Group, except BIGMOUTH STRIKES AGAIN (Smiths) / 20TH CENTURY BOY (T.Rex).

Album rating: PLACEBO (*9) / WITHOUT YOU I'M NOTHING (*8)

BRIAN MOLKO (b.1972) – vocals, guitars, bass / **STEFAN OLSDAL** – bass, guitars, keyboards / **ROBERT SCHULTZBERG** – drums, percussion, didgeridoo

		Fierce Panda	not iss.

Nov 95. (7") *(NING 13)* **BRUISE PRISTINE. / (Soup: 'Meltdown')**   □   –

		Deceptive	not iss.

Feb 96. (7") *(BLUFF 024)* **COME HOME. / DROWNING BY NUMBERS**   □   –
(cd-s+=) *(BLUFF 024CD)* – Oxygen thief.

—— **STEVE HEWITT** b. Northwich, England – drums; repl. Schultzberg.

		Elevator	Caroline

Jun 96. (7") *(FLOOR 001)* **36 DEGREES. / DARK GLOBE**   □   –
(cd-s+=) *(FLOORCD 001)* – Hare Krishna.

Jun 96. (cd/c/lp) *(CD/MC/LP FLOOR 002)* <7575> **PLACEBO**   40   Jul96
– Come home / Teenage angst / Bionic / 36 degrees / Hang on to you IQ / Nancy boy / I know / Bruise pristine / Lady of the flowers / Swallow. *(re-dist.Jan97 hit UK No.5; same)*

Sep 96. (7"/cd-s) *(FLOOR/+CD 003)* **TEENAGE ANGST. / BEEN SMOKING TOO LONG / HUG BUBBLE**   30
(7"m) *(FLOORX 003)* – ('A'-V.P.R.O. radio session) / Flesh mechanic (demo) / HK farewell.

Jan 97. (7") *(FLOOR 004)* **NANCY BOY. / SLACKERBITCH**   4
(cd-s+=) *(FLOORCD 004)* – Bigmouth strikes again / Hug bubble.
(cd-s) *(FLOORCDX 004)* – ('A'side) / Eyesight to the blind / Swallow (Brad Wood mix) / Miss Moneypenny.

May 97. (cd-s/cd-s) *(FLOOR MC/CD 005)* **BRUISE PRISTINE / THEN THE CLOUDS WILL OPEN FOR ME / BRUISE PRISTINE (One Inch Punch remix)**   14   –
(cd-s) *(FLOORCDX 005)* – ('A'side) / Waiting for the sun of man / Serenity (Lionrock remix).

		Elevator	Hut

Aug 98. (cd-ep) *(FLOORCD 6)* **PURE MORNING / MARS LANDING PARTY / LEELOO**   4   –
(cd-ep) *(FLOORCDX 6)* – ('A'-lp version) / Needledick / The innocence of sleep.

Sep 98. (c-s/cd-s) *(FLOOR C/CD 7)* <95363> **YOU DON'T CARE ABOUT US / 20TH CENTURY BOY / ION**   5   –
(cd-s) *(FLOORDX 7)* – ('A'side) / ('A'-Les Rhythmes Digitales remix) / ('A'-Howie B remix).

Oct 98. (cd/c/lp) *(CDFLOOR/FLOORMC/FLOORLP 8)* <46531> **WITHOUT YOU I'M NOTHING**   7   Nov98
– Pure morning / Brick shithouse / You don't care about us / Ask for answers / Without you I'm nothing / Allergic (to thoughts of Mother Earth) / The crawl / Every you every me / My sweet prince / Summer's gone / Scared of girls / Burger queen.

Jan 99. (7") *(FLOORLH 9)* **EVERY YOU EVERY ME. / NANCY BOY (Blue Amazon remix)**   11   –
(c-s+=/cd-s+=) *(FLOORCD 9)* – ('A'-Jimmy Cauty remix).
(cd-s) *(FLOORDX 9)* – ('A'side) / ('A'-Sneaker Pimps version) / ('A'-Brothers In Rhythm remix).

Aug 99. (cd-ep; featuring DAVID BOWIE) *(FLOORCD 10)* **WITHOUT YOU I'M NOTHING / ('A'-Unkle remix) / ('A'-Americruiser remix) / ('A'-Brothers In Rhythm remix)**   –   – nochart

PLAINSONG (see under ⇒ MATTHEWS, Iain)

Robert PLANT (see under ⇒ LED ZEPPELIN)

PLASMATICS (dig out; Great Alt & Indie . . .)

PLASTIC ONO BAND (see under ⇒ LENNON, John)

P.M. (see under ⇒ EMERSON, LAKE & PALMER)

P.M. DAWN

Formed: New Jersey City, New Jersey, USA . . . 1988 by Christian brothers, the weighty ATTRELL (PRINCE BE) and the more considerably slim JARRETT CORDES (MINUTEMIX), step-sons of BUCK, a KOOL AND THE GANG member. After a flop 'ODE TO A FORGETFUL MIND' early '91, they scored a massive international hit in 1991 with 'SET ADRIFT ON MEMORY BLISS', which hit top spot in US. It sampled (more than thoroughly) SPANDAU BALLET's No.1 smash 'TRUE'. These were taken from debut album 'OF THE HEART, OF THE SOUL AND OF THE CROSS: THE UTOPIAN EXPERIENCE' (1991), which surprisingly faired better in Britain, hitting Top 10, while in America it only managed a Top 50 placing. On a daisy-age mission, like that of DE LA SOUL and The JUNGLE BROTHERS, PM DAWN fitted neatly into the hip hop/rap movement of the early 90's. In 1992, they contributed a few songs to the soundtrack of Eddie Murphy's film 'Boomerang', while PRINCE BE appeared in a TV commercial endorsing Nike trainers. Their follow-up album in the spring of '93; 'THE BLISS ALBUM?', contained a duet with BOY GEORGE; 'MORE THAN LIKELY'. PRINCE BE and MINUTE MIX changed their names to JC THE ETERNAL and THE NOCTURNAL repectively, but this didn't rectify their two and a half year absence, which led to disappointing third album 'JESUS WEPT'. • **Songwriters:** ATTRELL is main pensmith, with JARRETT contributing. Covers: NORWEGIAN WOOD (THIS BIRD HAS FLOWN) (Beatles) / sampled many including U2's 'The Fly', HUSH (Deep Purple) on 1995 return single. • **Trivia:** In 1991, they lost their attire, when British Airways mislaid their gear.

Album rating: OF THE HEART, OF THE SOUL AND OF THE CROSS: THE UTOPIAN EXPERIENCE (*7) / THE BLISS ALBUM? (*6) / JESUS WEPT (*5)

PRINCE BE (b. ATTRELL CORDES, 19 May'70) – vocals / **DJ MINUTEMIX** (b. JARRETT CORDES, 17 Jul'71) – DJ

		Gee Street	Gee Street

Jan 91. (7") **ODE TO A FORGETFUL MIND. / ?**   –   –

May 91. (7"/c-s) *(GEE/+C 32)* **A WATCHER'S POINT OF VIEW (DON'T 'CHA THINK). / TWISTED MELLOW**   36
(12"+=/cd-s+=) *(GEE T/CD 32)* – ('A'radio mix) / ('A'acappella mix).

Aug 91. (7"/c-s) *(GEE/+C 33)* <866094> **SET ADRIFT ON MEMORY BLISS. / FOR THE LOVE OF PEACE**   3   –
(12"+=/cd-s+=) *(GEE T/CD 33)* – ('A'extended).

Sep 91. (c-s,cd-s) <866094> **SET ADRIFT ON MEMORY BLISS / A WATCHER'S POINT OF VIEW (DON'T 'CHA THINK)**   –   1

Sep 91. (cd/c/lp) *(GEE D/C/A 7)* <510276> **OF THE HEART, OF THE SOUL AND OF THE CROSS: THE UTOPIAN EXPERIENCE**   8   48
– Intro / Reality used to be a friend of mine / Paper doll / To serenade a rainbow / Comatose / A watcher's point of view (don't 'cha think) / Even after I die / In the presence of mirrors / Set adrift on memory bliss / Shake / If I wuz u / On a clear day / The beautiful. *(cd+=/c+=)* – Ode to a forgetful mind (the more than words mix) / Twisted mellow / For the love of peace / Reality (US mix). *(cd re-iss. Aug98; GEE 100152-2)*

Oct 91. (7"/c-s) *(GEE/+C 35)* **PAPER DOLL / ODE TO A FORGETFUL MIND (THE MORE THAN WORDS MIX)**   49   –
(12"+=/cd-s+=) *(GEE T/CD 35)* – ('A'radio mix) / ('A'instrumental) / ('A'club).

Jan 92. (c-s,cd-s) <866374> **PAPER DOLL / AS THE LOVE OF PEACE**   –   28

Feb 92. (7"/c-s) *(GEE/+C 37)* **REALITY USED TO BE A FRIEND OF MINE (mix). / COMATOSE**   29   □
(cd-s+=) *(GEECD 37)* – Set adrift on memory bliss.
(12"+=) *(GEET 37)* – A watcher's point of view (melody mix).

—— Below from the film 'Boomerang'.

Nov 92. (7"/c-s) *(GEE/+C 39)* <24034> **I'D DIE WITHOUT YOU. / ON A CLEAR DAY**   30   3 Aug92
(cd-s+=) *(GESCD 39)* – ('A'club mix).

Mar 93. (7"/c-s) *(GEE/+C 47)* **LOOKING THROUGH PATIENT EYES. / PLASTIC**   11   -
(12"+=/cd-s+=) *(GEET/GESCD 47)* – ('A'&'B'mixes).

Mar 93. (c-s,cd-s) <862024> **LOOKING THROUGH PATIENT EYES / ('A'version)**   -   6

Mar 93. (cd/c/lp) *(GEE D/C/A 9)* <514517> **P.M. DAWN THE BLISS ALBUM . . . ? (VIBRATIONS OF LOVE AND ANGER AND THE TOLERANCE OF LIFE AND EXISTENCE)**   9   30
– Intro / When the midnight sighs / So on and so on / Plastic / The ways of the wind / To love me more / About nothing (for the love of destiny) / Norwegian wood (this bird has flown) / Beyond infinite affections / Looking through patient eyes / Filthy rich (I don't wanna be) / More than likely / The nocturnal is in the house / When it's raining cats and dogs / I'd die without you. *(re-iss. Mar96 on 'Island' cd)(c; IMCD 222)(ICM 2085) (cd re-iss. Aug98; GEE 100153-2)*

Jun 93. (7"/c-s; PM DAWN featuring BOY GEORGE) *(GEE/+C 49)* **MORE THAN LIKELY. / WHEN IT'S RAINING CATS AND DOGS**   40   -
(cd-s+=) *(GESCD 49)* – ('A'mixes).
(cd-s) *(GESCDX 49)* – ('A'-strings mix) / You, me and the electric vibe / Fly me to the Moon / Frostbite.

Jul 93. (c-s/cd-s) <862475> **THE WAYS OF THE WIND / ('A'mix)**   -   54

Nov 93. (7"/c-s) *(GEE/+C 51)* **NORWEGIAN WOOD (THIS BIRD HAS FLOWN). / TAKE CARE OF MY HEART**
(cd-s+=) *(GESCD 51)* – Looking through patient eyes / When midnight sighs.

Sep 95. (c-s) *(GEEC 63)* <4408> **DOWNTOWN VENUS / SHE DREAMS PERSISTENT MAYBES**   58   48
(cd-s+=/12"+=) *(GEET/GESCD 63)* – ('A'-Kiss my wife remix) / ('A'-I want to be with you mix).

Oct 95. (cd/c/d-lp) *(GEE CD/MC/AD 16)* <524147-2/-4> **JESUS WEPT**
– A lifetime / Puppet show / Sonchenne / Why God loves you / Sometimes I miss you so much / Once in a lifetime - 1999 / Apathy . . . superstar!? / Downtown Venus / I'll be waiting for you / Forever damaged (the 96th) / Miles from anything / 9:45 wake-up dream / My own personal gravity. *(cd re-iss. Aug98; GEE 100154-2)*

—— Late in '95, DJ JARRETT was charged with aggreveted sexual assault on his 14 year-old cousin.

Mar 96. (c-s) *(GEEC 65)* <854476> **SOMETIMES I MISS YOU SO MUCH (DEDICATED TO THE CHRIST CONSCIOUSNESS) / THE PUPPET SHOW**   58   95 Dec95
(cd-s+=) *(GESCD 65)* – Looking through patient eyes / Set adrift on memory bliss / You got me floatin'.
(cd-s) *(GECDX 65)* –

Apr 98. (c-s; PRINCE BE featuring KY-MANI) *(GEE 5001375)* <33513> **GOTTA BE . . . MOVIN' ON UP /**   90 Mar98
(12"+=/cd-s+=) *(GEE 500137-6/-3)* –

Sep 98. (c-s,cd-s) <33535> **I HAD NO RIGHT /**   -   44

Oct 98. (c-s; as PM DAWN featuring KY-MANI) *(GEE 5003945)* **GOTTA BE . . . MOVIN' ON UP /**   68   -
(12"+=/cd-s+=) *(GEE 50039-56/-33)* –

POCO

Formed: Los Angeles, California, USA . . . August '68 as POGO, by ex-BUFFALO SPRINGFIELD members RICHIE FURAY and JIM MESSINA, plus ex-BOENZEE CRYQUE pardners, RUSTY YOUNG and GEORGE GRANTHAM. RANDY MEISNER (formerly a member of The POOR) was also a brief member, subsequently departing to join RICK NELSON's STONE CANYON BAND and later The EAGLES. Early in '69, POGO signed to 'Epic', soon altering their name due to legal threats from a comic strip of the same name. Their debut album 'PICKIN' UP THE PIECES' managed a US Top 75 placing, its hippy harmonising and folk/country embellished, mellow-rock stylings laying the foundations for The EAGLES' subsequent multi-platinum flight. An eventual replacement for MEISNER was found in TIMOTHY B. SCHMIT, who, ironically, had previously lost out to the former at an earlier audition. The eponymous second set followed in summer 1970, its laidback hooks again ensnaring critics and newly converted country-rock fans alike. Something of a one-off for a genre that wasn't exactly renowned for uncompromising experimentation, the whole of the album's second side was devoted to a latin-country workout catchily titled 'EL TONTO DE NADIE REGRASA'. But it was in the free flowing, dope smoking climes of the live arena where the likes of POCO excelled and, with Heads turning to country in droves (even The GRATEFUL DEAD were mellowing out on pedal steel), the band made the US Top 30 in early '71 with the concert set, 'DELIVERIN'. Fed up with touring, MESSINA quit for a life of MOR pop mush in (KENNY) LOGGINS & MESSINA, a new guitarist found in PAUL COTTON. This line-up remained steady for a further two years, during which time the band recorded a handful of albums including the acclaimed 'A GOOD FEELIN' TO KNOW' (1973). The exhilarating title track remains one of their best-loved and most enduring moments; at their best, POCO were certainly a match for high flying contemporaries, The EAGLES, FURAY becoming increasingly frustrated by his band's middling commercial returns. When he departed to form the short-lived supergroup, SOUTHER-HILLMAN-FURY, pedal steel maestro, RUSTY YOUNG, steered POCO through the remainder of the 70's with a succession of competent, if workmanlike efforts. One of the standout tracks from this period was undoubtedly 'ROSE OF CIMARRON', a UK radio staple which surprisingly failed to make much of an impression in the US Top 100. Ironically, it was only after yet another member, SCHMIT, had defected to the rival EAGLES camp that POCO scored a bonafide US chart hit with 'CRAZY LOVE', the attendant 'LEGEND' (1979) album also making the Top

20. This marked a last stand of sorts, however, as country-rock was relegated to a fairly lowly placing on the agenda of America's changing musical climate at the dawn of the 80's. The bedraggled troupe soldiered on before finally hanging up their saddles after the lacklustre 'INAMORATA' (1984). The inevitable reunion of original members, FURAY, MESSINA, GRANTHAM, MEISNER and YOUNG came together in 1989, the revamped POCO scoring a syrupy Top 40 hit with the RICHARD MARX-penned 'CALL IT LOVE'. The single was accompanied, of course, by a comeback album, 'LEGACY' (1989) and the obligatory tour; with FURAY now a man of the cloth, he was hardly suited to the rock'n'roll lifestyle and amid increasing tension with his bandmates, departed in the early 90's. POCO, meanwhile, sauntered on down the trail, YOUNG, as ever, leading the way. • **Songwriters:** Group penned together and individually, with FURAY and COTTON contributing the most. Covered BRASS BUTTONS (Gram Parsons) / etc. • **Trivia:** STEELY DAN's DONALD FAGEN provided them with synthesized sound on their 'INDIAN SUMMER' album.

Album rating: PICKIN' UP THE PIECES (*7) / POCO (*6) / DELIVERIN' (*6) / FROM THE INSIDE (*5) / A GOOD FEELIN' TO KNOW (*7) / CRAZY EYES (*6) / SEVEN (*6) / CANTAMOS (*5) / HEAD OVER HEELS (*7) / THE VERY BEST OF POCO compilation (*7) / LIVE (*4) / ROSE OF CIMMARON (*7) / INDIAN SUMMER (*7) / LEGEND (*6) / UNDER THE GUN (*5) / BLUE AND GRAY (*4) / COWBOYS & ENGLISHMEN (*3) / GHOST TOWN (*4) / INAMORATA (*4) / LEGACY (*5) / POCO: THE FORGOTTEN TRAIL 1969-1974 compilation (*6)

RICHIE FURAY (b. 9 May'44, Yellow Springs, Ohio) – guitar, vocals / **JIM MESSINA** (b. 5 Dec'47, Maywood, Calif.) – guitar, vocals / **RUSTY YOUNG** (b.23 Feb'46, Long Beach, Calif.) – pedal steel guitar / **GEORGE GRANTHAM** (b.20 Nov'47, Cordell, Oklahoma) – drums, vocals / **RANDY MEISNER** (b. 8 Mar'46, Scottsbluff, Nebraska) – bass, vocals (RANDY left before debut recording)

       Epic   Epic

Jun 69. (7") <10501> **PICKIN' UP THE PIECES. / FIRST LOVE**   -   -

Jun 69. (lp) <26460> **PICKIN' UP THE PIECES**   -   63
– Foreward – What a day / Nobody's fool / Calico lady / First love / Make me smile – Short change / Pickin' up the pieces / Grand junction / Just in case it happens / Tomorrow / Consequently so long. *(UK-iss.1974; EPC 65327) (re-iss. Mar86 on 'Edsel'; XED 161) (cd-iss. Jul95; EK 66227)*

Nov 69. (7") <10543> **MY KIND OF LOVE. / HARD LUCK**   -   -

—— added **TIMOTHY B. SCHMIT** (b.30 Oct'47, Sacramento, Calif.) – bass, vocals (ex-NEW BREED)

Jul 70. (lp) *(EPC 64082)* <26522> **POCO**   -   58 Jun90
– Hurry up / You better think twice / Honky tonk downstairs / Keep on believin' / Anyway bye bye / Don't let it pass by / Nobody's fool / El Tonto de Nadie Regrasa.

Aug 70. (7") *(EPC 5141)* <10636> **YOU BETTER THINK TWICE. / ANYWAY BYE BYE**   -   72

Feb 71. (lp) *(EPC 64204)* <30209> **DELIVERIN' (live)**   -   26
– I guess you made it / C'mon / Hear that music / Kind woman / Hard luck – Child's claim to fame / Pickin' up the pieces / You'd better think twice / A man like me / Just in case it happens, yes indeed / Grand junction / Consequently so long.

Apr 71. (7") *(EPC 7138)* <10714> **C'MON. / I GUESS YOU MADE IT**   -   69 Mar71

—— **PAUL COTTON** (b.26 Feb'43) – guitar, vocals (ex-ILLINOIS SPEED PRESS) repl. MESSINA. (He joined LOGGINS & MESSINA)

Nov 71. (7") *(EPC 7631)* <10804> **JUST FOR ME AND YOU. / OL' FORGIVER**   -   -

Dec 71. (lp) *(EPC 64543)* <30753> **FROM THE INSIDE**   -   52 Sep71
– Bad weather / Ol' forgiver / Railroad days / From the inside / Hoe down / Just for me and you / What am I gonna do / You are the one / Do you feel it too / What if I should say I love you.

Jan 72. (7") <10816> **RAILROAD DAYS. / YOU ARE THE ONE**   -   -

Jan 73. (7") *(EPC 8240)* <10890> **A GOOD FEELIN' TO KNOW. / EARLY TIMES**   -   -

Jan 73. (lp) *(EPC 65126)* <31601> **A GOOD FEELIN' TO KNOW**   -   69 Nov72
– And settling down / Ride the country / I can see everything / Go and say goodbye / Keeper of the fire / Early times / A good feelin' to know / Restrain / Sweet lovin'.

Jan 73. (7") <10958> **I CAN SEE EVERYTHING. / GO AND SAY GOODBYE**   -   -

Mar 73. (7") *(EPC 1344)* **AND SETTLING DOWN. / I CAN SEE EVERYTHING**   -   -

Nov 73. (lp) *(EPC 65631)* <32354> **CRAZY EYES**   -   38 Sep73
– Blue water / Fool's gold / Here we go again / Brass buttons / A right along / Crazy eyes / Magnolia / Let's dance tonight. *(cd-iss. Jul95; EK 66968)*

Nov 73. (7") <11055> **FOOL'S GOLD. / HERE WE GO AGAIN**   -   -

Feb 74. (7") <11092> **BLUE WATER. / MAGNOLIA**   -   -

—— Trimmed to a quartet when RICHIE formed SOUTHER-HILLMAN-FURAY

Jun 74. (lp) *(EPC 80082)* <32895> **SEVEN**   -   68 May74
– Skatin' / Drivin' wheel / You've got your reasons / Just call my name / Faith in the families / Krikkit's song (passing through) / Rocky mountain breakdown / Angel. *(cd-iss. Jul95; EK 66985)*

Jun 74. (7") <11141> **ROCKY MOUNTAIN BREAKDOWN. / FAITH IN THE FAMILIES**   -   -

Nov 74. (7") <50076> **BITTER BLUE. / HIGH AND DRY**   -   -

Dec 74. (lp) *(EPC 80596)* <33192> **CANTAMOS**   -   76 Nov74
– Sagebush serenade / Susannah / High and dry / Western Waterloo / One horse blue / Bitter blue / Another time around / Whatever happened to your smile / All the ways.

       A.B.C.   A.B.C.

Jul 75. (lp) *(ABCL 5137)* <890> **HEAD OVER HEELS**   -   43
– Keep on tryin' / Lovin' arms / Let me turn back to you / Makin' love / Down in the quarter / Sittin' on a fence / Georgia, bind my ties / Us / Flyin' solo / Dallas / I'll be back again.

Sep 75. (7") *(EPC 7631)* <12126> **KEEP ON TRYIN'. / GEORGIA, BIND MY TIES**   -   50

Feb 76. (7") *(ABC 4096)* <12159> **MAKIN' LOVE. / FLYIN' SOLO**   -   -

—— added **AL GARTH** – fiddle, saxophone (to YOUNG, GRANTHAM, SCHMIT & COTTON)

May 76. (lp) *(ABCL 5166)* <946> **ROSE OF CIMARRON**   -   89
– Rose of cimarron / Stealaway / Just like me / Company's comin' / Slow poke /

Too many nights too long / P.N.S. (when you come around) / Starin' at the sky / All alone together / Tulsa turnaround. (re-iss. Feb82 on 'M.C.A.'; MCL 1638) (re-iss. Apr92 cd/c; MCLD/MCLC 19015) (cd re-iss. Apr94 on 'One Way'; MCAD 22076)

Jul 76. (7") <12204> **ROSE OF CIMARRON. / TULSA TURNAROUND**   [-] [94]

Oct 76. (7") (ABC 4149) **STARIN' AT THE SKY. / P.N.S. (WHEN YOU COME AROUND)**   [ ] [-]

—— returned to a quartet when AL GARTH departed

Apr 77. (7") <12295> **INDIAN SUMMER. / ME AND YOU**   [-] [50]

Apr 77. (lp) (ABCL 5220) <989> **INDIAN SUMMER**   [ ] [57]
– Indian summer / Twenty years / Me and you / Downfall / Win or lose / Living in the band / Stay (night until noon) / Find out in time / The dance medley:- When the dance is over – Never gonna stop – When the dance is over (reprise).

May 77. (7") (ABC 4178) **INDIAN SUMMER. / FIND OUT IN TIME**   [ ] [-]

—— **CHARLIE HARRISON** (b. England) – bass, vocals (ex-AL STEWART) repl. TIM to EAGLES / **STEVE CHAPMAN** (b. England) – drums, vocals (ex-AL STEWART) repl. GEORGE to The SECRETS / added **KIM BULLARD** (b. Atlanta, Georgia) – keyboards (ex-CROSBY, STILLS & NASH) (US tour)

Jan 79. (lp) (ABCL 5264) <1099> **LEGEND**   [ ] [14] Nov78
– Boomerang / Spellbound / Barbados / Little darlin' / Love comes love goes / Heart of the night / Crazy love / The last goodbye / Legend. (re-iss. Jun88 on 'M.C.A.'; DMCL 1879) (re-iss. Jan93 cd/c; MCLD/MCLC 19143)

Jan 79. (7") (ABC 4240) <12439> **CRAZY LOVE. / BARBADOS**   [ ] [17]
                               M.C.A.   M.C.A.

Jun 79. (7") (MCA 509) <41023> **HEART OF THE NIGHT. / THE LAST GOODBYE**   [ ] [20] May79

Sep 79. (7") <41103> **LEGEND. / INDIAN SUMMER**   [-] [ ]

May 80. (7") (MCA 589) **LEGEND. / ROSE OF CIMARRON**   [ ] [-]

Jul 80. (7") (MCA 635) <41269> **UNDER THE GUN. / REPUTATION**   [ ] [48]

Aug 80. (lp) (MCF 3076) <5132> **UNDER THE GUN**   [ ] [46] Jul80
– Under the gun / While we're still young / The everlasting kind / Down to the wire / Footsteps of a fool / Reputation / Midnight rain / A fool's Paradise / Friends in the distance / Made of stone.

Oct 80. (7") <41326> **MIDNIGHT RAIN. / FOOL'S PARADISE**   [-] [74]

Jan 81. (7") <51034> **FRIENDS IN THE DISTANCE. / EVERLASTING KIND**   [ ] [-]

Jul 81. (7") <51172> **WIDOWMAKER. / DOWN ON THE RIVER AGAIN**   [ ] [-]

Jul 81. (lp) <5227> **BLUE AND GRAY**   [ ] [76]
– Glorybound / Blue and gray / Streets of Paradise / The writing on the wall / Down the river again / Please wait for me / Widowmaker / Here comes that girl again / Sometime / The land of glory. (UK cd-iss. Apr94 on 'One Way'; MCAD 22068)

Feb 82. (lp) <5288> **COWBOYS AND ENGLISHMEN**   [-] [ ]
– Sea of heartbreak / No relief in sight / There goes my heart / Ashes / Feudin' / Cajun Moon / Ribbon of darkness / If you could read my mind / While you're on your way / The price of love. (UK cd-iss. Apr94 on 'One Way'; MCAD 22067)

Mar 82. (7") <52001> **SEA OF HEARTBREAK. / FEUDIN'**   [-] [ ]
                         Atlantic   Atlantic

Oct 82. (7") <89970> **GHOST TOWN. / HIGH SIERRA**   [ ] [ ]

Oct 82. (lp) (K 50902) <80008> **GHOST TOWN**   [ ] [ ]
– Ghost town / How will you feel tonight / Shoot for the moon / The midnight rodeo / Cry no more / Break of hearts / Love's so cruel / Special care / When hearts collide / High Sierra.

Dec 82. (7") <89919> **SHOOT FOR THE MOON. / THE MIDNIGHT RODEO (IN THE LEAD TONIGHT)**   [-] [50]

Jun 83. (7") <89851> **BREAK OF HEARTS. /**   [-] [ ]

—— **FURAY** returned reforming early line-up with **GRANTHAM, COTTON, SCHMIT + YOUNG**

May 84. (lp) <80184> **INAMORATA**   [-] [ ]
– Days gone by / This old flame / Daylight / Odd man out / How many moons / When you love someone / Brenda X / Standing in the fire / Save a corner of your heart / The storm.

Apr 84. (7") <89674> **DAYS GONE BY. / DAYLIGHT**   [ ] [80]

Jun 84. (7") <89650> **THIS OLD FLAME. / SAVE A CORNER OF YOUR HEART**   [-] [ ]

Aug 84. (7") <89629> **THE STORM. / SAVE A CORNER OF YOUR HEART**   [-] [ ]

—— They split 1984 but reformed 5 years later. **FURAY, MESSINA, GRANTHAM, MEISNER + RUSTY YOUNG.**
                         R.C.A.   R.C.A.

Oct 89. (7") (PB 49339) <9038> **CALL IT LOVE. / LOVIN' YOU EVERY MINUTE**   [ ] [18] Aug89
(12"+=/cd-s+=) (PT/PD 49340) – Who else?.

Nov 89. (lp/c/cd) (PL/PK/PD 90395) <9694> **LEGACY**   [ ] [40] Sep89
– When it all began / Call it love / The nature of love / What do people know / Nothin' to hide / Look within * / Rough edges / Who else? / Lovin' you every minute / If it wasn't for you / Follow your dreams. (cd+= *)

Nov 89. (7") <9131> **NOTHIN' TO HIDE. / IF IT WASN'T FOR YOU**   [ ] [39]

– compilations, etc. –

Aug 75. (d-lp) Epic; (EPC 88135) <33537> **THE VERY BEST OF POCO**   [ ] [90] Jul75
<cd-iss. 1989; > – (omits 2 tracks).

Mar 76. (lp) Epic; (EPC 80705) <33336> **POCO LIVE (live late '74)**   [ ] [ ]
– Blue water / Fools gold / Rocky mountain breakdown / Bad weather / Ride the country / Angel / High and dry / Restrain / A good feelin' to know.

Nov 77. (12"ep) A.B.C.; (4130) **ROSE OF CIMARRON / INDIAN SUMMER. / KEEP ON TRYIN' / STARIN' AT THE SKY**   [ ] [-]

Mar 80. (lp) Epic; <36210> **POCO: THE SONGS OF PAUL COTTON** (his POCO compositions)   [-] [ ]

Mar 80. (lp/c) C.B.S.; (CBS/40 31781) / Epic; <36211> **POCO: THE SONGS OF RICHIE FURAY** (his POCO compositions)   [ ] [ ]

1989. (cd) M.C.A.; **CRAZY LOVING: THE BEST OF POCO 1975-1982**   [-] [ ]

Jan 90. (cd) CBS-Legacy; <487483-2> **POCO: THE FORGOTTEN TRAIL (1969-74)**   [-] [ ]
(UK-iss.Jun97; same)

Jun 97. (cd) Beat Goes On; (BGOCD 359) **FROM THE INSIDE / A GOOD FEELIN' TO KNOW**   [ ] [-]

Jun 97. (cd) Half Moon; (HMNCD 008) **THE ESSENTIAL COLLECTION**   [ ] [-]

POET & THE ROOTS
(see under ⇒ JOHNSON, Linton Kwesi)

POGUES

Formed: North London, England . . . late 1983 by Tipperary-raised SHANE MacGOWAN, SPIDER STACEY and JEM FINER. MacGOWAN had earlier been part of punk outfit, The NIPPLE ERECTORS through 1978-1981; this motley crew released a solitary single, 'KING OF THE BOP' before shortening their name to The NIPS. A further few singles appeared and even an album, 'ONLY AT THE END OF THE BEGINNING', recommended for diehard POGUES fiends only. POGUE MAHONE (Gaelic for "kiss my arse") was subsequently formed by MacGOWAN and JAMES FEARNLEY (also a NIP), adding drinking buddy, ANDREW RANKEN, plus female singer/bassist CAIT O'RIORDAN. By Spring '84, they'd formed their own self-titled label, issuing a classic debut single, 'DARK STREETS OF LONDON'. Boasting all the Celtic melancholy, romance and gritted-teeth attitude which marked the best of the band's work, the track rather unfairly but predictably received an official BBC radio ban (apparently after the beeb managed to translate their name). A month later they secured a deal with 'Stiff', opting instead for The POGUES. Their Stan Brennan-produced debut album, 'RED ROSES FOR ME', broke into the UK Top 100 as they acquired growing support from live audiences the length and breadth of the country. Whether interpreting trad Irish folk songs or reeling off brilliant originals, the POGUES were apt to turn from high-spirited revelry ('STREAMS OF WHISKEY') to menacing threat ('BOYS FROM THE COUNTY HELL') in the time it took to neck a pint of Guinness (in MacGOWAN's case, not very long at all). April '85 saw the release of perhaps their finest single (and first Top 20 hit), the misty-eyed, ELVIS COSTELLO-produced 'A PAIR OF BROWN EYES'. COSTELLO also oversaw the accompanying album, 'RUM, SODOMY & THE LASH' (1985), a debauched, bruisingly beautiful classic which elevated The POGUES to the position of modern day folk heroes. MacGOWAN's gift for conjuring up a feeling of time and place was never more vivid than on the likes of the aforementioned 'A PAIR..', the rousing 'SALLY MacLENNANE' and the cursing malice of 'THE SICK BED OF CUCHULAINN', while O'RIORDAN put in a spine-tingling performance as a Scottish laird on the traditional 'I'M A MAN YOU DON'T MEET EVERYDAY'. On the 16th of May '86, the latter married COSTELLO and when she subsequently left that November (after writing the Top 50 hit 'HAUNTED' for the Alex Cox film, 'Sid & Nancy'), a vital component of POGUES chemistry went with her. Around the same time, the group played 'The McMahon Gang' in Cox's movie 'Straight To Hell', meeting ex-CLASH singer JOE STRUMMER on the set: the veteran punk would subsequently deputise for the absent MacGOWAN on an early 1988 US tour. This period also saw them peak at No.3 in the album charts with 'IF I SHOULD FALL FROM GRACE WITH GOD', an album which spawned an unlikely No.2 Christmas 1987 hit in 'FAIRY TALE OF NEW YORK'. A drunken duet with KIRSTY MacCOLL, the track was certainly more subversive than the usual Yuletide fodder and for a brief period, The POGUES were bonafide pop stars, their rampant collaboration with The DUBLINERS on 'IRISH ROVER' earlier that year having already breached the Top 10. Live, the band were untouchable, MacGOWAN's errant, tin-tray wielding genius the stuff of legend, particularly for many who witnessed their storming Glasgow Barrowlands performances (needless to say, Rangers fans were mercifully thin on the ground at these celebratory Celtic shindigs). Inevitably, MacGOWAN's hard-drinking ways were beginning to affect his writing and 'PEACE AND LOVE' (1989) signalled a slow slide into mediocrity. 1990's 'HELL'S DITCH' carried on in much the same vein, although this was to be MacGOWAN's final album under The POGUES banner, his failing health incompatable with the demands of a successful major label band. While the gap-toothed frontman eventually got a solo career together, The POGUES bravely soldiered on with a surprisingly impressive hit single, 'TUESDAY MORNING', lifted from their 1993 UK Top 20 "comeback" album, 'WAITING FOR HERB'. Two years on, a nostalgically titled follow-up set, 'POGUE MAHONE', failed to rekindle their former glory, while MacGOWAN continued to dominate the limelight. In 1999, some of the POGUES (SPIDER, HUNT + RANKIN) got together as The WISEMEN, while FINER has emerged with the single LONGPLAYER. • **Songwriters:** Group compositions, except; THE BAND PLAYED WALTZING MATILDA (Eric Bogle) / DIRTY OLD TOWN (Ewan MacColl) / WILD ROVER + MADRA RUM (trad.) / MAGGIE MAY (Rod Stewart) / HONKY TONK WOMAN (Rolling Stones) / WHISKEY IN THE JAR (Thin Lizzy) / MISS OTIS REGRETS (Cole Porter) / GOT A LOT O' LIVIN' TO DO (Elvis Presley) / HOW COME (Ronnie Lane) / WHEN THE SHIP COMES IN (Bob Dylan). FINER became main writer in the mid-90's with others contributed some material. • **Trivia:** In the early '90s, they supplied the soundtrack for TV play 'A Man You Don't Meet Every Day'. The song 'Fiesta' was subsequently used on Vauxhall-Tigra TV ad after the rights were sold from their 1988 album.

Album rating: RED ROSES FOR ME (*8) / RUM, SODOMY & THE LASH (*9) / IF I SHOULD FALL FROM GRACE WITH GOD (*8) / PEACE AND LOVE (*6) / HELL'S DITCH (*6) / THE BEST OF THE POGUES compilation (*9) / THE BEST OF THE REST OF THE POGUES compilation (*7) / WAITING FOR HERB (*6) / POGUE MAHONE (*5)

NIPPLE ERECTORS

SHANE MacGOWAN (b.25 Dec'57, Kent, England) – vocals, guitar / **ADRIAN THRILLS** – guitar (NME journalist) / **SHANE 'HASLER' BRADLEY** – bass / **ARCANE** – drums / + others

		Soho	not iss.
Jun 78.	(7") *(SH 1/2)* **KING OF THE BOP. / NERVOUS WRECK**	☐	–

NIPS

LARRY HINDRICKS – guitar repl. THRILLS

—— **MARK HARRIS** – drums repl. ARCANE

Aug 79.	(7") *(SH 4)* **ALL THE TIME IN THE WORLD. / PRIVATE EYES**	☐	–

—— **GAVIN DOUGLAS** – drums repl. LARRY

—— **JAMES FEARNLEY** (b.10 Oct'54, Manchester, England) – accordion (appeared on album)

Feb 80.	(7") *(SH 9)* **GABRIELLE. / VENGEANCE** *(re-iss. 1980 on 'Chiswick'; CHIS 119)*	☐	–
		Test Press	not iss.
Oct 80.	(lp) *(HOHO 1)* **ONLY AT THE END OF THE BEGINNING**	☐	–
Oct 81.	(7") *(TP 5)* **HAPPY SONG. / NOBODY TO LOVE**	☐	–

—— split in 1982. HASLER was soon to join MEN THEY COULDN'T HANG.

– compilation –

Nov 87.	(m-lp) *Big Beat; (WIKM 66)* **BOPS, BABES, BOOZE & BOVVER**	☐	–

– King of the bop / Nervous wreck / So pissed off / Stavordale Rd. N5 / All the time in the world / Private eye / Gabrielle / Vengeance.

POGUES

MacGOWAN + FEARNLEY plus **SPIDER STACEY** (b.PETER, 14 Dec'58, Eastbourne, England) – tin whistle (ex-NIPS) / **JEM FINER** (b.JEREMY, 29 Jul'55, Stoke, England) – banjo, guitar / **CAIT O'RIORDAN** – bass, vocals / **ANDREW RANKEN** (b.13 Nov'53, London) – drums

		Pogue Mahone	not iss.
May 84.	(7"; as POGUE MAHONE) *(PM 1)* **DARK STREETS OF LONDON. / THE BAND PLAYED WALTZING MATHILDA** *(re-iss. Jun84 as The POGUES on 'Stiff'; BUY 207)*	☐	–
		Stiff	not iss.
Sep 84.	(lp) *(SEEZ 55)* **RED ROSES FOR ME**	89	–

– Transmetropolitan / The battle of Brisbane / The auld triangle / Waxie's dargle / Boys from the county Hell / Sea shanty / Dark streets of London / Streams of whiskey / Poor daddy / Dingle regatta / Greenland whale fisheries / Down in the ground where the dead men go / Kitty. *(cd-iss. May87; CDSEEZ 55)* *(re-iss. Jan89 on 'WEA' lp/c; WX 240/+C)* (cd re-iss. Jan89; 244494-2)

Oct 84.	(7") *(BUY 212)* **BOYS FROM THE COUNTY HELL. / REPEALING OF THE LICENSING LAWS** *(d7"+=)* *(BUY 212 – 207)* – (see debut 45).	☐	–
Mar 85.	(7"/7"pic-d) *(BUY/DBUY 220)* **A PAIR OF BROWN EYES. / WHISKEY YOU'RE THE DEVIL** *(12"+=)* *(BUYIT 22)* – Muirshin Durkin.	72	–

—— added p/t **PHIL CHEVRON** (b. RYAN, 17 Jun'57, Dublin, Ireland) – guitar, producer (ex-RADIATORS FROM SPACE)

Jun 85.	(7",7"green/7"sha-pic-d) *(BUY/PBUY 224)* **SALLY MacLENNANE. / WILD ROVER** *(12"+=)* *(BUYIT 224)* – The leaving of Liverpool. *(c-s+=)* *(BUYC 224)* – Wild cats of Kilkenny.	51	–
Aug 85.	(lp/c/cd) *(SEEZ/CSEEZ/CDSEEZ 58)* **RUM, SODOMY & THE LASH**	13	–

– The sick bed of Cuchulainn / The old main drag / Wild cats of Kilkenny / I'm a man you don't meet every day / A pair of brown eyes / Dirty old town / Jesse James / Navigator / Billy's bones / The gentleman soldier / And the band played waltzing Matilda. *(cd+=)* – A pistol for Paddy Garcia. *(re-iss. Jan89 on 'WEA' lp/c; WX 241/+C)* (cd re-iss. Jan89; 244495-2)

Aug 85.	(7"/7"pic-d) *(BUY/PBUY 229)* **DIRTY OLD TOWN. / A PISTOL FOR PADDY GARCIA** *(12"+=)* *(BUYIT 229)* – The parting glass.	62	–
Feb 86.	(7"ep/12"ep/c-ep/7"pic-ep) *(BUY/BUYIT/BUYC/PBUY 243)* **POGUETRY IN MOTION** – A rainy night in Soho / The body of an American / London girl / Planxty Noel Hill.	29	–
Aug 86.	(7") *(MCA 1084)* **HAUNTED. / JUNK THEME** *(12"+=)* *(MCAT 1084)* – Hot dogs with everything. (above single from the motion picture, 'Sid & Nancy' on 'MCA')	42	–

—— **DARRYL HUNT** (b. 4 May'50, Bournemouth, England) – bass (ex-PRIDE O' THE CROSS) repl. CAIT

Mar 87.	(7"; by The POGUES & THe DUBLINERS) *(BUY 258)* **THE IRISH ROVER. / THE RARE OLD MOUNTAIN DEW** *(12"+=)* *(BUYIT 258)* – The Dubliners fancy.	8	–

—— added **TERRY WOODS** (b. 4 Dec'47, Dublin) – banjo (now 8-piece)

		Pogue Mahone-EMI	Island
Nov 87.	(7"; The POGUES featuring KIRSTY MacCOLL) *(NY 7)* **FAIRYTALE OF NEW YORK. / BATTLE MARCH MEDLEY** *(12"+=)(cd-s+=)* *(NY 12)(CDNY 1)* – Shanne Bradley.	2	☐
Jan 88.	(cd/c/lp) *(CD/TC+/NYR 1)* <90872> **IF I SHOULD FALL FROM GRACE WITH GOD**	3	88

– If I should fall from grace with God / Turkish song of the damned / Bottle of smoke / Fairytale of New York (featuring KIRSTY MacCOLL) / Metropolis / Thousands are sailing / Fiesta / Medley:- The recruiting sergeant – The rocky road to Dublin – Galway races / Streets of Sorrow – Birmingham Six / Lullaby of London / Sit down by the fire / The broad majestic Shannon / Worms. *(cd+=)* – South

Australia / The battle march medley. *(re-iss. Jan89 on 'WEA' lp/c; WX 243/+C)* (cd-iss. Jan89; 244494-2)

Feb 88.	(7") *(FG 1)* **IF I SHOULD FALL FROM GRACE WITH GOD. / SALLY MacLENNANE (live)** *(12"red-ep)(cd-ep+=)* **ST. PATRICK'S NIGHT** *(SGG 1-12)(CDFG 1)* – A pair of brown eyes (live) / Dirty old town (live).	58	☐
Jul 88.	(7") *(FG 2)* **FIESTA. / SKETCHES OF SPAIN** *(12"+=)(cd-s+=)* *(FG 2-12)(CDFG 2)* – South Australia.	24	–
		WEA	Island
Dec 88.	(7") *(YZ 355)* **YEAH, YEAH, YEAH, YEAH, YEAH. / THE LIMERICK RAKE** *(12"+=/cd-s+=)* *(YZ 355 T/CD)* – ('A'extended) / Honky tonk woman.	43	–
Jun 89.	(7"/c-s) *(YZ 407/+C)* **MISTY MORNING, ALBERT BRIDGE. / COTTON FIELDS** *(12"+=)* *(YZ 407T)* – Young ned of the hill. *(3"cd-s++=)* *(YZ 407CD)* – Train of love.	41	–
Jul 89.	(lp/c)(cd) *(WX 247/+C)(246086-2)* <91225> **PEACE AND LOVE**	5	☐

– White City / Young ned of the hill / Misty morning, Albert Bridge / Cotton fields / Blue heaven / Down all the days / U.S.A. / Lorelei / Gartloney rats / Boat train / Tombstone / Night train to Lorca / London you're a lady / Gridlock.

Aug 89.	(7"/c-s) *(YZ 409/+C)* **WHITE CITY. / EVERY MAN IS A KING** *(12"+=)* *(YZ 409TX)* – Maggie May (live). *(cd-s+=)* *(YZ 409CD)* – The star of the County Down.	☐	–
May 90.	(7"/c-s; The POGUES & The DUBLINERS) *(YZ 500/+C)* **JACK'S HEROES. / WHISKEY IN THE JAR** *(12"+=/cd-s+=)* *(YZ 500 T/CD)* – ('B'extended).	63	–

—— (theme song used by Eire in World Cup)

Aug 90.	(7") *(YZ 519)* **SUMMER IN SIAM. / BASTARD LANDLORD** *(12"+=/cd-s+=)* *(YZ 519 T/CD)* – Hell's ditch (instrumental) / The Irish rover.	64	–
Sep 90.	(cd)(lp/c) *(9031 72554-2)(WX 366/+C)* <422846> **HELL'S DITCH**	12	☐

– The sunnyside of the street / Sayonara / The ghost of a smile / Hell's ditch / Lorca's novena / Summer in Siam / Rain street / Rainbow man / The wake of the Medusa / House of the gods / Five green onions and Jean / Maidria Rua / Six to go.

Apr 91.	(cd-s) **SAYONARA / CURSE OF LOVE / INFINITY**	–	–
Sep 91.	(7") *(YZ 603)* **A RAINY NIGHT IN SOHO (remix). / SQUID OUT OF WATER** *(12"+=)* *(YZ 603)* – Infinity. *(cd-s+=)* *(YZ 603CD)* – POGUETRY IN MOTION (ep).	67	–
Sep 91.	(cd)(lp/c) *(9031 75405-2)(WX 430/+C)* **THE BEST OF THE POGUES** (compilation) <US-title 'ESSENTIAL POGUES'>	11	☐

– Fairytale of New York / Sally MacLennane / Dirty old town / The Irish rover / A pair of brown eyes / Streams of whiskey / A rainy night in Soho / Fiesta / Rain street / Misty morning, Albert Bridge / White City / Thousand are sailing / The broad majestic Shannon / The body of an American.

Dec 91.	(7") *(YZ 628)* **FAIRYTALE OF NEW YORK. / FIESTA** *(12"+=/cd-s+=)* *(YZ 628 T/CD)* – A pair of brown eyes / Sick bed of Cuchulainn / Maggie May.	36	–

—— p/t JOE STRUMMER is deposed by member SPIDER who takes over vox.

May 92.	(7"/c-s) *(YZ 673/+C)* **HONKY TONK WOMAN. / CURSE OF LOVE** *(12"+=)* *(YZ 673T)* – Infinity. *(cd-s+=)* *(YZ 673CD)* – The parting glass.	56	–
Jun 92.	(cd)(lp/c) *(9031 77341-2)(WX 471/+C)* **THE BEST OF THE REST OF THE POGUES** (compilation out-takes)	☐	☐

– If I should fall from grace with God / The sick bed of Cuchulainn / The old main drag / Boys from the county Hell / Young Ned of the hill / Dark streets of London / The auld triangle / Repeal of the licensing laws / Yeah yeah yeah yeah yeah / London girl / Honky tonk women / Summer in Siam / Turkish song of the damned / Lullaby of London / The sunnyside of the street / Hell's ditch.

—— (Sep'91) MacGOWAN left when his health deteriorated (JOE STRUMMER deputised for him on tour)

—— added 8th member & producer **MICHAEL BROOK** – infinite guitar

		WEA	Chameleon
Aug 93.	(7"/c-s) *(YZ 758/+C)* **TUESDAY MORNING. / FIRST DAY OF FOREVER** *(cd-s+=)* *(YZ 758CD)* – Turkish song of the damned (live). *(cd-s)* *(YZ 758CDX)* – ('A'side) / London calling / I fought the law (both live with JOE STRUMMER).	18	☐
Sep 93.	(cd/c/lp) *(4509 93463-2/-4/-1)* <61598> **WAITING FOR HERB**	20	☐ Oct98

– Tuesday morning / Smell of petroleum / Haunting / Once upon a time / Sitting on top of the world / Drunken boat / Big city / Girl from the Wadi Hammamat / Modern world / Pachinko / My baby's gone / Small hours.

Jan 94.	(7"/c-s) *(YZ 771/+C)* **ONCE UPON A TIME. / TRAIN KEPT ROLLING ON** *(12"+=/cd-s+=)* *(YZ 771 T/CD)* – Tuesday morning / Paris St. Germain.	66	–

—— FEARNEY and WOODS departed, apparently due to the brief Christmas comeback of SHANE MacGOWAN

—— **SPIDER / JEM / DARRYL + RANKEN** added **JAMIE CLARKE** – banjo / **JAMES McNALLY** – accordion, uilleann pipes / **DAVID COULTER** – mandolin, tambourine

Sep 95.	(7"colrd/c-s) *(WEA 011 X/C)* **HOW COME. / EYES OF AN ANGEL** *(cd-s+=)* *(WX 011CD)* – Tuesday morning (live) / Big city (live).	☐	–
Oct 95.	(cd/c/lp) *(0630 11210-2/-4/-1)* **POGUE MAHONE**	☐	–

– How come / Living in a world without her / When the ship comes in / Anniversary / Amadie / Love you 'till the end / Bright lights / Oretown / Pont Mirabeau / Tosspint / Four o'clock in the morning / Where that love's been gone / The sun and the moon.

—— note:- The POGUES also appeared on the flip side to KIRSTY MacCOLL's Cole Porter tribute single, 'Miss Otis Regrets' on the track 'JUST ONE OF THOSE THINGS'.

POISON

Formed: Harrisburg, Pennsylvania, USA ... March '84 by former SPECTRES members BRET MICHAELS and RIKKI ROCKETT, the line-up completed by BOBBY DALL and C.C. DEVILLE. Like a cartoon bubblegum version of FASTER PUSSYCAT or HANOI ROCKS, this super-glam metal outfit exploded onto the US rock scene in a sea of peroxide bleach circa late '86, their aptly titled debut album, 'LOOK WHAT THE CAT DRAGGED IN' (1986) reaching No.3 in the US charts, aided and abetted by the singalong sleaze anthem, 'TALK DIRTY TO ME'. Needless to say, the rest of the album was painfully amateurish at best, hilarious at worst. Still, the Americans lapped it up and made sure the follow-up, 'OPEN UP AND SAY ... AAH!' (1988) climbed to No.2. The obligatory "sensitive" ballad, in this case 'EVERY ROSE HAS ITS THORN' was a massive hit on both sides of the Atlantic (US No.1), a lonesome strumathon that EXTREME would've been proud to call their own. The album spawned a further three Stateside singles, including a cover of the old LOGGINS & MESSINA chestnut, 'YOUR MAMA DON'T DANCE'. 'FLESH AND BLOOD' (1990) was the band's most successful album to date, going Top 5 in both the British and American charts, POISON making a conscious effort to distance themselves from their mascara'd days of old. Nevertheless, they retained the ability to release annoyingly pointless pop-metal nonsense like 'UNSKINNY BOP'. By the release of 1993's 'NATIVE TONGUE' opus, the MICHAELS and Co. were trying so painfully hard to create a credible image, they employed the TOWER OF POWER horn section! If they were under the illusion that this would give them instant soul power then POISON were clearly even more clueless than their music gave them credit for. The ploy didn't work and the album failed to sell as much as its predecessor, MICHAELS more newsworthy for his shortlived affair with PAMELA ANDERSON than his music. • **Trivia:** Late in 1990, BRET co-wrote and produced girlfriend SUSIE HATTON's debut album. He landed the lead role in the 1996 movie 'A Letter From Death Row'.

Album rating: LOOK WHAT THE CAT DRAGGED IN (*6) / OPEN UP AND SAY ... AAH! (*7) / FLESH & BLOOD (*7) / SWALLOW THIS LIVE (*5) / NATIVE TONGUE (*5) / GREATEST HITS 1986-1996 compilation (*7) /

BRET MICHAELS (b. BRET MICHAEL SYCHAK, 15 Mar'63) – vocals / **C.C. DEVILLE** (b. BRUCE ANTHONY JOHANNESSON, 14 May'62, Brooklyn, N.Y.) – lead guitar (ex-SCREAMING MIMI) repl. MATT SMITH / **BOBBY DALL** (b. ROBERT KUY KENDALL, 2 Nov'63, Miami, Florida) – bass / **RIKKI ROCKETT** (b. RICHARD REAM, 8 Aug'61, Mechanicsburg, Pennsylvania) – drums

		Music For Nations	Capitol
Oct 86.	(lp/pic-lp/c) *(MFN 69/+P/C) <12523>* **LOOK WHAT THE CAT DRAGGED IN**		3 Jul86

– Cry tough / I want action / I won't forget you / Play dirty / Look what the cat dragged in / Talk dirty to me / Want some, need some / Blame it on you / #1 bad boy / Let me go to the show. *(re-iss. Apr89 lp,pic-lp,c/cd.Apr89; same/MFN 69CD) (re-iss. Jul94 cd/c; same) (re-iss. May96 on 'EMI Gold' cd/c; CD/TC GOLD 1027)*

May 87.	(7") *(KUT 125) <5686>* **TALK DIRTY TO ME. / WANT SOME, NEED SOME**	67	9 Mar87

(12"pic-d+=/12"+=) *(P+/12KUT 125)* – (interview).

Jun 87.	(7") *<44004>* **I WANT ACTION. / PLAY DIRTY**	-	50
Aug 87.	(7") *(KUT 127)* **CRY TOUGH. / LOOK WHAT THE CAT DRAGGED IN**	-	-

(12"pic-d+=/12"+=) *(P+/12KUT 127)* – ('A'-U.S. remix). *(re-iss. Apr89; same)*

		Capitol	Capitol
Sep 87.	(7") *<44038>* **I WON'T FORGET YOU. / BLAME IT ON YOU**	-	13
Apr 88.	(7"/7"w-poster/7"s) *(CL/+P/Z 486) <44145>* **NOTHIN' BUT A GOOD TIME. / LOOK BUT YOU CAN'T TOUCH**	35	6

(12"+=/12"g-f+=) *(12CL/+G 486)* – Livin' for a minute.

May 88.	(lp/pic-lp/c)(c/cd)(pic-cd) *(EST/+P 2059)(TC/CD/+EST 2059) (CDP 748493L) <48493>* **OPEN UP AND SAY ... AAH!**	23	2

– Love on the rocks / Nothin' but a good time / Back to the rocking horse / Good love / Tearin' down the walls / Look but you can't touch / Fallen angel / Every rose has its thorn / Your mama can't dance / Bad to be good. *(re-iss. Mar94 cd/c; same)*

Oct 88.	(7"/7"s) *(CL/+S 500) <44191>* **FALLEN ANGEL. / BAD TO BE GOOD**	59	12 Jul88

(12"+=/12"pic-d+=) *(12CL/+P 500)* – (interview).

Oct 88.	(7") *<44203>* **EVERY ROSE HAS ITS THORN. / LIVING FOR THE MINUTE**	-	1
Jan 89.	(7"/7"s/7"sha-pic-d) *(CL/+S/P 520)* **EVERY ROSE HAS ITS THORN. / BACK TO THE ROCKING HORSE**	13	-

(12"+=/12"g-f+=) *(12CL/+G 520)(CDCL 520)* – Gotta face the hangman.

Apr 89.	(7"/7"green) *(CL/+S 523) <44203>* **YOUR MAMA DON'T DANCE. / TEARIN' DOWN THE WALLS**	13	10 Feb89

(12"+=/12"green+=)(cd-s+=) *(12CL/+B 523)(CDCL 523)* – Love on the rocks.

Jul 89.	(7"/7"s)(c-s) *(CL/+X 539)(TCCL 539)* **NOTHIN' BUT A GOOD TIME. / LIVIN' FOR THE MINUTE**	48	-

(12"+=/12"pic-d+=)(cd-s+=) *(12CL/+P 539)(CDCL 539)* – Look what the cat dragged in (live).

Jun 90.	(c-s/7") *(TC+/CL 582) <44584>* **UNSKINNY BOP. / SWAMP JUICE (SOUL-O)**	15	3

(12"+=/12"pic-d+=)(cd-s+=) *(12CL/+P 582)(CDCL 582)* – Valley of lost souls / Poor boy blues.

Jul 90.	(cd/c/lp) *(CD/TC/+EST 2126) <918132>* **FLESH & BLOOD**	3	2

– Strange days of Uncle Jack / Valley of lost souls / Unskinny bop / (Flesh and blood) Sacrifice / Swamp juice (soul-o) / Let it play / Life goes on / Come Hell or high water / Ride the wind / Don't give up an inch / Something to believe in / Ball and chain / Life loves a tragedy / Poor boy blues. *(re-iss. cd Sep94;)*

Oct 90.	(c-s/7") *(TC+/CL 594) <44617>* **SOMETHING TO BELIEVE IN. / BALL AND CHAIN**	35	4

(12"+=) *(12CL 594)* – Look what the cat dragged in / Your mama don't dance /

Every rose has its thorn.
(10"yellow+=/cd-s+=) *(10/CD CL 594)* – (Bret Michaels interview).

Jan 91.	(c-s,12") *<44616>* **RIDE THE WIND. / COME HELL OR HIGH WATER**	-	38
Apr 91.	(c-s,12") *<44705>* **LIFE GOES ON. / SOMETHING TO BELIEVE IN (acoustic)**	-	35
Nov 91.	(7"/7"clear) *(CL/+P 640)* **SO TELL ME WHY. / GUITAR SOLO**	25	

(12"+=/cd-s+=) *(12/CD CL 640)* – Unskinny bop (live) / Ride the wind (live).
(12"pic-d+=/pic-cd-s+=) *(12/CD CLP)* – Only time will tell / No more lookin' back (poison jazz).

Dec 91.	(cd/c/d-lp) *(CD/TC+/ESTU 2159) <98046>* **SWALLOW THIS LIVE** (live / studio tracks *)	52	51

– Intro / Look what the dragged in / Look but you can't touch / Good love / I want action / Something to believe in / Poor boy blues / Unskinny bop / Every rose has its thorn / Fallen angel / Your mama don't dance / Nothin' but a good time / Talk dirty to me / So tell me why* / Souls on fire* / Only time will tell* / No more lookin' back (poison jazz).

—— (Nov'91) DeVILLE left, and was replaced (Jun'92) by **RICKIE KOTZEN** (b. 3 Feb'70, Reading, Pennsylvania) – guitar

Feb 93.	(c-s/7") *(TC+/CL 679) <44905>* **STAND. / STAND (CHR edit)**	25	50 Jan93

(cd-s) *(CDCL 679)* – ('A'side) / Native tongue / The scream / Whip comes down / ('A'-lp version).

Feb 93.	(cd/c/lp) *(CD/TC+/ESTU 2190) <98961>* **NATIVE TONGUE**	20	16

– Native tongue / The scream / Stand / Stay alive / Until you suffer some (Fire and ice) / Body talk / Bring it home / 7 days over you / Richie's acoustic thang / Ain't that the truth / Theatre of the soul / Strike up the band / Ride child ride / Blind faith / Bastard son of a thousand blues.

Apr 93.	(7"pic-d/c-s) *(CLP/TCCL 685)* **UNTIL YOU SUFFER SOME (FIRE AND ICE). / STAND (acoustic)**	32	

(cd-s+=) *(CDCL 685)* – Bastard son of a thousand blues / ('A'mix).
(12"colrd+=) *(12CL 685)* – Strike up the band / ('A'mix).

—— **BLUES SRACENO** (b.17 Oct'71) – guitar repl.KOTZEN

—— look to have went their separate ways

– compilations, etc. –

Feb 97.	(cd) *Capitol; (<CTMCD 312)>* **GREATEST HITS 1986-1996**		

– Nothin' but a good time / Talk dirty to me / Unskinny bop / Every rose has its thorn / Fallen angel / I won't forget you / Stand / Ride the wind / Look what the cat dragged in / I want action / Life goes on / (Flesh and blood) acrifice / Cry tough / Your mama don't dance / So tell me why / Something to believe in / Sexual thing / Lay your body down.

POLICE

Formed: London, England ...early 1977 by drummer STEWART COPELAND, vocalist/bassist STING (b. GORDON SUMNER) and guitarist HENRY PADOVANI. In May '77, this line-up released a debut punk single, 'FALL OUT', for Miles Copeland's (brother of STEWART) indie label, 'Illegal'. Immediately after the record's release, they were invited by GONG member MIKE HOWLETT to join veteran guitarist ANDY SUMMERS in live band, STRONTIUM 90. Following PADOVANI's departure in August of the same year (to form the brilliantly monikered FLYING PADOVANI BROTHERS), SUMMERS took his place in The POLICE, this modified line-up initially sessioning on EBERHARD SCHOENER's 'Video Flashback' album. Like all the best 'punk' bands of the time, The POLICE weren't actually punk at all, the members all coming from some kind of 'muso' background, SUMMERS having noodled for the likes of KEVIN AYERS and KEVIN COYNE while COPELAND had drummed for prog-rock merchants, CURVED AIR and STING had plucked his bass for the jazzy LAST EXIT. Not exactly the best credentials for the 'anyone can play' ethos of punk but The POLICE succeeded by infusing their complex reggae-tinged pop/rock with insidiously catchy hooks and radio friendly melodies while keeping most of their songs down to an acceptable post-hippy playing time. They also cultivated a trendy bleached haired image, sporting their new blonde barnets on a Wrigley's Spearmint Gum TV ad. After supporting SPIRIT of all people, the group signed to 'A&M', releasing their debut single, 'ROXANNE', soon after. Initially, this paean to a lady of the night failed to score a chart position, although it was subsequently released a year later, reaching No.12 in the UK charts. The follow-up, 'CAN'T STAND LOSING YOU', was a minor chart hit as was the debut album, 'OUTLANDOS D'AMOUR' (1978). An impressive collection with a strong rhythmic thrust and a few token nods to punk, the album was finally given its due when it was resurrected the following year, reaching Top 10 in the Spring of '79. Later that summer The POLICE captured their first No.1 single with the power pop of the 'MESSAGE IN A BOTTLE' single, swiftly followed by a No.1 album in 'REGATTA DE BLANC' (aka WHITE REGGAE; 1979). Again the record illustrated the band's masterful grasp of dynamics, using time changes to enhance rather than detract from the pop appeal of their songs. From the space reggae of 'WALKING ON THE MOON' to the melodic lament of 'THE BED'S TOO BIG WITHOUT YOU', The POLICE were continually charting new musical territory. It was only a matter of time before the group broke through worldwide, including the lucrative American market. That break came with the 'ZENYATTA MONDATTA' (1980) album and its attendant hits, 'DON'T STAND SO CLOSE TO ME' and the lyrically rhythmic genius of 'DE DO DO DO, DE DA DA DA'. By the release of 'GHOSTS IN THE MACHINE' (1981), The POLICE were now a world beating act, once more delivering the goods with a more instrumentally diverse opus best sampled on the exotically effervescent 'EVERY LITTLE THING SHE DOES IS MAGIC'. STING's lyrics were also taking on a new depth, notably on 'INVISIBLE SUN', wherein the singer commented on the strife-torn Northern Ireland. Bearing in mind that STING's songs formed the bulk of the band's output – leading to simmering discontentment in the ranks – it's surprising how well the trio gel on their final release and undisputed masterpiece, 'SYNCHRONICITY' (1983). The brooding atmospherics of 'EVERY BREATH YOU TAKE' (a massive worldwide No.1) formed the album's centrepiece while the melancholy 'WRAPPED AROUND YOUR FINGER' and the pummelling 'SYNCHRONICITY 2' illustrated the band's ability to craft a consistently satisfying but varied musical palate. The aforementioned tensions ultimately led to the band's demise, although an official announcement wasn't made until 1986, the trio working on solo projects in the meantime. Predictably, STING was the only member who went on to any commercial success – massive success in the event – while COPELAND and SUMMERS lingered in relative obscurity. The former had already released a string of 7"s under the KLARK KENT moniker at the turn of the decade as well as scoring the soundtrack for cult film 'Rumblefish' (featuring vocals of ex-WALL OF VOODOO man, STAN RIDGWAY). During the mid-80's, he went on to make an album of African music, 'THE RHYTHMATIST' (1985) for 'A&M' and a one-off 7" with ADAM ANT, 'OUT OF BOUNDS'. More recently, COPELAND has scored various films including 'Talk Radio', 'Wall Street' and 'First Power', going on to form ANIMAL LOGIC with bassist STANLEY CLARKE and vocalist DEBORAH HOLLAND. SUMMERS, meanwhile, continued his collaboration with ROBERT FRIPP (they'd released the 'I ADVANCE MASKED' album in 1982) on 'BEWITCHED' (1984) before going on to release a series of eclectic solo albums.

Album rating: OUTLANDOS D'AMOUR (*8) / REGATTA DE BLANC (*7) / ZENYATTA MONDATTA (*7) / GHOST IN THE MACHINE (*7) / SYNCHRONICITY (*8) / EVERY BREATH YOU TAKE – THE SINGLES compilation (*9) / GREATEST HITS compilation (*9) / LIVE! collection (*4)

STING (b. GORDON SUMNER, 2 Oct'51, Wallsend, England) – vocals, bass (ex-LAST EXIT) / **HENRY PADOVANI** (b. Corsica) – guitar, vocals / **STEWART COPELAND** (b.19 Jul'52, Alexandria, Egypt) – drums, vocals (ex-CURVED AIR)

	Illegal	not iss.
May 77. (7") (IL 1) **FALL OUT. / NOTHING ACHIEVING**	-	-
(re-act.Dec79 reached UK No.47)		

—— **ANDY SUMMERS** (b. ANDREW SOMERS, 31 Dec'42, Blackpool, England) – guitar (ex-KEVIN AYERS, ex-KEVIN COYNE, ex-ERIC BURDON, ex-SOFT MACHINE) soon repl. HENRY (after brief spell as 4-piece) left to form his FLYING PADOVANI BROTHERS

	A&M	A&M
Apr 78. (7",12") (AMS 7348) **ROXANNE. / PEANUTS**		
(re-iss. Apr79; same) – hit UK No.12		
Aug 78. (7",sha-pic-d,7"in most colours) (AMS 7381) **CAN'T STAND LOSING YOU. / DEAD END JOB**	42	-
(re-iss. Jun79; same) – hit UK No.2		
Oct 78. (lp/blue-lp/c) (AMLH/AMLN/CAM 68502) <4753> **OUTLANDOS D'AMOUR**		23 Feb79
– Next to you / So lonely / Roxanne / Hole in my life / Peanuts / Can't stand losing you / Truth hits everybody / Born in the 50's / Be my girl – Sally / Masoko tanga. (resurrected Apr79 made No.6) (cd-iss. Mar89; CDA 68502) (re-iss. Oct92 cd/c; CD/C MID 126)		
Oct 78. (7") (AMS 7402) **SO LONELY. / NO TIME THIS TIME**		
(re-dist.Feb80; same) – hit UK No.6		
Jan 79. (7") <2096> **ROXANNE. / DEAD END JOB**	-	32
Apr 79. (7") <2147> **CAN'T STAND LOSING YOU. / NO TIME THIS TIME**	-	-
Sep 79. (7",7"green,7"sha-pic-d) (AMS 7474) <2190> **MESSAGE IN A BOTTLE. / LANDLORD**	1	74 Nov79
Oct 79. (lp/c) (AMLH/CAM 64792) <4792> **REGGATTA DE BLANC**	1	25
– Message in a bottle / Reggata de blanc / It's alright for you / Bring on the night / Deathwish / Walking on the Moon / On any other day / The bed's too big without you / Contact / Does everyone stare / No time this time. (cd-iss. Mar89; CDA 64792) (re-iss. Oct92 cd/c; Cd/C MID 127)		
Nov 79. (7"/12") (AMS/+P 7494) **WALKING ON THE MOON. / VISIONS OF THE NIGHT**	1	
Jan 80. (7") **BRING ON THE NIGHT. / VISIONS OF THE NIGHT**	-	
Sep 80. (7"/7"sha-pic-d) (AMS/+P 7564) **DON'T STAND SO CLOSE TO ME. / FRIENDS**	1	-
Oct 80. (lp/c) (AMLH/CAM 64831) <4831> **ZENYATTA MONDATTA**	1	5
– Don't stand so close to me / Driven to tears / When the world is running down, you make the best of what's still around / Canary in a coalmine / Voices in my head / Bombs away / De do do do, de da da da / Behind my camel / Man in a suitcase / Shadows in the rain / The other way of stopping. (cd-iss. Sep86; CDA 64831)		
Oct 80. (7") <2275> **DE DO DO DO, DE DA DA DA. / FRIENDS**	-	10
Dec 80. (7"/7"pic-d) (AMS/+P 7578) **DE DO DO DO, DE DA DA DA. / A SERMON**	5	-
Feb 81. (7") <2301> **DON'T STAND SO CLOSE TO ME. / A SERMON**	-	10
Sep 81. (7") (AMS 8164) **INVISIBLE SUN. / SHAMELLE**	2	-
Sep 81. (7") <2371> **EVERY LITTLE THING SHE DOES IS MAGIC. / SHAMBELLE**	-	3
Oct 81. (lp/c) (AMLK/CKM 63730) <3730> **GHOST IN THE MACHINE**	1	2
– Spirits in the material world / Every little thing she does is magic / Invisible sun / Hungry for love / emolition man / Too much information / Rehumanize yourself / One world (not three) / Omega man / Darkness / Omega man / Secret journey / Darkness. (cd-iss. 1983; CDA 63730)		
Oct 81. (7"/7"pic-d) (AMS/+P 8174) **EVERY LITTLE THING SHE DOES IS MAGIC. / FLEXIBLE STRATEGIES**	1	-
Dec 81. (7") (AMS 8194) **SPIRITS IN THE MATERIAL WORLD. / LOW LIFE**	12	-
Jan 82. (7") <2390> **SPIRITS IN THE MATERIAL WORLD. / FLEXIBLE STRATEGIES**	-	11

Apr 82. (7") <2408> **SECRET JOURNEY. / DARKNESS**	-	46
May 83. (7"/7"pic-d) (AM/+SP 117) <2542> **EVERY BREATH YOU TAKE. / MURDER BY NUMBERS**	1	1
(d7"+=) (AM 117) – Truth hits everybody / Man in a suitcase.		
Jun 83. (lp/c/cd) (AMLX/CXM/CDA 63735) <3735> **SYNCHRONICITY**	1	1
– Synchronicity / alking in your footsteps / O my God / Mother / Miss Gradenko / Synchronicity II / Every breath you take / King of pain / Wrapped around your finger / Tea in the sahara. (c+=/cd+=) – Murder by numbers. (re-iss. Mar93 cd/c; CD/C MID 186)		
Jul 83. (7"/7"pic-d-x3) (AM/+P 127) **WRAPPED AROUND YOUR FINGER. / SOMEONE TO TALK TO**	7	-
(12"+=/12"pic-d+=) (AMX/+P 127) – Message in a bottle (live) / I burn for you.		
Aug 83. (7") <2569> **KING OF PAIN. / SOMEONE TO TALK TO**	-	3
Oct 83. (7") (AM 153) <2571> **SYNCHRONICITY II. / ONCE UPON A DAYDREAM**	17	16
Jan 84. (7"/12") (AM/+X 176) **KING OF PAIN. / TEA IN THE SAHARA (live)**	17	
Jan 84. (7") <2614> **WRAPPED AROUND YOUR FINGER. / TEA IN THE SAHARA (live)**	-	8

—— Split up although not officially, until 1986. STING, ANDY SUMMERS and STEWART COPELAND

– compilations, etc. –

on 'A&M' unless otherwise mentioned

Jun 80. (6x7"box) (AMPP 6001) **SIX PACK**	17	
– (first 5 – A&M singles re-issued in blue vinyl, plus added 45 below) THE BED'S TOO BIG WITHOUT YOU. / TRUTH HITS EVERYBODY		
Sep 86. (7"/12") (AM/+Y 354) <2879> **DON'T STAND SO CLOSE TO ME '86. / (live version)**	24	46
Nov 86. (lp/c/cd) (EVERY/EVERC/EVECD 1) <3902> **EVERY BREATH YOU TAKE – THE SINGLES**	1	7
– Roxanne / Can't stand losing you / Message in a bottle / Walking on the Moon / Don't stand so close to me '86 / De do do do, de da da da / Every little thing she does is magic / Invisible Sun / Spirits in the material world / Every breath you take / King of pain / Wrapped around your finger. (c+=/cd+=) – So lonely. (re-iss. UK Mar92 hit No.31)		
Nov 86. (7"/12") (AM/+Y 363) **ROXANNE '86. / SYNCHRONICITY II**	-	-
Jan 87. (7") **WALKING ON THE MOON. / MESSAGE IN A BOTTLE**	-	-
Apr 88. (3"cd-ep) (AMCD 905) **COMPACT HITS**	-	-
– Roxanne / Can't stand losing you / Canary in a coalmine / Bed's too big without you.		
Jun 89. (d-c) (AMC 24103) **REGATTA DE BLANC / SYNCHRONICITY**	-	-
Oct 92. (cd/c/lp) (540030-2/-4/-1) **THE POLICE: GREATEST HITS** (like above)	10	-
Oct 93. (4xcd-box) <0150> **MESSAGE IN A BOX: THE COMPLETE RECORDINGS**	-	79
May 95. (7"sha-pic-d/12") (581037-7/-1) **CAN'T STAND LOSING YOU (live). / VOICES IN MY HEAD (mix)**	27	
(cd-s+=) (581037-2) – Roxanne live).		
(d12") (581061-1) – Voices in my head (8 remixes).		
May 95. (d-cd/d-c) (540222-2/-4) <0222> **THE POLICE LIVE! (live)**	25	86
– Next to you / So lonely / Truth hits everybody / Walking on the Moon / Hole in my life / Fall out / Bring on the night / Message in a bottle / The bed's too big without you / Peanuts / Roxanne / Can't stand losing you / Landlord / Born in the 50's / Be my girl – Sally / Synchronicity I / Synchronicity II / Walking in your footsteps / Message in a bottle / O my God / De do do do, de da da da / Wrapped around your finger / Tea in the Sahara / Spirits in the material world / King of pain / Don't stand so close to me / Every breathe you take / Roxanne / Can't stand losing you / So lonely.		

—— see also STING for combined STING & THE POLICE releases

Iggy POP

Born: JAMES JEWEL OSTERBERG, 21 Apr'47, Ypsilanti, Michigan, USA. The son of an English father and American mother, he joined The IGUANAS as a drummer in 1964. They issued a cover of Bo Diddley's 'MONA', which was limited to 1,000 copies sold at gigs. The following year, he became IGGY POP and joined The PRIME MOVERS with bassist RON ASHETON, although they folded, IGGY subsequently moving to Chicago. In 1967, he returned to Michigan and formed The (PSYCHEDELIC) STOOGES with RON and his drummer brother SCOTT. They were soon joined by DAVE ALEXANDER, IGGY making his celluloid debut in the avant-garde film, 'Francois De Moniere' with girlfriend NICO. In 1968, the band gigged constantly, on one occasion IGGY being charged with indecent exposure. The following year, A&R man Danny Fields, while looking to sign MC5, instead signed The STOOGES to 'Elektra', furnishing them with a $25,000 advance. Their eponymous debut (produced by JOHN CALE – another VELVET UNDERGROUND connection), later proved to be way ahead of its time. Tracks such as 'NO FUN', '1969' and 'I WANNA BE YOUR DOG', were howling proto-punk, garage classics, later covered by The SEX PISTOLS, SISTERS OF MERCY and SID VICIOUS! respectively. The album just failed to secure a Top 100 placing, the second album faring even worse commercially, although it was hailed by the more discerning critics of the day as a seminal work. From the primal nihilism of 'DIRT', to the psychedelic kiss-off, 'I FEEL ALRIGHT (1970)', it seemed, to The STOOGES at least, as if flower-power had never happened. They were subsequently dropped by their label, following drug-related problems and dissension in the ranks. IGGY moved to Florida, becoming a greenkeeper while taking up golf more seriously, a healthier pastime than his penchant for self-mutilation. In 1972, he had a chance meeting with DAVID BOWIE and manager TONY DeFRIES, who persuaded IGGY to reform his STOOGES and sign a MainMan management deal, this in turn leading to a 'C.B.S.' contract. After his/their flawed classic, 'RAW

POWER' (not one of BOWIE's best productions), they folded again, citing drugs as the cause. It was, however, even more of an embryonic punk record, the amphetamine rush of 'SEARCH AND DESTROY' highly influential on the "blank generation" that would trade-in their STEELY DAN albums for anything with two chords and a sneering vocal. In 1975, IGGY checked in to a psychiatric institute, weaning himself off heroin. His only true friend, BOWIE, who regularly visited him in hospital, invited him to appear on his 'LOW' album. He signed to 'R.C.A.' (home of BOWIE) in 1977, issuing the BOWIE-produced debut solo album, 'THE IDIOT', which, due to the recent "new wave" explosion, broke him into the UK Top 30 and US Top 75. It contained the first BOWIE/POP collaboration, 'CHINA GIRL', later a smash hit for BOWIE. His second solo release, 'LUST FOR LIFE' (also produced by BOWIE in '77), was another gem, again deservedly reaching the UK Top 30 (the title track was later resurrected in 1996 after appearing on the soundtrack to the cult Scottish movie, 'Trainspotting'). In 1979, IGGY moved to 'Arista' records, shifting through various infamous personnel, although his commercial appeal was on the wane. The first half of the 80's saw IGGY desperately trying to carve out a successful solo career while combating his continuing drug problems. Albums such as, 'SOLDIER' (1980), 'PARTY' (1981) and 'ZOMBIE BIRDHOUSE' (1982) marking the nadir of POP's chequered career. Finally teaming up again with BOWIE for 1986's 'BLAH BLAH BLAH', the proclaimed "Godfather Of Punk" at last gained some belated recognition, his revival of a 1957 Johnny O'Keefe hit, 'REAL WILD CHILD', gaving IGGY his first Top 10 hit (UK). Still with 'A&M' records and adding ex-SEX PISTOLS guitarist STEVE JONES, he consolidated his recovery with 'INSTINCT' (1988). His new lease of life prompted 'Virgin America' to give IGGY (who had recently taking up acting) a new contract, the 1990 set, 'BRICK BY BRICK' featuring the G N' R talents of SLASH and DUFF McKAGAN. To end the year, IGGY showed his caring side by duetting with former punkette, DEBORAH HARRY, on AIDS benefit single, 'WELL DID YOU EVAH!' (a bigger hit for NANCY Sinatra & LEE Hazlewood in 1971). He resurfaced once again in 1993 with 'AMERICAN CAESAR', a length set which contained some of his raunchiest tracks for some time, including 'WILD AMERICA', 'F*****' ALONE' and Richard Berry's 'LOUIE LOUIE'. Busying himself with more film work, he eventually broke his recording silence with an umpteenth album, 'NAUGHTY LITTLE DOGGIE' (1996). Mr. POP was back on song in the Autumn of '99, the album 'AVENUE B' delivering his usual raw power with all the finesse of a man taking a motorcycle ride to Hell. 'NAZI GIRLFRIEND', 'LONG DISTANCE' and even a cover of Johnny Kidd's 'SHAKIN' ALL OVER', all testament to a guy not yet ready to get out his pipe and slippers. • IGGY covered; SOMETHING WILD (John Hiatt) / LIVIN' ON THE EDGE OF THE NIGHT (Rifkin / Rackin) / SEX MACHINE (James Brown). • Trivia: In 1987, IGGY made a cameo appearance in the film, 'The Color Of Money'. In 1990, his film & TV work included, 'Cry Baby', 'Shannon's Deal', 'Tales From The Crypt' & 'Miami Vice'. In 1991, he starred in the opera! 'The Manson Family'.

Album rating: Stooges: THE STOOGES (*8) / FUN HOUSE (*10) / RAW POWER as Iggy & the Stooges (*7) / METALLIC K.O. (*5) / Iggy Pop: THE IDIOT (*9) / LUST FOR LIFE (*9) / TV EYE (*3) / NEW VALUES (*5) / SOLDIER (*5) / PARTY (*4) / ZOMBIE BIRDHOUSE (*4) / BLAH-BLAH-BLAH (*6) / INSTINCT (*5) / BRICK BY BRICK (*7) / AMERICAN CAESAR (*6) / NAUGHTY LITTLE DOGGIE (*5) / NUDE & RUDE: THE BEST OF IGGY POP compilation (*8) / AVENUE B (*7)

STOOGES

IGGY POP – vocals / **RON ASHETON** (b. RONALD RANKLIN ASHETON JR., 17 Jul'48, Washington, D.C.) – guitar / **DAVE ALEXANDER** (b. DAVID MICHAEL ALEXANDER, 3 Jun'47, Ann Arbor) – bass / **SCOTT ASHETON** (b. SCOTT RANDOLPH ASHETON, 16 Aug'49, Washington) – drums

		Elektra	Elektra
Sep 69.	(lp) <(EKS 74051)> **THE STOOGES**		Aug69

– 1969 / I wanna be your dog / We will fall / No fun / Real cool time / Ann / Not right / Little doll. (re-iss. Mar77; K 42032) <US cd-iss. 1988; 74051-2> (cd-iss. Nov93; 7559 60667-2)

Oct 69. (7") <EK 45664> **I WANNA BE YOUR DOG. / 1969**

—— added guests **STEVE MACKAY** – saxophone / **BILL CHEATHAM** – 2nd guitar

Dec 70. (lp) <(EKS 74071)> **FUN HOUSE**
– Down on the street / Loose / T.V. eye / Dirt / I feel alright (1970) / Fun house / L.A. blues. (re-iss. Mar77; K 42051) <US cd-iss. 1988; 74071-2> (cd-iss. Nov93; 7559 60669-2)

Dec 70. (7") <EKM 45695> **I FEEL ALRIGHT (1970). / DOWN ON THE STREET**

—— broke-up in 1972. **IGGY** re-formed the group with **SCOTT** and **RON** (now bass)

IGGY AND THE STOOGES

JAMES WILLIAMSON – guitar repl. DAVE (died 10 Feb'75)

		C.B.S.	Columbia
Jun 73.	(lp) (CBS 65586) <KC 32111> **RAW POWER**		May73

– Search and destroy / Gimme danger / Hard to beat * / Penetration / Raw power / I need somebody / Shake appeal / Death trip. (re-iss. Mar77 on 'CBS-Embassy'; 31464), hit UK No.44, *track repl. by – Your pretty face is going to Hell. (re-iss. Nov81; CBS 32081) <US cd-iss. 1988 on 'Columbia'; > (UK re-iss. May89 on 'Essential' cd/c/lp; ESS CD/MC/LP 005) (cd-iss. all tracks) (re-iss. May94 & Apr97 on 'Columbia' cd/c; 485176-2/-4) (lp re-iss. Jul98 on 'Simply Vinyl'; SVLP 33)

Jun 73. (7") <45877> **SEARCH AND DESTROY. / PENETRATION**

—— added **SCOTT THURSTON** – keyboards (on last 1974 tour, before disbanding) The ASHETONS formed The NEW ORDER (US version), with RON moving on to DESTROY ALL MONSTERS who had three 45's for UK label 'Cherry Red' in the late 70's.

– compilations, others, etc. –

1977. (white-d-lp) Visa; <IMP 1015> **METALLIC K.O.**
– Raw power / Head on / Gimme danger / Rich bitch / Cock in my pocket / Louie Louie. (originally issued 1976 on French 'Skydog'; SGIS 008) (re-iss. May88 as 'METALLIC KO x 2' on 'Skydog' lp/cd; 62232-1/2) (cd-iss. Sep94; same) (re-iss. Sep96 & May98 on 'Dressed To Kill'; DTKLP 001)

1977. (7"ep) Bomp; <EP 113> **I'M SICK OF YOU**
– I'm sick of you / Tight pants / Scene of the crime.

1977. (7"ep; by IGGY POP & JAMES WILLIAMSON) Bomp; <EP 114> **JESUS LOVES THE STOOGES**
– Jesus loves the Stooges / Consolation prizes / Johanna. (re-iss. 10"ep.Nov94;)

1977. (7") Siamese; <PM 001> **I GOT A RIGHT. / GIMME SOME SKIN**
(UK-iss.Dec95 on 'Bomp'; REVENGE 2)

Feb 78. (lp,green-lp; as IGGY POP with JAMES WILLIAMSON) Radar; (RAD 2) / Bomp; <BLP 4001> **KILL CITY** ☐ Nov77
– Sell your love / Kill city / I got nothin' / Beyond the law / Johanna / Night theme / Night theme reprise / Master charge / No sense of crime / Lucky monkeys / Consolation prizes. (re-iss. ! on 'Elektra';) (cd-iss. Feb89 on 'Line'; LICD 9.00131) (cd-iss. Jan93;) (re-iss. 10"lp Feb95 on 'Bomp'; BLP 4042-10) (cd-iss. ; BCD 4042)

Apr 78. (7") Radar; (ADA 4) **KILL CITY. / I GOT NOTHIN'**

1978. (7"ep) Skydog; (SGIS 12) **(I GOT) NOTHING** - France
– I got nothing / Gimme danger / Heavy liquid.

Aug 80. (lp/c) Elektra; (K/K4 52234) <EF 7095> **NO FUN** (1969-70 best of THE STOOGES)

1983. (lp) Invasion; <E 1019> **I GOT A RIGHT**

1987. (lp) Revenge; (MIG 2) **I GOT A RIGHT** - France

1987. (7") Revenge; (SS 1) **I GOT A RIGHT. / NO SENSE OF CRIME** - France

1987. (7") Revenge; (BF 50) **KILL CITY. / I'M SICK OF YOU** - France

Dec 87. (lp) Fan Club; (FC 037) **RUBBER LEGS** - France
– Rubber legs / Open up and bleed / Johanna / Cock in my pocket / Head on the curb / Cry for me. (free 7") – GIMME DANGER (live). / I NEED SOMEBODY (live) (cd-iss. Apr97 on 'Last Call'; 422248)

1988. (cd-ep) Revenge; (CAX 1) **PURE LUST** - France
– I got a right / Johanna / Gimme some skin / I got nothing.

1988. (cd-ep) Revenge; (CAX 2) **RAW POWER** - France
– Raw power / Head on the curb / Purple haze / Waiting for the man.

1988. (12"pink-ep,cd-ep) Revenge; (CAX 3) **GIMME DANGER** - France
– Gimme danger / Open up and bleed / Heavy liquid / I got nothing / Dynamite boogie.

1988. (7") Revenge; (SS 6) **JOHANNA. / PURPLE HAZE** - France

Sep 88. (pic-lp; as IGGY & THE STOOGES) Revenge; (LPMIG 6) **DEATH TRIP** - France

May 88. (cd; as IGGY & THE STOOGES) Revenge; (HTM 16) **OPEN UP AND BLEED** - France
(re-iss. Feb96 on 'Bomp' cd/lp; BCD/BLP 4051) (cd re-iss. Jul96; 890016)

Dec 88. (lp; as IGGY & THE STOOGES) Revenge; (MIG 7) **LIVE AT THE WHISKEY A GO-GO**
(cd-iss. Nov94 & Feb97; 895104F)

Dec 88. (lp; as IGGY & THE STOOGES) Electric; (190069) **RAW STOOGES VOL.1** - German

Dec 88. (lp; as IGGY & THE STOOGES) Electric; (190070) **RAW STOOGES VOL.2** - German

May 92. (cd) Line; (LICD 921175) **I'M SICK OF YOU / KILL CITY**

Jun 94. (cd; IGGY & THE STOOGES) New Rose; (890028) **MY GIRL HATES MY HEROIN**
(re-iss. Feb97 on 'Wrote Music'; 7890028) (re-iss. Sep97 on 'Revenge'; MIG 28)

Jul 94. (cd; IGGY & THE STOOGES) New Rose; (642100) **NIGHT OF DESTRUCTION**
(re-iss. as 6xcd-s-box on 'Wind'; WM 375)

Jul 94. (cd; IGGY & THE STOOGES) New Rose; (642042) **TILL THE END OF THE NIGHT**
(re-iss. Apr97; same) (re-iss. Sep97 on 'Revenge'; MIG 42)

Sep 94. (cd; IGGY & THE STOOGES) New Rose; (642011) **LIVE 1971 & EARLY LIVE RARITIES** (live)
(re-iss. Apr97; same)

Sep 94. (cd; IGGY & THE STOOGES) New Rose; (895002) **RAW MIXES VOL.1**

Sep 94. (cd; IGGY & THE STOOGES) New Rose; (895003) **RAW MIXES VOL.2**

Sep 94. (cd; IGGY & THE STOOGES) New Rose; (895004) **RAW MIXES VOL.3**

Feb 95. (10"lp/cd) Bomp; (BLP/BCD 4049) **ROUGH POWER**

—— Also in France; THE STOOGES(12"ep) / SHE CREATURES OF HOLLYWOOD HILLS

Jul 96. (cd) Revenge; (642050) **WILD ANIMAL (live 1977)**

Jul 96. (cd) Revenge; (893334) **PARIS HIPPODROME 1977 (live)**

Jul 96. (cd; as IGGY & THE STOOGES) Trident; (PILOT 008) **YOUR PRETTY FACE IS GOING TO HELL**

Mar 97. (cd; IGGY & THE STOOGES) Bomp; (BCD 4063) **YEAR OF THE IGUANA**

Apr 97. (cd; STOOGES) Arcade; (301563-2) **THE COMPLETE RAW MIXES**

Sep 97. (cd/lp; IGGY & THE STOOGES) Bomp; (BCD/BLP 4069) **CALIFORNIA BLEEDING**

Nov 97. (cd) King Biscuit; (88003) **KING BISCUIT FLOWER HOUR**

Mar 98. (cd) Snapper; (SMMCD 528) **LIVE IN L.A. 1973 (live)**

Apr 98. (cd) King Biscuit; (KBFHCD 001) **KING BISCUIT PRESENTS . . .**

May 88. (12"ep; IGGY & THE STOOGES) Revenge; (CAX 8MAXI) **I GOT NOTHIN. / SEARCH AND DESTROY / COCK IN MY POCKET**

Jun 98. (lp; IGGY & THE STOOGES) Get Back; (GET 33LP) **RUBBER**

Nov 99. (7"pic-d; as IGGY & THE STOOGES) Munster; (MR 7125) **I GOT NOTHING. /**

IGGY POP

— had already went solo, augmented by **DAVID BOWIE** – producer, keyboards / **RICKY GARDINER** – guitar / **TONY SALES** – bass / **HUNT SALES** – drums (latter 2; ex-TODD RUNDGREN) / guest **CARLOS ALOMAR** – guitar

	R.C.A.	R.C.A.
Feb 77. (7") <10989> SISTER MIDNIGHT. / BABY	-	
Mar 77. (lp/c) (PL/PK 12275) <2275> THE IDIOT	30	72

– Sister midnight / Nightclubbing / Fun time / Baby / China girl / Dum dum boys / Tiny girls / Mass production. *(re-iss. Apr90 on 'Virgin' lp/c/cd; OVED/OVEDC/CDOVD 277)*

May 77. (7") (PB 9093) CHINA GIRL. / BABY

— **STACEY HEYDON** – guitar / **SCOTT THURSTON** – keyboards repl. BOWIE + ALOMAR

Sep 77. (lp/c) (PL/PK 12488) <2488> LUST FOR LIFE	28	

– Lust for life / Sixteen / Some weird sin / The passenger / Tonight / Success / Turn blue / Neighbourhood threat / Fall in love with me. *(re-iss. 1984 lp/c; NL/NK 82488) (re-iss. Apr90 on 'Virgin' lp/c/cd; OVED/OVEDC/CDOVD 278) (lp re-iss. Nov97 on 'Virgin'; LPCENT 40)*

Oct 77. (7") (PB 9160) SUCCESS. / THE PASSENGER

— **IGGY** retained **THURSTON**, and recruited **SCOTT ASHETON** – drums / **FRED 'SONIC' SMITH** – guitar (ex-MC5) / **GARY RAMUSSEN** – bass (The SALES brothers later to BOWIE's TIN MACHINE)

Apr 78. (7") (PB 9213) I GOT A RIGHT (live). / SIXTEEN (live)

May 78. (lp/c) (PL/PK 12796) TV EYE (live 1977)

– T.V. eye / Funtime / Sixteen / I got a right / Lust for life / Dirt / Nightclubbing / I wanna be your dog. *(cd-iss. Jul94 on 'Virgin'; CDOVD 448)*

— **IGGY / THURSTON** now with **JAMES WILLIAMSON** – guitar, producer / **JACKIE CLARKE** – bass (ex-IKE & TINA TURNER) / **KLAUS KREUGER** – drums (ex-TANGERINE DREAM) / **JOHN HORDEN** – saxophone

	Arista	Arista
Apr 79. (lp/c) (SPART/TC-SPART 1092) <4237> NEW VALUES	60	

– Tell me a story / New values / Girls / I'm bored / Don't look down / The endless sea / Five foot one / How do ya fix a broken part / Angel / Curiosity / African man / Billy is a runaway. *(re-iss. Mar87; 1201144) (re-iss. Oct90 cd/lp; 260/210 997)*

May 79. (7") (ARIST 255) <0438> I'M BORED. / AFRICAN MAN

Jul 79. (7"/7"pic-d) (ARIP/+D 274) FIVE FOOT ONE. / PRETTY FLAMINGO

— **IGGY / KREUGER** recruited **IVAN KRAL** – guitar (ex-PATTI SMITH) / **PAT MORAN** – guitar / **GLEN MATLOCK** – bass (ex-SEX PISTOLS, ex-RICH KIDS) / **BARRY ANDREWS** – keyboards (ex-XTC, ex-LEAGUE OF GENTLEMEN) (THURSTON formed The MOTELS)

Jan 80. (lp/c) (SPART/TC-SPART 1117) <4259> SOLDIER	62	

– Knockin' 'em down (in the city) / I'm a conservative / I snub you / Get up and get out / Ambition / Take care of me / I need more / Loco mosquito / Mr. Dynamite / Play it safe / Dog food. <US re-iss. Oct87; 201160> *(cd-iss. Apr91; 251 160)*

Jan 80. (7") (ARIST 327) LOCO MOSQUITO. / TAKE CARE OF ME

— **IGGY / KRAL** now with **ROB DuPREY** – guitar / **MICHAEL PAGE** – bass / **DOUGLAS BROWNE** – drums (BARRY ANDREWS formed SHRIEKBACK)

May 81. (7") (ARIST 407) BANG BANG. / SEA OF LOVE

Jun 81. (lp/c) (SPART/TC-SPART 1158) <9572> PARTY

– Pleasure / Rock and roll party / Eggs on plate / Sincerity / Houston is hot tonight / Pumpin' for Jill / Happy man / Bang bang / Sea of love / Time won't let me. *(re-iss. Jan87 lp/c; 203/403 806) (cd-iss. Sep89 on 'R.C.A.'; 253 806)*

— **IGGY / DuPREY** found new people **CHRIS STEIN** – guitar, producer (ex-BLONDIE) / **CLEM BURKE** – drums (ex-BLONDIE)

	Animal-Chrysalis	Animal
Aug 82. (7") (CHFLY 2634) RUN LIKE A VILLAIN. / PLATONIC		
Sep 82. (lp/c) (CHR/ZCHR 1399) <APE 6000> ZOMBIE BIRDHOUSE		

– Run like a villain / The villagers / Angry hills / Life of work / The ballad of Cookie McBride / Ordinary bummer / Eat to be eaten / Bulldozer / Platonic / The horse song / Watching the news / Street crazies.

— In 1984, he sang the title song on Alex Cox's movie 'REPO MAN'. For the same director, he appeared in the 1985 film 'SID & NANCY' about SID VICIOUS.

— **IGGY** now with **ERDAL KIZILCAY** – drums, bass, synthesizers / **KEVIN ARMSTRONG** – guitar / **BOWIE + STEVE JONES** (guest writers)

	A&M	A&M
Sep 86. (7"/12") (AM/+Y 358) <2874> CRY FOR LOVE. / WINNERS & LOSERS		
Oct 86. (lp/c/cd) <(AMA/AMC/CDA 5145)> BLAH-BLAH-BLAH	43	75

– Real wild child (wild one) / Baby, it can't fail / Shades / Fire girl / Isolation / Cry for love / Blah-blah-blah / Hideaway / Winners and losers. *(cd+=)* – Little Miss Emperor. *(cd re-iss. 1989; 395 145-2) (re-iss. Jun91 cd/c; CD/C+/MID 159)*

Nov 86. (7"/12") (AM/+Y 368) <2909> REAL WILD CHILD (WILD ONE). / LITTLE MISS EMPEROR	10	

Feb 87. (7") (AM 374) SHADES. / BABY IT CAN'T FAIL

(12"+=) (AMY 374) – Cry for love.

Apr 87. (7"/12") (AM/+Y 392) FIRE GIRL. / BLAH-BLAH-BLAH (live)

Jun 87. (7") (AM 397) ISOLATION. / HIDEAWAY

(12"+=) (AMY 397) – Fire girl (remix).

— **IGGY** now with **STEVE JONES** – guitar / **PAUL GARRISTO** – drums (ex-PSYCHEDELIC FURS) / **SEAMUS BEAGHEN** – keyboards / **LEIGH FOXX** – bass

Jul 88. (lp/c/cd) <(AMA/AMC/ADA 5198)> INSTINCT	61	

– Cold metal / High on you / Strong girl / Tom tom / Easy rider / Power & freedom / Lowdown / Tuff baby / Squarehead.

Aug 88. (7") (AM 452) COLD METAL. / INSTINCT

(12"+=/12"pic-d+=) (AM Y/P 452) – Tuff baby.

Nov 88. (7") (AM 475) HIGH ON YOU. / SQUAREHEAD

(12"+=) (AMY 475) – Tuff baby (remix).

— **ALVIN GIBBS** – guitar (ex-UK SUBS) repl. STEVE JONES (continued solo) / **ANDY McCOY** – bass (ex-HANOI ROCKS) repl. FOXX (to DEBORAH HARRY)

Nov 88. (lp/c/cd) LIVE AT THE CHANNEL (live 17.9.88)	-	

(UK-iss.May94 on 'New Rose'; 642005) (re-iss. cd Sep97 on 'Revenge'; MIG 40-41)

— now with **SLASH** – guitar / **DUFF McKAGAN** – bass (both of GUNS N' ROSES) / **KENNY ARONOFF** – drums

	Virgin America	Virgin America
Jan 90. (7"/c-s) (VUS/+C¹ 18) <VSC 1228> LIVIN' ON THE EDGE OF THE NIGHT. / THE PASSENGER	51	

(12"+=/12"pic-d+=/cd-s+=) (VUS T/TE/CD 18) – Nightclubbing / China girl.

Jun 90. (7"/c-s) (VUS/+C 22) HOME. / LUST FOR LIFE

(12"+=/cd-s+=) (VUS T/CD 22) – Pussy power / Funtime.

Jul 90. (cd/c/lp) (CDVUS/VUSMC/VUSLP 19) <91381> BRICK BY BRICK	50	90

– Home / Main street eyes / I won't crap out / Candy / Butt town / The undefeated / Moonlight lady / Something wild / Neon forest / Stormy night / Pussy power / My baby wants to rock & roll / Brick by brick / Livin' on the edge of the night. *(c re-iss. Apr92; OVEDC 426)*

(below 'A'side featured **KATE PIERSON** – vox (of B-52's)

Oct 90. (7"/c-s) (VUS/+C 29) <98900> CANDY. / PUSSY POWER (acoustic demo)	67	28

(10"+=/cd-s+=) (VUS 29) – My baby wants to rock'n'roll (acoustic demos).
(12"/cd-s) (VUS T/CD 29) – ('A'side) / The undefeated / Butt town (acoustic demo).

— Oct 90, IGGY dueted with DEBORAH HARRY on UK Top 50 single 'DID YOU EVAH'; *Chrysalis; CHS 3646)*

— with **LARRY MULLEN** (U2) – drums, percussion / **HAL CRAGIN** – bass / **ERIC SCHERMERHORN** – guitar plus guests **MALCOLM BURN** – guitars, etc

Aug 93. (12"ep/c-ep/12"ep/cd-ep) (VUS/+C/T/CD 74) THE WILD AMERICA EP	63	

– Wild America / Credit card / Come back tomorrow / My angel.

Sep 93. (cd/c/lp) (CDVUS/VUSMC/VUSLP 64) AMERICAN CAESAR	43	

– Character / Wild America / Mixin' the colors / Jealousy / Hate / It's our love / Plastic & concrete / F***in' alone / Highway song / Beside you / Sickness / Boogie boy / Perforation / Problems / Social life / Louie Louie / Caesar / Girls of N.Y

May 94. (10"ep) (VUS A/C 77) BESIDE YOU / EVIL CALIFORNIA. / HOME (live) / FUCKIN' ALONE	47	

(cd-ep) (VUSCD 77) – ('A'side) / Les amants / Louie Louie (live) / ('A'acoustic).

Feb 96. (cd/c/lp) (CDVUS/VUSMC/VUSLP 102) NAUGHTY LITTLE DOGGIE		

– I wanna live / Pussy walk / Innocent world / Knucklehead / To belong / Keep on believing / Outta my head / Shoeshine girl / Heart is saved / Look away.

— IGGY featured in the film 'The Crow II'

Sep 99. (cd) (CDVUS 163) AVENUE B		

– No shit / Nazi girlfriend / Avenue B / Miss Argentina / Afraid to get close / Shakin' all over / Long distance / Corruption / She called me daddy / I felt the luxury / Espanol / Motorcycle / Facade.

Oct 99. (7") (VUS 155) CORRUPTION. / ROCK STAR GRAVE

(cd-s+=) (VUSCD 155) – Hollywood affair.

– compilations, etc. –

May 82. (7") RCA Gold; (GOLD 549) THE PASSENGER. / NIGHTCLUBBING		
Sep 84. (lp/c) R.C.A.; (PL/PK 84597) CHOICE CUTS		-
Apr 88. (cd-ep) A&M; (AMCD 909) COMPACT HITS		

– Real wild child (the wild one) / Isolation / Cry for love / Shades.

Jan 92. (cd) Arista; (262 178) POP SONGS		
Jan 93. (3xcd-box) Virgin; (TPAK 21) LUST FOR LIFE / THE IDIOT / BRICK BY BRICK		
Jun 93. (cd) Revenge; (642044) LIVE NYC RITZ '86 (live)		
Aug 93. (cd/c) Revenge; (642/644 050) SUCK ON THIS!		
Aug 95. (cd) Skydog; WE ARE NOT TALKING ABOUT COMMERCIAL SHIT		
Aug 95. (cd) Skydog; WAKE UP SUCKERS		
Aug 96. (cd) M.C.A.; (MCD 84021) THE BEST OF IGGY POP LIVE (live)		
Sep 96. (cd) Camden RCA; (74321 41503-2) POP MUSIC		
Oct 96. (cd/c/d-lp) Virgin; (CDVUS/VUSMC/VUSLP 115) NUDE & RUDE: THE BEST OF IGGY POP		

– I wanna be your dog / No fun / Search & destroy / Gimme danger / I'm sick of you / Funtime / Nightclubbing / China girl / Lust for life / The passenger / Kill city / Real wild child / Cry for love / Cold metal / Candy / Home / Wild America.

Nov 96. (7"colrd/c-s) Virgin; (VUS/+C 116) LUST FOR LIFE / (GET UP I FEEL LIKE BEING A) SEX MACHINE	26	

(cd-s+=) (VUSCD 116) – ('A'live) / I wanna be your dog (live).

Dec 96. (cd) The Network; (3D 013) POP MUSIC		-
Apr 97. (cd) Wotre; (642007) LIVE IN BERLIN '91		-
Sep 97. (d-cd) Snapper; (SMDCD 142) HEAD ON		-
Nov 97. (cd) Other People's Music; (OPM 2116CD) HEROIN HATES YOU		-
Nov 97. (cd) Eagle; (EABCD 011) THE MASTERS		-
Feb 98. (c-s) Virgin; (VSC 1689) THE PASSENGER /	22	

(12"+=/cd-s+=) (VS T/CDT 1689) –

Aug 98. (cd) A&M; (540943-2) BLAH BLAH BLAH / INSTINCT		-

POP GROUP

Formed: Bristol, England ... 1978 by MARK STEWART, JON WADDINGTON, DAVID WRIGHT, SEAN OLIVER and BRUCE SMITH. Inspired by punk's nihilistic energy and influenced by everyone from ROLAND KIRK to CAN and LEE PERRY, The POP GROUP harnessed their competing forces into a funky but defiant howl of rage at newly elected Prime Minister, Margaret Thatcher, with 1979's debut single, 'SHE IS BEYOND GOOD AND EVIL'. Issued on Jake Riviera's newly established 'Radar' label, the track was hailed as one of the most innovative releases of the post-punk era. With OLIVER and WRIGHT subsequently replaced by SIMON UNDERWOOD and GARETH SAGER – the latter introducing screeching free-jazz sax into the equation – The POP GROUP recorded a landmark debut album, 'Y' (1979). Produced by reggae veteran DENNIS

BOVELL, the record presaged the primal intensity of The BIRTHDAY PARTY with spontaneous layers of visceral noise, militant lyrics and tortured vocals underpinned by CHIC-style basslines and dub dynamics. NICK CAVE, for one, was irrevocably changed after witnessing The POP GROUP in full flight, recently confessing (early 1999) on Channel 4 that the seminal 'WE ARE ALL PROSTITUTES' was among the most "violent, paranoid" music he'd ever heard. Essential ingredients for decent rock'n'roll of course, the band's first single for 'Rough Trade' offering it up in spades. A second album, 'FOR HOW MUCH LONGER DO WE TOLERATE MASS MURDER' (1980), was, if anything, even more intense but hardly helped widen the band's limited appeal. Something had to give and inevitably it all ended in tears, the band subsequently embroiled in legal wrangles with their label and signing off after a split single with The SLITS. STEWART went on to work with The ON-U SOUND posse, issuing records as MARK STEWART & THE MAFFIA (and later solo in his own right), while SAGER went on to form RIP, RIG + PANIC. UNDERWOOD achieved brief but enduring acclaim as founder of PIGBAG while WADDINGTON formed MAXIMUM JOY. OLIVER, sadly, was to die of heart failure in 1990, having recently co-written TERENCE TRENT D'ARBY's massive 'Wishing Well'. As cult as they come, The POP GROUP are widely acknowledged as laying the foundations for a fertile Bristol music scene which would subsequently spawn such revered artists as MASSIVE ATTACK, NENEH CHERRY, NELLEE HOOPER, PORTISHEAD, TRICKY etc. • Songwriters: STEWART lyricist / group compositions.

Album rating: Y (*7) / FOR HOW MUCH LONGER . . . (*8) / WE ARE TIME (*5) / Mark Stewart: LEARNING TO COPE WITH COWARDICE (*6) / AS THE VENEER OF DEMOCRACY BEGINS TO FADE (*6) / MARK STEWART (*5) / METATRON (*5) / CONTROL DATA (*5)

MARK STEWART – vocals / **JOHN WADDINGTON** – guitar / **DAVID WRIGHT** – saxophone / **SEAN OLIVER** – bass / **BRUCE SMITH** – drums, percussion

		Radar	not iss.
Mar 79. (7"/12") *(ADA 29/1229)* **SHE IS BEYOND GOOD AND EVIL. / 3:38**		☐	-

—— **SIMON UNDERWOOD** – bass repl. OLIVER who joined ESSENTIAL LOGIC / **GARETH SAGER** – guitar, saxophone repl. WRIGHT who joined ESSENTIAL LOGIC

Apr 79. (lp) *(RAD 20)* **Y** ☐ -
– Thief of fire / Snowgirl / Blood money / Savage sea / We are time / Words disobey me / Don't call me Pain / The boys from Brazil / Don't sell your dreams. *(re-iss. cd/lp; SCAN CD/LP 14)(+=)* – She is beyond good and evil.

—— **DAN KATSIS** – bass (also of GLAXO BABIES) repl. SIMON who joined PIGBAG / added **TRISTAN HONSINGER** – cello

		Rough Trade	not iss.
Oct 79. (7") *(RT 023)* **WE ARE ALL PROSTITUTES. / OUR CHILDREN SHALL RISE UP AGAINST**		☐	-

—— **PAUL STUART** – drums; repl. SMITH who joined SLITS

Mar 80. (7") *(RT 039 – Y1)* **(In The Beginning – by SLITS). / WHERE THERE'S A WILL THERE'S A WAY** ☐ -
Mar 80. (lp) *(ROUGH 9 – Y2)* **FOR HOW MUCH LONGER DO WE TOLERATE MASS MURDER?** ☐ -
– Forces of oppression / Feed the hungry / One out of many / Blind faith / How much longer . . . / Justice / There are no spectators / Communicate / Rob a bank.
Dec 80. (lp) *(ROUGH 12 – Y5)* **WE ARE TIME (live)** ☐ -
– Kiss the book / Amnesty report / Springer / Sense of purpose / We are time / Trap / Thief of fire / Genius or lunatic / Colour blind / Spanish inquisition. *(re-iss. Aug84; same)*

—— split 1980, when GARETH formed RIP, RIG & PANIC with other ex-POP GROUP members, SEAN and BRUCE. WADDINGTON and CATSIS formed MAXIMUM JOY

MARK STEWART

		Y Records	not iss.
May 82. (10"/7"; as MOUTH 2) *(10+/Y 20)* **WHO'S HOT. / CATCH A CAB**		☐	-

—— with **CHARLES 'ESKIMO' FOX** – drums / **EVAR** – bass / **NOAH** – keyboards

		On-U-Sound	not iss.
Oct 82. (10"ep; as MARK STEWART & THE MAFFIA) *(ONUDP 5)* **JERUSALEM. / HIGH IDEALS AND CRAZY DREAMS / LIBERTY CITY**		☐	-

—— **FATFINGERS** – keyboards; repl. NOAH

Jun 83. (lp; as MARK STEWART & THE MAFFIA) *(ONULP 24)* **LEARNING TO COPE WITH COWARDICE** ☐ -
– Learning to cope with cowardice / Liberty city / Blessed are those / Who struggle / None dare / Call it conspiracy / Don't you ever lay down / Your arms / The paranoia of power / To have the vision / Jerusalem.

—— he again worked with **ADRIAN SHERWOOD** – producer / **KEITH LA BLANCA** – drums (ex-MALCOLM X) / **DOUG WIMBUSH** – bass / **SKIP McDONALD** – keyboards, guitar

		Mute	Mute
May 85. (7") *(7MUTE 37)* **HYPNOTISED. / DREAMERS**		☐	☐

(12"+=) (12MUTE 37) – The veneer of democracy starts to fade.
Nov 85. (lp) *(<STUMM 24>)* **AS THE VENEER OF DEMOCRACY BEGINS TO FADE** ☐ ☐
– Passcreation programme / Bastards / The resistance of the cell / As the veneer of democracy starts to fade / Hypnotised / Slave of love / The waiting room. *(cd-iss. Apr88 +=; CDSTUMM 24)* – Dreamers.
Sep 87. (7") *(MUTE 59)* **THIS IS STRANGER THAN LOVE. / ANGER IS HOLY** ☐ ☐
(12"+=) (12MUTE 59) – Survival / ('A'dub).
Oct 87. (cd/lp) *(<CD+/STUMM 43>)* **MARK STEWART** ☐ ☐

– Survival / Survivalist / Anger is holy / Hell is empty / Stranger / Forbidden colour – Forbidden dub / Fatal attraction / This is stranger than love.
Mar 90. (12"/cd-s) *(12/CD MUTE 92)* **HYSTERIA. /** ☐ -
Apr 90. (cd/c/lp) *(<CD/C+/STUMM 62>)* **METATRON** ☐ -
– Hysteria / Shame / Collision / Faith healer / These things happen / My possession / Possession dub / Mammon.
Mar 96. (12"/cd-s) *(12/CD MUTE 130)* **DREAM KITCHEN. /** ☐ -
Apr 96. (cd/d-lp) *(CD+/STUMM 93)* <69013> **CONTROL DATA** ☐ Jun96
– Dream kitchen / Forbidden love / Red zone / Scorpio / Consumed / Data blast / Digital justice / Simulacra / Half / Blood money 2.
Aug 98. (cd-s/12") *(CD+/MUTE 213)* **CONSUMED (remix). /** ☐ -

---

POPOL VUH (dig out; Great Psychedelic . . .)

John POPPER (see under ⇒ BLUES TRAVELLER)

POP WILL EAT ITSELF

Formed: Stourbridge, Midlands, England . . . early 1985 initially as WILD AND WANDERING by vocalist/guitarist CLINT MANSELL, guitarist/keyboardist ADAM MOLE, bassist RICHARD MARCH and drummer GRAHAM CRABB. After the wittily titled '2000 LIGHT ALES FROM HOME' EP, the band adopted the POP WILL EAT ITSELF moniker in early '86. Their debut release, 'POPPIES SAY GRRR . . . EP' was originally sold at a Dudley gig, although after this DIY effort was made more widely available, it subsequently became an NME single of the week and was playlisted on night time Radio One. Later that summer, the band signed to Craig Jennings' indie label, 'Chapter 22', Jennings becoming their manager after a few more singles (including a cover of SIGUE SIGUE SPUTNIK's brilliantly vacant 'LOVE MISSILE F1-11'). By the release of the impressive debut album, 'BOX FRENZY' (1987) these self-styled 'GREBO GURU's were in the process of progressing from their early guitar pop to a sample-driven hybrid of heavy punk (a la KILLING JOKE) and psyche-pop. While songs like 'BEAVER PATROL' were criticised for their schoolboy sexism, indie chart hits like the driven genius of 'THERE IS NO LOVE BETWEEN US ANYMORE' and the anthemic 'DEF CON ONE' proved they were major contenders. Fittingly then, they were duly signed up by 'R.C.A.' and scored further minor chart successes with 'CAN U DIG IT' and 'WISE UP! SUCKER', while a follow-up album, 'THIS IS THE DAY, THIS IS THE HOUR, THIS IS THIS' (1989) made the Top 30. By this point the band had long since abandoned a conventional drum kit for an electronic model and, in the Spring of 1990, PWEI turned out their most dance-friendly track to date in 'TOUCHED BY THE HAND OF CICCIOLINA'. A collaboration with the infamous Italian porn star-turned MP (only in Italy!) of the same name, the record was released just in time for the World Cup, complete with crowd noises and chanting. That year's album, 'THE POP WILL EAT ITSELF CURE FOR SANITY', confirmed the trend with 'DANCE OF THE MAD BASTARDS' and 'X, Y AND ZEE'. Nevertheless, by the release of 'THE LOOKS OR THE LIFESTYLE' (1992), the band had reverted back to a living, breathing human drummer in the form of FUZZ. Although the record spawned their biggest hit to date, the Top 10 'GET THE GIRL! KILL THE BADDIES', PWEI were subsequently dropped by RCA after the live 'WEIRD'S BAR & GRILL' (1993), the band also largely dismissed by a music press that had new fish to fry. Down but not out, the grebo troopers signed a new deal with the indie label, 'Infectious', hooking up with 'FUN-DA-MENTAL' in 1994 for the anti-nazi effort, 'ICH BIN EIN AUSLANDER'. The record was a minor hit, although their fifth studio effort, the harder-edged 'DOS DEDOS MIS AMIGOS' became their highest charting album to date, almost reaching the Top 10 and proving that they could get along just fine without a major label. If any more proof was needed, the defiantly titled remix album, 'TWO FINGERS MY FRIENDS', showed that PWEI were nothing if not resilient. • **Songwriters:** Group compositions except; LIKE AN ANGEL (Mighty Lemon Drops) / ORGONE ACCUMULATOR (Hawkwind) / EVERYTHING THAT RISES (Eno) / ROCK-A-HULA BABY (Elvis Presley).

Album rating: BOX FRENZY (*8) / NOW FOR A FEAST compilation (*7) / THIS IS THE DAY, THIS IS THE HOUR, THIS IS THIS (*7) / . . . CURE FOR SANITY (*5) / THE LOOKS OF THE LIFESTYLE (*6) / WEIRDS, BAR & GRILL (*4) / 16 DIFFERENT FLAVOURS OF HELL compilation (*7) / DOS DEDOS MIS AMIGOS (*5) / TWO FINGERS MY FRIENDS remixes (*5)

CLINT MANSELL (b. 7 Jan'63, Coventry, England) – vocals, guitar / **ADAM MOLE** (b. 8 Apr'62) – guitar, keyboards / **GRAHAM CRABB** (b.10 Oct'64, Sutton Coldfield, England) – drums / **RICHARD MARCH** (b. 4 Mar'65, York, England) – bass

		Iguana	not iss.
Feb 86. (12"ep; as WILD & WANDERING) *(VYK 14)* **2000 LIGHT ALES FROM HOME**			-

– Dust me down / Stand by me / Real cool time / Interlong / Apple tree (pt.1 & 2).

		Desperate	not iss.
May 86. (7"ep) *(SRT 1)* **THE POPPIES SAY GRRRR . . . EP**		☐	-

– I'm sticking with you hoo / Sick little girl / Mesmerized / There's a psychopath in my soup / Candydiosis. *(re-iss. Jun86; DAN 1)*

		Chapter 22	Rough Trade
Oct 86. (7"ep) *(CHAP 9)* **POPPIECOCK**		☐	-

– The Black country chainsaw massacreee / Monogamy / Oh Grebo I think I love you / Titanic clown / B-B-B-Breakdown.
(12"ep+=) (12CHAP 9) – THE POPPIES SAY GRRRR . . . EP.
Jan 87. (12"/7") *(12+/CHAP 11)* **SWEET SWEET PIE. / DEVIL INSIDE / RUNAROUND** ☐ -
May 87. (7") *(CHAP 13)* **LOVE MISSILE F1-11. / ORGONE ACCUMULATOR** ☐ -

(12"ep+=) **THE COVERS EP** *(12CHAP 13)* – Everything that rises / Like an angel.
(12"ep+=) *(L12CHAP 13)* – ('A'-Designer Grebo mix) / Everything that rises (new version).

Sep 87. (7"pink,7"clear/7") *(L+/CHAP 16)* **BEAVER PATROL. / BUBBLES**
(12"+=) *(12CHAP 16)* – Oh Grebo I think I love you (new version).

Oct 87. (lp/c/cd) *(CHAP LP/MC/CD 18)* <ROUGHUS 33/+C/CD> **BOX FRENZY**
– Grebo guru / Beaver patrol / Let's get ugly / U.B.L.U.D. / Inside you / Evelyn / There is no love between us anymore / She's surreal / Intergalactic love mission / Love missile F1-11 / Hit the hi-tech groove / Razorblade kisses.

Jan 88. (7"pic-d/7") *(L+/CHAP 20)* **THERE IS NO LOVE BETWEEN US ANYMORE. / PICNIC IN THE SKY** `66`
(12"+=) *(12CHAP 20)* – On the razor's edge / Kiss that girl.
(ext.12"+=) *(L12CHAP 20)* – ('A'-extended high mix) / Hit the hi-tech groove (the M&K mix).
(12") *(CLUBCHAP 20)* – (above 2 tracks).

Jul 88. (7") *(PWEI 001)* **DEF CON ONE. / INSIDE YOU (live)** `63`
(12"+=) *(PWEI 12-001)* – She's surreal (live) / Hit the hi-tech groove (live).
(12"+=) *(PWEIL 12-001)* – ('A'-Doomsday power mix) / She's surreal (live).

Dec 88. (lp/c/cd) *(CHAP LP/MC/CD 33)* **NOW FOR A FEAST** (compilation)
– The Black country chainstore massacreee / Monogamy / Oh Grebo I think I love you / Titanic clown / B-B-B-Breakdown / Sweet sweet pie / Like an angel / I'm sniffin' with you hoo / Sick little girl / Mesmerized / There's a psychopath in my soup / Candydiosis / The devil inside / Orgone accumulator.

Feb 89. (7"/7"orange,7"green/7"s) *(PB 42621/42619/42729)* **CAN U DIG IT. / POISON TO THE MIND**   R.C.A.   R.C.A. `38`
(cd-s+=) *(PD 42620)* – Radio PWEI (acapella) / ('A'-12"version).
(12"++=) *(PT 42620)* – The fuses have been lit.

Apr 89. (7"/7"pic-d) *(PB PB 42761/42793)* **WISE UP! SUCKER. / ORGYONE STIMULATOR** `41`
(c-s+=)(12"+=/cd-s+=) *(PK 42761)(PT/PD 42762)* – ('A'extended / Can u dig it (riffs mix).
(10") *(PJ 42762)* – ('A'side) / ('A'extended) / ('A'version).

May 89. (lp/c/cd) *(PL/PK/PD 74106)* <9742> **THIS IS THE DAY, THIS IS THE HOUR, THIS IS THIS** `24`
– PWEI is a four letter word / Preaching to the peverted / Wise up! sucker / Sixteen different flavours of Hell / Inject me / Can u dig it? / The fuses have been lit / Poison to the mind / Def con one / Radio PWEI / Shortwave transmission on up to the minuteman / Satellite ecstatica / Now we're busy / Wake up! time to die . . . *(cd+=)* – Wise up sucker (mix). *(re-iss. cd Nov93; 74321 15792-2)*

Aug 89. (7"ep)(7"g-f-ep)(7"sha-pic-ep)(c-ep)(12"ep)(cd-ep) *(PB 42883)(PB 43021)(PA 43022)(PK 43023)(PT 42884)(PD 42894)*
VERY METAL NOISE POLLUTION EP `45`
– Very metal noise pollution / P.W.E.I.-zation / 92° F / Def con one 1989 A.D.
(12") *(PT 43068)* – Def con 1989 AD including:- Twilight zone / Preaching to the peverted / P.W.E.I.-zation / 92° F.

May 90. (7"/c-s) *(PB/PK 43735)* **TOUCHED BY THE HAND OF CICCIOLINA. / THE INCREDI-BULL MIX** `28`
(12"+=) *(PT 43736)* – ('A'-Extra time mix).
(cd-s) *(PD 43736)* – ('A'-Extra time mix) / ('A'-Diva Futura mix) / ('A'-Renegade Soundwave mix – Smoothneck).
(12") *(PT 43738)* – ('A'-Diva Futura mix) / ('A'-Renegade Soundwave mix – Smoothneck).

Oct 90. (7"/c-s) *(PB/PK 44023)* **DANCE OF THE MAD. / PREACHING TO THE PEVERTED** `32`
(12"ep+=/cd-ep+=) **PWEI VS. THE MORAL MAJORITY EP** *(PT/PD 44023)* – ('A'other mix).

Oct 90. (cd/c/lp) *(PD/PK/PL 74828)* **CURE FOR SANITY** `33`
– Incredible PWEI vs. The Moral Majority / Dance of the mad bastards / 88 seconds . . . and still counting / X Y & Zee / City Zen radio 1990-2000 FM / Dr. Nightmares medication time / Touched by the hand of Cicciolina / 1000 x no! / Psycho sexual / Axe of men / Another man's rhubarb / Medicine man speaks with forked tongue / Nightmare at 20,000 feet / Very metal noise pollution / 92 degrees (the 3rd degree) / Lived in splendour, died in chaos / The beat that refused to die. *(re-iss. May91 pic-lp; PL 75041)* *(re-iss. cd Nov93; 74321 15791-2)*

Jan 91. (7"/c-s) *(PB/PK 44243)* **X Y & ZEE. / AXE OF MEN** `15`
(12"box+=) *(PT 44243)* – Psychosexual.
(12"+=/cd-s+=) *(PT/PD 44243)* – ('A'-Intergalactic mix) / ('A'-Sensory amp mix).

May 91. (7"/c-s) *(PB/PK 44555)* **92 DEGREES. / INCREDIBLE PWEI VS. DIRTY HARRY** `23`
(10"+=/12"+=/cd-s+=) *(PX/PT/PD 44555)* – Another man's rhubarb.

May 92. (7"/c-s) *(PB/PK 45467)* **KARMADROME. / EAT ME DRINK ME LOVE ME** `17`
(12"+=) *(PT 45467)* – Dread alert in the karmadrome / ('A'version).
(cd-s) *(PD 45467)* – ('A'side) / PWEI-zation (original metal noise pollution).
(12"pic-d+=) *(PTP 45467)* – PWEI-zation (original . . .) / Eat me drink me dub . . .

Aug 92. (7"pic-d/c-s+=) *(74321 11013-7/4)* **BULLETPROOF! / ('A'-On-U-Sound mix)** `24`
(12"pic-d+=/cd-s+=) *(74321 11013-6/-2)* – Good from far, far from good.
(12") *(74321 11013-8)* – ('A'-Mile high mix) / ('A'-No half measures mix).

Sep 92. (cd/c/lp) *(74321 10265-2/-4/-1)* **THE LOOKS OR THE LIFESTYLE** `15`
– England's finest / Eat me, drink me, love me, kill me / Mother / Get the girl, kill the baddies! / I've always been a coward baby / Spoken drug song / Karmadrome / Urban futuristic (son of South Central) / Pretty pretty / I was a teenage grandad / Harry Dean Stanton / Bulletproof!. *(re-iss. cd Nov93; 74321 15790-2)*

—— added 5th member **FUZZ TOWNSHEND** (b. JOHN TOWNSHEND, 31 Jul'64, Birmingham, England) – drums

Jan 93. (7"/c-s) *(74321 12880-7/-4)* **GET THE GIRL! KILL THE BADDIES!. / ('A'-Adrian Sherwood mix)** `9`
(12"+=/cd-s+=) *(74321 12880-6/-2)* – ('A'-Black country & western mix) or ('A'boilerhouse mix).
(cd-s) *(74321 12880-5)* – ('A'side) / Urban futuristic (live) / Can u dig it? (live) / Wise up! sucker! (live).

Feb 93. (cd/c/lp) *(74321 13343-2/-4/-1)* **WEIRD'S BAR AND GRILL (live)** `44`
– England's finest / Eat me drink me love me kill me / Get the girl, kill the baddies!! (live)

Wise up! sucker / 88 seconds and counting / Karmadrome / Token drug song mother / Preaching to the perverted / Axe of men / Nightmare at 20,000 feet / Always been a coward / Can U dig it / Bullet proof / Urban futuristic / There is no love between us anymore / Def con one. *(cd+=/c+=)* – Harry Dean Stanton teenage grandad.

Oct 93. (cd/c/lp) *(74321 15317-2/-4/-1)* **16 DIFFERENT FLAVOURS OF HELL** (compilation) `73`
– Def con one / Wise up! sucker / Can U dig it / Touched by the hand of Cicciolina (extra time mix) / Dance of the mad / X Y & Zee (sunshine mix) / 92 degrees (Boilerhouse The Birth mix) / Karmadrome / Bullet proof / Get the girl! kill the baddies! / Another man's rhubarb / Rockahula baby / Wise up sucker / Cicciolina (Renegade Soundwave mix) *(cd+=)* – Preaching to the perverted (remix) / Eat me drink me love me kill me / PWEi-zatin.

    Infectious   Nothing-Interscope

Oct 93. (c-s) *(INFECT 1MC)* <95887> **R.S.V.P. / FAMILUS HORRIBILUS** `27`   Feb94
(cd-ep+=) *(INFECT 1CD)* – ('B'remixes) / ('B'live).
(12"ep+=/cd-ep+=) *(INFECT 1/+CDX)* – ('A'side) / ('B'-Higher later space mix agency vocal).

Feb 94. (7"/7"pic-d) *(INFECT 4 G/P)* **ICH BIN EIN AUSLANDER. / CP1 #2** `28`
(12"+=/cd-s+=) *(INFECT 4/+CD)* – ('A'-Fun-Da-Mental instrumental) / ('A'-Fun-Da-Mental extra).
(12"+=) *(INFECT 4TX)* – ('A'-Drone ranger mix) / Intense.

Sep 94. (7"colrd) *(INFECT 9GG)* **EVERYTHING'S COOL. / LET IT FLOW** `23`
(7"colrd) *(INFECT 9SO)* – ('A'side) / Wild west.
(cd-s) *(INFECT 9CD)* – ('A'side) / ('A'-Youth remix) / R.S.V.P. (Fluke mix).
(cd-s) *(INFECT 9CDX)* – ('A'side) / Ich bin ein Auslander (live) / Familus horribilus (live) / R.S.V.P. (live).

Sep 94. (cd/c) *(INFECT 10 CD/MC)* <92393> **DOS DEDOS MIS AMIGOS** `11`
– Ich bin ein Auslander / Kick to kill / Familus horribilus / Underbelly / Fatman / Home / Cape connection / Menofearthereaper / Everything's cool / R.S.V.P. / Babylon. *(also d-lp/d-c/d-cd; INFECT 10 LPX/MCX/CDX)*

Mar 95. (d-cd/d-c) *(INFECT 10 CDR/MCR)* <22> **TWO FINGERS MY FRIENDS!** (remixes) `25`
– Ich bin ein Auslander (Fun-Da-Mental) / Kick to kill (Jim Foetus seersucker mix) / Familus horribilus (mega web 2) / Underbelly (Renegade Soundwave blackout mix) / Fatman (Hoodlum Priest Fatboy mix) / Home (Orb sweet sin and salvation mix) / Cape Connection (Transglobal Underground Cossack in UFO encounter mix) / Menofearthereaper (concrete no fee, no fear mix) / Everything's cool (safe as milk mix) / R.S.V.P. (made in Japan, live at the Budokan double live Gonzo F mix) / Babylon (Loop Guru Babylon a dub fire mix) / Ich bin ein Auslander (Die Krupps mix) / Familus horribilus (Hia Nyg vocal mix) / Cape Connection (golden claw versus clock and dagger mix) / Intense / C.P.I. #2 / Cape Connection (TGV aliens, bodacious aliens mix) / Everything's cool (Dragonfly mix) / RSVP (Fluke lunch mix) / Cape Connection (Secret Knowledge transfered up mix) / Underbelly (The Drum Club bugsong mix).

—— CRABB left to pursue own career. He formed The BUZZARD and other project, The Golden Claw Music.

– compilations, etc. –

Jun 96. (cd) *Camden; (74321 39339-2)* **WISE UP SUCKERS**

PORNO FOR PYROS (see under ⇒ JANE'S ADDICTION)

PORTISHEAD

Formed: Bristol, England . . . 1993 by duo GEOFF BARROW and BETH GIBBONS, who took their name from a local coastal town. After working as MASSIVE ATTACK's studio runner and writing one of the better songs on NENEH CHERRY's 'HOMEBREW' album, BARROWS recruited covers band stalwart GIBBONS and the band signed to 'Go! Discs' off-shoot 'Go! Beat'. Named after BARROW's faded seaside resort hometown of Portishead near Bristol, the group debuted with a short film, 'TO KILL A DEAD MAN'. A retro spy movie pastiche, the film (which starred PORTISHEAD in an acting capacity) and its accompanying soundtrack were indicative of the cinematic melodrama which would characterise the band's groundbreaking debut. Released in August '94 amid much anticipation, and preceded by the singles 'NUMB' and 'SOUR TIMES', 'DUMMY' was a wracked, claustrophobic melange of painfully slow hip hop rhythms, droning hammond, knife-edge guitar and rumbling bass. Spiced with a sprinkling of obscure samples and topped off by the sublime lament of GIBBONS' vocals, the sound PORTISHEAD had created was one of the most striking definitions of the phenomena that would come to be known as 'Trip Hop'. Along with MASSIVE ATTACK, TRICKY et all, the band insisted the label was a lazy attempt at pigeonholing but what really set PORTISHEAD apart was simply the otherness of their sound, a strange grace that made the unrelenting lyrical bleakness and despair bearable. Who knows, winning the Mercury Music Prize in 1995 may have cheered them up a bit, although it would be a long time before they would resurface (meanwhile, BARROW guested on EARTHLING's 'Radar' set). During the summer of '97, PORTISHEAD delivered their first product in over two years, albeit a limited-edition 12"-only single, 'COWBOYS'. Nevertheless, the track was indeed a modern day classic, subsequently appearing on the flip of their Top 10 single, 'ALL MINE' – BETH was never better. As for their sophomore parent album, 'PORTISHEAD' (1997) – which made No.2 and nearly the Top 20 in America! – people would have been better not to compare it with their debut. Just when the fans thought it would take until the year 2000 for a third set, a live stop-gap, 'PNYC', came out the following year. • **Songwriters:** BARROW-GIBBONS, but most with UTLEY. Sample; MORE MISSION IMPOSSIBLE (Lalo Schifrin) / SPIN

IT JIG (Smokey Brooks) / ELEGANT PEOPLE (Weather Report) / MAGIC MOUNTAIN (War) / I'LL NEVER FALL IN LOVE AGAIN (Johnnie Ray; at slow speed!) / ISAAC MOODS (Isaac Hayes). • **Trivia:** Have remixed for the likes of DEPECHE MODE (In Your Room) / RIDE (I Don't Know Where It Comes From) / GRAVEDIGGAZ (Nowhere To Run).

Album rating: DUMMY (*10) / PORTISHEAD (*8) / PNYC (*6)

BETH GIBBONS – vocals / **GEOFF BARROW** (b.1971) – programming, synthesizer with **ADRIAN UTLEY** – guitar, bass / **CLIVE DEAMER** – drums / **DAVE McDONALD** – nose flute / **RICHARD NEWELL** – drum programme / **NEIL SOLMAN** – synthesizers, organ / **ANDY HAGUE** – trumpet

		Go Beat	Polygram
Jun 94.	(c-s) *(GODMC 114)* <857561> **NUMB / NUMBED IN MOSCOW**		
	(12"+=/cd-s+=) *(GOD X/CD 114)* – Revenge of the numbed / Numb: Earth – Linger / Extra numb		
	(cd-s++=) *(GOLCD 114)* – A tribute to Monk and Cantella.		
Aug 94.	(c-s) *(GODMC 116)* **SOUR TIMES / SOUR SOUR TIMES**	57	-
	(12"+=) *(GODX 116)* – Lot more / Sheared times.		
	(re-iss. Apr95, hit UK No.13)		
	(cd-s++=) *(GODCD 116)* – Airbus reconstruction.		
	(cd-s) *(GOLCD 116)* – ('A'side) / It's a fire / Pedestal / Theme from 'To Kill A Dead Man'.		
Aug 94.	(cd/c/lp) *(<828552-2/-4/-1>)* **DUMMY**	2	79 Jan95
	– Mysterons / Sour times / Strangers / It could be sweet / Wandering star / Numb / Roads / Pedestal / Biscuit / Glory box.		
Oct 94.	(c-s) *(GODMC 120)* **GLORY BOX / TOY BOX**	13	
	(12"+=/cd-s+=) *(GOD X/CD 120)* – Scorn / Sheared box.		
Jan 95.	(cd-s) <857816> **SOUR TIMES (NOBODY LOVES ME) / AIRBUS RECONSTRUCTION**	-	53
Jun 97.	(12"ltd) *(571277-1)* **COWBOYS. / COWBOYS (instrumental)**		-
Sep 97.	(c-s) *(571597-4)* <871881> **ALL MINE / COWBOYS**	8	
	(12"+=/cd-s+=) *(571597-1-2)* – Cowboys (instrumental).		
Oct 97.	(cd/c) *(<539189-2/-4>)* **PORTISHEAD**	2	21
	– Cowboys / All mine / Undenied / Half day closing / Over / Humming / Mourning air / Seven months / Only you / Elysium / Western eyes.		
Nov 97.	(12"/cd-s) *(571993-1/-2)* **OVER. / OVER (remix) / OVER (instrumental)**	25	
	(cd-s) *(571995-2)* – ('A'side) / Half day closing (live) / Humming (live).		
Mar 98.	(c-s) *(569474-4)* **ONLY YOU / ELYSIUM (Parlour Talk remix)**	35	
	(12"+=/cd-s+=) *(569475-1/-2)* – Only you (NYC) / Only you.		
Nov 98.	(cd/c/d-lp) *(<559424-2/-4/-1>)* **PNYC (live)**	40	
	– Humming / Cowboys / All mine / Mysterons / Only you / Half day crossing / Over / Glory box / Sour times / Roads / Strangers.		

––– UTLEY moonlighted with the MOUNT VERNON ARTS LAB via a collaborative mini-set, 'WARMINSTER' (1999).

Cozy POWELL (dig out; Great Metal . . .)

POWERMAN 5000

Formed: Boston, Massachusetts, USA . . . 1990 by frontman SPIDER (incidently the younger brother of ROB ZOMBIE!) along with his spikey-topped mystery men ADAM, M.33, DORIAN 27 and AL 3. Firing up a large home-based following after their well-received debut album, 'THE BLOOD SPLAT RATING SYSTEM' (1995), POWERMAN 5000 found themselves being asked to sign for 'DreamWorks'. Re-issuing the record as 'MEGA!! KUNG FU RADIO' in February '97, the metal-rap band were subsequently invited to support the man OSBOURNE on his US 'Ozzfest' tour. With the comic-book obsessed quintet augmented by DJ LETHAL (of LIMP BIZKIT) and GINGER FISH (of MARILYN MANSON) on their 1999 follow-up, 'TONIGHT THE STARS REVOLT!', it was no surprise when the band smashed into the US Top 30.

Album rating: THE BLOOD SPLAT RATING SYSTEM – MEGA!! KUNG FU RADIO (*4) / TONIGHT THE STARS WILL REVOLT! (*5)

SPIDER – vocals / **ADAM** – guitar / **M.33** – guitar / **DORIAN 27** – bass / **AL 3** – drums

		not iss.	Conscience
1995.	(cd) **THE BLOOD SPLAT RATING SYSTEM**	-	-
		DreamWorks	DreamWorks
Feb 97.	(cd/c) <DRD 50005> **MEGA!! KUNG FU RADIO** (re-working of debut)		
	– Public menace, freak, human fly / Organized / Neckbone / Car crash / Earth vs. me / Swim with the sharks / 20 miles to Texas, 25 to Hell / Mega!! kung fu radio / Tokyo vigilante #1 / Boredwitcha / Standing 8 / Even Superman shot himself.		
Aug 99.	(cd) <(DRD 50107)> **TONIGHT THE STARS REVOLT!**	29	Jul99
	– The eye is upon you / Super nova goes pop / When worlds collide / Nobody's real / System 11:11 / Tonight the stars revolt! / AUTOmatic / Son of X-51 / Operate, annihilate / Blast off to nowhere / They know who you are / Good times roll / Watch the sky for me.		

– others, etc. –

Mar 97.	(cd) Curve Earth; <16> **TRUE FORCE**	-	-

POWER STATION (see under ⇒ DURAN DURAN)

PRAS (see under ⇒ FUGEES)

PREFAB SPROUT

Formed: Consett, Durham, England . . . 1982 by budding singer/songwriter and Newcastle University student, PADDY McALOON, along with his brother MARTIN on bass and drummer, MICK SALMON. A debut single, 'LIONS IN MY OWN GARDEN (EXIT SOMEONE)' was rejected by many major labels although its 1,000 copies (released on the self-financed 'Candle' label) shifted quickly enough for local man Keith Armstrong to sign them to the new independent label, 'Kitchenware'. After a respectable showing in the indie charts with the follow-up, 'THE DEVIL HAS ALL THE BEST TUNES', the label struck a deal with 'C.B.S.' who released the band's first Top 75 entry, 'DON'T SING' in early '84. The debut album, 'SWOON', was released the following month to sporadic critical fervour, an impressive collection of clever, jazz-tinged pop with eloquent, carefully crafted lyrics. Preceded by two unsuccessful issues of the wistful 'WHEN LOVE BREAKS DOWN', 'STEVE McQUEEN' (1985; re-titled 'TWO WHEELS GOOD' in America after an objection from McQUEEN's family) had the music press in rapture. Their first album was to be produced by 80's guru THOMAS DOLBY, the songs were more directly melodic than the debut, enhancing the dreamy romance of much of the material while the country-inflected 'FARON YOUNG' was the first of McALOON's fond tributes to his musical heroes. 'WHEN LOVE BREAKS DOWN' was eventually a hit third time round when it was issued later that year although it would be 1988 before a new PREFAB SPROUT album was on the shelves, the masterful 'FROM LANGLEY PARK TO MEMPHIS'. The writing and arranging were more ambitious than ever, McALOON effortlessly updating the extravagance of an earlier golden era on the likes of 'HEY MANHATTAN' and 'VENUS OF THE SOUP KITCHEN', the latter featuring gospel act The ANDRAE CROUCH SINGERS. STEVIE WONDER made an appearance with his inimitable harmonica playing on 'NIGHTINGALES', with PETE TOWNSHEND also guesting on the album, such was the ever burgeoning reputation of the PREFAB SPROUT frontman. The intoxicating 'CARS AND GIRLS' was aimed at BRUCE SPRINGSTEEN's alleged narrow song repertoire, although McALOON had obviously forgotten the boss's 'Nebraska'. 'THE KING OF ROCK'N'ROLL's irresistible hook saw the group score their first, and only, Top 10 hit single to date. While 'PROTEST SONGS' (1989) was a collection initially pencilled in for four years previous, 'JORDAN: THE COMEBACK' (1990) was the next PREFAB SPROUT album proper, a lengthy quasi-concept album partly dedicated to ELVIS PRESLEY, while also paying tribute to such unlikely figures as Jesse James and Fred Astaire, over a bewitching musical backdrop. 1992's compilation, 'A LIFE OF SURPRISES', filled in a large gap between their next set, 'ANDROMEDA HEIGHTS', which, finally released in '97 hit the UK Top 10 for a week.

Album rating: SWOON (*6) / STEVE McQUEEN (*8) / FROM LANGLEY PARK TO MEMPHIS (*7) / PROTEST SONGS (*6) / JORDAN: THE COMEBACK (*7) / A LIFE OF SURPRISES – THE BEST OF PREFAB SPROUT compilation (*9) / ANDROMEDA HEIGHTS (*5)

PADDY McALOON (b. 7 Jun'57) – vocals, guitar / **WENDY SMITH** (b.31 May'63) – some guitar, vocals / **MARTIN McALOON** (b. 4 Jan'62) – bass / **MICK SALMON** – drums

		Candle	not iss.
Aug 82.	(7") *(CANDLE 1)* **LIONS IN MY OWN GARDEN (EXIT SOMEONE). / RADIO LOVE**		-
	(re-iss. May83 on 'Kitchenware'; SK 4) (re-iss. May83 on 'Kitchenware-Rough Trade'; SK 4 – RT 141)		
		Kitchenware	Epic
Oct 83.	(7") *(SK 7)* **THE DEVIL HAS ALL THE BEST TUNES. / WALK ON**		-
	(Dec83:- 12"+=) *(SK 8)* – Lions in my own garden / Radio love.		
Jan 84.	(7") *(SK 9)* **DON'T SING. / GREEN ISAAC II**	64	-
	(12"+=) *(SK 9-12)* – He'll have to go.		

––– **GRAHAM LANT** – drums; repl. SALMON

Feb 84.	(lp/c) *(KW LP/C 1)* **SWOON**	22	
	– Don't sing / Cue fanfare / Green Isaac I / Here on the eerie / Cruel / Couldn't bear to be special / I never play basketball now / Ghost town blues / Elegance / Technique / Green Isaac II. *(re-iss. Mar88 on 'C.B.S.' lp/c/cd; 460908-1/-4/-2)* (re-iss. Mar93 & Feb97 cd/c; 460908-2/-4)		
Mar 84.	(7") *(SK 10)* **COULDN'T BEAR TO BE SPECIAL. / SPINNING BELINDA**		
	(12"+=) *(SK 10-12)* – Donna Summer.		

––– **NEIL CONTI** (b.12 Feb'59, London, England) – drums; repl. GRAHAM

Oct 84.	(7") *(SK 19)* **WHEN LOVE BREAKS DOWN. / DIANA**		-
	(d7"+=) *(SKDP 19)* – The yearning loins / Donna Summer.		
	(12"++=) *(SKK 19)* – Cruel.		
Mar 85.	(7") *(SK 21)* **WHEN LOVE BREAKS DOWN (remix). / THE YEARNING LOINS**		
	(d7"+=) *(SK 21-12)* – The Devil has all the best tunes / Walk on.		
	(d7"+=) *(SKDQ 21)* – Lions in my own garden (exit someone). / Radio love.		
Jun 85.	(7") *(SK 22)* **FARON YOUNG. / SILHOUETTES**	74	
	(d7"+=) *(SKDP 22)* – When love breaks down / The yearning loins.		
	(12") *(SKX 22)* – ('A'-Truckin' mix) / ('B'-full version).		
Jun 85.	(lp/c/cd) *(KW LP/C 3)*(CD 26522) <40100> **STEVE McQUEEN** <US-title 'TWO WHEELS GOOD'>	21	
	– Faron Young / Bonny / Appetite / When love breaks down / Goodbye Lucille (Johnny Johnny) / Hallelujah / Moving the river / Horsin' around / Desire as / Blueberry pies / When the angels. <US+=> – The yearning loins / He'll have to go / Faron (truckin' mix). *(re-iss. Mar90 & May97 on 'C.B.S.' cd/c/lp; 466336-2/-4/-1)*		
Aug 85.	(7") *(SK 23)* **APPETITE. / HEAVEN CAN WAIT**		
	(d12"+=) *(SKXDP 23)* – Oh, the Swiss / Faron Young (truckin' mix) / Silhouettes.		

Oct 85. (7") *(SK 21)* **WHEN LOVE BREAKS DOWN. / THE YEARNING LOINS** `25`
(12"+=) *(SK 21-12)* – Spinning Belinda / Donna Summer.
(d7"++=) *(SKD 21)* – He'll have to go.

Feb 86. (7"/7"sha-pic-d) *(SK/+X 24)* **JOHNNY JOHNNY. / WIGS** `64`
(12"+=) *(SKK 24)* – The guest who stayed forever.

Feb 88. (7") *(SK 35)* **CARS AND GIRLS. / VENDETTA** `44`
(10"+=) *(SKQ 35)* – Real life (just around the corner).
(12"++=/pic-cd-s++=) *(SKK/CDDSK 35)* – Faron Young (truckin' mix).

Mar 88. (lp/c/cd) *(KW LP/C/CD 9)* **FROM LANGLEY PARK TO MEMPHIS** `5`
– The king of rock'n'roll / Cars and girls / I remember that / Enchanted / Nightingales / Hey Manhattan! / Knock on wood / The golden calf / Nancy (let your hair down for me) / The Venus of the soup kitchen. *(cd re-iss. May97 on 'Columbia'; 460124-2)*

Apr 88. (7"/7"box) *(SKQ/SKB 37)* **THE KING OF ROCK'N'ROLL. / MOVING RIVER** `7`
(12"+=) *(SKX 35)* – Dandy of the blue river / Tin can pot.
(cd-s+=) *(CDDSK 35)* – Dandy of the blue river / He'll have to go.

Jul 88. (7"/7"box) *(SK/+B 38)* **HEY MANHATTAN! / TORNADO** `72`
(12"+=/12"g-f+=/cd-s+=) *(SKX/SKGT/CDSK 38)* – ('A'-JFK version) / Donna Summer.

Nov 88. (7") *(SK 39)* **NIGHTINGALES. / LIONS IN MY OWN GARDEN**
(d7"ep+=) *(SKEP 39)* – The Devil has all the best tunes.
(12"+=/cd-s+=) *(SKX/CDSK 39)* – Life of suprises / Bearpark.
(12") *(SKK 39)* – ('A'extended) / The king of rock'n'roll (live).

Feb 89. (7"/7"pic-d) *(SK/+P 41)* **THE GOLDEN CALF. / THE VENUS OF THE SOUP KITCHEN**
(12"+=/cd-s+=) *(SKX/CDSK 41)* – ('A'long version) / Bonny (live).
(below album was to have been released in 1985, thus its low cat.no.)

Jun 89. (lp/c/cd) *(KW LP/C/CD 4)* **THE PROTEST SONGS** `18`
– The world awake / Life of suprise / Horse chimes / Wicked things / Dublin / Tiffany's / Diana / Talkin' Scarlet / 'Till the cows come home / Pearly gates. *(cd re-iss. May91 & Mar93 & Feb97 on 'Columbia'; 465118-2)*

Aug 90. (7"/c-s) *(SK/+C 47)* **LOOKING FOR ATLANTIS. / MICHAEL** `51`
(12"+=) *(SKK 47)* – King of rock'n'roll / Cars and girls.
(cd-s++=) *(CDSK 47)* – When love breaks down.

Aug 90. (cd/c/lp) *(KW CD/C/LP 14)* **JORDAN: THE COMEBACK** `7`
– Looking for Atlantis / Wild horses / Machine gun Ibiza / We let the stars go / Carnival 2000 / Jordan: the comeback / Jesse James symphony / Jesse James bolero / Moon dog / All the world loves lovers / All boys believe anything / The ice maiden / Paris Smith / The wedding march / One of the broken / Michael / Mercy / Scarlet nights / Doo wop in Harlem. *(re-iss. May94 & May97 cd/c; 467161-2)*

Oct 90. (7"/c-s) *(SK/+C 48)* **LET THE STARS GO. / CRUEL** `50`
(12"+=) *(SKK 48)* – Don't sing / Couldn't bear to be special.
(cd-s+=) *(CDSK 48)* – Faron Young / Hey Manhattan (JFK version).

Dec 90. (7"ep/12"ep/cd-ep) *(SK/SKK/CDSK 49)* **JORDAN: THE EP** `35`
– Carnival 2000 / One of the broken / The ice maiden / Jordan: The comeback.

Jun 92. (7"/c-s) *(SK/+C 58)* **THE SOUND OF CRYING. / ONE OF THE BROKEN** `23`
(cd-s+=) *(CDSK 58)* – Nightingales / Faron Young.
(cd-s) *(CDSKX 58)* – ('A'full version) / The golden calf / Looking for Atlantis.

Jul 92. (cd/c/lp) *(471886-2/-4/-1)* **A LIFE OF SURPRISES – THE BEST OF PREFAB SPROUT** (compilation) `3`
– The king of rock'n'roll / When love breaks down / The sound of crying / Faron Young / Carnival 2000 / Goodbye Lucille 1 (Johnny Johnny) / I remember that / Cruel / Cars and girls / We let the stars go / Life of surprises / Appetite / If you don't love me / Wild horses / Hey Manhattan! / All the world loves lovers.

Jul 92. (7"/c-s) *(SK/+C 60)* **IF YOU DON'T LOVE ME.** / ('A'mix) `33`
(cd-s) *(CDSK 60)* – ('A'side) / ('A'-String driven thing mix) / Nero the zero / Real life (just around the corner).
(cd-s) *(CDSKX 60)* – ('A'side) / ('A'-No strings attached mix) / Lions in my own garden (exit someone) / Hey Manhattan (JFK mix).

Sep 92. (7"/c-s) *(SK/+C 62)* **ALL THE WORLD LOVES LOVERS. / MACHINE GUN IBIZA** `61`
(cd-s) *(CDSK 62)* – ('A'side) / Knock on wood / Desire as / Moondog.
(cd-s+=) *(CDSKX 62)* – Till the cows come home / Enchanted.

Jan 93. (7"/c-s) *(SK/+C 63)* **LIFE OF SURPRISES. / THE KING OF ROCK'N'ROLL** `24`
(cd-s+=) *(CDSK 63)* – If you don't love me.
(12") *(SKK 63)* – ('A'side) / If you don't love me (2 mixes).

Mar 93. (cd-s) *(SKCD 64)* **I REMEMBER THAT / THE WORLD AWAKE**

Apr 97. (c-s) *(SKC 70)* **A PRISONER OF THE PAST / WHERE THE HEART IS** `30` `–`
(cd-s+=) *(CDSK 70)* – Just because I can.
(cd-s) *(SKZD 70)* – ('A'side) / The king of rock'n'roll / Cars and girls.

May 97. (cd/c) *(KW CD/MC 30)* **ANDROMEDA HEIGHTS** `7`
– Electric guitars / A prisoner of the past / The mystery of love / Life's a miracle / Anne Marie / Whoever you are / Steal your thunder / Avenue of stars / Swans / The fifth horseman / Weightless / Andromeda heights.

Jul 97. (c-s) *(SKC 71)* **ELECTRIC GUITARS / DRAGONS** `53` `–`
(cd-s+=) *(SKCD 71)* – End of the affair.
(cd-s) *(SKZD 71)* – ('A'side) / Girl I'm here / Never trust a spell.

– compilations, etc. –

1988. (cd) *C.B.S.; (CDPS 241)* **SWOON / STEVE McQUEEN** `–`
(re-iss. May97 on 'Columbia'; PS 21CD)

Feb 93. (d-cd) *Columbia; (471886-2)* **A LIFE OF SURPRISES / STEVE McQUEEN** `–`

Feb 95. (cd) *Columbia; (478482-2)* **STEVE McQUEEN / FROM LANGLEY PARK TO MEMPHIS** `–`

May 97. (d-cd) *Columbia; (PS 22CD)* **FROM LANGLEY PARK TO MEMPHIS / JORDAN: THE COMEBACK** `–`

–––– PADDY McALOON also nearly issued a solo 7", 'HORSIN' AROUND' along with the help of LOUISE and DEIRDRE RUTKOWSKI of SUNSET GUN

PRESIDENTS OF THE UNITED STATES OF AMERICA

Formed: Seattle, Washington, USA ... late 1993 by long-time friends CHRIS BALLEW, JASON FINN and DAVE DEDERER. All veterans of the alternative rock scene in one way or another (BALLEW had even worked as part of BECK's backing band), this "wacky" outfit were akin to a head-on collision between The CARS and DEVO. Combining surreal animal-inspired lyrics and a youthfully enthusiastic, funky pop/punk approach, the band recorded their celebrated debut set. Initially released on the independent 'Pop Llama' label in 1994, the eponymous album was subsequently remixed and reissued the following year after 'Columbia' came out tops in the ensuing bidding war for their presidential signatures. Powered by the success of the 'LUMP' single, the album went on to sell well over a million copies in the States, eventually making the Top 10. The band also made a dent in the UK market, helped by the success of the bizarre 'PEACHES' single. A follow-up set, 'II', eventually appeared in 1996, although this time around they failed to capture the public's attention in quite the same fashion. Early in 1998, the band split up, leaving behind a couple of albums and a miserable leftovers collection, 'PURE FROSTING'. • **Songwriters:** BALLEW and group except KICK OUT THE JAMS (MC5) / WE ARE NOT GOING TO MAKE IT (Ben Reiser) / VIDEO KILLED THE RADIO STAR (Buggles) / CA PLANE POUR MOI (Plastic Bertrand) / DEVIL IN A SLEEPING BAG (Willie Nelson) / CLEVELAND ROCKS (Ian Hunter). • **Trivia:** PEACHES video was directed by ROMAN COPPOLA, son of FRANCIS FORD COPPOLA.

Album rating: PRESIDENTS OF THE UNITED STATES OF AMERICA (*5) / II (*7) / PURE FROSTING part compilation (*3)

CHRIS BALLEW – vocals, two-string basitar (ex-SUPERGROUP) / **DAVE DEDERER** – three-string guitbass, vocals (ex- LOVE BATTERY) / **JASON FINN** – drums, vocals (ex-SKIN YARD, ex-HELIOS CREED)

–––– released a single on 'Pop Llama' US Mar 95.

                                     Columbia Columbia

Oct 95. (cd/c) *(481309-2/-4)* *<67291>* **PRESIDENTS OF THE UNITED STATES OF AMERICA** `14` `6` Sep95
– Kitty / Feather pluckn / Lump / Stranger / Boll Weevil / Peaches / Dune buggy / We are not going to make it / Kick out the jams / Body / Back porch / Candy / Naked and famous. *(re-iss. cd Jul96; 484334-2) (yellow-lp Apr96; 481309-0)* – (2 extra). *(w/ free cd+=)* – Dune buggy / Kick / Peaches / Lump / Back porch (versions). *(lp re-iss. Jun98 on 'Munster'; MR 093)*

–––– <above album was originally issued on 'Pop Llama' in the US>

Dec 95. (7"pic-d/c-s) *(662496-7/-4)* **LUMP. / WAKE UP** `15` `–`
(cd-s+=) *(662496-2)* – Carolyn's bootie / Candy's cigarette.

Feb 96. (c-s,cd-s) *<78254>* **PEACHES / CANDY CIGARETTE** `–` `29`

Mar 96. (7") **FUCK CALIFORNIA. / CAROLYN'S BOOTIE** `–`
above on US label 'C/Z'

Apr 96. (7"pic-d/c-s) *(663107-7/-4)* **PEACHES. / CONFUSION** `8` `–`
(cd-s) *(663107-2)* – ('A'side) / Feather pluckin (live) / Boll Weevil (live) / Dune buggy (live).

Jul 96. (7"pic-d/c-s) *(663489-7/-4)* **DUNE BUGGY. / PEACHES (live)** `15` `–`
(cd-s) *(663489-3)* – ('A'side) / Back porch (live) / Kick out the jams (live) / Video killed the radio star (live).

Oct 96. (7"pic-d) *(663881-7)* **MACH 5. / BODY (live)** `29` `–`
(c-s) *(663817-4)* – ('A'side) / Carolyn's bootie.
(cd-s) *(663817-2)* – ('A'side) / Tremelo blooz / Tiki lounge god.

Nov 96. (cd/c/lp) *(485092-2/-4/-1)* *<67577>* **II** `36` `31`
– Ladies and gentlemen part 1 / Lunatic to love / Volcano / Mach 5 / Twig / Bug city / Bath of fire / Tiki god / L.I.P. / Froggie / Toob amplifier / Supermodel / Puffy little shoes / Ladies and gentlemen part 2 / Basketball dream.

–––– split leaving behind a few remnants below

Mar 98. (cd/c) *(489702-2/-4)* *<69201>* **PURE FROSTING** (part compilation)
– Love delicatessen / Video killed the radio star / Mobile home / Japan / Black porch / Man (deposable thumb) / Tiki lounge god / Teenage girl / Slip away / Tremolo blooz / Cleveland rocks / Lump.

Jul 98. (c-s/cd-s) *(W 0450 C/CD)* **VIDEO KILLED THE RADIO STAR / (other tracks by Ellen Dow & Sugarhill Gang / Culture Club** `52` `–`
(above issued on the 'Maverick/Warners' label)

–––– BALLEW was now in a band called, the GIRAFFES

Elvis PRESLEY

Born: ELVIS AARON PRESLEY, 8 Jan'35, Tupelo, Mississippi, USA. One of twin sons (the other Jesse was stillborn), he was raised in Memphis, Tennessee. Between the summer of '53 and '54, he spent time in Sam Phillips' 'Sun' studios, cutting demos. With the arrival of back-up session players, SCOTTY MOORE and BILL BLACK, his first single, a rousing cover of Arthur Crudup's 'THAT'S ALL RIGHT MAMA', gained local airplay even before its release on the 'Sun' label. After a brief flirtation with country, he opted for R&B after his young audiences lapped up his pelvic action. Although Sam Phillips initially thought ELVIS was a black blues singer, he still chose to feature ELVIS's country recordings on the flip sides. Colonel Tom Parker became his manager in 1955, soon securing a large 5-figure deal with 'R.C.A.', who also bought out his contract with 'Sun' records; the attention ELVIS's riotous stage shows had received prompted an intense bidding war. His major debut, 'HEARTBREAK HOTEL', sparked off a new phenomenom at the start of 1956 which soon gave him a massive selling No.1. PRESLEY appeared on many TV shows around this time, the newfound star going on to appear in his first feature film, 'Love Me Tender' (named after his song, see also further film discography). The constant demand for ELVIS's records saw many simultaneous releases clogging the charts; he scored a further nine US No.1's in the States (namely 'I WANT YOU, I NEED YOU, I LOVE YOU', 'DON'T BE CRUEL', 'HOUND DOG', 'LOVE ME TENDER', 'TOO MUCH', 'ALL SHOOK UP', 'LET ME BE YOUR TEDDY BEAR', 'JAILHOUSE ROCK' and 'DON'T'), before being controversially drafted into the army on the 24th of March '58. While serving his country over a two-year period, ELVIS suffered the death of his mother, Gladys, something which was to deeply affect him in the years to come. During this period, several singles were issued, the records (including chart-topping 'HARD HEADED WOMAN' and 'A BIG HUNK O LOVE') recorded just prior to his draft. After being promoted to Sergeant, his army time expired in March 1960, another US No.1, 'STUCK ON YOU', celebrating his return to "civvie" street. ELVIS returned to the Nashville studios and began working on a new ballad-esque style backed with an uptempo beat, a sound that was only vaguely reminiscent of his pre-army days. His films too, (around three a year in the 60's), contained a sort of manufactured pop, guided no doubt by the vast sums of money it stimulated. However, in spells between 1960 and 1965, ELVIS did create some truly wonderful pop records including 'IT'S NOW OR NEVER', 'ARE YOU LONESOME TONIGHT?', 'WOODEN HEART', 'RETURN TO SENDER', 'DEVIL IN DISGUISE', 'VIVA LAS VEGAS' and 'CRYING IN THE CHAPEL' to name but a few. In 1965, he also released the first of a series of gospel albums, 'HIS HAND IN MINE', while on the 1st of May '67, he married long-time girlfriend, Priscilla Beaulieu. After she bore him a child, Lisa Marie, in 1968, they separated in 1972 and divorced a year later (she subsequently became an actress, most notably on the 'Dallas' soap). In the late '60's, ELVIS revived a somewhat commercially declining singles career when 'IN THE GHETTO' then 'SUSPICIOUS MINDS' hit the Top 3. His work in the 70's showed him moving into the money-spinning cabaret circuit as his live appearances were mainly in Las Vegas and Hawaii. While "The King" was still a top performer, as loyal fans old and new flocked to see his larger frame (squeezing out of a white glitzy suit) churn out another exhaustive show, he was barely a shadow of the rock'n'roll hero he once was. A combination of a special diet, prescribed drugs, junk food (binges) and alcohol eventually proved too much for ailing heart and tragically on the 16th of August 1977, he was found dead in his Graceland home by girlfriend, Ginger Alden. His funeral saw over 75,000 fans/mourners flocking to the gates of his home in Gracelands. THE KING OF ROCK was dead. Following the death of ELVIS, many tabloids reported sightings of a living Elvis and speculation about his doomed life has been catapulted into the ridiculous. The KING should've been laid to rest in peace, his music the only thing to live on. • **Songwriters:** Covered (singles only mentioned):- THAT'S ALL RIGHT MAMA + MY BABY LEFT ME (Arthur 'Big Boy' Crudup) / BLUE MOON OF KENTUCKY (Bill Monroe) / BABY LET'S PLAY HOUSE (Arthur Gunter) / BLUE SUEDE SHOES (Carl Perkins) / TUTTI FRUTTI + RIP IT UP (Little Richard) / HOUND DOG (Freddie Bell . . . & Big Mama Thornton) / ALL SHOOK UP (Otis Blackwell) / ONE BROKEN HEART FOR SALE (Blackwell-Scott) / ONE NIGHT (Smiley Lewis) / A FOOL SUCH AS I (Hank Snow) / MY WISH CAME TRUE (Ivory Joe White) / IT'S NOW OR NEVER + SURRENDER + ASK ME (Italian trad.) / ARE YOU LONESOME TONIGHT? (Vaughn Deleath) / I FEEL SO BAD (Chuck Willis) / WITCHCRAFT (Spiders) / WHAT'D I SAY (Ray Charles) / BOSSA NOVA BABY (Lieber-Stoller) / SUCH A NIGHT (Johnnie Ray) / FRANKIE & JOHNNY (?) / LOVE LETTERS (Dick Haymes) / BIG BOSS MAN (Jimmy Reed) / U.S. MALE (Jerry Reed) / YOU'LL NEVER WALK ALONE (hit. Gerry & The Pacemakers) / IN THE GHETTO (Mac Davis) / SUSPICIOUS MINDS (Mark James) / THE WONDER OF YOU (Ray Peterson) / KENTUCKY RAIN (Eddie Rabbit) / YOU DON'T HAVE TO SAY YOU LOVE ME (Dusty Springfield) / THERE GOES MY EVERYTHING (Engelbert Humperdink) / I REALLY WANT TO KNOW (Les Paul & Mary Ford) / RAGS TO RICHES (Tony Bennett) / I JUST CAN'T HELP BELIEVIN' (B.J.Thomas) / UNTIL IT'S TIME FOR YOU TO GO (Buffy Sainte-Marie) / AN AMERICAN TRILOGY (Mickey Newbury) / BURNING LOVE (Arthur Alexander) / STEAMROLLER BLUES (James Taylor) / POLK SALAD ANNIE (Tony Joe White) / I'VE GOT A THING ABOUT YOU BABY (Billy Lee Riley) / PROMISED LAND (Chuck Berry) / MY BOY (hit. Richard Harris) / HURT (Timi Yuro) / GREEN, GREEN GRASS OF HOME (Tom Jones) / MY WAY (Paul Anka) / TOMORROW'S A LONG TIME (Bob Dylan) / etc. • **Filmography:** LOVE ME TENDER (1956) / LOVING YOU (1957) / JAILHOUSE ROCK (1957) / KING CREOLE (1958) / G.I.BLUES (1960) / WILD IN THE COUNTRY (1961) / FLAMING STAR (1961) / BLUE HAWAII (1961) / FOLLOW THAT DREAM (1962) / KID GALAHAD (1962) / GIRLS! GIRLS! GIRLS! (1962) / IT HAPPENED AT THE WORLD'S FAIR (1963) / FUN IN ACAPULCO (1963) / KISSIN' COUSINS (1964) / VIVA LAS VEGAS (1964) / ROUSTABOUT (1964) / GIRL HAPPY (1965) / TICKLE ME (1965) / HAREM HOLIDAY (1965, 'HARUM SCARUM'-US title) / FRANKIE AND JOHNNY (1966) / PARADISE, HAWAIIAN STYLE (1966) / CALIFORNIA HOLIDAY (1966, 'SPINOUT'-US title) / DOUBLE TROUBLE (1967) / CLAMBAKE (1968) / STAY AWAY JOE (1968) / SPEEDWAY (1968) / LIVE A LITTLE, LOVE A LITTLE (1968) / CHARRO (1969) / THE TROUBLE WITH GIRLS (1969) / CHANGE OF HABIT (1970) / (This was his last feature film, but many concerts were recorded)

Best CD compilation: PRESLEY – THE ALL-TIME GREATEST HITS (*10)

with **SCOTTY MOORE** – guitar / **BILL BLACK** – bass / + session drummers

		not iss.	Sun
Aug 54.	(7") <209> **THAT'S ALL RIGHT MAMA. / BLUE MOON OF KENTUCKY** <re-iss. Nov55 on 'R.C.A.'; 6380>	-	☐
Oct 54.	(7") <210> **GOOD ROCKIN' TONIGHT. / I DON'T CARE IF THE SUN DON'T SHINE** <re-iss. Nov55 on 'R.C.A.'; 6381>	-	☐
Jan 55.	(7") <215> **MILK COW BLUES BOOGIE. / YOU'RE A HEARTBREAKER** <re-iss. Nov55 on 'R.C.A.'; 6382>	-	☐
May 55.	(7") <217> **I'M LEFT, YOU'RE RIGHT, SHE'S GONE. / BABY LET'S PLAY HOUSE** <re-iss. Nov55 on 'R.C.A.'; 6383>	-	☐
Aug 55.	(7") <223> **MYSTERY TRAIN. / I FORGOT TO REMEMBER TO FORGET** <re-iss. Nov55 on 'R.C.A.'; 6357> (all UK rel.Feb59 & Mar64 on 'RCA')	-	☐

—— added **D.J. FONTANA** – drums (on tour and then on session)

—— now adding on session **FLOYD CRAMER** – piano / **CHET ATKINS** – guitar / **HANK GARLAND** – guitar / **'BOOTS' RANDOLPH** – saxophone

—— He was also backed and at times credited with The JORDANAIRES; GORDON STOKER, HOYT HAWKINS, NEAL MATTHEWS and HUGH JARRETT.

		H.M.V.	R.C.A.
Mar 56.	(7")(78) (7M 385)(POP 182) <47-6420> **HEARTBREAK HOTEL. / I WAS THE ONE**	2	1 19 Feb56
Mar 56.	(lp) <LPM 1254> **ELVIS PRESLEY** – Blue suede shoes* / I'm counting on you* / Money honey* / I got a sweetie (I got a woman)* / One sided love affair* / I'm gonna sit right down and cry over you* / Tryin' to get to you* / I love you because / Just because / Blue moon / I'll never let you go / Tutti frutti. (tracks * =on next album too) (UK-iss.Oct56;) (re-iss. Mar85 on 'R.C.A.' lp/c/cd; (NL/NK/ND 89046) (pic-lp.Oct88 on 'R.C.A.'; PD 1254)	-	1
May 56.	(7")(78) (7M 405)(POP 213) **BLUE SUEDE SHOES. / TUTTI FRUTTI**	9	-
Jul 56.	(7")(78) (7M 424)(POP 235) <47-6540> **I WANT YOU, I NEED YOU, I LOVE YOU. / MY BABY LEFT ME**	14	1 31 May56
Sep 56.	(7",78) (POP 249) <47-6604> **HOUND DOG. / DON'T BE CRUEL** (re-iss. Jun78 on 'R.C.A.'; PB 9265) – (hit UK No.24)	2	1 Jul56
Sep 56.	(7",78) (POP 253) <476643> **LOVE ME TENDER. / ANYWAY YOU WANT ME (THAT'S HOW I WILL BE)**	11	1 20 Oct56
Nov 56.	(lp) (CLP 1093) <LPM 1382> **ROCK'N'ROLL NO.1** <US title 'ELVIS'> – That's all right / Lawdy Miss Clawdy / Mystery train / Playing for keeps / Poor boy / Money honey / I'm counting on you / My baby left me / I was the one / Shake rattle and roll / I'm left, you're right, she's gone / You're a heartbreaker / Tryin' to get to you / Blue suede shoes. (re-iss. Mar59 as 'ELVIS'; CLP 1093) – (hit No.4) (re-iss. May72 as 'ROCK'N'ROLL' on 'R.C.A.'; SF 8233) – (hit No.34) (re-iss. Sep81 on 'R.C.A.' lp/c; NL/NK 89125)	*	1
Nov 56.	(7",78) (POP 272) **BLUE MOON. / I DON'T CARE IF THE SUN DON'T SHINE**	9	-
Feb 57.	(7",78) (POP 295) **MYSTERY TRAIN. / LOVE ME**	25	-
Mar 57.	(7",78) (POP 305) **RIP IT UP. / BABY LET'S PLAY HOUSE**	27	-
Apr 57.	(lp) (CLP 1105) **ROCK'N'ROLL NO.2** – Rip it up / When my blue moon turns to gold again / Love me / Long tall Sally / First in line / Old Shep / So glad you're mine / How's the world treating you / Any place is Paradise / Paralysed / Ready Teddy / How do think I feel. (re-iss. 1962 on 'R.C.A.' mono/stereo; RD/SF 7528) (re-iss. Jan84 on 'R.C.A.' lp/c; NL/NK 81382) (cd-iss. May90; ND 81382)	*	1
May 57.	(7",78) (POP 330) <47-6800> **TOO MUCH. / PLAYING FOR KEEPS**	6	1 21 Jan57
Jun 57.	(7",78) (POP 359) <47-6870> **ALL SHOOK UP. / THAT'S WHEN YOUR HEARTACHES BEGIN**	1	1 58 Mar57

—— ELVIS was now backed by a variety of session men. SCOTTY and BILL left. In Jun'58, **BOB MOORE** – bass / **HANK GARLAND** – guitar repl. them

		R.C.A.	R.C.A.
Jul 57.	(7",78) (RCA 1013) <47-7000> **(LET ME BE YOUR) TEDDY BEAR. / LOVING YOU**	3	1 20 Jun57
Aug 57.	(10"lp) (RC 24001) <LPM 1515> **LOVING YOU (film soundtrack)** – Mean woman blues / (Let me be your) Teddy bear / Loving you / Got a lot o' livin' to do / Lonesome cowboy / I need you so / Have I told you lately that I love you / True love / Party / Blueberry hill / Hot dog / Don't leave me now. (re-iss. Sep77 lp/c +=; PK/PL 42358) – (hit UK No.24) (re-iss. Aug81 on 'RCA International' INTS 5109) (re-iss. Jan84 lp/c; NL/NK 81515) (cd-iss. Oct87; ND 81515)	*	1 Jul57
Oct 57.	(7",78) (RCA 1020) **PARTY. / GOT A LOT OF LIVIN' TO DO**	2	1
Nov 57.	(7",78) (RCA 1025) **SANTA BRING MY BABY BACK TO ME. / SANTA CLAUS IS COMING TO TOWN**	7	1
Nov 57.	(lp) (RD 27052) <LOC 1035> **ELVIS' CHRISTMAS ALBUM** – Santa Claus is coming to town / White Christmas / Precious Lord it is no secret (what God can do) / Blue Christmas / Santa bring my baby back to me / I'll be home for Christmas / Here comes Santa (right down Santa Claus lane) / O little town of Bethlehem / Silent night / Take my hand / I believe / (There'll be) Peace in the valley (for me). (re-iss. Nov58; same) (re-iss. Nov71 on 'RCA International; INTS 1126) – (hit No.7) (re-iss. Jan84 lp/c; NL/NK 89116) (re-iss. Nov85; PL 85486) (re-iss. Oct79 on 'RCA-Camden' lp/c; CDS/CAM 1155) (re-iss. Nov75 on 'Pickwick' diff; CAM 462)		
Jan 58.	(7",78) (RCA 1028) <47-7035> **JAILHOUSE ROCK. / TREAT ME NICE** (re-iss. May77; PB 2695) – (hit UK No.44 Aug77) (re-iss. Jan83, hit No.27, also on 7"pic-d diff B-side THE ELVIS MEDLEY)	1	1 18 Oct57
Feb 58.	(7",78) (RCA 1043) <47-7150> **DON'T. / I BEG OF YOU**	2	1 8 Jan58

—— ELVIS was served US army draft notice in Dec'57. He finally – after much fan/film producer protest – joined army on 24 Mar'58. He has had enough time to record many songs and appeared on celluloid once again (aka KING CREOLE film).

Apr 58. (7",78) (RCA 1058) <47-7240> **WEAR MY RING ROUND YOUR NECK. / DON'T CHA THINK IT'S TIME** | 3 | 2 | 15 Jun58

Jul 58. (7",78) (RCA 1070) <47-7280> **HARD HEADED WOMAN. / DON'T ASK ME WHY** | 2 | 1 | 25 Jun58

Sep 58. (7",78) (RCA 1081) **KING CREOLE. / DIXIELAND ROCK** | 2 | –

Oct 58. (lp) (RD 27088) <LPM 1884> **KING CREOLE (film soundtrack)** | 4 | 2 Sep58
– King Creole / As long as I have you / Crawfish / Lover doll / Hard headed woman / Don't ask me why / Trouble / New Orleans / Dixieland rock / Steadfast, loyal and true / Young dreams. (re-iss. 1963 & Feb69; same) (re-iss. Aug81 on 'RCA International'; INTS 5013) (re-iss. Jan84 lp/c; NL/NK 83733) (cd-iss. Oct87; ND 83733)

Jan 59. (7",78) (RCA 1100) <47-7410> **ONE NIGHT. / I GOT STUNG** | 1 | 4 | 8 Oct58
(re-iss. May77; PB 2696)

Apr 59. (7",78) (RCA 1113) <47-7506> **(NOW AND THEN THERE'S) A FOOL SUCH AS I. / I NEED YOUR LOVE TONIGHT** | 1 | 2 | 4 Mar59
(re-iss. May77; PB 2697)

Jul 59. (7",78) (RCA 1136) <47-7600> **A BIG HUNK O' LOVE. / MY WISH CAME TRUE** | 4 | 1 | 12 Jun59

(all singles from Jul'57 were re-iss. Mar60)

—— ELVIS was now demobbed from the army 5 Mar'60. His session men now are **FLOYD CRAMER** – piano / **SCOTTY MOORE** – guitar

Mar 60. (7",78) (RCA 1187) <47-7740> **STUCK ON YOU. / FAME AND FORTUNE** | 3 | 1 | 17

Jun 60. (mono-lp)(stereo-lp) (RD 27171)(SF 5060) <LSP 2231> **ELVIS IS BACK!** | 1 | 2 May60
– Make me no it / The girl of my best friend / Dirty dirty / I will be home again / The thrill of your love / Feeling / Soldier boy / Such a night / It feels so right / Like a baby / Fever / Reconsider baby / The girl next door. (re-iss. Apr84 lp/c; NL/NK 89013) (cd-iss. Jul89; ND 89013)

Jul 60. (7") (RCA 1194) **A MESS OF BLUES. / THE GIRL OF MY BEST FRIEND** | 2 | –

Jul 60. (7") <47-7777> **IT'S NOW OR NEVER. / A MESS OF BLUES** | – | 1 | 32

Oct 60. (7") (RCA 1207) **IT'S NOW OR NEVER. / MAKE ME KNOW IT** | 1 | –
(re-iss. May77; PB 2698) – (hit UK No.39 in Aug77)

Dec 60. (mono-lp)(stereo-lp) (RD 27192)(SF 5078) <LSP 2256> **G.I. BLUES (Film soundtrack)** | 1 | 1 Oct60
– Tonight is so right for love / What's she really like / Big boots / Frankfurt special / Wooden heart / Shoppin' around / Pocketful of rainbows / G.I. blues / Doin' the best I can / Didja ever / Blue suede shoes. (re-iss. Sep77; same) – (hit UK No.14) (re-iss. Aug81 on 'RCA International'; INTS 5104) (re-iss. Jan84 lp/c; NL/NK 83735) (cd-iss. Oct87; ND 83735)

Jan 61. (7") (RCA 1216) <47-7810> **ARE YOU LONESOME TONIGHT? / I GOTTA KNOW** | 1 | 1 | 20 Nov60
(re-iss. May77; PB 2699) – (hit UK No.46 Aug77)

Mar 61. (7") (RCA 1226) **WOODEN HEART. / TONIGHT IS SO RIGHT FOR LOVE** | 1 | –
(re-iss. May77; PB 2700) – (hit UK No.49 Aug77)

May 61. (mono-lp)(stereo-lp) (RD 27211)(SF 5094) <LSP 2328> **HIS HAND IN MINE** | 3 | 13 Jan61
– His hand in mine / I'm gonna walk dem golden stairs / Milky white way / My father's house / Known only to him / Mansions over the hilltop / I believe in the sky / If we never meet again / Working on the building / Jesus knows what I need / Joshua fit the battle / Swing low sweet chariot. (re-iss. Aug81 on 'RCA International'; INTS 5105) (re-iss. Jan84 lp/c; NL/NK 83935) (cd-iss. Oct88; ND 83935)

May 61. (7") (RCA 1227) <47-7850> **SURRENDER (TORNA A SURRIENTO). / LONELY MAN** | 4 | 1 | 32 Feb61
(re-iss. May77; PB 2701)

Aug 61. (7") (RCA 1244) <47-7880> **WILD IN THE COUNTRY. / I FEEL SO BAD** | 4 | 26 | 5 May61

Oct 61. (7") (RCA 1258) <47-7908> **(MARIE'S THE NAME) HIS LATEST FLAME. / LITTLE SISTER** | 1 | 26 | 5 Aug61
(re-iss. May77; PB 2702)

Oct 61. (mono-lp)(stereo-lp) (RD 27224)(SF 5106) <LSP 2370> **SOMETHING FOR EVERYBODY** | 2 | 1 Jul61
– There's always me / Give me the right / Gently / It's a sin / Sentimental me / Starting today / I'm coming home / I slipped I stumbled I fell / Put the blame on me / I want you with me / Judy / In your arms. (re-iss. Jan84 lp/c; NL/NK 84116) (cd-iss. Dec90;)

Dec 61. (mono-lp)(stereo-lp) (RD 27238)(SF 5115) <LSP 2426> **BLUE HAWAII (Soundtrack)** | 1 | 1 Oct61
– Blue Hawaii / Almost always true / Moonlight swim / No more / Can't help falling in love / Rock a hula baby / Island of love / Hawaiian sunset / Hawaiian wedding song / Alohaoe / Beach boy blues / Slicin' sands / Ku ui Po / Ito eats. (re-iss. Sep77; SF 8145) – (hit UK No.26) (re-iss. Aug84 lp/c; NL/NK 83683) (cd-iss. Oct87; ND 83683)

Jan 62. (7") (RCA 1270) <47-7968> **ROCK-A-HULA-BABY. / CAN'T HELP FALLING IN LOVE** | 1 | 23 | 2 Dec61
(re-iss. May77; PB 2703)

May 62. (7") (RCA 1280) <47-7992> **GOOD LUCK CHARM. / ANYTHING THAT'S PART OF YOU** | 1 | 1 | 31 Mar62
(re-iss. May77; PB 2704)

Jun 62. (mono-lp) (stereo-lp) (RD 27265)(SF 5135) <LSP 2523> **POT LUCK** | 1 | 4
– Kiss me quick / Just for old times sake / Fountain of love / Gonna get back home somehow / Such an easy question / Night rider / Suspicion / Stepping out of line / I fell I've known you forever / That's someone you never forget / Something blue / I'm yours. (re-iss. Apr81 on 'RCA International'; INTS 5074) (re-iss. Jul84 lp/c; NL/NK 89098) (cd-iss. Apr88; ND 89098)

Aug 62. (7") (RCA 1303) <47-8041> **SHE'S NOT YOU. / JUST TELL HER JIM SAID HELLO** | 1 | 5 | 55 Jul62
(re-iss. May77; PB 2705)

Nov 62. (7") (RCA 1320) <47-8100> **RETURN TO SENDER. / WHERE DO YOU COME FROM** | 1 | 2 | 99 Oct62
(re-iss. May77; PB 2706) – (hit UK No.42 Aug77)

Jan 63. (lp; mono/stereo) (RD/SF 7534) <LSP 2621> **GIRLS! GIRLS! GIRLS! (Film soundtrack)** | 2 | 3 Dec62
– Girls! girls! girls! / I don't wanna be tired / Because of love / Return to sender / Where do you come from / I don't want to / We'll be together / A boy like me a girl like you / Song of the shrimp / The walls have ears / Earth boy / Thanks to the rolling sea / We're coming in loaded. (re-iss. Oct79; lp/c; PL/PK 42354) (re-iss. Aug81 on 'RCA International'; INTS 5107) (re-iss. Jun84 lp/c; NL/NK 89048) (re-iss. Sep86 on 'RCA-Camden' lp/c; CDS/CAM 1221)

Feb 63. (7") (RCA 1337) <47-8134> **ONE BROKEN HEART FOR SALE. / THEY REMIND ME TOT MUCH OF YOU** | 12 | 11 | 53

May 63. (lp; mono/stereo) (RD/SF 7565) <LSP 2697> **IT HAPPENED AT THE WORLD'S FAIR (Film Soundtrack)** | 4 | 4 Apr63
– Beyond the bend / Relax / Take me to the fair / Happy ending / They remind to much of you / One broken heart for sale / I'm falling in love tonight / Cotton candy land / A world of our own / How would you like to be. (re-iss. Aug81 on 'RCA International'; INTS 5033) (re-iss. Jan84 lp/c; NL/NK 82568)

Jun 63. (7") (RCA 1355) <47-8188> **(YOU'RE THE) DEVIL IN DISGUISE. / PLEASE DON'T DRAG THAT STRING AROUND** | 1 | 3
(re-iss. May77; PB 2707)

Oct 63. (7") (RCA 1374) <47-8243> **BOSSA NOVA. / WITCHCRAFT** | 13 | 8 | 32

Dec 63. (7") (RCA 1375) <447-0639> **KISS ME QUICK. / SOMETHING BLUE** | 14 | 34 Apr64

Dec 63. (lp; mono/stereo) (RD/SF 7609) <LSP 2756> **FUN IN ACAPULCO (Film Soundtrack)** | 9 | 3 Mar64
– Fun in Acapulco / The bullfighter was a lady / Margueritta / There's no room to rhumba in a sports car / Dinero y amor / Mexico / I think I'm gonna like it here / Bossa nova baby / Vino / El Toro / You can't say no to acapulco / Guadalajara / Love me tonight / Slowly but surely. (re-iss. Oct79 lp/c; PL/PKM 42357) (re-iss. Aug81 on 'RCA International'; INTS 5106)

Mar 64. (7") (RCA 1390) <47-8360> **VIVA LAS VEGAS. / WHAT'D I SAY** | 17 | 29 | 21 May64

Jun 64. (7") (RCA 1404) <47-8307> **KISSIN' COUSINS. / IT HURTS ME** | 10 | 12 | 29 Feb64

Jun 64. (lp; mono/stereo) (RD/SF 7645) <LSP 2894> **KISSIN' COUSINS (Film Soundtrack)** | 5 | 6 Apr64
– Kissin' cousins / Smokey mountain boy / Anyone could fall in love with you / Catchin' on fast / Tender feeling / Once is enough / (It's a) Long lonely highway / Barefoot ballet / Echoes of love / Kissin' cousins (reprise). (re-iss. Oct79 lp/c; PL/PK 42355) (re-iss. Aug81 on 'RCA International'; INTS 5108) (re-iss. Nov84 lp/c; NL/NK 84115) (re-iss. Sep86 on 'RCA Camden' lp/c; CDS/CAM 1222)

Aug 64. (7") (RCA 1411) <47-8400> **SUCH A NIGHT. / NEVER ENDING** | 13 | 16 Jul64

Oct 64. (7") (RCA 1422) <47-8440> **AIN'T THAT LOVIN' YOU BABY. / ASK ME** | 15 | 16 | 12

Nov 64. (7") (RCA 1430) <HO-0808> **BLUE CHRISTMAS. / WHITE CHRISTMAS** | 11 |

Jan 65. (lp; mono/stereo) (RD/SF 7678) <LSP 2999> **ROUSTABOUT (Film Soundtrack)** | 12 | 1 Nov64
– Roustabout / Little Egypt / Poison Ivy league / Hard knocks / It's a wonderful world / Big love big heartache / There's a brand new day on the horizon / Wheels of my heels / Carny town / One track heart / It's carnival time. (re-iss. Oct79 lp/c; PL/PK 42356) (re-iss. Aug81 on 'RCA International'; INTS 5110) (re-iss. Nov84 lp/c; NL/NK 89049)

Mar 65. (7") (RCA 1443) <47-8500> **DO THE CLAM. / YOU'LL BE GONE** | 19 | 21 Feb64

Apr 65. (lp; mono/stereo) (RD/SF 7714) <LSP 3338> **GIRL HAPPY (Film Soundtrack)** | 8 | 8
– Girl happy / Spring fever / Fort Lauderdale / You'll be gone / Chamber of commerce / Startin' tonight / Puppet on a string / Do not disturb / Cross my heart and hope to die / Wolf call / The meanest girl in town / I've got to find my baby / Do the clam. (re-iss. Aug81 on 'RCA International'; INTS 5034) (re-iss. Nov84 lp/c; NL/NK 83338)

May 65. (7") (RCA 1455) <447-0643> **CRYING IN THE CHAPEL. / I BELIEVE IN THE MAN IN THE SKY** | 1 | 3
(re-iss. May77; PB 2708) – (hit UK No.43 Aug77)

Jun 65. (7") <47-8585> **(SUCH AN) EASY QUESTION. / IT FEELS SO RIGHT** | – | 11 | 55

Sep 65. (7") <47-8657> **I'M YOURS. / (IT'S A) LONG LONELY HIGHWAY** | – | 11

Sep 65. (mono-lp) (RD 7723) **FLAMING STAR AND SUMMER KISSES** | 11 | –
– (compilation of 'FLAMING STAR' Film soundtrack EP + 'LOVING YOU' lp) (re-iss. Jun69 as 'FLAMING STAR' on 'RCA INternational'; INTS 1012) – (hit UK No.2) (re-iss. Apr79 on 'RCA Camden' lp/c; CDS/CAM 1185)

Nov 65. (7") <447-0650> **PUPPET ON A STRING. / WOODEN HEART** | – | 14

Nov 65. (7") (RCA 1489) **TELL ME WHY. / PUPPET ON A STRING** `15` `-`

Nov 65. (lp; mono/stereo) (RD/SF 7752) <LSP 3450> **ELVIS FOR EVERYONE!** `8` `10` Sep65
– You're cheatin' heart / Summer kisses / Winter tears / For the millionth and the last time / Finders keepers losers weepers / In my way / Tomorrow night / Forget me never / Met her tonight / Memphis Tennessee / Sound advice / Santa Lucia / When it rains it really pours. (re-iss. 1972; SF 8232) (re-iss. Apr84 lp/c; NL/NK 84232) (cd-iss. Apr95;)

Jan 66. (7") <47-8740> **TELL ME WHY. / BLUE RIVER** `-` `33` `95`

Jan 66. (lp; mono/stereo) (RD/SF 7767) <LSP 3468> **HAREM HOLIDAY (Film Soundtrack)** <US title 'HARUM SCARUM'> `11` `8` Nov65
– Harem holiday / My desert serenade / Go west young man / Hey little girl / Mirage / Shake that tambourine / Golden coins / So close yet so far (from Paradise) / Animal instinct / Wisdom of ages. (re-iss. Aug80 on 'RCA International'; INTS 5035) (re-iss. Apr84 lp/c; NL/NK 82558)

Feb 66. (7") (RCA 1504) **BLUE RIVER. / DO NOT DISTURB** `22` `-`

Mar 66. (7") (RCA 1509) <47-8780> **FRANKIE AND JOHNNY. / PLEASE DON'T STOP LOVING ME** `21` `25`

Apr 66. (lp; mono/stereo) (RD/SF 7793) <LSP 3553> **FRANKIE AND JOHNNY (Film Soundtrack)** `11` `20`
– Frankie and Johnny / Come along / What every woman lives for / Petunia the gardeners daughter / Beginners luck / Chesay / Down by the riverside / When the saints go marching in / Please don't stop loving me / Look out / Everybody come aboard / Shout it out / Hard luck. (re-iss. Aug80 on 'RCA International'; INTS 5036) (re-iss. Apr84 lp/c; NL/NK 82559)

Jun 66. (7") (RCA 1526) <47-8870> **LOVE LETTERS. / COME WHAT MAY** `6` `19`

Jul 66. (lp; mono/stereo) (RD/SF 7810) <LSP 3643> **PARADISE, HAWAIIAN STYLE (Film Soundtrack)** `7` `15`
– Paradise Hawaiian style / Queenie Wamine's papaya / Scratch my back (then I'll scratch yours) / House of sand / Datin' / Drums of the islands / A dogs life / Sand castles / This is my heaven. (re-iss. Aug80 on 'RCA International'; INTS 5037) (re-iss. Apr84 lp/c; NL/NK 89010)

Oct 66. (7") (RCA 1545) <47-8941> **ALL THAT I AM. / SPINOUT** `17` `40` B-side

Nov 66. (lp; mono/stereo) (RD/SF 7820) <LSP 3702> **CALIFORNIA HOLIDAY (Film Soundtrack)** <US-title 'SPINOUT'> `17` `18`
– Stop look and listen / Adam and evil / All that I am / Am I ready / Never say yes / Beach shack / Spinout / Smorgasbord / Tomorrow is a long time / Down in the alley / I'll be back / I'll remember you. (re-iss. Aug80 on 'RCA International' lp/c; INT S/K 5038)

Nov 66. (7") (RCA 1557) <47-8950> **IF EVERY DAY WAS LIKE CHRISTMAS. / HOW WOULD YOU LIKE TO BE** `13`

Feb 67. (7") (RCA 1565) <47-9056> **INDESCRIBABLY BLUE. / FOOLS FALL IN LOVE** `21` `33`

Apr 67. (lp; mono/stereo) (RD/SF 7867) <LSP 3758> **HOW GREAT THOU ART** `11` `18`
– How great thou art / In the garden / Without him / By and by / Somebody bigger than you and I / Stand by me / Farther along / Where could I go to but the Lord / Crying in the chapel / If the Lord wasn't by my side / So high / Run on / Where no one stands alone. (re-iss. Jul84 lp/c; NL/NK 83758) (cd-iss. Apr88; ND 83758)

May 67. (7") (RCA 1593) **YOU GOTTA STOP. / LOVE MACHINE** `38` `-`

Aug 67. (7") (RCA 1616) <47-9115> **LONG-LEGGED GIRL (WITH THE SHORT DRESS ON). / THAT'S SOMEONE YOU NEVER FORGET** `49` `63` `92`

Aug 67. (lp; mono/stereo) (RD/SF 7892) <LSP 3787> **DOUBLE TROUBLE (Film Soundtrack)** `34`
– Double trouble / Baby if you'll give me all your love / City by night / Could I fall in love / Old McDonald / I love only one girl / Long legged girl (with the short dress on) / It won't be long / There is so much world to see / Blue river / Never ending / What now what next where to. (re-iss. Aug80 on 'RCA International'; INTS 5039)

Sep 67. (7") (RCA 1628) <47-9287> **THERE'S ALWAYS ME. / JUDY** `56` `78`

Nov 67. (7") (RCA 1642) <47-9341> **BIG BOSS MAN. / YOU DON'T ME** `38` Oct67

Feb 68. (7") (RCA 1663) <47-9425> **GUITAR MAN. / HI-HEEL SNEAKERS** `19` `43`

Apr 68. (lp; mono/stereo) (RD/SF 7917) <LSP 3893> **CLAMBAKE (Film Soundtrack)** `19` `40` Feb68
– Clambake / Who needs money / A house that has everything / Confidence / Hey hey hey / You don't know me / Guitar man / The girl I never loved / How can you lose what you never had / Big boss man / Singing trees / Just call me lonesome. (re-iss. Aug80 on 'RCA International'; INTS 5040) (re-iss. Jan84 lp/c; NL/NK 82565)

May 68. (7") (RCA 1688) <47-9465> **U.S. MALE. / STAY AWAY** `15` `28` `67` Mar68

Jul 68. (7") (RCA 1714) <47-9547> **YOUR TIME HASN'T COME YET BABY. / LET YOURSELF GO** `22` `72` `71` Jun68

Aug 68. (lp; mono/stereo) (RD/SF 7957) <LSP 3989> **SPEEDWAY (Film Soundtrack)** `82`
– Speedway / There ain't nothing like a song / Your time hasn't come yet baby / Who are you (who am I) / He's your uncle not your dad / Let yourself go / Your groovy self (by NANCY SINATRA) / Western union / Five sleepy heads / Mine / Goin' home / Suppose. (re-iss. Aug81 on 'RCA International'; INTS 5041) (re-iss. Jan84 lp/c; NL/NK 85012)

Oct 68. (7") (RCA 1747) <47-9600> **YOU'LL NEVER WALK ALONE. / WE CALL ON HIM** `44` `90` Apr68

Nov 68. (7") <47-9670> **IF I CAN DREAM. / EDGE OF REALITY** `-` `12`

Dec 68. (7") (RCA 1768) <47-9610> **A LITTLE LESS CONVERSATION. / ALMOST IN LOVE** `69` `95` Sep68

Feb 69. (7") (RCA 1795) **IF I CAN DREAM. / MEMORIES** `11` `-`

Mar 69. (7") <47-9731> **MEMORIES. / CHARRO** `-` `35`

Jun 69. (7") (RCA 1831) <47-9741> **IN THE GHETTO. / ANY DAY NOW** `2` `3` May69

Aug 69. (lp; mono/stereo) (RD/SF 8029) <LSP 4155> **FROM ELVIS IN MEMPHIS** `1` `13` Jun69
– Wearin that loved-in look / Only the strong survive / I'll hold you in my heart / Long black limousine / It keeps right on a-turnin' / I'm moving on / Power of my love / Gentle on my mind / After loving you / True love travels on a gravel road / Any day now / In the ghetto. (cd-iss. Mar91;) (re-iss. Mar94 cd/c;)

Aug 69. (7") (RCA 1869) <47-9747> **CLEAN UP YOUR OWN BACK YARD. / THE FAIR'S MOVING ON** `21` `35` Jul69

Nov 69. (7") (RCA 1900) <47-9764> **SUSPICIOUS MINDS. / YOU'LL THINK OF ME** `2` `1` Sep69

Feb 70. (7") (RCA 1916) <47-9768> **DON'T CRY DADDY. / RUBBERNECKIN'** `8` `6` Nov69

—— His live band mid '69 for album **JAMES BURTON** – lead guitar / **JOHN WILKINSON** – guitar / **CHARLIE HODGE** – guitar / **JERRY SCHEFF** – bass / **LARRY MUHOBERAC** – keyboards / **RONNIE TUTT** – drums back up groups were The IMPERIALS and also The SWEET INSPIRATIONS

Mar 70. (d-lp) (SF 8080-1) <LSP 6020> **FROM MEMPHIS TO VEGAS – FROM VEGAS TO MEMPHIS** `3` `12` Nov69
– FROM MEMPHIS TO VEGAS (live at the International, Vegas) – Blue suede shoes / Johnny B. Goode / All shook up / Hound dog / Are you lonesome tonight / I can't stop loving you / Me babe / Medley; Mystery train – Tiger man / Words / In the ghetto / Suspicious minds / Can't help falling in love. FROM VEGAS TO MEMPHIS (studio sessions) – Elvis back in Memphis / Inherit the wind / This is the story / Stranger in my hometown / A little bit of green / The fair's moving on / And the grass don't pay no mind / From a jack to a king / You'll think of me / Without love (there's nothing). (re-iss. Jun84; NL 89068) (cd-iss. Dec91;) – (first lp only)

—— **GLEN D. HARDIN** – drums (ex-CRICKETS) repl. TUTT

May 70. (7") (RCA 1949) <47-9701> **KENTUCKY RAIN. / MY LITTLE FRIEND** `21` `16` Feb70

Jul 70. (7") (RCA 1974) <47-9835> **THE WONDER OF YOU. / MAMA LIKED THE ROSES** `1` `9` May70
(re-iss. May77; PB 2709) – (hit UK No.48)

Jul 70. (lp) (SF 8128) <LSP 4362> **ON STAGE – FEBRUARY 1970 (live)** `2` `13` Jun70
– See see rider blues / Release me (and let me live again) / Sweet Caroline / Runaway / The wonder of you / Polka salad Annie / Yesterday / Proud Mary / Walk a mile in my shoes / Let it be me (je't appartiens). (re-iss. Mar91 cd/c/lp;)

Nov 70. (7") (RCA 1999) <47-9873> **I'VE LOST YOU. / THE STEP IS LOVE** `9` `32` Aug70

Jan 71. (7") (RCA 2046) <47-9916> **YOU DON'T HAVE TO SAY YOU LOVE ME. / PATCH IT UP** `9` `11` Oct70

Jan 71. (lp) (SF 8162) <LSP 4445> **THAT'S THE WAY IT IS (live Las Vegas)** `12` `21` Dec70
– I just can't help believin' / Twenty days and twenty nights / How the web was woven / Patch it up / Mary in the morning / You don't have to say you love me / You've lost that lovin' feeling / I've lost you / Just pretend / Stranger in the crowd / The next step is love / Bridge over troubled water. (re-iss. Jan84 lp/c; NL/NK 84114) (re-iss. Jul93 cd/c;)

Mar 71. (7") (RCA 2060) <47-9960> **THERE GOES MY EVERYTHING. / I REALLY DON'T WANT TO KNOW** `6` `21` Dec70

Mar 71. (lp) (SF 8172) <LSP 4460> **ELVIS COUNTRY (I'M 10,000 YEARS OLD)** `6` `12` Jan71
– Snowbird / Tomorrow never comes / Little cabin on the hill / Whole lotta shakin' goin' on / Funny how time slips away / I really don't want to know / There goes my everything / It's your baby / You rock it / Fool / Faded love / I washed my hands in muddy water / Make the world go away / I was born about 10,000 years ago (re-iss. Aug84)(re-iss. cd+c Jul93)

May 71. (7") (RCA 2084) <47-9980> **RAGS TO RICHES. / WHERE DID THEY GO, LORD** `9` `33` Mar71

May 71. (7") <47-9985> **LIFE. / ONLY BELIEVE** `-` `53`

Jul 71. (lp) (SF 8202) <LSP 4530> **LOVE LETTERS FROM ELVIS** `7` `33` Jun71
– Love letters / When I'm over you / I'll never know / Got my mojo working / Heart of Rome / It ain't no big thing (but it's growing) / Only believe / This is our dance / Cindy Cindy / Life. (re-iss. Aug81 on 'RCA International'; INTS 5081) (re-iss. Nov84 lp/c; NL/NK 89011) (cd-iss. Jun88; NL 89011)

Sep 71. (7") (RCA 2125) <47-9998> **I'M LEAVIN'. / HEART OF ROME** `23` `36` Aug71

Oct 71. (7") <48-1017> **IT'S ONLY LOVE. / THE SOUND OF YOUR CRY** `-` `51`

Nov 71. (7") (RCA 2158) **I JUST CAN'T HELP BELIEVIN'. / HOW THE WEB WAS WOVEN** `6` `-`

Nov 71. (7") <74-0572> **MERRY CHRISTMAS BABY. / O COME, ALL YE FAITHFUL** `-`

Mar 72. (7") (RCA 2188) <74-0619> **UNTIL IT'S TIME FOR YOU TO GO. / WE CAN MAKE THE MORNING** `5` `40` Feb72

May 72. (lp) (SF 8266) <LSP 4671> **ELVIS NOW** `12` `43` Jan72
– Help me make it through the night / Miracle of the rosary / Hey Jude / Put your hand in the hand / Until it's time for you to go / We can make the morning / Early mornin' rain / Sylvia / Fools rush in (where angels feared to tread) / I was born about ten thousand years ago. (re-iss. Jul93 cd/c;)

Jun 72. (7") (RCA 2229) <74-0672> **AN AMERICAN TRILOGY. / THE FIRST TIME EVER I SAW YOUR FACE** `8` `66` Apr72

Jul 72. (lp) (SF 8296) <LSP 4776> **ELVIS AS RECORDED AT MADISON SQUARE GARDEN (live)** `3` `11`
– Introduction; / Theme from 2001 – a space odyssey / That's all right / Proud Mary / Never been to Spain / You don't have to say you love me / You've lost that lovin' feelin' / Polk salad Annie / Love me / All shook up / Heartbreak hotel / Medley; / (Let me your) Teddy bear – Don't be cruel – Love me tender – The impossible dream / Hound dog / Suspicious minds / For the good times / An American trilogy / Funny how time slips away / I can't stop loving you / Can't help falling in love.

Aug 72. (lp/c) (SF 8275) <LSP 4690> **HE TOUCHED ME** (gospel) `38` `79` Apr72
– He touched me / I've got confidence / Amazing Grace / Seeing is believing / He is my everything / Bosom of Abraham / An evening prayer / Lead me, guide me / There is no god but God / Thing called love / I, John / Reach out to Jesus.

Sep 72. (7") (RCA 2267) <74-0769> **BURNING LOVE. / IT'S A MATTER OF TIME** `7` `2` Aug72

Dec 72. (7") (RCA 2304) <74-0815> **ALWAYS ON MY MIND. / SEPARATE WAYS** `9` `20` B-side

Feb 73. (d-lp) (DPS 2040) <VPSX 6089> **ALOHA FROM HAWAII VIA SATELLITE** (TV special rec. 14th Jan '73) `11` `1`
– Theme from 2001 (a space odyssey) / See see rider / Burning love / Something / You gave me a mountain / Steamroller blues / My way / Love me Johnny B. Goode / It's over / I can't stop loving you / Blue suede shoes / I'm so lonesome I could cry /

Hound dog / What now my love / Fever / Welcome to my world / Suspicious minds / I'll remember you / Medley; Long lotta shakin' goin' on – An American trilogy – A big hunk o' love – I can't help falling in love. *(re-iss. Aug84 lp/c; PL/PK 82642) (cd-iss. Sep86; PD 8642) (cd re-iss. Oct95;)*

May 73. (7") (RCA 2359) **POLK SALAD ANNIE. / SEE SEE RIDER** — 23 | –

Jul 73. (7") (RCA 2393) <74-0910> **FOOL. / STEAMROLLER BLUES** — 16 | 17

Sep 73. (lp) (SF 8378) <APL 0283> **ELVIS** — 16 | 52
— Fool / Where do I go from here / Love me, love the life I lead / I'm still here / It's impossible / (That's what you get) For lovin' me / Padre / I'll take you home again Kathleen / I will be true / Don't think twice, it's alright. *(re-iss. Mar94;)*

Nov 73. (7") (RCA 2435) <APBO 0088> **RAISED ON ROCK. / FOR OL' TIMES SAKE** — 36 | 50

Nov 73. (lp) <(APL1 0388)> **RAISED ON ROCK**
— Raised on rock / Are you sincere / Find out what's happening / I miss you / Girl of mine / For 'ol times sake / If you don't come back / Just a little bit / Sweet Angeline / Three corn patches. *(re-iss. Mar94 cd/c;)*

Mar 74. (7") <APBO 0196> **TAKE GOOD CARE OF HER. / I'VE GOT A THING ABOUT YOU BABY** — 33 | 39 Mar74

May 74. (lp) <(APL1 0475)> **GOOD TIMES** — 42 | 90
— Take good care of her / Loving arms / I got a feeling in my body / If that isn't love / She wears my ring / I've got a thing about you baby / My boy / Spanish eyes / Talk about the good times / Good time Charlie got the blues. *(re-iss. Mar94 cd/c;)*

Jun 74. (7") <(APBO 0280)> **IF YOU TALK IN YOUR SLEEP. / HELP ME** — 40 | 17

Aug 74. (lp) <(APL1 0606)> **ELVIS AS RECORDED LIVE ON STAGE (live in Memphis)** — 44 | 33
— See see rider / I got a woman / Love me / Trying to get to you / Medley; Long tall Sally – Whole lotta shakin' goin on / Mama don't dance / Flip flop and fly / Jailhouse rock / Hound dog / Why me Lord / How great thou art / Blueberry hill / I can't stop loving you / Help me / An American trilogy / Let there be me / My baby left me / Lawdy Miss Clawdy / Can't help falling in love / Closing vamp.

Oct 74. (7") (RCA 2458) **MY BOY. / LOVING ARMS** — 5 | –

Dec 74. (7") <(PB 10074)> **PROMISED LAND / IT'S MIDNIGHT** — 9 | 14 Oct74

Jan 75. (7") (PB 10191) **MY BOY. / THINKING ABOUT YOU** — – | 20

Feb 75. (lp) <(APL1 0873)> **PROMISED LAND** — 21 | 47
— Promised land / There's a honky tonk angel (who will take me back in) / Help me / Mr. Songman / Love song of the year / It's midnight / Your love's been a long time comin' / If you talk in your sleep / Thinking about you / You ask me to. *(cd-iss. Dec91;)*

May 75. (7") (RCA 2562) <PB 10278> **T-R-O-U-B-L-E. / MR. SONGMAN** — 31 | 35

Jun 75. (lp) (RS 1011) <APL1 1039> **TODAY** — 48 | 57
— T.R.O.U.B.L.E. / And I love you so / Susan when she tried / Woman without love / Shake a hand / Pieces of my life / Fairy tale / I can help / Bringin' it back / Green green grass of home.

Oct 75. (7") <PB 10401> **BRINGING IT BACK. / PIECES OF MY LIFE** — – | 65

Nov 75. (7") (RCA 2635) **GREEN GREEN GRASS OF HOME. / THINKING ABOUT YOU** — 29 | –

Apr 76. (7") (RCA 2674) <PB 10601> **HURT. / FOR THE HEART** — 37 | 28

Jun 76. (lp) (RS 1060) <APL1 1506> **FROM ELVIS PRESLEY BOULEVARD, MEMPHIS, TENNESSEE** — 29 | 41
— Hurt / Never again / Blue eyes crying in the rain / Danny boy / The last farewell / For the heart / Bitter they are, harder they fall / Solitaire / Love coming down / I'll never fall in love again. *(re-iss. Jan85 lp/c; PL/PK 89266) (re-iss. Jul93 cd/c;)*

Feb 77. (7") (PB 857) <PB 10857> **MOODY BLUE. / SHE THINKS I STILL CARE** — 6 | 31

Jul 77. (7") (PB 998) <PB 10998> **WAY DOWN. / PLEDGING MY LOVE** — 1 | 18

——— On the 16th August 1977, ELVIS died of heart failure. Below are songs he recorded just prior to death.

Aug 77. (lp/c) (PL/PK 12428) <AFL 2428> **MOODY BLUE** (some live) — 3 | 3
— Unchained melody / If you love me (let me know) / Little darlin' / He'll have to go / Let me be there / Way down / Pledging my love / Moody blue / She thinks I still care. *(re-iss. Sep81 lp/c; RCA LP/K 3021) (re-iss. Jan85 lp/c; NL/NK 90252) (cd-iss. Oct88; ND 90252)*

– postumous compilations, others, etc. –

all below releases were issued on 'R.C.A.' until stated otherwise

Aug 77. (lp/c) (PL/PK 12274) <APL 2274> **WELCOME TO MY WORLD** — 7 | 44
— Welcome to my world / Help make it through the night / Release me (and let me love again) / I really don't know what to know / For the good times / Make the world go away / Gentle on my mind / I'm so lonesome I could cry / Your cheatin' heart / I can't stop loving you. *(re-iss. Sep81 lp/c; RCA LP/K 3020)*

Oct 77. (lp/c) (CPL1/APK1 0341) **A LEGENDARY PERFORMER VOL.1** — – | –

Oct 77. (lp/c) (CPL1/APK1 1349) **A LEGENDARY PERFORMER VOL.2** — – | –

Nov 77. (d-lp/d-c) (PL/PK 02587) <APL1 2587> **ELVIS IN CONCERT (live)** — 13 | 5 Oct77
— (Elvis' fans comment, and opening riff to 2001) / See see rider / That's alright / Are you lonesome tonight? / You gave me a mountain / Jailhouse rock / How great thou art / I really don't want to know / (Elvis introduces his father) / Hurt. *(re-iss. Jul93 cd/c;)*

Nov 77. (7") (PB 1165) <11165> **MY WAY (live). / AMERICA, THE BEAUTIFUL (live)** — 9 | 22

Apr 78. (lp/c) (PL/PK 12772) <AFL 2772> **HE WALKS BESIDE ME (gospel)** — 37 | –
— He is my everything / Miracle of the rosary / Where did they go Lord / Somebody bigger than you and I / An evening prayer / The impossible dream / If I can dream / Padre / Known only to him / Who am I / How great thou art.

May 78. (lp/c) (PL/PK 42101) **THE '56 SESSIONS VOL.1** — 47 | –
(re-iss. Sep81 lp/c; RCA LP/K 3025)

Jul 78. (lp) (CPL 2901) **ELVIS SINGS FOR CHILDREN AND GROWNUPS TOO!** — – | –

Nov 78. (lp/c) (PL/PK 42102) **THE '56 SESSIONS VOL.2** — – | –
(re-iss. Sep81 lp/c; RCA LP/K 3030)

Nov 78. (lp) (KKL 7065) **ELVIS – A CANADIAN TRIBUTE** — – | 86

Nov 78. (7") (PB 9334) **OLD SHEP. / PARALYZED** — – | –

Jan 79. (lp/c) (PL/PK 13082) <CPL 3082> **A LEGENDARY PERFORMER VOL.3** — 43 |

Apr 79. (lp/c) (PL/PK 13279) <AQL 3279> **OUR MEMORIES OF ELVIS** — 72 |

Sep 79. (lp/c) (PL/PK 13448) <AQL 3448> **OUR MEMORIES OF ELVIS VOL.2** — |

Oct 79. (d-lp) (NL 43054) **ELVIS PRESLEY** — |

Nov 79. (lp/c) (PL/PK 42371) **ELVIS SINGS THE WONDERFUL WORLD OF CHRISTMAS** — |

Dec 79. (7"/12") (PB/PC 9464) **IT WON'T SEEM LIKE CHRISTMAS (WITHOUT YOU). / MERRY CHRISTMAS BABY** — 13 |

Mar 80. (lp/c) (INTS/INTK 5001) **PICTURES OF ELVIS** — |

Jun 80. (lp/c) (INTS/INTK 5031) **ELVIS PRESLEY SINGS LEIBER AND STOLLER** — 32 |
(re-iss. Apr84 lp/c; NL/NK 89099)

Aug 80. (8xlp-box) (ELVIS 25) <CPL 3699> **ELVIS AARON PRESLEY** — 21 | 27
— (AN EARLY LIVE PERFORMANCE / AN EARLY BENEFIT PERFORMANCE / COLLECTOR'S GOLD FROM THE MOVIE YEARS / THE TV SPECIALS / THE LAS VEGAS YEARS / LOST SINGLES / ELVIS AT THE PIANO – THE CONCERT YEARS (PART 1) / THE CONCERT YEARS (concluded).

Aug 80. (7") (RCA 4) **IT'S ONLY LOVE. / BEYOND THE REEF** — 3 | –

Nov 80. (7") (RCA 16) **SANTA CLAUS IS BACK IN TOWN. / I BELIEVE** — 41 | –

Feb 81. (7") (RCA 43) <PB 12158> **GUITAR MAN (remix). / FADED LOVE** — 43 | 28

Mar 81. (lp/c) (RCA LP/K 5010) <AAL 3917> **GUITAR MAN** — 33 | 49
— Guitar man / After loving you / Too much monkey business / Just call me lonesome / Lovin' arms / You asked me to / Clean up your own backyard / She thinks I still care / Faded love / I'm movin' on.

Apr 81. (7") (RCA 48) **LOVING ARMS. / YOU ASKED ME TO** — 47 | –

May 81. (d-lp/d-c) (RCA LP/K 5029) <CPL 4031> **THIS IS ELVIS (Soundtrack)** — 47 |
(re-iss. May84 d-lp/d-c; BL/BK 84031)

Oct 81. (lp/c) (INTS/INTK 89024) **20 GREATEST HITS VOL.1** — |
(re-iss. Apr84 lp/c; NL/NK 89024)

Mar 82. (lp/c) (INTS/INTK 5116) **20 GREATEST HITS VOL.2** — |
(re-iss. Jan85 lp/c; NL/NK 89168) – (hit UK No.98)

Feb 82. (lp/c) (RCA LP/K 3060) **THE SOUND OF YOUR CRY** — 31 |

Feb 82. (7") (RCA 196) **ARE YOU LONESOME TONIGHT? (live version). / FROM A JACK TO A KING (live)** — 25 |

Mar 82. (11x7"ep-box) (EP 1) **THE EP COLLECTION** — 97 |

Jun 82. (7"/7"pic-d) (RCA/+P 232) **THE SOUND OF YOUR CRY. / I'LL NEVER KNOW** — 59 |

Aug 82. (d-lp/d-c) (RCA LP/K 1000) **ROMANTIC ELVIS 20 LOVE SONGS – ROCKIN' ELVIS 60's** — 62 |
(re-iss. May84 lp/c; PL/PK 89124)

Sep 82. (7"ep) **G.I. BLUES – THE ALTERNATIVE TAKES** — – |
— Shoppin' around / Big boots / Frankfurt special / Tonight's all right for love.

Oct 82. (11x7"ep-box) (EP 2) **THE EP COLLECTION VOL.2** — – |
— THE REAL ELVIS / ELVIS PRESLEY / LOVE ME TENDER / HEARTBREAK HOTEL / JAILHOUSE ROCK / LOVING YOU / KING CREOLE VOL.1 / SUCH A NIGHT / FOLLOW THAT DREAM / KID GALAHAD)

Nov 82. (7",7"pic-d) <PB 13351> **THE ELVIS MEDLEY: Jailhouse Rock-Teddy Bear-Hound Dog-Don't Be Cruel-Burning Love-Suspicious Minds. / JAILHOUSE ROCK** — – | 71

Nov 82. (lp) <AHL 4530> **THE ELVIS MEDLEY** — – |

Dec 82. (lp/c) (NL/NK 89025) **IT WON'T SEEM LIKE CHRISTMAS WITHOUT YOU** — 80 |
(re-dist.Nov84; same)

Feb 83. (pic-lp) **PICTURES OF ELVIS II** — – |

Apr 83. (pic-lp) (RCALP 9020) **JAILHOUSE ROCK / LOVE IN LAS VEGAS** — 40 |
— (compilation of music from the 2 films)

Apr 83. (7") (RCA 332) **(YOU'RE SO SQUARE) BABY, I DON'T CARE. / TRUE LOVE** — 61 |
(12"pic-d) (RCAP 332) – ('A'side) / One-sided love affair / Tutti frutti.

May 83. (c-ep) **CASSETTE EP** — – |
— I just can't help believin' / Always on my mind / Separate ways / I've lost you.

Jul 83. (c-ep) (RCXK 014) **FLIP HITS** — – |
— It's now or never / The girl of my best friend / Are you lonesome tonight? / Surrender.

Aug 83. (lp/c) (RCA LP/K 3105) <AHL 4678> **I WAS THE ONE** — 83 | May83

Nov 83. (7") (RCA 369) **I CAN HELP. / THE LADY LOVES ME (w/ ANN-MARGARET)** — 30 |
(10"pic-d+=) (RCAP 369) – If every day was like Christmas.

Nov 83. (lp/c) (PL/PK 84848) **A LEGENDARY PERFORMER VOL.4** — 91 |

Mar 84. (lp/c) (PL/PK 89287) **I CAN HELP** — 71 |

Apr 84. (lp/c) (PG/PH 89387) <3601> **ELVIS – THE FIRST LIVE RECORDINGS** — 69 | Mar84

May 84. (7"m) (RCA 405) **GREEN GREEN GRASS OF HOME. / RELEASE ME (AND LET ME LOVE AGAIN) (live) / SOLITAIRE (live)** — |

Jun 84. (c) (NK 89400) **MAGIC MOMENTS** — |

Aug 84. (d-lp/c) (NL/NK 45180) **THE COMPLETE SONGS** — |

Aug 84. (lp/c) (NL/NK 43730) **ELVIS IN GERMANY (live)** — |

Aug 84. (d-lp/d-c/cd) (NL/NK/PD 89388) **32 FILM HITS** — |

Oct 84. (7") (RCA 459) **THE LAST FAREWELL. / IT'S EASY FOR YOU** — 48 |
(12"+=) (RCAT 459) – Shake, rattle and roll / Flip, flop and fly / That's all right (mama) / My heart cries for you.

Nov 84. (6xlp-box/6xc-box) (PL/PK 85172) <5172> **ELVIS – A GOLDEN CELEBRATION** — | 80

Jan 85. (7") (RCA 476) **THE ELVIS MEDLEY. / BLUE SUEDE SHOES** — 51 |

Jan 85. (lp/c) (PL/PK 84941) **GOLDEN RECORDS VOL.5** — |
(cd-iss. 1986; PD 84941)

Feb 85. (lp) <AFL1 5353> **A VALENTINE GIFT FOR YOU** — – |

Mar 85. (lp/c) (PL/PK 89003) **RARE ELVIS VOL.1** — – |

Mar 85. (lp/c) (PL/PK 89019) **RARE ELVIS VOL.2** — – |

Mar 85. (lp/c) (PL/PK 89051) **RARE ELVIS VOL.3** — – |

Mar 85. (lp/c/cd) (PL/PK/PD 85182) <AFM 5182> **ROCKER** — | Nov84

May 85. (lp/c/cd) (PL/PK/PD 85418) **RECONSIDER BABY** | 92 | -
Jul 85. (d-lp/d-c/cd) (NL/NK/PD 89550) **32 FILM HITS VOL.2** | | -
Jul 85. (7") (PB 49943) **ALWAYS ON MY MIND. / TOMORROW NIGHT** | 59 | -
(12"+=) (PT 49943) – Ain't that loving you baby / Dark moon.
Jul 85. (lp/c/cd) (PL/PK/PD 85430) **ALWAYS ON MY MIND** | | -
Feb 86. (cd) (PD 89248) **ELVIS: THE COLLECTION VOL.1** | | -
Feb 86. (cd) (PD 89249) **ELVIS: THE COLLECTION VOL.2** | | -
Feb 86. (cd) (PD 89472) **ELVIS: THE COLLECTION VOL.3** | | -
Feb 86. (cd) (PD 89473) **ELVIS: THE COLLECTION VOL.4** | | -
(was originally issued w / same track in 1983 on 3xcd)
Jul 86. (lp/c) (NK 89004) **FOREVER** | | -
Dec 86. (lp/c/cd) (PL/PK/PD 89979) **ESSENTIAL ELVIS** | | -
Mar 87. (7") (ARON 1) **BOSSA NOVA BABY (remix). / AIN'T THAT LOVIN' YOU BABY** | 47 | -
(12"+=) (ARONT 1) – I'm coming home / Rock-a-hula baby.
(12") (PT 49745) – ('A'side) / ('A'-Stretch mix) / I'm coming home.
Aug 87. (d-lp/d-c/d-cd) (PL/PK/PD 90100) <6382> **PRESLEY – THE ALL TIME GREATEST HITS** <US title 'THE TOP TEN HITS'> | 4 |
– Heartbreak Hotel / Blue suede shoes / Hound dog / Love me tender / Too much / All shook up / Teddy bear / Paralysed / Party / Jailhouse rock / Don't / Wear my ring around your neck / Hard headed woman / King Creole / One night / A fool such as I / Big hunk o' love / Stuck on you / Girl of my best friend / It's now or never / Are you lonesome tonight? / Wooden heart / Surrender / His latest flame / Can't help falling in love / Good luck charm / She's not you / Return to sender / Devil in disguise / Crying in the chapel / Love letters / If I can dream / In the ghetto / Suspicious minds / Don't cry daddy / The wonder of you / I just can't help believing / American trilogy / Burning love / Always on my mind / My boy / Suspicion / Moody blue / Way down / It's only love.
Aug 87. (d-lp/d-cd) (PL/PK/PD 86414) **THE COMPLETE SUN SESSIONS** | | -
Aug 87. (7") (ARON 2) **LOVE ME TENDER. / TEDDY BEAR** | 56 |
(12"+=) (ARONT 2) – If I can dream / Bossa nova baby (extended).
Aug 87. (d-lp/d-cd) (PL/PK/PD 86221) **THE MEMPHIS ALBUM** | | -
Dec 87. (cd) (ND 89474) **I WISH YOU A MERRY CHRISTMAS** | | -
Jan 88. (7"/12"/cd-s) (PB 49595) **STUCK ON YOU. / ANYWAY YOU WANT ME** | 58 | -
Aug 88. (lp/c/cd) (PL/PK/PD 86985) **THE ALTERNATIVE ALOHA** | | -
Jan 89. (7") (PB 49473) **MEAN WOMAN BLUES. / I BEG OF YOU** | | -
(12"+=/cd-s+=) (PT/PD 49474) – ('A'dub version) / Party.
Jan 89. (lp/c/cd) (PL/PK/PD 90250) **ESSENTIAL ELVIS VOLUME 2: STEREO '57** | 60 |
Feb 89. (3"cd-ep) (PD 49467) **HEARTBREAK HOTEL / I WAS THE ONE / DON'T BE CRUEL / HOUND DOG** | | -
Jul 90. (cd/c/lp) (PD/PK/PL 90486) **ESSENTIAL ELVIS – VOLUME 3: HITS LIKE NEVER BEFORE** | 71 |
Aug 90. (cd)(c)(lp) **THE GREAT PERFORMANCES** | 62 |
Nov 90. (cd) **FOR THE ASKING** | |
Jul 91. (7") (PB 49177) **ARE YOU LONESOME TONIGHT? (live '69). / RUNAWAY (live)** | 68 | -
(12"+=/cd-s+=) (PT/PD 49177) – Baby, What You Want Me To Do (Live) / Reconsider Baby (Live)
Aug 91. (3xcd)(3xc) **COLLECTOR'S GOLD** | 57 |
Jul 92. (cd-box)(c-box)(lp-box) **THE COMPLETE 50's MASTERS** | |
1992. (cd)(c)(d-lp) **FROM THE HEART – HIS GREATEST LOVE SONGS** | 4 |
Aug 92. (7"/c-s) (74321 11077-7/-4) **DON'T BE CRUEL. / ALL SHOOK UP** | 42 | -
(cd-s+=) (74321 11077-2) – Jailhouse rock / I need your love tonight.
Mar 93. (cd) **KID GALAHAD / GIRLS! GIRLS! GIRLS!** | |
Mar 93. (cd) **IT HAPPENED AT THE WORLD'S FAIR / FUN IN ACAPULCO** | |
Mar 93. (cd) **VIVA LAS VEGAS / ROUSTABOUT** | |
Mar 93. (cd) **HARUM SCARUM / GIRL HAPPY** | |
Nov 93. (cd)(c) **THE DEFINITIVE R'N'R ALBUM** | |
Nov 93. (cd)(c) **THE DEFINITIVE GOSPEL ALBUM** | |
Nov 93. (cd)(c) **THE DEFINITIVE COUNTRY ALBUM** | |
Nov 93. (cd)(c) **THE DEFINITIVE FILM ALBUM** | |
Nov 93. (cd)(c) **THE DEFINITIVE LOVE ALBUM** | |
Nov 93. (cd)(c) **ELVIS' CHRISTMAS ALBUM** | |
Nov 93. (cd)(c) **ELVIS SINGS THE WONDERFUL WORLD OF CHRISTMAS** | |
below stuff on some 'RCA' subsidiaries, 'Camden, Golden Grooves, etc.
Sep 77. (lp)(c) **PICTURES OF ELVIS** | 52 | -
(re-iss. Apr80 on 'RCA Int.')
Apr 79. (lp)(c) **PLEASE DON'T STOP LOVING ME** | | -
Jan 80. (lp)(c) **DOUBLE DYNAMITE VOL.1** | | -
Jan 80. (lp)(c) **DOUBLE DYNAMITE VOL.2** | | -
(also iss. as d-lp/d-c on Jan80)
Jan 80. (lp)(c) **THE KING . . . ELVIS** | | -
Jan 81. (lp)(c) **ELVIS PRESLEY** | | -
Jan 81. (d-lp)(d-c) **THE WONDERFUL WORLD OF ELVIS** | | -
Jan 81. (lp)(c) **RETURN TO SENDER** | | -
Sep 81. (lp)(c) **IT'S NOW OR NEVER** | | -
Sep 81. (lp)(c) **HEARTBREAK HOTEL** | | -
Mar 82. (lp)(c) **ARE YOU LONESOME TONIGHT?** | | -
Mar 82. (lp)(c) **SUSPICIOUS MINDS** | | -
Apr 83. (lp)(c) **CAN'T HELP FALLING IN LOVE AND OTHER GREAT MOVIE HITS** | | -
Aug 83. (lp)(c) **LOVE SONGS** | | -
Nov 83. (lp)(c) **THE LEGEND** | | -
Sep 84. (lp)(c) **THE FIRST TEN YEARS** | | -
(cd-iss. 1984 in silver or gold box on 'RCA')
Apr 86. (lp)(c) **THE ROCK HITS** | |
Jul 81. (7") **I JUST CAN'T HELP BELIEVIN'. / BRIDGE OVER TROUBLED WATER (live)** | | -
Jul 81. (7") **AN AMERICAN TRILOGY. / SUSPICIOUS MINDS (live)** | |

Jul 81. (7") **THE GIRL OF MY BEST FRIEND. / SUSPICION** | | -
Aug 81. (7") **THAT'S ALL RIGHT (MAMA). / HARBOUR LIGHTS** | | -
Oct 81. (7") **GOOD ROCKIN' TONIGHT. / MYSTERY TRAIN** | | -
Nov 81. (7") **IF EVERY DAY WAS LIKE CHRISTMAS. / BLUE CHRISTMAS** | | -
May 82. (7") **WAY DOWN. / MOODY BLUE** | | -
Apr 88. (cd) **DIAMOND SERIES – ELVIS PRESLEY** | | -
Oct 77. (lp) Charly; **THE SUN YEARS** | 31 |
Aug 83. (lp) Charly; (SUN 1007) **THE FIRST YEAR** | |
(originally iss.ltd.Nov79 on 'Golden First') (re-iss. Jan85 on 'RCA')
Jan 88. (cd) Charly; **THE COMPLETE MILLION DOLLAR SESSIONS** | |
—— (above featured songs with JERRY LEE LEWIS, JOHNNY CASH, etc)
Mar 79. (lp) Ace; (RED 1) **THE ELVIS TAPES** (press conference 1957) | |
(cd-iss. Dec91)
Nov 84. (lp/c) Topline; (TOP 106/KTOP 106) **IN THE BEGINNING** | |
(cd-iss. Apr87)
Jun 85. (lp/c) Topline; **ELVIS, SCOTTY & BILL** | |
(actually iss.earlier 1979 on 'Virgin')(cd-iss. Feb93 on 'Charly')
Mar 82. (d-lp) Audio Fidelity; **PERSONALLY ELVIS** | |
Mar 84. (pic-lp) Audio Fidelity; **AN HISTORICAL DOCUMENTARY** | |
Jul 82. (lp/c) Everest; (CBR 1014/KCBR/1014) **ELVIS IN HOLLYWOOD** | |
Dec 83. (d-lp/d-c) Everest; (EPC 1000/EPK 1000) **BLUE RHYTHMS** | |
(both these re-iss. Dec84 on 'Premier')
Jun 78. (d-lp/d-c) Pickwick; (PDA 042/PDC 042) **ELVIS PRESLEY COLLECTION VOL.2** | |
Apr 79. (d-lp/d-c) Pickwick; (PDA 054/PDC 054) **ELVIS PRESLEY COLLECTION VOL.3** | |
Oct 79. (lp) Hammer; (HMR 9005) **THE KING SPEAKS** (dialogue) | |
(re-iss. Mar81)
Nov 79. (d-lp/d-c) K-Tel; (NE 1062/) **LOVE SONGS** | 4 |
Nov 80. (lp/c) K-Tel; (NE 1101/CE 2101) **INSPIRATION** (gospel) | 6 |
Nov 81. (lp/c) K-Tel; **THE ULTIMATE PERFORMANCE** | 45 |
Jun 82. (lp/c) K-Tel; (NE 1170/CE2170) **ROCK'N'ROLL REBEL (20 ROCK'N'ROLL ORIGINALS)** | |
Mar 81. (lp) Buttons; **ELVIS ANSWERS BACK** | |
Jan 85. (c) V.F.M.; **1935-1977** | |
Mar 85. (d-lp/d-c) Cambra; (CR 061/CRT 061) **IMAGES** | |
Oct 85. (lp/c/cd) Telstar; (STAR 2264/STAC 2264/TCD 2264) **BALLADS** | 23 |
All below on 'Old Gold' until otherwise mentioned.
Oct 86. (7") (OG 9616) **IN THE GHETTO. / SUSPICIOUS MINDS** | |
Oct 86. (7") (OG 9618) **PARTY. / A LOT O' LIVIN' TO DO** | |
Oct 86. (7") (OG 9620) **BLUE MOON. / I DON'T CARE IF THE SUN DON'T SHINE** | |
Oct 86. (7") (OG 9622) **HIS LATEST FLAME. / GIRL OF MY BEST FRIEND** | |
Oct 86. (7") (OG 9624) **AN AMERICAN TRILOGY. / UNTIL IT'S TIME FOR YOU TO GO (live)** | |
Apr 87. (7") (OG 9700) **HOUND DOG. / DON'T BE CRUEL** | |
Apr 87. (7") (OG 9702) **ARE YOU LONESOME TONIGHT?. / WOODEN HEART** | |
Apr 87. (7") (OG 9704) **HEARTBREAK HOTEL. / ALL SHOOK UP** | |
Apr 87. (7") (OG 9706) **WILD IN THE COUNTRY. / I FEEL SO BAD** | |
Jan 88. (7") (OG 9740) **JAILHOUSE ROCK. / TREAT ME NICE** | |
Jan 88. (7") (OG 9742) **IT'S NOW OR NEVER. / SURRENDER** | |
Jan 88. (7") (OG 9744) **ALWAYS ON MY MIND. / BURNING LOVE** | |
Jan 88. (7") (OG 9746) **LOVING YOU. / PARALYSED** | |
Jan 88. (7") (OG 9750) **KING CREOLE. / HARD HEADED WOMAN** | |
Jan 88. (7") (OG 9752) **DON'T. / WEAR MY RING AROUND YOUR NECK** | |
Jan 88. (7") (OG 9754) **CAN'T HELP FALLING IN LOVE. / ROCK-A-HULA BABY** | |
Jan 88. (7") (OG 9756) **MY BOY. / MY WAY (live)** | |
Jan 88. (7") (OG 9758) **WAY DOWN. / MOODY BLUE** | |
Jan 88. (7") (OG 9761) **THE WONDER OF YOU. / IF I CAN DREAM** | |
Nov 90. (5xcd-box) Reader's Digest; **THE LEGEND LIVES ON** | |
Mar 94. (cd) **KNOWN ONLY TO HIM: ELVIS GOSPEL 1957-1971** | |
Mar 94. (cd) (74321187542) **THE MEMPHIS RECORD** | |
Jun 94. (cd/c) (07863663602/7863663604) **FRANKIE & JOHNNY / PARADISE, HAWAIIAN STYLE** | |
Jun 94. (cd/c) (07863663612/7863663614) **SPINOUT / DOUBLE TROUBLE** | |
Jun 94. (cd/c) (07863663622/7863663624) **KISSIN' COUSINS / CLAMBAKE / STAY AWAY, JOE** | |
Sep 94. (cd/c/d-lp) (74321228712/74321228714/74321228711) **THE ESSENTIAL COLLECTION** | 6 |
Sep 94. (cd/c) **AMAZING GRACE** | |
Nov 94. (cd) (07863665062) **IF EVERY DAY WAS LIKE CHRISTMAS** | |
Jun 94. (cd) Javelin; (HADCD 151) **THE ONE AND ONLY** | |
Jun 95. (cd) Thunderbolt; **FROM CALYPSO TO CALLAPSO** | |
Jan 95. (d-cd) Simon & Schuster; **ELVIS: AN AUDIO SCRAPBOOK** | |
Nov 95. (cd-ep) (74321 32012-2) **THE TWELFTH OF NEVER** | 21 | -
May 96. (cd-ep) (74321 33686-2) **HEARTBREAK HOTEL / I WAS THE ONE** | 45 | -
May 97. (c-s) R.C.A.; (74321 48541-4) **ALWAYS ON MY MIND / SEPARATE WAYS** | 13 |
(cd-s) (74321 48541-2) – ('A'side) / Are you lonesome tonight? / Moody blue / Way down.
Jun 97. (cd/c) R.C.A.; (74321 48984-2/-4) **ALWAYS ON MY MIND – ULTIMATE LOVE SONGS** | 3 |
Jul 99. (3xcd-box/3xc-box) <(07863 67732-2/-4)> **ARTIST OF THE CENTURY** | |

Apr 95. (cd) (07863665572) **FLAMING STAR / WILD IN THE COUNTRY / FOLLOW THAT DREAM** | | -
Apr 95. (cd) (CDS 1146) **EASY COME EASY GO / SPEEDWAY** | | -
Apr 95. (cd) () **LIVE A LITTLE, LOVE A LITTLE / CHARRO / THE TROUBLE . . .** | | -

May 95. (cd/c) *Pickwick;* () **THE LEGEND BEGINS – LIVE 1954-56 (with interviews)** [ ] -
Jul 95. (d-cd) () **THE ESSENTIAL 60'S MASTERS VOLUME 2** [ ] -
Oct 95. (cd) () **THE COLLECTION 1** [ ]
Oct 95. (cd-ep) () **TWELFTH OF NEVER / BURNING LOVE / WALK A MILE IN MY SHOES** [21]
Jul 97. (cd) **PLATINUM: A LIFE IN MUSIC** [80]
Feb 98. (cd/c) (74321 55628-2/-4) **BLUE SUEDE SHOES (The Ultimate Rock'n'roll Collection)** [39]

– pre-death compilations, etc. –

on 'R.C.A.' unless mentioned otherwise
Mar 56. (7"ep) **ELVIS PRESLEY** [-] [20]
– Blue suede shoes No.20 / /
May 56. (7"ep) **HEARTBREAK HOTEL** [-]
Sep 56. (7"ep) **ELVIS PRESLEY (SHAKE, RATTLE AND ROLL)** [-]
Sep 56. (7"ep) **THE REAL ELVIS** [-]
– Don't be cruel / Hound dog / My baby left me / I want you, I need you, I love you. *(re-iss. Apr61 on 'RCA-Gold')*
Oct 56. (7"ep) **ANYWAY YOU WANT ME** [-]
Nov 56. (7"ep) **ELVIS, VOLUME 1** [-]
– Love me No. 2 / When my blue moon turns to gold again No.19 / (2 tracks).
Dec 56. (7"ep) (TEG 8199) **LOVE ME TENDER** [-]
– Love me tender / Let me / Poor boy No.24 / We're gonna move. *(UK re-iss. Mar60)*
Sep 57. (7"ep) (TEG 8256) **GOOD ROCKING TONIGHT** [-]
– Good rocking tonight / Blue Moon of Kentucky / Milkcow blues boogie / Just because.
Dec 56. (7"ep) **ELVIS, VOLUME 2** [-]
Jun 57. (7"ep) (RCX 101) **PEACE IN THE VALLEY** [3] Apr 57
– (There'll be) Peace in the valley (for me) No.25 / It is no secret / I believe / Take my hand precious Lord. *(UK re-iss. Mar60 + Oct82) (US re-iss. Apr61 on 'RCA Gold')*
Jun 57. (7"ep) **LOVING YOU** [-]
– Loving you / Let's have a party / Teddy bear / Gotta lotta lovin' to do. *(re-iss. Oct77)*
Jun 57. (7"ep) **LOVING YOU, VOLUME 2** [-] [18] lp-cht
Aug 57. (7"ep) **JUST FOR YOU** [-] [18] lp-cht
Oct 57. (7"ep) (RCX 104) **ELVIS PRESLEY** [-]
– I need you so / Have I told you lately that I love you / Blueberry Hill / Don't leave me now. *(re-iss. Mar60)*
Jan 58. (7"ep) (RCX 106) **JAILHOUSE ROCK** [18] Nov 57
– Jailhouse rock / Young and beautiful / Don't leave me now / Baby I don't care / I want to be free. *(re-iss. Mar60 + Feb82)*
Sep 58. (7"ep) (RCX 117) **KING CREOLE VOLUME 1** [-]
– King Creole / New Orleans / As long as I have you / Lover doll. *(re-iss. Mar60 + Feb82) (US re-iss. Apr61 on 'RCA Gold')*
Sep 58. (7"ep) (RCX 118) **KING CREOLE VOLUME 2** [-]
– Trouble / Young dreams / Crawfish / Dixieland rock. *(re-iss. Mar60 + Feb82) (US re-iss. Apr61 on 'RCA Gold')*
Oct 58. (lp) (RB 16069) <LPM 1707> **ELVIS' GOLDEN RECORDS** [3] Apr58
(re-iss. 1970; (SF 8129) (re-iss. Sep81 as 'VOL.1' on 'RCA International' lp/c; INTS/INTK 5143) (re-iss. Nov84 lp/c; NL/NK 81707) (cd-iss. 1988; PD 85196)
Nov 58. (7"ep) (RCX 121) **ELVIS SINGS CHRISTMAS SONGS** [ ] Nov57
– Santa bring my baby back to me / Blue Christmas / Santa Claus is back in town / I'll be home for Christmas.
Nov 58. (7"ep) (RCX 131) **ELVIS SAILS** (dialogue) [-] Mar59
Dec 58. (7"ep) **CHRISTMAS WITH ELVIS** [-]
Feb 59. (7"ep) (RCX 135) **ELVIS IN TENDER MOOD** [-]
– Young and beautiful / True love / Lover doll / Love me tender. *(re-iss. Mar60)*
Mar 59. (lp) **FOR LP FANS ONLY** [-] [19]
(cd-iss. Nov89)
Jul 59. (lp) **A DATE WITH ELVIS (early Sun recordings)** [4] [32] Sep59
– Blue Moon of Kentucky / Young and beautiful / Baby I don't care / Milk cow blues boogie / Baby let's play house / Good rockin' tonight / Is it so strange / I forgot to remember to forget. *(re-iss. Aug80 + Apr84) (cd-iss. Nov89)*
Dec 59. (7"ep) (RCX 1045) **A TOUCH OF GOLD, VOLUME 1** [ ] [-]
– Hard headed woman / Good rockin' tonight / Don't / Teddy bear. *(re-iss. Mar60 + Oct82)*
Feb 60. (7"ep) (RCX 175) **STRICTLY ELVIS** [26] Jan 57
– Old Shep / Any place is Paradise / Paralysed / Is it so strange.
Jun 60. (lp) (RD 27159) <LPM 2075> **50,000,000 ELVIS FANS CAN'T BE WRONG – ELVIS' GOLDEN RECORDS VOLUME 2** [4] [31] Feb60
(re-iss. Sep81 as 'ELVIS GOLDEN VOL.2' on 'RCA International' lp/c; INTS/INTK 5144) (cd-iss. Nov84;)
(these early collections vary in track listings UK/US).
1960. (7"ep) (RCX 1048) **A TOUCH OF GOLD, VOLUME 2** [-]
– Wear my ring around your neck / Treat me nice / One night / That's all right mama.
Nov 60. (7"ep) (RCX 190) **SUCH A NIGHT** [-]
– Such a night / It feels so right / Like a baby / Make me know it.
Apr 61. (7"ep) **ELVIS BY REQUEST** [ ]
– Flaming star No.14 / (3 tracks).
Jun 62. (7"ep) (RCX 211) **FOLLOW THAT DREAM** [34]
– Follow that dream No.15 / Angel / What a wonderful world / I'm not the marrying kind.
Jan 63. (7"ep) (RCX 7109) **KID GALAHAD** [16] Sep 62
– King of the whole wide world No.30 / This is living / Riding the rainbow / Home is where the heart is / I got lucky / Whistling tune.
Apr 64. (lp) (RD 7630) <LSP 2765> **ELVIS' GOLDEN RECORDS, VOLUME 3** [6] [3] Sep63
(re-iss. Sep81 on 'RCA International' lp/c; INTS/INTK 5145) (re-iss. Nov84 lp/c; NL/NK 82765) (cd-iss. Dec90)
Apr 64. (7"ep) (RCX 7141) **LOVE IN LAS VEGAS** [ ] [92]
– If you think I don't need you / I need somebody to lean on / C'mon everybody / Today tomorrow and forever.
May 64. (7"ep) (RCX 7142) **ELVIS FOR YOU VOLUME 1** [ ]
– Rip it up / Love me / When my blue moon turns to gold / Paralysed.
May 64. (7"ep) (RCX 7143) **ELVIS FOR YOU VOLUME 2** [ ]
– Long tall Sally / First in line / How do you think I feel / How's the world treating you.

Jul 65. (7"ep) (RCX 7173) **TICKLE ME VOLUME 1** [ ] [70]
– I feel that I've known you forever / Night rider / Slowly but surely / Dirty dirty feeling / Put the blame on me.
Jul 65. (7"ep) (RCX 7174) **TICKLE ME VOLUME 2** [ ] [ ]
– I'm yours / Long lonely highway / It feels so right / Such an easy question.
Sep 65. (lp) (RD 7762) **ELVIS FOR EVERYONE!** [8] [10]
(UK – ELVIS FOR EVERYBODY) (UK re-iss. +c.May72, hit No.48)
Jun 67. (7") (RCX 7187) **EASY COME EASY GO** [-]
– Easy come easy go / Yoga is as Yoga does / Sing you children / I'll take love.
Apr 68. (lp) (RD/SF 7924) <LSP 3921> **ELVIS' GOLD RECORDS, VOLUME 4** [33]
(re-iss. Sep81 on 'RCA International' lp/c; (NL/NK 83921) (re-iss. Apr84 lp/c; NL/NK 83921) (cd-iss. Dec90;)
Apr 69. (lp) (RD 8011) **ELVIS – N.B.C. TV SPECIAL** [2] [8] Jan69
(re-iss. UK Aug78 No.50) (re-iss. Aug81 & Nov84) (cd-iss. Mar91)
Feb 70. (lp) (RCA 555) **PORTRAIT IN MUSIC** [36]
Nov 70. (4xlp) (LPM 6401) **WORLD WIDE 50 GOLD AWARD HITS** [49] [45]
(c-iss.May72 – 2 Volumes 25 hits in each)
May 71. (c) **WORLD WIDE 25 GOLD AWARD HITS Vol.3** [ ]
Jul 71. (7"m) **HEARTBREAK HOTEL. / HOUND DOG / DON'T BE CRUEL** [10] [-]
Jul 71. (lp)(c) **C'MON EVERYBODY** [5]
—— (above & below album were budget, below on 'RCA Camden').
Jul 71. (lp/c) (CDS 1088/CAM 415) **YOU'LL NEVER WALK ALONE** (gospel) [20] Apr 71
Sep 71. (lp/c) () **ALMOST IN LOVE** [38]
Nov 71. (7"m) **JAILHOUSE ROCK. / ARE YOU LONESOME TONIGHT?. / (LET ME BE YOUR) TEDDY BEAR / STEADFAST, LOYAL AND TRUE** [42] [-]
Nov 71. (lp/c) (PL 42371/PK 42371) **ELVIS SINGS THE WONDERFUL WORLD OF CHRISTMAS** [7]
(cd-iss. Nov89)
Dec 71. (lp/c) (CDS 1154/CAM 496) **I GOT LUCKY** [26]
(re-iss. Nov75 on 'RCA Camden')
Feb 74. (lp/c) (CPL1 1349/APK1 1349) **A LEGENDARY PERFORMER VOL.1** [20]
Dec 74. (lp/c) (LPL 17527/LPK 17527) **HITS OF THE 70'S** [ ]
(re-iss. Sep77, hit No.30)
Mar 75. (lp)(c) () **HAVING FUN WITH ELVIS ON STAGE (live)** [ ]
Mar 75. (c) () **WORLD WIDE 25 GOLD AWARD HITS Vol.4** [ ]
Sep 75. (7"m) () **BLUE MOON / YOU'RE A HEARTBREAKER. / I'M LEFT, YOU'RE RIGHT, SHE'S GONE** [ ]
Sep 76. (7") (RCA 2729) **THE GIRL OF MY BEST FRIEND. / A MESS OF BLUES** [9] [-]
Nov 76. (7") (RCA 2768) **SUSPICION. / (IT'S A) LONG LONELY HIGHWAY** [9] [-]
Feb 77. (lp/c) (PL 42003/PK 42003) **ELVIS IN DEMAND** [12]
(re-iss. Sep81)
May 77. (7") (RCA 2694) **ALL SHOOK UP. / HEARTBREAK HOTEL** [41]
Jul 72. (lp/c) RCA Camden; (CDS 1110/CAM 423) **ELVIS SINGS HITS FROM HIS MOVIES, VOL.1** [ ]
Nov 72. (lp/c) RCA Camden; **BURNING LOVE AND HITS FROM HIS MOVIES, VOL.2** [22]
1973. (lp/c) RCA Camden; (CDS 1118/CAM 428) **SEPARATE WAYS** [46]
Jun 75. (lp/c) RCA Camden; (CDS 1150/CAM457) **U.S. MALE** [ ]
1975. (lp/c) RCA Camden; (CDS 1146/CAM 1146) **EASY COME EASY GO** [ ]
Aug 75. (lp/c) RCA Starcall; (NL 42757/NK 42757) **THE ELVIS PRESLEY SUN COLLECTION** [16]
(re-iss. Mar79) (re-iss. Oct83, cd-iss. Aug88 on 'RCA')
Jun 78. (d-lp/d-c) RCA Starcall; (PDA 042/PDC 042) **THE ELVIS PRESLEY COLLECTION VOL.2** [-]
Jun 75. (d-lp/d-c) Arcade; **40 GREATEST HITS** [1] [-]
(re-iss. Nov78 on 'RCA', hit No.40)
Jul 76. (d-lp/d-cd) Pickwick; (PDA 009/PDC 009) **ELVIS PRESLEY COLLECTION** [-]
– (50,000,000 FANS lp / +) (cd-iss. !)

PRETENDERS

Formed: London, England ... March '78 by American singer/songwriter CHRISSIE HYNDE together with Hereford based musicians, guitarist JAMES HONEYMAN-SCOTT, bassist PETE FARNDON and drummer GERRY MACKLEDUFF. Prior to forming the band, HYNDE had spent the early 70's at Kent State University before moving to London in 1973 and securing work as an NME journalist. The following year, she relocated to Paris, to join the cringingly titled FRENCHIES, meeting CHRIS SPEDDING who invited her to contribute backing vocals on his 1977 album, 'Hurt'. Prior to this, HYNDE had returned to her home in Ohio in 1975 to join R&B group, JACK RABBIT. On the move again, she returned to London the following year to form The BERK BROTHERS (DAVE & FRED), before they replaced her with JOHNNY MOPED. Her self-penned songs were strong enough, however, to attract the attention of DAVE HILL, (currently in the process of setting up his own label, 'Real') for whom she cut a demo tape in August '77. HILL subsequently asked HYNDE to form a band, and voila, The 'PRETENDERS' were born. Their first single was a cover of The Kinks' 'STOP YOUR SOBBING', produced by NICK LOWE (ex-BRINSLEY SCHWARZ) and garnering much critical acclaim for its fresh faced new wave/ power-pop in the wake of punk overload. Another minor hit followed in the emotionally fragile 'KID' before the group hit big at the tail end of '79 with 'BRASS IN POCKET'. A simmering, swaggering slice of white pop-funk, the record became a UK No.1 and HYNDE was fast gaining a reputation as one of the finest songwriters around with an evocatively sultry voice to match. If there were any doubters then 'PRETENDERS' (1980) silenced them, a brilliant debut with a consistently engaging stylistic diversity. In addition to the singles, the album boasted the reggae-esque 'PRIVATE LIFE' and the gorgeous 'LOVERS OF TODAY', the individual musicians acquitting themselves with impressive conviction, notably the talented HONEYMAN-SCOTT. The album made The PRETENDERS a household name, the band subsequently undertaking an US stadium tour. While in America, HYNDE met her hero, RAY DAVIES (ex-KINKS), the pair duly becoming lovers (while DAVIES would eventually become her common-law husband and father of her first child, Natalie, the pair were allegedly refused a marriage certificate when the registrar became annoyed by their constant arguing!). The much anticipated follow-up, 'PRETENDERS II' (1981), was eventually released in August '81 to mixed reviews. The singles, 'MESSAGE OF LOVE', 'TALK OF THE TOWN' along with the steamy 'THE ADULTRESS' were highlights, although overall the album lacked the energy and verve of the debut. Later that summer, FARNDON was kicked out due to his spiralling drug use, narcotics also to blame for the death of HONEYMAN-SCOTT, found dead in his London flat two days later. Picking up the pieces, HYNDE went back into the studio with temporary replacements, guitarist BILLY BREMNER (ex-DAVE EDMUNDS' ROCKPILE) and bassist TONY BUTLER (future BIG COUNTRY) to record the driving melancholy of 'BACK ON THE CHAIN GANG' (written for HONEYMAN-SCOTT). With semi-permanent members ROBBIE McINTOSH and MALCOLM FOSTER brought in on guitar and bass respectively, the band began a new chapter in early '83. Incredibly, tragedy struck again almost immediately with PETE FARNDON becoming another fatal drugs casualty. A single eventually surfaced towards the end of the year, the undulating '2,000 MILES', while a third album, 'LEARNING TO CRAWL', appeared in early '84. Though the album contained some stellar PRETENDERS moments, it once more met with mixed reviews and performed better in America than Britain. The following year was to be an eventful one for HYNDE, meeting and subsequently marrying JIM KERR (SIMPLE MINDS) as well as playing Live Aid and topping the UK charts via her UB40 collaboration, a remake of the old SONNY & CHER chestnut, 'I GOT YOU BABE'. HYNDE eventually re-emerged with a slightly modified PRETENDERS line-up and a new deal with 'WEA' in late '86, the group scoring their first Top 10 hit in years with the infectiously chugging 'DON'T GET ME WRONG'. This was swiftly followed by the 'GET CLOSE' (1986) album, a warmer sounding affair with HYNDE singing to her new daughter (born to KERR) on the lovely 'HYMN TO HER', while revealing an increasing political awareness with 'HOW MUCH DID YOU GET FOR YOUR SOUL'. Indeed, 1988 saw her billed on the Nelson Mandela concert alongside UB40 at Wembley Stadium (she also scored another Top 10 collaboration with the band that summer, 'BREAKFAST IN BED'), while also becoming involved in various animal rights activities. HYNDE eventually turned her hand to The PRETENDERS once more at the turn of the decade, now virtually solo with a revolving cast of musicians backing her on 'PACKED' (1990) and 'LAST OF THE INDEPENDENTS' (1994). While not scaling the giddy heights of old, these releases proved HYNDE was still capable of writing affectingly melodic pop/rock. The unplugged set was inevitable really, HYNDE releasing 'THE ISLE OF VIEW' in 1995, a collection of spartan reworkings of old classics. The PRETENDERS return album proper, 'VIVA EL AMOR!' (1999), saw CHRISSIE and her band find old favour with her 80's fanbase (it reached the UK Top 40), the opening track 'POPSTAR' truly a single that deserved better airplay. • Songwriters: Group compositions, except as said plus; MAY THIS BE LOVE (Jimi Hendrix) / IF THERE WAS A MAN (co-w/ John Barry) / NOT A SECOND TIME (Beatles) / CREEP (Radiohead). • Trivia: CHRISSIE caused controversy in June '89, when she attended a Greenpeace Rainbow Warriors press conference, telling how she (a staunch vegetarian) once firebombed McDonalds burger shop. The day after, one of their shops in Milton Keynes was firebombed and CHRISSIE was asked/told to sign a retracting statement, or be taken to court.

Album rating: PRETENDERS (*8) / PRETENDERS II (*7) / LEARNING TO CRAWL (*8) / GET CLOSE (*5) / THE SINGLES compilation (*8) / PACKED! (*4) / LAST OF THE INDEPENDENTS (*6) / THE ISLE OF VIEW (*5) / VIVA EL AMOR (*6)

CHRISSIE HYNDE (b. 7 Sep'51, Akron, Ohio) – vocals, guitar / **JAMES HONEYMAN-SCOTT** (b. 4 Nov'57, Hereford, England) – guitar, keyboards (ex-CHEEKS) / **PETE FARNDON** (b.1953, Hereford) – bass / **GERRY MACKLEDUFF** – drums

	Real	Sire
Jan 79. (7") (ARE 6) **STOP YOUR SOBBING. / THE WAIT**	34	-

—— **MARTIN CHAMBERS** (b. 4 Sep'51, Hereford) – drums repl. GERRY

	Real	Sire
Jun 79. (7") (ARE 9) **KID. / TATTOOED LOVE BOYS**	33	Jul 80
Nov 79. (7") (ARE 11) **BRASS IN POCKET. / SWINGING LONDON** (12"+=) (ARET 11) – Nervous but shy. (c-ep-iss.Apr81; SPC 5)	1	-
Jan 80. (lp/c) (RAL/+C 3) <6083> **PRETENDERS** – Precious / The phone call / Up the neck / Tattooed love boys / Space invader / The wait / Stop your sobbing / Kid / Private life / Brass in pocket / Lovers of today / Mystery achievement. (cd-iss. 1983 on 'WEA'; 256774-2)	1	9
Feb 80. (7") <49181> **BRASS IN POCKET. / SPACE INVADER**	-	14
Apr 80. (7") (ARE 12) **TALK OF THE TOWN. / CUBAN SLIDE AND SLIDE**	8	
May 80. (7") <49506> **STOP YOUR SOBBING. / PHONE CALL**	-	65
Feb 81. (7") (ARE 15) **MESSAGE OF LOVE. / PORCELAIN**	11	Apr81
Aug 81. (lp/c) (RAL/+C 3) <3572> **PRETENDERS II** – The adultress / Bad boys get spanked / Message of love / I go to sleep / Birds of Paradise / Talk of the town / Pack it up / Waste not, want not / Day after day / Jealous dogs / Waste not want not / English rose / Louie Louie. (cd-iss. Nov86 & Jul93 on 'WEA'; 256774-2)	7	10
Aug 81. (7") <49819> **LOUIE LOUIE. / IN THE STICKS**	-	

Aug 81. (7") (ARE 17) **DAY AFTER DAY. / IN THE STICKS** (12"+=) (ARE 17a) – The adultress.	45	-
Nov 81. (7") (ARE 18) **I GO TO SLEEP. / THE ENGLISH ROSE** (12"+=) (ARE 18T) – Waste not, want not.	7	-
Jan 82. (7") **I GO TO SLEEP. / WASTE NOT, WANT NOT**	-	

—— (Sep'82) **BILLY BREMNER** – guitar (ex-NICK LOWE, ex-DAVE EDMUNDS' ROCKPILE) repl. HONEYMAN-SCOTT who died of drug overdose 16 Jun'82 / **TONY BUTLER** – bass (of BIG COUNTRY) repl. FARNDON (died o.d. 14 Apr'83)

Sep 82. (7") (ARE 19) <29840> **BACK ON THE CHAIN GANG. / MY CITY HAS GONE** (12"+=) (ARE 19T) – ('A'-part 2).	17	5 Dec82

—— (Feb83) **HYNDE** and **CHAMBERS** brought in new members **ROBBIE McINTOSH** (25 Oct'57) – guitar (ex-MANFRED MANN'S EARTH BAND, ex-NIGHT) repl. BREMNER who rejoined NICK LOWE etc. / **MALCOLM FOSTER** (b.13 Jan'56) – bass repl. BUTLER who rejoined BIG COUNTRY

Nov 83. (7") (ARE 20) **2000 MILES. / THE LAW IS THE LAW** ('A'fast or slow versioned 12"+=) (ARE 20T) – Money (live).	15	-
Nov 83. (7") <29444> **MIDDLE OF THE ROAD. / 2,000 MILES**	-	19
Jan 84. (lp/c)(cd) (WX 2/+C)(923980-2) <23980> **LEARNING TO CRAWL** – Middle of the road / Back on the chain gang / Time the avenger / Watching the clothes / Show me / Thumbelina / My city was gone / Thin line between love and hate / I hurt you / 2000 miles.	11	5
Feb 84. (7"/12") (ARE 21/+T) **MIDDLE OF THE ROAD. / WATCHING THE CLOTHES**		-

—— added **PAUL CARRACK** – keyboards (ex-ACE, ex-ROXY MUSIC, ex-solo artist)

Mar 84. (7") <29317> **SHOW ME. / FAST OR SLOW (THE LAW IS THE LAW)**	-	28
Apr 84. (7") (ARE 22) <29249> **THIN LINE BETWEEN LOVE AND HATE. / TIME THE AVENGER** (12"+=) (ARE 22T) – Bad boys get spanked.	49	83 Jun84

—— Sep 85, CHRISSIE HYNDE guests on UB40's 'I Got You Babe' which hits No.1. Three years later the same team hit no.6 with 'Breakfast In Bed'. PRETENDERS regroup with **HYNDE, McINTOSH** and **TIM STEVENS** – bass / **BLAIR CUNNINGHAM** – drums (ex-HAIRCUT 100) repl. CHAMBERS (on some) and **BERNIE WORRELL** – keyboards

	W.E.A.	Warners
Sep 86. (7") (YZ 85) <28630> **DON'T GET ME WRONG. / DANCE** (12"+=) (YZ 85T) – ('A'extended).	10	10
Oct 86. (lp/c)(cd) (WX 34/+C)(240976-2) <25488> **GET CLOSE** – My baby / When I change my life / Light of the Moon / Dance * / Tradition of love / Don't get me wrong / I remember you / How much did you get for your soul / Chill factor / Hymn to her / Room full of mirrors. (c+=/cd+= *)	6	25
Nov 86. (7") (YZ 93) **HYMN TO HER. / ROOM FULL OF MIRRORS** (12"+=) (YZ 93T) – Stop your sobbing (demo).	8	-
Feb 87. (7") <28496> **MY BABY. / ROOM FULL OF MIRRORS**	-	64
Mar 87. (7") (YZ 110) **MY BABY. / TRADITION OF LOVE (remix)** (12"+=) (YZ 110T) – Thumbelina. (7"ep+=) (YZEP 110) – Private life / Middle of the road.	-	-
Apr 87. (7") **HYMN TO HER. / TRADITION OF LOVE**	-	
Aug 87. (7"; as PRETENDERS 007) (YZ 149) <28259> **IF THERE WAS A MAN. / INTO VIENNA** (12"+=) (YZ 149T) – Where has everybody gone.	49	
Oct 87. (lp/c)(cd) (WX 135/+C)(242229-2) <25664> **THE SINGLES** (compilation) – Stop your sobbing / Kid / Brass in pocket / Talk of the town / Back on the chain gang / Middle of the road / 2000 miles / Show me / Thin line between love and hate / Don't get me wrong / Hymn to her / My baby / I got you babe (w / UB40) / What you gonna do about it.	6	69
Oct 87. (7") (YZ 156) **KID (remix). / STOP YOUR SOBBING (original)** (12"+=/cd-s+=) (YZ 156 T/CD) – ('B' 1978 demo) / What you gonna do about it ('87 remix). Jun'88, she guested again with UB40 on hit single 'BREAKFAST IN BED'.	-	-

—— added guest **JOHNNY MARR** – guitar (ex-SMITHS) repl. McINTOSH

Apr 89. (7"/12"/3"cd-s) (PRE/+T/CD 69) **WINDOWS OF THE WORLD. / 1969**	-	-

—— (above from the film '1969', a one-off on label 'Polydor')

—— now virtually **CHRISSIE** solo, augmented by **BLAIR CUNNINGHAM** – drums / **BILLY BREMNER + DOMINIC MILLER** – guitar / **JOHN McKENZIE** – bass / plus others

May 90. (7"/c-s) (YZ 469/+C) <19820> **NEVER DO THAT. / NOT A SECOND TIME** (12"+=) (YZ 469T) – The wait. (cd-s++=) (YZ 469CD) – Spirit of life.	-	-
May 90. (cd)(lp/c) (9031 71403-2)(WX 346/+C) <26219> **PACKED!** – Never do that / Let's make a pact / Millionaires / May this be love / No guarantee / When will I see you / Sense of purpose / Downtown (Akron) / How do I miss you / Hold a candle to this / Criminal. (cd re-iss. Nov94; 9031 71403-2)	19	48
Oct 90. (7") (YZ 507) **SENSE OF PURPOSE. / SPIRIT OF LIFE** (12"+=) (YZ 507T) – Brass in pocket. (cd-s++=/cd-s++=) (YZ 507 CD/s) – Not a second time.	-	-

—— Oct 91, CHRISSIE's vox was credited on single 'SPIRITUAL HIGH', by MOOD SWINGS. It finally hit UK no. 47 early '93.

—— She wrote most with B. STEINBERG + T.KELLY. Covered; FOREVER YOUNG (Bob Dylan).

—— **CHRISSIE** + main band **MARTIN CHAMBERS** – drums / **ADAM SEYMOUR** – guitar / **ANDY HOBSON** – bass

Apr 94. (7"/c-s) (YZ 815/+C) <18160> **I'LL STAND BY YOU. / REBEL ROCK ME** (cd-s+=) (YZ 815CD1) – Bold as love. (cd-s) (YZ 815CD2) – ('A'side) / Message of love / Brass in pocket / Don't get me wrong.	10	16 Aug94
May 94. (cd)(lp/c) (4509 95822-2/-4/-1) <45572> **LAST OF THE INDEPENDENTS** – Hollywood perfume / Night in my veins / Money talk / 977 / Revolution / All my	8	41

dreams / I'll stand by you / I'm a mother / Tequila / Every mother's son / Rebel rock me / Love colours / Forever young.

May 94. (c-s,cd-s) <18163> **NIGHT IN MY VEINS / ANGEL OF THE MORNING** `-` `71`

Jun 94. (7"/c-s) (YZ 825/+C) **NIGHT IN MY VEINS. / BAD BOYS GET SPANKED** `25` `-`
(cd-s+=) (YZ 825CD) – My city was gone / Tattooed love boys.

Oct 94. (7"/c-s) (YZ 848/+C) **977. / I'LL STAND BY YOU (live)** `66`
(cd-s+=) (YZ 848CD1) – Hollywood perfume (live) / Kid (live).
(cd-s) (YZ 848CD2) – ('A'side) / Back on the chain gang (live) / Night in my veins (live) / Precious (live).

Sep 95. (c-s) (WEA 014C) **KID (acoustic) / THE ISLE OF VIEW (acoustic)** `73`
(cd-s+=) (WEA 014CD) – Creep (acoustic).

Oct 95. (cd/c) (0630 12059-2/-4) <46085> **THE ISLE OF VIEW (live acoustic)** `23` `100`
– Sense of purpose / Chill factor / Private life / Back on the chain gang / Kid / I hurt you / Criminal / Brass in pocket / 2000 miles / Hymn to her / Lovers of today / The phone call / I go to sleep / Revolution. (cd+=) – The Isle of View.

Nov 95. (c-s/cd-s) (WEA 024 C/CD) **2000 MILES (acoustic) / TEQUILA**
(cd-s+=) (WEA 024CDX) – Happy Christmas / Night in my veins.

Apr 97. (c-s/12"/cd-s) (NEG 104 C/T/CD) **GOIN' BACK. / (other track by The LA'S)**
(above issued on 'Blanco Y Negro')

May 99. (c-s) (WEA 207C) **HUMAN / THE HOMECOMING (Street version)** `33`
(cd-s+=) (WEA 207CD) – ('A'-Glass mix).

May 99. (cd/c) (<3984 27152-2/-4>) **VIVA EL AMOR!** `32`
– Popstar / Nails in the road / Human / From the heart down / Who's who / Dragway 42 / Baby's breath / One more time / Legalise me / Biker / Samurai / Rabo de nube.

Aug 99. (c-s) (WEA 219C) **POPSTAR / THE NEEDLE AND THE DAMAGE DONE**
(cd-s+=) (WEA 219CD) – Samurai.

– compilations, etc. –

Jul 94. (cd/c) Carlton; (4509 91885-2/-4) **DON'T GET ME WRONG** `-`

PRETTY THINGS

Formed: Dartford, Kent, England ... 1963 by DICK TAYLOR and PHIL MAY. The former had once been a member of LITTLE BOY BLUE & THE BLUE BOYS, an embryonic version of The ROLLING STONES. The pair added BRIAN PENDLETON, JOHN STAX and PETE KITLEY, the latter being replaced by drummer VIV PRINCE. Taking their name from a BO DIDDLEY song, they soon signed to 'Fontana', employing the management team of Bryan Morrison and James Duncan, the latter of whom wrote their summer '64 debut Top 50 hit, 'ROSALYN'. Their pure roots/R&B follow-up, 'DON'T BRING ME DOWN' (which drew inspiration from black American blues artists of the 50's) dented the UK Top 10, preceding their eponymous Top 10 album in early '65. Unlike the STONES (of whom they were dubbed by the press as uglier cousins), their hits had dried up by 1967, due to a misguided foray into psychedelia. Later that year, they moved to 'Columbia' records, releasing two flop 45's, before they embarked on their most ambitious project so far, 'S.F. SORROW'. It was the first ever "rock opera", inspiring PETE TOWNSHEND (The Who) to write his legendary 'Tommy'. The album was a commercial flop and critically lambasted by the press, although it has since become regarded as an innovative piece of work that was essential to the development of "rock" music. During its recording, TAYLOR left to become a producer, the band folding but regrouping for a heavier 'Harvest' set, 'PARACHUTE' (1970). They struggled on regardless, subsequently signing for LED ZEPPELIN's heavyweight 'Swan Song' label in '74. Two mediocre albums followed before the band split in '76 after their remaining founder member, MAY, departed. They reformed many times and still tread the boards on the blues circuit alongside members of The YARDBIRDS. • **Songwriters:** Most by PHIL MAY, except covers; PRETTY THING + ROADRUNNER + MONA (Bo Diddley) / CRY TO ME (Bert Berns) / A HOUSE IN THE COUNTRY (Ray Davies; Kinks) / REELIN' AND ROCKIN' (Chuck Berry) / I'M A KING BEE (Muddy Waters) / SHAKIN' ALL OVER (Johnny Kidd & The Pirates) / etc. • **Trivia:** The group made cameo appearances in the films, 'What's Good For The Goose' (1969 w /Norman Wisdom) and 'The Monster Squad' (1980 w /Vincent Price). They were given a tribute by BOWIE in 1973, when he covered their first two hits on his 'PIN-UPS' album.

Album rating: THE PRETTY THINGS (*7) / GET THE PICTURE (*6) / EMOTIONS (*6) / S.F. SORROW (*7) / PARACHUTE (*6) / FREEWAY MADNESS (*6) / SILK TORPEDO (*5) / SAVAGE EYE (*5) / CROSSTALK (*4) / LIVE AT THE HEARTBREAK HOTEL (*4) / OUT OF THE ISLAND (*4) / THE PRETTY THINGS 1967-1971 compilation (*7)

PHIL MAY (b. 9 Nov'44, Kent, England) – vocals / **DICK TAYLOR** (28 Jan'43) – lead guitar / **BRIAN PENDLETON** (b.13 Apr'44, Wolverhampton, England) – rhythm guitar / **JOHN STAX** (b.JOHN FULLEGAR, 6 Apr'44) – bass / **VIV PRINCE** (b. 9 Aug'44, Loughborough, Leicestershire, England) – drums (PETE KITLEY, then VIV ANDREWS sessioned on 1st-two 45's)

		Fontana	Fontana
Jun 64.	(7") (TF 469) <1916> **ROSALYN. / BIG BOSS MAN**	`41`	Oct64
Oct 64.	(7") (TF 503) <1941> **DON'T BRING ME DOWN. / WE'LL BE TOGETHER**	`10`	Jan65
Feb 65.	(7") (TF 537) <1508> **HONEY I NEED. / I CAN NEVER SAY**	`13`	
Mar 65.	(lp) (TL 5239) <67544> **THE PRETTY THINGS**	`6`	

– Roadrunner / Judgement day / 13 Chester street / Honey I need / Big city / Unkown

blues / Mama, keep your big mouth shut / Oh baby doll / She's fine she's mine / Don't you lie to me / The Moon is rising / Pretty thing. (re-iss. Jul90 lp/c/cd; 646054-1/-4/-2)

Jul 65.	(7") (TF 585) <1518> **CRY TO ME. / JUDGEMENT DAY**	`28`	
Dec 65.	(7") (TF 647) <1540> **MIDNIGHT TO SIX MAN. / CAN'T STAND THE PAIN**	`46`	
Dec 65.	(lp) (TL 5280) **GET THE PICTURE**		

– Get the picture / You don't believe me / We'll play house / Can't stand the pain / Rainin' in my heart / Buzz the jerk / London town / You'll never do it to me baby / Cry to me / I had a dream / Gonna find me a substitute / I want your love. (re-iss. Mar84; 6438 214) (cd-iss. Jul90; 846459-2)

— **SKIP ALAN** (b. ALAN ERNEST SKIPPER, 11 Jun'44) – drums repl. PRINCE on some

		Fontana	Blue Thumb
Apr 66.	(7") (TF 688) **COME SEE ME. / £.s.d.**	`43`	
Jul 66.	(7") (TF 722) **A HOUSE IN THE COUNTRY. / ME NEEDING YOU**	`50`	
Dec 66.	(7") (TF 773) **PROGRESS. / BUZZ IN THE JERK**		
Apr 67.	(7") (TF 829) **CHILDREN. / MY TIME**		
May 67.	(lp; stereo/mono) (S+/TL 5425) **EMOTIONS**		`-`

– Death of a socialite / Children / The sun / There will never be another day / House of ten / Out in the night / One long glance / Growing in my mind / Photographer / Bright lights of the city / Tripping / My time / A house in the country / Me needing you / Progress. (re-iss. Apr91;)

— **PHIL + DICK** were left to recruit new members **JOHN POVEY** (b.20 Aug'44) – keyboards, vocals (ex-FENMEN) repl. PENDLETON / **WALLY ALLEN** – bass, vocals (ex-FENMEN) repl. SKIP / **MITCH MITCHELL** – (session) drums repl. SKIP

		Columbia	Rare Earth
Nov 67.	(7") (DB 8300) **DEFLECTING GREY. / MR. EVASION**		`-`

— **BOBBIE GRAHAM** – drums (also on session) repl. MITCHELL

| Feb 68. | (7") (DB 8353) **TALKIN' ABOUT THE GOOD TIMES. / WALKING THROUGH MY DREAMS** | | `-` |

— **JOHN 'TWINK' ADLER** – percussion, vocals (ex-TOMORROW, etc) repl. GRAHAM

| Nov 68. | (7") (DB 8494) <5005> **PRIVATE SORROW. / BALLROOM BURNING** | | `-` |
| Dec 68. | (lp; mono/stereo) (SX/SCX 6306) <506> **S.F. SORROW** | | `Feb70` |

– S.F. sorrow / Bracelets of fingers / She says good morning / Private sorrow / Balloon burning / Death / Baron Saturday / I see you / The journey / Well of destiny / Trust / Old man going / Lonliest person. (re-press.1970; same) (re-iss. Oct87 on 'Edsel'; XED 236) (cd-iss. Oct90; ECDC 236)

— **SKIP ALAN** – drums, vocals (returned from SUNSHINE) repl. TWINK who joined PINK FAIRIES (new one below) **VICTOR UNITT** – guitar, vocals (ex-EDGAR BROUGHTON) repl. TAYLOR (⇒ producer)

		Harvest	Rare Earth
Apr 70.	(7") (HAR 5016) **THE GOOD MR. SQUARE. / BLUE SERGE BLUES**		
Jun 70.	(lp) (SHVL 774) <515> **PARACHUTE**	`43`	

– Parachute / Scene 1: The good Mr. Square, she was tall, she was high / Rare Earth / In the square, the letter, rain / Miss Fay regrets / Cries from the midnight circus / Grass / Sickle clowns / She's a lover / What's the use. (re-iss. Sep88 on 'Edsel' lp/cd; ED/+CD 289)

— **PETER TOLSON** (b.10 Sep'51, Bishops Stortford, England) – guitar, vocals (ex-EIRE APPARANT) repl. UNITT (who returned to EDGAR BROUGHTON BAND)

| Oct 70. | (7") (HAR 5031) **OCTOBER 26. / COLD STONE** | | |
| May 71. | (7"m) (HAR 5037) **STONE-HEARTED MAMA. / SUMMERTIME / CIRCUS MIND** | | |

— **STUART BROOKS** – bass, vocals repl. WALLY who went into producing

		Warners	Warners
Dec 72.	(lp) (K 46190) <2680> **FREEWAY MADNESS**		

– Love is good / Havana bound / Peter / Rip off train / Over the Moon / Religion's dead / Country road / All night sailor / Onion soup / Another bowl?

| Jan 73. | (7") **OVER THE MOON. / HAVANA BOUND** | `-` | `-` |

— added **GORDON EDWARDS** (b.26 Dec'46, Southport, England) – keyboards (to MAY, ALAN, POVEY, TOLSON and BROOKS)

		Swan Song	Swan Song
Oct 74.	(lp) (SSK 59400) <8411> **SILK TORPEDO**		

– Dream / Joey / Maybe you tried / Atlanta / L.A.N.T.A. / Is it only love / Come home / Bridge of God / Singapore silk torpedo / Belfast cowboy / Bruise in the sky.

| Dec 74. | (7") (K 19401) **JOEY. / IS IT ONLY LOVE** | | |
| Jun 75. | (7") (K 19403) **I'M KEEPING. / ATLANTA** | | |

— **JACK GREEN** (b.12 Mar'51, Glasgow, Scotland) – bass, vocals (also as EDWARDS, ex-SUNSHINE) repl. BROOKS

Aug 75.	(7") (K 19404) <70107> **JOEY. / COME HOME MOMMA**		
Feb 76.	(7") (K 19405) **SAD EYE. / REMEMBER THAT BOY**		`-`
Apr 76.	(7") **REMEMBER THAT BOY. / IT ISN'T ROCK'N'ROLL**	`-`	`-`
May 76.	(lp) (SSL 59401) <8414> **SAVAGE EYE**		`Feb 76`

– Under the volcano / My song / Sad eye / Remember that boy / It isn't rock'n'roll / I'm keeping / It's been so long / Drowned man / Theme for Michelle.

| May 76. | (7") (K 19406) **TONIGHT. / IT ISN'T ROCK'N'ROLL** | | `-` |

— Last original PHIL MAY went solo augmented by the FALLEN ANGELS (see below). POVEY also departed leaving only 4 (SKIP, PETER, JACK and GORDON) calling themselves METROPOLIS between mid '76-late'77. JACK also joined T.REX and GORDON went to The KINKS.

PHIL MAY & THE FALLEN ANGELS

with **MICKEY FINN** – guitar (ex-T.REX) / **BILL LOVELADY** – guitar / **BRIAN JOHNSTON** – keyboards (ex-STREETWALKERS) / **WALL ALLEN** – bass / **CHICO GREENWOOD** – drums / etc.

		Philips	not iss.
1978.	(lp) (6410 969) **PHIL MAY & THE FALLEN ANGELS**	`-`	`-` Dutch

– Fallen angels / California / 13 floor suicide / Dance again / Shine on baby / My good friend / Cold wind / I keep on / Dogs of war / Girl like you. (UK-iss.1982;) (re-iss. Feb85;)

PRETTY THINGS

re-formed ex-members in 1980. (**PHIL MAY, DICK TAYLOR, JOHN POVEY, PETER TOLSON, WALLY ALLEN** and **SKIP ALAN**)

	Warners	Warners
Aug 80. (lp) *(K 56842)* <3466> **CROSS TALK** – I'm calling / Edge of the night / Sea of blue / Office love / Lost that girl / Bitter end / Falling again / It's so hard / She don't / No future.	☐	☐
Aug 80. (7") *(K 17670)* **I'M CALLING. / SEA OF BLUE**	☐	☐

—— Disbanded 1981, but re-formed briefly as . . .

ZAC ZOLAR AND ELECTRIC BANANA

	Butt	not iss.
1984. (7") **TAKE ME HOME. / JAMES MARSHALL**		-

—— (above appeared on 'Minder' TV series) *(re-iss. Aug86 on 'Shanghai'; MGLS 2)*

PRETTY THINGS

re-formed by **MAY + TAYLOR** in 1984. Now with **JOE SHAW** – guitar / **DAVE WINTOUR** – bass / **KEVIN FLANAGAN** – saxophone / **JOHN CLARKE** – drums

	Big Beat	not iss.
Aug 84. (lp) *(WIK 24)* **LIVE AT THE HEARTBREAK HOTEL (live)** – Big boss man / Midnight to six man / I'm a king bee / Honey I need / Shakin' all over / Rosalyn / Roadrunner / Mama keep your big mouth shut / Raining in my heart / Reelin' and rockin' / Don't bring me down / Mona.	☐	-

—— **ROLF TER VELD** – bass + **BERTRAM ENGEL** – drums (ex-UDO LINDENBERG, ex-PANIKORCHESTER) repl.WINTOUR, FLANAGAN + CLARKE

	In-Akustik	not iss.
Jun 88. (cd) *(INAK 8708)* **OUT OF THE ISLAND** – Cry to me / Baby doll / She's fine, she's mine / Get the picture / Havana bound / Can't stop / Loneliest person / £.s.d. / Private sorrow / The moon is rising / Big city / Cause and effect / Well known blues / You don't believe me / Judement day. *(re-iss. May95; same)*	☐	-

—— **MAY + TAYLOR** again re-formed them again in 1989, with new **GLEN MATLOCK** – bass, vocals (ex-SEX PISTOLS, ex-RICH KIDS) / **FRANK HOLLAND** – guitar, keyboards / **BOBBY WEBB** – keyboards, vocals / **MARK ST. JOHN** – drums, bass, vocals

	Trax	not iss.
Sep 89. (7") *(7TX 12)* **EVE OF DESTRUCTION. / GOIN' DOWNHILL** (12"+=) *(12TX 12)* – Can't stop.	☐	-

—— (on tour) **STEVE BROWNING** – bass repl. MATLOCK

—— Re-formed again in 1991, with **PHIL MAY / DICK TAYLOR** (ex-MEKONS) / **JIMMY McCARTY** (ex-YARDBIRDS) / **RICHARD HITE** (ex-CANNED HEAT)

PRETTY THINGS & THE YARDBIRD BLUES BAND

Super-blues-group / collab with ex-YARDBIRDS and plenty covers

	Demon	not iss.
Oct 91. (cd) *(FIENDCD 708)* **CHICAGO BLUES JAM 1991** – Can't judge the book / Down in the bottom / Hush hush / Can't hold out / Spoonful / She fooled me / Time is on my side / Scratch my back / Long tall Shorty / Diddley daddy / Ain't got you / Caress my baby / Here's my picture / Chain of fools / Don't start crying now.	☐	-
Feb 94. (cd) *(FIENDCD 748)* **WINE, WOMEN & WHISKEY** – Wine, women and whiskey / Sure look good to me / No questions / The amble / It's all over now / Bad boy / Spoonful (bare bones remix) / French champagne / My back scratcher / Can't hold out (big city remix) / Diddley daddy (street corner remix) / I'm cryin' / Gettin' all wet.	☐	-

PRETTY THINGS 'N MATES
(WITH MATTHEW FISHER)

featuring a plethora of famous cover versions

	Kingdom	not iss.
May 94. (cd) *(CDKVL 9031)* **A WHITER SHADE OF DIRTY WATER** – He's waitin' / Strychnine / Pushing too hard / Kicks / Candy / Louie, Louie / 96 tears / Let's talk about girls / Sometimes good guys don't wear black / I'm a man / Red river rock / Midnight to 6 man '93.	☐	-

PRETTY THINGS

	not iss.	Medicine
1994. (7") **HAVANA BOUND. / RELIGION'S DEAD**	-	☐

—— re-formed again 1995, **MAY, TAYLOR, POVEY, ALEN, ALAN + HOLLAND**

	Fragile	not iss.
Oct 95. (d-cd) *(FRA 005D)* **UNREPENTANT – BLOODY BUT UNBOWED**	☐	-
Jun 96. (7"pic-d) *(FRPS 006)* **EVE OF DESTRUCTION. / ROSALYN / PASSION OF LOVE**	☐	-

– compilations, others, etc. –

Dec 64. (7"ep) *Fontana; (TE 17434)* **PRETTY THINGS**	☐	-
Aug 65. (7"ep) *Fontana; (TE 17442)* **RAINING IN MY HEART**	☐	-
Jan 66. (7"ep) *Fontana; (TE 17472)* **ON FILM**	☐	-
1967. (lp) *Wing; (WL 1167)* **BEST OF THE PRETTY THINGS**	☐	-
1968. (lp) *Phonogram;* **GREATEST HITS** *(cd-iss. 1991 on 'Carnaby';)*	☐	-
Jun 69. (7") *Fontana; (TF 1024)* **ROSALYN. / DON'T BRING ME DOWN**	☐	-
Jun 75. (d-lp) *Harvest; (SHDW 406) / Rare Earth; <R7 549>* **REAL PRETTY:- S.F. SORROW / PARACHUTE**	☐	☐ 1976

Jul 77. (lp) *Harvest; (SHSM 2022)* **SINGLES A's & B's**	☐	-
1976. (d-lp) *Sire; <SASH 37132>* **THE VINTAGE YEARS**	☐	-
1979. (lp; as ELECTRIC BANANA) *Butt; (NOTT 001)* **THE SEVENTIES** (with various artists)	☐	-
1980. (lp; as ELECTRIC BANANA) *Butt; (NOTT 003)* **THE SIXTIES** (with various artists)	☐	-

—— Film music lp's as ELECTRIC BANANA on 'De Wolfe':- 1967; ELECTRIC BANANA *(DWSLP 3280)* / 1968; MORE ELECTRIC BANANA *(DWSLP 3281)* / 1969; EVEN MORE ELECTRIC BANANA *(DWSLP 3282)* / 1973; THE RETURN OF THE ELECTRIC BANANA (DWSLP 3283) / 1973; HOT LICKS *(DWSLP 3284)*

Mar 82. (lp/c) *See For Miles; (CM/+K 103)* **THE PRETTY THINGS 1967-1971** *(cd-iss. Oct89; SEECD 103)*	☐	-
Jul 82. (7") *Old Gold; (OG 9237)* **DON'T BRING ME DOWN. / HONEY I NEED**	☐	-
Jun 84. (lp) *Edsel; (ED 139)* **LET ME HEAR THE CHOIR SING**	☐	-
Feb 86. (lp) *Bam Caruso; (KIRI 032)* **CLOSED RESTAURANT BLUES**	☐	-
May 86. (lp/c) *Harvest; (EMS/TCEMS 1119)* **CRIES FROM THE MIDNIGHT CIRCUS** (1968-1971)	☐	-
Nov 88. (cd) *Radioactive; (HORN 004)* **THE PRETTY THINGS**	☐	-
Aug 91. (cd) *Repertoire; (REP 4089WZ)* **MORE ELECTRIC BANANA**	☐	-
Apr 92. (cd) *Band Of Joy; (BOJCD 3)* **ON AIR**	☐	-
Mar 94. (cd/c) *Spectrum; (550 186-2/-4)* **MIDNIGHT TO 6**	☐	-
Jun 97. (cd) *See For Miles; (SEECD 476)* **THE EP COLLECTION**	☐	-

PRIMAL SCREAM

Formed: Glasgow, Scotland . . . mid-'84 by JESUS & MARY CHAIN drummer BOBBY GILLESPIE. Signing to JAMC's label, 'Creation', in 1985, they cut two singles, GILLESPIE leaving The 'MARY CHAIN after the debut, 'ALL FALL DOWN' (1985). The first album, 'SONIC FLOWER GROOVE' (1987), was recorded by the current band line-up core of ANDREW INNES, ROBERT 'THROB' YOUNG and MARTIN DUFFY (save MANI, ex-STONE ROSES, who joined up in 1996) along with an ever-changing array of additional musicians. Released on 'Creation' boss ALAN McGEE's 'WEA' subsidiary label, 'Elevation', the album saw the band pretty much live up to their name, a primitive take on raw ROLLING STONES, STOOGES etc. with a bit of BYRDS jingle jangle thrown in. This sound served the band well through their second album, 'PRIMAL SCREAM' (1989) until the release of 'LOADED' in early 1990. Back at 'Creation' and enamoured with the Acid House explosion, the band had enlisted the esteemed ANDREW WEATHERALL to remix 'I'M LOSING MORE THAN I'LL EVER HAVE' from the second lp. More a revolution than a remix, WEATHERALL created the stoned funk shuffle of 'LOADED', in the process bringing indie and rave kids together on the same dancefloor for the first time. PRIMAL SCREAM were now set on pushing the parameters of rock, releasing a trio of singles that defined an era; 'COME TOGETHER' (1990) was 90's style hedonist gospel that converted even the most cynical of rock bores while 'HIGHER THAN THE SUN' (1991) was perhaps the 'SCREAM's stellar moment, a narcotic lullaby beamed from another galaxy. Combining all the aforementioned tracks with a trippy 13TH FLOOR ELEVATORS cover, a heavyweight dub workout and a clutch of STONES-like beauties, 'SCREAMADELICA' (1991) was flawless. Opening with the euphoric 'MOVIN' ON UP' (the best song the 'STONES never wrote), the album effortlessly proved that dance and rock were essentially carved out of the same soulful root source, a seam that's been mined by any artist that's ever mattered. A landmark album, 'SCREAMADELICA' was awarded the Mercury Music prize in 1992 and for sheer breadth of vision the record has yet to meet its match in the 90's. Inevitably, then, the GEORGE DRAKOULIAS-produced follow-up, 'GIVE OUT BUT DON'T GIVE UP' (1994) was a disappointment in comparison. Recorded in MEMPHIS, the record saw PRIMAL SCREAM trying far too hard to achieve a roughshod R&B grit. Where before they had made The STONES' sound their own, now they came across as mere plagiarists, and over-produced plagiarists at that. Granted, the likes of 'JAILBIRD' and 'ROCKS' were funkier than any of the insipid indie competition around at the time and GILLESPIE's epileptic handclap routine was always more endearing than the run-of-the-mill rock posturing. Rumours of severe drug abuse abounded at this point and few were shocked when, in January 1994, it emerged that DUFFY had survived a near fatal stabbing in America. For the next couple of years, the band kept a fairly low profile, only a contribution to the 'Trainspotting' soundtrack and an unofficial Scottish 'Euro '96' single confirmed the 'SCREAM were still in existence. But while Scotland stumbled to defeat (again!!), PRIMAL SCREAM cleaned up their act and recorded the wonderful 'VANISHING POINT' (1997). Apparently cut as an alternative soundtrack to cult 70's road movie 'Kowalski', this album was the true follow-up/comedown to the psychedelic high of 'SCREAMADELICA'. 'OUT OF THE VOID' was the band's darkest moment to date while the title track and 'STUKA' were fractured, paranoid psych-outs. Only the vintage screenshow of 'GET DUFFY' and the mellow 'STAR' offered any respite. Big on dub and low on derivation, the album was a spirited return to form for one of Scotland's most enduring and groundbreaking bands. • **Songwriters:** GILLESPIE, YOUNG and BEATTIE, until the latter's replacement by INNES. Covered CARRY ME HOME (Dennis Wilson) / UNDERSTANDING (Small Faces) / 96 TEARS (? & The Mysterians) / KNOW YOUR RIGHTS (Clash) / MOTORHEAD (Motorhead).

Album rating: SONIC FLOWER GROOVE (*5) / PRIMAL SCREAM (*6) /

SCREAMADELICA (*10) / GIVE OUT BUT DON'T GIVE UP (*7) / VANISHING POINT (*8) / ECHO DEK (*6)

BOBBY GILLESPIE (b.22 Jun'64) – vocals (ex-WAKE) (also drummer of JESUS & MARY CHAIN) / **JIM BEATTIE** – guitar / **ROBERT YOUNG** – bass / **TOM McGURK** – drums / **MARTIN ST.JOHN** – tambourine

		Creation	not iss.
May 85. (7") *(CRE 017)* **ALL FALL DOWN. / IT HAPPENS** — / —

—— added **PAUL HARTE** – rhythm guitar (GILLESPIE left JESUS & MARY)
Apr 86. (7") *(CRE 026)* **CRYSTAL CRESCENT. / VELOCITY GIRL** — / —
    (12"+=) *(CRE 026T)* – Spirea X.

—— **STUART MAY** – rhythm guitar (ex-SUBMARINES) repl. HARTE (Dec86) / **ANDREW INNES** – rhythm guitar (of REVOLVING PAINT DREAM) repl. MAY / Guest drummers **PHIL KING** (studio) + **DAVE MORGAN** (tour) repl. McGURK

		Elevation	not iss.
Jun 87. (7") *(ACID 5)* **GENTLE TUESDAY. / BLACK STAR CARNIVAL** — / —
    (12"+=) *(ACID 5T)* – I'm gonna make you mine.
Sep 87. (7") *(ACID 5)* **IMPERIAL. / STAR FRUIT SURF RIDER** — / —
    (12"+=/s12"+=) *(ACID 5T/+W)* – So sad about us / Imperial (demo).
Oct 87. (lp/c)(cd) *(ELV 2/+C)(242-182-2)* **SONIC FLOWER GROOVE** 62 / —
    – Gentle Tuesday / Treasure trip / May the sun shine bright for you / Sonic sister love / Silent spring / Imperial / Love you / Leaves / Aftermath / We go down slowly. *(re-iss. Jul91)*

—— (Jun87) **GAVIN SKINNER** – drums repl. ST.JOHN

—— (Feb88) Now a trio **GILLESPIE, YOUNG + INNES** augmented by **JIM NAVAJO** – guitar. (BEATTIE formed SPIREA X, and SKINNER also left)

—— (Feb89) added **HENRY OLSEN** – bass (ex-NICO) / **PHILIP 'TOBY' TOMANOV** – drums (ex-NICO, ex-DURUTTI COLUMN, ex-BLUE ORCHIDS)

		Creation	Mercenary
Jul 89. (7") *(CRE 067)* **IVY IVY IVY. / YOU'RE JUST TOO DARK TO CARE** — / —
    (12"+=)(cd-s+=) *(CRE 067T)(CRESCD 067)* – I got you split wide open over me.
Sep 89. (lp/c/cd) *(CRE LP/C/CD 054)* <2100> **PRIMAL SCREAM** — / —
    – Ivy Ivy Ivy / You're just dead skin to me / She power / You're just too dark to care / I'm losing more than I'll ever have / Gimme gimme teenage head / Lone star girl / Kill the king / Sweet pretty thing / Jesus can't save me. *(free 7"ltd.)* – SPLIT WIDE OPEN (demo). / LONE STAR GIRL (demo)

—— trimmed to a trio again (**GILLESPIE, YOUNG + INNES**)

		Creation	Sire
Feb 90. (7") *(CRE 070)* **LOADED. / I'M LOSING MORE THAN I'LL EVER HAVE** 16 / —
    (ext.12"+=/'A'Terry Farley remix-12"+=)(ext.cd-s+=) *(CRE 070 T/X)(CRESCD 070)* – Ramblin' Rose (live).
Jul 90. (7"/c-s)(ext.12")(ext.cd-s) *(CRE/+CS 078)(CRE 078T(CRESCD 078)* <26384> **COME TOGETHER (Terry Farley mix). / COME TOGETHER (Andrew Weatherall mix)** 26 / Aug90
    (12") *(CRE 078X)* – ('A'-HypnotoneBrainMachine mix) / ('A'-BBG mix).
Jun 91. (7"/ext.12") *(CRE 096/+T)* **HIGHER THAN THE SUN. / ('A' American Spring mix)** 40 / —
    (cd-s+=) *(CRESCD 096)* – Higher than the Orb.

—— guest spot on above from **JAH WOBBLE** – bass
Aug 91. (7"/ext.12")(c-s) *(CRE 110/+T)(CRECS 110)* **DON'T FIGHT IT, FEEL IT. / ('A'scat mix featuring Denise Johnson)** 41 / —
    (cd-s+=) *(CRESCD 110)* – ('A'extended version).
Sep 91. (cd/c/d-lp) *(CRE CD/C/LP 076)* <26714> **SCREAMADELICA** 8 / —
    – Movin' on up / Slip inside this house / Don't fight it, feel it / Higher than the Sun / Inner flight / Come together / Loaded / Damaged / I'm comin' down / Higher than the Sun (a dub symphony in two parts) / Shine like stars.
Jan 92. (7"ep/c-ep) *(CRE/+CS 117)* <40193> **DIXIE-NARCO EP** 11 / —
    – Movin' on up / Carry me home / Screamadelica.
    (12"ep+=)(cd-ep+=) *(CRE 117T)(CRESCD 117)* – Stone my soul.

—— In Jan'94, MARTIN DUFFY was stabbed in Memphis, although he recovered soon after.

—— Line-up:- **GILLESPIE, YOUNG, INNES, DUFFY + DAVID HOOD + DENISE JOHNSON** + guest **GEORGE CLINTON** – vocals
Mar 94. (7"/c-s) *(CRE/+CS 129)* <18189> **ROCKS. / FUNKY JAM** 7 / Apr94
    (12")(cd-s) *(CRE 129T)(CRESCD 129)* – ('A'side) / Funky jam (hot ass mix) / Funky jam (club mix).
Apr 94. (cd/c/lp) *(CRE CD/C/LP 146)* <45538> **GIVE OUT, BUT DON'T GIVE UP** 2 / —
    – Jailbird / Rocks / (I'm gonna) Cry myself blind / Funky jam / Big jet plane / Free / Call on me / Struttin' / Sad and blue / Give out but don't give up / I'll be there for you.
Jun 94. (7"/c-s) *(CRE/+CS 145)* **JAILBIRD. / ('A'-Dust Brothers mix)** 29 / —
    (12"+=) *(CRE 145T)* – ('A'-Toxic Trio stay free mix) / ('A'-Weatherall dub chapter 3 mix).
    (cd-s++=) *(CRESCD 145)* – ('A'-Sweeney 2 mix).
Nov 94. (7"/c-s) *(CRE/+CS 183)* **(I'M GONNA) CRY MYSELF BLIND (George Drakoulias mix). / ROCKS (live)** 51 / —
    (cd-s+=) *(CRESCD 183)* – I'm losing more than I'll ever have (live) / Struttin' (back in our minds) (Brendan Lynch remix).
    (10") *(CRE 183X)* – ('A'side) / Struttin' (back in our minds) (Brendan Lynch remix) / Give out, but don't give up (Portishead remix) / Rockers dub (Kris Needs mix).
Jun 96. (c-s/cd-s; PRIMAL SCREAM, IRVINE WELSH AND ON-U SOUND PRESENT . . .) *(CRECS-CRESCD 194)* **THE BIG MAN AND THE SCREAM TEAM MEET THE BARMY ARMY UPTOWN (mixes:- full strength fortified dub / electric soup dub / a jake supreme)** 17 / —

—— In Oct'96, GILLESPIE, INNES, YOUNG & DUFFY were joined by **MANI MOUNFIELD** – bass (ex-STONE ROSES)

		Creation	Creation
May 97. (c-s) *(<CRECS 245>)* **KOWALSKI / 96 TEARS** 8 / —
    (cd-s+=) *(<CRESCD 245>)* – Know your rights / ('A'-Automator mix).
Jun 97. (c-s) *(CRECS 263)* **STAR / JESUS** 16 / —
    (cd-s+=) *(CRESCD 263)* – Rebel dub / How does it feel to belong.
    (12"+=) *(CRE 263T)* – ('A'mixes).
Jul 97. (cd/d-lp)(c) *(CRE CD/LP 178)(CCRE 178)* <46559> **VANISHING POINT** 2 / —
    – Burning wheel / Get Duffy / Kowalski / Star / If they move, kill 'em / Out of the void / Stuka / Medication / Motorhead / Trainspotting / Long life.
Oct 97. (7") *(CRE 272)* **BURNING WHEEL. /** 17 / —
    (12")(cd-s) *(CRE 272T)(CRESCD 272)* – ('A'side) / ('A'-Chemical Brothers remix) / Hammond connection / Higher than the sun (original).
Oct 97. (cd/7"box) *(CRE CD/L7 224)* **ECHO DEK** (remixes) 43 / —
    – Duffed up / Revolutionary / Ju-87 / First name unknown / Vanishing dub / Last train / Wise blood / Dub in vain.
Feb 98. (7") *(CRE 284)* **IF THEY MOVE, KILL 'EM. / BADLANDS** — / —
    (12"+=)(cd-s+=) *(CRE 284T)(CRESCD 284)* – ('A'-My Bloody Valentine Arkestra mix) / ('A'-Darklands 12"disco mix).

—— added on 1998 tour **JIM HUNT** – saxophone / **DUNCAN MACKAY** – trumpet / **DARREN MOONEY** – drums
Nov 99. (c-s) *(CRECS 326)* **SWASTIKA EYES / ('A'mix)** 22 / —
    (12"/cd-s) *(CRE 326T)(CRESCD 326)* – ('A'-Chemical Brothers mix) / ('A'-Spectre mix) / ('A'side).

– others, etc. –

Nov 97. (12") *Creation; (PSTLS 1)* **STUKA (Two Lone Swordsmen mixes)** — / —

PRIMITIVES (dig out; 4th edition or Great Alt & Indie . . .)

PRIMUS

Formed: Bay Area, San Francisco, USA . . . mid-80's by bassist/vocalist LES CLAYPOOL and guitarist TODD HUTH, initially as PRIMATE. Something of a cult phenomenon in their native city, the act's first release was a live affair, 'SUCK ON THIS' (1989), recorded at a local club and released on the band's own 'Prawnsong' label. By this point, JOE SATRIANI protege, LARRY LALONDE, had replaced HUTH who joined fellow Bay Area act, BLIND ILLUSION (CLAYPOOL had once been a member). PRIMUS were hardly purveyors of breakneck rifferama, however, CLAYPOOL's wayward muse fashioning instead a notoriously bizarre, bass-heavy fish stew of thrash, aquatic funk, avant-rock and surreal humour, CLAYPOOL's staccato-snorkle vocals colouring his marine-obsessed tales of fishermen and sturgeon. PRIMUS' first studio effort, 'FRIZZLE FRY' (1990), was released on the American independent label, 'Caroline' ('Virgin' in the UK), many of the songs from the debut reworked, including the brilliant 'JOHN THE FISHERMAN'. The band had also recruited a permanent drummer in TIM 'HERB' ALEXANDER, complementing CLAYPOOL's slippery, knottily intricate bass work. PRIMUS fitted in loosely with the burgeoning funk-metal scene of the day (supporting the likes of FAITH NO MORE, 24-7 SPYZ and LIVING COLOUR) and soon found themselves with a major label contract via 'Interscope', subsequently making their major label debut with the wonderfully titled 'SAILING THE SEAS OF CHEESE' (1991). The record's highlight was a reworked 'TOMMY THE CAT' (from the debut), complete with vocals courtesy of highly respected fellow weirdster, TOM WAITS. Touring with RUSH obviously hadn't damaged the band's street cred too much and the '93 follow-up, 'PORK SODA' made the US Top 10, proving that weird, in PRIMUS' case, was indeed wonderful. The same year, CLAYPOOL teamed up with old colleagues HUTH and JAY LANE to form a side project, SAUSAGE, releasing the album 'RIDDLES ARE ABOUND TONIGHT' (1993). A further (US) Top 10 PRIMUS album appeared in 1995, 'TALES FROM THE PUNCHBOWL', CLAYPOOL proving that he hadn't lost his technicolour, often flippant sense of humour with such lyrical vignettes as 'WYNONA'S BIG BROWN BEAVER'. Prior to the release of 'THE BROWN ALBUM' in '97, a rare line-up change occurred with BRIAN MANTIA replacing ALEXANDER. The following year saw the release of a largely disappointing covers album, 'RHINOPLASTY'; it looked like PRIMUS were sailing on cheese right enough. • **Covers:** MAKING PLANS FOR NIGEL + SCISSOR MAN (Xtc) / INTRUDER + THE FAMILY AND THE FISHING NET (Peter Gabriel) / HAVE A CIGAR (Pink Floyd) / TIPPY TOES (Meters) / SILLY PUTTY (Stanley Clarke) / AMOS MOSES (Jerry Reed) / BEHIND MY CAMEL (Police) / THE THING THAT SHOULD NOT BE (Metallica) / etc.

Album rating: SUCK ON THIS (*4) / FRIZZLE FRY (*7) / SAILING THE SEAS OF CHEESE (*7) / PORK SODA (*8) / TALES FROM THE PUNCH BOWL (*8) / THE BROWN ALBUM (*6) / RHINOPLASTY mini (*5) / ANTIPOP (*5) / Sausage: RIDDLES ARE ABOUND TONIGHT (*4)

LES CLAYPOOL (b.29 Sep'63, Richmond, Calif.) – vocals, bass (ex-BLIND ILLUSION) / **LARRY LaLONDE** (b.12 Sep'68, Richmond) – guitar (ex-POSSESSED) repl. TODD HUTH (b.13 Mar'63, San Leandro, Calif.) who joined BLIND ILLUSION / **JAY LANE** (b.15 Dec'64, San Francisco) – drums; repl. drum machine

		not iss.	Prawn Song
Jan 90. (lp) <CAROL 160-2> **SUCK ON THIS (live)** — / —
    – John the fisherman / Groundhog's day / The heckler / Pressman / Jelikit / Tommy the cat / Pudding time / Harold of the rocks / Frizzle fry. *(UK cd-iss. Mar92 on 'Atlantic'; 7567 91833-2)* *(re-iss. Jun97 on 'Caroline' lp/cd; CAR/+OLCD 1620)*

—— **TIM 'HERB' ALEXANDER** (b.10 Apr'65, Cherry Point, New Connecticut) – drums
repl. JAY who joined SAUSAGE

                                                        Virgin   Caroline

Jul 90. (cd/c/lp) *(CAR CD/C/LP 10)* <*CAROL 1619-2*> **FRIZZLE FRY**   ☐   ☐ Feb90
    – To defy the laws of tradition / Ground hog's day / Too many puppies / Mr.Know-
    it-all / Frizzle fry / John the fisherman / You can't kill Michael Malloy / The toys
    go winding down / Pudding time / Sathington Willoby / Spaghetti western / Harold
    of the rocks / To defy. *(cd re-iss. Jun97; CAROLCD 1619)*

                                              Atlantic Interscope

May 91. (cd/c/lp) <*7567 91659-2/-4/-1*> **SAILING THE SEAS OF**
CHEESE   ☐   ☐
    – Seas of cheese / Here come the bastards / Sgt. Baker / American life / Jerry was a
    race car driver / Eleven / Is it luck? / Grandad's lil ditty / Tommy the cat / Sathington
    waltz / Those damned blue collar tweekers / Fish on / Los bastardos. *(re-iss. Feb95;
    same)*

Jun 92. (cd-ep) *(A 6167CD)* **CHEESY EP 1** <US title
    'MISCELLANEOUS DEBRIS'>   ☐   ☐
    – Making plans for Nigel / Tommy the cat / Tippy toes / Have a cigar.
    (cd-ep) **CHEESY 2** *(A 6167CDX)* – (1st 2 tracks) / Sinister exaggerator / Intruder.

May 93. (cd/c/lp) <*7567 92257-2/-4/-1*> **PORK SODA**   56   7
    – Pork chop's little ditty / My name is mud / Welcome to this world / Bob /
    D.M.V. / The ol' Diamondback sturgeon (Fisherman's chronicles, part 3) / Nature
    boy / Wounded Knee / Pork soda / The pressman / Mr.Krinkle / The air is getting
    slippery / Hamburger train / Pork chop's little ditty / Hail Santa. *(cd re-iss. Jul96 on
    'Interscope'; IND 92257)*

Jun 95. (cd/c) <*(IND/INC 92553)*> **TALES FROM THE PUNCHBOWL**   8
    – Professor Nutbutter's house of treats / Mrs. Blaileen / Wynona's big brown beaver /
    Southbound pachyderm / Space farm / Year of the parrot / Hellbound 17 1/2 (theme
    from) / Glass sandwich / Del Davis tree farm / De Anza jig / On the tweak again /
    Over the electric grapevine / Captain Shiner. *(enhanced-cd re-iss. Jul96; IND 92665)*

Dec 95. (c-s) *(A 8129C)* **WYNONA'S BIG BROWN BEAVER / HELLO**
SKINNY – CONSTANTINOPLE   ☐   -
    (cd-s+=) *(A 8129CD)* – Have a cigar.
    (above issued on 'Atlantic' in the UK)

—— early '96, CLAYPOOL featured on ALEX LIFESON'S (Rush) VICTOR project

—— (Sep'96) **BRIAN 'Brain' MANTIA** – drums (ex-GODFLESH) repl. TIM

Jul 97. (cd/d-lp) <*(IND/ISC 90126)*> **BROWN ALBUM**   ☐   21
    – The return of Sathington Willoughby / Fisticuffs / Golden boy / Over the falls /
    Shake hands with beef / Camelback cinema / Hats off / Puddin' Taine / Bob's party
    time lounge / Duchess and the proverbial mind spread / Restin' bones / Coddington /
    Kalamazoo / Chastasing of renegade / Arnie.

Aug 98. (m-cd) <*(IND 90214)*> **RHINOPLASTY**   ☐   ☐
    – Scissor man / The family and the fishing net / Silly putty / Amos Moses / Behind
    my camel / Too many puppies / The thing that should not be / Tommy the cat / Bob's
    party time lounge.

Oct 99. (cd/c) <*(490414-2/-4)*> **ANTIPOP**   ☐   44
    – Intro / Electric Uncle Sam / Natural Joe / Laquerhead / Electric electric / Greet the
    sacred cow / Mama didn't raise no fool / Dirty drowning man / Ballad of bodacious /
    Power mad / Final voyage of the liquid sky / Coat tails of a dead man / Heckler.

SAUSAGE

LES CLAYPOOL – vocals, bass / **TODD HUTH** – guitar / **JAY LANE** – drums

                                             East West East West

Apr 94. (cd/c) <*(6544 92361-2/-4)*> **RIDDLES ARE ABOUND**
TONIGHT   ☐   ☐
    – Temporary phase / Girls for single men / Caution should be used while driving a
    motor vehicle or operating machinery / Shattering song / Prelude to fear / Riddles
    are abound tonight / Here's to the man / Toyz 1988 / Recreating.

PRINCE

Born: PRINCE ROGERS NELSON, 7 Jun'58, Minneapolis, Minnesota, USA. Named after his father JOHN's jazz band, The PRINCE ROGER TRIO (which featured his mother Mattie on vocals), one of the young PRINCE's earliest musical experiences was witnessing JAMES BROWN in concert at the age of ten, a performer whose approach to music would heavily influence PRINCE's future career. By the time (1972) he was invited to play in his cousin CHARLES SMITH'S high school band, GRAND CENTRAL, alongside ANDRE ANDERSON (by whose family PRINCE had been adopted), the musical prodigy had already mastered guitar and piano, in addition to writing his own material. The following year, the band evolved into CHAMPAGNE as PRINCE became the leader following the replacement of SMITH by MORRIS DAY. Being in control was something PRINCE would make central to his steep career trajectory as he grew older, although he was wise enough to learn the ropes first. His initial studio experience came when he played session guitar for Sound 80 Studios' PEPE WILLIE, subsequently cutting a demo with the help of CHRIS MOON who guided him in the ways of recording. MOON also introduced him to OWEN HUSNEY whose hustling skills eventually secured PRINCE a groundbreaking solo deal with 'Warners' in 1978, allowing him complete control over every step of the creative process. His debut effort, 'FOR YOU' was released in October, a fairly conventional collection of slinky soul that spawned an American R&B hit in 'SOFT AND WET', the lewdness of the lyrics fairly tame in light of what was to come. While PRINCE played all the instruments and produced the record himself, for the eponymous 'PRINCE' (1980), the diminutive one brought in a cast of musicians for a more rock-based approach, namely guitarist DEZ DICKERSON, keyboardist GAYLE CHAPMAN, bassist ANDRE CYMONE (the same ANDRE of PRINCE's childhood who had by now changed his name), drummer BOBBY Z and MATT FINK on more keyboards. The result was a US Top 20 single with the playful funk-pop of 'I WANNA BE YOUR LOVER', a song addressed to singer Patrice Rushen. Following the album's relative success, PRINCE took his new band out on the road for the first time, meeting with consistently positive

reviews. CHAPMAN was soon ousted in favour of LISA COLEMAN as the band previewed songs from the new album, 'DIRTY MIND' (1980), the first PRINCE release in which he gave free rein to his frequently sexually explicit lyrical muse. 'HEAD' was self-explanatory while 'SISTER' rather dodgily put forward the case for incest, the music moving ever further from the R&B of the debut and flirting with synth-heavy new wave. The album's lyrical frankness precluded any mainstream coverage although The ROLLING STONES were impressed enough to invite PRINCE to support them the following year. In the event, the shows were calamitous, The 'STONES infamously partisan crowd not taking too kindly to PRINCE's soulful androgyny. November of the same year saw the release of 'CONTROVERSY', an aptly titled album which divided the critics. While PRINCE once again dabbled with different styles and explored human desire on the likes of 'JACK U OFF', the record lacked the melodic immediacy of its predecessor. On a more positive note, PRINCE embarked on his most successful tour to date, building up a grassroots fanbase that would help make '1999' (1983) the biggest album of his career thus far. By the time of the record's release, PRINCE's backing band had evolved into The REVOLUTION with a couple of personnel changes along the way; the questionably named BROWN MARK replaced ANDRE who had departed for a solo career while WENDY MELVOIN was recruited in place of DICKERSON. '1999's synth- throb of a title track gave PRINCE his first real UK success while the infectiously commercial 'LITTLE RED CORVETTE' (his first Top 10 hit, boosted by heavy MTV rotation) proved PRINCE could write top pop material to rival any stars of the day. While the album's best moments could've probably been squeezed onto a single record, there was a marked maturity in the songwriting which reached fruition with 'PURPLE RAIN' (1984), arguably the most fully realised record of PRINCE's career. The album was actually the soundtrack to the near-autobiographical film of the same name, the first single to be lifted from it, 'WHEN DOVES CRY', giving PRINCE his first No.1 in May '84. This poignant portrayal of family strife also gave PRINCE his biggest UK hit to date, reaching No.4 later that summer. Other highlights of the album included the epic title track and the loose-limbed soul-rock of 'LET'S GO CRAZY', the latter complete with a searing HENDRIX-style guitar climax. The purple-clad genius' career subsequently went stratospheric, a Purple Rain tour breaking box office records with sales of the album running into the millions worldwide. As well as furnishing CHAKA KHAN with her first hit in years ('I FEEL FOR YOU'), PRINCE also wrote the controversial 'Sugar Walls' for Scottish-born SHEENA EASTON, a US Top 10 hit which further incensed the moral minority. Never the most communicative of stars, the mystique surrounding PRINCE grew deeper with the release of 'AROUND THE WORLD IN A DAY' (1985), a largely esoteric collection of psychedelic pop interspersed with the melodic brilliance of 'RASPBERRY BERET', possibly the finest song PRINCE has yet penned. This was also the album upon which PRINCE began attempting to reconcile the carnal with the spiritual, a preoccupation which would dominate his music in the years to come. 'AROUND THE WORLD . . .' was released on PRINCE's newly formed, Minneapolis-based record company (and lavish recording complex), 'Paisley Park', also home to friends like The FAMILY, SHEILA E. (who had also become part of PRINCE's touring band), GEORGE CLINTON etc. Concentrating on his new baby, PRINCE announced, BEATLES-style, that he was retiring from live work, only to later backtrack on his decision and undertake a tour in support of the 'PARADE' (1986) album. Another soundtrack, this time for PRINCE's derided 'Under The Cherry Moon', the music stood apart from the movie, taking the blueprint of its predecessor as a starting point and embroidering it with pop nous (notably on the sensuous 'GIRLS AND BOYS'). The record also provided PRINCE with his third No.1 single in the shape of 'KISS', a supple, teasing funk workout later famously covered by TOM JONES. At the end of the tour, PRINCE disbanded The REVOLUTION, going solo for the next few albums while recruiting a new band for live work. 'SIGN O' THE TIMES' (1987) was PRINCE's most thorough exploration of sex and religion, a satisfyingly diverse double set that marked the maturation of everything the artist had been working toward up to that point. While the gloriously dirty funk of the title track incorporated a comment on the degradation of the social fabric, the muted musical foreplay of 'IF I WAS YOUR GIRLFRIEND', and indeed the vast majority of tracks found PRINCE back on familiar lyrical territory. 'The BLACK ALBUM' concentrated almost solely on the mechanics of sex via some visceral uncut funk yet allegedly, PRINCE considered the album was 'immoral' (!) and recalled it from 'Warners' German pressing plant at the last minute. Officially released late in 1994, the album remained a favourite talking point for years among PRINCE obsessives and casual observers alike, bootleggers no doubt making a fortune. Presumably his white album, then, 'LOVESEXY' (1988) was the flipside to its predecessor's libidinous funk, the insistent pop of the title track a UK No.1. Though the album sold relatively poorly in the States, PRINCE's commercial fortunes were revived with the 'BATMAN' soundtrack, a multi-million seller which topped the charts on both sides of the Atlantic. If not exactly the most profound of his albums, it was certainly more listenable than the weak 'MUSIC FROM GRAFFITI BRIDGE' (1990). Thankfully, PRINCE seems to have let up on his film aspirations in recent years, though his musical output doesn't seem to have benefited that much. Nevertheless, the 90's started on a high note with the massive 'DIAMONDS AND PEARLS' (1991) album, credited to PRINCE & THE NEW POWER GENERATION. This band had already backed PRINCE on the 'GRAFFITI BRIDGE' project, this time around their playing injecting a more spontaneous live feel to proceedings. The sexy strut of 'CREAM' and the more intense funk lewdness of 'GET OFF' dominated the set (a remixed import single of the former hit the UK Top 40!), while 'MONEY DON'T MATTER 2 NIGHT' was deeply affecting, soul-baring stuff. Following the release of the '(SYMBOL)' (1992) album – a patchy collection partly redeemed by the jazzy leer of 'SEXY M.F.' – PRINCE bizzarely announced he was changing his name to 'symbol' (I can't get that damn sign on my computer!), followed by yet more rumours that he wished to be known as VICTOR, then finally T.A.F.K.A.P. (The Artist Formerly Known As PRINCE). More controversy followed with revelations that PRINCE wanted out of his contract with 'Warners', unhappy that he was restricted to one album a year. In protest, he took to wearing a mask onstage and painting the word 'Slave' on his face, subsequently releasing the lush charm of 'THE MOST BEAUTIFUL GIRL IN THE WORLD' on independent labels worldwide. Fulfilling his contract, T.A.F.K.A.P. released a further couple of largely uninspired albums, 'THE GOLD EXPERIENCE' (1995) and 'CHAOS AND DISORDER' (1996), before disbanding the N.P.G. and retreating into silence. Now regarded as something of a joke by the music press, it remains to be seen whether this eminently capable genius can regain the giddy heights of his early 80's domination. Stop press:- his last ("THE ARTIST") set, 'RAVE UN2 THE JOY FANTASTIC', did little to regain his diminishing audience (he covered Sheryl Crow's(!) 'EVERYDAY IS A WINDING ROAD'; sexfunk is dead. • **Songwriters:** A prolific pensmith, he also wrote songs under pseudonyms CAMILLE, JAMIE STARR, CHRISTOPHER, etc., and has written hits especially for SHEENA EASTON (Sugar Walls) and BANGLES (Manic Monday). Note: WENDY AND LISA wrote 'MOUNTAINS' before departing for own duo. In 1996, he covered; BETCHA BY GOLLY WOW! (Stylistics) / I CAN'T MAKE YOU LOVE ME (Bonnie Raitt) / LA LA MEANS I LOVE YOU (Delfonics) / ONE OF US (hit; Joan Osborne). • **Trivia:** In 1988, his sister TYKA NELSON signed for 'Chrysalis', although her album failed to take off.

Album rating: FOR YOU (*5) / PRINCE (*6) / DIRTY MIND (*7) / CONTROVERSY (*6) / 1999 (*8) / PURPLE RAIN (*8) / AROUND THE WORLD IN A DAY (*6) / PARADE (*7) / SIGN 'O' THE TIMES (*9) / LOVESEXY (*8) / BATMAN (*6) / GRAFITTI BRIDGE (*8) / DIAMONDS AND PEARLS (*8) / SYMBOL (UNTITLED) (*8) / THE HITS 1 compilation (*9) / THE HITS 2 compilation (*9) / EXODUS (*8; as New Power Generation) / THE BEAUTIFUL EXPERIENCE mini (*5) / COME (*4) / THE GOLD EXPERIENCE (*6) / CHAOS AND DISORDER (*5) / EMANCIPATION (*4) / NEW POWER SOUL (*5; as New Power Generation) / CRYSTAL BALL boxed-set (*5) / THE VAULT – OLD FRIENDS 4 SALE collection (*4) / RAVE UN2 THE JOY FANTASTIC (*5)

PRINCE – vocals, multi-instrumentalist, synthesizers, producer, everything

	Warners	Warners
Oct 78. (lp,c) <3150> **FOR YOU**	–	–
– For you / In love / Soft and wet / Crazy you / Just as long as we're together / Baby / My love is forever / So blue / I'm yours. (UK-iss.Sep86 lp/c; K/K4 56989) (cd-iss. Oct87; K2 56989)		
Nov 78. (7") <8619> **SOFT AND WET. / SO BLUE**	–	92
Jan 79. (7") <8713> **JUST AS LONG AS WE'RE TOGETHER. / IN LOVE**	–	–

—— **PRINCE** – vocals, guitar live back-ups **DEZ DICKERSON** – guitar / **GAYLE CHAPMAN** – keyboards / **ANDRE CYMONE** – bass / **MATT FINK** – keyboards / **BOBBY Z** – drums

Nov 79. (7") <49050> **I WANNA BE YOUR LOVER. / MY LOVE IS FOREVER**	–	11
Dec 79. (7") (K 17537) **I WANNA BE YOUR LOVER. / JUST AS LONG AS WE'RE TOGETHER**	41	–
Jan 80. (lp/c) (K/K4 56772) <3366> **PRINCE**	22	Oct79
– I wanna be your lover / Why you wanna treat me so bad? / Sexy dancer / When we're dancing close and slow / With you / Bambi / Still waiting / I feel for you / It's gonna be lonely. (cd-iss. 1986; K2 56772)		
Feb 80. (7") <49178> **WHY YOU WANNA TREAT ME SO BAD?. / BAD**	–	–

—— (Feb80) live **LISA COLEMAN** – keyboards repl. GAYLE

Apr 80. (7"/12") (K 17590/+T) **SEXY DANCER. / BAMBI**	–	–
May 80. (7") <49226> **STILL WAITING. / BAMBI**	–	–
Sep 80. (7") <49559> **UPTOWN. / CRAZY YOU**	–	–
Oct 80. (lp/c) (K/K4 56862) <3478> **DIRTY MIND**		45
– Dirty mind / When you were mine / Do it all night / Gotta broken heart again / Uptown / Head / Sister / Party up. (re-iss. 1989) (cd-iss. Dec85; K2 56862)		
Nov 80. (7") <49638> **DIRTY MIND. / WHEN WE'RE DANCING CLOSE AND SLOW**	–	–
Mar 81. (7"/12") (K 17768/+T) **DO IT ALL NIGHT. / HEAD**	–	–
Jun 81. (7") (K 17819) **GOTTA STOP (MESSIN' ABOUT). / UPTOWN (live)**		–
(12"+=) (K 17819T) – Head (live).		
(12") (K 17819TX) – ('A'side) / I wanna be your lover (live).		

—— (mid'81) live **BROWN MARK** – bass repl. ANDRE who ventured solo

Oct 81. (7"/12") (K 17866/+T) <49808> **CONTROVERSY. / WHEN YOU WERE MINE**		70
Nov 81. (lp/c) (K/K4 56950) <3601> **CONTROVERSY**		21
– Controversy / Sexuality / Do me, baby / Private joy / Ronnie talk to Russia / Let's work / Annie Christian / Jack u off. (cd-iss. 1984; K2 56950)		
Apr 82. (7"/12") (K 17922/+T) <50002> **LET'S WORK. / RONNIE TALK TO RUSSIA**		
(12") <50028> – ('A'side) / Gotta stop.		
Jun 82. (7") <29942> **DO ME, BABY. / PRIVATE JOY**	–	–

PRINCE & THE REVOLUTION

—— live **WENDY MELVOIN** – guitar repl. DEE

Jan 83. (7") (W 9896) <29896> **1999. / HOW COME U DON'T CALL ME ANYMORE**	25	44 Oct82
(free c-s w/7") (W 9896C) – 1999 / Controversy / Dirty mind / Sexuality.		
(12"+=) (W 9896T) – D.M.S.R. <US re-dist.Jun83 hit No.12>		

Feb 83. (lp/c) (W 3809/+C) <23720> **1999**		26
– 1999 / Little red Corvette / Delirious / Let's pretend we're married / D.M.S.R. * / Delirious / Automatic / Something in the water / Free / Lady cab driver / All the critics love u in New York / International lover. (re-iss. Nov83 as d-lp/d-c; 923720-1/-4) – hit UK No.30. (cd-iss. Sep84; 923720-2) – (omits *)		
Feb 83. (7") <29746> **LITTLE RED CORVETTE. / ALL THE CRITICS LOVE U IN NEW YORK**	–	6
Apr 83. (7") <29548> **LET'S PRETEND WE'RE MARRIED. / IRRESISTIBLE BITCH**	–	52
Apr 83. (7") (W 9688) **LITTLE RED CORVETTE. / LADY CAB DRIVER**	54	–
(12") – ('A'extended) / Automatic lover / International lover.		
Sep 83. (7") <29503> **DELIRIUS. / HORNY TOAD**	–	8
Nov 83. (7") (W 9436) **LITTLE RED CORVETTE. / HORNY TOAD**	66	–
(ext.12"+=) (W 9436) – D.M.S.R.		
Jun 84. (7"/12") (W 9296/+T) <29286> **WHEN DOVES CRY. / 17 DAYS**	4	1 May84
(d12"+=/c-s+=) (W 9296 T/C) – 1999 / D.M.S.R.		
Jul 84. (lp,purple-lp/c/cd) (925110-1/-4/-2) <25110> **PURPLE RAIN** (Music From The Motion Picture)	7	1
– Let's go crazy / Take me with u / The beautiful ones / Computer blue / Darling Nikki / When doves cry / I would die 4 U / Baby I'm a star / Purple rain. <US-iss.as d-lp, w/ += tracks by The TIME + APOLLONIA 6> (re-iss. Jan92 hit UK No.59) (re-iss. cd/c Feb95) (lp re-iss. Jun99; ame)		
Jul 84. (7") <29216> **LET'S GO CRAZY. / EROTIC CITY**	–	1
Sep 84. (7"/7"sha-pic-d) (W 9174/+P) <29174> **PURPLE RAIN. / GOD**	8	2
(12") (W 9174T) – ('A'side) / ('A'vocal + instrumental).		
Nov 84. (7") (W 9121) <29121> **I WOULD DIE 4 U. / ANOTHER LONELY CHRISTMAS**	58	8
(12"+=) (W 9121T) – Free.		
(12") (W 9121TE) – ('A'&'B' US remixes).		
Jan 85. (7"/12") (W 1999C) **1999. / LITTLE RED CORVETTE**	2	–
(free c-s w/7"+=) (W 1999C) – 1999 / Uptown / Controversy / D.M.S.R. / Sexy dancer.		
Feb 85. (7") (K 2000) **LET'S GO CRAZY. / TAKE ME WITH U**	7	–
(ext.12"+=) (K 2000T) – Erotic city.		
Feb 85. (7") <29079> **TAKE ME WITH U. / BABY I'M A STAR**	–	25

—— added live **SHEILA E.** (b.ESCOVEDO) – percussion, vocals / **ERIC LEEDS** – saxophone

	Paisley Park	Paisley Park
Apr 85. (lp/c/cd) (925286-1/-4/-2) <25286> **AROUND THE WORLD IN A DAY**	5	1
– Around the world in a day / Paisley Park / Condition of the heart / Raspberry beret / Tambourine / America / Pop life / The ladder / Temptation.		
May 85. (7"/7"sha-pic-d) (W 9052/+P) **PAISLEY PARK. / SHE'S ALWAYS IN MY HAIR**	18	–
(12"+=) (W 9052T) – ('A'extended).		
May 85. (7") <28972> **RASPBERRY BERET. / SHE'S ALWAYS IN MY HAIR**	–	2
Jul 85. (7"/12") (W 8929/+T) **RASPBERRY BERET. / HELLO**	25	–
Jul 85. (7") <28998> **POP LIFE. / HELLO**	–	7
Oct 85. (7") <28999> **AMERICA. / GIRL**	–	46
Oct 85. (7"/ext-12") (W 8858/+T) **POP LIFE. / GIRL**	60	–
Feb 86. (7"/7"pic-d/ext-12") (W 8751/+P/T) <28751> **KISS. / LOVE OR MONEY**	6	1
Apr 86. (lp,pic-lp/c/cd) (925395-1/-4/-2) <25395> **PARADE (Music from the film 'Under The Cherry Moon')**	4	3
– Christopher Tracey's parade / New position / I wonder u / Under the cherry moon / Girls and boys / Life can be so nice / Venus de Milo / Mountains / Do u lie / Kiss / Anotherloverholdenyohead / Sometimes it snows in April.		
May 86. (7") (W 8711) <28711> **MOUNTAINS. / ALEXA DE PARIS**	45	23
(10"white/12") (W 8711 TW/T) – ('A'&'B'extended).		
Aug 86. (7"/7"sha-pic-d) (W 8586/+P) **GIRLS AND BOYS. / UNDER THE CHERRY MOON**	11	–
(12"+=) (W 8586T) – Erotic city.		
(d7"+=) (W 8586F) – She's always in my hair / 17 days.		
Oct 86. (7") <28620> **ANOTHERLOVERHOLDENYOHEAD. / GIRLS AND BOYS**	–	63
Oct 86. (7"/ext-12"/ext-12"pic-d) (W 8521/+T/TP) **ANOTHERLOVERHOLDENYOHEAD. / I WANNA BE YOUR LOVER**	36	–
(d7"+=) (W 8521F) – Mountains / Alexa de Paris.		

PRINCE

—— solo, without WENDY & LISA who formed own duo. He retained live **FINK, LEEDS & SHEILA E.** adding **MICO WEAVER** – guitar / **BONI BOYER** – keyboards / **LEVI SEACER JR.** – bass / **CAT GLOVER** – dancer, vocals

Mar 87. (7") (W 8399) <28399> **SIGN 'O' THE TIMES. / LA LA LA HE HE HE HE**	10	3
(12"/12"pic-d) (W 8399/+T/TP) – ('A'&'B'extended).		
Mar 87. (d-lp/c)(cd) (WX 88/+C)(925577-2) <25577> **SIGN 'O' THE TIMES**	4	6
– Sign 'o' the times / Play in the sunshine / Housequake / Ballad of Dorothy Parker / It / Starfish and coffee / Slow love / Hot thing / Forever in my life / U got the look / If I was your girlfriend / Strange relationship / I could never take the place of your man / The cross / It's gonna be a beautiful night / Adore.		
Jun 87. (7"/7"peach/c-s/ext-12"/ext-12"pic-d) (W 8334/+E/C/T/TP) <28334> **IF I WAS YOUR GIRLFRIEND. / SHOCKADELICA**	20	May87

—— (next 'A'side featured backing vocals by solo artist SHEENA EASTON now living in California with all her well-invested millions!)

Aug 87. (7"/c-s) (W 8289/+C) <28289> **U GOT THE LOOK. / HOUSEQUAKE**	11	2 Jul87
('B'ext-12"/12"pic-d+=) (W 8289 T/TP) – ('A'long version).		
Nov 87. (7"/c-s) (W 8288/+C) <28288> **I COULD NEVER TAKE THE PLACE OF YOUR MAN. / HOT THING**	29	10 / 63
(12"+=/12"pic-d+=) (W 8288 T/TP) – ('B'extended).		

Apr 88. (7"/c-s) *(W 7900/+C)* <27900> **ALPHABET ST. / THIS IS NOT MUSIC, THIS IS A TRIP** | 9 | 8 |
(12"/cd-s) *(W 7900 T/CD)* – ('A'&'B'extended)

May 88. (lp/c)(cd) *(WX 164/+C)(925720-2)* <25720> **LOVESEXY** | 1 | 11 |
– I no / Alphabet St. / Glam slam / Anna Stesia / Dance on / Lovesexy / When 2 r in love / I wish U Heaven / Positivity. *(re-iss. cd/c Feb95)*

Jul 88. (7"/12") *(W 7806/+T)* **GLAM SLAM. / ESCAPE** | 29 | - |
(cd-s+=) *(W 7806CD)* – Escape (free yo mind from this rat race).

Oct 88. (7") *(W 7745)* **I WISH U HEAVEN. / SCARLET PUSSY (by 'Camille')** | 24 | - |
(12"+=/cd-s+=) *(W 7745 T/CD)* – ('A' pts.2 & 3).

Jun 89. (7"/c-s/ext-12"/ext-12"pic-dcd-s/3"cd-s) *(W 2924/+C/T/TP/CD/CDX)* <22924> **BATDANCE. / 200 BALLOONS** | 2 | 1 |
('A'-Batmix-12"+=) *(W 2924TX)* – ('A'-Vicki Vale mix).

Jun 89. (lp/c/cd/pic-lp) *(WX 281)* <25936> **BATMAN** | 1 | 1 |
– The future / Electric chair / The arms of Orion / Partyman / Vicki waiting / Trust / Lemon crush / Scandalous / Batdance. *(re-iss. cd/c Feb95)*

Aug 89. (7"/c-s/remix-12"/ext-12") *(W 2814/+C/T/TX)* <22814> **PARTYMAN. / FEEL U UP** | 14 | 18 |
(12"pic-d/cd-s) *(W 2814 TP/CD)* – ('A'video mix). / ('B'long stroke mix).

Oct 89. (7"/c-s; PRINCE with SHEENA EASTON) *(W 2757/+C)* <22757> **THE ARMS OF ORION. / I LUV U IN ME** | 27 | 36 |
(12"+=/cd-s+=/12"pic-d+=) *(W 2757 T/CD/TP)* – ('A'extended).

—— live **PATRICE RUSHDEN** – keyboards (solo artist) repl. BOYER + GLOVER / **MICHAEL BLAND** – drums repl. SHEILA E. / **CANDY DULFER** – saxophone repl. LEEDS

Jul 90. (7"/c-s) *(W 9751/+C)* <19751> **THIEVES IN THE TEMPLE. / (Part 2)** | 7 | 6 |
('A'remix; 12"+=/cd-s+=/12"pic-d+=) *(W 9751 T/CD/TP)* – ('A'dub).

Aug 90. (cd)(d-lp/c) *(927493-2)(WX 361/+C)* <27493> **MUSIC FROM GRAFFITI BRIDGE (soundtrack)** | 1 | 6 |
– Can't stop this feeling I got / New power generation / The question of U / Elephants and flowers / Joy in repetition / Tick, tock, bang / Thieves in the temple. *(also other tracks by 'The TIMES' etc.)*

Oct 90. (7"/c-s) *(W 9525/+C)* <19525> **NEW POWER GENERATION. / (Part 2)** | 26 | 64 |
(12"+=/cd-s+=/12"pic-d+=) *(W 9525 T/CD/TP)* – Melody cool (extended remix).

PRINCE & THE NEW POWER GENERATION

—— with **LEVI SEACER JR.** – guitar, vox / **TOMMY BARBARELLA** – keys, synths / **SONNY T.** – bass, vox / **ROSIE GAINES** – co-vocals, organ, synths / **MICHAEL B.** – drums / **TONY M.** – rap/vox / **KIRKY JOHNSON** – perc., vox / **DAMON DICKSON** – perc., vox

Aug 91. (7"/c-s/+C) *(W 0056/+C)* <19225> **GETT OFF (remix). / HORNY PONY** | 4 | 21 |
(12"+=) *(W 0056T)* – ('A'-Thrust mix).
(cd-s+=) *(W 0056CD)* – ('A'-Purple pump mix).
(above: as a m-lp, its US import hit UK chart! at No.33)

Sep 91. (7"/c-s) *(W 0061/+C)* <19175> **CREAM. / HORNY PONY** | 15 | 1 |
(12"+=/cd-s+=) *(W 0061 T/CD)* – Gangster glam.

Sep 91. (cd)(d-lp/c) *(925379-2)(WX 432/+C)* <25379> **DIAMONDS AND PEARLS** | 2 | 3 |
– Thunder / Daddy pop / Diamonds and pearls / Cream / Strollin' / Willing and able / Gett off / Walk don't walk / Jughead / Money don't matter 2 night / Push / Insatiable / Live 4 love. *(re-iss. cd/c Feb95)*

Nov 91. (7"/c-s) *(W 0075/+C)* <19083> **DIAMONDS AND PEARLS. / LAST DANCE** | 25 | 4 |
(cd-s+=) *(W 0075CD)* – 2 the wire (Grammy instrumental) / Do you dance (remix).

Dec 91. (c-s,cd-s) <19090> **INSATIABLE / I LOVE U IN ME** | - | 77 |

Mar 92. (7"/c-s/cd-s) *(W 0091/+C/CD)* <19020> **MONEY DON'T MATTER 2 NIGHT. / CALL THE LAW** | 19 | 23 |
(12"+=) *(W 0091T)* – Push.

Jun 92. (7"/c-s) *(W 0113/+C)* **THUNDER. / VIOLET THE ORGAN DRIVER** | 28 | - |
(12"+=/cd-s+=/12"pic-d+=) *(W 0113 T/CD/TP)* – Gett off (thrust dub).

—— **MAYTE** – vocals; repl. ROSIE

Jul 92. (7"/c-s) *(W 0123/+C)* <18817> **SEXY M.F. / STROLLIN'** | 4 | 66 |
(12"+=/cd-s+=) *(W 0123 T/CD)* – Daddy Pop.

Sep 92. (7"/c-s/+C) *(W 0132/+C)* **MY NAME IS PRINCE / 2 WHOM IT MAY CONCERN** | 7 | - |
(12"+=) *(W 0132T)* – Sexy mutha.
(cd-s++=) *(W 0132CD)* – ('A'extra mix).

Sep 92. (c-s,cd-s) <18707> **MY NAME IS PRINCE / SEXY MUTHA** | - | 36 |

Nov 92. (12"/cd-s) *(W 0142 T/CD)* **MY NAME IS PRINCE (remixes). / (other mixes)** | 51 | - |

Oct 92. (cd)(d-lp/c) *(9362 45037-2)(WX 490/+C)* <45037> **(SYMBOL)** | 1 | 5 |
– My name is Prince / Sexy MF / Love 2 the 9's / The morning papers / The Max / Segue / Blue light / I wanna melt with U / Sweet baby / The continental / Dawn U / Arrogance / The flow / 7 / And God created woman / 3 chains o' gold / Segue / The sacrifice of Victor.

Nov 92. (7"/c-s) *(W 0147/+C)* <18824> **7. / 7 (acoustic)** | 27 | 7 |
(cd-s+=) *(W 0147CD)* – ('A'other mixes).

Mar 93. (7"/c-s) *(W 0162/+C)* <18583> **THE MORNING PAPERS. / LIVE 4 LOVE** | 52 | 44 |
(cd-s+=) *(W 0162CD)* – Love 2 the 9's.

Sep 93. (cd/c/d-lp) *(9362 45431-2/-4/-1)* **THE HITS 1** (compilation) | 5 | 46 |
– When doves cry / Pop life / Soft and wet / I feel for you / Why you wanna treat me so bad? / When you were mine / Uptown / Let's go crazy / 1999 / I could never take the place of your man / Nothing compares 2 U / Adore / Pink cashmere / Alphabet St. / Sign 'o' the times / Thieves in the temple / Diamonds and pearls / 7.

Sep 93. (cd/c/d-lp) *(9362 45435-2/-4/-1)* **THE HITS 2** (compilation) | 5 | 54 |
– Controversy / Dirty mind / I wanna be your lover / Head / Do me, baby / Delirious / Little red Corvette / I would die 4 U / Raspberry beret / If I was your girlfriend / Kiss / Peach / U got the look / Sexy M.F. / Gett off / Cream / Pope / Purple rain.

Sep 93. (3xcd/3xc) *(9362 45440-2/-4)* **THE HITS / THE B-SIDES** | 4 | 19 |
– (all of above plus corresponding 'B'sides)

+ Hello / 200 balloons / Escape / Gotta stop (messin' about) / Horny toad / Feel U up / Girl / I love U in me / Erotic city / Shockadelica / Irresistable bitch / Scarlet pussy / La, la, la, he, he, hee / She's always in my hair / 17 days / How come U don't call me anymore / Another lonely Christmas / God / Tears in your eyes / Power fantastic.

Sep 93. (c-s,cd-s) <18371> **PINK CASHMERE / SOFT AND WET (remix)** | - | 50 |

Oct 93. (7"/c-s) *(W 0210/+C)* **PEACH. / WISH U HEAVEN** | 14 | - |
(cd-s+=) *(W 0210CD)* – Girls & boys / My name is Prince.
(cd-s) *(W 0210CD2)* – ('A'side) / Money don't matter 2 nite / Partyman / Mountains.

Dec 93. (7"pic-d/c-s) *(W 0215 P/C)* **CONTROVERSY. / THE FUTURE** | 5 | - |
(cd-s) *(W 0215CD1)* – ('A'side) / The future (remix) / Glam slam / D.M.S.R.
(cd-s) *(W 0215CD2)* – ('A'side) / Paisley Park / Anotherloverholenyohead / New power generation.

	Warners	Bellmark

Mar 94. (7"/c-s) *(NPG 60155/+C)* <72514> **THE MOST BEAUTIFUL GIRL IN THE WORLD. / BEAUTIFUL** | 1 | 3 |
(12"+=/cd-s+=) *(NPG 60155 T/CD)* – ('A'mixes).

May 94. (12"ep/c-ep/cd-ep) *(NPG 60212 T/C/CD)* <71003> **THE BEAUTIFUL EXPERIENCE** | 18 | 92 |
– (7 versions of last single)

—— Musicians: **PRINCE / MICHAEL B. / SONNY T. / TOMMY BARBARELLA / MR.HAYES / MAYLE**

	Warners	Warners

Aug 94. (cd/c/lp) *<9362 45700-2/-4/-1>* **COME** | 1 | 15 |
– Come / Space / Pheromone / Loose! / Papa / Race / Dark / Letitgo / Orgasm.

Aug 94. (7"pic-d/c-s) *(W 0260/+C)* <18074> **LETITGO. / SOLO** | 30 | 31 |
(cd-s+=) *(W 0260CD)* – Alexa de Paris / Pope.

Mar 95. (cd-ep) *(W 0289CD)* <17903> **PURPLE MEDLEY / PURPLE MEDLEY (extended) / PURPLE MEDLEY (Kirk J's B-side remix)** | 33 | 84 |

NEW POWER GENERATION

	N.P.G.	N.P.G.

Mar 95. (7"ep/c-ep/12"ep/cd-ep) *(NPG 0061045/+C/T/CD)* **GET WILD / BEAUTIFUL GIRL (sax version) / HALLUCINATION RAIN** | 19 | - |

Apr 95. (cd/c/lp) *(NPG 6103-2/-4/-1)* **EXODUS** | 11 | - |
– N.P.G. operator intro / Get wild / Segue / DJ gets jumped / New power soul / DJ seduces Sonny / Segue / Count the days / The good life / Cherry, Cherry / Segue / Return of the bump squad / Mashed potato girl intro / Segue / Big fun / New power day / Segue / Hallucination rain / N.P.G. bum rush the ship / The exodus has begun / Outro.

Aug 95. (c-s) *(NPG 0061515C)* **THE GOOD LIFE / ('a' MIXES)** | 29 | - |
(cd-s+=/12") *(NPG 0065151 CD/T)* – Free the music / Get wild (mixes) *(re-iss. Jun97; hit UK No.15; 006151 9/5/0 NPG)*

Oct 95. (c-s) *(NPG 6133-9)* **COUNT THE DAYS /** | | |
(cd-s) *(NPG 6133-5)* –

PRINCE (symbol)

or T.A.F.K.A.P. (The Artist Formerly Known As PRINCE)

	Warner-NPG	Warner-NPG

Sep 95. (c-s) *(W 0315C)* <17811> **EYE HATE U / ('A'mix)** | 20 | 12 |
(cd-s+=) *(W 0315CD)* – ('A'mixes).

Sep 95. (cd/c/lp) *<9362 45999-2/-4/-1>* **THE GOLD EXPERIENCE** | 4 | 6 |
– P control / npq operator / Endorphinmachine / Shhh / We march / npq operator / The most beautiful girl in the world / Dolphin / npq operator / Now / npq operator / 319 / npq operator / Shy / Billy Jack bitch / Eye hate u / npq operator / Gold.

Nov 95. (c-s) *(W 0325C)* <17715> **GOLD / ROCK AND ROLL IS ALIVE! (AND IT LIVES IN MINNEAPOLIS)** | 10 | 58 |
(cd-s+=) *(W 0325CD)* – Eye hate U (extended remix).

—— In Apr 96, he wrote music for the film soundtrack 'GIRL 6' hit US 75

—— performed by New Power Generation; **MR. HAYES, TONY BARBARELLA, SONNY T, MICHAEL B** plus **KIRK JOHNSON, ROSIE GAINES + NPG HORNS**

Jul 96. (cd/c) *<9362 46317-2/-4>* **CHAOS AND DISORDER** | 14 | 26 |
– Chaos and disorder / Dinner with Dolores / The same December / Right the wrong / Zannalee / I rock, therefore I am / Into the light / I will / Dig u better dead / Had u.

Jul 96. (c-s) *(9362 43742-4)* **DINNER WITH DOLORES / HAD U** | 36 | - |
(cd-s+=) *(9362 43742-2)* – Right the wrong.

The ARTIST with The NEW POWER GENERATION

	E.M.I.	NPG-Warner

Nov 96. (t-cd/t-c) *(CD/TC EMD 1102)* <NPG 54982> **EMANCIPATION** | 18 | 11 |
– Jam of the year / Right back here in my arms / Somebody's somebody's / Get yo groove on / Courtin' time / Betcha by golly wow / We gets up / White mansion / Darned if I do / I can't make U love me / Mr. Happy / In this bed I scream / Sex in the summer / One kiss at a time / Soul sanctuary / Emale / Curious child / Dreamin' about U / Joint 2 joint / The holy river / Let's have a baby / Saviour / The plan / Friend lover sister mother-wife / Slave / New world / The human body / Face down / La la la means I love you / Style / Sleep around / Da da da / My computer / One of us / The wow we make / Emancipation.

Dec 96. (c-s/cd-s) *(TC/CD EM 463)* **BETCHA BY GOLLY WOW! / RIGHT BACK HERE IN MY ARMS** | 11 | - |
(cd-s) *(CDEMS 463)* – ('A'mix).

Mar 97. (c-s/cd-s) *(TC/CD EM 467)* **THE HOLY RIVER / SOMEBODY'S SOMEBODY / THE MOST BEAUTIFUL GIRL IN THE WORLD** | 19 | |
(cd-s) *(CDEMS 467)* – ('A'side) / The most beautiful girl in the world (Mustang mix) / Somebody's somebody / On sale now!

	NPG	NPG

Mar 98. (4xcd-box) *<(BCT 9871CD)>* **CRYSTAL BALL** (out-takes & 4th cd new) | | 62 |
– Crystal ball / Dream factory / Acknowledge me / Ripopgodazippa / Lovesign (Shock G remix) / Hide the bone / 2morrow / So dark / Movie star / Tell me how u wanna be done // Interactive / Da bang / Calhoun Square / What's my name /

Crucial / An honest man / Sexual suicide / Cloreen bacon skin / Good love / Strays of the world // Days of wild / Last heart / Poom poom / She gave her angels / 18 & over / The ride / Get loose (remix) / P. control (club mix) / Make your mama happy / Goodbye // The truth / Don't play me / Circle of amour / 3rd eye / Dionne / Man in a uniform / Animal kingdom / The other side of the pillow / Fascination / One of your tears / Comeback / Welcome 2 the dawn (acoustic). <US mail-order cont.5th cd+=> – KAMASUTRA (instrumental ballet score).

(SYMBOL) THE NEW POWER GENERATION

——   now with **CHAKA KHAN, LARRY GRAHAM + DOUG E FRESH**

		NPG-RCA	NPG
Jul 98.	(cd/c) (74321 60598-2/-4) <9872> **NEWPOWER SOUL**	38	22

– New power soul / Mad sex / Until u're in my arms again / When U love somebody / Shoo-bed-ooh / Push it up / Freaks on this side / Come on / The one / (I like) Funky music.

Nov 98.	(c-s) (74321 63472-4) **COME ON / COME ON (late night mix)**		65	

(cd-s+=) (74321 63472-2) – Come on (The Artist remix).

The ARTIST

		Arista	Arista
Oct 99.	(c-s/cd-s) <13749> **THE GREATEST ROMANCE EVER SOLD**	-	63
Nov 99.	(cd) (74321 72574-2) <14624> **RAVE UN2 THE JOY FANTASTIC**		18

– Rave un2 the joy fantastic / Undisputed / The greatest romance ever sold / Segue / Hot wit U / Tangerine / So far so pleased / The sun and the moon and the stars / Everyday is a winding road / Segue / Man o war / Baby knows / I love you but I don't trust you anymore / Silly game / Strange but true / Wherever U go whatever U do / 1800 new funk ad.

– compilations, others, etc. –

on 'WEA/Warners' unless mentioned otherwise

Oct 88.	(cd-s) (921186-2) **WHEN DOVES CRY / PURPLE RAIN**		
Oct 88.	(cd-s) (921787-2) **LET'S GO CRAZY (extended) / TAKE ME WITH U**		
Oct 88.	(cd-s) (921842-2) **LITTLE RED CORVETTE (dance mix) / 1999 (extended)**		
Oct 88.	(cd-s) (921188-2) **KISS / GIRLS AND BOYS / UNDER THE CHERRY MOON**	36	47
Nov 94.	(cd/c) <(45793)> **THE BLACK ALBUM** (finally released!)		

– Le grind / Cindy C. / Dead on it / When 2 R in love / Bob George / Superfunkycalifragisexy / 2 nigs united for West Compton / Rockhard in a funky place.

Dec 98.	(c-s) (W 467C) **1999 / HOW COME U DON'T CALL ME ANYMORE**	10	

(12"+=/cd-s+=) (W 467 T/CD) – DMSR.
(re-iss. Dec99; same) – hit No.51

Feb 99.	(m-cd) <1999> **1999: THE NEW MASTERS EP**	-	
Aug 99.	(cd/c) <(9362 47522-2/-4)> **THE VAULT . . . OLD FRIENDS 4 SALE** (out-takes 1985-1994)	47	85

– The rest of my life / It's about that walk / She spoke 2 me / 5 women / When the lights go down / My little pill / There is lonely / Old friends 4 sale / Sarah / Extraordinary.

Nov 99.	(d-cd) Charly; (CDVAL 1112) **THE EARLY YEARS ('94 EAST)**		-

John PRINE

Born: 10 Oct'46, Maywood, Illinois, USA. The young JP learned guitar from his elder brother and started to both write and play in his early teens. Graduating from High School in 1964, he spent two years working as a postman before being drafted into the army. Although the Vietnam war was beginning to take its toll on America's young men, PRINE was lucky enough to be posted to Germany, where he whiled away his time in the motor pool and entertained his barrack-room buddies with his strikingly original and obliquely observed compositions. After his discharge from the army, he returned to work for the US mail and continued his songwriting although still on an amateur basis. He made his professional debut in a Chicago folk club ("the 5th Peg") in 1970 and was persuaded by the club's owner that his talents lay in the direction of music rather than mail delivery. Soon after, he was introduced to KRIS KRISTOFFERSON and 50's crooner, PAUL ANKA, to whom he played a few of his (now classic) compositions. Both were astounded by his mature writing style and the diverse range of emotions running through his subject matter. (Let's face it, songs on masturbation:- 'DONALD AND LYDIA', were not exactly thick on the ground in early 70's America). The pair arranged for him to make some demos and thereafter KRISTOFFERSON invited him to play a few songs on his show. In the audience that particular night was Jerry Wexler of Atlantic Records who was bowled over and immediately offered him a recording deal. The singer's eponymous debut album was immediately hailed as a groundbreaking record and met with great critical and grass-roots popular success although it performed poorly by way of sales. This was quickly followed by 'DIAMONDS IN THE ROUGH' (1972) which again showcased his wry observations of life's trials and tribulations. Once again, critical plaudits were huge, while commercial success was moderate. At the time, PRINE was being promoted – complete with denim jacket – as the "new Dylan", a term he felt less than happy about. However, he was beginning to acquire a solid groundbase of loyal fans. More importantly, leading artists were beginning to listen to – and include his songs on – their albums; everybody who was anybody in the US folk/country world wanted to cover a PRINE composition. Third album, 'SWEET REVENGE' (1973), disappointed both

fans and critics with a flawed attempt at exploring new horizons. However, this session did produce one popular song, 'DEAR ABBIE', demonstrating that his muse hadn't completely deserted him. 'COMMON SENSE' was released in 1975 and again it was generally agreed that PRINE had produced a "bummer!". Moreover, Atlantic Records had by now decided that he was definitely not the new Dylan. They almost immediately ended their 5-year association by mutual agreement. Three years passed while he took stock, subsequently composing and polishing enough material to impress the 'Asylum' label. The fruits of his labour finally emerged in the shape of 'BRUISED ORANGE' (1978), another PRINE classic regarded by many as a return to the promise he showed earlier in the decade. JP took a more lighthearted approach to his sixth album, 'PINK CADILLAC' (1979), an uncharacteristically electrified set which lacked the spark of its acoustic predecessor. This was followed by the more sedate 'STORM WINDOWS' (1979), which contained some remixed material from the previous sessions. This was to be JOHN's last effort for four years, although he continued to work on material and collaborations with other writers and artists. Around this time the man took the decision to start his own label, 'Oh Boy', an exercise that dug deep into his finances and time, resulting in his temporary, although somewhat lengthy absence from the spotlight. Fans were thrown a crumb of comfort in 1982 with the release of that rare PRINE curiosity, a Christmas single, 'I SAW MUMMY KISSING SANTA CLAUS' – backed unceremoniously by 'SILVER BELLS' (yuk!). The aptly titled 'AIMLESS LOVE' (1984) album was another lacklustre effort yet despite ignoring recording and concert work, PRINE's standing among his peers had never been higher and he continued to write, play and guest on various projects while still trying to kickstart his label. This he partly achieved with his ninth album, 'GERMAN AFTERNOONS', which received a nomination for Best Contemporary Folk Album of 1987; this was probably due to the NANCI GRIFFITHS cover of one of its better tracks, 'THE SPEED OF THE SOUND OF LONELINESS'. PRINE was back to something approaching his old style, although all was not going well in his personal life. A second marriage had failed (check the lyrics of the aforementioned!) and the recent death from cancer of his close friend, singer/songwriter and erstwhile collaborator, Steve Goodman, had left its mark. Once more, he disappeared into the shadows of depression with the only output being a double live album of old favourites, 'JOHN PRINE LIVE' (1987). It was rumoured in some camps that, following the death of his close friend, Prine had given up the business completely and it was to take three years coaxing and cajoling by his long-time musical buddies (including BONNIE RAITT, BRUCE SPRINGSTEEN, TOM PETTY, JOHN MELLENCAMP and DAVID LINDLEY), before he resurfaced with the well-received 'THE MISSING YEARS' (1991). Agents were once more beating a path to his door and his back catalogue was being rediscovered by new legions of fans. A resulting Grammy Award finally gave PRINE the recognition he undeniably deserved and vindicated both his fans and co-artists' loyalty over those "missing years"). More importantly, that elusive element, commercial success, had finally come within JOHN's grasp; he found himself very much in demand again for concerts, tours and other ventures. His soundtrack contribution to the movie, 'Falling from Grace', further enhanced his reputation; he even released a Christmas album (!). 'LOST DOGS AND MIXED BLESSINGS' (1995) took off in yet another direction, while he even hosted a TV series, 'Town and Country' for Channel 4. JOHN also re-married and relocated to the Irish Republic. After surviving a throat cancer operation, he returned in 1999 with 'IN SPITE OF OURSELVES', a covers album of duets with everyone from IRIS DeMENT to EMMYLOU HARRIS.

Album rating: JOHN PRINE (*9) / DIAMONDS IN THE ROUGH (*8) / SWEET REVENGE (*5) / COMMON SENSE (*3) / PRIME TIME - THE BEST OF JOHN PRINE compilation (*9) / BRUISED ORANGE (*8) / PINK CADILLAC (*5) / STORM WINDOWS (*3) / AIMLESS LOVE (*5) / GERMAN AFTERNOONS (*6) / JOHN PRINE LIVE (*6) / THE MISSING YEARS (*8) / GREAT DAYS: THE JOHN PRINE ANTHOLOGY compilation (*9) / A JOHN PRINE CHRISTMAS mini (*3) / LOST DOGS AND MIXED BLESSINGS (*5) / LIVE ON TOUR (*6) / IN SPITE OF OURSELVES (*6)

JOHN PRINE – vocals, guitar

		Atlantic	Atlantic
Sep 71.	(7") <2815> **SAM STONE. / BLUE UMBRELLA**	-	
Apr 72.	(lp) (K 40357) <SD 8296> **JOHN PRINE**		Dec71

– Illegal smile / Spanish pipedream / Hello in there / Sam stone / Paradise / Pretty good / Your flag Decal won't get you into Heaven anymore / Far from me / Angel from Montgomery / Quiet man / Donald and Lydia / Six o'clock news / Flashback blues. <US cd-iss. 1990; 19156-2> (UK cd-iss. Jul96 on 'Warners'; 7567 81541-2)

Apr 72.	(7") <2857> **ILLEGAL SMILE. / QUIET MAN**		
Nov 72.	(lp) (K 40427) <SD 7240> **DIAMONDS IN THE ROUGH**		Oct72

– Everybody / The torch singer / Souvenirs / The late John Garfield blues / Sour grapes / Billy the bum / The frying pan / Yes I guess they oughtta name a drink after you / Take the star out of the window / The great compromise / Clocks and spoons / Rocky mountain time / Diamonds in the rough. <cd-iss. 1990; 7240-2>

Jan 73.	(7") (K 10271) <2925> **EVERYBODY. / CLOCKS AND SPOONS**		Oct72
Jun 73.	(7") (K 10350) **SPANISH PIPEDREAM. / ILLEGAL SMILE**	-	
Feb 74.	(7") <3013> **GRANDPA WAS A CARPENTER. / ONOMATOPOEIA**	-	
May 74.	(lp) (K 40524) <SD 7274> **SWEET REVENGE**		Oct73

– Sweet revenge / Please don't bury me / Christmas in prison / Dear Abby / Blue umbrella / Often is a word I seldom use / Onomatopoeia / Grandpa was a carpenter / The accident (things could be worse) / Mexican home / A good time / Nine pound hammer. <cd-iss. 1990;7274-2>

1974.	(7") <3218> **QUIET MAN. / ILLEGAL SMILE**	-	
1975.	(lp) (K 50137) <SD 18127> **COMMON SENSE**		66 Apr75

– Middle man / Common sense / Come back to us Barbara Lewis Hare Krishna

Beauregard / Wedding day in Funeralville / Way down / My own best friend / Forbidden Jimmy / Saddle in the rain / That close to you / He was in Heaven before he died / You never can tell. *<cd-iss. 1990; 18127-2>*

Jun 75. (7") *<3276>* **MIDDLE MAN. / SADDLE IN THE RAIN**   [-] [☐]

Nov 75. (7") *<3297>* **COMMON SENSE. / COME BACK TO US BARBARA LEWIS HARE KRISHNA BEAUREGARD**   [-] [☐]

Jan 77. (lp) *<SD 18202>* **PRIME PRINE – THE BEST OF JOHN PRINE**
(compilation)
– Sam Stone / Saddle in the rain / Please don't bury me / The great compromise / Grandpa was a carpenter / Donald and Lydia / Illegal revenge / Dear Abby / Souvenirs / Come back to us Barbara Lewis Hare Krishna Beauregard / Hello in there. *(cd-iss. Feb95 on 'WEA'; 7567 81504-2)*

—— now with a plethora of session people

		Asylum	Asylum

Aug 78. (lp) *(K 53084)* *<6E 139>* **BRUISED ORANGE**   [☐] [☐ Jul78]
– Fish and whistle / There she goes / If you don't want my love / That's the way the world goes 'round / Bruised orange (chain of sorrow) / Sabu visits the twin cities alone / Aw heck / Crooked piece of time / Iron ore Betty / The hobo song. *<cd-iss. 1989 on 'Oh Boy'; OBRCD 6>*

Oct 78. (7") *(K 13136)* **THERE SHE GOES. / BRUISED ORANGE**   [☐] [☐]

Oct 79. (lp) *(K 52164)* *<6E 222>* **PINK CADILLAC**   [☐] [☐ Sep79]
– Chinatown / Automobile / Killing the blues / No name girl / Saigon / Cold war (this cold war with you) / Baby let's play house / Down by the side of the road / How lucky / Ubangi stomp. *<cd-iss. 1989 on 'Oh Boy'; OBRC 7>*

Aug 80. (lp) *<6E 286>* **STORM WINDOWS**   [☐] [☐]
– Shop talk / Living in the future / It's happening to you / Sleepy eyed boy / All night blue / Just wanna be with you / Storm windows / Baby Ruth / One red rose / I had a dream. *<cd-iss. 1989 on 'Oh Boy'; OBRCD 8>*

		Demon	Oh Boy

Nov 84. (7"red) *<OBR 001>* **I SAW MOMMY KISSING SANTA CLAUS. / SILVER BELLS**   [-] [☐]

Feb 85. (lp/c/cd) *(FIEND 84)* *<OBR 002/+C/CD>* **AIMLESS LOVE**   [☐] [☐ Nov84]
– Be my friend tonight / Aimless love / Me, myself and I / The oldest baby in the world / Slow boat to China / The bottomless lake / Maureen, Maureen / Somewhere someone's falling in love / People puttin' people down / Unwed fathers / Only love. *<cd-iss. 1987 on 'Mobile Fidelity'; MFCD 856>*

Aug 87. (lp/cd) *(FIEND/+CD 103)* *<OBR 003/+CD>* **GERMAN AFTERNOONS**   [☐] [☐ 1986]
– Lulu walls / Speed of the sound of loneliness / Sailin' around / If she were you / Linda goes to Mars / I just want you to dance with me / Love love love / Bad boys / They'll never take her love from me / Paradise.

Sep 87. (7"green) *<OBR 004>* **LET'S TALK DIRTY IN HAWAIIN. / KOKOMO**   [-] [☐]

Jan 88. (d-lp/c/cd) *<OBR/+C/CD 005>* **JOHN PRINE LIVE (live)**
– Come back to us Barbara Lewis Hare Krishna Beauregard / Six o'clock news / The oldest baby in the world / Angel from Montgomery / Grandpa was a carpenter / Blue umbrella / Fish and whistle / Sabu visits the twin cities alone / Living in the future / Illegal smile / Mexican home / Speed of the sound of loneliness / The accident (things could be worse) / Sam Stone / Souvenirs / Aw heck / Donald and Lydia / That's the way that the world goes round / Hello in there.

		This Way Up	Oh Boy

Jul 92. (cd/c) *(512774-2/-4)* *<OBR 009>* **THE MISSING YEARS**   [☐] [☐ Sep91]
– Picture show / All the best / The sins of Mephisto / Everybody wants to feel like you / It's a big old goofy world / I want to be with you always / Daddy's little pumpkin / Take a look at my heart / The great run / Way back then / Unlonely / You got cold / Everything is cool / Jesus: the missing years.

Nov 94. (m-cd) *<OBR 011>* **A JOHN PRINE CHRISTMAS**   [☐] [-]
– Everything is cool / All the best (live) / Silent night all day long / If you were the woman and I was the man / Silver bells / I saw mommy kissing Santa Claus / Christmas in prison / A John Prine Christmas.

		Rykodisc	Oh Boy

Sep 95. (cd) *(RCD 10333)* *<OBR 013>* **LOST DOGS & MIXED BLESSINGS**   [☐] [☐ Apr95]
– New train / Ain't hurtin' nobody / All the way with you / Lake Marie / We are the lonely / Humidity built the snowman / Day is done / Quit hollerin' at me / Big fat love / Same thing happened to me / This love is real / Leave the lights on / He forgot it was Sunday / I love you so much it hurts.

		Oh Boy	Oh Boy

May 97. (cd) *<(OBR 015)>* **LIVE ON TOUR (live)**   [☐] [☐ Apr97]
– Picture show / Quit hollerin' at me / You got gold / Unwed fathers / Space monkey / The late John Garfield blues / Storm windows / Jesus: the missing years / Humidity built the snowman / Illegal smile / Daddy's little pumpkin / Lake Marie / If I could / Stick a needle in my eye / You mean so much to me.

—— In Nov'98, PRINE's label released V/A set, 'Lucky 13', which included 3 tracks by himself, namely 'Let's talk dirty in Hawaiian', 'Beautiful World' and 'Kokomo'.

Sep 99. (cd) *<(OBR 019)>* **IN SPITE OF OURSELVES**
– We're not the jet set (w/ IRIS DeMENT) / So sad (to watch good love go bad) (w/ CONNIE SMITH) / Wedding bells – Let's turn back the years (w/ LUCINDA WILLIAMS) / When two worlds collide (w/ TRISHA YEARWOOD) / Milwaukee here I come (w/ MELBA MONTGOMERY) / I know one (w/ EMMYLOU HARRIS) / It's a cheating situation (w/ DOLORES KEANE) / Back street affair (w/ PATTY LOVELESS) / Loose talk (w/ CONNIE SMITH) / Let's invite them over (w/ IRIS DeMENT) / Til a tear becomes a rose (w/ FIONA PRINE) / In a town this size (w/ DOLORES KEANE) / We could (w/ IRIS DeMENT) / We must have been out of our minds (w/ MELBA MONTGOMERY) / In spite of ourselves (w/ IRIS DeMENT) / Dear John (I sent your saddle home).

– compilations, etc. –

Feb 94. (d-cd) *Rhino; (8122 71400-2)* **GREAT DAYS: THE JOHN PRINE ANTHOLOGY**   [☐] [☐ Aug93]
– Illegal smile / Spanish pipedream / Hello in there / Sam Stone / Paradise / Donald and Lydia / The late John Garfield blues / Yes I guess they ought to name a drink after you / The great compromise / Sweet revenge / Please don't bury me / Christmas in prison / Dear Abby (live) / Blue umbrella / Common sense / Come back to us Barbara Lewis Hare Krishna Beauregard / Saddle in the rain / He was in Heaven before he died / Fish and whistle / That's the way the world goes 'round / Bruised orange (chain of sorrow) / Sabu visits the twin cities alone / Automobile / Killing the blues / Down by the side of the road / Living in the future / It's happening to you / Storm windows / One red rose / Souvenirs / Aimless love / The oldest baby in

the world / People puttin' people down / Unwed fathers / Angel from Montgomery (live with BONNIE RAITT) / Linda goes to Mars / Bad boy / Speed of the sound of loneliness (live) / It's a big old goofy world (live) / The sins of Mephisto / All the best.

PROCOL HARUM

Formed: Southend, Essex, England . . . 1959 as The PARAMOUNTS, by five schoolboys; BOB SCOTT, GARY BROOKER, ROBIN TROWER, CHRIS COPPING and MICK BROWNLEE. They played a number of local gigs, BROOKER soon taking over vocal chores when SCOTT failed to show. In 1962, they left school and acquired manager Peter Martin. The following year, with a few personnel changes, the band signed to EMI's 'Parlophone' label, soon hitting the UK Top 40 with an R&B cover of The COASTERS' 'POISON IVY'. Their follow-up, a re-working of THURSTON HARRIS's 'LITTLE BITTY PRETTY ONE', failed to emulate their minor earlier success, and, after a few more covers, they folded in late summer '66. • **Note other covers:** I FEEL GOOD ALL OVER (Drifters) / I'M THE ONE WHO LOVES YOU (Major Lance) / BAD BLOOD (Coasters) / BLUE RIBBONS (Jackie DeShannon) / CUTTIN' IN (Johnny Guitar Watson) / YOU'VE NEVER HAD IT SO GOOD (P.F.Sloan). In 1967, BROOKER and lyricist KEITH REID advertised in the Melody Maker for musicians, soon settling with MATTHEW FISHER, RAY ROYER, DAVE KNIGHTS and BOBBY HARRISON. They became PROCOL HARUM (taking the name from the Latin "procul", meaning "far from these things"), and with help from producer Denny Cordell, they unleashed their mesmeric debut 45, 'A WHITER SHADE OF PALE', for 'Deram'. Adapted from a classical suite by BACH (No.3 in d major; 'Air On A G String'), its neo-gothic/baroque organ refrain combined with REID's extremely surreal lyrics to create a quasi-psychedelic million seller (stayed at No.1 for 6 weeks in the UK charts). With record company pressures to tour, ROYER and HARRISON departed from the group, replaced by former PARAMOUNTS; TROWER and WILSON. Later that year, they moved with producer CORDELL to 'Regal Zonophone', having another major stab at the Top 10 with 'HOMBURG'. They increasingly enjoyed greater success Stateside and by 1970, the band's line-up was identical to the earlier PARAMOUNTS of '63 (see above). In 1972, with their live album riding high in the charts, they resurrected their old 1967 number, 'CONQUISTADOR', subsequently a major hit on both sides of the Atlantic. PROCOL HARUM continued to gain respect from US and Canadian audiences, although the single, 'PANDORA'S BOX', in 1975, gave them a renewed UK chart thrust. Its parent album, 'PROCOL'S NINTH', also returned them to The Top 50, including a cover of The BEATLES' 'EIGHT DAYS A WEEK'. After another patchy album, BROOKER split the band, joining the ERIC CLAPTON BAND before going solo. Like many other rock dinosaurs, the band reformed for a one-off album in the early 90's, surprising many with its inclusion of ROBIN TROWER (he had already established himself as a guitar hero in the 70's & 80's).

Album rating: PROCOL HARUM (*6) / SHINE ON BRIGHTLY (*6) / A SALTY DOG (*6) / HOME (*6) / BROKEN BARRICADES (*7) / PROCOL HARUM LIVE IN CONCERT WITH THE EDMUNTON SYMPHONY ORCHESTRA (*6) / GRAND HOTEL (*6) / EXOTIC BIRDS AND FRUIT (*6) / PROCOL'S NINTH (*6) / SOMETHING MAGIC (*4) / THE PRODIGAL STRANGER (*3) / GREATEST HITS compilation (*7)

PARAMOUNTS

GARY BROOKER (b.29 May'45) – vocals, keyboards / **ROBIN TROWER** (b. 9 Mar'45) – guitar / **DIZ DERRICK** – bass repl. CHRIS COPPING who went to Leicester University (Sep63) / **B.J. WILSON** (b.18 Mar'47) – drums repl. MICK BROWNLEE (Jan63)

			Parlophone	not iss.
Dec 63.	(7") *(R 5093)* **POISON IVY. / I FEEL GOOD ALL OVER**		35	-
Feb 64.	(7") *(R 5107)* **LITTLE BIT PRETTY ONE. / A CERTAIN GIRL**		☐	-
Jun 64.	(7") *(R 5155)* **I'M THE ONE WHO LOVES YOU. / IT WON'T BE LONG**		☐	-
Nov 64.	(7") *(R 5187)* **BAD BLOOD. / DO I**		☐	-
Mar 65.	(7") *(R 5272)* **BLUE RIBBONS. / CUTTIN' IN**		☐	-
Oct 65.	(7") *(R 5351)* **YOU'VE NEVER HAD IT SO GOOD. / DON'T YA LIKE MA LOVE**		☐	-

PROCOL HARUM

BROOKER with also **MATTHEW FISHER** (b. 7 Mar'46) – organ (ex-SCREAMING LORD SUTCH) / **RAY ROYER** (b. 8 Oct'45) – guitar / **DAVE KNIGHTS** (b.28 Jun'45) – bass / **BOBBY HARRISON** (b.28 Jun'43) – drums / **KEITH REID** (b.10 Oct'46) – lyrics

			Deram	Deram
May 67.	(7") *(DM 126)* *<7507>* **A WHITER SHADE OF PALE. / LIME STREET BLUES** *<US re-iss. Jan73 on 'A&M'; 1389>*		1	5

—— **ROBIN TROWER** – guitar (ex-PARAMOUNTS) repl. ROYER who formed FREEDOM / **B.J. WILSON** – drums (ex-PARAMOUNTS) repl. HARRISON who also formed FREEDOM

			Regal Zonophone	A&M
Sep 67.	(7") *(RZ 3002)* *<885>* **HOMBURG. / GOOD CAPTAIN CLACK** *(re-iss. Oct75 on 'Fly'; BUG 2)*		6	34
Dec 67.	(lp) *(LRZ 1001)* *<18008>* **PROCOL HARUM**			47 Sep67

– A whiter shade of pale / Conquistador / She wandered through the garden fence / Something following me / Mabel / Cerdes (outside the gate of) / Homburg / Christmas camel / Kaleidoscope / Salad days / Good Captain Clack /

Repent Walpurgis. *(re-iss. May85 as 'A WHITER SHADE OF PALE' on 'Sierra' lp/c; FEDB/CFEDB 5008) (cd-iss. Jun97 as 'A WHITER SHADE OF PALE' on 'Repertoire'; RR 4666)*

Apr 68. (7") *(RZ 3007) <927>* **QUITE RIGHTLY SO. / IN THE WEE SMALL HOURS OF SIXPENCE** | 50 | ☐

Dec 68. (lp; stereo/mono) *(S+/LRZ 1004) <SP 4151>* **SHINE ON BRIGHTLY** | ☐ | 24 Oct68
– Quite rightly so / Shine on brightly / Skip softly (my moonbeams) / Wish me well / Rambling on / Magdalene (my regal zonophone) / In held twas I:- a) Glimpses of Nirvana – (b) Twas tea-time at the circus – (c) In the Autumn of my madness – (d) Look to your soul – (e) Grand finale. *(re-iss. Sep85 on 'Sierra' lp/c; FEDB/CFEDB 5026) (cd-iss. Nov92 on 'Castle'; CLACD 321) (cd re-iss. Jun97 on 'Repertoire'; RR 4667)*

May 69. (lp) *(SLRZ 1009) <SP 4179>* **A SALTY DOG** | 27 | 32
– A salty dog / The milk of human kindness / Too much between us / The Devil came from Arkansas / Boredom / Juicy John Pink / Wreck of the Hesperus / All this and more / Crucifiction Lane / Pilgrim's progress. *(re-iss. 1971 on 'Music For Pleasure'; MFP 5275) (re-iss. May85 on 'Sierra' lp/c; FEDB/CFEDB 5012) (cd-iss. 1986 on 'Mobile Fidelity'; MFCD 823) (cd re-iss. Jul92 on 'Castle'; CLACD 289)*

Jun 69. (7") *(RZ 3019)* **A SALTY DOG. / LONG GONE CREEK** | 44 | -
Jul 69. (7") *<1111>* **THE DEVIL CAME FROM KANSAS. / BOREDOM** | - | ☐

—— **CHRIS COPPING** – organ, bass (ex-PARAMOUNTS) repl. FISHER + KNIGHTS

Jun 70. (7") *<1218>* **WHISKEY TRAIN. / ABOUT TO DIE** | - | -
Jun 70. (lp) *(SLRZ 1014) <SP 4261>* **HOME** | 49 | 34
– Whiskey train / Dead man's dream / Still there'll be more / Nothing that I didn't know / About to die / Barnyard story / Piggy pig pig / Whaling stories / Your own choice. *(re-iss. Apr89 on 'Castle' lp/c/cd; CLA LP/MC/CD 142)*

                Chrysalis   A&M
Jun 71. (lp) *(ILPS 9158) <SP 4294>* **BROKEN BARRICADES** | 42 | 32 May71
– Simple sister / Broken barricades / Memorial drive / Luskus Delph / Power failure / Song for a dreamer / Playmate of the mouth / Poor Mohammed. *(re-iss. 1974 lp/c; CHS/ZCHS 1057)*

Jun 71. (7") *<1264>* **BROKEN BARRICADES. / POWER FAILURE** | - | -
Oct 71. (7") *<1287>* **SIMPLE SISTER. / SONG FOR A DREAMER** | - | -

—— **DAVE BALL** (b.30 Mar'50) – guitar repl. ROBIN TROWER (later solo) / added **ALAN CARTWRIGHT** (b.10 Oct'45) – bass (to **BROOKER, COPPING, WILSON, REID + BALL**)

Apr 72. (lp) *(CHR 1004) <SP 4335>* **PROCOL HARUM IN CONCERT WITH THE EDMUNTON SYMPHONY ORCHESTRA (live)** | 48 | 5
– Conquistador / Whaling stories / A salty dog / All this and more / In held 'twas I; a) Glimpses of Nirvana – (b) 'Twas teatime at the circus – (c) In the Autumn of my madness – (d) I know if I'd been wiser – (e) Grand finales.

May 72. (7") *<1347>* **CONQUISTADOR (live). / A SALTY DOG (live)** | - | 16
Jul 72. (7") *(CHR 2003)* **CONQUISTADOR (live). / LUSKUS DELPH** | 22 | -

                Chrysalis   Chrysalis
Mar 73. (lp/c) *(<CHR/ZCHR 1037>)* **GRAND HOTEL** | ☐ | 21
– Grand hotel / Toujours l'amour / A rum tale / T.V. Ceaser / A souvenir of London / Bringing home the bacon / Robert's box / For licorice John / Fires (which burnt brightly) / Robert's box. *(cd-iss. Oct95 on 'Essential'; ESMCD 290)*

Apr 73. (7") *(CHS 2010)* **ROBERT'S BOX. / A RUM TALE** | ☐ | -
Apr 73. (7") *<2011>* **BRINGING HOME THE BACON. / TOUJOURS L'AMOUR** | - | ☐
Aug 73. (7") *<2013>* **GRAND HOTEL. / FIRE'S (WHICH BURNT BRIGHTLY)** | - | ☐
Aug 73. (7") *(CHS 2015)* **A SOUVENIR OF LONDON. / TOUJOURS L'AMOUR** | - | -

—— **MICK GRABHAM** – guitar (ex-PLASTIC PENNY, ex-COCHISE) repl. BALL to BEDLAM

Apr 74. (lp/c) *(<CHR/ZCHR 1058>)* **EXOTIC BIRDS AND FRUIT** | ☐ | 86
– Nothing but the truth / Beyond the pale / As strong as Samson / The idol / The thin edge of the wedge / Monsieur R. Monde / Fresh fruit / Butterfly boys / New lamps for old. *(cd-iss. Oct95 on 'Essential'; ESMCD 291)*

Apr 74. (7") *(CHS <2032>)* **NOTHING BUT THE TRUTH. / DRUNK AGAIN** | ☐ | ☐
Jul 75. (7") *(CHS <2073>)* **PANDORA'S BOX. / THE PIPER'S TUNE** | 16 | ☐
Aug 75. (lp/c) *(<CHR/ZCHR 1080>)* **PROCOL'S NINTH** | 41 | 52
– Pandora's box / Fools gold / Taking the time / The unquiet zone / The final thrust / I keep forgetting / Without a doubt / The piper's tune / Typewriter torment / Eight days a week. *(cd-iss. Oct95 on 'Essential'; ESMCD 292)*

Oct 75. (7") *(CHS 2079)* **THE FINAL THRUST. / TAKING THE TIME** | ☐ | -
Jan 76. (7") *(CHS 2084)* **AS STRONG AS SAMSON. / THE UNQUIET ZONE** | ☐ | -

—— **PETE SOLLEY** – keyboards (ex-ARTHUR BROWN, ex-SNAFU, ex-CHRIS FARLOWE) repl. CARTWRIGHT (COPPING now bass only)

Jan 77. (7") *<2115>* **WIZARD MAN. / SOMETHING MAGIC** | - | -
Feb 77. (7") *(CHS 2138)* **WIZARD MAN. / BACKGAMMON** | ☐ | ☐
Mar 77. (lp/c) *(<CHR/ZCHR 1130>)* **SOMETHING MAGIC** | ☐ | ☐
– Something magic / Skating on thin ice / Wizard man / The mark of the claw / Strangers in space / The worm and the tree. *(cd-iss. Oct95 on 'Essential'; ESMCD 293)*

—— Disbanded mid-77. WILSON joined JOE COCKER. GRABHAM to MICKEY JUPP. GARY BROOKER joined ERIC CLAPTON band and went solo. PROCOL HARUM re-formed Oct'91, TIM RENWICK instead of TROWER.

—— re-formed in 1991. **BROOKER** – vocals, piano / **KEITH REID** – words / **ROBIN TROWER** – lead guitar / **MATTHEW FISHER** – hammond organ / with guests **DAVE BRONZE** – bass / **MARK BRZEZICKI** – drums (of BIG COUNTRY) / **JERRY STEVENSON** – mandolin, guitar

              Zoo-
              B.M.G.   Zoo
Feb 92. (cd/c/lp) *(HH CD/MC/LP 00589)* **THE PRODIGAL STRANGER** | ☐ | ☐
– The truth won't fade away / Holding on / Man with a mission / (You can't) Turn back the page / One more time / A dream in ev'ry home / The hand that rocks the cradle / The king of hearts / All our dreams are sold / Perpetual motion / Learn to fly / The pursuit of happiness.

—— in Jul'95, PROCOL HARUM members guested on a classical album, 'THE LONG GOODBYE' with The London Philharmonic Orchestra

– compilations, others, etc. –

Mar 64. (7"ep) *Parlophone; (GEP 8908)* **THE PARAMOUNTS** | ☐ | -
– Little bitty pretty one / A certain girl / Poison Ivy / I feel good all over.
1971. (lp) *Fly; (TON 4)* **THE BEST OF PROCOL HARUM** | ☐ | -
<US-iss.Oct73 on 'A&M'; 4401>
Apr 72. (7"m) *MagniFly; (ECHO 101)* **A WHITER SHADE OF PALE. / HOMBURG / A SALTY DOG** | 13 | -
Apr 72. (d-lp/d-c) *Cube; (TOOFA 7)* **PROCOL HARUM – A WHITER SHADE OF PALE / A SALTY DOG** | 26 | ☐
(re-iss. Jan75, Mar78, Oct81; same)
Mar 76. (lp) *Decca; (ROOTS 4)* **ROCK ROOTS** | ☐ | -
Mar 78. (7") *Fly; (BUG 77)* **A WHITER SHADE OF PALE. / CONQUISTADOR** | ☐ | -
(re-iss. Mar79; HBUG 77) (re-iss. Aug82 on 'Dakota'; BAK 1)
Mar 78. (d-lp/d-c) *Cube; (TOOFA/ZCTOF 10)* **SHINE ON BRIGHTLY / HOME** | ☐ | -
May 78. (lp) *Hallmark; (SHM 956)* **PROCOL HARUM'S GREATEST HITS** | ☐ | -
Aug 78. (7") *Chrysalis; (CHS 2244)* **CONQUISTADOR. / A SALTY DOG** | ☐ | -
Aug 78. (7"ep) *E.M.I.; (NUT 2834)* **THE PARAMOUNTS** | ☐ | -
– Poison Ivy / I feel glad all over / Blue ribbons / Cuttin' in.
Oct 81. (d-lp/c) *Cube; (PLAT/ZCPLT 1003)* **THE PLATINUM COLLECTION** | ☐ | -
Apr 82. (lp) *Ace; (6886555)* **PROCOL HARUM** (67-69) | ☐ | -
(re-iss. Apr82 on 'Impact'; 7486 552) (re-iss. Oct82 on 'Dakota'; COUNT/ZCCNT 13)
Aug 82. (7") *Dakota; (BAK 2)* **HOMBURG. / A SALTY DOG** | ☐ | -
Apr 83. (lp; by PARAMOUNTS) *Edsel; (ED 112)* **WHITER SHADES OF R'N'B** | ☐ | -
(cd-iss. Aug87 + Sep91; EDCD 112)
Oct 84. (d-lp/c) *Sierra; (FEDD/CFEDD 1004)* **OFF THE RECORD WITH PROCOL HARUM** | ☐ | -
Apr 86. (d-lp/d-c/cd) *Castle; (CCS LP/MC/CD 120)* **THE COLLECTION** | ☐ | -
– A whiter shade of pale / Homburg / Too much between us / A salty dog / The Devil came back from Kansas / Whaling stories / Good Captain Clack / All this and more / Quite rightly so / Shine on brightly / Grand hotel / Bringing home the bacon / Toujours l'armour / Broken barricades / Power failure / Conquistador (live) / Nothing but the truth / Butterfly boys / Pandora's box / Simple sister.
Feb 87. (7") *Old Gold; (OG 9692)* **CONQUISTADOR. / PANDORA'S BOX** | ☐ | -
Mar 88. (d-lp/c/cd) *That's Original; (TFO LP/MC/CD 5)* **SHINE ON BRIGHTLY. / A SALTY DOG** | ☐ | -
Mar 88. (cd-ep) *Special Edition; (CD 3-14)* **A WHITER SHADE OF PALE / HOMBURG / CONQUISTADOR / A SALTY DOG** | ☐ | -
Jun 88. (7") *Old Gold; (OG 9225)* **A WHITER SHADE OF PALE. / HOMBURG** | ☐ | ☐
Jun 88. (cd) *A&M; (CD 2515)* **CLASSICS** | ☐ | ☐
Jul 88. (lp/c/cd) *Knight; (KN LP/MC/CD 10005)* **NIGHTRIDING: PROCOL HARUM** | ☐ | -
Dec 88. (lp/c/cd) *Fun; (FUN/+C/CD 9028)* **20 GREATEST HITS** | ☐ | -
1991. (cd)(c/lp) *Chrysalis; (MPCD 1638)(Z+/CNW 4)* **PORTFOLIO** | ☐ | -
Feb 92. (cd-box) *Castle; (CLABX 910)* **3 ORIGINALS** | ☐ | -
– (HOME / A SALTY DOG / A WHITER SHADE OF PALE).
Jun 92. (cd) *Dojo; (EARLD 6)* **THE EARLY YEARS** | ☐ | -
Oct 94. (cd) *Disky; (CUCD 05)* **PROCOL HARUM** | ☐ | -
Jan 95. (cd) *B.R.Music; (BRCD 106)* **BEST OF PROCOL HARUM** | ☐ | -
Jul 95. (cd-ep) *Essential; **A WHITER SHADE OF PALE / A SALTY DOG / REPENT WALPURGIS*** | ☐ | -
Sep 95. (cd/c) *Essential; (ESS CD/MC 295)* **HOMBURG & OTHER HITS – THE BEST OF PROCOL HARUM** | ☐ | -

PRODIGY

Formed: Braintree, Essex, England ... early 90's by LIAM HOWLETT together with MC MAXIM REALITY, LEEROY THORNHILL and KEITH FLINT. With their roots in hip hop, this irrepressible quartet of techno terrorists spread their first waves of discontent through the harder end of the rave scene, releasing the 'WHAT EVIL LURKS' EP in March '91 on the (then) fledgling 'XL' label. One track, the rave call to arms of 'EVERYBODY IN THE PLACE' would rocket to No.2 the following Christmas, hot on the heels of the PRODIGY's seminal debut hit (No.3), 'CHARLY'. A masterstroke of genius, HOWLETT sampled a veteran Government TV ad warning children off playing with fire (a recurring lyrical obsession) and welded it to fuck-off, hoover synths and a juggernaut breakbeat. The mixed result: proof that ravers had a sense of humour/irony and a string of low-rent imitations sampling everything from 'Sesame Street' to 'Rhubarb and Custard'. Borrowing from ARTHUR BROWN's hoary old chestnut of the same name, 'FIRE' gave the PRODIGY their third Top 20 hit in a row, closely followed by 'THE PRODIGY EXPERIENCE' (1992). More assured and inventive than most of the weak cash-in albums to come out of the 12"-dominated rave scene, the record proffered alternate versions of the hits and killer new tracks like the brilliant breakbeat-skank, 'OUT OF SPACE'. By this point the group were also making waves with their formidable live show, still largely gracing raves yet a far cry from your average P.A. featuring a scantily clad diva miming to a 15-minute set. By 1993, HOWLETT was extending his horizons; a much in demand remixer, he worked on material for such diverse acts as DREAM FREQUENCY and FRONT 242 as well as poring over new PRODIGY tracks. The first of these, the wailing 'ONE LOVE' was initially realeased as a white label, apparently to keep in touch with their underground roots. The record still charted of course, going Top 10 in late '93 after a full release. 'NO GOOD START THE DANCE' was the sound of a group in transition, a speeded-up female vocal alternating with a thundering techno assault. The single made the Top 5 in Spring '94, but it was hardly representative of what lay in store on 'MUSIC FOR THE JILTED GENERATION' later that summer. Opening with a sinister tap-tapping typewriter and spoken word intro, then slamming into a dark, twisting techno groove, it was clear HOWLETT was no longer "luvved up". The album was breathtaking in its sweep, mapping out the future of techno, PRODIGY style, incorporating heavy riffing (on the two fingered salute to the Criminal Justice Bill, 'THEIR LAW', a collaboration with POP WILL EAT ITSELF), 70's style funky flute (the evocative '3 KILOS') and even a trio of tracks, 'THE NARCOTIC SUITE', climaxing the album in blistering form. Obvious highlights were the utterly compelling 'VOODOO PEOPLE' (riffs AND funky flute!; arguably The PRODIGY's finest moment to boot) and the military stomp of 'POISON' (complete with techno-gothic video; a must-see). The album was a UK No.1, establishing the band as major contenders who had far outstripped the narrow confines of 'dance', as was evidenced at their shows over the ensuing two years. White-gloved ravers blew their whistles hopefully, waiting in vain for 'CHARLY' or 'NO GOOD START THE DANCE', while more recent converts contorted and thrashed wildly to the new material (when, that is, they weren't threatening to shove the raver's eardrum-rupturing whistles where the sun doesn't shine!). By late '95/early '96, The PRODIGY were also showcasing new material at live gigs, including an incendiary little ditty entitled 'FIRESTARTER'. Primarily KEITH's baby, the 'song' was released as a single in Spring '96, giving The PRODIGY their first No.1. FLINT had, by now, fashioned his once flowing locks into a formidable luminous green mohican and had also developed a stage act that made IGGY POP (circa The STOOGES) look like a librarian. The fine, upstanding British public were subsequently treated to the new improved KEITH via the brilliant video (claustrophobically shot in the London Underground) on Top Of The Pops, resulting in an avalanche of complaints. Of course, the kids loved it, even toddlers were heard to garble 'I'm a twisted firestarter' while dragging their hapless mums into Woolies to bag a copy. As for the song itself, FLINT took a starring role, spitting out his demented cockney threats over depth charge beats. The next single, 'BREATHE', was even better, an ominous JOY DIVISION-esque guitar riff segueing into the hardest funkiest breakbeats this side of The CHEMICAL BROTHERS. Arguably the single of the year, the track raised expectations for the forthcoming PRODIGY opus to fever pitch. Almost inevitably, then, 'THE FAT OF THE LAND' (1997) was something of a letdown. There was nothing to match the dark majesty of 'BREATHE' (included on the album along with 'FIRESTARTER'), but there were plenty of other tracks to 'melt some brains' as HOWLETT put it. The insistent techno-hop of 'DIESEL POWER' (with KOOL KEITH guesting) attested to the group's love of hardcore rap, while the BEASTIE BOYS-sampling 'FUNKY SHIT' and MC MAXIM-led 'MINDFIELDS' were high-octane PRODIGY crowd pleasers. Minus points, however, for the dull collaboration with CRISPIAN MILLS (KULA SHAKER), 'NARAYAN' and the pointless cover of L7's 'FUEL MY FIRE'. Far more compelling was the insidiously funky 'CLIMBATIZE'. But it was the album's opener which had the nation's moral guardians and pro-women groups in a tizzy; whatever the inspiration for 'SMACK MY BITCH UP', The PRODIGY were as defiant and unapologetic as ever. Politics aside, the album may not have fully met expectations but it still trampled on the competition. Live, The PRODIGY remain a revelation, an electric maelstrom of colour and sound (and grimacing!), with an abiltiy to mobilise a crowd unmatched in the musical spectrum. In saying that, if they rely on punk cliches without pushing the boundaries of dance music – which is what they do best – they risk becoming a caricature of themselves.

• **Songwriters:** HOWLETT except samples of BABY D ('Casanova') on 'BREAK & ENTER', and KELLY CHARLES on 'YOU'RE NO GOOD FOR ME'. 'FULL THROTTLE' is also reminiscent of JOAN ARMATRADING's 'Me Myself I'.

Album rating: EXPERIENCE (*8) / MUSIC FOR THE JILTED GENERATION (*10) / THE FAT OF THE LAND (*7)

KEITH FLINT (b.17 Sep'69) – vocals, dancer / **LIAM HOWLETT** (b.21 Aug'71) – keyboards / **MC MAXIM REALITY** (b.KEITH PALMER, 21 Mar'67) – rapper-vox, dancer / **LEEROY THORNHILL** (b.7 Oct'69) – dancer, vocals

	X.L.	Elektra
Mar 91. (12"ep) (XLT 17) **WHAT EVIL LURKS / WE GONNA ROCK. / ANDROID / EVERYBODY IN THE PLACE**	☐	-
Aug 91. (7"/c-s) (XLS/XLC 21) <66411> **CHARLY. / CHARLY (original mix)**	3	☐
(12"+=/cd-s+=) (XLT/CDXLS 21) – Pandemonium / Your love.		
Dec 91. (7"/c-s) (XLS/XLC 26) **EVERYBODY IN THE PLACE. / G-FORCE (ENERGY FLOW)**	2	-
(12"+=) (XLT 26) – Crazy man / Rip up the sound system.		
(cd-s++=) (XLS 26CD) – ('A'remix).		
Sep 92. (7"/c-s) (XLS/XLC 30) <66370> **FIRE. / JERICHO (original mix)**	11	☐
(12"+=/cd-s+=) (XLT/XLS 30CD) – Fire (sunrise version) / Jericho (genaside II remix).		
Oct 92. (cd/c/lp) (XLCD/XLMC/XLLP 110) <61365> **EXPERIENCE**	12	☐
– Jericho / Music reach (1/2/3/4) / Wind it up / Your love (remix) / Hyperspeed (G-Force part 2) / Charly (trip into drum and bass version) / Out of space / Everybody in the place (155 and rising) / Weather experience / Fire (sunrise version) / Ruff in the jungle bizness / Death of the Prodigy dancers (live).		
Nov 92. (7"/c-s) (XLS/XLC 35) <66346> **OUT OF SPACE (remix). / RUFF IN THE JUNGLE BIZNESS (uplifting vibes remix)**	5	Dec92
(12"+=)(cd-s+=) (XLT/XLS 35CD) – ('A'techno underworld remix) / Music reach (1,2,3,4) (live).		
Apr 93. (7"/c-s) (XLS/XLC 39) <66319> **WIND IT UP (REWOUND). / WE ARE THE RUFFEST**	7	☐

(12"+=) (XLT 39) – Weather experience (remix).		
(cd-s++=) (XLS 39CD) – ('A'edit).		
Oct 93. (c-ep/12"ep/cd-ep) (XLC/XLT/XLS 47CD) **ONE LOVE / RHYTHM OF LIFE (original mix). / FULL THROTTLE (original mix) / ONE LOVE (Jonny L remix)**	8	-
May 94. (12"/c-s) (XLT/XLC 51) **NO GOOD (START THE DANCE) / NO GOOD (bad for you mix) / NO GOOD (CJ Bolland's museum mix)**	4	-
(cd-s+=) (XLS 51CD) – No Good (original mix).		
below album with **PHIL BENT** – flute / **LANCE RIDDLER** – guitar		

	X.L.	Mute
Jul 94. (cd/c/d-lp) (XLCD/XLMC/XLLP 114) <55642> **MUSIC FOR THE JILTED GENERATION**	1	Mar95
– Intro / Break & enter / Their law (featuring POP WILL EAT ITSELF) / Full throttle / Voodoo people / Speedway (theme from 'Fastlane') / The heat (the energy) / Poison / No good (start the dance) / One love (edit) – The narcotic suite / 3 kilos / Skylined / Claustrophobic sting.		
Sep 94. (12"ep) (XLT 54) <67007> **VOODOO PEOPLE (original mix) / VOODOO PEOPLE (Dust Brothers remix). / VOODOO PEOPLE (Haiti Island mix) / GOA (THE HEAT, THE ENERGY PART 2)**	13	☐
(cd-ep) (XLS 54CD) – (3rd track repl.by) ('A'edit).		
Mar 95. (c-s) (XLC 58) **POISON ('95) / ('A'-Rat Poison mix) / SCIENIDE**	15	☐
(12"+=/cd-s+=) (XLT/XLS 58CD) – ('A'-Environmental science dub mix).		

	X.L.	Geffen
Mar 96. (c-s) (XLC 70) <17387> **FIRESTARTER / MOLOTIV BITCH**	1	30 Jan97
(12"+=/cd-s+=) (XLT/XLS 70CD) – ('A'-Empiron mix) / ('A'instrumental).		

—— All singles re-issued Apr96 hitting UK Top 75.

Nov 96. (c-ep/12"ep) (XLC/XLT 80) **BREATHE / THEIR LAW featuring PWEI (live at Phoenix fesival '96). / POISON (live at the Tourhout & Werchter festival '96)**	1	☐
(cd-ep+=) (XLS 80CD) – The trick.		
Jul 97. (cd/c/lp) (XL CD/MC/LP 121) <46606> **THE FAT OF THE LAND**	1	1
– Smack my bitch up / Breathe / Diesel power / Funky shit / Serial thrilla / Mindfields / Narayan / Firestarter / Climbatize / Fuel my fire.		
Nov 97. (12"/c-s) (XLT/XLS 90) <43946> **SMACK MY BITCH UP. / NO MAN ARMY**	8	89
(cd-s+=) (XLS 90CD) – Minefields (heavy rock dub) / ('A'-DJ Hype remix).		

PRONG (dig out; Great Metal . . .)

PROPAGANDA (dig out; Great Alt & Indie . . .)

PROPELLERHEADS

Formed: Bath, England . . . 1995 by ALEX GIFFORD (once a part-time contributor of The GRID) and WILL WHITE. Signed to the super trendy London-based big beat label, 'Wall Of Sound', debuting in early '96 with the bouncy 'DIVE' (now on a TV ad for Adidas). Touring with dodgy dance outfit AGENT PROVOCATEUR, the duo upstaged said band almost every night, gradually incorporating live instruments (hammond organ, drums, percussion) to their set. With almost every major label knocking at their door, PROPELLERHEADS remained resolutely independent, flying high with the massive underground club smash, 'TAKE CALIFORNIA' (a minor UK chart hit). In 1997, they injected their floorquaking dance sound with some widescreen panache, taking 60's cinematic espionage as the inspiration for 'SPYBREAK!'. This Top 40 breaker helped convince soundtrack whizz kid DAVID ARNOLD to use them on his forthcoming collaborative James Bond project, 'Shaken And Stirred' (he/they lifted the single 'ON HER MAJESTIES SECRET SERVICE' from the album). SHIRLEY BASSEY, who sang the original version of one of the tracks, 'Diamonds Are Forever', was the guest chanteuse on The PROPELLERHEADS next single, 'HISTORY REPEATING' (another Top 20 hit).

Album rating: DECKSANDDRUMSANDROCKANDROLL (*8)

ALEX GIFFORD – saxophone, etc / **WILL WHITE** – drums, etc

	Wall Of Sound	Dreamworks
Mar 96. (12"ep/cd-ep) (WALL T/D 016) **DIVE EP**	☐	-
– Dive / Ron' theory / Lethal cat / Go faster.		
Nov 96. (12"/cd-s) (WALL T/D 024) **TAKE CALIFORNIA. / ('A'mixes) / ECHO AND BOUNCE**	69	-
May 97. (12"/cd-s) (WALL T/D 029) **SPYBREAK! / VELVET PANTS / CLANG / TAKE CALIFORNIA**	40	-
(cd-s) (WALLD 029X) – ('A'side) / Wide / Props got skilz.		

—— In Oct'97, the duo teamed up with DAVID ARNOLD on his UK Top 10 version of 'ON HER MAJESTIES SECRET SERVICE'.

Oct 97. (12"ltd.) (WALLT 034) **BANG ON! / DIVE**		-
Dec 97. (c-s/12"/cd-s; PROPELLERHEADS featuring MISS SHIRLEY BASSEY) (WALL CS/T/D 036) <GR 057> **HISTORY REPEATING / (Knee Length mix) / (Ankle Length mix) / (Hip Length mix)**	19	Apr98
Jan 98. (cd/c/d-lp) (WALL CD/C/P 015) <50031> **DECKSANDDRUMSANDROCKANDROLL**	6	100 Mar98
– Take California / Echo and bounce / Velvet pants / Better? / Oh yeah? / History repeating (featuring MISS SHIRLEY BASSEY) / Bang on! / A number of microphones / On her majesty's secret service / Bigger? / Cominagetcha / Spybreak!		
Jun 98. (12"/cd-s) (WALL T/D 039) **BANG ON! (short one) / VELVET PANTS (Spare Pair mix) / BANG ON! (wrecked)**	53	
Feb 99. (7") (WALLS 045) **CRASH! / YOU WANT IT BACK (featuring The JUNGLE BROTHERS)**	☐	

(12"+=) *(WALLT 045)* – Props vote of gratitude / 360° (oh yeah) – featuring DE LA SOUL.

(cd-s++=) *(WALLD 045)* – ('A'&'B'extended).

Aug 99. (ltd-12"; as PROPELLERHEADS featuring The JUNGLE BROTHERS) *(WALLT 057)* **TAKE CALIFORNIA. / . . . AND PARTY** ☐ –

PSYCHEDELIC FURS

Formed: London, England . . . 1977 by RICHARD and TIM BUTLER, JOHN ASHTON, ROGER MORRIS and DUNCAN KILBURN, who eventually completed the line-up with drummer VINCE ELY. Gaining a bit of much-needed credibilty via a Radio One John Peel session, the band signed to 'Epic-C.B.S.' in 1978 and released a debut single, 'WE LOVE YOU', late the following year. This was followed in early 1980 by a classic second single, 'SISTER EUROPE' and a Top 20 eponymous debut album. A vintage slice of post-punk miserabilism tracing the classic linage of VELVET UNDERGROUND, ROXY MUSIC, ~'BOWIE etc., the record's dischordant mesh of jagged melody, inwardly spiralling guitar and BUTLER's cracked monotone placed The PSYCHEDELIC FURS firmly at the forefront of the alternative rock scene. Subsequently relocating to New York, they worked on an even better follow-up, 'TALK TALK TALK' (1981), a record which might've made more concessions to pop/rock convention but made up for it with gloriously subversive songwriting; 'INTO YOU LIKE A TRAIN' was leeringly self explanatory, 'DUMB WAITERS' tripped out on a mangled STOOGES vibe while the lugubrious 'PRETTY IN PINK' provided the 'FURS with a near-Top 40 hit and remains their best-known track. With ex-BIRTHDAY PARTY man, PHIL CALVERT, replacing ELY (who teamed up with ROBYN HITCHCOCK), the band hooked up with TODD RUNDGREN for the disappointing 'FOREVER NOW' (1982), a combination that looked intersting on paper but somehow failed to translate on vinyl. The record nevertheless made the UK Top 20, as did 1984's 'MIRROR MOVES', by which time line-up changes had seen KEITH FORSEY and MARS WILLIAMS replace CALVERT and founding members KILBURN and MORRIS. Despite flashes of darkly melodic inspiration, a suffocatingly slick production erased any traces of mystery or danger, further testing the patience of many longtime fans. A re-released 'PRETTY IN PINK' (issued to coincide with the film of the same name, inspired by the song itself) illustrated just how lifeless the newer material was, while the terminally dull 'MIDNIGHT TO MIDNIGHT' (1987) showed no signs of an imminent return to form. With ELY back on the drum stool, a further late 80's effort, 'BOOK OF DAYS' (1989), attempted a more credible approach to diminishing commercial returns and minimal critical reaction. Finally, after 1991's 'WORLD OUTSIDE', the band hung up their 'FURS for good, BUTLER going on to form LOVE SPIT LOVE with RICHARD FORTUS and FRANK FERRER, releasing a one-off eponymous album for 'Imago-R.C.A.' in 1994. • **Songwriters:** RICHARD BUTLER + FURS, except MACK THE KNIFE (Bobby Darin).

Album rating: THE PSYCHEDELIC FURS (*8) / TALK TALK TALK (*7) / FOREVER NOW (*7) / MIRROR MOVES (*6) / MIDNIGHT TO MIDNIGHT (*5) / ALL OF THIS AND NOTHING compilation (*7) / BOOK OF DAYS (*4) / WORLD OUTSIDE (*4) / B-SIDES AND LOST GROOVES collection (*5)

RICHARD BUTLER (b. 5 Jun'56, Kingston-Upon-Thames, England) – vocals / **JOHN ASHTON** (b.30 Nov'57) – lead guitar / **ROGER MORRIS** – guitar / **TIM BUTLER** (b. 7 Dec'58) – bass / **DUNCAN KILBURN** – saxophone, keyboards / **VINCE ELY** – drums (ex-UNWANTED)

	Epic C.B.S.	not iss. Columbia
Oct 79. (7") *(EPC 8005)* **WE LOVE YOU. / PULSE**		–
Feb 80. (7") *(CBS 8179)* **SISTER EUROPE. / ******		
Mar 80. (lp/c) *(CBS/40 84084) <36791>* **THE PSYCHEDELIC FURS**	18	
– India / Sister Europe / Imitation of Christ / Fall / Pulse / We love you / Wedding song / Blacks / Radio / Flowers. *(re-iss. Mar83) (cd-iss. Apr89)*		
Oct 80. (7") *(CBS 9059)* **MR. JONES. / SUSAN'S STRANGE**		
Apr 81. (7") *(A 1166)* **DUMB WAITERS. / DASH**	59	
May 81. (lp/c) *(CBS/40 84892) <37339>* **TALK TALK TALK**	30	89
– Dumb waiters / Pretty in pink / I wanna sleep with you / No tears / Mr. Jones / Into you like a train / It goes on / So run down / All of this and nothing / She is mine. *(re-iss. Nov84 lp/c; CBS/40 32539) (cd-iss. Apr89; CD 32539) (cd re-iss. Mar96 on 'Columbia'; 483663-2)*		
Jun 81. (7"/7"pic-d) *(A/WA 1327)* **PRETTY IN PINK. / MACK THE KNIFE**	43	
(12"+=) *(A13 1327)* – Soap commercial.		

— **PHIL CALVERT** – drums (ex-BIRTHDAY PARTY) repl. ELY (to ROBYN HITCHCOCK)

Jul 82. (7") *(A 2549) <03197>* **LOVE MY WAY. / AEROPLANE (dance mix)**	42	
Sep 82. (lp/c) *(CBS/40 85909) <38261>* **FOREVER NOW**	20	61
– Love my way / President Gas / Sleep comes down / Forever now / Danger / You and I / Run and run / Merry-go-round / Goodbye / No easy street. *(c+=)* – Shadow. *(re-iss. Apr86 lp/c; CBS/40 85909)*		
Oct 82. (7") *(A 2665) <03340>* **DANGER. / (I DON'T WANT TO BE YOUR) SHADOW**		
(12"+=) *(TA 2665)* – Goodbye (mix).		
Feb 83. (7") *<03340>* **LOVE MY WAY. / SHADOW**	–	44
May 83. (7") *<03930>* **PRESIDENT GAS. / RUN AND RUN**	–	

— **KEITH FORSEY** – drums repl. CALVERT who joined CRIME & THE CITY SOLUTION / **MARS WILLIAMS** – saxophone (ex-WAITRESSES) repl. KILBURN + MORRIS

Mar 84. (7"/12") *(A/TA 4300)* **HEAVEN. / HEARTBEAT (remix)**	29	–

May 84. (lp/c) *(CBS/40 25950) <39278>* **MIRROR MOVES**	15	43
– The ghost in you / Here come cowboys / Heaven / Heartbeat / My time / Like a stranger / Alice's house / Only a game / Highwire days. *(re-iss. Jan87 lp/c; 450356-1/-4) (cd-iss. May87; CD 25950) (re-iss. Jun94 on 'Columbia' cd/c; 450356-2/-4)*		
May 84. (7"/7"pic-d) *(A/WA 4470) <04416>* **THE GHOST IN YOU. / CALYPSO DUB**	68	59
(12"+=) *(TA 4470)* – President Gas (live).		
Jul 84. (7") *<04577>* **HERE COME COWBOYS. / ANOTHER EDGE**	–	–
Sep 84. (7") *<04627>* **HEAVEN. / ALICE'S HOUSE**	–	–
Oct 84. (7"/12") *(A/TA 4654)* **HEARTBEAT (Mendelssohn mix). / MY TIME**		–
(d7"+=) *(DA 4654)* – Here comes cowboys / Heaven.		

— **PAUL GARISTO** – drums repl. DORSEY. <below 45 on 'A&M' US>

Apr 86. (7") *<2826>* **PRETTY IN PINK. / (dub)**	–	41
Aug 86. (7"/7"pic-d) *(A/WA 7242)* **PRETTY IN PINK (film version). / LOVE MY WAY**	18	
(12"+=) *(TA 7242)* – ('A'version).		
(d7"+=) *(DA 7242)* – Heaven / Heartbeat.		
Oct 86. (7") *(650183-7) <06420>* **HEARTBREAK BEAT. / NEW DREAM**		26 Mar87
(12"+=) *(650186-6)* – ('A'version).		
(free c-s w/7"+=) *(650183-0)* – Sister Europe / Into you like a train / President Gas.		
Jan 87. (7") *(FURS 3)* **ANGELS DON'T CRY. / NO RELEASE**		
(free c-s w/7"+=) *(FURSD 3)* – We love you / Pretty in pink / Love my way.		
Feb 87. (lp/c/cd) *(450256-1/-4/-2) <40466>* **MIDNIGHT TO MIDNIGHT**	12	29
– Heartbreak beat / Shock / Shadow in my heart / Angels don't cry / Midnight to midnight / One more word / Torture / All of the law / No release * / Petty in pink. *(cd+= *) (re-iss. Feb89 lp/cd; 463399-1/-4/-2)*		
Apr 87. (7") *<07224>* **SHOCK. / PRESIDENT GAS (live)**	–	
Jun 87. (7") **ANGEL'S DON'T CRY. / MACK THE KNIFE**		

— **VINCE ELY** – drums returned to repl. GARISTO (to CURE) + WILLIAMS

Jul 88. (7") *(FURS 4) <07974>* **ALL THAT MONEY WANTS. / BIRDLAND**	75	
(12"+=) *(FURST 4)* – No easy street (live).		
(d7"++=) *(FURSEP 4)* – Heaven (live).		
(cd-s++=) *(CDFURS 4)* – No tears (live).		
Aug 88. (lp/c/cd) *(461110-1/-4/-2) <44377>* **ALL OF THIS AND NOTHING** (compilation)	67	
– President Gas / All that money wants / Imitation of Christ / Sister Europe / Love my way / Highwire days / Dumb waiters / Pretty in pink / Ghost in you / Heaven / Heartbeat beat / All of this and nothing. *(cd+=)* – No easy street / She is mine. *(re-iss. Apr91 cd/c; 461110-2)*		
Nov 88. (7") *<38-08499>* **HEAVEN. / INDIA**	–	
Nov 89. (lp/c/cd) *(465982-1/-4/-2) <45412>* **BOOK OF DAYS**	74	
– Entertain me / Book of days / Should God forget / Torch / Parade / Mother-son / House / Wedding / I don't mine.		
Jan 90. (7"/7"pic-d) *(FURS/+P 5)* **HOUSE. / WATCHTOWER**		–
(10") *(FURSQT 5)* – ('A'side) / ('A'-Flashback mix) / Badman / Totch (electric).		
(cd-s+=) *(CDFURS 5)* – Badman / Torch (electric).		

— **BUTLER, ASHTON + BUTLER** recruited **DON YALLITCH** – drums repl. ELY

	East West	Epic
Jun 91. (7"/c-s) *(73855)* **UNTIL SHE COMES. / MAKE IT MINE**		–
(12"+=/cd-s+=) *(73855)* – Sometimes / ('A'remix).		
Jul 91. (c-s,cd-s) *<74055>* **UNTIL SHE COMES / SOMETIMES**	–	–
Jul 91. (cd)(lp/c) *(9031 74669-2)(WX 422/+C) <74669>* **WORLD OUTSIDE**	68	
– Valentine / In my head / Until she comes / Don't be a girl / Sometimes / Tearing down / There's a world / Get a room / Better days / All about you. *(re-iss. cd Feb95; same)*		
Sep 91. (7"/c-s) **DON'T BE A GIRL. / GET A ROOM (acoustic)**		
(12"+=/cd-s+=) – (2 'A'versions).		

— disbanded after above

– compilations, etc. –

on 'C.B.S.' unless mentioned otherwise

Nov 82. (c-ep) *(A 2909)* **GREATEST ORIGINAL HITS**		–
– Sister Europe / Pretty in pink / Dumb waiters / Love my way. *(re-iss. Mar83.as 7"ep.)*		
Sep 86. (c-ep) *(450130-4)* **THE 12" TAPE**		–
– Pretty in pink / Love my way / Heaven / Heartbeat / Ghost in you.		
Jan 92. (7") **PRETTY IN PINK. / (B-side by the Only Ones)**		–
(cd-s+=) – (other track by Only Ones).		
Oct 91. (cd) *Castle; (CCSCD 308)* **THE COLLECTION**		–
May 95. (cd) *Columbia; (480363-2) <57889>* **B SIDES AND LOST GROOVES**		Oct94
Feb 97. (cd) *Strange Fruit; (SFRSCD 003)* **RADIO ONE SESSIONS**		–

LOVE SPIT LOVE

RICHARD BUTLER – vocals / **RICHARD FORTUS** – guitar / **TIM BUTLER** – bass / **FRANK FERRER** – drums

	Imago-RCA	Imago-RCA
Oct 94. (cd/c) *(72787 21055-2/-4) <21030>* **LOVE SPIT LOVE**		
– Seventeen / Superman / Half a life / Jigsaw / Change in the weather / Wake up / Am I wrong / Green / Please / Codeine / St. Mary's gate / More.		
Oct 94. (c-s,cd-s) *<25073>* **AM I WRONG / CODEINE**	–	83

PSYCHIC TV   (dig out; Great Alt & Indie . . .)

PUBLIC ENEMY

Formed: New York, USA . . . early 80's by CHUCK D (b. CARLTON RIDENHOUR), a student at Adelphi University in Long Island. MC'ing for a local DJ crew, Spectrum City, CHUCK met the outfit's mainman, HANK SHOCKLEE (who would subsequently become PUBLIC ENEMY's co-producer), the pair subsequently teaming up for BILL STEPHNEY's rap show on WBAU. Producing rough mixes and co-hosting the show, CHUCK developed his hard hitting lyrical style while SHOCKLEE undertook his earliest experiments in creating funky noise collages. The inimitable FLAVOR FLAV (b. WILLIAM DRAYTON) was an avid listener, eventually joining the show as a co-host; the stage was set for the formation of PUBLIC ENEMY. Mulling over the offer of a record deal from 'Def Jam' via Rick Rubin, CHUCK eventually formulated the concept of the group alongside co-conspirators SHOCKLEE and STEPHNEY. With a brief to combine the caustic hip hop of RUN-D.M.C. and the radical attitude of The CLASH, they appointed DJ Terminator X (b. NORMAN RODGERS), PROFESSOR GRIFF (b. RICHARD GRIFFIN) as 'Minister Of Information' and a militaristic back-up troupe named the S1W's (Security Of The First World). They also set up a formidable production team, the aptly monikered BOMB SQUAD, consisting of CHUCK, ERIC 'VIETNAM' SADLER, HANK and his brother KEITH. Taking their name from an early demo track (included in reworked form on the debut album), 'PUBLIC ENEMY No.1', the group unleashed their debut album, 'YO! BUM RUSH THE SHOW' (1987). The intent was clear from the start; the sleeve depicted the crew standing menacingly over a turntable in a darkened basement, their faces semi-submerged in shadows while the PE logo featured a sniper surrounded by a mock rifle sight. The music inside was equally uncompromising, by 1987 standards anyway. Opening with the pre-driveby fury of 'YOU'RE GONNA GET YOURS' (still arguably PE's finest moment), the record combined 70's funk samples (METERS, FRED WESLEY etc.), punishing beats, noise collages and even a guitar solo by LIVING COLOR's VERNON REID ('SOPHISTICATED BITCH'). The political campaign was kickstarted with 'RIGHTSTARTER (MESSAGE TO A BLACK MAN)', CHUCK D possessing one of the loudest, most portentous voices in rap. This was clearly a man who meant business, not another mealy-mouthed hip hop boaster. 'IT TAKES A NATION OF MILLIONS TO HOLD US BACK' (1988) was PE's tour de force, hip hop's tour de force, even. With the BOMB SQUAD creating a multi-layered blanket of noise (a hybrid of their trademark, screeching JAMES BROWN horn stabs, incendiary political samples and dextrous scratching), CHUCK D raged through what amounted to a whole new black manifesto. In terms of emotional directness and righteous anger, this record makes even the most vicious "Gangsta" album sound like a cash-in thrown together during a lunch break. Among the highlights were 'BRING THE NOISE' (later the subject of a collaborative re-vamp with ANTHRAX), 'DON'T BELIEVE THE HYPE' and the pulsing paranoia of 'BLACK STEEL IN THE HOUR OF CHAOS'. PE even managed to make a SLAYER riff sound groovy, mangling it up on 'SHE WATCH CHANNEL ZERO' while The BOMB SQUAD seemingly provided the base material for MADONNA's 'JUSTIFY MY LOVE' with 'SECURITY OF THE FIRST WORLD'. The album went Top 10 in the UK, propelling PUBLIC ENEMY into the media spotlight. The group were already the subject of much controversy and following anti-semitic remarks made by PROFESSOR GRIFF in a newspaper interview, the media circus went into overdrive. Although GRIFF and PUBLIC ENEMY soon parted ways, these events informed much of the group's new material. CHUCK D's initial response was the inflammatory 'FIGHT THE POWER', the rapper railing against what he perceived to be a white, European conspiracy to wipe out the black race. The song was given added resonance after appearing in Spike Lee's 'Do The Right Thing' over scenes of race rioting. 'WELCOME TO THE TERRORDOME' was the next single, an awesome, intimidating narrative. Much of 'FEAR OF A BLACK PLANET' (1990) portrayed PE as victims, hounded by a predominantly white media and while there were accusations of racism, CHUCK had previously clearly stated that the group's agenda was not anti-white. Musically, the album wasn't quite as resourcefully ambitious as its predecessor, although tracks such as '911 IS A JOKE' and 'BURN, HOLLYWOOD, BURN' were classic PUBLIC ENEMY, the record becoming PE's biggest seller to date (Top 5 UK, Top 10 US). Later that year, it came to light that the group had been mentioned in an FBI report to Congress, underlining the scale of PE's influence. With SISTER SOULJAH now on board, 'APOCALYPSE '91 . . .THE ENEMY STRIKES BLACK' was as militant as ever, at least lyrically. Expressing outrage at the American state's refusal to celebrate Martin Luther King's birthday, 'BY THE TIME I GET TO ARIZONA' set swathes of towering funk against SOULJAH's almost gospel tones and CHUCK's irate rapping. Elsewhere, tracks like 'NIGHTTRAIN' and '1 MILLION BOTTLEBAGS' saw the rapper railing against the self-destructiveness of his own community. More commercial and with a cleaner production than PE's previous releases, the album reached the US Top 5. In the three years prior to the next album, FLAV (who had been arrested on a domestic charge) again found himself on the wrong side of the law in late '93, following an incident with his neighbour. After a spell in rehab for drug addiction, FLAV was back in action for 'MUSE SICK-N-HOUR MESS AGE' (1994), scoring with the funky 'GIVE IT UP' and 'SO WHATCHA GONNA DO NOW' wherein CHUCK berated the pointless negativity of gangsta rap. Although the record was a relative success, PUBLIC ENEMY felt they had taken the concept to its limit, calling it a day the following year (one of their last shows was an emotional affair at England's 'Phoenix Festival'). CHUCK D had always been peerless both as an entertainer and an educator, but it was the latter route that he subsequently chose for his post-PUBLIC ENEMY activities, lecturing on the college circuit as well as writing a book and hosting a news show on America's CNN. While this one-man think-tank is not on the ball 100% of time (some controversial comments on the Northern Ireland situation at a Glasgow Barrowlands gig spring to mind), he remains a fiercely articulate voice for the disenfranchised among

the black community. PUBLIC ENEMY's legacy meanwhile, transcends all boundaries of race and culture, no hip hop artists have yet come close. Of late (after a final set, 'HE GOT GAME' for their old label), PUBLIC ENEMY have emerged on the independent, 'Play It Again Sam', although 1999's 'THERE'S A POISON GOIN' ON', was poorly received; CHUCK D's 'CONFRONTATION CAMP' looked the more promising for the future.

Album rating: YO! BUMRUSH THE SHOW (*8) / IT TAKES A NATION OF MILLIONS TO HOLD US BACK (*9) / FEAR OF A BLACK PLANET (*9) / APOCALYPSE 91 . . . THE ENEMY STRIKES BACK (*8) / GREATEST MISSES part compilation (*4) / MUSE SICK-N-HOUR MESS AGE (*5) / HE GOT GAME (*5) / THERE'S A POISON GOIN' ON (*4)

CHUCK D (b. CARLTON RIDENHOUR, 1 Aug'60) – vocals / **FLAVOR FLAV** (b. WILLIAM DRAYTON, 16 Mar'59) – multi-instrumentalist, classically trained pianist / **TERMINATOR X** (b. NORMAN LEE RODGERS, 25 Aug'66) – DJ / **PROFESSOR GRIFF** (b. RICHARD GRIFFIN) – information-vocals / plus part-time **JAMES ALLEN + JAMES NORMAN**

<Please note they never released a 7" in US>

		Def Jam	Def Jam
Mar 87.	(7") (650497-7) **PUBLIC ENEMY No.1. / TIMEBOMB**	☐	☐
	(12"+=) (650497-6) <440671-9> – Son of Public Enemy No.1 (Flavor Whop version).		
Apr 87.	(lp/c/cd) (450482-1/-4/-2) <40658> **YO! BUMRUSH THE SHOW**	☐	☐
	– You're gonna get yours / Sophisticated bitch / Miuzi weighs a ton / Timebomb / Too much posse / Rightstarter (message to a black man) / Public enemy No.1 / M.P.E. / Yo! bumrush the show / Raise the roof / Megablast / Terminator X speaks with his hands. (cd re-iss. Sep93 & Jul95; 527441-2)		
Jun 87.	(7") (650975-7) **YOU'RE GONNA GET YOURS. / MIUZI WEIGHS A TON**	☐	☐
	(12"+=) (650975-6) <440686-1> – ('A'dub mix) / ('A'-Terminator X getaway mix) / Rebel without a pause.		
Nov 87.	(7"/7"pic-d) (651245-7/-0) **REBEL WITHOUT A PAUSE (vocal). / ('A'instrumental)**	37	-
	(12"+=) (651245-6) – Terminator X speaks with his hands / Sophisticated bitch.		
	(12"+=) (651245-8) – Bring the noise (noise version) / Sophisticated bitch.		
Dec 87.	(12"; by The BLACK FLAMES) <440749-1> **ARE YOU MY WOMAN? / BRING THE NOISE**	-	☐
	(12"+=) (440754-5) – ('A'-Noise version) / ('A'-acappella mix).		
Jan 88.	(7") (651335-7) **BRING THE NOISE. / SOPHISTICATED BITCH**	32	-
	(12"+=/s12"+=) (651335-6/-8) – ('A'noise versions) / ('A'acappella version) / ('A'-instrumental).		
Jun 88.	(7"/s7") (652833-7/-0) **DON'T BELIEVE THE HYPE. / PROPHETS OF RAGE**	18	☐
	(12"+=) (652833-6) – The rhythm, the rebel (acappella) / ('B'-power version).		
	(cd-s+=) (652833-2) – Bring the noise / ('B'-power version).		
Jul 88.	(lp/c/cd) (462415-1/-4/-2) <4303> **IT TAKES A NATION OF MILLIONS TO HOLD US BACK**	8	42
	– Countdown to armageddon / Bring the noise / Don't believe the hype / Cold lampin' with Flavor / Terminator X to the edge of panic / Mind terrorist / Louder than a bomb / Caught, can we get a witness / Show 'em whatcha got / She watch Channel Zero?! / Night of the living baseheads / Black steel in the hour of chaos / Security of the first world / Rebel without a pause / Prophets of rage / Party for your right to fight. (re-iss. cd Jul95; 527358-2)		
Oct 88.	(7"/s7") (653046-7/-0) **NIGHT OF THE LIVING BASEHEADS. / TERMINATOR X TO THE EDGE OF PANIC**	63	☐
	(12"+=/cd-s+=) (653046-8/-2) – ('A'-Anti high blood pressure mix) / ('A'-Terminator X meets DST and Chuck Chillout instrumental mix).		
	(s7") (653046-9) – ('A'side) / ('A'-Terminator X meets DST. . .).		
	(US-12"+=) <4408121> – Cold lampin' with Flavor.		
1989.	(12"ep) <4468216> **BLACK STEEL IN THE HOUR OF CHAOS (radio version) / ('A'instrumental). / TOO MUCH POSSE / CAUGHT, CAN I GET A WITNESS (dub mix) / B-SIDE WINS AGAIN**	-	☐
Jun 89.	(7") (ZB 42877) **FIGHT THE POWER. / ('A'version)**	29	
	(ext.12"+=/ext.cd-s+=) (ZT/ZD 42878) <MOT 4647> – ('A'-Flavor meets Spike Lee mix).		
	(above was issued on a one-off 'Motown' deal).		
Jan 90.	(7"/c-s) (655476-0/-4) **WELCOME TO THE TERRORDOME. / ('A'-Terromental version)**	18	☐
	(12"+=/cd-s+=) (655476-8/-2) <4473135> – Terrorbeat / Black steel in the hour of chaos.		

—— Trimmed when PROFESSOR GRIFF left permanently to go solo. He soon released debut 'PAWNS IN THE GAME' with his LAST ASIATIC DISCIPLES. A year later he followed this with second album 'KAD'S II WIZ *7* DOME'.

Apr 90.	(7"/c-s) (655837-7/-4) **911 IS A JOKE. / REVOLUTIONARY GENERATION**	41	☐
	(12"+=/cd-s+=) (655837-8/-2) <4473179> – ('A'&'B'-instrumentals).		
	(12") (655837-5) – ('A'side) / Son of Public Enemy (Flavor Whop version) / Bring the noise (no noise version) / Rebel without a pause.		
Apr 90.	(cd/c/lp) (466281-2/-4/-1) <45413> **FEAR OF A BLACK PLANET**	4	10
	– Contract on the world love jam / Brothers gonna work it out / 911 is a joke / Incident at 66.6 FM / Welcome to the terrordome / Meet the G that killed me / Pollywanacraka / Anti-nigger machine / Burn Hollywood burn / Power to the people / Who stole the soul / Fear of a black planet / Revolutionary generation / Can't do nuttin' for ya man / Reggae Jax / Leave this off your fuckin' charts / B side wins again / War at 33 1/3 / Final count of the collision between us and the damned. (re-iss. cd Jul95; 523446-2)		
Jun 90.	(7"/c-s) (656018-0/-4) **BROTHERS GONNA WORK IT OUT (remix). / WAR AT 33 1/3**	46	☐
	(12"+=/12"w-poster+=) (656018-6/-8) <4473391-1> – Bring the noise (no noise instrumental) / ('B'instrumental).		
	(cd-s+=) (656018-2) <44K73391> – Anti-nigger machine / Don't believe the hype.		

Oct 90. (7"/c-s) *(656385-7/-4)* **CAN'T DO NUTTIN' FOR YA MAN. /** **('A'-Bass in your face mix)**   `53` `-`
(12"+=/cd-s+=) *(656385-6/-2)* – ('A'-dub in your face mix).
(12") *(656385-8)* – ('A'-full rub mix) / Get the f . . . out of Dodge (uncensored) / Powersave / Burn Hollywood burn.

—— added **SISTER SOULJAH** – vocals

—— (May91) FLAVOR FLAV served 30 days in jail for an earlier incident in which he was said to have hit the mother of his 3 children Karen Ross.

—— Jun91, teamed up with ANTHRAX on a hit single version of 'BRING THE NOISE'.

Sep 91. (7"/c-s) *(657530-7/-4)* **CAN'T TRUSS IT (Goree Island Conga radio mix). / ('A'-Almighty raw 125th street bootleg mix**   `22` `50`
(cd-s+=) *(657530-7)* <44K73869> – Move! (censored radio mix).
(12"++=) *(657530-6)* – ('A'-instrumental).

Oct 91. (cd/c/d-lp) *(468751-2/-4/-1)* <47374> **APOCALYPSE 91 . . .THE ENEMY STRIKES BACK**   `8` `4`
– Lost at birth / Rebirth / Night train / Can't truss it / I don't wanna be called yo niga / How to kill a radio consultant / By the time I get to Arizona / Move! / 1 million bottlebags / More news at 11 / Shut 'em down / A letter to the New York post / Get the f . . . outta Dodge / Bring the noise (w/ ANTHRAX). *(re-iss. cd Jul95; 523479-2)*

Jan 92. (7"/c-s) *(657761-7/-4)* **SHUT 'EM DOWN (Pe-Te rock mixx). / BY THE TIME I GET TO ARIZONA**   `21`
(12"+=/12"pic-d+=/cd-s+=) *(657761-6/-8/-2)* <44K74165> – ('A'rock mixx instrumental) / ('A'bald beat acappella) / ('B'side dubbed).

Mar 92. (7"/c-s) *(657864-7/-4)* **NIGHT TRAIN (Pe-Te rock . . .mixx). / MORE NEWS AT 11 (Funk minister . . .mixx)**   `55`
(12"+=/12"pic-d+=) *(657864-6/-8)* – ('A'-Pete Rock LIRR Strong island mixx).
(cd-s++=) *(657864-2)* <44K74254> – ('A'instrumental mixx).

Sep 92. (cd/c/lp) *(472031-2/-4/-1)* <53014> **GREATEST MISSES** (part compilation)   `14` `13`
– Tie goes to the runner / Hitt da road Jack / Get off my back / Air hoodlum got to do what I gotta do / Hazy shade of criminal megablast (remix) / Louder than a bomb (telephone groove) / How to kill a radio consultant (DJ check chillout..) / Who stole the soul (mixx) / Party for your right to fight (metromix) / You're gonna get yours (version). *(cd+=)* – Shut 'em down (live in the UK). *(re-iss. cd Jul95; 523487-2)*

Mar 93. (cd/c) *(473052-2/-4)* **THE 12" MIXES**   `-`

—— PROFESSOR GRIFF, TERMINATOR X, and newcomer SISTER SOULJAH all had own releases for various labels from 1990 onwards.
FLAVOR FLAV was charged late '93, for drunkenly attempting to shoot his neighbour, after he allegedly thought his wife was committing adultery.

Jul 94. (c-s,cd-s) <853316> **GIVE IT UP / BEDLAM**   `-` `33`

Aug 94. (c-ep/12"ep/cd-ep) *(DEFMC/12DEF/DEFCD 1)* **GIVE IT UP. / ('A'-main version) / Bedlam (instrumental)**   `18` `-`
(cd-s+=) *(DEFDX 1)* – Live and undrugged (part 2) / Harry Allen interactive highway / Bedlam (instrumental).

Aug 94. (cd/c/lp) <(523362-2/-4/-1)> **MUSE SICK-N-HOUR MESS AGE**   `12` `14`
– Whole lotta love / Theatrical / Give it up / What side you on? / Body count / Stop in the name / What kind of power we got? / So watcha gone do now? / White Heaven – black Hell / Race against time / Used to call it dope / Aintnuthin' buttersong / Live & undrugged parts I & II / I ain't madd at all / Death of carjacka / I stand accused / Gold complexx / Hitler day / Harry Allen superhighway.

Dec 94. (12"ep/cd-ep) *(12DEF/DEFCD 2)* **I STAND ACCUSED / WHAT KIND OF POWER WE GOT**   `-` `-`
(cd-s+=) *(DEFCDX 2)* – I stand accused (Sleek'sschool of self-defence mix) / Mao Tse Tung.

—— On 26th May'95, FLAVOR was jailed for drug possession. He was sent to a rehab centre and given three years probation. While in Italy in July, he broke his leg in a motorcycle accident.

Jul 95. (c-s) *(DEFMC 5)* **SO WHATCHA GONNA DO NOW? / BLACK STEEL IN THE HOUR OF CHAOS**   `50`
(12"+=/cd-s+=) *(12DEF/DEFCD 5)* – ('A'-Drive by s**t mix) / ('A'-Drive by instrumental).

May 98. (cd/c/d-lp) <(558130-2/-4/-1)> **HE GOT GAME**   `50` `26`
– Resurrection / He got game / Unstoppable / Shake your booty / Is your god a dog / House of the rising sun / Revelation 33 1/3 revolutions / Game face / Politics of the Sneaker Pimps / What you need is Jesus / Super agent / Go cat go / Sudden death (interlude).

May 98. (c-s) *(568985-4)* **HE GOT GAME / ('A'mix)**   `16`
(12"+=/cd-s+=) *(568985-1/-2)* – Resurrection (mixes).

                          Play It   Play It
                   Again Sam   again Sam

Jul 99. (cd/c/d-lp) <(PIASX CD/MC/LP 004)> **THERE'S A POISON GOIN' ON**   `55`
– Dark side of the wall: 2000 / Do you wanna go our way / LSD / Here I go / 41.19 / Crash / Crayola / First the sheep then the shepherd? / World tour sessions / Last mass of the caballeros / I / What what / Kervorkian / Swinders list.

Sep 99. (12") *(PIASX 005T)* **DO YOU WANNA GO OUR WAY (extended). / (instrumental) / CRAYOLA**   `66`
(cd-s) *(PIASX 005CD)* – ('A'clean version) / I / ('A'video).

TERMINATOR X

                                       P.R.O. Div. P.R.O. Div

Dec 90. (12"ep) *(RAL 6564456)* **WANNA BE DANCIN'. / GROOVE WITH THE X-MAN / X-WHYLIN / ('A'instrumental)**

May 91. (cd/c/lp) *(RAL 468421-2/-4/-1)* <RAL 46896> **TERMINATOR X AND THE VALLEY OF THE JEEP BEATS** (with various help credited to that particular group or artist)   `97`

May 91. (12"ep) *<RAL 4473737>* **HONEY DON'T PLAY DAT (vocal & instrumental). / JUVENILE DELINQUINTZ (vocal & instrumental)**

Aug 91. (12"ep) *<RAL 4473903>* **JUVENILE DELINQUINTZ (two radio versions & instrumental). / BACK TO THE SCENE OF THE BASS (two versions & instrumental)**   `-`

Jun 94. (cd) <(523343)> **TERMINATOR X AND THE GODFATHERS OF THREATT: SUPER BAD**

—— (various artists like above)

—— SISTER SOULJAH also had US releases on 'Epic'; the singles 'THE FINAL SOULTION; SLAVERY'S BACK IN EFFECT' <497407-1> and 'THE HATE THAT HATE PRODUCED' <497421-0>. These just preceded April '92 album 'DEGREES OF POWER' <EK 48713360>.

CHUCK D

                            Mercury   Mercury

Oct 96. (c-s) *(MERMC 476)* **NO / (mixes)**   `55`
(12"/cd-s) *(MER X/CD 476)* – (album snippets)

Oct 96. (cd/c) *(532944-2/-4)* **AUTOBIOGRAPHY OF MISTACHUCK**
– Mistachuck / Free big Willie / No / Generation wrekked / Niggativity . . . do I dare disturb the universe / Talk show created the fool / But you can kill the nigger in you / Underdog / Paid / Endonesia / Pride / Horizontal heron.

PUBLIC IMAGE LTD.

Formed: London, England . . . July '78 by ex-SEX PISTOLS frontman, JOHNNY ROTTEN, who reverted to his real name, JOHN LYDON. He recruited local friends, guitarist KEITH LEVENE (ex-CLASH), bassist JAH WOBBLE and Canadian drummer JIM WALKER, re-signing to 'Virgin' in the process. 'PUBLIC IMAGE', both the debut single and the title track of the debut album was a raucous slice of post-PISTOLS sonic energy, the record coming wrapped in a mock-newspaper sleeve and reaching the UK Top 10 late in 1978. The album followed it into the Top 30 at the end of the year, hardly a departure from punk but a convincing statement of intent nevertheless; tracks such as 'RELIGION', 'ANNA LISA' and 'ATTACK' formed the basis for LYDON's subsequent experiments. Preceded by the bizarre 'DEATH DISCO' single, 'METAL BOX 1' (1979) was a strikingly different beast, its pristine packaging (three 12" 45's inside a metal film can, something much copied by record company marketing departments in the years to come) rather deceptively encasing a dark, often disturbing set of experimental, Eastern-influenced material. As far from punk as LYDON has ever ventured, the record utilised monotonic repitition, LEVENE's shards of splintered guitar dissecting the vague structures of WOBBLE's rubbery basslines while LYDON wailed and ranted like a damned soul. John Peel was a particular champion of the record, playlisting virtually all its disturbing but accessible tracks, 'CAREERING', 'POPTONES' and 'GRAVEYARD' highlighting what came to be regarded as one of the last classic "punk/alternative" albums of the 70's. Surely one of the most avant-garde releases to ever grace the Top 20, the album even hit the charts a second time (Top 50) when it was re-issued in double-album format as 'SECOND EDITION' two months later. Following a patchy live album, 'PARIS AU PRINTEMPS' (1980), WOBBLE departed on a sour note, leaving LYDON and LEVENE to mastermind 'FLOWERS OF ROMANCE' (1981). A comparatively weaker effort, the record nevertheless almost made the Top 10 and the more contrived moments were interspersed with a few gems, notably the Burundi-esque title track, a Top 30 hit single. LEVENE was also soon to leave in less than pleasant circumstances following the success of P.I.L.'s biggest hit single to date, the compelling 'THIS IS NOT A LOVE SONG'. LYDON subsequently completed the lacklustre 'THIS IS WHAT YOU WANT . . . THIS IS WHAT YOU GET' opus with the help of session musicians, disbanding the group around the time of the album's release in the summer of '84. By this point, LYDON had moved to Los Angeles and his career slowed up somewhat, although he subsequently reformed 'P.I.L.' in late '85. Using such respected (and glaringly un-punk) musos as STEVE VAI, RYUICHI SAKAMOTO, GINGER BAKER and RAVI SHANKAR, LYDON recorded the minimally titled 'ALBUM' (also released as 'CASSETTE' and 'COMPACT DISC', of course). The BILL LASWELL-produced effort remains his last consistent collection, the 'SINGLE', 'RISE', almost making the Top 10, a driving, resonating, infectiously commercial example of LYDON doing what he does best (although I could be wrong . . .). For the remainder of the 80's, LYDON was content to churn out formula 'JOHNNY ROTTEN'-to-order type material that often incorporated bland Americanised rock backing. This only served to further entrench him in the mire of self-parody. Albums like 'HAPPY?' (1987) and '9' (1989) achieved only minimal commercial success although LYDON was back in the Top 20 in 1990 with 'DON'T ASK ME', the punk veteran's comment on the topical subject of the environment. The single was cannily included by 'Virgin' on a best of set, the hopefully titled 'GREATEST HITS – SO FAR' (1990). Then again, LYDON proved he could still cut the mustard with his late '93 LEFTFIELD collaboration, 'OPEN UP'. When LYDON lets rip, as he does here (a blood curdling wail of 'Burn, Hollywood, burn'), he is still the most frightening man in rock, no contest. Just to prove it, he hooked up once more with the original SEX PISTOLS line-up for the aptly titled 'Filthy Lucre' tour, appearing on 'Top Of The Pops' and scaring young children all over again with his gravity-defying hairdo.

Album rating: PUBLIC IMAGE (*9) / METAL BOX 1 (*10) / FLOWERS OF ROMANCE (*5) / LIVE IN TOKYO (*5) / THIS IS WHAT YOU WANT . . . THIS IS WHAT YOU GET (*4) / ALBUM (*7) / HAPPY? (*6) / 9 (*5) / GREATEST HITS – SO FAR compilation (*8) / THAT WHAT IS NOT (*4) / PLASTIC BOX boxed set (*8) / John Lydon: PSYCHO'S PATH (*4)

JOHN LYDON (b.31 Jan'56, Finsbury Park, London, England) – vocals (ex-SEX PISTOLS) / **KEITH LEVENE** (b. London, England) – guitar (ex-CLASH) / **JAH WOBBLE** (b. JOHN WORDLE) – bass / **JIM WALKER** (b. Canada) – drums (ex-FURIES)

—— (most singles just credit "PiL")

	Virgin	Warners
Oct 78. (7") *(VS 228)* **PUBLIC IMAGE. / THE COWBOY SONG**	9	–
Dec 78. (lp/c) *(V/TCV 2114) <3288>* **PUBLIC IMAGE**	22	–

– Theme / Religion I / Religion II / Annalisa / Public image / Low life / Attack / Fodderstompf. *(re-iss. Apr86 lp/c; OVED/+C 160) (cd-iss. Jun88; CDV 2114)*

—— **DAVE CROWE** – drums repl. WALKER who joined The PACK (with KIRK BRANDON) added **JEANNETTE LEE** – keyboards, synthesizer

Jun 79. (7") *(VS 274)* **DEATH DISCO. / NO BIRDS DO SING**	20	–

(12"+=) *(VS 274-12)* – Death disco megamix.

Sep 79. (7"/ext.12") *(VS 299/+12)* **MEMORIES. / ANOTHER**	60	–
Dec 79. (3x12"box)<lp> *(METAL 1) <3288>* **METAL BOX 1** <US-title 'SECOND EDITION'>	18	Jul80

– Albatross / Memories / Swan lake/ / Poptones / Careering / No birds / Graveyard / The suit / Bad baby / Socialist – Chant – Radio 4. *(re-iss. Feb80 as 'SECOND EDITION' d-lp/c; VD/TCVD 2512); hit UK No.46) (cd-iss. Jun86; CDVD 2512) (original; cd-iss. Jun90; MTLLCD 1)*

—— **RICHARD DUDANSKI** – drums (ex-101'ERS, ex-BASEMENT 5) repl. CROWE

—— (he had joined during Apr-Sep'79) (below French titles of above songs)

Nov 80. (lp/c) *(V/TCV 2183)* **PARIS AU PRINTEMPS (live 'PARIS IN THE SPRING')**	61	–

– Theme / Psalmodie (Chant) / Precipitamment (Careering) / Sale bebe (Bad baby) / La vie ignoble (Low life) / Attaque (Attack) / Timbres de pop (Poptones). *(re-iss. Mar84 lp/c; OVED/+C 50)*

—— (Jul80) Trimmed to a quartet when JAH WOBBLE went solo. / **MARTIN ATKINS** (b. 19 Aug'59, Coventry, England) (aka BRIAN BRAIN) – drums repl. DUDANSKI who joined RAINCOATS. (ATKINS was sacked Jul80, most of drums by LYDON and LEVENE)

Mar 81. (7") *(VS 397)* **FLOWERS OF ROMANCE. / HOME IS WHERE THE HEART IS**	24	–

(12"+=) *(VS 397-12)* – ('A'instrumental).

Apr 81. (lp/c) *(V/TCV 2189) <3536>* **FLOWERS OF ROMANCE**	11	

– Four enclosed walls / Track 8 / Phenagen / Flowers of romance / Under the house / Hymie's him / Banging the door / Go back / Francis massacre. *(re-iss. Mar84 lp/c; OVED/+C 51) (cd-iss. Apr90 & Mar94; CDV 2189)*

—— **KEN LOCKIE** – keyboards (ex-COWBOYS INTERNATIONAL, ex-Solo) repl. LEE / added (May82) **MARTIN ATKINS** – drums / **PETE JONES** – bass

Aug 83. (7") *(VS 529)* **THIS IS NOT A LOVE SONG. / PUBLIC IMAGE**	5	–

(12"+=) *(VS 529-12)* – Blue water / ('A'remix). *(re-iss. Jun88 cd-ep; CDT 14)*

—— LYDON + ATKINS were joined by US session people from New Jersey; **JOSEPH GUIDA** – guitar / **TOM ZVONCHECK** – keyboards / **LOUIE BERNARDI** – bass

	Virgin	Elektra
Sep 83. (2x12"/c) *(VGD/+C 3508)* **LIVE IN TOKYO (live)**	28	

– Annalisa / Religion / Low life / Solitaire / Flowers of romance / This is not a love song / Death disco / Bad life / Banging the door / Under the house. *(cd-iss. 1986; VGDCD 3508)*

May 84. (7"/ext.12") *(VS 675/+12)* **BAD LIFE. / QUESTION MARK**	71	–
Jul 84. (lp/c) *(V/TCV 2309) <60365>* **THIS IS WHAT YOU WANT... THIS IS WHAT YOU GET**	56	

– Bad life / This is not a love song / Solitaire / Tie me to the length of that / The pardon / Where are you? / 1981 / The order of death. *(re-iss. 1986 lp/c; OVED/+C 176) (cd-iss. Apr90; CDV 2309)*

Aug 84. (lp; as KEITH LEVENE & PiL) <XYZ 007> **THE COMMERCIAL ZONE**		–

– (as last album, with LEVENE's guitar parts more obvious)

—— Disbanded mid'84, but reformed by LYDON late '85 with on session **STEVE VAI** – guitar (ex-ALCATRAZZ) / **RYUICHI SAKAMOTO** – keys (ex-YELLOW MAGIC ORCHESTRA) / **GINGER BAKER** (ex-CREAM, etc) / **TONY WILLIAMS** (ex-MILES DAVIES, etc) / **RAVI SHANKER** – violin

Jan 86. (7"/12") *(VS 841/+12)* **RISE. / ('A'instrumental)**	11	–
Feb 86. (cd/c/lp) *(CD/TC+/V 2366) <60438>* **ALBUM**	14	–

– FFF / Rise / Fishing / Round / Bags / Home / Ease. *(re-iss. 1989 lp/c; OVED/+C 245)*

Apr 86. (7") *(VS 855)* **HOME. / ROUND**	75	–

(12"+=) *(VS 855-12)* – ('A'-lp version).
(d7"+=) *(VSD 855)* – Rise / ('A'instrumental).

—— (Feb86) LYDON recruited **LU EDMUNDS** – guitar, keys (ex-DAMNED, ex-MEKONS) / **JOHN McGEOGH** – guitar (of ARMOURY SHOW, ex-SIOUXSIE & THE BANSHEES) / **ALAN DIAS** – bass / **BRUCE SMITH** – drums (ex-RIP, RIG & PANIC, ex-SLITS, ex-POP GROUP)

	Virgin	Virgin
Aug 87. (7") *(VS 988)* **SEATTLE. / SELFISH RUBBISH**	47	–

(12"+=/c-s+=) *(VS/+C 988-12)* – The suit.

Sep 87. (cd/c/lp) *(CD/TC+/V 2455) <90642>* **HAPPY?**	40	

– Seattle / Rules and regulations / The body / Save me / Hard times / Open and revolving / Angry / Fat chance hotel. *(re-iss. Apr90 lp/c; OVED/+C 299)*

Oct 87. (7") *(VS 1010)* **THE BODY. / RELIGION (new version)**	100	

(12"+=) *(VS 1010)* – Angry.
(12") *(VSR 1010)* – ('A'extended remix) / ('A'-U.S. remix) / Angry.

—— trimmed to a quartet when EDMUNDS dispersed.

Apr 89. (7") *(VS 1181)* **DISAPPOINTED. / SAME OLD STORY**	38	–

(ext.12"+=/12"pic-d+=/3"cd-s+=) *(VS T/TY/CD 181)* – ('A'version).

Jun 89. (cd/c/lp) *(CD/TC+/V 2588) <91062>* **9**	36	

– Happy / Disappointed / Warrior / U.S.L.S. 1 / Sand castles in the snow / Worry / Brave new world / Like that / Same old story / Armada.

Jul 89. (7"/7"g-f) *(VS 1195)* **WARRIOR. / U.S.L.S. 1**		–

(ext.12"+=) *(VST 1195)* – ('A'instrumental).
(3"cd-s+=) *(VSCD 1195)* – ('A'extended).
(12") *(VSTX 1195)* – ('A'-Dave Dorrell remix) / ('A'instrumental).

Oct 90. (7"/c-s) *(VS/+C 1231)* **DON'T ASK ME. / RULES AND REGULATIONS**	22	

(cd-s+=) *(VSCD 1231)* – Warrior (original).
(12") *(VST 1231)* – ('A'extended) / Warrior (remix).

Oct 90. (cd/c/lp) *(CD/TC+/V 2644)* **GREATEST HITS – SO FAR** (compilation)	20	

– Public image / Death disco / Memories / Careering / Flowers of romance / This is not a love song / Rise / Home / The body / Rules and regulations / Disappointed / Warrior / Don't ask me / Seattle.

—— **MIKE JOYCE** – drums (ex-SMITHS, ex-BUZZCOCKS) repl. BRUCE

Feb 92. (7") *(VS 1390)* **CRUEL. / LOVE HOPE**	49	–

(cd-s+=) *(VSCD 1390)* – Rise (live) / Home (live).
(10"+=) *(VST 1390)* – Happy (live).

Feb 92. (cd/c/lp) *(CD/TC+/V 2681) <86263>* **THAT WHAT IS NOT**	46	–

– Acid drops / Lucks up / Cruel / God / Covered / Love hope / Unfairground / Think tank / Emperor / Good things.

—— In Nov'93, LYDON was credited on acclaimed dance hit & UK No.19 'Open Up' by LEFTFIELD / LYDON on 'Hard Hands' records.

—— Stop press:- Early '96, JOHN LYDON (ROTTEN) re-grouped with The SEX PISTOLS for summer tours in Britain, Europe and America.

– compilations, etc. –

Mar 99. (4xcd-box) *Virgin; PILBOX 1)* **PLASTIC BOX**		–

JOHN LYDON

	Virgin America	Virgin America
Jun 97. (cd/c) *(CDVUS/VUSMC 130) <44209>* **PSYCHO'S PATH**		

– Grave ride / Dog / Psychopath / Sun / Another way / Dis-ho / Take me / No and a yes / Stump / Armies / Open up.

Jul 97. (12"/cd-s) *(VUS T/CD 122)* **SUN. / GRAVE RIDE / PSYCHOPATH**	42	–

PUFF DADDY

Born: SEAN COMBS, 1970, Harlem, New York, USA. Growing up near Mt. Vernon, the up and coming millionaire MC inforced his humble quest in becoming a businessman by applying to Howard University (in Washington) and persuading his childhood chum-cum-rapper HEAVY D to employ him at 'Uptown Records'. As the months passed by, COMBS had worked his way up from dogsbody to A&R man to executive producer on FATHER MC's hit album 'FATHER'S DAY' (1990). However, his time with the company was short-lived when in 1992 (at Uptown's peak, following the success of MARY J BLIGE and HEAVY D AND THE BOYZ), COMBS was fired, shattering all images of the bigtime. He reluctantly founded a new imprint 'Bad Boy' in 1993. Working from his apartment with little more than a workforce of five, remixing the odd track here and there for various artists in the small hours of the morning. By the end of 1993 he had signed two of the record company's main artists: CRAIG MACK and old friend the NOTORIOUS B.I.G. The following year, MACK's single 'FLAVA IN YA EAR' had become a huge hit in the States, boasting guest appearances from LL COOL J, BUSTA RYMES and NOTORIOUS. The single went platinum and went on to be Bad Boy's first major success. The words of NOTORIOUS B.I.G. were spreading like wildfire through America, and, in 1995 he achieved a Top 10 spot with his single 'Big Poppa', and a double Platinum certificate for his debut album 'Ready To Die'. COMBS signed two R&B acts, FAITH EVANS (who was the B.I.G. man's wife) and TOTAL (who was also connected to the aforementioned rapper), the pair both going on to sell double platinum. After COMBS had remixed tracks for BOYZ II MEN and MARIAH CAREY, a feud between Death Row's 2PAC SHAKUR and infamous label manager SUGE KNIGHT erupted when SHAKUR was rumoured to be sleeping with FAITH EVANS. Verbal abuse was constantly spat from America's two coasts, and in September 1996, SHAKUR was shot dead. Six months later, NOTORIOUS B.I.G. was also killed, his assailants unknown. After the death of NOTORIOUS, COMBS abandoned his PUFF DADDY solo project to mourn the once great seminal rapper. However, he subsequently exploded onto the hip hop scene early '97 with the brash 'CAN'T NOBODY HOLD ME DOWN'; the worldwide No.1, 'I'LL BE MISSING YOU' (a revamp of The Police's 'EVERY BREATH YOU TAKE') was attributed to B.I.G. and featured his widow FAITH EVANS. 'NO WAY OUT' the debut album, followed in 1998 and won the Grammy award for best rap album and best performance for the aforementioned 'I'LL BE MISSING YOU'. Along with a contribution to the 'Godzilla' soundtrack, 'COME WITH ME', which hit Top 5 for him and its maker, JIMMY PAGE (of LED ZEPPELIN), PUFF DADDY issued his sophomore set 'FOREVER' in 1999. Its sharp melodies and sublime, chilled out temperament, helped it climb up the American Billboard charts, the DADDY had now come of age.

Album rating: NO WAY OUT (*6) / FOREVER (*6)

PUFF DADDY – vocals, etc + guests

	Arista	Arista
Mar 97. (c-s; PUFF DADDY featuring MASE) *(74321 46455-4)* **CAN'T NOBODY HOLD ME DOWN / ('A'mix)**	19	1 Jan97

(12"+=/cd-s+=) *(74321 46455-2/-1)* – ('A'mixes).

Jun 97. (c-s; PUFF DADDY & FAITH EVANS featuring 112 & THE LOX) *(74321 49910-4)* **I'LL BE MISSING YOU / ('A'mix)**	1	1

(12"+=/cd-s+=) *(74321 49910-1/-2)* – ('A'mixes).
(above was a tribute to the recently deceased NOTORIOUS B.I.G.)

Jul 97. (cd/c/d-lp; PUFF DADDY & THE FAMILY) <(8612 73012-2/-4/-1)> **NO WAY OUT**	10	1

– No way out / Victory / Been around the world / What you gonna do? / Don't stop what you're doing / If I should die tonight / Do you know? / Young G's / I love you baby / It's all about the Benjamins / Pain / Is this the end? / I got the power / Friend / Senorita / I'll be missing you / Can't nobody hold me down.

Oct 97. (c-s; PUFF DADDY & THE FAMILY) (74321 53944-4)
<79130> **BEEN AROUND THE WORLD / ('A'mix)** | 20 | 2
(cd-s) (74321 53944-2) – ('A'mixes).
(cd-s) (74321 53946-2) – ('A'mixes) / It's all about the Benjamins (mixes).
(12") (74321 53944-1) – ('A'mixes).

Jan 98. (c-s; PUFF DADDY & THE FAMILY) (74321 56197-4)
IT'S ALL ABOUT THE BENJAMINS / IT'S ALL ABOUT THE BENJAMINS (DJ Ming & FS Drum & Bass mix) | 18 | 2 Nov97
(cd-s+=) (74321 56197-2) – ('A'-original) / ('A'-Dave Grohl mix 2).

Mar 98. (c-s,cd-s; PUFF DADDY & The FAMILY featuring THE NOTORIOUS B.I.G. & BUSTA RHYMES) <79155>
VICTORY / VICTORY (mixes) | - | 19

Jul 98. (cd-s; PUFF DADDY featuring JIMMY PAGE) (666079-2)
<78954> **COME WITH ME / ('A'mix)** | 2 | 4 Jun98
(cd-s) (666284-5) – ('A'mixes).
(cd-s) (666284-2) – ('A'mixes).
(above taken from the film, 'Godzilla', issued on 'Epic' records)

—— In Jul'98, he featured on MASE's US Top 10 hit, 'Lookin' At Me'.

—— In Apr'99, he featured on FAITH EVANS' Top 10 hit, 'All Night Long'.

Aug 99. (c-s; by PUFF DADDY featuring HURRICANE G) (74321 69479-4) **PE 2000 / MISSING YOU** | 13 |
(12"/cd-s) (74321 69447-1/69479-2) – ('A'side) / Gangsta shit.
(cd-s) (74321 69498-2) – ('A'side) / Victory.

Aug 99. (cd/c) (74321 68906-2/-4) <73033> **FOREVER** | 9 | 2
– Forever (intro) / What you want / I'll do this for you / Do you like it . . . do you want it . . . (with JAY-Z) / Satisfy you (with R KELLY) / Is this the end, pt.2 (with TWISTA) / I hear voices (with CARL THOMAS) / Fake thugs dedication (with REDMAN) / Daddy speaks! (interlude) / Angels with dirty faces (with BIZZY BONE) / Gangsta SH*T / P.S. 112 / Pain (with G-DEP) / Reverse / Real niggas (with NOTORIOUS B.I.G. & LIL' KIM) / Journey through the life (with NAS & BEANIE SEAGAL) / Best friend (with MARIO WINANS) / Mad rapper / P.E. 2000 (with HURRICANE G). (explicit version; 74321 68905-2/-4)

Sep 99. (c-s; as PUFF DADDY featuring R. KELLY) <79283>
SATISFY YOU | - | 2

Oct 99. (c-s; PUFF DADDY feat. MARIO WINIANS & MAD RAPPER) (74321 71231-4) **BEST FRIEND / SATISFY YOU** | 24 |
(cd-s+=) (74321 71232-2) – ('A'side) / Do you like it . . . do you want it.
(cd-s) (74321 71231-2) – ('A'mixes).

PULP

Formed: Sheffield, England . . . 1981 originally as ARABACUS PULP by JARVIS COCKER while still at school. Following on in the tradition of geek heart-throbs like BUDDY HOLLY, JARVIS COCKER achieved the knicker-wetting adulation he'd always aspired to through sheer hard graft and the determination of the downtrodden. His long road to stardom began in the mid-80's with the release of the 'IT' mini-lp and a prestigious JOHN PEEL session. Further releases like the 'LITTLE GIRL AND OTHER PIECES' (1985) and 'DOGS ARE EVERYWHERE' (1986) EP's saw COCKER developing as a wry and sharply observant chronicler of working class drudgery and sexual frustration, his inimitable brand of camped-up showmanship unhampered by a spell in a wheel chair (his injuries allegedly sustained after falling from a window when trying to show off to a woman!). By the release of 'FREAKS' (1987), the core of the latter day PULP was in place, violinist/guitarist RUSSELL SENIOR and keyboardist CANDIDA DOYLE beginning to move away from the band's early LEONARD COHEN/FALL hybrid to a more arty MONOCHROME SET/ULTRAVOX (John Foxx era!) type vibe. Most of the band moved to London in the late 80's, with bassist STEVE MACKAY and drummer NICHOLAS BANKS stabilising the line-up. In this incarnation, the sleek, new-look PULP recorded the 'SEPARATIONS' (1991) album, a more ambitious affair which spawned the enduringly glitter-tastic 'MY LEGENDARY GIRLFRIEND' single. The track's success encouraged PULP to set up their own label, 'Gift', through which they released a string of early 90's EP's, becoming critical darlings with some sections of the music press alongside fellow pop sculptors like SAINT ETIENNE. It wasn't long before the enigmatic JARVIS and crew were on the roster of 'Island', releasing their breakthrough 'HIS 'N' HERS' album in 1994. Previewed by the driving, tongue-in-cheek query of the 'DO YOU REMEMBER THE FIRST TIME?' single (a short film was released to tie in with the track, featuring various biz figureheads candidly talking about their "first time"), the album expertly dissected the sexual undertow of working class Britain with a incisive accuracy, mordant humour and lashings of glam posturing. The album made the UK Top 10, becoming a consistent seller and setting COCKER up as a fashion icon (Bri-Nylon, national health specs etc.). The singer was to become a star on the same scale as BRETT ANDERSON (Suede) following the success of the landmark 'COMMON PEOPLE' single. A classic pop song that almost made No.2 on the back of the Britpop zeitgeist, the single was a brilliant portrayal of the British class divide set to an almost 80's-style synth-led backdrop. After the headlining act dropped out, PULP stepped in to put in one of the most acclaimed performances of their career at the 1995 Glastonbury festival, releasing the 'DIFFERENT CLASS' album in October to round off the most successful year to date in the band's career. With the social commentary as cutting as ever (the controversial 'SORTED FOR E'S AND WHIZZ') and their gift for effortlessly poignant pop intact ('DISCO 2000'), PULP consolidated their position as Britain's leading exponents of home-grown pop genius. A more downbeat COCKER returned late in '97 with the Top 10 hit, 'HELP THE AGED' (all monies going to that particular charity), while Britain awaited with much anticipation the porn-inspired 'THIS IS HARDCORE' set in '98. • **Songwriters:** COCKER + SIMON HINKLER collaborated on

debut. COCKER, SENIOR, C. DOYLE, MANSELL penned, until 90's when COCKER was main contributor. • **Trivia:** COCKER and MACKAY directed videos for TINDERSTICKS and The APHEX TWIN. • **Note:** Not to be confused with other band fronted by ANDY BEAN + PAUL BURNELL, who released in 1979; LOW FLYING AIRCRAFT single.

Album rating: IT (*4) / FREAKS (*4) / SEPARATIONS (*5) / PULPINTRO – THE GIFT RECORDINGS compilation (*7) / HIS 'N' HERS (*9) / MASTERS OF THE UNIVERSE collecttion (*5) / DIFFERENT CLASS (*9) / THIS IS HARDCORE (*8)

JARVIS COCKER (b. Sep'62) – vocals, guitar, piano / **SIMON HINKLER** – keyboards, vocals repl. PETER DALTON / **PETER BOAM** – bass repl. JAMIE PINCHBECK who had repl. DAVID LOCKWOOD / **DAVID HINKLER** – keyboards, trombone / **GARY WILSON** – drums (of ARTERY) repl. WAYNE FURNISS who had repl. JIMMY SELLERS who had repl. MARK SWIFT

—— plus guests **SASKIA COCKER + GILL TAYLOR** – b.vox / **TIMM ALLCARD** – keyboards

	Red Rhino	not iss.

Apr 83. (m-lp) (REDLP 29) **IT**
– My lighthouse / Wishful thinking / Joking aside / Boats and trains / Blue girls / Love love / In many ways. (cd-iss. Mar94 on 'Cherry Red'; CDMRED 112 w/drawn) (cd+=) – Looking for life / Everybody's problem / There was. (re-iss. cd Dec94 on 'Fire'; REFIRE CD15) (cd+=) – Looking for life. <US cd-iss. 1997 on 'Velvel'; 79750>

May 83. (7") (RED 32) **MY LIGHTHOUSE (remix). / LOOKING FOR LIFE** | | -

Sep 83. (7") (RED 37) **EVERYBODY'S PROBLEM. / THERE WAS** | | -

—— **RUSSELL SENIOR** – guitar, violin, vocals repl. DAVID
CANDIDA DOYLE – keyboards, vocals repl. SIMON who joined ARTERY then the MISSION)

—— **MAGNUS DOYLE** – drums repl. GARY, SASKIA, GILL + TIMM

—— **PETER MANSELL** – bass repl. BOAM

	Fire	not iss.

Nov 85. (12"ep) (FIRE 5) **LITTLE GIRL AND OTHER PIECES** | | -
– Little girl (with blue eyes) / Simultaneous / Blue glow / The will to power. (re-iss. Oct91)

Jun 86. (12"ep) (BLAZE 10) **DOGS ARE EVERYWHERE / THE MARK OF THE DEVIL. / 97 LOVERS / ABORIGINE / GOODNIGHT** | | (re-iss. Oct91)

Jan 87. (7"/ext.12") (BLAZE 17/+T) **THEY SUFFOCATE AT NIGHT. / TUNNEL** | |

Mar 87. (7"/12") (BLAZE 21/+T) **MASTER OF THE UNIVERSE (sanitised version). / MANON / SILENCE** | | (re-iss. Oct91)

May 87. (lp) (FIRE LP5) **FREAKS** | |
– Fairground / I want you / Being followed home / Master of the universe / Life must be so wonderful / There's no emotion / Anorexic beauty / The never-ending story / Don't you know / They suffocate at night. (cd-iss. Apr93; FIRE CD5) <US cd-iss. 1997 on 'Velvel'; 79752>

—— **STEPHEN MACKAY** – bass repl. STEPHEN HAVENLAND who had repl. PETER

—— **NICHOLAS BANKS** – drums, percussion repl. MAGNUS

Sep 90. (12"ep) (BLAZE 44T) **MY LEGENDARY GIRLFRIEND. / IS THIS HOUSE? / THIS HOUSE IS CONDEMNED** | | (re-iss. Oct91)

Aug 91. (12"ep/cd-ep) (BLAZE 51 T/CD) **COUNTDOWN. / DEATH GOES TO THE DISCO / COUNTDOWN (edit)** | | (re-iss. Oct91)

Oct 91. (cd/c/lp) (FIRE 33/22/11 026) **SEPARATIONS** | | -
– Love is blind / Don't you want me anymore / She's dead / Separations / Down by the river / Countdown / My legendary girlfriend / Death II / This house is condemned. (re-iss. Jun92; same) <US cd-iss. 1995 on 'Razor & Tie'; 2090-2>

	Gift	not iss.

May 92. (12"ep/cd-ep) (GIF 1/+CD) **O.U. (GONE GONE) / SPACE / O.U. (GONE GONE) (radio edit)** | | -

Oct 92. (12"ep/cd-ep) (GIF 3/+CD) **BABIES. / STYLOROC (NIGHTS OF SUBURBIA) / SHEFFIELD – SEX CITY** | | -

Feb 93. (7") (7GIF 6) **RAZZAMATAZZ. / INSIDE SUSAN (abridged; Stacks – 59 Lynhurst Grove)** | | -
(12"ep+/cd-ep+=) (GIF 6/+CD) – (B-side; A STORY IN 3 PARTS).

	Island	Polygram

Oct 93. (cd/c)(lp) (IMCD/IMCT 159)(ILPM 2076) <2076-518451> **PULPINTRO – THE GIFT RECORDINGS** (compilation) | | -
– Space / O.U. (gone gone) / Babies / Styloroc (nights of suburbia) / Razzamatazz / Sheffield – Sex city / Medley of stacks: Inside Susan (a story in 3 songs) Stacks – Inside Susan – 59 Lyndhurst Grove.

Nov 93. (7") (IS 567) **LIPGLOSS. / YOU'RE A NIGHTMARE** | 50 |
(12"+=)(cd-s+=) (12IS/CID 567) – Deep fried in Kelvin. (re-iss. Aug96) (re-iss. Oct96 on 7"red)

Mar 94. (7"/c-s) (IS/CIS 574) **DO YOU REMEMBER THE FIRST TIME?. / STREET LITES** | 33 |
(12"+=)(cd-s+=) (12IS/CID 574) - The babysitter. (re-iss. Aug96, hit 73) (re-iss. Oct96 7"biege)

Apr 94. (cd/c/lp) (CID/ICT/ILPS 8025) <524006> **HIS 'N' HERS** | 9 | Jun94
– Joyriders / Lipgloss / Acrylic afternoons / Have you seen her lately? / She's a lady / Happy endings / Do you remember the first time? / Pink glove / Someone like the Moon / David's last summer.(cd,c+=) – Babies (remix).

May 94. (7"ep/c-ep/12"ep/cd-ep) (IS/CIS/12IS/CID 595) **THE SISTERS EP** | 19 | -
– Babies / Your sister's clothes / Seconds / His'n'hers. (re-iss. Aug96) (re-iss. Oct96 on white 7"ep)

May 95. (c-s) (CIS 613) **COMMON PEOPLE. / UNDERWEAR** | 2 | -
(cd-s+=) (CID 613) – ('A'-Motiv8 mix) / ('A'-Vocoda mix). (re-iss. Aug96) (re-iss. Oct96 7"yellow/12")
(cd-s) (CIDX 613) – ('A'side) / Razzmatazz (acoustic) / Dogs are everywhere (acoustic) / Joyriders (acoustic).

—— Below second side (double A) caused controversy with tabloids and parents, due to it's mis-use of drugs in JARVIS's lyrics. JARVIS was to become the hero to most and villain to the few early in 1996 at a certain awards ceremony (skinny J.C. vs. St.MICHAEL & the bouncers; who won – you decide).

Sep 95. (c-s) *(CIS 620)* **MIS-SHAPES / SORTED FOR E'S AND WIZZ** [2] [-]
(cd-s+=) *(CID 620)* – P.T.A. (Parent Teacher Association) / Common people (live at Glastonbury). *(re-iss. Oct96 7"blue/12")*
(cd-s+=) – Common people (Motiv8 mix). *(re-iss. Aug96)*

Oct 95. (cd/c/lp) *(CID/ICT/ILPS 8041)* *<524165>* **DIFFERENT CLASS** [1]
– Mis-shapes / Pencil skirt / Common people / I spy / Disco 2000 / Live bed show / Something changed / Sorted out for E's and wizz / F.E.E.L.I.N.G.C.A.L.L.E.D.L.O.V.E. / Underwear / Monday morning / Bar Italia.

Nov 95. (c-s) *(CIS 623)* **DISCO 2000 / ANSAPHONE** [7] [-]
(cd-s+=) *(CID 623)* – ('A'-Motiv8 Gimp dub & Discoid mixes). *(re-iss. Aug96)* *(re-iss. Oct96 7"orange/12")*
(cd-s+=) *(CIDX 623)* – Live bed show (extended).

Mar 96. (c-s) *(CIS 632)* **SOMETHING CHANGED / MILE END** [10] [-]
(cd-s+=) *(CID 632)* – F.E.E.L.I.N.G.C.A.L.L.E.D.L.O.V.E (The Moloko mix) / F.E.E.L.I.N.G.C.A.L.L.E.D.L.O.V.E. (live from Brixton Academy). *(re-iss. Aug96)* *(re-iss. Oct96 7"pink/12")*

──── now without SENIOR, who wanted to pursue new projects

Nov 97. (c-s/7") *(C+/IS 679)* **HELP THE AGED. / LAUGHING BOY** [8] [-]
(cd-s+=) *(CID 679)* – Tomorrow never lies.

Mar 98. (c-s) *(CIS 695)* **THIS IS HARDCORE / LADIES MAN** [12] [-]
(cd-s+=) *(CID 695)* – Professional.
(cd-s) *(CIDX 695)* – ('A'mixes).

Mar 98. (cd/c/d-lp) *(ILPSD/ICT/CID 8066)* *<524492>* **THIS IS HARDCORE** [1]
– The fear / Dishes / Party hard / Help the aged / This is hardcore / TV movie / A little soul / I'm a man / Seductive Barry / Sylvia / Glory days / Day after the revolution.

Jun 98. (c-s) *(CIS 708)* **A LITTLE SOUL / COCAINE SOCIALISM** [22] [-]
(cd-s+=) *(CID 708)* – Like a friend.
(cd-s) *(CIDX 708)* – ('A'alternative mix) / ('A'-Lafayette Velvet revisited mix) / That boy's evil.

Sep 98. (c-s/cd-s) *(CIS/CID 719)* *<572418>* **PARTY HARD / WE ARE THE BOYZ / THE FEAR** [29]
(cd-s) *(CIDX 719)* – ('A'mixes by Stretch'n'Vern & All Seeing I).

– compilations, etc. –

Jun 94. (cd/c/lp) *Fire; (FIRE CD/MC/LP 36)* **MASTERS OF THE UNIVERSE – PULP ON FIRE 1985-86** [-]
– Little girl (with blue eyes) / Simultaneous / Blue glow / The will to power / Dogs are everywhere / The mark of the Devil / 97 lovers / Aborigine / Goodnight / They suffocate at night / Tunnel / Master of the universe (sanitised version) / Manon.

Mar 96. (d-cd/c/d-lp) *Nectar; (NTM CDD/C/LP 521)* **COUNTDOWN 1992-1983** [10] [-]
– Countdown / Death goes to the disco / My legendary girlfriend / Don't you want me anymore / She's dead / Down by the river / I want you / Being followed home / Master of the universe / Don't you know / They suffocate at night / Dogs are everywhere / Mark of the Devil / 97 lovers / Little girl (with blue eyes) / Blue glow / My lighthouse / Wishful thinking / Blue girls / Countdown (extended).

Jul 98. (cd) *Connoisseur; (VSOPCD 256)* **DEATH GOES TO THE DISCO** [-]

Sep 98. (cd) *E.M.I.; <79737>* **FRESHLY SQUEEZED (EARLY YEARS)** [-] [ ]

Nov 95. (7") *(IS 619)* **FIRE. / YOU'RE ONLY TRYING TO TWIST MY ARM** [ ] [-]
(cd-s+=) *(CID 619)* – All star.

Apr 96. (7"/7"g-f) *(IS/+G 624)* **INDIA. / GUTTER GIRL** [ ] [-]
(cd-s+=) *(CID 624)* – Let down.

Apr 96. (cd/c/lp) *(CID/ICT/ILPS 8046)* **PURESSENCE** [-]
– Near distance / I suppose / Mr. Brown / Understanding / Fire / Traffic jam in memory lane / Casting lazy shadows / You're only trying to twist my arm / Every house on every street / India.

Jun 96. (cd-s) *(ISG/CIS 639)* **TRAFFIC JAM IN MEMORY LANE. / DIFFERENT SAND** [ ] [-]
(cd-s+=) *(CID 639)* – Sick of waiting.

Aug 96. (7"/c-s) *(IS/CIS 641)* **CASTING LAZY SHADOWS. / FIFTEEN YEARS** [ ] [-]
(cd-s+=) *(CID 641)* – Half the way you were.

May 98. (7") *(IS 688)* **THIS FEELING. / THINK OF THE TIMES** [33] [-]
(cd-s+=) *(CID 688)* – Walk on by.
(cd-s) *(CIDX 688)* – ('A'side) / Near distance (demo) / Northern framing company (demo) / London in the rain.

Jul 98. (7"/cd-s) *(IS 703)* **IT DOESN'T MATTER ANYMORE. / ANOTHER DAY ANOTHER NIGHT / TAKE A RIDE** [47] [-]
(cd-s) *(CIDX 703)* – ('A'side) / Drone / Deathtrap.

Aug 98. (cd/c/lp) *(CID/ICT/ILPS 8064)* **ONLY FOREVER** [36] [ ]
– Sharpen up the knives / This feeling / It doesn't matter anymore / Street lights / Standing in your shadow / All I want / Behind the man / Never be the same again / Hey hey I'm down / Past believing / Turn the lights out when I die / Gazing down.

Nov 98. (7") *(IS 722)* **ALL I WANT. / TURN THE LIGHTS (demo)** [39] [-]
(cd-s) *(CID 722)* – ('A'side) / Along the sure / This feeling.
(cd-s) *(CIDX 722)* – ('A'side) / Never be the same again / All I want (acoustic) / Casting lazy shadows (acoustic).

┌──┐
│ **PUSSY GALORE** (dig out; Great Alt & Indie . . .) │
└──┘

┌──┐
│ **PYRAMID (see under ⇒ MATTHEWS, Iain)** │
└──┘

PURESSENCE

Formed: Oldham, Lancashire, England . . . May '92 by JAMES MUDRICZKI, NEIL McDONALD, KEVIN MATTHEWS and TONY SZUMINSKI. Inspired by, or even idolising the STONE ROSES after their legendary 1990 Spike Island concert, PURESSENCE embarked on their own creative sojourn. In the summer of '92, their first of three singles over the course of the following year, the 'PETROL SKIN' EP, was issued by Northern imprint, '2 Damn Loud'. However, it wasn't until Island's Toby Chalmers took control, that the band's indie-rock direction started to take shape. In 1995, now signed to the aforementioned major, PURESSENCE found a larger fanbase with the much-improved 'I SUPPOSE' 45, having also supported MARION on tour. An eponymous debut set was in the shops by '96, although the track 'CASTING LAZY SHADOWS', should really have fared better when released as an accompanying single. However, the quartet finally made their long-awaited chart breakthrough when the track, 'THIS FEELING', burst into the UK Top 40 in 1998. Although the JOY DIVISION/MORRISSEY-laden, 'IT DOESN'T MATTER ANYMORE', just failed to do a similar feat, their second album, 'ONLY FOREVER', notched up sufficient sales. The high-pitched singer, JAMES, subsequently landed a bit-part in the movie, 'Molly's Idle Ways', which starred SHAUN RYDER (of BLACK GRAPE), while the long-struggling PURESSENCE were happening big time in the Mediterranean sunspots of Greece and Israel.

Album rating: PURESSENCE (*6) / ONLY FOREVER (*6)

JAMES MUDRICZKI – vocals / **NEIL McDONALD** – guitar / **KEVIN MATTHEWS** – bass / **TONY SZUMINSKI** – drums

		2 Damn Loud	not iss.
Jul 92.	(12"ep) *(2DM 01)* **PETROL SKIN EP**	[ ]	[-]
	– Telekenesis / Suck the knife / Polystyrene snow / Petrol skin.		
Jan 93.	(7") *(45rev 9)* **SIAMESE. / SCAPA FLOW**	[ ]	[-]
	(above issued for the 'Rough Trade' singles club)		
Apr 93.	(12"/cd-s) *(2DM/+CD 02)* **OFFSHORE. / NONE HANDED / MIST**	[ ]	[-]

		Island	not iss.
May 95.	(12"/cd-s) *(12IS/CID 612)* **I SUPPOSE. / LET IT ALL GO / FREEFALL**	[ ]	[-]

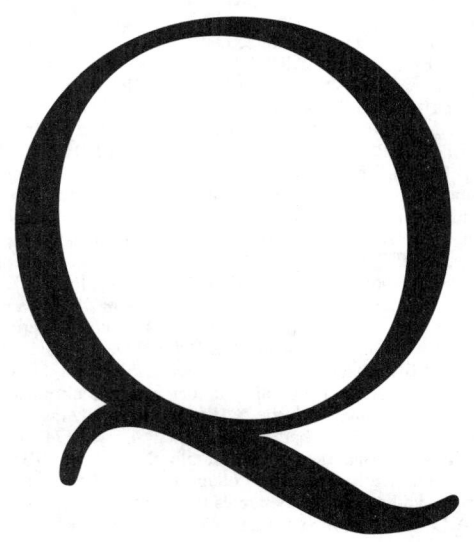

Suzi QUATRO

Born: SUZI QUATROCCHIO, 3 Jun'50, Detroit, Michigan, USA. Raised in a musical environment, she began playing in her father's jazz combo (the ART QUATRO TRIO) before she'd even reached her teens. At sweet sixteen she packed in school and formed her own garage band, SUZI SOUL & THE PLEASURE SEEKERS, with sisters NANCY, PATTI and ARLENE. An all-girl group in an almost exclusivly male domain, the quartet released a one-off single, 'NEVER THOUGHT YOU'D LEAVE ME', for the small 'Hideout' label in 1965. A further single, 'LIGHT OF LIFE', was issued on 'Mercury' the following year before the band changed their name to The CRADLE (without PATTI who later formed FANNY). In this incarnation, they were spotted by ace producer MICKIE MOST who duly signed up SUZI to his 'Rak' label at the dawn of the 70's. While the singer's flop 1972 debut single, 'ROLLING STONE' was self-penned, MOST quickly teamed her up with crack pop pensmiths/production duo, NICKY CHINN & MIKE CHAPMAN; the pair also worked with fellow 'Rak' artists MUD and SMOKIE and were already writing hits for SWEET. The latter act, along with SLADE, T.REX, etc., formed the vanguard of the 70's UK glam-rock scene within which QUATRO was to make her name. She hit paydirt in early 1973 with only her second single, 'CAN THE CAN', a million-selling No.1 hit that established her monster-hook, turbo-glitter sound and earthy sex appeal. The diminutive rock-chick sustained her assault on the charts with '48 CRASH' (Top 3) and 'DAYTONA DEMON' (Top 20) while her second million-selling No.1 arrived early the following year in the shape of the blistering 'DEVIL GATE DRIVE'. Yet amid all this UK success she was almost unknown in her native USA and an attempt to redress the situation was made in the mid-70's with QUATRO securing a high profile tour support slot to ALICE COOPER. A bad move all round, she was rewarded with only a couple of minor US hits while her absence from the British scene proved detrimental to her career. In 1977, QUATRO became more famous for her acting prowess in classic US comedy series 'Happy Days' (in which, surprise, surprise, she played a rock singer). This led to a new deal with 'R.S.O.' and three more major hit singles with 'IF YOU CAN'T GIVE ME LOVE', 'STUMBLIN' IN' (with SMOKIE'S CHRIS NORMAN), and the galloping pop gem, 'SHE'S IN LOVE WITH YOU' a year later. The 80's saw her make the transformation from leather-clad rebel to thespian as she increasingly concentrated on theatre work. • **Covered:** ALL SHOOK UP (Elvis Presley) / GLAD ALL OVER (Dave Clark Five) / etc. She and hubby TUCKLEY also wrote many songs. • **Trivia:** Her older brother MICHAEL QUATRO, a talented multi-instrumentalist, also released several lp's.

Best CD compilation: THE WILD ONE – THE GREATEST HITS (*6)

SUZI QUATRO – vocals, bass (with session people)

		Rak	Bell
Jul 72.	(7") *(RAK 134)* **ROLLING STONE. / BRAIN CONFUSION**	☐	-

—— SUZY was now augmented by future husband **LEN TUCKLEY** – guitar / **DAVE NEAL** – drums / **ALISTAIR McKENZIE** – keyboards

May 73.	(7") *(RAK 150)* **CAN THE CAN. / AIN'T YA SOMETHING HONEY**	1	-
Jul 73.	(7") *(RAK 158) <45-401>* **48 CRASH. / LITTLE BITCH BLUE**	3	-
Oct 73.	(7") *<45-416>* **48 CRASH. / CAN THE CAN**	-	-
Oct 73.	(lp/c) *(SRAK/TC-SRAK 505) <1302>* **SUZI QUATRO**	32	Mar74

– 48 crash / Glycerine queen / Shine my machine / Official suburban Superman / I wana be your man / Primitive love / Can the can / All shook up / Sticks and stones / Skin tight skin / Get back mamma / Shakin all over.

Oct 73.	(7") *(RAK 161)* **DAYTONA DEMON. / ROMAN FINGERS**	14	-

Feb 74.	(7") *(RAK 167) <45-609>* **DEVIL GATE DRIVE. / IN THE MORNING**	1	☐ Oct74
Jun 74.	(7") *(RAK 175)* **TOO BIG. / I WANNA BE FREE**	14	-
Aug 74.	(7") *<45-477>* **ALL SHOOK UP. / GLYCERINE QUEEN**	-	85
Sep 74.	(lp/c) *(SRAK/TC-SRAK 509) <1313>* **QUATRO**		

– The wild one / Keep a knockin' / Too big / Klondyke Kate / Savage silk / Move it / Hit the road Jack / Trouble / Cat's eyes / A shot of rhythm and blues / Friday / Devil gate drive.

Nov 74.	(7") *(RAK 185)* **THE WILD ONE. / SHAKE MY SUGAR**	7	-
Dec 74.	(7") *<45-615>* **KEEP A KNOCKIN'. / CAT'S EYE**	-	-

		Rak	Arista
Jan 75.	(7") *(RAK 191) <0106>* **YOUR MAMA WON'T LIKE ME. / PETER PETER**	31	☐
Apr 75.	(7") *(RAK 200)* **I BIT OFF MORE THAN I COULD CHEW. / RED HOT ROSIE**	☐	-
May 75.	(lp/c) *(SRAK/TC-SRAK 514) <4035>* **YOUR MAMA WON'T LIKE ME**	☐	-

– I bit off more than I could chew / Strip me / Paralysed / Prisoner of your imagination / Your mama won't like me / I can't trust love / New day woman / Fever / You can't make me want you.

Aug 75.	(7") *(RAK 215)* **I MAY BE TOO YOUNG. / DON'T MESS AROUND**	☐	-

—— **MIKE DEACON** – keyboards (ex-VINEGAR JOE) repl. McKENZIE

Feb 77.	(7") *(RAK 248)* **TEAR ME APART. / CLOSE ENOUGH FOR ROCK'N'ROLL**	27	-
Feb 77.	(lp/c) *(SRAK/TC-SRAK 525)* **AGGRO-PHOBIA**	☐	-

– Heartbreak hotel / Don't break my heart / Make me smile / What's it like to be loved / Tear me apart / Honky tonk downstairs / Half as much as me / Close the door / American lady / Wake up little Suzie.

Apr 77.	(7") *(RAK 256)* **ROXY ROLLER. / I'LL GROW ON YOU**	☐	-

—— In 1977 she featured on US TV series, 'Happy Days'.

		Rak	R.S.O.
Mar 78.	(7") *(RAK 271)* **IF YOU CAN'T GIVE ME LOVE. / CREAM DREAM**	4	-
Jul 78.	(7") *(RAK 278)* **THE RACE IS ON. / NON-CITIZEN**	43	-
Sep 78.	(lp/c) *(SRAK/TC-SRAK 532) <3044>* **IF YOU KNEW SUZI**	☐	37 Mar79

– Don't change my luck / Tired of waiting / Suicide / Evie / The race is on / If you can't give me love / Breakdown / Non-citizen / Rock'n'roll hoochie coo / Wiser than you. *(cd-iss. Apr96 on 'Laserlight'; 16159)*

Nov 78.	(7",7"clear; as SUZI QUATRO & CHRIS NORMAN) *(RAK 285) <917>* **STUMBLIN' IN. / STRANGER WITH YOU**	41	4 Jan79
May 79.	(7") *<929>* **IF YOU CAN'T GIVE ME LOVE. / NON-CITIZEN**	-	45
Sep 79.	(7") *<1001>* **I'VE NEVER BEEN IN LOVE. / SPACE CADET**	-	44

—— **BILL HURD** – keyboards, vocals + **JAMIE CRAMPTON** – guitar; repl. DEACON

Oct 79.	(7") *(RAK 299)* **SHE'S IN LOVE WITH YOU. / SPACE CADETS**	11	-
Nov 79.	(7") *<1014>* **SHE'S IN LOVE WITH YOU. / STARLIGHT LADY**	-	41
Nov 79.	(lp/c) *(SRAK/TC-SRAK 538) <3064>* **SUZI . . . AND OTHER FOUR LETTER WORDS**	☐	☐ Oct79

– I've never been in love / Mind demons / She's in love with you / Hollywood / Four letter words / Mama's boy / Starlight lady / You are my love / Space cadets / Love hurts.

Jan 80.	(7") *(RAK 303)* **MAMA'S BOY. / MIND DEMONS**	34	-
Mar 80.	(7") *(RAK 307)* **I'VE NEVER BEEN IN LOVE. / STARLIGHT LADY**	56	-
Apr 80.	(lp/c) *(EMTV/TC-EMTV 24)* **SUZI QUATRO'S GREATEST HITS** (compilation)	4	-

– Can the can / She's in love with you / 48 crash / Wild one / Too big / I may be too young / If you can't give me love / Devil gate drive / Daytona demon / Mama's boy / Tear me apart / The race is on / Your mama won't like me / I've never been in love. *(re-iss. Apr83; same)*

		Dreamland	Dreamland
Oct 80.	(7") *(DLSP 6)* **ROCK HARD. / STATE OF MIND**	68	☐
Oct 80.	(lp) *(2479 275) <5006>* **ROCK HARD**	☐	☐

– Rock hard / Glad all over / Love is ready / State of mind / Woman cry / Lipstick / Hard headed / Ego in the night / Lonely is the hardest / Lay me down / Wish upon me. *(re-iss. Apr90 on 'Connoisseur' cd/c/lp; 911 378/311/304) (re-iss. Jan91 on 'Document' cd/c/lp; CSAP CD/MC/LP 102)*

Jan 81.	(7") *(DLSP 8)* **GLAD ALL OVER. / EGO IN THE NIGHT**	☐	-
May 81.	(7") *<107>* **LIPSTICK. / WOMAN CRY**	☐	51 Jan81

—— **CHRIS ANDREWS** – keyboards, vocals; repl. HURD + CRAMPTON

		Polydor	not iss.
Nov 82.	(7") *(POSP 477)* **HEART OF STONE. / REMOTE CONTROL**	60	-
Nov 82.	(lp)(c) *(2311 159)(3100 647)* **MAIN ATTRACTION**	☐	-

– Heart of stone / Main attraction / Cheap shot / She knows / Two miles out of Georgia / Candy man / Remote control / Fantasy in stereo / Transparent / Oh baby.

Feb 83.	(7") *(POSP 555)* **MAIN ATTRACTION. / TRANSPARENT**	☐	-

—— In 1983, she re-signed to 'Rak' and hosted TV show, 'Gas'. She subsequently appeared in West End play, 'Annie Get Your Gun'.

		Rak	not iss.
Jul 84.	(7"/12") *(RAK/12RAK 372)* **I GO WILD. / I'M A ROCKER**	☐	-
Jul 85.	(7"/ext-12") *(RAK/12RAK 384)* **TONIGHT I COULD FALL IN LOVE. / GOOD GIRL (LOOKING FOR A BAD TIME)**	☐	-

		First Night	not iss.
Sep 86.	(7") *(SCORE 3)* **I GOT LOST IN HIS ARMS. / YOU CAN'T GET A MAN WITH A GUN**	☐	-

		WEA	not iss.
Jun 89.	(7") *(YZ 406)* **BABY YOU'RE A STAR. / ('A'instrumental)**	☐	-
	(12"+=) *(YZ 406T)* – ('A'extended).		

—— SUZY retired from music business, although she appeared in musicals 'Annie Get Your Gun' & 'Tallulah Who?' (the latter co-written w. Willy Russell). In the early 90's, she was still living in her Essex home with husband Len and children Laura and Richard; until '95 that is

		Now	not iss.
Dec 95.	(c-s/cd-s) (CA/CD WAG 248) **WHAT GOES AROUND /**	☐	-
Feb 96.	(cd/c) (WAG CD/MC 249) **WHAT GOES AROUND**	☐	-
Jun 96.	(cd-s) (CDWAG 252) **IF YOU CAN'T GIVE ME LOVE /**	☐	-

– compilations, etc. –

Jan 76.	(7") Big Tree; (16053) **CAN THE CAN. / DON'T MESS AROUND**	-	56
Jul 83.	(7") EMI Gold; (G45 35) **CAN THE CAN. / DEVIL GATE DRIVE**	☐	-
Nov 86.	(7"/ext-12") P.R.T.; (7P/12P 367) **WILD THING. / I DON'T WANT YOU (with REG PRESLEY)**	☐	-
Nov 87.	(lp) Biff!; (BIFF 4) **SATURDAY NIGHT SPECIAL** (cd-iss. Feb88 as 'ROCK 'TIL YA DROP'; BIFF 4CD)	☐	-
Apr 90.	(cd/c/lp) E.M.I.; (CD/TC+/EMS 1357) **THE WILD ONE – THE GREATEST HITS**		-

– Can the can / 48 crash / Daytona demon / Devil gate drive / Too big / The wild one / Your mama won't like me / I bit off more than I could chew / I may be too young / Tear me apart / Roxy roller / If you can't give me love / The race is on / She's in love with you / Mama's boy / I've never been in love. (cd+=) – Rolling stone / All shook up / Keep a knockin' / Wake up little Susie. (cd re-iss. Jul96 & Jun98 on 'Razor & Tie'; RE 2102-2) (cd re-iss. Mar99 on 'EMI Gold'; 499506-2)

Mar 96.	(cd/c) EMI Gold; (CD/TC GOLD 1004) **THE GOLD COLLECTION**	☐	-
Oct 97.	(cd/c) Go On Deluxe; (1018-2/-4) **THE VERY BEST OF SUZI QUATRO**	☐	-
Feb 98.	(cd) Disky; (WB 88586-2) **DAYTONA DEMON**	☐	-
Sep 98.	(cd) Connoisseur; (VSOPCD 260) **UNRELEASED EMOTION**	☐	-

Finlay QUAYE

Born: 1974, Leith, Edinburgh, Scotland ... to a native Scots mother who died of a heroin overdose when he was still at primary school; his Ghanian jazz-playing father was absent for most of FINLAY's troubled upbringing. Subsequently living between grandparents in Edinburgh and auntie/uncle in Manchester, he also spent a lot of his youth in London. With many notable industry connections stemming from his father's side of the family (i.e. uncle ERIC QUAYE, percussionist with OSIBISA, and half-brother CALEB QUAYE, a session man for the likes of ELTON JOHN), FINLAY naturally gravitated towards a career in music. Probably his most famous relative, TRICKY, is rather confusingly, actually QUAYE's nephew (his sister, MAXIN QUAYE is Tricky's mother!). The pair subsequently collaborated on a couple of tracks, one of which, 'DUPPY UMBRELLA' was a lengthy ode to magic mushrooms featuring a guest spot from IGGY POP (no relation!). One of his earliest musical endeavours was playing drums with the Rainbow Tribe hippy community in London, the reggae loving QUAYE eventually securing a deal with major 'Epic' records. In 1997, the fruits of his labour were revealed, the sun-kissed pop/reggae/hip-hop charm of his 'MAVERICK A STRIKE' album gaining him a wide cross-section of fans and a Top 3 UK chart placing. This acclaimed opus also spawned three major Top 30 hits, the biggest selling being 'EVEN AFTER ALL'. • **Songwriters:** Self-penned except; CROSSTOWN TRAFFIC (Jimi Hendrix).

Album rating: MAVERICK A STRIKE (*7)

FINLAY QUAYE – vocals; with session men

		Epic	Epic
Jun 97.	(c-s) (664455-4) **SUNDAY SHINING / MASHING UP LUCIFER: STONE THE DEVIL**	16	☐

(12"/cd-s) (664455-6/-2) – ('A'side) / Sunday best / I need a lover / Singing from the same hymn sheet.

Sep 97.	(c-s/cd-s) (664971-4/-2) **EVEN AFTER ALL / BURNING**	10	☐

(cd-s+=) (664971-5) – ('A'mixes).

Sep 97.	(cd/c/lp) (488758-2/-4/-1) **MAVERICK A STRIKE**	3	☐

– Ultra stimulation / It's great when you're together / Sunday shining / Even after all / Ride on and turn the people on / Way of the explosive / Your love gets sweeter / Supreme I preme / Sweet and loving man / Red rolled and seen / Failing / I need a lover / Maverick a strike. (cd re-iss. Jul98; same)

Nov 97.	(c-s) (665338-4) **IT'S GREAT WHEN WE'RE TOGETHER / MORNING PRACTICE**	29	☐

(cd-s+=) (665338-5) – ('A'mix) / Even after all (live).
(cd-s) (665338-2) – ('A'side) / ('A'mix) / Birds of one feather / Crosstown traffic.

Feb 98.	(c-s) (665606-4) **YOUR LOVE GETS SWEETER / EVERYBODY KNOWS**	16	☐

(cd-s+=) (665606-5) – Le saint des delinquents.
(cd-s) (665606-2) – ('A'side) / Can't be left alone / Maverick a dub.

Aug 98.	(cd-s) (666079-2) **ULTRA STIMULATION / WHITE PAPER**	51	☐

(c-s+=) (666079-4) – Colours dub.
(cd-s) (666079-5) – ('A'side) / Too many guns.

QUEEN

Formed: London, England ... early 1971 by guitarist BRIAN MAY, drummer ROGER TAYLOR and vocalist par excellence FREDDIE MERCURY, bassist JOHN DEACON completing the line-up. MAY had left school in 1963 (with a whopping ten O-levels), joining teen group The OTHERS who issued one single for 'Fontana' in 1965, 'OH YEAH'. Together with TAYLOR, he then went on to form SMILE in 1969, a project that met with little success although they did release one 45 for 'Mercury US', 'EARTH' / 'STEP ON ME'. The pair then hooked up with the African-born MERCURY and formed QUEEN in 1971, JOHN DEACON subsequently recruited on bass. After spending most

of 1972 in the studio, QUEEN were picked up by 'E.M.I.' when engineer John Anthony sent the company a demo tape. The group made their live debut in April '73 at London's famed Marquee club, but prior to any QUEEN release, FREDDIE MERCURY (as LARRY LUREX!) issued a one-off 'EMI' solo single that summer, 'I CAN HEAR MUSIC' / 'GOIN' BACK' (the former an old BEACH BOYS number). A month later, QUEEN simultaneously unleashed their eponymous Roy Thomas-Baker produced debut album, and single, 'KEEP YOURSELF ALIVE'. Influenced by LED ZEPPELIN and the more garish elements of glam-rock, the group had fashioned a unique, densely layered sound around MERCURY's impressive vocal acrobatics and MAY's fluid, coin-pick guitar style. Though the album didn't exactly set the charts alight, the band subsequently set out on a heavy touring schedule, supporting friends to be, MOTT THE HOOPLE, in late '73. Success eventually came with the piano-led bombast of the 'SEVEN SEAS OF RHYE' single, the track making the Top 10 in February '74 and paving the way for 'QUEEN II' the following month. The album reached No.5, consolidating QUEEN's new position as a headline act; while MERCURY was allegedly known to be fairly shy in real life, onstage he embodied everything that the word QUEEN implied with a passionate theatricality unmatched in rock music. The group really came into their own with the 'KILLER QUEEN' single, an infectious slice of jaunty high camp that reached No.2 in late '74. The following month, QUEEN released their strongest album to date, 'SHEER HEART ATTACK', an eminently listenable collage of killer hooks, neo-metal riffs, O.T.T. choruses and satin-clad dynamics that contained the likes of 'STONE COLD CRAZY' and the next single, 'NOW I'M HERE'. But QUEEN, to use a particularly crap pun, were finally crowned, commercially at least, with the 'BOHEMIAN RHAPSODY' single in late 1975. Surely one of the most annoyingly overplayed singles of all time next to 'Stairway To Heaven', the song was nevertheless something of an innnovation at the time, a grandiose epic that gave new meaning to the term 'rock opera'; forget concept albums, QUEEN could condense such lofty conceits into a meagre 6 minutes! The song was accompanied by what is widely regarded as the first promotional video, a quintessentially 70's affair that, in retrospect, resembles the title sequence of 'Doctor Who'. Nevertheless, the single gave QUEEN an astonishing nine-week run at the top of the charts over the Christmas period, ensuring similar success for the highly ambitious 'NIGHT AT THE OPERA' (1975) album. Apparently the most expensive project recorded up to that point, the record took QUEEN's bombastic pretensions to new limits, MERCURY's multi-tracked vocals setting new standards in studio mastery. While most of QUEEN's work was penned by MERCURY and MAY, TAYLOR and DEACON were also talented songsmiths, the latter contributing one of the group's loveliest songs, 'YOU'RE MY BEST FRIEND', its heartfelt simplicity counterbalancing some of the album's more excessive moments. 'NIGHT AT THE OPERA' also went Top 5 in the States, QUEEN having broken America with their irrepressible stage show earlier that year. Their ascent into world-beater status continued with 'A DAY AT THE RACES' (1976), another No.1 album which spawned a further massive hit in 'SOMEBODY TO LOVE' and contained the classic camp of 'GOOD OLD FASHIONED LOVER BOY'. The anthemic double header of the 'WE ARE THE CHAMPIONS' / 'WE WILL ROCK YOU' single reached No.2 the following year, presaging QUEEN's move away from operatic artifice to more straightahead chart rock. 'NEWS OF THE WORLD' (1977) and 'JAZZ' (1978) confirmed this, both albums selling well despite their lack of inventiveness. The riff-heavy 'FAT BOTTOMED GIRLS' could only have been recorded in the 70's, a gloriously unreconstructed paeon to shapely women that just wouldn't do in today's PC-controlled climate. While other rock monsters of the 70's were washed away on the tide of dour aggression that was punk, QUEEN looked to other musical forms to keep their sound fresh, namely 50's style rockabilly on the classic 'CRAZY LITTLE THING CALLED LOVE', MERCURY coming on like a camp ELVIS in the video, decked out in biker gear with a leather cap, of course, de rigeur. The group also flirted with disco on the bass-heavy 'ANOTHER ONE BITES THE DUST', a US No.1 that was later sampled by GRANDMASTER FLASH. Both tracks were featured on 'THE GAME' (1980), QUEEN'S most consistent album since the mid-70's and a transatlantic chart topper. After a partially successful sidestep into soundtrack work with 'FLASH GORDON' (1980), QUEEN rounded up the highlights of the preceding decade with a multi-platinum greatest hits set. While the band had been selling more records of late in the States than the UK, this trend was reversed with 'UNDER PRESSURE', a collaboration with DAVID BOWIE which toppped the British charts. 'HOT SPACE' (1982) ranks as one of QUEEN's dodgiest albums but with 'THE WORKS' (1984), QUEEN once again enjoyed a run of Top 10 singles with the likes of 'RADIO GA-GA' and 'I WANT TO BREAK FREE'. While these were listenable enough they lacked the pop brilliance of QUEEN's best 70's work. Live, QUEEN were still a massive draw, MERCURY's peerless ability to work a crowd evidenced on his famous Live Aid appearance in 1985. While the group's back catalogue subsequently clogged up the album charts, QUEEN returned with new material in the shape of 'A KIND OF MAGIC' (1986). Maybe Live Aid went to QUEEN's collective head, the album suffering from a kind of plodding stadium-friendly malaise that saw the group descending into self-parody. Nevertheless, the record made No.1, as QUEEN continued to tour the world and play to record-breaking audiences. The band returned to the fray with 'THE MIRACLE' in 1989, another No.1 album that contained few surprises. Nor did 'INNUENDO' (1991), although bearing in mind MERCURY's rumoured failing health, it'd be churlish to criticise what must have been a very difficult album for the singer to finish. On the 23rd of November, 1991, a matter of months after the album's release, MERCURY succumbed to AIDS. The following month, 'BOHEMIAN RHAPSODY' was re-released and once again topped the UK charts, raising money for research into the killer disease. A tribute concert was held the following Spring at Wembley Stadium, the cream of the music world's top-drawer stars paying their respects including ELTON JOHN, GUNS N' ROSES, GEORGE MICHAEL and DEF LEPPARD. Inevitably, QUEEN split although a posthumous album was released in 1995, featuring material that MERCURY had been working on prior to his death. While it didn't exactly add anything significant to QUEEN's stunning legacy, it tied up the loose ends, bringing the saga of one of music's most flamboyantly colourful bands to a dignified close.

• MERCURY covered: THE GREAT PRETENDER (Platters). The CROSS covered FOXY LADY (Jimi Hendrix), BRIAN MAY covered ROLLIN' OVER (Small Faces).

Album rating: QUEEN (*7) / QUEEN II (*6) / SHEER HEART ATTACK (*8) / A NIGHT AT THE OPERA (*7) / A DAY AT THE RACES (*5) / NEWS OF THE WORLD (*6) / JAZZ (*5) / LIVE KILLERS (*7) / THE GAME (*6) / HOT SPACE (*4) / FLASH (*3) / THE WORKS (*4) / A KIND OF MAGIC (*5) / LIVE MAGIC (*6) / THE MIRACLE (*6) / INNUENDO (*6) / QUEEN'S GREATEST HITS compilation (*9) / GREATEST HITS II compilation (*8)

FREDDIE MERCURY (b. FREDERICK BULSARA, 5 Sep'46, Zanzibar, Africa. In 1959, he moved with family to Feltham, Middlesex, England) – vocals, piano / **BRIAN MAY** (b.19 Jul'47, London, England) – guitar, vocals, keyboards / **ROGER MEDDOWS-TAYLOR** (b.26 Jul'49, King's Lynn, Norfolk, England) – drums, vocals / **JOHN DEACON** (b.19 Aug'51, Leicester, England) – bass, vocals

	E.M.I.	Elektra	
Jul 73. (7") (EMI 2036) <45863> **KEEP YOURSELF ALIVE. / SON AND DAUGHTER**			
Jul 73. (lp/c) (EMC/TCEMC 3006) <75064> **QUEEN**		83	Oct73

– Keep yourself alive / Doing all right / Great King Rat / My fairy king / The night comes down / Modern times rock'n'roll / Son and daughter / Jesus / Seven seas of rhye [US only] (hit UK No.24 Mar74) (re-iss. Aug82 on 'Fame' lp/c; FA/TCFA 3040) (cd-iss. Nov86; CDP 746204-2) (cd-iss. May88; CDFA 3040) <US cd-iss. Jun91 on 'Hollywood'+=; 61064-2> – Mad the swine, keep yourself alive (long lost retake) / Liar (1991 remix) (re-iss. Apr94 on 'Parlophone' cd/c; CD/TC PCSD 139)

	E.M.I.	Elektra	
Nov 73. (7") <45884> **LIAR. / DOING ALL RIGHT**	–		
Feb 74. (7") (EMI 2121) <45891> **SEVEN SEAS OF RHYE. / SEE WHAT A FOOL I'VE BEEN**	10		
Mar 74. (lp/c) (EMA/TCEMA 767) <75082> **QUEEN II**	5	49	May74

– Procession / Father to son / White queen (as it began) / Some day one day / The loser in the end / Ogre battle / The fairy feller's master-stroke / Nevermore / The march of the black queen / Funny how love is / Seven seas of rhye. (re-iss. Apr84 on 'Fame' lp/c; FA/TCFA 3099) (cd-iss. Nov86; CDP 746205-2) (re-iss. May88; CDFA 3099) <US cd-iss. Oct91 on 'Hollywood'+=; 61232-2> – See what a fool I've been / Ogre battle – 1991 remix / Seven seas of rhye – 1991 remix. (re-iss. Apr94 on 'Parlophone' cd/c; CD/TC PCSD 140)

	E.M.I.	Elektra	
Oct 74. (7") (EMI 2229) <45226> **KILLER QUEEN. / FLICK OF THE WRIST**	2	12	Jan75
Nov 74. (lp,red-lp/c-s) (EMC/TCEMC 3061) <1026> **SHEER HEART ATTACK**	2	12	Dec74

– Brighton rock / Killer Queen / Tenement funster / Flick of the wrist / Lily of the valley / Now I'm here / In the lap of the gods / Stone cold crazy / Dear friends / Misfire / Bring back that Leroy Brown / She makes me (stormtrooper in stilettoes) / In the lap of the gods . . . revisited. (re-iss. 1984 lp/c; ATAK/TCATAK 22) (cd-iss. 1984; CDP 746052-2) (cd-iss. Jun88; CDP 746206-2) <US cd-iss. Nov88 on 'Hollywood'+=; 61036-2> – Stone cold sober – 1991 remix) (re-iss. Aug93 on 'Parlophone' cd/c; CD/TC PCSD 129)

	E.M.I.	Elektra	
Jan 75. (7") (EMI 2256) **NOW I'M HERE. / LILY OF THE VALLEY**	11	–	
Apr 75. (7") <45268> **LILY OF THE VALLEY. / KEEP YOURSELF ALIVE**	–		
Nov 75. (7") (EMI 2375) <45297> **BOHEMIAN RHAPSODY. / I'M IN LOVE WITH MY CAR**	1	9	Dec75
Dec 75. (lp/c) (EMTC/TCEMTC 103) <1053> **A NIGHT AT THE OPERA**	1	4	

– Death on two legs (dedicated to . . .) / Lazing on a Sunday afternoon / I'm in love with my car / You're my best friend / '39 / Sweet lady / Seaside rendezvous / The prophet's song / Love of my life / Good company / Bohemian rhapsody / God save the Queen. (re-iss. 1984 lp/c; ATAK/TCATAK 27) (cd-iss. 1984; CDP 746050-2) (cd-iss. Jun88; CDP 746207-2) <US cd-iss. Aug91 on 'Hollywood'+=; 61065-2> – I'm in love with my car – 1991 remix / You're my best friend – 1991 remix. (re-iss. Aug93 on 'Parlophone' cd/c; CD/TC PCSD 130)

	E.M.I.	Elektra	
Jun 76. (7") (EMI 2494) <45318> **YOU'RE MY BEST FRIEND. / '39**	7	16	May76
Nov 76. (7") (EMI 2565) <45362> **SOMEBODY TO LOVE. / WHITE MAN**	2	13	
Dec 76. (lp/c) (EMTC/TCEMTC 104) <101> **A DAY AT THE RACES**	1	5	Jan77

– Tie your mother down / You take my breath away / Long away / The millionaire waltz / You and I / Somebody to love / White man / Good old fashioned lover boy / Drowse / Teo Torriate (let us cling together). (re-iss. 1984 lp/c; ATAK/TCATAK 28) (cd-iss. 1984; CDP 746051-2) (cd-iss. Jun88; CDP 746208-2) <US cd-iss. Mar91 on 'Hollywood'+=; 61035-2> – Tie your mother down – remix / Somebody to love – remix. (re-iss. Aug93 on 'Parlophone' cd/c; CD/TC PCSD 131) (lp re-iss. Nov97; LPCENT 29)

	E.M.I.	Elektra	
Mar 77. (7") (EMI 2593) **TIE YOUR MOTHER DOWN. / YOU AND I**	31	–	
Mar 77. (7") <45385> **TIE YOUR MOTHER DOWN. / DROWSE**	–	49	
May 77. (7"ep) (EMI 2623) **QUEEN'S FIRST EP**	17	–	

– Good old fashioned lover boy / Death on two legs (dedicated to . . .) / Tenement funster / White Queen (as it began).

	E.M.I.	Elektra	
Jun 77. (7") <45412> **LONG AWAY. / YOU AND I**	–		
Oct 77. (7") (EMI 2708) <45441> **WE ARE THE CHAMPIONS. / WE WILL ROCK YOU**	2	4	
Nov 77. (lp/c) (EMA/TCEMA 784) <112> **NEWS OF THE WORLD**	4	3	

– We will rock you / We are the champions / Sheer heart attack / All dead, all dead / Spread your wings / Fight from the inside / Get down make love / Sleeping on the sidewalk / Who needs you / It's late / My melancholy blues. (re-iss. 1984 lp/c; ATAK/TCATAK 20) (cd-iss. Jun88; CDP 746209-2) <US cd-iss. Mar91 on 'Hollywood'+=; 61037-2> – We will rock you – 1991 remix. (re-iss. Aug93 on 'Parlophone' cd/c; CD/TC PCSD 132)

	E.M.I.	Elektra	
Feb 78. (7") (EMI 2575) **SPREAD YOUR WINGS. / SHEER HEART ATTACK**	34	–	
Apr 78. (7") <45478> **IT'S LATE. / SHEER HEART ATTACK**	–	74	
Oct 78. (7") (EMI 2870) <45541> **BICYCLE RACE. / FAT BOTTOMED GIRLS**	11	24	Nov78
Nov 78. (lp/c) (EMA/TCEAM 788) <166> **JAZZ**	2	6	

– Mustapha / Fat bottomed girls / Jealousy / Bicycle race / If you can't beat them / Let me entertain you / Dead on time / In only seven days / Dreamer's ball / Fun it / Leaving home ain't easy / Don't stop me now / More of that jazz. (re-iss. 1984 lp/c; ATAK/TCATAK 24) (cd-iss. Jun88; CDP 746210-2) <US cd-iss. Jun91 on 'Hollywood'+=; 61062-2> – Fat bottomed girls – 1991 remix / Bicycle race – 1991 remix. (re-iss. Feb94 on 'Parlophone' cd/c; CD/TC PCSD 133)

	E.M.I.	Elektra	
Feb 79. (7") (EMI 2910) **DON'T STOP ME NOW. / IN ONLY SEVEN DAYS**	9	–	
Feb 79. (7") <46008> **DON'T STOP ME NOW. / MORE OF THAT JAZZ**	–	86	
Apr 79. (7") <46039> **JEALOUSY. / FUN IT**	–		
Jun 79. (d-lp/d-c) (EMSP/TC2EMSP 330) <702> **LIVE KILLERS (live)**	3	16	

– We will rock you / Let me entertain you / Death on two legs / Killer Queen / Bicycle race / I'm in love with my car / Get down, make love / You're my best friend / Now I'm here / Dreamer's ball / '39 / Keep yourself alive / Don't stop me now / Spread your wings / Brighton rock / Bohemian rhapsody / Tie your mother down / Sheer heart attack / We will rock you / We are the champions / God save the Queen. (re-iss. 1984 lp/c; ATAK/TCATAK 23) (cd-iss. Jun88; CDP 746211-2) <US cd-iss. Nov88 on 'Hollywood'; 61066-2> (re-iss. Apr94 on 'Parlophone' cd/c; CD/TC PCSD 138)

	E.M.I.	Elektra	
Jul 79. (7") (EMI 2959) **LOVE OF MY LIFE (live). / NOW I'M HERE (live)**	63	–	
Aug 79. (7") <46532> **WE WILL ROCK YOU (live). / LET ME ENTERTAIN YOU (live)**	–		
Oct 79. (7") (EMI 5001) **CRAZY LITTLE THING CALLED LOVE. / WE WILL ROCK YOU (live)**	2	–	
Dec 79. (7") <46579> **CRAZY LITTLE THING CALLED LOVE. / SPREAD YOUR WINGS**	–	1	
Feb 80. (7") (EMI 5022) **SAVE ME. / LET ME ENTERTAIN YOU (live)**	11	–	
Jun 80. (7") (EMI 5076) <46652> **PLAY THE GAME. / HUMAN BODY**	14	42	
Jul 80. (lp/c) (EMA/TCEMA 795) <513> **THE GAME**	1	1	

– Play the game / Dragon attack / Another one bites the dust / Need your loving tonight / Crazy little thing called love / Rock it (prime time) / Don't try suicide / Sail away sweet sister / Coming soon / Save me. (re-iss. 1984 lp/c; ATAK/TCATAK 21) (cd-iss. Jun88; CDP 746213-2) <US cd-iss. Jun91 on 'Hollywood'+=; 61063-2> – Dragon attack – 1991 remix. (re-iss. Feb94 on 'Parlophone' cd/c; CD/TC PCSD 134)

	E.M.I.	Elektra	
Aug 80. (7") (EMI 5102) **ANOTHER ONE BITES THE DUST. / DRAGON ATTACK**	7	–	
Aug 80. (7") <47031> **ANOTHER ONE BITES THE DUST. / DON'T TRY SUICIDE**	–	1	
Oct 80. (7") <47086> **NEED YOUR LOVING TONIGHT. / ROCK IT (PRIME JIVE)**	–	44	
Nov 80. (7") (EMI 5126) <47092> **FLASH. / FOOTBALL FIGHT**	10	42	Jan81
Dec 80. (lp/c) (EMC/TCEMC 795) <518> **FLASH GORDON (Soundtrack)**	10	23	

– Flash's theme / In the space capsule (the love theme) / Ming's theme (in the court of Ming the merciless) / The ring (hypnotic seduction of Dale) / Football fight / In the death cell (love theme reprise) / Execution of Flash / The kiss (Aura resurrects Flash) / Arboria (planet of the tree men) / Escape from the swamp / Flash to the rescue / Vultan's theme (attack of the hawk men) / Battle theme / The wedding march / The marriage of Dale and Ming (and Flash approaching) / Flash's theme reprise (victory celebrations) / The hero. (re-iss. 1984 lp/c; ATAK/TCATAK 26) (cd-iss. Jun88; CDP 746214-2) <US cd-iss. Aug91 on 'Hollywood'+=; 61203-2> – Flash – 1991 remix. (re-iss. Apr94 on 'Parlophone' cd/c; CD/TC PCSD 137)

	E.M.I.	Elektra	
Nov 81. (lp/c) (EMTV/TCEMTV 30) <564> **QUEEN'S GREATEST HITS** (compilation)	1	14	

– Bohemian rhapsody / Another one bites the dust / Killer queen / Fat bottomed girls / Bicycle race / You're my best friend / Don't stop me now / Save me [or US= Keep yourself alive / Under pressure] / Crazy little thing called love / Somebody to love / Now I'm here / Good old-fashioned lover boy / Play the game / Flash / Seven seas of Rhye / We will rock you / We are the champions. (cd-iss. Aug84; CDP 746033-2) (re-hit at No.7 – Dec91) (re-iss. Jun94 on 'Parlophone' cd/c; CD/TC PCSD 141)

	E.M.I.	Elektra	
Nov 81. (7"; by QUEEN and DAVID BOWIE) (EMI 5250) <47235> **UNDER PRESSURE. / SOUL BROTHER**	1	29	
Apr 82. (7") (EMI 5293) <47452> **BODY LANGUAGE. / LIFE IS REAL (SONG FOR LENNON)**	25	11	
May 82. (lp/c) (EMA/TCEMA 797) <60128> **HOT SPACE**	4	22	

– Staying power / Dancer / Back chat / Body language / Action this day / Put out the fire / Life is real (song for Lennon) / Calling all girls / Las Palabras de amor / Cool cat / Under pressure. (cd-iss. Jun88; CDP 746215-2) (re-iss. Aug89 on 'Fame' cd/c/lp; CDP/TC+/FA 3228) <US cd-iss. Mar91 on 'Hollywood'+=; 61038-2> – Body language – 1991 remix. (re-iss. Feb94 on 'Parlophone' cd/c; CD/TC PCSD 135)

	E.M.I.	Elektra	
Jun 82. (7") (EMI 5316) **LAS PALABRAS DE AMOR. / COOL CAT**	17	–	
Jul 82. (7") <69981> **CALLING ALL GIRLS. / PUT OUT THE FIRE**	–	60	
Aug 82. (7"/ext.12") (EMI/12EMI 5325) <69941> **BACKCHAT. / STAYING POWER**	40		

	E.M.I.	Capitol	
Jan 84. (7") (QUEEN 1) <5317> **RADIO GA GA. / I GO CRAZY** (ext.12") (12QUEEN 1) – ('A'dub version).	2	16	
Mar 84. (lp/c)(cd) (WORK/TCWORK 1)(CDP 7460160-2) <12322> **THE WORKS**	2	23	

– Radio ga ga / Tear it up / It's a hard life / Man on the prowl / Machines (or back to humans) / I want to break free / Keep passing the open windows / Hammer to fall / Is this he world we created?. <US cd-iss. Dec91 on 'Hollywood'+=; 61233-2> – Radio Ga Ga (12"mix) / I want to break free (12"mix) / I go crazy. (re-iss. Feb94 on 'Parlophone' cd/c; CD/TC PCSD 136)

	E.M.I.	Capitol	
Apr 84. (7"/ext.12") (QUEEN/12QUEEN 2) <5350> **I WANT TO BREAK FREE (remix). / MACHINES (OR BACK TO HUMANS)**	3	45	
Jul 84. (7"/12"pic-d) (QUEEN/12QUEENP 3) <5372> **IT'S A HARD LIFE. / IS THIS THE WORLD WE CREATED?**	6	72	

(12"+=) (12QUEEN 3) – ('A'extended remix).

Sep 84. (7"/'A'-Headbangers-12") (QUEEN/12QUEEN 4) <5424> **HAMMER TO FALL. / TEAR IT UP** — `13` `☐`

Dec 84. (7"/ext.12") (QUEEN/12QUEEN 5) **THANK GOD IT'S CHRISTMAS. / MAN ON THE PROWL / KEEP PASSING OPEN WINDOWS** — `21` `-`

—— In the mid 80's & before, each individual had also launched solo

Nov 85. (7"/ext-12") (QUEEN/12QUEEN 6) <5530> **ONE VISION. / BLURRED VISION** — `7` `61`

Feb 86. (7") <5568> **PRINCES OF THE UNIVERSE. / A DOZEN RED ROSES FOR MY DARLING** — `-` `☐`

Mar 86. (7"/ext.12"/ext.12"pic-d) (QUEEN/12QUEEN/12QUEENP 7) <5590> **A KIND OF MAGIC. / A DOZEN RED ROSES FOR MY DARLING** — `3` `42` Jun86

May 86. (lp/c)(cd) (EU/TCEU 3509)(CDP 746267-2) <12476> **A KIND OF MAGIC** — `1` `46`
– One vision / A kind of magic / One year of love / Pain is so close to pleasure / Friends will be friends / Who wants to live forever / Gimme the prize / Don't lose your head / Princes of the universe. (cd+=) – A kind of 'A kind of magic – Friends will be friends – Who wants to live forever. <US cd-iss. Jun91 on 'Hollywood'+=; 61152> – Forever, One vision.

Jun 86. (7"/7"pic-d) (QUEEN/+P 8) **FRIENDS WILL BE FRIENDS. / SEVEN SEAS OF RHYE** — `14` `-`
(12"+=) (12QUEEN 8) – ('A'extended mix).

Jul 86. (7") <5633> **DON'T LOSE YOUR HEAD. / PAIN IS SO CLOSE TO PLEASURE** — `-` `-`

Sep 86. (7") (QUEEN 9) **WHO WANTS TO LIVE FOREVER. / KILLER QUEEN** — `24` `-`
(12"+=) (12QUEEN 9) – ('A'-lp version) / Forever.

Dec 86. (d-lp/c)(cd) (EMC/TCEMC 3519)(CDP 746413-2) **LIVE MAGIC (live)** — `3` `☐`
– One vision / Tie your mother down / I want to break free / Hammer to fall / Seven seas of rhye / We are the champions / Another one bites the dust / Is this the world we created? / Bohemian rhasody / Radio Ga Ga / Friends will be friends / We will rock you / Under pressure / A kind of music / God save the Queen. (re-iss. Dec91 on 'Parlophone')

—— During this lull in QUEEN activity, FREDDIE MERCURY had released some solo singles and collaborated with MONTSERRAT CABALLE. TAYLOR had formed The CROSS

                                         Parlophone   Capitol

Apr 89. (c-s/7") (TC+/QUEEN 10) <44372> **I WANT IT ALL. / HANG ON IN THERE** — `3` `50`
(12"+=/cd-s+=) (12/CD QUEEN 10) – ('A'album version).

May 89. (lp/c/cd) (PCSD/TCPCSD/CDPCSD 107) <92357> **THE MIRACLE** — `1` `24`
– Party / Khashoggis ship / The miracle / I want it all / The invisible man / Breakthru / Rain must fall / Scandal / Was it all worth it / My baby does me. (cd+=) – Hang on in there / Chinese torture / The invisible man (ext). <US cd-iss. Oct91 on 'Hollywood' ++=; 61134-2> – Scandal (12"mix).

Jun 89. (c-s/7"/7"sha-pic-d) (TC+/QUEEN/+PD 11) **BREAKTHRU.' / STEALIN'** — `7` `-`
(12"+=/cd-s+=) (12/CD QUEEN 11) – ('A'extended).

Aug 89. (c-s/7"/7"clear) (TC+/QUEEN/+X 12) **INVISIBLE MAN. / HIJACK MY HEART** — `12` `-`
(cd-s+=/12"+=/12"clear+=) (CD/12 QUEEN/X 12) – ('A'extended).

Oct 89. (c-s/7") (TC+/QUEEN 14) <44457> **SCANDAL. / MY LIFE HAS BEEN SAVED** — `25` `☐`
(12"+=/cd-s+=) (12/CD QUEEN 14) – ('A'extended).

Dec 89. (c-s/7") (TC+/QUEEN 15) **THE MIRACLE. / STONE COLD CRAZY (live)** — `21` `☐`
(12"+=/cd-s+=) (12/CD QUEEN 15) – My melancholy blues (live).

                                        Parlophone Hollywood

Jan 91. (c-s/7") (TC+/QUEEN 16) **INNUENDO. / BIJOU** — `1` `☐`
('A'-Explosion mix; cd-s+=12"+=/12"pic-d+=) (CD/12 QUEEN/+P 16) – Under pressure (extended).

Feb 91. (cd/c/lp) (CD/TC/PCSD 115) <61020> **INNUENDO** — `1` `30`
– Innuendo / I'm going slightly mad / Headlong / I can't live with you / Don't try so hard / Ride the wild wind / All God's people / These are the days of our lives / Delilah / Hit man / Bijou / The show must go on.

Mar 91. (c-s/7"/7"sha-pic-d) (TC+/QUEEN/+P 17) **I'M GOING SLIGHTLY MAD. / HIT MAN** — `22` `☐`
(12"+=/cd-s+=) (12/CD QUEEN 17) – Lost opportunity.

May 91. (c-s/7") (TC+/QUEEN 18) **HEADLONG. / ALL GOD'S PEOPLE** — `14` `☐`
(cd-s+=/12"+=/12"pic-d+=) (CD/12 QUEEN/+P 18) – Mad the swine.

Oct 91. (c-s/7") (TC+/QUEEN 19) **THE SHOW MUST GO ON. / KEEP YOURSELF ALIVE** — `16` `☐`
(12"+=) (12QUEEN 19) – (Queen talks – interview).
(cd-s+++=) (CDQUEEN 19) – Body language.
(cd-s) – ('A'side) / Now I'm here / Fat bottomed girls / Los Palabras de amor.

Oct 91. (cd/c/d-lp) (CD/TC+/PMTV 2) <61311> **GREATEST HITS II** (compilation) (US title 'CLASSIC QUEEN') — `1` `4`
– A kind of magic / Under pressure / Radio Ga Ga / I want it all / I want to break free / Innuendo / It's a hard life / Breakthru / Who wants to live forever / Headlong / The miracle / I'm going slightly mad / Hammer to fall / Friends will be friends / The show must go on / One vision. (hit UK No.29 in May93) (US-version +=)– Bohemian rhapsody / Stone cold crazy / One year of love / Tie your mother down / These are the days of our lives / Keep yourself alive.

—— On the 23 Nov'91, FREDDIE lost his 2 year silent battle against AIDS. The previous day, it was announced in the news. The rumours had now ended.

Dec 91. (c-s/12"/cd-s/7") (TC/12/CD+/QUEEN 20) <64794> **BOHEMIAN RHAPSODY. / THESE ARE THE DAYS OF OUR LIVES** — `1` `2`

Jun 92. (12")(c-s) <64725> **WE WILL ROCK YOU. / WE ARE THE CHAMPIONS** — `-` `52`/`11`

Sep 92. (cd) <61265> **GREATEST HITS**

Apr 93. (c-ep/cd-ep/7"ep; by GEORGE MICHAEL & QUEEN) (TC/CD+/R 6340) <61479> **FIVE LIVE EP** — `1` `46` album

—— Somebody to love / Medley: Killer – Papa was a rollin' stone / These are the days of our lives (with LISA STANSFIELD) / Calling you.
(cd-ep) (CDRS 6340) – ('A'side) / Medley: Killer / Papa was a rollin' stone (with PM DAWN).
(12"+=) (12RS 6340) – Medley: Killer / Papa was a rollin' stone – instrumental.

—— <In the US, the EP's main track 'SOMEBODY TO LOVE', hit No.30; <64647>

—— In Feb'95, FREDDIE and BRIAN featured on EDDIE HOWELL's re-issued 1977 single 'THE MAN FROM MANHATTAN'.

Oct 95. (c-s) (TCQUEEN 21) **HEAVEN FOR EVERYONE / IT'S A BEAUTIFUL DAY** — `2` `☐`
(cd-s+=) (CDQUEEN 21) – ('A'-lp version).
(cd-s) (CDQUEENS 21) – ('A'side) / Keep yourself alive / Seven seas of rhye / Killer queen.

Nov 95. (cd/c/lp) (CD/TC+/PCSD 167) <62017> **MADE IN HEAVEN** — `1` `58`
– It's a beautiful day / Made in Heaven / Let me live / Mother love / My life has been saved / I was born to love you / Heaven for everyone / Too much love will kill you / You don't fool me / A winter's tale / It's a beautiful day (reprise) / Yeh / Track 13.

Dec 95. (c-s/7") (TC+/QUEEN 22) **A WINTER'S TALE. / THANK GOD IT'S CHRISTMAS** — `6` `☐`
(cd-s+=) (CDQUEEN 22) – Rock in Rio blues.
(cd-s) (CDQUEENS 22) – ('A'side) / Now I'm here / You're my best friend / Somebody to love.

Feb 96. (c-s/7") (TC+/QUEEN 23) **TOO MUCH LOVE WILL KILL YOU. / WE WILL ROCK YOU / WE ARE THE CHAMPIONS** — `15` `☐`
(cd-s+=) (CDQUEEN 23) – Spread your wings.

Jun 96. (c-s/7"pic-d) (TCQUEEN/QUEENP 24) **LET ME LIVE. / MY FAIRY KING / DOIN' ALRIGHT / LIAR** — `9` `☐`
(cd-s) (CDQUEEN 24) – ('A'side) / Fat bottomed girls / Bicycle race / Don't stop me now.

Nov 96. (c-s) (TCQUEEN 25) **YOU DON'T FOOL ME / ('A'remix)** — `17` `-`
(12") (12QUEEN 25) – ('A'-Freddie's club + revenge mixes).
(cd-s+=) (CDQUEEN 25) – ('A'-Dancing Divas mix) / ('A'-sexy club mix).

Nov 97. (cd/c/d-lp) (823091-2/-4/-1) **QUEEN ROCKS** — `7` `☐`
– No-one but you / We will rock you / Tie your mother down / Seven seas of rhye / I can't live with you / Hammer to fall / Stone cold crazy / Fat bottomed girls / Keep yourself alive / Tear it up / One vision / Killer queen / Sheer heart attack / I'm in love with my car / Put out the fire / Headlong / It's late / I want it all.

Jan 98. (c-s) (TCQUEEN 27) **NO-ONE BUT YOU / TIE YOUR MOTHER DOWN** — `13` `☐`
(12"+=/cd-s+=) (QUEENPD/CDQUEEN 27) – We will rock you (mix) / Gimme the prize (mix).

Nov 98. (c-s; by QUEEN / WYCLEF JEAN featuring PRAS MICHEL & FREE) (DRMC 22364) **ANOTHER ONE BITES THE DUST / (mix)** — `5` `☐`
(12"+=/cd-s+=) (DRM T/CD 22364) – (Wyclef Jean remix) / (Black Rock Star remix).
(above from the movie, 'Small Soldiers', released on 'Dreamworks')

Dec 99. (7"pic-d; QUEEN & DAVID BOWIE) (QUEENPD 28) **UNDER PRESSURE. / BOHEMIAN RHAPSODY** — `14` `☐`
(c-s+=/cd-s+=) (TC/CD QUEEN 28) – Thank God it's Christmas.
(cd-s) (CDQUEENS 28) – ('A'mixes).

– compilations, etc. –

on 'EMI'UK / 'Capitol'US, unless otherwise mentioned.
Dec 85. (14xlp-box) (QB 1) **THE COMPLETE WORKS** `☐` `☐`
Nov 88. (3"cd-ep) (QUECD 1) **SEVEN SEAS OF RHYE / SEE WHAT A FOOL I'VE BEEN / FUNNY HOW LOVE IS** `☐` `☐`
Nov 88. (3"cd-ep) (QUECD 2) **KILLER QUEEN / FLICK OF THE WRIST / BRIGHTON ROCK** `☐` `☐`
Nov 88. (3"cd-ep) (QUECD 3) **BOHEMIAN RHAPSODY / I'M IN LOVE WITH MY CAR / YOU'RE MY BEST FRIEND** `☐` `☐`
Nov 88. (3"cd-ep) (QUECD 4) **SOMEBODY TO LOVE / WHITE MAN / TIE YOUR MOTHER DOWN** `☐` `☐`
Nov 88. (3"cd-ep) (QUECD 5) **GOOD OLD FASHIONED LOVER BOY / DEATH ON TWO LEGS (DEDICATED TO . . .) / TENEMENT FUNSTER / WHITE QUEEN (AS IT BEGAN)** `☐` `☐`
Nov 88. (3"cd-ep) (QUECD 6) **WE ARE THE CHAMPIONS / WE WILL ROCK YOU / FAT BOTTOMED GIRLS** `☐` `☐`
Nov 88. (3"cd-ep) (QUECD 7) **CRAZY LITTLE THING CALLED LOVE / SPREAD YOUR WINGS / FLASH** `☐` `☐`
Nov 88. (3"cd-ep) (QUECD 8) **ANOTHER ONE BITES THE DUST / DRAGON ATTACK / LAS PALABRAS DE AMOR** `☐` `☐`
Nov 88. (3"cd-ep) (QUECD 9) **UNDER PRESSURE / SOUL BROTHER / BODY LANGUAGE** `☐` `☐`
Nov 88. (3"cd-ep) (QUECD 10) **RADIO GA GA / I GO CRAZY / HAMMER TO FALL** `☐` `☐`
Nov 88. (3"cd-ep) (QUECD 11) **I WANT TO BREAK FREE / MACHINES (OR BACK TO HUMANS) / IT'S A HARD LIFE** `☐` `☐`
Nov 88. (3"cd-ep) (QUECD 12) **A KIND OF MAGIC / A DOZEN RED ROSES FOR MY DARLING / ONE VISION** `☐` `☐`
Dec 89. (lp/c/cd) Band of Joy; (BOJ LP/MC/CD 001) **QUEEN AT THE BEEB (live)** `67` `☐`
Jun 92. (cd) Parlophone; <CDPCSD 725> / Hollywood; <61104> **QUEEN: LIVE AT WEMBLEY (live)** `2` `53`
– (above was originally issued UK on video)
Oct 94. (d-cd/d-c) Parlophone; (CD/TC PCSD 161) **GREATEST HITS 1 & 2** `37` `☐`
Dec 95. (20xcd-box) E.M.I.; (QUEENBOX 20) **ULTIMATE QUEEN** `☐` `☐`
Nov 99. (cd/c/d-lp) Parlophone; (523452-2/-4/-1) **GREATEST HITS III** (hits/collaborations & solo material) `5` `☐`
– The show must go on / Under pressure / Barcelona / Too much love / Somebody to love / You don't fool me / Heaven for everyone / Las palabras / Driven by you / Living on my own / Let me live / The great pretender / Princess of the universe / Another one bites the dust / No one but you / These are the days of our lives / Thank God it's Christmas.

FREDDIE MERCURY

	C.B.S.	Columbia

Sep 84. (7"/7"pic-d/ext.12") (A/WA/TA 4375) <04606> **LOVE KILLS. / ROT WANG'S PARTY** (by Giorgio Moroder) — **10** | **69**
(above from film 'Metropolis' & co-written w / Georgio Moroder)

Apr 85. (7"/ext.12") (A/TA 6019) <04869> **I WAS BORN TO LOVE YOU. / STOP ALL THE FIGHTING** — **11** | **76**
(d7"+=) (DA 6019) – Love kills (extended) / Stop all the fighting (extended).

May 85. (lp/c/cd) (CBS/+40/CD 86312) <40071> **MR. BAD GUY** — **6** |
– Let's turn it on * / Made in Heaven / I was born to love you * / Foolin' around / Mr. Bad guy / Man made Paradise / There must be more to life than this / Living on my own * / Your kind of lover / My love is dangerous / Love me like there's no tomorrow. (c+cd+=) – (* extended tracks).

Jul 85. (7"/7"sha-pic-d) (A/WA 6413) **MADE IN HEAVEN** (remix). / **SHE BLOWS HOT AND COLD** — **57** | **–**
(ext.12"+=) (TA 6413) – ('A'extended).

Sep 85. (7"/12"/12"g-f) (A/TA/GA 6555) <05455> **LIVING ON MY OWN. / MY LOVE IS DANGEROUS** — **50** | **–**

Oct 85. (7") **LIVING ON MY OWN. / SHE BLOWS HOT AND COLD** — **–** | **–**

Nov 85. (7"/ext.12") (A/TA 6725) **LOVE ME LIKE THERE IS NO TOMORROW. / LET'S TURN IT ON** — **–** | **–**
(below from Dave Clark musical 'Time')

	E.M.I.	not iss.
	Parlophone	Capitol

May 86. (7"/ext.12") (EMI/+12 5559) **TIME. / TIME** (instrumental) — |

Feb 87. (7"/7"sha-pic-d) (R/RP 6151) <5696> **THE GREAT PRETENDER. / EXERCISES IN FREE LOVE** — **4** |
(12"+=) (12R 6151) – ('A'extended).

FREDDIE MERCURY with MONTSERRAT CABALLE

—— (with female Spanish opera star)

	Polydor	Hollywood

Oct 87. (7") (POSP 887) **BARCELONA. / EXERCISES IN FREE LOVE** (her version) — **8** |
(c-s+=/12"+=/12"pic-d+=/cd-s+=) (POSP C/X/P/CD 887) – ('A'extended).

Oct 88. (lp/c)(cd) (POLH/+C 44)(837277-2) **BARCELONA** — **25** |
– Barcelona / La Japonaise / The fallen priest / Ensueno / The golden boy / Guide me home / How can I go on / Overture piccante. (re-iss. Aug92, hit UK No.15)

Oct 88. (7") (POSP 23) **THE GOLDEN BOY. / THE FALLEN PRIEST** — |
(12"+=)(cd-s+=) (POSPX 23)(PZ 23CD) – ('A'instrumental).

Jan 89. (7"/7"pic-d) (POSP/POSX 29) **HOW CAN I GO ON. / OVERTURE PICCANTE** — |
(12"+=)(cd-s+=) (POSPX 29)(PZ 29CD) – Guide me home.
(below were posthumous releases)

Jul 92. (7"/c-s/cd-s) (PO/+CS/CD 221) **BARCELONA. / EXCERCISES IN FREE LOVE** — **2** |
(12"+=) (P 221) – ('A'extended).

Oct 92. (7"/c-s) **HOW CAN I GO ON. / THE GOLDEN BOY** — |
(cd-s+=) – The fallen priest.
(12"+=/cd-s+=) – Guide me home / Overture piccante.

	Parlophone	Hollywood

Nov 92. (cd/c/lp) (CD/TC+/PCSD 124) **THE FREDDIE MERCURY ALBUM** (compilation) — **4** |
– The great pretender / Foolin' around / Time / Your kind of love / Exercises in free love / In my defence / Mr. Bad guy / Let's turn it on / Living on my own / Love kills / Barcelona (w / MONSERRAT CABALLEE).

Dec 92. (c-s/7") (TC+/R 6331) **IN MY DEFENCE. / LOVE KILLS** (original) — **8** |
(cd-s+=) (CDR 6331) – Mr. Bad guy / Living on my own (mix).

Jan 93. (c-s/7") (TC+/R 6336) **THE GREAT PRETENDER. / STOP ALL THE FIGHTING** — **29** |
(cd-s+=) (CDR 6336) – Exercises in free love / ('A'-Malouf mix).

Jul 93. (c-s/7") (TC+/R 6355) **LIVING ON MY OWN. / ('A'mix)** — **1** |
(12"+=/cd-s+=) (12R/CDR 6355) – ('A'mixes).

—— **JOHN DEACON** played bass on The IMMORTALS May'86 'M.C.A.' single 'NO TURNING BACK', from the film 'Biggles'.

BRIAN MAY

—— with **EDDIE VAN HALEN** – guitar / **PHIL CHEN** – bass / **FRED MANDEL** – keyboards / **ALAN GRATZER** – drums etc.

	E.M.I.	Capitol

Oct 83. (7"; as BRIAN MAY & FRIENDS) (EMI 5436) **STARFLEET. / SON OF STARFLEET** — **65** | **–**

Oct 83. (7"; as BRIAN MAY & FRIENDS) <B-5278> **STARFLEET. / STARFLEET** (extended) — **–** | **–**

Oct 83. (m-lp/c; as BRIAN MAY & FRIENDS) (SFLT 107806-1/-4) <15014> **STARFLEET PROJECT** — **35** |
– Starfleet / Let me out / Bluesbreakers.

—— In the Autumn of '89, BRIAN MAY wrote the song 'WHO WANTS TO LIVE FOREVER' and gave it to charity for single by youngsters IAN MEESON & BELINDA GHILETT; 'EMI' 7"/12" (ODO/12ODO 112)

	Parlophone	Hollywood

Nov 91. (7"/c-s) (R/TCR 6304) **DRIVEN BY YOU. / JUST ONE LIFE** (dedicated to the memory of Philip Sayer) — **6** |
(b-guitar version; 12"+=/cd-s+=) (12R/CDR 6034) – Driven by you (Ford Ad version).

Sep 92. (7"/c-s) (R/TCR 6320) **TOO MUCH LOVE WILL KILL YOU. / I'M SCARED** — **5** |
(cd-s+=/s-cd-s+=) (CDR/+S 6320) – Driven by you (feat. COZY POWELL + NEIL MURRAY).

Oct 92. (cd/c/lp) (CD/C+/PCSD 123) **BACK TO THE LIGHT** — **6** |
– The dark / Back to the light / Love token / Resurrection / Too much love will kill

you / Driven by you / Nothin' but blue / I'm scared / Last horizon / Let your heart rule your head / Just one life / Rollin' over. (re-iss. Jun93 in gold-cd; CDPCSDX 123)

—— In Oct'92, BRIAN featured on HANK MARVIN's (Shadows) version of QUEEN's song 'WE ARE THE CHAMPIONS'.

Nov 92. (7"/c-s) (R/TCR 6329) **BACK TO THE LIGHT. / NOTHING BUT BLUE** (guitar version) — **19** |
(B-guitar cd-s=) (CDR 6329) – Blues breaker.
(cd-s) (CDRX 6329) – ('A'side) / Star fleet / Let me out.

Jun 93. (c-s; by BRIAN MAY with COZY POWELL) (TCR 6351) **RESURRECTION / LOVE TOKEN** — **23** |
(12"pic-d+=/cd-s+=) (12RPF/CDRS 6351) – Too much love will kill you (live).
(cd-s) (CDR 6351) – ('A'side) / Driven by you (two) / Back to the light (live) / Tie your mother down (live).

Dec 93. (7"/c-s) (R/TCR 6371) **LAST HORIZON. / LET YOUR HEART RULE YOUR HEAD** — **51** |
(cd-s/s-cd-s) (CDR/+S 6371) – ('A'side) / ('A'live) / We will rock you (live) / ('A'album mix).

—— **MAY** – vox, guitar with **COZY POWELL** – drums / **NEIL MURRAY** – bass / **SPIKE EDNEY** – keyboards / **JAMIE MOSES** – guitar, vocals / **CATHY PORTER + SHELLEY PRESTON** – vox

Feb 94. (cd/c/d-lp; by BRIAN MAY BAND) (CD/C+/PCSD 150) **LIVE AT THE BRIXTON ACADEMY** (live London, 15th June 1993) — **20** |
– Back to the light / Driven by you / Tie your mother down / Love token / Headlong / Love of my life / '39 – Let your heart rule your head / Too much love will kill you / Since you've been gone / Now I'm here / Guitar extravagance / Resurrection / Last horizon / We will rock you / Hammer to fall.

May 98. (7") (R 6498) **THE BUSINESS** (Rock On Cozy mix). / **MAYBE BABY** — **51** |
(cd-s+=) (CDR 6498) – (Brian talks) / ('A'-CD-Rom video).

Jun 98. (cd/c/lp) (494973-2/-4/-1) **ANOTHER WORLD** — **23** |
– Space / The business / China belle / Why don't we try again / On my way up / Cyborg / Guv'nor / Wilderness / Slow down / One rainy wish / All the way from Memphis / Another world.

Aug 98. (c-s/cd-s) (TCR/CDR 6504) **WHY DON'T WE TRY AGAIN / ONLY MAKE BELIEVE / F.B.I.** — **44** | **–**

– (MAY) compilations, etc. –

Nov 95. (cd) Javelin; (HADCD 190) **THEMES AND DREAMS** — | **–**

Dec 95. (cd-s) Koch; (34337-2) **BLACK WHITE HOUSE** — | **–**

—— with APPICE (veteran drummer) + SLASH (of Guns N' Roses)

Feb 96. (cd-s; by BRIAN MAY with CARMINE APPICE'S GUITAR ZEUS) **NOBODY KNEW (BLACK WHITE HOUSE) / NOBODY KNEW (BLACK WHITE HOUSE) (long version)** — | **–**

ROGER TAYLOR

	E.M.I.	Elektra

Aug 77. (7") (EMI 2679) **I WANNA TESTIFY. / TURN ON THE T.V.** — | **–**

Apr 81. (7") (EMI 5157) **FUTURE MANAGEMENT. / LAUGH OR CRY** — **49** | **–**

Apr 81. (lp/c) (EMC/TCEMC 3369) <5E-522> **FUN IN SPACE** — **18** | **–**
– No violins / Laugh or cry / Future management / Let's get crazy / My country I & II / Good times are now / Magic is loose / Interlude in Constantinople / Airheads / Fun in space. (cd-iss. May96 on 'Parlophone'; CDPCS 7380)

Apr 81. (7") <E-47151> **LET'S GET CRAZY. / LAUGH OR CRY** — **–** | **–**

Jun 81. (7") (EMI 5200) **MY COUNTRY. / FUN IN SPACE** — |

	E.M.I.	Capitol

Jun 84. (7"/ext.12") (EMI/+12 5478) **MAN ON FIRE. / KILLING TIME** — **66** | **–**

Jul 84. (lp/c) (RTA/TCRTA 1) <EJ-240137-1> **STRANGE FRONTIER** — **30** |
– Strange frontier / Beautiful dreams / Man on fire / Racing in the street / Masters of war / Killing time / Abandon fire / Young love / It's an illusion / I cry for you (love, hope & confusion). (cd-iss. May96 on 'Parlophone'; CDPCS 7381)

Aug 84. (7") (EMI 5490) **STRANGE FRONTIER. / I CRY FOR YOU** (remix) — | **–**
(ext.12"+=) (EMI12 5490) – Two sharp pencils.

The CROSS

ROGER with **PETER NOONE** – bass / **CLAYTON MOSS** – guitar / **SPIKE EDNEY** – keyboards / **JOSH MacRAE** – drums

	Virgin	Virgin

Sep 87. (7"/ext.12")(cd-s) (VS/+T 1007)(CDEP 10) **COWBOYS AND INDIANS. / LOVE LIES BLEEDING** — **74** |
(c-s+=) (VSTC 1007) – ('A'extended).

Jan 88. (7") (VS 1026) **SHOVE IT. / ROUGH JUSTICE** — |
(ext.12"+=) (VS 1026-12) – ('A'-Metropolix mix).
(cd-s+=) (CDEP 20) – Cowboys and Indians / ('A'extended).

Jan 88. (lp/c/cd) (V/TCV/CDV 2477) **SHOVE IT** — **58** |
– Shove it / Heaven for everyone / Love on a tightrope (like an animal) / Cowboys and Indians / Stand up for love / Love lies bleeding (she was a wicked, wily waitress) / Contact. (cd+=) – Rough justice – 2nd shelf mix.

Mar 88. (7") (VS 1062) **HEAVEN FOR EVERYONE. / LOVE ON A TIGHTROPE (LIKE AN ANIMAL)** — |
(12"+=) (VST 1062) – Contact.

Jul 88. (7") (VS 1100) **MANIPULATOR. / STAND UP FOR LOVE** — |
(12"+=) (VS 1100-12) – ('A'extended).

	Parlophone	Capitol

Apr 90. (7") (R 6251) **POWER TO LOVE. / PASSION FOR TRASH** — |
(12"+=/cd-s+=) (12R/CDR 6251) – ('A'extended).

May 90. (cd/c/lp) (CD/TC+/PCS 7342) **MAD, BAD AND DANGEROUS TO KNOW** — |
– On top of the world ma / Liar / Closer to you / Breakdown / Penetration guru / Power to love / Sister blue / Better things / Old men (lay down) / Final destination. (cd+=) – Foxy lady.

ROGER TAYLOR

—— with **JASON FALLOON** – guitars / **PHIL SPALDING** – bass / **MIKE CROSSLEY** – piano, keyboards / **CATHERINE PORTER** – backing vocals / **JOSHUA J. MacRAE** – programming

		Parlophone	Capitol
Apr 94.	(c-s/7") (TC+/R 6379) **NAZIS 1994.** / ('A'radio mix) (12"red+=) (12R 6379) – ('A'extended) / ('A'-Big science mix). (cd-s++=) (CDR 6379) – ('A'kick mix) / ('A'-Schindler's extended mix).	22	
Sep 94.	(cd/c) (CD/TC PCSD 157) **HAPPINESS?** – Nazis 1994 / Happiness / Revelations / Touch the sky / Foreign sand / Freedom train / You had to be there / The key / Everybody hurts sometime / Loneliness . . . / Dear Mr. Murdoch / Old friends.	22	

—— Below featured a Japanese classically trained drummer, pianist & co-composer **YOSHIKI** plus **JIM CREGAN** – guitars / **PHIL CHEN** – bass / **DICK MARX** – strings arrangement

Sep 94.	(c-s/7"colrd; by ROGER TAYLOR & YOSHIKI) (TC+/R 6389) **FOREIGN SAND.** / ('A'mix) (12"pic-d+=/cd-s+=) (12R/CDR 6389) – You had to be there / Final destination.	26	
Nov 94.	(7") (R 6399) **HAPPINESS.** / **RIDE THE WILD WIND** (live) (12") (12R 6399) – ('A'side) / Dear Mr.Murdoch / Everybody hurts sometime (live) / Old friends (live). (cd-s) (CDR 6399) – ('A'side) / Loneliness / Dear Mr. Murdoch / I want to break free (live).	32	
Sep 98.	(7"/cd-s) (R/CDR 6507) **PRESSURE ON.** / **PEOPLE ON STREETS** (mashed) / **TONIGHT** (dub sangria)	45	–
Sep 98.	(cd/c/lp) (496724-2/-4/-1) **ELECTRIC FIRE** – Pressure on / Nation of haircuts / Believe in yourself / Surrender / People on the streets / Whispers / No more fun / Tonight / Where are you now / Working class hero / London town c'mon down.	53	
Mar 99.	(7") (R 6517) **SURRENDER.** / **LONDON TOWN, C'MON DOWN** (cd-s+=) (CDR 6517) – A nation of haircuts (club cut). (cd-s) (CDRS 6517) – ('A'live) / No more fun (live) / Tonight (live) / ('A'-CD-Rom video).	38	

QUEENS OF THE STONE AGE (see under ⇒ KYUSS)

QUEENSRYCHE

Formed: Bellevue, Seattle, Washington, USA . . . 1980 initially as The MOB by high school friends, CHRIS DE GARMO, MICHAEL WILTON, EDDIE JACKSON and SCOTT ROCKENFIELD. With the addition of classically trained vocalist GEOFF TATE, the act assumed the QUEENSRYCHE moniker after an enduring track on their eponymous debut EP. The 12" was released by record shop owners Kim and Diana Harris who had set up the independent '206' label expressly for this purpose. Following the record's underground success, 'EMI America' snapped the band up for a seven-album deal and promptly re-issued the record before setting them to work on a debut album with producer James Guthrie. The result was 'THE WARNING' (1984), a rather underwhelming affair handicapped by an unsympathetic final mix. 'RAGE FOR ORDER' (1986) was the first QUEENSRYCHE release to hint at the band's future cerebro-metal direction, TATE's impressive vocal muscle flexing a taster of what was in store with 'OPERATION MINDCRIME' (1988). One of the landmark metal releases of that year, the record was a 1984-style concept affair dealing with media brainwashing and social turmoil, conjuring up a convincingly chilling vision of a future gone wrong. Interspersed with snippets of dialogue, broadcasts etc., the songs effortlessly created an atmosphere of tension and portent, TATE veering between prophetic threat and despairing menace while the band's twin guitar attack raged and insinuated in equal measure. ' . . .MINDCRIME' subsequently went gold in America while selling over a million copies worldwide with nary a hit single to support it. Firmly established as the foremost thinking man's metal band, they could afford to be a bit more instinctive with their next release, the acclaimed 'EMPIRE' (1990). More a collection of set pieces, the record's highlight was the hypnotic 'SILENT LUCIDITY', a US Top 10 hit with heavy MTV rotation, the album itself reaching No.7. Other highlights included the brawny 'JET CITY WOMAN', the final single (save a re-release of 'SILENT LUCIDITY' which made the UK Top 20) before a period of relative inactivity. QUEENSRYCHE finally re-emerged in 1994 with 'PROMISED LAND', a more introspective and meditative effort which nevertheless made the US Top 3, cementing the band's position as prime purveyors of intelligent hard rock/metal. • **Trivia:** PAMELA MOORE was guest singer on 'SUITE SISTER MARY'. • **Songwriters:** DeGARMO or TATE / WILSON except; SCARBOROUGH FAIR – CANTICLE (Simon & Garfunkel) / GONNA GET CLOSE TO YOU (Lisa Diabello).

Album rating: THE WARNING (*5) / RAGE FOR ORDER (*7) / OPERATION: MINDCRIME (*8) / EMPIRE (*7) / PROMISED LAND (*6) / HEAR IN THE NEW FRONTIER (*6) / Q2K (*5)

GEOFF TATE (b.14 Jan'59, Stuttgart, Germany) – vocals / **CHRIS DeGARMO** (b.14 Jun'63, Wenatchee, Washington) – guitar / **MICHAEL WILTON** (b.23 Feb'62, San Francisco, Calif.) – guitar / **EDDIE JACKSON** (b.29 Jan'61, Robstown, Texas) – bass / **SCOTT ROCKENFIELD** (b.15 Jun'63, Seattle, Washington) – drums

		EMI America	EMI America
Sep 83.	(12"ep) (12EA 162) <19006> **QUEENSRYCHE** – Queen of the Reich / Nightrider / Blinded / The lady wore black. <first issued 1982 on '206' records; R 101>		81 m-lp

Sep 84.	(7") (EA 183) **TAKE HOLD OF THE FLAME.** / **NIGHTRIDER**		
Sep 84.	(lp/c) (EJ 240220-1/-4) <E2 46557> **THE WARNING** – The warning / En force / Deliverance / No sanctuary / NM 156 / Take hold of the flame / Before the storm / Child of fire / Roads to madness. (cd-iss. Mar87; CDP 746 557-2) (re-iss. Aug91 cd/c; QY 1) (re-iss. cd Oct94; CDP 746557-2)	61	
Jul 86.	(lp/c) (AML/TCAML 3105) <E2 46330> **RAGE FOR ORDER** – Walk in the shadows / I dream in infrared / The whisper / Surgical strike / Neue regel / Chemical youth (we are rebellion) / London / Screaming in digital / I will remember. (cd-iss. Feb87; CDP 746330-2)	66	47
Aug 86.	(7") (EA 22) **GONNA GET CLOSE TO YOU.** / **PROPHECY** (d7"+=) (EAD 22) – Queen of the Reich / Deliverance.		

		Manhattan	Manhattan
May 88.	(lp/c/cd) (MTL/TCMTL/CDMTL 1023) <48640> **OPERATION: MINDCRIME** – I remember now / Anarchy-X / Revolution calling / Operation: Mindcrime / Speak / Spreading the disease / The mission / Suite Sister Mary / The needle lies / Electric requiem / Breaking the silence / I don't believe in love / Waiting for 22 / My empty room / Eyes of a stranger. (re-iss. cd Oct94; CDP 748640-2)	58	50
Oct 88.	(10"ep) (10QP 1) **OVERSEEING THE OPERATION.** / **EXCERPTS FROM OPERATION MINDCRIME** – Suite sister Mary / I Remember Now / Revolution Calling / Operation: Mindcrime / Breaking The Silence / Eyes Of A Stranger.		
Apr 89.	(7") (MT 65) **EYES OF A STRANGER.** / **QUEEN OF THE REICH** (12"+=/12"g-f+=) (12MT/+G 65) – Walk in the shadows / Take hold of the flame. (cd-s+=) (CDMT 65) – Take hold of the flame / Prophecy.	59	

		E.M.I. USA	E.M.I.
Sep 90.	(7"/7"sha-pic-d) (MT/+PD 90) **EMPIRE.** / **SCARBOROUGH FAIR – CANTICLE** (12"+=/cd-s+=) (12/CD MT 90) – Prophecy.	61	
Sep 90.	(cd/c/d-lp) (CD/TC+/1058) <E2 92806> **EMPIRE** – Best I can do / The thin line / Jet city woman / Della Brown / Another rainy night (without you) / Empire / Resistance / Silent lucidity / Hand on heart / One and only / Anybody listening?	13	7
Apr 91.	(7"/7"box/c-s) (MT/MTS/TCMTP 94) <50345> **SILENT LUCIDITY.** / **THE MISSION** (live) (12"+=) (12MTP 94) – Eyes of a stranger. (cd-s+=) (CDMT 94) – Della Brown.	34	9 Mar91
Jun 91.	(7"/c-s) (MT/CTMT 97) **BEST I CAN.** / **I DREAM IN INFRARED** (acoustic remix) (10"+=) (10MT 97) – Prophecy. (cd-s++=) (CDMT 97) – ('A'radio edit).	36	
Aug 91.	(7"/7"sha-pic-d) (MT/+PD 98) **JET CITY WOMAN.** / **EMPIRE** (live) (12"+=) (12MTS 98) – Walk in the shadows (live). (cd-s) (CDMT 98) – ('A'side) / Walk in the shadows (live) / Queen of The Reich.	39	
Nov 91.	(cd+video) <97048> **OPERATION: LIVECRIME** (live)	–	38
Aug 92.	(7"/c-s) (MT/CTMT 104) **SILENT LUCIDITY.** / **I DON'T BELIEVE IN LOVE** (live) (12"pic-d) (12MTPD 104) – ('A'side) / Last time in Paris / Take hold of the fame. (cd-s) (CDMT 104) – ('A'side) / Suite Sister Mary (live) / Last time in Paris. (cd-s) (CDMTS 104) – ('A'side) / Eyes of a stranger (live) / Operation: Mindcrime.	18	–
Oct 94.	(cd/c/clear-lp) (CD/TC+/MTL 1081) <30711> **PROMISED LAND** – 9:28 a.m. / I am I / Damaged / Out of mind / Bridge / Promised land / Disconnected / Lady Jane / My global mind / One more time / Someone else?.	13	3
Jan 95.	(12"gold) (12MT 109) **I AM I.** / **REAL WORLD** / **SOMEONE ELSE?** (cd-s+=/s-cd-s+=) (CDMT/+S 109) – Dirty li'l secret.	40	
Mar 95.	(7"pic-d/c-s) (MTPD/TCMT 111) **BRIDGE.** / **THE KILLING WORDS** (live) (cd-s+=) (CDMTS 111) – The lady wore black (live) / Damaged (live). (cd-s) (CDMTSX 111) – ('A'side) / Silent lucidity (live) / My empty room (live) / Real world (live).	40	
Mar 97.	(cd/c) (CD/TC EMC 3764) **HEAR IN THE NEW FRONTIER** – Sign of the times / Cuckoo's nest / Get a life / Voice inside / Some people fly / Saved / You / Miles away / Reach / All I want / Hit the black / Anytime – anywhere / Spool.	46	19

		Atlantic	Atlantic
Nov 99.	(cd) <(7567 83225-2)> **Q2K** – Falling down / Sacred ground / One life / When the rain comes / How could I know / Beside you / Liquid sky / Breakdown / Burning man / Wot kinda man / Right side of my mind.	46	Sep99

– compilations, etc. –

1988.	(cd) E.M.I. USA; <CDP7 90615-2> **QUEENSRYCHE**	–	
Oct 99.	(d-cd) Axe Killer; (AXE 3052182CD) **OPERATION: MINDCRIME / QUEEN OF THE RYCHE**		–

? & THE MYSTERIANS (dig out; Great Psychedelic . . .)

QUICKSILVER MESSENGER SERVICE

Formed: San Francisco, California, USA . . . late 1964 by JIM MURRAY, JOHN CIPOLLINA, DAVID FREIBERG and CASEY SONOBAN. Also present at their early rehearsals were SKIP SPENCE and DINO VALENTI, who was later jailed for possession of drugs. In June '65, CIPOLLINA, MURRAY and FREIBERG were joined by GREG ELMORE and GARY DUNCAN (both from The BROGUES, who released a few US 45's in 1965). Two years later, they received a great reception at The Monterey

International Pop Festival, although MURRAY left when the group signed to 'Capitol'. They had previously recorded two tracks, 'CODINE' and 'BABE, I'M GONNA LEAVE YOU', for the (late '67) Various Artists soundtrack album, 'REVOLUTION' on 'United Artists'. In the summer of '68, they finally released their eponymous debut, which, amid much anticipation, reached the US Top 75. Their 1969 follow-up, 'HAPPY TRAILS', featuring a 25-minute improvised version of BO DIDDLEY's 'WHO DO YOU LOVE', crashed into the US Top 30. Apparently as close an approximation of what it was actually like to have your ears massaged/assaulted in the San Francisco ballrooms as you're likely to hear, the part-live album nevertheless sounds dated. Although NICKY HOPKINS impressed with THE ROLLING STONES, his addition to the QUICKSILVER line-up for 1969's 'SHADY GROVE' didn't create the musical spark the band needed and with VALENTE back in the fold after his stint in prison, things went downhill. He came to dominate the band's output over the remainder of their career, his average material dulling the spontaneity that had characterised QUICKSILVER's earlier work and effecting a transformation in their sound from psychedelic rock to workmanlike rock'n'roll. While the band had their sole top 50 hit with 'FRESH AIR' in 1970, the album it was taken from and the rest of their 70's output was bog-standard stuff which suffered from the aforementioned lack of honed songwriting and a constantly changing line-up. QUICKSILVER MESSENGER SERVICE finally delivered its last lacklustre communication in 1975 after a 3-year hiatus, CIPOLLINA going off to join MAN, FREIBERG joining STARSHIP. • **Songwriters:** CIPOLLINA + FREIBERG, until VALENTI's virtual take-over in 1970 as alter-ego JESSE ORIS FARROW (although others still individually contributed). • **Trivia:** Debut album was produced by NICK GRAVENITES and HARVEY BROOKS of ELECTRIC FLAG.

Album rating: QUICKSILVER MESSENGER SERVICE (*7) / HAPPY TRAILS (*8) / SHADY GROVE (*5) / JUST FOR LOVE (*5) / WHAT ABOUT ME (*6) / QUICKSILVER (*4) / COMIN' THRU (*4) / ANTHOLOGY compilation (*6) / SOLID SILVER (*4) / MAIDEN OF THE CANCER MOON collection (*5) / THE ULTIMATE JOURNEY compilation (*7) / PIECE BY PIECE (*1) / SONS OF MERCURY (1968-1975) compilation (*8)

JOHN CIPOLLINA (b.24 Aug'43, Berkeley, Calif.) – guitar, vocals (ex-DEACONS) / **GARY DUNCAN** (b. GARY GRUBB, 4 Sep'46) – guitar, vocals repl. SKIP SPENCE / **DAVID FREIBERG** (b.24 Aug'38, Boston, Mass.) – bass, vocals / **GREG ELMORE** (b. 4 Sep'46, San Diego, Calif.) – drums repl. CASEY SONOBAN

			Capitol	Capitol
May 68.	(lp) <(ST 2904)> **QUICKSILVER MESSENGER SERVICE**		☐	63

– Pride of man / Light your windows / Dino's song / Gold and silver / It's been too long / The fool. *(re-iss. Jul86 on 'Edsel'; ED 200) (cd-iss. Mar89; CDP 791146-2) (cd-iss. Jul92 on 'Edsel'; EDCD 200)*

Jun 68.	(7") <2194> **PRIDE OF MAN. / DINO'S SONG**		-	
Nov 68.	(7") <2320> **BEARS. / STAND BY ME**		-	
Mar 69.	(lp) <(EST 120)> **HAPPY TRAILS**		☐	27

– Who do you love suite:- Who do you love (pt.1) – Who do you love – Where do you love – How do you love – Which do you love – Who do you love (pt.2) / Mona / Maiden of the Cancer Moon / Calvary / Happy trails. *(re-iss. Jun81 on 'Greenlight' lp/c; GO/TC-GO 2012) (cd-iss. Mar89; CDP 791215-2) (cd re-iss. Dec92 on 'Beat Goes On'; BGOCD 151)*

Jul 69.	(7") <2557> **WHO DO YOU LOVE (edit). / WHICH DO YOU LOVE**		-	91

—— **NICKY HOPKINS** (b.24 Feb'44, London, England) – keyboards (ex-STEVE MILLER BAND) repl. DUNCAN

Nov 69.	(7") <2670> **HOLY MOLY. / WORDS CAN'T SAY**		-	
Dec 69.	(lp) <(EST 391)> **SHADY GROVE**		☐	25

– Shady Grove / Flute song / Three or feet from home / Too far / Holy Moly / Joseph's coat / Flashing lonesome / Words can't say / Edward, the mad shirt grinder. *(re-iss. Feb87 on 'Edsel'; XED 208) (cd-iss. Sep90; EDCD 208)*

Feb 70.	(7") <2800> **SHADY GROVE. / THREE OR FOUR FEET FROM HOME**		-	☐

—— added now officially ex-part time member **DINO VALENTI** (b. CHESTER POWERS, 7 Nov'43, Danbury, Connecticut) – guitar, vocals / **GARY DUNCAN** – guitar, vocals returned to 6-piece w / JOHN, NICKY, DAVID + GREG

Aug 70.	(lp) <(EA-ST 498)> **JUST FOR LOVE**		☐	27

– Wolf run (part 1) / Just for love (part 1) / Cobra / The hat / Freeway flyer / Gone again / Fresh air / Just for love (part 2) / Wolf run (part 2). *(cd-iss. Dec92 on 'Beat Goes On'; BGOCD 141)*

Sep 70.	(7") <2920> **FRESH AIR. / FREEWAY FLYER**		-	49

—— **MARK NATALFIN** – keyboards (ex-PAUL BUTTERFIELD) repl. (on 3 tracks) HOPKINS. Also on below lp: **JOSE RICO REYES** – percussion / **MARTINE FIERRO** – wind / **RON TAORMINA** – saxes / **FRANK MORIN** – sax / **PAT O'HARA** – trombone / **KEN BALZELL** – trumpet

Feb 71.	(lp) <(EA-ST 630)> **WHAT ABOUT ME**		26	Jan71

– What about me / Local color / Baby baby / Won't kill me / Long haired lady / Subway / Spindrifter / Good old rock and roll / All in my mind / Call on me. *(re-iss. Jul89 on 'Beat Goes On'; BGOLP 58) (cd-iss. Oct90; BGOCD 58)*

Mar 71.	(7") <3046> **WHAT ABOUT ME. / GOOD OLD ROCK AND ROLL**		-	100

—— Now a quintet when CIPOLLINA left to form COPPERHEAD / **MARK RYAN** – bass (ex-COUNTRY JOE & THE FISH) repl. DAVID to JEFFERSON STARSHIP

Nov 71.	(lp) <(SW 819)> **QUICKSILVER**		☐	☐

– Hope / I found love / Song for Frisco / Play my guitar / Rebel / Fire Brothers / Out of my mind / Don't cry my lady love / The truth. *(cd-iss. Jan94 on 'Beat Goes On'; BGOCD 217)*

Nov 71.	(7") <3233> **HOPE. / I FOUND LOVE**		-	☐

—— **CHUCK STEAKS** – organ repl. NATAFLIN

May 72.	(lp) <(ST 11002)> **COMIN' THRU**		☐	☐

– Doin' time in the U.S.A. / Chicken / Changes / California state correctional facility blues / Forty days / Mojo / Don't lose it. *(cd-iss. Jul91 on 'Beat Goes On' lp/cd; BGO/+CD 88)*

May 72.	(7") <3349> **DOIN' TIME IN THE U.S.A. / CHANGES**		-	☐

—— Mid'72, contributed 2 tracks for live lp 'The Last Days Of Fillmore'.

—— (May73) **JOHN NICHOLAS** – bass (ex-IT'S A BEAUTIFUL DAY) repl. RYAN / added **HAROLD ACEVES** – 2nd drummer (6-piece DINO, GARY, GREG + CHUCKS)

—— (Feb74) **BOB HOGAN** – keyboards (ex-MILES DAVIS) repl. STEAKS / **SKIP OLSEN** – bass repl. BOB FLURIE who had repl. JOHN NICHOLAS

—— (Mar75) **DINO, GARY, GREG, SKIP** plus the returning **JOHN CIP . . . + DAVID** on tour / added **MICHAEL LEWIS** – piano

Oct 75.	(lp) <(ST 11462)> **SOLID SILVER**		☐	89

– Gypsy lights / Heebie jeebies / Cowboy on the run / I heard you singing / Worryin' shoes / The letter / They don't know / Flames / Witches' moon / Bittersweet Moon. *(cd-iss. Sep93 on 'Edsel'; EDCD 376)*

Nov 75.	(7") (CL 15859) <4206> **GYPSY LIGHTS. / WITCHES MOON**		☐	☐

—— Had already broke-up, after brief re-union. CIPOLLINA joined MAN but was to die on 29th May '89 of emphysema lung disease. FREIBERG returned to STARSHIP. In 1987, GARY DUNCAN resurrected QUICKSILVER MESSENGER SERVICE with FREIBERG and others

Jul 86.	(lp) <12498> **PEACE BY PIECE**		-	☐

– Good thang / 24 hour deja vu / Midnight sun / Swamp girl / Wild in the city / Pool hall chili / Pistolero / Peace by piece.

—— Some original members, included others from The GRATEFUL DEAD, JEFFERSON AIRPLANE and (HUEY LEWIS &) THE NEWS, played a benefit in San Francisco; they subsequently issued 'SHAPESHIFTER'

– compilations, others, etc. –

Oct 73.	(lp) Capitol; (STSP 13) <ST 11165> **ANTHOLOGY**		☐	May73

– Pride of man / Dino's song / Fool / Bears / Mona / Edward, the mad shirt grinder / Three or four feet from home / Fresh air / Just for love / Spindrifter / Local color / What about me / Don't cry my lady love / Hope / Fire brothers / I found love. *(cd-iss. Jun95 on 'Beat Goes On'; BGOCD 270)*

Sep 83.	(d-lp) Psycho; (PSYCHO 10) **MAIDEN OF THE CANCER MOON** (live Fillmore, Jun'68)		☐	☐
Apr 86.	(lp) See For Miles; (SEE 61) **THE ULTIMATE JOURNEY**		☐	-

– Who do you love / Pride of man / Codine / Dino's song / Gold and silver / Joseph's coat / Shady grove / Fresh air / Too far / Stand by me / What about me / Mona. *(cd-iss. Aug93; SEECD 61)*

Aug 91.	(d-cd) Rhino; **SONS OF MERCURY (THE BEST OF QUICKSILVER MESSENGER SERVICE 1968-1975)**		-	☐

QUIET RIOT	(dig out; 4th edition or Great Metal . . .)

QUINTESSENCE	(dig out; Great Psychedelic . . .)

QUIREBOYS	(dig out; 4th edition or Great Metal . . .)

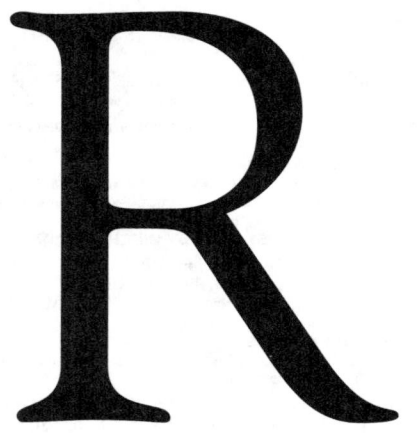

searing guitar line evoking a feeling of utter desolation and emptiness. Probably the best example of YORKE's self-acknowledged struggle to sound anything other than melancholy, the track was one of many highlights on 'OK COMPUTER' (1997), RADIOHEAD's feverishly anticipated follow-up to the poll-topping 'THE BENDS'. A densely complex, almost initally impenetrable album, 'OK..' was a demanding beast, previewed by the wildly ambitious 'PARANOID ANDROID', a kind of post-prog symphony in three parts. The oscillating guitar vibration of 'AIRBAG' kicked off proceedings in much the same fashion as 'PLANET TELEX', but then things started getting weird. 'SUBTERRANEAN HOMESICK ALIEN' was truly adrift in space, the guitars twinkling and shimmering like tiny constellations, while with 'EXIT MUSIC (FOR A FILM)' (written for the closing sequence of the revamped 'Romeo And Juliet' movie), YORKE's vocal was so eerily intimate, it sounded as if he was in the same room, the song building to a majestic climax via unearthly choral parts and swooning synths. 'LET DOWN' was an almost BYRDS-esque follow-up to 'CREEP', its pealing guitar and infectious melody framing a similar theme and creating what was conceivably the nearest the record came to conventional rock. Much of the album was vaguely reminiscent of the more cerebral moments on U2's 'Unforgettable Fire', although YORKE has never come so close to sounding like BONO as on 'CLIMBING THE WALLS', for once managing to avoid the bruised resignation that normally colours his voice. With 'NO SURPRISES', RADIOHEAD cleverly contrasted an almost child-like musical lullaby with lyrics expressing a hopeless world-weariness. Of their contemporaries, only SPIRITUALIZED and MOGWAI were making music this far out, RADIOHEAD once again almost sweeping the board at the end-of-year polls and bravely taking rock music into the future rather than fawning over a Union Jack-clad past.

Album rating: PABLO HONEY (*7) / THE BENDS (*8) / OK COMPUTER (*9)

THOM YORKE (b. 7 Oct'68) – vocals, guitar / **ED O'BRIEN** (b.15 Apr'68) – guitar, vocals / **JON GREENWOOD** (b. 5 Nov'71) – guitar / **COLIN GREENWOOD** (b.26 Jun'69) – bass / **PHIL SELWAY** (b.23 May'67) – drums

		Parlophone	Capitol
May 92.	(c-ep/12"ep/cd-ep) *(TCR/12R/CDR 6312)* **DRILL EP** – Prove yourself / Stupid car / You / Thinking about you.	☐	☐
Sep 92.	(c-ep/12"ep/cd-ep) *(TCR/12R/CDR 632?)* <15978? **CREEP / LURCEE. / INSIDE MY HEAD / MILLION $ QUESTION**	☐	☐ Apr93
Feb 93.	(c-ep/cd/cd-ep) *(TCR/12R/CDR 6333)* **ANYONE CAN PLAY GUITAR. / FAITHLESS, THE WONDER BOY / COKE BABIES**	32	–
Feb 93.	(cd/c/lp) *(CD/TC+/PCS 7360)* <81409> **PABLO HONEY** – You / Creep / How do you? / Stop whispering / Thinking about you / Anyone can play guitar / Ripcord / Vegetable / Prove yourself / I can't / Lurgee / Blow out.	25	32 Jun93
May 93.	(c-ep/12"ep/cd-ep) *(TCR/12R/CDR 6345)* **POP IS DEAD / BANANA CO. (acoustic). / CREEP (live) / RIPCORD (live)**	42	–
Jun 93.	(c-s,cd-s) <44932> **CREEP / FAITHLESS, THE WONDER BOY**	–	34
Sep 93.	(7"clear-ep/c-ep/cd-ep) *(RS/TCR/CDR 6359)* **CREEP / YES I AM. / BLOW OUT (remix) / INSIDE MY HEAD (live)**	7	–
	(12"ep) *(12RG 6359)* – ('A'-acoustic KROQ) / You (live) / Vegetable (live) / Killer cars (live).		
Oct 94.	(c-ep/12"ep) *(TCR/12R 6984)* <58274> **MY IRON LUNG / THE TRICKSTER / LEWIS (mistreated) / PUNCHDRUNK LOVESICK SINGALONG**	24	
	(cd-s) *(CDRS 6394)* – (1st & 4th track) / Lozenge of love.		
	(cd-s) *(CDR 6394)* – (1st & 2nd track) / Permanent daylight / You never wash up after yourself.		
Mar 95.	(c-s) *(TCR 6405)* <58537> **HIGH & DRY / PLANET TELEX**	17	Feb96
	(cd-s+=) *(CDR 6405)* – Killer cars / Planet Telex (LFO JD mix).		
	(cd-s+=) *(CDRS 6405)* – Maquiladora / Planet Telex (hexadecimal mix).		
	(12") *(12R 6405)* – Planet Telex (hexadecimal mix) / Planet Telex (LFO JD mix) / Planet Telex (hexadecimal dub) / High & dry.		
Mar 95.	(cd/c/lp) *(CD/TC+/PCS 7372)* <29626> **THE BENDS** – Planet Telex / The bends / High & dry / Fake plastic trees / Bones (nice dream) / Just / My iron lung / Bulletproof . . . I wish I was / Black star / Sulk / Street spirit (fade out).	6	88
May 95.	(c-ep/cd-ep) *(TCR/CDRS 6411)* <58424> **FAKE PLASTIC TREES / INDIA RUBBER / HOW CAN YOU BE SURE?**	20	Jul95
	(cd-s) *(CDR 6411)* – ('A'side) / ('A'acoustic) / Bulletproof..I wish I was (acoustic) / Street spirit (fade out) (acoustic).		
Aug 95.	(c-ep/12"ep) *(TCR/12R 6415)* **JUST / PLANET TELEX (Karma Sun Ra mix) / KILLER CARS (mogadon mix)**	19	–
	(cd-s) *(CDR 6415)* – ('A'side) / Bones (live) / Planet Telex (live) / Anyone can play guitar (live).		
Jan 96.	(7"white) *(R 6419)* <82523> **STREET SPIRIT (FADE OUT). / BISHOP'S ROBES**	5	☐
	(cd-s+=) *(CDRS 6419)* – Talk show host.		
	(cd-s) *(CDR 6419)* – ('A'side) / Banana co. / Molasses.		
Feb 96.	(c-s,cd-s) <58537> **HIGH AND DRY / FAKE PLASTIC TREES**	–	78
Jun 97.	(7") *(NODATA 01)* **PARANOID ANDROID. / POLYETHYLENE (PARTS 1 & 2)**	3	–
	(cd-s+=) *(CDNODATAS 01)* – Pearly.		
	(cd-s) *(CDNODATA 01)* – ('A'side) / A reminder / Melatonin.		
Jun 97.	(cd/c/d-lp) *(CD/TC+/NODATA 01)* <55229> **OK COMPUTER** – Airbag / Paranoid android / Subterranean homesick alien / Exit music (for a film) / Karma police / Electioneering / Climbing up the walls / No surprises / Lucky / The tourist.	1	21
Aug 97.	(cd-s) *(CDNODATA 03)* **KARMA POLICE / CLIMBING UP THE WALLS (Fila Brazillia & Zero 7 mixes)**	8	☐
	(12"+=) *(12NODATA 03)* – Meeting in the aisle.		
	(cd-s) *(CDNODATAS 03)* – ('A'side) / Meeting in the aisle / Lull.		
Jan 98.	(12") *(12NODATA 04)* **NO SURPRISES. / PALO ALTO**	4	☐
	(c-s+=/cd-s+=) *(TC/CD NODATA 04)* – How I made my millions.		
	(cd-s) *(CDNODATAS 04)* – ('A'side) / Airbag (live) / Lucky (live).		

RADAR BROS. (dig out; Great Alt & Indie . . .)

RADIOHEAD

Formed: Oxford, England . . . 1988 by frontman THOM YORKE, guitarist ED O'BRIEN and bassist COLIN GREENWOOD with drummer PHIL SELWAY completing the line-up. Dubbing themselves ON A FRIDAY, the band began gigging around Oxford, subsequently boasting a triple guitar attack following the addition of COLIN's brother, JONNY. Initially, the group also fleshed out their sound with a couple of sax0phone players (though it's now difficult to imagine what that must have sounded like). With the various members trooping off to complete their respective educations, the RADIOHEAD story really began in the summer of '91 when the band got back together and adopted the aforesaid moniker (after a TALKING HEADS song). Signed to the ever vigilant 'Parlophone', the band enjoyed some airplay with their first release, a Spring '92 EP with 'PROVE YOURSELF' as the lead track. Next up was the seminal 'CREEP', an incendiary anthem for anyone who'd ever felt rejected/alienated (and let's face it, that's most of the population), the song stiffing first time round but subsequently kickstarting RADIOHEAD's career. The track also used the group's trademark soft bit/quiet bit dynamics to stunning effect, a method which would come to form the basis for some of the band's best tracks. In the meantime, RADIOHEAD eventually scraped in to the lower regions of the Top 40 with the abrasive 'ANYONE CAN PLAY GUITAR', the debut album, 'PABLO HONEY' making the UK Top 30 around the same time in early '93. Though it had its moments, the album lacked consistency with YORKE seemingly searching for some kind of vocal identity. While the record found enthusiastic champions in some sections of the music press, by and large, RADIOHEAD were passed over. All that changed, however, when 'CREEP' exploded in the States, the record obviously striking a deep chord with the multitudes who weren't part of the 'American Dream'. Taking the first flight over there, RADIOHEAD capitalised on this surprise success, the band treated like homecoming heroes and selling out concerts night after night. In a bizarre reversal of the standard process, this US success laid the groundwork for the re-release of 'CREEP' in the UK, where it became a Top 10 hit, sales of the album also enjoying a healthy re-invigoration. With such a universal theme, it was no surprise that the track was also a massive hit all over the world, RADIOHEAD finding themselves in the strange position of being international pop stars yet, at the same time, regarded merely as a competent indie band in their home country. 'THE BENDS' (1995) convincingly silenced the doubters once and for all, a groundbreaking album with a spectral musical vision which rarely failed to take the breath away. Opening with the searing, reverbating 'PLANET TELEX' the record proceeded to juxtapose howling guitar menace against bleakly beautiful melodies, echoing synth and acoustic strumming, YORKE painting piercingly vivid images with his tortured musings on the nature of the human psyche. The fragile majesty of 'FAKE PLASTIC TREES' was RADIOHEAD at their most sublime, YORKE's ability to hit those high notes pivotal to the resigned melancholy of his vocals. The churning claustrophobia of 'BLACK STAR' sounded like the final fling of a condemned man, positively revelling in its own pain and misery, while the funereal 'STREET SPIRIT' was a ghostly coda, its award-winning video perfectly evoking the track's haunting feeling of time standing still. Basically, the album wiped the floor with the competition, laying waste to the snot-nosed chaff of Brit-pop and confirming that there was indeed a thinking man's alternative to OASIS. R.E.M. felt the same way, inviting the band to support them on tour later that year, something of a dream come true for RADIOHEAD who had long been massive fans of STIPE & Co. The summer of '95 also saw the release of the 'HELP' album, a project involving the cream of the British music scene with proceeds from album sales donated to the War Child charity (which raised money for war-torn Bosnia). RADIOHEAD contributed 'LUCKY', a song apparently written about the band's newfound position as one of the most highly regarded groups in the world. Stunning though the track is, it sounds more like a dirge than a celebration, the

Apr 98. (m-cd) *(858701-2)* **AIRBAG / PEARLY (remix) / MEETING IN THE AISLE / A REMINDER / POLYTHENE (parts 1 & 2) / MELATONIN / PALO ALTO**

☐	–

(above wasn't legitimate to chart in Britain)

Apr 98. (m-cd) *<58071>* **AIRBAG / HOW AM I DRIVING (EP)**

–	56

RAEKWON (see under ⇒ WU-TANG CLAN)

Gerry RAFFERTY

Born: 16 Apr '47, Paisley, Scotland. In 1968, he joined The HUMBLEBUMS, alongside TAM HARVEY and future comedian, BILLY CONNOLLY. The trio signed up to folk label, 'Transatlantic', recording two albums, 'HUMBLEBUMS' (1969) & 'OPEN UP THE DOOR' (1970), together before parting ways. RAFFERTY subsequently released a debut solo album, 'CAN I HAVE MY MONEY BACK', in 1971 before moving to London and forming STEALER'S WHEEL with RAB NOAKES and JOE EGAN. Signed to 'A&M', the band went through some major personnel upheavals prior to the release of their eponymous album in late '72, PAUL PILNICK, TONY WILLIAMS and ROB COOMBES replacing RAB NOAKES, IAN CAMPBELL and ROGER BROWN respectively. Overseen by veteran production duo, LEIBER & STOLLER, the album was characterised by gentle, folky harmonies and an unerring ear for pop melody, the haunting 'NEXT TO ME' resonating long after the first listen. Then of course, there was the 'Dylanesque' shuffle of 'STUCK IN THE MIDDLE WITH YOU', a transatlantic Top 10 upon its original 1973 release and later an integral, ingeniously effective part of Quentin Tarantino's infamous 'Reservoir Dogs' movie. There was almost as much confusion surrounding the identity of the STEALER'S WHEEL line-up as there was among Tarantino's panicked criminal pros, RAFFERTY leaving for a couple of months before returning in time for a follow-up. By this point, all the original members (who themselves had been temporarily replaced!) were gone and the core duo of EGAN and RAFFERTY roped in a crew of session players to complete 'FERGUSLIE PARK' (1973). Another set of consummate folk-pop, the record was nevertheless a commercial disappointment save for a minor Top 30 hit, 'STAR'. Disillusioned, the pair completed one further set, the equally impressive 'RIGHT OR WRONG' (1975), before permanently parting company and embarking on respective solo careers. After a number of years grappling with business problems, RAFFERTY emerged in early '78 with the 'CITY TO CITY' album. Changing tack to a more contemporary, MOR style, RAFFERTY scored a massive international hit (and a US No.1) with the 'BAKER STREET' single, RAPHAEL RAVENSCROFT's famous sax riff forming the basis of this world-weary classic. The track's success saw album sales go through the roof, RAFFERTY becoming something of a reluctant overnight superstar. Shunning the limelight and choosing not to promote the album in America (where it went platinum), RAFFERTY instead began work on a follow-up, 'NIGHT OWL' (1979). While failing to scale the commercial heights of its predecessor, the record was a sizeable success nonetheless, RAFFERTY's inimitably understated approach again delighting fans who put it into the UK Top 10. Subsequent albums such as 'SLEEPWALKING' (1982) and 'NORTH AND SOUTH' (1988) weren't quite as inspired, RAFFERTY taking a sabbatical during the mid-80's (although he did contribute to MARK KNOPFLER's 'Local Hero' soundtrack and produce The PROCLAIMERS' 1987 single, 'Letter From America'). He continued to record in the 90's, if sporadically, such seasoned hands as pedal steel player, B.J. COLE, lending their expertise to 1993's 'ON A WING AND A PRAYER', the record also featuring the backing vocal and co-writing talents of brother JIM.
• **Songwriters:** STEALER'S WHEEL was virtually a writing partnership for RAFFERTY and EGAN. GET OUT OF MY LIFE WOMAN (Allen Toussaint).

Album rating: CAN I HAVE MY MONEY BACK? (*6) / Stealer's Wheel: STEALER'S WHEEL (*7) / FERGUSLIE PARK (*7) / RIGHT OR WRONG (*6) / Gerry Rafferty: CITY TO CITY (*8) / NIGHT OWL (*7) / SNAKES AND LADDERS (*6) / SLEEPWALKING (*4) / NORTH AND SOUTH (*4) / RIGHT DOWN THE LINE – THE BEST OF GERRY RAFFERTY compilation (*6) / ON A WING & A PRAYER (*4) / OVER MY HEAD (*4) / ONE MORE DREAM – THE VERY BEST OF GERRY RAFFERTY compilation (*7)

GERRY RAFFERTY – vocals, guitar (with session people including future STEALER'S WHEEL members)

			Transatla.	Blue Thumb
1971.	(lp) *(TRA 241) <BTS 58>* **CAN I HAVE MY MONEY BACK**		☐	☐

– New street blues / Didn't I / Mr. Universe / Mary Skeffington / Long way round / Can I have my money back / Sign on the dotted line / Make you break you / To each and everyone / One drink down / Don't count me out / Half a chance / Where I belong. *<US re-iss. 1978; 6031>* (re-iss. Sep81 lp/c; TRS/KTRS 112) (re-iss. Apr85 on 'Autograph' c; ASK 769) (re-iss. cd+c Apr93 on 'Ariola Express')

1972.	(7") **CAN I HAVE MY MONEY BACK. / SO SAD THINKING**	☐	–
1972.	(7") **CAN I HAVE MY MONEY BACK. / SIGN ON THE DOTTED LINE**	–	☐

STEALER'S WHEEL

GERRY with **JOE EGAN** – vocals, keyboards / **PAUL PILNICK** – guitar (ex-BIG THREE) repl. RAB NOAKES who went solo / **TONY WILLIAMS** – bass repl. IAN CAMPBELL / **ROD COOMBES** – drums repl. ROGER BROWN

		A&M	A&M	
Oct 72.	(7") *(AMS 7033)* **LATE AGAIN. / I GET BY**	☐	–	
Nov 72.	(7") *(AMS 7036) <1416>* **STUCK IN THE MIDDLE WITH YOU. / JOSE**	☐	6	Feb73

(re-dist.May73, hit UK No.8)

Dec 72.	(lp) *(AMLH 68121) <4377>* **STEALER'S WHEEL**	☐	50

– Late again / Stuck in the middle with you / Another meaning / I get by / Outside looking in / Johnny's song / Next to me / Josie / Gets so lonely / You put something better inside of me.

Feb 73.	(7") *(AMS 7046)* **YOU PUT SOMETHING BETTER INSIDE OF ME. / NEXT TO ME**	☐	–

—— Group had disbanded when RAFFERTY had been replaced by **LUTHER GROSVENOR** (ex-SPOOKY TOOTH) for 2 months. **DELISLE HARPER** – bass repl. others

—— By mid'73, they were a basic duo (**RAFFERTY & EGAN**) augmented by **BERNIE HOLLAND** – guitar / **CHRIS MERCER** – saxophone / **ANDREW STEELE** – drums / **CHRIS NEILL** – harmonica and loads more sessioners.

Aug 73.	(7") *(AMS 7079)* **EVERYTHING'L TURN OUT FINE. / JOHNNY'S SONG**	33	–
Aug 73.	(7") *<1450>* **EVERYONE'S AGREED THAT EVERYTHING WILL TURN OUT FINE. / NEXT TO ME**	–	49
Nov 73.	(lp) *(AMLH 68209) <4419>* **FERGUSLIE PARK**	☐	☐

– Good businessman / Star / Wheelin' / Waltz (you know it makes sense!) / What more could you want / Over my head / Blind faith / Nothing's gonna change my mind / Steamboat row / Back on my feet again / Who cares / (Everyone's agreed that) Everything will turn out fine.

Dec 73.	(7") *(AMS 7094) <1483>* **STAR. / WHAT MORE COULD I WANT**	25	29
Apr 74.	(7") *<1529>* **WHEELIN'. / YOU PUT SOMETHING BETTER INSIDE OF ME**	–	–
Feb 75.	(7") *(AMS 7152)* **RIGHT OR WRONG. / THIS MORNING**	☐	☐
Feb 75.	(lp) *(AMLH 68293) <4517>* **RIGHT OR WRONG**	☐	☐

– Benediction / Found my way to you / This morning / Let yourself go / Home from home / Go as you please / Wishbone / Don't get me wrong / Monday morning / Right or wrong.

May 75.	(7") *(AMS 7170)* **FOUND MY WAY TO YOU. / WISHBONE**	☐	☐
May 75.	(7") *<1675>* **FOUND MY WAY TO YOU. / THIS MORNING**	–	☐

—— Broke again later in the year. JOE EGAN went solo, as did GERRY.

– compilations, etc. –

Sep 78.	(lp) *A&M; (AMLH 64708) <4708>* **THE BEST OF STEALER'S WHEEL**	☐	☐

(re-iss. 1981 on 'Music For Pleasure'; MFP 50501)

Sep 78.	(7") *A&M; <2075>* **(EVERYONE AGREED THAT) EVERYTHING'L TURN OUT FINE. / WHO CARES**	–	–
Mar 82.	(7") *Old Gold; (OG 9148)* **STUCK IN THE MIDDLE WITH YOU. / STAR**	☐	–

GERRY RAFFERTY

with many session people.

		U.A.	U.A.	
Oct 77.	(7") *(UP 36278)* **CITY TO CITY. / MATTIE'S RAG**	☐	1	
Jan 78.	(lp/c) *(UAS/TCK 30104) <840>* **CITY TO CITY**	6	1	

– he ark / Baker Street / Right down the line / City to city / Stealin' time / Mattie's rag / Whatever's written in your heart / Home and dry / Waiting for the day. *(re-iss. Mar85 on 'Fame' lp/c; FA/TC-FA 3119) (cd-iss. Jul89; CDFA 3119)*

Feb 78.	(7") *(UP 36346) <1192>* **BAKER STREET. / BIG CHANGE IN THE WEATHER**	3	2	Apr78

above featured **RAPHAEL RAVENSCROFT** – saxophone

May 78.	(7") *(UP 36403)* **WHATEVER'S WRITTEN IN YOUR HEART. / WAITING FOR THE DAY**	☐	–
Aug 78.	(7") *<1233>* **RIGHT DOWN THE LINE. / WAITING FOR THE DAY**	–	12
Sep 78.	(7") *(UP 36445)* **RIGHT DOWN THE LINE. / ISLAND**	–	☐
Nov 78.	(7") *<1266>* **HOME AND DRY. / MATTIE'S RAG**	–	28
May 79.	(7") *(UP 36512)* **NIGHT OWL. / WHY DON'T YOU TALK TO ME**	5	–
May 79.	(lp/c) *(UAK/TCK 30238) <958>* **NIGHT OWL**	9	29

– Days gone down (still got the light in your eyes) / Night owl / The way that you do it / Why won't you talk to me / Get it right next time / Take the money and run / Family tree / Already gone / The tourist / It's gonna be a long night. *(re-iss. 1985 on 'Liberty' lp/c; ATAK/TC-ATAK 37) (re-iss. Jul86 on 'Fame' lp/c; FA/TC-FA 3147) (cd-iss. Jul89; CDFA 3147)*

May 79.	(7") *<1298>* **DAYS GONE DOWN (STILL GOT THE LIGHT IN YOUR EYES). / WHY WON'T YOU TALK TO ME?**	–	17
Aug 79.	(7") *<BP 301) <1316>* **GET IT RIGHT NEXT TIME. / IT'S GONNA BE A LONG NIGHT**	30	21
Mar 80.	(7") *(BP 340)* **BRING IT ALL HOME. / IN TRANSIT**	54	15
Mar 80.	(lp/c) *(UAK/TCK 30298) <1039>* **SNAKES AND LADDERS**	15	61

– The Royal Mile / I was a boy scout / Welcome to Hollywood / Wastin' away / Look at the Moon / Bring it all home / The garden of England / Johnny's song / Didn't I / Syncopatin' Sandy / Cafe le Cabotin / Don't close the door. *(cd-iss. Mar89 on 'Liberty'; CZ 162)*

Oct 80.	(7") *(BP 354) <1366>* **THE ROYAL MILE (SWEET DARLIN') . / WASTIN' AWAY**	67	54	Jul80

		Liberty	Liberty	
Aug 82.	(7") *(BP 413)* **SLEEPWALKING. / WHEN I REST**	39	☐	
Sep 82.	(lp/c) *(LEG/TCG 30352)* **SLEEPWALKING**	☐	☐	

– Standing at the gates / Good intentions / A change of heart / On the way / Sleepwalking / Cat and mouse / The right moment / As wise as a serpent. *(re-iss. Sep84 on 'Fame' lp/c; FA/TC-FA 3113) (re-iss. Aug86 on 'E.M.I.' lp/c; ATAK/TC-ATAK 84) (cd-iss. Mar89; CZ 163)*

Nov 82.	(7") *(BP 415)* **A CHANGE OF HEART. / GOOD INTENTIONS**	☐	☐
Nov 82.	(7") **STANDING AT THE GATES. / GOOD INTENTIONS**	–	☐

—— Took some time off, although he did appear on MARK KNOPFLER's 'Local Hero' 1983 soundtrack and in 1987 produced 'Letter From America' by The PROCLAIMERS.

		London	London
Apr 88.	(7") *(LON 170)* **SHIPYARD TOWN. / HEARTS DESIRE**	☐	☐

(12"+=/cd-s+=) (LON X/CD 170) – ('A'lp version).

May 88. (lp/c)(cd) (LON LP/C 55)(828089-2) **NORTH AND SOUTH** `43` ☐
– North and south / Moonlight and gold / Tired of talking / Hearts run dry / A dangerous age / Shipyard town / Winter's come / Nothing ever happens down here / On a night like this / Unselfish love. (re-iss. Apr91; same)

—— now with **PAVEL ROSAK** – keyboards, drums, bass, percussion, programming / **HUGH BURNS** – electric guitars, co-producer / **MEL COLLINS** – sax / **B.J. COLE** – pedal guitar / **ARRAN AHMUN** – percussion / **MO FOSTER** – bass / **BRYN HAWORTH** – bottleneck guitar / etc. Note: Brother **JIM RAFFERTY** also provided backing vocals & co-songwriting.

<table>
<tr><td></td><td></td><td>A&M</td><td>A&M</td></tr>
</table>

Nov 92. (7"c-s/cd-s) **I COULD BE WRONG. / BAKER STREET / LIFE GOES ON**

Feb 93. (c/cd) (517495-2/-4) **ON A WING & A PRAYER** `73` ☐
– Time's caught up on you / I see red / It's easy to talk / I could be wrong / Don't speak of my heart / Get out of my life woman / Don't give up on me / Hang on / Love and affection / Does he know what he's taken on / The light of love / Life goes on.

Polydor Polydor

Jun 95. (cd) (523599-2) **OVER MY HEAD**
– Bajan moon / The waters of forgetfulness / Down and out / Over my head / The girl's got no confidence / Wrong thinking / Lonesome polecat / Right or wrong / Late again / Clear day / Out the blue / A new beginning / Her father didn't like me anyway.

– (his) compilations, others, etc. –

Apr 74. (lp) Transatlantic; (TRA 270) **GERRY RAFFERTY REVISITED** ☐ `-`
Jul 87. (cd) Transatlantic; (TRACD 601) **THE COLLECTION** ☐ `-`
Apr 78. (7") Logo; (GO 314) **MARY SKEFFINGTON. / SHOESHINE BOY** ☐ `-`
Sep 78. (lp) Logo; (VISA 7006) **GERRY RAFFERTY** ☐ `-`
Apr 84. (lp/c) Cambra; (CR/+T 132) **THE FIRST CHAPTER** ☐ `-`
Jun 88. (lp) Demon; (TRANDEM 3) **BLOOD AND GLORY** ☐ `-`
Nov 89. (cd/c/lp) E.M.I.; (CD/TC+/UAG 30333) **RIGHT DOWN THE LINE – THE BEST OF GERRY RAFFERTY** ☐ `-`
– Baker Street / Whatever's written in your heart / Bring it all home / Right down the line / Get it right next time / Night owl / A dangerous age / Family tree / Shipyard town / The right moment / Look at the Moon. (cd+=) – The way that you do it / Tired of talking / The garden of England / Sleepwalking / As wise as a serpent.
Feb 90. (7") E.M.I.; (EM 132) **BAKER STREET (remix). / NIGHT OWL (remix)** `53` `-`
(12"+=) (12EM 132) – ('A'extended).
(cd-s++=) (CDEM 132) – Bring it all home (remix).
Apr 95. (cd) Castle; (CCSCD 428) **THE TRANSATLANTIC YEARS** ☐ `-`
Oct 95. (cd/c) Polygram TV; (529279-2/-4) **ONE MORE DREAM – THE VERY BEST OF . . .** `17` `-`

RAGE AGAINST THE MACHINE

Formed: Los Angeles, California, USA . . . 1992 by rapper/vocalist ZACK DE LA ROCHA and guitarist TOM MORELLO along with bassist TIMMY C and drummer BRAD WILK. Signed to 'Epic' partly on the strength of their infamous live reputation, the band divebombed their way into the UK charts after performing the incendiary 'KILLING IN THE NAME OF' on cult 'yoof' TV show (now sadly missed), 'The Word'. One of the most visceral, angry and overtly political records of the 90's, the song formed the centrepiece of their pivotal 1993 eponymous debut album. A revelatory hybrid of monster riffing and knotty hip hop rhythms, the album was venom-spewing and utterly defiant. While detractors argued that the band's position on the roster of a major corporation was untenable, RATM countered that they had to get their message across to as wide an audience as possible. The vital point was that this was one SERIOUSLY angry young man, raging against all kinds of injustice, mainly the ruling white American capitalist system. Most of the tracks (highlights being 'BOMBTRACK', 'BULLET IN THE HEAD' and 'KNOW YOUR ENEMY') were positively seething with anger but, crucially, they were also funky as hell and this is where RATM scored over their square-jawed copyists. Music aside, how many bands in the 90's had the balls to be openly political?; or rather, how many bands even knew the meaning of protest? In a music world of drug-inspired vacancy, RATM provided a vital injection of reality. Putting their money where their mouth was, or rather putting their modesty thereabouts, the band walked on stage naked at a show in Philadelphia, the initials PMRC (Parent Music Resource Centre) scrawled across their respective chests in defiance of the risible censorship organisation. Political dissent was nothing new to either TOM or ZACK, MORELLO's father being a member of the Mau Mau (Kenyan guerillas) who fought for an end to British colonialism, while his uncle, JOMO KENYATTA, was imprisoned, later becoming the Kenyan president. LA ROCHA's father, meanwhile, was a noted L.A. muralist and political activist. While the band continued to stir up controversy with their live work (including a sold-out 1993 UK tour and blinding set at the 1994 Glastonbury Festival), a follow-up album wasn't released until 1996. When it eventually surfaced, 'EVIL EMPIRE' was something of a disappointment, lacking the focus and some of the funkiness of the debut, although it did hit US No.1. The cover art too, lacked the impact of the first album (a powerful photo of a buddhist monk setting himself on fire in protest at the Vietnam war). Nevertheless, the group put in a brilliant performance at that year's Reading Festival, whipping the crowd into a frenzy and almost upstaging headliners, The PRODIGY. The impressively talented and ever inventive MORELLO subsequently hooked up with the Essex electro-punks on the acclaimed 'NO MAN ARMY' track. Three years in the making (as per usual), the third album, 'THE BATTLE OF LOS ANGELES' (1999), once again pulled no punches and deservedly topped the US chart (only Top 30 in Britain!). Tracks such as the

single, 'GUERRILLA RADIO', 'MIC CHECK' and 'NEW MILLENNIUM HOMES', were certainly the highlights as the band undertook an extensive world tour.

Album rating: RAGE AGAINST THE MACHINE (*9) / EVIL EMPIRE (*7) / THE BATTLE OF LOS ANGELES (*7)

ZACK DE LA ROCHA (b.1970, Long Beach, Calif.) – vocals / **TOM MORELLO** (b.1964, New York City, NY) – guitars / **TIMMY C.** (b. TIM COMMERFORD) – bass / **BRAD WILK** (b.1968, Portland, Oregon) – drums

<table>
<tr><td></td><td></td><td>Epic</td><td>Epic</td></tr>
</table>

Feb 93. (7"/12"white/cd-s) (658492-7/-6/-2) **KILLING IN THE NAME. / CLEAR THE LANE / DARKNESS OF GREED** `25` `-`
Feb 93. (cd/c/lp) (472224-2/-4/-1) <52959> **RAGE AGAINST THE MACHINE** `17` `45` Nov92
– Bombtrack / Killing in the name / Take the power back / Settle for nothing / Bullet in the head / Know your enemy / Wake up / Fistful of steel / Township rebellion / Freedom. (lp re-iss. Feb99 on 'Simply Vinyl'; SVLP 69)
Apr 93. (7") (659258-7) **BULLET IN THE HEAD. / BULLET IN THE HEAD (remix)** `16` `-`
(12"/cd-s) (659258-6/-2) – Bullet in the head / Settle for nothing.
Sep 93. (7") (659471-7) **BOMBTRACK. / ('A'mix)** `37` `-`
(12"+=/cd-s+=) (659471-6/-2) – ('A'version).
Feb 94. (cd-s; w-drawn) (659821-2) **FREEDOM** `-` `-`
Apr 96. (7"colrd/cd-s) (663152-7/-2) **BULLS ON PARADE. / HADDA BE PLAYING ON THE JUKEBOX** `8` `1`
Apr 96. (cd/c/lp) (481026-2/-4/-1) <57523> **EVIL EMPIRE** `4` `1`
– People of the sun / Bulls on parade / Vietnow / Revolver / Snakecharmer / Tire me / Down rodeo / Without a face / Wind below / Roll right / Year of tha boomerang.
Aug 96. (7"orange) (663628-7) **PEOPLE OF THE SUN. / ZAPATA'S BLOOD (live)** `26` `-`
(cd-s+=) (663628-2) – Without a face (live).
(cd-s) (663628-5) – ('A'side) / Killing in the name (live) / Bullet in the head (live).

—— TIMMY C. now as **Y.tim.K**

Oct 99. (7") (668314-7) <79720> **GUERRILLA RADIO. / THE GHOST OF TOM JOAD** `32` `69`
(cd-s+=) (668314-2) – No shelter.
(cd-s) (668314-5) – ('A'side) / F*** tha police (live) / Freedom (live).
Nov 99. (cd/c) (491993-2/-4) <69630> **THE BATTLE OF LOS ANGELES** `23` `1`
– Testify / Guerrilla radio / Calm like a bomb / Mic check / Sleep now in the fire / Born of a broken man / Born as ghosts / Maria / Voice of the voiceless / New millennium homes / Ashes in the fall / War within a breath.

– compilations, etc. –

Apr 97. (10"ep) Revelation; (REV 056) **PEOPLE OF THE SUN (live) / WITHOUT A FACE (live) / INTRO BLACK STEEL IN THE HOUR OF CHAOS (live). / ZAPATA'S BLOOD (live) / BULLS ON PARADE / HADDA BE PLAYING ON THE JUKEBOX (live)** ☐ `-`

RAILWAY CHILDREN (dig out; Great Alt & Indie . . .)

RAINBOW

Formed: 1975 . . . by former DEEP PURPLE guitar guru, RITCHIE BLACKMORE. Recruiting New York band ELF wholesale, including the esteemed metal warbler RONNIE JAMES DIO, BLACKMORE recorded the eponymous debut album in the summer of '75. While 'PURPLE lumbered towards imminent implosion, BLACKMORE took the Brontosaurus-rock blueprint to mystical new heights, the classic 'MAN ON THE SILVER MOUNTAIN' being the prime example. By the release of the seminal 'RAINBOW RISING' (1976), the ubiquitous COZY POWELL was on the drum stool. The record (released under the slightly clipped moniker of BLACKMORE'S RAINBOW) featured such enduring BLACKMORE stage favourites as 'TAROT WOMAN', 'STARGAZER' and 'A LIGHT IN THE BLACK', arguably the most cohesive set of the guitarist's career. After a live album, more line-up changes ensued, BOB DAISLEY finally stepping in for MARK CLARKE, who had temporarily replaced BAIN (DAVID STONE was now the new keyboard man in place of TONY CAREY). Although 'LONG LIVE ROCK'N'ROLL' (1978) was another hard-rock classic, it wasn't until DIO had departed for BLACK SABBATH that the band enjoyed their greatest success. Recruiting ex-MARBLES vocalist, GRAHAM BONNET, as a replacement, and surprisingly enlisting old 'PURPLE mucker ROGER GLOVER on bass, the band hit the UK Top 10 twice in a row at the turn of the decade with 'SINCE YOU BEEN GONE' and 'ALL NIGHT LONG'. Watertight, marvellously crafted melodic rock, both songs featured on the 'DOWN TO EARTH' (1979) album. POWELL left the following year, as did BONNET, BLACKMORE recruiting JOE LYNN TURNER as frontman. Their next single, 'I SURRENDER', was their biggest hit to date, an epic slice of American-influenced rock that stands among metal's greatest moments. The album, 'DIFFICULT TO CURE' (1981) made the UK Top 5 although it was clear RAINBOW had adopted a more commercial approach in an attempt to break America, subsequent efforts failing to make much impact, however. With no pot of gold at the end of this particular rainbow, BLACKMORE eventually folded the band in 1984, with plans to resurrect the classic Mk.II DEEP PURPLE line-up. Ten years on, BLACKMORE (again leaving 'PURPLE) resurrected another version of RAINBOW, a 1995 album, 'STRANGER IN US ALL', purely for BLACKMORE diehards.

Album rating: RITCHIE BLACKMORE'S RAINBOW (*6) / RAINBOW RISING (*8) / LIVE ON STAGE (*4) / LONG LIVE ROCK'N'ROLL (*6) / DOWN TO EARTH (*6) / DIFFICULT TO CURE (*5) / THE BEST OF RAINBOW compilation (*7) /

STRAIGHT BETWEEN THE EYES (*5) / BENT OUT OF SHAPE (*4) / FINAL VINYL (*4) / STRANGER IN US ALL (*4) / THE VERY BEST OF RAINBOW compilation (*6)

RITCHIE BLACKMORE'S RAINBOW

RITCHIE BLACKMORE (b.14 Apr'45, Weston-Super-Mare, England) – guitar with (ex-ELF) men **RONNIE JAMES DIO** – vocals / **MICKEY LEE SOULE** – keyboards / **CRAIG GRUBER** – bass / **GARY DRISCOLL** – drums

		Oyster	Oyster
Aug 75.	(lp/c) *(OYA 2001)* <6049> **RITCHIE BLACKMORE'S RAINBOW**	11	30

– Man on the silver mountain / Self portrait / Black sheep of the family / Catch the rainbow / Snake charmer / Temple of the king / If you don't like rock'n'roll / Sixteenth century Greensleeves / Still I'm sad. *(re-iss. Aug81 on 'Polydor; 2490 141) (re-iss. Aug83 on 'Polydor' lp/c; SPE LP/MC 7) (cd-iss. 1988 & Jan93 on 'Polydor'; 825089-2)*

Oct 75. (7") *(OYR 103)* <14290> **MAN ON THE SILVER MOUNTAIN. / SNAKE CHARMER**

—— RITCHIE only retained **DIO**, recruiting new members **TONY CAREY** – keyboards / **JIMMY BAIN** – bass / **COZY POWELL** – drums

		Polydor	Oyster
May 76.	(lp/c; as BLACKMORE'S RAINBOW) *(2490 137)* <1601> **RAINBOW RISING**	11	48

– Tarot woman / Run with the wolf / Starstruck / Do you close your eyes / Stargazer / A light in the black. *(re-iss. Aug83 lp/c; SPE LP/MC 35) (cd-iss. Nov86; 823089-2)*

RAINBOW

Jul 77.	(d-lp) *(2657 016)* <1801> **RAINBOW ON STAGE (live)**	7	65

– Kill the king: (a) Man on a silver mountain, (b) Blues, (c) Starstruck / Catch the rainbow / Mistreated / Sixteenth century Greensleeves / Still I'm sad. *(re-iss. Jan84; SPDLP 6) (cd-iss. Nov86; 823656-2)*

Aug 77.	(7") *(2066 845)* **KILL THE KING: MAN ON THE SILVER MOUNTAIN. / MISTREATED**	44	-

(re-iss. Jul81; same) ; reached UK No.41

—— **MARK CLARKE** – bass (ex-COLOSSEUM, ex-URIAH HEEP) repl. BAIN who joined WILD HORSES / **BOB DAISLEY** – bass (ex-WIDOWMAKER, ex-CHICKEN SHACK) repl. CLARKE / **DAVID STONE** – keyboards (ex-SYMPHONIC SLAM) repl. CAREY

		Polydor	Polydor
Mar 78.	(7") *(2066 913)* <14481> **LONG LIVE ROCK'N'ROLL. / SENSITIVE TO LIGHT**	33	

(re-iss. Jul81; same)

Apr 78.	(lp/c) *(POLD/+C 5002)* <6143> **LONG LIVE ROCK'N'ROLL**	7	89

– Long live rock'n'roll / Lady of the lake / L.A. connection / Gates of Babylon / Kill the king / The shed (subtle) / Sensitive to light / Rainbow eyes. *(re-iss. Aug83 lp/c; SPE LP/MC 34) (cd-iss. Jan93; 825090-2)*

Sep 78.	(7"red) *(2066 968)* **L.A. CONNECTION. / LADY OF THE LAKE**	40	-

(re-iss. 7"black Jul81; same)

—— **BLACKMORE** retained only **COZY POWELL** / **GRAHAM BONNET** – vocals (ex-Solo artist, ex-MARBLES) repl. DIO who went solo / **ROGER GLOVER** – bass, vocals (ex-DEEP PURPLE) repl. DAISLEY / **DON AIREY** – keyboards repl. STONE

Aug 79.	(clear-lp/c) *(POLD/+C 5023)* <6221> **DOWN TO EARTH**	6	66

– All night long / Eyes of the world / No time to lose / Makin' love / Since you been gone / Love's no friend / Danger zone / Lost in Hollywood. *(re-iss. Apr84 lp/c; SPE LP/MC 69) (cd-iss. Dec86; 823705-2)*

Aug 79.	(7") *(POSP 70)* <2014> **SINCE YOU BEEN GONE. / BAD GIRLS**	6	57 Oct79

(re-iss. Jul81; same)

Feb 80.	(7") *(POSP 104)* <2060> **ALL NIGHT LONG. / WEISS HEIM**	5	

(re-iss. Jul81; same)

—— **JOE LYNN TURNER** – vocals, repl. BONNET who continued solo career. / **BOBBY RONDINELLI** – drums repl. POWELL who later joined E.L.P.

Jan 81.	(7") *(POSP 221)* **I SURRENDER. / MAYBE NEXT TIME**	3	-

(re-iss. Jul81; same)

Feb 81.	(lp/c) *(POLD/+C 5036)* <6316> **DIFFICULT TO CURE**	3	50

– I surrender / Spotlight kid / No release / Vielleicht das nachster zeit (Maybe next time) / Can't happen here / Freedom fighter / Midtown tunnel vision / Difficult to cure. *(re-iss. Aug84 lp/c)(cd; SPE LP/MC 76)(800-018-2)*

Jun 81.	(7") *(POSP 251)* **CAN'T HAPPEN HERE. / JEALOUS LOVER**	20	-
Nov 81.	(m-lp) *<502>* **JEALOUS LOVER**	-	

– Jealous lover / Can't happen here / I surrender / Weiss Helm.

—— **DAVE ROSENTHAL** – keyboards; repl. AIREY who joined OZZY OSBOURNE

		Polydor	Mercury
Mar 82.	(7"blue/ext-12"blue) *(POSP/+X 421)* <76146> **STONE COLD. / ROCK FEVER**	34	40

Apr 82.	(lp/c) *(POLD/+C 5056)* <4041> **STRAIGHT BETWEEN THE EYES**	5	30

– Death alley driver / Stone cold / Bring on the night (dream chaser) / Tite squeeze / Tearin' out my heart / Power / Miss Mistreated / Rock fever / Eyes of fire. *(cd-iss. Nov83; 800-028-2) (cd re-iss. Apr94; 521709-2)*

—— **BLACKMORE** still had in his ranks **GLOVER, TURNER, ROSENTHAL, /** and **CHUCK BURGI** – drums (ex-BRAND X) repl. RONDINELLI.

Aug 83.	(7"/7"pic-d) *(POSP/+P 631)* <815660> **STREET OF DREAMS. / IS ANYBODY THERE**	52	60

(12"+=) *(POSPX 631)* – Power (live).

Sep 83.	(lp/c)(cd) *(POLD/+C 5116)(<815-305-2>)* **BENT OUT OF SHAPE**	11	34

– Stranded / Can't let you go / Fool for the night / Fire dance / Anybody there / Desperate heart / Street of dreams / Drinking with the devil / Snowman / Make your move.

Oct 83.	(7"/7"sha-pic-d) *(POSP/+P 654)* **CAN'T LET YOU GO. / ALL NIGHT LONG (live)**	43	

(12"+=) *(POSPX 654)* – Stranded (live).

—— Split late '83 . . . BLACKMORE and GLOVER reformed DEEP PURPLE

RITCHIE BLACKMORE'S RAINBOW

—— re-formed for comeback concerts & an album. His new band:- **DOOGIE WHITE** – vocals / **PAUL MORRIS** – keyboards / **GREG SMITH** – bass / **JOHN O'REILLY** – drums

		Arista	Arista
Sep 95.	(cd/c) *(74321 30337-2/-4)* **STRANGER IN US ALL**		

– Wolf to the Moon / Cold hearted woman / Hunting humans (insatiable) / Stand and fight / Ariel / Too late for tears / Black masquerade / Silence / Hall of the mountain king / Still I'm sad.

– compilations, etc. –

Sep 78.	(d-lp) *Polydor; (268 3078)* **RITCHIE BLACKMORE'S RAINBOW / RAINBOW RISING**		-

Nov 81.	(d-lp/d-c) *Polydor; (POLDV/PODVC 2)* **THE BEST OF RAINBOW**	14	

– All night long / Man on the silver mountain / Can't happen here / Lost in Hollywood / Since you been gone / Stargazer / Catch the rainbow / Kill the king / 16th century Greensleeves / I surrender / Long live rock'n'roll / Eyes of the world / Starstruck / A light in the black / Mistreated. *(cd-iss. 1983; 800-074-2)*

Feb 83.	(d-c) *Polydor; (3574 141)* **DOWN TO EARTH / DIFFICULT TO CURE**		-

Feb 86.	(d-lp/d-c)(d-cd) *Polydor; (PODV/+C 8)(<827-987-2>)* **FINYL VINYL** (live 80's material)		87

– Spotlight kid / I surrender / Miss mistreated / Jealous lover / Can't happen here / Tearin' out my heart / Since you been gone / Bad girl / Difficult to cure / Stone cold / Power / Man on the silver mountain / Long live rock'n'roll / Weiss heim.

Feb 88.	(7") *Old Gold; (OG 9772)* **SINCE YOU BEEN GONE. / ALL NIGHT LONG**		

Oct 89.	(d-lp/c/cd) *Connoisseur; (RPVSOP LP/MC/CD 143)* **ROCK PROFILE VOL.1**		-

(above credited to RITCHIE BLACKMORE contains early sessions and PURPLE work) (cd.omits interview tracks + 1 song)

Dec 90.	(d-cd/c/d-lp) *Connoisseur; (DPVSOP CD/MC/LP 155)* **LIVE IN GERMANY 1976 (live)**		-

Jul 91.	(cd/d-lp) *Connoisseur; (RPVSOP CD/LP 157)* **ROCK PROFILE VOLUME 2**		-

(above also credited to RITCHIE BLACKMORE cont. RAINBOW material, etc.)

Jun 93.	(cd-s) *Old Gold; (OG)* **I SURRENDER / SINCE YOU BEEN GONE / ALL NIGHT LONG**		-
Jan 94.	(cd) *R.P.M.; (RPM 120)* **SESSION MAN**		-
Jun 94.	(cd) *R.P.M.; (PRM)* **TAKE IT! – SESSIONS 63-68**		-
Aug 97.	(cd) *Polydor; (537687-2)* **THE VERY BEST OF RAINBOW**		-

RAINCOATS (dig out; Great Alt & Indie . . .)

RAIN PARADE

Formed: Los Angeles, California, USA . . . 1981 as The SIDEWALKS by Minneapolis college mates DAVID ROBACK and MATT PIUCCI. They also numbered DAVID's younger brother STEVEN and WILL GLENN, before they opted for a name change. Their vinyl debut came with the BYRDS-like 'WHAT'S SHE DONE TO YOUR MIND' in 1982 while they found a permanent drummer in EDDIE KALWA. DAVID moonlighted with another project, RAINY DAY, but a disappointing covers album was soon forgotten when 'EMERGENCY THIRD RAIL POWER TRIP' hit the shops. Purveyors of the burgeoning "Paisley Underground" scene, the set was a throwback to the psychedelic sound of PINK FLOYD/KALEIDOSCOPE, while the guitar plucking was reminiscent of TELEVISION. The record gained a UK release on Demon's off-shoot 'Zippo' label, as did their 1984 mini-lp 'EXPLOSIONS IN THE GLASS PALACE'. The record was recorded without co-leader DAVID, however, who had left earlier in the year. 'Island' records gave them their break in '85 but surely damaged their growing reputation when they rush-released a live-set recorded in Japan, 'BEYOND THE SUNSET'. With MATT and STEVEN the sole remaining members, they recruited JOHN THOMAN and MARK MARCUM, although the 1986 album, 'CRASHING DREAM', was appropriately titled, 'Island' soon ditching them. They took a two-year hiatus before going back into the studio to finish off a double album. It never found its way to the shops, as PIUCCI joined a re-formed CRAZY HORSE, while the rest became VIVA SATURN. • **Songwriters:** All written by the ROBACKs and group, except AIN'T THAT NOTHIN' (Television).

Album rating: EMERGENCY THIRD RAIL POWER TRIP (*7) / EXPLOSIONS IN THE GLASS PALACE mini (*6) / BEYOND THE SUNSET (*6) / CRASHING DREAM (*6) / Viva Saturn: VIVA SATURN mini (*5) / SOUNDMIND (*6) / BRIGHTSIDE (*6)

DAVID ROBACK – vocals, guitar, percussion / **MATT PIUCCI** – guitar, vocals, sitar / **WILL GLENN** – keyboards / **STEVEN ROBACK** – bass, vocals / **EDDIE KALWA** – drums

		not iss.	Llama
1982.	(7") **WHAT'S SHE DONE TO YOUR MIND?. / ?**	-	-
		Zippo	Enigma

Aug 84.	(lp) *(ZING 001)* <ENIGMA 19> **EMERGENCY THIRD RAIL POWER TRIP**		1983

– Talking in my sleep / This can't be today / I look around / 1 hr. half ago / Carolyn's song / What she's done to your mind / Look at Merri / Saturday's asylum / Kaleidoscope / Look both ways.

—— trimmed to a quartet when DAVE left to form RAINY DAY (later OPAL). He is now part of duo MAZZY STAR

1984.	(m-lp) *(ZANE 003)* <71081> **EXPLOSIONS IN THE GLASS PALACE**		

– You are my friend / Prisoners / Blue / Broken horse / No easy way down.

Feb 85. (7") *(ZIPPO 45-1)* **YOU ARE MY FRIEND. / THIS CAN'T BE TODAY**

		1984

—— **MARK MARCUM** – drums repl. KALWA

—— added **JOHN THOMAN** – guitar, vocals

	Island	Restless

Jun 85. (lp/c) *(IMA/IMC 17)* *<72086>* **BEYOND THE SUNSET** (live in Tokyo 1984)

	Island	Restless
	78	

– Night shade / Prisoners / This can't be today / Blue / Eyes closed / Ain't that nothin' / Don't feel bad / 1 hr. 1/2 ago / Blue / No easy way down / Cheap wine.

	Island	Island

Oct 85. (lp/c) *(ILPS/ICT 9805)* *<90499-1/-4>* **CRASHING DREAM**
– Depending on you / My secret country / Don't feel bad / Mystic green / Sad eyes kill / Shoot down the railroad man / Fertile crescent / Invisible people / Gone west / Only business.

—— disbanded when PIUCCI formed GONE FISHIN' then joined CRAZY HORSE

– compilations, etc. –

Feb 92. (cd) *Mau Mau; (MAUCD 610)* **EMERGENCY THIRD RAIL POWER TRIP / EXPLOSIONS IN THE GLASS PALACE**

	-	

VIVA SATURN

STEVEN ROBACK – guitar, piano, vocals / **JOHN THOMAN** – guitar / **MARK MARCUM**

	World Service	Heyday

Jun 89. (m-lp) *(SERVS 003)* **VIVA SATURN**
– So glad / Brought it on yourself / Remember I'm dead / Old world / Wild town.

—— **MATT PIUCCI** – guitar, vocals; repl. MARK

—— added **ROSS INDEN** – bass / **CARLO NUCCIO** – drums

	Normal	Heyday

May 94. (cd) *(NORMAL 139CD)* *<ADE 009CD>* **SOUNDMIND**

	Normal	Heyday
		1992

– Still she waits / Love the sugar / Believe / Haven't felt like / Soundmind / Suicidal lamb / Raised / Better get your nerve Paradise / Mermaid / Waiting for the train.

	Restless	Restless

Jul 95. (cd) *<(72909-2)>* **BRIGHTSIDE**
– Send a message / Black cloud / Brightside / Here comes April / Abondoned car string me out a line / Mourn the light / Distracted / Nothing helps / Heart of you / One for my baby.

RAIN TREE CROW (see under ⇒ JAPAN)

RAINY DAY (see under ⇒ MAZZY STAR)

Bonnie RAITT

Born: 8 Nov'49, Burnbank, California. Brought up in a Quaker family (her dad John was also an actor!), she learned guitar as a young child, receiving the instrument as a Christmas present and subsequently catching the blues bug at college in Cambridge, Massachusetts (reading African studies). Branching out from her love of folk music (JOAN BAEZ was a favourite) to records by JOHN LEE HOOKER, SON HOUSE and MISSISSIPPI FRED McDOWELL, the young RAITT became a well known blues performer on the Northeastern circuit alongside bassist, DAN 'FREEBO' FRIEDBERG (sometimes sharing a stage with her idols, MISSISSIPPI JOHN HURT, HOWLIN' WOLF and SIPPIE WALLACE). Her boyfriend, Dick Waterman, became her manager and, influenced by BOB DYLAN, MUDDY WATERS and JOHN HAMMOND, RAITT began recording for 'Warner Brothers' in 1971. Establishing her own individual blend of country blues and LA-style soft rock, her eponymous debut album set the tone for her later work with a combination of self-penned songs and carefully selected covers (by the likes of JACKSON BROWNE, ROBERT JOHNSON and RANDY NEWMAN). Her second set, 'GIVE IT UP', followed in 1972 and featured the lusty Chris Smithers' cover, 'LOVE ME LIKE A MAN', Jackson Browne's 'UNDER THE FALLING SKY' and Eric Katz's 'LOVE HAS NO PRIDE'. Recorded after RAITT's relocation to LA, 1973's 'TAKIN' MY TIME' (with contributions from TAJ MAHAL, JIM KELTNER, BILL PAYNE and LOWELL GEORGE) featured such outstanding tracks as 'KOKOMO BLUES'. Over the ensuing decade, RAITT moved towards an out-and-out rock direction, exemplified in 1977's 'SWEET FORGIVENESS' (her most successful 'Warner Brothers' album, peaking at US 25), recorded with her regular touring band of WILL McFARLANE (guitar), JEFF LABES (keyboards), DENNIS WHITTED (drums), FREEBO (bass) and vocalists MICHAEL McDONALD and JOHN DAVID SOUTHER. The record provided RAITT with her first US Top 60 hit single, a rocking version of Del Shannon's 'RUNAWAY'. 1982's 'GREEN LIGHT' (a US Top 40 album) featured a new backing outfit, The BUMP BAND, which numbered ex-FACES keyboard man, IAN McLAGAN, drummer RICKY FATAAR (ex-BEACH BOYS), bassist RAY OHARA and guitarist JOHNNY LEE SCHELL. RAITT subsequently disappeared from the scene to undergo drugs and alcohol rehabilitation, resurfacing in 1985 when she took part in the ARTISTS AGAINST APARTHEID project. Her last album for 'Warners' was 'NINE LIVES', a modest selling record which included songs by KARLA BONOFF, TOM SNOW, BRYAN ADAMS, WILL JENNINGS, RICHARD KERR and ERIC KATZ. It also featured her old friend and blues mentor, SIPPIE WALLACE, singing on their version of Toots & The Maytals' 'TRUE LOVE IS HARD TO FIND'. In 1987, RAITT joined a programme for recovering alcoholics and after recovering, spent two days recording with

PRINCE in Minneapolis. Her benefit work also increased in 1987 when she took part in The July Fourth Disarmament Festival in the Soviet Union, Stop Contra Aid, Amnesty International, Farm Aid and a film about homeless awareness. Real success had been a long time coming, although she bounced back with 'BABY OF MINE' (a duet recorded with DON WAS) from the Disney covers album, 'Stay Awake' (1988); the single's release led to a new recording deal with 'Capitol'. Her first album for her new company, 1989's DON WAS-produced 'NICK OF TIME', (highlights being the self-penned title track, 'THE ROAD'S MY MIDDLE NAME' and JOHN HIATT's 'THING CALLED LOVE') was aimed at the AOR market, subsequently netting her three Grammy's and gave her a UK chart debut at number No.51 (a chart topper in America). This elevated her into the superstar bracket, leading to guest spots on projects by the likes of DAVID CROSBY, EMMYLOU HARRIS and B.B. KING to name but a few. RAITT's next album, 'LUCK OF THE DRAW' (1991), was an even bigger seller (US Top 3 and UK Top 40), although the songs (from the likes of JOHN HIATT, PAUL BRADY and herself) weren't quite as strong. RAITT's personal life became stable following her marriage to actor, MICHAEL O'KEEFE, in 1991 after years of singing about broken hearts and no-good men. 1994 saw a return to previous highs with 'LONGING IN THEIR HEARTS', an album that reaped more Grammy's and went deservedly multi-platinum. A concert set, 'ROAD TESTED' (1995), was incredibly her first such outing despite her legendary live status. Featuring duets with JACKSON BROWNE and BRUCE HORSNBY, it also contained a disappointing collaboration with BRYAN ADAMS, although excellent versions of Talking Heads' 'BURNING DOWN THE HOUSE' and John Prine's 'ANGEL FROM MONTGOMERY' were enough to save the album. Having started out in her long career using an acoustic, thumb-picking style of playing and progressing to slide guitar, she has become perhaps the only woman in the "rock" world to be recognised as a guitar virtuoso (RAITT was initially tutored by the late, great LOWELL GEORGE of LITTLE FEAT). • **Covered:** WALKING BLUES (Robert Johnson) / UNDER THE FALLING SKY (Jackson Browne) / LOVE HAS NO PRIDE (Eric Kaz) / GUILTY (Randy Newman) / WHAT IS SUCCESS (Allen Toussaint) / WOMEN BE WISE (Wallace-Beach) / MY FIRST NIGHT ALONE WITH YOU (. . . Vassey) / SUGAR MAMA (McClinton-Clark) / LOUISE (Paul Siebel) / NO WAY TO TREAT A LADY (Bryan Adams) / THE GLOW (. . . Hildebrand) / BUILT TO MAKE ME LEAVE HOME (. . . Randle) / WITH YA, WON'T CHAS (. . . Schell) / YOUR GOOD THING (Hayes-Porter) / YOUR GONNA GET WHAT'S COMING (Robert Palmer) / GOIN' WILD FOR YOU BABY (Snow-Batteau) / etc. In 1989 most were written by JOHN HIATT and others including SOMETHING TO TALK ABOUT (S.Eikhardt) / I CAN'T MAKE YOU LOVE ME (Reid / Shamblin).

Album rating: BONNIE RAITT (*5) / GIVE IT UP (*6) / TAKIN' MY TIME (*7) / STREETLIGHTS (*6) / HOME PLATE (*4) / SWEET FORGIVENESS (*5) / THE GLOW (*6) / GREEN LIGHT (*6) / NINE LIVES (*5) / NICK OF TIME (*8) / THE BONNIE RAITT COLLECTION compilation (*7) / LUCK OF THE DRAW (*8) / LONGING IN THEIR HEARTS (*7) / ROAD TESTED (*5) / FUNDAMENTAL (*5)

BONNIE RAITT – vocals, guitar, steel guitar / **FREEBO** – bass / **A.C.REID** – tenor sax / etc.

	Warners	Warners

Nov 71. (lp) *<(WS 1953)>* **BONNIE RAITT**
– Bluebird revisited / I'm a mighty tight woman / Thank you / Finest lovin' man / Any day woman / Big road / Walking blues / Danger heartbreak dead ahead / Since I fell for you / I ain't blue / Woman be wise. *(re-iss. Jun76; K 56255)*

Dec 71. (7") *<7554>* **BLUEBIRD. / WOMAN BE WISE**

	-	

Nov 72. (lp) *(K 46189)* *<BS 2643>* **GIVE IT UP**

		Oct72

– Give it up or let me go / Nothing seems to matter / I know / If you gotta be a fool of somebody / Love me like a man / Stayed too long at the fair / Under the falling sky / You got to know how / You told me baby / Love has no pride.

Dec 72. (79") *(K 16226)* *<7645>* **STAYED TOO LONG AT THE FAIR. / UNDER THE FALLING SKY**

—— now on session **LOWELL GEORGE / BILL PAYNE / JIM KELTNER + TAJ MAHAL**

Oct 73. (7") *<7758>* **YOU'VE BEEN IN LOVE TOO LONG. / EVERYBODY'S CRYIN' MERCY**

	-	

Nov 73. (lp) *(K 46261)* *<BS 2729>* **TAKIN' MY TIME**

	87	Oct73

– You've been in love too long / I gave my love a candle / Let me in / Everybody's cryin' mercy / Cry like a rainstorm / Wah she go do / I feel the same / I thought I was a child / Write me a few of your lines – Kokomo blues / Guilty. *(re-iss. Jun76; K 56254) (cd-iss. Feb93; 7599 27275-2)*

Oct 74. (7") *<8044>* **I GOT PLENTY. / YOU GOTTA BE READY FOR LOVE (IF YOU WANNA BE MINE)**

	-	

Nov 74. (lp) *(K 56075)* *<BS 2818>* **STREETLIGHTS**

	80	Oct74

– That song about the Midway / Rainy day man / Angel from Montgomery / I got plenty / Streetlights / What is success / Ain't nobody home / Everything that touches you / Got you on my mind / You gotta be ready for love (if you wanna be mine). *(cd-iss. 1989; 927286-2)*

Nov 75. (7") *<8166>* **MY FIRST NIGHT ALONE WITH YOU. / GOOD ENOUGH**

Dec 75. (lp/c) *(K/K4 56160)* *<BS 2864>* **HOME PLATE**

	43	Oct75

– What do you want the boy to do / Good enough / Run like a thief / Fool yourself / My first night alone with you / Walk out the front door / Sugar mama / Pleasin' each other / I'm blowin' away / Your sweet and shiny eyes. *(cd-iss. Feb93; 7599 27292-2)*

May 76. (7") *<8189>* **WALK OUT THE FRONT DOOR. / RUN LIKE A THIEF**

	-	

Jun 76. (7") *(K 16728)* **I'M BLOWIN' AWAY. / RUN LIKE A THIEF**

	-	-

—— In 1976, she duetted w/**GEOFF MULDAUR** on single 'WHEN YOU TOUCH ME THIS WAY' / 'SINCE I'VE BEEN WITH YOU BABE'.

—— Her touring band were **WILL McFARLANE** – guitar / **JEFF LABES** – keyboards / **DENNIS WHITTED** – drums / **FREEBO** – bass (as always) + guests **MICHAEL McDONALD + J.D.SOUTHER** on guest backing vocals

Apr 77. (lp/c) *(K/K4 56323)* *<BS 2990>* **SWEET FORGIVENESS**

	25	

– Sweet forgiveness / Gamblin' man / Two lives / Runaway / About to make me leave home / Three time loser / My opening farewell / Takin' my time / Home / Louise.

May 77. (7") <8382> **RUNAWAY. / LOUISE**　　| - | | 57 |
May 77. (7") (K 16953) **RUNAWAY. / HOME**　　| - | |
Aug 77. (7") <8430> **THREE TIME LOSER. / TWO LIVES**　　| - | |
Aug 77. (7") (K 17003) **THREE TIME LOSER. / LOUISE**　　| - | |
Nov 77. (7") <8485> **GAMBLIN' MAN. / ABOUT TO MAKE ME LEAVE HOME**　　| - | |
Oct 79. (lp/c) <3369> **THE GLOW**　　| | 30 |
　　– I thank you / Your good thing (is about to end) / Sleep's dark and silent gate / The glow / Bye bye baby / The boy can't help it / (I could have been your) Best old friend / You're gonna get what's coming / (Goin') Wild for you baby. (cd-iss. Feb93; 7559 27403-2)
Nov 79. (7") <49116> **YOU'RE GONNA GET WHAT'S COMING. / THE GLOW**　　| - | | 73 |
Mar 80. (7") <49185> **(I COULD HAVE BEEN YOUR) BEST OLD FRIEND. / (GOIN') WILD FOR YOU BABY**　　| - | |

—— In mid-80's, she released 'Asylum' 45; 'DON'T IT MAKE YOU WANNA DANCE'. At the same time she and J.D. SOUTHER issued 'ONCE IN A LIFETIME' / 'YOU'RE ONLY LONELY'.

—— next feat. **The BUMP BAND** incl. **IAN McLAGAN** – keyboards (ex-SMALL FACES) / **JOHNNY LEE SCHELL** – guitar / **RAY O'HARA** – bass / **RICKY FATAAR** – drums

Feb 82. (7") <50022> **CAN'T GET ENOUGH. / KEEP THIS HEART IN MIND**　　| - | |
Feb 82. (lp/c) (K/K4 56980) <BSK 3630> **GREEN LIGHT**　　| | 38 |
　　– Keep this heart in mind / River of tears / Can't get enough / Me and the boys / I can't help myself / Willya wontcha / Let's keep it between us / Baby come back / Talk to me / Green light.
Apr 82. (7") <29992> **ME AND THE BOYS. / RIVER OF TEARS**　　| - | |
Apr 82. (7") (K 17943) **ME AND THE BOYS. / KEEP THIS HEART IN MIND**　　| | - |

—— She semi-retired in 1982 to go through a period of drug rehabilitation and attend a form of alcoholics anonymous.

Sep 86. (lp/c/cd) (925486-1/-4/-2) <25486> **NINE LIVES**　　| | Aug 86 |
　　– No way to treat a lady / Runnin' back to me / Who but a fool / Crime of passion / All day, all night / Stand up to the night / Excited / Freezin' (for a little human love) / True love is hard to find / Angel.
Sep 86. (7") <28615> **NO WAY TO TREAT A LADY. / STAND UP TO THE NIGHT**　　| - | |
Feb 87. (7") <28450> **CRIMES OF PASSION. / STAND UP TO THE NIGHT**　　| - | |

—— In Oct '88, she teamed up with DON WAS of WAS (NOT WAS) on 'A&M' single 'BABY MINE'. Their vocalists **SWEAT PEA ATKINSON + SIR HARRY BOWENS** plus guests **DAVID CROSBY & GRAHAM NASH, FATAAR & SCHELL, KIM WILSON,** etc.

	Capitol	Capitol
Apr 89. (cd/c/lp) (CD/TC+EST 2095) <91268> **NICK OF TIME**	51	1

　　– Nick of time / A thing called love / Love letter / Cry on my shoulder / Real man / Nobody's girl / Have a heart / Too soon to tell / I will not be denied / I ain't gonna let you break my heart again / The road's my middle name. (re-dist.Apr90)
May 89. (7") (TC+/CL 530) <44364> **NICK OF TIME. / THE ROAD'S MY MIDDLE NAME**　　| | Aug89 |
　　(12"+=/cd-s+=) (12/CD CL 530) – I ain't gonna let you break my heart again. (re-dist.Mar90) <re-iss. May90; hit US No.92>
Mar 90. (7") <44501> **HAVE A HEART. / THE ROAD'S MY MIDDLE NAME**　　| - | 49 |
May 90. (7") (CL 576) **A THING CALLED LOVE. / NOBODY'S GIRL**　　| | - |
　　(12"+=/cd-s+=) (12/CD CL 576) – The road's my middle name.

—— next featured **HIATT** plus **BRUCE HORNSBY + RICHARD THOMPSON**

Jul 91. (cd/c/lp) (CD/TC+/EST 2145) <96111> **LUCK OF THE DRAW**　　| 38 | 2 |
　　– Something to talk about / Good man, good woman / I can't make you love me / Tangled and dark / Come to me / No business / One part of my lover / Not the only one / Papa come quick (Jody and Chico) / Slow ride / Luck of the draw / All at once.
Jul 91. (c-s/7") (TC+/CL 619) <44724> **SOMETHING TO TALK ABOUT. / ONE PART OF MY LOVER**　　| | 5 |
　　(12"+=) (12CL 619) – I ain't gonna let you break my heart again.
　　(cd-s++=) (CDCL 619) – Nick of time. (re-iss. Feb92; same)
Aug 91. (c-s/7") (TC/+CL 627) <44764> **NOT THE ONLY ONE. / COME TO ME**　　| | 34 Mar92 |
　　(12"+=/cd-s+=) (12/CD CL 627) – Papa come quick (Jody and Chico).
Dec 91. (c-s/7") (TC+/CL 639) <44729> **I CAN'T MAKE YOU LOVE ME. / COME TO ME**　　| 50 | 18 Nov91 |
　　(cd-s+=) (CDCL 639) – Tangled and dark.
Jun 92. (c-s/7") <44770> **GOOD MAN, GOOD WOMAN. / NICK OF TIME**　　| | |
　　(cd-s+=) – Thing called love / One part be my lover.
Apr 94. (c-s) (TCCL 713) <58125> **LOVE SNEAKIN' UP ON YOU / HELL TO PAY**　　| 69 | 19 Mar94 |
　　(cd-s+=) (CDCL 713) – Nick of time / Baby be mine.
Apr 94. (cd/c) (CD/TC EST 2227) <81427> **LONGING IN THEIR HEARTS**　　| 26 | 1 Mar94 |
　　– Love sneakin' up on you / Longing in their hearts / You / Cool, clear water / Circle dance / I sho do / Dimming of the day / Feeling of falling / Steal your heart away / Storm warning / Hell to pay / Shadow of doubt.
Jun 94. (c-s) (TCCL 718) **YOU / I CAN'T MAKE YOU LOVE ME**　　| 31 | - |
　　(cd-s+=) (CDCL 718) – I ain't gonna let you break my heart again / All at once.
　　(cd-s) (CDCLS 718) – ('A'side) / This thing called love / Longing in their hearts / Good man, good woman.
Jul 94. (c-s) <58195> **YOU / FEELING OF FALLING**　　| - | 92 |
May 95. (c-s) (74321 26624-4) <12795> **YOU GOT IT / FEELING OF FALLING**　　| | 33 Feb95 |
　　(cd-s+=) (74321 26624-2) – Circle dance.
　　(above single issued on 'Arista' & from movie 'Boys On The Side')
Nov 95. (c-s; BONNIE RAITT & BRYAN ADAMS) (TCCL 763)
　　<58500> **ROCK STEADY (live) / COME TO ME (live)**　　| 50 | 73 |
　　(cd-s+=) (CDCL 763) – Thing called love (live with BRUCE HORNSBY).
Nov 95. (cd/c) (CD/TC EST 2274) <33702> **ROAD TESTED (live)**　　| 69 | 44 |
　　– Thing called love / Something to talk about / Never make your move too soon /

Shake a little / Matters of the heart / Love me like a man / The Kokomo medley: Write me a few of your lines – Kokomo blues / My opening farewell / Dimming of the day / Longing in their hearts / Love sneakin' up on you / Burning down the house / I can't make you love me / I believe I'm in love / Rock steady / Angel from Montgomery.
Apr 96. (c-s) (TCCL 771) **BURNING DOWN THE HOUSE (live) / SHAKE A LITTLE (live)**　　| | |
　　(cd-s+=) (CDCL 771) – I can't make you love me (live) / Rock steady (live).
Apr 98. (cd) <(8 56397-2)> **FUNDAMENTAL**　　| | 17 |
　　– Fundamental things / Cure for love / Round and round / Spit of love / Lover's will / Blue for no reason / Meet me halfway / I'm on your side / Fearless love / I need love / One belief away.

– compilations, etc. –

Aug 90. (cd/c/lp) Warners; (26242) **THE BONNIE RAITT COLLECTION**　　| | 61 Jul90 |
　　– Finest lovin' man / Give it up or let me go / Women be wise (live with SIPPIE WALLACE) / Under the falling sky / Love me like a man / Love has no pride / I feel the same / Guilty / Angel from Montgomery / What is success / My first night alone without you / Sugar mama / Louise / About to make me leave home / Runaway / The glow / (Goin') Wild for you baby / Willya wontcha / True love is hard to find / No way to treat a lady.

RAKIM (see under ⇒ B, Eric & RAKIM)

RAMMSTEIN

Formed: Germany . . . 1994 by former East German Olympic swimmer, TILL LINDEMANN, plus his 30-something long-time companions, OLIVER RIEDEL, RICHARD KRUSPE, FLAKE, PAUL LANDERS and CHRISTOPH SCHEIDER. Naming themselves after the German airbase at Rammstein (originally going by the name of ORGASM DEATH GIMMICK), the industrial shock metallers, like a fusion of LAIBACH, MINISTRY and fellow countrymen, EINSTURZENDE NEUBAUTEN, RAMMSTEIN had five hit singles in their home country. This was due to their OTT stage extravaganzas which featured TILL singing (in his native tongue) covered in a metallic coat of fire before he unveiled to show off his muscular, naked body complete with very large dildo strapped upside his leather belt!. Meanwhile, the naked OLIVER (bar his white socks), RICHARD (wearing a white wedding dress) and the rest of the bare-cheeked crew played their aggro-rock to a backdrop of Leni Riefenstahl's (Hitler's fave!) controversial film, 'Olympiad'. A German-only released debut album was finally upstaged by a second, 'SEHNSUCHT' (1997), which went on to surprisingly sell over half a million copies in the States. In the Autumn of '98, RAMMSTEIN were at the centre of some accusations of neo Nazi-ism when English tabloids branded them with that unfortunate tag. Around the same time, the single 'DU HAST' (actually a cover of Depeche Mode's 'STRIPPED') was given a British release and it looked as if these brassnecked technoid show-offs were going to eventually invade our shores.

Album rating: SEHNSUCHT (*7)

TILL LINDEMANN – vocas / **RICHARD KRUSPE** – guitar / **PAUL LANDERS** – guitar / **OLIVER RIEDEL** – bass / **FLAKE** – keyboards / **CHRISTOPH SCHNEIDER** – drums

	London	Motor – Slash
Nov 97. (cd) (537304-2) <539901> **SEHNSUCHT**		45 Jan98

　　– Sehnsucht / Engel / Tier / Bestrafe mich / Du hast / Buck dich / Spiel mit mir / Klavier / Alter Mann / Eifersucht / Kuss mich (fellfrosch) / Engel / Du hast.
Nov 98. (cd-s) (LONCD 422) **DU HAST / (Jacob Hellner remix) / (Clawfinger remix)**　　| | |

RAMONES

Formed: Forest Hills, New York, USA . . . August '74 as a trio by JOHNNY, JOEY and DEE DEE, who all took the working surname RAMONE (although they were brothers only in the loosest sense of the term). One of the prime movers (many would subsequently cite them as the first) in the emergent US punk scene, the band began a residency at the legendary NY club, CBGB's, TOMMY coming in on the drum stool in order to free JOEY up for suitably deranged vocal duties. In June '75, the band were dealt a slight setback when they failed an audition for RICK DERRINGER's 'Blue Sky' label in front of 20,000 fans at a JOHNNY WINTER concert, although later that year manager, Danny Fields, found up-and-coming new wave label, 'Sire' (run by Seymour Stein) considerably more receptive. Released around the same time as their pivotal (and highly influential) London Roundhouse gig, the band's eponymous summer '76 debut album presented a sound every bit as exhilaratingly juvenile and humorously warped as their leering, mop-topped scruffiness might suggest. Ripping out gloriously dumb, two-minute buzz-saw classics on such perennial punk subjects as solvent abuse ('I WANNA SNIFF SOME GLUE'), girls (most of the album) and erm, chainsaws ('CHAIN SAW'), The RAMONES had invented themselves as larger than life, cartoon yob no-wavers well ahead of their time, their attitude alone copped by countless two-bit punk bands (and a few great ones) the length and breadth of the British Isles. Barely pausing for breath (or whatever it was these guys inhaled), the new yoik brudders followed up with 'LEAVE HOME' (1977), another strychnine-fuelled session of primitive but tuneful terrace-chant anthems, RAMONES-style; from this point onwards, the words 'Gabba Gabba Hey' would be forever carved in the stone of the punk lexicon. The album even managed a minor dent in the UK charts, a full-scale assault led later that year with the brilliantly throwaway 'SHEENA IS A PUNK ROCKER'. The climax of the early RAMONES blitzkreig came with 'ROCKET TO RUSSIA' (1977), the lads easing ever so slightly off the gas pedal and taking the credo of mangled, two-minute surf-pop to its dayglo conclusion; the hilarious 'CRETIN HOP', 'ROCKAWAY BEACH' and 'TEENAGE LOBOTOMY' remain among the most definitive moments in the RAMONES' dog-eared catalogue. A rather disappointing Top 60 placing failed to do the record justice, although by this stage the band were beginning to make some inroads into the home market. Further evidence, if any was needed, that The RAMONES' chief writer was at the peak of his powers came with the blistering 'Chinese Rocks', a HEARTBREAKERS track co-penned by DEE DEE. With the departure of TOMMY (into production work) the following year, ex-VOID-OID MARC BELL was recruited in his place, rechristened, of course, MARKY RAMONE. Incredibly, the tried and tested formula (with a few notable exceptions, a guitar solo (!) on 'GO MENTAL' and a ballad, 'QUESTIONINGLY') continued to excite with 'ROAD TO RUIN' (1978), their first album to break into the UK Top 40 and the resting place of the legendary 'I WANNA BE SEDATED'. The riotous 'IT'S ALIVE' (1979) captured the RAMONES concert experience head-on, neatly wrapping up the first stage of the boys' career and providing a handy overview of their career to date. Every punk band coped with the scene's fragmentation in their own way, The RAMONES not so wisely choosing to indulge their love of classic 60's pop via the genre's guru, Phil Spector. The result were predictably confused, many longtime RAMONES headbangers balking at their UK Top 10 cover of The Ronettes' 'BABY I LOVE YOU'. Subsequent 80's efforts such as 'PLEASANT DREAMS' (1981) and 'SUBTERRANEAN JUNGLE' (1983) lacked the ragged glory of their earlier work although with the replacement of MARKY with RICHIE (aka RICHARD REINHARDT) in 1984, 'TOO TOUGH TO DIE' (1985) found the band sharpening their attack and presenting a united front against the hardcore pretenders of the day. They couldn't keep it up though, and the limitations of their art really began to bite deep on the bedraggled 'ANIMAL BOY' (1986) and 'HALFWAY TO SANITY' (1987). DEE DEE bailed out after 'BRAIN DRAIN' (1989), replacement C.J. effecting something of a rejuvenation on 'MONDO BIZARRO' (1992). The following year's 'ACID EATERS' saw the band pay tribute to the 60's sounds which had inspired them, while in turn, many of the younger bands who had actually been inspired by The RAMONES would soon be calling the shots at America'a major labels. Yet despite this punk revival and the success of such acts as GREEN DAY and OFFSPRING, The RAMONES finally decided to call it a day in early 1996 following the release of the 'ADIOS AMIGOS' set and the accompanying tour. • Songwriters: DEE DEE and group, except; DO YOU WANNA DANCE (Bobby Freeman) / SURFIN' BIRD (Trashmen) / BABY I LOVE YOU (Ronettes; Phil Spector) / NEEDLES AND PINS (Searchers) / STREET FIGHTIN' MAN (Rolling Stones) / TAKE IT AS IT COMES (Doors) / R.A.M.O.N.E.S. (Motorhead) / ANY WAY YOU WANT IT (Dave Clark) / SPIDER-MAN (Harris-Webster) / etc. In '77, DEE DEE co-wrote 'CHINESE ROCKS' for The HEARTBREAKERS. • Trivia: The RAMONES featured in the films 'Blank Generation' (1976) & 'Rock'n'roll High School' (Roger Corman 1979).

Album rating: RAMONES (*9) / LEAVE HOME (*8) / ROCKET TO RUSSIA (*8) / ROAD TO RUIN (*7) / IT'S ALIVE (*6) / END OF THE CENTURY (*7) / PLEASANT DREAMS (*6) / SUBTERRANEAN JUNGLE (*6) / TOO TOUGH TO DIE (*7) / ANIMAL BOY (*6) / HALFWAY TO SANITY (*4) / RAMONES MANIA compilation (*9) / BRAIN DRAIN (*4) / LOCO LIVE (*3) / MONDO BIZARRO (*3) / ACID EATERS (*3) / ADIOS AMIGOS (*5) / WE'RE OUTTA HERE (*5)

JOEY RAMONE (b. JEFFREY HYMAN, 19 May'51) – vocals (was drummer) / **JOHNNY RAMONE** (b. JOHN CUMMINGS, 8 Oct'51, Long Island, N.Y.) – guitar, vocals / **DEE DEE RAMONE** (b. DOUGLAS COLVIN, 18 Sep'52, Fort Lee, Virginia) – bass, vocals / **TOMMY RAMONE** (b. TOM ERDELYI, 29 Jan'49, Budapest, Hungary) – drums

		Sire	Sire
Jul 76.	(lp) (9103 253) <7520> **RAMONES**		May76

– Blitzkrieg bop / Beat on the brat / Judy is a punk / I wanna be your boyfriend / Chain saw / Now I wanna sniff some glue / I don't wanna go down to the basement / Loudmouth / Havana affair / Listen to my heart / 53rd & 3rd / Let's dance / I don't wanna walk around with you / Today your love, tomorrow the world. (re-iss. Sep78; SRK 6020)

Jul 76.	(7") (6078 601) <725> **BLITZKRIEG BOP. / HAVANA AFFAIR**		May76
Oct 76.	(7"m) <734> **I WANNA BE YOUR BOYFRIEND. / CALIFORNIA SUN (live) / I DON'T WANNA WALK AROUND WITH YOU (live)**	-	
Feb 77.	(7"m) (6078 603) **I REMEMBER YOU. / CALIFORNIA SUN (live) / I DON'T WANNA WALK AROUND WITH YOU (live)**	-	
Mar 77.	(lp) (9103 254) <7528> **LEAVE HOME**	45	- Feb77

– Glad to see you go / Gimme gimme shock treatment / I remember you / Oh oh I love her so / Babysitter * / Suzy is a headbanger / Pinhead / Now I wanna be a good boy / Swallow my pride / What's your game / California sun / Commando / You're gonna kill that girl / You should never have opened that door / California sun. (re-iss. Jun77 'Carbona Not Glue' replaced *; other re-iss's same) (re-iss. Sep78; SRK 6031) (re-iss. Nov87 on 'Mau Mau'; MAU 602)

May 77.	(7"m,12"m) (6078 606) <746> **SHEENA IS A PUNK ROCKER. / COMMANDO / I DON'T CARE**	22	81
Jul 77.	(7"m) (6078 607) <738> **SWALLOW MY PRIDE. / PINHEAD / LET'S DANCE (live)**	36	- Mar77
Nov 77.	(7"m,12"m) (6078 611) **ROCKAWAY BEACH. / TEENAGE LOBOTOMY / BEAT ON THE BRAT**		-
Nov 77.	(7") <1008> **ROCKAWAY BEACH. / LOCKET LOVE**	-	66
Dec 77.	(lp) (9103 255) <6042> **ROCKET TO RUSSIA**	60	49 Nov77

– Cretin hop / Rockaway beach / Here today, gone tomorrow / Locket love / I don't care / Sheena is a punk rocker / We're a happy family / Teenage lobotomy / Do you

wanna dance? / I wanna be well / I can't give you anything / Ramona / Surfin' bird / Why is it always this way. (re-iss. Sep78; SRK 6042)

| Feb 78. | (7") <1017> **DO YOU WANNA DANCE? / BABYSITTER** | - | 86 |
| Mar 78. | (7"m) (6078 615) **DO YOU WANNA DANCE? / IT'S A LONG WAY BACK TO GERMANY / CRETIN HOP** | | - |

—— **MARKY RAMONE** (b. MARC BELL, 15 Jul'56) – drums (ex-RICHARD HELL & THE VOID-OIDS, ex-DUST) repl. TOMMY who continued producing others.

| Sep 78. | (7",7"yellow,12"yellow,12"red) (SRE 1031) <1025> **DON'T COME CLOSE. / I DON'T WANT YOU** | 38 | |
| Oct 78. | (yellow-lp) <(SRK 6063)> **ROAD TO RUIN** | 32 | |

– I just want to have something to do / I wanted everything / Don't come close / I don't want you / Needles and pins / I'm against it / I wanna be sedated / Go mental / Questioningly / She's the one / Bad brain / It's a long way back.

Nov 78.	(7") <1045> **NEEDLES AND PINS. / I WANTED EVERYTHING**		-
Jan 79.	(7") (SIR 4009) **SHE'S THE ONE. / I WANNA BE SEDATED**	-	-
May 79.	(d-lp/c) (SRK/SRC 26074) **IT'S ALIVE (live)**	27	-

– Rockaway beach / Teenage lobotomy / Blitzkrieg bop / I wanna be well / Glad to see you go / Gimme gimme shock treatment / You're gonna kill that girl / I don't care / Sheena is a punk rocker / Havana affair / Commando / Here today, gone tomorrow / Surfin' bird / Cretin hop / Listen to my heart / California sun / I don't wanna walk around with you / Pinhead / Do you wanna dance? / Chain saw / Today your love, tomorrow the world / Now I wanna be a good boy / Judy is a punk / Suzy is a headbanger / Let's dance / Oh oh I love her so / Now I wanna sniff some glue / We're a happy family. (cd-iss. Nov93 on 'Warners'; 7599 26069-2) (cd re-iss. Jan96; 9362 46045-2)
(above album features TOMMY on drums)

Sep 79.	(7") <1051> **DO YOU WANNA DANCE? / ROCK'N'ROLL HIGH SCHOOL**	-	-
Sep 79.	(7") (SIR 4021) **ROCK'N'ROLL HIGH SCHOOL. / SHEENA IS A PUNK ROCKER (live) / ROCKAWAY BEACH (live)**	67	-
Jan 80.	(lp/c) <(SRK/SRC 6077)> **END OF THE CENTURY**	14	44

– Do you remember rock'n'roll radio? / I'm affected / Danny says / Chinese rock / The return of Jackie and Judy / Let's go / Baby I love you / I can't make it on time / This ain't Havana / Rock'n'roll high school / All the way / High risk insurance. (re-iss. cd Mar94; 7599 27429-2)

Jan 80.	(7") (SIR 4031) <49182> **BABY, I LOVE YOU. / HIGH RISK INSURANCE**	8	
Apr 80.	(7") <49261> **DO YOU REMEMBER ROCK'N'ROLL RADIO? / LET'S GO**	-	
Apr 80.	(7") (SIR 4037) **DO YOU REMEMBER ROCK'N'ROLL RADIO?. / I WANT YOU AROUND**	54	-
Jul 81.	(7") (SIR 4051) <49812> **WE WANT THE AIRWAVES. / ALL'S QUIET ON THE EASTERN FRONT**		-
Jul 81.	(lp/c) <(SRK/SRC 3571)> **PLEASANT DREAMS**		58

– We want the airwaves / All's quiet on the Eastern front / The KKK took my baby away / Don't go / You sound like you're sick / It's not my place / She's a sensation / 7-11 / You didn't mean anything to me / Come on now / This business is killing me / Sitting in my room. (re-iss. cd Mar94; 7599 23571-2)

| Oct 81. | (7") (SIR 4052) **SHE'S A SENSATION. / ALL'S QUIET ON THE EASTERN FRONT** | | - |
| May 83. | (lp/c) (WX/+C 3800) <23800> **SUBTERRANEAN JUNGLE** | | 83 |

– Little bit o' soul / I need your love / Outsider / What'd ya do / Highest trails above / Somebody like me / Psycho therapy / Time has come today / My-my kind of girl / In the park / Time bomb / Everytime I eat vegetables It makes me think of you. (re-iss. cd Mar94; 7599 23800-2)

| Jun 83. | (7") (W 9606) **TIME HAS COME TODAY. / PSYCHO THERAPY** | | - |

(12"+=) (W 9606T) – Baby I love you / Don't come close.

—— **RICHIE RAMONE** (b. RICHARD REINHARDT, aka BEAU) – drums (ex-VELVETEENS) repl. MARC

		Beggars Banquet	Sire
Nov 84.	(7") <29107> **HOWLING AT THE MOON (SHA LA LA). / WART HOG**	-	-
Jan 85.	(lp/c) (BEGA/BEGC 59) <25187> **TOO TOUGH TO DIE**	63	Oct84

– Mama's boy / I'm not afraid of life / Too young to die / Durango 95 / Wart hog / Danger zone / Chasing the night / Howling at the Moon (sha-la-la) / Daytime dilemma (dangers of love) / Planet Earth 1988 / Human kind / Endless vacation / No go.

| Jan 85. | (7") (BEG 128) **HOWLING AT THE MOON (SHA-LA-LA). / CHASING THE NIGHT** | | - |

(d7"+=)(12"pic-d+=) (BEG 128D)(BEGTP 128) – Smash you / Street fighting man.

| Jun 85. | (7") (BEG 140) **BONZO GOES TO BITBURG. / DAYTIME DILEMMA (DANGERS OF LOVE)** | | - |

(12"+=) (BEG 140T) – Go home Annie.

| Apr 86. | (7") (BEG 157) **SOMETHING TO BELIEVE IN. / SOMEBODY PUT SOMETHING IN MY DRINK** | 69 | - |

(12"+=) (BEG 157T) – (You) Can't say anything nice.

| May 86. | (lp/c) (BEGA/BEGC 70) <25433> **ANIMAL BOY** | 38 | |

– Somebody put something in my drink / Animal boy / Love kills / Apeman hop / She belongs to me / Crummy stuff / My brain is hanging upside down (Bonzo goes to Bitburg) / She belongs to me / Mental hell / Eat that rat / Freak of nature / Hair of the dog / Something to believe in.

| Jun 86. | (7") <28599> **SOMETHING TO BELIEVE IN. / ANIMAL BOY** | | - |
| Jul 86. | (7") (BEG 167) **CRUMMY STUFF. / SHE BELONGS TO ME** | - | - |

(12"+=,12"red+=) (BEG 167 T) – I don't want to live this life.

—— **MARKY RAMONE** – drums returned to repl. CLEM BURKE (ex-BLONDIE) who had repl. RICKY (above now with originals JOEY, DEE DEE and JOHNNY)

| Sep 87. | (7") (BEG 198) **A REAL COOL TIME. / INDIAN GIVER** | | |

(12"+=) (BEG 198T) – Life goes on.

| Sep 87. | (7") (BEGA/BEGC 89) <25641> **HALFWAY TO SANITY** | 78 | |

– I wanna live / Bop 'til you drop / Garden of serenity / Weasel face / Go lil' Camaro go / I know better now / Death of me / I lost my mind / A real cool time / I'm not Jesus / Bye bye baby / Worm man. (cd-iss. Dec87 +=; BEGA 89CD) – Indian giver / Life goes on.

| Nov 87. | (7"/12") (BEG 201/+T) **I WANNA LIVE. / MERRY CHRISTMAS (I DON'T WANT TO FIGHT TONIGHT)** | | |

Aug 89. (lp/c/cd) *(CHR/ZCHR/CCD 1725)* <25905> **BRAIN DRAIN** — `Chrysalis` 75 / `Sire` Jun89
– I believe in miracles / Zero zero UFO / Don't bust my chops / Punishment fits the crime / All screwed up / Palisades Park / Pet sematary / Learn to listen / Can't get you outta my mind / Ignorance is bliss / Come back, baby / Merry Christmas (I don't want to fight tonight).

Sep 89. (7") *(CHS 3423)* **PET SEMATARY. / ALL SCREWED UP**
(12"+=) *(CHS12 3423)* – Zero zero UFO.

Sep 89. (7") <22911> **PET SEMATARY. / SHEENA IS A PUNK ROCKER** — - /

—— **C.J. RAMONE** (b. CHRISTOPHER JOSEPH WARD, 8 Oct'65, Long Island, N.Y.) – bass repl. DEE DEE who became rap artist DEE DEE KING

Oct 91. (cd/c/d-lp) *(CCD/ZCHR/CHR 1901)* **LIVE LOCO** (live)
– The good, the bad and the ugly / Django 95 / Teenage lobotomy / Psycho therapy / Blitzkrieg bop / Rock'n'roll radio / I believe in miracles / Gimme gimme shock treatment / Rock'n'roll high school / I wanna be sedated / The KKK took my baby away / I wanna live / Bonzo goes to Bitzburg / Too tough to die / Sheena is a punk rocker / Rockaway beach / Pet sematary / Don't bust my shape / Palisades park / Mama's boy / Animal boy / Wart hog / Surfin' bird / Cretin hop / I don't wanna walk around with you / Today your love, tomorrow the world / Pinhead / Somebody put something in my drink / Beat on the brat / Judy is a punk / Chinese rocks / Love kills / Ignorance is bliss.

Sep 92. (cd/c/lp) <(RAR D/C 10615)> **MONDO BIZARRO** — `Radioactive` / `Radioactive`
– Censorship / The job that ate my brain / Poison heart / Anxiety / Strength to endure / It's gonna be alright / Take it as it comes / Main man / Tomorrow she goes away / I won't let it happen again / Cabbies on crack / Heidi is a heartache / Touring.

Nov 92. (c-s/7"yellow) *(TC+/CHS 3917)* **POISON HEART. / CENSORSHIT** (live) — `Chrysalis` 69 / `Radioactive` -
(12"+=) *(12CHS 3917)* – Chinese rocks (live) / Sheena is a punk rocker (live).
(cd-s+=) *(CDCHS 3917)* – Rock and roll radio (live).

Dec 93. (cd/c/lp) *(CD/TC+/CHR 6052)* <10913> **ACID EATERS**
– Journey to the center of the mind / Substitute / Out of time / The shape of things to come / Somebody to love / When I was young / 7 and 7 is / My back pages / Can't seem to make you mine / Have you ever seen the rain / I can't control myself / Surf city.

—— Album of covers; SUBSTITUTE (Who) / I CAN'T CONTROL MYSELF (Troggs) / SURF CITY (Jan & Dean) / OUT OF TIME (Rolling Stones) / THE SHAPE OF THINGS TO COME (Headboys) / etc.

Jun 95. (cd/c/lp) *(CD/TC+/CHR 6104)* <11273> **ADIOS AMIGOS** — 62 /
– I don't want to grow up / I'm makin' monsters for my friends / It's not for me to know / The crusher / Life's a gas / Take the pain away / I love you / Cretin family / Have a nice day / Scattergun / Got a lot to say / She talks to rainbows / Born to die in Berlin.

—— split after tour early the following year, although they had a brief reunion on the 6th August, 1996 at The Palace, Los Angeles

Nov 97. (cd) *(EAGCD 010)* <11555> **WE'RE OUTTA HERE!** — `Eagle` / `Radioactive`
– Durango 95 / Teenage lobotomy / Psycho therapy / Blitzkrieg bop / Do you remember rock and roll radio / I believe in miracles / Gimme gimme shock treatment / Rock'n'roll high school / I wanna be sedated / Spider-man / The K.K.K. took my baby away / I just want to have something to do / Commando / Sheena is a punk rocker / Rockaway beach / Pet sematary / The crusher / Love kills / Do you wanna dance / Someone put something in my drink / I don't want you / Wart hog / Cretin hop / R.A.M.O.N.E.S. / Today your love, tomorrow the world / Pinhead / 53rd & 3rd / Listen to your heart / We're a happy family / Chinese rock / Beat on the brat / Any way you want it.

—— after what we think is their final release, MARKY RAMONE went solo

– compilations, etc. –

Aug 80. (7") R.S.O.; *(RSO 70)* / Sire; <2090 512> **I WANNA BE SEDATED. / THE RETURN OF JACKIE AND JUDY**

—— (above from Various Artists Film Soundtrack 'Rock'n'roll High School' also incl. 'Medley: Blitzkrieg bop – Teenage lobotomy – California sun – Pinhead – She's the one')

Nov 80. (7"ep) Sire; *(SREP 1)* **MELTDOWN WITH THE RAMONES**
– I just wanna have something to do / Questioningly / I wanna be your boyfriend / Here today, gone tomorrow.

Jun 88. (7") Sire; <27663> **I WANNA BE SEDATED. / (part 2)** — - /

Jun 88. (d-lp/c/cd) Sire; *(925709-1/-4/-2)* <25709> **RAMONES MANIA** — - /
– I wanna be sedated / Teenage lobotomy / Do you remember rock'n'roll radio? / Gimme gimme shock treatment / Beat on the brat / Sheena is a punk rocker / I wanna live / Pinhead / Blitzkrieg bop / Cretin hop / Rockaway beach / Commando / I wanna be your boyfriend / Mama's boy / Bop 'til you drop / We're a happy family / Bonzo goes to Bitzburg / Psycho therapy / Wart hog / Animal boy / Needles and pins / Howlin' at the Moon / Somebody put something in my drink / We want the airwaves / Chinese rocks / I just want to have something to do / The KKK took my baby away / Indian giver / Rock'n'roll high school.

Sep 90. (cd/c/d-lp) Sire; *(7599 2620-2/-4/-1)* **ALL THE STUFF (AND MORE)** (demos 1976-77, etc) — / -

—— JOEY also on "HOLLY & JOEY" 7" – 1982 'I Got You Babe' on 'Virgin'.

—— In August '88, JOHNNY teamed up with DEBBIE HARRY for 7" – 'Go Lil Camara Go'.

DEE DEE RAMONE

writes with **REY**

Jun 94. (cd/lp) *(1571757-2/-1)* **I HATE FREAKS LIKE YOU** — `World Dom.` / `World Dom.`
– I'm making monsters for my friends / Don't look in my window / Chinese bitch / It's not for me to know / Runaway / All's quiet on the Eastern Front / I hate it / Life is like a little smart Alleck / I hate creeps like you / Trust me / Curse on me / I'm seeing strawberry's again / Lass mich in Fuhe / I'm making monsters for my friends.

Sep 97. (cd-ep) *(OPM 2118CD)* **ZONKED E.P.** — `Other PM` / `Other PM`

Oct 97. (7") *(BLK 5008E7)* **I AM SEEING UFO'S. / BAD HOROSCOPE** — `Blackout` / `Blackout` -

Nov 97. (cd) *(BLK 5008ECD)* **AIN'T IT FUN**
– I'm zonked los hombres / Fix yourself up / I am seeing UFO's / Get off the scene / Never never again / Bad horoscope / It's so bizarre / Get out of the room / Someone who doesn't fit in / Victim of society / My Chico / Disguises / Why is everyone always against Germany / Please kill me.

Lee RANALDO (see under ⇒ SONIC YOUTH)

RANCID

Formed: Albany, California, USA ... 1987 as tattooed ska-punk act, OPERATION IVY, by TIM 'LINT' ARMSTRONG and MATT FREEMAN (alias MATT McCALL), who also numbered JESSE MICHAELS and DAVE MELLO in their ranks. This quartet would become a cult act of the late 80's, although they only managed to squeeze out one album, 'ENERGY', in 1989. ARMSTRONG and FREEMAN continued to work with various outfits, including MDC, a band that they often supported at the infamous Gilman Street Club in Berkeley. In 1990, the pair were joined by BRETT REED and thus RANCID were spawned. After the release of a self-financed EP, 'I'M NOT THE ONLY ONE' in '92, the trio inked a deal with BRETT GUREWITZ's 'Epitaph' records. They subsequently added second guitarist LARS FREDERIKSON, who was to swell the ranks following the release of their well-received eponymous debut in 1993. With the early 90's resurgence of punk and youthful peers such as OFFSPRING and GREEN DAY making commercial headway, RANCID were well placed to capitalise on their particular brand of gut-level hardcore. Following the release of a 1994 EP, 'RADIO RADIO RADIO' on FAT MIKE's (NOFX) independent 'Fat Wreck Chords' label, the band cracked the elusive US Top 100 with their second album, 'LET'S GO' (1994). The following year, RANCID scored with an even higher placed album, ' ... AND OUT COME THE WOLVES', a Top 60 success. In 1998, like The CLASH over 20 years before them, RANCID adopted some roots reggae and ska into their umpteenth set, 'LIFE WON'T WAIT' (Jamaican, BUJU BANTON and MIGHTY MIGHTY BOSSTONES' mainman DICKY BARRETT guested). The results surprisingly worked as the album went Top 40 in America and Britain. • **Trivia:** ARMSTRONG also set up his own label, 'Hellcat', his best signings being DROPKICK MURPHYS, The PIETASTERS, GADJITS, HEPCAT and US BOMBS.

Album rating: Operation Ivy: OPERATION IVY (*6) / Rancid: RANCID (*7) / LET'S GO (*6) / ...AND OUT COME THE WOLVES (*8) / LIFE WON'T WAIT (*7)

OPERATION IVY

TIM ARMSTRONG – vocals, guitar / **MATT FREEMAN** (as MATT McCALL) – bass / **JESSE MICHAELS** – vocals / **DAVE MELLO** – drums

Jan 88. (7"ep) **HECTIC EP** — `not iss.` - / `Lookout` -

Apr 91. (lp) <LOOKOUT 10> **OPERATION IVY** — - /
– Knowledge / Sound system / Jaded / Take warning / The crowd / Bombshell / Unity / Vulnerability / Bankshot / One of these days / Gonna find you / Bad town / Smiling / Caution / Freeze up / Artificial life / Room without a window / Big city / Missionary / Junkie's running dry / Here we go again / Hoboken / Yellin' in my ear / Sleep long / Healthy body / Officer / I got no. (UK-iss.Oct94 lp/c/cd+=; LOOKOUT 10/+MC/CD) – HECTIC EP

—— they had already split in May '89, DAVE hoined SCHLONG while JESSE became a Buddhist monk! but ten years later formed COMMON RIDER with members from SQUIRTGUN. ARMSTRONG and FREEMAN worked with the DANCE HALL CRASHERS and DOWNFALL, while both joined MDC, FREEMAN more so; he featured on the group's 1990 set, 'Hey Cop, If I Had A face Like Yours'.

RANCID

—— **ARMSTRONG + FREEMAN** added **BRETT REED** – drums (ex-SMOG)

1992. (7"ep) <LOOK 059> **RANCID** — `not iss.` - / `Lookout`
– I'm not the only one / etc
(UK-iss.Dec94 & Dec95; same as US)

1992. (7"ep) <FAT 509> **RADIO, RADIO, RADIO EP** — `not iss.` - / `Fat Wreck Chords`
(UK-iss.Apr94; same as US)

May 93. (cd/c/lp) <(E 86428-2/-4/-1)> **RANCID** — `Epitaph` / `Epitaph`
– Adina / hyena / Detroit / Rats in the hallway / Another night / Animosity / Otta my mind / Whirlwind / Rejected / Injury / The bottle / Trenches / Holiday sunrise / Unwritten rules / Get out of my way / (untitled).

—— added **LARS FREDERIKSON** – guitar (ex-UK SUBS)

Jan 95. (cd/c/d-10"lp) <(E 86434-2/-4/-1)> **LET'S GO** — 97 Jun94
– Nihilism / Radio / Sidekick / Salvation / Tenderloin / Let's go / As one / Burn / Ballad of Jimmy & Johnny / Gunshot / I am the one / Gave it away / Ghetto box / Harry Bridges / Black and blue / St. Mary / Dope sick girl / International cover-up / Solidarity / Midnight / Motorcycle ride / Name / 7 years down.

Jun 95. (7") **ROOTS RADICALS. / I WANNA RIOT** — - /

Aug 95. (cd/c/lp) <(E 86444-2/-4/-1)> **...AND OUT COME THE WOLVES** — 55 / 45
– Maxwell murder / 11th hour / Roots radicals / Time bomb / Olympia Wa. / Lock, step and gone / Junkie man / Listed M.I.A. / Ruby Soho / Daly city train / The way I feel / Avenues and alleyways / As wicked / You don't care nothin' / Wars end / Disorder and disarray / Old friend / She's automatic / Journey to the end of the East Bay.

Oct 95. (7"ep/cd-ep) (WOOS 8 S/CDS) **TIME BOMB / THE WAR'S END / BLAST 'EM** | 56 | - |
(above issued on 'Out Of Step')
May 96. (7"ep/cd-ep) (86464-7/-2) **RUBY SOHO. / THAT'S ENTERTAINMENT / DISORDER AND DISARRAY** | | - |
Jun 98. (d-cd/d-c/d-lp) (6497-2/-4/-1) <86497> **LIFE WON'T WAIT** | 32 | 35 |
– Intro / Bloodclot / Black lung / Life won't wait / New dress / Warsaw / Hooligan / Crane fist / Leicester Square / Backslide / Who would've thought / Cas culture and violence / Wolf / 1998 / Lady Liberty / Wrongful suspicion / Turntable / Something in the world today / Corazon de oro / Coppers.
Aug 98. (7"ep/cd-ep) (1005-7/-2) **BLOODCLOT. / ENDRINE / STOP** | | |
Dec 98. (7"ep/cd-ep) (1009-7/-2) **HOOLIGANS / CASH, CULTURE AND VIOLENCE (bass drop mix) / THINGS TO COME** (dance hall mix) | | |

RAPEMAN (see under ⇒ BIG BLACK)

RASCALS / YOUNG RASCALS (dig out; Great Psychedelic . . .)

RATS (see under ⇒ RONSON, Mick)

RATT (dig out; Great Metal . . .)

Paul RAVEN (see under ⇒ GLITTER, Gary)

Chris REA

Born: 4 Mar'51, Middlesborough, England . . . from Irish/Italian parentage. Taking up the guitar in the early 70's, by '73 REA had joined MAGDALENE, taking the place of DAVID COVERDALE who had departed for WHITESNAKE. The following year, the singer released a debut one-off solo single for 'Magnet', 'SO MUCH LOVE'. MAGDALENE, meanwhile, changed their name to The BEAUTIFUL LOSERS in 1975 and although they won a Melody Maker 'Best Newcomer Award', they subsequently split in '77. As well as guesting on HANK MARVIN's 'Guitar Syndicate' album, REA struck out on a long and fairly fruitful solo career, signing a new long-term deal with 'Magnet'. Almost instant success came the following year with 'FOOL IF YOU THINK IT'S OVER', REA's gravel-voiced AOR appeal sitting well within the American market where the single almost went Top 10. Later that Autumn, the track was re-promoted in the UK and REA scored his first domestic hit, narrowly scraping into the Top 30. Amid this early excitement, GUS DUDGEON produced the singer/songwriter's debut album, 'WHATEVER HAPPENED TO BENNY SANTINI?' (1978), the record's title referring to the frankly ridiculous name his label wanted him to adopt. This bluff northerner was assuredly his own man, however, soon building up a cult following and consistently nudging into the lower regions of the chart with early 80's albums like 'TENNIS' (1980), 'CHRIS REA' (1982) and 'WATER SIGN' (1983). Comparisons were often made with MARK KNOPFLER and indeed, they shared a certain slow-burning charm as well as similar audiences. By the release of 'SHAMROCK DIARIES' (1985), word was out, and REA finally began reaping significant commercial rewards with a Top 20 album (by this point, the singer had already achieved superstar status in Germany). Released in Spring '86, 'ON THE BEACH' was a great summer album, the sun-kissed jazzy noodling of the title track perfect driving music. The brassy 'LET'S DANCE' gave REA his biggest hit UK hit single to date late the following year (No.12), while the accompanying 'DANCING WITH STRANGERS' (1987) opus made No.2 in the album charts, REA further warming the cockles of many a housewife's heart with his perennial yuletide chestnut, 'DRIVING HOME FOR CHRISTMAS' (originally released the previous year). 1988 brought the first chapter of REA's career to some kind of conclusion, the singer signing a new deal with 'W.E.A.' and releasing a summation of the cream of his work to date, 'NEW LIGHT THROUGH OLD WINDOWS'. With 'THE ROAD TO HELL' (1989), REA's muse took him down to the proverbial crossroads where he presumably signed his musical soul away for a darkly intoxicating No.1 album of AOR spook-blues. His biggest selling album to date, REA was now in the major league alongside ERIC CLAPTON, PHIL COLLINS etc., 'AUBERGE' (1991) giving REA his second chart topping set. In the 90's the singer continued to be a regular chart fixture with the likes of 'GOD'S GREAT BANANA SKIN' (1992) and 'ESPRESSO LOGIC' (1993), while more recently he truly took the road to (comedy) hell, lining up with the other masochistic hopefuls to be abused by VIC and BOB on BBC 2's brilliant 'Shooting Stars'. • **Trivia:** He guested on CATHERINE HOWE's 1978 album, 'Truth Of The Matter'. In 1982, ELKIE BROOKS scored a UK Top 20 hit with her interpretation of 'FOOL'.

Album rating: WHATEVER HAPPENED TO BENNY SANTINI? (*6) / DELTICS (*5) / TENNIS (*4) / CHRIS REA (*4) / WATER SIGN (*4) / WIRED TO THE MOON (*5) / SHAMROCK DIARIES (*5) / ON THE BEACH (*7) / DANCING WITH STRANGERS (*7) / NEW LIGHT THROUGH OLD WINDOWS compilation (*7) / THE ROAD TO HELL (*8) / AUBERGE (*6) / GOD'S GREAT BANANA SKIN (*5) / ESPRESSO LOGIC (*5) / THE VERY BEST OF CHRIS REA compilation (*7) / LA PASSIONE soundtrack (*3) / THE BLUE CAFE (*4)

CHRIS REA – vocals, guitar (with various session people)

	Magnet	U.A.
May 74. (7") (MAG 10) **SO MUCH LOVE. / BORN TO LOSE**		-

—— Returned to MAGDALENE who changed their name to The BEAUTIFUL LOSERS in 1975. They won 'Melody Maker's Best Newcomers award', but in 1977, they disbanded. REA returned to solo work, re-signing longer term contract for 'Magnet'.

Apr 78. (7") (MAG 111) <1198> **FOOL (IF YOU THINK IT'S OVER). / MIDNIGHT LOVE** | | 12 | Jun78
(re-dist.UK Sep78, hit No.30)
Jun 78. (lp/c) (MAG/TC-MAG 5021) <879> **WHATEVER HAPPENED TO BENNY SANTINI?** | | 49 |
– Whatever happened to Benny Santini? / he closer you get / Because of you / Dancing with Charlie / Bows and bangles / Fool (if you think it's over) / Three angels / Just one of these days / Standing in your doorway / Fires of Spring. (re-iss. Jun83; MAGL 5021) (cd-iss. 1983; CDMAG 5021) (re-iss. Feb88 on 'WEA' lp/c; WX 184/+C) (cd re-iss. Feb88 on 'WEA'; 242368-2) (re-iss. Mar93 on 'Pickwick';) (re-iss. Sep95 on 'Warners')
Jun 78. (7",7"red) (MAG 121) <1252> **WHATEVER HAPPENED TO BENNY SANTINI? / THREE ANGELS** | | 71 | Nov78
Feb 79. (lp/c) (MAG/TC-MAG 5028) <UA 959> **DELTICS** | 54 | |
– Twisted wheel / The things lovers should do / Dance (don't think) / Raincoat and a rose / Cenotaph – Letter from Amsterdam / Deltics / Diamonds / She gave it away / Don't want your best friend / Diamonds / No qualifications / Seabird. (re-iss. +cd. Feb88 on 'WEA')
Mar 79. (7"/12") (MAG/+12 144) <1285> **DIAMONDS. / CLEVELAND CALLING** | 44 | 44 |
Jun 79. (7") (MAG 151) **RAINCOAT AND A ROSE. / NO QUALIFICATIONS** | | |

	Magnet	Columbia
Feb 80. (7") (MAG 163) **TENNIS. / IF YOU REALLY LOVE ME**		
Feb 80. (lp/c) (MAGL/TC-MAG 5032) <36435> **TENNIS**	60	

– Tennis / Since I don't see you anymore / Dancing girls / No work today / Everytime I see you smile / For ever and ever / Good news / Friends across the water / Only with you / Stick it / Tennis.
May 80. (7") (MAG 176) **DANCING GIRLS. / FRIENDS ACROSS THE WATER** | | |
Jan 82. (7") (MAG 215) <02727> **LOVING YOU. / LET ME BE THE ONE** | 65 | 88 | Mar88
Mar 82. (lp/c) (MAGL/ZC-MAGL 5040) <37664> **CHRIS REA** | 52 | |
– Loving you / If you choose to go / Guitar Street / Do you still dream / Every beat of my heart / Goodbye little Colombus / One sweet tender touch / Do it for love / Just want to be with you / Runaway / When you know your love has died. (re-iss. Sep87 on 'WEA' lp/c; WX 187/+C) (cd-iss. Feb88; 242371-2)
May 82. (7") (MAG 225) **EVERY BEAT OF MY HEART. / DON'T LOOK BACK** | | |
Jul 82. (7") (MAG 233) **LET IT LOOSE. / SIERRA SIERRA** | | |
(12"+=) (MAG12 233) – Urban Samurai.
(free-7"ep+=) (MAGD 233) – Fool (if you think it's over) / The closer you get / Diamonds / Guitar Street.
Apr 83. (7") (MAG 244) **I CAN HEAR YOUR HEARTBEAT. / FROM LOVE TO LOVE** | 60 | |
Jun 83. (lp/c) (MAGL/ZCMAGL 5084) **WATER SIGN** | 64 | |
– Nothing's happening by the sea / Deep water / Candles / Love's strange ways / Texas / Let it loose / I can hear your heartbeat / Midnight blue / Hey you / Out of the darkness. (re-iss. Sep87 on 'WEA' lp/c; WX 188/+C) (cd-iss. Feb88; 242372-2)
Jul 83. (7") (MAG 245) **LOVE'S STRANGE WAYS. / SMILE** | | |
Feb 84. (7"/12") (MAG 255) **I DON'T KNOW WHAT IT IS BUT I LOVE IT. / MYSTERY MAN** | 65 | - |
Apr 84. (lp/c) (MAGL/ZCMAGL 5057) **WIRED TO THE MOON** | 35 | |
– Bombollini / Touche d'amour / Shine, shine, shine / Wired to the Moon / easons / I don't know what it is but I love you / Ace of hearts / Holding out / Winning. (re-iss. Sep87 on 'WEA' lp/c; WX 189/+C) (cd-iss. Feb88; 242 373-2) (re-iss. +cd.Jul91 on 'East West')
May 84. (7") (MAG 259) **BOMBOLLINI. / TRUE LOVE** | | |
(12"+=) (MAGT 259) – Excerpts from Bombollini.
Jun 84. (7") (MAG 260) **TOUCHE D'AMOUR. / ('A'instrumental)** | | |
(ext.12"+=) (MAGT 260) – Let it loose – I can hear your heartbeat – I don't know what it is but I love it (medley).
Sep 84. (7") (MAG 269) **ACE OF HEARTS. / I CAN HEAR YOUR HEARTBEAT** | | |
(12"+=/c-s+=) (MAGT/ZCMAG 269) – From love to love / True love / Smile.
Mar 85. (7") (MAG 276) **STAINSBY GIRLS. / AND WHEN SHE SMILES** | 27 | |
(12"+=/c-s+=) (MAGT/ZCMAG 276) – Sunrise / Dancing shoes / September blue.
(d7"+=) (MAGD 276) – Bittersweet / Auf Immer und Ewig.
May 85. (lp/c/cd) (MAGL/ZCMAG/CDMAG 5062) **SHAMROCK DIARIES** | 15 | |
– Steel river / Stainsby girls / Chisel Hill / Josephine / One golden rule / All summer long / Stone / Shamrock diaries / Love turns to lies / Hired gun. (re-iss. Sep87 on 'WEA' lp/c; WX 190/+C) i(cd-iss. Feb88; 242374-2) (re-iss. Jul91 on 'East West')
Jun 85. (7") (MAG 280) **JOSEPHINE (remix). / DANCING SHOES** | 67 | - |
(12"+=) (MAGT 280) – Every time it rains.
Nov 85. (7") (MAG 269) **ACE OF HEARTS (remix). / I CAN HEAR YOUR HEARTBEAT (live)** | | |
(12"+=) (MAGT 269) – From love to love / True love / Smile.
Mar 86. (7") (MAG 283) **IT'S ALL GONE. / BLESS THEM ALL** | 69 | - |
(12"+=/c-s+=) (MAGT/ZCMAG 283) – Crack that mould / Look out for me / Let's dance.
Apr 86. (lp/c/cd) (MAGL/ZCMAG/CDMAG 5069) **ON THE BEACH** | 11 | |
– On the beach / Little blonde plaits / Giverny / Lucky day / Just passing through / It's all gone / Hello friend / Two roads / Light of hope / Auf immer and ewig. (c+=/cd+=) – Bless them all / Freeway / Crack that mould. (re-iss. Feb88 on 'WEA' lp/c; WX 191/+C) (re-iss. Jun91 on 'East West')
Jun 86. (7") (YZ 195) **ON THE BEACH. / IF ANYBODY ASKS YOU** | 57 | |
(12"+=) (YZ 195T) – ('A'extended remix).
(d7"+=) (YZ 195CD) – One golden rule (live) / Midnight blue (live).
Dec 86. (7") (MAG 298) **DRIVING HOME FOR CHRISTMAS. / HELLO FRIEND** | | - |
(d7"+=) (MAGD 298) – It's all gone (live) / Steel river (live).

	Magnet	Motown
May 87. (7"/c-s) (MAG 299) <1900> **LET'S DANCE. / I DON'T CARE ANYMORE**	12	81

(12"+=) (MAGT 299) – ('A'extended).
(cd-s+=) (CDMAG 29) – Josephine (French version).

Aug 87. (7") *(MAG 300)* **LOVING YOU AGAIN. / DONAHUE'S BROKEN WHEEL** `47` [ ]
(12"+=) *(MAGT 300)* – ('A'extended).

Sep 87. (lp/c/cd) *(MAGL/ZCMAG/CDMAG 5071)* **DANCING WITH STRANGERS** `2` [ ]
– Joys of Christmas / I can't dance to that / Windy Town / Gonna buy a hat / Curse of the traveller / Let's dance / Que sera / Josie's tune / Loving you again / That girl of mine / September blue. *(cd+=)* – I don't care anymore / Donahue's broken wheel / Danielle's breakfast. *(re-iss. +cd.Jul91 on 'East West')*

Nov 87. (7") *(MAG 314)* **JOYS OF CHRISTMAS. / DRIVING HOME FOR CHRISTMAS** `67` `-`
(12"+=) *(MAGT 314)* – Hello friend (remix).
(cd-s+=) *(CDMAG 314)* – Yes I do.

Jan 88. (7") *(MAG 318)* **QUE SERA. / SE SEQUI (instrumental)** `73` [ ]
(12"+=) *(MAGT 318)* – ('A'extended).
(cd-s+=) *(CDMAG 318)* – One sweet tender touch.

                                                  W.E.A.   **Motown**

Jul 88. (7") *(YZ 195)* **ON THE BEACH (SUMMER '88). / I'M TAKING THE DAY OUT** `12` [ ]
(12"+=/cd-s+=) *(YZ 195 T/CD)* – It's all gone (live).

Oct 88. (7") *(YZ 320)* **I CAN HEAR YOUR HEARTBEAT. / LOVING YOU AGAIN (live)** `74` [ ]
(12"+=/cd-s+=) *(YZ 320 T/CD)* – Giverny.

                                                  W.E.A.   **Geffen**

Oct 88. (lp/c)(cd) *(WX 200/+C)(243841-2) <24232>* **NEW LIGHT THROUGH OLD WINDOWS – THE BEST OF CHRIS REA** (new mixes) `5` `92`
– Let's dance / Working on it / Ace of hearts / Josephine / Candles / On the beach / Fool (if you think it's over) / I can hear your heartbeat / Shamrock diaries / Stainsby girls / Windy town / Driving home for Christmas / Steel river.

Dec 88. (d7"/12"ep/3"cd-ep) *(YZ 325 T/CD)* **DRIVING HOME FOR CHRISTMAS. / FOOTSTEPS IN THE SNOW // JOYS OF CHRISTMAS. / SMILE** `53` [ ]

Jan 89. (7") *(YZ 350)* **WORKING ON IT. / ONE GOLDEN RULE** `53` `-`
(12"+=) *(YZ 350T)* – ('A'extended.
(cd-s+=) *(YZ 350CD)* – Stainsby girls.

Mar 89. (7") *<27535>* **WORKING ON IT. / LOVING YOU AGAIN** `-` `73`

Sep 89. (7") *(YZ 431)* **THE ROAD TO HELL. / HE SHOULD KNOW BETTER** `10` [ ]
(12") *(YZ 431T)* – ('A'side) / The road to Hell (pt.2) / Josephine (French re-recorded).
(cd-s) *(YZ 431CD)* – (all 4 tracks).

Oct 89. (lp/c)(cd) *(WZ 317/+C)(246285-2) 24276>* **THE ROAD TO HELL** `1` [ ]
– The road to Hell (part 1 & 2) / You must be evil / Texas / Looking for a rainbow / Your warm and tender love / Daytona / That's what they all say / I just wanna be with you / Tell me there's a Heaven. *(re-iss. cd/c Feb95)*

Nov 89. (7"/c-s) *(YZ 448/+C)* **THAT'S WHAT THEY ALL SAY. / 1975** [ ] [ ]
(12"+=) *(YZ 448T)* – ('A'extended rainbow mix).
(cd-s++=) *(YZ 448CD)* – Driving home for Christmas.

Feb 90. (7"/c-s) *(YZ 455/+C)* **TELL ME THERE'S A HEAVEN. / AND WHEN SHE SMILES** `24` [ ]
(12"+=) *(YZ 455T)* – Curse of the traveller.
(cd-s+++=) *(YZ 455CD)* – Little blonde plaits.

Apr 90. (7"/c-s) *(YZ 468/+C)* **TEXAS. / LET'S DANCE** `69` [ ]
(12") *(YZ 468T)* – ('A'side) / ('B'live) / The road to Hell (part 1 & 2).
(cd-s+=) *(YZ 468CD)* – Working on it.

                                              East West   **East West**

Feb 91. (7"/c-s) *(YZ 555/+C)* **AUBERGE. / HUDSON'S DREAMS** `16` [ ]
(cd-s) *(YZ 555CD)* – ('A'side) / Let's dance / On the beach / The road to Hell (pt.2).

Feb 91. (cd)(lp/c) *(9031 75693-2) (WZ 407/+C) <91662>* **AUBERGE** [ ] [ ]
– Auberge / Gone fishing / You're not a number / Heaven / Set me free / Red shoes / Sing a song of love to me / Every second counts / Looking for the summer / And you my love / The mention of your name.

Apr 91. (7"/c-s) *(YZ 566/+C)* **HEAVEN. / THEME FROM THE PANTILE JOURNALS** `57` [ ]
(12"+=) *(YZ 566T)* – Teach me to dance.
(cd-s+=) *(YZ 566CD)* – ('A'side) / Stainsby girls / Josephine / Tell me there's a Heaven.

Jun 91. (7"/c-s) *(YZ 584/+C)* **LOOKING FOR THE SUMMER. / SIX UP** `49` [ ]
(12"+=/cd-s+=) *(YZ 584 T/CD)* – Urban Samurai / Theme from the Pantile / Teach me to dance.

Nov 91. (7"/c-s) *(YZ 629/+C)* **WINTER SONG. / FOOTPRINTS IN THE SNOW / TELL ME THERE'S A HEAVEN** `27` [ ]
(cd-s+=) *(YZ 629CD)* – True to you.

Oct 92. (7"/c-s) *(YZ 699/+C)* **NOTHING TO FEAR. / STRANGE DANCE** `16` [ ]
(cd-s+=) *(YZ 699CD)* – Daytona (live).
(cd-s) *(YZ 699CDX)* – ('A'side) / Road to Hell (live) / Working on it (live).

Nov 92. (cd)(lp/c) *(4509 90995-2)(WX 496/+C)* **GOD'S GREAT BANANA SKIN** `4` [ ]
– Nothing to fear / Miles is a cigarette / God's great banana skin / Nineties blues / Too much pride / Boom boom / I ain't the fool / There she goes / I'm ready / Black dog / Soft top hard shoulder.

Nov 92. (7"/c-s) *(YZ 706/+C)* **GOD'S GREAT BANANA SKIN. / I SAW YOU COMING** `31` [ ]
(cd-s+=) *(YZ 706CD)* – Just passing through (live).
(cd-s+=) *(YZ 706CDX)* – She's gonna change everything / You must be evil.

——— his band: **ROBERT AHWAI** – guitar / **MAX MIDDLETON** – piano, keyboards / **SYLVIN MARC** – bass / **MARTIN DITCHAM** – drums, percussion

Jan 93. (7"/c-s) *(YZ 710/+C)* **SOFT TOP HARD SHOULDER. / MELANCHOLY** `53` [ ]
(cd-s+=) *(YZ 710CD)* – The van stomp – Glasgow horizon.
(cd-s) *(YZ 710CDX)* – ('A'side) / One fine day / One seet & tended touch / Sierra Sierra.

Jul 93. (7"/c-s) *(YZ)* **TOO MUCH PRIDE (new version). / MUNICH 1993 IMPROVISED INTRO (live)** [ ] [ ]
(cd-s+=) – On the beach (live).
(cd-s) – ('A'side) / Gone fishing (live) / Nothing to fear (live) / Soft top, hard shoulder (live).

Oct 93. (7"/c-s) *(YZ 772/+C)* **JULIA. / I THOUGHT I WAS GOING TO LOSE YOU** `18` [ ]
(cd-s+=) *(YZ 772CD)* – Jordan 191.

Nov 93. (cd/c/lp) *(4509 94311-2/-4/-1)* **ESPRESSO LOGIC** `8` [ ]
– Espresso logic / Red / Soup of the day / Johnny needs a fast guitar / Between the Devil and the deep blue sea / Julia /Summer love / New way / Stop / She closed her eyes.

Dec 93. (7"/c-s) *(YZ 783/+C)* **ESPRESSO LOGIC. / WE DON'T HAVE A PROBLEM** [ ] `-`
(cd-s+=) *(YZ 783CD)* – That's the way it goes.

Oct 94. (cd/c) *(4509 98040-2/-4)* **THE VERY BEST OF CHRIS REA** (compilation) `3` [ ]
– The road to Hell / Josephine / Let's dance / Fool (if you think it's over) / Auberge / Julia / Stainsby girls / If you were me (with ELTON JOHN) / On the beach / Looking for the summer / I can hear your heartbeat / Go your own way / God's great banana skin / Winter song / Gone fishing / Tell me there's a Heaven.

Nov 94. (c-s) *(YZ 835C)* **YOU CAN GO YOUR OWN WAY. / ESPRESSO LOGIC (mixes)** `28` [ ]
(12"/cd-s) *(YZ 835 T/CD)* – ('A'side) / Ruby blue / Three little green candles.

Dec 94. (7"/c-s) *(YZ 885/+C)* **TELL ME THERE'S A HEAVEN. / AND WHEN SHE SMILES** `70` `-`
(cd-s+=) *(YZ 885CD)* – Curse of the traveller / Little blonde plaits.
(below from the film written by CHRIS REA himself)

Nov 96. (c-s; CHRIS REA & SHIRLEY BASSEY) *(EW 072C)* **'DISCO' LA PASSIONE / DINO** `41` [ ]
(12"/cd-s) *(EW 072 T/CD)* – Only to fly.

Nov 96. (cd/c) *(0630-16695-2/-4)* **LA PASSIONE (soundtrack)** `43` [ ]
– La passione (film theme) / Dov'e il signore? / Shirley do you own a Ferrari? / Girl in a sports car / When the grey skies turn to blue / Horses / Olive oil / Only to fly / You must follow / 'Disco' La passione / Dov'e il signore? part two / Le Mans.

May 97. (c-s) *(EW 103C)* **GIRL IN A SPORTSCAR. / LA PASSIONE** [ ] [ ]
(cd-s+=) *(EW 103CD)* – Olive Oil.

Jan 98. (cd/c) *(3984 21688-2/-4)* **THE BLUE CAFE** `10` [ ]
– Square peg, round hole / Since I found you / Miss your kiss / Shadows of the big man / Where do we go from here? / Thinking of you / As long as I have your love / Anyone quite like you / Sweet summer day / Stick by you / I'm still holding on / The blue cafe.

Feb 98. (c-s) *(EW 152C)* **SQUARE PEG, ROUND HOLE / THE MAN'S SO COOL** [ ] `-`
(cd-s+=) *(EW 152CD)* – ('A'-Front Room mix) / ('A'drum'n'bass).

Eddi READER

Born: SADENIA READER, 28 Aug'59, Glasgow, Scotland. She began her career after being invited to join DISC O'DELL's 'Y' records outfit, DISCONNECTION (also in their ranks, former PIGBAG guitarist JAMES JOHNSTONE and HI-TENSION bassman LEROY WILLIAMS), the quartet managing to release two singles, 'BALI HAI' in '82 and 'WE LOVE YOU' a few years later. In 1987, the now one-time backing singer for GANG OF FOUR, WATERBOYS, etc, formed FAIRGROUND ATTRACTION with English songwriter MARC B. NEVIN. After literally busking around city centres, they subsequently progressed to gigs, recruiting guitaron player (Mexican acoustic bass) SIMON EDWARDS and drummer ROY DODDS. Soon snapped up by 'R.C.A.' records, their early '88 debut single, 'PERFECT', swooned its way to No.1, paving the way for the Top 3 album, 'FIRST OF A MILLION KISSES'. An endearingly charming folk-jazz shuffle, the song was carried with READER's dreamy, angelic Scots brogue, a voice which dominated the rootsy pop of the album. Despite winning a couple of Brit Awards the following year, the band's lifespan was brief, subsequently splitting in 1990. While NEVIN joined MORRISSEY in '91 (later forming SWEETMOUTH), READER branched off into an acting career, scoring a major role in the acclaimed Scottish TV Country & Western comedy drama, 'Your Cheatin' Heart'. With DODDS remaining as drummer, READER hooked up with guitarists, NEIL MacCOLL and DOMINIC MILLER, along with double bassist, PHIL STERIOPULOS; they were now EDDI READER & The PATRON SAINTS OF IMPERFECTION. In this guise, she recorded the 'MIRMAMA' (1992) album, a well-received set that saw contributions from JOOLS HOLLAND on piano. Shifting labels to 'Warner' subsidiary, 'Blanco Y Negro', READER found herself high in the charts once more (No.4) with an eponymous solo album in 1994, the material written by another Scot, BOO HEWERDINE, former leader of The BIBLE.
• **Songwriters:** NEVIN penned all FAIRGROUND ATTRACTION, except YOU SEND ME (Sam Cooke) / MYSTERY TRAIN (Elvis Presley) / DO YOU WANT TO KNOW A SECRET (Beatles) / WALKING AFTER MIDNIGHT (Patsy Cline) / AY FOND KISS (trad. Robert Burns) / TRYING TIMES (Donny Hathaway) / SUNDAY MORNING (Velvet Underground) / JACK O'HAZLEDEAN (trad.Walter Scott) / OLE BUTTERMILK SKY (Hoagy Carmichael). EDDI READER solo:- MY OLD FRIEND THE BLUES (Steve Earle) / WHAT YOU DO (S.W. Kahn) / SPIRIT (Waterboys) / I LOVED A LAD (trad).

Album rating: Fairground Attraction: THE FIRST OF A MILLION KISSES (*5) / AY FOND FISS collection (*5) / PERFECT – THE BEST OF . . . compilation (*6) / Eddi Reader: MIRMAMA (*5) / EDDI READER (*6) / CANDYFLOSS AND MEDICINE (*5) / ANGELS AND ELECTRICITY (*5)

FAIRGROUND ATTRACTION

EDDI READER – vocals / **MARC B. NEVIN** – guitars / **SIMON EDWARDS** – guitaron (Mexican accoustic bass) / **ROY DODDS** – drums

		R.C.A.	R.C.A.
Mar 88.	(7") (PB 41845) <8789> **PERFECT. / MYTHOLOGY**	1	80 Nov88

(12"+=/cd-s+=) (PT/PD 41846) – Falling backwards / Mystery train.

May 88.	(lp/c/cd) (PL/PK/PD 71696) <8596> **THE FIRST OF A MILLION KISSES**

2 　Jan89
– A smile and a whisper / Perfect / Moon on the rain / Find my love / Fairground attraction / The wind knows my name / Clare / Comedy waltz / The moon is mine / Station street / Whispers / Allelujah. (cd+=) – Falling backwards / Mythology. (cd re-iss. May93; 74321 13439-2)

Jul 88.	(7") (PB 42079) **FIND MY LOVE. / WATCHING THE PARTY**	7

(12"+=/cd-s+=) (PT/PD 42080) – You send me / Ay fond kiss.

Nov 88.	(7") (PB 42249) **A SMILE AND A WHISPER. / WINTER ROSE**	75

(12"+=/cd-s+=) (PT/PD 42250) – Walkin' after midnight / Trying times.

Jan 89.	(7") (PB 42607) **CLARE. / GAMES OF LOVE**	49

(12"+=/cd-s+=) (PT/PD 42608) – Do you want to know a secret? / Jock O'Hazeldean.

May 90.	(7"/c-s) (PB 43654) **WALKIN' AFTER MIDNIGHT. / COMEDY WALTZ (live)**

(12"+=/cd-s+=) (PT/PD 43654) – Clare (live).

Jun 90.	(cd/c/lp) (PD/PK/PL 74596) **AY FOND KISS** (rare + demos, etc)	55

– Jock O'Hazeldean / The game of love / Walkin' after midnight / You send me / Trying times / Mystery train / Winter rose / Do you want to know a secret? / Allelujah (live) / Cajun band / Watching the party / Ay fond kiss. (cd re-iss. Apr94; 74321 19371-2)

----- had already disbanded early 1990; EDDI went into an acting career notably the Scottish TV 'C&W' drama, 'Your Cheatin' Heart'. NEVIN joined MORRISSEY in '91 and subsequently formed SWEETMOUTH.

– compilations, etc. –

Feb 93.	(7"/c-s) R.C.A.; (74321 13491-7/4) **PERFECT / CAPTURED (featuring BRIAN KENNEDY)**

(cd-s+=) (74321 13491-2) – Walkin' after midnight / You send me.

Sep 94.	(cd) R.C.A.; (74321 23251-2) **THE COLLECTION**
Apr 95.	(d-cd) R.C.A.; (74321 25959-2) **THE FIRST OF A MILLION KISSES / AY FOND KISS**
Jul 95.	(cd) R.C.A.; (74321 29277-2) **PERFECT – THE BEST OF FAIRGROUND ATTRACTION**
Apr 96.	(cd) RCA Camden; (74321 37541-2) **THE VERY BEST OF FAIRGROUND ATTRACTION**
	(re-iss. Feb97 cd/c; 74321 44675-2/-4)
May 96.	(cd-s) Old Gold; (1262 36379-2) **PERFECT / FIND MY LOVE**

EDDI READER

----- with The PATRON SAINTS OF IMPERFECTION: **ROY DODDS** – drums, percussion / **PHIL STERIOPULOS** – 5-string double bass / **NEIL MacCOLL** – guitar / **DOMINIC MILLER** – guitar / and guest **JOOLS HOLLAND** – piano

		R.C.A.	R.C.A.
Nov 91.	(7"ep/12"ep/c-ep) **ALL OR NOTHING EP**		-

– All or nothing / Sunday morning / Ole buttermilk sky / Broken vows.
(cd-ep) – (first & last track) / The blacksmith / The girl with the weight of the world in her hands.

Feb 92.	(7"/c-s) **WHAT YOU DO WITH WHAT YOU'VE GOT. / I WISH YOU WERE MY BOYFRIEND**		-

(cd-s+=) – Broken vows / Ole buttermilk sky (take 2).

Mar 92.	(cd/c/lp) (PD/PK/PL 75156) **MIRMAMA**	34	

– What you do with what you've got / Honeychild / All or nothing / Hello in there / Dolphins / The blacksmith / That's fair / Cinderellas downfall / Pay no mind / The swimming song / My old friend the blues. (cd re-iss. Sep94; 74321 15865-2)

Apr 92.	(7"/c-s) **HONEYCHILD. / SPIRIT (live)**		-

(cd-s+=) – All or nothing (live).

		Haven	not iss.
Mar 93.	(cd-ep; as READER, GREGSON & HEWERDINE) (HAVENT 3CD) **WONDERFUL LIE EP**		-

– Wonderful lie / Last night I dreamt somebody loved me / Who's your jailer now.

		Blanco Y Negro	Sire
May 94.	(7"/c-s) (NEG 68/+C) **PATIENCE OF ANGELS. / RED FACE BIG SKY**	33	-

(cd-s+=) (NEG 68CD) – Shirt & comb.

Jun 94.	(cd/c) (<4509 96177-2/-4>) **EDDI READER**	4	

– The right place / Patience of angels / Dear John / Scarecrow / East of us / Joke / The exception / Red face big sky / Howling in Ojai / When I watch you sleeping / Wonderful lie / Siren.

Aug 94.	(7"/c-s) (NEG 72/+C) **JOKE (I'M LAUGHING). / SATURDAY NIGHT**	42	-

(cd-s+=) (NEG 72CD) – Wonder boy.
(cd-s) (NEG 72CDX) – ('A'side) / Three crosses / Go and sit upon the grass.

Oct 94.	(7"/c-s) (NEG 75/+C) **DEAR JOHN. / BATTERSEA MOON**	48	-

(cd-s+=) (NEG 75CD) – When I watch you sleeping / What you do with what you've got / That's fair.

Sep 95.	(c-s) (NEG 82C) **NOBODY LIVES WITHOUT LOVE / WONDERFUL LIE**		-

(cd-s+=) (NEG 82CD) – Red face, big sky.

Jun 96.	(c-s) (NEG 90C) **TOWN WITHOUT PITY / LEAVE THE LIGHT ON**		-

(cd-s+=) (NEG 90CD1) – Wonderboy / Shall I be mother.
(cd-s) (NEG 90CD2) – ('A'side) / Sex lives boy / If you gotta minute.

Jul 96.	(cd/c) (<0630 15129-2/-4>) **CANDYFLOSS AND MEDICINE**	24	

– Glasgow star / Town without pity / Medicine / Rebel angel / Semi precious / Lazy heart / I loved a lad / Butterfly jar / Candyfloss / Darkhouse.

Aug 96.	(c-s) (NEG 95C) **MEDICINE / SUGAR ON THE PILL**		-

(cd-s) (NEG 95CD1) – Earlies / Nameless.
(cd-s) (NEG 95CD2) – ('A'side) / Green grow the rushes / John Anderson my Joe / Who knows where the time goes.

Apr 98.	(cd-s) (NEG 111CD) **KITEFLYER'S HILL / ST. CHRISTOPHER**		-
May 98.	(cd/c) (6398 422816-2/-4) **ANGELS AND ELECTRICITY**	49	

– Kiteflyer's hill / Prayer wheel / Postcard / Wings on my heels / On a whim / Hummingbird / Barcelona window / Bell, book and candle / California / Follow my tears / Psychic reader / Please don't ask me to dance / Clear.

RED CRAYOLA　(dig out; Great Psychedelic . . .)

Otis REDDING

Born: 9 Sep'41, Dawson, Georgia, USA. Singing in a gospel choir as a child and later winning a succession of talent contests with LITTLE RICHARD covers, REDDING's prescient abilities were noted by PHIL WALDEN who, at the time, was managing local R&B outfit, JOHNNY JENKINS & THE PINETOPPERS. OTIS soon became a driver/occasional singer with the act, his/their first release being the 'SHOUT BAMALAMA' single released on the 'Confederate' label in 1960. The following year, after OTIS' marriage to ZELDA, they issued 'GETTIN' HIP' on 'Alshire', while 1962 saw the release of a further single, 'LOVE TWIST' on 'Gerald' records. During this time, OTIS was only given the odd vocal spot, although this changed following the group's 'Atlantic'-sponsored recording session at the burgeoning 'Stax' studios. REDDING was allotted the time left over from JENKINS' session, putting it to good use and cutting two tracks, a soul shouter, 'HEY HEY BABY', and a ballad, 'THESE ARMS OF MINE'. Impressed, 'Stax' released the two tracks as a single on their subsidiary, 'Volt', the latter song becoming a minor US hit in mid '63. By mutual agreement and a special contract, 'Atlantic (aka Atco)' decided to allow the label to continue releasing REDDING material. Backed by 'Stax' house band, BOOKER T & THE MG's, the singer scored another minor hit with the lovesick ballad, 'PAIN IN MY HEART', releasing a similarly titled album the following year. REDDING led the way in 'Stax's back-to-basics soul crusade, the singer being widely credited with altering the sound of black music with his radically inventive horn parts. Though he wasn't an accomplished musician, he had an intuitive feel for rhythm and melody which he'd translate to his backing band, most of his material recorded spontaneously with a minimal number of takes. Co-written with MG, STEVE CROPPER, 'MR PITIFUL' was a slightly self-mocking caricature of REDDING as the king of soul heartbreak, its driving, emotive delivery overshadowing the baleful 'THAT'S HOW STRONG MY LOVE IS' when it was released as the B-side of the latter in the Spring of '65. REDDING's first real breakthrough, however, came with another poignant ballad, 'I'VE BEEN LOVING YOU TOO LONG', a near-Top 20 hit later that summer. After a follow-up album, 'THE GREAT OTIS REDDING SINGS SOUL BALLADS' (1965) failed to chart, REDDING had a surprise UK Top 20 hit towards the end of the year with a cover of The Temptations' 'MY GIRL', paving the way for the success of his seminal third album, 'OTIS BLUE (OTIS REDDING SINGS SOUL)', one of the most revered records in the soul canon. As well as featuring the enduring, much covered classic, 'RESPECT', the album boasted three SAM COOKE covers, including the uplifting 'CHANGE GONNA COME', as well as his famous cover of The Rolling Stones' 'I CAN'T GET NO SATISFACTION'. Though REDDING continued to sell respectably in the States, he was a massive crossover success in the UK, his profile heightened by an ecstatically received performance on hip 60's TV Show, 'Ready Steady Go'. By all accounts, REDDING was an inspirational live performer, his frenetic delivery and magnetic enthusiasm drawing rave reviews and striking fear into the heart of any act unlucky enough to have to follow him. REDDING returned to the UK in 1967, following the release of 'OTIS REDDING'S DICTIONARY OF SOUL' (which included the soul sophistication of 'TRY A LITTLE TENDERNESS' and a follow-up of sorts to 'MR. PITIFUL', the rhythmic punch of 'FA-FA-FA-FA-FA (SAD SONG)'), he and his band given a rapturous reception with many stars of the day present in the audience. In June, REDDING was the first black soul singer to perform at a predominantly white rock event, namely the Monterey Pop Festival. His acclaimed performance finally saw the singer gaining the Stateside respect that had long been his due. Later that summer, an album of duets with fellow 'Stax' artist, CARLA THOMAS, 'KING AND QUEEN' dented the US Top 40. Lifted from the record, the brilliant 'TRAMP', in which OTIS' backwoods country hick was pitted against the worldly-wise THOMAS, gave REDDING another American Top 30 single. Following an operation for throat problems, REDDING went back into the studio late in '67 and cut a final series of tracks, one song in particular, '(SITTIN' ON) THE DOCK OF THE BAY', becoming his epitaph; on the 10th of December, 1967, REDDING's private plane crashed into Lake Monona, Madison, the singer and four members of his backing band, The BAR-KAYS, subsequently drowning. As a stunned music world tried to come to terms with the tragedy, thousands attended REDDING's funeral in his hometown of Macon, the aforementioned 'SITTIN'..' subsequently scaling the American charts upon its posthumous release early in '68. REDDING's voice honey-sweet and fragile in contrast to the earthiness of old, the song was a heart-rendingly wistful acoustic folk/soul hybrid, the singer's death adding to its poignancy. The song reflected a new found maturity (also evident in the subsequent album of the same name) which indicated that REDDING was only beginning to realise his full potential, his contribution incalculable to not only black soul but music in general. • **Covered:** DOCK OF THE BAY (c. Steve Cropper) / MY GIRL (Temptations) / PAIN IN MY HEART (Irma

Thomas) / DAY TRIPPER (Beatles) / SHAKE! (Sam Cooke) / KNOCK ON WOOD (Eddie Floyd) / PAPA'S GOT A BRAND NEW BAG (James Brown) / A LOVER'S QUESTION (Clyde McPhatter) / AMEN (Impressions) / etc.
• **Trivia:** Late in 1973, his son DEXTER issued a single GOD BLESS. In the early 80's, he was joined by other son OTIS and their cousin MARK LOCKET who transpired as The REDDINGS. All on vocals and instruments, they released 2 albums, THE AWAKENING and CLASS on the 'Believe' label.
Album rating: PAIN IN MY HEART (*7) / THE GREAT OTIS REDDING SINGS SOUL BALLADS (*7) / OTIS BLUE – OTIS REDDING SINGS SOUL (*9) / THE SOUL ALBUM (*6) / COMPLETE & UNBELIEVABLE . . . THE OTIS REDDING DICTIONARY OF SOUL (*8) / KING AND QUEEN with Carla Thomas (*7) / OTIS REDDING LIVE IN EUROPE (*7) / HISTORY OF OTIS REDDING compilation (*8) / posthumous:- THE DOCK OF THE BAY (*6) / THE IMMORTAL OTIS REDDING (*5) / . . .IN PERSON AT THE WHISKY A GO GO (*6) / LOVE MAN compilation (*5) / THE BEST OF OTIS REDDING compilation (*7) / PURE OTIS (*5) / THE VERY BEST OF OTIS REDDING compilation (*7) / OTIS! THE DEFINITIVE OTIS REDDING compilation (*9)

OTIS REDDING – vocals (solo with session people)

			London	Volt
Oct 62.	(7") <103> **THESE ARMS OF MINE. / HEY HEY BABY**		-	85
Jul 63.	(7") <109> **THAT'S WHAT MY HEART NEEDS. / MARY'S LITTLE LAMB**		-	-
Nov 63.	(7") (HLK 9833) <112> **PAIN IN MY HEART. / SOMETHING IS WORRYING ME**			61

―――― His backing included BOOKER T. & THE MG'S plus JOHNNY JENKINS.

Mar 64.	(7") (HLK 9876) <116> **COME TO ME. / DON'T LEAVE ME THIS WAY**		-	69
Apr 64.	(lp) <161> **PAIN IN MY HEART**			-

– Pain in my heart / The dog / Stand by me / Hey hey baby / You send me / I need your lovin' / Louie Louie / These arms of mine / Something is worrying me / Security / That's what my heart needs / Lucille. (UK-iss.Apr67 on 'Atlantic', hit No.28) (cd-iss. Aug93)

May 64.	(7") (2091020) **SECURITY. / WONDERFUL WORLD**		-	-
Jun 64.	(7") <117> **SECURITY. / I WANT TO THANK YOU**		-	97
Oct 64.	(7") <121> **CHAINED AND BOUND. / YOUR ONE AND ONLY MAN**			70

		Atlantic	Volt
Apr 65.	(7") (4024) <124> **MR.PITIFUL. / THAT'S HOW STRONG MY LOVE IS**		41 / 74 Feb65
May 65.	(7") <126> **I'VE BEEN LOVING YOU TOO LONG (TO STOP NOW). / I'M DEPENDING ON YOU**	-	21
Aug 65.	(7") (2091062) **I'VE BEEN LOVING YOU TOO LONG. / RESPECT**		-
Sep 65.	(lp) (SD 33248) <411> **THE GREAT OTIS REDDING SINGS SOUL BALLADS**		Mar65

– That's how strong my love is / Chained and bound / A woman, a lover, a friend / Your one and only man / Nothing can change this love / It's too late / For your precious love / I want to thank you / Come to me / Home in your heart / Keep your arms around me / Mr. Pitiful. (hit UK chart No.30, Apr66) (re-iss. Jun88 on 'Atco', cd-iss. Jul91) (cd-iss. May93)

Sep 65.	(7") <128> **RESPECT. / OLE MAN TROUBLE**		35
Nov 65.	(7") (4050) **MY GIRL. / DOWN IN THE VALLEY**	11	-
Nov 65.	(7") <130> **JUST ONE MORE DAY. / I CAN'T TURN YOU LOOSE**	-	85
Feb 66.	(lp) (ATL 5041) <412> **OTIS BLUE (OTIS REDDING SINGS SOUL)**	6	75 Oct 65

– My girl / (I can't get no) Satisfaction / Respect / Shake! / I've been loving you too long / You don't miss your water / Rock me baby / Wonderful world / Down in the valley / Change gonna come / Ole man trouble. (UK re-iss. Jan67, hit No.7) (re-iss. 1974 + Dec83 +c) (cd-iss. Jun91 on 'Atco')

Mar 66.	(7") (4080) <132> **(I CAN'T GET NO) SATISFACTION. / ANY OLE WAY**	33	31
Jul 66.	(7") (584009) <136> **MY LOVER'S PRAYER. / DON'T MESS WITH CUPID**	37	61 Jun66
Jul 66.	(lp) (587-011) <413> **THE SOUL ALBUM**	22	54 Apr66

– Just one more day / It's growing / Cigarettes and coffee / Chain gang / Nobody knows you (when you're down and out) / Good to me / Scratch my back / Treat her right / Everybody makes a mistake / Any ole way / 634-5789. (cd-iss. Jul91 on 'Atco') (cd-iss. Jun93)

Aug 66.	(7") (584030) **I CAN'T TURN YOU LOOSE. / JUST ONE MORE DAY**	29	-
Nov 66.	(7") (584049) <138> **FA FA FA FA FA (SAD SONG). / GOOD TO ME**	23	29 Sep66
Jan 67.	(lp) (588-050) <415> **OTIS REDDING'S DICTIONARY OF SOUL**	23	73 Nov 66

– Fa-fa-fa-fa-fa (sad song) / I'm sick y'all / Tennessee waltz / Sweet Lorene / Try a little tenderness / Day tripper / My lover's prayer / She put the hurt on me / Ton of joy / You're still my baby / Hawg for you / Love have mercy. (re-iss. Jun88, cd-iss. Jul91 on 'Atco') (cd-iss. Jun93) (US-title 'COMPLETE AND UNBELIEVABLE . . . THE OTIS REDDING DICTIONARY OF SOUL')

Jan 67.	(7") (584070) <141> **TRY A LITTLE TENDERNESS. / I'M SICK Y'ALL**	46	25 Dec 66
Mar 67.	(7") (K 10051) **RESPECT. / THESE ARMS OF MINE** (re-iss. Feb72)		-

		Stax	Volt
Mar 67.	(7") (601005) **DAY TRIPPER. / SHAKE!**	43	-
Apr 67.	(7") (601007) <146> **LET ME COME ON HOME. / I LOVE YOU MORE THAN WORDS CAN SAY**	48	78 B-side
May 67.	(7"; by OTIS REDDING & CARLA THOMAS) <216> **TRAMP. / TELL IT LIKE IT IS**	-	26
Jun 67.	(7") (601011) **SHAKE (live). / 634-5789 (live)**	28	-
Jun 67.	(7") <149> **SHAKE. / YOU DON'T MISS YOUR WATER**	-	-

―――― Some releases on 'Stax' now with CARLA THOMAS, daughter of singer RUFUS.

Jun 67.	(lp; as OTIS REDDING & CARLA THOMAS) (589-007) <716> **KING AND QUEEN**	18	36 Apr67

– Knock on wood / Let me be good to you / Tramp / Tell it like it is / When something is wrong with my baby / Lovey dovey / New Year's resolution / It takes two / Are you lonely for me baby / Bring it on home to me / Ooh Carla, Ooh Otis. (re-iss. Jun88) (cd-iss. Jul91; 7567 82256-2)

Jul 67.	(7"; by OTIS REDDING & CARLA THOMAS) (601 012) **TRAMP. / OOH CARLA OOH OTIS**	18	-
Aug 67.	(7") (601 017) <152> **GLORY OF LOVE. / I'M COMING HOME**		60 Jul67
Sep 67.	(lp) <416> **LIVE IN EUROPE (live)**	-	32 Aug67

– Respect / Can't turn you loose / I've been loving you too long / My girl / Shame / Satisfaction / Fa-fa-fa-fa-fa (sad song) / These arms of mine / Day tripper / Try a little tenderness. (UK-iss.Mar68; 589 016) – hit No.2 (re-iss. Aug69 on 'Atco'; 228 017) (cd-iss. Aug93) (cd-iss. Feb95 & Sep95 on 'Warners')

Oct 67.	(7"; as OTIS REDDING & CARLA THOMAS) (601 021) <228> **KNOCK ON WOOD. / LET ME BE GOOD TO YOU**	35	30 Aug67
Nov 67.	(7") (601027) **SATISFACTION. / I'VE BEEN LOVING YOU TOO LONG**		-

―――― on the 10th of December '67, OTIS was killed in a plane crash

– posthumous releases, etc. –

Dec 67.	(lp/c) Volt; <(418)> **THE HISTORY OF OTIS REDDING** (re-iss. 1969 on 'Atco'; 228 001) below released on 'Volt'/ 'Stax' unless mentioned otherwise	2	9
Feb 68.	(7") (601 031) <157> **(SITTIN' ON) THE DOCK OF THE BAY. / MY SWEET LORENE**	3	1 Jan68
Mar 68.	(7"; by OTIS REDDING & CARLA THOMAS) (601 033) <244> **LOVEY DOVEY. / NEW YEAR'S RESOLUTION**		68 Feb68
May 68.	(lp) (230 001) <419> **DOCK OF THE BAY (late 1967 sessions)**	1	4 Mar68

– The dock of the bay / Home in your heart / I want to thank you / Your one and only man / Nothing can change this love / It's too late / For your precious love / Keep your arms around me / Come to me / A woman, a lover, a friend / Chained and bound / That's how strong my love is. (re-iss. Jul69 on 'Atco'; 228 022) (re-iss. Nov71)

May 68.	(7") (601 040) <163> **THE HAPPY SONG (DUM DUM). / OPEN THE DOOR** Below released on 'Atlantic' UK/ 'Atco' US unless mentioned.	24	25 Apr68
Feb 68.	(7") (K 10111) **MY GIRL. / MR. PITIFUL** (re-iss. 1972, 1980 & Mar84)	36	-
Jul 68.	(7") (584199) <6592> **HARD TO HANDLE. / AMEN**	15	36 B-side
Aug 68.	(lp) <252> **THE IMMORTAL OTIS REDDING** (re-iss. Jan72 on 'Atco') (cd-iss. Aug93; 7567 80270-2)	19	58 Jul68
Sep 68.	(7") <6612> **I'VE GOT DREAMS TO REMEMBER. / NOBODY'S FAULT BUT MINE**	-	41
Oct 68.	(7") (584220) <6636> **I'VE GOT DREAMS TO REMEMBER. / CHAMPAGNE AND WINE**	-	-
Nov 68.	(lp) (587148) <265> **OTIS REDDING IN PERSON AT THE WHISKEY A GO-GO (live 1966)**		82

– I can't turn you loose / Pain in my heart / Just one more day / Mr.Pitiful / (I can't get no) Satisfaction / I'm depending on you / Any ole way / These arms of mine / Papa's got a brand new bag / Respect. (cd-iss. Dec94 & Sep95 on 'Warners')

Dec 68.	(7") <6631> **MERRY CHRISTMAS BABY. / WHITE CHRISTMAS** (UK-iss.Dec72; K 10206)	-	-
Dec 68.	(7") (584234) <6636> **PAPA'S GOT A BRAND NEW BAG (live). / DIRECT ME** Below released on 'Atco' unless mentioned.		21 Nov 68
Mar 69.	(7") (584249) <6654> **A LOVER'S QUESTION. / YOU MADE A MAN OUT OF ME**		48 Feb 69
Apr 69.	(7") <6665> **WHEN SOMETHING IS WRONG WITH MY BABY (w/CARLA THOMAS) / OOH CARLA, OOH OTIS**	-	-
May 69.	(7") <6677> **LOVE MAN. / CAN'T TURN YOU LOOSE**	-	72
Jun 69.	(7") (226001) **LOVE MAN. / THAT'S HOW STRONG MY LOVE IS**	43	-
Jun 69.	(lp) (228 025) <289> **LOVE MAN** (re-iss. Nov71 on 'Atlantic') (cd-iss. Jul92 on 'Rhino')		46
Aug 69.	(7") <6700> **FREE ME. / (YOUR LOVE HAS LIFTED ME) HIGHER AND HIGHER**		-
Feb 70.	(7") (226012) <6723> **LOOK AT THE GIRL. / THAT'S A GOOD IDEA**		-
1970.	(7") <6742> **DEMONSTRATION. / JOHNNY'S HEARTBREAK**	-	-
1970.	(7") <6766> **GIVE AWAY NONE OF MY LOVE. / SNATCH A LITTLE PIECE**	-	-

– more compilations, etc. –

Feb 68.	(lp) Marble Arch; (MAL 772) **HERE COMES SOME SOUL FROM OTIS REDDING AND LITTLE JOE CURTIS (W / LITTLE JOE CURTIS)**	-	-
Jun 68.	(7") Pye Int.; (7N 25463) **SHE'S ALRIGHT. / GAMA LAMA**	-	-

―――― Above and below single rec.1959

Sep 69.	(7") Evolution; E 2442) **SHE'S ALRIGHT. / TUFF ENUFF**	-	-

―――― In Sep70, shared live lp with JIMI HENDRIX (rec.Jun67) 'MONTEREY INTERNATIONAL POP FESTIVAL' on 'Reprise', hit US No.16.
below releases on 'Atlantic' UK/ 'Atco' US unless mentioned otherwise

Jul 70.	(7") (2091 015) **I LOVE YOU. / I NEED YOU**		-
Jul 70.	(7") (2091 020) **WONDERFUL WORLD. / SECURITY**		-
Jan 71.	(lp) (2400 018) <333> **TELL THE TRUTH (rec.1967)**		Aug70

– Demonstration / Tell the truth / Out of sight / Give away none of my love / Wholesale love / I got the will / Johnny's heartbreak / Snatch a little piece / Slippin' and slidin' / The match game / A little time / Swingin' on a string. (cd-iss. Jul92 on 'Rhino')

Mar 71.	(7") (2091062) **I'VE BEEN LOVIN' YOU TOO LONG. / TRY A LITTLE TENDERNESS**		-
Aug 71.	(7"m) (2091112) **(SITTIN' ON) THE DOCK OF THE BAY. / RESPECT / MR.PITIFUL** (re-iss. Jan72, 1974, Jul84)		-
Aug 71.	(7") **MY GIRL. / GOOD TO ME**	-	-

Nov 71. (7") *(K 10206)* **WHITE CHRISTMAS. / MERRY CHRISTMAS BABY**		-
Jan 73. (7"m) *(K 10390)* **(SITTIN' ON) THE DOCK OF THE BAY. / SATISFACTION / I CANT TURN YOU LOOSE**		-
Feb 73. (7"; by OTIS REDDING & CARLA THOMAS) **TRAMP. / KNOCK ON WOOD**		-
Jul 73. (c) *(K4 60016)* **THE BEST OF OTIS REDDING** *(cd-iss. Mar87)*		**76** Sep72
Aug 73. (7") *(K 10601)* **MY GIRL. / HARD TO HANDLE**		-
Aug 74. (lp) *WEA;* **STAR COLLECTION**		-
Jun 79. (lp/c) *(K 50564)* **PURE OTIS**		
Apr 80. (12") **I CAN'T TURN YOU LOOSE. / (SITTIN' ON) THE DOCK OF THE BAY**		
May 81. (lp/c) **OTIS REDDING VOL.1**		
Apr 82. (lp/c) **RECORDED LIVE (live)**		
Apr 84. (lp/c) *Charly; (CRB/TCCRB 1077)* **COME TO ME**		
Jul 84. (lp/c) *WEA; (780171-1/-4)* **THE BEST OF OTIS REDDING**		
Oct 84. (7") *(A 9607)* **(SITTIN' ON) THE DOCK OF THE BAY. / YOU DON'T MISS YOUR WATER**		
Jan 85. (7") *Old Gold; (OG 9500)* **(SITTIN' ON) THE DOCK OF THE BAY. / MY GIRL**		-
May 87. (7") *(YZ 117)* **TRY A LITTLE TENDERNESS. / I'VE BEEN LOVING YOU TOO LONG** (12"+=) *(YZ 117T)* – Hard to handle.		
Jul 87. (lp/c/cd) *(241118-1/-4/-2)* **DOCK OF THE BAY – THE DEFINITIVE COLLECTION** *(re-iss. cd+c.Aug93,hit UK No.50)*		
Dec 88. (lp) *(SD 2807)* **THE OTIS REDDING STORY**		
Apr 91. (cd/c) *Knight; (KN CD/MC 12060)* **HEART AND SOUL OF OTIS REDDING** (below from film 'The Commitments')		-
Aug 91. (7"/c-s) *MCS;* **TRY A LITTLE TENDERNESS. / I'VE BEEN LOVING YOU TOO LONG** (12"+=/cd-s+=) –		
Sep 91. (cd) *Traditional Line;* **SOUL EXPLOSION**		-
Sep 91. (cd) *Traditional Line; (TL 1032)* **LIVE IN CONCERT 1965 (live)**		-
Oct 91. (cd) *Stax;* **1000 VOLTS OF STAX**		
Dec 91. (cd/c) *Stax; (CDSXD/SXDC 041)* **IT'S NOT JUST SENTIMENTAL**		
Jul 92. (cd/c) *Castle; (CCS CD/MC 339)* **THE COLLECTION** – My girl / Stand by me / Higher and higher / The happy song / I love you more than words can say / Amen / Fa-fa-fa-fa-fa (sad song) / I've been losing you too long / The glory of love / I've got dreams to remember / Love man / Free me / Papa's got a brand new bag / (Sittin' on) The dock of the bay.		-
Nov 92. (7"/c-s) *East West; (A 4432/+C)* **(SITTIN' ON) THE DOCK OF THE BAY. / SWEET LORRAINE** (12"+=/cd-s+=) *(A 4432 T/CD)* – Hard to handle / The glory of love.		-
May 93. (cd/lp) *Stax; (CDSX/SXD 089)* **GOOD TO ME – RECORDED LIVE AT THE WHISKEY A-GO-GO**		
Sep 93. (cd/c) *<9548 31709-2)>* **DOCK OF THE BAY – THE DEFINITIVE COLLECTION**	**50**	
Oct 93. (4xcd-box) *<(8122 71439-2)>* **OTIS – THE DEFINITIVE OTIS REDDING**		
Apr 94. (cd) *That's Soul; (TS 022)* **I'VE BEEN LOVIN' YOU TOO LONG**		
Apr 94. (c/cd) *Charly; (TC+/CRB 1077)* **COME TO ME**		
May 94. (7"/c-s) *Rhino;* **(SITTIN' ON THE) DOCK OF THE BAY. /**		
May 98. (cd) *Rhino-Atlantic; <(8122 72955-2)>* **LOVE SONGS**		

REDD KROSS (dig out; Great Alt & Indie . . .)

RED HOT CHILI PEPPERS

Formed: Hollywood, California, USA . . . 1983 after four years as ANTHEM, by schoolfriends ANTHONY KIEDIS (aka ANTWAN THE SWAN), Israeli-born HILLEL SLOVAK, MICHAEL 'FLEA' BALZARY and JACK IRONS. This motley bunch of funky funsters then proceeded to sign with 'E.M.I.' stark naked as part of a now famous publicity stunt. The exhibitionist streak was to be a mainstay of their early career, most famously on the cover for the ABBEY ROAD EP (1988), the lads wearing nought but one sock, strategically placed (no prizes for guessing where!) in a send-up of the classic Beatles' album of the same name. With IRONS and SLOVAK under contractual obligations to their own group, WHAT IS THIS?, drummer JACK SHERMAN (ex-CAPTAIN BEEFHEART) and guitarist CLIFF MARTINEZ (ex-WEIRDOS, ex-TEENAGE JESUS & THE JERKS) filled in on the 1984 eponymous debut album, a promising start which introduced the band's mutant funk-punk hybrid. Taking their cue from the cream of 70's funk (obvious reference points were SLY STONE, JAMES BROWN, the METERS, etc.) and injecting it with a bit of L.A. hardcore mayhem, the CHILI PEPPERS came up with such gonzoid grooves as 'GET UP AND JUMP' and 'POLICE HELICOPTER', although the most interesting track was the haunting 'GRAND PAPPY DU PLENTY', a kind of pre-'Twin Peaks' slice of instrumental noir. The GEORGE CLINTON-produced follow-up, 'FREAKY STYLEY' (1985), sounded more cohesive, most impressively on the galvanising defiance of the hypnotic title track. Alongside fairly faithful covers of Sly Stone's 'IF YOU WANT ME TO STAY' and The Meters' 'HOLLYWOOD (AFRICA)', the group "got down" with their own groove thang on the likes of 'JUNGLE MAN' and 'AMERICAN GHOST DANCE'. 'CATHOLIC SCHOOL GIRLS RULE' and 'SEX RAP', meanwhile, left no doubt as to the CHILI PEPPERS' feminist-baiting agenda. While these records were American-only affairs, the band's manic reputation was beginning to reach across the Atlantic, 'UPLIFT MOFO PARTY PLAN'

(1988) introducing the band to a receptive UK audience. Tougher than their earlier releases, the record consolidated the group's place at the forefront of the burgeoning funk-metal explosion, their brash, kaleidoscopic sound injecting a bit of colour and excitement to Blighty's rather dour rock scene. The party was cut somewhat short, however, with the death of SLOVAK in June, yet another victim of a heroin overdose. With KEIDIS also a heroin addict, IRONS (who subsequently formed the band, ELEVEN) obviously didn't like the way things were going and decided to bail out. Eventual replacements were found in guitarist JOHN FRUSCIANTE and drummer CHAD SMITH, the group throwing themselves into the recording of 'MOTHER'S MILK' (1989). Unfairly criticised in some quarters, the album contained some of the CHILI PEPPERS' finest moments to date. 'KNOCK ME DOWN' was an impassioned plea for sanity in the face of drugs hell, the group enjoying MTV exposure for the first time with the video. A brilliant, celebratory cover of Stevie Wonder's 'HIGHER GROUND' also scored with MTV, easing the band slowly out of cultdom. 'TASTE THE PAIN' was an uncharacteristically introspective (by the CHILIs' standards anyhow) song, no doubt also born of the band's recent troubles and showing a newfound maturity in songwriting. More trouble was to follow in April '90, when that young scamp, KIEDIS, was given a 60-day jail sentence for sexual battery and indecent exposure to a female student (the following year, FLEA and SMITH were both charged with offences of a similar nature). As well as clearly possessing red hot libidos, by the early 90's the band had become red hot property following the release of the RICK RUBIN-produced 'BLOOD SUGAR SEX MAGIK' (1991). Their first release for new label, 'Warners', at last the band had fulfilled their potential over the course of a whole album (a US Top 3). With another series of striking videos, the CHILI PEPPERS almost scored a US No.1 with the aching ballad, 'UNDER THE BRIDGE' while the body-jerk funk-rock of 'GIVE IT AWAY' made the UK Top 10. A multi-million seller, the album catapulted The RED HOT CHILI PEPPERS into the big league, the band subsequently securing a prestigious headlining slot on the 1992 Lollapalooza tour. Always an utterly compelling live proposition, the group's hyperactive stage show is the stuff of legend, what with KEIDIS' manic athletics and FLEA's (possibly) JIMI HENDRIX-inspired upside down bass playing, hanging feet-up by a rope!!!. By the release of 'ONE HOT MINUTE' (1995), a transatlantic Top 5, FRUSCIANTE had been replaced with DAVE NAVARRO (ex-JANE'S ADDICTION), adding a new dimension to the band's sound. For many, the album was the 'CHILI PEPPERS' peak achievement, from the dreamy 'WALKABOUT' to the japery of 'AEROPLANE', the latter becoming a UK hit single. While many of the group's funk-rock contemporaries folded or fell by the wayside when that scene went out of fashion, the RED HOT CHILI PEPPERS developed into one of America's most entertaining, and biggest selling 'alternative' acts through a combination of sheer hard work, talent and concrete self belief (and no doubt a hefty dose of shagging!). Never the most stable of bands, rumours of a 'PEPPERS split were rife in 1997, although they still managed to hit the UK Top 10 with their fantastic cover of The Ohio Players' 'LOVE ROLLERCOASTER' (straight from the Beavis & Butt-Head film). With the returning FRUSCIANTE out from the bench to replace NAVARRO, the band were back with a bang on 1999's 'CALIFORNICATION'. Meanwhile, another stab at the singles chart paid off with a transatlantic Top 20 hit, 'SCAR TISSUE'. • Songwriters: Group compositions except other covers; SUBTERRANEAN HOMESICK BLUES (Bob Dylan) / FIRE + CASTLES MADE OF SAND (Jimi Hendrix) / MOMMY WHERE'S DADDY (Frank Zappa) / THEY'RE RED HOT (Robert Johnson) / SEARCH AND DESTROY (Iggy Pop) / SUFFRAGETTE CITY (David Bowie) / WHY DON'T YOU LOVE ME (Hank Williams) / TINY DANCER (Elton John).

Album rating: RED HOT CHILI PEPPERS (*5) / FREAKY STYLEY (*5) / THE UPLIFT MOFO PARTY PLAN (*6) / MOTHER'S MILK (*7) / BLOOD SUGAR SEX MAGIK (*8) / WHAT HITS!? compilation (*7) / PLASMA SHAFT exploitation (*4) / OUT IN L.A. exploitation (*3) / ONE HOT MINUTE (*6) / CALIFORNICATION (*6)

ANTHONY KIEDIS (ANTWAN THE SWAN) (b. 1 Nov'62, Grand Rapids, Michigan) – vocals / **HILLEL SLOVAK** (b.13 Apr'62, Haifa, Israel) – guitar / **MICHAEL 'FLEA' BALZARY** (b.16 Oct'62, Melbourne, Australia) – bass / **JACK IRONS** (b.18 Jul'62, Los Angeles, California) – drums

		EMI America	EMI America
1984. (lp/c/cd) *(790616-1/-4/-2>* **THE RED HOT CHILI PEPPERS** – True men don't kill coyotes / Baby appeal / Buckle down / Get up and jump / Why don't you love me / Green heaven / Mommy where's daddy? / Out in L.A. / Police helicopter / You always sing / Grand pappy du plenty. *(UK-iss.Aug90 on 'EMI Manhattan' cd/c/lp; CD/TC+/MTL 1056) (re-iss. Jun93 on 'Fame' cd/c; CD/TC FA 3297) (lp re-iss. Dec99 on 'Simply Vinyl'; SVLP 156)*		-	
—— (Due to contractual reasons, SLOVAK and IRONS couldn't play on debut. They were deputised by session men **JACK SHERMAN** – guitar (ex-CAPTAIN BEEFHEART) / & **CLIFF MARTINEZ** – drums (ex-WEIRDOS, ex-TEENAGE JESUS & THE JERKS)			
—— **HILLEL SLOVAK** returned from WHAT IS THIS? to repl. SHERMAN guests included **MACEO PARKER + FRED WESLEY** (of FUNKADELIC / PARLIAMENT)			
1985. (lp/c/cd) *<790617-1/-4/-2>* **FREAKY STYLIE** – Jungle man / Hollywood (Africa) / American ghost dance / If you want me to stay / Never mind / Freaky stylie / Blackeyed blonde / The brothers cup / Battle ship / Lovin' and touchin' / Catholic school girls rule / Sex rap / Thirty dirty birds / Yertle the turtle. *(UK-iss.Aug90 on 'EMI Manhattan' cd/c/lp; CD/TC+/MTL 1057) (re-iss. Dec94 on 'Fame' cd/c; CD/TC FA 3309)*		-	
Aug 85. (7") *(EA 205)* **HOLLYWOOD (AFRICA). / NEVER MIND** (remixed-12"+=) *(12EA 205)* – ('A'dub version).			
—— **JACK IRONS** returned from WHAT IS THIS? to repl. MARTINEZ			
Jan 88. (7") *(EA 241)* **FIGHT LIKE A BRAVE. / FIRE** (12"+=/12"pic-d+=) *(12EA/+P 241)* – ('A'-Mofo mix) / ('A'-Knucklehead mix).			

		EMI Manhattan	EMI Manhattan

Mar 88. (cd/c/lp) *(CD/TC+/AML 3125)* <48036> **THE UPLIFT MOFO PARTY PLAN**   □   Nov87
– Fight like a brave / Funky crime / Me and my friends / Backwoods / Skinny sweaty man / Behind the sun / Subterranean homesick blues / Special secret song inside / No chump love sucker / Walkin' on down the road / Love trilogy / Organic anti-beat box band.

May 88. (7"ep) *(MT 41)* **THE ABBEY ROAD EP**   □   –
– Backwoods / Hollywood (Africa) / True men don't kill coyotes.
(12"ep+=) *(12MT 41)* – Catholic school girls rule.

──── **ANTWAN & FLEA** (now adding trumpet) brought in new lads **JOHN FRUSCIANTE** (b. 5 Mar'70, New York City) – guitar repl. HILLEL who died (of heroin OD) 25 Jun'88. **CHAD SMITH** (b.25 Oct'62, St. Paul, Minnesota) – drums repl. IRONS who later formed ELEVEN and joined PEARL JAM

		E.M.I. USA	E.M.I.

Aug 89. (7"/7"sha-pic-d/12"pic-d) *(MT/MTPD/12MTPD 70)* **KNOCK ME DOWN. / PUNK ROCK CLASSIC / PRETTY LITTLE DITTY**   □   □
(12") *(12MT 70)* – (first 2 tracks) / Special secret song inside / Magic Johnson.
(cd-s) *(CDMT 70)* – (first 2 tracks) / Jungle man / Magic Johnson.

Aug 89. (cd/c/lp) *(CD/TC+/MTL 3125)* <92152> **MOTHER'S MILK**   52   □
– Good time boys / Higher ground / Subway to Venus / Magic Johnson / Nobody weird like me / Knock me down / Taste the pain / Stone cold bush / Fire / Pretty little ditty / Punk rock classic / Sexy Mexican maid / Johnny kick a hole in the sky.

Dec 89. (7") *(MT 75)* **HIGHER GROUND. / MILLIONAIRES AGAINST HUNGER**   55   □
('A'-Munchkin mix-cd-s+=) *(CDMT 75)* – Mommy where's daddy / Politician (mini rap).
(12") *(12MT 75)* – ('A'-Munchkin mix) / ('A'dub mix) / Politician (mini rap) / Mommy where's daddy.
(12") *(12MTX 75)* – ('A'side) / ('A'-Munchkin mix) / ('A'dub mix) / Politician (mini rap).

Jun 90. (c-s/7") *(TC+/MT 85)* **TASTE THE PAIN. / SHOW ME YOUR SOUL**   29   □
(12"+=/9"square-pic-d+=) *(12/10 MT 85)* – Castles made of sand (live).
(cd-s++=) *(CDMT 85)* – Never mind.
(remixed-12"+=) *(12MTX 85)* – If you want me to stay / Never mind.

Aug 90. (c-s/7") *(TC+/MT 88)* **HIGHER GROUND. / FIGHT LIKE A BRAVE**   54   □
(12"+=/12"pic-d+=) *(12MT/+PD 88)* – ('A'-Daddy-O mix).
(cd-s+=) *(CDMT 88)* – Behind the sun / Out in L.A.

		Warners	Warners

Sep 91. (cd)(d-lp/c) *(7599 26681-2)(WX 441/+C) <26681>* **BLOOD SUGAR SEX MAGIK**   25   3
– The power of equality / If you have to ask / Breaking the girl / Funky monks / Suck my kiss / I could have lied / Mellowship slinky in B major / The righteous & the wicked / Give it away / Blood sugar sex magik / Under the bridge / Naked in the rain / Apache Rose peacock / The greeting song / My lovely man / Sir psycho sexy / They're red hot. *(re-iss. Mar92 cd/c; same)*

Dec 91. (c-s,cd-s) *<19147>* **GIVE IT AWAY / SEARCH AND DESTROY**   –   73

Mar 92. (c-s,cd-s) *<18978>* **UNDER THE BRIDGE / THE RIGHTEOUS AND THE WICKED**   –   2

Mar 92. (7"/s7"/c-s) *(W 0084/+W/C)* **UNDER THE BRIDGE. / GIVE IT AWAY**   26   –
(12"/cd-s) *(W 0084 T/CD)* – ('A'side) / Search and destroy / Soul to squeeze / Sikamikanico.

──── (the last track also featured on 'Wayne's World' film/single)

──── **ZANDER SCHLOSS** (THELONIUS MONSTER) – guitar, repl. FRUSCIANTE who went solo 'TO CLARA' in 1994 on 'American'.

Jun 92. (c-s,cd-s) **IF YOU HAVE TO ASK /**   –   □

Aug 92. (7"/c-s) *(W 0126/+C)* **BREAKING THE GIRL. / FELA'S COOK**   41   □
(12"+=/cd-s+=) *(W 0126 T/CD)* – Suck my kiss (live) / I could have lied (live).

──── (Aug'92) **ARIK MARSHALL** (b.13 Feb'67, Los Angeles) – guitar (ex-MARSHALL LAW) repl. SCHLOSS

Jun 93. (c-s) *(W 188C)* **GIVE IT AWAY / IF YOU HAVE TO ASK (Friday night fever blister mix)**   □   –
(12"+=/cd-s+=) *(W 188 TP/CD1)* – ('A'-extended + Rasta mixes).
(cd-s) *(W 188CD2)* – ('A'side) / ('A'-Disco Krisco mix) / ('A'-Scott & Garth mix).

Aug 93. (c-s,cd-s) *<18401>* **SOUL TO SQUEEZE / NOBODY WEIRD LIKE ME**   –   22

──── **DAVE NAVARRO** (b. 7 Jun'67, Santa Monica, Calif.) – guitar (ex-JANE'S ADDICTION) repl. MARSHALL

Jan 94. (c-s) *(W 0225C)* **GIVE IT AWAY / SOUL TO SQUEEZE**   9   □
(cd-s+=) *(W 0225CD1)* – ('A'-extended & Rasta mixes).
(cd-s) *(W 0225CD2)* – ('A'side) / If you have to ask (Friday night fever blister mix) / ('A'-Scott & Garth mix) / Nobody weird like me (live).
(12") *(W 0225T)* – ('A'extended) / ('A'-Rasta mix) / If you have to ask (disco krisco mix).

Apr 94. (7"blue/c-s) *(W 0237/+C)* **UNDER THE BRIDGE. / SUCK MY KISS (live)**   13   –
(cd-s+=) *(W 0237CD)* – Sikamikanico / Search and destroy (live).
(cd-s) *(W 0237CDX)* – ('A'side) / I could have lied (live) / Fela's cook / Give it away (in progress; demo).

Aug 95. (c-s) *(W 0316C)* **WARPED / PEA**   31   –
(cd-s+=) *(W 0316CD)* – Melancholy mechanics.

Sep 95. (cd/c/lp) *<(9362 45733-2/-4/-1)>* **ONE HOT MINUTE**   2   4
– Warped / Aeroplane / Deep kick / My friends / Coffee shop / Pea / One big mob / Walkabout / Tearjerker / One hot minute / Falling into grace / Shallow be thy name / Transcending.

Oct 95. (c-s) *(W 0317C)* **MY FRIENDS / LET'S MAKE EVIL**   29   –
(12"+=/cd-s+=) *(W 0317 TX/CD)* – Coffee shop / Stretch.

Feb 96. (c-s) *(W 0331C)* **AEROPLANE / SUFFRAGETTE CITY (live)**   11   –
(cd-s+=) *(W 0331CD)* – Suck my kiss (live).
(cd-s) *(W 0331CDX)* – ('A'side) / Backwoods (live) / Transcending (live) / Me and my friends (live).

──── FLEA + CHAD splintered with THERMIDOR, which was formed by ROBBIE ALLEN and DAVID KING. An album 'MONKEY ON RICO' was released in the Spring.

Jun 97. (7"/c-s/cd-s) *(GFS/+C/TD 22188)* **LOVE ROLLERCOASTER. / Engelbert Humperdinck: Lesbian Seagull**   7   –
(above from the 'Beavis & Butt-Head Do America' film; on 'Geffen')

──── (Apr'98) **JOHN FRUSCIANTE** returned to repl. NAVARRO (who formed SPREAD)

May 99. (c-s) *(W 490C) <16913>* **SCAR TISSUE / GONG LI**   15   9
(cd-s+=) *(W 490CD2)* – Instrumental No.1.

Jun 99. (cd/c) *<(9362 47386-2/-4)>* **CALIFORNICATION**   5   3
– Around the world / Parallel universe / Scar tissue / Otherside / Get on top / Californication / Easily / Porcelain / Emit remmus / Velvet glove / Savoir / Purple stain / Right on time / Road trippin'.

Aug 99. (c-s) *(W 500C)* **AROUND THE WORLD / YERTLE TRILOGY**   35   □
(cd-s+=) *(W 500CD2)* – Me and my friends.
(cd-s) *(W 500CD1)* – ('A'side) / Parallel universe / Teatro jam.

Dec 99. (cd-s) *(W 510CD1)* **OTHERSIDE / HOW STRONG / ROAD TRIPPIN' (without strings)**   □   –
(cd-s) *(W 510CD2)* – ('A'side) / My lovely man.

– compilations, others, etc. –

Oct 92. (cd/c/d-lp) *EMI USA; (CD/TC+/MTL 1071) <94762>* **WHAT HITS!?**   23   22
– Higher ground / Fight like a brave / Behind the Sun / Me & my friends / Backwoods / True men don't kill coyotes / Fire / Get up and jump / Knock me down / Under the bridge / Show me your soul / If you want me to stay / Hollywood / Jungle man / The brothers cup / Taste the pain / Catholic school girls rule / Johnny kick a hole in the sky.

Oct 94. (d-cd) *Warners; (9362 45649-2)* **PLASMA SHAFT** (rare mixes/live)   □   □

Nov 94. (cd/c/lp) *E.M.I.; (CD/TC+/MTL 1062)* **OUT IN L.A.** (rare remixes, demos & live)   61   82

Nov 95. (3xcd-box) *E.M.I.; (CDOMB 004)* **THE RED HOT CHILI PEPPERS / FREAKY STYLIE / THE UPLIFT MOFO PARTY PLAN**   □   □

Apr 98. (cd/c) *EMI-USA; <72434-94139-2/-4>* **ESSENTIAL RED HOT CHILI PEPPERS: UNDER THE COVERS**   –   □

RED HOUSE PAINTERS

Formed: San Francisco, California, USA ... 1989 by MARK KOZELEK (who had earlier sung in GOD FORBID) along with drummer ANTHONY KOUTSOS whom he met in 1989, after moving from Ohio to Atlanta. Relocating once again, this time to San Francisco, the pair duly recruited guitarist GORDON MACK and bassist JERRY VESSEL. The outfit was basically KOZELEK's baby, however, and his writing and distinctly melancholy musings dominated the group's work. Their debut album, 'DOWN COLOURFUL HILL', was virtually a bare demo which had arrived in the hands of '4 a.d.' supremo, Ivo Watts-Russell, via American Music Club miserabilist, MARK EITZEL. Spiritually akin to AMC, the debut showcased KOZELEK's moody pastel-rock introspections, downbeat but often hauntingly melodic. Though the press raved over it (comparisons were made with singer/songwriters like NEIL YOUNG and LOU REED), the album sold negligably. A further couple of RED HOUSE PAINTERS' releases followed in 1993, confusingly enough, both entitled 'RED HOUSE PAINTERS'. One was a sprawling double set building on the wistfulness of the debut while the other was a mini-album featuring such endearing covers as Paul Simon's 'I AM A ROCK' and 'THE STAR SPANGLED BANNER'. It would be another two years before the group's next album, KOZELEK and Co. undertaking a rare UK tour, their first British dates since an early appearance at London's 'Borderline'. 'OCEAN BEACH' (1995) was a more robust set, KOZELEK illustrating the breadth of his influences with a YES cover, 'LONG DISTANCE RUNAROUND', no doubt a crime punishable by public flogging in most indie bands' book. Though the critical plaudits continued to roll in, the album again failed to sell in any great quantity. With a move to 'Island' in 1996, surely a better home for the sparse melancholy of the bulk of KOZOLEK's material, the group released 'SONGS FOR THE BLUE GUITAR?'. • **Songwriters:** All by KOZELE K, except 'DRAGONFLIES' by ROBYN RIEL-NAIL. Covers; STAR SPANGLED BANNER (US National Anthem) / SHOCK ME (Kiss). • **Trivia:** Their UK first gig (very rare) was at The Borderline in London in the Autumn of '92.

Album rating: DOWN COLORFUL HILL (*7) / RED HOUSE PAINTERS double-set (*9) / RED HOUSE PAINTERS mini-set (*6) / OCEAN BEACH (*7) / SONGS FOR A BLUE GUITAR (*6) / RETROSPECTIVE compilation (*8)

MARK KOZELEK – vocals / **GORDON MACK** – guitar / **JERRY VESSEL** – bass / **ANTHONY KOUTSOS** – drums

		4 a.d.	4ad- Warners

Sep 92. (cd)(lp/c) *(CAD 2014CD)(CAD/+C 2014) <45062>* **DOWN COLORFUL HILL**   □   □
– 24 / Medicine bottle / Down colourful hill / Japanese to English / Lord kill the pain / Michael.

May 93. (cd)(d-lp/c) *(DAD 3008CD)(DAD/+C 3008) <45256>* **RED HOUSE PAINTERS**   63   □
– Grace cathedral park / Down through / Katy song / Mistress / Things mean a lot / Funhouse / Take me out / Rollercoaster / New Jersey / Dragonflies / Mistress (piano version) / Mother / Strawberry hill / Brown eyes.

Oct 93. (cd)(m-lp/c) *(CAD 3016CD)(CAD/+C 3016) <45441>* **RED HOUSE PAINTERS**   68   □
– Evil / Bubble / I am a rock / Helicopter / New Jersey / Uncle Joe / Blindfold / Star spangled banner.

Feb 94. (12"ep/cd-ep) *(BAD 4004/+CD)* **SHOCK ME / SHOCK ME (mix). / SUNDAYS AND HOLIDAYS / THREE-LEGGED CAT** ☐ -

Mar 95. (cd)(c)(2x10"lp) *(CAD 5005CD)(CADC 5005)(DAD 5005)* *<45859>* **OCEAN BEACH** ☐ ☐
– Cabezon / Summer dress / San Geronimo / Shadows / Over my head / Red carpet / Brockwell Park / Moments / Drop. *(lp+=)* – Long distance runaround.

                                                 Island   Polygram

Jul 96. (cd/c) *(CID/ICT 8050)* *<531061>* **SONGS FOR A BLUE GUITAR** ☐ ☐
– Have you forgotten / Song for a blue guitar / Make like paper / Priest alley song / Trailways / Feel the rain fall / Long distance runaround / All mixed up / Revelation Big Sur / Silly love songs / Another song for a blue guitar.

Jul 99. (d-cd) *(DAD 9013CD)* **RETROSPECTIVE** (compilation) ☐ ☐
– Shock me / Grace cathedral park / Katy song / Summer dress / New Jersey / Medicine bottle / Michael / San Geronimo / Bubble / Mistress / Drop / Evil / Roller-coaster / Funhouse / Waterkill / Uncle Joe / Helicopter / Brown eyes / Dragonflies / Japanese to English / Shock me (mix) / Over my head / Brockwell Park / Shadows / Mistress (piano version) / Summer dress / Instrumental.

RED NOISE (see under ⇒ NELSON, Bill)

REDSKINS (dig out; Great Alt & Indie . . .)

RED SNAPPER (dig out; Great Alt & indie . . .)

Dan REED NETWORK (dig out; Great Metal . . .)

Lou REED

Born: LOUIS FIRBANK, 2 Mar'42, Freeport, Long Island, New York, USA. In 1958, he formed The JADES, who released two REED-penned singles, 'LEAVE HER FOR ME' / 'SO BLUE' and 'LEAVE HER FOR ME' / 'BELINDA' for 'Time' and 'Dot' respectively. Late in '64, he joined the 'Pickwick' stable of writers, achieving a local minor hit when The PRIMITIVES issued his 'THE OSTRICH' / 'SNEAKY PETE' 45. Later in the year, he helped with the seminal VELVET UNDERGROUND. An integral part of the group's songwriting prowess, he departed in September 1970, going solo and signing to 'R.C.A.'. His eponymous 1972 debut (with Richard Robinson on production), scraped into the US Top 200, gaining nothing in renewed respect. Later that year, helped by stablemates DAVID BOWIE and MICK RONSON, he unleashed 'TRANSFORMER', giving him his first major triumph when it reached the Top 30 on both sides of the Atlantic. It was boosted by 'WALK ON THE WILD SIDE' (a superb Top 20 single), the piano-led melancholy of 'PERFECT DAY', the raw glam of 'VICIOUS' and one-that-got-away 'SATELLITE OF LOVE'. His next album, 'BERLIN' (1973), although unfairly panned by US critics, still managed a Top 10 placing in Britain. On reflection, its subject matter of suicide and child neglect ('THE BED' and 'THE KIDS') didn't help win any new friends and it still stands as one of the most unrelentingly bleak listens in the history of rock. After the claustrophobic confessions of BERLIN, the live 'ROCK 'N' ROLL ANIMAL' (1974) album must have come as something of a relief to R.C.A. A technically faultless back-up band roared through a selection of old VELVETS numbers with REED hollering over the top, and while the set represented something of a concession to commercial credibility (by REED's standards anyway), it captured little of the VELVET UNDERGROUND's subtlety. It also saw REED sinking further into self-parody, hamming up his studied image of sleazy decadence to the max. 'SALLY CAN'T DANCE', released later the same year, was REED in full emotionless flight, an icy collection of biting cynicism that included the infamous 'ANIMAL LANGUAGE' track. But laughing LOU hadn't played his ace card yet, that musical two-fingered salute fell to 1975's 'METAL MACHINE MUSIC', the one everyone talks about but have never had the will or mental endurance to listen to the whole way through. A double album of impenetrable feedback noise interspersed with inhuman screams, hums etc., the record successfully alienated most of REED's long suffering fans amid critical meltdown. In true contrary style, he sashayed sweetly back with the mellow 'CONEY ISLAND BABY' (1976), although the lyrics remained as brutally frank as ever. His first record for 'Arista', 'ROCK 'N' ROLL HEART' (1976) was indeed as vacantly awful as the title suggests, though the punk-inspired 'STREET HASSLE' (1978) showcased a re-energised REED, most impressively on the malicious guitar workout of 'DIRT' and the swaggering title track. After a tedious live album, REED started to show uncharacteristic signs of maturity in both his music and lyrics with 'THE BELLS' (1979) and 'GROWING UP IN PUBLIC' (1980). At the turn of the 80's, he hooked up with former Void-Oid, ROBERT QUINE, a partnership that resulted in one of the most consistent and accomplished sets in REED's solo career, 'THE BLUE MASK'. Newly married and back at his original stable, 'R.C.A.', REED proffered more domestic lyrical fare alongside darker musings. QUINE remained for one more studio album, the similarly focused 'LEGENDARY HEARTS', before breaking ranks. 1984's 'NEW SENSATIONS' was fairly low-key while 'MISTRIAL' (1986) saw REED introduce a few drum-machine tracks in typical 80's style. These were competent albums but hardly essential and only the most devout REED believer could've predicted the creative, commercial and critical renaissance that would ensue with 1989's 'NEW YORK' album. A skeletal strum-athon, this was LOU REED in the raw with the sparsest of musical accompaniment. Back on familiar territory, his sardonic tales of the Big Apple's seedier side made for compelling listening. 'SONGS

FOR DRELLA' (1990), a collaboration with JOHN CALE, was a heartfelt tribute to ANDY WARHOL, while 'MAGIC AND LOSS' (1992) was a sincere series of stark meditations on life and death. Despite an ill-advised VELVET UNDERGROUND reunion, REED retained critical favour, going on to release another well-received album in 1996, 'SET THE TWILIGHT REELING'.
• **Songwriters:** REED compositions except, SEPTEMBER SONG (Kurt Weill) / SOUL MAN (Sam & Dave). In 1979 and 1980, he co-wrote with MICHAEL FORFARA plus other group members. The single, 'CITY LIGHTS', was co-written with NILS LOFGREN. • **Trivia:** Surprisingly in 1973, WALK ON THE WILD SIDE was not banned from airplay. It contained the lyrics "giving head", which had been overlooked by unstreet-wise cred. radio producers. LOU has been married twice, first to cocktail waitress, Betty on the 9th of January '73, then to Sylvia Morales on the 14th of February '80. He played guitar and composed four tracks on NICO's 'Chelsea Girl' lp in 1967. Nine years later he produced NELSON SLATER's 'Wild Angel' album, also contributing guitar, piano and vocals. In 1979 and 1981 he co-composed with NILS LOFGREN and KISS on their 'NILS' and 'THE ELDER' albums respectively. In the late 80's, he guested for RUBEN BLADES and his old friend MAUREEN TUCKER. He was also backing vocalist on SIMPLE MINDS' 'This is Your Land' / DION's 'King of The New York Streets' and TOM TOM CLUB's version of 'Femme Fatale'.

Album rating: LOU REED (*5) / TRANSFORMER (*9) / BERLIN (*7) / ROCK'N'ROLL ANIMAL (*6) / SALLY CAN'T DANCE (*5) / LOU REED LIVE (*5) / METAL MACHINE MUSIC (*1) / CONEY ISLAND BABY (*7) / ROCK AND ROLL HEART (*4) / WALK ON THE WILD SIDE – THE BEST OF LOU REED compilation (*7) / STREET HASSLE (*7) / LIVE – TAKE NO PRISONERS (*3) / THE BELLS (*5) / GROWING UP IN PUBLIC (*4) / ROCK AND ROLL DIARY 1967-1980 compilation (*6) / THE BLUE MASK (*6) / LEGENDARY HEARTS (*6) / LIVE IN ITALY (*4) / NEW SENSATIONS (*7) / MISTRIAL (*5) / NEW YORK (*8) / RETRO compilation (*7) / SONGS FOR DRELLA with John Cale (*7) / MAGIC AND LOSS (*7) / BETWEEN THOUGHT AND EXPRESSION: THE LOU REED ANTHOLOGY boxed-compilation (*7) / SET THE TWILIGHT REELING (*5)

LOU REED – vocals, guitar (ex-VELVET UNDERGROUND) / with **STEVE HOWE** – guitar / **RICK WAKEMAN** – keyboards (both of YES) / **CLEM CATTINI** – drums (ex-TORNADOES)

		R.C.A.	R.C.A.
Jun 72. (7") *<0727>* **GOING DOWN. / I CAN'T STAND IT**		-	
Jul 72. (lp) *(SF 8281)* *<4701>* **LOU REED**			Jun72

– I can't stand it / Going down / Walk and talk it / Lisa says / Berlin / I love you / Wild child / Love makes you feel / Ride into the Sun / Ocean.

Aug 72. (7") *(RCA 2240)* *<0784>* **WALK AND TALK IT. / WILD CHILD** ☐ ☐

now with MICK RONSON – guitar / **HERBIE FLOWERS + KLAUS VOORMANN** – bass / **JOHN HALSEY + RITCHIE DHARMA + BARRY DE SOUZA** – drums / **RONNIE ROSS** – saxophone / **DAVID BOWIE** – backing vocals, producer

Nov 72. (lp) *(LSP 4807)* *<4807>* **TRANSFORMER**	13	29

– Vicious / Andy's chest / Perfect day / Hangin' round / Walk on the wild side / Make up / Satellite of love / Wagon wheel / New York telephone conversation / I'm so free / Goodnight ladies. *(re-iss. Feb81 lp/c; INT S/K 5061; hit UK No.91)* *(re-iss. 1984 lp/c; NL/NK 83806)* *(cd-iss. 1985 + Oct87; PD 83806)*

Nov 72. (7") *(RCA 2303)* *<0887>* **WALK ON THE WILD SIDE. / PERFECT DAY**	10	16

(re-iss. May79 on 'RCA Gold'; GOLD 5)

Feb 73. (7") *<0964>* **SATELLITE OF LOVE. / WALK AND TALK IT**	-	
Mar 73. (7") *(RCA 2318)* **SATELLITE OF LOVE. / VICIOUS**	-	
Apr 73. (7") *<0054>* **VICIOUS. / GOODNIGHT LADIES**	-	

all new band **DICK WAGNER + STEVE HUNTER** – guitar (both ex-ALICE COOPER) / **STEVE WINWOOD** – keyboards / **JACK BRUCE** – bass / **AYNSLEY DUNBAR** – drums / etc.

Oct 73. (7") *<0172>* **HOW DO YOU THINK IT FEELS. / LADY DAY**	-	
Oct 73. (lp) *(RS 1002)* *<0207>* **BERLIN**	7	98

– Berlin / Lady day / Men of good fortune / Caroline says I / How do think it feels / Oh Jim / Caroline says II / The kids / The bed / Sad song. *(re-iss. Oct81 lp/c; INT S/K 5150)* *(re-iss. 1984 lp/c; NL/NK 84388)* *(cd-iss. Jun86; PD 84388)*

Feb 74. (7") *(APBO 0221)* **CAROLINE SAYS I. / CAROLINE SAYS II** ☐ -

PRAKASH JOHN – bass (ex-ALICE COOPER) repl. TONY LEVIN / **JOSEF CHIROWSKY** – keyboards / **WHITNEY GLEN** – drums (ex-ALICE COOPER)

Feb 74. (lp/c) *(APL 1/4 0472)* *<0472>* **ROCK'N'ROLL ANIMAL (live)**	26	45

– (intro) – Sweet Jane / Heroin / White light – white heat / Lady day / Rock and roll. *(re-iss. May81 lp/c; INT S/K 5086)* *(re-iss. 1984 lp/c; NL/NK 83664)* *(cd-iss. Jun86; PD 83664)*

Apr 74. (7") *<(APBO 0238)>* **SWEET JANE (live). / LADY DAY (live)** ☐ ☐

MICHAEL FORFARA – keyboards repl. JOSEF

Aug 74. (7") *<10053>* **SALLY CAN'T DANCE / VICIOUS**	-	
Sep 74. (lp/c) *(APL 1/4 <0611>)* **SALLY CAN'T DANCE**		10

– Ride Sally ride / Animal language / Baby face / N.Y. stars / Kill your sons / Billy / Sally can't dance / Ennui. *(re-iss. Mar87; PD 80611)* *(re-iss. cd Feb89; ND 90308)*

Oct 74. (7") *(RCA 2467)* *<10081>* **SALLY CAN'T DANCE. / ENNUI**	☐	
Mar 75. (lp) *(RS 1007)* *<0959>* **LOU REED LIVE (live)**		62

– Walk on the wild side / I'm waiting for the man / Vicious / Oh Jim / Satellite of love / Sad song. *(re-iss. Feb81 lp/c; INT S/K 5071)* *(cd-iss. Mar87 + Feb90; ND 83752)*

LOU now used synthesizer only.

Jul 75. (d-lp) *<(CPL2 1101)>* **METAL MACHINE MUSIC – (THE AMINE B RING)** ☐ ☐
– Metal machine music A1 / A2 / A3 / A4. *(re-iss. Mar91 on 'Great Expectations' cd/d-c/d-lp; PIPD C/M/L 023)*

Band now featured **MICHAEL SUCHORSKY** – percussion / **BOB KULICK** – guitar / **BRUCE YAW** – bass

Jan 76. (lp) *(RS 1035)* *<0915>* **CONEY ISLAND BABY**	52	41

– Crazy feeling / Charley's girl / She's my best friend / Kicks / A gift / Oooh baby / Nobody's business / Coney island baby. *(re-iss. Mar81 lp/c; INT S/K 5082)* *(re-iss. 1984 lp/c; NL/NK 83807)* *(cd-iss. Dec86 & Sep89; PD 83807)*

Mar 76. (7") *(RCA 2666) <10573>* **CHARLEY'S GIRL. / NOWHERE AT ALL**

May 76. (7") *<10648>* **CRAZY FEELING. / NOWHERE AT ALL**

	Arista	Arista

Nov 76. (lp/c) *(ARTY/TC-ARTY 142) <4100>* **ROCK AND ROLL HEART** — 64
 – I believe in love / Banging on my drum / Follow the leader / You wear it so well / Ladies pay / Rock and roll heart / Temporary thing.

Nov 76. (7") *<0215>* **I BELIEVE IN LOVE. / SENSELESSLY CRUEL**

Apr 77. (7") *(105)* **ROCK AND ROLL HEART. / SENSELESSLY CRUEL** — -

—— **STUART HEINRICH** – guitar, vocals repl. KULICK / **MARTY FOGEL** – saxophone repl. YAW

Apr 78. (lp/c) *(SPART/TC-SPART 1045) <4169>* **STREET HASSLE** — 89
 – Gimme some good times / Dirt / Street hassle / I wanna be black / Real good time together / Shooting star / Leave me alone / Wait.

Apr 78. (12") **STREET HASSLE. / (same track)** — -

Jul 78. (12"ep) *(ARIST12 198)* **STREET HASSLE. / Waiting For The Man + Venus In Furs (by "The VELVET UNDERGROUND")** — -

—— **ELLARD BOLES** – bass, guitar repl. HEINRICH. (Below released 'RCA' UK)

Mar 79. (d-lp)<red,blue-lp> *(XL 03066) <8502>* **LIVE – TAKE NO PRISONERS (live)** — Nov78
 – Sweet Jane / I wanna be black / Satellite of love / Pale blue eyes / Berlin / I'm waiting for the man / Coney island baby / Street hassle / Walk on the wild side / Leave me alone.

—— **REED** now with **FORFARA, BOLES, SUCHORSKY, FOGEL** and **DON CHERRY** – trumpet

Oct 79. (lp/c) *(SPART/TC-SPART 1093) <4229>* **THE BELLS** — May 79
 – Stupid man / Disco mystic / I want to boogie with you / With you / Looking for love / City lights / All through the night / Families / The bells. *(cd-iss. Aug92; 262 918)*

Jun 79. (7") *<0431>* **CITY LIGHTS. / I WANT TO BOOGIE WITH YOU** — -

Oct 79. (7") *(ARIST 308)* **CITY LIGHTS. / SENSELESSLY CRUEL** — -

—— **CHUCK HAMMER** – synthesizer, guitar repl. FOGEL & CHERRY

May 80. (lp/c) *(SPART/TC-SPART 1131) <9522>* **GROWING UP IN PUBLIC**
 – How do you speak to an angel / My old man / Keep away / Growing up in public / Standing on ceremony / So alone / Love is here to stay / The power of positive drinking / Smiles / Think it over / Teach the gifted children. *(cd-iss. Aug92; 262 917)*

Jun 80. (7") *<0535>* **THE POWER OF POSITIVE DRINKING. / GROWING UP IN PUBLIC** — -

—— now with **ROBERT QUINE** – guitar / **FERNANDO SAUNDERS** – bass, vocals / **DOANE PERRY** – drums

	R.C.A.	R.C.A.

Mar 82. (lp/c) *(RCA LP/K 6028) <4221>* **THE BLUE MASK** — Feb82
 – My house / Women / Underneath the bottle / The gun / The blue mask / Average guy / The heroine / Waves of fear / The day John Kennedy died / Heavenly arms.

Mar 83. (lp/c) *(RCA LP/K 6071) <4568>* **LEGENDARY HEARTS**
 – Legendary hearts / Don't talk to me about work / Make up mind / Martial law / The last shot / Turn out the light / ow wow / Betrayed / Bottoming out / Home of the brave / Rooftop garden. *(re-iss. Oct86 lp/c; NL/NK 89843) (re-iss. Apr91 cd/c; ND/NK 89843)*

Apr 83. (7") *<13558>* **MARTIAL LAW. / DON'T TALK TO ME ABOUT WORK** — -

Jan 84. (d-lp/c) *(PL/PK 89156)* **LIVE IN ITALY (live)** — -
 – Sweet Jane / I'm waiting for the man / Martial law / Satellite of love / Kill your sons / Betrayed / Sally can't dance / Waves of fear / Average guy / White light – white heat / Some kinda love / Sister Ray / Walk on the wild side / Heroin / Rock and roll.

—— line-up now **SAUNDERS** plus **FRED MAHER** – drums / **PETER WOOD** – piano, synthesizer, accordion / **L. SHANKER** – electric violin

Mar 84. (7") *<13841>* **I LOVE YOU SUZANNE. / MY FRIEND GEORGE** — -

May 84. (12") *<13849>* **MY RED JOY STICK. / ('A' remix)** — -

May 84. (lp/c) *(PL/PK 84998) <4998>* **NEW SENSATIONS** — 92 | 56
 – I love you, Suzanne / Endlessly jealous / My red joystick / Turn to me / New sensations / Doin' the things that we want to / What becomes a legend most / Fly into the Sun / High in the city / My friend George / Down at the arcade. *(cd-iss. Jul86; PD 84998)*

May 84. (7") *(RCA 417)* **I LOVE YOU, SUZANNE. / VICIOUS** — -
 (12"+= (RCAT 417) – Walk on the wild side.

Apr 86. (12") *<14427>* **THE ORIGINAL WRAPPER. / (2 'A' versions)** — -

Apr 86. (lp/c/cd) *(PL/PK/PD 87190) <7190>* **MISTRIAL** — 69 | 47
 – Mistrial / No money down / Outside / Don't hurt a woman / Video violence / Spit it out / The original wrapper / Mama's got a lover / I remember you / Tell it to your heart. *(re-iss. Oct88 lp/c/cd; NL/NK/ND 90253)*

Jun 86. (7") *(RCA 501) <14368>* **NO MONEY DOWN. / DON'T HURT A WOMAN**
 (12"+= (RCAT 501) <14388> – ('A'dub version).

—— Next from the film 'Soul Man'.

	A&M	A&M

Jan 87. (7"; LOU REED & SAM MOORE) *(AM 364)* **SOUL MAN. / Sweet Sarah (by 'Tom Scott')** — 30
 <US-12"+=> – My love is chemical.

—— new band **MIKE RATHKE** – guitar / **ROB WASSERMAN** – bass / **FRED MAHER** – drums / **MAUREEN TUCKER** – drums on 2 (ex-VELVET UNDERGROUND)

	Sire	Sire

Jan 89. (lp/c)(cd) *(WX 246/+C)(925 829-2) <25829>* **NEW YORK** — 14 | 40
 – Romeo had Juliette / Halloween parade / Dirty Blvd. / Endless cycle / There is no time / The last great American whale / Beginning of a great adventure / Busload of faith / Sick of you / Hold on / Good evening Mr. Waldheim / Xmas in February / Strawman / Dime store mystery. *(re-iss. Feb95 cd/c;)*

Feb 89. (7") **ROMEO HAD JULIETTE. / BUSLOAD OF FAITH (live)** — -

Feb 89. (7") *(W 7547)* **DIRTY BLVD. / THE LAST GREAT AMERICAN WHALE** — -
 (12"+= (W 7547T) – The room.

Apr 90. (cd)(lp/c; by LOU REED / JOHN CALE) *(7599 <26140-2)>(WX 345/+C)* **SONGS FOR DRELLA** — 22
 – Smalltown / Open house / Style it takes / Work / Trouble with classicists / Starlight / Faces and names / Images / Slip away (a warning) / It wasn't me / I believe / Nobody but you / A dream / Forever changed / Hello it's me. *(re-iss. Feb91 & Jan97; same)*
 (above re-united the two VELVET UNDERGROUND members, tributing the recently deceased ANDY WARHOL)

—— **MICHAEL BLAIR** – percussion, drums, vocals repl. MAHER

Jan 92. (cd/lp/c) *(7599 <26662-2>)(WX 435/+C)* **MAGIC AND LOSS** — 6 | 80
 – Dorita – the spirit / What's good – the thesis / Power and glory – the situation / Magician – internally / Sword of Damocles – eternally / Goodby mass – in a chapel bodily termination / Cremation – ashes to ashes / Dreamin' – escape / No chance – regret / Warrior king – revenge / Harry's circumcision – reverie gone astray / Gassed and stoked – loss / Power and glory part II – magic transformation / Magic and loss – the summation. *(cd re-iss. Jan97; same)*

Mar 92. (7"/c-s) **WHAT'S GOOD. / THE ROOM**
 (12"+=/cd-s+=) – Mary's circumcision / A dream.

—— now with just **FERNANDO SAUNDERS** – basses / **TONY 'Thunder' SMITH** – drums / + guest **LAURIE ANDERSON** – backing vocals

	WEA	Reprise

Feb 96. (cd/c) *<(9362 46159-2/-4)>* **SET THE TWILIGHT REELING** — 26
 – Egg cream / NYC man / Finish line / Trade in / Hang on to your emotions / Sex with your parents (motherfucker) part II (live) / Hooky wooky / The proposition / Adventurer / Riptide / Set the twilight reeling.

May 96. (c-s) *(W 0351C)* **HOOKY WOOKY / ON THE RUN**
 (cd-s) (W 0351CD) – ('A'side) / This magic moment / You'll never know you loved.

– compilations, others, etc. –

—— Below releases issued on 'RCA' unless mentioned otherwise

Apr 77. (lp/c) *(PL/PK 12001) <2001>* **WALK ON THE WILD SIDE – THE BEST OF LOU REED**
 (cd-iss. Mar87; PD 83753)

Jan 79. (lp/c) *(NL/NK 42731)* **VICIOUS**

Dec 80. (d-lp) *Arista; (DARTY 8)* **ROCK AND ROLL DIARY 1967-1980**
 – (above featured 8 tracks by Velvet Underground)

Aug 81. (7") *RCA Gold; (GOLD 523)* **WALK ON THE WILD SIDE. / VICIOUS** — -
 (re-iss. Oct86 & Mar89 on 'Old Gold'; OG 9635)

Sep 82. (lp) *(SF 8281)* **I CAN'T STAND IT**

Oct 85. (7") *A&M; (AM 283)* **SEPTEMBER SONG. / Oh Heavenly Action (by 'Mark Bingham with Johnny Adams & Aaron Neville')**

May 86. (c) *(NK 89895)* **MAGIC MOMENTS**

Sep 86. (lp/c) *Fame; (FA/TC-FA 3164)* **NEW YORK SUPERSTAR**

Feb 89. (3"cd-ep) *(PD 49453)* **WALK ON THE WILD SIDE / PERFECT DAY / SATELLITE OF LOVE / VICIOUS**

Sep 89. (lp/c/cd) *(PL/PK/PD 90389)* **RETRO** — 29
 – Walk on the wild side / Satellite of love / I love you Suzanne / Wild child / How do you think it feels / Lady day / Coney Island baby / Sweet Jane (live) / Vicious / Sally can't dance / Berlin / Caroline says II / Kill your sons / White light – white heat (live). *(cd+=)* – I'm waiting for the man (VELVET UNDERGROUND) / Heroin (VELVET UNDERGROUND).

Mar 92. (3xcd-box/3xc-box) *(PD/PK 90621)* **BETWEEN THOUGHT AND EXPRESSION: THE LOU REED ANTHOLOGY** — Apr92

REEF

Formed: London-based from Bath, England . . . 1994 by GARY STRINGER, KENWYN HOUSE, JACK BESSANT and DOMINIC GREENSMITH. Following a PAUL WELLER support slot, REEF were snapped up by corporate giants, 'Sony', hitting the ears of the nation in 1995, when a Minidisc TV commercial featured one of their tracks, 'NAKED'. This became their second! Top 30 hit, although they shunned STILTSKIN-like now-made-it-through-TV-ad comparisons. Their debut album, 'REPLENISH' followed later that summer, a decidedly un-Brit-poppy hybrid of loudmouthed funky, heavy country/blues fusing the rootsy sounds of BLACK CROWES or LENNY KRAVITZ with LED ZEPPELIN. The record crashed into the UK Top 10, REEF wowing festival audiences as well as playing a riotous gig on Newquay beach. The year ended with further controversy when the band made an in-store appearance at Tower Records in Birmingham, STRINGER allegedly inciting the crowd to loot CD's from the racks and the show breaking down in confusion as the electricity cut out. After a relatively quiet start to '96, the group returned with the anthemic 'PLACE YOUR HANDS ON' which stormed into the charts at No.6 in October, the track becoming the band's signature tune as well as one of Chris Evans' themes on his 'TFI Friday' show. A follow-up album, the GEORGE DRAKOULIAS-produced 'GLOW', topped the charts in early '97, another rootsy, Glastonbury via American Deep South melange of raunchy, soulful pop with the odd mellow moment like 'CONSIDERATION'. Consolidating their position as Britain's foremost purveyors of unreconstructed 70's via 90's rock, the band undertook another round of festival appearances, including a homecoming gig at rain-drenched Glastonbury. With growing confidence and a two-year lay-off, REEF coasted back in '99 with their third and most critically acclaimed set to date, 'RIDES' (notable for the guest appearance by BECK (HANSEN)'s dad, DAVID CAMPBELL on string arrangements!).

Album rating: REPLENISH (*6) / GLOW (*7) / RIDES (*8)

GARY STRINGER – vocals / **KENWYN HOUSE** – guitar / **JACK BESSANT** – bass / **DOMINIC GREENSMITH** – drums

Apr 95. (c-s) *(661360-4)* **GOOD FEELING / WAKE**   **Sony-S2** [24] **Sony** ☐
(cd-s+=) *(661360-2)* – End.
(12"pic-d++=) *(661360-6)* – Water over stone.

May 95. (7"colrd/c-s) *(662062-7/-4)* **NAKED. / CHOOSE TO LIVE**   [11] ☐
(cd-s+=) *(662062-2)* – Fade.

Jun 95. (cd/c/lp) *(480698-2/-4/-1)* **REPLENISH**   [9] ☐
– Feed me / Naked / Good feeling / Repulsive / Mellow / Together / Replenish / Choose to live / Comfort / Loose / End / Reprise.

Jul 95. (7"colrd/c-s) *(662277-7/-4)* **WEIRD. / ACOUSTIC ONE**   [19] ☐
(cd-s+=) *(662277-2)* – ('A'side) / Sunrise shakers / Together / End (live).

—— Sep'96, STRINGER sustained a gash in his hand when attacked by a gang in a pub.

Oct 96. (c-s) *(663571-4)* **PLACE YOUR HANDS / UNCOMFORTABLE**   [6] ☐
(cd-s+=) *(663571-2)* – The snob / Weird (Australian edit).
(cd-s) *(663571-5)* – ('A'side) / Repulsive (live) / Speak lark (live) / Naked (live).

Jan 97. (c-s) *(664097-4)* **COME BACK BRIGHTER / RESIGNATION**   [8] ☐
(cd-s+=) *(664097-2)* – It's not what I need / Hawaiian tooth.
(cd-s) *(664097-5)* – ('A'side) / Back into line / Dom and Gary / Robot part.

Feb 97. (cd/c/lp) *(486940-2/-4/-1)* **GLOW**   [1] ☐
– Place your hands / I would have left you / Summer's in bloom / Lately stomping / Consideration / Don't you like it? / Come back brighter / Higher vibration / I'm not scared / Robot riff / Yer old / Lullaby.

Mar 97. (7"red/c-s) *(664312-7/-4)* **CONSIDERATION / ALLOTMENT**   [13] ☐
(cd-s+=) *(664312-2)* – New thinking / ('A'radio mix).
(cd-s) *(664312-5)* – ('A'side) / Claypits / Higher vibration (live) / Come back brighter (live).

Jul 97. (c-s) *(664703-4)* **YER OLD / SUMMER'S IN BLOOM (live)**   [21] ☐
(cd-s+=) *(664703-2)* – Place your hands (live) / Yer old (Young version).
(cd-s) *(664703-5)* – ('A'side) / Higher vibration (live) / Lately stomping (live) / ('A'live).

Mar 99. (c-s) *(666954-4)* **I'VE GOT SOMETHING TO SAY / FOOT ONE**   [15] ☐
(cd-s+=) *(666954-2)* – Buried.
(cd-s) *(666954-5)* – ('A'side) / Who are you / Choose to live (live).

Apr 99. (cd/c/lp) *(492882-2/-4)* **RIDES**   [3] ☐
– New bird / I've got something to say / Wandering / Metro / Hiding / Sweety / Locked inside / Back in my place / Undone & sober / Who are you / Love feeder / Moaner snap / Funny feeling / Electric Sunday.

May 99. (c-s) *(667373-4)* **SWEETY / TRIUMPHANT ANTHEM**   [46] ☐
(cd-s+=) *(667373-2)* – Bullitt.
(cd-s) *(667373-5)* – ('A'side) / New bird (version) / This day.

Aug 99. (7") *(667851-7)* **NEW BIRD. / BACK IN MY PLACE**   [73] ☐
(cd-s+=) *(667851-2)* – Sweety (video).

Martha REEVES (see under ⇒ MARTHA & THE VANDELLAS)

REGULAR FRIES (dig out; Great Alt & Indie . . .)

Terry REID (dig out; Great 4th edition)

Vernon REID (see under ⇒ LIVING COLOUR)

R.E.M.

Formed: Athens, Georgia, USA ... Spring 1980 by MICHAEL STIPE and PETER BUCK, who, once meeting MIKE MILLS and BILL BERRY, played at a local party under the name TWISTED KITES. In 1981, through manager Jefferson Holt, they released their debut MITCH EASTER-produced 45, 'RADIO FREE EUROPE'. With its soaring melody and jangly guitar playing off STIPE's low-key vocals, the sound was unique and caught the ears of 'I.R.S.' label boss, MILES COPELAND. The latter duly signed them up and retained EASTER for the mini-lp 'CHRONIC TOWN' (1982). The five-song set was received with gushing enthusiasm and set the scene for R.E.M.'s first album proper, 'MURMUR' (1983). Co-produced by EASTER and DON DIXON, the album was a stunning debut which sharpened the hooks, honed the pealing guitar sound and generally engendered a compelling air of mystique. Much of this was down to STIPE's impenetrable lyrics and vague execution which enhanced rather than detracted from the melodic melancholy of songs like 'TALK ABOUT THE PASSION'. While this inventiveness wasn't quite consolidated with 'RECKONING' (1984), the album was slightly more accessible, leading to a Top 30 placing in the American charts. Boasting the ambling country poignancy of '(DON'T GO BACK TO) ROCKVILLE', what the record lacked in innovation it made up for in songwriting skill. Never content to tread water, the band recorded 'FABLES OF THE RECONSTRUCTION' (1985) in London with veteran folk producer JOE BOYD, an interesting pairing which made for a trippy, heavily atmospheric sound. Even the poppier 'DRIVER 8' wasn't free of the edginess which characterised the record. Dextrously combining sonic exploration and heart-melting melodies, 'LIFE'S RICH PAGEANT' (1986) was a bold step forward. Tracks like 'FALL ON ME', 'I BELIEVE' and 'CUYAHOGA' showed an assured poise which the band were undoubtedly developing through their ceaseless touring and snowballing critical acclaim. 'DOCUMENT' (1987) was even more focused, STIPE actually beginning to sound comprehensible. The sardonic, brooding 'THE ONE I LOVE' single gave R.E.M. their first US Top 10 hit, while the band's 'Warners' debut, 'GREEN' (1988), finally saw them become a mainstream act, in terms of commercial success at least. The unashamed jaunty pop of 'STAND' (1989) gave the band their biggest hit to date while 'ORANGE CRUSH' (1989) echoed the muted moodiness of

'THE ONE I LOVE'. Elsewhere, gems like 'WORLD LEADER PRETEND' were artful examples of that rare ability to create subtle, intelligent songs that were still annoyingly hummable. After 'GREEN's release, R.E.M. undertook a mammoth world tour with the result that the next album, 'OUT OF TIME', didn't hit the shelves until 1991. For most people it was well worth the wait. Preceded by the starkly melancholy 'LOSING MY RELIGION' with its mournful mandolin refrain, 'OUT OF TIME' was a multi-million seller, hitting the top spot on both sides of the Atlantic. While 'SHINY HAPPY PEOPLE' was a mite sickly sweet after 10,000 listens, and 'RADIO' was an ill-advised foray into rap, acoustic flavoured diamonds like 'HALF A WORLD AWAY', 'COUNTRY FEEDBACK' and 'ME IN HONEY' rendered the album a classic. Equally successful but much harder going, 1992's 'AUTOMATIC FOR THE PEOPLE' was a moody masterpiece. Focusing on the more painful aspects of human existence, the album wasn't as immediate as its predecessor, but the lucid beauty of tracks like 'NIGHTSWIMMING' and 'MAN ON THE MOON' (written about their tragic comic-hero, Andy Kaufman, and later made into a film starring Jim Carrey, c.1999) soon slipped insidiously into your subconscious. Silencing rumours that MICHAEL STIPE was suffering from Aids, R.E.M. bounced back with the grungy 'MONSTER' (1994) album. Despite confident hits like 'WHAT'S THE FREQUENCY KENNETH?' and 'CRUSH WITH EYELINER', R.E.M. were capable of more imaginative fare. The subsequent tour (the first since the late 80's) came to a premature halt when BILL BERRY suffered a brain haemorrhage. After a successful recovery, the band reconvened to record 1996's 'NEW ADVENTURES IN HI-FI' (sadly, the last with BERRY). Written mainly on the road, the album was a return to more familiar R.E.M. territory, rich in imagery and possessed of all the qualities that make R.E.M. one of rock's most respected bands. Between ' . . .HI-FI' and 98's slightly disappointing Top 3 set 'UP', BUCK took up posts in MINUS 5 (with YOUNG FRESH FELLOWS' SCOTT McCAUGHEY) and lounge-pop/jazz supergroup, TUATARA. The aforementioned 'UP' was certainly their most pensive and melancholy record to date, UK Top 30 singles such as 'DAYSLEEPER', 'LOTUS' and 'AT MY MOST BEAUTIFUL', sitting alongside their use of LEONARD COHEN lyrics on 'HOPE'. • **Songwriters:** Group compositions except 'B'side covers; THERE SHE GOES AGAIN + PALE BLUE EYES + FEMME FATALE (Velvet Underground) / TOYS IN THE ATTIC (Aerosmith) / KING OF THE ROAD (Roger Miller) / CRAZY (Pylon) / AFTER HOURS (Lou Reed) / LOVE IS ALL AROUND (Troggs) / FIRST WE TAKE MANHATTAN (Leonard Cohen) / LAST DATE (Floyd Cramer) / TIGHTEN UP (Booker T. & The MG's) / SEE NO EVIL (Television) / ACADEMY EIGHT SONG (Mission of Burma) / SUMMERTIME (Gershwin) / BABY BABY (Vibrators) / WHERE'S CAPTAIN KIRK? (Spizz) / PARADE OF WOODEN SOLDIERS (Tchaikovsky) / MOON RIVER (Henry Mancini) / THE ARMS OF YOU (Robyn Hitchcock) / THE LION SLEEPS TONIGHT (Tokens) / DARK GLOBE (Syd Barrett) / SPONGE (Vic Chesnutt). • **Trivia:** R.E.M. stands for Rapid Eye Movement.

Album rating: CHRONIC TOWN mini (*6) / MURMUR (*9) / RECKONING (*9) / FABLES OF THE RECONSTRUCTION (*8) / LIFE'S RICH PAGEANT (*8) / DEAD LETTER OFFICE compilation (*7) / DOCUMENT (*8) / EPONYMOUS compilation (*7) / GREEN (*8) / THE BEST OF R.E.M. compilation (*9) / OUT OF TIME (*9) / AUTOMATIC FOR THE PEOPLE (*10) / MONSTER (*7) / NEW ADVENTURES IN HI-FI (*8) / UP (*7) / Hindu Love Gods: HINDU LOVE GODS (*5)

MICHAEL STIPE (b. JOHN MICHAEL STIPE, 4 Jan'60, Decatur, Atlanta) – vocals / **PETER BUCK** (b. 6 Dec'56, Oakland, Calif.) – guitar / **MIKE MILLS** (b.17 Dec'58, Orange County, Calif.) – bass, keyboards, vocals / **BILL BERRY** (b.31 Jul'58, Duluth, Minnesota) – drums, vocals

			not iss.	**Hib-Tone**
Jul 81.	(7") *(HT-0001)* **RADIO FREE EUROPE. / SITTING STILL**		–	☐
			I.R.S.	**I.R.S.**
Aug 82.	(m-lp) *<SP 70502>* **CHRONIC TOWN**		–	☐

– Wolves, lower / 1,000,000 / Gardening at night / Stumble / Carnival of sorts (box cars). *(re-iss. Feb85; IRS 70502)*

Aug 83. (7") *(PFP 1017) <9916>* **RADIO FREE EUROPE. / THERE SHE GOES AGAIN**   ☐ [78] Jul83

Aug 83. (lp/c) *(SP/CS 70604) <70604>* **MURMUR**   ☐ [36] May83
– Radio free europe / Pilgrimage / Laughing / Talk about the passion / Moral kiosk / Perfect circle / Catapult / Sitting still / 9-9 / Shaking through / We walk / West of the fields. *(cd-iss. 1988; CDA 7014) (cd re-iss. Mar91 ++; CDMID 129)* – There she goes again / 9-9 (live) / Gardening at night (live) / Catapult (live).

Nov 83. (7") *(PFP 1026)* **TALK ABOUT THE PASSION. / SHAKING THROUGH**   ☐ –
(12"+=) *(PFSX 1026)* – Carnival of sorts (box cars) / 1,000,000.

Mar 84. (7") *(IRS 105) <9927>* **S). CENTRAL RAIN (I'M SORRY). / KING OF THE ROAD**   ☐ [85] Jun84
(12") *(PFSX 105)* – ('A'side) / Voice of Harold / Pale blue eyes.

Apr 84. (lp/c) *(IRS A/CS 70044) <70044>* **RECKONING**   [91] [27]
– Harborcoat / 7 Chinese Bros. / So. central rain (I'm sorry) / Pretty persuasion / Time after time (Annelise) / Second guessing / Letter never sent / Camera / (Don't go back to) Rockville / Little America. *(cd-iss. 1988 on 'A&M'; CDA 7045) (re-iss. Oct94 on 'A&M' cd/c;)*

Jun 84. (7") *(IRS 107)* **(DON'T GO BACK TO) ROCKVILLE. / WOLVES**   ☐ –
(12"+=) *(IRSX 107)* – 9 minus 9 (live) / Gardening at night (live).

Jun 84. (7") *<IR 9931>* **(DON'T GO BACK TO) ROCKVILLE. / CATAPULT (live)**   – –

Jul 85. (7") *(IRM 102)* **CAN'T GET THERE FROM HERE. / BANDWAGON**   – –
(12"+=) *(IRT 102)* – Burning Hell.

Jul 85. (lp/c) *(MIR F/C 1003) <5592>* **FABLES OF THE RECONSTRUCTION – RECONSTRUCTION OF THE FABLES**   [35] [28] Jun85
– Feeling gravitys pull / Maps and legends / Driver 8 / Life and how to live it /

Old Man Kensey / Can't get there from here / Green grow the rushes / Kokoutek / Auctioneer (another engine) / Good advices / Wendell Gee. (cd-iss. Apr87; DMIRF 1003) (re-iss. cd Jan90; DMIRL 1503)

Oct 85. (7") <52678> **DRIVER 8. / CRAZY** `-` `-`

Oct 85. (7") (IRM 105) **WENDELL GEE. / CRAZY** `-` `-`
(d7"+=) (IRMD 105) – Ages of you / Burning down.
(12"+=) (IRT 105) – Driver 8.

Aug 86. (7") (IRM 121) <52883> **FALL ON ME. / ROTARY TEN** `-` `94`
(12"+=) (IRMT 121) – Toys in the attic.

Aug 86. (lp/c) (MIRG /+C 1014) <5783> **LIFE'S RICH PAGEANT** `43` `21`
– Begin the begin / These days / Fall on me / Cuyahoga / Hyena / Underneath the bunker / The flowers of Guatemala / I believe / What if we give it away? / Just a touch / Swan swan H / Superman. (cd-iss. Dec86; DMIRG 1014) (re-iss. cd Sep91; DMIRL 1507)

Mar 87. (7") (IRM 128) **SUPERMAN. / WHITE TORNADO** `-` `-`
(12"+=) (IRMT 128) – Femme fatale.

Aug 87. (7") (IRM 145) **IT'S THE END OF THE WORLD AS WE KNOW IT (AND I FEEL FINE). / THIS ONE GOES OUT (live)** `-` `-`
(12"+=) (IRMT 145) – Maps and legends (live).

Sep 87. (7") <53171> **THE ONE I LOVE. / MAPS AND LEGENDS (live)** `-` `9`

Oct 87. (lp/c/cd) (MIRG/MIRGC/DMIRG 1025) <42059> **DOCUMENT** `28` `10` Sep87
– Finest worksong / Welcome to the occupation / Exhuming McCarthy / Disturbance at Heron House / Strange / It's the end of the world as we know it (and I feel fine) / The one I love / Fireplace / Lightnin' Hopkins / King of birds / Oddfellows local 151. (cd re-iss. Sep91 +=; DMIRL 1508) – Finest worksong (other mix) / Last date / The one I love (live) / Time after time etc. (live) / Disturbance at the Heron house (live) / Finest worksong (lengthy club mix). (lp re-iss. Apr99; 499466-1)

Nov 87. (7") (IRM 146) **THE ONE I LOVE. / LAST DATE** `51` `-`
(12"+=/cd-s+=) (IRMT/DIRM 146) – Disturbance at the Heron House (live).

Jan 88. (7") (IRM 161) **FINEST WORKSONG. / TIME AFTER TIME, ETC.** `50` `-`
(12"+=) (IRMT 161) <23850> – ('A'-lengthy club mix).
(cd-s+=) (DIRM 161) – It's the end of the world and we know it (and I feel fine).

Jan 88. (7") <53220> **IT'S THE END OF THE WORLD AS WE KNOW IT (AND I FEEL FINE). / LAST DATE** `-` `69`

	Warners	Warners

Nov 88. (lp/c/cd) (WX 234/+C) <(7599-25795-2)> **GREEN** `27` `12`
– Pop song '89 / Get up / You are the everything / Stand / World leader pretend / The wrong child / Orange crush / Turn you inside-out / Hairshirt / I remember California / Untitled song. (lp re-iss. Jul99; same)

Jan 89. (7"/s7") (W 7577/+X) <27688> **STAND. / MEMPHIS TRAIN BLUES** `51` `6`
(12"+=/3"cd-s+=/3"s-cd-s+=) (W 7577 T/CD/CDX) – (The eleventh untitled song).

Mar 89. (7"/s7"/7"box/c-s) (W 2960/+X/B/C) **ORANGE CRUSH. / GHOST RIDERS** `28` `-`
(12"+=/3"cd-s+=) (W 2960 T/CD) – Dark globe.

Jun 89. (7") <27640> **POP SONG '89 / ('A'acoustic)** `-` `86`

Jul 89. (7"/s7") (W 2833/+W) **STAND. / POP SONG '89 (acoustic)** `48` `-`
(12"+=/3"cd-s+=/3"s-cd-s+=) (W 2833 T/CD/CDX) – Skin tight (live).

—— (all above 7"singles were re-iss. in 4xbox Dec89)

Sep 89. (7") <7-22791> **GET UP. / FUNTIME** `-` `-`

—— R.E.M. toured early '91 as BINGO HAND JOB.

Feb 91. (7"/c-s) (W 0015/+C) <19392> **LOSING MY RELIGION. / ROTARY ELEVEN** `19` `4` Mar91
(12"+=/cd-s+=) (W 0015 T/CD) – After hours (live).
(cd-s) (W 0015CDX) – ('A'side) / Stand (live) / Turn you inside-out (live) / World leader pretend (live).

Mar 91. (cd/c/lp) <(7599 26496-2/-4/-1)> **OUT OF TIME** `1` `1`
– Radio song / Losing my religion / Low / Near wild Heaven / Endgame / Shiny happy people / Belong / Half a world away / Texarkana / Country feedback / Me in honey. (lp re-iss. Jul99; same)

—— (the album feat. PETER HOLSAPPLE – guitar (ex-DB'S) / KRS-1 – rapper) MICHAEL STIPE released album with KRS-1 'CIVILIZATION VS.TECHNOLOGY' Oct91.

May 91. (7"/c-s) (W 0027/+C) <19242> **SHINY HAPPY PEOPLE. / FORTY SECOND SONG** `6` `10` Jul91
(12"+=/cd-s+=) (W 0027 T/CD) – Losing my religion (live acoustic).
(cd-s) (W 0027CDX) – ('A'side) / I remember California (live) / Get up (live) / Pop song '89 (live).
(above 'A'side feat. KATE PIERSON of The B-52'S)

Aug 91. (7"/c-s) (W 0055/+C) **NEAR WILD HEAVEN. / POP SONG '89** `27` `-`
(12"+=) (W 0055T) – Half a world away (live).
(cd-s) (W 0055CDX) – ('A'side) / Tom's diner (live) / Low (live) / Endgame (live).

Nov 91. (7"/c-s) (W 0072/+C) **RADIO SONG. / LOVE IS ALL AROUND (live)** `28` `-`
(12"+=) (W 0072T) – Shiny happy people (music mix).
(cd-s) (W 0072CD) – ('A'side) / You are my everything (live) / Orange crush (live) / Belong (live).

Oct 92. (7"/c-s) (W 0136/+C) **DRIVE. / WORLD LEADER PRETEND** `11` `-`
(cd-s+=) (W 0136CD) – First we take Manhattan /
(cd-s) (W 0136CDX) – ('A'side) / It's a free world, baby / Winged mammal theme / First we take Manhattan.

Oct 92. (c-s,cd-s) <18729> **DRIVE / WINGED MAMMAL THEME** `-` `28`

Oct 92. (cd)(lp/c) <(9362 45055)>(WX 488/+C) **AUTOMATIC FOR THE PEOPLE** `1` `2`
– Drive / Try not to breathe / The sidewinder sleeps tonight / Everybody hurts / New Orleans instrumental No.1 / Sweetness follows / Monty got a raw deal / Ignoreland / Star me kitten / Man on the Moon / Nightswimming / Find the river.

Nov 92. (7"/c-s) (W 0143/+C) **MAN ON THE MOON. / TURN YOU INSIDE-OUT** `18` `-`
(cd-s+=) (W 0143CD) – Arms of love.
(cd-s) (W 0143CDX) – ('A'side) / Fruity organ / New Orleans instrumental /2 / Arms of love.

Jan 93. (c-s,cd-s) <18642> **MAN ON THE MOON / NEW ORLEANS INSTRUMENTAL #2** `-` `30`

Feb 93. (7"/c-s) (W 0152/+C) **THE SIDEWINDER SLEEPS TONIGHT. / GET UP** `17` `-`
(cd-s) (W 0152CD1) – ('A'side) / The lion sleeps tonight (live) / Fretless.
(cd-s) (W 0152CD2) – ('A'side) / Organ song / Star me kitten (demo).

Apr 93. (7"/c-s) (W 0169/+C) **EVERYBODY HURTS. / POP SONG '89** `7` `-`
(cd-s) (W 0169CD1) – ('A'side) / Mandolin strum / New Orleans instrumental No.1 (long version).
(cd-s) (W 0169CD2) – ('A'side) / Dark globe / Chance (dub).

Jul 93. (7"/c-s) (W 0184/+C) **NIGHTSWIMMING. / LOSING MY RELIGION (live)** `27` `-`
(one-sided-12"pic-d/cd-s) (W 0184 TP/CD) – ('A'side) / World leader pretend (live) / Low (live) / Belong (live).

Aug 93. (c-s) <18638> **EVERYBODY HURTS / MANDOLIN STRUM** `-` `29`
(12"orange+=) <9362 40989-04> – Belong / Orange crush (live).
(12"white or blue)(cd-ep) <9362 40992-08> – ('A'side) / Star me kitten (demo) / Losing my religion (live) / Organ song.

Dec 93. (7"/c-s) (W 0211/+C) **FIND THE RIVER. / EVERYBODY HURTS (live)** `54` `-`
(cd-s+=) (W 0211CD1) – World leader pretend (live).
(cd-s) (W 0211CD2) – Orange crush (instrumental).

Sep 94. (7"/c-s) (W 0265/+C) <18050> **WHAT'S THE FREQUENCY, KENNETH? / ('A'instrumental)** `9` `21`
(cd-s) (W 0265CD) – ('A'side) / Monty got a raw deal (live) / Everybody hurts (live) / Man on the Moon (live).

Oct 94. (cd/c/lp) <(9362 45740-2/-4/-1)> **MONSTER** `1` `1`
– What's the frequency, Kenneth? / Crush with eyeliner / King of comedy / I don't sleep I dream / Star 69 / Strange currencies / Tongue / Bang and blame / I took your name / Let me in / Circus envy / You.

Nov 94. (7"/c-s) (W 0275/+C) <17994> **BANG AND BLAME / ('A'instrumental)** `15` `19`
(cd-s) (W 0275CD) – ('A'side) / Losing my religion (live) / Country feedback (live) / Begin the begin (live).

Jan 95. (7"/c-s) (W 0281 X/C) **CRUSH WITH EYELINER. / ('A'instrumental)** `23` `-`
(cd-s) (W 0281CD) – ('A'side) / Calendar bag / Fall on me (live) / Me in honey (live) / Finest worksong (live).

—— On 1st March, 1995, BILL BERRY suffered a brain haemorrhage, after collapsing during a concert in Switzerland. Thankfully, he steadily recovered during the following few months.

Apr 95. (7"/c-s) (W 0290 X/C) <17900> **STRANGE CURRENCIES. / ('A'instrumental)** `9` `47`
(cd-s) (W 0290CD) – ('A'side) / Drive (live) / Funtime (live) / Radio free Europe (live).

Jul 95. (c-s) (W 0308 X/C) **TONGUE / ('A'instrumental)** `13` `-`
(cd-s) (W 0308CD) – ('A'side) / Bang and blame (live) / What's the frequency, Kenneth? (live) / I don't sleep, I dream (live).

Aug 96. (c-s) (W 0369C) <17529> **E-BOW THE LETTER / TRICYCLE** `4` `49`
(cd-s+=) (W 0369CD) – Wall of death / Departure.

Sep 96. (cd/cd-lp) <(9362 46320-2/-4/-1)> **NEW ADVENTURES IN HI-FI** `1` `2`
– How the west was won and where it got us / The wake-up bomb / New test leper / Undertow / E-bow the letter / Leave / Departure / Bittersweet me / Be mine / Binky the doormat / Zither / So fast, so numb / Low desert / Electrolite.

Oct 96. (c-s) (W 0377C) <17490> **BITTERSWEET ME / UNDERTOW (live)** `19` `46`
(cd-s+=) (W 0377CD) – Wichita lineman (live) / New test leper (acoustic).

Dec 96. (c-s) (W 0383C) <43810> **ELECTROLITE / THE WAKE-UP BOMB (live)** `29` `96`
(cd-s+=) (W 0383CD) – King of comedy (808 State mix) / Binky the doormat (live).

—— now without BERRY whose place was taken up by guests

Oct 98. (c-s) (W 0455C) <17129> **DAYSLEEPER / EMPHYSEMA** `6` `57`
(cd-s+=) (W 0455CD) – Why not smile (Oxford American version).
(3"cd-s) (W 0466CDX) – Daysleeper / Sad professor (live in the studio).

Oct 98. (cd/c/lp) (9362 47151-2/-4/-1) <47112> **UP** `2` `3`
– Airportman / Lotus / Suspicion / Hope / At my most beautiful / The apologist / Sad professor / You're in the air / Walk unafraid / Why not smile / Daysleeper / Diminished / Parakeet / Falls to climb.

Dec 98. (c-s) (W 466CD) **LOTUS / SURFING THE GANGES** `26` `-`
(cd-s+=) (W 466CD) – Lotus (weird mix).
(3"cd-s) (W 466CDX) – Lotus / Suspicion (live in the studio).

Mar 99. (cd-s) (W 477CD) **AT MY MOST BEAUTIFUL / THE PASSENGER (live at 'Later With Jools Holland') / COUNTRY FEEDBACK (live at 'Later With Jools Holland')** `10` `-`
(3"cd-s) (W 477CDX) – ('A'live) / So. central rain (live at 'Later With Jools Holland').

Jun 99. (cd-s) (W 488CD) **SUSPICION / ELECTROLITE ('Later With Jools Holland' version) / MAN ON THE MOON ('Later With Jools Holland' version)** `-` `-` tour
(3"cd-s+=) (W 488CDX) – ('A'live) / Perfect circle ('Later With Jools Holland' version).

Dec 99. (-) <radio cut> **THE GREAT BEYOND** `-` `72`
(above was taken from the movie/soundtrack, 'Man In The Moon', in which they contributed several other tracks)

– compilations, others, etc. –

—— on 'I.R.S.' unless mentioned otherwise

May 87. (lp/c/cd) <(SP/CS/CDA 70054)> **DEAD LETTER OFFICE** `60` `52`
(b-sides, rarities, etc.)
– Crazy / There she goes again / Burning down / Voice of Harold / Burning Hell / White tornado / Toys in the attic / Windout / Ages of you / Pale blue eyes / Rotary ten / Bandwagon / Femme fatale / Walters theme / King of the road. (cd+=) – CHRONIC TOWN (re-iss. Oct94 on 'A&M' cd/c; CD/MID 195)

Oct 88. (lp/c/cd) (MIRG/MIRGC/DMIRG 1038) <6262> **EPONYMOUS** `69` `44`
– Radio free Europe / Gardening at night / Talk about the passion / So. central rain /

(Don't go back to) Rockville / Can't get there from here / Driver 8 / Romance / Fall on me / The one I love / Finest worksong / It's the end of the world as we know it (and I feel fine).

Oct 88. (7") (IRM 173) **THE ONE I LOVE. / FALL ON ME** [ ] [-]
(12"+=/cd-s+=) (IRMT/DIRM 173) – So. central rain (I'm sorry).

May 90. (c) A&M; (AMC 24109) **MURMUR / RECKONING**

Sep 91. (cd/c/lp) (DMIRH/MIRHC/MIRH 1) **THE BEST OF R.E.M.** [7] [-]
– Carnival of sorts / Radio free Europe / Perfect circle / Talk about the passion / So. central rain / (Don't go back to) Rockville / Pretty persuasion / Green grow the rushes / Can't get there from here / Driver 8 / Fall on me / I believe / Cuyahoga / The one I love / Finest worksong / It's the end of the world as we know it (and I feel fine).

Sep 91. (7"/c-s) (IRM/+C 178) **THE ONE I LOVE. / CRAZY** [16] [ ]
(cd-s) (DIRMT 178) – ('A'side) / This one goes out (live) / Maps and legends (live).
(cd-s) (DIRMX 178) – ('A'side) / Driver 8 (live) / Disturbance at the Heron House (live).

Dec 91. (7"/c-s) (IRM/+C 180) **IT'S THE END OF THE WORLD (AS WE KNOW IT). / RADIO FREE EUROPE** [39]
(cd-s+=) (DIRMT 180) – Time after time, etc. (live).

—— When MICHAEL STIPE went off guesting for groups incl. GOLDEN PALOMINOS; others splintered off into . . .

HINDU LOVE GODS

                       not iss.   I.R.S.

Sep 85. (7") **NARRATOR. / GONNA HAVE A GOOD TIME TONIGHT** [-] [ ]

—— with **WARREN ZEVON** – vocals They guested on his late '89 album; SENTIMENTAL HYGIENE.

                       Reprise   Giant

Nov 90. (7") **RASPBERRY BERET. / WANG DANG DOODLE** [ ] [ ]
(12"+=/cd-s+=) – Mannish boy.

Nov 90. (cd/c/lp) <(7599 24406-2/-4/-1)> **HINDU LOVE GODS**
– Walkin' blues / Travelin' riverside blues / Raspberry beret / Crosscut saw / Junco pardner / Mannish boy / Wang dang doodle / Battleship chains / I'm a one woman man / Vigilante man.

—— (all above HINDU songs were covers)

RENAISSANCE (dig out; 4th edition . . .)

RENTALS (see under ⇒ WEEZER)

REO SPEEDWAGON

Formed: Champaign, Illinois, USA . . . 1968 by NEAL DOUGHTY and ALAN GRATZER, who soon recruited GARY RICHRATH, TERRY LUTTRELL and GREG PHILBIN. With help from manager Irving Azoff, they signed to 'Epic' records in 1971, releasing their eponymous debut album soon after. Through constant touring and a highly productive recording schedule, the band built up a hefty national following, although early albums like 'LOST IN A DREAM' (1975) and 'THIS TIME WE MEAN IT' (featuring contributions from SLY STONE, of all people; 1975) only managed minor US chart placings. However, by the release of 'R.E.O.' in 1976, frontman CRONIN had returned following a brief period as a solo artist, his co-writing skills (along with RICHRATH) contributing to the band's subsequent breakthrough. The live 'YOU GET WHAT YOU PLAY FOR' (1977) was the group's first multi-million seller while the appallingly titled 'YOU CAN TUNE A PIANO, BUT YOU CAN'T TUNA FISH' (1978) followed suit, their first US Top 30 placing. The group were also moving away from the rather faceless snooze-rock of old to a more poppy, hook-laden style, the shift paying off in 1981 when the 'SPEEDWAGON scored dual US No.1's with the melancholic balladry of single, 'KEEP ON LOVING YOU' and accompanying album, 'HI INFIDELITY'. An AOR classic in the mould of JOURNEY, STYX, BOB SEGER or KANSAS, 'HI . . .' was highly melodic, infectious and endearing despite the rather sappy vocal delivery and the group's chronic unfashionability. Tunes like 'TOUGH GUYS' and 'TAKE IT ON THE RUN' made great driving material, though you'd never admit as much to your mates. The follow-up, 'GOOD TROUBLE' (1982) was by all accounts a disappointment although the band were back on track by the mid-80's with the 'WHEELS ARE TURNIN'' (1984) album and its attendant No.1 single, 'CAN'T FIGHT THIS FEELING'. REO SPEEDWAGON continued to enjoy fair to middling US success throughout the remainder of the decade although since the departure of RICHRATH in 1990, the band have struggled to make an impact on the charts. • **Songwriters:** RICHRATH until 1976 when CRONIN returned to co-write most. • **Trivia:** Took their name from a 1911 fire truck.

Album rating: REO SPEEDWAGON (*6) / R.E.O. T.W.O. (*7) / RIDIN' THE STORM OUT (*6) / LOST IN A DREAM (*5) / THIS TIME WE MEAN IT (*5) / R.E.O. (*4) / REO SPEEDWAGON LIVE – YOU GET WHAT YOU PAY FOR (*5) / YOU CAN TUNE A PIANO, BUT YOU CAN'T TUNA FISH (*6) / NINE LIVES (*5) / A DECADE OF ROCK AND ROLL 1970 TO 1980 compilation (*6) / HI INFIDELITY (*6) / GOOD TROUBLE (*4) / LIFE AS WE KNOW IT (*4) / THE HITS compilation (*6) / THE EARTH, A SMALL MAN, HIS DOG AND A CHICKEN (*3) / A SECOND DECADE OF ROCK AND ROLL 1981-1991 compilation (*5) / BUILDING THE BRIDGE (*3)

GARY RICHRATH (b.18 Oct'49, Peoria, Illinois) – lead guitar / **NEAL DOUGHTY** (b.29 Jul'46, Evanston, Illinois) – keyboards, organ / **ALAN GRATZER** (b. 9 Nov'48, Syracuse, N.Y.) – drums / **TERRY LUTTRELL** – vocals / **GREG PHILBIN** – bass

                                      Epic   Epic

Jan 72. (7") <10827> **PRISON WOMEN. / SOPHISTICATED LADY** [-] [ ]

Jun 72. (7") <10847> **157 RIVERSIDE AVENUE. / FIVE MEN WERE KILLED TODAY**

Jul 72. (lp) (EPC 64813) <31089> **REO SPEEDWAGON** [ ] Dec71
– Gypsy woman's passion / 157 Riverside Avenue / Anti-establishment man / Lay me down / Sophisticated lady / Five men were killed today / Prison women / Dead at last. (re-iss. Nov81 on 'C.B.S.'; CBS 32096) (re-iss. Jun93 on 'Sony Collectors' cd/c; 982967-2/-4)

Aug 72. (7") <10892> **GYPSY WOMAN'S PASSION. / LAY ME DOWN** [-]

—— **KEVIN CRONIN** (b. 6 Oct'51, Evanston) – vocals, guitar repl. LUTTRELL

Dec 72. (7") <31745> **R.E.O. T.W.O.** [ ] [-]
– Let me ride / How the story goes / Little Queenie / Being kind / Music man / Like you do / Flash tan queen / Golden country.

Apr 73. (7") <10975> **GOLDEN COUNTRY. / LITTLE QUEENIE** [-]

—— **MIKE MURPHY** – vocals repl. CRONIN who became unrecorded solo artist

Jan 74. (lp) <32378> **RIDIN' THE STORM OUT** [-]
– Ridin' the storm out / Whiskey night / Oh woman / Find my fortune / Open up / Movin' / Son of a poor man / Start a new life / It's everywhere / Without expression.

Feb 74. (7") <11078> **RIDIN' THE NIGHT STORM. / WHISKEY NIGHT** [-]

Jun 74. (7") <11132> **OPEN UP. / START A NEW LIFE** [-]

Nov 74. (lp) <32948> **LOST IN A DREAM** [-] [98]
– Give me a ride / Throw the chains away / Sky blues / You can fly / Lost in a dream / Down by the dam / Do your best / Wild as the western wind / They're on the road / I'm feeling good.

Apr 75. (7") <50059> **THROW THE CHAINS AWAY. / SKY BLUES** [-] [ ]

—— **KEVIN CRONIN** returned to repl. MURPHY

Aug 75. (7") <50120> **OUT OF CONTROL. / RUNNING BLIND** [-]

Jul 75. (lp) <33338> **THIS TIME WE MEAN IT** [-] [74]
– Reelin' / Headed for a fall / River of life / Out of control / You better realise / Gambler / Candalera / Lies / Dance / Dream weaver.

Nov 75. (7") <50180> **HEADED FOR A FALL. / REELIN'** [-]

Jun 76. (7") <50254> **KEEP PUSHIN' / TONIGHT** [-]

Jun 76. (lp) <34143> **R.E.O.** [-]
– Keep pushin' / Any kind of love / Summer love / Our time is gonna come / Breakaway / Flying turkey trot / Tonight / Lightning.

Nov 76. (7") <50288> **FLYING TURKEY TROT. / KEEP PUSHIN'**

May 77. (7") <50367> **RIDIN' THE STORM OUT (live). / BEING KIND (live)** [-] [94]

Aug 77. (d-lp) (EPC 88265) <34494> **REO SPEEDWAGON LIVE / YOU GET WHAT YOU PLAY FOR (live)** [72] Mar77
– Like you do / Lay me down / Any kind of love / Being kind (can hurt someone sometimes) / Keep pushin' / (Only) A summer love / Son of a poor man / (I believe) Our time is gonna come / Flying turkey trot / Gary's guitar solo / 157 Riverside Avenue / Ridin' the storm out / Music man / Little Queenie / Golden country.

Aug 77. (7") <50459> **FLYING TURKEY TROT (live). / KEEP PUSHIN' (live)** [-] [ ]

—— **BRUCE HALL** (b. 3 May'53) – bass repl. PHILBIN

Jul 78. (lp) (EPC 82554) <35082> **YOU CAN TUNE A PIANO, BUT YOU CAN'T TUNA FISH** [29] Apr78
– Roll with the changes / Time for me to fly / Runnin' blind / Blazin' your own trail again / Sing to me / Lucky for you / Do you know where your woman is tonight / The unidentified flying tuna trot / Say you love me or say goodnight. (re-iss. Sep82; EPC 32115)

Jun 78. (7") (EPC 6415) <50545> **ROLL WITH THE CHANGES. / THE UNIDENTIFIED FLYING TUNA TROT** [58] May78

Jul 78. (7") <50582> **TIME FOR ME TO FLY. / RUNNIN' BLIND** [-] [56]

Jul 79. (7") <50764> **EASY MONEY. / I NEED YOU TONIGHT** [-]

Aug 79. (lp/c) (EPC/40 83647) <35988> **NINE LIVES** [33]
– Heavy on your love / Drop it (an old disguise) / Only the strong survive / Easy money / Rock'n 'roll music / Take me / I need you tonight / Meet me on the mountain / Back on the road again.

Oct 79. (7") (EPC 7918) <50790> **ONLY THE STRONG SURVIVE. / DROP IT (AN OLD DISGUISE)**

Aug 80. (7") (EPC 8903) **ONLY THE STRONG SURVIVE. / MEET ME ON THE MOUNTAIN**

Nov 80. (7") <50953> **KEEP ON LOVING YOU. / TIME FOR ME TO FLY** [1]

Feb 81. (7") (EPC 9544) **KEEP ON LOVING YOU. / FOLLOW MY HEART** [7] [-]

Apr 81. (lp/c) (EPC/40 84700) <36844> **HI INFIDELITY** [6] [1] Dec80
– Don't let him go / Keep on loving you / Follow my heart / In your letter / Take it on the run / Tough guys / Out of season / Shakin' it loose / Someone tonight / I wish you were there. (re-iss. Nov84 lp/c; EPC/40 32538) (cd-iss. 1988 on 'C.B.S.'; CD 84700)

Jun 81. (7") (EPC 1207) <01054> **TAKE IT ON THE RUN. / SOMEONE TONIGHT** [19] [5] Mar81

Jun 81. (7") <02127> **DON'T LET HIM GO. / I WISH YOU WERE THERE** [-] [24]

Sep 81. (7") (EPC 1562) <02457> **IN YOUR LETTER. / SHAKIN' IT LOOSE** [20] Aug81

Jul 82. (7") (EPC 2495) <02967> **KEEP THE FIRE BURNIN'. / I'LL FOLLOW YOU** [7] Jun82

Jul 82. (lp/c) (EPC/40 85789) <38100> **GOOD TROUBLE** [29] [7]
– Keep the fire burnin' / Sweet time / Girl with the heart of gold / Every now and then / I'll follow you / The key / Back in my heart again / Let's bebop / Stillness of the night / Good trouble. (re-iss. 1986; EPC 32789)

Sep 82. (7") (EPC 2715) <03175> **SWEET TIME. / STILLNESS OF THE NIGHT** [26] Aug82

Oct 82. (7") (EPC 2889) <03400> **THE KEY. / LET'S BEBOP**

Oct 84. (7") <04659> **I DO'WANNA KNOW. / ROCK AND ROLL STAR** [29]

Nov 84. (lp/c/cd) (EPC/40/CD 26137) <39593> **WHEELS ARE TURNIN'** [29] [7]
– I do'wanna know / One lonely night / Thru the window / Rock and roll star / Live every moment / Can't feel more / Break his spell / Wheels are turnin'.

Jan 85. (7") <04713> **CAN'T FIGHT THIS FEELING. / BREAK HIS SPELL** | - | 1
Feb 85. (7") (A 4880) **CAN'T FIGHT THIS FEELING. / ROCK AND ROLL STAR** | 16 | -
(12"+=) (TA 4880) – Keep on loving you.
May 85. (7") (A 6225) <04848> **ONE LONELY NIGHT. / WHEELS ARE TURNIN'** | | 19 Mar85
(12"+=) (TA 6225) – Take it on the run.
Jul 85. (7") (A 6466) <05412> **LIVE EVERY MOMENT. / GOTTA FEEL MORE** | | 34
Nov 85. (7") (A 6673) **WHEREVER YOU'RE GOING. / SHAKIN' IT LOOSE** | | -
Mar 87. (7") (650390-7) <06656> **THAT AIN'T LOVE. / ACCIDENTS CAN HAPPEN** | | 16 Jan87
Apr 87. (lp/c/cd) (450380-1/-4/-2) <> **LIFE AS WE KNOW IT** | | 28 Feb87
– New way to love / That ain't love / In my dreams / One too many girlfriends / Variety tonight / Screams and whispers / Can't get you out of my heart / Over the edge / Accidents can happen / Tired of getting nowhere.
May 87. (7") <07055> **VARIETY TONIGHT. / TIRED OF GETTING NOWHERE** | - | 60
Oct 87. (7") (651040-7) <07255> **IN MY DREAMS. / OVER THE EDGE** | | 19 Jul87
——— **GRAHAM LEAR** – drums (ex-SANTANA) repl. GRATZER
Sep 88. (7") (651646-7) <07901> **HERE WITH ME. / WHEREVER YOU'RE GOIN' (IT'S ALRIGHT)** | | 20 Jun88
(12"+=/cd-s+=) (651646-6/-2) – Keep on loving you / Take it on the run.
Nov 88. (7") <08030> **I DON'T WANT TO LOSE YOU. / ON THE ROAD AGAIN** | - |
——— (Apr'89) **MILES JOSEPH** – guitar (ex-PLAYER) repl. RICHRATH
——— (1990) **CRONIN, DOUGHTY & HALL** brought in new members **DAVE AMATO** – lead guitar, vocals (ex-TED NUGENT) repl. MILES JOSEPH / **BRYAN HITT** – drums (ex-WANG CHUNG) repl. LEAR / added **JESSE HARMS** – keyboards, vocals (ex-JOHN HIATT, ex-RY COODER)
Aug 90. (7") <73499> **LIVE IT UP. /** | - |
Sep 90. (cd/c/lp) (467013-1/-4/-2) <> **THE EARTH, A SMALL MAN, HIS DOG AND A CHICKEN** | | Aug90
– Love is a rock / The heart survives / Live it up / All Heaven broke loose / Love in the future / Half way / Love to hate / You won't see me / Can't lie to my heart / L.I.A.R. / Go for broke.
Oct 90. (c-s,cd-s) <73540> **LOVE IS A ROCK. / GO FOR BROKE** | - | 65
Jan 91. (7") <73659> **L.I.A.R. / HALF WAY** | - |
——— split some time in 1991 before re-forming later

	not iss.	Essential
Jul 96. (cd) <119> **BUILDING A BRIDGE**
– Can't stop rockin' / I still love you / Building the bridge / When I get home / Then I met you / Look the other way / After tonight / Hey wait a minute / One true man / She's gonna love me / Ballad of the Illinois Opry.

– compilations, etc. –

Below releases on 'Epic' unless mentioned.
May 80. (7") <50858> **TIME FOR ME TO FLY. / LIGHTNING** | - | 77
Jul 80. (d-lp/d-c) (EPC/40 22131) <36444> **A DECADE OF ROCK'N'ROLL 1970 TO 1980** | | 55 Apr80
– Sophisticated lady / Music man / Golden country / Son of a poor man / Lost in a dream / Reelin' / Keep pushin' / Our time is gonna come / Breakaway / Lightning / Like you do / Flying turkey trot / 157 Riverside Avenue / Ridin' the storm out / Roll with the changes / Time for me to fly / Say you love me or say goodnight / Only the strong survive / Back on the road again. (re-iss. Jul82; same)
Apr 83. (7") <03846> **KEEP THE FIRE BURNIN'. / TAKE IT ON THE RUN** | - |
Apr 83. (7") <03847> **IN YOUR LETTER. / DON'T LET HIM GO** | - |
Aug 84. (7"ep/c-ep) Scoop; (7SR/7SC 5049) **6 TRACK HITS** | - |
– Only the strong survive / Meet me on the mountain / Shakin' it loose / In your letter / I need you tonight / Roll with the changes.
Nov 85. (lp/c) (EPC/40 26640) **BEST FOOT FORWARD – THE BEST OF REO SPEEDWAGON**
(re-iss. Jan92 cd/c; 468603-2/-4) (cd re-iss. Oct94; 477510-2)
Feb 86. (7"ep) Old Gold; (OG 4010) **KEEP ON LOVIN' YOU. / (2 other tracks by 'Journey' & 'Meat Loaf')**
Jun 88. (lp/c/cd) (460856-1/-4/-2) <44202> **THE HITS** | | 56
Aug 88. (3"cd-s) <> **KEEP ON LOVIN' YOU. / TIME FOR ME TO FLY** | - |
Oct 91. (cd/c/lp) (468958-2/-4/-1) **A SECOND DECADE OF ROCK'N'ROLL 1981-1991**
– Don't let him go / Tough guys / Take it on the run / Shakin' it loose / Keep the fire burnin' / Roll with the changes / I do wanna know / Can't fight this feeling / Live every moment / That ain't love / One too many girlfriends / Variety tonight / Back on the road again / Keep on loving you '89 / Love is a rock / All Heavens broke loose / L.I.A.R. / Live it up.

REPLACEMENTS

Formed: Minneapolis, Minnesota, USA ... 1980 originally as The IMPEDIMENTS by the STINSON brothers – TOMMY and BOB – along with CHRIS MARS and chief songwriter/frontman, PAUL WESTERBERG. Legendary purveyors of ramshackle three-chord punk rock, The REPLACEMENTS' early efforts were so lo-fi they were off the end of the scale. Signed to Minneapolis indie stalwart, 'Twin Tone', the band debuted with 'SORRY MA, FORGOT TO TAKE OUT THE TRASH' (1981), the record's raw-nerve attitude, cathartic melodies and twisted humour shining through the garden shed (and a particularly dilapidated one at that) production. The following year's 'STINK' stepped on the gas and upped the nihilism ('GIMME NOISE', 'FUCK SCHOOL') although 'HOOTENANNY' (1983) and 'LET IT BE' (1984) used the hormonal energy to more satisfying and constructive ends. The latter set, especially, saw

WESTERBERG's breathtakingly intuitive way with a melody reach fruition; granted, the likes of 'GARY'S GOT A BONER' didn't suggest another ELVIS COSTELLO in the ascendant but the bruised beauty of 'SIXTEEN BLUE' put WESTERBERG head and shoulders above most of his contemporaries (with the honourable exception of, perhaps, HUSKER DU). The record's charms were powerful enough to attract the major label attentions of 'Sire' and in late '85, The REPLACEMENTS released the Tommy Erdelyi (formerly TOMMY RAMONE)-produced 'TIM'. Furnished with a bigger budget, the group tempered their ragged sound while retaining much of the threadbare authenticity, the hooks as razor sharp as ever. It was to be the last album to feature the departing BOB, the band's notoriously shambolic live appearances robbed of the man's more, erm, eccentric tendencies (playing in a dress – radical for the time! – or indeed in the nude, was not uncommon). With ROBERT 'SLIM' DUNLAP brought in as a replacement (ha!), the band recorded what many fans and critics alike regard as their finest hour, 'PLEASED TO MEET ME' (1987). More musically adventurous in line with their growing eclecticism, the album also found WESTERBERG's songwriting prowess at its unprecedented best, 'SKYWAY' soaring heavenward while 'CAN'T HARDLY WAIT' was the killer pop song he'd been threatening to pen since the band's inception. Criminally, the rave reviews and positive momentum surrounding the album's release failed to translate into sales, The REPLACEMENTS sounding strangely muted on 1989's 'DON'T TELL A SOUL', despite the return of BOB STINSON. While the minor concessions to commerciality resulted in a Top 60 US chart entry, the band were on their last legs and 1990's 'ALL SHOOK DOWN' was a WESTERBERG solo effort in all but name. The split eventually came in 1992, TOMMY forming BASH & POP (who released an album, 'FRIDAY NIGHT IS KILLING ME' the following year), while WESTERBERG worked on his solo debut proper, '14 SONGS' (1993). Although the writing was faultless, the record lacked the unkempt charm of old, any chance of a full REPLACEMENTS reunion suffering a serious setback as BOB succumbed to a drugs overdose the following year. In the latter half of the 90's (while MARS was also delivering the odd album), WESTERBERG found acceptance – in the way of US chart fame – via two further sets, 'EVENTUALLY' (1996) and 'SUICAINE GRATIFACTION' (1999). • **Songwriters:** Penned by WESTERBERG, except; I WILL DARE (Kiss) / ROUTE 66 (Nelson Riddle Orchestra) / 20TH CENTURY BOY (T-Rex) / HEY GOOD LOOKING (Bo Diddley) / CRUELLA DE VILLE (from '1001 Dalmations'). • **Trivia:** Were quoted after a tour as saying 'Better hours, 9 to 5; 9 at night to 5 in the morning, that is'. Their '87 single 'ALEX CHILTON', was dedicated to legendary BOX TOPS leader.

Album rating: SORRY MA, FORGOT TO TAKE OUT THE TRASH (*4) / STINK mini (*4) / HOOTENANNY (*6) / BOINK!! compilation (*7) / LET IT BE (*8) / TIM (*7) / PLEASED TO MEET ME (*8) / DON'T TELL A SOUL (*6) / ALL SHOOK DOWN (*6) / Paul Westerberg: 14 SONGS (*5) / EVENTUALLY (*6) / SUICAINE GRATIFACTION (*7) / Chris Mars: HORSESHOES AND HAND GRENADES (*5) / 75% LESS FAT (*5) / TENTERHOOKS (*6) / ANONYMOUS BOTCH (*5)

PAUL WESTERBERG (b.31 Dec'60) – vocals, rhythm guitar / **BOB STINSON** (b.17 Dec'59) – lead guitar / **TOMMY STINSON** (b. 6 Oct'66, San Diego, Calif.) – bass / **CHRIS MARS** (b.26 Apr'61) – drums

	not iss.	Twin Tone
1981. (lp) <TTR 8123> **SORRY MA, FORGOT TO TAKE OUT THE TRASH** | - | |
– Takin' a ride / Careless / Customer / Hanging downtown / Kick your door down / Otto / I bought a headache / Rattlesnake / I hate music / Johnny's gonna die / Shiftless when idle / More cigarettes / Don't ask why / Something to do / I'm in trouble / Love you till Friday / Shut up / Raised in the city. (UK-iss.Mar88 on 'What Goes On'; GOES ON 017) (cd-iss. Apr93 on 'Roadrunner'; RR 9089-2) (cd re-iss. Mar95; TTR 8123-2)
1981. (7") <TTR 8120> **I'M IN TROUBLE. / IF ONLY YOU WERE LONELY** | | |
1982. m-(lp) <TTR 8228> **STINK** | | |
– Kids don't follow / Fuck school / Stuck in the middle / God damn job / White and lazy / Dope smokin' moron / Go / Gimme noise. (UK-iss.Mar88 on 'What Goes On'; GOES ON 020) (cd-iss. Apr93 on 'Roadrunner'; RR 9090-2) (cd re-iss. Mar95; 8228-2)
1983. (lp) <TTR 8332> **HOOTENANNY** | | |
– Hootenanny / Run it / Color me impressed / Will power / Take me down to the hospital / Mr. Whirly / Within your reach / Buck hill / Lovelines / You lose / Hayday / Treatment bound. (UK-iss.Mar88 on 'What Goes On'; GOES ON 021) (cd-iss. Apr93 on 'Roadrunner'; RR 9091-2) (cd re-iss. Feb95; TTR 8332-2)
1984. (12") <TTR 8440> **I WILL DARE. / 20TH CENTURY BOY / HEY GOOD LOOKING (live)** | | |

	Zippo	Twin Tone
Oct 84. (lp) (ZONG 002) <TTR 8441> **LET IT BE** | | |
– I will dare / We're comin' out / Tommy gets his tonsels out / Black diamond / Androgynous / Unsatisfied / Seen your video / Gary's got a boner / Sixteen blue / Answering machine. (cd-iss. Apr93 on 'Roadrunner'; RR 9092-1) (cd re-iss. Mar95)
1985. (c) **THE SHIT HITS THE FAN (live bootleg)** | | |

	Sire	Sire
Nov 85. (lp/c) (K 925330-1/-4) <25330> **TIM** | | |
– Hold my life / I'll buy / Kiss me on the bus / Dose of thunder / Waitress in the sky / Swingin' party / Bastards of young / Left of the dial / Litle mascara / Here comes a regular. (cd-iss. Jul93; 7599 25330-2)
Mar 86. (7") (W 8727) **SWINGIN' PARTY. / LEFT OF THE DIAL** | | - |
May 86. (7") (W 8679) **KISS ME ON THE BUS. / LITTLE MASCARA** | | - |

——— **ROBERT 'SLIM' DUNLAP** (b.14 Aug'51, Plainview, Minnesota) – keyboards repl. BOB (he was to die on the 18th of February 1995 o.d.)
Apr 87. (lp/c/cd) (K 925557-1/-4/-2) <25557> **PLEASED TO MEET ME** | | |
– I.O.U. / Alex Chilton / I don't know / Nightclub jitters / The ledge / Never mind / Valentine / Shooting dirty pool / Red red wine / Skyway / Can't hardly wait. (cd re-iss. Jul93; 7599 25557-2)

Jun 87. (7") *(W 8297)* **ALEX CHILTON. / ELECTION DAY** ☐ -
(12"+=) *(W 8297T)* – Nightclub jitters / Route 66.
Jul 87. (7") *<28151>* **CAN'T HARDLY WAIT. / COOL WATER** - ☐
—— **BOB STINSON** – guitar returned to repl. SLIM who went solo
Jan 89. (lp/c/cd) *(K 925721-1/-4/-2) <25721>* **DON'T TELL A SOUL** ☐ 57
– Talent show / Back to back / We'll inherit the Earth / Achin' to be / They're blind / Anywhere's better than here / Asking me lies / I won't / Rock'n'roll ghost / Darlin' one. *(cd re-iss. Jul93; 7559 25831-2)*
Apr 89. (7") *<22992>* **I'LL BE YOU. / DATE TO CHURCH (with** - 51
TOM WAITS)
(below w/ guests **STEVE BERLIN / MICHAEL BLAIR / BELMONT TENCH / JOHN CALE** / etc.
Sep 90. (cd/c/lp) *(<7599 26298-2/-4/-1)>* **ALL SHOOK DOWN** 69
– Merry go round / One wink at a time / Nobody / Bent out of shape / Sadly beautiful / Someone takes the wheel / When it began / All shook down / Attitude / Happy town / Torture / My little problem / The lost. *(cd re-iss. Jul93 & Feb95; same)*
—— (Mar'91) **STEVE FOLEY** – drums; repl. MARS who went solo
—— disbanded late in 1991, TOMMY formed BASH & POP, while WESTERBERG and MARS went solo

– compilations, others, etc. –

Apr 86. (m-lp/m-c) *Glass; (MGA LP/MC 016)* **BOINK!!** ☐ -
– Color me impressed / White and lazy / Within your reach / If only you were lonely / Kids don't follow / Nowhere is my home / Take me down to the hospital / Go.

BASH & POP

TOMMY STINSON – vocals, guitar / **KEVIN FOLEY** – bass, vocals / **STEVE FOLEY** – drums / **MARY ANN DIBS** – check

	not iss.	Warners

Jan 93. (cd) *<45133>* **FRIDAY NIGHT IS KILLING ME** - ☐
– Never aim to please / Hang ups / Loose ends / One more time / Tickled to tears / Nothing / Fast & hard / Friday night (is killing me) / He means it / Tiny pieces / First steps.

PAUL WESTERBERG

	Sire	Warners

Jun 93. (cd/c) *<9362 45255-2/-4>* **14 SONGS** ☐ 44
– Knockin' on mine / First glimmer / World class fad / Runaway wind / Dice behind your shades / Even here we are / Silver naked ladies / A few minutes of silence / Someone I once knew / Black eyed Susan / things / Something is me / Mannequin shop / Down love.
Jul 93. (7"/c-s) *(W 0183/+C)* **WORLD CLASS FAD. / SEEING HER** ☐ ☐
(12"/cd-s) *(W 0183 T/CD)* – ('A'side) / Men without ties / Down love.
Oct 93. (7"/c-s) *(W 0209/+C)* **WORLD CLASS FAD. / CAN'T HARDLY WAIT (live)** ☐ ☐
(cd-s+=) *(W 0209CD1)* – Left of the dial (live) / Another girl another planet (live).
(cd-s) *(W 0209CD2)* – ('A'side) / Waiting for somebody / Dyslexic heart / Answering machine (live).
Apr 96. (cd/c) *(9362 46251-2/-4) <46176>* **EVENTUALLY** ☐ 50
– These are the days / Century / Love untold / Ain't got me / You've had it with you / Mamadaddydid / Hide n seekin' / Once around the weekend / Trumpet clip / Angels walk / Good day / Time flies tomorrow.
Apr 99. (cd/c) *(499145-2/-4) <59004>* **SUICAINE GRATIFACTION** ☐ ☐Mar99
– It's a wonderful lie / Self defence / The best thing that ever happened / Lookin' out forever / Born for me / The final hurrah / Tears rolling up our sleeves / The fugitive kind / Sunrise always listens / Whatever makes you happy / Actor in the street / Bookmark.

CHRIS MARS

plays multi-instruments + augmented by some guests

	not iss.	Polygram

1992. (cd) *<513198>* **HORSESHOES AND HAND GRENADES** - ☐
– Reverse status / Popular creeps / Outer limits / Before it began / Get out of my life / Monkey sees / Ego maniac / Midnight carnival / I, me, we, us, them / Don't you see it / Happy disconnections / Better days / City lights on Mars / Last drop.

	not iss.	Smash

1993. (cd) *<8004>* **75% LESS FAT** - ☐
– Stuck in rewind / No bands / Weasel / Public opinion / All figured out / Whining horse / Car camping / Skipping school / Bullshit detector / Candy liquor / Demolition / No more mud / Nightcap.

	not iss.	Bar/None

1995. (cd) *<52A>* **TENTERHOOKS** - ☐
– White Patty rap / Forkless tree / Mary / Lizard brain / Hate it / Brother song / Water biscuits / E.I.B. negative / Haunted town / Floater.
Sep 96. (cd) *<85A>* **ANONYMOUS BOTCH** - ☐
– Conquering cow farmer / Sheep spine shimmy / Narrow / Down drag / Black days / Two dreams / It's a long life / Janet's new kidney / Weather / Where and why / Funeral hymn of the small critter / I'll be gone / Cadaver dogs / New day.

REPUBLICA

Formed: Windsor, Berkshire, England ... 1994 by Nigerian-born singer and former ballet dancer SAFFRON, along with former FLOWERED UP keyboard player TIM DORNEY; the latter initiated the group after striking up a partnership with remixer ANDY TODD. JONNY MALE and ANDY DAVE BARBAROSSA would subsequently be added (all five veterans of the capital's 80's/90's indie/dance/baggy scene having played in the likes of SOUL FAMILY SENSATION and the SHAMEN). Signing with dance-orientated label, 'DeConstruction' and delivering debut CD-single, 'BLOKE'),

they scored a minor UK and US hit with their second single, 'READY TO GO', a high-octane Brit-pop/techno hybrid which subsequently became a much-aired backdrop on various sports/fashion TV shows after its more successful re-release in early '97. Initially issued in the States, their eponymous debut album (also featuring another re-vamped UK chartbuster, 'DROP DEAD GORGEOUS') proceeded to sell a quarter million copies before it was successfully delivered in Britain. • **Songwriters:** Group mainly except SAFFRON solo on her version of ARE FRIENDS ELECTRIC (Tubeway Army).
Album rating: REPUBLICA (*6) / SPEED BALLADS (*6)

SAFFRON (b. SAMANTHA SPRACKLING, 3 Jun'68, Lagos, Nigeria) – vocals / **JONNY MALE** (b.10 Oct'63, Windsor, England) – guitar / **TIM DORNEY** (b.30 Mar'65, Ascot, England) – keyboards (ex-FLOWERED UP) / **TODDY** (b. ANDY TODD) – keyboards / **DAVE BARBAROSSA** – drums (ex-BOW WOW WOW, ex-ADAM & THE ANTS)

	Deconstr.- BMG	Deconstr.- RCA

Jan 95. (cd-s) *(74321 25154-2)* **BLOKE / mixes:– extended / Blame it on the vodka (Jack Daniels)** ☐ ☐
Apr 96. (c-s) *(74321 32613-4) <64540>* **READY TO GO / (A'original)** 43 56 Jul96
(12"/cd-s) *(74321 32613-1/-2)* – ('A'mixes).
(re-iss. Feb97; same) – hit UK No.13
Jul 96. (c-s) *(74321 38694-4)* **DROP DEAD GORGEOUS / OUT OF THIS WORLD** ☐ 93 Jan97
(cd-s+=) *(74321 40843-2)* – Bitch (mix).
(cd-s+=) *(74321 38694-2)* – Mutha / Holly.
Mar 97. (cd/c) *(<74321 41052-2/-4>)* **REPUBLICA** 4 ☐
– Ready to go / Bloke / Bitch / Get off / Picture me / Drop dead gorgeous / Out of the darkness / Wrapp / Dont you ever / Holly / Ready to go (original mix). *(d-cd re-iss. Nov97 +=; 74321 53633-2)* – Drop dead gorgeous (live) / Bloke (live) / Get off (live) / Ready to go (live) / Out of the darkness (live) / Holly (live).
Apr 97. (c-s/cd-s) *(74321 88694-4/-2)* **DROP DEAD GORGEOUS / ('A'mix)** 7 ☐
(cd-s) *(74321 40832-2)* – ('A'mixes).
—— trimmed to a trio of **SAFFRON, TIM + ANDY**
Sep 98. (c-s) *(74321 61047-4)* **FROM RUSH HOUR WITH LOVE / CLONE MY SOUL** 20 ☐
(cd-s+=) *(74321 61047-2)* – World ends in the morning.
(ltd-7"colrd) *(74321 61047-7)* – ('A'side) / House special.
Oct 98. (cd/c) *(<74321 61046-2/-4>)* **SPEED BALLADS** 37 ☐
– From rush hour with love / Fading of the man / Try everything / Luxury cage / Faster faster / Nothing's feeling new / Millennium / Pretty girl hate / Kung Fu movies / Pub pusher.

RESIDENTS

Formed: Shreveport, Louisiana, USA ... 1966 by mysterious line-up. Soon relocating to San Mateo, California in the early 70's, they made a few untitled homemade recordings. They subsequently sent these to Hal Haverstadt of 'Warners' who promptly returned them, the address marked; 'for the attention of the residents'. Adopting the latter as their moniker, they later issued the two newly named tapes in the early 70's, 'RUSTY COAT HANGER FOR THE DOCTOR' and 'THE BALLAD OF STUFFED TRIGGER' respectively. In 1972, they shifted base to San Francisco, founding the independently distributed 'Ralph' records. Their "real" debut lp, 'MEET THE RESIDENTS' was issued in 1974, its title and cover art a tongue-in cheek take-off of The BEATLES. They then released a series of very limited edition lp's, 'THIRD REICH AND ROLL' in 1976, a collection of mangled 50's and 60's covers, carrying on where FRANK ZAPPA left off (albeit in a much weirder fashion). Later in the year, The RESIDENTS and DEVO competed for the best re-constructed version of The STONES' 'SATISFACTION'; however, the latter won out in the end. After more comical parodying of The BEATLES and others, they unleashed the 'ESKIMO' set in 1979. This seminal meisterwork was recorded over a lengthy period of time; weird in the extreme, it featured tribal rhythms behind sub-lingual voices (VIC REEVES in "club style" must have taken inspiration). In 1980, the 'COMMERCIAL ALBUM' was released; containing forty tracks of exactly one minute in length, it was another to explore the barren frontiers of possibilities in music. They continued throughout the 80's with even more obscurity than their earlier 70's work. They were infamous for their hilarious head disguises, which included giant eyeballs, etc. • **Songwriters:** Group penned, except tribute/covers lp's of ELVIS PRESLEY, HANK WILLIAMS, GEORGE GERSHWIN and JAMES BROWN material.
Album rating: MEET THE RESIDENTS (*7) / THE THIRD REICH AND ROLL (*6) / FINGERPRINCE (*6) / NOT AVAILABLE (*6) / DUCK STAB – BUSTER AND GLEN (*7) / ESKIMO (*8) / NIBBLES compilation (*6) / THE COMMERCIAL ALBUM (*8) / MARK OF THE MOLE (*6) / THE TUNES OF TWO CITIES (*4) / INTERMISSION mini (*4) / RESIDUE OF THE RESIDENTS (*4) / TITLE IN LIMBO with Renaldo & The Loaf (*4) / GEORGE AND JAMES (*4) / RALPH BEFORE '84 – VOLUME 1 compilation (*6) / WHATEVER HAPPENED TO VILENESS FATS (*4) / RALPH BEFORE '84 – VOLUME 2 compilation (*6) / THE BIG BUBBLE – PART 4 OF THE MOLE TRILOGY (*4) / THE PAL TV LP (*4) / HEAVEN? collection (*6) / HELL? collection (*6) / 13th ANNIVERSARY SHOW (*5) / STARS AND HANK FOREVER – THE AMERICAN COMPOSERS SERIES VOL.2 (*4) / GOD IN THREE PERSONS (*4) / THE MOLE SHOW earlier recording (*4) / THE KING AND EYE (*4) / FREAKSHOW (*4) / PRESENT OUR FINEST FLOWERS (*4) / GINGERBREAD MAN (*4) / RESIDUE DEUX (*4)

The RESIDENTS (4) – instruments, vocals, noises / assisted by **SNAKEFINGER** (b. PHILIP LITHMAN) (ex-CHILLI WILLI & THE RED HOT PEPPERS)

not iss.   Ralph

Dec 72. (d-7"ltd) <RR 1272> **SANTA DOG**
– Aircraft damage (credited to ARR + OMEGA) / The COLLEGE WALKERS – Lightning /

Feb 74. (lp-ltd) <RR 0274> **MEET THE RESIDENTS**
– Boots . . . Numb erone . . . Guylum Bardot . . . Breath and length . . . Consuelo's departure . . . Smelly tongues . . . Rest aria . . . Skratz . . . Spotted pinto bean . . . Infant tango . . . Seasoned greetings . . . N-er-gee (crisis blues). (re-iss. re-mixed Aug77; RR 0677) – (lost 7 minutes). (re-iss. Dec88 on 'Torso' cd/lp; CD/40 416)

—— In Oct'75, they issued 500 copies US of lp 'BLORP ESETTE' for 'LAFMS'; 005>

Feb 76. (lp-ltd) <RR 1075> **THE THIRD REICH AND ROLL**
– Hitler was a vegetarian / Hey Jude / Swastikas on parade / The twist / Land of 1000 dances / Hanky panky. <re-iss. 1978; same>

Sep 76. (7"ltd) <RR 0776> **SATISFACTION. / LOSER = WEED**
<re-iss. Aug78 as 7"yellow; RR 7803>

Jan 77. (7"ep-ltd) <RR 0377> **BABYFINGERS**
<re-iss. 1979 on 'W.E.I.R.D.' 7"pink; 1>

Feb 77. (lp-ltd) <RR 1276> **FINGERPRINCE**
– You yesyesyes / Home age conversation / Godsong / March de la winni / Bos sy / Boo who / Tourniquet of roses / You yesyesyes again / Six things to a cycle. (re-iss. twice 1978; same) (cd-iss. Dec87 on 'Torso'; TORSOCD 047)

Aug 77. (7") <RR 0577> **(THE BEATLES PLAY THE RESIDENTS AND THE RESIDENTS PLAY THE BEATLES)**
– Beyond the valley of a day in the life /

Feb 78. (7"ep) <RR 1177> **DUCK STAB EP**

Oct 78. (lp) <RR 1174> **NOT AVAILABLE**
– Edweena / The making of a soul / Ships a going down / Never known questions epilogue. (UK-iss.cd Sep94 on 'Indigo'; 7539-2)

Nov 78. (lp) <RR 0278> **DUCK STAB / BUSTER AND GLEN**
– Constantinople / Sinister exaggerator / The Booker tease / Blue rosebuds / Laughing song / Bach is dead / Elvis and his boss / Lizard lady / Semolina / Birthday boy / Weight-lifting Lulu / Krafty cheese / Hello skinny / The electrocutioner. (cd-iss. Jul87 on 'Torso'; TORSOCD 406)

Dec 78. (7") <RR 7812> **SANTA DOG 78. / SANTA DOG**

Aug 79. (lp) <SM 7908> **SUBTERRANEAN MODERN**

—— more guests **CHRIS CUTLER** – percussion / **DON PRESTON** – synth

Sep 79. (lp,white-lp) <ESK 7906> **ESKIMO**
– The walrus hunt / Birth / Arctic hysteria / The angry Angakok / A spirit steals a child / The festival of death. (cd-iss. Jul87 on 'Torso'; TORSOCD 404) (cd re-iss. 1996 on 'Ralph Euro'; CD 016)

Virgin   Ralph

Sep 79. (lp; with SNAKEFINGER) (VR 3) <DJ 7901> **NIBBLES** <US title 'PLEASE DO NOT STEAL IT' – DJ compilation>   Mar79
– Yesyesyesyes / Santa dog '78 / Gloria / Rest aria / Semolina / The spot / Never known questions / Constantinople / Laughing song / The mocking of a soul / Skratz / Good lovin' / Blue rosebuds / Six things to a cycle / The electrocutioner.

Pre   Ralph

Oct 80. (lp) (PREX 2) <6559> **THE RESIDENTS COMMERCIAL ALBUM**
– Easter woman / Perfect love / Picnic boy / End of home / Amber / Japanes watercolour / Red rider / My second wife / Suburban bathers / Floyd / Dimples and toes / The nameless souls / Die in terror / Love leaks out / Act of being polite / Medicine man / Tragic bells / Loss of innocence / The simple song / Ups and downs / Possessions / Give it someone else / Phantom / Less not more / My work is so behind / Birds in the trees / Handful of desire / Moisture / Love is . . . / Troubled man / La la loneliness / Nice old man / The talk of creatures / Fingertips / In between dreams / Margaret Freeman / The coming of the crow / When we were young.

Oct 80. (7"ep) (PRE 009) **THE RESIDENTS COMMERCIAL SINGLE**
– Amber / Red rider / Picnic boy / When we were young / Phantom / Moisture.

1980. (12"ep) <RZ 8006-D> **DISKOMO**
– Diskomo / Goosebump: Disasterplants – Farmers – Twinkle.

1981. (lp) <8152> **MARK OF THE MOLE**
– Hole-worker at the mercies of nature / Voices of the air / The ultimate disaster / Won't you keep us working / First warning / Back to normality / The sky falls / Why are we crying / The tunnels are filling / It never stops / Migration / March to the sea / The observer / Hole-worker's new hymn / Hole-worker's vs Man and machine / Another land / Rumors / Arrival / Deployment / Saturation / The new machine / Idea / Construction / Failure / Reconstruction / Success / Final confrontation / Success / Final confrontation / Driving the moles away / Don't tread on me / The short war / Resolution. (UK cd-iss. Sep94 on 'Indigo'; 7540-2)

Ralph   Recommended

May 82. (lp) (RZ 8202) **THE TUNES OF TWO CITIES**   Mar82
– Serenade for Missy / Mousetrap / Smack your lips clap your teeth / A maze of jigsaws / God of darkness / Smokebams / Mourning the undead / Song of the wild / Happy home / The secret seed / The evil disposer.

Jul 83. (12"ep) (RALPH 1) <RZ 8252> **INTERMISSION**
– Lights out / Shorty's lament / Moles are coming / Would we be alive / New hymn. (lp-iss.1989 on 'Torso'; TORSO 33-055)

1983. (lp) <RZ 8302> **RESIDUE OF THE RESIDENTS**
– The sleeper / Whoopy snorp / Kamakazi lady / Boy in love / Shut up! shut up! / Anvil forest / Diskomo / Jailhouse rock / Up & down / Walter Westinghouse / Saint Nix / Open up.

New Ralph   New Ralph

Jan 84. (lp; with RENALDO & THE LOAF) (RR 8351) **TITLE IN LIMBO**

Korova   Recommended

Jul 84. (7") (KOW 36) **IT'S A MAN'S MAN'S MAN'S WORLD. / I'LL GO CRAZY**

Aug 84. (lp/c) (KODE/CODE 9) <RZ 8402> **GEORGE & JAMES** (some live)
– Rhapsody in blue / I got rhythm / Summertime / Live at the Apollo: I'll go crazy / Try me / Think / I don't mind / Lost someone / Please please please / Night train. (c+=) – (extra track). (cd-iss. Sep94 on 'Indigo'; 2122-2)

DoubleVision   Ralph

Dec 84. (lp) (DV 9) <RZ 8452> **WHATEVER HAPPENED TO VILENESS FATS**
– Whatever happened to Vileness Fats / Atomic shopping carts / Adventures of a troubled heart / Search for the short man / The importance of evergreen / Broccoli and saxophone / Disguised as meat / Thoughts busily

betraying / Lord, it's lonely / The knife fight. (UK cd-iss. Sep94 on 'Indigo'; 7537-2)

1985. (lp) <RZ 8552> **THE BIG BUBBLE – PART 4 OF THE MOLE TRILOGY**
– Sorry / Hop a little / Go where ya wanna go / Gotta gotta get / Cry for the fire / Die stay-go / Vinegar / Fire fly / The big bubble / Fear for the future / Kula bocca says so. (cd-iss. Sep94 on 'Indigo'; 7541-2)

Sep 85. (red-lp) (DVR 17) **THE PAL TV LP**

Torso   Torso

Oct 86. (d-lp) (TORSO 33-018) <2614220> **13TH ANNIVERSARY SHOW (live in Japan & Holland)**
– Jailhouse rock / Where is she? / Picnic in the jungle / I got rhythm / Passing in the bottle / Monkey and Bunny / This is a man's man's man's world / Walter Westinghouse / Easter woman guitar solo / Diskomo / Hello skinny / Constantinople / Hop a little / Cry for the fire / Kamikaze. (cd-iss. Sep94 on 'Indigo'; 7534-2)

Nov 86. (lp) (TORSO33 022) <2614202> **STARS & HANK FOREVER! – THE AMERICAN COMPOSER'S SERIES VOL.II (THE MUSIC OF HANK WILLIAMS AND JOHN PHILIP SOUSA)**
– Hank Williams:- Hey good lookin' / Six more miles (to the graveyard) / Kaw-liga / Ramblin' man / Jambalaya / John Philip Sousa:- Sousaside: a) Nobles of the mystic shrine, b) The stars & stripes forever, c) El capitan, d) The liberty bell, e) Semper fidelis, f) The Washington post. (re-iss. Sep94 on 'Indigo'; 7530-1)

Dec 86. (7"/12") (TORSO 7/12 022) **KAW-LIGA. /**
(re-iss. Mar89; cd-s; TORSOCD 322)

Jun 87. (7"/12") (TORSO 7/12 032) **HIT THE ROAD. /**

Aug 88. (d-lp/cd/dat) (TORSO 33/CD/DAT 055) <2614226> **GOD IN THREE PERSONS**
– Hard and tenderly / Devotion / The thing about them / Their early yearsx / Loss of a loved one / The touch / The service / Confused / Fine fat flies / Time / Silver sharp / Kiss of flesh / Pain and pleasure. (re-iss. lp Sep94 on 'Indigo'; 7531-1)

1989. (lp/cd) <2614262> **THE MOLE SHOW LIVE (live)**
– Voices of the air / The secret seed / Narration / The ultimate disaster / God of darkness / Migration / Smack your lips clap your feet / Another land / The new machine / Call of the wild / Final confrontation / Satisfaction / Happy home. (UK cd-iss. Sep94 on 'Indigo'; 7542-2)

1989. (3"pic-cd-ep) (TORSOCD 355) **DOUBLE SHOT / LOSS OF LOVED ONE (extended) / KISS OF FLESH (instrumental)**

1989. (lp/cd) <14263-26> **THE KING AND EYE**
– Blue suede shoes / Don't be cruel / Heartbreak hotel / All shook up / Return to sender / Teddy bear / Devil in disguise / Stuck on you / Big hunk o' love / A fool such as I / Little sister / His latest flame / Burning love / Viva Las Vegas / Love me tender / Hound dog. (UK cd-iss. Sep94 on 'Indigo'; 7535-2)

1989. (cd-ep) (TORSOCD 421) **DISKOMO / WHOOPY SNORP / SAINT NIX / DISKOMO LIVE**

May 90. (7"ep/12"ep/cd-ep) **DON'T BE CRUEL. / DISKOMO / DISCO WILL NEVER DIE**

Indigo   East Side Digital

1991. (cd,lp) <80602> **FREAKSHOW**
– Everyone comes to the freak show / Harry the head / Herman the human mole / Wanda the worm woman / Jack the boneless boy / Benny the bouncing bum / Mickey the mumbling midget / Lillie / Nobody laughs when they leave. (re-iss. Sep94 on 'Indigo' cd)(lp; 2125-2)(7532-1)

1995. (cd) <8107> **GINGERBREAD MAN**

—— returned in 1998

Sep 98. (cd) (8535-2) <81332> **WORMWOOD: CURIOUS STORIES FROM THE BIBLE**   Oct98
– In the beginning / Fire fall / They are the meat / Melncholy clumps / How to get a head / Cain and Abel / Mr. Misery / Tent peg in the temple / God's magic finger / Spilling the seed / Dinah and the unclean skin / Bathsheba bathes / Bridegroom of blood / Hanging by his hair / Seven ugly cows / Burn baby burn / Kill him / I hate Heaven / Judas slaves / Revelation.

– others, etc. –

Sep 94. (lp)(cd) Torso; (TORSO 33-199)(7536-2) **CUBE E**

Sep 94. (cd) Indigo; (2124-2) **POOR KAW LIGA'S PAIN**

Sep 94. (cd/lp) Indigo; (7543-2/-6) **POOR KAW LIGA (housey mix)**

Oct 94. (cd) Cargo; (2129-2) **THE RESIDENTS**

– compilations, etc.

Oct 84. (lp/c) Korova; (KODE/CODE 10) **RALPH BEFORE '84 – VOLUME 1**
– It's a man's man's man's world / Diskomo / Hello skinny / (I left my heart in) San Francisco / Happy home / Smack your lips / Yesyesyesyes / Jailhouse rock / Monkey and Bunny / Festival of death.

Jan 85. (lp) Korova; (KODE 12) **RALPH BEFORE '84 – VOLUME 2**
– Eva's warning / Halloween / Evolution / What use / Mahogany wood / Same ole me / Tritone / Melvyn's repose / Yeti: what are you / Nelda danced at day break / Norrgarden nyvia.

Jan 86. (cd) Rykodisc; <RCD 20012> **HEAVEN?**
– The importance of evergreen / It's a man's man's man's world / H.E.L.L. no! / Japanese watercolours / I got rhythm / Ups and downs / Serenade for Missy / Eastern woman / Amber / The census taker / Happy home / Crashing / Redrider / Floyd / The moles are coming / Resolution / Mahogany wood / Simple song / Kula bocca says no / Love leaks out / New hymn / Whater happened to Vileness Fats / Twinkle / Festival of death (excerpt).

Jan 86. (cd) Rykodisc; <RCD 20013> **HELL?**
– The ultimate disaster (excerpt) / Lights out / Where is she? / The coming of the crow / Lizard lady / Die interior / Shut up! shut up! / Shorty's lament / Hello skinny / Kamikaze lady / Secret seed / Sonny / Smelly tongues / Monkey and Bunny / Farmers / Satisfaction / Sinister exaggerator / Loss of innocence / The sleeper / Final confrontation (excerpt).

Nov 92. (cd/c/lp) Euro Ralph; (80782) **PRESENT OUR FINEST FLOWERS**
– Gone again / Sour song / Six amber things / Mr. Lonely / Perfect goat / Blue tongues / Jungle bunny / I'm dreaming of a white sailor / Or maybe a marine / Kick a picnic / Dead wood / Baby sister / Forty-four no more / He also serves / Ship of fools / Be kind to U-web footed friends. (re-iss. cd Sep94 on 'Indigo'; 2121-2)

May 97. (4xcd-box) Cargo; (RESBOX 1) **25th ANNIVERSARY BOX SET**

Apr 98. (cd) *East Side Digital*; *<8132-2>* **RESIDUE DEUX** [-] [ ]
– Sleeper / Whoopy snorp / Kamikazi lady / A boy in love / Shut up! shut up! / Anvil forest / Diskomo / Jailhouse rock / Ups and downs / Scent of mint / Saint Nix / Open up / From the plains of Mexico / In San Francisco / Dumbo the clown / Is he really bringing roses? / Time's up / Daydream believer / Prelude for a toddler / Toddler's lullaby / Sagety is cootie wootie / Daydream in space.

Martin REV (see under ⇒ SUICIDE)

REVENGE (see under ⇒ NEW ORDER)

REVOLTING COCKS (see under ⇒ MINISTRY)

REZILLOS / REVILLOS (dig out; Great Alt & Indie . . .)

Keith RICHARDS (see under ⇒ ROLLING STONES)

RICH KIDS (dig out; Great Alt & Indie . . .)

Jonathan RICHMAN

Born: 16 May'51, Boston, Massachusetts, USA. After a period in the late 60's working as a contributor for local music papers, 'Vibrations' & 'Fusion', he formed his first real band, MODERN LOVERS, in 1971. With the help of producer KIM FOWLEY, they recorded a successful demo for 'Warners' in 1972, although the label subsequently shelved their JOHN CALE-produced debut album and soon dropped the group. RICHMAN & Co. finally split in late '74, only to re-form again six months later and record a debut single, 'ROADRUNNER', for 'United Artists'. They then moved to West Coast label 'Beserkley', who bought the unreleased 'Warners' tapes and finally packaged the songs as an eponymous album in 1976. Featuring the classic MODERN LOVERS line-up of JERRY HARRISON, ERNIE BROOKS and DAVID ROBINSON, the album was one of the more genuine efforts to lay claim to the vastly oversubscribed 'first punk album' tag. Carrying on where his heroes The VELVET UNDERGROUND left off, RICHMAN fashioned an idiosyncratic update of late 60's garage-rock, his REED-y vocals carrying epistles of adolescent angst over a simplistic but effective musical backing. While UK Top 20 hit, 'ROADRUNNER', may have whetted fans' appetites for more of the same, a belated follow-up album, 'JONATHAN RICHMAN & THE MODERN LOVERS' (1977) was a different beast altogether. While HARRISON and BROOKS were now tending greener new-wave pastures with The TALKING HEADS and The CARS respectively, the revamped MODERN LOVERS line-up of ROBINSON, LEROY RADCLIFFE and GREG KERANEN were following RICHMAN's more whimsically eccentric path, cutting retro pop, acoustic-based tracks about aliens, insects and, erm, abominable snowmen. A second album that year, 'ROCK'N'ROLL WITH THE MODERN LOVERS', confirmed RICHMAN's new strategy, hitting the British Top 50 despite itself and spawning a second hit (Top 5) in the bizarre instrumental, 'EGYPTIAN REGGAE'. Critics were divided, some hailing the man as a wayward genius, some confounded at what they perceived as a waste of good talent. Whatever, after a late 70's lay-off, RICHMAN continued to plow his singular furrow throughout the following decade with an ever-changing cast of musicians and different labels. Amid the grating childishness, the man was still capable of a wistful charm and the occasional sting of biting poignancy, fans and critics alike generally agreed that 'JONATHAN SINGS!' (1984) remains his finest release from this period. Towards the end of the decade, he recruited BRENDAN TOTTEN and JOHNNY AVILA for the leaner 'MODERN LOVERS '88' before abandoning the backup for good and going it alone. His 1989 eponymous solo debut was followed up with a misguided attempt at C&W, 'JONATHAN GOES COUNTRY' (1990), while a Spanish-language set, '!JONATHAN, TE VAS A EMOCIONAR!' (1994) surely tested the patience of even his most loyal fans. Much more promising were 1995's 'YOU MUST ASK THE HEART' and the following year's 'SURRENDER TO JONATHAN', the latter his first for a major label ('WEA') after years in the commercial wilderness. During the latter half of the 90's, RICHMAN stuck to his task of coming up with the odd album, 1999's 'I'M SO CONFUSED', a slight return to the old fun JONNO of yore. • **Songwriters:** RICHMAN compositions. • **Trivia:** JOHN CALE (ex-Velvet Underground), went on to record his brilliant 'PABLO PICASSO'.

Album rating: THE MODERN LOVERS (*8) / JONATHAN RICHMAN & THE MODERN LOVERS (*7) / ROCK'N'ROLL WITH THE MODERN LOVERS (*6) / THE MODERN LOVERS LIVE (*5) / BACK IN YOUR LIFE (*6) / THE JONATHAN RICHMAN SONGBOOK compilation (*7) / JONATHAN SINGS! (*6) / ROCKIN' AND ROMANCE (*5) / IT'S TIME FOR JONATHAN RICHMAN & THE MODERN LOVERS (*5) / MODERN LOVERS '88 (*5) / JONATHAN RICHMAN (*4) / JOHNATHAN GOES COUNTRY (*4) / 23 GREAT RECORDINGS BY JONATHAN RICHMAN & THE MODERN LOVERS compilation (*8) / HAVING A PARTY WITH JONATHAN RICHMAN collection (*6) / I, JONATHAN (*6) / JONATHAN, TE VAS A EMOCIONAR! (*5) / YOU MUST ASK THE HEART (*5) / SURRENDER TO JONATHAN (*6) / I'M SO CONFUSED (*6)

MODERN LOVERS

were formed by **RICHMAN** – vocals, guitar / with **JERRY HARRISON** – keyboards, vocals / **ERNIE BROOKS** – bass, vocals / **DAVID ROBINSON** – drums (left Nov73 to DMZ, after recording debut)

	U.A.	U.A.
	Beserkley	Beserkley
Jun 75. (7") *(UP 36006)* **ROADRUNNER. / IT WILL STAND**	[ ]	[ ]
Oct 76. (7") *<5701>* **ROADRUNNER. / Friday On My Mind (by Earthquake)**	[-]	[ ]
Oct 77. (lp/c) *(BSERK/BSERC 1) <BZ/+CA 0050>* **THE MODERN LOVERS** (1972 demos)	[ ]	[ ] Oct76

– Roadrunner / Astral plane / Old world / Pablo Picasso / I'm straight / She cracked / Hospital / Someone I care about / Girlfriend / Modern world. *(re-iss. Nov87; same) <re-iss. Nov89 on 'Rhino'; RNLP 70091> (cd-iss. Feb93 on 'Rev-Ola'+=; CREV 007CD)* – (3 extra tracks).

—— HARRISON (also to TALKING HEADS) and BROOKS joined ELLIOTT MURPHY

JONATHAN RICHMAN & THE MODERN LOVERS

with also **LEROY RADCLIFFE** – guitar, vox / **GREG KERANEN** – bass, vox / **DAVID ROBINSON** – drums

Feb 77. (7") *<5743>* **NEW ENGLAND. / HERE COME THE MARTIAN MARTIANS**	[-]	[ ]
Jun 77. (7") *(BZZ 1)* **ROADRUNNER (once). / ROADRUNNER (twice)** *(re-iss. Jul82 on 'Old Gold'; OG 9113)*	[11]	[-]
Oct 77. (lp/c) *(BSERK/BSERC 2) <BZ/+CA 0048>* **JONATHAN RICHMAN & THE MODERN LOVERS**	[ ]	[ ] Jul76

– Rockin' shopping center / Back in the U.S.A. / Important in your life / New England / Lonely financial zone / Hi dear / Abominable snowman in the market / Hey there little insect / Here comes the Martian Martians / Springtime / Amazing Grace. *<re-iss. Nov87; same> (cd-iss. Feb93 on 'Rev-Ola'; CREV 008CD)*

Aug 77. (lp/c) *(BSERK 9) <BZ/+CA 0053>* **ROCK'N'ROLL WITH THE MODERN LOVERS**	[50]	[ ]

– The sweeping wind (kwa ti feng) / Ice cream man / Rockin' rockin' leprechauns / Summer morning / Afternoon / Fly into the mystery / South American folk song / Roller coaster by the sea / Dodge veg-o-matic / Egyptian reggae / Coomyah / The wheels on the bus / Angels watching over you. *<re-iss. Nov87; same> (cd-iss. Feb93 on 'Rev-Ola'; CREV 009CD)*

Sep 77. (7") *(BZZ 2)* **EGYPTIAN REGGAE. / ROLLER COASTER BY THE SEA**	[5]	[ ]

—— **D.SHARPE** – drums repl. ROBINSON / **ASA BREMNER** – bass repl. KERANEN

Dec 77. (lp/c) *(BSERK/BSERC 12) <BZ/+CA 055>* **THE MODERN LOVERS LIVE** (live)	[ ]	[ ]

– I'm a little airplane / Hey there little insect / Egyptian reggae / Ice cream man / I'm a little dinosaur / My little kookenhaken / South American folk song / New England / Morning of our lives. *<re-iss. Nov87; same> (cd-iss. Feb93 on 'Rev-Ola'; CREV 010CD) (cd re-iss. Apr97 on 'Wooded Hill'; HILLCD 15)*

Jan 78. (7"; as MODERN LOVERS) *(BZZ 7)* **MORNING OF OUR LIVES (live). / ROADRUNNER (thrice) (live)**	[28]	[ ]
Apr 78. (7"; as MODERN LOVERS) *(BZZ 14)* **NEW ENGLAND. / ASTRAL PLANE (live)**	[ ]	[-]
Jul 78. (7") *(BZZ 19)* **ABDUL & CLEOPATRA. / OH CAROL**	[ ]	[ ]
Dec 78. (7") *(BZZ 25)* **BUZZ BUZZ BUZZ. / HOSPITAL (live)**	[ ]	[ ]
Feb 79. (lp/c) *(BSERK/BSERC 17) <BZ/+CA 0060>* **BACK IN YOUR LIFE**	[ ]	[ ]

– Abdul and Cleopatra / (She's gonna) Respect me / Lover please / Affection / Buzz buzz buzz / Back in your life / Party in the woods tonight / My love is a flower (just beginning to bloom) / I'm nature's mosquito / Emaline / Lydia / I hear you calling me. *<re-iss. Nov87; same> (cd-iss. Feb93 on 'Rev-Ola'; CREV 011CD) (cd re-iss. Apr97 on 'Wooded Hill'; HILLCD 14)*

Mar 79. (7") *(BZZ 28)* **LYDIA. / IMPORTANT IN YOUR LIFE**	[ ]	[ ]

JONATHAN RICHMAN

Jan 80. (lp) *(DSERK 19)* **JONATHAN RICHMAN SONGBOOK – THE BEST OF . . .** (compilation)		

—— JONATHAN retired in the late 70's, until 1982. Joining him were **KEN FORFIA** – keyboards / **BETH HARRINGTON** – guitar / **GREG KERANEN** – bass, vocals / **MICHAEL GUARDABASCIO** – drums, vocals / **ELLIE MARSHALL** – backing vocals

	Rough Trade	Sire
Aug 84. (lp/c) *(ROUGH/+C 52)* **JONATHAN SINGS!**	[ ]	[ ]

– That summer feeling / This kind of music / The neighbors / Somebody to hold me / These conga drums / Stop this car / Not yet three / Give Paris one more chance / You're the one for me / When I'm walking.

May 85. (7") *(RT 152)* **THAT SUMMER FEELING. / THIS KIND OF MUSIC** *(12"+=) (RTT 152)* – The tag game.	[ ]	[ ]

—— re-formed again with **JONATHAN, ELLIE, MICHAEL** and newcomer **ANDY PALEY** – toy piano

Jun 85. (lp/c) *(ROUGH/+C 72)* **ROCKIN' AND ROMANCE**	[ ]	[ ]

– The beach / My jeans / Bermuda / The U.F.O. man / Down in Bermuda / V. Van Gogh / Walter Johnson / I'm just beginning to live / The fenway / Chewing gum wrapper / The Baltimores / Up in the sky sometime / Now is better than before.

Aug 85. (7") *(RT 154)* **I'M JUST BEGINNING TO LIVE. / CIRCLE I** *(12"+=) (RTT 154)* – Shirin & Fahrad.	[ ]	[ ]

JONATHAN RICHMAN & THE MODERN LOVERS

Feb 86. (lp/c) *(ROUGH/+C 92)* **IT'S TIME FOR JONATHAN RICHMAN & THE MODERN LOVERS**	[ ]	[ ]

– It's you / Let's take a trip / This love of mine / Neon sign / Double chocolate malted / Just about seventeen / Corner store / The desert / Yo Jo Jo / When I dance / Shirin & Fahrad / Ancient and long ago.

—— JONATHAN recruited complete new line-up **BRENDAN TOTTEN** – guitar / **JOHNNY AVILA** – drums

	Demon	Rounder
Feb 88. (lp/cd) *(FIEND/+CD 106) <ROUNDER/+CD 9014>* **MODERN LOVERS '88**	[ ]	[ ]

– Dancin' late at night / When Harpo played his harp / Gail loves me / New kind of neighborhood / African lady / I love hot nights / California desert party / Everything's gotta be right / Circle 1 / I have come out to play / The theme from 'Moulin Rouge'!.

JONATHAN RICHMAN

		Special Delivery	Rounder

Aug 89. (lp/c/cd) <(SPD/+C/CD 1024)> **JONATHAN RICHMAN** [ ] [ ]
– Malagueno de Jojo / Action packed / Everyday clothes / Fender Stratocaster / Blue Moon / Closer / I eat with Gusto / Damn!! you bet / Miracles will start to happen / Sleepwalk / Que reste t'll de nos amours / A mistake today for me / Cerca.

—— now with **TOM BRUMLEY** – guitar

Aug 90. (lp/c/cd) <(SPD/+C/CD 1037)> **JONATHAN GOES COUNTRY** [ ] [ ]
– Since she started to ride / Reno / You're the one for me / Your good girl's gonna go bad / I must be king / You're crazy for takin' the blues / Rodeo wind / Corner store / The neighbours / Men walks among us / I can't stay mad at you / Satisfied mind.

		Rounder	Rounder

Dec 92. (cd/c) <(ROU CD/C 9036)> **I, JONATHAN** [ ] [ ]
– Parties in the U.S.A. / Tandem jump / You can't talk to the dude / Velvet underground / I was dancing in the lesbian bar / Rooming house on Venice beach / That summer feeling / Grunion run / A higher power / Twilight in Boston.

May 94. (cd) <(ROUCD 9040)> **JONATHAN, TE VAS A EMOCIONAR!** [ ] [ ]
– Pantomima de el amor Brujo / Harpo en su Harpa / No te oye / No mas por fun / Papel de chicle / Los vecinos / Compadrito corazon / Melodia tradicional Ecuadoriana / Shirin y Farad / Reno / Cerca / El U.F.O. man / Ahora es Mejor / Sabor A.Mi / Una Fuerza alla.

May 95. (cd/c) <(ROU CD/C 9047)> **YOU MUST ASK THE HEART** [ ] [ ]
– To hide a little thought / The heart of Saturday night / Vampire girl / Just because I'm Irish / That's how I feel / Let her go into darkness / The rose / You must ask the heart / Nothing can change this love / Amorcito corazon / City vs. country / Walter Johnson / Nishi.

		Vapor – Warners	Vapor – Warners

Sep 96. (cd/c) <(9362 46296-2/-4)> **SURRENDER TO JONATHAN** [ ] [ ]
– Just look at me / That little sleeper car / Not just a plus list on the guest list anymore / My little girl's got a full time daddy now / Rock'n'roll drummer straight from the hospy-tel / atisfy / When she kisses me / Egyptian reggae / To hide a little thought / I was dancing in the lesbian bar / Surrender / Floatin' / French style.

—— next with **DARRYL JENIFER** – bass / **TOMMY LARKINS** – drums

Feb 99. (cd) <(9362 47086-2/-4)> **I'M SO CONFUSED** [ ] [ ]
– When I dance / Nineteen in Naples / I'm so confused / True love is not nice / Love me like I love / Hello from Cupid / If she don't love me / The lonely little thrift store / Affection / I can hear her fighting with herself / The night is still young / I can't find my best friend.

– compilations, etc. –

Oct 81. (lp) Bomp; <LBOM 1> **THE ORIGINAL MODERN LOVERS** [-]
(UK-iss.Jun87 on 'Link'; 400.310)

Jul 82. (7") Old Gold; (OG 9112) **EGYPTIAN REGGAE. / MORNING OF OUR LIVES (live)** [-]

1987. (cd) Rhino; <RNCD 75889> **THE BEST OF JONATHAN RICHMAN AND THE MODERN LOVERS** [-]

1988. (cd) Rounder; (CDS1) **JONATHAN RICHMAN & BARRENCE WHITFIELD** [-]

Feb 91. (cd/c/lp) Essential; (ESS CD/MC/LP 128) **23 GREAT RECORDINGS BY JONATHAN RICHMAN AND THE MODERN LOVERS** [-]
– Roadrunner / Dignified & old / Pablo Picasso / I'm straight / Astral plane / Girl friend / Government centre / New teller / It will stand / Morning of our lives / Abominable snowman in the market / Important in your life / My little kookenhaken / Dodge veg-o-matic / Lonely financial zone / Roller coaster by the sea / New England / Egyptian reggae / Ice cream man / Buzz buzz buzz / Abdul & Cleopatra / Roadrunner (twice). (c+=) – She cracked / Hospital. (re-iss. cd Sep93 on 'Castle'; CSCD 397)

1991. (lp) Ubik; <BAKTUN 004> **ORIGINAL MODERN LOVERS** [-]
(UK-iss.Feb97 on 'Bomp'; BLP 4021)

Nov 91. (cd) Cheree; (CHEREE 22) **HAVING A PARTY WITH JONATHAN RICHMAN (live US tour in '83)** [-]
– The girl stands up to me now / Cappuccino bar / my career as a homewrecker / She doesn't laugh at my jokes / When she kisses me / They're not tryin' on the dance floor / At night / When I say wife / 1963 / Monologue about bermuda / Our swingin' pad / Just for fun.

Apr 94. (cd) Castle; **THE COLLECTION** [ ] [-]

Apr 95. (cd; by MODERN LOVERS) Rounder; (ROUCD 9042) **PRECISE MODERN LOVERS ORDER** [ ] [-]
(originally issued in 1992 on French 'Fan Club'; 422439)

Jun 95. (cd) Nectar; (NPMCD 506) **A PLEA FOR TENDERNESS** [ ] [-]

RIDE

Formed: Oxford, England ... 1988 by local art college students MARK GARDENER, ANDY BELL and LAURENCE COLBERT. They drafted in STEVE QUERALT and journalist/manager Dave Newton who subsequently secured them some London gigs. These led to a deal with 'Creation' records and they released their eponymous debut EP early in 1990, the record quickly selling out of its limited number and squeezing into the UK Top 75. The disc showcased the band's spiralling guitar-scapes and contained an early classic in the cathartic 'DRIVE BLIND'. It was hotly pursued by two further Top 40 EP's, 'PLAY' and 'FALL', the latter containing their best track to date (at that point) in 'TASTE'. Come October, with the "shoegazing" scene in full flow, they nearly secured a Top 10 place with their stunning debut album, 'NOWHERE'. 1991 was spent in the studio (excluding Reading Festival), and the fruits were heard early in '92 on their superb 8-minute single 'LEAVE THEM ALL BEHIND'. This slow-burning psychedelic epic gave them their

first Top 10 entry and was a prelude to their second, more BYRDS-esque album, 'GOING BLANK AGAIN'. The record went Top 5, despite being derided by certain music critics. Frictions began to appear and it was thought a two-year sabbatical would solve the problem. BELL took time off to help out his Swedish wife and stablemate IDHA (OVELIUS) on her debut album. In 1994, RIDE were back with 'CARNIVAL OF LIGHT', but again they received lukewarm reviews. Early the next year, GARDENER took off to the States, leaving them all behind (ouch!). Their swansong, 'TARANTULA' was annoyingly deleted after one week, as BELL and GARDENER considered separate solo ventures. • **Songwriters:** Lyrics MARK or ANDY / group compositions except covers EIGHT MILES HIGH (Byrds) / THE MODEL (Kraftwerk) / HOW DOES IT FEEL TO FEEL (Creation) / THAT MAN (Small Faces) / UNION CITY BLUE + ATOMIC (Blondie). • **Trivia:** In 1991, they headlined the Slough Music Festival in front of over 8,000 fans.

Album rating: NOWHERE (*8) / GOING BLANK AGAIN (*7) / CARNIVAL OF LIGHT (*6) / TARANTULA (*6)

MARK GARDENER – vocals, guitar / **ANDY BELL** – guitar, vocals / **STEPHAN QUERALT** – bass / **LAURENCE COLBERT** – drums

				Creation	Sire

Jan 90. (12"ep)(cd-ep) (CRE 072T)(CRESCD 072) **RIDE** [71] [-]
– Chelsea girl / Drive blind / Close my eyes / All I can see. (re-iss. Oct90; same)

Apr 90. (12"ep)(cd-ep) (CRE 075T)(CRESCD 075) **PLAY** [32] [-]
– Like a daydream / Silver / Furthest sense / Perfect time.

Jun 90. (m-cd,m-c) <26390> **SMILE** (first two EP's) [-] [ ]
(UK-iss.Nov92; CRECD 126)

Oct 90. (12"ep)(cd-ep) (CRE 087T)(CRESCD 087) **FALL** [34] [ ]
– Dreams burn down / Taste / Here and now / Nowhere.

Oct 90. (cd/lp)(c) (CRE CD/LP 74)(CREC 74) <26462> **NOWHERE** [11] [ ] Dec90
– Seagull / Kaleidoscope / Polar bear / Dreams burn down / In a different place / Decay / Paralysed / Vapour trail. (cd+=) – Taste / Here and now / Nowhere.

Jan 91. (cd-ep) <40055> **VAPOUR TRAIL** [-] [ ]

Mar 91. (c-ep)(12"ep)(cd-ep) (CRECS 100)(CRE 100T)(CRESCD 100) **TODAY FOREVER** [14] [-]
– Unfamiliar / Sennen / Beneath / Today.

Feb 92. (c-ep)(12"ep)(cd-ep) (CRECS 123)(CRE 123T)(CRESCD 123) <40332> **LEAVE THEM ALL BEHIND. / CHROME WAVES / GRASSHOPPER** [9] [ ]

Mar 92. (cd/2x12"lp)(c) (CRE CD/LP 124)(CCRE 124) <26836> **GOING BLANK AGAIN** [5] [ ]
– Leave them all behind / Twisterella / Not fazed / Chrome waves / Mouse trap / Time of her life / Cool your boots / Making Jusy smile / Time machine / OX4.

Apr 92. (c-ep)(12"ep)(cd-ep) (CRECS 150)(CRE 150T)(CRESCD 150) <40448> **TWISTERELLA / GOING BLANK AGAIN. / HOWARD HUGHES / STAMPEDE** [36] [ ]

—— In Oct'93, 'Fright' records issued 'UNION CITY BLUE' (FRIGHT 060) (re-iss. Apr97; same)

Apr 94. (12"ep/12"clear-ep)(cd-ep) (CRE 155T/+C)(CRESCD 155) **BIRDMAN / ROLLING THUNDER 2. / LET'S GET LOST / DON'T LET IT DIE** [38] [-]

Jun 94. (7"/c-s) (CRE/+MC 184) **HOW DOES IT FEEL TO FEEL? / CHELSEA GIRL** [58] [-]
(12")(cd-s) (CRES 184T)(CRESCD 184) – ('A'side) / Walkabout / At the end of the universe.

Jun 94. (pic-cd-d-lp)(c) (CRE CD/LP 147)(C-CRE 147) <45610> **CARNIVAL OF LIGHT** [5] [ ]
– Moonlight medicine / 1000 miles / From time to time / Natural grace / Only now / Birdman / Crown of creation / How does it feel to feel? / Endless road / Magical spring / Rolling thunder / I don't know where it comes from.

Sep 94. (c-s) (CRECS 189) **I DON'T KNOW WHERE IT COMES FROM. / TWISTERELLA** [46] [ ]
(12")(cd-s) (CRE 189T)(CRESCD 189) – ('A'side) / Drive blind / From time to time / How does it feel to feel (live w / The CREATION).
(cd-s) (CRESCD 189R) – ('A'-Apollo 11 mix) / Moonlight medicine (ride on the wire mix by Portishead) / A journey to the end of the universe (version).

—— split officially early '96. MARK citing ANDY's near takeover of vocal duties.

Feb 96. (12"ep/cd-ep) (CRE 199T)(CRESCD 199) **BLACK NITE CRASH** [67] [-]
– Black nite crash / Nothing lasts forever / Slave / A trip down Ronnie Lane

Mar 96. (cd/lp)(c) (CRE CD/LP 180)(CCRE 180) <61893> **TARANTULA** [21] [ ]
– Black nite crash / Sunshine – Nowhere to run / Dead man / Walk on water / Deep inside my pocket / Mary Anne / Castle on the hill / Gonna be alright / Dawn patrol / Ride the wind / Burnin' / Starlight motel.
above was only available for 1 week only

—— On the 30th of June '96, MARK GARDENER released his limited solo cd-single 'MAGDALEN SKY / CAN'T LET IT DIE (demo)' for Oxford-based 'Shifty Disco' (DISCO 9706). (re-iss. Jun97; same)

– compilations, etc. –

Oct 95. (cd,c) Elektra; <61884> **LIVE LIGHT (live)** [-] [ ]
– Seagull / Magical Spring / From time to time / Chelsea girl / Birdman / Only now / Leave them all behind / Let's get lost.

RIFF RAFF (see under ⇒ BRAGG, Billy)

RIGOR MORTIS (see under ⇒ WHO)

Minnie RIPERTON

Born: 8 Nov'47, Chicago, Illinois, USA. Having studied music in her teens, RIPERTON subsequently secured a job as receptionist for legendary blues/soul label, 'Chess', with whom she also recorded as a member of girl group The GEMS. Formed in 1961, the latter outfit released a few singles as well as providing backing vocals for such luminaries as FONTELLA BASS and ETTA JAMES. Following a one-off solo single, 'LONELY GIRL' (under the nom de plume, ANDREA DAVIS), RIPERTON became lead singer of psychedelic soul outfit, The ROTARY CONNECTION. Beginning with an eponymous 1968 debut album on the 'Cadet Concept' label, the group proceeded to release a total of six albums over the ensuing four years. Although a few of their songs – most notably 'AMEN' – enjoyed heavy rotation on FM radio, they never crossed over to the mainstream in the same way as contemporaries like SLY STONE. By the time the 'CONNECTION had delivered their final album, 'HEY LOVE' (1971), RIPERTON had already initiated her solo career via the 'Janus' label with 'COME TO MY GARDEN' (1970); her spine-tingling 5-octave singing voice was especially dazzling on the sublime 'LES FLEUR'. RIPERTON susbsequently attracted the attention of STEVIE WONDER, for whom she sang backing vocals on his 1974 album, 'Fulfillingness' First Finale'. She also toured with WONDER as a member of his WONDERLOVE backing band and the soul superstar co-produced (under the pseudonym, EL TORO NEGRO) a couple of tracks on her 'Epic' sophomore effort, 'PERFECT ANGEL' (1974). Alongside the orgasmic 'EVERY TIME HE COMES AROUND', the album featured pop-soul classic, 'LOVIN' YOU', furnishing MINNIE with a US chart topper (UK No.2) and finally giving her the exposure she deserved. It wasn't to last though and, inexplicably, neither 'ADVENTURES IN PARADISE' (1975) nor 'STAY IN LOVE' (1977) made much commercial headway outside America. Tragically, RIPERTON was revealed to be suffering from breast cancer (undergoing a mastectomy in 1976), the singer devoting much of her time throughout her final years to the American Cancer Society. Although her illness became progressively worse, she continued to perform and record during this time, a final album, entitled simply 'MINNIE', released by 'Capitol' in 1979. With her death on July 12th the same year, soul music had lost one of its most talented, beautiful and original singers. Like former SUPREME, FLORENCE BALLARD, she'd been cut down in her prime, aged only 31. A posthumous collection of previously unreleased vocals with newly recorded instrumental backing, 'LOVE LIVES FOREVER', was released by 'Capitol' and hit the Top 40 in 1980.

Album rating: COME TO MY GARDEN (*6) / PERFECT ANGEL (*7) / ADVENTURES IN PARADISE (*5) / STAY IN LOVE (*5) / MINNIE (*5) / LOVE LIVES FOREVER (*5) / THE BEST OF MINNIE RIPERTON compilation (*7)

MINNIE RIPERTON – vocals (with various sessioners)

		not iss.	G.R.T.
1970's.	(lp) *<30001>* **COME TO MY GARDEN** (rec.1969)	-	

– Les fleur / Completeness / Come to my garden / Memory band / Rainy day in Centerville / Close your eyes and remember / Oh, by the way / Expecting / Only when I'm dreaming. *<re-iss. Nov74 on 'Janus'; 7011> (UK cd-iss. May95 on 'Blue Moon'; CDBM 080) (UK cd re-iss. May97 on 'Aim'; AIM 1060)*

		Epic	Epic
Jun 74.	(7") *<11139>* **EVERY TIME HE COMES AROUND. / REASONS**	-	
Sep 74.	(7") *(EPC 2660) <50020>* **SEEING YOU THIS WAY. / THE EDGE OF A DREAM**		Aug74

(re-iss. Jan75; same)

Oct 74.	(lp/c) *(EPC/40 80426) <32561>* **PERFECT ANGEL** (hit UK chart May75)	33	4 Aug74

– Perfect angel / Every time he comes around / Lovin' you / Our lives / Reasons / It's so nice / Take a little trip / Seeing you this way / The edge of a dream.

Mar 75.	(7") *(EPC 3121) <50057>* **LOVIN' YOU. / THE EDGE OF A DREAM**	2	1 Jan75
Jun 75.	(7") *(EPC 3360)* **SEEING YOU THIS WAY. / IT'S SO NICE TO SEE OLD FRIENDS**		-
Jun 75.	(lp/c) *(EPC/40 69142) <33454>* **ADVENTURES IN PARADISE**		18 May75

– Baby, this love I have / Feelin' that your feelin's right / When it comes down to it / Minnie's lament / Love and its glory / Adventures in Paradise / Inside my love / Alone in Brewster Bay / Simple things / Don't let anyone bring you down.

Sep 75.	(7") *(EPC 3574) <50128>* **INSIDE MY LOVE. / DON'T LET ANYONE BRING YOU DOWN**		76 Jul75
Oct 75.	(7") *<50155>* **WHEN IT COMES DOWN TO IT. / MINNIE'S LAMENT**	-	
Jan 76.	(7") *<50166>* **SIMPLE THINGS. / MINNIE'S LAMENT**	-	
Jan 76.	(7") *(EPC 3796)* **WHEN IT COMES DOWN TO IT. / LOVE AND IT'S GLORY**	-	
Apr 76.	(7") *<50190>* **ADVENTURES IN PARADISE. / WHEN IT COMES DOWN TO IT**	-	
Mar 77.	(7") *(EPC 5032) <50337>* **STICK TOGETHER. / (part 2)**	-	
Mar 77.	(lp/c) *(EPC/40 81457) <34191>* **STAY IN LOVE**		71

– Young, willing and able / Could it be I'm in love / Oh darlin' . . . life goes on / Can you feel I'm saying? / Gettin' ready for your love / Stick together / Wouldn't matter where you are / How could I love you more / Stay in love.

Jun 77.	(7") *<50394>* **WOULDN'T MATTER WHERE YOU ARE. /**	-	
Sep 77.	(7") *<50427>* **YOUNG, WILLING AND ABLE. / HOW COULD I LOVE YOU MORE**	-	

		Capitol	Capitol
May 79.	(7") *(CL 16082) <4706>* **MEMORY LANE. / I'M A WOMAN**		

—— on the 12th of July '79 (aged 30) MINNIE died of cancer

Aug 79.	(lp/c) *<(EST/TCEST 11936)>* **MINNIE**		29 May79

– Memory lane / Lover and friend / Return to forever / Love hurts / Dancin' & acting crazy / Never existed before / I'm a woman / Light my fire. *(re-iss. May82 on 'Fame' lp/c; FA/TCFA 3027)*

Sep 79.	(7") *(CL 16102) <4761>* **LOVER AND FRIEND. / RETURN TO FOREVER**		
Nov 79.	(7") *<4902>* **HERE WE GO. / RETURN TO FOREVER**	-	

(below album recorded 1978 with new accompaniment)

Oct 80.	(lp/c) *<(EST/TCEST 12097)>* **LOVE LIVES FOREVER**		35 Aug80

– Here we go / I'm in love again / Strange affair / Island in the Sun / Give me time / You take my breath away / Song of life (la-la-la).

Jan 81.	(7") *<4955>* **ISLAND IN THE SUN. / GIVE ME TIME**	-	-
Apr 81.	(7") *(CL 16165)* **ISLAND IN THE SUN. / LIGHT MY FIRE**	-	-

(12"+=) *(12CL 16165)* – Lover and friend.

– compilations, etc. –

Nov 81.	(lp/c) *Capitol; (EST/TC-EST 12189)* **THE BEST OF MINNIE RIPERTON**		

– Perfect angel / Memory lane / Loving you / Can you feel what I'm saying / Here we go / Inside my love / Lover and friend / Woman of heart and mind / Young, willing and able / You take my breath away / Adventures in Paradise.

Nov 87.	(7") *Old Gold; (OG 9725)* **LOVING YOU. / INSIDE MY LOVE**		
Aug 93.	(cd) *Capitol; <(CDP 780516-2)>* **CAPITOL GOLD: THE BEST OF MINNIE RIPERTON**		

– Perfect angel / Lover and friend / Memory lane / Woman of heart and mind / Loving you / Young, willing and able / Can you feel what I'm saying / Stick together / Wouldn't matter where you are / Stay in love / Inside my love / Here we go / Give me time / You take my breath away / Adventures in Paradise / Simple things / Light my fire.

Feb 98.	(cd) *Chess-M.C.A.; <(MCD 0939-2)>* **HER CHESS YEARS**		

RIP, RIG + PANIC   (dig out; Great Alt & Indie . . .)

Robbie ROBERTSON

Born: JAMIE ROBERTSON, 4 Jul'44, Toronto, Canada. An integral part of The BAND (as guitarist and songwriter), one of America's most revered rock groups, ROBERTSON diversified into acting and production (he'd already overseen NEIL DIAMOND's 'Beautiful Noise' album in 1976) following the group's demise in the late 70's. His most high profile project during this period was 'Carny', a film about American freak shows for which he wrote the score as well as starring in. Passing up the opportunity to become part of a reformed BAND in the mid-80's, ROBERTSON instead concentrated on developing a belated solo career. Co-produced by mood master, Daniel Lanois and boasting the likes of U2, PETER GABRIEL, NEIL YOUNG and even the GIL EVANS horn formation, the album steered clear of the roots-rock of The BAND, opting instead for a highly original blend of atmospheric sophistication best sampled on the sultry 'SOMEWHERE DOWN THE CRAZY RIVER'. The latter track was an unexpected UK Top 20 hit, while the album itself sold respectably, making the lower regions of the British Top 50 and the American Top 40. Hardly the most prolific of artists, it would be another four years before the release of a follow-up, 'STORYVILLE' (1991). This time around mining the rich seam of New Orleans music in tandem with assorted METERS and NEVILLE BROTHERS, he moved seamlessly through a variety of Crescent City styles incorporating blues, gospel and R&B via his trademark half-spoken vocal style. Despite widespread critical acclaim and a Top 30 UK chart position, the record failed to launch ROBERTSON into the major league of adult rock. Moving back into film, the singer hooked up with The RED ROAD ENSEMBLE for the soundtrack to US TV documentary, 'The Native Americans', released on disc in 1994. • Trivia: Other film parts; 'The Coal Miner's Daughter' (1980) + 'The Right Stuff' (1983).

Album rating: ROBBIE ROBERTSON (*7) / STORYVILLE (*6) / MUSIC FOR THE NORTH AMERICANS (*5) / CONTACT FROM THE UNDERWORLD OF RED BOY (*5)

ROBBIE ROBERTSON – vocals, guitar, keyboards / with **BILL DILLON** – guitar / **TONY LEVIN** – bass / **MANU KATCHE** – drums, percussion / **DANIAL LANOIS** – percussion, guitar, bass, co-producer / **PETER GABRIEL** – vocals / **U2** / **GARTH HUDSON** + **RICK DANKO**, etc

		Geffen	Geffen
Oct 87.	(7") *<28175>* **SHOWDOWN AT THE BIG SKY. / HELL'S HALF ACRE**	-	
Oct 87.	(lp/c/cd) *(WX 133/+C)(924160-2) <24160>* **ROBBIE ROBERTSON**	47	38

– Fallen angel / Showdown at the big sky / Broken arrow / Sweet fire of love / American roulette / Somewhere down the crazy river / Hell's half acre / Sonny get caught in the moonlight / Testimony. *(re-iss. Jan91 lp/c/cd; GEF/+C/D 24160) (re-iss. cd Oct95; GFLD 19294)*

Oct 87.	(7") *(GEF 32)* **FALLEN ANGEL. / HELL'S HALF ACRE**		

(12"+=) *(GEF 32T)* – Tailgate.

Nov 87.	(7") *<28111>* **SOMEWHERE DOWN THE CRAZY RIVER. / HELL'S HALD ACRE**	-	-
Jun 88.	(7") *(GEF 40)* **SOMEWHERE DOWN THE CRAZY RIVER. / BROKEN ARROW**	15	-

(12"+=) *(GEF 40T)* – Tailgate.

Sep 88.	(7") *(GEF 46)* **FALLEN ANGEL. / HELL'S HALF ACRE**		

(12"+=/cd-s+=) *(GEF 46 T/CD)* – Tailgate.

Sep 91.	(lp/c/cd) *<(GEF/+C/D 24303)>* **STORYVILLE**	30	69

– Night parade / Hold back the dawn / Go back to your woods / Soap box preacher / Day of reckoning (burnin' for you) / What about now / Shake this town / Break in the rules / Resurrection / Sign of the rainbow. *(re-iss. cd Oct95; GFLD 19295)*

		Capitol	Capitol
Oct 94.	(cd/c; ROBBIE ROBERTSON & The RED ROAD ENSEMBLE) *(CD/TC EST 2238) <28295>* **(MUSIC FOR) THE NATIVE AMERICANS**		

– Coyote dance / Mahk tchi (heart of the people) / Ghost dance / The vanishing breed / It's a good day to die / Golden feather / Akua Tutu / Words of fire, deeds of blood / Cherokee morning song / Skinwalker / Ancestor song / Twisted hair.

Mar 98.	(cd) *(854243-2)* **CONTACT FROM THE UNDERWORLD OF RED BOY**		

– The sound is fading / The code of Handsome Lake / Making a noise / Unbound / Sacrifice / Rattlebone / Peyote healing / In the blood / Stomp dance (unity) / The lights / Take your partner by the hand.

Smokey ROBINSON (see under ⇒ MIRACLES)

Tom ROBINSON

Born: 1 Jun'50, Cambridge, England. Sent to reform school as a lad, the young ROBINSON met guitarist DANNY KUSTOW and subsequently formed DAVANQ in the early 70's. Duly relocating to London, ROBINSON put together cabaret-folk outfit, CAFE SOCIETY, releasing an eponymous solo album on RAY DAVIES' (KINKS) 'Konk' label in 1974. Relations between the band and DAVIES soon soured, the project falling by the wayside as ROBINSON formed his own outfit, The TOM ROBINSON BAND. With a stable line-up cementing around KUSTOW, MARK AMBLER and DOLPHIN TAYLOR, the group were signed up by 'E.M.I.', immediately hitching a ride on the emerging punk juggernaut with stompalong classic, '2-4-6-8 MOTORWAY'. The track's UK Top 5 success was followed with the live EP, 'RISING FREE', ROBINSON's radical political manifesto introduced with the celebratory 'SING IF YOU'RE GLAD TO BE GAY' and the defiant 'DON'T TAKE NO FOR AN ANSWER'. Adopted by the music press as something of a new wave cause celebre, TRB, along with the likes of The CLASH, espoused a more positive strand of protest than the bleak nihilism of many punk acts, their anti-racist, pro-individual freedom stance represented by the clenched fist logo on debut album, 'POWER IN THE DARKNESS' (1978). Brimming with anthemic rallying cries for the disaffected yet rarely lapsing into laboured preaching, the album confirmed ROBINSON's credentials as an articulate spokesman for the punk generation. And it wasn't just empty rhetoric, ROBINSON putting his politics where his mouth was and playing a host of benefit gigs (chiefly anti-racism and gay/lesbian rights events) both at home and in the States where he was something of a minor hero on the college circuit. Following the departure of AMBLER and TAYLOR, however, ROBINSON struggled through a TODD RUNDGREN-produced follow-up set, 'TRB 2' (1979). Preceded by the flop PETER GABRIEL collaboration, 'BULLY FOR YOU', the album's bland sloganeering was met with a frosty critical reception and relatively poor sales (despite a UK Top 20 placing); the TOM ROBINSON BAND fell apart, its mainman subsequently suffering a nervous breakdown. Upon his recovery, the singer formed a new outfit, SECTOR 27, initiating his own label, 'Panic' and releasing an eponymous album in 1980. A more experimental post-punk affair, the album was well received but failed to sell and again, ROBINSON changed his plans. Moving to Hamburg, Germany in early '82, he cut his first solo album proper, 'NORTH BY NORTHWEST', another strong effort which found him developing a more conventional singer/songwriter style. This paid dividends the following year when 'WAR BABY' made the UK Top 10, its laidback, swinging sophistication contrasting with the three-chord assault of old. An equally classy follow-up, 'LISTEN TO THE RADIO: ATMOSPHERICS', just nudged into the Top 40 later that year, another collaboration with PETER GABRIEL. Together with a further minor hit in Steely Dan's 'RIKKI DON'T LOSE THAT NUMBER', the singles were included on the fine 1984 set, 'HOPE AND GLORY', ROBINSON's most successful album since the late 70's. 'STILL LOVING YOU' (1986) saw the man's muse become increasingly mellow as he entered fatherhood (it emerged that he was actually bi-sexual, not homosexual) although the album failed to match even its predecessor's limited success. Throughout the remainder of the 80's and on into the 90's, ROBINSON regularly performed with original members of TRB as well as touring, writing and recording as a solo artist. Featuring such disparate guests as CHRIS REA and T.V. SMITH, 1994's 'LOVE OVER RAGE' album boasted ROBINSON's most confident set of songs in almost a decade, proving that he didn't have to rely on mere nostalgia to make a living.

Album rating: POWER IN THE DARKNESS (*8) / TRB TWO (*5) / SECTOR 27 (*4; by SECTOR 27) / TOM ROBINSON BAND compilation (*7) / NORTH BY NORTHWEST (*7) / HOPE AND GLORY (*6) / STILL LOVING YOU (*5) / WE NEVER HAD IT SO GOOD with Jakko M. Jakszuk (*4) / LIVING IN A BOOM TIME (*5) / LOVE OVER RAGE (*5) / HAVING IT BOTH WAYS (*5) / RISING FREE – THE BEST OF TOM ROBINSON compilation (*7)

TOM ROBINSON BAND

TOM ROBINSON – vocals, bass (ex-CAFE SOCIETY, ex-DAVANQ) / **DANNY KUSTOW** – guitar (ex-DAVANQ) / **MARK AMBLER** – keyboards repl. ANTON MAUVE, BRET SINCLAIR & MARK GRIFFITHS / **DOLPHIN TAYLOR** – drums, vocals repl. NICK TREVISICK (ex-CAFE SOCIETY)

		E.M.I.	Harvest
Oct 77.	(7") *(EMI 2715)* <4533> **2-4-6-8 MOTORWAY. / I SHALL BE RELEASED**	5	
Feb 78.	(7"ep) *(EMI 2749)* **RISING FREE (live)**	18	
	– Don't take no for an answer / Right on sister / Sing if you're glad to be gay / Martin.		
May 78.	(7") *(EMI EMI 2787)* **UP AGAINST THE WALL. / I'M ALRIGHT JACK**	33	-
May 78.	(lp/c) *(EMC/TC-EMC 3226)* <11930> **POWER IN THE DARKNESS**	4	
	– Up against the wall / Grey Cortina / Too good to be true / Ain't gonna take it / Long hot summer / Winter of 79 / Man you never saw / Better decide which side you're on / You gotta survive / Power in the darkness / 2-4-6-8 Motorway. *(re-iss. Aug83 lp/c; EMS/TC-EMS 106668-1/-4)* *(re-iss. Oct94 on 'Cooking Vinyl' cd/c; COOK C/CD 076)* *(cd re-iss. Aug96 on 'Razor & Tie'; RE 2018)*		
Aug 78.	(7") *(EMI 2847)* **TOO GOOD TO BE TRUE. / POWER IN THE DARKNESS**		-

Sep 78.	(7") <4568> **RIGHT ON SISTER. / GLAD TO BE GAY**		-	
——	(mid'78) **IAN PARKER** – keyboards repl. NICK PLYTAS (ex-ROOGALATOR) who had repl. AMBLER (Apr'78).			
——	(Dec78) **PRESTON HEYMAN** – drums (ex-BRAND X) repl. DOLPHIN who joined STIFF LITTLE FINGERS.			
Mar 79.	(7") *(EMI 2916)* <4726> **BULLY FOR YOU. / OUR PEOPLE**	68		
Mar 79.	(lp/c) *(EMC/TC-EMC 3296)* <11930> **TRB TWO**	18		
	– All right all night / Why should I mind / Black angel / Let my people be / Blue murder / Bully for you / Crossing over the road / Sorry Mr. Harris / Law and order / Days of rage / Hold out. *(re-iss. Aug83 lp/c; EMS/TC-EMS 165215-1/-4)* *(re-iss. Oct94 on 'Cooking Vinyl' cd/c; COOK CD/C 077)* *(cd re-iss. Aug96 on 'Razor & Tie'; RE 2019)*			
May 79.	(7"; w-drawn) *(EMI 2946)* **ALRIGHT ALL NIGHT. / BLACK ANGEL**		-	
——	**CHARLIE MORGAN** – drums repl. the returning TREVISICK who had repl. HEYMAN. The latter joined KATE BUSH. **GEOFF SHARKEY** – guitar repl. KUSTOW / added **GRAHAM COLLIER** – double bass / **GEOFF DALY** – saxophone			
Aug 79.	(7"; TOM ROBINSON & THE VOICE SQUAD) *(EMI 2967)* **NEVER GONNA FALL IN LOVE (AGAIN). / GETTING TIGHTER**		-	
——	Disbanded late summer '79. **TOM ROBINSON** now vocals, guitar went solo with back-up from SECTOR 27. **STEVE BLANCHARD** – guitar / **DEREK QUINTON** – drums / **JO BURT** – bass (recorded one withdrawn lp, 'SECTOR 27', on 'Regal Zonophone')			

SECTOR 27

—— were now given full billing.

		Panic	not iss.
Jul 80.	(7") *(SEC 27)* **NOT READY. / CAN'T KEEP AWAY**		-
Oct 80.	(7") *(SEC 28)* **INVITATION, WHAT HAVE WE GOT TO LOSE? / DUNGANNON**		-

		Fontana	I.R.S.
Nov 80.	(lp) *(6359 039)* <70013> **SECTOR 27**		
	– Invitation / Not ready / Mary Lynne / Looking at you / 523 / Total recall / Where can we go tonight / Take it or leave it / Bitterly disappointed / One fine day. *(cd-iss. Jun96 +=; 532642-2)* – (extra tracks).		

		Panic	not iss.
Jan 81.	(7") *(SEC 29)* **TOTAL RECALL. / STORNOWAY**		-
May 81.	(7") *(SEC 30)* **MARTIN'S GONE. / CHRISTOPHER CALLING**		-

TOM ROBINSON

—— went solo again. (SECTOR 27 as a trio branched out on own). **TOM** added **STEVE LAURIE** – drums / **RICHARD MAZDA** – guitar, producer / etc

		Panic	Geffen
Jun 82.	(lp) **NORTH BY NORTHWEST**		
	– Now Martin's gone / Atmospherics / Can't keep away (part 2) / Looking for a bonfire / Merrily up on high / Those days / In the cold / The night tide / Dungannon / Love comes. *(re-iss. 1986 on 'Castle' lp/c/cd; CLA LP/MC/CD 128)* *(cd-iss. Jun97 on 'Castaway Northwest'+=; CNWVP 003CD)* – Tango an der wand / Now Richard's gone / Airtraum tango dob / Any favours / Out to lunch.		
Jul 82.	(7") *(NIC 1)* **NOW MARTIN'S GONE. / ATMOSPHERICS**		-
	(re-iss. Feb83 as 5-track-12"ep; NIC 1-12) – ATMOSPHERICS		
Jun 83.	(7") *(NIC 2)* **WAR BABY. / HELL YES**	6	Sep84
	(12"+=) *(NIC 2-12)* – Martin's gone (original).		
Nov 83.	(7") *(NIC 3)* **LISTEN TO THE RADIO: ATMOSPHERICS. / DON'T DO ME ANY FAVOURS**	39	
	(12"+=) *(NIC 3-12)* – Out to lunch.		

		Castaway-RCA	Geffen
Jun 84.	(7") *(TR 1)* **BACK IN THE OLD COUNTRY. / BEGGIN'**		
	(12"+=) *(TRT 1)* – ('A'live version).		
Sep 84.	(7"/12") *(TR/+T 2)* **RIKKI DON'T LOSE THAT NUMBER. / CABIN BOY (live)**	58	-
Sep 84.	(lp/c) *(ZL/ZK 70483)* **HOPE AND GLORY**	21	-
	– War baby / Atmospherics: Listen to the radio / Cabin boy / Blond and blue / Hope and glory / Murder at the end of the day / Prison / Rikki don't lose that number / Old friend / Looking for a bonfire.		
May 85.	(7"/12") *(ZB/ZT 400 19/20)* **PRISON. / MORE LIVES THAN ONE**		-
——	TOM brought back **BLANCHARD + BURT** plus **RED** – drums		
Jul 86.	(7") *(TR 3)* **(IT AIN'T NOTHIN' LIKE) THE REAL THING. / THE WEDDING**		-
	(12"+=) *(TRT 3)* – ('A'extended).		
Sep 86.	(lp/c/cd) *(ZL/ZK/ZD 71129)* **STILL LOVING YOU**		-
	– Feels so good – Hurt so bad / (It ain't nothin' like) The real thing / Still loving you / Take me home again / You tattooed me / Drive all night / Living in a love town / Spain / This little romance / The wedding.		
Sep 86.	(7"/12") *(TR/+T 4)* **STILL LOVING YOU. / THE SATURDAY DISCO**		-
Jan 87.	(7"; TOM ROBINSON & KIKI DEE) *(TR 5)* **FEELS SO GOOD. / NORTHERN RAIN**		-
	(12"+=) *(TRT 5)* – You tattooed me / Change.		
Jun 87.	(7") *(ZB 41333)* **SPAIN. / DRIVE ALL NIGHT**		
	(12"+=) *(ZT 41333)* – (It ain't nothin' like) The real thing.		

		Musidisc	not iss.
Oct 90.	(cd/c/lp; TOM ROBINSON & JAKKO M. JAKSZUK) *(10666-2/-4/-1)* **WE NEVER HAD IT SO GOOD**		-
	– We never had it so good / Drinking through the desert / Blood brother / What have I ever done to you / The baby rages on / Tomboy / Kiss and roll over / Hard cases / Can't stop: Peter's theme / My own sweet way.		
Nov 90.	(7"; as TOM ROBINSON & JAKKO M. JAKSZUK) **BLOOD BROTHER. / ('A'version)**		-
	(12"+=) – What have I ever done to you / Rigging.		

		Cooking Vinyl	Scarface
Sep 92.	(lp/c/cd) (COOK/+C/CD 052) **LIVING IN A BOOM TIME**		-

– Folk song (intro) / Living in a boom time / More lives than one / Yuppie scum / My own sweet way / Castle island / Digging it up / The Brits / War baby / Back in the old country. *(re-iss. Mar94 cd/c; same)*

| Jan 93. | (c-ep/cd-ep) **WAR BABY. / BLOOD BROTHER / WE DIDN'T KNOW WHAT WAS GOING ON / WAR BABY** | | - |

— now w / **ROBIN MILLAR** – rhythm guitar / **CHRIS REA** – slide guitar / **MARK AMBLER** – keyboards / **WINSTON BLISSETT** – bass / **MARTIN DITCHAM** – drums / **MARK RAMSDEN** – saxophone / **T.V.SMITH + ANDY MITCHELL** – backing vocals

| May 94. | (lp/c/cd) (COOK/+CD 066) <53913> **LOVE OVER RAGE** | | - |

– Roaring / Hard / Loved / Days / Driving / Green / DDR / Fifty / Silence / Chance.

Jun 94.	(cd-ep) (FRYCD 028) **HARD / GREEN / LIVING IN A BOOM TIME / PORTOBELLO TERRACE**		-
Jul 94.	(cd-ep) (FRYCD 029) **LOVED / FIFTY / YUPPY SCUM / GLAD TO BE GAY '94**		-
Sep 94.	(cd-ep) (FRYCD 031) **DAYS (THAT CHANGED THE WORLD) / ROARING / THE BRITS COME ROLLING BACK**		-
May 96.	(cd/c) (COOK CD/C 097) **HAVING IT BOTH WAYS**		-

– Disrespect / One / Rum thunderbird / Cold cold ground / Fool to myself / Hot dog / Sorry / Raining in Connecticut / Congo blue / Castaway / The last word.

| Jul 96. | (cd-ep) (FRYCD 050) **RAINING IN CONNECTICUT / DISRESPECT / RUM THUNDERBIRD / RAINING IN CONNECTICUT (mix)** | | - |

– compilations, etc. –

| Dec 81. | (lp) E.M.I.; (EMS 1005) **TOM ROBINSON BAND** | | - |

(re-iss. May82 on 'Fame'; FA 3028)

Nov 82.	(lp) Panic; (ROBBO 2) **CABARET '79 (live)**		-
Oct 83.	(7") Old Gold; (OG 9379) **2-4-6-8 MOTORWAY. / DON'T TAKE NO FOR AN ANSWER**		-
Apr 87.	(lp/c; TOM ROBINSON & THE CREW) Dojo; (DOJO LP/CD 51) **MIDNIGHT AT THE FRINGE (live)**		-
Sep 87.	(7") E.M.I.; (EM 28) **2-4-6-8 MOTORWAY (live). / ('A'original)**		-

(12"+=) (12EM 28) – Sing if you're glad to be gay.

Sep 87.	(cd/c/lp) E.M.I.; (CD/TC+/EMC 3540) **COLLECTION 77-87**		-
Mar 89.	(lp/cd) Line; (MS LP/CD9.00695) **GLAD TO BE GAY CABARET**		-
Jun 89.	(cd) Line; (LICD 9.005888) **LAST TANGO**		-
Oct 89.	(d-lp/c/cd) Connoisseur; (VSOP LP/MC/CD 138) **BACK IN THE OLD COUNTRY**		-

– Listen to the radio: Atmospherics / Too good to be true / Up against the wall / Northern rain / I shall be released / 2-4-6-8 motorway / Drive all night / Don't take no for an answer / Where can we go tonight / Back in the old country / Alright all night / War baby / Days / Crossing over the road / Rikki don't lose that number / Looking for a bonfire / Hard cases / Still loving you / Not ready / Bully for you / Long hot summer. *(d-lp/c+=)* – Mary Lynne / Bitterly disappointed.

| Jun 92. | (d-cd) Line; (LICD 921215) **GLAD TO BE GAY / LAST TANGO** | | - |

(re-iss. Aug95; same)

Aug 92.	(cd) Pop Almanac; (PACD 7005) **WINTER OF '89**		-
Jun 93.	(cd/c) Optima; (OPTM CD/C 012) **TOM ROBINSON**		-
Jul 94.	(cd) Music De-Luxe; (MSCD 6) **MOTORWAY**		-
Mar 96.	(cd/c) EMI Gold; (CD/TC GOLD 1015) **THE GOLD COLLECTION**		-
Jun 97.	(cd) EMI Gold; (CDGOLD 1098) **RISING FREE – THE BEST OF TOM ROBINSON**		-
Jun 97.	(cd; with JAKKO M. JAKSZUK) Castaway Northwest; (CNWVP 001CD) **BLOOD BROTHER**		-

(above was virtually 'WE NEVER HAD IT SO GOOD' & extra tracks)

| Jul 97. | (cd) Castaway Northwest; (CNWVP 002CD) **LAST TANGO / MIDNIGHT AT THE FRINGE** | | - |
| Aug 97. | (cd) Castaway Northwest; (CNWVP 004CD) **GLAD TO BE GAY (CABARET '79)** | | - |

ROCKET FROM THE CRYPT

Formed: San Diego, California, USA … 1989 by half-Portuguese singer, SPEEDO (JOHN REIS), alongside PETEY X, ATOM, JC 2000 and ND. REIS left school and joined PITCHFORK, a hardcore band who rapidly evolved into DRIVE LIKE JEHU (other members of this outfit being RICK FROBERG, MIKE KENNEDY and MARK TROMBINO), the frontman continuing to moonlight for the latter outfit through his early career with the 'CRYPT. Kick-ass speedball R&R punks/greasers drawing on the earthiest of 50's tradition, ROCKET FROM THE CRYPT were as suave as Vegas-era ELVIS with the attitude and sound of their heroes, The MISFITS (whom they initially supported). In a further bid to boost their street cred, RFTC also claimed to have opened for two of the most legendary figures in black music, JAMES BROWN and SUN RA. On the recording front, the lads issued a plethora of singles for various hip US underground labels (the tracks were later collected together for UK consumption as 'ALL SYSTEMS GO!'), along the way releasing a debut album, 'PAINT AS A FRAGRANCE' (1991) and picking up sax player, APOLLO NINE. They unearthed a second album, 'CIRCA: NOW!', a year later and although the ROCKET-fuelled formula varied little, there was an audible improvement in the musicianship. While their mid-90's release schedule was as prolific as ever, they finally settled on a long-term deal with 'Interscope' ('El-e-mental' in the UK) in 1995. Towards the end of that year, they finally made their critical breakthrough on the UK alt-rock scene with the 'SCREAM, DRACULA, SCREAM!' album. It also lent them a modicum of commercial success, scraping into the UK Top 40 and spawning no less than three hit singles, the last of which, 'ON A ROPE', found them threatening the Top 10. In the best tradion of the DEAD BOYS or the SAINTS, however, ROCKET FROM THE CRYPT were in their element on stage blasting out

their visceral, three-chord mainline rock'n'roll, NME recognising their talent by bestowing upon them a Brat Award for Best Newcomer. In the summer of '98, the slicked-back six-piece resurfaced with their second major label album, 'RFTC', a slightly subdued, more pop/rock-orientated affair that only just scraped into the UK Top 75. • **Songwriters:** Group, except GOLD (MC5). • **Trivia:** SPEEDO recently married ND's sister.

Album rating: PAINT AS A FRAGRANCE (*5) / CIRCA: NOW! (*5) / ALL SYSTEMS GO compilation (*7) / THE STATE OF ART IS ON FIRE mini (*5) / HOT CHARITY mini (*4) / SCREAM, DRACULA, SCREAM! (*8) / RFTC (*6) / ALL SYSTEMS GO 2 compilation (*7)

SPEEDO (b. JOHN REIS) – vocals, guitar / **ND** (aka ANDY) – guitar / **PETEY X** – bass, bass vocals / **ATOM** (aka ADAM) – drums / **JC 2000** (aka JAY) – trumpet, percussion, organ, vocals

		not iss.	Pushead
1990.	exist? (7"red) <200772> **CUT IT LOOSE. / GLAZED**	-	

		Helter Skelter	not iss.
1991.	(7"ep) <HS 92712> **YUM KIPPERED EP**		Italian

– Bad Ninja / Goodbye / Kill the funk (there will be no funk in Outer Space). *(UK-iss.Apr95 c-s/cd-s; same)*

		not iss.	Headhunter
Feb 91.	(lp/c/cd) <HED 003/+MC/CD> **PAINT AS A FRAGRANCE**	-	

– French guy / Maybellene / Shy boy / Basturds / Velvet touch / Evil party / Stinker / Jiggy jig / Weak superhero / Thumbmaster. *(cd-iss. Mar93; same +UK)*

— added **APOLLO NINE** (aka PAUL) – saxophone, vocals

		not iss.	Sympathy F
Jun 92.	(7"m) <SFTRI 179> **BOY CHUCKER. / JUMPER K. BALLS / LEFTY**	-	

		not iss.	Sub Pop
Jun 92.	(7"blue-ep) <SP 154> **NORMAL CARPET RIDE / WHERE ARE THE FUCKERS. / SLUMBER QUEEN / FLIP THE BIRD**	-	

		not iss.	Drunken Fish
Jul 92.	(one-sided-7"gold) <DF 02> **GOLD**	-	

		not iss.	Standard
Oct 92.	(7") <SR 72> **CHA CHA CHA. / (other track by DEADBOLT)**	-	

		not iss.	Merge
Nov 92.	(7") <MRG 035> **PIGEON EATER. / (THE) PASTE THAT YOU LOVE**	-	

		not iss.	Pussheads
Dec 92.	(d7") **PUSS MORT. / (other by SEPTIC DEATH)**	-	

		Headhunter	Headhunter
Jan 93.	(lp/c/cd) <(HED 015/+MC/CD)> **CIRCA: NOW!**		Nov92

– Short lip fuser / Hippy dippy do / Ditch digger / Don't Darlene / Killy kill / Hairball alley / Sturdy wrists / March of dimes / Little arm / Dollar / Glazed.

		not iss.	Drunken Fish
Apr 93.	(7",7"clear) <DF 05> **PURE GENIUS. / LIFT AND LOVE**	-	

		not iss.	Merge
Feb 94.	(12") <1994> **BURNT MOUTH OFF LIAR. / UFO UFO UFO**	-	

		Bacteria Sour	not iss.
May 94.	(7") (SOUR 2V/3V) **BLOODY THIRSTY BUTCHERS. /**	-	

		not iss.	Sympathy F
1995.	(10"ep) <SFTRI 320> **THE STATE OF THE ART IS ON FIRE**	-	

– Light me / A+ in arson class / Rid or ride / Human torch / Ratsize / Human spine / Trouble / Masculine intuition.

		El-e-mental	Interscope
Oct 95.	(m-lp) (ELM 27LP) <92595> **HOT CHARITY**		Aug95

– Pushed / Guilt free / Poison eye / My arrow's aim / Feathered friends / Cloud over Branson / Lorna Doom / Shucks / Pity yr paws.

| Dec 95. | (cd/c)<lp> (ELM 34 CD/MC) <92596-2/-4> <Hed 54> **SCREAM, DRACULA, SCREAM!** | 40 | | Oct95 |

– Middle / Born in '69 / On a rope / Young livers / Drop out / Used / Ball lightning / Fat lip / Suit city / Heater hands / Misbeaten / Come see, come saw / Salt future / Burnt alive.

		El-e-mental	Interscope
Jan 96.	(7"/cd-s) (ELM 32 S/CD) **BORN IN '69. / CIAO PATSY**	68	-
Apr 96.	(7"/c-s) (ELM 33 S/MC) **YOUNG LIVERS / BURNING ARMY MEN**	67	-

(cd-s+=) (ELM 33CD) – Lumps.

| Sep 96. | (cd-ep) (ELM 38CD1) **ON A ROPE / ALONE / WHO NEEDS YOU / YOUNG LIVERS (Mark Radcliffe session)** | 12 | - |

(cd-ep) (ELM 38CD2) – ('A'-White Room version) / Allergic reaction / Transcendent crankiness / Suit city (Mark Radcliffe session).

(cd-ep) (ELM 38CD3) – ('A'-Ghetto box mix) / You and I / Intro – Don't Darlene (Mark Radcliffe session) / Lorna Doom (Mark Radcliffe session).

| Nov 96. | (7"ep) (SFTRI 373) **PLAYS THE MUSIC MACHINE EP** | | Oct96 |

(above on 'Sympathy For The Record Industry' / 'Kill Rock Stars' US)

| Jun 98. | (10"pic-d-ep) (ELM 47TPIC) **WHEN IN ROME (DO THE JERK). / TARZAN / TIGER FEET TONITE** | | |
| Jul 98. | (cd/c/lp) (ELM 50 CD/MC/LP) <90167> **RFTC** | 63 | | Jun98 |

– Eye on you (with HOLLY GOLIGHTLY) / Break it up / I know / Panic scam / Made for you / Lipstick / You gotta move / Your touch / Let's get busy / Dick on a dog / Back in the state / When in Rome / Run kid run. *(also ltd-cd; ELM 50CDQ)*

| Aug 98. | (10") (ELM 48TEN) **LIPSTICK. / HOT HEART** | 64 | |

(cd-s) (ELM 48CDS1) – ('A'side) / Heads are gonna roll / Cheetah.

(cd-s) (ELM 48CD2) – ('A'side) / When in Rome (do the jerk) / Stranglehold.

— In Oct'98, the group were on a split 7" with JULIAN Y SUS HERMANOIS for 'Vinyl Communication' (VC 76)

| Nov 98. | (7") (ELM 49S) **BREAK IT UP. / TURKISH REVENGE** | | - |

(cd-s+=) (ELM 49CDS1) – Crack attack.

(cd-s) (ELM 49CDS2) – ('A'side) / U.S. Army / Raped by ape.

		Flapping Jet	Flapping Jet
Oct 99.	(m-lp) <(FJ 010)> **5 SONG EP**		

– compilations, etc. –

Dec 93. (lp/cd) *Sympathy For The Record Industry; (SFTRI 558/+CD) / Hedhunter; <Hed 023>* **ALL SYSTEMS GO**
– Live the funk / Bad song Ninja / Goodbye / Boy chucker / Jumper K. balls / Lefty / Normal carpet ride / Where are the fuckers / Slumber queen / Flip the bird / Cha cha cha / Pressure's on / Pigeon eater / (The) Paste that you love / Pure genius / Lift and love / Press darlings / Filly fill again / Chantilly face. *(cd re-iss. Dec98; same)*

Oct 99. (lp/cd) *Swami; <(SWA 2001/+CD)>* **ALL SYSTEMS GO 2**
– Tarzan / UFO x3 / Birdman / Ciao Patsy / Heads are gonna roll / Cheetah / Turkish revenge / US aim / Raged by an age / Crack party / Stranglehold / 10 forward / Call it a clue / Hot heart / I drink blood / Slow / Who needs you / Allergic reaction / You and I / Transcendent crankiness / Lose your clown / Burning army man / Ballot fire / Nobobby / Ushering in a new age of quarrel.

DRIVE LIKE JEHU

JOHN REIS – guitar / **RICK FROBERG** – vocals, guitar / **MIKE KENNEDY** – bass / **MARK TROMBINO** – drums

	not iss.	Merge
1992. (7") <MRG 023> **HAND OVER FIST. / BULLET TRAIN TO VEGAS**	–	□

	Headhunter	Headhunter
Jan 93. (lp/cd) <(HED/+CD 008)> **DRIVE LIKE JEHU**	□	Dec91

– Caress / Spikes to you / Step on chameleon / O pencil sharp / Atom Jack / If it kills you / Good luck in jail / Turn it off / Future home of Stucco monstrosity.

	El-e-mental	Cargo
May 94. (cd) <(ELM 22CD) /EFA 17690-2> **YANK CRIME**	□	□

– Here come the Rome plows / Do you compute / Golden brown / Luau / Super unison / New intro / New math / Human interest / Sinews. *(lp-iss.Aug94 on 'Cargo'; HED 037)*

ROCKET FROM THE TOMBS
(see under ⇒ PERE UBU)

ROCKETS (see under ⇒ CRAZY HORSE)

ROCKPILE (see under ⇒ EDMUNDS, Dave)

Nile RODGERS (see under ⇒ CHIC)

Paul RODGERS

Born: 17 Dec'49, Middlesborough, England. The grits 'n' honey voice behind both FREE and BAD COMPANY, RODGERS struck out on a solo career following the demise of the latter band in the early 80's. Recorded at RODGERS' home studio with the singer laying down all the instrumental parts himself, 'CUT LOOSE' (1983) was largely unremarkable fare from a man eminently capable of R&B/hard-rock genuis. His next project, The FIRM (a collaboration with JIMMY PAGE and ROBERT PLANT), also failed to do the business over the course of two average albums in the mid-80's. Declining to join a reformed BAD COMPANY in 1986, RODGERS eventually resurfaced in the early 90's as one half of The LAW with ex-WHO drummer KENNY JONES. Releasing a sole lacklustre album, 'THE LAW' (1991), the duo certainly didn't rewrite any rules and a general lack of interest saw the group locked away for good. RODGERS' emerged again a couple of years later with the star-studded 'MUDDY WATERS BLUES: A TRIBUTE TO MUDDY WATERS' (1993). As the title suggested, the record was an interpretation of RODGERS' fave blues numbers featuring the likes of JEFF BECK, STEVE MILLER, NEAL SCHON and BUDDY GUY to name but a few. His most consistent effort since the BAD COMPANY days, the album surprisingly made the UK Top 10. The following year saw the release of a live EP featuring a trio of Hendrix covers, namely 'PURPLE HAZE', 'STONE FREE' and 'LITTLE WING'. A set of original material, 'NOW' (1997), eventually appeared in 1997 on the 'S.P.V.' label, released around the same time as a live set running through old FREE and BAD COMPANY classics.

Album rating: CUT LOOSE (*4) / MUDDY WATERS BLUES (*7) / NOW (*5) / LIVE (*4) / the Law: THE LAW (*4)

PAUL RODGERS – vocals, instruments

	Atlantic	Atlantic
Nov 83. (lp/c) (780 121-1/-4) <80121> **CUT LOOSE**	□	□

– Fragile / Cut loose / Live in peace / Sweet sensation / Rising sun / Boogie mama / Morning after the night before / Northwinds / Superstar woman / Talking guitar blues.

Nov 83. (7") (A 9749) <89749> **CUT LOOSE. / TALKING GUITAR BLUES**	□	□
Jan 84. (7") <89709> **MORNING AFTER THE NIGHT BEFORE. / NORTHWINDS**	–	□

—— Early in 1985, he joined The FIRM (see under ⇒ LED ZEPPELIN). In the 90's he returned to the studio.

The LAW

RODGERS wrote some material w/ **BRYAN ADAMS / DAVID GILMORE / CHRIS REA**. Covered: MISS YOU IN A HEARTBEAT (Def Leppard).

RODGERS – vocals / **KENNY JONES** – drums (ex-WHO, ex-SMALL FACES)

	Atlantic	Atco
Mar 91. (7") **LAYING DOWN THE LAW. / TOUGH LOVE**	□	□

(12"+=/cd-s+=) – That's when you fall.

Apr 91. (cd/c/lp) <(7567 82195-2/-4/-1)> **THE LAW**	61	□

– For a little ride / Miss you in a heartbeat / Stone cold / Come save me (Julianne) / Laying down the law / Nature of the beast / Stone / Anything for you / Best of my love / Tough love / Missing you bad girl.

Paul RODGERS

(solo) with **JASON BONHAM** – drums / **PINO PALLADINO** – bass / **IAN HATTON** – rhythm guitar / plus **JIMMIE WOOD** – harmonica / **RONNIE FOSTER** – organ / **MARK T.WILLIAMS** – bass drum and guest lead guitarists on each of the 15 tracks; **BUDDY GUY / TREVOR RABIN / BRIAN SETZER / JEFF BECK / JEFF BECK / STEVE MILLER / TREVOR RABIN / DAVID GILMOUR / SLASH / GARY MOORE / BRIAN MAY / JEFF BECK / NEAL SCHON / RICHIE SAMBORA / NEAL SCHON**

	Victory	Victory
Jun 93. (cd/c) (828424-2/-4) <480013> **MUDDY WATERS BLUES: A TRIBUTE TO MUDDY WATERS**	9	91

– Muddy Water blues (acoustic version) / Louisiana blues / I can't be satisfied / Rollin' stone / Good morning little school girl (part 1) / I'm your hoochie coochie man / She's alright / Standing around crying / The hunter / She moves me / I'm ready / I just want to make love to you / Born under a bad sign / Good morning little school girl (part 2) / Muddy Water blues (electric version). *(free-cd 'THE HISTORY'; re-recordings of FREE and BAD COMPANY hits)* – All right now / Wishing well / Fire & water / Bad company / Feel like making love / Can't get enough.

—— Album 'MUDDY WATER BLUES' songs stemming from MUDDY WATERS, RODGERS, SONNY BOY WILLIAMSON, WILLIE DIXON or BOOKER T. JONES.

Jan 94. (7"ep/c-ep/cd-ep) (ROG ER/MC/CD 1) **MUDDY WATER BLUES / PURPLE HAZE (live) / STONE FREE (live) / LITTLE WING (live)**	45	–

(cd-ep) (ROCDP 1) – ('A'side) / The hunter (live) / Stone free (live) / Nature of the beast (live) .

—— More covers; PURPLE HAZE + STONE FREE + LITTLE WING (Jimi Hendrix).

	S.P.V.	S.P.V.
Jan 97. (cd-s) (<SPV 0554462-3>) **SOUL OF LOVE / ALL RIGHT NOW (live) / FEEL LIKE MAKIN' LOVE / SOUL OF LOVE (version)**	□	□
Feb 97. (cd) (SPV 085-4466-2) **NOW**	30	□

– Soul of love / Overloaded / Heart of fire / Saving grace / All I want is you / Chasing shadows / Nights like this / Shadow of the sun / Holding back the storm.

Mar 97. (cd) (SPV 085-4467-2) **LIVE (The Loreley Tapes)**	□	□

– Little bit of love / Be my friend / Feel like making love / Louisiana blues / Muddy Waters blues / Rolling stone / I'm ready / Wishing well / Mister Big / Fire and water / The hunter / Cant get enough / Alright now.

ROLLING STONES

Formed: London, England ... mid-1962 by JONES, JAGGER and RICHARDS. After a residence at Richmond blues club, 'The Crawdaddy', the band were signed by A&R man DICK ROWE to 'Decca', who had just rejected The BEATLES. Their debut single, a cover of CHUCK BERRY's 'COME ON', almost hit top 20, and the band were well on the way to crystallising their image as the original bad boys of rock. Hairier, uglier and more rebellious (publicly anyway) than The BEATLES, manager/hustler extrordinaire, ANDREW LOOG OLDHAM, wasted no time in playing the outlaw card for all it was worth. Working the press like a true pro, he elicited a string of publicity-grabbing headlines, culminating with the infamous "Would you let your daughter marry a ROLLING STONE?" Which, of course, made the band even more desirable in the eyes of those self-same teenage daughters. As the 'STONES snaked their way across the country the following year on a joint headlining tour with The RONETTES, what had begun as hysteria and isolated fisticuffs had escalated into full-on rioting with promoters quaking in their boots. That summer, they scored their first No.1 single with a cover of BUDDY HOLLY's 'NOT FADE AWAY', now beginning to usurp The BEATLES as the UK's premier knicker-wetting phenomenon. As for the music, the early 'STONES' sound was a fairly derivative take on black America yet it possessed a primal, sexual intensity that made their Merseyside rivals sound like choirboys. Rhythm was everything and in full flight WATT'S fluid, unswerving backbeat locked in perfect unholy union with WYMAN'S bass and RICHARDS' demonic guitar grooves. JONES, meanwhile, casually lashed out searing slide guitar and JAGGER, the blueprint for decades of wannabes to come, pouted, preened and snarled in equal measure. The first three albums, 'THE ROLLING STONES' (1964), '12 x 5' (1964) and 'THE ROLLING STONES NOW' (1965) were made up largely of R&B and blues covers, the latter marginally topping the other two with the most focused number JAGGERS/RICHARDS had come up with by that point, 'HEART OF STONE' and an electrifying reading of WILLIE DIXON's 'LITTLE RED ROOSTER'. Apparently revealed to KEITH RICHARDS in a dream, one of the most recognisable and famous riffs in rock history formed the core of The 'STONES' breakthrough hit, '(I CAN'T GET NO) SATISFACTION'. Despite the controversial lyrics which earned a boycott from US radio and further enhanced their reputation as leering malcontents, the record hit the top of the charts on both sides of the Atlantic during the summer of '65. This opened the floodgates for a wave of No.1 singles: 'GET OFF MY CLOUD' (1965), '19TH NERVOUS BREAKDOWN' (1966) and 'PAINT IT BLACK' (1966), the latter a brooding psychedelic-tinged stampede that featured some nifty sitar playing by a cross-legged BRIAN JONES. 'AFTERMATH' (1966) was a huge step forward with JONES adding exotic touches in line with his growing admiration for the JouJouka musicians of Morocco. Meanwhile, the JAGGER/RICHARDS songwriting partnership was blossoming, tackling social issues with trenchant ease; 'MOTHER'S LITTLE HELPER' as well as the usual sexual politics; 'UNDER MY THUMB'. It was around this time that JAGGER began assuming the multitude of different masks he would use onstage and off, as one journalist aptly pointed out; "MICK JAGGER was an interesting bunch of guys". His cocky, chameleon-like affectations stood in stark contrast to KEITH RICHARDS' sullen, slightly aloof distance but it was exactly this homo-erotic chemistry that fuelled The STONES and fashioned the decadent legend of 'The Glimmer Twins' as they'd come to be known in the 70's. 'BETWEEN THE BUTTONS' (1967) contained another salacious rebel anthem in 'LET'S SPEND THE NIGHT TOGETHER' alongside the ebb-and-flow wistfulness of 'RUBY TUESDAY'. By this time, though, the powers that be had had just about enough of these unkempt subversives and their dubious morals. The infamous Redlands drug bust in February '67 was probably the most famous of all The 'STONES' run-in's with the law, although by no means the most serious and in the end, RICHARDS' conviction was quashed on appeal while JAGGER was given a year's probation. Yet only a few days later, MICK talked defiantly to the press about revolution and The 'STONES recorded their acerbic reply to The BEATLES' 'ALL YOU NEED IS LOVE'. With LENNON and McCARTNEY collaborating, the band cut 'WE LOVE YOU'. Allegedly written by JAGGER in jail as a tribute to the fans who had stood by him, it came out sounding like a deliciously snide riposte to the authorities, complete with the sounds of heavy footsteps and a cell door clanging shut. While they were successful with occasional ventures into warped psychedelia, The 'STONES remained first and foremost a rock'n'roll band and their attempt at a psychedelic concept album, 'THEIR SATANIC MAJESTIES REQUEST' (1967), was always destined to sound half-baked at best. The stellar '2000 LIGHT YEARS FROM HOME' and 'SHE'S A RAINBOW' saved the album from being a complete failure although it didn't even come close to rivalling 'SGT. PEPPERS'. A more honest response to The BEATLES' magnum opus, 'BEGGARS BANQUET' (1968) was the first album in a staggering burst of creativity that would see The ROLLING STONES release four of the best albums in the history of rock over a five-year period. Preceded by the much needed No.1 hit, 'JUMPIN' JACK FLASH', (which marked the beginning of a fruitful partnership with JIMMY MILLER), the album saw the band realign themselves with roots music to startling effect. At this point The 'STONES were not simply imitating their heroes of the American South, they had made the music truly their own. Inspired by Mikhail Bulgakov's novel, 'The Master And Margarita', 'SYMPATHY FOR THE DEVIL' was pure malevolent genius, MICK casting himself gleefully in the role of Beelzebub over an irresistible voodoo funk. Similarly controversial were the topical 'STREET FIGHTIN' MAN' and the leering 'STRAY CAT BLUES' which centred on a rock star and an obliging 15-year-old groupie, the grinding rhythm oozing illicit sex. These subversive broadsides were alternated with threadbare country blues numbers that, save for JAGGER's barrow boy via Louisiana vocals, sounded so authentic you could almost smell the corn bread. During sessions for the follow-up, 'LET IT BLEED' (1969), BRIAN JONES had left the band and was found dead in controversial circumstances a month later on the 3rd of July, 1969, at his Pooh Corner home. He had never really recovered from having control of the band wrestled from him and his unstable personality buckled under a frightening drug intake. Preceded by The 'STONES' last No.1 single, 'HONKY TONK WOMAN', 'LET IT BLEED' was eventually released the same fateful month as the Altamont disaster and possessed a vivid essence of brooding portent, most obvious on the opening track 'GIMME SHELTER', with its thundering rhythm and near-hysterical urging. 'MIDNIGHT RAMBLER' was equally chilling while RICHARDS made his vocal debut on 'YOU GOT THE SILVER', his voice a ragged sliver of emotive simplicity that stood in direct contrast to MICK's affectations. Closing with the aching desolation of 'YOU CAN'T ALWAYS GET WHAT YOU WANT', the album was another example, if one was needed at all, that The 'STONES preferred harsh realism to dopey idealism and had never really embraced the hippy philosophy. Perhaps it was fitting then, that The 'STONES were, quite literally, centre stage when that hopeful euphoria of the 60's finally came to an end during the last bitterly cold days of 1969. As the band played a free gig at a barren speedway track in Altamont, Northern California, poor organisation and delays contributed to bad vibes which were exacerbated by brutal, acid-crazed Hells Angels. Supposedly acting in a security capacity, one of their number ended up stabbing an innocent fan to death while many others were beaten up. The 'STONES' ferried out by helicopter in fear of their lives. By the release of 'STICKY FINGERS' (1971), the dark potency of the previous albums had gone, save for a few tracks, notably MARIANNE FAITHFULL's bleakly beautiful 'SISTER MORPHINE'. The band had pushed things to the limit and from here on in they retreated. Nevertheless, the best was yet to come, and 'STICKY FINGERS' kept up the momentum. 'DEAD FLOWERS' was a rollicking country hoedown shot through with typically twisted humour while JAGGER assumed his inimitable Delta Bluesman mantle for the inspired cover of MISSISSIPPI FRED McDOWELL's 'YOU GOT TO MOVE'. Elsewhere, tracks like 'BROWN SUGAR' and 'BITCH' were quintessential 'STONES, revelling in their own mythology. This was also the first studio material to feature ex-BLUESBREAKER, MICK TAYLOR, who'd joined in '69 as a replacement for BRIAN JONES. Although his distinctive style was an integral part of the band's early 70's sound, he'd later leave amid growing dissatisfaction with the JAGGER/RICHARDS domination of the band. 'EXILE ON MAIN STREET' (1972) remains one of the best double

albums ever released and quite possibly staking a claim for the best album, bar none, ever released. Big claims, yet this was the pure, unadulterated essence of that cliched thing called rock'n'roll, no cobwebbed history lecture, but a living, breathing, sweating justification for white boys playing the blues. Recorded in a dank, humid basement in RICHARDS' villa in the South of France, the production is so murky that JAGGER's vocals verge on the indecipherable at points and the whole thing seems continually on the brink of collapse. Yet this only serves to enhance the unerringly strong material and elegantly wasted mood of the record. From the aural massage of 'TUMBLING DICE' to the raggedy-assed beauty of 'LOVING CUP', the down-home gospel of 'SHINE A LIGHT' to KEITH RICHARDS' off-the-cuff anthem 'HAPPY', The 'STONES, or rock music, for that matter, would never sound so spiritually debauched again. In comparison, 'GOAT'S HEAD SOUP' (1973) was inevitably a let-down, the band sounding tired and listless, although JAGGER at least sounded half-convincing on his tender ballad, 'ANGIE'. MICK TAYLOR's last album, 'IT'S ONLY ROCK'N'ROLL' (1974) was 'STONES by numbers and didn't bode well for the coming decade. 'BLACK AND BLUE' (1976) saw ex-FACE, RON WOOD brought into the fold and a half hearted attempt at reggae stylings. By this point, the band were a massive live draw but often sloppy on stage due in no small part to the band's colossal drug intake. It came as little surprise to even the most casual 'STONES observer when, in February 1977, RICHARDS was busted in Toronto holding serious amounts of Class A. Amid alleged rumours of a huge pay-off, KEITH was eventually let off fairly leniently and, yet again, the 'STONES lived to fight another day, another 20 years in fact, and counting. Too long some might say, as 'SOME GIRLS' (1978) was the last 'STONES album that actually sounded like they meant it. Although the disco experimentalism of 'MISS YOU' was rather lukewarm, the album contained the last great JAGGER/RICHARDS song, 'BEAST OF BURDEN'. 'EMOTIONAL RESCUE' (1980) was dull and formulaic while 1981's 'TATTOO YOU' redeemed itself slightly with a rawer sound and the sprightly, if cliched hit 'START ME UP'. THE ROLLING STONES were, by now, one of the biggest acts on the stadium rock circuit, particularly in the U.S.A. and although their studio output was stagnating, the band's live show was still worth the admission price, especially now that KEITH had cleaned up his act and could get through a whole set without falling asleep on stage. 'UNDERCOVER' (1984) was a typically ill-advised 80's attempt at experimentation and as such, an unmitigated disaster, while 'DIRTY WORK' (1986) was only marginally less tedious. After a brief lull, the band returned with 1989's 'STEEL WHEELS' and while the single 'MIXED EMOTIONS' was their best in a decade, the album favoured glossy production and slick professionalism over content. With a move to 'Virgin' amid million-pound deals, 'VOODOO LOUNGE' (1994) was touted as a dangerous return to form, although it was their first as a quartet as WYMAN departed. In the event, it was as flaccid and cliched as anything the band had done. The pared-down, semi-acoustic 'STRIPPED' (1995) was listenable, although as the prospect of a creative rebirth grows ever more remote, maybe one more album would suffice. This came in the shape of 1997's 'BRIDGES TO BABYLON', another commercial success that spawned a few minor hits, the near 60-year-olds still drawing the crowds (not in Britain though as the taxman became their enemy once again). • **Trivia:** JAGGER's relationship with singer MARIANNE FAITHFULL ended in 1970, when he met Nicaraguan model, Bianca Rosa Perez-Mora and later married her on the 12th of May '71. They split in 1978, probably over Marsha Hunt's allegations that MICK was the father of her child. After a long relationship with Jerry Hall (formerly Bryan Ferry's girlfriend), he later married her on the 21st November '90. JAGGER's film work included:- NED KELLY (1969) / PERFORMANCE (1970) / FITZCARALDO (1981, but cutting-room floor only!). WYMAN's marriage (since 1959) ended abruptly in the mid-80's, after his 2-year relationship with 16-year-old, Mandy Smith, was revealed in The News Of The World. They married relatively quietly on the 2nd of June '89, but controversially divorced in 1992, with the now famous Mandy allegedly suing for half a million. • **Songwriters:** JAGGER-RICHARDS mostly except covers; NOT FADE AWAY (Buddy Holly) / ROUTE 66 (Nelson Riddle Orchestra) / I JUST WANT TO MAKE LOVE TO YOU (Willie Dixon) / HONEST I DO (Jimmy Reed) / I NEED YOU BABY (Bo Diddley) / POISON IVY (Coasters) / NOW I'VE GOT A WITNESS . . . (Gene Pitney) / LITTLE BY LITTLE (Pitney / Spector) / COME ON + CAROL + YOU CAN'T CATCH ME + TALKIN' 'BOUT YOU + LITTLE QUEENIE + AROUND AND AROUND + BYE BYE JOHNNY (Chuck Berry) / CAN I GET A WITNESS (Holland-Dozier-Holland) / MONEY (Barrett Strong) / I WANNA BE YOUR MAN (Beatles) / LITTLE BY LITTLE (w/Spector) / YOU CAN MAKE IT IF YOU TRY (Gene Allison; hit) / WALKING THE DOG (Rufus Thomas) / SUSIE Q (Dale Hawkins) / UNDER THE BOARDWALK (Drifters) / I CAN'T BE SATISFIED + MANNISH BOY (Muddy Waters) / DOWN HOME GIRL (Jerry Butler) / IT'S ALL OVER NOW (Valentinos) / LITTLE RED ROOSTER (Willie Dixon) / PAIN IN MY HEART + MY GIRL (Otis Redding) / EVERYBODY NEEDS SOMEBODY TO LOVE (Solomon Burke) / DOWN THE ROAD APIECE (?. Raye) / TIME IS ON MY SIDE (Irma Thomas) / SHE SAID YEAH (Jackson/Christy) / I DON'T KNOW WHY (Stevie Wonder) / MERCY, MERCY (Don Covay) / GOOD TIMES (Sam Cooke) / CRY TO ME (Betty Harris; hit) / HITCH HIKE (Marvin Gaye) / THAT'S HOW STRONG MY LOVE IS (?. Jamison) / OH BABY . . . (?. Ozen) / PRODIGAL SON (Robert Wilkins) / YOU BETTER MOVE ON (Arthur Alexander) / LOVE IN VAIN (Robert Johnson; trad.) / AIN'T TOO PROUD TO BEG + JUST MY IMAGINATION (Temptations) / I'M A KING BEE + SHAKE YOUR HIPS (Slim Harpo) / CHERRY OH BABY (? reggae) / GOING TO A GO-GO (Smokey Robinson / Miracles) /

HARLEM SHUFFLE (Bob & Earl) / TWENTY FLIGHT ROCK (Eddie Cochran) / CORRINA (Taj Mahal) / etc. KEITH RICHARDS solo wrote with JORDAN. RONNIE WOOD covered TESTIFY (Parliaments) / AM I GROOVIN' YOU (Bert Berns) / SEVEN DAYS (Bob Dylan) / SHOW ME (J. Williams).

Album rating (UK): THE ROLLING STONES (*8) / THE ROLLING STONES NO.2 (*8) / OUT OF OUR HEADS (*7) / AFTERMATH (*7) / BIG HITS (HIGH TIDE AND GREEN GRASS) compilation (*8) / GOT LIVE IF YOU WANT IT (*5) / BETWEEN THE BUTTONS (*7) / THEIR SATANIC MAJESTIES REQUEST (*5) / BEGGARS BANQUET (*9) / THROUGH THE PAST, DARKLY (BIG HITS VOL.2) compilation (*8) / LET IT BLEED (*9) / GET YER YA-YA'S OUT! (*7) / STONE AGE exploitation (*7) / STICKY FINGERS (*8) / GIMME SHELTER exploitation (*6) / HOT ROCKS 1964-1971 compilation US (*10) / MILESTONES exploitation (*6) / EXILE ON MAIN ST. (*10) / ROCK 'N' ROLLING STONES exploitation (*5) / GOAT'S HEAD SOUP (*6) / IT'S ONLY ROCK'N'ROLL (*6) / MADE IN THE SHADE compilation (*7) / METAMORPHOSIS exploitation (*5) / ROLLED GOLD - THE VERY BEST OF THE ROLLING STONES compilation (*10) / BLACK AND BLUE (*6) / LOVE YOU LIVE (*5) / GET STONED exploitation (*7) / SOME GIRLS (*7) / EMOTIONAL RESCUE (*5) / TATTOO YOU (*6) / STILL LIFE (AMERICAN CONCERTS 1981) (*3) / STORY OF THE STONES exploitation (*6) / UNDERCOVER (*5) / REWIND 1971-1984 (THE BEST OF THE ROLLING STONES) compilation (*7) / DIRTY WORK (*6) / STEEL WHEELS (*6) / FLASHPOINT (*4) / JUMP BACK - THE BEST OF THE ROLLING STONES 1971-1993 compilation (*8) / VOODOO LOUNGE (*8) / STRIPPED (*6) / BRIDGES TO BABYLON (*6) / Mick Jagger: SHE'S THE BOSS (*5) / PRIMITIVE COOL (*4) / WANDERING SPIRIT (*6) / Keith Richards: TALK IS CHEAP (*6) / ...LIVE AT THE HOLLYWOOD PALLADIUM (*5) / MAIN OFFENDER (*5)

MICK JAGGER (b.26 Jul'43, Dartford, Kent, England) – vocals, harmonica / **KEITH RICHARDS** (b.18 Dec'43, Dartford) – rhythm guitar / **BRIAN JONES** (b.28 Feb'43, Cheltenham, England) – lead guitar / **CHARLIE WATTS** (b. 2 Jun'41, Islington, London) – drums (ex-BLUES INC.) / **BILL WYMAN** (b.WILLIAM PERKS, 24 Oct'36, Lewisham, London) – bass repl. DICK TAYLOR who later joined PRETTY THINGS / **IAN STEWART** – piano (was 6th member, pushed to the background by manager)

			Decca	London
Jun 63.	(7") (F 11675) **COME ON. / I WANT TO BE LOVED**		21	-
Nov 63.	(7") (F 11764) <9641> **I WANNA BE YOUR MAN. / STONED**		12	- Jan64
Feb 64.	(7") (F 11845) **NOT FADE AWAY. / LITTLE BY LITTLE**		3	-
Mar 64.	(7") <9657> **NOT FADE AWAY. / I WANNA BE YOUR MAN**		-	48
Apr 64.	(lp) (LK 4605) <375> **THE ROLLING STONES** (US-title 'ENGLAND'S NEWEST HITMAKERS – THE ROLLING STONES')		1	11 Jun64

– (Get your kicks on) Route 66 / I just want to make love to you / Honest I do / I need you baby (Mona) / Now I've got a witness (like uncle Phil and uncle Gene) / Little by little / I'm a king bee / Carol / Tell me (you're coming back) / Can I get a witness / You can make it if you try / Walking the dog. (US) – Not fade away. / Mona (re-iss. Jul84 lp/c; LKD/KSDC 4605) (cd-ss.1985 on 'London'; 820 047-2) (re-iss. Jun95 on 'London' cd/c/lp; 844460-2/-4/-1)

Jun 64.	(7") (F 11934) <9687> **IT'S ALL OVER NOW. / GOOD TIMES, BAD TIMES**		1	26 Aug64
Jul 64.	(7") <9682> **TELL ME (YOU'RE COMING BACK). / I JUST WANT TO MAKE LOVE TO YOU**		-	24
Oct 64.	(7") <9708> **TIME IS ON MY SIDE. / CONGRATULATIONS**		-	6
Nov 64.	(7") (F 12014) **LITTLE RED ROOSTER. / OFF THE HOOK**		1	-
Nov 64.	(lp) <402> **12 x 5**		-	3

– Around and around / Confessin' the blues / Empty heart / Time is on my side / Good times bad times / It's all over now / 2120 South Michigan Avenue / Under the boardwalk / Congratulations / Grown up wrong / If you need me / Susie Q. (UK-iss.Aug88 lp/c; LKD/KDKHAC 5335) (cd-iss. Nov84 on 'London'; 820 048-2) (re-iss. Jun95; 844461-2/-4/-1)

| Jan 65. | (lp) (LK 4661) **THE ROLLING STONES No.2** | | 1 | - |

– Everybody needs somebody to love / Down home girl / You can't catch me / Time is on my side / What a shame / Grown up wrong / Down the road apiece / Under the boardwalk / I can't be satisfied / Pain in my heart / Off the hook / Susie Q. (re-iss. 1986;)

Jan 65.	(7") <9725> **HEART OF STONE. / WHAT A SHAME**		-	19
Feb 65.	(7") (F 12104) <9741> **THE LAST TIME. / PLAY WITH FIRE**		1	9 / 96 Mar65
Mar 65.	(lp) <420> **THE ROLLING STONES NOW!**		-	5

– Everybody needs somebody to love / You can't catch me / Heart of stone / I need you baby (Mona) / Down the road apiece / Off the hook / Pain in my heart / Oh baby (we got a good thing goin') / Little red rooster / Surprise surprise. (UK-iss.Aug88 cd; 820133-2) (re-iss. Jun95 on 'London' cd/c/lp; 844462-2/-4/-1)

May 65.	(7") (F 12220) **(I CAN'T GET NO) SATISFACTION. / THE SPIDER AND THE FLY**		1	-
Jun 65.	(7") <9766> **(I CAN'T GET NO) SATISFACTION. / THE UNDER ASSISTANT WEST COAST MAN**		-	1
Sep 65.	(lp; mono/stereo) (LK/SKL 473) <429> **OUT OF OUR HEADS**		2	1 Aug 65

– She said yeah * / Mercy, mercy / Hitch hike / That's how strong my love is / Good times / Gotta get away * / Talkin' 'bout you * / Cry to me / Oh baby (we got a good thing going) * / Heart of stone / The under assistant west coast man / I'm free. *UK tracks above * were repl. by in US* – I'm alright (live) / (I can't get no) Satisfaction / Play with fire / The spider and the fly / One more try. (re-iss. Jul84 lp/c/cd; LKD/LSLSC 5336)(820 049-2) (re-iss. Jun95 on 'London' cd/c/lp; 844463-2/-4/-1)

Sep 65.	(7") <9792> **GET OFF OF MY CLOUD. / I'M FREE**		-	1
Oct 65.	(7") (F 12263) **GET OFF OF MY CLOUD. / THE SINGER NOT THE SONG**		1	-
Nov 65.	(lp) <451> **DECEMBER'S CHILDREN (AND EVERYBODY'S)**		-	4

– She said yeah / Talkin' 'bout you / You better move on / Look what you've done / The singer not the song / Route 66 (live) / Get off of my cloud / I'm free / As tears go by / Gotta get away / Blue turns to grey / I'm movin' on (live). (UK-iss.Aug88 cd; 820 135-2) (re-iss. Jun95 on 'London' cd/c/lp; 844464-2/-4/-1)

Dec 65.	(7") <9808> **AS TEARS GO BY. / GOTTA GET AWAY**		-	6
Feb 66.	(7") (F 12331) **19th NERVOUS BREAKDOWN. / AS TEARS GO BY**		1	-
Feb 66.	(7") <9823> **19th NERVOUS BREAKDOWN. / SAD DAY**		-	2

| Apr 66. | (lp; mono/stereo)(c) (LK/SKL 4786)(KSKC 4786) <451> **AFTERMATH** | | 1 | 2 Jul66 |

– Mother's little helper / Stupid girl / Lady Jane / Under my thumb / Doncha bother me / Goin' home / Flight 505 / High and dry / Out of time / It's not easy / I am waiting / Take it or leave it / Think / What to do. (US version+=) – Paint it black. (re-iss. May85 lp/c/cd; SKLD/4786)(820 050-2) (re-iss. Jun95 on 'London' cd/c/lp; 844466-2/-4/-1)

May 66.	(7") <901> **PAINT IT BLACK. / STUPID GIRL**		-	1
May 66.	(7") (F 12395) **PAINT IT BLACK. / LONG LONG WHILE**		1	-
Jul 66.	(7") <902> **MOTHER'S LITTLE HELPER. / LADY JANE**		-	8 / 24
Sep 66.	(7") (F 12497) <903> **HAVE YOU SEEN YOUR MOTHER BABY, STANDING IN THE SHADOW?. / WHO'S DRIVING YOUR PLANE?**		5	9
Nov 66.	(lp; mono/stereo)(c) (TXL/TXS 101)(KSKC 101) <1> **BIG HITS (HIGH TIDE AND GREEN GRASS)** (compilation)		4	3 Apr 66

– Have you seen your mother baby, standing in the shadows? / Paint it black / It's all over now / The last time / Heart of stone / Not fade away / Come on / (I can't get no) Satisfaction / Get off my cloud / As tears go by / 19th nervous breakdown / Lady Jane / Time is on my side / Little red rooster. (re-iss. Jun95 on 'London' cd/c/lp; 844465-2/-4/-1)

| Dec 66. | (lp) <493> **GOT LIVE IF YOU WANT IT** (live, Royal Albert Hall) | | - | 6 |

– Under my thumb / Get off of my cloud / Lady Jane / Not fade away / I've been loving you too long (to stop now) (studio) / Fortune teller (studio) / The last time / 19th nervous breakdown / Time is on my side / I'm alright / Have you seen your mother baby, standing in the shadow? / (I can't get no) Satisfaction. (UK-iss.Aug88 cd; 820 137-2) (re-iss. Jun95 on 'London' cd/c/lp; 844467-2/-4/-1)

| Jan 67. | (7") (F 12546) <904> **LET'S SPEND THE NIGHT TOGETHER. / RUBY TUESDAY** | | 3 | 55 / 1 |
| Jan 67. | (lp; mono/stereo)(c) (LK/SKL 4852)(KSKC 4852) <499> **BETWEEN THE BUTTONS** | | 3 | 2 Feb67 |

– Yesterday's papers / My obsession / Back street girl* / Connection / She smiled sweetly / Cool, calm and collected / All sold out / Please go home* / Who's been sleeping here? / Complicated / Miss Amanda Jones / Something happened to me yesterday. (US version*; = tracks repl. by)
– Let's spend the night together / Ruby Tuesday. (cd-iss. Jul85; 820 138-2) (re-iss. Dec91 on 'UFO' with free booklet) (re-iss. Jun95 on 'London' cd/c/lp; 844468-2/-4/-1)

| Jul 67. | (lp) <509> **FLOWERS** (compilation) | | - | 3 |

(UK cd-iss. Aug88; 820 139-2) (re-iss. cd Jun95 on 'London')

Aug 67.	(7") (F 12654) <905> **WE LOVE YOU. / DANDELION**		8	50 / 14
Nov 67.	(7") <906> **SHE'S A RAINBOW. / 2,000 LIGHT YEARS FROM HOME**		-	25
Dec 67.	(lp; mono/stereo)(c) (TXL/TXS 103)(KTXC 103) <2> **THEIR SATANIC MAJESTIES REQUEST**		3	2

– Sing this all together / Citadel / In another land / 2,000 man / Sing this all together (see what happens) / She's a rainbow / The lantern / Gomper / 2,000 light years from home / On with the show. (re-iss. Feb86 lp/c/cd; 820 129-1/-4/-2) (re-iss. Jun95 on 'London' cd/c/lp; 844469-2/-4/-1)

Dec 67.	(7"; by BILL WYMAN) <907> **IN ANOTHER LAND. / THE LANTERN**		-	87
May 68.	(7") (F 12782) <908> **JUMPIN' JACK FLASH. / CHILD OF THE MOON**		1	3
Aug 68.	(7") <909> **STREET FIGHTING MAN. / NO EXPECTATIONS**		-	48
Dec 68.	(lp; mono/stereo)(c) (LK/SKL 4955)(KSKC 4955) <539> **BEGGARS BANQUET**		3	5

– Sympathy for the Devil / No expectations / Dear doctor / Parachute woman / Jigsaw puzzle / Street fighting man / Prodigal son / Stray cat blues / Factory girl / Salt of the Earth. (cd-iss. Jan83; 800 084-2) (re-iss. Jul84 lp/c; SKDL/KSKC 4955) (re-iss. Jun95 on 'London' cd/c/lp; 844471-2/-4/-1)

—— (Jun69) **MICK TAYLOR** (b.17 Jan'48, Hertfordshire, England) – lead guitar (ex-JOHN MAYALL's BLUESBREAKERS) repl. BRIAN JONES who was found dead by his girlfriend on 3 Jul'69, after a heavy drink/drugs binge.

| Jul 69. | (7") (F 12952) <910> **HONKY TONK WOMEN. / YOU CAN'T ALWAYS GET WHAT YOU WANT** | | 1 | 1 |
| Sep 69. | (lp; mono/stereo)(c) (LK/SKL 5019)(KSKC 5019) <3> **THROUGH THE PAST DARKLY (BIG HITS VOL.2)** (compilation) | | 2 | 2 |

– Jumping Jack Flash / Mother's little helper / 2,000 light years from home / Let's spend the night together / You'd better move on / Street fighting man / She's a rainbow / Ruby Tuesday / Dandelion / Sittin' on the fence / Honky tonk women. (re-iss. Jun95 on 'London' cd/c/lp; 844472-2/-4/-1)

—— (all UK singles so far were re-iss. Mar82)

| Dec 69. | (lp/c) (SLK/KSKC 5025) <4> **LET IT BLEED** | | 1 | 3 |

– Gimme shelter / Love in vain / Country honk / Live with me / Let it bleed / Midnight rambler / You got the silver / Monkey man / You can't always get what you want. (cd-iss. Feb86; 820 052-2) (re-iss. Jun95 UK+US on 'London' cd/c/lp; 844473-2/-4/-1)

—— Mid'70, MICK JAGGER finally took the starring role in the film 'Ned Kelly'.

| Sep 70. | (lp/c) (SKL/KSKC 5065) <5> **GET YER YA'S OUT** (live, New York, Nov'69) | | 1 | 6 Oct69 |

– Jumpin' Jack Flash / Carol / Stray cat blues / Love in vain / Midnight rambler / Sympathy for the Devil / Live with me / Little Queenie / Honky tonk women. (cd-iss. Aug88; 820 131-2) (re-iss. Jun95 on 'London' cd/c/lp; 844474-2/-4/-1)

—— In 1970, MICK JAGGER starred in his second feature film 'Performance'. Below single was his first solo 45 from the film.

| Nov 70. | (7"; by MICK JAGGER) (F 13067) **MEMO FROM TURNER.** / ('B'side by 'Jack Nitzsche') | | 32 | - |
| Apr 71. | (lp/c) (SKL/KSKC 5084) **STONE AGE** (compilation) | | 4 | - |

– Look what you've done / It's all over now / Confessin' the blues / One more try / As tears go by / The spider and the fly / My girl / Paint it black / If you need me / The last time / Blue turns to grey / Around and around.

			Rolling Stones	Rolling Stones
Apr 71.	(7"m) (RS 19100) **BROWN SUGAR. / BITCH / LET IT ROCK**		2	-
Apr 71.	(lp/c) (<COC/KCOC 59100>) **STICKY FINGERS**		1	1

– Brown sugar / Sway / Wild horses / Can't you hear me knocking? / You gotta move / Bitch / I got the blues / Sister Morphine / Dead flowers / Moonlight mile. *(re-iss. Nov79 on 'E.M.I.'; CUN 59100) <US re-iss. 1980; MFSL 1-060> (cd-iss. Nov86 on 'C.B.S.', CK 40488) (re-iss. Nov89 on 'CBS' UK/US lp/c/cd; 450 195-1/-4/-2) (re-iss. cd Jun94 on 'Virgin' UK+US; 7243-8-39504-2-3) (re-iss. Aug94 on 'Virgin' cd/c; CDV/TCV 2730) (lp re-iss. Nov97 on 'Virgin'; LPCENT 38)*

Date	Release	UK	US
Apr 71.	(7") <19100> **BROWN SUGAR. / BITCH**	-	1
Jun 71.	(7") <RS 19101> **WILD HORSES. / SWAY**	-	28
Apr 72.	(7") (<RS 19103>) **TUMBLING DICE. / SWEET BLACK ANGEL**	5	7
Jun 72.	(d-lp/c) (COC/KCOC 69100) <2900> **EXILE ON MAIN ST.**	1	1

– Rocks off / Rip this joint / Shake your hips / Casino boogie / Tumbling dice / Sweet Virginia / Torn and frayed / Sweet black angel / Loving cup / Happy / Turd on the run / Ventilator blues / I just want to see his face / Let it loose / All down the line / Stop breaking down / Shine a light / Soul survivor. *(re-iss. Nov79 on 'E.M.I.'; CUNSP 69100) (re-iss. Nov89 on 'CBS' lp/c/cd UK/US; 450 196-1/-4/-2) (re-iss. Aug94 on 'Virgin' cd/c; CDV/TCV 2731)*

Date	Release	UK	US
Jun 72.	(7") <19104> **HAPPY. / ALL DOWN THE LINE**	-	22
Aug 73.	(7") (RS <19105>) **ANGIE. / SILVER TRAIN**	5	1
Sep 73.	(lp/c) (<COC/KCOC 59101>) **GOAT'S HEAD SOUP**	1	1

– Dancing with Mr.D / 100 years ago / Coming down again / Doo doo doo doo doo (heartbreaker) / Angie / Silver train / Hide your love / Winter / Can you hear the music / Star star. *(re-iss. Nov79 on 'E.M.I.'; CUN 59101) (re-iss. Nov89 on 'CBS' UK/US; 450 207-1/-4/-2) (re-iss. Aug94 on 'Virgin' cd/c; CDV/TCV 2735)*

Date	Release	UK	US
Jan 74.	(7") <19109> **DOO DOO DOO DOO DOO (HEARTBREAKER). / DANCING WITH MR.D**	-	15
Jul 74.	(7") (RS 19114) <19304> **IT'S ONLY ROCK'N'ROLL. / THROUGH THE LONELY NIGHTS**	10	16
Oct 74.	(lp/c) (COC/KCOC 59103) <79101> **IT'S ONLY ROCK'N'ROLL**	2	1

– If you can't rock me / Ain't too proud to beg / It's only rock'n'roll / Till the next goodbye / Time waits for no one / Luxury / Dance little sister / If you really want to be my friend / Short and curlies / Fingerprint file. *(re-iss. Nov79 on 'E.M.I.'; CUN 59103) (re-iss. Nov89 on 'CBS' UK/US lp/c/cd; 450 202-1/-4/-2) (re-iss. Aug94 on 'Virgin' cd/c; CDV/TCV 2733)*

Date	Release	UK	US
Oct 74.	(7") (19302) **AIN'T TOO PROUD TO BEG. / DANCE LITTLE SISTER**	-	17
Jun 75.	(lp/c) (COC/KCOC 59104) <79102> **MADE IN THE SHADE** (compilation)	14	6

– Brown sugar / Tumbling dice / Happy / Dance little sister / Wild horses / Angie / Bitch / It's only rock'n'roll (but I like it) / Doo doo doo doo doo (heartbreaker) / Rip this joint.

— (Apr-Dec75) **RON WOOD** – lead guitar (ex-FACES, ex-CREATION, etc) repl. MICK TAYLOR who left Dec74 and later joined JACK BRUCE BAND

Date	Release	UK	US
Apr 76.	(7") (RS 19121) **FOOL TO CRY. / CRAZY MAMA**	6	-
Apr 76.	(7") <19304> **FOOL TO CRY. / HOT STUFF**	-	10
May 76.	(lp/c) (COC/KCOC 59106) <79104> **BLACK AND BLUE**	2	49 / 1

– Hot stuff / The hand of fate / Cherry oh baby / Memory motel / Hey Negrita / Melody / Fool to cry / Crazy mama. *(re-iss. Nov79 on 'E.M.I.'; CUN 59106) (re-iss. Nov89 on 'C.B.S.' UK/US; 450 203-1/-4/-2) (re-iss. Aug94 on 'Virgin' cd/c; CDV/TCV 2736)*

Date	Release	UK	US
Sep 77.	(d-lp/d-c) (COC/KCOC 89101) <9001> **LOVE YOU LIVE (live)**	3	5

– Fanfare for the common man / Honky tonk woman / If you can't rock me / Get off of my cloud / Happy / Hot stuff / Star star / Tumbling dice / Fingerprint file / You gotta me / You can't always get what you want / Mannish boy / Crackin' up / Little red rooster / Around and around / It's only rock'n'roll / Brown sugar / Jumpin' Jack Flash / Sympathy for the Devil. *(re-iss. Nov79 on 'E.M.I.'; CUNSP 69101) (re-iss. Nov89 on 'C.B.S.' UK/US d-lp/c/cd; 450 208-1/-4/-2) (cd re-iss. Apr98 on 'Virgin'; CDV 2857)*

Date	Release	UK	US
May 78.	(7"/ext.12"pink) (EMI/12EMI 2802) <19307> **MISS YOU. / FARAWAY EYES**	3	1
Jun 78.	(lp/c) (<CUN/TCCUN 39108>) **SOME GIRLS**	2	1

– Miss you / When the whip comes down / Just my imagination / Some girls / Lies / Far away etes / Respectable / Before they make me run / Beast of burden / Shattered. *(re-iss. Nov89 on 'C.B.S' UK/US lp/c/cd; 450 197-1/-4/-2) (re-iss. Aug94 on 'Virgin' cd/c;)*

Date	Release	UK	US
Sep 78.	(7") <19309> **BEAST OF BURDEN. / WHEN THE WHIP COMES DOWN**	-	8
Sep 78.	(7") (EMI 2861) **RESPECTABLE. / WHEN THE WHIP COMES DOWN**	23	-
Dec 78.	(7") <19310> **SHATTERED. / EVERYTHING IS TURNING TO GOLD**	-	31
Jun 80.	(7") (RSR 105) <20001> **EMOTIONAL RESCUE. / DOWN IN THE HOLE**	9	3
Jul 80.	(lp/c) (CUN/TCCUN 39111) <16015> **EMOTIONAL RESCUE**	1	1

– Dance (pt.1) / Summer romance / Send it to me / Let me go / Indian girl / Where the boys go / Down in the hole / Emotional rescue / She's so cold / All about you. *(re-iss. Nov89 on 'C.B.S.' UK/US; 450 206-1/-4/-2) (re-iss. Aug94 on 'Virgin' cd/c; CDV/TCV 2737)*

Date	Release	UK	US
Sep 80.	(7") (RSR 106) <21001> **SHE'S SO COLD. / SEND IT TO ME**	33	26
Mar 81.	(lp/c) (CUN/TCCUN 39112) <16028> **SUCKING IN THE 70'S** (compilation + new)	15	

– Shattered / Everything is turning to gold / Hot stuff / Time waits for no one / Fool to cry / Mannish boy / When the whip comes down (live) / I was a dancer (part 2) / Crazy mama / Beast of burden. *(re-iss. Nov89 on 'C.B.S.' UK/US; 450 205-1/-4/-2)*

Date	Release	UK	US
Aug 81.	(7") (RSR 108) <21003> **START ME UP. / NO USE IN CRYING**	7	2
Sep 81.	(lp/c) (CUN/TCCUN 39114) <16052> **TATTOO YOU**	2	1

– Start me up / Hang fire / Slave / Little T & A / Black limousine / Neighbours / Worried about you / Tops / Heaven / No use in crying / Waiting on a friend. *(re-iss. Nov89 on 'C.B.S.' UK/US; 450 198-1/-4/-2) (re-iss. Aug94 on 'Virgin' cd/c; CDV/TCV 2732)*

Date	Release	UK	US
Nov 81.	(7") (RSR 109) <21004> **WAITING ON A FRIEND. / LITTLE T & A**	50	13
Mar 82.	(7") (21300) **HANG FIRE. / NEIGHBORS**	-	20
Jun 82.	(7") (RSR 110) <21301> **GOING TO A GO-GO (live). / BEAST OF BURDEN (live)**	26	25
Jun 82.	(lp/pic-lp/c) (CUN/CUNP/TCCUN 39115) <39113> **STILL LIFE (AMERICAN CONCERTS 1981)**	4	5

– Under my thumb / Let's spend the night together / Shattered / Twenty flight rock / Going to a go-go / Let me go / Time is on my side / Just my imagination / Start me up / (I can't get no) Satisfaction / Take the A train / Star-spangled banner. *(re-iss. Nov89 on 'C.B.S.' UK/US lp/c/cd; 450 204-1/-4/-2) (cd re-iss. Apr98 on 'Virgin'; CDV 2856)*

Date	Release	UK	US
Sep 82.	(7") (RSR 111) <99978> **TIME IS ON MY SIDE (live). / TWENTY FLIGHT ROCK (live)**	62	
	(12"+=) (12RSR 111) – Under my thumb (live).		
Nov 83.	(7") (RSR 113) <99813> **UNDERCOVER OF THE NIGHT. / ALL THE WAY DOWN**	11	9
	(ext.12"+=) (12RSR 113) – Feel on baby (instrumental dub).		
Nov 83.	(lp/c/cd) (CUN 165436-1/-4/-2) <90120> **UNDERCOVER**	3	4

– Undercover of the night / She was hot / Tie you up / Wanna hold you / Feel on baby / Too much blood / Pretty beat up / Too tough / All the way down / It must be hell. *(re-iss. Nov89 on 'C.B.S.' UK/US; 450 200-1/-4/-2) (re-iss. Aug94 on 'Virgin' cd/c; CDV/TCV 2741)*

Date	Release	UK	US
Jan 84.	(7"/12"sha-pic-d) (RSR/+P 114) <99788> **SHE WAS HOT. / I THINK I'M GOING MAD**	42	44
Apr 84.	(7") <99724> **TOO TOUGH. / MISS YOU**	-	
Jul 84.	(lp/c/cd) (CUN 1) <90176> **REWIND 1971-1984 (THE BEST OF THE ROLLING STONES)** (compilation)	23	86

– Brown sugar / Undercover of the night / Start me up / Tumbling dice / It's only rock'n'roll (but I like it) / She's so cold / Hang fire / Miss you / Beast of burden / Fool to cry / Waiting on a friend / Angie / Emotional rescue. *(cd+= 2 extra) (re-iss. Nov89 on 'C.B.S.' UK/US; 450 199-1/-4/-2)*

— In 1984, JAGGER guested dual vocals w / MICHAEL JACKSON on The JACKSONS' 'State Of Shock'. He also recorded debut solo album 'She's The Boss', which was released 1985. Later mid'85, he appeared at LIVE AID with DAVID BOWIE duetting on (Martha & The Vandellas) song 'DANCING IN THE STREET'. When issued as a charity single, it made UK No.1 / US No.7 (see BOWIE ⇒).

— 12th Dec'85, IAN STEWART their long-serving 6th member died of a heart attack.

C.B.S.   Rolling Stones

Date	Release	UK	US
Mar 86.	(7"/7"w-poster) (A/QA 6864) <05802> **HARLEM SHUFFLE. / HAD IT WITH YOU**	13	5
	('A'-New York mix; 12"+=/12"w-poster+=) (TA/QTA 6864) – ('A'-London mix).		
Mar 86.	(lp/c/cd) (CUN/40/CD 86321) <40250> **DIRTY WORK**	4	4

– One hit (to the body) / Fight / Harlem shuffle / Hold back / Too rude / Winning ugly / Back to zero / Dirty work / Had it with you / Sleep tonight. *(re-iss. Nov89 on 'C.B.S.' UK/US; 465 953-1/-4/-2) (re-iss. Aug94 on 'Virgin' cd/c; CDV/TCV 2743)*

Date	Release	UK	US
May 86.	(7"/'A'-London mix-12") (A/TA 7160) <05906> **ONE HIT (TO THE BODY). / FIGHT**		28

— During this lull in group activity, JAGGER and RICHARDS ventured solo amidst rumours of disbandment. In 1989, they re-surfaced.

Date	Release	UK	US
Aug 89.	(7"/c-s) (655 193-7/-4) <69008> **MIXED EMOTIONS. / FANCY MAN BLUES**	36	5
	(cd-s+=) (655 193-2) – Tumbling dice / Miss you.		
	(cd-s+=) (655 214-2) – Shattered / Waiting on a friend.		
	(12"+=) (655 193-8) – ('A'-Chris Kimsey's mix).		
Sep 89.	(lp/c/cd) (465 752-1/-4/-2) <45333> **STEEL WHEELS**	2	3

– Sad sad sad / Mixed emotions / Terrifying / Hold on to your hat / Hearts for sale / Blinded by love / Rock and a hard place / Can't be seen / Almost hear you sigh / Continental drift / Break the spell / Slipping away. *(cd re-iss. Dec92;) (re-iss. Aug94 on 'Virgin' cd/c; CDV/TCV 2742)*

Date	Release	UK	US
Nov 89.	(7"/c-s) (655 422-7/-4) <73057> **ROCK AND A HARD PLACE. / COOK COOK BLUES**	63	23
	('A'dance-12"+=) (655 422-8) – ('A'-Oh-oh hard dub mix).		
	(cd-s+=) (655 448-2) – It's only rock'n'roll / Rocks off.		
	(cd-s+=) (655 448-5) – Emotional rescue / Some girls.		
	(12") (655 422-5) – ('A'-Michael Brauer mix) / ('A'side) / ('A'-bonus beats mix).		
Jun 90.	(7") <73093> **ALMOST HEAR YOU SIGH. / BREAK THE SPELL**	-	50
Jun 90.	(7"/c-s) (656 065-7/-4) **ALMOST HEAR YOU SIGH. / WISH I'D NEVER MET YOU**	31	-
	(c-s+=) (656 065-2) – Mixed emotions.		
	(cd-s+=) (656 065-5) – Miss you / Waiting on a friend.		
	(12")(cd-s) – ('A'side) / Beast of burden / Angie / Fool to cry.		
Aug 90.	(7"/c-s) (656 122-7/-4) **TERRIFYING (remix). / ROCK AND A HARD PLACE (remix)**		
	('A'-dance-12"+=) (656 122-6) – Harlem shuffle (London mix).		
	(cd-s+=) (655 122-5) – ('A'side) / Start me up / Shattered / If you can't rock me.		

Sony   Sony

Date	Release	UK	US
Mar 91.	(7"/c-s) (656 756-7/-4) <73742> **HIGHWIRE. / 2000 LIGHT YEARS FROM HOME (live)**	29	57
	(12"+=/cd-s+=) (656 756-6/-2) – Sympathy for the Devil (live) / I just want to make love to you (live).		
	(cd-s+=) (656 756-5) – Play with fire (live) / Factory girl (live).		
Apr 91.	(d-cd/cd/c/lp) (468 135-9/-2/-4/-1) <47456> **FLASHPOINT (live)**	6	16

– Start me up / Sad sad girl / Miss you / Ruby Tuesday / Tou can't always get what you want / Factory girl / Little red rooster / Paint it black / Sympathy for the Devil / Brown sugar / Jumpin' Jack Flash / (I can't get no) Satisfaction / Sexdrive (studio) / High wire (studio). *(cd+=) – Rock and a hard place / Can't be seen. (cd re-iss. Apr98 on 'Virgin'; CDV 2855)*

Date	Release	UK	US
May 91.	(7"/c-s) (656 892-7/-4) **RUBY TUESDAY (live). / PLAY WITH FIRE (live)**	59	-
	(12"+=) (656 892-6) – You can't always get what you want (live) / Rock and a hard place (live).		
	(3"cd-s+=) (656 892-1) – You can't always get what you want (live) / Undercover of the night (live).		
	(cd-s) (656 892-5) – ('A'side) / Harlem shuffle / Winning ugly London mix).		

— In Nov'91, The STONES signed to 'Virgin', and BILL WYMAN soon quit.

Virgin   Virgin

Date	Release	UK	US
Nov 93.	(d-lp/c/cd) (V/TCV/CDV 2726) **JUMP BACK: THE BEST OF THE ROLLING STONES 1971-1993** (compilation)	16	-

– Start me up / Brown sugar / Harlem shuffle / It's only rock'n'roll (but I like it) / Mixed emotions / Angie / Tumbling dice / Fool to cry / Rock and a hard place / Miss you / Hot stuff / Emotional rescue / Respectable / Beast of burden / Waiting on a friend / Wild horses / Bitch / Undercover of the night. *(re-iss. Oct94 & Jun95;)*

— WYMAN replaced by sessioners **DARRYL JONES** – bass / **CHUCK LEAVELL** – piano

Date	Release	UK	US
Jul 94.	(7"/c-s) (VS/+C 1503) <38446> **LOVE IS STRONG. / THE STORM**	14	91

(cd-s+=) *(VSCDT 1503)* – So young / ('A'-Bob Clearmount mix).
(cd-s) *(VSCDX 1503)* – ('A'-Teddy Riley mixes; 5 mixes + other).

Jul 94. (cd/c/d-lp) *(8397821-2/-4/1)* *<39782>* **VOODOO LOUNGE**   `1` `2`
– Love is strong / You got me rocking / Sparks will fly / The worst / New faces / Moon is up / Out of tears / I go wild / Brand new car / Sweethearts together / Suck on the jugular / Blinded by rainbows / Baby break it down / Thru and thru.
(cd-rom-iss.Jun95; VMED 2)

Oct 94. (7"/c-s) *(VS/+C 1518)* **YOU GOT ME ROCKING. / JUMP ON TOP OF ME**   `23`
(cd-s+=) *(VSCDG 1518)* – ('A'-Perfecto mix) / ('A'-sexy dub mix).
(12") *(VST 1518)* – ('A'-Perfecto mix) / ('A'-sexy dub) / ('A'-trance).

Dec 94. (7"/c-s) *(VS/+C 1524)* *<38459>* **OUT OF TEARS. / I'M GONNA DRIVE**   `38` `60` Oct94
(cd-s+=/s-cd-s+=) *(VSCD T/X 1524)* – Sparks will fly / ('A'-Bob Clearmountain remix).

Jul 95. (7"/c-s) *(VSP/VSC 1539)* **I GO WILD. / ('A'-Scott Litt remix)**   `29` `–`
(cd-s+=) *(VSCDX 1539)* – ('A'version) / ('A'-Luis Resto straight vocal mix).

Nov 95. (c-s) *(VSC 1562)* **LIKE A ROLLING STONE / BLACK LIMOUSINE / ALL DOWN THE LINE**   `12` `–`
(cd-s+=) *(VSCDT 1562)* – ('A'edit).

Nov 95. (cd/c/d-lp) *(CD/TC+/V 2801)* *<41040>* **STRIPPED (live)**   `9` `9`
– Street fighting man / Like a rolling stone / Not fade away / Shine a light / The spider and the fly / I'm free / Wild horses / Let it bleed / Dead flowers / Slipping away / Angie / Love in vain / Sweet Virginia / Little baby.

Sep 97. (7"pic-d/c-s) *(VS/+C 1653)* **ANYONE SEEN MY BABY? / ('A'-Soul Solution remix)**   `22`
(12"+=/cd-s+=) *(VSCDT 1653)* – ('A'-Armand's Rolling Steelo).

Oct 97. (cd/c) *(CD/TC+/V 2840)* **BRIDGES TO BABYLON**   `6` `3`
– Flip the switch / Anybody seen my baby? / Low down / Already over me / Gunface / You don't have to mean it / Out of control / Saint of me / Might as well get juiced / Always suffering / Too tight / Thief in the night / How can I stop.

Jan 98. (7"pic-d) *(VSY 1667)* *<38626>* **SAINT OF ME. / ANYWAY YOU LOOK AT IT**   `26` `94` Feb98
(cd-s+=) *(VSCDX 1667)* – ('A'-Deep Dish grunge garage remix).
(cd-s) *(VSCDT 1667)* – Gimme shelter (live) / Anybody seen my baby? (Phil Jones remix) / ('A'-Deep Dish grunge garage remix).
(d12"+=) *(VSTX 1667)* – ('A'mixes incl. Armand's Rolling Steelo mix of 'B'side).
(d12"+=) *(VSTDT 1667)* – ('A'mixes; Deep Dish & Garage).

Aug 98. (7"pic-d) *(VSY 1700)* **OUT OF CONTROL. / ('A'-In Hand With Fluke mix)**   `51` `–`
(cd-s+=) *(VSCDT 1700)* – ('A'-In hand with Fluke instrumental).
(pic-cd-s) *(VSCDX 1700)* – ('A'-Saber final mix) / ('A'-Bi-Polar At The Controls mix) / ('A'-Bi-Polar's Fat Controller mix).

—— next featured guests, DAVE MATTHEWS and TAJ MAHAL

Nov 98. (cd/c/lp) *(CD/TC+/V 2880)* *<46740>* **NO SECURITY (live 1997)**   `67` `34`
– (intro) / You got me rocking / Gimme shelter / Flip the switch / Memory hotel / Corinna / Saint of me / Waiting on a friend / Sister morphine / Live with me / Respectable / Thief in the night / The last time / Out of control.

—— In Dec'99, a VARIOUS ARTISTS version of 'IT'S ONLY ROCK'N'ROLL' made the UK Top 20

– compilations, etc. –

—— Below releases issued on 'Decca' UK/ 'Abkco' US unless mentioned

Jan 64. (7"ep) *(DFE 8560)* **THE ROLLING STONES**   `–`
– Bye bye Johnny / Money / You better move on / Poison Ivy. *(re-iss. Mar82)* *(12"ep-iss.Dec83)*

Aug 64. (7"ep) *(DFE 8590)* **5 X 5**   `–`
– If you need me / Empty heart / 2120 South Michegan Avenue / Confessin' the blues / Around and around. *(re-iss. Mar82)* *(12"ep-iss.Dec83)*

Jun 65. (7"ep) *(DFE 8620)* **GOT LIVE IF YOU WANT IT! (live)**   `–`
– We want the Stones / Everybody needs somebody to love / Pain in my heart / Route 66 / I'm moving on / I'm alright. *(re-iss. Mar82)* *(12"ep-iss.Dec83)*

Jul 71. (7"m) *(F 13195)* **STREET FIGHTING MAN. / SURPRISE SURPRISE / EVERYBODY NEEDS SOMEBODY TO LOVE**   `21` `–`

Aug 71. (lp/c) *(SLK/KSKC 5101)* **GIMME SHELTER**   `19` `–`

Jan 72. (d-lp/c) *<606-7>* **HOT ROCKS 1964-1971**   `–` `4`
(UK cd-iss. 1983 on 'Decca'; 800 083-2) *(re-iss. Jul90 cd/c/lp; 820 140-2/-4/-1)* *<US cd-iss. 1989 on 'Abko'>* *(re-iss. Jun95 on 'London' cd/c/d-lp; 844475-2/-4/-1)*

Feb 72. (lp/c) *(SKL/KSKC 5098)* **MILESTONES**   `14` `–`

Jun 72. (7") *(export)* **EVERYBODY NEEDS SOMEBODY TO LOVE. / SURPRISE SURPRISE**   `–`

Nov 72. (lp/c) *(SKL/KSKC 5149)* **ROCK'N'ROLLING STONES**   `41` `–`

Dec 72. (lp/c) *<626-7>* **MORE HOT ROCKS (BIG HITS & FAZED COOKIES)**   `–` `9`
(UK cd-iss. Aug88; 820 515-2) *(re-iss. cd Nov90;)* *(re-iss. Jun95 on 'London' cd/c; 844478-2/-4)*

Apr 73. (7") *(F 13404)* **YOU CAN'T ALWAYS GET WHAT YOU WANT. / SAD DAY**   `42`

Oct 73. (lp/c) *(SKL/KSKC 5173)* **NO STONE UNTURNED**   `–`

May 75. (7") *(F 13584)* **I DON'T KNOW WHY. / TRY A LITTLE HARDER**   `42`

Jun 75. (lp/c) *(SKL/KSKC 5212)* **METAMORPHISIS (early demos)**   `45` `8`

Sep 75. (7") *(F 13597)* **OUT OF TIME. / JIVING SISTER FANNY**   `45` `81`

Nov 75. (d-lp)(d-c) *(ROST 1-2)(K2R 26)* **ROLLED GOLD – (THE VERY BEST OF THE ROLLING STONES)**   `7` `–`
– Come on / I wanna be your man / Not fade away / Carol / It's all over now / Little red rooster / Time is on my side / The last time / (I can't get no) Satisfaction / Get off my cloud / 19th nervous breakdown / As tears go by / Under my thumb / Lady Jane / Out of time / Paint it black / Have you seen your mother baby, standing in the shadows? / Let's spend the night together / Ruby Tuesday / Yesterday's papers / We love you / She's a rainbow / Jumpin' Jack Flash / Honky tonk women / Sympathy for the Devil / Street fighting man / Midnight rambler / Gimme shelter.

Apr 76. (7") *(F 13635)* **HONKY TONK WOMEN. / SYMPATHY FOR THE DEVIL**   `–`
(re-iss. Mar82)

Oct 79. (lp/c) *Arcade; (ADE P/C 32)* **GET STONED**   `13` `–`

May 79. (lp) *Rolling Stones; (COC 59107)* **TIME WAITS FOR NO ONE**

Aug 80. (12x7"box) *(STONE 1-12)* **BOXED SET SINGLES 1963-1969**
– COME ON. / I WANNA BE YOUR MAN // IT'S ALL OVER NOW. / I WANT TO BE LOVED // (I CAN'T GET NO) SATISFACTION. / LITTLE BY LITTLE / NOT FADE AWAY. / LITTLE RED ROOSTER // THE LAST TIME. / PAINT IT BLACK // GET OFF OF MY CLOUD. PLAY WITH FIRE // JUMPIN' JACK FLASH. / AS TEARS GO BY // 19TH NERVOUS BREAKDOWN. / HAVE YOU SEEN YOUR MOTHER BABY, STANDING IN THE SHADOWS? // LET'S SPEND THE NIGHT TOGETHER. / YOU CAN'T ALWAYS GET WHAT YOU WANT // HONKY TONK WOMAN. / RUBY TUESDAY STREET FIGHTING MAN. / OUT OF TIME // SYMPATHY FOR THE DEVIL. / GIMME SHELTER

Oct 80. (lp/c) *(TAB/KTBC 1)* **SOLID ROCK**   `–`

Nov 81. (lp/c) *(TAB/KTBC 30)* **SLOW ROLLERS**   `–`

Oct 82. (d-lp/d-c) *K-Tel; (NE2/CE2 201)* **THE STORY OF THE STONES**   `24` `–`

Jun 84. (7"/7"sha-pic-d) *Rolling Stones; (SUGAR/+P 1)* **BROWN SUGAR. / BITCH**   `–`

Jan 86. (cd) *(820 141-2)* **HOT ROCKS 1**   `1985`

Jan 86. (cd) *(820 142-2)* **HOT ROCKS 2**   `1985`

Sep 89. (d-lp/d-c/d-cd) *(820 900-1/-4/-2)* */ Abkco; <1218>* **SINGLES COLLECTION: THE LONDON YEARS**   `91`
(re-iss. Jun95)

Jun 90. (7") *(LON/+CS 264)* **PAINT IT BLACK. / HONKY TONK WOMAN**   `61`
(12"+=/remix-12"+=) *(LONX/+R 264)* – Sympathy for the Devil.

Jul 90. (3xcd-box) *Columbia; (466918-2)* **COLLECTOR'S EDITION**

Mar 92. (cd/c/lp/video) *Circus;* **LIVE AT THE HOLLYWOOD PALLADIUM DECEMBER 15, 1988 (live)**

-solo releases-

MICK JAGGER

(see also other single late 1970)

		C.B.S.	Columbia
Feb 85. (7") *(A 4722)* *<04743>* **JUST ANOTHER NIGHT. / TURN THE GIRL LOOSE** ('A'extended-12"+=) *(TA 4722)* – ('A'dub version).		32	12
Mar 85. (lp/c/cd) *(CBS/40/CD 86310)* **SHE'S THE BOSS**		6	13

– Lonely at the top / Half a loaf / Hard woman / Lucky in love / Secrets / Just another night / She's the boss / Running out of luck / Turn the girl loose. *(re-iss. cd Aug95 on 'East West'; 7567 82553-2)*

Apr 85. (7"/12") *(A/TA 6213)* *<04893>* **LUCKY IN LOVE. / RUNNING OUT OF LUCK**   `38`

Jul 86. (7") *<34-06211>* **RUTHLESS PEOPLE. / I'M RINGING**   `–` `51`
(above from the film 'Ruthless People', issued on 'Epic' records)

Aug 87. (7"/s7") *(651028-7/-0)* *<07306>* **LET'S WORK. / CATCH US CATCH CAN**   `31` `39`
(12"+=) *(651028-6)* – ('A'dance mix).

Sep 87. (lp/c/cd) *(460 123-1/-4/-2)* **PRIMITIVE COOL**   `26` `41`
– Throwaway / Let's work / Radio control / Say you will / Primitive cool / Kow Tow / Shoot off your mouth / Party doll / War baby. *(re-iss. cd Aug95 on 'East West'; 7567 82554-2)*

Nov 87. (7"/7"pic-d) *(THROW/+P 1)* *<07653>* **THROWAWAY. / PEACE FOR THE WICKED**   `67`
('A'remixed; 12"+=/cd-s+=) *(THROW T/C 1)* – ('A'vocal dub mix).

Feb 88. (7") *<07703>* **SAY YOU WILL. / SHOOT OFF YOUR MOUTH**   `–`

		Atlantic	Atlantic
Jan 93. (7"/c-s) *(A 7401/+C)* *<87410>* **SWEET THING. / WANDERING SPIRIT** (12"+=/cd-s+=) *(A 7410 T/CD)* – ('A'dub mix).		24	84
Feb 93. (cd/c/lp) *(<7567 82436-2/-4/-1>)* **WANDERING SPIRIT**		12	11

– Wired all night / Sweet thing / Out of focus / Don't tear me up / Put me in the trash / Use me / Evening gown / Mother of a man / think / Wandering spirit / Hang on to me tonight / I've been lonely for so long / Angel in my heart / Handsome Molly. *(re-iss. cd Aug95 on 'East West'; same)*

Apr 93. (7"/c-s) *(A 7368/+C)* **DON'T TEAR ME UP. / EVERYBODY KNOWS ABOUT MY GOOD THING**   `–`
(12"+=/cd-s+=) *(A 7368 T/CD)* – Sweet thing (funky guitar edit).

Jul 93. (7"/c-s) *(A 7332/+C)* **OUT OF FOCUS. / HIPGRASS**
(12"+=/cd-s+=) *(A 7332 T/CD)* – ('A'mix).

KEITH RICHARDS

(covers 'A'side= Chuck Berry / 'B'= Jimmy Cliff)

		Rolling Stones	Rolling S.
Nov 78. (7") *(RSR 102)* *<19311>* **RUN RUDOLPH RUN. / THE HARDER THEY COME**			

		Virgin	Virgin
Oct 88. (lp/c/cd) *(V/TCV/CDV 2554)* **TALK IS CHEAP**		37	24

– Talk is cheap / Take it so hard / Struggle / I could have stood you up / Make no mistake / You don't move me / It means a lot / Whip it up / How I wish / Rock awhile / Locked away. *(re-iss. Sep90 on 'Virgin' lp/c/cd; OVED/+C/CD 338)*

Oct 88. (7") *(VS 1125)* *<99297>* **TAKE IT SO HARD. / I COULD HAVE STOOD YOU UP**
(12"+=/3"cd-s+=) *(VST/VSCD 1125)* – It means a lot.

Apr 89. (7") *(VS 1179)* *<99240>* **MAKE NO MISTAKE. / IT MEANS A LOT**
(12"+=/cd-s+=) *(VST/VSCD 1179)* – ('A'extended).

		Virgin	Virgin
Nov 91. (cd/c/lp) *(CDVUS/VUSMC/VUSLP 45)* **KEITH RICHARDS AND THE X-PENSIVE WINOS LIVE AT THE HOLLYWOOD, PALLADIUM, DECEMBER 15, 1988 (live)**			

– Take it so hard / How I wish / I could have stood you up / Too rude / Make no mistake / Time is on my side / Big enough / Whip it up / Locked away / Struggle / Happy / Connection / Rockawhile.

Oct 92. (cd/c/lp) *(CDVUS/VUSMC/VUSLP 59)* *<86499>* **MAIN OFFENDER**   `45` `99`
– 999 / Wicked as it seems / Eileen / Words of wonder / Yap yap / Bodytalks / Hate it when you leave / Runnin' too deep / Will but you don't / Demon.

—— RICHARDS writes with JORDAN and some with WACHTEL.

Henry ROLLINS

Born: HENRY GARFIELD, 13 Feb'61, Washington DC, USA. After cutting his teeth in the 'straight edge' (militantly clean living) hardcore punk scene of the late 70's, ROLLINS made his name with the seminal BLACK FLAG. Recruited in time for their 'DAMAGED' (1981) opus, ROLLINS added a manic intensity to the brilliant 'SIX PACK' as well as new numbers like 'LIFE OF PAIN' and the title track. So extreme was the record that MCA's top man, Al Bergamo, tried to block the record's release even though thousands of copies had already been pressed. ROLLINS honed his writing and performing talents over a further series of albums, eventually going solo after the release of 'LOOSE NUT' (1985). 'HOT ANIMAL MACHINE' (1987) was a crudely visceral debut, ROLLINS indicating that, if anything, his solo career was going to be even more uncompromising than his work with BLACK FLAG. Later the same year, the singer released the mini album, 'DRIVE BY SHOOTING' under the pseudonym, HENRIETTA COLLINS AND THE WIFE-BEATING CHILD HATERS, a taste of ROLLINS' particularly tart brand of black humour. By 1988, The ROLLINS BAND line-up had solidified around guitarist CHRIS HASKETT (who'd played on the earlier releases), bassist ANDREW WEISS and drummer SIMON CAIN, releasing the IAN MACKAYE (of hardcore gurus, FUGAZI)-produced 'LIFE TIME' (1988) album later that year. An incendiary opus, the record was The ROLLINS BAND blueprint, setting the agenda for future releases with a lyrical incisiveness and musical ferocity that would be hard to equal. Following a slot on the hugely successful 1991 Lollapalooza tour, The ROLLINS BAND moved from cult status to a major label deal with 'Imago/RCA', releasing 'THE END OF SILENCE' in early '92. Fiercely self-analytic, ROLLINS had always used the stage and the rock medium, to a certain extent, as a kind of therapy, dredging up his childhood demons and tackling them head on. With '. . .SILENCE', ROLLINS had penned his most introspective work to date, leaving no stone unturned. The fact that he'd seen his best friend, Joe Cole, gunned down in cold blood had obviously deeply affected the singer and subsequently the material on the album. This intensely personal exorcism is what made ROLLINS' shows so damn compelling; for ROLLINS, this was far beyond mere entertainment, for the most part at least, and this was no doubt a major contributing factor in the band's constant live work. As well as a punishing regime of physical exercise, ROLLINS found time to run his own publishing company, '2.13.61' (showcasing work of underground authors as well as ROLLINS' own material, including his acclaimed collection of short stories, 'Black Coffee Blues'), and tour his darkly observant, often hilarious and ultimately inspiring spoken word sets. A choice selection of the latter were included on the double-set, 'BOXED LIFE' (1993). The ROLLINS BAND, meanwhile, returned in 1994 with 'WEIGHT', their most commercially successful set to date, and a record which finally made inroads into the UK market, almost making the Top 20. Musically, the album was more accessible than its predecessor, firmly establishing ROLLINs & Co. as 'alternative rock' heavyweights. More recently, ROLLINS has expanded his jack-of-all-trades CV with another burst of acting (he'd made his onscreen debut alongside LYDIA LUNCH in 1991's 'Kiss Napoleon Goodbye'), appearing in 'The Chase' and 'Johnny Mnemonic' as well as scoring a cameo in the much heralded De Niro/Pacino face-off, 'Heat'. In mid '96, ROLLINS was the subject of a lawsuit (an 8-figure sum) by 'Imago' for allegedly signing with 'Dreamworks' while under contract, the singer claiming he was let go by the major distributors of the label, 'B.M.G.'. Despite all this, the singer returned to the fray in 1997 with a new album, 'COME IN AND BURN', the record actually appearing on 'Dreamworks'. With ROLLINS becoming something of an all-round celebrity, it remains to be seen whether he can retain the outsider intensity of old (though it wouldn't be an idea to argue with the man!).
• **Covers:** GHOST RIDER (Suicide) / EX-LION TAMER (Wire) / DO IT (Pink Fairies) / LET THERE BE ROCK (Ac-Dc) / FRANKLIN'S TOWER (Grateful Dead).

Album rating (music only): HOT ANIMAL MACHINE (*6) / LIFE TIME (*5) / DO IT! (*6) / HARD VOLUME (*6) / TURNED ON (*6) / THE END OF SILENCE (*8) / WEIGHT (*7) / BLACK COFFEE BLUES mini (*5) / COME IN AND BURN (*5)

HENRY ROLLINS – vocals (ex-BLACK FLAG, ex-SOA) / with **CHRIS HASKETT** (b. Leeds, England) – guitar (ex-SURFIN' DAVE) / **BERNIE WANDEL** – bass / **MICK GREEN** – drums

		Fundam.	Texas Hotel
Jul 87.	(lp) (SAVE 024) <TXH 001> **HOT ANIMAL MACHINE**		

– Black and white / Followed around / Lost and found / There's a man outside / Crazy lover / A man and a woman / Hot animal machine I / Ghost rider / Move right in / Hot animal machine 2 / No one. (cd-iss. Oct88 +=; SAVE 024CD) – . (cd re-iss. Mar94 on 'Intercord'; 986976)

—— In Oct'87, he shared 'LIVE' lp with GORE, released on Dutch 'Eksakt' label; *EKSAKT 034*

| Dec 87. | (lp; solo) <TXH 005> **BIG UGLY MOUTH** (spoken word live early '87) | - | |

(UK cd-iss. Mar93 on '1/4 Stick'; QS 9CD)
(below saw him do a reverse MICHAEL JACKSON and black-up)

| Jan 88. | (12"ep; as HENRIETTA COLLINS AND THE WIFEBEATING CHILDHATERS featuring HENRY ROLLINS) (HOLY 5) <TXH 03> **DRIVE BY SHOOTING** | | Aug87 |

– Drive by shooting (watch out for that pig) / Ex-lion tamer / Hey Henriezza / Can you speak this? / I have come to kill you / Men are pigs.

ROLLINS BAND

retained **HASKETT** and recruited **ANDREW WEISS** – bass / **SIMEON CAIN** – drums

| Sep 88. | (lp/cd) (SAVE 065/+CD) <TXH > **LIFE TIME** | | |

– Burned beyond recognition / What am I doing here / 1000 times blind / Lonely / Wreck-age / Gun in mouth blues / You look at you / If you're alive / Turned out. (cd+=) – What am I doing here? / Burned beyond recognition / Move right in / Hot animal machine 2. (cd re-iss. Mar94 on 'Intercord'; 986977)

		World Service	Texas Hotel
Jan 89.	(lp) (SERVM 004) <TXH 013CD> **DO IT!** (live/studio)		Apr89

– Do it / Move right in / Next time / Joe is everything, everything is Joe / Black and white / Lost and found / Followed around / Wreck age / Lonely / Hot animal machine #1 / You look at you / Gun in mouth blues / Turned out / Thousand times blind / No one. (re-iss. cd Mar94 on 'Intercord'; 986978)

| Apr 89. | (d-lp; solo) <TXH 015> **SWEATBOX** (spoken word live) | - | |

(UK d-cd-iss. Mar93 on '1/4 Stick'; QS 10CD)

| Nov 89. | (m-lp/cd) (SERV 010 LP/CD) <TXH > **HARD VOLUME** | | |

– Hard / What have I got / I feel like this / Planet Joe / Love song / Turned inside out / Down and away. (cd+=) – Joyriding with Frank. (cd-iss. Mar94 on 'Intercord'; 986979)

—— In 1989, a Swiss cassette found its way into UK; 'READINGS: SWITZERLAND' on 'Action' *ACTIONK 001*

—— In 1990, WARTIME was an extra-curricular activity headed by ROLLINS and ANDREW WEISS. An cd-ep surfaced 'FAST FOOD FOR THOUGHT' on 'Chrysalis'; *MPCD 1753*

| 1990. | (lp; solo) <TXH > **LIVE AT McCABE'S** (spoken word live) | - | |

(UK cd-iss. Mar93 on '1/4 Stick'; QS 11CD)

		not iss.	Sub Pop
1990.	(7",7"red,7"pink) <SP 72> **I KNOW YOU. / EARACHE MY EYE**	-	

		1/4 Stick	1/4 Stick
Nov 90.	(lp/cd) <(QS 02/+CD)> **TURNED ON** (live '89)		

– Lonely / Do it / What have I got / Tearing / Out there / You didn't need / Hard / Followed around / Mask / Down & away / Turned inside out / The Dietmar song / Black & white / What do you do / Crazy lover.

—— in July '91, HENRY ROLLINS & The HARD-ONS released their collaboration 'LET THERE BE ROCK' issued on 'Vinyl Solution' (VS 30/+CD)

		Imago-RCA	Imago-RCA
Feb 92.	(12") (PT 49113) **LOW SELF OPINION. / LIE, LIE, LIE**		
Feb 92.	(cd/c/d-lp) (PD/PK/PL 90641) <21006> **THE END OF SILENCE**		

– Low self opinion / The end of silence / Grip / Tearing / You didn't need / Almost real / Obscene / What do you do? / Blues jam / Another life / Just like you.

| Aug 92. | (7") (72787 87250-18-7) **TEARING. / EARACHE IN MY EYE** (live) | 54 | |

(12"+=/cd-s+=) (72787 87250-18-1/-2) – (There'll be no) Next time / Ghost rider.

| Jan 93. | (2xcd-box/2xc-box) (72787 21009-2/-4) **THE BOXED LIFE** (compilation of alter-ego workings) | | |

—— In early '94, he acted in the film 'The Chase', and was about to be seen in 'Johnny Mnemonic'.

—— **MELVIN GIBBS** – bass repl. HASKINS who left in 1993.

| Apr 94. | (cd/c/clear d-lp) <(72787 21034-2/-4/-1)> **WEIGHT** | 22 | 33 |

– Disconnect / Fool / Icon / Civilized / Divine object of hatred / Liar / Step back / Wrong man / Volume 4 / Tired / Alien blueprint / Shine.

| Aug 94. | (7"/c-s) (74321 213057-7/-4) **LIAR. / DISCONNECT** | 27 | |

(cd-s+=) (74321 213057-2) – Right here too much / Nightsweat.

		not iss.	Thirsty Ear
Apr 97.	(m-cd) <21321> **BLACK COFFEE BLUES**	-	

– Black coffee blues / Invisible woman blues / Monster / Exhaustion blues / I know you.

		Dreamworks	Dreamworks
Apr 97.	(cd/c) <(DRD/DRC 50011)> **COME IN AND BURN**		Mar97

– Shame / Starve / All I want / The end of something / On my way to the cage / Thursday afternoon / During a city / Neon / Spilling over the side / Inhale exhale / Saying goodbye again / Rejection / Disappearing act.

| Jul 97. | (7") (DRMS 22271) **THE END OF SOMETHING. / ALSO RAN** | | - |

(cd-s) (DRMCD 22271) – ('A'side) / ('A'-We Change remix) / Threshold.
(cd-s) (DRMXD 22271) – ('A'side) / ('A'-Grooverider remix) / Stray.

– compilations, etc. –

| Mar 93. | (d-cd) 1/4 Stick; (QS 12CD) **HUMAN BUTT** (book readings) | | 1991 |
| Mar 93. | (cd-box) 1/4 Stick; (QS 13CD) **DEEP THROAT** | | |

– (all 4 spoken word releases)

Nov 94.	(d-cd) Imago; <(74321 24238-2)> **GET IN THE VAN** (book readings; life on the road with BLACK FLAG)		
Nov 94.	(book) Imago; **HENRY: PORTRAIT OF A SINGER SINGER** (spoken word)		
Jul 96.	(cd) Thirsty Ear; <2.13.61> **EVERYTHING** (spoken word)	-	

RONETTES

Formed: New York City, New York, USA . . . 1959 by mixed-race sisters VERONICA 'RONNIE' and ESTELLE BENNETT together with cousin NEDRA TALLEY. In 1961, they gained valuable exposure via an appearance – as The DOLLY SISTERS – in the dance-craze movie, 'Twist Around The Clock'. Their dance routines were witnessed by top NY DJ, Murray K, who invited them to becmome regulars at his club nights. 1961 also saw the release of a one-off debut single for 'Colpix', 'I WANT A BOY', this time under the moniker RONNIE & THE RELATIVES. Finally plumping for the The RONETTES, the trio cut a further series of sides for the 'May' label including 'I'M GONNA QUIT WHILE I'M AHEAD' and 'MY GUIDING ANGEL'.

At this point, RONNIE & Co were merely one of many cooing girl groups attempting to woo the pop charts with cutesy harmonies and beehive hairdos; it took the genius of pioneering producer PHIL SPECTOR to briefly turn their fortunes around and, in the process, create one of the 60's most timeless pieces of sonic art. SPECTOR had initially wanted to sign RONNIE to his 'Philles' label as a solo singer but, being family, the group were loathe to be split. After a period providing backup for other artists on the label, The RONETTES captured the nation's heart with the thundering 'teen symphony' of 'BE MY BABY'. Possibly SPECTOR's most effective 'Wall Of Sound' creation, the track (a transatlantic No.5 hit in October '63) pitched RONNIE's shrill but sensual vibrato against his trademark mass of discordant overload and set it off against heart-rending harmonies. Songwriters Jeff Barry and Ellie Greenwich were also responsible for the early '64 follow-up, 'BABY I LOVE YOU', a single almost as good but not nearly as successful as its predecessor. '(THE BEST PART OF) BREAKIN' UP' and 'DO I LOVE YOU?' followed into the Top 40 but even the epic Mann-Weill composition, 'WALKIN' IN THE RAIN' couldn't crack the Top 20 as SPECTOR's tried and tested formula looked to be losing its public appeal. While the producer went on to further success with The RIGHTEOUS BROTHERS, The RONETTES' brief period of fame was all but over. After a final flop single, 'I CAN HEAR MUSIC', the trio split in 1966, the same year PHIL married RONNIE (after a three-year romance). Mrs SPECTOR eventually re-emerged in a solo capacity as The RONETTES featuring The Voice of VERONICA, releasing a one-off 1969 solo single, 'YOU CAME, YOU SAW, YOU CONQUERED' for 'A&M'. A further one-off – as simply RONNIE SPECTOR – for 'Apple', 'TRY SOME, BUY SOME' met with little success in 1971. Two years later she appeared at a revival show in New York with a couple of new RONETTES (DENISE EDWARDS and CHIP FIELDS) and released another couple of unsuccessful singles for 'Buddah'. 1973 was also the year she divorced SPECTOR and escaped back to New York, later revealing that the increasingly unstable producer had virtually made her a prisoner in their L.A. mansion. While she continued to record and tour (hitting the road with BRUCE SPRINGSTEEN's band in 1976) sporadically through the 70's and 80's, she hit the charts only once, with the (1986) US Top 5 EDDIE MONEY duet, 'TAKE ME HOME TONIGHT'.

Best CD compilation: THE BEST OF THE RONETTES (*7)

VERONICA 'Ronnie' BENNETT (b.10 Aug'43) – lead vocals / **ESTELLE BENNETT** (b.22 Jul'44) – vocals / **NEDRA TALLEY** (b.27 Jan'46) – vocals

	not iss.	Colpix
Jul 61. (7"; as RONNIE & THE RELATIVES) <601> **I WANT A BOY. / SWEET 16**	-	
Jan 62. (7") <646> **I'M GONNA QUIT WHILE I'M AHEAD. / I'M ON THE WAGON**	-	

	not iss.	May
Feb 62. (7"; as RONNIE & THE RELATIVES) <111> **MY GUIDING ANGEL. / I'M GONNA QUIT WHILE I'M AHEAD**	-	
Apr 62. (7") <114> **SILHOUETTES. / YOU BET I WOULD**	-	
Aug 62. (7") <138> **GOOD GIRLS. / MEMORIES**	-	

	not iss.	Dimension
Nov 62. (7") <1046> **RECIPE FOR LOVE. / HE DID IT**	-	

	London	Philles
Oct 63. (7") (HLU 9793) <116> **BE MY BABY. / TEDESCO AND PITMAN**	4	2 Aug63
Jan 64. (7") (HLU 9826) <118> **BABY I LOVE YOU. / MISS JOAN AND MR. SAM**	11	24 Dec63

—— in Apr'64, RONNIE BENNETT issued the single 'SO YOUNG'

Jun 64. (7") <121> **DO I LOVE YOU? / BEBE & SUSAN**	-	34
Aug 64. (7") (HLU 9905) <120> **(THE BEST PART OF) BREAKIN' UP. / BIG RED**	43	39 Mar64
Oct 64. (7") (HLU 9922) **DO I LOVE YOU? / WHEN I SAW YOU**	35	-
Nov 64. (7") (HLU 9931) <123> **(WALKING) IN THE RAIN. / HOW DOES IT FEEL?**		23 Oct64
Feb 65. (7") (HLU 9952) <126> **BORN TO BE TOGETHER. / BLUES FOR BABY**		52 Jan65
May 65. (lp) (HA-U 8212) <4006> **(PRESENTING) THE FABULOUS RONETTES (FEATURING VERONICA)**		96 Dec64
– Walking in the rain / Do i love you / So young / Breakin' up / I wonder / What'd I say / Be my baby / Baby i love you / How does it feel / When i saw you / Chapel of love. |||

May 65. (7") <128> **IS THIS WHAT I GET FOR LOVING YOU? / OH, I LOVE YOU**	-	75
Jul 65. (7") (HLU 9976) **IS THIS WHAT I GET FOR LOVING YOU?. / YOU BABY**		-

—— (Aug'65) cousin **ELAINE BENNETT** – lead vocals; repl. VERONICA who married PHIL SPECTOR

Oct 66. (7") <133> **I CAN HEAR MUSIC. / WHEN I SAW YOU**	-	100

—— they split later in '66; ESTELLE and NEDRA quit the music scene. Meanwhile, RONNIE SPECTOR (aka VERONICA BENNETT) went solo as . . .
below as The RONETTES featuring The Voice of VERONICA

	A&M	A&M
Mar 69. (7") <1040> **YOU CAME, YOU SAW, YOU CONQUERED. / OH I LOVE YOU**	-	-
Apr 69. (7") (AM 748) **YOU CAME, YOU SAW, YOU CONQUERED. / I CAN HEAR MUSIC**		-

	Apple	Apple
Apr 71. (7"; by RONNIE SPECTOR) (APPLE 33) <1832> **TRY SOME, BUY SOME. / TANDOORI CHICKEN**		

—— her proposed album produced by PHIL and co-penned with GEORGE HARRISON was shelved

—— re-form with **RONNIE** recruiting **DENISE EDWARDS + CHIP FIELDS** – backing vocals

	not iss.	Buddah
Nov 73. (7"; as RONNIE & The RONETTES) <384> **LOVER, LOVER. / GO OUT AND GET IT**	-	
May 74. (7"; as RONNIE & The RONETTES) <408> **I WISH I NEVER SAW THE SUNSHINE. / I WONDER WHAT HE'S DONE**	-	
below was actually by The RONETTES |||

	not iss.	Warner-Spector
1975. (7"; as RONNIE SPECTOR) <0409> **PARADISE. / WHEN I SAY YOU**	-	

—— late in '76, RONNIE joined BRUCE SPRINGSTEEN & THE E-STREET SHUFFLE on tour

	Epic	Epic
Apr 77. (7"; as RONNIE & The RONETTES) (EPC 5185) <50374> **SAY GOODBYE TO HOLLYWOOD. / BABY PLEASE DON'T GO**		

RONNIE SPECTOR

	not iss.	Tom Cat
1977. (7") <10380> **YOU'D BE GOOD FOR ME. / SOMETHING TELLS ME**	-	

	not iss.	Alston
1978. (7") <3738> **IT'S A HEARTACHE. / I WANNA COME OVER**	-	

	Red Shadow	Polish
Jan 81. (7") <202> **DARLIN'. / TONIGHT**		
Jan 81. (7") (MS 488) **DARLIN'. / SETTIN' THE WOODS ON FIRE**		-
Jan 81. (lp) (LP 002) **SIREN**		
– Here today, gone tomorrow / Darlin' / Any way that you want me / Tonight / Boys will be boys / Hell of a nerve / Settin' the woods on fire / Let your feelings show / Dynamite / Happy birthday rock'n'roll. |||
Mar 81. (7") (REDS 11) **HERE TODAY GONE TOMORROW. / HELL OF A NERVE**		-

	C.B.S.	Columbia
Jun 87. (7"/12") (650823-7/-6) <07082> **WHO CAN SLEEP. / WHEN WE DANCED**		
Jul 87. (lp/c) (450823-1/-4) **UNFINISHED BUSINESS**		
– Who can sleep / Love on a rooftop / Dangerous / Burning love / Unfinished business / (If I could) Walk away / Heart song / True to you / When we danced / Good love is hard to find. |||
Jan 88. (7") <07300> **LOVE ON A ROOFTOP. / GOOD LOVE IS HARD TO FIND**	-	

—— In 1990, RONNIE disclosed untold events in her book 'Be My Baby'.

– (RONETTES) compilations, etc. –

on 'Phil Spector Int.' unless mentioned otherwise

Jun 65. (lp) Colpix; <486> **THE RONETTES**	-	
Jan 69. (7") London; (HLU 10240) **BE MY BABY. / BABY I LOVE YOU**	-	
1974. (7"m) **FROSTY THE SNOWMAN. / (2 by CRYSTALS)** (re-iss. Dec82; 2010 010)		
Jul 75. (7") (2010 003) **BE MY BABY. / OH, I LOVE YOU**		
Sep 75. (lp) (2307 003) **THE RONETTES SING THEIR GREATEST HITS**		-
Oct 75. (7") (2010 009) **I'M A WOMAN IN LOVE. / WHEN I SAW YOU**		-
Mar 76. (7") (2010 014) **I CAN HEAR MUSIC. / HOW DOES IT FEEL**		-
Jul 76. (7") (2010 017) **(WALKING) IN THE RAIN. / I WONDER**		-
Nov 81. (7") Polydor; (POSP 377) **DO I LOVE YOU. / (THE BEST PART OF) BREAKIN' UP**		-

—— Also featured on VOL.II of a multi-'Phil Spector' boxed set WALL OF SOUND.

Aug 87. (lp) Murray Hill; (000156) **THE COLPIX YEARS 1961-63**		-
Aug 92. (cd) Sequel; (NEMCD 620) **THE COLPIX AND BUDDAH YEARS**		-
Oct 92. (cd/c) <(PSCD/PSTC 1006)> **THE BEST OF THE RONETTES**		-
– Be my baby / Why don't they let us fall in love / I wonder / Baby, I love you / (The best part of) Breakin' up / So young / When i saw you / Do i love you? / You baby / How does it feel? / WAlking in the rain / Born to be together / Is this what I get for loving you? / Paradise / Here I sit / I wish I never saw the sunshine / Everything under the Sun / You came, you saw, you conquered. |||

Mick RONSON

Born: 1946, Hull, England. In 1964, he formed his first band, The RATS, although after a couple of singles over the next few years, they laid low. RONSON re-surfaced the band for a one-off psychedelic track, 'THE RISE AND FALL OF BERNIE GRIPPLESTONE', which, recorded in late '67, only made it to the demo stage. Guitarist RONSON subsequently went into session work, notably for MICHAEL CHAPMAN on his 'Fully Qualified Survivor' album, before his initial association with BOWIE under the group name, HYPE. Around the same time (1971), RONNO made a prog-rock attempt, although the single '4TH HOUR OF MY SLEEP', failed miserably. Alongside drummer WOODY WOODMANSEY on BOWIE's 'Man Who Sold The World', they soon became known as The SPIDERS FROM MARS, named after BOWIE's 1972 album, 'Ziggy Stardust & The Spiders From Mars'. RONSON left for a solo career in 1974 after featuring on late 1973 album, 'Bowie Pin-Ups'. Retained by 'MainMan' productions & 'RCA' records, he issued a solo debut, 'SLAUGHTER ON 10th AVENUE', which featured a version of ELVIS' 'LOVE ME TENDER' and RONSON's most famous track, 'ONLY AFTER DARK'. In between this and his 1975 follow-up,

'PLAY DON'T WORRY', he had a short spell with MOTT THE HOOPLE, who were shortly to disband soon after. Their frontman, IAN HUNTER, whom MICK had also toured alongside, formed a partnership with him as The HUNTER-RONSON BAND. For the next decade and a half, RONSON was his guitarist, a dual album, 'YUI ORTA', finally being issued in 1990. MICK's work during this period had included stints with BOB DYLAN on his ROLLING THUNDER REVUE of '75-'76, where he met ROGER McGUINN of The BYRDS. MICK subsequently produced his 'Cardiff Rose' album. He also went on to work in the late 70's for JOHN COUGAR (Chestnut Street Incident), RICH KIDS (Ghosts Of Princes In Towers) and DAVID JOHANSEN (In Style). After a lean spell in the 80's, RONSON returned in 1992, producing MORRISSEY's 'Your Arsenal', and guesting alongside old mates BOWIE and HUNTER at FREDDIE MERCURY's Wembley Tribute that April. It was rumoured at the time, that MICK was suffering from cancer and he was to die on the 30th of April, 1993, prior to completing most of his long-awaited third album, 'FROM HEAVEN TO HULL', released in 1994. • **Songwriters:** Self-penned except; THE GIRL CAN'T HELP IT (Little Richard) / WHITE LIGHT WHITE HEAT (Velvet Underground) / GROWING UP AND I'M FINE + MOONAGE DAYDREAM (live encore) (Bowie). The RATS covered; PARCHMAN FARM (Mose Allison) / EVERY DAY I HAVE THE BLUES (Arthur Alexander) / SPOONFUL (Willie Dixon) / I'VE GOTTA SEE MY BABY EVERYDAY (Chris Andrews). • **Trivia:** His sister, MARGARET RONSON, provided backing vocals for his debut album. MICK's 80's production work was for the obscure outfits, The PAYOLAS and LOS ILLEGALS.

Album rating: SLAUGHTER ON 10th AVENUE (*6) / PLAY DON'T WORRY (*5) / HEAVEN AND HULL (*4)

RATS

MICK RONSON – guitar / + unknown

		Oriole	not iss.
Nov 64.	(7") (CB 1967) **PARCHMAN FARM. / EVERY DAY I HAVE THE BLUES**	☐	-

—— **WOODY WOODMANSEY** – drums repl. ? / (entire new members with RONSON) / included JOHN CAMBRIDGE

		Columbia	not iss.
Mar 65.	(7") (DB 7483) **SPOONFUL. / I'VE GOT MY EYES ON YOU BABY**	☐	-
Jun 65.	(7") (DB 7607) **I GOTTA SEE MY BABY EVERYDAY. / HEADIN' BACK (TO NEW ORLEANS)**	☐	-

—— Disbanded. (see biography for BOWIE details, etc.)

RONNO

MICK RONSON – guitar / **BENNY MARSHALL** / etc.

		Vertigo	Vertigo
Jul 71.	(7") (6059 029) <100> **4th HOUR OF MY SLEEP. / POWERS OF DARKNESS**	☐	☐

—— He then played on BOWIE albums 'ZIGGY STARDUST', 'ALADDIN SANE' & 'PIN-UPS'.

MICK RONSON

solo with **AYNSLEY DUNBAR** – drums / **TREVOR BOLDER** – bass / **MIKE GARSON** – piano

		R.C.A.	R.C.A.
Jan 74.	(7") (APBO 212) <0212> **LOVE ME TENDER. / ONLY AFTER DARK**	☐	☐
Mar 74.	(lp/c) (APL/APK 1-0353) **SLAUGHTER ON 10th AVENUE**	9	☐

– Love me tender / Growing up and I'm fine / Only after dark / Music is lethal / I'm the one / Medley: Pleasure man – Hey ma get papa / Slaughter on 10th Avenue.

Apr 74.	(7") (APBO 5022) <0291> **SLAUGHTER ON 10th AVENUE. / LEAVE MY HEART ALONE**	☐	☐

—— From Sep-Dec'74, RONSON joined MOTT THE HOOPLE, and featured on only one single 'SATURDAY GIGS'. He continued on already recorded 2nd solo album.

Feb 75.	(7") (RCA 2482) <10237> **BILLY PORTER. / HAZY DAYS**	☐	☐
Feb 75.	(lp/c) (APL/APK 1-0681) **PLAY DON'T WORRY**	29	☐

– Billy Porter / Angel No.9 / This is for you / White light – white heat / Play don't worry / Hazy days / The girl can't help it / Empty bed (lo me ne andrail) / Woman.

—— MICK lost contract, and went off to play for BOB DYLAN, IAN HUNTER, and produce many (see biography). In 1990 he was on record again with IAN HUNTER on album 'YUI ORTA'. (see under ⇒)

		Epic	Epic
Apr 94.	(c-s) (660358-4) **DON'T LOOK DOWN. / SLAUGHTER ON 10th AVENUE**	55	☐

(12"+=/cd-s+=) (660358-6/-2) – Billy Porter / Love me tender. (above with JOE ELLIOTT of DEF LEPPARD on vocals).

May 94.	(cd/c/lp) (474742-2/-4/-1) **HEAVEN AND HULL**	☐	☐

– Don't look down / Like a rolling stone / When the world falls down / Trouble with me / Life's a river / You and me / Colour me / Takes a long line / Midnight love / All the young dudes.

– compilations, etc. –

May 82.	(7") (RCA Gold; (GOLD 546) **BILLY PORTER. / SLAUGHTER ON 10th AVENUE**	☐	-
Sep 94.	(d-cd) Trident; (GY 003) **ONLY AFTER DARK**	☐	☐

Linda RONSTADT

Born: 15 Jul'46, Tucson, Arizona, USA. Raised by Mexican/German parents, the young RONSTADT grew up singing a combination of country/rock'n'roll covers and Mexican folk songs. After hearing The BYRDS, she was inspired to relocate to L.A. in the mid-60's where she hooked up with guitarist, BOB KIMMEL, in folk-rock band, The STONE PONEYS. Through manager, Herb Cohen, the group eventually secured a deal with 'Capitol', releasing three flop albums, though they're probably best remembered for their one-off, MIKE NESMITH-penned hit,'DIFFERENT DRUM', the single making the US Top 20 in late '67. The group's final effort was completed by RONSTADT after KIMMEL and third member, KENNY EDWARDS both bailed out. Thrown into the solo deep end, RONSTADT subsequently struggled through a turbulent, commercially barren period in the early 70's, struggling to find a niche. Setting up home in L.A.'s Topanga Canyon alongside the countrified, singer/songwriter elite (NEIL YOUNG, JONI MITCHELL etc.), RONSTADT went through a series of producers, managers and backing musicians, hiring the (future) EAGLES for her 1972 eponymous solo debut. Along with those aforementioned purveyors of chart-smooth country-rock, RONSTADT signed to 'Asylum' in 1973, a new label set up by biz maestro, David Geffen. Her debut for the label, 'DON'T CRY NOW', was largely produced by fellow Topangan-ite and EAGLES collaborator, J.D. SOUTHER, with whom RONSTADT subsequently became romantically entwined. With the album failing to be completed on schedule, Englishman PETER ASHER (previously of 60's pop duo, PETER & GORDON) was brought in to finish the project. Eventually released in late '73, the album kickstarted RONSTADT's career, ASHER subsequently becoming her manager and guiding her towards superstardom. In ASHER, she'd finally found a mentor who could package her crystal-pure voice and dusky looks for a mainstream market, RONDSTADT finally covering material that was sympathetic to her vocal style. A version of Betty Everett's 'YOU'RE NO GOOD' became a Christmas US No.1 the following year, the 'HEART LIKE A WHEEL' (1975) album following suit and finally establishing RONSTADT among the rock hierarchy. The album was a considered mix of rootsy oldies and similarly accented current material (affecting readings of James Taylor's 'YOU CAN CLOSE YOUR EYES' and Little Feat's 'WILLIN'), a winning combination which would serve her well over the later 70's period. On subsequent albums, however, she increasingly moved away from the country/folk bias of her earlier work, incorporating Motown soul/R&B into 'PRISONER IN DISGUISE' (1976) and covering a trio of songs by the (then) unknown KARLA BONOFF on 'HASTEN DOWN THE WIND'. With 'SIMPLE DREAMS' (1977), RONSTADT was back at No.1, covering a couple of songs by cult L.A. gunslinger, WARREN ZEVON, the sardonic 'POOR, POOR, PITIFUL ME' and the raw beauty of 'CARMELITA'. With the punk wars raging in an attempt to break the stranglehold of a perceived decadent rock aristocracy (the back-slapping L.A. mob were particularly reviled), RONSTADT bravely attempted a cover of Elvis Costello's 'ALISON' on 1978's 'LIVING IN THE USA'. While COSTELLO was reportedly none too impressed with the result, RONSTADT made a rather ill-advised attempt to get hip with the new breed on 'MAD LOVE' (1980), covering a further three COSTELLO songs on a set which met with critical derision. The fact that RONSTADT's backing band were called The CRETONES (!) says it all really. 'GET CLOSER' received an even rougher ride from the press and it was clear RONSTADT needed a speedy rethink as to where her career was going. In a shrewd move, the singer made a stylistic U-turn, subsequently recording three albums of orchestrated, easy-listening standards. Predictably, 'WHAT'S NEW' (1983), 'LUSH LIFE' (1984) and 'FOR SENTIMENTAL REASONS' (1986) were all big sellers, resurrecting her ailing career. Equally successful was the 'TRIO' (1987) album, a country set recorded with friends EMMYLOU HARRIS and DOLLY PARTON, RONSTADT scoring a Transatlantic Top 10 hit later that summer via a syrupy duet with JAMES INGRAM, 'SOMEWHERE OUT THERE'. RONSTADT made another stylistic volte-face in the late 80's/early 90's, going back to her roots and recording a couple of albums of Mexican/Spanish folk, 'CANCIONES DE MI PADRE (MY FATHER'S SONG)' (1987) and 'MAS CANCIONES' (1991). These releases were interspersed with a more conventional pop set, 'CRY LIKE A RAINSTORM – HOWL LIKE THE WIND' (1989), the drippy duet with AARON NEVILLE, 'DON'T KNOW MUCH' giving RONSTADT her biggest UK hit to date. In the 90's, RONSTADT once again found herself in the commercial fringes, 'WINTER LIGHT' (1993) and 'FEELS LIKE HOME' (1995) barely making the (US) Top 100. Nevertheless, she remains a consistent live draw and a widely respected vocalist with the ability to effortlessly slide between genres. • **Songwriters:** Owes much to other artists' material; I'LL BE YOUR BABY TONIGHT (Bob Dylan) / SILVER THREADS AND GOLDEN NEEDLES (Springfields) / DESPERADO (Eagles) / WHEN WILL I BE LOVED (Everly Brothers) / IT DOESN'T MATTER ANYMORE + THAT'LL BE THE DAY + IT'S SO EASY (Buddy Holly) / THE TRACKS OF MY TEARS (Miracles) / HEATWAVE (Martha & The Vandellas) / CRAZY (Patsy Cline) / SOMEONE TO LAY DOWN BESIDE ME (Karla Bonoff) / TUMBLING DICE (Rolling Stones) / BLUE BAYOU (Roy Orbison) / BACK IN THE USA (Chuck Berry) / LOVE ME TENDER (Elvis Presley) / OOH BABY BABY (Smokey Robinson) / JUST ONE LOOK (Doris Troy) / GIRLS TALK (Elvis Costello) / HURT SO BAD (Little Anthony & The Imperials) / I KNEW YOU WHEN (Billy Joe Royal) / EASY FOR YOU TO SAY + SHATTERED (Jimmy Webb) / DON'T KNOW MUCH (Bill Medley) / WHEN SOMETHING IS WRONG WITH MY BABY (Sam & Dave) / FEELS LIKE HOME (Randy Newman) /

AFTER THE GOLDRUSH (Neil Young) / THE WAITING (Tom Petty) / etc.
• **Trivia:** In 1980, she made her acting debut on stage production of 'The Pirates Of Penzance'. In 1983, she starred in the film version.
Album rating: HAND SOWN HOME GROWN (*4) / SILK PURSE (*5) / LINDA RONSTADT (*4) / DON'T CRY NOW (*6) / DIFFERENT DRUM compilation (*6) / HEART LIKE A WHEEL (*8) / PRISONER IN DISGUISE (*6) / HASTEN DOWN THE WIND (*6) / GREATEST HITS compilation (*7) / A RETROSPECTIVE exploitation (*6) / SIMPLE DREAMS (*7) / LIVING IN THE USA (*5) / MAD LOVE (*5) / GREATEST HITS, VOLUME 2 compilation (*6) / GET CLOSER (*4) / WHAT'S NEW (*6) / LUSH LIFE (*5) / FOR SENTIMENTAL REASONS (*5) / TRIO with Dolly Parton & Emmylou Harris (*7) / CANCIONES DE MI PADRE (*5) / CRY LIKE A RAINSTORM – HOWL LIKE THE WIND (*5) / MAS CANCIONES (*5) / FRENESI (*4) / WINTER LIGHT (*6) / FEELS LIKE HOME (*5) / DEDICATED TO THE ONE I LOVE (*5) / WESTERN WALL – THE TUCSON SESSIONS with Emmylou Harris (*5)

STONE PONEYS

featured **LINDA** – vocals / plus **BOB KIMMEL** – guitar / + **KENNY EDWARDS** with sessioners / **BILLY MUNDI** – drums

		not iss.	Sidewalk
1966.	(7") <937> **SO FINE. / EVERYBODY HAS THEIR OWN IDEAS**	-	-

		Capitol	Capitol
Mar 67.	(lp) <ST 2666> **THE STONE PONEYS**	-	-

– Sweet summer blue and gold / If I were you / Just a little bit of rain / Bicycle song (soon now) / Orion / Wild about my lovin' / Back home / Meredith (on my mind) / Train and the river / All the beautiful things / 2:10 train.
Mar 67. (7") <5838> **ALL THE BEAUTIFUL THINGS. / SWEET SUMMER BLUE AND GOLD**
Jun 67. (7") <5910> **EVERGREEN. / ONE FOR ALL**

—— She was now credited/billed with The STONE PONEYS.
Dec 67. (7") (CL 15523) <2004> **DIFFERENT DRUM. / I'VE GOT TO KNOW** — 13 Nov67
Jun 67. (lp) <ST 2763> **EVERGREEN – THE STONE PONEYS VOLUME 2** — 100
– December dream / Song about the rain / Autumn afternoon / I've got to know / Evergreen (parts 1 & 2) / Different drum / Driftin' / One for one / Back on the street again / Toys in time / New hard times.
Feb 68. (7") <2110> **UP TO MY NECK IN MUDDY WATER. / CARNIVAL BEAR** — 93
Apr 68. (lp) <ST 2863> **LINDA RONSTADT, STONE PONEYS & FRIENDS: VOL.3** —
– Golden song / Merry-go-round / Love is a child / By the fruits of their labors / Hobo (morning glory) / Star and a stone / Let's stick together / Up to my neck in muddy water / Aren't you the one / Wings / Some of Shelly's blues / Stoney end.
May 68. (7") <2195> **SOME OF SHELLY'S BLUES / HOBO (MORNING GLORY)** —

—— When EDWARDS left, the group folded

LINDA RONSTADT

went solo, after she made a US Christmas 45 with the TURTLES.

		Capitol	Capitol
Apr 69.	(lp) (E-ST 208) **HAND SOWN – HOME GROWN**		

– Baby you've been on my mind / Silver threads and golden needles / Bet no one ever hurt this bad / A number and a name / The only mamma that'll walk the line / Break my mind / I'll be your baby tonight / It's about time / We need a lot more of Jesus (and a lot less of rock and roll) / The dolphins. (US re-iss. 1975)
Apr 69. (7") (CL 15590) <2438> **THE DOLPHINS. / THE WRONG WAY AROUND**
Oct 69. (7") (CL 15612) **BABY YOU'VE BEEN ON MY MIND. / I'LL BE YOUR BABY TONIGHT**
Sep 70. (lp) (E-ST 407) <407> **SILK PURSE**
– Lovesick blues / Are my thoughts with you? / Will you love me tomorrow? / Nobody's / Louise / Long long time / Mental revenge / I'm leaving it all up to you / He darkens the Sun / Life is like a mountain railway.
Sep 70. (7") (CL 15657) <2846> **LONG LONG TIME. / NOBODY'S** 25 Aug70
Dec 70. (7") <2767> **WILL YOU LOVE ME TOMORROW?. / LOVESICK BLUES** —
Jan 71. (7") <3021> **(SHE'S A) VERY LOVELY WOMAN. / THE LONG WAY AROUND** 70

—— She recruited tour/studio band of future EAGLES / **BERNIE LEADON** – guitar / **GLEN FREY** – guitar / **RANDY MEISNER** – bass / **DON HENLEY** – drums
Feb 72. (lp) (EA-ST 635) <635> **LINDA RONSTADT**
– Rock me on the water / Crazy arms / I won't be hangin' around / I still miss someone / In my reply / I fall to pieces / Ramblin' round / Birds / Rescue me. (re-iss. May82 on 'Fame')
Apr 72. (7") (CL 15717) <3273> **ROCK ME ON THE WATER. / CRAZY ARMS** 85 Feb 72
Apr 72. (7") <3210> **I FALL TO PIECES. / CAN IT BE TRUE?** —
(She now used numerous sessioners)

		Asylum	Asylum
Nov 73.	(lp) (SYL 9012) <5064> **DON'T CRY NOW**		45

– I can almost see it / Love has no pride / Silver threads and golden needles / Desperado / Don't cry now / Sail away / Colorado / The fast one / Everybody loves a winner / I believe in you. (re-iss. Jun76)
Dec 73. (7") <11026> **LOVE HAS NO PRIDE. / I CAN ALMOST SEE IT** — 51
Apr 74. (7") <11032> **SILVER THREADS AND GOLDEN NEEDLES. / DON'T CRY FOR NOW** — 67

—— With PETE ASHER for the second time producing, she had to make contractual album for 'Capitol'. Augmented by **ANDREW GOLD** – guitar, keyboards, etc.
Dec 74. (7") <3990> **YOU'RE NO GOOD. / WHEN WILL I BE LOVED** — 1

Jan 75.	(lp) (E-ST 11358) <11358> **HEART LIKE A WHEEL**	1	Nov 74

– You're no good / It doesn't matter anymore / Faithless love / The dark end of the street / Heart like a wheel / When will I be loved / Willin' / I can't help it (if I'm still in love with you) / Keep me blowing away / You can close your eyes. (re-iss. Dec86)
Jan 75. (7") (CL 15804) **YOU'RE NO GOOD. / I CAN'T HELP IT** —
Apr 75. (7") (CL 15820) <4050> **WHEN WILL I BE LOVED. / IT DOESN'T MATTER ANYMORE** 2 / 47

		Asylum	Asylum
Oct 75.	(7") (AYM 550) <45282> **HEAT WAVE. / LOVE IS A ROSE**	5	63

Nov 75. (7") <45271> **SILVER BLUE. / LOVE IS A ROSE** —
Jan 76. (lp) (SYL 1045) <1045> **PRISONER IN DISGUISE** 4 Sep 75
– Love is a rose / Hey mister, that's me up on the jukebox / Roll um easy / The tracks of my tears / Prisoner in disguise / Herat wave / Many rivers to cross / The sweetest gift / You tell me that I'm falling down / I will always love you / Silver blue.
Jan 76. (7") <45295> **THE TRACKS OF MY TEARS. / THE SWEETEST GIFT** — 25
Mar 76. (7") (K 13034) **THE TRACKS OF MY TEARS. / PRISONER IN DISGUISE** 42 —
Aug 76. (lp) (K 53045) <1072> **HASTEN DOWN THE WIND** 32 3
– Lose again / The tattler / If he's ever near / That'll be the day / Lo siento mi vida / Hasten down the wind / Rivers of Babylon / Give one heart / Try me again / Crazy / Down so low / Someone to lay down beside me. (cd-iss. Sep89)
Sep 76. (7") (K 13053) <45340> **THAT'LL BE THE DAY. / TRY ME AGAIN** 11 Aug 76
Oct 76. (7") (K 13065) <45402> **LOSE AGAIN. / LO SIENTO MI VIDA** 76 May77
Dec 76. (lp) (K 53055) <1092> **GREATEST HITS** (compilation) 37 6
– You're no good / Silver threads and golden needles / Desperado / Love is a rose / That'll be the day / Long long time / Different drum / When will I be loved? / Love has no pride / Heat wave / It doesn't matter anymore / Tracks of my tears. (cd-iss. 1984)
Feb 77. (7") (K 13071) <45361> **SOMEONE TO LAY DOWN BESIDE ME. / CRAZY** 42 Dec 76
Sep 77. (7") <45431> **BLUE BAYOU. / OLD PAINT** — 3
Sep 77. (7") (K 13094) **POOR POOR PITIFUL ME. / OLD PAINT** — —
Oct 77. (7") <45438> **IT'S SO EASY. / LO SIENTO MI VIDA** — 5
Nov 77. (lp) (K 53065) <104> **SIMPLE DREAMS** 15 1 Sep77
– It's so easy / Carmelita / Simple man, simple dream / Sorrow lives here / I will never marry / Blue bayou / Poor poor pitiful me / Maybe I'm right / Tumbling dice / Old paint. (cd-iss. Jan87)
Nov 77. (7") (K 13100) **IT'S SO EASY. / SORROW LIVES HERE** — —
Jan 78. (7") (K 13106) **BLUE BAYOU. / MAYBE I'M RIGHT** 35 —
Feb 78. (7") <45462> **POOR POOR PITIFUL ME. / SIMPLE MAN, SIMPLE DREAM** — 31
Mar 78. (7") (K 13120) **TUMBLING DICE. / CARMELITA** — —
May 78. (7") <45479> **TUMBLING DICE. / I WILL NEVER MARRY** — 32
Sep 78. (7") (K 13133) <45519> **BACK IN THE U.S.A. / WHITE RHYTHM & BLUES** 16 Aug 78
Oct 78. (lp) (K 53085) <155> **LIVING IN THE U.S.A.** 39 1 Sep 78
– Back in the U.S.A. / When I grow too old to dream / Just one look / Alison / White rhythm & blues / All that you dream / Ooh baby baby / Mohammed's radio / Blowing away / Love me tender.
Oct 78. (7") <45546> **OOH BABY BABY. / BLOWIN' AWAY** — 7
Nov 78. (7") (K 13139) **OOH BABY BABY. / BLACK ROSES** — —
Feb 79. (7") <46011> **JUST ONE LOOK. / LOVE ME TENDER** — 44
Apr 79. (7",7"pic-disc) (K 13149) **ALISON. / ALL THAT YOU DREAM** 66 —
Apr 79. (7") <46034> **ALISON. / MOHAMMED'S RADIO** — —
Feb 80. (7") (K 12419) <46602> **HOW DO I MAKE YOU. / RAMBLER GAMBLER** 10 Jan 80
Feb 80. (lp) (K 52210) <510> **MAD LOVE** 65 3
– Mad love / Party girl / How do I make you / I can't let go / Hurt so bad / Look out for my love / Cost of love / Justine / Girls talk / Talking in the dark. (above has backing from The CRETONES)
Jun 80. (7") (K 12444) <46624> **HURT SO BAD. / JUSTINE** 8 Apr 80
Jul 80. (7") <46654> **I CAN'T LET GO. / LOOK OUT FOR MY LOVE** — 31
Nov 80. (lp) (K 52255) <516> **GREATEST HITS, VOLUME 2** (compilation) 26
– It's so easy / I can't let go / Hurt so bad / Blue bayou / How do I make you / Back in the U.S.A. / Ooh baby baby / Poor poor pitiful me / Tumbling dice / Just one look / Someone to lay down beside me. (cd-iss. 1983)

—— (next featured **J.D. SOUTHER** – vocals)

		Elektra	Elektra
Oct 82.	(7") (9969948) <69948> **GET CLOSER. / SOMETIMES YOU JUST CAN'T WIN**		29

Oct 82. (lp) (E 0185) <60185> **GET CLOSER** 31
– Get closer / The Moon is a harsh mistreess / I knew you when / Easy for you to say / People gonna talk / Talk to me of Mendocino / I think it's gonna work out fine / Mr. Radio / Lies / Tell him / Sometimes you just can't win / My blue tears. (cd-iss. Jan84)
Jan 83. (7"/12") (E 9853/+T) <69853> **I KNEW YOU WHEN. / TALK TO ME OF MENDOCINO** 37
Mar 83. (7"/12") (E 9877/+T) **TELL HIM. / MR. RADIO** —
Apr 83. (7") <69838> **EASY FOR YOU TO SAY. / MR. RADIO** — 54

—— next 2 albums credit The NELSON RIDDLE ORCHESTRA.
Nov 83. (lp/c/cd) (960 260-1/-4/-2) <60260> **WHAT'S NEW** 31 3
– What's new / I've got a crush on you / Guess I'll hang my tears out to dry / Crazy he calls me / Someone to watch over me / I don't stand a ghost of a chance with you / What'll I do / Lover man (oh where can you be) / Good-bye. (re-iss. Nov 86)
Mar 84. (7") (E 9780) <69780> **WHAT'S NEW. / CRAZY HE CALLS ME** 53 Nov83
Dec 84. (lp/c) (960 387-1/-4) <60387> **LUSH LIFE** 100 13 Nov84
– When I fall in love / Skylark / It never entered my mind / Mean to me / When your lover has gone / I'm a fool to want you / You took advantage of me / Sophisticated lady / Can't we be friends / My old flame / Falling in love again / Lush life. (cd-iss. Jun87)

Jan 85. (7") (E 9667) **FALLING IN LOVE AGAIN. / SOPHISTICATED LADY** ☐ ☐

──── next credited NELSON RIDDLE & HIS ORCHESTRA (NELSON died mid-80's)

Sep 86. (lp/c/cd) (960 474-1/-4/-2) <60474> **FOR SENTIMENTAL REASONS** ☐ ☐
– When you wish upon a star / Bewitched, bothered & bewildered / You go to my head / But not for me / My funny valentine / I get along without you very well / Am I blue / I love you for sentimental reasons / Straighten up and fly right / Little girl blue / 'Round midnight.

Jun 87. (7"; as LINDA RONSTADT & JAMES INGRAM)
(MCA 1132) <52973> **SOMEWHERE OUT THERE. /**
('A'instrumental) **8** **2** Dec86
(12"+=) (MCAT 1132) – ('A'version).
(above 45 on 'MCA' and lifted from the film 'An American Tail')

──── in Mar'87, she teamed up with DOLLY PARTON & EMMYLOU HARRIS (⇒) on album TRIO. It hits No.6 in the States, and a number of 45's are lifted from it by Warners.

Nov 87. (lp/c/cd) (960 765-1/-4/-2) <60765> **CANCIONES DE MI PADRE (MY FATHER'S SONG)** ☐ **42**
– Por un amor / Los Laureles / Hay unos ojos / La cigarra / Tu solo tu / Y andale / Rogaciano el huapanguero / La charreada / Dos arbolitos / Corrido de cananea / La barca de guaymas / La calandria / El sol que tu eres. (re-iss. cd Nov93)

	Elektra	Elektra

Oct 89. (lp/c)(cd) (EKT 76/+C)(960872-2) <60872> **CRY LIKE A RAINSTORM – HOWL LIKE THE WIND** **43** **7**
– Still within the sound of my voice / Cry like a rainstorm / All my life / I need you / Don't know much / Adios / Trouble again / I keep it hid / So right, so wrong / Shattered / When something is wrong with my baby / Goodbye my friend. (below with AARON NEVILLE)

Nov 89. (7"/-c-s) (EKR 101/+C) <69261> **DON'T KNOW MUCH. / HURT SO BAD** **2** **2** Sep89
(12"+=/cd-s+=) (EKR 101 T/CD) – I can't let go.

Jan 90. (7") (EKR 105) <64987> **ALL MY LIFE. / SHATTERED** ☐ **11**
(12"+=/cd-s+=) (EKR 105 T/CD) – Love has no pride.

May 90. (7"; LINDA RONSTADT featuring AARON NEVILLE) <64968> **WHEN SOMETHING IS WRONG WITH MY BABY. / TRY ME AGAIN** **-** **78**

──── Oct 91, she again duetted with AARON NEVILLE on his 'A&M' 45, 'CLOSE YOUR EYES'

Nov 91. (cd/c) (7559 61239-2/-4) <61239> **MAS CANCIONES** ☐ **88**
– Tata dios / El Toro Relajo / Mi ranchito / La Mariquita / Gritenme Piedras del Campo / Siempre hace Frio / El Curcifijo de Piedra / Palomita de ojos negros / Pena de los amores / El Camino / El Gustito / El Sueno.

Aug 92. (cd/c) <81383> **FRENESI** **-**
– Frenesi / Mentira Salome / Alma adentro / Entre abismos / Cuando me querias tu / Piel canela / Verdad amarga / Despojos / En mi soledad / Piensa en mi / Quiereme mucho / Perfidia / Te quiero dijiste.

Nov 93. (7"/c-s) (EKR 177/+C) **WINTER LIGHT. / DON'T KNOW MUCH** ☐ ☐
(cd-s+=) (EKR 177CD) – Blue bayou / Alison.

Dec 93. (cd/c) <(7559 61545-2/-4)> **WINTER LIGHT** ☐ **92**
– Heartbeats accelerating / Do what you gotta do / Anyone who had a heart / Don't talk (put your head on my shoulder) / Oh no, not my baby / It's too soon to know / I just don't know what to do with myself / A river for him / Adonde voy / You cant treat the wrong man right / Winter light.

Feb 94. (c-s) (EKR 179C) **HEARTBEATS ACCELERATING / THE SECRET GARDEN** ☐ ☐
(cd-s+=) (EKR 179CD) – ('A'side) / Don't know much / Desperado / A river for him.

Mar 95. (cd/c) <(7559 61703-2/-4)> **FEELS LIKE HOME** ☐ **75**
– The waiting / Walk on / High Sierra / After the gold rush / The blue train / Feels like home / Teardrops will fall / Morning blues / Women 'cross the river / Lover's return.

Mar 95. (c-s) **THE WAITING / DESPERADO** ☐ ☐
(cd-s+=) – Poor poor pitiful me / Cry like a rainstorm.

Jul 96. (cd/c) <(7599 61916-2/-4)> **DEDICATED TO THE ONE I LOVE** ☐ **78**
– Dedicated to the one I love / Be my baby / In my room / Devoted to you / Baby, I love you / Angel baby / We will rock you / Winter light / Brahms' lullaby / Good night.

Sep 99. (cd/c; as LINDA RONSTADT & EMMYLOU HARRIS) <(7559 62408-2/-4)> **WESTERN WALL – THE TUCSON SESSIONS** ☐ **73**
– Loving the highwayman / Raise the dead / For a dancer / Western wall / 1917 / He was mine / Sweet spot / Sisters of mercy / Fallin' down / Valerie / This is to mother you / All I left behind / Across the border.

– compilations, etc. –

(STONE PONEYS =*)
1972. (lp/c) Pickwick; (SPC 3298) **STONEY END** * ☐ **-**
Jun 75. (lp) Capitol; <ST 11383> **THE STONE PONEYS FEATURING LINDA RONSTADT** * **-** **-**
Apr 77. (lp/c) Capitol; <11269> **DIFFERENT DRUM** * **-** **92** Feb74
Jul 77. (7") Capitol; (CL 15933) **DIFFERENT DRUM. / IT DOESN'T MATTER ANYMORE** **-**
Jul 77. (d-lp) Capitol; (CAPSP 102) <11629> **A RETROSPECTIVE** ☐ May77
Sep 76. (7") Asylum; (K 13049) **DESPERADO. / SILVER THREADS AND GOLDEN NEEDLES** **-**
Nov 86. (cd-box) Asylum; <(60489-2)> **'ROUND MIDNIGHT WITH NELSON RIDDLE AND HIS ORCHESTRA** ☐ ☐
– (WHAT'S NEW / LUSH LIFE / FOR SENTIMENTAL REASONS)
Dec.99 (4xcd-box) <(7559 62472-2)> **THE LINDA RONSTADT BOX SET** ☐ ☐

ROOTS

Formed: Philadelphia, Pennsylvania, USA ... 1989 by rappers TARIQ TROTTER (aka BLACK THOUGHT) and AHMIR-KHALIB THOMPSON (aka ?UESTLOVE), who subsequently recruited a live band around LEON HUBBARD (aka HUB) and MALIK B. Taking the form back to basics, these dedicated hip-hop purists proceeded to build up a sizeable grassroots following through constant live work. Word soon spread and the group were subsequently signed to 'Geffen', releasing their first full-length album, the well-received 'DO YOU WANT MORE', in late '94. Feted by such rap luminaries as CHUCK D and GENIUS/GZA, The ROOTS were finally afforded their due commercial success when their third release, 'ILLADELPH HALFLIFE' (1996) almost made the US Top 20. They achieved further Stateside success in Spring of the following year when the 'WHAT THEY DO' single was a Top 40 hit. • **note:** not to be confused with the similarly named reggae group.

Album rating: FROM THE GROUND UP mini (*5) / DO YOU WANT MORE?!!!??! (*6) / ILLADELPH HALFLIFE (*6) / THINGS FALL APART (*8) / ROOTS COME ALIVE (*5)

TARIQ TROTTER (aka BLACK THOUGHT) – rapper / **AHMIR-KHALIB THOMPSON** (aka ?UESTLOVE) – drums / **LEON 'HUB' HUBBARD** – bass / **MALIK ABDUL-BASIT** – rapper

	Talkin' Loud	Geffen

Jun 94. (m-cd/m-lp) (518941-2/-1) **FROM THE GROUND UP** ☐ ☐
– Worldwide / Do you want more / It's comin' / Distortion to static / Mellow my man / Dat scat. (cd+=) – Do you want more (Beat mix).

──── guests included RAHZEL THE GODFATHER OF NOYZE + SCOTT STORCH

	Geffen	Geffen

Nov 94. (cd/c/lp) <(GED/GEC/GEF 24708)> **DO YOU WANT MORE?!!!??!** ☐ Jan95
– (intro) – There's somethin' goin' on / Proceed / Distortion to static / Mellow my man / I remain calm / Datskat / Lazy afternoon / ? vs Rahzel / Do you want more?!!!??! / What goes on (part 7) / Essaywhuman / Swept away / You ain't fly / Silent treatment / Lesson (part 1) / Unlocking. (cd re-iss. Sep97; same)

Feb 96. (cd-s) **CLONES / SECTION** **-**
Nov 96. (cd) (GED 24972) **ILLADELPH HALFLIFE** ☐ **21** Sep96
– Intro / Respond – React / Section / Panic!!!!!!! / It just don't stop / Episodes / Push up ya lighter / What they do / ? vs. Scratch (the token D.J. cut) / Concerto of the desperado / Clones / Universe at war / No alibi / Dave vs. us / No great pretender / Hypnotic / Itai (the universal side) / One shine / Adventures in Wonderland / (outro).

	M.C.A.	M.C.A.

Apr 97. (12"/cd-s) (GFST/+D 22240) **WHAT THEY DO. / RESPOND – REACT ('A'+'B' versions)** ☐ **34** Dec96

Feb 99. (12"/cd-s; The ROOTS featuring ERYKAH BADU) (MCST/+D 48110) <55539> **YOU GOT ME. / ADRENALINE / ('A'mix)** **31** **39**
Mar 99. (cd)(d-lp) (MCD 11830)<(MCA 2-11948)> **THINGS FALL APART** ☐ **4**
– Things fall apart / Table of contents / Next movement / Step into the realm / Spark / Dynamite / Without a doubt / Ain't sayin' nothin' new / Double trouble / The love of my life / 100% Dundee / Dierdre vs Dice / Adrenaline / Electric boogaloo / You got me / Don't see us / Return to innocence lost.
Nov 99. (d-cd/d-c) <112059> **THE ROOTS COME ALIVE (live)** **-** **50**
– Live at the T-Connection / Next movement / Step into the realm / Proceed / Mellow my man – Jusufckwithis / Love of my life / Ultimate / Don't see us / 100% Dundee / Adrenaline! / Essaywhuman?!!!!! / Silent treatment / Notice / You got me / Encore / What you want / We got you / Lesson – part III (it's over now) / All I know / Ya'll know who / For the love of money.

Tim ROSE

Born: September 1940, Washington DC, USA. Prior to striking out on his own, ROSE's credentials as a folkie were already pretty hip, having played with everyone from JOHN PHILIPS and SCOTT McKENZIE (in The JOURNEYMEN) to CASS ELLIOT (in The BIG THREE). ROSE became a solo singer in his own right following the latter group's demise in 1964, eventually securing a contract with 'Columbia' in 1966 and releasing a debut single, 'I'M GONNA BE STRONG', at the end of the year. This was trailed in Spring the following year by ROSE's finest moment, the classic one-that-got-away, 'MORNING DEW', a further two singles (including pacifist rallying cry, 'COME AWAY MELINDA') following before the release of an eponymous debut album in early '68. Featuring such noted sessioners as FELIX PAPPALARDI and BERNARD PURDIE and containing all the aforementioned singles, the album was an impressive showcase for ROSE's gritty larynx and foreboding, almost apocalyptic delivery, particularly on his tortured reworking of the traditional 'HEY JOE', cited as the inspiration for JIMI HENDRIX's subsequent hit version. Yet the record failed to translate cult acclaim into sales, a comparatively lacklustre follow-up, 'THROUGH ROSE COLOURED GLASSES' (1969) failing to remedy the situation. Subsequently signing with 'Capitol', ROSE released 'LOVE – A KIND OF HATE STORY' (1971) before opting for the less commercially demanding confines of independent label, 'Playboy'. Perhaps hoping to repeat the artistic triumph of his debut, he released yet another 'TIM ROSE' in 1974, covering The Beatles' 'HIDE YOUR LOVE AWAY' and Tim Hardin's 'IF I WERE A CARPENTER' in his own inimitable style. Subsequently relocating to London, ROSE hooked up with HARDIN (a similarly struggling and underrated singer/songwriter) to form a live duo, although this pairing was also doomed to failure. After a final album for 'Atlantic', 'THE MUSICIAN' (1975), ROSE faded into obscurity for the best part of fifteen years, finally re-emerging in 1991 with 'THE GAMBLER'. More recently, there has been a bit of a mini TIM ROSE revival, what with the CD reissue of his first two albums (on 'BGO'), the patronage of none other than murder balladeer, NICK CAVE, and a suitably scary rendition of 'HEY JOE' on BBC 1's 'Later With Jools'.

Album rating: TIM ROSE (aka MORNING DEW) (*7) / THROUGH ROSE COLOURED GLASSES (*6) / LOVE – A KIND OF HATE STORY (*4) / TIM ROSE (*4) / THE MUSICIAN (*4) / THE GAMBLER (*4) / HAUNTED (*5) / HIDE YOUR LOVE AWAY (THE COLLECTION 1970-1974) compilation (*6)

TIM ROSE – vocals, guitar; with session people **HUGH McCRACKEN + JAY BERLINER** – guitar / **FELIX PAPPALARDI** – bass, producer (CREAM producer) / **BERNARD PURDIE** – drums

		C.B.S.	Columbia
Dec 66.	(7") <43958> **I'M GONNA BE STRONG. / I GOT A LONELINESS**	-	
Mar 67.	(7") (202631) <44031> **MORNING DEW. / YOU'RE SLIPPING AWAY FROM ME** (re-iss. 1970; 2631)		
Nov 67.	(7") <44387> **COME AWAY MELINDA. / LONG TIME MAN**	-	
Feb 68.	(7") (3277) **I GOT A LONELINESS. / LONG TIME MAN**	-	
Feb 68.	(lp; stereo/mono) (S+/BPG 63168) <9577> **TIM ROSE**		

– I got a loneliness / I'm gonna be strong / I gotta do things my way / Fare thee well / Eat, drink and be merry / Hey Joe / Morning dew / Where was I / You're slipping away from me / Long time man / Come away, Melinda. (re-iss. Apr88 as 'MORNING DEW' on 'Edsel' lp/cd; ED/+CD 267)

| May 68. | (7") (3478) **I GUESS IT'S OVER. / HELLO SUNSHINE** | | |
| Jul 68. | (7") (3598) **LONG-HAIRED BOY. / LOOKING AT MY BABY** | | |

—— now totally solo.

Apr 69.	(7") <44792> **ANGELA. / WHATCHA GONNA DO**	-	
Jun 69.	(7") (4209) <44849> **ROANOKE. / BABY YOU TURN ME ON**		
Jul 69.	(lp) (63636) <9772> **THROUGH ROSE COLOURED GLASSES**		

– The days back when / Roanoke / Hello sunshine / When I was a young man / Whatcha gonna do / Let there be love / Baby you turn me on / Apple truck swamper / Angela / You'd laugh / You ain't my girl no more.

		Capitol	Capitol
Jan 71.	(7") <3001> **I'VE GOTTA GET A MESSAGE TO YOU. / JAMIE SUE**	-	
Feb 71.	(7") (CL 15664) **I'VE GOTTA GET A MESSAGE TO YOU. / ODE TO AN OLD BALL**		-
Feb 71.	(lp) (ST 22673) <673> **LOVE – A KIND OF HATE STORY**		Nov70

– I've gotta get a message to you / Dimlight / Where do you go to my lovely / You can't stop yourself / Sad song / Georgia by morning / Ode to an old ball / Sympathy / I know these two people / Jamie Sue.

—— added **GARY WRIGHT** – keyboards, producer / **MICK JONES** – guitar / **ARCHIE LEGGETT** – bass / **BRYSON GRAHAM** – drums

		Dawn	Playboy
1972.	(7") (50005> **IT TAKES A LITTLE LONGER. / HIDE YOUR LOVE AWAY**	-	
1973.	(7") <50012> **GOIN' DOWN TO HOLLYWOOD. /**	-	
1974.	(lp) (DNLS 3062) <101> **TIM ROSE**		1972

– It takes a little longer / You can't keep me / Hide your love away / Boogie woogie / If I were a carpenter / Cryin' shame / Darling you were all that I had / Cotton growin' man / Goin' down in Hollywood.

| Sep 74. | (7") (DNS 1085) **HIDE YOUR LOVE AWAY. / IF I WERE A CARPENTER** | | - |

now with a plethara of musicians.

		Atlantic	not iss.
1975.	(lp) (K 50183) **THE MUSICIAN**		-

– 7:30 song / Small town talk / The musician / Loving arms / Old man / It's not my life that's been changin' / The day I spent with you / Second avenue / Now you're a lady / Where is the good life. (cd-iss. Nov95 on 'Edsel';)

| Oct 75. | (7") (K 10667) **THE MUSICIAN. / 7:30 SONG** | | - |

—— retired from music business until below.

		President	not iss.
Nov 91.	(cd/c) (PCOM/PTLC 1117) **THE GAMBLER**		-

– I just wanna make love to you / He was born to be a lady / Dance on ma belle / It'll be alright on the night / Runaway / Moving targets / The gambler / Blow me back Santa Ana / So much to lose / Is there something 'bout the way I hold my gun / Bowery Avenue / Laurie.

		Best Dressed	Best Dressed
May 98.	(cd) <(SKIRT 51)> **HAUNTED**		Nov97

– (Hey Joe) Blu steel '44 / Give your lovin' to the livin' / He never was a hero / Natural thing / Mite confused? / I ain't had no lovin' / Because you're rich / Dealer / Come away, Melinda / Haunted / Four dancin' queens / Hanging tree / I sold it with my cat / Morning dew.

– compilations, etc. –

Dec 87.	(lp) See For Miles; (SEE 213) **I'VE GOTTA GET A MESSAGE TO YOU**		-
Nov 97.	(cd) Beat Goes On; (BGOCD 378) **TIM ROSE / THROUGH ROSE COLOURED GLASSES**		-
Jul 98.	(cd) Flying Thorn; (MMR 700) **HIDE YOUR LOVE AWAY (THE COLLECTION 1970-1974)**		-

Diana ROSS (see under ⇒ SUPREMES)

Ricky ROSS (see under ⇒ DEACON BLUE)

Francis ROSSI (see under ⇒ STATUS QUO)

ROSSINGTON-COLLINS BAND (see under ⇒ LYNYRD SKYNYRD)

David Lee ROTH

Born: 10 Oct'55, Bloomington, Indiana, USA. Suffering from hyperactivity from an early age, he attended a child clinic at the age of eight. His family subsequently moved to Pasadena, where he later joined the group, MAMMOTH, in 1973. Two years later, this outfit had evolved into VAN HALEN, ROTH taking centre stage as their inimitably OTT frontman over a period of ten years. During this time, the group became one of the biggest hard rock/metal acts in the world as well as regularly hitting the pop charts. By the mid-80's, however, ROTH was getting restless, recording a mini solo album, 'CRAZY FROM THE HEAT', as a side project in early '85. Scoring a US Top 3 hit with one of its singles, a memorable cover of The Beach Boys' 'CALIFORNIA GIRLS', 'Diamond' DAVE finally decided to take the plunge and leave VAN HALEN later that summer. Enlisting a cast of crack rock troopers including guitarist STEVE VAI (ex-FRANK ZAPPA) and much touted bassist, BILLY SHEEHAN (ex-TALAS, future MR. BIG), ROTH cut a fully fledged solo album, 'EAT 'EM AND SMILE'. Released in the summer of '86, the album was roundly praised in the rock press, making the US Top 5. Alive with the singer's infectious enthusiasm and natural talent for showmanship, the record was a consistently entertaining listen, the brilliant 'YANKEE ROSE' making the US Top 20. Its follow-up, 'SKYSCRAPER', duly appeared a couple of years later, the sleeve depicting DAVE in the throes of his latest obsession, rock climbing. Fittingly then, there was a lofty, widescreen sound to much of the album, the soaring 'JUST LIKE PARADISE' giving ROTH his first solo UK Top 10 hit. By the release of 'A LITTLE AIN'T ENOUGH' (1991), both VAI and SHEEHAN had departed, the album missing their instrumental spark and underlining ROTH's increasingly formulaic approach. Though the album made the US Top 5, it failed to spawn any hit singles, ROTH subsequently sacking his band and heading for New York. Not that he fared much better in the Big Apple, the singer running into personal problems and failing to kickstart his ailing career with the poor 'YOUR FILTHY LITTLE MOUTH' (1994). Not a man to be held down for long, motormouth DAVE subsequently re-united with VAN HALEN. • **Songwriters:** ROTH written (most with STEVE VAI '86-88), except JUST A GIGOLO (Ted Lewis) / I AIN'T GOT NOBODY (Marian Harris) / THAT'S LIFE (hit; Frank Sinatra) / TOBACCO ROAD (Nashville Teens).

Album rating: CRAZY FROM THE HEAT mini (*5) / EAT 'EM AND SMILE (*7) / SKYSCRAPER (*5) / A LITTLE AIN'T ENOUGH (*4) / YOUR FILTHY LITTLE MOUTH (*3)

DAVID LEE ROTH – vocals (ex-VAN HALEN) with **DEAN PARKS + EDDIE MARTINEZ + SID McGINNIS** – guitar / **EDGAR WINTER** – keyboards, sax, synthesizers, vocals / **JAMES NEWTON HOWARD** – synthesizers / **WILLIE WEEKS** – bass / **JOHN ROBINSOB** – drums / **SAMMY FIGUEROA** – percussion / **BRIAN MANN** – synthesizers

		Warners	Warners
Feb 85.	(7") (W 9102> <29102> **CALIFORNIA GIRLS. / ('A'remix)**	68	3 Jan85

(above featured CARL WILSON of The BEACH BOYS on backing vocals)

| Feb 85. | (m-lp/m-c) (925222-1/-4) <25222> **CRAZY FROM THE HEAT** | 91 | 15 |

– Easy street / Just a gigolo – I ain't got nobody / Coconut Grove / California girls.

| Apr 85. | (7") (W 9040> <29040> **JUST A GIGOLO – I AIN'T GOT NOBODY. / ('A'remix)** | | 12 Mar85 |

—— **STEVE VAI** – guitar (ex-FRANK ZAPPA) / **BILLY SHEEHAN** – bass (ex-TALAS) / **BRETT TUGGLE** – keyboards / **GREGG BISSONETTE** (b. 9 Jun'59) – drums

| Jul 86. | (7"/7"sha-pic-d) (W 8656/+P) <28656> **YANKEE ROSE. / SHYBOY** | | 16 |

(12"+=) (W 8656T) – Easy street.

| Jul 86. | (lp/c)(cd) (WX 56/+C)(925470-2) <25470> **EAT 'EM AND SMILE** | 28 | 4 |

– Yankee Rose / Shyboy / I'm easy / Ladies' nite in Buffalo? / Goin' crazy! / Tobacco Road / Elephant gun / Big trouble / Bump and grind / That's life.

| Sep 86. | (7") <28584> **GOIN' CRAZY! / OOCO DEO CALOR (Spanish version)** | - | 66 |
| Nov 86. | (7") <28511> **THAT'S LIFE. / BUMP AND GRIND** | - | 85 |

—— **MATT BISSONETTE** – bass repl. SHEEHAN who joined OZZY OSBOURNE

| Jan 88. | (lp/c)(cd) (WX 140/+C)(925671-2) <25671> **SKYSCRAPER** | 11 | 6 |

– Knucklebones / Just like paradise / The bottom line / Skyscraper / Damn good / Hot dog and a shake / Stand up / Hina / Perfect timing / Two fools a minute. (cd+=) – California girls / Just a gigolo – I ain't got nobody. (re-iss. Jan89 lp/c)(cd; WX 236/+C)(925824-2)

| Feb 88. | (7") (W 8119) <28119> **JUST LIKE PARADISE. / THE BOTTOM LINE** | 27 | 6 Jan88 |

(12"pic-d+=/3"cd-s+=) (W 8119 TP/CD) – Yankee Rose.

Apr 88.	(7") <28108> **STAND UP. / KNUCKLEBONES**	-	64
Jul 88.	(7") <27825> **DAMN GOOD. / SKYSCRAPER**	-	
Jul 88.	(7"/12") (W 7753/+T) **DAMN GOOD. / STAND UP**	72	-
Nov 88.	(7") (W 7650) **CALIFORNIA GIRLS. / JUST A GIGOLO**	-	

(12"+=) (W 7650T) – I ain't got nobody.
(cd-s++=) (W 7650CD) – Yankee Rose.

—— (Apr'89-Jan'90) **ROCKY RICHETTE** – guitar (ex-STEPPENWOLF, ex-BLACK ROSE) repl. STEVE VAI who went solo and joined WHITESNAKE

—— (Oct'90) **TODD JENSEN** – bass (ex-HARLOW) repl. MATT / **DEZZI REXX + JOE HOLMES** – guitar repl. JASON BECKER + ROCKY RICHETTE

		W.E.A.	Warners
Dec 90.	(7"/c-s) (W 0002/+C) **A LITTLE AIN'T ENOUGH. / BABY'S ON FIRE**	32	

(12"+=/cd-s+=) (W 0002 T/CD) – Tell the truth.

| Jan 91. | (cd)(lp/c) <(7599 26477-2)>(WX 403/+C) **A LITTLE AIN'T ENOUGH** | 4 | 18 |

– A little ain't enough / Shoot it / Lady Luck / Hammerhead shark / Tell the truth / Baby's on fire / 40 below / Sensible shoes / Last call / The dogtown shuffle / It's showtime! / Drop in the bucket.

Mar 91. (7"/5"sha-pic-d) *(W 0016/+P/C)* **SENSIBLE SHOES. / A LIL AIN'T ENOUGH**
(12"/cd-s) *(W 0016 T/CD)* – ('A'side) / California girls / Just a gigolo / I ain't got nobody.

Feb 94. (7"/c-s) *(W 0229/+C)* **SHE'S MY MACHINE. / MISSISSIPPI POWER** `64`
(cd-s+=) *(W 0229CD1)* – Land's edge / Yo breathin' it.
(cd-s+=) *(W 0229CD2)* – ('A'mixes).

Mar 94. (cd/c/lp) *<(9362 45391-2/-4/-1)>* **YOUR FILTHY LITTLE MOUTH** `28` `78`
– She's my machine / Everybody's got the monkey / Big train / Experience / A little luck / Cheatin' heart cafe / Hey, you never know / No big 'ting / Yo breathin' it / Your filthy little mouth / Land's edge / Night life / Sunburn / You're breathin' it (urban NYC mix).

May 94. (7"/c-s) *(W 0249/+C)* **NIGHT LIFE. / JUMP (live)** `72`
(cd-s+=) *(W 0249CD1)* – She's my machine (live).
(cd-s+=) *(W 0249CD2)* – ('A'side) / Panama (live) / Big train (live) / Experience (live).

—— returned to VAN HALEN in 1996.

– compilations, etc. –

Nov 97. (cd/c) *Warners; <(8122 72941-2/-4/)>* **THE BEST OF DAVID LEE ROTH**
– Don't piss me off / Yankee rose / A lil' ain't enough / Just like Paradise / Big train / Big trouble / It's showtime / Hot dog and a shake / Skyscraper / Shyboy / She's my machine / Stand up / Tobacco road / Easy street / California girls / Just a gigolo / I ain't got nobody / Sensible shoes / Goin' crazy / Ladies nite in Buffalo / Land's edge.

Kevin ROWLAND (see under ⇒ DEXY'S MIDNIGHT RUNNERS)

ROXETTE

Formed: Halmstad, Sweden … 1984 by long-time sweethearts, singer MARIE FREDRIKSSON and songwriter PER GESSLE. This 80's power ballad duo met whilst recording in a local studio with separate bands; GESSLE's pedigree was fronting rock band GYLLENE TIDER. For the next two years, he began writing for the likes of FRIDA LYNGSTAD (ex-ABBA), who recorded a few numbers for her 1984 album. They immediately found that they shared similar ambitions of becoming hugely successful in a pop/rock group. The two set out to make what was to become their debut set, 'PEARLS OF PASSION', in 1986. This sold relativley well on their home turf but died a death when it received no backing for a release abroad. It displayed the usual 80's synth and MOR guitar riffs backed by FREDRIKSSON's histrionic and terribly irritating vocals; the cheesy lyrics could also make a grown man cry. Nevertheless, the two pop divas returned in 1988 with the sophomore set, 'LOOK SHARP!', which climbed high in the Swedish charts, but, like the aforementioned debut, didn't sell too well outside of ROXETTE's native country. It wasn't until an American student took an import of singles 'THE LOOK' and 'LISTEN TO YOUR HEART' into his college radio station, that the tracks – with soaring choruses and serious rock guitar et al – began receiving airplay around the US and subsequently Europe. Inevitably, the former was released by 'E.M.I.', who catapulted the band into the limelight and the UK Top 10 having achieved No.1 in the States; now released worldwide, 'LOOK SHARP!' went on to sell a staggering 7 million copies. The following year saw the pair return to Sweden after notching up further US No.1 successes, 'LISTEN TO YOUR HEART' and 'IT MUST HAVE BEEN LOVE' (the latter taken from the 'Pretty Woman' soundtrack). The follow-up, 'JOYRIDE', was finally issued in March '91 to great commercial acclaim, although the critics (me included!) were still apparently dumbfounded. The same format remained, a few poppish rock songs (the title track, for example) neatly juxtapositioned between crass ballads ('CHURCH OF YOUR HEART') and sweeping laments … not for the faint hearted (!). 'TOURISM (SONGS FROM STUDIOS, STAGES, HOTEL ROOMS AND OTHER STRANGE PLACES)' reared its ugly head in the Spring of 1992. The album was obviously a collection of live performances, studio sessions and basic songs that had been thrown into the proverbial melting pot; the only high point of 'TOURISM …' was its harder-edged live songs. Two years later, the group reappeared with 'CRASH! BOOM! BANG!', their "mature" album, which was mostly filled with soft, soothing acoustic pop ballads, something that you wouldn't expect by the use of onomatopoeia in the title. 'DON'T BORE US … GET TO THE CHORUS' (a greatest hits package), was released the following year. This tongue-in-cheek title (we think!?) could have been what was so unappealing about ROXETTE: instead of feeling and thought and true emotion, sprung from or inspired by real life experiences, FREDRIKSSON and GESSLE had little to say in the way of expressing visions both musically and lyrically. However, the duo kept the hits coming (although now only minor and in the UK), ROXETTE discovering that the fickle lifespan of pop in the rock market was harder than just churning out the same sounding pap. GESSLE even ventured solo in 1997 before ROXETTE re-emerged once again in '99 with more pop drivel. • **Trivia:** CLARENCE OFWERMAN, the 3rd member, was also their producer. In 1991, Sweden used their heads on a new postage stamp.

Album rating: PEARLS OF PASSION (*4) / LOOK SHARP! (*6) / JOYRIDE (*5) / TOURISM (*4) / CRAH! BOOM! BANG! (*3) / DON'T BORE US … GET TO THE CHORUS: GREATEST HITS VOL.1 compilation (*7) / HAVE A NICE DAY (*6) / Gessle: THE WORLD ACCORDING TO GESSLE (*4)

MARIE FREDRIKSSON (b. 30 May'58) – vocals / **PER GESSLE** (b. 12 Jun'59) – guitar, vocals

			unknown	not iss.
1986.	(lp/c) *(136245-1/-4)* **PEARLS OF PASSION**		–	– Swedish
1987.	(m-lp) *(136261-1)* **DANCE PASSION** (remix)		–	– Sweden

—— with band, CLARENCE OFWERMAN – keyboards, prog. / JONAS ISACSSON – guitars / PELLE ALSING – drums / ERIK HAUSLER – sax / ANDERS HERRLIN – bass, prog., engineer / JALLE LORENSSON – harmonica / JANIE OLDAEUS – slide guitar / ERIK BORELIUS – Spanish guitar and sessioners on 3 GRAHAM EDWARDS – bass / ADAM McCULLOCH – sax / MORRIS MICHAEL – guitar / ANDREW WRIGHT – keyboards

		E.M.I.	E.M.I.
Feb 89. (c-s/7") *(TC+/EM 87)* *<50190>* **THE LOOK. / SILVER BLUE**		7	1

(12"+=/cd-s+=) *(12/CD EM 87)* – ('A'-Heddrum mix).

Mar 89. (cd/c/lp) *(CD/TC+/EMC 3557)* *<91098>* **LOOK SHARP!** `45` `23`
– The look / Dressed for success / Sleeping single / Paint / Dance away / Cry / Chances / Dangerous / Half a woman, half a shadow / View from a hill / Shadow of a doubt / Listen to your heart. (cd+=) – (I could never) Give you up. *(hit No.4 in the UK, Jun90) (re-iss. cd+c Sep94)*

May 89. (7") *<50204>* **DRESSED FOR SUCCESS. / THE LOOK (version)** `–` `14`

Jun 89. (c-s/7") *(TC+/EM 96)* **DRESSED FOR SUCCESS. / THE VOICE** `48` `–`
(12"+=) *(12EM 96)* – The look (version).
(cd-s+=) *(CDEM 96)* – ('A'-Big red mix).

Aug 89. (7") *<50223>* **LISTEN TO YOUR HEART. / HALF A WOMAN, HALF A SHADOW** `–` `1`

Oct 89. (c-s/7") *(TC+/EM 108)* **LISTEN TO YOUR HEART. / (I COULD NEVER) GIVE YOU UP** `62` `–`
(12"+=) *(12EM 108)* – Dressed for success (mix).
(cd-s+=) *(CDEM 108)* – Dressed for success (radio mix) / ('A'-Swedish mix).

Dec 89. (c-s,12") *<50233>* **DANGEROUS. / ('A'extended)** `–` `2`
Apr 90. (c-s) *<50283>* **IT MUST HAVE BEEN LOVE / CHANCES** `–` `1`
May 90. (c-s/7") *(TC+/EM 141)* **IT MUST HAVE BEEN LOVE. / PAINT** `3` `–`
(12"+=) *(12EM 141)* – Cry (live).
(cd-s+=) *(CDEM 141)* – Surrender (live).

Jul 90. (c-s/7") *(TC+/EM 149)* **LISTEN TO YOUR HEART. / DANGEROUS** `6` `–`
(12"+=) *(12EM 149)* – Dangerous (US club mix).
(cd-s++=) *(CDEM 149)* – ('A'-Swedish mix) / ('A'-US club mix).

Oct 90. (c-s/7") *(TC+/EM 162)* **DRESSED FOR SUCCESS. / THE VOICE** `18` `–`
(12"+=/cd-s+=) *(12/CD EM 162)* – The look (big red mix).

—— they still retained OFWERSON + ISACSSON

Mar 91. (c-s/7") *(TC+/EM 177)* *<50342>* **JOYRIDE. / COME BACK (BEFORE YOU LEAVE)** `4` `1`
(12"+=) *(12EM 177)* – ('A'magic friend mix).
(cd-s++=) *(CDEM 177)* – ('A'-US remix).

Apr 91. (cd/c/lp) *(CD/TC+/EMD 1019)* *<94435>* **JOYRIDE** `2` `12`
– Joyride / Hotblooded / Fading like a flower (every time you leave) / Knockin' on every door / Spending my time / I remember you *[not on lp]* / Watercolours in the rain / The big L / Soul deep / (Do you get) Excited? / Church of your heart *[not on lp]* / Small talk / Physical fascination / Things will never be the same / Perfect day.

May 91. (c-s/7") *(TC+/EM 190)* *<50355>* **FADING LIKE A FLOWER (EVERY TIME YOU LEAVE). / I REMEMBER YOU** `12` `2`
(12"+=) *(12EM 190)* – The look.
(cd-s+=) *(CDEM 190)* – Physical fascination (guitar solo).

Aug 91. (c-s/7") *(TC+/EM 204)* **THE BIG L. / ONE IS SUCH A LONELY NUMBER (demo)** `21`
(cd-s+=) *(CDEM 204)* – ('A'-Better mix) / It must have been love.
(12"+=) *(CDEMS 204)* – ('A'-US mix) / It must have been love.

Nov 91. (c-s/7") *(TC+/EM 215)* *<50366>* **SPENDING MY TIME. / LISTEN TO YOUR HEART (Swedish)** `22` `32` Oct91
(cd-s+=) *(CDEM 215)* – The sweet hello, the sad goodbye / ('A'-Electric dance mix) / Listen to your heart.

Mar 92. (c-s/7") *(TC+/EM 227)* *<50380>* **CHURCH OF YOUR HEART. / ROXETTE MEGAMIX** `21` `36` Feb92
(cd-s+=) *(CDEM 227)* – Soul deep.
(cd-s) *(CDEMS 227)* – ('A'side) / I call your name / Come back (before you leave) / Fading like a flower (every time you leave).

—— Basically same line-up as before

Jul 92. (c-s/7") *(TC+/EM 241)* *<50410>* **HOW DO YOU DO! / FADING LIKE A FLOWER (EVERY TIME YOU LEAVE)** `13` `58` Sep92
(cd-s+=) *(CDEM 241)* – How do you do! (mix) / Knockin' on Heaven's door.

Jul 92. (cd/c/d-lp) *(CD/TC+/EMD 1036)* *<99929>* **TOURISM (live *)** `2`
– How do you do! / Fingertips / The look * / The heart shaped sea / The rain / Keep me waiting / It must have been love * / Cinnamon street / Never is a long time / Silver blue / Here comes the weekend * / So far away * / Come back (before you leave) / Things will never be the same / Joyride * / Queen of rain.

Nov 92. (c-s/7") *(TC+/EM 253)* **QUEEN OF RAIN. / PEARLS OF PASSION** `28`
(cd-s) *(CDEM 253)* – ('A'side) / It must have been love / Paint / Dangerous.
(cd-s+=) *(CDEMS 253)* – (interview).

Jul 93. (c-s/7") *(TC+/EM 268)* *<44942>* **ALMOST UNREAL. / THE HEART SHAPED SEA** `7` `94` Jun93
(cd-s+=/12"pic-d+=) *(CD/12 EM 268)* – Fingertips '93 / ('A'-AC mix). (above single from the movie 'Super Mario Bros.' on 'Capitol')

Sep 93. (c-s/7") *(TC+/EM 285)* **IT MUST HAVE BEEN LOVE (remix). / DANGEROUS** `10`
(cd-s+=) *(CDEM 285)* – 2 Cinnamon Street / How do you do.

Mar 94. (c-s/7") *(TC+/EM 314)* *<58143>* **SLEEPING IN MY CAR. / THE LOOK (unplugged version)** `14` `50` Jun94
(cd-s+=) *(CDEM 314)* – ('A'demo) / Almost unreal.

Apr 94. (cd/c/lp) *(CD/TC+/EMD 1056)* **CRASH! BOOM! BANG!** `3`
– Harleys & Indians (riders in the sky) / Crash! boom! bang! / Fireworks / Run to you / Sleeping in my car / Vulnerable / The first girl on the Moon / Place your love / I love the sound of crashing guitars / What's she like / Do you wanna go the whole way? / Lies / I'm sorry / Love is all (shine your light on me) / Go to sleep.

May 94. (c-s/7") (TC+/EM 324) **CRASH! BOOM! BANG! / JOYRIDE (unplugged)** `26` `-`
(cd-s+=) (CDEM 324) – The look.
(cd-s=) (CDEMS 324) – ('A'side) / Run to you / It must have been love.

Aug 94. (c-s/7") (TC+/EM 345) **FIREWORKS. / CRASH! BOOM! BANG!** `30`
(cd-s+=) (CDEM 345) – Dangerous (MTV unplugged) / The rain (demo).
(cd-s) (CDEMS 345) – ('A'side) / ('A'mixes) / I'm sorry (demo) / Sleeping in my car.

Nov 94. (c-s/7") (TC+/EM 360) **RUN TO YOU. / LOVE IS ALL (SHINE YOUR LIGHT ON ME)** `27`
(cd-s) (CDEM 360) – ('A'side) / Don't believe in accidents (demo) / Crash! boom! bang! (demos) / Almost unreal (demo).
(cd-s) (CDEMS 360) – ('A'side) / Listen to your heart / How do you do! / Joyride.

Mar 95. (c-s) (TCEM 369) **VULNERABLE / THE SWEET HELLO, THE SAD GOODBYE** `44`
(cd-s+=) (CDEM 369) – ('A'mix.)

Oct 95. (cd/c) (CD/TC EMTV 98) **DON'T BORE US . . . GET TO THE CHORUS! – GREATEST HITS VOL.1** (compilation) `5` `-`
– June afternoon / You don't understand me / The look / Dressed for success / Listen to your heart / Dangerous / It must have been love / Joyride / Fading like a flower / The big L / Spending my time / How do you do? / Almost unreal / Sleeping in my car / Crash! boom! bang! / Vulnerable / She doesn't live anymore / I don't want to get hurt.

Nov 95. (c-s) (TCEM 406) **THE LOOK '95 (remix) / ('A'mix)** `28`
(cd-s+=) (CDEM 406) – ('A'mixes – 2).
(cd-s) (CDEMS 406) – ('A'side) / The look (original) / Crazy about you / Dressed for success (U.S. version).

Mar 96. (c-s) (TCEM 418) **YOU DON'T UNDERSTAND ME / THE SWEET HELLO, THE SAD GOODBYE** `42`
(cd-s+=) (CDEM 418) – Almost unreal (demo) / Harleys and Indians (riders in the sky).
(cd-s) (CDEMS 418) – ('A'side) / The look (acoustic) / Listen to your heart (acoustic) / You don't understand me (acoustic).

Jul 96. (c-s) (TCEM 437) **JUNE AFTERNOON / SEDUCE ME** `52`
(cd-s+=) (CDEM 437) – It must have been love / Listen to your heart.

Mar 99. (c-s) (TCEM 537) **WISH I COULD FLY / HAPPY TOGETHER** `11`
(cd-s+=) (CDEM 537) – ('A'-Tee's In House mix).
(cd-s) (CDEMS 537) – ('A'side) / ('A'-Tee's radio mix) / ('A'-Stonebridge R&B mix) / ('A'-Stonebridge club mix).

Mar 99. (cd/c) (499461-2/-4) **HAVE A NICE DAY** `28`
– Crush on you / Wish I could fly / You can't put your arms around what's already gone / Waiting for the rain / Anyone / It will take a long long time / 7 twenty 7 / I was so lucky / Stars / Salvation / Pay the price / Cooper / Staring at the ground / Beautiful.

Jul 99. (c-s/cd-s) (TCEM/CDEM 543) **ANYONE / LISTEN TO YOUR HEART (Abbey Road session) / THE LOOK (Abbey Road session)**

Sep 99. (c-s/cd-s) (TCEM/CDEM 550) **STARS / ANYONE**
(cd-s+=) (CDEMS 550) – ('A'mixes; Almighty radio / Almighty 12" definitive / X-treme extended).

(Per) GESSLE

May 97. (cd) (CDEMD 1105) **THE WORLD ACCORDING TO GESSLE**
– (You make me feel so) Stupid / Do you wanna be my baby / Saturday / Elvis in Germany / I want you to know / The reporter / B any 1 U wanna B / Wish you the best / Kix / T-T-Take it / It'll be alright / There is my baby / Lay down your arms.

Nov 97. (cd-s) (CDEM 501) **KIX (mixes) / LOVE DOESN'T LIVE HERE**
(cd-s) (CDEMS 501) – ('A'side) / Blue umbrella / Jupiter calling / Let's party.

ROXY MUSIC

Formed: Newcastle, England . . . 1970 by art school graduate and teacher, BRYAN FERRY alongside GRAHAM SIMPSON. Early in 1971, they invited ANDY MACKAY and electronic wizard BRIAN ENO to join, finally settling with the debut album line-up a year later, when they added PHIL MANZANERA and PAUL THOMPSON. The concept of ROXY MUSIC was the brainchild of FERRY, who attempted to realise his vision of a musical equivalent to the pop art he'd become fascinated with at college. Fashioning the band in an outlandish hybrid of decadent glamour and future shock experimentalism, FERRY made sure ROXY MUSIC would be hot property after only a handful of gigs. At this point, the other prime mover behind ROXY MUSIC was BRIAN ENO, who shaped the band's pioneering sound by wrenching all manner of bizarre electronic noises from his mini-moog, feeding the rest of the instruments through an EMS modular synth and masterminding pre-recorded special effects. Signed to 'Island', the band released their self-titled debut in the summer of 1972. Produced by PETE SINFIELD (the KING CRIMSON lyricist), the album effortlessly fused FERRY's suave crooning, a pulsing rhythm section and ENO's inspired electronic experimentation, garnering rave reviews and defying any attempts to pigeonhole the band's sound. But it was the follow-up single, 'VIRGINIA PLAIN' (1972), which launched the band into pop stardom. A careering blast of avant-pop that managed to incorporate a lyric focussing on one of FERRY's surrealist paintings, the single breached the upper echelons of the charts. By this juncture, SIMPSON had been given his marching orders and the band went through a bewildering succession of personnel changes, FERRY retaining strict control throughout. After another top ten hit with 'PYJAMARAMA' in 1973, ROXY MUSIC released their second album, 'FOR YOUR PLEASURE' later the same year. Juxtaposing the ironic wig-out of tracks like 'DO THE STRAND' and 'BEAUTY QUEEN' with the vivid desolation of 'IN EVERY DREAM

HOME A HEARTACHE', the album distilled the essence of FERRY's original vision. ENO left soon after, his more extreme experimental leanings at odds with the direction in which FERRY wanted to take the band. FERRY also began a solo career around this time which he ran in tandem with the band, releasing an album of covers, 'THESE FOOLISH THINGS', in 1973. ROXY MUSIC, meanwhile, released their third masterpiece, 'STRANDED', a month later. The first album to feature new recruit EDDIE JOBSON (ex-CURVED AIR), the record was less confrontational but more assured in terms of songwriting, FERRY excelling himself with the haunted romanticism of 'MOTHER OF PEARL' and the sweeping grandeur of 'A SONG FOR EUROPE'. A typically ROXY slice of ambiguous, discordant pop, the single, 'STREET LIFE', gave the band yet another Top 10 hit. By the following summer, FERRY had another solo album on the shelves; 'ANOTHER TIME, ANOTHER PLACE' saw him revelling in the role of slicked-back sophisticate, while ROXY's 'COUNTRY LIFE' saw the band in rock-out mode on tracks like 'THE THRILL OF IT ALL', while still buffing the sound with an ironic sheen. Despite a promising single, 'LOVE IS THE DRUG', 'SIREN' (1975) found FERRY's studied musings sounding jaded. Less then a year later, the band split, with McKAY and MANZANERA off to work on solo projects while JOBSON joined FRANK ZAPPPA. FERRY, meanwhile, concentrated on his burgeoning solo career, hitting Top 5 with the funky 'LET'S STICK TOGETHER', following it up with the good-time album of the same name, for once going a bit easier on the irony. 'IN YOUR MIND' (1977) kept up the momentum, spawning the hit, 'TOKYO JOE', and seeing FERRY branch out into original material. Recorded in L.A. with aging session musicians, the sober tones of 'THE BRIDE STRIPPED BARE' (1978) were never going to gain much headway during the height of the punk explosion, yet it remains one the more accessible of FERRY's solo albums. The same year, he cannily reformed ROXY MUSIC, 'MANIFESTO' (1979) heralding a smoother, cleaner sound with the emphasis on FERRY's wistful crooning. The singles 'ANGEL EYES' and 'DANCE AWAY' were the first in a string of tortured pop nuggets that breached the upper reaches of the charts at the turn of the decade, the band finally reaching No.1 with their sublime cover of JOHN LENNON's 'JEALOUS GUY' in 1981. 'FLESH AND BLOOD' (1980) and 'AVALON' (1982) were commercial but finely honed and exquisitely melodic, the latter a quintessentially 80's piece of synthesizer sophistication which inspired many 'New wave-futurist' bands of the 80's. On this high note, FERRY disbanded ROXY MUSIC finally in 1982 and resumed his solo career, carving out a niche as a purveyor of refined, complex adult-orientated pop on albums 'BOYS AND GIRLS' (1985) and 'BETE NOIR' (1987). 'TAXI' (1993) saw him return to covers material while 'MAMOUNA' (1994) was an accomplished, mature set of original material. • **Songwriters:** FERRY / MANZANERA with contributions from MACKAY and ENO, until the latter bailed out. They covered; IN THE MIDNIGHT HOUR (Wilson Pickett) / EIGHT MILES HIGH (Byrds) / JEALOUS GUY (John Lennon) / LIKE A HURRICANE (Neil Young). • **FERRY's solo covers:-** A HARD RAIN'S A-GONNA FALL (Bob Dylan) / SYMPATHY FOR THE DEVIL (Rolling Stones) / DON'T EVER CHANGE (Crickets) / THESE FOOLISH THINGS (Col Porter?) / PIECE OF MY HEART (hit; Janis Joplin) / I LOVE HOW YOU LOVE ME (Paris Sisters) / DON'T WORRY BABY (Beach Boys) / TRACKS OF MY TEARS (Miracles) / IT'S MY PARTY (Leslie Gore) / BABY I DON'T CARE (Leiber-Stoller) / WALK A MILE IN MY SHOES (Joe South) / THE IN-CROWD (Dobie Gray) / WHAT A WONDERFUL WORLD (Sam Cooke) / YOU ARE MY SUNSHINE (Ray Charles) / SMOKE GETS IN YOUR EYES (Platters) / HELP ME MAKE IT THROUGH THE NIGHT (Kris Kristofferson) / FINGERPOPPIN' (Hank Ballard) / FUNNY HOW TIME SLIPS AWAY (Jimmy Ellidge) / LET'S STICK TOGETHER (Wilbert Harrison) / THE PRICE OF LOVE (Everly Brothers) / IT'S ONLY LOVE (Barry White) / SHAME SHAME SHAME (Shirley & Company) / HEART ON MY SLEEVE (Gallagher & Lyle) / SHE'S LEAVING HOME + YOU WON'T SEE ME (Beatles) / WHEN SHE WALKS IN THE ROOM (Searchers) / TAKE ME TO THE RIVER (Al Green) / YOU DON'T KNOW (Sam & Dave) / PARTY DOLL (Buddy Knox) / FEEL THE NEED (Detroit Emeralds). Note:- JOHNNY MARR (ex-Smiths) co-wrote THE RIGHT STUFF in 1987. FERRY returned in 1993 with a covers album 'TAXI'. • **Trivia:** FERRY married model, Lucy Helmore, on the 26th of June '82 after a 70's relationship with Jerry Hall had finished. He was said to have turned down the Keith Forsey-penned song, 'DON'T YOU FORGET ABOUT ME', a No.1 for SIMPLE MINDS.

Album rating: ROXY MUSIC (*8) / FOR YOUR PLEASURE (*9) / STRANDED (*8) / COUNTRY LIFE (*7) / SIREN (*6) / VIVA! ROXY MUSIC (*5) / GREATEST HITS compilation (*8) / MANIFESTO (*6) / FLESH + BLOOD (*5) / AVALON (*7) / THE HIGH ROAD mini (*4) / THE ATLANTIC YEARS 1973-1980 compilation (*5) / Bryan Ferry: THESE FOOLISH THINGS (*7) / ANOTHER TIME, ANOTHER PLACE (*5) / LET'S STICK TOGETHER (*6) / IN YOUR MIND (*5) / THE BRIDE STRIPPED BARE (*6) / BOYS AND GIRLS (*7) / BETE NOIRE (*5) / TAXI (*4) / MAMOUNA (*5) / AS TIME GOES BY (*3) / Bryan Ferry & Roxy Music compilations:- STREET LIFE: 20 GREAT HITS (*9) / THE ULTIMATE COLLECTION (*8) / MORE THAN THIS – THE BEST OF . . . (*8)

BRYAN FERRY (b.26 Sep'45, Washington, Durham, England) – vocals, piano / **ANDY MACKAY** (b.23 Jul'46, London, England) – saxophone, oboe, wind inst. / (BRIAN) **ENO** (b.15 May'48, Woodbridge, Suffolk, England) – synthesizers-keyboards / **GRAHAM SIMPSON** – bass, vocals / **PHIL MANZANERA** (b. PHILIP TARGETT-ADAMS, 31 Jan'51, London) – guitar (ex-QUIET SUN) repl. DAVID O'LIST (ex-NICE) who had repl. original ROGER BUNN (Jul'71). / **PAUL THOMPSON** (b.13 May'51, Jarrow, Northumberland, England) – drums repl. original DEXTER LLOYD (Jul71).

ROXY MUSIC (cont)

	Island	Reprise
Jun 72. (lp/c) *(ILPS/ICT 9200)* <*RS 2114*> **ROXY MUSIC**	10	

– Bitters end / The bob / Chance meeting / If there is something / Ladytron / Re-make/re-model / 2HB / Would you believe? / Sea breezes. *(re-iss. Feb77 on 'Polydor' lp)(c; 2302 048)(3100 348) (re-iss. Jan87 on 'E.G.' lp/c/cd+=; EG LP/MC/CD 6)* – Virginia Plain. *(re-iss. Sep91 on 'EG';)*

—— (May72) **RIK KENTON** (b.31 Oct'45) – bass repl. SIMPSON

	Island	Reprise
Aug 72. (7") *(WIP 6144)* <*1124*> **VIRGINIA PLAIN. / THE NUMBERER**	4	

—— (Jan73) **JOHN PORTER** – bass repl. KENTON who went solo

	Island	Warners
Mar 73. (7") *(WIP 6159)* **PJAMARAMA. / THE PRIDE AND THE PAIN**	10	
Mar 73. (lp/c) *(ILPS/ICT 9232)* <*2696*> **FOR YOUR PLEASURE**	4	

– Do the strand / Beauty queen / Strictly confidential / Editions of you / In every dream home a heartache / The bogus man / Grey lagoons / For your pleasure. *(re-iss. Feb77 on 'Polydor' lp)(c; 2302 049)(3100 349) (re-iss. Jan87 on 'E.G.' lp/c/cd; EG LP/MC/CD 8) (cd+c.Sep91 on 'EG') (re-iss. Feb97 on 'E.M.I.'; LPCENT 19)*

Jul 73. (7") <*7719*> **DO THE STRAND. / EDITIONS OF YOU**

—— (Jul73) **EDDIE JOBSON** (b.28 Apr'55, Billingham, Teeside, England) – keyboards, violin (ex-CURVED AIR) repl. ENO who went solo. session bassmen **JOHN GUSTAFSON** (studio) / **SAL MAIDA** (tour)repl. PORTER (other 5= FERRY, MANZANERA, MACKAY, JOBSON & THOMPSON)

	Island	Atco
Nov 73. (7") *(WIP 6173)* **STREET LIFE. / HULA KULA**	9	-
Nov 73. (lp/c) *(ILPS/ICT 9252)* <*7045*> **STRANDED**	1	

– Street life / Just like you / Amazona / Psalm / Serenade / A song for Europe / Mother of pearl / Sunset. *(re-iss. Feb77 on 'Polydor' lp)(c; 2302 050)(3100 350) (re-iss. Jan87 on 'E.G.' lp/c/cd; EG LP/MC/CD 10) (cd+c. Sep91 on 'EG')*

—— brought in **JOHN WETTON** (b.1949, Derby, England) – tour bass (ex-FAMILY, ex-KING CRIMSON, etc.) repl. MAIDA

	Island	Atco
Oct 74. (7") *(WIP 6208)* **ALL I WANT IS YOU / YOUR APPLICATIONS FAILED**	12	-
Nov 74. (lp/c) *(ILPS/ICT 9303)* <*106*> **COUNTRY LIFE**	3	37 Jan75

– The thrill of it all / Three and nine / All I want is you / Out of the blue / If it takes all night / Bitter-sweet / Triptych / Casanova / A really good time / Prairie rose. *(re-iss. Feb77 on 'Polydor' lp)(c; 2302 051)(3100 351) (re-iss. Jan87 on 'E.G.' lp/c/cd; EG LP/MC/CD 16) (cd+c.Sep91 on 'EG')*

	Island	Atco
Nov 74. (7") <*7018*> **THE THRILL OF IT ALL. / YOUR APPLICATIONS FAILED**	-	
Sep 75. (7") *(WIP 6248)* **LOVE IS THE DRUG. / SULTANESQUE**	2	
Oct 75. (lp/c) *(ILPS/ICT 9344)* <*127*> **SIREN**	4	50

– Love is the drug / End of the line / Sentimental fool / Whirlwind / She sells / Could it hapen to me / Both ends burning / Nightingale / Just another high. *(re-iss. Feb77 on 'Polydor' lp)(c; 2302 052)(3100 352) (re-iss. Jan87 on 'E.G.' lp/c/cd; EG LP/MC/CD 20) (cd+c.Sep91 on 'EG')*

	Island	Atco
Dec 75. (7") *(WIP 6262)* **BOTH ENDS BURNING. / FOR YOUR PLEASURE**	25	
Dec 75. (7") <*7042*> **LOVE IS THE DRUG. / BOTH ENDS BURNING**	-	30

—— **RICK WILLS** – tour bass repl. WETTON who stayed on with FERRY

—— Disbanded officially mid'76, leaving behind one more album

	Island	Atco
Jul 76. (lp/c) *(ILPS/ICT 9400)* <*139*> **VIVA! ROXY MUSIC (live 1973-1975)**	6	81

– Out of the blue / Pjamarama / The bogus man / Chance meeting / Both ends burning / If there is something / In every dream home a heartache / Do the strand. *(re-iss. Feb77 on 'Polydor' lp)(c; 2302 053)(3100 353) (re-iss. Jan87 on 'E.G.' lp/c/cd; EG LP/MC/CD 25) (cd+c.Sep91 on 'EG')*

—— After split ANDY MACKAY continued solo work, as did PHIL MANZANERA. EDDIE JOBSON joined FRANK ZAPPA.

BRYAN FERRY

also had simultaneous solo career. (same labels). He used various session people, including many members of ROXY MUSIC.

	Island	
Sep 73. (7") *(WIP 6170)* **A HARD RAIN'S GONNA FALL. / 2 HB**	4	
Oct 73. (lp/c) *(ILPS/ICT 9249)* <*7304*> **THESE FOOLISH THINGS**	5	

– A hard rain's a-gonna fall / River of salt / Don't ever change / Piece of my heart / Baby I don't care / It's my party / Don't worry baby / Sympathy for the Devil / Tracks of my tears / You won't see me / I love how you love me / Loving you is sweeter than ever / These foolish things. *(re-iss. Aug84 on 'Polydor' lp/c;) (re-iss. Jan87 on 'E.G.' lp/c/cd; EG LP/MC/CD 9)*

	Island	
May 74. (7") *(WIP 6196)* **THE IN-CROWD. / CHANCE MEETING**	13	-
Jul 74. (lp/c) *(ILPS/ICT 9284)* <*18113*> **ANOTHER TIME, ANOTHER PLACE**	4	

– The in-crowd / Smoke gets in your eyes / Walk a mile in my shoes / Funny how time slips away / You are my sunshine / (What a) Wonderful world / It ain't me babe / Fingerpoppin' / Help me make it through the night. *(re-iss. Aug84 on 'Polydor' lp/c;) (re-iss. Jan87 on 'E.G.' lp/c/cd; EG LP/MC/CD 14)*

	Island	
Aug 74. (7") *(WIP 6205)* **SMOKE GETS IN YOUR EYES. / ANOTHER TIME, ANOTHER PLACE**	17	
Jun 75. (7") *(WIP 6234)* **YOU GO TO MY HEAD. / RE-MAKE RE-MODEL**		

—— Solo again, with ex-ROXY MUSIC men **PAUL THOMPSON + JOHN WETTON**. Added **CHRIS SPEDDING** – guitar (ex-SHARKS)

	Island	Atlantic
Jun 76. (7") *(WIP 6307)* **LET'S STICK TOGETHER. / SEA BREEZES**	4	-
Aug 76. (7"ep) *(IEP 1)* **EXTENDED PLAY**	7	-

– The price of love / Shame shame shame / Heart on my sleeve / It's only love.

	Island	Atlantic
Sep 76. (lp/c) *(ILPS/ICT 9367)* <*18187*> **LET'S STICK TOGETHER**	19	

– Let's stick together / Casanova / Sea breeze / Shame shame shame / 2HB / The price of love / Chance meeting / It's only love / You go to my head / Re-make/re-model / Heart on my sleeve. *(re-iss. Aug84 on 'Polydor' lp/c;) (re-iss. Jan87 on 'E.G.' lp/c/cd; EG LP/MC/CD 24)*

	Island	Atlantic
Nov 76. (7") <*3364*> **HEART ON MY SLEEVE. / RE-MAKE/RE-MODEL**	-	86

—— added **PHIL MANZANERA** – guitar / **ANN ODELL** – keyboards / **MEL COLLINS** – sax / plus many backing singers.

	Polydor	Atlantic
Jan 77. (7") *(2001 704)* **THIS IS TOMORROW. / AS THE WORLD TURNS**	9	
Feb 77. (lp/c) *(2302/3100 055)* <*18216*> **IN YOUR MIND**	5	

– This is tomorrow / All night operator / One kiss / Love me madly again / Tokyo Joe / Party doll / Rock of ages / In your mind. *(re-iss. Jan87 on 'E.G.' lp/c/cd; EG LP/MC/CD 27)*

	Polydor	Atlantic
Apr 77. (7") *(2001 711)* **TOKYO JOE. / SHE'S LEAVING HOME**	15	-
Jun 77. (7") **TOKYO JOE. / AS THE WORLD TURNS**	-	

—— FERRY continued to use many different musicians, too many to mention.

	Polydor	Atlantic
Apr 78. (7") *(POSP 3)* **WHAT GOES ON. / CASANOVA**	67	
Apr 78. (lp/c) *(POLD/+C 5003)* **THE BRIDE STRIPPED BARE**	13	

– Sign of the times / Can't let go / Hold on (I'm coming) / The same old blues / When she walks in the room / Take me to the river / What goes on / Carrickfergus / That's how strong my love is / This island Earth. *(re-iss. Jan87 on 'E.G.' lp/c/cd; EG LP/MC/CD 36)*

	Polydor	Atlantic
Jul 78. (7") *(2001 798)* **SIGN OF THE TIMES. / FOUR LETTER LOVE**	37	
Nov 78. (7") **SIGN OF THE TIMES. / CAN'T LET GO**		
Nov 78. (7") *(2001 834)* **CARRICKFERGUS. / WHEN SHE WALKS IN THE ROOM**		

ROXY MUSIC

re-formed with **FERRY, MANZANERA, MACKAY, THOMPSON**, plus **PAUL CARRACK** – studio keyboards (ex-ACE) / **DAVID SKINNER** – tour keyboards / **GARY TIBBS** – bass (ex-VIBRATORS)

	Polydor-EG	Atco
Feb 79. (7") *(POSP 32)* **TRASH. / TRASH 2**	40	23
Mar 79. (lp/c)(pic-lp) *(POLH/+C 001)(EGPD 001)* <*114*> **MANIFESTO**	7	

– Manifesto / Trash / Angel eyes / Still falls the rain / Stronger through the years / Ain't that so / My little girl / ance away / Cry cry cry / Spin me round. *(re-iss. Jan87 on 'E.G.' lp/c/cd+=; EG LP/MC/CD 38)* – Angel eyes (12"disco version).

	Polydor-EG	Atco
Apr 79. (7") *(POSP 44)* **DANCE AWAY. / CRY CRY CRY**	2	
Apr 79. (7") <*7100*> **DANCE AWAY. / TRASH 2**	-	44
Aug 79. (7"/ext.12") *(POSP/+X 67)* **ANGEL EYES. / MY LITTLE GIRL**	4	
May 80. (7") *(POSP 93)* **OVER YOU. / MANIFESTO**	5	
May 80. (lp/c) *(POLH/+C 002)* <*102*> **FLESH + BLOOD**	1	35

– In the midnight hour / Oh yeah (on the radio) / Same old scene / Flesh and blood / My only love / Over you / Eight miles high / Rain rain rain / No strange delight / Running wild. *(re-iss. Jan87 on 'E.G.' lp/c/cd; EG LP/MC/CD 46)*

	Polydor-EG	Atco
May 80. (7") <*7301*> **OVER YOU. / MY ONLY LOVE**	-	80
Jul 80. (7") *(2001 972)* **OH YEAH (ON THE RADIO). / SOUTH DOWNS**	5	
Nov 80. (7") *(ROXY 1)* **SAME OLD SCENE. / LOVER**	12	
Dec 80. (7") **IN THE MIDNIGHT HOUR. /**	-	

—— Earlier 1980, CARRACK joined SQUEEZE, and TIBBS joined ADAM & THE ANTS. Session men used at the time **NEIL HUBBARD** – guitar / **ALAN SPENNER** – bass / **ANDY NEWMARK** – drums repl. THOMPSON

	E.G.	Warners
Feb 81. (7") *(ROXY 2)* <*7329*> **JEALOUS GUY. / TO TURN YOU ON**	1	
Apr 82. (7"/12") *(ROXY/+X 3)* **MORE THAN THIS. / INDIA**	6	
May 82. (lp/c) *(EGHP/+C 50)* <*23686*> **AVALON**	1	53

– More than this / The space between / India / While my heart is still beating / Main thing / Take a chance with me / Avalon / To turn you on / True to life / Tara. *(re-iss. Jan87 on 'E.G.' lp/c/cd; EG LP/MC/CD 50) (re-iss. Apr92 on 'Virgin' lp/c; OVED/+C 397)*

	E.G.	Warners
Jun 82. (7") *(ROXY 4)* **AVALON. / ALWAYS UNKNOWING**	13	
Sep 82. (7"/12") *(ROXY/+X 5)* **TAKE A CHANCE WITH ME. / THE MAIN THING**	26	
Sep 82. (7") <*29978*> **TAKE A CHANCE ON ME. / INDIA**	-	
Nov 82. (7") <*29912*> **MORE THAN THIS. / ALWAYS UNKNOWING**	-	

—— added **GUY FLETCHER + JIMMY MAELEN** – keyboards / **MICHELLE COBBS + TAWATHA AGEE**

	E.G.	Warners
Mar 83. (m-lp/c) *(EGM LP/MC 1)* <*23808*> **THE HIGH ROAD (live)**	26	67

– Can't let go / My only love / Like a hurricane / Jealous guy.

—— Had already disbanded again late 1982. MANZANERA and MACKAY became The EXPLORERS, and FERRY went solo again.

BRYAN FERRY

	E.G.	Warners
May 85. (7") *(FERRY 1)* **SLAVE TO LOVE. / VALENTINE (instrumental)**	10	

(12"+=) *(FERRYX 1)* – ('A'instrumental).

	E.G.	Warners
Jun 85. (lp/c/cd) *(EG LP/MC/CD 62)* <*25082*> **BOYS AND GIRLS**	1	63

– Sensation / Slave to love / Don't stop the dance / A wasteland / Windswept / The chosen one / Valentine / Stone woman / Boys and girls. *(re-iss. Jan87; same) (re-iss. cd+c.Sep91)*

	E.G.	Warners
Aug 85. (7") *(FERRY 2)* **DON'T STOP THE DANCE. / NOCTURNE**	21	

(12"+=) *(FERRYX 2)* – Windswept (instrumental).

	E.G.	Warners
Nov 85. (7"/7"pic-d) *(FERRY/FEREP 3)* **WINDSWEPT. / CRAZY LOVE**	46	

(12"+=) *(FERRYX 3)* – Feel the need / Broken wings.

	E.G.	Warners
Mar 86. (7") *(FERRY 4)* **IS YOUR LOVE STRONG ENOUGH. / WINDSWEPT (instrumental)**	22	

(12"+=) *(FERRYX 4)* – ('A'mix).

	E.G.	Warners
Jul 86. (7") **HELP ME. / BROKEN WINGS**	-	

	Virgin	Reprise
Sep 87. (7"/12") *(VS 940/+12)* **THE RIGHT STUFF. / ('A'instrumental)**	37	

(c-s+=) *(VSC 940)* – ('A'extended) / ('A'dub version).

	Virgin	Reprise
Nov 87. (cd/c/lp) *(CD/TC+/V 2474)* <*25598*> **BETE NOIRE**	9	63

– Limbo / Kiss and tell / New town / Day for night / Zamba / The right stuff / Seven deadly sins / The name of the game / Bete noire. *(cd re-iss. Dec88; CDVP 2474)*

	Virgin	Reprise
Feb 88. (7") *(VS 1034)* <*28117*> **KISS AND TELL. / ZAMBA**	41	31

(12"+=)(cd-s+=) *(VST 1034)(CDEP 19)* – ('A'&'B'remixes).

Jun 88. (7") (VS 1066) **LIMBO (Latin mix). / BETE NOIRE (instrumental)**
(12"+=/cd-s+=) (VS T/CD 1066) – ('A'mix).

Feb 93. (7"/c-s) (VS/+C 1400) **I PUT A SPELL ON YOU. / THESE FOOLISH THINGS** | 18 |
(cd-s+=) (VSCDX 1400) – Ladytron (live) / While my heart is still beating (live).
(cd-s) (VSCDG 1400) – ('A'-5 mixes).

Mar 93. (cd/c/lp) (CD/TC+/V 2700) <45246> **TAXI** | 2 | 79 |
– I put a spell on you / Will you love me tomorrow / Answer me / Just one look / Rescue me / All tomorrow's parties / Girl of my best friend / Amazing Grace / Taxi / Because you're mine.

May 93. (7"/c-s) (VS/+C 1455) **WILL YOU LOVE ME TOMMOROW. / A HARD RAIN'S A-GONNA FALL** | 23 |
(cd-s+=) (VSCDT 1455) – A wasteland (live) / Windswept (live).
(cd-s) (VSCDG 1455) – ('A'side) / Crazy love / Feel the need / When she walks in the room.

Aug 93. (c-s) (VSC 1468) **GIRL OF MY BEST FRIEND / NOCTURNE** | 57 |
(cd-s+=) (VSCDT 1468) – Are you lonesome tonight? / Valentine.
(cd-s) (VSCDG 1468) – Let's stick together / Boys and girls (live) / The bogus man (live).

—— now with a plethora of musicians

		Virgin	Virgin

Sep 94. (cd/c/lp) (CD/TC+/V 2751) <39838> **MAMOUNA** | 11 | 94 |
– Don't want to know / N.Y.C. / Your painted smile / Mamouna / The only face / The 39 steps / Which way to turn / Wildcat days / Gemini Moon / Chain reaction.

Oct 94. (7"/c-s) (VS/+C 1508) **YOUR PAINTED SMILE. / DON'T STOP THE DANCE**
(cd-s+=) (VSCDG 1508) – In every dream home a heartache (live) / Bete noire (live).

Feb 95. (c-s) (VSC 1528) **MAMOUNA / THE 39 STEPS (Brian Eno mix)** | 57 |
(cd-s+=) (VSCDG 1528) – Jealous guy (live) / Slave to love (live).

Oct 99. (cd/c) (CD/TC VIR 89) **AS TIME GOES BY** | 16 |
– As time goes by / The way you look tonight / Easy living / I'm in the mood for love / Where or when / When somebody thinks you're wonderful / Sweet and lovely / Miss Otis regrets / Time on my hands / Lover come back to me / Falling in love again / Love me or leave me / You do something to me / Just one of those things / September song.

– (FERRY) compilations, others, etc. –

Jun 88. (3"cd-ep) E.G.; (CDT 10) **LET'S STICK TOGETHER / SHAME SHAME SHAME / CHANCE MEETING / SEA BREEZES** | – |

Oct 88. (7") E.G.; (EGO 44) **LET'S STICK TOGETHER ('88 remix). / TRASH** | 12 |
(12"+=) (EGOX 44) – Shame shame shame / Angel eyes.
(cd-s+=) (EGOCD 44) – Casanova / Sign of the times.

Nov 88. (lp/c/cd/pic-cd; BRYAN FERRY & ROXY MUSIC) E.G.; (EG TV/MTV/CTV/CPTV 7) **THE ULTIMATE COLLECTION** | 6 |
– Let's stick together ('88 remix) / The in-crowd / Angel eyes (ROXY MUSIC) / He'll have to go / Tokyo Joe / All I want is you (ROXY MUSIC) / Jealous guy (ROXY MUSIC) / The price of love / Don't stop the dance / Love is the drug (ROXY MUSIC) / This is tomorrow / Slave to love / Help me / Avalon (ROXY MUSIC) / Dance away (ROXY MUSIC).

Feb 89. (7") E.G.; (EGO 46) **THE PRICE OF LOVE (R&B mix). / LOVER** | 49 |
(12"+=) (EGOX 46) – Don't stop the dance (remix) / Nocturne.
(cd-s+=) (EGOCD 46) – Don't stop the dance (remix) / Slave to love (remix).

Apr 89. (7") E.G.; (EGO 48) **HE'LL HAVE TO GO. / CARRICKFERGUS** | 63 |
(cd-s+=) (EGOCD 48) – Take me to the river / Broken wings.
(12") (EGOX 48) – ('A'side) / Windswept / Is your love strong enough.

Dec 89. (3xc-box/3xcd-box) E.G.; (EGBM/EGBC 5) **THESE FOOLISH THINGS / LET'S STICK TOGETHER / BOYS AND GIRLS** (free w / Island Various Artists compilations)

Oct 95. (cd/c/d-lp) Virgin; (CD/TC+/V 2791) **MORE THAN THIS – THE BEST OF BRYAN FERRY & ROXY MUSIC** | 15 |

– (ROXY MUSIC) compilations, etc. –

—— on 'E.G.' unless mentioned otherwise

Oct 77. (7") Polydor; (2001 739) **VIRGINIA PLAIN. / PJAMARAMA** | 11 |

Nov 77. (lp)(c) Polydor; (2303 073)(3100 407) **GREATEST HITS** | 20 |
– Virginia Plain / Do the strand / All I want is you / Out of the blue / Pjamarama / Editions of you / Love is the drug / Mother of pearl / Song for Europe / Thrill of it all / Street life. (re-iss. Jan87 on 'E.G.' lp/cd; EG LP/CD 31)

Jan 78. (7") Polydor; (2001 756) **DO THE STRAND. / EDITIONS OF YOU** | – |

Dec 81. (7xlp-box/7xc-box) (EG BS/BC 1) **THE FIRST SEVEN ALBUMS** | – |
– (ROXY MUSIC / FOR YOUR PLEASURE / STRANDED / COUNTRY LIFE / SIREN / MANIFESTO / FLESH AND BLOOD).

Nov 83. (lp/c)(cd) (EG LP/MC 54)(815 849-2) / Atco; <90122> **THE ATLANTIC YEARS 1973-1980** | 23 |

Apr 86. (d-lp/c)(cd) (BRYAN FERRY & ROXY MUSIC) (EGTV/EGMTV/EGCTV 1) <25857> **STREET LIFE: 20 GREAT HITS** | 1 | 100 | Aug89 |
– Virginia plain / A hard rain's a-gonna fall (BRYAN FERRY) / Do the strand / These foolish things (BRYAN FERRY) / Street life / Let's stick together (BRYAN FERRY) / Smoke gets in your eyes (BRYAN FERRY) / Love is the drug / Sign of the times (BRYAN FERRY) / Dance away / Angel eyes / Oh yeah / Over you / Same old scene / The midnight hour / More than this / Avalon / Slave to love (BRYAN FERRY) / Jealous guy.

Jun 88. (3"cd-ep) (CDT 8) **JEALOUS GUY / LOVER / SOUTHDOWN**

Dec 89. (3xc-box/3xcd-box) (EGBM/EGBC 3) **ROXY MUSIC – THE EARLY YEARS**
– (ROXY MUSIC / FOR YOUR PLEASURE / STRANDED).

Dec 89. (3xc-box/3xcd-box) (EGBM/EGBC 4) **ROXY MUSIC – THE LATER YEARS**
– (MANIFESTO / FLESH AND BLOOD / AVALON).

Oct 90. (cd/c/d-lp) (EG CD/MC/LP 77) **HEART STILL BEATIN' (live in France '82)**

Oct 90. (7") **LOVE IS THE DRUG (live). / EDITIONS OF YOU (live)** | – |
(12"+=/cd-s+=) – Do the strand (live).

Oct 94. (3xcd-box) **THE COMPACT COLLECTION**

Nov 95. (4xcd-box) Virgin; (CDBOX 5) **THE THRILL OF IT ALL – ROXY MUSIC 1972-1982**

Apr 96. (c-ep/12"ep/cd-ep) Virgin; (VS C/T/CDT 1580) **LOVE IS THE DRUG (Rollo & Sister Bliss Monster mixes; 3) / ('A'-original version)** | 33 |

ROYAL TRUX (dig out; Great Alt & Indie . . .)

RTZ (see under ⇒ BOSTON)

RUNAWAYS

Formed: Los Angeles, California, USA . . . mid-1974 by the notorious solo star turned record producer KIM FOWLEY (along with teen lyricist, KARI KROME), who set out to create a female RAMONES. After successfully applying to his music paper ad, JOAN JETT became the first to join, followed soon after by SANDY WEST and MICKI STEELE. With a few gigs under their belt, STEELE was replaced by CHERIE CURRIE, while the line-up was finalised with the addition of LITA FORD and JACKIE FOX. This was the formation that played a rooftop session on a Los Angeles apartment block in early 1976, an event that helped secure a record deal with 'Mercury'. While their eponymous debut was hitting the shops, the girls (average age 16) made their New York debut at CBGB's in September '76 supporting TELEVISION and TALKING HEADS. Dragging glam-metal by the pubic hair and injecting it with punk energy, tracks such as 'CHERRY BOMB' and 'HOLLYWOOD' saw The RUNAWAYS lumped in with the fermenting US New Wave scene. Early in '77, they released a second album, 'QUEENS OF NOISE', and like its predecessor it too failed to capitalize on the hype. Internal tensions were coming to a head around the time of the Japanese-only (The RUNAWAYS were huge in the Far East) live set, VICKI BLUE standing in for the worn out JACKIE FOX, while the blonde CURRIE finally split for a solo career (JOAN JETT taking over vocal duties). Adopting a harder-edged approach, the new line-up released yet another album, 'WAITIN' FOR THE NIGHT' (1978), the last to feature LITA FORD (another RUNAWAY to go onto a semi-successful solo career) and VICKI BLUE (who had attempted suicide). Although LAURIE McCALLISTER was brought in as a brief replacement, she didn't play on a posthumous covers set, 'AND NOW . . . THE RUNAWAYS', the band having already finally split. JOAN JETT was the third and most successful member to carve out a solo niche. However, FOWLEY subsequently resurrected the name (minus any original members!) for a less than impressive 1987 set, 'YOUNG AND FAST'. • **Trivia:** The JOAN JETT & THE RUNAWAYS album was entirely made up of covers; Slade's 'MAMA WEER ALL CRAZEE NOW' being one of them.

Album rating: THE RUNAWAYS (*7) / QUEENS OF NOISE (*6) / LIVE IN JAPAN (*5) / WAITIN' FOR THE NIGHT (*4) / AND NOW . . . THE RUNAWAYS (*3) / THE BEST OF THE RUNAWAYS compilation (*6) / YOUNG AND FAST (*3)

CHERIE CURRIE (b.1960) – vocals who repl. MICKI STEELE (was part-time vox, bass) / **LITA FORD** (b.23 Sep'59, London, England) – lead guitar, vocals / **JOAN JETT** (b.22 Sep'60, Philadelphia, Pennsylvania) – rhythm guitar, vocals / **JACKIE FOX** – bass / **SANDY WEST** (b.1960) – drums

		Mercury	Mercury

Sep 76. (7") (6167 392) <73819> **CHERRY BOMB. / BLACKMAIL** | | | Jun 76 |
Nov 76. (lp) (9100 029) <SRM1 1090> **THE RUNAWAYS**
– Cherry bomb / You drive me wild / Is it day or night? / Thunder / Rock and roll / Lovers / American nights / Blackmail / Secrets / Dead end justice.

Feb 77. (lp) (9100 032) <SRM1 1126> **QUEENS OF NOISE** | | | Jan 77 |
– Queens of noise / Take it or leave it / Midnight music / Born to be bad / Neon angels on the road to ruin / Midnight music / I love playin' with fire / California Paradise / Hollywood heartbeat / Johnny Guitar.

Feb 77. (7") <73890> **HEARTBEAT. / NEON ANGELS ON THE ROAD TO RUIN** | – | – |
Feb 77. (7") (6167 493) **QUEENS OF NOISE. / BORN TO BE BAD** | – | – |

Oct 77. (lp) (9100 046) **LIVE IN JAPAN (live)**
– Queens of noise / California Paradise / All right you guys / Wild thing / Gettin' hot / Rock and roll / You drive me wild / Neon angels on the road to ruin / I wanna be where the boys are / Cherry bomb / American nights / C'mon.

—— (Jul'77) **VICKI BLUE** – bass repl. FOX who suffers from nervous exhaustion. **JETT** took over lead vocals, when CURRIE left to go solo.

Oct 77. (7") (6167 587) **SCHOOL DAYS. / WASTED**
Dec 77. (lp) (9100 047) <SRM1 3075> **WAITIN' FOR THE NIGHT**
– Little sister / Wasted / Gotta get out tonight / Wait for me / Fantasies / School days / Trash can murders / Don't go away / Waitin' for the night / You're too possessive.

—— **LAURIE McALLISTER** – bass repl. VICKI BLUE when she attempted suicide. Split late 1978, when LITA FORD went solo after the recording of final album below.

		Cherry Red	not iss.

Jul 79. (lp,colrd-lp) (ARED 3) **AND NOW . . . THE RUNAWAYS** | | | – |
– Saturday night special / Eight days a week / Mama weer all crazee now / I'm a million / Right now / Takeover / My buddy and me / Little lost girls / Black leather. <re-iss. US 1981 as 'LITTLE LOST GIRLS' on 'Rhino' lp><pic-lp; RNLP 70861><RNDF 250> <cd-iss. US 1987; R2 70861> (cd-iss. Jul93 on 'Anagram'; CDGRAM 63)

Aug 79. (7") (CHERRY 8) **RIGHT NOW. / BLACK LEATHER** | – | – |

—— JOAN JETT went solo backed by her BLACKHEARTS

– compilations, others, etc. –

Feb 80.	(lp) *Cherry Red; (BRED 9)* **FLAMING SCHOOLGIRLS** (live/studio)	☐	-
Sep 82.	(lp/c) *Mercury; (MERB/+C 12)* **THE BEST OF THE RUNAWAYS**		
1981.	(12"ep) *Rhino; <RNEP 602>* **MAMA WEER ALL CRAZEE NOW**		
Apr 82.	(pic-lp/lp; JOAN JETT & THE RUNAWAYS) *Cherry Red; (P+/LAKER 1)* **I LOVE PLAYING WITH FIRE**	☐	-
1992.	(cd) *Mercury; <838 583-2>* **NEON ANGELS**	-	
Jun 94.	(10"lp) *Marilyn; (FM 1004)* **BORN TO BE BAD**	-	- France

Todd RUNDGREN

Born: 22 Jun'48, Upper Darby, Pennsylvania, USA. In 1967, he and another ex-WOODY'S TRUCK STOP member, CARSTEN VAN OSTEN, formed The NAZZ (taking the name from a YARDBIRDS b-side). In 1968, after supporting The DOORS a year previously, they signed to 'Screen Gems/Columbia'. An eponymous debut album sold moderately, RUNDGREN leaving the band in the middle of '69, after the completion of two further albums of psychedelic metal. In 1970, he became an in-house producer for Albert Grossman's 'Bearsville', his first job being for The AMERICAN DREAM. Later in the year, he formed his own band, RUNT (his nickname), releasing an album of the same name which spawned his first Top 20 hit, 'WE GOTTA GET YOU A WOMAN'. Following a further RUNT album, he decided to use his own name for future releases. In 1972, after taking over the production duties from GEORGE HARRISON on BADFINGER's 'Straight Up' set, he unleashed a truly wonderful solo debut, 'SOMETHING / ANYTHING?'. The double album reached the Top 30, a cut from it, 'I SAW THE LIGHT', making the US Top 20 (a year later Top 40 in the UK). Playing every instrument himself, it encompassed almost every style in the pop/rock pantheon. Among the many highlights were; the aforementioned single, 'HELLO IT'S ME', 'MARLENE', 'COULDN'T I JUST TELL YOU' and 'COLD MORNING LIGHT'. His next effort, 'A WIZARD, A TRUE STAR' was a wildly ambitious concept piece that attempted to reconstruct psychedelia. Although the record overreached itself, failing commercially as a result, it nevertheless contained a smattering of RUNDGREN gems including 'JUST ONE VICTORY'. Prolific in his songwriting, he returned after only nine months with yet another double set, 'TODD', an unrelentingly snooze-worthy affair. To complement his wide-ranging solo work under many styles, TODD formed a band, UTOPIA, who were a much more free-flowing, progressive rock/jazz outfit. Their first self-titled outing was released at the end of '74, while RUNDGREN himself worked on his monumental 'INITIATION'. Released in '75, it was largely lambasted by the press, although inside the hour-long lp was the minor classic hit, 'REAL MAN' and the 30-odd minute 'A TREATISE ON COSMIC FIRE' (which was split into three parts). RUNDGREN increasingly seemed to lose his penchant for experimentalism, although UTOPIA's 'RA' album was the exception. The album, 'OOPS! WRONG PLANET' (also 1977), took a more commercial direction, while at the same time, TODD was painstakingly producing MEAT LOAF's grandiose 'Bat Out Of Hell'. For the remainder of the 70's and throughout the first half of the 80's, TODD combined his solo output with UTOPIA releases. Most of these were well-received commercially, although critically, he was often unfairly savaged by the music press. • **Songwriters:** Phenomenal pensmith, although he did fit in a number of near perfect covers: DO YA (Move) / GOOD VIBRATIONS (Beach Boys) / LOVE OF THE COMMON MAN (from West Side Story?) / MOST LIKELY TO GO YOUR WAY (Bob Dylan) / TIN SOLDIER (Small Faces) / STRAWBERRY FIELDS FOREVER + RAIN (Beatles) / IF SIX WAS NINE (Jimi Hendrix) / HAPPENINGS TEN YEARS TIME AGO (Yardbirds) / etc? • **Trivia:** In 1983, TODD co-wrote the Top 20 hit 'KISSING WITH CONFIDENCE' for WILL POWERS (see under Carly SIMON). TODD's others major productions have included GRAND FUNK (1973) / HALL & OATES (1974) / TOM ROBINSON (1978) / TUBES (1979) / PSYCHEDELIC FURS (1982) / etc. Note:- TODD released in 1992 a compilation album of his production work.

Album rating: Nazz: NAZZ (*6) / NAZZ NAZZ (*5) / NAZZ III (*5) / compilation:- THE BEST OF NAZZ (*7) / Todd Rundgren: RUNT (*6; as Runt) / THE BALLAD OF TODD RUNDGREN (*7; as Runt) / SOMETHING – ANYTHING? (*9) / A WIZARD, A TRUE STAR (*6) / TODD (*4) / TODD RUNDGREN'S UTOPIA (*4; as Todd Rundgren's Utopia) / INITIATION (*8) / ANOTHER LIVE (*4; as Todd Rundgren's Utopia) / FAITHFUL (*6) / RA (*7; as Utopia) / OOPS! WRONG PLANET (*6; as Utopia) / HERMIT OF MINK HOLLOW (*8) / BACK TO THE BARS (*5) / ADVENTURES IN UTOPIA (*6; as Utopia) / DEFACE THE MUSIC (*6; as Utopia) / HEALING (*5) / SWING TO THE RIGHT (*4; as Utopia) / UTOPIA (*4; as Utopia) / THE EVER POPULAR TORTURED ARTIST EFFECT (*7) / OBLIVION (*4; as Utopia) / POV (*4; as Utopia) / A CAPPELLA (*4) / NEARLY HUMAN (*6) / SECOND WIND (*4) / REDUX '92: LIVE IN JAPAN (*4; as Utopia) / NO WORLD ORDER – LITE (*3) / greatest compilation:- THE BEST OF TODD RUNDGREN "GO AHEAD, IGNORE ME." (*9)

NAZZ

TODD RUNDGREN – lead guitar, vocals, composer / **ROBERT 'Stewkey' ANTONI** (b.17 Nov'47, Rhode Island, N.Y.) – vocals, piano / **CARSTEN VAN OSTEN** (b.24 Sep'46, New Jersey) – bass, vocals / **THOM MOONEY** (b. 5 Jan'48, Pennsylvania) – drums

		Screen Gems	Screen Gems
Sep 68.	(7") *(SGC 219 001) <001>* **HELLO IT'S ME. / OPEN MY EYES**	☐	66
Apr 69.	(lp) *(SGC 221 001) <SD 5001>* **NAZZ**	☐	☐ Oct68

– Open my eyes / See what you can be / Back of your mind / Hello it's me / Wildwood blues / If that's the way you feel / When I get my plane / The lemming song / Crowded / She's goin' down. *<US re-iss. Oct83 on 'Rhino'; >*

Apr 69.	(7") *(SGC 219 002) <002>* **HELLO IT'S ME. / CROWDED**	☐	-
May 69.	(lp,red-lp) *<SD 5002>* **NAZZ NAZZ**	-	80

– Forget all about it / Not wrong long / Rain rider / Gonna cry today / Meridian Leeward / Under the ice / Hang on Paul / Kiddie boy / Letters don't count / A beautiful song. *<US re-iss. Oct83 on 'Rhino'; RNLP 109>*

May 69.	(7") *(SGC 219 003) <006>* **NOT WRONG LONG. / UNDER THE ICE**	☐	☐
Nov 70.	(7") *<009>* **SOME PEOPLE. / MAGIC ME**	☐	☐
Dec 70.	(lp,green-lp) *<SD 5003>* **NAZZ III**	☐	☐

– Some people / Only one winner / Kicks / It's not that easy / Old time lovemaking / Magic me / Loosen up / Take the hand / How can you call that beautiful / Plenty of lovin' / Christopher Colombus / You are my window. *<US re-iss. Nov83 on 'Rhino'; RNLP 111)*

—— Had already disbanded early 1970, after completion of III'rd album.

RUNT

was formed by **RUNDGREN** now on – lead vocals, guitar / **TONY SALES** – bass / **HUNT SALES** – drums

		not iss.	Ampex
Nov 70.	(7") *<31001>* **WE GOTTA GET YOU A WOMAN. / BABY LET'S SWING**	-	20
Dec 70.	(lp) *<10105>* **RUNT**	-	☐

– Broke down and busted / Believe in me / We gotta get you a woman / Who's that man / Once burned / Devil's bite / I'm in the cliche / There are no words / Baby let's swing / The last thing you said / Don't tie my hands / Birthday carol. *(UK-iss.Apr72 on 'Bearsville'; K 44505) <US re-iss. Oct87 on 'Rhino'; > (cd-iss. May93 on 'Rhino-Bearsville'; 812270686-2)*

—— **N.D.SMART** – drums repl. HUNT who later joined IGGY POP then TIN MACHINE

May 71.	(7") *<31002>* **BE NICE TO ME. / BROKE DOWN AND BUSTED**	-	71
May 71.	(lp) *<10116>* **THE BALLAD OF TODD RUNDGREN**	-	☐

– Long flowing robe / The ballad / Bleeding / Wailing wall / The range war / Chain letter / A long time, a long way to go / Boat on the Charles / Be nice to me / Hope I'm around / Parole / Remember me. *(UK-iss.Apr72 on 'Bearsville'; K 45506) <US re-iss. Oct87 on 'Rhino'; > (cd-iss. May93 on 'Rhino-Bearsville'; 812271109-2)*

Aug 71.	(7") *<31004>* **A LONG TIME, A LONG WAY TO GO. / PAROLE**	-	92

TODD RUNDGREN

now completely solo except for one side of the d-lp which was frequented by session people.

		Bearsville	Bearsville
Mar 72.	(d-lp) *(K 65501) <2066>* **SOMETHING / ANYTHING?**	☐	29

– I saw the light / It wouldn't have made any difference / Wolfman Jack / Cold morning light / It takes two to tango (this is for the girls) / Sweeter memories / (intro) Breathless / The night the carousel burned down / Saving grace / Marlene / Song of the Viking / I went to the mirror / Black Maria / One more day (one word) / Couldn't I just tell you / Torch song / Little red lights / Dust in the wind / Piss Aaron / Hello it's me / Some folks is even whiter than me / You left me sore / Slut. *<US re-iss. Nov87 on 'Rhino'; > (re-iss. Jul89 on 'Essential' d-lp/c/cd; ESD LP/MC/CD 007) (re-iss. Jun93 on 'Rhino-Bearsville'; 812271107-2)*

Mar 72.	(7") *<0003>* **I SAW THE LIGHT. / BLACK MARIA**	-	16
Mar 72.	(7") *(K 15502)* **I SAW THE LIGHT. / MARLENE**	-	☐
Jul 72.	(7") *<0007>* **COULDN'T I JUST TELL YOU. / WOLFMAN JACK**	-	93
May 73.	(7"m) *(K 15506)* **I SAW THE LIGHT. / BLACK MARIA / LONG FLOWING ROBE**	36	-
	(re-iss. Nov76)		
Jun 73.	(lp) *(K 45513) <213>* **A WIZARD, A TRUE STAR**	☐	86

– International feel / Never never land / Tic tic tic it wear off / You need your head / Rock and roll pussy / Dogfight giggle / You don't have to camp around / Flamingo / Zen archer / Just another onionhead – Da da Dali / When the shit hits the fan – Sunset Blvd. / Le feel internacionale / Sometimes I don't know what to feel / Does anybody love you? / I'm so proud – Ooh ooh baby – La la means I love you – Cool jerk / Is it my name? / Just one victory. *(re-iss. Nov80 on 'Island'; IRSP 10) (re-iss. Apr89 on 'Castle' lp/c/cd; CLA LP/MC/CD 134) (re-iss. May93 on 'Rhino-Bearsville' cd; 812270864-2)*

Oct 73.	(7") *(K 15509)* **WE GOTTA GET YOU A WOMAN. / COULDN'T I JUST TELL YOU**	☐	-
Dec 73.	(7") *(K 15513) <0009>* **HELLO IT'S ME. / COLD MORNING LIGHT**	☐	5 Sep73
Dec 73.	(7") *<0015>* **SOMETIMES I DON'T KNOW WHAT TO FEEL. / DOES ANYONE LOVE YOU?**	-	☐

—— He now used many musicians that were to appear as first UTOPIA incarnation

Mar 74.	(d-lp) *(K 85501) <6952>* **TODD**	☐	54

– How about a little fanfare? / I think you know / The spark of life / An elpee's worth of toons / A dream goes on forever / Lord Chancelor's nightmare song / Drunken blue rooster / The last ride / Everybody's going to Heaven / King Kong reggae / Number one lowest common denominator / Useless begging / Sidewalk cafe / Izzat love / Heavy metal kids / In and out of Chakras we go / Don't you ever learn / Sons of 1984. *(re-iss. Dec89 on 'Castle' d-lp/c/cd; CLD LP/MC/CD 177) (re-iss. May93 on 'Rhino-Bearsville' cd; 812271108-2)*

May 74.	(7") *(K 15515) <0020>* **A DREAM GOES ON FOREVER. / HEAVY METAL KIDS**	☐	69

—— **TODD** formed UTOPIA with **MOODY KLINGMAN** – keyboards / **RALPH SHUCKETT** – bass / **JOHN SIEGLER** – bass, cello / **M.FROG LABAT** – synthesizers (TODD also released solo material)

Nov 74.	(lp; by TODD RUNDGREN'S UTOPIA) *(K 55501) <6954>* **TODD RUNDGREN'S UTOPIA**	☐	34

– Utopia (theme) / Freak parade / Freedom fighter / The ikon. *(re-iss. cd May93 on 'Rhino-Bearsville'; 812270865-2)*

Feb 75.	(7") *(K 15519) <0301>* **WOLFMAN JACK. / BREATHLESS**	☐	1974

Jun 75. (lp) (*K 55504*) <*6981*> **INITIATION** ☐ **86**
– Real man / Born to synthesize / The death of rock and roll / Eastern intrigue / Initiation / Fair warning / A treatise on cosmic fire: Intro-Prana, (ii) The fire of mind – or solar fire, (iii) The fire of spirit – or electric fire, (i) The internal fire – or fire by friction (Muladhara – The dance of Kundalini / Svadhishthana – Bam, bham, mam, yam, ram, lam, thank you mahm / Manipura – seat of fire / Anahata – the hals of air / Vishudda – sounds beyond ears / Anja – sights beyond eyes / Brahmarandhra – nirvana shakti) / Outro-Prana. (*cd-iss. May93 on 'Rhino-Bearsville'; 812270866-2*)

Sep 75. (7") (*K 15521*) <*0304*> **REAL MAN. / PRANA** ☐ **83**

──── trimmed slightly when LABAT departed.

Oct 75. (lp; as TODD RUNDGREN'S UTOPIA) (*K 55508*) <*6961*> **ANOTHER LIVE (live)** **66**
– Another life / The wheel / The seven rays / (intro) – Mister Triscuts / West Side Story theme / Something's coming / Just one victory / Heavy metal kids / Do ya / Just one victory. (*cd-iss. Aug93 on 'Rhino-Bearsville'; 812270867-2*)

Apr 76. (lp) (*K 55510*) <*6963*> **FAITHFUL** **54**
– Happenings ten years time ago / Good vibrations / Rain / Most likely you go your way and I'll go mine / If six was nine / Strawberry fields forever / Black and white / Love of the common man / When I pray / Cliche / The verb "to love" / Boogies (hamburger hell). (*cd-iss. Jun93 on 'Rhino-Bearsville'; 812270868-2*)

Jun 76. (7") <*0309*> **GOOD VIBRATIONS. / WHEN I PRAY** – **34**

Jun 76. (7") (*K 15524*) **LOVE OF THE COMMON MAN. / GOOD VIBRATIONS** –

Nov 76. (7") <*0310*> **LOVE OF THE COMMON MAN. / BLACK AND WHITE** –

UTOPIA

with TODD now completely changed line-up into **ROGER POWELL** – keyboards (from late '75) / **JOHN 'WILLIE' WILCOX** – drums / **KASIM SULTON** – bass

Jan 77. (lp) (*K 55514*) <*6965*> **RA** **27** **79**
– (overture) / Communion with the sun / Magic dragon theatre / Jealousy / Eternal love / Sunburst finish / Hiroshima / Singing and the glass guitar. (*cd-iss. May93 on 'Rhino-Bearsville'; 812270869-2*)

Feb 77. (7") (*K 15531*) <*0317*> **COMMUNION WITH THE SUN. / SUNBURST FINISH** ☐

──── TODD played/produced 'BAT OUT OF HELL' album for MEAT LOAF, which included some UTOPIANS and was massive seller from 1978 onwards.

Sep 77. (lp) (*K 55517*) <*6970*> **OOPS! WRONG PLANET** **59** **73**
– Trapped / Windows / Love in action / Crazy lady blue / Back on the street / Marriage of Heaven and Hell / The martyr / Abandon city / Gangrene / My angel / Rape of the young / Love is the answer. (*cd-iss. Jun93 on 'Rhino-Bearsville'; 812270870-2*)

Oct 77. (7") (*K 15536*) <*0321*> **LOVE IS THE ANSWER. / THE MARRIAGE OF HEAVEN AND HELL** ☐

TODD RUNDGREN

Apr 78. (lp) (*K 55521*) <*6981*> **HERMIT OF MINK HOLLOW** **42** **36**
– All the children sing / Can we still be friends / Hurting for you / Too far gone / Onomatopoeia / Determination / Bread / Bag lady / You cried wolf / Lucky guy / Out of control / Fade away. (*cd-iss. May93 on 'Rhino-Bearsville'; 812270784-2*)

May 78. (7") (*K 15539*) <*0324*> **CAN WE STILL BE FRIENDS. / DETERMINATION** ☐ **29**
<*some US copies had 'OUT OF CONTROL' on B-side*>

Jul 78. (7") <*0330*> **YOU CRIED WOLF. / ONOMATOPOEIA** –

Nov 78. (7") (*K 15543*) **ALL THE CHILDREN SING. / BAG LADY** ☐

Dec 78. (d-lp) (*K 65511*) <*6986*> **BACK TO THE BARS (live)** **75**
– Real man / Love of the common man / The verb "to love" / Love in action / A dream goes on forever / Sometimes I just don't know what to think / The range war / Black and white / The last ride / Cliche / Don't you ever learn / Never never land / Black Maria / Zen archer / Medley: I'm so proud – Ooh ooh baby – La la means I love you / I saw the light / It wouldn't have made any difference / Eastern intrigue / Initiation / Couldn't I just tell you / Hello it's me. (*cd-iss. Jun93 on 'Rhino-Bearsville'; 812271109-2*)

Feb 79. (7") <*0335*> **IT WOULDN'T HAVE MADE ANY DIFFERENCE. / DON'T YOU EVER LEARN** –

UTOPIA

	Island	Bearsville

Jan 80. (lp/c) (*ILPS/ZCI 9602*) <*6991*> **ADVENTURES IN UTOPIA** **57** **32**
– The road to Utopia / You make me crazy / Second nature / Set me free / Caravan / Last of the new wave riders / Shot in the dark / The very last time / Love alone / Rock love. (*cd-iss. May93 on 'Rhino-Bearsville'; 812270872-2*)

Mar 80. (7") (*WIP 6581*) <*49180*> **SET ME FREE. / UMBRELLA MAN** **27**

May 80. (7") <*49247*> **THE VERY LAST TIME. / LOVE ALONE** – **76**

Oct 80. (lp) (*ILPS 9642*) <*3487*> **DEFACE THE MUSIC** **65**
– I just want to touch you / Crystal ball / Where does the world go to hide / Silly boy / Alone / That's not right / Take it home / Hoi poloi / Life goes on / Feel too good / Always late / All smiles / Everybody else is wrong. (*cd-iss. May93 on 'Rhino-Bearsville'; 812270873-2*)

Oct 80. (7") <*49545*> **SECOND NATURE. / YOU MAKE ME CRAZY** –

Nov 80. (7"ep) (*IEP 12*) **I JUST WANT TO TOUCH YOU EP**
– I just want to touch you / Silly boy / Life goes on / All smiles.

Dec 80. (7") <*49579*> **I JUST WANT TO TOUCH YOU. / ALWAYS LATE** –

TODD RUNDGREN

Feb 81. (7") <*49696*> **TIME HEALS. / TINY DEMONS** –

Feb 81. (lp) (*ILPS 9567*) <*3522*> **HEALING** **48**
– Healer / Pulse / Flesh / Golden goose / Compassion / Shine / Healing (part 1, 2 & 3). (*free-7"ltd.w.a.*) – TIME HEALS. / TINY DEMONS (*re-iss. Dec81 on 'Avatar' lp/c; AALP/BHS 3522*) (*cd-iss. May93 on 'Rhino-Bearsville'; 812270874-2*)

Jan 82. (7") <*49771*> **COMPASSION. / HEALING** –

UTOPIA

	Avatar	Bearsville

Mar 82. (lp) (*BRK* <*3666*>) **SWING TO THE RIGHT** ☐
– Swing to the right / Lysistrata / The up / Junk rock (million monkeys) / Shinola / For the love of money / Last dollar on Earth / Fahrenheit 451 / Only human / One world. (*cd-iss. Mar93 on 'Rhino-Bearsville'; 812270785-2*)

Apr 82. (7") <*50062*> **ONE WORLD. / SPECIAL INTEREST** –

May 82. (7") (*AAA 126*) **ONE WORLD. / JUNK ROCK (MILLION MONKEYS)** –

Jun 82. (7") <*29947*> **LYSISTRATA / JUNK ROCK (MILLION MONKEYS)** –

Nov 82. (7"ep) (*AVAB 1*) **TIME HEALS / TINY DEMONS / I SAW THE LIGHT / CAN WE STILL BE FRIENDS** –

	Epic	Network

Nov 82. (7") (*EPCA 2972*) <*69859*> **FEET DON'T FAIL ME NOW. / FORGOTTEN BUT NOT GONE** **82**

Nov 82. (lp/c) (*EPC/40 25207*) <*60183*> **UTOPIA** **84**
– Libertine / Bad little actress / Feet don't fail me now / Neck on up / Say yeah / Call it what you will / I'm looking at you but I'm talking to myself / Hammer in the heart / Burn three times / There goes my inspiration. (*w/ free UK+US m-lp*) – Princess of the universe / Infrared and ultraviolet / Forgotten but not gone / Private Heaven / Chapter and verse. (*cd-iss. Aug93 on 'Rhino-Bearsville'; 812270713-2*)

Jan 83. (7") <*69859*> **HAMMER IN MY HEART. / I'M LOOKING AT YOU BUT I'M TALKING TO MYSELF** –

TODD RUNDGREN

	Lambourghini	Bearsville

Mar 83. (7") <*29686*> **BANG THE DRUM ALL DAY. / CHANT** – **63**

Aug 83. (lp/c) (*LMGLP/ZCLMG 2000*) <*23732*> **THE EVER POPULAR TORTURED ARTIST EFFECT** **66** Feb83
– Hideaway / Influenza / Don't hurt yourself / There goes my baybay / Tin soldier / Emperor of the highway / Bang the drum all day / Drive / Chant. (*cd-iss. Jun93 on 'Rhino-Bearsville'; 812270876-2*)

Aug 83. (7") (*LMG 1*) **BANG THE DRUM ALL DAY. / DRIVE** ☐

Sep 83. (7") <*29759*> **HIDEAWAY. / EMPEROR OF THE HIGHWAY** –

UTOPIA

	W.E.A.	Passport

Apr 84. (lp/c) (*WX 4/+C*) <*6029*> **OBLIVION** **74**
– Itch in my brain / Love with a thinker / Bring me my longbow / If I didn't try / Too much water / Maybe I could change / Crybaby / Welcome to my revolution / Winston Smith takes it on the jaw / I will wait.

May 84. (7") (*YZ 5*) <*7923*> **CRYBABY. / WINSTON SMITH TAKES IT ON THE JAW** ☐

Jul 84. (7") (*YZ 11*) **LOVE WITH A THINKER. / WELCOME TO MY REVOLUTION** ☐ –

	Food For Thought	Passport

Jun 85. (lp/c) (*GRUB 5*) <*6044*> **POV** May 85
– Play this game / Style / Stand for something / Secret society / Zen machine / Mated / Wildlife / Mimi gets mad / Mystified / More light.

Jun 85. (7") (*YUM 107*) **MATED. / MAN OF ACTION**

Jun 85. (7") <*7927*> **MATED. / STAND FOR SOMETHING** –

──── (Oct85) TODD is credited on duet with BONNIE TYLER on single 'LOVING YOU IS A DIRTY JOB'.

TODD RUNDGREN

	Warners	Warners

Oct 85. (7") (*W 8852*) <*28821*> **SOMETHING TO FALL BACK ON. / LOCKJAW**
(12"+=) (*WT 8862*) – ('A'dance mix).

Nov 85. (lp/c) (*925128-1/-4*) <*25128*> **A CAPPELLA**
– Blue Orpheus / Johnee Jingo / Pretending to care / Hodja / Lost horizon / Something to fall back on / Miracle in the bazaar / Lockjaw / Honest work / Mighty love.

──── Early in 1986, UTOPIA split and ROGER POWELL went solo. TODD returned to solo work in 1988 augmented by **ROSS VALORY** – bass (ex-JOURNEY) / **PRAIRIE PRINCE** – drums (ex-TUBES) (same label)

May 89. (lp/c/cd) (*K 92588-1/-4/-2*) <*25881*> **NEARLY HUMAN** ☐
– The want of a nail / The waiting game / Parallel lines / Can't stop running / Unloved children / Fidelity / Feel it / Hawking / I love my life. (*cd+=*) – Two little Hitlers.

May 89. (7") <*22868*> **PARALLEL LINES. / I LOVE MY LIFE** –

Feb 91. (cd/c/lp) (*7599-26478-2/-4/-1*) <*26478*> **SECOND WIND**
– Change myself / Love science / Who's sorry now / The smell of money / If I have to be alone / Love in disguise / Kindness / Public servant / Goya's eyes / Second wind.

Jun 93. (cd/c) <*8122-71185-2/-4*> **REDUX '92: LIVE IN JAPAN (Utopia live)**
– Fix your gaze / Zen machine / Trapped / Princess of the universe / Abandon city / Hammer in my heart / Swing to the right / Ikon / Hiroshima / Back on the street / Only human / Love in action / Caravan / Last of the new wave riders / One world / Love is the answer.

	Food For Thought	Warners

Sep 94. (d-cd/d-c) (*CD/C+/GRUB 30*) **NO WORLD ORDER / LITE**
– Worldwide epiphany / No world order / Worldwide epiphany / Day job / Property / Fascist Christ / Love thing / Time stood still / Proactivity / No world order / World epiphany / Time stood still / Love thing / Time stood still / World made flesh / Fever broke. (*d-cd+=*) – (10 different versions of above).

1995. (cd) **THE INDIVIDUALIST**
– Tables will turn / If not now, when? / Family values / The ultimate crime / Espresso (all jacked up) / The individualist / Cast the first stone / Beloved infidel / Temporary sanity / Woman's world.

	E.M.I.	E.M.I.

Oct 97. (cd) <*(859866-2)*> **WITH A TWIST** (re-workings in acoustic/lounge style)

– I saw the light / Influenza / Can we still be friends / Mated / It wouldn't have made any difference / Love is the answer / Fidelity / Never neverland / Hello it's me / I want you / The dream goes on forever.

– compilations, etc. –

1984.	(lp; by NAZZ) *Rhino; <RNLP 116>* **THE BEST OF NAZZ**	-	
Nov 87.	(lp/c/cd; UTOPIA) *Passport; <PB/+C/CD 6053>* **TRIVIA**	-	
Feb 88.	(d-lp/c/cd; by TODD RUNDGREN) *Raw Power; (RAW LP/TC/CD 035)* **ANTHOLOGY**		1989

– Can we still be friends / All the children sing / Too far gone / Sweet memories / It wouldn't have made any difference / Hello it's me / I saw the light / Just one victory / Love of the common man / The verb 'to love' / Sometimes I don't know what to feel / Couldn't I just tell you / Tiny demons / Initiation / Real man / A long time a long way to go / Long flowing robe / Compassion / We gotta get you a woman / A dream goes on forever / The last ride / Don't you ever learn / Bang the drum all day / Zen archer.

Mar 88.	(d-lp/d-c/d-cd; by RUNT /+/ TODD RUNDGREN) *That's Original; (TFO LP/MC/CD 3)* **RUNT / HERMIT OF MINK HOLLOW**		-
Mar 88.	(d-lp/d-c/d-cd; by UTOPIA) *That's Original; (TFO LP/MC/CD 9)* **OOPS! SORRY WRONG PLANET / ADVENTURES IN UTOPIA**		-
Jun 88.	(d-lp/d-c/d-cd; by UTOPIA) *Castle; (CCS LP/MC/CD 181)* **THE UTOPIA COLLECTION**		-

– Where does the world go to hide / Freedom fighters / All smiles / Lysistrata / Always late / Love in action / Rock love / Set me free / The seven rays / Traped / Swing to the right / One world / Heavy metal kids / The very last time / Crazy lady blue / Feel too good / Love alone / Love is the answer.

Sep 88.	(cd-ep) *Special Edition; (CD 3-6)* **BANG THE DRUM ALL DAY / I SAW THE LIGHT / CAN WE STILL BE FRIENDS / ALL THE CHILDREN SING**		
Oct 88.	(7") *Old Gold; (OG)* **I SAW THE LIGHT. / (other artist)**		-
1989.	(d-lp; by TODD RUNDGREN) *Rhino; <R1 71491>* **ANTHOLOGY (1968-1985)**	-	
	(UK-iss.d-cd Aug93 on 'Rhino-Bearsville';)		
Apr 92.	(cd) *Rhino; <R2>* **AN ELPEE'S WORTH OF PRODUCTIONS** (various)		
May 95.	(cd; by UTOPIA) *Rhino; (8122 70892-2)* **ANTHOLOGY**		
Jul 96.	(cd; as UTOPIA) *Rhino; (8122 72287-2)* **THE PASSPORT COLLECTION**		
Apr 98.	(cd) *Canyon; (PCCY 01121)* **UP AGAINST IT**		

RUN-D.M.C.

Formed: Hollis, New York, USA . . . 1982 by JOE SIMMONS (aka RUN) and MC D. (aka DARRYL McDANIELS) along with DJ JAM-MASTER JAY (aka JASON MIZEL) These schoolboy friends had persuaded JOE's brother, RUSSELL (owner of 'Rush' productions and future co-chairman of the seminal 'Def Jam' label) to let them make a record, the result being the seminal 1983 single, 'IT'S LIKE THAT' / 'SUCKER M.C.'S'. Oft quoted as the record which kickstarted modern hip-hop, 'SUCKER M.C.'S' substituted the conventional live backing band of the day for stripped-down, pulverising drum machine beats. RUN-D.M.C. also had attitude aplenty, their leather-clad, sneaker-obsessed B-Boy image more accurately reflecting street culture and what was going down in the underground clubs. With the help of RUSSELL, they signed to 'Profile', releasing their eponymous debut the following year. Underscoring their uncompromising vision, the record introduced the group's pioneering marriage of metal and rap on the stinging 'ROCK BOX', subsequently going gold. 1985 saw the group make an appearance in the film, 'Krush Groove' (based on the life of RUSSELL) alongside the likes of KURTIS BLOW and The BEASTIE BOYS as well as releasing a follow-up album, 'KING OF ROCK' (1985), taking their rock/rap hybrid to new extremes. But it was 'RAISING HELL' (1986) which really put RUN-D.M.C. on the map, their genius collaborative effort with AEROSMITH (then in a career trough) on the latter's 'WALK THIS WAY' making them chart stars (Top 5 UK, Top 10 US). From the style frenzy of 'MY ADIDAS' to the vocal wordplay of 'PETER PIPER' and 'IT'S TRICKY' the record led the mid-80's hip hop zeitgeist, becoming the first rap album to go platinum. The BEASTIE BOYS' 1986 debut, 'License To Ill' followed suit, a multi-million seller which topped the US chart, whilst an anarchic joint tour with the BEASTIE's further consolidated RUN-D.M.C.'s reputation as the kings of rap. A year is a long time in hip hop, and by the release of 'TOUGHER THAN LEATHER' (1988), hard hitting young upstarts like PUBLIC ENEMY were crossing over to the lucrative white audience with a vengeance. Although tracks like 'RUN'S HOUSE' and 'BEATS TO THE RHYME' stood up among the best of their earlier work, the record lacked the fire of old, while a film of the same name failed miserably at the box office. 'BACK FROM HELL' (1990) barely scraped into the US charts and though the record had its moments, it failed to remedy the group's critical and commercial decline. A difficult period for them, SIMMONS and McDANIELS had undergone various personal problems, the latter suffering from alcoholism while SIMMONS was accused of rape. They eventually re-emerged three years later on 'DOWN WITH THE KING' (1993), its title a reference to their recent religious conversion. With contributions from the cream of the rap fraternity, the album was a reasonable success, their first foray into the US Top 10 in five years. However, along with the likes of the once-mighty JUNGLE BROTHERS, RAKIM etc., RUN-D.M.C. have failed to re-invent themselves (like old buddies The BEASTIE BOYS), their sound now somewhat dated in a hip hop scene which thrives on constant flux.

Album rating: RUN-D.M.C. (*8) / KING OF ROCK (*7) / RAISING HELL (*8) / TOUGHER THAN LEATHER (*6) / BACK FROM HELL (*6) / RUN-D.M.C.'S GREATEST HITS TOGETHER FOREVER 1983-1991 compilation (*8) / DOWN WITH THE KING (*6)

RUN (b. JOSEPH SIMMONS, 14 Nov'64) – vocals / **D.M.C.** (b. DARRYL McDANIELS, 31 May'64) – vocals / **JAM-MASTER JAY** (b. JASON MIZELL, 21 Jan'65) – turntables, programming

		4th & Broad	Profile
1983.	(7") **IT'S LIKE THAT. / SUCKER M.C.'s**	-	
Jun 84.	(lp) *(1202)* **RUN-D.M.C.**	-	53

– Hard times / Rock box / Jam-master Jay / Hollis Crew (krush-groove 2) / Sucker M.C.'s (krush-groove 1) / It's like that / Wake up / 30 days / Jay's game. (*UK-iss.May85 lp/c; BR LP/CA 506) (cd-iss. 1990 on 'London'; 846 561-2) (re-iss. Apr91 on 'Profile' cd/c/lp; FILE CD/CT/R 202)*

Jun 84.	(7") *(BRW 8)* **ROCK BOX. / ('A'vocal dub)**		
	(12"+=) – *(12BRW 8)* – ('A'dub version).		
Sep 84.	(7") **30 DAYS. / (instrumental)**	-	
Jan 85.	(7") **HOLLIS CREW. / (instrumental)**		
Feb 85.	(lp/c)(pic-lp) *(BR LP/CA 504)(PBRLP 504) <1205>* **KING OF ROCK**		52

– Rock the house / King of rock / You talk too much / Jam-master jammin' / Roots, rap, reggae / Can you rock it like this / You're blind / It's not funny / Daryll and Joe (krush-groove 3). *(cd-iss. May88; BRCD 504) (re-iss. Apr91 on 'Profile' cd/c; FILE CD/CT 205)*

Mar 85.	(7") *(BRW 21)* **KING OF ROCK. / JAM MASTER JAMMIN'**		
	(12"+=) – *(12BRW 21)* – You talk too much.		
Mar 86.	(7") *(BRW 25)* **YOU TALK TOO MUCH. / DARRYL AND JOE (KRUSH-GROOVE 3)**		
	(12"+=) – *(12BRW 25)* – ('A'instrumental) / Sucker M.C.'s (krush-groove 1).		
Apr 86.	(7") **JAM-MASTER JAMMIN'. / (part 2)**	-	
May 86.	(7") **CAN YOU ROCK IT LIKE THIS. / TOGETHER FOREVER**	-	

		London	Profile
Jun 86.	(7") *(LON 101)* **MY ADIDAS. / PETER PIPER**	62	
	(12"+=) – *(LONX 101)* – ('A'instrumental).		
Jul 86.	(lp/c)(cd) *(LON LP/C 21)(828018-2) <1217>* **RAISING HELL**	41	3 Jun86

– Peter Piper / It's tricky / My Adidas / Walk this way / Is it live / Perfection / Hit it run / Raising hell / You be illin' / Dumb girl / Son of Byford / Proud to be black.

Jul 86.	(7") *<5112>* **WALK THIS WAY. / KING OF ROCK**	-	4
Aug 86.	(7"; RUN-D.M.C. featuring AEROSMITH) *(LON 104)* **WALK THIS WAY. / ('A'instrumental)**	8	-
	(12"+=) – *(LONX 104)* – My Adidas.		
Feb 87.	(7") *(LON 118) <5119>* **YOU BE ILLIN'. / HIT IT RUN**	42	29 Oct86
	(12"+=) – *(LONX 118)* – ('A'instrumental).		
May 87.	(7") *(LON 130) <5131>* **IT'S TRICKY. / PROUD TO BE BLACK**	16	57 Feb87
	(12"+=) – *(LONX 130)* – ('A'club tempo mix) / ('A'-Scratchappella) / ('A'reprise).		
Sep 87.	(7") *(LON 154)* **PETER PIPER. / MY ADIDAS**		-
	(12"+=) – *(LONX 154)* – Walk this way / King of rock.		
Nov 87.	(7"/7"g-f) *(LON/+G 163)* **XMAS IN HOLLIS. / PETER PIPER**	56	-
	(12"+=) – *(LONX 163)* – My Adidas / Walk this way / King of rock.		
Apr 88.	(7"/7"pic-d) *(LON/+P 177)* **RUN'S HOUSE. / BEATS TO THE RHYME**	37	
	(12"+=/cd-s+=) – *(LON X/CD 177)* – ('A'&'B'instrumental).		
Jun 88.	(lp/c)(cd) *(LON LP/C 38)(828070-2) <1265>* **TOUGHER THAN LEATHER**	13	9 May88

– Run's house / Mary, Mary / They call us Run DMC / Beats to the rhyme / Radio station / Papa crazy / Tougher than leather / I'm not going out like that / How d'ya do it Dee? / Miss Elaine / Soul to rock and roll / Ragtime. *(re-iss. Nov92 on 'Profile' cd/c; PCD/PCT 1265)*

Jul 88.	(7") *<5211>* **MARY, MARY. / ROCK BOX**	-	75
Aug 88.	(7"/7"s) *(LON/+S 191)* **MARY, MARY. / RAISING HELL**	-	-
	(12"+=) – *(LONX 191)* – ('A'instrumental).		

		M.C.A.	Profile
Aug 89.	(7"/c-s) *(MCA/+C 1360) <PROF 262>* **GHOSTBUSTERS THEME II. / ('A'instrumental)**	65	
	(12"+=/cd-s+=) – *(MCA T/CD 1360) <PRO FT/CD 262>* – Pause.		

		Profile	Profile
Nov 90.	(7"/c-s) *<(PROF/+C 315)>* **WHAT'S IT ALL ABOUT. / THE AVE**	48	
	(12"+=) – *<(PROFT 315)>* – ('A'&'B'instrumentals).		
	(cd-s+=) – *<(PROCD 315)>* – ('A'instrumental) / ('A'version).		
Nov 90.	(cd/c/lp) *<(FILE CD/CT/R 1401)>* **BACK FROM HELL**	81	

– Back from hell / Bob your head / Livin' in the city / Sucker DJs / What's it all about / Word is born / Pause / Not just another groove / P upon a tree / Party time / Naughty / Kick the frama lama lama / Groove to the sound / Don't stop.

Mar 91.	(7"/c-s) **FACES. / BACK FROM HELL (remix)**		
	(12"+=) – ('A'radio mix) / ('A'instrumental).		
	(cd-s) – (2 'A'versions see above) / (2 'B'versions).		
	(12") – (4 'A'mixes – 3 above).		
Nov 91.	(cd/c/lp) *<(FILE CD/CT/R 1419)>* **RUN DMC GREATEST HITS TOGETHER FOREVER 1983-1991** (compilation)		

– Sucker M.C.'s (krush groove 1) / Walk this way / Together forever (krush groove 4) (live at Hollis Park '84) / King of rock / Run's house / It's tricky / Pause / You be illin' / My Adidas / Here we go (live at The Funhouse) / Rock box / What's it all about / Hard times / Beats to the rhyme / Jam-master Jay / Peter Piper / It's like that / Christmas in Hollis.

—— Earlier 1991, JOSEPH SIMMONS was charged with raping a 22-year female fan.

Mar 93.	(12"/cd-s) *(PROF T/CD 39) <5391>* **DOWN WITH THE KING. / ('A'instrumental)**	69	21
	(re-iss. Nov93 UK; same)		
May 93.	(cd/c/lp) *<(FILE CD/CT/R 1440)>* **DOWN WITH THE KING**	44	7

– Down with the king / C'mon everybody / Can I get it to yo / Hit 'em hard / To the maker / In the head / Ooh, what ya gonna do / Big Willie / Three little Indians / In the house / Kick it (can I get a witness) / Get open / What's next / Wreck shop / For ten years.

Jul 93.	(12"/cd-s) **OOH, WHATCHA GONNA DO. / ('A'mixes)**		
Apr 94.	(12"/cd-s) **WHAT'S NEXT. / CAN I GET IT, YO / PIED PIPER**		

– compilations, etc. –

Sep 86. (7") *4th & Broadway; (BRW 56)* **KING OF ROCK. / ROCK BOX (vocal)** — | —
(12"+=) *(12BRW 56)* – Jam master Jay.
(12"+=) *(12BRWX 56)* – ('A'-Cut-up version) / Jay's game / Rock box.

Nov 95. (10x12"box) *Profile; (12" box)* **12" SINGLES BOX SET** — | —

Sep 97. (cd-s; RUN-DMC VS JASON NEVINS) *Smile; (SM 9065-2)* **IT'S LIKE THAT (mixes)** — |

Feb 98. (12"/cd-s; RUN-DMC VS JASON NEVINS) *Columbia; <665293-6/-2>* **IT'S LIKE THAT (mixes)** **63** |
(yes! the above version actually hit the UK charts! before it gained another official release)

Mar 98. (10"/c-s/12"/cd-s; RUN-DMC VS JASON NEVINS) *Smile (SM 9065/+4/1/2)* **IT'S LIKE THAT (mixes)** **1** |

Mar 98. (12"; RUN-DMC VS JASON NEVINS) *Time; (TIME 094)* **IT'S LIKE THAT (mixes)** — | —

May 98. (12"; RUN-DMC VS JASON NEVINS) *Epidrome; (EPD 66665698)* **IT'S TRICKY (mixes)** — | —

May 98. (cd) *Profile; (FILECD 474)* **TOGETHER FOREVER – GREATEST HITS 1983-1998** **31** |
– (same as earlier compilation + add recent hit remixes).

RUNRIG (dig out; 4th edition)

RUSH

Formed: Toronto, Canada . . . 1969 by ALEX LIFESON, GEDDY LEE and JOHN RUTSEY. Initially a hard-rock power outfit in the classic British mould of CREAM and LED ZEPPELIN, they toured local bars and clubs, culminating in a hometown support slot with The NEW YORK DOLLS. Immediately prior to this (1973), RUSH formed their own label, 'Moon', issuing a cover of Buddy Holly's 'NOT FADE AWAY' as their debut 45. An eponymous debut followed in early '74 and was soon picked up by DJ, Donna Halper, who sent a copy to Cliff Burnstein at 'Mercury' records. The company signed RUSH for a 6-figure sum, re-mixing (courtesy of Terry 'Broon' Brown) and re-releasing the record to minor US success (bubbled under the Top 100). Although a tentative start, GEDDY's helium-laced shrill was employed to stunning effect on tracks such as 'WORKING MAN', 'FINDING MY WAY' and 'WHAT YOU'RE DOING'. However, with drummer NEIL PEART replacing RUTSEY, RUSH began to develop the unique style which would characterise their classic 70's work. As well as being a consummate sticksman, PEART masterminded the band's lyrical flights of fantasy, beginning with 'FLY BY NIGHT' (1975). With the conceptually similar YES still world-beating favourites, RUSH found it difficult to progress commercially. Creatively, however, the trio attempted to wrestle the symphonic-rock crown from their transatlantic neighbours with such mystical, grandiose fare as 'BY-TOR AND THE SNOW DOG'. Later the same year, they released the under-par 'CARESS OF STEEL', which featured the self-indulgently lengthy 'FOUNTAIN OF LAMNETH'. This stage of RUSH's career reached its zenith in 1976 with the concept album, '2112', based on the work of novelist and philosopher Ayn Rand. Boasting a spectacular side-long 20-minute title track/overture, this feted prog-rock/sci-fi classic gave RUSH their long-awaited breakthrough, the record almost achieving a US Top 60 placing. In the course of the previous three years, the band's fanbase had swelled considerably, enabling them to get away with releasing a live double set, 'ALL THE WORLD'S A STAGE'. Featuring electrifying renditions of RUSH's most exquisite material to date, the album was hailed as an instant classic, its Top 40 success in the States leading to massive import sales in Europe. This persuaded the band to bring their live show to Britain/Europe, their wildly enthusiastic reception encouraging them to stay on in Wales and record 'A FAREWELL TO KINGS'. Not surprisingly, the album made the UK (& US) Top 40, its success boosted by a UK Top 40 hit/EP, 'CLOSER TO THE HEART' early the following year. 1978's 'HEMISPHERES' set was the last to feature PEART's trademark epics, the album consolidating the band's growing UK support, while their native Canada lavished upon them the title, 'Ambassadors Of Music'. While many bands of their ilk floundered critically, RUSH began the 80's on a high note, scoring a rare UK Top 20 hit single with 'SPIRIT OF RADIO'. Taken from their million-selling 'PERMANENT WAVES' opus, the track was characteristic of the shorter, leaner sound that RUSH would pursue throughout the coming decade. Not escaping the increasing technological influence of 80's music, the band adopted a more keyboard-orientated approach on albums such as 'MOVING PICTURES' (1981), 'SIGNALS' (1982), 'GRACE UNDER PRESSURE' (1984) and 'POWER WINDOWS' (1985). Finally parting company with their longstanding producer, TERRY BROWN, they further refined their sound on the 1987 album, 'HOLD YOUR FIRE', which spawned a near UK Top 40 single, 'TIME STAND STILL' (credited AIMEE MANN of 'TIL TUESDAY). After the compulsory live set, 'A SHOW OF HANDS', the band opted for a fresh start with 'Atlantic', 'PRESTO' (1989) being the first fruits of this new alliance. Incredibly, despite regular critical derision from the trendier sections of the music press, RUSH went on to even greater success in the 90's, both 'ROLL THE BONES' (1991) and 'COUNTERPARTS' (1993) making the US Top 5 (now only Top 30 in Britain!). Certainly, PRIMUS' well-documented admiration has done the band no harm, LIFESON even bringing in the latter band's LES CLAYPOOL for a guest spot on his ill-advised VICTOR project. The same year (1996), RUSH released their umpteenth set, 'TEST FOR ECHO', the band looking good for their 30th anniversary just prior to the millennium. • **Trivia:** Early in 1982, GEDDY guested for BOB & DOUG

McKENZIE (aka Rick Moranis & Dave Thomas) on their US Top 20 single 'Take Off'.

Album rating: RUSH (*6) / FLY BY NIGHT (*6) / CARESS OF STEEL (*5) / 2112 (*8) / ALL THE WORLD'S A STAGE (*8) / A FAREWELL TO KINGS (*7) / HEMISPHERES (*6) / PERMANENT WAVES (*6) / MOVING PICTURES (*7) / EXIT . . . STAGE LEFT (*5) / SIGNALS (*6) / GRACE UNDER PRESSURE (*5) / POWER WINDOWS (*5) / HOLD YOUR FIRE (*5) / A SHOW OF HANDS (*5) / PRESTO (*5) / CHRONICLES compilation (*7) / ROLL THE BONES (*5) / COUNTERPARTS (*4) / TEST FOR ECHO (*5) / DIFFERENT STAGES live compilation (*5) / Alex Lifeson: VICTOR (*3)

GEDDY LEE (b. GARY LEE WEINRIB, 29 Jul'53, Willowdale, Toronto, Canada) – vocals, bass, keyboards / **ALEX LIFESON** (b. ALEX ZIVOJINOVICH, 27 Aug'53, Surnie, British Columbia, Canada) – lead guitar / **JOHN RUTSEY** – drums

		not iss.	Moon
1973.	(7") **NOT FADE AWAY. / YOU CAN'T FIGHT IT**	—	—
		Mercury	Mercury
Aug 74.	(7") <73623> **FINDING MY WAY. /**	—	
Feb 75.	(lp) (9100 011) <1011> **RUSH**		Jul74

– Finding my way / Need some love / Take a friend / Here again / What you're doing / In the mood / Before and after / Working man. *(c-iss.Apr82; 7142 365) (re-iss. Jun83 lp/c; PRICE/PRIMC 18) (cd-iss. Apr87; 822 541-2)*

| Feb 75. | (7") <73647> **WHAT YOU'RE DOING. / IN THE MOOD** | — | |

—— (Autumn '74) **NEIL PEART** (b.12 Sep'52, Hamilton, Ontario, Canada) – drums, vocals, lyrics repl. RUTSEY

| Apr 75. | (lp) (9100 013) <1023> **FLY BY NIGHT** | | Feb75 |

– Anthem / Best I can / Beneath, between and behind / By-Tor & the snowdog: (i) At the tobes of Hades – (ii) Across the Styx – (iii) Of the battle – (iv) Epilogue / Fly by night / Making memories / Rivendell / In the end. *(c-iss.Apr82; 7142 389) (re-iss. Jun83 lp/c; PRICE/PRIMC 19) (cd-iss. Apr87; 822 542-2)*

May 75.	(7") <73681> **FLY BY NIGHT. / ANTHEM**	—	
	<re-iss. Dec77; 73990>		
Nov 75.	(7") <73737> **BASTILLE DAY. / LAKESIDE PARK**	—	
Mar 76.	(lp) (9100 018) <1046> **CARESS OF STEEL**		Oct75

– Bastille day / I think I'm going bald / Lakeside Park / The necromancer: (I) Unto darkness – (II) Under the shadow – (III) REturn of the prince / In the valley / Didacts and narpets / No one at the bridge / Panacea / Bacchus plateau / The fountain. *(c-iss.Apr82; 7142 421) (re-iss. Jun83 lp/c; PRICE/PRIMC 20) (cd-iss. Apr87; 822 543-2)*

| Jun 76. | (lp) (9100 039) <1079> **2112** | | 61 Apr76 |

– Overture / The temples of Syrinx / Discovery / Presentation / Oracle. The dream / Soliliquy / Grand finale / A passage to Bangkok / The twilight zone / Lessons / Tears / Something for nothing. *(re-iss. Jan85 lp/c; PRICE/PRIMC 79) (cd-iss. Apr87; 822 545-2)*

| Jun 76. | (7") <73803> **LESSONS. / THE TWILIGHT ZONE** | — | |
| Mar 77. | (d-lp) (6672 015) <7508> **ALL THE WORLD'S A STAGE (live)** | | 40 Sep76 |

– Bastille day / Anthem / Fly by night / In the mood / Something for nothing / Lakeside park / Overture / The temple of Syrinx / Presentation / Soliloquy / Grand finale / By-Tor and the snowdog / In the end / Working man / Finding my way / What you're doing. *(c-iss.Apr78; 7553 047) (re-iss. Sep84 d-lp/d-c; PRID/+C 1) (cd-iss. Apr87 – = a few tracks; 822 552-2)*

Dec 76.	(7") <73873> **FLY BY NIGHT (live). / IN THE MOOD (live) / SOMETHING FOR NOTHING (live)**	—	88
Feb 77.	(7") <73912> **THE TEMPLES OF SYRINX. / MAKING MEMORIES**	—	
Sep 77.	(lp) (9100 042) <1184> **A FAREWELL TO KINGS**	22	33

– A farewell to kings / Xanadu / Closer to the heart / Cinderella man / Madrigal / Cygnus X-1. *(re-iss. Apr86 lp/c; PRICE/PRIMC 92) (cd-iss. Apr87; 822 546-2)*

Nov 77.	(7") <73958> **CLOSER TO THE HEART. / MADRIGAL**	—	76
Jan 78.	(7"ep) (RUSH 7) **CLOSER TO THE HEART. / BASTILLE DAY / THE TEMPLES OF SYRINX**	36	—
	(12"ep+=) (RUSH 12) – Anthem.		
Nov 78.	(lp)(c)<US-pic-lp> (9100 059)(7142 647) <3743> **HEMISPHERES**	14	47

– Prelude / Apollo (bringer of wisdom) Hemispheres / Dionysus (bringer of love) / Armageddon (the battle of heart and mind) / Cygnus (bringer of balance) / The sphere (a kind of dream) / Circumstances / The trees / La villa Strangiato. *(cd-iss. Apr87; 822 547-2) (re-iss. Mar88 lp/c; PRICE/PRIMC 118)*

| Jan 79. | (7") <74051> **CIRCUMSTANCES. / THE TREES** | — | — |
| Jan 80. | (lp)(c) (9100 071)(7142 720) <4001> **PERMANENT WAVES** | 3 | 4 |

– Spirit of radio / Freewill / Jacob's ladder / Entre nous / Different strings / Natural science. *(cd-iss. Apr87; 822 548-2)*

Feb 80.	(7") <76044> **SPIRIT OF RADIO. / CIRCUMSTANCES**	—	51
Feb 80.	(7") (RADIO 7) **SPIRIT OF RADIO. / THE TREES**	13	
	(12"+=) (RADIO 12) – Working man.		
Apr 80.	(7") <76060> **DIFFERENT STRINGS. / ENTRE NOUS**	—	—
Feb 81.	(7") <76095> **LIMELIGHT. / XYZ**	—	55
Feb 81.	(lp/c) (6337/7141 160) <4013> **MOVING PICTURES**	3	3

– Tom Sawyer / Red Barchetta / XYZ / Limelight / The camera eye / Witch hunt (part III of fear) / Vital signs. *(cd-iss. 1983; 800 048-2)*

Mar 81.	(7") (VITAL 7) **VITAL SIGNS. / IN THE MOOD**	41	
	(12"+=) (VITAL 12) – A passage to Bangkok / Circumstances.		
May 81.	(7") <76109> **TOM SAWYER. / WITCH HUNT**	—	44
Oct 81.	(7") <76124> **FREEWILL (live). / CLOSER TO THE HEART (live)**	—	
Oct 81.	(d-lp/d-c) (6619/7558 053) <7001> **EXIT . . . STAGE LEFT (live)**	6	10

– The spirit of radio / Red Barchetta / YYZ / A passage to Bangkok *[not on cd]* / Closer to the heart / Beneath, between and behind / Jacob's ladder / Broon's bane / The trees / Xanadu / Freewill / Tom Sawyer / La villa Strangiato. *(cd-iss. Apr87; 822 551-2)*

Oct 81.	(7") (EXIT 7) **TOM SAWYER (live). / A PASSAGE TO BANGKOK (live)**	25	—
	(12"+=) (EXIT 12) – Red Barchetta (live).		
Dec 81.	(7") (RUSH 1) <76124> **CLOSER TO THE HEART (live). / THE TREES (live)**		69
Aug 82.	(7") (RUSH 8) <76179> **NEW WORLD MAN. / VITAL SIGNS (live)**	42	21
	(12"+=) (RUSH 8-12) – Freewill (live).		

Sep 82. (lp/c) *(6337/7141 243)* <403> **SIGNALS** `3` `10`
– Subdivisions / The analog kid / Chemistry / Digital man / The weapon / New world man / Losing it / Countdown. (cd-iss. 1983; 810 002-2)

Oct 82. (7") <76196> **SUBDIVISIONS. / COUNTDOWN** `-` ` `

Oct 82. (7"/7"pic-d) *(RUSH/+P 9)* **SUBDIVISIONS. / RED BARCHETTA (live)** `53` `-`
(12"+=) *(RUSH 9-12)* – Jacob's ladder (live).

Apr 83. (7"/7"sha-pic-d) *(RUSH 10/+PD)* **COUNTDOWN. / NEW WORLD MAN** `36`
(12"+=) *(RUSH 10-12)* – Spirit of radio (live) / (interview excerpts).

Apr 84. (lp/c)(cd) *(VERH/+C 12)(818 476-2)* <818476> **GRACE UNDER PRESSURE** `5` `10`
– Distant early warning / After image / Red sector A / The enemy within / The body electric / Kid gloves / Red lenses / Between the wheels.

May 84. (7") *(RUSH 11)* **THE BODY ELECTRIC. / THE ANALOG KID** `56`
(10"red+=/12"+=) *(RUSH 11 10/12)* – Distant early warning.

Oct 85. (7") *(RUSH 12)* <884191> **THE BIG MONEY. / TERRITORIES** `45`
(12"+=) *(RUSH 12-12)* – Red sector A (live).
(d7"+=) *(RUSHD 12)* – Closer to the heart / Spirit of radio.
(7"g-f) *(RUSHG 12)* – ('A'side) / Middletown dreams.

Nov 85. (lp/pic-lp/c)(cd) *(VERH/+P/C 31)(826 098-2)* <826098> **POWER WINDOWS** `9` `10` Oct85
– The big money / Grand designs / Manhattan project / Marathon / Territories / Middletown dreams / Emotion detector / Mystic rhythms.

Oct 87. (7") *(RUSH 13)* **TIME STAND STILL. / FORCE TEN** `41`
(12"pic-d+=) *(RUSHP 13-12)* – The enemy within (live).
(12"++=) *(RUSH 13-12)* – Witch hunt (live).

Nov 87. (lp/c)(cd) *(VERH/+C 47)(832 464-2)* <832464> **HOLD YOUR FIRE** `10` `13` Sep87
– Force ten / Time stand still / Open secrets / Second nature / Prime mover / Lock and key / Mission / Turn the page / Tai Shan / High water.

Mar 88. (7") *(RUSH 14)* **PRIME MOVER. / TAI SHAN**
(12"+=) *(RUSH 14-12)* – Open secrets.
(12"++=) *(RUSHR 14-12)* – New world man (live).
(cd-s+=) *(RUSHCD 14)* – Distant early warning (live) / New world man (live).
(7"white) *(RUSHR 14)* – ('A'side) / Distant early warning (live).

Jan 89. (d-lp/c/cd) *(836 346-1/-4/-2)* <836346> **A SHOW OF HANDS (live)** `12` `21`
– (intro) / The big money / Subdivisions / Marathon / Turn the page / Manhattan project / Mission / Distant early warning / Mystic rhythms / Witch hunt (part III of fear) / The rhythm method / Force ten / Time stand still / Red sector A / Closer to the heart.

Atlantic　Atlantic

Dec 89. (lp/c)(cd) *(WX 327/+C)(782 040-2)* <82040-1/-4/-2> **PRESTO** `27` `16` Nov89
– Show don't tell / Chain lightning / The pass / War paint / Scars / Presto / Superconductor / Anagram (for Mongo) / Red tide / Hand over fist / Available light.

Jan 90. (7") **SHOW DON'T TELL. /**

Sep 91. (cd)(lp/c) <(7567 82293-2)>(WX 436/+C) **ROLL THE BONES** `10` `3`
– Dreamline / Bravado / Roll the bones / Face up / Where's my thing? (part IV 'Gangster Of Boats' trilogy) / The big wheel / Heresy / Ghost of a chance / Neurotica / You bet your life.

Feb 92. (7") *(A 7524)* **ROLL THE BONES. / SHOW DON'T TELL** `49`
(cd-s+=) *(A 7524CD)* – (interviews) / Anagram.
(7"sha-pic-d) *(A 7524TE)* – ('A'side) / The pass / It's a rap part 1.

Apr 92. (7") *(A 7491)* **GHOST OF A CHANCE. / DREAMLINE**
(cd-s+=) *(A 7491CD)* – Chain lightning / Red tide.

Oct 93. (cd/c/lp) <(7567 82528-2/-4/-1)> **COUNTERPARTS** `14` `2`
– Animate / Stick it out / Cut to the chase / Nobody's hero / Between sun & moon / Alien shore / The speed of love / Double agent / Leave that thing alone / Cold fire / Everyday glory.

Sep 96. (cd/c) <(7567 82925-2/-4)> **TEST FOR ECHO** `25` `5`
– Test for echo / Driven / Half the world / The color of right / Time and motion / Totem / Dog years / Virtuality / Resist / Limbo / Carve away the stone.

Nov 98. (t-cd/d-c) *(7567 80921-2/-4)* <83122> **DIFFERENT STAGES (live history)** `35`
– Dreamline / Limelight / Driven / Bravado / Animate / Show don't tell / Trees / Nobody's hero / Closer to the heart / 2112 – Overture / Temples in Syrinx – Discovery – Presentation – Oraci (the dream – Soliloquy – Grand finale) / Test for echo / Analog kid / Freewill / Roll the bones / Stick it out / Resist / Leave that thing alone / Neil's solo / Natural science / Spirit of radio / Tom Sawyer / XYZ / Bastille day / By Tor and the snow dog / Xanadu / Farewell to kings / Something for nothing / Cygnus X-1 / Anthem / Working man / Fly by night / In the mood / Cinderella man.

– compilations, others, etc. –

on 'Mercury' unless otherwise mentioned

May 78. (t-lp)(d-c) *(6641 779)(7649 103)* <9200> **ARCHIVES** Apr78
– (RUSH / FLY BY NIGHT / CARESS OF STEEL)

Sep 81. (lp/c) <6337/7141 171> **RUSH THROUGH TIME** `-`

Feb 88. (7") Old Gold; *(OG 9767)* **SPIRIT OF RADIO. / CLOSER TO THE HEART** `-`

Oct 90. (d-cd/d-c/t-lp) Vertigo; *(838 936-2/-4/-1)* / Mercury; <838936> **CHRONICLES** `42` `51` Sep90
– Finding my way / Working man / Fly by night / Anthem / Bastille day / Lakeside park / 2112: a) Overture, b) The temples of Syrinx / What you're doing (live) / A farewell to kings / Closer to the heart / The trees / La villa Strangiato / Freewill / Spirit of radio / Tom Sawyer / Red barchetta / Limelight / A passage to Bangkok (live) / Subdivisions / New world man / Distant early warning / Red sector A / The big money / Manhattan project / Force ten / Time stand still / Mystic rhythms (live) / Show don't tell.

VICTOR

ALEX LIFESON – guitar, bass, keyboards / **BILL BELL** – wobble & slide guitar, co-writer / **PETER CARDINALI** – bass / **BLAKE MANNING** – drums / + guests EDWIN – vocals (of I MOTHER EARTH) + LES CLAYPOOL – bass (of PRIMUS)

Atlantic　Atlantic

Feb 96. (cd/c) <(7567-82852-2/-4)> **VICTOR** `99` Jan96
– Don't care / Promise / Start today / Mr. X / At the end / Sending a warning / Shut up shuttin' up / Strip and go naked / The big dance / Victor / I am the spirit.

Leon RUSSELL

Born: HANK WILSON, 2 Apr'41, Lawton, Oklahoma, USA. Having learned to play the piano at an early age, he soon mastered a string of other instruments and by the late 50's – still in his teens – had progressed to nightclubs, augmenting RONNIE HAWKINS and JERRY LEE LEWIS. By the early 60's, RUSSELL had relocated to California where he secured session work under the name of RUSSELL BRIDGES. He became a regular contributor to PHIL SPECTOR's "wall of sound", other sessions including HERB ALPERT's 'Taste Of Honey' & The BYRDS 'Mr. Tambourine Man'. In the mid-60's, he arranged a hit for GARY LEWIS & THE PLAYBOYS, 'This Diamond Ring', while also also signing a solo deal with 'A&M' records. His work for others continued, including sessions for GENE CLARK (ex-Byrds) and arranging a hit single, 'Feelin' Groovy', for HARPER'S BIZARRE. In 1968 he formed ASYLUM CHOIR with MARC BENNO, releasing an eponymous album which found a cult audience but little critical acclaim. Subsequently befriending rootsy soul duo, DELANEY & BONNIE, RUSSELL produced their 'Accept No Substitute' (1969) album as well as augmenting them on their 'Friends' tour (later 'friends' would include such luminaries as ERIC CLAPTON and GEORGE HARRISON). That year also saw JOE COCKER taking RUSSELL's 'DELTA LADY' into the UK Top 10, the workaholic jack-of-all-musical trades the brains behind COCKER's celebrated 'Mad Dogs and Englishmen' tour the following year. Incredibly, he also found time to start up his own label, 'Shelter', along with A&M producer, Denny Cordell, the first releases being a follow-up ASYLUM CHOIR effort and RUSSELL's own eponymous 1970 debut. Performed in his own inimitable blues/gospel drenched, backwoods bayou style, RUSSELL's chunky piano chords graced a clutch of covers (including Screamin' Jay Hawkins' 'I PUT A SPELL ON YOU' and a rather more unlikely 'GIVE PEACE A CHANCE') alongside enjoyable originals. As well as launching RUSSELL's own career, 'Shelter' was instrumental in setting out J.J.CALE, amongst others, on a long and illustrious (if low key) career. With exposure from the 'Mad Dogs..' tour doing him no harm, RUSSELL's debut made a minor dent in the US charts, although the superior follow-up, 'LEON RUSSELL AND THE SHELTER PEOPLE' (1971) broke the American Top 20 and the British Top 30, another mix of hard hitting interpretations (this time a handful of scorching DYLAN covers; 'HARD RAIN'S A-GONNA FALL', 'IT TAKES A LOT TO LAUGH, IT TAKES A TRAIN TO CRY' and 'IT'S ALL OVER NOW, BABY BLUE') and idiosyncratic self-penned material. August '71 saw him joining the fray for GEORGE HARRISON's 'Concert For Bangladesh', while the following year's 'CARNEY' was an even bigger success, a near US-No.1 which saw the impressively bearded singer/songwriter using his chequered history in the music business as inspiration. Despite the clown symbolism which he used on the record, RUSSELL's services were in demand constantly, the pianist even writing and producing two tracks with DYLAN, 'Watching The River Flow' and 'When I Paint My Masterpiece'. He also lent a hand to his wife, MARY MCREARY, releasing her solo debut, 'Butterflies In Heaven', in 1973, as well as working with her on 1976's 'THE WEDDING ALBUM'. 'HANK WILSON'S BACK' (1973) introduced RUSSELL's country alter-ego, a direction he would subsequently pursue with WILLIE NELSON as well as forming his own bluegrass combo at the turn of the decade. While the bulk of RUSSELL's latter 70's output met with minimal critical and commercial success, the 'WILLIE AND LEON' (1979) set made the US Top 30 and spawned a massive country hit with the cover of Elvis Presley's 'HEARTBREAK HOTEL'. The 80's saw RUSSELL's solo recording activities take a back seat, 'HANK WILSON VOL.II' (1984) his last album for almost a decade. He eventually returned in 1992 with the BRUCE HORNSBY-produced 'ANYTHING CAN HAPPEN', an aptly titled effort which saw RUSSELL's experimental excursions receive a frosty reception from critics. Nevertheless, he remains something of a backroom legend in the music industry, his place in the annals of rock history assured. **Covers:** BEWARE OF DARKNESS (George Harrison) / THE BATTLE OF NEW ORLEANS (Jimmy Driftwood) / MASTERS OF WAR + THE MIGHTY QUINN (Bob Dylan) / ROLL IN MY SWEET ARMS BABY (Lester Flatt) / IF I WERE A CARPENTER (Tim Hardin) / JAMBALAYA + I'M SO LONESOME I COULD CRY (Hank Williams) / and other covers from 'HANK WILSON'S BACK'.JUMPING JACK FLASH (Rolling Stones) / YOUNG BLOOD + IDOL WITH THE GOLDEN HEAD (Leiber-Stoller) / SWEEPING THROUGH THE CITY (. . . Casal) / I SERVE A LIVING SAVIOR (. . . Watson) / SOME DAY (. . . Henderson) / TOO MUCH MONKEY BUSINESS (Chuck Berry) / JEZEBEL (. . . Shanklin) / etc. • **Trivia:** In 1977, his song 'THIS MASQUERADE', won a Grammy award for GEORGE BENSON.

Album rating: LEON RUSSELL (*7) / LEON RUSSELL & THE SHELTER PEOPLE (*7) / CARNEY (*7) / LEON LIVE (*6) / HANK WILSON'S BACK, VOL.1 (*6; as Hank Wilson) / STOP ALL THAT JAZZ (*4) / WILL O' THE WISP (*5) / WEDDING ALBUM with Mary Russell (*5) / BEST OF LEON compilation (*7) / MAKE LOVE TO THE MUSIC with Mary Russell (*4) / AMERICANA (*4) / ONE FOR THE ROAD with Willie Nelson (*5) / LIFE & LOVE (*5) / THE LIVE ALBUM with the New Grass Revival (*4) / HANK WILSON VOL.II (*3; as Hank Wilson) / ANYTHING CAN HAPPEN (*5) / GIMME SHELTER compilation (*8)

LEON RUSSELL – vocals, piano, trumpet, guitar, etc.

not iss.　A&M

1964. (7") <734> **MISTY. / CINDY** `-` ` `
Dot　Dot

Nov 65. (7") *(DS 16771)* **EVERYBODY'S TALKIN' 'BOUT THE YOUNG. / IT'S ALRIGHT WITH ME**

—— LEON joined ASYLUM CHOIR with MARC BENNO. They made two albums in the late 60's. Early in 1970, RUSSELL augmented both DELANEY & BONNIE plus JOE COCKER before returning to solo work.

A&M / Shelter

May 70. (7") *<301>* **ROLL AWAY THE STONE. / HUMMINGBIRD**

Jun 70. (lp) *(AMLS 982) <8901>* **LEON RUSSELL** — 60 Dec69
– A song for you / Dixie lullaby / I put a spell on you / Shoot out on the plantation / Hummingbird / Delta lady / Prince of peace / Old masters / Give peace a chance / Hurt somebody / Pisces apple lady / Roll away the stone. *(re-iss. Apr76 on 'Island'; ISA 5005) (cd-iss. Nov90 on 'Sequel'; NEXCD 146)*

May 71. (7") **THE BALLAD OF MAD DOGS AND ENGLISHMEN. / LET IT BE**

A&M / Shelter

May 71. (lp) *(AMLS 65003) <8903>* **LEON RUSSELL AND THE SHELTER PEOPLE** — 29 / 17
– Stranger in a strange land / Of thee I sing / Hard rain's a-gonna fall / Crystal closet queen / Home sweet Oklahoma / Alcatraz / The ballad of mad dogs and Englishmen / It takes a lot to laugh, it takes a train to cry / She smokes like a river / Sweet Emily / Beware of darkness. *(re-iss. Apr76 on 'Island'; ISA 5006) (cd-iss. 1991 on 'Sequel'+=; NEXCD 137)* – It's all over now, baby blue / Love minus zero – No limit / She belongs to me.

May 71. (7") *<7302>* **HOME SWEET OKLAHOMA. / IT TAKES A LOT TO LAUGH, IT TAKES A TRAIN TO CRY**

Apr 72. (7") *<7305>* **ME AND BABY JANE. / A HARD RAIN'S A-GONNA FALL**

Jun 72. (7") *<7316>* **A SONG FOR YOU. / A HARD RAIN'S A-GONNA FALL**

Aug 72. (lp) *(AMLH 68911) <8911>* **CARNEY** — 2 Jul72
– Tight rope / Out in the woods / Me and baby Jane / Manhattan island serenade / Cajun love song / Roller derby / Carney / Acid Annapolis / If the shoe fits / My cricket / This masquerade / Magic mirror. *(cd-iss. Nov90 on 'Sequel'; NEXCD 147)*

Aug 72. (7") *<7325>* **TIGHT ROPE. / THIS MASQUERADE** — 11

Sep 72. (7") *(AMS 7026)* **TIGHT ROPE. / DELTA LADY**

Dec 72. (7") *(AMS 7045) <7328>* **SLIPPING INTO CHRISTMAS. / CHRISTMAS IN CHICAGO** — Xmas
(re-iss. Dec76 on 'Island'; WIP 6365)

Aug 73. (t-lp) *<8917>* **LEON LIVE (live Long Beach Arena)** — 9 Jul73
– Medley:- I'll take you there – Idol with the golden head – The mighty Quinn – I serve a living savior – The mighty Quinn / Shoot out on the plantation / Dixie lullaby / Queen of the roller derby / Roll away the stone / It's been a long time baby / Great day / Alcatraz / Crystal closet queen / Prince of peace / Sweet Emily / Stranger in a strange land / Out in the woods / Some day / Sweeping through the city / Medley:- Jumping Jack Flash – Young blood / Medley:- Of thee I sing – Yes I am – Delta lady / It's all over now, baby blue. *(UK-iss.Jan92 on 'Sequel' d-cd; NEDCD 172)*

Aug 73. (7") *<7337>* **QUEEN OF THE ROLLER DERBY (live). / ROLL AWAY THE STONE** — 89

Sep 73. (lp; as HANK WILSON) *(AMLS 68923) <8923>* **HANK WILSON'S BACK** — 28
– Roll in my sweet baby's arms (part 1 & 2) / She thinks I still care / I'm so lonesome I could cry / I'll sail my ship alone / Jambalaya / A six pack to go / Battle of New Orleans / Uncle Pen / Am I that easy to forget / Truck drivin' man / The window up above / Lost highway / Goodnight Irene. *(cd-iss. Oct90 on 'Sequel'; REXCD139)*

Sep 73. (7"; as HANK WILSON) *<7336>* **ROLL IN MY SWEET BABY'S ARMS. / I'M SO LONESOME I COULD CRY** — 78

Nov 73. (7"; as HANK WILSON) *<7338>* **UNCLE PEN. / SIX PACK TO GO**

Apr 74. (7") *(AMS 7107) <40210>* **IF I WERE A CARPENTER. / WILD HORSES** — 73

Jul 74. (lp) *(AMLS 68262) <2108>* **STOP ALL THAT JAZZ** — 34
– If I were a carpenter / Smashed / Leaving Whipporwhill / Spanish Harlem / Streaker's ball / Working girl / Time for love / The ballad of Hollis Brown / Mona Lisa please / Stop all that jazz. *(re-iss. Apr76 on 'Island'; ISA 5009) (cd-iss. Apr91 on 'Sequel'; NEXCD 151)*

Jul 74. (7") *<40277>* **TIME FOR LOVE. / LEAVING WHIPPORWHILL**

Jun 75. (lp) *(AMLS 68309) <2138>* **WILL O' THE WISP** — 30
– Will o' the wisp / Little hideaway / Make you feel good / Can't get over losing you / My father's shoes / Stay away from sad songs / Back to the island / Down on deep river / Bluebird / Laying right here in Heaven / Lady blue. *(re-iss. Apr76 on 'Island'; ISA 5012) (cd-iss. Apr91 on 'Sequel'; NEXCD 157)*

Aug 75. (7") *(AMS 7199) <40378>* **LADY BLUE. / LAYING RIGHT HERE IN HEAVEN** — 14

Dec 75. (7") *<40483>* **BACK TO THE ISLAND. / LITTLE HIDEAWAY** — 53

Feb 76. (7") *<62004>* **BLUEBIRD. / BACK TO THE ISLAND**

LEON & MARY RUSSELL

Mary was his wife. **MARY McCREARY** – vocalist with LITTLE SISTER (ex-SLY & THE FAMILY STONE).

Paradise / Paradise

Jun 76. (lp) *(K 56244) <2943>* **THE WEDDING ALBUM** — 34 Apr76
– Rainbow in your eyes / Like a dream come true / Love's supposed to be that way / Fantasy / Satisfy you / You are on my mind / Lavender blue / Quiet nights / Windsong / Daylight.

Jun 76. (7") *<8208>* **RAINBOW IN YOUR EYES. / LOVE'S SUPPOSED TO BE THAT WAY** — 52

Sep 76. (7") *<8274>* **SATISFY YOU. / WINDSONG**

Jun 77. (lp) *<3066>* **MAKE LOVE TO THE MUSIC**
– Easy love / Joyful noise / Now now boogie / Say you will / Make love to the music / Love crazy / Love is in your eyes / Hold on to this feeling / Island in the sun.

Jun 77. (7") *<8369>* **SAY YOU WILL. / LOVE CRAZY**

Oct 77. (7") *<8438>* **EASY LOVE. / HOLD ON TO THIS FEELING**

LEON RUSSELL

—— solo again on same label

Aug 78. (lp) *(K 56534) <3172>* **AMERICANA**
– Let's get started / Elvis and Marilyn / From Maine to Mexico / When a man loves a woman / It's only me / Midnight lover / Housewife / Ladies of the night / Shadow and me / Jesus on my side.

Oct 78. (7") *(K 17244) <8667>* **ELVIS AND MARILYN. / ANITA BRYANT**

Jan 79. (7") *<8719>* **FROM MAINE TO MEXICO. / MIDNIGHT LOVER**

—— Mid'79, he partners WILLIE NELSON for d-lp 'WILLIE AND LEON', see further.

1979. (lp) *(K 56891) <3341>* **LIFE & LOVE**
– One more love song / You girl / Struck by lightning / Strange love / Life and love / On the first day / High horse / Sweet mystery / On the borderline.

Warners / Paradise

Jan 81. (7") *<49662>* **OVER THE RAINBOW. / I'VE JUST SEEN A FACE**

Mar 81. (lp; as LEON RUSSELL & THE NEW GRASS REVIVAL) *(K 56891) <3532>* **THE LIVE ALBUM (live)**
– Over the rainbow / I've just seen a face / One more love song / I believe to my soul / Pilgrim land / Georgia blues / Prince of peace / Rollin' in my sweet baby's arms / Stranger in a strange land / I want to be at the meeting / Wild horses / Jambalaya / Caribbean / Jumpin' Jack Flash.

1984. (lp; as HANK WILSON) *<0002>* **HANK WILSON VOL.II**

—— retired from solo music biz, until 1992, when he co-wrote songs with BRUCE HORNSBY.

Virgin Am. / Virgin

May 92. (cd/c) *(CDVUS/VUSMC 50)* **ANYTHING CAN HAPPEN**
– Anything can happen / Black halos / No man's land / Too much monkey business / Angel ways / Life of the party / Stranded on Easy Street / Jezebel / Love slave / Faces of the children.

Eldorado / ARKK

May 98. (cd) *(ELDCD 004) <ARK 1002-2>* **LEGEND IN MY TIME: HANK WILSON VOL.3**
– Sixteen tons / Night life / Act naturally / Sweet dreams / Daddy sang bass / He stopped loving her today / Mama don't let your babies grow up to be / Funny how time slips away / Okie from Muskogee / Crazy / Love's gonna live here / He'll have to go / Legend in my time.

– compilations, others, etc. –

Jan 72. (7" by 'ASYLUM CHOIR') *Shelter;* **STRAIGHT BROTHER. / TRYIN' TO STAY ALIVE**

1974. (lp) *Olympic; <7112>* **LOOKING BACK**

Jan 77. (lp) *Island; (ISA 5004) / Shelter; <52004>* **THE BEST OF LEON** — 40 Oct76

Jan 77. (7") *Island; (WIP 6290)* **TIGHT ROPE. / THIS MASQUERADE**

Jan 92. (cd/c) *Castle; (CCS CD/MC 313)* **THE COLLECTION**
– A song for you / Lady blue / Tight rope / Blue bird / This masquerade / Roll away the stone / Beware of darkness / Crystal closet queen / Delta lady / Back to the island / Stranger in a strange land / Hummingbird / Queen of the roller derby / Of thee I sing / Streaker's ball / Roll in my sweet baby's arms / Magic mirror / If I were a carpenter / Out in the woods / The battle of New Orleans.

Nov 96. (d-cd) *E.M.I.; <52644>* **GIMME SHELTER: THE BEST OF LEON RUSSELL**
– Hello little friend / Sweet home Chicago / Tryin' to stay 'live / Ballad for a soldier / Song for you / Dixie lullaby / Hummingbird / Delta lady / Pisces apple lady / Old masters (masters of war) / Home, sweet Oklahoma / She smiles like a river / Beware of darkness / Tight rope / Me and baby Jane / Manhattan island serenade / Magic mirror / This masquerade / Roll away the stone / Prince of peace / Sweet Emily / Roll in my sweet baby's arms / She thinks I still care / In the jailhouse now / If I were a carpenter... / Leaving Whiporwhill / Time for love / Will o' the wisp / Little hideaway / Back to the island / Bluebird / Lady blue / She belongs to me / Wild horses / Anything can happen / Faces of the children / Everybody's talkin' 'bout the young / It's alright with me.

WILLIE NELSON & LEON RUSSELL

C.B.S. / Columbia

Jun 79. (7") *<11119>* **TROUBLE IN MIND. / ONE MORE FOR MY BABY AND ONE FOR THE ROAD**

Jul 79. (d-lp) *(CBS 88461) <36064>* **WILLIE AND LEON – ONE FOR THE ROAD (live)** — 25
– Detour / I saw the light / Heartbreak hotel / Let the rest of the world go by / Trouble in mind / Don't fence me in / Wild side of life / Ridin' down the canyon / Sioux City Sue / You are my sunshine / Danny boy / Always / Summertime / Because of you / Am I blue / Tenderly / Far away places / That lucky old Sun / Stormy weather / One for my baby.

Jul 79. (7") **HEARTBREAK HOTEL. / SIOUX CITY SUE**

Mike RUTHERFORD (see under ⇒ GENESIS)

RUTS (dig out; Great Alt & Indie . . .)

Mitch RYDER (dig out; Great Psychedelic . . .)

Buffy SAINTE-MARIE

Born: 20 Feb'41, Piapot Reservation, Saskatchewan, Canada. Although adopted by a white family at a very early age, Cree Indian SAINTE-MARIE never strayed far from her roots, incorporating Native American styles into her musical approach and actively campaigning for her beleaguered brethren. Moving to the American East coast during the 60's, she was discovered by 'Vanguard' producer, Maynard Solomon and subsequently signed to the label, a hub of the burgeoning folk-protest movement. With PATRICK SKY (a solo artist for the same label) and ART DAVIS accompanying her, the singer/songwriter made her recording debut in 1964 with 'IT'S MY WAY!', a promising set which included some of SAINTE-MARIE's most enduring tracks. While her distinctive vocal style took a bit of getting used to, there was no disputing the quality of her songs; DONOVAN took protest anthem, 'UNIVERSAL SOLDIER' into the Top 20 the following year, while 'COD'INE' was memorably covered by QUICKSILVER MESSENGER SERVICE amongst others. Though chart success eluded her, the singer continued to make her mark on the counter-culture scene with increasingly diverse albums. 1968's 'I'M GONNA BE A COUNTRY GIRL AGAIN' saw her adopt a C&W approach with mixed results, while 'ILLUMINATIONS' (1969) dabbled with electronics. SAINTE-MARIE scored a belated UK Top 10 hit in 1971 with 'SOLDIER BLUE', the theme tune to the movie of the same name. That year's album 'SHE USED TO WANNA BE A BALLERINA', was one of the most robust sets of her career, featuring the backing talents of RY COODER and CRAZY HORSE although, despite the success of the single, it failed to make the charts. Early the following year, she scored a further UK Top 40 hit with a re-released 'I'M GONNA BE A COUNTRY GIRL AGAIN', while, incredibly, 'MISTER CAN'T YOU SEE' (from the 'MOONSHOT' album) gave SAINTE-MARIE her only US Top 40 hit a few months later. Her later albums for 'M.C.A.', 'BUFFY' (1974) and 'CHANGING WOMAN' (1975), lacked focus and despite a return to her roots on 'SWEET AMERICA' (1976), the singer retired from the studio for the remainder of the 70's and the whole of the following decade. As well as her continuing work for Native American causes and children's charities, SAINTE-MARIE was invited to appear on US kids' show, 'Sesame Street', in the late 70's, remaining there for the best part of five years and helping to shape the programme's anti-racist educational slant. She also co-wrote (along with husband JACK NITZSCHE) 'UP WHERE WE BELONG', a massive 1982 hit for JOE COCKER & JENNIFER WARNES. Newly signed to 'Chrysalis' ('Ensign' in the UK), SAINTE-MARIE eventually returned to the recording front in her own right with 1992's 'COINCIDENCE AND LIKELY STORIES'. The record proved she was far from a spent musical force, receiving encouraging reviews and even making the UK Top 40. • **Covers:** UNTIL IT'S TIME FOR YOU TO GO (hit; Elvis Presley) / etc. She herself covered THE CIRCLE GAME + SONG TO A SEAGULL (Joni Mitchell) / YOU'RE GONNA NEED SOMEBODY ON YOUR BOND (Robert Johnson) / and some traditional material, etc.

Album rating: IT'S MY WAY (*6) / MANY A MILE (*6) / LITTLE WHEEL SPIN AND SPIN (*6) / FIRE & FLEET & CANDLELIGHT (*6) / I'M GONNA BE A COUNTRY GIRL AGAIN (*5) / ILLUMINATIONS (*6) / THE BEST OF BUFFY SAINTE-MARIE compilation (*7) / SHE USED TO WANNA BE A BALLERINA (*7) / MOONSHOT (*6) / QUIET PLACES (*5) / BUFFY (*4) / THE BEST OF BUFFY SAINTE-MARIE VOL.II compilation (*6) / NATIVE NORTH AMERICAN CHILD: AN ODYSSEY compilation (*6) / CHANGING WOMAN (*4) / SWEET AMERICA (*4) / COINCIDENCE AND LIKELY STORIES (*7) /

BUFFY SAINTE-MARIE – vocals, guitar with **PATRICK SKY** (b.Oct'40 near Atlanta, Georgia, USA) – guitar (also a solo artist for same label) / **ART DAVIS** – bass

			Fontana	Vanguard
1964.	(lp) *(TFL 6040)* <VSD 79142> **IT'S MY WAY!**		□	□

– Now that the buffalo's gone / The old man's lament / Ananias / Mayoo sto hoon / Cod'ine / Cripple creek / Universal soldier / Babe in arms / He lived alone in town / You're gonna need somebody on your bond / The incest song / Eyes of amber / It's my way. *(re-iss.May69 on 'Vanguard'; SVRL 19030) (cd-iss. Feb93 on 'Vanguard';)*

RUSS SAVAKUS – bass + **DADDY BONES** – guitar repl. DAVIS

Jun 65.	(7") *(TF 574)* <35028> **UNTIL IT'S TIME FOR YOU TO GO. / THE FLOWER AND THE APPLE TREE**	□	□
1965.	(lp) *(TFL 6047)* <VSD 79171> **MANY A MILE**		

– Must I go bound / Los Pescadores / Groundhog / On the banks of red roses / Fixin' to die / Until it's time for you to go / The Piney Wood Hills / Welcome welcome emigrante / Brokedown girl / Johnny be fair / Maple sugar boy / Lazarus / Come all ye fair and tender girls / Many a mile. *(re-iss. Apr69 on 'Vanguard'; SVRL 19031)*

Sep 65.	(7") *(H 614)* **THE UNIVERSAL SOLDIER. / CRIPPLE CREEK**	□	-

---

BRUCE LANGHORNE + ERIC WEISSBERG – guitar repl. BONES

May 66.	(7") *(H 695)* **TIMELESS LOVE. / LADY MARGARET**	□	-
May 66.	(lp) *(STFL 6071)* <VSD 79211> **LITTLE WHEEL SPIN AND SPIN**	□	**97**

– Little wheel spin and spin / Waly Waly / Rolling log blues / My country 'tis of thy people you're dying / Men of the fields / Timeless love / Sir Patrick Spens / Poor man's daughter / Lady Margaret / Sometimes when I get to thinkin' / Winter boy. *(re-iss. Apr69 on 'Vanguard'; SVRL 19023) (cd-iss. Feb93;)*

Jan 67.	(7") <35050> **JUSQU'AU JOUR OU TU PARTIRAS. / UNTIL IT'S TIME FOR YOU TO GO**	-	□

AL ROGERS – drums / **MONTE DUNN** – mandolin / **BOB SIGGINS** – banjo repl. SKY + WEISSBERG. From the 1968 onwards, her albums featured heap many session people.

Jul 67.	(lp) <VSD 79250> **FIRE & FLEET & CANDLELIGHT**	-	□

– The seeds of brotherhood / Summer boy / The circle game / Lyke wake dirge / Song to a seagull / Doggett's gap / The wedding song / 97 men in this here town would give a half a grand in silver just to follow me down / Lord Randall / The carousel / T'es pas un autre / Little boy dark eyes / Reynardine – a vampire legend / Hey, little boy. *(UK-iss.Jan72; same)*

Jul 67.	(7") <35053> **THE CIRCLE GAME. / UNTIL IT'S TIME FOR YOU TO GO**	-	□
Jun 68.	(7") <35064> **THE PINEY WOOD HILLS. / SOULFUL SHADE OF BLUE**	-	□
Jul 68.	(lp) <VSD 79280> **I'M GONNA BE A COUNTRY GIRL AGAIN**	-	□

– I'm gonna be a country girl again / He's a pretty good man if you ask me / Uncle Joe / A soulful shade of blue / From the bottom of my heart / Sometimes when I get to thinkin' / The Pine Wood Hills / How that the buffalo's gone / They outta quit kickin' my dawg around / Tall trees in Georgia / The love of a good man / Take my hand for awhile / Gonna feel much better when you're gone. *(UK-iss.Apr72; same) (cd-iss. Oct96; VMD 79280)*

Nov 68.	(7") <35072> **BETTER TO FIND OUT FOR YOURSELF. / SOMETIMES WHEN I GET TO THINKIN'**	-	□
1969.	(7") <35075> **I'M GONNA BE A COUNTRY GIRL AGAIN. / FROM THE BOTTOM OF MY HEART**	-	□
Dec 69.	(lp) <VSD 79300> **ILLUMINATIONS**	-	

– God is alive, magic is a foot / Mary / Better to find out for yourself / The vampire / Adam / The dream tree / Suffer the little children / The angel / With you honey / Guess who I saw in Paris / He's a keeper of the fire / Poppies. *(UK-iss.Dec71 on 'Vanguard'; same) (cd-iss. Feb93 on 'Vanguard';)*

Dec 69.	(7") <35091> **HE'S A KEEPER OF THE FIRE. / BETTER TO FIND OUT FOR YOURSELF**	-	□
Aug 70.	(7") <35108> **BETTER TO FIND OUT FOR YOURSELF. / THE CIRCLE GAME**	-	□
Feb 71.	(7") <35116> **SOLDIER BLUE. / UNTIL IT'S TIME FOR YOU TO GO**	-	□

(below 45 from the 1970 film 'Soldier Blue')

		R.C.A.	R.C.A.
May 71.	(7") *(RCA 2081)* **SOLDIER BLUE. / MORATORIUM**	**7**	-
		Vanguard	Vanguard
Jul 71.	(7") <35127> **SHE USED TO WANNA BE A BALLERINA. / MORATORIUM**		
Sep 71.	(lp) <(VSD 79311)> **SHE USED TO WANNA BE A BALLERINA**		Apr71

– Rollin' mill man / Smack water Jack / Sweet September morning / She used to be a ballerina / Bells / Helpless / Moratorium – Bring our brothers home / The surfer / Song of the French partisans / Soldier blue / Now you've been gone a long time. *(cd-iss. Oct95; VMD 79311)*

Sep 71.	(7") <35135> **HELPLESS. / NOW YOU'VE BEEN GONE A LONG TIME**	-	□
Oct 71.	(7") *(VAN 1001)* **SHE USED TO WANNA BE A BALLERINA. / UNTIL IT'S TIME FOR YOU TO GO**	□	-
Jan 72.	(7") <(VRS 35143)> **I'M GONNA BE A COUNTRY GIRL AGAIN. / THE PINEY WOOD HILLS**	**34**	**98** Nov71
Jun 72.	(7") <(VRS 35151)> **MISTER CAN'T YOU SEE.**		**38** Mar72
Jul 72.	(lp) <(VSD 79312)> **MOONSHOT**		May72

– Not the lovin' kind / You know how to turn on those lights / I wanna hold your hand forever / He's an Indian cowboy in the rodeo / Lay it down / Moonshot / Native North American child / My baby left me / Sweet memories / Jeremiah / Mister can't you see. *(cd-iss. Feb93;)*

Aug 72.	(7") <(VRS 35156)> **HE'S AN INDIAN COWBOY IN THE RODEO. / NOT THE LOVIN' KIND**	-	**98**
Feb 73.	(7") <35172> **JEREMIAH. / I WANNA HOLD YOUR HAND FOREVER**		
Nov 73.	(lp) <(VSD 79330)> **QUIET PLACES**		

– Why you been gone so long / No one told me / For free / She'll be comin' 'round the mountain when she comes / Clair Vol's young son / Just that kind of man / Quiet places / Have you seen my baby / There's no gone in the world like Caleb / Civilization / Eventually / The jewels of Hanalei. *(cd-iss. Jan94 & Oct96; VMD 79330)*

		M.C.A.	M.C.A.
Feb 74.	(7") <40193> **CAN'T BELIEVE THE FEELING. / WHEN YOU'RE GONE**	□	□
Mar 74.	(7") *(MCA 127)* **CAN'T BELIEVE THE FEELING. / WAVES**	□	-
Mar 74.	(lp) *(MCG 3517)* **BUFFY**	□	

– Can't believe the feeling when you're gone / I've really fallen for you / Sweet little Vera / Star boy / Sweet, fast hooker blues / Generation / Hey, baby howdja do me this way / I can't take it no more / Waves / That's the way you fall in love.

May 74.	(7") <40216> **WAVES. / SWEET LITTLE VERA**	□	□

Jul 74. (7") <40286> **I CAN'T TAKE IT NO MORE. / NATIVE NORTH AMERICAN CHILD: AN ODYSSEY**

Sep 74. (7") <40347> **GENERATION. / SWEET, FAST HOOKER BLUES**

Mar 75. (MCA 183) <40368> **LOVE'S GOT TO BREATHE AND FLOWER. / NOBODY WILL EVER KNOW IT'S REAL BUT YOU**

Mar 75. (lp) (MCF 2594) **CHANGING WOMAN**
– Eagle man – Changing woman / Can't you see the way I love you / Love's got to breathe and fly / You take me away / 'Til I see you again / Mongrel pup / The beauty way / Nobody will ever know it's real but you / All around the world / A man.

Feb 76. (lp) (ABCL 5168) **SWEET AMERICA**
– Sweet America / Wynken, Blynken and Nod / Where poets go / Free the lady / America my home / Look at the facts / I don't need no city life / Sweet January / Q'appelle Valley, Saskatchewan / Honey can you hang around / I been down / Starwalker / Ain't no time for the worryin' blues.

Mar 76. (7") <12183> **STARWALKER. / FREE THE LADY**

Apr 76. (7") (ABC 4113) **SWEET AMERICA. / STAR WALKER**

Jul 76. (7") (ABC 4132) <12203> **LOOK AT THE FACTS. / WHERE POETS GO**

—— She retired from the studio, but in the late 70's was invited to appear on US children's show 'Sesame Street'. She stayed on the show for over 5 years, helping to initiate their attitude to racism in America. She returned to the studio in 1991 with new band **ROGER JACOBS** – bass, drums, percussion / **CHRIS BIRETT** – samples / **RICK MARVIN** – keyboards / etc.

		Ensign	Chrysalis
Jan 92. (7"/c-s) (ENY/+MC 650) **THE BIG ONES GET AWAY. / I'M GOING HOME** (12"pic-d+=/cd-s+=) (ENY X/CD 650) – Contralosophy.		39	
Mar 92. (cd)(lp/c) (CCD 1920)(CHEN/TCCHEN 23) **COINCIDENCE AND LIKELY STORIES**		39	

– The big ones get away / Fallen angels / Bad end / Emma Lee / Starwalker / The priests of the golden bull / Disinformation / Getting started / I'm going home / Bury my heart at Wounded Knee / Goodnight.

Jun 92. (7"/c-s) **FALLEN ANGELS. / SOLDIER BLUE**
(cd-s+=) – ('A'mixes).

– compilations, others, etc. –

Note; on 'Vanguard' until otherwise mentioned.

May 73. (d-lp) <(VSD 3-4)> **THE BEST OF BUFFY SAINTE-MARIE**
– Soulful shade of blue / Soldier blue / Universal soldier / Better to find out for yourself / Cod'ine / He's a keeper of the fire / Take my hand for a while / Ground hog / The circle game / My country 'tis of thy people you're dying / Many a mile. (re-iss. Mar89 on 'Start' lp/c/cd; VM LP/TC/CD 5309) <US re-iss. Nov84; same>

1974. (d-lp) (VSD 33-44) **THE BEST OF BUFFY SAINT-MARIE VOL.II**

1974. (7") <35180> **SOLDIER BLUE. / ('A'version)**

Oct 74. (lp) <(VSD 79340)> **NATIVE NORTH AMERICAN CHILD: AN ODYSSEY**

Jul 75. (7") (VS 5002) **I'M GONNA BE A COUNTRY GIRL AGAIN. / NOW THAT THE BUFFALO'S GONE**

Mar 76. (7") (VS 5004) **TAKE MY HAND FOR A WHILE. / TALL TREES IN GEORGIA**

Oct 76. (lp) Golden Hour; (GH 825) **A GOLDEN HOUR OF BUFFY SAINTE-MARIE**

Nov 81. (d-lp/d-c) P.R.T.; (SPOT/ZCSPT 1018) **SPOTLIGHT ON BUFFY SAINTE-MARIE**

Jan 83. (7") Flashback; (FBS 17) **SOLDIER BLUE. / I'M GONNA BE A COUNTRY GIRL AGAIN**
(re-iss. Jan90 on 'Old Gold'; OG 9932)

Mar 96. (cd) Premier-EMI; (CDEMC 3745) **UP WHERE WE BELONG**
– Darling don't cry / Up where we belong / Piney Wood hills / Cripple creek / God is alive / Until it's time for you to go / Universal soldier / Goodnight / Dance me around / He's an Indian cowboy in the rodeo / Now that the buffalo's gone / Soldier blue / Eagle man – Changing woman / Bury my heart at Wounded Knee / Starwalker.

SAINT ETIENNE

Formed: North London, England ... early 90's by music journo, BOB STANLEY and PETE WIGGS. Naming themselves after French football team, St. Etienne, after originally toying with the name, REARDON (the snooker player!), they signed to up-and-coming indie label 'Heavenly'. With MOIRA LAMBERT on vocals (borrowed from FAITH OVER REASON), the outfit's first vinyl foray was a sublime dub/indie-dance cover of Neil Young's 'ONLY LOVE CAN BREAK YOUR HEART'. Re-released after securing their first minor hit, 'NOTHING CAN STOP US', the track brought ST. ETIENNE to the attention of both the dance and indie scene. By this point however, a full-time vocalist (guest DONNA SAVAGE of the DEAD FAMOUS PEOPLE featured on their version of the Field Mice's 'KISS AND MAKE UP') had been recruited in the shape of SARAH CRACKNELL, whose sensuous, playful voice graced the bulk of 'FOXBASE ALPHA' (1991). A stunning debut album mixing and matching disco samples, trippy bass-lines and airy atmospherics into a pot-pourri of kitschy pop genius, the record was released to rave reviews and its relatively lowly chart position barely reflected its importance. With word now out, the group narrowly missed the UK Top 20 with their next single, 'JOIN OUR CLUB', although by early 1993 they found themselves bonafide pop stars when 'YOU'RE IN A BAD WAY' became their biggest hit to date. The accompanying album, 'SO TOUGH', cemented SAINT ETIENNE's position as top swoon-pop ironists, a masterfully sampledelic set featuring such classy compositions as 'HOBART PAVING', 'AVENUE' (also a Top 40 hit) and 'CALICO'. Following CRACKNELL's high profile collaboration with TIM BURGESS (Charlatans) for the Xmas

hit, 'I WAS BORN ON CHRISTMAS DAY', the oufit completed their fourth set, 'TIGER BAY', a record which slightly disappointed their fan/fox base with its more experimental approach. Although the future of the group seemed in doubt with CRACKNELL working on solo material, a brilliant return to form with the 'HE'S ON THE PHONE' single boded well for the future. • **Songwriters:** STANLEY-WIGGS except a few with CRACKNELL plus outside covers WHO DO YOU THINK YOU ARE (Scott-Dyer) / MY CHRISTMAS PRAYER (Billy Fury) / WESTERN WIND (trad.) / STRANGER IN PARADISE (hit; Tony Bennett) / IS IT TRUE (Marc Bolan) / HOW I LEARNED TO LOVE THE BOMB (TV Personalities). • **Trivia:** Sang a version of RIGHT SAID FRED's 'I'M TOO SEXY' on a 1992 'Heavenly' compilation ep.

Album rating: FOXBASE ALPHA (*8) / SO TOUGH (*7) / YOU NEED A MESS OF HELP TO STAND ALONE compilation (*6) / TIGER BAY (*6) / TOO YOUNG TO DIE – THE SINGLES compilation (*7) / CASINO CLASSICS (*6) / GOOD HUMOR (*6) / Sarah Cracknell: LIPSLIDE (*5)

BOB STANLEY (b.25 Dec'64, Horsham, Sussex) – keyboards / **PETE WIGGS** (b.15 May'66, Reigate, Surrey) – keyboards, synthesizers / **MOIRA LAMBERT** – vocals (of FAITH OVER REASON)

		Heavenly	Warners
Jul 90. (7"/12") (HVN 2/212) **ONLY LOVE CAN BREAK YOUR HEART. / ('A'version)** (12") (HVN 212R) – ('A'-A mix of two halves mix by Andy Weatherall) / The Official Saint Etienne world cup theme.			-

—— **DONNA SAVAGE** – vocals (of DEAD FAMOUS PEOPLE) repl. MOIRA

Sep 90. (7"/12") (HVN 4/412) **KISS AND MAKE UP. / SKY'S DEAD**
(cd-s+=) (HVN 412R) – ('A'extended).
(12") (HVN 4CD) – ('A'mixes by Pete Helber incl. dub version).

—— **SARAH CRACKNELL** – vocals repl. DONNA

May 91. (7"/12") (HVN 9/912) **NOTHING CAN STOP US. / SPEEDWELL** (cd-s+=) (HVN 9CD) – ('A'instrumental). (12"++=) (HVN 912R) – ('B'-Flying mix) / ('B'-Project mix) / 3-D tiger. below A-side featured MOIRA LAMBERT / B-side featured Q-TEE		54	
Aug 91. (7"/12"/c-s) (HVN 12/+12/+CS) **ONLY LOVE CAN BREAK YOUR HEART. / FILTHY** (cd-s+=) (HVN 12CD) – ('A'-A mix of two halves).		39	-
Oct 91. (cd/c/lp) (HVN CD/MC/LP 1) <26793> **FOXBASE ALPHA**		34	Jan92

– This is Radio Etienne / Only love can break your heart / Wilson / Carnt sleep / Girl VII / Spring / She's the one / Stoned to say the least / Nothing can stop us / Etienne gonna die / London belongs to me / Like the swallow / Dilworth's theme.

Jan 92. (12"ep) <0-40395> **NOTHING CAN STOP US (mixes) / SPEEDWELL**

Feb 92. (c-s) <19078> **ONLY LOVE CAN BREAK YOUR HEART / STONED TO SAY THE LEAST** (12"+=) <0-40196> – ('A'mixes).		-	97
May 92. (7"/c-s) (HVN 15/+CS) **JOIN OUR CLUB. / PEOPLE GET REAL** (12"+=/cd-s+=) (HVN 15 12/CD) – ('A'-Chemically friendly zoom mix) / Scene '93.		21	-
Sep 92. (c-ep/12"ep/cd-ep) (HVN 23 CS/12/CD) **AVENUE / SOME PLACE ELSE. / PAPER / JOHNNY IN THE ECHO CAFE** (cd-s) (HVN 23CDR) – ('A'club mix) / ('A'-Marshall mix) / ('A'-Venusian mix) (all remixed by A.R. KANE or GORDON KING).		40	-

—— added **IAN CATT** – guitar, programmer

Feb 93. (7"/c-s) (HVN 25/+CS) **YOU'RE IN A BAD WAY. / CALIFORNIA SNOW STORY** (12"+=/cd-s+=) (HVN 25 12/CD) – Archway people / Duke Duvet.		12	-
Mar 93. (cd/c/lp) (HVN CD/MC/LP 6) <45166> **SO TOUGH**		7	

– Mario's cafe / Railway jam / Date with Spelman / Calico / Avenue / You're in a bad way / Memo to Pricey / Hobart paving / Leafhound / Clock milk / Conchita Martinez / No rainbows for me / Here come clown feet / Junk the morgue / Chicken soup. (re-iss. Jun93 with free ltd.cd 'YOU NEED A MESS OF HELP TO STAND ALONE' compilation; HVN CDX 6) – Who do you think you are / Archway people / California snow storm / Kiss and make up / Duke duvet / Filthy / Join our club / Paper / Some place else / Speedwell.

May 93. (7"/c-s) (HVN 29/+CS) **HOBART PAVING. / WHO DO YOU THINK YOU ARE** (12"+=/cd-s+=) (HVN 29 12/CD) – Your head my voice (voix revirement) / Who do you think you are (Quex-Rd) (Aphex Twin remixes).		23	-
Jun 93. (12"/cd-s) <40910> **WHO DO YOU THINK YOU ARE (mixes)**		-	-
Dec 93. (7"/c-s) (HVN 36/+CS) **I WAS BORN ON CHRISTMAS DAY. / MY CHRISTMAS PRAYER** (12"+=/cd-s+=) (HVN 36 12/CD) – Snowplough / Peterloo. (above 'A' featured dual vocals with TIM BURGESS of The CHARLATANS)		37	-
Dec 93. (cd/c/lp) (HVN CD/MC/LP 7) **YOU NEED A MESS OF HELP TO STAND ALONE** – (see last album)			
Feb 94. (7"/c-s) (HVN 37/+CS) **PALE MOVIE. / HIGHGATE ROAD INCIDENT** (12"/cd-s) (HVN 37 12/CD) – ('A'side) / ('A'-Stentorian dub) / ('A'-Secret Knowledge trouse assassin mix) / ('A'-Lemonentry mix).		28	-
Feb 94. (cd/c/lp) (HVN CD/MC/LP 8) <45634> **TIGER BAY**		8	Jun94

– Urban clearway / Former lover / Hug my soul / Like a motorway / On the shore / Marble lions / Pale movie / Cool kids of death / Western wind / Tankerville / Western wind / Boy scouts of America.

May 94. (7"/c-s) (HVN 40/+CS) **LIKE A MOTORWAY. / YOU KNOW I'LL MISS YOU WHEN YOU'RE GONE / SUSHI RIDER** (12"/cd-s) (HVN 40 12/CD) – ('A'side) / ('A'-Chekhov warp mix) / ('A'-David Holmes mix) / (Skin up, you're already dead) (Dust Brothers mix).		47	-
Sep 94. (c-ep/cd-ep) (HVN 42 CS/CD) <41591> **HUG MY SOUL / I BUY AMERICAN RECORDS / HATE YOUR DRUG / LA POUPEE QUI FAIT NON (NO, NO, NO) (live)**		32	

(12"ep) *(HVN 4012)* – ('A'side) / ('A'-Sure Is Pure) / ('A'-Motiv8) / ('A'-Secret Knowledge).
(cd-ep+=) *(HVN 42CDR)* – (above tracks) / ('A'-Juan "Kinky" Hernandez mix).

Feb 95. (fan club-cd) *(HVNCD 9)* **I LOVE TO PAINT** | - | - |
        Heavenly   M.C.A.

Oct 95. (c-s) *(HVN 50CS)* *<55268>* **HE'S ON THE PHONE /**
('A'-Motiv8 mix) | 11 | | Jan96
(cd-s=) *(HVN 50CDR)* – Cool kids of death (Underworld mix) / How I learned to love the bomb.
(cd-s) *(HVN 50CD)* – ('A'side) / Groveley Road / Is it true / The process.

Nov 95. (cd/c/d-lp) *(HVN CD/MC/LP 10)* **TOO YOUNG TO DIE – THE**
SINGLES (compilation) | 17 | - |
– Only love can break your heart / Kiss and make up / Nothing can stop us / Join our club / People get real / Avenue / You're in a bad way / Who do you think you are / Hobart paving / I was born on Christmas day / Pale movie / Like a motorway / Hug my soul / He's on the phone. *(cd w/cd 'THE REMIX ALBUM'; HVN LP 10CDR)(+=)* – (9 remixes).

—— next with French dance artist ETIENNE DAHO and on 'Dindisc'/'Alex'US.

Jan 96. (m-cd; as ST. ETIENNE DAHO) *(DINSD 150)* *<5567>*
RESERECTION | 50 | - | Feb96
Oct 96. (d-cd/d-c/t-lp) *(HVNLP 16 CD/MC/LP)* **CASINO CLASSICS** | 34 | - |
– remixes by Chemical Brothers / PFM / Underworld / Way out West / Andrew Weatherall / Lionrock / David Holmes / Monkey Mafia / Death In Vegas / Sure Is Pure / Billy Nasty / Gordon King / Secret Knowledge / The Aloof / Broadcast / Aphex Twin / Primax / Psychonauts / Balearico.

—— SARAH had already tried out a solo career

SARAH CRACKNELL

          Gut   not iss.

Jul 96. (c-s/cd-s) *(CA/CD GUT 3)* **ANYMORE / OH BOY, THE**
FEELING WHEN YOU HELD MY HAND | 39 | - |
(cd-s+=) *(CXGUT 3)* – Fifth floor / Anymore (mix).
Apr 97. (c-s) *(CAGUT 7)* **GOLDIE / ('A'mix)** | | |
(cd-s+=) *(CDGUT 7)* – ('A'mixes).
May 97. (cd/c) *(GUT CD/MC 2)* **LIPSLIDE** | | - |
– Ready or not / Desert baby / Coastal town / Home / Anymore / How far / Goldie / Taxi / Taking off for France / If you leave me / Penthouse girl, basement boy / Can't stop now.

SAINT ETIENNE

—— SARAH returned to the fold in 1997

          Creation   not iss.

Jan 98. (c-s) *(CRECS 279)* **SYLVIE / AFRAID TO GO HOME** | 12 | - |
(cd-s+=) *(CRESCD 279)* – Zipcode / Hill street connection.
(cd-s) *(CRESCD 279X)* – ('A'mixes).
Apr 98. (c-s) *(CRECS 290)* **THE BAD PHOTOGRAPHER / HIT THE . . .** | 27 | - |
(cd-s+=) *(CRESCD 290)* – Swim swan swim / Madelaine.
(cd-s) *(CRESCD 290X)* – ('A'side) / 4.35 in the morning (Kid Loco remix) / Foto (Bronx Dogs mix) / Uri Geller bent my boyfriend (Add N To X mix).
May 98. (cd/lp) *(CRE CD/LP 225)* **GOOD HUMOR** | 18 | - |
– Woodcabin / Sylvie / Split screen / Mr Donut / Goodnight Jack / Lose that girl / The bad photographer / Been so long / Postman / Erica America / Dutch TV. *(also ltd-cd; CRECD 225L)*

          Kung Fu Fighting   not iss.

Feb 99. (ltd-7") *(CHANME 02)* **LOVER PLAY THE BASS** | - | - |
          Amberley   not iss.
Sep 99. (ltd-7") *(AMY 009)* **SATURDAY** | - | - |

| **SAINTS** (dig out; Great Alt & Indie . . .) |

| **SALAD** (dig out; 4th edition or Great Alt & Indie . . .) |

| **SALAKO** (dig out; Great Alt & Indie . . .) |

SALT-N-PEPA

Formed: Queens, New York, USA . . . 1985 by female rappers, CHERYL 'SALT' JAMES and SANDY 'PEPA' DENTON alongside DJ PAMELA GREENE. Their break came when JAMES' boyfriend, HURBY 'LUV BUG' AZOR, asked them to rap on his 'SHOW STOPPA' single, (a response to DOUG E. FRESH and SLICK RICK's 'THE SHOW'), the track credited to SUPER NATURE upon its release by 'Pop Art' records. The single was a minor hit on the US R&B charts, inspiring the duo to adopt the SALT-N-PEPA moniker and seek out a deal with US indie, 'Next Plateau'. Produced by AZUR, who had also become the girls' manager, their debut album, 'HOT, COOL AND VICIOUS' (1987) marked a blueprint for feisty feminine hip hop, SALT-N-PEPA trading sassy lines with sly humour on their ingenious update of the OTIS REDDING and CARLA THOMAS duet, 'TRAMP', while the hip-grinding sexiness of 'PUSH IT' would go on to become a massive UK hit in re-mixed form the following year. Released in June to tie in with SALT-N-PEPA's appearance at the Nelson Mandela 70th birthday concert in London's Wembley Stadium, the single made No.2, setting the scene for the Top 20 success of the follow-up album, 'A SALT WITH A DEADLY PEPA' (1988). The record carried on where the earlier material had left off, once again fearlessly revamping golden oldies like The Isley Brothers' 'TWIST AND SHOUT' and 'IT'S YOUR THING' (as 'SHAKE YOUR THANG') alongside bolshy originals. The record also featured the cut 'n' scratch skills of DJ SPINDERELLA (aka DEIRDRE ROPER) who had replaced GREENE. With

'BLACK'S MAGIC' (1990), SALT-N-PEPA addressed their Afro-American roots as well as confronting the largely taboo subject of female sexuality head-on with 'LET'S TALK ABOUT SEX', a huge transatlantic hit which the duo re-recorded a couple of years later as part of an AIDS awareness campaign. The album consolidated SALT-N-PEPAs as the foremost female rap outfit, notching up considerable album sales in both the UK and US markets. In 1993, the insistent skank of 'SHOOP' gave them their first US Top 5 single, the album 'VERY NECESSARY' (1993) achieving a similar feat, its American-sounding grooves giving SALT-N-PEPA more success than ever in their home country while a collaboration with EN VOGUE, the romantic manifesto of 'WHATTA MAN' almost made the US Top spot. With SALT, PEPA and SPINDERELLA all entering motherhood in the early 90's, the group remained out of the spotlight for a few years, eventually returning in 1996 with the sassy, classy 'CHAMPAGNE' (a track that recalled the bass-heavy groove of The OHIO PLAYERS), included on their 'BRAND NEW' (1997) album.
Album rating: HOT, COOL & VICIOUS (*7) / A SALT WITH A DEADLY PEPA (*6) / BLACKS' MAGIC (*6) / GREATEST HITS compilation (*6) / RAPPED IN REMIXES (*5) / VERY NECESSARY (*7) / BRAND NEW (*4)

CHERYL JAMES (b. 8 Mar'64, Brooklyn, NY) – vocals / **SANDI DENTON** (b. 9 Nov'61, Kingston, Jamaica) – vocals / **PAMELA GREENE** – DJ

          Champion   Next Plateau

Feb 87. (7") *(CHAMP 39)* **MY MIKE SOUNDS NICE. / ('A'mix)** | | |
(12"+=) *(CHAMP12 39)* – ('A'mixes).
Jul 87. (7") *(CHAMP 51)* **TRAMP (remix). / PUSH IT** | | |
(12"+=) *(CHAMP12 51)* – Idle chatter / I'll take your man.
Jul 87. (lp/c/cd) *(CHAMP/+K/CD 1007)* *<1007>* **HOT, COOL &**
VICIOUS | | 26 |
– Beauty and the beat / Tramp / I'll take your man / It's all right / Chick on the side / I desire / The showstopper / My mike sounds nice. *(re-iss. Nov91 on 'Ffrr' cd/c; 828296-2/-4)*
Nov 87. (12") *<NP 5007-1>* **I AM DOWN. / ('A'mix)** | | - |

—— **DEIDRE 'DEE DEE' SPINDERELLA** (b. 3 Aug'??, New York City) – DJ; repl. PAMELA

          Ffrr   Next Plateau

Feb 88. (7"/7"pic-d) *(FFR/+315)* **PUSH IT. / I AM DOWN** | 41 | 19 | Nov87
(12"+=/7"ep+=) *(FFR X/EE 2)* – Hit 'em with this / ('A'mixes).
Jun 88. (7") *(FFRR 2)* **PUSH IT. / TRAMP** | 2 | |
(12"+=) *(FFRRX 2)* – ('A'-US remix) / ('A'extended).
(also a hit on 'Champion' 12"/cd-s; CHAMP X/CD 51)
Jul 88. (lp/c)(cd) *(FFR LP/MC 3)(828102-2)* *<1011>* **A SALT WITH**
A DEADLY PEPA | 19 | 38 |
– Intro jam / A Salt with a deadly Pepa / I like it like that / Solo power (let's get paid) / Shake your thang / I gotcha / Let the rhythm run (remix) / Everybody get up / Spinderella's not a fella (but a girl DJ) / Solo power (syncopated soul) / Twist and shout / Hyped on me mic / Push it. *(re-iss. May93 on 'Entertainment Today' cd/c; 550041-2/-4)*
Aug 88. (7"/7"g-f; SALT-N-PEPA featuring E.U.) *(FFR/+G 11)* **SHAKE YOUR THANG (IT'S YOUR THING). /**
SPINDERELLA'S NOT A FELLA (BUT A GIRL DJ) | 22 | |
(12"+=/12"pic-d+=cd-s+=) *(FFR X/XP/CD 11)* – ('A'club mix) / ('A'-Instru-pella mix) / ('B'-Instru-pella).
Oct 88. (7"/7"pic-d) *(FFR/+B 16)* **TWIST AND SHOUT. /**
EVERYBODY GET UP | 4 | |
(12"+=/cd-s+=) *(FFR X/CD 16)* –
Feb 89. (7") *(FFR 20)* **I LIKE IT LIKE THAT. / PUSH IT** | | |
(12"+=) *(FFRX 20)* – ('A'mix).
Jan 90. (7"/c-s) *(F/+CS 127)* *<329>* **EXPRESSION. / ('A'-Half Step**
mix) | 40 | 26 | Feb90
(12"+=) *(FX 127)* – ('A'-Brixton dub) / ('A'-Brixton bass mix).
(cd-s++=) *(FCD 127)* – ('A'-Upso mix).
Apr 90. (cd/c/lp) *(828164-2/-4/-1)* *<1019>* **BLACKS' MAGIC** | | 38 | Mar90
– Expression / Doper than dope / Negro wit' an ego / You showed me / Do you want me / I like to party / Blacks' magic / Start the party / Let's talk about sex / I don't know / Live and let die / Independent. *(cd+=/c+=)* – Expression (Brixton bass mix).
May 91. (7") *(F 151)* *<331>* **DO YOU WANT ME. /('A'remix)** | 5 | 21 | Mar91
(12"+=/cd-s+=) *(FX/FCD 151)* – ('A'remixes).

—— They featured on PEBBLES' No.73 US hit 'Backyard' on 'M.C.A.'
Jun 91. (cd/c/lp) *(828249-2/-4/-1)* **A BLITZ OF SALT-N-PEPA HITS**
(re-mixes) | 70 | - |
Aug 91. (7"; SALT-N-PEPA featuring PSYCHOTROPIC) *(F 162)*
<333> **LET'S TALK ABOUT SEX. / ('A'original mix)** | 2 | 13 |
(12"+=/cd-s+=) *(FX/FCD 162)* – ('A'mixes).
Oct 91. (cd/c/lp) *(828291-2/-4/-1)* **GREATEST HITS** (compilation) | 6 | - |
– Push it / Expression / Independent / Shake your thang (it's your thang) / Twist and shout / Let's talk about sex / I like it like that / Tramp / Do you want me / My mic sounds nice / I'll take your man / I gotcha / I am down / You showed me.
Nov 91. (7") *(F 174)* *<50165>* **YOU SHOWED ME. /('A'mix)** | 15 | 47 | Jan92
(12"+=/cd-s+=) *(FX/FCD 174)* – ('A'mixes).
Mar 92. (7") *(F 182)* **EXPRESSION (re-mix). / ('A'mix)** | 23 | - |
(12"+=/cd-s+=) *(FX/FCD 182)* – ('A'mixes).
Apr 92. (cd/c) *(828297-2/-4)* **RAPPED IN REMIXES** | 37 | - |
– Push it / Expression / Shake your thang (it's your thing) / Twist and shout / Let's talk about sex / Do you want me / You showed me / Tramp / Let's talk about sex (remix) / You showed me (remix).
Sep 92. (7") *(F 196)* **START ME UP. / ('A'mix)** | 39 | - |
(12"+=/cd-s+=) *(FX/FCD 196)* – ('A'mixes).
Sep 93. (7"/c-s) *(F/+CS 219)* *<857314>* **SHOOP. / EMPHATICALLY**
NO | 29 | 4 |
(12"+=/cd-s+=) *(FX/FCD 219)* – Let's talk about AIDS.
Oct 93. (cd/c) *(828454-2/-4)* *<828392>* **VERY NECESSARY** | | 4 |
– Groove me / No one does it better / Somebody's gettin' on my nerves / Whatta man (with EN VOGUE) / None of your business / Step / Shoop / Heaven or Hell / Big shot / Sexy noises turn me on / Somma time man / Break of dawn / PSA we

talk / Shoop (Danny D's radio mix) / Start me up. *(re-dist.Apr94, hit UK No.36) (cd re-iss. Aug98; same)*

Mar 94.	(7"/c-s; SALT-N-PEPA with EN VOGUE) *(F/+CS 222)* <857390> **WHATTA MAN. /** ('A'mix) (12"+=) *(FX 222)* – (2-'A'mixes). (cd-s++=) *(FCD 222)* – (2-'A'mixes).	**7**	**3**
May 94.	(7"/c-s) *(F/+CS 234)* **SHOOP (re-mix). /** ('Amix) (12"+=/cd-s+=) *(FX 234)* – ('A'mix)	**13**	**–**
Oct 94.	(c-s/cd-s) *(FCS/FCD 244)* <857776> **NONE OF YOUR BUSINESS / HEAVEN 'N HELL** (12"+=) *(FX/FCD 244)* –	**19**	**32** Jul94
Oct 95.	(c-s,12") <850346> **AIN'T NUTHIN' BUT A SHE THING. /** ('A'remix)	**–**	**38**
Dec 96.	(c-s) *(MCS 48025)* **CHAMPAGNE /** ('A'instrumental) (12"+=/cd-s+=) *(MCST/+D 48025)* – ('A'remixes). (above issued on 'M.C.A.')	**23**	**–**
Nov 97.	(c-s) *(FCS 322)* **R U READY /** (12"+=/cd-s+=) *(FX/FCD 322)* – (cd-s) *(FCDP 322)* – ('A'side) / Shoop / Whatta man / Let's talk about sex.	**24**	
Nov 97.	(cd/c/lp) <828959-2/-4/-1)> **BRAND NEW /** – R U ready / Good life / Do me right / Friends / Say ooh / Imagine / Knock knock / Gitty up / Boy toy / Brand new / Silly of you / The clock is tickin' / Hold on.		**37**
Mar 98.	(c-s,cd-s) <570100> **GITTY UP /**	**–**	**50**
Nov 99.	(c-s/cd-s) *(FCS/FCD 373)* **THE BRICK TRACK VERSUS GITTY UP /** (mixes) (cd-s) *(FCDP 373)* – ('A'mixes).	**22**	

SAM & DAVE

Formed: Miami, Florida, USA ... 1961 by SAM MOORE and DAVE PRATER. Both fairly experienced vocalists on the gospel circuit, the pair decided to pool their resources after a chance meeting at Miami's King Of Hearts club. As SAM & DAVE they cut a handful of sides for the small 'Roulette' label before being signed to 'Atlantic' by ace producer/A&R man, Jerry Wexler. He subsequently transferred them to the more sympathetic environs of 'Atlantic'-affiliate, 'Stax', the Memphis-based label which served as a laboratory for the 60's 'Southern Soul' sound. With the help of house band, BOOKER T & THE MG's and the crack songwriting/production team of ISAAC HAYES and DAVID PORTER, SAM & DAVE became one of the genre's most exciting proponents. Although their first two singles ('A PLACE NOBODY CAN FIND' and 'I TAKE WHAT I WANT') flopped, they hit the R&B Top 10 for the first time with 1966's 'YOU DON'T KNOW LIKE I KNOW'. A few months later they went one better by topping the R&B chart and entering the pop Top 30 with 'HOLD ON! I'M A COMIN'. This opened the floodgates for a string of mid-60's soul belters; while not particularly innovative, the likes of 'SAID I WASN'T GONNA TELL NOBODY', 'YOU GOT ME HUMMIN', 'WHEN SOMETHING IS WRONG WITH MY BABY' and the definitive 'SOUL MAN' (a near US No.1) were as gritty, earthy, impassioned and propulsively brassy as the Southern Soul sound came. Although the duo scored a further US Top 10 hit in early '68 with 'I THANK YOU', the termination of the 'Stax'-'Atlantic' partnership later that year was to have a profound effect; no longer able to avail themselves of the Stax musicians or writers, SAM & DAVE struggled through the latter years of their career. To make matters worse, the pair's personal off-stage relationship was deteriorating badly. A classic case of tension channeled creatively, SAM & DAVE (or 'Double Dynamite') were famous for having one of the most thrillingly kinetic, charged live shows in the history of soul, yet in the real world they could apparently hardly look at each other. The inevitable break-up came in 1970 and, although the duo sporadically reunited several times, they consistently failed to recapture their chart glory. Their legacy was subsequently given a bit of a dusting-down in 1979 as actors/comedians John Belushi and Dan Ackroyd initiated their hugely successful BLUES BROTHERS routine; clearly inspired by SAM & DAVE, the duo's party piece was the Southern Soul sound came. In 1987, while MOORE was joined by LOU REED(!) on a UK Top 30 duet of 'SOUL MAN', PRATER was arrested on a drugs charge, escaping a prison term only to die in a car crash the following year (9th April). MOORE later resurfaced in 1992 when he sang back-up vocals on BRUCE SPRINGSTEEN's 'Human Touch' album.

Best CD compilation: THE VERY BEST OF SAM & DAVE (*8)

SAM MOORE (b.12 Oct'35, Miami) – vocals / **DAVE PRATER** (b. 9 May'37, Ocilla, Georgia, USA) – vocals

		not iss.	Roulette
1962.	(7") <4419> **I NEED LOVE. / KEEP A WALKIN'**	**–**	
1962.	(7") <4445> **NO MORE PAIN. / MY LOVE BELONGS TO YOU**	**–**	
1962.	(7") <4461> **SHE'S ALRIGHT. / IT FEELS SO NICE**	**–**	
1963.	(7") <4480> **IT WAS SO NICE WHILE IT LASTED. / YOU AIN'T NO BIG THING BABY**	**–**	
1963.	(7") <4508> **IF SHE'LL STILL HAVE ME. / LISTENING FOR MY NAME**	**–**	
1964.	(7") <4533> **I FOUND OUT. / I GOT A THING GOIN' ON**	**–**	

		Atlantic	Stax
Jan 66.	(7") *(AT 4066)* <180> **YOU DON'T KNOW LIKE I KNOW. / BLAME ME (DON'T BLAME MY HEART)** *(re-iss. Mar67; 584 086)*		**90**
May 66.	(7") *(584 003)* <189> **HOLD ON! I'M A COMIN'. / I GOT EVERYTHING I NEED**		**21** Apr66

Sep 66.	(7") *(584 047)* <198> **IF YOU GOT THE LOVING (I GOT THE TIME). / SAID I WASN'T GONNA TELL NOBODY**		**64** Aug66
Dec 66.	(lp; mono/stereo) *(587/588 045)* <708> **HOLD ON, I'M COMING** – Hold on! I'm a comin' / If you got the lovin' / I take what I want / I got everything I need / Don't make it so hard on me / It's a wonder / Don't help me out / Just me / You got it made with me / Blame me (don't blame my heart). *(cd/c-iss.Jan91; 7567 80255-2/-4)*	**35**	**45** Jul66
Jan 67.	(7") *(584 064)* <204> **YOU GOT ME HUMMIN'. / SLEEP GOOD TONIGHT**		**77** Nov66

		Stax	Stax
Mar 67.	(7") *(601 004)* **SOOTHE ME. / SWEET PAINS**	**35**	**–**
Apr 67.	(lp) *(589 003)* <712> **DOUBLE DYNAMITE** – You got me hummin' / Said I wasn't gonna tell nobody / That's the way it's gotta be / When something is wrong with my baby / I'm your puppet / Soothe me / Just can't get enough / Sweet pains / Sleep good tonight / I don't need nobody / Home at last / Use me.	**28**	Jan67
May 67.	(7") *(601 006)* <210> **WHEN SOMETHING IS WRONG WITH MY BABY. / A SMALL PORTION OF YOUR LOVE**		**42** Feb67
Jun 67.	(7") <218> **SOOTHE ME (live). / I CAN'T STAND UP FOR FALLING DOWN**	**–**	**56**
Oct 67.	(7") *(601 023)* <231> **SOUL MAN. / MAY I BABY**	**24**	**2** Aug67
Mar 68.	(7") *(601 030)* <242> **I THANK YOU. / WRAP IT UP**	**34**	**9** Jan68
Mar 68.	(lp) *(589 015)* <725> **SOUL MEN**	**32**	**62** Nov67
	– Soul man / May I baby / Broken down piece of man / Let it be me / Hold it baby / I'm with you / Don't knock it / Just keep holding on / The good runs the bad way / Rich kind of poverty / I've seen what loneliness can do. *(re-iss. Aug69; 588 185) (cd-iss. Jul93; 8122 70296-2)*		

		Atlantic	Atlantic
Jun 68.	(7") *(584 192)* <2517> **YOU DON'T KNOW WHAT YOU MEAN TO ME. / THIS IS YOUR WORLD**		**48** May68
Sep 68.	(7") *(584 211)* <2540> **CAN'T YOU FIND ANOTHER WAY (OF DOING IT). / STILL IS THE NIGHT**		**54** Jul68
Nov 68.	(7") *(584 228)* <2568> **EVERYBODY'S GOT TO BELIEVE IN SOMEBODY. / IF I DIDN'T HAVE A GIRL LIKE YOU**		**73** Oct68
Jan 69.	(7") *(584 237)* <2590> **SOUL SISTER, BROWN SUGAR. / COME ON IN**	**15**	**41** Dec68
Jan 69.	(lp) *(588 154)* <8205> **I THANK YOU**		Jun68
	– I thank you / Everybody got to believe in somebody / These arms of mine / Wrap it up / If I didn't have a girl like you / You don't know what you mean to me / Don't turn your heater on / Talk to the man / Love is after me / Ain't that a lot of love / Don't waste that love / Lucky old sun. *(cd-iss. Mar93 on 'WEA'; 8122 71012-2)*		
Mar 69.	(7") <2608> **BORN AGAIN. / GET IT**	**–**	**92**
Apr 69.	(7") *(584 247)* **YOU DON'T KNOW LIKE I KNOW. / HOLD ON! I'M A COMIN'**		**–**
Jun 69.	(lp; mono/stereo) *(587/588 181)* **DOUBLE TROUBLE**		**–**
Nov 69.	(lp) *(588 155)* <8218> **THE BEST OF SAM & DAVE** (compilation)		**87** Feb69
	– Hold on! I'm a comin' / When something is wrong with my baby / You don't know like I know / May I baby / Soul man / Soothe me / Wrap it up / I thank you / I take what I want / You don't know what you mean to me / A small portion of your love / You got me hummin' / Can't you find another way / Said I wasn't gonna tell nobody. *(re-iss. 1972; K 40027) (re-iss. Apr82; K 50748) (re-iss. Aug84 on 'WEA'; 881202-1) (cd-iss. Oct87 on 'WEA'; 781219-2)*		
Nov 69.	(7") *(584 303)* <2668> **OOH, OOH, OOH. / HOLDIN' ON**		
Mar 70.	(7") *(584 324)* <2714> **BABY, BABY, DON'T STOP NOW. / I'M NOT AN INDIAN GIVER**		
May 70.	(7") <2728> **ONE PART LOVE, TWO PARTS PAIN. / WHEN YOU STEAL FROM ME**		
1970.	(7") <2733> **YOU EASILY EXCITE ME. / WHEN YOU STEAL FROM ME (YOU'RE ONLY HURTING YOURSELF)**	**–**	

—— the pair split with DAVE PRATER signing to 'Alston' for a one-off

—— SAM MOORE was now a solo artist (for next three singles)

1971.	(7"; by SAM MOORE) <2762> **TENNESSEE WALTZ. / GIVE YOU PLENTY LOVIN'**	**–**	
1971.	(7"; by SAM MOORE) <2791> **STOP. / KEEP ON SOCKIN' IT TO ME**	**–**	
1972.	(7"; by SAM MOORE) <2814> **IF I SHOULD LOSE YOU LOVE. / SHOP AROUND**	**–**	
1972.	(7") <2839> **DON'T PULL YOUR LOVE. / JODY RYDER GOT KILLED**	**–**	

		U.A.	U.A.
Sep 75.	(7") *(UP 36008)* **UNDER THE BOARDWALK. / GIVE IT WHAT YOU CAN**		
Oct 75.	(lp) *(UAS 29694)* <LA 524> **BACK AT'CHA**		
	– Come into my life / When my love hand comes down / A little bit of good / Party in my heart / Under the boardwalk / Shoo rah, shoo rah / Queen of the ghetto / Blinded by love / Give it what you can / Don't close the curtain.		

		Contempo	not iss.
Feb 77.	(7") *(CS 2109)* **WHY DO YOU DO IT. / DON'T MESS WITH MY MONEY**		**–**
Aug 77.	(7"m) *(CS 2124)* **WE CAN WORK IT OUT. / YOU DON'T KNOW LIKE I KNOW / HOLD ON~ I'M A COMIN'**		**–**

		Gusto	Gusto
Jan 80.	(lp) <(GT 0045)> **SWEET AND FUNKY GOLD** (versions) *(cd-iss. 1988; CD 1018)*		Sep79

		Polydor	Boiling Point
Nov 85.	(7"/12") *(POSP/+X 775)* **MEDLEY – SOUL REVIEW. / HOLD ON**		

		A&M	A&M
Jan 87.	(7"; by SAM MOORE & LOU REED) *(AM 364)* **SOUL MAN. /**	**30**	

—— after being arrested then sentenced on a drugs charge a year earlier, DAVE died (9th of April, 1988) when his car veered off the road

– compilations, others, etc. –

1966.	(7") *Roulette;* <4671> **IT FEELS SO NICE. / IT WAS NICE WHILE IT LASTED**	-	
1966.	(7") *King; (KG 1041)* **NO MORE PAIN. / YOU AIN'T NO BIG THING BABY**		-
1966.	(lp) *King; (KGL 4001) / Roulette;* <R 25323> **SAM & DAVE** (early singles)		
	(re-iss. Jul68 on 'Major Minor'; MCP 5000) (cd-iss. Jun94 on 'Edsel'; EDCD 388)		
May 72.	(7") *Atlantic; (K 10180)* **SOUL MAN. / I THANK YOU / SOOTHE ME**		-
Oct 72.	(7"ep) *Atlantic; (K 10240)* **SOUL SISTER, BROWN SUGAR / SAID I WASN'T GONNA TELL NOBODY. / YOU GOT ME HUMMIN' / WHEN SOMETHING IS WRONG WITH MY BABY**		-
1974.	(7"m) *Atlantic; (K 10391)* **HOLD ON! I'M A COMIN'. / SOUL MAN / I THANK YOU**		-
Aug 75.	(7") *Atlantic; (K 10594)* **YOU DON'T KNOW LIKE I KNOW. / SAID I WASN'T GONNA TELL NOBODY**		-
Nov 80.	(7"m) *Atlantic; (K 11616)* **HOLD ON! I'M A COMIN'. / SOOTHE ME / SOUL SISTER, BROWN SUGAR**		-
May 84.	(lp) *Edsel; (ED 133)* **CAN'T STAND UP FOR FALLING DOWN**		-
Jan 85.	(7") *Old Gold; (OG 9498)* **HOLD ON! I'M A COMIN'. / (other track by Eddie Floyd)**		-
Apr 86.	(lp/c) *Castle; (SHLP/SHTC 119)* **GREATEST HITS** *(cd-iss. Dec87; SHCD 119)*		-
Feb 87.	(lp/c) *Topline; (TOP/KTOP 163)* **SWEET SOUL MUSIC** *(re-iss. Aug91 on 'Laserlight' cd)/c; 15076)(79526)*		-
May 87.	(12") *Perfect; (PER12 8604)* **SOUL MAN.**		-
Jul 87.	(cd) *Look Back; (120 106)* **GREATEST HITS**		-
Aug 87.	(cd) *The Collection; (OR 0010)* **THE ORIGINAL SOUL MAN**		-
Dec 88.	(cd) *Spectrum; (SPEC 85033)* **20 GREATEST HITS**		-
Jan 90.	(cd/c/lp) *Mainline; (266/116/226 224)* **20 GREATEST HITS**		-
Mar 92.	(c) *Entertainers; (ENTMC 13061)* **HOLD ON I'M COMING**		-
Oct 92.	(cd/c) *Muskateer; (MU 5/4 034)* **SOUL MAN: GREATEST HITS**		-
Oct 92.	(cd) *Carlton; (SMS 057)* **SOUL KINGS VOL.2**		-
Oct 93.	(cd/c) *Realisation; (RLB TC/TM 001)* **R&B**		-
Dec 93.	(d-cd) *Warners;* <(8122 71253-2)> **SWEAT AND SOUL** (rare stuff)		Jul93
Jul 94.	(cd) *Wisepack; (LECD 063)* **SAM & DAVE: LEGENDS IN MUSIC**		-
Nov 94.	(cd) *BAM; (KLMCD 035)* **SAM & DAVE**		-
Feb 95.	(cd) *Rhino;* **THE VERY BEST OF SAM & DAVE**	-	-
Mar 95.	(cd) *K-Tel; (ECD 3212)* **SWEET SOUL MUSIC**		-
Jun 95.	(cd) *Charly; (CDCD 1244)* **SOUL BROTHERS**		-
Jul 96.	(cd) *Javelin; (HADCD 208)* **TWO GREAT SOUL MEN**		-
May 97.	(cd) *Aim; (AIM 2003CD)* **SOUL MAN: THE BEST OF SAM & DAVE**		-
Aug 97.	(cd/c) *Hallmark; (30769-2/-4)* **SOUL MEN**		-

Richie SAMBORA (see under ⇒ BON JOVI)

SAMSON (dig out; Great Metal . . .)

SANTANA

Formed: San Francisco, California, USA . . . October '66 as The SANTANA BLUES BAND, by Mexican-born/Tijuana-raised CARLOS SANTANA. The guitarist's distinctly pure, fluid sound was backed by a constantly changing personnel over the years, though the best work was driven by the powerhouse rhythm section of drummer, MICHAEL SHRIEVE, and percussionist JOSE 'CHEPITO' AREAS. A compelling fusion of Latin stylings and psychedelic-tinged blues jamming, the band's early work has often been copied but rarely equalled. In 1968, the BLUES BAND part of the name was jettisoned and under the more effective moniker of SANTANA they played San Francisco's Fillmore West. Later the same year, CARLOS guested on the album, 'THE LIVE ADVENTURES OF AL KOOPER AND MIKE BLOOMFIELD' which brought him to the attention of 'Columbia' records. Following a show-stopping performance at The Woodstock Festival, their long-awaited eponymous debut album cracked the US Top 5 in late '69. The record, together with their next two follow-up albums, 'ABRAXAS' (1970) and 'SANTANA III' (1971), secured SANTANA's position as one of US rock's leading lights, the latter two sets hitting No.1 in America as well as spawning the hits 'BLACK MAGIC WOMAN', 'EVERYBODY'S EVERYTHING' and a dazzling, frenetic cover of TITO PUENTE's 'OYE COMO VA'. Following an indulgent live set featuring BUDDY MILES, SANTANA released 'CARAVANSERAI' in 1972, a transitional piece that signalled a tentative move away from blues towards the jazz-fusion that would come to characterise most of the band's later 70's output. Around this time CARLOS became a devotee of Indian guru, SRI CHIMNOY, recording the 'LOVE DEVOTION SURRENDER' (1973) album with the similarly converted JOHN McLAUGHLIN. A contemplative piece of ethereal jazz, it had a spiritual partner in the following year's 'ILLUMINATIONS', recorded with CHIMNOY disciple and jazz composer ALICE COLTRANE. Meanwhile, the SANTANA band released 'WELCOME' (1973) and 'BORBOLETTA' (1974), which further explored complex jazz textures, although 1976's 'AMIGOS' returned to a more grounded Latin-rock sound. It was short-lived though, and late 70's albums such as 'MOONFLOWER' (1977) and 'INNER SECRETS' (1978) bordered on the snooze-worthy with their directionless experimentation. 'ZEBOP' (1981) began the new decade on a high note, a masterful set that spawned the US hit single, 'WINNING'. The

80's also saw a solo effort, 'HAVANA MOON' (1983) and the grammy-award winning 'BLUES FOR SALVADOR' (1987) as well as a film score for 'La Bamba'. Following a deal with 'Island', SANTANA has continued his prolific output, releasing the 'BROTHERS' album in 1994 – a collaboration with sibling JORGE. When the phrase "re-inventing yourself" was thought up, they must have had CARLOS SANTANA in mind because what happened by the end of the decade transformed the SANTANA we once knew into Latino Blues stars of the new millennium. The record in question, 'SUPERNATURAL' (1999), was inspired by the gods and only CARLOS could hand-pick a team of guest singers/musicians (DAVE MATTHEWS, EVERLAST, LAURYN HILL, WYCLEF JEAN, EAGLE EYE CHERRY and ERIC CLAPTON) to complement this "tight" masterwork. However, it would be Matchbox20's ROB THOMAS who stole some of the spotlight, providing cooler than cool vocal chords on multi-million selling single, 'SMOOTH'; it would be no surprise when SANTANA cleaned up most of the top awards in the next year's Grammys. • **Songwriters:** CARLOS penned with group, except covers:- JIN-GO-LA-BA (Michael Babatunde Olatunji) / BLACK MAGIC WOMAN (Fleetwood Mac) / GYPSY WOMAN (Curtis Mayfield) / PEACE ON EARTH (Alice Coltrane) / STORMY (Classics IV) / SHE'S NOT THERE (Zombies) / WELL ALL RIGHT (Buddy Holly) / ONE CHAIN (Four Tops) / WINNING (Russ Ballard) / THIRD STONE FROM THE SUN (Jimi Hendrix) / WHO'S THAT LADY (Isley Brothers) / FULL MOON (Paola Rustichelli) / RIGHT ON (Marvin Gaye) / I'VE BEEN TO THE MOUNTAIN TOP (. . . King) / etc. • **Trivia:** In 1973, CARLOS married Urmila, a Sri Chimnoy devotee. He also became highly religious, changing his name to DEVADIP, which means 'The Light Of The Lamp Supreme'. In the mid-70's, Bill Graham took over the management of SANTANA. For lovers of anything SANTANA, his brother JORGE (in Latin-rock band MALO) had success in April '72 with an eponymous album, which hit US No.14. A single lifted from it, 'SALI VECITO', made No.18. MALO went on to release three more 'Warner Bros.' albums; DOS (1972) / EVOLUTION (1973) + ASCENSION (1974).

Album rating: SANTANA (*7) / ABRAXAS (*8) / SANTANA III (*7) / CARLOS SANTANA & BUDDY MILES! LIVE! solo/collaboration with Buddy Miles (*4) / CARAVANSERAI (*8) / LOVE DEVOTION SURRENDER solo/collaboration with Mahavishnu John McLaughlin (*6) / WELCOME (*6) / ILLUMINATIONS solo/collaboration with Turiya Alice Coltrane (*4) / SANTANA'S GREATEST HITS compilation (*8) / BORBOLETTA (*6) / LOTUS (*6) / AMIGOS (*7) / FESTIVAL (*6) / MOONFLOWER (*6) / INNER SECRETS (*4) / ONENESS: SILVER DREAMS – GOLDEN REALITY solo as Devadip (*5) / MARATHON (*5) / THE SWING OF DELIGHT solo (*4) / ZEBOP! (*6) / SHANGO (*5) / HAVANA MOON solo (*5) / BEYOND APPEARANCES (*4) / FREEDOM (*6) / BLUES FOR SALVADOR solo (*6) / VIVA! SANTANA boxed-compilation (*8) / SPIRITS DANCING IN THE FLESH (*5) / MILAGRO (*5) / SACRED FIRE – LIVE IN SOUTH AMERICA (*4) / BROTHERS as Santana Brothers (*4) / DANCE OF THE RAINBOW SERPENT boxed-set (*7) / SUPERNATURAL (*7)

CARLOS SANTANA (b.20 Jul'47, Autlan de Navarro, Mexico) – lead guitar / **GREGG ROLIE** (b.17 Jun'47, Seattle, Washington) – keyboards, vocals / **DAVID BROWN** (b.15 Feb'47, New York) – bass repl. GUS RODRIGUES (in 1967) / **MIKE SHRIEVE** (b. 6 Jul'49, San Francisco) – drums repl. BOB LIVINGSTONE (in '67). He had repl. ROD HARPER / **JOSE CHEPITO AREAS** (b.25 Jul'46, Leon, Nicaragua) – percussion / **MIKE CARABELLO** (b.18 Nov'47, San Francisco) – congas repl. TOM FRAZER – guitar

		C.B.S.	Columbia	
Oct 69.	(7") *(CBS 4593)* **PERSUASION. / SAVOR**	-	-	
Oct 69.	(7") *<45010>* **JIN-GO-LA-BA. / PERSUASION**	-	56	
Nov 69.	(lp) *(CBS 63015)* <9781> **SANTANA**	26	4	Sep69
	– Waiting / Evil ways / Shades of time / Savor / Jin-go-la-ba / Persuasion / Treat / You just don't care / Soul sacrifice. *(re-iss. Mar70; CBS 63815) (re-iss. Mar81 lp/c; CBS/40 32003) (cd-iss. May87; CD 63815) (cd re-iss. May92 & Apr98 on 'Columbia'; 489542-2)*			
Jan 70.	(7") *<45069>* **EVIL WAYS. / WAITING**	-	9	
Apr 70.	(7") *(CBS 4940)* **EVIL WAYS. / JIN-GO-LA-BA**		-	
Nov 70.	(lp) *(CBS 64087)* <30130> **ABRAXAS**	7	1	Sep 70
	– Singing winds / Oye como va / Incident at Neshabur / Se a cabo / Mother's daughter / Samba pa ti / Hope you're feeling better / El Nicoya. *(re-iss. Mar81 lp/c; CBS/40 32032) (cd-iss. Mar86; CD 64087) (cd re-iss. Mar91; CD 32032) (cd re-iss. Apr98 on 'Columbia'; 489543-2)*			
Dec 70.	(7") *(CBS 5325)* <45270> **BLACK MAGIC WOMAN. / HOPE YOU'RE FEELING BETTER**		4	Nov70
Mar 71.	(7") *(CBS 7046)* <45330> **OYE COMO VA. / SAMBA PA TI**		13	Feb71
	added **NEAL SCHON** (b.27 Feb'54) – guitar / **COKE ESCOVEDO** (b. THOMAS ESCOVEDO, 30 Apr'41, Calif.) – percussion			
Oct 71.	(lp) *(CBS 69015)* <30595> **SANTANA III**	6	1	
	– Batuka / No one to depend on / Taboo / Toussaint l'overture / Everybody's everything / Guajira / Everything's coming our way / Jungle strut / Para los rumberos. *(re-iss. Mar82 lp/c; CBS/40 32058) (cd-iss. Mar81; CD 69015) (re-iss. Jun94 on 'Columbia' cd/c; 476830-2) (cd re-iss. Apr98; 489554-2)*			
Nov 71.	(7") *(CBS 7546)* <45472> **EVERYBODY'S EVERYTHING. / GUAJIRA**		12	Oct71
Mar 72.	(7") *(CBS 7842)* <45552> **NO ONE TO DEPEND ON. / TABOO**		36	Feb72
Jul 72.	(lp; by CARLOS SANTANA & BUDDY MILES) *(CBS 65142)* <31308> **CARLOS SANTANA & BUDDY MILES! LIVE! (live)**	29	8	
	– Marbles / Lava / Evil ways / Faith interlude / Them changes / Free form funkafide filth. *(re-iss. Sep84 lp/c; CBS/40 32271)*			
Oct 72.	(7"; by CARLOS SANTANA & BUDDY MILES) *(CBS 8338)* <45666> **EVIL WAYS (live). / THEM CHANGES (live)**		84	Aug72
	ARMANDO PERAZA – percussion repl. CARABELLO and ESCOVEDO (latter died 4 Apr'85) / **TOM RUTLEY** – bass repl. BROWN			
Nov 72.	(lp) *(CBS 65299)* <31610> **CARAVANSERAI**	6	8	
	– Eternal caravan of reincarnation / Waves within / Look up (to see what's coming down) / Just in time to see the sun / Song of the wind / All the love of the universe / Future primitive / Stone flower / La fuente del ritmo /			

Every step of the way. *(re-iss. Nov81 lp/c; CBS/40 32060) (cd-iss. 1988; CD 65299)*

Jan 73. (7") <45753> **LOOK UP (TO SEE WHAT'S COMING DOWN). / ALL THE LOVE OF THE UNIVERSE** — [ ]

Jul 73. (lp; by CARLOS DEVADIP SANTANA AND MAHAVISHNU JOHN McLAUGHLIN) (CBS 69073) <32034> **LOVE DEVOTION SURRENDER** [7] [14]
— A love supreme / Naima / The lie divine / Let us go into the house of the Lord / Meditation. *(re-iss. Oct92 & Jun94 on 'Columbia' cd/c; 982830-2/-4)*
(above album featured below newcomers (**RAUCH + LEWIS**) + **PERAZA, JAN HAMMER** – keyboards / **BILLY COBHAM** – drums / **LARRY YOUNG** – keyboards)

—— **CARLOS** retained **AREAS, PERAZA + SHRIEVE** and brought in newcomers **TOM COSTER** – keyboards, vocals repl. ROLIE who formed JOURNEY / **RICHARD KERMODE** – keyboards repl. SCHON who also formed JOURNEY / **DOUG RAUCH** – bass repl. RUTLEY / added **LEON THOMAS** – vocals / **JAMES MINGO LEWIS** – congas

Nov 73. (lp) (CBS 69040) <32445> **WELCOME** [8] [25]
— Going home / Love, devotion and surrender / Samba de sausalito / When I look into your eyes / Yours is the light / Mother Africa / Light of life / Flame-sky / Welcome. *(re-iss. 1984 lp/c; CBS/40 32194)*

Nov 73. (7") (CBS 1925) <45999> **WHEN I LOOK INTO YOUR EYES. / SAMBA DE SAUSALITO** [ ]

Sep 74. (lp; by TURIYA ALICE COLTRANE & DEVADIP CARLOS SANTANA) (CBS 69063) <32900> **ILLUMINATIONS** [40] [79]
— Guru Sri Chimnoy aphorism / Angel of air – Angel of water / Bliss: The eternal now / Angel of sunlight / Illuminations. *(cd-iss. Mar96 on 'Columbia; 483810-2)* above w/ **ALICE** – keyboards, etc.

—— **GREG WALKER** – vocals + sessioners repl. KERMODE, LEWIS and THOMAS

Nov 74. (lp/c) (CBS/40 69084) <33135> **BORBOLETTA** [18] [20] Oct74
— Spring manifestations / Canto de los flores / Life is anew / Give and take / One with the Sun / Aspirations / Practice what you preach / Mirage / Here and now / Flor de canela / Promise of a fisherman / Borboletta. *(re-iss. Nov83 lp/c; CBS/40 32157) (re-iss. cd Nov93 on 'Sony Collectors';)*

Nov 74. (7") (CBS 2829) **PRACTICE WHAT YOU PREACH. / CANTO DE LOS FLORES** [ ] [ ]

Jan 75. (7") (CBS 3005) <10073> **MIRAGE. / FLOR DE CANELA** [ ] [ ]

Mar 75. (7") <10088> **GIVE AND TAKE / LIFE IS ANEW** [ ]

—— (Below triple album was issued initially in Japan 1973)

Dec 75. (t-lp) (CBS 66325) **LOTUS (live)** [ ] [ ]
— Meditation / Going home / A-1 funk / Every step of the way / Black magic woman – Gypsy queen / Oye como va / Yours is the light / Batuka / Xibaba (she-ba-ba) / Savor / Stone flower / (introduction) / Castillos de arena (pt.1) / Waiting / Se a cabo / Samba pa ti / Toussaint l'overture / Incident at Neshabur. *(re-iss. Dec90 d-cd/d-c; 467943-2/)*

—— **LEON NDUGU CHANCLER** – drums repl. SHRIEVE and AREAS / **IVORY STONE** – bass repl. RAUCH

Mar 76. (7") (CBS 4143) <10421> **EUROPA. / TAKE ME WITH YOU** [ ] Nov76

Apr 76. (lp/c) (CBS/40 86005) <33576> **AMIGOS** [21] [10]
— Dance sister dance (baila mi Hermana) / Take me with you / Let me / Gitano / Tell me are you tired / Europa (Earth's cry, Heaven's smile) / Let it shine. *(re-iss. Jun84 lp/c; CBS/40 32476) (cd-iss. Mar87; CD 86005) (re-iss. cd Jun92)*

May 76. (7") (CBS 4335) <10336> **LET IT SHINE. / TELL ME ARE YOU TIRED** [ ] [77]

Aug 76. (7") (CBS 4512) <10353> **DANCE SISTER DANCE (BAILA MI HERMANA). / LET ME** [ ]

—— **JOSE AREAS** returned to repl. PERAZA / **PABLO TELEZ** – bass repl. STONE

Dec 76. (lp/c) (CBS/40 86020) <34423> **FESTIVAL** [27] [27]
— Carnaval / Let the children play / Jugando / Carnival / Give me love / Verao Vermelho / Let the music set you free / Revelations / Reach up / The river / Try a little harder / Maria Caracoles.

Jan 77. (7") (CBS 4927) **REVELATIONS. / REACH UP** [ ] [ ]

Jan 77. (7") <10524> **REVELATIONS. / GIVE ME LOVE** [ ]

Mar 77. (7") (CBS 5102) <10481> **LET THE CHILDREN PLAY. / CARNAVAL** [ ]

—— Trimmed slightly when CHANCLER vacated

Sep 77. (7") (CBS 5671) <10616> **SHE'S NOT THERE. / ZULU** [11] [27]

Oct 77. (d-lp/c) (CBS/40 88272) <34914> **MOONFLOWER (live + studio)** [7] [10]
— Dawn – Go within / Carnaval / Let the children play / Jugando / I'll be waiting / Zulu / Bahia / Black magic woman – Gypsy queen / Dance sister dance (baila mi Hermana) / Europa (Earth's cry, Heaven's smile) / She's not there / Flor de Luna (Moonflower) / Soul sacrifice / Heads, hands & feet / El Morocco / Transcendance / Savor / Toussaint l'overture. *(re-iss. Apr85 d-lp/c; CBS/40 86098) (cd-iss. Apr89; CD 33280) (re-iss. cd Jun96; 463370-2)*

Jan 78. (7") (CBS 6055) **BLACK MAGIC WOMAN (live). / TRANSCENDANCE** [ ] [ ]

Jan 78. (7") <10677> **BLACK MAGIC WOMAN (live). / I'LL BE WAITING (live)** [ ] [ ]

Aug 78. (7"; by CARLOS SANTANA) (CBS 6520) **I'LL BE WAITING. / FLOR DE LUNA (MOONFLOWER)** [ ] [ ]

—— **CARLOS** retained only **WALKER + COSTER** and introduced **ARMANDO PERAZA** returned to repl. AREAS / **DAVID MARGEN** – bass repl. TELLEZ / added **GRAHAM LEER** – drums / **CHRIS RHYME** – keyboards / **RAUL REKOW** – percussion / **CHRIS SOLBERG** – guitar, keyboards, vocals

Oct 78. (7") <10839> **WELL ALL RIGHT / JERICHO** [ ] [69]

Oct 78. (7") (CBS 6755) **WELL ALL RIGHT. / WHAM!** [53] [ ]
(12"+=) – (CBS12-6755) – Life is a lady – Holiday.

Nov 78. (lp/c) (CBS/40 86075) <35600> **INNER SECRETS** [17] [27]
— Dealer / Spanish rose / Well all right / One chain (don't make no prison) / Stormy / Open invitation / Wham! / The facts of love / Life is a lady – Holiday / Move on. *(cd-iss. 1986 & Jun92; CD 86075)*

Jan 79. (7") (CBS 6998) **ONE CHAIN (DON'T MAKE NO PRISON). / MOVE ON** [ ] [ ]

Jan 79. (7") <10873> **STORMY. / MOVE ON** [ ] [32]

Mar 79. (lp/c; as DEVADIP) (CBS/40 86037) <35686> **ONENESS: SILVER DREAMS, GOLDEN REALITY** [55] [87]
— The chosen hour / Arise awake / Light versus darkness / Jim Jeannie /

Transformation day / Victory / Silver dreams golden smiles / Cry of the wilderness / Guru's song / Oneness / Life is just a passing parade / Golden dawn / Free as the morning sun / Song for Devadip. *(cd-iss. Mar97 on 'Columbia'; 487238-2)*

Apr 79. (7") <10938> **ONE CHAIN (DON'T MAKE NO PRISON). / LIFE IS A HOLIDAY** [ ] [59]

—— **ALEX LIGERTWOOD** – vocals (ex-BRIAN AUGER) repl. WALKER / **ALAN PASQUE** – keyboards, vocals repl. COSTER + RHYME

Oct 79. (7") (CBS 7971) <11144> **YOU KNOW THAT I LOVE YOU. / AQUA MARINE** [ ] [35]

Oct 79. (lp/c) (CBS/40 86098) <36154> **MARATHON** [28] [25]
— Marathon / Lightning in the sky / Aqua marine / You know that I love you / All I ever wanted – Runnin' / Summer lady / Love / Stay / Hard times. *(cd-iss. May87; CD 86098)*

Feb 80. (7") (CBS 8160) **ALL I EVER WANTED. / LOVE** [57] [ ]

Feb 80. (7") <11218> **ALL I EVER WANTED. / LIGHTNING IN THE SKY** [ ] [ ]

Jun 80. (7") (CBS 8649) **AQUA MARINE. / STAND UP – RUNNIN'** [ ] [ ]

Sep 80. (d-lp/d-c; by CARLOS SANTANA) (CBS/40 84514) <36590> **THE SWING OF DELIGHT** [65] [65]
— Swapan tari / Love theme from 'Sparticus' / Phuler Matan / Song for my brother / Jharna kala / Gardenia / La Llave / Golden hours / Shere Khan, the tiger.
(above featured The MILES DAVIS QUINTET of the 60's)

—— added **ORESTES VILATO** – percussion / **RICHARD BAKER** – keyboards

Apr 81. (7") (A-1139) <01050> **WINNING. / BRIGHTEST STAR** [ ] [17]

Apr 81. (lp/c) (CBS/40 84946) <37158> **ZEBOP!** [33] [9]
— Changes / E papa re / Primera invasion / Searchin' / Over and over / Winning / Tales of Kilimanjaro / The sensitive kind / American gypsy / I love you much too much / Brightest star / Hannibal. *(cd-iss. Dec85; CD 84946)*

Jun 81. (7") (A-1388) **CHANGES. / AMERICAN GYPSY** [ ] [ ]

Sep 81. (7") (A-1556) <02178> **THE SENSITIVE KIND. / AMERICAN GYPSY** [56] Jul81

Jan 82. (7") <02519> **SEARCHIN'. / TALES OF KILIMANJARO** [ ] [ ]

—— **CARLOS** retained only **LEAR, MARGEN, BAKER + VILATO**

Aug 82. (lp/c) (CBS/40 85915) <38122> **SHANGO** [35] [22]
— The Nile / Hold on / Night hunting time / Nowhere to run / Nueva York / Oxun / Body surfing / What does it take / Let me inside / Warrior / Shango. *(cd-iss. 1983; CD 85914)*

Aug 82. (7") <03160> **HOLD ON. / OXUN** [ ] [15]

Nov 82. (7") <03376> **NOWHERE TO RUN. / NUEVA YORK** [ ] [66]

CARLOS SANTANA

solo, featuring **WILLIE NELSON, BOOKER T.JONES & The FABULOUS THUNDERBIRDS**

Apr 83. (7") <03925> **WATCH YOUR STEP. / TALES OF KILIMANJARO** [ ] [ ]

Apr 83. (7") (A-3330) **WATCH YOUR STEP. / LIGHTNIN'** [ ] [ ]

Apr 83. (lp/c) (CBS/40 25350) <38642> **HAVANA MOON** [84] [31]
— Watch your step / Lightnin' / Who do you love / Mudbone / One with you / Ecuador / Tales of Kilimanjaro / Havana Moon / Daughter of the night / They all went to Mexico / Vereda tropical. *(cd-iss. May87' CD 25350)*

May 83. (7") (A-3359) **THEY ALL WENT TO MEXICO. / MUDBONE** [ ] [ ]

Jun 83. (7") <04034> **HAVANA MOON. / LIGHTNIN'** [ ] [ ]

SANTANA

CARLOS only retained **VILATO** plus sessioners

Mar 85. (7") (A-4514) <04758> **SAY IT AGAIN. / TOUCHDOWN RAIDERS** [ ] [46] Feb85
(12"+=) – (TA-4514) – She's not there / ('A'instrumental).

Mar 85. (lp/c) (CBS/40 86307) <39527> **BEYOND APPEARANCES** [58] [50]
— Breaking out / Written in sand / How long / Brotherhood / Spirit / Say it again / Who loves you / I'm the one who loves you / Touchdown raiders / Right now. *(cd-iss. Mar86; CD 86307)*

May 85. (7") (A-6284) **HOW LONG. / RIGHT NOW** [ ] [ ]
(12"+=) – (TA-6284) – She's not there.

May 85. (7") <04912> **I'M THE ONE WHO LOVES YOU. / RIGHT NOW** [ ] [ ]

—— **CARLOS** re-united **GREGG ROLIE, MIKE SHRIEVE, JOSE AREAS** +sessioners

Feb 87. (lp/c/cd) (450 500-1/-4/-2) <40272> **FREEDOM** [ ] [95]
— Vera Cruz / She can't let go / Once it's gotcha / Love is you / Songs of freedom / Deeper, dig deeper / Praise / Mandela / Before we go / Victim of circumstance.

May 87. (7"/12") (650417-7/-6) <06654> **VERA CRUZ. / MANDELA** [ ] Mar87

May 87. (7") <07038> **VERA CRUZ (remix). / MANDELA** [ ] [ ]

Jul 87. (7") <07140> **PRAISE. / LOVE IS YOU** [ ] [ ]

—— SANTANA touring band **ROLIE, CHESTER THOMPSON** – keyboards / **TOM COSTER** – synthesizers / **ALFONSO JOHNSON** – bass / **GRAHAM LEER** – drums / **BUDDY MILES** – vocals / **ARMANDO PERAZA, PAUL REKOW + ORESTES VILATO** – percussion

Nov 87. (lp/c/cd; by CARLOS SANTANA) (460 258-1/-4/-2) <40875> **BLUES FOR SALVADOR** [ ] [ ]
— Bailando / Aquatic park / Bella / I'm gone / 'Trane / Deeper, dig deeper / Mingus / Now that you know / Hannibal / Blues for Salvador.
(above featured mainly session people)

—— **CARLOS** retained **THOMPSON + PERAZA**, plus recruited **BENNY RIETVELD** – bass / **ALEX LIGERTWOOD** – vocals, guitar / **WALFREDO REYES** – drums, timbales, perc with host of guests (over 15).

Jun 90. (cd/c/lp) (466913-2/-4/-1) <46065> **SPIRITS DANCING IN THE FLESH** [68] [85]
— Let there be light – Spirits dancing in the flesh / Gypsy woman / It's a jungle out there / Soweto (African light) / Choose / Peace on Earth . . . Mother Earth . . . Third stone from the Sun / Full Moon / Who's that lady / Jin-go-la-ba / Goodness and mercy.

Jun 90. (7") (656027-7) **GYPSY WOMAN. / GOODNESS AND MERCY** [ ] [ ]
(12"+=/cd-s+=) (656027-6/-2) – Black magic woman (live) / Oye como va (live) / She's not there (live).

—— Next with samples from MILES DAVIS and JOHN COLTRANE.

	Polydor	Polydor

Apr 92. (cd/c/d-lp) *(513197-2/-4/-1)* <513197> **MILAGRO**
– Medley:- Introduction by BILL GRAHAM – Milagro / Medley:- I've been to the mountain top – Somewhere in Heaven / Medley:- Saja – Right on / Your touch / Life is for living / Red prophet / Aqua que va ceer / Make somebody happy / Free all the people (South Africa) / Medley:- Gypsy – Grajoonca / We don't have to wait / Adios.

Nov 93. (cd/c) *(521 082-2/-4)* **SACRED FIRE** (live in S. America)
– Angels all around us / Vive le Vada (life is for living) / Esperando / No one to depend on / Black magic woman – Gypsy queen / Oye como va / Samba pa ti / Guajira / Make somebody happy / Toussaint l'overture / Soul sacrifice / Don't try this at home / Europa / Jingo-la-ba.

—— with brother **JORGE** – guitar (ex-MALO) + **CARLOS HERNANDEZ**

	Island	Island

Sep 94. (cd/c; by SANTANA BROTHERS) *(CID/ICT 8034)* <523677> **BROTHERS**
– Transmutation industrial / Thoughts / Luz amor y vida / En aranjouz con tu amour / Contigo / Blues Latino / La olaza / Brujo / The trip / Reflections / Morning in Marin.

	Arista	Arista

Aug 99. (cd/c) <(07822 19080-2/-4)> **SUPERNATURAL** | 33 | 1 Jun99 |
– Da le Yaleo / Love of my life (w/ DAVE MATTHEWS) / Put your lights on (w/ EVERLAST) / Africa bamba / Smooth (w/ ROB THOMAS) / Do you like the way (w/ LAURYN HILL) / Maria Maria (w/ WYCLEF JEAN) / Migra / Corazon Espinado / Wishing it was (w/ EAGLE EYE CHERRY) / El farol / Primavera / Calling (w/ ERIC CLAPTON).

Oct 99. (c-s/cd-s; SANTANA featuring ROB THOMAS) *(74321 70949-4/-2)* <13718> **SMOOTH / EL FAROL** | 75 | 1 Jul99 |

– compilations, others, etc. –

on 'CBS/ Columbia' until mentioned otherwise.

Mar 73. (7") *(CBS 1155)* **OYE COMO VA. / BLACK MAGIC WOMAN**
(re-iss. Feb76; CBS 3950)

Aug 74. (lp/c) *(CBS/40 69081)* <3050> **SANTANA'S GREATEST HITS** | 14 | 17 Jul74 |
– Evil ways / Jin-go-la-ba / Hope you're feeling better / Samba pa ti / Persuasion / Black magic woman / Oye como va / Everything's coming up roses / Se a cabo / Everybody's everything. *(cd-iss. Jun87; CD 69081) (re-iss. Feb88 lp/c; CBS/40 32386) (cd re-iss. Jul99 on 'Columbia'; CDZ 32386)*

Sep 74. (7") *(CBS 2561)* <46067> **SAMBA PA TI. / INCIDENT AT NESHABUR** | 27 | |
(re-iss. Feb79; CBS 7063)

Oct 80. (t-lp) *(CBS 66354)* **BOX SET** (first 3 albums)

Jul 84. (7") *(A-4587)* **SHE'S NOT THERE. / SAMBA PA TI**

Feb 86. (12"ep) *Old Gold; (OG 4005)* **SAMBA PA TI / JIN-GO-LA-BA. / SHE'S NOT THERE / EVIL WAYS**

Oct 86. (lp/c/cd) *K-Tel; (NE1/CE2/NCD3 338)* **VIVA! SANTANA – THE VERY BEST OF SANTANA** | 50 | - |

Jan 88. (7") *Old Gold; (OG 9753)* **SAMBA PA TI. / SHE'S NOT THERE**

May 88. (cd) *Arcade; (ADEHCD 828-0)* **THE VERY BEST OF SANTANA – VOLUME ONE**

May 88. (cd) *Arcade; (ADEHCD 828-1)* **THE VERY BEST OF SANTANA – VOLUME TWO**

Jun 88. (d-lp/c/d-cd) *That's Original; (TFO LP/MC/CD 14)* **WELCOME / CARLOS SANTANA & BUDDY MILES LIVE**

Oct 88. (t-lp/d-c/d-cd) *(462500-1/-4/-2)* <44344> **VIVA! SANTANA** (best + live)
– Everybody's everything / Black magic woman – Gypsy queen / Guajira / Jungle strut / Jingo / Ballin' / Bambara / Angel Negro / Incident at Neshabur / Just let the music speak / Super boogie – Hong Kong blues / Song of the wind / Abi cama / Vitalo / Paris finale / Brotherhood / Open invitation / Aqua marine / Dance, sisters, dance / Europa / Peraza 1 / She's not there / Bambele / Evil ways / Daughter of the night / Peraza II / Black magic woman – Gypsy woman (live) / Oyo como va / Persuasion / Soul sacrifice. *(d-cd re-iss. Jun97; same)*

May 89. (3"cd-ep) **BLACK MAGIC WOMAN / SAMBA PA TI / OYE COMO VA / JIN-GO-LA-BA**

Jun 89. (lp/cd) *Thunderbolt; (THBVL/CDTB 071)* **PERSUASION**
(cd re-iss. Apr98 on 'MagMid'; MM 003)

Jan 90. (lp/cd) *Thunderbolt; (THBVL/CDTB 079)* **LATIN TROPICAL**
(cd re-iss. Jun98 on 'MagMid'; MM 007)

Oct 90. (cd) *Thunderbolt; (CDTB 087)* **ACAPULCO SUNRISE**
(re-iss. May97 on 'C.M.C.'; 100182) (re-iss. Mar99 on 'MagMid'; MM 024)

May 92. (cd) *Traditional Line; (TL 1315)* **LIVE IN MONTREUX 1971** (live)

Jun 92. (cd/c) *(468267-2/-4)* **THE BEST OF SANTANA**
(re-iss. Oct94; same)

Mar 93. (d-cd) *(465221-2)* **SANTANA / ABRAXAS**

May 93. (cd) *F.N.A.C.;* **NINETEEN SIXTY EIGHT**

Sep 93. (cd/c) *Sony Collectors; (983259-2/-4)* **SALSA, SAMBA & SANTANA**

Nov 93. (d-cd) *Sound Wings; (ACD 23057-2)* **SAMBA PA TI**

Feb 94. (cd) *Thunderbolt; (CDTB 502)* **EVOLUTION**

Mar 94. (cd) *Charly; (CDCD 1168)* **SOUL SACRIFICE**

Apr 94. (3xcd) *Pulsar;* **THE SUPER COLLECTION**

Jul 94. (cd/c) *Success;* **AS YEARS GO BY**

Jul 94. (cd/c) *Success;* **SANTANA JAM**

Jul 94. (cd/c) *Success;* **EVERY DAY I HAVE THE BLUES**

Jul 94. (cd/c) *Success;* **WITH A LITTLE HELP FROM MY FRIENDS**

Oct 94. (cd) *Charly; (CDCD 1187)* **LATIN ROCK FUSIONS**

Feb 95. (cd/c) *B.A.M.;* **PEARLS OF THE PAST**

Apr 95. (cd/c) *Muskateer; (MU 5/4 025)* **THE EARLY YEARS**

Sep 95. (3xcd-box) *Legacy-Columbia; (C3K 64605)* **DANCE OF THE RAINBOW SERPENT**

Oct 95. (cd/c) *Collectors Choice; (462563-2/-4)* **SAMBA PA TI**

Nov 95. (3xcd-box) *The Collection; (KBOX 346)* **THE COLLECTION**

Mar 97. (d-cd) *Legacy; (485106-2)* **LIVE ROCK . . . AT FILLMORE** (live)

Apr 97. (cd) *(CDX 32386)* **THE VERY BEST**

May 97. (cd) *C.M.C.; (101182)* **LIVE**

May 97. (d-cd) *Laserlight; (24359)* **SANTANA**

May 97. (cd) *Experience; (EXP 027)* **SANTANA VOL.1**

May 97. (cd) *Experience; (EXP 028)* **SANTANA VOL.2**

Mar 98. (d-cd) *Charly; (CPCD 83312)* **AWAKENING**

Aug 98. (cd/c) *Sony TV; (SONYTV 47 CD/MC)* **THE ULTIMATE COLLECTION** | 23 | |

Jun 99. (cd) *Columbia; (494678-2)* **BLACK MAGIC WOMAN – THE BEST OF SANTANA**

Jul 99. (cd) *Akarma; (AK 068CD)* **SF MISSION DISTRICT LIVE (live)**

Jul 99. (d-cd) *Yeaah; (YEAAH 4)* **FRIED NECKBONES AND HOME FRIES**

—— Note: Most albums up to 1974 were also issued on quad-lp. SUCH IS LIFE album late '93, must have been by other band of same name.

Joe SATRIANI

Born: 15 Jul'57, Bay Area, San Francisco, California, USA, although he was raised in Carle Place, Long Island. In addition to working as a guitar teacher (STEVE VAI and METALLICA's KIRK HAMMETT are among his more famous ex-pupils), six-string maestro SATRIANI played in various rock outifts (i.e. The SQUARES), before eventually making his vinyl debut in 1985 with an eponymous EP. A debut album, 'NOT OF THIS EARTH' (1987) followed soon after, introducing SATRIANI as more then yet another fretboard acrobat; conventional song structures and strong melodies were given just as much emphasis as the (admittedly impressive) soloing and flying-fingered technicality. So it was then, that SATRIANI attracted conventional rock fans and guitar freaks alike, a follow-up effort, 'SURFING WITH THE ALIEN' (1987), hitting the US Top 30, a remarkable feat for an instrumental opus. A master of mood, SATRIANI's forte was the ability to segue smoothly from grinding jazz-tinged raunch rock like 'SATCH BOOGIE' into the beautiful lilt of 'ALWAYS WITH YOU, ALWAYS WITH ME'. 'FLYING IN A BLUE DREAM' (1989) developed this approach, a flawless album which took in everything from dirty boogie ('BIG BAD MOON') to PRINCE-esque white funk ('STRANGE') as well as the obligatory ballad (the corny yet heartfelt 'I BELIEVE'), careering guitar juggernauts ('BACK TO SHALLA-BAL') and even a back-porch banjo hoedown (!), 'THE PHONE CALL'. The album also introduced SATRIANI the singer, and as might be expected, his vocal talents didn't quite match his celebrated axe skills. Nevertheless, it was a brave attempt to advance even further down the song-centric route and his voice did have a certain sly charm although the most affecting tracks on the album remained the new-agey efforts where SATRIANI was talking through his instrument (so to speak!), just listen to the likes of 'THE FORGOTTEN', lie back and melt! A third effort followed in 1992, 'THE EXTREMIST' almost making the UK Top 10 and consolidating SATRIANI's reputation as one of the foremost players of his era. A double set, 'TIME MACHINE' (1993) collected rare and previously released material with a smattering of new tracks while a fourth album proper was eventually released in the form of the eponymous 'JOE SATRIANI' (1995), following the guitarist's brief stint in DEEP PURPLE. In 1997, a live set appeared although this was shared alongside fellow guitar troopers STEVE VAI and ERIC JOHNSON. • Trivia: JOE also guested on ALICE COOPER's 'Hey Stoopid' and SPINAL TAP's 'Break Like The Wind'.

Album rating: NOT OF THIS EARTH (*6) / SURFING WITH THE ALIEN (*7) / FLYING IN A BLUE DREAM (*8) / THE EXTREMIST (*5) / TIME MACHINE part compilation (*6) / JOE SATRIANI (*6) / G3 LIVE IN CONCERT with Eric Johnson & Steve Vai (*7) / CRYSTAL PLANET (*6)

JOE SATRIANI – guitar, bass, keyboards, percussion, etc. / with band **JEFF CAMPITELLI** – drums, percussion, DX / **JOHN CUNIBERTI** – percussion, vocals / **BONGO BOB SMITH** – electronics, drums / **JEFF KREEGER** – synthesizer

	not iss.	Rubina

1985. (12"ep) **JOE SATRIANI** | - | |

	Food For Thought	Combat

Feb 87. (lp) *(GRUB 7)* <88561-8110-2> **NOT OF THIS EARTH** | | Nov86 |
– Not of this Earth / The snake / Rubina / Memories / Brother John / The enigmatic / Driving at night / Hordes of locusts / New day / The headless horseman. *(re-iss. Sep88 cd/c; CD/T GRUB 7) (re-iss. Feb93 cd/c/lp; CD/T+/GRUB 7X) (re-iss. May93 on 'Relativity' cd/c; 462962-2/-4)*

—— he was now joined by **STU HAMM** – bass / **JONATHAN MOVER** – drums

	Food For Thought	Relativity

Nov 87. (lp) *(GRUB 8)* <8195> **SURFING WITH THE ALIEN** | | 29 |
– Surfing with the alien / Ice 9 / Crushing day / Always with you, always with me / Satch boogie / Hill of the skull / Circles / Lords of Karma / Midnight / Echo. *(re-iss. Sep88 cd/c; CD/T GRUB 8) (re-iss. Feb93 cd/c/lp; CD/T+/GRUB 8X) (re-iss. May93 on 'Relativity' cd/c; 462973-2/-4)*

Jun 88. (7") *(YUM 112)* **ALWAYS WITH YOU, ALWAYS WITH ME. / SURFING WITH THE ALIEN**

Dec 88. (12"ep) *(YUMT 114)* <8265> **DREAMING #11** | | 42 m-lp |
– The crush of love / Ice 9 / Memories (live) / Hordes of locusts (live). *(re-iss. May93 on 'Relativity' cd-ep/c-ep; 473604-2/-4)*

—— SATRIANI now on vocals for 6 tracks & returned to original line-up

Nov 89. (cd/c/lp) *(CD/T+/GRUB 14)* <1015> **FLYING IN A BLUE DREAM** | | 23 |
– Flying in a blue dream / The mystical potato head groove thing / Can't slow down / Headless / Strange / I believe / One big rush / Big bad moon / The feeling / The phone call / Day at the beach (new rays from an ancient Sun) / Back to Shalla-bal / Ride / The forgotten (part one) / The forgotten (part two) / The bells of Lal (part one) ? The bells of Lal (part two) / Into the light. *(re-iss. Feb93 cd/c/lp; CD/T+/GRUB 14X) (re-iss. May93 on 'Relativity' cd/c; 465995-2/-4)*

Mar 90. (7") *(YUM 118)* **BIG BAD MOON. / DAY AT THE BEACH (NEW RAYS FROM AN ANCIENT SUN)** | | Nov89 |
(12"+=/cd-s+=) *(YUMT 118)* – ('A'extended).

Mar 91. (7") **I BELIEVE. / FLYING IN A BLUE DREAM** ☐ ☐
(12"+=/cd-s+=) – ('A'remix).

—— now with **ANDY JOHNS** on production, etc.

		Epic	Relativity
Aug 92.	(cd/c/lp) *(471672-2/-4/-1)* <1053> **THE EXTREMIST**	13	22

– Friends / The extremist / War / Cryin' / Rubina's blue sky happiness / Summer song / Tears in the rain / Why / Motorcycle driver / New blues.

Feb 93. (12"ep/cd-ep) *(658953-2/-4)* **THE SATCH EP** `53` ☐
– The extremist / Cryin' / Banana mango / Crazy.

Nov 93. (2xcd/2xc/3xlp) *(474515-2/-4/-1)* <1177> **TIME MACHINE** `32` `95`
(out-takes & new)
– Time machine / The mighty turtle head / All alone (a.k.a. left alone) / Banana mango 11 / Thinking of you / Crazy / Speed of light / Baroque / Dweller of the threshold / Banana mango / Dreaming #11 / I am become death / Saying goodbye / Woodstock jam / Satch boogie / Summer song / Flying in a blue dream / Cryin' / The crush of love / Tears in the rain / Always with me, always with you / Big bad Moon / Surfing with the alien / Rubina / Circles / Drum solo / Lords of Karma / Echo.

Oct 95. (cd/c) *(481102-2/-4)* <1500> **JOE SATRIANI** `21` `51`
– Cool #9 / If / Down down down / Luminous flesh giants / SMF / Look my way / Home / Moroccan sunset / Killer bee bop / Slow down blues / (You're) My world / Sittin' 'round.

May 97. (cd/c; shared with ERIC JOHNSON & STEVE VAI)
(487539-2/-4) **G3 LIVE IN CONCERT (live 2nd November, 1996 at Northrop Auditorium, Minneapolis)** ☐ ☐
– Cool No.9 / Flying in a blue dream / Summer song / (tracks by ERIC JOHNSON) / (tracks by STEVE VAI) / The jam songs (featuring all 3 G's):- Going down.
(video+=) – My guitar wants to kill your mama / Red house.

Mar 98. (cd/c) *(489473-2/-4)* <68018> **CRYSTAL PLANET** `32` `50`
– Up in the sky / House full of bullets / Crystal planet / Love thing / Trundrumbalind / Lights of Heaven / Raspberry jam delta-V / Ceremony / With Jupiter in mind / Secret player / A train of angels / A piece of liquid / Psycho monkey / Time / Z.Z.'s song.

– compilations, etc. –

Oct 94. (3xcd-box) *Relativity;* (477519-2) **NOT OF THIS EARTH / SURFING WITH THE ALIEN / FLYING IN A BLUE DREAM** ☐ ☐

SAUSAGE (see under ⇒ PRIMUS)

SAVOY BROWN (dig out; 4th edition)

SAW DOCTORS

Formed: Tuam, Galway, Ireland . . . 1987 by Irish punk veteran LEO MORAN and former BLAZE X man DAVY CARTON; both had performed together in an embryonic SAW DOCTORS since the late 70's. The splendid sound of The SAW DOCTORS (which also boasted LEO MORAN, TONY LAMBERT and PEARSE DOHERTY) could be described as a hybrid cross between The POGUES' drunken punk and traditional Irish rock, with a working-class ethic thrown in for good measure. Throughout the years in which the band have been active, they have almost outsold U2 and are on their way to becoming the second most successful band in Ireland. They began their road to stardom when The WATERBOYS' lead singer, MIKE SCOTT, invited the small local band for support on their UK tour. This happened around the release of The SAW DOCTORS' debut single 'N17' (produced by MIKE SCOTT) which was quite successfully imported into Britain. After the tour had finished, sophomore single 'I USETA LOVE HER' (a rip-roaring track about the perils of Catholic love) generated so much hype that it went straight to No.1 (in Ireland) and stayed there for a further nine weeks – becoming the largest-selling Irish record of all time. The band subsequently re-issued their debut single (which also reached No.1) and released the humorous and delightful full-length set 'IF THIS IS ROCK AND ROLL I WANT MY OLD JOB BACK' (1991). Following the release of 'ALL THE WAY FROM TUAM' (1992), 'A SMALL BIT OF LOVE' became the group's first British hit and went on to reach the Top 30. To celebrate their country's appearance in the 1994 World Cup, the lads attributed their national team with their single, 'TO WIN JUST ONCE'. Early in 1996, the SAW DOCTORS finally issued their third long-player 'SAME OUL' TOWN', and advanced their UK cred when the album reached the Top 10. The following year, 'SING A POWERFUL SONG' (a collection of earlier material) was released to their usual fanfare, as was 'SHE SAYS', an EP written for the BBC sitcom 'Give my head peace'. The SAW DOCTORS' finally achieved some recognition in America when the single, 'NEVER MIND THE STRANGERS', received some airplay. The track was co-written by drummer PADRAIG STEVENS, who had left the group at the time of the single's release. The popularity surrounding the song was mainly credited to its accompanying Guinness advert. Fourth album proper, 'SONGS FROM SUN STREET' (1998) sold well enough to hit the UK Top 30, the two founding members (plus mainstay PEARSE DOHERTY) adding the current line-up which includes JOHN DONNELLY and DEREK MURRAY.
• **Songwriters:** Most by MORAN-CARTON or group, except THE WEST'S AWAKE (trad) / TEENAGE KICKS (Undertones).
Album rating: IF THIS IS ROCK'N'ROLL, I WANT MY OLD JOB BACK (*5) / ALL THE WAY FROM TUAM (*5) / SAME OUL' TOWN (*5) / SING A POWERFUL SONG collection (*5) / SONGS FROM SUN STREET (*4)

JOHN BURKE – mandolin, organ, guitars, vocals / **DAVY CARTON** – vocals, guitars / **LEO MORAN** – guitars, vocals, organ, etc / **TONY LAMBERT** – accordion, organ / **PEARSE DOHERTY** – bass, vocals, piano, flute / guest **JOHN DONNELLY** – drums, percussion

		Solid	WEA
1989.	(7") **n17. / ?**	–	Ireland

Oct 90. (7"m) **I USETA LOVE HER. / CAPTAIN JOE FIDDLE'S / I USED TO LOVER HER BLAZE X** ☐ ☐

May 91. (cd/c/lp) *(ROC D/C/K 7)* **IF THIS IS ROCK'N'ROLL, I WANT MY OLD JOB BACK** `69` ☐
– I useta lover / Only one girl / Why do I always want you / It won't be tonight / Irish post / Sing a powerful song / Freedom fighters / That's what she said last night / Red Cortina / Presentation boarder / Don't let me down / £25 / What a day / n17 / I hope you meet again. *(re-iss. Dec93 cd/c; ROC DG/CG 7)* (re-iss. Dec94 on 'Shamtown' cd/c; SAWDOC 001 CD/MC)

Jul 91. (7"/c-s) **n17. / n17 LIVE (including PADDY'S POEM)** ☐ ☐
(cd-s+=) – At least pretend.

Nov 91. (7"/c-s) *(ROK/+C 751)* **THAT'S WHAT SHE SAID LAST NIGHT. / HAY WRAP: HAY WRAP – THE WEST'S AWAKE – HAY WRAP** ☐ ☐
(cd-s+=) *(ROKCD 751)* – The trip to Tipp.

		W.E.A.	Warners
Oct 92.	(cd/c/lp) *(<4509 91146-2/-4/-1>)* **ALL THE WAY FROM TUAM**	33	☐

– Green & red of Mayo / You got me on the run / Pied piper / My heart is livin' in the sixties still / Hay wrap / Wake up sleeping / Midnight express / Broke my heart / Exhilarating sadness / All the way from Tuam / Music I love / Yvonne / Never mind the strangers. *(re-iss. Dec93 on 'Solid' cd/c; ROC D/C 11)* (re-iss. Dec94 on 'Shamtown' cd/c; SAWDOC 002 CD/MC)

Feb 93. (7"/c-s) *(YZ 731/+C)* **WAKE UP SLEEPING. / JOE WALL BROKE MY HEART** ☐ ☐
(cd-s+=) *(YZ 731CD)* – Thank God it's a Tuesday / I hope you melt again.
(cd-s) *(YZ 731CDX)* – ('A'side) / Why do I always want you (live) / What a day (live) / N17 (live).

—— **ANTO THISTLETHWAITE** – saxophone, etc (ex-WATERBOYS, ex-solo artist 1993 album; AESOP WROTE . . .) repl. BURKE

May 94. (7"/c-s/cd-s) **TO WIN JUST ONCE. / ?** ☐ – Ireland

—— Above was the unofficial Irish World Cup theme.

—— now without THISTLETWAITE who was now solo. 5th member on below album
DEREK MURRAY – keyboards, accordion, guitar, mandolin, banjo

		Shamtown	Warners
Oct 94.	(c-ep/cd-ep) *(SAW 001 MC/CD)* **SMALL BIT OF LOVE / MICHAEL D. ROCKING IN THE DAIL / I'D LOVE TO KISS THE BANGLES / WHERE'S THE PARTY (live)**	24	☐
Jan 96.	(c-ep/cd-ep) *(SAW 002 MC/CD)* **WORLD OF GOOD / BLESS ME FATHER / LETTER FROM LOUISE / TUAM BEAT**	15	☐
Feb 96.	(cd/c) *(SAWDOC 004 CD/C)* **SAME OUL' TOWN**	6	☐

– All the one / Same oul' town / To win just once / Everyday / World of good / Back to Tuam / Mercy gates / Macnas parade / Share the darkness / I want you more / All over now / Clare Island.

Jul 96. (c-ep/cd-ep) *(SAW 004 MC/CD)* **TO WIN JUST ONCE / SOUND SHAM / WINTER'S JUST A DREAM / GREEN & RED OF MAYO** `14` ☐
(cd-ep) *(SAW 004CDX)* – ('A'side) / Teenage kicks (live) / I useta lover (live) / Clare Island (live).

Nov 97. (cd/c) *(SAWDOC 005 CD/MC)* **SING A POWERFUL SONG** ☐ ☐
– Green & red of Mayo / It won't be tonight / Wake up sleeping / Macnas parade / What a day / Hay wrap / N17 / Exhilarating sadness / Red Cortina / Clare island / To win just once / Share the darkness / I useta lover.

Nov 97. (c-s) *(SAW 006MC)* **SIMPLE THINGS /** `56` ☐
(cd-s+=) *(SAW 006CD)* –

Oct 98. (cd/c/lp) *(SAWDOC 006 CD/MC/LP)* **SONGS FROM SUN STREET** `24` ☐
– Good news / Sugar town / Galway and Mayo / Carry me away / Heading for the sunshine / Catriona tell lies / Blah blah blah / D'ya wanna hear my guitar / Joyce country ceili band / High Nellie / Best of friends / Will it ever stop raining / Tommy K / Away with the fairies / I'll be on my way / Apples sweets or chocolate.

– compilations, etc. –

1994. (cd) *Warners;* **FRIENDS, DEMOS & B-SIDES** ☐ –

SAXON (dig out; 4th edition or Great Metal . . .)

Boz SCAGGS

Born: WILLIAM ROYCE SCAGGS, 8 Jun'44, Ohio, USA. In the late 50's, having learnt guitar from Texas schoolpal, STEVE MILLER, he joined The MARKSMEN. The pair soon enrolled at Wisconsin University where they joined The ARDELLS, an outfit which mutated into FABULOUS NIGHT TRAIN. In 1963, SCAGGS returned to Texas where he formed The WIGS, moving to the UK the following year. He then relocated to Sweden where he released the eponymous 1966 'Polydor' lp, 'BOZ'. In September '67, he joined The STEVE MILLER BAND and played on two albums, 'Children Of The Future' and 'Sailor', before going on to solo work again. Signing to 'Atlantic', SCAGGS recorded his eponymous debut proper at the famed 'Muscle Shoals' studio, the record (released in 1969) introducing a more soulful blues/R&B sound which he'd polish over the coming decade. A stand-out track for the bulk of fans and critics alike was the smoking 'LOAN ME A DIME', SCAGGS's oak-rich vocals pleading poverty over the late DUANE ALLMAN's blistering slide guitar. Switching labels to 'C.B.S.', recruiting a backing band (JOACHIM JIMMY YOUNG, GEORGE RAINS and DAVID BROWN) and hooking up with producer Glyn Johns, SCAGGS attempted to develop his soul/rock hybrid with 'MOMENTS' and 'BOZ SCAGGS AND BAND', both albums released in 1971. While these were minor US chart successes, SCAGGS opted for a full-on white-soul ballad approach on 'SLOW DANCER' (1974), employing such noted players as sax man, JACK SCHROER (who'd been part of VAN MORRISON's legendary Caledonia Soul Orchestra) and roping in ex-Motown man Johnny Bristol to augment Johns on production duties. But SCAGGS didn't really nail the sound he was after until 1976's 'SILK DEGREES', an album which almost topped the US chart and made the UK Top 20. Utilising a superslick core of backing musicians (who would develop into AOR crown kings, TOTO), SCAGGS achieved a fine balance between orchestrated gloss and grainy soulfulness, 'LOWDOWN' making the US Top 3 and 'WHAT CAN I SAY!' becoming the man's only Top 10 hit. A further single, 'LIDO SHUFFLE', provided him with more transatlantic success although the aptly titled 'HARD TIMES' (from the 1977 set, 'DOWN TWO, THEN LEFT') lingered in the lower regions of the chart as SCAGGS struggled to match the form displayed only a year earlier. While his 'MIDDLE MAN' (1980) album made the US Top 10 and he scored a one-off Top 20 hit with 'MISS SUN', SCAGGS subsequently retired from the music business in the early 80's to run a Southern style restaurant in his adopted hometown of San Francisco. Returning to the studio in 1987, he cut the disappointing 'OTHER ROADS' (1988), scoring a minor hit single with 'HEART OF MINE' (co-written with JIM CARROLL). He finally returned to performing full-time as part of DONALD FAGEN's 'New York Rock and Soul Revue' in the early 90's, subsequently inking a new contract with 'Virgin' and releasing 'SOME CHANGE' (1994) and 'COME ON HOME' (1997). • Trivia: RITA COOLIDGE reached both US + UK Top 10's, with her version of 'WE'RE ALL ALONE'.

Album rating: BOZ (*4) / BOZ SCAGGS (*7) / MOMENTS (*6) / BOZ SCAGGS & BAND (*5) / MY TIME (*6) / SLOW DANCER (*6) / SILK DEGREES (*8) / DOWN TWO THEN LEFT (*5) / MIDDLE MAN (*6) / HITS! compilation (*7) / OTHER ROADS (*5) / SOME CHANGE (*5) / COME ON HOME (*6) / A BOZ SCAGGS ANTHOLOGY compilation (*7)

BOZ SCAGGS – vocals, guitar (with session people)

		Polydor	not iss.
1966.	(lp) (LPHM 46253) **BOZ**	-	- Sweden

—— SCAGG joined The STEVE MILLER BAND for two albums; then solo again with Muscle Shoals session people plus **DUANE ALLMAN** – slide guitar

		Atlantic	Atlantic
Jul 69.	(7") <2692> **I'M EASY. / I'LL BE LONG GONE**		-
Aug 69.	(lp) (588205) <8239> **BOZ SCAGGS**		-

– I'm easy / I'll be long gone / Another day (another letter) / Now you're gone / Finding her / Love what I got / Waiting for a train / Loan me a dime / Sweet release. <re-iss. 1971; 19166> <re-iss. Jul74; 8239> (re-iss. Jul74; K 40419) (cd re-iss. 1989 on 'WEA'; 781545-2) (cd re-iss. May93; 7567 81545-2)

—— now with **JOACHIM JIMMY YOUNG** – keyboards / **GEORGE RAINS** – drums / **DAVID BROWN** – bass / + many others

		C.B.S.	Columbia
Apr 71.	(7") (CBS 7219) <45353> **WE WERE ALWAYS SWEETHEARTS. / PAINTED BELLS**		61
Jun 71.	(lp) (CBS 64248) <30454> **MOMENTS**		Apr71

– We were always sweethearts / Downright woman / Painted bells / Alone, alone / Near you / I will forever sing (the blues) / Moments / Hollywood blues / We been away / Can I make it last (or will it just be over).

Aug 71.	(7") (CBS 7401) <45408> **NEAR YOU. / DOWNRIGHT WOMAN**		
Dec 71.	(lp) (CBS 64431) <30796> **BOZ SCAGGS & BAND**		96 Jun71

– Monkey time / Runnin' blue / Up to you / Love anyway / Flames of love / Here to stay / Nothing will take your place / Why why / You're so good. (re-iss. Oct80 lp/c; CBS/40 31848)

Jan 72.	(7") **HERE TO STAY. / RUNNIN' BLUE**	-	
Feb 72.	(7") (CBS 7803) **UP TO YOU. / RUNNIN' BLUE**		
Sep 72.	(lp) (CBS 64975) <31384> **MY TIME**		

– Dinah Flo / Slowly in the west / Full lock power-slide / Old time lovin' / Might have to cry / Hello my lover / Freedom for the stallion / He's a fool for you / We're gonna roll / My time.

Sep 72.	(7") (CBS 8341) <45670> **DINAH FLO. / HE'S A FOOL FOR YOU**		86

—— toured with guests STEVE MILLER and GEORGE RAINS. Late 1972, his new band were **LES DUDEK** – guitar / **JIMMY YOUNG** – keyboards / **TOM RUTLEY** – bass / **RICK SCHLOSSER** – drums / **JACK SCHROEDER** – sax

Apr 74.	(7") (CBS 2321) **YOU MAKE IT SO HARD (TO SAY NO). / THERE IS SOMEONE ELSE**		-
Apr 74.	(lp) (CBS 65953) <32760> **SLOW DANCER**		81 Mar74

– You make it so hard (to say no) / Slow dancer / Angel lady (come just in time) / There is someone else / Hercules / Pain of love / Let it happen / Sail on white moon / I got your number / Take it for granted. (re-iss. Mar82 lp/c; CBS/40 32072) (re-iss. cd Apr94 on 'Sony Collectors'; 982986-2)

Jul 74.	(7") (CBS 2305) **I GOT YOUR NUMBER. / SLOW DANCER**		
Jul 74.	(7") **PAIN OF LOVE. / SLOW DANCER**	-	

—— next with guests & future members of TOTO (aka the PORCARO's and STEVE LUKATHER)

Apr 76.	(7") (CBS 4214) **GEORGIA. / JUMP STREET**		-
Jun 76.	(7") (CBS 4338) <10319> **IT'S OVER. / HARBOUR LIGHTS**		38 Mar76
Jun 76.	(7") <10367> **LOWDOWN. / HARBOR LIGHTS**	-	3
Aug 76.	(lp/c) (CBS/40 81193) <33920> **SILK DEGREES**	20	2 Mar76

– What can I say / Georgia / Jump street / What do you want the girl to do? / Harbor lights / Lowdown / It's over / Love me tomorrow / Lido shuffle / We're all alone. (re-iss. Mar81; CBS 32036) (re-iss. Oct92 on 'Carlton' cd/c; 982840-2/-4) (cd re-iss. Feb95 on 'Columbia'; CK 64420) (cd re-iss. Feb97 on 'Columbia'; 471968-2) (lp re-iss. Jun99 on 'Simply Vinyl'; SVLP 73)

Oct 76.	(7") (CBS 4563) **LOWDOWN. / JUMP STREET**	28	-
Nov 76.	(7") <10440> **WHAT CAN I SAY. / WE'RE ALL ALONE**		42
Jan 77.	(7") (CBS 4869) **WHAT CAN I SAY. / HARBOUR LIGHTS**	10	-
Apr 77.	(7") (CBS 5136) <10491> **LIDO SHUFFLE. / WE'RE ALL ALONE**	13	11 Mar77
Nov 77.	(7") (CBS 5828) <10606> **HARD TIMES. / WE'RE WAITING**		58 Oct77
Nov 77.	(lp/c) (CBS/40 86028) <34729> **DOWN TWO THEN LEFT**	55	11

– Still falling for you / Hard times / A clue / Whatcha gonna tell your man? / We're

waiting / Hollywood / Then she walked away / Gimme the goods / 1993 / Tomorrow never came / Tomorrow never came (reprise).

Nov 77.	(7") (CBS 5836) **HOLLYWOOD. / WE'RE WAITING**	33	-
Jan 78.	(7") <10679> **HOLLYWOOD. / A CLUE**	-	49
Feb 78.	(7") (CBS 6096) **1993. / A CLUE**	-	-
Sep 78.	(7") (CBS 4693) **IT'S OVER. / LOVE ME TOMORROW**		-
Apr 80.	(7") (CBS 8501) <11241> **BREAKDOWN DEAD AHEAD. / ISN'T IT TIME**	15	Mar80
May 80.	(lp/c) (CBS/40 86094) <36106> **MIDDLE MAN**	52	8 Apr80

– JoJo / Breakdown dead ahead / Simone / You can have me anytime / Middle man / Do like you do in New York / Angel you / Isn't it time / You got some imagination.

Jun 80.	(7") (CBS 8740) <11281> **JOJO. / DO LIKE YOU DO IN NEW YORK**		17
Jul 80.	(7") (CBS 8828) **SIMONE. / DO LIKE YOU DO IN NEW YORK**		-
Aug 80.	(7") <11349> **LOOK WHAT YOU'VE DONE TO ME. / SIMONE**	-	14
Oct 80.	(7") (CBS 9034) **LOOK WHAT YOU'VE DONE TO ME. / YOU GOT SOME IMAGINATION**		-
Dec 80.	(lp/c) (CBS/40 84706) <36106> **HITS!** (compilation)		24 Nov80

– Lowdown / You make it so hard (to say no) / Miss Sun / Lido shuffle / We're all alone / Breakdown dead ahead / Look what you've done to me / What can I say / Dinah Flo / You can have me anytime.
(below featured b.vox by LISA DAL BELLO)

Jan 81.	(7") (CBS 9424) <11406> **MISS SUN. / DINAH FLO**		14 Nov80
Mar 81.	(7") **YOU CAN HAVE ME ANYTIME. / GEORGIA**	-	

—— BOZ retired from the music scene to run Southern style restaurant in San Francisco. He returned to the studio in 1987.

May 88.	(7") (CBS 651559-7) <07780> **HEART OF MINE. / YOU'LL NEVER KNOW**		35 Apr88

(12"+=) (651559-8) – We're all alone / Slow dancer.
(cd-s+=) (651559-2) – Soul to soul / What can I say.

Jun 88.	(lp/c/cd) (461112-1/-4/-2) <40463> **OTHER ROADS**		47 JMay88

– What's number one? / Claudia / Heart of mine / Right out of my head / I don't hear you / Mental shakedown / Crimes of passion / Funny / Cool running / The night of Van Gogh.

Jul 88.	(7") **COOL RUNNING. / YOU'LL NEVER KNOW**	-	
Sep 88.	(7") **WHAT'S NUMBER ONE? / CLAUDIA**	-	

—— In 1990, SCAGGS produced the debut album for local group SMOKING SECTION before getting back to solo work later

		Virgin America	Virgin
Jun 94.	(cd/c) (CDVUS/VUSMC 73) <39489> **SOME CHANGE**		91 Apr94

– You got my letter / Some change / I'll be the one / Call me / Fly like a bird / Sierra / Lost it / Time / Illusion / Follow that man.

Apr 97.	(cd) (CDVUS 124) **COME ON HOME**		94

– It all went down the drain / Ask me 'bout nothin' (but the blues) / Don't cry no more / Found love / Come home / Pictures of a broken heart / Love letters / I've got your love / Early in the morning / Your good thing (is about to end) / T-bone shuffle / Sick and tired / After hours / Goodnight Louise.

– compilations, etc. –

Feb 83.	(d-c) C.B.S.; **SLOW DANCER / SILK DEGREES**		
Feb 89.	(7") Old Gold; (OG 9862) **WHAT CAN I SAY. / LIDO SHUFFLE**		
Oct 97.	(d-cd) Columbia; (487397-2) **MY TIME (BOZ SCAGGS ANTHOLOGY 1969-1997)**		

Michael SCHENKER (GROUP)

Born: 10 Jan'55, Savstedt, Germany. Famous for forming teutonic rockers The SCORPIONS with his brother RUDOLF in 1971, he went on to join English band, UFO, with whom he cut four albums (PHENOMENON / FORCE IT / NO HEAVY PETTIN' / LIGHTS OUT). SCHENKER subsequently returned to Germany in 1978 where he briefly rejoined The SCORPIONS for the 1979 album, 'LOVEDRIVE', augmenting them live before striking out on his own and forming the MICHAEL SCHENKER GROUP. Recruiting GARY BARDEN, MO FOSTER, SIMON PHILIPS and ex-COLOSSEUM II keyboard whizz, DON AIREY, the guitarist released an eponymous debut in 1980. Dominated by SCHENKER's sizzling axework, the album smashed into the UK Top 10, the guitarist's impressive pedigree ensuring healthy sales. For the subsequent tour, however, SCHENKER made the first personnel changes (PAUL RAYMOND, CHRIS GLEN and COZY POWELL replacing AIREY, FOSTER and PHILIPS respectively) in what would become a familiar pattern and no doubt contribute to the group's eventual spiral into mediocrity. This was the line-up which played on 'MSG' (1981), SCHENKER ripping out what could be his theme tune in 'ATTACK OF THE MAD AXEMAN'. Like The SCORPIONS, MSG enjoyed obsessive adulation in Japan, as witnessed on 1982's barnstorming double live set, 'ONE NIGHT AT BUDOKAN'. More line-up changes ensued, chief among them being ex-RAINBOW vocalist, GRAHAM BONNET replacing BARDEN, while former RORY GALLAGHER sticksman, TED McKENNA, was recruited in place of POWELL (who joined WHITESNAKE). With BONNET's earthier tones and significant songwriting input, the resulting album, 'ASSAULT ATTACK' (1982) was a bluesier affair albeit with SCHENKER's stinging guitar still vying for attention. Following BONNET's resumption of his solo career, BARDEN was welcomed back into the fold for 'BUILT TO DESTROY' (1983) and 'ROCK WILL NEVER DIE' (1984), two lacklustre albums which didn't exactly do much for SCHENKER's reputation. Inevitably, the group splintered, with the guitarist going back to Germany to reconsider his battle plan. When he resurfaced in late '87 with 'PERFECT TIMING', the 'M' in MSG now stood for McAULEY, SCHENKER having teamed up with former FAR CORPORATION / GRAND PRIX vocalist ROBIN McCAULEY for a

more accessible melodic rock approach. The group enjoyed moderate success although by the release of 1992's 'M.S.G.', they seemed bankrupt of ideas and the record was roundly slated by critics. Marginally more inspired was the 'CONTRABAND' (1991) project, a collaboration with the likes of TRACII GUNS and BOBBY BLOTZER. The days of the guitar hero may well be over, however, and SCHENKER has been conspicuous by his absence from the metal scene for most of the 90's; perhaps he's taken up the flugelhorn . . .
• **Trivia:** CONTRABAND covered Mott The Hoople's 'ALL THE WAY FROM MEMPHIS'.

Album rating: MICHAEL SCHENKER GROUP (*5) / MSG (*4) / ONE NIGHT AT BUDOKAN (*6) / ASSAULT ATTACK (*4) / BUILT TO DESTROY (*4) / ROCK WILL NEVER DIE (*4) / PORTFOLIO compilation (*6) / McAuley-Schenker Group: PERFECT TIMING (*5) / SAVE YOURSELF (*4) / MSG (*4)

MICHAEL SCHENKER – lead guitar (ex-SCORPIONS, ex-UFO) / **GARY BARDEN** – vocals / **DON AIREY** – keyboards (ex-COLOSSEUM II) / **MO FOSTER** – bass / **SIMON PHILLIPS** – drums

			Chrysalis	Chrysalis
Aug 80.	(lp/c) (<CHR/ZCHR 1302>) **MICHAEL SCHENKER GROUP**		8	100

– Armed and ready / Cry for the nations / Victim of illusion / Bijou pleasurette / Feels like a good thing / Into the arena / Looking out from nowhere / Tales of mystery / Lost horizons. (re-iss.Jun84 on 'Fame' lp/c; FA41 3105-1/-4)

| Aug 80. | (7"colrd) (CHS 2455) **ARMED AND READY. / BIJOU PLEASURETTE** | | 53 | |
| Oct 80. | (7"clear) (CHS 2471) **CRY FOR THE NATIONS. / INTO THE ARENA** (live) | | 56 | |

(12"+=) (CHS12 2471) – Armed and ready (live).

—— **PAUL RAYMOND** – keyboards (ex-UFO, etc.) repl. AIREY / **CHRIS GLEN** – bass (ex-SENSATIONAL ALEX HARVEY BAND) repl. FOSTER / **COZY POWELL** – drums (ex-RAINBOW, ex-Solo artist) repl. PHILLIPS

| Aug 81. | (7"clear) (CHS 2541) **READY TO ROCK. / ATTACK OF THE MAD AXEMAN** | | | |
| Sep 81. | (lp/c) (<CHR/ZCHR 1336>) **MSG** | | 14 | 81 |

– Ready to rock / Attack of the mad axeman / On and on / Let sleeping dogs lie / But I want more / Never trust a stranger / Looking for love / Secondary motion. (cd-iss. May86; CCD 1336)

| Feb 82. | (d-lp/d-c) (<CTY/ZCTY 1375>) **ONE NIGHT AT BUDOKAN** (live) | | 5 | |

– Armed and ready / Cry for the nations / Attack of the mad axeman / But I want more / Victim of illusion / Into the arena / On and on / Never trust a stranger / Let sleeping dogs lie / Courvoisier concert / Lost horizons / Doctor doctor / Are you ready to rock. (d-cd-iss. Sep91; CCD 1375) (cd re-iss. Jun96 on 'Beat Goes On'; BGOCD 312)

—— **GRAHAM BONNET** – vocals (ex-RAINBOW, ex-Solo, ex-MARBLES) repl. BARDEN + RAYMOND / **TED McKENNA** – drums (ex-SENSATIONAL ALEX HARVEY BAND, ex-RORY GALLAGHER) repl. COZY who joined WHITESNAKE

| Sep 82. | (7"clear,7"pic-d) (CHS 2636) **DANCER. / GIRL FROM UPTOWN** | | 52 | |

(12"+=) (CHS12 2636) – ('A'extended).

| Oct 82. | (lp/c/pic-lp) (<CHR/ZCHR/PCHR 1393>) **ASSAULT ATTACK** | | 19 | |

– Assault attack / Rock you to the ground / Dancer / Samurai / Desert song / Broken promises / Searching for a reason / Ulcer. (cd-iss. Aug96 on 'Beat Goes On'; BGOCD 321)

—— **GARY BARDEN** – vocals returned to repl. BONNET who went solo / added **DEREK ST. HOLMES** – keyboards (ex-TED NUGENT) (on tour **ANDY NYE** – keyboards)

| Sep 83. | (lp/c/pic-lp) (<CHR/ZCHR/PCHR 1441>) **BUILT TO DESTROY** | | 23 | |

– Rock my nights away / I'm gonna make you mine / The dogs of war / Systems failing / Captain Nemo / Still love that little devil / Red sky / Time waits (for no one) / Walk the stage. (cd-iss.Jan97 on 'Beat Goes On'; BGOCD 344)

| Jun 84. | (lp/c) (<CUX/ZCUX 1470>) **ROCK WILL NEVER DIE** (live) | | 24 | |

– Captain Nemo / Rock my nights away / Are you ready to rock / Attack of the mad axeman / Into the arena / Rock will never die / Desert song / I'm gonna make you mine / Doctor, doctor.

—— When CHRIS GLEN departed, most of others also departed

McAULEY-SCHENKER GROUP

—— added **ROBIN McAULEY** (b.20 Jan'53, County Meath, Eire) – vox (ex-FAR CORPORATION) / **MITCH PERRY** – guitar / **ROCKY NEWTON** – bass / **BOBO SCHOPF** – drums

			E.M.I.	Capitol
Oct 87.	(7") (EM 30) <44079> **GIMME YOUR LOVE. / ROCK TILL YOU'RE CRAZY**			

(12"+=/12"remix+=) (12EM/+S 30) – ('A'extended).

| Oct 87. | (cd/c/lp) (CD/TC+/EMC 3539) <46985> **PERFECT TIMING** | | 65 | 95 |

– Gimme your love / Here today, gone tomorrow / Don't stop me now / No time for losers / Follow the night / Get out / Love is not a game / Time / I don't wanna lose / Rock 'til you're crazy.

| Jan 88. | (7"/12"/12"remix) (EM/12EM/12EMS 40) <44113> **LOVE IS NOT A GAME. / GET OUT** | | | |
| Apr 88. | (7") <44156> **FOLLOW THE NIGHT. / DON'T STOP ME NOW** | | – | |

—— **McAULEY & SCHENKER** now with **BOBO SCHOPF** – drums / **STEVE MANN** (b.9 Aug'56) – rhythm guitar / **ROCKY NEWMAN** (b.11 Sep'57) – bass (ex-LIONHEART)

| Oct 89. | (cd/c/lp) (CD/TC+/EMC 3567) <92752> **SAVE YOURSELF** | | | 92 |

– Save yourself / Bad boys / Anytime / Get down to bizness / Shadow of the night / What we need / I am your radio / There has to be another way / This is my heart / Destiny. (cd+=) – Take me back.

| Apr 90. | (c-s/7") (TC+/EM 127) <44471> **ANYTIME. / WHAT WE NEED** | | | |

(12"+=/12"pic-d+=/cd-s+=) (12EM/12EMPD/CDEM 127) – ('A'version).

—— **SCHENKER** with **ROBIN McAULEY** – vocals / **JEFF PILSON** – bass (ex-DOKKEN) / **JAMES KOTTAK** – drums (ex-KINGDOM COME)

			E.M.I.	Impact
Feb 92.	(12"ep/cd-ep) **NEVER ENDING NIGHTMARE**			
Feb 92.	(cd)(c/lp; as SCHENKER – McAULEY) (CDP 798487-2)(EUS MC/LP 3) <10385> **M.S.G.**			

– Eve / Paradise / When I'm gone / The broken heart / We believe in love / Crazy / Invincible / What happens to me / Lonely nights / This night is gonna last forever / Never ending nightmare.

– compilations, etc. –

| Jun 87. | (lp/c)(cd) Chrysalis; (CNW/ZCNW 1)(MPCD 1598) **PORTFOLIO** | | | – |

– Doctor doctor (UFO) / Rock bottom (UFO) / Rock will never die / Armed and ready / Ready to rock / Assault attack / Ulcer / Attack of the mad axeman / I'm a loser / Reasons to love / Too hot to handle / Only you can rock me (UFO) / Lights out (UFO) / Arbory hill / Love drive (SCORPIONS) / Searching for a reason / Rock my nights away / Captain Nemo.

Jul 91.	(cd/c) Castle; (CCS CD/MC 294) **THE COLLECTION**			–
Oct 92.	(cd/c) Chrysalis; (CD/TC CHR 1949) **THE ESSENTIAL MICHAEL SCHENKER GROUP**			–
Apr 93.	(cd) Connoisseur; (VSOPCD 185) **ANTHOLOGY**			–

– (with UFO tracks) (re-iss. Aug95 on 'Griffin';)

Nov 93.	(cd) Windsong; (WINCD 043) **BBC RADIO 1 LIVE IN CONCERT** (live)			–
Apr 94.	(cd) Chrysalis; (CDCHR 6071) **THE STORY OF MICHAEL SCHENKER GROUP**			–
Jun 94.	(cd/c) Music Club; (MC CD/TC 160) **ARMED AND READY – THE BEST OF MICHAEL SCHENKER GROUP**			
Jul 96.	(cd) Beat Goes On; (BGOCD 316) **MICHAEL SCHENKER GROUP / MSG**			
Mar 97.	(cd; SCHENKER & McAULEY GROUP) Disky; (CR 86993-2) **CHAMPIONS OF ROCK**			

Fred SCHNEIDER (see under ⇒ B-52's)

Neal SCHON & Jan HAMMER (see under ⇒ JOURNEY)

SCORPIONS

Formed: Hanover, Germany . . . 1971 by the SCHENKER brothers (MICHAEL and RUDOLPH) together with KLAUS MEINE, LOTHAR HEINBERG and WOLFGANG ZIONY. After a well-received debut, 'LONESOME CROW' (1973), on the domestic 'Brain' records, the band underwent a turbulent series of personnel changes which resulted in ULRICH ROTH replacing MICHAEL (who went on to join U.F.O.), JURGEN ROSENTHAL replacing ZIONY and FRANCIS BUCHHOLZ coming in for the departing LOTHAR. Signing worldwide to 'R.C.A.', the new-look SCORPIONS released a follow-up, 'FLY TO THE RAINBOW' in 1974. Archetypal German hard-rock, The SCORPIONS' sound consisted of initially jazz-inflected, lumbering riffs punctuated with piercing solos and topped off with MEINE's strangely accessible nasal whine. They developed this approach over a number of 70's albums, 'IN TRANCE' (1976), erm.. 'VIRGIN KILLERS' (1977), etc. The live 'TOKYO TAPES' (1979) brought the first half of the group's career to a neat close, ROTH subsequently departing to form ELECTRIC SUN, disillusioned at the band's increasingly commercial direction. His replacement was MATHIAS JABS although MICHAEL SCHENKER returned briefly, guesting on three tracks for the 'LOVEDRIVE' (1979) set. Now signed to 'Harvest' ('Mercury' in the States), the group had produced their most radio-friendly collection to date, the album taking them into the UK (Top 40) and US (Top 60) charts for the first time. 'ANIMAL MAGNETISM' (1980) fared even better, almost breaking the UK Top 20 with the NWOBHM in full swing, the record also featuring the anthemic live favourite, 'THE ZOO'. 'BLACKOUT' (1982) finally broke the group in America, achieving double platinum status. 1984's 'LOVE AT FIRST STING' fared even better, selling twice as many as its predecessor and spawning a Top 30 hit single with the stop-start riffing of 'ROCK YOU LIKE A HURRICANE'. The SCORPIONS were now seemingly tailoring their music for the US market, concentrating more on melody and hooklines with each successive release. Save for the massive-selling concert set,'WORLD WIDE LIVE' (1985), it was to be a further four years before the group released a new album as they became the first Western rock group to play in the Soviet Union, 'SAVAGE AMUSEMENT' finally surfacing in 1988. The SCORPIONS' anthemic rock continued to attract a bigger audience Stateside than in Britain, the group scoring a Top 5 US hit single (and a worldwide No.1) in 1991 with the lighter-waving ballad, 'WIND OF CHANGE'. Sadly not referring to MEINE finally having that awful mullet cut off, the song instead dealt with the sweeping changes in the communist bloc (a version was actually recorded in Russian!). They continued to eschew tales of loose women and 'crazy' nights for more serious political matters on 'FACE THE HEAT' (1993), exploring the social effect of their country's reunification.

Album rating: ACTION (or) LONESOME CROW (*4) / FLY TO THE RAINBOW (*4) / IN TRANCE (*6) / VIRGIN KILLERS (*6) / TAKEN BY FORCE (*4) / TOKYO TAPES (*5) / LOVEDRIVE (*6) / ANIMAL MAGNETISM (*5) / BLACKOUT (*6) / LOVE AT FIRST STING (*6) / WORLD WIDE LIVE (*6) / SAVAGE AMUSEMENT (*5) / CRAZY WORLD (*4) / FACE THE HEAT (*3) / LIVE BITES (*3) / DEADLY STING compilation (*6) / PURE INSTINCTS (*4) / EYE TO EYE (*3)

KLAUS MEINE (b.25 May'52) – vocals / **MICHEL SCHENKER** (b.10 Jan'55, Savstedt, Germany) – lead guitar / **RUDOLF SCHENKER** (b.31 Aug'52, Hildesheim, Germany) – guitar (ex-COPERNICUS) / **LOTHAR HEIMBERG** – bass / **WOLFGANG DZIONY** – drums

1973. (lp) <1001> **LONESOME CROW**

	Brain	not iss.
	-	- German

– It all depends / Action / Lonesome crow / I'm goin' mad / Leave me / In search of the peace of mind / Inheritance. *(re-iss.Aug74 as 'I'M GOIN' MAD & OTHERS' on 'Billingsgate'; 1004) (re-iss. Nov77 as 'GOLD ROCK' on 'Brain'; 004 0016) (re-iss. May80 as 'ACTION' on 'Brain'; 0040 150) (UK-iss.Nov82 on 'Heavy Metal' lp/c/pic-lp; HMI LP/MC/PD 2) (cd-iss. 1988 on 'Brain'; 825 739-2) (re-iss. Jul91 on 'Metal Masters' cd/c/lp; METAL MCD/K/PS 114)*

—— (Jun'73) **ULRICH ROTH** – lead guitar repl. MICHAEL who joined UFO / **JURGEN ROSENTHAL** – drums repl. WOLFGANG / **FRANCIS BUCHHOLZ** (b.19 Feb'50) – bass repl. LOTHAR

Nov 74. (lp) (RS 1023) <APL-1 4025> **FLY TO THE RAINBOW**

	R.C.A.	R.C.A.

– Speedy's coming / They need a million / Drifting Sun / Fly people fly / This is my song / Fly away / Fly to the rainbow. *(re-iss. Oct85 lp/c; NL/NK 70084) (cd-iss. Apr88; ND 70084)*

Apr 75. (7") <10574> **SPEEDY'S COMING. / THEY NEED A MILLION**

	-	

—— (1975) **RUDY LENNERS** – drums repl. JURGENS

Mar 76. (lp) (RS 1039) <PPL-1 4028> **IN TRANCE**

	-	

– Dark lady / In trance / Life's like a river / Top of the bill / Living and dying / Robot man / Evening wind / Sun in my hand / Longing for fire / Night lights. *(re-iss. Jun83; INTS 5251) (re-iss. 1984 NL/c; NL/NK 70028) (cd-iss. Feb90; ND 70028)*

Nov 76. (7") <10691> **IN TRANCE. / NIGHT LIGHTS**

	-	-

Feb 77. (lp) (PPL1 4225) <APL-1 4225> **VIRGIN KILLERS**

	-	-

– Pictured life / Catch your train / In your park / Backstage queen / Virgin killer / Hell cat / Crying days / Polar nights / Yellow raven. *(re-iss. Apr88 lp/cd; NL/ND 70031)*

—— **HERMAN RAREBELL** (b.18 Nov'53, Lubeck, Germany) – drums (ex-STEPPENWOLF) repl. RUDY

Apr 78. (lp/c) (PL/PK 28309) <APL-1 2628> **TAKEN BY FORCE**

– Steamrock fever / We'll burn the sky / I've got to be free / The riot of your time / The sails of Charon / Your light / He's a woman she's a man / Born to touch your feelings. *(re-iss. Sep81 lp/c; RCA LP/K 3024) (re-iss. Oct88 lp/c/cd; NL/NK/ND 70081)*

Feb 79. (d-lp) (NL 28331) **THE TOKYO TAPES** (live)

– All night long / Pictured life / Backstage queen / Polar nights / In trance / We'll burn the sky / Suspender love / In search of the peace of mind / Fly to the rainbow / He's a woman, she's a man / Speedy's coming / Top of the bill / Hound dog / Long tall Sally / Steamrock fever / Dark lady / Kojo no tsuki / Robot man. *(re-iss. 1984 lp/c; NL/NK 70008) (d-cd-iss. Nov88; PD 70008)*

—— (Dec'78) **MATHIAS JABS** (b.25 Oct'56) – lead guitar repl. ULRICH who formed ELECTRIC SUN. **MICHAEL SCHENKER** also guested on 3 tracks on next album, joining **KLAUS, RUDOLF, HERMAN, FRANCIS + MATHIAS**

Mar 79. (7") <76008> **LOVING YOU SUNDAY MORNING. / COAST TO COAST**

	Harvest	Mercury
	-	-

Apr 79. (lp/c) (SHSP/TC-SHSP 4097) <3795> **LOVEDRIVE**

	36	55

– Loving you Sunday morning / Another piece of meat / Always somewhere / Coast to coast / Can't get enough / Is there anybody there? / Lovedrive / Holiday. *(re-iss. Nov83 on 'Fame' lp/c; FA41 3080-1/-4) (cd-iss. Nov88; CDFA 3080)*

May 79. (7") (HAR 5185) **IS THERE ANYBODY THERE? / ANOTHER PIECE OF MEAT**

	39	-

Aug 79. (7"/12") (HAR/12HAR 5188) **LOVEDRIVE. / COAST TO COAST**

	69	-

Apr 80. (lp/c) (SHSP/TC-SHSP 4113) <3825> **ANIMAL MAGNETISM**

	23	52

– Make it real / Don't make no promises (your body can't keep) / Hold me tight / Twentieth century man / Lady starlight / Fallin' in love / Only a man / The zoo / Animal magnetism. *(re-iss. Aug85 on 'E.M.I.'; ATAK/TC-ATAK 48) (re-iss. May89 on 'Fame' cd/c/lp; CD/TC+/FA 3217)*

May 80. (7") (HAR 5206) <76070> **MAKE IT REAL. / DON'T MAKE NO PROMISES (YOUR BODY CAN'T KEEP)**

	72	-

Jul 80. (7") <76084> **LADY STARLIGHT. /**

Aug 80. (7") (HAR 5212) **THE ZOO. / HOLIDAY**

	75	-

—— In 1981, MICHAEL SCHENKER briefly returned to repl. JABS while MEINE had throat surgery. Everything resumed as 1980 line-up re-appeared in 1982.

Mar 82. (lp/c) (SHVL/TC-SHVL 823) <4039> **BLACKOUT**

	11	10

– Blackout / Can't live without you / No one like you / You give me all I need / Now! / Dynamite / Arizona / China white / When the smoke is going down. *(re-iss. May85 on 'Fame' lp/c; FA/TCFA 3126) (re-iss. Nov88; CDFA 3126)*

Mar 82. (7"/7"pic-d) (HAR/+P 5219) <76153> **NO ONE LIKE YOU. / NOW!**

	64	65 Jun82

Jul 82. (7") (HAR 5221) **CAN'T LIVE WITHOUT YOU. / ALWAYS SOMEWHERE**

	63	-

Feb 84. (7") (HAR 5225) <818440> **ROCK YOU LIKE A HURRICANE. / COMING HOME**

	-	25

Mar 84. (lp/c) (SHSP 24-0007-1/-4) <814981> **LOVE AT FIRST STING**

	17	6

– Bad boys running wild / Rock you like a hurricane / I'm leaving you / Coming home / The same thrill / Big city nights / As soon as the good times roll / Crossfire / Still loving you. *(re-iss. Nov87 on 'E.M.I.' lp/c; ATAK/TC-ATAK 69) (re-iss. Aug89 on 'Fame' cd/c/lp; CD/TC+/FA 3224)*

Aug 84. (7"/12"/12"pic-d) (HAR/12HAR/12HARP 5231) **BIG CITY NIGHTS. / BAD BOYS RUNNING WILD**

		-

Mar 85. (7") (HAR 5232) <880082> **STILL LOVING YOU. / HOLIDAY**

		64 Jun84

(12"+=) (12HAR 5232) – Big city nights.

Jun 85. (d-lp/d-c) (SCORP/TC-SCORP 1) <824344> **WORLD WIDE LIVE** (live)

	18	14

– Countdown / Coming home / Blackout / Bad boys running wild / Loving you Sunday morning / Make it real / Big city nights / Coast to coast / Holiday / Still loving you / Rock you like a hurricane / Can't live without you / Another piece of meat / Dynamite / The zoo / Can't get enough (part 1) / Six string sting / Can't get enough (part 2). *(d-cd-iss. Feb86; CDP 746155-2)*

Jun 85. (7") (HAR 5237) **NO ONE LIKE YOU (live). / THE ZOO (live)**

		-

Apr 88. (cd/c/lp)(pic-lp) (CD/TC+/SHSP 4125) <832963> **SAVAGE AMUSEMENT**

	18	5

– Don't stop at the top / Rhythm of love / Passion rules the game / Media overkill / Walking on the edge / We let it rock ... you let it roll / Every minute every day / Love on the run / Believe in love. *(pic-lp-iss.May88; SHSPP 4125)*

May 88. (7"/7"box/7"pic-d) (HAR/+X/P 5240) <870323> **RHYTHM OF LOVE. / WE LET IT ROCK ... YOU LET IT ROLL**

	59	75

(12"+=) (12HAR 5240) – Love on the run (mix).

Aug 88. (7"/7"pic-d) (HAR 5241) **BELIEVE IN LOVE. / LOVE ON THE RUN**

(12"+=) (12HAR 5241) – ('A'version).

Feb 89. (7") (HAR 5242) **PASSION RULES THE GAME. / EVERY MINUTE EVERY DAY**

	74	

(12"+=)/(12"pic-d+=) (12HAR/+P 5242) – Is there anybody there?
(cd-s++=) (CDHAR 5242) – ('A'extended).

Nov 90. (cd/c/lp) (846908-2/-4/-1) <846908> **CRAZY WORLD**

	Vertigo	Mercury
		21

– Tease me please me / Don't believe her / To be with you in Heaven / Wind of change / Restless nights / Lust or love / Kicks after six / Hit between the eyes / Money and fame / Crazy world / Send me an angel. *(re-dist.Oct91; hit UK No.27)*

Dec 90. (7"/c-s) (VER/+MC 52) **DON'T BELIEVE HER. / KICKS AFTER SIX**

(12"+=)/(12"g-f+=)/(cd-s+=) (VER X/XG/CD 52) – Big city nights / Holiday (live).

Mar 91. (7"red/c-s) (VER/+MC 54) **WIND OF CHANGE. / RESTLESS NIGHTS**

	53	-

(12"red+=) (VERXP 54) – The zoo (live).
(cd-s+=) (VERCD 54) – To be with you in Heaven / Blackout (live).
(12"red+=) (VERPX 54) – Zoo (live).

May 91. (c-s,cd-s) <868180> **WIND OF CHANGE / MONEY AND FAME**

	-	4

Sep 91. (7"/c-s) (VER/+MC 58) **WIND OF CHANGE. / RESTLESS NIGHTS**

	2	-

(12"pic-d+=) VERX 58) – Hit between the eyes / Blackout (live).
(cd-s+=) (VERCD 58) – Blackout (live) / To be with you in Heaven.

Nov 91. (c-s,cd-s) <868956> **SEND ME AN ANGEL / RESTLESS NIGHTS**

	-	44

Nov 91. (7"/c-s) (VER/+MC 60) **SEND ME AN ANGEL. / WIND OF CHANGE (Russian)**

	27	-

(12"+=/cd-s+=) (VER X/CD 60) – Tease me, please me (live) / Lust or love (live).

—— (May'92) BUCHHOLZ departed repl. by **RALPH RIECKERMANN** (b. 8 Aug'??, Lubeck) – bass

Sep 93. (cd/c/lp) (<518280-2/-4/-1>) **FACE THE HEAT**

	Mercury	Mercury
	51	24

– Alien nation / No pain, no gain / Someone to touch / Under the same sun / Unholy alliance / Woman / Hate to be nice / Taxman woman / Ship of fools / Nightmare Avenue / Lonely nights / Destin / Daddy's girl.

Nov 93. (c-s) (MERMC 395) **UNDER THE SAME SUN / SHIP OF FOOLS**

(12"+=) (12MER 395) – Alien nation / Rubber fucker.
(cd-s++=) (MERCD 395) – Partners in crime.

Apr 95. (cd) (526903-2) **LIVE BITES** (live)

– Tease me, please me / Is anybody / Rhythm of love / In trance / No pain no gain / When the smoke is going down / Ave Maria no morro / Living for tomorrow / Concerto in V / Alien nation / Hit between the eyes / Crazy world / Wind of change / Heroes don't cry / White dove.

—— line-up **KLAUS, RUDOLF, MATTHIAS + RALPH** were joined by **CURT CRESS + PITTI HECHT** – drums / **LUKE HERZOG + KOEN VAN BAEL** – keyboards

May 96. (cd/c/lp) (0630 14524-2) <82913> **PURE INSTINCT**

	East West	Atlantic
		99

– Wild child / But the best for you / Does anyone know / Stone in my shoe / Soul behind the face / Oh girl (I wanna be with you) / When you came into my life / Where the river flows / Time will call your name / You and I / Are you the one?

Jun 96. (c-s/cd-s) (W 0042 C/CD) **YOU AND I / SHE'S KNOCKING AT MY DOOR / YOU AND I (extended)**

		-

Mar 99. (7"pic-d) (COLA 074) **TO BE NO.1. / MIND LIKE A TREE**

	Coalition – eastwest	Coalition – eastwest

(cd-s+=) (COLA 074CD) – ('A'-CD-Rom version).

Mar 99. (cd) <(3984 26830-2)> **EYE TO EYE**

– Mysterious / To be No.1 / Obsession / 10 light years away / Mind like a tree / Eye to eye / What you give you get back / Skywriter / Yellow butterfly / Freshly squeezed / Priscilla / Du bist so schmutzig / Aleyah / Moment is a million years.

– compilations, etc. –

on 'R.C.A.' unless mentioned otherwise

Nov 79. (12"ep) (PC 9402) **ALL NIGHT LONG / FLYING TO THE RAINBOW. / SPEEDY'S COMING / IN TRANCE**

		-

Sep 81. (lp/c) (RCA LP/K 3035) <3516> **THE BEST OF THE SCORPIONS**

		Nov79

– Steamrock fever / Pictured life / Robot man / Backstage queen / Speedy's coming / Hell-cat / He's a woman, she's a man / In trance / Dark lady / The sails of Charon / Virgin killer. *(re-iss. Feb89 lp/c/cd; NL/NK/ND 74006)*

Nov 89. (cd/c/lp) E.M.I.; (CD/TC+/EMD 1014) / Mercury; <842002> **BEST OF ROCKERS 'N' BALLADS**

		43

(re-iss. Sep91 on 'Fame'; CD/TC FA 3262)

Feb 90. (lp/c/cd) (NL/NK/ND 74517) <5085> **THE BEST OF THE SCORPIONS, VOL.2**

		Jul84

Feb 90. (cd) (ND 70672) **HOT AND HEAVY**

Nov 90. (cd/c/lp) E.M.I.; (CD/TC+/EMC 3586) **STILL LOVING YOU** *(re-iss. Feb92 cd/c/lp; CD/TC+/EMD 1031)*

Dec 90. (cd/c/lp) Connoisseur; (VSOP CD/MC/LP 156) **HURRICANE ROCK**

		-

Oct 91. (3xcd-box) E.M.I.; (CDS 797963-2) **SCORPIONS 3 CD SET**
– (WORLDWIDE LIVE / SAVAGE AMUSEMENT / ROCKERS 'N' BALLADS)

Dec 91. (cd/c) (ND/NK 75029) **HOT AND SLOW (THE BEST OF THE BALLADS)**

		-

Sep 93. (cd) (74321 15119-2) **HOT AND HARD**

Feb 95. (cd) E.M.I.; (CDEMC 3698) **DEADLY STING**

		-

Mike SCOTT (see under ⇒ WATERBOYS)

Gil SCOTT-HERON

Born: 1 Apr'49, Chicago, Illinois, USA. The son of a footballer father (who enjoyed a spell with Glasgow Celtic) and a librarian mother, SCOTT-HERON spent the bulk of his childhood in Jackson, Tennessee, raised by his grandmother following his parents' separation. By the time GIL was back living with his mother in New York and attending high school, he had already begun to master piano, his precocious talent for writing subsequently recognised by one of his teachers and leading to SCOTT-HERON completing his studies at noted private school, Fieldston. From there he moved on to Lincoln University, following in the footsteps of his literary hero, Langston Hughes, and subsequently taking a year out to write his first novel, 'The Vulture' (recently republished by the illustrious Canongate Books imprint, Payback Press!). Musically, SCOTT-HERON cited influences as diverse as RICHIE HAVENS, BILLIE HOLIDAY, OTIS REDDING and JOSE FELICIANO; more obvious was the radical style of THE LAST POETS (who, after witnessing their show in Ohio, allegedly inspired SCOTT-HERON to take up performing) as well as the melting pot of African and Latin sounds that echoed through the Chelsea district of New York where he lived. GIL made his recording debut with 'SMALL TALK AT 125th AND LENOX' (1972), a set largely comprised of poems set to a sparse percussive backing, released on Bob Thiele's 'Flying Dutchman' label. Updating the tradition of the African griot, SCOTT-HERON laid out an uncompromising manifesto for the black man, executed with mordant humour and sly wit and railing against consumerism, drug-addled hippies, false prophets and white oppression. The record's worth hearing for the brilliant 'WHITEY ON THE MOON' alone, that's if you can stomach the rampant homophobia of 'THE SUBJECT WAS FAGGOTS'; clearly, SCOTT-HERON's vision of a brighter tomorrow had no place for gay men. Nevertheless, 'PIECES OF A MAN' (1973) was a stunning, often tenderly poignant follow-up, benefiting from a fuller sound courtesy of keys player/co-writer, BRIAN JACKSON, along with such notable players as BERNARD PURDIE, RON CARTER and flautist HUBERT LAWS. 'LADY DAY AND JOHN COLTRANE' remains one of GIL's most uplifting songs, the singer stepping off the soapbox for once and celebrating the power of music. In stark contrast, 'THE REVOLUTION WILL NOT BE TELEVISED' was SCOTT-HERON at his most glaringly effective, ominously intoning the death-knell for white, middle class inertia over a hypnotic, stinging bassline. Often cited as one of the earliest prototype rap tracks, its most readily identifiable antecedent was 'Television, Drug Of The Nation' by THE DISPOSABLE HEROES OF HIP HOPRISY, a group closer in spirit to SCOTT-HERON's work than many rap acts. But the man was most affecting when he addressed the everyday tragedies of human experience; any listener not moved by the likes of 'PIECES OF A MAN' and 'HOME IS WHERE THE HATRED IS' must have a heart of steel. Following his departure from 'Flying Dutchman', SCOTT-HERON recorded 'WINTER IN AMERICA' (1974) on the US independent, 'Strata East'. As well as the atmospheric lament of the title track, the album featured one of the singer's most famous tracks, 'THE BOTTLE' a much covered, funky, flute-driven testament to the dangers of alcohol. The following year, he signed to the newly formed 'Arista', scoring a Top 30 album with 'THE FIRST MINUTE OF A NEW DAY' (1975). Co-credited to BRIAN JACKSON, the album was the first to feature The MIDNIGHT BAND, a backing troupe which the pair led right through into the 80's with varying line-ups. The record also provided a minor US R&B hit with the disco-influenced 'JOHANNESBURG', once again conclusively proving that dancefloor didn't necessarily mean braindead. Throughout the latter part of the 70's and on into the early 80's, SCOTT-HERON maintained an impressively consistent, unusually prolific recording schedule, his coffee-rich vocals and enduring blend of jazz, blues and soul providing an often lone voice of sanity in the decadent, coke-fuelled music scene of the time. As well as documenting the very real threat of nuclear power ('WE ALMOST LOST DETROIT', 'SHUT 'EM DOWN'), he continued to address the concerns of working-class blacks ('INNER CITY BLUES', 'BLUE COLLAR') and the contentious issue of drugs ('ANGEL DUST'). His scathing political commentary also continued apace, 'B-MOVIE', from the acclaimed 'REFLECTIONS' (1981) set, nailing the newly elected REAGAN with pinpoint accuracy. It's all the more ironic, then, that SCOTT-HERON releases petered out after the early 80's, the singer falling prey to the drug and alcohol abuse he'd spoken out so militantly against throughout his career. Maybe the state of politics (US and British) was just too much for him to take. After all, if SCOTT-HERON's articulate defence of humanist principles was ever needed at all, it was in the moral wasteland of that vilified decade. Though a belated comeback album, 'SPIRITS' (1994), failed to impress many fans, SCOTT-HERON continues to tour ceaselessly, his live show still impressive if you're lucky enough to catch him on a good night. Though his golden period may be over, arguably, GIL has nothing left to prove, his back catalogue standing up amongst the cream of black music history. • **Covered:** INNER CITY BLUES (Marvin Gaye) / GRANDMA'S HANDS (Bill Withers). GIL was the original voice-over for the "You know you've been Tangoed" TV ad. LaBELLE covered his song 'THE REVOLUTION WILL NOT BE TELEVISED' in 1974.

Album rating: SMALL TALK AT 125th AND LENOX (*6) / FREE WILL (*7) / PIECES OF A MAN (*7) / WINTER IN AMERICA (*7) / THE REVOLUTION WILL NOT BE TELEVISED compilation (*8) / THE FIRST MINUTE OF A NEW DAY with Brian Jackson (*7) / FROM SOUTH AFRICA TO SOUTH CAROLINA with Brian Jackson (*7) / IT'S YOUR WORLD with Brian Jackson (*6) / BRIDGES with Brian Jackson (*6) / SECRETS with Brian Jackson (*6) / 1980 with Brian Jackson (*6) / REAL

EYES (*6) / REFLECTIONS (*7) / MOVING TARGET (*5) / THE BEST OF GIL SCOTT-HERON compilation (*7) / THE TALES OF GIL SCOTT-HERON AND THE AMNESIA EXPRESS (*6) / SPIRITS (*8) / GHETTO STYLE compilation (*8)

GIL SCOTT-HERON – vocals, piano, guitar

		Philips	Flying Dutchman
1970.	(lp) **SMALL TALK AT 125th AND LENOX** (rap poems)	-	☐

– Introduction – The revolution will not be televised / Omen / Brother / Comment #1 / Small talk at 125th & Lenox / The subject was faggots / Evolution (and flashback) / Plastic pattern people / Whitey on the moon / The vulture / Enough / Paint it black / Who'll pay reparations on my soul? / Everyday. *(cd-iss. Jun97 on 'RCA Victor'; 07863 66611-2)*

1972.	(lp) *<10153>* **FREE WILL**	-	☐

– Free will / The middle of your day / The get out of the ghetto blues / Speed kills / Did you hear what they said? / The King Alfred plan / No knock / Wiggy / Ain't no new thing / Bill Green is dead / Sex education: ghetto style / . . .And then he wrote (meditations).

— added **BRIAN JACKSON** – keyboards / **DANNY BOWENS** – bass / **BOB ADAMS** – drums

Apr 73.	(lp) *(6369 415) <10143>* **PIECES OF A MAN**	☐	☐

– Lady Day and John Coltrane / When you are who you are / The revolution will not be televised / Home is where the hatred is / I think I'll call it morning / Save the children / The needle's eye / Pieces of a man / A sign of the ages / Or down you fall / The prisoner.

Apr 73.	(7") *(6073 705)* **WHEN YOU ARE WHO YOU ARE. / LADY DAY AND JOHN COLTRANE**	☐	☐

		R.C.A.	Flying Dutchman
Jul 75.	(lp) *(SF 8428) <BXL1-0613>* **THE REVOLUTION WILL NOT BE TELEVISED**	☐	Mar74

– The revolution will not be televised / Sex education: ghetto style / The get out of the ghetto blues / No knock / Lady Day and John Coltrane / Pieces of a man / Home is where the hatred is / Brother / Save the children / Did you hear what they said? *(cd-iss. May89 on 'Bluebird-RCA' lp/c/cd+=; NL/NK/ND 86994)* – (extra track).

		not iss.	Stata East
1974.	(lp) *<19742>* **WINTER IN AMERICA**	-	☐

– Peace go with you brother / Rivers of my father / A very precious time / Back home / The bottle / Song for Bobby Smith / Your daddy loves you / H2o gate blues / Peace go with you brother. *(cd-iss. Sep92; 66051015) (cd re-iss. Mar99 on 'Charly'; CDGR 225)*

GIL SCOTT-HERON & BRIAN JACKSON

— next featured The MIDNIGHT BAND

— **JOSEF BLOCKER + REGGIE BRISBANE** – drums repl. ADAMS

		Arista	Arista
Jul 75.	(lp) *(ARTY 106) <4030>* **THE FIRST MINUTE OF A NEW DAY**	☐	30 Jun75

– Offering / The liberation song (red, black and green) / Must be something / Ain't no such thing as Superman / Pardon our analysis (we beg your pardon America) / Winter in America / Guerilla / Western sunrise / Alluswe. *(cd-iss. Feb99 on 'TVT'; 4350)*

Jul 75.	(7") *<0117>* **AIN'T NO SUCH THING AS SUPERMAN. / WE BEG YOUR PARDON AMERICA**	-	☐
Oct 75.	(7") *(ARIST 23) <0152>* **(WHAT'S THE WORD) JOHANNESBURG. / FELL TOGETHER**	☐	☐
Jan 76.	(lp) *(ARTY 121) <4044>* **FROM SOUTH AFRICA TO SOUTH CAROLINA**	☐	Oct75

– (What's the word) Johannesburg / A toast to the people / The summer of '42 / Beinnings (first minute of a new day) / South Carolina (Barnwell) / Essex / Fell together / A lovely day.

Nov 76.	(7") *<0225>* **THE BOTTLE. /**	-	-
Nov 76.	(lp) *(DARTY 1) <5001>* **IT'S YOUR WORLD (live)**	☐	☐

– Seventeenth street / Tomorrow's trane (gospel trane) / Must be something / It's your world / New York City / The bottle / Possum Slim / Home is where the hatred is / Bicentennial blues / Sharing.

— **JOSEF BLOCKER + REGGIE BRISBANE** – drums repl. ADAMS

Dec 77.	(lp) *(SPARTY 1031) <4147>* **BRIDGES**	☐	Oct77

– Hello Sunday! hello road! / Song of the wind / Racetrack in France / Vildgolia (deaf, dumb and blind) / Under the hammer / We almost lost Detroit / Tuskeegee No.626 / Delta man (where I'm coming from) / 95 South (all of the places we've been).

Dec 77.	(7") *(ARIST 169)* **HELLO SUNDAY, HELLO ROAD. / THE BOTTLE (live)**	☐	-
Dec 77.	(7") *<0285>* **HELLO SUNDAY, HELLO ROAD. / SONG OF THE WIND**	-	☐
Mar 78.	(7") *<0317>* **UNDER THE HAMMER. / RACETRACK IN FRANCE**	-	☐

— **GREG PHILLINGANES** – keyboards repl. BOWENS

Jul 78.	(7") *<0366>* **ANGEL DUST. / THIRD WORLD REVOLUTION**	-	☐
Sep 78.	(lp) *(SPARTY 1073) <4189>* **SECRETS**	☐	61

– Angel dust / Madison Avenue / Cane / Third world revolution / Better days ahead / Three miles down / Angola, Louisiana / Show bizness / A prayer for everybody / To be free.

Oct 78.	(7") *(ARIST 215) <0390>* **SHOW BIZNESS. / BETTER DAYS AHEAD**	☐	☐

— retained only **JACKSON** + recruited **ED GRADY** – guitar / **KENNY POWELL** – drums / **GLEN TURNER** – keyboards / **CARL CORNWALL + VERNON JAMES** – tenor sax, flute / **KENNY SHEFFIELD** – trumpet

Feb 80.	(lp) *<9514>* **1980**	-	82

– Shut 'um down / Alien / Willing / Corners / 1980 / Push comes to shove / Shah mot / Late last night. *(UK-iss.Jul85; 201733)*

Mar 80.	(7"/ext-12") *<0488>* **SHUT 'UM DOWN. / BALTIMORE**	-	☐
May 80.	(7") *<0505>* **WILLIN'. /**	-	☐

GIL SCOTT-HERON

Dec 80. (lp) <9540> **REAL EYES**
 – The train from Washington / Not needed / Waiting for the axe to fall / Combinations / A legend in his own mind / You could be my brother / The Klan / Your daddy loves you.

Dec 80. (7") <0583> **LEGEND IN HIS OWN MIND. /**

Aug 81. (7") <0634> **STORM MUSIC. /**

Oct 81. (7") <0647> **B-MOVIE. /**

Dec 81. (lp) (SPARTY 1180) <9566> **REFLECTIONS**
 – Storm music / Grandma's hands / Is that jazz? / Morning thoughts / Inner city blues (poem – The siege of New Orleans) / Gun / B-movie. (cd-iss. Feb97; 254094)

Feb 82. (7") (ARIST 452) **STORM MUSIC. / B-MOVIE**
 (12"+=) (ARIST12 452) – Gun.

Sep 82. (7") **FAST LANE. / BLUE COLLAR**

Sep 82. (lp) (204921) <9606> **MOVING TARGET**
 – Fast lane / Washington D.C. / No exit / Blue collar / Ready or not / Explanations / Black history – The word. (cd-iss. Feb97; 254921)

May 83. (7") (ARIST 527) **(WHAT'S THE WORD) JOHANNESBURG. / WAITING FOR THE AXE TO FALL**
 (12"+=) (ARIST12 527) – B-Movie (intro, poem, song).

Aug 84. (7") (ARIST 573) **RE-RON, / B-MOVIE**
 (12") (ARIST12 573) – Re-Ron (the missing brain mix). / B-Movie (intro, poem, song).

Sep 84. (lp/c) (206/406 618) **THE BEST OF GIL SCOTT-HERON**
 (compilation)
 – The revolution will not be televised / The bottle / Winter in America / Ain't no such thing as Superman / Re-Ron / Shut 'em down / Angel dust / B-movie. (cd-iss. Apr88; 256 618)

Nov 85. (7"/10") (ARIST/+10 643) **WINTER IN AMERICA. / JOHANNESBURG**

——— now with **ROBBIE GORDON** – bass, percussion / **RON HOLLOWAY** – saxophone

	Essential	Rykodisc

Mar 90. (7") (GILL 003) **SPACE SHUTTLE (vocal). / ('A'original mix)**
 (12"+=) (GILT 003) – ('A'deep club mix) / Pieces of gold – medley.
 (12"+=) (GILTY 003) – ('A'deep club dub) / War is very ugly.
 (cd-s+=) (GILTX 003) – The bottle / Pieces of gold – medley.

Mar 90. (cd/c/d-lp) (ESD CD/MC/LP 201) **THE TALES OF GIL SCOTT-HERON AND HIS AMNESIA EXPRESS (live)**
 – Washington DC / Save the children / Angel dust / Gun / Blue collar / Amen (hold on to your dream) / Three miles down / The bottle.

	Mother	T.V.T.

Jul 94. (cd/c) (MUM CD/C 9415) <TVT 43102> **SPIRITS**
 – Message to the messengers / Spirits / Give her a call / Laly's song / Spirits past / The other side (parts 1-3) / Work for peace / Don't give up. (lp-iss.Mar99 on 'TVT'; same as US)

Oct 94. (12"/cd-s) **DON'T GIVE UP. / MESSAGE TO THE MESSENGERS / THE BOTTLE (live)**

– others, etc. –

Jul 80. (7"/12"; GIL SCOTT-HERON & BRIAN JACKSON)
 Inferno; (HEAT 23/+12) **THE BOTTLE (drunken mix). / THE BOTTLE (sober mix)**
 (re-iss. Jan81 on 'Champagne' 7"/12"; VAT/+S 302)

1981. (lp) Audio Fidelity; (1017) **THE BOTTLE (1973)**

Mar 88. (12"m) Old Gold; (OG 4054) **THE BOTTLE. / JOHANNESBURG / WINTER IN AMERICA**

Nov 90. (d-cd) Arista; (353913) **GLORY (THE GIL SCOTT-HERON COLLECTION)**

Apr 94. (cd/c) Castle; (CCS CD/MC 403) **MINISTRY OF INFORMATION (live)**
 – Winter in America / Alien / The bottle / Is that jazz / Washington DC / Gun / B-movie.

Nov 98. (cd) Camden-BMG; (74321 628062) **GHETTO STYLE**
 – The revolution will not be televised / Or down you fall / The needle's eye / I think I'll call it morning / When you are who you are / Save the children / Did you hear what they said? / Free will / Speed kills / Middle of your day / Pieces of a man / A sign of the ages / The get out of the ghetto blues / Lady day & John Coltrane / Home is where the hatred is / No knock / The revolution will not be televised (early version) / Sex education ghetto style / Small talk at 125th & Lenox / King Alfred plan / Billy Green is dead.

Oct 99. (12")(cd-s) Joeboy; (JBV 008)(JBCD 017) **THE BOTTLE**

SCREAMING BLUE MESSIAHS (dig out; Great Alt & Indie . . .)

SCREAMING TREES

Formed: Ellensburg, Washington, USA . . . 1985 by girthsome brothers VAN and GARY LEE CONNER along with frontman MARK LANEGAN and drummer MARK PICKEREL. Following early effort, 'CLAIRVOYANCE' (1986) for the tiny 'Velvetone' label, the group signed to respected US indie, 'S.S.T.', making their debut with the convincing 'EVEN IF AND ESPECIALLY WHEN' (1987). Fuelled by raging punk, The SCREAMING TREES were nevertheless characterised by the spectral hue of 60's psychedelia running through much of their music, LANEGAN's exotic, JIM MORRISON-esque vocals adding an air of brooding mystery on the likes of fans favourite, 'TRANSFIGURATION'. Another couple of stirring sets, 'INVISIBLE LANTERN' (1988) and 'BUZZ FACTORY' (1989) followed before the band released a one-off EP for 'Sub Pop'. With the emerging grunge phenomenon in nearby Seattle on the cusp of world domination, The SCREAMING TREES were obviously a promising prospect for major label A&R and it came as little surprise when they signed for 'Epic'. That same year, prior to their debut for the label, the various 'TREES occupied themselves with solo projects,

GARY LEE forming PURPLE OUTSIDE and releasing 'MYSTERY LANE', while brother VAN issued the eponymous 'SOLOMON GRUNDY' set the same year, both appearing on 'New Alliance'. Best of the lot, however, was LANEGAN's windswept 'WINDING SHEET', an intense, largely acoustic collection featuring a cover of Leadbelly's 'WHERE DID YOU SLEEP LAST NIGHT' (as later covered in frightening style by KURT COBAIN). Co-produced by CHRIS CORNELL, the subsequent SCREAMING TREES effort, 'UNCLE ANAESTHASIA' (1991), saw the group moving towards a more overt 70's rock sound, while 'SWEET OBLIVION' (1992) saw PICKEREL replaced with BARRETT MARTIN on a more low-key set which stood at odds with the grunge tag unwillingly forced on the band. Augmented by such Seattle "luminaries" as TAD and DAN PETERS (MUDHONEY) along with DINOSAUR JR.'s J. MASCIS, LANEGAN cut an acclaimed solo follow-up, 'WHISKEY FOR THE HOLY GHOST' (1993), before beginning the long and arduous work on the material which would eventually come to make up 'DUST' (1996). Widely held up as the group's most affecting work to date, the George Drakoulias-produced album perfectly captured their threadbare grit and world-weary mysticism, the disparate elements of their sound finally fusing in harmony and exorcising the lingering spirit of grunge. During the latter part of the 90's, LANEGAN was again a solo artist, two albums for 'Sub Pop' ('Beggars Banquet' in Britain), 'SCRAPS AT MIDNIGHT' (1998) and 'I'LL TAKE CARE OF YOU' (1999), being released to mixed response and sliding out of the hard/grunge-rock circle. • **Covered:** SLIDE MACHINE (13th Floor Elevators). • **Note:** Not to be confused with the English band on 'Native' records.

Album rating: OTHER WORLDS mini (*4) / EVEN IF AND ESPECIALLY WHEN (*7) / INVISIBLE LANTERN (*5) / BUZZ FACTORY mini (*5) / UNCLE ANAESTHESIA (*6) / ANTHOLOGY – THE S.S.T. YEARS 1985-1989 compilation (*7) / SWEET OBLIVION (*7) / DUST (*9) / Mark Lanegan: THE WINDING SHEET (*6) / WHISKEY FOR THE HOLY GHOST (*7) / SCRAPS AT MIDNIGHT (*6) / I'LL TAKE CARE OF YOU (*8)

MARK LANEGAN (b.25 Nov'64) – vocals / **GARY LEE CONNER** (b.22 Aug'62, Fort Irwin, Calif.) – guitar, vocals / **VAN CONNER** (b.17 Mar'67, Apple Valley, Calif.) – bass, vocals / **MARK PICKEREL** – drums, percussion

	not iss.	Velvetone

1986. (m-lp) **CLAIRVOYANCE**

	S.S.T.	S.S.T.

Feb 87. (m-lp/m-cd) <SST/+C/CD 105> **OTHER WORLDS**
 – Like I said / Pictures in my mind / Turning / Other worlds / Barriers / Now your mind is next to mine. (UK-iss.May93; same as US)

Sep 87. (lp/cd) <SST 132/+CD> **EVEN IF AND ESPECIALLY WHEN**
 – Transfiguration / Straight out to any place / World painted / Don't look down / Girl behind the mask / Flying / Cold rain / Other days and different planets / The pathway / You know where it's at / Back together / In the forest. (cd re-iss. May93; same)

Sep 88. (lp/c/cd) <SST 188/+C/CD)> **INVISIBLE LANTERN**
 – Ivy / Walk through to the other side / Line & circles / Shadow song / Grey diamond desert / Smokerings / The second I awake / Invisible lantern / Even if / Direction of the sun / Night comes creeping / She knows.

Mar 89. (m-lp/m-cd) <SST 248/+CD> **BUZZ FACTORY**
 – Where the twain shall meet / Windows / Black sun morning / Too far away / Subtle poison / Yard trip / Flower web / Wish bringer / Revelation revolution / The looking glass cracked / End of the universe.

	Glitterhouse	Sub Pop

Dec 89. (d7"w /1-white) (GR 80) <SP 48B> **CHANGE HAS COME. / DAYS / / FLASHES. / TIME SPEAKS HER GOLDEN TONGUE**
 (re-iss. Dec90 cd-ep+=; GRCD 80) – I've seen you before. (re-iss. May93; same)

——— LEE CONNER also formed PURPLE OUTSIDE in 1990, releasing 'MYSTERY LANE'. Brother VAN with SOLOMON GRUNDY issued eponymous same year also for 'New Alliance'.

	Epic	Epic

Oct 90. (12"ep) <73539> **UNCLE ANAESTHESIA / WHO LIES IN DARKNESS. / OCEAN OF CONFUSION / SOMETHING ABOUT TODAY (numb inversion version)**

Jun 91. (cd/c/lp) (467 307-2/-4/-1) <EK 46800> **UNCLE ANAESTHESIA**   Mar91
 – Beyond this horizon / Bed of roses / Uncle anaesthesia / Story of her fate / Caught between / Lay your head down / Before we arise / Something about today / Alice said / Time for light / Disappearing / Ocean of confusion / Closer.

——— **BARRETT MARTIN** (b.14 Apr'67, Olympia, Washington) – drums repl. PICKEREL who later joined TRULY

Oct 92. (cd/c/lp) (471 724-2/-4/-1) <48996> **SWEET OBLIVION**
 – Shadow of the season / Nearly lost you / Dollar bill / More or less / Butterfly / For celebrations past / The secret kind / Winter song / Troubled times / No one knows / Julie Paradise.

Feb 93. (12"ep/pic-cd-ep) (658 237-6/-2) **NEARLY LOST YOU. / E.S.K. / SONG OF A BAKER / WINTER SONG (acoustic)**   50   -

Apr 93. (7"pic-d) (659 179-7) **DOLLAR BILL. / (THERE'LL BE) PEACE IN THE VALLEY FOR ME (acoustic)**   52   -
 (12"colrd+=/cd-s+=) (659 179-6/-2) – Tomorrow's dream.

Jul 96. (cd/c/lp) (483 980-2/-4/-1) <64178> **DUST**   32
 – Halo of ashes / All I know / Look at you / Dying days / Make my mind / Sworn and broken / Witness / Traveler / Dime western / Gospel plow.

Sep 96. (7") (663 351-7) **ALL I KNOW. / WASTED TIME**
 (cd-s+=) (663 351-2) – Silver tongue.
 (cd-s) (663 351-5) – ('A'side) / Dollar bill / Nearly lost you / Winter song (acoustic).

Nov 96. (7"white) (663 870-7) **SWORN AND BROKEN. / BUTTERFLY**   -
 (cd-s+=) (663 870-2) – Dollar bill (U.S. radio session) / Caught between – The secret kind (U.S. radio session).

——— on a long holiday from each other, maybe for ever, VAN CONNER now moonlighting in VALIS with DAN PETERS of MUDHONEY, while BARRETT plays on tour with R.E.M., while joining PETER BUCK's supergroup, TUATARA. LANEGAN continued solo (see below)

– compilations, others, etc. –

Nov 91. (d-lp/d-cd) <(SST 260/+CD)> **ANTHOLOGY . . . THE S.S.T. YEARS 1985-1989**

MARK LANEGAN

—— with on first **MICHAEL JOHNSON** – guitar / **JACK ENDINO** – bass, guitar / **KURT COBAIN** – guitar, vocals / **CHRIS NOVOSELIC** – bass / **MARK PICKEREL** – drums / **STEVE FISK** – keyboards

               Glitterhouse Sub Pop

May 90. (red-lp/cd) (GR 085/+CD) <SP 61> **THE WINDING SHEET**
– Mockingbirds / Museum / Undertow / Ugly Sunday / Down in the dark / Wild flowers / Eyes of a child / The winding sheet / Woe / Ten feet tall / Where did you sleep last night? / Juarez / I love you little girl. (c+cd+=) – I love you little girl. (re-iss. Apr94 & Oct99; same).
Sep 90. (7") **DOWN IN THE DARK. /**

—— next w / **J.MASCIS + MARK JOHNSON** (Dinosaur Jr.) / **TAD DOYLE** (Tad) / **DAN PETERS** (Mudhoney) / **KURT FEDORA** (Gobblehoof)

               Sub Pop   Sub Pop

Jan 94. (lp/cd) <(SP/+CD 78249)> **WHISKEY FOR THE HOLY GHOST**
– The river rise / Borracho / House a home / Kingdoms of rain / Carnival / Riding the nightingale / El Sol / Dead on you / Shooting gallery / Sunrise / Pendulum / Jesus touch / Beggar's blues. (cd re-iss. Oct99; SPCD 132)
May 94. (cd-ep) <(SPCD 131-327)> **HOUSE A HOME / SHOOTING GALLERY / UGLY SUNDAY / SUNRISE**

               Beggars
               Banquet   Sub Pop

Jul 98. (cd) (BBQCD 204) <SP 419> **SCRAPS AT MIDNIGHT**
– Hospital roll call / Hotel / Stay / Black bell ocean / Last one in the world / Wheels / Waiting on a train / Day and night / Praying ground / Because of this.
Sep 98. (7"colrd) (BBQ 328) **STAY. / SLIDE MACHINE**
(cd-s+=) – (BBQ 328CD) – Death don't have no mercy.
Sep 99. (cd/lp) (BBQ CD/LP 215) **I'LL TAKE CARE OF YOU**
– Carry home / I'll take care of you / Shiloh town / Creeping coastline of lights / Ba dee da / Consider me / On Jesus program / Little Sadie / Together again / Shanty man's life / Boogie boogie.

SCRITTI POLITTI

Formed: London, England . . . late '77 by Leeds art student (and former Young Communist), 'GREEN' GARTSIDE, along with NIAL JINKS and TOM MORLEY. Politically motivated punks, their first release, 'SKANK BLOC BOLOGNA' (issued on their own 'St. Pancras' label) created enough interest for a John Peel session, the tracks subsequently released on 'Rough Trade' in 1979. By the time of the release of the classic 'SWEETEST GIRL' single in summer '81, only MORLEY remained from the original line-up, GREEN now steering the band in an altogether more endearing new-wave art-pop/white reggae vein. The track (which featured the piano talents of ROBERT WYATT) was a minor chart hit, likewise the follow-up singles, 'FAITHLESS' and 'JERUSALEM'. All three were included on the much anticipated debut set, 'SONGS TO REMEMBER' (1982), GREEN's dreamy falsetto, musical eclecticism and unerring way with an insidious pop hook (not to mention clever-clever lyrics) making him – by this juncture SCRITTI POLITTI were basically a studio vehicle for GREEN – a critical darling and one of 'Rough Trade's most unlikely success stories; the album almost made the UK Top 10, becoming the label's biggest selling release to date. Subsequently relocating to New York and moving up to 'Virgin', GREEN sought out such accomplished US musicians as MARCUS MILLER (former bassist for MILES DAVIS), who accompanied him on his first (UK) Top 10 hit, 'WOOD BEEZ (PLAY LIKE ARETHA FRANKLIN)' in 1984. A succession of different sessioners played on subsequent singles, 'ABSOLUTE', 'HYPNOTISE' and 'THE WORD GIRL', although FRED MAHER and DAVID GAMSON went on to augment GREEN on the follow-up album, 'CUPID AND PSYCHE' '85 (1985). Again including all the singles, this slick set of Arif Mardin-produced dancefloor pop-soul also included 'PERFECT WAY', the track which broke SCRITTI POLITTI (albeit briefly) in the States and was later given the honour of a cover by aforementioned jazz legend, MILES DAVIS. The trumpeter also contributed to 'OH PATTI (DON'T FEEL SORRY FOR LOVERBOY)', GREEN's first single after three years of beavering away in the studio. The accompanying album, 'PROVISION' (1988), further refined the man's luxuriant pop vision with an altogether more straightforward approach, GAMSON again providing the lush synth textures. Despite the quality, further singles, 'FIRST BOY IN TOWN (LOVESICK)' and 'BOOM! THERE SHE WAS' lingered in the lower regions of the singles chart. After another interminable lay-off, GREEN returned in 1991 for a Top 20 collaborative cover of The Beatles' 'SHE'S A WOMAN' with ragga loveman, SHABBA RANKS, while a further duet with SWEETIE IRIE (a version of Gladys Knight's hit, 'TAKE ME IN YOUR ARMS') was not quite so successful. With no album forthcoming in the early/mid 90's, it did seem as if GREEN had finally abandoned SCRITTI POLITTI as a front for his musical activities, although seemed likely that this pop maverick would emerge at one point in one form or another. Ah, to see a prophecy come true. Re-inventing himself as a bearded rapper type (well his backing group were anyhow), GREEN and SCRITTI POLITTI came storming back from oblivion on the long-awaited fourth set, 'ANOMIE AND BONHOMIE' (1999). • **Trivia:** SCRITTI POLITTI is nearly Italian for political writing. MADNESS had a 1986 hit with 'THE SWEETEST GIRL'.

That year also saw GREEN and GAMSON write the title track for AL JARREAU's album, 'L IS For Lover'.

Album rating: SONGS TO REMEMBER (*8) / CUPID & PSYCHE (*7) / PROVISION (*4) / ANOMIE AND BONHOMIE (*6)

GREEN (b. GREEN STROHMEYER-GARTSIDE, 22 Jun'56, Cardiff, Wales) – vox, guitar / **TOM MORLEY** – linn drum / **MATTHEW 'K'** – programme organiser / **NIAL JINKS** – bass

               St.Pancras   not iss.

Nov 78. (7") (SCRIT 1) **SKANC BLOG BOLOGNA. / IS AND OUGHT OF THE WESTERN WORLD**

               Rough Trade   not iss.

Sep 79. (12"ep) (RT 027T) **4 A SIDES**
– Doubt beat / Confidences / Bibbly O'tek / P.A.'s.
Nov 79. (7"ep) (SCRIT 2 – RT 034) **WORK IN PROGRESS** (PEEL SESSIONS)
– Hegamony / Scritlocks door / Opec-Immac / Messthetics.

—— added **MIKE MacEVOY** – synthesizers, vocoder / **MGOTSE** – d.bass / guest **ROBERT WYATT** – piano

Aug 81. (7"/12") (RT 091/+T) **THE SWEETEST GIRL. / LIONS AFTER SLUMBER**   64   –

—— **JOE CANG** – bass repl. NIAL / **STEVE SIDWELL** – trumpet / **JAMIE TALBOT** – saxophone repl. MGOTSE

Apr 82. (7"/12") (RT 107/+T) **FAITHLESS. / FAITHLESS PART II (instrumental)**   56   –
Jul 82. (7"/7"pic-d) (RT 111/+P) **ASYLUMS IN JERUSALEM. / JAQUES DERRIDA**   43   –
(12"+=) (RT 111T) – ('A'extended).
Aug 82. (lp) (ROUGH/+C 20) **SONGS TO REMEMBER**   12   –
– Asylums in Jerusalem / A slow soul / Jacques Derrida / Lions after slumber / Faithless / Sex / Rock-a-boy blue / Gettin' havin' & holdin' / The sweetest girl. (cd-iss. May87; ROUGH/+CD 20)

—— **GREEN** recruited US musicians **MARCUS MILLER** – bass (ex-MILES DAVIS) / **STEVE FERRONE** – drums (ex-BRIAN AUGER) / **PAUL JACKSON Jnr.** – guitar / (MORLEY went solo and released one 1985 single for 'Zarjazz', 'WHO BROKE THE LOVE?')

               Virgin   Warners

Mar 84. (7"/7"pic-d) (VS 657/+P) <28811> **WOOD BEEZ (PLAY LIKE ARETHA FRANKLIN). / ('A'dub)**   10   91 Jan86
(12"+=) (VS 657T) – ('A'extended).

—— **GREEN** with **ROBBIE BUCHANAN + DAVID FRANK** – keyboards / **FRED MAHER** – drums

Jun 84. (7"/7"pic-d) (VS 680/+P) **ABSOLUTE. / ('A'version)**   17
(12"+=) (VS 680T) – ('A'extended).

—— **GREEN** now with **DAVID GAMSON** – keyboards / **ALLAN MURPHY** – guitar

Nov 84. (7"/7"pic-d) (VS 725/+P) **HYPNOTISE. / ('A'version)**   68
(12"+=) (VS 725T) – ('A'extended).

—— **NICK MOROCH** – guitar was added to above guests for album below.

May 85. (7"/7"sha-pic-d) (VS 747/+P) **THE WORD GIRL. / FLESH AND BLOOD**   6
(12"+=) (VS 747-12) – ('A'&'B'versions).
Jun 85. (lp/c/cd) (V/TCV/CDV 2350) <25302> **CUPID AND PSYCHE '85**   5   50
– The word girl / Small talk / Absolute / A liitle knowledge / Don't work that way / Perfect way / Lover to fall / Wood beez (pray like Aretha Franklin) / Hypnotize. (cd+=)– (other versions). (re-iss. Apr90 lp/c; OVED/C 294)
Aug 85. (7") (VS 780) <28949> **PERFECT WAY. / ('A'version)**   48   11
(12"+=) (VS 780-12) – ('A'extended).

—— **GREEN** with numerous session people, + guest **MILES DAVIS**

Apr 88. (7") (VS 1006) **OH PATTI (DON'T FEEL SORRY FOR LOVERBOY). / ('A'instrumental)**   13
(12"+=/12"pic-d+=) (VST/+P 1006) – ('A'extended).
(cd-s+=) (VSCD 1006) – Best thing ever.
(c-s++=) (VSTC 1006) – ('A'-Drumless mix).
Jun 88. (lp/c/cd) (V/TCV/CDV 2515) <25686> **PROVISION**   8
– Boom! there she was / Overnite / First boy in this town / All that we are / Best thing ever / Oh Patti (don't feel sorry for loverboy) / Bam salute / Sugar and spice / Philosophy now. (cd+=) – Oh Patti (extended) / Boom! . . . (dub). (re-iss. Aug91 cd/c;)
Jul 88. (7") (VS 1082) **FIRST BOY IN TOWN (LOVESICK). / WORLD COME BACK TO LIFE**   63
(12"+=) (VST 1082) – ('A'instrumental).
(cd-s+=) (VSCD 1082) – ('A'extended remix).
Oct 88. (7") (VS 1143) <27973> **BOOM! THERE SHE WAS. / PHILOSOPHY NOW**   55   53 Jun88
(12"+=/3"cd-s+=) (VS T/CD 1143) – ('A'mix) / ('A'dub version).
Mar 91. (7"/c-s; SCRITTI POLITTI & SHABBA RANKS) (VS/+C 1333) **SHE'S A WOMAN. / LITTLE WAY (different)**   20
(12"+=) (VST 1333) – ('A'-Apollo 440 remix).
(cd-s+=) (VSCD 1333) – Wood beez (pray like Aretha Franklin).
(12") (VSTX 1333) – ('A'-William Orbit remix) / ('A'-Tutology business mix).
Jul 91. (7"/c-s) (VS/+C 1346) **TAKE ME IN YOUR ARMS. / ('A'instrumental) / ('A'mix)**   47
(12"+=/cd-s+=) (VS T/CD 1346) – She's a woman.
above single credited SWEETIE IRIE on the sleeve. GREEN abandoned SCRITTI although he still writes for and with others until . . .
Jul 99. (cd-s) (VSCDT 1731) **TINSEL TOWN TO THE BOOGIEDOWN / DEAD CERTAINTY**   46
(12"/cd-s) (VST/VSCDX 1731) – ('A'mixes).
Jul 99. (cd/c) (CDV/TCV 2884) **ANOMIE AND BONHOMIE**   33
– Umm / Tinsel town to the boogiedown / First goodbye / Die alone / Mystic handyman / Smith n' slappy / Born to be / World you understand is over and over / Here come July / Prince among men / Brushed with oil dusted with powder.

– compilations, others, etc. –

on 'Virgin' unless mentioned otherwise

Jun 88.	(3"cd-ep) *(CDT 13)* **THE WORD GIRL / FLESH AND BLOOD** / ('A'-Turntable mix)	☐ —
Nov 88.	(3"cd-ep) *(CDT 34)* **WOOD BEEZ (PRAY LIKE ARETHA FRANKLIN)** / ('A'dub) / **SMALL TALK**	☐ —
Apr 90.	(3"cd-ep) *(VVCS 1)* **ABSOLUTE** / (3 tracks by other artists)	☐ —

SEAHORSES

Formed: based London, England ... 1996 by ex-STONE ROSES guitarist JOHN SQUIRE who allegedly 'discovered' frontman CHRIS HELME busking in his native Yorkshire. With STUART FLETCHER and ANDY WATTS completing the line-up, the band hooked up with producer Tony Visconti and quickly entered a studio in L.A. to begin work on their debut set, 'DO IT YOURSELF'. In stark contrast to the infamously drawn-out sessions for the final 'ROSES album, all the tracks were laid down inside a month and the record was in the shops by Spring '97. Inevitably, the hype surrounding the whole thing tended to obscure the question of whether the record was actually any good or not; the bulk of critics (perhaps only too eager to get the boot into SQUIRE, a previously unassailable indie guitar god) thought not, or at least panned the set for its inoffensive blandness. Certainly, there was nothing to match the quality of any track from the STONE ROSES sublime debut, although on its own terms, the record's vaguely enjoyable, bluesy indie-rock would've counted as a decent debut by a new band. Somewhat akin to a folk-ish cross between IAN BROWN and LIAM GALLAGHER (who, incidentally, co-penned 'LOVE ME AND LEAVE ME'), HELME's singing, as with SQUIRE's guitar flash, was as competent yet ultimately forgettable as any second division Brit-rock outfit. With the album lacking any real songwriting magic (bar say 'LOVE IS THE LAW' and 'BLINDED BY THE SUN'), some fans began to wonder just who put the mysterious X factor into the STONE ROSES (and talk is that IAN BROWN's forthcoming solo album might just have the self-same critics who ridiculed the last STONE ROSES performance eating their ludicrously exaggerated words), although enough people thought differently to take the album to No.2 in the UK chart. With a string of successful singles and festival appearances also now under their belt, British sales of the debut are approaching the half million mark; SQUIRE may at last be achieving the success that has long seemed his due, ironically, with the most underwhelming material of his career. However, the SEAHORSES were treading water (so to speak!) during the latter half of '98, HELME expressing to mainman SQUIRE he wanted more of a say in the music/lyrics he was to sing. Inevitably, with more of a whimper than a bang, the band were no more, leading to tabloid rumours of yet another STONE ROSES reformation; HELME was meanwhile plotting his own solo career.

Album rating: DO IT YOURSELF (*7)

JOHN SQUIRE (b.24 Nov'62, Broadheath, Lancashire, England) – guitar / **CHRIS HELME** – vocals, acoustic guitar / **STUART FLETCHER** – bass / **ANDY WATTS** – drums, vocals

		Geffen	Geffen
May 97.	(7"/c-s/cd-s) *(GFS/+C/TD 22243)* **LOVE IS THE LAW. / DREAMER / SALE OF THE CENTURY**	3	—
May 97.	(cd/c/lp) *(<GED/GEC/GEF 25134>)* **DO IT YOURSELF** – I want you to know / Blinded by the sun / Suicide drive / The boy in the picture / Love is the law / Happiness is eggshaped / Love me and leave me / Round the universe / 1999 / Standing on your head / Hello.	2	—
Jul 97.	(7"/c-s/cd-s) *(GFS/+C/TD 22266)* **BLINDED BY THE SUN. / KILL PUSSYCAT KILL / MOVING ON**	7	—
Sep 97.	(7"/c-s/cd-s) *(GFS/+C/TD 22282)* **LOVE ME AND LEAVE ME. / SHINE / FALLING IS EASY**	16	—
Dec 97.	(7"/c-s/cd-s) *(GFS/+C/TD 22297)* **YOU CAN TALK TO ME. / DON'T TRY / 3 WIDE**	15	—

—— **MARK HEANEY** – drums; repl. WATTS

—— in Feb'99, the SEAHORSES announced they had split

SEAL

Born: SEALHENRY SAMUEL, 13 Feb'63, Paddington, London, England of Nigerian/Brazilian parentage. After beginning his performing career singing in the Capital's pubs, SEAL took off for the Far East and Asia. Upon his return to Britain, SEAL hooked up with techno boffin, ADAMSKI, the pair penning the seminal 'KILLER' track, an evocative house/soul epic which topped the UK chart in 1990. With SEAL on vocal duties, his rich, mahogany tones gained widespread exposure, laying the groundwork for a highly successful solo career. Swiftly netted by 'Z.T.T.', SEAL began work on his eponymous debut with veteran producer, Trevor Horn. Previewed by the massive worldwide hit, 'CRAZY', 'SEAL' (1991) established the soul/rock/pop giant (six and a half foot!) as a household name, deftly turning his hand to a variety of styles with a voice that could probably turn lead into gold. Later that year the singer scored a further UK Top 10 with a revamped, rockier 'KILLER', complete with a B-side cover of 'HEY JOE', a track made famous by JIMI HENDRIX amongst others. The HENDRIX connection continued with SEAL reworking 'MANIC DEPRESSION' alongside JEFF BECK for the 1993 tribute album, 'STONE FREE'. Laden with awards, including an Ivor Novello, SEAL subsequently went to ground, again working with Trevor Horn on a follow-up album. Incredibly, again titled 'SEAL' (1994), the record's contents nevertheless

belied its unimaginative title, the singer working with a plethora of respected musicians including WENDY & LISA, JONI MITCHELL, WILLIAM ORBIT and the aforementioned JEFF BECK. Another UK No.1, the record finally broke SEAL in America after 'KISS FROM A ROSE' was included on the 'Batman Forever' soundtrack. • Covered: THE WIND CRIES MARY (Jimi Hendrix).

Album rating: SEAL (*7) / SEAL (2) (*7) / HUMAN BEING (*5)

SEAL – vocals, acoustic guitar (ex-ADAMSKI) with many session people

		Z.T.T.	Sire	
Nov 90.	(7"/c-s) *(ZANG 8/+C)* <19298> **CRAZY. / SPARKLE** (12"+=/cd-s+=) *(ZANG 8 T/CD)* – ('A'extended).	2	7	May91
Apr 91.	(7"ep/c-ep) *(ZANG 11/+C)* **THE FUTURE LOVE EP** – Future love paradise / A minor groove / Violet. (12"+=/cd-s+=) *(ZANG 11 T/CD)* – ('A'extended).	12	☐	
May 91.	(cd/c/lp) *(ZTT 9 CD/C/LP)* <26627> **SEAL** – The beginning / Deep water / Crazy / Killer / Whirlpool / Future love Paradise / Wild / Show me / Violet.	1	24	Jun91
Jul 91.	(7"/c-s) *(ZANG 21/+C)* **THE BEGINNING. / DEEP WATER (acoustic)** (cd-s+=) *(ZANG 21CD)* – ('A'-Giro mix) / ('A'remix) (12") *(ZANG 21T)* – ('A'remix) / ('A'dub mix).	24	☐	
Nov 91.	(7"ep/c-ep) *(ZANG 12/+C)* <19119> **KILLER EP** – Killer / Hey Joe / Come see what love has done. (12"+=/cd-s+=) *(ZANG 23 T/CD)* – ('A'-Killer . . . on the loose remixes).	8	100	Mar92
Feb 92.	(7"/7"sha-pic-d/c-s) *(ZANG 27/+PD/C)* **VIOLET. / WILD** (cd-s+=) *(ZANG 27CD)* – Show me / Whirlpool.	39	☐	

—— with a plethora of musicians, the principals being; **GUS ISIDORE, WENDY MELVOIN, LISA COLEMAN & JAMIE MUHOBERAC** (the first 3 co-writers). Guests incl. **JEFF BECK, JONI MITCHELL, LUIS JARDIM, ANNE DUDLEY, ANDY NEWMARK, WILLIAM ORBIT, PINO PALLADINO, GAVIN WRIGHT, BETSY COOK** + producer **TREVOR HORN**

May 94.	(7"/c-s) *(ZANG 51/+C)* <18138> **PRAYER FOR THE DYING. / DREAMING IN METAPHORS** (cd-s+=) *(ZANG 51CD)* – Crazy (acoustic) / ('A'acoustic).	14	21	
May 94.	(cd/c/lp) *(4509 96256-2/-4/-1)* <45415> **SEAL** – Bring it on / Prayer for the dying / Dreaming in metaphors / Don't cry / Fast changes / Kiss from a rose / People asking why / Newborn friend / If I could / I'm alive / Bring it on (reprise).	1	16	Jun94
Jul 94.	(c-s) *(ZANG 52C)* **KISS FROM A ROSE. / I'M ALIVE (SON OF BONTEMPI)** (7"+=/12"+=/cd-s+=) *(ZANG 52/+T/CD2)* – (2 'A'mixes). (cd-s+=) *(ZANG 52CD1)* – ('A'side) / The wind cries Mary / Blues in E.	20	—	
Oct 94.	(c-s) *(ZANG 58C)* **NEWBORN FRIEND / ('A'mix)** (12"+=) *(ZANG 58T)* – ('A'mix). (cd-s++=) *(ZANG 58CD)* – ('A'mix).	45	☐	
Jul 95.	(c-s) *(ZANG 70C)* <17896> **KISS FROM A ROSE / I'M ALIVE (SON OF BONTEMPI)** (12"+=/cd-s+=) *(ZANG 70 T/CD)* – I'm alive (Sasha & BT remix).	5	1	Jun95
Nov 95.	(c-s) *(ZANG 75C)* **DON'T CRY / PRAYER FOR THE DYING / DON'T CRY (YOU'RE NOT ALONE)** (cd-s+=) *(ZANG 75CD)* – ('B'extended).	51	—	
Feb 96.	(c-s,cd-s) <17708> **DON'T CRY / FAST CHANGES** (below from the movie 'Space Jam' on 'Warner Sunset' US)	—	33	
Mar 97.	(c-s) *(ZEAL 1C)* <87046> **FLY LIKE AN EAGLE / ('A'instrumental)** (12") *(ZEAL 1T)* – ('A'mixes). (cd-s) *(ZEAL 1CD)* – ('A'mixes).	13	10	Nov96

		Warners	Warners	
Nov 98.	(c-s) *(W 464C)* **HUMAN BEINGS / PRINCESS** (cd-s+=) *(W 464CD)* – Human beings (reprise).	50	☐	
Nov 98.	(cd/c/lp) *(<9362 46828-2/-4>)* **HUMAN BEING** – Human beings / State of grace / Latest craze / Just like you said / Princess / I have lost my faith / Excerpts from / When a man is wrong / Colour / Still love remains / No easy way / Human beings (reprise).	44	22	

SEARCHERS

Formed: Kirkdale, Liverpool, England ... 1961 by MIKE PENDER and JOHN McNALLY, who soon found TONY JACKSON and NORMAN McGARRY (the latter being replaced by CHRIS CURTIS). Naming themselves after the famous film starring John Wayne, they became the backing band of club singer, JOHNNY SANDON. Like The BEATLES, they played The Cavern and recorded at The Star-Club in Germany in 1962/63, and were soon signed to 'Pye' by A&R man, TONY HATCH. Their first 45, 'SWEETS FOR MY SWEET' (written by DOC POMUS & MORT SHUMAN for The DRIFTERS), hit the UK top spot, the first of a string of hits over the next three years, many of which competed for chart space with the aforementioned BEATLES. These included such classy harmony-laden pop ditties as 'SUGAR AND SPICE' (another written by HATCH) and their second No.1 smash, 'NEEDLES AND PINS' (written by JACK NITZSCHE and SONNY BONO). Their third chart topper, 'DON'T THROW YOUR LOVE AWAY', was issued in Spring '64, this time around penned by The ORLONS. However, JACKSON subsequently departed to form his own outfit, taking his characteristic falsetto voice with him. His replacement, FRANK ALLEN, made sure that the hits kept flowing however, a version of Jackie DeShannon's 'WHEN YOU WALK IN THE ROOM' hitting No.3. The SEARCHERS had already found an audience in the States, scoring their biggest hit to date (Top 3) with the US-only 'LOVE POTION NUMBER NINE'. The times they were a-changin' however, The SEARCHERS' star beginning to fade with their attempt at protest folk-pop, 'WHAT HAVE THEY DONE TO THE RAIN' (written by MALVINA REYNOLDS) only hitting No.13 in the UK (Top 30 US). Although CURTIS and PENDER were still writing some hits, the group had their last stand late in 1966 with 'HAVE YOU EVER LOVED SOMEBODY'. After three flops the following year (an injustice for the first of them, 'POPCORN DOUBLE FEATURE' – later re-hashed by The FALL), they were dropped by 'Pye'. The band subsequently fell by the wayside and into the cabaret scene during the 70's, although they returned with an ill-advised attempt at "new wave" in 1979. A few years later, they played a Royal Variety Show performance alongside the likes/dislikes (delete according to taste) of CLIFF RICHARD, LONNIE DONEGAN and ADAM & THE ANTS. MIKE PENDER continues to tour on the golden oldies circuit, refusing to let go of the jingly-jangly 60's. • **Other cover versions:** SOME DAY WE'RE GONNA LOVE AGAIN (Barbara Lewis) / LOVE POTION NUMBER NINE (Clovers) / BUMBLE BEE (LaVern Baker) / TAKE ME FOR WHAT I'M WORTH (P.F. Sloan) / TAKE IT OR LEAVE IT (Rolling Stones) / and loads of lp tracks.

Best CD compilation: THE ULTIMATE COLLECTION (*7)

MIKE PENDER (b. MICHAEL JOHN PRENDERGAST, 3 Mar'42) – vocals, lead guitar / **JOHN McNALLY** (b.30 Aug'41) – vocals, rhythm guitar / **TONY JACKSON** (b.16 Jul'40) – vocals, bass / **CHRIS CURTIS** (b. CHRISTOPHER CRUMMEY, 26 Aug'41, Oldham, England) – vocals, drums; repl. NORMAN McGARRY who joined RORY STORME & THE HURRICANES replacing RINGO STARR

		Pye	Mercury
Jun 63.	(7") *(7N 15533)* <72172> **SWEETS FOR MY SWEET. / IT'S ALL BEEN A DREAM**	1	Mar64
Aug 63.	(lp) *(NPL 18086)* **MEET THE SEARCHERS**	2	–

– Sweets for my sweet / Alright / Love potion No.9 / Farmer John / Stand by me / Money / Da doo ron ron / Ain't gonna love ya / Since you broke my heart / Tricky Dickey / Where have all the flowers gone / Twist and shout. *(re-iss.1966 on 'Golden Guinea'; GGL 0349) (re-iss. Feb81 on 'P.R.T.'; same) (re-iss. Oct87 on 'P.R.T.' lp/c/cd; PYL/PYM/PYC 6014) (cd re-iss. Dec89 on 'Castle'; CLACD 165)*

		Pye	Liberty
Oct 63.	(7") *(7N 15566)* <55646> **SUGAR AND SPICE. / SAINTS AND SEARCHERS**	2	Dec63

<US re-iss. Apr64; 55689> hit No.44>

Nov 63.	(lp) *(NPL 18089)* **SUGAR AND SPICE**	5	–

– Sugar and spice / Don't cha know? / Some other guy / One of these days / Listen to me / Unhappy girls / (Ain't that) Just like me / Oh my lover / Saints and searchers / Cherry stones / All my sorrows / Hungry for love. *(re-iss. 1967 on 'Marble Arch'; MAL 704) (re-iss. Feb81 on 'P.R.T.'; same) (re-iss. Oct87 on 'P.R.T.' lp/c/cd; PYL/PYM/PYC 6015) (cd re-iss. Dec89 on 'Castle'; CLACD 166)*

		Pye	Kapp
Jan 64.	(7") *(7N 15594)* <577> **NEEDLES AND PINS. / SATURDAY NIGHT OUT**	1	13 Feb64
Mar 64.	(lp) <3363> **MEET THE SEARCHERS – NEEDLES AND PINS**	–	22

– (tracks from last 2 albums plus title track)

Mar 64.	(7") <584> **AIN'T THAT JUST LIKE ME. / AIN'T GONNA KISS YA**	–	61
Apr 64.	(7") *(7N 15630)* <593> **DON'T THROW YOUR LOVE AWAY. / I PRETEND I'M WITH YOU**	1	16 May64
May 64.	(lp) *(NPL 18092)* <3412> **IT'S FAB! IT'S GEAR! IT'S THE SEARCHERS**	4	–

– Sea of heartbreak / Glad all over / It's in her kiss / Livin' lovin' wreck / Where have you been / Shimmy shimmy / Needles and pins / This empty place / Gonna send you back to Georgia / I count the tears / High heel sneakers / Can't help forgiving you / Sho' know a lot about love / Don't throw your love away. *(re-iss. 1968 on 'Marble Arch'; MAL 798) (re-iss. Feb81 on 'P.R.T.'; same) (re-iss. Oct87 on 'P.R.T.' lp/c/cd; PYL/PYM/PYC 6016) (cd re-iss. Dec89 on 'Castle'; CLACD 167)*

Jul 64.	(7") *(7N 15670)* <609> **SOMEDAY WE'RE GONNA LOVE AGAIN. / NO ONE ELSE COULD LOVE YOU**	11	34 Aug64

–––– **FRANK ALLEN** (b. FRANCIS RENAUD McNEICE, 14 Jul'43, Hayes, England) – vocals, bass (ex-CLIFF BENNETT & THE REBEL ROUSERS) repl. JACKSON, who formed TONY JACKSON & VIBRATIONS

Sep 64.	(7") *(7N 15694)* <618> **WHEN YOU WALK IN THE ROOM. / I'LL BE MISSING YOU**	3	35 Oct64
Oct 64.	(lp) <3409> **THIS IS US**	–	97

– (near same track listing as above album)

Nov 64.	(7") *(7N 15739)* <644> **WHAT HAVE THEY DONE TO THE RAIN. / THIS FEELING INSIDE**	13	29 Jan65
Dec 64.	(7") <Winners Circle; 27> **LOVE POTION NO.9. / HI HEEL SNEAKERS**	–	3
Feb 65.	(7") *(7N 15794)* <658> **GOODBYE MY LOVE. / TILL I MET YOU**	4	52 Mar65

–––– <US-title of above 'GOODBYE MY LOVER GOODBYE'>

Mar 65.	(lp) *(NPL 18111)* <3412> **SOUNDS LIKE SEARCHERS**	8	

<US-title 'THE NEW SEARCHERS'>
– Everybody come and clap your hands / If I could fine someone / Magic potion / I don't want to go on without you / Bumble bee / Something you got baby / Let the good times roll / A tear fell / Till you say you'll be mine / You wanna make her happy / Everything you do / Goodnight baby. *(re-iss. Feb81 on 'P.R.T.'; same) (re-iss. Oct87 on 'P.R.T.' lp/c/cd; PYL/PYM/PYC 6017)*

Mar 65.	(7") <Winners Circle; 49> **BUMBLE BEE. / A TEAR FELL**	–	21
Jul 65.	(7") *(7N 15878)* <686> **HE'S GOT NO LOVE. / SO FAR AWAY**	12	79
Oct 65.	(lp) <3449> **THE SEARCHERS No.4**	–	

– (virtually the same as next album)

Oct 65.	(7") *(7N 15950)* **WHEN I GET HOME. / I'M NEVER COMING BACK**	35	–
Oct 65.	(7") <706> **DON'T YOU KNOW WHY. / YOU CAN'T LIE TO A LIAR**	–	
Nov 65.	(7") *(7N 15992)* <729> **TAKE ME FOR WHAT I'M WORTH. / TOO MANY MILES**	20	76 Jan66
Nov 65.	(lp) *(NPL 18120)* <3477> **TAKE ME FOR WHAT I'M WORTH**		1966

– I'm ready / I'll be doggone / Does she really care for me / It's time / Too many miles / You can't lie to a liar / Don't you know why / I'm your loving man / Each time / Be my baby / Four strong winds / Take me for what I'm worth. *(re-iss. Feb81 on 'P.R.T.'; same)*

–––– **JOHN BLUNT** (b.28 Mar'47, London, England) – drums repl. CURTIS

Apr 66.	(7") *(7N 17094)* **TAKE IT OR LEAVE IT. / DON'T HIDE IT AWAY**	31	–
Oct 66.	(7") *(7N 17170)* <783> **HAVE YOU EVER LOVED SOMEBODY. / IT'S JUST THE WAY LOVE WILL COME AND GO**	48	94
Jan 67.	(7") *(7N 17225)* <811> **POPCORN DOUBLE FEATURE. / LOVERS**		
Apr 67.	(7") *(7N 17308)* **WESTERN UNION. / I'LL CRY TOMORROW**		–
Nov 67.	(7") *(7N 17424)* **SECONDHAND DEALER. / CRAZY DREAMS**		–

		Liberty	World Pacific
Nov 68.	(7") *(LBF 15159)* <77908> **UMBRELLA MAN. / OVER THE WEEKEND**		
Jul 69.	(7") *(LBF 15340)* **KINKY KATHY ABERNATHY. / SUZANNA**	–	

–––– (Late 1969) **BILLY ADAMSON** – drums, vocals repl. BLUNT

		R.C.A.	R.C.A.
Aug 71.	(7") *(RCA 2057)* <74-0484> **DESDEMONA. / THE WORLD IS WAITING FOR TOMORROW**		94
Oct 71.	(7") *(RCA 2139)* <0652> **LOVE IS EVERYWHERE. / AND A BUTTON**		
Apr 72.	(7") *(RCA 2231)* **SING SINGER SING. / COME ON BACK TO ME**		
Aug 72.	(7"m) *(RCA 2248)* **NEEDLES AND PINS. / WHEN YOU WALK IN THE ROOM / COME ON BACK TO ME**		
Oct 72.	(7") *(RCA 2288)* **VAHEVALA. / MADMAN**		
Nov 72.	(lp) *(SF 8289)* **SECOND TAKE**		

– Sugar and spice / Don't throw your love away / Farmer John / Come on back to me / When you walk in the room / Needles and pins / Goodbye my love / Love potion No.9 / Sweets for my sweet / Take me for what I'm worth / What have they done to the rain.

Feb 73.	(7") *(RCA 2330)* **SOLITAIRE. / SPICKS AND SPECKS**		

–––– Resigned themselves to oldies circuit in the US.

		Sire	Sire
Oct 79.	(7") *(SIR 4029)* **HEARTS IN HER EYES. / DON'T HANG ON**		
Feb 80.	(7") *(SIR 4036)* **IT'S TOO LATE. / THIS KIND OF LOVE AFFAIR**		
Feb 80.	(7") **IT'S TOO LATE. / DON'T HANG ON**	–	
Mar 80.	(lp) *(SRK <6082>)* **THE SEARCHERS**		

– Hearts in her eyes / Switchboard Susan / Feeling fine / Back to the war / This kind of love affair / Lost in your eyes / It's too late / Love's melody / No dancing / Love's gonna be strong / Don't hang on. <US tracks differed>

Jul 80.	(7") *(SIR 4046)* **LOVE'S MELODY. / CHANGING**		
Mar 81.	(7") *(SIR 4049)* **ANOTHER NIGHT. / BACK TO THE WAR**		
May 81.	(lp) *(SRK 3523)* **PLAY FOR TODAY** <US title 'LOVE'S MELODIES'>		

– Another night / September girls / Murder in my heart / She made a fool of you / Silver / Sick and tired / Radio romance / Infatuation / Almost Saturday night / Everything but a heartbeat / Little bit of Heaven / New day.

May 81.	(7") <49665> **LOVE'S MELODY. / LITTLE BIT OF HEAVEN**	–	–

–––– Around mid-80's, group dispersed into 2 sections (aka MIKE PENDER'S SEARCHERS and other SEARCHERS). The others took MIKE to court in 1988. **SPENCER JAMES** – guitar, vocals repl.PENDER

		Arista	Coconut
Apr 90.	(cd/c/lp) *(259/409/209 459)* **HUNGRY HEART**		

– Forever in love (near to Heaven) / Love lies bleeding / Lonely weekend / Somebody told me / Every little tear / Sweets for my sweet (new 1988 version) / No other love / This boy's in love / Fooled myself once again / Baby, I do / Push, push / Needles and pins.

– compilations, others, etc. –

on 'Pye' unless stated otherwise

Sep 63.	(7") *Philips; (BF 1274)* **SWEET NUTHINS (live in Hamburg). / WHAT'D I SAY**	48	–
Oct 63.	(7"ep) *(NEP 24177)* **AIN'T GONNA KISS YA**	12	–
Dec 63.	(7"ep) *(NEP 24183)* **SWEETS FOR MY SWEETS**		–
Jan 64.	(7"ep) *(NEP 24184)* **HUNGRY FOR LOVE**		–
Apr 64.	(7") *Mercury; <72390>* **(AIN'T THAT) JUST LIKE ME. / I CAN TELL**		
Jun 64.	(lp) *Mercury; <SR 60916>* **HEAR! HEAR! (live in Hamburg)**	–	
1964.	(7"ep) *(NEP 24201)* **THE SEARCHERS PLAY THE SYSTEM**		
1964.	(7"ep) *(NEP 24204)* **WHEN YOU WALK IN THE ROOM** *(re-iss. Jul80 on 'Flashback-Pye'; FBEP 105)*		
1965.	(7"ep) *(NEP 24218)* **BUMBLE BEE**		
1965.	(7"ep) *(NEP 24222)* **SEARCHERS '65**		
Nov 65.	(7"ep) *(NEP 18120)* **TAKE ME FOR WHAT I'M WORTH**		
1966.	(7"ep) *(NEP 24228)* **FOUR BY FOUR**		
1967.	(lp) *Marble Arch; (MAL 640)* **SMASH HITS**		
1967.	(lp) *Marble Arch; (MAL 673)* **SMASH HITS VOL.2**		
1970.	(lp/c) *Golden Hour; (GH/ZCGH 541)* **THE GOLDEN HOUR OF THE SEARCHERS** *(re-iss. May90 on 'Knight' cd/c; KGH CD/MC 101)*		
1971.	(lp) *Hallmark; (HMA 203)* **NEEDLES AND PINS**		
1973.	(lp/c) *Golden Hour; (GH/ZCGH 564)* **THE GOLDEN HOUR OF THE SEARCHERS VOL.2** *(re-iss. Dec90 on 'Knight' cd/c; KGH CD/MC 132)*		
May 76.	(7") *(7N 45598)* **NEEDLES AND PINS. / SUGAR AND SPICE**	–	–
1976.	(lp) *Mercury; <501>* **HISTORY OF BRITISH POP**	–	
1976.	(lp) *Mercury; <508>* **HISTORY OF BRITISH POP VOL.2**	–	
Jan 77.	(12"ep) *Big Deal; (BD 113)* **WHEN YOU WALK IN THE ROOM / NEEDLES AND PINS. / DON'T THROW YOUR LOVE AWAY / GOODBYE MY LOVE**		
Nov 77.	(d-lp/d-c) *(FILD/ACFLD 002)* **THE SEARCHERS FILE**		
Jul 78.	(7") *(7N 46110)* **WHEN YOU WALK IN THE ROOM. / DON'T THROW YOUR LOVE AWAY**		
Apr 79.	(7") *Flashback; (FBS 4)* **NEEDLES AND PINS. / SWEETS FOR MY SWEET**		–

Jan 80. (d-lp/d-c) *P.R.T.; (SPOT/ZCSPT 1014)* **SPOTLIGHT ON THE SEARCHERS**

May 80. (lp/c) *(NSPL/ZCP 18617)* **WHEN YOU WALK IN THE ROOM**

Jun 82. (c) *P.R.T.; (ZCTON 103)* **100 MINUTES OF THE SEARCHERS**

Jul 82. (7") *Old Gold; (OG 9141)* **NEEDLES AND PINS. / DON'T THROW YOUR LOVE AWAY**

Nov 82. (7") *P.R.T.; (7P 250)* **I DON'T WANT TO BE THE ONE. / HOLLYWOOD**

Jul 83. (10"lp/c) *P.R.T.; (DOW/TC-DOW 11)* **LOVE LIES BLEEDING**

Jul 84. (7") *Old Gold; (OG 9409)* **SWEETS FOR MY SWEET. / WHEN YOU WALK IN THE ROOM**

Dec 85. (lp/c) *Flashback; (FBLP/ZCFBL 8084)* **SWEETS FOR MY SWEET**

Jan 86. (lp) *Rhino; <RNLP 162>* **GREATEST HITS**

Apr 86. (lp/c) *Showcase; (SH LP/TC 135)* **GREATEST HITS**

Apr 87. (7"/12") *P.R.T.; (7P/12P 371)* **WHEN YOU WALK IN THE ROOM. / BE MY BABY**

Apr 87. (cd/c/lp) *P.R.T.; (CD/ZC+/NRT 2)* **SILVER SEARCHERS**
(*re-iss. Jul91 as 'THE SILVER COLLECTION' on 'Woodford' cd/c; WM CD5/MC4 597*)

Sep 87. (lp/c/cd) *P.R.T.; (PYL/PYM/PYC 4002)* **THE HIT COLLECTION**

Oct 87. (lp/c/cd) *P.R.T.; (PYL/PYM/PYC 6019)* **THE SEARCHERS PLAY THE SYSTEM** (rare b-sides, etc)

1988. (d-c) *Ditto; (DTO 10225)* **NEEDLES AND PINS**

Nov 88. (cd-s) *Old Gold; (OG 6103)* **NEEDLES AND PINS / SWEETS FOR MY SWEET / WHEN YOU WALK IN THE ROOM**

Dec 88. (d-lp/c/cd) *Castle; (CCS LP/MC/CD 208)* **THE COMPLETE COLLECTION**
– Sweets for my sweet / Listen to me / When you walk in the room / Goodbye my love / Don't want to go on without you / What have they done to the rain / Don't throw your love away / Ain't gonna kiss ya / Since you broke my heart / Goodnight baby / Hungry for love / When I get home / Needles and pins / (Ain't that) Just like me / Take it or leave it / Bumble bee / Someday we're gonna love again / Farmer John / Sugar and spice / Have you ever loved somebody / Take me for what I'm worth / Western Union / He's got no love / Love potion No.9. (*re-iss. Nov91 cd/c; CCS CD/MC 303*)

Mar 89. (lp/cd) *Legacy; (C90/GHCD 2)* **THE SEARCHERS**

Apr 89. (lp/cd) *Legacy; (C90/GHCD 4)* **C90 COLLECTOR SERIES**

Jul 89. (lp/c/cd) *See For Miles; (SEE/+K/CD 275)* **THE EP COLLECTION**

May 90. (lp/c/cd) *Castle; (CTV CD/MC/LP 003)* **THE ULTIMATE COLLECTION**

Mar 91. (cd/c) *O.N.N.; (ONN 81 CD/MC)* **MIKE PENDER'S SEARCHERS** (cd re-iss. Jan93 on 'Tring'; GRF 185)

Aug 91. (cd/c) *Carlton; (WK S/MC 4076)* **THE BEST OF THE SEARCHERS 1963-1964**

Aug 91. (cd) *Repertoire; (REP 4102)* **GERMAN, FRENCH AND RARE RECORDINGS**

Oct 91. (cd/c) *Music For Pleasure; (CD/TC MFP 5922)* **THE SEARCHERS**

Feb 92. (3xcd-box) *Sequel; (NEXCD 170)* **30th ANNIVERSARY COLLECTION**

Feb 92. (3xcd-box) *Castle; (CLABX 913)* **THE SEARCHERS CD BOX SET**

Nov 92. (cd) *See For Miles; (SEECD 359)* **THE EP COLLECTION VOL.2**

May 94. (cd/c) *Prima; (PMM 0567-2/-4)* **NEEDLES & PINS**

Jul 94. (cd/c) *Sucess; (550 741-2/-4)* **DON'T THROW YOUR LOVE AWAY**

Sep 94. (cd/c) *Spectrum; (550 741-2/-4)* **SWEETS FOR MY SWEET**

Feb 95. (cd) *B.A.M.; (KLMCD 031)* **PEARLS OF THE PAST**

May 97. (cd) *Music Club; (MCCD 291)* **THE BEST OF THE SEARCHERS**

SEBADOH

Formed: Boston, Massachusetts, USA … 1989 by LOU BARLOW, lo-fi overlord and former DINOSAUR JR member. After a less than amicable break from DINOSAUR mainman, J. MASCIS, BARLOW began writing and recording material with sticksman, ERIC GAFFNEY. Released on 'Homestead' over two albums, 'THE FREED MAN' (1989) and 'WEED FORESTIN' (1990), these acoustic sketches (released in 1992 as a single CD package, 'FREED WEED') were a taster for the fully fledged pop subversion of 'SEBADOH III' (1991). With the addition of bassist/guitarist, JASON LOWENSTEIN, the trio ventured into raucous electric territory, while keeping one foot in the acoustic camp, reconciling their love of lo-fi noise with barbed indie-folk. Though a US-only affair, the album was given a belated UK release in 1994; in the meantime, SEBADOH's output became more readily available following a deal with 'Sub Pop', the mini-set, 'ROCKIN' THE FOREST' (1992), boasting the semi-classic self-parody of 'GIMME INDIE ROCK', previously only available as an import 7". A second mini-album that year, 'SEBADOH VS HELMET', found BARLOW and Co. bravely tackling a Nick Drake cover (the timeless 'PINK MOON') with interesting results, while 'BUBBLE AND SCRAPE' (1992) was the band's most commercially successful release to date, making the UK Top 75. BARLOW continued to express his more lo-fi urges via side projects, releasing material as The FOLK IMPLOSION with (former PALACE) guitarist JOHN DAVIS and working on his own as LOU BARLOW AND HIS SENTRIDOH. Industriously (and confusingly for discographers!) prolific in the best indie tradition, BARLOW continued apace with his SEBADOH duties, releasing the acclaimed 'BAKESALE' in 1994. Though GAFFNEY had been replaced by BOB FAY, his playing still featured on an album which came as close to conventional alternative rock as anything BARLOW has yet recorded, the sound less self-consciously muted. It also marked their entry into the UK Top 40, just, while 1996's 'HARMACY' was even more accessible without compromising their indie/grunge ethos. BARLOW even had a hit single on his hands following the inclusion of FOLK IMPLOSION's 'NATURAL

ONE' in Larry Clark's hotly debated 'Kids' movie, proving conclusively that lo-fi didn't necessarily entail lo-sales. Towards the end of a busy 90's for BARLOW, he delivered three excellent long-players, 'DARE TO BE SURPRISED' (1997) and 'ONE PART LULLABY' (1999) – both from the FOLK IMPLOSION – squeezed either side of SEBADOH's eponymous 'THE SEBADOH' (1999). The last-named sold enough in its first week to crack the UK Top 50, while one of its highlights, 'FLAME', hit No.30(!).
• **Songwriters:** BARLOW and GAFFNEY (until latter repl. by FAY), some by LOWENSTEIN after 1992. Covered REJECT (Negros) / SICKLES AND HAMMERS (Minutemen) / WONDERFUL! WONDERFUL! (Edwards-Raleigh) / EVERYBODY'S BEEN BURNED (Byrds) / PINK MOON (Nick Drake) / RUN TO YOU (Bryan Adams) / BLONDE IN THE BLEACHERS (Joni Mitchell) / NAIMA (John Coltrane?). FOLK IMPLOSION covered SCHOOL (Nirvana) / WON'T BACK DOWN (Tom Petty) / I SMELL A RAT (Bags).

Album rating: THE FREED MAN (*5) / WEED FORRESTIN' (*4) / SEBADOH III (*7) / ROCKIN' THE FOREST (*4) / SEBADOH VS. HELMET (*5) / SMASH YOUR HEAD ON THE PUNK ROCK collection (*5) / BUBBLE AND SCRAPE (*7) / BAKESALE (*8) / HARMACY (*7) / THE SEBADOH (*8) / Lou Barlow & His Sentridoh: COLLECTION OF HOME RECORDINGS (*4) / ANOTHER COLLECTION OF HIS HOME RECORDINGS (*4) / LOU BARLOW & HIS SENTRIDOH (*5) / Folk Implosion: TAKE A LOOK INSIDE … mini (*5) / DARE TO BE SURPRISED (*6) / ONE PART LULLABY (*8)

LOU BARLOW (b.17 Jul'66, Northampton, Massachusetts) – vocals, guitar (ex-DINOSAUR JR) / **ERIC GAFFNEY** – drums

		Homestead	Homestead
Dec 89.	(lp/c) *<HMS 145-1/-4>* **THE FREED MAN**	-	

– Temporary dream / New worship / Subtle holy gift / My own religion / Ride the darker wave / More simple / Jealous of Jesus / Mr. Genius eyes / Perfect power / Feeding evil / Sexual confusion / Three times a day / Gate to hell / Broken / Whiley peach / I can't see / Take my hand / Pound my skinny head / I believe in fate / Waited forever / Slightest suggestion / It's so hard to fall in love / Brand new love.

Nov 90.	(lp/c) *<HMS 158-1/-4>* **WEED FORESTIN'**	-	

– Healthy sick / Burning out / Little man / Punch in the nose / Loose 'n' screw / Jealous evil / Moldy bread / Solid brownies / The bridge was you / Bolder / Slit your wrists / True hardcore / Stop the wheel / Made real / Close enough / Level anything / Soul mate / Nest / Narrow stories / Ladybugs / Yellow submarine / Wall of doubt / Crumbs / Growin' up with you. (*UK cd-iss. Nov92 & Mar99 of above two as 'FREED WEED'; HMS 158-2*)

—— added **JASON LOEWENSTEIN** – bass, guitar, drums, vocals

Jul 91.	(7") *<HMS 165>* **GIMME INDIE ROCK. /** (*UK-iss.Apr97; same*)	-	
Sep 91.	(cd/lp) *<HMS 168-2/-1>* **SEBADOH III**	-	

– Freed pig / Sickles and hammers / Total peace / Violet execution / Scars, our eyes / Truly great thing / Kath / Perverted world / Wonderful! wonderful! / Limb by limb / Smoke a bowl / Black haired girl / Hoppin' up and down / Supernatural force / Rockstar / Downmind / Renaissance man / God told me / Holy picture / Hassle / No different / Spoiled / As the world does, the eyes of God. (*UK-iss.Jul94 & Jun98 & Mar99; same*)

		not iss.	Siltbreeze
Nov 91.	(7") **OVEN IS MY FRIEND. /**	-	

—— In 1991, Sonic Life fanzine issued 'SPLIT WITH BIG STICK' for 'Blast First'.

		not iss.	Vertical
1992.	(7") **ASSHOLE. /**	-	

		Domino	Sub Pop
Aug 92.	(m-cd/m-lp) *(WIG CD/LP 2)* **ROCKIN' THE FOREST**		-

– Gimme indie rock / Ride the darker wave / It's so hard to fall in love / Cry sis / Really insane II / Vampire / Junk bands / Mind-held.

—— Sep 92; split an EP release w/ AZALIA SNAIL on 'Dark Beloved Cloud'; *DBC 001*)

Oct 92.	(m-cd/m-lp) *(WIG CD/LP 3)* **SEBADOH VS HELMET**		-

– Notsur dnuora selcric / Brand new love / Mean distance / … Burned / New worship / Good things, proud man / P.Moon / Cecilia chime in Melee / Soulmate.

Nov 92.	(cd) *<SP 176>* **SMASH YR HEAD ON PUNK ROCK** (compilation of above 2)	-	

– Crisis / Brand new love / Notsur dnuora selcric / Vampire / Good things / Cecelia chime in Melee / Everybody's been burned / Junk bonds / New worship / Pink moon / Mind meld. (*UK-iss.May98; same as US*)

Mar 93.	(7") *(RUG 4)* **SOUL AND FIRE. / FANTASTIC DISASTER** (amateur mix)		

(*12"+=/cd-s+=*) *(RUG 4 T/CD)* – Emma get wild / Reject.

Apr 93.	(cd/c/lp) *(WIG CD/MC/LP 4) <SP 192>* **BUBBLE AND SCRAPE**	63	

– Soul and fire / Two years two days / Telecosmic alchemy / Fantastic disaster / Happily divided / Sister / Cliche / Sacred attention / Elixir is Zog / Emma get wild / Sixteen / Homemade / Forced love / No way out / Bouquet for a siren / Think (let tomorrow be) / Flood.

Dec 93.	(7") *(RUG 17)* **REBOUND. / CAREFUL**		-

(*12"ep+=/cd-ep+=*) **FOUR SONGS EP** *(RUG 17)* – Mar backlash / Not a friend / Foreground / Naima / 40203 / Mystery man / Drumstick jumble / Lime kiln.

—— **BOB FAY** – drums; repl. GAFFNEY who went solo (although still on below album)

Jul 94.	(7"ep/cd-ep) *(RUG 22/+CD)* **SKULL. / PUNCHING MYSELF IN THE FACE REPEATEDLY, PUBLICLY / SING SOMETHING – PLATE O'HATRED**		-
Aug 94.	(cd/c/lp) *(WIG CD/MC/LP 11) <SP 260>* **BAKESALE**	40	

– License to confuse / Careful / Magnet's coil / Not a friend / Not too amused / Dreams / Skull / Got it / S. soup / Give up / Rebound / Mystery man / Temptation tide / Drama mine / Together or alone. (*ltd. w / free 7"*)

Jun 95.	(7"/cd-s) *(RUG 38/+CD)* **NOT TOO AMUSED. / HANK WILLIAMS**		-
Jul 96.	(7"ep/10"ep/cd-ep) *(RUG 47/+T/CD)* **BEAUTY OF THE RIDE / SIXTEEN. / RIDING / SLINTSTRUMENTAL**	74	
Aug 96.	(cd/c/d-lp) *(WIG CD/MC/LP 26) <SP 370>* **HARMACY**	38	

– On fire / Prince – S / Ocean / Nothing like you / Crystal gypsy / Beauty of the ride / Mind reader / Sferzando! / Willing to wait / Hillbilly II / Zone doubt / Too pure / Worst thing / Love to fight / Perfect way / Can't give up / Open ended / Weed against speed / I smell a rat.

Oct 96. (7") *(RUG 50)* **OCEAN (Tim O'Heir's Ocean way remix). / WORST THING (Osterville version)** [ ] [-]
(cd-s+=) *(RUG 50CD)* – Third generation deadline / Portrait of the artist on the phone.

—— **RUSS POLLARD** – drums; repl. FEY

	Domino	Sire
Jan 99. (7") *(RUG 80)* **FLAME (remix). / FLAME (4-track) / SWEET SURRENDER**	30	-

(cd-s) *(RUG 80CD1)* – ('A'side) / Loss of soul and shoe / Television nitelite.
(cd-s) *(RUG 80CD2)* – ('A'side) / Crystal crossed / Saltwater garden.

	Domino	Sire
Feb 99. (cd/c/lp) *(WIG CD/MC/LP 57)* <31044> **THE SEBADOH**	45	-

– It's all you / Weird / Bird in the hand / Break free / Tree / Nick of time / Flame / So long / Love is stronger / Decide / Colorblind / Thrive / Cuban / Sorry / Drag down.

Jun 99. (7") *(RUG 89)* **IT'S ALL YOU. / EMMETT PIG** [ ] [ ]
(cd-s+=) *(RUG 89CD)* – Mind reader.

– compilations, others, etc. –

Feb 97. (cd) *Cortex; (CORX 016CD)* **MAGNET'S COIL** [ ] [-]

LOU BARLOW AND HIS SENTRIDOH

—— - vocals, guitar

	not iss.	Sub Pop
1993. (7"; as LOU BARLOW) **I AM NOT MOCKING YOU. /**	-	

	not iss.	Smells Like
1992. (7") **LOSERCORE. / REALLY INSANE**	-	

	not iss.	Little Bro.
1993. (7"ep) **THE MYSTERIOUS SENTRIDOH**	-	

	Smells Like	Smells Like
Jun 94. (cd; LOU BARLOW'S ACOUSTIC SENTRIDOH) <SLR 08> **COLLECTION OF HOME RECORDINGS**	-	

– Stronger / Chokechain / Only losers / Breakdown day / Rise below slowly / Dragdown memory / Not nice to be nice / Mellow, cool and painfully aware / Crackers and coffee / High school /

Oct 94. (cd; SENTRIDOH) <(SM 11CD)> **WINNING LOSERS** [ ] [ ]
Oct 94. (cd; LOU BARLOW & FRIENDS) <(SM 12CD)> **ANOTHER COLLECTION OF HOME RECORDINGS**
– Run to you / Puffin / Queen of the shore / Blonde in the bleachers / What would it be like / Feel good / Symbiosis / Option / Alone to decide / Cranky / Machinery / Synthstrument.

—— Also cd on 'Shrimper' cd+d-lp 'LOSING YEARS'.

	City Slang	City Slang
1995. (cd/d-lp) <(EFA 04940-2/-1)> **LOU BARLOW AND HIS SENTRIDOH**		

– I am not mocking you / Survival / Helpless heartbreak / Dirty mind / Forever instant / Natural nature / Don't need / Endless tease / Paranoid revolution / Same old, say mold / Good in others / Spirit that kills / Weakness is the secret / Cold love / No one taught me / No matter what / Feel good / Symbiosis / Option / Alone to decide / Cranky / Machinery / Synthstrument.

the FOLK IMPLOSION

LOU BARLOW + JOHN DAVIS

	Chocolate	Drunken F.
1993. (c) **FOLK IMPLOSION**		

(5 tracks were featured in Sep94 on cd+10"m-lp 'TAKE A LOOK INSIDE THE FOLK IMPLOSION' om 'Tupelo-Communion'UK / 'Shrimper'US)

	imported	Drunken F.
Aug 94. (7"ep) **WALK THRU THIS WORLD WITH THE FOLK IMPLOSION**	-	

– My head really hurts / End of the first side / Won't back down / School.

	Communion	Communion
Sep 94. (m-cd/m-lp) *(COMM 32)* **TAKE A LOOK INSIDE . . . . . .**		

– Blossom / Sputnik's down / Slap me / Chicken squawk / Spiderweb / Butterfly / Had to find out / Better than allrite / Why do they they hide / Winter's day / Boyfriend, girlfriend / Shake a little Heaven / Waltin' with yor ego / Take a look inside / Start again.

1996. (7") **PALM OF MY HAND. /** [ ] [ ]

	Domino	Domino
Mar 96. (7"; as DELUXX FOLK IMPLOSION) *(RUG 44)* **DADDY NEVER UNDERSTOOD. /**		

	London	London
May 96. (12") *(LONX 382)* <0430> **NATURAL ONE. / ('A'-Unkle mix) / (Unkle instrumental)**	45	29 Nov95

(cd-s+=) *(LONCD 382)* – ('A'-Unkle No Skratch mix).
(above single taken from the movie, 'Kids')

	Communion	Communion
Feb 97. (7") <(COMM 47)> **POLE POSITION. / OPENING DAY**		

(cd-s+=) <(COMM 47CD)> – Summer's over.
Apr 97. (7") <(COMM 46)> **INSINUATION. / KEEPING SCORE** [ ] [ ]
(cd-s+=) <(COMM 46CD)> – Trail burn.
Jun 97. (lp/cd) <(COMM 45/+CD)> **DARE TO BE SURPRISED** [ ] [ ]
– Pole position / Wide web / Insinuation / Barricade / That's the trick / Checking in / Cold night / Park dub / Burning paper / (Blank paper) / Ball and chain / Fall into November / Dare to be surprised / River devotion.

	Domino	Interscope
Oct 99. (cd/d-lp) *(WIG CD/LP 72)* <490336> **ONE PART LULLABY**		Sep99

– My ritual / One part lullaby / Free to go / Serge / East L.A. / Mechanical men / Kingdom of lies / Gravity / Changed to the moon / Merry go round / Someone to love / No need to worry / Back to the sunrise.

JOHN DAVIS

	not iss.	Shrimper
1993. (c) **STARS & SONGS**	-	
1994. (cd) **PURE NIGHT**	-	

	Communion	Communion
May 95. (lp/cd) <COMM 37/+CD> **LEAVE HOME**	-	

(UK-iss.Dec96; same)

	Shrimper	Shrimper
Jan 96. (m-lp/m-cd; as JOHN DAVIS & DENNIS CALLACI) <SHR 74/+CD> **ROOM FOR SPACE**	-	

– Take a walk / Room for space / Sea shore / Unclean / Saddle / Needle drag / Stand tall / Sail away. (UK-iss.Dec96; same as US)

Nov 96. (m-cd) <(SHR 85CD)> **I'LL BURN** [ ]
– I'll burn (album version) / Long range view / Topanga road / Vivid life / Automatic as apples / Circus / Endless soft hits / I'll burn (home version).
Jan 97. (lp/cd) <(SHR 90/+CD)> **BLUE MOUNTAINS** [ ]
– Jeep Cherokee / I took flight / I'll burn / Blue mountains / Narrow / Knock out / Face to the storm / Tethers / Startle / I freaked out like a big truck / Zowie pop / The way you touch me makes me laugh / Ready / Eloped – Elated.

SECRETS (see under ⇒ WARD, Clifford T.)

SEEDS / Sky SAXON
(dig out; 4th edition or Great Psychedelic . . .)

Bob SEGER

Born: 6 May'45, Michigan, USA. Coming from an impoverished working-class background, SEGER began developing his hard-hitting brand of rock'n'roll in the early 60's, eventually joining (DOUG BROWN &) THE OMENS as a keyboard player. Tha material was co-written by SEGER and BROWN, the pair even managing a spoof of BARRY SADLER's 'The Ballad Of The Green Berets' under the pseudonym of The BEACH BUMS in early '66. The OMENS subsequently became BOB SEGER & THE LAST HEARD, the hard gigging troupe garnering a hardcore local following and releasing a handful of singles on the small 'Hideout' and 'Cameo' labels. Early in '68, Eddie 'Punch' Andrews became their manager as the band were now billed as The BOB SEGER SYSTEM; with a 'Capitol' contract in hand, a line-up of SEGER, DAN HONAKER, TONY NEME, BOB SCHULTZ and PEP PERRINE scored a US Top 20 hit with the blistering white R&B of 'RAMBLIN' GAMBLIN' MAN', a fitting title track for the freewheeling 1969 debut album. The group's Motor City following helped place the record in the lower reaches of the American chart although subsequent singles failed to build on this initial success. Disbanding The SYSTEM, SEGER replaced the departing SCHULTZ and NEME, recording his solo debut set, 'MONGREL' (1970). The musical chairs continued as the singer hooked up with musicians DAVE TEEGARDEN, SKIP VANWINKLE KNAPE and MICHAEL BRUCE for 72's 'SMOKIN' O.P.'s', a set of eclectic covers with the added bluster of a revamped 'HEAVY MUSIC' and the distinction of being SEGER's first album issued on his own label, 'Palladium'. The rootsy 'BACK IN '72' (1973), despite boasting the backing talents of JJ CALE and one MARCY LEVY (later reborn as MARCELLA DETROIT of SHAKESPEAR'S SISTER fame), failed to raise SEGER above cult acclaim. Likewise 'SEVEN' (1974), although it did spawn a minor hit in the brawny 'GET OUT OF DENVER'. SEGER's hard-bitten determination finally began to pay off in the mid-70's as he formed his finest backing unit to date in The SILVER BULLET BAND (namely DREW ABBOTT, ROBIN ROBBINS, CHRIS CAMPBELL, ALTO REED and CHARLIE ALLEN MARTIN) and returned to 'Capitol' for the 'BEAUTIFUL LOSER' album. Combining his trademark JOHN FOGERTY-esque grit with a newfound maturity and precision, SEGER was hailed in some quarters as the new BRUCE SPRINGSTEEN; certainly, in America at least, the singer's hard-driving, pretension-free nuggets of everyday wisdom went down a storm and the superior 'NIGHT MOVES' (1977), SEGER at last found himself in the Top 10. Proving that he was now as equally adept at delivering more sensitive material as high-octane rock'n'roll, the singer breached the US Top 5 with the album's moving title track. 'STRANGER IN TOWN' (1978) kept up the momentum, again, like its predecessor, utilising The MUSCLE SHOALS' rhythm section for added authenticity. Brushing aside the new wave pretenders, SEGER was now something of an American institution, finally topping the charts in 1980 with the ballad-heavy 'AGAINST THE WIND' album. The record also saw him making the UK Top 30 for the first time, although his British sales would never match the multi-platinum success afforded him in the States. Though hardly prolific in the 80's, his two studio albums, 'THE DISTANCE' (1982) and 'LIKE A ROCK' (1986) both made the US Top 5, dependable million-sellers which satisfied his loyal fans if not exactly breaking any new ground. SEGER was naturally in his element in the live environment, a scathing in-concert cover of Creedence Clearwater Revival's 'FORTUNATE SON' making the latter set an essential purchase. With The SILVER BULLET BAND whittled away to its barest bones throughout the 80's, SEGER's work may lack the intensity of old, though his two most recent albums, 'THE FIRE INSIDE' (1991) and 'IT'S A MYSTERY' (1995) illustrated that SEGER himself was far from a spent force. • **Songwriters:** SEGER wrote most except, RIVER DEEP MOUNTAIN HIGH + NUTBUSH CITY LIMITS (Ike & Tina Turner) / BO DIDDLEY (Bo Diddley) / IF I WERE A CARPENTER (Tim Hardin) / LOVE THE ONE YOU'RE WITH (Stephen Stills) / BLIND LOVE + 16 SHELLS

FROM A 30.6 (Tom Waits) / SHE CAN'T DO ANYTHING WRONG (C. Davis-Richmond) / C'EST LA VIE (Chuck Berry) / etc. • **Trivia:** SEGER's songs have been covered by many including ROSALIE (Thin Lizzy) / GET OUT OF DENVER (Eddie & The Hot Rods) / WE'VE GOT TONITE (Kenny Rogers & Sheena Easton).

Album rating: RAMBLIN' GAMBLIN' MAN (*6) / NOAH (*6) / MONGREL (*5) / BRAND NEW MORNING (*5) / BACK IN '72 (*5) / SMOKIN' O.P.'s (*6) / SEVEN (*6) / BEAUTIFUL LOSER (*7) / 'LIVE' BULLET (*7) / NIGHT MOVES (*8) / STRANGER IN TOWN (*7) / AGAINST THE WIND (*6) / NINE TONIGHT (*6) / THE DISTANCE (*6) / LIKE A ROCK (*6) / THE FIRE INSIDE (*6) / THE FIRE INSIDE (*5) / GREATEST HITS compilation (*8) / IT'S A MYSTERY (*5)

BOB SEGER & The LAST HEARD

BOB SEGER – vocas, guitar with **DAN HONAKER** – bass, guitar, vocals / **PEP PERRINE** – drums, vocals / **DOUG BROWN** – keyboards

			not iss.	Hideout
May 66.	(7") <1013> **EAST SIDE STORY. / EAST SIDE SOUND**		-	☐

— <above & below 45's, were soon distributed by 'Cameo' 438 + 465>

| Jul 66. | (7") <1014> **PERSECUTION SMITH. / CHAIN SMOKIN'** | | - | ☐ |

			not iss.	Cameo
Dec 66.	(7") <444> **SOCK IT TO ME, SANTA. / FLORIDA TIME**		-	☐
1967.	(7") <473> **VAGRANT WINTER. / VERY FEW**		☐	☐
1967.	(7") <494> **HEAVY MUSIC (part 1). / HEAVY MUSIC (part 2)**		-	☐

BOB SEGER SYSTEM

— repl. BROWN with **BOB SCHULTZ** – keyboards, saxophone / **TONY NEME** – guitar, keyboards

		Capitol	Capitol
Jan 68.	(7") <2145> **2 + 2 = WHAT?. / DEATH ROW**	-	☐
Dec 68.	(7") (CL 15574) <2297> **RAMBLIN' GAMBLIN' MAN. / TALES OF LUCY BLUE**		17
Jan 69.	(lp) <172> **RAMBLIN' GAMBLIN' MAN**	-	62

– Ramblin' gamblin' man / Tales of Lucy Blue / Ivory / Gone / Down home / Train man / White wall / Black eyed girl / 2 + 2 = what? / Doctor Fine / The lost song (love needs to be loved). (UK-iss.Nov77; CAPS 1013) (re-iss. Jun81 on 'Greenlight'; GO 2018)

May 69.	(7") <2480> **IVORY. / LOST SONG (LOVE NEEDS TO BE LOVED)**		☐
Jan 70.	(7") <2576> **LENNIE JOHNSON. / NOAH (or) OUT LOUD**	-	97
Mar 70.	(7") <2640> **INNERVENUS EYES. / LONELY MAN**		☐
Apr 70.	(7") <236> **NOAH**		☐
May 70.	(7") (CL 15642) <2748> **LUCIFER. / BIG RIVER**		84 Mar70
Oct 70.	(lp) <499> **MONGREL**		☐

– Song to Rufus / Evil Edna / Highway child / Big river / Mongrel / Lucifer / Teachin' blues / Leavin' on my dream / Mongrel too / River deep mountain high. (UK-iss.Nov77; CAPS 1010) (re-iss. Jun81 on 'Greenlight'; GO 2022) (re-iss. Jul83 on 'Fame' lp/c; FA/TC-FA 3072)

BOB SEGER

— added **DON WATSON** – keyboards to repl SCHULTZ + NEME

— now with **DAVE TEEGARDEN** – drums / **SKIP VANWINKLE KNAPE** – keyboards, bass / **MICHAEL BRUCE** – guitar

| Nov 71. | (lp) <731> **BRAND NEW MORNING** | | - |
| Nov 71. | (7") <3187> **LOOKIN' BACK. / HIGHWAY CHILD** | - | 96 |

		Reprise	Palladium
Jul 72.	(7") <1079> **IF I WERE A CARPENTER. / JESSE JAMES**	-	76
Aug 72.	(lp) (K 44214) <2109> **SMOKIN' O.P.'s**		Jul72

– Bo Diddley / Love the one you're with / If I were a carpenter / Hummingbird / Let it rock / Turn on your love light / Jesse James / Someday / Heavy music. (re-iss. Apr80; 11746)

| Nov 72. | (7") <1117> **TURN ON YOUR LOVE LIGHT. / Bo Diddley: BO DIDDLEY** | - | ☐ |

— SEGER's back-up back included **DICK SIMS** – keyboards / **TOM CARTMELL** – sax / **JAMIE OLDAKER** – drums / **SERGIO PASTORA** – percussion / **MARCY LEVY** – backing vocals

| Mar 73. | (lp) (K 44227) <2126> **BACK IN '72** | | ☐ |

– Midnight rider / So I wrote you a song / Stealer / Rosalie / Turn the page / Back in '72 / Neon sky / I've been working / I've got time.

| Apr 73. | (7") <1143> **ROSALIE. / NEON SKY** | | ☐ |
| Nov 73. | (7") (K 14243) **ROSALIE. / BACK IN '72** | | ☐ |

His band all left to join ERIC CLAPTON. Newcomers **KENNY BUTTREY** – drums / **RANDY MEYERS** – drums / **RICK MANSKA** – keyboards / **TOMMY COGBILL** – bass / + guitars.

| Jun 74. | (7") <1171> **NEED YA. / SEEN A LOT OF FLOORS** | | ☐ |
| Jul 74. | (lp) (K 44262) <2184> **SEVEN / CONTRASTS** | | ☐ |

– Get out of Denver / Long song comin' / Need ya / School teacher / Cross of gold / U.M.C. (Upper Middle Class) / Seen a lot of floors / 20 years from now / All your love. (re-iss. Apr80; 11748) (re-iss. Jun81 on 'Greenlight'; GO 2006)

| Aug 74. | (7") (K 14364) <1205> **GET OUT OF DENVER. / LONG SONG COMIN'** | | 80 |
| Nov 74. | (7") <1316> **U.M.C. (UPPER MIDDLE CLASS). / THIS OLD HOUSE** | - | ☐ |

— new line-up consisted of **DREW ABBOTT** – guitar / **ROBIN ROBBINS** – keyboards / **CHRIS CAMPBELL** – bass / **ALTO REED** – saxophone / **CHARLIE ALLEN MARTIN** – drums

		Capitol	Capitol
May 75.	(7") <4062> **BEAUTIFUL LOSER. / FINE MEMORY**	-	☐
Aug 75.	(lp/c) <(EST/TC-EST 11378)> **BEAUTIFUL LOSER**		Apr75

– Beautiful loser / Black night / Katmandu / Jody girl / Travellin' man / Momma / Nutbush city limits / Sailing nights / Fine memory. (re-iss. Jun85 on 'Fame'; FA41 3117-1)

| Aug 75. | (7") (CL 15831) <4116> **KATMANDU. / BLACK NIGHT** | ☐ | 43 |
| Nov 75. | (7") <4183> **NUTBUSH CITY LIMITS. / TRAVELIN' MAN** | - | ☐ |

BOB SEGER & THE SILVER BULLET BAND

| Aug 76. | (d-lp/d-c) <(ESTSP/TC-ESTSP 16)> <11523> **LIVE BULLET (live Detroit)** | ☐ | 34 Apr76 |

– Nutbush city limits / Travellin' man / Beautiful loser / Jody girl / Lookin' back / Get out of Denver / Let it rock / I've been workin' / Turn the page / U.M.C. (Upper Middle Class) / Heavy music / Katmandu. (cd-iss. Oct88; CDP 746085-2) (cd re-iss. Feb95)

| Jun 76. | (7") <4269> **NUTBUSH CITY LIMITS (live). / LOOKIN' BACK** | - | 69 May76 |
| Aug 76. | (7") CL 15884) <4300> **TRAVELLIN' MAN (live). / BEAUTIFUL LOSER (live)** | ☐ | ☐ |

— Next 2 albums also credited The MUSCLE SHOALS RHYTHM SECTION on one side apiece. They were **DAVID HOOD** – bass / **ROGER HAWKINS** – drums / **BARRY BECKETT** & **JIMMY JOHNSON** – horns / **DOUG RILEY** – keyboards / **PETE CARR** – guitar / + **GLENN FREY**

| Nov 76. | (7") (CL 15895) **MAINSTREET. / COME TO POPPA** | ☐ | 8 Nov76 |
| Mar 77. | (lp/c) <(EST/TC-EST 11557)> **NIGHT MOVES** | | ☐ |

– Rock and roll never forgets / Night moves / The fire down below / Sunburst / Sunspot baby / Mainstreet / Come to poppa / Ship of fools / Mary Lou. (re-iss.May82 on 'Fame' lp/c; FA/TC-FA 3022) (cd-iss. Oct88; CDP 746075-2) (cd re-iss. Feb95)

Mar 77.	(7") (CL 15904) <4369> **NIGHT MOVES. / SHIP OF FOOLS**	-	4 Dec76
Apr 77.	(7") <4422> **MAINSTREET. / JODY GIRL**		24
Jul 77.	(7") <4449> **ROCK AND ROLL NEVER FORGETS. / THE FIRE DOWN BELOW**	-	41
Sep 77.	(7") (CL 15938) **ROCK AND ROLL NEVER FORGETS. / SHIP OF FOOLS**	☐	☐

— **DAVE TEEGARDEN** – drums (ex-STK) repl. CHARLIE (was paralysed from car crash)

| May 78. | (silver-lp/c) <(EST/TC-EST 11698)> **STRANGER IN TOWN** | 31 | 4 |

– Hollywood nights / Still the same / Old time rock & roll / Till it shines / Feel like a number / Ain't got no money / We've got tonite / Brave strangers / The famous final scene. (cd-iss. Oct88' CDP 746074-2) (cd re-iss. Feb95)

May 78.	(7") (CL 15990) <4581> **STILL THE SAME. / FEEL LIKE A NUMBER**		4
Jul 78.	(7") <4618> **HOLLYWOOD NIGHTS. / BRAVE STRANGERS**	-	☐
Aug 78.	(7"silver+=) (CL 16004) **HOLLYWOOD NIGHTS. / OLD TIME ROCK & ROLL**	42	-
Jan 79.	(7") (CL 16028) <4653> **WE'VE GOT TONITE. / AIN'T GOT NO MONEY**	41	13 Oct78
Mar 79.	(7") (CL 16073) **TILL IT SHINES. / BEAUTIFUL LOSER** (12"+=) (12CL 16073) – Get out of Denver.	-	☐
Apr 79.	(7") <4702> **OLD TIME ROCK & ROLL. / SUNSPOT BABY**	-	28
Mar 80.	(7") (CL 16130) <4836> **FIRE LAKE. / LONG TWIN SILVER LINE**		6 Feb80
Mar 80.	(lp/c) <(EST/TC-EST 12041)> **AGAINST THE WIND**	26	1

– The horizontal bop / You'll accomp'ny me / Her strut / No man's land / Long twin silver line / Against the wind / Good for me / Betty Lou's getting out tonight / Fire Lake / Shinin' brightly. (cd-iss. 1986 & Feb95)

May 80.	(7") (CL 16143) <4863> **AGAINST THE WIND. / NO MAN'S LAND**	☐	5 Apr80
Aug 80.	(7") (CL 16163) <4904> **YOU'LL ACCOMP'NY ME. / BETTY LOU'S GETTING OUT TONIGHT**	☐	14 Jul80
Oct 80.	(7"m) (CL 16174) **AGAINST THE WIND. / GET OUT OF DENVER / NUTBUSH CITY LIMITS**	☐	-
Nov 80.	(7") <4951> **THE HORIZONTAL BOP. / HER STRUT**		42
Sep 81.	(d-lp/d-c) <(ESTSP/TC2-ESTSP 23)> <12182> **NINE TONIGHT (live)**	24	3

– Nine tonight / Tryin' to live my life without you / You'll accomp'ny me / Hollywood nights / Old time rock & roll / Mainstreet / Against the wind / The fire down below / Her strut / Feel like a number / Fire Lake / Betty Lou's gettin' out tonight / We've got tonight / Night moves / Rock and roll never forgets / Let it rock. (cd-iss. Feb95)

Sep 81.	(7") <5042> **TRYIN' TO LIVE MY LIFE WITHOUT YOU (live). / BRAVE STRANGERS (live)**		5
Oct 81.	(7"/12") (CL/12CL 223) **HOLLYWOOD NIGHTS (live). / BRAVE STRANGERS (live)**	49	-
Dec 81.	(7") (CL 235) **WE'VE GOT TONIGHT (live). / FEEL LIKE A NUMBER (live)** (12"+=,12"red+=) (12CL 235) – Brave strangers (live).	60	-
Dec 81.	(7") <5077> **FEEL LIKE A NUMBER (live). / HOLLYWOOD NIGHTS (live)**	-	48

— SEGER retained **CHRIS CAMPBELL** + **ALTO REED**, and recruited **ROY BITTAN** – keyboards (of BRUCE SPRINGSTEEN's E-STREET BAND) / **RUSS KUNKEL** – drums / **WADDY WACHTEL** – guitar / **CRAIG FROST** – keyboards (ex-GRAND FUNK RAILROAD)

| Dec 82. | (7") (CL 275) <5187> **SHAME ON THE MOON. / HOUSE BEHIND A HOUSE** | | 2 |
| Dec 82. | (lp/c) <(EST/TC-EST 12254)> **THE DISTANCE** | 45 | 5 |

– Even now / Makin' Thunderbirds / Boomtown blues / Shame on the Moon / Love's the last to know / Roll me away / House behind a house / Comin' home / Little victories. (cd-iss. Oct88; CDP 746 005-2)

Mar 83.	(7") (CL 284) <5213> **EVEN NOW. / LITTLE VICTORIES** (d7"+=/c-s+=) (CLD/TCCL 284) – We've got tonight / Brave strangers.	73	12
Jun 83.	(7") (CL 297) <5235> **ROLL ME AWAY. / BOOMTOWN BLUES** (below 'A'side was used on the film 'Teachers')	☐	27 May83
Jan 85.	(7") (CL 350) <5413> **UNDERSTANDING. / EAST L.A.** (12"+=) – We've got tonite.	☐	11 Nov84

— **DON BREWER** – drums (ex-GRAND FUNK RAILROAD) repl. KUNKEL

| Mar 86. | (7") (CL 396) <5532> **AMERICAN STORM. / FORTUNATE SON** (12"+=) (12CL 396) – Hollywood nights (live). (d7"++=) (CLD 396) – Hollywood nights. | ☐ | 13 |
| Apr 86. | (lp/c) <(EST/TC-EST 2011)> <12398> **LIKE A ROCK** | 35 | 3 |

– American storm / Like a rock / Miami / The ring / Tightrope / The aftermath / Sometimes / It's you / Somewhere tonight. *(cd-iss. Oct88 +=; CDP 746195-2)* – Living inside my heart / Like a rock / Like a rock (edit) / Fortunate son (live).

Jul 86.	(7") *(CL 408)* <5592> **LIKE A ROCK. / LIVING INSIDE MY HEART** (12"+=) *(12CL 408)* – Katmandu.		12 May86
Aug 86.	(7") <5623> **IT'S YOU. / THE AFTERMATH**	-	52
Nov 86.	(7") <5658> **MIAMI. / SOMEWHERE TONIGHT** (below solo 45 from the 'Beverley Hills Cop II' film on 'M.C.A.')	-	70
Aug 87.	(7"/12") *(MCA/T 1172)* <53094> **SHAKEDOWN. / THE AFTERMATH**		1 May87
Sep 91.	(cd/c/lp) *(CD/TC+/EST 2149)* <91134> **THE FIRE INSIDE** – Take a chance / The real love / Sightseeing / Real at the time / Always in my heart / The fire inside / Which way / New coat of paint / The mountain / The long way home / Blind love / She can't do anything wrong.	54	7
Aug 91.	(c-s,cd-s) <44743> **THE REAL LOVE / THE MOUNTAIN**	-	24
Sep 91.	(7") **THE REAL LOVE. / WHICH WAY** (cd-s+=) – Hollywood nights.	-	-
Mar 92.	(c-s/cd-s/7") *(TC/CD+/648)* **THE FIRE INSIDE. / THE REAL LOVE**		
Jan 95.	(7") *(CL 734)* **WE'VE GOT TONIGHT. / HOLLYWOOD NIGHTS** (c-s+=/cd-s+=) *(TC/CD+/CL 734)* – C'est la vie. (cd-s) *(CDCLS 734)* – ('A'side) / Night moves (live) / Nutbush city limits (live).	22	-
Feb 95.	(c/d/c/lp) *(CD/TC+/EST 2241)* <30334> **GREATEST HITS** (compilation) – Roll me away / Night moves / Turn the page / You'll accomp'ny me / Hollywood nights / Still the same / Old time rock & roll / We've got tonight / Against the wind / Main street / The fire inside / Like a rock / C'est la vie / In your time.	6	8 Nov94
Apr 95.	(c-s) *(CCCL 741)* **NIGHT MOVES / EVEN NOW / WE'VE GOT TONIGHT (live)** (cd-s+=) *(CDCL 741)* – American storm. (cd-s) *(CDCLS 741)* – ('A'side) / Katmandu (live) / The fire down below / The refamous final scene.	50	-
Jul 95.	(c-s/cd-s) *(TC/CD CL 749)* **HOLLYWOOD NIGHTS / ROCK AND ROLL NEVER FORGETS / HOLLYWOOD NIGHTS (live)** (cd-s) *(CDCLS 749)* – ('A'side) / Come to poppa / Fire lake.	52	-
Nov 95.	(cd/c) *(CD/TC EST 2271)* <99774> **IT'S A MYSTERY** – Rite of passage / Lock and load / By the river / Manhattan / I wonder / It's a mystery / Revisionism street / Golden boy / I can't save you, Angelene / 16 shells from a 30.6 / West of the Moon / Hands in the air.		27
Feb 96.	(c-ep/cd-ep) *(TC/CD CL 765)* **LOCK AND LOAD / THE FIRE INSIDE / LIKE A ROCK / MANHATTAN** (cd-ep) *(CDCLS 765)* – ('A'side) / It's a mystery / Roll me away / Mainstreet.	57	

– compilations, etc. –

on 'Capitol' unless mentioned otherwise

Jun 77.	(7"ep) *Reprise; (K 14476)* **EXTENDED PLAY** – Get out of Denver / Back in '72 / Midnight rider / Rosalie.		-
Nov 77.	(7"m) *(CL 15956)* **TURN THE PAGE. / GET OUT OF DENVER (live) / HEAVY MUSIC (live)**		-
Sep 83.	(7") <5276> **OLD TIME ROCK & ROLL. / TILL IT SHINES**	-	48
Mar 84.	(7") *(CL 326)* **OLD TIME ROCK & ROLL. / ROLL ME AWAY** (12"+=) *(12CL 326)* – Makin' Thunderbirds.	-	-

SELECTER

Formed: Birmingham, England . . . mid '79 by NOEL DAVIS with help from JOHN BRADBURY of The SPECIAL A.K.A. who wanted a B-side instrumental for the 'Gangsters' 45. The single made the UK Top 10 with 'THE SELECTER' getting a fair whack of the airplay and prompting a proper band set-up. Retained on '2-Tone' by JERRY DAMMERS, who had arranged a co-deal with 'Chrysalis', the group branched out on their own, keyboard player DESMOND BROWN and guitarist KEVIN HARRIS recruiting an entire new band from scratch (BRADBURY was busy with The SPECIALS, DAVIS had returned to his day job). Foremost among this new bunch of ska hopefuls was PAULINE BLACK, one of the few female vocalists on the ska scene. Her playfully distinctive tones virtually made the first real SELECTER hit, 'ON MY RADIO', an irrepressibly boisterous pop stomper which gatecrashed the Top 10 in late '79. 'THREE MINUTE HERO' followed in much the same fashion, preceding the Top 5 debut album, 'TOO MUCH PRESSURE' early in 1980. An effervescent companion piece to The SPECIALS' more radical debut, the album featured all the hits including 'MISSING WORDS' and the high-octane ska freak-out of the title track. It seemed The SELECTER star had initially burned too brightly, however, the naive charm of the debut supplanted with more lugubrious state-of-the-nation musing on the 1981 follow-up, 'CELEBRATE THE BULLET'. This coincided with the once vibrant '2-Tone' scene reaching its natural conclusion and the group split soon after the album's release. BLACK later resurfaced as presenter of kids TV quiz show, 'Hold Tight' before eventually re-joining a revamped SELECTER in the early 90's, initally as a touring project. 1994 saw the first album release for thirteen years, however, ironically enough entitled 'THE HAPPY ALBUM'. • **Songwriters:** All written by DAVIS and group, except JAMES BOND (John Barry) / TRAIN TO SKAVILLE (Ethiopians) / RAINY DAY WOMAN (Bob Dylan) / SUGAR TOWN (Lee Hazlewood) / etc. PAULINE BLACK also covered singles once hits of Johnny Nash and Betty Wright.
Album rating: TOO MUCH PRESSURE (*7) / CELEBRATE THE BULLET (*5) / THE HAPPY ALBUM (*4) / PUCKER! (*4) / GREATEST HITS compilation (*7) / CRUEL BRITANNIA (*3)

JOHN BRADBURY – drums (of The SPECIAL AKA) / **DESMOND BROWN** – keyboards / **NOEL DAVIS** – guitar / **KEVIN HARRISON** – guitar / **STEVE** – bass

		2-Tone	not iss.
Jul 79.	(7") *(TT 1-2)* **Gangsters (by The Special AKA). / THE SELECTER**	6	-

—— **DESMOND + KEVIN** recruited entire new band. (BRADBURY re-to SPECIALS) / new **PAULINE BLACK** – vocals / **CHARLEY ANDERSON** – bass / **COMPTON AMANOUR** – guitar / **CHARLEY 'H' BEMBRIDGE** – drums / **ARTHUR 'GAPS' HENDRICKSON** – vocals

		Chrysalis– 2-Tone	Chrysalis
Oct 79.	(7") *(CHSTT 4)* **ON MY RADIO. / TOO MUCH PRESSURE**	8	-
Jan 80.	(7") *(CHSTT 8)* **THREE MINUTE HERO. / JAMES BOND**	16	-
Feb 80.	(lp/c) *(CDLTT/ZCDLTT 5)* <CHR 1274> **TOO MUCH PRESSURE** – Three minute hero / Every day / They make me mad / Missing words / Danger / Street feeling / My Collie (not a dog) / On my radio / Too much pressure / Murder / Out on the streets / Carry go bring home / Black and blue / James Bond.	5	
Mar 80.	(7") *(CHSTT 10)* **MISSING WORDS. / CARRY GO BRING HOME**	23	-

—— **ADAM WILLIAMS** – bass; repl. ANDERSON / **JAMES MACKIE** – keyboards, sax; repl. BROWN

		Chrysalis	Chrysalis
Aug 80.	(7") *(CHSS 1)* **THE WHISPER. / TRAIN TO SKAVILLE** (12"+=) *(CHS12S 1)* – ('A'extended).	36	-

—— **NORMAN WATT-ROY** – bass; (ex-IAN DURY . . .) repl. WILLIAMS

Feb 81.	(7") *(CHSS 2)* **CELEBRATE THE BULLET. / LAST TANGO**		-
Feb 81.	(lp/c) *(<CHR/ZCHR 1306>)* **CELEBRATE THE BULLET** – Celebrate the bullet / Tell me what's wrong / (Who likes) Facing situations / Bristol and Miami / Their dream goes on / Cool blue lady / Red reflections / Bombscare / Washed up and left for dead / Selling out your future / Deep water.	41	

—— disbanded mid '81 (PAULINE BLACK released two flop 45's) although they reformed a decade later. BLACK / DAVIES + MARTIN STEWART – keyboards / NICK WELSH – bass / PERRY MELIUS – drums (below with PRINCE BUSTER)

		Triple X	not iss.
Jan 94.	(cd-ep) **THE MADNESS EP** – Madness / Madness (mix) / The Selecter / On my radio.		

		Demon	not iss.
Jul 94.	(cd) *(FIENDCD 751)* **THE HAPPY ALBUM** – Reselecterisation / Whip them down / Sweet and dandy / Neurotica / California screaming / I want justice / Trout / Copasetic / Mother knows best / Ladders. *(re-iss. Nov97 on 'Diablo'; DIAB 841)*		

		Triple X	Triple X
Aug 95.	(cd-ep) *(<TX 51214CD>)* **HAIRSPRAY EP** – Hairspray / Die happy / On my radio (live) / Missing words (live).		

		Dojo	Triple X
Aug 95.	(cd) *(DOJOCD 218)* **PUCKER!** – My perfect world / Hearsay / Die happy / Sugar town / Hairspray / Chocolate whip / Not so tall / Then she did / Rainy day women / Vicky's magic garden.		

		Madfish	Madfish
Nov 98.	(cd) *(<SMACD 812>)* **CRUEL BRITANNIA** – Cruel Britainnia / Respect yourself / Musical servent / How can I win / Better must come / Viper / Never said I love you / What a confusion / Bad dog / Lyrical sniper / The blind leading the blind.		

– compilations, others, etc. –

Feb 87.	(7") *Old Gold; (OG 9681)* **ON MY RADIO. / THREE MINUTE HERO** (12"+=) *(OG 4017)* – Missing words / The whisper.		-
Mar 92.	(cd/c/lp) *Receiver; (RR CD/MC/LP 156)* **OUT IN THE STREETS** *(re-iss. Oct93; same)* <US cd-iss. Aug95 on 'Triple X'>		-

—— In Dec'92, shared an album with The SPECIALS 'BBC RADIO 1 LIVE IN CONCERT'

—— the following year, the SELECTER scraped into the UK Top 30 with the 'ON MY RADIO' EP from '2-Tone' alongside SPECIALS, MADNESS & The BEAT

Nov 94.	(cd) *Blue Moon; (CDBM 103)* **PRIME CUTS VOL.1**		-
Nov 94.	(cd) *Dojo; (DOJOCD 199)* **RARE SELECTER**		-
Mar 95.	(cd) *Dojo; (DOJOCD 201)* **RARE SELECTER VOLUME TWO**		-
May 95.	(cd) *Dojo; (DOJOCD 205)* **RARE SELECTER VOLUME 3 – VERSIONS**		-
May 96.	(cd/c) *EMI Gold; (CD/TC GOLD 1034)* **GREATEST HITS** – Three minute hero / Too much pressure / Celebrate the bullet / Bomb scare / Deep water / Time hard / They make me mad / Bristol and Miami / Missing words / James Bond / On my radio / The whisper / Carry go bring home / Murder / Washed up and left for dead / Last tango in dub.		
Jun 96.	(cd) *Blue Moon; (CDBM 106)* **PRIME CUTS VOL.2**		-
Jun 96.	(cd) *Blue Moon; (CDBM 108)* **LIVE INJECTION (live)** *(re-iss. Jan98 on 'Summit')* <US cd-iss. SUMCD 4156>		-
Oct 96.	(cd/c) *Emporio; (EMPR CD/MC 663)* **GREATEST HITS LIVE (live)**		-
Oct 96.	(cd) *Dojo; (DOJOCD 270)* **SELECTERIZED – THE BEST OF THE SELECTER 1991-1996**		-
Nov 96.	(cd) *Blue Moon; (CDBM 108)* **LIVE AT ROSKLIDE (live)**		
May 97.	(d-cd) *Snapper; (SMDCD 138)* **TOO MUCH PRESSURE**		
Nov 97.	(cd) *Triple X; (<TX 51238CD>)* **THE VERY BEST OF THE SELECTER**		
Feb 98.	(cd) *Receiver; (RRCD 252)* **I WANT JUSTICE (live)**		
Oct 98.	(cd) *E.M.I.; (497792-2)* **THE BBC SESSIONS – LIVE AT PARIS THEATRE 1979 (live)**		
Mar 99.	(cd) *Mayo-Harry May; (MAYOCD 109)* **TOO MUCH PRESSURE (some live)**		
Oct 99.	(cd) *Receiver; (RRCD 274)* **THE TROJAN SONGBOOK**		
Nov 99.	(cd) *Receiver; (RRCD 275)* **MY PERFECT WORLD**		

SEMISONIC

Formed: Minneapolis, Minnesota, USA . . . mid 90's by DAN WILSON and JOHN MUNSON, who had previously played with the indie-pop band, TRIP SHAKESPEARE. The aforementioned quartet (other two members being MATT WILSON and ELAINE HARRIS) completed four well-received but commercially dismissed albums, 'THE APPLEHEAD MAN' (1988), 'ARE YOU SHAKESPEARIENCED?' (1989), 'ACROSS THE UNIVERSE' (1990) and 'LULU' (1991); covers set 'VOLT' (1992) was their final mini-CD release before they moved on. Song credits:- WHAT'S SO FUNNY ABOUT PEACE, LOVE AND UNDERSTANDING (Nick Lowe) / SOMETHING IN THE AIR (Thunderclap Newman) / BALLAD OF EL GOODO / TIME OF THE SEASON (Zombies) / DEAD SET ON DESTRUCTION (Husker Du) / HELPLESS (Neil Young). Shortly afterwards, WILSON and MUNSON drafted in drummer JACOB SLICHTER and thus SEMISONIC were born. In 1995, the trio delivered their first release, the EP 'PLEASURE', which was followed in '96 by their debut album, 'GREAT DIVIDE', a perfect piece of pop melancholia. A second set for 'M.C.A.', 'FEELING STRANGELY FINE', won over a large fanbase in the States and made the Top 50 due to its well-structured songwriting ability especially in the MTV friendly track, 'CLOSING TIME' – by mid 1999 it was peaking in the British charts.

Album rating: Trip Shakespeare: APPLEHEAD MAN (*5) / ARE YOU SHAKESPEARIENCED? (*5) / ACROSS THE UNIVERSE (*6) / LULU (*4) / VOLT mini (*4) / Semisonic: GREAT DIVIDE (*6) / FEELING STRANGELY FINE (*7)

TRIP SHAKESPEARE

DAN WILSON (b.1965) – vocals, guitar, piano / **JOHN MUNSON** – vocals, bass, harmonica, etc / **MATT WILSON** – guitar, vocals, piano / **ELAINE HARRIS** – percussion, drums

			not iss.	Twin/Tone
1988.	(lp/cd) <89177> **APPLEHEAD MAN**		-	

– Fangs / Rose / Stop the winter / Necklace / Applehead man / Washington Bridge / Pearle / Fireball / Highway in the sun / Beatle.

1989.	(lp/cd) <89180> **ARE YOU SHAKESPEARIENCED?**		-	

– Diane / The lake / Swing / Two wheeler, four wheeler / Spirit / The tief / Toolmaster of Brainerd / Vines / Reception.

			A&M	A&M
Jul 90.	(7") (AM 572) **GONE, GONE, GONE.** /			
	(12"+=) (AMY 572) –			
Aug 90.	(cd/c/lp) (395294-2/-4/-1) <75021-5294-2/-4/-1> **ACROSS THE UNIVERSE**			

– Turtledove / Pearle / Snow days / Drumming like me / Gone, gone, gone / The slacks / Unlucky lady / The nail / The crane / Late / Honey tree.

1990.	(cd-ep) **THE CRANE EP**		-	
1991.	(cd) **LULU**		-	

– None of the regular rules were true / Lulu / Bachelorette / Your mouth / Will you be found / Down my block / Jill can drive / Look at the Moon / Graveyard / Bonneville / Today you move / Patricia / Down the dusty road / If you miss me.

1992.	(m-cd) <89248> **VOLT**		-	

– What's so funny about peace, love and understanding / Something in the air / Ballad of El Goodo / Time of the season / Dead set on destruction / Helpless.

—— disbanded after the relative failure of above

SEMISONIC

WILSON + MUNSON / + JACOB SLICHTER – drums

			not iss.	Elektra
1995.	(cd-ep) **PLEASURE**		-	
			M.C.A.	M.C.A.
1996.	(cd) <11414> **GREAT DIVIDE**		-	

– FNT / If I run / Delicious / Down in flames / Across the great divide / Temptation / Prize / No one else / Brand new baby / Falling / In another life / I'll feel for you. (UK-iss.Nov99; same)

Oct 98.	(c-s) (MCSC 48098) **CLOSING TIME / FALLING (live)**			
	(cd-s+=) (MCSTD 48098) – The air that I breathe			
Oct 98.	(cd) <(MCD 11733)> **FEELING STRANGELY FINE**		43	Mar98

– Closing time / Singing in my sleep / Made to last / Never you mind / Secret smile / DND / Completely pleased / This will be my year / All worked out / California / She spreads her wings / Gone to the movies. (re-dist.Jul99, hit UK No.16)

Jun 99.	(c-s) (MCSC 40210) **SECRET SMILE / TAKE ME WITH YOU (live)**		13	
	(cd-s+=) (MCSXD 40210) – Singing in my sleep (remix).			
	(cd-s) (MCSTD 40210) – ('A'side) / Completely pleased / Erotic city.			
Oct 99.	(c-s) (MCSC 40221) **CLOSING TIME / THE AIR THAT I BREATHE (live)**		25	
	(cd-s+=) (MCSXD 40221) – FNT (live acoustic).			
	(cd-s) (MCSTD 40221) – ('A'side) / Falling (live) / Long way from home (live).			

SENSATIONAL ALEX HARVEY BAND
(see under ⇒ HARVEY, Alex)

SENSELESS THINGS
(dig out; 4th edition or Great Alt & Indie . . .)

SENSER (dig out; 4th edition or Great Alt & Indie . . .)

SENTRIDOH (see under ⇒ SEBADOH)

SEPULTURA

Formed: Belo Horizonte, Brazil . . . 1983 by brothers MAX and schoolboy IGOR CAVALERA alongside JAIRO T. and PAOLO JR., taking the name SEPULTURA from the MOTORHEAD song, 'Dancing On Your Grave' (Sepultura meaning 'grave' in Portuguese). Influenced largely by black metal bands such as VENOM, as well as British punk, SEPULTURA's earliest release was a split album with fellow Brazilian death metallers, OVERDOSE, entitled 'BESTIAL DEVASTATION' (1984). Another rudimentary thrash effort followed in 'MORBID VISIONS' (1985), again released on the small 'Cogumelo' label. It was nevertheless enough to see the band snapped up by 'Roadrunner', who released the 'SCHIZOPHRENIA' set in early '87. With ANDREAS KISSER replacing JAIRO T, SEPULTURA at last began to focus some of their unbridled sonic savagery, MAX's trademark growl assuming the bowel quaking chill it had always threatened as the ubiquitous Scott Burns worked his magic at the mixing desk. With BURNS in a production capacity, the masterful 'BENEATH THE REMAINS' (1989) finally signalled the arrival of a major force on the international metal scene. Breathtakingly dynamic, the album twisted and turned like a joyrider on speed, switching from breakneck thrash to pummeling sludge-riffing with untramelled ferocity. Though you still couldn't actually make out what CAVALERA was saying, the unearthly roar of his voice was a revelation, almost an instrument in itself with its own rhythmic thrust. And while many thrash acts gave the impression of playing aggressively purely because that's what was expected of them, the likes of 'INNER SELF' and 'STRONGER THAN HATE' reeked of the genuine frustration, despair and disillusionment of growing up in an impoverished third world country. One of the last great thrash albums of the 80's, the record marked the end of the first stage in SEPULTURA's development; the next album, 'ARISE' (1991), was released as the scene was in its death throes and on this showing it was clear they weren't going to be left behind. On many tracks, the pace was slowed to a seismic turbo-Sabbath grind, gut wrenchingly heavy and immensely powerful; SEPULTURA were redefining the boundaries of metal with each successive release. Already massive in Brazil (SEPULTURA had played the huge 'Rock In Rio' festival in 1990), the group narrowly missed the UK Top 10 with 'CHAOS A.D.' (1993). Taking the more basic approach of its predecessor even further, the record adopted a markedly more political lyrical stance than anything they'd released to date, the anger ferociously focused into bitter diatribes like 'SLAVE NEW WORLD'. Having previously injected a malignant power to MOTORHEAD's 'Orgasmatron' (which even LEMMY couldn't muster) a couple of years back, here SEPULTURA steamrollered NEW MODEL ARMY's 'The Hunt', proving that punk was as close as metal, if not more so, to the group's charred heart. But SEPULTURA really guaranteed their place in the rock hall of fame with 'ROOTS' (1996), voted by Kerrang! magazine as one of the best metal albums ever released. Stunning in both its stylistic breadth and unrelenting intensity, this was the masterpiece SEPULTURA had been working towards from the beginning of their career. Leaving most of their peers banging their heads on the starting post, the record embraced the cultural heritage of their native Brazil (with the help of rainforest tribe, the Xavantes) to concoct a haunting fusion of ethno-metal and hypnotic tribal spiritualism. The rock world was stunned when SEPULTURA disbanded early in 1997, one of the few metal acts to quit while they were on top (MAX has since formed SOULFLY, taking up where 'ROOTS' more rhythmic sound left off). However, that was certainly not the end, as SEPULTURA regrouped the following year complete with new frontman, DERRICK GREEN. An excellent comeback set, 'AGAINST', astonished most hardcore fans, GREEN's earthy vocal chords giving the group another dimension. • Songwriters: Group penned, except DRUG ME (Dead Kennedys) / SYMPTOM OF THE UNIVERSE (Black Sabbath) / CLENCHED FIST (Ratos De Porao) / INTO THE CRYPT OF RAYS + PROCREATION (OF THE WICKED) (Celtic Frost) / GENE MACHINE – DON'T BOTHER ME (Bad Brains).

Album rating: MORBID VISIONS (*4) / SCHIZOPHRENIA (*7) / BENEATH THE REMAINS (*9) / ARISE (*6) / CHAOS A.D. (*7) / ROOTS (*9) / BLOOD-ROOTED compilation (*7) / AGAINST (*8)

MAX CAVALERA (b.MASSIMILANO A. CAVALERA, 4 Aug'69) – vocals, guitar / **JAIRO T** – guitar / **PAULO JR.** (b.PAULO XISTO PINTO JR., 30 Apr'69) – bass / **IGOR CAVALERA** (b.4 Sep'70) – drums

			Cogumelo	not iss.
Nov 84.	(m-lp; shared with OVERDOSE) (803248) **BESTIAL DEVASTATION**		-	Brazil

– Bestial devastation / Antichrist / Necromancer / Warriors of death. (cd-iss. Mar97 on 'Bestial'; SBD 001)

Nov 85.	(lp) **MORBID VISIONS**		-	-

– Morbid visions / Mayhem / Troops of doom / War / Crucifixion / Show me the wrath / Funeral rites / Empire of the damned / The curse. (UK-iss.Apr89 on 'Shark' German; SHARK 004) (UK-iss.Nov91 on 'Roadracer' w/ 'BESTIAL DEVASTATION' cd/c/lp; RO 9276-2/-4/-1) (re-iss. Apr94 + Aug95 on 'Roadrunner'; same)

—— **ANDREAS KISSER** (b.24 Aug'68, Sao Bernado Do Campo, Brazil) – lead guitar; repl. JAIRO T

			Shark	New Renaissance
Feb 88.	(lp/cd) (SHARK/+CD 006) **SCHIZOPHRENIA**		-	German

– Intro / From the past comes the storms / To the wall / Escape to the void / Inquisition symphony / Screams behind the shadows / Septic schizo / The abyss / R.I.P. (Rest In Pain). (c+=/cd+=) – Troops of doom. (re-iss. cd/c/lp Apr94 + Aug95 on 'Roadrunner'; same)

Apr 89. (lp/c/cd) <(RO 9511-1/-4/-2)> **BENEATH THE REMAINS**

Roadracer	Roadracer

– Beneath the remains / Inner self / Stronger than hate / Mass hypnosis / Sarcastic existence / Slaves of pain / Lobotomy / Hungry / Primitive future. *(re-iss. Apr94 & Aug95 on 'Roadrunner'; same)*

Mar 91. (cd/c/lp/pic-lp) <(RO 9328-2/-4/-1/-8)> **ARISE** [40]
– Arise / Dead embryonic cells / Desperate cry / Murder / Subtraction / Altered state / Under siege (regnum Irae) / Meaningless movements / Infected voice. (pic-lp+=) – Orgasmatron. *(re-iss. Apr94 & Aug95 on 'Roadrunner'; same)*

Mar 91. (c-ep/12"ep/cd-ep) (RO 2424-4/-6/-3) **UNDER SIEGE (REGNUM IRAE). / TROOPS OF DOOM (re-recorded) / ORGASMATRON**

Feb 92. (c-ep/12"ep/cd-ep) (RO 2406-4/-6/-3) **ARISE. / INNER SELF (live) / TROOPS OF DOOM (live)**

Roadrunner	Epic

Sep 93. (7"pic-d-ep/c-ep/12"ep/cd-ep) (RR 2382-7/-4/-6/-3) **TERRITORY. / POLICIA / BIOTECH IS GODZILLA** [66]

Oct 93. (cd/c/lp) (RR 9000-2/-4/-1) <57458> **CHAOS A.D.** [11] [32]
– Refuse-Resist / Territory / Slave new world / Amen / Kaiowas / Propaganda / Biotech is Godzilla / Nomad / We who are not as others / Manifest / The Hunt / Clenched fist *(cd-tin-box.Mar94; 9000-0)* (+=) – Policia / Inhuman nature. *(re-iss. Aug95+=; same)* – Chaos B.C. / Kaiowas (tribal jam) / Territory (live) / Amen – Inner self (live). *(re-iss. Oct96; same)*

—— Early in '94, MAX was arrested and fined for stamping on the Brazilian flag. He is said to have done it accidentally.

Feb 94. (7"ep/c-ep/12"ep/12"purple-ep/cd-ep/s-cd-ep) (RR 2377-7/-4/-6/-8/-3/-5) **REFUSE – RESIST. / INHUMAN NATURE / PROPAGANDA** [51]

May 94. (cd-s) (RR 2374-3) **SLAVE NEW WORLD / DESPERATE CRY** [46]
(c-ep/etched-12"ep/cd-ep) (RR 2374-4/-8/-5) – ('A'side) / Crucificados Pelo systema / Drug me / Orgasmatron. (live).

Feb 96. (7"colrd) (RR 2320-7) **ROOTS BLOODY ROOTS. / SYMPTOM OF THE UNIVERSE** [19]
(cd-s) (RR 2320-2) – ('A'side) / Procreation (of the wicked) / Refuse – resist (live) / Territory (live).
(cd-s) (RR 2320-5) – ('A'side) / Propaganda (live) / Beneath the remains (live) / Escape to the void (live).

Feb 96. (cd/c/lp) <(RR 8900-2/-4/-1)> **ROOTS** [4] [27]
– Roots bloody roots / Attitude / Cut-throat / Ratamahatta / Breed apart / Straighthate / Spit / Lookaway / Dusted / Born stubborn / Jasco / Itsari / Ambush / Endangered species / Dictatorshit. (cd+=) – Chaos B.C. / Symptom of the universe / Kaiowas (live). *(re-iss. Oct96 as 'THE ROOTS OF SEPULTURA' cd w/ bonus cd of 20 unreleased + rare tracks; RR 8900-8)*

Aug 96. (7") (RR 2314-7) **RATAMAHATTA. / MASS HYPNOSIS (live)** [23]
(cd-s) (RR 2314-2) – ('A'side) / War / Slave new world (live) / Amen – Inner self (live).
(cd-s) (RR 2314-5) – ('A'side) / War / Roots bloody roots (demo) / Dusted (demo).

Dec 96. (7") (RR 2299-7) **ATTITUDE. / DEAD EMBRYONIC CELLS (live)** [46]
(cd-s) (RR 2299-2) – ('A'side) / Lookaway (master vibe mix) / Mine.
(cd-s) (RR 2299-5) – ('A'side) / Kaiowas (tribal jam) / Clenched fist (live) / Biotech is Godzilla (live).

—— split late '96, when MAX was told he was no longer wanted. He subsequently formed SOULFLY, while SEPULTURA went to ground for a year. They returned with a new singer **DERRICK GREEN** (ex-ALPHA JERK)

Oct 98. (cd/c/lp) (<RR 8700-2/-4/-1>) **AGAINST** [40] [82]
– Against / Choke / Rumors / Old earth / Floaters in mud / Boycott / Tribus / Common bonds / F.O.E. / Reza / Unconscious / Kamaitachi / Drowned out / Hatred aside / T3rcermillennium.

Nov 98. (cd-s) (RR 2219-3) **CHOKE / GENE MACHINE (demo) / DON'T BOTHER ME (demo) / AGAINST (demo)**

Jul 99. (cd-s) (RR 2169-3) **AGAINST / THE WASTE / TRIBUS / COMMON BONDS (Alternate mix)**

– compilations, etc. –

Nov 89. (cd) Shark; (CDSHARK 012) **MORBID VISIONS / CEASE TO EXIST** [-] [-] German

May 90. (c) Shark; (SHARKMC 017) **SCHIZOPHRENIA / MORBID VISIONS** [-] [-] German

Aug 97. (cd) Roadrunner; (<RR 8821-2>) **BLOOD ROOTED**
– Procreation (of the wicked) / Inhuman nature / Policia / War / Criucificados pelo sistema / Symptom of the universe / Mine / Lobotomy / Dusted / Roots bloody roots / Drug me / Refuse – resist / Slave new world / Propaganda / Beneath the remains / Escape to the void / Kaiowas / Clenched fist / Biotech is Godzilla.

NAILBOMB

MAX CAVALERA + ALEX NEWPORT (of FUDGE TUNNEL)

Roadrunner	Epic

Mar 94. (cd/c/lp) (RR 9055-2/-4/-1) **POINT BLANK** [62]
– Wasting away / Vai toma no cu / 24 hour bullshit / Guerillas / Blind and lost / Sum of your achievements / Cockroaches / For f***'s sake / World of shit / Exploitation / Religious cancer / Shit panata / Sick life. *(re-iss. Aug95; same)*

Oct 95. (cd/c/lp) (RR 8910-2/-4/-1) **PROUD TO COMMIT COMMERCIAL SUICIDE**
– Wasting away / Guerrillas / Cockroaches / Vai toma no co / Sum of your achievements / Religious cancer / Police truck / Exploitation / World of shit / Blind and lost / Sick life / While you sleep, I destroy your world / Zero tolerance.

Will SERGEANT (see under ⇒ ECHO & THE BUNNYMEN)

SEVENDUST

Formed: Atlanta, Georgia, USA . . . 1994 initially as CRAWLSPACE by MORGAN ROSE, VINCE HORNSBY, CLINT LOWERY, JOHN CONNOLLY and LAJON WITHERSPOON, the last two a black funk singer poached from his brother COREY's band (now a STUCK MOJO member). One single, 'MY RUIN' was independently issued under this moniker (also appeared on V/A set 'Mortal Kombat: More Kombat') and was to subsequently surface on the SEVENDUST debut album. Under the wing of manager, JAY JAY FRENCH (ex-TWISTED SISTER), the band signed to 'TVT', although it was by sheer chance as the label's A&R men were detoured by a hard-of-hearing cab driver who took them to one of their gigs, not a strip club as requested. Their bruising, aggro-rock sound (with similarities between LIVING COLOUR and/or MINISTRY) was soon being given radio airplay in the States via an excellent eponymous set in '97. A second set, 'HOME' (1999) repeated the riff-laden formula, only this time it payed off with a US Top 20 placing. MORGAN, meanwhile (who'd married COAL CHAMBERS' RAYNA FOSS), was possibly up for a bit of paternity leave following the subsequent birth of their new baby.

Album rating: SEVENDUST (*6) / HOME (*6)

LAJON WITHERSPOON – vocals / **CLINT LOWERY** – guitar / **JOHN CONNOLLY** – guitar / **VINCE HORNSBY** – bass / **MORGAN ROSE** – drums

		TVT	TVT

Sep 98. (cd/c) <(TVT 5730-2/-4)> **SEVENDUST** [ ] [Apr97]
– Black / Bitch / Terminator / Too close to hate / Wired / Prayer / Face / Speak / Will it bleed / My ruin / Born to die.

		Loud-Epic	TVT

Oct 99. (cd/c) (4961579) <5820> **HOME** [ ] [19]
– Home / Denial / Headtrip / Insecure / Reconnect / Waffle / Rumble fish / Licking cream / Grasp / Crumble / Feel so / Grasshopper / Bender.

SEVEN MARY THREE

Formed: Orlando, Florida, USA . . . 1992 by the 4-piece of JASON ROSS, JASON POLLOCK, CASEY DANIEL and GITI KHALSA. Signed to 'Atlantic' records on the strength of an independently released debut 'CHURN' (1995), the band cruised into the US Top 40 with the 'CUMBERSOME' single. Taken from the Top 30 album, 'AMERICAN STANDARD', the track's title accurately described the band's post-grunge sound, akin to a heavy COUNTING CROWS or even COLLECTIVE SOUL. The aforesaid album caused considerable controversy with artwork depicting a farmer about to behead a chicken with an axe. In the summer of '97, SMT returned with a third effort, 'ROCKCROWN', although this only managed to dent the US Top 75.

Album rating: CHURN (*6) / AMERICAN STANDARD (*7) / ROCKCROWN (*6) / ORANGE AVE. (*5)

JASON ROSS – vocals, guitar / **JASON POLLOCK** – guitar / **CASEY DANIEL** – bass / **GITI KHALSA** – drums

	not iss.	Independent

1995. (cd) **CHURN** [-] [-]

	Mammoth–Atlantic	Mammoth–Atlantic

Apr 96. (7"/c-s) (A 5688/+C) <98111> **CUMBERSOME. / SHELF LIFE** [ ] [39] Jan96
(cd-s+=) (A 5688CD) – ('A'acoustic).

Apr 96. (cd/c) <(7567 92633-2/-4)> **AMERICAN STANDARD** [ ] [24] Jan96
– Cumbersome / Favorite dog / Punch in punch out / Margaret / Devil boy / My my / Lame / Anything / Headstrong / Roderigo / Water's edge.

Jun 97. (cd/c) <(7567 83018-2/-4)> **ROCKCROWN** [ ] [75]
– Lucky / Rockcrown / Needle can't burn / Honey of generation / Home stretch / People like new / Make up your mind / Gone away / Times like these / I could be wrong / Angry blue / Houdini's angels / This evening's great excuse / Player piano / Oven.

Jul 98. (cd,c) <83114> **ORANGE AVE.** [-] [ ]
– Peel / Over your shoulder / Chasing you / Each little mystery / In-between / Joliet / Super-related / Flagship Eleanor / Southwestern state / Hang on / Blessing in disguise / Devil's holy joke.

Nov 98. (cd-s) **OVER YOUR SHOULDER** [-] [ ]

SEX PISTOLS

Formed: London, England . . . summer 1975 out of The SWANKERS by PAUL COOK, STEVE JONES and GLEN MATLOCK, the latter two regular faces at MALCOLM McLAREN's 'Sex' boutique on the capital's King's Road. With the NEW YORK DOLLS already on his CV, McLAREN was well qualified to mastermind the rise and fall of The SEX PISTOLS as he dubbed his new plaything, the entrepeneur/svengali installing another 'Sex' customer, the green-haired JOHN LYDON, as a suitably sneering frontman. JONES soon renamed the latter JOHNNY ROTTEN, informing his farting rear-end, "You're rotten, you are"; the tone of the SEX PISTOLS was set. After a few local gigs, the group supported JOE STRUMMER's 101'ers in April '76, their bedraggled, low-rent bondage chic troupe of followers including the likes of SIOUXSIE SIOUX (later of BANSHEES fame) and one SID VICIOUS, allegedly the perpetrator behind the infamous glass-throwing incident at the 100 Club punk all-dayer in which a girl was partially blinded. Controversy, intentional or otherwise, hung around the group like a bad smell and made The SEX PISTOLS into minor legends with barely one single under their belts. Signed to 'E.M.I.' for £40,000, their debut release, 'ANARCHY IN THE U.K.'

(having already shocked those of a sensitive disposition after being aired on the 'So It Goes' TV pop show) was finally released in November '76. An inflammatory slice of primal nihilism which surpassed even The STOOGES' finest efforts, the track initially climbed into the Top 40 before being unceremoniously withdrawn following the band's riotous appearance on a local chat/news programme, 'Today'. With JONES swearing copiously at presenter Bill Grundy, the tabloids had a field day, stirring up the moral majority and prompting more "must we subject our pop kids to this filth" editorials than you could shake a snotty stick at. 'E.M.I.' of course, bailed out (writing off the advance as a particularly bad debt) early the following year, MATLOCK was fired around the same time for being, well, er . . . too nice. His replacement was the aforementioned VICIOUS, a suitably violent and abusive character who duly became more of a punk anti-hero/caricature than McLAREN could ever have dreamed. After a short period in label limbo, The 'PISTOLS signed to 'A&M' in March '77 for another six figure sum; the honeymoon period was probably the shortest in recording history as the band's infamous antics at the post-signing party, together with protests from other artists on the label saw the UK's foremost punk band once again minus a recording contract. Once again, the band retained the loot from the advance and once again, a single, 'GOD SAVE THE QUEEN', was withdrawn (some copies did find their way into circulation and now fetch considerably more than the original 50p price tag). Arguably The 'PISTOLS defining moment, this jaw-clenching two-fingered salute to the monarchy and everything it represented was to truly make the band public enemy No.1, its release coinciding sweetly with her highness' silver jubilee year. Re-released by new label 'Virgin' (virtually the only company willing to take the band on-for a meagre £15,000 advance), the single was predictably banned by the BBC, though that didn't prevent it from outselling the official No.1 at the time, Rod Stewart's 'I Don't Want To Talk About It'. That long, hot summer also saw the band hiring a boat and sailing up and down the Thames in a publicity stunt which ended in chaos; cue yet more controversy and howls of derision from the nation's moral guardians. Knuckle-headed English royalists decided to take matters into their own hands, both COOK and ROTTEN attacked in separate incidents as another blankly brilliant single, 'PRETTY VACANT', gatecrashed the Top 10. Previewed by the seething, squalling outrage of 'HOLIDAYS IN THE SUN', the legendary debut album, 'NEVER MIND THE BOLLOCKS, HERE'S THE SEX PISTOLS' was finally released at the end of the year. While the record undeniably contained some filler, it remains the classic punk statement, the blistering 'BODIES' and the gleeful kiss-off to their former employers, 'E.M.I.', almost standing up against the intensity of the singles (included in their entirety). As ever, controversy clouded its release, the album reaching No.1 in spite of the word 'Bollocks' – a near contravention of the 1889 Indecent Advertisements Act(!) – resulting in boycotts from many major outlets. Constantly on the verge of falling apart, the band subsequently flew to America for a string of chaotic dates, the final round of blanks in The 'PISTOLS depleted armoury. Amid sporadic showdowns with Deep South cowboys and SID's ever worsening heroin problem, ROTTEN (bowing out on stage in San Francisco with the immortal phrase "Ever get the feeling you've been cheated") effectively ended the whole sorry affair with his departure after the final gig. While LYDON (the name he now reverted back to) went on to form PUBLIC IMAGE LTD., McLAREN had other ideas for the splintered remains of the band, namely jetting off to Rio De Janeiro to record a single with exiled trainrobber, RONNIE BIGGS. The result, 'NO ONE IS INNOCENT (A PUNK PRAYER BY RONNIE BIGGS)', made the Top 10 in summer '78, although VICIOUS was absent from the recording, holed up in New York with his similarly addicted girlfriend, Nancy Spungen. He did find time to record a peerless rendition of Paul Anka's 'MY WAY', the single taking on an added poignancy following his untimely but hardly surprising death early the following year; out on bail after being charged with the murder of Spungen in October, VICIOUS succumbed to a fatal heroin overdose on the 2nd of February '79. The following month saw the belated release of McLAREN's pet project, an artistically licensed celluloid account of The SEX PISTOLS' history entitled 'THE GREAT ROCK'N'ROLL SWINDLE'. Widely criticised for its blatant exclusion of GLEN MATLOCK, the glaring absence of ROTTEN as an active participant and its paper-thin storyline, the movie was nevertheless an occasionally exhilarating, often hilarious trip through the misspent youth of Britain's best-loved punk band. While a perfunctory cover of Eddie Cochran's 'C'MON EVERYBODY' (a posthumous VICIOUS recording) made the Top 10 later that summer and 'Virgin' continued to flog The SEX PISTOLS' dead corpse with a variety of exploitation jobs, COOK and JONES formed the short-lived PROFESSIONALS. Although they didn't invent punk, The SEX PISTOLS certainly helped popularise it and while they were at least partly responsible for an avalanche of unlistenably amateurish shit, the band's uncompromising approach permanently altered the machinations of the music industry and took three-chord rock'n'roll to its ultimate conclusion. Despite the fact that original fans had long since given up on the UK ever descending into anarchy, the original 'PISTOLS line-up of LYDON, MATLOCK, JONES and COOK reformed in summer '96 for a handful of outdoor gigs and an accompanying live album. Opinion was divided as to whether this blatantly commercial venture (billed as "The Filthy Lucre Tour") was in keeping with the original punk spirit; probably not, although few paying punters complained about what was subsequently hailed as one of the events of the summer and it was certainly a safer bet than the new GREEN DAY album . . . • **Songwriters:** Group compositions, until COOK & JONES took over in 1978. They also covered; NO FUN (Stooges) / ROCK AROUND THE CLOCK (Bill Haley) / JOHNNY B. GOODE (Chuck Berry) / STEPPING STONE (Boyce-Hart) / etc. • **Trivia:** In 1979, they took McLAREN to court for unpaid royalties. In 1986,

the official receiver, through McLAREN paid a 7-figure out of court settlement to LYDON, JONES, COOK and SID's mother.

Album rating (selective): NEVER MIND THE BOLLOCKS, HERE'S THE SEX PISTOLS (*10) / THE GREAT ROCK'N'ROLL SWINDLE soundtrack (*8) / FLOGGING A DEAD HORSE compilation (*8) / KISS THIS compilation (*8) / FILTHY LUCRE LIVE (*6)

JOHNNY ROTTEN (b. JOHN LYDON, 31 Jan'56) – vocals / **STEVE JONES** (b. 3 Sep'55) – guitar / **GLEN MATLOCK** (b.27 Aug'56) – bass / **PAUL COOK** (b.20 Jul'56) – drums

	E.M.I.	not iss.
Nov 76. (7") (EMI 2566) **ANARCHY IN THE U.K. / I WANNA BE ME**	38	-

— (Feb'77) **SID VICIOUS** (b.JOHN RITCHIE, 10 May'57) – bass, vocals (ex-SIOUXSIE & THE BANSHEES) repl. MATLOCK who soon formed RICH KIDS

	A&M	not iss.
Mar 77. (7"w-drawn) (AMS 7284) **GOD SAVE THE QUEEN. / NO FEELINGS**	-	-

— Were soon paid off yet again. Above copies filtered through and soon became a collectors item).

	Virgin	Warners
May 77. (7") (VS 181) **GOD SAVE THE QUEEN. / DID YOU NO WRONG**	2	-

— (above was banned by the BBC, and outsold the official No.1 at the time; Rod Stewart's 'I Don't Want To Talk About It'.)

Jul 77. (7") (VS 184) **PRETTY VACANT. / NO FUN**	6	-
Oct 77. (7") (VS 191) **HOLIDAYS IN THE SUN. / SATELLITE**	8	-
Nov 77. (7") **PRETTY VACANT. / SUBMISSION**	-	
Nov 77. (lp/c) (V/TCV 2086) <3147> **NEVER MIND THE BOLLOCKS, HERE'S THE SEX PISTOLS**	1	106

– Holidays in the sun / Bodies / No feelings / Liar / God save the Queen / Problems / Seventeen / Anarchy in the UK / Submission / Pretty vacant / New York / E.M.I. (7" free w/some copies of 'Submission'; SPOTS 001) – SUBMISSION (one-sided). (pic-lp Jan78; VP 2086) (re-iss. Oct86 lp/c; OVED/+C 136) (cd-iss. Oct86; CDV 2086) (re-iss. cd May93; CDVX 2086) (re-iss. 1996 on cd w/ free 'SPUNK' bootleg tracks) <cd-iss. Jul96 on 'Alex; 5695>

— ROTTEN left, reverted to JOHN LYDON and created new band PUBLIC IMAGE LTD. His place was temporarily taken by **RONNIE BIGGS** (the Great Train Robber escapee now exiled in Brazil) 'A'-side vocals / **SID VICIOUS** – 'B'side vocals

Jun 78. (7") (VS 220) **NO ONE IS INNOCENT (A PUNK PRAYER BY RONNIE BIGGS). / MY WAY**	7	-

(12") (VS 220-12 A1/2) – The biggest blow (a punk prayer by Ronnie Biggs) / My way.
(12"+=) (VS 220-12 A3) – (above listing) / (interview).

— On 11 Oct'78, SID was charged with the murder of girlfriend NANCY SPUNGEN. MALCOLM McLAREN/'Virgin' bailed him out, but he died 2 Feb'79 of drug overdose. The 1979/80 singles were all taken from THE GREAT ROCK'N'ROLL SWINDLE film.

Feb 79. (7") (VS 240) **SOMETHING ELSE. / FRIGGIN' IN THE RIGGIN'**	3	-
Mar 79. (d-lp/d-c) (VD/TCV 2510) <45083> **THE GREAT ROCK'N'ROLL SWINDLE (Film Soundtrack)**	7	

– God save the Queen symphony / Rock around the clock / Johnny B. Goode / Roadrunner / Black Arabs / Watcha gonna do about it (* on some) / Who killed Bambi? / Silly thing / Substitute / No lip / (I'm not your) Stepping stone / Lonely boy / Somethin' else / Anarchie pour le UK / Einmal war Belsen vortrefflich / No one is innocent / My way / C'mon everybody / E.M.I. / The great rock'n'roll swindle / You need hands / Friggin' in the riggin'. (re-iss. 1-lp May80; V 2168) (re-iss. Apr89 lp/c; OVED/+C 234) (d-cd iss.Jul86; CDVD 2510) (re-iss. cd May93; CDVDX 2510)

Apr 79. (7") (VS 256) **SILLY THING. / WHO KILLED BAMBI?**	6	

— (above 'A'vocals – **STEVE JONES**, 'B'vocals – **EDDIE TENPOLE TUDOR**) (below 'A'vocals – **SID VICIOUS**)

Jun 79. (7") (VS 272) **C'MON EVERYBODY. / GOD SAVE THE QUEEN SYMPHONY / WATCHA GONNA DO ABOUT IT**	3	-
Aug 79. (lp/c) (VR/ 2) **SOME PRODUCT: CARRI ON SEX PISTOLS**	6	-

– The very name (the Sex Pistols) / From beyond the grave / Big tits across America / The complex world of Johnny Rotten / Sex Pistols will play / Is the Queen a moron / The fuckin' rotter. (cd-iss. May93; CDVR 2)

Oct 79. (7") (VS 290) **THE GREAT ROCK'N'ROLL SWINDLE. / ROCK AROUND THE CLOCK**	21	
Dec 79. (lp/c; by SID VICIOUS) (V/TCV 2144) **SID SINGS**	30	-

– Born to lose / I wanna be your dog / Take a chance on me / (I'm not your) Stepping stone / My way / Belsen was a gas / Somethin' else / Chatterbox / Search and destroy / Chinese rocks / My way. (re-iss. Aug88 lp/c; OVED/+C 85) (cd-iss. Feb89; CDV 2144)

— There were other SID VICIOUS exploitation releases later.

Feb 80. (lp/c) (V/TCV 2142) **FLOGGING A DEAD HORSE**	23	-

– (singles compilation) (re-iss. Apr86 lp/c; OVED/+C 165) (cd-iss. Oct86; CDV 2142)

Jun 80. (7") (VS 339) **(I'M NOT YOUR) STEPPING STONE. / PISTOLS PROPAGANDA**	21	-

— COOK and JONES were now The PROFESSIONALS

– compilations, exploitation releases –

Note; on 'Virgin' until mentioned otherwise.

Jan 80. (lp) Flyover; (YX 7247) **THE BEST OF . . . AND WE DON'T CARE**		
Dec 80. (6x7"box) (SEX 1) **PISTOLS PACK**		

– GOD SAVE THE QUEEN. / PRETTY VACANT // HOLIDAYS IN THE SUN. / MY WAY / SOMETHING ELSE. / SILLY THING // C'MON EVERYBODY. / THE GREAT ROCK'N'ROLL SWINDLE // STEPPING STONE. / ANARCHY IN THE U.K. // BLACK LEATHER. / HERE WE GO AGAIN (below 45 credited EDDIE TENPOLE TUDOR)

Sep 81. (7") (VS 443) **WHO KILLED BAMBI?. / ROCK AROUND THE CLOCK**		-

1983.   (7") *(VS 609)* **ANARCHY IN THE UK. / NO FUN**
        (12"+=) *(VS 609-12)* – E.M.I.

Jan 85. (7"/7"pic-d)(12") *Cherry Red; (PISTOL 76P)(12PISTOL 76)*
        **LAND OF HOPE AND GLORY. ("EX-PISTOLS") / FLOWERS
        OF ROMANSK** | 69 | - |

Jan 85. (m-lp) *Chaos; (MINI 1)* **THE MINI-ALBUM**
        (pic-m-lp.Jan86; AMPL 37) (cd-iss. Mar89; APOCA 3)

Mar 87. (7",7"yellow,7"pink) *Chaos; (DICK 1)* **SUBMISSION. / NO
        FEELINGS**
        (12",12"colrd) *(EXPORT 1)* – ('A'side) / Anarchy in the U.K.

Feb 85. (lp) *Receiver; (RRLP 101)* **THE ORIGINAL PISTOLS LIVE
        (live)**
        *(pic-lp Jun86 on 'American Phono.'; APKPD 13) (re-iss. Jan89 on 'Dojo'; DOJOLP
        45) (re-iss. May86 on 'Fame' lp/c; FA 41-3149-1/-4) (cd-iss. Jul89; CDFA 3149)*

1985.   (lp) *Receiver; (RRLP 102)* **AFTER THE STORM**
        (above with tracks by NEW YORK DOLLS) (cd-iss. Jul91; RRCD 102)

Aug 85. (lp) *Konnexion;* **LIVE WORLDWIDE (live)**

Nov 85. (lp) *Receiver;* **WHERE WERE YOU IN '77**

Nov 85. (lp/pic-lp) *Bondage;* **BEST OF SEX PISTOLS LIVE (live)**

Nov 85. (lp) *Hippy;* **NEVER TRUST A HIPPY**

Nov 85. (lp) *'77 Records;* **POWER OF THE PISTOLS**

Feb 86. (lp) *McDonald-Lydon; (JOCK 1)* **THE LAST SHOW ON EARTH
        (live)**

Apr 86. (12") *McDonald-Lydon; (JOCK 1201)* **ANARCHY IN THE U.K.
        (live). / FLOGGING A DEAD HORSE**

Aug 86. (lp) *McDonald-Lydon; (JOCKLP 3)* **THE SEX PISTOLS 10th
        ANNIVERSARY ALBUM**

Aug 86. (12"ep) *Archive 4; (TOF 104)* **ANARCHY IN THE UK / I'M
        A LAZY SOD. / PRETTY VACANT / SUBSTITUTE**

Jan 87. (6xlp-box) *McDonald-Lydon; (JOCK BOX1)* **THE FILTH AND
        THE FURY**
        – FILTH & THE FURY / LAST SHOW ON EARTH / 10th ANNIVERSARY
        ALBUM / ITALIAN DEMOS / NO FUTURE USA / THE REAL SID & NANCY

May 88. (lp/cd) *Restless; <72255-1/-2>* **BETTER LIVE THAN DEAD
        (live)**

Jun 88. (cd/lp) *M.B.C.; (JOCK/+LP 12)* **IT SEEMED TO BE THE END
        UNTIL THE NEXT BEGINNING**

Jun 88. (3"cd-s) *(CDT 3)* **ANARCHY IN THE U.K. / E.M.I. / NO
        FUN**

Oct 88. (m-lp) *Specific; (SPAW 101)* **ANARCHY WORLDWIDE**

Oct 88. (cd-ep) *Specific; (SPCFC 102)* **CASH FOR CHAOS**
        – Submission (live) / God save the Queen / Liar.

Oct 88. (cd-ep) *Classic Tracks; (CDEP 13C)* **THE ORIGINAL PISTOLS
        (live)**
        – Anarchy in the U.K. / Pretty vacant / No fun / Substitute.

Dec 88. (3"cd-s) *(CDT 37)* **GOD SAVE THE QUEEN / DID YOU NO
        WRONG / DON'T GIVE ME NO LIP CHILD**

Jun 89. (lp,pink-lp,green-lp/c) *Link; (LINK LP/MC 063)* **LIVE AND
        LOUD (live)**
        (cd-iss. Oct92; LINKCD 063)

Dec 89. (lp/c/cd,pic-cd) *Receiver; (RR LP/MC/CD 117)* **NO FUTURE
        U.K.?**

Feb 90. (cd/c) *Action Replay; (CDAR/ARLC 1008)* **THE BEST OF AND
        THE REST OF THE SEX PISTOLS**

1990.   (12"blue-ep) *Receiver; (REPLAY 3012)* **THE EARLY YEARS
        LIVE**
        – Anarchy in the U.K. / Pretty vacant / Liar / Dolls (aka 'New York').

Jan 91. (d-lp) *Receiver; (RRLD 004)* **PRETTY VACANT**
        (d-cd-iss. Jul93; RRDCD 004)

Sep 92. (7"/c-s) *(VS/+C 1431)* **ANARCHY IN THE U.K. / I WANNA
        BE ME** | 33 | |
        (cd-s+=/s-cd-s+=) *(VSCD T/X 1431)* – ('A'demo).

Oct 92. (cd) *Streetlink; (STRCD 019)* **EARLY DAZE – THE STUDIO
        COLLECTION**
        (re-iss. May93 on 'Dojo'; DOJOCD 119)

Oct 92. (cd/c/d-lp) *V/TC/CDV 2702) / Alex; <2931>* **KISS THIS** | 10 | |
        – Anarchy in the UK / God save the Queen / Pretty vacant / Holidays in ther Sun / I
        wanna be me / Did you no wrong / No fun / Satellite / Don't give me no lip child /
        (I'm not your) Stepping stone / Bodies / No feelings / Liar / Problems / Seventeen /
        Submission / New York / E.M.I. / My way / Silly thing. // *(cd w/bonus cd+=)* **LIVE IN
        TRONDHEIM 21st JULY 1977** :- Anarchy in the UK / I wanna be me / Seventeen /
        New York / E.M.I. / No fun / No feelings / Problems / God save the Queen.

Nov 92. (7") *(VS 1448)* **PRETTY VACANT. / NO FEELINGS (demo)** | 56 | |
        (12"+=) *(VST 1448)* – Satellite (demo) / Submission (demo).
        (cd-s+=) *(VSCDG 1448)* – E.M.I. (demo) / Satellite (demo).
        (cd-s) *(VSCDT 1448)* – ('A'side) / Seventeen (demo) / Submission (demo) / Watcha
        gonna do about it?

Mar 93. (cd) *Dojo; (DOJOCD 66)* **LIVE AT CHELMSFORD PRISON**

Nov 93. (cd) *Dojo; (DOJOCD 73)* **BETTER LIVE THAN DEAD**

Jul 95. (cd) *Dojo; (DOJOCD 216)* **WANTED – THE GOODMAN
        TAPES**

Oct 95. (d-cd) *Essential; (ESDCD 321)* **ALIVE**

Jan 96. (cd) *Dojo; (DOJOCD 222)* **PIRATES OF DESTINY**

Jan 97. (7") *Man's Ruin; (MR 053)* **split with the UGLYS**

Mar 97. (7") *Man's Ruin; (MR 056)* **split with the SOPHISTICATES**

Jun 97. (cd) *Emporio; (EMPRCD 716)* **RAW**

─── The original SEX PISTOLS re-formed at the back end of '95. Messrs LYDON,
     JONES, COOK + MATLOCK finally returned live on 24th June 1996, with packed
     out Finsbury Park concert. Embarked on their 'Filthy Lucre' tour soon after.

		Virgin America	Caroline

Jul 96. (7"silver) *(VUS 113)* **PRETTY VACANT – LIVE. / NO FEELING
        (demo)** | 18 | - |
        (cd-s+=) *(VUSCD 113)* – EMI (demo) / Satellite (demo)

Aug 96. (cd/c/lp) *(41926) <7541>* **FILTHY LUCRE LIVE (live)** | 26 | - |
        – Seventeen / New York / Did you no wrong / God save the Queen / Liar / Satellite /
        (I'm not your) Stepping stone / Holidays in the sun / Submission / No feelings /
        Pretty vacant / E.M.I. / Problems / Anarchy in the UK / No fun.

─── JONES was also part-member of trans-Atlantic supergroup, NEUROTIC
     OUTSIDERS, alongside DUFF McKAGAN and MATT SORUM (Guns N' Roses)
     and JOHN TAYLOR (Duran Duran). They released an eponymous album for
     'Maverick' in August '96 and from it they lifted the single, 'JERK'.

Ron SEXSMITH

Born: RONALD ELDON SEXSMITH, 1964, St. Catherine's, nr. Niagara
Falls, Canada. Subsequently relocating to Toronto, the babyfaced 30-
something singer/songwriter held down a day job as a courier while amassing
the material he hoped would secure him a record deal. Word got out with the
release of a cassette-only affair (as RON SEXSMITH AND THE UNCOOL)
in 1991, 'GRAND OPERA LANE'. A refreshingly unpretentious troubadour
with a crystal vocal style reminiscent of AARON NEVILLE (with perhaps
the hesitant fragility of TIM HARDIN and the bite of ELVIS COSTELLO),
SEXSMITH hooked up with noted producer, MITCHELL FROOM for his
eponymous solo debut proper. Released on 'Interscope' at the tail end of '95
(Spring '96 in Britain), the record received almost unanimous praise from
the press, especially from the more adult-muso end of the media spectrum.
Dedicated to the late HARRY NILSSON, the record revealed SEXSMITH
to be a songwriter in the truly classic sense of the term, maintaining the
sparsest of acoustic backing and relying on subtlety and mood rather than
vulgar confessionals. A writer's writer (ELVIS COSTELLO, JOHN HIATT and
RICHARD THOMPSON number among his biggest fans), the man continued
along the same unassuming path for 1997's 'OTHER SONGS', a largely
downbeat, monochromatic collection of snapshots from the humble lens of one
of rock's most unlikely heroes. People were asking of his 'WHEREABOUTS'
(1999) long before the set's release date. Puns aside, the Canadian's overtly
DYLAN-esque fourth album was much of the same as his last recordings. It
would seem he was getting stuck in a kind of 60's/70's time warp, although it
was popular with the bedsitter brigade.

Album rating: GRAND OPERA LANE (*5) / RON SEXSMITH (*6) / OTHER SONGS
(*6) / WHEREABOUTS (*6)

RON SEXSMITH – vocals, guitars; with MITCHELL FROOM, JERRY MARETTA,
BRAD JONES (2nd lp guest SHERYL CROW)

		not iss.	No Label

1991.   (c; as RON SEXSMITH AND THE UNCOOL) **GRAND
        OPERA LANE** | - | |

		Interscope	Interscope

May 96. (cd/c) *<(IND/INC 92485)>* **RON SEXSMITH** | | Nov95 |
        – Secret heart / There's a rhythm / Words we never use / Summer blowin' town /
        Lebanon, Tennessee / Speaking with the angel / In place of you / Heart with no
        companion / Several miles / From a few streets over / First chance I get / Wastin'
        time / Galbraith Street.

Aug 96. (cd-s) *(IND 95507)* **SECRET HEART /**

Jun 97. (cd/c) *<(IND/INC 90123)>* **OTHER SONGS**
        – Thinking out loud / Strawberry blonde / Average Joe / Thinly veiled disguise /
        Nothing good / Pretty little cemetery / It never fails / Clown in broad daylight / At
        different times / Child star / Honest mistake / So young / While you're waiting /
        April after all.

Jun 98. (cd-ep) *(IND 95564)* **STRAWBERRY BLONDE / SAME OLD
        EYES / YOU WERE THERE / REAQUAINTED**

Jun 99. (cd) *<(INTD 90299)>* **WHEREABOUTS** | | May99 |
        – Still time / Right about now / Must have heard it wrong / Riverbed / Feel for you /
        In a flash / Idiot boy / Beautiful view / One grey morning / Doomed / Every passing
        day / Seem to recall.

SHACK

Formed: Liverpool, England ... mid-80's out of semi-successful indie-pop
outfit The PALE FOUNTAINS. MICK HEAD, his brother JOHN HEAD
and CHRIS McCAFFREY, almost immediately recruited THOMAS 'JOCK'
WHELAN and ANDY DIAGRAM (the latter from DISLOCATION DANCE
and The DIAGRAM BROS) to form the seminal, tragedy struck PALE
FOUNTAINS. Their debut single, '(THERE'S ALWAYS) SOMETHING ON
MY MIND', set the tone for their melancholy, melodic, 60's-inspired alt-
pop, like a cross between The BEATLES and LOVE. 'Virgin' were quick off
the mark to sign them, their contract off to a promising start when follow-
up single, 'THANK YOU', hit the Top 50 late in '82. However, sales of
subsequent 45's and debut album, 'PACIFIC STREET' (1984), didn't quite
meet expectations, its brassy tropical feel (with colourful image to match) a
touch exotic for the average indie fan. A second album, the IAN BROUDIE-
produced ' ...FROM ACROSS THE KITCHEN TABLE', emerged early the
following year, the pleasant but hardly inspiring 'JEAN'S NOT HAPPENING'
summing up PALE FOUNTAINS appeal. With their chart potential having
almost completely dried up, The PALE FOUNTAINS split as the brothers
HEAD re-emerged as SHACK. Along with new boys, DAVE BUTCHER,
JUSTIN SMITH and MICHAEL CURTIS, they were the first act to sign for
the 'Ghetto Recording Company', the first fruits of their efforts being the
1988 set, 'ZILCH'. Displaying an even stronger BEATLES influence, the
album was a sterling slab of subtle, intelligent indie-pop. However, it took
all of two years for the band to return, the single 'I KNOW YOU WELL'
calling to mind The BEATLES' 'Taxman' with its knotty stop-start rhythms.
A solitary single, 'AL'S VACATION', arrived in Spring '91 and although an
album was completed, a studio fire destroyed what was thought to be the only
existing master tape. Fortunately, producer Chris Allison unearthed a DAT
master, although he subsequently lost it again after leaving it in a hired car.

Incredibly, the fabled tape later turned up in Germany (!), the belated album finally issued in '95 (prior to that, the HEAD brothers kept themselves busy by supporting ARTHUR LEE in 1992 at Liverpool) as 'WATERPISTOL' by 'Marina' records. MICHAEL HEAD was back in a solo capacity in 1998, members of SHACK backing him up on his inaugural release, 'THE MAGICAL WORLD OF THE STRANDS'. A year later, acclaim had finally reached SHACK, with the release of the poignant 'HMS FABLE'. Described as a cross between MERCURY REV's 'Deserter's Songs' and the BEATLES' 'Abbey Road', the set documented the highs and lows in the last few years of the HEAD brothers. From heroin addiction to musical misfortune, it was all there; of course, a SHACK album wouldn't have been complete without any of these things! In turn, the music press went crazy at this stunning comeback, the result being that the album entered the British charts at No.25. Singles such as 'NATALIE'S PARTY' and 'COMEDY' furthered the band's reputation, even if the general public didn't pay much attention to this wonderful discovery. 'HMS FABLE' also topped many magazines' 'Album Of the Year' polls – a well deserved reward for a hard working but unlucky outfit.

Album rating: Pale Fountains: PACIFIC STREET (*6) / ...FROM ACROSS THE KITCHEN TABLE (*4) / Shack: ZILCH (*7) / WATERPISTOL (*6) / Michael Head: THE MAGICAL WORLD OF THE STRANDS (*6) / Shack: HMS FABLE (*9)

PALE FOUNTAINS

MICK HEAD (b.28 Nov'61) – vocals, guitar / **JOHN HEAD** (b. 4 Oct'65) – lead guitar / **CHRIS McCAFFREY** – bass / **ANDY DIAGRAM** – trumpet (ex-DISLOCATION DANCE, ex-DIAGRAM BROS) / **THOMAS 'JOCK' WHELAN** – drums, percussion / + 6th member **M. BARRADAS** – oil drums, percussion

	Operation Twilight	not iss.
Jul 82. (7") (OPT 09) **(THERE'S ALWAYS) SOMETHING ON MY MIND. / JUST A GIRL**		-

	Virgin	not iss.
Oct 82. (7") (VS 557) **THANK YOU. / MEADOW OF LOVE**	48	-
May 83. (7"/12") (VS 568/+12) **PALM OF MY HAND. / LOVE'S A BEAUTIFUL PLACE**		-
Jan 84. (7"/12") (VS 614/+12) **UNLESS. / NATURAL**		-
Feb 84. (lp/c) (V/TCV 2274) **PACIFIC STREET**		-

– Reach / Something on my mind / Unless / Southbound excursion / Natural / Faithful pillow (part 1) / (Don't let your love) Start a war / Beyond Friday's field / Abergele next time / Crazier / Faithful pillow (part 2). (re-iss. Aug87 lp/c; OVED/+C 143) (cd-iss. Nov89; CDV 2274)

Mar 84. (7"/12") (VS 668/+12) **(DON'T LET YOUR LOVE) START A WAR. / LOVE SITUATION**		-

—— now without BARRADAS

Jan 85. (7"/12") (VS 735/+12) **JEAN'S NOT HAPPENING. / BICYCLE THIEVES**		-
Feb 85. (lp/c) (V/TCV 2333) **...FROM ACROSS THE KITCHEN TABLE**		-

– Shelter / Stole the love / Jean's not happening / Bicycle thieves / Limit / 27 ways to get back home / Bruised arcade / These are the things / It's only hard / ...From across the kitchen table / Hey / September sting. (re-iss. Apr86 lp/c; OVED/+C 164) (cd-iss. Jul89; CDV 2333)

Jun 85. (7") (VS 750) **...FROM ACROSS THE KITCHEN TABLE. / BICYCLE THIEVES**		-

(12"+=) (VS 750-12) – Thank you.
(d7"++=) (VS 750) – Just a girl.

—— disbanded when DIAGRAM returned to DISLOCATION DANCE (sadly, McCAFFREY was to die in August '89)

SHACK

—— **MICK HEAD + JOHN HEAD** with **DAVE BUTCHER** – keyboards / **JUSTIN SMITH** – bass / **MICHAEL KURTIS** – drums

	Ghetto	not iss.
Mar 88. (7") (GTG 1) **EMERGENCY. / LIBERATION**		-

(12"+=) (GTGT 1) – Faith.
(cd-s+=) (CDGTG 1) – What's it like.

Mar 88. (lp/c/cd) (GHETT/+C/D 1) **ZILCH**		-

– Emergency / Someone's knocking / John Kline / Realization / I need you / High rise, low life / Who killed Clayton Square? / Who'd believe it? / What's it like . . . / The believers.

Jun 88. (7") (GTG 2) **HIGH RISE LOW LIFE. / WHO KILLED CLAYTON SQUARE?**		-

(12"+=/cd-s+=) (GTGT/CDGTG 2) – ('A'-Bert Hardy mix).

Jul 90. (7") (GTG 11) **I KNOW YOU WELL. / FEEL NO WAY**		-

(ext.12") (GTG 11T) – ('A'-If you want it mix).
(cd-s++=) (CDGTG 11) – ('A'extended).

Apr 91. (7") **AL'S VACATION. /**		-

(12"+=/cd-s+=) –

—— an album was recorded but destroyed after a studio fire (see above).

	Marina	not iss.
Nov 95. (cd) (MAR 16) **WATERPISTOL**		-

– Sgt. Major / Neighbours / Stranger / Dragonfly / Mood of the morning / Walter's song / Time machine / Mr. Appointment / Undecided / Hazy / Hey mama / London town. (re-iss. Feb98 & Jul99; same)

MICHAEL HEAD

—— with other members of SHACK as backing

	Megaphone	not iss.
Feb 98. (cd/lp) (CD/LP MEGA 01) **THE MAGICAL WORLD OF THE STRANDS**		-

– Queen Matilda / Something like you / And luna / X hits the spot / The prize /

Undecided (reprise) / Glynys and Jaqui / It's harvest time / Loaded man / Hocken's hey / Fontilan.

Apr 98. (7") (7MEGA 02) **SOMETHING LIKE YOU. /**		-

(cd-s=) (CDMEGA 02) –
(re-iss. Oct98; same)

SHACK

	London	
Jun 99. (c-s) (LONCS 427) **COMEDY / UNCLE DELANEY / COMEDY (No Strings)**	44	

(cd-s) (LONCD 427) – (first two tracks) / Petroleum.
(cd-s) (LONCDP 427) – ('A'side) / 24 hours / Solid gold.

Jun 99. (cd/c) (556113-2/-4) **HMS FABLE**	25	

– Natalie's party / Comedy / Pull together / Lend's some dough / Captain's table / Streets of Kenny / Reinstated / I want you / Cornish town / Since I met you / Daniella.

Aug 99. (c-s) (LONCS 436) **NATALIE'S PARTY /**	63	

(cd-s) (LONCD 436) –
(cd-s) (LONCDP 436) –

SHADOWS

Formed: London, England ... 1958 as THE FIVE CHESTERNUTS by HANK MARVIN, BRUCE WELCH and PETE CHESTER (son of comedian Charlie Chester) along with GERALD HURST and NEIL JOHNSON. Following a one-off flop single, 'TEENAGE LOVE', for 'Columbia' in Autumn of that year, they were spotted by CLIFF RICHARD manager, John Foster, who needed a replacement for guitarist KEN PAVEY. Six-string wizard MARVIN agreed to join on the condition that WELCH was also hired, the susbsequent addition of IAN SAMWELL and TERRY SMART fleshing out a unit which was now trading under The DRIFTERS. In November '58, CLIFF replaced SAMWELL (who became their manager in 1959) with JET HARRIS and the new-look beat combo backed up RICHARD on his famous 'LIVIN' LOVIN' DOLL' single. More upheaval followed at the tail end of the year as TONY MEEHAN replaced SMART (who went off to join the merchant navy!). By this point, the quartet had managed a further couple of singles in their own right, 'FEELIN' FINE' and 'JET BLACK'. Neither was successful and to compound their problems, the band had an injuction slapped on them by the US soul/R&B outfit of the same name. After a final flop 45 at the tail end of the year (featuring a rare vocal) things took a serious turn for the better the following summer as the rumbling Wild West-style guitar atmospherics of 'APACHE' saw them topping the UK chart. A benchmark track that saw the bespectacled MARVIN embraced by many young wannabe guitar heros as a role model, the song was subsequently turned into a 70's funk/breakbeat classic by MICHAEL VINER'S INCREDIBLE BONGO BAND. It also signalled the beginning of an incredible (largely instrumental) chart run that lasted right through until the hippy revolution of the mid-late 60's. 'MAN OF MYSTERY', 'F.B.I.', 'FRIGHTENED CITY', 'THE SAVAGE' and 'KON TIKI' all went Top 10 over '60/'61, the last track giving them their second No.1 while their eponymous album also topped the charts. A more laid-back, quintessentially English counterpoint to the surf instrumentals sweeping the American West Coast, the SHADOWS sound was hugely influential on many young guitarists who snapped up their records in droves; 1962 saw the band score three No.1's in a row with 'WONDERFUL LAND', the 'OUT OF THE SHADOWS' album and 'DANCE ON', topping it with another No.1 in '63, 'FOOT TAPPER'. By this point JET HARRIS and TONY MEEHAN had both been replaced (by BRIANs, BENNETT and LOCKING respectively), the pair going on to score three 1963 UK Top 5 singles in their own right (i.e. 'DIAMONDS', 'SCARLETT O'HARA' and 'APPLEJACK'). While still a regular fixture on the chart, The SHADOWS' began losing their identity as they added more vocals to their repertoire towards the middle of the decade. By 1967, their (lone) star was really beginning to fade and after the October '68 release of joint CLIFF RICHARD set, 'ESTABLISHED 1958', the band split to concentrate on solo projects. While BENNETT's material failed to spark much interest, MARVIN's eponymous 1969 solo set made the UK Top 20. 1969 also saw MARVIN duetting with CLIFF on Top 10 hit, 'THROW DOWN A LINE', following it up in 1970 with 'JOY OF LIVING'. The SHADOWS also returned that year on 'Parlophone' with a flop album of pop/rock standards, 'SHADES OF ROCK', only to disband the same year. MARVIN and WELCH then got together with Aussie guitarist, JOHN FARRAR to form a vocal trio although the project again proved relatively short-lived and commercially unsuccessful. The SHADOWS re-formed for a second time in 1973 with a line-up of MARVIN, WELCH, FARRAR and BENNETT, WELCH undertaking vocal duties for their 1975 Eurovision entry (!), 'LET ME BE THE ONE'. Although the song was runner-up it did furnish them with a much needed Top 20 hit. This pushed the brilliantly titled 'SPECS APPEAL' (1975) album into the Top 30. The late 70's brought another mini-revival with a Top 5 cover of 'DON'T CRY FOR ME ARGENTINA' (from the musical, 'Evita'), a Top 10 reading of 'THEME FROM THE DEER HUNTER (CAVATINA)', a Top 5 CLIFF collaboration, 'THANK YOU VERY MUCH' and a No.1 album of covers from all walks of musical life (everything from Blondie's 'HEART OF GLASS' to Art Garfunkel's 'BRIGHT EYES'). Though they wouldn't hit the singles chart again, The SHADOWS stepped into middle-age with a winning formula of fine but not specy-tacular (sorry) renditions of classics from every genre and era of music history, making regular appearances in the Top 10 album chart throughout the 80's. MARVIN also carried his solo career into the 80's/90's to occasional success, working with the likes of BRIAN MAY and MARK KNOPFLER. • **Songwriters:** First songs written by/with PETE CHESTER or IAN SAMWELL. The group, mainly MARVIN and WELCH pen some, but mainly use other worldly sources; JERRY LORDAN wrote APACHE / WONDERFUL LAND / etc. His wife PETRINA penned A PLACE IN THE SUN. Their producer NORRIE PARAMOUR wrote THE FRIGHTENED CITY + THE SAVAGE. MAN OF MYSTERY + KON-TIKI (Michael Carr). They also covered ('A'singles only, there were loads more); DANCE ON (Avons) / DON'T MAKE MY BABY BLUE (hit; Frankie Laine) / THE WARLORD (Jerome Moross) / MAROC 7 + LET ME BE THE ONE (Paul Ferris; a friend) / SLAUGHTER ON 10th AVENUE (Richard Rodgers) / DON'T CRY FOR ME ARGENTINA (Tim Rice-Andrew Lloyd Webber) / DEER HUNTER (John Williams) / RODRIGO'S GUITAR CONCERTO (Manuel; Geoff Love) / RIDERS IN THE SKY (Stan Jones; hit, Ramrods) / EQUINOXE V (Jean-Michel Jarre) / MOZART FORTE (Mozart; hit, Waldo De La Rios) / TELSTAR (Tornados) / TREAT ME NICE (Elvis Presley) / MISSING (Vangelis) / GOIN' HOME (Mark Knopfler) / MOONLIGHT SHADOW (Mike Oldfield) / DANCING IN THE DARK (Bruce Springsteen) / EASTENDERS-HOWARD'S WAY + PULASKI (TV themes) / SNOWMAN (hit; Aled Jones) / etc, etc, etc. • **Trivia:** WELCH was married in 1959, although he left his wife eight years later for singer OLIVIA NEWTON JOHN. The group appeared in CLIFF's films; THE YOUNG ONES / SUMMER HOLIDAY (title track penned by MARVIN & BENNETT) / WONDERFUL LIFE / ALADDIN . . . + CINDERELLA (wrote and performed the pantomines).

Best CD compilation: 20 GOLDEN GREATS (*8)

HANK MARVIN (b.BRIAN RANKIN, 28 Nov'41, Newcastle, England) – lead guitar / **BRUCE WELCH** (b.CRIPPS, 2 Nov'41, Bognor Regis, England) – rhythm guitar / **GERALD HURST** – vocals / **PETER CHESTER** – drums / **NEIL JOHNSON** – bass

	Columbia	not iss.
Aug 58. (7",78; as FIVE CHESTERNUTS) (DB 4165) **TEENAGE LOVE. / JEAN DOROTHY**		-

—— (Oct'58) they were also the backing for CLIFF RICHARD

IAN SAMWELL – bass + **TERRY SMART** – drums; repl. all bar **MARVIN + WELCH** (Oct-Dec'58) / **JET HARRIS** (b.TERRENCE, 6 Jul'39, London) – bass (ex-VIPERS) repl. IAN SAMWELL who became their manager in 1959) / **TONY MEEHAN** (b. DANIEL, 2 Mar'43, London) – drums (ex-VIPERS) repl. TERRY SMART who joined the merchant navy

Feb 59. (7",78; as DRIFTERS) (DB 4263) **FEELIN' FINE. / DON'T BE A FOOL WITH LOVE**		
Jul 59. (7"; as DRIFTERS) (DB 4325) **JET BLACK. / DRIFTIN'** (above single released in the US as "The Four Jets")		

—— the SHADOWS name was taken to avoid confusion with American soul/R&B group, they also remained as CLIFF RICHARD's backers

	Columbia	Atlantic
Dec 59. (7",78) (DB 4387) **SATURDAY DANCE. / LONESOME FELLA** (above 'A'side featured vocals by BRUCE)		-
Jul 60. (7") (DB 4484) **APACHE. / QUARTERMASTER'S STORES**	1	-
Oct 60. (7") (DB 4530) **MAN OF MYSTERY. / THE STRANGER**	5	-
Jan 61. (7") (DB 4580) **F.B.I. / MIDNIGHT**	6	-
May 61. (7") (DB 4637) **FRIGHTENED CITY. / BACK HOME**	3	-
Jun 61. (7") **FRIGHTENED CITY. / F.B.I.**	-	
Aug 61. (7") (DB 4698) **KON TIKI. / 36-24-36**	1	-
Sep 61. (lp; mono/stereo) (33SX 1374/SCX 3414) **THE SHADOWS** – Shadoogie / Nivram / Blue star / Theme from a filletted plaice / Sleepwalk / See you in my dreams / Stand up and say that / All my sorrows / That's my desire / Find me a golden street / Big boy / Gonzales / My resistance is low / Baby my heart. (re-iss. +c.May83 on 'Fame')	1	-

BRIAN BENNETT (b. 9 Feb'40, London) – drums; repl. MEEHAN

Nov 61. (7") (DB 4726) **THE SAVAGE. / PEACE PIPE**	10	
Feb 62. (7") (DB 4790) **WONDERFUL LAND. / STARS FELL ON STOCKTON**	1	

BRIAN 'Licorice' LOCKING – bass; repl. JET HARRIS (who still featured on next LP's tracks) to own duo with MEEHAN

Jul 62. (7") (DB 4870) **GUITAR TANGO. / WHAT A LOVELY TUNE**	4	
Oct 62. (lp; mono/stereo) (33SX 1458/SCX 3449) **OUT OF THE SHADOWS** – The rumble / The bandit / Perfidia / Cosy / Some are lonely / Little B / Spring is nearly here / Bo Diddley / Kinda cool / 1861 / South of the border / Are they all like you / Tales of a raggy tramline. (re-iss. +c.Aug86 on 'Awareness')	1	-
Dec 62. (7") (DB 4948) **DANCE ON. / ALL DAY**	1	-
Dec 62. (7") **DANCE ON. / RUMBLE**	-	
Mar 63. (7") (DB 4984) **FOOT TAPPER. / THE BREEZE AND I**	1	-
May 63. (7") (DB 7047) **ATLANTIS. / I WANT YOU TO BUY ME**	2	-
Jun 63. (lp) (33SX 1522) **GREATEST HITS** (compilation) – Apache / Man of mystery / F.B.I. / Midnight / Frightened city / Kon-tiki / 36-24-36 / The savage / Peace pipe / Wonderful land / Stars fell on Stockton / Guitar tango / The boys / Dance on / The stranger. (re-iss. Aug71 / re-iss. May74, hit No.48) (cd-iss. May89 on 'E.M.I.')	2	
Sep 63. (7") (DB 7106) **SHINDIG. / IT'S BEEN A BLUE DAY**	6	-

JOHN ROSTILL (b.16 Jun'42, Birmingham, England) – bass (ex-INTERNS) repl. LOCKING; they shared duties on below album

Nov 63. (7") (DB 7163) **GERONIMO. / SHAZAM**	11	-
Feb 64. (7") (DB 7231) **THEME FOR YOUNG LOVERS. / THIS HAMMER**	12	-
May 64. (7") (DB 7261) **THE RISE & FALL OF FLINGEL BUNT. / IT'S A MAN'S WORLD**	5	-
May 64. (lp; mono/stereo) (33SX 1619/SCX 3511) **DANCE WITH THE SHADOWS** – Chattanooga choo choo / Blue shadows / Fandango / Tonight / That's the way it goes / Don't it make you feel good / Big 'B' / Dakota / In the mood / The lonely bull / French dressing / The high and the mighty / Zambesi / Temptation.	2	-

Jun 64. (7") **THE RISE AND FALL OF FLINGEL BUNT. / THEME FOR YOUNG LOVERS**	-	
Aug 64. (7") (DB 7342) **RHYTHM AND GREENS. / THE MIRACLE**	22	
Nov 64. (7") (DB 7416) **GENIE WITH THE LIGHT BROWN LAMP. / PRINCESS**	17	-

—— Next with vocals as was alternate singles until MAROC 7 instrumental

HANK + BRIAN also added keyboards to repertoire

Feb 65. (7") (DB 7476) **MARY ANNE. / CHU-CHI**	17	-
May 65. (7") (DB 7588) **STINGRAY. / ALICE IN SUNDERLAND**	19	-
Jul 65. (lp; mono/stereo) (33SX 1736/SCX 3554) **SOUND OF THE SHADOWS** – A little bitty tear / Five hundred miles / Let it be me / Brazil / Blue sky, blue sea, blue me / Bossa roo / Cotton pickin' / Santa Ana / The windjammer / Deep purple / Dean's theme / Breakthru / National provincial samba.	4	-
Jul 65. (7") (DB 7650) **DON'T MAKE MY BABY BLUE. / MY GRANDFATHER**	10	-
Nov 65. (7") (DB 7769) **WARLORD. / WISH I COULD SHIMMY**	18	-
Dec 65. (lp; mono/stereo) (33SX 1791/SCX 3578) **MORE HITS!** (compilation) – Foot tapper / Atlantis / Shindig / Theme for young lovers / Geronimo / Shazam / The rise and fall of Flingel Bunt / Genie with the light brown lamp / Mary-Anne / Stingray / Rhythms and greens / Don't make my baby blue / Lute number / Drum number. (re-iss. Aug85) (cd-iss. May89 on 'E.M.I.')		
Mar 66. (7") (DB 7853) **I MET A GIRL. / LATE LAST NIGHT**	22	-
May 66. (lp; mono/stereo) (33SX/SCX 6041) **SHADOW MUSIC** – Razzamatazz / I only want to be with you / Babes in the wood / Only one way to love / Stay around / In the past / Bento-San / Fly me to the Moon / 4th street / A sigh (un sospero) / Don't stop now / March to Drina / The magic doll / Now that you're gone / Maid Marion's theme.	5	-
Jun 66. (7") (DB 7952) **A PLACE IN THE SUN. / WILL YOU BE THERE**	24	-
Oct 66. (7") (DB 8034) **THE DREAMS I DREAM. / SCOTCH ON THE SOCKS**	42	-
Mar 67. (7") (DB 8170) **MAROC 7. / BOMBAY DUCK**	24	-
Jul 67. (lp) (SCX 6148) **JIGSAW** – Prelude in E major / Jigsaw / Waiting for Rosie / With a hym hym on my knee / Chelsea boot / Winchester cathedral / Green eyes / Stardust / Marie Elena / Tennessee waltz / Trains and boats and planes / Cathy's clown / Semi-detached Mr.James / Friday on my mind. (re-iss. Apr90 on 'Beat Goes On')	8	-
Sep 67. (7") (DB 8264) **TOMORROW'S CANCELLED. / SOMEWHERE**		
Dec 67. (lp) (SCX 6199) **FROM HANK, BRUCE, BRIAN AND JOHN** – Snap, crackle and how's your dad / Evening glow / A thing of beauty / Naughty Nippon nights / The wild roses / The letter / San Francisco / The day I met Marie / Holy cow / I'm a believer. (re-iss. Apr90 on 'Beat Goes On';)		
Jan 68. (7"; as HANK MARVIN & THE SHADOWS) (DB 8326) **LONDON'S NOT TOO FAR. / RUNNING OUT OF THE WORLD**		-
Mar 68. (7") (DB 8372) **DEAR OLD MRS. BELL. / TRYING TO FORGET THE ONE YOU LOVE**		-

—— The SHADOWS split late '68, after release in October of shared lp 'ESTABLISHED 1958' with CLIFF RICHARD.

SHADOWS

—— re-formed in mid'69. **ALAN HAWKSHAW** – guitar, keyboards repl. WELCH (see further below)

	Parlophone	not iss.
Oct 69. (7"; by HANK MARVIN) **SLAUGHTER ON 10th AVENUE. / MIDNIGHT COWBOY**		-

—— augmented by bassmen; **HERBIE FLOWERS, DAVE RICHMOND + BRIAN HODGES**

Oct 70. (lp) (SCX 6420) **SHADES OF ROCK** – Proud Mary / My babe / Lucille / Johnny B.Goode / Paperback writer / (I can't get no) Satisfaction / Bony Moronie / Get back / Something / River deep, mountain high / Memphis / What'd I say.		

—— they disbanded again in 1970; ROSTILL rejoined the TOM JONES band but was tragically electrocuted on the 26th November '73 when playing guitar in his home

MARVIN, WELCH & FARRAR

—— formed trio (**FARRAR** – b. Australia), augmented by **HAWKSHAW, RICHMOND / CLEM CATTINI** – drums / **PETER VINCE** – organ

	Regal Zonophone	not iss.
Jan 71. (7") (RZ 3030) **FAITHFUL. / MR. SUN**		-
Feb 71. (lp) (SRZA 8502) **MARVIN, WELCH & FARRAR** – You're burning bridges / A thousand conversations / Brownie Kentucky / My home town / Silvery rain / Throw down a line / Baby I'm calling you / Faithful / Mistress Fate & Father Time / Take her away / Wish you were here / Mr. Sun / Strike a light. (cd-iss. Aug91 on 'See For Miles';) – (extra tracks).	30	-

—— the trio now augmented by **BENNETT, HAWKSHAW + RICHMOND**

May 71. (7") (RZ 3035) **LADY OF THE MORNING. / TINY ROBIN**		-
Nov 71. (lp) (SRZA 8504) **SECOND OPINION** – Black eyes / Tiny Robin / Ronnie / Far away falling / Lady of the morning / Let's say goodbye / Lonesome mole / The time to come / Thank Heaven's I've got you / Come back to natre / All day, all night blues. (cd-iss. Aug91 on 'See For Miles';) – (extra tracks)		-
Apr 72. (7") (RZ 3048) **MARMADUKE. / STRIKE A LIGHT**		-

—— early in 1972, when WELCH's girlfriend (OLIVIA NEWTON-JOHN) broke off engagement, he attempted suicide. The remaining 5 members became part of

MARVIN & FARRAR

	E.M.I.	not iss.
Aug 73. (7") (EMI 2044) **MUSIC MAKES MY DAY. / SKIN DEEP**		
Aug 73. (lp) (EMA 755) **HANK MARVIN AND JOHN FARRAR** – So hard to live with / Music makes my day / Skin deep / If I rewrote yesterdays /		

Galadrie / Love oh love / Help me into your wagon / Small and lonely night / You never can tell / Nobody cares / Lord how it's hurting. *(cd-iss. Aug91 on 'See For Miles' with extra tracks)*

SHADOWS

—— re-formed (**MARVIN, WELCH, FARRAR + BENNETT**)

	E.M.I.	not iss.
Nov 73. (7") *(EMI 2081)* **TURN AROUND AND TOUCH ME. / JUNGLE JAM**		-

—— added **ALAN TARNEY** – bass

Dec 73. (lp/c) *(EMA/TCEMA 762)* **ROCKIN' WITH CURLY LEADS** — `45` / `-`
– Pinball wizard – See me, feel me / Years away / Deep roots / Humbucker / Jungle jam / Gracie / Good vibrations / Rockin' with curly leads / Turn around and touch me / Wide mouthed frog / Gutbucket / Jumpin' Jack input.

Apr 74. (7"; by BRUCE WELCH) *(EMI 2141)* **PLEASE MR. PLEASE. / SONG OF YESTERDAY** — / `-`

—— same 5-piece, but **WELCH** now vocals, **TARNEY** – piano

Mar 75. (7") *(EMI 2269)* **LET ME BE THE ONE. / STAND UP LIKE A MAN** — `12` / `-`

Apr 75. (lp/c) *(EMC/TCEMC 3066)* **SPECS APPEAL** — `30` / `-`
– God only knows / Cool clear air / Rose, Rose / This house runs on sunshine / Colorado songbird / No no Nina / Don't throw it all away / Honourable puff-puff / Spider juice / Let me be the one / Like strangers / Stand up like a man.

Jun 75. (7") *(EMI 2310)* **RUN BILLY RUN. / HONOURABLE PUFF-PUFF** — / `-`

Oct 75. (7"; as MARVIN & FARRAR) **SMALL AND LONELY NIGHT. / GALADRIEL (SPIRIT OF STARLIGHT)** — / `-`

Nov 75. (lp) *(EMC 3095)* **LIVE AT THE PARIS OLYMPIA (live April'75)** — / `-`
– The rise and fall of Flingel Bunt / Man of mystery / Lady of the morning / Nivram / Tiny Robin / Sleepwalk / Guitar tango / Honourable puff-puff / Apache / Shadoogie / Marmaduke / Somewhere / Little 'B' / Medley (Lucille – Rip it up – Blue suede shoes). *(re-iss. Apr81 on 'M.F.P.', w/free other live at Sankei Hall) (cd-iss. Feb92)*

Jun 76. (7") *(EMI 2461)* **IT'LL BE ME BABE. / LIKE STRANGERS** — / `-`

—— In Jan'77, the TV advertised compilation '20 GOLDEN GREATS' hit No.1

—— **FRANCIS MONKMAN** – keyboards repl. FARRAR who went to solo & Australia. / **ALAN JONES** – bass repl. TARNEY

Jul 77. (7") *(EMI 2660)* **ANOTHER NIGHT. / CRICKET BAT BOOGIE** — / `-`

Aug 77. (lp/c) *(EMC/TCEMC 3195)* **TASTY** — / `-`
– Cricket bat boogie / Return to the Alamo / Another night / Goodbye yellow brick road / Honky tonk woman / Montezuma's revenge / Walk don't run / Superstar / Bermuda triangle / The most beautiful girl in the world / Creole nights.

Aug 78. (7") *(EMI 2838)* **LOVE DE LUXE. / SWEET SATURDAY NIGHT** — / `-`

—— **CLIFF HALL** – keyboards (ex-CLIFF RICHARD Band) repl. MONKMAN to SKY They were now virtually a trio of **MARVIN, WELCH & BENNETT**

Nov 78. (7") *(EMI 2890)* **DON'T CRY FOR ME ARGENTINA. / MONTEZUMA'S REVENGE** — `5` / `-`

—— In Feb79, their album with CLIFF 'THANK YOU VERY MUCH' hit No.5.

Apr 79. (7") *(EMI 2939)* **THEME FROM 'THE DEER HUNTER'. / BERMUDA TRIANGLE** — `9` / `-`

Sep 79. (lp/c) *(EMC/TCEMC 3310)* **STRING OF HITS** — `1` / `-`
– Riders in the sky / Parisienne walkways / Heart of glass / Classical gas / You're the one that I want / Theme from 'The Deer Hunter' / Bridge over troubled water / Don't cry for me Argentina / Song for Duke / Bright eyes / Rodrigo's guitar de Aranjuez / Baker street. *(re-iss. Sep85 on 'M.F.P.', re-iss. Sep88) (cd-iss. Oct87)*

Oct 79. (7") *(EMI 5004)* **RODRIGO'S GUITAR CONCERTO. / SONG FOR DUKE** — / `-`

Jan 80. (7") *(EMI 5027)* **RIDERS IN THE SKY. / RUSK** — `12` / `-`

Jul 80. (7") *(EMI 5083)* **HEART OF GLASS. / RETURN OF THE ALAMO** — / `-`

	Polydor	not iss.
Aug 80. (7") *(POSP 148)* **EQUINOXE V. / FENDER BENDER**	`50`	`-`
Sep 80. (lp)(c) *(2442 179)(3184 147)* **CHANGE OF ADDRESS**	`17`	`-`

– Mozart forte / Midnight creeping / Change of address / Just the way you are / Indigo-Outdigo / Arty's party / Albatross / Hello Mr. W.A.M. / Temptation / If you leave me now / Equinoxe V. *(re-iss. Aug83)*

Nov 80. (7") *(POSP 187)* **MOZART FORTE. / MIDNIGHT CREEPING** — / `-`

Apr 81. (7") *(POSP 255)* **THE THIRD MAN. / THE FOURTH MAN** — `44` / `-`

Sep 81. (7") *(POSP 316)* **TELSTAR. / SUMMER LOVE '59** — / `-`

Sep 81. (lp/c) *(POLD/+C 5046)* **HITS RIGHT UP YOUR STREET** — `15` / `-`
– Telstar / Chi Mai (theme from 'The Life & Times Of David Lloyd George') / We don't talk anymore / Imagine; Woman / Hats off to Wally / One day I'll fly away / Summer love '59 / Misty / This ole house / The winner takes all / Sailing / Nut rocker / Thing-me-jig / More than I can say / Cowboy cafe / The third man.

Nov 81. (7") *(POSP 376)* **IMAGINE; WOMAN. / HATS OFF TO WALY** — / `-`

May 82. (7") *(POSP 439)* **TREAT ME NICE. / SPOT THE BALL** — / `-`

Jul 82. (7") *(POSP 485)* **THE THEME FROM 'MISSING'. / THE SHADY LADY** — / `-`

Sep 82. (2xlp/d-c) *(SHAD S/C 1)* **LIFE IN THE JUNGLE** — `24` / `-`
– Life in the jungle / High noon / The theme from 'Missing' / Treat me nice / Cat'n'mouse / Chariots of fire / No dancing / Riders of the range / The old romantics / You rescue me / Lili Marlene / Raunchy. *(re-iss. as lp May89)* **LIVE AT ABBEY ROAD (live)** – The third man / Thing-me-jig / Runaway / All I have to do is dream / It doesn't matter anymore / Johnny B.Goode / Over in a flash / Summer love '59 / Oh! boy / Crying in the rain / Arty's party. *(cd-iss. May89)*

Aug 83. (7") *(POSP 629)* **DIAMONDS. / ELEVEN IS** — / `-`

Oct 83. (lp/c) *(POLD/+C 5120)* **XXV** — `34` / `-`
– Africa / Goin' home (theme from 'Local Hero') / Up where we belong / You don't have to say you love me / The modern way / Diamonds / Time is tight / Memory / Liverpool days / Queen of hearts / A whiter shade of pale. *(cd-iss. 1988)*

Oct 83. (7") *(POSP 647)* **GOIN' HOME. / CAT'N'MOUSE** — / `-`

Aug 84. (7") *(POSP 694)* **ON A NIGHT LIKE THIS. / THING-ME-JIG** — / `-`

Nov 84. (lp/c) *(POLD/+C 5169)* **GUARDIAN ANGEL** — `98` / `-`
– How do I love thee / Hammerhead / The Saturday western / On a night like this /

Look back on love / Johnny Staccato / I will return / (I'm gonna be your) Guardian angel / Can't play your game / Turning point / Our Albert. *(cd-iss. Nov86; 823797-2)*

May 86. (7") *(POSP 792)* **MOONLIGHT SHADOW. / JOHNNY STACCATO** — / `-`

May 86. (lp/c)(cd) *(PRO LP/MC 8)(829358-2)* **MOONLIGHT SHADOWS** — `6` / `-`
– Moonlight shadow / Walk of life / I just called to say I love you / Hello / Every breath you take / Nights in white satin / The power of love / Three times a lady / Against all odds / Hey Jude / Dancing in the dark / Imagine / I know him so well / Memory / Sailing / A whiter shade of pale. *(re-iss. cd/c Apr95)*

Aug 86. (7") *(POSP 808)* **DANCING IN THE DARK. / TURNING POINT** — / `-`
(12"+=) *(POSPX 808)* – ('A'version).

Nov 86. (7") *(POSP 847)* **EASTENDERS; HOWARD'S WAY. / NO DANCING!** — / `-`

Oct 87. (7") *(POSP 886)* **PULASKI. / CHANGE OF ADDRESS** — / `-`

Oct 87. (lp/c)(cd) *(SHAD/+C 1)(833682-2)* **SIMPLY SHADOWS** — `11` / `-`
– I knew you were waiting (for me) / We don't need another hero / Theme from 'The Snowman' / Careless whisper / Don't give up / I guess that's why they call it the blues / A heart will break tonight / The lady in red / Pulaski / Take my breath away / Eastenders / I want to know what love is / Skye boat song / Jealous guy / Chain reaction / Howard's way.

Nov 87. (7") *(POSP 898)* **THEME FROM THE SNOWMAN. / OUTDIGO** — / `-`

Apr 89. (7") *(PO 47)* **MOUNTAINS OF THE MOON. / STACK-IT** — / `-`
(cd-s+=) *(PZCD 47)* – Turning point.

May 89. (lp/c)(cd) *(SHAD/+C 30)(839357-2)* **STEPPIN' TO THE SHADOWS** — `11` / `-`
– You win again / I wanna dance with somebody (who loves me) / He ain't heavy, he's my brother / Candle in the wind / Farewell my lovely / Mountains of the Moon / Nothing's gonna change my love for you / Heaven is a place on Earth / When the going gets tough / Alone / All I ask of you / Stack-it / Shoba / You keep me hangin' on / Some people / One moment in time. *(re-iss. cd+c May93 on 'Spectrum')*

Oct 90. (cd/c/lp) *(847120-2/-4/-1)* **REFLECTION** — `6` / `-`
– Eye of the tiger / Crockett's theme / Right here waiting / Every little thing she does is magic / Sealed with a kiss / Uptown girl / Strawberry fields forever / Riders in the sky '90 / Flashdance / Something's gotten hold of my heart / Love changes everything / Nothing's gonna stop us now / Bilitis / You'll never walk alone / Always on my mind / Megamix.

Oct 91. (cd/c/lp) *(511374-2/-4/-1)* **THEMES AND DREAMS** — `21` / `-`
– Crockett's theme / Up where we belong / Take my breath away / Theme from The Deerhunter / Walking in the air / If you leave me now / One day I'll fly away / Africa / Every breath you take / Memory / Nights in white satin / Candle in the wind / You win again / Sailing / Just the way you are / Moonlight shadow.

– compilations, etc. –

on 'Columbia' unless mentioned otherwise

1961.	(7"ep) *(SEG 8061)* **THE SHADOWS**		-
1961.	(7"ep) *(SEG 8094)* **THE SHADOWS TO THE FORE**		-
1962.	(7"ep) *(SEG 8135)* **SPOTLIGHT ON THE SHADOWS**		-
1962.	(7"ep) *(SEG 8148)* **THE SHADOWS (No.2)**		-
1962.	(7"ep) *(SEG 8166)* **THE SHADOWS NO.3**		-
1962.	(7"ep) *(SEG 8171)* **WONDERFUL LAND OF THE SHADOWS**		-
1962.	(7"ep) *(SEG 8193)* **THE BOYS**		-
1963.	(7"ep) *(SEG 8218)* **OUT OF THE SHADOWS**		-
1963.	(7"ep) *(SEG 8233)* **DANCE ON WITH THE SHADOWS**		-
1963.	(7"ep) *(SEG 8249)* **OUT OF THE SHADOWS NO.2**		-
1963.	(7"ep) *(SEG 8268)* **FOOT TAPPING WITH THE SHADOWS**		-
1963.	(7"ep) *(SEG 8278)* **LOS SHADOWS**		-
1963.	(7"ep) *(SEG 8286)* **SHINDIG WITH THE SHADOWS**		-
1964.	(7"ep) *(SEG 8321)* **THOSE BRILLIANT SHADOWS**		-
1964.	(7"ep) *(SEG 8342)* **DANCE WITH THE SHADOWS**		-
1964.	(7"ep) *(SEG 8362)* **RHYTHM AND GREENS**		-
1964.	(7"ep) *(SEG 8375)* **DANCE WITH THE SHADOWS NO.2**		-
1965.	(7"ep) *(SEG 8396)* **THEMES FROM "ALADDIN AND HIS WONDERFUL LAMP"**		-
1965.	(7"ep) *(SEG 8408)* **DANCE WITH THE SHADOWS NO.3**		-
1965.	(7"ep) *(SEG 8445)* **ALICE IN SUNDERLAND**		-
1965.	(7"ep) *(SEG 8459)* **THE SOUND OF THE SHADOWS**		-
1966.	(7"ep) *(SEG 8473)* **THE SOUND OF THE SHADOWS NO.2**		-
1966.	(7"ep) *(SEG 8494)* **THE SOUND OF THE SHADOWS NO.3**		-
1966.	(7"ep) *(SEG 8500)* **THOSE TALENTED SHADOWS**		-
1966.	(7"ep) *(SEG 8510)* **THUNDERBIRDS ARE GO! (with Cliff Richard)**		-
1967.	(7"ep) *(SEG 8528)* **THE SHADOWS ON STAGE AND SCREEN**		-
Nov 69.	(lp) *Regal Starline; (SRS 5012)* **SOMETHIN' ELSE**		-
Oct 72.	(lp) *Music For Pleasure; (MFP 5266)* **MUSTANG**		-
Nov 72.	(7"m) *Parlophone; (DB 8958)* **APACHE. / WONDERFUL LAND / F.B.I.**		-
	(re-iss. Feb77 on 'E.M.I.'; EMI 2573)		
Jan 75.	(lp) *Ember; (SE 8031)* **THE SHADOWS**		-
Nov 76.	(lp/c) *Nut-EMI; (NUT/TCNUT 2)* **RARITIES**		-
	(cd-iss. Mar93)		
Jan 77.	(lp/c) *E.M.I.; (EMTV/TCEMTV 3)* **20 GOLDEN GREATS**	`1`	-

– Apache / Frightened city / Guitar tango / Kon-tiki / Genie with the light brown lamp / The warlord / A place in the Sun / Atlantis / Wonderful land / F.B.I. / The savage / Geronimo / Shindig / Stingray / Theme for young lovers / The rise and fall of Flingel Bunt / Maroc 7 / Dance on / Man of mystery / Foot tapper. *(cd-iss. Aug87; CDP 746243-2)*

Jan 78.	(lp) *Music For Pleasure; (MFP 50347)* **THE SHADOWS AT THE MOVIES**		-
Feb 80.	(lp/c) *Music For Pleasure; (MFP/TCMFP 50468)* **ROCK ON WITH THE SHADOWS**		-
Jul 80.	(lp/c) *E.M.I.; (EMC/TCEMC 3339)* **ANOTHER STRING OF HOT HITS**		-
	(re-iss. Nov83 on 'M.F.P.', cd-iss. Oct87)		
Aug 83.	(d-lp) *E.M.I.; (EDP 1546323)* **SOUND OF THE SHADOWS / DANCE WITH THE SHADOWS**		-

(re-iss. Sep86 on 'Music For Pleasure' lp/c; DL/TCDL 1092) (cd-iss. Mar91 on 'E.M.I.')

Release	Details	UK	US
Sep 83.	(d-lp) *Tellydisc;* **SHADOWS SILVER ALBUM**		-
May 84.	(lp/c) *E.M.I.; (EG 260075-1/-4)* **THE SHADOWS' VOCALS**		-
Sep 84.	(cd) *Polydor; (823080-2)* **COMPACT SHADOWS**		-
Jan 85.	(c) *VFM; VCA 016)* **HITS OF THE SHADOWS VOLUME 1**		-
May 86.	(c) *Hour Of Pleasure; (HR 8123)* **AN HOUR OF THE SHADOWS**		-
1987.	(pic-lp) *Exclusive; (AR 30086)* **DRIFTIN'**		-
Jun 87.	(lp/c) *Pathe Marconi; (156810-3/-9)* **DOUBLE ALBUM**		-
Jan 89.	(lp/c/cd) *See For Miles; (SEE/+K/CD 246)* **THE EP COLLECTION**		-
May 89.	(cd) *CMP; (CC 240)* **LISTEN TO THE SHADOWS**		-
Sep 89.	(cd/c/lp) *Music For Pleasure; (CD/TC+/MFP 5873)* **THE SHADOWS IN THE 60'S**		-
Nov 86.	(cd; as MARVIN, WELCH & FARRAR) *See For Miles; (SEE 78)* **STEP FROM THE SHADOWS** *(cd-iss. Nov89; SEECD 78) (re-iss. cd/lp Apr93)*		-
Dec 89.	(lp/c)(cd) *Pickwick; (CN/+4 2104)(PWKS 559)* **THE COLLECTION**		-
Dec 89.	(lp/c/cd) *Polydor; (841520-1/-4/-2)* **AT THEIR VERY BEST**		-
Dec 89.	(7"ep/cd-ep) *Polydor; (PD/PZCD 61)* **SHADOWMIX** – Apache – Wonderful land – Rise and fall of Flingel Bunt – Kon Tiki – F.B.I. – Man of mystery – Apache.		-
Feb 90.	(d-cd/d-c/d-lp) *E.M.I.; CD/TC+/EM 1354)* **THE ORIGINAL CHART HITS 1960-1980** *(d-cd+=) – (11 tracks).*		-
Sep 90.	(lp/c/cd) *See For Miles; (SEE/+K/CD 296)* **THE EP COLLECTION VOL.2**		-
Sep 90.	(lp/c/cd) *Pickwick; PWK LPS/MCS/S 4018P)* **DIAMONDS**		-
Mar 91.	(cd) *E.M.I.; (CZ 378)* **THE SHADOWS / OUT OF THE SHADOWS**		-
Apr 91.	(cd/c) *Pickwick; (PWK S/MC 4031P)* **DANCING IN THE DARK**		-
Sep 91.	(cd-box) *E.M.I.; (CDSHAD 1)* **THE EARLY YEARS**		-
Feb 92.	(cd) *E.M.I.; (CZ 477)* **SHADOW MUSIC / SHADES OF ROCK**		-
Jul 92.	(3xcd-box) *Magpie;* **THE EP COLLECTIONS** – (1 EP is by CLIFF RICHARD & THE SHADOWS)		-
Mar 93.	(cd) *E.M.I.; (CDEMC 3651)* **EVERYTHING OF VALUE (RARITIES II)**		-
May 93.	(cd/c) *Polygram TV; (843798-2/-4)* **SHADOWS IN THE NIGHT – 16 CLASSIC TRACKS**	22	-
Oct 93.	(cd/c) *Spectrum; (550094-2/-4)* **DREAMTIME**		-
Oct 93.	(cd) *See For Miles; (SEECD 375)* **THE EP COLLECTION VOLUME 3**		-
Nov 93.	(d-cd/d-c) *E.M.I.;* **THE DEFINITIVE GUITAR ALBUM**		-
May 94.	(cd/c) *BR Music; (BR/+MC 137-2/-4)* **THE SHADOWS AND FRIENDS**		-
Oct 94.	(cd/c) *Polygram TV; (523821-2/-4)* **THE BEST OF HANK MARVIN & THE SHADOWS**	19	-
May 95.	(3xcd-box) *E.M.I.; (CDSHAD 2)* **THE FIRST 20 YEARS AT THE TOP – 75 ORIGINALS 1959-1979**		-
Aug 95.	(cd) *Ichiban;* **THE DARK SIDE OF THE SHADOWS**		-
Oct 95.	(cd) *Laserlight; (16090)* **DANCE ON**		-
Nov 98.	(cd; as HANK MARVIN & THE SHADOWS) *Polygram TV; (559211-2/-4)* **THE FIRST 40 YEARS**	56	-

SHADOWS OF KNIGHT

(dig out; 4th edition or Great Psychedelic . . .)

SHAKESPEAR'S SISTER

Formed: London, England . . . 1988 by ex-BANANARAMA singer, SIOBHAN FAHEY, who teamed up with former session guitarist and American singer, MARCELLA DETROIT (aka MARCY LEVY, she'd already released a debut solo set, 'MARCELLA' on 'Epic' in 1982). Taking their name from the SMITHS single of the same name, the group signed to 'London' subsidiary, 'FFRR', in '88 after initial gigs in Leningrad. Although a debut single, 'BREAK MY HEART', flopped, the group scored a UK Top 10 the following summer with the sassy 'YOU'RE HISTORY'. The debut album, 'SACRED HEART', followed into the Top 10 soon after, although this odd couple's rather strenuous attempts at 'weird' art-pop sounded largely contrived and half-baked. Further singles stiffed and the pair went back to the drawing board, eventually resurfacing in Autumn '91 with 'GOODBYE CRUEL WORLD'. Once again, the single failed to break the Top 40. Then, seemingly out of nowhere, SHAKESPEAR'S SISTER rocketed to the top of the charts in early '92 with 'STAY', the single perched at the top of the tree for a staggering (and eventually tedious!) two months. An epic pop weepie with dark overtones, it was certainly the strangest No.1 for many a moon, the goth-spook video generating almost as much interest as the song itself. A follow-up album, 'HORMONALLY YOURS' (1992), made the UK Top 3, a definite improvement on the debut spawning a further two Top 20 hits with 'I DON'T CARE' and the evocative 'HELLO (TURN YOUR RADIO ON)'. Remixed for the dancefloor, 'BLACK SKY' also became a brooding fixture in the nation's trendier clubs. That summer, SHAKESPEARS SISTER's success went transatlantic when 'STAY' hit the US Top 5, the group seemingly poised for global pop dominance. It wasn't to be, however, as the couple slowly became estranged, FAHEY withdrawing from the music business at large amid health problems. DETROIT released a belated second solo set in 1994, 'JEWEL', a Top 20 effort boasting contributions from the likes of JOOLS HOLLAND and PHIL MANZANERA. • **Songwriters:** STEWART/DETROIT collaborated with FERRARA/FELDMAN/SEYMOUR, except COULD YOU BE LOVED (Bob Marley) / AIN'T NOTHING LIKE THE REAL THING

(Ashford & Simpson) / I WANT TO TAKE YOU HIGHER (Sly & The Family Stone) / OUT OF MY MIND (Lance Aston). • **Trivia:** SIOBHAN married The EURYTHMICS mainman DAVE STEWART on 1st August '87.

Album rating: SACRED HEART (*5) / HORMONALLY YOURS (*6)

SIOBHAN STEWART (b. SIOBHAN FAHEY, 10 Sep'58, Dublin, Ireland) – vox, etc. / **MARCELLA DETROIT** (b.21 Jun'59, Detroit) – guitar (ex-ERIC CLAPTON Band) with 3rd member **RICHARD FELDMAN** – keyboards

		London	London
Nov 88.	(7") *(LON 200)* **BREAK MY HEART (YOU REALLY). / HEROINE** (ext-12"+=) *(LONX 200)* – ('A'-Acidic mix). (cd-s+=) *(LONCD 200)* – ('A'-Shep Pettibone house mix). (12") *(LONXR 200)* – ('A'-Shep Pettibone house mix) / (~'B'-Heavenly remix) / ('A'-dub mix).		-

		ffrr-London	London
Jul 89.	(7"/7"pic/d/c-s) *(F/+PD/CS 112)* **YOU'RE HISTORY. / DIRTY MIND** (12"+=/cd-s+=) *(FX/FCD 112)* – Heroine / You're history (parts 2-4).	7	
Aug 89.	(lp/c/cd) *(<828131-1/-4/-2>)* **SACRED HEART** – Heroine / Run silent, run deep / Dirty mind / Sacred heart / Heaven is in your arms / Twist the knife * / You're history / Break my heart / Red rocket / Electric Moon / Primitive love / Could you be loved / You made me come to this *. *(cd+= * remixed)*	9	
Sep 89.	(7"/c-s) *(F/+CS 119)* **RUN SILENT. / MR. WRONG** (12"+=/cd-s+=/box-cd-s+=) *(FX/FCD/FBCD 119)* – ('A'-the Run Deep mix).	54	
Feb 90.	(7") *(F 128)* **DIRTY MIND. / ('A'-1990 version)** (12"+=/c-s+=/cd-s+=) *(FX/FCS/FCD 128)* – Electric Moon.	71	

—— now with **MICK COZZI** – guitar (on 1) / **JONATHON PERKINS** – keyboards / **IAN MAIDMAN** – bass, keyboards / **STEVE FERRARA** – drums, keyboards / **ED SHEAMUR** – keyboards

		London	London
Sep 91.	(7"/c-s) *(LON/+CS 309)* **GOODBYE CRUEL WORLD. / BLACK SKY (mix)** (12"+=) *(LONX 309)* – ('A'dub versions) / ('B'-Black widow mix). (cd-s+=) *(LONCD 309)* – You're history.	59	-
Jan 92.	(7") *(LON 314)* *<869730>* **STAY. / THE TROUBLE WITH ANDRE** (c-s+=/cd-s+=) *(LON CS/CD 314)* – Remixes: Run silent / Dirty mind / ('A'-lp sample).	1	4 Jun92
Feb 92.	(cd/c/lp) *(<828266-2/-4/-1>)* **HORMONALLY YOURS** – Goodbye cruel world / I don't care / My 16th apology / Are we in love yet / Emotional thing / Stay / Black sky / The trouble with Andre / Moonchild / Catwoman / Let me entertain you / Hello (turn your radio on). *(cd re-iss. Sep99; 3984 28239-2)*	3	56
Mar 92.	(7"/c-s) *(LON/+CS 318)* **I DON'T CARE. / REMEMBER MY NAME** (pic-cd-s+=) *(LONCD 318)* – You're history / Catwoman.	7	-
Jul 92.	(7"/c-s) *(LON/+CS 322)* **GOODBYE CRUEL WORLD. / MOONCHILD** (cd-s+=) *(LONCD 322)* – Are we in love yet?	32	
Oct 92.	(7"/c-s) *(LON/+CS 330)* **HELLO (TURN YOUR RADIO ON). / STAY (remix)** (cd-s+=) *(LONCD 330)* – Black sky (dubextravaganza) / Goodbye cruel world (bio remix).	14	
Nov 92.	(c-s,cd) *<869946>* **I DON'T CARE / STAY (acoustic)**	-	55
Feb 93.	(7"/c-ep/cd-ep) *(LON/+CS/CD 337)* **MY 16th APOLOGY EP** – My 16th apology / Catwoman / Dirty mind / Hot love. (cd-s+=) *(LONCDX 337)* – ('A'-alternative piano mix) / ('A'version).		-

—— split early in '93 after which the admittedly volatile SIOBHAN admitted herself into a psychiatric unit. Meanwhile, MARCELLA DETROIT carved out own successful career, culminating in UK Top 20 album 'JEWEL'

—— now just **SIOBHAN** + Scottish musicians (writes w/ DAVID A. STEWART)

Jun 96.	(7"red/c-s) *(LON/+CS 383)* **I CAN DRIVE / OH NO, IT'S MICHAEL** (cd-s+=) *(LONCD 383)* – Suddenly.	30	-

—— a proposed album was shelved and SIOBHAN packed it in

SHAMEN

Formed: Aberdeen, Scotland . . . 1984 as ALONE AGAIN OR (named after a LOVE track from '67) by COLIN ANGUS and McKENZIE brothers DEREK and KEITH. After two singles (one for 'Polydor'; DREAM COME TRUE), they became The SHAMEN, releasing the singles 'YOUNG TILL YESTERDAY' (1986) and 'SOMETHING ABOUT YOU' (1987) on their own 'Moksha' label. The debut album, 'DROP' (1987), followed soon after and at this point the band were touting a fairly derivative indie take on classic West coast psychedelia combined with overtly political/drug orientated lyrics. As Angus became increasingly preoccupied with the nascent dance scene, however, DEREK McKENZIE split ranks and was replaced by WILL SINOTT. After the controversial single, 'JESUS LOVES AMERIKA' (1988), ANGUS and SINOTT relocated to LONDON, immersing themselves in the burgeoning acid house scene. The 'SHAMEN VS BAM BAM' (1988) moved the duo ever further into electronic territory and though the 'IN GORBACHEV WE TRUST' (1989) album fitted with the indie/dance crossover zeitgeist, The SHAMEN were one of the only acts to take the phenomenon to its ultimate conclusion. After a last outing for 'Moksha', the band signed to the 'One Little Indian' label in 1989. Their second single for the label, 'PROGEN' (1990), finally saw The SHAMEN make their mark on the dance scene. Although it barely scraped into the charts, the track was huge on the club scene and climbed to No.4 upon its re-release (in remixed form) the following year. In addition to this pivotal track, the album 'EN-TACT' (1990), contained the liquid psychedelia of 'HYPERREAL' (featuring the velvet tones of Polish singer PLAVKA) and the dancefloor manifesto of 'MAKE IT MINE', both minor hit singles. Having initially had DJ EDDIE RICHARDS play acid house ar their gigs, The SHAMEN had now developed the 'Synergy' live experience, a pioneering integration of live electronica and top flight DJ's (including the likes of MIXMASTER MORRIS and PAUL OKENFOLD) that attmepted to create a cultural fusion between the excitement of live performance and the communal vibe of the party scene. Just as the band were beginning to realise their dreams, WILL SINOTT drowned while swimming off the coast of The Canary Islands in May '91. ANGUS eventually decided to carry on and recruited RICHARD WEST aka Mr C, a veteran of the house scene, having DJ'd at the seminal RIP club. He was a natural choice, having rapped on the revamped 'PROGEN' single and collaborated on the 'Synergy' gigs, his inimitable cockney patois possessing a ragamuffin charm. He was also visually striking and along with SOUL FAMILY SENSATION singer JHELISSA ANDERSON, would become the public face of the The SHAMEN, ANGUS cannily content to communicate with the media via E-mail. The 'L.S.I. (LOVE, SEX, INTELLIGENCE)' (1992) single introduced a more commercial sound to the new look SHAMEN, as did the unashamed pop/dance of controversial hit, 'EBENEEZER GOODE' (1992) (the question of whether Mr C did actually sing 'E's are good' was endlessly debated by those tireless moral guardians of the nation's wellbeing). Many longtime fans couldn't stomach the new sound although the band gained a whole new following of pop kids enamoured with cheeky chappy Mr C. The million selling 'BOSS DRUM' (1992) album combined the aforementioned chart fodder with typically SHAMEN-esque communiques on ~'Archaic Revivals' and the like (i.e.'RE-EVOLUTION', the title track etc.). 1995 saw ex-SOUL II SOUL chanteuse VICTORIA WILSON JAMES replace ANDERSON and a new album in the shops, 'AXIS MUTATIS'. Although the record included the celebratory dance pop of single 'DESTINATION ESCHATON', overall it was more cerebral with a companion ambient album, 'ARBOR BONA/ARBOR MALA', released at the same time. 'HEMPTON MANOR' (1996) carried on The SHAMEN's overriding theme of transformation through mind altering substances and although the media profile of the band has shrunk considerably over the last couple of years, The SHAMEN have kept fans abreast of their activities with a rather fabby self-produced internet web-site, 'Nemeton'. • **Songwriters:** All written by COLIN and DEREK, until the latter's departure and replacement by the late WILL SINNOTT. ANGUS & WEST took over in '91. Covered; GRIM REAPER OF LOVE (Turtles) / FIRE ENGINE + SLIP INSIDE THIS HOUSE (13th Floor Elevators) / LONG GONE (Syd Barrett) / SWEET YOUNG THING (Monkees) / PURPLE HAZE (Jimi Hendrix). • **Trivia:** In Apr'88, they were dropped from a McEwans lager TV ad, because of their then anti-commercial approach.

Album rating: DROP (*5) / IN GORBACHEV WE TRUST (*7) / PHORWARD mini (*6) / EN-TACT (*9) / BOSS DRUM (*8) / AXIS MUTATIS (*7) / ARBOR BONA – ARBOR MALA (*7) / HEMPTON MANOR (*6) / THE SINGLES COLLECTION compilation (*8)

ALONE AGAIN OR

COLIN ANGUS (b.24 Aug'61) – keyboards / **DEREK McKENZIE** (b.27 Feb'64) – vocals, guitar / **KEITH McKENZIE** (b.30 Aug'61) – drums

	All One	not iss.
Dec 84. (7") (ALG 1) **DRUM THE BEAT (IN MY SOUL). / SMARTIE EDIT**	☐	-

	All One – Polydor	not iss.
Mar 85. (7") (ALG 2) **DREAM COME TRUE. / SMARTER THAN THE AVERAGE BEAR**	☐	-

(12") (ALGX 2) – ('A'-Splintered version) / ('B'-Ursa Major) / Drum the beat (shall we dance?).

SHAMEN

—— added **ALISON MORRISON** – bass, keyboards

	One Big Guitar	not iss.
Apr 86. (12"ep) (OBG 003T) **THEY MAY BE RIGHT . . . BUT THEY'RE CERTAINLY WRONG**	☐	-

– Happy days / Velvet box / I don't like the way the world is turning.

—— **PETER STEPHENSON** (b. 1 Mar,62, Ayrshire) – keyboards repl. ALISON

	Moksha	not iss.
Nov 86. (7"m) (SOMA 1) **YOUNG TILL YESTERDAY. / WORLD THEATRE / GOLDEN HAIR**	☐	-

(12"m) (SOMA 1T) – (first 2 tracks) / It's all around / Strange days dream.

May 87. (7"m) (SOMA 2) **SOMETHING ABOUT YOU. / DO WHAT YOU WILL**	☐	-

(12"+=) (SOMA 2T) – Grim reaper of love.

Jun 87. (lp/c) (SOMA LP/C 1) **DROP**	☐	-

– Through with you / Something about you / Four letter girl / The other side / Passing away / Young till yesterday / Happy days / Where do you go / Through my window / I don't like the way the world is turning / World theatre / Velvet box. (c+=) – Do what you will. (cd-iss. Nov88 ++=; SOMACD 1) – Strange days dream. (re-iss. Jan92 on 'Mau Mau' lp/c/cd; MAU/+MC/CD 613)

Sep 87. (7") (SOMA 3) **CHRISTOPHER MAYHEW SAYS. / SHITTING ON BRITAIN**	☐	-

(12"+=) (SOMA 3T) – Fire engine / Christopher Mayhew says a lot.

—— **WILL SINNOTT** (b.23 Dec'60, Glasgow, Scotland) – bass repl. DEREK (COLIN now vocals, guitar)

Feb 88. (7") (SOMA 4) **KNATURE OF A GIRL. / HAPPY DAYS**	☐	-

(12"+=) (SOMA 4T) – What's going down / Sub knature of a girl.

	Ediesta	not iss.
Jun 88. (7") (CALC 069) **JESUS LOVES AMERIKA. / DARKNESS IN ZION**	☐	-

(12"+=) (CALCT 069) – Do what you will.
(cd-s++=) (CALCCD 069) – Sub knatural dub.

—— now a duo of **COLIN + WILL**

	Desire	not iss.
Nov 88. (12"; as SHAMEN VS BAM BAM) (WANTX 10) **TRANSCENDENTAL. / ('A'-housee mix)**	☐	-

	Demon	Demon
Jan 89. (lp/c/cd) (<FIEND/+C/CD 666>) **IN GORBACHEV WE TRUST**	☐	-

– Synergy / Sweet young thing / Raspberry infundibulum / War prayer / Adam Strange / Jesus loves Amerika / Transcendental / Misinformation / Raptyouare / In Gorbachev we trust / (Fundamental). (c+=) – Resistance (once again). (cd+=) – Yellow cellaphane day / Mayhew speaks out.

—— added **SANDRA** – percussion

	Moksha	not iss.
Apr 89. (7") (SOMA 6) **YOU, ME & EVERYTHING. / RERAPTYOUARE**	☐	-

('A'-Evil edits; 12"+=/cd-s+=) (SOMA 6 T/CD) – Ed's bonus beats.

May 89. (10"m-lp/c/cd) (SOMA LP/C/CD 3) **PHORWARD**	☐	-

– You, me & everything (else) / Splash 2 / Negation state / Reraptyouare / SDD 89 / Phorward. (free 7") – (The S&N Sessions) (c+=/cd+=) – Happy days / Knature of a girl.

—— **JOHN DELAFONS** – percussion repl. SANDRA

	One Little Indian	Epic
Nov 89. (12"ep/cd-ep) (30TP 12/7CD) **OMEGA AMIGO / OMEGA A. / OMEGA PRE-MIX / PH 1**	☐	-

Mar 90. (7") (36 TP7) **PRO>GEN (Beatmasters mix). / ('A'dub version)**	55	-

(12") (36 TP12L) – ('A'-C-mix F+) / ('B'side) / Lightspan (Ben Chapman mix).
(c-s+=) (36 TP7C) – ('A'-Paul Oakenfold 'Land Of Oz' mix).
(12") (36 TP12) – (above mix) / Lightspan (Ben Chapman mix).
(cd-s) (36 TP7CD) – (above + 2 mixes) / ('A'-Steve Osborne mix).

Sep 90. (7"/c-s) (46 TP7/+C) **MAKE IT MINE (Lenny D vox). / ('A'-Evil Ed mix)**	42	Feb92

(12"/cd-ep) (46TP 12/7CD) <742 36/41> – ('A'-Lenny D mix) / ('A'-Progress mix) / ('A'-Lenny D vox) / Something wonderful.
(12") (46 TP12L) – ('A'-Evil Ed mix) / ('A'-Outer Limits mix) / Pro>gen (Land of Oz mix) / ('A'-Micro minimal mix).

Oct 90. (cd)(c)(2x12"lp) (TPLP 22 CD/MC/SP) <48722> **EN-TACT**	31	

– Human N.R.G. / Pro>gen (land of Oz) / Possible worlds / Omega amigo / Evil is even / Hyperreal / Lightspan / Make it mine V 2.5 / Oxygen restriction / Here are my people (orbital delays expected). (cd+=) – (Oxygen reprise (V 2.0 mix) / Human NRG (Massey mix) / Make it mine (pirate radio mix) / (etc.). (re-iss. Nov90 lp; TPLP 22)

Mar 91. (7"/c-s) (48 TP7/+C) **HYPERREAL (William Orbit mix). / ('A'-lp version)**	29	-

(12") (48 TP12) – ('A'versions incl. Maguire + dub) / In the bag.
(cd-s) (48 TP7CD) – ('A'versions incl. Meatbeat Manifesto mix) / In the bag.
(12") (48 TP12L) – ('A'-Meatbeat Manifesto mixes) / ('A'-Maguire + Dirty dubbing mixes).
(above featured **PLAVKA** (b. Poland) – vocals)

—— On the 23 May'91, WILL drowned while on holiday in Ibiza.

Jul 91. (7"/c-s) (52 TP7/+C) <74044> **MOVE ANY MOUNTAIN – PROGEN '91 (Beatmasters edit). / ('A'-The Goat From The Well Hung Parliament mix)**	4	38 Nov91

(12") (52 TP12) <74043> – ('A'-mixes; Landslide / Devil / Rude / R.I.P. in the Land Of Oz).
(cd-s) (52 TP7CD) <74044> – ('A'mixes; Beatmasters / Landslide / F2 Mello / Mountains in the sky).

Sep 91. (3xlp/c/cd) (TPLP 32/+MC/CD) **PROGENCY 2(8 versions)**	23	-

—— New line-up COLIN plus **MR.C** – vocals, rhythm / + **JHELSA ANDERSON** – backing vox (ex-SOUL FAMILY SENSATION) / **BOB BREEKS** – live keyboards / **GAVIN KNIGHT** – live drums / **RICHARD SHARPE** – occasional analogue

Jun 92. (7"/12") (68 TP 7/12) <74437> **L.S.I. (LOVE SEX INTELLIGENCE). / POSSIBLE WORLDS**	6	

(c-s+=/cd-s+=) (68 TP 7 C/CD) – Make it mine (Moby mix).

Aug 92. (7"/c-s) (78 TP7/+C) **EBENEEZER GOODE. / ('A'dub)**	1	

(12"+=/cd-s+=) (78 TP 12/7CD) – ('A'mix) / L.S.I. (mix).

Oct 92. (lp/c/cd) (TPLP 42/+C/CD) <52925> **BOSS DRUM**	3	

– Boss drum / L.S.I.: Love Sex Intelligence / Space time / Librae solidi denari / Ebeneezer Goode (Beatmasters mix) / Comin' on / Phorever people / Fatman / Scientas / Re: evolution.

Oct 92. (7"/c-s) (88 TP 7/+C) <74953> **BOSS DRUM. / OMEGA AMIGO**	4	Apr93

(cd-s+=) (88 TP7CD) – (3 'A'mixes).
(12"-2 diff.) (88 TP12) – (5 'A'mixes either J.Robertson or Beatmasters).
(cd-s++=) (88 TP7CDL) – ('A'-Steve Osbourne mixes & Youth).

Dec 92. (7"ep/c-ep/12"ep/cd-ep) (98 TP 7/7C/12/CD) <74889> **PHOREVER PEOPLE. / ('A'dub + 'A'-Hyperreal orbit mix)**	5	

(cd-s++=) (98 TP7CDL) – ('A'mixes).

Feb 93. (c-s; as SHAMEN with TERENCE McKENNA) (118 TP7C) **RE:EVOLUTION / ('A'mix)**	18	

(12"+=/cd-s+=) (118 TP 12/7CD) – ('A'mixes).

Oct 93. (c-ep/12"ep/cd-ep) (108 TP 7C/12/7CD) **THE S.O.S. EP**	14	

– Comin' on / Make it mine / Possible worlds.
(cd-ep) (108 TP7CDL) – ('A'mixes).

—— now with vocalist **VICTORIA WILSON-JAMES**

Aug 95. (c-s) (128 TP7C) <78038> **DESTINATION ESCHATON (Beatmasters mix) / ('A'-Deep melodic mix)**	15	

(cd-s) (128 TP7CD) – ('A'-Shamen acid: Escacid) / (2 'A'-Hardfloor mixes).
(cd-s) (128 TP7CDL) – (2 'A'-Basement Boys mixes) / (3 'A'-Beatmasters mixes).

Oct 95. (c-s) *(138 TP7C)* **TRANSAMAZONIA (Beatmasters mix) /** **('A'-Visnadi mix) / ('A'-Watershed instrumental) / ('A'-LTJ Bukin mix)** | 28 | |
(12"+=) *(138 TP12)* – ('A'-Deep dish mix).
(cd-s) *(138 TP7CD)* – (6 'A'mixes including; Alex Party Aguirre / Zion Train).
(cd-s+=) *(138 TP7CDL)* – ('A'-Nuv Idol mix).

Oct 95. (d-lp/c/cd) *(TPLP 52/+C/CD)* <57796> **AXIS MUTATIS** | 27 | |
– Destination Eschaton / Transamazonia / Conquistador / Mauna Kea to Andromeda / Neptune / Prince of Popacatapertl / Heal the separation / Persephone's quest / Moment / Axis mundi / Eschaton omega (deep melodic techno).
(cd/c/d-lp with other cd/c/d-lp) *(TPLP 52 CDL/CL/L)* **ARBOR BONA / ARBOR MALA** – Asyptotic Escaton / Sefirotic axis (a)(b)(c) Formation (d) Action / Extraterrestrial / Deneter / Beneath the underworld / Xochipilis return / Rio Negro / Above the underworld / A moment in dub / Pizarro in Paradiso / West of the underworld / Anticipation Escaton (be ready for the storm) / Out in the styx.

Feb 96. (c-s) *(158 TP7C)* **HEAL (THE SEPARATION) / ('A'mix)** | 31 | |
(cd-s) *(158 TP7CD)* – ('A'mixes; organ / science park / PM Dawn / Steve Osborne ambient – H.E.L.P. breakfast / Beatmasters / foul play vocal).
(cd-s) *(158 TP7CDL)* – ('A'mixes; mighty organ / live '95) / Boss drum (Lionrock dub) / Phorever people (Todd Terry).

Oct 96. (3x12"lp/c/cd) *(TPLP 62/+C/CD)* **HEMPTON MANOR** | | - |
– Freya / Urpflanze / Cannabeo / Khat / Bememe / Indica / Rausch / Kava / El-fin / Monoriff.

Dec 96. (c-s) *(169 TP7C)* **MOVE ANY MOUNTAIN '96 / ('A'mix)** | 35 | |
(12"/cd-s) *(169 TP 12P/7CD)* – (mixes; Beatmasters radio / Tony De Vit edit) / Indica / L.S.I. (Beat edit).
(cd-s) *(169 TP7CDL)* – (mixes:- Tomka / Tony De Vit / Sneaker Pimps / Beatmasters 12").

Jan 97. (cd/c) *(TPLP 72 CD/C)* **THE SHAMEN COLLECTION** (compilation) | | |

Jan 97. (cd/c) *(TPLP 72 CDR/CR)* **THE SHAMEN REMIX COLLECTION – STARS ON 45** (compilation) | | |
(both above re-iss. Apr98 d-cd/d-c; TPLP 72 CDE/CE) – hit UK No.26

Moksha   Moksha

Oct 98. (cd-ep) *(<MOKSHA 3CD>)* **UNIVERSAL (mixes:- 1999 vocal / 187 B.P. metamix (major) / 1999 dance vocal / Sharp trade life dub / Mr.C tech house mix / 187 Lockdown dark dub)** | | Nov98 |

– compilations, others, etc. –

Aug 88. (lp/c)(cd) *Materiali Sonori; (MASO 33041/+C)(MASOCD 9008)* **STRANGE DAY DREAMS** | - | - | Italy
(re-iss. cd Oct91 imported) (re-iss. Jan93; same)

Dec 89. (m-lp/cd) *Communion; (COMM 4 LP/CD)* **WHAT'S GOING DOWN** | | - |

Nov 93. (cd/c/lp) *Band Of Joy; (BOJ CD/MC/LP 006)* **ON AIR (live BBC sessions)** | 61 | - |
(cd re-iss. Mar98 on 'Strange Fruit'; SFRSCD 055)

Mar 98. (12") *Moksha; (AGC 002)* **U-NATIONS** | | - |

SHAM 69

Formed: London, England ... 1976 by JIMMY PURSEY, ALBIE SLIDER, MARK CAIN and DAVE PARSONS (the last two replacing original members BILLY BOSTIK and NEIL HARRIS – who himself had replaced the curiously monikered JOHN GOODFORNOTHING – respectively). Inspired by The SEX PISTOLS, PURSEY set out making pogo-friendly, dumbly anthemic punk with a fiercely working class agenda, issuing a statement of intent with an independently released, JOHN CALE-produced single, 'I DON'T WANNA'. Subsequently signing with 'Polydor', the band made their major label debut with the inimitable 'BORSTAL BREAKOUT' in early '77, following it up with a partly live album, 'TELL US THE TRUTH'. What really took their terrace chant appeal to the masses, however, was the subsequent trio of hit singles led by 'ANGELS WITH DIRTY FACES'; 'HURRY UP HARRY' and 'IF THE KIDS ARE UNITED' followed into the Top 10 shortly after, the last track (complete with hilarious chirpy cockney intro) a well meant but naive call for youthful brotherhood. Which kind of summed up SHAM 69's fate; PURSEY's idealistic working class warrior philosophy backfired as the air-punching punk-by-numbers began attracting more and more face-punching neo-Nazi skinheads. Despite a considered attempt to brush up on the lads-on-the-loose formula with their third set, 'THE ADVENTURES OF THE HERSHAM BOYS' (1979), Top 10 success only seemed to make the situation worse. PURSEY finally disbanded SHAM 69 in the summer of '79 only to reform a couple of months later for a final album, 'THE GAME' (1980). This failed to chart and PURSEY subsequently pursued a low key solo career, initially with 'Polydor' (who released his 1980 debut set, 'IMAGINATION CAMOUFLAGE') then with 'Epic', before going on to record a series of one-off singles for various indie labels. With this going nowhere fast, PURSEY and PARSONS resurrected SHAM 69 in 1987, releasing a largely ignored album, 'VOLUNTEER' the following year. Retreating from view for a further four years, they were back yet again in the 90's, releasing a string of albums for the diehards and playing regular gigs on the punk nostalgia circuit. • **Songwriters:** Penned by PURSEY-PARSONS except; YOU'RE A BETTER MAN THAN I (Yardbirds) / WITH A LITTLE HELP FROM MY FRIENDS (Beatles). The WANDERERS covered THE TIMES THEY ARE A-CHANGIN' (Bob Dylan). • **Trivia:** PURSEY appeared on Various Artists lp, 'The Whip', in '83.

Album rating: TELL US THE TRUTH (*6) / THAT'S LIFE (*5) / ADVENTURES OF THE HERSHAM BOYS (*5) / THE GAME (*4) / THE FIRST, THE BEST AND THE LAST compilation (*7) / VOLUNTEER (*2) / INFORMATION LIBRE (*2) / KINGS AND QUEENS (*3) / SOAPY WATER & MR MARMALADE (*1)

JIMMY PURSEY (b. Hersham, Surrey, England) – vocals / **DAVE PARSONS** – guitar repl. NEIL HARRIS who had repl. JOHNNY GOODFORNOTHING / **ALBIE SLIDER** (b. ALBERT MASKAIL) – bass, vocals / **MARK CAIN** – drums repl. BILLY BOSTIK

		Step Forward	not iss.
Oct 77. (7"m/12"m) *(SF 4/+12)* **I DON'T WANNA. / RED LONDON / ULSTER** *(re-iss. 1979; same)*			-

—— **DAVE TREGANNA** – bass, vocals repl. ALBIE

	Polydor	Sire
Jan 78. (7") *(2058 966)* **BORSTAL BREAKOUT. / HEY LITTLE RICH BOY**		-
Feb 78. (lp) *(2383 491)* <6060> **TELL US THE TRUTH** (some live)	25	-

– We gotta fight / Rip off / Ulster / George Davis is innocent / They don't understand / Borstal breakout / Family life / Hey little rich boy / I'm a man, I'm a boy / What about the lonely / Tell us the truth / It's never too late / Whose generation. *(re-iss. Mar89 on 'Receiver'; RRD 001) (cd-iss. Mar96 on 'Dojo'; DOJOCD 256)*

Apr 78. (7") *(2059 023)* **ANGELS WITH DIRTY FACES. / COCKNEY KIDS ARE INNOCENT**	19	-
Jul 78. (7") *(2059 050)* **IF THE KIDS ARE UNITED. / SUNDAY MORNING NIGHTMARE**	9	-
Oct 78. (7") *(POSP 7)* **HURRY UP HARRY. / NO ENTRY**	10	-
Nov 78. (lp) *(2442 158)* **THAT'S LIFE**	27	-

– Leave me alone / Who gives a damn / Everybody's right, everybody's wrong / That's life / Win or lose / Hurry up Harry / Evil way (live) / Reggae pick up (part 1) / Sunday morning nightmare / Reggae pick up (part 2) / Angels with dirty faces / Is this me or is this you. *(re-iss. Jul88 on 'Skunx'; SHAMX 1) (cd-iss. Mar96 on 'Dojo'; DOJOCD 257)*

| Mar 79. (7"m) *(POSP 27)* **QUESTIONS AND ANSWERS. / I GOTTA SURVIVE (live) / WITH A LITTLE HELP FROM MY FRIENDS** | 18 | - |
| Jul 79. (7"m) *(POSP 64)* **HERSHAM BOYS. / I DON'T WANNA (live) / TELL US THE TRUTH (live)** | 6 | - |

(12"m+=) *(POSPX 64)* – I'm a man, I'm a boy (live).

| Sep 79. (lp) *(POLD/+C 5025)* **THE ADVENTURES OF THE HERSHAM BOYS** | 8 | - |

– Money / Fly dark angel / Joey's on the street / Cold blue in the night / You're a better man than I / Hersham boys / Lost on Highway 46 / Voices / Questions and answers / What have we got. *(free 12") (2812 045)* – IF THE KIDS ARE UNITED. / BORSTAL BREAKOUT *(cd-iss. Mar96 on 'Dojo'; DOJOCD 258)*

| Oct 79. (7") *(POSP 82)* **YOU'RE A BETTER MAN THAN I. / GIVE A DOG A BONE** | 49 | - |

—— Disbanded for two months Jul'79. **MARK GOLDSTEIN** – drums repl. CAIN

| Mar 80. (7") *(POSP 136)* **TELL THE CHILDREN. / JACK** | 45 | - |
| May 80. (lp) *(2442 173)* **THE GAME** | | - |

– The game / Human zoo / Lord of the flies / Give a dog a bone / In and out / Tell the children / Spray it on the wall / Dead or alive / Simon / Deja vu / Poor cow / Run wild run free / Unite and win. *(re-iss. Mar89 on 'Receiver'; RRLD 002) (cd-iss. Mar96 on 'Dojo'; DOJOCD 259)*

| Jun 80. (7") *(2059 259)* **UNITE AND WIN. / I'M A MAN** | | - |
| Nov 80. (lp) *(2383 596)* **THE FIRST, THE BEST AND THE LAST** (compilation) | | - |

– Borstal breakout / Hey little rich boy / Angels with dirty faces / Cockney kids are innocent / If the kids are united / Sunday morning nightmare / Hurry up Harry / Questions and answers / Give the dog a bone / Hersham boys / Tell the children / Unite & win. *(free 7"ep live) (RIOT 1 – 2816 028) (cd-iss. Apr94; 513429-2).*

—— Had already splintered, with PURSEY going solo

—— re-formed in '87. (PURSEY, PARSONS, +2)

	Legacy	Legacy
Jul 87. (7") *(LGY 69)* **RIP AND TEAR. / THE GREAT AMERICAN SLOWDOWN**		-
Feb 88. (7") *(LGY 71)* **OUTSIDE THE WAREHOUSE. / ('A'version)**		-

(12"+=) *(LGY/+T 71)* – How the west was won.

| Jun 88. (lp/c) *(<LLP/LLK 117>)* **VOLUNTEER** | | |

– Outside the warehouse / Wicked tease / Wallpaper / Mr.Know it all / As black as sheep / How the west was won / That was the day / Rip and tear / Bastard club / Volunteer. *(cd-iss. Dec89; LLCD 117) (cd re-iss. Mar92 on Castle'; CLACD 274)*

	Rotate	not iss.
Nov 92. (cd/lp) *(ROT CD/LP 006)* **INFORMATION LIBRE**		

– Break on through / Uptown / Planet trash / Information libertaire / Caroline's suitcase / Feel it / King Kong drinks Coca-Cola / Saturdays and Strangeways / Breeding dinosaurs / Wild and wonderful. *(cd re-iss. Nov95 on 'Dojo'; DOJOCD 236)*

	C.M.P.	not iss.
Nov 92. (12") **M25. /**		-
Mar 93. (7") **UPTOWN. / BORSTAL BREAKOUT**		-

(12"+=) – Flowers / Wild and wonderful.

| Nov 93. (cd) **KINGS & QUEENS** | | |

– Action time vision / I don't wanna / Ulster boy / They don't understand / Tell us the truth / Borstal breakout / Family life / The kids are united / Hurry up Harry / Hey little rich boy / Bosnia / Reggae giro. *(re-iss. Jul95 on 'Dojo';)*

| Oct 93. (cd-ep) *(CMCCD 002)* **ACTION TIME & VISION / BOSNIA / HEY LITTLE RICH BOY / REGGAE GIRO** | | |

	Red Cat	not iss.
Jul 95. (cd) *(A1CD 001)* **SOAPY WATER & MR. MARMALADE**		-

– compilations, others, etc. –

Oct 82. (12"ep) *Polydor; (POSPX 602)* **ANGELS WITH DIRTY FACES / BORSTAL BREAKOUT. / HURRY UP HARRY / IF THE KIDS ARE UNITED**		-
Nov 86. (lp/c) *Receiver; (RRLP/RRLC 104)* **ANGELS WITH DIRTY FACES – THE BEST OF SHAM 69**		-
Dec 87. (lp) *Link; (LINKLP 004)* **LIVE AND LOUD (live)**		-
Apr 88. (lp) *Link; (LINKLP 025)* **LIVE AND LOUD VOL.2**		-
May 89. (cd/c/lp) *Receiver; (RRLP/CD 112)* **THE BEST OF THE REST OF SHAM 69**		-
Oct 89. (cd/c/lp) *Castle; (CLA CD/MC/LP 153)* **COMPLETE LIVE (live)**		-

Apr 90.	(cd/c) *Action Replay; (CDAR/ARLC 1011)* **SHAM 69 LIVE** (live)	☐ -
Aug 90.	(cd/lp) *Receiver;* **LIVE AT THE ROXY** (live tapes '77)	☐ -
Jul 91.	(cd) *Dojo; (DOJOCD 62)* **LIVE AT THE CBGB'S**	☐ -
Apr 93.	(cd) *Dojo; (DOJOCD 95)* **SHAM'S LAST STAND**	☐ -
Oct 93.	(cd) *Dojo; (DOJOCD 105)* **LIVE IN JAPAN** (live)	☐ -
Nov 93.	(cd) *Windsong; (WINCD 049)* **BBC RADIO 1 LIVE IN CONCERT** (Live)	☐ -
Mar 95.	(cd; shared with 999) *Step-1;* **LIVE AND LOUD**	☐ -
Sep 95.	(cd) *Emporio; (EMPRCD 582)* **SHAM 69 LIVE**	☐ -
Dec 95.	(cd) *Essential; (ESDCD 350)* **LIVE / THE BEST OF SHAM 69**	☐ -
Jun 96.	(cd/c) *Hallmark; (30446-2/-4)* **UNITED**	☐ -
Oct 98.	(7"; shared with DIE TOTEN HOSEN) *M Tradegy; (MT 385)* **SAWBLADE SERIES #19**	☐ -

SHANGRI-LA'S

Formed: Andrew Jackson High, Queens, New York, USA ... as The BON BONS by sisters BETTY & MARY WEISS along with twins MARY-ANN and MARGIE GANSER. The girls were handed their big music biz break after being discovered by producer GEORGE 'SHADOW' MORTON who changed their name and signed them to 'Red Bird', the label owned by NY songwriters Jerry Leiber and Mike Stoller. MORTON himself penned 'REMEMBER (WALKING IN THE SAND)', an eerily melodramatic ballad with an ambitious production that cast SHADOW as an East Coast version of PHIL SPECTOR. The single hit the US Top 5 (UK Top 20) in September '64 and primed The SHANGRI-LA'S for their entrance into pop legend with 'LEADER OF THE PACK'. A half-spoken/half-sung (in MARY's trademark emotionally loaded, cheerleader-style NY accent) tale of tearful teen love, rebellion and death complete with revving motorbike/smashing glass sound effects, the track topped the US chart in late '64 and established a new benchmark in pop artistry. Further brilliantly overwrought creations followed over the next two years although only the more customary girly 'GIVE HIM A GREAT BIG KISS' and the runaway anguish of 'I CAN NEVER GO HOME ANYMORE' were significant hits. Following summer 66's unsettling spoken monologue, 'PAST, PRESENT AND FUTURE', the girls moved to 'Mercury' for a greatest hits package and a final couple of singles, 'THE SWEET SOUND OF SUMMER' and 'TAKE YOUR TIME'. The SHANGRI-LA'S split in 1967 amid legal problems with both the GANSER twins subsequently meeting unpleasant deaths (MARY ANN from encephalitis and MARGE from a drugs overdose). MORTON, meanwhile, went on to work with the likes of MOTT THE HOOPLE and The NEW YORK DOLLS.

Best CD compilation: THE BEST OF THE SHANGRI-LA'S (*8)

MARY WEISS – lead vocals / **BETTY WEISS** – vocals / **MARY-ANN GANSER** – vocals / **MARGE GANSER** – vocals

		Red Bird	Red Bird
Sep 64.	(7") <*RB10 008*> **REMEMBER (WALKING IN THE SAND). / IT'S EASIER TO CRY**	14	5 Aug64
Dec 64.	(7") <*RB10 014*> **LEADER OF THE PACK. / WHAT IS LOVE?**	11	1 Oct64
Jan 65.	(7") <*RB10 018*> **GIVE HIM A GREAT BIG KISS / TWIST AND SHOUT**		18 Dec64
Jan 65.	(7") <*RB10 019*> **MAYBE. / SHOUT**		91 Dec64
1965.	(lp) <*RB20 101*> **THE SHANGRI-LAS – LEADER OF THE PACK**		Mar65
	– Give him a great big kiss / Leader of the pack / Bull dog / It's easier to cry / What is love? / Remember (walking in the sand) / Twist and shout / Maybe / So much in love / Shout / Good night, my love / Pleasant dreams / You can't sit down. (*re-iss. 1983 on 'Charly'; CRM 2028*)		
1965.	(7") <*RB10 025*> **OUT IN THE STREETS. / THE BOY**		53 Mar65
1965.	(7") <*RB10 030*> **GIVE US YOUR BLESSINGS. / HEAVEN ONLY KNOWS**		29 May65
1965.	(7") <*RB10 036*> **RIGHT NOW AND NOT LATER. / TRAIN FROM KANSAS CITY**		99 Sep65
1965.	(lp) <*RB20 014*> **SHANGRI-LAS '65**	-	
	– Right now and not later / Never again / Give us your blessings / Sophisticated boom boom / I'm blue / Heaven only knows / The train from Kansas City / Out in the streets / What's a girl supposed to do / The dum dum ditty / You cheated, you lied / The boy. (*UK-iss.Mar84 on 'Charly'; CRM 2029*)		
Jan 66.	(7") <*RB10 043*> **I CAN NEVER GO HOME ANYMORE. / BULLDOG**		6 Nov65
Mar 66.	(7") <*RB10 048*> **LONG LIVE OUR LOVE. / SOPHISTICATED BOOM BOOM**		33 Jan66
——	now without MARGE		
May 66.	(7") <*RB10 053*> **HE CRIED. / DRESSED IN BLACK**		65 Apr66
Aug 66.	(7") <*RB10 068*> **PAST, PRESENT AND FUTURE. / PARADISE**		59 Jun66
		Mercury	Mercury
1966.	(lp) (*MCL 20096*) <*61099*> **GOLDEN HITS** (compilation)		
	– Leader of the pack / The train from Kansas City / Heaven only knows / Remember (walking in the sand) / I can never go home anymore / What is love? / Past, present and future / Out in the streets / Give him a great big kiss / Long live our love / Give us your blessings / Sophisticated boom boom. (*re-iss. 1973 on 'Philips' lp)(c; 6336 215)(7175 031)*		
1967.	(7") (*MF 962*) **THE SWEET SOUND OF SUMMER. / I'LL NEVER LEARN**		
1967.	(7") (*MF 979*) **TAKE YOUR TIME. / FOOTSTEPS ON THE ROOF**		
——	Split in 1967. In 1971 MARY ANN died of encephalitis. MARGE died of a drug overdose.		

– compilations, etc. –

1965.	(7"ep) *Red Bird; (RB 40002)* **THE SHANGRI-LAS**	☐ -
1971.	(7") *Philips; (6061 027)* **PAST, PRESENT AND FUTURE. / THE TRAIN FROM KANSAS CITY**	☐ -
Oct 72.	(7") *Kama Sutra; (2013 024)* **LEADER OF THE PACK. / REMEMBER (WALKING IN THE SAND)** (*re-iss. Jul82 & Jun88 on 'Old Gold'; OG 9085*)	3
1973.	(7"m) *Buddah; (2011 164)* **GIVE HIM A GREAT BIG KISS. / NEW YORK IS A LONELY TOWN / THE BOY FROM NEW YORK CITY**	☐ -
May 76.	(7") *Charly; (CYS 1009)* **LEADER OF THE PACK. / GIVE HIM A GREAT BIG KISS**	7
May 76.	(7") *Contempo; (CS 9032)* **LEADER OF THE PACK. / REMEMBER (WALKING IN THE SAND)**	7
1976.	(7"ep) *Charly; (CEP 109)* **REMEMBER (WALKING IN THE SAND) / LEADER OF THE PACK. / GIVE HIM A GREAT BIG KISS / PAST, PRESENT AND FUTURE** (*cd-ep iss.Feb89; CDS 3*)	☐ -
Aug 76.	(7"m) *Philips; (6160 051)* **PAST, PRESENT AND FUTURE. / GIVE HIM A GREAT BIG KISS / REMEMBER (WALKING IN THE SAND)**	☐ -
Sep 78.	(7") *Charly; (CYS 1041)* **LEADER OF THE PACK. / THE BOY FROM NEW YORK CITY**	☐ -
1978.	(lp) *Charly; (CRM 2005)* **TEEN ANGUISH VOL.2**	☐ -
Nov 84.	(lp/c) *Topline; (TOP/KTOP 100) / Astan; <20/40 097>* **LEADER OF THE PACK**	☐ -
May 87.	(cd) *Topline; (TOPCD 519)* **GREATEST HITS**	☐ -
Aug 87.	(cd) *The Collection; (OR 0012)* **SHANGRI-LAS**	☐ -
Jun 88.	(cd) *Spectrum; (U 4063)* **GREATEST HITS**	☐ -
Feb 89.	(cd-s) *Old Gold; (OG 6114)* **LEADER OF THE PACK / REMEMBER (WALKING IN THE SAND) / CHAPEL OF LOVE**	☐ -
Mar 89.	(cd) *Crusader; (RMB 5633)* **LEADER OF THE PACK**	☐ -
Feb 90.	(cd/c/lp) *Instant; (CD/TC+/INS 5021)* **REMEMBER**	☐ -
	– Leader of the pack / Give him a great big kiss / Maybe / Out in the streets / Give us your blessings / Right now and not later / Remember (walking in the sand) / I can never go home anymore / Long live our love / Past, present and future / The train from Kansas City / Shout / Twist and shout / I'm blue / You cheated, you lied / So much in love. (*re-iss. Apr96 on 'Hallmark' cd/c; 30412-2/-4*)		
Apr 94.	(cd) *Disky; (DISK 4512)* **HIT SINGLE COLLECTABLES**	☐ -
Mar 95.	(cd) *The Collection; (COL 043)* **THE COLLECTION**	☐ -
Apr 95.	(cd) *R.P.M.; (RPM 136)* **MYRMIDONS OF MELODRAMA**	☐ -

Del SHANNON

Born: CHARLES WEEDON WESTOVER, 30 Dec'34, Coopersville, Michegan, USA. Although he'd learned the guitar while still in his teens, his break didn't come until 1960 when he met keyboard player, MAX CROOK. The pair formed CHARLIE JOHNSON & HIS LITTLE BIG SHOW BAND, in turn attracting the attention of DJ Ollie McLaughlin who introduced them to 'Big Top' label owners Harry Balk and Irving Micahnik. CHARLES was signed solo as DEL SHANNON with CROOK remaining as his co-writer sidekick, the duo hitting paydirt almost immediately with 1961's classic 'RUNAWAY'. A transatlantic No.1, the single segued from SHANNON's brooding, bitter verses into a rollercoaster falsetto-vocal chorus, the whole thing driven along on minor chords and underpinned by CROOK's trademark 'Musitron' organ. It was a striking musical formula that saw follow-up single, 'HATS OFF TO LARRY', make the Top 10 in both Britain and America. Yet as his Stateside profile waned, so he became more popular in Britain where his tough yet melodic sound and uncompromising self-penned material found a more appreciative audience. Over his golden period of '62-'63, both 'HEY! LITTLE BABY' and 'THE SWISS MAID' narrowly missed the UK No.1 spot while 'LITTLE TOWN FLIRT' and 'TWO KINDS OF TEARDROPS' went Top 5. SHANNON subsequently met and played alongside The BEATLES on a 1963 tour and became the first American artist to cover a Fab Four track, releasing 'FROM ME TO YOU' in summer '63. That year also saw him sever ties with Balk and Micahnik, the singer briefly setting up his own label ('Berlee') amid the ensuing legal battle. He then relocated to New York and signed to the 'Amy' imprint where he scored his last significant hit with the blistering 'KEEP SEARCHIN'. 1965 found British duo PETER & GORDON covering SHANNON's 'I GO TO PIECES' while DEL himself was breaking the mould by cutting a whole album of HANK WILLIAMS tunes. The following year he signed to L.A.'s 'Liberty' where producer Snuff Garrett and arranger LEON RUSSELL were fresh from turning twee teensters GARY LEWIS & THE PLAYBOYS into lucrative chart material. An attempt to groom SHANNON for teen idol status was doomed to failure, the label subsequently shelving an ambitious album of orchestrated ('AND THE MUSIC PLAYS ON') pop/rock which the singer had recorded alongside JIMMY PAGE, JOHN PAUL JONES and NICKY HOPKINS. With his chart days clearly behind him, SHANNON moved into production work towards the end of the decade, taking the helm for The SHIRELLES and BRIAN HYLAND. The early 70's found him label-hopping with various comeback single attempts, even releasing an Australian-only single in 1975. Throughout the latter half of the decade the singer struggled with alcoholism although by the early 80's he'd recovered sufficiently to have a final crack at the US Top 40 with the country-style, TOM PETTY-produced 'SEA OF LOVE' single. Further sporadic singles emerged before SHANNON began work on a new album with JEFF LYNNE in 1990. Tragically, by the time 'ROCK ON' (1991) was released, SHANNON was dead; he'd committed suicide (by shooting himself) on 8th February 1990 after reportedly suffering severe depression. His death was made all the more poignant with the revelation that he'd been mooted as a replacement for ROY ORBISON in The TRAVELING WILBURYS. • **Covered:** THE SWISS MAID (Roger Miller) / HANDY MAN (Jimmy Jones) / DO YOU WANT TO DANCE? (Bobby Freeman) / MEMPHIS (Chuck Berry) / TWIST AND SHOUT (Isley Brothers) / CRYING + RUNNING SCARED + PRETTY WOMAN (Roy Orbison) / NEEDLES AND PINS + WHEN YOU WALK IN THE ROOM (Searchers) / RAG DOLL (Four Seasons) / A WORLD WITHOUT LOVE (hit; Peter & Gordon) / THE BIG HURT (Toni Fisher) / UNDER MY THUMB (Rolling Stones) / KICKS (Paul Revere) / RED RUBBER BALL (Cyrkle) / PIED PIPER (Crispian St. Peters) / SUMMER IN THE CITY (Lovin' Spoonful) / SUNNY (Bobby Hebb) / TELL HER NO (Zombies).

Best CD compilation: GREATEST HITS (*7)

DEL SHANNON – vocals (with session people incl. MAX CROOK – keyboards)

		London	Big Top	
Apr 61.	(7") (HLX 9317) <3067> **RUNAWAY. / JODY**	1	1	Feb61
Sep 61.	(7") (HLX 9402) <3075> **HATS OFF TO LARRY. / DON'T GILD THE LILY, LILY**	6	5	May61
Nov 61.	(7") (HLX 9462) <3083> **SO LONG BABY. / THE ANSWER TO EVERYTHING**	10	28	Sep61
Nov 61.	(lp) (HA-X 2402) <1303> **RUNAWAY WITH . . .**			

– Misery / Daydreams / His latest flame / The prom / The search / Runaway / I wake up crying / Wide wide world / I'll always love you / Lies / He doesn't care / Jody.

		London	Big Top	
Nov 61.	(7") <3091> **HEY! LITTLE GIRL. / I DON'T CARE ANYMORE**	-	38	
Mar 62.	(7") (HLX 9515) **HEY! LITTLE BABY. / YOU NEVER TALKED ABOUT ME**	2	-	
Mar 62.	(7") <3098> **GINNY IN THE MIRROR. / I WON'T BE THERE**	-		
Aug 62.	(7") (HLX 9587) <3112> **CRY MYSELF TO SLEEP. / I'M GONNA MOVE ON**	29	99	Jun62
Sep 62.	(7") <3117> **THE SWISS MAID. / YOU NEVER TALKED ABOUT ME**	-	64	
Oct 62.	(7") (HLX 9609) **THE SWISS MAID. / GINNY IN THE MIRROR**	2	-	
Jan 63.	(7") (HLX 9653) <3131> **LITTLE TOWN FLIRT. / THE WAMBOO**	4	12	Dec62
Apr 63.	(7") (HLX 9710) <3143> **TWO KIND OF TEARDROPS. / KELLY**	5	50	
May 63.	(lp) (8071) **HATS OFF TO LARRY** (compilation)			

– The Swiss maid / Cry myself to sleep / Ginny in the mirror / You never talked about me / Don't gild the lily, Lily / I won't be there / Hats off to Larry / The answer to everything / Hey little girl / I'm gonna move on / I don't care anymore / So long baby.

		London	Big Top	
Jun 63.	(7") <3152> **FROM ME TO YOU. / TWO SILHOUETTES**	-	77	
Aug 63.	(7") (HLX 9761) **TWO SILHOUETTES. / MY WILD ONE**	23	-	
Oct 63.	(lp) (HA-X 8091) <1308> **LITTLE TOWN FLIRT**	15	12	Jun63

– Two kind of teardrops / Dream baby / Happiness / Two silhouettes / She thinks I still care / My wild one / Runaround Sue / From me to you / Kelly / Hey baby / Go away little girl / Little town flirt.

		London	Berlee
Oct 63.	(7") (HLU 9800) <501> **SUE'S GONNA BE MINE. / SINCE SHE'S GONE**	21	71
Mar 64.	(7") (HLU 9858) <502> **THAT'S THE WAY LOVE IS. / TIME OF THE DAY**		

		Stateside	Amy
Mar 64.	(7") (SS 269) <897> **MARY JANE. / STAINS ON MY LETTER**	35	
Jul 64.	(7") (SS 317) <905> **HANDY MAN. / GIVE HER LOTS OF LOVIN'**	36	22
Oct 64.	(7") (SS 349) <911> **DO YOU WANT TO DANCE? / THIS IS ALL I HAVE TO GIVE**		43 Sep64
Jan 65.	(lp) (SL 10115) <8003> **HANDY MAN**		Nov64

– Memphis / That's the way love is / Ruby baby / I'll be lonely tomorrow / I can't fool around anymore / Handy man / Crying / Mary Jane / A world without love / I ran all the way home / Give her lots of lovin' / Twist and shout.

		Stateside	Amy
Jan 65.	(7") (SS 368) <915> **KEEP SEARCHIN' (WE'LL FOLLOW THE SUN). / BROKEN PROMISES**	3	9 Nov64
Mar 65.	(7") (SS 395) <919> **STRANGER IN TOWN. / OVER YOU**	40	30 Feb65
May 65.	(lp) (SL 10130) <8004> **DEL SHANNON SINGS HANK WILLIAMS**		

– Your cheatin' heart / Kaw-liga / I can't help it / Honky tonk blues / (See I hear) That lonesome whistle / You win again / Ramblin' man / Hey good looking / Long gone lonesome blues / Weary blues / I'm so lonesome, I could cry / Cold cold heart.

		Stateside	Amy
Jun 65.	(7") (SS 430) <925> **BREAK UP. / WHY DON'T YOU TELL HIM**		95 May65
Sep 65.	(7") (SS 452) <937> **MOVE IT ON OVER. / SHE STILL REMEMBERS TONY**		
Sep 65.	(lp) (SL 10140) <8006> **1,661 SECONDS WITH DEL SHANNON**		

– Stranger in town / She cried / Needles and pins / Broken promises / Why don't you tell him / Do you wanna dance / I go to pieces / I'm gonna be strong / Rag doll / Over you / Running scared / Keep searchin'.

		Liberty	Liberty
Mar 66.	(7") (SS 494) <947> **I CAN'T BELIEVE MY EARS. / I WISH IT WASN'T ME TONIGHT**		
Apr 66.	(7") (LIB 55866) <55866> **THE BIG HURT. / I GOT IT BAD**		94
Jun 66.	(7") (LIB 55889) <55889> **FOR A LITTLE WHILE. / HEY LITTLE STAR**		
Sep 66.	(7") <55894> **SHOW ME. / NEVER THOUGHT I COULD**	-	
Nov 66.	(7") <55904> **UNDER MY THUMB. / SHE WAS MINE**	-	
Nov 66.	(lp; stereo/mono) (S+/LBY 1320) <LST 7452> **THIS IS MY BAG**		

– Lightnin' strikes / The cheater / Kicks / Action / It's too late / Never thought I could / The big hurt / Everybody loves a clown / Hey! little star / When you walk in the room / For a little while / Oh pretty woman.

		Liberty	Liberty
Jan 67.	(7") (LIB 55939) <55939> **SHE. / WHAT MAKES YOU RUN**		
Feb 67.	(lp; stereo/mono) (S+/LBY 1335) <LST 4779> **TOTAL COMMITMENT**		

– Under my thumb / Red rubber ball / She was mine / Where were you when I needed you / The joker went wild / The Pied Piper / Sunny / Show me / Time won't let me / What makes you run / I can't be true / Summer in the city.

		Liberty	Liberty
Jun 67.	(7") (LIB 10277) **MIND OVER MATTER. / LED ALONG**		
Jun 67.	(7") <55961> **LED ALONG. / I CAN'T BE TRUE**	-	
Oct 67.	(7") <55993> **RUNAWAY (live '67). / HE CHEATED**	-	
Oct 67.	(7") (LBF 15020) **RUNAWAY '67. / SHOW ME**	-	

—— early in '68, 'Liberty' shelved the album 'AND THE MUSIC PLAYS ON'. It featured session men JIMMY PAGE, JOHN PAUL JONES + NICKY HOPKINS.

Mar 68.	(7") (LBF 15061) <56018> **THINKIN' IT OVER. / RUNNING ON BACK**		
May 68.	(7") (LBF 15079) <56036> **GEMINI. / MAGICAL MUSICAL BOX**		
Jul 68.	(lp) (LBL/LBS 83114E) <LST 7539> **THE FURTHER ADVENTURES OF CHARLES WESTOVER**		

– Thinkin' it over / Be my friend / Silver birch / I think I love you / River cool / Colour flashing hair / Gemini / Runnin' on back / Conquer / Been so long / Magical music box / New Orleans (Mardi Gras). (cd-iss. Aug98 on 'Beat Goes On'+=; BGOCD 402) – She / Runaway / What's the matter baby / Early in the morning / In my arms again.

		Stateside	Dunhill
Feb 69.	(7") **RAINDROPS. / YOU DON'T LOVE ME**	-	
Sep 69.	(7") (SS 8025) <4193> **COMIN' BACK TO ME. / SWEET MARY LOU**		

		U.A.	U.A.
Mar 70.	(7") (SS 8040) <4224> **SISTER ISABELLE. / COLORADO RAIN**		
Oct 72.	(7") (UP 35460) **WHAT'S A MATTER, BABY. / EARLY IN THE MORNING**		
May 73.	(7") (UP 35535) **KELLY. / COOPERSVILLE YODEL**		
Jun 73.	(lp) (UAS 29474) <LA 151> **LIVE IN ENGLAND** (live)		

– Hats off to Larry / Handy man / The Swiss maid / Hey! little girl / Little town flirt / Kelly / Crying / Two kinds of teardrops / Coopersville yodel / The answer to everything / Keep searchin' (We'll follow the sun) / What's a matter, baby / So long baby / Runaway. (re-iss. May82 on 'Fame' lp/c; FA/TCFA 3020)

		U.A.	U.A.
Oct 74.	(7") (UP 35740) **AND THE MUSIC PLAYS ON. / IN MY ARMS AGAIN**		-

		not iss.	Island
1975.	(7") <021> **TELL HER NO. / RESTLESS**	-	-
1975.	(7") <038> **CRY BABY CRY. / IN MY ARMS AGAIN**	-	-

—— between 1975-76, he issued Australian 45; OH HOW HAPPY. / THE GHOST. Retired for the rest of the 70's, but returned in the early 80's after a bout of alcoholism. First batch of releases co-produced with TOM PETTY.

		Demon	Network
Dec 81.	(7") <47951> **SEA OF LOVE. / MIDNIGHT TRAIN**	-	33
Apr 82.	(7") <48006> **TO LOVE SOMEONE. / LIAR**	-	
May 83.	(lp) (FIEND 8) <568> **DROP DOWN AND GET ME**		Dec81

– Sea of love / Life without you / Out of time / Sucker for your love / To love someone / Drop down and get me / Maybe tomorrow / Liar / Never stop tryin' / Midnight train. (UK-version +=) – Cheap love. (cd-iss. Jun98 on 'Varese Sarabande'; VAR 5927)

		Demon	Network
May 83.	(7") (D 1017) **CHEAP LOVE. / DISTANT GHOST**	-	-
Nov 83.	(7") (D 1019) **SEA OF LOVE. / HELP ME**	-	

		not iss.	Warners
1985.	(7") <29098> **IN MY ARMS AGAIN. / YOU CAN'T FORGIVE ME**	-	-
1985.	(7") <28853> **STRANGER ON THE RUN. / WHAT YOU GONNA DO WITH THAT BEAUTIFUL MODY OF YOURS**	-	-

—— after another Australian-only single (WALK AWAY) in 1987, he signed to 'Silvertone' in the UK 1989. Tragically, after more fits of depression, he committed suicide on 8th of February 1990.

		Silvertone	M.C.A.
Mar 91.	(7") **WALK AWAY. / NOBODY'S BUSINESS**	-	-

(cd-s+=) – Let's dance.

		Silvertone	M.C.A.
Apr 91.	(cd/c/lp) (ORE CD/MC/LP 514) **ROCK ON!**		

– Walk away / Who left who / Are you lovin' me too / Callin' out my name / I go to pieces / Lost in a memory / I got you / What kind of fool do you think I am? / When I had you / Let's dance. (re-iss. cd/c Apr94; same)

		Silvertone	M.C.A.
Jun 91.	(7") **ARE YOU LOVIN' ME TOO. / ONE WOMAN MAN**	-	-

(cd-s+=) – Who left who.

– compilations, etc. –

Jan 62.	(7"ep) London; (RE-X 1332) **RUNAWAY WITH DEL SHANNON**		-
Feb 63.	(7"ep) London; (RE-X 1346) **DEL SHANNON No.2**		-
Oct 63.	(7"ep) London; (RE-X 1383) **DEL'S OWN FAVOURITES**		-
Nov 63.	(7"ep) London; (RE-X 1387) **FROM DEL TO YOU**		-
May 65.	(7"ep) Stateside; (SE 1029) **DEL SHANNON HITS**		-
Mar 67.	(7"ep) Liberty; (LEP 2272) **THE NEW DEL SHANNON**		-
Apr 71.	(lp) Sunset; (SLS 50211) **TENTH ANNIVERSARY ALBUM**		-
Jun 73.	(lp) Contour; (2870 323) **THE BEST OF DEL SHANNON**		-
Nov 74.	(7"ep) Cooltempo; (CS 9013) **THE SWISS MAID. / HEY! LITTLE GIRL**		-
Jan 75.	(7") Cooltempo; (CS 9021) **RUNAWAY. / KEEP SEARCHIN' (WE'LL FOLLOW THE SUN)**		-
Mar 75.	(7") Cooltempo; (CS 9033) **KELLY. / THE ANSWER TO EVERYTHING**		-
Jul 75.	(d-lp) Cooltempo; (CRMD 1001) **THE VERY BEST OF DEL SHANNON**		-
Aug 76.	(7"ep) D.J.M.; (DJS 10700) **RUNAWAY**		-
Mar 78.	(lp) Sunset; (SLS 50412) **AND THE MUSIC PLAYS ON** (unissued lp from 1968)		-

– It's the feeling / Mind over matter / Silently / Cut and come again / My love has gone / Led along / Life is but nothing / And the music plays on / Easy to say, easy to do / Friendly with you / Raindrops / He cheated / Leaving you behind / Runaway '67.

Jun 79.	(7") *Creole;* (CR 196) **RUNAWAY (new version). / HATS OFF TO LARRY (new version)**	☐	-
Jun 80.	(7") *J.B.;* (001) **RUNAWAY. / KEEP SEARCHIN' (WE'LL FOLLOW THE SUN)** *(re-iss. Jan81 on 'London'; HL 10580)*	☐	-
Jun 80.	(7") *J.B.;* (005) **HATS OFF TO LARRY. / LITTLE TOWN FLIRT**	☐	-
Jul 80.	(lp) *London;* (HAR 8545) **THE DEL SHANNON HIT PARADE**	☐	-
Oct 82.	(lp/c) *Dakota;* (COUNT/ZCCNT 8) **DEL SHANNON**	☐	-
Apr 83.	(7") *Old Gold;* (OG 9256) **RUNAWAY. / JODY**	☐	-
Apr 83.	(7") *Old Gold;* (OG 9257) **HATS OFF TO LARRY. / HEY! LITTLE GIRL**	☐	-
Apr 83.	(7") *Old Gold;* (OG 9258) **THE SWISS MAID. / SO LONG BABY**	☐	-
Apr 83.	(7") *Old Gold;* (OG 9259) **LITTLE TOWN FLIRT. / TWO KIND OF TEARDROPS**	☐	-
Apr 83.	(7") *Old Gold;* (OG 9260) **KEEP SEARCHIN' (WE'LL FOLLOW THE SUN). / KELLY**	☐	-
1983.	(lp) *Audio Fidelity;* (AFEMP 1048) **20 GREATEST HITS**	☐	-
Mar 84.	(lp) *Edsel;* (XED 121) **RUNAWAY HITS** *(cd-iss. Nov86; EDCD 121)*	☐	-
Apr 86.	(lp) *Edsel;* (ED 174) **I GO TO PIECES** *(cd-iss. 1990; EDCD 174)*	☐	-
Apr 86.	(lp) *Music For Pleasure;* (MFP/TCMFP 5746) **ROCK'N'ROLL GREATS: DEL SHANNON**	☐	-
May 88.	(lp/c) *Flashback;* (3/6 4044) **GREATEST HITS**	☐	-
Oct 88.	(lp/c) *BR Music;* (BR LP/MC 51) **GREATEST HITS**	☐	-
Dec 88.	(cd) *Line;* (IMCD 9.00436) **THE COLLECTION**	☐	-
Feb 89.	(cd-s) *Old Gold;* (OG 6113) **RUNAWAY / HATS OFF TO LARRY / KEEP SEARCHIN' (WE'LL FOLLOW THE SUN)**	☐	-
Jul 91.	(cd/c) *Connoisseur;* (VSOP CD/MC 161) **LOOKING BACK: HIS BIGGEST HITS**		-

– Runaway / Hats off to Larry / Don't gild the lily / So long baby / The answer to everything / Hey little girl / I don't care anymore / You never talked about me / I won't be there / Ginny in the mirror / cry myself to sleep / Swiss maid / Little town flirt / Two kinds of teardrops / Kelly / Two silhouettes / From me to you / Sue's gonna be mine / That's the way love is / Mary Jane / Handy man / World without love / Do you wanna dance / Keep searchin' / Broken promises / I go to pieces / Stranger in town / Break up / Why don't you tell him / Move it on over.

Aug 91.	(cd) *E.M.I.;* (CZ 427) **THE LIBERTY YEARS**	☐	-
Oct 92.	(cd/c) *Muskateer;* (MU 5/4 017) **20 GREATEST HITS**	☐	-
Oct 93.	(cd) *Charly;* (CPCD 8001) **DEL SHANNON'S GREATEST HITS**	☐	-
Nov 93.	(cd/c) *Remember;* (RMB 7/4 5027) **RUNAWAY**	☐	-
Nov 93.	(cd) *B.A.M.;* (KLMCD 002) **PEARLS OF THE PAST**	☐	-
Jun 95.	(cd) *Beat Goes On;* (BGOCD 280) **LIVE IN ENGLAND / . . .AND THE MUSIC PLAYS ON**	☐	-
Mar 96.	(cd) *Beat Goes On;* (BGOCD 307) **THIS IS MY BAG / TOTAL COMMITMENT**	☐	-
Apr 96.	(cd/c) *Music;* (CD6/MC7 011) **THE BEST OF DEL SHANNON**	☐	-
Aug 96.	(cd) *Gold;* (GOLD 051) **DEL SHANNON: GOLD**	☐	-
Nov 96.	(cd) *Tring;* (QED 098) **ALL THE HITS AND MORE**	☐	-
Jul 97.	(cd/c) *Carlton;* (303600079-2/-4) **RUNAWAY – THE ULTIMATE COLLECTION**	☐	-
Sep 97.	(cd) *Beat Goes On;* (BGOCD 367) **RUNAWAY WITH DEL SHANNON / HATS OFF TO LARRY**	☐	-
Oct 97.	(d-cd) *Charly;* (COCD 8315-2) **THE DEFINITIVE COLLECTION**	☐	-
Nov 97.	(d) *Music Club;* (MCCD 326) **THIS IS DEL SHANNON**	☐	-
Feb 98.	(d-cd) *Raven;* (RVCD 51) **DEL SHANNON 1961-1990 (A COMPLETE ANTHOLOGY)**	☐	-
Feb 98.	(cd) *Disky;* <(WB 88551-2)> **THE VERY BEST OF DEL SHANNON**	☐	-
Mar 98.	(cd) *Beat Goes On;* (BGOCD 388) **LITTLE TOWN FLIRT / HANDY MAN**	☐	-
Aug 98.	(cd) *Beat Goes On;* (BGOD 404) **SINGS HANK WILLIAMS / 1,661 SECONDS OF . . .**	☐	-

Feargal SHARKEY (see under ⇒ UNDERTONES)

Sandie SHAW

Born: SANDRA GOODRICH, 26 Feb'47, Dagenham, Essex, England. A protege of pop singer ADAM FAITH (who introduced her to his manager, Eve Taylor), SANDIE SHAW made her debut in summer '64 with 'AS LONG AS YOU'RE HAPPY BABY'. While this flop single failed to capture the public imagination, the teenage singer struck gold with her BACHARACH & DAVID-penned follow-up '(THERE'S) ALWAYS SOMETHING THERE TO REMIND ME'. Appearing barefoot on Top Of The Pops, SANDIE's girl-next-door image and distinctive vocal performance helped propel the track to the top of the British chart. A subsequent link-up with songwriter/producer CHRIS ANDREWS (also on the books on Taylor) initiated a string of major hits beginning with 'GIRL DON'T COME'. 'LONG LIVE LOVE' became her second UK No.1 in the summer of '65, establishing her in the top flight of new young female singers alongside DUSTY SPRINGFIELD, CILLA BLACK and LULU. SHAW's last ANDREWS-penned effort 'MESSAGE UNDERSTOOD' was another sizeable British hit, although her lightweight pop appeal didn't translate well to the American market. Post 1965, her career began to flag, until that is, an opportunity knocked in the form of an invite to sing for Blighty in the 1967 Eurovision Song Contest. Penned by Bill Martin & Phil Coulter, the infectiously jerky 'PUPPET ON A STRING' walked away with the top prize and subsequently furnished SANDIE with a third and final No.1. Yet again the barefoot babe's career took a slight nosedive thereafter, her

only Top 10 hit coming in the shape of 1969's 'MONSIEUR DUPONT'. An attempt to move even further into the mainstream with cabaret and TV work was doomed to failure as the new decade began with her marriage on the rocks and her reputation dragged through the press quagmire. However, SHAW was rediscovered and introduced to a new audience in the early 80's courtesy of HEAVEN 17 offshoot B.E.F.; they collaborated on a cover of 'ANYONE WHO HAD A HEART', originally a chart-topper for CILLA BLACK. Another 80's figure to sing SANDIE's praises was MORRISSEY, who – in his position as lead singer of up and coming indie mavericks The SMITHS – was instrumental in rejuvenating her career. In the Spring of '84, the ever youthful SHAW hit the Top 30 (and the indie charts for 'Rough Trade'!) with a cover of 'HAND IN GLOVE', MORRISSEY, MARR and Co backing her on a Top Of the Pops performance. This exposure led her to 'Polydor', for whom she released two 1986 singles, 'ARE YOU READY TO BE HEARTBROKEN' (penned by LLOYD COLE) and 'FREDERICK' (a PATTI SMITH cover). Towards the end of the decade she was back at 'Rough Trade' for a whole album, 'HELLO ANGEL' (1988), singing material by The SMITHS and even The JESUS & MARY CHAIN(!). One of the album's better tracks, 'NOTHING LESS THAN BRILLIANT' was issued as a single, although it didn't crack the charts for another six years by which time 'Virgin' had taken over the reins. In fact, her new label released a long overdue retrospective under the same title in 1994. A few years later, the cult icon of 60's pop helped set up London's Arts Clinic while regular TV appearances helped establish her as a minor celeb. • **Covered:** ROUTE 66 (hit; Nelson Riddle) / HOMEWARD BOUND + SCARBOROUGH FAIR (Simon & Garfunkel) / (I CAN'T GET NO) SATISFACTION (Rolling Stones) / WORDS (Bee Gees) / WHAT NOW MY LOVE (hit; Shirley Bassey) / MAMA ROUX (Dr. John) / SYMPATHY FOR THE DEVIL (Rolling Stones) / YOUR TIME IS GONNA COME (Led Zeppelin) / LOVE ME DO (Beatles) / THOSE WERE THE DAYS (hit; Mary Hopkin) / MAYBE I'M AMAZED (Paul McCartney) / WALKIN' THE DOG (Rufus Thomas) / LAY LADY LAY (Bob Dylan) / ROSE GARDEN (hit; Lynn Anderson) / FATHER AND SON (Cat Stevens) / etc.

Best CD compilation: NOTHING LESS THAN BRILLIANT (*7)

SANDIE SHAW – vocals (with session people)

		Pye	Reprise
Jul 64.	(7") *(7N 15671)* **AS LONG AS YOU'RE HAPPY BABY. / YA-YA-DA-DA**	☐	☐
Sep 64.	(7") *(7N 15704) <0320>* **(THERE'S) ALWAYS SOMETHING THERE TO REMIND ME. / DON'T YOU KNOW**	1	52 Nov64
Dec 64.	(7") *(7N 15743) <0342>* **GIRL DON'T COME. / I'D BE FAR BETTER OFF WITHOUT YOU**	3	42 Feb65
Feb 65.	(7") *(7N 15783)* **I'LL STOP AT NOTHING. / YOU CAN'T BLAME HIM**	4	-
Feb 65.	(lp) *(NPL 18110) <6166>* **SANDIE** <US-title 'SANDIE SHAW'>	3	100 Jun65

– Everybody loves a lover / Gotta see my baby every day / Love letters / Stop feeling sorry for yourself / Always / Don't be that way / It's in his kiss / Downtown / You won't forget me / Lemon tree / Baby, I need your loving / Talk about love. *(cd-iss. Nov95 on 'See For Miles'+=; SEECD 436)* – ME

May 65.	(7") *(7N 15841) <0375>* **LONG LIVE LOVE. / I'VE HEARD ABOUT HIM**	1	97 Jun65
Sep 65.	(7") *(7N 15940)* **MESSAGE UNDERSTOOD. / DON'T YOU COUNT ON IT**	6	☐
Nov 65.	(7") *(7N 15987)* **HOW CAN YOU TELL. / IF EVER YOU NEED ME**	21	☐
Nov 65.	(lp) *(NSPL 18121)* **ME**		

– You don't love me no more / I don't need that kind of lovin' / Down dismal ways / Oh, no, he don't / When I was a child / Do you mind / (You don't know) How glad I am / Do you mind / I know / Till the night begins to die / Too bad you don't want me / One day / When I fall in love.

Jan 66.	(7") *(7N 17036)* **TOMORROW. / HURTING YOU**	9	☐
May 66.	(7") *(7N 17086)* **NOTHING COMES EASY. / STOP BEFORE YOU START**	14	☐
Aug 66.	(7") *(7N 17163)* **RUN. / LONG WALK HOME**	32	☐
Nov 66.	(7") *(7N 17212)* **THINK SOMETIMES ABOUT ME. / HIDE ALL EMOTION**	32	☐
Jan 67.	(7") *(7N 17239)* **I DON'T NEED ANYTHING. / KEEP IN TOUCH**	50	☐
Mar 67.	(7") *(7N 17272)* **PUPPET ON A STRING. / TELL THE BOYS**	1	☐
Apr 67.	(lp; w-drawn) *(NPL 18182)* **PUPPET ON A STRING** *(cd-iss. Aug91 on 'Repertoire'; REP 4092)*	-	-
Jul 67.	(7") *(7N 17346)* **TONIGHT IN TOKYO. / YOU'VE BEEN SEEING HER AGAIN**	21	☐
Sep 67.	(7") *(7N 17378)* **YOU'VE NOT CHANGED. / MAKE ME CRY**	18	☐
Dec 67.	(lp) *(NSPL 18205)* **LOVE ME, PLEASE LOVE ME**		-

– Love me, please love me / One note samba / Smile / Yes, my darling daughter / Ne me quitte pas / Ev'ry time we say goodbye / The way that I remember him / Hold 'im down / I get a kick out of you / Time after time / That's why / By myself. *(cd-iss. Mar94 on 'R.P.M.'+=; RPM 124)* – Tonight in Tokyo / You've been seeing her again / You've not changed / Make me cry / Today / London / Don't run away / Stop.

Jan 68.	(7") *(7N 17441)* **TODAY. / LONDON**	27	☐
Apr 68.	(7") *(7N 17504)* **DON'T RUN AWAY. / STOP**	☐	☐
Jun 68.	(7") *(7N 17564)* **SHOW ME. / ONE MORE LIFE**	☐	☐
Aug 68.	(7") *(7N 17587)* **TOGETHER. / TURN ON THE SUNSHINE**	☐	☐
Oct 68.	(7") *(7N 17611)* **THOSE WERE THE DAYS. / MAKE IT GO**	☐	☐
Nov 68.	(lp) *(NSPL 18232)* **THE SANDIE SHAW SUPPLEMENT**	☐	☐

– Route 66 / Homeward bound / Scarborough fair / Right to cry / Same thing / Our song of love / (I can't get no) Satisfaction / Words / Remember me / Change of heart / Aranjuez mon amour / What now my love. *(cd-iss. Nov93 on 'R.P.M.'+=; RPM 112)* – Show mw / One more lie / Together / Turn on the sunshine / Those were the days / Make it go / Monsieur Dupont / Voice in the crowd.

Feb 69. (7") *(7N 17675)* **MONSIEUR DUPONT. / VOICE IN THE CROWD** — 6

May 69. (7") *(7N 17726)* **THINK IT ALL OVER. / SEND ME A LETTER** — 42

May 69. (lp) *(NSPL 18323)* **REVIEWING THE SITUATION**
 – Reviewing the situation / Lay lady lay / Mama roux / Sun in my eyes / Walkin' the dog / Love me do / Oh gosh / Your time is gonna come / Coconut groove / Sympathy for the Devil. *(cd-iss. Jan92 on 'R.P.M.'+=; RPM 101)* – Think it all over / Send me a letter / Heaven knows I'm missing him now / So many things to do / By tomorrow / Maple village / Wight is Wight / That's the way he's made / Rose garden / Maybe I'm amazed.

Sep 69. (7") *(7N 17821)* **HEAVEN KNOWS I'M MISSING HIM NOW. / SO MANY THINGS TO DO** — -

Jan 70. (7") *(7N 17894)* **BY TOMORROW. / MAPLE VILLAGE** — -

1970. (7") *(7N 17954)* **WIGHT IS WIGHT. / THAT'S THE WAY HE'S MADE** — -

1971. (7") *(7N 45040)* **ROSE GARDEN. / MAYBE I'M AMAZED** — -

1971. (7") *(7N 45073)* **THE POWER AND THE GLORY. / DEAR MADAME** — -

1972. (7") *(7N 45118)* **WHERE DID THEY GO. / LOOK AT ME** — -

1972. (7") *(7N 45164)* **FATHER AND SON. / PITY THE SHIP** — -

	C.B.S.	not iss.

Jun 77. (7") *(CBS 5371)* **ONE MORE NIGHT. / STILL SO YOUNG** — -

Aug 77. (7") *(CBS 5513)* **JUST A DISILLUSION. / YOUR MAMA WOULDN'T LIKE IT** — -
below was credited with B.E.F. (aka HEAVEN 17)

	Virgin	not iss.

Apr 82. (7") *(VS 484)* **ANYONE WHO HAD A HEART. / (instrumental)** — -

	Palace	not iss.

Apr 83. (7") *(3)* **WISH I WAS. / LIFE IS LIKE A STAR** — -

May 83. (lp) *(PR 2002)* **CHOOSE LIFE** — -
 – Dragon gate / Dragon king's daughter / The mermaid / Let down your hair / East meets west / Treasure tower / Bark bark at dogs / Life is like a star / Moontalk / Sister sister / Wish I was. *(cd-iss. Jun95 on 'Retro'; RETRO 801)*

—— next was accompanied by The SMITHS

	Rough Trade	not iss.

Apr 84. (7") *(RT 130)* **HAND IN GLOVE. / I DON'T OWE YOU ANYTHING** — 27 —
 (12"+=) *(RTT 130)* – Jeanne.

	Polydor	not iss.

May 86. (7") *(POSP 793)* **ARE YOU READY TO BE HEARTBROKEN. / STEVEN (YOU DON'T EAT MEAT)** — 68 —
 (12"+=) *(POSPX 793)* – Hand in glove.

Jul 86. (7") *(POSP 811)* **FREDERICK. / GO JOHNNY GO** — -
 (12"+=) *(POSPX 811)* – Girl don't come.

	Rough Trade	Rough Trade

Sep 88. (7") *(RT 220)* **PLEASE HELP THE CAUSE AGAINST LONELINESS. / I WILL REMAIN (alt mix)** — -
 (12"+=/cd-s+=) *(RTT 220/+CD)* – Jeanne / Lover of the century.

Oct 88. (lp/c/cd) *(ROUGH/+C/CD 110)* **HELLO ANGEL**
 – Nothing less than brilliant / Take him / Hello angel / A girl called Johnny / Strange bedfellows / Please help the cause against loneliness / Hand in glove / Cool about you / Flesh and blood / Comrade in arms / I will remain.

Nov 88. (7") *(RT 230)* **NOTHING LESS THAN BRILLIANT. / LOVE PEACE** — -
 (12"+=/cd-s+=) *(RTT 230/+CD)* – I don't owe you anything / Where were you.

	Virgin	Virgin

Nov 94. (c-s) *(VSC 1521)* **NOTHING LESS THAN BRILLIANT / (THERE'S) ALWAYS SOMETHING THERE TO REMIND ME** — 66 —
 (cd-s+=) *(VSCDT 1521)* – Are you ready to be heartbroken.
 (cd-s+=) *(VSCDX 1521)* – Comrade in arms.

Nov 94. (cd/c) *(VTCD 34)* **NOTHING LESS THAN BRILLIANT** (compilation) — 64
 – (There's) Always something there to remind me / Long live love / Girl don't come / Message understood / Nothing less than brilliant / Hand in glove / Are you ready to be heartbroken? / A girl called Johnny / I'll stop at nothing / Heaven knows I'm missing him now / You've not changed / Monsieur Dupont / I don't owe you anything / Anyone who had a heart (with B.E.F.) / Comrade in arms / Hello angel / Strange bedfellows / Words / Ev'ry time we say goodbye / Your time is gonna come / Frederick / Please help the cause against loneliness / Tomorrow / Nothing comes easy / Puppet on a string. *(re-iss. Apr97 cd/c; CD/TC VIP 183)*

– compilations, etc. –

1964. (7"ep) *Pye; (NEP 24208)* **(THERE'S) ALWAYS SOMETHING THERE TO REMIND ME** — -

1965. (7"ep) *Pye; (NEP 24220)* **LONG LIVE LOVE** — -

1965. (7"ep) *Pye; (NEP 24232)* **TALK ABOUT LOVE** — -

1965. (7"ep) *Pye; (NEP 24234)* **SANDIE** — -

1966. (7"ep) *Pye; (NEP 24236)* **MESSAGE UNDERSTOOD** — -

1966. (7"ep) *Pye; (NEP 24247)* **TOMORROW** — -

Apr 66. (lp) *Golden Guinea; (GGL 0360)* **THE GOLDEN HITS OF SANDIE SHAW** — -
 (re-iss. 1968 on 'Marble Arch'; MALS 781)

1966. (7"ep) *Pye; (NEP 24254)* **NOTHING COMES EASY** — -

1966. (7"ep) *Pye; (NEP 24264)* **RUN WITH SANDIE SHAW** — -

1967. (7"ep) *Pye; (NEP 24271)* **SANDIE SHAW IN FRENCH** — -

1967. (7"ep) *Pye; (NEP 24273)* **SANDIE SHAW IN ITALIAN** — -

1967. (7"ep) *Pye; (NEP 24281)* **TELL THE BOYS** — -

1967. (lp) *Golden Guinea; (GGL 0378)* **SANDIE SINGS** — -

1974. (lp) *Golden Hour; (GH 533)* **THE GOLDEN HOUR OF . . .** — -
 (cd/c-iss.Apr90 on 'Knight'; KGH CD/MC 108)

Nov 77. (d-lp/d-c) *P.R.T.; (FILD/ZCFLD 007)* **THE SANDIE SHAW FILE** — -

Jul 80. (7") *Flashback-Pye; (FBEP 109)* **PUPPET ON A STRING** — -
 – Puppet on a string / Long live love / Girl don't come / (There's) Always something there to remind me.

Jul 82. (7") *Old Gold; (OG 9133)* **PUPPET ON A STRING. / LONG LIVE LOVE** — -

Jul 82. (7") *Old Gold; (OG 9144)* **(THERE'S) ALWAYS SOMETHING THERE TO REMIND ME. / GIRL DON'T COME** — -

Apr 83. (10"lp/c) *P.R.T.; (DOW/ZCDOW 8)* **REMINDING YOU** — -

Apr 86. (lp/c) *Bulldog; (BDL/BDC 2051)* **20 GOLDEN PIECES** — -

Nov 87. (12"ep) *Nighttracks; (SFNT 2)* **NIGHT TRACKS** — -

1988. (cd) *K-Tel; (NCD 3409)* **THE COLLECTION** — -

Apr 89. (7"/12") *P.R.T.; (PYS/PYT 25)* **(THERE'S) ALWAYS SOMETHING THERE TO REMIND ME. /** — -

May 89. (cd) *Bulldog; (BDCD 2051)* **GOLDEN CD COLLECTION** — -

Mar 90. (cd/c/lp) *(CCS CD/MC/LP 251)* **THE COLLECTION** — -

Nov 90. (lp/cd) *See For Miles; (SEE/+CD 305)* **THE E.P. COLLECTION** — -

Apr 91. (cd/c) *Knight; (KGH CD/MC 145)* **THE GOLDEN HOUR OF . . . VOL.2** — -

Jun 91. (cd/c) *Music For Pleasure; (CD/TC MFP 5918)* **THE BEST OF SANDIE SHAW** — -

Jun 91. (cd/c) *Woodford Music; (WM CD/MC 5611)* **LONG LIVE LOVE** — -

Jul 92. (c/cd) *Tring; (MC+/JHD 048)* **CLASSIC ARTISTS: SANDIE SHAW** — -

May 93. (d-cd) *Sequel; (NEDCD 230)* **THE COMPLETE SANDIE SHAW – THE 64-67 SETS** — -

Mar 94. (cd/c) *Prima; (PMM 0556-2/-4)* **PUPPET ON A STRING** — -
 (re-iss. Sep94 on 'Spectrum'; 550255-2/-4)

Jan 95. (cd) *Collection; (COL 067)* **THE COLLECTION** — -

Nov 95. (cd/c) *Emporio; (EMPR CD/MC 625)* **COVER TO COVER** — -

Aug 96. (cd) *Disky; <(DC 86981-2)* **LONG LIVE LOVE (ALL HER HITS)** — -

Aug 96. (cd/c) *Autograph; (MAC CD/MC 171)* **GREATEST HITS OF SANDIE SHAW** — -

Sep 96. (cd) *Tring; (QED 133)* **ALWAYS SOMETHING THERE TO REMIND ME** — -

Mar 97. (cd) *Disky; (WB 87860-2)* **ALWAYS SOMETHING THERE TO REMIND ME** (different) — -

Apr 97. (cd) *BR Music; (RM 1545)* **GREATEST HITS** — -

Sep 97. (cd) *Laserlight; (21038)* **PUPPET ON A STRING** — -

Feb 98. (cd) *R.P.M.; (RPM 181)* **COOL ABOUT YOU** — -

Aug 99. (cd) *Castle Pie; (PIESD 048)* **SANDIE SHAW** — -

Sep 99. (cd) *Bear Family; (BCD 16353)* **DEIN ANDERES GESICHT – IHRE DEUTSCH AUFNAHMEN** — -

SHED SEVEN

Formed: York, England . . . late 1991 by RICK WITTER, PAUL BANKS, TOM GLADWIN and ALAN LEACH. Signing to 'Polydor' in 1994, the group were initially grouped in with the hopelessly contrived "new wave of new wave" scene alongside run-of-the-mill pseudo-punk revivalists like S*M*A*S*H and THESE ANIMAL MEN. Resisting the lure of the Big Smoke, the lads preferred to stay in their native York, their sound a more glam/mod retro pastiche lying somewhere between SUEDE and The CHARLATANS. A debut single, 'MARK', had certain sections of the music press tipping them for big things and they finally assaulted the Top 30 later that summer with the 'DOLPHIN' and 'SPEAKEASY' singles. While SHED SEVEN's music was no great shakes really, the diminutive WITTER had a remarkable voice, somewhat akin to a sleazy liaison between BRETT ANDERSON and ADAM ANT (!?). They also had attitude in abundance, something which translated well in the live arena, SHED SEVEN becoming a regular attraction in the UK's sweatier venues. A debut album, 'CHANGE GIVER' (1994), wasn't exactly groundbreaking although it consolidated their limited appeal. Only a couple of unremarkable singles followed in the next year and a half, before the band returned with 'GETTING BETTER' in 1996, their biggest hit single to date. While the accompanying album, 'A MAXIMUM HIGH' (1996), drew some critical praise it ultimately failed to drag the band out of the indie second division ghetto. However, their albums were still reaching the Top 10 and singles such as 'THE HEROES' and 'DEVIL IN YOUR SHOES' weren't doing too bad either; a stop-gap 'greatest hits' package, 'GOING FOR GOLD' (1999) followed the aforementioned trend. • **Songwriters:** WITTER lyrics / group compositions. Covered JUMPING JACK FLASH (Rolling Stones). • **Trivia:** Said to have taken their group name, after it was revealed by ALAN the drummer that he lost his virginity in a shed aged only 7. (eh!)

Album rating: CHANGE GIVER (*6) / A MAXIMUM HIGH (*7) / LET IT RIDE (*5) / GOING FOR GOLD – THE GREATEST HITS compilation (*6)

RICK WITTER (b.1973) – vocals / **PAUL BANKS** (b.1973) – guitar / **TOM GLADWIN** (b.1973) – bass / **ALAN LEACH** (b.1970) – drums

	Polydor	Atlantic

Mar 94. (7"green) *(YORK 1)* **MARK. / CASINO GIRL** — 77 —
 (12"+=/cd-s+=) *(YORK X/CD 1)* – Mobile 10.

Jun 94. (7"/c-s) *(YORK/YORCS 2)* **DOLPHIN. / IMMOBILITIES** — 28 —
 (12"+=/cd-s+=) *(YORK X/D 2)* – ('A'remix).

Aug 94. (7"/c-s) *(YORK/YORCS 3)* **SPEAKEASY. / AROUND YOUR HOUSE** — 24 —
 (12"+=/cd-s+=) *(YORKX/YORCD 3)* – Your guess is as good as mine / Dolphin.

Sep 94. (cd/c/lp) *(523 615-2/-4/-1) <4063>* **CHANGE GIVER** — 16
 – Dirty soul / Speakeasy / Long time dead / Head and hands / Casino girl / Missing out / Dolphin / Stars in your eyes / Mark / Ocean pie / On an island with you.

Nov 94. (7"/c-s) *(YORK/YORCS 4)* **OCEAN PIE. / NEVER AGAIN** — 33 —
 (12"+=/cd-s+=) *(YORKX/YORCD 4)* – Sleepeasy / Sensitive.

Apr 95. (7"green/c-s) *(YORK/YORCS 5)* **WHERE HAVE YOU BEEN TONIGHT? / SWING MY WAVE** — 23 —
 (cd-s+=) *(YORCD 5)* – This is my house.

	Polydor	Polygram
Jan 96. (7"/c-s) *(577 890-7/-4)* **GETTING BETTER. / ONLY DREAMING**	14	-

(cd-s+=) *(577 890-2)* – Song seven.

Mar 96. (7"/c-s) *(576 215-7/-4)* **GOING FOR GOLD. / MAKING WAVES**	8	-

(cd-s+=) *(576 215-2)* – Barracuda.

Apr 96. (cd/c/lp) *(<531 039-2/-4/-1>)* **A MAXIMUM HIGH**	8	

– Getting better / Magic streets / Where have you been tonight? / Going for gold / On standby / Out by my side / Lies / This day was ours / Ladyman / Falling from the sky / Bully boy / Parallel lines. *(d-cd re-iss. Sep96; 533 416-2)* – (includes THE B-SIDES).

May 96. (7"ep/c-ep) *(576 596-7/-4)* **BULLY BOY / WHERE HAVE YOU BEEN TONIGHT?** (live). **/ DOLPHIN** (live) **/ SPEAKEASY** (live)	22	-

(cd-ep) *(576 596-2)* – ('A'side) / Mark (live) / Ocean pie (live) / Getting better (live).

Aug 96. (7"/c-s) *(575 188-7/-4)* **ON STANDBY. / JUMPING JACK FLASH**	12	-

(cd-s+=) *(575 273-2)* – Killing time.
(cd-s) *(575 188-2)* – ('A'side) / Long time dead (version) / Stepping on hearts.

Nov 96. (7"/c-s) *(575 929-7/-4)* **CHASING RAINBOWS. / IN COMMAND**	17	-

(cd-s+=) *(575 928-2)* – The skin I'm in.

Mar 98. (7") *(569540-7)* **SHE LEFT ME ON FRIDAY. / BOTTOM UPWARDS**	11	

(cd-s+=) *(569541-2)* – Melpomene.
(cd-s) *(569543-2)* – ('A'side) / Mispent youth / You.

May 98. (7"/c-s) *(569916-7/-4)* **THE HEROES. / SLINKY LOVE THEME**	18	-

(cd-s+=) *(569917-2)* – She left me on Friday (live).
(cd-s) *(569923-2)* – ('A'side) / She left me on Friday (live) / Forever (isn't such a long time) (live)(.

Jun 98. (cd/c/lp) *(557359-2/-4/-1)* **LET IT RIDE**	9	-

– Return / Let it ride / The heroes / Halfway home / Devil in your shoes / She left me on Friday / Hole / Drink your love / Stand up and be counted / Chasing rainbows / Goodbye.

Aug 98. (7") *(567207-7)* **DEVIL IN YOUR SHOES. / DUMB SCENE**	37	-

(cd-s+=) *(567207-2)* – Better late than never.
(cd-s) *(567205-2)* – ('A'side) / Happy now / Better late than never.

—— now as **SHED 7**

May 99. (c-s) *(563874-4)* **DISCO DOWN / HANDS UP**	13	-

(cd-s+=) *(563875-2)* – Your guess is as good as mine.
(cd-s) *(563877-2)* – ('A'side) / Another hole / Catapult.

May 99. (cd/c) *(547 442-2/553-4)* **GOING FOR GOLD – THE GREATEST HITS** (compilation)	7	-

– Going for gold / Disco down / Getting better / Chasing rainbows / Speakeasy / She left me on Friday / On standby / Dolphin '99 / High hopes / Bully boy / Devil in your shoes / Where have you been tonight? / Ocean pie / Mark / The heroes. *(ltd d-cd; 547609-2)* – Disco down / Going for gold / The heroes / Missing out / Wired for sound / Eye in the sky / Jumping Jack Flash.

SHEEP ON DRUGS (dig out; Great Alt & Indie . . .)

SHELLAC (see under ⇒ BIG BLACK)

Pete SHELLEY (see under ⇒ BUZZCOCKS)

Michelle SHOCKED

Born: KAREN MICHELLE JOHNSTON, 24 Feb'62, Gilmer, East Texas, USA. After a childhood spent moving around army bases with her stepfather, SHOCKED experienced a turbulent adolescence which included a spell in a psychiatric hospital (committed by her Mormon mother) and a stint as an anarcho-punk squatter in San Francisco, all grist for the songwriting mill (and inspiration for her adoption of the SHOCKED moniker) of this radical post-folk singer. Her break came in 1986 when she was talent-spotted at the Kerrville Folk Festival by 'Cooking Vinyl' bod, Pete Lawrence, the eagle-eared Englishman recording an informal campfire-side set on a walkman. It was a break which SHOCKED was initially unsure about, however, the singer understandably suspicious of the machinations of the music industry. The recordings were eventually released in late '86 as 'THE TEXAS CAMPFIRE TAPES', MICHELLE no doubt, erm . . . shocked (ouch!) to find herself at the top of the UK indie charts. Once again with much trepidation, the singer eventually relented to a deal with the massive 'Polygram' corporation, signing with 'London' in Britain, 'Mercury' in the States. In keeping with her fiercely held beliefs and constant striving for integrity, SHOCKED reportedly made sure that she retained some creative control, the singer vindicated by the critical and commercial success of her debut album, 'SHORT SHARP SHOCKED' (1988). As the title and cover (SHOCKED in a police stranglehold) might suggest, the record was a defiant rabble of engaging protest songs combining roots folk with rock and pop accessibility. Among the highlights were the lilting 'ANCHORAGE' and the affecting 'GRAFFITI LIMBO', an elegy for murdered street artist, Michael Stewart. While the record made the UK Top 40 and garnered a groundswell of support, a follow-up album, 'CAPTAIN SWING' (1989) was way off the mark, moving away from her lone acoustic approach in favour of more ambitious arrangements. While SHOCKED was criticised in some quarters for political preaching, her more hardcore fans thought the record wasn't radical enough. Casting these complaints aside, SHOCKED went off on a musical pilgrimage of sorts, touring America Woody Guthrie-style and recording with an array of respected roots musicians including TAJ MAHAL, POPS

STAPLES, DOC WATSON and the brilliant UNCLE TUPELO. Issued as 'ARKANSAS TRAVELER' (1992), the set reclaimed some of the singer's lost critical ground although it failed to make much of an impact on the charts. Unhappy with the way she was being treated by her record label, SHOCKED subsequently sued the company and self-financed her next album, 'KIND HEARTED WOMAN' (1994), the record receiving a belated UK release two years later. • **Songwriters:** Writes all material and borrows some trad., except ZIP-A-DEE-DOO-DAH (Wrubel-Gilbert) / GOODNIGHT IRENE (Leadbelly).

Album rating: THE TEXAS CAMPFIRE TAPES (*7) / SHORT SHARP SHOCKED (*8) / CAPTAIN SWING (*5) / ARKANSAS TRAVELER (*7) / KIND HEARTED WOMAN (*5) / ARTISTS MAKES LOUSY SLAVES (*5) / MERCURY POISE: 1988-1995 compilation (*6)

MICHELLE SHOCKED – vocals, acoustic guitar

	Cooking Vinyl	Mercury
Nov 86. (lp/c) *(COOK/+C 002)* *<834581-1/-4>* **THE TEXAS CAMPFIRE TAPES**		

– 5 a.m. in Amsterdam / The secret admirer / The incomplete image / Who cares? / Down on St. Thomas St. / Fogtown / Steppin' out / The hepcat / Necktie / (Don't you mess around with) My little sister / The ballad of Patch eye & Meg / The secret to a long life (is knowing when it's time to go). *(cd-iss. Apr88+=' COOKCD 002)* – The chain smoker / Stranded in a limousine / Goodnight Irene. *(re-iss. Nov93 cd/c; same as US)*

Jun 87. (7") *(FRY 002)* **DISORIENTATED. / IF LOVE WAS A TRAIN**		-

(12"+=) *(FRY 002T)* – Chain smoker / Stranded in a limousine / Goodnight Irene.

—— now added numerous session people

	London	Mercury
Aug 88. (lp/c)(cd) *(CV LP/MC 1)<(834924-2)>* **SHORT SHARP SHOCKED**	33	73

– When I grow up / Hello Hopeville / Memories of East Texas / (Making the run to) Gladewater / Graffiti limbo / If love was a train / Anchorage / The L&N don't stop here anymore / V.F.D. / Black widow.

Sep 88. (7") *(LON 193)* **ANCHORAGE. / FOGTOWN**	60	-

(10"+=) *(LONT 193)* – Remodelling the Pentagon / Penny Evans (live).
(12"+=/cd-s+=) *(LON X/CD 193)* – Strawberry jam (live) / Penny Evans (live).

Nov 88. (7") *<870611>* **ANCHORAGE. / ('A'live)**	-	66

Dec 88. (7") *(LON 212)* **IF LOVE WAS A TRAIN. / MEMORIES OF EAST TEXAS**	63	

(12"+=) *(LONX 212)* – Graffiti limbo (live).
(cd-s+=) *(LONCD 212)* – V.F.D. / Jambouree queen.

Feb 89. (7") *(LON 219)* **WHEN I GROW UP. / 5 A.M. IN AMSTERDAM** (live)	67	

(12"+=) *(LONX 219)* – Goodnight Irene.
(cd-s+=) *(LONCD 219)* – Camper crusade.

Nov 89. (lp/c/cd) *<(838 878-1/-4/-2)>* **CAPTAIN SWING**	31	95

– God is a real estate developer / On the greener side / Silent ways / Sleep keeps me awake / The cement lament / (You don't mess around with) My little sister / Looks like Mona Lisa / Too little too late / Street corner ambassador / Must be luff.

Nov 89. (7"/c-s) *(LON 245)* **ON THE GREENER SIDE. / RUSSIAN ROULETTE**		

(12"+=/cd-s+=) *(LON X/CD 245)* – The Titanic / Old paint.

Mar 92. (7"/c-s) **COME A LONG WAY. / OVER THE WATERFALL**		

(cd-s+=) – Contest coming / Jump Jim Crow-Zip-a-dee-doo-dah.
(cd-s+=) – Worth the weight / Shaking hands (soldier's toy).

Apr 92. (cd/c/lp) *(512 189-2/-4/-1)* **ARKANSAS TRAVELER**	46	

– 33 r.p.m. soul / Come a long way / Secret to a long life / Contest coming (Cripple Creek) / Over the waterfall / Shaking hands (Soldier's joy) / Medley:- Jump Jim crow – Zip-a-dee-doo-dah / Hold me back / Strawberry jam / Prodigal daughter (Cotton-eyed Joe) / Blackberry blossom / Weaving way / Arkansas traveler / Woody's rag.

May 92. (7") **33 R.P.M. SOUL. / BLACKBERRY BLOSSOM** (live)		

(cd-s+=) – Over the waterfall (live) / ('A'live).

	Private-BMG	Private
Nov 96. (cd/c) *<(01005 82145-2/-4)>* **KIND HEARTED WOMAN**		

– Stillborn / Homestead / Winter wheat / Cold comfort / Eddie / Child like Grace / Fever breaks / Silver spoon / Hard way / No sign of rain.
(above was independently distributed in 1994)

	not iss.	Independ.
1996. (cd) *<none>* **ARTISTS MAKE LOUSY SLAVES**	-	

– compilations, etc. –

Nov 96. (cd/c) *London; <(532960-2/-4)>* **MERCURY POISE: 1988-1995**		

– On the greener side / Anchorage / Come along way / Quality of mercy / Street corner ambassador / Too little too late / If love was a train / When I grow up / Prodigal daughter / Over the waterfall / Holy spirit / Stillborn.

SHONEN KNIFE

Formed: Osaka, Japan . . . 1981 by sisters ATSUKO and NAOKO YAMANO with fellow school student MICHIE NAKATANI. Punkette "kewpie-doll" pop heavily influenced by western culture rock and pop (like X-RAY SPEX meeting PHIL SPECTOR's RONETTES via FRANCOISE HARDY), the youthful looking trio released several albums throughout the 80's, finding their way onto many a Stateside turntable. The American interest was down to the efforts of CALVIN JOHNSON (of the BEAT HAPPENING), who had discovered them on their home turf and later distributed 1983's 'BURNING FARM' via his own 'K' label. 1986 saw the band's first bonafide US release in the shape of the album 'PRETTY LITTLE BAKA GUY', an eponymous compilation set following in 1990. KURT COBAIN, for one, was a big fan and the girls actually supported NIRVANA, subsequently moving to America around the same time. The Grunge era also saw a host of bands (including SONIC YOUTH and HOLE) paying tribute to the diminutive threesome via an album, 'Every Band Has A Shonen Knife Who Loves Them'. SHONEN KNIFE rounded off their most successful year to date with the festive frenzy, 'SPACE CHRISTMAS'. Subsequently signing to UK Creation off-shoot label, 'August' ('MCA-Victor' in the States), they issued 'LET'S KNIFE' towards the end of '92. Athough the press hype diminished, the girls kept plugging away with their trademark nursery school lyrics and day-glo buzz-pop via albums such as 'WE ARE VERY HAPPY YOU CAME' (1993), 'ROCK ANIMALS' (1994), 'BRAND NEW KNIFE' (1997) and 'HAPPY HOUR' (1998). • Covered: (LIVE IS LIKE A) HEAT WAVE (Martha & The Vandellas) / TOP OF THE WORLD (Carpenters) / PARADISE (Nilsson) / BOYS (Dixon-Farrell) / TILL THE END OF THE DAY (Kinks) / DON'T HURT MY LITTLE SISTER (Beach Boys) / DAYDREAM BELIEVER (hit; Monkees).

Album rating: BURNING FARM mini (*6) / YAMANO ATCHAN mini (*5) / PRETTY LITTLE BAKA GUY (*6) / SHONEN KNIFE compilation (*8) / 712 (*6) / LET'S KNIFE (*5) / WE ARE VERY HAPPY YOU CAME (*5) / ROCK ANIMALS (*4) / BRAND NEW KNIFE (*6) / HAPPY HOUR (*4)

NAOKO YAMANO (b.18 Dec'61) – vocals / **ATSUKO YAMANO** (b.22 Feb'60) – drums / **MICHIE NAKATANI** (b. 8 Oct'61) – bass

	X.A.	not iss.
Aug 82. (c) **MINNA TANOSHIKU SHONEN KNIFE**	–	– Japan

	Zero	K
Jul 83. (8"m-lp) **BURNING FARM**		– Japan
May 84. (8"m-lp) **YAMANO ATCHAN**	–	Jun85

—— Dec'84, also released Jap comp 'HUDDLE NO TROUBLE' for 'Balcony'

	Zero	Subversive
Jun 86. (8"m-lp) **PRETTY LITTLE BAKA GUY**		Oct86

<US re-iss. Dec90 on 'Rockville' cd+=/c+=; 6053-2/-4> – LIVE IN JAPAN

—— Jan 90, another Jap comp 'FLOWER WORLD' was issued on cassette.

	not iss.	Giant
May 90. (cd/c/lp) <6047-2/-4/-1> **SHONEN KNIFE** (compilation)	–	

	Seminal Twang	Rockville
Mar 91. (7") **LAZYBONE. / BLUE OYSTER CULT** (Jap version)	–	
Jul 91. (cd/c) <ROCK 6065-2/-4> **712** (also on 'Nippon Crown' in Japan)		–
Jul 91. (7") **NEON ZEBRA. / BEAR UP BISON** (above single issued for 'Sub Pop')		–
Nov 91. (7") **SPACE CHRISTMAS. / BEAR UP BISON** (cd-s+=) – Christmas message '91.		–
Nov 92. (7") <6075-7> **SPACE CHRISTMAS. / CHRISTMAS MESSAGE '91**	–	

	August	Capitol
Oct 92. (cd/c/lp) (RUST 001 CD/MC/LP) <86638> **LET'S KNIFE**		Jan93

– Riding the rocket / Bear up bison / Twist Barbie / Tortoise theme 2 / Antonio baka guy / Ah Singapore / Flying jelly attack / Black bass / Cycling is fun / Watchin' girl / I am a cat / Tortoise theme 1 / Devil house / Insect collector / Burning farm. (cd+=) – Space Christmas / Bear up bison / Mickey Way / Do the Bartman.

Nov 92. (7") (CAUG 001) **RIDING ON THE ROCKET. / NEON ZEBRA** (**English version**) | | – |
(12"/cd-s) (CAUG 001 T/CD) – ('A'side) / Milky Way / Burning farm (long version) / ('A'reprise).

Jan 93. (7") (CAUG 003) **GET THE WOW. / TWIST BARBIE** | | – |
(12"+=/cd-s+=) (CAUG 003 T/CD) – Fruit loop dreams / Don't hurt my little sister. (cd-s) (CAUG 003CDL) – ('A'side) / Animal song / Ice cream city (John Pel session) / Neon zebra (English version).

Apr 93. (cd/lp) (RUST 004 CD/LP) **WE ARE VERY HAPPY YOU CAME** (live) | | – |
– Lazybone / Public bath / Goose steppin' mama / I wanna eat choco bars / Suzy is a headbanger / Boys / Red Kross.

	August	Virgin
Jan 94. (cd-ep) <38414> **BROWN MUSHROOMS / BUTTERFLY BOY / STRAWBERRY CREAM PUFF / TILL THE END OF THE DAY**		
Jan 94. (cd/c) (RUST 009 CD/MC) <39063> **ROCK ANIMALS**	–	

– Quavers / Concrete animals / Butterfly boy / Little tree / Catnip dream / Tomato head / Another day / Brown mushrooms / Johnny, Johnny, Johnny / Cobra versus mongoose / Music square.

	M.C.A.	Big Deal
May 94. (cd-s) <38433> **TOMATO HEAD /**	–	
Sep 97. (d-cd) (MCD 80071) <9035> **BRAND NEW KNIFE**		Mar97

– Explosion! / Wind your spring / The perfect world / E.S.P. / Loop di loop / Wonder wine / Magic Joe / Fruit & vegetables / Tower of the sun / Keep on rockin' / Frogphobia / Buddha's face / One week.

	Big Deal	Big Deal
Nov 97. (cd-ep) <(BD 9047-2)> **EXPLOSION!**		
– Explosion! / Explosion! / E.S.P. / Loop-di-loop / Wind your spring / One week.
| 1998. (cd) <BD 9055> **HAPPY HOUR** | – | |

– Shonen Knife planet / Konnichiwa / Cookie day / Hot chocolate / Sushi bar song / Fish eyes / Banana chips / Dolly / Jackalope / Gyoza / Catch your bus / People traps / His pet / Daydream believer.

– compilations, others, etc. –

May 94. (cd) Tec Tones; (19422) **KNIFE COLLECTORS**	–	– Japan
Mar 96. (cd) Virgin; <41414> **THE BIRDS AND THE B-SIDES**	–	

– (Love is like a) Heat wave / Gomi day / Top of the world / Ice cream city / Paradise / Little tree / Space Christmas / Fruit loop dreams / Boys / Till the end of the day / Elmer elevator / Don't hurt my little sister / Strawberry cream puff / Neon zebra / Lazybone / Public bath / I wanna eat choco bars / Redd Kross.

Apr 96. (cd) Tec Tones; (SHONEN) **FAN CLUB CD**	–	– Japan

Jane SIBERRY (dig out; Great Alt & Indie . . .)

SIGUE SIGUE SPUTNIK (dig out; Great Alt & Indie . . .)

SILVER APPLES (dig out; Great Psychedelic . . .)

SILVERCHAIR

Formed: Newcastle, Australia . . . 1992 by schoolmates DANIEL JOHNS, his songwriting partner BEN GILLIES and CHRIS JOANNOU. After winning a national talent contest, SILVERCHAIR were lucky enough to have one of their tracks, 'TOMORROW', playlisted by Australia's foremost "alternative" radio stations. Released as a single in summer 1994, the song scaled the domestic charts, the pubescent schoolboys becoming overnight sensations. A follow-up, 'PURE MASSACRE' repeated the feat, as did their debut album, 'FROGSTOMP', its enjoyable, if cliched grunge/rock stylings proving a massive (Top 10) hit in the States. Finally given a British release in late summer '95, the album squeezed into the Top 50, although it didn't have quite the same impact. Early the following year, their track 'ISRAEL'S SON' was cited by the lawyer of two teenage Americans who were charged with murdering one of their own relatives. The SILVERCHAIR rollercoaster continued early in 1997 with the 'FREAKSHOW' album, a set that once again took its cue from the cream of American alt-rock (i.e. PEARL JAM, STONE TEMPLE PILOTS, etc.) and predictably performed well in the US charts. The lads even began to progress a little further in Britain, the Top 40 album spawning two similarly successful singles, 'FREAK' and 'ABUSE ME'. Returning with a third album, 'NEON BALLROOM' (1999), SILVERCHAIR sold out to the mainstream and bypassed their metallic roots for a more tuneful, string-laden style. However, the record still coined in enough sales for it to dent the US Top 50 (UK Top 30), although the boyz to men development had certainly not worked critically.

Album rating: FROGSTOMP (*7) / FREAKSHOW (*5) / NEON BALLROOM (*4)

DANIEL JOHNS – vocals, guitar / **CHRIS JOANNOU** – bass / **BEN GILLIES** – drums

	Columbia	Columbia
Jul 95. (12") (662264-6) **PURE MASSACRE. / STONED** (cd-s+=) (662264-2) – Acid rain / Blind.	71	
Sep 95. (7"/c-s) (662395-7/-4) **TOMORROW. / BLIND** (live) (cd-s) (662395-2) – ('A'side) / Leave me out (live) / Undecided (live).	59	
Sep 95. (cd/c) (480340-2/-4) <67247> **FROGSTOMP**	49	9 Aug95

– Israel's son / Tomorrow / Faultline / Pure massacre / Shade / Blind / Leave me out / Suicidal dream / Madman / Undecided / Cicada / Findaway.

Feb 97. (cd/c/pic-lp) (487103-2/-4/-1) <67905> **FREAKSHOW**	38	12

– Slave / Freak / Abuse me / Lie to me / No association / Cemetry / Pop song for us rejects / Door / Learn to hate / Petrol and chlorine / Roses / Nobody came.

Mar 97. (10"/cd-s) (664076-0/-5) **FREAK. / SLAVE / (interview)** (cd-s) (664076-2) – ('A'side) / New race / Punk song #2 / (interview with Daniel, Ben & Chris).	34	
Jul 97. (c-s/cd-s) (664790-4/-2) **ABUSE ME / FREAK (Remix for us rejects) / BLIND** (cd-s) (664790-5) – ('A'side) / Surfin' bird / Slab (Nick Launoise mix).	40	

Feb 99. (7"/cd-s) (667088-7/-2) **ANTHEM FOR THE YEAR 2000. / MILLENNIUM BUG**		–
Mar 99. (cd/c) (493309-2/-4) <69816> **NEON BALLROOM**	29	50

– Emotion sickness / Anthem for the year 2000 / Ana's song (open fire) / Spawn again / Miss you love / Dearest helpless / Do you feel the same / Black tangled heart / Point of view / Satin sheets / Paint pastel princess / The steam will rise.

May 99. (7") (667345-7) **ANA'S SONG (OPEN FIRE). / ('A'-acoustic)** (cd-s+=) (667345-5) – Trash. (cd-s) (667345-2) – ('A'side) / Anthem for the year 2000 (Paul Mac remix) / London's burning.	45	
Aug 99. (cd-ep) **MISS YOU LOVE / WASTED / FIX ME / MINOR THREAT**		–

SILVER SUN

Formed: Camden, London, England . . . 1995 as SUN..! by songwriter JAMES BROAD and RICHARD KANE who met at a record store. The pair soon found RICHARD SAYCE and PAUL SMITH, changing their name to SILVER SUN (a German metal band was already named SUN) and signing to 'Polydor' the same year. Fusing JELLYFISH, WEEZER and the anthemic rush of SLADE with sugar-coated indie glam-pop, these post-pubescent alt-rockers scored a minor hit with 'LAVA' towards the end of '96. Early the following year, they cracked the Top 50 with 'LAST DAY', entering a purple patch as they went on to notch up three further hits and a Top 30 eponymous album. However, a summery 1998 cover of Johnny Mathis' (!!!) 'TOO MUCH, TOO LITTLE, TOO LATE' was more attuned to a teeny-pop audience, no doubt putting off many of their more diserning fans and possibly accounting for the lowly chart position (No.74) afforded sophomore effort, 'NEO WAVE' (1998). • Covered: XANADU (Rush) / I'M A DICK (Muffs) / YOU MAKE ME REALISE (My Bloody Valentine).

Album rating: SILVER SUN (*6) / NEO WAVE (*5)

JAMES BROAD – vocals / **PAUL SMITH** – guitar, vocals / **RICHARD KANE** – bass, vocals / **RICHARD SAYCE** – drums, vocals

	Polydor	Polygram
Jul 96. (7"ep/c-ep; as SUN..!) (575112-7/-4) **E.P.**		–

– There will never be another me / etc.
(cd-ep+=) (575113-2) –

Oct 96. (7"/c-s) *(575686-7/-4)* **LAVA. / CHANGING** `54` `-`
(cd-s+=) *(575687-2)* – Streets are paved with tarmac.

Feb 97. (7"/c-s) *(573242-7/-4)* **LAST DAY. / TRICKLE DOWN** `48` `-`
(cd-s+=) *(cd-s+=)* *(573243-2)* – Gossip.

Apr 97. (7"pink) *(573826-7)* **GOLDEN SKIN. / SHE'LL DO** `32` `-`
(cd-s) *(573829-2)* – ('A'side) / 17 times / In nature.
(cd-s) *(573827-2)* – ('A'side) / Hight times / It couldn't be you.

May 97. (cd/c/lp) *(537208-2/-4/-1)* **SILVER SUN** `30` `-`
– Test / Golden skin / Dumb / Julia / Far out / Last day / Service / Yellow light / Lava / 2 digits / This 'n' that / Wonderful / Bad haircut / Nobody / Animals feets.

Jun 97. (7"/c-s) *(571174-7/-4)* **JULIA. / REASONS TO LIVE** `51` `-`
(cd-s+=) *(571175-2)* – American metal.
(cd-s) *(571177-2)* – ('A'side) / Angel eyes / Made for you.

Oct 97. (7") *(571422-7)* **LAVA. / CHANGING / STREETS ARE PAVED
WITH TARMAC** `35` `-`
(cd-s) *(571422-2)* – ('A' side) / Tokyo E Ikitai / Fifteen / Lava (acoustic).
(cd-s) *(571424-2)* – ('A' side) / Built in a day / Click / Last day of your life (bedroom demo).

Jun 98. (7"/c-s) *(569968-7/-4)* **TOO MUCH, TOO LITTLE, TOO LATE. /
XANADU** `20` `-`
(cd-s+=) *(569915-2)* – You made me realise / I'm a dick.

Sep 98. (c-s) *(<567452-4>)* **I'LL SEE YOU AROUND / FOR YOUR
ART** `26` `Nov98`
(cd-s+=) *(567455-2)* – Disguise.
(cd-s) *(<567453-2>)* – ('A'side) / Missed / Jessica.

Oct 98. (cd/c/lp) *(559085-2/-4/-1)* **NEO WAVE** `74` `-`
– Cheerleading / I'll see you around / Would've if I could've / Too much, too little, too late / Scared / There goes summer / Sharks / The prophet of the prairie / Mustard / Pixie, pixie / Hey girl friend / Only a girl / Special powers / Fire & blood / Patients / Dead end.

Nov 98. (7") *(563118-7)* **SHARKS. / WAYS OF LOVE** `☐` `-`
(cd-s+=) *(563118-2)* – Hey girlfriend (live).
(cd-s) *(563119-2)* – ('A'side) / I can't wait (live) / Animals feet (live).
(cd-s) *(563118-4)* – ('A'side) / Too much too little too late / Lava.

—— now without RICHARD SAYCE who left Feb'99

Gene SIMMONS (see under ⇒ KISS)

Carly SIMON

Born: 25 Jun'45, New York, New York City, USA. In 1963, CARLY formed folk duo, The SIMON SISTERS along with older sister, LUCY. The pair recorded a few 45's and a children's album on the 'Kapp' label, before branching out on her own in 1966. CARLY subseqently went solo in the early 70's after signing to 'Elektra', an eponymous debut album (in which she worked with film critic, Jacob Brackman) hitting the shops the following year. A Top 30 success as was the follow-up, 'ANTICIPATION' (1971), she went on to work with producer, Richard Perry, beefing up her sound and inspiring both her singing ability and songwriting skills; one of her greatest songs (to this day!) 'YOU'RE SO VAIN' topped the American charts and was apparently about Warren Beaty. This classic transatlantic hit previewed the accompanying chart-topping 'NO SECRETS' album, generally regarded as her finest hour. The striking singer/songwriter married her male counterpart, JAMES TAYLOR, at the height of her fame and the couple were to subsequently hook up on a version of Charlie & Inez Foxx's 'MOCKINGBIRD'; released in 1974 it featured on yet another top selling album, 'HOTCAKES'. Her mid 70's work was much in the mould of the typically slick L.A. sound, although she did excel herself on the classy 'NOBODY DOES IT BETTER' (written by Marvin Hamlisch & Carole Bayer Sager for the Bond film, 'The Spy Who Loved Me') in 1977. More US Top 50 albums were to follow, although only the single, 'JESSE' gave her any notable chart success. It was around this time that her showcase marriage began to hit the rocks. Having separated in '82, she and TAYLOR were divorced the following year, CARLY, like most artists of her generation, losing her way in the unforgiving 80's. Nevertheless, early '87 saw her 'COMING AROUND AGAIN' (from the movie, 'Heartburn' starring Meryl Streep) with her Top 20 hit of the same name, a short-lived revival seeing the similarly-titled album making the US Top 30. Over the ensuing decade, CARLY continued to release the odd album, each selling moderately well and seeing her move further into the adult/contemporary bracket. • **Covered:** IT KEEPS YOU RUNNING (Doobie Brothers) / DEVOTED TO YOU (Everly Brothers) / WHY (Chic) / etc. She recorded 2 standards/covers albums TORCH and MY ROMANCE. CARLY also collaborated on several numbers.

Album rating: CARLY SIMON (*5) / ANTICIPATION (*6) / NO SECRETS (*7) / HOTCAKES (*6) / PLAYING POSSUM (*5) / THE BEST OF CARLY SIMON compilation (*7) / ANOTHER PASSENGER (*5) / BOYS IN THE TREES (*6) / SPY (*5) / COME UPSTAIRS (*5) / TORCH (*4) / HELLO BIG MAN (*5) / SPOILED GIRL (*4) / COMING AROUND AGAIN (*6) / GREATEST HITS LIVE (*5) / MY ROMANCE (*4) / HAVE YOU SEEN ME LATELY? (*4) / LETTERS NEVER SENT (*5) / CLOUDS IN MY COFFEE boxed-set (*6) / FILM NOIR (*5) / THE VERY BEST OF CARLY SIMON compilation (*7)

SIMON SISTERS

CARLY & LUCY – dual vocals

	London	Kapp
Apr 64. (7") *(HLR 9893)* *<586>* **WINKIN', BLINKIN' AND NOD. / SO GLAD I'M HERE**	☐	`73`
Aug 65. (7") *(HLR 9984)* **CUDDLEBUG. / NO ONE TO TALK MY TROUBLES TO**	☐	☐

—— Split in 1966, when LUCY went off to get married. The following year, CARLY

moved to France but returned to sign for Albert Grossman management. After dispute with him, she met producer JAC HOLZMAN who signed her to 'Elektra' in 1969.

CARLY SIMON

CARLY – vocals, piano, guitar was augmented by session musicians.

	Elektra	Elektra
Apr 71. (lp) *(K 42077)* *<74082>* **CARLY SIMON** – That's the way I've always heard it should be / Alone / One more time / The best thing / Just a sinner / Dan, my fling / Another door / Reunions / Rolling down the hills / The love's still growing. *(quad-lp iss.Apr77)* *(cd-iss. Jan96; 7559 60672-2)*	☐	`30`
May 71. (7") *(K 12232)* *<45724>* **THAT'S THE WAY I'VE ALWAYS HEARD IT SHOULD BE. / ALONE**	☐	`10` Apr71
Dec 71. (lp) *(K 42101)* *<75016>* **ANTICIPATION** – Anticipation / Legend in your own time / Our first day together / The girl you think you see / Summer's coming around again / Share the end / Three days / Julie through the glass / I've got to have you. *(cd-iss. Oct89; 960 679-2)*	☐	`30` Nov71
Dec 71. (7") *<45759>* **ANTICIPATION. / THE GARDEN**	☐	`13`
Mar 72. (7") *(K 12043)* *<45774>* **LEGEND IN YOUR OWN TIME. / JULIE THROUGH THE GLASS**	☐	`50`
Sep 72. (7") **SHARE THE END. / THE GIRL YOU THINK YOU SEE**	☐	☐
Nov 72. (7") *(K 12077)* *<45824>* **YOU'RE SO VAIN. / HIS FRIENDS ARE MORE THAN FOND OF ROBIN**	`3`	`1`
Jan 73. (lp/c) *(K/K4 42127)* *<75049>* **NO SECRETS** – The right thing to do / The Carter family / You're so vain / His friends are more than fond of Robin / We have no secrets / Embrace me you child / Waited so long / It was so easy / Night owl / When you close your eyes. *(quad-lp Apr77)* *(cd-iss. Jul93; 7559 60684-2)*	`3`	`1` Dec72
Mar 73. (7") *<45843>* **THE RIGHT THING TO DO. / WE HAVE NO SECRETS**	☐	`17`
Mar 73. (7") *(K 12232)* **THE RIGHT THING TO DO. / THE WAY I'VE ALWAYS HEARD IT SHOULD BE**	`17`	☐
Jan 74. (7") *(K 12145)* *<45887>* **HAVEN'T GOT TIME FOR THE PAIN. / MIND ON MY MAN**	☐	`14` May74
Mar 74. (lp/c) *(K/K4 52005)* *<1002>* **HOTCAKES** – Just not true / Hotcakes / Misfit / Forever my love / Mockingbird / Grown up / Haven't got time for the pain / Safe and sound / Mind on my man / Think I'm gonna have a baby / Older sister. *(quad-lp iss.Apr77)*	`19`	`3` Jan74
Mar 74. (7"; CARLY SIMON & JAMES TAYLOR) *(K 12134)* *<45880>* **MOCKINGBIRD. / GROWN UP**	`34`	`5` Jan74
May 75. (lp/c) *(K/K4 52020)* *<1033>* **PLAYING POSSUM** – After the storm / Love out on the street / Look me in the eyes / More and more / Slave / Attitude dancing / Waterfall / Sons of summer / Are you ticklish / Playing possum. *(quad-lp iss.Apr77)*	☐	`10`
Jun 75. (7") *(K 12178)* *<45246>* **ATTITUDE DANCING. / ARE YOU TICKLISH**	☐	`21` May75
Jun 75. (7") *<45248>* **LOOK ME IN THE EYES. / SLAVE**	☐	`-`
Aug 75. (7") *(K 12187)* *<45263>* **WATERFALL. / AFTER THE STORM**	☐	`78` Jul75
Oct 75. (7") *<45278>* **MORE AND MORE. / LOVE OUT IN THE STREET**	☐	`94`
Dec 75. (lp/c) *(K/K4 52025)* *<1048>* **THE BEST OF CARLY SIMON** (compilation) – That's the way I've always heard it / Should be / The right thing to do / Mockingbird / Legend in our own time / Haven't you got time for the pain / You're so vain / No secrets / Night owl / Anticipation / Attitude dancing. *(cd-iss. 1983; K2 52025)* *(re-iss. + cd.May91)*	☐	`17`
Jun 76. (7") *<45323>* **IT KEEPS YOU RUNNIN'. / LOOK ME IN THE EYES**	☐	`46`
Jun 76. (7") *(K 12217)* **IT KEEPS YOU RUNNIN'. / BE WITH ME**	☐	`-`
Jun 76. (lp/c) *(K/K4 52036)* *<1064>* **ANOTHER PASSENGER** – Half a chance / It keeps you runnin' / Fairweather father / Cowtown / He likes to roll / In times when my head / One love stand / Riverboat gambler / Darkness 'til dawn / Dishonesty modesty / Libby / Be with me.	☐	`29`
Aug 76. (7") *(K 12237)* *<45341>* **HALF A CHANCE. / LIBBY**	☐	☐
Jul 77. (7") *(K 12261)* *<45413>* **NOBODY DOES IT BETTER. / AFTER THE STORM** (above single from the James Bond film 'The Spy Who Loved Me')	`7`	`2`
Apr 78. (7") *(K 12289)* *<45477>* **YOU BELONG TO ME. / IN A SMALL MOMENT**	☐	`6`
Apr 78. (lp/c) *(K/K4 52066)* *<128>* **BOYS IN THE TREES** – You belong to me / Boys in the trees / Back down to Earth / Devoted to you / De bat (fly in me face) / Haunting / Tranquillo (melt my heart) / You're the one / In a small moment / One man woman / For old times sake.	☐	`10`
Aug 78. (7") *(K 12315)* **TRANQUILLO (MELT MY HEART). / FOR OLD TIMES SAKE**	☐	`-`
Nov 78. (7"; CARLY SIMON & JAMES TAYLOR) *(K 12313)* *<45506>* **DEVOTED TO YOU. / BOYS IN THE TREES**	☐	`36` Aug78
Feb 79. (7") *<45544>* **TRANQUILO (MELT MY HEART). / BACK DOWN TO EARTH**	☐	`-`
Jun 79. (lp/c) *(K/K4 52147)* *<506>* **SPY** – Vengeance / We're so close / Just like you do / Coming to get you / Never been gone / Pure sin / Love you by heart / Spy / Memorial day.	☐	`45`
Jun 79. (7") *(K 12362)* *<46051>* **VENGEANCE. / I LOVE YOU BY HEART**	☐	`48`
Aug 79. (7") *(K 12380)* *<46514>* **SPY. / PURE SIN**	☐	☐

	Warners	Warners
Jun 80. (7") *(K 17644)* **COME UPSTAIRS. / JAMES**	☐	☐
Jul 80. (lp/c) *(K/K4 56828)* *<3443>* **COME UPSTAIRS** – Come upstairs / Stardust / Them / Jesse / James / In pain / The three of us in the dark / Take me as I am / The desert.	☐	`36`
Nov 80. (7") *(K 17689)* *<49518>* **JESSE. / STARDUST**	☐	`11` Jul80
Sep 81. (lp/c) *(K/K4 56935)* *<3592>* **TORCH** – Blue of blue / I'll be around / I got it bad and that ain't good / I get along without you very well / Body and soul / Hurt / Spring is here / Pretty strange / What shall we do with the child / Not a day goes by.	☐	`50`
Jan 82. (7") *(K 17898)* *<49880>* **HURT. / FROM THE HEART**	☐	☐
Jul 82. (7") *(K 79300)* *<4051>* **WHY. / WHY (instrumental)** (12"+=) *(K 79300T)* – ('A'extended). *(re-iss. Jun89; U 7501/+T)* – (hit UK 56)	`10`	`74`

(above single from the film 'Soup For One' on 'Mirage' records). In Aug'83, she provided the singing part on UK No.17 hit single 'Kissing With Confidence' by WILL POWERS.

Sep 83. (lp/c) *(923886-1/-4)* <23886> **HELLO BIG MAN**   [ ] [69]
– You know what to do / Menemsha / Damn you get to me / Is this love / Orpheus / It happens everyday / Such a goody boy / Hello big man / You don't feel the same / Floundering. *(cd-iss. Jul86; 923886-2)*

Sep 83. (7") <29484> **YOU KNOW WHAT TO DO. / ORPHEUS**   [–] [83]

Feb 84. (7") <29428> **HELLO BIG MAN. / DAMN YOU GET TO ME**   [–]
                                                        not iss.   Planet

1984.   (7") **SOMEONE WAITS FOR YOU. / ('A'version)**   [–]
                                                        Epic   Epic

Jun 85. (7"/12") *(A/TA 6388)* <05419> **TIRED OF BEING BLONDE. / BLACK HONEYMOON**   [ ] [70]

Aug 85. (lp/c/cd) *(CBS/40/CD 26376)* <39970> **SPOILED GIRL**   [ ] [88] Jul85
– My new boyfriend / Come back home / Tonight and forever / Spoiled girl / Tired of being blonde / The wives are in Connecticut / Anyone but me / Interview / Make me feel something / Can't give it up. *(c+=/cd+=)* – Black honeymoon. *(cd re-iss. Jun91)*

Aug 85. (7"/12") *(A/TA 6654)* <05596> **MY NEW BOYFRIEND. / THE WIVES ARE IN CONNECTICUT**   [ ] [ ]
next 45 was from film 'Heartburn'.
                                                        Arista   Arista

Jan 87. (7") *(ARIST 687)* <9525> **COMING AROUND AGAIN. / ITSY BITSY SPIDER**   [12] [18] Oct86
(12"+=) *(ARIST12 687)* – If it wasn't love.

Apr 87. (7") *(RIS 8)* <9587> **GIVE ME ALL NIGHT. / TWO HOT GIRLS (ON A HOT SUMMER'S NIGHT)**   [ ] [61]
(12"+=) *(RIST 8)* – Hold what you've got.

Jun 87. (lp/c/cd) *(208/408/258 140)* <8443> **COMING AROUND AGAIN**   [25] [25] Apr87
– Coming around again / Give me all night / As time goes by / Do the walls come down / It should have been me / The stuff that dreams are made of / Two hot girls (on a hot summer's night) / You have to hurt / All I want is you / Hold what you've got / Itst bitsy spider. *(re-iss. Nov90 cd/c; 261/411 038)*

Aug 87. (7") *(RIS 33)* <9619> **THE STUFF THAT DREAMS ARE MADE OF. / AS TIME GOES BY**   [ ] [ ]
(12"+=) *(RIST 33)* – Sleight of hand.

Oct 87. (7") <9653> **ALL I WANT IS YOU. / TWO HOT GIRLS (ON A HOT SUMMER NIGHT)**   [ ] [ ]

Nov 87. (7") *(RIS 47)* **ALL I WANT IS YOU. / YOU HAVE TO HURT**   [–] [54]

Sep 88. (lp/c/cd) *(209/409/259 196)* <8526> **GREATEST HITS LIVE (live)**   [49] [87]
– You're so vain / Nobody does it better / Coming around again / It happens every day / Anticipation / Right thing to do / Do the walls come down / You belong to me / Two hot girls (on a hot summer night) / All I want is you / Never been gone. *(re-iss. cd Oct95)*

Sep 88. (7")<US-c-s> *(111 701)* **YOU'RE SO VAIN (live). / DO THE WALLS COME DOWN (live)**   [ ] [ ]
(12"+=/cd-s+=) *(611/661 701)* – Coming around again (live) / Itsy bitsy spider (live).

Nov 88. (7") *(111 807)* **NOBODY DOES IT BETTER (live). / ALL I WANT IS YOU (live)**   [ ] [ ]
(12"+=/cd-s+=) *(611/661 807)* – Never been gone (live).

——   Below 45 was from the movie, 'Working Girl'.
Feb 89. (7") <9793> **LET THE RIVER RUN. / THE TURN OF THE TIDE**   [–] [49]

Mar 89. (7"/c-s) *(112 124)* **LET THE RIVER RUN. / CARLOTTA'S HEART**   [ ] [–]
(12"+=/cd-s+=) *(612/662 124)* – Medley: Coming around again – Itsy bitsy spider.

Mar 90. (cd/c/lp) *(210/410/260 602)* <8582> **MY ROMANCE**   [ ] [46]
– My romance / By myself / I see your face / When your lover is gone / In the wee small hours / My funny valentine / Something wonderful / Little girl blue / He was good to me / What has she got / Bewitched / Danny boy / Time after time. *(re-iss. May92 cd/c; 262/412 019)*

Oct 90. (cd/c/lp) *(261/411/211 044)* <8650> **HAVE YOU SEEN ME LATELY?**   [ ] [60]
– Better not tell her / Didn't I? / Have you seen me lately? / Life is eternal / Waiting at the gate / Happy birthday / Holding me tonight / It's not like him / Don't wrap it up / Fisherman's song / We just got here.

Oct 90. (c-s,cd-s) <2083> **BETTER NOT TELL HER. / HAPPY BIRTHDAY**   [ ] [–]

Jan 91. (c-s,cd-s) <2164> **LIFE IS ETERNAL / WE JUST GOT HERE**   [ ] [–]

Nov 94. (cd/c) <07822 18752-2/-4)> **LETTERS NEVER SENT**   [ ] [ ]
– (intro) / Letters never sent / Lost in your love / Like a river / Time works on all the wild young men / Touched by the Sun / Davy / Halfway 'round the world / What about a holiday / The reason / Private / Catch it like a fever / Born to break my heart / I'd rather it was you.

Dec 95. (3xcd-box/3xc-boxc) <07822 18798-2/-4)> **CLOUDS IN MY COFFEE** (compilation)   [ ] [ ]

Oct 97. (cd/c) <(07822 18984-2/-4)> **FILM NOIR**   [ ] [84]
– You won't forget me / Ev'rytime we say goodbye / Lili Marlene / Last night when we were young (with JIMMY WEBB) / Spring will be a little late this year / Film noir / Laura / I'm a fool to want you / Fools coda / Two sleepy people (with JOHN TRAVOLTA) / Don't smoke in bed / Somewhere in the night.

– compilations, etc. –

On 'Elektra' unless otherwise mentioned.
Sep 76. (7") *(K 12233)* **YOU'RE SO VAIN. / ANTICIPATION**   [ ] [–]
(re-iss. Sep85 on 'Old Gold'; OG 9521)

Sep 76. (7") **MOCKINGBIRD. / LEGEND IN**   [ ] [–]

Apr 81. (lp/c) *Hallmark; (SHM/HSC 3062)* **YOU'RE SO VAIN**   [ ] [ ]

Oct 82. (d-c) **ANTICIPATION / NO SECRETS**   [ ] [ ]

Dec 82. (7") *Mirage; (CARLY 1)* **COME UPSTAIRS. / JESSE**   [ ] [ ]
(12"+=) *(CARLY 1T)* – ('A'version).

Apr 91. (7"/c-s) *(EKR 123/+C)* **YOU'RE SO VAIN. / DO THE WALLS COME DOWN**   [41] [–]

(12"+=) *(EKR 123T)* – Coming around again / Itsy bitsy spider.
(cd-s) *(EKR 123CD)* – ('A'side) / The girl you think you see / Anticipation.

May 91. (lp/c/cd) *(EKT 86/+C/CD)* **THE BEST OF CARLY SIMON**   [ ] [ ]

Mar 99. (cd/c) *Global TV; <(RAD CD/MC 103)>* **THE VERY BEST OF CARLY SIMON**   [22] [ ] Oct98
– You're so vain / Nobody does it better / Why / Coming around again / The right thing to do / We have no secrets / You belong to me / That's the way I've always heard it should be / Mockingbird / Anticipation / Legend in your own time / The street that dreams are made of / All I want is you / Give me all night / Like a river / Better not tell her / Angel from Montgomery / Let the river run.

Paul SIMON (see under ⇒ SIMON & GARFUNKEL)

SIMON AND GARFUNKEL

Formed: New York, USA . . . 1957 as TOM & JERRY by ART GARFUNKEL (b. ARTHUR GARFUNKEL, 5 Nov'41, Queens, New York) and PAUL SIMON (b.13 Oct'41, Newark, New Jersey). Though the pair scored their first hit in 1957 with the lightweight rock'n'roll of 'HEY SCHOOLGIRL', it would be almost a decade later before they met with any real success. In the meantime, SIMON released a series of obscure singles under various pseudonyms including TRUE TAYLOR (!) and JERRY LANDIS, wisely opting for a plain and simple PAUL SIMON as his songs began to take on a more folky hue. GARFUNKEL, meanwhile, had gone back to college, although by 1964 the duo had reunited, subsequently signing with 'C.B.S.' and recording a tentative debut album, 'WEDNESDAY MORNING 3 A.M.' The record's dismal sales figures prompted SIMON to return to Europe, where he'd been living the previous year. He duly recorded an eponymous solo album in London, the set featuring many SIMON compositions (including the evocative 'HOMEWARD BOUND', the railway station weighing so heavily on SIMON's homesick heart actually being Widnes in England) which he'd later re-record with GARFUNKEL and which would become mainstays of the S&G repertoire. Back in New York, producer Tom Wilson had taken it upon himself to revamp the acoustic 'SOUND OF SILENCE' (from 'WEDNESDAY. . .') in an electric folk-rock style, de rigeur in 1965. The result was stunning, as powerful and revelatory as the BYRDS' re-working of 'Mr. Tambourine Man', the track storming to the top of the US charts (The BACHELORS subsequently took the track to No.3 in Britain). SIMON returned from Blighty poste-haste, hooking up with GARFUNKEL once again for what would become the most commercially successful period of his career. 'SOUND OF SILENCE' the album was hurriedly released to consolidate the duo's new found fame, a set largely comprising folk-rock reworkings of SIMON's back catalogue and spawning two further US Top 5 hits in the shape of bedsit classic, 'I AM A ROCK' and the aforementioned 'HOMEWARD BOUND', a worldwide smash. 'PARSLEY, SAGE, ROSEMARY & THYME' (1966) polished up the clean-cut harmonies and witnessed SIMON's songwriting develop apace; 'SCARBOROUGH FAIR / CANTICLE' was an inventive attempt to splice two traditional songs, while '7 O'CLOCK NEWS / SILENT NIGHT' fairly effectively overlaid the traditional Christmas carol with bad tidings in the form of a grim newscast. 'FOR EMILY, WHEREVER I MAY FIND HER', meanwhile, arguably ranks as one of SIMON's most emotive and personal performances. The following summer saw SIMON play a major hand in organising the Monterey Pop Festival, SIMON & GARFUNKEL subsequently headlining the first day of the event. The summer of '68, meanwhile, finally saw S&G break big-time in Britain, both with the evergreen pop fizz of 'MRS. ROBINSON' (written as part of the soundtrack which S&G penned for 'The Graduate', a cult flick turned blockbuster starring Dustin Hoffman and Anne Bancroft) and their biggest album to date, 'BOOKENDS'. A transatlantic No.1, the record is still regarded by many as representing the peak of S&G's career, an even more ambitious set than its predecessor, encompassing everything from the autumnal melancholy of 'HAZY SHADE OF WINTER' to the BEATLES-esque 'OLD FRIENDS'. Even greater success was to come though, the duo making rock/pop history in 1970 when 'BRIDGE OVER TROUBLED WATER' simultaneously made the UK and US Top spot in both its single and album format, the latter staying in the UK chart for an incredible 300 weeks. Its title track was the album's main selling point, an epic, exquisitely arranged ballad sung by GARFUNKEL, the song becoming the group's signature tune, even more so than say, 'MRS ROBINSON'. Other highlights included the celebratory 'CECILIA', 'THE BOXER' and the adapted Peruvian folk tune, 'EL CONDOR PASA'. GARFUNKEL was dissatisfied, however, both with the direction in which SIMON was steering the group and the fact that the latter dominated the songwriting front. At the peak of their fame, then, S&G disbanded, creating a legend in their wake. While GARFUNKEL concentrated on acting, SIMON continued with the solo career he'd begun in 1965, scoring almost immediately with the buoyant pop-reggae of 'MOTHER AND CHILD REUNION', a transatlantic Top 5 hit single in early 1972. The track was released the same month as the album, his second effort to bear an eponymous title and a UK No.1 to boot. Widely acclaimed, the record proved conclusively that SIMON could fashion his own distinct musical identity, experimenting with an array of musical styles on the likes of 'ME AND JULIO DOWN BY THE SCHOOLYARD' and 'DUNCAN'. 'THERE GOES RHYMIN' SIMON' (1973) and the Grammy Award-winning 'STILL CRAZY AFTER ALL THESE YEARS' (1975) were even more successful, if more overtly commercial, the latter featuring a rare duet with GARFUNKEL, 'MY LITTLE TOWN'. SIMON suffered a critical roasting, however, with 'ONE TRICK PONY' (1980), the ambitious soundtrack to his flop film of the same name. Reuniting briefly with GARFUNKEL in 1981, the pair gave a hugely popular free concert in New York's Central Park (released as a double album the following year), although a mooted studio project was abandoned. Left to his own devices, SIMON came with up 'HEARTS AND BONES' (1983), a patchy effort which nevertheless included some of SIMON's most affecting material. With 'GRACELAND' (1986), the singer/songwriter changed tack again, looking to African rhythms and musicians for inspiration. The result was a highly infectious, exotic fusion of SIMON's innate feel for pop melody and traditional African sounds, recorded in collaboration with the likes of LADYSMITH BLACK MAMBAZO. Despite the initial fuss over SIMON's supposed breach of the anti-apartheid cultural boycott (through recording and touring the album in South Africa), the groundbreaking charm of tracks like 'THE BOY IN THE BUBBLE', 'DIAMONDS ON THE SOLES OF HER SHOES' and 'YOU CAN CALL ME AL' was eventually recognised when the album won a Grammy. The record also resurrected SIMON's UK career, making No.1, as did the follow-up, 'THE RHYTHM OF THE SAINTS' (1990), a similar project, constructed around compelling Brazilian percussion. More recently, SIMON has been working on 'SONGS FROM THE CAPEMAN', a concept project based on the life of Salvador Agron, a Puerto Rican criminal turned writer. Working with Nobel-prize winning poet/playwright, Derek Walcott, the album was one of SIMON's most ambitious recordings to date. ART GARFUNKEL, meanwhile, balanced his acting work with a recording career, releasing a string of albums throughout the 70's and 80's, 'ANGEL CLARE' (1973) and 'BREAKAWAY' (1975) being the most successful, the latter featuring a fine cover of Stevie Wonder's 'I BELIEVE (WHEN I FALL IN LOVE IT WILL BE FOREVER)'. The angelic voiced singer was at his best performing other people's material, his most famous hit coming in early '79 with the poignant 'BRIGHT EYES' (penned by none other than Wombling free MIKE BATT), the theme tune from animated film, 'Watership Down'. Chart success eluded GARFUNKEL in the 80's although he continues to record for 'Columbia', releasing an album as recently as 1993, 'UP UNTIL NOW', duetting on one track with JAMES TAYLOR. • Covered: THE TIMES THEY ARE A-CHANGIN' (Bob Dylan) / BYE BYE LOVE (Everly Brothers). PAUL SIMON covered GO TELL IT TO THE MOUNTAIN (trad). GARFUNKEL covered loads including ALL I KNOW (Jimmy Webb) / SECOND AVENUE (Tim Moore) / BREAKAWAY (Gallagher & Lyle) / I ONLY HAVE EYES FOR YOU (Flamingos) / WONDERFUL WORLD (Sam Cooke) / SINCE I DON'T HAVE YOU (Skyliners) / SO MUCH IN LOVE (Tymes) / MISS YOU NIGHTS (Cliff Richard) / WHEN A MAN LOVES A WOMAN (Percy Sledge) / RAG DOLL (Four Seasons) / etc. • ART's filmography: CATCH 22 (1970 with Alan Arkin) / CARNAL KNOWLEDGE (1971 w/Ann-Margret, Candice Bergen & Jack Nicholson) / BAD TIMING (1979 w/Teresa Russell) / ILLUSIONS (1980) / GOOD TO GO (1986) / MOTHER GOOSE ROCK'N'RHYME (1989 TV Disney musical with PAUL). Note PAUL cameoed in the 1977 Woody Allen film 'Annie Hall'. • Trivia: PAUL's video for the 1986 single, 'YOU CAN CALL ME AL', featured comic actor Chevy Chase.

Album rating: WEDNESDAY MORNING 3 A.M. (*6) / SOUNDS OF SILENCE (*7) / PARSLEY, SAGE, ROSEMARY & THYME (*7) / THE GRADUATE soundtrack (*5) / BOOKENDS (*8) / BRIDGE OVER TROUBLED WATER (*9) / SIMON AND GARFUNKEL'S GREATEST HITS compilation (*10) / THE CONCERT IN CENTRAL PARK (*7) / THE DEFINITIVE SIMON AND GARFUNKEL compilation (*10) / Paul Simon:- THE PAUL SIMON SONGBOOK (*6) / PAUL SIMON (*8) / THERE GOES RHYMIN' SIMON (*7) / LIVE RHYMIN' (*5) / STILL CRAZY AFTER ALL THESE YEARS (*8) / GREATEST HITS, ETC compilation (*7) / ONE-TRICK PONY (*5) / HEARTS AND BONES (*4) / GRACELAND (*8) / NEGOTIATIONS AND LOVE SONGS 1971-1986 compilation (*8) / THE RHYTHM OF THE SAINTS (*7) / PAUL SIMON'S CONCERT IN THE PARK (*7) / 1964-1993 boxed set (*6) / SONGS FROM THE CAPEMAN (*4) / Art Garfunkel: ANGEL CLARE (*7) / BREAKAWAY (*6) / WATERMARK (*5) / FATE FOR BREAKFAST (*4) / SCISSORS CUT (*4) / LEFTY (*4) / THE ART GARFUNKEL ALBUM compilation (*6) / UP 'TIL NOW (*4) / THE VERY BEST OF – ACROSS AMERICA (*4) / SONGS FROM A PARENT TO A CHILD (*5)

TOM AND JERRY

TOM = ART GARFUNKEL / JERRY = PAUL SIMON

	Gala	Big
Dec 57. (7") <613> **HEY! SCHOOLGIRL.** / **DANCIN' WILD** <US re-iss. 1960 on 'King'; 5167>	-	49
1958. (7") <616> **OUR SONG.** / **TWO TEENAGERS**	-	
1958. (7") <618> **DON'T SAY GOODBYE.** / **THAT'S MY STORY** <US re-iss. 1959 on 'Hunt' & flipped over; 319>	-	
1959. (7") <621> **BABY TALK.** / **TWO TEENAGERS** <US re-iss. 1971 on 'Bell' w/ diff.B-side by RONNIE LAWRENCE; 120>	-	
1959. (GSP 806) **BABY TALK.** / (b-side by PAUL SHELDON)		

	Pye Int.	Ember
May 63. (7") (7N 25202) <1094> **I'M LONESOME.** / **LOOKING AT YOU**		1962

	not iss.	ABC Para..
1962. (7") <10363> **SURRENDER, PLEASE SURRENDER.** / **FIGHTING MAD**	-	
1966. (7") <10788> **THAT'S MY STORY.** / **TIA-JUANA BLUES**	-	

PAUL SIMON under pseudonyms

TRUE TAYLOR

	not iss.	Big
1958. (7") <614> **TRUE OR FALSE.** / **TEENAGE FOOL**	-	

JERRY LANDIS

	not iss.	M.G.M.
1959. (7") <12822> **ANNA BELLE.** / **LONELINESS**	-	

	not iss.	Warwick
1959. (7") <522> **SWANEE.** / **TOOT, TOOT TOOTSIE GOODBYE**	-	
1960. (7") <552> **SHY.** / **JUST A BOY**	-	
1960. (7") <588> **ID LIKE TO BE THE LIPSTICK ON YOUR COLLAR.** / **JUST A BOY**	-	
1961. (7") <619> **PLAY ME A SAD SONG.** / **IT MEANS A LOT TO THEM**	-	

	not iss.	Canadian A
1961. (7") <130> **I'M LONELY.** / **I WISH I WEREN'T IN LOVE**	-	

	not iss.	Amy
Dec 62. (7") <875> **THE LONE TEEN RANGER.** / **LISA** <re-iss. 1963 on 'Jason Scott'; 2>	-	97

	Oriole	Tribute
May 64. (7"; in US- by PAUL KANE) (CB 1930 <128> **CARLOS DOMINGUEZ.** / **HE WAS MY BROTHER**		

TICO & THE TRIUMPHS

	not iss.	Madison
Dec 61. (7") <169> **MOTORCYCLE.** / **I DON'T BELIEVE THEM** <re-iss. Dec61 on 'Amy'; 835> <hit US No.99>	-	

	not iss.	Amy
1962. (7") <845> **EXPRESS TRAIN.** / **WILDFLOWER**	-	
1962. (7") <860> **CRY, LITTLE BOY, CRY.** / **GET UP & DO THE WONDER**	-	
Feb 63. (7"; by TICO) <876> **CARDS OF LOVE.** / **NOISE**	-	

ARTIE GARR

pseudonym of ART GARFUNKEL

	not iss.	Warwick
1959. (7") <515> **DREAM ALONE.** / **BEAT LOVE**	-	

	not iss.	Octavia
1960. (7") <8002> **PRIVATE WORLD.** / **FORGIVE ME**	-	

PAUL SIMON

released solo below.

	C.B.S.	Columbia
May 65. (lp) <62579> **THE PAUL SIMON SONGBOOK** – I am a rock / Leaves that are green / A church is burning / April come she will / The sound of silence / Patterns / A most peculiar man / He was my brother / Kathy's song / The side of a hill / A simple desultory Philippic / Flowers never bend with the rainfall. (cd-iss. Jan88)		
Jul 65. (7") (201797) **I AM A ROCK.** / **LEAVES THAT ARE GREEN**		

SIMON AND GARFUNKEL

both vocals, acoustic guitar

	C.B.S.	Columbia
Oct 64. (lp) <9049> **WEDNESDAY MORNING 3 A.M.** – You can tell the world / Last night I had the strangest dream / Bleecker Street / Sparrow / Benedictus / The sound of silence / He was my brother / Peggy-O / Go tell it to the mountain / The sun is burning / The times they are a-changin' / Wednesday morning 3 a.m. (US re-dist.Jan66, hit No.30) (UK-iss.Nov68; 63370) – hit No.24. (re-iss. Nov85 lp/c; CBS/40 32575) (cd-iss. Dec85; CD 63370)	-	
Jul 65. (7"ep) (EP 6053) **SIMON AND GARFUNKEL** – Bleecker Street / Sparrow / Wednesday morning 3 a.m. / The sound of silence.		
Dec 65. (7") (201977) <43396> **THE SOUND OF SILENCE.** / **WE'VE GOT A GROOVY THING GOIN'**	1	Nov65
Mar 66. (lp) (BPG 62690) <9269> **SOUND OF SILENCE** – The sound of silence / Leaves that are green / Blessed / Kathy's song / Somewhere they can't find me / Anji / Homeward bound / Richard Cory / A most peculiar man / April come she will / We've got a groovy thing goin' / I am a rock. (re-iss. Mar81 lp/c; CBS/40 32020) (cd-iss. Dec85; CD 62690)	13	21 Feb66
Mar 66. (7") (202045) <43511> **HOMEWARD BOUND.** / **LEAVES THAT ARE GREEN**	9	5 Feb66
Jun 66. (7") (202303) <43617> **I AM A ROCK.** / **FLOWERS NEVER BEND WITH THE RAINFALL** (7"ep+=) (EP 6074) – The sound of silence / Blessed.	17	3 May66
Sep 66. (7") (202285) <43728> **THE DANGLING CONVERSATION.** / **THE BIG BRIGHT GREEN PLEASURE MACHINE**		25 Aug66
Oct 66. (lp) (BPG 62860) <9363> **PARSLEY, SAGE, ROSEMARY & THYME** – Dangling conversation / Scarborough fair – Canticle / Patterns / For Emily, whenever I may find her / The big bright green pleasure machine / A poem on the underground all / Cloudy / A simple desultory Philippic (or how I was Robert McNamara'd into submission) / Flowers never bend with the rainfall / 7 o'clock news – Silent night / Parsley, sage, Rosemary and thyme. (UK re-dist.Aug68, hit No.13) (re-iss. Mar81 lp/c; CBS/40 32031) (cd-iss. Jul87; CD 62825) (cd re-iss. Apr89; CD 32031)		4
Nov 66. (7") (202378) <43873> **A HAZY SHADE OF WINTER.** / **FOR EMILY, WHENEVER I MAY FIND HER**		13
Mar 67. (7") (202608) <44046> **AT THE ZOO.** / **THE 59th STREET BRIDGE SONG (FEELIN' GROOVY)**		16
Jun 67. (7"ep) (EP 6360) **FEELIN' GROOVY** – The 59th Street bridge song (feelin' groovy) / The big bright green pleasure machine / A hazy shade of winter / Homeward bound.		-
Aug 67. (7") (2911) <44232> **FAKIN' IT.** / **YOU DON'T KNOW WHERE YOUR INTEREST LIES**		23 Jul67
Mar 68. (7") (3317) <44465> **SCARBOROUGH FAIR; CANTICLE.** / **APRIL COME SHE WILL**		11 Feb68

Jul 68. (7") *(3443)* <44511> **MRS. ROBINSON. / OLD FRIENDS; BOOKENDS** — [4] [1] Apr68

Jul 68. (lp) *(BPG 63101)* <9529> **BOOKENDS** — [1] [1] May 68
– Bookends theme / Save the life of my child / America / Overs / (voices of old people) – Old friends / Bookends / Fakin' it / Punky's dilemma / Mrs. Robinson / A hazy shade of winter / At the zoo. *(re-iss. Nov82 lp/c; CBS/40 32073) (cd-iss. Dec85; CD 63101)*

Oct 68. (lp) *(BPG 70042)* <3180> **THE GRADUATE (Film Soundtrack; with tracks by DAVE GRUISIN *)** — [3] [1] Mar68
– The sound of silence / The singleman party foxtrot * / On the strip * / Sunporch cha-cha-cha * / Mrs.Robinson / A great effect * / Scarborough fair – Canticle / April come she will / Whew * / The folks * / The big bright green pleasure machine. *(re-iss. Feb84 lp/c; Dec85; CD 32359) (cd-iss. Dec85; CD 70042) (cd re-iss. Apr89; CD 32359) (cd-iss. Apr91 on 'Sequel';) (re-iss. Feb94 on 'Columbia' cd/c; CD/40 32359)*

Dec 68. (7"ep) *(EP 6400)* **MRS. ROBINSON** — [9] [-]
– Mrs.Robinson / April come she will / Scarborough fair – Canticle / The sound of silence.

Apr 69. (7") *(4162)* <44785> **THE BOXER. / BABY DRIVER** — [6] [7]

Feb 70. (7") *(4790)* <45079> **BRIDGE OVER TROUBLED WATER. / KEEP THE CUSTOMER SATISFIED** — [1] [1]
(re-iss. Feb78 + Jul84; CBS 4596)

Feb 70. (lp) *(63699)* <9914> **BRIDGE OVER TROUBLED WATER** — [1] [1]
– Bridge over troubled water / El Condor Pasa / Cecilia / Keep the customer satisfied / So long, Frank Lloyd Wright / The boxer / Baby driver / The only living boy in New York / Why don't you write me / Bye bye love / Song for the asking. *(re-iss. on quad 1974; CQ 30995) (cd-iss. Dec82; CD 63699) (cd re-iss. Sep93 cd/c; 462485-2/-4) (cd re-iss. Dec95 on 'Columbia'; 480418-2)*

Apr 70. (7") *(4916)* <45133> **CECILIA. / THE ONLY LIVING BOY IN NEW YORK** — [ ] [4]

Sep 70. (7") <45237> **EL CONDOR PASA. / WHY DON'T YOU WRITE ME** — [-] [18]

—— Both went solo, after ART wanted to concentrate on acting career.

– compilations, exploitation, etc. –

Note; Released on 'CBS/ Columbia' unless otherwise mentioned.

Sep 70. (7") *(5172)* **THE SOUND OF SILENCE. / THE 59th STREET BRIDGE SONG** — [ ] [-]

Jul 72. (lp/c) *(CBS/40 69003)* <31350> **SIMON AND GARFUNKEL'S GREATEST HITS** — [2] [5] Jun72
– Mrs.Robinson / For Emily, wherever I may find her / The boxer / Feelin' groovy / The sound of silence / I am a rock / Scarborough fair (Canticle) / Homeward bound / Bridge over troubled water / America / Kathy's song / If I could / Bookends / Cecilia. *(cd-iss. Mar87; CD 69003)*

Sep 72. (7") *(8336)* <45663> **AMERICA. / FOR EMILY, WHENEVER I MAY FIND HER** — [25] [97] [53]

Apr 73. (7") *(1159)* **MRS. ROBINSON. / SCARBOROUGH FAIR; CANTICLE**

Mar 76. (7") *(3949)* **HOMEWARD BOUND. / THE SOUND OF SILENCE** — [ ] [-]

Nov 81. (lp/c) *(CBS/40 24005)* **THE SIMON AND GARFUNKEL COLLECTION** — [4] [-]
– I am a rock / Homeward bound / America / 59th Street Bridge song / Wednesday morning 3 a.m. / El condor pasa / At the Zoo / Scarborough fair (Canticle) / The boxer / The sound of silence / Mrs.Robinson / Keep the customer satisfied / Song for the asking / Hazy shade of winter / Cecilia / Old friends / Bookends / Bridge over troubled water. *(cd-iss. Apr85 + 1988; CD 24005)*

Dec 81. (7") *(A 1938)* **HOMEWARD BOUND. / THE 59TH STREET BRIDGE SONG** — [ ] [-]

—— SIMON AND GARFUNKEL re-united for one-off concert 20 Dec'81.

	Geffen	Warners

Mar 82. (d-lp/d-c) *(GEF/40 96008)* <3654> **THE CONCERT IN CENTRAL PARK (live)** — [6] [6]
– Mrs. Robinson / Homeward bound / America / Scarborough fair / Me and Julio down by the schoolyard / Wake up little Susie / April come she will / Slip slidin' away / Still crazy after all these years / American tune / 50 ways to leave your lover / Late in the evening / Bridge over troubled water / A heart in New York / The 59th Street bridge song (feelin' groovy) / The sound of silence / Kodachrome / Old friends: bookends / Maybellene / The boxer. *(re-iss. May88 lp/c/cd; GEF/40/CD 96008)*

Mar 82. (7") *(GEF 2287)* **WAKE UP LITTLE SUSIE (live). / THE BOXER (live)** — [ ] [-]

Mar 82. (7") <50053> **WAKE UP LITTLE SUSIE (live). / ME AND JULIO DOWN BY THE SCHOOLYARD (live)** — [-] [27]

Jun 82. (7") *(GEF 2221)* **MRS. ROBINSON (live). / BRIDGE OVER TROUBLED WATER (live)**

– other compilations, etc. –

1966. (lp) *Pickwick; <SPC-3059>* **THE HIT SOUNDS OF SIMON & GARFUNKEL** (early TOM & JERRY material) — [ ] [ ]
<re-iss. 1969 as 'SIMON & GARFUNKEL' on 'Sears'; <435>

1967. (lp) *Allegro; (ALL 836)* **SIMON AND GARFUNKEL** (early) — [ ] [-]

1988. (cd) *(CDSG 241)* **BRIDGE OVER TROUBLED WATER / PARSLEY, SAGE, ROSEMARY & SAGE**

May 88. (cd) *Arcade; (01280061)* **COLLECTION** — [ ] [-]

Nov 91. (7"/c-s/cd-s) *(657 653-7/-4/-2)* **A HAZY SHADE OF WINTER. / SILENT NIGHT – SEVEN O'CLOCK NEWS (Medley)** — [30]

Nov 91. (lp/c/cd) *Sony-Columbia; (MOOD/+C/D 21)* **THE DEFINITIVE SIMON & GARFUNKEL** — [8]
– Wednesday morning 3 a.m. / The sound of silence / Homeward bound / Cathy's song / I am a rock / For Emily wherever I may find her / Scarborough fair (canticle) / The 59th Street bridge song (feelin' groovy) / Seven o'clock news – Silent night / A hazy shade of winter / El condor pasa (If I could) / Mrs.Robinson / America / At the zoo / Old friends / Bookends theme / Cecilia / The boxer / Bridge over troubled water / Song for the asking. *(hit UK No.12 in Aug'97)*

Feb 92. (7") *Sony-Columbia; (657 806-7)* **THE BOXER. / CECILIA** — [75] [ ]
(cd-ep+=/cd-ep+=) (657 806-2/-5) –

Aug 92. (2xcd-box) *Sony;* **PARSLEY, SAGE, ROSEMARY & SAGE / BOOKENDS** — [ ] [ ]

Oct 96. (3xcd-box) *(485324-2)* **BRIDGE OVER TROUBLED WATER / SOUNDS OF SILENCE / THE GRADUATE** — [ ] [-]

PAUL SIMON

(solo with session people)

	C.B.S.	Columbia

Feb 72. (7") *(7793)* <45547> **MOTHER AND CHILD REUNION. / PARANOIA BLUES** — [5] [4]

Feb 72. (lp/c) *(CBS/40 69007)* <30750> **PAUL SIMON** — [1] [4]
– Mother and child reunion / Duncan / Everything put together falls apart / Run that body down / Armistice day / Me and Julio down by the schoolyard / Peace like a river / Papa hobo / Hobo's blues / Paranoia blues / Congratulations. *(re-iss. 1974 on quad; CQ 30750) (re-iss. Dec87 on 'WEA' lp/c/cd; 925588-1/-4/-2)*

Apr 72. (7") *(7264)* <45585> **ME AND JULIO DOWN BY THE SCHOOLYARD. / CONGRATULATIONS** — [15] [22]

Jul 72. (7") <45638> **DUNCAN. / RUN THAT BODY DOWN** — [-] [52]

May 73. (lp/c) *(CBS/40 69035)* <32280> **THERE GOES RHYMIN' SIMON** — [4] [2]
– Kodachrome / Tenderness / Take me to the Mardi Gras / Something so right / One man's ceiling is another man's floor / American tune / Was a sunny day / Learn how to fall / St. Judy's comet / Loves me like a rock. *(re-iss. 1974 on quad; CQ 32280) (re-iss. Dec87 on 'WEA' lp/c/cd; 925589-1/-4/-2)*

May 73. (7") <45859> **KODACHROME. / TENDERNESS** — [-] [2]

May 73. (7") *(1578)* **TAKE ME TO THE MARDI GRAS. / KODACHROME** — [7] [ ]

Sep 73. (7") *(1700)* <45907> **LOVES ME LIKE A ROCK. / LEARN HOW TO FALL** — [39] [2] Aug73

Feb 74. (7") *(1979)* <45900> **AMERICAN TUNE. / ONE MAN'S CEILING IS ANOTHER MAN'S FLOOR** — [ ] [35] Nov73

—— Below in concert with URUBOMBA and The JESE DIXON SINGERS.

Mar 74. (lp/c) *(CBS/40 69059)* <32855> **PAUL SIMON IN CONCERT / LIVE RHYMIN' (live)** — [ ] [33]
– Jesus is the answer / The boxer / Duncan / El Condor pasa (if I could) / Me and Julio down by the schoolyard / American tune / Homeward bound / America / Mother and child reunion / Loves me like a rock / Bridge over troubled water / The sound of silence. *(re-iss. Dec87 on 'WEA' lp/c/cd; 925590-1/-4/-2)*

May 74. (7") *(2349)* <46038> **THE SOUND OF SILENCE (live). / MOTHER AND CHILD REUNION (live)** — [ ] [ ]

Nov 74. (7") *(2822)* **SOMETHING SO RIGHT. / TENDERNESS** — [ ] [ ]

Aug 75. (7") <10197> **GONE AT LAST (w/ PHOEBE SNOW). / TAKE ME TO THE MARDI GRAS** — [-] [23]

Oct 75. (7"; PAUL SIMON & PHOEBE SNOW with The JESSE DIXON SINGERS) *(3594)* **GONE AT LAST. / TENDERNESS** — [ ] [-]

Oct 75. (lp/c) *(CBS/40 86001)* <33540> **STILL CRAZY AFTER ALL THESE YEARS** — [6] [1]
– Still crazy after all these years / My little town / I do it all for love / 50 ways to leave your lover / Night game / Gone at last / Some folks lives roll easy / Have a good time / You're kind / Silent eyes. *(re-iss. 1976 on quad; Q 86001) (cd-iss. Dec85; CD 86001) (re-iss. Dec87 on 'WEA' lp/c/cd; 925591-1/-4/-2)*

Oct 75. (7"; SIMON & GARFUNKEL) <10230> **MY LITTLE TOWN. / Art Garfunkel: RAG DOLL** — [-] [9]

Nov 75. (7"m; SIMON & GARFUNKEL) *(3712)* **MY LITTLE TOWN. / Art Garfunkel: RAG DOLL / YOU'RE KIND**

Dec 75. (7") *(3887)* <10270> **50 WAYS TO LEAVE YOUR LOVER. / SOME FOLKS LIVES ROLL EASY** — [23] [1]

Apr 76. (7") <10332> **STILL CRAZY AFTER ALL THESE YEARS. / I DO IT FOR YOUR LOVE** — [-] [40]

Apr 76. (7") *(4188)* **STILL CRAZY AFTER ALL THESE YEARS. / SILENT EYES** — [ ] [-]

Nov 77. (7") *(5770)* <10630> **SLIP SLIDIN' AWAY. / SOMETHING SO RIGHT** — [36] [5] Oct77

Nov 77. (lp/c) *(CBS/40 10007)* <35032> **GREATEST HITS, ETC. (part compilation)** — [6] [18]
– Slip slidin' away / Stranded in a limousine / Still crazy after all these years / Have a good time / Duncan / Me and Julio down by the schoolyard / Something so right / Kodachrome / I do it for your love / 50 ways to leave your lover / American tune / Mother and child reunion / Loves me like a rock / Take me to the Mardi Gras. *(re-iss. Nov86 lp/c; 450166-1/-4) (cd-iss. Mar87; CD 69003)*

—— See ART GARFUNKEL discography further on for other single

May 78. (7") *(6290)* <10711> **STRANDED IN A LIMOSINE. / HAVE A GOOD TIME** — [ ] [ ]

	Warners	Warners

Aug 80. (lp/c) *(K/K4 56846)* <3472> **ONE-TRICK PONY** — [17] [12]
– Late in the evening / That's why God made the movies / One-trick pony / How the heart approaches what it yearns / Oh, Marion / Ace in the hole / Nobody / God bless the absentee / Jonah / Long, long day. *(cd-iss. 1987; K2 56846)*

Aug 80. (7") *(K 17666)* <49511> **LATE IN THE EVENING. / HOW THE HEART APPROACHES WHAT IT YEARNS** — [58] [6]

Nov 80. (7") *(K 17715)* <49601> **ONE TRICK PONY. / LONG, LONG DAY** — [ ] [40] Oct80

Jan 81. (7") *(K 17745)* <49675> **OH, MARION. / GOD BLESS THE ABSENTEE** — [ ] [ ]

—— See ART GARFUNKEL discography again for duet A HEART IN NEW YORK single

—— Early '83, PAUL collaborated with RANDY NEWMAN on US No.51 single THE BLUES

Nov 83. (lp/c/cd) *(923942-1/-4/-2)* <23942> **HEARTS AND BONES** — [34] [35]
– Allergies / Hearts and bones / When numbers get serious / Think too much (part 1) / Song about the Moon / Think too much (part 2) / Train in the distance / Renee and Georgette Margritte with the dog after the war / Cars are cars / The late great Johnny Ace.

Nov 83. (7") *(W 9453)* <29453> **ALLERGIES. / THINK TOO MUCH** — [ ] [44]

Feb 84. (7") <29333> **SONG ABOUT THE MOON. / THINK TOO MUCH** — [-] [ ]

Aug 86. (7")(12") *(W 8667)* <28667> **YOU CAN CALL ME AL. / GUMBOOTS** — [4] [44]
<re-iss. Mar87 US, hit No.23>

Sep 86. (lp/c)(cd) *(WX 52/+C)(925477-2) <25447>* **GRACELAND** `[1]` `[3]`
– The boy in the bubble / Graceland / I know what I know / Gumboots / Diamonds on the sole of her shoes / You can call me Al / Under African skies / Homeless / Crazy love Vol.2 / That was your mother / All around the world of the myth of fingerprints.

Nov 86. (7") *(W 8509)* **THE BOY IN THE BUBBLE.** / ('A'remix) `[33]` `[-]`
(12"+=) *(W 8509T)* – Hearts and bones.

Dec 86. (7") *<28522>* **GRACELAND.** / **HEARTS AND BONES** `[-]` `[81]`
(re-iss. US 1988)

Feb 87. (7") *<28460>* **THE BOY IN THE BUBBLE.** / **CRAZY LOVE VOL.2** `[-]` `[86]`

Apr 87. (7"/12") *() <28389>* **DIAMONDS ON THE SOLES OF HER SHOES.** / **ALL AROUND THE WORLD OF THE MYTH OF FINGERPRINTS** `[-]` `[-]`

Apr 87. (7") *(W 8349)* **GRACELAND.** / **CRAZY LOVE VOL.2** `[-]` `[-]`
(12"+=) *(W 8349T)* – The late great Johny Ace.

Aug 87. (7") *(W 8221) <28221>* **UNDER AFRICAN SKIES.** / **I KNOW WHAT I KNOW** `[-]` `[-]`
(12"+=) *(W 8221T)* – Homeless. (above w/LINDA RONSTADT)

Oct 90. (7") *(W 9549) <19549>* **THE OBVIOUS CHILD.** / **THE RHYTHM OF THE SAINTS** `[15]` `[92]`
(12"+=) *(W 9549T)* – You can call me Al.
(cd-s++=) *(W 9549CD)* – The boy in the bubble.

Oct 90. (cd)(lp/c) *(926098-2)(WX 340/+C) <26098>* **THE RHYTHM OF THE SAINTS** `[1]` `[4]`
– The obvious child / Can't run but / The coast / Proof / Further to fly / She moves on / Born at the right time / The cool cool river / Spirit voices / The rhythm of the saints.

Feb 91. (7")(c-s) **PROOF.** / **THE OBVIOUS CHILD** `[ ]` `[ ]`
(12"/cd-s) – ('A'side) / The cool cool river / American tune.

Apr 91. (7") **BORN AT THE RIGHT TIME.** / **FURTHER TO FLY** `[ ]` `[ ]`
(12"+=) – You can call me Al.
(cd-s++=) – Me and Julio down by the schoolyard / 50 ways to leave your lover.

Nov 91. (cd)(d-lp/c) *(926737-2)(WX 448/+C) <26737>* **THE CONCERT IN THE PARK – AUGUST 15th 1991 (live)** `[60]` `[ ]`
– The obvious child / The boy in the bubble / She moves on / Kodachrome / Born at the right time / Train in the distance / Me and Julio down by the schoolyard / I know what I know / Cool cool river / Bridge over troubled water / Proof / Coast / Graceland / You can call me Al / Still crazy after all these years / Loves me like a rock / Diamonds on the sole of her shoes / Hearts and bones / Later in the evening / America / The boxer / Cecelia / Sound of silence.

Nov 97. (cd/c) *(9362 46814-2/-4)* **SONGS FROM THE CAPEMAN** `[42]`
(The Broadway Musical)
– Adios Hermanos / Born in Puerto Rico / Satin summer nights / Bernadette / The vampires / Quality / Can I forgive him / Sunday afternoon / Killer wants to go to college / Time is an ocean / Virgil / Killer wants to go to college II / Trailways bus.

– (PAUL SIMON) compilations, others, etc. –

on 'C.B.S.' / 'Columbia' unless mentioned otherwise
Nov 88. (d-lp/c/cd) *(WX 223/+C)(925789-2) <25789>* **NEGOTIATIONS AND LOVE SONGS** `[17]` `[ ]`
– Mother and child reunion / Me and Julio down by the schoolyard / Something so right / St.Judy's comet / Loves me like a rock / Have a good time / 50 ways to leave your lover / Still crazy after all these years / Late in the evening / Slip slidin' away / Hearts and bones / Train in the distance / Rene and Georgette Magritte with their dog after the war / Diamonds on the soles on her shoes / You can call me Al / Kodachrome. *(d-lp+=)* – Graceland.

Nov 88. (7") *(W 7655)* **MOTHER AND CHILD REUNION.** / **TRAIN IN THE DISTANCE** `[ ]` `[ ]`
(12"+=/cd-s+=) *(W 7655 T/CD)* – The boy in the bubble.

Feb 89. (c) *Venus; (VENUMC 5)* **THE MAGIC OF PAUL SIMON** `[ ]` `[ ]`

May 93. (cd) *Royal; (RC 82112)* **PAUL SIMON & FRIENDS** `[ ]` `[-]`

Sep 93. (3xcd-box) *Warners; (9362 45474-2)* **1964-1993** `[ ]` `[ ]`

Sep 93. (cd/c) *Warners; (9362 45408-2/-4)* **ANTHOLOGY** `[ ]` `[ ]`

ART GARFUNKEL

(solo with session people)

	C.B.S.	Columbia
Sep 73. (7") *(1777) <45926>* **ALL I KNOW.** / **MARY WAS AN ONLY CHILD**		9
Oct 73. (lp/c) *(CBS/40 89021) <31472>* **ANGEL CLARE**	14	5 Sep73

– Travelling boy / Down in the willow garden / I shall sing / Old man / Feuilles oh! – Do spacemen pass dead souls on their way to the Moon? / All I know / Woyaya / Mary was an only child / Barbara Allen / Another lullaby. *(also on quad-lp; CQ 31474)* *(cd-iss. 1988; CD 69021)* *(re-iss. Jul89 on 'Pickwick'; 982185)*

| Feb 74. (7") *(2013) <45983>* **I SHALL SING.** / **FEUILLES OH! – DO SPACEMEN PASS DEAD SOULS ON THEIR WAY TO THE MOON?** | | |
| Sep 74. (7") *(2672) <10020>* **SECOND AVENUE.** / **WOYAYA** | | 38 Dec 73 / 34 |

—— (above 1973/74 releases as "GARFUNKEL")

| Sep 75. (7") *(3575) <10190>* **I ONLY HAVE EYES FOR YOU.** / **LOOKING FOR THE RIGHT ONE** | 1 | 18 Aug75 |
| Oct 75. (lp/c) *(CBS/40 86002) <33700>* **BREAKAWAY** | 7 | 7 |

– I believe (when I fall in love it will be forever) / Rag doll / Breakaway / Disney girls / Waters of March / My little town / I only have eyes for you / Looking for the right one / 99 miles from L.A. / The same old tears on a new background. *(re-iss. Nov85 lp/c; CBS/40 32574) (cd-iss. Apr86; CD 86002) (re-iss. Sep89 on 'Pickwick' lp/c/cd; 902199-1/-4/-2) (cd re-iss. Sep93 on 'Sony Collectors';) (cd re-iss. Feb87; 468873-2)*

—— See PAUL SIMON section, for their hit duet MY LITTLE TOWN.

Dec 75. (7") *<10273>* **BREAKAWAY.** / **DISNEY GIRLS** `[-]` `[ ]`

Jan 76. (7") *(3888)* **BREAKAWAY.** / **THE SAME OLD TEARS ON A NEW BACKGROUND** `[-]` `[ ]`

May 76. (7") *(4348)* **I BELIEVE (WHEN I FALL IN LOVE IT WILL BE FOREVER).** / **WATERS OF MARCH** `[ ]` `[-]`

Nov 77. (7") *(5683) <10608>* **CRYING IN MY SLEEP.** / **MR.SHUCK'N'JIVE** `[ ]` `[ ]`

Jan 78. (7"; ART GARFUNKEL, PAUL SIMON & JAMES TAYLOR) *(6061) 19676>* **(WHAT A) WONDERFUL WORLD.** / **WOODEN PLANES** `[ ]` `[17]`

Feb 78. (lp/c) *(CBS/40 86054) <34975>* **WATERMARK** `[25]` `[19]`
– Crying in my sleep / Marionette / Shine it on me / Watermark / Saturday suit / All my love's laughter / (What a) Wonderful world / Mr. Shuck 'n' jive / Paper chase / She moved through the fair / Someone else (1958) / Wooden planes. *(re-iss. Jan87 lp/c; 450378-1/-4) (cd-iss. Apr94 on 'Sony')*

Apr 78. (7") *(6325)* **MARIONETTE.** / **ALL MY LOVE'S LAUGHTER** `[ ]` `[ ]`

Feb 79. (7") *(6847)* **BRIGHT EYES.** / **KEHAAR'S THEME** `[1]` `[ ]`
(above from animated film 'Watership Down') *(re-iss. Jul84)*

Mar 79. (7") *<10933>* **AND I KNOW.** / **IN A LITTLE WHILE (I'LL BE ON MY WAY)** `[-]` `[ ]`

Apr 79. (lp/c) *(CBS/40 86090) <35780>* **FATE FOR BREAKFAST** `[2]` `[67]`
– In a little while (I'll be on my way) / Since I don't have you / And I know / Sail on a rainbow / Miss you nights / Bright eyes / Finally a reason / Beyond the tears / Oh how happy / When someone doesn't want you / Take me away. *Cd-iss.Jul97 on 'Columbia'; 487946-2)*

May 79. (7") *<10999>* **SINCE I DON'T HAVE YOU.** / **WHEN SOMEONE DOESN'T WANT YOU** `[-]` `[53]`

Jun 79. (7") *(7371)* **SINCE I DON'T HAVE YOU.** / **AND I KNOW** `[38]` `[ ]`

Aug 79. (7") **BRIGHT EYES.** / **SAIL ON A RAINBOW** `[-]` `[ ]`

Aug 81. (7"; ART GARFUNKEL & PAUL SIMON) *(A 1495) <02307>* **A HEART IN NEW YORK.** / **IS THIS LOVE** `[ ]` `[66]`

Sep 81. (lp/c) *(CBS/40 85259) <37392>* **SCISSORS CUT** `[51]` `[ ]`
– Scissors cut / A heart in New York / Up in the world / Hang on in / So easy to begin / Can't turn my heart away / The French waltz / The romance / In cars / That's all I've got to say.

Oct 81. (7") *(A 1708)* **SCISSORS CUT.** / **SO EASY TO BEGIN** `[ ]` `[-]`

—— Late 1981, he had re-united with PAUL SIMON for live one-off album.

Oct 84. (7") *(A 4674)* **SOMETIME WHEN I'M DREAMING.** / **SCISSORS CUT** `[ ]` `[-]`

Nov 84. (lp/c/cd) *(CBS/40/CD 10046)* **THE ART GARFUNKEL ALBUM** `[12]` `[ ]`
(compilation)
– Bright eyes / Break away / A heart in New York / I shall sing / 99 miles from L.A. / All I know / I only have eyes for you / Watermark / Sometimes when I'm dreaming / Travelin' boy / The same old tears on a new background / (What a) Wonderful world / I believe (when I fall in love it will be forever) / Scissors cut. *(cd re-iss. Oct90; 466333-2)*

Nov 86. (7"; with AMY GRANT) **CAROL OF THE BIRDS.** / **THE DECREE** `[-]` `[ ]`

Dec 86. (lp/c) *(CBS/40 26704) <40212>* **THE ANIMALS' CHRISTMAS** `[ ]` `[ ]`
– The annunciation / The creatures of the field / Just a simple little tune / The decree / Incredible phat / The friendly beasts / The song of the camel / Words from an old Spanish carol / Carol of the birds / The frog / Herod / Wild geese.

Jan 88. (7") *<07711>* **SO MUCH IN LOVE.** / **KING OF TONGA** `[-]` `[ ]`

Feb 88. (7") *(651 450-7)* **SO MUCH IN LOVE.** / **SLOW BREAKUP** `[ ]` `[-]`
(12"+=/cd-s+=) *(651 450-6/-2)* – (What a) Wonderful world / I only have eyes for you.

Mar 88. (7") *<07949>* **THIS IS THE MOMENT.** / **SLOW BREAKUP** `[ ]` `[ ]`

Mar 88. (lp/c/cd) *(460694-1/-4/-2) <40942>* **LEFTY** `[ ]` `[ ]`
– This is the moment / I have a love / So much in love / Slow breakup / Love is the only chain / When a man loves a woman / I wonder why / King of Tonga / If love takes you away / The promise.

May 88. (7") *(651 632-7)* **WHEN A MAN LOVES A WOMAN.** / **KING OF TONGA** `[ ]` `[-]`

May 88. (7") *<08511>* **WHEN A MAN LOVES A WOMAN.** / **I HAVE A LOVE** `[-]` `[-]`

	Columbia	Columbia

Nov 93. (cd/c/lp) *(474853-2/-4)* **UP 'TIL NOW**
– Crying in the rain (w/ JAMES TAYLOR) / All I know / Just over the Brooklyn Bridge / The sound of silence / The breakup / Skywriter / The decree / It's all in the game / One less holiday / Since I don't have you / Two sleepy people / Why worry / All my love's daughter.

	Virgin	Virgin
Dec 96. (cd/c) *(VT CD/MC 113) <20001>* **ACROSS AMERICA (live)**	59	May97

– Heart in New York / Crying in the rain / Scarborough fair / Poem on the underground wall / Homeward bound / All I know / Bright eyes / El condor pasa (If i could) / Bridge over troubled water / Mrs. Robinson / 59th Street Bridge song (feelin' groovy) / I will / April come she will / Sound of silence / Grateful / Goodnight my love.

– (ART GARFUNKEL) compilations, etc. –

Oct 79. (3xlp-box) *(C.B.S.;)* **ART GARFUNKEL** `[ ]` `[ ]`
(first 3 albums)

1984. (7") *Columbia;* **BRIGHT EYES.** / **THE ROMANCE** `[ ]` `[ ]`

Jun 97. (cd) *<67674>* **SONGS FROM A PARENT TO A CHILD** `[-]` `[ ]`
(covers)

SIMPLE MINDS

Formed: Gorbals, Glasgow, Scotland … early 1978 after four members (frontman JIM KERR, guitarists CHARLIE BURCHILL and DUNCAN BARNWELL and drummer BRIAN McGEE) had left punk band, JOHNNY & THE SELF ABUSERS. Taking the group name from a line in a BOWIE song, the band gigged constantly at Glasgow's Mars Bar, finally being signed on the strength of a demo tape by local Edinburgh music guru and record store owner, Bruce Findlay. Also becoming the band's manager, Findlay released their debut album, 'LIFE IN A DAY' (1979) on his own 'Zoom' label, the record scoring a Top 30 placing. Its minor success led to a deal with 'Arista' who released the follow-up, 'REEL TO REEL CACOPHONY' (1979), a set of post-punk, electronic experimentation best sampled on the evocative synth spirals of 'FILM THEME'. SIMPLE MINDS took another about turn with 'EMPIRES AND DANCE' (1980), an album heavily influenced by the harder end of the Euro-disco movement, the abrasive electro pulse of the 'I TRAVEL' single becoming a cult dancefloor hit. Initially released as a double set, 'SONS AND FASCINATION' / 'SISTER FEELINGS CALL' (1981), marked the first fruits of a new deal with 'Virgin' and gave the group their first major success, peaking at No.11 in the UK chart on the back of the Top 50 single, 'LOVE SONG'. SIMPLE MINDS were beginning to find their niche, incorporating their artier tendencies into more conventional and melodic song structures. This was fully realised with 'NEW GOLD DREAM (81-82-83-84)' (1982), a record which marked the pinnacle of their early career and one which arguably, they've since failed to better. Constructed with multiple layers of synth, the band crafted a wonderfully evocative and atmospheric series of undulating electronic soundscapes, often married to pop hooks, as with 'GLITTERING PRIZE' and 'PROMISED YOU A MIRACLE' (the group's first Top 20 hits), but more effectively allowed to veer off into dreamier territory on the likes of 'SOMEONE SOMEWHERE IN SUMMERTIME'. While SIMPLE MINDS and U2 were often compared in terms of their anthemic tendencies, a closer comparison could be made, in spirit at least, between 'NEW GOLD..' and U2's mid-80's experimental classic, 'The Unforgettable Fire'. The album reached No.3 in the UK charts, a catalyst for SIMPLE MINDS' gradual transformation from an obscure cult act to stadium candidates, this process helped along nicely by the success of 'SPARKLE IN THE RAIN' (1984), the band's first No.1 album. Though it lacked the compelling mystery of its predecessor, the record featured such memorable SIMPLE MINDS' moments as 'UP ON THE CATWALK', 'SPEED YOUR LOVE TO ME' and an inventive cover of Lou Reed's 'STREET HASSLE'. For better or worse, the album also boasted SIMPLE MINDS' first truly BIG anthem, the sonic bombast of 'WATERFRONT'. But the track that no doubt finally alienated the old faithful was 'DON'T YOU (FORGET ABOUT ME)', the theme tune for quintessentially 80's movie, 'The Breakfast Club' and surely one of the most overplayed records of that decade. The song had stadium-friendly written all over it, subsequently scaling the US charts and paving the way for the transatlantic success of 'ONCE UPON A TIME' (1985). Unashamedly going for the commmercial pop/rock jugular, the album was heady, radio orientated stuff, the likes of 'ALIVE AND KICKING', 'SANCTIFY YOURSELF' and 'OH JUNGLELAND' among the most definitive anthems of the stadium rock genre. Predictably, the critics were unimpressed, although they didn't really stick the knife in until the release of the overblown 'BELFAST CHILD', a UK No.1 despite its snoozeworthy meandering and vague political agenda. The accompanying album, 'STREET FIGHTING YEARS' (1989) brought more of the same, although it cemented SIMPLE MINDS' position among the coffee table elite. Down to a trio of KERR, BURCHILL and and drummer, MEL GAYNOR, the group hired a team of session players for their next album, 'REAL LIFE' (1991), the record almost spawning a Top 5 hit in the celebratory 'LET THERE BE LOVE'. Although the album narrowly missed the UK top spot, it held nothing new, nor did their most recent release, 'GOOD NEWS FROM THE NEXT WORLD' (1995). You can't help feeling a little sorry for JIM KERR, not only does a young pretender like LIAM GALLAGHER hook up with his wife (PATSY KENSIT), but his band have become something of an anachronism in the ever changing world of 90's music. While U2 have at least made an attempt to move with the times, however embarassing, SIMPLE MINDS' sound is so deeply rooted in the 80's that it seems inconceivable they could ever make any kind of relevant departure. • **Songwriters:** All group compositions except KERR-BURCHILL. Covered BIKO (Peter Gabriel) / SIGN O' THE TIMES (Prince) / DON'T YOU FORGET ABOUT ME (Keith Forsey-Steve Chiff). • **Trivia:** On the 5th May'84, JIM KERR married CHRISSIE HYNDE. SIMPLE MINDS have played both LIVE AID and MANDELA DAY concerts in 1985 and 1988 respectively.

Album rating: LIFE IN A DAY (*7) / REAL TO REAL CACOPHONY (*5) / EMPIRES AND DANCE (*8) / SONS AND FASCINATION – SISTER FEELING CALL (*8) / CELEBRATION compilation (*7) / NEW GOLD DREAM (81-82-83-84) (*8) / SPARKLE IN THE RAIN (*8) / ONCE UPON A TIME (*8) / LIVE IN THE CITY OF LIGHT (*6) / STREET FIGHTING YEARS (*5) / REAL LIFE (*5) / GLITTERING PRIZE – SIMPLE MINDS 81-92 compilation (*8) / GOOD NEWS FROM THE NEXT WORLD (*4) / NEAPOLIS (*3)

JOHNNY & THE SELF ABUSERS

JIM KERR (b. 9 Jul'59) – vocals / **CHARLIE BURCHILL** (b.27 Nov'59) – guitar / **DUNCAN BARNWELL** – guitar / **BRIAN McGEE** – drums / + 3 future CUBAN HEELS members.

		Chiswick	not iss.
Nov 77.	(7") (NS 22) **SAINTS AND SINNERS. / DEAD VANDALS**	☐	–

SIMPLE MINDS

—— (**KERR, BURCHILL + McGEE**) recruited **MICK McNEILL** (b.20 Jul'58) – keyboards / **DEREK FORBES** (b.22 Jun'56) – bass

		Zoom	not iss.
Apr 79.	(7") (ZUM 10) **LIFE IN A DAY. / SPECIAL VIEW**	62	–
Apr 79.	(lp) (ZULP 1) **LIFE IN A DAY**	30	–

– Someone / Life in a day / Sad affair / All for you / Pleasantly disturbed / No cure / Chelsea girl / Wasteland / Destiny / Murder story. (re-iss. Oct82 on 'Virgin' lp/c; VM/+C 6) (re-iss. 1985 on 'Virgin' lp/c; OVED/+C 95) (cd-iss. Jul86; VMCD 6)

			–
Jun 79.	(7") (ZUM 11) **CHELSEA GIRL. / GARDEN OF HATE**	☐	–
		Arista	Arista
Nov 79.	(lp/c) (SPART/TC-SPART 1109) **REAL TO REAL CACOPHONY**	☐	☐

– Real to real / Naked eye / Citizen (dance of youth) / Carnival (shelter in a suitcase) / Factory / Cacophony / Veldt / Premonition / Changeling / Film theme / Calling your name / Scar. (re-iss. Oct82 on 'Virgin' lp/c; V/TCV 2246) (re-iss. 1985 on 'Virgin' lp/c; OVED/+C 124) (cd-iss. May88; CDV 2246)

Jan 80.	(7") (ARIST 325) **CHANGELING. / PREMONITION (live)**	☐	–
Sep 80.	(lp/c) (SPART/TC-SPART 1140) **EMPIRES AND DANCE**	41	

– I travel / Today I died again / Celebrate / This fear of gods / Capital city / Constantinople line / Twist-run-repulsion / Thirty frames a seconds / Kant-kino / Room. (re-iss. Oct82 on 'Virgin' lp/c; V/TCV 2247) (cd-iss. May88; CDV 2247)

Oct 80.	(7") (ARIST 372) **I TRAVEL. / NEW WARM SKIN**		
	(w/ free 7"blue flexi) – KALEIDOSCOPE. / FILM DUB THEME		
	(12") (ARIST 12-372) – ('A'side) / Film dub theme.		
Feb 81.	(7") (ARIST 394) **CELEBRATE. / CHANGELING (live)**	☐	☐
	(12"+=) (ARIST 12-394) – I travel (live).		
		Virgin	A&M
May 81.	(7"/remix.12") (VS 410/+12) **THE AMERICAN. / LEAGUE OF NATIONS**	59	–

—— **KENNY HYSLOP** (b.14 Feb'51, Helensburgh, Scotland) – drums (ex-SKIDS, ex-ZONES, ex-SLIK) repl. McGee, who in 1994 became a songwriter for LES McKEOWN (ex-BAY CITY ROLLERS)

Aug 81.	(7"/12") (VS 434/+12) **LOVE SONG. / THE EARTH THAT YOU WALK UPON** (instrumental)	47	–
Sep 81.	(2xlp/d-c) (V/TCV 2207) **SONS AND FASCINATION / SISTER FEELINGS CALL**	11	

– SONS AND FASCINATION – In trance as mission / Sweat in bullet / 70 cities as love brings the fall / Boys from Brazil / Love song / This Earth that you walk upon / Sons and fascination / Seeing out the angels. SISTER FEELINGS CALL – Theme for great cities * / The American / 20th Century promised land / Wonderful in young life / League of nations / Careful in career / Sound in 70 cities. (issued separately Oct81; V 2207 / OVED 2) (cd-iss. Apr86 + Apr90; CDV 2207) – (omits tracks *)

Oct 81.	(7") (VS 451) **SWEAT IN BULLET. / 20th CENTURY PROMISED LAND**	52	–
	(d7"+=) (VSD 451) – League of nations (live) / Premonition (live).		
	(12"+=) (VS 451-12) – League of nations (live) / In trance as mission (live).		
Apr 82.	(7") (VS 488) **PROMISED YOU A MIRACLE. / THEME FOR GREAT CITIES**	13	–
	(12"+=) (VS 488-12) – Seeing out the angel (instrumental mix).		

—— **MIKE OGLETREE** – drums repl. HYSLOP who formed SET THE TONE

Aug 82.	(7"/12") (VS 511/+12) **GLITTERING PRIZE. / GLITTERING THEME**	16	☐

—— **MEL GAYNOR** (b.29 May'59) – drums (ex-sessions) repl. MIKE who joined FICTION FACTORY

Sep 82.	(lp/c)<gold-lp> (V/TCV 2230) <4928> **NEW GOLD DREAM (81-82-83-84)**	3	69 Jan83

– Someone, somewhere in summertime / Colours fly and the Catherine wheel / Promised you a miracle / Big sleep / Somebody up there likes you / New gold dream (81-82-83-84) / Glittering prize / Hunter and the crowd. (cd-iss. Jul83 & Apr92; CDV 2230) (re-iss. Apr92 lp/c; OVED/+C 393)

Nov 82.	(7"/7"pic-d) (VS/+Y 538) **SOMEONE, SOMEWHERE IN SUMMERTIME. / KING IS WHITE AND IN THE CROWD**	36	
	(12"+=) (VS 538-12) – Soundtrack for every Heaven.		
Nov 82.	(7") **PROMISED YOU A MIRACLE. / THE AMERICAN**	–	
Nov 83.	(7"/12") (VS 636/+12) **WATERFRONT. / HUNTER AND THE HUNTED** (live)	13	
Jan 84.	(7"/7"pic-d) (VS/+Y 649) **SPEED YOUR LOVE TO ME. / BASS LINE**	20	
	(12"+=) (VS 649-12) – ('A'extended).		
Feb 84.	(cd/c/lp,white-lp) (CD/TC+/V 2300) <4981> **SPARKLE IN THE RAIN**	1	64

– Up on the catwalk / Book of brilliant things / Speed your love to me / Waterfront / East at Easter / White hot day / Street hassle / "C" Moon cry like a baby / The kick inside of me / Shake off the ghosts. (re-iss. cd Mar91; same)

Mar 84.	(7"/7"pic-d)(12") (VS/+Y 661)(VS 661-12) **UP ON THE CATWALK. / A BRASS BAND IN AFRICA**	27	☐
Apr 85.	(7"/7"sha-pic-d)(12") (VS/+S 749)(VS 749-12) <2703> **DON'T YOU (FORGET ABOUT ME). / A BRASS BAND IN AFRICA**	7	1 Feb85
	(re-iss. Jun88 cd-s; CDT 2)		

—— **KERR, BURCHILL, McNEILL + GAYNOR** brought in new member **JOHN GIBLING** – bass (ex-PETER GABRIEL sessions) to repl. FORBES

Oct 85.	(7"/12") (VS 817/+12) **ALIVE AND KICKING. / ('A'instrumental)**	7	–
	(12"+=) (VS 817-13) – Up on the catwalk (live).		
Oct 85.	(cd/c/lp,pic-lp) (CD/TC+/V 2364) <5092> **ONCE UPON A TIME**	1	10

– Once upon a time / All the things she said / Ghost dancing / Alive and kicking / Oh jungleland / I wish you were here / Sanctify yourself / Come a long way.

Oct 85.	(7") <2783> **ALIVE AND KICKING. / UP ON THE CATWALK (live)**	–	3
Jan 86.	(7") (SM 1) <2810> **SANCTIFY YOURSELF. / ('A'instrumental)**	10	14
	(d7"+=) (SMP 1) – Love song (live) / Street hassle (live).		
	(12") (SM 1-12) – ('A'mix). / ('A'dub instrumental).		
Apr 86.	(7") (VS 860) <2828> **ALL THE THINGS SHE SAID. / DON'T YOU (FORGET ABOUT ME)**	9	28
	(12"+=) (VS 860-12) – Promised you a miracle (US mix).		
Nov 86.	(7") (VS 907) **GHOSTDANCING. / JUNGLELAND (instrumental)**	13	☐
	(12"+=/cd-s+=) (VS/MIKE 907-12) – ('A'instrumental) / ('B'instrumental).		
May 87.	(d-cd/d-c/d-lp) (CDVSM/SMDCX/SMDLX 1) <6850> **LIVE IN THE CITY OF LIGHT** (live)	1	96 Jul87

– Ghostdancing / Big sleep / Waterfront / Promised you a miracle / Someone somewhere in summertime / Oh jungleland / Alive and kicking / Don't you (forget about me) / Once upon a time / Book of brilliant things / East at Easter / Sanctify yourself / Love song / Sun City – Dance to the music / New gold dream (81-82-83-84).

Jun 87.	(7"/10") (SM 2/+10) **PROMISED YOU A MIRACLE (live). / BOOK OF BRILLIANT THINGS** (live)	19	
	(12"+=/c-s+=) (SM/+C 2-12) – Glittering prize (live) / Celebrate (live).		

—— **KERR, BURCHILL + McNEILL** were basic trio, w/other 2 still sessioning.

Feb 89. (7") *(SMX 3)* **BELFAST CHILD. / MANDELA DAY** | 1 | |
(c-s+=/12"ep+=/12"box-ep+=/cd-ep+=) **BALLAD OF THE STREETS** *(SMX C/T/C/CD 3)* – Biko.
Apr 89. (7") *(SMX 4)* **THIS IS YOUR LAND. / SATURDAY GIRL** | 13 | |
(c-s=/12"+=/12"g-f+=/3"cd-s+=) *(SMX C/T/TG/CD 4)* – Year of the dragon.
May 89. (cd/c/lp) *(MIND D/C/S 1) <3927>* **STREET FIGHTING YEARS** | 1 | 70 |
– Soul crying out / Wall of love / This is your land / Take a step back / Kick it in / Let it all come down / Biko / Mandela day / Belfast child / Street fighting years. *(re-iss. Dec89 box-cd/c +=; SMBX D/C 1)* – (interview cassettes).
Jul 89. (7"/c-s) *(SMX/+C 5)* **KICK IT IN. / WATERFRONT ('89 mix)** | 15 | |
(12"+=/cd-s+=) *(SMX T/CD 5)* – Big sleep (live).
(12"g-f+=) *(SMXTG 5)* – ('A'mix).
Dec 89. (7"ep/c-ep/12"ep/cd-ep) *(SMX/+C/T/CD 6)* **THE AMSTERDAM EP** | 18 | |
– Let it all come down / Sign o' the times / Jerusalem.
(12"ep+=/cd-ep+=) *(SMX TR/X 6)* – Sign o' the times (mix).
—— KERR, BURCHILL + GAYNOR brought in sessioners **MALCOLM FOSTER** – bass / **PETER JOHN VITESSE** – keyboards / **STEPHEN LIPSON** – bass, keyboards / **ANDY DUNCAN** – percussion / **GAVIN WRIGHT** – string leader / **LISA GERMANO** – violin
Mar 91. (7"/c-s) *(VS/+C 1332)* **LET THERE BE LOVE. / GOODNIGHT** | 6 | |
(12"+=) *(VST 1332)* – Alive and kicking (live).
(cd-s+=) *(VSCD 1332)* – East at Easter (live).
Apr 91. (cd/c/lp) *(CD/TC/V 2660) <5352>* **REAL LIFE** | 2 | 74 |
– Real life / See the lights / Let there be love / Woman / Stand by love / African skies / Let the children speak / Ghostrider / Banging on the door / Travelling man / Rivers of ice / When two worlds collide.
May 91. (7"/c-s) *(VS/+C 1343)* **SEE THE LIGHTS. / THEME FOR GREAT CITIES ('91 edit)** | 20 | – |
(12"+=/cd-s+=) *(VS T/CD 1343)* – Soul crying out (live).
May 91. (c-s/cd,cd) *<1553>* **SEE THE LIGHTS / GOODNIGHT** | – | 40 |
Aug 91. (7"/c-s) *(VS/+C 1358)* **STAND BY LOVE. / KING IS WHITE AND IN THE CROWD (live)** | 13 | |
(12"+=/cd-s+=) *(VS T/CD 1358)* – Let there be love (live).
Oct 91. (7"/c-s) *(VS/+C 1382)* **REAL LIFE. / SEE THE LIGHTS** | 34 | |
(ext.12"+=) *(VST 1382)* – Belfast child (extended).
(cd-s+=) *(VSCD 1382)* – Ghostrider.
Oct 92. (7"/c-s) *(VS/+C 1440)* **LOVE SONG. / ALIVE AND KICKING** | 6 | |
(ext.cd-s+=) *(VSCDG 1440)* – ('B'instrumental).
(cd-s+=) *(VSCDX 1440)* – Travelling man / Oh jungleland.
Oct 92. (cd/c/lp) *(SMTV D/C/S 1)* **GLITTERING PRIZE – SIMPLE MINDS 81-92** (compilation) | 1 | – |
– Waterfront / Don't you (forget about me) / Alive and kicking / Sanctify yourself / Love song / Someone somewhere in summertime / See the lights / Belfast child / The American / All the things she said / Promised you a miracle / Ghostdancing / Speed your love to me / Glittering prize / Let there be love / Mandela Day.
—— KERR + BURCHILL with guests **MARK BROWNE, MALCOLM FOSTER, MARCUS MILLER + LANCE MORRISON** – bass / **MARK SCHULMAN, TAL BERGMAN + VINNIE COLAIUTA** – drums

	Virgin	Virgin
Jan 95. (7"/c-s/cd-s) *(VS/+C/+DG 1509) <38467>* **SHE'S A RIVER. / E55 / ('A'mix)** | 9 | 52 |
(cd-s) *(VSCDX 1509)* – ('A'side) / Celtic strings / ('A'mix).
Jan 95. (cd/c/lp) *(CD/TC+/V 2760) <39922>* **GOOD NEWS FROM THE NEXT WORLD** | 2 | 87 |
– She's a river / Night music / Hypnotised / Great leap forward / 7 deadly sins / And the band played on / My life / Criminal world / This time.
Mar 95. (7"/c-s) *(VS/+C 1534)* **HYPNOTISED. / #4** | 18 | – |
(cd-s+=) *(VSCDX 1534)* – ('A'-Tim Simenon extended remixes) / ('A'-Malfunction mix).
(cd-s) *(VSCDT 1534)* – ('A'side) / Up on the catwalk (live) / And the band played on (live) / She's a river (live).
—— KERR + BURCHILL brought back **DEREK FORBES** – bass / **MEL GAYNOR** – drums / also **HAMI LEE** – additional programming

	Chrysalis	not iss.
Mar 98. (c-s) *(TCCHS 5078)* **GLITTERBALL / WATERFRONT (Union Jack mix)** | 18 | – |
(cd-s+=) *(CDCHSS 5078)* – Love song (Philadelphia Bluntz mix).
(cd-s) *(CDCHS 5078)* – ('A'side) / Don't you forget about me (Jam & Spoon mix) / Theme for great cities (Fila Brazillia mix).
Mar 98. (cd/c) *(493712-2/-4)* **NEAPOLIS** | 19 | – |
– Song for the tribes / Glitterball / War babies / Tears of a guy / Superman v supersoul / Lightning / If I had wings / Killing Andy Warhol / Androgyny.
May 98. (ext;c-s/7") *(TC+/CHS 5088)* **WAR BABIES. / I TRAVEL (Utah Saints mix)** | 43 | – |
('A'-Bascombe mix;cd-s+=) *(CDCHS 5088)* – Theme for great cities '98 (Fluke's Atlantis mix) / ('A'-Johnson Somerset extended mix).

– compilations, others, etc. –

on 'Virgin' unless otherwise mentioned
Jan 82. (7") *Arista; (ARIST 448)* **I TRAVEL. / THIRTY FRAMES A SECOND (live)** | | – |
(12"+=) *(ARIST12 448)* – ('A'live).
Feb 82. (lp/c) *Arista; (SPART/TCSPART 1183)* **CELEBRATION** | 45 | |
(re-iss. Oct82 on 'Virgin' lp/c; V/TCV 2248) (re-iss. Apr89 on 'Virgin' lp/c; OVED/+C 275) (cd-iss. Aug89; CDV 2248)
Apr 83. (12") *(VS 578-12)* **I TRAVEL (mix). / FILM THEME** | | – |
Aug 90. (5xcd-box-ep) **THEMES – VOLUME ONE** | | |
– (Apr79 – LIFE IN A DAY – Apr82 – PROMISED YOU A MIRACLE singles)
Sep 90. (5xcd-box-ep) **THEMES – VOLUME TWO** | | |
– (Aug82 – GLITTERING PRIZE – Apr85 – DON'T YOU (FORGET ABOUT ME) singles)
Oct 90. (5xcd-box-ep) **THEMES – VOLUME THREE** | | |
– (Oct85 – ALIVE AND KICKING – Jun87 – PROMISED YOU A MIRACLE (live) singles)
Nov 90. (5xcd-box-ep) **THEMES – VOLUME FOUR** | | |
– (Feb89 – BELFAST CHILD, Dec89 – THE AMSTERDAM EP)
Nov 90. (3xcd-box) *(TPAK 2)* **COLLECTOR'S EDITION** | | – |
– (LIFE IN A DAY / REEL TO REAL CACOPHONY / EMPIRES AND DANCE)

SIMPLY RED

Formed: Manchester, England …1984 by the flame haired MICK HUCKNALL, who had cut his teeth in power-punk outfit, The FRANTIC ELEVATORS. The band released four independent singles in all, the last of which, 'HOLDING BACK THE YEARS' would go on to become a massive SIMPLY RED hit. Hooking up with manager Elliot Rashman, HUCKNALL formed an early incarnation of SIMPLY RED with EDDIE SHERWOOD, OJO and MOG, these musicians soon replaced with former DURUTTI COLUMN men, TONY BOWERS, CHRIS JOYCE and TIM KELLET. Subsequently signing with 'Elektra', the band scored immediately with a biting pop/funk cover of The VALENTINE BROTHERS' 'MONEY'S TOO TIGHT (TO MENTION)', political sentiments many people could identify with in Thatcher's brutal economic regime of the 80's. The single deservedly made the Top 20 in the summer of '85, introducing HUCKNALL's dynamic vocal acrobatics and paving the way for a Top 40 album, 'PICTURE BOOK' (1985). Though a second single, the uptempo 'COME TO MY AID' stiffed in the lower regions of the chart, a ponderous remake of the aforementioned 'HOLDING …' became a US No.1 the following Spring, giving the debut album a whole new lease of life. The ballad also narrowly missed the top of the UK charts, establishing HUCKNALL as a distinctive fixture in pop's rich tapestry as well as an unlikely sex symbol. In early '87, SIMPLY RED were back in the Top 20 with 'THE RIGHT THING', preceding a follow-up album, 'MEN AND WOMEN'. Partly co-penned with seasoned Motown writer, LAMONT DOZIER, the album was a more ambitious attempt at updating classic soul for the 80's. Though the rather dull cover of COLE PORTER's 'EV'RY TIME WE SAY GOODBYE' was another big hit, another couple of singles flopped and SIMPLY RED's position in the major league wasn't yet assured. That honour came with 'A NEW FLAME' (1989), an unashamed effort to capture the coffee table middle ground between pop, soul, rock and jazz which furnished SIMPLY RED with their first UK No.1 placing. The album's centrepiece was a tepid reading of the old HAROLD MELVIN chestnut, 'IF YOU DON'T KNOW ME BY NOW', a huge worldwide hit. In between dating models and fending off the tabloids, HUCKNALL subsequently took time out from his new found fame to pen the best selling and most consistent album of his career, 'STARS' (1991). Previewed by the sassy 'SOMETHING GOT ME STARTED', the record found HUCKNALL revelling in his role of dreadlocked love god, his voice swooning and keening over a set of impressive originals. Though SIMPLY RED were constantly harangued by the more cynical factions of the music press, the group had amassed legions of devoted fans, their support making 'STARS' one of the most popular albums of the 90's. Following a couple of years of heavy touring and some time out, SIMPLY RED returned in 1995 with 'FAIRGROUND', something of a departure with its dancefloor backing track nicked from The GOODMEN's club smash, 'GIVE IT UP'. The single gave SIMPLY RED their first No.1, closely followed by yet another No.1 album, 'LIFE' (1995), consolidating the group's position as one of the UK's most popular musical exports. The following year, HUCKNALL illustrated his love of reggae, hooking up with SLY & ROBBIE for a smoking version of the dub standard, 'NIGHT NURSE'. • Songwriters: HUCKNALL compositions, some with LAMONT DOZIER. Covered:- LET ME HAVE IT ALL (Sly Stone) / EV'RY TIME WE SAY GOODBYE (Cole Porter) / LOVE FIRE (Bunny Wailer) / IT'S ONLY LOVE (Barry White; c. J & V Cameron).

Album rating: PICTURE BOOK (*7) / MEN AND WOMEN (*8) / A NEW FLAME (*9) / STARS (*9) / LIFE (*7) / GREATEST HITS (HOLDING BACK THE YEARS 1985-96) compilation (*9) / BLUE (*5) / LOVE AND THE RUSSIAN WINTER (*4)

FRANTIC ELEVATORS

MICK HUCKNALL – vocals, guitar / **NEIL MOSS** – guitar, piano / **BRIAN TURNER** – piano, bass / **KEVIN WILLIAMS** – drums

	T.J.M.	not iss.
Jun 79. (7"m) *(TJM 5)* **VOICE IN THE DARK. / PASSION / EVERY DAY I DIE** | | – |

	Eric's	not iss.
Jan 80. (7"demo) *(TJM 6)* **HUNCHBACK OF NOTRE DAME. / SEE NOTHING AND EVERYTHING / DON'T JUDGE ME** | | – |

	Crackin'Up	not iss.
Nov 80. (7") *(ERICS 006)* **YOU KNOW WHAT YOU TOLD ME. / PRODUCTION PREVENTION** | | – |

	No Waiting	not iss.
Apr 81. (7") *(CRACK 1)* **SEARCHING FOR THE ONLY ONE. / HUNCHBACK OF NOTRE DAME** | | – |

Oct 82. (7") *(WAIT 1)* **HOLDING BACK THE YEARS. / PISTOLS IN MY BRAIN** | | – |
—— HUCKNALL formed SIMPLY RED

– compilations, etc. –

Sep 87. (m-lp) *T.J.M.; (TJM 101)* **THE EARLY YEARS** | | – |
(re-iss. Jul88 by "MICK HUCKNALL & FRANTIC ELEVATORS" on 'Receiver' cd/lp; CD+/KNOB 2)
1992. (cd) *Classic Artists; (MER 004)* **SIMPLY MICK HUCKNALL** | | – |

SIMPLY RED

MICK HUCKNALL (b. 8 Jun'60) – vocals (ex-FRANTIC ELEVATORS) / **DAVID FRYMAN** – guitar (originals EDDIE SHERWOOD – ex-BITING TONGUES, OJO & MOG repl. by below) / **TONY BOWERS** – bass (ex-DURUTTI COLUMN, ex-MOTHMEN) / **CHRIS**

JOYCE – drums (ex-DURUTTI COLUMN, ex-MOTHMEN, ex-PINK MILITARY) / **FRITZ McINTYRE** – guitar / **TIM KELLETT** – brass (ex-DURUTTI COLUMN)

	Elektra	Elektra

Jun 85. (7"/7"pic-d) (EKR 9/+P) **MONEY$ TOO TIGHT (TO MENTION). / OPEN UP THE RED BOX** — `13` —
- (ext.12"+=) (EKR 9T) – Every bit of me.
- (12") (EKR 9TX) – ('A'-Cutback mix) / ('A'dub) / ('B'side).

Aug 85. (7") (EKR 19) **COME TO MY AID. / VALENTINE** — `66` —
- (ext.12"+=) (EKR 19T) – Granma's hand.
- ('A'-Survival mix-12"++=) (EKR 19TX) – ('A'heavy dub mix).

—— **SYLVAN RICHARDSON** – guitar repl. FRYMAN (but on below lp)

Oct 85. (lp/c)(cd) (EKT 27/+C)(960 452-2) <60452> **PICTURE BOOK** `34` `16` Apr86
- – Come to my aid / Sad old Red / Look at you now / Heaven / Jericho / Money$ too tight (to mention) / Holding back the years / Open up the red box / No direction / Picture book. (pic-lp iss.May86; EKT 27P) (hit UK No.2 in May87) (re-mast.cd Feb92 on 'East West'; 9031-76993-2, hit UK No.39)

Nov 85. (7"/7"sha-pic-d/7"gf) (EKR 29/+P/F) <69564> **HOLDING BACK THE YEARS. / I WON'T FEEL BAD** `51` `1` Mar86
- (ext.12"+=) (EKR 29T) – Drowning in my own tears.

	WEA	Elektra

Feb 86. (7"/7"red) (YZ 63/+R) **JERICHO. / JERICHO THE MUSICAL** `53` —
- (ext.12"+=) (YZ 63T) – Money$ too tight (to mention) (live) / Heaven (live).

May 86. (7") (YZ 70) **HOLDING BACK THE YEARS. / DROWNING IN MY OWN TEARS** `2` –
- (ext.12"+=) (YZ 70T) – Picture book in dub.

Jul 86. (7") <69528> **MONEY$ TOO TIGHT (TO MENTION). / PICTURE BOOK (dub)** – `28`

Jul 86. (7"/7"box) (YZ 75/+B) **OPEN UP THE RED BOX (remix). / LOOK AT YOU NOW (live)** `61` —
- (d7"+=) (YZ 75F) – Holding back the years / Drowning in my own tears.
- (ext.12"+=) (YZ 75T) – Heaven the movie (live).
- (d12"+++=) (YZ 75TF) – (all above) / Picture book in dub.

—— **AZIZ IBRAHIM** – guitar repl. SYLVAN / added **IAN KIRKHAM** – saxophone / **JANETTE SEWELL** – b.vocals

Feb 87. (7"/7"s) (YZ 103/+V) <69487> **THE RIGHT THING. / THERE'S A LIGHT** `11` `27`
- (d7"+=) (YZ 103F) – Holding back the years / Drowning in my own tears.
- (ext.12"+=/ext.12"clear-pic-d+=) (YZ 103 T/TP) – Ev'ry time we say goodbye.

Mar 87. (lp/c)(cd) (WX 85/+C)(242-071-2) <60727> **MEN AND WOMEN** `2` `31`
- – The right thing / Infidelity / Suffer / I won't feel bad / Ev'ry time we say goodbye / Let me have it all / Love fire / Move on out / Shine / Maybe someday . . . (re-mast.Feb95;)

May 87. (7") (YZ 114) **INFIDELITY. / LADY GODIVA'S ROOM** `31` —
- (12"/12"pic-d) (YZ 114 T/TP) – ('A'-Stretch mix) / Love fire (Massive Red mix) / ('B'side).

Jul 87. (7") (YZ 141) **MAYBE SOMEDAY . . . / LET ME HAVE IT ALL (remix)** — —
- (12"+=) (YZ 141T) – Broken man. (US; b-side)

Nov 87. (7") (YZ 161) **EV'RY TIME WE SAY GOODBYE. / LOVE FOR SALE (live in studio)** `11` –
- (10"+=) (YZ 161TE) – Sad old Red / Broken man.
- (12"+=/12"s+=) (YZ 161 T/TW) – ('A'live in studio).
- (cd-s++=) (YZ 161CD) – Sad old Red.

Mar 88. (7") (YZ 172) **I WON'T FEEL BAD. / LADY GODIVA'S ROOM** `68` —
- (12"+=) (YZ 172T) – ('A'-Arthur Baker remix).
- (cd-s++=) (YZ 172CD) – The right thing.

Jul 88. (7") **LET ME HAVE IT ALL. / SUFFER** – —

—— **HEITOR T.P.** – guitar repl. IBRAHIM and SEWELL

Jan 89. (7") (YZ 349) <69317> **IT'S ONLY LOVE. / TURN IT UP** `13` `57`
- ('A'-Valentine mix-10"+=) (YZ 349TE) – I'm gonna lose you.
- (12") (YZ 349T) – ('A'-Valentine mix) / ('B'side) / X.
- (Valentine-3"cd-s+=/3"cd-s+=) (YZ 349CD/+X) – The right thing.

Feb 89. (lp/c)(cd) (WX 242/+C)(244 689-2) <60828> **A NEW FLAME** `1` `22`
- – It's only love / A new flame / You've got it / To be with you / More / Turn it up / Love lays its tune / She'll have to go / If you don't know me by now / Enough. (re-mast.Feb92; , hit UK No.44)

Apr 89. (7") (YZ 377) <69297> **IF YOU DON'T KNOW ME BY NOW. / MOVE ON OUT (live)** `2` `1`
- (12"+=) (YZ 377T) – Shine (live).
- (3"cd-s++=/cd-s++=) (YZ 377CD/+X) – Sugar daddy.
- (10"+=) (377TE) – The great divide (S.H.T.G.).

Jul 89. (7"/c-s) (YZ 404/+C) **A NEW FLAME. / MORE** `17` —
- (10"+=) (YZ 404TE) – I asked her for water (live) / Funk on out (live).
- (12"+=/3"cd-s+=) (YZ 404 T/CD) – I asked her for water (live) / Resume (live).

Oct 89. (7"/c-s) (YZ 424/+C) **YOU'VE GOT IT. / HOLDING BACK THE YEARS (live acoustic)** `46` –
- (12"+=/cd-s+=) (YZ 424 T/CD) – I wish.
- (10"++=) (YZ 424TE) – I know you got soul.

Oct 89. (7") **YOU'VE GOT IT. / SHE'LL HAVE TO GO** – —

—— **HUCKNALL, McINTYRE, KELLETT, HEITOR + KIRKHAM** recruit newcomers **GOTA** – drums, percussion, programs repl. JOYCE / **SHAUN WARD** – bass repl. BOWERS / added guest **JESS BAILEY** – programmer

	East West	East West

Sep 91. (7"/c-s) (YZ 614/+C) **SOMETHING GOT ME STARTED. / A NEW FLAME** `11` `27`
- ('A'-Perfecto mix-12"+=) (YZ 614T) – ('A'instrumental).
- (cd-s+++=) (YZ 614CD) – Come on in my kitchen.

Oct 91. (cd)(lp/c) (9031-75284-2)(WX427/+C) <91773> **STARS** `1` `76`
- – Something got me started / Stars / Thrill me / Your mirror / She's got it bad / For your babies / Model / How could it fall / Freedom / Wonderland.

Nov 91. (7"/c-s) (YZ 626/+C) <98636> **STARS. / STARS (PM-Ized mix)** `8` `44` Jan92
- ('A'-Comprende mix-12"+=) (YZ 626T) – Ramblin' on my mind / Something got me started (Hurley's House mix).

Feb 92. (7")(c-s)(9031-76339-4) **FOR YOUR BABIES. / ('A'-French version)** `9`
- (12"+=) (YZ 642T) – Freedom (Perfecto mix).
- (cd-s++=) (YZ 642CDX) – Me & the Devil blues / Freedom (how long mix).

Apr 92. (7"/c-s) (YZ 671/+C) **THRILL ME. / ('A'-Nellie Hooper mix)** `33`
- (cd-s+=) (YZ 671CD) – ('A'live) / When you've got a good friend.
- (12") (YZ 671T) – ('A'-Connoisseur mix) / ('A'-Stewart Levine's club mix) / ('A'-Nellie Hooper dub).

Jul 92. (7") (YZ 689) **YOUR MIRROR. / ('A'live)** `17`
- (c-s) (YZ 689C) – ('A'side) / More live) / Something got me started.
- (cd-s) (YZ 689CD) – ('A'side) / Same old Red (live) / She's got it bad (live).

Nov 92. (7"ep/c-ep/cd-ep/s-cd-ep) (YZ 716/+C/CD/CDX) **MONTREAUX EP (live)** `11`
- – Love for sale / Drowning in my own tears / Granma's hand / Lady Godiva's room.

—— **DEE JOHNSON** – backing vocals repl.TIM

Sep 95. (c-s) (EW 001C) **FAIRGROUND / ('A'extended)** `1`
- (cd-s+=) (EW 001CD1) – Stars (live) / The right thing (live).
- (cd-s+=) (EW 001CD2) – ('A'-In the Garden mix) / ('A'-Too precious mix) / ('A'-Rollo and Sister Bliss remix).

Oct 95. (cd/c/lp) (0630-12069-2/-4/-1) <61853> **LIFE** `1` `75`
- – You make me believe / So many people / Lives and loves / Fairground / Never never love / So beautiful / Hillside avenue / Remembering the first time / Out on the range / We're in this together.

Dec 95. (c-s/cd-s) (EW 015 C/CD1) **REMEMBERING THE FIRST TIME / ENOUGH (live) / A NEW FLAME (live)** `22`
- (cd-s) (EW 015CD2) – ('A'-radio disco mix) / ('A'-Hucknall – Herrington remix) / ('A'-Self Preservation Society remix) / ('A'-Satoshi Tomiie remix) / ('A'-Too Precious remix).

Feb 96. (c-s/cd-s) (EW 029 C/CD1) **NEVER NEVER LOVE / ('A'-Too Precious mix) / ('A'-DJ Muggs mix))** `18`
- (cd-s2) (EW 029CD2) – ('A'side) / Fairground (live) / You make me believe (mix) / Groovy situation.

—— In Apr'96 as SIMPLY RED & WHITE, they released football version of 'DAYDREAM BELIEVER (CHEER UP PETER REID)', which hit No.41.

Jun 96. (c-s/cd-s) (EW 046 C/CD) **WE'RE IN THIS TOGETHER / SOMETHING'S GOT ME STARTED (live) / MONEY'S TOO TIGHT TO MENTION (live)** `11`
- (cd-s) (EW 046CDX) – ('A'side) / You make me believe (live) / Hillside Avenue (live).

Oct 96. (cd/c) (0630 16552-2/-4) **GREATEST HITS (HOLDING BACK THE YEARS 1985-1996)** (compilation) `1`
- – Holding back the years / Money's too tight to mention / The right thing / It's only love / A new flame / You've got it / If you don't know me by now / Stars / Something got me started / Thrill me / Your mirror / For your babies / So beautiful / Angel / Fairground.

Oct 96. (c-s) (EW 074C) **ANGEL / MONEY$ TOO TIGHT TO MENTION (disco vocal)** `4`
- (cd-s+=) (EW 074CD2) – ('A'-live from Montreux) / +1
- (cd-s) (EW 074CD1) – ('A'side) / ('A'-Mousse T soul mix) / ('A'-Rubbadubb mix) / (2 other 'A'mixes).

—— In Sep'97, they teamed up with SLY & ROBBIE on the No.13 hit 'NIGHT NURSE' (East West EW 129 C/CD1/CD2)

May 98. (c-s) (EW 164C) **SAY YOU LOVE ME / SO JUNGIFUL** `7`
- (cd-s+=) (EW 164CD) – So many people / Never never never (live).

May 98. (cd/c/lp) (3984 23097-2/-4/-1) **BLUE** `1`
- – Mellow my mind / Blue / Say you love me / To be free / The air that I breathe / Someday in my life / The air that I breathe reprise / Night nurse / Broken man / Come get me angel / Ghetto girl / Love has said goodbye again / High fives.

Aug 98. (c-s/cd-s) (EW 181 C/CD2) **THE AIR THAT I BREATHE / LOVE HAS SAID GOODBYE AGAIN** `6`
- (cd-s) (EW 181CD1) – ('A'side) / Tu sei dentro di me (Someday in my life).

Nov 98. (c-s/cd-s) (EW 191 C/CD2) **GHETTO GIRL / SO BEAUTIFUL (live) / SAY YOU LOVE ME (live)** `34`
- (cd-s) (EW 191CD1) – ('A'mixes).

Oct 99. (c-s) (EW 208C) **AIN'T THAT A LOT OF LOVE /** `14`
- (cd-s+=) (EW 208CD1) – ('A'mixes).
- (cd-s) (EW 208CD2) – ('A'mixes).
- (12") (EW 208T) – ('A'side) / Come on in my kitchen.

Nov 99. (cd/c/lp) (3984 29942-2/-4/-1) **LOVE AND THE RUSSIAN WINTER** `6`
- – Spirit of love / Ain't that a lot of love / Your eyes / Sky is a gypsy / Back into the universe / Words for girlfriends / Thank you / Man made the gun / Close to you / More than a dream / Wave the old world goodbye.

SIOUXSIE & THE BANSHEES

Formed: London, England . . . September '76 by SIOUXSIE SIOUX and STEVE SEVERIN, both members of the infamous 'Bromley Contingent' punk troupe who religiously followed The SEX PISTOLS during the turbulent early years of their career; an early incarnation of The BANSHEES even featured future PISTOL, SID VICIOUS on drums, the outfit mangling the Lord's Prayer at the legendary 100 Club punk all-dayer in summer '76. SIOUX gained further notoriety following her appearance (as a fan) on the fateful edition of Bill Grundy's 'Today' programme wherein his tete-a-tete with the 'PISTOLS outraged the country's more upstanding citizens. Cutting a striking dash through the punk scene with her Nazi chic and proto-goth garb, SIOUXSIE and her BANSHEES (who, after much to-ing and fro-ing, were eventually completed by JOHN McKAY amd KENNY MORRIS) toured constantly throughout 1977, eventually signing to 'Polydor' the following year after their original label, 'Track', went bust. A debut single, 'HONG KONG GARDEN' was a sprightly slice of oriental flavoured post-punk which hit the Top 10 with ease and introduced the band outwith the confines of the London scene. 'THE SCREAM' (1978) was instantly hailed as a classic upon its release a few months later, the record's queasy, churning goth-psychedelia breaking new ground and spearheading a new direction for many bands inspired by a movement already dying on its feet. For many recent converts, then, 'JOIN HANDS' (1979) was a disappointment, a turgid affair which lacked the bite of its predecessor and presaged a band breakdown; McKAY and MORRIS upped sticks and left mid-tour, ROBERT SMITH (The Cure) briefly deputising before a new guitarist was eventually found in erstwhile MAGAZINE man, JOHN McGEOGH. The drum seat, meanwhile, was taken by ex-SLITS man, BUDGIE, who would subsequently become SIOUXSIE's beau and eventual husband. The revamped line-up bounced back in 1980 with the enchanting 'HAPPY HOUSE' (a Top 20 hit that Spring) and an accompanying Top 5 album, 'KALEIDOSCOPE', investing their sound with a newly acquired accessibility and ensuring a degree of crossover success for SIOUXSIE's icy sensuality. 'JU JU' (1981) further refined the group's subtle gothic tapestries, again taking the band into the UK Top 10 and spawning a clutch of minor hits while 'ONCE UPON A TIME – THE SINGLES' neatly rounded up the first instalment in The BANSHEES' career. More overtly experimental was the following year's 'A KISS IN THE DREAMHOUSE', utilising strings and flirting with club sounds. 1983 saw a flurry of side project activity as SIOUXSIE and BUDGIE formed The CREATURES, releasing 'FEAST', the first of two albums together (they also had a major hit with Mel Torme's 'RIGHT NOW'). SEVERIN, meanwhile, formed The GLOVE with SMITH (who had also rejoined the BANSHEES ranks as a part-time, temporary replacement for the departing McGEOGH), releasing the 'BLUE SUNSHINE' album the same year. No new BANSHEES material surfaced, although an atmospheric cover of The Beatles' 'DEAR PRUDENCE' hit No.3 and gave them their biggest selling single to date. The track featured on 1983's live set, 'NOCTURNE', while the following year's 'HYAENA', saw SMITH making his presence felt over the course of a haunting set that was unfairly panned by the critics. With SMITH subsequently finding the demands of a dual lifestyle too tiring, ex-CLOCKDVA man, JOHN CARRUTHERS was drafted in for 'TINDERBOX' (1986), an album which carried on in much the same vein, spawning a sizeable hit with the infectious 'CITIES IN DUST'. Perhaps the band really were running out of ideas as their detractors suggested, a suitably gothic Top 20 rendition of Bob Dylan's 'THIS WHEEL'S ON FIRE' trailing a whole album's worth of competent but hardly inspiring cover versions. Featuring yet another guitarist, JON KLEIN, 1988's 'PEEPSHOW' was a much more compelling proposition, a perversely eclectic selection best sampled on the mutant dancefloor hit, 'PEEK-A-BOO'. Now something of an alternative institution, SIOUXSIE & THE BANSHEES cruised into the 90's with their most chart-friendly original material to date, the swooning 'KISS THEM FOR ME' (the band's first – and to date only – major US hit) single and attendant 'SUPERSTITION' (1991) album. Despite the latter set's commercial and critical success, the group reached the end of its natural lifespan in the mid-90's, bowing out on a high with the majestic 'THE RAPTURE'. Officially splitting in April '96, SIOUXSIE was working on new CREATURES material with spouse BUDGIE, while SEVERIN scored the soundtrack for the movie, 'Visions Of Ecstasy'. The aforementioned CREATURES finally resurfaced via 'ANIMA ANIMUS' (1999), an album that boasted a few minor hits; SIOUXSIE was now looking rather Elizabeth Taylor-ish although when she wailed and her BUDGIE drummed it was safe there was no lasting comparison. • **Songwriters:** All written by SIOUXSIE / SEVERIN except; HELTER SKELTER (Beatles) / 20th CENTURY BOY (T.Rex) / IL EST NE LE DIVIN ENFANT (French festive song) / ALL TOMORROW'S PARTIES (Velvet Underground). THROUGH THE LOOKING GLASS was a covers album containing THE PASSENGER (Iggy Pop) / YOU'RE LOST LITTLE GIRL / GUN (John Cale) / THIS TOWN AIN'T BIG ENOUGH FOR THE BOTH OF US (Sparks) / SEA BREEZES (Roxy Music) / STRANGE FRUIT (Billie Holiday) / WALL OF MIRRORS (Kraftwerk) / LITTLE JOHNNY JEWEL (Television) / TRUST IN ME ('Jungle Book' animated film). • **Trivia:** SEVERIN produced ALTERED IMAGES debut 45 'Dead Pop Stars'.

Album rating: THE SCREAM (*9) / JOIN HANDS (*7) / KALEIDOSCOPE (*7) / JU JU (*7) / ONCE UPON A TIME – THE SINGLES compilation (*9) / A KISS IN THE DREAMHOUSE (*7) / NOCTURNE (*5) / HYAENA (*7) / TINDERBOX (*7) / THROUGH THE LOOKING GLASS (*5) / PEEP SHOW (*5) / SUPERSTITION (*5) / TWICE UPON A TIME compilation (*7) / THE RAPTURE (*5) / Creatures: FEAST (*5) / BOOMERANG (*4) / ANIMA ANIMUS (*6) / Glove: BLUE SUNSHINE (*5)

SIOUXSIE SIOUX (b. SUSAN DALLION, 27 May'57) – vocals / **STEVEN SEVERIN** (b. STEVEN BAILEY, 25 Sep'55) – bass / **JOHN McKAY** – guitar repl. PT FENTON who had repl. MARCO PIRRONI (he joined MODELS and later ADAM & THE ANTS) / **KENNY MORRIS** – drums repl. SID VICIOUS who later became bassman for SEX PISTOLS

	Polydor	Polydor
Aug 78. (7") (2059 052) **HONG KONG GARDEN. / VOICES**	7	-
Oct 78. (7") **HONG KONG GARDEN. / OVERGROUND**	-	-
Nov 78. (lp/c) (POLD/+C 5009) <6207> **THE SCREAM**	12	
– Pure / Jigsaw feeling / Overground / Carcass / Helter skelter / Mirage / Metal postcard / Nicotine stain / Suburban relapse / Switch. (cd-iss. Mar89 & Mar95 on 'Wonderland'; 839 008-2) (cd re-iss. Mar95)		
Mar 79. (7") (POSP 9) **THE STAIRCASE (MYSTERY). / 20th CENTURY BOY**	24	-
Jun 79. (7") (POSP 59) **PLAYGROUND TWIST. / PULLED TO BITS**	28	-
Sep 79. (lp/c) (POLD/+C 5024) **JOIN HANDS**	13	-
– Poppy day / Regal zone / Placebo effect / Icon / Premature burial / Playground twist / Mother / Oh mein papa / The Lord's prayer. (cd-iss. Mar89 & Mar95 on 'Wonderland'; 839004-2)		
Sep 79. (7") (2059 151) **MITTAGEISEN (METAL POSTCARD). / LOVE IN A VOID**	47	-

BUDGIE (b.PETER CLARK, 21 Aug'57, St.Helens, England) – drums (ex-SLITS, ex-PLANETS, ex-BIG IN JAPAN, etc.) repl. MORRIS who bailed out (he subsequently released a solo 12", 'LA MAIN MORTE', for 'Temple' records in '86) / **JOHN McGEOGH** (b. 1955, Greenock, Scotland) – guitar (of MAGAZINE) finally repl. ROBERT SMITH (of The Cure) + JOHN CARRUTHERS who repl. McKAY (he finally formed ZOR GABOR in 1986 – with vocalist LINDA CLARK – and released one single, 'TIGHTROPE', for 'In-Tape' early '87)

	Polydor	Polydor
Mar 80. (7") (POSP 117) **HAPPY HOUSE. / DROP DEAD**	17	-
May 80. (7") (2059 249) **CHRISTINE. / EVE WHITE EVE BLACK**	24	-
Aug 80. (lp/c) (2442 177)(3184 146) **KALEIDOSCOPE**	5	-
– Happy house / Tenant / Trophy / Hybrid / Lunar camel / Christine / Desert kisses / Red light / Paradise place / Skin. (cd-iss. Mar89 & Mar95 on 'Wonderland'; 839006-2)		
Nov 80. (7"/dance-12") (POSP/+X 205) **ISRAEL. / RED OVER WHITE**	41	-
May 81. (7") (POSP 273) **SPELLBOUND. / FOLLOW THE SUN**	22	-
(12"+=) (POSPX 273) – Slap dash snap.		
Jun 81. (lp/c) (POLS/+C 1034) **JU JU**	7	-
– Spellbound / Into the light / Arabian knights / Halloween / Monitor / Night shift / Sin in my heart / Head cut / Voodoo dolly. (cd-iss. Mar89 & Mar95 on 'Wonderland'; 839005-2)		
Jul 81. (7") (POSP 309) **ARABIAN KNIGHTS. / SUPERNATURAL THING**	32	-
(12"+=) (POSPX 309) – Congo conga.		

──── SIOUXSIE & BUDGIE as The CREATURES hit Top 30 with WILD THINGS EP.

	Polydor	Polydor
Dec 81. (lp/c) (POLS/+C 1056) **ONCE UPON A TIME – THE SINGLES**	21	-
– Hong Kong garden / Mirage / The staircase (mystery) / Playground twist / Happy house / Christine / Israel / Spellbound / Arabian knights / Fireworks. (cd-iss. Mar89 on 'Wonderland'; 831542-2)		
May 82. (7") (POSPG 450) **FIREWORKS. / COAL MIND**	22	-
(12"+=) (POSPX 450) – We fall.		
Sep 82. (7") (POSP 510) **SLOWDIVE. / CANNIBAL ROSES**	41	-
(12"+=) (POSPX 510) – Obsession II.		
Nov 82. (lp/c) (POLD/+C 5064) **A KISS IN THE DREAMHOUSE**	11	-
– Cascade / Green fingers / Obsession / She's a carnival / Circle / Melt! / Painted bird / Cocoon / Slowdive. (cd-iss. Apr89 & Mar 95 on 'Wonderland'; 839007-2)		
Nov 82. (7") (POSP 539) **MELT! / IL EST NE LE DIVIN ENFANT**	49	
(12"+=) (POSPX 539) – A sleeping rain.		

──── ROBERT SMITH – guitar (of The Cure) returned part-time to repl. McGEOGH who later joined The ARMOURY SHOW.

──── In 1983, SMITH and SEVERIN had also splintered into The GLOVE, with SIOUXSIE and BUDGIE re-uniting as The CREATURES (see further on).

	Wonderland – Polydor	Geffen
Sep 83. (7") (SHEG 4) **DEAR PRUDENCE. / TATTOO**	3	-
(12"+=) (SHEX 4) – There's a planet in my kitchen.		
Nov 83. (d-lp/c) (SHAH/+C 1) **NOCTURNE (live)**	29	-
– Intro – The rite of Spring / Israel / Dear Prudence / Paradise place / Melt! / Cascade / Pulled to bits / Night shift / Sin in my heart / Slowdive / Painted bird / Happy house / Switch / Spellbound / Helter skelter / Eve white eve black / Voodoo dolly. (cd-iss. Apr89 & Mar95; 839009-2)		
Mar 84. (7") (SHE 6) **SWIMMING HORSES. / LET GO**	28	-
(12"+=) (SHEX 6) – The humming wires.		
May 84. (7") (SHE 7) **DAZZLE. / I PROMISE**	33	-
(12"+=) (SHEX 7) – Throw them to the lions / ('A'mix).		
Jun 84. (lp/c)(cd) (SHEH P/C 1)(821510-2) <24030> **HYAENA**	15	
– Dazzle / We hunger / Take me back / Belladonna / Swimming horses / Bring me the head of the preacher man / Running town / Pointing bone / Blow the house down. (re-iss. cd Mar95; same)		

──── JOHN CARRUTHERS – guitar (ex-CLOCKDVA, ex-JEFFREY LEE PIERCE) returned to repl. SMITH who had CURE commitments.

Oct 84. (12"ep) (SHEEP 8) **THE THORN (live)**	47	-
– Voices / Placebo effect / Red over white / Overground.		
Oct 85. (7") (SHE 9) **CITIES IN DUST. / AN EXECUTION**	21	-
(12"+=) (SHEX 9) – Quarter drawing of the dog.		
Feb 86. (7") (SHE 10) **CANDYMAN. / LULLABY**	34	-
(12"+=) (SHEX 10) – Umbrella.		
Apr 86. (lp/c)(cd) (SHE LP/MC 10)(829145-2) <24092> **TINDERBOX**	13	88
– Candyman / The sweetest chill / This unrest / Cities in dust / Cannons / Partys fall / 92° / Lands End. (cd+=) – An execution / Quarter drawing of the dog / Lullaby / Umbrella / Candyman (extended). (re-iss. cd Mar95; same)		
Jan 87. (7") (SHE 11) **THIS WHEEL'S ON FIRE. / SHOOTING SUN**	14	-
(12"+=) (SHEX 11) – Sleepwalking (on the high wire).		
Feb 87. (lp/c)(cd) (SHE LP/MC 13)(831474-2) <24134> **THROUGH THE LOOKING GLASS**	15	
– Hall of mirrors / Trust in me / This wheel's on fire / Strange fruit / This town ain't big enough for the both of us / You're lost little girl / The passenger / Gun / Sea breezes / Little Johnny Jewel. (re-iss. cd Mar95; same)		
Mar 87. (7") (SHE 12) **THE PASSENGER. / SHE'S CUCKOO**	41	-
(12"+=) (SHEX 12) – Something blue.		

──── JON KLEIN (b. 9 May'??, Bristol, England) – guitar (ex-SPECIMEN) repl. CARRUTHERS / added **MARTIN McCARRICK** (b.29 Jul'??) – cello, keyboards (ex-MARC ALMOND, ex-The GLOVE) (to SIOUXSIE, SEVERIN, BUDGIE + KLEIN)

Jul 87. (7"/7"pic-d/c-s) (SHE/+P/+PC 13) **SONG FROM THE EDGE OF THE WORLD. / THE WHOLE PRICE OF BLOOD**	59	-
(12"+=) (SHEX 13) – Mechanical eyes.		
Jul 88. (7"/7"g-f) (SHE/+G 14) <27760> **PEEK-A-BOO. / FALSE FACE**	16	53
(c-s+=/cd-s+=) (SHE CS/CD 14) – Catwalk / ('A'-Big suspender mix).		
(12"+=) (SHEXR 14) – ('A'-2 other mixes).		
Sep 88. (lp/c)(cd) (SHE LP/MC 5)(837240-2) <24205> **PEEPSHOW**	20	68
– Peek-a-boo / Killing jar / Scarecrow / Carousel / Burn-up / Ornaments of gold / Turn to stone / Rawhead and bloodydbones / The last beat of my heart / Rhapsody. (re-iss. cd Mar95; same)		
Sep 88. (7"/7"g-f/7"pic-d) (SHE/+G/P 15) **KILLING JAR. / SOMETHING WICKED (THIS WAY COMES)**	41	-
(12"+=/cd-s+=) (SHE X/CD 15) – Are you still dying, darling.		

Nov 88. (7"/7"g-f) *(SHE/+G 16)* **THE LAST BEAT OF MY HEART. /
EL DIABLO LOS MUERTOS** `44` `☐`
(12"+=) *(SHEX 16)* – Sunless.
(cd-s++=) *(SHECD 16)* – ('B'mix).

—— In Autumn'89, The CREATURES issued singles and 'BOOMERANG' album.
May 91. (7"/c-s) *(SHE/+CS 19)* <19031> **KISS THEM FOR ME. /
RETURN** `32` `23`
(ext-12"+=/12"pic-d+=) *(SHE X/XD 19)* – Staring back.
(cd-s++=) *(SHECD 19)* – ('A'side).
Jun 91. (cd/c/lp) *(847731-2/-4/-1))* <24387> **SUPERSTITION** `25` `65`
– Kiss them for me / Fear (of the unknown) / Cry / Drifter / Little sister /
Shadowtime / Silly thing / Got to get up / Silver waterfalls / Softly / The ghost in
you. *(re-iss. cd Mar95; same)*
Jul 91. (7"/c-s) *(SHE/+CS 20)* **SHADOWTIME. / SPIRAL TWIST** `57` `☐`
(12"+=/cd-s+=) *(SHE X/CD 20)* – Sea of light. / ('A'-Eclipse mix).

—— Below single from the film 'Batman Returns'.
Jul 92. (7"/c-s) *(SHE/+CS 21)* **FACE TO FACE. / I COULD BE AGAIN** `21` `☐`
(cd-s+=) *(SHECD 21)* – ('A'-catatonic mix) / Hothead.
(12") *(SHEX 21)* – ('A'side) / ('A'-catatonic mix) / Hothead.
Oct 92. (cd/c/lp) *(517160-2/-4/-1)* **TWICE UPON A TIME – THE THING** `26` `☐`
– Fireworks / Slowdive / Melt / Dear Prudence / Swimming horses / Dazzle /
Overground (from The Thorn) / Cities in dust / Candyman / This wheel's on fire /
The passenger / Peek-a-boo / The killing jar / The last beat of my heart / Kiss them
for me / Shadowtime / Fear (of the unknown) / Face to face. *(re-iss. cd Mar95; same)*

—— In Aug 94, SIOUXSIE partnered MORRISSEY on his single, 'INTERLUDE'.
Dec 94. (c-s) *(SHECS 22)* **O BABY. / OURSELVES** `34` `-`
(cd-s+=) *(SHECD 22)* – ('A'-Manhattan mix).
(cd-s) *(SHECDX 22)* – ('A'side) / Swimming horses (live) / All tomorrow's parties
(live).
Jan 95. (cd/c/lp) *(523725-2/-4/-1)* <24630> **THE RAPTURE** `33` `☐`
– O baby / Tearing apart / Stargazer / Fall from grace / Not forgotten / Sick child /
The lonely one / Falling down / Forever / The rapture / The double life / Love out
me.
Feb 95. (7"/c-s) *(SHE/+CS 23)* **STARGAZER. / HANG ME HIGH** `64` `☐`
(cd-s+=) *(SHECD 23)* – Black Sun.
(cd-s) *(SHECDX 23)* – ('A'-Mambo sun) / ('A'-Planet queen mix) / ('A'-Mark
Saunders mix).

—— Split Apr'96 although SIOUXSIE and BUDGIE recorded a third album as The
CREATURES. SEVERIN has written for the film 'Visions Of Ecstacy'.

– compilations, etc. –

Feb 87. (12"ep) *Strange Fruit; (SFPS 012)* **THE PEEL SESSIONS
(29.11.77)** `☐` `-`
– Love in a void / Mirage / Suburban relapse / Metal postcard. *(c-ep-iss.Jun87;
SFPSC 012) (cd-ep-iss.Mar88; SFPSCD 012)*
Feb 89. (12"ep/cd-ep) *Strange Fruit; (SPPS/+CD 066)* **THE PEEL
SESSIONS (Feb78)** `☐` `-`
– Hong Kong garden / Carcass / Helter skelter / Overground.

CREATURES

(SIOUXSIE & BUDGIE)

	Polydor	not iss.
Sep 81. (d7"ep/d7"gf-ep) *(POSP D/G 354)* **WILD THINGS** `24` `-`
– Mad-eyed screamer / So unreal / But not them / Wild thing / Thumb.

	Wonderland	Geffen
May 83. (7") *(SHE 2)* **MISS THE GIRL. / HOT SPRING IN THE
SNOW** `21` `-`
May 83. (lp/c) *(SHE LP/MC 1)* **FEAST** `17` `-`
– Morning dawning / Inoa 'ole / Ice house / Dancing on glass / Gecko / Sky train /
Festival of colours / Miss the girl / A strutting rooster / Flesh.
Jul 83. (7") *(SHE 2)* **RIGHT NOW. / WEATHERCADE** `14` `-`
(12"+=) *(SHEX 2)* – Festival of colours.
Oct 89. (7") *(SHEP 17)* **STANDING THERE. / DIVIDED** `53` `-`
(12"+=/cd-s+=) *(SH X/CD 17)* – Solar choir / ('A'-Andalucian mix).
('A'-La Frontera mix-10"+=) *(SHET 17)* – Solar choir.
Nov 89. (lp/c/cd) *(841463-1/-4/-2)* <24275> **BOOMERANG** `☐` `☐`
– Standing there / Manchild / You! / Pity / Killing time / Willow / Pluto drive / Solar
choir * / Speeding * / Fury eyes / Fruitman / Untiedundone * / Simoom * / Strolling
wolf / Venus sands / Morriha. *(extra tracks on cd= *)*
Feb 90. (7"/7"box) *(SHE/+B 18)* **FURY EYES. / ABSTINENCE** `☐` `☐`
(12"/cd-s) *(SHE P/CD 18)* – ('A'-20/20 mix) / ('A'dub) / ('A'-Fever mix).

	Sioux	Record Of Substance
Jun 98. (7") *(SIOUX 1)* **SAD CUNT. / SAD CUNT (chix'n'dix mix)** `☐` `-`
Aug 98. (10"ep/cd-ep) *(SIOUX 2 V/CD)* <1> **ERASER CUTS** `☐` `☐`
– Pinned down / Guillotine / Thank you / Slipping away.
Oct 98. (7"green) *(SIOUX 3V)* **2ND FLOOR. / TURN IT ON** `☐` `-`
(12"on 'Hydrogen Jukebox'+=)(cd-s+=) *(DUKE 044DJV)(SIOUX 3CD)* – ('A'-Girl
eats boy mix) / ('A'-Emperor Sly mix).
Dec 98. (cd-ep) *(SIOUX 5CD)* **EXTERMINATING ANGEL** `-` `-` mail-o
– Exordium (one night in France) / Interim (NYC & Paris) / Remake (the James
Hardway) / Remodel (album mix).
Feb 99. (cd/c/2x10"lp) *(SIOUX 4 CD/C/V)* **ANIMA ANIMUS** `☐` `☐`
– 2nd floor / Disconnected / Turn it on / Take mine / Say / I was me / The prettiest
thing / Exterminating angel / Another planet / Don't go to sleep without me.
Mar 99. (7"clear) *(SIOUX 6V)* **SAY. / ALL SHE COULD ASK FOR** `72` `☐`
(cd-s) *(SIOUX 6CD)* – ('A'side) / Broken.
(cd-s) *(SIOUX 6CDX)* – ('A'-Witchman remix) / ('A'-Justice & Endemic void
remix).
Mar 99. (12"ltd) *(DUKE 055DJV)* **SAY (Witchman 4x4 mix). /
THANK YOU (Dub Pistols brings you joy mix)** `☐` `-`
Jul 99. (12"ltd) *(DUKE 064DJV)* **DISCONNECTING (Beloved's
mix). / PRETTIEST THING (Super Chumbo's mix)** `☐` `-`
(above singles on 'Hydrogen Dukebox')

Sep 99. (10"blue/cd-s) *(SIOUX 9 V/CD)* **THE PRETTIEST THING
(mixes)** `☐` `-`
(cd-s) *(SIOUX 9CDX)* – ('A'mixes).
Nov 99. (cd/d-lp) *(DUKE 066 CD/DJV)* **HYBRIDS** (remixes) `☐` `☐`

The GLOVE

(SEVERIN & ROBERT SMITH) also incl. **MARTIN McCARRICK** – cello / **ANNE
STEPHENSON + GINNY HEWES** – strings / **ANDY ANDERSON** – drums / (JEANETTE)
LANDRAY – dual vocals w/**SMITH**

	Wonderland	Rough Trade
Aug 83. (7") *(SHE 3)* **LIKE AN ANIMAL. / MOUTH TO MOUTH** `52` `-`
(12"+=) *(SHEX 3)* – Animal (club mix).
Aug 83. (lp/c) *(SHE LP/MC 2)* <ROUGHUS 85> **BLUE SUNSHINE** `35` `-`
– Like an animal / Looking glass girl / Sex-eye-make-up / Mr. Alphabet says / A
blues in drag / Punish me with kisses / This green city / Orgy / Perfect murder /
Relax. *(re-iss. Sep90 lp/c/cd+=; 815019-1/-4/-2)* – Mouth to mouth / The tightrope /
Like an animal (club mix).
Nov 83. (7") *(SHE 5)* **PUNISH ME WITH KISSES. / THE TIGHTROPE** `☐` `-`

SIREN (see under ⇒ COYNE, Kevin)

SISTERS OF MERCY

Formed: Leeds, England ... 1980 by frontman/lyricist extraordinaire,
ANDREW ELDRITCH along with guitarist, GARY MARX. The original
"goth" combo, ELDRITCH and Co. were among the first acts to define
the genre in its lasting image of black clad, po-faced rockers meditating on
dark, impenetrable lyrics, decipherable only for those willing to substitute
make-up for flour or wear pointy boots (and, more importantly, never to
emerge in daylight!). For their early releases, the group employed a drum
machine, christened Doktor Avalanche, issuing material on their self-financed
label, 'Merciful Release'. Following the debut single, 'DAMAGE DONE',
ELDRITCH and MARX recruited guitarist BENN GUNN and bassist CRAIG
ADAMS, fleshing out the sound on a further series of 7 and 12"s, the 'ALICE'
EP drawing widespread interest with its goth/alternative/dance fusion. GUNN
was then replaced with ex-DEAD OR ALIVE guitarist, WAYNE HUSSEY, for
the piledriving theatrics of 'TEMPLE OF LOVE'. During this time, the group
had also built up a live reputation, supporting the likes of The BIRTHDAY
PARTY and The PSYCHEDELIC FURS as well as appearing at the Leeds
Futurama festival. Word was spreading, and in 1984, The SISTERS OF
MERCY and their label were signed to a worldwide deal with 'WEA'. A debut
album, 'FIRST AND LAST AND ALWAYS', appeared the following year, a
worthwhile effort which saw the group almost break into the UK Top 10. Yet
only a month after the record's release, the band announced they were to split,
tension between ELDRITCH and MARX resulting in the latter leaving the
group first. After a final concert at London's Royal Albert Hall, a bitter legal
battle ensued between ELDRITCH and ADAMS/HUSSEY. At stake was the
SISTERS OF MERCY moniker, ELDRITCH eventually winning out, though
not before he'd hastily released a single and album, 'GIFT' (1986), under
The SISTERHOOD, primarily to prevent ADAMS and HUSSEY using the
title. The latter two subsequently formed The MISSION while ELDRITCH
relocated to Berlin/Hamburg, retaining ex-GUN CLUB bassist, PATRICIA
MORRISON (who'd played on 'GIFT') and recording 'FLOODLAND' (1987)
with the help of his ever faithful drum machine. The preceding single,
'THIS CORROSION' was suitably grandiose, all ominous vocals and OTT
production courtesy of JIM STEINMAN, the single giving ELDRITCH his
first UK Top 10 hit. The album achieved a similar feat, incorporating
a more overtly rhythmic feel to create a kind of doom-disco sound
(perfect for goths who couldn't dance anyway!). MORRISON subsequently
left, ELDRITCH recruiting an array of diverse musicians including TIM
BREICHENO, ANDREAS BRUHN and punk veteran, TONY JAMES (ex-
SIGUE SIGUE SPUTNIK, ex-GENERATION X) to record 'VISION THING'
(1990). Employing a more commercial hard rock sound, 'MORE' was one
of The SISTERS' most effective singles to date while again the album was a
Top 20 success. Further acclaim came in 1992 with the surprisingly consistent
retrospective, 'SOME GIRLS WANDER BY MISTAKE' (1992), and its
attendant single, a brilliant re-vamp of 'TEMPLE OF LOVE', Israeli warbler,
OFRA HAZA, adding that extra mystical touch. After a 1991 joint tour with
PUBLIC ENEMY (nice idea, but probably taking the Lollapollooza ethic a bit
too far) was abandoned after poor ticket sales, not much has been heard from
The SISTERS OF MERCY. ELDRITCH remains an enigmatic figure, any
significant activity normally resulting in intense interest from the music press.
The odds are that he'll return, though whether in the guise of The SISTERS
OF MERCY remains to be seen. • **Covered:** EMMA (Hot Chocolate) /
1969 (Stooges) / GIMME SHELTER (Rolling Stones) / KNOCKIN' ON
HEAVEN'S DOOR (Bob Dylan).

Album rating: FIRST AND LAST AND ALWAYS (*8) / GIFT (*7; as Sisterhood) /
FLOODLAND (*8) / VISION THING (*7) / SOME GIRLS WANDER BY MISTAKE
compilation (*8) / GREATEST HITS VOLUME 1 – A SLIGHT CASE OF
OVERBOMBING compilation (*7)

ANDREW ELDRITCH (b. ANDREW TAYLOR, 15 May'59, East Anglia, England) –
vocals / **GARRY MARX** (b. MARK PEARMAN) – guitar / + drum machine DOKTOR
AVALANCHE

	Merciful Release	not iss.
1980. (7"m) *(MR 7)* **THE DAMAGE DONE. / WATCH / HOME
OF THE HITMAN** `☐` `-`

—— added **BEN GUNN** (b. BENJAMIN MATTHEWS) – guitar / **CRAIG ADAMS** (b. 4 Apr'62) – bass (ex-EXPELAIRES)

		C.N.T.	not iss.
Feb 82.	(7") *(CNT 002)* **BODY ELECTRIC. / ADRENOCHROME**		

		Merciful	BrainEater
Nov 82.	(7") *(MR 015)* **ALICE. / FLOORSHOW**		
Mar 83.	(7") *(MR 019)* **ANACONDA. / PHANTOM**		
Apr 83.	(12"ep) *(MR 021)* **ALICE. / FLOORSHOW / 1969 / PHANTOM**		
May 83.	(12"ep) *(MR 023)* **THE REPTILE HOUSE** – Kiss the carpet / Lights / Valentine / Burn / Fix. *(re-iss. Apr94)*		

—— **WAYNE HUSSEY** (b. JERRY LOVELOCK, 26 May'58, Bristol, England) – guitar (ex-DEAD OR ALIVE, ex-HAMBI & THE DANCE) repl. BEN

Oct 83.	(7") *(MR 027)* **TEMPLE OF LOVE. / HEARTLAND**		
	(ext.12"+=) *(MRX 027)* – Gimme shelter.		
Jun 84.	(7"; as The SISTERS) *(MR 029)* **BODY AND SOUL. / TRAIN**	46	-
	(12"+=) *(MR 029T)* – After hours / Body electric.		

		Merciful Release	Elektra
Oct 84.	(7") *(MR 033)* **WALK AWAY. / POISON DOOR** (above w/free 7"flexi) *(MR 033 – SAM 218)* – Long Train.	45	-
	(12"+=) *(MR 033T)* – On the wire.		
Feb 85.	(7") *(MR 035)* **NO TIME TO CRY. / BLOOD MONEY**	63	-
	(12"+=) *(MR 035T)* – Bury me deep.		
Mar 85.	(7" L/c) *(MR 337 L/C)* <60405> **FIRST AND LAST AND ALWAYS**	14	

– Black planet / Walk away / No time to cry / A rock and a hard place / Marian / First and last and always / Possession / Nine while nine / Amphetamine logic / Some kind of stranger. *(cd-iss. Jul88; 240616-2) (re-iss. re-mastered.Jul92 on 'East West' lp/c; MR 571 L/C) (cd re-mast.Jun92; 9031 77379-2)*

—— disbanded mid-'85 . . . GARRY MARX helped form GHOST DANCE. HUSSEY and ADAMS formed The MISSION after squabbles with ANDREW over use of group name.

—— **ELDRITCH** with ever faithful drum machine adopted

The SISTERHOOD

—— recruited **PATRICIA MORRISON** (b.14 Jan'62) – bass, vocals (ex-FUR BIBLE, ex-GUN CLUB) / **JAMES RAY** – guitar / **ALAN VEGA** – synthesizers (ex-SUICIDE) / **LUCAS FOX** – drums (ELDRITCH moved to Berlin, Germany)

		Merciful	not iss.
Feb 86.	(7") *(SIS 001)* **GIVING GROUND (remix). / GIVING GROUND (album version)**		-
Jul 86.	(lp/c) *(SIS 020/+C)* **GIFT**	90	-

– Jihad / Colours / Giving ground / Finland red, Egypt white / Rain from Heaven. *(cd-iss. Sep89; SIS 020CD) (re-iss. Jul94 cd/c; 1131684-2/-4)*

—— JAMES RAY went solo (backed with The PERFORMANCE), subsequently issuing a couple of 45's, 'MEXICO SUNDOWN BLUES' and 'TEXAS', for 'Merciful Release'. At the turn of the decade, he and his new outfit, JAMES RAY'S GANGWAR, issued a few more, 'DUSTBOAT' and 'WITHOUT CONSCIENCE', the former from a part compilation set, 'A NEW KIND OF ASSASSIN' (1989). In 1992 and '93, the band delivered two more, 'DIOS ESTA DE NUESTRO LADO' and 'THIRD GENERATION'.

The SISTERS OF MERCY

—— were once again **ELDRITCH + MORRISON** obtaining rights to name

		Merciful-WEA	Elektra
Sep 87.	(7") *(MR 39)* **THIS CORROSION. / TORCH**	7	
	(c-s+=/12"+=/cd-s+=) *(MR 39 C/T/CD)* – Colours.		
Nov 87.	(lp/c)(cd) *(MR 441 L/C)(242246-2)* <60762> **FLOODLAND**	9	

– Dominion / Mother Russia / Flood I / Lucretia my reflection / 1959 / This corrosion / Flood II / Driven like the snow / Neverlan. *(c+=)*– Torch. *(cd-s++=)* – Colours.

Feb 88.	(7") *(MR 43)* **DOMINION. / SANDSTORM / UNTITLED**	13	-
	(d12"+=) *(MR 43TB)* – Emma.		
	(c-s+=/3"cd-s+=) *(MR 43 C/CD)* – Ozy-Mandias.		
May 88.	(7"/ext.12"/ext.3"cd-s) *(MR 44/+T/CD)* **LUCRETIA MY REFLECTION. / LONG TRAIN**	20	

—— (Feb'90) **ELDRITCH** w/drum machine, recruited complete new line-up / **TONY JAMES** (b.1956) – bass, vocals (ex-SIGUE SIGUE SPUTNIK, ex-GENERATION X) / **ANDREAS BRUHN** (b. 5 Nov'67, Hamburg, Germany) – guitar / **TIM BRICHENO** (b. 6 Jul'63, Huddersfield, England) – guitar (ex-ALL ABOUT EVE) / guests were **MAGGIE REILLY** – b.vocals (ex-MIKE OLDFIELD) / **JOHN PERRY** – guitar (ex-ONLY ONES)

Oct 90.	(7"/c-s) *(MR 47/+C)* <66595> **MORE. / YOU COULD BE THE ONE**	21	
	(cd-s+=/cd-s+=) *(MR 47CD/+X)* – ('A'extended).		
Oct 90.	(cd)(c/lp) *(9031 72663-2)(MR 449 C/L)* <61017> **VISION THING**	11	

– Vision thing / Ribons / Destination Boulevard / Something fast / When you don't see me / Doctor Jeep / More / I was wrong.

Dec 90.	(7") *(MR 51)* **DOCTOR JEEP. / KNOCKIN' ON HEAVEN'S DOOR (live)**	37	
	(12"+=/cd-s+=) *(MR 51 T/CD)* – ('A'extended).		
	(ext.12") *(MR 51TX)* – Burn (live) / Amphetamine logic (live).		

—— (Oct91) **TONY JAMES** split from ELDRITCH amicably.

—— Next featured vocals by **OFRA HAZA**

		East West	Elektra
Apr 92.	(7") *(MR 53)* **TEMPLE OF LOVE (1992). / I WAS WRONG (American fade)**	3	
	(ext.12"+=) *(MR 53T)* – Vision thing (Canadian club mix).		
	(cd-s+=) *(MR 53CD)* – When you don't see me (German release).		
Apr 92.	(cd)(c/d-lp) *(9031 76476-2)(MR 449 C/L)* <61306> **SOME GIRLS WANDER BY MISTAKE** (1980-1983 material)	5	

– Alice / Floorshow / Phantom / 1969 / Kiss the carpet / Lights / Valentine / Fix /

Burn / Kiss the carpet (reprise) / Temple of love / Heartland / Gimme shelter / Damage done / Watch / Home of the hitmen / Body electric / Adrenochrome / Anaconda.

—— now just **ANDREW ELDRITCH** on own with guests

Aug 93.	(7"/c-s) *(MR 59/+C)* **UNDER THE GUN. / ALICE (1993)**	19	-
	(12"+=/cd-s+=) *(MR 59 T/CD)* – ('A'-Jutland mix).		
Aug 93.	(cd/c/d-lp) *(4509 93579-2/-4/-1)* <61399-2/-4> **GREATEST HITS VOLUME 1 – A SLIGHT CASE OF OVERBOMBING** (compilation)	14	

– Under the gun / Temple of love (1992) / Vision thing / Detonation boulevard / Doctor Jeep / More / Lucretia my reflection / Dominion – Mother / This corrosion / No time to cry / Walk away / Body and soul.

—— ELDRITCH and his gang seem to have split from the music scene

– compilations, etc. –

Jan 94.	(cd) *Cleopatra; (CLEO 6642CD)* **FIRST, LAST FOREVER**		-

---

60 FT DOLLS   (dig out; Great Alt & Indie . . .)

Roni SIZE (REPRAZENT)

Born: 29 Oct'69, Bristol, England. Kicked out of school at the age of 16, SIZE became a DJ on the thriving late 80's Bristol club/music scene as well as running a music workshop at the 'Basement Project', a local youth centre. Familiarising himself with the complexities of samplers and drum machines, the budding producer progressed to cutting his own dub plates and after releasing his debut on the label ('V' records) run by fellow Bristolian drum'n'bass purveyor, DJ KRUST, SIZE subsequently initiated his own imprint, 'Full Cycle'. Developing his style over a string of 12" vinyl releases, both on 'V' (notably the sabre rattling snares and chunky basslines of '94's 'TIMESTRETCH') and 'Full Cycle', this dreadlocked pioneer eventually arrived at the tough but soulful drum'n'bass sophistication of the massively acclaimed 'NEW FORMS' (1997) album. Though masterminded by SIZE, the record was recorded via an eclectic posse of stalwarts known as REPRAZENT i.e. silky voiced chanteuse, ONALLEE, MC DYNAMITE, longtime musical collaborators DJ's KRUST, DIE and SUV along with a trio of conventional musicians; bassist SI JOHN (of groundbreaking Bristolian acid-jazzers, The FEDERATION), guitarist STEVE GRAHAM and PORTISHEAD sticksman, CLIVE DEAMER. Released on the ever hip 'Talkin' Loud' label and surprise winner of the prestigious 'Mercury' music award, the aptly titled 'NEW FORMS' took the genre into uncharted territory, as equally innovative as the work of GOLDIE and LTJ BUKEM yet more readily accessible. Clocking in at over two hours, the album was perhaps too much to take in one sitting although given time, its charms soon revealed themselves; a self-acknowledged fan of funk and soul (QUINCY JONES was a much cited influence), SIZE had managed to craft a record that was synapse-shatteringly futuristic yet retained an organic warmth missing in much modern dance music. The Top 20 charting single, 'BROWN PAPER BAG' was as fine a taster as any, its seismic bass depth charges and free flowing rapping more than justifying the not inconsiderable hype (it's now a backing recording used by the BBC on some of their TV programmes – listen out!). With a plethora of side projects in the pipeline and artists queuing up for remix work, it seems that for once, SIZE really does matter. BREAKBEAT ERA was RONI and DJ DIE's next musical operation, jazzy drum'n'bass were obviously still the concept although singer-songwriter LEONIE LAWS had joined the posse. Having delivered a one-off set, 'ULTRA OBSCENE' (1999), RONI RIZE was scheming yet another futuristic assault.

Album rating: NEW FORMS (*9) / Breakbeat Era: ULTRA-OBSCENE (*7)

RONI SIZE – vocals (with various technicians)

		V	not iss.
1992.	(12"; RONI SIZE & D.J. DIE) *(V 005)* **IT'S A JAZZ THING. / PLAY IT FOR ME (DJ DIE)**		-
	(re-iss. Dec94; same) (re-iss. Apr97; V 022) (re-iss. May98 on 'Ultra'; UL 020)		
1993.	(12") *(V 006)* **MUSIC BOX**		-
Nov 94.	(12") *(V 007)* **TIMESTRETCH**		-
May 95.	(12") *(V 008R)* **ALL THE CREW (Big Up remix)**		-
Jun 95.	(12") *(V 010)* **FASHION**		-

		Full Cycle	not iss.
Jun 95.	(12"; RONI SIZE & D.J. KRUST) *(FCY 2)* **DAYLIGHT. / TOUCH**		-
Jun 96.	(12") *(FCY 9)* **BRUTE FORCE**		-
	(re-iss. Apr97; same)		

—— early in '97, a SKYLAB vs RONI SIZE 12"/cd-s/12"remix 'THE TRIP' was issued by the 'Eye Q' imprint; (EYEUK 011/+CD/R)

RONI SIZE REPRAZENT

RONI SIZE – vocals / **ONALLEE** (TRACIE) – vocals (ex-BLUE AEROPLANES, ex-SOURMASH) / **DYNAMITE MC** (DOMINIC) – rap / **FI JOHNS** – bass (of The FEDERATION) / **CLIVE DEAMER** – drums (of PORTISHEAD, ex-HAWKWIND) / **STEVE GRAHAM** – acoustic guitar / **DJ DIE** – turntables / **DJ KRUST** – turntables / **DJ SUV** – turntables

		Talkin' Loud	Polygram
Jun 97.	(12"/cd-s) *(TLX/TLCD 21)* **SHARE THE FALL / NEW FORMS (featuring BAHAMADIA)**	37	
	(12") *(TLXX 21)* – ('A'mixes by; Grooverider / Krust / Way Out West).		

Jun 97. (cd/c/d-lp) (<534 933-2/-4/-1>) **NEW FORMS**   8   Oct97
– Railing / Brown paper bag / New forms / Let's get it on / Digital / Matter of fact /
Mad cat / Heroes / Share the fall / Watching windows / Beatbox / Morse code /
Destination. *(some w/free cd/c/d-lp+=)* – Intro / Hi potent / Trust me / Change my
life / Share the fall / Down / Jazz / Ballet dance.
Aug 97. (12"/cd-s) *(TL X/CD 25)* **HEROES. / ELECTRIKA**   31
(12") *(TLXX 25)* – ('A'mixes).
Oct 97. (12") *(TLX 28)* <568.203-2> **BROWN PAPER BAG. /**
WESTERN   20   -
(cd-s+=) *(TLCC 28)* – Hi potent.
(12") *(TLXX 28)* – ('A'mixes).
Mar 98. (12"/cd-s) *(TLX/TLCD 31)* **WATCHING WINDOWS (vocal**
mix) / (Ed Rush & Optical mixes) / (DJ Die mix) /
(Nuyorican mix)   28
(12"/cd-s) *(TLDD/TLXX 31)* – ('A'remixes).
Dec 98. (ltd-12") *(566589-1)* **WATCHING WINDOWS (DJ Die mixes)**   -

BREAKBEAT ERA

RONI SIZE / **DJ DIE** / + **LEONIE LAWS** – vocals / with **ADRIAN UTLEY** + **JEFF ROSE** +
ROB CHANT – guitar / **TOBY PASCOE** – drums

		X.L.	Interscope
Jul 98.	(c-s)(12")(cd-s) *(XLC 95)(XLT 95)(XLS 95CD)* **BREAKBEAT ERA. / BREAKBEAT ERA**	38	-
Aug 99.	(12") *(XLT 107)* <97124> **ULTRA-OBSCENE. / OUR DISEASE**	48	

(cd-s+=) *(XLS 107CD2)* – Rancid (Rinse revamp).
(cd-s) *(XLS 107CD)* – ('A'side) / Life is my friend / Love to be loved.
Aug 99. (cd/lp) *(XLDCD/XLLP 130)* <90428> **ULTRA-OBSCENE**   31   Sep99
– Past life / Rancid / Ultra-obscene / Bulitproof / Breakbeat era / Time 4 breaks /
Anti-everything / Late morning / Our disease / Maz / Control freak / Terrible funk /
Sex change / Life is my friend. *(also 7x12"box+=; XLDX 130)* – Rancid (rinse
revamp) / Our disease (remix) / Control freak (instrumental).
Nov 99. (12") *(<FH 719-12>)* **BULLITPROOF (remixes)**
(above issued on 'Under One Sun')

RONI SIZE

		Full Cycle	not iss.
Nov 99.	(12") *(FCY 020)* **26 BASS. / SNAPSHOT**		-

SKID ROW

Formed: Dublin, Ireland . . . 1968 by 16 year-old guitarist GARY MOORE
with PHIL LYNOTT (vocals, bass), ERIC BELL (guitar) and BRIAN
DOWNEY (drums), the line-up being dramatically altered a year later, when
all but MOORE departed to form THIN LIZZY. These future "Vagabonds
Of The Western World" were replaced by BRENDAN "BRUSH" SHIELS
and NOEL BRIDGEMAN, the revamped band releasing a couple of Irish
45's, before signing to 'C.B.S.' in 1970. Their debut album grazed the UK
Top 30, its promising fusion of hard-edged power blues and progressive
jazz-rock landing US support slots to the likes of CANNED HEAT and
SAVOY BROWN. A follow-up set, '34 HOURS' surfaced in 1971, although
it soon became clear that MOORE's talents were mushrooming beyond the
group's limited parameters. PAUL CHAPMAN was subsequently secured as
MOORE's replacement, his tenure short-lived as the group finally crashed the
following year.
Album rating: SKID (*6) / 34 HOURS (*5)

BRUSH SHIELS – vocals, bass / **GARY MOORE** – guitar, vocals / **NOEL BRIDGEMAN** –
drums, vocals

		Song	not iss.
1969.	(7") **NEW PLACES, OLD FACES. / MISDEMEANOR DREAM FELICITY**	-	- Irish
1969.	(7") **SATURDAY MORNING MAN. / MERVYN ALDRIDGE**	-	- Irish

		C.B.S.	Columbia
1970.	(7") *(CBS 4893)* **SANDIE'S GONE. / (part 2)**		
Oct 70.	(lp) *(CBS 63965)* **SKID ROW**	30	-

– Mad dog woman / Virgo's daughter / Heading home again / An awful lot of
woman / Unco-up showband blues / For those who do / After I'm gone / The man
who never was / Felicity. *(cd-iss. Aug94 on 'Columbia'; 477360-2)*
Apr 71. (7") *(CBS 7181)* **NIGHT OF THE WARM WITCH. / MR.**
DELUXE
1971. (lp) *(CBS 64411)* <30913> **34 HOURS**
– "Night of the warm witch" including (a. The following morning) / "First thing in
the morning" including (a. The last thing at night) / "Mar" / "Go, I'm never gonna let
you" (part 1) including ("Go, I'm never gonna let you" part 2) / "Lonesome still" /
"The love story" (part 1) including ("The love story" part 2) ("The love story" part
3) ("The love story" part 4). *(cd-iss. 1990's on 'Repertoire'; REP 4073) (cd re-iss.
May95 on 'Columbia'; 480525-2)*

──── **PAUL CHAPMAN** – guitar, vocals, repl. GARY MOORE who joined folkies DR.
STRANGELY STRANGE before going solo, etc in 1973. BRIDGEMAN later
sessioned for CLANNAD and joined The WATERBOYS.

– compilations, etc. –

Jun 76. (lp) *Release; (RRL 8001)* **ALIVE & KICKING**   -   - Irish
Apr 87. (lp/c; as GARY MOORE / BRUSH SHIELS / NOEL
BRIDGEMAN) *C.B.S.; (450 263-1/-4)* **SKID ROW**
– Benedict's cherry wine / Saturday morning man / Crystal ball / Mr. Deluxe / Girl
called winter / Morning star avenue / Silver bird. *(cd-iss. Jun94 on 'Castle'; CLACD
343)*

SKID ROW

Formed: New Jersey, New York, USA . . . late '86 by DAVE 'Snake' SABO
and RACHEL BOLAN (male!). Following the addition of SCOTTI HILL,
ROB AFFUSO and Canadian born frontman SEBASTIAN BACH, the band
line-up was complete, a subsequent management deal (with Doc McGhee)
and a support slot on BON JOVI's 1989 US tour a result of SABO's personal
connection with JON BON JOVI. Signed worldwide to 'Atlantic' in 1988,
the group enjoyed heavy MTV coverage of their summer '89 debut single,
'YOUTH GONE WILD', BACH's blonde-haired good looks and brattish
behaviour proving a compelling focal point. Combining the metallic glam of
MOTLEY CRUE / L.A. GUNS with the nihilistic energy of the SEX PISTOLS,
their eponymous debut album narrowly missed the US Top 5, going on to sell
a staggering four million copies. Sales were boosted by the Top 10 success
of subsequent singles, the angst-ridden '18 AND LIFE' and token ballad, 'I
REMEMBER YOU'. Controversy followed after BACH was charged with
assault (following a bottle throwing incident), the singer escaping jail with
three years probation. With their reputation as rock bad boys complete, the
group stormed into the US No.1 slot (UK No.5) with a follow-up, 'SLAVE
TO THE GRIND' (1991). A more aggressive affair, the punk influence was
more pronounced, with the group even releasing a fiery cover of the 'Pistols'
'HOLIDAYS IN THE SUN' (originally recorded as part of the 1989 metal
compilation, 'Stairway To Heaven, Highway To Hell') as the B-side of the
'WASTED TIME' single. No hits were forthcoming, however, and the record
failed to match sales of the debut. A third album eventually appeared in 1995,
'SUBHUMAN RACE', the record faring better in the UK (Top 10) than
their native USA where it barely made the Top 40. • **Songwriters:** BOLAN
w/ SNAKE + BACH or BOLAN w / AFFUSO + HILL. Covered PSYCHO
THERAPY (Ramones) / C'MON AND LOVE ME (Kiss) / DELIVERING
THE GOODS (Judas Priest) / WHAT YOU'RE DOING (Rush) / LITTLE
WING (Jimi Hendrix).
Album rating: SKID ROW (*6) / SLAVE TO THE GRIND (*6) / B-SIDE OURSELVES
collection (*4) / SUBHUMAN RACE (*5) / 40 SEASONS – THE BEST OF SKID ROW
compilation (*6)

SEBASTIAN BACH (b. SEBASTIAN BIERK, 3 Apr'68, Bahamas) – vocals; repl. MATT
FALLON / **DAVE 'Snake' SABO** (b.16 Sep'62) – guitar / **SCOTTI HILL** (b.31 May'64) –
guitar / **RACHEL BOLAN** (b. 9 Feb'64) – bass / **ROB AFFUSO** (b. 1 Mar'63) – drums

		Atlantic	Atlantic
Nov 89.	(7"/7"sha-pic-d) *(A 8935/+P)* <88935> **YOUTH GONE WILD. / SWEET LITTLE SISTER**	42	99 May89

(12"+=/cd-s+=) *(A 8935T)* – Makin' a mess (live).
Dec 89. (lp/c/cd) *(K 781936-1/-4/-2)* <81936> **SKID ROW**   30   6 Feb90
– Big guns / Sweet little sister / Can't stand the heartache / Piece of me / 18 and
life / Rattlesnake shake / Youth gone wild / Here I am / Makin' a mess / I remember
you / Midnight – Tornado. *(cd re-iss. Feb95; same)*
Jan 90. (7"one-sided/7"sha-pic-d) *(A 8883/+P)* <88883> **18 AND**
LIFE. / MIDNIGHT – TORNADO   12   4 Jul89
(12"+=/cd-s+=) *(A 8883 T/CD)* – Here I am (live).
Mar 90. (7"/7"s/c-s) *(A 8886/+X/C)* <88886> **I REMEMBER YOU. /**
MAKIN' A MESS   36   6 Nov89
(12"+=/cd-s+=) *(A 8886 TW/CD)* – Big guns.
(10"+=) *(A 8886T)* – ('A'live).

		East West	Atlantic
Jun 91.	(7"sha-pic-d/c-s) *(A 7673/+C)* <87673> **MONKEY BUSINESS. / SLAVE TO THE GRIND**	19	

(12"+=/cd-s+=) *(A 7673 TW/CD)* – Riot act.
Jun 91. (cd)(lp/c) *(7567 82242-2)*(WX 423/+C) **SLAVE TO THE**
GRIND   5   1
– Monkey business / Slave to the grind / The threat / Quicksand Jesus / Psycho love /
Get the fuck out / Livin' on a chain gang / Creepshow / In a darkened room / Riot
act / Mudkicker / Wasted time.
Sep 91. (7"/c-s) *(A 7603/+C)* **SLAVE TO THE GRIND. / C'MON**
AND LOVE ME   43   -
(12") *(A 7603TX)* – ('A'side) / Creepshow / Beggar's day.
(cd-s++=) *(A 7603CD)* – (above 'B'side).
Nov 91. (7") *(A 7570)* **WASTED TIME. / HOLIDAYS IN THE SUN**   20   -
(12"+=) *(A 7570T)* – What you're doing / Get the fuck out (live).
(cd-s+=) *(A 7570CD)* – Psycho love / Get the fuck out (live).
(12"pic-d) *(A 7570TP)* – ('A'side) / Psycho love.
Dec 91. (c-s,cd-s) <87565> **WASTED TIME / C'MON AND LOVE**
ME   -   88
Aug 92. (7"/c-s) *(A 7444/+C)* **YOUTH GONE WILD. / DELIVERIN'**
THE GOODS   22   -
(12"+=/cd-s+=) *(A 7444 T/CD)* – Get the funk out / Psycho therapy.
Sep 92. (m-cd/m-c) <(7567 82431-2/-4)> **B-SIDE OURSELVES**   58
– Psychotherapy / C'mon and love me / Deliverin' the goods / What you're doing /
Little wing.
Mar 95. (cd/c/lp) <(7567 82730-2/-4/-1)> **SUBHUMAN RACE**   8   35
– My enemy / Firesign / Bonehead / Beat yourself blind / Eileen / Remains to be
seen / Subhuman race / Frozen / Into another / Face against my soul / Medicine jar /
Breakin' down / Ironwill.
Nov 95. (7"colrd) *(A 7135)* **BREAKIN' DOWN. / RIOT ACT (live)**   48
(cd-s) *(A 7135CD1)* – ('A'side) / Firesign (demo) / Slave to the grind (live) /
Monkey business (live).
(cd-s) *(A 7135CD2)* – ('A'side) / Frozen (demo) / Beat yourself blind (live) /
Psychotherapy (live).

──── split early in 1996, but will reform under a new banner in '98/'99. **SEAN McCABE**
– vocals; repl. BACH who went solo

– compilations, etc. –

Jul 98. (cd/c) *Atlantic; <(7567 83103-2/-4)>* **40 SEASONS – THE BEST OF SKID ROW** [ ] [-]
– Youth gone wild / 18 and life / Piece of me / I remember you / Threat / Psycho love / Monkey business / Quicksand Jesus / Slave to the grind / Into another (mix) / Frozen / My enemy / Breakin' down (mix) / Beat yourself blind (live) / Forever / Fire in the hole.

SKIDS

Formed: Dunfermline, Scotland . . . Spring 1977 by RICHARD JOBSON and STUART ADAMSON together with BILL SIMPSON and TOM KELLICHAN. Careering into the wreckage of the post-punk music scene with the self-financed 'CHARLES' single, the band soon found themselves with a deal courtesy of the ever eclectic 'Virgin' label. After a couple of minor hit singles, the group hit the UK Top 10 with 'INTO THE VALLEY', a shining example of The SKIDS' anthemic, new wave warriors style. In addition to JOBSON's highly distinctive, affected vocals and ADAMSON's strident axework (which he'd later perfect in BIG COUNTRY), The SKIDS were notable for their clever visual image (i.e. JOBSON's kick-dance and ultra-slick wavey hairdo). A debut album, 'SCARED TO DANCE' (1979), made the UK Top 20 and established the group as a more tasteful Caledonian alternative to The BAY CITY ROLLERS. Later that Spring, The SKIDS scored another Top 20 hit single with 'MASQUERADE', a highlight of the BILL NELSON-produced follow-up album, 'DAYS IN EUROPA' (1979), alongside the almost militaristic clarion call of 'WORKING FOR THE YANKEE DOLLAR'. All wasn't well within The SKIDS camp, however, personnel upheaval (leading to an all-new rhythm section of RUSSELL WEBB and MIKE BAILLIE) adding to criticisms of JOBSON's increasing lyrical complexities and the group's more schitzo pop/experimental sound. Despite all this, a third album, 'THE ABSOLUTE GAME' (1980) saw a return to form of sorts, furnishing the group with their one and only Top 10 set. ADAMSON became increasingly disillusioned, however, and finally departed the following summer. Left to his own devices, JOBSON dominated The SKIDS' final album, 'JOY' (1981), an at times trad/folk concept effort which met with a frosty critical reception and signalled the subsequent demise of the group early in '82. While ADAMSON went on to massive success with "bagpipe"-guitar rockers, BIG COUNTRY, JOBSON concentrated on a solo career which extended to writing (and recording) poetry. He then went on to form the short-lived and critically derided ARMOURY SHOW along with ex-MAGAZINE men, JOHN McGEOGH and JOHN DOYLE, releasing a sole album, 'WAITING FOR THE FLOODS' (1985). More recently, JOBSON's recording career has taken a backseat to his more successful forays into modelling and TV journalism. • **Songwriters:** JOBSON lyrics/group compositions, except ALL THE YOUNG DUDES (hit; Mott The Hoople) / BAND PLAYED WALTZING MATILDA (Australian trad.). • **Trivia:** In 1981, JOBSON published book of poetry, 'A MAN FOR ALL SEASONS'.

Album rating: SCARED TO DANCE (*8) / DAYS IN EUROPA (*6) / THE ABSOLUTE GAME (*6) / JOY (*4) / DUNFERMLINE compilation (*7) / SWEET SUBURBIA – THE BEST OF THE SKIDS compilation (*8)

RICHARD JOBSON (b. 6 Apr'60) – vocals, guitar / **STUART ADAMSON** (b.WILLIAM STUART ADAMSON, 11 Apr'58, Manchester, England) – lead guitar, vocals / **BILL SIMPSON** – bass / **TOM KELLICHAN** – drums

	No-Bad	not iss.
Mar 78. (7"m) *(NB 1)* **CHARLES.** / REASONS / TEST-TUBE BABIES	[ ]	[-]
	Virgin	not iss.
Sep 78. (7",7"white) *(VS 227)* **SWEET SUBURBIA.** / OPEN SOUND	70	[-]
Oct 78. (7"red-ep/12"red-ep) *(VS 232/+12)* **WIDE OPEN**	48	[-]

– The saints are coming / Of one skin / Confusion / Night and day.

Feb 79. (7",7"white) *(VS241)* **INTO THE VALLEY.** / T.V. STARS	10	[-]
Feb 79. (lp/c) *(V/TCV 2116)* **SCARED TO DANCE**	19	[-]

– Into the valley / Scared to dance / Of one skin / Dossier (of fallibility) / Melancholy soldiers / Hope and glory / The saints are coming / Six times / Calling the tune / Integral plot / Charles / Scale. *(re-iss. Apr84 lp/c; OVED/+C 41) (cd-iss. Jun90+=; CDV 2116)* – Sweet suburbia / Open sound / TV stars / Night and day / Contusion / Reasons / Test tube babies. *<US cd-iss. 1991 on 'Caroline'; CAROL 1817-2>*

May 79. (7") *(VS 262)* **MASQUERADE.** / OUT OF TOWN	14	[-]

(d7"+=) *(VS 262-12)* – Another emotion / Aftermath dub.

———— **RUSTY EGAN** – drums (ex-RICH KIDS) repl. KELLICHAN

Sep 79. (7") *(VS 288)* **CHARADE.** / GREY PARADE	31	[-]
Oct 79. (lp/c) *(V/TCV 2138)* **DAYS IN EUROPA**	32	[-]

– Animation * / Charade / Dulce et decorum (pro patria mor) / Pros and cons / Home of the saved / Working for the yankee dollar / The olympian / Thanatos / Masquerade / A day in Europa / Peaceful times. *(re-dist.Mar80 += *) (re-iss. Mar84 lp/c; OVED/+C 42)*

Nov 79. (7") *(VS 306)* **WORKING FOR THE YANKEE DOLLAR.** / VANGUARD'S CRUSADE	20	[-]

(d7"+=) *(VS 306)* – All the young dudes / Hymns from a haunted ballroom.

———— **RUSSELL WEBB** – bass, vocals (ex-ZONES, ex-SLIK) repl. SIMPSON / **MIKE BAILLIE** – drums (ex-INSECT BITES) repl. EGAN who joined VISAGE

Feb 80. (7") *(VS 323)* **ANIMATION.** / PROS AND CONS	56	[-]
Jul 80. (7") *(VS 359)* **CIRCUS GAMES.** / ONE DECREE	32	[-]
Sep 80. (lp/c) *(V/TCV 2174)* **THE ABSOLUTE GAME**	9	[-]

– Circus games / Out of town / Goodbye civilian / The children saw the shame / A woman in winter / Hurry on boys / Happy to be with you / The Devil's decade / One decree / Arena. *(free-lp w.a.) (VDJ 333)* **STRENGTH THROUGH JOY** *(re-iss. Mar84 lp/c; OVED/+C 43)*

Oct 80. (7"/7"pic-d) *(VS/+P 373)* **GOODBYE CIVILIAN.** / MONKEY McGUIRE MEETS SPECKY POTTER BEHIND THE LOCHORE INSTITUTE	52	[-]
Nov 80. (7") *(VSK 101)* **A WOMAN IN WINTER.** / WORKING FOR THE YANKEE DOLLAR (live)	49	[-]

———— **KENNY HYSLOP** (b.14 Feb'51, Helensburgh, Scotland) – drums (ex-ZONES, ex-SLIK) repl. BAILLIE who joined EPSILON

Aug 81. (7"/12") *(VS 401/+12)* **FIELDS.** / BRAVE MAN	[ ]	[-]

———— **JOBSON + WEBB** recruited **PAUL WISHART** – saxophone, flute to repl. ADAMSON who formed BIG COUNTRY and HYSLOP who joined SIMPLE MINDS. Session people on album incl. **J.J. JOHNSON** – drums / **The ASSOCIATES / VIRGINIA ASTLEY / MIKE OLDFIELD** – guitar / **KEN LOCKIE / TIM CROSS** – piano / **ALAN DARBY** – guitar

Oct 81. (7") *(VS 449)* **IONA.** / BLOOD AND SPOIL	[ ]	[-]
Nov 81. (lp/c) *(V/TCV 2217)* **JOY**	[ ]	[-]

– Blood and soil / A challenge, the wanderer / Men of mercy / A memory / Iona / In fear of fire / Brothers / And the band played Waltzing Matilda / The men of the fall / The sound of retreat (instrumental) / Fields. *(re-iss. 1988 lp/c; OVED/+C 200)*

———— folded early '82 with JOBSON already concentrating on poetry & solo work

– compilations, etc. –

on 'Virgin' unless mentioned otherwise

May 82. (lp/c) *(VM/+C 2)* **FANFARE**	[ ]	[-]
May 83. (12"ep) *(VS 591-12)* **INTO THE VALLEY / MASQUERADE. / SCARED TO DANCE / WORKING FOR THE YANKEE DOLLAR**	[ ]	[-]
Jul 87. (cd) *(CDVM 9022)* **DUNFERMLINE (THE SKIDS' FINEST MOMENTS)**	[ ]	[-]
Feb 92. (m-cd) *Windsong; (<WINCD 008>)* **BBC RADIO 1 LIVE IN CONCERT** (live)	[ ]	[-]
Jan 95. (cd) *(CDOVD 457)* **SWEET SUBURBIA – THE BEST OF THE SKIDS**	[ ]	[-]

– Into the valley / Charles / The saints are coming / Scared to dance / Sweet suburbia / Of one skin / Night and day / Animation / Working for the yankee dollar / Charade / Masquerade / Circus games / Out of town / Goodbye civilian / A woman in winter / Hurry on boys / Iona / Fields.

SKIN (dig out; Great Metal . . .)

SKUNK ANANSIE

Formed: London, England . . . early 1994 by striking, shaven-headed black lesbian frontwoman, SKIN and bassist CASS LEWIS. With ACE and ROBBIE FRANCE completing the line-up, SKUNK ANANSIE kicked up enough of a stink to get themselves signed after only a handful of gigs. Their first single, however, was an unofficial limited edition mail order affair lifted from a BBC Radio One Evening Session, 'LITTLE BABY SWASTIKKKA'. A debut single proper, 'SELLING JESUS' hit the shops and the Top 50 in March '95, its controversial content attracting even more interest than the band's burgeoning live reputation. A further couple of furious indie-metallic missives followed in the shape of 'I CAN DREAM' and 'CHARITY', while the band hooked up with labelmate BJORK on her 'Army Of Me' single. Surely one of the most radical acts to ever be associated with the metal scene, the intense interest surrounding scary SKIN and her uncompromising musical vision/political agenda guaranteed a Top 10 placing for the debut album, 'PARANOID & SUNBURNT' (1995). One of the record's most soul-wrenching tracks, 'WEAK', became their biggest hit to date (Top 20) the following January, SKIN's cathartic howl akin to a more soulful PATTI SMITH. Temporary replacement LOUIS was succeeded in turn by MARK RICHARDSON prior to their next Top 20 hit, 'ALL I WANT', one of the many highlights on their second set, 'STOOSH' (1996). Even more scathing than their debut, this angst-ridden collection saw SKUNK ANANSIE championed by Kerrang!, the lead track, 'YES IT'S FUCKING POLITICAL' summing things up perfectly. Riding high in the end of year polls, the Top 10 album contained a further three hit singles, 'TWISTED (EVERYDAY HURTS)', 'HEDONISM (JUST BECAUSE YOU FEEL GOOD)' and 'BRAZEN (WEEP)'. Subsequently signing to 'Virgin' records, SKIN and her band previewed their excellent third album, 'POST ORGANIC CHILL' (1999), with yet another Top 20 single, 'CHARLIE BIG POTATO'; sonic ballads 'SECRETLY' and 'LATELY' followed it into the UK charts shortly afterwards. • **Songwriters:** SKIN – ARRAN, some with other two.

Album rating: PARANOID & SUNBURNT (*7) / STOOSH (*9) / POST ORGANIC CHILL (*8)

SKIN (b. DEBORAH DYER, 3 Aug'67, Brixton, London) – vocals / **ACE** (b. MARTIN KENT, 30 Mar'67, Cheltenham, England) – guitar / **CASS LEWIS** (b. RICHARD LEWIS, 1 Sep'60) – bass / **ROBBIE FRANCE** – drums

	One Little Indian	Sony
Mar 95. (10"white/c-s) *(101 TP10/TP7C)* **SELLING JESUS. / THROUGH RAGE / YOU WANT IT ALL**	46	[-]
(cd-s+=) *(101 TP7CD)* – Skunk song. *(re-iss. Mar99; same)*		
Jun 95. (10"lime/c-s) *(121 TP10/TP7C)* **I CAN DREAM. / AESTHETIC ANARCHIST / BLACK SKIN SEXUALITY**	41	[-]
(cd-s+=) *(121 TPCD)* – Little baby Swastikkka. *(re-iss. Mar99; same)*		

———— **LOUIS** – drums; repl. ROBBIE

Aug 95. (c-s) *(131 TP7C)* **CHARITY / I CAN DREAM (version)** | 40 | - |
(cd-s+=) *(131 TP7CD)* – Punk by numbers.
(cd-s+=) *(131 TP7CDL)* – Kept my mouth shut.
(10"colrd) *(131 TP10)* – ('A'side) / Used / Killer's war.
(re-iss. Mar99; same)

Sep 95. (lp/c/cd) *(TPLP 55/+C/CD)* <67216> **PARANOID &** **SUNBURNT** | 8 | |
– Selling Jesus / Intellectualise my blackness / I can dream / Little baby swastikkka / All in the name of pity / Charity / It takes blood & guts to be this cool but I'm still just a cliche / Weak / And here I stand / 100 ways to be a good girl / Rise up. *(cd re-iss. same)*

Jan 96. (c-s) *(141 TP7C)* **WEAK / TOUR HYMN** | 20 | - |
(cd-s+=) *(141 TP7CD)* – Selling Jesus ('Strange Days' film version).
(cd-s) *(141 TP7CDL)* – ('A'side) / Charity (clit pop mix) / 100 ways to be a good girl (anti matter mix) / Rise up (Banhamoon mix).
(re-iss. Mar99; same)

Apr 96. (c-s) *(151 TP7C)* **CHARITY / I CAN DREAM (live)** | 20 | - |
(cd-s+=) *(151 TP7CD)* – Punk by numbers (live).
(cd-s) *(151 TP7CDL)* – ('A'side) / And here I stand (live) / It takes blood & guts to be this cool but I'm still just a cliche (live) / Intellectualise my blackness (live).
(re-iss. Mar99; same)

────── **MARK RICHARDSON** (b.28 May'70, Leeds, England) – drums; repl. LOUIS

Sep 96. (7") *(161 TP7)* **ALL I WANT. / FRAGILE** | 14 | - |
(cd-s+=) *(161 TP7CD)* – Punk by numbers / Your fight.
(cd-s) *(161 TP7CDL)* – ('A'side) / But the sex was good / Every bitch but me / Black skinhead coconut dogfight.
(re-iss. Mar99; same)

Oct 96. (lp/c/cd) *(TPLP 85/+C/CD)* <67555> **STOOSH** | 9 | |
– Yes it's fucking political / All I want / She's my heroine / Infidelity (only you) / Hedonism (just because you feel good) / Twisted (everyday hurts) / We love your apathy / Brazen (weep) / Pickin on me / Milk is my sugar / Glorious pop song.

Nov 96. (c-s) *(171 TP7C)* **TWISTED (EVERYDAY HURTS) / SHE'S** **MY HEROINE (polyester & cotton mix)** | 26 | - |
(cd-s+=) *(171 TP7CD1)* – Milk in my sugar (cement mix) / Pickin on me (instrumental pick'n'mix).
(cd-s) *(171 TP7CD2)* – ('A'-Cake mix) / Pickin on me (pick'n'mix) / Milk in my sugar (instrumental cement mix) / Yes it's fucking political (comix).
(re-iss. Mar99; same)

Jan 97. (c-ep/cd-ep) *(181 TP7C/+D)* **HEDONISM (JUST BECAUSE** **YOU FEEL GOOD) / SO SUBLIME / LET IT GO / STRONG** | 13 | - |
(cd-ep) *(181 TP7CDL)* – ('A'side) / Song recovery / Contraband / I don't believe.
(re-iss. Mar99; same)

Jun 97. (cd-ep) *(191 TP7CD1)* **BRAZEN (WEEP) / TWISTED** **(EVERYDAY HURTS) (radio 1 session) / ALL I WANT** **(radio 1 session) / IT TAKES BLOOD & GUTS TO BE THIS** **COOL BUT I'M STILL JUST A CLICHE (radio 1 session)** | 11 | - |
(cd-ep) *(191 TP7CD2)* – ('A'-Dreadzone remix) / ('A'-Hani's Weeping club mix) / ('A'-Ventura's Underworld mix) / ('A'-Stealth Sonic Orchestra remix) / ('A'-Cutfather & Joe electro mix).
(cd-ep) *(191 TP7CD3)* – ('A'-Junior Vasquez's Arena anthem) / ('A'-Paul Oakenfold & Steve Osborne mix) / ('A'-Dreadzone's instrumental mix) / ('A'-Junior Vasquez's riff dub) / ('A'-Hani's Hydro instrumental mix). *(re-iss. Mar99; same)*

| | Virgin | Virgin |
Mar 99. (c-s) *(VSC 1725)* **CHARLIE BIG POTATO / FEEL / 80'S** **MELLOW DRONE** | 17 | |
(cd-s+=) *(VSCDT 1725)* – ('A'-CD-Rom video).
(cd-s) *(VSCDX 1725)* – ('A'side) / Sane / Jack knife ginal.

Mar 99. (cd/c/lp) *(CD/TC+/V 2881)* **POST ORGANIC CHILL** | 16 | |
– Charlie big potato / On my hotel T.V. / We don't need who you think you are / Tracey's flaw / The skank heads / Lately / Secretly / Good things don't always come to you / Cheap honesty / You'll follow me down / And this is nothing that I thought I had / I'm not afraid.

May 99. (c-s/cd-s) *(VSC/+DT 1733)* **SECRETLY / KING PSYCHEDELIC** **SIZE / PAINKILLERS** | 16 | |
(cd-s) *(VSCDX 1733)* – ('A'side) / Breathing / ('A'-Optical vocal mix).

Jul 99. (c-s/cd-s) *(VSC/+DT 1738)* **LATELY / THE DECADENCE OF** **YOUR STARVATION / CHARLIE BIG POTATO (Smokin'** **Jo skin up mix)** | 33 | |
(cd-s) *(VSCDX 1738)* – ('A'side) / This pill's too painful / Secretly (Armand Van Helden's mix).

Oct 99. (c-s/cd-s) *(VSC/+DT 1754)* **YOU'LL FOLLOW ME DOWN /** **YOU'LL FOLLOW ME DOWN (The Rollo & Sister Bliss** **mix) / YOU'LL FOLLOW ME DOWN (Golden Ashes mix)** | | - |
(cd-s) *(VSCDX 1754)* – ('A'side) / Hedonism (just because you make me feel good) (live) / The skank heads (live).

SLADE

Formed: Wolverhampton, Midlands, England . . . 1964 as The VENDORS, by DAVE HILL and DON POWELL, becoming The IN-BE-TWEENS the following year and recording a demo EP for French label, 'Barclay'. Their official debut 45, 'YOU BETTER RUN' (with newcomers NODDY HOLDER and JIMMY LEA), flopped late in '66, the group retiring from studio activity until 1969 when they became AMBROSE SLADE at the suggestion of Fontana's Jack Baverstock. A belated debut album, 'BEGINNINGS', sold poorly although ex-ANIMALS bass player, CHAS CHANDLER, recognised the band's potential after spotting them performing in a London night club (the band now residing in the capital) and subsequently became their manager/producer. Kitted out in bovver boots, jeans, shirt and braces, SLADE topped their newly adopted 'ard look with skinheads all round, CHANDLER moulding the band's image and sound in an attempt to distance them from the fading hippy scene. Although they attracted a sizable grassroots following, SLADE's appropriately titled first album, 'PLAY IT LOUD' (on 'Polydor') failed to translate into sales. However, they finally cracked the UK Top 20

in May 1971 via a rousing cover of Bobby Marchan's 'GET DOWN AND GET WITH IT', the track bringing SLADE into the living rooms of the nation through a Top Of The Pops appearance. By this point, HOLDER and Co. had grown some hair, painted their boots sci-fi silver and initiated the roots of "Slademania" (foot-stomping now all the rage). The noisy, gravel-throated HOLDER (complete with tartan trousers, top hat and mutton-chop sideburns), the bare-chested, glitter-flecked HILL and the not so flamboyant LEA and POWELL, became part of the glam-metal brigade later in the year, 'COZ I LUV YOU' hitting the top of the charts for 4 weeks. Competing with the likes of GARY GLITTER, T. REX and SWEET, the lads amassed a string of anthemic UK chart toppers over the ensuing two years, namely 'TAKE ME BACK 'OME', 'MAMA WEER ALL CRAZEE NOW', 'CUM ON FEEL THE NOIZE', 'SKWEEZE ME PLEEZE ME' and the perennial festive fave 'MERRY XMAS EVERYBODY'. The noize level was markedly lower on the pop-ballad, 'EVERYDAY' (1974), a song that only hit No.3, glam-rock/pop shuddering to a halt around the same time. Their chart-topping albums, 'SLAYED?' (1972), 'SLADEST' (1973) and 'OLD NEW BORROWED AND BLUE' (1974) were now shoved to the back of people's record collections, PINK FLOYD, MIKE OLDFIELD and GENESIS now vying for the attention of the more discerning rock fan. Late '74 saw the release of a film/rockumentary 'SLADE IN FLAME'; issued as an album, it only managed a Top 10 placing. SLADE found it even harder to compete with the burgeoning punk/new wave scene, only re-emerging into the Top 10 in 1981 with 'WE'LL BRING THE HOUSE DOWN', released on their own 'Cheapskate' records. Three years later, the loveable rogues with the 'Bermingham' accent scored yet again, 'MY OH MY' just narrowly missing the No.1 spot, while the follow-up, 'RUN RUNAWAY' made the Top 10. Both records surprised observers by cracking the elusive US charts, the former hitting No.37, the latter No.20; a year previously, metal act, QUIET RIOT had taken Slade's 'CUM ON FEEL THE NOIZE' into the US Top 5 and subsequently charted with another, 'MAMA WEER ALL CRAZEE NOW'. SLADE continued on their merry way, untroubled by the fashion crimes of the 80's. The following decade saw the band chart once more, 'RADIO WALL OF SOUND' blasting out HOLDER's frantic yell to an appreciative Kerrang!- friendly audience. The jovial HOLDER has regained his footing as a celebrity in the 90's, VIC REEVES and BOB MORTIMER giving him and SLADE the highest accolade by inventing a whole series of irreverent sketches based around the band. OASIS, too, have contributed to the cult of NODDY, regularly performing 'CUM ON FEEL THE NOIZE' on stage. • **Songwriters:** HOLDER-LEA or LEA-POWELL penned except IN-BETWEENS:- TAKE A HEART (Sorrows) / CAN YOUR MONKEY DO THE DOG (Rufus Thomas) / YOU BETTER RUN (Rascals). AMBROSE SLADE:- BORN TO BE WILD (Steppenwolf) / AIN'T GOT NO HEAT (Frank Zappa) / IF THIS WORLD WERE MINE (Marvin Gaye) / FLY ME HIGH (Justin Hayward) / MARTHA MY DEAR (Beatles) / JOURNEY TO THE CENTER OF MY MIND (Ted Nugent). SLADE:- THE SHAPE OF THINGS TO COME (Max Frost & The Troopers; Mann-weill) / ANGELINA (Neil Innes) / COULD I (Griffin-Royer) / JUST A LITTLE BIT (?) / DARLING BE HOME SOON (Lovin' Spoonful) / LET THE GOOD TIMES ROLL (Shirley & Lee) / MY BABY LEFT ME – THAT'S ALL RIGHT (Elvis Presley) / PISTOL PACKIN' MAMA (Gene Vincent) / SOMETHIN' ELSE (Eddie Cochran) / OKEY COKEY (seasonal; trad) / HI HO SILVER LINING (Jeff Beck) / STILL THE SAME (Bob Seger) / YOU'LL NEVER WALK ALONE (Rogers-Hammerstein) / AULD LANG SYNE (trad.) / SANTA CLAUS IS COMING TO TOWN (festive) / LET'S DANCE (Chris Montez) / etc.

Best CD compilation: FEEL THE NOIZE: THE VERY BEST OF SLADE (*8)

The IN-BE-TWEENS

JOHNNY HOWELLS – vocals / **MICKEY MARSTON** – guitar / **DAVE HILL** (b. 4 Apr'52, Fleet Castle, Devon, England) – guitar / **DAVE JONES** – bass / **DON POWELL** (10 Sep'50, Bilston, Staffordshire) – drums

			Barclay	not iss.
1965.	(7"ep) **TAKE A HEART / LITTLE NIGHTINGALE.** / (2 tracks by 'The Hills')		-	- France
1965.	(7"ep) **TAKE A HEART. / CAN YOUR MONKEY DO THE DOG / OOP OOP I DO**		-	- France

────── **NODDY HOLDER** (b. NEVILLE HOLDER, 15 Jun'50, Walsall, England) – vox, guitar repl. HOWELLS / **JIM LEA** (b.14 Jun'52, Wolverhampton) – bass, piano repl. MARSTON + JONES

		Columbia	not iss.
Nov 66.	(7"; as N' BETWEENS) *(DB 8080)* **YOU BETTER RUN. / EVIL WITCHMAN**		

AMBROSE SLADE

(HOLDER, HILL, LEA + POWELL)

		Fontana	Fontana
Apr 69.	(lp) *(STL 5492)* <67592> **BEGINNINGS**		
	– Genesis / Everybody's next one / Knocking nails into my house / Roach daddy / Ain't got no heat / Pity the mother / Mad dog Cole / Fly me high / If this world were mine / Martha my dear / Born to be wild / Journey to the centre of my mind. *(re-iss. Jun91 on 'Polydor' cd/c; 849 185-2/-4)*		
May 69.	(7") *(TF 1015)* **GENESIS. / ROACH DADDY**		-

SLADE

(same line-up + label)

Oct 69.	(7") *(TF 1056)* **WILD WINDS ARE BLOWING. / ONE WAY HOTEL**		-

(Polydor / Cotillion)

Mar 70. (7") (TF 1079) **SHAPE OF THINGS TO COME. / C'MON C'MON** — | -

Sep 70. (7") (2058 054) **KNOW WHO YOU ARE. / DAPPLE ROSE** — | -

Nov 70. (lp) (2383 026) <9035> **PLAY IT LOUD**
– Raven / See us here / Dapple rose / Could I / One way hotel / The shape of things to come / Know who you are / I remember / Pouk Hill / Angelina / Dirty joker / Sweet box. (re-iss. Jun91 cd/c; 849 178-2/-4)

(Polydor / Polydor)

May 71. (7"m) (2058 112) <44128> **GET DOWN AND GET WITH IT. / DO YOU WANT ME / THE GOSPEL ACCORDING TO RASPUTIN** — 16

Oct 71. (7") (2058 155) **COZ I LUV YOU. / LIFE IS NATURAL** — 1

Jan 72. (7") (2058 195) <15041> **LOOK WOT YOU DUN. / CANDIDATE** — 4

Jan 72. (7") <15044> **COZ I LOVE YOU. / GOTTA KEEP A-ROCKIN' (live)** — -

Mar 72. (lp) (2383 101) <5508> **SLADE ALIVE! (live)** — 2
– Hear me calling / In like a shot from my gun / Darling be home soon / Know who you are / Gotta keep on rockin' / Get down and get with it / Born to be wild. (re-iss. Nov84 lp/c; SPE LP/MC 84) (re-iss. Jun91 cd/c; 841 114-2/-4)

May 72. (7") (2058 231) <15046> **TAKE ME BAK 'OME. / WONDERIN'** — 1 | 97 Sep72

Aug 72. (7") (2058 274) <15053> **MAMA WEER ALL CRAZEE NOW. / MAN WHO SPEAKS EVIL** — 1 | 76 Nov72

Nov 72. (7") (2058 312) <15060> **GUDBUY T'JANE. / I WON'T LET IT 'APPEN AGAIN** — 2 | 68 Mar73

Dec 72. (lp)(c) (2383 163) <5524> **SLAYED?** — 1 | 69
– How d'you ride / The whole world's goin' craze / Look at last nite / I won't let it 'appen again / Move over / Gudbuy t'Jane / Gudbuy gudbuy / Mama weer all crazee now / I don't mind / Let the good times roll. (cd-iss. May91; 849 180-2)

Feb 73. (7") (2058 339) <15069> **CUM ON FEEL THE NOIZE. / I'M MEE, I'M NOW AN' THAT'S ORL** — 1 | 98 May73

Jun 73. (7") (2058 377) **SKWEEZE ME PLEEZE ME. / KILL 'EM AT THE HOT CLUB TONITE** — 1

(Polydor / Reprise)

Jul 73. (7") <15080> **LET THE GOOD TIMES ROLL. / FEEL SO FINE – I DON' MINE** — - | -

Sep 73. (7") (2058 407) **MY FRIEND STAN. / MY TOWN** — 2

Sep 73. (lp) (2442 119) <2173> **SLADEST (compilation)** — 1
– Wild things are blowing / Shape of things to come / Know who you are / Pounk Hill / One way hotel / Get down and get with it / Coz I luv you / Look wot you dun / Tak me bak ome / Mama weer all crazee now / Gudbuy t'Jane / Look at last night / Cum on feel the noize / Skweeze me pleeze me. (cd-iss. Mar93; 837 103-2)

(Polydor / Warners)

Sep 73. (7") <1182> **SKWEEZE ME PLEEZE ME. / MY TOWN** —

Dec 73. (7") (2058 422) <7759> **MERRY XMAS EVERYBODY. / DON'T BLAME ME** — 1
(re-iss. Dec80, Dec81 (No.32), Dec82 (No.67), Dec83 (No.20), Dec84 (No.47).)

Feb 74. (lp) (2383 200) <2770> **OLD NEW BORROWED AND BLUE** <US title 'STOMP YOUR HANDS, CLAP YOUR FEET'> — 1
– Just want a little bit / When the lights are out / My town / Find yourself a rainbow / Miles out to sea / We're really gonna raise the roof / Do we still do it / How can it be / Don't blame me / My friend Stan / Everyday / Good time gals. (cd-iss. May91; 849 181-2)

Mar 74. (7") (2058 453) <7777> **EVERYDAY. / GOOD TIME GALS** — 3

Jun 74. (7") (2058 492) **THE BANGIN' MAN. / SHE DID IT TO ME** — 3

Jul 74. (7") <7808> **WHEN THE LIGHTS ARE OUT. / HOW CAN IT BE** —

Oct 74. (7") (2058 522) **FAR FAR AWAY. / OK YESTERDAY WAS YESTERDAY** — 2

Nov 74. (lp) (2442 126) <2865> **SLADE IN FLAME (Film Soundtrack)** — 6 | 93
– How does it feel? / Them kinda monkeys can't swing / So far so good / Summer song (wishing you were here) / O.K. yesterday was yesterday / Far far away / This girl / Lay it down / Standin' on the corner. (re-iss. Nov82 on 'Action Replay'; REPLAY 1000) (cd-iss. May91; 849 182-2)

Feb 75. (7") (2058 547) **HOW DOES IT FEEL. / SO FAR SO GOOD** — 15

Apr 75. (7") <8134> **HOW DOES IT FEEL. / O.K. YESTERDAY WAS YESTERDAY** — -

May 75. (7") (2058 585) **THANKS FOR THE MEMORY (WHAM BAM THANK YOU MAM). / RAINING IN MY CHAMPAGNE** — 7

Nov 75. (7") (2058 663) **IN FOR A PENNY. / CAN YOU JUST IMAGINE** — 11

Jan 76. (7") (2058 690) **LET'S CALL IT QUITS. / WHEN THE CHIPS ARE DOWN** — 11

Mar 76. (lp) (2383 377) <2936> **NOBODY'S FOOLS** — 14
– Nobody's fools / Do the dirty / Let's call it quits / Pack up your troubles / In for a penny / Get on up / L.A. jinx / Did your mama ever tell ya / Scratch my back / I'm a talker / All the world is a stage. (cd-iss. May91; 849 183-2)

Apr 76. (7") (2058 716) **NOBODY'S FOOL. / L.A. JINX** —

Apr 76. (7") <8185> **NOBODY'S FOOL. / WHEN THE CHIPS ARE DOWN** — -

(Barn-Polydor / not iss.)

Feb 77. (7") (2014 105) **GYPSY ROADHOG. / FOREST FULL OF NEEDLES** — 48

Mar 77. (lp) (2314 103) **WHATEVER HAPPENED TO SLADE**
– Be / Lightning never strikes twice / Gypsy roadhog / Dogs of vengeance / When fantasy calls / One eyed Jacks with moustaches / Big apple blues / Dead men tell no tales / She's got the lot / It ain't love but it ain't bad / The soul, the fall and the motion. (cd-iss. May93; 849 184-2)

Apr 77. (7") (2014 106) **BURNING IN THE HEAT OF LOVE. / READY STEADY KIDS** —

Oct 77. (7") (2014 114) **MY BABY LEFT ME – THAT'S ALL RIGHT (Medley). / O.H.M.S.** — 32

Mar 78. (7") (2014 121) **GIVE US A GOAL. / DADDIO** —

Oct 78. (7") (2014 127) **ROCK'N'ROLL BOLERO. / MY BABY'S GOT IT** —

(Barn / not iss.)

Nov 78. (lp) (2314 106) **SLADE ALIVE VOL.2** — -
– Get on up / Take me bak 'ome / Medley: My baby left me – That's all right / Be / Mama weer all crazee now / Burning in the heat of love / Everyday / Gudbuy t'Jane / One-eyed Jacks with moustaches / C'mon feel the noize. (cd-iss. May93; 849 179-2)

Mar 79. (7" yellow) (BARN 002) **GINNY GINNY. / DIZZY MAMA** — -

Oct 79. (7") (BARN 010) **SIGN OF THE TIMES. / NOT TONIGHT JOSEPHINE** —

Oct 79. (lp) (NARB 003) **RETURN TO BASE**
– Wheels ain't coming round / Hold on to your hats / Chakeeta / Don't waste your time / Sign of the times / I'm a rocker / Nuts, bolts and screws / My baby's got it / I'm mad / Lemme love into ya / Ginny, Ginny.

Dec 79. (7") (BARN 011) **OKEY COKEY. / MY BABY'S GOT IT** —

(Cheapskate / not iss.)

Sep 80. (7"ep) (CHEAP 5) **SLADE ALIVE AT READING '80 (live)** — 44
– When I'm dancing I ain't fightin' / Born to be wild / Somethin' else / Pistol packin' mama / Keep a rollin'.

Nov 80. (7") (CHEAP 11) **MERRY XMAS EVERYBODY. / OKEY COKEY / GET DOWN AND GET WITH IT** — 70

Jan 81. (7") (CHEAP 16) **WE'LL BRING THE HOUSE DOWN. / HOLD ON TO YOUR HATS** — 10

Mar 81. (lp/c) (SKATE/KAT 1) **WE'LL BRING THE HOUSE DOWN** — 25
– Night starvation / Wheels ain't coming down / I'm a rocker / Nuts, bolts and screws / We'll bring the house down / Dizzy mama / Hold on to your hats / Lemme love into ya / My baby's got it / When I'm dancing I ain't fightin'. (cd-iss. Nov96 on 'Castle'; CLACD 418) (cd re-iss. Sep99; 547412-2)

Mar 81. (7") (CHEAP 21) **WHEELS AIN'T COMING DOWN. / NOT TONIGHT JOSEPHINE** — 60

May 81. (7") (CHEAP 24) **KNUCKLE SANDWICH NANCY. / I'M MAD** —

(R.C.A. / CBS-Assoc.)

Sep 81. (7") (RCA 124) **LOCK UP YOUR DAUGHTERS. / SIGN OF THE TIMES** — 29

Nov 81. (lp/c) (RCA LP/K 6021) **TILL DEAF US DO PART**
– Rock and roll preacher (hallelujah I'm on fire) / Ruby red / Lock up your daughters / Till deaf us do part / That was no lady that was my wife / She brings out the devil in me / A night to remember / M'hat m'coat / It's your body not your mind / Let the rock and roll out of control / Knuckle sandwich Nancy / Till deaf resurrected. (cd-iss. Apr93 & Nov96 on 'Castle'; CLACD 377 & 415) (cd re-iss. Sep99; 547407-2)

Mar 82. (7") (RCA 191) **RUBY RED. / FUNK PUNK AND JUNK** — 51
(d7"+=) (RCAD 191) – Rock'n'roll preacher (live) / Take me back 'ome (live).

Nov 82. (7") (RCA 291) **(AND NOW – THE WALTZ) C'EST LA VIE. / MERRY XMAS EVERYBODY (ALIVE & KICKIN')** — 50

Dec 82. (lp/c) (RCA LP/K 3107) **ON STAGE (live)** —
– Rock and roll preacher / When I'm dancing I ain't fightin' / Tak me bak 'ome / Everyday / Lock up your daughters / We'll bring the house down / A night to remember / Mama weer all crazee now / Gudbuy t'Jane / You'll never walk alone. (cd-iss. Jul93 & Nov96 on 'Castle'; CLACD 380 & 420) (cd re-iss. Sep99; 547413-2)

Nov 83. (7"m) (RCA 373) **MY OH MY. / MERRY XMAS EVERYBODY (live) / KEEP YOUR HANDS OFF MY POWER SUPPLY** — 2

Dec 83. (lp/c) (PL/PK 70116) **THE AMAZING KAMIKAZE SYNDROME** — 49
– Slam the hammer down / In the doghouse / Run runaway / High and dry / My oh my / Cocky rock boys / Ready to explode / (And now – The waltz) C'est la vie / Cheap 'n' nasty love / Razzle dazzle man. (cd-iss. Apr93 & Nov96 on 'Castle'; CLACD 381 & 419) (cd re-iss. Sep99; 547411-2)

Jan 84. (7"/12") (RCA/+T 385) **RUN RUNAWAY. / TWO TRACK STEREO, ONE TRACK MIND** — 7

Apr 84. (lp) (39336) **KEEP YOUR HANDS OFF MY POWER SUPPLY** <cd-iss. 1988; ZK 3936> — - | 33

Apr 84. (7") <04398> **RUN RUNAWAY. / DON'T TAME A HURRICANE** — - | 20

Jul 84. (7") <04528> **MY OH MY. / HIGH AND DRY** — - | 37

Nov 84. (7") (RCA 455) **ALL JOIN HANDS. / HERE'S TO . . . (THE NEW YEAR)** — 15
(12"+=) (RCAT 455) – Merry xmas everybody (live & kickin').

Jan 85. (7") (RCA 475) **7 YEAR (B)ITCH. / LEAVE THEM GIRLS ALONE** — 60
(12"+=) (RCAT 475) – We'll bring the house down (live).

Mar 85. (lp/c) (PL/PK 70604) <39976> **ROGUES GALERY**
– Hey ho wish you well / Little Sheila / Harmony / Myzsterious Mizster Jones / Walking on water, running on alcohol / 7 year (b)itch / I'll be there / I win, you lose / Time to rock / All join hands. (cd-iss. Sep99; 547406-2)

Mar 85. (7",7"pic-d) (PB 40027) **MYZSTERIOUS MIZSTER JONES. / MAMA NATURE IS A ROCKER** — 50
(ext.12"+=) (PT 40028) – My oh my (piano and vocal version).

Apr 85. (7") <04865> **LITTLE SHEILA. / LOCK UP YOUR DAUGHTERS** — - | 86

Nov 85. (7") (PB 40449) **DO YOU BELIEVE IN MIRACLES. / MY OH MY (swing version)** — 54
(d7"+=) (PB 40549) – (see below d12" for extra tracks)
(12"+=) (PT 40450) – Time to rock.
(12"++=) (PT 40550) – Santa Claus is coming to town / Auld lang syne / You'll never walk alone.

Feb 87. (7"/12") (PB 4113 7/8) **STILL THE SAME. / GOTTA GO HOME** — 73
(d7"+=) (PB 41147D) – The roaring silence / Don't talk to me about love.

Apr 87. (7") (PB 41271) **THAT'S WHAT FRIENDS ARE FOR. / WILD WILD PARTY**
(12"+=) (PT 41272) – Hi ho silver lining / Lock up your daughters (live).

Apr 87. (lp/c/cd) (PL/PK/PD 71260) **YOU BOYZ MAKE BIG NOIZE**
– Love is like a rock / That's where friends are for / Still the same / Fools go crazy / She's heavy / We won't give in / Won't you rock with me / Ooh la la in L.A. / Me and the boys / Sing shout (knock yourself out) / The roaring silence / It's hard having fun nowadays / You boyz make big noize / Boyz (instrumental). (cd re-iss. Apr93 & Nov96 on 'Castle'; CLACD 379 & 417) (cd re-iss. Sep99; 547408-2)

	Cheapskate-RCA	not iss.
Jun 87. (7") (BOYZ 1) **YOU BOYZ MAKE BIG NOIZE.** / ('A'instrumental) (12"+=) (TBOYZ 1) – ('A'-USA mix).	☐	-
Nov 87. (7") (BOYZ 2) **WE WON'T GIVE IN.** / **LA LA IN L.A.**	☐	-
Nov 88. (7") (BOYZ 3) **LET'S DANCE (1988 remix).** / **STANDING ON THE CORNER** (cd-s+=) (BOYZCD 3) – Far far away / How does it feel.	☐	-

	Polydor	not iss.
Oct 91. (7"/c-s) (PO/+CS 180) **RADIO WALL OF SOUND.** / **LAY YOUR LOVE ON THE LINE** (cd-s+=) (PZCD 180) – Cum feel the noize.	21	-
Nov 91. (cd/c/lp) (511 612-2/-4/-1) **WALL OF HITS** (compilation & new hits)	34	

– Get down and get with it / Coz I luv you / Look wot you dun / Take me bak 'ome / Gudbuy t'Jane / Cum on feel the noize / Skweeze me pleeze me / My friend Stan / Everyday / Bangin' man / Far far away / Let's call it quits / My oh my / Run run away / Radio wall of sound / Universe / Merry Xmas everybody. (cd/c+=) – How does it feel / Thanks for the memory (wham bam thank you mam).

	Polydor	not iss.
Nov 91. (7"/c-s) **UNIVERSE.** / **MERRY CHRISTMAS EVERYBODY** (12"+=/cd-s+=) – Gypsy roadhog.	☐	-

—— no new material as yet

– compilations, etc. –

on 'Polydor' unless stated otherwise

Jun 80. (12"ep) Six Of The Best; (SUPER45 3) **SIX OF THE BEST**	☐	-

– Night starvation / When I'm dancing I ain't fightin' / I'm a rocker / Don't waste your time / Wheels ain't coming down / Nine to five.

Nov 80. (lp) (POLTV 13) **SLADE SMASHES**	21	-
Apr 81. (d-lp/d-c) (2689/3539 101) **THE STORY OF SLADE** (cd-iss. VOL.1 & VOL.2 Nov90 on 'Bear Tracks'; BTCD 97941-1/-2)		-
Dec 81. (7"ep) (POSP 399) **CUM ON FEEL THE NOIZE / COZ I LUV YOU. / TAKE ME BAK 'OME / GUDBUY T'JANE** (12"ep+=) (POSPX 399) – Coz I luv you.	☐	-
Dec 82. (7"/7"pic-d) Speed; (SPEED/+P 201) **THE HOKEY COKEY.** / **GET DOWN AND GET WITH IT**	☐	-
May 84. (lp/c) (SLAD/+C 1) **SLADE'S GREATS**	☐	☐
Nov 85. (7"/12") (POSP/+X 780) **MERRY CHRISTMAS EVERYBODY (remix).** / **DON'T BLAME ME** (re-iss. Dec86, hit No.71)	48	☐
Nov 85. (lp/c) Telstar; (STAR/STAC 2271) **CRACKERS – THE SLADE CHRISTMAS PARTY ALBUM**	34	
1988. (cd-ep) Counterpoint; (CDEP 12C) **HOW DOES IT FEEL / FAR FAR AWAY** / (2 tracks by Wizzard)	☐	
Mar 89. (3"cd-ep) R.C.A.; (PD 42637) **MY OH MY / KEEP YOUR HANDS OFF MY POWER SUPPLY / RUNAWAY / ONE TRACK STEREO, ONE TRACK MIND**		-
Apr 91. (cd/c/lp) R.C.A.; (ND/NK/NL 74926) **COLLECTION 81-87** (re-iss. Apr93 on 'Castle' cd/c; CCS CD/MC 372) (cd re-iss. Sep99 on 'Polydor'; 547410-2)		-
Dec 95. (c) Prestige; (CASSGP 0253) **KEEP ON ROCKIN'**		-
Jan 97. (cd/c) (537 105-2/-4) **GREATEST HITS – FEEL THE NOIZE**	19	-

– Get down and get with it / Coz I luv you / Look wot you dun / Take me bak 'ome / Mama weer all crazee now / Gudbuy t'Jane / Cum on feel the noize / Skweeze me pleeze me / My friend Stan / Everyday / Bangin' man / Far far away / How does it feel to feel / In for a penny / We'll bring the house down / Lock up your daughters / Oh my my / Run run away / All join hands / Radio wall of sound / Merry Xmas everybody. (re-iss. Dec99 as 'GREATEST HITS – FEEL THE NOIZE'; same)

Mar 97. (cd) Music Corp; (TMC 9606) **THE GENESIS OF SLADE**	☐	-
Dec 98. (c-s; SLADE VS FLUSH) Polydor; (563352-4) **MERRY XMAS EVERYBODY '98 REMIX** / ('A'remix) (12"+=) (563353-1) – ('A'mix). (cd-s+=) (563353-2) – Cum on feel the noize.	30	-

---

SLAPP HAPPY (dig out; Great Psychedelic . . .)

SLAYER

Formed: Los Angeles, California, USA . . . late 1981 by TOM ARAYA, JEFF HANNEMAN, KERRY KING and former jazz drummer, DAVE LOMBARDO. One of the heaviest, fastest and generally more extreme outfits to emerge from the initial wave of thrash-metal, SLAYER recorded their first couple of releases, 'SHOW NO MERCY' (1984) and the 'HAUNTING THE CHAPEL' EP (1984) for the 'Metal Blade' label. A largely unfocussed blurr of manic drumming and powerdrill guitar shredding, these early efforts also showcased a lyrical excess to match the 'music', heralding a new era in which initially thrash outfits, then death-metal merchants, trawled new depths of goriness (the PMRC would probably use the term depravity). 'HELL AWAITS' (1985) followed in much the same fashion and it wasn't until the epochal 'REIGN IN BLOOD' (1987) that SLAYER began to assume the status of metal demi-gods. Cannily signed up by RICK RUBIN to the ultra-hip 'Def Jam' (home to such groundbreaking rap outfits as The BEASTIE BOYS and PUBLIC ENEMY), SLAYER not only benefitted from the added kudos of a 'street' label but were touted by the rock press as having produced the ultimate speed-metal album. From its trademark black-period Goya-esque artwork to the breakneck precision of the playing and the wildly controversial lyrical fare ('NECROPHOBIC', 'RAINING BLOOD' etc.), 'REIGN IN BLOOD' was a landmark metal release, which in many respects has never been bettered in its respective field. The biggest fuss, however, was reserved for 'ANGEL OF DEATH', a track detailing the horrific atrocities of Nazi butcher, Joseph Mengele. 'Def Jam's distributor, 'Columbia' refused to handle the album, with 'Geffen' stepping in to facilitate the group's first Top 100 (US) entry. While

SLAYER allegedly hold right-wing political views, the disturbingly soft-spoken ARAYA maintains that his lyrics do not promote war or violence but merely reflect the darker aspects of humanity. Whatever, there was no denying the power of SLAYER's music, especially on the more composed 'SOUTH OF HEAVEN' (1988). No doubt finally realising that only too often they sacrificed effectiveness for speed, SLAYER took their proverbial foot off the accelerator. Sure, there were still outbursts of amphetamine overkill, but with the likes of the apocalyptic title track, the chugging fury of 'MANDATORY SUICIDE' (complete with chilling spoken word outro) and a raging cover of Judas Priest's 'DISSIDENT AGGRESSOR', SLAYER had at last harnessed the malign potential which they had always promised. The record brought the band an unprecedented UK Top 30 chart placing, proof that the group were now being taken seriously as major thrash contenders alongside METALLICA, MEGADETH and ANTHRAX. The acclaimed 'SEASONS IN THE ABYSS' (1990) confirmed that SLAYER were not merely contenders but challengers for the thrash throne. With 'SEASONS..', the group succeeded in combining their instinct for speed with a newfound maturity, resulting in one of the most intense yet accessible metal records ever released. The doom-obsessed, bass-crunching likes of 'EXPENDABLE YOUTH', 'SKELETONS OF SOCIETY' and the brooding title track recalled the intensity of prime 70's BLACK SABBATH while even the harder tracks like 'WAR ENSEMBLE' and 'BLOOD RED' displayed traces of melody. The obligatory lyrical shock tactics came with 'DEAD SKIN MASK' an eery meditation reportedly inspired by serial killer, Ed Gein. Again produced by RUBIN and released on his fledgling 'Def American' label, the album made the UK Top 20 and finally broke the group into the US Top 40. Promoting the record with the legendary 'Clash Of The Titans' tour (also featuring MEGADETH, SUICIDAL TENDENCIES and TESTAMENT), SLAYER had finally made it into the metal big league and summing up the first blood-soaked chapter of their career, the group duly released the live double set, 'DECADE OF AGGRESSION' (1991). Amid much rumour and counter-rumour, LOMBARDO finally left the band for good in Spring '92, ex-FORBIDDEN sticksman, PAUL BOSTOPH, drafted in as a replacement. A long-awaited sixth set, 'DIVINE INTERVENTION', finally arrived in 1994, a consolidation of SLAYER's hallowed position in the metal hierarchy and the group's first assault on the US Top 10. The heaviest band ever (as Kerrang! readers acclaimed them!) spewed back with 'UNDISPUTED ATTITUTE' (1996), although it was 1998's 'DIABOLUS IN MUSICA' (apparently a "devilish" musical scale banned by churches in the 15th century!) which brought their brutal gore back to the fore. • **Songwriters:** ARAYA words / HANNEMAN music, also covered IN-A-GADDA-DA-VIDA (Iron Butterfly) / DISORDER + WAR + UK 82 (as 'US 92'; 3 from 1993 film 'Judgment Night') (Exploited). 'UNDISPUTED ATTITUTE' album all covers; ABOLISH GOVERNMENT (TSOL) / I WANNA BE YOUR DOG (Iggy Pop) / (GBH) / GUILTY OF BEING WHITE (Minor Threat) / other covers from (Verbal Abuse), (D.I.), (Dr Know) and (DRI).

Album rating: SHOW NO MERCY (*5) / HELL AWAITS (*7) / REIGN IN BLOOD (*9) / SOUTH OF HEAVEN (*9) / SEASONS IN THE ABYSS (*8) / DECADE OF AGGRESSION (*8) / DIVINE INTERVENTION (*7) / UNDISPUTED ATTITUDE (*6) / DIABOLUS IN MUSICA (*5)

TOM ARAYA (b. 6 Jun'61, Chile) – vocals, bass / **JEFF HANNEMAN** (b.31 Jan'64) – lead guitar / **KERRY KING** (b. 3 Jun'64, Huntington Park, Calif.) – lead guitar / **DAVE LOMBARDO** (b.16 Feb'65) – drums

	Roadrunner	Metal Blade
Jun 84. (lp) (RR 9868) <MBR 1013> **SHOW NO MERCY**	☐	Feb84

– Evil has no boundaries / The antichrist / Die by the sword / Fight till death / Metalstorm – Face the slayer / Black magic / Tormentor / The final command / Crionics / Show no mercy. <US re-iss. pic-lp Dec88; 72214-1> (re-iss. Aug90 on 'Metal Blade' cd/c/lp; CD/T+/ZORRO 7) (cd re-iss. Feb96 on 'Metal Blade'; 3984 14032CD)

	Roadrunner	
Oct 84. (12"ep) (RR12 55087) **HAUNTING THE CHAPEL.** / **CHEMICAL WARFARE / CAPTOR OF SIN** (re-iss. Oct89 as cd-ep; RR 2444-2)	☐	☐

	Roadrunner	Enigma
May 85. (lp/c) (RR 9795-1/-4) <72297> **HELL AWAITS**	☐	☐

– Hell awaits / Kill again / At dawn they sleep / Praise of death / Necrophiliac / Crypts of eternity / Hardening of the arteries. (cd-iss. Feb89; RR34 9795) (re-iss. Aug90 on 'Metal Blade' cd/c/lp; CD/T+/ZORRO 8) (cd re-iss. Feb96 on 'Metal Blade'; 3984 14031CD)

	London	Def Jam
Apr 87. (lp/c/pic-lp) (LON LP/C/PP 34) <24131> **REIGN IN BLOOD**	47	94 Oct86

– Angel of death / Piece by piece / Necrophobic / Alter of sacrifice / Jesus saves / Criminally insane / Reborn / Epidemic / Post mortem / Raining blood. (cd-iss. Dec94 on 'American'; 74321 24848-2)

	London	Def Jam
May 87. (7"red) (LON 133) **CRIMINALLY INSANE (remix).** / **AGGRESSIVE PERFECTER** (12"+=) (LONX 133) – Post mortem.	64	☐
Jun 88. (lp/c)(cd) (LON LP/C 63)(828 820-2) <24203> **SOUTH OF HEAVEN**	25	57

– South of heaven / Silent scream / Live undead / Behind the crooked cross / Mandatory suicide / Ghosts of war / Read between the lies / Cleanse the soul / Dissident aggressor / Spill the blood. (cd re-iss. Dec94 on 'American'; 74321 24849-2)

Sep 88. (12") (LONX 201) **MANDATORY SUICIDE.** / **IN-A-GADDA-DA-VIDA**	☐	-

	American	Def American
Oct 90. (cd/c/lp) (849 6871-2/-4/-1) <24307> **SEASONS IN THE ABYSS**	18	40

– War ensemble / Blood red / Spirit in black / Expendable youth / Dead skin mask / Hallowed point / Skeletons of society / Temptation / Born of fire / Seasons in the abyss. (cd re-iss. Dec94 on 'American'; 74321 24850-2)

Oct 91.   (d-cd/d-c/d-lp) (510 605-2/-4/-1) <26748> **DECADE OF**
AGGRESSION (live) | 29 | |
– Hell awaits / The anti-Christ / War ensemble / South of Heaven / Raining blood /
Altar of sacrifice / Jesus saves / Dead skin mask / Seasons in the abyss / Mandatory
suicide / Angel of death / Hallowed paint / Blood red / Die by the sword / Black
magic / Captor of sin / Born of fire / Post mortem / Spirit in black / Expendable
youth / Chemical warfare. (cd re-iss. Dec94; 74321 24851-2)

Oct 91.   (7") (DEFA 9) **SEASONS IN THE ABYSS (live). /**
AGGRESSIVE PERFECTOR (live) | 51 | |
(12"+=) (DEFA 9-12) – Chemical warfare.
(12"pic-d+=)(cd-s+=)(DEFAP 9-12)(DEFAC 9) – ('A'-experimental).

——   (May'92) **PAUL BOSTAPH** (b. 4 Mar'65, Hayward, Calif.) – drums repl.
LOMBARDO

Oct 94.   (cd/c/lp) (74321 23677-2/-4/-1) <26748> **DIVINE**
INTERVENTION | 15 | 8 |
– Killing fields / Sex. murder. art / Fictional reality / Dittohead / Divine intervention /
Circle of beliefs / SS-3 / Serenity in murder / 213 / Mind control.

Sep 95.   (7"ep) (74321 26234-7) **SERENITY IN MURDER / RAINING**
BLOOD. / DITTOHEAD / SOUTH OF HEAVEN | | - |
(cd-s) (74321 26234-2) – ('A'side) / At dawn they sleep (live) / Dead skin mask
(live) / Divine intervention (live).
(cd-s) (74321 31248-2) – ('A'side) / Angel of death / Mandatory suicide / War
ensemble.

——   (after below) **JOHN DETTE** – drums (ex-TESTAMENT) repl. BOSTOPH

May 96.   (cd/c/10"d-lp) (74321 35759-2/-4/-1) <43072> **UNDISPUTED**
ATTITUDE | 31 | 34 |
– Disintegration – Free money / Verbal abuse – Leeches / Abolish government –
Superficial love / Can't stand you / Ddamm / Guilty of being white / I hate you /
Filler – I don't want to hear it / Spiritual law / Sick boy / Mr. Freeze / Violent
pacification / Richard hung himself / I wanna be your god / Gemini. (cd w/ free
cd+=)(74321 38325-2) – Witching hour / Dittohead / Divine intervention.

Aug 96.   (7") <(SP 368)> **ABOLISH GOVERNMENT. /**   Sub Pop Sub Pop

——   there was also a SLAYER tribute album released Nov95; 'SLATANIC
SLAUGHTER' on 'Black Sun' cd/lp; BS 003 CD/LP)

Jun 98.   (cd/c/lp) (491302-2/-4/-1) <69192> **DIABOLUS IN MUSICA** | Columbia 27 | Columbia 31 |
– Bitter peace / Death's head / Stain of mind / Overt enemy / Perversions of pain /
Love to hate / Desire in the name of God / Screaming from the sky / Wicked / Point /
Scrum.

– compilations, etc. –

Dec 88.   (lp/c) Roadrunner; (RR/+34 9574) / Enigma; <72015-1> **LIVE**
UNDEAD (live 1984) | | Oct87 |
– Black magic / Die by the sword / Captor of sin / The antichrist / Evil has no
boundaries / Show no mercy / Aggressive perfector / Chemical warfare. (re-iss.
Sep91 on 'Metal Blade' cd/c/lp; CD/T+/ZORRO 29) (cd re-iss. Feb96 on 'Metal
Blade'+=; 3984 14011CD) – HAUNTING THE CHAPEL

SLEATER-KINNEY (dig out; Great Alt & Indie . . .)

Percy SLEDGE

Born: 25 Nov'40, Leighton, Alabama, USA. Another soul legend to begin his
singing career in the church, SLEDGE subsequently moved into the secular
music world in the early-mid 60's as part of The ESQUIRES COMBO. His
break came in 1966 when local DJ Quin Ivy helped produce SLEDGE's
landmark classic, 'WHEN A MAN LOVES A WOMAN'. With its ardent,
intense vocals and proclamation of love's eternal endurance, the song quickly
became a hallowed soul standard and a new benchmark for aspiring balladeers.
As well as hiring SPOONER OLDHAM for the sombre farfisa organ part, Ivy
released the record independently before licensing it to budding Southern Soul
sponsors, 'Atlantic'. Unsurprisingly, it topped the US chart and broke the UK
Top 5, announcing the arrival of yet another rich talent from the ever fertile
American south. Follow-up, 'WARM AND TENDER LOVE', proved it was
no mercurial one-off, making the US Top 20 and preceding a whole album of
heartfelt romantic testament named after his debut hit. Working with the cream
of country-soul writers such as OLDHAM, DAN PENN and CHIPS MOMAN,
SLEDGE scored a further US Top 20 hit, 'IT TEARS ME UP', later that year.
Increasingly, however, the man's chart placings failed to reflect the quality
of his work. While his superior version of the OLDHAM/MOMAN classic,
'DARK END OF THE STREET' (from 1967's 'THE PERCY SLEDGE WAY'
album) somehow never made it onto 7" vinyl, SLEDGE did score one further
Top 20 hit in Spring '68 with the sublime 'TAKE TIME TO KNOW HER'.
While not attempting as daring a marriage as say, RAY CHARLES, SLEDGE
was one of the era's most subtle interpreters of the link between country and
soul; having already covered Charlie Rich's 'BEHIND CLOSED DOORS' on
his debut album, SLEDGE went on to perform Kris Kristofferson's 'HELP
ME MAKE IT THROUGH THE NIGHT', released as a single in 1970. By
this point, however, his career was in commercial decline and although he
subsequently signed to Phil Walden's Southern Rock bastion, 'Capricorn',
he could only manage one last minor hit with 1974's 'I'LL BE YOUR
EVERYTHING'. Although he was dogged by ill health, SLEDGE made a
successful living on the golden oldies circuit over the forthcoming decades, his
famous debut single resurrected in 1987 when it hit the UK Top 5 all over again
after being used in a Levi's jeans ad. In 1994 he released his first new material
in over a decade in the shape of the 'BLUE NIGHT' album, featuring guest
spots by the likes of STEVE CROPPER and BOBBY WOMACK. • **Trivia:**
In 1991, poodle-haired howler, MICHAEL BOLTON, also took 'WHEN A
MAN . . .' into the UK Top 10.

Best CD compilation: THE ULTIMATE COLLECTION – THE BEST OF . . . (*7)

PERCY SLEDGE – vocals (with session people)

		Atlantic	Atlantic
May 66.	(7") (584 001) **WHEN A MAN LOVES A WOMAN. / LOVE ME LIKE YOU MEAN IT** (re-iss. 1974) (12"iss.Apr80)	4	1 Mar66
Jul 66.	(7") (584 034) <2342> **WARM AND TENDER LOVE. / SUGAR PUDDIN'**	34	17
Jul 66.	(lp; mono/stereo) (587/588 105) <8125> **WHEN A MAN LOVES A WOMAN**		37 May66
	– When a man loves a woman / You're pouring water on a drowning man / Love makes the world go round / Love me like you meant it / Put a little lovin' on me / Love me all the way / When she touches me / Thief in the night / You fooled me / Success. (re-iss. 1970)		
Oct 66.	(7") <2358> **IT TEARS ME UP. / HEART OF A CHILD**	-	20
Nov 66.	(7") (584 055) **HEART OF A CHILD. / MY ADORABLE ONE**	-	-
Jan 67.	(7") (584 071) **IT TEARS ME UP. / OH HOW HAPPY**	-	
Feb 67.	(lp; mono/stereo) (587/588 048) <8132> **WARM AND TENDER SOUL**		Nov66
	– Make it good and make it last / When a man loves a woman / Walkin' in the Sun / Warm and tender love / The God love / Out of left field / Behind closed doors / Just out of reach / I believe in you / I believe in you / Take time to know her. (re-iss. +c.Aug86 on 'Blue Moon')		
Feb 67.	(7") (584 083) <2383> **BABY, HELP ME. / YOU'VE LOST THAT SOMETHING WONDERFUL**		87
Apr 67.	(7") (584 108) <2396> **OUT OF LEFT FIELD. / IT CAN'T BE STOPPED**		59
Jun 67.	(7") <2414> **LOVE ME TENDER. / WHAT AM I LIVING FOR**	-	40 91
Aug 67.	(7") <2434> **JUST OUT OF REACH (OF MY TWO EMPTY ARMS). / HARD TO BELIEVE**	-	66
Oct 67.	(7") (584 140) **PLEDGING MY LOVE. / YOU DON'T MISS YOUR WATER**		
Nov 67.	(lp; mono/stereo) (587/588 081) <8146> **THE PERCY SLEDGE WAY**		Aug67
	– Dark end of the street / You send me / I had a talk with my woman / What am I living for / I've been loving you too long / Drown in my own tears / My special prayer / Just out of reach / Pledging my love / You don't miss your water . . .		
Nov 67.	(7") <2453> **COVER ME. / BEHIND EVERY GREAT MAN THERE IS A WOMAN**	-	42
Apr 68.	(7") (584 177) <2490> **TAKE TIME TO KNOW HER. / IT'S ALL WRONG BUT IT'S ALRIGHT**		11 Mar68
May 68.	(lp) <8180> **TAKE TIME TO KNOW HER**	-	
	– Take time to know her / Feed the flame / Out of left field / Cover me / Come softly to me / Sudden stop / Spooky / Baby help me / It's all wrong but it's alright / High cost of leaving / Between these arms / I love everything about you.		
Jul 68.	(7") <2539> **SUDDEN STOP. / BETWEEN THESE ARMS**	-	63
Sep 68.	(7") <2563> **YOU'RE ALL AROUND ME. / SELF PRESERVATION**	-	
Nov 68.	(7") (584 225) **COME SOFTLY TO ME. / YOU'RE ALL AROUND ME**	-	-
Jan 69.	(7") <2594> **MY SPECIAL PRAYER. / BLESS YOUR SWEET LITTLE SOUL**	-	93
May 69.	(7") (584 264) <2616> **ANY DAY NOW. / THE ANGELS LISTENED IN**		86 Apr69
Aug 69.	(7") (584 286) <2646> **KIND WOMAN. / WOMAN OF THE NIGHT**		
Nov 69.	(7") (584 300) <2679> **TRUE LOVE TRAVELS ON A GRAVEL ROAD. / FAITHFUL AND TRUE**		
Nov 69.	(lp; mono/stereo) (587/588 153) <8210> **THE BEST OF PERCY SLEDGE** (compilation)		Feb69
	– When a man loves a woman / Out of left field / Take time to know her / Warm and tender / Just out of reach (of my two empty arms) / Dark end of the street / Cover me / Sudden stop / Baby help me / It tears me up / My special prayer / You're all around me. (re-iss. 1972 & 1980)		
Feb 70.	(7") <2719> **TOO MANY RIVERS TO CROSS. / PUSHING MY PRIDE AGAIN**	-	-
May 70.	(7") <2754> **HELP ME MAKE IT THROUGH THE NIGHT. / THIEF IN THE NIGHT**	-	
Aug 70.	(7") <2826> **THAT'S THE WAY I WANT TO LIVE MY LIFE. / STOP THE WORLD TONIGHT**	-	-
1970.	(lp) <9257> **IN SOUTH AFRICA (live)**	-	-
	– My special prayer / Cover me / Heart of a child / Take time to know her / Warm and tender love / I gotta get a message to you / Silent night / Come softly to me / What am I living for / When a man loves a woman.		
1971.	(7") <2886> **SUNDAY BROTHER. / EVERYTHING YOU'LL EVER NEED**	-	
Mar 72.	(7") (K 10144) **RAINBOW ROAD. / STANDING ON THE MOUNTAIN**	-	
Jun 72.	(7"m) **BABY HELP ME. / WARM AND TENDER LOVE / TAKE TIME TO KNOW HER**		
Aug 73.	(7") (K 10358) <2963> **SUNSHINE. / UNCHANGING LOVE**		
		Capricorn	Capricorn
Oct 74.	(7") <0209> **I'LL BE YOUR EVERYTHING. / BLUE WATER**	-	62
Nov 74.	(7") (2089 009) **I'LL BE YOUR EVERYTHING. / WALKIN' IN THE SUN**	-	-
Nov 74.	(lp) <0147> **I'LL BE YOUR EVERYTHING**	-	-
	– Walkin' in the sun / Behind closed doors / Make it good and make it last / The good love I believe in you / I'll be your everything / If this is the last time / Hard to be friends / Blue water / Love among people.		
Feb 75.	(7") <0220> **BEHIND CLOSED DOORS. / IF THIS IS THE LAST TIME**	-	-
1977.	(7") <0273> **WHEN A BOY BECOMES A MAN. / WHEN SHE TOUCHES ME**	-	-

——   PERCY retired for a while after being dogged by ill health

		Monument	Monument
1983.	(7") SHE'S TOO PRETTY TO CRY. / ?	-	-

1983. (lp) <(MNT 25369)> PERCY
– Bring your lovin' to me / You had to be there / All night rain / She's too pretty to cry / I still miss someone / The faithful kind / Home type thing / Personality / I'd put angels around you / Hard lovin' woman. (re-iss. Jul87 on 'Charly' lp/c; CRB/TCCRB 1152) (cd-iss. Jul87; CDCHARLY 95)

		Demon	
Jul 89.	(lp/cd) (FIEND/+CD 140) WANTED AGAIN (rec.1986-87)		

– Keep the fire burning / Wanted again / Kiss an angel good morning / Hey good lookin' / If you've got the money honey / He'll have tp go / Today I started lovin' you again / She thinks I still care / Wabash cannonball / For the good times. (cd re-iss. Jun98 on 'Diablo'; DIAB 859)

		Virgin – Pointblank	Virgin – Pointblank
Nov 94.	(cd/c) <(VPB CD/TC 21)> BLUE NIGHT		

– You got away with love / Love come knockin' / Why did you stop / I wish it would rain / Blue night / These ain't teardrops / Your love will save the world / First you cry / Going home tomorrow / The grand blvd. / I've got dreams to remember.

– compilations, etc. –

Apr 80.	(7"ep) Atlantic; (ATM 3) WHEN A MAN LOVES A WOMAN		-
	– When a man loves a woman / Warm and tender love / (+ 2 by BEN E. KING).		
Jun 81.	(lp/c) Hallmark; (SHM/HSC 3064) WHEN A MAN LOVES A WOMAN		-
	(cd-iss. Oct89 on 'Pickwick'; PWKS 547)		
Mar 84.	(lp/c) Charly; (CRB/TCCRB 1078) ANY DAY NOW		-
Aug 84.	(c) Goldmasters; (GM 0204) GREATEST HITS		-
Jan 85.	(7") Old Gold; (OG 9496) WHEN A MAN LOVES A WOMAN. / WARM AND TENDER LOVE		-
	(re-iss. Mar90; same)		
Jan 85.	(lp/c) Topline; (TOP/KTOP 113) WHEN A MAN LOVES A WOMAN		-
	(cd-iss. Apr87; TOPCD 502)		
Jul 86.	(cd) Timeless; (810) HIS TOP HITS		-
Aug 86.	(lp) Blue Moon; (BMM 006) WARM AND TENDER LOVE		-
Jan 87.	(7"/12") Atlantic; (YZ 96/+T) WHEN A MAN LOVES A WOMAN. / WARM AND TENDER LOVE	2	-
	(cd-s+=) (500 068) –		
Feb 87.	(lp/c)(cd) Atlantic; (WX 89/+C)(780212-2) WHEN A MAN LOVES A WOMAN (THE ULTIMATE COLLECTION)	36	

– When a man loves a woman / It tears me up / Take time to know her / My special prayer / Baby help me / It's all wrong but it's right / You're all around me / Dark end of the street / Warm and tender love / Love me tender / Out of left field / Come softly to me / What am I living for? / You're pouring water on a drowning man / Just out of reach / Cover me / Sudden stop / You really got a hold on me / That's how strong my love is / Put a little lovin' in me.

May 87.	(7"/12") Atlantic; (YZ 199/+T) COVER ME. / IT TEARS ME APART		-
Aug 87.	(cd) The Collection; (OR 0013) WHEN A MAN LOVES A WOMAN		-
Aug 87.	(lp) Charly; (CRB 1137) IF LOVING YOU IS WRONG		-
	(cd-iss. Feb93; CDCD 1064)		
Nov 87.	(pi-lp) Exclusive; (AR 30065) WHEN A MAN LOVES A WOMAN		-
——	also shared an album SOUL SENSATION in Dec 87 with ARETHA FRANKLIN		
Feb 88.	(7") Sonet; (SON 2335) JUST CAN'T STOP.		-
May 88.	(lp/c) Streetlife; (226/216 2212) GREATEST HITS		-
Dec 88.	(cd) Spectrum; (SPEC 85027) / Gusto; <CD 1023> GREATEST HITS		-
Dec 88.	(cd) Magnum Force; (510439-2) WHEN A MAN LOVES A WOMAN		-
Oct 90.	(lp) President; (BDL 3007) OUT OF LEFT FIELD		-
	(re-iss. 1992 on 'T.K.O.' cd/c; TKO CD/CS 008)		
Apr 91.	(cd/c) Knight; (KNCD/KNMC 12061) HEART AND SOUL		-
Feb 92.	(cd/c) Muskateer; (MU 5/4 016) 20 GREATEST HITS		-
Mar 93.	(cd) Rhino-WEA; <(8122 70285-2)> IT TEARS ME UP: THE BEST OF PERCY SLEDGE		Mar92
May 93.	(cd) Prestige; (CDSPG 044) GREATEST HITS		-
Feb 94.	(cd/c) Javelin; (HAD CD/MC 125) SPOTLIGHT ON . . .		-
Jul 94.	(cd/c) Success; WHEN A MAN LOVES A WOMAN		-
Aug 94.	(cd) Legends In Music; (LECD 065) PERCY SLEDGE		-
Jan 95.	(cd/c) K-Tel; (ECD3/EMC2 087) WHEN A MAN LOVES A WOMAN		-
Jun 95.	(cd) Collection; (COL 048) THE COLLECTION		-
Feb 96.	(cd) Music De-Luxe; MSCD 026) BEHIND CLOSED DOORS		-
Nov 96.	(cd) Summit; (SUMCD 4009) A LITTLE TENDERNESS		-
May 97.	(cd) A-Play; (10058-2) WHEN A MAN LOVES A WOMAN		-
Jul 97.	(cd) Koch Int.; (322698) WHEN A MAN LOVES A WOMAN		-
Jan 98.	(cd; shared with OTIS REDDING) Members Edition; (UAE 3009-2) PERCY SLEDGE & OTIS REDDING		-

SLEEPER

Formed: Ilford, Essex, England . . . 1993 by LOUISE WENER and her boyfriend JON STEWART, the pair duly recruiting ANDY McCLURE and DIID OSMAN. Signing to upcoming 'R.C.A.'-offshoot, 'Indolent', SLEEPER released their debut EP in late '93, 'ALICE IN VAIN', WENER causing controversy from the off with an attack on the sacred cow of feminism. If she brought the wrath of the more radical in the female population, then she no doubt scored a few brownie points with the boys, indie lads increasingly besotted by her saucer-eyed cuteness as well as her outspoken personality. Another couple of EP's, 'SWALLOW', and 'DELICIOUS', followed in quick succession, their sexual frankness further endearing WENER to the more hormonal element of her audience. The singer had already

acquired a burgeoning reputation for her lippy diatribes by the time the 'INBETWEENER' single broke the Top 20 in early '95 and the attendant interest in all things WENER ensured the debut album, 'SMART', a Top 5 placing. Getting down to the nitty gritty i.e. the music, were SLEEPER actually any good? Well, they could certainly hold their own among the Brit-pop competition although that wasn't saying much; basically they were a competent spiky guitar outfit with the odd ear-catching tune, notably the dreamy bit/noisy bit pop rush of 'VEGAS', arguably their finest moment. Later that year, the group scored a second Top 20 hit with the lightweight indie-pop of 'WHAT DO I DO NOW?' followed by 'SALE OF THE CENTURY', their first Top 10 single, though by no means their best. WENER's profile was at an all-time high, her forthright views offending and delighting in equal measure; there was no middle ground with this lass, you either admired her or wished she would sod off (the aptly named SLEEPER also proved that work and pleasure were actually compatible after all). Predictably, then, a follow-up album, 'THE IT GIRL' (1996), met with decidedly mixed reviews although it sold respectably. A backlash was inevitable, however, a third set, 'PLEASED TO MEET YOU' (1997) only produced universal indifference, both critically and commercially. Being ignored is probably one thing which WENER never counted on, although it's doubtful such a feisty babe will bow out without a fight, or at least a controversial word or two. • **Songwriters:** Most by WENER or some w/ STEWART. Covered OTHER END OF THE TELESCOPE (Elvis Costello & Aimee Mann) / ATOMIC (Blondie); used on 'Trainspotting' film.

Album rating: SMART (*8) / THE IT GIRL (*6) / PLEASED TO MEET YOU (*6)

LOUISE WENER (b.30 Jul'68) – vocals, guitar / **JON STEWART** (b.12 Sep'67, Sheffield, England) – lead guitar / **DIID OSMAN** (b. KENEDIID, 10 Apr'68, Mogadishu, Somalia) – bass / **ANDY MacCLURE** (b. 4 Jul'70, Manchester, England) – drums, percussion

		Indolent	Arista
Nov 93.	(7"ep/12"ep/cd-ep) (SLEEP 001/+T/CD) THE ALICE EP		-
	– Alice in vain / Ha ha you're dead / Big nurse.		
Feb 94.	(7"ep/cd-ep) (SLEEP 002/+CD) SWALLOW. / TWISTED / ONE GIRL DREAMING		-
May 94.	(7"ep/cd-ep) (SLEEP 003/+CD) DELICIOUS. / LADY LOVE YOUR COUNTRYSIDE / BEDSIDE MANNERS	75	-
	(12"ep+=) (SLEEP 003T) – Tatty.		
Oct 94.	(7"mail-order) BUCKET AND SPADE (live)	-	-
	– Bedhead / Alice in vain / Swallow.		
Jan 95.	(7"/c-s) (SLEEP 006/+MC) INBETWEENER. / LITTLE ANNIE	16	-
	(cd-s+=) (SLEEP 006CD) – Disco Duncan.		
	(12"++=) (SLEEP 006T) – Bank.		
Feb 95.	(cd/c/lp) (SLEEP CD/MC/LP 007) <25825> SMART	5	Mar95

– Inbetweener / Swallow / Delicious / Hunch / Amuse / Bedhead / Lady love your countryside / Vegas / Poor flying man / Alice in vain / Twisted / Pyrotechnician.

Mar 95.	(7"blue/c-s) (SLEEP 008/+MC) VEGAS. / HYMN TO HER	33	-
	(12"pic-d/cd-s+=) (SLEEP 008 T/CD) – It's wrong to breed / Close.		
Sep 95.	(7"/c-s) (SLEEP 009/+MC) WHAT DO I DO NOW? / PAINT ME	14	-
	(cd-s+=) (SLEEP 009CD1) – Room at the top.		
	(cd-s) (SLEEP 009CD2) – ('A'side) / Vegas (live) / Amuse (live) / Disco Duncan (live).		
Apr 96.	(7"colrd/c-s/cd-s) (SLEEP 011/+MC/CD1) SALE OF THE CENTURY. / ATOMIC	10	-
	(cd-s) (SLEEP 011CD2) – ('A'side) / Package holiday / Oh well.		
May 96.	(cd/c/lp) (SLEEP CD/MC/LP 012) <18824> THE IT GIRL	5	-

– Lie detector / Sale of the century / What do I do now? / Good luck Mr. Gorsky / Feeling peaky / Shrinkwrapped / Dress like your mother / Statuesque / Glue ears / Nice guy Eddie / Stop your crying / Factor 41 / Click . . . off . . . gone.

Jul 96.	(7"/c-s) (SLEEP 013/+MC) <3064> NICE GUY EDDIE. / INBETWEENER	10	-
	(cd-s+=) (SLEEP 013CD) – Poker face / Blazer sleeves.		
Sep 96.	(7") (SLEEP 014) STATUESQUE. / SHE'S A SWEETHEART	17	-
	(cd-s+=) (SLEEP 014CD1) – Spies.		
	(cd-s) (SLEEP 014CD2) – ('A'side) / ('A'-The Boxed Off mix) / Other end of the telescope / Atomic (Wubble U mix).		
——	**CHRIS GIAMMALVO** – bass (of MADDER ROSE) repl. OSMAN		
Sep 97.	(7"/c-s) (SLEEP 015/+MC) SHE'S A GOOD GIRL. / COME ON COME ON	28	-
	(cd-s+=) (SLEEP 015CD) – I'm a man.		
Oct 97.	(cd/c/lp) (SLEEP CD/MC/LP 016) PLEASED TO MEET YOU	7	-

– Please please please / She's a good girl / Rollercoaster / Miss you / Romeo me / Breathe / You got me / Superclean / Firecracker / Because of you / Nothing is changing / Motorway man / Traffic accident.

Nov 97.	(7"clear) (SLEEP 017) ROMEO ME. / C**T LONDON	39	-
	(cd-s) (SLEEP 017CD1) – ('A'side) / This is the sound of someone else / What do I get? / Nice guy Eddie (Peel session).		
	(cd-s) (SLEEP 017CD2) – ('A'side) / When will you smile? / What do I now? (radio 1 evening session) / Motorway man (Arctic mix).		

—— now with new temp bassist **DAN KAUFMANN**

—— early '98, they split with WENER and McCLURE forming other band

SLINT

Formed: Louisville, Kentucky, USA . . . 1988 by former SQUIRREL BAIT partners, BRIAN McMAHAN and BRITT WALFORD, who had already teamed up with DAVID PAJO and ETHAN BUCKLER prior to the latter band's division into BASTRO and SLINT. The influential noiseniks made their debut the following year with the self-financed, STEVE ALBINI-produced album, 'TWEEZ', a wilfully weird clutch of mainly instrumental guitar/bass-led creations named after their family members (including a dog!). While WALFORD (aka SHANNON DOUGHTY) moonlighted on The BREEDERS' first album, 'Pod', BUCKLER would subsequently leave to form KING KONG, replacement TODD BRASHER installed as work commenced on a BRIAN PAULSON-produced follow-up set, 'SPIDERLAND'. Upon its release (on 'Touch & Go') in '91, the album generated a healthy amount of column inches praising its uncategorisable guitar-scapes, Scotland's own MOGWAI later citing the record as a pivotal reference point. While rumours circulated that the album's recording had almost sent SLINT over the edge, the individual members were obviously sane enough to work on various projects including WILL OLDHAM's PALACE BROTHERS (WALFORD, McMAHAN and BRASHER) and TORTOISE (PAJO). A final postscript to the SLINT story came in 1993 with the release of double-A side ("untitled") single, 'GLENN' / 'RHODA' (the latter a cut from '89), with McMAHAN, however, embarking on his own adventure, The FOR CARNATION with SLINT buddy PAJO; other members DOUGLAS McCOMBS, GRANT BARGER and JOHN HERNDON. This quintet released the EP, 'FLIGHT SONGS' (1995), while the mini-set 'MARSHMALLOWS' (1996) was without the much in-demand PAJO. Not released in Britian, it finally surfaced in 1997 as 'PROMISED WORKS', containing the debut EP tracks. Like in SLINT, McMAHAN enforced the dizzy guitars and whispering sung/spoken vocals that made the aforementioned group sound so interesting, GALAXIE 500 and GASTR DEL SOL were also names that were thrown in as noteworthy comparisons. Adding LEONARD COHEN-esque incoherence to the mix, a slightly surreal view of life encouraged McMAHAN's lyrics and influence to reach higher dynamic points within his sound and vision. With his brother MICHAEL on guitar, BOB BRUNO, TODD COOK and moonlighting RADAR BROS drummer STEVE GOODFRIEND, The FOR CARNATION were reborn for an album which was scheduled for release early 2000. Meanwhile, following PAJO's stint with avant-jazz combo, TORTOISE, the musical Jack-of-all trades followed a similar dusty path to the aforementioned WILL OLDHAM, on his eponymous 1997 debut solo set (released under the AERIAL-M moniker), foregoing vocals in favour of backporch strumming. Licensed from 'Drag City' to 'Domino' in the UK, the rootsy homegrown affair showed a mellower side to the normally uncompromising guitarist and paved the way for two further releases over the course of the following year. Neither single, 'M IS . . .' and 'OCTOBER', featured on the album, although they may well make an appearance on the anticipated follow-up.

Album rating: TWEEZ (*7) / SPIDERLAND (*8) / Aerial-M: AERIAL-M (*7) / For Carnation: PROMISED WORKS collection of US EP's (*6)

BRIAN McMAHAN – vocals, guitar (ex-SQUIRREL BAIT) / **DAVID PAJO** – guitar / **ETHAN BUCKLER** – bass / **BRITT WALFORD** – drums (ex-SQUIRREL BAIT)

	Jennifer Hartman	Jennifer Hartman
Sep 89. (lp) <(JHR 136)> **TWEEZ**		

– Ron / Nan ding / Carol / Kent / Charlotte / Darlene / Warren / Pat / Rhoda. <(re-iss. May93 on 'Touch & Go' lp/cd; TG 138/+D)>

——— **TODD BRASHER** – bass; BUCKLER who formed KING KONG

	Touch & Go	Touch & Go
Mar 91. (lp/cd) <(T&Glp*64/+cd)> **SPIDERLAND**		

– Breadcrumb trail / Nosferatu man / Don, Aman / Washer / For dinner . . . / Good morning, captain. (re-iss. Sep98; same)

Sep 94. (10"/cd-s) <(T&G*132/+cd)> **SLINT**		

– Glenn / Rhoda.

——— had already disbanded in 1992, WALFORD + McMAHAN later joined the PALACE BROTHERS; the latter also formed The FOR CARNATION. PAJO (a part-timer with TFC) subsequently joined TORTOISE before forming AERIAL-M.

The FOR CARNATION

BRIAN McMAHAN with **DAVID PAJO** – guitar / **DOUGLAS McCOMBS** – bass / **JOHN HERNDON** – drums / **GRANT BARGER** – engineer, co-writer

	Matador	Matador
Jun 95. (cd-ep) <(OLE 131-2)> **FIGHT SONGS EP**		Apr95

– Grace beneath the pines / How I beat the Devil / Get and stay get March.

——— **BRAD WOOD, JOHN WEISS + TIM RUTH** repl. PAJO

Mar 96. (m-cd/m-lp) <(OLE 172-2/-1)> **MARSHMALLOWS**	-	

– On the swing / I wear the gold / Imyr, marshmallow / Winter lair / Salo / Preparing to receive you.

	Runt	not iss.
Jun 97. (cd) (RUNT 30) **PROMISED WORKS** (compilation of the EP and mini-set)		-

——— **McMAHAN** recruited his brother **MICHAEL McMAHAN** – guitar / **BOBB BRUNO** – guitar, sampler, keyboards / **TODD COOK** – bass / **STEVE GOODFRIEND** – drums / forthcoming set in March 2000 also incl. **KIM DEAL** – vocals (ex-PIXIES) / **RACHEL HAYDEN** – vocals (of that dog.) + **JOHN McENTIRE** – (who else?, on production)

AERIAL-M

DAVID PAJO – guitars

	Domino	Drag City
1996. (7") **SAFELESS.** /	-	
Dec 96. (7"; split with MONADE) **VOL DE NUIT.** /	-	
Sep 97. (cd/lp) (WIG CD/LP 037) <DC 114> **AS PERFORMED BY . . . AERIAL-M**		Aug97

– Dazed and awake / Aass / Wedding song No.2 / Rachmaninoff / Skrak theme / Compassion for M / Always farewell.

Feb 98. (7"m)<cd-ep> (RUG 062)<DC 144CD> **M IS . . . / WEDDING THEME NO.3 / MOUNTAINS HAVE EARS**		Dec97
Jun 98. (7") (RUG 070) <DC 155> **OCTOBER**		Feb99

– Vivea / Last caress.

SLIPKNOT

Formed: Des Moines, Iowa, USA . . . 1995 by members 0, 1, 2, 3, 4, 5, 6, 7 and 8 – aka DJ SID WILSON, JOEY JORDISON, PAUL GRAY, CHRIS FEHN, JAMES ROOT, CRAIG JONES, SHAWN CRAHAN, MIC THOMPSON and singer (or screamer) COREY TAYLOR. The menacing 9-piece recorded and released the now rare album 'MATE, FEED, KILL, REPEAT' in 1996, receiving mass attention from record labels in the process. The ensemble signed with 'Roadrunner' in 1997 and released their self-titled debut album in 1999. The album (predictably) gained a huge cult following from the widespread majority of disfunctional teens all over the globe. In a way, it's not hard to describe SLIPKNOT's music: fast, heavy, vicious, ferocious, venomous and crude – in fact a few journos made them out to be Rock's answer to 'The Texas Chainsaw Massacre'. The mask-clad spooksters have found their niche within the flow of sports metal in the US, bands such as KORN and white chumps LIMP BIZKIT thrive off the money made from these double-bass drum pedallers. But as a band, the angsty punk-metallers are not bad, mixing in a blend of tricky, thumping and downright blastferic lyrics along with the pounding guitars and drums. It's what grandmothers have nightmares about.

Album rating: SLIPKNOT (*8)

COREY TAYLOR – vocals / **MIC THOMPSON** – guitar / **JIM ROOT** – guitar / **PAUL GRAY** – bass / **JOEY JORDISON** – drums / **CHRIS FEHN** – percussion / **SHAWN CRAHAN** – percussion / **CRAIG JONES** – samples, programmes / **SID WILSON** – DJ

	not iss.	unknown
1996. (cd) **MATE, FEED, KILL, REPEAT**	-	
	Roadrunner	Roadrunner
Jun 99. (cd) <(RR 8655-2)> **SLIPKNOT**	37	

– 74261000027 / Eyel ESS / Wait and bleed / Surfacing / Spit it out / Tattered and torn / Frail limb nursery / Purity / Liberate / Prosthetics / No life / Diluted / The only one. (other cd+=; RR 8655-5) – Me inside / Get this / Interloper (demo) / Despise (demo).
(above will break into the US Top 100 early 2000)

SLITS

Formed: London, England . . . early 1977 as the foremost all-girl outfit on the punk scene (until BUDGIE joined that is) and initially comprising ARI UP (aka ARIANNA FOSTER), KATE KORUS, SUZI GUTSY and PALMOLIVE. By the time the group had secured a support slot on The CLASH's Spring 1977 tour, KORUS and GUTSY had been replaced by VIV ALBERTINE and TESSA POLLITT respectively, the band's infamously amateurish approach compensated by their bolshy hardline feminist attitude. Although they had two John Peel sessions under their belts, The SLITS didn't actually sign a deal until 1979, having turned down the 'Real' label (home to The HEARTBREAKERS and PRETENDERS) the previous year. In the event the not-so "TYPICAL GIRLS" signed with 'Island' and set to work on a debut album with reggae producer, Dennis Bovell, the aforementioned BUDGIE (PETER CLARK) coming in as a replacement for PALMOLIVE who departed midway through the recording sessions. A Top 30 hit upon its release in late '79, the seminal 'CUT' showcased ARI's distinctive vocal phrasing against a compelling backdrop of unorthodox tribal rhythms and raw guitar abrasion, the sleeve's cover shot of the lasses getting butt naked and muddy generating almost as much interest as the music. With BUDGIE decamping to SIOUXSIE & THE BANSHEES, BRUCE SMITH was recruited in his place and despite the presence of respected jazz trumpeter, DON CHERRY (father of NENEH), a dreadful untitled bootleg/jam affair did the band no favours. Much more enjoyable was the subsequent cover of John Holt's 'MAN NEXT DOOR', released as a single a couple of months later in the summer of 1980. A further single followed on the 'Human' label before The SLITS signed to 'C.B.S.' for a final disappointing patchy album, 'RETURN OF THE GIANT SLITS' (1981), the group disbanding in early '82. While SMITH joined Bristolian avant-funk collective RIP, RIG & PANIC, the remaining members (minus POLLITT) went on to be part of colossus ensemble, The NEW AGE STEPPERS.
• **Songwriters:** Group compositions, except I HEARD IT THROUGH THE GRAPEVINE (Marvin Gaye). • **Trivia:** Early in 1978, they were sighted in the punk film, 'Jubilee'.

Album rating: CUT (*9) / UNTITLED (*1) / RETURN OF THE GIANT SLITS (*6) / DOUBLE PEEL SESSIONS collection (*7)

ARI UP (b. ARIANNA FOSTER) – vocals / **VIVIEN ALBERTINE** – guitar (ex-FLOWERS OF ROMANCE) repl. KATE KORUS to KLEENEX (Feb77) / **TESSA POLLITT** – bass repl. SUZI GUTSY who formed The FLICKS. / **PALMOLIVE** – drums (ex-FLOWERS OF ROMANCE) was repl. (Oct78) by **BUDGIE** (b. PETER CLARK, 21 Aug'??, St.Helens, England) – percussion, drums (ex-BIG IN JAPAN, ex-SECRETS,etc)

	Island	Antilles
Sep 79. (lp/c) (ILPS/ZC1 9573) <7072> **CUT**	30	

– Instant hit / So tough / Spend spend spend / Shoplifting / FM / Newtown / Ping pong affair / Love and romance / Typical girls / Adventures close to home. (cd-iss. Apr90; IMCD 89)

Sep 79. (7") (WIP 6505) **TYPICAL GIRLS.** / **I HEARD IT THROUGH THE GRAPEVINE**	60	

(12"+=) (12WIP 6505) – Typical girls (brink style) / Liebe and romanze.

——— **BRUCE SMITH** – drums (of POP GROUP) repl. BUDGIE to SIOUXSIE & BANSHEES jazz-trumpeter **DON CHERRY** guested

		Y – Rough Trade	not iss.
Mar 80.	(7") *(Y1 – RT 039)* **IN THE BEGINNING THERE WAS RHYTHM. / (B-side by the Pop Group)**		-
May 80.	(lp) *(Y3LP)* **UNTITLED (Y3LP)** (bootleg demo jam)		-

– A boring life / Slime / Or what it is / No.1 enemy / Once upon a time in a living room / Bongos on the lawn / Face place / Let's do the split / Mosquitos / Vaseline / No more rock and roll for you.

| Jun 80. | (7") *(Y4 – RT 044)* **MAN NEXT DOOR. / MAN NEXT DOOR (dub version)** | | - |

—— added guest **STEVE BERESFORD** – keyboards, guitar (of FLYING LIZARDS)

		Human C.B.S.	not iss. Epic
Nov 80.	(7") *(HUM 4)* **ANIMAL SPACE. / ANIMAL SPACIER**		
1981.	(12"m) **ANIMAL SPACE. / ANIMAL SPACIER / IN THE BEGINNING THERE WAS RHYTHM**	-	-
Aug 81.	(7") *(A 1498)* **EARTHBEAT. / BEGIN AGAIN RHYTHM** (12"+=) *(A13 1498)* – Earthdub.		-
Oct 81.	(lp/c) *(CBS/40 85269)* **RETURN OF THE GIANT SLITS**		

– Earthbeat / Or what it is? / Face place / Walkabout / Difficult fun / Animal space – Spacier / Improperly dressed / Life on Earth. *(free-7"w/ lp) (XPS 125)* – AMERICAN RADIO INTERVIEW (Winter 1980). / FACE DUB

| Dec 81. | (7") *(49-02567)* **EARTHBEAT. / OR WHAT IT IS?** | - | - |

—— Parted ways early 1982. BRUCE joined RIP, RIG & PANIC. All except TESSA were part of colossus band NEW AGE STEPPERS.

– compilations, others, etc. –

on 'Strange Fruit' unless otherwise mentioned

| Feb 87. | (12"ep) *(SFPS 021)* **THE PEEL SESSION** (19.9.77) | | - |

– Love and romance / Vindictive / Newtown / Shoplifting.

| Nov 88. | (m-lp/cd) *(SFPMA/+CD 207)* **DOUBLE PEEL SESSIONS** | | - |

SLOWDIVE (dig out; Great Alt & Indie . . .)

SLY & THE FAMILY STONE

Formed: San Francisco, California, USA . . . 1966, initially as The STONERS by former DJ/Producer, SLY STONE (born SYLVESTER STEWART) with brother FREDDIE, sister ROSEMARY and cousin LARRY GRAHAM. They adopted the name SLY & THE FAMILY STONE after gigging around local bars/clubs in Oakland and in 1967 they signed to 'Epic', releasing their debut album, 'A WHOLE NEW THING'. The record introduced the superfly new sound created by one of the first inter-racial, inter-gender and inta-drugs outfits to emerge between the rock/soul divide. With SLY casting himself HENDRIX-like in the role of Afro-American uber-hippie, he and his family were pioneers of the "Psychedelic Soul" movement, re-influencing old hands like The TEMPTATIONS and The ISLEY BROTHERS. Their breakthrough came with the 1968 single, 'DANCE TO THE MUSIC', a skilfully honed melange of doo-wop, soul and acid-funk that shook even the most stoned of hippy asses. The album of the same name followed later that year, crystallising the bands distinctive cross-over sound. Possibly their finest moment, the irresistable swing of 'EVERYDAY PEOPLE' was almost gospel-like in its passionate intensity. The single's B-side, 'SING A SIMPLE SONG', was similarly evangelical and illustrated that musically, at least, in The FAMILY STONE all the soul brothers and sisters were born equal. Each family member was given a fair deal in the mix, both instrumentally and vocally, and along with the band's unique hybrid of styles, this musical equanimity defined their sound. The classic 'STAND' (1969) album fully captured this collective, celebratory fanfare, including the aforementioned tracks as well as the 15-minute bass-heavy pulse of 'SEX MACHINE'. It also introduced SLY's penchant for mordant humour with 'DON'T CALL ME NIGGER, WHITEY'. As the 60's dream turned sour, this penchant would become ever more pronounced, 'HOT FUN IN THE SUMMERTIME' (1969) a wry observation on America's summer of discontent. Come 1970, SLY had moved to L.A. where he immersed himself in cocaine and the vacuum of the back-slapping Hollywood elite. 'THANK YOU (FALLETTINME BE MICE ELF AGIN)' (1970) was an edgy piece of taut funk that indicated the way SLY was headed. Partly composed in SLY's infamous drug den of a motorhome, where he lived gypsy-style around L.A., 'THERE'S A RIOT GOIN' ON' finally appeared in 1971. Reflecting the drug-induced paranoia and detachment of the recording sessions, most of the tracks were blurred snatches of dirty, slow burning funk, topped off by SLY's ravaged vocal chords. The deceptively laid-back groove of 'FAMILY AFFAIR' belied a grim lyrical content which extended to the whole album. From his embalming cocoon of Grade-A narcotics, SLY gave a hazily cynical commentary on the decline of American civilisation, and the album remains a darkly brooding classic. With drug busts, financial pressures and hassles from militant black nationalists who didn't care for SLY's racially mixed philosophy, it was two years before 'FRESH' (1973) was released. While the sound recalled the band's effervescent charisma of old, a distinct edginess remained in the watertight grooves. The cool pop-funk of 'IF YOU WANT ME TO STAY' (1973) was the 'FAMILY STONE's last top 20 single. 'SMALL TALK' (1974) was almost overwhelmingly bland save for the title track and from there on in, SLY lost it big time. A drug casualty of the saddest order, SLY's latter 70's output was unremarkable at best. • **Songwriters:** All by SLY and group except; I CAN'T TURN YOU LOOSE (Otis Redding) / YOU REALLY GOT ME (Kinks). • **Trivia:** On the 5th of June '74, SLY married Kathy Silva on stage at Madison Square Garden. Two months earlier, she had borne him his first child, Bubb Ali (all three pictured on the album cover of 'SMALL TALK'). She divorced SLY in '75, and he filed for bankruptcy early '76.

Album rating: A WHOLE NEW THING (*5) / DANCE TO THE MUSIC (*6) / LIFE (*6) / STAND! (*9) / GREATEST HITS compilation (*8) / THERE'S A RIOT GOIN' ON (*9) / FRESH (*7) / SMALL TALK (*6) / HIGH ON YOU (*5; by Sly Stone) / HEARD YA MISSED ME, WELL I'M BACK (*4) / BACK ON THE RIGHT TRACK (*4) / AIN'T BUT THE ONE WAY (*4) / TAKIN' YOU HIGHER – THE BEST OF SLY & THE FAMILY STONE compilation (*8)

SLY STONE

SLY STONE's early US recordings under various pseudonyms

—— first 2 with brother FREDDIE and sister ROSE? (most doo-wop sound)

1959.	(7"; by STEWART BROTHERS) *<Ensign; 4032>* **THE RAT. / RA RA ROO**	-	
1960.	(7"; by STEWART BROTHERS) *<Keen; 2113>* **SLEEP ON THE PORCH. / YUM YUM YUM**	-	
1961.	(7"; by DANNY STEWART) *<Luke 1008>* **A LONG TIME ALONE. / I'M JUST A FOOL**	-	
1961.	(7"; by SYLVESTER STEWART) *<G&P; 901>* **A LONG TIME ALONE. / HELP ME WITH MY BROKEN HEART**	-	
1961.	(7"; by the VISCANES) *<Tropo; 101>* **STOP WHAT YOU ARE DOING. / I GUESS I'LL BE**	-	
1961.	(7"; by the VISCANES) *<VPM; 1006>* **YELLOW MOON. / UNCLE SAM NEEDS YOU**	-	
1961.	(7"; by SLY STEWART) **YELLOW MOON. / HEAVENLY ANGEL**	-	
1964.	(7"; by SLY STEWART) *<Autumn; 3>* **I JUST LEARNED HOW TO SWIM. / SCAT SWIM**	-	
1965.	(7"; by SLY) *<Autumn; 14>* **BUTTERMILK. / (part 2)**	-	
1965.	(7"; by SLY) *<Autumn; 26>* **TEMPTATION WALK. / (part 2)**	-	

—— SLY at this time was producing Autumn acts The BEAU BRUMMELS, BOBBY FREEMAN and The MOJO MEN. He also became well-known local DJ for K-DIA.

SLY & THE FAMILY STONE

SLY STONE (b. SYLVESTER STEWART, 15 Mar'44, Dallas, Texas) – vox, guitar, keyboards (ex-SLY & THE MOJO MEN) / **FREDDIE STONE** (b. FRED STEWART, 5 Jun'46, Dallas) – guitar / **CYNTHIA ROBINSON** (b.12 Jan'46, Sacramento, Calif.) – trumpet / **ROSEMARY STONE** (b. ROSEMARY STEWART, 21 Mar'45, Vallejo, Calif.) – vocals, piano / **LARRY GRAHAM** (b.14 Aug'46, Beaumont, Texas) – bass / **JERRY MARTINI** (b. 1 Oct'43, Colorado) – saxophone / **GREG ERRICO** (b. 1 Sep'46) – drums

		not iss. Columbia	Loadstone Epic
1966.	(7") *<3951>* **I AIN'T GOT NOBODY. / I CAN'T TURN YOU LOOSE**	-	
1967.	(lp) *<30333>* **A WHOLE NEW THING**	-	

– Underdog / If this room could talk / Run run run / Turn me loose / Let me hear it from you / Advice / I cannot make it / Trip to your heart / I hate to love her / Bad risk / That kind of person / Day. *(cd-iss. Jul95 on 'Epic'; EK 66424)*

| 1967. | (7") *<10229>* **(I WANT TO TAKE YOU) HIGHER. / UNDERDOG** | - | |

		Direction	Epic
Mar 68.	(7") *(DB 8369)* *<10256>* **DANCE TO THE MUSIC. / LET ME HEAR IT FROM YOU**		8 Jan68
Jun 68.	(7") *(58-3568)* **DANCE TO THE MUSIC. / LET ME HEAR IT FROM YOU**	7	-
Sep 68.	(lp) *(8-63412)* *<26371>* **DANCE TO THE MUSIC**		Apr68

– Dance to the music / (I want to take you) Higher / I ain't got nobody (for real) / Dance to the medley: Music is alive – Dance in – Music lover / Ride the rhythm / Color me true / Are you ready / Don't burn baby / I'll never fall in love again. *(re-iss. Oct73 on 'Embassy'; EMB 31030) (cd-iss. Jul94 on 'Epic'; 480906-2)*

| Sep 68. | (7") *(58-3707)* *<10353>* **M'LADY. / LIFE** | 32 | 93
93 Jun68 |
| Jan 69. | (lp) *(8-63461)* *<26397>* **M'LADY** (US-title 'LIFE') | | Nov68 |

– Dynamite! / Chicken / Plastic Jim / Fun / Into my own thing / Harmony / Life / Love city / I'm an animal / M'lady / Jane is a groupie.

| Mar 69. | (7") *(58-3938)* *<10407>* **EVERYDAY PEOPLE. / SING A SIMPLE SONG** | 36 | 1
89 Nov68 |
| May 69. | (7") *(58-4279)* *<10450>* **STAND!. / I WANT TO TAKE YOU HIGHER** | | 22
60 Apr69 |

<re-prom.May70 but flipped over, hit US No.38>

| Jul 69. | (lp) *(8-63655)* *<26456>* **STAND!** | | 13 Apr69 |

– Stand! / Don't call me nigger, Whitey / I want to take you higher / Somebody's watching you / Sing a simple song / Everyday people / Sex machine / You can make it if you try. *(cd-iss. Feb95 on 'Epic'; EK 64422)*

| Aug 69. | (7") *(58-4471)* *<10497>* **HOT FUN IN THE SUMMERTIME. / FUN** | | 2 |
| Feb 70. | (7") *(58-4782)* *<10555>* **THANK YOU (FALLETTINME BE MICE ELF AGIN). / EVERYBODY IS A STAR** | | 1 Dec69 |

		C.B.S.	Epic
May 70.	(7") *(5054)* **I WANT TO TAKE YOU HIGHER. / YOU CAN MAKE IT IF YOU TRY**		-
Jan 71.	(lp) *(EPC 69002)* *<30325>* **GREATEST HITS** (compilation)		2 Oct70

– I want to take you higher / Everybody is a star / Stand / Life / Fun / You can make it if you try / Dance to the music / Everyday people / Hot fun in the summertime / M'lady / Sing a simple song / Thank you (falletinme be mice elf agin). *(<quad-lp 1975; EQ 30325>) (re-iss. Mar81 on 'Epic'; EPC 32029) (re-iss. Jun90 on 'Epic' cd/c/lp; EPC 462524-2/-4/-1)*

		Epic Epic	
Nov 71.	(7") *(EPC 7632)* *<10805>* **FAMILY AFFAIR. / LUV 'N' HAIGHT**	15	1 Oct71
Jan 72.	(lp/c) *(EPC/40 64613)* *<30986>* **THERE'S A RIOT GOIN' ON**	31	1 Nov71

– Luv 'n' haight / Just like a baby / Poet / Family affair / Africa talks to you 'The Asphalt Jungle' / Brave & strong / Smilin' / Time / Spaced cowboy / Runnin' away / Thank you for talkin' to me Africa. *(UK-iss.w/free ltd.7"ep & newspaper) (re-iss. Feb86 on 'Edsel' lp/c; XED/CED 165) (cd-iss. Jan91; EDCD 165) (re-iss. May94 cd/c; 467063-2/-4)*

Mar 72. (7") (EPC 7810) <10829> **RUNNIN' AWAY. / BRAVE & STRONG** — 17 | 23 Jan72

Apr 72. (7") <10850> **SMILIN'. / LUV 'N' HAIGHT** — - | 42

—— (Jan73) **RUSTEE ALLEN** – bass repl. LARRY (formed GRAHAM CENTRAL STATION) **ANDY NEWMARK** – drums repl. ERRICO. / added **PAT RICCO** – saxophone

Jun 73. (lp/c) (EPC/40 69039) <32134> **FRESH**   [ ] | 7
– In time / If you want me to stay / Let me have it all / Frisky / Thankful 'n' thoughtful / The skin I'm in / I don't know (satisfaction) / Keep on dancin' / Que sera sera / If it were left up to me / Babies makin' babies. *(re-iss. May87 on 'Edsel' lp/c/cd; XED/CED/EDCD 232) (cd re-iss. Sep96 on 'Columbia'; 485170-2)*

Aug 73. (7") (EPC 1655) <11017> **IF YOU WANT ME TO STAY. / THANKFUL 'N' THOUGHTFUL**   [ ] | 12 Jun73

Oct 73. (7") <11060> **FRISKY. / IF IT WERE LEFT UP TO ME**   - | 79

Jan 74. (7") (EPC 1981) **QUE SERA SERA. / IF IT WERE LEFT UP TO ME**   [ ] | -

—— **BILL LORDAN** – drums repl. NEWMARK who became session man

Jul 74. (lp/c) (EPC/40 69070) <32930> **SMALL TALK**   [ ] | 15
– Small talk / Say you will / Mother beautiful / Time for livin' / Can't strain my brain / Loose booty / Holdin' on / Wishful thinking / Better thee than me / Livin' while I'm livin' / This is love.

Jul 74. (7") (EPC 2530) <11140> **TIME FOR LIVIN'. / SMALL TALK**   [ ] | 32

Jan 75. (7") (EPC 1882) <50033> **LOOSE BOOTY. / CAN'T STRAIN MY BRAIN**   [ ] | 84 Oct84

SLY STONE

Oct 75. (lp/c) <EPC/40 69165> <33835> **HIGH ON YOU**   [ ] | 45
– I get high on you / Crossword puzzle / That's lovin' you / Who do you love / Green-eyed monster girl / Organize / Le lo li / My world / So good to me / Greed.

Oct 75. (7") (EPC 3596) <50135> **I GET HIGH ON YOU. / THAT'S LOVIN' YOU**   [ ] | 52 Sep75

Dec 75. (7") <50175> **LE LO LI. / WHO DO YOU LOVE**   [ ] | -

Mar 76. (7") <50201> **CROSSWORD PUZZLE. / GREED**   [ ] | -

SLY & THE FAMILY STONE

—— reformed with last line-up

Dec 76. (lp/c) (EPC/40 81641) <33698> **HEARD YA MISSED ME, WELL I'M BACK**   [ ] | [ ]
– Heard ya missed me, well I'm back / What was I thinkin' / In my head / Sexy situation / Blessing in disguise / Everything in you / Mother is a hippie / Let's be together / The thing / Family again.

Feb 77. (7") <50331> **FAMILY AGAIN. / NOTHING LESS THAN HAPPINESS**   - | [ ]

Warners / Warners

Sep 79. (7") (K 17474) <49062> **REMEMBER WHO YOU ARE. / SHEER ENERGY**   [ ] | [ ]

Oct 79. (lp/c) (K/K4 56640) <3303> **BACK ON THE RIGHT TRACK**   [ ] | [ ]
– Remember who you are / Back on the right track / If it's not addin' up . . . / The same thing (makes you laugh, makes you cry) / Shine it on / It takes all kinds / Who's to say / Sheer energy. *(cd-iss. Jan96; 7599 26858-2)*

Dec 79. (7") <49132> **THE SAME THING (MAKES YOU LAUGH, MAKES YOU CRY). / WHO'S TO SAY**   - | [ ]

—— In 1981, SLY guested on album 'THE ELECTRIC SPANKING OF WAR BABIES' by George Clinton's FUNKADELIC.

– compilations, etc. –

—— on 'Epic' unless stated otherwise

1972. (lp; by SLY STONE) *Sculpture*; <SCP 2001> **RECORDED IN SAN FRANCISCO: 1964-67**   - | -

Mar 73. (7") (EPC 1148) **FAMILY AFFAIR. / DANCE TO THE MUSIC**   - | -

Feb 75. (7"ep) (EPC 3048) **DANCE TO THE MUSIC / COLOUR ME TRUE. / STAND! / RIDE THE RHYTHM**   [ ] | -

May 75. (d-lp/c) (EPC 22004) <33462> **HIGH ENERGY**   [ ] | [ ]
– (A WHOLE NEW THING / LIFE)

1975. (7") <50119> **HOT FUN IN THE SUMMERTIME. / FUN**   - | [ ]

1975. (7") (152282) **DANCE TO THE MUSIC. / LIFE**   [ ] | -

1975. (7") (152302) **HOT FUN IN THE SUMMERTIME. / M'LADY**   [ ] | -

1975. (7") (152317) **FAMILY AFFAIR. / RUNNIN' AWAY**   [ ] | -

1975. (7") (152331) **IF YOU WANT ME TO STAY. / FRISKY**   [ ] | -

Jan 77. (7") <EPC 4879> **DANCE TO THE MUSIC. / I WANT TO TAKE YOU HIGHER**   [ ] | -

Mar 79. (7") (EPC 7070) **DANCE TO THE MUSIC. / STAND!**   [ ] | -

Nov 79. (7") (EPC 8017) <50795> **DANCE TO THE MUSIC. / SING A SIMPLE SONG**   [ ] | -

Jan 80. (lp) (EPC 83640) <35974> **TEN YEARS TOO SOON** (disco remixes)   [ ] | -

Aug 80. (7") (EPC 8853) **DANCE TO THE MUSIC. / EVERYDAY PEOPLE**   [ ] | -
(re-iss. Jul82 on 'Old Gold'; OG 9188)

May 82. (d-lp) (EPC 22119) <37071> **ANTHOLOGY**   [ ] | [ ] Dec81
(re-iss. Sep87 lp/c; 460175-1/-4)

Sep 87. (7") *Portrait*; (SLY 1) **DANCE TO THE MUSIC. / FAMILY AFFAIR**   [ ] | [ ]
(12"+=) (SLYT 1) – Everyday people / Runnin' away.

Apr 91. (cd/c) *Thunderbolt*; (CDTB/THBC 119) **FAMILY AFFAIR**   [ ] | -

Nov 91. (cd/c) *Castle*; (CCS CD/MC 307) **THE COLLECTION**   [ ] | -

Dec 91. (cd) *Thunderbolt*; (CDTB 129) **IN THE STILL OF THE NIGHT**   [ ] | -

Jul 92. (cd/c/lp) *Sony*; (471758-2/-4) **TAKIN' YOU HIGHER – THE BEST OF SLY & THE FAMILY STONE**   [ ] | -
– Dance to the music / I want to take you higher / Family affair / Thank you (falletinme be mice elf agin) / I get high on you / Stand / M'lady / Skin I'm in / Everyday people / Sing a simple song / Hot fun in the summertime / Don't call me nigger, Whitey / Brave & strong / Life / Everybody is a star / If you want me to stay / (You caught me) Smilin' / Que sera sera / Running away / Family affair (remix). *(cd re-iss. Oct94 on 'Epic'; 477506-2)*

Feb 94. (cd/c) *Javelin*; (HAD CD/MC 119) **SPOTLIGHT ON SLY & THE FAMILY STONE**   [ ] | [ ]

Mar 94. (cd) *Charly*; **REMEMBER WHO YOU ARE**   [ ] | [ ]

Sep 94. (cd) *Ace*; (CDCHD 539) **PRECIOUS STONE: IN THE STUDIO WITH SLY STONE** (rec.1963-65)   [ ] | [ ]

Dec 94. (cd/c) *Prestige*; (CD/CAS SGP 0125) **EVERY DOG HAS IT'S DAY**   [ ] | [ ]

Feb 95. (cd; by SLY STONE & THE MOJO MEN) (KLMCD 005) **PEARLS FROM THE PAST**   [ ] | [ ]

—— Thunderbolt records issued 2 albums of SLY STONE productions in Apr87 + Oct87 respectively, named 'DANCE TO THE MUSIC' & 'FAMILY AFFAIR'.

SLY STONE

Warners / Warners

Mar 83. (lp) (923700-1) <23700-1> **AIN'T BUT THE ONE WAY**   [ ] | [ ]
– L.O.V.I.N.U. / One way / Ha ha, hee hee / Hobo Ken / Who in the funk do you think we are / You really got me / Sylvester / We can do it / High, y'all. *(cd-iss. Jan96; 7599 23700-2)*

—— In 1984, SLY joined BOBBY WOMACK on tour. He later guested on JESSE JOHNSON's 'A&M' US No.53 hit single 'Crazay' (Oct86) *AM 360 /<2878>.*

not iss. / A&M

Oct 86. (7") <2890> **EEK-A-BO-STATIK. / BLACK GIRLS (RAE DAWN CHONG)**   - | -

Dec 86. (7"w/ MARTHA DAVIS) **STONE LOVE AND AFFECTION. / BLACK GIRLS (RAE DAWN CHONG)**   - | -

SMALL FACES

Formed: East London, England . . . mid '65 by RONNIE LANE, KENNY JONES and JIMMY WINSTON, who subsequently found lead singer and ex-child actor, STEVE MARRIOTT. After a successful residency at Leicester Square's Cavern Club, the band were snapped up by 'Decca' records as potential usurpers to The WHO's mod crown. Their debut single, 'WHATCHA GONNA DO ABOUT IT' (1965) graced the Top 20 with its roughshod R&B and amid the ensuing attention the band received, WINSTON was kicked out after shamelessly trying to promote himself as the lynchpin of the group. With IAN McLAGAN drafted in as a replacement, the band hit Top 3 with the 'SHA LA LA LA LEE' (1966) single. Despite the cliched boy-meets-girl lyric, the record was a wildly exhilarating rush of amphetamine pop and suddenly The SMALL FACES were big news. After another Top 10 single and a critically acclaimed eponymous debut album, the band were being mentioned in the same breath as The BEATLES and The ROLLING STONES. Indeed, in August '66 they deposed The Fab Four's 'ELEANOR RIGBY' at the top of the charts with 'ALL OR NOTHING'. Come 1967, the band had left 'Decca' and signed with ANDREW LOOG-OLDHAM's 'Immediate' label, releasing 'HERE COMES THE NICE'. The single marked a change in direction and in keeping with the times, was vaguely psychedelic. After a similarly adventurous second album that bore a decidedly unadventurous title ('SMALL FACES' yet again), the band released their most well-known track, the slightly twee, deeply dippy 'ITCHYCOO PARK' (later reduced to dross by M-PEOPLE). Next came the abrasive 'TIN SOLDIER' (1967) single after which the band began working on their psychedelic masterpiece, 'OGDEN'S NUT GONE FLAKE' (1968). An engaging blend of trippy R&B and cockney charm, the album's influence was far reaching and it gets re-issued with the same tireless regularity as 'OCEAN WELLER SCENE' namedrop the band. Timeless as it was, the record proved to be the group's swansong and after a few singles, including the gorgeous 'AFTERGLOW (OF YOUR LOVE)' (1969), the band split, with MARRIOTT flouncing off to form HUMBLE PIE. Meanwhile JONES, LANE and McLAGAN ditched the psychedelic overtones, recruited RON WOOD and ROD STEWART, renaming the band The FACES; lad-rock was born! The FACES peddled a distinctive strain of ramshackle, boozy, bluesy rock that was apparently best heard in a live setting surrounded by sweaty males. Their debut, 'FIRST STEP' (1970), was a boisterous statement of intent which included the ragged charm of 'THREE BUTTON HAND ME DOWN' and a raw cover of DYLAN's 'WICKED MESSENGER'. 'LONG PLAYER' (1971) was equally ballsy, while 'A NOD IS AS GOOD AS A WINK . . .TO A BLIND HORSE' (1971) saw the band in full flight, WOOD going hell for leather on 'MISS JUDY'S FARM' and the gloriously un-PC raunch of 'STAY WITH ME'. The McLAGAN/LANE penned 'YOU'RE SO RUDE' was a leering gem and LANE excelled himself with the lovely 'DEBRIS'. As STEWART's solo career skyrocketed, the band began to splinter, unbalanced by ROD's high profile. After the slightly disappointing 'OOH LA LA' (1973) album, LANE left to go solo, The FACES basically becoming STEWART's backing band and after a final below-par live album, RON WOOD left for The ROLLING STONES. There was a brief SMALL FACES reunion (minus LANE) in the late 70's and although the band had a deal with 'Atlantic', no commercial success was forthcoming. JONES went on to join The WHO, while MARRIOTT re-formed HUMBLE PIE but any chances of a further reunion were dealt a fatal blow in 1991 when MARRIOTT tragically died in a fire at his Essex home. After a respectable, if hardly commercial solo career, RONNIE LANE finally succumbed to Multiple Sclerosis earlier this year (1997). A sad end for two pioneering musicians who, through both The FACES and The SMALL FACES, heavily influenced the course of popular music; stand up BLUR, PULP, OASIS, PRIMAL SCREAM, The BLACK CROWES etc.
• **Songwriters:** MARRIOTT and LANE except; WHATCHA GONNA DO ABOUT IT (Ian Samwell-Smith; their early producer) / SHA-LA-LA-LA-LEE

(c.Kenny Lynch & Mort Schuman) / EVERY LITTLE BIT HURTS (Brenda Holloway) / TAKE THIS HURT OFF ME (Don Covay) / YOU'VE REALLY GOT A HOLD ON ME (Miracles) / etc. The FACES covered MAYBE I'M AMAZED (Paul McCartney) / I WISH IT WOULD RAIN (Temptations) / etc.
• **Trivia:** The FACES had come together initially as the supergroup, QUIET MELON, which included ART WOOD, LONG JOHN BALDRY and JIMMY HOROWITZ.

Album rating: THE SMALL FACES (*6) / FROM THE BEGINNING out-takes (*6) / SMALL FACES (*5) / THERE ARE BUT FOUR SMALL FACES (*7) / OGDENS' NUT GONE FLAKE (*8) / THE AUTUMN STONE collection (*5) / Faces: FIRST STEP (*6) / LONG PLAYER (*6) / A NOD'S AS GOOD AS A WINK (TO A BLIND HORSE) (*7) / OOH LA LA (*6) / COAST TO COAST – OVERTURE FOR BEGINNERS (*5; as Rod Stewart & The Faces) / SNAKES AND LADDERS: THE BEST OF THE FACES compilation (*7) / Small Faces: PLAYMATES (*3) / 78 IN THE SHADE (*4) / THE ULTIMATE COLLECTION compilation (*8)

STEVE MARRIOTT (b.30 Jan'47, Bow, London) – vocals, guitar (ex-solo artist) / **JIMMY WINSTON** (b. JAMES LANGWITH, 20 Apr'45, Stratford, London) – organ / **RONNIE LANE** (b. 1 Apr'45, Plaistow, London) – bass, vocals / **KENNEY JONES** (b.16 Sep'48, Stepney, London) – drums

		Decca	Press
Aug 65.	(7") (F 12208) <45-9794> **WHATCHA GONNA DO ABOUT IT?. / WHAT'S A MATTER, BABY**	14	Jan66

—— **IAN McLAGAN** (b.12 May'45, Hounslow, England) – keyboards repl. WINSTON who went solo

Nov 65.	(7") (F 12276) **I'VE GOT MINE. / IT'S TOO LATE**		-
Jan 66.	(7") (F 12317) <45-9826> **SHA-LA-LA-LA-LEE. / GROW YOUR OWN**	3	Apr66
May 66.	(7") (F 12393) <45-5007> **HEY GIRL. / ALMOST GROWN**	10	Jul66
May 66.	(lp) (LK 4790) **SMALL FACES**	3	-

– Shake / Come on children / You better believe it / It's too late / One night stand / Whatcha gonna do about it? / Sorry she's mine / E to D / You need loving / Don't stop what you're doing / Own up / Sha-la-la-la-lee. (cd-iss.Jul88 on 'London' += 820 572-2) – What's a matter baby / I've got mine / Grow your own / Almost grown.

		Decca	RCA Victor
Aug 66.	(7") (F 12470) <47-8949> **ALL OR NOTHING. / UNDERSTANDING**	1	Sep66
Nov 66.	(7") (F 12500) <47-9055> **MY MIND'S EYE. / I CAN'T DANCE WITH YOU**	4	Dec66
Feb 67.	(7") (F 12565) **I CAN'T MAKE IT. / JUST PASSING**	26	-
Apr 67.	(7") (F 12619) **PATTERNS. / E TO D**		-
May 67.	(lp) (LK 4879) **FROM THE BEGINNING** (out-takes, demos, etc)	17	-

– Runaway / My mind's eye / Yesterday, today and tomorrow / That man / My way of giving / Hey girl / Tell me have you ever seen me? / Come back and take this hurt off me / All or nothing / Baby don't do it / Plum Nellie / Sha-la-la-la-lee / You really got a hold on me / Whatcha gonna do about it?. (re-iss.Aug84; DOA 2) (cd-iss.Jan89 on 'London' w/ extra tracks; 820 766-2)

		Immediate	Immediate
Jun 67.	(7") (IM 050) <1902> **HERE COMES THE NICE. / TALK TO YOU**	12	
Jun 67.	(lp; mono/stereo) (IMLP/IMSP 008) **SMALL FACES**	12	-

– Green circles / Become like you / Get yourself together / All our yesterdays / Talk to you / Show me the way / Up the wooden hills to Bedfordshire / Eddie's dreaming / (Tell me) Have you ever seen me / Something I want to tell you / Feeling lonely / Happy boys happy / Things are going to get better / My way of giving. (cd-iss. May91 as 'GREEN CIRCLES (FIRST IMMEDIATE ALBUM)' on 'Sequel'; NEXCD 163) (+=) – Green circles (take 2) / Donkey rides, a penny, a glass / Have you ever seen me (take 2). (cd re-iss.Apr97 on 'Essential'; ESMCD 476)

| Aug 67. | (7") (IM 052) <501> **ITCHYCOO PARK. / I'M ONLY DREAMING** | 3 | 16 Nov67 |
| Nov 67. | (7") (IM 062) <5003> **TIN SOLDIER. / I FEEL MUCH BETTER** | 9 | 73 Mar68 |

(re-iss.May75; IMS 100)

| Feb 68. | (lp) <Z12-52-002> **THERE ARE BUT FOUR SMALL FACES** | | |

– Here comes the nice / All or nothing / Lazy Sunday / Sha-la-la-la-lee / Collibosher / The Autumn stone / Whatcha gonna do about it? / My mind's eye / Itchycoo Park / Hey girl / The universal / Runaway / Call it something nice / I can't make it / Afterglow (of your love) / Tin soldier.

| Apr 68. | (7") (IM 064) <5007> **LAZY SUNDAY. / ROLLIN' OVER** | 2 | |

(re-iss.Oct82; same)

| Jun 68. | (lp; mono/stereo) (IMLP/IMSP 012) <Z12-52-008> **OGDENS' NUT GONE FLAKE** | 1 | |

– Ogden's nut gone flake / Afterglow (of your love) / Long agos and worlds apart / Rene / Son of a baker / Lazy Sunday / Happiness Stan / Rollin' over / The hungry intruder / The journey / Mad John / Happy days / Toy town. <US re-iss.Mar73 on 'Abkco'; 4225> (re-iss.Dec75; IML 1001) (re-iss.Jun77; IML 2001) (re-iss. export Aug78 on 'Charly'; CR 300015) (re-iss. Mar80 on 'Virgin'; V 2159) (re-iss. Oct86 on 'Castle' lp/cd+=; CLA LP/CD 116) – Tin soldier (live). (re-cd-iss. in box Feb91 on 'Castle'; CLACT 016) (re-iss. Feb97 on 'Original Recordings'; ORRLP 001) (cd re-iss.Apr97 on 'Essential'; ESMCD 477)

Jul 68.	(7") (IM 069) <5009> **THE UNIVERSAL. / DONKEY RIDES, A PENNY, A GLASS**	16	
Nov 68.	(7") <5012> **THE JOURNEY. / MAD JOHN**	-	
Mar 69.	(7") (IM 077) <5014> **AFTERGLOW (OF YOUR LOVE). / WHAM BAM, THANK YOU MAM**	36	
Mar 69.	(d-lp) (IMAL 01/02) **THE AUTUMN STONE** (rarities, live, etc)		

– Here comes the nice / The Autumn stone / Collibosher / All or nothing / Red balloon / Lazy Sunday / Rollin' over / If I were a carpenter / Every little bit hurts / My mind's eye / Tin soldier / Just asking / Call it something nice / I can't make it / Afterglow (of your love) / Sha-la-la-la-lee / The universal / Itchycoo Park / Hey girl / Wide eyed girl / On the wall / Whatcha gonna do about it / Wham bam thank you mam. (re-iss.Jul84; IMLD 1) (re-iss. May86 on 'Castle' lp/c/cd; CLA LP/MC/CD 114) (re-iss. 1991) (cd re-iss.Apr97 on 'Essential'; ESMCD 478)

—— Disbanded Mar'69. STEVE MARRIOTT formed HUMBLE PIE. The remaining members became The FACES.

The FACES

alongside **ROD STEWART** (b.10 Jan'45, London) – vocals (also Solo artist, ex-JEFF BECK) / **RON WOOD** (b. 1 Jun'47, Hillingdon, England) – guitar (ex-JEFF BECK GROUP, ex-CREATION)
(note: in the US, debut lp still credited to The SMALL FACES)

		Warners	Warners
Feb 70.	(7") (WB 8005) **FLYING. / THREE-BUTTON HAND-ME-DOWN**		-
Mar 70.	(lp) (WS 3000) **FIRST STEP**	45	-

– Wicked messenger / Devotion / Shake, shudder, shiver / Stone / Around the plynth / Flying / Pineapple and the monkey / Nobody knows / Looking out the window / Three-button hand-me-down. (re-iss.Dec71 lp/c; K/K4 46053) (re-iss. Jul87 on 'Edsel'; ED 240) (cd-iss. Sep91; EDCD 240) (cd re-iss. Sep93; 7599 26376-2)

| Mar 71. | (7") (WB 8018) **HAD ME A REAL GOOD TIME. / REAR WHEEL SKID** | | - |
| Mar 71. | (lp) (WS 3011) <1892> **LONG PLAYER** | 31 | 29 |

– Bad 'n' ruin / Tell everyone / Sweet lady Mary / Richmond / Maybe I'm amazed / Had a real good time / On the beach / I feel so good / Jerusalem. (re-iss.Dec71 lp/c; K/K4 46064) (cd-iss. Sep93; 7599 26191-2)

Apr 71.	(7") **MAYBE I'M AMAZED. / OH LORD I'M BROWNED OFF**		-
Nov 71.	(7") (K 16136) **STAY WITH ME. / DEBRIS**	6	-
Nov 71.	(lp/c) (K/K4 56006) <2574> **A NOD IS AS GOD AS A WINK . . . TO A BLIND HORSE**	2	6

– Miss Judy's farm / You're so rude / Love lives here / Last orders please / Stay with me / Debris / Memphis / Too bad / That's all I need. (cd-iss. Sep93; 7599 25929-2)

Dec 71.	(7") <7545> **STAY WITH ME. / YOU'RE SO RUDE**	-	17
Feb 73.	(7") (K 16247) <7681> **CINDY INCIDENTALLY. / SKEWIFF**	2	48
Apr 73.	(lp/c) (K/K4 56011) <2665> **OOH LA LA**	1	21

– Silicone grown / Cindy incidentally / Flags and banners / My fault / Borstal boys / Fly in the ointment / If I'm on the late side / Glad and sorry / Just another monkey / Ooh la la. (cd-iss. Sep93; 7599 26368-2)

| May 73. | (7") **OOH LA LA. / BORSTAL BOYS** | - | |

—— **TETSU YAMAUCHI** (b.21 Oct'47, Fukuoka, Japan) – bass (ex-FREE) repl. RONNIE LANE who went solo

| Nov 73. | (7") (K 16341) **POOL HALL RICHARD. / I WISH IT WOULD RAIN** | 8 | |

ROD STEWART & THE FACES

due to ROD's solo successes

		Mercury	Mercury
Jan 74.	(lp) (9100 011) <1-697> **COAST TO COAST – OVERTURE FOR BEGINNERS** (live)	3	63

– It's all over now / Cut across Shorty / Too bad / Every picture tells a story / Angel / Stay with me / I wish it would rain / I'd rather go blind / Borstal boys / Amazing Grace / Jealous guy. (cd-iss. Nov87; 832 128-2)
(above also featured ROD's songs from solo career)

		Warners	Warners
Nov 74.	(7") (K 16494) **YOU CAN MAKE ME DANCE SING OR ANYTHING. / AS LONG AS YOU TELL HIM**	12	

—— Late '75, crumbled again, as ROD STEWART enjoyed overwhelming solo stardom. RON WOOD went off to join The ROLLING STONES.

– their compilations, others, etc. –

| Oct 75. | (d-lp) Warners; (K 66027) **TWO ORIGINALS OF THE FACES** | | - |

– (FIRST STEP / LONG PLAYER)

| Apr 77. | (lp/c) Riva; (K/K4 56172) <2897> **SNAKES AND LADDERS – THE BEST OF THE FACES** | 24 | |

– Pool hall Richard / Cindy incidentally / Ooh la la / Sweet Lady Mary / Flying / Pineapple and the monkey / You can make me dance, sing or anything / Had me a real good time / Stay with me / Miss Judy's farm / Silicone grown / That's all you need.

| May 77. | (7"ep) Riva; (RIVA 8) **THE FACES** | 41 | |

– Cindy incidentally / Stay with me / Memphis / You can make me dance, sing or anything.

Sep 80.	(lp/c) Pickwick; (SSP/SSC 3074) **THE FACES FEATURING ROD STEWART**		-
Nov 92.	(cd/c) Mercury; (514 180-2/-4) **THE BEST OF ROD STEWART & THE FACES**	58	
May 93.	(cd/c; ROD STEWART & THE FACES) Spectrum; (550026-2/-4) **AMAZING GRACE**		-

SMALL FACES

SMALL FACES re-formed by **JONES, McLAGAN** + re-instated **MARRIOTT** incomer **RICKY WILLS** – bass (ex-Peter FRAMPTON'S CAMEL, ex-ROXY MUSIC, etc)

		Atlantic	Atlantic
Jul 77.	(7") (K 10983) **LOOKIN' FOR A LOVE. / KO'D (BY LUV)**		
Aug 77.	(lp/c) (K/K4 50375) <SD 19113> **PLAYMATES**		

– High and happy / Never too late / Tonight / Say larvee / Find it / Lookin' for a love / Playmates / Drive in romance / This song's just for you / Smilin' in tune. (cd-iss.Jun92 on 'Repertoire';)

| Nov 77. | (7") (K 11043) **STAND BY ME (STAND BY YOU). / HUNGRY AND LOOKING** | | |

—— added on tour **JIMMY McCULLOCH** (b.1953, Glasgow, Scotland) – guitar (of WINGS)

| Jun 78. | (7") (K 11173) **FILTHY RICH. / OVER TOO SOON** | | |
| Sep 78. | (lp/c) (K/K4 50468) <SD 19171> **78 IN THE SHADE** | | |

– Over too soon / Too many crossroads / Let me down gently / Thinkin' about love / Stand by you / Brown man do / Soldier / Reel sour / You ain''t seen nothin' yet / Filthy rich. (cd-iss.Nov93 on 'Repertoire';)

—— Disbanded again mid'78. KENNY JONES joined The WHO. McCULLOCH died 27th Sep'79. MARRIOTT re-formed HUMBLE PIE. He was to tragically die in his Essex home after it went on fire 20 Apr'91. More recently, in fact just as this books deadline approached, founder member RONNIE LANE finally died in June '97, after 18 years suffering from multiple sclerosis.

– compilations, others, etc. –

Jun 72.	(7") *Pride; <1006>* **RUNAWAY./ SHAKE**	-	
Jul 72.	(lp) *Pride; <PRD 0001>* **EARLY YEARS**	-	
Dec 72.	(lp) *Pride; <PRD 0014>* **THE HISTORY OF THE SMALL FACES**		-
1974.	(lp) *M.G.M.; <M3P 4955>* **ARCHETYPES**		-
Jun 77.	(lp) *Decca; (ROOTS 5)* **ROCK ROOTS: THE SMALL FACES** ('A'&'B'sides)		-
Sep 77.	(7"m) *Decca; (F 13727)* **SHA-LA-LA-LA-LEE. / WHAT'CHA GONNA DO ABOUT IT / ALL OR NOTHING** (re-iss. Mar82)		-
Sep 79.	(7"ep) *Decca; (FR 13864)* **THE LONDON BOYS EP** – (shared EP w/ DAVID BOWIE, DOBIE GRAY, BIRDS)		-
Mar 81.	(lp) *Decca; (TAB 16)* **SHA-LA-LA-LA-LEE**		-
Nov 75.	(7") *Immediate; (IMS 102)* **ITCHYCOO PARK. / MY MIND'S EYE**	9	-
Dec 75.	(7") *Immediate; (IMS 701)* **LAZY SUNDAY. / THE AUTUMN STONE** (re-iss. Sep81; same)		-
Mar 76.	(7") *Immediate; (IMS 106)* **LAZY SUNDAY. / (TELL ME) HAVE YOU EVER SEEN ME**	36	
Jul 76.	(lp) *Immediate; (IML 1008)* **MAGIC MOMENTS**		-
Jan 78.	(lp/c) *Immediate; (IML/IMC 2008)* **GREATEST HITS**		-
May 75.	(d-lp) *Sire; (3709/2)* **VINTAGE YEARS – THE IMMEDIATE STORY VOL.2**	-	
Aug 78.	(lp) *Charly; (CR 300025)* **LIVE UK 1969** (live)		-
May 80.	(lp) *New World; (NW 6001)* **THE SMALL FACES** (shared w / AMEN CORNER)		-
Jul 80.	(lp/c) *Virgin; (V/TCV 2166)* **BIG HITS**		-
Jul 80.	(7"m) *Virgin; (VS 367)* **TIN SOLDIER. / TIN SOLDIER** (live) / **RENE** (live)		-
Oct 80.	(lp) *Virgin; (T/TCV 2178)* **FOR YOUR DELIGHT THE DARLINGS OF WAPPING WHARF LAUNDERETTE**		-
1982.	(lp) *Accord; (SN 7157)* **BY APPOINTMENT**		-
Oct 83.	(7") *Old Gold; (OG 9343)* **ALL OR NOTHING. / MY MIND'S EYE**		-
Oct 83.	(7") *Old Gold; (OG 9344)* **SHA-LA-LA-LA-LEE. / WHAT'CHA GONNA DO ABOUT IT**		-
1984.	(d-lp) *Compleat; <672 004-1>* **BIG MUSIC – A COMPLEAT COLLECTION**	-	
Nov 84.	(lp) *Astan; (20049)* **GOLDEN HITS**		-
Jan 85.	(7") *Old Gold; (OG 9465)* **LAZY SUNDAY. / TIN SOLDIER**		-
Jan 85.	(7") *Old Gold; (OG 9466)* **ITCHYCOO PARK. / HERE COMES THE NICE**		-
Oct 85.	(lp) *Platinum; (PLP 29/LP 24045)* **SORRY SHE'S MINE**		-
Nov 85.	(d-lp/c/cd) *Castle; (CCS LP/MC/CD 108)* **SMALL FACES COLLECTION** (re-iss. cd Oct91; same)		-
Jun 86.	(12"ep) *Archive 4; (TOF 103)* **CLASSIC CUTS** – Itchycoo park / Lazy Sunday / Here comes the nice / Sha-la-la-la-lee.		-
Sep 86.	(lp/c) *Showcase; (SHLP 145)* **QUITE NATURALLY** (cd-iss. Dec87; SHCD 145)		-
Jan 88.	(lp/cd) *Big Time; (261 552-1/-2)* **20 GREATEST HITS**		-
May 88.	(3"cd-ep) *Castle Special Edition; (CD 3-9)* **ITCHYCOO PARK / LAZY SUNDAY / ALL OR NOTHING** (live) / **AUTUMN STONE**		-
Jul 88.	(lp/c) *Knight; (KN LP/C 10007)* **NIGHTRIDING**		-
Feb 89.	(cd-ep) *Old Gold; (OG 6119)* **ITCHYCOO PARK / LAZY SUNDAY / TIN SOLDIER**		-
Apr 89.	(lp/c/cd) *Castle; (CLA LP/MC/CD 146)* **GREATEST HITS**		-
Jan 90.	(cd) *O.N.N. Range; (ONN 65)* **GREATEST HITS**		-
May 90.	(cd/c/d-lp) *Castle TV; (CTV CD/MC/LP 004)* **THE ULTIMATE COLLECTION** (cd re-iss. Dec91 as 'THE COMPLETE COLLECTION'; CCSCD 302)		-
Jun 90.	(cd/c/lp) *See For Miles; (SEE 293/+C/CD)* **THE SINGLES A's & B's** (cd+ = extra tracks)		-
Sep 90.	(cd) *Success; (SUC 2198)* **LAZY SUNDAY** (re-iss. Sep92 on 'Pickwick';)		-
1990.	(cd) *Ariola Express; (ARICD 973)* **LAZY SUNDAY**		-
Aug 91.	(cd) *Dojo; (DOJOCD 60)* **QUITE NATAURALLY RARE**		-
1992.	(cd) *Sony; <52427>* **ALL OR NOTHING**		-
May 93.	(cd/c) *Spectrum; (550 047-2/-4)* **IT'S ALL OR NOTHING**		-
Sep 93.	(cd/c) *Laserlight; (CD/MC 12208)* **ITCHYCOO PARK**		-
Mar 94.	(cd/c) *Laserlight; (CD/MC 12221)* **HERE COMES THE NICE**		-
Apr 94.	(cd-ep) *Disky; (DISK 4504)* **HIT SINGLE COLLECTABLES** – Itchycoo Park / Tin soldier / Lazy Sunday.		-
May 94.	(cd) *Arc; (TOP 940500)* **GREATEST HITS**		-
Mar 95.	(cd) *Mastertone; (10065)* **ITCHYCOO PARK**		-
Jul 95.	(cd) *Summit; (SUMCD 4001)* **THE BEST OF THE SMALL FACES**		-
Aug 95.	(cd) *It's Music; (22579)* **THE SMALL FACES**		-
Jul 95.	(cd) *Repertoire; (REP 4429-WO)* **BOXED**		-
Oct 95.	(cd) *Abracadabra; (AB 3034)* **ITCHYCOO PARK**		-
Nov 95.	(4xcd-box) *Charly; (IMMBOX 1)* **THE IMMEDIATE YEARS**		-
May 96.	(cd/d-cd/d-cd/d-lp) *Deram; (844583-2/-4/-1)* **THE DECCA ANTHOLOGY 1965-1967**	66	-
Jan 97.	(d-cd) *Charly; (CPCD 82602)* **THE VERY BEST OF THE SMALL FACES**		-

---

S*M*A*S*H (dig out; Great Alt & Indie . . .)

SMASHING PUMPKINS

Formed: Chicago, Illinois, USA . . .late 80's by BILLY CORGAN, JAMES IHA, D'ARCY WRETZKY. The son of a jazz guitarist and former member of local goth band, The MARKED, CORGAN initiated The SMASHING PUMPKINS as a three-piece using a drum machine, before the band recruited sticksman, JIMMY CHAMBERLAIN. After a debut single for a local label, 'I AM ONE', and the inclusion of two tracks on a local compilation album, the group came to the attention of influential Seattle label, 'Sub Pop'. After only one single, 'TRISTESSA', The SMASHING PUMPKINS moved once more, signing to Virgin subsidiary, 'Hut', in the UK, 'Caroline' in America. Produced by BUTCH VIG, a debut album, 'GISH', was released in early '92, its grunge pretensions belying a meandering 70's/psychedelic undercurrent which distanced the band from most of their contemporaries. Nevertheless, the group amassed a sizable student/grassroots following which eventually saw the debut go gold in the States, a re-released 'I AM ONE' sneaking into the UK Top 75 later that year. With the masterful 'SIAMESE DREAM' (1993), the band went from underground hopefuls to alternative rock frontrunners, the album fully realising the complex 'PUMPKINS sound in a delicious wash of noise and gentle melody. Influenced by acoustic LED ZEPPELIN fused with slices of 70's PINK FLOYD, CORGAN's croaky but effective voice was at its best on the pastel, NIRVANA-esque classics, 'TODAY' and 'DISARM', while the 'PUMPKINS went for the jugular on the likes of 'CHERUB ROCK', 'ROCKET' and 'GEEK U.S.A.'. The album made the Top 5 in Britain, Top 10 in the States, selling multi-millions and turning the band into a 'grunge' sensation almost overnight, despite the fact that their mellotron stylings and complex arrangements marked them out as closer in spirit to prog-rock than punk. Amidst frantic touring, the band released the outtakes/B-sides compilation, 'PISCES ISCARIOT' (1994), the next album proper surfacing in late '95 as the sprawling double set, 'MELLON COLLIE AND THE INFINITE SADNESS'. Dense and stylistically breathtaking, the album veered from all-out grunge/thrash to acoustic meandering and avant-rock doodlings, a less cohesive whole than its predecessor but much more to get your teeth into. Inevitably, there were criticisms of self-indulgence, though for a two-hour set there was a surprising, compelling consistency to proceedings; among the highlights were 'BULLET WITH BUTTERFLY WINGS', 'TONIGHT, TONIGHT' and the visceral rage of '1979'. The record scaled the US charts, where The SMASHING PUMPKINS were almost reaching the commercial and critical heights of NIRVANA, the group also taking Britain by storm, headlining the 1995 Reading Festival. Never the most stable of bands, disaster struck the following year when new boy (keyboard player) JONATHAN MELVOIN died of a drugs overdose and heroin addict CHAMBERLAIN was finally kicked out. More recently (early 1998), IHA released an acclaimed solo album of acoustic strumming ('LET IT COME DOWN') while the others recorded fresh songs with a drum machine, taking things full circle. That summer, the 'PUMPKINS showed a softer side to their character when the mournful but still effective album, 'ADORE', hit the Top 5. 1999 saw two major personnel changes via the return of CHAMBERLAIN and the departure of D'ARCY (who was replaced by ex-HOLE bassist MELISSA); one last set would appear in 2000. • **Songwriters:** CORGAN, except several with IHA. Covered; A GIRL NAMED SANDOZ (Eric Burdon & The Animals) / LANDSLIDE (Fleetwood Mac) / DANCING IN THE MOONLIGHT (Thin Lizzy) / NEVER LET ME DOWN (Depeche Mode) / YOU'RE ALL I'VE GOT TONIGHT (Cars) / CLONES (WE'RE ALL) (Alice Cooper) / DREAMING (Blondie) / A NIGHT LIKE THIS (Cure) / DESTINATION UNKNOWN (Missing Persons) / SAD PETER PAN with Red Red Meat (Vic Chesnutt). • **Miscellaneous:** IHA and D'ARCY set up their own label, 'Scratchie', for whom the outfit, FULFLEJ recorded an album ('Wack-Ass Tuba Riff') in 1996 with the pair making guest appearances.

Album rating: GISH (*6) / SIAMESE DREAM (*9) / MELLON COLLIE AND THE INFINITE SADNESS (*9) / PISCES ISCARIOT compilation (*5) / THE AEROPLANE FLIES HIGH boxed set (*6) / ADORE (*5) / James Iha: LET IT COME DOWN (*5)

BILLY CORGAN (b.17 Mar'67) – vocals, guitar / **JAMES IHA** (b.26 Mar'68, Elk Grove, Illinois) – guitar / **D'ARCY (WRETZKY)** (b. 1 May'68, South Haven, Michigan) – bass, vocals / **JIMMY CHAMBERLIN** (b.10 Jun'64, Joliet, Illinois) – drums

		not iss.	Limited Potential
Apr 90.	(7") *<Limp 006>* **I AM ONE. / NOT WORTH ASKING**	-	

		Glitterhouse	Sub Pop
Dec 90.	(7",7"pink) *<SP 90>* **TRISTESSA. / LA DOLLY VITA** (UK-12"+=; May93) *(SP 10-137)* – Honeysbee.	-	

		Hut	Caroline
Aug 91.	(12") *(HUTT 6)* **SIVA. / WINDOW PAINE**		-
Feb 92.	(12"ep/cd-ep) *(HUTT/CDHUT 10)* **LULL EP** – Rhinoceros / Blue / Slunk / Bye June (demo).		-
Feb 92.	(cd/c/lp) *(HUT CD/MC/LP 002) <1705>* **GISH** – I am one / Siva / Rhinoceros / Bury me / Crush / Suffer / Snail / Tristessa / Window paine / Daydream. (re-iss. May94; diff.versions cd/lp; HUT CDX/LPX 002)		Aug91
Jun 92.	(c-ep/12"ep/cd-ep) *(HUT C/T/CD 17)* **PEEL SESSIONS** – Siva / A girl named Sandoz / Smiley.		-
Aug 92.	(12"ep/cd-ep) *(HUTT/CDHUT 18)* **I AM ONE. / PLUME / STARLA** (10"ep) *(HUTTEN 18)* – ('A'side) / Terrapin (live) / Bullet train to Osaka.	73	-
Jun 93.	(7"clear) *(HUT 31)* **CHERUB ROCK. / PURR SNICKETY** (12"/cd-s) *(HUTT/CDHUT 31)* – ('A'side) / Pissant / French movie theme / (Star spangled banner).	31	
Jul 93.	(cd/c/d-lp) *(HUT CD/MC/LP 011) <88267>* **SIAMESE DREAM**	4	10

– Cherub rock / Quiet / Today / Hummer / Rocket / Disarm / Soma / Geek U.S.A. / Mayonaise / Spaceboy / Silverfuck / Sweet sweet / Luna.

Sep 93. (7"red) (HUT 37) **TODAY.** / APATHY'S LAST KISS   44   –
(c-s/12"/cd-s) (HUTC/HUTT/CDHUT 37) – ('A'side) / Hello kitty kat / Obscured.
Feb 94. (7"purple) (HUT 43) **DISARM.** / SIAMESE DREAM   11   –
(12"/cd-s) (HUT T/CD 43) – ('A'side) / Soothe (demo) / Blew away.
(cd-s) (HUTDX 43) – ('A'side) / Dancing in the moonlight / Landslide.
Oct 94. (cd/c/gold-lp) <39834> **PISCES ISCARIOT** (compilation of   –   4
B-sides & rarities)
– Soothe / Frail and bedazzled / Plume / Whir / Blew away / Pissant / Hello Kitty
Kat / Obscured / Landslide / Starla / Blue / A girl named Sandoz / Spaced. <w/ free gold-7"; CAR 1767-7> **NOT WORTH ASKING.** / HONEY SPIDER
II (UK-iss.Oct96 cd/c/lp; HUT CD/MC/LP 41)
                                                                       Hut   Virgin
Dec 94. (7"peach) (HUTL 48) **ROCKET.** / NEVER LET ME DOWN   –   –
(4x7"box-set) (SPBOX 1) **SIAMESE SINGLES** – (last 3 singles 1993-94 + above)
Oct 95. (c-s/cd-s) (HUT C/CD 63) <38522> **BULLET WITH BUTTERFLY**
WINGS / . . .SAID SADLY   20   25
Oct 95. (d-cd/d-c) (CD/TC HUTD 30) <40861> **MELLON COLLIE**
AND THE INFINITE SADNESS   4   1
– DAWN TO DUSK:- Mellon Collie and the infinite sadness / Tonight, tonight /
Jellybelly / Zero / Here is no why / Bullet with butterfly wings / To forgive / An
ode to no one / Love / Cupid de Locke / Galapogos / Muzzle / Porcelina of the vast
oceans / Take me down. // TWILIGHT TO STARLIGHT:- Where boys fear to tread /
Bodies / Thirty-three / In the arms of sleep / 1979 / Tales of a scorched Earth / Thru
the eyes of Ruby / Stumbleine / X.Y.U. / We only come out at night / Beautiful /
Lily (my one and only) / By starlight / Farewell and goodnight. (re-iss. Apr96 as
t-lp+=; HUTTLP 30) – Tonight reprise / Infinite sadness.

─── added on tour **JONATHAN MELVOIN** – keyboards (ex-DICKIES) (brother of
WENDY; ex-WENDY & LISA, ex-PRINCE)

Jan 96. (c-ep/12"ep/cd-ep) (HUT C/T/CD 67) <38547> **1979 /**
UGLY. / BELIEVE / CHERRY   16   12
(12"ep/cd-ep; Mar96) (HUT TX/CDX 67) – 1979 REMIXES: Vocal / Instrumental /
Moby / Cement.
May 96. (c-ep) (HUTC 69) <38547> **TONIGHT, TONIGHT /**
MELADORI MAGPIE / ROTTEN APPLES   7   36   Jun96
(cd-ep+=) (HUTCD 69) – Medellia of the gray skies.
(cd-ep) (HUTDX 69) – ('A'side) / Jupiter's lament / Blank / Tonite (reprise).

─── On 12th Jul'96, MELVOIN died of a heroin overdose. CHAMBERLIN, who found
him dead, was charged with drug offences and sacked by the remaining trio who
were said to be sick of his long-lasting drug addiction. In August, they were replaced
for tour by **DENNIS FLEMION** – keyboards (ex-FROGS) + **MATT WALKER** – drums
(of FILTER)

Sep 96. (m-cd) (HUTCD 73) <38545> **ZERO EP**   –   46   May96
– Zero / God / Mouths of babes / Tribute to Johnny / Marquis in spades / Pennies /
Pastichio medley: (excerpts).
Nov 96. (cd-ep) (HUTCD 78) <38574> **THIRTY THREE / THE LAST**
SONG / THE AEROPLANE FLIES HIGH (TURNS LEFT,
LOOKS RIGHT) / TRANSFORMER   21   39
(cd-ep) (HUTDX 78) – ('A'side) / The bells / My blue Heaven.
Nov 96. (5xcd-ep;box) <SPBOX 2> **THE AEROPLANE FLIES HIGH**   –   42
– (BULLET WITH BUTTERFLY WINGS / 1979 / TONIGHT, TONIGHT /
THIRTY THREE / ZERO)

─── early in '97, CORGAN provided six songs for 'RANSOM' film soundtrack credited
to conductor JAMES HORNER (Hollywood HR 62086-2)

Jun 97. (c-s) (W 0404C) **THE END IS THE BEGINNING IS THE END /**
THE BEGINNING IS THE BEGINNING IS THE END   10   –
(cd-s+=) (W 0404CD) – The ethers tragic / The guns of love disastrous.
(12"/cd-s) (W 0410 T/CD) – ('A'mixes; 2 Fluke mixes / 2 Rabbit in The Moons
mixes / Hallucination Gotham mix).
(above from the film 'Batman And Robin' on 'Warners')
May 98. (7") (HUT 101) <38647> **AVA ADORE.** / CZARINA   11   42   Jun98
(c-s+=/cd-s+=) (HUT C/CD 101) – Once in a while.
Jun 98. (cd/c/d-lp) (CDHUT/TCHUT/HUTDLP 51) <45879> **ADORE**   5   2
– To Sheila / Ava adore / Perfect / Daphne decends / Once upon a time / Tear /
Crestfallen / Appels + oranjes / Pug / The tale of Dusty and Pistol Pete / Annie-dog /
Shame / Behold! the night mare / For Martha / Blank page / 17.
Sep 98. (c-s/cd-s) (HUT C/CD 106) <38650> **PERFECT / SUMMER /**
PERFECT (Nellee Hooper mix)   24   54
(cd-s) (HUTDX 106) – ('A'side) / Daphne descends (Oakenfold Perfecto mix) /
Daphne descends (Kerry B mix).

─── **CHAMBERLAIN** was now back in the fold

JAMES IHA

JAMES IHA – vocals, guitar / **NEAL CASAL** – guitar / **ADAM SCHLESINGER** – piano (of
FOUNTAINS OF WAYNE) / **GREG LEISZ** – steel guitar / **JOHN GINTY** – hammond organ /
SOLOMON SNYDER – bass / **MATT WALKER** – drums / **NINA GORDON** (of VERUCA
SALT) also a part of initial basement set-up
Feb 98. (cd/c/lp) (CDHUT/HUTMC/HUTLP 47) <45411> **LET IT COME**
DOWN   –   –
– Be strong now / Sound of love / Beauty / See the sun / Country girl / Jealousy /
Lover, lover / Silver string / Winter / One and two / No one's gonna hurt you.
Feb 98. (12"ep/cd-ep) (HUT T/CD 99) **BE STRONG NOW / MY**
ADVICE. / TAKE CARE / FALLING   –   –

SMASH MOUTH

Formed: San Jose, California, USA . . . 1994 by frontman STEVE HARWELL
with guitarist GREG CAMP, bassist PAUL DE LISLE and drummer KEVIN
COLEMAN. Signing to 'Interscope', the band made the Top 20 in late '97 with
their annoyingly catchy debut single, 'WALKIN' ON THE SUN'. Imagine the
bastard child of The DOORS and The STEREO MC's reared on a strict diet
of 'nutty' ska and you're probably nowhere near it. The debut album, 'FUSH
YU MANG' followed soon after, a more intense collection of pogo pop that

was as unmistakably American as it was infectious. The speedy HARWELL
and Co skated their way back up the charts via a sophomore set, 'ASTRO
LOUNGE' (1999), an overrated "teenager type" record that delivered two hit
singles, 'ALL STAR' plus 'AND THEN THE MORNING COMES'.

Album rating: FUSH MU MANG (*6) / ASTRO LOUNGE (*4)

STEVE HARWELL – vocals / **GREG CAMP** – guitar / **PAUL DE LISLE** – bass / **KEVIN
COLEMAN** – drums
                                                           Interscope Interscope
Oct 97. (c-s) <(INC 95555)> **WALKIN' ON THE SUN** / SORRY
ABOUT YOUR PENIS   19   Jan98
(cd-s+=) (IND 95555) – Dear Inez / Push.
Oct 97. (cd) <(IND 90142)> **FUSH YU MANG**   19   Jul97
– Flo / Beer goggles / Walkin' on the sun / Let's rock / Heave-ho / The Fonz / Pet
names / Padrino / Nervous in the alley / Disconnect the dots / Push / Why can't we
be friends.
Apr 98. (c-s) (INC 95585) **THE FONZ / BEER GOGGLES**   –   –
(cd-s+=) (IND 95585) – Walkin' on the sun (live) / Disconnect the dots (live).
Jul 99. (c-s) (497100-4) <radio cut> **ALL STAR / WALKIN' ON THE**
SUN   24   4   May99
(cd-s+=) (497118-2) – Can't get enough of you baby / ('A'-CD-Rom enhanced).
(cd-s) (497117-2) – ('A'side) / Walkin' on the sun (Sun E delight remix) / The Fonz.
Aug 99. (cd/c) (IND/INC 90316) <490316> **ASTRO LOUNGE**   6   Jun99
– Who's there / Diggin' your scene / I just wanna see / Waste / All star / Satellite
radio / Stoned / Then the morning comes / Road man / Fallen horses / Defeat you /
Come on come on / Home / Can't get enough of you baby.
Nov 99. (-) <album cut> **THEN THE MORNING COMES**   –   14

Elliott SMITH

Born: 1970, Dallas, Texas, USA, although raised from a young age by his
father in Portland, Oregon, after his parents divorced. The singer/songwriter
relocated to university digs in Brooklyn, New York, playing in mid-90's noisy
alternative rock band, HEATMISER. They released four rare albums, 'DEAD
AIR' (1993), 'YELLOW NO.5' (1994; a mini-set), 'COP AND SPEEDER'
(1995) and 'MIC CITY SONS' (1996), while ELLIOTT, meantime had opted
for a more sedate solo career. He delivered three very well received albums for
the 'Kill Rock City' imprint', namely 'ROMAN CANDLE' (1994), 'ELLIOTT
SMITH' (1995) and 'EITHER/OR' (1997) – all licensed in 1998 to the UK arm
of 'Domino' – before he inked a deal with 'DreamWorks'. This was due to the
plaudits heaped upon him after appearing on stage alongside CELINE DION
and TRISHA YEARWOOD at the "Oscars" ceremony! An unlikely story you
may think, although the truth is, he provided part of the soundtrack to one of
the best films of the year, 'Good Will Hunting'. His unfashionable (especially
his taste in clothing and headgear – sometimes a tammy) approach was slightly
reminiscent of SIMON & GARFUNKEL, BIG STAR or the lo-fi RICHARD
DAVIES (of CARDINAL). His fourth album, 'XO', hit the shops later in 1998
and ELLIOTT looked certain to make his impact on the music scene.

Album rating: Heatmiser: DEAD AIR (*6) / COP AND SPEEDER (*7) / MIC
CITY SONS (*6) / Elliott Smith: ROMAN CANDLE (*7) / ELLIOTT SMITH (*7) /
EITHER/OR (*8) / XO (*7)

HEATMISER

ELLIOTT SMITH – vocals / **NEIL GUST** – guitar, vocals / **SAM COOMES** – bass / **TONY LASH**
– drums
                                                         Frontier Frontier
Jul 93. (cd/c) <(31057-2/-4)> **DEAD AIR**   –   –   Jun93
– Still / Candyland / Mock up / Dirt / Bottle rocket / Blackout / Stray / Can't be
touched / Cannibal / Don't look down / Sands hotel / Low life / Buick / Dead air.
Jul 94. (m-cd) <(31062-2)> **YELLOW NO.5**   –   –
– Wake / Fortune 500 / The corner seat / Idler / Junior mint / Yellow No.5.
Apr 95. (cd) <(31063-2)> **COP AND SPEEDER**   –   –
– Disappearing ink / Bastard John / Flamel / Temper / Why did I decide to stay? /
Collect to NYC / Hitting on the waiter / Busted lip / Antonio Carlos Jobim / It's not
a prop / Something to lose / Sleeping pill / Trap door / Nightcap.
                                                         Caroline Cavity
                                                                   Search
Oct 96. (cd) (CAR 75402) <CSR 35-2> **MIC CITY SONS**   –   –
– Get lucky / Plainclothes man / Low flying jets / Rest my head against the wall /
Fix is in / Eagle eye / Cruel reminder / You gotta move / Pop in G / Blue highway /
See you later.

─── split after SMITH was already making a name for himself as a solo act, while
COOMES was in a duo with JANET WEISS called QUASI.

ELLIOTT SMITH

- vocals, drums, bass saxophones, etc.
                                                         not iss. Suicide
                                                                   Squeeze
1994.   (7") <5> **DIVISION DAY.** / NO NAME #6   –   –
                                                         not iss. Cavity
                                                                   Search
Dec 94. (cd) <CSR 13-2> **ROMAN CANDLE**   –   –
– Roman candle / Condor avenue / No name #I / No name #II / No name #III / Drive
all over town / No name #IV / The last call / Kiwi mad-dog 20-20. (UK-iss.Mar98
on 'Cavity Search'; same as US) (re-iss. Aug98 on 'Domino' cd/lp; REWIG CD/LP
002)
                                                         Kill Rock Kill Rock
                                                         Stars   Stars
Feb 95. (7") <(KRS 239)> **NEEDLE IN THE HAY.** /   –   –
Jul 95. (lp/cd) <KRS 246/+CD> **ELLIOTT SMITH**   –   –
– Needle in the hay / Christian brother / Clementine / Southern belle / Single file /
Coming up roses / Satellite / Alphabet town / St.Ides heaven / Good to go / White

lady loves you more / Biggest lie. (UK-iss.Mar98; same) (re-iss. Aug98 on 'Domino' cd/lp; REWIG CD/LP 001)

Oct 96. (7") <(KRS 266)> **SPEED TRIALS.** /

Mar 97. (lp/cd) <(KRS 269/+CD)> **EITHER/OR**
– Speed trials / Alameda / Ballad of big nothing / Between the bars / Pictures of me / No name No.5 / Rose parade / Punch and Judy / Angeles / Cupid's trick / 2:45 am / Say yes. (UK-iss.Jun98 on 'Domino' cd/lp; WIG CD/LP 51)

Jun 98. (7") (RUG 74) **BALLAD OF BIG NOTHING. / SOME SONG / DIVISION DAY**
(cd-s+=) (RUG 74CD) – Angeles.

	Damaged Goods	not iss.

Jul 98. (7") (DAMGOOD 152) **.** / (track by the PEECHEES) | | - |

—— now with a plethora of session people + strings

	DreamWorks	DreamWorks

Aug 98. (cd/c) <(DRD/DRC 50048)> **XO**
– Sweet Adeline / Tomorrow tomorrow / Waltz #2 (XO) / Baby Britain / Pitseleh / Independence day / Bled white / Waltz #1 / Amity / Oh well, okay / Bottle up and explode! / A question mark / Everybody cares, everybody understands / I didn't understand. <(lp-iss.on 'Bongload'; BL 35)>

Dec 98. (c-s/cd-s) (DRM S/CD 22347) **WALTZ #2 (XO) / OUR THING / HOW TO TAKE A FALL** | 52 | | Feb99

Apr 99. (7") (DRMS7 50953) **BABY BRITAIN. / WALTZ No.1** | 55 | |
(cd-s+=) (DRMDC 50950) – The enemy is you.
(cd-s) (DRMDC 50951) – ('A'side) / Some song / Bottle up and explode.

Patti SMITH

Born: 31 Dec'46, Chicago, Illinois, USA. She started to write for New York magazine 'Rock' in 1969, having earlier being shipped around by her family between Paris and London. In the early 70's, PATTI began writing poetry full-time and met fellow rock-scribe, LENNY KAYE, who provided guitar accompaniment for her beat-poet monologues at readings/gigs. By 1971 she was writing for 'Creem' magazine and soon developed a professional musical partnership with playwright, SAM SHEPHERD. A prolific time for SMITH, come Christmas '72 she had two books of poetry, 'Witt' and '7th Heaven' in the stores and, after contributing to TODD RUNDGREN's 'A WIZARD, A TRUE STAR' album, he credited her for nicknaming him 'Runt'. RICHARD SOHL was recruited alongside SMITH and KAYE for a one-off single in 1974, 'HEY JOE / PISS FACTORY' on the small 'MER' label. A suitably caustic slice of proto-punk, it later gained airplay after being picked up by 'Sire' records. Meanwhile, SMITH completed the line-up of what would become The PATTI SMITH GROUP with IVAN KRAAL and JAY DEE DAUGHERTY, signing to 'Arista' and starting work on the 'HORSES' (1975) album with JOHN CALE producing. From the monochrome androgyny of the cover shot to the DIY three chord thrash which formed the bulk of the musical backing, the album was a blueprint for a generation of both American and British punk/new wave artists. Although SMITH's vocals were something of an acquired taste, her distinctive intonation was a perfect vehicle for the image-rich symbolism of her free flowing lyrics. 'GLORIA' and 'LAND OF 1,000 DANCES' were transformed into wired, beat-inspired flashes of nervous energy, while quieter moments like the intro to 'REDONDO BEACH' and 'FREE MONEY' possessed a stark beauty. After this alternative tour de force, the follow-up, 'RADIO ETHIOPIA' (1976), came as something of a departure. Possessing a more straightforward hard-rock approach save for the chaotic feedback-drenched exploration of the title track, the album received mixed reviews. After SMITH survived breaking her neck after falling from the stage at a gig, it was to be another two years before the release of her next album. 'EASTER' (1978) was a confident comeback which moved even further into commercial rock territory without extinguishing the livewire spark that had made 'HORSES' so compelling. The record contained an unlikely collaboration with BRUCE SPRINGSTEEN, 'BECAUSE THE NIGHT', which saw SMITH breach the upper reaches of the singles charts on both sides of the Atlantic and propelled the album to similar success. 'WAVE' (1979) sounded slightly unfocused although it attained a higher chart placing Stateside than its predecessor. After a final tour in 1979, SMITH bowed out of the music business for domestic bliss with her new husband FRED 'SONIC' SMITH (ex-MC5). Together with her spouse, SOHL and DOUGHERTY, she recorded a low-key comeback album in 1988, 'DREAM OF LIFE', although tragedy struck in the 90's when both SOHL and her husband died from heart failure. With many artists namechecking her as an influence, SMITH recorded 'GONE AGAIN' (1996) amid a mini-renaissance. A tribute to FRED, it was filled with a sense of loss and yearning, echoing the intensity of her earlier work. • **Songwriters:** Lyrics PATTI, some music KAYE. Covered HEY JOE (Jimi Hendrix) / LAND OF A THOUSAND DANCES (Cannibal & The Headhunters) / MY GENERATION (The Who) / GLORIA (Them) / SO YOU WANNA BE A ROCK'N'ROLL STAR (Byrds) / 5-4-3-2-1 (Manfred Mann) / DOWNTOWN TRAIN (Tom Waits) / WICKED MESSENGER (Bob Dylan). • **Trivia:** In 1974, she co-wrote with ex-boyfriend ALLEN LANIER, his groups' (BLUE OYSTER CULT) 'Career Of Evil'. Her albums were produced by JOHN CALE (1st) / JACK DOUGLAS (2nd) / JIMMY IOVINE (3rd) / TODD RUNDGREN (4th) / FRED SMITH and JIMMY IOVINE (1988).

Album rating: HORSES (*9) / RADIO ETHIOPIA (*7) / EASTER (*7) / WAVE (*6) / DREAM OF LIFE (*5) / GONE AGAIN (*6) / PEACE AND NOISE (*6)

PATTI SMITH – vocals, poetry / with **LENNY KAYE** – guitar / **RICHARD SOHL** – piano

	not iss.	M.E.R.

Aug 74. (7") <601> **HEY JOE. / PISS FACTORY** | - | |
(UK-iss.Mar78 on 'Sire'; SRE 1009)

—— added **IVAN KRAL** – bass, guitar, piano / **JAY DEE DAUGHERTY** – drums

	Arista	Arista

Dec 75. (lp) (ARTY 122) <4066> **HORSES** | | 47 |
– Gloria / Redonda Beach / Birdland / Free money / Kimberly / Break it up / Land: Horses – Land of a thousand dances – La mer (de) / Elegie. (re-iss. Aug88 lp/c/cd; 201/401/252-112) (cd re-iss. Jul96+=; 18827-2) – My generation (live).

Apr 76. (7") (ARIST 47) <AS 0171> **GLORIA. / MY GENERATION (live)**
(re-iss. 12"-Sep77; ARIST 12135)

Oct 76. (lp/c) (SPARTY/TCSPARTY 1001) <4097> **RADIO ETHIOPIA**
– Ask the angels / Ain't it strange / Poppies / Pissing in the river / Pumping (my heart) / Distant fingers / Radio Ethiopia / Abyssinia. (re-iss. Aug88 lp/c/cd; 201/401/251-117) (re-iss. cd Jul96; 18825-2)

—— Her tour featured **LEIGH FOXX** – bass repl. SOHL. Others augmenting at the time **ANDY PALEY** (ex-ELLIOT MURPHY) + **BRUCE BRODY** – keyboards (ex-JOHN CALE)

PATTI SMITH GROUP

with **KAYE, KRAAL, DAUGHERTY, BRODY + SOHL**

Mar 78. (7") (ARIST 181) <AS 0318> **BECAUSE THE NIGHT. / GOD SPEED** | 5 | 13 |

Mar 78. (lp/c) (SPARTY/TCSPARTY 1043) <4171> **EASTER** | 16 | 20 |
– Till victory / Space monkey / Because the night / Ghost dance / Babelogue / Rock'n'roll nigger / Privilege (set me free) / We three / 25th floor / High on rebellion / Easter. (re-iss. Jan83 on 'Fame' lp/c; FA/TCFA 3058) (re-iss. Aug88 lp/c/cd; 201/401/251-128) (re-iss. cd Jul96; 18826-2)

Jun 78. (7") (ARIST 191) **PRIVILEGE (SET ME FREE). / ASK THE ANGELS** | 72 | - |
(12"+=) (ARIST 12191) – 25th floor (live) / Bablefield (live).

—— **FRED 'Sonic' SMITH** – drums (ex-MC5) repl. DAUGHERTY to TOM VERLAINE

May 79. (7") (ARIST 264) **FREDERICK. / FIRE OF UNKNOWN ORIGIN** | 63 | |

May 79. (lp/c) (SPART/TCART 1086) <4221> **WAVE** | 41 | 18 |
– Frederick / Dancing barefoot / Citizen ship / Hymn / Revenge / So you want to be a rock'n'roll star / Seven ways of going / Broken flag / Wave. (re-iss. Aug88 lp/c/cd; 201/401/251-139) (re-iss. cd Jul96; 18829-2)

Jun 79. (7") <AS 0427> **FREDERICK. / FREDERICK (live)** | - | 90 |

Jul 79. (7") (ARIST 281) **DANCING BAREFOOT. / 5-4-3-2-1 (live)** | - | - |

Aug 79. (7"m) <AS 0453> **SO YOU WANT TO BE A ROCK'N'ROLL STAR. / 5-4-3-2-1 / FIRE OF UNKNOWN ORIGIN** | - | |

Sep 79. (7") (ARIST 291) **SO YOU WANT TO BE A ROCK'N'ROLL STAR. / FREDERICK (live)** | | - |

—— PATTI retired Mar'80 with her new husband FRED SMITH to bring up children. BRUCE BRODY was another to join ex-TELEVISION singer TOM VERLAINE's band.

PATTI SMITH

re-appeared in 1988 with still **SOHL, DAUGHERTY & SONIC**

	Fierce	Fierce

Feb 88. (7"m) (white label) **BRIAN JONES. / STOCKINGED FEET / JESUS CHRIST** | | - |

	Arista	Arista

Jul 88. (7")<US-c-s> (109877) <AS1/CAS 9689> **PEOPLE HAVE THE POWER. / WILD LEAVES**
(12"+=) (609877)<AD1 9688> – Where duty calls.
(cd-s++=) (659877) – ('A'-album version).

Jul 88. (lp/c/cd) (209/409/259-172) <8453> **DREAM OF LIFE** | 70 | 65 |
– People have the power / Going under / Up there, down there / Paths that cross / Dream of life / Where duty calls / (I was) Looking for you / The Jackson song. (re-iss. cd.Apr92;) (cd re-iss. Jul96; 18828-2)

—— RICHARD SOHL was to die from a cardiac arrest on 3 Jun'90. PATTI returned to reciting and recording her poetry in 1995. Now with some of her original group (**DAUGHERTY + KAYE**), **TONY SHANAHAN** – bass / **LUIS RESTO** – keyboards and on some **TOM VERLAINE** – guitar (ex-TELEVISION) / **OLIVER RAY** – guitars. Album featured guest spots from JOHN CALE, JEFF BUCKLEY and JANE SCARPANTONI – cello

Jul 96. (cd/c) (74321 38474-2/-4) <18747> **GONE AGAIN** | 44 | 55 |
– Gone again / Beneath the Southern Cross / About a boy / My madrigal / Summer cannibals / Dead to the world / Wing / Ravens / Wicked messenger / Fireflies / Farewell reel.

Aug 96. (cd-ep) (74321 40168-2) **SUMMER CANNIBALS / COME BACK LITTLE SHEEBA / GONE AGAIN (live) / PEOPLE HAVE THE POWER**
(cd-ep) (74321 40299-2) – ('A'side) / People have the power (live) / Beneath the Southern cross / Come in my kitchen.

—— **OLIVER RAY** ; repl. RESTO

Nov 97. (cd/c) <(07822 18986-2/-4)> **PEACE AND NOISE** | | | Sep97
– Waiting underground / Whirl away / 1959 / Spell / Don't say nothing / Dead city / Blue poles / Death singing / Memento Mori / Last call.

– compilations, others, etc. –

Apr 83. (7") Arista; (ARIST 513) **BECAUSE THE NIGHT. / GLORIA** | | - |
(12") (ARIST 12513) – ('A'side) / Redondo beach / Dancing barefoot / Free money.

Jul 84. (7") Old Gold; (OG 9458) **BECAUSE THE NIGHT. / GLORIA** | | |

Sep 91. (3xcd-box) R.C.A.; (354.226) **BOX SET** | | - |
– (RADIO ETHIOPIA / HORSES / WAVE albums)

SMITHEREENS   (dig out; Great Alt & Indie . . .)

SMITHS

Formed: Manchester, England ... late '82 by (STEPHEN PATRICK) MORRISSEY and JOHNNY MARR. An intellectually intense, budding pop scholar and music journalist, MORRISSEY had previously had a book, 'James Dean Isn't Dead', published by 'Babylon' and had served a stint as UK president of The NEW YORK DOLLS fan club. MARR, meanwhile, had cut his six-string teeth in a variety of Manc beat combos, the pair initially forming a songwriting partnership and subsequently bringing in drummer MIKE JOYCE and bassist ANDY ROURKE to realise their vision of The SMITHS. Kicking off at The Ritz in Manchester, the group played a series of debut gigs around the country, earning rave reviews and attracting the interest of indie label, 'Rough Trade'. Turning down a deal with the local 'Factory', The SMITHS recorded a one-off single for 'Rough Trade', 'HAND IN GLOVE', the track championed by John Peel and subsequently topping the indie charts. Wooed by the majors, MORRISSEY and Co. stuck to their principles and inked a long-term contract with 'Rough Trade'. Later that year saw the release of the Top 30 hit, 'THIS CHARMING MAN', the first real glimpse of the The SMITHS' strange allure, MARR's rhythmic exuberance buoying MORRISSEY's morose verbal complexities. This was also the first time the Great British public were treated to the legendary sight of MORRISSEY sashaying and shimmying across the Top Of The Pops stage sporting a hearing aid and a back pocketfull of gladioli. Defiantly original, The SMITHS rapidly amassed a large, fiercely partisan fanbase with MORRISSEY as chief deity, MARR running a close second. A follow-up single, 'WHAT DIFFERENCE DOES IT MAKE', narrowly missed the Top 10 in early '84 with the breathlessly anticipated debut, 'THE SMITHS', hitting the shelves the following month. It didn't disappoint, a darkly ruminating kick in the eye for the tosspot music scene of the mid-80's and a compelling showcase for the unbounded potential of the MORRISSEY/MARR writing partnership. While the album missed the No.1 slot by a whisker, a high profile scrape with the tabloids followed soon after, the press hounds rounding on what they supposed to be ambiguous references to child abuse. The highly articulate MORRISSEY vocally put matters to right, the singer finally vindicated when a mother of one of the Moors murder victims openly supported the 'SUFFER THE LITTLE CHILDREN' track, another target of press speculation. The SMITHS were nothing if not controversial, MORRISSEY's pro-miserablist, anti-royalist and openly celibate stance making him the first real 'bedsit' non-pop star and drawing more and more attention to the group. No bad thing of course, when the music was as good as 'HEAVEN KNOWS I'M MISERABLE NOW' and 'WILLIAM, IT WAS REALLY NOTHING', another couple of fine Top 20 singles released later that summer. Both were included on the brilliant 'HATFUL OF HOLLOW' (1984) set along with a number of BBC session recordings and a few new tracks, notably the haunting 'PLEASE PLEASE PLEASE LET ME GET WHAT I WANT' and one of The SMITHS' trump cards, 'HOW SOON IS NOW' (previously released as a B-side to 'WILLIAM . . .' and subsequently as a single in its own right in early '85), a churning mantra presumably laying bare the depths of MORRISSEY's tortured soul with its bitter lyrical plea; that pop/dance outfit SOHO later managed to incorporate its ominous guitar reverb into a club hit is surely one of the great wonders of modern music. The following month saw the release of the acclaimed 'MEAT IS MURDER', MORRISSEY partly substituting the navel gazing of old for a more socially-pointed stance; slap happy headmasters, teenage thugs, child abusers and of course, those partial to a bit of steak, being the prime targets of the frontman's razor-sharp lyrical barbs. MORRISSEY wasn't hogging all the limelight, however, MARR's nimble fingered genius on the likes of 'THAT JOKE ISN'T FUNNY ANYMORE' seeing him touted as the greatest British guitarist since ERIC CLAPTON. The album gave the group their first No.1, solidifying their position as the biggest "indie" band of the decade, The SMITHS now at the peak of their powers. Next up was the irrepressible 'THE BOY WITH THE THORN IN HIS SIDE' and the scathing wit of 'BIGMOUTH STRIKES AGAIN', both featured on, and acting as preludes to 'THE QUEEN IS DEAD' (1986). Though the album was delayed due to record company hassles, with personnel difficulties (ROURKE briefly kicked out for heroin abuse, the addition of CRAIG GANNON also arising, it remains The SMITHS' magnum opus and, for many, the album of the decade. Effortlessly segueing from the darkly claustrophobic (the stinging social commentary of the title track and to a lesser extent, the lugubrious 'NEVER HAD NO ONE EVER') to the whimsically witty ('VICAR IN A TUTU') and on to the heartbreakingly poignant ('THERE IS A LIGHT THAT NEVER GOES OUT), the album was breathtaking in its emotional sweep and musical focus. Though they would never quite reach those heights again, The SMITHS' highly prolific recording schedule continued apace with the anthemic 'PANIC' (indie kids delighting in its clarion call of 'Hang the DJ') and the breezy 'ASK', probably The SMITHS most commercial moment. The fact that, like most of their singles, it failed to break the Top 10, led to the group announcing a split with 'Rough Trade' and a new deal with 'E.M.I.'. Further controversy followed around this time as CRAIG GANNON was sacked, the guitarist duly sueing the group. Early '87 saw the release of another semi-compilation of old and new material, 'THE WORLD WON'T LISTEN', essential if only for the classic MORRISSEY angst of 'HALF A PERSON' and the sublime 'OSCILLATE WILDLY'. Though the wellspring of the MORRISSEY/MARR muse was seemingly bottomless, relations between the pair were reaching breaking point and by the release of the 'STRANGEWAYS HERE WE COME' (1987) opus, The SMITHS had already split. The album's morbid, fractured sound apparently confirmed the growing musical differences between the group's main protagonists, an inevitability perhaps, for such a

consistently intense and prefectionist band. A posthumous live album, 'RANK' (1988) appeared the following year, documenting the London stop on The SMITHS' final frenzied tour of 1986. Various compilations were released in successive years, especially after 'Warners' secured the rights to The SMITHS back catalogue in 1992, heralding a period when, ironically, most of the material was only available on US import! While MARR sessioned for the likes of The PRETENDERS and BRYAN FERRY before working with THE THE and forming ELECTRONIC with NEW ORDER's BERNARD SUMNER, MORRISSEY went on to a relatively successful, if comparitively drab solo career. As is so often the case, the sum of The SMITHS' parts was always greater than the whole, the group's influence on modern rock music incalculable, their unique sound echoing through the strains of countless indie success stories and untold hopefuls alike. • **Songwriters:** Lyrics – MORRISSEY / music – MARR, except HIS LATEST FLAME (Elvis Presley) / GOLDEN LIGHTS (Twinkle).

Album rating: THE SMITHS (*10) / HATFUL OF HOLLOW part compilation (*9) / MEAT IS MURDER (*10) / THE QUEEN IS DEAD (*10) / THE WORLD WON'T LISTEN part compilation (*8) / STRANGEWAYS HERE WE COME (*8) / LOUDER THAN BOMBS import (*8) / RANK (*7) / BEST . . . I compilation (*10) / BEST II compilation (*9)

MORRISSEY (b. STEPHEN PATRICK MORRISSEY, 22 May'59) – vocals (ex-NOSEBLEEDS) / **JOHNNY MARR** (b. JOHN MAHER, 31 Oct'63) – guitar, harmonica, mandolins, piano / **ANDY ROURKE** (b.1963) – bass / **MIKE JOYCE** (b. 1 Jun'63) – drums

			Rough Trade	Sire
May 83.	(7") *(RT 131)* **HAND IN GLOVE. / HANDSOME DEVIL**		–	–
Nov 83.	(7") *(RT 136)* **THIS CHARMING MAN. / JEANE**		25	–
	(12") *(RTT 136)* – ('A'side) / Accept yourself / Wonderful woman.			
Jan 84.	(7") *(RT 146)* **WHAT DIFFERENCE DOES IT MAKE?. / BACK TO THE OLD HOUSE**		12	–
	(12"+=) *(RTT 146)* – These things take time.			
Feb 84.	(lp/c) *(ROUGH/+C 61)* <25065> **THE SMITHS**			
	– Reel around the fountain / You've got everything now / Miserable lie / Pretty girls make graves / The hand that rocks the cradle / Still ill / Hand in glove / What difference does it make? / I don't owe you anything / Suffer little children. *(cd-iss. May87; ROUGHCD 61) (cd re-iss. 1989 on 'Line'; LICD 9.00308) (re-iss. cd/c)(ltd-10"lp Nov93 on 'WEA'; 4509 91892-2/-4)(SMITHS 1)*			
May 84.	(7") *(RT 156)* **HEAVEN KNOWS I'M MISERABLE NOW. / SUFFER LITTLE CHILDREN**		10	
	(12"+=) *(RTT 156)* – Girl afraid.			
Aug 84.	(7") *(RT 166)* **WILLIAM, IT WAS REALLY NOTHING. / PLEASE PLEASE PLEASE LET ME GET WHAT I WANT**		17	
	(12"+=) *(RTT 166)* – How soon is now?			
Nov 84.	(lp/c) *(ROUGH/+C 76)* **HATFUL OF HOLLOW** (with BBC sessions *)		7	–
	– William, it was really nothing / What difference does it make? * / These things take time * / This charming man * / How soon is now? / Handsome devil * / Hand in glove / Still ill * / Heaven knows I'm miserable now / This night has opened my eyes * / You've got everything now * / Accept yourself * / Girl afraid / Back to the old house * / Reel around the fountain * / Please please please let me get what I want. *(cd-iss. May87; ROUGHCD 76) (re-iss. cd/c)(ltd-d10"lp Nov93 on 'WEA'; 4509 91893-2/-4)(SMITHS 2)*			
Jan 85.	(7") *(RT 176)* **HOW SOON IS NOW?. / WELL I WONDER**		24	–
	(12"+=) *(RTT 176)* – Oscillate wildly.			
Feb 85.	(7") *(RT 176)* **HOW SOON IS NOW?. / THE HEADMASTER RITUAL**		–	
Feb 85.	(lp/c) *(ROUGH/+C 81)* <25269> **MEAT IS MURDER**		1	
	– The headmaster ritual / Barbarism begins at home / Rusholme ruffians / I want the one I can't have / What she said / Nowhere fast / That joke isn't funny anymore / Well I wonder / Meat is murder. *(cd-iss. May87; ROUGHCD 81) (re-iss. cd/c)(ltd-d10"lp Nov93 on 'WEA'; 4509 91895-2/-4)(SMITHS 3)*			
Mar 85.	(7") *(RT 181)* **SHAKESPEARE'S SISTER. / WHAT SHE SAID**		26	
	(12"+=) *(RTT 181)* – Stretch out and wait.			
Jul 85.	(7") *(RT 186)* **THAT JOKE ISN'T FUNNY ANYMORE. / MEAT IS MURDER (live)**		49	
	(12"+=) *(RTT 186)* – Nowhere fast / Shakespeare's siste / Stretch out and wait (all live).			
Sep 85.	(7") *(RT 191)* **THE BOY WITH THE THORN IN HIS SIDE. / ASLEEP**		23	
	(12"+=) *(RTT 191)* – Rubber ring.			
——	added **CRAIG GANNON** – guitar, bass (ex-AZTEC CAMERA, ex-BLUEBELLS)			
May 86.	(7") *(RT 192)* **BIGMOUTH STRIKES AGAIN. / MONEY CHANGES EVERYTHING**		26	
	(12"+=) *(RTT 192)* – Unloveable.			
Jun 86.	(lp/c) *(ROUGH/+C 96)* <25426> **THE QUEEN IS DEAD**		2	70
	– Frankly Mr. Shankly / I know it's over / Never had no one ever / Cemetery gates / Big mouth strikes again / Vicar in a tutu / There is a light that never goes out / Some girls are bigger than others / The queen is dead / The boy with the thorn in his side. *(cd-iss. May87; ROUGHCD 96) (re-iss. cd/c)(ltd-d10"lp Nov93 on 'WEA'; 4509 91896-2/-4)(SMITHS 4)*			
Jul 86.	(7") *(RT 193)* **PANIC. / VICAR IN A TUTU**		11	
	(12"+=) *(RTT 193)* – The draize train.			
Oct 86.	(7") *(RT 194)* **ASK. / CEMETRY GATES**		14	
	(12"+=/c-s+=) *(RTT 194/+C)* – Golden lights.			
——	Reverted to a quartet, when GANNON left to join The CRADLE.			
Feb 87.	(7") *(RT 195)* **SHOPLIFTERS OF THE WORLD UNITE. / HALF A PERSON**		12	
	(12"+=) *(RTT 195)* – London.			
Feb 87.	(lp/c/cd) *(ROUGH/+C/CD 101)* **THE WORLD WON'T LISTEN** (part compilation)		7	–
	– Panic / Ask / London / Big mouth strikes again / Shakespeare's sister / There is a light that never goes out / Shoplifters of the world unite / The boy with the thorn in his side / Asleep / Unloveable / Half a person / Stretch out and wait / That joke isn't funny anymore / Oscillate wildly / You just haven't earned it yet baby / Rubber ring. *(c+=)* – Money changes everything. *(re-iss. cd/c)(ltd-d10"lp Nov93 on 'WEA'; 4509 91898-2/-4)(SMITHS 5)*			

Apr 87. (7") (RT 196) **SHEILA TAKE A BOW. / IS IT REALLY SO STRANGE?** `10` `☐`
(12"+=) (RTT 196) – Sweet and tender hooligan.

Jun 87. (d-lp/d-c/d-cd) (ROUGH/+C/CD 255) <25569> **LOUDER THAN BOMBS** (compilation) `38` `62` Apr87
– Is it really so strange? / Sheila take a bow / Sweet and tender hooligan / Shoplifters of the world unite / Half a person / London / Panic / Girl afraid / Shakespeare's sister / William, it was really nothing / You just haven't earned it yet, baby / Golden lights / Ask / Heaven knows I'm miserable now / Unloveable / Asleep / Oscillate wildly / These things take time / Rubber ring / Back to the old house / Hand in glove / Stretch out and wait / This night has opened my eyes / Please, please, please, let me get what I want. (cd re-iss. Feb95 on 'WEA'; 4509 93833-2)

Aug 87. (7") (RT 197) **GIRLFRIEND IN A COMA. / WORK IS A FOUR-LETTER WORD** `13` `☐`
(12"+=/c-s+=) (RTT 197/+C) – I keep mine hidden.

Sep 87. (lp/c/cd) (ROUGH/+C/CDR 106) <25649> **STRANGEWAYS HERE WE COME** `2` `55`
– A rush and a push and the land is ours / I started something I couldn't finish / Death of a disco dancer / Girlfriend in a coma / Stop me if you think you've heard this one before / Last night I dreamt that somebody loved me / Unhappy birthday / Paint a vulgar picture / Death at one's elbow / I won't share you. (re-iss. cd/c)(ltd-d10" lp Nov93 on 'WEA'; 4509 91899-2/-4)(SMITHS 6)

Oct 87. (7") **STOP ME IF YOU THINK YOU'VE HEARD THIS ONE BEFORE. / I KEEP MINE HIDDEN** `-` `☐`

Nov 87. (7") (RT 198) **I STARTED SOMETHING I COULDN'T FINISH. / PRETTY GIRLS MAKE GRAVES** `23` `☐`
(12"+=) (RTT 198) – Some girls are bigger than others (live).
(c-s++=) (RTT 198C) – What's the world (live).

Dec 87. (7") (RT 200) **LAST NIGHT I DREAMT THAT SOMEBODY LOVED ME. / NOWHERE FAST (BBC version)** `30` `☐`
(12"+=) (RTT 200) – Rusholme Russians (BBC version).
(cd-s++=) (RTT 200CD) – William, it was really nothing (BBC version).

——— they broke-up in August '87, ROURKE and JOYCE splintered with ADULT NET before joining MORRISSEY when he went solo.

– compilations, etc. –

Note; on 'Rough Trade' UK / 'Sire' US, unless otherwise mentioned.

Aug 88. (lp/c/cd/dat) (ROUGH/+C/CD 126) <25786> **RANK (live October '86)** `2` `77`
– The queen is dead / Panic / Vicar in a tutu / Ask / Rusholme ruffians / The boy with the thorn in his side / What she said / Is it really so strange? / Cemetry gates / London / I know it's over / The draize train / Still ill / Bigmouth strikes again / (Marie's the name) His latest flame – Take me back to dear old blighty. (re-iss. cd/c)(ltd-d10"lp Nov93 on 'WEA'; 450991900-2/-4)(SMITHS 7)

Nov 88. (3"cd-ep) (RTT 215CD) **THE HEADMASTER RITUAL / NOWHERE FAST (live) / MEAT IS MURDER (live) / STRETCH OUT AND WAIT (live)** `☐` `-`

Nov 88. (3"cd-ep) (RTT 171CD) **BARBARISM BEGINS AT HOME / SHAKESPEARE'S SISTER / STRETCH OUT AND WAIT** `☐` `-`

——— (Note:- 12"singles from Jan84 / May84 / Sep85 / Jul86 / Oct86 were issued on 3"cd-ep Nov88 – add suffix of CD to cat no.).

Oct 88. (12"ep/cd-ep) Strange Fruit; (SFPS/+CD 055) **THE PEEL SESSIONS** (18.5.83) `☐` `-`
– What difference does it make? / Reel around the fountain / Miserable lie / Handsome devil.

——— Note; Below on 'WEA' UK/ 'Sire' US unless otherwise mentioned.

Jul 92. (7"/c-s) (YZ 0001/+C) **THIS CHARMING MAN. / WONDERFUL WOMAN / ACCEPT YOURSELF** `8` `-`
(cd-s+=) (YZ 0001CD) – Jeane.

Aug 92. (cd)(lp/c) (4509 90044-2)(SMITHS 8/+C) <45042> **BEST . . . 1** `1`
– This charming man / William, it was really nothing / What difference does it make / Stop me if you think you've heard it before / Girlfriend in a coma / Half a person / Rubber ring / How soon is now? / Hand in glove / Shoplifters of the world unite / Sheila take a bow / Some girls are bigger than others / Panic / Please please please let me get what I want.

Sep 92. (7"/c-s) (YZ 0002/+C) **HOW SOON IS NOW. / HAND IN GLOVE** `16` `-`
(cd-s+=) (YZ 0002CD1) – The queen is dead / Handsome devil / I started something I couldn't finish.
(cd-s+=) (YZ 0002CD2) – I know it's over / Suffer little children / Back to the old house.

Oct 92. (7"/c-s) (YZ 0003/+C) **THERE IS A LIGHT THAT NEVER GOES OUT. / HANDSOME DEVIL (live)** `25` `☐`
(cd-s+=) (YZ 0003CD1) – I don't owe you anything / Hand in glove / Jeane.
(cd-s+=) (YZ 0003CD2) – Money changes everything (live) / Some girls are bigger than others (live) / Hand in glove (live).

Nov 92. (cd)(lp/c) (4509 90406-2)(SMITHS 9/+C) **BEST II** `29` `☐`
– The boy with a thorn in his side / The headmaster ritual / Heaven knows I'm miserable now / Ask / Oscillate wildly / Nowhere fast / Still ill / That joke isn't funny anymore / Shakespeare's sister / Girl afraid / Reel around the fountain / Last night somebody loved me / There is a light that never goes out.

Feb 95. (7"/c-s) (YZ 0004/+C) **ASK. / CEMETARY GATES** `62` `-`
(cd-s+=) (YZ 0004CD) – Golden lights.

Mar 95. (cd/c) (4509 99090-2/-4) **"SINGLES"** `5`
– Hand in glove / This charming man / What difference does it make? / Heaven knows I'm miserable now / William, it was really nothing / How soon is now? / Shakespeare's sister / That joke isn't funny anymore / The boy with the thorn in his side / Bigmouth strikes again / Panic / Ask / Shoplifters of the world unite / Sheila take a bow / Girlfriend in a coma / I started something I couldn't finish / Last night I dreamt that somebody loved me / There is a light that never goes out.

SMOG

Formed: Silver Springs, Maryland, USA . . . 1988 by sole member, BILL CALLAHAN. The painfully introverted grandaddy of the American lo-fi scene (although he professes to loathe that particular term), CALLAHAN began releasing his bedroom creations in the late 80's as a series of mainly

instrumental cassette-only affairs. All issued on his own 'Disaster' imprint, 'MACRAME GUNPLAY' (1988), 'COW' (1989), 'A TABLE SETTING' (1990) and 'TIRED MACHINE' (1990) set the tone for a debut album proper, 'SEWN TO THE SKY' (1991). This was originally released only in the States on the 'Drag City' label and carried on in the same vein as its skeletal predecessors; CALLAHAN only really began taking SMOG in a more conventionally song-structured direction with the 'FORGOTTEN FOUNDATION' (1992) album and only really started whetting critical appetites with 1993's acclaimed 'JULIUS CAESAR'. The latter set was recorded with sometime collaborator CYNTHIA 'CINDY' DALL, boasting sharper, more robust songwriting embellished with string flourishes and synth tinkling although the lyrical misery continued unabated. The mood blackened further on 1994's mini-album, 'BURNING KINGDOM', the reclusive pessimeister making WILL OLDHAM sound like a circus clown. Yet while CALLAHAN's sad-eyed music could be overbearingly claustrophobic, it was more often genuinely moving, the painstakingly recounted tales of everday heartbreak/failure featured on 'WILD LOVE' (1995) and the 'KICKING A COUPLE AROUND' EP offering up an almost voyeuristic view into the man's insular world. The bitter fruit of 'THE DOCTOR CAME AT DAWN' (1996) and 'RED APPLE FALLS' (1997) further confirmed BILL as the crown prince of sad-core, a label he'd no doubt detest even more than lo-fi. 'KNOCK KNOCK' (1999) was described as an album for teenagers and definitely one of his best, SMOG were now becoming the most popular one-mam band in America.

Album rating: SEWN TO THE SKY (*6) / FORGOTTEN FOUNDATION (*7) / JULIUS CAESAR (*8) / BURNING KINGDOM mini (*5) / WILD LOVE (*7) / THE DOCTOR CAME AT DAWN (*8) / RED APPLE FALLS (*7) / KNOCK KNOCK (*8)

BILL CALLAHAN (b.1966) – vocals, guitar, etc

			not iss.	Disaster
1988.	(c) <none> **MACRAME GUNPLAY**		-	
1989.	(c) <none> **COW**		-	
1990.	(c) <none> **A TABLE SETTING**		-	
1990.	(c) <none> **TIRED TAPE MACHINE**		-	

			not iss.	#1 Records
1991.	(7") <none> **MY SHELL. / (track by other artist)**		-	

			Matador	Drag City
1991.	(7"ep) <DC 6> **FLOATING EP**		-	
1991.	(lp/cd) <DC 74/+CD> **SEWN TO THE SKY**		-	

– Souped up II / Kings tongue / Garb / Hollow out cakes / Confederate bills and pinball slugs / Coconut cataract / Fruit bats / Peach pit / Disgust / Russian winter / Polio shimmy / Smog / Lost my key / Fried piper / Fables / Puritan work ethic / A jar of sand / I want to tell you about a man / Olive drab spectre / The weightlifter. (UK-iss.Nov95 on 'Drag City'; same as US)

1992.	(lp/cd) <DC 13> **FORGOTTEN FOUNDATION**		-	

– Burning kingdom / Filament / High school freak / Your dress / Barometric pressure / Guitar innovator / Evil tyrant / Head of stone I / Head of stone II / Long gray hair / Kiss your lips (with LISA CARVER) / Bad ideas for country songs I / Bad ideas for country songs II / Dead river / Bad investment / Brown bag / Let me have that jar back / This insane cop / 97th street / Do the bed / I'm smiling / With a green complexion. *cd re-iss. Jan96; same)

——— now with **CINDY DALL** – vocals, etc

Jul 94.	(cd/lp) (OLE 097-2/-1) <DC 31> **JULIUS CAESAR**		☐	Nov93

– Strawberry rash / Your wedding / 37 push ups / Stalled on the tracks / One less star / Golden / When you talk / I am star wars / Connections / When the power goes out / Chosen one / What kind of angel / Stick in the mud.

			City Slang	Drag City
Nov 94.	(m-cd/m-lp) (EFA 04946-2/-1) <DC 41> **BURNING KINGDOM**		☐	Sep94

– My shell / Renee died 1:45 / My family / Drunk on the stars / Not lonely anymore / Desert.

Mar 95. (7"yellow) (EFA 04951-7) **A HIT. / WINE STAINED LIPS** `☐` `-`

Apr 95.	(cd/lp) (EFA 04952-2/-1) <DC 60> **WILD LOVE**		☐	Mar95

– Bathysphere / Wild love / Sweet Smog children / Bathroom floor / Emperor / Limited capacity / It's rough / Sleepy Joe / Candle / Be hit / Prince alone in the studio / Goldfish bowl.

			Domino	Drag City
May 96.	(12"ep/cd-ep) (RUG 45 T/CD) <DC 81> **KICKING A COUPLE AROUND EP**		☐	Apr96

– Your new friend / Back in school / I break horses / The orange glow of a stranger's living room.

Sep 96. (cd/lp) (WIG CD/LP 27) <DC 95> **THE DOCTOR CAME AT DAWN** `☐` `☐`
– You moved in / Somewhere in the night / Lize / Spread your bloody wings / Carmelite light / Everything you touch becomes a crutch / All your women things / Whistling teapot (rag) / Four hearts in a can / Hangman blues.

Nov 96. (7") (HM 19) **CAME BLUE. / SNAKEY VINES** `-` `-` German
(above issued on 'Hausmusik') <below on 'Shrimper'>

1997. (d7") <SHR7 04> **SWING SET** `-` `-`

May 97. (cd/lp) (WIG CD/LP 35) <DC 116> **RED APPLE FALLS** `☐` `☐`
– Morning papers / Blood red bird / Red apples / I was a stranger / To be of use / Red apple falls / Ex-con / Inspirational / Finer days.

Oct 97. (7") (RUG 58) **EX-CON. / JUST LIKE NAPOLEON** `☐` `☐`
(cd-s+=) (RUG 58CD) – Little girl shoes / Duckpond blues.

Feb 99. (cd/lp) (WIG CD/LP 60) <DC 161> **KNOCK KNOCK** `☐` `☐` Jan99
– Let's move to the country / Held / River guard / No dancing / Teenage spaceship / Cold bloodied old times / Sweet treat / Hit the ground running / I could drive forever / Left only with love.

May 99. (7") (RUG 83) **HELD. / LOOK NOW / THE ONLY MOTHER** `☐` `-`
(cd-s+=) (RUG 83CD) – Held (acoustic).

Oct 99. (7") (RUG 98) **COLD BLOODED OLD TIMES. / ('A'acoustic)** `☐` `-`
(cd-s+=) (RUG 98CD) – I break horses / Chosen one.

SNEAKER PIMPS

(dig out; 4th edition or Great Alt & Indie . . .)

SNOOP DOGGY DOGG

Born: CALVIN BROADUS, 20 Oct'72, Long Beach, California, USA; he was given his nickname by his mother(!). Unleashed in 1993 when his debut DR. DRE (ex-N.W.A.) produced album 'DOGGYSTYLE' created furore amongst the moral majority in America, SNOOP swaggered his way to the forefront of the new G-funk strain of Gangsta-rap like a doberman on heat. Signed to DRE's 'Death Row' label (he also guested on the man's 'Nuthin' But A G Thang'), the canine sensation sniffed out a Top 10 position for the 'WHAT'S MY NAME' single before notching up record-breaking sales of his chart-topping debut album. Before the record's release (August '93), however, SNOOP (a convicted teenage drug dealer) was arrested when a local hood was killed; shots were allegedly fired by his bodyguard MALIK out of SNOOP's car. The rapper was released after being bailed for $1m and early in 1994, he hit London under a storm of protest, not least from tabloid press; The Daily Star's memorable front page headline ran; 'KICK THIS EVIL BASTARD OUT!'. Of course, this only spurred on Brit youngsters' enthusiasm, especially after he was premiered on C4's 'The Word', complete with interview; a film 'Murder Was The Case' (based around a track SNOOP was famous for) hit Stateside No.1 in November '94. Never out of the headlines on drug charges, etc, SNOOP was finally acquitted of murder and manslaughter early '96 (a mis-trial was the judge's verdict). Later that year, the rapper delivered his sophomore set, 'THA DOGGFATHER', another chart-topper (Top 20 in the UK). SNOOP DOGG was indeed back on the prowl, the man even delighting his pop fans with a hit cover of the Gap Band's 'Snoop's UPSIDE YOUR HEAD'. From 1997-1999, SNOOP was never far from some sort of controversial headlines (either drug busts, shootings or whatever) and it was amazing he found the time to deliver two further long-players, 'DA GAME IS TO BE TOLD, NOT TO BE SOLD' (1998) and 'NO LIMIT TOP DOGG' (1999).

Album rating: DOGGYSTYLE (*7) / THA DOGGFATHER (*7) / DA GAME IS TO BE TOLD, NOT TO BE SOLD (*6) / NO LIMIT TOP DOGG (*8)

SNOOP DOGGY DOGG – vocals / with The DOGG POUND & The DRAMATICS plus **WARREN G / KURUPT / NANCY FLETCHER / DAT NIGGA DAZ / D.O.C. RBX / THE LADY OF RAGE / LIL HERSHEY LOC (MALIK) / NATE DOGG**

		Death Row-West	Death Row-Interscope	
Dec 93.	(7"/c-s) (A 8337/+C) <98340> **WHAT'S MY NAME?** / ('A'club mix) (12"+=/cd-s+=) (A 8337 T/CD) – ('A'-Explicit mix) / ('A'instrumental) / Who am I (what's my name?).	20	8	Nov93
Dec 93.	(cd/c) <(IND/INC 92279)> **DOGGYSTYLE** – Bathtub / G funk intro / Gin and juice / Tha shiznit / Lodi dodi / Murder was the case / Seria killa / Who am I (what's my name)? / For all my niggaz & bitches / Aint no fun (if the homies cant have none) / Doggy Dogg world / GZ and hustlas / Pump pump.	38	1	Nov93
Feb 94.	(7"/c-s) (A 8316/+C) <98318> **GIN AND JUICE** / ('A'-Laid back mix) (12"+=/cd-s+=) (A 8316 T/CD) – (2-'A'mixes).	39	8	
Aug 94.	(c-s) (A 8289C) **DOGGY DOGG WORLD** / ('A'-Perfecto mix) (12"+=/s12"+=/cd-s+=) (A 8289 T/TX/CD) – ('A'-Dr.Dre mix) / ('A'-Perfecto x-rated mix).	32	-	

—— He is still to stand trial for murder on the 13th of January '95. At the end of '94, he and 3 band members (RICHARD BROWN, DARRYL DANIEL + DELMAR ARNAUDE) were arrested and charged with possession of drugs. In Oct'95, SNOOP'S trial finally got underway, due to his attorney Johnnie Cochran being slightly busy with the O.J. Simpson case!. THA DOGG POUND album hit US No.1 in November '95. He was cleared of murder and attempted manslaughter early '96. While on bail, he had guested on 2 PAC's 'All Eyez on Me' album. Other credits were with NATE DOGG on his late 1996 US Top 40 single, 'Never Leave Me Alone'.

| Nov 96. | (cd/c/lp) <(IND/INC/INTLP 90038)> **THA DOGGFATHER** – Intro / Tha doggfather / Ride 4 me / Up jump tha boogie / Freestyle conversation / When I grow up / Snoop bounce / Gold rush / (Tear 'em off) Me & my doggz / You thought / Vapors / Blueberry / 2001 / Sixx minutes / (O.J.) Wake up / Snoops upside ya head / Groupie / Traffic jam / Doggyland / Downtown assassins / Outro. | 15 | 1 | |
| Dec 96. | (c-s) (INC 95520) **SNOOPS UPSIDE YA HEAD** / ('A'mix) (cd-s+=) (IND 95520) – ('A'mixes). (12"+=) (INT 95520) – ('A'mixes). | 12 | - | |

—— In Apr'97, SNOOP partnered the late 2PAC on a UK Top 20 single, 'WANTED DEAD OR ALIVE'.

Apr 97.	(c-s/12"/cd-s) (INC/INT/IND 95530) **VAPORS.** / ('A'live) / **SNOOPS UPSIDE YA HEAD**	18		
Sep 97.	(c-s/cd-s) (664990-4/-5) **WE JUST WANNA PARTY WITH YOU** (mixes with JD NAS) / **ESCOBAR 97** (cd-s+=) (664990-2) – Some cow fonque (more tea vicar). (above on 'Columbia')	21		
Jan 98.	(c-s) (INC 95550) **THA DOGGFATHER** / ('A'mix) (cd-s) (IND 95550) – ('A'mixes). (cd-s) (INT 95550) – ('A'mixes).	36		

—— shortened his moniker to SNOOP DOGG

		Priority	No Limit	
Aug 98.	(cd/d-lp) (CDPTY/PTYLP 153) <50000> **DA GAME IS TO BE SOLD, NOT TO BE TOLD** – Show me love / See ya when I get there / Whatcha gon do / Tru tank dogs / Don't let go / Don't let go / Hustle n' ball / Gin and juice (part 2) / Still a G thang / I can't take the heat / DP gangsta / Woof / 20 dollars to my name / Game of life / Pay for P / Picture this / Doggz gonna get ya / Hoss money and clout / Get 'bout it and rowdy / DOG's get lonely 2 / Ain't nut'in personal.	28	1	

| Aug 98. | (c-s/cd-s) <53450> **STILL A G THANG** | - | 19 | |
—— In Oct'98, SNOOP was credited on the massive US hit (minor UK one in November) for KEITH SWEAT, 'Come And Get With Me'.
Dec 98.	(c-s/cd-s; as SNOOP DOGG featuring MYSTIKAL & FIEND) <53462> **WOOF / WOOF (instrumental) / IT'S ALL A T'T**	-	62	
May 99.	(cd) (CDPTY 171) <50052> **NO LIMIT TOP DOGG** – Dolomite intro / Buck 'em (with STICKY FINGERS) / Trust me (with SYLK E. FINE) / Sug free / My heart goes boom / Dolomite / Snoopfella / In love with a thug / 6 bedtime stories / Down 4 my N's (with C-MURDER) / Magic / Betta days / Somethin' 'bout yo bizness (with RAPHAEL) / B- please (with XZIBIT & NATE DOGG) / Doin' too much / Gangsta ride (with SILKK THE SHOCKER) / Ghetto symphony (with MIA X & FIEND) / Party with ADPG / Buss n' rocks / Just dippin' (with DR. DRE) / Jewell / Don't tell (with WARREN G & MAUSEBURG) / 20 minutes (with GOLDIE LOC) / I love my momma.	48	2	
Sep 99.	(-; as SNOOP DOGG featuring XZIBIT & NATE DOGG) <radio cut> **B-PLEASE**	-	77	
—— SNOOP DOGG was also part of the team augmenting DR. DRE

– compilations, etc. –

| Aug 99. | (cd-book) Star Profile; (8246) **STAR PROFILE** | | - |

SOCIAL DISTORTION

(dig out; 4th edition or Great Alt & Indie . . .)

S.O.D. (see under ⇒ ANTHRAX)

SOFT BOYS (see under ⇒ HITCHCOCK, Robyn)

SOFT CELL (see under ⇒ ALMOND, Marc)

SOFT MACHINE

Formed: Canterbury, England . . . 1966 by ex-WILDE FLOWERS members ROBERT WYATT and KEVIN AYERS, who met up with Australian beatnik, DAEVID ALLEN and former Oxford University student MIKE RATLEDGE. The others members of The WILDE FLOWERS (PYE HASTINGS & RICHARD COUGHLAN) went on to form CARAVAN. A trip to Majorca in 1966 by ALLEN and AYERS led to a chance meeting with a monied, freak-friendly American by the name of Wes Brunson, who agreed to finance the first incarnation of SOFT MACHINE, the fondly named MR. HEAD. Moving to London, the band regrouped and after phoning WILLIAM BURROUGHS to ask his permission, adopted the SOFT MACHINE moniker. Together with PINK FLOYD, the band formed the vanguard of the psychedelic revolution, playing such legendary London gigs as the International Times launch at the Roundhouse. Early in 1967, they were signed to 'Polydor' by CHAS CHANDLER, who employed the services of SOFTS fan JIMI HENDRIX on the B-side of their debut single, 'LOVE MAKES SWEET MUSIC' (1967). The single was basically a pop song and not entirely representative of the band's live free-form improvisation that took its cue from the avant-jazz of artists like ORNETTE COLEMAN and JOHN COLTRANE. After a gig in St. Tropez (where they played an hour long version of AYERS' 'WE DID IT AGAIN' to the assembled Parisian elite), ALLEN was refused re-entry to the UK due to an expired visa, remaining in France and subsequently forming uber-hippies, GONG. Pared down to a trio, SOFT MACHINE underwent a gruelling tour of America supporting JIMI HENDRIX. During a short break in the middle of the tour, the band recorded their eponymous debut for 'PROBE' records, a US-only affair which incredibly, still hasn't had a full UK release almost 30 years on. A pioneering hybrid of psychedelic jazz improvisation, the album was the first and last to feature KEVIN AYERS, who took off for IBIZA at the end of the US tour. Recruiting HENDRIX roadie HUGH HOPPER, the band recorded another album for 'Probe' to fulfill contractual obligations. 'SOFT MACHINE VOL.2' (1969) was another idiosyncratic classic, containing a backwards rendition of the alphabet and a multitude of highbrow cultural references. Employing such live instrumentation as saxophone, trombone and cornet, the band increasingly moved towards jazz fusion and 'THIRD' (1970) was largely instrumental, save for WYATT's sublime meditation, 'MOON IN JUNE'. The other band members refused to have any serious involvement with the song, a crucial factor in WYATT's eventual split from the group. As SOFT MACHINE moved further into tepid jazz-rock territory, WYATT became increasingly frustrated and was eventually pushed out after 'FOURTH' (1971). While WYATT went on to form MATCHING MOLE before going solo, SOFT MACHINE released a further clutch of noodling albums before splitting in 1981. • **Songwriters:** Either AYERS (on debut lp only), WYATT (on first four albums only), or RATLEDGE and group. • **Trivia:** A John Peel session was recorded on the 21st of June '69 with their seminal 7-piece line-up. They were the first "rock" act to play the normally orchestrated 'Proms' at London's Albert Hall (1970). Non-originals, RATLEDGE and JENKINS became ADIEMUS, who had a UK Top 50 hit with their self-titled single (the theme from the TV ad for Delta Airlines), which featured vocalist MIRIAM STOCKLEY.

Album rating: THE SOFT MACHINE (*6) / SOFT MACHINE VOL.2 (*6) / THIRD (*7) / FOURTH (*6) / SOFT MACHINE FIFTH (*5) / SIX (*5) / SEVEN (*4) / BUNDLES (*4) / SOFTS (*4) / ALIVE AND WELL IN PARIS (*3) / THE LAND OF

COCKAYNE (*3) / JET-PROPELLED PHOTOGRAPH early stuff (*6) / THE PEEL SESSIONS (*6) / AS IF . . . (*4) / RUBBER RIFF (*4) / VIRTUALLY (*4)

MIKE RATLEDGE – keyboards / **DAEVID ALLEN** (b. Australia) – guitar / **KEVIN AYERS** (b.16 Aug'45, Herne Bay, England) – bass, vocals (ex-WILDE FLOWERS) / **ROBERT WYATT** (b. ROBERT ELLIDGE, Bristol, England) – drums, vocals (ex-WILDE FLOWERS) / Note:- Other original American-born guitarist LARRY NOLAN left before debut 45.

	Polydor	not iss.
Feb 67. (7") (56151) **LOVE MAKES SWEET MUSIC. / FEELIN' REELIN' SQUEELIN'**	☐	-

—— trimmed to a trio, when DAEVID ALLEN went to France to form GONG. He was deputised on tour only by ANDY SUMMERS. First 2 albums guest **BRIAN HOPPER** – saxophone (ex-WILDE FLOWERS)

	Probe	Probe
Nov 68. (7") <452> **JOY OF A TOY. / WHY ARE WE SLEEPING**	-	☐
Dec 68. (lp) <PLP 4500> **THE SOFT MACHINE**	-	☐

– Hope for happiness / Joy of a toy / Hope for happiness (reprise) / Why am I so short? / So boot if at all / A certain kind / Save yourself / Priscilla / Lullabye letter / We did it again / Plus belle qu'une poubele / Why are we sleeping / Box 25-4 LID. *(UK-iss.Mar87 on 'Big Beat' lp/c; WIK A/C 57)*

—— **HUGH HOPPER** – bass (ex-WILDE FLOWERS) repl. AYERS who'd went solo

Apr 69. (lp) (SPB 1002) <PLP 4505> **SOFT MACHINE VOL.2**
– Pataphysical introduction (part I) / A concise British alphabet (part I) / Hibou, Anemone and bear / A concise British alphabet (part II) / Hulloder / Dada was here / Thank you Pierrot Lunaire / Have you ever been green? / Pataphysical introduction (part II) / Out of tunes / As long as he lies perfectly still / Dedicated to you but you weren't listening / Fire engine passing with bells clanging / Pig / Orange skin food / A door opens and closes / 10.30 returns to the bedroom. *(re-iss. 1974 on 'ABC'; ABCL 5004) (re-iss. May87 on 'Big Beat' lp/c; WIK A/C 58)*

—— added **ELTON DEAN** – saxophone (ex-BLUESOLOGY) / **LYN DOBSON** – flute, sax / **NICK EVANS** – trombone + **MARK CHARIG** – cornet (ex-BLUESOLOGY) both left before 3rd album. Added guests **JIMMY HASTINGS** – wind / **A.B. SPALL** – violin

	C.B.S.	Columbia
Jun 70. (d-lp) (66246) <30339> **THIRD**	18	☐

– Facelift / Slightly all the time / Moon in June / Out-Bloody-Rageous. *(re-iss. Jun88 on 'Decal' lp/c; LIKD/TCLIKD 35) (re-iss. Mar93 on 'Beat Goes On'; BGOCD 180) (cd re-iss. Jul96 on 'Columbia'; 471407-2)*

—— Now quartet, when LYN departed. Guests **HASTINGS + ALAN SKIDMORE** – sax

Feb 71. (lp) (64280) <30754> **FOURTH**	32	☐

– Teeth / Kings and queens / Fletcher's blemish / Virtually (parts 1-4). *(cd-iss. Apr95 on 'Sony Europe') (re-iss. cd Oct95 on 'One Way')*

—— **JOHN MARSHALL + PHIL HOWARD** – drums (shared) repl. WYATT who went solo. **ELTON DEAN** added electric piano + **ROY BABBINGTON** – double bass (guested 3)

Jun 72. (lp) (64806) <31604> **FIFTH**
– All white / Drop / Mc / As if / LBO / Pigling bland / Bone. *(re-iss. 1979 on 'CBS-Embassy'; 31748) (cd-iss. Apr93 on 'Sony Europe') (re-iss. Sep95 on 'One Way')*

—— **KARL JENKINS** – piano, saxophone repl. DEAN who stayed with JUST US (above newcomer alongside **RATLEDGE, HOPPER + MARSHALL**)

Feb 73. (d-lp) (68214) <32260> **SIX** (half live)
– Fanfare / All white / Between / Riff / 37 and a half / Geseolveut / E.P.V. / Lefty / Stumble / 5 from 13 (for Phil Seaman with love and thanks) / Riff II / The soft weed factor / Stanley stamps gibbon album (for B.O.) / Chloe and the pirates / 1983. *(cd-iss. Apr93 on 'Sony Europe')*

—— **ROY BABBINGTON** – bass (guest) repl. HUGH HOPPER who went solo

Oct 73. (lp) (65799) <32716> **SEVEN**
– Nettle bed / Carolyn / Day's eye / Bone fire / Tarabos / D.I.S. / Snodland / Penny hitch / Block / Down the road / The German lesson / The French lesson. *(cd-iss. Apr93 on 'Sony Europe')*

—— added **ALAN HOLDSWORTH** – guitar

	Harvest	not iss.
Apr 75. (lp) (SHSP 4044) **BUNDLES**	☐	

– Hazard profile (parts 1-5) / Gone sailing / Bundles / Land of the bag snake / The man who waved at trains / Peff / Four gongs two drums / The floating world. *(re-iss. 1989 on 'See For Miles' lp/cd; SEE/+CD 283)*

—— With last original RATLEDGE going solo and HOLDWORTH joining GONG, the remainder (**BABBINGTON, JENKINS + MARSHALL**) were joined by **ALAN WAKEMAN** – saxophone + **JOHN ETHERIDGE** – guitar

Jun 76. (lp) (SHSP 4056) **SOFTS** | ☐ | - |
– Aubade / The tale of Taliesyn / Bab ban Caliban / Song of Aeolus / Out of season / Second bundle / Kayoo / The Camden tandem / Nexus / One over the eight / Etika. *(reiss.Jan90 on 'See For Miles' lp/cd; SEE/+CD 285)*

—— **RIC SAUNDERS** – violin + **STEVE COOKE** – bass repl. WAKEMAN + BABBINGTON

Mar 78. (lp) (SHSP 4083) **ALIVE AND WELL - RECORDED IN PARIS** | ☐ | - |
– White kite / Eos / Odds, bullets and blades (part 1 & 2) / Song of the sunbird / Puffin, huffin' / Number three / The nodder / Surrounder silence / Soft space. *(cd-iss. Mar90 on 'See For Miles'; SEECD 290) (cd re-iss. Nov95 on 'One Way';)*

Apr 78. (7") (HAR 5155) **SOFT SPACE. / (part 2)** | ☐ | - |

—— Folded 1979, but re-formed for one-off studio outing below. Musicians:- **ETHRIDGE, MARSHALL, HOLDSWORTH** plus sessioners **DICK MORRISSEY** – saxophone / **ALAN PARKER** – guitar / **JOHN TAYLOR** – keyboards / **RAY WARLEIGH** – flute / **JACK BRUCE** – bass

	E.M.I.	not iss.
Mar 81. (lp) (EMC 3348) **THE LAND OF COCKAYNE**	☐	-

– Over 'n' above / Lotus groves / Isle of the blessed / Panoramania / Behind the crystal curtain / Palace of glass / Hot biscuit slim / (Black) Velvet mountain / Sly monkey / A lot of what you fancy.

—— finally disbanded after above – until . . .

	Elite	not iss.
May 91. (cd/c) (ELITE 006 CD/MC) **AS IF . . .**	☐	-

– Facelift / Slightly all the time / Kings and queens / Drop / Chloe and the pirates / As if. *(cd-iss. Sep93; same)*

– compilations, others, etc. –

Oct 74. (d-lp) A.B.C.; (ABC 602) **THE SOFT MACHINE COLLECTION**	☐	-

– (1st 2 albums) *(cd-iss. Sep89 on 'Big Beat'; CDWIKD 920)*

1976. (lp) De Wolfe; (3331) **RUBBER RIFF** | | - |
– Crunch / Pavan / Jombles / A little floating music / Hi-power / Little Miss B / Splot / Rubber riff / Sam's short shuffle / Melina / City steps / Gentle turn / Porky / Travelogue. *(cd-iss. Nov94 on 'Voiceprint'; VP 190CD) (cd re-iss. Sep97 on 'Blueprint'; BP 190CD)*

Jan 77. (lp) Charly; (CR 30014) **AT THE BEGINNING** | ☐ | - |
– That's how much I need you now / Save yourself / I should've / Jet propelled photographs / When I don't want you / Memories / You don't remember / She's gone / I'd rather be with you. *(re-iss. Mar83; CR 30196) (re-iss. Sep87 as 'JET PROPELLED PHOTOGRAPH' on 'Decal'; LIK 35) (cd-iss. Sep89 as 'JET PROPELLED PHOTOGRAPH' on 'Decal'; LIKCD 197) (re-iss. cd Jul97 on 'Charly'; CDGR 188)*

Mar 77. (t-lp) Harvest; (SHTW 800) **TRIPLE ECHO** | ☐ | - |
Aug 88. (cd/lp) Reckless; (CD+/RECK 5) **LIVE AT THE PROMS** (live) | ☐ | - |
Sep 90. (cd/c/d-lp) Strange Fruit; (SFR CD/MC/LP 201) **THE COMPLETE PEEL SESSIONS** | ☐ | - |
Dec 90. (cd/c/d-lp) Castle; (CCS CD/MC/LP 281) **THE UNTOUCHABLE COLLECTION (75-78)** | ☐ | - |
Aug 92. (3xcd-box) Magpie; (MAGPIE 2) **SOFTS / ALIVE & WELL / BUNDLES** | ☐ | - |
Apr 93. (m-cd) Windsong; (WINCD 031) **BBC RADIO 1 LIVE IN CONCERT** (live) | ☐ | - |
Jun 94. (cd) Windsong; (WINCD 056) **BBC RADIO 1 LIVE IN CONCERT** (live) | ☐ | - |
Jan 95. (cd) Movieplay Gold; (MPG 74033) **LIVE AT THE PARADISO** (re-iss. Oct96 on 'Blueprint'; BP 193CD) | ☐ | - |
Jun 95. (cd) C5; (C5MCD 623) **THE BEST OF SOFT MACHINE: THE HARVEST YEARS** (re-iss. May97; same) | ☐ | - |
Nov 96. (cd) Cuniform; (RUNE 90) **SPACED** | ☐ | - |
Jun 97. (cd; with MARK LEEMAN & DAVEY GRAHAM) Spalax; (14557) **LONDON 1967** | ☐ | - |
Jun 98. (cd) Blueprint; (BP 290CD) **LIVE 1970** (live) | ☐ | - |
Jun 98. (cd) Cuniform; (RUNE 100) **VIRTUALLY** (live in Bremen) | ☐ | - |

SONIC BOOM (see under ⇒ SPACEMEN 3)

SONIC YOUTH

Formed: New York City, New York, USA . . . early 1981 by THURSTON MOORE and KIM GORDON. They replaced an early embryonic rhythm section with LEE RANALDO and RICHARD EDSON. After numerous releases on various US indie labels (notably Glenn Branca's 'Neutral' records), they signed to 'Blast First' in the U.K. First up for the label was 'BAD MOON RISING' in 1985, showing them at their most menacing and disturbing, especially on the glorious 'DEATH VALLEY 69' (a macabre reference to killer Charles Manson) with LYDIA LUNCH providing dual vox. They subsequently secured a US deal with 'S.S.T.', heralding yet another socially passionate thrash effort with 'EVOL'. A sideline project, CICCONE YOUTH, saw KIM and the lads plus MIKE WATT (of fIREHOSE), take off MADONNA's 'INTO THE GROOVE(Y)', which became a surprise dancefloor fave. Two more classic pieces, 'SISTER' (1987) & 'DAYDREAM NATION' (1988), finally secured them a major deal with 'D.G.C.' (David Geffen Company). In the early 90's, they smashed into the UK Top 40 with the album 'GOO', featuring a cameo by CHUCK D (of PUBLIC ENEMY) on the track/single 'KOOL THING'. The album, which sweetened their garage-punk/art-noise collages with melodic hooks, also included their deeply haunting tribute to KAREN CARPENTER, 'TUNIC (SONG FOR KAREN)'. They supported PUBLIC ENEMY that year, also stepping out with NEIL YOUNG on his 'Ragged Glory' tour in '91 (much to the distaste of YOUNG's more conservative fans!). In 1992, many thought 'DIRTY' to be a disappointment, the record being overproduced and overtaken by their new rivals and labelmates NIRVANA. By the mid-late 90's, they had returned to ground roots with acoustic psychedelia and the albums, 'EXPERIMENTAL JET SET' (1994), 'WASHING MACHINE' (1995) and 'A THOUSAND LEAVES' (1998) were again lauded by the alternative music press. All members had also taken on side solo projects, KIM featuring in all-star punk-grunge affair, FREE KITTEN. SONIC YOUTH returned towards the end of the decade with an appropriately-titled set, 'GOODBYE 20th CENTURY' (1999), a record in which they took on the works of avant-garde composers CHRISTIAN WOLFF, JOHN CAGE and CORNELIUS CARDEW. • **Songwriters:** MOORE / RANALDO / GORDON compositions, except I WANNA BE YOUR DOG (Stooges) / TICKET TO RIDE + WITHIN YOU WITHOUT YOU (Beatles) / BEAT ON THE BRAT + others (Ramones) / TOUCH ME, I'M SICK (Mudhoney) / ELECTRICITY (Captain Beefheart) / COMPUTER AGE (Neil Young). Their off-shoot CICCONE YOUTH covered INTO THE GROOVE (Madonna) / ADDICTED TO LOVE (Robert Palmer) / IS IT MY BODY (Alice Cooper) / PERSONALITY CRISIS (New York Dolls) / CA PLANE POUR MOI (Plastic Bertrand) / MOIST VAGINA = (MV) (Nirvana). FREE KITTEN covered: OH BONDAGE UP YOURS (X-Ray Spex). • **Trivia:** Early in 1989, they were featured on an hour-long special TV documentary for Melvyn Bragg's 'The South Bank Show'.

Album rating: CONFUSION IS SEX (*6) / KILL YR IDOLS (*4) / BAD MOON RISING (*8) / EVOL (*8) / SISTER (*9) / DAYDREAM NATION (*9) / GOO (*9) / DIRTY (*7) / EXPERIMENTAL JET SET, TRASH AND NO STAR (*6) / WASHING MACHINE (*8) / A THOUSAND LEAVES (*6) / GOODBYE 20th CENTURY (*7) / Lee Ranaldo: FROM HERE TO INFINITY (*4) / EAST JESUS (*7) / Thurston Moore: PSYCHIC HEARTS (*8) / ROOT (*7)

THURSTON MOORE (b.25 Jul'58, Coral Gables, Florida) – vocals, guitar / **KIM GORDON** (b.28 Apr'53, Rochester, N.Y.) – vocals, bass / **LEE RANALDO** (b. 3 Feb'56, Glen Cove, N.Y.) – vocals, guitar repl. ANN DEMARIS / **RICHARD EDSON** – drums repl. DAVE KEAY

		Neutral	not iss.
Feb 84.	(m-lp) *(ND 01)* **SONIC YOUTH** (live)	-	- German

– The burning spear / I dreamt I dreamed / She's not alone / I don't want to push it / The good and the bad. *(re-iss. cd Oct87 on 'S.S.T.'; SSTCD 097)*

—— **JIM SCLAVUNOS** – drums repl. EDSON

Feb 84.	(lp) *(ND 02)* **CONFUSION IS SEX**	-	- German

– Inhuman / The world looks red / Confusion is next / Making the nature scene / Lee is free / (She's in a) Bad mood / Protect me you / Freezer burn / I wanna be your dog / Shaking Hell. *(re-iss. cd Oct87 on 'S.S.T.'; SSTCD 096)*

—— **BOB BERT** – drums repl. SCLAVUNOS (still featured on 2 tracks)

		Zensor	not iss.
Oct 83.	(m-lp) *(ZENSOR 10)* **KILL YR. IDOLS**	-	- German

– Protect me you / Shaking Hell / Kill yr. idols / Brother James / Early American.

		not iss.	Ecstatic Peace
1984.	(c) *<none>* **SONIC DEATH** (SONIC YOUTH LIVE)		

– Sonic Death (side 1) / Sonic Death (side 2). *(UK cd-iss. Jul88 on 'Blast First'; BFFP 32CD>*

		not iss.	Iridescence
Dec 84.	(12"; by SONIC YOUTH & LYDIA LUNCH) *<1-12>* **DEATH VALLEY '69. / BRAVE MEN (RUN IN MY FAMILY)**	-	

		Blast First	Homestead
Mar 85.	(lp) *(BFFP 1)* *<HMS 016>* **BAD MOON RISING**		

– Intro / Brave men rule / Society is a hole / I love her all the time / Ghost bitch / I'm insane / Justice is might / Death Valley '69. *(cd-iss. Nov86+=; BFFP 1CD)* – Satan is boring / Flower / Halloween. *<US cd re-iss. 1995 on 'Geffen'; 24512>*

Jun 85.	(12"ep; by SONIC YOUTH & LYDIA LUNCH) *(BFFP 2)* *<HMS 012>* **DEATH VALLEY '69. / I DREAMT I DREAMED / INHUMAN / BROTHER JAMES / SATAN IS BORING**		
Jan 86.	(12",12"yellow) *(BFFP 3)* **HALLOWEEN. / FLOWER**	-	
Jan 86.	(7") *(BFFP 3)* **FLOWER. / REWOLF** (censored)	-	
	(12") – ('A'side) / Satan is boring (live).		
Mar 86.	(etched-12") *(BFFP 3-B)* **HALLOWEEN II**	-	

—— **STEVE SHELLEY** (b.23 Jun'62, Midland, Michigan) – drums repl. BOB BERT who joined PUSSY GALORE

		Blast First	S.S.T.
May 86.	(lp/c) *(BFFP 4/+C)* *<SST/+C/CD 059>* **EVOL**		

– Green light / Star power / Secret girl / Tom Violence / Death to our friends / Shadow of a doubt / Marilyn Moore / In the kingdom / Madonna, Sean and me. *(cd-iss. Nov86+=; BFFP 4CD)* – Bubblegum. *<US cd re-iss. 1995 on 'Geffen'; 24513>*

Jul 86.	(7") *(BFFP 7)* **STAR POWER. / BUBBLEGUM**		
	(12"+=) *(BFFP 7T)* – Expressway.		

—— added guest **MIKE WATT** – bass (of fIREHOSE)

Nov 86.	(12"; as CICCONE YOUTH) *(BFFP 8)* **INTO THE GROOVE(Y). / TUFF TITTY RAP / BURNIN' UP**		
Jun 87.	(lp/c/cd) *(BFFP 20/+C/CD)* *<SST/+C/CD 134>* **SISTER**		

– White cross / (I got a) Catholic block / Hot wire my heart / Tuff gnarl / Kotton crown / Schizophrenia / Beauty lies in the eye / Stereo sanctity / Pipeline – killtime / PCH. *(cd+=)* – Master-Dik (original). *<US cd re-iss. 1995 on 'Geffen'; 24514>*

Jan 88.	(m-lp) *(BFFP 26T)* **MASTER-DIK**		

– Master-Dik / Beat on the brat / Under the influence of the Jesus & Mary Chain: Ticket to ride / Ringo – He's on fire – Florida oil / Chines jam / Vibrato – Guitar lick – Funky fresh / Our backyard / Traffik.

		Blast First	Capitol
Jan 88.	(lp/c/cd; as CICCONE YOUTH) *(BFFP 28/+C/CD)* *<C1/C4/C2 75402>* **THE WHITEY ALBUM**	63	

– Needle-gun (silence) / G-force / Platoon II / Macbeth / Me & Jill / Hendrix Cosby / Burnin' up / Hi! everybody / Children of Satan / Third fig / Two cool rock chicks / Listening to Neu! / Addicted to love / Moby-Dik / March of the Ciccone robots / Making the nature scene / Tuff titty rap / Into the groovey. *<US cd re-iss. 1995 on 'Geffen'; 24516>*

Feb 88.	(d-one-sided-7"on 'Fierce') *(FRIGHT 015-016)* **STICK ME DONNA MAGICK MOMMA / MAKING THE NATURE SCENE** (live)		-
	(also soon issued as normal-7")		

		Blast First	Torso
Oct 88.	(d-lp/c/cd) *(BFFP 34/+C/CD)* *<2602339>* **DAYDREAM NATION**	99	

– Teenage riot / Silver rocket / The sprawl / 'Cross the breeze / Eric's trip / Total trash / Hey Joni / Providence / Candle? / Rain king / Kissability / Trilogy: The wonder – Hyperstation – Eliminator Jr.

—— Late in '88, KIM teamed up with LYDIA LUNCH and SADIE MAE to form one-off project HARRY CREWS. Their live appearences were issued in Apr 90 as 'NAKED IN GARDEN HILLS' for 'Big Cat' UK + 'Widowspeak' US.

Feb 89.	(12") *(BFFP 46)* **TOUCH ME, I'M SICK. / (Halloween; by MUDHONEY)**		

		W.E.A.	D.G.C.
Jun 90.	(cd/c/lp) *<7599 24297-2/-4/-1)>* **GOO**	32	96

– Dirty boots / Tunic (song for Karen) / Mary-Christ / Kool thing / Mote / My friend Goo / Disappearer / Mildred Pierce / Cinderella's big score / Scooter + Jinx / Titanium expose. *(re-iss. cd Oct95 on 'Geffen'; GFLD 19297)*

Sep 90.	(7"/c-s) **KOOL THING. / THAT'S ALL I KNOW (RIGHT NOW)**		-
	(12"+=) – ('A'demo version).		
	(cd-s++=) – Dirty boots (rock & roll Heaven version).		

—— In Autumn '90, THURSTON was part of 'Rough Trade' supergroup VELVET MONKEYS.

		D.G.C.	D.G.C.
Apr 91.	(m-lp/m-c/m-cd) *(DGC/+C/D 21634)* **DIRTY BOOTS** (all live, except the title track)	69	-

– Dirty boots / The bedroom / Cinderella's big scene / Eric's trip / White kross. *(re-iss. cd Apr92; DGLD 19060)*

—— Early in '92, THURSTON and STEVE also teamed up with RICHARD HELL's off-shoot group The DIM STARS.

Jun 92.	(7") *(DGCS 11)* **100%. / CREME BRULEE**	28	-
	(10"orange+=/12"+=) *(DGC V/T 11)* – Hendrix necro.		
	(cd-s++=) *(DGCTD 11)* – Genetic.		
Jul 92.	(d-lp/c/cd) *(DGC/+C/D 24485)>* **DIRTY**	6	83

– 100% / Swimsuit issue / Theresa's sound-world / Drunken butterfly / Shoot / Wish fulfillment / Sugar Kane / Orange rolls, angel's spit / Youth against fascism / Nic fit / On the strip / Chapel Hill / JC / Purr / Creme brulee. *(d-lp+=)* – Stalker. *(re-iss. cd Oct95; GFLD 19296)*

		Geffen	D.G.C.
Oct 92.	(7") *(GFS 26)* **YOUTH AGAINST FASCISM. / PURR**	52	-

(10"colrd+=) *(GFSV 26)* – ('A'version).
(12"++=/cd-s++=) *(GFST/+D 26)* – The destroyed room (radio version)

Apr 93.	(7"/c-s) *(GFS/+C 37)* **SUGAR KANE. / THE END OF THE END OF THE UGLY**	26	-
	(10"blue+=/cd-s+=) *(GFS V/TD 37)* – Is it my body / Personality crisis.		
Apr 94.	(10"silver/c-s/cd-s) *(GFS V/C/TD 72)* **BULL IN THE HEATHER. / RAZORBLADE**	24	-
May 94.	(cd/c/blue-lp) *<(GED/GEC/GEF 24632)>* **EXPERIMENTAL JET SET, TRASH AND NO STAR**	10	34

– Winner's blues / Bull in the heather / Starfield road / Skink / Self-obsessed and sexxee / Bone / Androgynous mind / Quest for the cup / Waist / Doctor's orders / Tokyo eye / In the mind of the bourgeois reader / Sweet shine.

—— In Sep 94; 'A&M' released CARPENTERS tribute album, which contained their single 'SUPERSTAR'. It was combined with also another cover from REDD KROSS, and reached UK No.45.

Oct 95.	(cd/c/d-lp) *<(GED/GEC/GEF 24925)>* **WASHING MACHINE**	39	58

– Becuz / Junkie's promise / Saucer-like / Washing machine / Unwind / Little trouble girl / No queen blues / Panty lies / Becuz coda * / Skip tracer / The diamond sea. *(cd+= *)*

Apr 96.	(12"/cd-s) *(GRS T/D 22132)* **LITTLE TROUBLE GIRL. / MY ARENA / THE DIAMOND SEA** (edit)		-
Feb 98.	(12"ep/cd-ep; SONIC YOUTH & JIM O'ROURKE) *(SYR 003/+CD)* **INVITO AL CIELO EP**		

– Invito al cielo / Hungara vivo / Radio-Amatoroj.
(above issued on own 'Sonic Youth Records')

May 98.	(d-cd/d-lp) *<(GED/GEF 25203)>* **A THOUSAND LEAVES**	38	85

– Contre le sexisme / Sunday / Female mechanic now on duty / Wildflower soul / Hoarfrost / French tickler / Hits of sunshine (for Allen Ginsberg) / Karen Koltrane / The ineffable me / Snare / Girl / Heather angel.

Jun 98.	(7") *(GFS 22332)* **SUNDAY. / MOIST VAGINA**	72	-
	(cd-s+=) *(GFSTD 22332)* – Silver panties / ('A'edit).		

—— THURSTON collaborated with DON FLEMING and JIM DUNBAR on the freeform/experimental project, FOOT, releasing 'S/T' for 'God Bless'

		Smells Like	Smells Like
Nov 99.	(d-lp/cd) *<(SYR 04/+CD)>* **GOODBYE 20th CENTURY**		

– Edges / Six / Six for new time for Sonic Youth / + - / Voice piece for soprano / Pendulum music // Having never written a note for percussion / Six / Burdocks / Four / Piano piece #3 / Piece enfantine / Treatise.

– compilations, others, etc. –

Feb 92.	(cd) *Sonic Death; <(SD 13001)>* **GOO DEMOS LIVE AT THE CONTINENTAL CLUB** (live)		- Nov89
Mar 95.	(m-lp/c) *Blast First; (BFFP 113 CD/C)* **CONFUSION IS SEX / KILL YR IDOLS**		-
Mar 95.	(cd) *Warners-Rhino; (8122 71591-2)* **MADE IN THE U.S.A.** (1986 soundtrack)		
Apr 95.	(cd) *Blast First; (BFFP 119CD)* **SCREAMING FIELDS OF SONIC LOVE**		-
May 97.	(pic-lp) *Sonic Death; (SYLB 1)* **LIVE IN BREMEN** (live)		
Jun 97.	(12"ep/cd-ep) *Sonic Youth; (SYR 1/+CD)* **SYR VOL.1**		
	– Anagrama / Improvisation ajout'e / Tremens / Mieux: de corrosion.		
Jul 98.	(cd) *S.K.R.; (SKR 1)* **SILVER SESSION FOR JASON KNUTH**		
Aug 98.	(cd) *Goofin' (GOO 2CD)* **HOLD THAT TIGER** (live 1987)		

LEE RANALDO

		Blast First	S.S.T.
Jul 87.	(m-lp/c) *(BFFP 9/+C)* *<SST 113>* **FROM HERE ⇒ ETERNITY**		

– Time stands still / Destruction site / Ouroboron / Slodrown / New groove loop / Florida flower / Hard left / Fuzz-locusts / To Mary / Lathe speaks / The resolution / King's egg. *(re-iss. May93 on 'S.S.T.' lp/c/cd; same as US)*

		not iss.	Blast First
Oct 95.	(cd) *<BFFPCD 103>* **EAST JESUS**		

– Bridge / Time stands still / Destruction site / Oroboron / Slo drone / Some distortion / Live #1 / New groove loop / Some hammering . . . / Walker grooves / Fuxx – Locusts / To Mary (x2) / Lathe speaks / Deva, Spain / Resolution – King's Ogg.

FREE KITTEN

KIM GORDON – vocals, bass, guitar / **JULIE CAFRITZ** – vocals, guitar (ex-PUSSY GALORE)

		Wiiija	Ecstatic Peace
1992.	(7") **OH BONDAGE UP YOURS. /**		

—— there were other singles collected on their compilation, see below

1992.	(m-cd) *<E#22>* **CALL NOW**		-
	– Falling backwards / + 5		

—— added **MARK IBOLD** – bass (of PAVEMENT) + **YOSHIMI** – drums, trumpet

Jun 94.	(cd) *(WIJ 036CD)* **UNBOXED** (compilation)		

– Skinny butt / Platinumb / Smack / Falling backwards / Oneness / Dick / Yoshimi Vs. Mascis / Oh bondage up yours / 1-2-3 / Party with me punker / John Stark blues / Guilty pleasures / Sex boy / Cleopatra / Loose lips / Oh baby.

Jan 95.	(7"one-sided) *(LTD 002)* **HARVEST SPOON**		-
Feb 95.	(cd/lp) *(WIJ 041 CD/V)* **NICE ASS**		

– Harvest sppon / Rock of ages / Proper band / What's fair / Kissing well / Call back / Blindfold test / Greener pastures / Revlon liberation orchestra / The boaster / Scratch the D.J. / Secret sex friend / Royal flush / Feelin' / Alan Licked has ruined music for an entire generation.

Feb 96. (7"ep) *(WIJ 047V)* **PUNKS SUING PUNKS EP**   ☐ ☐ –
– Kitten bossa nova / Punk v. punk / Coco's theme.

Oct 97. (12"ep) *(WIJ 074)* **CHINATOWN EXPRESS. / NEVER GONNA SLEEP / GAA**   ☐ ☐ –

Oct 97. (cd/lp) *(WIJ CD/LP 1076)* **SENTIMENTAL EDUCATION**
– Teenie weenie boppie / Top 40 / Never gonna sleep / Strawberry milk / Played yrself / Dr. Spooky's spatialized Chinatown express / Bouwerie's boys / Records sleep / Picabo who / Sentimental education / One forty five / Eat cake / Gaa / Daddy long legs / Noise doll.

THURSTON MOORE

	Geffen	D.G.C.
May 95. (cd/c/d-lp;colrd 3-sides) *<(GEF/GEC/GED 24810)>* **PSYCHIC HEARTS**   ☐ ☐
– Queen bee and her pals / Ono soul / Psychic hearts / Pretty bad / Patti Smith math scratch / Blues from beyond the grave / See-through play-mate / Hang out / Feathers / Tranquilizor / Staring statues / Cindy (rotten tanx) / Cherry's blues / Female cop / Elergy for all dead rock stars.

	Forced Exposure	Forced Exposure
Dec 96. (cd; by JIM SAUTER, DON DIETRICH & THURSTON MOORE) *<(FE 015)>* **BAREFOOT IN THE HEAD** (rec. 1988)   ☐ ☐
– All doors look alike / Tanned moon / On the phrase "ass-backwards" / The date-reduced loaf / Concerning the sun as a cool solid.

	Victo	Victo
Mar 97. (cd) *<(VICTOCD 045)>* **PIECE FOR JETSUN DOLMA**   ☐ ☐

	Corpus Hermeticum	Corpus Herme
Apr 97. (cd) *(HERMES 011)* **KLANGFARBENMELODIE**   ☐ ☐

	Father Yod	Father Yod
May 97. (cd; by THURSTON MOORE & PHIL MILSTEIN) *(HOTYOD 1)* **SONGS WE TAUGHT THE LORD VOL.2**   ☐ –

	Little Brother	Little Brother
Jul 97. (cd; by THURSTON MOORE & NELS CLINE) *<(LB 011CD)>* **PILLOW WAND**   ☐ ☐
(re-iss. Feb99 on 'Skycap'; RTD 3012002-2)

	Xeric	Xeric
Aug 98. (cd/lp; by LOREN MAZZACANE CONNORS, JEAN-MARC MONTERA, THURSTON MOORE & LEE RANALDO) *<(X 99 0/5)>* **mmmr**   ☐ ☐
– (untitled) / (untitled) / (untitled).

	Lo Record.	Lo Record.
Oct 98. (cd/lp) *<(LCD/LLP 011)>* **ROOT** (V/A remixes)   ☐ ☐

	Fourth Dimension	Fourth Dimension
Feb 99. (10"lp) *<(FDCD 57)>* **NOT ME. / LYDIA's MOTH**   ☐ ☐

	Materiali Sonori	Materiali Sonori
Mar 99. (cd; by THURSTON MOORE, EVAN PARKER & WALTER PRATI) *<(MASDO 90106)>* **THE PROMISE**   ☐ ☐
– The promise / Is / Our future / Our promise / Are / Children / All children.
(lp-iss.Apr99 on 'Get Back'; FT 803)

SONNY & CHER (see under ⇒ CHER)

SON VOLT (see under ⇒ UNCLE TUPELO)

SOUL ASYLUM

Formed: Minneapolis, Minnesota, USA . . . 1981 as LOUD FAST RULES, by ex-AT LAST guitarist DAN MURPHY and ex-SHITS frontman DAVE PIRNER, who were subsequently joined by KARL MUELLER then PAT MORLEY. Very much in the mould of HUSKER DU and The REPLACEMENTS, SOUL ASYLUM joined the latter at 'Twin Tone' records, while the former's BOB MOULD produced their 1984 debut album, 'SAY WHAT YOU WILL'. Later that year, MORLEY departed while the rest of the band took a break, SOUL ASYLUM subsequently returning in 1986 with GRANT YOUNG on their follow-up, 'MADE TO BE BROKEN'. A fusion of 60's pop and 70's punk, the album (also produced by MOULD) showed PIRNER blossoming into a cuttingly perceptive lyricist. Later that year, the band delivered another fine set, 'WHILE YOU WERE OUT', the record attracting major label attention in the form of 'A&M'. Fulfilling their contract with 'Twin Tone', SOUL ASYLUM cut a covers set, 'CLAM DIP AND OTHER DELIGHTS', displaying their wide range of tastes from Barry Manilow's 'MANDY' to Foreigner's 'JUKEBOX HERO'. In 1988, A&M issued the LENNY KAYE and ED STASIUM produced album, 'HANG TIME', an endearing collection of gleaming power-pop nuggets that occasionally veered off the beaten track into country. Their second and final release for A&M, 'SOUL ASYLUM AND THE HORSE THEY RODE IN ON' (1990), saw PIRNER spiral into despair despite the album's critical acclaim. Disillusioned with the major label inertia, the frontman took a break from amplified noise while his colleagues resumed their day jobs. Staking their chances on yet another major label, SOUL ASLYUM subsequently signed to 'Columbia' and achieved almost instant success with the album 'GRAVE DANCERS UNION' in 1992. This was mainly due to the massive interest in the TOM PETTY-esque 'RUNAWAY TRAIN', a single that hit the American Top 5 in the summer of '93. The track's radio-friendly success

paved the way for more typically abrasive numbers as 'SOMEBODY TO SHOVE' and 'BLACK GOLD', PIRNER landing on his feet as he wooed sultry actress, Winona Ryder (he appeared with her in the film, 'Generation X'). SOUL ASYLUM subsequently became MTV darlings and friends of the stars, such luminaries as BOB DYLAN, PETER BUCK and GUNS N' ROSES professing to fan status. In 1995, they returned with a new drummer, STERLING CAMPBELL, and a new album, 'LET YOUR DIM LIGHT SHINE', another worldwide seller which spawned the melancholy Top 30 gem, 'MISERY'. MURPHY and PIRNER (latter part-time) had also moonlighted in the countrified GOLDEN SMOG with among others the JAYHAWKS' GARY LOURIS and MARC PERLMAN. An EP of covers in '92 was finally followed up by an album in '96, 'DOWN BY THE OLD MAINSTREAM'. A few years later y'all supergroup added BIG STAR's JODY STEPHENS to replace the drumming PIRNER, a second set, WEIRD TALES', gaining many plaudits. • **Covers:** MOVE OVER (Janis Joplin) / RHINESTONE COWBOY (Glen Campbell) / BARSTOOL BLUES (Neil Young) / SEXUAL HEALING (Marvin Gaye) / ARE FRIENDS ELECTRIC (Tubeway Army) / SUMMER OF DRUGS (Victoria Williams) / WHEN I RAN OFF AND LEFT HER (Vic Chesnutt).

Album rating: SAY WHAT YOU WILL (*6) / MADE TO BE BROKEN (*6) / WHILE YOU WERE OUT (*6) / HANG TIME (*5) / CLAM DIP AND OTHER DELIGHTS (*5) / SOUL ASYLUM AND THE HORSE THEY RODE IN ON (*8) / GRAVE DANCERS UNION (*7) / LET YOUR DIM LIGHTS SHINE (*6) / CANDY FROM A STRANGER (*5)

DAVE PIRNER (b.16 Apr'64, Green Bay, Wisconsin) – vocals, guitar / **DAN MURPHY** (b.12 Jul'62, Duluth, Minnesota) – guitar, vocals / **KARL MUELLER** (b.27 Jul'63) – bass / **PAT MORLEY** – drums, percussion

	Rough Trade	Twin Tone
Aug 84. (m-lp) *<TT 8439>* **SAY WHAT YOU WILL**   ☐ ☐
– Long day / Voodoo doll / Money talks / Stranger / Sick of that song / Walking / Happy / Black and blue / Religiavision. *<US re-iss. May89+=; same>* – Dragging me down / Do you know / Spacehead / Broken glass / Masquerade. *(UK cd-iss. Mar93 as 'SAY WHAT YOU WILL CLARENCE . . . KARL SOLD THE TRUCK' on 'Roadrunner'; RR 9093-2) (cd re-iss. Mar95 on 'Twin Tone'; TTR 8439-2)*

—— **GRANT YOUNG** (b. 5 Jan'64, Iowa City, Iowa) – drums, percussion; repl. MORLEY

Sep 86. (lp) *(ROUGH 102) <TT 8666>* **MADE TO BE BROKEN**   ☐ ☐
– Tied to the tracks / Ship of fools / Can't go back / Another world another day / Made to be broken / Never really been / Whoa! / New feelings / Growing pain / Lone rider / Ain't that tough / Don't it (make your troubles seem small). *(cd-iss. Mar93 on 'Roadrunner'+=; RR 9094-2)* – Long way home. *(cd re-iss. Sep98 on 'R.C.A.'; 74321 60573-20)*

Sep 86. (7") **TIED TO THE TRACKS. /**   ☐ –

	What Goes On	Twin Tone
Mar 88. (lp) *(GOES ON 16) <TT 8691>* **WHILE YOU WERE OUT**   ☐ 1987
– Freaks / Carry on / No man's land / Crashing down / The judge / Sun don't shine / Closer to the stars / Never too soon / Miracles mile / Lap of luxury / Passing sad daydream. *(cd-iss. Mar93 on 'Roadrunner'; RR 9096-2) (cd re-iss. Feb95 on 'Twin Tone'; TTR 8691-2)*

May 88. (m-lp) *(GOES ON 22) <TT 8814>* **CLAM DIP AND OTHER DELIGHTS**   ☐ 1987
– Just plain evil / Chains / Secret no more / Artificial heart / P-9 / Take it to root / Jukebox hero / Move over / Mandy / Rhinestone cowboy. *(cd re-iss. Mar93 on 'Roadrunner'; RR 9097-2) (cd re-iss. Feb95 on 'Twin Tone'; TTR 8814-2)*

—— split but re-formed adding guest **CADD** – sax, piano

	A&M	A&M
Jun 88. (7"/12") *(AM/+Y 447)* **SOMETIME TO RETURN. / PUT THE BOOT IN**   ☐ –
(12"-iss.Jun91 +=; same) – Marionette.
Jun 88. (lp/c/cd) *(AMA/AMC/CDA 5197) <395197-1/-4/-2>* **HANG TIME**   ☐ ☐
– Down on up to me / Little too clean / Sometime to return / Cartoon / Beggars and choosers / Endless farewell / Standing in the doorway / Marionette / Jack of all trades / Twiddly dee / Heavy rotation. *(re-iss. Sep93 cd/c; CD/C MID 189)*
Aug 88. (7") *(AM 463)* **CARTOON. / TWIDDLY DEE**   ☐ –
(12"+=) *(AMY 463)* – Standing in the doorway.
Sep 90. (cd/c/lp) *(395318-2/-4/-1)* **SOUL ASYLUM & THE HORSE THEY RODE IN ON**   ☐ 1989
– Spinnin' / Bitter pill / Veil of tears / Nice guys (don't get paid) / Something out of nothing / Gullible's travels / Brand new shine / Grounded / Don't be on your way / We / All the king's friends. *(re-iss. Sep93 cd/c; CD/C MID 190)*
Jan 91. (7") **EASY STREET. / SPINNING**   ☐ ☐
(12"+=) – All the king's friends / Gullible's travels.

	Columbia	Columbia
Oct 92. (cd/c/lp) *(472253-2/-4/-1) <48896>* **GRAVE DANCERS UNION**   ☐ 11
– Somebody to shove / Black gold / Runaway train / Keep it up / Homesick / Get on out / New world / April fool / Without a trace / Growing into you / 99% / The Sun maid. *(re-iss.Jul93; hit UK No.52) (UK No.27 early '94)*
Mar 93. (10"ep/cd-ep) *(659 088-0/-2)* **BLACK GOLD. / BLACK GOLD (live) / THE BREAK / 99%**   ☐ ☐
May 93. (c-s/cd-s) *<74966>* **RUNAWAY TRAIN / NEVER REALLY BEEN** (live)   – 5
Jun 93. (7"/c-s) *(659 390-7/-4)* **RUNAWAY TRAIN. / BLACK GOLD** (live)   37 –
(12"+=) *(659 390-6)* – By the way / Never really been (live).
(cd-s++=) *(659 390-2)* – Everybody loves a winner. (- Black Gold).
(above single returned into UK chart Nov'93 to hit No.7)
Aug 93. (12"ep/cd-ep) *(659 649-6/-2)* **SOMEBODY TO SHOVE / SOMEBODY TO SHOVE (live). / RUNAWAY TRAIN (live) / BY THE WAY** (demo)   34 –
(c-ep) *(659 649-4)* – ('A'side) / Black gold (live) / Runaway train (live).
Jan 94. (7"/c-s) *(659 844-7/-4)* **BLACK GOLD. / SOMEBODY TO SHOVE**   26 –
(cd-s+=) *(659 844-2)* – Closer to the stairs / Square root.

(cd-s+=) *(659 844-5)* – Runaway train (live).

Mar 94. (7"/c-s) *(660 224-7/-4)* **SOMEBODY TO SHOVE. / BY THE WAY**   `32`   `-`
(cd-s+=) *(660 224-2)* – Stranger (unplugged) / Without a trace (live).
(cd-s++=) *(660 224-5)* – ('A'mix).

—— **STERLING CAMPBELL** – drums; repl. YOUNG

Jun 95. (cd/c) *(480 320-2/-4)* <57616> **LET YOUR DIM LIGHT SHINE**   `22`   `6`
– Misery / Shut down / To my own devices / Hopes up / Promises broken / Bittersweetheart / String of pearls / Crawl / Caged rat / Eyes of a child / Just like anyone / Tell me when / Nothing to write home about / I did my best.

Jun 95. (c-s,cd-s) <77959> **MISERY / HOPE**   `-`   `20`

Jul 95. (7"white/c-s) *(662 109-7/-4)* **MISERY. / STRING OF PEARLS**   `30`   `-`
(cd-s+=) *(662 109-2)* – Hope (demo) / I did my best.

Nov 95. (c-s) *(662 478-4)* **JUST LIKE ANYONE / DO ANYTHING YOU WANNA DO (live)**   `52`   `-`
(cd-s+=) *(662 478-2)* – Get on out (live).
(cd-s) *(662 478-5)* – ('A'side) / You'll live forever (demo) / Fearless leader (demo).

Feb 96. (c-s,cd-s) <78215> **PROMISES BROKEN / CAN'T EVEN TELL (live)**   `-`   `63`

—— now a trio of PIRNER, MURPHY + MUELLER

May 98. (cd/c) *(487265-2/-4)* <67618> **CANDY FROM A STRANGER**   `☐`
– Creatures of habit / I will still be laughing / Close / See you later / No time for waiting / Blood into wine / Lies of hate / Draggin' out the lake / Blackout / The game / Cradle chain.

SOUL COUGHING (dig out; Great Alt & Indie . . .)

SOULFLY

Formed: based – Phoenix, Arizona, USA . . . 1997 by ex-SEPULTURA mainman, MAX CAVALERA, the Brazilian enlisting the aid of LUCIO (JACKSON BANDIERA), MARCELLO D RAPP and punk rocker, ROY MAYORGA. MAX had recently found faith in God after his step-son, Dana (also son of wife/manager, Gloria) died; his other sons, Zyon and Igor also had serious illnesses. The man never changed his "ungod"-like vocal chords though, and SOULFLY (under the production of Ross Robinson) unleashed their thrillingly diverse eponymous set in the Spring of '98. The contrast between the tribal 'UMBABARAUMA' and the grinding 'NO' somehow worked, the latter's refreshingly metal assault on the ears and the line, "no motherf***in' HOOTIE & THE BLOWFISH", supplying the definitive "ROCK!!!" highlight of the year!

Album rating: SOULFLY (*8)

MAX CAVALERA – vocals, 4-string guitar (ex-SEPULTURA) / **JACKSON BANDIERA** (aka LUCIO) – guitars (ex-CHICO SCIENCE) / **MARCELLO D. RAPP** – bass (ex-MIST) / **ROY "RATA" MAYORGA** – drums (ex-AGNOSTIC FRONT, ex-SHELTER, ex-NAUSEA, ex-CHAOS USA)

                                  Roadrunner Roadrunner

Mar 98. (ltd;cd-ep) *(RR 2238-3)* **BLEED / NO HOPE = NO FEAR / CANGACEIRO / AIN'T NO FEEBLE BASTARD**   `☐`   `-`

Apr 98. (cd/c/lp) *(<RR 8748-2/-4/-1>)* **SOULFLY**   `16`   `79`
– Eye for an eye / No hope = no fear / Bleed / Tribe / Bumba / First commandment / Bumbklaatt / Soulfly / Umbabarauma / Quilombo / Fire / The song remains insane / No / Prejudice / Karmageddon. *(special cd+=; RR 8748-9)* – Cangaceiro / Ain't no feeble bastard / The possibility of life's destruction. *(re-iss. May99 d-cd+=; RR 8748-8)*– Tribe (fuck shit up mix) / Qilombo (extreme ragga dub mix) / Umbabaraumba (World Cup remix) / No hope = no fear (live) / Bleed (live) / Quilombo (live) / The song remains the insane (live) / Eye for an eye (live) / Tribe (tribal terrorism mix) / Umbabaraumba (Brasilia '70 remix) / Quilombo (Zumbi dub remix) / Soulfly (eternal spirit remix).

Jun 98. (ltd;cd-ep) *(RR 2231-3)* **UMBABARAUMA / UMBABARAUMA (World Cup mix) / TRIBE (extended) / UMBABARAUMA (World Cup instrumental)**   `☐`   `-`

May 99. (cd-s) *(RR 2203-3)* **TRIBE (fuck shit up mix) / QUILOMBO (Zumbi dub mix) / TRIBE (tribal terrorism mix)**   `☐`   `-`

SOUL II SOUL

Formed: South London, England . . . 1982 by BERESFORD ROMEO (aka JAZZIE B) and PHILIP 'DADDAE' HARVEY. Initially operating purely as a sound system, SOUL II SOUL began branching out with the arrival of producer/arranger and erstwhile WILD BUNCH man, NELLEE HOOPER. Having landed a residency at Covent Garden's Africa Centre, the trio began shopping demos around the major labels and were subsequently taken on by 'Virgin' offshoot, 'Ten'. While the outfit's earliest efforts, 'FAIRPLAY' and 'FEEL FREE' only just scraped into the UK Top 75, March 89's sublime 'KEEP ON MOVIN' made the Top 5 and added pop star to a JAZZIE B CV that already included radio presenter (with soon-to-be-commercial pirate station, Kiss FM), record shop proprietor and clothes merchandiser; the collective's famous 'Funky Dred' logo became synonymous with the rise of the club scene in the late 80's. Having whetted peoples' appetites, SOUL II SOUL served up a gourmet platter in the shape of UK No.1 platinum-selling album, 'CLUB CLASSICS VOL.1' (1989); for once the title was no idle boast and an exquisite combination of lavish strings, way heavy dub-style basslines, molten hip hop beats and Afro influences heralded one of the key developments in the British soul/R&B scene. There was also the small matter of CARON WHEELER's steamy diva-esque vocals (alongside other guest singers ROSE WINDROSS and DO'REEN), her tonsils gracing both the aforementioned 'KEEP ON MOVIN' and subsequent No.1 single, 'BACK TO

LIFE (HOWEVER DO YOU WANT ME)'. The track's creamy R&B appeal even translated to the States where the record made the Top 5, a rare feat for an English club-orientated act. While WHEELER went on to a solo career, JAZZIE B and HOOPER used the success as a springboard for high profile production work, their biggest credit coming in early 1990 with SINEAD O'CONNOR's PRINCE-penned No.1, 'Nothing Compares 2 U'. Sophomore album, 'VOL II, A NEW DECADE 1990' arrived the same year, again making No.1 and spawning the singles, 'A DREAM'S A DREAM' and 'MISSING YOU'. With VICTORIA WILSON-JAMES performing on the former and KYM MAZELLE undertaking vocal duties on the latter, SOUL II SOUL had once again perfectly matched up singer and song while the album itself benefited from the talents of COURTNEY PINE and legendary rapper FAB 5 FREDDIE. 1991 saw HOOPER work with old mates MASSIVE ATTACK on their epochal 'Unfinished Sympathy', arguably the pinnacle of his career (although he went on to work with everyone from BJORK to U2) but also the end of his partnership with JAZZIE B & Co. SOUL II SOUL were back in the Top 5 the following year with 'JOY', their first single to feature a male vocalist (RICHIE STEPHENS). The accompanying album, 'JUST RIGHT VOLUME III' (1992) made the Top 3 but met with a lukewarm critical reception as did 'VOLUME V – BELIEVE' (1995), SOUL II SOUL's parting shot for 'Virgin'. Although the crew moved on to 'Island/4th & Broadway', 'SOUL II SOUL VOL.6 – TIME TO CHANGE' (1997) failed to chart and suggested that the concept had grown just the tiniest bit stale.

Album rating: CLUB CLASSICS – VOLUME ONE (*8) / VOL.II, A NEW DECADE 1990 (*6) / JUST RIGHT VOLUME III (*5) / VOLUME IV – THE CLASSIC SINGLES 88-93 compilation (*7) / VOLUME V – BELIEVE (*5) / SOUL II SOUL VOL.6 – TIME TO CHANGE (*4)

JAZZIE B. (BERESFORD ROMEO) – keyboards, vocals / **NELLEE HOOPER** – keyboards

                                 10-Virgin   Virgin

May 88. (7") *(TEN 228)* **FAIRPLAY. / ('A'radio mix)**   `63`   `☐`
(12"+=) *(TENX 228)* – ('A'bonus beats).
(12") *(TENR 228)* – ('A'side) / Ambition (rap) / ('A'-freestyle horns mix).
above singer & co-composer ROSE WINDROSS

Sep 88. (7") *(TEN 239)* **FEEL FREE. / FAIRPLAY**   `64`   `☐`
(12"+=/cd-s+=) *(TEN X/CD 239)* – ('A'instrumental).
(12"+=) *(TENR 239)* – ('A'-unlimited remix).
above singer DO'REEN

Mar 89. (7"/7"w/poster/c-s) *(TEN/+P/C 263)* <99205> **KEEP ON MOVIN'. / ('A'instrumental)**   `5`   `11` Jun89
(12") *(TENX 263)* – ('A'club mix) / ('A'-Big beat acappella) / ('A'-Pianopella) / ('A'instrumental).
(12"/3"cd-s) *(TENR/+D 263)* – ('A'-New York mix) / ('A'-First Movement mix) / ('A'-A dub in the sun mix).
(3"cd-s) *(TENCD 263)* – ('A'side) / ('A'club mix) / Feel free.
above & below singer CARON WHEELER (solo artist she co-wrote below 45)

Apr 89. (cd/c/lp) *(DIX/CDIX/DIXCD 82)* <91267> **CLUB CLASSICS – VOLUME ONE** <US-title 'KEEP ON MOVIN'>   `1`   `14`
– Keep on movin' (featuring CARON WHEELER) / Fairplay (featuring ROSE WINDROSS) / Holdin' on / Feeling free (live rap) / African dance / Dance / Feel free (featuring DO'REEN) / Happiness (dub) / Back to life (acapella) (featuring CARON WHEELER) / Jazzie's groove. *(cd+=)* – Back to life (however do you want me).

Jun 89. (7"/c-s) *(TEN/+C 265)* <99171> **BACK TO LIFE (HOWEVER DO YOU WANT ME). / BACK TO LIFE (version)**   `1`   `4` Sep89
(12"/c-s) *(TEN X/W 265)* <965370> – ('A'club) / ('A'-Jam on the groove) / ('A'back to the beats).
(3"cd-s) *(TENCD 265)* – ('A'side) / ('A'club) / ('A'-Jam on the groove).

Nov 89. (7"/c-s) *(TEN/+C 284)* <98981> **GET A LIFE. / JAZZIE'S GROOVE (new version)**   `3`   `54` Apr90
('A'club-12"+=) *(TENX 284)* – ('A'bonus beats)/ ('A'piano version).
(ext-12"/12"w/poster) *(TEN R/P 284)* – Back to life (one world mix).
(cd-s+=) *(TENCD 284)* – ('A'club) / Keep on movin' (Teddy Riley remix).
above singer MARCIE LEWIS who repl. WHEELER (became solo star)

Apr 90. (7"/c-s/7"box) *(TEN/+C/B 300)* <98955> **A DREAM'S A DREAM. / ('A'instrumental)**   `6`   `85` Jun90
(12"/cd-s) *(TEN X/CD 300)* – ('A'-A night at the opera mix) / ('A'club dub) / Courtney blows (with COURTNEY PINE).
above singer VICTORIA WILSON-JAMES

May 90. (cd/c/lp) *(DIXCD/CDIX/DIX 90)* <91367> **VOL II – A NEW DECADE – 1990**   `1`   `21`
– Get a life / Love comes through to you / People / Missing you / Courtney blows / 1990 (a new decade) / A dream's a dream / Time / In the heat of the night / Our time has come now.

—— ('PEOPLE' vox – MARCIE)

Oct 90. (7"/c-s) *(TEN/+C 345)* **MISSING YOU. / ('A'instrumental)**   `22`   `☐`
(12"+=) *(TENX 345)* – ('A'-thumpin' bass mix) / ('A'-humanity mix) / People (club).
(12") *(TENR 345)* – ('A'remake) / ('A'-blow Mr. hornsman blow mix) / ('A'-thumpin' bass mix).
(cd-s) *(TENCD 345)* – (the 4 tracks except 7"-b-side).
above singer KYM MAZELLE

Apr 92. (7"/c-s) *(TEN/+C 350)* **JOY. / ('A'radio mix)**   `4`   `☐`
(12"+=) *(TENX 350)* – ('A'instrumental) / ('A'club mix).
(12"++=/cd-s++=) *(TEN R/CD 350)* – ('A'-Brand New Heavies remix).
above singer RICHIE STEPHENS

Apr 92. (cd/c/lp) *(BMCDIXD/BMCDIX/10DIX 100)* <91771> **JUST RIGHT – VOLUME III**   `3`   `88` May92
– Joy / Take me higher / Storm / Direction / Just right / Move me no mountain / Intelligence / Future / Mood / Everywhere.
below featured band JELLYFISH

Jun 92. (7"/c-s) *(TEN/+C 400)* **MOVE ME NO MOUNTAIN. / ('A'mix)**   `31`   `☐`
(12"/cd-s) *(TEN X/CD 400)* – ('A'side) / ('A'club) / ('A'-Hackney E9 mix) / ('A'dub mix) / ('A'removed club mix) / ('A'dum dum dub).
above singer KOFI

Sep 92. (7"/c-s) *(TEN/+C 410)* **JUST RIGHT. / ('A'jinx mix)** `38` ☐
(club;12"+=/cd-s+=) *(TEN X/GD 410)* – ('A'-funky dred mix) / ('A'-Intelligence (9 a.m. mix) / Intelligence (Jazzie II guru mix).
above singer & co-composer **RICK CLARKE**

<table>
<tr><td></td><td></td><td>Virgin</td><td>Virgin</td></tr>
</table>

Oct 93. (7"/c-s) *(VS/+C 1480)* **WISH. / BACK TO LIFE (Masters At Work remix)** `24` ☐
(10"+=/cd-s+=) *(VST/VSCDG/VSCDT 1480)* – (2 original mixes).
above singer **MELISSA BELL**

Nov 93. (cd/c)(d-lp) *(CD/TC+/V 2724)* **VOLUME IV – THE CLASSIC SINGLES 88-93** (compilation) `10` ☐
– Back to life (however do you want me) / Keep on movin' / Get a life / A dream's a dream / Missing you / Just right / Move me no mountain / People / Fairplay / Jazzie's groove / Wish / Joy / Keep on movin' (Mafia & Fluxy mix) / Fairplay (Ethnic Boys mix) / Back to life (bonus beats). *(cd+=)* – Keep on movin' (Q & Dobie mix)/ Back to life (Masters at work & R&B mixes).

—— now with **PENNY FORD** – vocals (ex-SNAP)

Jul 95. (12"/c-s) *(VST/VSCDG 1527)* **LOVE ENUFF / ('A'-New York mix) / ('A'-4 wheel drive mix) / ('A'-Todd Terry house mix) / ('A'-Todd Terry horns mix)** `12` ─
(cd-s) *(VSCDT 1527)* – ('A'mixes near as above).

Jul 95. (cd/lp) *(CD/TC+/V 2739)* **VOLUME V – BELIEVE** `13` ☐
– Love enuff / Ride on / How long / Feeling / Universal / Being a man / Zion / Don't you dream / Gane dunn / Sundays / Pride / I care (Soul II Soul) / B groove / Believe.

Oct 95. (c-s) *(VSC 1560)* **I CARE (SOUL II SOUL) / ('A'-12"master)** `17` ☐
(12") *(VST 1560)* – ('A'side) / ('A'-Maserati mix) / ('A'-Fred freaky mix) / ('A'-Nu Soul mix) / ('A'-Secret weapon mix).
(cd-s+=) *(VSCDT 1560)* – (includes c-s b-side).

Oct 96. (c-s) *(VSC 1612)* **KEEP ON MOVIN'** (remix) / `31` ☐
(cd-s+=) *(VSCDT 1612)* –

<table>
<tr><td></td><td></td><td>4th & Broad</td><td>Island</td></tr>
</table>

Aug 97. (c-s) *(BRCA 357)* **REPRESENT /** `39` ☐
(12"/cd-s) *(12BRW/BRCD 357)* –

<table>
<tr><td></td><td></td><td>Island</td><td>Island</td></tr>
</table>

Sep 97. (cd/c/lp) *(CID/ICT/ILPS 8060)* **SOUL II SOUL VOL.6 – TIME TO CHANGE** ☐
– Camdino soul / Pleasure dome / Thank you / Dare to differ / Get away / Love ain't around / Represent / Time for change / I feel love / The limit is the sky.

Oct 97. (c-s) *(CIS 669)* **PLEASURE DOME / ('A'-Booker T mix)** `51` ☐
(12"+=/cd-s+=) *(12IS/CID 669)* – ('A'-Tuff Jam's UVF mix) / ('A'-Dream Team dub).

SOUNDGARDEN

Formed: Seattle, Washington, USA ... 1984 by lead singer CHRIS CORNELL, guitarist KIM THAYIL and bassist HIRO YAMAMOTO. With the addition of drummer MATT CAMERON in '86, the band became one of the first to record for the fledgling 'Sub Pop' label, releasing the 'HUNTED DOWN' single in summer '87. Two EP's, 'SCREAMING LIFE', and 'FOPP' followed, although the group signed to 'S.S.T.' for their debut album, 'ULTRAMEGA OK' (1988). Despite its lack of focus, the record laid the foundations for what was to follow; a swamp-rich miasma of snail-paced, bass-crunch uber-riffing, wailing vocals and punk attitude shot through with bad-trip psychedelia (i.e. not something to listen to last thing at night). And with the Grammy-nominated 'LOUDER THAN LOVE' (1989), the group's major label debut for 'A&M', SOUNDGARDEN harnessed their devilish wares onto infectious melodies and fuck-off choruses; one listen to the likes of 'HANDS ALL OVER', 'LOUD LOVE' and the tongue-in-cheek brilliance of 'BIG DUMB SEX' was enough to convince you that these hairy post-metallers were destined for big, grunge-type things. Success wasn't immediate however, the album failing to make a dent beyond the Sub-Pop in-crowd and a few adventurous metal fans. YAMAMOTO departed soon after the record's release, his replacement being ex-NIRVANA guitarist JASON EVERMAN, who was succeeded in turn by BEN SHEPHERD. CORNELL and CAMERON subsequently got together with future PEARL JAM members, EDDIE VEDDER, STONE GOSSARD and JEFF AMENT to form TEMPLE OF THE DOG, releasing an eponymous album in early '91 to critical acclaim. SOUNDGARDEN, meanwhile, finally got their break later that year when 'BADMOTORFINGER' broke the US/UK Top 40. An even more accessible proposition, the record combined a tighter, more driven sound with pop/grunge hooks and their trademark cerebral lyrics to create such MTV favourites as 'JESUS CHRIST POSE' and 'OUTSHINED'. 'RUSTY CAGE' was another juggernaut riffathon, while 'SEARCHING WITH MY GOOD EYE CLOSED' meted out some of the most brutal psychedelia this side of MONSTER MAGNET. A high profile support slot on GUNS N' ROSES' 'Lose Your Illusion' tour afforded the band valuable exposure in the States, their crossover appeal endearing them to the metal hordes on both sides of the Atlantic. Previewed by the Top 20 'SPOONMAN' single, SOUNDGARDEN's masterful fourth set, 'SUPERUNKNOWN' (1994), finally gave the group long overdue success, scaling the US charts and going Top 5 in Britain. Constructed around a head-spinning foundation of acid-drenched retro-rock and JIM MORRISON-esque doom, this epic album spawned the Grammy-winnning 'BLACK HOLE SUN' while 'FELL ON BLACK DAYS' stands as one of their most realised pieces of warped psychedelia to date. Following a world tour with the likes of The SMASHING PUMPKINS, the group began work on 'DOWN ON THE UPSIDE' (1996). Another marathon set boasting sixteen tracks, the record inevitably failed to garner the plaudits of its predecessor; the claustrophobia of old had given way to a marginally more strightforward melodic grunge sound, evidenced to best effect on the likes of 'BURDEN IN MY HAND'. Subversiveness was still the key word; 'TY COBB's

mutant country-punk and gonzoid expletive-filled attitude was reminiscent of MINISTRY's seminal 'Jesus Built My Hotrod'. The album ultimately proved to be their swan song, SOUNDGARDEN subsequently pushing up the daisies as of April '97. CORNELL (now in his mid-30's!) returned as a solo artist a few years later, although a largely timid soft-rock debut, 'EUPHORIA MORNING' (1999) – featuring the JEFF BUCKLEY tribute, 'WAVE GOODBYE' – saw the man lose his "metal" credentials. • **Songwriters:** Most by CORNELL and group permutations. Covered SWALLOW MY PRIDE (Ramones) / FOPP (Ohio Players) / INTO THE VOID tune only (Black Sabbath) / BIG BOTTOM (Spinal Tap) / EARACHE MY EYE (Cheech & Chong) / I CAN'T GIVE YOU ANYTHING (Ramones) / HOMOCIDAL SUICIDE (Budgie) / I DON'T CARE ABOUT YOU (Fear) / CAN YOU SEE ME (Jimi Hendrix) / COME TOGETHER (Beatles).

Album rating: ULTRAMEGA OK (*7) / LOUDER THAN LOVE (*8) / BADMOTORFINGER (*9) / SUPERUNKNOWN (*9) / DOWN ON THE UPSIDE (*6) / A-SIDES compilation (*8) / Chris Cornell: EUPHORIA MORNING (*4) / Temple Of The Dog: TEMPLE OF THE DOG (*7)

CHRIS CORNELL (b.20 Jul'64) – vocals, guitar / **KIM THAYIL** (b. 4 Sep'60) – lead guitar / **HIRO YAMAMOTO** (b.13 Apr'61) – bass / **MATT CAMERON** (b.28 Nov'62, San Diego, Calif.) – drums, percussion

<table>
<tr><td></td><td></td><td>not iss.</td><td>Sub Pop</td></tr>
</table>

Jun 87. (7"blue) *<SP 12a>* **NOTHING TO SAY. / HUNTED DOWN** ─ ☐

Oct 87. (12"ep,orange-12"ep) *<SP 12>* **SCREAMING LIFE** ─ ☐
– Hunted down / Entering / Tears to forget / Nothing to say / Little Joe / Hand of God.

Aug 88. (12"ep) *<SP 17>* **FOPP** ─ ☐
– Fopp / Fopp (dub) / Kingdom of come / Swallow my pride.

<table>
<tr><td></td><td></td><td>S.S.T.</td><td>S.S.T.</td></tr>
</table>

Nov 88. (m-lp/c/cd) *<(SST 201/+C/CD)>* **ULTRAMEGA OK** ─ ☐
– Flower / All your lies / 665 / Beyond the wheel / 667 / Mood for trouble / Circle of power / He didn't / Smokestack lightning / Nazi driver / Head injury / Incessant mace / One minute of silence. *(re-iss. Oct95;*

May 89. (12"ep/c-ep/cd-ep) *<(SST 231/+C/CD)>* **FLOWER. / HEAD INJURY / TOY BOX** ─ ☐

<table>
<tr><td></td><td></td><td>A&M</td><td>A&M</td></tr>
</table>

Sep 89. (lp/c/cd) *<(AMA/AMC/CDA 5252)>* **LOUDER THAN LOVE** ─ ☐
– Ugly truth / Hands all over / Gun / Power trip / Get on the snake / Full on Kevin's mom / Loud love / I awake / No wrong no right / Uncovered / Big dumb sex / Full on (reprise).

Apr 90. (10"ep/cd-ep) *(AM X/CD 560)* **HANDS ALL OVER** ─ ☐
– Hands all over / Heretic / Come together / Big dumb sex.

Jul 90. (7"ep/12"ep) *(AM/+Y 574)* **THE LOUD LOVE E.P.** ─ ☐
– Loud love / Fresh deadly roses / Big dumb sex (dub) / Get on the snake.

—— **JASON EVERMAN** (b.16 Aug'67) – bass (ex-NIRVANA) repl. HIRO who later formed TRULY after working in a bike shop.

Oct 90. (7",7"purple/green) *<SP 83>* **ROOM A THOUSAND YEARS WIDE. / H.I.V. BABY** ─ ☐
(above issued on 'Sub Pop')

—— **BEN SHEPHERD** (b. HUNTER SHEPHERD, 20 Sep'68, Okinawa, Japan) – bass repl. JASON

Oct 91. (cd/c/lp) *(395374-2/-4/-1) <5374>* **BADMOTORFINGER** `39` `39`
– Rusty cage / Outshined / Slaves & bulldozers / Jesus Christ pose / Face pollution / Somewhere / Searching with my good eye closed / Room a thousand years wide / Mind riot / Drawing flies / Holy water / New damage.

Mar 92. (7") *(AM 862)* **JESUS CHRIST POSE. / STRAY CAT BLUES** `30` ─
(cd-s+=) *(AMCD 862)* – Into the void (stealth).

Jun 92. (7"pic-d) *(AM 874)* **RUSTY CAGE. / TOUCH ME** `41` ─
(12"+=/cd-s+=) *(AM Y/CD 874)* – Show me.
(cd-s+=) *(AMCDX 874)* – Big bottom / Earache my eye.

Nov 92. (7") *(AM 0102)* **OUTSHINED. / I CAN'T GIVE YOU ANYTHING** `50` ─
(12"+=/cd-s+=) *(AM 0102 T/CD)* – Homocidal suicide.
(cd-s+=) *(AM 0102CDX)* – I don't care about you / Can't you see me.

Feb 94. (7"pic-d/c-s) *(580 538-7/-4)* **SPOONMAN. / FRESH TENDRILS** `20` ─
(12"clear+=/cd-s+=) *(580 539-1/-2)* – Cold bitch / Exit Stonehenge.

Mar 94. (cd/c/orange-d-lp) *(540215-2/-4/-1) <0198>* **SUPERUNKNOWN** `4` `1`
– Let me drown / My wave / Fell on black days / Mailman / Superunknown / Head down / Black hole Sun / Spoonman / Limo wreck / The day I tried to live / Kickstand / Fresh tendrils / 4th of July / Half / Like suicide / She likes surprises.

Apr 94. (7"pic-d/c-s) *(580594-7/-4)* **LIKE SUICIDE (acoustic)** `42` ─
(12"etched+=/cd-s+=) *(580595-1/-2)* – Kickstand (live).

Aug 94. (7"pic-d/c-s) *(580736-7/-4)* **BLACK HOLE SUN. / BEYOND THE WHEEL (live) / FELL ON BLACK DAYS (live)** `12` ─
(pic-cd-s+=) *(580753-2)* – Birth ritual (demo).
(cd-s) *(580737-2)* – ('A'side) / My wave (live) / Jesus Christ pose (live) / Spoonman (remix).

Jan 95. (7"pic-d/c-s) *(580947-7/-4)* **FELL ON BLACK DAYS. / KYLE PETTY, SON OF RICHARD / MOTORCYCLE LOOP** `24` ─
(cd-s) *(580947-2)* – ('A'side) / Kyle Petty, son of Richard / Fell on black days (video version).
(cd-s) *(580947-5)* – ('A'side) / Girl u want / Fell on black days (early demo).

May 96. (7"red/cd-s) *(581620-7/-4)* **PRETTY NOOSE. / JERRY GARCIA'S FINGER** `14` ─
(cd-s) *(581620-2)* – ('A'side) / Applebite / An unkind / (interview with Eleven's Alain and Natasha).

May 96. (cd/c/d-lp) *(540526-2/-4/-1) <0526>* **DOWN ON THE UPSIDE** `7` `2`
– Pretty noose / Rhinosaur / Zero chance / Dusty / Ty Cobb / Blow up the outside world / Burden in my hand / Never named / Applebite / Never the machine forever / Tighter & tighter / No attention / Switch opens / Overfloater / An unkind / Boot camp.

Sep 96. (7"/cd-s) *(581854-7/-2)* **BURDEN IN MY HAND. / KARAOKE** `33` ─
(cd-s) *(581855-2)* – ('A'side) / Bleed together / She's a politician / (Chris Cornell interview).

Dec 96. (7") *(581986-7)* **BLOW UP THE OUTSIDE WORLD. / DUSTY**   `38`   `-`
(cd-s+=) *(581987-2)* – Gun.
(cd-s) *(581986-2)* – ('A'side) / Get on the snake / Slice of spacejam.

—— split on the 9th of April 1997

– compilations, etc –

Oct 93. (cd) *A&M; (CDA 24118)* **LOUDER THAN LOUD /**
BADMOTORFINGER
Oct 93. (c/cd) *Sub Pop; (SP/+CD 12)* **SCREAMING LIFE / FOPP**
Nov 97. (cd) *A&M; (540833-2) <0833>* **A-SIDES**   `63`
– Nothing to say / Flower / Loud love / Hands all over / Get on the snake / Jesus
Christ pose / Outshined / Rusty cage / Spoonman / The day I tried to live / Black hole
sun / Fell on black days / Pretty noose / Burden in my hand / Blow up the outside
world / Ty Cobb / Bleed together.

CHRIS CORNELL

Sep 99. (cd/c) *<(490412-2/-4)>* **EUPHORIA MORNING**   `31`   `18`
– Can't change me / Flutter girl / Preaching the end of the world / Follow my
way / When I'm down / Mission / Wave goodbye / Moonchild / Sweet euphoria /
Disappearing one / Pillow of your bones / Steel rain.
Oct 99. (7") *(497173-7)* **CAN'T CHANGE ME. / FLUTTER GIRL**   `62`
(cd-s+=) *(497173-2)* – Nowhere but you.
(cd-s) *(497174-2)* – ('A'side) / When I'm down / ('A'-video).

TEMPLE OF THE DOG

splinter-group feat. **CORNELL + CAMERON** plus **STONE GOSSARD / JEFF AMENT** (both
ex-MOTHER LOVE BONE, future PEARL JAM)

	A&M	A&M

Jun 92. (cd/c/lp) *(395 350-2/-4/-1) <5350>* **TEMPLE OF THE DOG**   `5`
– Say hello to Heaven / Reach down / Hunger strike / Pushing forward back / Call
me a dog / Times of trouble / Wooden Jesus / Your saviour / 4-walled world / All
night thing.
Oct 92. (7"pic-d/c-s) *(AM 0091/+C)* **HUNGER STRIKE. / ALL NIGHT**
THING   `51`
(12"+=/cd-s+=) *(AM 0091 T/CD)* – Your saviour.

HATER

MATT + BEN

	Sub Pop	Sub Pop

Aug 93. (7") *<(SP 233)>* **CIRCLES. / GENOCIDE**

	A&M	A&M

Sep 93. (cd/c) *(540 137-2/-4) <0137>* **HATER**
– Mona bone jakon / Who do I kill? / Tot finder / Lion and lamb / Roadside / Down
undershoe / Circles / Putrid / Blistered / Sad McBain. *(re-iss. cd May95; same)*

SOUP DRAGONS   (dig out; Great Alt & Indie . . .)

SOUTHERN DEATH CULT (see under ⇒ CULT)

SPACE

Formed: Liverpool, England . . . 1993 by TOMMY SCOTT, JAMIE
MURPHY, FRANNY GRIFFITHS and ANDY PARLE, all seasoned
campaigners of the local music scene (TOMMY and FRANNY played in
The AUSTRALIANS, whose track, 'THE GIRL WHO LOVED HER MAN
ENOUGH TO KILL HIM' appeared on the 'Hit The North' various artists
compilation). After a one-off single on the independent 'Home', the band were
snapped up by 'Gut', a label which brought us the bare-arsed "pop thrills" of
RIGHT SAID FRED. Equally camp in a more masculine kind of Scouse way,
SPACE were light years removed from the shower of Brit-pop retro merchants
doing the rounds in the mid-90's; the 'NEIGHBOURHOOD' single sounded
like ENNIO MORRICONE waltzing round the last chance saloon to an acid-
fried Mariachi soundtrack, SCOTT's robotic vocal affectations carrying lyrics
cut from the same cloth as PETE SHELLEY's (Buzzcocks) creations. For all
his little-boy-lost charm, SCOTT sounded pretty damn scary throughout much
of the 'SPIDERS' (1996) album, his tales of losers, freaks and paranoid killers
balancing black humour with unhinged Liverpudlian menace. Preceded by
the voodoo-xylophone pop genius of 'FEMALE OF THE SPECIES' (a Top
20 hit and arguably one of the singles of the year) and the brassy, bouncy
life affirming 'ME & YOU VERSUS THE WORLD' (about as commercial
as SPACE get and a nod to native forebears, The Fab Four), the debut was
released in late '96 to encouraging reviews and a subsequent Top 5 chart
placing. Running the gamut of the band's many influences, from SINATRA
and KRAFTWERK to 'South Pacific' and 'Midnight Cowboy', the album
even catered for MURPHY's avowed love of techno with an acid freakout,
'GROWLER', bolted on as the closing track. Armed with a further two Top 20
hits in a re-released 'NEIGHBOURHOOD' and 'DARK CLOUDS', SPACE
were ready to explore the final frontier where no (sensible) band had gone
before i.e. the festival circuit. 1997 proved to be an even more hectic year,
one that nearly broke them; JAMIE (at only 21, the stress of it all had played
havoc with his peace of mind) pulled out on the eve of an American tour
in February, TOMMY mysteriously lost his voice for a couple of months as
well as being stalked and the general pressures of slogging round the world
turned them into emotional wrecks. No doubt the experiences which formed

the basis for follow-up Top 3 album, 'TIN PLANET' (1998), the cadets
safely back on earth and ready for a new mission that resulted in two Top 10
hits, 'AVENGING ANGEL' and the tongue-in-cheek duet with CATATONIA's
CERYS, 'THE BALLAD OF TOM JONES'. • **Songwriters:** Perm any
SCOTT / GRIFFITHS / MURPHY and group except WE GOTTA GET OUT
OF THIS PLACE (Animals).
Album rating: SPIDERS (*7) / TIN PLANET (*7)

TOMMY SCOTT – vocals, guitar / **JAMIE MURPHY** – guitar, vocals / **FRANNY GRIFFITHS**
– bass / **ANDY PARLE** – drums

	Home	not iss.

Oct 95. (c-s) *(CAHOME 1)* **MONEY / KILL ME**   `-`
(cd-s+=) *(CDHOME 1)* – ('A'club) / ('B'club).
(12") *(12HOME 1)* – ('A'-Lost in space remix) / ('A'-Still lost in space & safe bass
mix) / ('A'-Space club mix) / ('A'-instrumental).

	Gut	Uptown – Universal

Mar 96. (c-s) *(CAGUT 1)* **NEIGHBOURHOOD / REJECTS**   `56`   `-`
(cd-s+=) *(CDGUT 1)* – Turn me on to spiders.
(12") *(12GUT 1)* – ('A'-Live it! club) / ('A'-Live it! instrumental club) / ('A'-Pissed
up stomp).
Jun 96. (c-s) *(CAGUT 2)* **FEMALE OF THE SPECIES / LOONEY**
TUNE   `14`   `-`
(12"+=/cd-s+=) *(12/CD GUT 2)* – ('A'radio) / Give me something.
Aug 96. (c-s) *(CAGUT 4)* **ME & YOU VERSUS THE WORLD /**
SPIDERS   `9`   `-`
(cd-s+=) *(CDGUT 4)* – Life of a miser / Blow your cover.
(cd-s) *(CXGUT 4)* – ('A'mixes).
Sep 96. (cd/c/lp) *(GUT CD/MC/LP 1) <53028>* **SPIDERS**   `5`   `Jan97`
– Neighbourhood / Mister Psycho / Female of the species / Money / Me & you vs the
world / Lovechild of the queen / No-one understands / Voodoo roller / Drop dead /
Dark clouds / Major pager / Kill me / Charlie M. / Growler.

—— added **DAVE PALMER** – bass

Oct 96. (c-s) *(CAGUT 5) <1152>* **NEIGHBOURHOOD / ONLY HALF**
AN ANGEL   `11`
(cd-s+=) *(CDGUT 5)* – Crisis / Shut your mouth.
(cd-s) *(CXGUT 5)* – ('A'side) / Welcome to the neighbourhood / Nighthood /
Neighbourhood (pissed up stomp mix).
Feb 97. (c-s) *(CAGUT 6)* **DARK CLOUDS / HAD ENOUGH**   `14`   `-`
(cd-s+=) *(CDGUT 6)* – Children of the night / Influenza.
(cd-s) *(CXGUT 6)* – ('A'side) / Darker clouds / Storm clouds.

	Gut	Imprint

Dec 97. (7"blue) *(7GUT 16)* **AVENGING ANGELS. / I AM UNLIKE**
A LIFEFORM YOU'VE NEVER MET   `6`   `-`
(c-s) *(CAGUT 16)* – ('A'side) / Bastard me, bastard you.
(cd-s++=) *(CDGUT 16)* – Theme from "Baretta Vendetta".
(cd-s) *(CXGUT 16)* – ('A'side) / ('A'mixes:- John 'OO' Fleming Theramin mix /
Ultra Vegas mix / The Jumping Soundboy mix / Franny's 'Peaceful Devil' mix /
Brainbasher's 'Kick Ass Angel' mix / Jonnie Newman's 'Altered State' mix).

—— **LEON CAFFREY** – drums (ex-PROPER) repl. PARLE

Feb 98. (7"red; with CERYS of CATATONIA) *(7GUT 18)* **THE**
BALLAD OF TOM JONES. / NOW SHE'S GONE   `4`   `-`
(c-s+=) *(CAGUT 18)* – Happy endings.
(cd-s++=) *(CDGUT 18)* – Stress transmissions.
(cd-s) *(CXGUT 18)* – ('A'mixes:- Cocktail Lounge mix / Dirty Beatniks mix / Sound
5 mix / Sure Is Pure dub mix / SX Dub Scratching Cuckoo mix / Tom Jones Axe
To Your Head mix).
Mar 98. (cd/c/lp) *(GUT CD/MC/LP 5) <110683>* **TIN PLANET**   `3`   `Jul98`
– Begin again / Avenging angels / The ballad of Tom Jones / 1 o'clock / Be there /
The man / A liddle biddy help from Elvis / The unluckiest man in the world / Piggies /
Bad day's / There's no you / Disco dolly / Fran in Japan.
Jun 98. (c-s/cd-s) *(CA/CD GUT 19)* **BEGIN AGAIN / YOU**
ROMANTIC FOOL / NUMB THE DOUBT / INFLUENZA
(flu mix)   `21`
(cd-s) *(CXGUT 19)* – ('A'side) / The ballad of Tom Jones (live) / Female of the
species (live) / Avenging angels (live).
Nov 98. (c-s) *(CAGUT 22)* **BAD DAYS EP**   `20`
– Bad days / We gotta get out of this place / The unluckiest man in the world.
(cd-s+=) *(CDGUT 22)* – Cold in the city.
(cd-s+=) *(CXGUT 22)* – Yeah right!

SPACEHOG   (dig out; 4th edition or Great Alt & Indie . . .)

SPACEMEN 3

Formed: Rugby, Warwickshire, England . . . 1983 by SONIC BOOM (PETE
KEMBER) and JASON PIERCE. They enlisted PETE BAINES and ROSCO
as a rhythm section and through their manager, Gerald Palmer, they signed to
indie label, 'Glass'. In 1986, they debuted with 'SOUND OF CONFUSION',
a primal embryo for "shoegazers" to come. Their follow-up, 'THE PERFECT
PRESCRIPTION', set the world alight (well! the indie world anyway), with
some clever pulsating, psychedelic garage-noise intertwined with melancholy
bursts of beauty and experimentation, i.e 'WALKIN WITH JESUS' (again!),
'TRANSPARENT RADIATION' and 'TAKE ME TO THE OTHER SIDE'. In
1989, they were back again with a third set, 'PLAYING WITH FIRE', featuring
the 10-minute squall of 'SUICIDE', and 'REVOLUTION' (later covered by
MUDHONEY). SONIC BOOM's heroin addiction was taking its toll during
the early 90's and with JASON having founded SPIRITUALIZED, the group
were heading for their own proverbial rocketship to oblivion. Their final
outing, 'RECURRING' (1991), recorded amid escalating tension, was a slight
disappointment. By this time, SONIC had gone solo, subsequently going under
the guise of SPECTRUM. His debut was followed by two albums of patchy,

yet somewhat appealing albums, 'SOUL KISS (GLIDE DIVINE)' (1992) and 'HIGH LOWS AND HEAVENLY BLOWS' (1994). The ever prolific KEMBER went on play with mid 90's outfit, JESSAMINE, who to date have released a string of albums including 1997's 'ANOTHER FICTIONALIZED HISTORY'. Around the same, KEMBER/SONIC simultaneously resurfaced with a SPECTRUM set, 'FOREVER ALIEN', released on the '3rd Stone' imprint. • **Songwriters:** KEMBER or PIERCE material until the 90's when KEMBER penned all. Covered; IT'S ALRIGHT (Bo Diddley) / CHE + ROCK'N'ROLL IS KILLING MY LIFE (Suicide) / WHEN TOMORROW HITS (Mudhoney) / COME TOGETHER + STARSHIP (MC5) / MARY-ANNE (. . .Campbell) / ROLLER COASTER (13th Floor Elevators).

Album rating: SOUND OF CONFUSION (*7) / THE PERFECT PRESCRIPTION (*8) / PLAYING WITH FIRE (*8) / RECURRING (*8) / PERFORMANCE posthumous (*7) / DREAM WEAPON – ECSTASY IN SLOW MOTION posthumous: (*7) / TAKING DRUGS TO MAKE MUSIC TO TAKE DRUGS TO posthumous (*5) / SPACEMEN ARE GO! posthumous (*3) / FOR ALL THE FUCKED UP CHILDREN IN THE WORLD posthumous (*4) / TRANSLUCENT FLASHBACKS collection (*6) / Sonic Boom: SPECTRUM (*5) / Spectrum: SOUL KISS (GLIDE DIVINE) (*6) / HIGH LOWS AND HEAVENLY BLOWS (*6) / FOREVER ALIEN (*6)

SONIC BOOM (b. PETE KEMBER, 19 Nov'65) – vocals / **JASON PIERCE** (b.19 Nov'65) – guitar / **STEWART (ROSCO) ROSSWELL** – keyboards / **PETE (BASSMAN) BAINES** – bass

		Glass	not iss.
Jun 86.	(lp) (GLA 018) **SOUND OF CONFUSION**		–
	– Losing touch with my mind / Hey man / Roller coaster / Mary Anne / Little doll / 2:35 / O.D. catastrophe. (re-iss.Sep89 on 'Fire' lp/c/cd; REFIRE CD/MC/LP 5) <US cd-iss. 1994 on 'Taan~g!'; 93>		
Dec 86.	(12"m) (GLAEP 105) **WALKIN' WITH JESUS (SOUND OF CONFUSION). / ROLLERCOASTER / FEEL SO GOOD**		–
Jul 87.	(12"m) (GLAEP 108) **TRANSPARENT RADIATION / ECSTASY SYMPHONY / TRANSPARENT RADIATION (FLASHBACK). / THINGS'LL NEVER BE THE SAME / STARSHIP**		–
Aug 87.	(lp/c) (GLA LP/MC 026) **THE PERFECT PRESCRIPTION**		–
	– Take me to the other side / Walking with Jesus / Ode to street hassle / Ecstasy – Symphony / Feel so good / Things'll never be the same / Come down easy / Call the doctor / Soul 1 / That's just fine. (re-iss.Dec89 on 'Fire' lp/c/cd; REFIRE LP/MC/CD 6) <US cd-iss. 1994 on 'Taang!'; 94>		
Mar 88.	(12") (GLASS 12-054) **TAKE ME TO THE OTHER SIDE. / SOUL 1 / THAT'S JUST FINE**		–
Jul 88.	(lp/cd) (GLA LP/CD 030) **PERFORMANCE** (live 1988 Holland)		–
	– Mary-Anne / Come together / Things'll never be the same / Take me to the other side / Roller coaster / Starship / Walkin' with Jesus. (re-iss.May91 on 'Fire' cd/c/lp; REFIRE CD/MC/LP 11)		

      WILLIE B. CARRUTHERS – bass / **JON MATLOCK** – drums repl. ROSCO + BAINES who formed The DARKSIDE

		Fire	not iss.
Nov 88.	(7") (BLAZE 29S) **REVOLUTION. / CHE**		–
	(12"+=/cd-s+=) (BLAZE 29 T/CD) – May the circle be unbroken.		
Feb 89.	(lp/c/cd) (FIRE LP/MC/CD 16) **PLAYING WITH FIRE**		–
	– Honey / Come down softly to my soul / How does it feel? / I believe it / Revolution / Let me down gently / So hot (wash away all my tears) / Suicide / Lord can you hear me. (free-12"ep/cd-ep+=) – Starship / Revolution / Suicide (live) / Repeater / Live intro theme (xtacy). <US cd-iss. 1994 on 'Taang~'; 97>		
Jul 89.	(7") (BLAZE 36S) **HYPNOTIZED. / JUST TO SEE YOU SMILE HONEY (part 2)**		–
	(12"+=/3"cd-s+=) (BLAZE 36 T/CD) – The world is dying. (free 7"flexi w.a) (CHEREE 5) – EXTRACTS FROM A CONTEMPORARY SITAR EVENING (with other artists).		
Jan 91.	(7") (BLAZE 41) **BIG CITY. / DRIVE**		–
	(12"+=/cd-s+=) (BLAZE 41 T/CD) – Big City (everybody I know can be found here). (12"w-drawn) (BLAZE 41TR) – ('A'remix) / I love you (remix).		
Feb 91.	(cd/lp)(s-lp) (FIRE CD/LP 23)(FIRELP 23S) **RECURRING**	46	–
	– Big city (everybody I know can be found here) / Just to see you smile (orchestral) / I love you / Set me free / I've got the key / Set me free (reprise) / Feel so bad (reprise) / Hypnotized / Sometimes / Feelin' just fine (head full of shit) / Billy Whizz – blue 1. (cd+=) – When tomorrow hits / Why couldn't I see / Just to see you smile (instrumental) / Feel so sad (demo) / Drive.		

      Had already folded June '90.

– compilations, etc. –

Dec 90.	(cd/d-lp) Fierce; (FRIGHT 042/+CD) **DREAM WEAPON / ECSTASY IN SLOW MOTION**		–
	(re-iss. Nov95 on 'Space Age' cd/d-lp; ORBIT 001 CD/LP)		
Jun 94.	(cd/lp) Taang!; <TAANG 96 CD/LP> **THE SINGLES**		–
Nov 94.	(cd) Bomp; (<BCD 4047>) **TAKING DRUGS TO MAKE MUSIC TO TAKE DRUGS TO** (demos of 1986)		–
May 95.	(cd/lp) Sympathy For The Record Industry; (<SFTRI 1368 CD/LP>) **FOR ALL FUCKED UP CHILDREN OF THE WORLD WE GIVE YOU . . .** (debut recording session)		–
May 95.	(cd) Bomp; (<BCD 4044>) **SPACEMEN ARE GO!**		–
Jun 95.	(cd/d-lp) Fire; (FLIP CD/DLP 003) **TRANSLUCENT FLASHBACKS**		–
Sep 95.	(cd) Taang~; <TAANG 95CD> **LIVE AT THE MILKWEG 6/2/88** (live)		–
	– Mary Ann / Come together / Things'll never be / Take me to the other side / Rollercoaster / Walking with Jesus / Repeater / Starship / Revolution / Suicide.		
Oct 95.	(cd) Fierce; (FRIGHT 063) **THE CHOICE IS REVOLUTIONORHERION**		–
Nov 95.	(cd/d-lp) Space Age; (ORBIT 002 CD/LP) **LIVE IN EUROPE 1989** (live)		–
Mar 97.	(d-cd) Nectar; (NTMCDD 534) **1 + 1 = 3**		–

SONIC BOOM

(**PETE KEMBER** solo with **WILLIE B. CARRUTHERS** and also **PHIL PARFITT + JO WIGGS** of PERFECT DISASTER)

		Silvertone	not iss.
Oct 89.	(12"ep/cd-ep) (ORE/+CD 11) **ANGEL. / ANGEL (version) / HELP ME PLEASE**		–
Feb 90.	(cd/c/lp) (ORE CD/MC/LP 506) **SPECTRUM**	65	–
	– Pretty baby / If I should die / Lonely avenue / Help me please / Angel / Rock'n'roll is killing my life / You're the one. (free 10" w-lp) (SONIC 1) – DRONE DREAM EP: OCTAVES. / TREMELOS <US-iss.Oct97 as 'WHEN CAME BEFORE AFTER' on 'Sympathy For The Record Industry'; SFTRI 493>		
Apr 91.	(7"; gig freebie) (SONIC 2) **(I LOVE YOU) TO THE MOON AND BACK. / CAPO WALTZ** (live)		–

      SONIC BOOM has now featured in E.A.R. (EXPERIMENTAL AUDIO RESEARCH), who after first low-key album 'MESMERISED' in 1994 on 'Sympathy For The Record Industry), released for 'Big Cat' the 1996 lp/cd 'BEYOND THE PALE' (ABB 96/+CD). It featured KEVIN SHIELDS (of; we still think; MY BLOODY VALENTINE),KEVIN MARTIN (of GOD) and EDDIE PREVOST. SONIC BOOM and E.A.R. released a split 7" in Jul'98 on 'Earworm' (WORM 22)

      In Mar 92, HONEY TONGUE (aka MATTOCK + WIGGS) released lp 'NUDE NUDES' on 'Playtime'; AMUSE 012CD)

SPECTRUM

KEMBER, CARRUTHERS, etc

		Silvertone	Warners
Jun 92.	(7") (ORE 41) **HOW YOU SATISFY ME. / DON'T GO (instrumental 2)**		–
	(12"clear+=/cd-s+=) (ORE 41 T/CD) – My life spins around your every smile / Don't go (instrumental 1).		
Jun 92.	(cd/c/lp) (ORE CD/C/LP 518) <41501> **SOUL KISS (GLIDE DIVINE)**		–
	– How you satisfy me / Lord I don't even know my name / The drunk suite (overture) / Neon sigh / Waves wash over me / (I love you) To the Moon and back / My love for you never died away but my soul gave out and wit / Sweet running water / Touch the stars / Quicksilver glide divine / The drunk suite / Phase me out (gently). (re-iss. Apr95; same)		
Sep 92.	(7") (ORE 44) **TRUE LOVE WILL FIND YOU IN THE END. / MY LIFE SPINS AROUND YOUR EVERY SMILE**	70	–
	(12"/cd-s) (ORE T/CD 44) – ('A'side) / To the moon and back / Waves wash over me.		
Aug 93.	(7") (ORE 56) **INDIAN SUMMER. / BABY DON'T YOU WORRY (California lullabye)**		–
	(12"+=/cd-s+=) (ORE T/CD 56) – It's alright / True love will find you in the end.		
Oct 94.	(12"ep/cd-ep) (ORE T/CD 65) **UNDO THE TABOO / IN THE FULLNESS OF TIME. / TURN THE TIDE (SUB AQUA) / GO TO SLEEP**		–
Nov 94.	(cd/lp) (ORE CD/LP 532) **HIGHS, LOWS AND HEAVENLY BLOWS**		–
	– Undo the taboo / Feedback / Then I just drifted away / Take your time / Soothe me / All night long / Don't pass me by / I know they say / Take me away.		

		not iss.	Sympathy F
Oct 96.	(10"ep) <SFTRI 278> **CALIFORNIA LULLABY EP**		–

      SONIC BOOM also became part of JESSAMINE, an outfit who released a few albums including 'Another Fictionalized History' in '97.

		3rd Stone	Warners
Oct 96.	(cd-ep) <46303> **SONGS FOR OWLSLEY**		–
Aug 97.	(lp/cd) (ORBIT 008/+CD) <46715> **FOREVER ALIEN**		–
	– Feels like I'm slipping away / The stars are so far (how does it feel?) / Close your eyes and you'll see / Delia Derbyshire / Owsley / Forever alien / Matrix / Like . . . / The new Atlantis / End.		
Sep 97.	(cd-s) (ORBIT 010CD) **FEELS LIKE I'M SLIPPING AWAY**		–
	– Feels like I'm slipping away / Forever alien / Dream time / What comes before after?		

      Note; Not to be confused with dance outfit, who released 'SKY ABOVE' & 'BRAZIL'.

SPAIN

Formed: Los Angeles, California, USA . . . 1993 by JOSH HADEN (son of jazz legend CHARLIE HADEN, brother of PETRA and RACHEL from THAT DOG). A singer-songwriter and bass player rolled into one, JOSH cut his teeth very early (at 14!) with 'S.S.T.' hardcore jazz-rock trio, THREACHEROUS JAYWALKERS; three sets were delivered, 'SUNRISE' (1987), 'GOOD MEDICINE' (1989) and 'LA ISLA BONITA' (1990), before they folded. Bursting back onto the scene in 1995 with the cult and brooding 'THE BLUE MOODS OF . . .', the quartet (which included PETRA) established themselves as a good studio act that were apparently 90% shy of live audiences. The album, released on the 'Restless' label was predictably compared with early COWBOY JUNKIES and THE VELVET UNDERGROUND's self titled third album, its sparse Saturday night blues feel and moody jazz homage artwork reflected HADEN's vocals brilliantly, while the rest of the band could be heard in the background strumming quietly away as if they were trying not to wake the neighbours. As SPAIN's members lived in different cities in the States, a reformation wasn't apparent until 1999, when (and just at the height of Alt Country), the group recorded the spine tingling 'SHE HAUNTS MY DREAMS'. Ten whispering tracks about lost love, high hopes and broken hearts in true country style, proved that SPAIN were the peers for such similar artists as NADINE, WHISKEYTOWN and HAZLEDINE. JOEY WARONKER, who can be heard doing the same sort of stuff on BECK's

'MUTATIONS', supplied the endless stream of rimshots and slow brushed snares while ESBJORN SVENSSON provided the occasional, but sublime, honky-tonk piano over HADEN's twenty-a-day vocals. It would be hard to imagine that in the future, SPAIN could return with an album that provoked such images of beauty and still upheld such works of passion. • **Note:** Not to be confused with two different acts that released 'SAETAS – CANTE DE LA SEMANA SANTA ANDALUZA' album and 'SOMETHING TO FEEL' single in the mid-90's respectively.

Album rating: Treacherous Jaywalkers: SUNRISE mini (*3) / GOOD MEDICINE (*4) / LA ISLA BONITA mini (*4) / Spain: THE BLUE MOODS OF SPAIN (*6) / SHE HAUNTS MY DREAMS (*8)

TREACHEROUS JAYWALKERS

JOSH HADEN – vocals, bass, keyboards / **QUINN HABER** – guitar / **JAMES FENTON** – drums, vocals

		S.S.T.	S.S.T.
Sep 87.	(m-lp/m-c) <(SST 126/+C)> **SURNISE**		

– Detonate / Can you afford the pleasure? / Sunrise / Helicopters in the sunrise. <(re-iss. May93 lp/c/cd; SST 126/+C/CD)>

Dec 89. (lp/c) <(SST 207/+C)> **GOOD MEDICINE**
– Dishes / Los tumbos / In the world / Vision pit / Pave the way / Long forgotten summer / Have you ever seen the sunrise? / Encomienda 1988 / Papa Greg / Fake / Gaze. <(re-iss. May93; same)>

below featured **SYLVIA JUNCOSA** – vocals, keyboards (ex-LEAVING TRAINS)

May 90. (m-lp/m-cd) <(SST 217/+CD)> **LA ISLA BONITA**   Mar90
– La Isla Bonita / Ezag / Have you ever seen the sundance? / Sand / L-O-V-E / Sunride.

—— hit the proverbial road after above

SPAIN

JOSH HADEN – vocals, bass / with **PETRA HADEN** – violin, vocals (of THAT DOG) / **EVAN HARTZELL** – drums

		Restless-BMG	Restless
Sep 95.	(cd) <(72910-2)> **THE BLUE MOODS OF SPAIN**		

– It's so true / Ten nights / Dreaming of love / Untitled #1 / Her used-to-been / Ray of light / World of blue / I lied / Spiritual.

—— **JOSH** now with **MERLO PODLEWSKI** – acoustic guitar / **JOEY WARONKER** – drums / plus **ESBJORN SVENSSON** – keyboards / **BJORN OLSSON** – guitar / **STEVIE KLASSON** – steel guitars / **KEN BOUDAKIAN** – guitar

Jun 99. (cd) (74321 67030-2) <72929-2> **SHE HAUNTS MY DREAMS**
– I'm leaving you / It's all over / Before it all went wrong / Hoped and prayed / Waiting for you to come / Easy lover / Bad woman blues / Nobody has to know / Every time I try / Our love is gonna live forever.

SPANDAU BALLET

Formed: Islington, London, England . . . late 1979 by brothers GARY and MARTIN KEMP alongside TONY HADLEY, JOHN KEEBLE and STEVE NORMAN. With their kilts swishing and their fringes flapping, SPANDAU BALLET were initially darlings of the London 'New Romantic' scene, their earliest recordings as haughtily pretentious as their awful moniker. With help from VISAGE man, STEVE STRANGE and RUSTY EGAN (Skids), they found a manager going by the unlikely name of Steve Dagger. The latter famously turned down a deal with 'Island' records, helping the band set up their own label instead, 'Reformation'. A canny move, the group's subsequent output duly being licensed by 'Chrysalis' and a debut single, 'TO CUT A LONG STORY SHORT', making the UK Top 5. This was basically the sole high point of their overwrought debut album, 'JOURNEYS TO GLORY' (1981), one of the first "New Romantic" long players to break the UK Top 5. Their biggest hit to date came later that summer via a collaboration with funksters, BEGGAR & CO., 'CHANT No.1 (I DON'T NEED THIS PRESSURE ON)', a taster for the more commercial leanings of the 'DIAMOND' (1982) opus. The album spawned a further three Top 20 hits, although it was only with the No.1 'TRUE' (1983) album that SPANDAU BALLET really found their calling in musical life; white boy soul/lounge pop with a polished veneer. The new sound was defined with the title track, a massive transatlantic smash upon its release as a single and the SPANDAU's first No.1 hit. 'GOLD' followed suit, a more upbeat effort with HADLEY's coffee table croon no less effective, while 'ONLY WHEN YOU LEAVE' gave the group their third Top 3 hit in succession. 'PARADE' (1984) carried on much the same vein and was almost as successful, providing a further trio of UK Top 20 hits. Its dismal performance in the States, however, led to the group sueing 'Chrysalis' for lack of promotion, the legal battle keeping SPANDAU BALLET occupied for the whole of 1985. The group eventually re-emerged in late '86 with the embarrassing 'FIGHT FOR OURSELVES', newly signed to 'C.B.S.'. The lighter waving ballad, 'THROUGH THE BARRICADES', gave them their last Top 10 hit, preceding the album of the same name. Though the set also made the Top 10, it was to be the group's final taste of real chart action. Subsequent singles stiffed and 'sunk like a stone' would've been a more accurate title for their 1989 effort, 'HEART LIKE A SKY'. Clearly, SPANDAU BALLET were now a glaring anachronism as the 80's gave way to some decent music in the new decade, wisely splitting in 1990. The KEMP brothers found success in acting, both garnering plaudits for their double lead role in 'The Krays', the 1989 film based on the infamous East End gangsters. GARY subsequently appeared in 'The Bodyguard' alongside Whitney Houston, marrying actress Sadie Frost in real life. He wasn't quite

so successful musically, however, a 1995 solo effort predictably stiffing as did HADLEY's early 90's efforts on 'E.M.I.'. The KEMP's were back on show in 1999, while MARTIN (who'd recently suffered a life or death brain operation) starred in Eastenders, GARY was sued by the rest of SPANDAU BALLET for unpaid songwriter royalties; that April, a judge threw out the unwritten agreement in favour of GARY. • **Songwriters:** All written by the KEMP brothers. TONY HADLEY used writers SINFIELD-HILL, CLIMIE-FISHER or DIANE WARREN. HADLEY Covered: ROCK'N'ROLL SUICIDE (David Bowie) / THE BOYS OF SUMMER (Don Henley).

Album rating: JOURNEYS TO GLORY (*5) / DIAMOND (*4) / TRUE (*6) / PARADE (*5) / THE SINGLES COLLLECTION compilation (*7) / THROUGH THE BARRICADES (*6) / HEART LIKE A SKY (*3) / THE BEST OF SPANDAU BALLET compilation (*6)

TONY HADLEY (b. 2 Jun'59) – vocals, synthesizers / **GARY KEMP** (b.16 Oct'60) – keyboards, guitar / **STEVE NORMAN** (b.25 Mar'60) – saxophone, guitar / **MARTIN KEMP** (b.10 Oct'61) – bass / **JOHN KEEBLE** (b. 6 Jul'59) – drums

		Chrysalis	Chrysalis
Nov 80.	(7"/12") (CHS/+12 2473) **TO CUT A LONG STORY SHORT. / ('A'instrumental)**	5	
Jan 81.	(7"/ext.12") (CHS/+12 2486) **THE FREEZE. / ('A'instrumental)**	17	
Mar 81.	(lp/c) (<CHR/ZCHR 1331>) **JOURNEYS TO GLORY**	5	

– To cut a long story short / Reformation / Mandolin / Musclebound / Age of blows / The freeze / Confused / Toys. (cd-iss. Dec82; CCD 1331) (cd re-iss. Jul96 on 'EMI Gold'; CDGOLD 1046)

Mar 81.	(7"/12") (CHS/+12 2509) **MUSCLEBOUND. / GLOW**	10	
	(c-ep) (ZCHL 2509) **ACT 1** – ('A'side) / To cut a long story short / The freeze.		
Jul 81.	(7"/12") (CHS/+12 2528) **CHANT NO.1 (I DON'T NEED THIS PRESSURE ON). / FEEL THE CHANT**	3	
Nov 81.	(7"/12") (CHS/+12 2560) **PAINT ME DOWN. / MAN WITH GUITAR (RE-PAINT)**	30	
Jan 82.	(7"/12") (CHS/+12 2585) **SHE LOVED LIKE DIAMOND. / ('A'version)**	49	
Mar 82.	(lp/c/4x12"box) (<CHR/ZCHR/C-BOX 1353>) **DIAMOND**	15	

– Chant No.1 (I don't need this pressure on) / Instinction / Paint me down / Coffee club / She loved like diamond / Pharoah / Innocence and science / Missionary. (cd-iss. Dec82; CDL 1353)

Apr 82.	(7",7"pic-d) (CHS 2602) **INSTINCTION. / GENTLY**	10	
	(12"+=) (CHS/+12 2602) – Chant No.1 (remix).		
Sep 82.	(7"/7"pic-d/12") (CHS/+P/12 2642) **LIFELINE. / LIVE AND LET LIVE**	7	
Feb 83.	(7"/7"pic-d) (CHS/+P 2668) **COMMUNICATION. / COMMUNICATION (part 2)**	12	-
	(12"+=) (CHR12 2668) – ('A'-edited club mix).		
Mar 83.	(lp/c) (<CDL/ZCDL 1403>) **TRUE**	1	19 May83

– Pleasure / Communication / Code of love / Gold / Lifeline / Heaven is a secret / Foundation / True. (cd-iss. 1986; CCD 1403) (cd re-iss. Mar94; CD25CR 11)

		Reformation	Chrysalis
Apr 83.	(7"/7"pic-d) (SPAN/+P 1) **TRUE. / LIFELINE**	1	
	(12"+=) (SPANX 1) – Lifeline (a capella).		
Jul 83.	(7") <42720> **TRUE. / GENTLY**	-	4
Aug 83.	(7"/7"pic-d) (SPAN/+P 2) **GOLD. / GOLD (part 2)**	2	-
	(12"+=) (SPANX 2) – Foundation.		
Nov 83.	(7") <42743> **GOLD. / GOLD (live)**	-	29
Mar 84.	(7") <42770> **COMMUNICATION. / ONLY WHEN YOU LEAVE**	-	59
May 84.	(7"/7"pic-d) (SPAN/+P 3) **ONLY WHEN YOU LEAVE. / PAINT ME DOWN (live)**	3	34 Jul84
	(12"+=) (SPANX 3) – ('A'live).		
Jun 84.	(lp/c) (<CDL/ZCDL 1473>) **PARADE**	2	50 Aug84

– Only when you leave / Highly strung / I'll fly for you / Nature of the beast / Revenge for love / Always in the back of my mind / With the pride / Round and round. (cd-iss. Jun87; CCD 1473) (re-iss. Mar96 on 'EMI Gold' cd/c; CD/TC GOLD 1010)

Aug 84.	(7"/7"pic-d; 5-different) (SPAN/+P 4) **I'LL FLY FOR YOU. / TO CUT A LONG STORY SHORT (live)**	9	
	(12"+=) (SPANX 4) – ('A'live).		
Oct 84.	(7"silver) (SPAN 5) **HIGHLY STRUNG. / (part 2)**	15	
	(12"+=) (SPANX 5) – ('A'extended).		
Nov 84.	(7") (SPAN 6) **ROUND AND ROUND. / TRUE (live)**	18	
	(12"+=,12"gold+=) (SPANX 6) – Gold (live).		
Nov 85.	(lp/c) (SBTV/ZSBTV 1) **THE SINGLES COLLECTION** (compilation)	3	-

– Gold / Lifeline / Round and round / Only when you leave / Instinction / Highly strung / True / Communication / I'll fly for you / To cut a long story short / Chant No.1 (I don't need this pressure on) / She loved like diamond / The freeze / Musclebound. (w/free 7") (c+= extra mixes) (cd-iss. Apr86; CCD 1498)

		C.B.S.	Epic
Jun 86.	(7") (QA 7264) **FIGHT FOR OURSELVES. / FIGHT . . . THE HEARTACHE**	15	-
	(12"+=) (QTA 7264) – ('A'extended).		
Oct 86.	(7") (SPANDS 1) **THROUGH THE BARRICADES. / WITH THE PRIDE**	6	-
	(12"+=) (SPANDST 1) – ('A'extended).		
Nov 86.	(lp/c/cd) (450259-1/-4/-2) **THROUGH THE BARRICADES**	7	

– Barricades – introduction / Cross the line / Man in chains / How many lies / Virgin / Swept / Fight for ourselves / Swept / Snakes and lovers / Through the barricades.

Jan 87.	(7") (SPANDS 2) **HOW MANY LIES. / COMMUNICATION**	34	-
	(12"+=) (SPANDST 2) – ('A'extended).		
Mar 87.	(7") **HOW MANY LIES. / SNAKES AND LOVERS**	-	-
May 87.	(7") **THROUGH THE BARRICADES. / SNAKES AND LOVERS**	-	
Aug 87.	(7"/7"pic-d) (SPANS/+P 3) **RAW. / RAW (flip)**	47	
	(12"+=/cd-s+=) (SPANS T/C 3) – Raw (extended).		
	(pic-cd-s+=) (SPANSD 3) – Raw (amnesia mix).		

Aug 89. (7") *(SPANS 4)* **BE FREE WITH YOUR LOVE. / ('A'-dance mix edit)** `42` ☐
(cd-s+=) *(SPANSC 4)* – Through the barricades.
(pic-cd-s+=) *(SPANSD 4)* – Raw (extended).
(12"+=) *(SPANST 4)* – ('A'dub version).
Sep 89. (lp/c/cd) *(463318-1/-4/-2)* **HEART LIKE A SKY** `31` ☐
– Be free with your love / Crashed into love / Big feeling / A matter of time / Motivator / Raw / Empty spaces / Windy town / A handful of dust.
Nov 89. (7"/c-s) *(SPANS/+M 5)* **EMPTY SPACES. / WITH THE PRIDE – GOLD (live)** ☐
(cd-s+=) *(SPANSC 5)* – Chant No.1 (live).
(pic-cd-s+=) *(SPANSD 5)* – True (live).
(12"+=) *(SPANST 5)* – Fight for ourselves (live).
Feb 90. (7"/c-s) *(SPANS/+M 6)* **CRASHED INTO LOVE. / HOW MANY LIES (live)** ☐
(12"+=/cd-s+=) *(SPANS T/C 6)* – Through the barricades (live).
(cd-s) *(SPANSD 6)* – ('A'side) / With the pride – Gold (live) / True (live).

—— split when the KEMP's became 'The Krays' in the 1990 film. GARY went on to act in 'The Bodyguard' and married actress Sadie Frost before embarking on a solo career in 1995

– compilations, etc. –

(on 'Chrysalis' unless otherwise stated)
Dec 82. (d-c) *(ZCDP 103)* **JOURNEYS TO GLORY / DIAMOND** ☐ -
Nov 86. (lp/c) *(SBD/ZSBD 1)* **THE 12" MIXES** ☐ -
(cd-iss. Apr87; CCD 1574)
Feb 87. (7") *Old Gold; (OG 9677)* **TO CUT A LONG STORY SHORT. / CHANT NO.1 (I DON'T NEED THIS PRESSURE ON)** ☐ -
Feb 87. (7") *Old Gold; (OG 9679)* **TRUE. / GOLD** ☐ -
(cd-s iss. Aug95; OG 6319)
Nov 87. (c+book) *(THPA 1232)* **GREATEST HITS** ☐ -
Jan 88. (12") *Old Gold; (OG 4037)* **COMMUNICATION. / LIFELINE** ☐ -
Aug 91. (7"/c-s) **TRUE. / LIFELINE** ☐ -
(12"+=/cd-s+=) – Heaven is a secret / Pleasure.
Sep 91. (cd/c/lp) *(CCD/ZCHR/CHR 1353)* **THE BEST OF SPANDAU BALLET** `44` -
– (as THE SINGLES COLLECTION +) Fight for ourselves / Through the barricades / How many lies / Raw / Be free with your love.

SPARKLEHORSE

Formed: Richmond, Virginia, USA ... 1995 by MARK LINKOUS. Early releases on 'Slow River', including 'CHORDS I'VE KNOWN' and 'HAMMERING THE CRAMPS' introduced this drawling southern singer-songwriter. Subsequently securing a deal with 'Capitol', LINKOUS supported labelmates RADIOHEAD in late '95 prior to the release of a debut single, 'SOMEDAY I WILL TREAT YOU GOOD' early the following year. A second single, a re-issue of 'HAMMERING THE CRAMPS', appeared a few months later, both tracks featuring on the tongue twistingly titled debut album, 'VIVADIXIESUBMARINETRANSMISSIONPLOT' (1996). Determinedly lo-fi, melancholic alt-country characterised by LINKOUS' catatonic vocals and influenced by the likes of TOM WAITS, NEIL YOUNG and The AFGHAN WHIGS, the album was an instant hit with the critics and even made a Top 60 showing in the UK charts. A former heroin addict, LINKOUS' health was almost the end of him when he collapsed with a heart attack and badly damaged his legs (he was also confined to a wheelchair for three months) following SPARKLEHORSE's live UK debut. When he eventually resurfaced in 1998 with the acclaimed 'GOOD MORNING SPIDER', several critics suggested that LINKOUS's near-death experience was perhaps a key factor in the vitality of the music. A record of strange beauty, 'GOOD MORNING..' segued from distorted sample-driven noise to passages of forlorn majesty with LINKOUS singing his blues against a lonely acoustic strum. Along with the likes of WILL OLDHAM and SMOG's BILL CALLAHAN, LINKOUS has become an unlikely figurehead for the lo-fi Americana scene with SPARKLEHORSE pushing the genre's boundaries while others are content to recycle. • **Covered:** WISH YOU WERE HERE (Pink Floyd) / WEST OF ROME (Vic Chesnutt).
Album rating: VIVADIXIESUBMARINETRANSMISSIONPLOT (*9) / GOOD MORNING SPIDER (*8)

MARK LINKOUS – vocals, guitar (ex-DANCING HOODS) / **BOB RUPE** or **ARMSTEAD WELLEFORD** – bass / **DAVID BUSH** or **JOHNNY HOTT** – drums / **DAVID CHARLES** – electric guitar, producer

	not iss.	Slow River
Apr 95. (7"ep) *<SRR 14>* **CHORDS I'VE KNOWN EP**	-	☐

– Heart of darkness / Almost lost my mind / Midget in a junkyard / Dead opera star / Hatchet song.

1995. (7") *<SRR 74>* **HAMMERING THE CRAMPS. /**	-	☐

(UK-iss. Oct96; same)

	Capitol	Capitol
Feb 96. (7") *(CL 766)* **SOMEDAY I WILL TREAT YOU GOOD. / LONDON**	☐	☐

(cd-s+=) *(CDCL 766)* – In the dry.

Apr 96. (7") *(CL 770)* **HAMMERING THE CRAMPS. / SPIRIT DITCH**	☐	☐

(cd-s+=) *(CDCL 770)* – Dead opera star / Midget in a junkyard.
May 96. (cd/c/d-lp) *(CD/TC+/EST 2280)* *<72438 32816-2/-4>*
VIVADIXIESUBMARINETRANSMISSIONPLOT `58` ☐ Nov95
– Homecoming queen / Weird sisters / 850 double pumper Holley / Rainmaker / Spirit ditch / Tears on fresh fruit / Saturday / Cow / Little bastard choo choo / Hammering the cramps / Most beautiful widow in town / Heart of darkness / Ballad of a cold lost marble / Someday I will treat you good / Sad and beautiful world / Gasoline horseys.

—— LINKOUS brought in **SCOTT MINOR, PAUL WATSON + SCOTT FITZSIMMONS**

Aug 96. (7") *(CL 777)* **RAINMAKER. / I ALMOST LOST MY MIND** `61` -
(cd-s) *(CDCLS 777)* – Intermission.
(cd-s) *(CDCL 777)* – ('A'side) / Homecoming queen (live on KCRW) / Gasoline horseys (live on KCRW).
Feb 98. (7") **COME ON IN. /** - ☐
(above an old release on 'Slow River')

—— virtually **LINKOUS** with **MINOR, WATSON + SOFIA MITCHALITSIANOS** – cello / **MELISSA MOORE** – violin / **JOHNNY HOTT** – drums, piano / guests **STEPHEN McCARTHY + DAVID LOWERY + VIC CHESNUTT**
Jul 98. (cd-ep) *(CDCL 806)* **PAINBIRDS / MARIA'S LITTLE ELBOWS / THE DIRT BIKE WRECK (enhanced) / WISH YOU WERE HERE** ☐
Jul 98. (cd/lp) *(496014-2/-1)* *<36671>* **GOOD MORNING SPIDER** `30` ☐ Feb99
– Pig / Painbirds / Saint Mary / Good morning spider / Sick of goodbyes / Box of stars (part one) / Sunshine / Chaos of the galaxy – Happy man / Hey, Joe / Come on in / Maria's little elbows / Cruel sun / All night home / Ghost of his smile / Hundreds of sparrows / Box of stars (part two) / Junebug.
Oct 98. (7"clear) *<(CL 808)>* **SICK OF GOODBYES. / GOOD MORNING SPIDER (session version)** `57` ☐
(cd-s) *<(CDCL 808)>* – ('A'side) / I shot a dog / Gasoline horseys.
(cd-s) *<(CDCLS 808)>* – ('A'side) / Happy place / Happy pig (session version).

SPARKS

Formed: Los Angeles, California, USA ... 1968 as HALFNELSON by brothers RON and RUSSELL MAEL. TODD RUNDGREN was sufficiently impressed with a demo tape to get them signed up for Albert Grossman's 'Bearsville' label where he worked as an in-house producer. With EARLE MANKEY, RALPH OSWALD and JOHN HENDERSON completing the line-up, the outfit recorded the eponymous 'HALFNELSON' (1972) under RUNDGREN's guidance. The record sold poorly, however, and the duo changed their name to SPARKS, replacing the rhythm section with JIM MANKEY and HARVEY FEINSTEIN. The resulting 'A WOOFER IN TWEETER'S CLOTHING' (1973) was equally unsuccessful and following an encouraging UK live reception, the brothers relocated to London in 1974, signing to 'Island'. Recruiting a new troupe of backing musicians, RON and RUSSELL were a massive hit (No.2) almost immediately with the pseudo-operatic glam melodrama of 'THIS TOWN AIN'T BIG ENOUGH FOR THE BOTH OF US'. Strikingly eccentric, both visually (RON's unnerving Hitler-esque moodiness and RUSSELL's flouncing, near-falsetto androgyny were quite a match) and musically, it was small wonder the duo were doomed to failure in the States. With Muff Winwood at the controls, the accompanying 'KIMONO MY HOUSE' (1974) developed their arch glam-pop over a whole album and drew inevitable if somewhat inaccurate comparisons with ROXY MUSIC. 'PROPAGANDA' (1974) carried on in the same vein, another Top 10 success which spawned a further two Top 20 hit singles in 'NEVER TURN YOUR BACK ON MOTHER EARTH' and 'SOMETHING FOR THE GIRL WITH EVERYTHING'. By the release of the Tony Visconti-produced 'INDISCREET' (1975), the formula was wearing thin and an expensively disastrous attempt at sub-metal posturing with 'BIG BEAT' (1976) marked the end of the brothers' tenure with 'Island' and a move back to Los Angeles. Meeting electro disco guru, GIORGIO MORODER in Germany the following year, SPARKS collaborated with him on comeback set, 'NUMBER ONE IN HEAVEN' (1979). Released by their new bosses, 'Virgin', the album spawned a couple of major UK hits in 'THE NUMBER ONE SONG IN HEAVEN' and the itchy disco-funk of 'BEAT THE CLOCK', despite barely scraping into the Top 75 itself. Although many 80's outfits owed an obvious debt to SPARKS' innovations, the decade saw them confined to the margins; while they were popular in France, the brothers failed to notch up any hits at all in Britain during this period. Bizarrely enough, SPARKS enjoyed some belated success in the States with the warbling 'ANGST IN MY PANTS' (1982) and 'SPARKS IN OUTER SPACE' (1983) sets. The MAELS' influence on the late 80's/early 90's house scene saw them release a one-off 12" for Scotland's very own 'Finflex' label, 'NATIONAL CRIME AWARENESS WEEK' with dance imprint, 'Logic' subsequently picking them up for the oh-so-cleverly titled 'GRATUITOUS SAX & SENSELESS VIOLINS' (1994). The latter opus actually spawned two minor Top 40 hits, 'WHEN DO I GET TO SING "MY WAY"' and 'WHEN I KISS YOU (I HEAR CHARLIE PARKER PLAYIN')'. With a career incredibly spanning almost thirty years, SPARKS are still showing no signs of pulling the plug, a collaborative revamp (with the late FAITH NO MORE) of the enduring 'THIS TOWN..' making the Top 40 in late '97. • **Songwriters:** RON MAEL wrote lyrics / music, and they also covered; I WANT TO HOLD YOUR HAND (Beatles) / FINGERTIPS (Stevie Wonder) / etc. • **Trivia:** In 1979, they produced NOEL's album 'Is There More To Life Than Dancing'. They also worked for ADRIAN MUSSEY, BIJOU + TELEX.

Album rating: HALFNELSON (*4; as Halfnelson) / A WOOFER IN TWEETER'S CLOTHING (*5) / KIMONO MY HOUSE (*7) / PROPAGANDA (*6) / INDISCREET (*5) / BIG BEAT (*5) / THE BEST OF SPARKS compilation (*7) / INTRODUCING SPARKS (*3) / NUMBER ONE IN HEAVEN (*5) / TERMINAL JIVE (*4) / WHOMP THAT SUCKER (*4) / ANGST IN MY PANTS (*5) / SPARKS IN OUTER SPACE (*4) / INTERIOR DESIGN (*3) / MAEL INTUITION: THE BEST OF SPARKS 1974-1976 compilation (*7) / GRATUITOUS SAX AND SENSELESS VIOLINS (*4) / PLAGIARISM (*4)

RUSSELL MAEL (b. 5 Oct'55, Santa Monica, Calif.) – vocals, bass / **RON MAEL** (b.12 Aug'50, Culver City, Calif.) – keyboards / **EARLE MANKEY** – guitar / with **RALPH OSWALD** – bass / **JOHN HENDERSON** – drums

Bearsville   Bearsville

Feb 72. (lp; as HALFNELSON) <2048> **HALFNELSON**
– Wonder girl / Fa la fa lee / Roger / High C / Fletcher Honorama / Simple ballet / Slowboat / Biology 2 / Saccharin and the war / Big bands / Mr.Nice guys. (UK-iss.Oct74 as 'SPARKS'; K 45511) (UK cd-iss. Aug93 on 'Rhino'; 8122 71300-2)

——— **JIM MANKEY** – bass + **HARVEY FEINSTEIN** – drums repl. RALPH and JOHN

Nov 72. (7") (K 15505) **WONDER GIRL. / (NO MORE) MR.NICE GUYS**

Feb 73. (7") (K 45510) **A WOOFER IN TWEETER'S CLOTHING**
– Girl from Germany / Beaver O'Lindy / Nothing is sacred / Here comes Bob / Moon over Kentucky / Do re mi / Argus desire / Underground / The louvre / Batteries not incuded / Whippings and apologies. (cd-iss. Aug91 on 'Repertoire'; REP 4051)

——— The **MAELS** moved to London and recruited British musicians **ADRIAN FISHER** – guitar / **MARTIN GORDON** – bass, vocals / **DINKY DIAMOND** – drums / **PETER OXENDALE** – keyboards

Island   Island

May 74. (7") (WIP 6193) <IS 001> **THIS TOWN AIN'T BIG ENOUGH FOR THE BOTH OF US. / BARBECUTIE** `2` Aug74

May 74. (lp/c) <(ILPS/ICT 9272)> **KIMONO MY HOUSE** `4`
– This town ain't big enough for the both of us / Amateur hour / Falling in love with myself again / Here in Heaven / Thank God it's not Christmas / Hasta manana Monsieur / Talent is an asset / Complaints / In the family / Equator. (cd-iss. Aug94; IMCD 198)

Jul 74. (7") (WIP 6203) **AMATEUR HOUR. / LOST AND FOUND** `7` `-`

Oct 74. (7") <IS 009> **TALENT IS AN ASSET. / LOST AND FOUND** `-`

——— **TREVOR WHITE** – guitar repl. PETER / **IAN HAMPTON** – bass (ex-JOOK) repl. MARTIN who joined JET

Oct 74. (7") (WIP 6211) **NEVER TURN YOUR BACK ON MOTHER EARTH. / ALABAMY NIGHT** `13` `-`

Nov 74. (lp/c) <(ILPS/ICT 9312)> **PROPAGANDA** `9` `63` Feb75
– Propaganda / At home, at work, at play / Reinforcements / B.C. / Thanks but no thanks / Don't leave me alone with her / Never turn your back on Mother Earth / Something for the girl with everything / Achoo / Who don't like kids / Bon voyage. (cd-iss. Aug94; IMCD 199)

Jan 75. (7") (WIP 6221) **SOMETHING FOR THE GIRL WITH EVERYTHING. / MARRY ME** `17` `-`

Mar 75. (7") <IS 023> **SOMETHING FOR THE GIRL WITH EVERYTHING. / ACHOO** `-`

Jul 75. (7") (WIP 6236) **GET IN THE SWING. / PROFILE** `27` `-`

Sep 75. (7") (WIP 6249) **LOOKS, LOOKS, LOOKS. / PINEAPPLE** `26` `-`

Oct 75. (lp/c) <(ILPS/ICT 9345)> **INDISCREET** `18`
– Hospitality on parade / Happy hunting ground / Without using hands / Get in the swing / Under the table with her / How are you getting home / Pineapple / Tits / It ain't 1918 / The lady is lingering / In the future / Looks, looks, looks / Miss the start, miss the end. (cd-iss. Aug94; IMCD 200)

Nov 75. (7") <IS 043> **LOOKS, LOOKS, LOOKS. / THE WEDDING OF JACQUELINE KENNEDY TO RUSSELL MAEL** `-`

Mar 76. (7"; w-drawn) (WIP 6282) **I WANT TO HOLD YOUR HAND. / ENGLAND** `-`

——— The **MAELS** used session people incl. **SAL MAIDA** – bass (ex-ROXY MUSIC)

Oct 76. (7") (WIP 6337) **BIG BOY. / FILL 'ER UP** `-`

Oct 76. (7") <(ILPS/ICT 9445)> **BIG BEAT**
– Big boy / I want to be like everybody else / Nothing to do / I bought the Mississippi River / Fill 'er up / Everybody's stupid / Throw her away / Confusion / Screwed up / White women / I like girls. (cd-iss. Aug94; IMCD 201)

Dec 76. (7") (WIP 6377) **I LIKE GIRLS. / ENGLAND** `-`

C.B.S.   Columbia

Sep 77. (7") (CBS 5593) **A BIG SURPRISE. / FOREVER YOUNG**

Oct 77. (lp/c) (CBS/40 82284) **INTRODUCING SPARKS**
– A big surprise / Occupation / Ladies / I'm not / Forever young / Goofing off / Girls on the brain / Over the summer / Those mysteries.

——— augmented by **GIORGIO MORODER** – electronics, producer

Virgin   Elektra

Mar 79. (7",7"green/12"red,12"blue) (VS 244/+12) **THE NUMBER ONE SONG IN HEAVEN. / ('A'-long version)** `14` `-`

Mar 79. (lp/c) (V/TCV 2115) **NO.1 IN HEAVEN** `73`
– Tryouts for the human race / Academy award performance / La dolce vita / Beat the clock / My other voice / The number one song in Heaven. (re-iss. Aug82 on 'Fame' lp/c; FA/TCFA 3035)

Jul 79. (7"/12",12"various colrd) (VS 270/+12) **BEAT THE CLOCK. / ('A'-long version)** `10` `-`

Oct 79. (7"/12",12"colrd pic-d) (VS 289/+12) **TRYOUTS FOR THE HUMAN RACE. / ('A'-long version)** `-`

Nov 79. (7") **TRYOUTS FOR THE HUMAN RACE. / NO. 1 SONG IN HEAVEN** `-`

Jan 80. (7") (VS 319) **WHEN I'M WITH YOU. / ('A'-long version)** `-`

Feb 80. (lp/c) (V/TCV 2137) **TERMINAL JIVE** `-`
– When I'm with you / Just because you love me / Rock and roll people in a disco world / When I'm with you (instrumental) / Young girls / Noisy boys / Stereo / The greatest show on Earth.

Apr 80. (7"/ext.12") (VS 343/+12) **YOUNG GIRLS. / JUST BECAUSE YOU LOVE ME** `-`

——— added (ex-BATES MOTEL members) **BOB HAAG** – guitar / **LESLIE BOHEM** – bass / **DAVID KENDRICK** – drums

Why-Fi   R.C.A.

Apr 81. (7"/12") (WHY/+T 1) **TIPS FOR TEENS. / DON'T SHOOT ME**

May 81. (lp) (WHO 1) <4091> **WHOMP THAT SUCKER**
– Tips for teens / Funny face / Where's my girl / Upstairs / I married a Martian / The willys / Don't shoot me / Suzie safety / That's not Nastassia / Wacky women.

Sep 81. (7") (WHY 4) **FUNNY FACE. / THE WILLYS**

——— The **MAELS** + MORODER added **JAMES GOODWIN** – synths.

Atlantic   Atlantic

Jun 82. (7") (K 11740) <4030> **I PREDICT. / MOUSTACHE** `60` May82

Jun 82. (lp/c) (K/K4 50888) <19347> **ANGST IN MY PANTS**
– Angst in my pants / I predict / Sextown U.S.A. / Sherlock Holmes / Nicotina /

Mickey mouse / Moustache / Instant weight loss / Tarzan and Jane / The decline and fall of me / Eaten by the monster of love.

1982. (7") **EATEN BY THE MONSTER OF LOVE. / MICKEY MOUSE** `-`

Jun 83. (7"; SPARKS & JANE WIEDLIN) () <89866> **COOL PLACES. / SPORTS** `49` Apr83

Jun 83. (lp/c) (K 780055-1/-4) 80055> **SPARKS IN OUTER SPACE** `88`
– Cool places / Popularity / Prayin' for a party / All you ever think about is sex / Please, baby please / Rockin' girls / I wish I looked a little better / Lucky me, lucky you / A fun bunch of guys from Outer Space / Dance godammit.

Nov 83. (7") <86990> **ALL YOU EVER THINK ABOUT IS SEX. / I WISH I LOOKED A LITTLE BETTER** `-`
(12") <86990> – ('A'club) / Dance goddamit (club version) / With all my might (extended club).

Jun 84. (lp/c) <7-80160-1/-4> **PULLING RABBITS OUT OF A HAT** `-`

——— MORODER moved on to produce PHIL OAKEY

Jun 84. (7") <7-89616> **PRETENDING TO BE DRUNK. / KISS ME QUICK** `-`

London   Curb-MCA

Jun 85. (7"/12") (LON/+X 69) **CHANGE. / THIS TOWN AIN'T BIG ENOUGH FOR THE BOTH OF US (acoustic)**

——— **JOHN THOMAS** – keyboards repl. GOODWIN

Consolidated M.C.A.

Nov 86. (7"/ext.12") (TOON/+T 2) **MUSIC THAT YOU CAN DANCE TO. / FINGERTIPS**

Nov 86. (lp/c) (TOONLP 2) **MUSIC THAT YOU CAN DANCE TO** Aug86
– Music that you can to / Rosebud / Fingertips / Armies of the night / The scene / Shopping mall of love / Modesty plays (new version) / Let's get funky. <US version; 'Armies of the night'; repl. Change>

Feb 87. (7") (TOON 3) **ROSEBUD. / ('A'-Cinematic version)**
(12") <TOONT 4> – ('A'extended) / ('A'-FM mix).

——— The **MAELS** retained **THOMAS** + **DAVID KENDRICK** ?, introducing **SPENCER SIRCOMBE** – guitar / **HANS CHRISTIAN REUMSCHUSSEL** – bass / **PAMELA STONEBROOK** – vocals

Carrere   Fine Art

Jul 88. (7") (CAR 427) **SO IMPORTANT. / BIG BRASS RING**
(12"+=) (CART 427) – ('A'extremely important mix).
(cd-s++=) (CARCD 427) – Madonna.

——— In Aug 88, SPARKS collaborated on 'SINGING IN THE SHOWER'. / 'SMOG' single by French husband and wife duo LES RITA MITSOUKO on 'Virgin' label.

Carrere   Rhino

Jul 88. (lp/c/cd) <R1/R4/R2 70841> **INTERIOR DESIGN** Aug88
– So important / Just got back from Heaven / Lots of reasons / You got a hold of my heart / Love o rama / The toughest girl in town / Let's make love / Stop me if you've heard this before / A walk down memory lane / Madonna. (cd+=) – Madonna (French – German – Spanish; versions) / The big brass ring / So important. (UK-iss.cd Aug92 on 'Thunderbolt'; CDTB 141)

Aug 89. (7") (CAR 431) **SO IMPORTANT. / JUST GOT BACK FROM HEAVEN** `-`
(12"+=) (CART 431) – ('A'-Extremely Important mix).

——— In 1991, the MAELS were working on own feature film 'Mai The Psychic Girl',

Fineflex   Fineflex

Nov 93. (12") (FF 1004) **NATIONAL CRIME AWARENESS WEEK. / (13 MINUTES OF HEAVEN) / ('A'-Perkins playtime mix)**
(cd-s) (FFCD 1004) – ('A'side) / (3 other mixes).

**Logic-   BMG
BMG**

Oct 94. (12"/c-s/cd-s) (74321 3446-1/-4/-2) **WHEN DO I GET TO SING MY WAY. / ('A'-Grid mix) / ('A'-Rapino Brrothers mix)** `38`
(cd-s) (74321 3447-2) – ('A'side) / ('A'-Vince Clarke mixes).

Nov 94. (cd/c) (74321 23267-2/-4) **GRATUITOUS SAX & SENSELESS VIOLINS**
– Gratutous sex / When do I get to sing 'My Way' / (When I kiss you) I hear Charlie Parker playing / Frankly Scarlett I don't give a damn / I thought I told you to wait in the car / Hear no evil, see no evil, speak no evil / Now that I own the BBC / Tsui Hark (featuring TSUI HARK & BILL KONG) / The ghost of Liberace / Let's go surfing / Senseless violins.

Feb 95. (c-s) (74321 26427-4) **WHEN I KISS YOU (I HEAR CHARLIE PARKER PLAYIN') / ('A'-Beatmasters mix)** `36`
(cd-s+=) (74321 26428-2) – This town ain't big enough for the both of us.
(12"+=/cd-s+=) (74321 26427-1/-2) – ('A'-Bernard Butler mix).

May 95. (c-s) (74321 27400-4) **WHEN DO I GET TO SING 'MY WAY' / ('A'-Grid mix)** `32`
(12"+=) (74321 27400-1) – National crime awareness week.
(cd-s++=) (74321 27400-2) – (2 extra 'A'mixes).

Feb 96. (c-s) (74321 34867-4) **NOW THAT I OWN THE BBC / BEAT THE CLOCK (live)** `60`
(cd-s) (74321 34867-2) – ('A'side) / ('A'mixes) / She's an anchorman.

Roadrunner   Roadrunner

Oct 97. (12"/cd-s) (RR 2262-6/-9) **THE NUMBER ONE SONG IN HEAVEN. / ('A'mix)** `70` `-`
(cd-s) (RR 2262-3) – ('A'remixes with Jimmy Somerville).

Oct 97. (cd) <(RR 8791-2)> **PLAGIARISM** (remixes)
– Pulling rabbits out of a hat / This town ain't big enough for the both of us / The number one song in Heaven / Funny face / When do I get to sing 'My Way' / Angst in my pants / Change / Popularity / Something for the girl with everything / This town ain't big enough for the both of us / Beat the clock / Big brass ring / Amateur hour / Propaganda / When I'm with you / Something for the girl with everything / Orchestral collage / The number one song in Heaven / Never turn your back on Mother Earth.

Dec 97. (cd-ep; as SPARKS VS FAITH NO MORE) (RR 2251-3) **THIS TOWN AIN'T BIG ENOUGH FOR THE BOTH OF US / ('A'version) / SOMETHING FOR THE GIRL WITH EVERYTHING / THE GREAT LEAP FORWARD** `40` `-`

– compilations, others, etc. –

Jul 74. (7") *Bearsville; (K 15516)* **GIRL FROM GERMANY. / BEAVER O'LINDY** □ -

Mar 76. (d-lp) *Bearsville; (K 85505)* **TWO ORIGINALS OF SPARKS** – (the albums from 1972 + 1973) □ -

Mar 77. (lp/c) *Island; (ILPS/ICT 9493)* **THE BEST OF SPARKS** □ -
– This town ain't big enough for the both of us / Hasta mañana monsieur / Tearing the place apart / At home, at work, at play / Never turn your back on Mother Earth / Get in the swing / Amateur hour / Looks, looks, looks / Thanks but no thanks / Gone with the wind / Something for the girl with everything / Thank God it's not Christmas. *(re-iss. Sep79; same) (cd-iss. Feb90; CID 9493)*

Sep 79. (7") *Island; (WIP 6532)* **THIS TOWN AIN'T BIG ENOUGH FOR THE BOTH OF US. / LOOKS, LOOKS, LOOKS** □ -

May 83. (12"ep) *Virgin; (VS 590-12)* **THE NUMBER ONE SONG IN HEAVEN / BEAT THE CLOCK. / WHEN I'M WITH YOU / YOUNG GIRLS** □ -

Nov 81. (lp) *Underdog;* **THE HISTORY OF THE SPARKS** - - French

May 90. (cd) *(IMCD 88)* **MAEL INTUITION** □ -

Jun 91. (d-cd) *Rhino; <R2 70731>* **PROFILE: IT'S A MAEL MAEL MAEL MAEL WORLD** □ □
(above was re-issue of BEST OF SPARKS)

May 93. (cd/c) *Spectrum; (550065-2/-4)* **IN THE SWING** □ □

Oct 93. (cd) *Sony;* **THE HEAVEN COLLECTION** □ □

Oct 93. (cd) *Sony;)* **THE HELL COLLECTION** □ □
(above also issued both as d-cd)

Mar 94. (cd) *DLoma; (LOMACD 23)* **SPARKS / A WOOFER IN TWEETER'S CLOTHING** □ -

Jul 94. (cd/c) *Success;* **JUST GOT BACK FROM HEAVEN** □ -

Oct 95. (cd) *Laserlight; (12571)* **SO IMPORTANT** □ -

SPARROW (see under ⇒ STEPPENWOLF)

SPEARHEAD (see under ⇒ DISPOSABLE HEROES OF HIPHOPRISY)

SPEAR OF DESTINY / THEATRE OF HATE
(dig out; 4th edition or Great Alt & Indie . . .)

SPECIAL EFFECT (see under ⇒ MINISTRY)

SPECIALS

Formed: Coventry, Midlands, England . . . 1978 by keyboardist JERRY DAMMERS, guitarist LYNVAL GOULDING and bassist HORACE GENTLEMAN. After a brief spell with CLASH manager, Bernie Rhodes, DAMMERS formed the seminal '2-Tone' label in in 1979, releasing a debut single, 'GANGSTERS' (based on the Prince Buster track, 'Al Capone') under The SPECIAL A.K.A. moniker. By this point, the line-up had widened to include frontman TERRY HALL, vocalist/percussionist NEVILLE STAPLES, guitarist RODDY RADIATION and drummer JOHN BRADBURY. Issued as a split single with fellow ska revivalists, The SELECTER, the track almost made the UK Top 5 in the summer of '79, the label – with its unmistakable rude boy logo – quickly becoming the hippest namedrop in Britain as MADNESS debuted with 'The Prince' later that summer. Adding trombonist RICO RODRIGUEZ, the group released a follow-up, 'A MESSAGE TO YOU, RUDY', the mellow warmth of RICO's brass virtually making the track, a socially aware message, as ever, belying the song's easy going feel. An eponymous ELVIS COSTELLO-produced album was released the same month, the record blowing a breath of fresh air through the ashes of the punk scene and heralding one of the most exciting periods in British music since the SEX PISTOLS' heyday. The stand-out track was 'TOO MUCH TOO YOUNG', a frenetic stomp railing against teenage pregnancies and showcasing perfectly the compelling mash-up of reggae, ska, punk and pop which became synonymous with the '2-Tone' label along with a number of covers including Harry J. All Stars' 'LIQUIDATOR' and Symarip's wonderfully titled 'SKINHEAD MOONSTOMP', the record giving the group their first No.1. Two further Top 10 hits followed in 1980 with 'RAT RACE' and 'STEREOTYPES', along with a second album, 'MORE SPECIALS'. The group's defining moment, however, came during the long hot summer of '81, with the eerily evocative 'GHOST TOWN', the track's plea of "why must the youth fight among themselves?" echoing against a backdrop of inner city rioting in both London and Liverpool. Though the track was easily the best No.1 single released that year, the band splintered soon after, GOULDING, STAPLES and HALL forming The FUN BOY THREE, while RADIATION formed The TEARJERKERS and RICO went solo. DAMMERS and BRADBURY re-adopted the SPECIAL A.K.A. moniker, recruiting RHODA DAKAR, NICKY SUMMERS, JOHN SHIPLEY and DICK CUTHELL. After a couple of minor hits with 'The BOILER' and 'RACIST FRIEND', DAMMERS & Co. were back in the Top 10 with 'FREE NELSON MANDELA' (1984), arguably one of the best pop singles of the 80's, an incredibly inspiring, heartfelt plea for the imprisoned ANC leader, almost gospel-like in its intensity and funky as hell to boot. The accompanying album, 'IN THE STUDIO', wasn't so successful and DAMMERS subsequently split the band, putting his creative talent into political activism. In 1985 he turned up on the 'STARVATION' reggae charity project, formed Artists Against Apartheid in 1986 and played a major role in oraganising the Nelson Mandela 70th Birthday concert at Wembley Stadium in 1988. While a re-

---

formed SPECIALS appeared in 1995, the absence of both DAMMERS (who retired from live work after developing tinnitus) and HALL meant the project lacked credibility. Though they recorded a relatively small body of work, The SPECIALS remain one of the most influential and pivotal bands of the last 20 years. • **Covered:** GUNS OF NAVARONE (Skatelites) / CONCRETE JUNGLE (Bob Marley) / LONG SHOT KICK DE BUCKET (Pioneers) / MONKEY MAN (Maytals) / MAGGIE'S FARM (Bob Dylan).

Album rating: THE SPECIALS (*8) / MORE SPECIALS (*6) / IN THE STUDIO (*6) / THE SPECIALS SINGLES compilation (*9) / TODAY'S SPECIALS (*3)

TERRY HALL (b.19 Mar'59) – vocals / **NEVILLE STAPLES** – vocals, percussion / **LYNVAL GOULDING** (b.24 Jul'51) – guitar, vocals / **JOHN BRADBURY** – drums / **JERRY DAMMERS** (b. GERALD DANKIN, 22 May'54, India) – keyboards / **RODDY RADIATION** (b. RODERICK BYERS) – guitar / **HORACE GENTLEMAN** (b. HORACE PANTER) – bass

			2-Tone	not iss.
Jul 79.	(7"; SPECIAL A.K.A.) *(TT 1 – TT2)* **GANGSTERS. / The Selecter: THE SELECTER**		6	-

— added (on some) guest **RICO RODRIQUEZ** – trombone

			Chrysalis – 2-Tone	Chrysalis
Oct 79.	(7") *(CHSTT 5)* **A MESSAGE TO YOU RUDY. / NITE CLUB**		10	-
Oct 79.	(lp/c) *(CDLTT/ZCDTL 5001) <1265>* **SPECIALS**		4	84

– A message to you Rudy / Do the dog / It's up to you / Nite club / Doesn't make it alright / Concrete jungle / Too hot / Monkey man / (Dawning of a) New era / Blank expression / Stupid marriage / Too much too young / Little bitch / You're wondering now. *(US-version with +=)* – Gangsters. *(re-iss. Nov84 on 'Fame' lp/c; FA41 3116-1/-4) (cd-iss. 1991; CCD 5001) (cd re-iss. Mar94; CD25CR 02)*

Jan 80.	(7"ep) *(CHSTT 7)* **THE SPECIAL A.K.A. LIVE EP** (live)		1	

– Too much too young / Guns of Navarone / Long shot kick de bucket / The liquidator / Skinhead moonstomp.

May 80.	(7") *(CHSTT 11)* **RAT RACE. / RUDE BOYS OUTA JAIL**		5	
Sep 80.	(7") *(CHSTT 13)* **STEREOTYPES (part 1). / INTERNATIONAL JET SET**		6	
Sep 80.	(lp/c) *(CHRTT/ZCHRT 5003) <1303>* **MORE SPECIALS**		5	98

– Enjoy yourself (it's later than you think) / Man at C & A / Hey little rich girl / Do nothing / Pearl's café / Sock it to 'em J.B. / Stereotypes / Stereotypes (part 2) / Holiday fortnight / I can't stand it / International jet set / Enjoy yourself (reprise). *(with free 7"; TT 999)* – Roddy Radiation & The Specials: BRAGGIN' AND TRYIN' NOT TO LIE. / Judge Roughneck: RUDE BUOYS OUTA JAIL *(cd-iss. 1991; CCD 5003)*

Jan 81.	(7") *(CHSTT 16)* **DO NOTHING. / MAGGIE'S FARM**		4	
Jun 81.	(7"m/12"m) *(CHSTT/+12 17)* **GHOST TOWN. / WHY / FRIDAY NIGHT, SATURDAY MORNING**		1	

— Only two originals (DAMMERS & BRADBURY) remained, as GOULDING, STAPLES & HALL formed The FUN BOY THREE. RADIATION formed TEARJERKERS. RICO went solo. All repl. by **RHODA DAKAR** – vocals + **NICKY SUMMERS** – bass (ex-BODYSNATCHERS) / **JOHN SHIPLEY** – guitar / **DICK CUTHELL** – saxophone

Jan 82.	(7"; RHODA with The SPECIAL A.K.A.) *(CHSTT 18)* **THE BOILER. / THEME FROM THE BOILER**		35	-

The SPECIAL A.K.A.

— **HORACE PANTER** – bass returned to repl. SUMMERS who joined The BELLE STARS / **STAN CAMPBELL** (b. 2 Jan'62) – vocals / **NICK PARKER** – violin repl. CUTHELL (same label)

Dec 82.	(7"/10") *(CHSTT/+10 23)* **WAR CRIMES (THE CRIME IS STILL THE SAME). / WAR CRIMES**		□	-

— **RODDY RADIATION** – guitar returned with newcomer **EGIDIO NEWTON** – vox

Aug 83.	(7"/7"pic-d) *(CHSTT/CHSTPTT 25)* **RACIST FRIEND. / BRIGHT LIGHTS**		60	

— **GARY McMANUS** – bass repl. PANTER who joined GENERAL PUBLIC guested on album **DICK CUTHELL** – cornet / **ANDY ADERINTO** – saxophone

Mar 84.	(7"/12") *(CHSTT/+12 26)* **NELSON MANDELA. / BREAK DOWN THE DOOR**		9	
Jun 84.	(lp/c) *(CHRTT/ZCHRT 5008)* **IN THE STUDIO**		34	

– Bright lights / Lonely crowd / House bound / War crimes / What I like most about you is your girlfriend / Night on the tiles / Nelson Mandela / War crimes / Rascist friend / Alcohol / Break down the door. *(cd-iss. 1991; CCD 5008)*

Aug 84.	(7"/12") *(CHSTT/+12 27)* **WHAT I LIKE MOST ABOUT YOU IS YOUR GIRLFRIEND. / CAN'T GET A BREAK**		51	

— Folded late '84, STAN CAMPBELL went solo and BRADBURY formed The JB's ALL STARS. DAMMERS turned up on a charity single by STARVATION early 1985.

— In Oct'93, SPECIALS were credited on DESMOND DEKKER single 'Jamaica Sky'.

— re-form with **GOLDING, STAPLES + RADIATION** + featuring **SHEENA STAPLE + KENDELL**

			Kuff	not iss.
Jan 96.	(c-s/12"/cd-s) *(KUFF C/T/D 3)* **HYPOCRITE / (mixes)**		66	-

above a Bob Marley cover and below a Toots & The Maytals number.

Mar 96.	(c-s/cd-s) *(KUFF C/D 4)* **PRESSURE DROP / (mixes)**		□	-
Apr 96.	(cd/c) *(KUFF CD/MC 2)* **TODAY'S SPECIALS**		□	-

– Take five / Pressure drop / Hypocrite / Goodbye girl / Little bit / The time has come / Somebody got murdered / 007 / Simmer down / Maga dog / Bad boys.

– compilations, etc. –

on 'Chrysalis' unless mentioned otherwise

Dec 82.	(d-c) *(ZCDP 104)* **SPECIALS / MORE SPECIALS**		□	-
Feb 87.	(12"ep) *Strange Fruit; (SFPS 018)* **THE PEEL SESSIONS** (23.5.79)		□	-

– Gangsters / Too much too young / Concrete jungle / Monkey man.

Feb 87.	(7"0 *Old Gold; (OG 9683)* **TOO MUCH TOO YOUNG (live). / RAT RACE**		□	-

Feb 87. (7") *(OG 9686)* **GHOST TOWN. / RAT RACE** ☐ -

Jun 88. (7"/12") *(CHS/+12 3276)* **FREE NELSON MANDELA – 70th Birthday re-make). / ('A'original)** ☐ -

Aug 91. (cd/c/lp) *(CHRTT/ZCHRT/CCD 5010)* **THE SPECIALS SINGLES** [10] -
– Gangsters / A message to you Rudy / Nite club / Too much too young – Guns of Navarone / Rat race / Rude boys outta jail / Stereotype / International jet set / Do nothing / Ghost town / Why? / Friday night, Saturday morning / Racist friend / Free Nelson Mandela / What I like most about you is your girlfriend.

Oct 91. (7"/cd-s) **GHOST TOWN (REVISITED. / ('A'dub version)** ☐ -
(12"+=) – Why / ('A'demo version).

Apr 92. (cd/c/lp) *(CCD/ZCHRITT/CHRITT 5011)* **LIVE AT THE MOONLIGHT CLUB (live)** ☐ -

Apr 92. (cd/c/lp) *Receiver;* **TOO MUCH TOO YOUNG** ☐ -

—— next shared with The SELECTER.

Dec 92. (cd) *Windsong; (WINCD 030)* **BBC RADIO 1 LIVE IN CONCERT (live)** ☐ -

Sep 93. (12"ep/c-ep/cd-ep; Various) *(CHS TT/TC/CD)* **THE TWO-TONE EP** [30] -
– Gangsters (SPECIAL AKA) / The Prince (MADNESS) / On my radio (SELECTER) / Tears of a clown (BEAT).

Sep 93. (cd) *Receiver; (RR CD/LP 178)* **DAWNING OF A NEW ERA** ☐ -

May 96. (cd/c) *EMI Gold; (CD/TC GOLD 1022)* **TOO MUCH TOO YOUNG** ☐ -

SPECTRUM (see under ⇒ SPACEMEN 3)

SPEECH (see under ⇒ ARRESTED DEVELOPMENT)

Alexander SPENCE (see under ⇒ MOBY GRAPE)

Jon SPENCER BLUES EXPLOSION

Formed: New York City, New York, USA … 1991 by former PUSSY GALORE namesake, JON SPENCER and ex-HONEYMOON KILLERS, JUDAH BAUER and RUSSELL SIMINS. Hardly blues in the conventional sense, SPENCER rather puts the emphasis on EXPLOSION, grinding out a bass-less groove-noise and howling out lip-curled soundbites. It was a formula that had its roots in the primal sludge of PUSSY GALORE and the first instalment in the JSBX saga carried on where that band left off, kind of. Released by 'Caroline' in the States and Virgin subsidiary, 'Hut', in Britain, the eponymous STEVE ALBINI-produced album surfaced in Spring '92, showcasing SPENCER's newly adopted blues drawl and revelling in defiantly dishevelled guitar abuse. Although some critics argued that SPENCER was all mouth and no trousers, so to speak, the man answered in strutting style on the likes of 'BELLBOTTOMS', one of the highlights from 1994's acclaimed 'ORANGE' album; that record, together with its 1993 predecessor, 'EXTRA WIDTH' (both released on 'Matador') really set out the band's manifesto of fractured 70's groove-funk, semi-detached melodies, hand claps, sweat dripping testimonial and sheer distorted noise. Sure, it might've been a style over substance white trash/noise interpretation of delta blues in the loosest sense but SPENCER's tongue was planted firmly in his cheek and following MTV exposure and a tour with The BEASTIE BOYS, JSBX were suddenly big news. A subsequent remix EP roped in such luminaries as BECK and if a move to 'Mute' seemed a little strange, there was no denying the blistering potential of 'NOW I GOT WORRY' (1996). From the delirious swagger of '2KINDSA LOVE' (surely a companion piece, if there ever was one, to MUDHONEY's 'Touch Me I'm Sick') to the disembodied static of Dub Narcotic's 'FUCK SHIT UP', SPENCER sounded as if he'd finally cut that deal down at the crossroads. Still, the man's recorded work only tells half the story; if you really want a baptism by BLUES EXPLOSION fire then you'll have to catch them live. 1998's STEVE ALBINI-produced set, 'ACME', was another adrenalin-fuelled taste of rock'n'roll blues although experimental sidesteps were always on show. Of late, an 'ACME +' remix LP has surfaced while his collaboration with the DUB NARCOTIC SOUND SYSTEM, 'SIDEWAYS SOUL', has also been issued. • **Songwriters:** SPENCER/ group except; LOVIN' UP A STORM (Willie Dixon)

Album rating: A REVERSE WILLIE HORTON (aka JON SPENCER BLUES EXPLOSION) (*5) / CRYPT-STYLE collection (*5) / EXTRA WIDTH (*6) / ORANGE (*7) / MO' WIDTH collection (*5) / NOW I GOT WORRY (*7) / ACME (*7) / ACME PLUS out-takes (*5) /

JON SPENCER – vocals, guitar / **JUDAH BAUER** – guitar / **RUSSELL SIMINS** – drums

		not iss.	In The Red
Oct 91.	(7") *<ITR 007>* **SHIRT JAC. / LATCH-ON**		-
Jan 92.	(7") *<ITR 011>* **SON OF SAM. / BENT**		-
Mar 92.	(7") *<ITR 019>* **TRAIN NO.3. / TRAIN NO.1**		-

		not iss.	Public Popcam
Feb 92.	(lp) *<PORK 1>* **A REVERSE WILLIE HORTON**	-	

– Write a song / IEV / Exploder / Rachel / Chicken walk / White tail / '78 style / Changed / What to do / Eye to eye / Eliza Jane / History of sex / Come back / Support-a-man / Maynard Ave. / Feeling of love / Vacuum of loneliness / Intro A / Biological / Water man. *<cd-iss.Apr92 as 'BLUES EXPLOSION' on 'Caroline'; CAROLCD 1719>* (UK-iss.Dec93 on 'Hut' cd/lp; HUT CD/LP 3) (cd re-iss. Jun97 & Sep98 on 'Caroline'; same as US)

		not iss.	Clawfist
Jun 92.	(7") *<13>* **HISTORY OF SEX. / WRITE A SONG / SMOKE CIGARETTES**	-	- mail-o

		not iss.	Sub Pop
Nov 92.	(7"green) *<SP 180>* **BIG YULE LOG BOOGIE. / MY CHRISTMAS WISH**	-	

		Matador	Matador
Aug 93.	(cd/c/lp; as BLUES EXPLOSION) *<(OLE 052-2/-4/-1)>* **EXTRA WIDTH**		Nov93

– Afro / History of lies / Black slider / Soul letter / Soul typecast / Pant leg / Hey mom / Big road / Train No.2 / Inside the world of the blues explosion / The world of sex.

Feb 94.	(7",7"white; as BLUES EXPLOSION) *<(OLE 077-7)>* **AFRO. / RELAX-HER** ☐ Jul93
Oct 94.	(cd/c/lp) *<(OLE 105-2/-4/-1)>* **ORANGE** ☐

– Bellbottoms / Ditch / Dang / Very rare / Sweat / Cowboy / Orange / Brenda / Dissect / Blues x men / Full grown / Flavor / Greyhound.

Feb 95.	(7"white) *(OLE 111-7)* **BELLBOTTOMS. / MISS ELAINE** ☐ -
	(12") *(OLE 111-1)* – ('A'remix) / Flavor 1 / Flavor 2.
	(cd-s+=) *(OLE 111-2)* – Soul typecast / Greyhound (part 1 & 2).
	(the REMIXES ep of above iss.May95)

		Mute	Matador – Capitol
Sep 96.	(cd/c/lp) *(cd/c+/stumm 132)* *<OLE 193 – 53553>* **NOW I GOT WORRY**	[50]	

– Skunk / Identify / Wail / Fuck shit up / 2Kindsa love / Love all of me / Chicken dog / Rocketship / Dynamite lover / Hot shot / Can't stop / Firefly child / Eyeballin / R.L. got soul / Get over here / Sticky. *(re-iss. May97; same)*

Oct 96.	(7") *(MUTE 202)* **2 KINDSA LOVE. / LET'S SMERF** ☐
	(cd-s) *(CDMUTE 202)* – ('A'side) / Fish sauce / Cool Vee.
Apr 97.	(7"m) *(MUTE 204)* **WAIL. / JUDAH LOVE THEME / RADIO SPOT** [66]
	(7"m) *(LMUTE 204)* – ('A'-Mario C remix) / Afro (live) / Flavor (live).
	(cd-s) *(CDMUTE 204)* – ('A'video mix) / Yellow eyes / Buscemi / Turn up Greene.
Oct 98.	(cd/lp) *(CD+/STUMM 154)* *<OLE 322 – 95566>* **ACME** [72] ☐

– Calvin / Magical colours / Do you wanna get heavy? / High gear / Talk about the blues / I wanna make it all right / Lovin' machine / Bernie / Blue green Olga / Give me a chance / Desperate / Torture / Attack.

Nov 98.	(7"yellow) *(MUTE 222)* **MAGICAL COLOURS. / CONFUSED** ☐ ☐
	(cd-s) *(CDMUTE 222)* – ('A'side) / Bacon / Get down lover.
Mar 99.	(7"orange) *(MUTE 226)* **TALK ABOUT THE BLUES. / WAIT A MINUTE (Moby mix)** ☐ ☐
	(12") *(12MUTE 226)* – ('A'side) / Lovin' machine (Automator mix) / Calvin (zebra ranch) / ('A'-Saints and sinners remix).
	(cd-s+=) *(CDMUTE 226)* – ('A'-video).
Jun 99.	(cd/lp) *(SMALL 004)* **NEW YEAR (DESTROYER). / other track by Barry Adamson** ☐ -
	(above issued on 'Slut Smalls')
Aug 99.	(7") *(MUTE 239)* **HEAVY. / GIVE YA SOME HELL** ☐ ☐
	(12") *(12MUTE 239)* – ('A'side) / 2 kindsa love (Duck rock remix) / Attack (Detroit) / Do you wanna get heavy? (Duck rock hip'n'bass remix).
	(cd-s) *(CDMUTE 239)* – ('A'side) / 2 kindsa love / Blues power / Attack (Detroit).
Sep 99.	(cd/d-lp) *(CD+/STUMM 184)* **ACME PLUS (out-takes)** ☐ ☐

– Wait a minute / Get down lover / Confused / Magical colors (31 flavors) / Not yet / Get old / Bacon / Blue green / Olga (remix) / Heavy (remix) / Lap dance / Right place, wrong time / Leave me alone so I can rock again / Soul trance / Electricity / New year / Chowder / TATB (for the saints and sinners mix) / Hell / I wanna make it alright (Zebra ranch).

– compilations, others, etc. –

Mar 94.	(cd/lp) *Crypt; (EFA 11502-2/-1)* *<29>* **CRYPT-STYLE (rec.1991 NYC)** ☐ Apr92

– Lovin' up a storm / Support a man / White tail / Maynard Ave. / '78 style / Chicken walk / Mo' chicken – Let's get funky / Watermain / Like a hawk / Big headed baby / Write a song / Eye to eye / Feeling of love / Kill a man / Rachel / History of sex / Comeback / The vacuum of loneliness.

Nov 96.	(7") *In The Red;* *<(ITR 42)>* **GET WITH IT. / DOWN LOW** ☐ ☐
Feb 97.	(lp/cd) *Au Go Go; <(ANDA 166/+CD)>* **MO' WIDTH** ☐ Jan95

– Afro / Out of luck / Cherry lime / Rob K / Ole man trouble / Wet cat blues / Johnson / There stands the glass / Lion cut / Beat of the traps / Memphis soul typecast.

Oct 97.	(7") *Au Go Go; <(ANDA 231)>* **ROCKETSHIP. / CHOCOLATE JOE** - - Austra

(cd-s) *<(ANDA 231CD)>* – ('A'side) / Down low / Dynamite lover / Flavor / Full grown.

SPICE GIRLS

Formed: London, England … early 1994 as TOUCH by the father and son management team of Chris and Bob Herbert, who auditioned some four hundred girls before deciding on GERI HALLIWELL (aka GINGER SPICE), MELANIE BROWN (aka MEL B and SCARY SPICE), MELANIE CHISHOLM (aka MEL C and SPORTY SPICE), VICTORIA ADAMS (aka POSH SPICE) and MICHELLE STEPHENSON. Unfortunately, MICHELLE didn't stick around long enough to earn the obligatory Spice nickname, leaving later that summer to be replaced by EMMA LEE BUNTON (aka BABY SPICE). After a year of perfecting their act in Herbert's Surrey studio, the girls left for Simon Fuller's '19 Management'. Fuller duly paired them up with three of the pop industry's most successful writing teams while the girls themselves were instrumental in netting a contract with 'Virgin'; the rest, as they say, is history. A marketing masterstroke, the SPICE GIRLS were presented as a female alternative to the chart domination of countless boy bands. Spicing up their strategy was the manufacture of five distinct personalities as opposed to the bland uniformity of the boy bands; add to this a pinch of quasi-feminist "girl power" and you had a recipe for not just British but worldwide chart domination. So successful, in fact, was the initial media campaign that the girls' summer '96 debut single, 'WANNABE', became the first record by an all-female act to enter the UK chart at No.1, subsequently going on to top charts all over Europe, the USA and beyond. Sassy, upwardly mobile role models for the girls, feisty sex symbols for the boys, soon everyone had a favourite Spice girl. But what about the actual music? Well, despite comprising the usual teen fodder of watered down R&B, pseudo-rap, etc, 'WANNABE' had an anthemic quality and a funky charisma that was hard to resist even for hardened cynics. With the media machine going into overdrive (nude photos from GERI's modelling past were a particular coup for the tabloids), follow-up single, 'SAY YOU'LL BE THERE', was never going to enter the chart at anything less than No.1. Likewise the pristine pop of debut album, 'SPICE' (1996); a major factor in the continuing success was their musical versatility and while the likes of '2 BECOME 1', 'MAMA' and 'SPICE UP YOUR LIFE' (all No.1 singles) were never going to help them win the Mercury Music prize, they kept their sound fresh. From mushy balladry to flashy Euro-pop, the girls carried it off effortlessly every time. While the debut album had its fair share of filler, 'SPICEWORLD' (1997) was more adventurous, from the Latin-tinged adrenalin of the title track to the retro girl-group soul of 'STOP' (which ironically "stopped" at No.2). By this point, each member had begun forming a separate musical identity as opposed to merely cosmetic, each playing to their own particular strengths. Accompanying the album was a full-length feature film as The SPICE GIRLS became not just a music biz cash cow but a cultural phenomenon; while 'Virgin' clocked up the sales, broadsheet scribes were analysing the implications and effects of "girl power". The group was once again at the epicentre of a media frenzy upon GERI's sudden departure in May '98. Amid the usual rumours and allegations, HALLIWELL took time out with her mate GEORGE MICHAEL before making a successful solo comeback. Despite the absence of GERI's dominating presence, The SPICE GIRLS continued to tour successfully before taking a break themselves. While POSH SPICE became a regular in 'Hello' mag after hooking up with Man Utd golden boy, David Beckham, MEL G scored a No.1 solo single, 'I WANT YOU BACK', in collaboration with top hip hop chanteuse, MISSY 'MISDEMEANOUR' ELLIOTT. SPORTY proved the most musically prolific of the lot, duetting with BRYAN ADAMS and scoring a UK Top 3 hit at Christmas '98 with 'WHEN YOU'RE GONE'. Underlining her position as the most "alternative" SPICE GIRL (if that's not a contradiction in terms), MELANIE C released her own album of vaguely indie-minded pop in the shape of 'NORTHERN STAR' (1999), while EMMA LEE BUNTON collaborated with TIN TIN OUT on a near chart-topping version of Eddi Brickell's 'WHAT I AM'. • **Covered:** WE ARE FAMILY (Sister Sledge) / SISTER (ARE DOIN' IT FOR THEMSELVES) (Aretha Franklin & The Eurythmics).

Album rating: SPICE (*6) / SPICEWORLD (*5) / Melanie C: NORTHERN STAR (*5)

GINGER SPICE (b. GERI HALLIWELL, 7 Aug'72, Watford, England) – vocals / **SCARY SPICE (MEL B)** (b. MELANIE BROWN, 29 May'75, Leeds, England) – vocals / **SPORTY SPICE (MEL C)** (b. MELANIE CHISHOLM, 12 Jan'76, Liverpool, England) – vocals / **BABY SPICE** (b. EMMA LEE BUNTON, 21 Jan'76, London, England) – vocals; repl. MICHELLE STEPHENSON / **POSH SPICE** (b. VICTORIA ADDAMS, 7 Apr'75, Cuffley, England) – vocals

		Virgin	Virgin	
Jul 96.	(7"/c-s) (VSLH/VSC 1588) <38579> **WANNABE. / BUMPER TO BUMPER**	1	1	Jan97

(cd-s+=) (VSCDT 1588) – ('A'-Vocal slam mix).
(cd-s) (VSCXD 1588) – ('A'side) / ('A'-Dave Way alternative mix) / ('A'instrumental).

Oct 96.	(7"/c-s) (VSLH/VSC 1601) <38592> **SAY YOU'LL BE THERE. / TAKE ME HOME**	1	3	May97

(cd-s+=) (VSCDT 1601) – ('A'-Junior's Main Pass mix) / ('A'instrumental).
(cd-s) (VSCDG 1601) – ('A'side) / (3-'A'mixes).

Oct 96.	(cd/c/lp) (CD/TC+/V 2812) <42174> **SPICE**	1	1	Feb97

– Wannabe / Say you'll be there / 2 become 1 / Love thing / Last time lover / Mama / Who do you think you are / Something kinda funny / Naked / If U can't dance.

Dec 96.	(7"/c-s) (VSLH/VSC 1607) **2 BECOME 1. / ONE OF THESE GIRLS**	1	4	Jul97

(cd-s+=) (VSCDT 1607) <38604> – ('A'orchestral) / Wannabe (Junior Vasquez remix).
(cd-s) (VSCDX 1607) <38609> – ('A'side) / ('A'-Dave Way remix) / Sleigh ride.

Mar 97.	(7"/c-s) (VSLH/VSC 1623) **MAMA. / WHO DO YOU THINK YOU ARE**	1	-	

(cd-s+=) (VSCDT 1623) – (2-'A'-David Morales mixes).

Oct 97.	(7"/c-s) (VSLH/VSC 1660) <38620> **SPICE UP YOUR LIFE. / SPICE INVADERS**	1	18	

(cd-s+=) (VSCDT 1660) – ('A'mixes).
(cd-s) (VSDG 1660) – ('A'mixes).

Nov 97.	(cd/c/lp) (CD/TC+/V 2850) <45111> **SPICEWORLD**	1	3	

– Spice up your life / Stop / Too much / Saturday night divas / Never give up on the good times / Move over / Do it / Denying / Viva forever / Lady is a vamp.

Dec 97.	(7"/c-s) (VSLH/VSC 1669) <38630> **TOO MUCH. / WALK OF LIFE**	1	9	Jan98

(cd-s+=) (VSCDX 1669) – ('A'mix).
(cd-s) (VSCDT 1669) – ('A'side) / Outer space girls / Spice up your life.

Mar 98.	(7"/c-s) (VSLH/VSC 1679) **STOP. / SOMETHING KINDA FUNNY**	2		Jun98

(cd-s+=) (VSCDT 1679) – Mama / Love thing.
(cd-s) (VSCDX 1679) <39642> – ('A'side) / (3 other mixes).

—— on the 31st of May '98, the five were now four when GERI HALLIWELL left the group; the following May she was at UK No.2 with her debut solo single, 'LOOK AT ME'. In June her album, 'SCHIZOPHONIC' made No.4 while follow-up singles, 'MI CHICO LATINO' and 'LIFT ME UP' both hit No.1 in August and November (1999) respectively. The latter kept EMMA BUNTON (who featured on TIN TIN OUT's cover of 'WHAT I AM') off the top spot.

Jul 98.	(c-s) (VSC 1692) **VIVA FOREVER / WHO DO YOU THINK YOU ARE**	1	-	

(cd-s+=) (VSCDT 1692) – Say you'll be there.
(cd-s) (VSCDX 1692) – ('A'mixes).

—— Dec'98, also saw MELANIE C hit the UK Top 3 when BRYAN ADAMS and the Sporty one dueted on 'WHEN YOU'RE GONE'

Dec 98.	(c-s) (VSC 1721) <38652> **GOODBYE / WE ARE FAMILY (live) / CHRISTMAS WRAPPING**	1	11	

(cd-s) (VSCDT 1721) – (first & third tracks) / ('A'version).
(cd-s) (VSCDX 1721) – (first two tracks) / Sisters (are doing it for themselves) (live).

– compilations, etc. –

Aug 97.	(d-cd) Metro Independent; (OTR 1100057) **OLD SPICE – THE EARLY YEARS** (Documentary & Music)		-
Oct 97.	(cd/c) Summit; (SUM CD/MC 4150) **SINGALONGA SPICE**		-
Nov 97.	(cd) Metro Independent; (10027) **BIOGRAPHY SERIES**		-
Aug 99.	(cd+book) Hallmark; (8168) **STAR PROFILE**		-

MELANIE G

—— after her solo debut (see below) she altered her moniker when she married Jimmy Gulzar (13th September, 1998).

		Virgin	Virgin
Sep 98.	(c-s; as MELANIE B featuring MISSY 'MISDEMEANOR' ELLIOTT) (VSC 1716) **I WANT YOU BACK / (mixes)**	1	-

(cd-s+=/12"+=) (VSCDT/VST 1716) – ('A'mixes).

Jul 99.	(7"/c-s) (VSLH/VSC 1735) **WORD UP. / ('A'-Tim's dance mix)**	14	-

(cd-s+=) (VSCDT 1735) – Sophisticated lady / ('A'-CD-Rom video).

MELANIE C

		Virgin	Virgin
Oct 99.	(c-s/cd-s) (VSC/+DT 1744) <896257> **GOIN' DOWN / GA GA / ANGEL ON MY SHOULDER**	4	Nov99
Oct 99.	(cd/c) (CD/TC VX 2893) <48510> **NORTHERN STAR**	10	Nov99

– Go / Northern star / Goin' down / I turn to you / If that were me / Never be the same again / Why / Suddenly Monday / Ga ga / Be the one / Closer / Feel the sun.

Nov 99.	(c-s/cd-s) (VSC/+DT 1748) <896388> **NORTHERN STAR / FOLLOW ME**	4	Dec99

(cd-s) (VSCDX 1748) – ('A'-full version) / (CD-Rom version).

SPIDERS (see under ⇒ COOPER, Alice)

SP!N (see under ⇒ GENE)

SPIN DOCTORS

Formed: New York City, New York, USA ... 1989 by bearded singer CHRIS BARRON, ERIC SCHENKMAN (who had both been in the band TRUCKING COMPANY alongside JOHN POPPER, later of BLUES TRAVELER) and AARON COMESS, all students at The New School Of Jazz in New York. With MARK WHITE completing the line-up, the group embarked on a heavy gigging schedule, cementing their good-time mesh of funky 70's style pop/blues and subsequently signing to 'Epic' in 1990. Fittingly, the band were introduced to the record buying public by way of a live EP, 'UP FOR GRABS', a couple of years later. Fuelled by MTV coverage of the 'LITTLE MISS CAN'T BE WRONG' single and the success of the insanely catchy 'TWO PRINCES', the debut album, 'POCKET FULL OF KRYPTONITE' (1993) slowly but surely made its way to both the US and UK Top 5. The rootsy pop-rock contained within its grooves drew inevitable comparisons with prime STEVE MILLER BAND, although other 70's stalwarts like FREE or even RANDY NEWMAN also sprang to mind. Spiritually at least, comparisons could also be made with the GRATEFUL DEAD, the band forming a central part of the new wave of 'jam' bands alongside the likes of PHISH and the aforementioned BLUES TRAVELER. While 'POCKET FULL ...' sold over two million copies, the group's third effort, 'TURN IT UPSIDE DOWN' (1994) was a relative disappointment (live stop-gap 'HOMEBELLY GROOVE', just might've been mistimed), although it hit the Top 30. Worse to come was their third studio set, 'YOU'VE GOT TO BELIEVE IN SOMETHING' (1996), a failure both critically and commercially. In August 1999, it was announced that BARRON could no longer sing, due to a rare disease that limited his vocal chords. • **Songwriters:** Group penned except WOODSTOCK (Joni Mitchell) / THAT'S THE WAY I LIKE IT (K.C. & The Sunshine Band) / STOP BREAKING DOWN (Robert Johnson).

Album rating: POCKET FULL OF KRYPTONITE (*7) / HOMEBELLY GROOVE live (*4) / TURN IT UPSIDE DOWN (*5) / YOU'VE GOT TO BELIEVE IN SOMETHING (*4)

CHRIS BARRON (b. CHRISTOPHER BARRON GROSS, 5 Feb'68, Hawaii) – vocals / **ERIC SCHENKMAN** (b.12 Dec'63, Massachusetts) – guitar / **MARK WHITE** (b. 7 Jul'62) – bass / **AARON COMESS** (b.24 Apr'68, Arizona) – drums

		Epic	Epic
Nov 91.	(cd-ep) **UP FOR GRABS**	-	
Feb 93.	(7"/c-s) (658489-7/-4) <74473> **LITTLE MISS CAN'T BE WRONG. / WHAT TIME IS IT?** (live)		17 Sep92

(cd-s+=) (658489-2) – Big fat funky booty – At this hour (live).
(re-iss. Jul93; same) – (hit UK No.23)

Mar 93.	(cd/c) (468250-2/-4) <47461> **POCKET FULL OF KRYPTONITE**	2	3 Jun92

– Jimmy Olsen's blues / What time is it? / Little Miss can't be wrong / forty or fifty / Refrigerator car / More than she knows / Two princes / Off my line / How could you want him (when you know you could have me?) / Shinbone alley – Hard to exist.

May 93. (7"/c-s) (659145-7/-4) <74804> **TWO PRINCES. / OFF MY LINE (live)** `3` `7` Jan93
(cd-s) (659145-2) – ('A'side) / Yo mamas a pajama (live) / Little miss can't be wrong (live).

Sep 93. (c-s,cd-s) <74929> **JIMMY OLSEN'S BLUES / YO MAMAS A PAJAMA** `-` `78`

Sep 93. (7"/c-s) (659758-7/-4) **JIMMY OLSEN'S BLUES. / AT THIS HOUR (live)** `40` `-`
(cd-s+=) (659758-2) – Rosetta stone (live).

Nov 93. (7"/c-s) (659955-7/-4) **WHAT TIME IS IT? / ('A'live)** `56` `-`
(cd-s+=) (659955-2) – Two princes (live) / Forty or fifty (live).

Dec 93. (cd/c) (472896-2/-4) <53309> **HOMEBELLY GROOVE (live)** ` ` ` `
– What time is it? – Off my line / Freeway of the plains – Lady Kerosene / Yo baby / Little Miss can't help it / Shinbone alley / Refrigerator car / Sweet widow / Stepped on a crack / Yo mamas a pajama / Rosetta Stone.

Jun 94. (7"pic-d/c-s) (660419-7/-4) <77525> **CLEOPATRA'S CAT. / URANIUM CENTURY** `29` `84`
(cd-s+=) (660419-2) – Stop breaking down (live).

Jun 94. (cd/c/lp) (476886-2/-4/-1) <52907> **TURN IT UPSIDE DOWN** `3` `28`
– Big fat funky booty / You let your heart go too fast / Cleopatra's cat / Hungry Hamed's / Biscuit head / Indifference / Bags of dirt / Mary Jane / More than meets the ear / Laraby's gang / At this hour / Someday all this will be road / Beasts in the woods.

Jul 94. (7"/c-s) (660661-4) <77600> **YOU LET YOUR HEART GO TOO FAST. / PIECE OF GLASS** `66` `42`
(cd-s+=) (660661-2) – I can't.

Oct 94. (c-s) (660977-4) **MARY JANE / WOODSTOCK** `55` ` `
(cd-s+=) (660977-2) – Hungry Hamed's.

—— **ANTHONY KRIZAN** (b.25 Aug'65, Plainfield, New Jersey) – guitar repl. ERIC

Jun 96. (c-s) (663268-4) **SHE USED TO BE MINE / MARCY OF THE AIR** `55` ` `
(cd-s+=) (663268-2) – Two princes.
(cd-s) (663268-5) – ('A'side) / Miss America / Little miss can't be wrong.

Jul 96. (cd/c) (483817-2/-4) **YOU'VE GOT TO BELIEVE IN SOMETHING** ` ` ` `
– You've got to believe in something / House / Dogs on a doe / I can't believe you're still with her / She used to be mine / She's not you / To make me blue / 'Bout a train / Where angels fear to tread / If wishes were horses / Sister Sisyphus. *(hidden track+=)* – That's the way I like it.

—— they disappeared from the music biz (see above)

SPIRIT

Formed: Los Angeles, California, USA ... 1964 as The RED ROOSTERS, by RANDY CALIFORNIA and his middle-aged, shaven-headed stepfather, ED CASSIDY. The band split in late '65 and later reformed as SPIRITS REBELLIOUS in the Spring of '67, CALIFORNIA returning from New York where he'd traded axe licks with, and been heavily influenced by, a young JIMI HENDRIX. Along with ex-ROOSTERS, MARK ANDES, JOHN LOCKE and JAY FERGUSON, the band became SPIRIT and signed to LOU ADLER's 'Ode' records. Their eponymous debut was released soon after, a mellow melange of jazz and trippy, bluesy rock that marked the band out from the bulk of the folk-rock pack in the L.A. of 1968. SPIRIT also looked different, CASSIDY resembling some ageing hippy Kojak. With the exuberant 'I GOT A LINE ON YOU' single from the follow-up album, 'THE FAMILY THAT PLAYS TOGETHER' (1969), the band scored an unexpected Top 30 hit, although the bulk of the record explored the grey area where jazz, rock and psychedelia met. 'CLEAR SPIRIT' (1969) displayed a harder-edged sound but the band didn't really come into their own until they were paired with NEIL YOUNG producer DAVID BRIGGS and recorded the psychedelic masterwork, 'TWELVE DREAMS OF DR. SARDONICUS' (1971). From the pastoral psychedelia of 'NATURE'S WAY' to the more direct approach of 'MORNING WILL COME' and 'MR. SKIN', this was CALIFORNIA at his most creative in terms of both songwriting and guitar playing. Although it was critically acclaimed upon release, it failed to sell in any great quantity and FERGUSON left shortly after to form JO JO GUNNE. With CALIFORNIA laid up after a road accident and ED CASSIDY the only original remaining member involved in the 'FEEDBACK' (1972) album, it came as no surprise when the record was a resounding failure, creatively, critically and commercially. This was, in effect, the end of the line for the band although a bogus SPIRIT sprang up to haunt them, fronted by the STAEHELY brothers who'd played on 'FEEDBACK'. Meanwhile, CALIFORNIA recorded a minor classic of a solo album, 'KAPT. KOPTER AND THE (FABULOUS) TWIRLYBIRDS'. A rough-hewn set of psychedelic garage-rock, the record featured some inspired covers including The BEATLES' 'RAIN ' and 'DAY TRIPPER'. The original SPIRIT line-up reformed in the mid-70's and recorded a series of albums for 'Mercury', which tried and failed to capture the original vibe. After yet another split and reformation, the band resurrected Kapt. Kopter and recorded a cod-concept album, 'JOURNEY TO POTATOLAND', in 1981 before breaking up again. In the way of these things, the band reformed with differing line-ups throughout the 80's, CALIFORNIA also recording two solo albums. The long 'SPIRIT'-ual journey finally came to an end when CALIFORNIA was tragically drowned off the coast of the Hawaiian island of Molokai, on the 1st January of 1997.
• **Songwriters:** CALIFORNIA and group, except YESTERDAY (Beatles) / HEY JOE (hit; Jimi Hendrix; c.William Roberts). CALIFORNIA covered solo:- MOTHER AND CHILD REUNION (Paul Simon) / ALL ALONG THE WATCHTOWER (Bob Dylan) / WILD THING (Troggs). • **Trivia:** MARK ANDES played on BORIS PICKETT & THE CRYPT KICKER

5's hit single, 'Monster Mash'. LED ZEPPELIN (Jimmy Page), must have listened to 1968 track, 'TAURUS', before writing 'Stairway To Heaven' (listen?).

Album rating: SPIRIT (*7) / THE FAMILY THAT PLAYS TOGETHER (*7) / CLEAR SPIRIT (*7) / TWELVE DREAMS OF DR SARDONICUS (*8) / FEEDBACK (*4) / THE BEST OF SPIRIT compilation (*8) / SPIRIT OF '76 (*5) / SON OF SPIRIT (*5) / FARTHER ALONG (*5) / FUTURE GAMES (A MAGICAL KAHUANA DREAM) (*4) / SPIRIT LIVE (*3) / JOURNEY TO POTATOLAND (*8) / THE THIRTEENTH DREAM remixes (*4) / Randy California: KAPTAIN KOPTER AND THE (FABULOUS) TWIRLY BIRDS (*5) / EURO AMERICAN (*4) / RESTLESS (*5) / SHATTERED DREAMS (*4) / Randy California's Spirit: RAPTURE IN THE CHAMBERS (*4) / TENT OF MIRACLES (*4) / LIVE AT LA PALOMA (*5) / CALIFORNIA BLUES (*4)

RANDY CALIFORNIA (b. RANDALL CRAIG WOLFE, 20 Feb'51) – guitar, vox / **JAY FERGUSON** (b. JOHN ARDEN FERGUSON, 10 May'47, Burbank, Calif.) – vocals / **MARK ANDES** (b.19 Feb'48, Philadelphia) – bass (ex-YELLOW BALLOON, w/JAY) / **ED CASSIDY** (b. 4 May'22, Chicago, Illinois) – drums (ex-NEW JAZZ TRIO) / **JOHN LOCKE** (b.25 Sep'43) – keyboards (ex-NEW WORLD JAZZ CO.)

		C.B.S.	Ode

Jun 68. (lp) (63278) <44004> **SPIRIT** ` ` `31` Jan68
– Fresh garbage / Uncle Jack / Mechanical world / Taurus / Straight arrow / Topango windows / Gramophone man / Water woman / Great canyon fire in general / Elijah / Girl in your eyes. *(re-iss. Apr79 as 'THE FIRST OF SPIRIT' on 'CBS-Embassy'; 31693) (re-iss. Apr89 on 'Edsel' lp/c/cd; ED/+MC/CD 311) (re-iss. cd Aug95; 480965-2)*

Jun 68. (7") (3523) <257-108> **UNCLE JACK. / MECHANICAL WORLD** ` ` ` `

Feb 69. (7") (3880) <257-115> **I GOT A LINE ON YOU. / SHE SMILED** `25` Dec68

Apr 69. (lp) (63523) <44014> **THE FAMILY THAT PLAYS TOGETHER** `22` Jan69
– I got a line on you / Poor Richard / Aren't you glad / It shall be / The drunkard / It's all the same / Dream within a dream / Jewish / So little to say / Silky Sam. <US re-iss. Jul72; > (re-iss. Mar86 on 'Edsel' lp/c/cd+=; XED/CED/EDCD 162) – She smiles / Darlin'. (cd re-iss. Sep94 on 'Rewind';)

Aug 69. (7") (4511) **DARK EYED WOMAN. / ICE** ` ` `-`

Sep 69. (7") (4565) <257-122> **DARK EYED WOMAN. / NEW DOPE AT TOWN** ` ` ` `

Oct 69. (lp) (63729) <44016> **CLEAR SPIRIT** ` ` `55` Jul69
– Dark eyed woman / Apple orchard / So little time to fly / Groundhog / Cold wind / Policeman's ball / Ice / Give a life, take a life / I'm truckin' / Clear / Caught / New dope in town. *(re-iss. Mar88 on 'Edsel' lp/cd; ED/+CD 268)*

		C.B.S.	Epic

Jan 70. (7") (4773) <257-128> **1984. / SWEET STELLA BABY** ` ` `69` Dec69

Sep 70. (7") (5149) <10648> **ANIMAL ZOO. / RED LIGHT, ROLL ON** ` ` `97` Aug70

Oct 70. (7") <10685> **MR. SKIN. / SOLDIER** `-` ` `

		Epic	Epic

Feb 71. (lp) (EPC 64191) <30267> **TWELVE DREAMS OF DR. SARDONICUS** ` ` `63` Dec70
– Nothing to hide / Nature's way / Animal zoo / Love has found a way / Why can't I be free / Mr. Skin / Space child / When I touch you / Sweet worm / Life has just begun / Morning will come / Soldier. *(re-iss. Mar81 lp/c; EPC/40 32006) (re-iss. Apr89 on 'Edsel' lp/c/cd; ED/+MC/CD 313) (re-iss. cd Aug93; 468030-2) (re-iss. cd Apr94; 476603-2)*

—— (Dec70) **JOHN ARLISS** – bass repl. FERGUSON and ANDES who formed JO JO GUNNE (May71) CASSIDY + LOCKE recruited new men **AL STAEHELY** – bass (ex-PUMPKIN) / **J.CHRISTIAN** (b.CHRIS STAEHELY) – guitar repl. ARLISS + RANDY who went solo

May 72. (7") (EPC 8083) **CADILLAC COWBOYS. / DARKNESS** ` ` `-`

Jun 72. (lp) (EPC 64507) <31175> **FEEDBACK** ` ` `63` Mar72
– Chelsea girl / Uncle Jack / Cadillac / Cowboys / Puesta del scam / Ripe and ready / Darkness / Earth shaker / Mellow morning / Trancas fog-out / The witch.

—— (Aug72) Now a totally 'bogus' SPIRIT, fronted by The STAEHELY brothers. **STU PERRY** – drums repl. CASSIDY (see further below), and LOCKE who went solo. An album 'STA-HAY-LEE', included CASSIDY and LOCKE surfaced in US later? CHRIS was another to join JO JO GUNNE. Regarded as the 'real SPIRIT'

RANDY CALIFORNIA

(solo!) with **TIM McGOVERN** – drums, vocals / **CHARLIE BUNDY** – bass, b.vox / **HENRY MANCHOVITZ** (aka MITCH MITCHELL) – drums / **CLIT McTORIUS** (aka NOEL REDDING) – bass / guests **CASS STRANGE** (aka ED CASSIDY) – bass / **FUZZY KNIGHT** (aka ARRY WEISBER) – keyboards

Sep 72. (7") <10927> **WALKIN' THE DOG. / LIVE FOR THE DAY** `-` ` `

Sep 72. (lp) (EPC 65381) <31755> **KAPTAIN KOPTER AND THE (FABULOUS) TWIRLY BIRDS** ` ` ` `
– Downer / Devil / I don't want nobody / Day tripper / Mother and child reunion / Things yet to come / Rain / Rainbow. *(re-iss. Jun80 on 'C.B.S.' lp/c; CBS/40 31829) (re-iss. Nov85 on 'Edsel'+=; ED 164) – Walkin' the dog / Live for the day. (cd-iss. Aug93 & May97 on 'Edsel'; EDCD 164)*

—— In 1973, CALIFORNIA attempted suicide by jumping off Chelsea Bridge.

SPIRIT

—— after a few other line-up's in 1974, settled with **CASSIDY, CALIFORNIA + MARK ANDES** who repl. FUZZY KNIGHT. **JOHN LOCKE** re-joined for short spell, until he went into sessions. Also ANDES (who joined FIREFALL) were repl. by **BARRY KEANE** – bass

		Mercury	Mercury

Jun 75. (d-lp) (6672 012) <804> **SPIRIT OF '76** ` ` ` `
– America the beautiful / The times they are a-changin' / Victim of society / Lady of the lakes / Tampa man / Mounalo / What do I have / Sunrise / Walking the dog / Joker on the run / When? / Like a rolling stone / Once again / Feeling in time / Happy / Jack Bond (part 1) / Mr. Road / Thank you Lord / Urantia / Guide me / Veruska / Hey Joe / Jack Bond (part 2) / The star spangled banner. *(re-iss. May88 on 'Edsel'; DED 251) (cd-iss. Mar93;)*

Aug 75. (7") <73697> **AMERICA THE BEAUTIFUL. / THE TIMES THEY ARE A-CHANGIN' / LADY OF THE LAKES** | - | |

—— added **MATT ANDES** – guitar (ex-JO JO GUNNE)

Oct 75. (lp) <SRM1 1053> **SON OF SPIRIT** | - | |
– Holy man / Looking into darkness / Maybe you'll find / Don't go away / Family / Magic fairy princess / Circle / The other song / Yesterday / It's time now. *(UK-iss.May89 on 'Great Expectations' lp/cd; PIP LP/CD 2)*

Oct 75. (7") <73722> **HOLY MAN. / LOOKING INTO DARKNESS** | - | |

Jul 76. (lp) <(SRM1 1094)> **FARTHER ALONG** | - | |
– Farther along / Atomic boogie / World eat world dog / Stoney night / Pineapple / Colossus / Mega star / Phoebe / Don't look up your door / Once with you / Diamond spirit / Nature's way.

Sep 76. (7") <73837> **FARTHER ALONG. / ATOMIC BOOGIE** | - | |

—— Now just a trio, when MARK re-joined FIREFALL and MATT & JOHN also left.

Apr 77. (lp) (9100 036) <SRM1 1133> **FUTURE GAMES (A MAGICAL KAHUANA DREAM)** | - | |
– CB talk / Stars are love / Kahouna dream / Brued my brain / Bionic unit / So happy now / All along the watchtower / Would you believe / Jack Bond speaks / Star Trek dreaming / Interlude XM / China doll / Hawaiian times / Gorn attack / Interlude 2001 / Detroit City / Freak out frog / The Romulan experiences / Monkey see, monkey do / Mt. Olympus / The journey of Nomad / Ending. *(re-iss. May89 on 'Great Expectations' lp/c/cd; PIP LP/MC/CD 3)*

May 77. (7") (6167 519) **ALL ALONG THE WATCHTOWER. / FURTHER ALONG** | | - |

—— **LARRY KNIGHT** – bass returned to repl. KEENE

	Illegal	Potato
Dec 78. (7") (IL 007) **NATURE'S WAY (live). / STONE FREE (live)** | | - |

Jan 79. (lp) (ILP 001) <PR 2001> **SPIRIT LIVE** (live 11th Mar'78, Rainbow, London)
– Rock and roll planet / Nature's way / Animal zoo / 1984 / Looking down / It's all the same / I got a line on you / These are words / Hollywood dream.

—— disbanded yet again late 1978; RANDY formed own band with **STEVE LAURA** – bass / **JACK WILLOUGHBY** – drums

—— they re-formed to re-record old unissued lost album below. **CALIFORNIA & CASSIDY** (alias KAPTAIN KOPTER & COMMANDER CASSIDY) enlisted **GEORGE VALUCK, JOHN LOCKE, MIKE BUNNELL + KARI NILE** – keys / **JEFF JARVIS, MIKE THORNBURGH + CHUCK SNYDER** – horns / **JOE GREEN** – strings

	Beggars Banquet	Rhino
Apr 81. (lp) (BEGA 23) **JOURNEY TO POTATOLAND** | 40 | |
– We've got a lot to learn / Potatoland theme / Open up your heart / Morning light / Potatoland prelude / Potatoland intro / Turn to the right / Donut house / Fish fry road / Information / My friend. *(re-iss. 1988 += on 'Chord' lp/c/cd; CHORD/+TC/CD 010) (re-iss. cd Jan91 on 'Line'; LICD 90009-2)*

Apr 81. (7") (BEGA 45) **WE'VE GOT A LOT TO LEARN. / FISH FRY ROAD** | | - |

Jun 81. (7") (BEGA 56) **TURN TO THE RIGHT. / POTATOLAND THEME** | | - |

—— Band toured 1981:- **CALIFORNIA, CASSIDY, VALUCK + STEVE LAURA** (aka LIBERTY)

RANDY CALIFORNIA

—— solo including all present SPIRIT members and some past.

Apr 82. (lp) (BEGA 36) **EURO-AMERICAN**
– Easy love / Fearless leader / Five in the morning / Skull and crossbones / Breakout / Hand gun (toy guns) / This is the end / Mon ami / Rude reaction / Calling you / Wild thing. *(free w/7")* – SHATTERED DREAMS. / MAGIC WAND

Apr 82. (7") (BEG 76) **HAND GUNS (TOY GUNS). / THIS IS THE END** | | |

Aug 82. (7") (BEG 82) **ALL ALONG THE WATCHTOWER. / RADIO MAN** | | |
(12"+=) (BEG 82T) – Breakout / Killer weed.

SPIRIT

—— originals re-formed re-recording material from that era.

	Mercury	Mercury
Jan 84. (7") (MER 151) **1984. / ELIJAH** | | |
(12"+=) (MERX 151) – I got a line on you.

Mar 84. (lp) (MERL 35) **THE THIRTEENTH DREAM** (remixes)
– Black satin nights / Mr. Skin / Mechanical world / Pick it up / All over the world / 1984 / Uncle Jack / Natures way / Fresh garbage / I got a line on you. *(c+=)* – Elijah. *(cd-iss. Jul84; 818 514-2)*

Apr 84. (7"/6") (MER 162/+6) **FRESH GARBAGE. / MR. SKIN** | | |

RANDY CALIFORNIA

—— solo with live + studio **MIKE SHEPHERD** – bass / **NEIL MURRAY + ADRIAN LEE + NEAL DOUGHTY** – keyboards / **CURLY SMITH** – drums live: **SCOTT MONAHAN** – keys / **LES WARNER** – drums

	Vertigo	Mercury
May 85. (7") (VER 16) **RUN TO YOUR LOVER. / SECOND CHILD** | | |
(12"+=) (VERX 16) – Shane.

Jun 85. (lp/c) (VERL 19) **RESTLESS**
– Run to your lover / Restless nights / Second child / Jack Rabbit / Shane / One man's Heaven / Murphy's law / Camelot / Battle march of the overlords / Childhood's end.

Jun 85. (7") (VER 21) **JACK RABBIT. / SUPER CHILD** | | |

	Line	not iss.
1986. (lp) **SHATTERED DREAMS** | - | - | German
– Hey Joe (live) / Shattered dreams / All along the watchtower / Don't bother me / Downer / Second child / Man at war / Killer weed / Hand guns (toy guns) / Radio man / Run to your lover.

—— In Apr'89, RANDY appeared on Various Artists live d-lp,c,cd,video 'NIGHT OF THE GUITAR', which was on next label.

RANDY CALIFORNIA'S SPIRIT

—— gigged with various line-ups, until in 1989 settled with **RANDY, ED + SCOTT** plus **MIKE BUNNELL** – bass

	I.R.S.	I.R.S.
Jun 89. (7") (EIRS 117) **HARD LOVE. / THE PRISONER** | | |
(12"+=) (EIRST 117) – Hey Joe.

Aug 89. (lp/c/cd) (EIRS A//CD 1014) **RAPTURE IN THE CHAMBERS** | | |
– Hard love / Love tonight / Thinking of / Rapture in the chambers / Mojo man / Contact / The prisoner / One track mind / Enchanted forest / Human sexuality / Shera, princess of power / End suite.

—— now without BUNNELL, repl. by **MIKE NILE**

	not iss.	Dolphin
1991. (cd) <DRG 22001> **TENT OF MIRACLES** | - | |
– Borderline / Zandu / Love from here / Ship of fools / Burning love / Tent of miracles / Logical answers / Old black magic / Neglected emotion / Imaginary mask / Stuttgart says good-bye / Deep in this land.

	not iss.	C.R.E.W.
1995. (cd) <22003> **LIVE AT LA PALOMA** (live) | - | |
– Life has just begun / Sadana / Mr. Skin / Hey Joe / I got a line on you / Prelude – Nothin' to hide / Like a rolling stone / Going back to Jones / Living in this world / Magic wand / Give a life take a life / La Paloma jam / 1984 / Jamaica jam / Super la Paloma jam / Nature's way.

—— SCOTT repl. by **MATT ANDES** – slide guitar / **STEVE LORIA** – bass / **RACHEL ANDES** (daughter of MATT) – vocals

1996. (cd) **CALIFORNIA BLUES** | - | |
– California blues / Look over yonder / The river / Call on me / Crossroads / Song for Clyde / Pawn shop blues / Sigar mama / Red house / Gimme some lovin' / We believe / One world / Like a dog / oem for John Lennon / Shoes back on (live '67) / Tell everyone (live '67) / Soundtrack for a moth (live '67).

—— On 1st January '97, RANDY was drowned while surfing

– compilations, others, etc. –

—— on 'Epic' unless mentioned otherwise

Aug 73. (d-lp) <31457> **SPIRIT. / CLEAR SPIRIT** | - | |

Oct 73. (7") (EPC 7082) <10701> **MR. SKIN / NATURE'S WAY** | | 92 |

Oct 73. (lp) (EPC 65585) <32271> **THE BEST OF SPIRIT** | | Jul73 |
(re-iss. Sep84; EPC 32516) <US re-iss. May89; >

Dec 91. (d-cd/d-c) Columbia; (471268-2/-4) **TIME CIRCLE (1968-72)**
– (first 4 albums)

Jan 92. (cd/c) Castle; (CCS CD/MC 319) **THE COLLECTION** | | |

Feb 92. (cd) Outline; (OLCD 991133) **CHRONICLES 1967-1982** | - | - |

Mar 94. (cd) Line; (LICD 9000920) **ADVENTURES OF KAPTAIN KOPTER & COMMANDER CASSIDY IN POTATOLAND** | | |

SPIRITUALIZED

Formed: Rugby, England ... 1990, initially as a side project for JASON 'SPACEMAN' PIERCE, who was soon to split from SONIC BOOM and SPACEMEN 3. He retained JON MATTOCK and WILLIE B. CARRUTHERS from the latter outfit and set about getting to grips with a new 90's psychedelia. Their first release was a version of The Troggs' 'ANYWAY THAT YOU WANT ME', which squeezed into the UK Top 75. The debut album, 'LAZER GUIDED MELODIES', was awash with VELVET-tones, recycled, and heavily distorted. A three year hiatus did not deter the British buying public, who also assured the follow-up, 'PURE PHASE', of a Top 30 placing in 1995. It was blessed with a more soulful vibe, while the majestic, lo-fi rhythm lifted it from an ambient crypt. In June '97, they returned to the fold (albeit a month after schedule) with their third album, 'LADIES AND GENTLEMEN WE ARE FLOATING IN SPACE B P'. The delay was due to ELVIS PRESLEY's team of whatnots objecting to the sample of 'Can't Help Falling In Love'. Nevertheless, the album, complete with bizarre prescription pill cd packaging, duly floated into the UK Top 5. Described by one reviewer as 'album of the decade', the record met with almost universal praise while its blissful melange of retro-psych, ambient noise and gospel was a heady tonic for the Dad-rock by numbers peddled by most 'indie' bands. • **Songwriters:** PIERCE, except more covers; BORN NEVER ASKED (Laurie Anderson) / WALKING WITH JESUS (Spacemen 3) / OH HAPPY DAY (Edwin Hawkins Singers). • **Trivia:** In the early 90's, they headlined at the ICA Rock Week sponsored by Irn Bru.

Album rating: LAZER GUIDED MELODIES (*8) / PURE PHASE (*8) / LADIES AND GENTLEMEN WE ARE FLOATING IN SPACE B P (*10) / ROYAL ALBERT HALL OCTOBER 10 1997 (*8)

JASON PIERCE – guitar / **WILLIE B. CARRUTHERS** – bass / **JON MATTOCK** – drums plus girlfriend **KATE RADLEY** – organ, keyboards, vocals / **MARK REFOY** – guitar, dulcimer

	Dedicated	R.C.A.
Jun 90. (7") (ZB 43783) **ANYWAY THAT YOU WANT ME. / STEP INTO THE BREEZE** | 75 | - |
(12"+=/cd-s+=) (ZT/ZD 43784) – ('B'-part 2).
(12") (ZT 43780) – ('A'remix) / ('B'-parts 2-3) / ('A'demo).

Jun 91. (7") (FRIGHT 053) **FEEL SO SAD. / I WANT YOU** | | - |
(above is a gig freebie given away by 'Fierce' re-iss. Apr97)

Aug 91. (7") (SPIRIT 002) **RUN. / I WANT YOU** | 59 | - |
(12"+=/cd-s+=) (SPIRIT 002 T/CD) – Luminescent (stay with me) / Effervescent.

Nov 91. (7") (SPIRIT 003) **WHY DON'T YOU SMILE NOW. / SWAY** | | - |
(12"+=/cd-s+=) (SPIRIT 003 T/CD) – ('A'extended).

Apr 92. (cd/c/2x12"lp) (DED CD/MC/LP 004) <66035-2/-4> **LAZER GUIDED MELODIES** | 27 | |
– You know it's true / If I were with her now / I want you / Run / Smiles / Step into the breeze / Symphony space / Take your time / Shine a light / Angel sigh / Sway / 200 bars. *(free-7" at 'Chain With No Name' shops)* – ANY WAY THAT YOU WANT ME / WHY DON'T YOU SMILE NOW *(re-iss. Jul97; same)*

Jul 92. (7"red) *(SPIRIT 005)* **MEDICATION. / SMILES (Peel session)** `55` `-`
(12"+=) *(SPIRIT 005T)* – Feel so sad (Peel session) / Angel sigh.
(cd-s++=) *(SPIRIT 005CD)* – Space (instrumental).
Jun 93. (mail-order cd) *(SPIRIT 006CD)* **F***ED UP INSIDE** `-` `-`
Oct 93. (7") *(SPIRIT 007)* **GOOD TIMES / LAY BACK IN THE SUN** `49` `-`
(12"ep+=/cd-ep+=) *(SPIRIT 008 T/CD)* – Electric Mainline 1 + 2.
—— now without REFOY, who formed SLIPSTREAM. They issued two albums for 'Che' in 1995; 'SLIPSTREAM' & 'SIDE EFFECTS'.

SPIRITUALIZED ELECTRIC MAINLINE

—— **SPACEMAN (JASON) + KATE RADLEY** – keyboards, vox / **SEAN COOK** – bass, harmonica / plus **MARK REFOY** – guitar (guest only) / **JON MATTOCK** – percussion / **LEON HUNT** – banjo / **STEWART GORDON** – violin / **THE BALANESCU QUARTET** – strings / + others on wind instruments

                                            Dedicated   Arista

Jan 95. (cd-ep) *(SPIRIT 009CD)* **LET IT FLOW / DON'T GO / STAY WITH ME / DON'T GO / STAY WITH ME (THE INDIVIDUAL)** `30` `-`
(cd-ep) *(SPIRIT 009CD2)* – ('A'side) / Take good care of it / Things will never be the same. / Clear rush.
(cd-ep) *(SPIRIT 009CD3)* – ('A'side) / Medication / Take your time / Smile.
(3xbox-cd-ep/10"ep) *(SPIRIT 009BOX/T)* – (all above).
Feb 95. (cd/c/d-lp) *(DED CD/MC/LP 017) <26035>* **PURE PHASE** `20` Mar95
– Medication / The slide song / Electric phase / All of my tears / These blues / Let it flow / Take good care of it / Born never asked / Electric mainline / Lay back in the sun / Good times / Pure phase / Spread your wings / Feel like goin' home. *(re-iss. Jul97; same)*
Nov 95. (cd-ep) *(74321 31178-2)* **LAY BACK IN THE SUN / THE SLIDE SONG / SPREAD YOUR WINGS / LAY BACK IN THE SUN** `☐` `☐`

SPIRITUALIZED

—— **DAMON REECE** – percussion + guests, repl. MATTOCK, HUNT + GORDON
Jun 97. (cd/c/lp) *(DED CD/MC/LP 034) <18974>* **LADIES AND GENTLEMEN WE ARE FLOATING IN SPACE** `4` `-`
– Ladies and gentlemen we are floating in space / Come together / I think I'm in love / All of my thoughts / Stay with me / Electricity / Home of the brave / The individual / Broken heart / No god only religion / Cool waves / Cop shoot cop . . . *(re-iss. Jan98 as 12xcd-s box; DEDCD 034A)*
Jul 97. (7") *(SPIRIT 012)* **ELECTRICITY. / COOL WAVES (instrumental)** `32` `-`
(cd-s+=) *(SPIRIT 012CD1)* – Take your time (live) / All of my tears (live).
(cd-s) *(SPIRIT 012CD2)* – ('A'album version) / Cop shoot cop (live) / Shine a light (live) / Electric mainline (live).
Feb 98. (7") *(SPIRIT 014)* **I THINK I'M IN LOVE. / ('A'version)** `27` `-`
(12"+=/cd-s+=) *(SPIRIT 014 T/CD)* – ('A'-Chemical Brothers vocal & instrumental mixes).
May 98. (7") *(SPIRIT 015) <13508>* **THE ABBEY ROAD EP** `39` `☐`
– Come together / Broken heart.
(cd-s+=) *(SPIRIT 015CD)* – Broken heart (instrumental).
(12"+=) *(SPIRIT 015T)* – ('A'-Richard Fearless remix) / ('A'-Two Lone Swordsmen remix).
—— **J(ASON) SPACEMAN, DAMON REECE, SEAN COOK, MICHAEL MOONEY, THIGHPAULSANDRA + RAYMOND (MOONSHAKE) DICKATY**
Oct 98. (d-cd/d-lp) *(74321 62285-2/1) <19032>* **ROYAL ALBERT HALL OCTOBER 10 1997 (live)** `38` Nov98
– Intro / Shine a light / Electric mainline / Electricity / Home of the brave / The individual / Medication / Walking with Jesus / Take your time / No God only religion / Broken heart / Come together / I think I'm in love / Cop shoot cop / Oh happy day.
—— COOK, REECE + MOONEY were sacked in June '99 and subsequently formed their own "real" band, LUPINE HOWL, who signed to 'Vinyl Hiss' for releases in early 2000

SPLIT ENZ (see under ⇒ CROWDED HOUSE)

SPOOKY TOOTH

(dig out; 4th edition or Great Psychedelic . . .)

Dusty SPRINGFIELD

Born: MARY O'BRIEN, 16 Apr '39, Hampstead, London, England. Taking her early inspiration from the likes of PEGGY LEE, O'BRIEN'S intitial music industry experience came as a member of the LANA SISTERS, an all-female trio who released a handful of singles for 'Fontana'. More successful were The SPRINGFIELDS, a PETER, PAUL & MARY-style folk trio which comprised DUSTY, her brother TOM and friend TIM FIELD. A string of UK hits (inlcuding 'BREAKAWAY', 'BAMBINO', 'ISLAND OF DREAMS' and 'SAY I WON'T BE THERE') established them as one of the most popular British acts of the era and in 1962 the trio even cracked the US Top 20 with 'SILVER THREADS AND GOLDEN NEEDLES'. A subsequent trip to the States introduced DUSTY to the burgeoning girl group craze, and heavily influenced by both Motown and the 'teen symphonies' of PHIL SPECTOR, she embarked on a solo career in 1963. Arranger Ivor Raymonde helped her realise her ambitions and later that year, she hit the UK Top 10 (US Top 20) courtesy of 'I ONLY WANT TO BE WITH YOU', a dizzying pop-soul classic in the trademark SPECTOR mould. A series of transatlantic hits ensued including 'STAY AWHILE', 'I JUST DON'T KNOW WHAT TO DO WITH MYSELF', 'LOSING YOU', 'LITTLE BY LITTLE' and 'WISHIN' AND HOPIN', the last-named being one of her most successful US singles (Top 10). With an earthier, huskier style than most of the girl groups, SPRINGFIELD was equally adept at carrying off rockier material and the 'British Invasion' led by The BEATLES only served to increase her popularity in the States. While bringing her trademark emotional punch to material by the cream of US writers such as Bacharach & David, Goffin & King, etc., SPRINGFIELD topped the UK chart (US Top5) in 1966 with the epic 'YOU DON'T HAVE TO SAY YOU LOVE ME'. By the late 60's, however, the rise of the "serious" rock artist meant it wasn't enough to simply churn out superior interpretations of other people's songs. Nevertheless, SPRINGFIELD gave it her best – many say greatest – shot with 1969's 'DUSTY IN MEMPHIS' album. Newly signed to 'Atlantic' and ensconced in a Deep South studio with country-soul guru, Jerry Wexler (alongside Tom Dowd and Arif Mardin), the singer reeled off a thrilling set of sultry, smoky soul-pop that invested the work of the aforementioned Bacharach/David, Goffin/King, along with Randy Newman and Mann-Weil (amongst others) with a rare emotional resonance. While supplying SPRINGFIELD with her last major hit (US/UK Top 10) in the classic 'SON OF A PREACHER MAN' (later DUSTY'd down for a new generation courtesy of Quentin Tarantino's 'Pulp Fiction' soundtrack) and the reverence of rock crtics, the album itself was a commercial failure destined for cult acclaim. Subsequently teaming up with the soon-to-be famous Philly writers, Gamble & Huff, she recorded another respectable set of blue-eyed soul in 1970's 'A BRAND NEW ME'. No major hits were forthcoming, however, SPRINGFIELD relocating to L.A. where she recorded one more album, 'CAMEO' (1973) before withdrawing from view as she tackled her spiralling drug dependency. Save for some backing vocals on soulstress ANNE MURRAY's 'Together' album, DUSTY was out of the picture until the late 70's when she made a failed comeback attempt with 'BEGINS AGAIN' (1978) and 'LIVING WITHOUT YOUR LOVE' (1979). Although she did score a minor UK hit with one-off single, 'BABY BLUE', a US-only comeback album, 'WHITE HEAT' (1982), fell flat. It would take the patronage of The PET SHOP BOYS to finally see DUSTY back in the spotlight, the camp synth-pop duo employing her services on their 1987 international smash, 'WHAT HAVE I DONE TO DESERVE THIS'. Early in '89, she had her first Top 20 hit in her own right since the late 60's with 'NOTHING HAS BEEN PROVED', a cut taken from the controversial UK movie, 'Scandal'. The accumulated exposure helped ensure a UK Top 20 placing for her long awaited 'REPUTATION' (1990) album, upon which NEIL TENNANT and CHRIS LOWE returned the favour by producing a couple of tracks. Going way back to her roots, the singer returned to Nashville for 1995's 'A VERY FINE LOVE'. Tragedy struck, however, as she was diagnosed with breast cancer during the album's recording. Sadly, after years of battling, she succumbed to the disease on 2 March, 1999, aged 59. One of the UK's most gifted and charismatic female vocalists, SPRINGFIELD was both loved and respected by fans, musicians and critics across the pop/rock/soul spectrum. It came as little surprise then, when she was inducted into the Rock And Roll Hall Of Fame shortly after her death.

Album rating: A GIRL CALLED DUSTY (*7) / EVERYTHING'S COMING UP DUSTY (*6) / WHERE AM I GOING (*7) / DUSTY DEFINITELY (*6) / DUSTY IN MEMPHIS (*9) / A BRAND NEW ME ((*6) / SEE ALL HER FACES (*5) / CAMEO (*4) / IT BEGINS AGAIN (*5) / LIVING WITHOUT YOUR LOVE (*5) / WHITE HEAT (*4) / REPUTATION (*6) / A VERY FINE LOVE (*4) / GOIN' BACK – THE VERY BEST OF DUSTY SPRINGFIELD compilation (*8)

SPRINGFIELDS

DUSTY SPRINGFIELD – vocals (ex-LANA SISTERS) / **TOM SPRINGFIELD** – vocals / **TIM FIELD** – vocals

		Philips	Philips
May 61. (7") *(PB 1145)* **DEAR JOHN. / I DONE WHAT THEY TOLD ME TO**			
Aug 61. (7") *(PB 1168)* **BREAKAWAY. / GOOD NEWS**		`31`	`-`
Nov 61. (7") *(PB 1178)* **BAMBINO. / STAR OF HOPE**		`16`	`-`
Dec 61. (7"ep) *(SBBE 9068)* **THE SPRINGFIELDS EP**			`-`
– Dear John / I done what they told me to / Breakaway / Good news.			
Jan 62. (7") *(PB 1220)* **GOODNIGHT IRENE. / FARAWAY PLACES**			`-`
Apr 62. (7") *(PB 1241) <40038>* **SILVER THREADS AND GOLDEN NEEDLES. / AUNT RHODY**			`20` Jul62
Apr 62. (lp) *(SBBE 6068) <052>* **KINDA FOLKSY** <US-title 'SILVER THREADS AND GOLDEN NEEDLES'>			`91` Oct62
– Mambo wimoweh *[not US]* / The black hills of Dakota / Row, row, row *[not US]* / The green leaves of summer / Silver dollar / Allentown jail / Lonesome traveller / Dear hearts and gentle people / They took John away *[not US]* / Eso es al amor *[not US]* / Two brothers / Tzena, tzena, tzena *[not US]*. <US+=> – Gotta travel on / Aunt Rhody.			
May 62. (7"ep) *(433622 BE)* **KINDA FOLKSY**		`☐`	`-`
May 62. (7"ep) *(433623 BE)* **KINDA FOLKSY NO.2**		`☐`	`-`
May 62. (7"ep) *(433624 BE)* **KINDA FOLKSY NO.3**		`☐`	`-`
Aug 62. (7") *(326536 BF)* **SWAHILI PAPA. / GOTTA TRAVEL ON**		`☐`	`-`
Oct 62. (7") *<40072>* **DEAR HEARTS AND GENTLE PEOPLE. / GOTTA TRAVEL ON**		`-`	`95`
Nov 62. (7") *(326557 BF)* **ISLAND OF DREAMS. / THE JOHNSTON BOYS**		`5`	`-`
Feb 63. (7") *<40092>* **LITTLE BY LITTLE. / WAF-WOOF**		`-`	`-`
Mar 63. (7") *(326577 BF)* **SAY I WON'T BE THERE. / LITTLE BOAT**		`5`	`-`
Apr 63. (7"ep) *(BBE 12538)* **HIT SOUNDS FROM THE SPRINGFIELDS**		`☐`	`-`
Apr 63. (7") *<40099>* **ISLAND OF DREAMS. / FOGGY MOUNTAIN TOP**		`-`	`-`
May 63. (lp) *(632304 BL)* **FOLK SONGS FROM THE HILLS**		`-`	`-`
– Settle down / There's a big wheel / Greenback dollar / Midnight special / Wabash cannonball / Alone with you / Cottonfields / Foggy mountain top / Little by little / Maggie / Darling Allalee / Mountain boy.			
Jul 63. (7") *(BF 1263)* **COME ON HOME. / PIT-A-PAT**		`31`	`-`
Nov 63. (7") *<40121>* **LITTLE BOAT. / SAY I WON'T BE THERE**		`-`	`-`

Jan 64.   (7") *(BF 1306)* **IF I WAS DOWN AND OUT. / MARACAMBA** ☐ –

——   The SPRINGFIELDS split when DUSTY went solo (TOM also went solo)

1964.   (d-lp) *(BET 606)* **THE SPRINGFIELDS STORY** ☐ –

DUSTY SPRINGFIELD

		Philips	Philips
Nov 63.	(7") *(BF 1292)* <40162> **I ONLY WANT TO BE WITH YOU. / ONCE UPON A TIME**	4	12 Jan64
Feb 64.	(7") *(BF 1313)* <40180> **STAY AWHILE. / SOMETHING SPECIAL**	13	38 Mar64
Apr 64.	(lp; stereo/mono) *(S+/BL 7594)* <PHS600 133> **A GIRL CALLED DUSTY** <US-title 'STAY WHILE / I ONLY WANT TO BE WITH YOU'>	6	62 Jun64

– Mama said / You don't own me / Do re mi / When the lovelight starts shining thru his eyes / My colouring book / Mockingbird / 24 hours from Tulsa / Nothing / Anyone who had a heart / Will you love me tomorrow / Wishin' and hopin' / Don't you know. *(cd re-iss. 1988 on 'Beat Goes On'; BGO 46) (re-iss. May89 cd/c; 842699-2/-4) (cd re-mast.Feb97 on 'Mercury'; 534520-2)*

Jun 64.	(7") <40207> **WISHIN' AND HOPIN'. / DO RE MI (FORGET ABOUT THE DO AND THINK ABOUT ME)**	–	6
Jun 64.	(7") *(BF 1348)* **I JUST DON'T KNOW WHAT TO DO WITH MYSELF. / MY COLOURING BOOK**	3	–
Sep 64.	(7") *(BF 1369)* **ALL CRIED OUT. / I WISH I'D NEVER LOVED YOU**	–	41
Oct 64.	(7") *(BF 1369)* **LOSING YOU. / SUMMER IS OVER**	5	–
Nov 64.	(7") *(BF 1382)* **OH HOLY CHILD. / Springfields: JINGLE BELLS**		
Nov 64.	(lp) <PHS600 156> **DUSTY**	–	
Jan 65.	(7") <40265> **GUESS WHO? / LIVE IT UP**		
Feb 65.	(7") *(BF 1396)* **YOUR HURTIN' KINDA LOVE. / DON'T SAY IT BABY**	37	–
Mar 65.	(7") <40270> **LOSING YOU. / HERE SHE COMES**	–	91
Jun 65.	(7") *(BF 1418)* <40303> **IN THE MIDDLE OF NOWHERE. / BABY, DON'T YOU KNOW**	8	Jul65
Sep 65.	(7") *(BF 1430)* **SOME OF YOUR LOVIN'. / I'LL LOVE YOU FOR A WHILE**	8	–
Oct 65.	(lp; stereo/mono) *(S+/RBL 1002)* <PHS600 210> **EVERYTHING'S COMING UP DUSTY** <US-title 'YOU DON'T HAVE TO SAY YOU LOVE ME'>		77 Jun66

– Won't be long / Oh no! not my baby / Long after tonight is all over / Who can I turn to? (when nobody needs me) / Doodlin' *[UK only]* / If it don't work out / That's how heartaches are made *[UK only]* / It was easier to hurt him / I've been wrong before / I can't hear you / I had a talk with my man / Packin' up *[UK only]*. <US+=> – You don't have to say you love me. *(re-iss. Sep89 on 'Beat Goes On' lp/c/cd; BGO LP/MC/CD 74) (cd re-mast.Mar98 on 'Mercury'; 536852-2)*

Nov 65.	(7") <40319> **I JUST DON'T KNOW WHAT TO DO WITH MYSELF. / SOME OF YOUR LOVIN'**	–	
Jan 66.	(7") *(BF 1466)* **LITTLE BY LITTLE. / IF IT HADN'T BEEN FOR YOU**	17	–
Mar 66.	(7") *(BF 1482)* **YOU DON'T HAVE TO SAY YOU LOVE ME. / EVERY OUNCE**	1	–
May 66.	(7") *(40371)* **YOU DON'T HAVE TO SAY YOU LOVE ME. / LITTLE BY LITTLE**	–	4
Jul 66.	(7") *(BF 1502)* **GOIN' BACK. / I'M GONNA LEAVE YOU**	10	–
Sep 66.	(7") *(BF 1510)* **ALL I SEE IS YOU. / GO AHEAD ON**	9	–
Sep 66.	(7") <40396> **ALL I SEE IS YOU. / I'M GONNA LEAVE YOU**	–	20
Oct 66.	(lp; stereo/mono) *(S+/BL 7737)* <PHS600 220> **GOLDEN HITS** (compilation)	2	Dec66

– All I see is you / Wishin' and hopin' / In the middle of nowhere / My colouring book / Goin' back / All cried out / You don't have to say you love me / I only want to be with you / Little by little / Losing you / Stay awhile / I just don't know what to do with myself.

Feb 67.	(7") *(BF 1553)* <40439> **I'LL TRY ANYTHING. / THE CORRUPT ONES**	13	40 Mar67
May 67.	(7") *(BF 1577)* <40465> **GIVE ME TIME. / THE LOOK OF LOVE**	24	76 / 22
Sep 67.	(7") *(BF 1608)* <40498> **WHAT'S IT GONNA BE. / SMALL TOWN GIRL**		49 Nov67
Nov 67.	(lp; stereo/mono) *(S+/BL 7820)* **WHERE AM I GOING**	40	

– Bring him back / Don't let me lose this dream / I can't wait until I see my baby's face / Take me for a little while / Chained to a memory / Sunny / They long to be close to you / Welcome home / Come back to me / If you go away / Broken blossoms / Where am I going. *(cd/c-iss.May90; 846050-2/-4) (cd re-mast.Mar98; 536962-2)*

Dec 67.   (lp) <PHS600 256> **THE LOOK OF LOVE**

– What's it gonna be / The look of love / Give me time / They long to be close to you / If you go away / Sunny / Come back to me / Welcome home / Small town girl / Take me for a little while / Chained to a memory.

Apr 68.	(7") <40547> **SWEET RIDE. / NO STRANGER AM I**	–	
Jun 68.	(7") *(BF 1682)* **I CLOSE MY EYES AND COUNT TO TEN. / NO STRANGER AM I**	4	
Jul 68.	(7") <40553> **I CLOSE MY EYES AND COUNT TO TEN. / LA BAMBA**	–	
Sep 68.	(7") *(BF 1706)* **I WILL COME TO YOU. / THE COLOUR OF YOUR EYES**	–	
Nov 68.	(lp; stereo/mono) *(S+/BL 7864)* **DUSTY . . . DEFINITELY**	30	–

– Ain't no sun since you've been gone / Take another little piece of my heart / Another night / Mr. Dream merchant / I can't give back the love I feel for you / Love power / This girl's in love with you / I only wanna laugh / Who (will take my place) / I think it's gonna rain today / Morning / Second time around. *(re-iss. May90 cd/c; 846049-2/-4)*

		Philips	Atlantic
Nov 68.	(7") *(BF 1730)* <2580> **SON OF A PREACHER MAN. / JUST A LITTLE LOVIN' (EARLY IN THE MORNING)**	9	10
Feb 69.	(7") <2606> **DON'T FORGET ABOUT ME. / BREAKFAST IN BED**	–	64 / 91

| Apr 69. | (7") <2623> **THE WINDMILLS OF YOUR MIND. / I DON'T WANT TO HEAR IT ANYMORE** | – | 31 |
| Apr 69. | (lp) *(SBL 7889)* <SD 8214> **DUSTY IN MEMPHIS** | | 99 Mar69 |

– Just a little lovin' / So much love / Son of a preacher man / I don't want to hear it anymore / Don't forget about me / Breakfast in bed / Just one smile / The windmills of your mind / In the land of make believe / No easy way down / I can't make it alone. *(re-iss. Sep80 on 'Mercury' lp/c+=; PRICE/PRIMC 83) (cd. Jun89; 836840-2) (cd re-iss. Jul90; 846252-2) (cd re-iss. Sep95 on 'Mercury' +=; 528687-2)*

Jul 69.	(7") <2647> **WILLIE & LAURA MAE JONES. / THAT OLD SWEET ROLL (HI-DE-HO)**	–	78
Sep 69.	(7") <2673> **IN THE LAND OF MAKE BELIEVE. / SO MUCH LOVE**	–	
Sep 69.	(7") *(BF 1811)* **AM I THE SAME GIRL. / EARTHBOUND GYPSY**	43	
Nov 69.	(7") *(BF 1826)* <2685> **A BRAND NEW ME. / BAD CASE OF THE BLUES**		24

——   In Feb'70, she and brother TOM released 'MORNING PLEASE DON'T COME'

| Feb 70. | (7") <2705> **SILLY, SILLY, FOOL. / JOE** | – | 76 |
| Apr 70. | (lp) *(SBL 7927)* <SD 8249> **FROM DUSTY . . . WITH LOVE** <US-title 'A BRAND NEW ME'> | 35 | Feb70 |

– Lost / Bad case of the blues / Never love again / Let me in your way / Let's get together soon / A brand new me / Silly, silly, fool / The star of my show / Let's talk it over.

May 70.	(7") <2729> **LET ME IN YOUR WAY. / I WANNA BE A FREE GIRL**	–	
Jul 70.	(7") <2739> **NEVER LOVE AGAIN. / LOST**	–	
Sep 70.	(7") *(6006 045)* **HOW CAN I BE SURE. / SPOOKY**	36	–
Nov 70.	(7") <2771> **WHAT GOOD IS I LOVE YOU. / WHAT DO YOU DO WHEN LOVE DIES**	–	
Oct 71.	(7") <2825> **HAUNTED. / NOTHING IS FOREVER**	–	
Dec 71.	(7") <2841> **SOMEONE WHO CARED. / I BELIEVE IN YOU**	–	

		Philips	Dunhill
May 72.	(7") *(6006 214)* **YESTERDAY WHEN I WAS YOUNG. / I START COUNTING**		
Nov 72.	(lp) *(6308 117)* **SEE ALL HER FACES**		

– Mixed up girl / Crumbs off the table / Let me down easy / Comfort dream / Girls can't do what the guys do / I start counting / Yesterday when I was young / Girls it ain't easy / What good is I love you / Willie & Laura Mae Jones / Someone who cares / Nothing is forever / See all her faces / That old sweet roll.

| Apr 73. | (7") *(6006 295)* **WHO GETS YOUR LOVE. / OF ALL THE THINGS** | | Feb73 |
| Apr 73. | (lp) *(6308 152)* **CAMEO** | | |

– Who gets your love / Breakin' up a happy home / Easy evil / Mama's little girl / The other side of life / Coming and going / I just wanna be there / Who could be loving other than me / Tupelo honey / Of all the things / Learn to say goodbye.

Jun 73.	(7") <4357> **LEARN TO SAY GOODBYE. / MAMA'S LITTLE GIRL**	–	–
Aug 73.	(7") *(6006 325)* **LEARN TO SAY GOODBYE. / EASY EVIL**	–	–
Mar 74.	(7") *(6006 350)* **WHAT'S IT GONNA BE. / BRING HIM BACK**	–	–

		Mercury	U.A.
Feb 78.	(lp)(c) *(9109 607)(7109 323)* **IT BEGINS AGAIN**	41	

– Turn me around / Checkmate / I'd rather leave while I'm in love / A love like yours (don't come knocking every day) / Love me by name / Sandra / I found love with you / Hollywood movie girls / That's the kind of love I've got for you.

Mar 78.	(7") *(DUSTY 1)* **A LOVE LIKE YOURS (DON'T COME KNOCKING EVERY DAY). / HOLLYWOOD MOVIE GIRLS**		
Mar 78.	(7") <XW 1205> **SANDRA. / CHECKMATE**		
Jun 78.	(7") *(DUSTY 2)* **THAT'S THE KIND OF LOVE I'VE GOT FOR YOU. / SANDRA**		
Jul 78.	(7") <XW 1225> **GIVE ME THE NIGHT. / CHECKMATE**		
Mar 79.	(lp)(c) *(9109 617)(7231 432)* **LIVING WITHOUT YOUR LOVE**		

– You've really got a hold on me / You can do it / Be somebody / Closet man / Living without your love / Save me, save me / Get yourself to love / I just fall in love again / Dream on / I'm coming home again.

Apr 79.	(7") *(DUSTY 3)* **I'M COMING HOME AGAIN. / SAVE ME SAVE ME**		–
Jul 79.	(7") <XW 1255> **LIVING WITHOUT YOUR LOVE. / GET YOURSELF TO LOVE**	–	
Sep 79.	(7"/disc-12") *(DUSTY 4/+12)* **BABY BLUE. / GET YOURSELF TO LOVE**	61	–
Jan 80.	(7") *(DUSTY 5)* **YOUR LOVE STILL BRINGS ME TO MY KNEES. / I'M YOUR CHILD**	–	
Jan 80.	(7") <XW 1006> **LET ME LOVE YOU ONCE BEFORE YOU GO. / I'M YOUR CHILD**	–	

		not iss.	20th Century
1981.	(7") <2457> **IT GOES LIKE IT GOES. / I WISH THAT LOVE WOULD LAST** (above from the movie, 'Norma Rae')		–

		not iss.	Casablanca
1982.	(7") <2356> **DONNEZ MOI (GIVE IT TO ME). / I AM CURIOUS**		–
1982.	(lp) <NBLP 7271> **WHITE HEAT**		–

– Donnez moi (give it to me) / I don't think we could ever be friends / Blind sheep / Don't call it love / Time and time again / I am curious / Sooner or later / Losing you / Gotta get used to you / Soft core.

——   In Mar'84, she duetted with SPENCER DAVIS on the single 'PRIVATE NUMBER' for 'Allegiance'; (ALES 3)

		Hippodrome	not iss.
Aug 85.	(7") *(HIPPO 103)* **SOMETIMES LIKE BUTTERFLIES. / I WANNA CONTROL YOU** (12"+=) *(12HIPPO 103)* – ('A'extended).		–

——   In Aug'87, DUSTY was nearly back at the top when she duetted with The PET SHOP BOYS on their 'WHAT HAVE I DONE TO DESERVE THIS'.

—— On a slightly lesser note, she augmented RICHARD CARPENTER on his single, 'SOMETHING IN YOUR EYES'.

		Parlophone	Enigma
Feb 89.	(7"/7"g-f) *(R/RG 6207)* <*75042*> **NOTHING HAS BEEN PROVED.** / (instrumental)	16	☐
	(12"+=/cd-s+=) *(12R/CDR 6207)* – ('A'dance mix).		
Nov 89.	(c-s/7") *(TC+/R 6234)* **IN PRIVATE.** / (instrumental)	14	-
	(cd-s+=) *(CDR 6234)* – ('A'extended).		
	(12") *(12R 6234)* – ('A'remix) / (~'A'dub) / ('A'bonus beats).		
May 90.	(7") *(R 6253)* **REPUTATION. / REP U DUB 1**	38	-
	('A'mix-12"+=) *(12R 6253)* – Rep U dub 2.		
Jun 90.	(cd/c/lp) *(CD/TC+/PCSD 111)* **REPUTATION**	18	☐
	– Reputation / Send it to me / Arrested by you / Time waits for no one / I was born this way / In private / Daydreaming / Nothing has been proved / I want to stay here / Occupy your mind. *(cd re-iss. Apr95 on 'Fame'; CDFA 3320)*		
Sep 90.	(c-s/7") *(TC+/R 6266)* **ARRESTED BY YOU.** / (instrumental)	70	-
	(ext-12"+=) *(12R 6266)* – Born this way (mix).		
	(ext-cd-s++=) *(CDR 6266)* – Getting it right.		

		Columbia	Columbia
Oct 93.	(7"; by CILLA BLACK & DUSTY SPRINGFIELD) *(659856-7)* **HEART AND SOUL.** / (other track by CILLA BLACK)	75	-
	(cd-s+=) *(659856-2)* – (a capella mix & instrumental).		
Jun 95.	(c-s; by DUSTY SPRINGFIELD & DARYL HALL) *(662059-4)* **WHEREVER WOULD I BE / ALL I HAVE TO OFFER YOU IS LOVE**	44	☐
	(cd-s+=) *(662059-2)* – Reputation (alternative mix) / ('A'solo).		
	(cd-s) *(662059-5)* – ('A'side) / Daydreaming / Arrested by you / ('A'mix).		
Jun 95.	(cd/c/lp) *(478508-2/-4/-1)* **A VERY FINE LOVE**	43	-
	– Roll away / A very fine love / Wherever would I be / Go easy on me / You are the storm / I can't help the way I don't feel / All I have to offer you is love / Lovin' proof / Old habits die hard / Where is A.		
Oct 95.	(c-s) *(662368-4)* **ROLL AWAY / OLD HABITS DIE HARD**	68	-
	(cd-s+=) *(662368-2)* – Your love still brings me to my knees / Born this way.		
	(cd-s+=) *(662368-5)* – Baby blue / What's it gonna be.		

—— sadly, on the 2nd March, 1999, DUSTY died of cancer (see above)

– compilations, etc. –

Mar 64.	(7"ep) *Philips; (BE 12560)* **I ONLY WANT TO BE WITH YOU**	☐	-
Sep 64.	(7"ep) *Philips; (BE 12564)* **DUSTY**	☐	-
Apr 65.	(7"ep) *Philips; (BE 12572)* **DUSTY IN NEW YORK**	☐	-
Jul 65.	(7"ep) *Philips; (BE 12579)* **MADEMOISELLE DUSTY**	☐	-
Aug 68.	(7"ep) *Philips; (BE 12605)* **IF YOU GO AWAY**	☐	-
Jun 76.	(lp/c) *Contour; (CN/+4 2016)* **YOU DON'T HAVE TO SAY YOU LOVE ME**	☐	-
Oct 79.	(lp)(c) *Mercury; (9109 629)(7231 442)* **GREATEST HITS** *(re-iss. Oct83 lp/c; PRICE/PRIMC 45)*	☐	-
Oct 81.	(lp/c) *K-Tel; (NE1/CE2 139)* **THE VERY BEST OF . . .**	☐	-
Jul 82.	(7") *Old Gold; (OG 9242)* **I ONLY WANT TO BE WITH YOU.** /		-
Feb 84.	(lp/c) *Spotlight; (SPR/SPC 8539)* **SON OF A PREACHER MAN**	☐	-
Jul 89.	(cd) *Pickwick; (PWK 120)* **LOVE SONGS**	☐	-
Jan 88.	(lp/c)(cd) *Philips; (DUST V/C 1)(834128-2)* **DUSTY – THE SILVER COLLECTION**	☐	-
1988.	(d-c) *Ditto; (DTO 10275)* **DUSTY'S SOUNDS OF THE 70's**	☐	-
May 90.	(lp/c)(cd) *Pickwick; (CN/+4 2107)(PWKS 580)* **SONGBOOK**	☐	-
May 93.	(cd/c) *Spectrum; (550005-2/-4)* **BLUE FOR YOU**	☐	-
May 94.	(cd/c) *Philips; (848789-2/-4)* **GOIN' BACK – THE VERY BEST OF DUSTY SPRINGFIELD**	5	
Aug 94.	(4xcd-box) *Philips; (522254-2)* **THE LEGEND OF DUSTY SPRINGFIELD**	☐	
Mar 96.	(cd/c) *Spectrum; (552093-2/-4)* **AM I THE SAME GIRL**	☐	-
Apr 96.	(d-cd) *Mercury; (528818-2)* **SOMETHING SPECIAL**	☐	-
Sep 97.	(cd) *EMI Gold; (CDGOLD 1077)* **REPUTATION AND RARITIES** <*re-iss. Feb98 on 'Disky' <(DC 88612-2)>*	☐	-
Oct 97.	(cd) *Spectrum; (537549-2)* **HITS COLLECTION**	☐	-
Feb 98.	(cd) *Mercury; (552863-2)* **THE SONGBOOKS**	☐	-
Apr 99.	(cd-s) *Classic; (CR 50051-2)* **THE LOOK OF LOVE**	☐	-

Bruce SPRINGSTEEN

Born: 23 Sep'49, Freehold, New Jersey, USA. While still attending college, SPRINGSTEEN formed the short-lived STEEL MILL, three members ('LITTLE STEVEN' VAN ZANDT, DANNY FEDERICI and VINI LOPEZ) subsequently becoming part of his 10-piece back-up group. In May '72, the singer signed to 'Columbia' with the help of legendary A&R man, John Hammond, who had previously signed BOB DYLAN to the same label a decade earlier. The connection didn't stop there, SPRINGSTEEN duly heralded as the latest successor to ZIMMERMAN's singer/songwriter mantle upon the release of his debut album, 'GREETINGS FROM ASBURY PARK, N.J.' Released in early '73, it originally sold poorly, as did the follow-up, 'THE WILD, THE INNOCENT & THE E-STREET SHUFFLE'. Following the latter set's completion, SPRINGSTEEN concentrated on heavy touring with the newly formed E-STREET BAND, the subsequent exposure resurrecting, to some degree, the commercial fortunes of his first two releases, both hitting the US Top 60 in mid-75. It was with much anticipation, then, that a third album, 'BORN TO RUN', eventually hit the shelves later that year. Co-producer and future manager, Jon Landau, had steered the project towards a suitably grandiose sound, the starry-eyed romanticism of SPRINGSTEEN's lyrical themes complementing the lavish arrangements. The title track best summed up the mood of the album, teenage rebels following their dreams on the open road; not exactly an original take on rock'n'roll but one which the singer would refine

and subvert as his career unfolded. Reaching Top 3 in the USA, the album gave SPRINGSTEEN his first real breakthrough, in the States at least, 'The Boss' (as the Americans soon took to calling him) undertaking a full scale US tour. It would be almost three years before another album as SPRINGSTEEN became embroiled in a legal battle with his former manager, Mike Appel. The latter had attempted to prevent his client working with Landau, an out of court settlement eventually bringing matters to a close and allowing the beleaguered singer to begin recording 'DARKNESS ON THE EDGE OF TOWN' (1978). As the title suggested, the album was an altogether more bleak affair, no doubt inspired by the legal traumas of the preceding few years. Yet it remains one of SPRINGSTEEN's most enduring efforts, establishing him as a sympathetic and cuttingly accurate observer of the gritty realities, hopes and dreams facing ordinary Americans. The spartan echoes of tracks like 'ADAM RAISED A CAIN' would resonate through SPRINGSTEEN's more introspective work throughout his subsequent career. Though the record again made the US Top 5, consolidating SPRINGSTEEN's position as a firm critics' favourite, he only really made a substantial breakthrough with 'THE RIVER' (1980), his first US No.1. A double set, the record could easily have been trimmed down to a single album, brimming as it was with workaday rockers centering on cars, girls, cars and, erm . . . more cars (see 'CADILLAC RANCH', 'RAMROD', 'CRUSH ON YOU', 'DRIVE ALL NIGHT' etc). One of the record's few redeeming factors was the title track, an aching ode to doomed love which indicated the direction of SPRINGSTEEN's next effort, 'NEBRASKA' (1982). Arguably one of the most darkly powerful modern folk albums of the past twenty years, the record's stark, sublime beauty stood in glaring contrast to the banal excess of its predecessor and could've conceivably been recorded by a different man. Accompanied by a lone acoustic guitar and occasional wailing harmonica, SPRINGSTEEN explored the boundaries between good and evil, right and wrong, through a series of deeply affecting character studies, his whisky throated voice wracked with doubt, frustration and pain. Although the record was a transatlantic Top 3 hit, it somewhat predictably failed to spawn any successful singles. Nevertheless, any readers basing their opinion of 'The Boss' solely on 'BORN IN THE U.S.A.' (1984) and suchlike are urged to give 'NEBRASKA' a spin. 'BORN . . .' saw SPRINGSTEEN's career finally go stratospheric, a record that came to define 80's America as much as it came to define the singer's stadium sound and blue collar image. Though SPRINGSTEEN had simplified his dark musings on the American dream for a wider audience, the message still wasn't clear enough for some people, Ronald Reagan included. Following the latter's attempt to hijack the supposed patriotic sentiments of the record, SPRINGSTEEN made his political allegiances public by supporting environmental and civil right groups. He'd also previously played a number of benefits for Vietnam war veterans, a subject he addressed in the album's raging title track. Elsewhere, songs like 'DOWNBOUND TRAIN' and 'I'M ON FIRE' centred on familiar SPRINGSTEEN themes of human suffering while 'DANCING IN THE DARK' gave him his biggest US hit to date. Despite the lyrical content, however, the bulk of the album was upbeat, infectious and highly commercial, a multi-million seller which precipitated the most extensive touring of SPRINGSTEEN's career. The massive-selling live boxed set, 'LIVE 1977-1985' neatly chalked out the end of an era, a markedly different SPRINGSTEEN surfacing in 1987 with 'TUNNEL OF LOVE'. With his marriage under strain, the album was a more personal affair exploring the vagaries of romance. While the likes of 'TOUGHER THAN THE REST' were touchingly direct, overall the album lacked the fire of old. Despite finally parting ways with the E STREET BAND, the concurrently released 'HUMAN TOUCH' and 'LUCKY TOWN' (1992) sets failed to satisfy critics or fans with their formulaic material. More endearing was the poignant 'STREETS OF PHILADELPHIA', which SPRINGSTEEN contributed to the film, 'Philadelphia', a subsequent Grammy Award winner and the singer's biggest hit single for over a decade. The following year saw the low key release of 'THE GHOST OF TOM JOAD' (1995). This was SPRINGSTEEN back doing what he does best, strumming desolate tales of America's lost underclass. With a title taken from Steinbeck's 'Grapes Of Wrath', WOODY GUTHRIE was mentioned in more than one review. It's a comparison not too far off the mark, SPRINGSTEEN never giving up the ghost on documenting the trials of the downtrodden. Many rank the stripped down, one-man shows that accompanied the album's release as among the best of SPRINGSTEEN's career, the singer achieving a new-found authority and maturity. • **Covered:** JERSEY GIRL (Tom Waits) / WAR (Edwin Starr) / SANTA CLAUS IS COMING TO TOWN (festive trad.) / VIVA LAS VEGAS (Elvis Presley) etc. • **Trivia:** SPRINGSTEEN produced two albums by GARY U.S. BONDS 'Dedication' (1981) and 'On The Line' (1982), records that featured The BOSS's songs. He also provided songs for; SPIRIT IN THE NIGHT + BLINDED BY THE LIGHT for (Manfred Mann's Earth Band) / SANDY (Hollies) / FIRE (Robert Gordon) + (Pointer Sisters) / BECAUSE THE NIGHT (Patti Smith) / FOR YOU (Greg Kihn) / FROM SMALL THINGS (Dave Edmunds) / DANCING IN THE DARK (Big Daddy) / THERE'S A RIOT GOIN' ON (Sly & The Family Stone) / etc. On the 13th of May '85, BRUCE married model/actress, Julianne Phillips, although she filed for divorce in August 1988 after seeing photographic newspaper evidence of a burgeoning relationship between BRUCE and backing singer, PATTI SCIALFA. The latter bore him a child, Evan James, on the 25th of July '90.

Album rating: GREETINGS FROM ASBURY PARK, N.J. (*6) / THE WILD, THE INNOCENT & THE E-STREET SHUFFLE (*6) / BORN TO RUN (*9) / DARKNESS ON THE EDGE OF TOWN (*8) / THE RIVER (*7) / NEBRASKA (*9) / BORN IN THE U.S.A. (*8) / LIVE 1977-1985 (*6) / TUNNEL OF LOVE (*6) / HUMAN TOUCH (*5) / LUCKY TOWN (*5) / IN CONCERT – MTV PLUGGED (*5) / GREATEST

HITS compilation (*8) / THE GHOST OF TOM JOAD (*7) / TRACKS early material (*5)

BRUCE SPRINGSTEEN – vocals, guitar / **DAVID SANCIOUS + DANNY FEDERICI** – keyboards / **GARRY TALLENT** – bass / **VINI LOPEZ** – drums / **CLARENCE CLEMENS** – saxophone / **STEVE VAN ZANDT** – lead guitar (left before recording of debut album)

			C.B.S.	Columbia
Feb 73.	(7") <45805> **BLINDED BY THE LIGHT. / ANGEL**		-	
Mar 73.	(lp/c) *(CBS/40 65480)* <31903> **GREETINGS FROM ASBURY PARK, N.J.**			Jan73

– Blinded by the light / Growin' up / Mary Queen of Arkansas / Does this bus stop at 82nd Street / Lost in the flood / The angel / For you / Spirit in the night / It's hard to be a saint in the city. *<hit No.60 in the US; Jul75>* (re-iss. Nov82 lp/c; CBS/40 32210) – hit No.41 in Jun85) (cd-iss. 1986; CD 65480)

| May 73. | (7") <45864> **SPIRIT IN THE NIGHT. / FOR YOU** | | - | |

—— For live appearances The BRUCE SPRINGSTEEN BAND now The E-STREET SHUFFLE. **ERNEST CARTER** – drums repl. LOPEZ

| Feb 74. | (lp/c) *(CBS/40 65780)* <32432> **THE WILD, THE INNOCENT & THE E-STREET SHUFFLE** | | | Nov73 |

– The E-Street shuffle / 4th of July, Asbury Park (Sandy) / Kitty's back / Wild Billy's circus story / Incident on 57th Street / Rosalita (come out tonight) / New York City serenade. *<hit No.59 in the US; Jul75>* (re-iss. Nov83 lp/c; CBS/40 32363) – (hit No.33 in Jun85) (cd-iss. Apr89; CD 32363)

—— **ROY BITTAN** – piano / **MAX WEINBERG** – drums / and the returning **VAN ZANDT** repl. SANCIOUS and CARTER

| Oct 75. | (lp/c) *(CBS/40 69170)* <33795> **BORN TO RUN** | | 17 | 3 Sep75 |

– Thunder road / Tenth Avenue freeze-out / Night / Backstreets / Born to run / She's the one / Meeting across the river / Jungleland. (re-iss. Jan87 boxed; BRUCE B2) (w / free-7") **BECAUSE THE NIGHT. / SPIRIT IN THE NIGHT** (cd-iss. 1983; CD 69170) (cd re-iss. 1988; CD 80959) (re-iss. cd.Jun93) (lp re-iss. Feb99 on 'Classic'; PC 33795)

Oct 75.	(7") *(A 3661)* <10209> **BORN TO RUN. / MEETING ACROSS THE RIVER**			23 Sep75
Feb 76.	(7") *(A 3940)* <10274> **TENTH AVENUE FREEZE-OUT. / SHE'S THE ONE**			83 Jan76
Jun 78.	(7") *(A 6424)* <10763> **PROVE IT ALL NIGHT. / FACTORY**			33
Jun 78.	(lp/c/US-pic-d) *(CBS/40 86061)* <35318> **DARKNESS ON THE EDGE OF TOWN**		16	5

– Badlands / Adam raised a Cain / Something in the night / Candy's room / Racing in the street / Promised land / Factory / Streets of fire / Prove it all night / Darkness on the edge of town. (cd-iss. Jul84; CD 66061) (re-iss. Nov84 lp/c; CBS/40 32542)

Jul 78.	(7") <10801> **BADLANDS. / STREETS OF FIRE**		-	42
Jul 78.	(7") *(A 6532)* **BADLANDS. / SOMETHING IN THE NIGHT**		-	-
Oct 78.	(7") *(A 6720)* **PROMISED LAND. / STREETS OF FIRE**		-	-
Oct 80.	(d-lp/d-c) *(CBS/40 88510)* <36854> **THE RIVER**		2	1

– The ties that bind / Sherry darling / Jackson cage / Two hearts / Independence day / Hungry heart / Out in the street / Crush on you / You can look (but you better not touch) / I wanna marry you / The river / Point blank / Cadillac ranch / I'm a rocker / Fade away / Stolen car / Ramrod / The price you pay / Drive all night / Wreck on the highway. (d-cd-iss. 1985; CD 88510) (re-iss. d-cd+d-c Oct94 on 'Columbia')

Nov 80.	(7") *(A 9309)* <11391> **HUNGRY HEART. / HELD UP WITHOUT A GUN**		44	5
Jan 81.	(7") <11431> **FADE AWAY. / BE TRUE**		-	20
Feb 81.	(7") *(A 9568)* **SHERRY DARLING. / BE TRUE**		-	-
May 81.	(7") *(A 1179)* **THE RIVER. / INDEPENDENCE DAY**		35	-
	(12") *(A13 1179)* – ('A'side) / Born to run / Rosalita.			
Aug 81.	(7") **CADILLAC RANCH. / WRECK ON THE HIGHWAY**			
Sep 82.	(lp/c) *(CBS/40 25100)* <38358> **NEBRASKA**		3	3

– Nebraska / Atlantic City / Mansion on the hill / Johnny 99 / Highway patrolman / State trooper / Used cars / Open all night / My father's house / Reason to believe. (cd-iss. 1983; CD 25100) (re-iss. Feb89 lp/c/cd; 463360-1/-4/-2)

| Oct 82. | (7") *(A 2794)* **ATLANTIC CITY. / MANSION ON THE HILL** | | | |
| Nov 82. | (7") **OPEN ALL NIGHT. / THE BIG PAYBACK** | | | |

—— **NILS LOFGREN** – lead guitar (Solo artist) repl. VAN ZANDT to solo as LITTLE STEVEN / added **PATTI SCIALFA** – backing vox (ex-SOUTHSIDE JOHNNY)

May 84.	(7"/7"sha-pic-d/12") *(A/TA/WA 4436)* <04463> **DANCING IN THE DARK. / PINK CADILLAC**		28	2
	(re-entered UK charts in Jan85, hit No.4)			
Jun 84.	(lp/c/cd/pic-lp) *(CBS/40/CD/11 86304)* <38653> **BORN IN THE U.S.A.**		1	1

– Born in the U.S.A. / Cover me / Darlington County / Working on the highway / Downbound train / I'm on fire / No surrender / Bobby Jean / I'm goin' down / Glory days / Dancing in the dark / My hometown.

Sep 84.	(7") *(A 4662)* <04561> **COVER ME. / JERSEY GIRL (live)**		38	7 Aug84
	(d7"+=) *(DA 4662)* – Dancing in the dark / Pink Cadillac.			
	(12"+=) *(TA 4662)* – Dancing in the dark (dub version).			
Nov 84.	(7") <04680> **BORN IN THE U.S.A. / SHUT OUT THE LIGHTS**		-	9
Jan 85.	(7") <04772> **I'M ON FIRE. / JOHNNY BYE BYE**		-	6
Mar 85.	(7"/7"sha-pic-d) *(A/WA 4662)* **COVER ME. / JERSEY GIRL (live)**		16	-
	(12"+=) *(QTA 4662)* – Dancing in the dark (dub) / Shut out the light / Cover me (dub).			
May 85.	(7"/7"sha-pic-d) *(A/WA 6342)* **I'M ON FIRE. / BORN IN THE U.S.A. (Freedom mix)**		5	-
	(12"+=) *(TA 6342)* – Rosalita / Bye Bye Johnny.			
Jul 85.	(7") *(A 6375)* <04924> **GLORY DAYS. / STAND ON IT**		17	5 May85
	(12"+=) *(QTA 6375)* – Sherry darling / Racing in the street.			
Aug 85.	(7") <05603> **I'M GOIN' DOWN. / JANEY, DON'T YOU LOSE HEART**		-	9
Dec 85.	(7") *(A 6773)* <05728> **MY HOMETOWN. / SANTA CLAUS IS COMIN' TO TOWN**		9	6
Nov 86.	(7") *(650 193-7)* <06432> **WAR (live). / MERRY XMAS BABY (live)**		18	8
	(12"+=) *(650 193-6)* – Incident on 57th Street (live).			
	(d7"+=) *(650 193-0)* – My home town (live) / Santa Claus is coming to town (live).			
Dec 86.	(5xlp-box/3xc-box/3xcd-box) *(450227-1/-4/-2)* <40588> **LIVE 1977-1985 (live)**		4	1 Nov86

– Thunder road / Adam raised a Cain / Fire / Spirit in the night / 4th of July – Asbury Park (Sandy) / Paradise by the 'C' / Growin' up / It's hard to be a saint in the city / Backstreets / Rosalita (come out tonight) / Raise your hand / Hungry heart / Two hearts / Cadillac ranch / You can look (but you better not touch) / War / Candy's room / Badlands / Because the night / Independence day / Johnny 99 / Darkness on the edge of town / Racing in the street / Nebraska / This land is your land / Working on the highway / Reason to believe / Born in the U.S.A. / Seeds / The river / Born to run / Darlington County / Jersey girl / Bobby Jean / Cover me / My hometown / No surrender / I'm on fire / The promised land.

Jan 87.	(7") <06657> **FIRE (live). / INCIDENT ON 57TH STREET**		-	46
Jan 87.	(7") *(650 381-7)* **FIRE (live). / FOR YOU (live)**		54	-
	(12"+=) *(650 381-6)* – Born to run (live) / No surrender (live) / Tenth avenue freeze-out (live).			
May 87.	(7"/7"s) *(BRUCE/+BP 2)* **BORN TO RUN (live). / JOHNNY 99 (live)**		16	-
	(d7"+=) *(BRUCEB 2)* – Spirit in the night / Because the night (live).			
	(cd-s+=) *(BRUCEC 2)* – Spirit in the night (live) / Seeds (live).			
Sep 87.	(7"/7"g-f/12") *(651 141-7/-0/-6)* <07595> **BRILLIANT DISGUISE. / LUCKY MAN**		20	5
Oct 87.	(lp/c/cd/pic-lp/pic-cd) *(460 270-1/-4/-2/-0/-9)* <40999> **TUNNEL OF LOVE**		1	1

– Ain't got you / Tougher than the rest / All that Heaven will allow / Spare parts / Cautious man / Walk like a man / Tunnel of love / Two faces / Brilliant disguise / One step up / When you're alone / Valentine's day.

Dec 87.	(7"/7"sha-pic-d) *(651 295-7/-0)* <07663> **TUNNEL OF LOVE. / TWO FOR THE ROAD**		45	9
	(cd-s+=) *(651 295-6/-2)* – Santa Claus is comin' to town.			
Mar 88.	(7") *(651 442-7)* <07716> **ONE STEP UP. / ROULETTE**		-	13 Feb88
	(12"+=/cd-s+=) *(651 442-6/-2)* – Lucky man.			
Jun 88.	(7") *(BRUCE 3)* **TOUGHER THAN THE REST. / ROULETTE**		13	-
	(12"+=) *(BRUCEQ 3)* – Born to run (live) / Be true (live).			
	(cd-s+=) *(BRUCEC 3)* – ('A'live) / Born to run (live).			
Oct 88.	(7") *(BRUCE 4)* **SPARE PARTS. / PINK CADILLAC**		32	-
	(cd-s+=/s-cd-s+=) *(BRUCE C/B 4)* – ('A'live version) / Chimes of freedom (live).			
	(12") *(BRUCEQ 4)* – ('A'side) / Cover me (live) / ('A'live) / I'm on fire (live).			

—— new band:- **SHANE FONTAYNE** – guitar / **ZACHERY ALFORD** – drums / **TOMMY SIMMS** – bass / **ROY BITTAN** – keyboards / **CRYSTAL TALIEFERO** – guitar, percussion, vocals / + backing vocalists

			Columbia	Columbia
Mar 92.	(c-s,cd-s) <74273> **HUMAN TOUCH / BETTER DAYS**		-	16
Mar 92.	(7"/c-s) *(657872-7/-4)* **HUMAN TOUCH. / SOULS OF THE DEPARTED**		11	-
	(12"+=/cd-s+=/pic-cd-d+=) *(657872-1/-2/-0)* – Long goodbye.			
Mar 92.	(cd/c/lp) *(471423-2/-4/-1)* <53000> **HUMAN TOUCH**		1	2

– Human touch / Soul driver / 57 channels and nothin' on) / Cross my heart / Gloria's eyes / With every wish / Roll of the dice / Real world / All or nothin' at al / Man's job / I wish I were blind / Long goodbye / Real man / Pony boy.

| Mar 92. | (cd/c/lp) *(471424-2/-4/-1)* <53001> **LUCKY TOWN** | | 2 | 3 |

– Better days / Lucky town / Local hero / If I should fall apart / Leap of faith / Big Muddy / Living proof / Book of dreams / Souls of the departed / My beautiful reward.

May 92.	(7"/c-s) *(657890-7/-4)* **BETTER DAYS. / TOUGHER THAN THE REST**		34	-
	(12"+=/cd-s+=) *(657890-1/-2)* – Part man, part monkey.			
Jun 92.	(c-s/cd-s) <74273> **57 CHANNELS (AND NOTHIN' ON). / PART MAN, PART MONKEY**		-	68
Jul 92.	(c-s) *(658138-7/-4)* **57 CHANNELS (AND NOTHIN' ON). / STAND ON IT**		32	-
	(cd-s+=) *(658138-5)* – Janey don't you lose heart.			
	(cd-s) *(658138-2)* – ('A'side) / Little Steven mix version 1 / Little Steven mix version 2 / There's a riot goin' on.			
Oct 92.	(7"/c-s) *(658369-7/-4)* **LEAP OF FAITH. / ('A'version)**		46	-
	(cd-s+=) *(658369-2)* – Shut out the light / The big payback.			
	(cd-s) *(658369-5)* – ('A'side) / 30 days out.			
Apr 93.	(7"/c-s) *(659228-7/-4)* **LUCKY TOWN (live). / ('A' version)**		48	-
	(cd-s+=) *(659228-2)* – Human touch (live).			
Apr 93.	(cd/c/lp) *(473860-2/-4/-1)* **IN CONCERT – MTV PLUGGED (live)**		4	-

– Red headed woman / Better days / Atlantic city / Darkness on the edge of town / Man's job / Human touch / Lucky town / I wish I were blind / Thunder Road / Light of day / If I should fall behind / Living proof / My beautiful reward.

—— his wife PATTI had their child on the 5th Jan '94.
below from the film 'Philadelphia', which won an Oscar for Tom Hanks.

Mar 94.	(7"/c-s/12") *(660065-7/-4/-1)* <77354> **STREETS OF PHILADELPHIA. / IF I SHOULD FALL BEHIND**		2	9 Feb94
	(cd-s+=) *(660065-2)* – Growing up (live) / The big Muddy (live).			
Feb 95.	(cd/c/lp) *(478555-2/-4/-1)* <67060> **GREATEST HITS (compilation)**		1	1

– Born to run / Thunder road / Badlands / The river / Hungry heart / Atlantic city / Dancing in the dark / Born in the U.S.A. / My hometown / Glory days / Brilliant disguise / Human touch / Better days / Streets of Philadelphia / Secret garden / Murder incorporated / Blood brothers / This hard land.

Apr 95.	(c-s) *(661295-4)* <77847> **SECRET GARDEN / THUNDER ROAD (plugged live version)**		44	63
	(cd-s+=) *(661295-2)* – Murder incorporated.			
	(cd-s) *(661295-5)* – ('A'side) / Because the night / Pink Cadillac / 4th Of July, Asbury Park (Sandy).			
Oct 95.	(7"pic-d/c-s) *(662625-7/-4)* **HUNGRY HEART. / STREETS OF PHILADELPHIA**		28	-
	(cd-s+=) *(662 625-2)* – ('A'-Berlin '95 version) / Thunder Road.			
Nov 95.	(cd/c/lp) *(481650-2/-4/-1)* <67484> **THE GHOST OF TOM JOAD**		16	11

– The ghost of Tom Joad / Straight time / Highway 29 / Youngstown / Sinaola cowboys / The line / Balboa Park / Dry lightning / The new timer / Across the border / Galveston Bay / The best was never good enough.

Apr 96.	(7"pic-d) *(663031-7)* **THE GHOST OF TOM JOAD. / STRAIGHT TIME (live)**		26	-
	(cd-s+=) *(663031-2)* – Sinaloa cowboys (live) / Darkness on the edge of town (live).			
	(cd-s) *(663031-5)* – ('A'side) / Meeting across the river / One step up / Nebraska.			

Apr 97. (c-s) *(664324-4)* **SECRET GARDEN / HIGHWAY 29** | 17 | | 19 | Jan97
(cd-s+=) *(664324-2)* – Missing / High hopes.
(cd-s) *(664324-5)* – ('A'side) / Ghost of Tom Joad / Blood brothers / Streets of Philadelphia.

– compilations, others, etc. –

Nov 85. (4x12"box) *C.B.S.; (BRUCE 1)* **BOXED SET 12" SINGLES** | | |
Nov 88. (d-cd) *C.B.S.; (CDBOS 241)* **NEBRASKA / BORN IN THE U.S.A.** | | |
Mar 93. (d-cd) *Columbia; (471607-2)* **DARKNESS ON THE EDGE OF TOWN / NEBRASKA** | | |
(re-iss. Feb95; same)
Jan 94. (d-cd/d-c/d-lp) *Dare Int.;* **PRODIGAL SON** | | |
Oct 96. (3xcd-box) *Columbia; (485325-2)* **DARKNESS ON THE EDGE OF TOWN / GREETINGS FROM ASBURY, N.J. / THE WILD, THE INNOCENT & THE E-STREET SHUFFLE** | | - |
Nov 98. (4xcd-box) *Columbia; (492605-2) <69475>* **TRACKS** (collection of outtakes, B-sides & rarities) | 50 | | 27 |
– Mary Queen of Arkansas / It's hard to be a saint in the city / Growin' up / Does this bus stop at 52nd Street / Bishop danced / Santa Ana / Seaside bar song / Zero & Blind Terry / Linda let me be the one / Thundercrack / Rendezvous / Give the girl a kiss / Iceman / Bring on the night / So young and in love / Hearts of stone / Don't look back // Restless nights / A good man is hard to find (Pittsburgh) / Roulette / Dollhouse / Where the bands are / Loose ends / Living on the edge of the world / Wages of sin / Take 'em as they come / Be true / Ricky wants a man of her own / I wanna be with you / Mary Lou / Stolen car / Born in the U.S.A. / Johnny bye-bye / Shut out the light // Cynthia / My love will not let you down / This hard land / Frankie / TV movie / Stand on it / Lion's den / Car wash / Rockaway the days / Brothers under the bridges ('83) / Man at the top / Pink Cadillac / Two for the road / Janey don't you lose heart / When you need me / The wish / The honeymooners / Lucky man / Leavin' train / Seven angels / Gave it a name / Sad eyes / My lover man / Over the rise / When the lights go out / Loose change / Trouble in Paradise / Happy / Part man, part monkey / Goin' Cali / Back in your arms / Brothers under the bridge.
Apr 99. (cd/c) *(494200-2/-4) <69476>* **18 TRACKS** | 23 | | 64 |
May 99. (c-s) *(667491-4)* **SAD EYES / I WANNA BE WITH YOU** | | |
(cd-s+=) *(667491-2)* – Man at the top.
(cd-s) *(667491-5)* – ('A'side) / Born in the USA / Pink Cadillac.

SQUEEZE

Formed: Deptford, South London, England ... March '74 by CHRIS DIFFORD and GLENN TILBROOK, the pair initially forming a writing partnership whereby the former penned the lyrics with the latter writing the music. Their genius was subsequently incorporated into a group format as the pair recruited ace pianist, JOOLS HOLLAND, bassist HARRY KAKOULLI and drummer PAUL GUNN, forming SQUEEZE in the process. Early 1977 saw the group's vinyl debut on the independent 'B.T.M.' label with the mock-Egyptian new wave pop/rock of 'TAKE ME I'M YOURS'. Despite the single being subsequently withdrawn, the group replaced GUNN with GILSON LAVIS and proceeded to release the JOHN CALE-produced 'PACKET OF THREE' EP on the 'Deptford Fun City' label. This duly attracted the attentions of 'A&M', keen to get in on the new wave act after their abortive signing of the SEX PISTOLS earlier that year. Immediate Top 20 chart success came with the re-release of 'TAKE ME..', an eponymous debut surfacing soon after. With the addition of JOHN BENTLEY on bass as a replacement for the departing KAKOULLI, the group narrowly missed No.1 in Spring '79 with the cockney wide-boy rap of 'COOL FOR CATS', a similarly titled follow-up album almost breaking the Top 40. The record consolidated the growing reputation of the DIFFORD/TILBROOK songwriting axis; their sagely observed, often darkly amusing social commentary drew inevitable comparisons with prime RAY DAVIES, definitely more accurate than the fanciful LENNON & McCARTNEY references. 'UP THE JUNCTION' was a perfect example, a compelling, hard-bitten tale of love on the breadline leading to broken-hearted disillusionment, a swooning, deceptively melancholy keyboard refrain holding the whole thing together. The song clearly struck a chord in the populace at large, SQUEEZE once again coming within a whisker of No.1. 'ARGYBARGY' (1980) gave the group their first Top 40 album, although the comparatively lowly placings afforded SQUEEZE's long players never really reflected the enduring quality of the songs contained within. Tracks like 'PULLING MUSSELS (FROM THE SHELL)', a brilliant slice of pop genius featuring a rollicking piano break courtesy of the illustrious HOLLAND. The latter left soon after to follow his boogie-woogie muse with JOOLS HOLLAND AND THE MILLIONAIRES and more famously, to present Channel 4's legendary music show, 'The Tube', alongside a young Paula Yates. Finding a replacement in respected vocalist/pianist, PAUL CARRACK (ex-ACE, ex-FRANKIE MILLER etc.), SQUEEZE cut their most successful album to date, 'EAST SIDE STORY' (1981). Co-produced by ELVIS COSTELLO, the album had a rootsier feel, CARRACK's COCKER-esque vocals gracing the grittily soulful 'TEMPTED', while the poignant 'LABELLED WITH LOVE' proved SQUEEZE could 'do' country better than most country artists. The latter song (Top 5) marked the end of their reign as a singles band, however, with the evocative 'BLACK COFFEE IN BED' not even breaching the Top 40. By this point CARRACK had left for a solo career, DON SNOW brought in for a final, patchy album, 'SWEETS FROM A STRANGER' (1982). Though the group were at the height of their popularity, creatively they were beginning to stall and wisely decided to quit while they were still on top. Later that year, the compilation, 'THE SINGLES – 45 AND UNDER', brought the era neatly to a close, a seminal record (no household

is complete without a copy!) illustrating why SQUEEZE have aged better than many "new wave" bands of the era. This wasn't the end, though, and after a solo 'DIFFORD & TILBROOK' (1984) album, the pair reunited with HOLLAND, recruiting KEITH WILKINSON on bass. A new album, 'COSI FAN TUTTI FRUTTI' appeared in summer '85, although they didn't really recapture anything resembling the old magic until 'BABYLON AND ON' (1987). That album gave SQUEEZE their first UK Top 20 hit in years with 'HOURGLASS', as well as some belated US chart action, the single reaching No.15 in the States while the album made the Top 40. 'FRANK' (1989) failed to capitalise on the momentum and SQUEEZE were subsequently dealt a double blow when HOLLAND left once again to concentrate on TV work and A&M finally let the band go. The band soldiered on, releasing a sole album, the acclaimed 'PLAY' (1991), for 'Reprise' before eventually regrouping with CARRACK and re-signing with 'A&M' for a further couple of 90's albums, 'SOME FANTASTIC PLACE' (1993) and 'RIDICULOUS' (1995). • **Songwriters:** Mostly DIFFORD & TILBROOK compositions, and some by CARRACK who joined late 1980. Covered END OF THE CENTURY (Blur).

Album rating: SQUEEZE (*6) / COOL FOR CATS (*7) / ARGYBARGY (*8) / EAST SIDE STORY (*7) / SWEETS FROM A STRANGER (*4) / THE SINGLES – 45 AND UNDER compilation (*8) / DIFFORD & TILBROOK (*5; as Difford & Tilbrook) / COSI FAN TUTTI FRUTTI (*6) / BABYLON AND ON (*5) / FRANK (*4) / A ROUND AND A BOUT early live (*3) / PLAY (*5) / GREATEST HITS compilation (*8) / SOME FANTASTIC PLACE (*6) / RIDICULOUS (*7) / DOMINO (*5)

CHRIS DIFFORD (b. 4 Nov'54) – vocals, guitar / **GLENN TILBROOK** (b.31 Aug'57) – vocals, guitar / **JOOLS HOLLAND** (b.JULIAN, 24 Jan'58) – keyboards / **HARRY KAKOULLI** – bass / **PAUL GUNN** – drums (below 45 withdrawn from release)

		B.T.M.	not iss.
Jan 77.	(7"; w-drawn) *(SBT 107)* **TAKE ME I'M YOURS. / NO DISCO KID, NO**	-	-

—— GILSON LAVIS (b.27 Jun'51) – drums (ex-MUSTARD) repl. GUNN

		Deptford Fun City	not iss.
Aug 77.	(7"ep,12"ep) *(DFC 01)* **PACKET OF THREE** – Cat on a wall / Back track / Night ride. *(re-iss. Nov79 12"ep; same)*		

		A&M	A&M
Feb 78.	(7"/12") *(AMS/+P 7335)* **TAKE ME, I'M YOURS. / NIGHT NURSE**	19	
Mar 78.	(lp/c) *(AMLH/CAM 68465) <4687>* **SQUEEZE** – Sex master / Bang bang / Strong in reason / Wild sewerage tickles Brazil / Out of control / Take me, I'm yours / The call / Model / Remember what / First thing wrong / Hesitation (rool Britania) / Get smart. *(re-iss. Mar82 lp/c; AMID/CMID 122)*		
May 78.	(7",7"green) *(AMS 7360)* **BANG BANG. / ALL FED UP**	49	-

—— JOHN BENTLEY (b.16 Apr'51) – bass; repl. KAKOULLI who went solo (he released an album, 'EVEN WHEN I'M NOT', in 1980 and subsequently released a handful of singles in the first half on the 80's)

Nov 78.	(7") *(AMS 7398)* **GOODBYE GIRL. / SAINTS ALIVE**	63	-
Mar 79.	(7",7"pale pink,7"pink,7"red/12"pink) *(AMS/+P 7426)* **COOL FOR CATS. / MODEL**	2	
Apr 79.	(lp/c) *(AMLH/CAM 68503) <4759>* **COOL FOR CATS** – Slap and tickle / Revue / Touching me, touching you / It's not cricket / It's so dirty / The knack / Hop, skip and jump / Up the junction / Hard to find / Slightly drunk / Goodbye girl / Cool for cats. *(cd-iss. Mar91; CDMID 131)*	45	
May 79.	(7",7"lilac) *(AMS 7444)* **UP THE JUNCTION. / IT'S SO DIRTY**	2	
Jun 79.	(7") *<2168>* **SLIGHTLY DRUNK. / GOODBYE GIRL**		
Aug 79.	(7",7"red) *(AMS 7466)* **SLAP AND TICKLE. / ALL'S WELL**	24	
Nov 79.	(7",7"white) *(AMS 7495)* **CHRISTMAS DAY. / GOING CRAZY**		
Jan 80.	(7",7"clear) *(AMS 7507)* **ANOTHER NAIL IN MY HEART. / PRETTY THING**	17	-
Feb 80.	(7") *<2229>* **IF I DIDN'T LOVE YOU. / PRETTY ONE**		
Feb 80.	(lp/c) *(AMLH/CAM 64802) <4802>* **ARGYBARGY** – Pulling mussels (from the shell) / Another nail in my heart / Separate beds / Misadventure / I think I'm go go / Farfisa beat / Here comes that feeling / Vicky Verky / If I didn't love you / Wrong side of the Moon / There at the top.	32	71
Apr 80.	(7",7"red) *(AMS 7523)* **PULLING MUSSELS (FROM THE SHELL). / WHAT THE BUTLER SAW**	44	-
Jun 80.	(7") *<2247>* **PULLING MUSSELS (FROM THE SHELL). / PRETTY ONE**	-	
Sep 80.	(7"m) *<2263>* **ANOTHER NAIL IN MY HEART. / GOING CRAZY / WHAT THE BUTLER SAW** *<re-iss. Sep82>*	-	

—— PAUL CARRACK (b. Apr'51, Sheffield, England) – keyboards (ex-ACE, ex-FRANKIE MILLER, ex-ROXY MUSIC) repl. JOOLS who formed his own MILLIONAIRES

Apr 81.	(7") *(AMS 8129)* **IS THAT LOVE. / TRUST**	35	-
May 81.	(lp/c) *(AMLH/CAM 64854) <4854>* **EAST SIDE STORY** – In quintessence / Someone else's heart / Tempted / Piccadilly / There's no tomorrow / A woman's world / Is that love / F-hole / Labelled with love / Someone else's bell / Mumbo jumbo / Vanity fair / Messed around. *(cd-iss. Jan87; CDA 3253) (re-iss. cd Mar91; same)*	19	44
Jul 81.	(7") *(AMS 8147)* **TEMPTED. / YAP YAP YAP** (free 5"w.a.) **ANOTHER NAIL IN MY HEART. / IF I DIDN'T LOVE YOU**	40	-
Jul 81.	(7") *<2345>* **TEMPTED. / TRUST**	-	49
Sep 81.	(7") *(AMS 8166)* **LABELLED WITH LOVE. / SQUABS ON FORTY FAB**	4	
Oct 81.	(7") *<2377>* **MESSED AROUND. / YAP YAP YAP**	-	

—— DON SNOW (b.13 Jan'57, Kenya) – keyboards (ex-VIBRATORS, ex-SINCEROS) repl. CARRACK (now solo)

Apr 82.	(7",7"pic-d) *(AMS 8219) <2424>* **BLACK COFFEE IN BED. / THE HUNT**	51		Jul82
Apr 82.	(12") *<2413>* **WHEN THE HANGOVER STRIKES. / I'VE RETURNED**	-		

May 82. (lp/c) *(AMLH/CAM 64899) <4899>* **SWEETS FROM A STRANGER** `37` `32`
– Out of touch / I can't hold on / Points of view / Stranger than the stranger on the shore / Onto the dance floor / When the hangover strikes / Black coffee in bed / I've returned / Tongue like a knife / His house her home / The very last dance / The elephant ride.

Jul 82. (7",7"pic-d) *(AMS 8237)* **WHEN THE HANGOVER STRIKES. / THE ELEPHANT RIDE** `☐` `-`

Oct 82. (7") *(AMS 8259) <2518>* **ANNIE GET YOUR GUN. / SPANISH GUITAR** `43` `Feb83`

Nov 82. (lp/c) *(AMLH/CAM 68552) <4922>* **SINGLES – 45 AND UNDER** (compilation) `3` `47`
– Take me I'm yours / Goodbye girl / Cool for cats / Up the junction / Slap and tickle / Another nail in my heart / Pulling mussels (from the shell) / Tempted / Is that love / Labelled with love / Black coffee in bed / Annie get your gun. *(cd-iss. Dec84; CDA 64922)*

Dec 82. (7") *<2534>* **ANOTHER NAIL IN MY HEART. / GOING CRAZY – WHAT THE BUTLER SAW** `-` `☐`

—— Split at same time of compilation.

DIFFORD & TILBROOK

—— carried on as duo, augmented by **KEITH WILKINSON** (b.24 Sep'54, Southfield, England) – bass / + other musicians

Jun 84. (7"/ext.12") *(AM/+X 193)* **LOVE'S CRASHING WAVES. / WITHIN THESE WALLS OF WITHOUT YOU** `57` `-`

Jun 84. (lp/c) *(AMLX/CXM 64985) <4985>* **DIFFORD & TILBROOK** `47` `55`
– Action speaks faster / Love's crashing waves / Picking up the pieces / On my mind tonight / Man for all seasons / Hope fell down / Wagon train / You can't hurt the girl / Tears for attention / The apple tree.

Jun 84. (7") *<2648>* **PICKING UP THE PIECES. / WITHIN THESE WALLS OF WITHOUT YOU** `-` `☐`

Oct 84. (7"/12") *(AM/+X 219)* **HOPE FELL DOWN. / ACTION SPEAKS FASTER** `☐` `-`

SQUEEZE

—— re-formed '78 line-up except **KEITH WILKINSON** – bass (- HARRY)

Jun 85. (7"/12") *(AM/+Y 255)* **LAST TIME FOREVER. / SUITE FROM FIVE STRANGERS** `45` `☐`

Aug 85. (lp/c/cd) *(AMLH/AMC/CDA 5085) <5085>* **COSI FAN TUTTI FRUTTI** `31` `57`
– Big bang / By your side / King George Street / I learnt how to pray / Last time forever / No place like home / Heartbreakin' world / Hits of the year / Break my heart / I won't ever go drinking again.

Sep 85. (7") *<2776>* **HITS OF THE YEAR. / THE FORTNIGHT SAGA** `-` `☐`

Sep 85. (7") *(AM 277)* **NO PLACE LIKE HOME. / THE FORTNIGHT SAGA**
(12"+=) *(AMY 277)* – Last time forever.

Nov 85. (7") *(AM 291)* **HEARTBREAKING WORLD. / BIG BANG** `☐` `-`
(10"+=) *(AMY 291)* – Tempted (live) / By your side (live).

Apr 86. (7") *(AM 306)* **KING GEORGE STREET. / LOVE'S CRASHING WAVES** (live) `☐` `-`
(12"+=) *(AMY 306)* – Up the junction (live).

—— added **ANDY METCALFE** – keyboards (ex-SOFT BOYS)

Aug 87. (7") *(AM 400) <2967>* **HOURGLASS. / WEDDING BELLS** `16` `15`
(12"+=) *(AMY 400)* – Splitting into three.

Sep 87. (lp/c/cd) *(<AMA/CDA 5161>)* **BABYLON AND ON** `14` `36`
– Hourglass / Footprints / Tough love / The prisoner / 853-5937 / In today's room / Trust me to open my mouth / Striking matches / Cigarette of a single man / Who are you? / The waiting game / Some Americans.

Sep 87. (7") *(AM 412)* **TRUST ME TO OPEN MY MOUTH. / TAKE ME, I'M YOURS** (live) `72` `-`
(12"+=) *(AMY 412)* – Black coffee in bed (live).

Nov 87. (7") *(AM 420)* **THE WAITING GAME. / LAST TIME FOREVER**
(12"+=) *(AMY 420)* – The prisoner.

Dec 87. (7") *<2994>* **853-5937. / TAKE ME I'M YOURS** (live) `-` `32`

Jan 88. (7"/ext.12") *(AM/+Y 426)* **853-5937. / TOUGH LOVE** `-` `-`

Apr 88. (7") *<3021>* **FOOTPRINTS. / BLACK COFFEE IN BED** (live) `-` `☐`

Jun 88. (7") *(AM 450)* **FOOTPRINTS. / STRIKING MATCHES (INSTANT BUFF)**
(ext.12"+=) *(AMY 450)* – In today's room.

—— Reverted back to 5-piece when METCALFE departed.

Sep 89. (7") *(AM 350) <1457>* **IF IT'S LOVE. / FRANK'S BAG** `☐` `-`
(12"+=/cd-s+=) *(AMY/CDEE 350)* – Vanity fair (piano version).

Sep 89. (lp/c/cd) *(<AMA/AMC/CDA 5278>)* **FRANK** `58`
– Frank / If it's love / Peyton Place / Rose I said / Slaughtered, gutted and heartbroken / (This could be) The last time / She doesn't have to shave / Love circles / Melody hotel / Can of worms / Dr. Jazz / Is it too late.

Jan 90. (7") *(AM 535)* **LOVE CIRCLES. / RED LIGHT** `☐` `-`
(12"+=/cd-s+=) *(AMY/CDEE 535)* – Who's that?

	Deptford Fun City	I.R.S.
Mar 90. (cd/c/lp) *(DFC CD/MC/LP 1) <82040>* **A ROUND AND A BOUT** (live 1974-1989) `50` `☐`
– Footprints / Pulling mussels (from the shell) / Black coffee in bed / She doesn't have to shave / Is that love / Up the junction / Slaughtered, gutted and heartbroken / Is it too late / Cool for cats / Take me, I'm yours / If it's love / Hourglass / Labelled with love / Annie get your gun / Boogie woogie country girl / Tempted. *(free 7"ep 'PACKET OF THREE')*

—— JOOLS left again to go solo and take up more TV work. In 1991 he was repl. by **MATT IRVING + STEVE NIEVE** – keyboards / **TONY BERG** – guitar, keyboards / **BRUCE HORNSBY** – accordion

	Reprise	Reprise
Jul 91. (7"/c-s) *(W 0054/+C)* **SUNDAY STREET. / MAIDSTONE** `-` `-`
(12"+=/cd-s+=) *(W 0054 T/CD)* – Mood swings.

Aug 91. (lp)(c)(cd) *(WX 428/+C)(<7599 26644-2>)* **PLAY** `41` `☐`

—— Satisfied / Crying in my sleep / Letting go / The day I get home / The truck / House of love / Cupid's toy / Gone to the dogs / Walk a straight line / Sunday street / Wicked and cruel / There is a voice. *(re-iss. cd Feb95; same)*

Nov 91. (7"/c-s) *(W 0071/+C)* **SATISFIED. / HAPPINESS IS KING** `☐` `-`
(12"+=/cd-s+=) *(W 0071 T/CD)* – Laughing in my sleep.

—— **DIFFORD + TILBROOK + WILKINSON** plus returning **PAUL CARRACK** – keyboards / **PETE THOMAS** – drums

	A&M	A&M
Jul 93. (7"/c-s) *(580334-7/-4)* **THIRD RAIL. / COOL FOR CATS – STRONG IN REASON** (live medley) `39` `-`
(cd-s+=) *(580335-2)* – Take me I'm yours (Paul Dakeyne remix).
(cd-s) *(580337-2)* – ('A'side) / The truth (live) / Melody hotel (live) / Walk a straight line (live).

Aug 93. (7"/c-s) *(580376-7/-4)* **SOME FANTASTIC PLACE. / JUMPING** `73` `-`
(cd-s+=) *(580377-2)* – Dark saloons / Discipline.
(cd-s) *(580379-2)* – ('A'side) / Is that the time? / Don't be a stranger / Stark naked.

Sep 93. (cd/c/lp) *(<540140-2/-4/-1>)* **SOME FANTASTIC PLACE** `26`
– Everything in the world / Some fantastic place / Third rail / Loving you tonight / It's over / Cold shoulder / Talk to him / Jolly comes home / Images of loving / True colours (the storm) / Pinocchio.

Oct 93. (7"/c-s/12") *(580412-7/-4/-1)* **LOVING YOU TONIGHT. / ('A'edit)** `☐` `-`
(cd-s+=) *(580413-2)* – Tempted (session) / Third rail (session).

Feb 94. (7"/c-s) *(580506-7/-4)* **IT'S OVER. / IS THAT LOVE** (live) `☐` `-`
(cd-s+=) *(580507-2)* – Pulling mussels (from the shell) (live) / Goodbye girl (live).

—— they were joined by drummer **KEVIN WILKINSON** (b.1957, Swindon)

	A&M	IRS-Capitol
Aug 95. (c-s) *(581189-4)* **THIS SUMMER / GOODBYE GIRL** (live) `47` `-`
(cd-s+=) *(581191-2)* – All the king's horses.
(cd-s) *(581189-2)* – ('A'side) / End of a century (live acoustic) / Periscope.

Nov 95. (c-ep/cd-ep) *(581271-4/-2)* **ELECTRIC TRAINS / CRACKER JACK / FIGHTING FOR PEACE / COLD SHOULDER** (live) `44` `-`
(cd-ep) *(581269-2)* – ('A'side) / Some fantastic place / It's over / Hour glass.

Nov 95. (cd/c) *(540440-2/-4) <38304>* **RIDICULOUS** `50` `☐`
– Electric trains / Heaven knows / Grouch of the day / Walk away / This summer / Got to me / Long face / I want you / Daphne / Lost for words / Great escape / Temptation for love / Sound asleep / Fingertips. *(re-iss. Sep97 cd/c; same)*

Jun 96. (cd-s) *(581605-2)* **HEAVEN KNOWS / GOODBYE GIRL (live) / LABELLED WITH LOVE (live) / IS THAT LOVE? (live)** `27` `-`
(cd-s) *(581607-2)* – ('A'side) / Tempted (live) / Walk away (live) / Some fantastic place (live).
(cd-s) *(581609-2)* – ('A'side) / Take me I'm yours (live) / Annie get your gun (live) / Slap and tickle (live).

Aug 96. (cd-s) *(581837-2)* **THIS SUMMER (remix) / ELECTRIC TRAINS / HEAVEN KNOWS / THIS SUMMER** `32` `-`
(cd-s) *(581839-2)* – ('A'side) / Cool for cats / Up the junction / Black coffee in bed.
(cd-s) *(581841-2)* – ('A'side) / Sweet as a nut / In another lifetime / Never there.

—— **DIFFORD, TILBROOK** with **CHRIS HOLLAND** – keyboards, vocals / **HILAIRE PENDA** – bass / **ASHLEY SOAN** – drums, vocals

	Quixotic	Quixotic
May 98. (cd-s) *(QRCSQ 098)* **DOWN IN THE VALLEY / DOWN IN THE VALLEY** (mixes; crowd / jug band / instrumental) `☐` `☐`

Nov 98. (cd) *()* **DOMINO** `☐` `Sep99`
– Play on / Bonkers / What's wrong with this picture? / Domino / To be a dad / Donkey talk / Sleeping with a friend / Without you here / In the morning / A moving story / Little king / Short break.

—— tragedy struck, when former member KEVIN was to hang himself on 17 Jul'99

– compilations, etc. –

1981. (10"m-lp) *A&M; <SP 3413>* **SIX SQUEEZE SONGS CRAMMED ONTO ONE TEN INCH RECORD** `-` `☐`

Oct 83. (7") *Old Gold; (OG 9364)* **TAKE ME, I'M YOURS. / UP THE JUNCTION**

Sep 85. (7") *Old Gold; (OG 9546)* **COOL FOR CATS. / LABELLED WITH LOVE**

Apr 92. (7"/c-s) *A&M; (AM/+MC 860)* **COOL FOR CATS. / TRUST ME TO OPEN MY MOUTH** `62`
(cd-s+=) *(AMCD 860)* – Squabs on forty fab (medley hits).

May 92. (cd/c/d-lp) *A&M (397181-2/-4/-1)* **GREATEST HITS** `6`
– (as THE SINGLES 45 AND UNDER +) Take me, I'm yours / Goodbye girl / Cool for cats / Up the junction / Slap and tickle / Another nail in my heart / Pulling mussels (from the shell) / Tempted / Is that love / Labelled with love / Black coffee in bed / Annie get your gun / King George Street / Last time forever / No place like home / Hourglass / Trust me to open my mouth / Footprints / If it's love / Love circles.

Oct 93. (cd) *A&M; (CDA 24120)* **BABYLON AND ON / EAST SIDE STORY** `☐` `☐`

Aug 96. (cd) *A&M;* **PICCADILLY COLLECTION** `-` `☐`

Nov 96. (d-cd) *A&M; (540651-2)* **EXCESS MODERATION** `☐` `☐`

Oct 97. (6xcd-box) *(540801-2)* **SIX OF ONE** `☐` `☐`

Billy SQUIER (dig out; Great Metal . . .)

Chris SQUIRE (see under ⇒ YES)

SQUIRREL BAIT

Formed: Louisville, Kentucky, USA . . . 1985 by DAVID GRUBBS, PETER SEARCY, BRIAN McMAHAN, BRITT WALFORD and ETHAN BUCKLER (the last two subsequently made way for BEN DAUGHTREY and CLARK JOHNSON respectively during debut session cuts). A seminal indie hardcore act with a neat line in adolescent humour, SQUIRREL BAIT set their first musical trap in early '86 with an eponymous HUSKER DU-esque album for Steven Joerg's 'Homestead' imprint. Their lifespan was brief however, the band effectively extinct as college captured them following the release of the excellent 'SKAG HEAVEN' (1987). While most of the posse were buried in their books, SEARCY formed The BIG WHEEL and GRUBBS (with JOHNSON) worked on a trio of thrash-metal/noise sets as BASTRO, the latter two surprisingly featuring drummer, JOHN McENTIRE, before he crawled off to form TORTOISE. The most famous by-product of SQUIRREL BAIT, however, was SLINT, an influential indie outfit formed from the ashes of the former band's final line-up (i.e. McMAHAN, WALFORD, DAVID PAJO and ETHAN BUCKLER). In 1991, GRUBBS initiated GASTR DEL SOL, a more intelligent, musically complex proposition which originally saw him working with BUNDY K BROWN and the ubiquitous McENTIRE (in a guest capacity) on the 1993 mini-set, 'THE SERPENTINE SIMILAR'. The latter sticksman also featured on the following single, '20 SONGS LESS', a collaboration with GRUBBS and JIM O'ROURKE (BUNDY had already joined TORTOISE). Having been part of the 'TeenBeat' operation, GASTR DEL SOL signed with 'Drag City' for 1994's acclaimed long-player, 'CROOKT, CRACKT, OR FLY', a subtle, spellbinding record that made genuine innovations in the use of dense acoustic guitar textures and traversed the boundaries of standard indie-rock structures. Never one to shirk a challenge, GRUBBS (and some local friends/musicians) took it upon himself to create a mini-orchestral suite scored to the usual freeform rules, the resulting 17-minute long 'HARP FACTORY ON LAKE STREET' (1995), taking the post-rock ethos into uncharted territory. The following year, GASTR DEL SOL returned to a more song-based approach on 'UPGRADE & AFTERLIFE', a slightly disappointing set which featured a cover of John Fahey's 'DRY BONES IN THE VALLEY'. The partnership of GRUBBS and O'ROURKE was tied up with the 'CAMOUFLEUR' (1998) album, an impressive swansong that found the pair in a more reflective mood, dabbling in a cinematic mix of folk and avant-jazz influences. Around the same time, GRUBBS was carving out his own "new age" solo career, releasing three albums, 'BANANA CABBAGE . . .' (1997), 'THE THICKET' (1998) and with MATS GUSTAFSSON, 'APERTURA' (1999), before the turn of the century.

Album rating: SQUIRREL BAIT (*6) / SKAG HEAVEN (*7) / Bastro: RODE HARD AND PUT UP WET (*4) / DIABLO GUAPO (*4) / SING THE TROUBLED BEAST (*5) / Gastr Del Sol: THE SERPENTINE SIMILAR mini (*5) / CROOKT, CRACKT, OR FLY (*7) / UPGRADE & AFTERLIFE (*5) / CAMOUFLEUR (*7) / David Grubbs: BANANA CABBAGE POTATO LETTUCE ONION ORANGE (*3) / THE THICKET (*5) / THE COXCOMB (*5) / APERTURA with Mats Gustafson (*5)

PETER SEARCY – vocals / **BRIAN McMAHAN** – guitar, vocals / **DAVID GRUBBS** – guitar / **CLARK JOHNSON** – bass; repl. ETHAN BUCKLER / **BEN DAUGHTREY** – drums; repl. BRITT WALFORD (played on two debut tracks)

		Homestead	Homestead
Jan 86.	(lp) <(HMS 028-1)> **SQUIRREL BAIT**		

– Hammering so hard / Thursday / Sun god / When I fall / The final chapter / Mixed blessing / Disguise.

Nov 86.	(7") **KID DYNAMITE. / SLAKE TRAIN COMING**		
Mar 87.	(lp/cd) <(HMS 072-1/-2)> **SKAG HEAVEN**		

– Kid Dynamite / Vigil's return / Black light poster child / Choose your poison / Short straw wins / Too close to the fire / Slake train coming / Rose Island road / Tape to California. (cd-iss. w/ debut)

—— split in 1988, singer SEARCY forming BIG WHEEL with guitarist and co-songwriter, GLENN TAYLOR, along with the rhythm section of MIKE BRADEN and SCOTT LANKFORD. The quartet released hard-rock/metal album, 'EAST END' for 'Giant' records in 1989, while two further albums, 'HOLIDAY MANOR' (1992) and 'SLOWTOWN' (1993) surfaced for 'Mammoth'.

BASTRO

—— meanwhile, **GRUBBS + JOHNSON** formed this outfit

		Homestead	Homestead
Sep 88.	(m-lp/m-c) <(HMS 111/+C)> **RODE HARD AND PUT UP WET**		

—— added **JOHN McENTIRE** – drums

Apr 89.	(7") <(HMS 137)> **SHOOT ME A DEAR. /**		
Jul 89.	(lp/c/cd) <(HMS 132-1/-4/-2)> **DIABLO GUAPO**		

– Tallow waters / Filthy five filthy ten / Guapo / Flesh-coloured house / Short-haired robot / Can of whoopass / Decent skin / Engaging the reverend / Wurlitzer / Pretty smart on my part / Hoosier logic / Shoot me a dear.

1990.	(cd/c/lp) <HMS 164-2/-4/-1> **SING THE TROUBLED BEAST**	-	

– Demons begone / Krakow, Illinois / I come from a long line of ship-builders / Tobacco in the sink / Recidivist / Floating home / Jefferson-in-drag / The sifter / Noise – Star / Recidivist.

—— disbanded after above, McENTIRE later formed TORTOISE

GASTR DEL SOL

DAVID GRUBBS – vocals, guitar, piano / **BUNDY K. BROWN** – bass (of TORTOISE) / with **JOHN McENTIRE** – percussion (of TORTOISE)

		not iss.	Teenbeat
Aug 93.	(m-cd/m-lp) <TB 95> **THE SERPENTINE SIMILAR**	-	-

– Watery Kentucky / Easy company / Jar of fat / Ursus arctos wonderfilis / Eye street / For Soren Mueller / The serpentine orbit / Even the odd orbit. <re-iss. 1997 on 'Drag City'; DC 106> (UK-iss.Jun97 on 'Dexter's Cigar' cd/lp; DEX 13 CD/LP)

—— **GRUBBS** now with **JIM O'ROURKE** – guitar / guests were McENTIRE + STEVE BUTTERS – percussion

Dec 93.	(7") <TB 125> **20 SONGS LESS. /**	-	

		Drag City	Drag City
Nov 94.	(cd/c) <DC 43 CD/C> **CROOKT, CRACKT, OR FLY**	-	

– Wedding in the park / Work from smoke / Parenthetically / Every five miles / Thos. Dudley ah old must dye / Is that a rifle when it rains? / C in cake / Wrong soundings. (UK-iss.Dec96; same as US)

Jan 95.	(12"ep/cd-ep) <DC 54/+CD> **MIRROR REPAIR**		

– Photographed yawning / Eight corners / Dictionary of handwriting / Why sleep / Mirror repair.

below with help from **McENTIRE, JEB BISHOP + BOB WESTON**

Aug 95.	(cd-s) <19> **HARP FACTORY ON LAKE STREET**	-	

—— <above issued on 'Table Of Elements'>

—— now the pair had guests **TONY CONRAD + KEVIN DRUMM**

Dec 96.	(d-lp/cd) <DC 90/+CD> **UPGRADE AND AFTERLIFE**		Jun96

– Our exquisite replica of "eternity" / Rebecca Sylvester / Sea incertain / Hello spiral / Relay / Crappie tactics / Dry bones in the valley.

—— the duo with past musicians

		Domino	Drag City
Feb 98.	(cd/lp) (WIG CD/LP 44) <DG 133> **CAMOUFLEUR**		Jan98

– Seasons reverse / Blues subtitled no sense of wonder / Black horse / Each dream is an example / Mouth canyon / Puff dew / Bauchrednr.

DAVID GRUBBS

—— with various people incl. **JOHN McENTIRE, TONY CONRAD, BUNDY K BROWN, MARY ANN STEWART, JOSHUA ABRAMS + JED BISHOP**

		Table Of Elements	Table Of Elements
Mar 97.	(cd) <(ZINC 30)> **BANANA CABBAGE POTATO LETTUCE ONION ORANGE**		

		Drag City	Drag City
Sep 98.	(lp/cd) <(DC 160/+CD)> **THE THICKET**		

– The thicket / Two shades of blue / Fool summons train / Orange disaster / Amleth's gambit / 40 words on worship / Swami vivekananda way / Buried in the wall / On worship.

		Rectangle	not iss.
Feb 99.	(12"ep) (RECAA 1) **THE COXCOMB**		-

		Blue Chopsticks	not iss.
Jul 99.	(cd; by DAVID GRUBBS & MATS GUSTAFSSON) (BC 2CD) **APERTURA**		-

SQUIRREL NUT ZIPPERS

Formed: Chapel Hill, North Carolina, USA . . . 1993 by JIM MATHUS and KATHARINE WHALEN; they apparently moved from their native soil to develop their artistic expression in a farmhouse somewhere in the south. MATHUS and WHALEN's obsession with Detroit Big Band and Ragtime Jazz had inspired bassist DON RALEIGH, vocalist/guitarist/saxophonist KEN MOSHER, clarinet player TOM MAXWELL and trumpet player JE WINDENHOUSE to join this theatrical showboat in the small and peaceful town of Efland. The group began to carve their own style of camp jazz, which seemed more to be taking the mickey rather than a serious attempt at a tribute crossover. It was around this period that they established the moniker The SQUIRREL NUT ZIPPERS, which was acquired from an authentic sweet shop. Frequent gigs in the Chapel Hill area enabled the band to attract a huge cult following, and in 1994, after much major label wranglings, the group signed to 'Mammoth'. They seemed duly impressed by the SNZ's surreal and vague attempts at recreating 1930's Berlin. Their debut set, 'THE INEVITABLE', appeared in 1995, although this failed to generate big league success. However, they continued to tour issuing a second album, 'HOT', two years later in '97. The set boasted dizzy guitars alongside theatrical brass sections, one of its highlights being novelty single, 'HELL', which went on to gain heavy rotation airplay throughout the American college radio. MTV soon caught on to the bandwagon, and before you could say "Charleston two-step", the single had spread across international radioland like a bad case of retro-flu. The album went gold while The SQUIRREL NUT ZIPPERS reached international stardom, although sophomore single, 'PUT A LID ON IT' failed to maintain the heights of its predecessor. It could be fair to say that the band were finding it hard to deliver a hit single!, although on the albums front, ~'PERENNIAL FAVORITES' (1998) and 'CHRISTMAS CARAVAN' (1998) were giving them recognition. They subsequently made a welcome appearance in the Neve Campbell film soundtrack project, 'Three To Tango'.

Album rating: THE INEVITABLE (*6) / HOT (*7) / PERENNIAL FAVORITES (*6) / CHRISTMAS CARAVAN (*4)

JIM MATHUS – vocals, guitar, trombone / **KATHARINE WHALEN** – vocals, banjo / **KEN MOSHER** – guitar, saxophone, vocals / **DON RALEIGH** – bass / **CHRIS PHILLIPS** – drums, percussion / **KEN MAXWELL** – vocals, guitar, baritone sax, clarinet / **JE WINDENHOUSE** – trumpet

		Mammoth	Mammoth
Apr 95.	(cd/lp) <(MR 0105-2/-1)> **THE INEVITABLE**		Mar95

– Lover's lane / Danny Diamond / I've found a new baby / Anything but love / Good enough for grandad / Wished for you / La grippe / Lugubrious whing whang / Club limbo / Wash Jones / You're drivin' me crazy / Plenty more. (cd re-iss. Nov98; 559257-2)

Jan 97.	(cd/c) <MR 0137-2/-4> **HOT**	-	27

– Got my own thing now / Put a lid on it / Memphis exorcism / Twilight / It ain't you / Prince Nez / Hell / Meant to be / Bad businessman / Flight of the passing fancy / Blue angel / Interlocutor. (UK-iss.cd Mar98 on 'Polydor'; 557038-2)

Sep 97.	(cd-ep) <MR 0177CD> **SOLD OUT EP**	-	

– Put a lid on it / Pallin' with Al / etc.

Oct 97.	(cd-ep) (MRG 057CD) **ROASTED RIGHT EP**		-

– Little mother-in-law / (You are my) Radio / Anything but live / Wish Jones. (above issued on 'Merge')

Aug 98. (cd/c) <980-169> **PERENNIAL FAVORITES**   [-] [18]
– The suits are picking up the bill / Low down man / The ghost of Stephen Foster / Pallin' with Al / The fat cat keeps getting fatter / Trou Macacq / My drag / Soon / Evening at Lafitte's / Kraken / That fascinating thing / It's over.

Oct 98. (cd) **CHRISTMAS CARAVAN** (festive)   [-] [ ]
– Winter weather / Indian giver / Johnny Ace / My evergreen / Sleigh ride / I'm coming home for Christmas / Carolina Christmas / Gift of the Magi / Hot Christmas / Hanging up my stockings.

                       Polygram   not iss.

Jan 99. (cd-s) <569613-2> **HELL**   [-] [ ]

STANDELLS (dig out; Great Psychedelic . . .)

Paul STANLEY (see under ⇒ KISS)

Vivian STANSHALL (see under ⇒ BONZO DOG BAND)

Ringo STARR

Born: RICHARD STARKEY, 7 Jul'40, Liverpool, England. Taking up the drums professionally in his late teens, STARKEY played with various skiffle outfits before being invited into The BEATLES fold in August '62. So named due to his predeliction for wearing rings, STARR filled the band's drum stool right through till their messy demise in 1969, occasionally doing a lead vocal and finally penning his own track with the endearing 'DON'T PASS ME BY' (from 1968's classic double set, 'THE BEATLES'). Early in '69, just prior to the band's split, STARR appeared in the movie version of Terry Southern's novel, 'Candy', taking a role alongside Peter Sellers the following year in another Southern adaptation, 'The Magic Christian'. A busy year for the budding actor, STARR also released two post-BEATLES solo albums, 'SENTIMENTAL JOURNEY' and 'BEAUCOUPS OF BLUES'. While the former was a string-laden, George Martin-produced set of Tin Pan Alley standards which made the UK Top 10 (and the US Top 30), the latter was a Nashville-recorded country affair, STARR immersing himself in a genre with which he obviously felt at home (he'd previously sung the few country/rockabilly tunes The BEATLES attempted, while the honky tonk fiddle of the aforementioned 'DON'T PASS..' was an indication of the direction he was headed). Although these sets failed to spawn any hit singles, STARR scored a string of transatlantic Top 10 hits in 1971 with the hard hitting 'IT DON'T COME EASY', 'BACK OFF BOOGALOO' and 'PHOTOGRAPH'. A US chart topper, the last-named was featured on the eponymous 'RINGO' (1973), his most successful solo album by a mile. Boasting the musical and songwriting talents of all three former BEATLES, the album was also STARR's most consistent, spawning a further sizeable hit in 'YOU'RE SIXTEEN'. The following year's 'GOODNIGHT VIENNA' included the Top 5 cover of Hoyt Axton's novelty number, 'NO NO SONG', while 'BLAST FROM YOUR PAST' (1975) summed up the first half of STARR's solo career. This half decade was also a purple patch for his acting career, STARR taking a lead role in 'That'll Be The Day' alongside DAVID ESSEX and even making his directing debut with 'Born To Boogie' a rockumentary of MARC BOLAN and T. REX. STARR subsequently signed with 'Atlantic' in 1976, 'RINGO'S ROTOGRAVURE' failing to match the success of his previous efforts, while 'RINGO THE 4TH' (1977) was a commercial failure. An album for 'Portrait', 'BAD BOY' (1978), failed to reverse his ailing fortunes and while he scored a Top 40 hit in 1981 with 'WRACK MY BRAIN', 1983's 'OLD WAVE' was only released in Germany. The 80's proved a difficult time for STARR as he struggled with alcohol and drug abuse, retiring completely from recording and concentrating on TV/film work; he famously narrated celebrated children's TV series, 'Thomas The Tank Engine' in 1984. STARR eventually returned to music full-time at the turn of the decade with 'RINGO STARR & HIS ALL-STARR BAND' (1990), a live set of favourites and cover versions performed with the formidable line-up of DR. JOHN, BILLY PRESTON, NILS LOFGREN, JOE WALSH, RICK DANKO, JIM KELTNER, LEVON HELM and CLARENCE CLEMONS. While STARR's vocal talent may be basic, his patter and wit more often than not makes up for it, and while he displays little of the technical flash of his BEATLES heyday, he remains one of the most solidly reliable drummers in the business. • **Filmography:** BLINDMAN (1971) / 200 MOTELS (1971 with Frank Zappa) / LISZTOMANIA (1975) / SCOUSE THE MOUSE (1977) / PRINCESS DAISY (1983 TV mini-soap with Barbara) / GIVE MY REGARDS TO BROAD STREET (Paul McCartney's film 1984) / WATER (1985) / WILLIE AND THE POOR BOYS (1985 Bill Wyman video) / ALICE IN WONDERLAND (1985 TV). • **Covered:** YOU'RE SIXTEEN (Johnny Burnette) / ONLY YOU (Platters) / SNOOKEROO (Elton John / Bernie Taupin) / IT'S ALL DOWN TO GOODNIGHT VIENNA (John Lennon) / HEY BABY (Bruce Channel). His 1978 album BAD BOY was another covers album. • **Trivia::** In the early 80's, he met actress Barbara Bach, whom he married on 27th of April '81.

Album rating: SENTIMENTAL JOURNEY (*5) / BEAUCOUPS OF BLUES (*5) / RINGO (87) / GOODNIGHT VIENNA (*5) / BLAST FROM YOUR PAST compilation (*6) / RINGO'S ROTOGRAVURE (*5) / RINGO THE 4th (*4) / BAD BOY (*4) / STOP AND SMELL THE ROSES (*5) / OLD WAVE (*3) / STARRSTRUCK: RINGO'S BEST compilation (*6) / RINGO STARR AND HIS ALL-STARR BAND (*6) / TIME TAKES TIME (*6) / RINGO STARR AND HIS ALL-STARR BAND, VOL.2 - LIVE FROM MONTREUX (*5) / VERTICAL SMILE (*5)

RINGO STARR – vocals, drums, etc (with session people)

			Apple	Apple
Mar 70.	(lp) (PCS 7101) <3365> **SENTIMENTAL JOURNEY**		7	22

– Sentimental journey / Night and day / Whispering grass / Bye bye blackbird / I'm a fool to care / Stardust / Blue, turning grey over you / Love is a many splendoured thing / Dream / You always hurt the one you love / Have I told you lately that I love you / Let the rest of the world go by. (cd-iss. May95 on 'E.M.I.';)

| Sep 70. | (lp) (PAS 10002) <3368> **BEAUCOUPS OF BLUES** | | | 65 |

– Beaucoups of blues / Love don't last long / Fastest growing heartache in the west / Without her / Woman of the night / I'd be talking all the time / $15 draw / Wine, women and loud happy songs / I wouldn't have you any other way / Loser's lounge / Waiting / Silent homecoming. (cd-iss. May95 on 'E.M.I.';)

Oct 70.	(7") <2969> **BEAUCOUPS OF BLUES. / COOCHY COOCHY**		-	87
Apr 71.	(7") (R 5898) <1831> **IT DON'T COME EASY. / EARLY 1970**		4	4
Mar 72.	(7") (R 5944) <1849> **BACK OFF BOOGALOO. / BLINDMAN**		2	9
Oct 73.	(7") (R 5992) <1865> **PHOTOGRAPH. / DOWN AND OUT**		8	1
Nov 73.	(lp/c) (PCTC 252) <3413> **RINGO**		7	2

– You and me (babe) / I'm the greatest / Have you seen my baby / Photograph / Sunshine life for me / You're sixteen / Oh my my / Step lightly / Six o'clock * / Devil woman. (US track *= extended) (re-iss. Nov80 on 'Music For Pleasure'; MFP 50508) (re-iss. Mar91 on 'E.M.I.' lp/cd;)

Feb 74.	(7") (R 5995) <1870> **YOU'RE SIXTEEN. / DEVIL WOMAN**		4	8 Dec73
Mar 74.	(7") <1872> **OH MY MY. / STEP LIGHTLY**		-	5
Nov 74.	(7") (R 6000) <1876> **ONLY YOU. / CALL ME**		28	6
Nov 74.	(lp) (PCS 7168) <3417> **GOODNIGHT VIENNA**		30	8

– It's all down to goodnight Vienna / Occapella / Oo-wee / Husbands and wives / Snookeroo / All by myself / Call me / No no song / Only you / Easy for me / Goodnight Vienna (reprise).

Feb 75.	(7") (R 6004) **SNOOKEROO. / OO-WEE**			
Feb 75.	(7") <1880> **NO NO SONG. / SNOOKEROO**		-	3
Jun 75.	(7") <1882> **IT'S ALL DOWN TO GOODNIGHT VIENNA. / OO-WEE**		-	31
Dec 75.	(lp/c) (PCS 7170) <3422> **BLAST FROM YOUR PAST** (compilation)			30

– You're sixteen / No no song / It don't come easy / Photograph / Back off boogaloo / Only you / Beacoups of blues / Oh my my / Early 1970 / I'm the greatest. (re-iss. Nov81 on 'Music For Pleasure'; MFP 50524) (cd-iss. 1987 on 'E.M.I.'; CDP 746663-2)

| Jan 76. | (7") (R 6011) **OH MY MY. / NO NO SONG** | | | - |

           Polydor   Atlantic

| Sep 76. | (7") (2001 694) <3361> **A DOSE OF ROCK'N'ROLL. / CRYIN'** | | | 26 |
| Sep 76. | (lp/c) (2382 040) <18193> **RINGO'S ROTOGRAVURE** | | | 28 |

– A dose of rock'n'roll / Hey baby / Pure gold / Cryin' / You don't know me at all / Cookin' / I'll still love you / This be called a song / La brisas / Lady Gaye. (re-iss. Jun82 lp/c; 2485 235/3201 743)

Nov 76.	(7") (2001 699) <3371> **HEY BABY. / LADY GAYE**			74
Sep 77.	(7") <3412> **DROWNING IN THE SEA OF LOVE. / GROWING**			-
Sep 77.	(7") (2001 734) **DROWNING IN THE SEA OF LOVE. / JUST A DREAM**			-
Sep 77.	(lp/c) (2310 556) <19108> **RINGO THE 4th**			

– Drowning in the sea of love / Tango all night / Wings / Gave it all up / Out on the streets / Can she do it like she dances / Sneaking Sally through the alley / It's no secret / Gypsies in flight / Simple love song.

| Oct 77. | (lp) (2480 429) **SCOUSE THE MOUSE** | | | |

– (8 children's songs)

| Nov 77. | (7") <3429> **WINGS. / JUST A DREAM** | | - | |

          Polydor   Portrait

| Apr 78. | (lp/c) (2310 599) <35378> **BAD BOY** | | | |

– Who needs a heart / Bad boy / Lipstick traces / Heart on my sleeve / Where did our love go / Hard times / Tonight / Monkey see monkey do / Old time relovin' / A man like me.

May 78.	(7"w-drawn) (2001 782) <70015> **OLD TIME RELOVIN'. / LIPSTICK TRACES (ON A CIGARETTE)**		-	-
Jun 78.	(7") (2001 795) **TONIGHT. / OLD TIME RELOVIN'**		-	
Jan 79.	(7") <70018> **HEART ON MY SLEEVE. / WHO NEEDS A HEART**			-

—— with NILSSON as COLONEL DOUG BOGIE, he released US single 'OKEY COKEY' / 'AWAY IN A MANGER'; <ABC Paramount; 12148>

          R.C.A.   Boardwalk

| Nov 81. | (7") (RCA 166) <130> **WRACK MY BRAIN. / DRUMMING IS MY MADNESS** | | | 38 |
| Nov 81. | (lp/c) (LP/K 6022) <33246> **STOP AND SMELL THE ROSES** | | | 98 |

– Private property / Wrack my brain / Drumming is my madness / Attention / Stop and take the time to smell the roses / Dead giveaway / You belong to me / Sure to fall (in love with you) / Nice way / Back off boogaloo.

| Feb 82. | (7") <134> **STOP AND TAKE TIME TO SMELL THE ROSES. / PRIVATE PROPERTY** | | - | - |

          Bellaphon   not iss.

| Jun 83. | (7") (100.16.012) **IN MY CAR. / AS FAR AS WE CAN GO** | | - | - German |
| Jun 83. | (lp) (260.16.029) **OLD WAVE** | | - | - German |

– In my car / Hopeless / Alibi / Be my baby / She's about a mover / Keep forgettin' / Picture show life / As far as we can go / Everybody's in a hurry but me / I'm going down.

—— Retired from solo work, guesting on ex-BEATLES' (PAUL McCARTNEY & GEORGE HARRISON solo). In '84, he narrated for children TV series 'Thomas The Tank Engine'. Returned to studio for 1990 album

---

RINGO STARR & HIS ALL-STAR BAND

DR.JOHN + BILLY PRESTON – keyboards / **NILS LOFGREN + JOE WALSH** – guitar / **RICK DANKO** – bass / **JIM KELTNER** – drums / **LEVON HELM** – percussion / **CLARENCE CLEMONS** – saxophone

			E.M.I.	Arista
Nov 90.	(cd/c/lp) (CD/TC+/EMC 1375) **RINGO STARR AND HIS ALL-STARR BAND** (live)			

– It don't come easy / The no-no song / Iko Iko / The weight / Shine silently / Honey don't / You're sixteen, you're beautiful, and you're mine / Quarter to three / Raining in my heart / Will it go round in circles / Life in the fast lane / Photograph.

		Private	Private
May 92. (12") (115392) **WEIGHT OF THE WORLD. / AFTER ALL THESE YEARS**		74	
May 92. (cd/c) <82097-2/-4> **TIME TAKES TIME**		-	

– Weight of the world / Don't know a thing about love / Don't go where the road don't go / Golden blunders / All in the name of love / After all these years / I don't believe you / Runaways / In a heartbeat / What goes around.

		Rykodisc	Rykodisc
Oct 93. (cd/c) (<RCD2/RAC 0264>) **RINGO STARR AND HIS ALL-STARR BAND, VOL.2: LIVE FROM MONTREUX (live)**			

– Really serious introduction (QUINCY JONES & RINGO) / I'm the greatest (RINGO) / Don't go where the rain don't go (RINGO) / Desperado (JOE WALSH) / I can't tell you why (TIMOTHY B.SCHMIT) / Girls talk (DAVE EDMUNDS) / Weight of the world (RINGO) / Bang the drum all day (TODD RUNDGREN) / Walking nerve (NILS LOFGREN) / Black Maria (TODD RUNDGREN) / In the city (JOE WALSH) / American woman (BURTON CUMMINGS) / Boys (RINGO) / With a little help from my friends (RINGO).

—— now with **DUDAS, GRAKAL + HUDSON**

		Mercury	Mercury
Aug 98. (cd/c) (558598-2/-4) <558400> **VERTICAL SMILE**		61	Jun98

– One / What in the . . . world / Mindfield / King of broken hearts / Love me do / Vertical man / Drift away / I was walking / De da / Without understanding / I'll be fine anywhere / Puppet / I'm yours.

– compilations, etc. –

May 84. (7") *EMI Gold;* (G45 13) **IT DON'T COME EASY. / BACK OFF BOOGALOO**			-
Feb 89. (lp/c/cd) *Rhino;* <R1/R4/R2 70135> **STARRSTRUCK: RINGO'S BEST** (1976-1983)		-	-

– Wrack my brain / In my car / Cookin' (in the kitchen of love) / I keep forgettin' / Hard times / Hey baby / Attention / A dose of rock'n'roll / Who needs a heart / Private property / Can she do it like she dances / Heart on my sleeve. (cd+=) – Sure to fall (in love with you) / Hopeless / You belong to me / She's about a mover.

STARSHIP (see under ⇒ JEFFERSON AIRPLANE)

STATUS QUO

Formed: London, England . . . 1962 as The SPECTRES, by schoolboys ALAN LANCASTER, ALAN KEY, MIKE ROSSI (aka FRANCIS) and JESS JAWORSKI. They subsequently added JOHN COGHLAN to replace BARRY SMITH, and, by the mid-60's were playing a residency at Butlin's holiday camp, where ROY LYNES took over from JESS. In July '66, they signed to 'Piccadilly' records but failed with a debut 45, a Leiber & Stoller cover, 'I (WHO HAVE NOTHING)'. They released two more flops, before they changed name in March '67 to The TRAFFIC JAM. After one 45, they chose an alternative moniker, The STATUS QUO, due to the more high profile TRAFFIC making the charts. In October '67, MIKE ROSSI reverted back to his real Christian name, FRANCIS, the band adding a second guitarist, RICK PARFITT. Now re-signed to 'Pye' records, they unleashed their first single, 'PICTURES OF MATCHSTICK MEN', giving them a breakthrough into the UK Top 10 (it also hit No.12 in the States – their only Top 50 hit). This was an attempt to cash-in on the hugely popular psychedelic scene, an enjoyable pastiche nevertheless, which remains one of their most enduring, timeless songs. The following year, they were again in the Top 10 with 'ICE IN THE SUN', another taken from the same blueprint. Soon after, the band shed their psychedelic trappings, opting instead for a blues/boogie hard rock sound a la CANNED HEAT. After two more Top 30 hits in the early 70's, their biggest and best being, 'DOWN THE DUSTPIPE', they jumped ship in 1972, signing to 'Vertigo' records. With their trademark blue jeans and (sometimes) white T-shirts, they became one of the top selling bands of the 70's. Their 3-chord-wonder barrage of rock'n'roll had few variations, a disappointing 1971 set, 'DOG OF TWO HEAD' nevertheless hiding a minor classic in 'MEAN GIRL' (a hit two years later). Flying high once more in early '73, STATUS QUO hit the Top 10 with 'PAPER PLANE', the single lifted from the accompanying album, 'PILEDRIVER' (which featured a cover of The Doors' 'ROADHOUSE BLUES'!). The 'QUO said 'HELLO' in fine fashion nine months later, the chart-topping album widely regarded as ROSSI and Co.'s 12-bar tour de force, the hit single 'CAROLINE' also making the Top 5. The following year, another Top 10'er, 'BREAK THE RULES' (from the 'QUO' album), saw the band rather ironically sticking steadfastly to their tried and tested formula. This same formula served them well throughout the mid 70's, their commercial peak coming with 'DOWN DOWN', a No.1 single from the similarly successful 'ON THE LEVEL' album. They followed this with 'BLUE FOR YOU', a set that was lapped up by the massed ranks of the 'QUO army and featured two classy, almost credible hit singles, 'RAIN' and 'MYSTERY SONG'. A hairy eight-legged hit machine, the band just kept on rockin' oblivious to the punk upstarts; perhaps the song most readily identifiable with STATUS QUO, the cover of John Fogerty's 'ROCKIN' ALL OVER THE WORLD' "rocked" the nation in 1977, everyone from housewives to headbangers getting down with their air-guitar. Although they kept their notoriously die-hard following, the band became something of a reliable joke in the music journals as they veered more and more into R&B-by-numbers pop-rock territory, 1984's cover of Dion's 'THE WANDERER' being a prime example. Two years previous, COGHLAN departed (possibly after hearing the same three chords just once too many), the group bringing

in PETE KIRCHNER until 1986 when JEFF RICH replaced him. That same year, yet another founder member, LANCASTER, bailed out, keyboard player, ANDY BOWN (a part-time member since '74) become a full-time fifth member. Hardly recognisable as a 'QUO single, the dreary 'IN THE ARMY NOW' almost took ROSSI, PARFITT and Co. back to the top of the charts in '86 (having earlier wowed the world at LIVE AID). STATUS QUO's past musical misdemeanours paled dramatically against the unforgivable early 90's medley, entitled 'ANNIVERSARY WALTZ' (25th unfortunately). The song found them vying for the knees-up-Mother Brown position previously held by cockney "entertainers", CHAS & DAVE. Enough said. • **Songwriters:** LANCASTER (until his departure) or ROSSI and PARFITT. In the early 70's, ROSSI and tour manager BOB YOUNG took over duties. Covered; SPICKS AND SPECKS (Bee Gees) / GREEN TAMBOURINE (Lemon Pipers) / SHEILA (Tommy Roe) / ICE IN THE SUN + ELIZABETH DREAMS + PARADISE FLAT + others (Marty Wilde – Ronnie Scott) / JUNIOR'S WAILING (Steamhammer) / DOWN THE DUSTPIPE (Carl Grossman) / THE PRICE OF LOVE (Everly Brothers) / WILD SIDE OF LIFE (Tommy Quickly) / IN THE ARMY NOW (Bolland-Bolland) / RESTLESS (Jennifer Warnes) / WHEN YOU WALK IN THE ROOM (Jackie DeShannon) / FUN, FUN, FUN (Beach Boys) / I CAN HEAR THE GRASS GROW (Move) / YOU NEVER CAN TELL (Chuck Berry) / GET BACK (Beatles) / SAFETY DANCE (Men Without Hats) / RAINING IN MY HEART (Buddy Holly) / DON'T STOP (Fleetwood Mac) / PROUD MARY (Creedence Clearwater Revival) / LUCILLE (Little Richard) / JOHNNY AND MARY (Robert Palmer) / GET OUT OF DENVER (Bob Seger) / THE FUTURE'S SO BRIGHT (Timbuk 3) / ALL AROUND MY HAT (Steeleye Span) / etc.

Album rating: PICTURESQUE MATCHSTICKABLE MESSAGES FROM THE STATUS QUO (*5) / SPARE PARTS (*4) / MA KELLY'S GREASY SPOON (*4) / DOG OF TWO HEAD (*6) / PILEDRIVER (*6) / HELLO! (*7) / QUO (*6) / ON THE LEVEL (*6) / BLUE FOR YOU (*5) / STATUS QUO LIVE! (*6) / ROCKIN' ALL OVER THE WORLD (*6) / IF YOU CAN'T STAND THE HEAT (*6) / WHATEVER YOU WANT (*6) / 12 GOLD BARS compilation (*6) / JUST SUPPOSIN' (*6) / NEVER TOO LATE (*5) / 1+9+8+2 (*5) / FROM THE MAKERS OF . . . compilation/live (*6) / BACK TO BACK (*4) / 12 GOLD BARS, VOL.2 compilation (*6) / IN THE ARMY NOW (*6) / AIN'T COMPLAINING (*5) / PERFECT REMEDY (*3) / ROCKIN' ALL OVER THE YEARS compilation (*7) / ROCK 'TIL YOU DROP (*5) / LIVE ALIVE QUO (*4) / THIRSTY WORK (*4) / DON'T STOP (*3) / UNDER THE INFLUENCE (*3) / Francis Rossi: KING OF THE DOGHOUSE (*3)

MIKE ROSSI (b. FRANCIS, 29 Apr'49, Forest Hill, London) – vocals, guitar / **ROY LYNES** (b.25 Oct'43, Surrey, Kent) – organ, vocals repl. JESS JAWORSKI / **ALAN LANCASTER** (b. 7 Feb'49, Peckham, London) – bass, vocals / **JOHN COGHLAN** (b.19 Sep'46, Dulwich, London) – drums repl. BARRY SMITH

		Piccadilly	not iss.
Sep 66. (7"; as The SPECTRES) (7N 35339) **I (WHO HAVE NOTHING). / NEIGHBOUR, NEIGHBOUR**			-
Nov 66. (7"; as The SPECTRES) (7N 35352) **HURDY GURDY MAN. / LATICA**			-
—— (above was not the DONOVAN song)			
Feb 67. (7"; as The SPECTRES) (7N 35368) **(WE AIN'T GOT) NOTHIN' YET. / I WANT IT**			-
Jun 67. (7"; as TRAFFIC JAM) (7N 35386) **ALMOST THERE BUT NOT QUITE. / WAIT JUST A MINUTE**			-

The STATUS QUO

—— added **RICK PARFITT** (b. RICHARD HARRISON, 12 Oct'48, Woking, Surrey) – guitar, vocals / MIKE now **FRANCIS ROSSI**

		Pye	Cadet Concept
Nov 67. (7") (7N 17449) <7001> **PICTURES OF MATCHSTICK MEN. / GENTLEMAN JOE'S SIDEWALK CAFE**		7	12 May68
Apr 68. (7") (7N 17497) <7015> **BLACK VEILS OF MELONCHOLY. / TO BE FREE**			Jul69
Aug 68. (lp) (NSPL 18220) <LSP 315> **PICTURESQUE MATCHSTICKABLE MESSAGES FROM THE STATUS QUO** (US-title 'MESSAGES FROM THE STATUS QUO')			

– Black veils of meloncholy / When my mind is not live / Ice in the Sun / Elizabeth dreams / Gentleman Joe's sidewalk cafe / Paradise flat / Technicolour dreams / Spicks and specks / Sheila / Sunny cellophane skies / Green tambourine / Pictures of matchstick men. (re-iss.Oct87 on 'P.R.T.' lp/c/cd; PYL/PYM/PYC 6020) (cd re-iss. Dec89 on 'Castle'; CLACD 168)

		Pye	Cadet Concept
Aug 68. (7") (7N 17581) <7006> **ICE IN THE SUN. / WHEN MY MIND IS NOT ALIVE**		8	70
Jan 69. (7"w-drawn) (7N 17650) **TECHNICOLOR DREAMS. / PARADISE FLAT**		-	-
Feb 69. (7") (7N 17665) **MAKE ME STAY A BIT LONGER. / AUNTIE NELLIE**			-
Mar 69. (7") <7010> **TECHNICOLOR DREAMS. / SPICKS AND SPECKS**		-	-
May 69. (7") (7N 17728) **ARE YOU GROWING TIRED OF MY LOVE. / SO ENDS ANOTHER LIFE**		46	-
Sep 69. (lp) (NSPL 18301) **SPARE PARTS**			

– Face without a soul / You're just what I'm looking for / Mr.Mind detector / Antique Angelique / So ends another life / Are you growing tired of my love / Little Miss Nothing / Poor old man / The clown / Velvet curtains / When I awake / Nothing at all. (re-iss.Oct87 on 'P.R.T.' lp/c/cd; PYL/PYM/PYC 6021) (re-iss.Aug90 on 'Castle' cd/c/lp; CLA CD/MC/LP 205) (re-mast.Aug98 on 'Essential'+=; ESMCD 625) – (extra tracks).

Oct 69. (7") (7N 17825) <7017> **THE PRICE OF LOVE. / LITTLE MISS NOTHING**			
		Pye	Janus
Mar 70. (7") (7N 17907) <127> **DOWN THE DUSTPIPE. / FACE WITHOUT A SOUL**		12	

Sep 70. (lp) *(NSPL 18344)* <3018> **MA KELLY'S GREASY SPOON** ☐ ☐
– Spinning wheel blues / Daughter / Everything / Shy fly / (April) Spring, Summer and Wednesdays / Junior's wailing / Lakky lady / Need your love / Lazy poker blues / (a) Is it really me – (b) Gotta go home. *(re-iss. Oct87 on 'P.R.T.'; PYL/PYM/PYC 6022) (cd re-iss. Dec89 on 'Castle'; CLACD 169)*

STATUS QUO

—— now a quartet of **ROSSI, PARFITT, LANCASTER + COGHLAN** when LYNES departed

			Pye	Pye
Oct 70.	(7") *(7N 17998)* <141> **IN MY CHAIR. / GERDUNDULA** *(re-iss. Jun79)*		21	☐
Jun 71.	(7") *(7N 45077)* <65000> **TUNE TO THE MUSIC. / GOOD THINKING**		☐	☐
Dec 71.	(lp/c) *(NSPL 18371)* <3301> **DOG OF TWO HEAD**		☐	☐

– Umleitung / Nanana / Something going on in my head / Mean girl / Nanana / Gerdundula / Railroad / Someone's learning / Nanana. *(cd-iss. 1986 on 'P.R.T.'; CDMP 8837) (re-iss. Oct87 on 'P.R.T.' lp/c/cd; PYL/PYM/PYC 6023) (re-iss. Aug90 on 'Castle' cd/c/lp; CLA CD/MC/LP 206) (re-mast.Aug98 on 'Essential' +=; ESMCD 626) – (extra tracks)*

			Vertigo	A&M
Jan 73.	(7") *(6059 071)* **PAPER PLANE. / SOFTER RIDE**		8	☐
Jan 73.	(lp) *(6360 082)* <4381> **PILEDRIVER**		5	

– Don't waste my time / O baby / A year / Unspoken words / Big fat mama / Paper plane / All the reasons / Roadhouse blues. *(re-iss. May83 lp/c; PRICE/PRIMC 17) (cd-iss. Feb91; 848 176-2)*

May 73.	(7") <1425> **DON'T WASTE MY TIME. / ALL THE REASONS**		–	
Jul 73.	(7") <1443> **PAPER PLANE. / ALL THE REASONS**		–	
Sep 73.	(7") *(6059 085)* **CAROLINE. / JOANNE**		5	–
Sep 73.	(lp) *(6360 098)* <3615> **HELLO!**		1	

– Roll over lay down / Claudie / A reason for living / Blue eyed lady / Caroline / Softer ride / And it's better now / Forty-five hundred times. *(re-iss. May83 lp/c; PRICE/PRIMC 16) (cd-iss. Feb91; 848 172-2)*

Feb 74.	(7") <1510> **CAROLINE. / SOFTER RIDE**		–	
Apr 74.	(7") *(6059 101)* **BREAK THE RULES. / LONELY NIGHT**		8	–
May 74.	(lp/c) *(9102/7231 001)* <3649> **QUO**		2	

– Backwater / Just take me / Break the rules / Drifting away / Don't think it matters / Fine fine fine / Lonely man / Slow train. *(re-iss. Aug83 lp/c; PRICE/PRIMC 38)*

			Vertigo	Capitol
Nov 74.	(7") *(6059 114)* <4039> **DOWN DOWN. / NIGHT RIDE**		1	
Feb 75.	(lp/c) *(9102/7231 002)* <11381> **ON THE LEVEL**		1	

– Little lady / Most of the time / I saw the light / Over and done / Nightride / Down down / Broken man / What to do / Where I am / Bye bye Johnny. *(re-iss. Aug83 lp/c; PRICE/PRIMC 39) (cd-iss. Feb91; 848 175-2)*

| Apr 75. | (7") <4125> **BYE BYE JOHNNY. / DOWN DOWN** | | – | – |
| May 75. | (7"ep) *(QUO 13)* **STATUS QUO LIVE!** (live) | | 9 | – |

– Roll over lay down / Gerdundula / Junior's wailing.

| Feb 76. | (7") *(6059 133)* **RAIN. / YOU LOST THE LOVE** | | 7 | |
| Mar 76. | (lp/c) *(9102/7231 006)* <11509> **BLUE FOR YOU** <US title 'STATUS QUO'> | | 1 | |

– Is there a better way / Mad about the boy / Ring of a change / Blue for you / Rain / Rolling home / That's a fact / Ease your mind / Mystery song. *(re-iss. Dec83 lp/c; PRICE/PRIMC 55)*

Jul 76.	(7") *(6059 146)* **MYSTERY SONG. / DRIFTING AWAY**		11	
Dec 76.	(7") *(6059 153)* **WILD SIDE OF LIFE. / ALL THROUGH THE NIGHT**		9	
Mar 77.	(d-lp)(d-c) *(6641 580)(7599 171)* <11623> **LIVE!** (live)		3	

– Junior's wailing / (a) Backwater, (b) Just take me / Is there a better way / In my chair / Little lady / Most of the time / Forty-five hundred times / Roll over lay down / Big fat mama / Caroline / Bye bye Johnny / Rain / Don't waste my time / Roadhouse blues. *(re-iss. Sep84; d-lp/d-c; PRID/+C 5) (d-cd-iss. Feb92 & Aug98; 510 334-2)*

| Oct 77. | (7") *(6059 184)* **ROCKIN' ALL OVER THE WORLD. / RING OF A CHANGE** | | 3 | |
| Nov 77. | (lp)(c) *(9102 014)(7231 012)* <11749> **ROCKIN' ALL OVER THE WORLD** | | 5 | |

– Hard time / Can't give you more / Let's ride / Baby boy / You don't own me / Rockers rollin' / Rockin' all over the world / Who am I? / Too far gone / For you / Dirty water / Hold you back. *(re-iss. Aug85 lp/c; PRICE/PRIMC 87) (cd-iss. Feb91; 848 173-2)*

| Aug 78. | (7") *(QUO 1)* **AGAIN AND AGAIN. / TOO FAR GONE** | | 13 | – |
| Oct 78. | (lp)(c) *(9102 027)(7231 017)* **IF YOU CAN'T STAND THE HEAT** | | 3 | – |

– Again and again / I'm giving up my worryin' / Gonna teach you to love me / Someone show me home / Long legged Linda / Oh! what a night / Accident prone / Stones / Let me fly / Like a good girl. *(cd-iss. see-compilations)*

Nov 78.	(7") *(QUO 2)* **ACCIDENT PRONE. / LET ME FLY**		36	–
Sep 79.	(7") *(6059 242)* **WHATEVER YOU WANT. / HARD RIDE**		4	–
Oct 79.	(lp/c) *(9102 037/7231 025)* **WHATEVER YOU WANT**		3	–

– Whatever you want / Shady lady / Who asked you / Your smiling face / Living on an island / Come rock with me / Rockin' on / Runaway / High flyer / Breaking away. *(cd-iss. see-compilations)*

| Nov 79. | (7") *(6059 248)* **LIVING ON AN ISLAND. / RUNAWAY** | | 16 | – |
| Apr 80. | (lp/c) *(QUO TV/MC 1)* **12 GOLD BARS** (compilation) | | 3 | – |

– Rockin' all over the world / Down down / Caroline / Paper plane / Break the rules / Again and again / Mystery song / Roll over lay down / Rain / The wild side of life / Whatever you want / Living on an island. *(cd-iss. Nov83; 800 062-2)*

| Oct 80. | (7") *(QUO 3)* **WHAT YOU'RE PROPOSIN'. / AB BLUES** | | 2 | – |
| Oct 80. | (lp/c) *(6302/7144 057)* **JUST SUPPOSIN'** | | 4 | – |

– What you're proposin' / Run to mummy / Don't drive my car / Lies / Over the edge / The wild ones / Name of the game / Coming and going / Rock'n'roll.

Dec 80.	(7") *(QUO 4)* **DON'T DRIVE MY CAR. / LIES**		11	–
Feb 81.	(7") *(QUO 5)* **SOMETHING 'BOUT YOU BABY I LIKE. / ENOUGH IS ENOUGH**		7	–
Mar 81.	(lp/c) *(6302/7144 104)* **NEVER TOO LATE**		2	–

– Never too late / Something 'bout you baby I like / Take me away / Falling in falling out / Carol / Long ago / Mountain lady / Don't stop me now / Enough is enough / Riverside. *(cd-iss. Oct83; 800 053-2)*

| Nov 81. | (7"m) *(QUO 6)* **ROCK'N'ROLL. / HOLD YOU BACK / BACKWATER** | | 8 | – |

—— **PETE KIRCHNER** – drums (ex-ORIGINAL MIRRORS, ex-HONEYBUS, etc.) repl. COUGHLAN who formed PARTNERS IN CRIME

| Mar 82. | (7") *(QUO 7)* **DEAR JOHN. / I WANT THE WORLD TO KNOW** | | 10 | – |
| Apr 82. | (lp/c) *(6302/7144 189)* **1+9+8+2** | | 1 | |

– She don't fool me / Young pretender / Get out and walk / Jealousy / I love rock and roll / Resurrection / Dear John / Doesn't matter / I want the world to know / I should have known / Big man. *(cd-iss. Oct83; 800 035-2)*

| Jun 82. | (7") *(QUO 8)* **SHE DON'T FOOL ME. / NEVER TOO LATE** | | 36 | – |
| Oct 82. | (7"/7"pic-d) *(QUO/+P 10)* **CAROLINE (live). / DIRTY WATER (live)** | | 13 | – |

(12"+=) *(QUO 10-12)* – Down down (live).

| Nov 82. | (t-lp/3xlp-box) *(PRO LP/BX 1)* **FROM THE MAKERS OF . . .** (compilation & 2 lp-sides live) | | 4 | – |

– Pictures of matchstick men / Ice in the Sun / Down the dustpipe / In my chair / Junior's wailing / Mean girl / Gerdundula / Paper plane / Big fat mama / Roadhouse blues / Break the rules / Down down / Bye bye Johnny / Rain / Mystery song / Blue for you / Is there a better way / Again and again / Accident prone / The wild side of life / Living on an island / What you're proposing / Rock and roll / Something 'bout you baby I like / Dear John / Caroline / Roll over lay down / Backwater / Little lady / Don't drive my car / Whatever you want / Hold you back / Rockin' all over the world / Over the edge / Don't waste my time.

| Sep 83. | (7"/7"blue) *(QUO/+B 11)* **OL' RAG BLUES. / STAY THE NIGHT** | | 9 | – |

(ext.12"+=) *(QUO 11-12)* – Whatever you want (live).

| Oct 83. | (lp/c)(cd) *(VERH/+C 10)(814 662-2)* **BACK TO BACK** | | 9 | – |

– A mess of blues / Ol' rag blues / Can't be done / Too close to the ground / No contrast / Win or lose / Marguerita time / Your kind of love / Stay the night / Going down town tonight. *(cd re-iss. see-compilations)*

| Oct 83. | (7") *(QUO 12)* **A MESS OF BLUES. / BIG MAN** | | 15 | – |

(ext.12"+=) *(QUO 12-12)* – Young pretender.

| Dec 83. | (7"/7"pic-d) *(QUO/+P 14)* **MARGUERITA TIME. / RESURRECTION** | | 3 | – |

(d7"+=) *(QUO 14-14)* – Caroline / Joanne.

May 84.	(7") *(QUO 15)* **GOING DOWN TOWN TONIGHT. / TOO CLOSE TO THE GROUND**		20	–
Oct 84.	(7"/12"clear) *(QUO/+P 16)* **THE WANDERER. / CAN'T BE DONE**		7	–
Nov 84.	(d-lp/c)(cd) *(QUO TV/MC 2)(822 985-2)* **12 GOLD BARS VOL.2** (compilation)		12	–

– What you're proposing / Lies / Something 'bout you baby I like / Don't drive my car / Dear John / Rock and roll / Ol' rag blues / Mess of the blues / Marguerita time / Going down town tonight / The wanderer. / (includes VOL.1).

—— **ROSSI + PARFITT** enlisted **ANDY BOWN** – keyboards (ex-HERD) (He was p/t member since 1974) / **JEFF RICH** – drums (ex-CLIMAX BLUES BAND) repl. KIRCHNER / **RHINO EDWARDS** (r.n.JOHN) – bass (ex-CLIMAX BLUES BAND) repl. LANCASTER

| May 86. | (7"/7"sha-pic-d) *(QUO/+PD 18)* **ROLLIN' HOME. / LONELY** | | 9 | – |

(12"+=) *(QUO 18-12)* – Keep me guessing.

| Jul 86. | (7") *(QUO 19)* **RED SKY. / DON'T GIVE IT UP** | | 19 | – |

(12"+=)(12"w-poster+=) *(QUO 19-12)(QUOPB 19-1)* – The Milton Keynes medley (live).
(d7"+=) *(QUOPD 19)* – Marguerita time.

| Aug 86. | (lp/c)(cd) *(VERH/+C 36)(830 049-2)* **IN THE ARMY NOW** | | 7 | – |

– Rollin' home / Calling / In your eyes / Save me / In the army now / Dreamin' / End of the line / Invitation / Red sky / Speechless / Overdose.

| Sep 86. | (7"/7"pic-d) *(QUO/PD 20)* **IN THE ARMY NOW. / HEARTBURN** | | 2 | – |

(d7"+=) *(QUODP 20)* – Marguerita time / What you're proposin'.
('A'-military mix.12"+=) *(QUO 20-12)* – Late last night.

| Nov 86. | (7") *(QUO 21)* **DREAMIN'. / LONG-LEGGED GIRLS** | | 15 | – |

('A'-wet mix.12"+=) *(QUO 21-12)* – The Quo Christmas cake mix.

| Mar 88. | (7"/7"s) *(QUO/+H 22)* **AIN'T COMPLAINING. / THAT'S ALRIGHT** | | 19 | – |

(ext.12"+=) *(QUO 22-12)* – Lean machine.
(cd-s++=) *(QUOCD 22)* – In the army now (remix).

| May 88. | (7"/7"s) *(QUO/+H 23)* **WHO GETS THE LOVE?. / HALLOWEEN** | | 34 | – |

(ext.12"+=) *(QUO 23-12)* – The reason for goodbye.
(cd-s++=) *(QUOCD 23)* – The wanderer (Sharon the nag mix).

| Jun 88. | (lp/c)(cd) *(VERH/+C 58)(834 604-2)* **AIN'T COMPLAINING** | | 12 | – |

– Ain't complaining / Everytime I think of you / One for the money / Another shipwreck / Don't mind if I do / I know you're leaving / Cross that bridge / Cream of the crop / The loving game / Who gets the love? / Burning bridges / Magic.

—— (Below single was a re-working of 'ROCKIN' ALL . . . ' for Sport Aid)

| Aug 88. | (7") *(QUAID 1)* **RUNNING ALL OVER THE WORLD. / MAGIC** | | 17 | – |

(12"+=) *(QUAID 1-12)* – ('A'extended).
(cd-s++=) *(QUACD 1)* – Whatever you want.

| Nov 88. | (7") *(QUO 25)* **BURNING BRIDGES (ON AND OFF AND ON AGAIN). / WHATEVER YOU WANT** | | 5 | – |

(ext.12"+=/cd-s+=) *(QUO 25-12/CD25)* – Marguerita time.

| Oct 89. | (7"/c-s) *(QUO/+MC 26)* **NOT AT ALL. / GONE THRU THE SLIPS** | | 50 | – |

(12"+=)(cd-s+=) *(QUO 26-12/CD26)* – Every time I think of you.

| Nov 89. | (lp/c/cd) *(842 098-1/-4/-2)* **PERFECT REMEDY** | | 49 | – |

– Little dreamer / Not at all / Heart on hold / Perfect remedy / Address book / The power of rock / The way I am / Tommy's in love / Man overboard / Going down for the first time / Throw her a line / 1,000 years.

| Dec 89. | (7"/7"pic-d/c-s) *(QUO/+P/MC 27)* **LITTLE DREAMER. / ROTTEN TO THE BONE** | | ☐ | – |

(12"+=)(cd-s+=) *(QUO 27-12)(QUO X/CD 27)* – Doing it all for you.

| Oct 90. | (7"/7"silver/c-s) *(QUO/+G/MC 28)* **THE ANNIVERSARY WALTZ – (PART 1). / THE POWER OF ROCK** | | 2 | – |

(12"+=/cd-s+=) *(QUO 28-12/CD28)* – Perfect remedy.

| Oct 90. | (cd/c/d-lp) *(846 797-2/-4/-1)* **ROCKIN' ALL OVER THE YEARS** (compilation) | | 2 | – |

– Pictures of matchstick men / Ice in the Sun / Paper plane / Caroline / Break the rules / Down down / Roll over lay down / Rain / Wild side of life / Whatever you want / What you're proposing / Something 'bout you baby I like / Rock'n'roll / Dear John / Ol' rag blues / Marguerita time / The wanderer / Rollin' home / In the army now / Burning bridges / Anniversary waltz (part 1).

Dec 90. (7"/c-s) *(QUO/+MC 29)* **THE ANNIVERSARY WALTZ – (PART 2). / DIRTY WATER (live)** `16` `-`
(12"+=/cd-s+=) *(QUO 29-12/CD29)* – Pictures of matchstick men – Rock'n'roll music – Lover please – That'll be the day – Singing the blues.

Aug 91. (7"/c-s) *(QUO/+MC 30)* **CAN'T GIVE YOU MORE. / DEAD IN THE WATER** `37` `-`
(12"+=/cd-s+=) *(QUO 30-12/CD30)* – Mysteries from the ball.

Sep 91. (cd/c/lp) *(510 341-2/-4/-1)* **ROCK 'TIL YOU DROP** `10` `-`
– Like a zombie / All we really wanna do (Polly) / Fakin' the blues / One man band / Rock 'til you drop / Can't give you more / Warning shot / Let's work together / Bring it on home / No problems. *(cd+=/c+=)* / Good sign / Tommy / Nothing comes easy / Fame or money / Price of love / Forty-five hundred times. *(re-iss. Feb93)*

Jan 92. (7"/c-s) *(QUO/+MC 32)* **ROCK 'TIL YOU DROP. / Awards Medley:- CAROLINE – DOWN DOWN – WHATEVER YOU WANT – ROCKIN' ALL OVER THE WORLD** `38` `-`
(12"+=/cd-s+=) *(QUO 32-12/CD32)* – Forty-five hundred times.

                                             Polydor   not iss.

Oct 92. (7"/c-s) *(QUO/+MC 33)* **ROADHOUSE MEDLEY (ANNIVERSARY WALTZ 25). / ('A'extended)** `21` ☐
(cd-s+=) *(QUOCD 33)* – (A'mix).
(cd-s+=) *(QUODD 33)* – Don't drive my car.

Nov 92. (cd/c/lp) *(517 367-2/-4/-1)* **LIVE ALIVE QUO (live)** `37` `-`
– Roadhouse medley:- Roadhouse blues – The wanderer – Marguerita time – Living on an island – Break the rules – Something 'bout you baby I like – The price of love – Roadhouse blues / Whatever you want / In the army now / Burning bridges / Rockin' all over the world / Caroline / Don't drive my car / Hold you back / Little lady.

—— In May 94; their 'BURNING BRIDGES' tune, was used for Manchester United Football Squad's UK No.1 'Come On You Reds'.

Jul 94. (7"colrd/c-s) *(QUO/+MC 34)* **I DIDN'T MEAN IT. / WHATEVER YOU WANT** `21` `-`
(cd-s+=) *(QUODD 34)* – Down down / Rockin' all over the world.
(cd-s) *(QUOCD 34)* – ('A'side) / ('A'-Hooligan version) / Survival / She knew too much.

Aug 94. (cd/c/lp) *(523607-2/-4/-1)* **THIRSTY WORK** `13` `-`
– Goin' nowhere / I didn't mean it / Confidence / Point of no return / Sail away / Like it or not / Soft in the head / Queenie / Lover of the human race / Sherri don't fail me now! / Rude awakening time / Back on my feet / Restless / Ciao ciao / Tango / Sorry.

Oct 94. (7"colrd/c-s) *(QUO/+MC 35)* **SHERRI DON'T FAIL ME NOW!. / BEAUTIFUL** `38` `-`
(cd-s+=) *(QUOCD 34)* – In the army now.
(cd-s) *(QUODD 34)* – ('A'side) / Tossin' and turnin' / Down to you.

Nov 94. (7"/c-s/cd-s) *(QUO/+MC/CD 36)* **RESTLESS (re-orchestrated). / AND I DO** `39` `-`

                              PolygramTV   not iss.

Oct 95. (7"/c-s) *(577 512-7/-4)* **WHEN YOU WALK IN THE ROOM. / TILTING AT THE MILL** `34` `-`
(cd-s+=) *(577 512-2)* – ('A'version).

Feb 96. (7"/c-s; STATUS QUO with The BEACH BOYS) *(576 262-7/-4)* **FUN FUN FUN. / MORTIFIED** `24` `-`
(cd-s+=) *(576 262-2)* – ('A'mix).
below album features all covers. They sued Radio One for not playing the above hit on their playlist after it charted. The QUO finally lose out in court and faced costs of over £50,000.

Feb 96. (cd/c) *(531 035-2/-4)* **DON'T STOP** `2` `-`
– Fun, fun, fun (with The BEACH BOYS) / When you walk in the room / I can hear the grass grow / You never can tell (it was a teenage wedding) / Get back / Safety dance / Raining in my heart (with BRIAN MAY) / Don't stop / Sorrow / Proud Mary / Lucille / Johnny and Mary / Get out of enver / The future's so bright (I gotta wear shades) / All around my hat (with MADDY PRIOR).

Apr 96. (7"/c-s) *(576 634-7/-4)* **DON'T STOP. / TEMPORARY FRIEND** `35` `-`
(cd-s+=) *(576 635-2)* –

Oct 96. (7"/c-s; STATUS QUO with MADDY PRIOR) *(575 944-7/-4)* **ALL AROUND MY HAT. / I'LL NEVER GET OVER YOU** `47` `-`
(cd-s+=) *(575 945-2)* – Get out of Denver.

—— FRANCIS ROSSI also issued solo releases, the album 'KING OF THE DOGHOUSE' was out in Sept'96

                              Eagle   Spitfire

Mar 99. (c-s) *(EAGCS 075)* **THE WAY IT GOES / UNDER THE INFLUENCE** `39` `-`
(cd-s) *(EAGXS 075)* – ('A'side) / Sea cruise.

Mar 99. (cd/c) *(EAG CD/MC 076)* <5035> **UNDER THE INFLUENCE** `26` ☐ Jul99
– Twenty wild horses / Under the influence / Round and round / Shine on / Little white lies / Keep 'em coming / Little me and you / Making waves / Blessed are the meek / Roll the dice / Not fade away.

May 99. (c-s) *(EAGCS 101)* **LITTLE WHITE LIES / I KNEW THE BRIDE** `47` `-`
(cd-s+) *(EAGXS 101)* – Pictures of matchstick men (1999).
(cd-s) *(EAGXA 101)* –

Sep 99. (c-s) *(EAGCS 105)* **TWENTY WILD HORSES / ANALYSE TIME** `53` `-`
(cd-s+=) *(EAGXS 105)* – Destruction day.

– more compilations, etc. –

Dec 69. (lp) *Marble Arch; (MALS 1193)* **STATUS QUOTATIONS** `-`
Mar 73. (7") *Pye; (7N 45229) / <65017>* **MEAN GIRL. / EVERYTHING** `20` `-`
May 73. (lp/c) *Pye; (NSPL/ZCP 18402)* **THE BEST OF STATUS QUO** `32` `-`
– Down the dustpipe / Gerdundula / In my chair / Umleitung / Lakky lady / Daughter / Railroad / Tune to the music / April, Spring, Summer and Wednesdays / Mean girl / Spinning wheel blues. *(cd-iss. 1986 on 'P.R.T.'; CDNSP 7773)*

Jun 73. (lp/c) *Golden Hour; (GH/ZCGH 556)* **A GOLDEN HOUR OF . . .** ☐ `-`
(re-iss. Apr90 on 'Knight' cd/c; KGH CD/MC 110)

Jul 73. (7") *Pye; (7N 45253)* **GERDUNDULA. / LAKKY LADY** ☐ `-`

1975. (lp) *Starline;* **ROCKIN' AROUND WITH** ☐ `-`
Oct 75. (lp/c) *Golden Hour; (GH/ZCGH 604)* **DOWN THE DUSTPIPE: THE GOLDEN HOUR OF . . . VOL.2** `20` `-`
Sep 76. (lp/c) *Pye; (PKL/ZCPKB 5546)* **THE REST OF STATUS QUO** ☐ `-`
Jan 77. (lp/c) *Pye; (FILD 005)* **THE STATUS QUO FILE SERIES** ☐ `-`
(re-iss. Sep79 on 'P.R.T.';)
Apr 77. (12"ep) *Pye; (BD 103)* **DOWN THE DUSTPIPE / MEAN GIRL. / IN MY CHAIR / GERDUNDULA** ☐ `-`
Apr 78. (lp) *Hallmark; (HMA 257)* **PICTURES OF MATCHSTICK MEN** ☐ `-`
May 78. (lp)(c) *Marble Arch; (HMA 260)(HSC 322)* **STATUS QUO** ☐ `-`
Aug 78. (d-lp/d-c) *Pickwick; (PDA/PDC 046)* **THE STATUS QUO COLLECTION** ☐ `-`
May 79. (7"yellow) *Flashback-Pye; (FBS 2)* **PICTURES OF MATCHSTICK MEN. / DOWN IN THE DUSTPIPE** ☐ `-`
(re-iss. 7"black Apr83 on 'Old Gold'; OG 9298)
Jun 79. (lp,orange-lp/c) *Pye; (NPSL/ZCP 18607)* **JUST FOR THE RECORD** ☐ `-`
Jun 80. (d-lp/d-c) *P.R.T.; (SPOT/ZCSPT 1028)* **SPOTLIGHT ON . . .** ☐ `-`
Sep 80. (d-lp/d-c) *Pickwick; (SSD/+C 8035)* **STATUS QUO** ☐ `-`
Oct 81. (10"lp/c) *P.R.T.; (DOW/ZCDOW 2)* **FRESH QUOTA** (rare) `74` `-`
Jun 82. (c) *P.R.T.; (ZCTON 101)* **100 MINUTES OF . . .** ☐ `-`
Jul 82. (7") *Old Gold; (OG 9142)* **MEAN GIRL. / IN MY CHAIR** ☐ `-`
Oct 82. (lp/c) *P.R.T.; (SPOT/ZCSPT 1028)* **SPOTLIGHT ON . . . VOL.II** ☐ `-`
Apr 83. (lp/c) *Contour; (CN/+4 2062)* **TO BE OR NOT TO BE** ☐ `-`
(cd-iss. Apr91 on 'Pickwick'; PWKS 4051P)
Jul 83. (10"lp/c) *P.R.T.; (DOW/ZCDOW 10)* **WORKS** ☐ `-`
Jul 84. (lp/c) *Vertigo; (818 947-2/-4)* **LIVE AT THE N.E.C. (live)** `83` `-` Dutch
(UK cd-iss. Jul91; 818 947-2)
Sep 85. (7") *Old Gold; (OG 9566)* **CAROLINE. / DOWN DOWN** ☐ `-`
Oct 85. (lp/c) *Flashback; (FBLP/ZCFBL 8082)* **NA NA NA** ☐ `-`
Nov 85. (7") *Old Gold; (OG 9567)* **ROCKIN' ALL OVER THE WORLD. / PAPER PLANE** ☐ `-`
(re-iss. Aug89 & Sep90)
Nov 85. (d-lp/c) *Castle; (CCS LP/MC 114)* **THE COLLECTION** ☐ `-`
(cd-iss. 1988; CCSCD 114)
Oct 87. (lp/c/cd) *P.R.T.; (PYL/PYM/PYC 6024)* **QUOTATIONS VOL.1 – (THE EARLY YEARS)** ☐ `-`
Oct 87. (lp/c/cd) *P.R.T.; (PYL/PYM/PYC 6025)* **QUOTATIONS VOL.2 – (ALTERNATIVES)** ☐ `-`
Sep 88. (lp/pic-lp/c/c/cd) *P.R.T.; (PYZ/PYX/PYM/PYC 4007)* **FROM THE BEGINNING (1966-67)** ☐ `-`
Apr 89. (c)(cd) *Legacy; (C 903)(GHCD 3)* **C90 COLLECTOR** ☐ `-`
Sep 90. (cd/c/d-lp) *Castle; (CCS CD/MC/LP 271)* **B SIDES AND RARITIES** ☐ `-`
Dec 90. (3xcd-box/3xlp-box) *Essential; (ESS CD/LP 136)* **THE EARLY WORKS** ☐ `-`
Feb 91. (cd) *Vertigo; (848 087-2)* **WHATEVER YOU WANT / JUST SUPPOSIN'** ☐ `-`
Feb 91. (cd) *Vertigo; (848 088-2)* **NEVER TOO LATE / BACK TO BACK** ☐ `-`
Feb 91. (cd) *Vertigo; (848 089-2)* **QUO / BLUE FOR YOU** ☐ `-`
(re-iss. Sep97; same)
Feb 91. (cd) *Vertigo; (848 090-2)* **IF YOU CAN'T STAND THE HEAT / 1+9+8+2** ☐ `-`
Sep 91. (d-cd) *Decal; (CDLIK 81)* **BACK TO THE BEGINNING** ☐ `-`
Nov 91. (cd) *Pickwick; (PWKS 4087P)* **THE BEST OF STATUS QUO 1972-1986** ☐ `-`
May 93. (cd/c) *Spectrum; (550002-2/-4)* **A FEW BARS MORE** ☐ `-`
Feb 94. (cd) *Dojo; (EARLD 8)* **THE EARLY YEARS** ☐ `-`
Aug 94. (cd/c) *Matchstick; (MAT CD/MC 291)* **STATUS QUO** ☐ `-`
Sep 94. (cd/c) *Spectrum; (550190-2/-4)* **IT'S ONLY ROCK'N'ROLL** ☐ `-`
Mar 95. (cd) *Connoisseur; (VSOPCD 213)* **THE OTHER SIDE OF STATUS QUO** ☐ `-`
May 95. (cd/c) *Spectrum; (550727-2/-4)* **PICTURES OF MATCHSTICK MEN** ☐ `-`
Jun 95. (cd/c) *Savanna; (SSL CD/MC 204)* **ICE IN THE SUN** ☐ `-`
(re-iss. Apr97 on 'Pulse' cd/c; PLS CD/MC 206)
Jul 96. (cd/c) *Truetrax; (TRT CD/MC 198)* **THE BEST OF STATUS QUO** ☐ `-`
Oct 97. (d-cd/d-c) *Polygram TV; (553507-2/-4)* **WHATEVER YOU WANT – THE VERY BEST OF** `13` `-`
Mar 99. (cd) *Castle Select; (SELCD 555)* **MATCHSTICK MEN – THE PSYCHEDELIC YEARS** ☐ `-`
Mar 99. (cd) *Spectrum; (554891-2)* **THE ESSENTIAL STATUS QUO VOL.1** ☐ `-`

FRANCIS ROSSI & BERNARD FROST

                              Vertigo   not iss.

Apr 85. (7")(ext-12") *(VER 17)(PROS 1)* **MODERN ROMANCE (I WANT TO FALL IN LOVE AGAIN). / I WONDER WHY** `54` `-`
Oct 85. (7") **JEALOUSY. / WHERE ARE YOU NOW** ☐ `-`
(ext.12"+=) – That's all right.

FRANCIS ROSSI

                              Virgin   not iss.

Jul 96. (7"pic-d/c-s) *(VSP/VSC 1594)* **GIVE MYSELF TO LOVE / KING OF THE DOGHOUSE** `42` `-`
(cd-s+=) *(VSCDT 1594)* – Someone show me.
Sep 96. (cd/c) *(CDV/TCV 2809)* **KING OF THE DOGHOUSE** ☐ `-`
– King of the doghouse / I don't know / Darling / Give myself to love / Isaac Ryan / Happy town / Wherever you go / Blue water / The fighter / Someone show me.

STEALER'S WHEEL (see under ⇒ RAFFERTY, Gerry)

STEELEYE SPAN

Formed: St. Albans, England ... 1969 by ex-FAIRPORT CONVENTION bassist, ASHLEY HUTCHINGS, who teamed up with folk duos, MADDY PRIOR / TIM HART and GAY & TERRY WOODS. Under the direction of manager/producer Sandy Robertson, the outfit signed to 'R.C.A.' and recorded a debut album, 'HARK! THE VILLAGE WAIT' (1970). The record consisted largely of traditional reworkings, laying down a blueprint for the distinctive folk-rock hybrid which the group fashioned through the early to mid 70's. By the time sessions had begun on a follow-up, the WOODS had been replaced by PETER KNIGHT and the respected MARTIN CARTHY (the progenitor of the ever impressive CARTHY folk dynasty), the resulting 'PLEASE TO SEE THE KING' (1971) and 'TEN MAN MOP OR MR. RESERVOIR BUTLER RIDES AGAIN' (1972) seeing the fruition of their experimentation with semi-electrified Olde England folk tunes like 'BLACKSMITH' and 'CAPTAIN COULSTON', the band also overhauling jigs and reels with merry abandon. 1972 saw major changes as CARTHY went solo and founder member, HUTCHINGS, pursued a more traditional folk vocation with The ALBION COUNTRY BAND. Rock scene veterans BOB JOHNSON and RICK KEMP were repectively recruited as replacements and the new-look 'SPAN signed to Chrysalis' for the 'BELOW THE SALT' (1972) album. Both this set and 1973's 'PARCEL OF ROGUES' saw the band further stretching the boundaries of the genre, the latter album making the UK Top 30 and even spawning a Top 20 Christmas hit in 'GAUDETTE'. With drummer NIGEL PEGRUM now on board, the band's more rock-centric dynamics were endearing them to a more mainstream audience, 'NOW WE ARE SIX' (1974) making the UK Top 20 and 'COMMONER'S CROWN' (1975) not far behind. It was 1975's Mike Batt-produced 'ALL AROUND MY HAT', however, that became the record most people associate with STEELEYE SPAN, both the album and Top 5 title track cementing the band's name in the public consciousness. Ironically, however, just as the band reached their commercial peak, they began to tread water artistically with the disappointing 'ROCKET COTTAGE' (1976). Even the return of CARTHY for 'STORM FORCE TEN' (1977) couldn't remedy matters and the band officially split in May '78. While the various members went on to further achievements in the folk scene, there were occasional STEELEYE SPAN reformations over the years, most recently in 1989 with the 'TEMPTED AND TRIED' album. While MADDY PRIOR had more or less maintained a solo career simultaneously with STEELEYE SPAN (both with her TIM HART collaborations and the 1976 'SILLY SISTERS' project with JUNE TABOR), she went on to form the MADDY PRIOR band in the 80's, recording for various labels before going solo once more the following decade.
• **Songwriters:** All members through the years contributed their own songs; i.e. HUTCHINGS, PRIOR & HART, The WOODS, CARTHY, JOHNSON, etc. They also covered traditional Olde England folk tunes, reels and jigs, plus more regular classics RAVE ON (Buddy Holly) / GAUDETE (trad.Latin hymn) / TO KNOW HIM IS TO LOVE HIM (Teddy Bears) / TWINKLE TWINKLE LITTLE STAR (children's song) / etc. MADDY covered RAG DOLL (Four Seasons) / WHO'S SORRY NOW? (Connie Francis) / SWIMMING SONG (Loudon Wainwright III) / BOYS OF BEDLAM (Nick Jones-Dave Morgan) / WINTER WAKENETH (M.Kiszco). • **Trivia:** Their 1974 Top 20 album, 'NOW WE ARE SIX', was produced by IAN ANDERSON (Jethro Tull), and featured DAVID BOWIE playing sax solo on track, 'TO KNOW HIM IS TO LOVE HIM'. Their following album 'COMMONER'S CROWN', saw actor PETER SELLERS play ukelele on 'NEW YORK GIRLS'.

Album rating: HARK! THE VILLAGE WAIT (*7) / PLEASE TO SEE THE KING (*7) / TEN MAN MOP (OR MR. RESERVOIR BUTLER STRIKES AGAIN) (*5) / INDIVIDUALLY AND COLLECTIVELY compilation (*6) / BELOW THE SALT (*8) / PARCEL OF ROGUES (*6) / NOW WE ARE SIX (*8) / COMMONER'S CROWN (*5) / ALL AROUND MY HAT (*6) / ROCKET COTTAGE (*4) / ORIGINAL MASTERS compilation (*7) / STORM FORCE TEN (*5) / LIVE AT LAST (*4) / SAILS OF SILVER (*5) / THE BEST OF STEELEYE SPAN compilation (*7) / BACK IN LINE (*5) / TEMPTED AND TRIED (*5) / TIME (*4)

MADDY PRIOR (b.14 Aug'47, Blackpool, England) – vocals / **TIM HART** (b. 9 Jan'48, Lincoln, England) – guitar, vocals / **GAY WOODS** – vocals, concertina / **ASHLEY HUTCHINGS** (b. ? Jan'45, London) – bass (ex-FAIRPORT CONVENTION) / **TERRY WOODS** – guitar, vocals with guest drummers **GERRY CONWAY + DAVE MATTACKS**

			R.C.A.	Chrysalis
Jun 70.	(lp)	(SF 8133) **HARK! THE VILLAGE WAIT**		1976

– A calling / On song / The blacksmith / Fisherman's wife / Blackleg miner / Dark-eyed sailor / Copshawholme fair / All things are quite silent / The hills of Greenmore / My Johnny was a shoemaker / Lowlands of Holland / Twa corbies / One night as I lay on my bed. *(re-iss. Mar76 on 'Mooncrest'; CREST 22) (re-iss. Jan91 lp/cd; CREST/+CD 003)*

—— **MARTIN CARTHY** (b.21 May'41, Hatfield, England) – electric guitar / **PETER KNIGHT** – fiddle repl. TERRY & GAY who formed own self-named duo.

			B&C	Chrysalis
Mar 71.	(lp)	(CAS 1029) **PLEASE TO SEE THE KING**	45	1976

– Blacksmith / Cold, haily, windy night / Bryan O'Lynn (jig) / The hag with the money / Prince Charlie Stuart / Boys of Bedlam / False knight on the road / The lark in the morning / Female drummer / The king / Lonely on the water. *(re-iss. Mar76 on 'Mooncrest'; CREST 8) (re-iss. Mar91 lp/cd; CREST/+CD 003)*

| Oct 71. | (7") | (CB 164) **RAVE ON. / REELS / FEMALE DRUMMER** | | - |

			Pegasus	Chrysalis
Jan 72.	(lp)	(PEG 9) **TEN MAN MOP (OR MR. RESERVOIR STRIKES AGAIN)**		-	1976

– Marrowbones / Captain Coulston / Reels: Dowd's favourite – 10 float – The morning dew / Wee weaver / Skewball / Gower wassail / Jigs: Paddy Clancy's jig – Willie Clancy's fancy / Four nights drunk / When I was on horseback. *(re-iss. Aug91 on 'Mooncrest' lp/cd; CREST/+CD 009)*

—— **BOB JOHNSON** – guitar, vocals repl. CARTHY who went solo / **RICK KEMP** (b.15 Nov'41) – bass repl. HUTCHINGS who joined ALBION COUNTRY BAND

			Chrysalis	Chrysalis
Aug 72.	(lp/c)	(<CHR/ZCCHR 1008>) **BELOW THE SALT**	43	

– Spotted cow / Rosebuds in June / Jigs / Sheepcrook and black dog / Royal forester / King Henry / John Barleycorn / Saucy sailor. *(cd-iss. Jan97 on 'Beat Goes On'; BGOCD 324)*

Sep 72.	(7")	(CHS 2005) **JOHN BARLEYCORN. / JIGS**		
Nov 73.	(7")	**GAUDETTE. / ROYAL FORESTER**	-	
Apr 73.	(lp/c)	(<CHR/ZCCHR 1046>) **PARCEL OF ROGUES**	26	

– Alison Gross / One misty moisty morning / The bold poacher / The ups and downs / Robbery with violins / The wee wee man / Cam ye o'er fae France / The weaver and the factory maid / Rogues in a nation / Hares on a mountain. *(cd-iss. Dec96 on 'Beat Goes On'; BGOCD 323)*

| Nov 73. | (7") | (CHS 2026) **GAUDETE. / THE HOLLY & THE IVY** | 14 | |

—— **PRIOR, HART, KNIGHT, JOHNSON + KEMP** added **NIGEL PEGRUM** – drums, percussion

| Feb 74. | (lp/c) | (<CHR/ZCCHR 1053>) **NOW WE ARE SIX** | 13 | |

– Thomas the rhymer / Two magicians / Edwin / Twinkle twinkle little star / Seven hundred elves / The mooncoin jig / Drink down the Moon / Long a-growing / Now we are six / To know him is to love him. *(cd-iss. Jun91 on 'Beat Goes On'; BGOCD 157)*

| Feb 74. | (7") | (CHS 2026) **THOMAS THE RHYMER. / THE MOONCOIN JIG** | | |
| Jan 75. | (lp/c) | (<CHR/ZCCHR 1071>) **COMMONER'S CROWN** | 21 | |

– Little Sir Hugh / Bach goes to Limerick / Long Lankin / Dogs and ferrets / Galtee farmer / Demon lover / Elf call / Weary cutters / New York girls. *(cd-iss/Sep96 on 'Beat Goes On'; BGOCD 315)*

Mar 75.	(7")	(CHS 2061) **NEW YORK GIRLS. / TWO MAGICIANS**		
Oct 75.	(7")	(CHS 2078) **ALL AROUND MY HAT. / BLACK JACK DAVY**	5	
Oct 75.	(lp/c)	(<CHR/ZCCHR 1091>) **ALL AROUND MY HAT**	7	

– Black Jack Davy / Hard times of old England / Cadgwith anthem / Sum waves (tunes) / The wife of Usher's Well / Gamble gold (Robin Hood) / All around my hat / Dance with me / Batchelor's hall. *(re-iss. Jul85 on 'M.F.P.'; 41-57061) (re-iss. Dec92 on 'Beat Goes On'; BGOCD 158) (cd re-iss. Mar94 on 'E.M.I.'; CDP 828785-2) (cd re-iss. Mar96; CDGOLD 1009)*

Jan 76.	(7")	(CHS 2085) **HARD TIMES OF OLD ENGLAND. / CADGWITH ANTHEM**		
Sep 76.	(7")	(CHS 2107) **LONDON. / SLIGO MAID**		
Oct 76.	(lp/c)	(<CHR/ZCCHR 1123>) **ROCKET COTTAGE**	41	

– London / The Bosnian hornpipes / Orfeo / Nathan's reel / The twelve witches / The brown girls / Fighting for strangers / Sligo maid / Sir James the rose / The drunkard. *(cd-iss. Oct96 on 'Beat Goes On'; BGOCD 318)*

| Nov 76. | (7") | (CHS 2125) **FIGHTING FOR STRANGERS. / THE BOSNIAN HORNPIPES** | | |

—— **MARTIN CARTHY** – guitar, vocals returned to repl. JOHNSON / **JOHN KIRKPATRICK** – accordion repl. KNIGHT who formed duo with JOHNSON. They made one album 'KING OF ELFLAND'S DAUGHTER' in 1978 for 'Chrysalis'.

| Nov 77. | (7") | (CHS 2192) **THE BOAR'S HEAD CAROL / GAUDETE / SOME RIVAL** | - | - |
| Nov 77. | (lp/c) | (<CHR/ZCCHR 1151>) **STORM FORCE TEN** | | |

– Awake, awake / Sweep, chimney sweep / The wife of the soldier / The victory / The black freighter / Some rival / Treadmill song / Seventeen come Sunday. *(cd-iss. Apr97 on 'Beat Goes On'; BGOCD 337)*

| Nov 78. | (lp/c) | (<CHR/ZCCHR 1199>) **LIVE AT LAST! (live)** | | |

– The Atholl highlanders / Walter Bulwer's polka / Saucy sailor / The black freighter / The maid and the palmer / Hunting the wren / Montrose / Bonnets so blue / The false knight on the road. *(cd-iss. Apr97 on 'Beat Goes On'; BGOCD 342)*

| Nov 78. | (7") | **RAG DOLL. / HUNTING THE WREN** | - | |

—— Split May '78 until reformation 1980, **KNIGHT & JOHNSON** returned 1974 line-up

			Chrysalis	Tacoma
Nov 80.	(7")	(CHS 2479) **SAILS OF SILVER. / SENIOR SERVICE**		
Nov 80.	(lp/c)	(<CHR/ZCCHR 1304>) **SAILS OF SILVER**		

– Sails of silver / My love / Barnet fair / Senior service / Gone to America / Where are they now / Let her go now / Longbone / Marigold – Harvest home / Tell me why.

| Feb 81. | (7") | (CHS 2503) **GONE TO AMERICA. / LET HER GO DOWN** | | - |

—— Disbanded 1981, MADDY PRIOR and TIM HART continued with solo work.

—— **STEELEYE SPAN** returned sporadically in the 80's now without HART.

			Flutterby	Shanachie
Nov 85.	(7")	(FLUT 1) **SOMEWHERE IN LONDON. / LANERCROST**		
May 86.	(lp)	(FLUT 2) **BACK IN LINE**		

– Edward / Lanercrost / Lady Diamond / Isabel / A cannon by Telemann / Blackleg miner / Peace on the border / Scarecrow / Take my heart / White man. *(cd re-iss. Aug91 on 'Park'+=; PRKCD 8)* – Spotted cow / One misty moisty morning.

| Apr 89. | (7") | (FLUT 3) **PADSTOW: THE FIRST HOUSE IN CONNAUGHT – SAILOR'S BONNET** | | |
| Sep 89. | (7") | (FLUT 4) **FOLLOWING ME. / TWO BUTCHERS** | | |

			Dover-Chrysalis	Shanachie
Sep 89.	(lp/cd)	(ADD/CCD 9) **TEMPTED AND TRIED**		

– Padstow / The fox / Two butchers / Following me / Seagull / The cruel mother / Jack Hall / Searching for lambs / Shaking of the sheets / Reels: The first house in Connaught – Sailor's bonnet – Betsy Bell and Mary Gray.

			Parkway	not iss.
Sep 92.	(cd/lp)	(PRK CD/M 010) **TONIGHT'S THE NIGHT, LIVE (live)**	-	

—— **GAY WOODS** re-joined

| Mar 96. | (cd/c) | (PRK CD/MC 34) **TIME** | | |

– The prickly bush / The old maid in the Garrett (b. Tam Lin (reel)) / Harvest of the moon / Underneath her apron / The Cutty Wren / Go from my window / The elf-knight / The water is wide / You will burn / Corbies / The song will remain.

—— In the same year, MADDY augmented STATUS QUO on their version of 'ALL AROUND MY HAT'.

– compilations, others, etc. –

1972.	(lp) *Charisma*; (CS 5) **INDIVIDUALLY AND COLLECTIVELY**	☐	-
Sep 76.	(7") *Mooncrest*; (MOON 50) **RAVE ON. / FALSE KNIGHT ON THE ROAD**	☐	-
1977.	(d-lp) *Mooncrest*; (CRD 1) **TIMESPAN**	☐	-
May 77.	(d-lp) *Chrysalis*; (CJT 3) **ORIGINAL MASTERS**	☐	-
	(cd-iss. Jan97 on 'Beat Goes On'; BGOCD 322)		
Nov 82.	(7"ep) *Chrysalis*; (CHS 2658) **ALL AROUND MY HAT / FIGHTING FOR STRANGERS. / GAUDETE / BOAR'S HEAD CAROL**	☐	-
Dec 82.	(d-c) *Chrysalis*; **ALL AROUND MY HAT / ROCKET COTTAGE**	☐	-
Mar 84.	(lp/c) *Chrysalis*; (CHR/ZCCHR 1467) **THE BEST OF STEELEYE SPAN**	☐	-
	(cd-iss. Jul85; CCD 1467)		
Oct 88.	(d-lp/c/cd) *Chrysalis*; (CNW 7) **PORTFOLIO**	☐	-
Nov 79.	(c) *Folktracks*; **FOLK ELECTRIC FOLK**	☐	-
May 80.	(lp) *Hallmark*; (SHM 3040) **STEELEYE SPAN**	☐	-
1980.	(7") *P.E.L.*; **JIGS AND REELS (REELS MEDLEY). / ('A'version)**	☐	-
Sep 84.	(d-lp/d-c) *Cambra*; (CR 5154) **STEELEYE SPAN**	☐	-
Feb 87.	(7") *Old Gold*; (OG 9690) **ALL AROUND MY HAT. / GAUDETE**	☐	-
Apr 89.	(d-lp/c/cd) *Connoisseur*; (VSOP LP/MC/CD 132) **EARLY YEARS**	☐	-
Apr 90.	(cd) *Action Replay*; (CDAR 1012) **THE BEST OF AND THE REST OF STEELEYE SPAN**	☐	-
Aug 91.	(cd/c) *Castle*; (CCS CD/MC 292) **THE COLLECTION**	☐	-
	– Thomas the rhymer / Alison Gross / John Barleycorn / King Henry / One misty moisty morning / The mooncoin jig / Long Lankin / The fox / Shaking of the sheets / Rougues in a nation / Galtee farmer / All around my hat / Sailor's bonnet / Black Jack Davy / Gaudete / Seven hundred elves / Sligo maid / Following me / Robbery with violins / Seventeen come Sunday.		
Nov 94.	(cd) *Park*; (PRKCD 027) **THE COLLECTION: STEELEYE SPAN IN CONCERT** (live)	☐	-
Mar 95.	(d-cd) *Chrysalis*; (CDCHR 6093) **SPANNING THE YEARS**	☐	-
Sep 96.	(cd) *Mooncrest*; (CRESTCD 022) **THE KING: THE BEST OF STEELEYE SPAN**	☐	-
Sep 96.	(cd) *Emporio*; (EMPRCD 668) **A STACK OF STEELEYE SPAN**	☐	-

---

STEEL PULSE (dig out; 4th edition)

STEELY DAN

Formed: New York, USA . . . by DONALD FAGEN and WALTER BECKER, initially as a writing partnership after leaving Bard's college in 1969. At the turn of the decade the pair toured with JAY & THE AMERICANS as backing musicians as well as recording a soundtrack for the movie, 'YOU GOTTA WALK IT LIKE YOU TALK IT' (starring Richard Pryor). Attempts to hawk their songs to Big Apple publishers proved fruitless however and it was only through meeting independent producer Gary Katz that the duo found their way into a staff job at L.A.'s 'Dunhill-ABC' label. Katz was also the catalyst for what would become STEELY DAN, a studio outfit comprising FAGEN, BECKER, vocalist DAVID PALMER, DENNY DIAS (a rhythm guitarist with whom they'd previously recorded early demos), ex-HOLY MODAL ROUNDERS guitarist JEFF 'SKUNK' BAXTER and drummer JIM HODDER, famously naming themselves after a steam-powered(!) dildo in William Burroughs' novel, 'Naked Lunch'. Although a debut single, 'DALLAS', made little impact, the simmering latin-funk rock of 'DO IT AGAIN' made the US Top 10. It also introduced FAGEN's inimitable lyrical wit, a cynical DLYAN-esque worldview which mocked L.A.'s pretensions and would see STEELY DAN hailed as one of the most cuttingly accurate commentators of the 70's. 'CAN'T BUY A THRILL' (1973) nailed the point home with consummate ease, laying down the jazz-rooted, FM-slick blueprint that was endlessly tweaked, polished and perfected with each successive album. The enduring 'REELIN' IN THE YEARS' was lifted as a second single and gave the group another major hit, the track's searing guitar solo, as with 'KINGS', provided by session man, ELLIOTT RANDALL; if there was one critical niggle it was that PALMER couldn't always carry the subtle insinuations of the lyrics. BECKER and FAGEN subsequently took up the task themselves on 'COUNTDOWN TO ECSTASY' (1973), combining even more opaque themes with densely layered, immaculately executed musicianship. Without the help of a hit single, however, the record only just made the Top 40; 'RIKKI DON'T LOSE THAT NUMBER' redressed the balance in fine style, a gorgeously lovelorn Top 5 hit inspired by a HORACE SILVER piano riff and a track which formed the centerpiece of 'PRETZEL LOGIC' (1974). More obviously jazz-influenced (included was a droll cover of Duke Ellington's 'EAST ST. LOUIS TOODLE-OO', while 'PARKER'S BAND' was a tribute to be-bop legend, CHARLIE PARKER) yet more immediately accessible, the album further enhanced their reputation among rock/pop connoiseurs. And it was a reputation that mushroomed without the PR of touring, BECKER and FAGEN refusing to play live after 1974 – although a tour was planned to promote the forthcoming 'KATY LIED' (1975), the idea was abandoned in its early stages. With STEELY DAN now basically a studio entity, both HODDER and BAXTER departed, the latter joining The DOOBIE BROTHERS (ironically enough, an easy rocking, all-American, all-touring hit machine that was essentially the antithesis of the whole SD concept). Coincidentally, BAXTER's replacement was MICHAEL McDONALD, a silky voiced future DOOBIES mentor whose harmony vocals helped sweeten the bite of the aforementioned 'KATY..'. 1976's 'THE ROYAL SCAM' was even more scathing in its lyrical ferocity, taking no prisoners in its portrayal of American society's inherent hypocrisy and monetary greed. But

if the sentiments were getting darker, the music was getting slicker; by this point, BECKER and FAGAN were employing the cream of the city's session musicians, recording 'AJA' (1977) in numerous different studios and endlessly remixing it prior to release. Painstakingly crafted but rarely overdone, 'AJA' – for many fans and critics alike – remains the definitive STEELY DAN opus, its dense, lush arrangements rewarding repeated listening. It was also their best seller, a transatlantic Top 5 (at the height of punk in the UK) later plundered by hip hopper's DE LA SOUL ('PEG'), Scotland's very own DEACON BLUE even taking their name from one of its tracks. With 'A.B.C.' coming under the auspices of 'M.C.A.', legal problems led to a three year wait for the final album of STEELY DAN's career, 'GAUCHO' (1980). Criticised for what many detractors saw as cloying slickness, the record was nevertheless another masterstroke of detached observation; the likes of 'BABYLON SISTERS' and 'GLAMOUR PROFESSION' were aimed squarely at the decadence of L.A.'s showbiz elite while 'THIRD WORLD MAN' remains one of the most haunting STEELY DAN compositions. After more than a decade of living in each other's pocket, BECKER and FAGAN parted company; while BECKER went into production, FAGAN penned a solo masterpiece in 'THE NIGHTFLY' (1982), trading in irony for surprisingly upbeat youthful reminiscences. The album's critical and commercial success didn't seem to spur him on to further glories, however, an incredible eleven year gap preceding a belated 90's follow-up, 'KAMAKIRIAD'. FAGAN returned BECKER's production favour on the latter's one and only solo effort, 'ELEVEN TRACKS OF WHACK' (1994), a hard-bitten affair borne of the kind of narcotic strife which would've finished a lesser talent. After appearing live as part of the New York Rock and Soul Revue in the early 90's, BECKER and FAGEN finally reformed STEELY DAN for a series of feverishly anticipated US live dates. Documented on 1995's 'ALIVE IN AMERICA' alive, the tour was an unqualified success despite the duo's misgivings; a new album, 'TWO AGAINST NATURE', will be issued in March 2000. • **Trivia:** In 1985, BECKER produced CHINA CRISIS' album 'Flaunt The Imperfection'.

Album rating: CAN'T BUY A THRILL (*8) / COUNTDOWN TO ECSTASY (*8) / PRETZEL LOGIC (*9) / KATY LIED (*8) / THE ROYAL SCAM (*6) / AJA (*8) / GREATEST HITS compilation (*9) / GAUCHO (*6) / STEELY DAN GOLD compilation (*8) / REELIN' IN THE YEARS – THE VERY BEST compilation (*9) / ALIVE IN AMERICA (*4) / Donald Fagen: THE NIGHTFLY (*6) / KAMAKIRIAD (*7) / Walter Becker: ELEVEN TRACKS OF WHACK (*5)

DONALD FAGEN (b.10 Jan'48, Passaic, New Jersey) – keyboards, vocals / **WALTER BECKER** (b.20 Feb'50, New York) – bass, vocals / **DAVID PALMER** – vocals (ex-MIDDLE CLASS) / **DENNY DIAS** – rhythm guitar / **JEFF BAXTER** – guitar (ex-HOLY MODAL ROUNDERS) / **JIM HODDER** – drums (ex-BEAD GAME)

		Probe	A.B.C.
Sep 72.	(7") (PRO 562) <11323> **DALLAS. / SAIL THE WATERWAY**	☐	
Nov 72.	(7") (PRO 577) <11338> **DO IT AGAIN. / FIRE IN THE HOLE**	☐	6
	(re-iss. Sep75 on 'A.B.C.'; 4075); hit UK No.39		
Jan 73.	(lp) (SPB 1062) <758> **CAN'T BUY A THRILL**	☐	17 Nov72
	– Do it again / Dirty work / Kings / Midnite cruiser / Only a fool would say that / Reeling in the years / Fire in the hole / Brooklyn (owes the charmer and me) / Change of the guard / Turn that heartbreak over again. (re-iss. Sep75 on 'A.B.C.' lp/c; ABCL/+C 5034); hit UK No.38) (re-iss. 1983 on 'M.C.A.' lp/c; MCL/+C 1769) (cd-iss. Jul88; DMCL 1769) (cd re-iss. Apr92; MCLD 19017)		
Mar 73.	(7") (PRO 587) <11352> **REELING IN THE YEARS. / ONLY A FOOL WOULD SAY THAT**	☐	11

──── **BECKER & FAGEN** now on lead vocals, when PALMER left to BIG WHA-KOO

Jul 73.	(7") (PRO 602) <11382> **SHOWBIZ KIDS. / RAZOR BOY**	☐	61
Jul 73.	(lp) (SPB 1079) <779> **COUNTDOWN TO ECSTASY**	☐	35
	– Bodhizattva / Razor boy / The Boston rag / Your gold teeth / Showbiz kids / My old school / Pearl of the quarter / King of the world. (re-iss. Feb82 on 'M.C.A.' lp/c; MCL/+C 1654) (re-iss. Jul83 on 'Fame' lp/c; FA/TC-FA 3069) (cd-iss. Dec88; DMCL 1654) (cd re-iss. Apr92; MCLD 19018)		
Oct 73.	(7") (PRO 606) <11396> **MY OLD SCHOOL. / PEARL OF THE QUARTER**	☐	63
Mar 74.	(lp) (SPBA 6282) <808> **PRETZEL LOGIC**	37	8
	– Rikki don't lose that number / Night by night / Any major dude will tell you / Barrytown / East St.Louis toodle-oo / Parker's bad / Through with buzz / Pretzel logic / With a gun / Charlie Freak / Monkey in your soul. (re-iss. Oct74 on 'A.B.C.' lp/c; ABCL/+C 5045) (re-iss. Feb84 on 'M.C.A.' lp/c; MCL/+C 1781) (cd-iss. Aug88 on 'M.C.A.'; DIDX 371) (cd re-iss. May90; DMCL 1781) (cd re-iss. Jun92; MCLD 19081)		
May 74.	(7") (PRO 622) <11439> **RIKKI DON'T LOSE THAT NUMBER. / ANY MAJOR DUDE WILL TELL YOU**	☐	4
	(re-iss. Oct78 on 'A.B.C.'; ABC 4241); hit UK No.58		

		A.B.C.	A.B.C.
Oct 74.	(7") (ABC 4019) <12033> **PRETZEL LOGIC. / THROUGH WITH BUZZ**	☐	57

──── **MICHAEL McDONALD** (b.12 Feb'52, St. Louis, Missouri) – keyboards, vocals repl. BAXTER to DOOBIE BROTHERS / **JEFF PORCARO** (b. 1 Apr'54) – drums repl. HODDER

Apr 75.	(lp/c) (ABCL/+C 5094) <846> **KATY LIED**	13	13
	– Black Friday / Bad sneakers / Rose darling / Daddy don't live in that New York City no more / Doctor Wu / Everyone's gone to the movies / Your gold teeth II / Chain lightning / Any world (that I'm welcome to) / Throw back the little ones. (re-iss. Jun84 on 'M.C.A.' lp/c; MCL/+C 1800) (cd-iss. Aug88; DIDX 373) (cd re-iss. Sep90 & Jun92; MCLD 19082)		
May 75.	(7") (ABC 4058) <12101> **BLACK FRIDAY. / THROW BACK THE LITTLE ONES**	☐	37
Sep 75.	(7") <12128> **BAD SNEAKERS. / CHAIN LIGHTNING**	-	37

──── When McDONALD joined DOOBIE BROTHERS and PORCARO left later joining TOTO, **BECKER & FAGEN** employed session people incl. **DENNY DIAS** part-time

May 76.	(lp/c) (ABCL/+C 5161> **THE ROYAL SCAM**	11	15
	– Kid Charlemagne / Caves of Altamira / Don't take me alive / Sign in stranger /		

The fez / Green earrings / Haitian divorce / Everything you did / The royal scam. *(re-iss. Sep82 on 'M.C.A.' lp/c; MCL/+C 1708) (cd-iss. Aug88; DIDX 370) (cd re-iss. Sep91 & Jun92; MCLD 19083)*

May 76. (7") *(ABC 4124) <12195>* **KID CHARLEMAGNE. / GREEN EARRINGS** — 82
Sep 76. (7") *<12222>* **THE FEZ. / SIGN IN STRANGER** - 59
Nov 76. (7") *(ABC 4152)* **HAITIAN DIVORCE. / SIGN IN STRANGER** 17 -
Sep 77. (lp/c) *(ABCL/+C 5225) <1006>* **AJA** 5 3
 – Black cow / Aja / Deacon blues / Peg / Home at last / I got the news / Josie. *(re-iss. 1983 on 'M.C.A.' lp/c; MCL/+C 1745) (cd-iss. 1985; DIDX 55) (cd re-iss. Sep91 & Jul92; MCLD 19145)*
Nov 77. (7") *(ABC 4207) <12320>* **PEG. / I GOT THE NEWS** — 11
Apr 78. (7"/12") *(ABC/+12 4217) <12355>* **DEACON BLUES. / HOME AT LAST** — 19 Mar78
Aug 78. (7") *<12404>* **JOSIE. / BLACK COW** - 26

M.C.A.   M.C.A.

Jul 78. (7") *(MCA 374) <40894>* **FM (NO STATIC AT ALL). / FM (Reprise)** 49 22 Jun78
Nov 80. (lp/c) *(ABCD/+C 616) <6102>* **GAUCHO** 27 9
 – Babylon sisters / Hey nineteen / Glamour profession / Gaucho / Time out of mind / My rival / Third world man. *(cd-iss. Jan85; DIDX 56) (re-iss. Sep86 lp/c; MCL/+C 1814) (cd re-iss. Sep91 & Jul92; MCLD 19146)*
Nov 80. (7") *(MCA 659) <51036>* **HEY NINETEEN. / BODHISATTVA (live)** — —
Mar 81. (7") *(MCA 680)* **BABYLON SISTERS. / TIME OUT OF MIND** — 10
Mar 81. (7") *<51082>* **TIME OUT OF MIND. / BODHISATTVA** - 22

—— Parted ways after album. FAGEN went solo and BECKER to production.

– compilations, others, etc. –

on 'M.C.A.' unless otherwise mentioned
Jan 78. (12"ep) *A.B.C.; (ABE 12-003)* **+ FOUR** -
 – Do it again / Haitian divorce / Dallas / Sail the waterway.
Mar 78. (lp; by BECKER & FAGEN) *Spark; (SRLP 124) <Visa; 7005>* **YOU GOTTA WALK IT (Film Soundtrack)** 1971
 (cd-iss. Sep92 on 'See For Miles')
Nov 78. (d-lp/c) *A.B.C.; (ABCD/+C 616) <1107>* **GREATEST HITS 1972-78** 41 30
 (re-iss. Mar82 on 'M.C.A.'; MCLD/+C 608)
Apr 82. (d-c) *(MCA2 101)* **CAN'T BUY A THRILL / AJA** -
Jun 82. (lp/c) *(MCF/+C 3145) <5324>* **GOLD** 44 -
 (w/ free-12") (re-iss. Aug91 cd/c; MCAD 10387)
Jul 82. (7") *(MCA 786)* **FM (NO STATIC AT ALL). / FM (REPRISE)** -
 (12"+=) (MCAT 786) – East St. Louis toodle-oo.
Apr 83. (7") *Old Gold; (OG 9321)* **DO IT AGAIN. / RIKKI DON'T LOSE THAT NUMBER** -
Oct 83. (d-c) *(MCA2 109)* **KATY LIED / THE ROYAL SCAM** -
Dec 83. (12"ep) *(MCAT 852)* **HAITIAN DIVORCE / DO IT AGAIN. / REELING IN THE YEARS / RIKKI DON'T LOSE THAT NUMBER** -
Mar 84. (lp) *Aero; <ML 8101>* **THE EARLY YEARS – WALTER BECKER & DONALD FAGEN**
Sep 84. (d-c) *(MCA2 115)* **COUNTDOWN TO ECSTACY / PRETZEL LOGIC** -
Aug 85. (cd) *(DIDX 306)* **DECADE OF STEELY DAN – THE BEST OF STEELY DAN** -
Oct 85. (lp/c) *(DAN TV/TC 1)* **REELIN' IN THE YEARS – THE VERY BEST OF STEELY DAN** 43 -
 – Do it again / Reelin' in the years / My old school / Bodhisattva / Show biz kids / Rikki don't lose that number / Pretzel logic / Black Friday / Bad sneakers / Doctor Wu / Haitian divorce / Kid Charlemagne / The fez / Peg / Josie / Deacon blues / Hey nineteen / Babylon sisters. *(re-iss. Dec92 d-cd/c; MCLD/MCLC 19147)*
Nov 85. (7") *(MSAM 32)* **REELING IN THE YEARS. / RIKKI DON'T LOSE THAT NUMBER** -
Apr 86. (c) *Showcase; (SHTC 128)* **SUN MOUNTAIN** (early demos) -
 (cd-iss. Oct92 on 'Thunderbolt'; CDTB 139)
May 86. (lp)(cd) *Bellaphon; (230-07-065)(288 07014)* **BERRYTOWN** (demos) - German
May 87. (lp/c/cd) *Thunderbolt; (THBL/THBL/CDTB 040)* **OLD REGIME** (early material) -
 (re-iss. Mar94 on 'Prestige' cd/c;)
Oct 87. (7") *(MCA 1214)* **RIKKI DON'T LOSE THAT NUMBER. / DO IT AGAIN** -
Oct 87. (lp/c/cd) *Telstar; (STAR//TCD 2297)* **DO IT AGAIN – THE VERY BEST OF STEELY DAN** 64 -
Apr 88. (lp)cd) *Thunderbolt; (THBL 054)(CDTB 056)* **STONE PIANO** (early material) -
Jun 88. (d-lp) *Castle; (CCSLP 193)* **BECKER AND FAGEN – THE COLLECTION** -
 (cd-iss. Nov93; CLACD 365)
Jul 93. (cd/c) *Charly; (CD CD/MC 116)* **ROARING OF THE LAMB** -
Sep 93. (cd/c; as WALTER BECKER & DONALD FAGEN) *Remember; (RMB 7/4 5004)* **FOUNDERS OF STEELY DAN** -
Nov 93. (cd/c) *(MCD/MCC 10967)* **REMASTERED – THE BEST OF STEELY DAN** 49
Dec 93. (4xcd-box) *(MCAD 410981)* **CITIZEN STEELY DAN (1972-1980)**
Feb 94. (cd/c) *Javelin; (HAD CD/MC 103)* **SPOTLIGHT ON STEELY DAN**
Jun 94. (d-cd) *Thunderbolt; (CDTB 503)* **CATALYST (THE ORIGINAL RECORDINGS 1968-71)** -
Feb 95. (cd; BECKER & FAGEN) *B.A.M.;* **PEARLS OF THE PAST** -
1995. (cd/c) *O.N.N.; (ONN 54 CD/MC)* **STEELY DAN (FEATURING WALTER BECKER & DONALD FAGEN)** -

DONALD FAGEN

Warners   Warners

Oct 82. (lp/c) *(923696-1/-4) <23696>* **THE NIGHTFLY** 44 11
 – New frontier / Walk between the raindrops / Maxine / Green flower street / The goodbye look / The nightfly / I.G.Y. (what a wonderful world). *(cd-iss. Jul88; 923696-2)*
Oct 82. (7") *(W 9900) <29900>* **I.G.Y. (WHAT A WONDERFUL WORLD). / WALK BETWEEN THE RAINDROPS** — 26
Jan 83. (7") *(W 9792) <29792>* **NEW FRONTIER. / MAXINE** — 70
 (12"+=) (W 9792T) – The goodbye look.
Apr 83. (7") *(W 9674)* **RUBY BABY. / WALK BETWEEN THE RAINDROPS**
 (below single from the film 'Bright Lights, Big City')
Apr 88. (7") *(W 7972) <27972>* **CENTURY'S END. / SHANGHAI CONFIDENTIAL (instrumental)** 83 Mar88
 (3"cd-s+=) (W 7972CD) – The nightfly / The goodbye look.

—— with **WALTER BECKER** – bass, solo guitar, co-writer some / **GEORGE WADENIUS** – guitar / **PAUL GRIFFIN** – hamond organ / **LEROY CLOUDEN or CHRISTOPHER PARKER** – drums / **BASHIRI JOHNSON** – percussion / **RANDY BRECKER + others** – horns

Reprise   Reprise

May 93. (cd/c/lp) *<(9362 45230-2/-4/-1)>* **KAMAKIRIAD** 3 10
 – Trans-island skyway / Countermoon / Springtime / Snowbound / Tomorrow's girls / Florida room / On the dunes / Teahouse on the tracks.
Jun 93. (7"/-c-s) *(W 0180/+C)* **TOMORROW'S GIRL. / SHANGHAI CONFIDENTIAL** 46
 (cd-s+=) (W 0180CDX) – Confide in me.
Aug 93. (7"/-c-s) *(WO 196/+C)* **TRANS-ISLAND SKYWAY. / BIG NOISE, NEW YORK**
 (12"+=/cd-s+=) (WO 196 T/CD) – Home at last (live).
Nov 93. (7"/-c-s) *(W 0216/+C)* **SNOWBOUND. / TRANS-ISLAND SKYWAY**
 (cd-s+=) (W 0216CD) – ('A'mix).

WALTER BECKER

Giant-RCA   Giant

Nov 94. (cd/c) *<(74321 22609-2/-4)>* **ELEVEN TRACKS OF WHACK**
 – Down in the bottom / Junkie girl / Surf and or die / Book of liars / Lucky Henry / Hard up case / Cringemaker / Girlfriend / My Waterloo / This moody bastard / Hat too flat.

STEELY DAN

—— duo re-formed for live appearances in the States. They had featured on various album 'LIVE AT THE BEACON' with The NEW YORK ROCK AND SOUL REVUE.

Giant-RCA   Giant

Oct 95. (cd/c) *(74321 28691-2/-4) <24634>* **ALIVE IN AMERICA (live 1994)** 62 40
 – Babylon sister / Green earrings / Bodhisattva / Reelin' in the years / Josie / Book of liars / Peg / Third World man / Kid Charlemagne / Sign in stranger / Aja.

> **Jim STEINMAN** (dig out; 4th edition or Great Metal . . .)

> **Martin STEPHENSON** (dig out; Great Alt & indie . . .)

STEPPENWOLF

Formed: Toronto, Canada . . . 1966 as blues band SPARROW, by JOHN KAY, plus MICHAEL MONARCH, GOLDY McJOHN, RUSHTON MOREVE and JERRY EDMONTON. After one-off 45 for 'Columbia', they soon relocated to Los Angeles following a brief stay in New York. There, they met producer Gabriel Mekler, who suggested the STEPPENWOLF name (after a Herman Hesse novel). They quickly signed to 'Dunhill' and recorded their eponymous 1968 debut, which included that summer's No.2 classic biker's anthem, 'BORN TO BE WILD'. This success resurrected the album's appeal, which finally climbed to the higher echelons of the charts. The track was subsequently used on the 1969 film, 'Easy Rider', alongside another from the debut, 'THE PUSHER'. While both songs were enjoyable, hot-wired romps through dusty blues-rock terrain, the pseudo-intellectual musings and less than inspired songwriting of JOHN KAY made the multitude of subsequent STEPPENWOLF releases hard going. Nevertheless, the band hit US Top 3 with the colourful psychedelia of the 'MAGIC CARPET RIDE' (1968) single, its parent album, 'STEPPENWOLF THE SECOND' (1969) notching up a similar placing in the album charts. By the early 70's, the band were experiencing diminishing chart returns and split after the 1972 concept album, 'FOR LADIES ONLY'. KAY recorded a couple of solo albums before reforming STEPPENWOLF in 1974. Signed to 'C.B.S.' then 'Epic', the band failed to resurrect their early momentum, although they continued to inflict their tired biker-rock on an oblivious music world right up until the 90's. • **Songwriters:** KAY written, except; THE PUSHER + SNOW BLIND FRIEND (Hoyt Axton) / SOOKIE SOOKIE (Grant Green) / BORN TO BE WILD (Dennis Edmonton; Jerry's brother) / I'M MOVIN' ON (Hank Snow) / HOOCHIE COOCHIE MAN (Muddy Waters). • **Trivia:** BORN TO BE WILD coined a new rock term in the their lyrics "heavy metal thunder". Early in 1969, they contributed some songs to another cult-ish film, 'Candy'.

Album rating: STEPPENWOLF (*6) / THE SECOND (*6) / AT YOUR BIRTHDAY PARTY (*6) / MONSTER (*7) / STEPPENWOLF 'LIVE' (*5) / STEPPENWOLF 7 (*5) / STEPPENWOLF GOLD – THEIR GREAT HITS compilation (*7) / FOR LADIES ONLY (*5) / FORGOTTEN SONGS AND UNSUNG HEROES (*5; by John Kay) / REST IN PEACE collection (*4) / 16 GREATEST HITS compilation (*7) / MY SPORTIN' LIFE (*4; by John Kay) / SLOW FLUX (*4) / HOUR OF THE WOLF (*3) / SKULLDUGGERY (*3) / REBORN TO BE WILD (*3) / ALL IN GOOD TIME (*3; by John Kay) / John Kay & Steppenwolf: LIVE IN LONDON (*4) / WOLF TRACKS (*3) / ROCK & ROLL REBELS (*4) / RISE & SHINE (*4) / BORN TO BE WILD: A RETROSPECTIVE compilation (*7)

JOHN KAY (b. JOACHIM F. KRAULEDAT, 12 Apr'44, Tilsit, Germany) – vox, guitar / **MICHAEL MONARCH** (b. 5 Jul'50, Los Angeles, California, USA) – guitar / **GOLDY McJOHN** (b. JOHN GOADSBY, 2 May'45) – organ / **RUSHTON MOREVE** (b.1948, Los Angeles) – bass / **JERRY EDMONTON** (b. JERRY McCROHAN, 24 Oct'46, Canada) – drums, vocals

		C.B.S.	Columbia
1966.	(7"; as The SPARROW) (202342) <43755> **TOMORROW'S SHIP. / ISN'T IT STRANGE**		
1967.	(7"; as The SPARROW) <43960> **GREEN BOTTLE LOVER. / DOWN GOES YOUR LOVE LIFE**	-	
1967.	(7"; as JOHN KAY) <44769> **TWISTED. / SQUAREHEAD PEOPLE**	-	

—— **JOHN RUSSELL MORGAN** – bass repl. MOREVE. He was killed in car crash on 1st Jul'81.

		R.C.A.	Dunhill
Nov 67.	(7") <4109> **A GIRL I KNOW. / THE OSTRICH**	-	
Apr 68.	(7") (RCA 1679) <4123> **SOOKIE SOOKIE. / TAKE WHAT YOU NEED**		Jan68
May 68.	(lp; mono/stereo) (RD/SF 7974) <50029> **STEPPENWOLF**	6	Jan68

– Sookie Sookie / Everybody's next one / Berry rides again / Hoochie coochie man / Born to be wild / Your wall's too high / Desperation / The pusher / A girl I knew / Take what you need / The ostrich. (re-iss. Apr70 on 'Stateside'; SSL 5020); hit No.59 (re-iss. Jun87 on 'M.C.A.' lp/c; MCL/+C 1857) (cd-iss. Jul87; CMCAD 31020) (re-iss. Apr92 cd/c; MCL D/C 19019)

Aug 68.	(7") (RCA 1735) <4138> **BORN TO BE WILD. / EVERYBODY'S NEXT ONE**		2 Jun68

(re-iss. May69 on 'Stateside'; SS 8017); hit No.30

		Stateside	Dunhill
Oct 68.	(7") (SS 8003) <4160> **MAGIC CARPET RIDE. / SOOKIE SOOKIE**		3 Sep68

(re-iss. Sep69; SS 8027)

Jan 69.	(lp; stereo/mono) (S+/SL 5003) <50053> **STEPPENWOLF THE SECOND**		3 Nov68

– Faster than the speed of life / Tighten up your wig / None of your doing / Spiritual fantasy / Don't step on the grass, Sam / 28 / Magic carpet ride / Disappointment number (unknown) / Lost and found by trial and error / Hodge, podge strained through a Leslie / Resurrection / Reflections. (cd-iss. Jun87 on 'M.C.A.'; CMCAD 31021)

—— **LARRY BYROM** (b.27 Dec'48, USA) – guitar repl. MONARCH / **NICK St.NICHOLAS** (b. KLAUS KARL KASSBAUM, 28 Sep'43, Pion, Germany) – bass repl. RUSSELL

Mar 69.	(7") (SS 8013) <4182> **ROCK ME. / JUPITER CHILD**		10 Feb69
Jun 69.	(lp; stereo/mono) (S+/SL 5011) <50060> **AT YOUR BIRTHDAY PARTY**		7 Mar69

– Don't cry / Chicken wolf / Lovely meter / Round and down / It's never too late / Sleeping dreaming / Jupiter child / She'll be better / Cat killer / Rock me / God fearing man / Mango juice / Happy birthday.

May 69.	(7") <4192> **IT'S NEVER TOO LATE. / HAPPY BIRTHDAY**	-	51
Aug 69.	(7") <4205> **MOVE OVER. / POWER PLAY**	-	31
Dec 69.	(7") <4221> **MONSTER. / BERRY RIDES AGAIN**	-	39
Jan 70.	(7") (SS 8035) **MONSTER. / MOVE OVER**		
Jan 70.	(lp) (SSL 5021) <50066> **MONSTER**	43	17 Nov69

– Monster / Suicide / America / Draft resister / Power play / Move over / Fag / What would you do (if I did that to you) / From here to there eventually. (cd-iss. Sep91 on 'Beat Goes On'; BGOCD 126)

Mar 70.	(7") (SS 8038) **THE PUSHER. / YOUR WALL'S TOO HIGH**		-
Jun 70.	(7") (SS 8049) <4234> **HEY LAWDY MAMA. / TWISTED**		35 Apr70
Jun 70.	(d-lp) (SSL 5029) <50075> **STEPPENWOLF 'LIVE'**	16	7 Apr70

– Sooki, Sooki / Don't step on the grass Sam / Tighten up your wig / Hey lawdy mama / Magic carpet ride / The pusher / Corina, Corina / Twisted / From here to there eventually / Born to be wild. (re-iss. Oct74 on 'A.B.C.'; ABCL 5007) (cd-iss. Aug98 on 'Beat Goes On'; BGOCD 412)

Sep 70.	(7") (SS 8056) <4248> **SCREAMING NIGHT HOG. / SPIRITUAL FANTASY**		62 Aug70

		Probe	Dunhill
Nov 70.	(7") (PRO 510) <4261> **WHO NEEDS YA. / EARSCHPLITTENLOUDENBOOMER**		54
Nov 70.	(lp) (SPBA 6254) <50090> **STEPPENWOLF 7**		19

– Ball crusher / Forty days and forty nights / Fat Jack / Renegade / Foggy mental breakdown / Snow blind friend / Who needs ya / Earschplittenloudenboomer / Hippo stomp.

Mar 71.	(7") (PRO 525) <4269> **SNOW BLIND FRIEND. / HIPPO STOMP**		60 Feb71

—— **KENT HENRY** – guitar repl. BYROM

—— **GEORGE BIONDO** (b. 3 Sep'45, Brooklyn, N.Y.) – bass repl. NICK

Jul 71.	(7") (PRO 534) <4283> **RIDE WITH ME. / FOR MADMEN ONLY**		52
Oct 71.	(7") (PRO 544) <4292> **FOR LADIES ONLY. / SPARKLE EYES**		64
Oct 71.	(lp) (SPBA 6260) <50110> **FOR LADIES ONLY**		54

– For ladies only / I'm asking / Shackles and chains / Tenderness / The night time's for you / Jadet strumpet / Sparkle eyes / Black pit / Ride with me / In hopes of a garden.

—— disbanded Feb'72, EDMUNTON and McJOHN formed MANBEAST

JOHN KAY

went solo, augmented by **KENT HENRY + GEORGE BIONDO** plus **HUGH SULLIVAN** – keyboards / **PENTII WHITNEY GLEN** – drums / etc. (same label)

Apr 72.	(lp) (1054) <50120> **FORGOTTEN SONGS AND UNSUNG HEROES**		

– Many a mile / Walk beside me / You win again / To be alive / Bold marauder / Two of a kind / Walking blues / Somebody / I'm moving on.

Apr 72.	(7") <4309> **I'M MOVIN' ON. / WALK BESIDE ME**	-	52
Jul 72.	(7") <4319> **YOU WIN AGAIN. / SOMEBODY**	-	
Jul 73.	(7") <4351> **MOONSHINE. / NOBODY LIVES HERE ANYMORE**	-	
Jul 73.	(lp) (6274) <50147> **MY SPORTIN' LIFE**	-	

– Moonshine / Nobody lives here anymore / Drift away / Heroes and devils / My sportin' life / Easy evil / Giles of the river / Dance to my song / Sing with the children.

Sep 73.	(7") (PRO 601) <4360> **EASY EVIL. / DANCE TO MY SONG**		

STEPPENWOLF

re-formed (**KAY, McJOHN, EDMUNTON, BIONDO**) plus **BOBBY COCHRAN** – guitar repl. KENT (first and last with horn section)

		C.B.S.	Mums
Oct 74.	(lp) (80358) <33093> **SLOW FLUX**		47 Sep74

– Gang war blues / Children of the night / Justice don't be slow / Get into the wind / Jeraboah / Straight shootin' woman / Smokey factory blues / Morning blue / A fool's factory / Fishin' in the dark.

Oct 74.	(7") (MUM 2679) <6031> **STRAIGHT SHOOTIN' WOMAN. / JUSTICE DON'T BE SLOW**		29 Sep74
Jan 75.	(7") <6034> **GET INTO THE WIND. / MORNING BLUE**	-	
Apr 75.	(7") (MUM 3147) <6036> **SMOKEY FACTORY BLUES. / A FOOL'S FANTASY**		

—— **ANDY CHAPIN** – keyboards repl. McJOHN who went solo

Aug 75.	(7") (MUM 3470) <6040> **CAROLINE (ARE YOU READY). / ANGEL DRAWERS**		
Sep 75.	(lp) (69151) <33583> **HOUR OF THE WOLF**		

– Caroline (are you ready for the outlaw world) / Annie, Annie over / Two for the love of one / Just for tonight / Hard rock road / Someone told a lie / Another's lifetime / Mr. Penny pincher.

—— **WAYNE COOK** – keyboards repl. ANDY

		Epic	Epic
May 77.	(lp) (81328) <34120> **SKULLDUGGERY**		

– Skullduggery / Roadrunner / Rock and roll song / Train of thought / Life is a gamble / Pass it on / Sleep / Lip service.

Dec 77.	(lp) <34382> **REBORN TO BE WILD** (remixes)	-	

– Straight shootin' woman / Hard rock road / Another's lifetime / Mr. Penny pincher / Smokey factory blues / Caroline / Get into the wind / Gang war blues / Children of night / Skullduggery.

—— Disbanded yet again.

JOHN KAY

with **LARRY BYROM** – slide guitar / **MAC McANALLY** – guitar / **CLAYTON IVEY** – keyboards / **BOB WRAY** – bass / **ROGER CLARK** – drums

		Mercury	Mercury
Jun 78.	(lp) (9110 054) <1-3715> **ALL IN GOOD TIME**		

– Give me some news I can use / The best is barely good enough / That's when I think of you / Ain't nobody home (in California) / Ain't nothin' like it used to be / Business is business / Show me how you'd like it done / Down in New Orleans / Say you will / Hey, I'm alright.

Jun 78.	(7") <74004> **GIVE ME SOME NEWS I COULD USE. / SAY YOU WILL**	-	-
Jun 78.	(7") (6167 683) **GIVE ME SOME NEWS I CAN USE. / BUSINESS IS BUSINESS**		-

—— In the early 80's, KAY and group toured as

JOHN KAY & STEPPENWOLF

with **MICHAEL PALMER** – guitar / **BRETT TUGGLE** – keyboards / **CHAD PERRY** – bass / **STEVEN PALMER** – drums

		not iss.	Allegiance
Dec 81.	(lp) **LIVE IN LONDON** (live)	-	

– Sookie Sookie / Give me news I can use / You / Hot night in a cold town / Ain't nothin' like it used to be / Magic carpet ride / Five finger discount / Hey lawdy mama / Business is business / Born to be wild / The pusher.

Dec 81.	(7") <3909> **HOT TOME IN A COLD TOWN. /**	-	-

—— **WELTON GITE** – bass repl. CHAD / added **MICHAEL WILK** – keyboards

		not iss.	CBS-Sony
1983.	(lp) <DIDZ 10010> **WOLFTRACKS**		

– All I want is all you got / None of the above / You / Every man for himself / Five finger discount / Hold your head up / Hot night in a cold town / Down to earth / For rock'n'roll / The balance. (UK-iss.May97 as 'FIVE FINGER DISCOUNT' on 'C.M.C.'; 10045-2)

—— now with **ROCKET RITCHOTTE** – guitar, vocals + **MICHAEL WILK** – keyboards, bass / **RON HURST** – drums, vocals. Finally issued new material 1988.

		Disky	Qwil
May 88.	(lp/c/cd) (979209-1/-4/-2) <1560> **ROCK & ROLL REBELS**		Sep87

– Give me life / Rock and roll rebels / Hold on (never give up, never give in) / Man on a mission / Everybody knows you / Rock steady (I'm rough and ready) / Replace the face / Turn out the lights / Give me news I can use / Rage.

		I.R.S.	I.R.S.
Aug 90.	<(cd/c/lp)> (EIRSA 1037) <241066-2/-4/-1) **RISE & SHINE**		

– Let's do it all / Time out / Do or die / Rise & shine / The wall / The daily blues / Keep rockin' / Rock'n'roll war / Sign on the line / We like it, we love it (we want more of it).

– compilations, others, etc. –

—— on 'Probe' UK / 'Dunhill' US unless mentioned otherwise

Jul 69. (lp) *Stateside; (5015)* / *Dunhill; <50060>* **EARLY STEPPENWOLF** | | 29 |
(live from 1967 as The SPARROW)
– Power play / Howlin' for my baby / Goin' upstairs / Corina Corina / Tighten up your wig / The pusher.

Mar 71. (lp) *(SPB 1033) <50099>* **STEPPENWOLF GOLD** | | 24 |
– Born to be wild / It's never too late / Rock me / Hey lawdy mama / Move over / Who needs ya / Magic carpet ride / The pusher / Sookie Sookie / Jupiter's child / Screaming night hog. *(re-iss. Oct74 on 'A.B.C.'; ABCL 8613) (re-iss. Aug80 on 'M.C.A.'; 1502) (re-iss. Aug81 lp/c; MCM/+C 1619) (re-iss. Jan83 on 'Fame' lp/c; FA/TCFA 3052)*

Jul 72. (lp) *(SPB 1059) <50124>* **REST IN PEACE** | 62 | Jun72 |

Mar 73. (lp) *(SPB 1071) <50135>* **16 GREATEST HITS** | | Feb73 |
(re-iss. Oct74 on 'A.B.C.'; ABCL 5028) (cd-iss. Feb91 on 'M.C.A.'; MCAD 37049)

Jun 80. (7") *M.C.A. (MCA 614)* **BORN TO BE WILD. / THE PUSHER** | | |
(re-iss. Apr83 on 'Old Gold'; OG 9323)

Jul 85. (lp/c) *M.C.A.; (MCM/+C 5002)* **GOLDEN GREATS** | | |
– Born to be wild / It's never too late / Rock me / Hey lawdy mama / Move over / Who needs ya / Monster / Snow blind friend / Magic carpet ride / The pusher / Sookie sookie / Jupiter's child / Screaming dog night / Ride with me / For ladies only / Tenderness.

1991. (cd) *M.C.A.; <MCA 10389>* **BORN TO BE WILD: A RETROSPECTIVE**

Aug 91. (cd/c) *Knight; (KN CD/MC 10022)* **NIGHTRIDING** | - | - |

Apr 93. (cd) *Movieplay Gold; (MPG 74016)* **BORN TO BE WILD** | - | - |

Jan 94. (cd) *Legacy;* **TIGHTEN UP YOUR WIG – THE BEST OF JOHN KAY & SPARROW**

May 97. (cd) *Experience; (EXP 029)* **STEPPENWOLF**

Feb 99. (c-s/cd-s) *M.C.A.; (MCS C/TD 48104)* **BORN TO BE WILD / MAGIC CARPET RIDE / ROCK ME** | 18 | |

Feb 99. (cd) *M.C.A.; (MCLD 19386)* **THE BEST OF STEPPENWOLF** | | - |

Mar 99. (cd) *Beat Goes On; (BGOCD 450)* **STEPPENWOLF / STEPPENWOLF II** | | - |

JOHN KAY

| | | not iss. |

May 97. (cd) *(CD 10045-2)* **FIVE FINGERS DISCOUNT** | - | |
– Five fingers discount / You / All I want is what you got / None of the above / Balance / Down to earth / Hot night in a cold town / Hold your head up / For rock'n'roll / Every man for himself.

STEREOLAB

Formed: South London, England ... late 1990, by ex-indie stalwart TIM GANE (mainman for McCARTHY), who invited girlfriend LAETITIA SADIER to join. They soon completed the initial line-up with MARTIN KEAN and JOE DILWORTH (other past indie veterans), subsequently forming their own label, 'Duophonic Super 45s'. The group released three 45's ('SUPER 45', 'SUPER ELECTRIC' & 'STUNNING DEBUT ALBUM') in 1991, the second of which was for the 'Too Pure' label (these have re-instated vinyl as worthy product, whether for limited edition collectors or just vinyl junkies who hate cd's). The following year, the eclectic ambient-boogie machine that was STEREOLAB topped the indie charts with their actual "stunning debut album", 'PENG!'. The record ran the gamut of the band's minimalist influences including VELVET UNDERGROUND, JOHN CAGE, NEU! and SPACEMEN 3. During this period, the couple introduced four new members; MARY HANSEN, SEAN O'HAGAN, DUNCAN BROWN and ANDY RAMSAY, who helped them with a busy touring schedule. In 1993, they signed to 'Elektra' in the States for a 6-figure sum, while in the UK, they released several more 45's! and an album, 'TRANSIENT RANDOM NOISE BURSTS WITH ANNOUNCEMENTS', which, like the classy single, 'JENNY ONDIOLINE', scraped into the UK charts (the track was premiered on Channel 4's "The Word" programme). 1994 saw them unsurprisingly hit the UK Top 20 with another double album, 'MARS AUDIAC QUINTET'. Two years later, with their best offering to date, 'EMPEROR TOMATO KETCHUP', they had established themselves as leaders of the "Metronomic Underground" scene, as the opening track suggested. Over the course of the last three years (including 1997's excellent 'DOTS AND LOOPS'), the band's sound had become increasingly characterised by the dreamy French-style vocals of LAETITIA (pronounced Le-ti-seaya), akin to a spacier SARAH CRACKNELL (of SAINT ETIENNE). Returning to the fold in August '99, STEREOLAB (complete with Gallic songstress, BRIGITTE FONTAINE) issued one of their special limited singles, 'CALIMERO', although it was not a feature on their accompanying album, 'COBRA AND PHASES GROUP PLAY VOLTAGE IN THE MILKY NIGHT'. Officially previewed with yet another single, 'THE FREE DESIGN' (inspired by the obscure outfit of the same name!), the album was a little too twee and lightweight for some, one slightly perturbed (or disturbed?) NME critic in particular panning it enough to give it zero out of ten! (a hanging offence in anyone's book). • **Songwriters:** GANE songs / SADIER lyrics.

Album rating: SWITCHED ON! collection (*6) / PENG! (*7) / THE GROOP PLAYED "SPACE AGE BATCHELOR PAD MUSIC" (*5) / TRANSIENT RANDOM NOISE BURSTS WITH ANNOUNCEMENTS (*8) / REFRIED ELECTOPLASM (SWITCHED ON, VOL.2) compilation (*6) / MUSIC FOR THE AMORPHOUS BODY STUDY CENTER (*8) / MARS AUDIO QUINTET (*8) / EMPEROR TOMATO KETCHUP (*9) / DOTS AND LOOPS (*8) / COBRA AND PHASES GROUP PLAY VOLTAGE IN THE MILKY NIGHT (*6)

TIM GANE (b.12 Jul'64) – guitar, vox organ, guitar (ex-McCARTHY) / **LAETITIA SADIER** (b. 6 May'68, Paris, France) – vocals, vox organ, guitar, tambourine, moog / **REBECCA MORRIS** – vocals / **JOE DILWORTH** – drums (of TH' FAITH HEALERS)

| | Duophonic | not iss. |

May 91. (10"ep-mail order) *(DS45-01)* **SUPER 45**
– The light (that will cease to fail) / Au grand jour / Brittle / Au grand jour!.

—— added **MARTIN KEAN** (b.New Zealand) – guitar (ex-CHILLS) / **RUSSELL YATES** – live guitar (of MOOSE). **MICK CONROY** (ex-MOOSE) was also a live member early '92.

Nov 91. (7"clear,7"colrd) *(DS45-02)* **STUNNING DEBUT ALBUM: Doubt / Changer** | | |

| | Too Pure | Slumberland |

Sep 91. (10"ep) *(PURE 4)* **SUPERELECTRIC / HIGH EXPECTATION. / THE WAY WILL BE OPENING / CONTACT**

Apr 92. (cd-ltd.) *(31022) <Slumberland 22>* **SWITCHED ON** (compilation)
– Superelectric / Doubt / Au grand jour / The way will be opening / Brittle / Contract / Au grand jour / High expectation / The light that will cease to fail / Changer. *(re-iss. Mar97 on 'Dupophonic' cd/lp; TBC 25/24) (cd/lp re-iss. Mar99 on 'Too Pure'; PUREL 78 CD/LP)*

—— GINA departed after above. (when did she join?)

| | Too Pure | American |

May 92. (cd,c,lp) *(PURE 11) <43018>* **PENG!** | | |
– Super falling star / Orgiastic / Peng! 33 / K-stars / Perversion / You little shits / The seeming and the meaning / Mellotron / Enivrez-vous / Stomach worm / Surrealchemist.

—— added **MARY HANSEN** – vocals, tambourine, guitar / **ANDY RAMSAY** – percussion, vox organ, bazouki repl. DILWORTH

Sep 92. (10"ep,10"clear-ep,cd-ep) *(PURE 14)* **LOW FI** | | |
– Et de votre coeur endormi / (Varoom!) / Laisser-faire / Elektro – He held the world in his iron grip.

—— added **SEAN O'HAGAN** – vox organ, guitar (ex-MICRODISNEY, ex-HIGH LLAMAS)

Feb 93. (7",7"pink) *<Slumberland 24>* **JOHN CAGE BUBBLEGUM. / ELOGE D'EROS** | - | |

—— added **DUNCAN BROWN** – bass, guitar, vocals

Mar 93. (cd,c,m-lp) *(PURE 19) <43013>* **THE GROOP PLAYED "SPACE AGE BACHELOR PAD MUSIC"** | | |
– Avant-garde M.O.R. / Space age bachelor pad music (mellow) / The groop play chord X / Space age bachelor pad music (foamy) / Ronco symphony / We're not adult orientated / UHF-MFP / We're not adult orientated (new wave live).

| | Duophonic | Elektra |

Aug 93. (10"ep/cd-ep) *(DUHF D/CD 01) <8815>* **JENNY ONDIOLINE / FRUCTION / GOLDEN BALL / FRENCH DISCO** | 75 | |

Sep 93. (cd/c/2xlp) *(DUHF CD/DMC/D 02) <61536>* **TRANSIENT RANDOM-NOISE BURSTS WITH ANNOUNCEMENTS** | 62 | |
– Tone burst / Our trinitone blast / Pack yr romantic mind / I'm going out of my way / Golden ball / Pause / Jenny Ondioline / Analogue rock / Crest / Lock-groove lullaby.

Nov 93. (7") *(DUHF D01P)* **FRENCH DISKO (new version). / JENNY ONDIOLINE** | | - |

—— added **KATHERINE GIFFORD** – synthesizers, keyboards

Jul 94. (7"ltd) *(DUHFD 04S)* **PING PONG. / MOOGIE WONDERLAND** | 45 | - |
(10"+=/cd-s+=) *(DUHF D/CD 04)* – Pain et spectacles / Transcoma (live).

Aug 94. (cd/c/d-lp) *(DUHF CD/MC/D 05) <61669>* **MARS AUDIAC QUINTET** | 16 | |
– Three-dee melodie / Wow and flutter / Transona five / Des etoiles electroniques / Ping pong / Anamorphose / Three longers later / Nihilist assault group / International colouring contest / The stars of our destination / Transporte sans bouger / L'enfer des formes / Outer accelerator / New orthophony / Fiery yellow. *(free clear-7" w /d-lp + cd-s on cd) (DUHF D/CD 05X)* – Klang-tang / Ulaan batter.

Oct 94. (7"ltd) *(DUHFD 07S)* **WOW AND FLUTTER. / HEAVY DENIM** | 70 | - |
(10"+=/cd-s+=) *(DUHF D/CD 07)* – Nihilist assault group / Narco Martenot.

Apr 95. (10"ep/cd-ep) *(DUHF D/CD 08)* **AMORPHOUS BODY STUDY CENTRE** | 59 | - |
– Pop quiz / The extension trip / How to explain your internal organs overnight / The brush descends the length / Melochord seventy five / Space moment.

Sep 95. (cd/c/colrd-d-lp) *(DUHF CD/MC/D 09) / Drag City; <DC 82>* **REFRIED ECTOPLASM (SWITCHED ON – VOLUME II)** (compilation) | 30 | |
– Harmonium / Lo boob oscillator / Mountain / Revox / French disko / Exploding head movie / Eloge d'eros / Tone burst (country) / Animal or vegetable (a wonderful wooden reason) / John Cage bubblegum / Cybele's reverie.

—— **GANE / SADIER / HANSEN / RAMSAY + BROWN** added **MORGANE LHOTE** (guests; SEAN O'HAGAN / JOHN McENTIRE (of TORTOISE) + RAY DICKARTY)

—— KATHERINE GIFFORD formed indie supergroup SNOWPONY

Feb 96. (7") *(DUHFD 10S)* **CYBELE'S REVERIE. / BRIGITTE** | 62 | |
(10"+=/cd-s+=) *(DUHF D/CD 10)* – Les yper yper sound / Young lungs.

Mar 96. (d-lp/c/cd) *(DUHF D/MC/CD 11) <61640>* **EMPEROR TOMATO KETCHUP** | 27 | Apr96 |
– Metronomic underground / Cybele's reverie / Percolator / Les ypersound / Spark plug / Olv 26 / The noise of carpet / Tomorrow is already here / Emperor tomato ketchup / Monstre sacre / Motoroller scalatron / Slow fast Hazel / Anonymous collective.

Apr 96. (12"ltd.) *(DS 3311)* **SIMPLE HEADPHONE MIND. / (other track by NURSE WITH WOUND)** | | - |
(re-iss. Jun97; same)

—— now without BROWN, who was repl. by **RICHARD HARRISON**

Sep 96. (7";on 'Lissys') *(LISS 15)* **SHE USED TO CALL ME SADNESS.** | | - |

Nov 96. (7"ep)(12"ep/cd-ep) *(DUHFD 14S)(DUHF D/CD 14)* **FLUORESCENCES EP** | | - |
– Fluorescences / Pinball / You used to call me sadness / Soop groove *2.

Dec 96. (12"; STEREOLAB & WAGON CHRIST) *(DUHFD 15)*
METROGNOMIC UNDERGROUND. /   `[ ]` `[ - ]`
Sep 97. (7") *(DUHFD 16S)* **MISS MODULAR. / ALLURES**   `[ 60 ]` `[ - ]`
(12"+=/cd-s+=) *(DUHF D/CD 16)* – Off-on / Spinal column.
Sep 97. (cd/c/d-lp) *(DUHF CD/C/D 17)* <62065> **DOTS AND LOOPS**   `[ 19 ]` `[ ]`
– Brakhage / Miss Modular. / The flower called Nowhere / Prisoner of Mars /
Rainbo conversation / Refractions in the plastic pulse / Parsec / Ticker-tape of the
unconscious / Contronatura.

—— **SADIER, GANE, HANSEN, RAMSEY + LHOTE** were joined by **SIMON JOHNS** – bass
(ex-CLEARSPOT) / **KEV HOOPER** – musical saw (ex-STUMP) / **ROB MAZUREK**
– cornet / **DOMINIC MURCOTT** – marimba / plus guests **JOHN McENTIRE** (of
TORTOISE) / **JIM O'ROURKE + SEAN O'HAGAN**
Aug 99. (7"/cd-s; STEREOLAB & BRIGITTE FONTAINE)
(DS45/+CD 25) **CALIMERO. /** (other track 'Cache Cache'   `[ ]` `[ - ]`
by MONADE)
Sep 99. (7") *(DUHFD 22S)* **THE FREE DESIGN. / ESCAPE POD**
(FROM THE WORLD OF MEDICAL OBSERVATIONS)   `[ ]` `[ - ]`
(cd-s+=) *(DUHFCD 22)* – With friends like these / Les aimes des memes.
Sep 99. (cd) *(DUHFCD 23)* **COBRA AND PHASES GROUP PLAY**
VOLTAGE IN THE MILKY NIGHT   `[ ]` `[ - ]`
– Fuses / People do it all the time / The free design / Blips drips and strips / Italian
shoes continuum / Infinity girl / The spiracles / Op hop detonation / Puncture in
the radah permutation / Velvet water / Blue milk / Caleidoscopic gaze / Strobo
acceleration / The emergency kisses / Come and play in the milky night.

– more very limited singles, etc. –

Jun 92. (7"pink) B.M.I.; *(BMI 025)* **THE LIGHT (THAT WILL CEASE**
TO FAIL). / AU GRAND JOUR   `[ ]` `[ - ]`
Jul 92. (7"colrd) Duophonic; *(DS45-04)* **HARMONIUM. / FARFISA**   `[ ]` `[ - ]`
Oct 93. (10"ep) Clawfist; *(Clawfist 20)* **CRUMB DUCK (with NURSE**
WITH WOUND)   `[ ]` `[ - ]`
– Animal or vegetable / Exploding head movie.
Oct 93. (7"clear) Sub Pop; *(<SP 107/283>)* **LE BOOB OSCILLATOR. /**
TEMPTER   `[ ]` `[ - ]`
Nov 93. (7") Teenbeat; <Teenbeat 121> **MOUNTAIN. /** ('B'by Unrest) `[ - ]` `[ - ]`
Oct 98. (d-cd/d-lp) <DC 159> **ALUMINIUM TUNES: SWITCHED**
ON VOL.3   `[ - ]` `[ ]`
– Pop quiz – The extension trip / How to play your internal organs / Brush descends
the length / Melochord seventy-five / Space moment / Speedy car / Golden atoms /
Olan bator / One small step / Iron man / Long hair of death / You used to call me
sadness / New orthophony / One note samba – Surfboard / Cadriopo / Klang tone /
Get Carter / 1000 miles an hour / Percolations / Seeperbold / Check and double
check / Munich madness / Metronumro underground / Incredible He-woman.

STEREO MC'S

Formed: Clapham, London, England . . . 1985 by DJ/producer NICK
HALLAM (aka THE HEAD) and rapper ROB BIRCH. After landing £7,000
from property developers who wanted them to vacate their flat, the enterprising
pair used the cash to start up their own label, 'Gee Street'. The operation
subsequently gained the backing of New York's '4th & Broadway', as well as
a UK deal with 'Island', the duo released their first single, 'MOVE IT', for
the label in Spring '88. Although DJ CESARE was initially an integral part
of the STEREO MC's set up, he soon departed for a solo career. The debut
album, '33-45-78' (1989) introduced the group's distinctive British hip hop
sound, earning them a support slot on a HAPPY MONDAYS American tour
where they eventually scored their first chart success, 'ELEVATE MY MIND'
breaking the US Top 40 singles list in the summer of '91. A follow-up album
had appeared the previous year, 'SUPERNATURAL', the record also spawning
the classic 'LOST IN MUSIC', still one of the group's best loved tracks. By
1992, the STEREO MC's move towards a completely organic hip hop sound
was complete, backing vocalists VERONICA and ANDREA augmenting
drummer OWEN IF and vocal stalwart, CATH COFFEY. Previewed by the
hypnotic skank of the 'CONNECTED' single, the album of the same name
propelled STEREO MC's into the big league. A seamless amalgam of hip hop,
soul and funk, the record was a massive crossover hit, pulling in clubbers, rap
fiends, indie and pop fans alike, eventually earning the band a Brit Award in
1994 for best group and best album (dance section). One of the few success
stories in British rap, the group's universal appeal is obviously grounded in
solid songwriting, as well as a fearsome live reputation. The STEREO MC's
have also maintained a concurrent career as esteemed remixers, servicing
everyone from The JUNGLE BROTHERS to U2, whom they supported for
part of their 'Zooropa' tour. With their foot squarely in the MY BLOODY
VALENTINE/STONE ROSES studio camp, however, it's now verging on
seven years since the group's last release, only the occasional remix keeping
the STEREO MC's name alive. • **Songwriters:** BIRCH-HALLAM, except
SALSA HOUSE (Richie Rich) / BLACK IS BLACK (Jungle Brothers) /
DANCE 4 ME (Queen Lafitah).

Album rating: 33-45-78 (*5) / SUPERNATURAL (*6) / CONNECTED (*8)

ROB B (b. ROBERT BIRCH, 11 Jun'61, Nottingham, England) – vocals / **THE HEAD** (b.
NICK HALLAM, 11 Jun'60, Nottingham) – DJ/producer / **OWEN IF** (b. IAN ROSSITER,
20 Mar'59, Newport, Wales) – drums / **CATH COFFEY** (b. 1965, Kenya) – vocals

		4th & Broad	4th & Broad
Mar 88.	(7"; STEREO MC'S & CESARE) *(BRW 94)* **MOVE IT. / FEEL SO GOOD**	`[ ]`	`[ - ]`

(12"+=) *(12BRW 94)* – ('A'mix).
above with CESARE although he left soon after.
Oct 88. (7") *(BRW 119)* **WHAT IS SOUL?** / ('A'-Rob B mix)   `[ ]` `[ - ]`
(12"+=) *(12BRW 119)* – ('A'vocal mix) / ('A'instrumental) / ('A'acappella mix).

Jun 89. (7"/c-s) *(BRW/BRCA 134)* **ON 33. / GEE STREET**   `[ ]` `[ - ]`
(10"+=) *(10BRW 134)* – Non stop.
(12"+=) *(12BRW 134)* – ('A'-DJ Mark the 45 King mix).
Jul 89. (lp/c/cd) *(BR LP/CA/CD 532)* **33-45-78**   `[ ]` `[ - ]`
– On 33 / Use it / Gee Street / Neighbourhood / Toe to toe / What is soul? / Use it
(part 2) / Outta touch / Sunday 19th March / This ain't a love song / Ancient concept /
On the mike / Back to the future.
Aug 89. (7") *(BRW 148)* **LYRICAL MACHINE. / ON THE MIKE**   `[ ]` `[ - ]`
(12"+=) *(12BRW 148)* – Mechanical / Bring it on.
Sep 90. (7") *(BRW 186)* **ELEVATE MY MIND. / SMOKIN' WITH THE**
MOTHERMAN   `[ 74 ]` `[ - ]`
(12"+=/cd-s+=) *(12BRW/BRCD 186)* – ('A'dub).
Sep 90. (cd/c/lp) *(BR CD/CA/LP 556)* **SUPERNATURAL**   `[ ]` `[ - ]`
– I'm a believer / Scene of the crime / Declaration / Elevate my mind / Watcha
gonna do / Two horse town / Ain't got nobody / Goin' back to my roots / Lost in
music / Life on the line / The other side / Set me loose / What's the word / Early
one morning. (cd+=/c+=) – Smokin' with the motherman / Relentless. (cd re-iss.
Apr94 on 'Island'; IMCD 185)
Mar 91. (7"/c-s) *(BRW/BRCA 198)* **LOST IN MUSIC (Ultimatum**
remix). / EARLY ONE MORNING   `[ 46 ]` `[ ]`
(cd-s+=) *(BRCD 198)* – ('A'instrumental).
(12") *(12BRW 198)* – ('A'side) / ('A'-B.B. mix) / ('A'-B.B. instrumental).
May 91. (c-s,12",cd-s) <447519> **ELEVATE MY MIND. / ('A'-12"**
version)   `[ - ]` `[ 39 ]`

—— now a 6-piece, added **VERONICA + ANDREA** – backing vox

		4th & Broad	Gee Street
Sep 92.	(7"/c-s) *(BRW/BRCA 262)* <864744> **CONNECTED. / FEVER**	`[ 18 ]`	`[ 20 ]` Mar93

(cd-s+=) *(BRCD 262)* – ('A'-full version) / Disconnected.
Oct 92. (cd/c/lp) *(BR CD/CA/LP 589)* <514061> **CONNECTED**   `[ 2 ]` `[ 92 ]`
– Connected / Ground level / Everything / Sketch / Fade away / All night long / Step
it up / Playing with fire / Pressure / Chicken shake / Creation / The end.
Nov 92. (7"/c-s) *(BRW/BRCA 266)* <862308> **STEP IT UP. /** ('A'mix)   `[ 12 ]` `[ 58 ]` Jun93
(12"+=/cd-s+=) *(12BRW/BRCD 266)* – Lost in music (US mix).
Feb 93. (7"/c-s) *(BRW/BRCA 268)* **GROUND LEVEL. / EVERYTHING**
(EVERYTHING GROOVES pt.1)   `[ 19 ]` `[ ]`
(12"+=/cd-s+=) *(12BRW/BRCD 268)* – ('B'mixes pt.2).
May 93. (7"/c-s) *(BRW/BRCA 276)* **CREATION. /** ('A'-Ultimation
mix)   `[ 19 ]` `[ ]`
(12"+=) *(12BRW 276)* – ('A'instrumental).
(cd-s+=) *(BRCD 276)* – All night long.

—— it seems like the group have split, although only time will tell

STEREOPHONICS

Formed: Cwmaman, Mid-Glamorgan, Wales . . . late 80's as The TRAGIC
LOVE COMPANY by songwriter KELLY JONES, RICHARD JONES and
STUART CABLE, initially treading the boards as a teenage covers band. The
trio proved they were more than capable of spearheading Richard Branson's
new 'V2' label with the release of debut single, 'LOOKS LIKE CHAPLIN',
a melodic riffathon that had more in common with trad 70's rock and Seattle
grunge than the still dominant Britpop. A Spring '97 follow-up, 'LOCAL BOY
IN THE PHOTOGRAPH', came within breathing distance of the Top 50, a
dizzying amalgam of the MANICS, RADIOHEAD, OASIS and BUFFALO
TOM that managed to sound simultaneously contemporary and classic. JONES
confirmed his newfound status as one of Britain's most promising young
songwriters as The STEREOPHONICS embarked on an impressive chart run
with the Top 40-breaking 'MORE LIFE IN A TRAMP'S VEST'. Late summer
saw them nudge closer to the Top 20 with 'A THOUSAND TREES', the
opening track on debut album, 'WORD GETS AROUND'. A massive selling
UK Top 10 success, the record featured in the upper reaches of many end-of-
year polls, helping to net the band a Brit Award (Best New Group) in early
'98. Having seen out '97 with the moody magnificence of 'TRAFFIC', JONES
and Co began the new year with a Top 20 re-issue of 'LOCAL BOY' prior
to a summer of heavy touring. Towards Christmas, The STEREOPHONICS
became a household name with Top 3 hit, 'THE BARTENDER & THE
THIEF', proving that despite the continued predictions of its imminent demise,
good old fashioned guitar-rock and solid songwriting was alive and well in
Wales. The following year saw the trio peak both critically and commercially,
three massive hits, 'JUST LOOKING', 'PICK A PART THAT'S NEW' and
'I WOULDN'T BELIEVE YOUR RADIO', all squeezed out of an excellent
sophomore set, 'PERFORMANCE AND COCKTAILS' (1999). Welsh pop
idol, TOM JONES, also called up the services of his fellow countrymen to
duet with him on a Top 10 hit of 'Mama Told Me Not To Come'. • **Covered:**
SUNNY AFTERNOON (Kinks) / POSITIVELY 4th STREET (Bob Dylan) /
SOMETHING IN THE WAY (Nirvana) / THE OLD LAUGHING LADY (Neil
Young).

Album rating: WORD GETS AROUND (*7) / PERFORMANCE AND COCKTAILS
(*8)

KELLY JONES (b. 3 Jun'74, Aberdare, Wales) – vocals, guitar / **RICHARD JONES** (b.23
May'74, Aberdare) – bass / **STUART CABLE** (b.19 May'70, Aberdare) – drums

		V2	V2
Nov 96.	(7") *(SPH 1)* **LOOKS LIKE CHAPLIN. / MORE LIFE IN A TRAMP'S VEST**	`[ ]`	`[ - ]`

(cd-s+=) *(SPHD 1)* – Raymond's shop.
Mar 97. (7") *(SPH 2)* **LOCAL BOY IN THE PHOTOGRAPH. / TWO**
MANY SANDWICHES   `[ 51 ]` `[ - ]`
(cd-s+=) *(SPHD 2)* – Buy myself a small plane.
May 97. (7") *(SPH 4)* **MORE LIFE IN A TRAMP'S VEST. /**
RAYMOND'S SHOP   `[ 33 ]` `[ - ]`
(cd-s+=) *(SPHD 4)* – Poppy day.

(cd-s) *(SPHDX 4)* – ('A'side) / Looks like Chaplin (live) / Too many sandwiches (live) / Last of the big time drinkers (live).

Aug 97. (7"/c-s) *(VVR 500044-7/-5)* **A THOUSAND TREES. / CARROT CAKE AND WINE**　`22`　`-`
(cd-s+=) *(VVR 500044-3)* – ('A'live).
(cd-s) *(VVR 500044-8)* – ('A'acoustic) / Home to me (acoustic) / Looks like Chaplin (acoustic) / Summertime (acoustic).

Aug 97. (cd/c/lp) *(VVR 100043-2/-4/-9)* <27006> **WORD GETS AROUND**　`6`
– A thousand trees / Looks like Chaplin / More life in a tramps vest / Local boy in the photograph / Traffic / Not up to you / Check my eyelids for holes / Same size feet / Last of the big time drinkers / Goldfish bowl / Too many sandwiches / Billy Daveys daughter.

Nov 97. (7"/c-s) *(VVR 500094-7/-5)* **TRAFFIC. / TIE ME UP TIE ME DOWN**　`20`　`-`
(cd-s+=) *(VVR 500094-3)* – Chris Chambers / ('A'version).
(cd-s) *(VVR 500094-8)* – ('A'side) / More life in a tramp's vest (live) / A thousand trees (live) / Local boy in the photograph (live).

Feb 98. (7"/c-s) *(VVR 500126-7/-5)* **LOCAL BOY IN THE PHOTOGRAPH (remix). / WHO'LL STOP THE RAIN**　`14`　`-`
(cd-s+=) *(VVR 500126-3)* – Check my eyelids for holes / ('A'-CD-Rom video).
(cd-s) *(VVR 500126-8)* – ('A'side) / Not up to you (live in session) / The last resort / Traffic (CD-rom video live).

Nov 98. (7"/c-s) *(VVR 500467-7/-5)* **THE BARTENDER AND THE THIEF. / SHE TAKES HER CLOTHES OFF**　`3`　`-`
(cd-s+=) *(VVR 500465-3)* – Fiddler's green.
(cd-s) *(VVR 500466-3)* – ('A'live) / Traffic (live) / Raymond's shop (live).

Feb 99. (7"/c-s) *(VVR 500532-7/-5)* **JUST LOOKING. / POSTMEN DO NOT GREAT MOVIE HEROES MAKE (featuring Marco Migliani)**　`4`　`-`
(cd-s+=) *(VVR 500530-3)* – Sunny afternoon.
(cd-s) *(VVR 500530-0)* – ('A'side) / Local boy in the photograph (live) / Same size feet (live).

Mar 99. (cd/c/lp) *(VVR 100449-2/-4/-9)* **PERFORMANCE AND COCKTAILS**　`1`
– Roll up and shine / The bartender and the thief / Hurry up and wait / Pick a part that's new / Just looking / Half the lies you tell ain't true / I wouldn't believe your radio / T-shirt sun tan / Is yesterday, tomorrow, today? / A minute longer / She takes her clothes off / Plastic California / I stopped to fill my car up. (special cd+=; VVR 100449-8)

May 99. (7"/c-s) *(VVR 500677-7/-5)* **PICK A PART THAT'S NEW. / NICE TO BE OUT (demo)**　`4`　`-`
(cd-s+=) *(VVR 500677-3)* – Positively 4th street / ('A'-CD-Rom video).
(cd-s) *(VVR 500677-8)* – ('A'acoustic) / In my day / Something in the way.

Aug 99. (7"/c-s) *(VVR 500882-7/-5)* **I WOULDN'T BELIEVE YOUR RADIO. / THE BARTENDER AND THE THIEF (bar version)**　`11`
(cd-s+=) *(VVR 500882-3)* – The old laughing lady.
(cd-s) *(VVR 500882-8)* – ('A'live) / Pick a part that's new (live) / T-shirt suntan (live).

Nov 99. (7"/c-s) *(VVR 500932-7/-5)* **HURRY UP AND WAIT. / ANGIE**　`11`　`-`
(cd-s+=) *(VVR 500932-3)* – I wouldn't believe your radio.
(cd-s) *(VVR 500932-8)* – ('A'live) / I stopped to fill my car up (live) / Billy Davey's daughter (live) / ('A'-video).

Cat STEVENS

Born: STEVEN DEMETRI GEORGIOU, 21 Jul'47, Soho, London, England. Son of Greek restaurant owner and Swedish mother. While studying at Hammersmith college in 1966 he met Mike Hurst (ex-SPRINGFIELDS). He produced first single 'I LOVE MY DOG', after which CAT was signed by Tony Hall to new Decca subsidiary label 'Deram'. It reached the UK Top 30, but was surpassed the next year when follow-up 'MATTHEW AND SON' hit No.2. His songs were soon being covered by many, including P.P.ARNOLD (First Cut Is The Deepest) & TREMELOES (Here Comes My Baby). After a barren chart spell and recuperation from TB two years previous, he signed new deal with 'Island' in 1970 (A&M in America). He scored a comeback Top 10 hit with 'LADY D'ARBANVILLE', which leant on the production skills of ex-YARDBIRD Keith Relf. He stayed for the follow-up to 'MONA BONE JAKON', the 1970 classic album 'TEA FOR THE TILLERMAN'. CAT went on to become one of the biggest stars of the 70's although his output became increasingly stale. 'TEASER AND THE FIRECAT' (1971) was another collection of pleasant but ultimately unsatisfying singer songwriter musings while 'CATCH BULL AT FOUR' (1972) and 'FOREIGNER' (1973) sounded overwrought and cluttered, a failing that marked the remainder of his output for 'Island' until his musical retirement in 1979 when he converted to the muslim faith and changed his name to YUSEF ISLAM. • **Songwriters:** Self-penned except; MORNING HAS BROKEN (Eleanor Farjeon) / ANOTHER SATURDAY NIGHT (Sam Cooke). • **Trivia:** Other STEVENS' songs given new light were; WILD WORLD (Jimmy Cliff – 1970, Maxi Priest – 1988) / FIRST CUT IS THE DEEPEST (Rod Stewart) / PEACE TRAIN (10,000 Maniacs).

Album rating: MATTHEW AND SON (*6) / NEW MASTERS (*5) / MONA BONE JAKON (*6) / TEA FOR THE TILLERMAN (*8) / TEASER AND THE FIRECAT (*9) / CATCH BULL AT FOUR (*7) / FOREIGNER (*5) / BUDDHA AND THE CHOCOLATE BOX (*6) / GREATEST HITS compilation (*9) / NUMBERS (*3) / IZITSO (*4) / BACK TO EARTH (*3) / FOOTSTEPS IN THE DARK – GREATEST HITS, VOL.2 compilation (*6) / THE VERY BEST OF CAT STEVENS compilation (*9)

CAT STEVENS – vocals, guitar, keyboards with orchestra

		Deram	Deram
Sep 66. (7") *(DM 102)* **I LOVE MY DOG. / PORTOBELLO ROAD**	`28`		
Dec 66. (7") *(DM 110)* **MATTHEW AND SON. / GRANNY**	`2`		
(re-iss. Aug81 on 'Decca')			

Mar 67. (lp; mono/stereo) *(DML/SML 1004)* <18005> **MATTHEW AND SON**　`7`
– Matthew and son / I love my dog / Here comes my baby / Bring another bottle baby / Portobello road / I've found a love / I see a road / Baby get your head screwed on / Granny / When I speak to the flowers / The tramp / Come on and dance / Hummingbird / Lady. (cd-iss. Jul88 on 'London'; 820 560-2)

Mar 67. (7") *(DM 118)* **I'M GONNA GET ME A GUN. / SCHOOL IS OUT**　`6`

Jul 67. (7") *(DM 140)* **A BAD NIGHT. / THE LAUGHING APPLE**　`20`

Dec 67. (7") *(DM 156)* **KITTY. / BLACKNESS OF THE NIGHT**　`47`

Dec 67. (lp; mono/stereo) *(DML/SML 1018)* <18010> **NEW MASTERS**
– Kitty / I'm so sleepy / Northern wind / The laughing apple / Smash your heart / Moonstone / The first cut is the deepest / I'm gonna be king / Ceylon city / Blackness of the night / Come on baby / I love them all. (re-iss. Nov84; DOA 5) (cd-iss. Apr89 +=; 820 767-2) – Image of Hell / Lovely city / Here comes my wife / The view from the top / It's a supa dupa life / Where are you / A bad night.

Feb 68. (7") *(DM 178)* **LOVELY CITY. / IMAGE OF HELL**

—— Around early 1968, CAT slowly recovered from tuberculosis.

Oct 68. (7") *(DM 211)* **HERE COMES MY WIFE. / IT'S A SUPA DUPA LIFE**

Jun 69. (7") *(DM 260)* **WHERE ARE YOU. / THE VIEW FROM THE TOP**　`-`　`-`

—— recruited band; **ALUN DAVIES** – guitar / **JOHN RYAN** – bass / **HARVEY BURNS** – drums

		Island	A&M
Jun 70. (7"m) *(WIP 6086)* **LADY D'ARBANVILLE. / TIME / FILL MY EYES**	`8`		
Jun 70. (lp) *(ILPS 9118)* <4260> **MONA BONE JAKON**	`63`		

– Lady D'Arbanville / Maybe you're right / Pop star / I think I see the light / Trouble / Mona bone jakon / I wish, I wish / Katmandu / Time – Fill my eyes / Lilywhite. (re-iss. 1974 & Jan78; same) (cd-iss. Apr87; CID 9118) (cd re-iss. Nov89; IMCD 35)

Nov 70. (lp) *(ILPS 9135)* <4280> **TEA FOR THE TILLERMAN**　`20`　`8` Feb71
– Where do the children play / Hard headed woman / Wild world / Sad Lisa / Miles from nowhere / But I might die tonight / Longer boats / Into white / On the road to find out / Father and son / Tea for the tillerman. (re-iss. 1974 & Jan78; same) (re-iss. Oct86 lp/c/cd; ILPM/ICM/CID 9135) (cd re-iss. Nov89; IMCD 36) (re-iss. lp Jan94 + May94; same)

Feb 71. (7") <1231> **WILD WORLD. / MILES FROM NOWHERE**　`-`　`11`

—— **LARRY STEELE** – bass repl. RYAN

Jun 71. (7") *(WIP 6092)* <1265> **MOON SHADOW. / FATHER AND SON**　`22`　`30`

Sep 71. (7") *(WIP 6102)* **TUESDAY'S DEAD. / MILES FROM NOWHERE**

Sep 71. (7") <1291> **PEACE TRAIN. / WHERE DO THE CHILDREN PLAY?**　`-`　`7`

Sep 71. (lp) *(ILPS 9154)* <4313> **TEASER AND THE FIRECAT**　`3`　`2`
– The wind / Ruby love / If I laugh / Changes IV / How can I tell you / Tuesday's dead / Morning has broken / Bitterblue / Moon shadow / Peace train. (re-iss. 1974 & Jan78; same) (re-iss. Oct86 lp/c/cd; ILPM/ICM/CID 9154) (cd re-iss. Mar90; IMCD 104)

(below 'A'side featured **RICK WAKEMAN** – piano)

Dec 71. (7") *(WIP 6121)* <1335> **MORNING HAS BROKEN. / I WANT TO LIVE IN A WIGWAM**　`9`　`6` Mar72

—— In Apr'72, STEVENS contributed tracks to film 'Harold And Maude'.

—— added **JEAN ROUSELL** – piano / **CAT** – some synthesizers repl. WAKEMAN. **ALAN JAMES** – bass repl. LARRY

Sep 72. (lp) *(ILPS 9206)* <4365> **CATCH BULL AT FOUR**　`2`　`1`
– Sitting / Boy with a moon and star on his head / Angel sea / Silent sunlight / Can't keep it in / 18th Avenue / Freezing steel / O Caritas / Sweet Scarlet / Ruins. (re-iss. 1974 & Jan78; same) (cd-iss. Oct86; CID 9206) (cd re-iss. Jul89; IMCD 34)

Nov 72. (7") *(WIP 6152)* **CAN'T KEEP IT IN. / CRAB DANCE**　`13`

Nov 72. (7") <1396> **SITTING. / CRAB DANCE**　`-`　`16`

—— CAT now became a tax exile in Brazil and donated money to charity

—— now w / **ROUSSEL, DAVIS, LYNCH + CONWAY** plus loads of sessioners

Jul 73. (7") *(WIP 6163)* <1418> **THE HURT. / SILENT SUNLIGHT**　`-`　`31`

Jul 73. (lp) *(ILPS 9240)* <4391> **FOREIGNER**　`3`　`3`
– Foreigner suite / The hurt / How many times / Later / 100 I dream. (re-iss. quad.1974) (cd-iss. Nov89; IMCD 72)

—— **BRUCE LYNCH** – bass repl. PAUL

Mar 74. (7") *(WIP 6190)* <1503> **OH VERY YOUNG. / 100 I DREAMS**　`10`

Mar 74. (lp/c) *(ILPS/ICT 9274)* <3623> **BUDDAH AND THE CHOCOLATE BOX**　`3`　`2`
– Music / Oh very young / Sun – C79 / Ghost town / Jesus / Ready / King of trees / Bad penny / Home in the sky. (cd-iss. Nov89; IMCD 70)

Aug 74. (7") *(WIP 6206)* <1602> **ANOTHER SATURDAY NIGHT. / HOME IN THE SKY**　`19`　`6`

Sep 74. (lp) **SATURDAY NIGHT (live)**　`-`
– Wild world / Oh very young / Sitting / Where do children play / Lady D'Arbanville / Another saturday night / Hard-headed woman / Peace train / Father & son / King of trees / A bad penny / Bitter blue.

Dec 74. (7") <1645> **READY. / I THINK I SEE THE LIGHT**　`-`　`26`

Jul 75. (7") *(WIP 6238)* <1700> **TWO FINE PEOPLE. / BAD PENNY**　`-`　`33`

Jul 75. (lp/c) *(ILPS/ICT 9310)* <4519> **GREATEST HITS** (compilation)　`2`　`6`
– Wild world / Oh very young / Can't keep it in / Hard headed woman / Moonshadow / Two fine people / Peace train / Ready / Father and son / Sitting / Morning has broken / Another saturday night. (cd-iss. Apr87; CID 9310) (cd-iss. Mar93; IMCD 168)

—— now w / **ROUSSEL, DAVIS, LYNCH + CONWAY** plus loads of sessioners

Dec 75. (lp/c) *(ILPS/ICT 9370)* <4555> **NUMBERS**　`13`
– Whistlestar / Novim's nightmare / Majik of majiks / Dry wood / Banapple gas / Land o' free love and goodbye / Jzero / Home / Nomad's anthem.

Mar 76. (7") *(WIP 6276)* <1785> **BANAPPLE GAS. / GHOST TOWN**　`41` Feb76

Mar 76. (7") <1924> **LAND O' FREE LOVE AND GOODBYE. / (I NEVER WANTED) TO BE A STAR**　`-`　`-`

Apr 77. (lp/c) *(ILPS/ICT 9451)* <4702> **IZITSO**　`18`　`7`
– (Remember the days of the) Old schoolyard / Life / Killin' time / Kypros / Bonfire / To be a star / Crazy / Sweet Jamaica / Was Dog a doughnut / Child for a day.

Jun 77. (7") *(WIP 6387)* **(REMEMBER THE DAYS OF THE) OLD SCHOOLYARD. / DOVES** — `44` / `-`

Jun 77. (7") *<1948>* **(REMEMBER THE DAYS OF THE) OLD SCHOOLYARD. / LAND O' FREE LOVE AND GOODBYE** — `-` / `33`

Nov 77. (7") *<1971>* **WAS DOG A DOUGHNUT. / SWEET JAMAICA** — `-` / `70`

Jan 79. (7") *<2109>* **BAD BRAKES. / NASCIMENTO** — `-` / `83`

Jan 79. (lp/c) *(ILPS/ICT 9565) <4735>* **BACK TO EARTH** — `33` Dec 78
– Just another night / Daytime / Bad brakes / Randy / The artist / Last love song / Nascimento / Father / New York times / Never.

Feb 79. (7") *(WIP 6465)* **LAST LOVE SONG. / NASCIMENTO** — `-`

Apr 79. (7") *<2126>* **RANDY. / NASCIMENTO** — `-`

—— He retired from the music scene, due to newfound Muslim religion. He changed his name to YUSEF ISLAM and married Fouzia Ali in Sep'79. They lived in London where he taught his faith to local school. In the late 80's, he was back in the limelight, when he condoned the Muslim sanction for the assassination of writer Salman Rushdie.

– compilations, etc. –

Nov 70. (lp) *Decca; (SPA 93)* **THE WORLD OF CAT STEVENS** — / `-`

Mar 71. (d-lp) *Deram; <18005>* **MATTHEW AND SON / NEW MASTERS** — `-` /
(UK-iss.May75 as 'VIEW FROM THE TOP'; DPA 3019-20)

Jan 72. (lp) *Deram; <18061>* **VERY YOUNG AND EARLY SONGS** — / `94`

Nov 73. (7") *Deram; (DM 406)* **I LOVE MY DOG. / MATTHEW AND SON** — / `-`
(re-iss. Oct83 on 'Old Gold'; OG 9336)

Aug 80. (7"ep) *Deram; (DM 435)* **MATTHEW AND SON / I LOVE MY DOG. / A BAD NIGHT / I'M GONNA GET ME A GUN** — / `-`

Aug 81. (lp/c) *Rock Echoes; (TAB/KTAB 25)* **THE FIRST CUT IS THE DEEPEST** — / `-`

Nov 83. (7") *Island; (IS 123)* **MORNING HAS BROKEN. / MOON SHADOW** — / `-`

Jan 85. (lp/c) *Island; <(ILPS/ICT 3736)>* **FOOTSTEPS IN THE DARK – GREATEST HITS VOL. 2** — / Dec84
(US version +=) – (3 extra tracks). (cd-iss. 1988; CD 3736)

Apr 86. (d-lp/c) *Castle; (CCS LP/MC 127)* **THE COLLECTION** — / `-`
(cd-iss. Sep92; CCSCD 127)

Apr 86. (c) *Spot; (SPC 8574)* **CAT STEVENS** — / `-`

Jan 88. (cd) *Deram; (820 561-2)* **FIRST CUTS** — / `-`

Feb 90. (cd)(lp/c) *Island; (840 148-2)(CATV/+C 1)* **THE VERY BEST OF CAT STEVENS** — `4` /
– Where do the children play / Wild world / Tuesday's dead / Lady D'Arbanville / The first cut is the deepest / Oh very young / Rubylove / Morning has broken / Moonshadow / Matthew and son / Father and son / Can't keep it in / Hard headed woman / (Remember the days of the) Old school yard / I love my dog / Another Saturday night / Sad Lisa / Peace train.(re-iss. Jul92; same)

Nov 92. (d-cd) *Island; (ITSCD 12)* **TEA FOR THE TILLERMAN / TEASER & THE FIRECAT** — / `-`

Apr 93. (cd) *Pulsar;* **WILD WORLD** — / `-`

Sep 93. (cd/c) *Spectrum; (550108-2/-4)* **EARLY TAPES** — / `-`

Sep 95. (d-cd/d-c; as YUSEF ISLAM) *Voiceprint; (MOL 7001 CD/MC 3)* **THE LIFE OF THE LAST PROPHET** — / `-`

Nov 99. (cd/c) *Island; (CID/ICT 8079)* **REMEMBER – THE ULTIMATE COLLECTION** — `31` /
– Moon shadow / Father and son / Norning has broken / Wild world / The first cut is the deepest / Lady D'Arbanville / Oh very young / Matthew and son / Sitting / Hard headed woman / I love my dog / Rubylove / Don't be shy / Can't keep it in / Here comes my baby / Into white / REmember the days of the old schoolyard / Where do the children play / Land o' freelove and goodbye / Another Saturday night / Foreigner suite / Just another night / Peace train / If you want to sing, sing out.

AL STEWART

Born: 5 Sep'45, Glasgow, Scotland. Moving to Bournemouth with his widowed mother as a toddler, STEWART later learned guitar alongside ROBERT FRIPP. In the mid-60's, after briefly sharing a flat with fellow (then) budding singer/songwriter folkie, PAUL SIMON, he released a one-off 45, 'THE ELF', for 'Decca', one JIMMY PAGE (then a session musician) playing lead guitar. Signing to 'C.B.S.' in 1967, he debuted with the 'BED-SITTER IMAGES' album the same year, which if nothing else, helped invent the concept of the down-at-heel songwriter poring over angst-ridden ruminations in the safety of his room. STEWART's navel-gazing tales of doomed romance were given free rein on 'ZERO SHE FLIES' (1970) and 'ORANGE' (1972), punctuated by the odd track written from a more historical vein. 1973's quasi-concept affair, 'PAST, PRESENT & FUTURE', took the latter approach to its conclusion and in 'NOSTRADAMUS', featured one of STEWART's most compelling tracks. Subsequently relocating to California, the singer's more Americanised latter 70's output saw him become a fairly major Stateside star. STEWART's first effort for 'R.C.A.', 'YEAR OF THE CAT' (1976) made the US Top 5 (UK Top 40) on the strength of the infectious title track, an American Top 10 hit in its own right. Produced by ALAN PARSONS, the record saw STEWART's fragile, understated style presented in a more accessible pop-folk framework, as did its (almost equally commericaly fruitful) successor, 'TIME PASSAGES' (1978). 1980's '24 CARROTS' didn't perform quite so well, STEWART embroiled in business problems for much of the 80's. Comeback set, 'LAST DAYS OF THE CENTURY' (1988), was a synth-enhanced affair embracing STEWART's increasingly fanciful lyrical themes, the singer moving to 'E.M.I.', then 'Permanent' in the 90's for whom he continues to record consistent, if commercially limited material.

Album rating: BEDSITTER IMAGES (*4) / LOVE CHRONICLES (*7) / ZERO SHE FLIES (*6) / ORANGE (*6) / PAST, PRESENT AND FUTURE (*7) / MODERN TIMES

(*6) / YEAR OF THE CAT (*8) / TIME PASSAGES (*6) / 24 CARROTS (*5) / LIVE INDIAN SUMMER (*5) / RUSSIANS & AMERICANS (*5) / LAST DAYS OF THE CENTURY (*5) / CHRONICLES: THE BEST OF AL STEWART compilation (*7) / RHYMES IN ROOMS (*5) / FAMOUS LAST WORDS (*5) / BETWEEN THE WARS (*5)

AL STEWART – vocals, guitar with orchestra

Jul 66. (7") *(F 12467)* **THE ELF. / TURN INTO STONE**
Decca / not iss. — `-` (C.B.S. / Columbia)

Sep 67. (7") *(CBS 3034)* **BEDSITTER IMAGES. / SWISS COTTAGE MANOEUVRES** — / `-`

Oct 67. (lp; stereo/mono) *(S+/BPG 63087)* **BED-SITTER IMAGES** — / `-`
– Bedsitter images / Swiss Cottage manoeuvres / Scandinavian girl * / Pretty golden hair * / Denise at 16 / Samuel, oh how you've changed! / Cleave to me * / A long way down from Stephanie / Ivich / Beleeka doodle day. *(re-iss. Jun70 as 'THE FIRST ALBUM (BED-SITTER IMAGES)'; CBS 64023) – Lover man / Clifton in the rain. (repl. * tracks)*

Jan 69. (lp; stereo/mono) *(S+/63460)* **LOVE CHRONICLES** — / `-`
– In Brooklyn / Old Compton Street blues / Ballad of Mary Foster / Life and life only / You should've listened to Al / Love chronicles. *(re-is.May82 on 'RCA International' lp/c; INT S/K 5120)*

Mar 70. (7") *(CBS 4843)* **ELECTRIC LOS ANGELES SUNSET. / MY ENEMIES HAVE SWEET VOICES** — / `-`

Mar 70. (lp) *(CBS 64023)* **ZERO SHE FLIES** — `40` /
– My enemies have sweet voices / A small fruit song / Gethsemane again / Burbling / Electric Los Angeles sunset / Manuscript / Black hill / Anna / Room of roots / Zero she flies. *(re-iss. Oct85 on 'R.C.A.' lp/c; NL/NK 70874)*

Dec 71. (7") *(CBS 5351)* **THE NEWS FROM SPAIN. / ELVASTON PLACE** — / `-`

Feb 72. (7") *(CBS 7763)* **YOU DON'T EVEN KNOW ME. / I'M FALLING** — / `-`

Feb 72. (lp) *(CBS 64739)* **ORANGE** — / `-`
– You don't even know me / Amsterdam / Songs out of clay / The news from Spain / I don't believe you / Once an orange, always an orange / I'm falling / Night of the 4th of May. *(re-iss. Nov81 lp/c; CBS/40 32061) (cd-iss. Jul96 on 'Columbia'; 484441-2)*

Apr 72. (7") *(CBS 7992)* **AMSTERDAM. / SONGS OUT OF CLAY** — / `-`
C.B.S. / Janus

Sep 73. (7") *(CBS 1791)* **TERMINAL EYES. / LAST DAYS OF JUNE 1934** — / `-`

Oct 73. (lp) *(CBS 65726) <3063>* **PAST, PRESENT & FUTURE** — / `-` Jan74
– Old admirals / Warren Harding / Soho (needless to say) / Last days of June 1934 / Post World War Two blues / Roads to Moscow / Terminal eyes / Nostradamus. *(re-iss. Jun81 lp/c; CBS/40 32026) <US cd-iss. 1987 on 'Arista'; ARCD 8359> (cd-iss. Nov92 on 'Beat Goes On'; BGOCD 155)*

Apr 74. (7") *<243>* **NOSTRADAMUS. / TERMINAL EYES** — `-` /

—— Around Spring'74, toured with backing band HOME

Jun 74. (7") *(CBS 2397)* **NOSTRADAMUS. / SWALLOW WIND** — / `-`

—— backed w/ **GERRY CONWAY / SIMON NICOL / PAT DONALDSON & SIMON ROUSSEL**

Mar 75. (7") *<250>* **CAROL. / SIRENS OF TITAN** — `-` /

Apr 75. (7") *(CBS 3254)* **CAROL. / NEXT TIME** — `-` /

Apr 75. (lp/c) *(CBS/40 80477) <7012>* **MODERN TIMES** — / `30` Feb75
– Carol / Sirens of Titan / What's going on / Not the one / Next time / Apple cider / Re-constitution / The dark and rolling sea / Modern times. *(re-iss. Mar81 lp/c; CBS/40 32019) (cd-iss. Jan93 on 'Beat Goes On'; BGOCD 156)*

Oct 76. (lp/c) *(RS/ 1082) <7022>* **YEAR OF THE CAT**
R.C.A. / Janus — `38` / `5`
– Lord Grenville / On the border / Midas shadow / Sand in your shoes / If it doesn't come naturally, leave it / Flying sorcery / Broadway Hotel / One stage before / Year of the cat. *(re-iss. Sep81 lp/c; RCA LP/K 3015) (cd-iss. Nov84; ND 71493) (re-iss. Dec87 lp/c; NL/NK 71493) (re-iss. Apr91 on 'Fame' cd/c; CD/TC FA 3253)*

Jan 77. (7") *(RCA 2771) <266>* **YEAR OF THE CAT. / BROADWAY HOTEL** — `31` / `8` Nov76

Apr 77. (7") *(PB 5019) <267>* **ON THE BORDER. / FLYING SORCERY** — `42` /
R.C.A. / Arista

Sep 78. (lp/c) *(PL/PK 25173) <4190>* **TIME PASSAGES** — `39` / `10`
– Time passages / Valentina way / Life in dark water / A man for all seasons / Almost Lucy / Palace of Versailles / Timeless skies / Song on the radio / End of the day. *(re-iss. Sep81 lp/c; RCA LP/K 3026) (re-iss. Aug84 lp/c; PL/PK 70274) (cd-iss. Dec86; PD 70274) (cd-iss. Oct91 on 'Fame'; CDFA 3312)*

Sep 78. (7") *<0362>* **TIME PASSAGES. / ALMOST LUCY** — `-` / `7`

Feb 79. (7") *(PB 5139) <0389>* **SONG ON THE RADIO. / A MAN FOR ALL SEASONS** — / `29` Jan79

Aug 80. (7") *(RCA 2)* **MONDO SINISTRO. / MERLIN'S TIME** — `-` /

Aug 80. (lp/c) *(PL/PK 25306) <9520>* **24 CARROTS** — `55` / `37`
– Running man / Midnight rocks / Constantinople / Merlin's time / Mondo sinistro / Murmansk run – Ellis Island / Rocks in the ocean / Paint by numbers / Optical illusion. *(re-iss. Sep81 lp/c; RCA LP/K 3042) (cd-iss. Aug92 on 'E.M.I.'; CZ 512)*

Aug 80. (7") *<0552>* **MIDNIGHT ROCKS. / CONSTANTINOPLE** — `-` / `24`

Nov 80. (7") *(RCA 17)* **PAINT BY NUMBERS. / OPTICAL ILLUSION** — / `-`

Jan 81. (7") *<0585>* **RUNNING MAN. / MERLIN'S TIME** — / `-`

Oct 81. (7") *(RCA 149) <0639>* **INDIAN SUMMER. / PANDORA** — / `-`

Nov 81. (d-lp/d-c) *(RCA LP/K 70257) <8607>* **LIVE – INDIAN SUMMER (live)** — / `-`
– Here in Angola / Pandora / Indian summer / Princess Olivia / Running man / Time passages / Merlin's time / If it doesn't come naturally, leave it / Roads to Moscow / Nostradamus (part 1) – World goes to Riyadah – Nostradamus (part 2) / Soho (needless to say) / On the border / Valentina way / Clarence Frogman Henry / Year of the cat. *(re-iss. 1984 lp/c; PL/PK 70257)*

May 84. (lp/c) *(PL/PK 70307)* **RUSSIANS AND AMERICANS**
R.C.A. / Passport — / `83`
– Strange girl / Russians and Americans / Cafe society / One, two, three / The candidate / 1-2-3 / Lori, don't go right now * / Rumours of war / The gypsy and the rose * / Accident on 3rd Street <US repl. * track> – The one that got away / Night meeting. *(cd-iss. Jul93 on 'E.M.I.'; CZ 523)*

Jun 84. (7") *(RCA 414)* **LORI, DON'T GO RIGHT NOW. / ACCIDENT ON 3rd STREET** — / `-`

May 85. (lp/c) *(PL/PK 70715)* **THE BEST OF AL STEWART**
(compilation)
– Year of the cat / On the border / If it doesn't come naturally, leave it / Time passages / Almost lucky / Merlin's theme / Valentina way / Running man / Roads to Moscow / Here in Angola / Rumours of war. *<US cd 1988; ARCD 8433> (cd-iss. Feb97 on 'E.M.I.'; CTMCD 310)*

Enigma   Enigma

Sep 88. (lp/c/cd) *(ENVLP/TCENV/CDENV 505)* **LAST DAYS OF THE CENTURY**
– Last days of the century / Real and unreal / King of Portugal / Red toupee / Where are they now / Bad reputation / Josephine Baker / License to steal / Fields of France / Antartica / Ghostly horses of the plain. *(cd+=)* – Helen and Cassandra. *(re-iss. Jul90 cd/c/lp; 773 316-2/-4/-1)*

Oct 88. (7") *(ENV 4)* **KING OF PORTUGAL. / JOSEPHINE BAKER**
(12"+=) *(ENVT 4)* – Bad reputation.
(3"cd-s+=) *(ENVCD 4)* – ('A'-rock mix version).

E.M.I.   Mesa

Feb 92. (cd/c/lp) *(CD/TC+/EMC 3613)* **RHYMES IN ROOMS (live)**
– Flying sorcery / Soho (needless to say) / Time passages / Josephine Baker / Nostradamus / On the border / Fields of France / Medley:- Clifton in the rain – A small fruit song / Broadway hotel / If it doesn't come naturally, leave it / Year of the cat. *(re-iss. cd Feb95 on 'Fame'; CDFA 3315)*

Mar 92. (7") **RHYMES IN ROOMS (live). / YEAR OF THE CAT (live)**
(cd-s+=) – Songs on the radio.

Permanent   Mesa

Oct 93. (cd/c) *(PERM CD/MC 15)* **FAMOUS LAST WORDS**   Feb94
– Feel like / Angels of mercy / Don't forget me / Peter on the white sea / Genie on a table top / Trespasser / Trains / Necromancer / Charlotte Corday / Hippo song / Night rolls on.

E.M.I.   Mesa

Jun 95. (cd/c) *(CD/TC EMC 3710)* **BETWEEN THE WARS**
– Night train to Munich / The age of rhythm / Sampan / Lindy comes to town / Three mules / A league of notions / Between the wars / Betty Boop's birthday / Marion the Chatelaine / Joe the Georgian / Always the cause / Laughing into 1939 / The black Danube.

– compilations, etc. –

Apr 78. (lp/c) *R.C.A.; (PL/PK 25131) / Arista; <US-d-lp>* **THE EARLY YEARS** (1967-1970)
(re-iss. Oct81 lp/c; INT S/K 5156) (re-iss. Sep86 on 'Fame' lp/c; FA/TC-FA 3165)

1985. (7") *Arista;* **YEAR OF THE CAT / TIME PASSAGES**

Nov 86. (7") *Old Gold; (OG 9642)* **THE YEAR OF THE CAT. / (other track by Climax Blues Band)**

Jun 91. (cd/c) *E.M.I.; (CD/TC EMC 3590)* **CHRONICLES: THE BEST OF AL STEWART (1976-81)**
– Year of the cat / On the border / If it doesn't come naturally, leave it / Time passages / Almost Lucy / Song on the radio * / Running man * / Merlin's time / In Brooklyn / Soho (needless to say) * / A small fruit song / Manuscript / Roads to Moscow (live) / Nostradamus (part 1) – World goes to Riyadh – Nostradamus (part 2). *(cd+= *)*

Oct 93. (d-cd) *E.M.I.; (CDEM 1511)* **TO WHOM IT MAY CONCERN (1966-1970)**

Apr 97. (3xcd-box) *E.M.I.; (CDOMB 020)* **THE ORIGINALS**
– (YEAR OF THE CAT / TIME PASSAGES / RUSSIANS AND AMERICANS)

Dave STEWART (see under ⇒ EURYTHMICS)

Mark STEWART (see under ⇒ POP GROUP)

Rod STEWART

Born: RODERICK DAVID STEWART, 10 Jan'45, Highgate, London. Of Scottish parentage, STEWART remains a passionate Scotland supporter and considers himself an adopted Scot. In addition to music, obviously, the singer's other passion is football, the young ROD initially biding his time as an apprentice for Brentford F.C. The lure of the itinerant troubadour lifestyle proved irresistible, however, and STEWART subsequently hooked up with folk singer, WIZZ JONES, busking/learning his trade around Europe before eventually being deported for vagrancy in 1963. Upon his return, STEWART threw himself headlong into the burgeoning Brit R&B scene as part of West Midlands group, JIMMY POWELL & The FIVE DIMENSIONS. He then took his feted harmonica blowing skills to London, playing on a live effort by JOHN BALDRY & THE HOOCHIE COOCHIE MEN. This in turn, led to ROD developing his vocal talents and releasing a one-off single for 'Decca' in 1964, 'GOOD MORNING LITTLE SCHOOLGIRL', before briefly joining BALDRY's new outfit (also featuring BRIAN AUGER, JULIE DRISCOLL and MICK WALLER, the latter a future STEWART collaborator), STEAMPACKET, the following year. After a dispute with BALDRY, STEWART then added a stint with SHOTGUN EXPRESS (alongside a star-studded line-up which boasted a young PETER GREEN and MICK FLEETWOOD amongst others) to his increasingly impressive CV. The big break finally came in 1967, when JEFF BECK recruited him as a lead singer, ROD's vocals gracing two albums, 'TRUTH' (1968) and 'BECK-OLA' (1969). While still a member of the JEFF BECK GROUP, STEWART signed a solo deal with 'Phonogram', debuting with 'AN OLD RAINCOAT WON'T EVER LET YOU DOWN' in early 1970 (US title, 'THE ROD STEWART ALBUM'). The record was a revelation, the years of practice finally coming together with STEWART rasping his way through a rootsy solo blueprint of folk, country, blues and R&B. Rapidly establishing himself as one of the finest white soul vocalists in the history of rock, STEWART's voice was a unique, compelling combination of bourbon-throated abrasiveness and blue-eyed crooning, equally at home on choice cover material (EWAN MacCOLL's 'Dirty Old Town' and MIKE D'ABO's 'Handbags And Gladrags') as his own brilliant originals, highlights being the gritty 'CINDY'S LAMENT' and the title track. Simultaneously, ROD had joined The FACES (formerly The SMALL FACES) along with RON WOOD, the pair forming the central writing core of the band as they grew from a laddish club act into stadium headliners, WOOD also becoming STEWART's right-hand writing partner through the pioneering early years of the singer's solo career. 'GASOLINE ALLEY' (1970) was a FACES album in all but name, if a bit more downbeat, WOOD, RONNIE LANE and KENNY JONES (IAN McLAGAN absent due to a 'bus strike', apparently!) all playing on a record which launched STEWART in the States (Top 30) and musically, was a companion piece to The FACES' acclaimed 'A Nod Is As Good As A Wink To A Blind Horse' (1971). Kicking in with the plaintive slide guitar moan and emotive reverie of the title track through a cover of ELTON JOHN's 'Country Comfort' and STEWART's own 'LADY DAY', the album also featured the first of his DYLAN cover versions, a sympathetic reading of 'ONLY A HOBO'. With the amplified acoustic double whammy of the 'MAGGIE MAY' / 'REASON TO BELIEVE' single in summer '71, ROD went from critical darling to international superstar overnight, the attendant transatlantic No.1 album, 'EVERY PICTURE TELLS A STORY' (1971) representing the creative pinnacle of his career. Featuring regular contributors such as guitarist, MARTIN QUITTENTON alongside the likes of DANNY THOMPSON and Scot, MAGGIE BELL, the album was a masterclass in roots rock boasting one of his most perfectly conceived originals in the lovely 'MANDOLIN WIND'. The choice of cover material was, as ever, impeccable, STEWART cutting a dash through ARTHUR CRUDUP's 'That's All Right' (a track originally made famous by ELVIS PRESLEY) and wringing a pathos from TIM HARDIN's aforementioned 'Reason To Believe' which even its doomed composer couldn't muster. 'NEVER A DULL MOMENT' (1972) was almost as good, the record taking STEWART's boisterous-lad-with-a-sensitive-side persona to its ultimate conclusion by interspersing a trio of worldly-wise rockers (including the classic 'TRUE BLUE') with a beautiful cover of BOB DYLAN's 'Mama You Been On My Mind', the record also spawning another UK No.1 single with 'YOU WEAR IT WELL'. By 1974, The FACES were buckling under the pressure of STEWART's massive successful solo career although, ironically, this also began to slide inexorably downhill, creatively at least, with the disappointing 'SMILER' set. This was the sound of ROD going through the motions, only 'LOCHINVAR' and 'DIXIE TOOT' approaching previous standards. Worse was to come though, as STEWART jacked in London for America, hooking up with sex-bomb actress, Britt Ekland and effecting one of the most extensive and needless musical turnarounds of the 70's. Many rock artists have been accused of 'selling-out' over the years but few managed it with such thoroughness and dearth of integrity. 'ATLANTIC CROSSING' (1975) and 'A NIGHT ON THE TOWN' (1976) had their moments (a cover of DANNY WHITTEN's 'I Don't Want To Talk About It' on the former and a definitive reading of CAT STEVEN's 'The First Cut Is The Deepest' on the latter), although danger signs were on the horizon. While the engaging ballad, 'THE KILLING OF GEORGIE' saw ROD acknowledging his sizeable gay following and the lilting 'TONIGHT'S THE NIGHT' (both major hits from 'A NIGHT . . .') proved ROD could still pen a decent love song, such tasteless nonsense as 'HOT LEGS' and 'D'YA THINK I'M SEXY' saw the singer living his sexist image up to the full as well as indulging his growing passion for pseudo-disco MOR. Predictably, by the release of 'BLONDES HAVE MORE FUN' (1978), STEWART was enjoying more success in America than his home country, the singer trawling a creative trough in the early 80's with the likes of 'FOOLISH BEHAVIOUR' and 'TONIGHT I'M YOURS'. His sales figures remained relatively undiminished however, STEWART enjoying the life of the rock aristocrat, his string of relationships with high profile blondes never far from the gossip columns. Tellingly, the singer's best work of the decade came via a reunion with JEFF BECK, the pair getting together for a brilliant reworking of CURTIS MAYFIELD's 'People Get Ready' (Top 50). The 90's saw STEWART regain at least some critical ground with 'VAGABOND HEART' (1991) while the obligatory 'UNPLUGGED . . . AND SEATED' (1993) saw an entertaining reunion with WOOD. Bizarrely enough, ROD has also exhibited a penchant for covering songs by arch weirdo, TOM WAITS, the latest of which, 'HANG ON ST. CHRISTOPHER', appeared on 'A SPANNER IN THE WORKS' (1995). While this alone signalled that STEWART hadn't completely lost the musical plot, the prospect of him ever returning to the down-home brilliance of old looked slim. However, 1998 saw Rod the Mod turn out a fine batch of covers (bar one of his own) under the title 'WHEN WE WERE THE NEW BOYS'. • **Songwriters:** ROD's cover versions:- STREET FIGHTING MAN (Rolling Stones) / RUBY TUESDAY / SWEET SOUL MUSIC (Arthur Conley) / I KNOW I'M LOSING YOU (Temptations) / IT'S ALL OVER NOW (Valentinos) / MY WAY OF GIVING (Small Faces) / CUT ACROSS SHORTY (hit; Eddie Cochran) / ANGEL (Jimi Hendrix) / AMAZING GRACE (trad. / hit; Judy Collins) / I'D RATHER GO BLIND (Etta James) / ONLY A HOBO / SWEETHEART LIKE YOU (Bob Dylan) / TWISTIN' THE NIGHT AWAY + BRING IT ON HOME TO ME + YOU SEND ME + HAVING A PARTY + SOOTHE ME (Sam Cooke) / OH NO NOT MY BABY + PRETTY FLAMINGO (Manfred Mann) / COUNTRY COMFORTS + YOUR SONG (Elton John) / WHAT MADE MILWAKEE FAMOUS (hit; Jerry Lee Lewis) / SAILING (Sutherland Brothers) / THIS OLD HEART OF MINE (Isley Brothers) / GET BACK (Beatles) / YOU KEEP ME HANGIN' ON (Supremes) / I DON'T WANT TO TALK ABOUT IT (Crazy Horse member Danny Whitten) / SOME GUYS HAVE ALL THE LUCK (Robert Palmer) / HOW LONG (Ace) / SWEET LITTLE ROCK'N'ROLLER + LITTLE QUEENIE (Chuck Berry) / THE GREAT PRETENDER (Platters) / ALL RIGHT NOW (Free) / TRY A LITTLE TENDERNESS (Otis Redding) / THE MOTOWN SONG (L.J.McNally) / IT TAKES TWO (Marvin Gaye & Tammi Terrell) / DOWNTOWN TRAIN + TOM TRAUBERT'S BLUES (Tom Waits) / BROKEN ARROW (Robbie Robertson) / HAVE I TOLD YOU LATELY THAT I LOVE YOU (Van Morrison) / PEOPLE GET READY (Curtis Mayfield) / SHOTGUN WEDDING (Roy C) / WINDY TOWN (Chris Rea) / DOWNTOWN LIGHTS (Blue Nile) / LEAVE VIRGINIA ALONE (Tom Petty) / OOH LA LA (with The Faces) / CIGARETTES & ALCOHOL (Oasis) / ROCKS (Primal Scream) / SUPERSTAR (Superstar) / SECRET HEART (Ron Sexsmith) / HOTEL CHAMBERMAID (Graham Parker) / SHELLY MY LOVE (Nick Lowe) / WEAK (Skunk Anansie) / WHAT DO YOU WANT ME TO DO (Mike Scott). SIMON CLIMIE began writing for him from 1988. YOU'RE THE STAR single written by Livesey, Lyle & Miller. **Trivia/Blondeography:** BRITT EKLAND (marriage 5 Mar'75-1978) / ALANA HAMILTON (marriage 1979-1984) / KELLY EMBERG (1985-1990) / RACHEL HUNTER (marriage 1990-1999).

Album rating: AN OLD RAINCOAT WILL NEVER LET YOU DOWN (*7) / GASOLINE ALLEY (*7) / EVERY PICTURE TELLS A STORY (*9) / NEVER A DULL MOMENT (*8) / SING IT AGAIN ROD (*5) / SMILER (*4) / ATLANTIC CROSSING (*7) / A NIGHT ON THE TOWN (*6) / FOOT LOOSE AND FANCY FREE (*4) / BLONDES HAVE MORE FUN (*5) / GREATEST HITS VOL.1 compilation (*8) / FOOLISH BEHAVIOUR (*3) / TONIGHT I'M YOURS (*4) / ABSOLUTELY LIVE (*3) / BODY WISHES (*3) / CAMOUFLAGE (*3) / EVERY BEAT OF MY HEART (aka ROD STEWART) (*4) / OUT OF ORDER (*5) / STORYTELLER – THE BEST OF ROD STEWART 1964-1990 compilation (*8) / VAGABOND HEART (*6) / UNPLUGGED . . . AND SEATED (*7) / A SPANNER IN THE WORKS (*6) / IF WE FALL IN LOVE TONIGHT (*6) / WHEN WE WERE THE NEW BOYS (*7)

ROD STEWART – vocals with session people

		Decca	Press
Oct 64.	(7") (F 11996) **GOOD MORNING LITTLE SCHOOLGIRL. / I'M GONNA MOVE TO THE OUTSKIRTS OF TOWN** (re-iss.Mar82)		

In 1965, he joined STEAMPACKET, but they issued no 45's, and split Mar'66.

		Columbia	not iss.
Nov 65.	(7") (DB 7766) **THE DAY WILL COME. / WHY DOES IT GO ON**		
Apr 66.	(7") (DB 7892) **SHAKE. / I JUST GOT SOME**		

A month previous, he had joined SHOTGUN EXPRESS who released one 45, 'I COULD FEEL THE WHOLE WORLD TURN AROUND' Oct66 on 'Columbia'.

		Immediate	not iss.
Nov 67.	(7") (IM 060) **LITTLE MISS UNDERSTOOD. / SO MUCH TO SAY** (re-iss.Sep80 on 'Virgin') (re-iss.Feb83)		

In 1968, he joined JEFF BECK GROUP, appearing on 2 albums; 'TRUTH' & 'BECK-OLA'. Similtaneously joined The FACES and returned to solo work 1969.

		Vertigo	Mercury
Feb 70.	(lp) (VO 4) <61237> **AN OLD RAINCOAT WON'T EVER LET YOU DOWN** <US-title 'THE ROD STEWART ALBUM'> – Street fighting man / Man of constant sorrow / Blind prayer / Handbags and gladrags / An old raincoat won't ever change a thing / Cindy's lament / Dirty old town. (re-iss.Aug83 on 'Mercury' lp/c; PRICE/PRIMC 27) (cd-iss.Nov87 & Sep95; 830 572-2) (cd re-iss.Aug98; 558058-2)		
Feb 70.	(7") <73009> **AN OLD RAINCOAT WON'T LET YOU DOWN. / STREET FIGHTING MAN**		–
May 70.	(7") (73031) **HANDBAGS AND GLADRAGS. / MAN OF CONSTANT SORROW** <re-iss.Feb72; 73031> – hit No.42.		–
Sep 70.	(7") (6086 002) <73095> **IT'S ALL OVER NOW. / JO'S LAMENT**		
Sep 70.	(lp) (6360 500) <61264> **GASOLINE ALLEY** – Gasoline alley / It's all over now / My way of giving / Country comfort / Cut across Shorty / Lady day / Jo's lament / I don't want to discuss it. (re-iss.Aug83 on 'Mercury' lp/c; PRICE/PRIMC 28) (cd-iss.Oct84 + Sep95; 824 881-2) (cd re-iss.Aug98; 558059-2)	62	27 Jun70
Nov 70.	(7") <73115> **GASOLINE ALLEY. / ONLY A HOBO**		–
Jan 71.	(7") <73156> **CUT ACROSS SHORTY. / GASOLINE ALLEY**		–
Mar 71.	(7") <73175> **MY WAY OF GIVING. /**		–
May 71.	(7") <73196> **COUNTRY COMFORT. / GASOLINE ALLEY**		–

		Mercury	Mercury
Jul 71.	(7") (6052 097) <73224> **MAGGIE MAY. / REASON TO BELIEVE**	1 / 19	1 / 62

(above was flipped over for BBC Radio One playlist. MAGGIE MAY was now the bigger played hit) (re-iss.Oct84)

Jul 71.	(lp) (6338 063) <609> **EVERY PICTURE TELLS A STORY** – Every picture tells a story / Seems like a long time / That's all right / Tomorrow is such a long time / Amazing Grace / Henry / Maggie May / Mandolin wind / (I know) I'm losing you / Reason to believe. (re-iss.May83 lp/c; PRICE/PRIMC 15) (cd-iss.Nov87 & Sep95; 822 385-2) (cd re-iss.Aug98; 558060-2)	1	1 Jun71
Nov 71.	(7") <73244> **(I KNOW) I'M LOSING YOU. / MANDOLIN WIND**	–	24
Jul 72.	(lp) (6499 153) <646> **NEVER A DULL MOMENT** – True blue / Lost paraguayos / Mama you been on my mind / Italian girls / Angel / Interludings / You wear it well / I'd rather go blind / Twisting the night away. (re-iss.May83 lp/c;) (cd-iss.Nov87 & Sep95; 826 263-2) (cd re-iss.Aug98; 558061-2)	1	2
Aug 72.	(7") (6052 171) **YOU WEAR IT WELL. / LOST PARAGUAYOS**	1	
Aug 72.	(7") <73330> **YOU WEAR IT WELL. / TRUE BLUE**	–	13

Sep72, a ROD STEWART early recording with PYTHON LEE JACKSON; 'In A Broken Dream' hits UK No.3 / US No.56.

| Nov 72. | (7") (6052 198) **ANGEL. / WHAT MADE MILWAUKEE FAMOUS (HAS MADE A LOSER OUT OF ME)** | 4 | – |
| Nov 72. | (7") <73344> **ANGEL. / LOST PARAGUAYOS** | – | 40 |

May73, older JEFF BECK & ROD STEWART recording 'I'VE BEEN DRINKIN' ' hit 27.

Aug 73.	(7") <73412> **TWISTING THE NIGHT AWAY. / TRUE BLUE – LADY DAY**	–	59
Aug 73.	(lp)(c) (6499 484)(7142 183) <680> **SING IT AGAIN ROD** (compilation of covers) – Reason to believe / You wear it well / Mandolin wind / Country comforts / Maggie May / Handbags and gladrags / Street fighting man / Twisting the night away / Lost Paraguayos / (I know) I'm losing you / Pinball wizard / Gasoline alley. (cd-iss.Oct84; 824882-2) (cd re-iss.Aug98; 558062-2)	1	31 Jul73
Aug 73.	(7") (6052 371) <73426> **OH! NO NOT MY BABY. / JODIE**	6	59 Oct73
Sep 74.	(7") (6167 033) **FAREWELL. / BRING IT ON HOME TO ME – YOU SEND ME (Medley)**	7	–
Oct 74.	(lp)(c) (9104 001) <1017> **SMILER** – Sweet little rock'n'roller / Lochinvar / Farewell / Sailor / Bring it on home to me – You send me (medley) / Let me be your car / A natural man / A natural man / Dixie toot / Hard road / I've grown accustomed to her face / Girl of the North Country / Mine for me. (cd-iss.Nov87 & Sep95; 832 056-2) (cd re-iss.Aug98; 558063-2)	1	13
Nov 74.	(7") <73636> **MINE FOR ME. / FAREWELL**	–	91
Jan 75.	(7") <73660> **LET ME BE YOUR CAR. / SAILOR**	–	–

		Warners	Warners
Aug 75.	(7") (K 16600) **SAILING. / STONE COLD SOBER** (re-activated Sep76, hit UK No.3, re-iss.Jan84) (re-iss.Jun77 on 'Riva') (re-iss.Mar87 for Channel Ferry disaster fund, hit No.41)	1	–
Aug 75.	(lp/c) (K/K4 56151) <2875> **ATLANTIC CROSSING** – Three time loser / Alright for an hour / All in the name of rock'n'roll / Drift away / Stone cold sober / I don't want to talk about it / It's not the spotlight / This old heart of mine / Still love you / Sailing. (re-iss.Jan78 on 'Riva' lp/c; RV LP/4 4) (cd-iss.Feb87; K2 56151) (blue-lp Jul77)	1	9
Aug 75.	(7") <8146> **SAILING. / ALL IN THE NAME OF ROCK'N'ROLL**	–	58

		Riva	Warners
Nov 75.	(7") (1) **THIS OLD HEART OF MINE. / ALL IN THE NAME OF ROCK'N'ROLL**	4	–
Jan 76.	(7") <8170> **THIS OLD HEART OF MINE. / STILL LOVE YOU**	–	83
May 76.	(7") (RIVA 3) **TONIGHT'S THE NIGHT. / THE BALLTRAP**	5	–
Jun 76.	(lp/c) (RV LP/4 1) <2938> **A NIGHT ON THE TOWN** – Tonight's the night / The first cut is the deepest / Fool for you / The killing of Georgie (part 1 & 2) / The balltrap / Pretty flamingo / Big bayou / The wild side of life / Trade winds. (re-iss.Jun83 on 'Warner Bros' lp/c; K/K4 56234) (cd-iss.1989 on 'WEA'; K2 56234) (cd re-iss.Jun93; 7599 27339-2)	1	2
Aug 76.	(7") (RIVA 4) **THE KILLING OF GEORGIE. / FOOL FOR YOU**	2	–
Sep 76.	(7") <8262> **TONIGHT'S THE NIGHT. / FOOL FOR YOU**	–	1
Nov 76.	(7") (RIVA 6) **GET BACK. / TRADE WINDS**	11	–
Feb 77.	(7") <8321> **THE FIRST CUT IS THE DEEPEST. / THE BALLTRAP**	–	21
Apr 77.	(7") (RIVA 7) **THE FIRST CUT IS THE DEEPEST. / I DON'T WANT TO TALK ABOUT IT**	1	–
Apr 77.	(7") <8396> **THE KILLING OF GEORGIE. / ROSIE**	–	30
Oct 77.	(7") (RIVA 11) <8476> **YOU'RE IN MY HEART. / YOU GOT A NERVE**	3	4
Nov 77.	(lp/c) (RV LP/4 5) <3092> **FOOT LOOSE AND FANCY FREE** – Hot legs / You're insane / You're in my heart / Born loose / You keep me hangin' on / (If loving you is wrong) / You got a nerve / I was only joking. (re-iss.Jun83 on 'Warner Bros.' lp/c; K/K4 56423) (cd-iss.Jun89; K2 56423)	3	2
Jan 78.	(7") (RIVA 10) **HOT LEGS. / I WAS ONLY JOKING**	5	–
Feb 78.	(7") <8535> **HOT LEGS. / YOU'RE INSANE**	–	28
Apr 78.	(7") <8568> **I WAS ONLY JOKING. / BORN LOOSE**	–	22
May 78.	(7"; by ROD STEWART with the SCOTLAND WORLD CUP SQUAD) (RIVA 15) **OLE OLA (MUHLER BRASILEIRA). / I'D WALK A MILLION MILES FOR ONE OF YOUR GOALS**	4	–
Nov 78.	(7") (RIVA 17) **D'YA THINK I'M SEXY?. / DIRTY WEEKEND**	1	–
Dec 78.	(7") <8734> **D'YA THINK I'M SEXY?. / SCARRED AND SCARED**	–	1
Dec 78.	(lp/c)<US-pic-lp> (RV LP/4 8) <3261> **BLONDES HAVE MORE FUN** – D'ya think I'm sexy / Dirty weekend / Ain't love a bitch / The best days of my life / Is that the thanks I get / Attractive female wanted / Blondes (have more fun) / Last summer / Standing in the shadows of love / Scarred and scared. (re-iss.Jun83 on 'Warner Bros.' lp/c; K/K4 56572) (cd-iss.Jan91 on 'Warners'; 7599 27376-2)	3	1
Jan 79.	(7") (RIVA 18) **AIN'T LOVE A BITCH. / SCARRED AND SCARED**	11	–
Apr 79.	(7") <8810> **AIN'T LOVE A BITCH. / LAST SUMMER**	–	22
Apr 79.	(7") (RIVA 19) **BLONDES (HAVE MORE FUN). / THE BEST DAYS OF MY LIFE**	63	–
Nov 79.	(lp/c) (RODTV/+4 1) <3373> **GREATEST HITS VOLUME 1** (compilation) – Hot legs / Maggie May / a ya think I'm sexy / You're in my heart / Sailing / I don't want to talk about it / Tonight's the night / The killing of Georgie (parts 1 & 2) / Maggie May / The first cut is the deepest / I was only joking. (re-iss.Jun83 lp/c; K/K4 56744) (cd-iss.Jan84 on 'Warner Bros.'; K2 56744)	1	22
Dec 79.	(7") <49138> **I DON'T WANT TO TALK ABOUT IT. / THE BEST DAYS OF MY LIFE**	–	46
May 80.	(7") (RIVA 23) **IF LOVING YOU IS WRONG (I DON'T WANT TO BE RIGHT). / LAST SUMMER**	23	–
Nov 80.	(7"/ext.12") (RIVA 26/+T) <49617> **PASSION. / BETTER OFF DEAD**	17	5
Nov 80.	(lp/c) (RV LP/4 11) <3485> **FOOLISH BEHAVIOR** – Better off dead / Foolish behaviour / My girl / She won't dance with me / Gi' me wings / So soon we change / Somebody special / Passion / Say it ain't true / Oh God, I wish I was home tonight. (re-iss.Jun83 on 'Warner Bros.' lp/c; >)	4	12
Dec 80.	(7") (RIVA 28) **MY GIRL. / SHE WON'T DANCE WITH ME**	32	–

Mar 81. (7"/c-s) *(RIVA 29/+M)* **OH GOD, I WISH I WAS HOME TONIGHT. / SOMEBODY SPECIAL** ☐ –

Mar 81. (7") *<49686>* **SOMEBODY SPECIAL. / SHE WON'T DANCE WITH ME** – 71

Oct 81. (7") *<49843>* **YOUNG TURKS. / SONNY** – 5

Oct 81. (7") *(RIVA 33)* **TONIGHT I'M YOURS (DON'T HURT ME). / SONNY** 8 –

Nov 81. (lp/c) *(RV LP/4 14) <3602>* **TONIGHT I'M YOURS** 8 11
– Tonight I'm yours (don't hurt me) / Only a boy / Just like a woman / How long / Never give up on a dream / Jealous / Tora, Tora, Tora (out with the boys) / Young Turks / Tear it up / Sonny. (re-iss. Jun83 lp/c; K/K4 56951) (cd-iss. Jun93 on 'Warners'; 7599 23602-2)

Dec 81. (7") *(RIVA 34)* **YOUNG TURKS. / TORA, TORA, TORA (OUT WITH THE BOYS)** 11 –

Jan 82. (7") *<49886>* **TONIGHT I'M YOURS (DON'T HURT ME). / TORA, TORA, TORA (OUT WITH THE BOYS)** – 20

Feb 82. (7") *(RIVA 35) <50051>* **HOW LONG. / JEALOUS** 41 49 Apr82

Nov 82. (d-lp/d-c) *(RV LP/4 17) <23743>* **ABSOLUTELY LIVE (live)** 35 46
– The stripper / Tonight I'm yours / Sweet little rock'n'roller / Hot legs / Tonight's the night / The great pretender / Passion / She won't dance with me / Little Queenie / You're in my heart / Rock my plimsoul / Young Turks / Guess I'll always love you / Gasoline alley / Maggie May / Tear it up / D'ya think I'm sexy / Sailing / I don't want to talk about it / Stay with me. (re-iss. Mar84 on 'Warner Bros.' d-lp/dc; 923743-1/-4) (cd-iss. Mar87; 923743-2)

Nov 82. (7") *<29874>* **GUESS I'LL ALWAYS LOVE YOU (live). / ROCK MY PLIMSOUL (live)** – –

Warners Warners

May 83. (7") *(W 9608) <29608>* **BABY JANE. / READY NOW** 1 14
(12"+=) *(W 9608T)* – If loving you is wrong (live).

Jun 83. (lp/c) *(K 923977-1/-4) <23877>* **BODY WISHES** 5 30
– Dancin' alone / Baby Jane / Move me / Body wishes / Sweet surrender / What am I gonna do / Ghetto blaster / Ready now / Strangers again / Satisfied. (cd-iss. Jul84; K 923977-2)

Aug 83. (7"/12") *(W 9564/+T) 29564>* **WHAT AM I GONNA DO?. / DANCIN' ALONE** 3 35

Dec 83. (7"/67"pic-d) *(W 9440/+P)* **SWEET SURRENDER. / GHETTO BLASTER** 23 –
(12"+=) *(W 9440T)* – Oh God I wish I was home tonight.

May 84. (7") *(W 29256)* **INFATUATION. / SHE WON'T DANCE WITH ME** – 6

May 84. (7") *(W 9256)* **INFATUATION. / THREE TIME LOSER** 27 –
(12"+=) *(W 9256T)* – Tonight's the night.

Jun 84. (lp/c/cd) *(925095-1/-4/-4) <25095>* **CAMOUFLAGE** 8 18
– Infatuation / All right now / Some guys have all the luck / Can we still be friends / Bad for you / Heart is on the line / Camouflage / Trouble. (free 1-sided 7"pic-d w.a.) – INFATUATION / (interview).

Jul 84. (7") *(W 9204) <29215>* **SOME GUYS HAVE ALL THE LUCK. / I WAS ONLY JOKING** 15 10
(12"+=) *(W 9204T)* – The killing of Georgie.

Nov 84. (7") *(W 9115)* **TROUBLE. / TORA, TORA, TORA (OUT WITH THE BOYS)** – –
(12"+=) *(W 9115T)* – This old heart of mine.

Dec 84. (7") *<29112>* **ALL RIGHT NOW. / DANCIN' ALONE** – 72

—— In 1985, he was credited on 45 'PEOPLE GET READY' by JEFF BECK.

Jun 86. (7") *(W 8668) <28668>* **LOVE TOUCH. / HEART IS ON THE LINE** 27 6 May86
(12"pic-d+=) *(W 8668TP)* – Hard lesson to learn.

Jun 86. (lp/c)(cd) *(WX 53/+C)(925446-2) <25446>* **EVERY BEAT OF MY HEART** <US-title 'ROD STEWART'> 5 28
– Here to eternity / Another heartache / A night like this / Who's gonna take me home / Red hot in black / Love touch / In my own crazy way / Every beat of my heart / Ten days of rain / In my life. (cd+=) – Every beat of my heart (remix).

Jul 86. (7") *(W 8625) <28625>* **EVERY BEAT OF MY HEART. / TROUBLE** 2 83 Nov86
(12"+=) *(W 8625)* – ('A'mix).
(12"pic-d+=) *(W 8625TE)* – Some guys have all the luck (live)

Sep 86. (7") *(W 8631) <28631>* **ANOTHER HEARTACHE. / YOU'RE IN MY HEART** 54 52
(12"+=) *(W 8631T)* – ('A'extended).

Jul 87. (7") *<28303>* **TWISTING THE NIGHT AWAY. / LET'S GET SMALL** – 80
above was issued on 'Geffen' and on film 'Innerspace'.

May 88. (7"/US-c-s) *(W 7927) <27927>* **LOST IN YOU. / ALMOST ILLEGAL** 21 12
(12"+=/12"pic-d+=) *(W 7927 T/TP)* – ('A'extended).
(cd-s+=) *(W 7927CD)* – Baby Jane / Every beat of my heart.

May 88. (lp/c)(cd) *(WX 152/+C)(925684-2) <25684>* **OUT OF ORDER** 11 20
– Lost in you / The wild horse / Lethal dose of love / Forever young / My heart can't tell you no / Dynamite / Nobody loves you when you're down and out / Crazy about her / Try a little tenderness / When I was your man.

Jul 88. (7") *(W 7796) <27796>* **FOREVER YOUNG. / DAYS OF RAGE** 57 12
(12"+=) *(W 7796)* – ('A'extended).
(cd-s+=) *(W 7796CD)* – Every beat of my heart.

Jan 89. (7") **TRY A LITTLE TENDERNESS. / MY HEART CAN'T TELL YOU NO** ☐ ☐

Apr 89. (7") *(W 7729) <27729>* **MY HEART CAN'T TELL YOU NO. / THE WILD HORSE** 49 4 Nov88
(12"+=/12"pic-d+=/cd-s+=) *(W 7729 T/TP/CD)* – Passion (live).

May 89. (7"/c-s) *<27657>* **CRAZY ABOUT HER. / DYNAMITE** – 11

Nov 89. (7"/7"pic-d/c-s; with RONALD ISLEY) *(W 2686/+P) <19983>* **THIS OLD HEART OF MINE. / TONIGHT I'M YOURS (DON'T HURT ME)** 51 –
(12"+=/cd-s+=/12"pic-d+=) *(W 2686 T/TP/CD)* – Ain't love a bitch.

Nov 89. (d-lp/d-c/d-cd) *(925987-2/-4/-1) <25987>* **STORYTELLER – THE BEST OF ROD STEWART 1964-1990** (compilation) 3 54

—— (was also issued UK on (7xlp)(4xc)(4xcd).

Jan 90. (7"/c-s) *(W 2647/+C) <22685>* **DOWNTOWN TRAIN. / THE KILLING OF GEORGIE** (pt.1 & 2) 10 3 Nov89
(12"/cd-s) *(W 2647 T/CD)* – ('A'side) / Hot legs.
(12"+=) *(W 2647TE)* – ('A'side) / Cindy incidentally / To love somebody.

Mar 90. (7"; with RONALD ISLEY) *<19983>* **THIS OLD HEART OF MINE. / YOU'RE IN MY HEART** – 10

Mar 90. (cd/c) *<26158>* **DOWNTOWN TRAIN – SELECTIONS FROM STORYTELLER** (compilation) – 20

Nov 90. (7"/c-s; ROD STEWART & TINA TURNER) *(ROD 1/+C)* **IT TAKES TWO. / HOT LEGS (live)** 5 ☐
(12"+=) *(ROD 1 T/CD)* – ('A'extended remix).

Mar 91. (7"/c-s) *(W 0017) <19366>* **RHYTHM OF MY HEART. / MOMENT OF GLORY** 3 5 Feb91
(12"+=) *(W 0017 T/CD)* – I don't want to talk about it (re-recording).

Apr 91. (cd)(lp/c) *(<7599 26596-2>)(WX 408/+C)* **VAGABOND HEART** 2 10
– Rhythm of my heart / Rebel heart / Broken arrow / It takes two / When a man's in love / You are everything / The Motown song / Go out dancing / No holding back / Have I told you lately that I love you / Moment of glory / Downtown train / If only.

Jun 91. (7"/c-s) *(W 0030/+C) <19322>* **THE MOTOWN SONG. / SWEET SOUL MUSIC (live)** 10 10
(12"+=/cd-s+=) *(W 0030 T/CD)* – Try a little tenderness.

Aug 91. (7"/c-s) *(W 0059/+C)* **BROKEN ARROW. / I WAS ONLY JOKING** 54 ☐
(10"+=/cd-s+=) *(W 0059 T/CD)* – The killing of Georgie (parts 1 & 2).

Oct 91. (c-s,cd-s) *<19274>* **BROKEN ARROW / THE WILD HORSE** – 20

Apr 92. (c-s,cd-s) *<865944>* **YOUR SONG / MANDOLIN WIND** – 48

—— <above issued on 'Polydor' US>

Apr 92. (7"/c-s) *(W 0104/+C)* **YOUR SONG. / BROKEN ARROW** 41 –
(12"+=/cd-s+=) *(W 0104 T/CD)* – Mandolin wind / The first cut is the deepest.

Nov 92. (7"/c-s) *(W 0104/+C)* **TOM TRAUBERT'S BLUES (WALTZING MATILDA). / NO HOLDING BACK** 6 –
(cd-s+=) *(W 0104CD)* – Downtown train.
(cd-s) *(W 0104CDX)* – ('A'side) / Sailing / I don't want to talk about it / Try a little tenderness.

Feb 93. (cd/c/lp) *(<9362 45258-2>)(WX 503/+C)* **ROD STEWART, LEAD VOCALIST** (part compilation) 3 ☐
– I ain't superstitious / Handbags & gladrags / Cindy incidentally / Stay with me / True blue / Sweet Mary lady / Hot legs / Stand back / Ruby Tuesday / Shotgun wedding / First I look at the purse / Tom Traubert's blues.

Feb 93. (7"/c-s) *(W 0158/+C)* **RUBY TUESDAY. / YOU'RE IN MY HEART** 11 –
(cd-s+=) *(W 0158CD)* – Out of order / Passion.
(cd-s) *(W 0158CDX)* – Crazy about her / Passion.

Apr 93. (7"/c-s) *(W 0171/+C)* **SHOTGUN WEDDING. / EVERY BEAT OF MY HEART** 21 –
(cd-s+=) *(W 0171CD)* – Sweet soul music (live).
(cd-s) *(W 0171CDX)* – ('A'side) / Memphis / Maybe I'm amazed / Had me a real goodtime (all 3 by ROD STEWART & THE FACES).
below with special guest **RONNIE WOOD** – guitar plus others **JEFF GOLUB** – guitar / **CARMINE ROJAS** – bass / **CHARLES KENTISS III** – piano, organ / **KEVIN SAVIGAR** – piano, organ & accordion / **JIM CREGAN** – guitar / **DON TESCHNER** – guitar, violin & mandolin / **PHIL PARLAPIANO** – accordion & mandolin / & backing singers

May 93. (cd/c/lp) *(<9362 45289-2/-4/-1>)* **UNPLUGGED . . . AND SEATED (live)** 2 2
– Hot legs / Tonight's the night / Handbags and gladrags / Cut across Shorty / Every picture tells a story / Maggie May / Reason to believe / People get ready / Have I told you lately / Tom Traubert's blues (waltzing Matilda) / The first cut is the deepest / Mandolin wind / Highgate shuffle / Stay with me / Having a party.

Jun 93. (7"/c-s) *(W 0185/+C) <18511>* **HAVE I TOLD YOU LATELY THAT I LOVE YOU? / GASOLINE ALLEY** 5 5 Apr93
(cd-s+=) *(W 0185CD)* – ('A'side) / Love wars / One night.
(cd-s) *(W 0185CDX)* – ('A'side) / Love wars / One night.

Aug 93. (7"/c-s) *(W 0198/+C) <18427>* **REASON TO BELIEVE (unplugged). / IT'S ALL OVER NOW (unplugged)** 51 19
(cd-s+=) *(W 0198CD1)* – Love in the right hands.
(cd-s) *(W 0198CD2)* – ('A'side) / Cindy incidentally / Stay with me (both w / FACES).

—— In Dec '93, ROD & STING, teamed up with BRYAN ADAMS on his US Top 5 hit 'All For Love'.

Dec 93. (7"/c-s) *(W 0226/+C)* **PEOPLE GET READY. / I WAS ONLY JOKING** 45 –
(cd-s) *(W 0226CD1)* – ('A'side) / Tonight's the night / If loving you is wrong (I don't want to be right).
(cd-s) *(W 0226CD2)* – ('A'side) / Da ya think I'm sexy / Sweet little rock'n'roller (live) / Baby Jane.

—— Late '93, ROD, BRYAN ADAMS and STING teamed up on a song from 'The Three Musketeers' film; 'ALL FOR LOVE', which hit UK No.2 (early '94) + US No.1.

Dec 93. (c-s,cd-s; ROD STEWART with RONNIE WOOD) *<18427>* **HAVING A PARTY (live unplugged) / SWEET LITTLE ROCK AND ROLLER (live acoustic)** – 36

May 95. (c-s) *(W 0296C)* **YOU'RE THE STAR / SHOCK TO THE SYSTEM** 19 –
(cd-s+=) *(W 0296CD)* – Have I told you lately.

May 95. (cd/c/lp) *(<9362 45867-2/-4/-1>)* **A SPANNER IN THE WORKS** 4 35
– Windy town / Downtown lights / Leave Virginia alone / Sweetheart like you / This / Lady luck / Muddy, Sam and Otis / Hang on St. Christopher / Delicious / Soothe me / Purple heather.

Jun 95. (c-s,cd-s) *<17847>* **LEAVE VIRGINIA ALONE / SHOCK TO THE SYSTEM** – 52

Aug 95. (c-s) *(W 0310C)* **LADY LUCK / HOT LEGS** 56 –
(cd-s+=) *(W 0310CD1)* – The groom still waiting at the altar / Young Turks.
(cd-s) *(W 0310CD2)* – ('A'side) / The killing of Georgie / Sailing / The first cut is the deepest.

Jun 96. (c-s/cd-s) *(W 0354 C/CD)* **PURPLE HEATHER / EVERY BEAT OF MY HEART** 16 ☐

—— The official song for Scotland's Euro '96 football campaign. All proceeds were donated to the families of the Dunblane tragedy.

Nov 96. (cd/c) *(<9362 46467-2/-4>)* **IF WE FALL IN LOVE TONIGHT** `8` `19`
– If we fall in love tonight / Sometimes when we touch / I don't want to talk about it / For the first time / When I need you / Broken arrow / Have I told you lately / Tonight / Forever young / My heart can't tell you no / First cut is the deepest / Tonight's the night / You're in my heart.

Dec 96. (c-s) *(W 0380C) <17459>* **IF WE FALL IN LOVE TONIGHT / TOM TRAUBERT'S BLUES (WALTZING MATILDA)** `58` `54` Nov96
(cd-s) *(W 0380CD)* – ('A'side) / So far away / I was only joking / Ten days of rain.

—— N-TRANCE featured ROD on their version of 'DA YA THINK I'M SEXY?', which hit UK No.7 in Nov'97.

May 98. (c-s) *(W 0446C) <17195>* **OOH LA LA / A NIGHT LIKE THIS** `16` `39` Jun98
(cd-s+=) *(W 0446CD)* – Ten days of rain.

Jun 98. (cd/c) *(<9362 46792-2/-4>)* **WHEN WE WERE THE NEW BOYS** `2` `44`
– Cigarettes and alcohol / Ooh la la / Rocks / Superstar / Secret heart / Hotel chambermaid / Shelly my love / When we were the new boys / Weak / What do you want me to do?

Aug 98. (c-s) *(W 0452C)* **ROCKS / STAY WITH ME (live)** `55`
(cd-s+=) *(W 0452CD2)* – Maggie May (live).
(cd-s) *(W 0452CD1)* – ('A'side) / Hot legs (live) / Da ya think I'm sexy? (live).

Dec 98. (c-s) *(W 465C)* **SUPERSTAR /**
(cd-s+=) *(W 465CD)* –

Apr 99. (c-s) *(UNC 56235)* **FAITH OF THE HEART / Mark Shainman: MAIN TITLE SCORE** `60`
(cd-s+=) *(UND 56235)* – Front porch.
(above issued on 'Universal')

– compilations, etc. –

Sep 72. (7"; by PYTHON LEE JACKSON) *Youngblood; (YB 1017) / GNP Crescendo; <449>* **IN A BROKEN DREAM. / THE BLUES** `3` `56`
(re-iss. Jul80 /12"+=) – Cloud 9. (re-iss. Aug87 as "PYTHON LEE JACKSON / ROD STEWART" on 'Bold Reprieve')

—— PYTHON LEE JACKSON was in fact an Australian 5-piece of the late 60s, headed by keyboard player **DAVID BENTLEY**, who employed ROD to sing on 3 tracks from their lp 'IN A BROKEN DREAM'.

1979. (7") *Lightning;* **IN A BROKEN DREAM. / IF THE WORLD STOPS STILL TONIGHT** `-`
Below releases on 'Mercury' until otherwise mentioned.

Feb 76. (d-lp/c) *(6672 013)* **THE VINTAGE YEARS 1969-70**
Feb 76. (7") *(6086 02)* **IT'S ALL OVER NOW. / HANDBAGS AND GLADRAGS** `-`
1976. (7") **EVERY PICTURE TELLS A STORY. / WHAT MADE MILWAUKEE FAMOUS (HAS MADE A LOSER OUT OF ME)** `-`
Jul 76. (lp/c) **RECORDED HIGHLIGHTS AND ACTION REPLAYS** `-` `-`
Jun 77. (7"m) *(6160 007)* **MANDOLIN WIND. / GIRL FROM THE NORTH COUNTRY / SWEET LITTLE ROCK'N'ROLLER** `-`
Jun 77. (d-lp)(d-c) *(6643 030)(7599 141) <7507>* **THE BEST OF ROD STEWART** `18` `90`
(re-iss. Sep85 lp/c; PRID/+C 10)
Jul 77. (c) *(714506-1)* **THE MUSIC OF ROD STEWART (1970-71)** `-`
Aug 77. (d-lp/d-c) *(661903-1/-4)* **THE BEST OF ROD STEWART VOLUME 2** `-`
Nov 79. (7") *(6160 006)* **MAGGIE MAY. / YOU WEAR IT WELL** `-`
(re-iss. Apr88 on 'Old Gold';)
Sep 80. (lp) *(646306-1)* **HOT RODS** `-`
May 81. (lp) *(927913-2)* **BEST OF THE BEST** `-`
Nov 87. (cd) *(925466-2)* **THE ROD STEWART ALBUM** `-`
Jun 89. (lp/c/cd) *(830784-1/-4/-2)* **THE ROCK ALBUM** `-`
Jun 89. (cd) *(830785-2)* **THE BALLAD ALBUM** `-`
Feb 91. (cd/c) *(846 988-2/-4)* **GASOLINE ALLEY / SMILER** `-`
Oct 92. (7"/c-s) **YOU WEAR IT WELL / I WOULD RATHER GO BLIND**
(cd-s+=) – Angel.
Dec 78. (lp) *St.Michael;* **REASON TO BELIEVE** `-`
Sep 81. (lp/c) *Contour; (CN/+4 2045)* **MAGGIE MAY** `-`
(cd-iss. Jul90 on 'Pickwick'; PWKS 586)
Oct 82. (lp/c) *Contour; (CN/+4 2059)* **ROD STEWART** `-`
Sep 85. (lp/c) *Contour; (CN/+4 2077)* **THE HITS OF ROD STEWART** `-`
Jan 87. (lp/c) *Contour; (CN/+4 2082)* **JUKE BOX HEAVEN (14 ROCK'N'ROLL GREATS)** `-`
Jul 83. (d-c) *Cambra;* **ROD STEWART** `-`
Nov 83. (d-c) *Warners; (923955-2)* **ATLANTIC CROSSING / A NIGHT ON THE TOWN** `-`
Nov 84. (lp/c) *Astan; (2/4 0119)* **CAN I GET A WITNESS** `-`
Jul 88. (lp/c) *Knight; (KNLP/KNMC 10002)* **NIGHTRIDIN'** `-`
Feb 89. (c) *Venus; (VENUMC 3)* **THE MAGIC OF ROD STEWART** `-`
Oct 89. (lp/c/cd) *K-Tel;* **IN A BROKEN DREAM** `1988`
Dec 92. (cd/c) *M Classics; (CJES D/C 2)* **JUST A LITTLE MISUNDERSTOOD** `-`
Feb 93. (cd; ROD STEWART & STEAMPACKET) *Charly;* **THE FIRST SUPER GROUP** `-`
Jul 93. (cd/c) *Telstar; (CDSR/TCSR 014)* **THE FACE OF THE SIXTIES** `-`
Jul 94. (cd/c) *Success;* **COME HOME BABY** `-`
Aug 95. (cd/c) *Spectrum; (551110-2/-4)* **MAGGIE MAY – THE CLASSIC YEARS** `-`
Oct 95. (d-cd) *Mercury; (528 823-2)* **HANDBAGS AND GLADRAGS (The Mercury Recordings 1970-1974)** `-`
May 97. (cd) *Experience; (EXP 030)* **ROD STEWART** `-`
Jul 97. (cd) *Going For A Song; (GFS 061)* **ROD STEWART** `-`
Aug 98. (cd) *Mercury; (558873-2)* **THE VERY BEST OF ROD STEWART** `-`

STIFF LITTLE FINGERS

Formed: Belfast, N.Ireland ... 1977 by teenagers JAKE BURNS, HENRY CLUNEY, ALI McMORDIE and GORDON BLAIR, the last soon being replaced by BRIAN FALOON. Famously taking their name from a line in a VIBRATORS' b-side, the group began life as a CLASH covers band. Taken under the wing of journalist, GORDON OGILVIE (who subsequently became both band manager and BURNS' writing partner), the group began to rely on original material, releasing their incendiary 1978 debut single, 'SUSPECT DEVICE'. / 'WASTED LIFE' on the self-financed 'Rigid Digits' label. Wound tight, both lyrically and musically, with the frustration and anger of living in war-torn Belfast, the record introduced SLF as one of the most visceral and compelling punk bands since The SEX PISTOLS. Championed by the ever vigilant John Peel, the single led to a deal with 'Rough Trade' who jointly released a follow-up single, 'ALTERNATIVE ULSTER', the track rapidly assuming legendary status, although it was originally penned for release as a magazine flexi-disc. A debut album, 'INFLAMMABLE MATERIAL', followed in early '79, a raging, politically barbed howl of punk protest which lined up all the aforementioned tracks alongside such definitive SLF material as 'STATE OF EMERGENCY' and 'JOHNNY WAS'. Storming into the Top 20, the album expanded their already voracious fanbase, the group undertaking their first major headlining tour to promote it. The insistent, bass-heavy pop-punk dynamics of 'GOTTA GETAWAY' marked the debut of JIM REILLY (replacing the departing FALOON on the drum stool) and no doubt fuelled a thousand teenage runaway fantasies while the vicious 'STRAW DOGS' marked the group's major label debut for 'Chrysalis'. Early the following year, SLF scored their sole Top 20 hit with 'AT THE EDGE', another seething account of BURNS' troubled youth in Northern Ireland and arguably one of the group's finest moments. 'NOBODY'S HEROES' (1980) saw a move towards a more varied musical palate and a distinctly melodic feel, notably on the title track although 'TIN SOLDIERS' was as brutal as ever. The seminal live album, 'HANX!' (1980) gave the band their only Top 10 success later that year, surprising given the band's increasingly commercial approach as witnessed on the infectious 'JUST FADE AWAY' (possibly the only song ever written about a woman harassing a man!). A centrepiece of the 'GO FOR IT' (1981) set, the single stood in stark contrast to the insipid cod-reggae that so many punk bands, SLF unfortunately included, were now falling back on. 'NOW THEN' (1982) was an uncomfortable attempt to branch out even further into uncharted pop/rock territory, BURNS leaving soon after to form JAKE BURNS & THE BIG WHEEL. This effectively spelled the end for the band, and after a farewell tour, they called it a day. The live demand for SLF was so strong, however, that they were able to regroup in 1987, new material eventually surfacing in 1991 following the replacement of the disillusioned McMORDIE with ex-JAM bassist BRUCE FOXTON. The album in question, 'FLAGS AND EMBLEMS', hardly set the rock world alight, gigs predictably characterised by diehard fans shouting for old favourites. 'GET A LIFE' (1994) was similarly formulaic and, without being precious, one can't help but wonder how such a vital, influential band are now reduced to basically retreading past glories for a greying audience. • **Songwriters:** BURNS penned, some with OGILVIE. They also covered JOHNNY WAS (Bob Marley) / RUNNING BEAR (Johnny Preston) / WHITE CHRISTMAS (Bing Crosby) / LOVE OF THE COMMON PEOPLE (Nicky Thomas) / THE MESSAGE (Grandmaster Flash). • **Trivia:** JAKE once applied for a job of a Radio 1 producer.

Album rating: INFLAMMABLE MATERIAL (*8) / NOBODY'S HEROES (*7) / HANX! (*6) / GO FOR IT (*5) / NOW THEN (*5) / ALL THE BEST compilation (*8) / NO SLEEP TILL BELFAST (*5) / SEE YOU UP THERE! (*5) / FLAGS AND EMBLEMS (*5) / GET A LIFE (*4) / TINDERBOX (*4)

JAKE BURNS – vocals, lead guitar / **HENRY CLUNEY** – guitar / **ALI McMORDIE** – bass / **BRIAN FALOON** – drums; repl. GORDON BLAIR who later joined RUDI

	Rigid Digits	not iss.
Mar 78. (7") *(SRD-1)* **SUSPECT DEVICE. / WASTED LIFE** `-`
(re-iss. Jun78) (re-iss. Mar79 on 'Rough Trade'; RT 006)

	Rough Trade	not iss.
Oct 78. (7") *(RT 004)* **ALTERNATIVE ULSTER. / '78 R.P.M.** `-`
Feb 79. (lp) *(ROUGH 1)* **INFLAMMABLE MATERIAL** `14`
– Suspect device / State of emergency / Here we are nowhere / Wasted life / No more of that / Barbed wire love / White noise / Breakout / Law and order / Rough trade / Johnny was / Alternative Ulster / Closed groove. (re-iss. Mar89 on 'E.M.I.' lp/c(cd); EMC/TC-EMC 3554)(CDP 792105-2) <US cd-iss. 1992 on 'Restless'; 72363>

—— JIM REILLY – drums repl. FALOON

May 79. (7") *(RT 015)* **GOTTA GETAWAY. / BLOODY SUNDAY** `-`

	Chrysalis	Chrysalis
Sep 79. (7") *(CHS 2368)* **STRAW DOGS. / YOU CAN'T SAY CRAP ON THE RADIO** `44`
Feb 80. (7") *(CHS 2406)* **AT THE EDGE. / SILLY ENCORES: RUNNING BEAR – WHITE CHRISTMAS** `15`
Mar 80. (lp/c) *(CHR/ZCHR 1270)* **NOBODY'S HEROES** `8`
– Gotta getaway / Wait and see / Fly the flag / At the edge / Nobody's hero / Bloody dub / Doesn't make it alright / I don't like you / No change / Suspect device / Tin soldiers. (re-iss. Mar89 on 'E.M.I.' lp/c(cd); EMC/TC-EMC 3555)(CDP 792106-2) <US cd-iss. 1992 on 'Restless'; 72364>
May 80. (7") *(CHS 2424)* **TIN SOLDIERS. / NOBODY'S HERO** `36`
Jul 80. (7") *(CHS 2447)* **BACK TO FRONT. / MR FIRE COAL-MAN** `49`
Sep 80. (lp/c) *(CHR/ZCHR 1300)* **HANX! (live)** `9`
– Nobody's hero / Gotta getaway / Wait and see / Barbed wire love / Fly the flag / Alternative Ulster / Johnny was / At the edge / Wasted life / Tin soldiers / Suspect device. (re-iss. Feb89 on 'Fame-EMI' lp/c/cd; FA/TC-FA/CD-FA 3215) <US cd-iss. 1992 on 'Restless'; 72365>

Mar 81. (7"m) *(CHS 2510)* **JUST FADE AWAY. / GO FOR IT /**

DOESN'T MAKE IT ALRIGHT (live) `47` `-`

Apr 81. (lp/c) *(CHR/ZCHR 1339)* **GO FOR IT** `14` `-`
– Roots, radicals, rockers and reggae / Just fade away / Go for it / The only one / Hits and misses / Kicking up a racket / Safe as houses / Gate 49 / Silver lining / Piccadilly Circus. *(re-iss. Feb89 on 'Fame-EMI' lp/c/cd+=; FA/TC-FA/CD-FA 3216)* – Back to front. *<US cd-iss. 1992 on 'Restless'; 72366>*

May 81. (7") *(CHS 2517)* **SILVER LINING. / SAFE AS HOUSES** `68` `-`

—— **BRIAN 'DOLPHIN' TAYLOR** – drums (ex-TOM ROBINSON BAND) repl. REILLY

Jan 82. (7"ep) *(CHS 2580)* **R.E.P. PAY 1.10 OR LESS EP** `33` `-`
– Listen / Sad-eyed people / That's when your blood bumps / Two guitars clash.

Apr 82. (7") *(CHS 2601)* **TALK BACK. / GOOD FOR NOTHING** `-` `-`

Aug 82. (7"/12") *(CHS/+12 2637)* **BITS OF KIDS. / STANDS TO**

REASON `73` `-`

Sep 82. (lp/c) *(CHR/ZCHR 1400)* **NOW THEN** `24` `-`
– Falling down / Won't be told / Love of the common people / The price of admission / Touch and go / Stands to reason / Bits of kids / Welcome to the whole week / Big city night / Talkback / Is that what you fought the war for. *(cd-iss. Dec94 on 'Fame'; CDFA 3306) (cd re-iss. Apr97 on 'EMI Gold'; CDGOLD 1090)*

Jan 83. (d-lp/d-c) *(CTY/ZCTY 1414)* **ALL THE BEST** (compilation) `19` `-`
– Suspect device / Wasted life / Alternative Ulster / '78 R.P.M. / Gotta getaway / Bloody Sunday / Straw dogs / You can't say crap on the radio / At the edge / Running bear / White Christmas / Nobody's hero / Tin soldiers / Back to front / Mr. Fire coal-man / Just fade away / Go for it / Doesn't make it alright / Silver lining / Safe as houses / Sad eyed people / Two guitars clash / Listen / That's when your blood bumps / Good for nothing / Talkback / Stand to reason / Bits of kids / Touch and go / The price of admission / Silly encores *[not on cass]*. *(d-cd-iss. Jun88; CCD 1414) (re-iss. Sep91 on 'E.M.I.' d-cd/d-c; CD/TC EM 1428) <US d-cd-iss. 1995 on 'One Way'; 18429>*

Feb 83. (7") *(CHS 2671)* **THE PRICE OF ADMISSION. / TOUCH**

AND GO `-` `-`

—— Had already disbanded late 1982. McMORDIE joined FICTION GROOVE and DOLPHIN joined SPEAR OF DESTINY after stint with GO WEST.

JAKE BURNS & THE BIG WHEEL

—— were formed by **JAKE** plus **NICK MUIR** – keyboards / **SEAN MARTIN** – bass / **STEVE GRANTLEY** – drums

Survival not iss.

Jul 85. (7"/12") *(SRD/+T 2)* **ON FORTUNE STREET. / HERE COMES**

THAT SONG AGAIN `-` `-`

Mar 86. (7"/12") *(SRD/+T 3)* **SHE GREW UP. / RACE YOU TO THE**

GRAVE `-` `-`

Jive not iss.

Feb 87. (7"/ext.12") *(JIVE/+T 139)* **BREATHLESS. / VALENTINE'S**

DAY `-` `-`

STIFF LITTLE FINGERS

—— re-formed in 1987 by **BURNS, TAYLOR, CLUNEY & McMORDIE**

Link not iss.

Apr 88. (d-lp,green-d-lp) *(LP 026)* **LIVE AND LOUD** (live) `-` `-`
– Alternative Ulster / Roots radicals rockers and reggae / Silver lining / Wait and see / Gotta getaway / Just fade away / Wasted life / The only one / Nobody's hero / At the edge / Listen / Barbed wire love / Fly the flag / Tin soldiers / No sleep till Belfast / Suspect device / Johnny was. *(re-iss. May88 as 'NO SLEEP TILL BELFAST' on 'Kaz' c/cd; KAZ MC/CD 6) (cd-iss. Sep89; CD 026)*

Skunx not iss.

Jun 88. (12"ep) *(SLFX 1)* **NO SLEEP TILL BELFAST** (live) `-` `-`
– Suspect device / Alternative Ulster / Nobody's hero.

Virgin Caroline

Mar 89. (12"ep/cd-ep) *(SLF/+CD 1)* **ST.PATRIX** (the covers live) `-` `-`
– The wild rover / Love of the common people / Johnny Was.

Apr 89. (d-lp/d-c/d-cd) *(VGD/+C/CD 3515) <CAROL 1377-1/-4/-2>*

SEE YOU UP THERE! (live) `-` `-`
– (intro: Go for it) / Alternative Ulster / Silver lining / Love of the common people / Gotta getaway / Just fade away / Piccadilly Circus / Gate 49 / Wasted life / At the edge / Listen / Barbed wire love / Fly the flag / Tin soldiers / The wild rover / Suspect device / Johnny was.

—— (Mar91) **BRUCE FOXTON** – bass (ex-JAM, ex-solo) repl. McMORDIE

Essential Taang!

Oct 91. (cd/c/lp)(pic-lp) *(ESS CD/MC/LP 171)(EPDLP 171)* **FLAGS &**

EMBLEMS `-` `-`
– (It's a) Long way to Paradise (from here) / Stand up and shout / Each dollar a bullet / The cool / Beirut Moon / The game of life / Human shield / Johnny 7 / Dread burn / No surrender. *(cd re-iss. Jul95 on 'Dojo';)*

Oct 91. (cd-ep) *(ESSX 2007)* **BEIRUT MOON / STAND UP AND**

SHOUT / (JAKE interview) `-` `-`

Jan 94. (12"ep) *(ESS 2035)* **CAN'T BELIEVE IN YOU. / SILVER**

LINING (unplugged) / **LISTEN** (unplugged) / **WASTED**

LIFE (unplugged) `-` `-`
(cd-ep) *(ESSX 2035)* – ('A'side) / ('A'extended) / Alternative Ulster (featuring RICKY WARWICK of The ALMIGHTY) / Smithers-Jones (live with BRUCE FOXTON vocals).

Feb 94. (cd/c) *(ESS CD/MC 210) <TAANG 100>* **GET A LIFE** `-` Oct94
– Get a life / Can't believe in you / The road to kingdom come / Walk away / No laughing matter / Harp / Forensic evidence / Baby blue ((what have they been telling you?) / I want you / The night that the wall came down / Cold / When the stars fall from the sky / What if I want more? i(re-iss. Apr97; ESMCD 488)

Jun 94. (12"/cd-s) **HARP. / SHAKE IT OFF / NOW WHAT WE**

WERE (PRO PATRIA MORI) `-` `-`

—— **STEVE GRANTLEY** – drums (ex-JAKE BURNS . . .) repl. TAYLOR

Spitfire Taang!

Jun 97. (cd/lp) *(SLF 100 CD/LP) <T 137>* **TINDERBOX** `-` Jul97
– You never hear the one that hits you / (I could) Be happy yesterday / Tinderbox / Dead of night / The message / My ever changing moral stance / Hurricane / You can move mountains / River flowing / You don't believe in me / In your hand / Dust in my eye / Roaring boys (part 1) / Roaring boys (part 2).

– compilations, etc. –

Sep 86. (12"ep) *Strange Fruit; (SFPS 004)* **THE PEEL SESSIONS**

(12.9.78) `-`
– Johnny was / Law and order / Barbed wire love / Suspect device. *(c-ep-iss.May87; SFPSC 004) (cd-ep-iss.Jul88; SFPCD 004)*

Nov 89. (lp/c/cd) *Strange Fruit; (SFR LP/MC/CD 106) / Dutch East India; <8103>* **THE PEEL SESSIONS** `-`

Oct 89. (12"ep) *Link; (LINK 1203)* **THE LAST TIME. / MR.FIRE-COAL**

MAN / TWO GUITARS CLASH `-`

Apr 91. (cd) *Streetlink; (STRCD 010)* **GREATEST HITS LIVE** (live) `-`

Oct 91. (cd) *Link; (AOK 103)* **ALTERNATIVE CHARTBUSTERS** `-`

Oct 89. (cd/green-lp) *Limited Edition; (LTD EDT 2 CD/LP)* **LIVE IN**

SWEDEN (live) `-`

Dec 92. (cd) *Dojo; (<DOJOCD 75>)* **FLY THE FLAGS – LIVE AT**

BRIXTON ACADEMY (27/9/91) `Oct94`

Aug 93. (cd) *Windsong; (<WINCD 037>)* **BBC RADIO 1 LIVE IN**

CONCERT (live) `-`

Mar 95. (cd) *Dojo; (DOJOCD 224)* **PURE FINGERS LIVE – ST.PATRIX**

1993 `-`

Stephen STILLS / MANASSAS
(see under ⇒ CROSBY, STILLS, NASH & YOUNG)

STILTSKIN (dig out; 4th edition or Great Metal . . .)

STING

Born: GORDON MATTHEW SUMNER, 2 Oct'51, Wallsend, nr.Newcastle, England. In the early 70's he gave up his job as a primary school teacher and joined a local group, gaining his nickname in honour of his famous black and yellow hooped T-shirt. STING joined jazz combo, LAST EXIT, in 1974, where he became lead singer on a single, 'WHISPERING VOICES'. Around the same time, the man enrolled with RADA and began occasional TV ad work (he was later to become a successful actor in the 70's). Early in 1977, he formed The POLICE, one of the world's top selling outfits until their demise (and his failed marriage to actress, Frances Tomelty) in 1983. STING had earlier branched out on a solo career, starring in, and scoring the soundtrack for the Dennis Potter film, 'Brimstone & Treacle'. It wasn't until 1985, however, that he released his first solo long player, 'DREAM OF THE BLUE TURTLES'. Employing such noted musicians as BRANFORD MARSALIS and WEATHER REPORT's OMAR HAKIM, STING crafted an endearing set of jazz-influenced, infectiously off-kilter pop songs, highlights being the gaslit noir of 'MOON OVER BOURBON STREET' and the two minor hit singles, 'IF YOU LOVE SOMEBODY SET THEM FREE' and 'SEVENTH WAVE'. The record was a Transatlantic Top 3 hit, STING subsequently touring/promoting with most of the musicians who'd played on the project, 'BRING ON THE NIGHT' (1986) documenting events. Again featuring MARSALIS, in addition to contributions from such luminaries as ERIC CLAPTON, MARK KNOPFLER, GIL EVANS and former colleague, ANDY SUMMERS, 'NOTHING LIKE THE SUN' (1987) was a largely introspective, instrumentally dextrous collection dedicated to STING's recently departed mother. 'AN ENGLISHMAN IN NEW YORK' was quintessential STING, a wry observation on cultural disparity, while the likes of 'FRAGILE' saw STING's work take on a more self-consciously political hue alongside contemporaries like U2 and SIMPLE MINDS. Indeed, most of '89 saw the singer campaigning for Brazilian rainforest projects, STING also championing the efforts of human rights organisation, Amnesty International. Commendable as all this was, many factions of the music press gave the singer a roasting for what they perceived as an often lofty and self-righteous attitude, BONO also coming in for similar flak. Brushing aside such criticism, STING eventually returned to recording with 'THE SOUL CAGES' (1991), a sombre affair informed this time around by the death of his father. Again retaining MARSALIS, STING also employed folk player, KATHRYN TICKELL, her uillean pipes adding to the often bleak atmospherics. Despite its dearth of hit singles, the album gave STING his second UK No.1 in succession, paving the way for the massive selling, and markedly more upbeat 'TEN SUMMONER'S TALES' (1993). As strong a set of songs as STING has yet penned, the record spawned two of his most enduring singles in 'IF I EVER LOSE MY FAITH IN YOU' and the pastoral beauty of 'FIELDS OF GOLD'. Later that year, the singer was back in the upper reaches of the singles chart with the theme tune from the film 'Demolition Man' and a three way collaboration with BRYAN ADAMS and ROD STEWART on the vomit-inducing 'ALL MY LOVE' (the theme from 'The Three Musketeers'. STING even attempted a country/reggae crossover together with PATO BANTON on 'THIS COWBOY SONG', a track culled from 94's greatest hits set, 'FIELDS OF GOLD – THE BEST OF STING 1984-1994'. Not exactly the most prolific of artists, STING's most recent release was the 'MERCURY FALLING' album in 1996. As well as being something of an older guy sex symbol, STING continues to court controversy, his recent comments on the benefits of Ecstasy coming under particular scrutiny. 'BRAND NEW DAY' (1999), was a slight return to his more conventional pop songwriting days, the Top 5 album featuring a title track hit that was certainly his finest number for a long time – it's now used on a TV ad. • **Covered:** SPREAD A LITTLE HAPPINESS + SOMEONE TO WATCH OVER ME (George Gershwin) / TUTTI FRUTTI (Little Richard) /

NEED YOUR LOVE SO BAD (Little Willie John) / MACK THE KNIFE (Bertold Brecht) / PURPLE HAZE (Jimi Hendrix) / SISTERS OF MERCY (Leonard Cohen) w/ CHIEFTAINS. • **Trivia:** In 1985, he dueted on singles MONEY FOR NOTHING (Dire Straits), which he co-wrote, plus LONG WAY TO GO (Phil Collins). That year, STING also guested on MILES DAVIS' album, 'You're Under Arrest'. He was also another one of the stars on BAND AID and LIVE AID. **Filmography:** QUADROPHENIA (1979) / RADIO ON (1980) / ARTEMIS (1981 TV movie) / BRIMSTONE AND TREACLE (1982) / DUNE (1984) / THE BRIDE (1985) / PLENTY (1985) / STORMY MONDAY (1988) / JULIA JULIA (1987). In 1988, he also narrated Stravinsky's 'Soldier's Tale', which was soon issued on own 'Pangaea' label. He followed this by writing score for the documentary about Quentin Crisp, 'Crisp City'.

Album rating: THE DREAM OF THE BLUE TURTLES (*6) / BRING ON THE NIGHT (*5) / NOTHING LIKE THE SUN (*8) / THE SOUL CAGES (*7) / TEN SUMMONER'S TALES (*8) / FIELDS OF GOLD – THE BEST OF STING 1984-1994 compilation (*8) / MERCURY FALLING (*6) / THE VERY BEST OF STING & THE POLICE compilation (*8) / BRAND NEW DAY (*7)

STING – vocals, bass, etc. (with on set session people)

                                               A&M   A&M

Aug 82. (7") (AMS 8242) **SPREAD A LITTLE HAPPINESS. / ONLY YOU**   `16` ☐
    (above from the film soundtrack 'BRIMSTONE AND TREACLE', released Sep'82 and containing other STING tracks)

—— Enlisted US musicians **KENNY KIRKLAND** – keyboards / **BRANFORD MARSALIS** – sax, percussion / **DARRYL JONES** – bass (ex-MILES DAVIS) / **OMAR HAKIM** – drums (WEATHER REPORT)

May 85. (7") (AM 258) <2738> **IF YOU LOVE SOMEBODY SET THEM FREE. / ANOTHER DAY**   `26` `3`
    (12"+=) (AMY 258) – ('A'-Torch song mix) / ('A'-Jellybean dance mix).

Jun 85. (lp)(c/cd)(DREAM 1)(DRE MC/MD 1) <3750> **THE DREAM OF THE BLUE TURTLES**   `3` `2`
    – If you love somebody set them free / Love is the seventh wave / Russians / Children's crusade / Shadows in the rain / We work the black seam / Consider me gone / The dream of the blue turtles / Moon over Bourbon Street / Fortress around your heart. (pic-lp Jan86; DREAMP 1) (lp re-iss. Sep99 on 'Simply Vinyl'; SVLP 116)

Aug 85. (7"/12") (AM/+Y 272) **LOVE IS THE SEVENTH WAVE. / CONSIDER ME GONE (live)**   `41` –

Aug 85. (7") <2767> **FORTRESS AROUND YOUR HEART. / CONSIDER ME GONE (live)**   – `8`

Oct 85. (7"/12") (AM/+Y 286) **FORTRESS AROUND YOUR HEART. / SHADOWS IN THE RAIN**   `49` –

Oct 85. <2787> **LOVE IS THE SEVENTH WAVE. / DREAM OF THE BLUE TURTLES**   – `17`

Dec 85. (7") (AM 292) <2799> **RUSSIANS. / GABRIEL'S MESSAGE**   `12` `16`
    (12"+=) (AMY 292) – I burn for you (live).

Feb 86. (7") (AM 305) **MOON OVER BOURBON STREET. / MACK THE KNIFE**   `44` ☐
    (12"+=) (AMY 305) – Fortress around your heart.

Jul 86. (d-lp/c/cd) (BRIN G/C/D 1) **BRING ON THE NIGHT (live)**   `16` –
    – Bring on the night – When the world is running down you make the best of what's still around / Consider me gone / Low life / We work the black seam / Driven to tears / The dream of the blue turtles / Demolition man / One world (not three) / Love is the seventh wave / Moon over Bourbon street / I burn for you / Another day / Children's crusade / Down so long / Tea in the Sahara.

—— he retained **KIRKLAND + MARSALIS**, and recruited **MANU KATCHE** – drums / **MINO CINELU** – percussion, vocoder / **ANDY NEWMARK** – 2nd drummer / plus guests **ERIC CLAPTON, MARK KNOPFLER, ANDY SUMMERS + GIL EVANS**

Oct 87. (7") (AM 410) <2983> **WE'LL BE TOGETHER. / CONVERSATION WITH A DOG**   `41` `7`
    (12"+=/3"cd-s+=) (AM Y/CD 410) – ('A'extended) / ('A'instrumental).

Oct 87. (d-lp/c/cd)(AMA/AMC/CDA 6402) <6402> **NOTHING LIKE THE SUN**   `1` `9`
    – The Lazarus heart / Be still my beating heart / Englishman in New York / History will teach us nothing / They dance alone (gueca solo) / Fragile / We'll be together / Straight to my heart / Rock steady / Sister Moon / Little wing / The secret marriage.

Jan 88. (7") <2992> **BE STILL MY BEATING HEART. / GHOST IN THE STRAND**   – `15`

Jan 88. (7") (AM 431) **ENGLISHMAN IN NEW YORK. / GHOST IN THE STRAND (instrumental)**   `51` –
    (12"+=/3"cd-s+=) (AM Y/CD 431) – Bring on the night – When the world is running down (live).

Mar 88. (7") <1200> **ENGLISHMAN IN NEW YORK. / IF YOU'RE THERE**   – `84`

Mar 88. (7") (AM 439) **FRAGILE. / FRAGIL (Portuguese mix)**   `70` –
    (12"+=/cd-s+=) (AM Y/CD 439) – Fragilidad (Spanish mix) / Mariposa libre.

Sep 88. (7") (AM 458) **THEY DANCE ALONE. / ELLAS DAMZON SOLAS (GUECA SOLO)**   ☐ ☐
    (12"+=/cd-s+=) (AM Y/CD 458) – Si estamos juntos.

Aug 90. (7"/c-s) (AM/+MC 580) **ENGLISHMAN IN NEW YORK (Ben Liebrand mix). / IF YOU LOVE SOMEBODY SET THEM FREE**   `15` –
    (12"+=/cd-s+=/pic-cd-s+=) (AM Y/CD/CDR 580) – ('A'original mix) / ('A'-Jellybean dance mix).

—— he retained **MARSALIS, KIRKLAND, KATCHE**. New **DOMINIC MILLER** – guitar / **DAVID SANCIOUS** – keyboards / **KATHRYN TICKELL** – pipes / **PAOLA PAPAREUE** – oboe / **RAY COOPER, VINK, BILL SUMMERS, MUNYUNGO JACKSON, SKIP BURNEY, TONY VALCA** – percussion.

Dec 90. (7"/c-s) (AM/+MC 713) **ALL THIS TIME. / I MISS YOU KATE (instrumental)**   `22` `5`
    (12"+=/cd-s+=/pic-cd-s+=) (AM Y/CD/CDR 713) <1541> – King of pain (live).

Jan 91. (cd/c/lp) (396 405-2/-4/-1) <6405> **THE SOUL CAGES**   `1` `2`
    – Island of souls / All this time / Mad about you / Jeremiah blues (pt.1) / Why should I cry for you / Saint Agnes and the burning train / The wild wild sea / The soul cages / When the angels fall.

Feb 91. (7"/c-s) (AM/+MC 721) **MAD ABOUT YOU (remix). / TEMPTED (live)**   `56` ☐
    (12"+=/cd-s+=) (AM Y/CDR 721) – If you love somebody set them free (live).

Apr 91. (7"/c-s) (AM/+MC 759) **THE SOUL CAGES. / OH LA LA HUGH**   `57` ☐
    (cd-s+=) (AMCD 759) – Walking in your footsteps (live).
    (12"++=) (AMY 759) – Don't stand so close to me (live).
    (12") (AMYR 759) – ('A'side) / Walking in your footsteps (live) / The Lazarus heart (live) / Too much inforation (live).

Aug 92. (7"/c-s/cd-s; by STING with ERIC CLAPTON) (AM/+MC/CD 883) **IT'S PROBABLY ME. / ('A'-long version)**   `30` ☐

—— retained on album **MILLER, SANCIOUS & TICKELL** and brought in **VINNIE COLAIUTA** – drums / **LARRY ADLER + BRENDAN POWER** – chromatic harmonicas / **SIAN BELL** – cello / **DAVE HEATH** – flute / **PAUL FRANKLIN** – pedal steel / **JAMES BOYD** – viola / **KATHRYN GREELEY + SIMON FISCHER** – violins / **GUY BARKER + JOHN BARCLAY** – trumpets / **RICHARD EDWARDS + MARK NIGHTINGALE** – trombone / **DAVID ROXXE** – narration

Feb 93. (7"/c-s) (AM/+MC 0172) <0111> **IF I EVER LOSE MY FAITH IN YOU. / ALL THIS TIME (unplugged)**   `14` `17`
    (cd-s+=) (AMCD 0172) – Mad about you (live) / Every breath you take (live).
    (cd-s) (AMCDR 0172) – ('A'side) / Message in a bottle (live) / Tea in the Sahara (live) / Walking on the moon (live).

Mar 93. (cd/c/lp) (540 074-2/-4/-1) <0070> **TEN SUMMONER'S TALES**   `2` `2`
    – Prologue (If I ever lose my faith in you) / Love is stronger than justice (the magnificent seven) / Fields of gold / Heavy cloud no rain / She's too good for me / Seven days / Saint Augustine in Hell / It's probably me / Everybody laughed but you / Shape of my heart / Something the boy said / Epilogue (Nothing 'bout me).

Apr 93. (7"/c-s) (580 222-7/223-4) **SEVEN DAYS. / JANUARY STARS**   `25` –
    (cd-s+=) (580 223-2) – Mad about you (live) / Ain't no sunshine (live).
    (cd-s) (580 225-2) – ('A'side) / Island of souls (live) / The wild wild sea (live) / The soul cages (live).

Jun 93. (7"/c-s) (580 301-7/302-4) <0258> **FIELDS OF GOLD. / WE WORK THE BLACK SEAM**   `16` `23`
    (cd-s) (580302-2) – ('A'side) / King of pain (live) / Fragile (live) / Purple haze (live).
    (cd-s) (580303-2) – ('A'side) / Message in a bottle (live) / Fortress around your heart (live) / Roxanne (live).

Aug 93. (7"/c-s) (580353-7/-4) **SHAPE OF MY HEART. / WALKING ON THE MOON**   `57` –
    (cd-s) (580353-2) – ('A'side) / The soul cages / The wild wild sea / All this time.

Nov 93. (7"/c-s) (580450-7/-4) **DEMOLITION MAN. / ('A'mix)**   `21` –
    (cd-s+=) (580451-2) – King of pain (live) / Shape of my heart (live).
    (cd-s) (580453-2) – ('A'side) / It's probably me (live) / A day in the life of (live).

—— Late 1993, he teamed up with BRYAN ADAMS & ROD STEWART to sing theme from 'The Three Musketeers'; ALL FOR LOVE, which hit UK No.2 & US No.1.

Feb 94. (7"/12"/c-s) (580529-7/-1/-4) <0350> **NOTHING 'BOUT ME. / IF I EVER LOSE MY FAITH IN YOU**   `32` `57` Sep93
    (cd-s+=) (580529-2) – ('B'mixes) / Demolition man (soul power mix).

Oct 94. (c-s) (580858-4) **WHEN WE DANCE / FORTRESS AROUND YOUR HEART**   `9` –
    (cd-s) (580859-2) – ('A'side) / If you love somebody set them free (remix) / ('A'remix).
    (12"/cd-s) (580861-1/-2) – ('A'remixes).

Oct 94. (c-s,cd-s) <0846> **WHEN WE DANCE / DEMOLITION MAN**   – `38`

Nov 94. (cd/c/d-lp) (540307-2/-4/-1) <0269> **FIELDS OF GOLD – THE BEST OF STING 1984-1994** (compilation)   `2` `7`
    – When we dance / If you love somebody set them free / Fields of gold / All this time / Englishman in New York / Mad about you / They dance alone / If I ever lose my faith in you / Fragile / We'll be together / Nothing 'bout me / Love is the seventh wave / Russians / Seven days / Demolition man / This cowboy song.

—— Around same time, Spanish crooner JULIO IGLESIAS covered his 'FRAGILE', which he accompanied with STING.
    (below single featured PATO BANTON)

Jan 95. (c-s) (580957-4) **THIS COWBOY SONG / IF YOU LOVE SOMEBODY SET THE FREE (Brothers In Rhythm mix)**   `15` –
    (cd-s+=) (580957-2) – Demolition man (Soul Power mix).
    (12"++=) (AMY 759) – If you love somebody set them free (extended).
    (cd-s) (580957-1) – ('A'side) / ('A'extended) / When we dance (classic) / Take me to the sunshine.

—— Jan 96, featured on PATO BANTON's UK Top 40 version of POLICE hit 'SPIRITS IN THE MATERIAL WORLD' from the film 'Ace Ventura II'.

—— with band: **MILLER, COLAIUTA, + KENNY KIRKLAND** – keyboards

Feb 96. (c-s) (581330-4) <1456> **LET YOUR SOUL BE YOUR PILOT / THE BED'S TOO BIG WITHOUT YOU**   `15` `86`
    (cd-s+=) (581331-2) – Englishman in New York.
    (12") (581527-1) – ('A'mixes).

Mar 96. (cd/c/lp) (540486-2/-4/-1) <0483> **MERCURY FALLING**   `4` `5`
    – The hounds of winter / I hung my head / Let your soul be your pilot / I was brought to my senses / You still touch me / I'm so happy I can't stop crying / All four seasons / Twenty five to midnight / La belle dame sans regrets / Valparaiso / Lithium sunset.

Apr 96. (c-s/cd-s) (581545-4/-2) <1582> **YOU STILL TOUCH ME / TWENTY FIVE TO MIDNIGHT (US version)**   `27` `60`
    (12"+=/cd-s+=) (581547-1/-2) – ('A' mixes) / Lullaby to an anxious child / Beneath a desert moon.

Jun 96. (c-ep/cd-ep) (581761-4/-2) **LIVE AT TFI FRIDAY EP**   `53` –
    – You still touch me / Lithium sunset / Message in a bottle.

Sep 96. (c-s/cd-s) (581890-4/-2) **I WAS BROUGHT TO MY SENSES (Steve Lipson remix) / WHEN WE DANCE / IF I EVER LOSE MY FAITH IN YOU / IF YOU LOVE SOMEBODY SET THEM FREE**   `31` –
    (cd-s) (581889-2) – ('A'side) / This was never meant to be / The pirate's bride.

Oct 96. (c-s,cd-s) <1982> **I'M SO HAPPY I CAN'T STOP CRYING / THIS WAS NEVER MEANT TO BE**   – `94`

Nov 96. (c-s) (582029-4) **I'M SO HAPPY I CAN'T STOP CRYING / FRAGILIDAD**   `54` –

(cd-s+=) *(582029-2)* – Fields of gold / Englishman in New York.
(cd-s) *(582031-2)* – ('A'side) / Seven days / Moonlight / Giacomo's blues.

—— In Dec'97, STING featured on TOBY KEITH's version of 'I'm So Happy I Can't Stop Crying'.

Sep 99. (c-s) *(497153-4)* **BRAND NEW DAY / (lp version)** `13` ☐
(cd-s) *(497152-2)* – ('A'side) / Windmills of your mind / End of the game (long version).
(cd-s) *(497153-2)* – ('A'side) / Fields of gold / Englishman in New York.

Sep 99. (cd/c) *(490425-2/-5)* <490443> **BRAND NEW DAY** `5` `15`
– Desert rose / Perfect love / Brand new day / After the rain / A thousand years / Ghost story / Big lie small world / Tomorrow we'll see / Fill her up / End of the game.

– compilations, others, etc. –
on 'A&M' unless mentioned otherwise

Jul 88. (cd-ep) *(AMCD 911)* **COMPACT HITS** ☐ -
– Someone to watch over me / Englishman in New York / If you love somebody set them free / Spread a little happiness.

Feb 90. (d-c) *(AMC 24110)* **DREAM OF THE BLUE TURTLES / NOTHING LIKE THE SUN** ☐ ☐

Nov 91. (cd-box) *(397 171-2)* **ACOUSTIC LIVE IN NEWCASTLE – LIMITED EDITION BOXED SET** ☐ ☐

Nov 97. (cd/c; STING & THE POLICE) *(540428-2/-4)* **THE VERY BEST OF STING & THE POLICE** `11` `100`
– Message in a bottle / Can't stand losing you / Englishman in New York / Every breath you take / Seven days / Walking on the moon / Fields of gold / Fragile / Every little thing she does is magic / De do do do de da da da / If you love somebody set them free / Let your soul be your pilot / Russians / If I ever lose my faith in you / When we dance / Don't stand so close to me / Roxanne / Roxanne '97 (Puff Daddy remix).

Dec 97. (c-s; STING & The POLICE) *(582455-4)* <582449> **ROXANNE '97 (Puff Daddy remix) / ROXANNE (original)** `17` `59`
(12"+=/cd-s+=) *(582455-1/-2)* – Walking on the moon (Roger Sanchez mix).

Sly STONE (see under ⇒ **SLY & THE FAMILY STONE**)

STONE PONEYS (see under ⇒ **RONSTADT, Linda**)

STONE ROSES

Formed: Sale & Chorley, Gtr. Manchester, England … 1984 by IAN BROWN, JOHN SQUIRE, RENI, ANDY COUZENS and PETER GARNER who took their name from a group called ENGLISH ROSE and The ROLLING STONES. After a MARTIN HANNETT produced 45, they signed a one-off deal with 'Black' records and in 1988, were snapped up by ANDREW LAUDER's 'Jive' subsidiary, 'Silvertone'. They soon became darlings of the music press after the indie success of the single, 'ELEPHANT STONE' (1988), a gloriously uplifting piece of pristine pop. Propelled by RENI's consummate drumming and featuring SQUIRE's dizzy, spiralling guitar, the track was a blueprint for the group's eponymous debut album, released the following year. Surely a contender for album of the decade, the record was flawless, from the ominous opening bass rumble of 'I WANNA BE ADORED' to the orgasmic finale of 'I AM THE RESURRECTION'. This life-affirming hybrid of BYRDS-style psychedelia and shuffling rhythmic flurries remains the definitive indie album, its all-pervading influence more pronounced with each successive crop of guitar bands. Incredibly, the band topped the magic of their debut with the 'FOOL'S GOLD' single, which exploded into the Top 10 later that year. A seminal guitar-funk workout, it was the crowning glory of the 'Baggy' movement with which The STONE ROSES had become so closely affiliated, and marked a creative highpoint in their career. After a few one-off shows (that have since achieved almost mythical status) and a solitary single, 'ONE LOVE', the following year, the band went to ground. In the five years that followed, the band fought a protracted court battle with 'Silvertone', eventually signing with 'Geffen' for a reported record sum of $4,000,000. After much speculation and intrigue into when or if a follow-up would finally appear, the appropriately title 'SECOND COMING' was eventually released in 1994. A month previously, they had enjoyed a return to the singles chart with the ZEPPELIN-esque 'LOVE SPREADS'. On the album, the effervescent pop of old took second place to riff-heavy guitar workouts, alienating many of their original fans. Nevertheless, the blistering funk-rock of 'BEGGING YOU' partly made up for any excess noodling by SQUIRE. As the STONE ROSES faithful dusted down their flares and beany hats in readiness for the band's headlining spot at the 1995 Glastonbury festival, they were again bitterly disappointed. At the last minute the band pulled out, apparently due to SQUIRE breaking his collarbone, young pretenders OASIS stealing the show in their absence. They had failed to seize the moment and from here on in, it was all downhill. Despite an ecstatically received Winter tour, SQUIRE shocked the music world by departing the following Spring (RENI had already quit a year earlier). BROWN and MANI bravely soldiered on for a headlining appearance at the 1996 Reading Festival but were given a critical mauling (particularly by the NME), finally splitting later that year. It was a sorry, messy end for a band that had seemed, at one point, to be on the brink of world domination and it remains a bitter irony that their duller Manchester progeny, OASIS, seem to have inherited the success that tragically eluded the 'ROSES. While SQUIRE has gone on to relative success with The SEAHORSES, their sound pales next to the magic of The STONE ROSES, a band that remains as fondly remembered as any in the history of rock. In early '98, IAN BROWN launched his solo career (via a new deal with 'Polydor') by releasing the single, 'MY STAR', a

taster from his debut album, 'UNFINISHED MONKEY BUSINESS', which also reached the Top 5. However, BROWN subsequently landed himself in deep water when he was charged with threatening behaviour on a flight between Paris and Manchester. Astonishingly sentenced to four months in prison at the end of October, the singer was released a couple of months early that Christmas eve. Back in circulation the following year, BROWN guested for 'Mo Wax' duo U.N.K.L.E. on the track, 'BE THERE'. Album No.2, 'GOLDEN GREATS', was completed and in the Top 20 towards the end of 1999. Previewed by the hit single, 'LOVE LIKE A FOUNTAIN', the set showed IAN (and co-writer DAVE McCRACKEN) venturing away from the staid and into every funkin' Rock genre under the sun. • **Songwriters:** Mainly SQUIRE but with other members also collaborating. The SEAHORSES was mainly SQUIRE, except a few by HELME. one with FLETCHER. NOEL GALLAGHER (Oasis) co-wrote 'LOVE ME AND LEAVE ME'. • **Trivia:** Their debut album artwork was a pastiche of a Jackson Pollock splatter job painted by the multi-talented SQUIRE.

Album rating: THE STONE ROSES (*10) / TURNS INTO STONE collection (*6) / SECOND COMING (*7) / THE COMPLETE STONE ROSES compilation (*8) / GARAGE FLOWER exploitation (*5) / Ian Brown: UNFINISHED MONKEY BUSINESS (*6) / GOLDEN GREATS (*7)

IAN BROWN (b.20 Feb'63, Ancoats, Manchester) – vocals / **JOHN SQUIRE** (b.24 Nov'62, Broadheath, Manchester) – guitar, vocals / **PETER GARNER** – rhythm guitar / **ANDY COUZENS** – bass / **RENI** (b. ALAN WREN, 10 Apr'64) – drums

			Thin Line	not iss.
Sep 85.	(12") *(THIN 001)* **SO YOUNG. / TELL ME**		☐	-

—— now a quartet when PETER departed

			Revolver	not iss.
May 87.	(12"m) *(12REV 36)* **SALLY CINNAMON. / HERE IT COMES / ALL ACROSS THE SAND**		☐	-

(re-iss. Feb89; same) (re-iss. Dec89 cd-ep+=; CDREV 36); hit No.46) – ('A'demo).

—— (1987) **GARY 'Mani' MOUNFIELD** (b.16 Nov'62, Crumpsall, Manchester) – bass, vocals repl. COUZENS who later joined The HIGH.

			Silvertone	Silvertone
Oct 88.	(7") *(ORE 1)* **ELEPHANT STONE. / THE HARDEST THING IN THE WORLD**		☐	-

(12"+=) *(ORE 1T)* – Full fathoms five. *(re-iss. Feb90 c-s/cd-s; ORE 1 C/CD); hit No.8. (cd-s re-iss. Oct96; same)*

Mar 89.	(7") *(ORE 2)* **MADE OF STONE. / GOING DOWN**		☐	-

(12"+=) *(ORE 2T)* – Guernica. *(re-iss. Mar90 c-s/cd-s; ORE 2 C/CD); hit No.20. (cd-s re-iss. Oct96; same)*

Apr 89.	(lp/c/cd) *(ORE LP/MC/CD 502)* <1184-1/-4/-2> **THE STONE ROSES**		`19`	`86`

– I wanna be adored / She bangs the drum / Waterfall / Don't stop / Bye bye badman / Elizabeth my dear / (Song for my) Sugar spun sister / Made of stone / Shoot you down / This is the one / I am the resurrection. *(re-iss. Aug91 as 2x12"+=; OREZLP 502)* – Elephant stone / Fool's gold. *(cd re-iss. Mar97; same) (d-cd re-iss. as 10th ANNIVERSARY EDITION; 059124-2)* – (w/ extra tracks). – (hit UK No.26)

Jul 89.	(7"/7"s) *(ORE/+X 6)* **SHE BANGS THE DRUM. / STANDING HERE**		`36`	-

(12"+=/12"s+=) *(ORE T/Z 6)* – Mersey Paradise.
(c-s++=/cd-s++=) *(ORE C/CD 6)* – Simone. *(re-entered chart Mar90; hit No.34) (cd-s re-iss. Oct96; same)*

			Silvertone	Jive
Nov 89.	(7"/ext.12") *(ORE/+T 13)* <1315-1> **FOOL'S GOLD. / WHAT THE WORLD IS WAITING FOR**		`8`	Mar90

(c-s++=/cd-s++=) *(ORE C/CD 13)* – ('A'extended). *(flipped over re-entered chart Sep90; hit No.22) (re-iss. remix May92, hit No.73) (cd-s re-iss. Oct96; same)*
(12") *(ORET 13)* – ('A'-The Top Won mix) / ('A'-The Bottom Won mix).

Nov 89.	(12"ep) <1301> **I WANNA BE ADORED / (long version) / GOING DOWN / SIMONE**		-	☐

Jul 90.	(7"/c-s/12"/cd-s) *(ORE/+C/T/CD 17)* <1399-1/-2> **ONE LOVE. / SOMETHING'S BURNING**		`4`	

(cd-s re-iss. Oct96; same)

Sep 91.	(7"/c-s) *(ORE/+C 31)* **I WANNA BE ADORED. / WHERE ANGELS PLAY**		`20`	

(12"+=/cd-s+=) *(ORE T/CD 31)* – Sally Cinnamon (live).
(cd-s re-iss. Oct96; same)

Jan 92.	(7"/c-s) *(ORE/+C 35)* **WATERFALL (remix). / ONE LOVE (remix)**		`27`	

(12"+=/cd-s+=) *(ORE T/CD 35)* – ('A'&'B'extended versions).
(cd-s re-iss. Oct96; same)

Apr 92.	(7"/c-s) *(ORE/+C 40)* **I AM THE RESURRECTION. / ('A'-Pan & scan radio version)**		`33`	

(12"+=) *(ORET 40)* – Fool's gold (The Bottom Won mix).
(cd-s++=) *(ORECD 40)* – ('A'-5:3 Stoned Out club mix).
(cd-s re-iss. Oct96; same)

Jul 92.	(cd/c/lp) *(ORE CD/C/LP 521)* **TURNS INTO STONE** (demos & rare)		`32`	

– Elephant stone / The hardest thing in the world / Going down / Mersey Paradise / Standing here Where angels play / Simone / Fools gold / What the world is waiting for / One love / Something's burning. *(cd re-iss. Mar97 & Mar99; same)*

			Geffen	Geffen
Nov 94.	(7"/c-s) *(GFS/+C 84)* **LOVE SPREADS. / YOUR STAR WILL SHINE**		`2`	

(cd-s+=) *(GFST 84)* – Breakout.
(12"++=) *(GFSTD 84)* – Groove harder.

Dec 94.	(cd/c/lp) <(GED/GEC/GEF 24503)> **SECOND COMING**		`4`	`47` Jan95

– Breaking into Heaven / Driving south / Ten storey love song / Daybreak / Your star will shine / Straight to the man / Begging you / Tightrope / Good times / Tears / How do you sleep? / Love spreads. *(cd+=)* – (untitled hidden track No.90). *(lp re-iss. Aug99 on 'Simply Vinyl'; SVLP 111)*

Feb 95.	(7"/c-s) *(GFS/+C 87)* **TEN STOREY LOVE SONG. / RIDE ON**		`11`	☐

(12"+=/cd-s+=) *(GFST/+D 87)* – Moses.

—— In Apr'95, RENI quit and was replaced by **ROBERT MADDIX** (ex-GINA GINA).

Oct 95. (c-s) *(GFSC 22060)* **BEGGING YOU / ('A'-Chic mix)** `15` `☐`
(cd-s+=) *(GFSTD 22060)* – ('A'-Stone Corporation mix) / ('A'-Lakota mix) / ('A'-Young American primitive remix).
(12") *(GFST 22060)* – ('A'-Carl Cox mix) / ('A'-Development Corporation mix).

—— Late in March '96, SQUIRE left to pursue new venture, The SEAHORSES. The STONE ROSES continued on and in Aug'96, they recruited **AZIZ IBRAHIM** (ex-SIMPLY RED) / **NIGEL IPPINSON** – keyboards

—— They officially split in Nov'96, after MANI joined PRIMAL SCREAM. IBRAHIM would join IAN BROWN and eventually issue his solo album in 1999, thoughtfully titled 'AZIZ'.

– compilations, etc. –

on 'Silvertone' unless mentioned; who else?

Jan 92. (8xcd-s-box-set) *(SRBX 1)* **SINGLES BOX** `☐` `-`
Nov 92. (10x12"box-set) *(SRBX 2)* **SINGLES BOX** `☐` `-`
Apr 95. (c-s) *(OREC 71)* **FOOL'S GOLD '95 / ('A'extended mix)** `23` `☐`
(12"+=/cd-s+=) *(ORE T/CD 71)* – ('A'-Tall Paul remix) / (A'-Cricklewood Ballroom mix).
May 95. (cd/c/lp) *(ORE CD/C/ZLP)* **THE COMPLETE STONE ROSES** `4` `☐`
Nov 96. (cd/c/lp) *(GARAGE CD/C/LP 1)* **GARAGE FLOWER** (early demos) `58` `-`
(cd re-iss. Augg99; same)
Jun 97. (7"ep) *Fierce; (FRIGHT 044)* **SPIKE ISLAND EP** (interviews, etc.) `☐` `-`
Feb 99. (c-s/cd-s) *Jive Electro; (052309-4/-2)* **FOOL'S GOLD / FOOL'S GOLD** (Grooverider mix) / **RABBIT IN THE MOON** `25` `-`

IAN BROWN

on mostly all vocals/instruments except co-writers **AZIZ IBRAHIM** – guitars, etc / **SIMON MOORE** – drums / **NIGEL IPPINSON** – keyboards, bass / guests **MANI MOUNFIELD** + **NOEL GALLAGHER** + **DENISE JOHNSON** + cp-writer/mixer **ROBBIE MADDIX**

Polydor   not iss.

Jan 98. (7"/c-s/cd-s) *(571 987-7/-4/-2)* **MY STAR. / SEE THE DAWN / FOURTEEN** `5` `☐`
Feb 98. (cd/c/lp) *(539 565-2/-4/-1)* **UNFINISHED MONKEY BUSINESS** `4` `☐`
– Intro under the paving stones: The beach / My star / Can't see me / Ice cold cube / Sunshine / Lions / Corpses in their mouths / What happened to ya part 1 / What happened to ya part 2 / Nah nah / Deep pile dreams / Unfinished monkey business.
Mar 98. (7"/c-s/cd-s) *(569 654-7/655-4/657-2)* **CORPSES. / JESUS ON THE MOVE / COME AGAIN** (part one) `14` `-`
Jun 98. (7") *(567 092-7)* **CAN'T SEE ME** (Bacon & Quarmby remix). / **CAN'T SEE ME** (Bacon & Quarmby vocal dub) `21` `-`
(cd-s+=) *(044 045-2)* – Under the paving stone: The beach (Gabriel's 13th dream remix).
(cd-s) *(044 047-2)* – ('A'side) / ('A'-Harvey's invisible mix) / Come again part two / My star (CD-ROM video).
(12"++=) *(044 047-6)* – ('A'exclusive mix).
Oct 99. (7") *(561516-7)* **LOVE LIKE A FOUNTAIN. / THE FISHERMAN** `23` `☐`
(cd-s+=) *(561516-2)* – ('A'-CD-Rom mix).
(cd-s) *(561517-2)* – ('A'side) / ('A'-Stereo MC's mix) / ('A'-Grand Central mix).
Nov 99. (cd/c/lp) *(543141-2/-4/-1)* **GOLDEN GREATS** `14` `☐`
– Getting high / Love like a fountain / Free my way / Set my baby free / So many sisters / Golden gaze / Dolphins were monkeys / Neptune / First world / Babasonicos.

STONE TEMPLE PILOTS

Formed: Los Angeles, California, USA . . . 1987 as MIGHTY JOE YOUNG by WEILAND and ROBERT DeLEO. Recruiting DeLEO's brother, DEAN and ERIC KRETZ, they opted for the less frenetic San Diego as a musical base, changing their moniker to STONE TEMPLE PILOTS (thankfully changed from the considerably more controversial SHIRLEY TEMPLE'S PUSSY). After a few years on the hard/alternative rock circuit, they finally signed to 'Atlantic', the fruits of their labour, 'CORE' released in '92. Critical raves saw the album climb up the US chart (eventually reaching Top 3), songs like 'SEX TYPE THING' and 'PLUSH' drawing inevitable comparisons to PEARL JAM; WEILAND's vocals especially, were from the EDDIE VEDDER school of gravel-throated cool. After the aforementioned tracks were issued as UK singles, the album surfaced in the British Top 30 a full year on from its original release date, WEILAND's carrot-topped mop marking him out as a distinctive focal point for the band. LED ZEPPELIN and ALICE IN CHAINS were other obvious reference points, a second album, 'PURPLE' (1994), building on these influences to create a more cerebral post-grunge sound. The fact that the album rocketed into the American charts at No.1 was a measure of the group's lofty standing in the echelons of US alt-rock. WEILAND's love of nose candy and associated pleasures was no secret in the music world, the frontman narrowly avoiding a sizeable prison stretch for possession. Early in 1996, STP delivered a third (Top 5) album, 'TINY MUSIC . . . SONGS FROM THE VATICAN GIFT SHOP', accompanying touring commitments severely disrupted when WEILAND was ordered by the court to attend a rehab centre while awaiting trial (he was later cleared). The following year, WEILAND continued his self-destructive behaviour, STP's future looking bleak as the remaining band members formed TALK SHOW. A WEILAND solo effort, '12 BAR BLUES' (1998), was poorly received by critics and fans alike, while a long 18 months (and after more WEILAND arrests!) saw the group back together on a 'NO.4' set in 1999 – needless to say this type of music had died in Britain ages ago.
• **Songwriters:** Lyrics: WEILAND + R. DeLEO / KRETZ most of music except covers DANCING DAYS (Led Zeppelin).

Album rating: CORE (*7) / PURPLE (*7) / TINY MUSIC . . . SONGS FROM THE VATICAN GIFT SHOP (*7) / NO.4 (*4) / Talk Show: TALK SHOW (*5) / Scott Weiland: 12 BAR BLUES (*5)

(SCOTT) WEILAND (b.27 Oct'67, Santa Cruz, Calif.) – vocals / **DEAN DeLEO** (b.23 Aug'61, New Jersey) – guitar / **ROBERT DeLEO** (b. 2 Feb'66, New Jersey) – bass / **ERIC KRETZ** (b. 7 Jun'66, Santa Cruz) – drums

Atlantic   Atlantic

Nov 92. (cd/c/lp) *<(7567 82418-2/-4/-1)>* **CORE** `☐` `3`
– Dead and bloated / Sex type thing / Wicked garden / No memory / Sin / Creep / Piece of pie / Naked Sunday / Plush / Wet my bed / Crackerman / Where the river goes. *(re-dist.Sep93, hit UK No.27)*
Mar 93. (12"/cd-s) *(A 5769 T/CD)* **SEX TYPE THING. / PIECE OF ME** `60` `-`
Aug 93. (7"/c-s) *(A 7349/+C)* **PLUSH. / SEX TYPE THING** (swing version) / **PLUSH** (acoustic) `23` `-`
(12"+=/cd-s+=) *(A 7349 T/CD)* – ('A'side) / ('B'live version) / Sin.
Nov 93. (7"/c-s) *(A 7293/+C)* **SEX TYPE THING. / WICKED GARDEN** `55` `-`
(12"+=/cd-s+=) *(A 7293 TP/CD)* – Plush (acoustic).
(cd-s+=) *(A 7293CDX)* –
Jun 94. (cd/c/purple-lp) *<(7567 82607-2/-4/-1)>* **PURPLE** `10` `1`
– Meatplow / Vasoline / Lounge fly / Interstate love song / Still remains / Pretty penny / Silvergun Superman / Big empty / Unglued / Army ants / Kitchenware & candybar!. *(cd+=/c+=)* – Gracious melodies.
Aug 94. (c-ep/12"ep/cd-ep) *(A 5650 C/T/CD)* **VASOLINE / MEATPLOW. / ANDY WARHOL / CRACKERMAN** `48` `-`
Dec 94. (7"purple/c-s) *(A 7192 K/C)* **INTERSTATE LOVE SONG. / LOUNGE FLY** `53` `-`
(cd-s+=) *(A 7192CD)* – ('A'live).
(cd-s++=) *(A 7192CDX)* – Vasoline (live).

—— In summer '95, WEILAND was credited on a MAGNIFICENT BASTARDS single, 'Mockingbird Girl'; other tracks by Devo & Stomp.

Mar 96. (cd/c/lp) *<(7567 82871-2/-4/-1)>* **TINY MUSIC . . . SONGS FROM THE VATICAN GIFT SHOP** `31` `4`
– Press play / Pop's love suicide / Tumble in the rough / Big bang baby / Lady picture show / And so I know / Tripping on a hole in a paper heart / Art school girl / Adhesive / Ride the cliche / Daisy / Seven caged tigers.
Apr 96. (c-s) *(A 5516C)* **BIG BANG BABY / ADHESIVE** `☐` `-`
(cd-s+=) *(A 5516CD)* – Daisy.

—— the group had to cancel promotion tours due to WEILAND being ordered by a Pasadena court to attend a live-in drug rehabilitation programme. He discharged himself for a few days in July '96 and gave himself up to the LAPD who had issued a warrant for his arrest; WEILAND was subsequently cleared. The other members (ROBERT DeLEO + KRETZ) started working on a side-project VITAMIN, which became TALK SHOW after recruiting frontman DAVID COUTTS

TALK SHOW

—— **ERIC KRETZ** + **ROBERT DeLEO** + **DEAN DeLEO** / + **DAVE COUTTS** – vocals (ex-TEN INCH MEN)
Oct 97. (cd/c) *<(7567 83040-2/-4)>* **TALK SHOW** `☐` `☐`
– Ring twice / Hello hello / Everybody loves my car / Peeling an orange / So long / Wash me down / End of the world / John / Behind / Morning girl / Hide / Fill the fields.

SCOTT WEILAND

plays nearly every instrument, SHERYL CROW guests on accordion!
May 98. (cd/c) *<(7567 83084-2/-4)>* **12 BAR BLUES** `☐` `42` Apr98
– Desperation #5 / Barbarella / About nothing / Where's the man / Divider / Cool kiss / The date / Son / Jimmy was a stimulator / Lady, your roof brings me down / Mockingbird girl / Opposite octave reaction.
Jun 98. (7"pink/c-s) *(AT 0035/+C)* **BARBARELLA. / MOCKINGBIRD GIRL** `☐` `☐`
(cd-s+=) *(AT 0035CD)* – ('A'-album version).

STONE TEMPLE PILOTS

—— re-formed for what will probably be their final outing
Oct 99. (cd/c) *<(7567 83255-2/-4)>* **NO.4** `☐` `6`
– Down / Heaven and hot rods / Pruno / Church on Tuesday / Sour girl / No way out / Sex and violence / Glide / I got you / MC5 / Atlanta.

STOOGES (see under ⇒ POP, Iggy)

STORM (see under ⇒ JOURNEY)

STRANGELOVE

(dig out; 4th edition or Great Alt & Indie . . .)

STRANGLERS

Formed: Chiddington, Surrey, England . . . Autumn 1974 as The GUILDFORD STRANGLERS by ex-science teacher, HUGH CORNWELL, history graduate JEAN-JACQUES BURNEL and jazz drummer JET BLACK. Augmented by organist DAVE GREENFIELD in the Spring of '75, they commenced gigging around the pub-rock circuit, developing their boorish, black-clad brand of DOORS/ELECTRIC PRUNES/DR.FEELGOOD retro rock with scant encouragement from the press. Late in '76, after supporting the likes of The FLAMIN' GROOVIES and The RAMONES, The STRANGLERS were signed to 'United Artists' and initially lumped in with the fermenting punk/new wave scene. Released early the following year, '(GET

A) GRIP (ON YOURSELF)' found the band at their sneering, leering best, GREENFIELD's churning organ characterising a sound with which they'd stick fairly closely over the early part of their career. The single stalled outside the UK Top 40 – reportedly due to a chart mistake – although its controversial follow-up, 'PEACHES', made the Top 10 and immediately brought the band into conflict with feminists and the more liberal contingent of the music press. It was also banned by the BBC (a slightly modified version was later deemed acceptable), the surrounding controversy the first of many throughout the band's career and one which certainly didn't harm sales of the classic debut album, 'STRANGLERS IV – RATTUS NORVEGICUS' (1977). A Top 5 success comprising both singles and the enduring STRANGLERS' favourite, 'HANGING AROUND', the record met with enthusiastic reviews as the group enjoyed the briefest of honeymoon periods with the press. A not entirely convincing attempt at political comment, 'SOMETHING BETTER CHANGE', gave the band a second Top 10 hit later that summer, closely followed by the vicious momentum of 'NO MORE HEROES'. Also released in '77, the album of the same name narrowly missed No.1, another solid set which armed their detractors with more ammunition in the form of 'BRING ON THE NUBILES'; a notorious, stripper-enhanced gig at Battersea Park didn't help matters and The STRANGLERS' were firmly tarred as sexist yobs. Not that their fans cared, helping put a further two singles, 'FIVE MINUTES' and 'NICE 'N' SLEAZY', into the Top 20, both tracks featuring on the album, 'BLACK AND WHITE' (1978). The latter set came free with a limited edition 7" featuring the lads' interesting cover of the BACHARACH/DAVID standard, 'WALK ON BY' tastefully placed side by side with the inimitable 'TITS'. More promising and certainly more memorable was the surprisingly melodic 'DUCHESS', a Top 20 hit lifted from accompanying album, 'THE RAVEN' (1979). That year also saw the release of solo albums from both J.J. BURNEL and HUGH CORNWELL (with ROBERT WILLIAMS), the former's 'EUROMAN COMETH' barely making the Top 40 while the latter's 'NOSFERATU' failed to make any impression on the charts. Worse was to come for CORNWELL when, on the 7th of January 1980, the singer was found guilty of drug possession and sentenced to three months in prison. Later that year, the whole band fell foul of the law, this time in the South of France where they were accused of inciting a riot; although threatened with serious jail terms, they were susbsequently let off with fines, later claiming it was 'NICE IN NICE' on 1986's 'DREAMTIME' album. The STRANGLERS' commercial fortunes didn't fare much better with 'THE MEN IN BLACK' (1981), a tongue-in-cheek (but critically derided nonetheless) pseudo-concept affair about alien undercover agents. Boasting the exquisite harpsichord stylings of 'GOLDEN BROWN', 'LA FOLIE' (1981) was a considerably more successful album, if somewhat pretentious. In line with the prevailing trend, The STRANGLERS' moved perilously closer to synth-pop as the 80's wore on, 'Epic' albums such as 'FELINE' (1983) and 'AURAL SCULPTURE' (1984) seeing the band's hardcore fanbase dwindle. Even a return to their former stamping ground (and the UK Top 10) with a musclebound run-through of The Kinks' 'ALL DAY AND ALL OF THE NIGHT' couldn't rejuvenate them and the subsequent studio album, '10' (1990) was the last to feature CORNWELL. Deciding to carry on with new frontman, JOHN ELLIS, the band recorded for various indie labels in the 90's and although the likes of 'STRANGLERS IN THE NIGHT' (1992) and 'ABOUT TIME' (1995) made the Top 40, most commentators (and many fans) were agreed that the band's glory days were definitely behind them. • **Songwriters:** Mostly CORNWALL-penned except some by BURNEL. They also covered; 96 TEARS (? & The Mysterians).

Album rating: STRANGLERS IV – RATTUS NORVEGICUS (*8) / NO MORE HEROES (*7) / BLACK AND WHITE (*7) / LIVE (X CERT) (*5) / THE RAVEN (*6) THE MEN-IN-BLACK (*5) / LA FOLIE (*7) / THE COLLECTION 1977-1982 compilation (*7) / AURAL SCULPTURE (*6) / DREAMTIME (*6) / ALL LIVE AND ALL OF THE NIGHT (*4) / '10' (*5) / THE STRANGLERS' GREATEST HITS compilation (*9) / STRANGLERS IN THE NIGHT (*4) / SATURDAY NIGHT SUNDAY MORNING (*3) / ABOUT TIME (*4) / WRITTEN IN RED (*4) / THE HIT MEN – THE COMPLETE SINGLES 1977-1990 compilation (*8) / COUP DE GRACE (*4) / JJ Burnel: EUROMAN COMETH (*3) / Dave Greenfield & Jean-Jacques Burnel: FIRE AND WATER (*4) / Hugh Cornwall & Robert Williams: NOSFERATU (*2)

HUGH CORNWALL (b.28 Aug'48, London, England) – vocals, guitar / **JEAN-JAQUES BURNEL** (b.21 Feb'52, London; French parents) – bass, vocals / **DAVE GREENFIELD** (b.29 Mar'49, Brighton, England) – keyboards / **JET BLACK** (b. BRIAN DUFFY, 26 Aug'43, Ilford, England) – drums

		U.A.	A&M
Jan 77.	(7") (UP 36211) **(GET A) GRIP (ON YOURSELF). / LONDON LADY**	44	-
Apr 77.	(lp/c) (UAG/UAC 30045) <4648> **STRANGLERS IV – RATTUS NORVEGICUS**	4	

– Sometimes / Goodbye Toulouse / London lady / Princess of the streets / Hanging around / Peaches / (Get a) Grip (on yourself) / Ugly / Down in the sewer: (a) Falling – (b) Down in the sewer – (c) Trying to get out again – (d) Rats rally. (*free ltd.7"w.a.*) **CHOOSEY SUSIE. / IN THE BIG SHITTY (live)** (re-iss. May82 on 'Fame' lp/c; FA/TC-FA 3001) (cd-iss. Apr88; CDFA 3001) (cd-iss. Feb88 on 'Liberty'; CZ 85)

May 77.	(7") (UP 36248) **PEACHES. / GO BUDDY GO**	8	-

—— Jun77; They backed CELIA & THE MUTATIONS on cover single 'MONY MONY'.

Jul 77.	(7") (UP 36277) **SOMETHING BETTER CHANGE. / STRAIGHTEN OUT**	9	-
Sep 77.	(7") (UP 36300) **NO MORE HEROES. / IN THE SHADOWS**	8	-
Oct 77.	(lp/c) (UAG/UAC 30200) <4659> **NO MORE HEROES**	2	-

– I feel like a wog / Bitching / Dead ringer / Dagenham Dave / Bring on the nubiles / Something better change / No more heroes / Peasant in the big shitty / Burning up time / English towns / School mam / In the shadows. (re-iss. 1985 lp/c; ATAK/TC-

ATAK 32) (cd-iss. Feb88 on 'E.M.I.'; CDP 746613-2) (re-iss. Sep87 on 'Fame' lp/c; FA/TC-FA 3190) (cd-iss. Aug88; CDFA 3190)

Nov 77.	(7"pink-ep) **SOMETHING BETTER CHANGE / STRAIGHTEN OUT. / GRIP / HANGIN' AROUND**	-	
Jan 78.	(7") (UP 36350) **FIVE MINUTES. / ROK IT TO THE MOON**	11	-
Apr 78.	(7") (UP 36379) **NICE 'N' SLEAZY. / SHUT UP**	18	Aug78
May 78.	(lp/c)<US-grey-lp> (UAK/TCK 30222) <4706> **BLACK AND WHITE**	2	

– Tank / Nice 'n' sleazy / Outside Tokyo / Mean to me / Hey! (rise of the robots) / Sweden (all quiet on the Eastern Front) / Toiler on the sea / Curfew / Threatened / Do you wanna? / Death and night and blood (Yukio) / Enough time. (*free ltd.7"w.a.*) (FREE 9) **WALK ON BY. / TITS / MEAN TO ME** (re-iss. Jan86 on 'Epic' lp/c; EPC/40 26439) (cd-iss. Jul88 on 'E.M.I.' +=; CZ 109) – (free 7" tracks).

		U.A.	I.R.S.
Jul 78.	(7"m) (UP 36429) **WALK ON BY. / OLD CODGER / TANK**	21	-
Mar 79.	(lp/c) (UAG/TCK 30224) <70011> **X-CERT (live)**	7	

– (Get a) Grip (on yourself) / Dagenham Dave / Burning up time / Dead ringer / Hanging around / I feel like a wog / Straighten out / Do you wanna – Death and night and blood (Yukio) / Five minutes / Go buddy go. (re-iss. 1985 lp/c; ATAK/TC-ATACK 33) (cd-iss. Jul88 +=; CZ 110) – In the shadows / Peasant in the big shitty.

Aug 79.	(7") (BP 308) **DUCHESS. / FOOLS RUSH OUT**	14	
Sep 79.	(lp/c) (UAG/TCK 30262) **THE RAVEN**	4	-

– Longships / The raven / Dead Loss Angeles / Ice / Baroque bordello / Nuclear device / Shah shah a go go / Don't bring Harry / Duchess / Meninblack / Genetix. (re-iss. Sep85 on 'Fame' lp/c; FA/TC-FA 3131) (cd-iss. Aug88; CDFA 3131) (cd-iss. Oct87 on 'EMI' +=; CZ 20) – Bear cage.

Oct 79.	(7") (BP 318) **NUCLEAR DEVICE (THE WIZARD OF AUS). / YELLOWCAKE UF6**	36	-
Nov 79.	(7"ep) (STR 1) **DON'T BRING HARRY**	41	

– Don't bring Harry / Wired / Crabs (live) / In the shadows (live).

		Liberty	I.R.S.
Jan 80.	(7") **DUCHESS. / THE RAVEN**		-
Jan 80.	(lp) <SP 70011> **STRANGLERS IV**		-

– (5 tracks from 'THE RAVEN', plus recent singles) (above w/ free 7"ep) – Do The European / Choosie Suzie / Wired / Straighten out.

Mar 80.	(7"/12") (BP/12BP 344) **BEAR CAGE. / SHAH SHAH A GO GO**	36	-
May 80.	(7") (BP 355) **WHO WANTS THE WORLD. / MENINBLACK**	39	-
Jan 81.	(7") (BP 383) **THROWN AWAY. / TOP SECRET**	42	-
Feb 81.	(lp/c) (LBG/TC-LBG 30313) **THE MEN• IN• BLACK**	8	-

– Waltzinblack / Just like nothing on Earth / Second coming / Waiting for the meninblack / Turn the centuries, turn / Two sunspots / Four horsemen / Thrown away / Manna machine / Hallo to our men. (re-iss. 1985 lp/c; ATAK/TC-ATAK 34) (re-iss. Sep88 on 'Fame' lp/c/cd; FA/TCFA/CDFA 3208) – Top secret / Maninwhite.

Mar 81.	(7") (BP 393) **JUST LIKE NOTHING ON EARTH. / MANINWHITE**		
Nov 81.	(7") (BP 405) **LET ME INTRODUCE YOU TO THE FAMILY. / VIETNAMERICA**	42	-
Nov 81.	(lp/c) (LBG/TC-LBG 30342) **LA FOLIE**	11	-

– Non stop / Everybody loves you when you're dead / Tramp / Let me introduce you to the family / The man they love to hate / Pin up / It only takes two to tango / Golden brown / How to find true love and happiness in the present day / La folie. (re-iss. Nov83 on 'Fame' lp/c; FA/TC-FA 3083) (cd-iss. Aug88; CDFA 3083) (cd-iss. Feb88 +=; CZ 86) – Cruel garden.

Jan 82.	(7") (BP 407) **GOLDEN BROWN. / LOVE 30**	2	-
Apr 82.	(7") (BP 410) **LA FOLIE. / WALTZINBLACK**	47	-
Jul 82.	(7") (BP 412) **STRANGE LITTLE GIRL. / CRUEL GARDEN**	7	-
Sep 82.	(lp/c) (LBG/TC-LBG 304353) **THE COLLECTION 1977-1982** (compilation)	12	-

– (Get a) Grip (on yourself) / Peaches / Hanging around / No more heroes / Duchess / Walk on by / Waltzinblack / Something better change / Nice'n'sleazy / Bear cage / Who wants the world / Golden brown / Strange little girl / La folie. (cd-iss. 1985; CDP 746066-2) (re-iss. Aug89 on 'Fame' cd/c/lp; CD/TC+/FA 3230)

		Epic	Epic
Nov 82.	(7"/7"pic-d) (EPCA/+11 2893) **THE EUROPEAN FEMALE. / SAVAGE BEAST**	9	
Jan 83.	(lp/c) (EPC/40 25237) <38542> **FELINE**	4	

– Midnight summer dream / It's a small world / Ships that pass in the night / The european female / Let's tango in Paris / Paradise / All roads lead to Rome / Blue sister / Never say goodbye. (*free ltd.one-sided-7"w.a.*) **AURAL SCULPTURE** (re-iss. Apr86 lp/c; EPC/40 32711) <US lp+=> – Golden brown. (cd-iss. Dec92)

Feb 83.	(7"/12") (A/+13 3167) **MIDNIGHT SUMMER DREAM. / VLADIMIR AND OLGA**	35	-
Jul 83.	(7") (A 3387) **PARADISE. / PAWSHER**	48	-
	(12"+=) (A13 3387) – Permission.		
Jul 83.	(12") **MIDNIGHT SUMMER DREAM. / PARADISE**	-	
Sep84.	(7") (A 4738) **SKIN DEEP. / HERE AND NOW**	15	-
	(12"+=) (TA 4738) – Vladimir and the beast.		
Nov 84.	(lp/c) (EPC/40 26220) <39959> **AURAL SCULPTURE**	14	

– Ice queen / Skin deep / Let me down easy / No mercy / North winds / Uptown / Punch & Judy / Spain / Laughing / Souls / Mad Hatter. (re-iss. May87 lp/c; 450488-1/-4) (cd-iss. 1987; 450488-2) (cd-iss. cd Sep93 on 'Sony Collectors') (cd re-iss. Feb97; 474676-2)

Nov 84.	(7"/7"sha-pic-d) (A/WA 4921) **NO MERCY. / IN ONE DOOR**	37	-
	(12"+=) (TA 4921) – Hot club (riot mix).		
	(d7"++=) (GA 4921) – Head on the line.		
Feb 85.	(7") (A 6045) **LET ME DOWN EASY. / ACHILLES HEEL**	48	-
	(12"+=) (TA 6045) – Place des victories.		
	(12"++=) (QTA 6045) – Vladimir goes to Havana / The aural sculpture manifesto.		
Aug 86.	(7"/12"/7"sha-pic-d) (650055-7/-6/-0) **NICE IN NICE. / SINCE YOU WENT AWAY**	30	
Oct 86.	(7"/7"sha-pic-d) (SOLAR/+P 1) **ALWAYS THE SUN. / NORMAN NORMAL**	30	
	(12"+=) (SOLART 1) – Soul.		
	(d7"+=) (SOLARD 1) – Nice in nice / Since you went away.		
Oct 86.	(lp/c/cd/pic-lp) (EPC/40/CD/11 26648) <40607> **DREAMTIME**	16	

– Always the sun / Dreamtime / Was it you? / You'll always reap what you sow / Ghost train / Nice in nice / Big in America / Shakin' like a leaf / Mayan skies / Too precious. (re-iss. Feb89 lp/c/cd; 463366-1/-4/-2)

Dec 86. (7"/7"sha-pic-d) *(HUGE/+P 1)* **BIG IN AMERICA. / DRY DAY** `48` `-`
(12"+=) *(HUGET 1)* – Uptown.
(d7"+=) *(HUGED 1)* – Always the sun / Norman normal.

Feb 87. (7"/7"sha-pic-d) *(SHEIK/+P 1)* **SHAKIN' LIKE A LEAF. / HIT MAN** `58` `-`
('A'-Jelly mix-12"+=) *(SHEIKQ 1)* – Was it you?
('A'live-12") *(SHEIKB 1)* – (an evening with Hugh Cornwall).

Dec 87. (7"/7"sha-pic-d) *(VICE/+P 1)* **ALL DAY AND ALL OF THE NIGHT (live). / VIVA VLAD** `7` `-`
(12"+=) *(VICET 1)* – Who wants the world (live).
(cd-s+=) *(CDVICE 1)* – Strange little girl.

Feb 88. (lp/c/cd) *(460259-1/-4/-2)* <44209> **ALL LIVE AND ALL OF THE NIGHT (live)** `12` `-`
– No more heroes / Was it you? / Down in the sewer / Always the sun / Golden brown / North winds / The European female / Strange little girl / Nice 'n' sleazy / Toiler on the sea / Spain / London lady / All day and all of the night.

Feb 90. (7"/c-s) *(TEARS/+M 1)* **96 TEARS. / INSTEAD OF THIS** `17` `-`
(12"+=/cd-s+=/pic-cd-s+=) *(TEARS T/C/P 1)* – Poisonality.

Mar 90. (cd/c/lp/pic-lp) *(466483-2/-4/-1/-0)* **10** `15` `-`
– The sweet smell of success / Someone like you / 96 tears / In this place / Let's celebrate / Man of the Earth / Too many teardrops / Where I live / Out of my mind / Never to look back. *(re-iss. cd Dec92)*

Apr 90. (7"/c-s/7"pic-d) *(TEARS/+M/P 2)* **THE SWEET SMELL OF SUCCESS. / MOTORBIKE** `65` `-`
(12"+=/cd-s+=) *(TEARS T/C 2)* – Something.

Nov 90. (cd/c/lp/pic-cd) *(467541-2/-4/-1/-9)* <47081> **THE STRANGLERS' GREATEST HITS 1977-1990** (compilation) `4` `-`
– Peaches / Something better change / No more heroes / Walk on by / Duchess / Golden brown / Strange little girl / The European female / Skin deep / Nice in Nice / Always the sun / Big in America / All day and all of the night / 96 tears / No mercy.

Dec 90. (7"/c-s) *(656 430-7/-4)* **ALWAYS THE SUN. / BURNHAM BEECHES** `29` `-`
(12"+=) *(656 430-6)* – Straighten out.
(cd-s) – ('A'side) / Nuclear device (live) / All day and all of the night (live) / Punch and Judy (live).

Mar 91. (7"/c-s) *(656 761-7/-4)* **GOLDEN BROWN (re-mix). / YOU** `68` `-`
(cd-s+=) *(656 761-2)* – Skin deep (extended) / Peaches.

—— (late 1990) **JOHN ELLIS** (b. 1 Jun'52, London) – guitar, vocals (once p/t member) (ex-VIBRATORS, etc.) repl. CORNWALL who has already ventured solo.

—— (Jan'91) also added **PAUL ROBERTS** (b.31 Dec'59, London) – vocals (ex-SNIFF 'N' THE TEARS)

		China	Viceroy

Aug 92. (7") *(WOK 2025)* **HEAVEN OR HELL. / DISAPPEAR** `46` `-`
(12"+=/c-s+=/cd-s+=) *(WOK T/C/CD 2025)* – Brainbox / Hanging around.

Sep 92. (lp/c/cd) *(WOL/+MC/CD 1030)* <8007> **STRANGLERS IN THE NIGHT** `33` `Feb93`
– Time to die / Sugar bullets / Heaven or Hell / Laughing at the rain / This town / Brainbox / Southern mountains / Gain entry to your soul / Grand canyon / Wet afternoon / Never see / Leave it to the dogs.

		Psycho	not iss.

Oct 92. (7"/c-s) *(PSY/+MC 002)* **SUGAR BULLETS. / SO UNCOOL** `` `-`
(cd-s+=) *(PSYCD 002)* – ('A'version).

—— **TIKAKE TOBE** – drums repl. JET BLACK

		Essential	Viceroy

Jun 93. (cd/c/lp) *(ESS CD/MC/LP 194)* <ESM 388> **SATURDAY NIGHT SUNDAY MORNING (live)** `` `Mar96`
– Toiler on the sea / 96 Tears / Always the sun / No more heroes / Golden brown / Tank / Strange little girl / Something better change / Hanging around / All day and all of the night / Duchess / *Medley / Was it you? / Down in the sewer.

—— In Jun'93, old Stranger HUGH CORNWALL released album 'WIRED' on 'Transmission' label. Nearly a year earlier as CCW, he, ROGER COOK & AND WEST issued cd 'CCW FEATURING HUGH CORNWALL • ROGER COOK • ANDY WEST' on 'UFO'.

—— **JET BLACK** returned

		When!	Beacon

May 95. (cd/c/lp) *(WEN CD/MC/LP 001)* <51568> **ABOUT TIME** `31` `Jan96`
– Golden boy / Money / Sinister / Little blue lies / Still life / Paradise row / She gave it all / Lies and deception / Lucky finger / And the boat sails by.

Jun 95. (12"/cd-s) *(WEN T/X 1007)* **LIES AND DECEPTION. / SWIM / DANNY COOL** `` `-`
(cd-s) *(WENX 1008)* – ('A'side) / Kiss the world goodbye / Bed of nails.

Jan 97. (pic-cd/cd/c) *(WEN PD/CD/MC 009)* **WRITTEN IN RED** `52` `-`
– Valley of the birds / In Heaven she walks / In a while / Silver into blue / Blue sky / Here / Joy de viva / Miss you / Daddy's riding the range / Summer in the city / Wonderful land.

Feb 97. (c-s/cd-s) *(WEN N/X 1018)* **IN HEAVEN SHE WALKS / GOLDEN BROWN (live)** `` `-`
(cd-s) *(WENX 1020)* – ('A'side) / Grip (live) / Something better change (live).

		Eagle	Festival

Oct 98. (cd) *(EAGCD 042)* <31965> **COUP DE GRACE** `` `Mar99`
– God is good / You don't think that what you've done is wrong / Tonight / Jump over my shadow / Miss you / Coup de grace (S-O-S) / In the end / No reason / Known only unto God / The light.

– compilations, etc. –

Mar 84. (7") *EMI Gold; (G45 6)* **GOLDEN BROWN. / STRANGE LITTLE GIRL** `` `-`
Sep 86. (lp/c) *Liberty; (LBG/TCLBG 5001)* **OFF THE BEATEN TRACK** `80` `-`
Nov 88. (lp/c) *Liberty; (EMS/TCEMS 1306)* **RARITIES** `` `-`
Jan 89. (7"/7"red) *E.M.I.; (EM/+R 84)* **GRIP '89. / WALTZINBLACK** `33` `-`
(12"+=) *(12EM 84)* – Tomorrow was thereafter.
(cd-s++=) *(CDEM 84)* – ('A'mix).
Feb 89. (cd/c/lp) *E.M.I.; (CD/TC+/EM 1314)* **THE SINGLES** `57` `-`

Jun 89. (12"ep) *Nightracks; (SFNT/+CD 020)* **RADIO 1 SESSION (1982)** `` `-`
– The man they love to hate / Nuclear device / Genetix / Down in the sewer.

Dec 90. (3xcd-box) *Epic; (467395-2)* **FELINE / AURAL SCULPTURE / DREAMTIME** `` `

Feb 92. (cd/c/d-lp) *Newspeak; (SPEAK CD/MC/LP 101)* **THE EARLY YEARS 74-75-76, RARE LIVE & UNRELEASED** `` `

Mar 92. (cd/c) *Epic; (471416-2/-4)* **ALL TWELVE INCHES** `` `

May 92. (cd/c) *(CDGO/TCGO 2033)* **LIVE AT THE HOPE AND ANCHOR (live)** `` `
(cd re-iss. Feb95 on 'Fame'; CDFA 3316)

Jul 92. (d-cd) *Epic; (466835-2)* **FELINE / DREAMTIME** `` `

Dec 92. (4xcd-box) *E.M.I.; CDS 799924-2)* **THE OLD TESTAMENT – THE U.A. STUDIO RECORDINGS (demos)** `` `

May 94. (cd) *Receiver; (<RRCD 187>)* **DEATH AND NIGHT AND BLOOD** `` `

Jun 94. (cd) *Castle; (CLACD 401)* **THE EARLY YEARS 1974-76** `` `

Feb 95. (cd) *Receiver; (RRCD 195)* **LIVE IN CONCERT (live w/ FRIENDS)** `` `

Nov 95. (cd) *Essential; <ESM 283>* **RADIO ONE** `` `-`
Nov 95. (cd-s) *Old Gold; (12623 6339-2)* **GOLDEN BROWN / NO MORE HEROES** `` `

Feb 97. (cd/c) *E.M.I.; (CD/TC EMC 3759)* **THE HIT MEN (The Complete Singles 1977-1990)** `` `

Dec 97. (cd) *Rialto; (<220>)* **LIVE IN LONDON (live)** `` `

Feb 98. (cd) *Cleopatra; <206>* **FRIDAY THE THIRTEENTH** `` `

Jul 98. (cd) *Voiceprint; <1>* **ACCESS ALL AREAS (live)** `` `-`

STRAWBERRY ALARM CLOCK   (dig out; Great Psychedelic . . .)

STRAWS

Formed: London, England . . . 1967 as The STRAWBERRY HILL BOYS by Leicester University student, DAVE COUSINS and schoolfriend TONY HOOPER, who, along with mandolin player ARTHUR PHILLIPS, initially traded in American-style bluegrass. With the addition of KEN GUDMAND, RON CHESTERMAN and a young SANDY DENNY, they moved towards a British folk revival sound and recorded the 'ALL OUR OWN WORK' album in 1968. This didn't actually see the light of day until 1974 when it was given a full release and credited to SANDY DENNY & THE STRAWBS, by that time of course, DENNY having carved out quite a career for herself. She originally left for FAIRPORT CONVENTION in '69, a core of COUSINS, HOOPER and CHESTERMAN completing 'THE STRAWBS' (1969) with the help of session men. Released on 'A&M', the album was highly regarded among the folk fraternity with its EWAN MacCOLL influenced compositions and exemplary playing. A follow-up, 'DRAGONFLY' (1970) wasn't so well received and the group subsequently pursued a new direction with the addition of ex-VELVET OPERA members, RICHARD HUDSON and JOHN FORD. Another star in the making, RICK WAKEMAN, was also a new addition, the classically trained keyboardist's impetus taking the band closer to electric prog-rock on 1970's 'JUST A COLLECTION OF ANTIQUES AND CURIOS'. Although alienating some of their more traditional fans, the record took The STRAWBS into the UK Top 30 for the first time. 'FROM THE WITCHWOOD' (1971) carried on in much the same vein, although WAKEMAN was feeling increasingly constricted and duly decamped to fledgling prog legends, YES. Ex-AMEN CORNER man, BLUE WEAVER, took his place for the acclaimed 'GRAVE NEW WORLD' (1972), an album which surprisingly failed to spawn a hit single depite its near Top 10 success. Recorded during a temporary split with the band, DAVE COUSINS' solo set, 'TWO WEEKS LAST SUMMER', was released just prior to The STRAWBS' first hit single, 'LAY DOWN'. This was almost immediately followed by the witty 'PART OF THE UNION' early in '73, a track lifted from the band's most creatively and commercially successful (near No.1) album of their career, 'BURSTING AT THE SEAMS'. With HOOPER already out of the picture by this point, internal tensions reached a head during an ill-fated US tour and led to the departure of HUDSON, FORD and WEAVER, a line-up of COUSINS, DAVE LAMBERT (who'd replaced HOOPER prior to 'BURSTING..'), CHAS CRONK, ROD COOMBES and JOHN HAWKEN going on to record a series of increasingly disappointing and poor selling albums right up until 1978. A re-formed STRAWBS, featuring COOPER, HOOPER and HUDSON with a cast of new faces, recorded the lacklustre 'DON'T SAY GOODBYE' in 1987, while varying permutations of the band continued to tour. • **Songwriters:** COUSINS or HUDSON-FORD (the latter pair between 1970 + 1973). • **Trivia:** Off-shoot duo, HUDSON-FORD, had a major Top 10 hit in 1973 with 'PICK UP THE PIECES', followed by a No.15 hit, 'BURN BABY BURN', in '74.

Album rating: STRAWBS (*7) / DRAGONFLY (*6) / JUST A COLLECTION OF ANTIQUES AND CURIOS (*6) / FROM THE WITCHWOOD (*6) / GRAVE NEW WORLD (*8) / BURSTING AT THE SEAMS (*7) / HERO AND HEROINE (*6) / STRAWBS BY CHOICE compilation (*6) / GHOSTS (*5) / NOMADNESS (*5) / DEEP CUTS (*5) / BURNING FOR YOU (*5) / DEADLINES (*5) / THE BEST OF THE STRAWBS compilation (*6) / DON'T SAY GOODBYE (*4) / A CHOICE SELECTION OF STRAWBS compilation (*8) / HALYCON DAYS: THE VERY BEST OF . . . compilation (*7)

DAVE COUSINS (b. 7 Jan'45, Leicester, England) – vocals, guitar, banjo / **TONY HOOPER** – guitar, vocals / **KEN GUDMAND** – drums / **RON CHESTERMAN** – bass / **ARTHUR PHILLIPS** – mandolin / added **SANDY DENNY** (b. 6 Jan'47, Wimbledon, England) – vocals

They recorded album 'ALL OUR OWN WORK' as SANDY DENNY & THE STRAWBS which was issued by 'Hallmark' in 1974. DENNY joined FAIRPORT

CONVENTION. **DAVE, TONY & RON** employed session men **RONNIE WERRELL** – drums / **ALAN PARKER** – guitar / **ALAN NEIGHBOUR** – bass

		A&M	A&M
Jun 68.	(7") (AMS 725) **OH HOW SHE CHANGED. / OR AM I DREAMING**		–
Nov 68.	(7") (AMS 738) **THE MAN WHO CALLED HIMSELF JESUS. / POOR JIMMY WILSON**		–
May 69.	(lp) (AMLS 936) **STRAWBS**		–

– The man who called himself Jesus / That which was once mine / All the little ladies / Pieces of 79 & 15 / Tell me what you see in me / Oh how she changed / Or am I dreaming / Where is this dream of your youth / Poor Jimmy Wilson / Where am I – I'll show you where to sleep / The battle.

—— basic trio added **CLAIRE DENIZ** – cello

| Jul 70. | (7") (AMS 791) **FOREVER. / ANOTHER DAY** | | – |
| Jul 70. | (lp) (AMLS 970) **DRAGONFLY** | | – |

– The weary song / Dragonfly / I turned my face into the wind / Josephine, for better or for worse / Another day / Till the sun comes shining through / Young again / The vision of the lady of the lake / Close your eyes.

—— **RICHARD HUDSON** (b. 9 May'48, London) – drums / **JOHN FORD** (b. 1 Jul'48, London) – bass (both ex-VELVET OPERA) / **RICK WAKEMAN** (b.18 May'48) – keyboards (who guested on last lp) repl. RON + CLAIRE

| Nov 70. | (lp) (AMLS 994) **JUST A COLLECTION OF ANTIQUES AND CURIOS** | 27 | |

– Martin Luther King's dream / The antique suite: The reaper – We must cross the river – Antiques and curios – Hey, it's been a long time / Temperament of mind / Fingertips / Song of a sad little girl / Where is this dream of your youth (live).

| Jan 71. | (7") **WHERE IS THE DREAM OF YOUR YOUTH (live). /** | | |
| Jul 71. | (lp) (AMLH 64304) **FROM THE WITCHWOOD** | 39 | |

– A glimpse of Heaven / Witchwood / Thirty days / Flight / The hangman & the papist / Sheep / Canon Dale / The shepherd's song / In amongst the roses / I'll carry on beside you. (re-iss. 1974)

—— **BLUE WEAVER** (b.11 Mar'48, Cardiff, Wales) – keyboards (ex-AMEN CORNER) repl. WAKEMAN who joined YES

| Feb 72. | (lp) (AMLH 68078) <4344> **GRAVE NEW WORLD** | 11 | |

– Benedictus / Hey little man ...Thursday's child / Queen of dreams / Heavy disguise / New world / Hey little man ...Wednesday's child / The flower and the young man / Tomorrow / On growing older / Ah me, ah my / Is it today, Lord? / The journey's end.

Feb 72.	(7") (AMS 874) **BENEDICTUS. / KEEP THE DEVIL OUTSIDE**		–
Apr 72.	(7") (AMS 7002) **HERE IT COMES. / TOMORROW**		–
Jun 72.	(7") <13645> **BENEDICTUS. / HEAVY DISGUISE**	–	

—— In Sep72, DAVE COUSINS issued a solo single GOING HOME. / WAYS AND MEANS plus an album TWO WEEKS LAST SUMMER for 'A&M'.

—— **DAVE LAMBERT** (b. 8 Mar'49, Hounslow, England) – guitar, vocals repl. HOOPER

Oct 72.	(7") (AMS 7035) **LAY DOWN. / BACKSIDE**	12	–
Jan 73.	(7") (AMS 7047) **PART OF THE UNION. / WILL YOU GO**	2	–
Feb 73.	(lp/c) (AMLH/CAM 68144) <4383> **BURSTING AT THE SEAMS**	2	

– Flying / Lady Fuchsia / Stormy down / Down by the sea / The river / Part of the union / Tears and Pavan medley / The winter and the summer / Lay down / Thank you.

| Apr 73. | (7") <1419> **PART OF THE UNION. / TOMORROW** | – | |
| Aug 73. | (7") <1451> **LAY DOWN. / THE WINTER AND THE SUMMER** | – | |

—— **COUSINS + LAMBERT** recruited new members **CHAS CRONK** – bass / **ROD COOMBES** – drums (ex-STEALER'S WHEEL) repl. HUDSON-FORD who formed own band **JOHN HAWKEN** – keyboards (ex-NASHVILLE TEENS, ex-RENAISSANCE, ex-VINEGAR JOE) repl. BLUE WEAVER

Aug 73.	(7") (AMS 7082) <1476> **SHINE ON SILVER SUN. / AND WHEREFORE**	34	Nov73
Apr 74.	(7") (AMS 7105) **HERO AND HEROINE. / WHY**		–
Apr 74.	(7") <1519> **ROUND AND ROUND. / HEROINE'S THEME**		–
Apr 74.	(lp/c) (AMLH/CAM 63607) <3607> **HERO AND HEROINE**	35	94 Feb74

– Autumn: (a) Heroine's theme – (b) Deep summer sleep – (c) The winter long / Sad young man / Just love / Shine on silver sun / Hero and heroine / Midnight sun / Out in the cold / Round and round / Lay a little light on me / Hero's theme.

| May 74. | (7") (AMS 7117) **HOLD ONTO ME (THE WINTER LONG). / WHERE DO YOU GO** | | |
| Aug 74. | (lp/c) (AMLH/CAM 68259) **BY CHOICE** (compilation) | | |

– The man who called himself Jesus / Another day / Forever / Song of a sad little girl / The shepherd's song / Benedictus / Here it comes / The actor / Lay down / Lay a little light on me.

| Nov 74. | (7") (AMS 7139) **GRACE DARLING. / CHANGES ARRANGES** | | – |
| Nov 74. | (lp/c) (AMLH/CAM 68277) <4506> **GHOSTS** | | 47 Feb75 |

– Ghosts: Sweet dreams – Night light – Guardian angel / Lemon pie / Starshine – Angel wine / Where do you go (when you need a hole to crawl in) / The life auction: Impressions of Southall from the train – The auction / Don't try to change me / Remembering / You and I / Grace darling.

Apr 75.	(7") (AMS 7161) **LEMON PIE. / DON'T TRY TO CHANGE ME**		–
Jun 75.	(7") <1687> **LEMON PIE. / WHERE DO YOU GO (WHEN YOU NEED A HOLE TO CRAWL IN)**	–	
Nov 75.	(7") <1747> **LITTLE SLEEPY. / THE GOLDEN SALAMANDER**	–	
Nov 75.	(lp/c) (AMLH/CAM 68331) <4544> **NOMADNESS**		Oct75

– To be free / Little sleepy / The golden salamander / Absent friend (how I need you) / Back on the farm / So shall our love die? / Tokyo Rosie / A mind of my own / Hanging in the gallery / The promised land.

		Oyster- Polydor	Oyster
Jul 76.	(7") (2066 705) **I ONLY WANT MY LOVE TO GROW IN YOU. / THINKING OF YOU**		–
Sep 76.	(lp/c) (2391-234) <1603> **DEEP CUTS**		

– I only want my love to grow in you / Turn me round / Hard, hard winter / My friend Peter / The soldier's tale / Simple visions / Charmer / (Wasting my time) Thinking of you / Beside the Rio Grande / So close and yet so far away.

| Oct 76. | (7") (2066 74) **CHARMER. / BESIDE THE RIO GRANDE** | | – |
| Dec 76. | (7") (2066 751) **SO CLOSE AND YET SO FAR AWAY. / THE SOLDIER'S TALE** | | – |

| May 77. | (7") (2066 818) **BACK IN THE OLD ROUTINE. / BURNING FOR ME** | | – |
| Jun 77. | (lp/c) (2391 287) <1604> **BURNING FOR YOU** | | – |

– Burning for me / Cut like a diamond / I feel your loving coming on / Barcarole / Alexander The Great / Keep on trying / Back in the old routine / Heartbreaker / Carry me home / Goodbye.

| Aug 77. | (7") (2066 846) **KEEP ON TRYING. / SIMPLE VISIONS** | | – |

		Arista	Arista
Jan 78.	(7") (ARIST 159) **JOEY AND ME. / DEADLY NIGHTSHADE**		–
Feb 78.	(lp/c) (SPART/TCARTY 1036) **DEADLINES**		–

– Deadlines (no return) / Joey and me / Sealed with a traitor's kiss / I don't want to talk about it / The last resort / Time and life / New beginnings / Deadly nightshade / Words of wisdom.

Mar 78.	(7") (ARIST 179) **NEW BEGINNINGS. / WORDS OF WISDOM**		–
Apr 78.	(7") (ARIST 179) **I DON'T WANT TO TALK ABOUT IT. / WORDS OF WISDOM**	–	
Oct 78.	(7") (ARIST 183) **I DON'T WANT TO TALK ABOUT IT. / THE LAST RESORT**		–

—— Folded in 1978. In Sep79, on 'Slurp' records, COUSINS made another solo album 'OLD SCHOOL SONGS' augmented by guitarist **BRIAN WILLOUGHBY**. In mid'83, COUSINS + HOOPER re-formed The STRAWBS with **CHAS CRONK** – bass / **TONY FERNANDEZ** – drums (both of RICK WAKEMAN's band). (below 45 feat. MADDY PRIOR)

		L.O.	not iss.
Nov 80.	(7") (LO 1) **THE KING. / RINGING DOWN THE YEARS**		–

—— Early in 1987, COUSINS, HOOPER, WILLOUGHBY, HUDSON brought in **CHRIS PARREN** – keyboards (ex-HUDSON-FORD) / **ROD DEMICK** – bass (ex-WHEELS)

| Feb 87. | (7") **THAT'S WHEN THE CRYING STARTS. / WE CAN MAKE IT TOGETHER** (released on 'Virgin Canada') | | – |

		Toots	not iss.
May 87.	(lp) (TOOTS 3) **DON'T SAY GOODBYE**		–

– A boy and his dog / Let it rain / We can make it together / Tina dei fada / Big brother / Something for nothing / Evergreen / That's when the crying starts / Beat the retreat. (re-iss. Oct88 on 'Chord' lp/cd; STRAWBS 001/ CD009)

		Chord	not iss.
Nov 88.	(7") (STRAWBS 101) **LET IT RAIN. / TINA DEI FADA**		–

		Road Goes On Forever	not iss.
Oct 93.	(cd) (RGFCD 015) **GREATEST HITS – LIVE** (live 1990)		–

– Cut like a diamond / Something for nothing / The hangman and the papist / Ringing down the years / Stormy down / Afraid to let you go / Grace darling / The river / Down by the sea / Lay down / Part of the union / Hero & heroine. (re-iss. Jul95;)

—— line-up:- COUSINS / CRONK / RICHARDS / FERNANDEZ

| Jul 95. | (cd) **HEARTBREAK HILL** | | |

– Something for nothing / Another day without you / We can make it together / Heartbreak Hill / Starting over / Two separate people / Desert song / Let it rain.

– compilations, etc. –

Sep 78.	(d-lp) A&M; (AMLH 66005) **THE BEST OF THE STRAWS**		
Mar 79.	(7") A&M; (AMS 7425) **PART OF THE UNION. / LAY DOWN** (re-iss. Jul82 on 'Old Gold'; OG 9149)		–
Oct 92.	(cd) A&M; (CDMID 173) **A CHOICE SELECTION OF STRAWBS**		

– Lay down / Lemon pie / Lady Fuschia / Autumn:- 1- Heroine's theme – 2- Deep summer's sleep – 3- The winter long / A glimpse of Heaven / The hangman and the papist / New world / Round and round / I only want my love to grow in you / Benedictus / Hero and heroine / Song of a sad little girl / Tears and Pavan:- 1- Tears – 2- Pavan / To be free / Part of the union / Down by the sea.

May 73.	(lp; SANDY DENNY & THE STRAWBS) Hallmark; (SHM 813) **ALL OUR OWN WORK** (re-iss. 1991 on 'Hannibal';)		
1992.	(d-cd) Road Goes On Forever; (DCD 003) **PRESERVES UNCANNED**		
Mar 95.	(cd) Windsong; (WINCD 069) **STRAWBS IN CONCERT** (live)		–

STREETWALKERS (see under ⇒ FAMILY)

Joe STRUMMER (see under ⇒ CLASH)

Dan STUART (see under ⇒ GREEN ON RED)

STYLE COUNCIL (see under ⇒ WELLER, Paul)

STYX

Formed: Chicago, Illinois, USA . . . 1964 as The TRADEWINDS by DENNIS DE YOUNG and neighbours, the PANOZZO twins (CHUCK and JOHN). After meeting JOHN CURULEWSKI at university and duly recruiting him as guitarist, the group briefly changed their name to TW4 before eventually settling on STYX (after the mythical Greek river). With the line-up augmented by a second guitarist, JAMES YOUNG, the group came to the attention of Bill Traut, who signed them to his 'Wooden Nickel' label. Initially touting a classical/art-rock fusion with overblown vocal arrangements, the group debuted with the eponymous 'STYX' in 1972. Although the album spawned a US Hot 100 single in 'BEST THING', subsequent sets such as 'THE SERPENT IS RISING' (1974) and 'MAN OF MIRACLES' (1974), failed to yield any chart action. Things changed in the mid-70's as CURULEWSKI was replaced with guitarist/vocalist/co-writer, TOMMY SHAW, who, along with DE YOUNG, would help steer the band in a more commercial direction.

Widely credited with inventing pomp-rock, STYX only really started to take their falsetto-warbling excess to the masses following a move to 'R.C.A.'. Almost instantaneous success came in late '74/early '75 when the label re-issued 'LADY' (from 1972's 'STYX II'), a strident slice of bombastic pop which marched into the US Top 10. Follow-up sets, 'EQUINOX' (1976) and 'CRYSTAL BALL' (1976) appeared on 'A&M', STYX slowly but surely swelling their fanbase with widescale touring and an increasingly radio-friendly sound. The big break finally came in 1977 with the multi-million selling 'THE GRAND ILLUSION' album and accompanying Top 10 crossover hit, 'COME SAIL AWAY'. The following year's 'PIECES OF EIGHT' (1978) achieved a fine balance between melody, power and stride-splitting vocal histrionics, although it was 'CORNERSTONE' (1980) which furnished the group with their sole No.1 single, the syrupy 'BABE'. A lavishly packaged pomp concept piece, 'PARADISE THEATER' (1980) became the group's first (and only) No.1, even making the Top 10 in Britain(!) Arguably among the group's most affecting work, the record spawned two US Top 10 singles, 'THE BEST OF TIMES' and 'TIME ON MY HANDS'. Yet another concept piece (centering on the increasingly controversial issue of censorship), 'KILROY WAS HERE' (1983), appeared in 1983, the last STYX studio album of the decade. The following year saw both DE YOUNG and SHAW releasing solo debuts, 'DESERT MOON' and 'GIRLS WITH GUNS' respectively. Both sets performed relatively well, although DE YOUNG's poppier affair spawned a Top 10 hit single with the title track. Subsequent mid to late 80's efforts (DE YOUNG's 'BACK TO THE WORLD' and 'BOOMCHILD', SHAW's 'WHAT IF' and 'AMBITION') failed to capture the public's imagination and the inevitable STYX reformation album was released in 1990. Despite the absence of SHAW (his replacement being GLEN BURTNIK), who had joined DAMN YANKEES, 'EDGE OF THE CENTURY' was a relative success, housing a massive US Top 3 hit in 'SHOW ME THE WAY'.

Album rating: STYX (*4) / STYX II (*5) / THE SERPENT IS RISING (*5) / MAN OF MIRACLES (*6) / EQUINOX (*6) / CRYSTAL BALL (*6) / THE GRAND ILLUSION (*7) / PIECES OF EIGHT (*7) / THE BEST OF STYX compilation (*6) / CORNERSTONE (*7) / PARADISE THEATER (*8) / KILROY WAS HERE (*6) / CAUGHT IN THE ACT – LIVE (*4) / EDGE OF THE CENTURY (*5) / GREATEST HITS compilation (*8) / RETURN TO PARADISE (*3)

DENNIS DeYOUNG (b.18 Feb'47) – vocals, keyboards / **JOHN CURULEWSKI** – guitar / **JAMES YOUNG** (b.14 Nov'48) – guitar / **CHUCK PANOZZO** (b.20 Sep'47) – bass / **JOHN PANOZZO** – drums

			not iss.	Wooden Nickel
Sep 72.	(lp) <BXLI 1008> **STYX**		-	

– Movement for the common man: Children of the land – Street collage – Fanfare for the common man / Mother Nature's matinee / Right away / What has come between us / Best thing / Quick is the beat of my heart / After you leave me. (UK-iss.Jul80 as 'STYX 1' on 'R.C.A.'; 3593)

			not iss.	Wooden Nickel
Sep 72.	(7") <0106> **BEST THING. / WHAT HAS COME BETWEEN US**		-	82
Jul 73.	(7") <0111> **I'M GONNA MAKE YOU FEEL IT. / QUICK IS THE BEAT OF MY HEART**		-	
Jul 73.	(lp) <BXLI 1012> **STYX II**		-	

– You need love / Lady / A day / You better ask / Little fugue in "G" / Father O.S.A. / Earl of Roseland / I'm gonna make you feel it. <re-dist.Jan75, hit US No.20> (UK-iss.Jul80 as 'LADY' on 'R.C.A.'; 3594)

			not iss.	Wooden Nickel
Sep 73.	(7") <0116> **LADY. / YOU BETTER ASK**		-	
Feb 74.	(lp) <BXLI 0287> **THE SERPENT IS RISING**		-	

– Witch wolf / The grove of Eglantine / Young man / As bad as this / Winner take all / 22 years / Jonas Psalter / The serpent is rising / Krakatoa / Hallelujah chorus. (UK-iss.Jul80 on 'R.C.A.'; 3595)

			not iss.	Wooden Nickel
Oct 74.	(7") <10027> **LIES. / 22 YEARS**		-	
Nov 74.	(lp) <BWLI 0638> **MAN OF MIRACLES**		-	

– Rock & roll feeling / Havin' a ball / Golden lark / A song for Suzanne / A man like me / Best thing / Evil eyes / Southern woman / Christopher Mr. Christopher. (UK-iss.Jul80 on 'R.C.A.'; 3596)

			R.C.A.	R.C.A.
Feb 75.	(7") (RCA 2518) <10102> **LADY. / CHILDREN OF THE LAND**		-	6 Dec74
Jul 75.	(7") <0252> **YOUNG MAN. / UNFINISHED SONG**		-	
May 75.	(7") <10272> **YOU NEED LOVE. / YOU BETTER ASK**		-	88
Nov 75.	(7") <10329> **BEST THING. / HAVIN' A BALL**		-	

			A&M	A&M
Feb 76.	(lp) (AMLH 64559) <4559> **EQUINOX**		-	58 Dec75

– Light up / Lorelei / Mother dear / Lonely child / Midnight ride / Born for adventure / Prelude 12 / Suite Madame Blue.

			A&M	A&M
Mar 76.	(7") (AMS 7220) <1786> **LORELEI. / MIDNIGHT RIDE**			27 Feb76
Jul 76.	(7") <1818> **LIGHT UP. / BORN FOR ADVENTURE**			

—— **TOMMY SHAW** (b.11 Sep'53, Montgomery, Alabama) – lead guitar repl. CURULEWSKI

Oct 76.	(lp) (AMLH 64604) <4604> **CRYSTAL BALL**			66

– Put me on / Mademoiselle / Jennifer / Crystal ball / Shooz / This old man / Clair de Lune – Ballerina.

Jan 77.	(7") (AMS 7273) <1877> **MADEMOISELLE. / LIGHT UP**			36 Nov76
Feb 77.	(7") <1900> **JENNIFER. / SHOOZ**			-
Jun 77.	(7") (AMS 7299) <1931> **CRYSTAL BALL. / PUT ME ON**			
Aug 77.	(lp/c) (AMLH/CAM 64637) <4637> **THE GRAND ILLUSION**			6 Jul77

– The grand illusion / Fooling yourself (the angry young man) / Superstars / Come sail away / Miss America / Man in the wilderness / Castle walls / The grand finale. (cd-iss.Jul87; CDA 3223)

Oct 77.	(7") (AMS 7321) <1977> **COME SAIL AWAY. / PUT ME ON**			8 Sep77
Mar 78.	(7") <2007> **FOOLING YOURSELF (THE ANGRY YOUNG MAN). / THE GRAND FINALE**			29 Feb78
Sep 78.	(lp/c)<US-pic-d> (AMLH/CAM 64724) <4724> **PIECES OF EIGHT**			6

– Great white hope / I'm O.K. / Sing for the day / The message / Lords of the ring / Blue collar man (long nights) / Queen of spades / Renegade / Pieces of eight / Aku-aku.

Oct 78.	(7"/12"colrd) (AMS/+P 7388) <2087> **BLUE COLLAR MAN (LONG NIGHTS). / SUPERSTARS**			21 Sep78
Mar 79.	(7",7"red) (AMS 7446) <2110> **RENEGADE. / SING FOR THE DAY**			16
				41
Sep 79.	(7") (AMS 7489) <2188> **BABE. / I'M OK**		6	1 Sep79
Jan 80.	(lp/c) (AMLK/CKM 63711) <3711> **CORNERSTONE**		36	2 Oct79

– Lights / Why me / Babe / Never say never / Boat on the river / Borrowed time / First time / Eddie / Love in the moonlight.

Dec 79.	(7") <2206> **WHY ME. / LIGHTS**		-	26
Mar 80.	(7") <2228> **BORROWED TIME. / EDDIE**		-	64
Mar 80.	(7") (AMS 7512) **BOAT ON THE RIVER. / COME SAIL AWAY**			-
May 80.	(7") (AMS 7528) **LIGHTS. / RENEGADE**			
Jan 81.	(lp/c) (AMLK/CKM 63719) <3719> **PARADISE THEATER**		8	1

– A.D. 1928 / Rockin' the Paradise / State street Sadie / Too much time on my hands / She cares / Snowblind / Nothing ever goes as planned / The best of times / Half-penny, two-penny / A.D. 1958. (cd-iss.Jun84; CDA 63719) (re-iss.Oct92 cd/c; CD/C MID 154)

Jan 81.	(7") (AMS 8102) <2300> **THE BEST OF TIMES. / LIGHT** (d-lazer-etched-7") – ('A'side) / PARADISE THEATER		42	3
Mar 81.	(7",7"colrd) (AMS 8118) <2323> **TOO MUCH TIME ON MY HANDS. / QUEEN OF SPADES**			9
Jul 81.	(7") <2348> **NOTHING EVER GOES AS PLANNED. / NEVER SAY NEVER**		-	54
Nov 81.	(7") (AMS 8175) **ROCKIN' THE PARADISE. / SNOWBLIND**		-	
Feb 83.	(lp/c) (AMLX/CAM 63734) <3734> **KILROY WAS HERE**		67	3

– Mr. Roboto / Cold war / Don't let it end / High time / Heavy metal poisoning / Just get through this night / Double life / Haven't we been here before / Don't let it end (reprise). (cd-iss.Apr84; CDA 63734)

Mar 83.	(7") (AMS 8308) <2525> **MR. ROBOTO. / SNOWBLIND**			3 Feb83
May 83.	(7"/7"sha-pic-d) (AM/+P 120) <2543> **DON'T LET IT END. / ROCKIN' THE PARADISE**		56	6 Apr83
Jun 83.	(7") <2560> **HAVEN'T WE BEEN HERE BEFORE. / DOUBLE LIFE**		-	
Aug 83.	(7") <2568> **HIGH TIME. / DOUBLE LIFE**		-	48
Apr 84.	(d-lp/d-c) (AMLH/CAM 66704) <6514> **CAUGHT IN THE ACT – LIVE** (live)		44	31

– Music time / Mr. Roboto / Too much time on my hands / Babe / Snowblind / The best of times / Suite Madame Blue / Rockin' the Paradise / Blue collar man (long night) / Miss America / Don't let it end / Fooling yourself (the angry young man) / Crystal ball / Come sail away.

May 84.	(7") (AM 197) <2625> **MUSIC TIME (live). / HEAVY METAL POISONING (live)**			40

—— the band rested activities while their main members DeYOUNG and SHAW went solo

—— STYX were back, although without SHAW (who joined DAMN YANKEES, and later SHAW BLADES), who was deposed by **GLEN BURTNIK** – lead guitar

Nov 90.	(cd/c/lp) (395327-2/-4/-1) <5327> **EDGE OF THE CENTURY**			63 Oct90

– Love is the ritual / Show me the way / Edge of the century / Love at first sight / All in a day's work / Not dead yet / World tonite / Carrie Ann / Homewrecker / Back to Chicago.

Dec 90.	(7"/7"pic-d) (AM/+X 709) <1525> **LOVE IS THE RITUAL. / HOMEWRECKER** (12"+=/cd-s+=) (AM Y/CD 709) – Babe.			80 Oct90
Feb 91.	(7"/c-s) <1536> **SHOW ME THE WAY. / BACK TO CHICAGO** (12"+=/cd-s+=) – Don't let it end.			3 Dec90
Mar 91.	(c-s,cd-s) <1548> **LOVE AT FIRST SIGHT / WORLD TONITE**		-	25

—— re-formed again with DeYOUNG, SHAW, YOUNG + PANOZZO

			S.P.V.	C.M.C.
Aug 98.	(d-cd) (SPV 0852918-2) <86212> **RETURN TO PARADISE** (live)			May97

– On my way / Paradise / Rockin' the paradise / Blue collar man / Lady / Too much time on my hands / Snowblind / Suite Madame blue / Crystal ball / The grand illusion / Foolish yourself (the angry young man) / Show me the way / Boat on the river / Lorelei / Babe / Miss America / Come sail away / Renegade / Best of times / Dear John.

– compilations, others, etc. –

Oct 79.	(lp/c) R.C.A.; (PL/PK 13116) <3597> **THE BEST OF STYX**			

– You need love / Lady / I'm gonna make you feel it / What has come between us / Southern woman / Rock & roll feeling / Winner take all / Best thing / Witch wolf / The grove of Eglantine / Man of miracles. (cd-iss. 1992; PD 83597)

Apr 78.	(7"ep) A&M; (AMS 7355) **MADEMOISELLE / COME SAIL AWAY. / CRYSTAL BALL / LORELEI**			-
1978.	(7") Wooden Nickel-RCA; <11205> **BEST THING. / WINNER TAKE ALL**		-	-
Sep 85.	(7") Old Gold; (OG 9545) **BABE. / THE BEST OF TIMES**		-	-
Jan 87.	(12"ep) Old Gold; (OG 4013) **BABE / THE BEST OF TIMES. / (2 by The Tubes)**		-	-
Apr 88.	(cd-ep) A&M; (AMCD 904) **COMPACT HITS**			

– Babe / Come sail away / Rockin' the Paradise / The best of times.

May 95.	(cd) A&M; (396959-2) **BOAT ON THE RIVER**			
Jul 97.	(cd) A&M; (540465-2) **THE BEST OF TIMES – THE BEST OF STYX**			

SUBLIME

Formed: Long Beach, California, USA ... 1988 by BRAD NOWELL, ERIC WILSON and FLOYD 'BUD' GAUGH. Signing to M.C.A. off-shoot 'Gasoline Alley', two albums passed virtually unoticed until the untimely drugs death of BRADLEY on 25th of May '96; at least they made it on to MTV while also gaining US radio play for the single, 'WHAT I GOT'. This became a minor hit, a ska-punk semi-classic which only served to underline what might've been, the accompanying eponymous third set going on to sell over two million copies Stateside. • **Songwriters:** NOWELL except RIVERS OF BABYLON

(Brent Dowe & James McNaughton; hit for Boney M) / TRENCHTOWN ROCK (Bob Marley). • **Trivia:** NO DOUBT's GWEN STEFANI guested on the track, 'SAW RED'. • **Note:** Don't get confused with UK group of the late 80's and another dance-orientated outfit from '93.

Album rating: 40 oz. TO FREEDOM (*5) / ROBBIN' THE HOOD (*6) / SUBLIME (*7) / SECOND-HAND SMOKE posthumous (*5) / SUBLIME LIVE – STAND BY YOUR VAN (*4) / ACOUSTIC: BRADLEY NOWELL (*4) / GREATEST HITS compilation (*6)

BRAD NOWELL (b. 1968) – vocals, guitar / **ERIC WILSON** – bass / **BUD** (b. FLOYD GAUGH) – drums

		not iss.	Gasoline Alley
1993.	(cd) <GASD 11413> **40oz TO FREEDOM**	-	

– What I got / Pawn shop / Same in the end / Caress me down / Doin' time / April 29, 1992 (Miami) / Ballad of Johnny Butt / Burritos / Garden grove / Seed / Paddle out / Under my voodoo / Get ready / Jailhouse / Santeria / What I got (reprise). <re-iss. mid-96 as 'SUBLIME' hit US No.13> (UK-iss.Jan98; same)

1994.	(cd) <GASD 11475> **ROBBIN' THE HOOD**	-	

– Waiting for Bud / Steady B loop dub / Raleigh sililoquy part I / Pool shark / Steppin' razor / Greatest-hits / Free loop dub / Q-ball / Saw red / The work that we do / Lincoln highway dub / Pool shark / Cisco kid / Raleigh soliloquy part II / S.T.P. / Boss D.J. / I don't care too much for reggae / Falling idols / All you need / Freeway time in la county jail / Mary / Raleigh soliloquy part III. (UK-iss.Jan98; same)

—— tragically, BRAD died of a heroin overdose on 25th May '96 leaving behind a wife, a child and their final recordings below.

		M.C.A.	Gasoline Alley
Jun 97.	(7"yellow/c-s) <MCS/+C 48045> **WHAT I GOT (Super No Mofo edit). / RIVERS OF BABYLON**	71	-

(cd-s+=) <MCSTD 48045> – All you need / What I got (reprise).

Sep 97.	(m-cd) <GASD 11678> **WHAT I GOT . . . THE 7 SONG EP**	-	

– What I got / 40 oz. to freedom / D.J.S. / All you need / Same in the end / The work that we do / Doin' time.

Nov 97.	(cd/c) <GAS D/C 11714> **SECOND-HAND SMOKE** (collection of out-takes)	-	28

– Doin' time / Get out! / Romeo / New realization / Don't push / Slow ride / Chick on my tip / Had a date / Trenchtown rock / Badfish / Drunk drivin' / Saw red / Garbage grove / April 29th, 1992 / Superstar punami / Legal dub / What's really goin' wrong / Doin' time / Thanx dub.

Dec 97.	(cd-ep) <55390> **DOIN' TIME /**	-	87
Jun 98.	(cd/c) <GAS D/C 11798> **STAND BY YOUR VAN: SUBLIME LIVE . . . (live)**	-	49

– Don't push / Right back / New thrash / Let's go get stoned / Greatest hits / Date rape / S.T.P. / Badfish / D.J.S. / The work that we do / Pool shark / Ebin / All you need / Waiting for my Ruca / Caress me down / KRS-One.

Nov 98.	(cd) <11889> **ACOUSTIC: BRADLEY NOWELL & FRIENDS**	-	

– Wrong way / Saw red / Foolish fool / Don't push / Mary / Big salty tears / Boss D.J. / Garden grove / Rivers of Babylon / Little district / KRS-One / Marley medley: Guava jelly – This train / What happened / The eye of Fatima / Freeway time in L.A. county jail / Pool shark / It's who you know.

Nov 99.	(cd/c) <12125> **GREATEST HITS** (compilation)	-	

– What I got / The wrong way / Santeria / 40 oz. to freedom / Smoke two joints / Date rape / Saw red / Badfish / Doin' time / Poolshark.

SUEDE

Formed: London, England . . . 1989 by BRETT ANDERSON, who, by 1992 had put together the final line-up of guitarist BERNARD BUTLER, bassist MATT OSMAN and drummer SIMON GILBERT (ELASTICA prime mover, JUSTINE FRISCHMANN, had also been an early member). After a single, 'BE MY GOD' / 'ART', failed to appear in 1990 on 'RML' (this lost recording was famous for featuring ex-SMITHS drummer, MIKE JOYCE), the band signed to 'Nude', precipitating a storm of media hype and adulation. Featured on the cover of NME before they had even released their debut single, the band became press darlings of a post-grunge/pre-Brit pop music scene desperate for a bit of cheap glamour. Widely touted as spiritual antecedents of The SMITHS, the group were actually closer in style to the camp affectations of mid-period BOWIE, although there was definitely a MORRISSEY-like archness to the lyrics, the glum one actually taking to covering 'MY INSATIABLE ONE' (the B-side of SUEDE's acclaimed debut effort, 'THE DROWNERS') live. Another couple of singles followed, 'METAL MICKEY' and 'ANIMAL NITRATE', these scoring successively higher chart positions. The media support, together with ANDERSON's sleazy, androgynous posturing, made him, and his band, instant heroes for a new generation of crazy, mixed up kids, the eponymous 1993 debut album quickly reaching No.1. 'Nude's takeover by 'Sony' in early that year gave the act a bit of major label muscle, ironically helping them on their way to becoming one of the biggest "indie" bands in Britain. At the beginning of '94, the band scored their biggest hit single to date with the epic 'STAY TOGETHER', the track peaking at No.3. Later that Spring, gay drummer SIMON bravely went to the House Of Commons to air his views on the homosexual laws of consent, which were to be lowered from 21 to either 16 (the heterosexual age) or 18, as it finally turned out. Around the same time, more controversy dogged the group when an American jazz singer called SUEDE won her lawsuit against the band in the US, the upshot of the affair being that from that point on, the band were to be known in America as LONDON SUEDE (lucky for them they didn't come from Leatherhead!). Meantime, the group had won the Mercury Music Prize for their acclaimed debut album and were well on the way to releasing a follow-up, 'DOG MAN STAR' (1994). The last album to feature the departing BUTLER (heralded by some as the UK's most promising guitarist since JOHNNY MARR, BUTLER subsequently went on to a successful, if short lived, collaboration with DAVID

McALMONT before signing to 'Creation' and embarking on a solo career), it marked something of a departure in the band's sound, a dense, ambitious set which met with a mixed critical reception. Unbowed, SUEDE swaggered on, recruiting the teenage RICHARD OAKES as BUTLER's replacement and providing a welcome diversion from the laddish excesses of Brit-pop. SUEDE's next effort, 'COMING UP' proved to be their most consistent set to date, spawning the brilliant lowlife anthem, 'TRASH' along with the similarly infectious, organic glam of 'FILMSTAR' and the dislocated melancholy of 'SATURDAY NIGHT'. A stop-gap but worthy collection of rarities and B-sides, 'SCI-FI LULLABIES' (1997) marked time before their return in the Spring of '99. 'ELECTRICITY' sparked off proceedings, the UK Top 5 single also the opening track on their No.1 Steve Osborne-produced 4th album proper, 'HEAD MUSIC' (1999). Three other retro-fied 45's ('SHE'S IN FASHION', 'EVERYTHING WILL FLOW' and 'CAN'T GET ENOUGH') were delivered to an eager kitsch fanbase who were still "into" all things glam:- BOWIE, ROXY, NUMAN, HUMAN . . . • **Songwriters:** ANDERSON / BUTLER, except; BRASS IN POCKET (Pretenders).

Album rating: SUEDE (*8) / DOG MAN STAR (*7) / COMING UP (*7) / SCI-FI LULLABIES collection (*6) / HEAD MUSIC (*7)

BRETT ANDERSON (b.27 Sep'67, Haywards Heath, Sussex, England) – vocals / **BERNARD BUTLER** (b. 1 May'70) – guitar, piano / **MATT OSMAN** (b. 9 Oct'67) – bass / **SIMON GILBERT** (b.23 May'65) – drums

		Nude	not iss.
Apr 92.	(7") (nud 1s) **THE DROWNERS. / TO THE BIRDS**	49	-

(12"+=/cd-s+=) (nud 1 t/cd) – My insatiable one.

Sep 92.	(7"/c-s) (nud 3 s/mc) **METAL MICKEY. / WHERE THE PIGS DON'T FLY**	17	-

(12"+=/cd-s+=) (NUD 3 t/cd) – He's dead.

		Nude-Sony	Columbia
Feb 93.	(7"/c-s) (NUD 4 s/mc) **ANIMAL NITRATE. / THE BIG TIME**	7	-

(12"+=/cd-s+=) (nud 4 t/cd) – Painted people.

Apr 93.	(cd/c/lp) (NUD 1 cd/mc/lp) <53792> **SUEDE**	1	

– So young / Animal nitrate / She's not dead / Moving / Pantomime horse / The drowners / Sleeping pills / Breakdown / Metal Mickey / Animal lover / The next life.

May 93.	(7"/c-s) (nud 5 s/mc) **SO YOUNG. / HIGH RISING**	22	-

(12"+=/cd-s+=) (nud 5 t/cd) – Dolly.

Sep 93.	(cd-ep) <44K 77172> **THE DROWNERS / MY INSATIABLE ONE / TO THE BIRDS / THE BIG TIME / HE'S DEAD** (live)	-	
Feb 94.	(7"/c-s) (nud 9 s/mc) **STAY TOGETHER. / THE LIVING DEAD**	3	-

(ext;12"+=/cd-s+=) (nud 9 t/cd) – My dark star.

—— In Spring 1994, gay drummer SIMON went to House Of Commons, to air his views on the homosexual laws of consent, which were to be lowered from 21 to either 16 (the heterosexual age) or 18, as it turned out to be. Around the same time, an American jazz singer called SUEDE won her lawsuit against the band in the US. They are now to be called LONDON SUEDE, but thankfully only in the States.

Mar 94.	(cd-ep) <CK 64382> **STAY TOGETHER / THE LIVING DEAD / MY DARK STAR / DOLLY HIGH RISING / STAY TOGETHER (extended)**	-	
Sep 94.	(7"/c-s) (nud 10 s/mc) **WE ARE THE PIGS. / KILLING OF A FLASH BOY**	18	-

(12"+=/cd-s+=) (nud 10 t/cd) – Whipsnade.

Oct 94.	(cd/c/d-lp) (nude 3 cd/mc/lp) <66769> **DOG MAN STAR**	3	

– Introducing the band / We are the pigs / Heroine / The wild ones / Daddy's speeding / The power / New generation / This Hollywood life / The 2 of us / Black or blue / The asphalt world / Still life. <US-version +=> – Modern boys.

—— BUTLER left July '94 and was repl. by 17 year-old **RICHARD OAKES** after recording album.

Nov 94.	(c-s) (nud 11mc) **THE WILD ONES / MODERN BOYS**	18	-

(cd-s+=) (nud 11cd1) – This world needs a father.
(12") (nud 11t) – ('A'side) / Eno's introducing the band.
(cd-s) (nud 11cd2) – (above 2) / Asda town.

Jan 95.	(7"/c-s) (nud 12mc) **NEW GENERATION. / TOGETHER**	21	-

(12"+=/cd-s+=) (nud 12 t/cd) – Bentswood boys.
(cd-s) (nud 12cd2) – ('A'side) / Animal nitrate (live) / The wild ones (live) / Pantomime horse (live).

—— added new member **NEIL CODLING** – keyboards, vocals

Jul 96.	(c-s) (nud 2mc) **TRASH / EUROPE IS OUR PLAYGROUND**	3	-

(cd-s+=) (nud 21cd1) – Every Monday morning comes.
(pic-cd-s) (nud 21cd2) – ('A'side) / Have you ever been this low? / Another no one.

Sep 96.	(cd/c/lp) (nude 6 cd/mc/lp) <67911> **COMING UP**	1	

– Trash / Filmstar / Lazy / By the sea / She / Beautiful ones / Starcrazy / Picnic by the motorway / The chemistry between us / Saturday night.

Oct 96.	(c-s) (nud 23mc) **BEAUTIFUL ONES / BY THE SEA (demo)**	8	-

(cd-s) (nud 23 cd1) – Young men / The sound of the streets.
(cd-s) (nud 23 cd2) – ('A'side) / Money / Sam.

Jan 97.	(c-s) (nud 24mc) **SATURDAY NIGHT / PICNIC BY THE MOTORWAY (live)**	6	-

(cd-s) (nud 24cd1) – ('A'side) / W.S.D. / Jumble sale mums.
(cd-s) (nud 24cd2) – ('A'side) / This time / ('A'demo).
(d7") (nud 24s) – ('A'side) / This time / Beautiful ones / The sound of the streets.

Apr 97.	(c-s) (nud 27mc) **LAZY / SHE (live)**	9	-

(cd-s) (nud 27cd1) – ('A'side) / These are the sad songs / Feel.
(cd-s) (nud 27cd2) – ('A'side) / Sadie / Digging a hole.

Aug 97.	(7") (nud 30s) **FILMSTAR / ('A'original demo)**	9	-

(cd-s) (nud 30cd1) – ('A'side) / Graffiti women / Duchess. (w/ free video footage; Beautiful ones / Coming up.
(cd-s) (nud 30cd2) – ('A'side) / Rent / Saturday night / Saturday night (cd-rom).

Oct 97.	(d-cd) (nude 9cd) <68857> **SCI-FI LULLABIES** (flipsides)	9	

– My insatiable one / To the birds / Where the pigs don't fly / He's dead / The big time / High rising / The living dead / My star / Killing of a flash boy / Whipsnade / Modern boys / Together / Bentswood boys / Europe is our playground // Every Monday morning comes / Have you ever been this low? / Another no one / Young men / The sound of the streets / Money / W.S.D. / This time / Jumble sale mums / These are the sad songs / Sadie / Graffiti women / Duchess.

Apr 99. (c-s) *(NUD 43MC)* **ELECTRICITY / IMPLIMENT, YEAH!** | 5 | - |
(cd-s) *(NUD 43CD1)* – ('A'side) / Popstar / Killer.
(cd-s) *(NUD 43CD2)* – ('A'side) / See that girl / Waterloo.

May 99. (cd/c/d-lp) *(NUDE 14 CD/MC/LP)* **HEAD MUSIC** | 1 | |
– Electricity / Savoir faire / Can't get enough / Everything will flow / Down / She's in fashion / Asbestos / Head music / Elephant man / Hi-fi / Indian strings / He's gone / Crack in the Union Jack.

Jun 99. (c-s) *(NUD 44MC)* **SHE'S IN FASHION / DOWN (demo)** | 13 | - |
(cd-s) *(NUD 44CD1)* – ('A'side) / Bored / Pieces of my mind.
(cd-s) *(NUD 44CD2)* – ('A'side) / Jubilee / God's gift.

Sep 99. (c-s) *(NUD 45MC)* **EVERYTHING WILL FLOW / BEAUTIFUL ONES (live)** | 24 | - |
(cd-s) *(NUD 45CD1)* – ('A'side) / Weight of the world / Leaving.
(cd-s) *(NUD 45CD2)* – ('A'side) / Crackhead / Seascape.

Nov 99. (cd-s) *(NUD 47CD1)* **CAN'T GET ENOUGH / LET GO / SINCE YOU WENT AWAY** | 23 | |
(cd-s) *(NUD 47CD2)* – ('A'side) / Situations / Read my mind.
(cd-s) *(NUD 47CD3)* – ('A'side) / Everything will flow (Rollo's vocal mix) / She's in fashion (Lironi version) / ('A'-CD video).

SUGAR

Formed: Minneapolis, USA . . . 1992 by former HUSKER DU frontman/co-writer, BOB MOULD. Upon the demise of the latter act in 1987, MOULD signed to 'Virgin America' and subsequently entered PRINCE's 'Paisley Park' studios to lay down his first solo set, 'WORKBOOK' (1989). Augmented by the former PERE UBU rhythm section of ANTON FIER and TONY MAIMONE and employing cellists JANE SCARPANTONI and STEVE HAIGLER, MOULD confounded expectations with a largely acoustic affair trading in melodic distortion for fragments of contemplative melancholy; only the closing 'WHICHEVER WAY THE WIND BLOWS' acknowledged the sonic assault of prime HUSKER DU. Despite the guaranteed critical plaudits and the more accessible nature of the material, 'WORKBOOK's sales were modest. Perhaps as a reaction, the following year's 'BLACK SHEETS OF RAIN' – again recorded with FIER and MAIMONE – was a searing return to bleaker, noisier pastures; 'HANGING TREE' remains among the most tormented work of MOULD's career, while the likes of 'HEAR ME CALLING' and 'IT'S TOO LATE' combined keening melody with blistering soloing/discordant riffing in patented MOULD fashion. When this album also failed to take off, the singer parted comapny from 'Virgin' and undertook a low-key acoustic tour. His wilderness period was brief, however, the emerging grunge vanguard citing HUSKER DU as a massive influence and inspiring MOULD to form another melodic power trio. Comprising fellow songwriter/bassist, DAVE BARBE and drummer MALCOLM TRAVIS, SUGAR signed to 'Creation' and proceeded to cut one of the most feted albums of the era in 'COPPER BLUE' (1992). Leaner, tighter and cleaner, the record's bittersweet pop-hardcore crunch finally provided MOULD with a springboard for commercial success; a UK Top 10 hit, the album even spawned a Top 30 hit single in the sublime 'IF I CAN'T CHANGE YOUR MIND'. 'BEASTER', 1993's mini-album follow-up, took tracks from the 'COPPER BLUE' sessions and buried them in a multi-layered blanket of howling distortion. Unsurprisingly it failed to spawn a hit, although its Top 3 success was no doubt sweet for the ever contrary MOULD, his follow-up proper, 'FILE UNDER EASY LISTENING (F.U.E.L.)' (1994), suggesting that he'd become bored with the whole concept. MOULD eventually disbanded the project in Spring '96, releasing a third solo album the same year, simply titled 'BOB MOULD'. • **Songwriters:** MOULD and now some with others. Covered; SHOOT OUT THE LIGHTS (Richard Thompson).

Album rating: Bob Mould: WORKBOOK (*7) / BLACK SHEETS OF RAIN (*6) / Sugar: COPPER BLUE (*9) / BEASTER mini (*7) / FILE UNDER: EASY LISTENING (*7) / BESIDES collection (*6) / Bob Mould: BOB MOULD (*8) / THE LAST DOG AND PONY SHOW (*7)

BOB MOULD

BOB MOULD – vocals, guitar, etc (ex-HUSKER DU) / with **ANTON FIER** – drums / **TONY MAIMONE** – bass, (both ex-PERE UBU) / **JANE SCARPANTONI** – cello (of TINY LIGHTS) / **STEVE HAIGLER** – cello

		Virgin	Virgin
Jun 89. (7") *(VUS 2)* **SEE A LITTLE LIGHT. / ALL THOSE PEOPLE KNOW**			-

(12"+=/cd-s+=) *(VUS 2T/CD2)* – Shoot out the lights / Composition for the young and the old (live).

Jul 89. (lp/cd) *(VUS LP/CD 2)* <91240> **WORKBOOK** | | Apr89 |
– Sunspots / Wishing well / Heartbreak a stranger / See a little light / Poison years / Sinners and their repentances / Lonely afternoon / Brasilia crossed the Tranton / Compositions for the young and old / Dreaming, I amd / Whichever way the wind blows. *(re-iss. Sep90; OVED 340)*

Aug 90. (cd/c/lp) *(VUS CD/MC/LP 21)* <91395> **BLACK SHEETS OF RAIN** | | May90 |
– Black sheets of rain / Stand guard / It's too late / One good reason / Stop your crying / Hanging tree / The last night / Hear me calling / Out of your life / Disappointed / Sacrifice – let there be peace.

		Virgin	Virgin
May 94. (cd) *(CDVM 9030)* <39587> **THE POISON YEARS** (compilation from first two sets)			Jul94

SUGAR

BOB MOULD – vox, guitar, keyboards, percussion / **DAVE BARBE** – bass (ex-MERCYLAND) / **MALCOLM TRAVIS** – drums, percussion (ex-ZULUS)

		Creation	Rykodisc
Jul 92. (cd-ep) *<1024>* **HELPLESS / NEEDLE HITS E / IF I CAN'T CHANGE YOUR MIND / TRY AGAIN**		-	
Aug 92. (12"ep)(cd-ep) *(CRE 126T)(CRESCD 126)* **CHANGES / NEEDLE HITS E. / IF I CAN'T CHANGE YOUR MIND / TRY AGAIN**			
Sep 92. (cd/lp)(c) *(CRE CD/LP 129)(C-CRE 129)* <RCD/RACS 10239> **COPPER BLUE**	10		

– The act we act / A good idea / Changes / Helpless / Hoover dam / The slim / If I can't change your mind / Fortune teller / Slick / Man on the Moon.

Oct 92. (7"ep/c-ep) *(CRE/+CS 143)* <1030> **A GOOD IDEA. / WHERE DIAMONDS ARE HALOS / SLICK** | 65 | |
(12"ep+=)(cd-ep+=) *(CRE 143T)(CRESCD 143)* – Armenia city in the sky.

Jan 93. (7"/c-s) *(CRE/+CS 149)* **IF I CAN'T CHANGE YOUR MIND. / CLOWN MASTER** | 30 | |
(12"+=) *(CRE 149T)* <1031> – Anyone (live) / Hoover dam (live).
(cd-s) *(CRESCD 149)* <1032> – ('A'side) / The slim / Where diamonds are halos.

Apr 93. (m-cd/m-lp)(m-c) *(CRE CD/LP 153)(C-CRE 153)* <50260> **BEASTER** | 3 | |
– Come around / Tilted / Judas cradle / JC auto / Feeling better / Walking away.

Aug 93. (7") *(CRE 156)* **TILTED. / JC AUTO (live)** | 48 | - |

Aug 94. (7"/c-s) *(CRE/+CS 186)* **YOUR FAVORITE THING. / MIND IS AN ISLAND** | 40 | |
(12"+=)(cd-s+=) *(CRE 186T)(CRESCD 186)* <1038> – Frustration / And you tell me (T.V. mix).

Sep 94. (cd/lp)(c) *(CRE CD/LP 172)(C-CRE 172)* <10300> **FILE UNDER EASY LISTENING (F.U.E.L.)** | 7 | 50 |
– Gift / Company book / Your favorite thing / What you want it to be / Gee angel / Panama city hotel / Can't help it anymore / Granny cool / Believe what you're saying / Explode and make up.

Oct 94. (7"/c-s) *(CRE/+CS 193)* **BELIEVE WHAT YOU'RE SAYING. / GOING HOME** | 73 | |
(cd-s+=) *(CRESCD 193)* <1039> – In the eyes of my friends / And you tell me.

Dec 94. (cd-ep) *<RCD5 1040>* **GEE ANGEL / EXPLODE AND MAKE UP / SLIM / AFTER ALL THE ROADS HAVE LED TO . . .** | - | |

Jul 95. (d-cd) *<10321>* **BESIDES** (compilation of b-sides, live, etc) | - | |

disbanded and BARBE formed BUZZHUNGRY / TRAVIS went to CUSTOMIZED

BOB MOULD

		Creation	Rykodisc
Apr 96. (cd/lp) *(CRE CD/LP 188)* <10342> **BOB MOULD**			

– Anymore time between / I hate alternative rock / Fort Knox, King Solomon / Next time that you leave / Egoverride / Thumbtack / Hair stew / Hair stew / Deep karma canyon / Art crisis / Roll over and die.

now with **MATT HAMMON** – drums / **ALISON CHESLEY** – cello

Aug 98. (7") *(CRE 206)* **CLASSIFIEDS. / MOVING TRUCKS** | | - |
Aug 98. (cd/lp) *(CRE CD/LP 215)* <10443> **THE LAST DOG AND PONY SHOW** | 58 | |
– New #1 / Moving trucks / Taking everything / First drag of the day / Classifieds / Who was around? / Skintrade / Vaporub / Sweet serene / Megamaniac / Reflecting pool / Along the way / (interview).

SUGARCUBES (see under ⇒ BJORK)

SUGAR RAY

Formed: Los Angeles, California, USA . . . 1989 out of cover outfit The SHRINKY DINX by MARK McGRATH (of Irish parentage), RODNEY SHEPPARD, MURPHY KARGES, STAN FRAZIER and DJ HOMOCIDE (aka CRAIG BULLOCK). Signed to Atlantic offshoot label 'Lava' in 1994, this dayglo bunch of funky pop-metal funsters debuted the following year with the 'LEMONADE & BROWNIES' set. While that record hinted at an endearing BEASTIES-esque charm, the group only really hit their saucy stride on follow-up set, 'FLOORED' (1997). Trading in hood-down, shout-along metal/rap with a winking undercurrent of dancefloor cheesiness, the record didn't come within a whisker of taking itself seriously (on the majority of tracks anyhow), stretching the limits of good natured fun with a cover of 'STAND AND DELIVER' (Adam & The Ants). While the album received encouraging reviews and the 'FLY' single was an MTV favourite, SUGAR RAY had still to capture the hearts (and groins) of the rock scene at large. Kicking off 1999 with a proverbial bang and now complete with sneakers and loud shirts, SUGAR RAY had a couple of massive American hits beginning with 'EVERY MORNING'. Taken from their sunkissed album, '14:59' (which also contained second Top 10'er, 'SOMEDAY'), the band could do no wrong. For now! • **Covered:** ABRACADABRA (Steve Miller Band).

Album rating: LEMONADE & BROWNIES (*6) / FLOORED (*6) / 14:59 (*6)

MARK McGRATH (b.1969) – vocals / **RODNEY SHEPPARD** (b.1966) – guitar / **MURPHY KARGES** (b.1966) – bass (ex-WEIRDOS) / **STAN FRAZIER** (b. CHARLES STANTON FRAZIER, 1968) – drums / **DJ HOMOCIDE** (b. CRAIG BULLOCK, 1971) – turntables (ex-ALCHOLIKS)

		Atlantic	Atlantic
Aug 95. (7"/c-s) *(A 7143/+C)* **MEAN MACHINE. / WANGO TANGO**			

(cd-s+=) *(A 7143CD)* – White minority / Wasted. *(re-iss. May96; same)*

Sep 95. (cd) <*(7567 82743-2)*> **LEMONADE & BROWNIES** | | |
– Snug harbor / Iron mic / Rhyme stealer / Hold your eyes / Big black woman /

Dance party USA / Danzig needs a hug / 10 seconds down / Streaker / Scuzzboots / Caboose / Drive by / Mean machine / Greatest.

Feb 96. (7"/c-s) (A 7111/+C) **IRON MIC. / CABOOSE**
(cd-s+=) (A 7111CD) – Mean machine (live) / Dr J (live).

Aug 97. (cd) (7567 83006-2) **FLOORED** | 12 | Jun97
– R.P.M. / Breathe / Anyone / Fly / Speed home California / High anxiety / Tap, twist, snap / American pig / Stand and deliver / Cash / Invisible / Right direction / Fly (reprise).

Jan 98. (7"/c-s+C) **FLY. / FLY (rock)** | 58 |
(cd-s+=) (AT 008CD) – Tap, twist, snap.

May 99. (c-s/cd-s) (AT 0065 C/CD) **EVERY MORNING / RIVERS / AIM FOR ME** | 10 | 3 | Jan99

Jun 99. (cd/c) (<7567 83151-2/-4)> **14:59** | 60 | 17 | Jan99
– New direction / Every morning / Falls apart / Personal space invader / Live and direct / Someday / Aim for me / Ode to the lonely hearted / Burning dog / Even though / Abracadabra / Glory.

Oct 99. (c-s) (AT 0071C) <84536> **SOMEDAY / EVERY MORNING (acoustic)** | 7 | Jun99
(cd-s) (AT 0071CD) – ('A'acoustic).

SUGGS (see under ⇒ MADNESS)

SUICIDAL TENDENCIES
(dig out; 4th edition or Great Alt & Indie . . .)

SUICIDE

Formed: New York, USA . . . 1971 by ALAN VEGA and ex-jazz band organist MARTIN REV. After a series of sporadic, performance art-style gigs in the early 70's, the duo laid low until the emergence of the CBGB's punk/new wave scene a few years later. Signed to US independent, 'Red Star' (run by Marty Thau, former manager of The NEW YORK DOLLS), the duo released one of the most influential records of the era in 1977's eponymous 'SUICIDE'. Delivering shock screams and whispered goth-rockabilly vocals over brooding, churning Farfisa organ, the duo laid the foundations for the industrial/electro experimentation of the following decade and in 'ROCKET U.S.A.' and 'FRANKIE TEARDROPS', penned two of the most compelling compositions in the NY avant-garde pantheon. Now almost universally heralded as being ahead of their time, punters of the day weren't always so appreciative; SUICIDE performances were infamous for audience stand-off's, a tour with the CLASH running into trouble while a gig in Belgium ended in a full-on riot (the same gig documented on the 1978 "official bootleg", '24 MINUTES OVER BRUSSELS'). Unperturbed, the pair moved to 'Ze' records ('Island' in the UK) and recorded a follow-up, 'ALAN VEGA / MARTIN REV – SUICIDE' (1980). Produced by CARS mainman, RIC OCASEK, the record presented a slightly more palatable version of SUICIDE's patented synth apocalypse, although sales remained minimal. Subsequently embarking on solo careers, the pair met with little more than cult success, although VEGA's eponymous 1980 solo debut spawned a Top 5 hit in France, 'JUKEBOX BABE'. Following his eponymous 1980 solo debut, REV devoted his time to sculpture with his work exhibited in 1982-83. VEGA continued working with OCASEK, also bringing in a young AL JOURGENSEN (later of MINISTRY fame) for 1983's 'SATURN STRIP' (featuring an unlikely but entertaining cover of Hot Chocolate's 'EVERYONE'S A WINNER') and guesting for SISTERS OF MERCY re-incarnation, The SISTERHOOD in 1986. VEGA and REV eventually reformed SUICIDE in 1988 and recorded 'A WAY OF LIFE' (1989) for 'Wax Trax!' (licensed to 'Chapter 22' in the UK), a label heavily indebted to the duo's pioneering electronics. With the album afforded little interest, VEGA resumed his solo activites on through the 90's, collaborating with STEPHEN LIRONI on his REVOLUTIONARY CORPS OF TEENAGE JESUS project and also ALEX CHILTON on their 1997 set, 'Cubist Blues'. Ironically, there's been something of an upsurge of interest in SUICIDE of late, the duo receiving renewed press attention after their performances with critical darlings SPRITUALIZED.

Album rating: SUICIDE (*8) / ALAN VEGA – MARTIN REV (*5) / HALF ALIVE exploitation (*6) / GHOST RIDERS exploitation (*5) / A WAY OF LIFE (*7) / Y.B. BLUE (*4) / Alan Vega: ALAN VEGA (*4) / COLLISION DRIVE (*5) / SATURN STRIP (*7) / JUST A MILLION DREAMS (*4) / DEUCE AVENUE (*5) / POWER ON TO ZERO HOUR (*4) / NEW RACEION (*4) / DUJANG PRANG (*3) / CUBIST BLUES with Alex Chilton & Ben Vaughn (*5)

ALAN VEGA (b. 1948) – vocals / **MARTIN REV** – keyboards, percussion

	Bronze	Red Star

Nov 77. (lp) (BRON 508) <RS 1> **SUICIDE**
– Ghost rider / Rocket U.S.A. / Cheree / Frankie Teardrops / Johnny / Girl / Che.
(re-iss. Sep86 on 'Demon'; FIEND 74) (cd-iss. Jun88; FIENDCD 74)

Jul 78. (7",12") (BRO 57) **CHEREE. / I REMEMBER**
(re-iss.Nov86 on 'Demon' 12"; D 1046T)

1978. (lp-ltd; official bootleg) (FRANKIE 1) **24 MINUTES OVER BRUSSELS (live)**

	Island	Ze

Nov 79. (ext.12"/7") (12+/WIP 6543) **DREAM BABY DREAM. / RADIATION**

May 80. (lp) (ILPS 7007) <7080> **ALAN VEGA / MARTIN REV - SUICIDE**
– Diamonds, furcoats, champagne / Mr. Ray / Sweetheart / Fast money music / Touch me / Harlem / Be bop kid / Las Vegas man / Shadazz / Dance.

—— Split partnership in the early 80's and both went solo.

ALAN VEGA
with **PHIL HAWK** – guitar

	not iss.	P.V.C.

1980. (lp) <PVC 7915> **ALAN VEGA**
– Jukebox babe / Fireball / Kung Foo cowboy / Love cry / Speedway / Ice drummer / Bye bye bayou / Lonely.

—— w/band 81-83 **MARK KUGH** – guitar / **LARRY CHAPLAN** – bass / **SESU COLEMAN** – drums

	Island	Island

Nov 81. (lp) <(ILPS 9692)> **COLLISION DRIVE**
– Magdalena 82 / Be bop a lula / Outlaw / Raver / Ghost rider / I believe / Magdalena 83 / Rebel / Viet vet.

Nov 81. (ext.12"/7") (12+/WIP 6744) **JUKEBOX BABE. / LONELY**

—— added **AL JOURGENSEN** – keyboards (of MINISTRY) / **STEPHEN GEORGE** – drums / **GREG HAWKES** – synth, sax (of CARS) / **RIC OCASEK** – guitar, producer (of CARS)

	Elektra	Elektra

Sep 83. (lp) (K 960259-1) <60259-1> **SATURN STRIP**
– Saturn drive / Video babe / American dreamer / Wipeout beat / Je t'adore / Angel / Kid Congo / Goodbye darling / Every 1's a winner.

—— retained OCASEK + added **KENNAN KEATING** – guitar / **CHRIS LORD** – synth

Oct 85. (7") (EKR 24) **ON THE RUN. / CRY FIRE**
(12"+=) (EKR 24T) – Rah rah baby.

Dec 85. (lp/c) (EKT 15/+C) <60434-1/-4> **JUST A MILLION DREAMS**
– On the run / Shooting for you / Hot fox / Too late / Wild heart / Creation / Cry fire / Ra ra baby.

—— In 1986, VEGA guested for SISTERS OF MERCY re-incarnation, SISTERHOOD

MARTIN REV

	not iss.	Infidelity

Feb 80. (lp) <228> **MARTIN REV**
– Mari / Baby o baby / Nineteen 86 / Temptation / Jomo / Asia.

	New Rose	Red Star

Mar 85. (lp) (ROSE 52) **CLOUDS OF GLORY**
– Rodeo / Clouds of glory / Metatron / Whisper / Rocking horse / Parade / Island.
(cd-iss. 1997 on 'Mau Mau'; MAUCD 648)

SUICIDE
re-formed in 1988

	Chapter 22	Wax Trax!

Jan 89. (lp/cd) (CHAP LP/CD 35) <WAX/+CS/CD 7072> **A WAY OF LIFE**
– Wild in blue / Surrender / Jukebox baby 96 / Rain of ruin / Sufferin' in vain / Dominic Christ / Love so lonely / Devastation.

Feb 89. (12") (12CHAP 36) **RAIN OF RUIN. / SURRENDER**

	Brake Out	Brake Out

Jun 92. (cd) <(OUT 108-2)> **Y B BLUE**
– Why be blue / Cheat-cheat / Hot ticket / Universe / The last time / Play the dream / Pump it / Flashy love / Chewy-chewy / Mujo.

ALAN VEGA
returned to solo work for the 90's. **LIZ LAMERA** – drums

	Chapter 22	Infinite Zero

Feb 90. (cd/lp) (CHAP CD/LP 45) <43032> **DEUCE AVENUE**
– Body bop jive / Sneaker gun fire / Jab Gee / Bad scene / La la bola / Deuce avenue / Faster blaster / Sugee / Sweet sweet money / Love on / No tomorrow / Future sex.
(re-iss. Jun90 on 'Musicdisc' cd/c/lp; 10558-2/-4/-1)

	Musidisc	Warners

Jul 91. (cd/c/lp) (10812-2/-4/-1) <43027> **POWER ON TO ZERO HOUR**
– Bring in the year 2000 / Sucker / Fear / Doomo dance / Automatic terror / Jungle justice / Full force of them nuclear shoes / Believe it / Cry a sea of tears / Quasi.

May 93. (cd/c) (11012-2/-4) <43051> **NEW RACEION**
– The pleaser / Christ dice / Gamma pop / Viva the legs / Do the job / Junior's little sister's dropped ta cheap / How many lifetimes / Holy skips / Keep it alive / Go Trane go / Just say.

—— next with **LIZ LAMERE** – keyboards, vocals

	Thirsty Ear	Thirsty Ear

Dec 96. (cd) <(21308)> **DUJANG PRANG** | | Jul96 |
– Dujang prang / Hammered / Chennaroka / Saturn drive 2 (subtalk) / Jaxson gnome / Life ain't life / Flowers, candles, crucifixes / Big daddy stat's livin' on Tron / Sacrifice / Kiss.

	Last Call	Thirsty Ear

May 97. (cd; ALAN VEGA, ALEX CHILTON, BEN VAUGHN) (422466) <21314> **CUBIST BLUES** | | Oct96 |
– Fat city / Fly away / Freedom / Candyman / Come on Lord / Promised land / Lover of love / Sister / Too late / Do not do not / Werewolf / Dream baby revisited.

– (SUICIDE) compilations, etc. –

Dec 81. (c) R.O.I.R.; <(A 103)> **HALF-ALIVE (half studio)**
Oct 86. (c) R.O.I.R.; <(A 145)> **GHOST RIDERS (live)**
(cd-iss. Apr90 on 'Danceteria'; DANCD 029) (cd-iss. Feb95 on 'ROIR Europe'; RE 145CD)

1995. (cd; by MARTIN REV) Alive; <1006> **CHEYENNE**
Jan 96. (cd; by MARTIN REV) R.O.I.R.; <(RUSCD 8220)> **SEE ME RIDIN'**
Mar 96. (cd; by ALAN VEGA) Infinite Zero; <43069> **JUKEBOX BABE / COLLISION DRIVE**
Jan 98. (12"ep) Blast First; (BFFP 115) **CHEREE. / HARLEM / I REMEMBER**

—— Their classic 'FRANKIE TEARDROP' was used by STEPHEN LIRONI (producer and ex- ALTERED IMAGES guy) on project REVOLUTIONARY CORPS, etc

---

SULTANS OF PING F.C.   (dig out; Great Alt & Indie . . .)

SUNDAYS

Formed: London, England . . . 1988 by HARRIET WHEELER, DAVID GAVURIN and PAUL BRINDLEY, initially playing with a drum machine before recruiting sticksman PATRICK 'Patch' HANNAN. Subsequently signing to 'Rough Trade', the band's fawning music press hype was justified with the release of the semi-classic 'CAN'T BE SURE' single in early '89. A luscious slice of sugary indie, the track's reverberating guitar and fragile, bone-china vocals (courtesy of WHEELER) brought comparisons with "shoegazing" forebears The COCTEAU TWINS, some critics also mentioning THROWING MUSES. Yet The SUNDAYS were in seemingly little hurry to follow-up this indie chart topper (and minor Top 40 hit), almost a full year passing before the release of much anticipated debut album, 'READING, WRITING AND ARITHMETIC' (1990). Its glistening jangle-pop didn't disappoint and The SUNDAYS suddenly found themselves in the UK Top 5, the US Top 40 and the glare of the world's media. An ensuing continent-straddling tour together with the collapse of the band's label conspired to slow down the band's already notoriously relaxed attitude to songwriting and it was late '92 before they re-emerged via a new 'Parlophone' deal. The resulting single, 'GOODBYE', displayed a more world-weary sound (the band even covering The Rolling Stones' mournful classic, 'WILD HORSES' on the B-side) and the accompanying album, 'BLIND', sounded frayed at the edges. While the record's Top 20 placing and the success of the attendant tour suggested that The SUNDAYS' fans hadn't lost interest, their patience would be tested with a subsequent five year gap prior to a third album. When 'STATIC & SILENCE' (1997) finally arrived, critics found fault with what they saw as musical stagnation although loyal fans helped put it into the UK Top 10, proving their enduring appeal. • **Trivia:** An instrumental piece was used on the 1993 series for comedy duo, Newman & Baddiel.

Album rating: READING, WRITING AND ARITHMETIC (*8) / BLIND (*7) / STATIC & SILENCE (*6)

HARRIET WHEELER (b.26 Jun'63, Maidenhead, England) – vocals (ex-JIM JIMINEE) / **DAVID GAVURIN** (b. 4 Apr'63) – guitar / **PAUL BRINDLEY** (b. 6 Nov'63, Loughborough, England) – bass / **PATRICK 'Patch' HANNAN** (b. 4 Mar'66) – drums repl. drum machine

		Rough Trade	D.G.C.
Feb 89.	(7") *(RT 218)* **CAN'T BE SURE. / I KICKED A BOY**	45	–
	(12"+=/cd-s+=) *(RT 218 T/CD)* – Don't tell your mother.		
Jan 90.	(lp/c/cd) *(ROUGH/+C/CD 148)* <24277> **READING, WRITING AND ARITHMETIC**	4	39
	– Skin & bones / Here's where the story ends / Can't be sure / I won / Hideous towns / You're not the only one I know / A certain someone / I kicked a boy / My finest hour / Joy. (re-iss.May96 cd/c; CD/TC PCS 7378)		
Jan 90.	(7") **HERE'S WHERE THE STORY ENDS. / SKIN AND BONES**	–	–
		Parlophone	D.G.C.
Sep 92.	(c-s/7") *(TC+/R 6319)* **GOODBYE. / WILD HORSES**	27	–
	(cd-s+=) *(CDR 6319)* – Noise.		
Oct 92.	(cd/c/lp) *(CD/TC+/PCSD 121)* <24479> **BLIND**	15	
	– I feel / Goodbye / Life and soul / Marc / On Earth / God made me / Love / What do you think? / Blood on my hands / Medieval. (re-iss. Mar94; same)		
Sep 97.	(7") *(R 6475)* **SUMMERTIME. / NOTHING SWEET**	15	–
	(cd-s+=) *(CDR 6475)* – Gone.		
	(cd-s) *(CDRS 6475)* – ('A'side) / Skin & bones (live) / Here's where the story ends (live).		
		Capitol	Geffen
Sep 97.	(cd/c/lp) *(CD/TC+/EST 2300)* <25131> **STATIC & SILENCE**	10	33
	– Summertime / Homeward / Folk song / She / When I'm thinking about you / I can't wait / Another flavour / Leave this city / Your eyes / Cry / Monochrome.		
Nov 97.	(c-s) *(TCR 6487)* **CRY / THROUGH THE DARK**	43	–
	(cd-s+=) *(CDR 6487)* – Life goes on.		
	(cd-s) *(CDRS 6487)* – ('A'side) / Can't be sure (demo) / You're not the only one I know (demo).		

SUN RA

Born: HERMAN BLOUT, 22 May 1914, Birmingham, Alabama, USA. A child prodigy, he was bought a piano for his 10th birthday by his parents, which he immediately learned to play, while composing some early songs. Majoring at Alabama A&M University, he later went under the name SONNY LEE, playing with a swing band led by FLETCHER HENDERSON. In 1948, he changed his name by deedpoll to LE SONNY'RA, soon shortened to SUN RA. Around this time, he claimed to have been born on Saturn and despatched to Earth as the "creator of the omniverse". By the mid-50's, he had assembled his "ARKESTRA", which included a nucleus of talented musicians; JOHN GILMORE, MARSHALL ALLEN and PAT PATRICK, fusing together be-bop jazz (influenced by THELONIUS MONK or DUKE ELLINGTON), with exotic worldly avant-garde. His/their first recordings were rare, free-form jazz affairs, the band's sound evolving following his move to New York in the early 60's. SUN RA's cult appeal grew, especially after introducing the Moog synthesizer when recording for underground 'E.S.P.' label (home of FUGS).

His concerts were of the cosmic funk variety, subsequently developed by the great FUNKADELIC via GEORGE CLINTON. In 1974, the death of his idol DUKE ELLINGTON, seemed to inspire an onslaught of shows, reviving the great man's work (albeit faster and more furiously uptempo). In the late 80's, after releasing many albums over the previous two decades, he signed to UK indie, 'Blast First' (at the time, home to such indie noise merchants as SONIC YOUTH, DINOSAUR JR and The BUTTHOLE SURFERS!), which issued his 1989 and retrospective and a new live album, 'OUT THERE A MINUTE' and 'LIVE IN LONDON 1990' respectively. This led to a contract with his first major, 'A&M', although it was clear his health was fading after suffering a few strokes. On the 4th of July '92, he opened for SONIC YOUTH at New York's Central Park, entering the stage on a wheelchair. He returned to his birthplace late in '92 after he suffered a third stroke, and on the 30th of May that year, he died. However, his band, under GILMORE's leadership, continued to play SUN RA's music.

Album rating (selective): THE HELIOCENTRIC WORLDS OF SUN RA, I (*9) / THE HELIOCENTRIC WORLDS OF SUN RA II (*8) / SUNRISE IN DIFFERENT DIMENSIONS (*7) / COSMIC TONES FOR MENTAL THERAPY (*7) / BLUE DELIGHT (*8)

SUN RA – piano (with session people)

		not iss.	Saturn
1955.	(7"; by The COSMIC RAYS) *<SR 401/402>* **DREAMING. / DADDY'S GONNA TELL YOU NO LIE**	–	
1956.	(7"; by The COSMIC RAYS with LE SUN RA and his ARKESTRA) *<B 222/223?>* **BYE BYE. / SOMEBODY'S IN LOVE**	–	
1956.	(7"; as LE SUN-RA and his ARKESTRA) *<Z 222>* **MEDICINE FOR A NIGHTMARE. / URNACK**	–	
1956.	(7") **A CALL FOR ALL DEMONS. / EMON'S LULLABY**	–	
1956.	(7") **SATURN. / SUPERSONIC JAZZ**	–	
1956.	(7") *<Z 1111>* **SUPER BLONDE. / SOFT TALK**	–	
1957.	(lp) *<H70 P0216>* **SUPER-SONIC JAZZ**	–	
	– India / Sunology / Advice to medics / Sunology part II / Kingdom of Not / Portrait of the living sky / Blues at midnight / El is a sound of joy. <cd-iss. May92 on 'Evidence'; ECD 22015>		
1959.	(7") **SATURN. / VELVET**	–	
1959.	(7") **'ROUND MIDNIGHT. / BACK IN YOUR OWN BACKYARD**	–	
1959.	(lp) *<K 70 P 359 0-1>* **JAZZ IN SILHOUETTE**	–	
	– Hours after / Horoscope / Images / Blues at midnight / Enlightenment / Saturn / Velvet / Ancient Aiethopia. (cd-iss. May92 on 'Evidence'; 22012-2)		

—— note:- SUN RA & HIS ARKESTRA also backed YOCHANAN on a few singles

1960.	(7") *<874>* **OCTOBER. / ADVENTUR IN SPACE**	–	
1960.	(7") *<SA-1001>* **THE BLUE SET. / BIG CITY BLUES**	–	
1961.	(7") *<L08W-0114-5>* **SPACE LKONELINESS. / STATE STREET**	–	
1961.	(lp) *<HK 5445>* **SUN RA AND HIS SOLAR ARKESTRA VISIT PLANET EARTH; WE TRAVEL THE SPACEWAYS**	–	
	– Eve / Interplanetary music / Tapestry from an asteroid / Velvet / We travel the spaceways / Space loneliness.		
1964.	(lp) *<408>* **COSMIC TONES FOR MENTAL THERAPY**	–	
	– And otherness / Thither and yon / Adventure – Equation / Moon dance / Voice of space.		
1964.	(lp) *<KH 9876>* **OTHER PLANES OF THERE**	–	
	– Other planes of there / Sound spectra / Sketch / Pleasure / Spiral galaxy. <cd-iss. Nov92 on 'Evidence'; ECD 22037-2>		
1960's.	(lp) *<9954>* **SECRETS OF THE SUN**	–	
	– Friendly galaxy / Solar differentials / Space aura / Love in outer space / Reflects motion / Solar symbols.		
1960's.	(lp) *<9956>* **ART FORMS OF DIMENSION TOMORROW**	–	
	– Cluster of galaxies / Ankh / Solar drums / The outer heavens / Infinity of the universe / Lights on a satellite / Kosmos in blue.		

		not iss.	E.S.P.
1965.	(lp) *(ESP 1014)* **THE HELIOCENTRIC WORLDS OF SUN RA, VOLUME I**	–	
	– Heliocentric / Outer nothingness / Other worlds / The cosmos / Of heavenly things / Nebulae / Dancing in the sun. (UK-iss.Apr81; same) (cd-iss. Dec94; ESP 1014-2) (re-iss. Apr97 on 'Get Back'; GET 1004)		
1966.	(lp) *(ESP 1017)* **THE HELIOCENTRIC WORLDS OF SUN RA, VOLUME II**	–	
	– The sun myth / A house of beauty / Cosmic chaos. (UK-iss.Apr81; same) (cd-iss. Dec94; ESP 1017-2) (re-iss. Apr97 on 'Get Back'; GET 1005)		
1968.	(lp) *(ESP 1045)* **NOTHING IS** (rec.May '66)		–
	– Dancing shadows / Imagination / Exotic forest / Sun Ra and his band from outer space / Shadow world / Theme of the stargazers / Outer spaceways incorporated / Next stop Mars. (UK-iss.Sep84 as 'DANCING SHADOWS' on 'Happy Bird'; B 90130) (cd-iss. Sep92 on 'Giants Of Jazz And Blues'; 30013) (original:- re-iss. Apr97 on 'Get Back'; GET 1007)		

		not iss.	Saturn
1968.	(7") *<3066>* **THE BRIDGE. / ROCKET NUMBER NINE**	–	
1968.	(7") *<911-AR>* **BLUES ON PLANET MARS. / SATURN MOON**	–	
1969.	(lp) *(ESR 507)* **ATLANTIS** (rec.1967)	–	
	– Atlantis / Mu / Lemuria / Yucatan / Bimini. (UK cd-iss. Nov93 on 'Evidence'+=; ECD 22067-2) – Yucatan (Impulse version).		
1969.	(lp) *(ESR 508)* **HOLIDAY FOR SOUL DANCE**	–	
	– Early Autumn / But not for me / Day by day / Holiday for strings / Dorothy's dance / I loves you orgy / Body and soul / Keep your sunny side up. (UK cd-iss. May92 on 'Evidence'; ECD 22011-2)		
1969.	(lp) *<SR 509>* **MONORAILS AND SATELLITES** (rec.1966)	–	
	– Spacetowers / Cognition / Skylight / The alter destiny / Easy street / Blue differentials / Monorails and satellites / The galaxy way. (UK cd-iss. May92 on 'Evidence'; ECD 22013-2)		
1970's.	(lp) *<SR 512>* **SOUND SUN PLEASURE!!** (rec.1959)	–	
	– 'Round midnight / You never told me that you care / Hour of parting / Back in your own backyard / I could have danced all night. (UK cd-iss. May92 on 'Evidence'; ECD 22014-2)		

1970's. (lp) <SR 519> **MONORAILS AND SATELLITES VOL.II**
(rec.1966)
– Astro vision / The ninth eye / Solar boats / Perspective prisms of Is / Calundronius.

1970's. (lp) <ESR 520> **CONTINUATION** (rec.1968-69)
– Continuation to / Jupiter festival / Biosphere blues / Intergalaxtic research / Earth primitive Earth / New planet.

1970's. (lp) <ESR 521> **MY BROTHER THE WIND**
– My brother the wind / Intergalactic II / To nature's god / The code of independence.

1970's. (lp) <ESR 523> **MY BROTHER THE WIND, VOLUME II**
– Somewhere else / Contrast / The wind speaks / Sun thoughts / Journey to the stars / World of the myth "I" / The design cosmos II / Otherness blue / Somebody else's world / Pleasant twilight / Walking on the Moon. (UK cd-iss. Nov92 on 'Evidence'; ECD 22040-2)

1970's. (lp) <ESR 532> **BAD AND BEAUTIFUL** (rec.late '61)
– The bad and the beautiful / Ankh / Search light blues / Exotic two / On the blue side / And this is my beloved.

Byg Actuel   not iss.

1972. (lp; as SUN RA & HIS SOLAR-MYTH ARKESTRA)
(529.340) **THE SOLAR MYTH APPROACH VOL.1** (rec.1968-1970)   France
– Spectrum / Realm of lightning / The satellites are spinning / Legend / Seen III, took 4 / They'll come back / The adventures of Bugs Hunter. (UK-iss.Feb78 on 'Infinity'; AFF 10)

1971. (lp; as SUN RA & HIS SOLAR-MYTH ARKESTRA)
(529.341) **THE SOLAR MYTH APPROACH VOL.2** (rec.1968-70)   France
– Scene 1, take 1 / Outer spaceways incorporated / The utter nots / Interpretation / Ancient Ethiopia / Strange worlds / Pyramids. (UK-iss.1983 on 'Affinity'; AFF 76)

Delmark   Delmark

1974. (lp; as SUN RA ARKESTRA) *(DL 411)* **SUN SONG**
– Brainville / Call for all emons / Transition / Possession / Street named Hell / Lullaby for Brainville / Future / Swing a little taste / New horizons / Fall off the log / Sun song. <US-iss.Dec94; DDCD 411>

1974. (lp; as SUN RA ARKESTRA) *(DL 414)* **SOUND OF JOY**
<US-iss.Dec94; DDCD 414>

Improvising Artists   not iss.

1978. (lp) *(37.38-50)* **SOLO PIANO, VOLUME 1**
– Sometimes I feel like a motherless child / Cosmo rhythmatic / Yesterdays / Romance of two planets / Irregular galaxy / To a friend. (cd-iss. Nov92; 123850-2)

1978. (lp) *(37.38-58)* **ST. LOUIS BLUES: SOLO PIANO (VOLUME 2)**
– Ohosnisixaeht / St. Louis blues / Three little words / Sky and sun / I am we are I / Thoughts on thoth. (cd-iss. Nov93; 123858-2)

Cobra   not iss.

1979. (lp; as SUN RA ARKESTRA) *(COB 37001)* **COSMOS EQUATION** (rec.August '76)
– The mystery of two / Interstellar low ways / Neo project No.2 / Cosmos / Moonship journey / Journey among the stars / Jazz from an unknown planet. (cd-iss. Sep92 on 'Giants Of Jazz And Blues'; 30011)

Inner City   not iss.

Apr 79. (lp) *(IC 1039)* **SUN RA**
– For the sunrise / Of the other tomorrow / From out where others dwell / On sound infinity spheres / The house of eternal being / Gos of the thunder rain / Lights on a satellite / Take the 'A' train / Prelude / El is the sound of joy / Encore 1 / Encore 2 / We travel the spaceways.

not iss.   Hat Hut

1980. (lp; as SUN RA ARKESTRA) <2R 17> **SUNRISE IN DIFFERENT DIMENSIONS**
– Lights from a hidden sun / Pin-points of spiral prisms / Silhouettes of the shadow world / Cocktails for two / 'Round midnight / Lady bird – Half Nelson / Big John's special / Yeah man! / Love in outer space * / Provocative celestials / Disguised gods in skullduggery rendezvous / Queer notions / Limehouse blues / King Porter stomp / Take the A train / Lightnin' / On Jupiter * / A helio-hello and goodbye too!. (cd-iss. Dec91 – =*; ARTCD 6099)

Y   not iss.

Sep 82. (lp) *(Y 19LP)* **STRANGE CELESTIAL ROAD** (rec.July '79)
– Celestial road / Say / I'll wait for you. <US-iss.1988 on 'Rounder' lp/c; ROUNDER 3035/+C> (cd-iss. 1990's cd/c; ROU CD/C 3035)

Nov 83. (12"; as SUN RA ARKESTRA) *(RA 1)* **NUCLEAR WAR. / SOMETIMES I'M HAPPY**

Affinity   not iss.

1983. (lp) *(AFF 76)* **SOLAR-MYTH APPROACH VOL.2**
– The utter nots / Outer spaceways (inc. Scene 1, take 1) / Pyramids / Interpretation / Ancient Ethiopia / Strange worlds. (cd-iss. both VOLS Jan90; CDAFF 76)

Praxis   not iss.

May 84. (lp) *(CM 106)* **SUN RA ARKESTRA MEETS SALAM RAGAB IN EGYPT**   Greece
– Egypt strut / Dawn / (three others by SALAH RAGAB and The CAIRO JAZZ BAND)

Happy Bird   not iss.

Sep 84. (lp) *(B 90131)* **OTHER WORLDS**
– Heliocentric / Other nothingness / Other worlds / The cosmos / Of heavenly things / Nebulae dancing in the sun.

Sep 84. (lp) *(B 90132)* **THE SUN MYTH**
– The sun myth / House of beauty / Cosmic chaos. (cd-iss. Sep92 on 'Giants Of Jazz And Blues'; 30012)

Saturn – Recommended   not iss.

Feb 86. (lp) *(SRRRD 1)* **COSMOS SUN CONNECTION** (live 1984)
– Fate in a pleasant mood / Cosmo journey blues / Cosmo sun connection / Cosmonaut astronaut rendezvous / As space ships aproach / Pharoah's den.

not iss.   Meltdown

1987. (lp) <MPA-1> **JOHN CAGE MEETS SUN RA**
– John Cage meets Sun Ra. <cd-iss. Jan97; MPA-1CD>

Sep 87. (lp; as SUN RA & HIS COSMO DISCIPLINE ARKESTRA) Leo; *(LR 149)* **NIGHT IN EAST BERLIN (live June '86)**
– Mystic prophecy / Beyond the wilderness of shadows / Prelude to a kiss / Interstellar low ways / Space is the place – We travel the spaceways / The shadow world / Rocket number nine – Second stop is Jupiter. (cd-iss. 1987 on 'Leo'; LR 149)

Black Saint   not iss.

1987. (cd) *(120 101-2)* **REFLECTIONS IN BLUE**   Italy
– State street Chicago / Nothin' from nothin' / Yesterdays / Say it isn't so / I dream too much / Reflection in blue.

1987. (cd) *(120 111-2)* **HOURS AFTER**   Italy
– But not for me / Hours after / Beautiful love / Dance of the extra terrestrians / Love on a faraway planet.

A&M   A&M

Feb 89. (lp/c/cd) *(AMA/AMC/CDA 5260)* **BLUE DELIGHT**
– Blue delight / Out of nowhere / Sunrise / They dwell on other planes / Gone with the wind / Your guest is as good as mine / Nashira / Days of wine and roses.

Jul 90. (cd) *(75021 5324)* **PURPLE NIGHT**
– Journey towards stars / Friendly galaxy / Love in outer space / Stars fell on Alabama / Of invisible them / Neverness / Purple night blues.

not iss.   Leo

1991. (cd) <LR 188> **FRIENDLY GALAXY**
– Intro percussion / Prelude to a kiss / Blue Lou / Lights on a satellite / Alabama / Fate in a pleasant mood / We travel the spaceways / Space is the place / Saturn rings / Friendly galaxy / They'll come back.

1991. (d-cd) <LR 210/211> **PLEIADES**
– Pleiades / Mythic / Sun procession / Lights on a satellite / Love in outer space / Planet Earth day / Mythic 2 / Blue Lou / Prelude #7 in A major.

1991. (d-cd) <LR 214/215> **LIVE AT THE HACKNEY EMPIRE (live)**
– Astro black / Other voices / Planet Earth day / Prelude to a kiss / Hocus pocus / Love in outer space / Blue Lou / Face the music / String singhs / Discipline 27-II / I'll wait for you / East of the sun / Somewhere over the rainbow / Frisco fog / Sunset on the Nile / Skimming and loping / Yeah man! / We travel the spaceways / They'll come back.

1992. (cd) <LR 230> **SECOND STAR TO THE RIGHT (SALUTE TO WALT DISNEY)** (rec.April '89)
– The forest of no return / Someday my prince will come / Frisco fog / Wishing well / Zip-adee-doo-dah / Second star to the right / Heigh ho! heigh ho! / Whistle while you work.

Black Saint   not iss.

Jan 92. (cd) *(12012-2)* **MAYAN TEMPLES** (rec.1990)   Italy
– Dance of the language barrier / Bygone / Discipline No.1 / Alone together / Prelude to stargazers / Mayan temples / I'll never be the same / Stardust from tomorrow / El is a sound of joy / Time after time / Opus in springtime / Theme of the stargazers / Sunset on the Nile.

Blast First   not iss.

Jan 92. (cd-s; w/2 videos) *(BFFPCD 101)* **COSMIC VISIONS**
– I am the instrument.

not iss.   Enja

Jul 92. (cd) <7071> **DESTINATION UNKNOWN** (rec. Switzerland)
– Carefree / Echoes of the future / Prelude to a kiss / Hocus pocus / Theme of the stargazers / Interstellar low ways / Destination unknown / The satellites are spinning / S'wonderful / Space is the place – We travel the spaceways.

—— SUN RA died on the 30th of May 1993.

not iss.   Rounder

Jan 94. (cd) <ROU 3124> **AT THE VILLAGE VANGUARD (live)**
– 'Round midnight / Sun Ra blues / Autumn in New York / S'wonderful / Theme of the stargazers.

– others, etc –

—— In Sep'79, he and WALT DICKERSON released 'VISIONS' rec.11 Jul'78 on Steeplechase'; SCS 1126)

Jan 85. (lp; as SUN RA & HIS ARKESTRA) Black Lion; *(BLP 30103)* **PICTURES OF INFINITY – IN CONCERT (live 1968)**
– Somewhere there / Outer spaceways incorporated / Saturn / Song of the sparer / Spontaneous simplicity. (cd-iss. Feb94+=; BLCD 760191) – Intergalactic motion (aka- Ankhnaton).

Mar 88. (lp; as SUN RA & HIS ARKESTRA) Leo; *(LR 154)* **LOVE IN OUTER SPACE (live in Utrecht December '83)**
– Along came Ra / Discipline 27 / Blues Ra / Big John's special / Fate in a pleasant mood / 'Round midnight / Love in outer space – Space is the place. (cd-iss. Sep88; CDLR 154)

Mar 89. (lp/c/cd) Blast First; *(BFFP 42/+C/CD)* **OUT THERE A MINUTE** (rec.in New York 1965-)
– Love in Outer Space / Somewhere in Space / Dark clouds with silver linings / Jazz and romantic sounds / When angels speak of love / Cosmo enticement / Song of tree and forest / Other worlds / Journey outward / Lights on a satellite / Starships and solar boats / Out there a minute.

May 92. (cd) Jazz View; *(COD 007)* **FOUNDATION NIGHTS VOL.2**   German

Nov 92. (cd) Evidence; <ECD 22036-2> **COSMIC TONES FOR MENTAL THERAPY / ART FORMS OF DIMENSIONS TOMORROW**

Nov 92. (cd) Evidence; <ECD 22038-2> **WE TRAVEL THE SPACEWAYS / BAD AND BEAUTIFUL**

Nov 92. (cd) Evidence; <ECD 22039-2> **SUN RA VISITS PLANET EARTH / INTERSTELLAR LOW WAYS** (rec.1956-58)
– Two tones / Saturn / Reflections in blue / El Viktor / Planet Earth / Eve / Overtones of China.

May 93. (cd) Savoy Jazz; *(SV 0213)* **THE FUTURISTIC SOUNDS OF SUN RA** (rec.Oct'61)
– Bassism / Of sounds and something else / What's that? / Where is tomorrow? / The beginning / China gate / New day / Tapestry from an asteroid / Jet flight / Looking outward / Space jazz reverie.

1993. (cd/c) Rounder; *(ROU CD/C 3036)* **SOMEWHERE ELSE**
– Priest / Discipline – Tall trees in the sun / S'wonderful / Hole in the sky / Somewhere else (part 1 & 2) / Stardust for tomorrow / Love in outer space / Everything is space / Tristar.

Nov 93. (cd) Evidence; <ECD 22066-2> **ANGELS AND DEMONS AT PLAY / THE NUBIANS OF PLUTONIA** (rec.1956-60)

Nov 93. (cd) Evidence; <ECD 22068-2> **FATE IN A PLEASANT MOOD / WHEN SUN COMES OUT** (1960-63)

Nov 93. (cd) Evidence; <ECD 22069-2> **THE MAGIC CITY** (rec.1965)
– The magic city / The shadow world / Abstract "I" / Abstract eye.

Nov 93. (cd) Evidence; <ECD 22070-2> **SPACE IS THE PLACE (original soundtrack)** (rec.1972)
– It's after the end of the world / Under diferent stars / Discipline 33 / Watusi / Calling planet Earth / I am the alter-destiny / The satellites are spinning (take 1) /

Cosmic forces / Outer spaceways incorporated (take 3) / We travel the spaceways / The overseer / Blackman – Love in outer space / Mysterious crystal / I am the brother of the wind / We'll wait for you / Space is the place.

Feb 94. (d-cd; as SUN RA ARKESTRA) *D.I.W.; (DIW 388-2)* **LIVE FROM SOUNDSCAPE (live November 1979)** `[ ]` `–` `–` Japan
– The possibility of altered destiny / Astro black / Pleiades / We're living in the space age / Keep your sunny side up / Discipline #27 / Untitled improvisation / Watusi / Space is the place / We travel the spaceways / Angel race / Destination unknown / On Jupiter.

1994. (7"; 33rpm) *<DEP 1-1>* **QUEER NOTIONS. / PRELUDE No.7** `–` `–` Japan

1994. (7"; 33rpm) *<DEP 1-2>* **EAST OF THE SUN. / FRISCO FOG** `–` `–` Japan

1994. (7"; 33rpm) *<DEP 1-3>* **OPUS SPRINGTIME. / COSMOS SWING BLUES** `–` `–` Japan

Mar 94. (cd) *D.I.W., (DIW 824)* **COSMO OMNIBUS IMAGIABLE ILLUSION: LIVE AT PIT-INN, TOKYO (live 8 August, 1988)** `[ ]` `–` Japan
– Introduction – Cosmo approach prelude / Angel race – I'll wait for you / Can you take it? / If you came from nowhere here / Astro black / Prelude to a kiss / Interstellar low ways.

Jun 96. (cd) *Blast First; (BFFP 60CD)* **LIVE IN LONDON 1990 (live at The Mean Fiddler, 11 June 1990)** `[ ]` `–`
– Frisco / Shadow world / For the blue people / Prelude to a kiss / Down here on the ground / Blue delight / Cosmo song / Space chants.

May 97. (d-cd; SUN RA & HIS INTERGALACTIC ARKESTRA) *Leo; (CDLR 235-236)* **STARDUST FROM TOMORROW** `[ ]` `–`

SUPERCHUNK (dig out; Great Alt & Indie . . .)

SUPER FURRY ANIMALS

Formed: Cardiff, Wales . . . 1993 by GRUFF RHYS, DAFYDD IEUAN, CIAN CIARAN, GUTO PRYCE and HUW BUNFORD. Emerging from the Welsh underground scene in the mid-90's with a wholly unpronounceable EP on their native 'Ankst' label, the band whipped up a fair bit of interest from the London-based media and industry insiders alike. Alan McGee's 'Creation' subsequently took them on with the proviso that the bulk of their work be in English, the 'FURRY' famously stipulating that they never be made to work on St. David's day. Their first single for the label, 'HOMETOWN UNICORN' appeared in early '96 and dented the Top 50, while the dayglo rampage of 'GOD! SHOW ME MAGIC' made the Top 40 a couple of months later. Hailed by critics as one of the debuts of the year, the accompanying 'FUZZY LOGIC' (1996) album thrilled jaded Brit-pop fans with its dayglo showcase of deranged prog-retro pop/rock; 'MARIO MAN' was their most definitive slice of pseudo psychedelia to date while 'HANGIN' WITH HOWARD MARKS' gave them instant cool – the record's cover art depicted the various guises of "nice guy" one-time drug smuggler, MARKS. A Top 30 hit, the album spawned a further two singles in 'SOMETHING 4 THE WEEKEND' and 'IF YOU DON'T WANT ME TO DESTROY YOU', while the blase brilliance of 'THE MAN DON'T GIVE A FUCK' (repetitive line from the STEELY DAN number, 'Showbiz Kids') drew a swaggering close to a successful but inevitably controversial year, the group having been earlier banned from the Welsh BAFTA awards after a skirmish in the crowd. 1997's follow-up set, 'RADIATOR', made the Top 10, its less intense but equally compelling shenanigans threatening to take the band into the big league (they played the festival circuit that including a return to the rainy 'T In The Park' – Muddy Waters was not even invited). In May '98, after two further Top 30 hits, 'PLAY IT COOL' and 'DEMONS', the band had their biggest hit to date (#12) via non-album cut, 'ICE HOCKEY HAIR'. To end the year, 'OUT-SPACED' (a selection of rare B-sides, etc), marked time as GRUFF RHYS and his crew plotted their return. The 'NORTHERN LITES' single (which reached No.11), previewed unquestionably their finest hour to date, 'GUERILLA' (1999), a Top 10 album that featured xylophones, Caribbean brass, steel guitars, etc over some "way-out" experimental jugband psychedelia.

Album rating: FUZZY LOGIC (*8) / RADIATOR (*7) / OUTSPACED collection (*6) / GUERILLA (*9)

GRUFF RHYS (b.18 Jul'70) – vocals, guitars (ex-EMILY, ex-FFA COFFI PAWB) / **CIAN CIARAN** (b.16 Jun'76) – keyboards / **HUW 'Bumpf' BUNFORD** (b.15 Sep'67, Bath, England) – guitars, vocals / **GUTO PRYCE** (b. 4 Sep'72) – bass / **DAFYDD IEUAN** (b. 1 Mar'69) – drums, percussion, vocals (ex-ANHREFN, ex-FFA COFFI PAWB)

                                  Ankst   not iss.

Jun 95. (7"ep/cd-ep) *(ANKST 057/+CD)* **LLANFAIRPWLLGWYNGYLLGOGERYCHWYNDROBW-LLANTYSILIOGOGOGOCHOCYNYGOFOD (IN SPACE) EP** `[ ]` `–`
– Organ yn dy geg / Fix idris / Crys Ti / Blerwytirhwng? *(re-iss. May97; same)*

Oct 95. (7"ep/cd-ep) *(ANKST 062/+CD)* **MOOG DROOG EP** `[ ]` `–`
– Pam V / God! show me magic / Sali Mali / Focus pocus – Debiel. *(re-iss. May97; same)*

                                  Creation   Sony

Feb 96. (7"/c-s) *(CRE/+CS 222)* **HOMETOWN UNICORN. / DON'T BE A FOOL, BILLY** `47` `–`
(cd-s+=) *(CRESCD 222)* – Lazy life (of no fixed identity).

Apr 96. (7"/c-s) *(CRE/+CS 231)* **GOD! SHOW ME MAGIC. / DIM BENDITH** `33` `–`
(cd-s+=) *(CRESCD 231)* – Death by melody.

May 96. (cd/lp)(c) *(CRE CD/LP 190)(CCRE 190) <67827>* **FUZZY LOGIC** `23` `[ ]`
– God! show me magic / Fuzzy birds / Something 4 the weekend / Frisbee /

Hometown unicorn / Gathering moss / If you don't want me to destroy you / Bad behaviour / Mario man / Hangin' with Howard Marks / Long gone / For now and ever.

Jul 96. (7"/c-s) *(CRE/+CS 235)* **SOMETHING 4 THE WEEKEND. / WAITING TO HAPPEN** `18` `–`
(cd-s+=) *(CRESCD 235)* – Arnofio / Glow in the dark.

Sep 96. (7"/c-s/cd-s) *(CRE/+CS/SCD 243)* **IF YOU DON'T WANT ME TO DESTROY YOU. / GUACAMOLE** `18` `–`
(cd-s+=) *(CRESCD 243)* – (Nid) Hon yw'r gan sy'n mynd I achub yr iaith (This song will save the Welsh language) (not).

Dec 96. (one-sided-7"blue) *(CRE 247)* **THE MAN DON'T GIVE A FUCK** `22` `–`
(cd-s+=) *(CRESCD 247)* – ('A'-Matthew 'Herbert' Herbert mix) / ('A'-Howard Marks mix).
(12"++=) *(CRE 247T)* – ('A'-Darren Price mix).

—— In Feb'97, HUW BUNFORD was fined £700 on an earlier drug possession charge

                                  Creation   Flydaddy

May 97. (7"/c-s) *(CRE/+CS 252)* **HERMANN LOVES PAULINE. / CALIMERO** `26` `–`
(cd-s+=) *(CRESCD 252)* – Trons Mr. Urdd.

Jul 97. (7"/c-s) *(CRE/+CS 269)* **THE INTERNATIONAL LANGUAGE OF SCREAMING. / WRAP IT UP** `24` `–`
(cd-s+=) *(CRESCD 269)* – Foxy music / O.K.

Aug 97. (cd/c/lp) *(CRECD/CCRE/CRELP 214) <FLY 34CD>* **RADIATOR** `8` `[ ]`
– Furryvision / The placid casual / The international language of screaming / Demons / Short painkiller / She's got spies / Play it cool / Hermann love's Pauline / Chupacabras / Torra fy ngwallt yn hir / Bass tuned to D.E.A.D. / Down a different river / Download / Mountain people.

Sep 97. (7"/c-s) *(CRE/+CS 275)* **PLAY IT COOL. / PASS THE TIME** `27` `–`
(cd-s+=) *(CRESCD 275)* – Cryndod yn dy lais.

Nov 97. (7"/c-s) *(CRE/+CS 283)* **DEMONS. / HIT AND RUN** `27` `–`
(cd-s+=) *(CRESCD 283)* – Carry the can.

May 98. (7"/c-s) *(CRE/+CS 288)* **ICE HOCKEY HAIR. / SMOKIN'** `12` `–`
(12"+=)(cd-s+=) *(CRE 288T)(CRESCD 288)* – Mu-tron / Let's quit smokin'.

Nov 98. (cd/lp) *(CRE CD/LP 229)* **OUT SPACED (selected B-sides & rarities 1994-1998)** `44` `–`
– The man don't give a fuck / Dim brys dim chwys / Smokin' / Dim bendith / Arnofio – Glo in the dark / Guacamole / Don't be a fool, Billy / Focus pocus – Debiel / Fix Idris / Pam V / Pass the time / Carry the can / Blerwytirhwng? *(ltd-cd; CRECD 229L) (cd re-iss. Sep99; same)*

May 99. (7"/c-s) *(CRE/+CS 314)* **NORTHERN LITES. / RABID DOG** `11` `–`
(cd-s+=) *(CRESCD 314)* – This, that and the other.

Jun 99. (cd/c/lp) *(CRECD/CCRE/CRELP 242)* **GUERILLA** `10` `[ ]`
– Check it out / Do or die / The turning tide / Northern lites / Night vision / Wherever I lay my phone (that's my home) / A specific ocean / Some things come from nothing / The door to this house remains open / The teacher / Fire in my heart / The sound of life today / Chewing chewing gum / Keep the cosmic trigger happy.

Aug 99. (7"/c-s) *(CRE/+CS 323)* **FIRE IN MY HEART. / THE MATTER OF TIME** `25` `–`
(cd-s+=) *(CRESCD 323)* – Mrs Spector.

SUPERGRASS

Formed: Oxford, England . . . 1991 as The JENNIFERS by schoolboy GAZ COOMBES and DANNY GOFFEY along with brother NICK and ANDY DAVIES. After a sole EP on 'Nude' (home to SUEDE), DAVIES went off to university, COOMBES and DANNY subsequently recruiting MICKEY QUINN and forming SUPERGRASS. Their raucous debut single, 'CAUGHT BY THE FUZZ', complete with a STIFF LITTLE FINGERS-like intro and a snotty, shouty vocal rampage recounting the teenage trauma of being busted for cannabis, could've conceivably come straight out of 1977. Initially released on the small 'Backbeat' label in 1994, the single was eventually re-released by 'Parlophone' after the label promptly snapped the group up in 1994. Although the track narrowly missed the Top 40, a 1995 follow-up, 'MANSIZE ROOSTER', made the Top 20, the MADNESS comparisons inevitable as SUPERGRASS wore their influences proudly on their retro sleeves. Another couple of singles followed in quick succession, 'LOSE IT' as a limited 'Sub Pop' singles club release and 'LENNY' as the group's first Top 10 hit. Few were surprised, then, when the debut album, 'I SHOULD COCO' (1995) made No.1 the following month, a proverbial grab-bag of musical styles from 60's harmony pop to sneering punk. The record's indisputable highlight was 'ALRIGHT', a perfectly formed BEACH BOYS via The YOUNG ONES' pop romp guaranteed to bring a smile to your face and proving that "Brit-pop" didn't necessarily mean second rate STRANGLERS/BLONDIE rip-offs. The song, and especially the Raleigh Chopper-riding exploits of the video, did much to crystallise The SUPERGRASS image, carefree, fun-loving lads with GAZ's wildly impressive sideburns adding to the cartoon appeal. Steven Spielberg was apparently even moved to offer the band the opportunity of starring in a 90's remake of The MONKEES! This was turned down, as was an offer for GAZ to model for Calvin Klein, the group preferring to concentrate solely on the music and downplay the novelty factor. Instead, there were two gems hidden away at the end of 'I SHOULD..' which indicated the direction SUPERGRASS were headed; the intoxicating, slow rolling 70's groove of 'TIME' and the dreamy psychedelia of 'SOFA (OF MY LETHARGY). Save a few live appearances and a solitary single, 'GOING OUT', SUPERGRASS were notably absent in 1996, tucked away once more at Sawmill Studios crafting their acclaimed follow-up, 'IN IT FOR THE MONEY'. Eventually released in Spring '97, the record was something of a departure to say the least. The impetuous buzzsaw punk-pop of old had been replaced by the dark assault of 'RICHARD III' while the bulk of the album fed off warped neo-psychedelia and stark introspection. Horn flourishes were sighted here and there, most satisfyingly on the lazy

chug of the aforementioned 'GOING OUT', while parping organs and acoustic strumming were the order of the day. The enigmatic shadow of The BEATLES' 'White Album' loomed large over proceedings, especially on 'YOU CAN SEE ME' and the oom-pa-pa eccentricity of 'SOMETIMES I MAKE YOU SAD'. In fact, the only glimpse of the old SUPERGRASS came with 'SUN HITS THE SKY', a soaring, handclapping, spirit-lifting celebration of good times and faraway places. No matter though, the record's dark charm ensured the band remained a critical favourite, if not quite consolidating the commercial heights of the debut. Clearly, SUPERGRASS were looking at a long term, albums-based career, and on the strength of 'IN IT . . .', the future seemed promising. In May '99, the glam BOWIE-esque 'PUMPING ON YOUR STEREO' was the first of three hit singles, the second 'MOVING' ('Dogs' by PINK FLOYD might've been "pumping on their stereo" at the time!?) previewing their self-titled third Top 3 album. However, several critics rated this as a drop in form. ALI G (Boo-y aka SACHA BARON COHEN) subsequently demolished the er, "Super-tramp" GAZ on his cult TV show; the 'SUN HITS THE SKY', indeed.
• **Covered:** STONE FREE (Jimi Hendrix) / ITCHYCOO PARK (Small Faces) / SOME GIRLS ARE BIGGER THAN OTHERS (Smiths).

Album rating: I SHOULD COCO (*9) / IN IT FOR THE MONEY (*8) / SUPERGRASS (*6)

JENNIFERS

GAZ COOMBES (b. GARETH, 8 Mar'76, Brighton, England) – vocals, guitar / **NICK GOFFEY** – guitar / **ANDY DAVIES** – bass / **DANNY GOFFEY** (b. DANIEL, 7 Feb'75, London, England) – drums

		Nude-Sony	not iss.
Aug 92.	(12"ep/cd-ep) *(NUD2 T/CD)* **JUST GOT BACK TODAY / ROCKS AND BOULDERS. / DANNY'S SONG / TOMORROW'S RAIN**	☐	-

—— **MICKEY QUINN** (b. MICHAEL, 17 Dec'69) – guitar; repl. TARA MILTON who had repl. NICK

SUPERGRASS

—— now without DAVIES who went to Bristol University

		Parlophone	Capitol
Oct 94.	(7"/c-s) *(R/TCR 6396)* <81769> **CAUGHT BY THE FUZZ. / STRANGE ONES** (cd-s+=) *(CDR 6396)* – Caught by the fuzz (acoustic).	43	☐ Feb95
Feb 95.	(7"/7"red/c-s) *(R/RS/TCR 6402)* <81964> **MANSIZE ROOSTER. / SITTING UP STRAIGHT** (cd-s+=) *(CDR 6402)* – Odd.	20	☐ Jun95
Mar 95.	(7"yellow) *(<SP 281>)* **LOSE IT. / CAUGHT BY THE FUZZ (acoustic)** (above on 'Sub Pop' also feat. on Jul95 box-set 'HELTER SHELTER') *(re-iss. Sep99; same)*	75	☐
Apr 95.	(7"blue/c-s) *(RS/TCR 6401)* **LENNY. / WAIT FOR THE SUN** (cd-s+=) *(CDR 6410)* – Sex!.	9	-
May 95.	(cd/c/lp) *(CD/TC+/PCS 7373)* <33350> **I SHOULD COCO** – I'd like to know / Caught by the fuzz / Mansize rooster / Alright / Lose it / Lenny / Strange ones / Sitting up straight / She's so loose / We're not supposed to / Time / Sofa (of my lethargy) / Time to go. *(7"free w/ ltd lp)* **STONE FREE. / ODD?**	1	☐ Jul95
Jul 95.	(c-s/7"colrd) *(TC+/R 6413)* <82277> **ALRIGHT / TIME** (cd-s+=) *(CDR 6413)* – Condition / Je suis votre papa sucre. (cd-s+=) *(CDRX 6413)* – Lose it.	2	☐
Feb 96.	(c-s/7"burgundy) *(TC+/R 6428)* **GOING OUT. / MELANIE DAVIS** (cd-s+=) *(CDR 6428)* – Strange ones (live).	5	-
Apr 97.	(cd-s/7"yellow) *(CD/+R 6461)* <83820> **RICHARD III. / NOTHING MORE'S GONNA GET IN MY WAY** (cd-s+=) *(CDRS 6461)* – 20ft halo. (cd-s) *(CDRS 6461)* – ('A'side) / Sometimes you make me very sad / Sometimes we're very sad.	2	☐
Apr 97.	(cd/c/lp) *(CD/TC+/PCS 7388)* <55228> **IN IT FOR THE MONEY** – In it for the money / Richard III / Tonight / Late in the day / G-song / Sun hits the sky / Going out / It's not me / Cheapskate / You can see me / Hollow little reign / Sometimes I make you sad.	2	☐ May97
Jun 97.	(c-s/7") *(TC+/R 6469)* <84187> **SUN HITS THE SKY. / SOME GIRLS ARE BIGGER THAN OTHERS** (cd-s+=) *(CDR 6469)* – ('A'extended.	10	☐
Oct 97.	(7"gold) *(R 6484)* <84758> **LATE IN THE DAY. / WE STILL NEED MORE (THAN ANYONE CAN GIVE)** (cd-s+=) *(CDRS 6484)* – It's not me (demo). (cd-s) *(CDR 6484)* – ('A'side) / Don't be cruel / The animal.	18	☐

—— while SUPERGRASS took a break from the biz, DANNY moonlighted with the indie superband, LODGER, who issued a few singles in '98

May 99.	(c-s) *(TCR 6518)* **PUMPING ON YOUR STEREO / YOU'LL NEVER WALK AGAIN** (cd-s+=) *(CDRS 6518)* – Sick. (cd-s) *(CDR 6518)* – ('A'side) / What a shame / Lucky (no fear).	11	☐
Sep 99.	(7") *(R 6524)* **MOVING. / BELIEVER** (c-s+=/cd-s+=) *(TCR/CDR 6524)* – Faraway (acoustic). (cd-s) *(CDRS 6524)* – ('A'side) / You too can play alright / Pumping on your stereo (CD-Rom).	9	☐
Sep 99.	(cd/c) *(522056-2/-4)* **SUPERGRASS** – Moving / Your love / What went wrong (in your head) / Beautiful people / Shotover hill / Eon / Mary / Jesus came back from outta space / Pumping on your stereo / Born again / Faraway / Mama and papa.	3	☐
Nov 99.	(7"silver) *(R 6531)* **MARY / PUMPING ON YOUR STEREO (live)** (c-s+=/cd-s+=) *(TCR/CDR 6531)* – Strange ones (live). (cd-s+=) *(CDRS 6531)* – Richard III (live) / Sun hits the sky (live).	36	☐

SUPERNATURALS

Formed: Glasgow, Scotland . . . mid-90's by JAMES McCOLL, KEN McALPINE, DEREK McMANUS, ALAN TILSTON and MARK GUTHRIE. The Scottish equivalent to HERMAN'S HERMITS, The SUPERNATURALS took the softer elements of TEENAGE FANCLUB and smiled their way WET WET WET-style into the hearts of the nation's less discerning retro-pop fans. Although the aforementioned 'SMILE' failed to chart first time round in '96, the frighteningly annoying follow-up, 'LAZY LOVER' gave them their first Top 40 hit. Spookily enough, the band notched up a further series of Top 30 sub-DODGY hits the following year, all included on their debut long-player, 'IT DOESN'T MATTER ANYMORE' (you could well be right, lads!).

Album rating: IT DOESN'T MATTER ANYMORE (*6) / A TUNE A DAY (*6)

JAMES McCOLL – vocals, guitar / **KEN McALPINE** – keyboards, tambourine / **DEREK McMANUS** – guitar, vocals / **ALAN TILSTON** – drums / **MARK GUTHRIE** – bass

		Food	not iss.
Jul 96.	(7") *(FOOD 79)* **SMILE. / CAN'T GET BACK TO NORMAL** (cd-s+=) *(CDFOOD 79)* – Mint choc chip.	☐	-
Oct 96.	(c-s/7") *(TC+/FOOD 85)* **LAZY LOVER. / JOSEPHINE** (cd-s+=) *(CDFOOD 85)* – Caterpillar song.	34	-
Jan 97.	(7") *(FOOD 88)* **THE DAY BEFORE YESTERDAY'S MAN. / HONK WILLIAMS** (cd-s+=) *(CDFOOD 88)* – Ken's song. (cd-s) *(CDFOODS 88)* – ('A'side) / Deep in my heart I know I'm a slob / Brontosaurus.	25	-
Apr 97.	(7") *(FOOD 92)* **SMILE. / STALINGRAD** (cd-s+=) *(CDFOOD 92)* – Childhood sweetheart. (cd-s) *(CDFOOD 92)* – ('A'side) / Can't get back to normal / Mint choc chip.	23	-
May 97.	(cd/c) *(FOOD CD/MC/LP 21)* **IT DOESN'T MATTER ANYMORE** – Please be gentle with me / Smile / Glimpse of the light / Lazy lover / Love has passed away / Dung beetle / Stammer / I don't think so / Pie in the sky / The day before yesterday's man / Prepare to land / Trees.	9	-
Jul 97.	(c-s) *(TCFOOD 99)* **LOVE HAS PASSED AWAY / THE DAY BEFORE YESTERDAY'S MAN / LAZY LOVER** (cd-s) *(CDFOODS 99)* – ('A'side) / Scandinavian girlfriend / That's not me. (cd-s) *(CDFOOD 99)* – ('A'side) / Trying too hard / Rupert the bear.	38	-
Oct 97.	(7") *(FOOD 106)* **PREPARE TO LAND. / STUPID LOVESONG** (cd-s+=) *(CDFOOD 106)* – Skyway. (cd-s) *(CDFOODS 106)* – ('A'side) / High tension at Boghead / Take some time out.	48	-
Jul 98.	(c-s/cd-s) *(TCFOOD/CDFOODS 112)* **I WASN'T BUILT TO GET UP / ROBOT SONG / I JUST CAN'T GO ON LIKE THIS** (cd-s) *(CDFOOD 112)* – ('A'side) / Star wars / Bubblegum hill.	25	-
Aug 98.	(cd/c) *(856893-2/-4)* **A TUNE A DAY** – You take yourself too seriously / Monday mornings / Submarine song / I wasn't built to get up / Country music / Motorcycle parts / Sheffield song (I love her more than I love you) / VW song / Idiot / Magnet / Still got that feeling / Let me know / It doesn't matter anymore / Everest.	21	-
Oct 98.	(c-s/cd-s) *(TCFOOD/CDFOODS 115)* **SHEFFIELD SONG (I LOVE HER MORE THAN I LOVE YOU) / I DON'T THINK IT'S OVER / X COUNTRY SONG** (cd-s) *(CDFOOD 115)* – ('A'side) / Boys in the band / Hang out with you.	45	-
Mar 99.	(c-s) *(TCFOOD 119)* **EVEREST / YOU'RE MY BEST FRIEND** (cd-s+=) *(CDFOOD 119)* – Smile (demo). (cd-s) *(CDFOODS 119)* – ('A'side) / Let it bleat / Tomato man.	52	☐

SUPERTRAMP

Formed: London, England . . . 1969 by RICHARD DAVIES. Through the sponsorship of Dutch millionaire, Stanley Miesegaes, he enlisted RICHARD PALMER, BOB MILLER and co-writer, ROBERT HODGSON through a music paper ad. Signing to 'A&M', the band released a largely ignored and directionless eponymous debut in summer 1970, the record's poor critical and commercial reception engendering a personnel reshuffle; HODGSON switched to guitar, recruiting a new rhythm section of FRANK FARRELL and KEVIN CURRIE and adding sax player, DAVE WINTHROP. The resulting album, 'INDELIBLY STAMPED' (1971) was more notable for the tasteless cover shot (a heavily tattooed bust) than any of the music contained within and the group packed it in later that summer. While WINTHROP later joined SECRET AFFAIR, DAVIES and HODGSON resurrected SUPERTRAMP a couple of years later, enlisting the former BEES MAKE HONEY rhythm section of DOUGIE THOMPSON and BOB C. BENBERG along with sax/clarinet player JOHN ANTHONY HELLIWELL. The musical chemistry finally clicked and 1974's 'CRIME OF THE CENTURY' album propelled SUPERTRAMP to major league prog-rock/pop status. Complex, insidious and intelligently crafted, the record married conceptually depressing lyrical fare to infectiously melodic hooklines with surprising results. The album itself made the Top 5 while 'DREAMER' was a Top 20 hit single. 'CRISIS? WHAT CRISIS?' (1975) and 'EVEN IN THE QUIETEST MOMENTS' (1977) utilised the same musicians and carried on in much the same vein, solidifying their growing cult fanbase (especially in the US) and even spawning a transatlantic hit single in the acoustic-based 'GIVE A LITTLE BIT'. Increasingly catering to the American AOR market, SUPERTRAMP finally broke through big style with the multi-million selling (US No.1) 'BREAKFAST IN AMERICA' (1979) and its attendant US hits. A living, breathing example of all that punk set out to destroy, this perhaps remains one of the album's charms; while the vocals may have erred towards limp posturing and the lyrics towards irrelevance, there was no denying the record's lasting pop appeal, especially the pompous yet evocative title track. ' . . .FAMOUS LAST WORDS' (1982) was the next studio set, carrying on in much the same inoffensive vein without the saving grace of its predecessor's charm. HODGSON left soon after (subsequently recording two mid-80's solo albums, 'IN THE EYE OF THE STORM' and 'HAI HAI'), leaving SUPERTRAMP to complete a further two studio sets, 'BROTHER WHERE YOU BOUND' (1985) and 'FREE AS A BIRD' (1987) amid increasing disinterest. Although they finally folded after a 1988 live effort, they reformed a mere eight years later and recorded an album for 'Chrysalis', 'SOME THINGS NEVER CHANGE' (1997). Unfortunately for SUPERTRAMP, the music scene had changed irrevocably and the record barely scraped a Top 75 placing. • **Songwriters:** HODGSON and/or DAVIE, except I'M YOUR HOOCHIE COOCHIE MAN (John Lee Hooker). • **Trivia:** They took their name from a 1910 W.H. Davies book, 'The Autobiography Of A Supertramp'.

Album rating: SUPERTRAMP (*4) / INDELIBLY STAMPED (*4) / CRIME OF THE CENTURY (*8) / CRISIS? WHAT CRISIS? (*6) / EVEN IN THE QUIETEST MOMENTS (*6) / BREAKFAST IN AMERICA (*7) / PARIS (*5) / . . .FAMOUS LAST WORDS (*6) / BROTHER WHERE YOU BOUND (*4) / THE AUTOBIOGRAPHY OF SUPERTRAMP compilation (*8) / FREE AS A BIRD (*4) / LIVE '88 (*4) / SOME THINGS NEVER CHANGE (*5)

RICHARD DAVIES (b.22 Jul'44) – vocals, keyboards (ex-The JOINT) / **ROGER HODGSON** (b.21 Mar'50) – bass, keyboards, vocals / **RICHARD PALMER** – guitar / **BOB MILLER** – drums

	A&M	A&M
Aug 70. (lp) *(AMLS 981)* **SUPERTRAMP**		

– Surely / It's a long road / Aubade / And I am not like other birds of prey / Words unspoken / Maybe I'm a beggar / Home again / Nothing to show / Shadow song / Try again / Surely (reprise). *<US-iss.Mar78; 4665> (re-iss. Mar82 lp/c; AMID/CMID 123) (re-iss. May84 on 'Hallmark' lp/c; SHM/HSC 3139) (cd-iss. 1988; CDA 3129) (re-iss. c Jan93)*

(May'71) HODGSON now also lead guitar, vox / **FRANK FARRELL** – bass / **KEVIN CURRIE** – drums repl. PALMER + MILLER / added **DAVE WINTHROP** (b.27 Nov'48, New Jersey) – saxophone

Jun 71. (lp/c) *(AMLS 64306)* **INDELIBLY STAMPED**		

– Your poppa don't mind / Travelled / Rosie had everything planned / Remember / Forever / Potter / Coming home to see you / Times have changed / Friend in need / Aries. *(cd-iss. 1988; CDA 3149) (re-iss. c Jan93)*

Oct 71. (7") *<1305>* **FOREVER. / YOUR POPPA DON'T MIND**	-	

Disbanded late Summer 1971, WINTHROP later joined SECRET AFFAIR. **DAVIES + HODGSON** re-formed them Aug'73. Recruited **DOUGIE THOMPSON** (b.24 Mar'51, Glasgow, Scotland) – bass (ex-BEES MAKE HONEY) / **BOB C. BENBERG** (b.SIEBENBERG) – drums (ex-BEES MAKE HONEY) / **JOHN ANTHONY HELLIWELL** (b.15 Feb'45, Todmorden, England) – saxophone, clarinet, vocals (ex-ALAN BOWN SET)

Mar 74. (7") *(AMS 7101)* **LAND HO. / SUMMER ROMANCE**		-
Sep 74. (lp/c) *(AMLS/CAM 68258) <3647>* **CRIME OF THE CENTURY**	4	38

– School / Bloody well right / Hide in your shell / Asylum / Dreamer / Rudy / If everyone was listening / Crime of the century. *(cd-iss. Apr86; CDA 68258) (cd re-iss. May97; 393647-2)*

Dec 74. (7") *(AMS 7152) <1660>* **DREAMER. / BLOODY WELL RIGHT**	13	35 Mar75

<above B-side was US A-side>

Nov 75. (lp/c) *(AMLH/CAM 68347) <4560>* **CRISIS? WHAT CRISIS?**	20	44

– Easy does it / Sister Moonshine / Ain't nobody but me / A soapbox opera / Another man's woman / Lady / Poor boy / Just a normal day / The meaning / Two of us. *(cd-iss. Apr86; CDA 4560) (cd re-iss. May97; 394560-2)*

Nov 75. (7") *(AMS 7201) <1793>* **LADY. / YOU STARTED LAUGHING (WHEN I HELD YOU IN MY ARMS)**		
Jun 76. (7") *<1814>* **SISTER MOONSHINE. / AIN'T NOBODY BUT ME**	-	
Apr 77. (lp/c) *(AMLK/CAM 64634) <4634>* **EVEN IN THE QUIETEST MOMENTS**	12	16

– Give a little bit / Lover boy / Even in the quietest moments / Downstream / Babaji / From now on / Fool's overture. *(cd-iss. Apr86; CDA 4634) (cd re-iss. May97; 394634-2)*

Jun 77. (7") *(AMS 7293) <1938>* **GIVE A LITTLE BIT. / DOWNSTREAM**	29	15
Nov 77. (7") *<1981>* **FROM NOW ON. / DREAMER**	-	
Nov 77. (7") *(AMS 7326)* **BABAJI. / FROM NOW ON**		
Mar 79. (lp/c) *(AMLK/CAM 63708) <3708>* **BREAKFAST IN AMERICA**	3	1

– Gone Hollywood / The logical song / Goodbye stranger / Breakfast in America / Oh darling / Take the long way home / Lord is it mine / Just another nervous wreck / Casual conversations / Child of vision. *(cd-iss. 1983; CDA 63708) (cd re-iss. May97; 393708-2)*

Mar 79. (7") *(AMS 7427) <2128>* **THE LOGICAL SONG. / JUST ANOTHER NERVOUS WRECK**	7	6
Jun 79. (7") *(AMS 7451)* **BREAKFAST IN AMERICA. / GONE HOLLYWOOD**	9	-
Sep 79. (7") *(AMS 7481) <2162>* **GOODBYE STRANGER. / EVEN IN THE QUIETEST MOMENTS**	57	15 Jul79
Oct 79. (7") *(AMS 7560)* **TAKE THE LONG WAY HOME. / FROM NOW ON**		-
Oct 79. (7") *<2193>* **TAKE THE LONG WAY HOME. / RUBY**	-	10
Sep 80. (d-lp/d-c) *(AMLM/CLM 66702) <6702>* **PARIS** (live 29-11-79)	7	8

– School / Ain't nobody but me / The logical song / Bloody well right / Breakfast in America / You started laughing / Hide in your shell / From now on / Dreamer / Rudy / A soapbox opera / Asylum / Take the long way home / Fool's overture / Two of us / Crime of the century. *(cd-iss. Apr86; CDD 6702)*

Sep 80. (7") *<2269>* **DREAMER (live). / FROM NOW ON** (live)	-	15
Nov 80. (7") *(AMS 7576)* **DREAMER (live). / YOU STARTED LAUGHING** (live)		
Nov 80. (7") *<2292>* **BREAKFAST IN AMERICA (live). / YOU STARTED LAUGHING** (live)	-	62
Oct 82. (7") *(AMS 8255) <2502>* **IT'S RAINING AGAIN. / BONNIE**	26	11
Oct 82. (lp/c) *(AMLK/CKM 63732) <3732>* **. . .FAMOUS LAST WORDS**	6	5

– Crazy / Put on your brown school shoes / It's raing again / Bonnie / Know who

you are / My kind of lady / C'est la bon / Waiting so long / Don't leave me now. *(cd-iss. 1983; CDA 63732)*

Jan 83. (7") *(AMS 8301) <2517>* **MY KIND OF LADY. / KNOW WHO YOU ARE**		31

(Nov82) Now a quartet when HODGSON departed to go solo. (Re-joined briefly late'86 tour). HODGSON solo albums: IN THE EYE OF THE STORM ('84) / HAI HAI ('87).

Apr 85. (7") *(AMS 248) <2731>* **CANNONBALL. / EVER OPEN DOOR**		28
May 85. (lp/c/cd) *(<AMA/AMC/CDA 5014>)* **BROTHER WHERE YOU BOUND**	20	21

– Cannonball / Still in love / No inbetween / Better days / Brother where you bound / Ever open door. *(re-iss. Jan93)*

Jul 85. (7") *(AMS 265) <2720>* **STILL IN LOVE. / NO INBETWEEN**		Feb85
(12"+=) – Cannonball (dance mix).		
Sep 85. (7") *<2760>* **BETTER DAYS. / NO INBETWEEN**	-	
Nov 86. (lp/c/cd) *(TRAMP/TRAMC/TRACD 1)* **THE AUTOBIOGRAPHY OF SUPERTRAMP** (compilation)	9	-

– Goodbye stranger / The logical song / Bloody well right / Breakfast in America / Take the long way home / Crime of the century / Dreamer / From now on / Give a little bit / It's raining again / Cannonball / Ain't nobody but me / Hide in your shell / Rudy. *(cd= 3 extra) (re-iss. cd Jan93 as 'THE VERY BEST OF SUPERTRAMP'+=)*– School.

Oct 87. (7"/12") *(AM/+Y 415)* **I'M BEGGIN' YOU. / NO INBETWEENS**		
Oct 87. (lp/c/cd) *(<AMA/AMC/CDA 5181>)* **FREE AS A BIRD**	93	

– It's alright / Not the moment / It doesn't matter / Where I stand / Free as a bird / I'm beggin' you / You never can tell with friends / Thing for you / An awful thing to waste.

Feb 88. (7") *<2996>* **FREE AS A BIRD. / THING FOR YOU**	-	
Feb 88. (7") *(AM 430)* **FREE AS A BIRD. / I'M BEGGIN' YOU**	-	
Oct 88. (lp/c/cd) *(MA/AMC/CDA 3923)* **LIVE '88** (live)		

– You started laughing / It's alright / Not the moment / Oh darling / Breakfast in America / From now on / Just another nervous wreck / The logical song / I'm your hoochie coochie man / Crime of the century / Don't you lie to me. *(re-iss. cd Jan93)*

Folded after above, although they reformed 8 years later. Line-up:- **RICK DAVIES** – vocals, keyboards / **MARK HART** – vocals, keyboards, guitars / **JOHN HELLIWELL** – saxophones, woodwind / **CLIFF HUGO** – bass / **BOB SIEBENBERG** – drums / **LEE R. THORNBURG** – trumpet, trombone, vocals / **CARL VERHEYEN** – guitars / **TOM WALSH** – percussion

	Chrysalis	Chrysalis
Apr 97. (cd/c) *(CD/TC CHR 6121)* **SOME THINGS NEVER CHANGE**	74	

– It's a hard world / You win, I lose / Get your act together / Live to love you / Some things never change / Listen to me please / Sooner or later / Help me down that road / And the light / Give me a chance / C'est what? / Where there's a will.

– compilations, etc. –

on 'A&M' unless mentioned otherwise

May 81. (d-c) A&M; *(CAMCR 7)* **CRISIS? WHAT CRISIS? / EVEN IN THE QUIETEST MOMENTS**	-	-
Sep 85. (7") Old Gold; *(OG 9542)* **DREAMER. / GIVE A LITTLE BIT**	-	-
Sep 86. (7") *(AM 357)* **THE LOGICAL SONG. / GOODBYE STRANGER**	-	-
Aug 88. (cd-ep) *(AMCD 914)* **COMPACT HITS**	-	-

– The logical song / Breakfast in America / Goodbye stranger / Hide in your shell.

Jul 92. (7")(c-s) **GIVE A LITTLE BIT (for Telethon). / ('A' original version)**		

(cd-s+=) – Breakfast in America.

Aug 92. (cd/c) *(TRA CD/MC 1992)* **THE VERY BEST OF SUPERTRAMP**	24	

– Schhol / Goodbye stranger / The logical song / Bloody well right / Breakfast in America / Rudy / Take the long way home / Crime of the century / Dreamer / Ain't nobody but me / Hide in your shell / From now on / It's raining again / Give a little bit / Cannonball. *(re-iss. Sep97 hit UK No.8)*

Apr 94. (cd) Compact Club; *(CCV 8919)* **THE SUPERTRAMP SONGBOOK**		-

SUPREMES

Formed: Detroit, Michigan, USA . . . 1959 as The PRIMETTES by PRIMES (an outfit that included future members of The TEMPTATIONS) manager, Milton Jenkins who originally employed by the then quartet of DIANA ROSS, FLORENCE BALLARD, MARY WILSON and BETTY TRAVIS to augment his act on stage. Making a name for themselves around town by guesting on records by established artists, the girls were eventually signed to 'Motown' where label owner, Berry Gordy took them under his wing, renamed them The SUPREMES and singled them out for special treatment. By the release of debut single, 'I WANT A GUY', in late 1960, BETTY had been replaced by BARBARA MARTIN who herself departed the following summer after the release of a second track, 'BUTTERED POPCORN'. Reduced to a trio, the group released a combination of minor hit singles and flops over the ensuing two years including 'LET ME GO THE RIGHT WAY' and 'MY HEART CAN'T TAKE NO MORE'. Many of these tracks had showcased BALLARD's earthy vocal style and the hits only really began piling up when ROSS' cooler, more seductive tones were pushed to the fore. Set to work on material by the crack songwriting team of HOLLAND/DOZIER/HOLLAND, the group scored their first Top 30 hit in late '63 with 'WHEN THE LOVELIGHT STARTS SHINING THROUGH HIS EYES'. The following summer they hit the US top spot (and the UK Top 3) with 'WHERE DID OUR LOVE GO' and over the coming decade racked up an incredible run of classic No.1 singles, becoming in the process the most successful act of the girl group era. Schooled in the legendary Motown way (i.e. choreography, etiquette etc,), The SUPREMES outshone their contemporaries in every department i.e. more glamorous, more professional, more adaptable, more urbane. Above all they had the best tunes and, in DIANA ROSS, a secret weapon of a singer capable of transforming even mediocre material into gold-dust. The run of US No.1's included 'BABY LOVE', 'STOP IN THE NAME OF LOVE', 'BACK IN MY ARMS AGAIN', 'I HEAR A SYMPHONY', 'YOU CAN'T HURRY LOVE' and 'YOU KEEP ME HANGIN' ON', many of these records coming to define the sound of quintessential 60's Motown pop-soul. The classic line-up's final No.1 came with 'THE HAPPENING' in 1967 after which BALLARD departed in messy circumstances (one of Motown's truly tragic characters, she was subsequently cheated out of her severance money and died amid depression, alcoholism and personal problems on the 22nd February '76, aged only 32). Although ex-PATTI LaBELLE & THE BLUE BELLES singer CINDY BIRDSONG was drafted in as a replacement, the next single, 'REFLECTIONS', was released as DIANA ROSS & THE SUPREMES, an indication of ROSS' impending solo career. Having dispensed with the services of HOLLAND/DOZIER/HOLLAND, the hits became thinner on the ground although the social commentary of 'LOVE CHILD' gave them a No.1 in late '68, the group teaming up with old buddies The TEMPTATIONS for a transatlantic Top 3 hit, 'I'M GONNA MAKE YOU LOVE ME' around the same time. Ironically, 'SOMEDAY WE'LL BE TOGETHER' marked their final No.1 in late '69 prior to ROSS' final appearance with the group at a Las Vegas farewell show in early 1970. JEAN TERRELL was the initial replacement, herself succeeded three years later by SCHERRIE PAYNE. In the meantime, the group had only scored one Top 10 hit (discounting the late 1970 collaboration with The FOUR TOPS on a cover of 'RIVER DEEP/MOUNTAIN HIGH') with 'STONED LOVE' in early 1971. LYNDA LAWRENCE had also replaced BIRDSONG and the pattern of personnel upheaval continued amid diminishing chart returns and the indifference of 'Motown' until they finally gave up the ghost in 1977. ROSS, meanwhile, had been paired with ASHFORD & SIMPSON, who produced her first run of solo hits beginning with 'REACH OUT AND TOUCH (SOMEBODY'S HAND)' in 1970. The eponymous debut album also contained her No.1 cover of 'AIN'T NO MOUNTAIN HIGH ENOUGH' (previously a Top 20 hit in 1967 for MARVIN GAYE & TAMMI TERRELL), setting her up as a polished soul diva in the making. • Trivia: Their hits have been covered successfully by many acts. The most popular being YOU CAN'T HURRY LOVE (Phil Collins) / YOU KEEP ME HANGIN' ON (Vanila Fudge) / NATHAN JONES (Bananarama).

Best CD compilation: 40 GOLDEN MOTOWN GREATS (*9)

DIANA ROSS (b.26 Mar'44) – lead vocals / **FLORENCE BALLARD** (b.30 Jun'43) – vocals / **MARY WILSON** (b. 6 Mar44, Greenville, Missouri) – vocals / **BARBARA MARTIN** – vocals; repl. BETTY TRAVIS in 1960

		Oriole	Motown
Dec 60.	(7") <54038> **I WANT A GUY. / NEVER AGAIN**	-	□
Jul 61.	(7") <54045> **BUTTERED POPCORN. / WHO'S LOVING YOU**	-	□

—— slimmed to a trio when BARBARA left

Jul 62.	(7") <1027> **YOUR HEART BELONGS TO ME. / (HE'S) SEVENTEEN**	-	95
Nov 62.	(7") <1034> **LET ME GO THE RIGHT WAY. / TIME CHANGES THINGS**	-	90
Apr 63.	(7") <1040> **MY HEART CAN'T TAKE NO MORE. / YOU BRING BACK MEMORIES**	-	□
Jul 63.	(7") <1044> **A BREATH TAKING GUY. / (THE MAN WITH THE) ROCK AND ROLL BANJO BAND**	-	75

                Stateside Motown

Dec 63.	(7") (SS 257) <1051> **WHEN THE LOVELIGHT STARTS SHINING THROUGH HIS EYES. / STANDING AT THE CROSSROADS OF LOVE**	-	□
Feb 64.	(lp) <606> **MEET THE SUPREMES**		23 Nov63

– Where did our love go / Your heart belongs to me / Buttered popcorn / Baby, don't go / (The man with) Rock and roll banjo band / I want a guy / When the lovelight starts shining through his eyes / You bring back memories / Play a sad song / Time changes things / Never again / Standing at the crossroads of love. (UK-iss.Nov64; SL 10109) – hit No.8

Mar 64.	(7") <1054> **RUN, RUN, RUN. / I'M GIVING YOU YOUR FREEDOM**	-	93
Aug 64.	(7") (SS 327) <1060> **WHERE DID OUR LOVE GO. / HE MEANS THE WORLD TO ME**	3	1 Jun64

(re-iss.Aug74) (re-iss. as were most major hit singles; Oct81)

Sep 64.	(lp) <623> **WHERE DID OUR LOVE GO**	-	2

– Where did our love go / Run, run, run / Baby love / When the lovelight starts shining through his eyes / Come see about me / Long gone lover / I'm giving you your freedom / A breath taking guy / He means the world to me / Standing at the crossroads of love / Your kiss of fire. (re-iss. Oct81)

Oct 64.	(7") (SS 350) <1066> **BABY LOVE. / ASK ANY GIRL**	1	1 Sep64
Jan 65.	(7") (SS 376) <1068> **COME SEE ABOUT ME. / (YOU'RE GONE BUT) ALWAYS IN MY HEART**	27	1 Nov64

           Tamla
           Motown Motown

Jan 65.	(lp) (TML 11002) <623> **WITH LOVE – FROM US TO YOU** <US-title 'A BIT OF LIVERPOOL'>		21 Nov64

– How do you do it / World without love / House of the rising sun / A hard day's night / Because / You've really got a hold on me / You can't do that / Do you love me / Can't buy me love / I want to hold your hand / Bits and pieces.

Mar 65.	(7") (TMG 501) <1074> **STOP! IN THE NAME OF LOVE. / I'M IN LOVE AGAIN**	7	1 Feb65
May 65.	(7") (TMG 516) <1075> **BACK IN MY ARMS AGAIN. / WHISPER YOU LOVE ME BOY**	40	1 Apr65
Jul 65.	(lp) (TML 11012) <629> **WE REMEMBER SAM COOKE**		75 Apr65

– You send me / Nothing can change this love / Cupid / Chain gang / Bring it on home to me / Only sixteen / Havin' a party / Shake / Wonderful world / A change is gonna come / (Ain't that) Good news. (re-iss.May86 lp/c; WL/WK 72445)

Jul 65.	(7") (TMG 527) <1080> **NOTHING BUT HEARTACHES. / HE HOLDS HIS OWN**		11
Aug 65.	(lp) (TML 11018) <625> **THE SUPREMES SING COUNTRY WESTERN AND POP**		79 Mar65

– Funny how time slips away / My heart can't take it no more / It makes no difference now / You didn't care / Tears in vain / Tumbling tumbleweeds / Lazy bones / You need me / Baby doll / Sunset / (The man with the) Rock and roll banjo band.

Sep 65.	(lp) (TML 11020) <627> **MORE HITS BY THE SUPREMES** (compilation)		6 Aug65

– Ask any girl / Nothing but heartaches / Mother dear / Honey boy / Back in my arms again / Whisper you love me, boy / The only time I'm happy / He holds his own / Who could ever doubt my love / Heartaches don't last always / I'm in love again.

Nov 65.	(7") (TMG 543) <1083> **I HEAR A SYMPHONY. / WHO COULD EVER DOUBT MY LOVE**	39	1 Oct65
Dec 65.	(7") <1085> **TWINKLE, TWINKLE LITTLE ME. / CHILDREN'S CHRISTMAS SONG**	-	
Dec 65.	(lp) <638> **MERRY CHRISTMAS** (festive songs)		

(UK-iss.Nov82 lp/c; STMS/CSTMS 5084) (re-iss. 1986 lp/c; WL/WK 72117)

Jan 66.	(lp; stereo/mono) (S+/TML 11026) <636> **THE SUPREMES AT THE COPA** (live)		11 Nov65

– Opening introduction: Put on a happy face / I am woman / Baby love / Stop! in the name of love / The boy from Ipanema / Make someone happy / Come see about me / Rock-a-bye your baby with a dixie melody / Queen of the house / Group intro – Somewhere / Back in my arms again / Sam Cooke medley / You're nobody til somebody loves you. (re-iss. Mar82 lp/c; STMS/CSTMS 5045)

Feb 66.	(7") (TMG 548) <1089> **MY WORLD IS EMPTY WITHOUT YOU. / EVERYTHING IS GOOD ABOUT YOU**		5 Jan66
May 66.	(lp; stereo/mono) (S+/TML 11028) <643> **I HEAR A SYMPHONY**		8 Mar66

– Stranger in Paradise / Yesterday / I hear a symphony / Unchained melody / With a song in my heart / My world is empty without you / A lover's concerto / Any girl in love (knows what I'm going through) / Wonderful, wonderful / Everything is good about you / He's all I got. (re-iss. Oct81 lp/c; STMS/CSTMS 5012)

May 66.	(7") (TMG 560) <1094> **LOVE IS LIKE AN ITCHING IN MY HEART. / HE'S ALL I GOT**		9 Apr66
Aug 66.	(7") (TMG 575) <1097> **YOU CAN'T HURRY LOVE. / PUT YOURSELF IN MY PLACE**	3	1
Oct 66.	(7") <1101> **YOU KEEP ME HANGIN' ON. / REMOVE THIS DOUBT**	-	1
Nov 66.	(7") (TMG 585) **YOU KEEP ME HANGIN' ON. / COME SEE ABOUT ME**	8	-
Dec 66.	(lp; stereo/mono) (S+/TML 11039) <649> **THE SUPREMES A-GO-GO**	15	1 Sep66

– Love is like an itching in my heart / This old heart of mine (is weak for you) / You can't hurry love / Shake me, wake up (when it's over) / Baby I need your loving / These boots are made for walking / I can't help myself / Get ready / Put yourself in my place / Money (that's what I want) / Come and get these memories / Hang on Sloopy. (re-iss. Oct81 lp/c; STMS/CSTMS 5013) (re-iss. 1986; WL 72072)

Feb 67.	(7") (TMG 597) <1103> **LOVE IS HERE AND NOW YOU'RE GONE. / THERE'S NO STOPPING US NOW**	17	1 Jan67
Apr 67.	(lp; stereo/mono) (S+/TML 11047) <650> **THE SUPREMES SING MOTOWN** <US-title 'THE SUPREMES SING HOLLAND-DOZIER-HOLLAND'>	15	6 Feb67

– You keep me hangin' on / You're gone, but always in my heart / Love is here and now you're gone / Mother, you smother me / I guess I'll always love you / I'll turn to stone / It's the same old song / Going down for the third time / Love is in our hearts / Remove the doubt / There's no stopping us now / Heatwave. (re-iss. Oct81 lp/c; STMS/CSTMS 5014) (cd-iss. Sep95)

May 67.	(7") (TMG 607) <1107> **THE HAPPENING. / ALL I KNOW ABOUT YOU**	6	1 Apr67
Sep 67.	(lp; stereo/mono) (S+/TML 11054) <659> **THE SUPREMES SING RODGERS AND HART**	25	20 Jun67

– The lady is a tramp / Mountain greenery / This can't be love / Where or when / Lover / My funny valentine / My romance / My heart stood still / Falling in love with love / Thou swell / Dancing on the ceiling / Blue moon. (cd-iss. Nov87; same) – (extra tracks).

—— (May'67) **CINDY BIRDSONG** (b.15 Dec'39, Camden, New Jersey) – vocals (ex-PATTI LaBELLE & THE BLUEBELLES) repl. BALLARD who went solo

DIANA ROSS & THE SUPREMES

Aug 67.	(7") (TMG 616) <1111> **REFLECTIONS. / GOING DOWN FOR THE THIRD TIME**	5	2
Nov 67.	(7") (TMG 632) <1116> **IN AND OUT OF LOVE. / I GUESS I'LL ALWAYS LOVE YOU**	13	9
Jan 68.	(lp<d-lp>; stereo/mono) (S+/TML 11063) <663> **DIANA ROSS & THE SUPREMES' GREATEST HITS** (compilation)	1	1 Sep67

(re-iss. Jan79 & Jun83)

Mar 68.	(lp; stereo/mono) (S+/TML 11070) <676> **LIVE AT LONDON'S TALK OF THE TOWN** (live)	6	57 Sep68

– With a song in my heart / Stranger than Paradise / Wonderful, wonderful / Without a song / Stop! in the name of love / Come and see about me / My world is empty without you / Baby love / Love is here and now you're gone / More / You keep me hangin' on / Michelle / Yesterday / In and out of love / The lady is a tramp / Let's get away from it all / The happening / Thoroughly modern Millie / Second hand Rose / Mame / Reflections / You're nobody till somebody loves you / I hear a symphony. (re-iss. Jan80 on 'Music For Pleasure'; MFP 50447)

Mar 68.	(7") (TMG 650) <1122> **FOREVER CAME TODAY. / TIME CHANGES THINGS**	28	28
Jun 68.	(7") (TMG 662) <1126> **SOME THINGS YOU NEVER GET USED TO. / YOU'VE BEEN SO WONDERFUL TO ME**	34	30
Jul 68.	(lp; stereo/mono) (S+/TML 11073) <665> **REFLECTIONS**	30	18 Apr68

– Reflections / I'm gonna make it (I will wait for you) / Forever came today / I can't make it alone / In and out of love / Bah-bah-bah / What the world needs now is love / Up, up and away / Love (makes me do foolish things) / Then / Misery makes its home in my heart / Ode to Billie Joe. (re-iss. Mar85 lp/c; WL/WK 72368)

Nov 68.	(lp; stereo/mono) (S+/TML 11088) <672> . . .**SING AND PERFORM FUNNY GIRL** (from the musical)	-	Sep68
Nov 68.	(7") (TMG 677) <1135> **LOVE CHILD. / THIS WILL BE THE DAY**	15	1 Oct68

Jan 69. (lp; stereo/mono) (S+/TML 11095) <670> **LOVE CHILD**   `8`   `14` Dec68
– Love child / Keep an eye / How long has the evening train been gone / Does your mama know about me / Honey bee (keep on stinging me) / Something you never get used to / He's my sunny boy / You've never been so wonderful to me / (Don't break these) Chains of love / You ain't living til you're lovin' / I'll set you free / Can't shake it loose. (re-iss. Aug82 lp/c; STMS/CSTMS 5070)

—— Late 1968, The SUPREMES re-united with The TEMPTATIONS on cross-Atlantic Top 3 hit 'I'M GONNA MAKE YOU LOVE ME'. Throughout 1969, they recorded and released a number of other hit 45's and lp's.

Apr 69. (7") (TMG 695) <1139> **I'M LIVIN' IN SHAME. / I'M SO GLAD I GOT SOMEBODY (LIKE YOU AROUND)**   `14`   `10` Jan69

Apr 69. (7") <1146> **THE COMPOSER. / THE BEGINNING OF THE END**   `-`   `27`

Jun 69. (lp; stereo/mono) (S+/TML 11114) <689> **LET THE SUNSHINE IN**   `24`
– The composer / Everyday people / No matter what sign you are / Hey Western Union man / What becomes of the broken hearted? / I'm livin' in shame / Aquarius (medley: Let the sun shine in (in the flesh failures)- Let the music play / With a child's heart / Discover me (and you'll discover love) / Will this be the day / I'm so glad I got somebody (like you around).

Jul 69. (7") (TMG 704) <1148> **NO MATTER WHAT SIGN YOU ARE. / THE YOUNG FOLKS**   `37`   `31` `69` Jun69

Dec 69. (7") (TMG 721) <1156> **SOMEDAY WE'LL BE TOGETHER. / HE'S MY SUNNY BOY**   `13`   `1` Oct69

Jan 70. (lp; stereo/mono) (S+/TML 11137) <694> **CREAM OF THE CROP**   `33` Nov69
– Someday we'll be together / Can't you see it's me / You gave me love / Hey Jude / The young folks / Shadows of society / Loving you is better than ever / When it's to the top (still I won't stop giving you love) / Till Johnny comes / Blowin' in the wind / The beginning of the end.

May 70. (lp) (STML 11146) <702> **DIANA ROSS & THE SUPREMES' GREATEST HITS VOL.3** (compilation)   `31` Jan70
– Reflections / Love is here and now you're gone / Someday we'll be together / Love child / Some things you never get used to / Forever came today / In and out of love / The happening / I'm livin' in shame / No matter what sign you are / The composer. (re-iss. Jul76, Oct81)

May 70. (d-lp) (STML 11154) <708> **FAREWELL** (final concert 14 Jan'70)   `46`
– T.C.B. / Medley: Stop! in the name of love – Come see about me – My world is empty without you / Baby love / Medley: The lady is a tramp – Let's get away from it all / Love is here and now you're gone / I'm gonna make you love me / Can't take my eyes off you / Reflections / My man / Didn't we / It's alright with me / Big spender / Falling in love with love / Love child / Aquarius – Let the sunshine in (the flesh failures) / The impossible dream / Someday we'll be together / (closing dialogue from group).

The SUPREMES

—— when DIANA ROSS left to go solo (Jan'70) she was replaced by **JEAN TERRELL** (b.26 Nov'44, Texas) – lead vocals

Apr 70. (7") (TMG 735) <1162> **UP THE LADDER TO THE ROOF. / BILL, WHEN ARE YOU COMING BACK**   `6`   `10` Mar70

Jun 70. (lp) (STML 11157) <705> **RIGHT ON**   `25` May70
– Up the ladder on the roof / Then we can try again / Everybody's got the right to love / Wait a minute before you leave me / You move me / But I love you more / I got hurt / Baby baby / Take a closer look at me / Then I met you / Bill, when are you coming back / Loving country.

Jul 70. (7") (TMG 747) <1167> **EVERYBODY'S GOT THE RIGHT TO LOVE. / BUT I LOVE YOU MORE**   `21`

Nov 70. (lp) (STML 11175) <720> **NEW WAYS BUT LOVE STAYS**   `68` Oct70
– Together we can make such sweet music / Stoned love / It's time to break down / Bridge over troubled water / I wish I were your mirror / Come together / Is there a place (in his heart for me) / Na na hey hey, kiss him goodbye / Shine on me / Thank him for today.

—— late 1970, they collaborated with another 'Motown' group The FOUR TOPS. They were to hit US/UK Top 20 with their version of RIVER DEEP – MOUNTAIN HIGH. A few other hits followed in 1971, accompanied by parent albums THE MAGNIFICENT 7 / THE RETURN OF THE MAGNIFICENT 7 / DYNAMITE

Jan 71. (7") (TMG 760) <1172> **STONED LOVE. / SHINE ON ME**   `3`   `7` Nov70

Aug 71. (7") (TMG 782) <1182> **NATHAN JONES. / HAPPY IS A BUMPY ROAD**   `5`   `16` May71

Sep 71. (lp) (STML 11189) <737> **TOUCH**   `40`   `85` Jun71
– This is the story / Nathan Jones / Here comes the sunrise / Love, it came to me first time / Johnny Raven / Have I lost you / Time and love / Touch / Happy (is a bumpy road) / It's so hard for me to say goodbye. (cd-iss. Nov93; 530211-2)

Sep 71. (7") <1190> **TOUCH. / IT'S SO HARD FOR ME TO SAY GOODBYE**   `-`   `71`

Feb 72. (7") (TMG 804) <1195> **FLOY JOY. / THIS IS THE STORY**   `9`   `16` Jan72

Jun 72. (lp) (STMLK 11210) <751> **FLOY JOY**   `54` May72
– Your wonderful sweet sweet love / Floy joy / A heart like mine / Over and over / Precious little things / Now the bitter, now the sweet / Automatically sunshine / The wisdom of time / Oh be my love.

Jun 72. (7") (TMG 821) <1200> **AUTOMATICALLY SUNSHINE. / PRECIOUS LITTLE THINGS**   `10`   `37` May72

—— **LYNDA LAWRENCE** – vocals; repl. BIRDSONG who was now married

Jul 72. (7") <1206> **YOUR WONDERFUL, SWEET SWEET LOVE. / THE WISDOM OF TIME**   `-`   `59`

Aug 72. (7") (TMG 835) **YOUR WONDERFUL, SWEET SWEET LOVE. / LOVE IT CAME TO ME THIS TIME**   `-`

Nov 72. (lp) (STML 11222) <756> **THE SUPREMES (PRODUCED BY JIM WEBB)**
– I guess I'll miss the man / 5:30 plane / Tossin' and turnin' / When can Brown begin / Beyond myself / Silent voices / All I want / Once in the morning / I keep it hid / Paradise / Cheap lovin'.

Mar 73. (7") (TMG 847) **BAD WEATHER. / IT'S SO HARD FOR ME TO SAY GOODBYE**   `37`   `-`

May 73. (7") <1225> **BAD WEATHER. / OH BE MY LOVE**   `-`   `87`

Jun 73. (7") (TMG 859) **TOSSIN' AND TURNIN'. / OH BE MY LOVE**   `-`

Jan 74. (7") (TMG 884) <1213> **I GUESS I'LL MISS THE MAN. / OVER AND OVER**   `85` Oct72

—— (Jul'73) **MARY + LYNDA** enlisted newcomer **SCHERRIE PAYNE** (b.14 Nov'44) – vocals repl. TERRELL

Jun 75. (lp) (STML 11293) <828> **THE SUPREMES**
– He's my man / Eary morning love / Where is it I belong / It's been said before / This is why I believe in you / You can't stop a girl in love / Colour my world blue / Give out, but don't give up / Where do I go from here / You turn me around.

Aug 75. (7") (TMG 950) <1358> **HE'S MY MAN / GIVE OUT, BUT DON'T GIVE UP**   `-`

Nov 75. (7") (TMG 1012) **EARLY MORNING LOVE. / WHERE IS IT I BELONG**   `-`

—— (1976) **SUSAYNE GREENE** – vocals; repl. CINDY who had repl. LYNDA

—— former member FLORENCE BALLARD tragically died on 22nd of Feb'76

May 76. (7") <1391> **I'M GONNA LET MY HEART DO THE WALKING. / EARLY MORNING LOE**   `-`   `40`

Jun 76. (lp) (STML 12027) <863> **HIGH ENERGY**   `42` May76
– High energy / I'm gonna let my heart do the walking / Only you (can love me like you love me) / You keep me moving on / Don't let my teardrops better you / Till the boat sails away / I don't want to lose you / You're what's missing in my life.

Jul 76. (7") (TMG 1029) **I'M GONNA LET MY HEART DO THE WALKING. / COLOUR MY WORLD BLUE**   `-`

Nov 76. (7") <1407> **YOU'RE MY DRIVING WHEEL. / YOU'RE WHAT'S MISSING IN MY LIFE**   `-`   `85`

Dec 76. (lp) (STML 12047) <873> **MARY, SCHERRIE & SUSAYNE**
– You're my driving wheel / Sweet dream machine / Let yourself go / Come into my life / We should be closer together / I don't want to be tied down / You are the heart of me / Love I never knew you could feel so good.

Feb 77. (7") <1415> **LET YOURSELF GO. / YOU ARE THE HEART OF ME**   `-`

Mar 77. (7") (TMG 1064) **LOVE I NEVER KNEW I COULD FEEL SO GOOD. / THIS IS WHY I BELIEVE IN YOU**   `-`

—— **KAREN JACKSON** – vocals; repl. MARY WILSON who later toured as MARY WILSON & THE SUPREMES; the real SUPREMES split 1977. On 16th May '83, DIANA, MARY and CINDY re-united for one-off Motown anniversary gig

– compilations, etc. –

Note; on 'Tamla Motown' unless otherwise mentioned

Jun 74. (t-lp) (TMSP 6001) <794> **ANTHOLOGY (1962-1969)**   `66` (d-cd-iss. Apr93)

Jul 74. (7") (TMG 915) **BABY LOVE. / ASK ANY GIRL**   `12`   `-`

Nov 74. (7") (TMG 925) **WHERE DID OUR LOVE GO. / NOTHING BUT HEARTACHES**   `-`

Sep 76. (7") (TMG 1046) **NATHAN JONES. / STONED LOVE**   `-`

Mar 77. (lp) (STMX 6001) **MOTOWN SPECIAL**   `-`

Sep 77. (lp/c) (EMTV/CEMTV 5) **DIANA ROSS & THE SUPREMES' 20 GOLDEN GREATS**   `1` (re-iss. Oct81, cd-iss. May86)

Jan 79. (lp/c) Music For Pleasure; (MFP/TC-MFP 50421) **STONED LOVE**   `-`

Apr 80. (7"ep/12"ep) (TMG/+12 1180) **SUPREMES MEDLEY EP. / Diana Ross: LOVE HANGOVER**   `-`

Oct 80. (7") (TMG 956) **YOU CAN'T HURRY LOVE. / THE HAPPENING**   `-`

Oct 80. (7") (TMG 960) **REFLECTIONS. / LOVE CHILD**   `-`

Oct 80. (lp) (STMR 9008) **THE EARLY YEARS 1961-1964**   `-`

Oct 81. (7") **BABY LOVE. / STOP! IN THE NAME OF LOVE**   `-`

Oct 81. (7") (TMG 964) **UP THE LADDER TO ROOF. / AUTOMATICALLY SUNSHINE**   `-`

Oct 81. (7") (TMG 971) **RIVER DEEP – MOUNTAIN HIGH. / YOU GOTTA HAVE LOVE IN YOUR HEART**   `-`

Oct 82. (7") (TMG 974) **FLOY JOY. / BAD WEATHER**   `-`

Nov 82. (lp/c) (STMS/CSTMS 5084) **MERRY CHRISTMAS**   `-`

Mar 83. (7") (TMG 981) **LOVE IS HERE AND NOW YOU'RE GONE. / BACK IN MY ARMS AGAIN**   `-`

Apr 85. (7"/12") (TMG/+T 992) **YOU KEEP ME HANGIN' ON. / COME SEE ABOUT ME**   `-`

Apr 86. (7") (ZB 40709) **YOU KEEP ME HANGIN' ON. / COME SEE ABOUT ME**   `-`
(12"+=) (ZT 40710) – I hear a symphony / Your love is like an itching in my heart.

Jul 86. (t-lp/d-c/d-cd) <5381> **25th ANNIVERSARY**   `-`

Oct 86. (cd) (ZD 72423) **COMPACT COMMAND PERFORMANCES – 20 GREATEST HITS**   `-`
– When the lovelight starts shining through his eyes / Where did our love go / Baby love / Come see about me / My world is empty without you / Stop in the name of love / Back in my arms again / I hear a symphony / You can't hurry love / Love is like an itching in my heart / You keep me hangin' on / Love is here now you're gone / Reflections / Love child / I'll try something new / I'm gonna make you love me / Someday we'll be together / The ladder to the roof / Stoned love / Nathan Jones.

Nov 86. (cd) (ZD 72459) **WHERE DID OUR LOVE GO. / I HEAR A SYMPHONY**   `-`

Nov 86. (cd) (ZD 73485) **LOVE CHILD / SUPREMES A GO-GO**   `-`

Dec 86. (cd) (ZD 72496) **LET THE SUNSHINE IN / CREAM OF THE CROP**   `-`

Feb 88. (cd) (WD 72597) **EVERY GREAT NO.1 HIT**   `-`

Feb 88. (cd) (WD 72600) **NEVER BEFORE RELEASED MASTERS**   `-`

Jan 89. (lp/c/cd) (ZL/ZK/ZD 72701) **LOVE SUPREME**   `10`
– You can't hurry love / Baby love / The happening / Automatically sunshine / Up the ladder to the roof / Stoned love / Where did our love go? / Love is here and now you're gone / Reflections / In and out of love / Stop! in the name of love / Come see about me / I'm gonna make you love me / Love child / I'm living in shame / Floy joy / You keep me hangin' on / I second that emotion / Nathan Jones / Someday we'll be together.

Feb 89. (7") (ZB 41963) **STOP! IN THE NAME OF LOVE. / AUTOMATICALLY SUNSHINE**   `62`   `-`
(12"+=) (ZT 41964) – Automatically sunshine medley.

Jul 92. (cd) **70's GREATEST HITS AND RARE CLASSICS**   `-`

May 93. (cd/c) *Spectrum; (550071-2/-4)* **STOP IN THE NAME OF LOVE**	☐	-
May 93. (cd/c) *Spectrum; (550075-2/-4)* **I'M GONNA MAKE YOU LOVE ME**	☐	-
Jun 97. (cd/c) *Hallmark; 30774-2/-4)* **THE HITS**	☐	-
Oct 98. (d-cd/d-c) *Polygram TV; (530961-2/-4)* **40 GOLDEN MOTOWN GREATS**	35	-

DIANA ROSS & THE SUPREMES WITH THE TEMPTATIONS

Jan 69. (7") *(TMG 685)* <1137> **I'M GONNA MAKE YOU LOVE ME. / A PLACE IN THE SUN**	3	2	Nov68
Jan 69. (lp; stereo/mono) *(S+/TML 11096)* <679> **DIANA ROSS & THE SUPREMES JOIN THE TEMPTATIONS**	1	2	Nov68

– I'm gonna make you love me / My guy / My girl / Uptight (everything's alright) / Sweet inspiration / I'll try something new / Ain't no mountain high enough / I second that emotion / Why must we fall in love / For better or worse / The weight / I'll be doggone / Stubborn kind of fellow. *(re-iss. Jul81 & Oct82)*

Mar 69. (7",7"red) <1146> **I'LL TRY SOMETHING NEW. / THE WAY YOU DO THE THINGS YOU DO**	-	25	
Jun 69. (lp; stereo/mono) *(S+/TML 11110)* <682> **TCB** (original soundtrack TV)	11	1	Dec68

– T.C.B. / Stop, in the name of love / You keep me hangin' on / Get ready / The way you do the things you do / A taste of honey / Eleanor Rigby / Do you know the way to San Jose / Mrs.Robinson / Respect / Somewhere / Ain't too proud to beg / Hello young lovers / For once in my life / I know I'm losing you / With a song in my heart / Come see about me / My world is empty without you / Baby love / I hear a symphony / The impossible dream. *(re-iss. Mar82)*

Jul 69. (7";w-drawn) <1150> **STUBBORN KIND OF FELLOW. / TRY IT BABY**	-	-	
Sep 69. (7") *(TMG 709)* **I SECOND THAT EMOTION. / THE WAY YOU DO THE THINGS YOU DO**	18	-	
Sep 69. (7") <1153> **THE WEIGHT. / FOR BETTER OR WORSE**	-	46	
Nov 69. (lp) <699> **ON BROADWAY** (TV Show)	-	38	
Feb 70. (lp) *(STML 11122)* <692> **TOGETHER**	28	28	Oct69

– Stubborn kind of fellow / I'll be doggone / The weight / Ain't nothing like the real thing / Uptight (everything's alright) / Sing a simple song / My guy, my girl / For better or worse / Can't take my eyes off you / Why (must we fall in love).

Mar 70. (7") *(TMG 730)* **WHY (MUST WE FALL IN LOVE). / UPTIGHT (EVERYTHING'S ALRIGHT)**	31	-

SUPREMES & THE FOUR TOPS

Nov 70. (7") <1173> **RIVER DEEP – MOUNTAIN HIGH. / TOGETHER WE CAN MAKE SUCH SWEET MUSIC**	-	14	
Jun 71. (7") *(TMG 777)* **RIVER DEEP – MOUNTAIN HIGH. / IT'S GOT TO BE A MIRACLE**	11	-	
Jun 71. (lp) *(STML 11179)* <717> **THE MAGNIFICENT 7**	6	-	Oct70

– River deep – mountain high / Knock on my door / For your love / Without the one you love / Reach out and touch (somebody's hand) / Stoned soul picnic / Baby (you've got what it takes) / Ain't nothing like the real thing / Everyday people / It's got to be a miracle (this thing called love) / A taste of honey / Together we can make such sweet music. *(re-iss. Oct81)*

Nov 71. (7") *(TMG 793)* <1181> **YOU GOTTA HAVE LOVE IN YOUR HEART. / I'M GLAD ABOUT IT**	25	55	Jul71
Nov 71. (lp) *(STML 11192)* <736> **THE RETURN OF THE MAGNIFICENT 7**	☐	☐	Jun71
Jan 72. (lp) *(STML 11203)* <745> **DYNAMITE**	☐	☐	

– It's impossible / The bigger you love (the harder you fall) / Hello stranger / Love the one you're with / Good lovin' ain't easy to come by / Melodie / If / If I could build my whole world around you / Don't let me lose this dream / Do you love me just a little honey.

SURVIVOR (dig out; Great Metal . . .)

SWANS (dig out; Great Alt & Indie . . .)

SWEET

Formed: London, England . . . early 1968 as SWEETSHOP, by BRIAN CONNOLLY and MICK TUCKER (former members of Harrow bubblegum-pop band, WAINWRIGHT'S GENTLEMEN). Completing the line-up with STEVE PRIEST and FRANK TORPY, SWEET released a one-off 45 for 'Fontana', 'SLOW MOTION', before MICK STEWART replaced TORPY. A further three throwaway pop singles (on 'Parlophone') followed with little interest, prior to the band finding a more steady guitarist in ANDY SCOTT and hooking up with the now famous hitmaking/songwriting team of (NICKY) CHINN and (MIKE) CHAPMAN through producer PHIL WAINMAN. Signing to 'R.C.A.', SWEET emerged from their sticky patch with a handful of chartbustin' pure pop nuggets between 1971/72, including 'FUNNY FUNNY', 'CO-CO', 'POPPA JOE', 'LITTLE WILLY' (also a Top 3 Stateside success!) and 'WIG WAM BAM'. One of the pivotal bands of the glam-pop era, SWEET, as with their music, took sugary fashion excess to gender-bending new limits. Early in '73, they followed in the high-heeled footstompin' steps of GARY GLITTER, SLADE, etc, by adopting a slightly harder-edged anthemic approach for the chart-topping 'BLOCKBUSTER'. They repeated this winning formula over the next twelve months, three more singles, 'HELLRAISER', 'BALLROOM BLITZ' and 'TEENAGE RAMPAGE' enjoying a tantalisingly close shave with the No.1 spot. Surprisingly banned from many British ballrooms/concert halls, SWEET subsequently toning down their OTT effeminate image for a more mature "harder" look. The resulting album, 'SWEET FANNY ADAMS' hit the UK Top 30, although no tracks were issued as singles. However, they did score

a Top 10 hit later that year with 'THE SIX TEENS' (they also suffered their first flop in some years, 'TURN IT DOWN'), both songs taken from another Top 30 album, 'DESOLATION BOULEVARD'. Early in '75, now without CHINN and CHAPMAN, they partially resurrected their flagging public profile with the self-penned 'FOX ON THE RUN', the single hitting No.2 (and later in the year No.5 in America, 'BALLROOM BLITZ' having achieved a similar feat a few months previous). Alienated from most of their former teenbop fans, SWEET's career began to turn sour, that is, until 'LOVE IS LIKE OXYGEN' breathed some fresh air into their newfound AOR/hard-rock sound, the single a Top 10 transatlantic smash. The internal tensions that had simmered through SWEET's career finally boiled over in 1979, CONNOLLY (younger brother of actor, MARK 'Taggart' McMANUS) striking out on a solo career, while the remaining members recruited GARY MOBERLEY for a handful of forgettable albums, including the aptly-titled 'IDENTITY CRISIS'. The 80's were characterised by countless reformations, tussles over the group name, etc, SWEET effectively finished as a chart commodity and opting instead to trawl the cabaret circuit while SCOTT released a few records under the ANDY SCOTT'S SWEET moniker. Meanwhile, CONNOLLY's health was in terminal decline, any SWEET fans witnessing the relevant TV documentary no doubt shocked by his ravaged appearance. Sadly, CONNOLLY died of heart failure on the 10th of February '97 (he'd previously survived a number of heart attacks) shortly after the programme was made.

Best CD compilation: BALLROOM BLITZ – THE VERY BEST OF SWEET (*8)

BRIAN CONNOLLY (b. 5 Oct'49, Hamilton, Scotland) – vocals (ex-WAINWRIGHT'S GENTLEMEN) / **STEVE PRIEST** (b.23 Feb'50, Hayes, Middlesex, England) – bass / **MICK TUCKER** (b.17 Jul'49, Harlesden, London) – drums, vox (ex-WAINWRIGHT'S GENTLEMEN) / **FRANK TORPY** – guitar

	Fontana	not iss.
Jul 68. (7") *(TF 958)* **SLOW MOTION. / IT'S LONELY OUT THERE**	☐	-

―――― **MICK STEWART** – guitar repl. FRANK

	Parlophone	not iss.
Sep 69. (7") *(R 5803)* **LOLLIPOP MAN. / TIME**	☐	-
Jan 70. (7") *(R 5826)* **ALL YOU'LL EVER GET FROM ME. / THE JUICER**	☐	-

(re-iss. May71 flipped over; R 5902)

Jun 70. (7") *(R 5848)* **GET ON THE LINE. / MR. McGALLAGHER**	☐	-

―――― **ANDY SCOTT** (b.30 Jun'51, Wrexham, Wales) – guitar (ex-ELASTIC BAND) repl. STEWART. (employed session people in 71-72)

	R.C.A.	Bell
Mar 71. (7") *(RCA 2051)* **FUNNY FUNNY. / YOU'RE NOT WRONG FOR LOVING ME**	13	☐
Jun 71. (7") *(RCA 2087)* **CO-CO. / DONE ME WRONG ALRIGHT**	2	☐
Jul 71. (7") *<45126>* **CO-CO. / YOU'RE NOT WRONG FOR LOVING ME**	-	99
Oct 71. (7") *(RCA 2121)* **ALEXANDER GRAHAM BELL. / SPOTLIGHT**	33	-
Nov 71. (lp) *(SF 8288)* **FUNNY HOW SWEET CO-CO CAN BE**	☐	-

– Co-Co / Chop chop / Reflections / Honeysuckle love / Santa Monica sunshine / Daydream / Funny funny / Tom Tom turnaround / Jeanie / Sunny sleeps late / Spotlight / Done me wrong all right.

Jan 72. (7") *(RCA 2164)* **POPPA JOE. / JEANIE**	11	-	
Jun 72. (7") *(RCA 2225)* *<45251>* **LITTLE WILLY. / MAN FROM MECCA**	4	3	Jan73
Sep 72. (7") *(RCA 2260)* **WIG-WAM BAM. / NEW YORK CONNECTION**	4		Dec73
Dec 72. (lp) *(SF 8316)* **SWEET'S BIGGEST HITS** (compilation)	☐	-	

– Wig-wam bam / Little Willy / Done me wrong alright / Poppa Joe / Funny funny / Co-Co / Alexander Graham Bell / Chop chop / You're not wrong for loving me / Jeanie / Spotlight / Tom Tom turnaround.

Jan 73. (7") *(RCA 2305)* *<45361>* **BLOCKBUSTER. / NEED A LOT OF LOVIN'**	1	73	Jun73
Apr 73. (7") *(RCA 2357)* **HELL RAISER. / BURNING**	2	-	
Jul 73. (lp) *<1125>* **THE SWEET**	☐	-	

– Little Willy / New York connection / Wig-wam bam / Done me wrong alright / Hell raiser / Blockbuster / Need a lot of lovin' / Man from Mecca / Spotlight / You're not wrong for loving me. *<re-iss. 1976 on 'Kory'; KK 3009>*

	R.C.A.	Capitol
Sep 73. (7") *(RCA 2403)* **BALLROOM BLITZ. / ROCK'N'ROLL DISGRACE**	2	-
Jan 74. (7") *(LPBO 5004)* **TEENAGE RAMPAGE. / OWN UP, TAKE A LOOK AT YOURSELF**	2	-
Apr 74. (lp) *(LPLI 5039)* **SWEET FANNY ADAMS**	27	-

– Set me free / Heartbreak today / No you don't / Rebel rouser / Peppermint twist / Sweet F.A. / Restless / Into the night / AC-DC.

Jul 74. (7") *(LPBO 5037)* **THE SIX TEENS. / BURN ON THE FLAME**	9	-	
Nov 74. (7") *(RCA 2480)* **TURN IT DOWN. / SOMEONE ELSE WILL**	41	-	
Nov 74. (lp) *(LPLI 5080)* *<11395>* **DESOLATION BOULEVARD**		25	Jul75

– The six teens / Solid gold brass / Turn it down / Medusa / Lady Starlight / Man with the golden arm / Fox on the run / Breakdown / My generation. *<US – version incl. tracks from 'SWEET FANNY ADAMS'>* *(re-iss. Feb90 on 'Castle' cd/lp; CLA CD/LP 170)*

Mar 75. (7") *(RCA 2524)* **FOX ON THE RUN. / MISS DEMEANOR**	2	-	
Jun 75. (7") *<4055>* **BALLROOM BLITZ. / RESTLESS**	-	5	
Jul 75. (7") *(RCA 2578)* **ACTION. / SWEET F.A.**	15	-	
Nov 75. (d-lp) *(SPC 0001)* **STRUNG UP** (live rec. Dec'73 + hits, etc.)	☐	-	

– Hell raiser / Burning / Someone else will / Rock'n'roll disgrace / Need a lot of lovin' / Done me wrong alright / You're not wrong for loving me / The man with the golden arm / Action / Fox on the run / Set me free / Miss Deameanour / Ballroom blitz / Burn on the flame / Solid gold brass / The six teens / I wanna be committed / Blockbuster.

Nov 75. (7") *<4157>* **FOX ON THE RUN. / BURN ON THE FLAME**	-	5	
Jan 76. (7") *(RCA 2641)* **THE LIES IN YOUR EYES. / COCKROACH**	35	-	
Feb 76. (7") *<4220>* **ACTION. / MEDUSA**	-	20	

Mar 76. (lp) *(RS 1036) <11496>* **GIVE US A WINK** — — **27**
– The lies in your eyes / Cockroach / Keep it in / 4th of July / Action / Yesterday's rain / White mice / Healer. *(re-iss. Aug91 on 'Repertoire' cd+=)(pic-lp; REP4084WZ)(REP 2084)* – Fox on the run / Lady Starlight / Sweet Fanny Adams / Miss Demeanor.

Oct 76. (7") *(RCA 2748)* **LOST ANGELS. / FUNK IT UP**   ☐ ☐

Feb 77. (7") *(PB 5001)* **FEVER OF LOVE. / DISTINCT LACK OF ANCIENT**   ☐ –

Mar 77. (lp/c) *(PL/PK 25072) <11636>* **OFF THE RECORD**   ☐ –
– Fever of love / Lost angels / Midnight to daylight / Windy city / Live for today / She gimme lovin' / Laura Lee / Hard times / Funk it up (David's song). *(pic-cd.Aug91 on 'Repertoire'+=; REP4085WZ)* – Distinct lack of ancient / Stairway to the stars / Why don't you do it to me.

Mar 77. (7") *<4429>* **FEVER OF LOVE. / HEARTBREAK TODAY**   – ☐

Jul 77. (7",12") *<4454>* **FUNK IT UP (DAVID'S SONG). / ('A'disco mix)**   – **88**

Aug 77. (7") *(PB 5046)* **STAIRWAY TO THE STARS. / WHY DON'T YOU DO IT TO ME**   ☐ –

Oct 77. (lp/c) *(PL/PK 25111)* **SWEET'S GOLDEN GREATS** (compilation)   ☐ –
– Blockbuster / Hell raiser / Ballroom blitz / Teenage rampage / The six teens / Turn it down / Fox on the run / Action / Lost angels / The lies in your eyes / Fever of love / Stairway to the stars.

	Polydor	Capitol
Jan 78. (7") *(POSP 1) <4549>* **LOVE IS LIKE OXYGEN. / COVER GIRL**	**9**	**8** Feb78
Jan 78. (lp/c) *(POLD/+C 5001) <11744>* **LEVEL HEADED**		**52**

– Dream on / Love is like oxygen / California nights / Strong love / Fountain / Anthem No.1 / Silverbird / Lettres d'amour / Anthem No.2 / Air on "A" tape loop. *(cd-iss. Aug91 on 'Repertoire'+=; REP 4234WP)* – Love is like oxygen (single) / Cover girl / California nights (single) / Show the way.

Jul 78. (7") *<4610>* **CALIFORNIA NIGHTS. / DREAM ON**   – **76**

—— **GARY MOBERLEY** – keyboards repl. CONNOLLY who went solo & later formed The NEW SWEET. (ANDY SCOTT was now on lead vocals)

Mar 79. (7") *(POSP 36)* **CALL ME. / WHY DON'T YOU**   ☐ ☐

Apr 79. (7") *<4730>* **MOTHER EARTH. / WHY DON'T YOU**   – ☐

Aug 79. (7") *(POSP 73)* **BIG APPLE WALTZ. / WHY DON'T YOU**   ☐ –

Oct 79. (lp/c) *(POLD/+C 5022) <11929>* **CUT ABOVE THE REST**   ☐ Apr79
– Call me / Play all night / Big apple waltz / Dorian Gray / Discophony / Eye games / Mother Earth / Hold me / Stay with me.

Apr 80. (7") *(POSP 131)* **GIVE THE LADY SOME RESPECT. / TALL GIRLS**   ☐ –

Apr 80. (lp/c) *(POLS/+C 1021)* **WATER'S EDGE** (US-title 'SWEET IV')   ☐ ☐
– Sixties man / Getting in the mood for love / Tell the truth / Own up / Too much talking / Thank you for loving me / At midnight / Water's edge / Hot shot gambler / Give the lady some respect.

Sep 80. (7") *(POSP 160)* **THE SIXTIES MAN. / OH YEAH**   ☐ ☐

Sep 80. (7") *<4908>* **THE SIXTIES MAN. / WATER'S EDGE**   – ☐

—— **MICK STEWART** – guitar returned to guest on next album.

Nov 82. (lp) *(2311 179)* **IDENTITY CRISIS**   ☐ –
– Identity crisis / New shoes / Two into one / Love is the cure / It makes me wonder / Hey mama / Falling in love / I wish you would / Strange girl.

—— They had already split Spring 1981, with PRIEST going to the States and SCOTT going into production for heavy metal bands like IRON MAIDEN. He also went solo (see further below). The SWEET re-formed in the mid-80's, with SCOTT, TUCKER plus **PAUL MARIO DAY** – vocals (ex-WILD FIRE) / **PHIL LANZON** – keyboards (ex-GRAND PRIX) / **MAL McNULTY** – bass repl. PRIEST

—— CONNOLLY died of heart failure in the mid 90's

– compilations, etc. –

Dec 70. (lp; one-side by The PIPKINS) *Music For Pleasure; (MFP 5248)* **GIMME DAT THING**   ☐ –

Jul 78. (lp) *Camden-RCA; (CDS 1168)* **THE SWEET**   ☐ –

Jun 80. (7"ep) *R.C.A.; (PE 5226)* **FOX ON THE RUN / HELLRAISER. / BLOCKBUSTER / BALLROOM BLITZ**   ☐ –

Aug 81. (7") *RCA Gold; (524)* **BLOCKBUSTER. / HELLRAISER**   ☐ –

May 82. (7") *RCA Gold; (551)* **BALLROOM BLITZ. / WIG-WAM BAM**   ☐ –

Aug 84. (pic-lp/lp) *Anagram; (P+/GRAM 16)* **SWEET 16 – IT'S ... IT'S ... SWEET'S HITS**   **49** –

Sep 84. (7") *Anagram; (ANA 27)* **THE SIX TEENS. / ACTION** (12"+=) *(12ANA 27)* – Teenage rampage.   ☐ –

Dec 84. (7"/12") *Anagram; (ANA/12ANA 28)* **IT'S ... IT'S ... THE SWEET MIX** (Medley; Blockbuster – Fox on the run – Teenage rampage – Hell raiser – Ballroom blitz). **/ FOX ON THE RUN**   **45** ☐

May 85. (7"/12") *Anagram; (ANA/12ANA 29)* **SWEET 2TH – THE WIG-WAM WILLY MIX. / THE TEEN ACTION MIX**   ☐ –

Apr 87. (7") *Old Gold; (OG 9707)* **BLOCKBUSTER. / LITTLE WILLY**   ☐ –

Apr 87. (7") *Old Gold; (OG 9709)* **FOX ON THE RUN. / BALLROOM BLITZ**   ☐ –

Jul 87. (cd/lp) *Zebra; (CDM+/ZEB 11)* **HARD CENTRES – THE ROCK YEARS**   ☐ –
(re-iss. cd Oct95; CDMZEB 11)

Jan 88. (7") *Old Gold; (OG 9760)* **WIG-WAM BAM. / CO-CO**   ☐ –

Jan 88. (7") *Old Gold; (OG 9762)* **TEENAGE RAMPAGE. / HELLRAISER**   ☐ –

Nov 89. (7") *R.C.A.; (PB 43337)* **WIG-WAM BAM. / LITTLE WILLY**   ☐ –

Dec 89. (lp/c/cd) *R.C.A.; (NL/NK/ND 74313)* **BLOCKBUSTERS**   ☐ –
– Ballroom blitz / Hell raiser / New York connection / Little Willy / Burning / Need a lot of lovin' / Wig-wam bam / Blockbuster / Rock'n'roll disgrace / Chop chop / Alexander Graham Bell / Poppa Joe / Co-Co / Funny funny.

Dec 89. (d-lp/c/cd) *Castle; (CCS LP/MC/CD 230)* **SWEET COLLECTION**   ☐ –

Jul 92. (cd-ep) *Old Gold; (OG 6174)* **WIG-WAM BAM / CO-CO / LITTLE WILLY**   ☐ –

Feb 93. (cd) *Receiver; (RRCD 169)* **ROCKIN' THE RAINBOW**   ☐ –

Feb 93. Receiver; (cd) *(RRCD 171)* **LAND OF HOPE AND GLORY**   ☐ –

Jul 93. (cd) *Repertoire; (REP 4140WZ)* **FIRST RECORDINGS 1968-1971**   ☐ –

Dec 93. (cd) *Receiver; (RRCD 175)* **LIVE FOR TODAY**   ☐ –

Jul 94. (cd) *Receiver; (RRCD 189)* **BREAKDOWN – THE SWEET LIVE** (live)   ☐ –

Nov 94. (cd) *Start;* **IN CONCERT**   ☐ –

Apr 95. (cd) *Receiver; (RRCD 198)* **SET ME FREE**   ☐ –

Jul 95. (cd) *Aim; (AIM 1041)* **GREATEST HITS LIVE**   ☐ –

Jan 96. (cd/c) *Polygram; (<535001-2/-4>)* **BALLROOM HITZ – THE VERY BEST OF SWEET**   **15**

Jan 96. (cd) *Happy Price; (HP 9346-2)* **IN CONCERT**   ☐ –

Jan 96. (cd) *Music De-Luxe; (MDCD 013)* **BLOCKBUSTER** (live on stage)   ☐ –

Aug 96. (cd) *KFG; (CDEC 5)* **HITZ, BLITZ, GLITZ**   ☐ –

SWEET 75 (see under ⇒ NIRVANA)

SWELL MAPS (dig out; Great Alt & Indie . . .)

SWERVEDRIVER (dig out; Great Alt & Indie . . .)

David SYLVIAN (see under ⇒ JAPAN)

SYMPOSIUM

Formed: Kensington, London, England . . . early '96 by fresh-faced youths and former Catholic school choirboys, ROSS CUMMINS, HAGOP TCHAPARIAN (part Armenian), WOJTEK GODZISZ (fully Polish), WILL McGONAGLE and JOSEPH BIRCH. Taking their cue from the noisy pop-punk fusion of GREEN DAY and ASH, these religiously fanatic QPR (a West London football club) fans bounded onto the indie scene in 1996 with the 'DRINK THE SUNSHINE' single, their debut effort for 'Infectious' (home of ASH). The lads proceeded to gatecrash the Top 30 with their follow-up, 'FAREWELL TO TWILIGHT', a taster from their spunky, CLIVE LANGER/ALAN WINSTANLEY-produced Top 30 debut set, 'ONE DAY AT A TIME' (1997). • **Songwriters:** GODZISZ or CUMMINGS except HARD DAY'S NIGHT (Beatles).

Album rating: ONE DAY AT A TIME mini (*7) / ON THE OUTSIDE (*8)

ROSS CUMMINS – vocals / **HAGOP TCHAPARIAN** – guitar / **WILL McGONAGLE** – guitar / **WOJTEK GODZISZ** – bass / **JOSEPH BIRCH** – drums

	Infectious	not iss.
Oct 96. (7") *(infect 30s)* **DRINK THE SUNSHINE. / DISAPPEAR** (cd-s+=) *(infect 30cd)* – Smiling.	☐	–
Mar 97. (7") *(infect 34s)* **FAREWELL TO TWILIGHT. / XANTHEIN** (7") *(infect 34sx)* – ('A'side) / Song. (cd-s++=) *(infect 34cd)* – Easily scared.	**25**	–
May 97. (7") *(infect 37s)* **ANSWER TO WHY I HATE YOU. / JIM** (cd-s+=) *(infect 37cd)* – Natural. (cd-s) *(infect 37cdx)* – ('A'side) / Torquoise / Keeping the secret.	**32**	–
Aug 97. (7") *(infect 44s)* **FAIRWEATHER FRIEND. / ('A'live)** (cd-s+=) *(infect 44cd)* – Greeting song / Just so. (cd-s+=) *(infect 44cdx)* – The answer to why I love you (live) / Disappear (live).	**25**	–
Oct 97. (m-cd/m-c/m-lp) *(infect 49 cd/mc/lp)* **ONE DAY AT A TIME** – Drink to the sunshine / Farewell to twilight / Puddles / Fairweather friend / One day at a time / Fizzy / Girl with brains in her feet / Smiling.	**29**	–
Nov 97. (7"purple) *(infect 50s)* **DRINK THE SUNSHINE. / FIZZY**	☐	–
Mar 98. (7") *(infect 52s)* **AVERAGE MAN. / TWIST** (cd-s) *(infect 52cd)* – ('A'side) / Journey / Little things / Me. (cd-s) *(infect 52cdx)* – ('A'side) / Hard day's night (live).	**45**	–
May 98. (7"pic-d) *(infect 55s)* **BURY YOU. / SCHOSTAKOWICH** (cd-s) *(infect 55cd)* – ('A'side) / Serenade the idiot / Standing honoured / Higher. (cd-s) *(infect 55cdx)* – ('A'side) / Fluorescent / Mairamout / ('A'-CD-ROM video clip).	**41**	–
May 98. (cd/c/lp) *(infect 56 cd/mc/lp)* **ON THE OUTSIDE** – Impossible / The answer to why I hate you / Bury you / Blue / The end / Nothing special / Circles squares and lines / Stay on the outside / Paint the stars / Obsessive compulsive disorder / Natural / Way.	**32**	–
Jul 98. (7") *(infect 57s)* **BLUE. / LIFE OF RILEY** (cd-s+=) *(infect 57cd)* – Carnival. (cd-s) *(infect 57cdx)* – ('A'side) / Cartwheels / Ode to the frogs.	**48**	–

	Curveball	not iss.
May 99. (7") *(SYMP 001S)* **KILLING POSITION. / WALL OF SILENCE / THE END** (live) (cd-s+=) *(SYMP 001CD)* – Hard day's night (live at Reading).	☐	–

– compilations, etc. –

Nov 99. (cd) *Strange Fruit; (SFRSCD 088)* **LIVE AND IN SESSION**   ☐ –

SYSTEM 7 (see ⇒ HILLAGE, Steve)

TAD (dig out; Great Alt & Indie . . .)

TALKING HEADS

Formed: Manhattan, New York, USA . . . May'75 by former art & design students DAVID BYRNE, TINA WEYMOUTH and CHRIS FRANTZ. Their first gig was supporting The RAMONES at the CBGB's club in New York, circa mid '75. The band were soon spotted by Seymour Stein, who duly signed them to his new US label, 'Sire' and in late 1976 they released their debut 45, 'LOVE GOES TO A BUILDING ON FIRE'. Although this flopped, the following year's '77 album sold well enough to reach the lower regions of the album chart. The record's centrepiece was the spastic, new wave-funk of 'PSYCHO KILLER', BYRNE's compelling eccentricity making the number a live favourite. By this point the band were well established as one of the leading lights in the New York art-punk scene, firing subversively intelligent broadsides at the overblown rock establishment. The follow-up album, 'MORE SONGS ABOUT BUILDINGS AND FOOD' (1978) was produced by BRIAN ENO whom the band had met on a British tour the previous year. Sharing ENO's disregard for the workmanlike, the band were spurred on to new heights, FRANTZ and WEYMOUTH fashioning intricate but gloriously funky rhythms, BYRNE turning around Al Green's 'TAKE ME TO THE RIVER' with his wonderfully idiosyncratic vocal style. ENO stuck around for 'FEAR OF MUSIC' (1979), an album which saw them experimenting with complex ethnic rhythms and instrumentation, an area that was further explored on the BYRNE/ENO collaboration, 'MY LIFE IN THE BUSH OF GHOSTS' (1981). Bolstered by a crew of esteemed session musicians, the band cut 'REMAIN IN LIGHT' (1980). Swathed in giddy funk and rooted by African polyrhythms, the album spawned the wondrous 'ONCE IN A LIFETIME' single. The band had now established themselves as a top live draw and were notching up increasing record sales, although it was to be three years before the next TALKING HEADS studio album as the band divided their time between solo projects and live work. Worth the wait, 'SPEAKING IN TONGUES' (1983) was another classy outing, spawning the trance-rock of the 'SLIPPERY PEOPLE' (1984) single and the jittery 'BURNING DOWN THE HOUSE' (1983) which went top 10 in the UK. The Jonathon Demme-directed concert movie 'STOP MAKING SENSE' contained some of the most innovative live footage ever commited to celluloid and further increased The TALKING HEADS' burgeoning reputation. Another groundbreaking piece of film came with the video for 'ROAD TO NOWHERE' (1985), the band's biggest chart hit to date. Its parent album, 'LITTLE CREATURES' (1985), marked a return to a more basic sound. From this point on, the band began to spend an increasing amount of time on solo projects. 'TRUE STORIES' (1986) was a patchy TALKING HEADS version of the soundtrack to the DAVID BYRNE film of the same name while 'NAKED' (1986) came on like an over-produced version of 'REMAIN IN LIGHT'. Following this album, the various 'HEADS went on to do their own thing, BYRNE concentrating on his solo career. The band officially split in 1991, although The HEADS (as WEYMOUTH, FRANTZ and HARRISON were now known) made a comeback album of sorts in '96 entitled 'NO TALKING, JUST HEAD', a record that utilised an array of vocal talent including SHAUN RYDER on the minor hit single, 'DON'T TAKE MY KINDNESS FOR WEAKNESS'. • **Songwriters:** Group compositions except; TAKE ME TO THE RIVER (Al Green) / SLIPPERY PEOPLE (Staple Singers). TOM TOM CLUB:- UNDER THE BOARDWALK (Drifters) / FEMME FATALE (Velvet Underground) / YOU SEXY THING (Hot Chocolate). DAVID BYRNE: – GREENBACK DOLLAR (Hoyt Axton) / GIRLS ON MY MIND (Toquinnho Vinicius) / DON'T FENCE ME IN (Cole Porter). • **Trivia:** FRANTZ and WEYMOUTH (later TOM TOM CLUB) married on the 18th of June '77. BYRNE produced The B-52's on their 1982 album, 'Mesopotamia' and FUN BOY THREE on their 1983, 'Waiting' album. HARRISON produced The VIOLENT FEMMES on 1986 album, 'The Blind Leading The Naked'. TOM TOM CLUB started out producing in 1988 with ZIGGY MARLEY, later working with HAPPY MONDAYS.

Album rating: TALKING HEADS '77 (*9) / MORE SONGS ABOUT BUILDINGS AND FOOD (*8) / FEAR OF MUSIC (*8) / REMAIN IN LIGHT (*8) / THE NAME OF THIS BAND IS TALKING HEADS (*6) / SPEAKING IN TONGUES (*7) / STOP MAKING SENSE (*7) / LITTLE CREATURES (*7) / TRUE STORIES soundtrack (*5) / NAKED (*5) / ONCE IN A LIFETIME – THE BEST OF TALKING HEADS compilation (*9) / Tom Tom Club: TOM TOM CLUB (*5) / CLOSE TO THE BONE (*4) / BOOM BOOM CHI BOOM BOOM (*3) / DARK SNEAK LOVE ACTION (*3) / Jerry Harrison: THE RED AND THE BLACK (*4) / CASUAL GODS (*4) / WALK ON WATER (*4) / Heads: NO TALKING, JUST HEADS (*4) / David Byrne: SONGS FROM 'THE CATHERINE WHEEL' (*6) / MUSIC FOR THE KNEE PLAYS (*6) / REI MOMO (*7) / THE FOREST soundtrack (*4) / UH-OH (*5) / DAVID BYRNE (*4) / FEELINGS (*5)

DAVID BYRNE (b.14 May'52, Dumbarton, Scotland) – vocals, guitar / **TINA WEYMOUTH** (b.22 Nov'50, Coronado, Calif.) – bass, vocals / **CHRIS FRANTZ** (b. CHARLTON CHRISTOPHER FRANTZ, 8 May'51, Fort Campbell, Kentucky) – drums

			Sire	Sire
Feb 77.	(7") (6078 604) <737>	**LOVE GOES TO A BUILDING ON FIRE. / NEW FEELING**	☐	☐

—— added **JERRY HARRISON** (b.21 Feb'49, Milwaukee, Wisconsin) – guitar, keyboards (ex-JONATHAN RICHMAN & THE MODERN LOVERS)

Sep 77.	(lp) (9103 328) <SR 6306>	**TALKING HEADS '77**	60	97

– Uh-oh, love comes to town / New feeling / Tentative decisions / Happy day / Who is it? / No compassion / The book I read / Don't worry about the government / First week – last week . . . carefree / Psycho killer / Pulled up. (re-iss. Sep78; SR 6036) (cd-iss. Feb87; K2 56647)

Oct 77.	(7") <1002>	**UH-OH, LOVE COMES TO TOWN. / I WISH YOU WOULDN'T SAY THAT**	–	☐
Dec 77.	(7") (6078 610)	**PSYCHO KILLER. / I WISH YOU WOULDN'T SAY THAT**	☐	–

(12"+=) (same) – Psycho killer (acoustic).

Jan 78.	(7") <1013>	**PSYCHO KILLER. / PSYCHO KILLER (acoustic)**	–	92
May 78.	(7") (6078 620)	**PULLED UP. / DON'T WORRY ABOUT THE GOVERNMENT**	☐	–
Jul 78.	(lp/c) (K/K4 56531) <SR 6058>	**MORE SONGS ABOUT BUILDINGS AND FOOD**	21	29

– Thank you for sending me an angel / With our love / The good thing / Warning sign / Girls want to be with the girls / Found a job / Artists only / I'm not in love / Stay hungry / Take me to the river / The big country. (double-play cass. includes debut album) (cd-iss. Jan87; K2 56531)

Oct 78.	(7") <1032>	**TAKE ME TO THE RIVER. / THANK YOU FOR SENDING ME AN ANGEL**	–	26
Jun 79.	(7") (SIR 4004)	**TAKE ME TO THE RIVER. / FOUND A JOB**	–	–

(d7"+=) (SAM 87) – Love goes to a building on fire / Psycho killer.

Aug 79.	(lp/c) (K/K4 56707) <SRK 6076>	**FEAR OF MUSIC**	33	21

– Air / Animals / Cities / Drugs / Electric guitar / Heaven / I Zimbra / Life during wartime / Memories can't wait / Mind / Paper. (re-iss. Sep79 lp/c; SRK/SRC 6076) (w/ free 7") – PSYCHO KILLER (live). / NEW FEELING (live) (cd-iss. Jul84; K2 56707)

Oct 79.	(7") (SIR 4027) <49075>	**LIFE DURING WARTIME. / ELECTRIC GUITAR**	☐	80
Feb 80.	(7") (SIR 4033)	**I ZIMBRA. / PAPER**	☐	–
Jun 80.	(7") (SIR 4040)	**CITIES. / CITIES (live)**	☐	–

(12"+=) (SIR 4040T) – Artists only.

—— basic 4 added **BUSTA CHERRY JONES** – bass / **ADRIAN BELEW** – guitar / **BERNIE WORRELL** – keyboards / **STEVEN SCALES** – percussion / **DONETTE McDONALD** – backing vox

Oct 80.	(lp/c) <(SRK/SRC 6095)>	**REMAIN IN LIGHT**	21	19

– The great curve / Crosseyed and painless / Born under punches / Houses in motion / Once in a lifetime / Listening wind / Seen and not seen / The overlord. (cd-iss. Mar84; K2 56867)

Feb 81.	(7"/ext.12") (SIR 4048/+T) <40649>	**ONCE IN A LIFETIME. / SEEN AND NOT SEEN**	14	☐
May 81.	(7") <49734>	**HOUSES IN MOTION (remix). / THE OVERLORD**	–	☐
May 81.	(7") (SIR 4050)	**HOUSES IN MOTION (remix). / AIR**	50	–

(ext.12"+=) (SIR 4050T) – ('A'live).

—— In 1981, all 4 diversed into own projects

Mar 82.	(7") (SIR 4055)	**LIFE DURING WARTIME (live). / LIFE DURING WARTIME**	☐	–

(12"+=) (SIR 4055T) – Don't worry about the government (live).

Apr 82.	(d-lp/d-c) <(SRK/SRC 23590)>	**THE NAME OF THIS BAND IS TALKING HEADS (live)**	22	31

– I Zimbra / Drugs / Houses in motion / Life during wartime / Take me to the river / The great curve / Cross-eyed and painless / New feeling / A clean break / Don't worry about the government / Pulled up / Psycho killer / Artists only / Stay hungry / Air / Building on fire / Memories can't wait. (cd-iss. May87; K2 66112)

Jun 83.	(lp,clear-lp/c/cd) (923883-1/-4/-2) <23883>	**SPEAKING IN TONGUES**	21	15

– Burning down the house / Making flippy floppy / Girlfriend is better / Slippery people / I get wild – Wild gravity / Swamp / Moon rocks / Pull up the roots / This must be the place (naive melody). (c+=/cd+=) – (6 extra mixes).

Jul 83.	(7") (W 9565) <29565>	**BURNING DOWN THE HOUSE. / I GET WILD – WILD GRAVITY**	☐	9

(12"+=) (W 9565T) – Moon rocks.

Jan 84.	(7") (W 9451) <29451>	**THIS MUST BE THE PLACE (NAIVE MELODY). / MOON ROCKS**	51	62 Oct83

(ext.d12"+=) (W 9451T / SAM 176) – Slippery people (remix) / Making flippy floppy (remix).

Feb 84.	(7") <29163>	**ONCE IN A LIFETIME (live). / THIS MUST BE THE PLACE (live)**	–	☐

			E.M.I.	Sire
Oct 84.	(7"/ext.12") (EMI/12EMI 5504)	**SLIPPERY PEOPLE (live). / THIS MUST BE THE PLACE (NAIVE MELODY) (live)**	68	–
Oct 84.	(lp/c) (TAH/+TC 1) <25121>	**STOP MAKING SENSE (live)**	37	41

– Psycho killer / Swamp / Slippery people / Burning down the house / Girlfriend is better / Once in a lifetime / What a day that was / Life during wartime / Take me to the river. (cd-iss. Feb85; CDP 746064-2) (c+=/cd+=) – (extra tracks) (re-iss. Mar90 cd)(c/lp; CZ 289)(TC+/ATAK 147) (re-iss. Nov93 on 'Fame' cd/c; CD/TC FA 3302)

Nov 84. (7"/ext.12") *(EMI/12EMI 5509)* **GIRLFRIEND IS BETTER (live). / ONCE IN A LIFETIME (live)** [ ] [-]

Dec 84. (7") *<29080>* **STOP MAKING SENSE (GIRLFIREND IS BETTER) (live). / HEAVEN** [-] [ ]

May 85. (7"/ext.12") *(EMI/12EMI 5520)* **THE LADY DON'T MIND. / GIVE ME BACK MY NAME** [ ] [-]
(d12"+=) *(12EMID 5520)* – Slippery people (live) / This must be the place (naive melody) (live).

Jun 85. (lp/c)(cd) *(TAH/+TC 2)(CDP 746158-2) <25035>* **LITTLE CREATURES** [10] [20]
– And she was / Give me back my name / Creatures of love / The lady don't mind / Perfect world / Stay up late / Walk it down / Television man / Road to nowhere. (c+=) – The lady don't mind (extended). (re-iss. Mar90 cd/c/lp; CZ 287)(TC+/ATAK 146) (re-iss. Nov93 on 'Fame' cd/c; CD/TC FA 3301)

Jun 85. (7") *<28987>* **ROAD TO NOWHERE. / GIVE ME BACK MY NAME** [-] [ ]

Sep 85. (7") *<28917>* **AND SHE WAS. / ('A'dub)** [-] [54]

Sep 85. (7"/7"pic-d) *(EMI/+P 5530)* **ROAD TO NOWHERE. / TELEVISION MAN** [6] [-]
(d12"+=) *(12EMID 5530)* – Slippery people (extended live) / This must be the place (naive melody) (live).

Feb 86. (7") *(EMI 5543)* **AND SHE WAS. / PERFECT WORLD** [17] [-]
(12"pic-d+=) *(12EMIP 5543)* – ('A'extended).

Apr 86. (7") *<29163>* **ONCE IN A LIFETIME (live). / THIS MUST BE THE PLACE (live)** [-] [91]
(above re-generated from 1984 album & taken from 'Down And Out In Beverly Hills')

Aug 86. (7") *(EMI 5567) <28629>* **WILD WILD LIFE. / PEOPLE LIKE US (movie version)** [43] [25]
(12"+=/12"pic-d+=) *(12EMI/+P 5567)* – ('A'extended).

Sep 86. (lp/c)(cd) *(EU/TCEU 3511)(CDP 746345-2) <25512>* **TRUE STORIES** [7] [17]
– Love for sale / Puzzlin' evidence / Hey now / Radio head / Papa Legba / Wild wild life / Radio head / Dream operator / People like us / City of dreams. (cd+=) – Wild (ET mix). (re-iss. Sep89 on 'Fame' cd/c/lp; CD/TC+/FA 3231)

Nov 86. (7") *<28497>* **LOVE FOR SALE. / HEY NOW** [-] [ ]

Nov 86. (lp/c) *(ENC/TCENC 3520)* **SONGS FROM 'TRUE STORIES' (Original DAVID BYRNE Film Soundtrack; w/ other artists)** [ ] [ ]
– Cocktail desperado / Road song / Freeway son / Brownie's theme / Mall muzak: Building a highway – Puppy polka – Party girls / Dinner music / Disco hits / City of steel / Love theme from 'True Stories' / Festa para um Rei Negro / Buster's theme / Soy de Tejas / I love metal buildings / Glass operator.

Apr 87. (7") *(EM 1)* **RADIO HEAD. / HEY NOW (movie version)** [52] [-]
(d7"+=)(12"+=/cd-s+=) *(EMD 1)(12/CD EM 1)* – ('A'remix) / ('B'-Milwaukee remix).

Mar 88. (cd/c/lp) *(CD/TC+/EMD 1005) <26654>* **NAKED** [3] [19]
– Blind / Mr. Jones / Totally nude / Ruby dear / (Nothing but) Flowers / The Democratic circus / The facts of life / Mommy daddy you and I / Big daddy / Cool water. (other cd+=; CDP 790156-2) – Bill. (re-iss. Nov93 on 'Fame' cd/c; CD/TC FA 3300)

Aug 88. (c-s/7") *(TC+/EM 68) <27948>* **BLIND. / BILL** [59] [ ]
(ext.12"+=/cd-s+=) *(12/CD EM 68)* – ('A'-Def, dub & blind mix).

Oct 88. (c-s/7") *(TC+/EM 53) <27992>* **(NOTHING BUT) FLOWERS. / RUBY DEAR** [ ] [ ] Apr88
(10"+=) *(10EM 53)* – Facts of life / Mommy, daddy, you and I.
(12") *(12EM 53)* – ('A'extended) / ('B'-Lillywhite mix).
(cd-s) *(CDEM 53)* – ('A'side) / ('B'-bush mix) / Mommy, daddy, you and I / ('A'-Lillywhite mix).

—— cease to function as a group, after last recording. Officially split 1991.

– compilations, others, etc. –

on 'E.M.I.' UK / 'Sire' US unless mentioned otherwise

Apr 81. (c-s) *WEA; (SPC 9)* **TAKE ME TO THE RIVER / PSYCHO KILLER** [ ] [-]

1989. (3"cd-ep) *Sire; (921 135-2)* **LOVE GOES TO A BUILDING ON FIRE / PSYCHO KILLER / ONCE IN A LIFETIME / BURNING DOWN THE HOUSE** [ ] [ ]

Oct 92. (c-s/7") *(TC+/EM 250)* **LIFETIME PILING UP. / ROAD TO NOWHERE** [50] [ ]
(cd-s+=) *(CDEM 250)* – Love for sale / The lady don't mind (extended).
(cd-s) *(250)* – ('A'side) / Stay up late / Radio head / Take me to the river.

Oct 92. (d-cd/d-c/d-lp) *(CD/TC+/EQ 5010) <26760>* **POPULAR FAVOURITES 1976-1992** [7] [ ]
– ONCE IN A LIFETIME:- Psycho killer / Take me to the river / Once in a lifetime / Burning down the house / This must be the place (naive melody) / Slippery people (live) / Life during wartime (live) / And she was / Road to nowhere / Wild wild life / Blind / (Nothing but) Flowers / Lifetime piling up. // SAND IN MY VASELINE:- Sugar on my tongue / I want to live / Love goes to a building on fire / I wish you wouldn't say that / Don't worry about the government / The big country / No compassion / Warning sign / Heaven / Memories can't wait / I Zimbra / Crosseyed and painless / Swamp / Girlfriend is better (live) / Stay up late / Love for sale / City of dreams / Mr. Jones / Gangster of love / Popsicle.

Nov 95. (3xcd-box) *(CDOMB 003)* **THE ORIGINALS** [ ] [-]
– (STOP MAKING SENSE / LITTLE CREATURES / TRUE STORIES). (re-iss. Mar97; same)

DAVID BYRNE

Early in 1981, he had collaborated with BRIAN ENO ⇒ on album 'MY LIFE IN THE BUSH OF GHOSTS'.

	Sire	Sire

Dec 81. (7") *(SIR 4054)* **BIG BLUE PLYMOUTH (EYES WIDE OPEN). / CLOUD CHAMBER** [ ] [-]
(12") *(SIR 4054T)* – ('A'side) / Leg bells / Light bath.

Jan 82. (lp/c) *(SRK/SRC 3645)* **SONGS FROM 'THE CATHERINE WHEEL' (Stage score)** [ ] [ ] Dec81
– His wife refused / Two soldiers / The red house / My big hands (fall through the cracks) / Big business / Eggs in a briar patch / Poison / Cloud chamber / What a day

that was / Big blue Plymouth (eyes wide open). *<US d-lp+=>* – Ade / Walking / Under the mountain / Dinosaur / Wheezing / Black flag / Combat / Leg bells / The blue flame / Danse beast / Five golden sections. (cd-iss. Jan93; 7599 27418-2)

Feb 82. (12"ep) *<50034>* **THREE BIG SONGS**
– Big business (remix) / My big hands (fall through the cracks) / Big blue Plymouth (eyes wide open).

	E.M.I.	ECM

Sep 85. (lp/c) *(EJ 240381-1/-4) <ECM 25022>* **MUSIC FOR THE KNEE PLAYS** [ ] [ ] May 85
– Tree (today is an important occasion) / In the upper room / The sound of business / Social studies / (The gift of sound) Where the sun never goes down / Theadora is dozing / Admiral Perry / I bid you goodnight / I've tried / Winter / Jungle book / In the future.

—— Recorded collaboration with RYUICHI SAKAMOTO on film 'THE LAST EMPEROR'.

—— BYRNE now used a plethora of Brazilian musicians, after compiling various artists BELEZA TROPICAL', 'O SAMBA', etc.

	Luaka Bop-Sire	Luaka Bop

Oct 89. (lp/c)(cd) *(WX 319/+C)(K 925990-2) <25990>* **REI MOMO** [52] [71]
– Independence day / Make believe mambo / The call of the wild / Dirty old town / The rose tattoo / The dream police / Don't want to be part of your world / Marching through the wilderness / Lie to me / Women vs. men / Carnival eyes / I know sometimes a man is wrong.

Dec 89. (7"/ext.12") **MAKE BELIEVE MAMBO. / LIE TO ME** [ ] [ ]

Jun 91. (cd) *(7599 26584-2)* **THE FOREST (instrumental)** [ ] [ ]
– Ur / Kish / Dura Europus / Nineveh / Ava / Machu picchu / Teotihuacan / Asuka.

Mar 92. (cd)(lp/c) *(7599 26799-2)(WX 464/+C) <26799>* **UH-OH** [26] [ ]
– Now I'm your mom / Girls on my mind / Something ain't right / She's mad / Hanging upside down / Twistin' in the wind / A walk in the dark / The cowboy mambo (hey lookit me now) / Tiny town / Somebody. (re-iss. Feb95 cd/c;)

Apr 92. (7"/c-s) **GIRLS ON MY MIND. / MONKEY MAN** [ ] [ ]
(12"+=/cd-s+=) – Cantode oxum.

May 92. (7"/c-s) **HANGING UPSIDE DOWN. / TINY TOWN** [ ] [ ]
(cd-s) – ('A'side) / Dirty old town (live) / (Nothing but) Flowers (live) / Girls on my mind (live).
(cd-s) – ('A'side) / Something ain't right (live) / Who we're thinking of (live) / Rockin' in the free world (live).

Jul 92. (7"/c-s) **SHE'S MAD. / SOMEBODY** [ ] [ ]
(12") – ('A'side) / Butt naked / Greenback dollar.
(cd-s++=) – ('A'side) / Now I'm your man.

—— with **PAUL SOCOLOW** – bass, vocals / **TODD TURKISHER** – drum, percussion / **VALERIE NARANJO** – percussion, tambourine (live: **MAURO REFOSCO** – percussion) / **BILL WARE** – marimba / **ARTO LINDSAY** – guitar / **JOHN MEDESKI** – organ / **BASHIRI JOHNSON** – congas, bongos / **BEBEL GILBERTO** – vocals

May 94. (cd/c) *(9362 45558-2/-4) <45558>* **DAVID BYRNE** [44] [ ]
– A long time ago / Angels / Crash / A self-made man / Back in the box / Sad song / Nothing at all / My love is you / Lillies of the valley / You & eye / Strange ritual / Buck naked.

Jun 94. (7"/c-s) *(W 0253/+C)* **ANGELS. / PRINCESS** [ ] [ ]
(12"+=/cd-s+=) *(W 0253 T/CD)* – Ready for this world.

Sep 94. (c-s/cd-s) *(W 0263 C/CD)* **BACK IN THE BOX / GYPSY WOMAN (live) / GIRLS ON MY MIND (live)** [ ] [ ]

May 97. (cd/c) *<(9362 46605-2/-4)>* **FEELINGS** [ ] [ ]
– Fuzzy freaky / Miss America / A soft seduction / Dance on vaseline / The gates of Paradise / Amnesia / You don't know me / Daddy go down / Finite = alright / Wicked little doll / Burnt by the sun / The civil wars / They are in love.

Jun 97. (cd-s) *(W 0401CD)* **MISS AMERICA / (mixes)** [ ] [-]

TOM TOM CLUB

CHRIS FRANTZ + TINA WEYMOUTH plus her 2 sisters + **STEVE SCALES** – percussion / **ALEX WEIR** – guitar / **TYRON DOWNIE** – keyboards

	Island	Sire

Jun 81. (7") *(WIP 6694)* **WORDY RAPPINGHOOD. / YOU DON'T STOP (WORDY RAP)** [7] [ ]
(12"+=) *(12WIP 6694)* – L'elephant.

Sep 81. (7") *(WIP 6735) <49882>* **GENIUS OF LOVE. / LORELEI (instrumental)** [65] [31] Jan82
(12"+=) *(12WIP 6735)* – Rappa rappa rhythm / Yella. (re-iss. Oct82; same)

Oct 81. (lp/c) *(ILPS/ICT 9686) <SRK 3628>* **TOM TOM CLUB** [78] [23]
– Wordy rappinghood / Genius of love / Tom Tom theme / L'elephant / As above, so below / Lorelei / On, on, on, on . . . / Booming and zooming. (re-iss. Oct86 lp/c; ILPM/ICM 9686) (cd-iss. May87; CID 9686) (re-iss. cd Apr90; IMCD 103)

Jul 82. (7") *(WIP 6762)* **UNDER THE BOARDWALK. / ON, ON, ON, ON . . . (remix)** [22] [ ]
(12"+=) *(12WIP 6762)* – Lorelei (remix).

Jul 83. (7"/12") *(IS/12IS 117)* **THE MAN WITH THE 4-WAY HIPS. / ('A'dub version)** [ ] [73]

Aug 83. (lp/c) *(ILPS/ICT 9738) <23916>* **CLOSE TO THE BONE** [ ] [ ]
– Pleasure of love / On the line again / This is a foxy world / Bamboo town / The man with the 4-way hips / Measure up / Never took a penny / Atsababy! (life is great).

Dec 83. (7") **NEVER TOOK A PENNY. / PLEASURE OF LOVE** [-] [ ]

—— **TINA + CHRIS** added **GARY POZNER** – keyboards / **MARK ROULE** – guitar, percussion

	Fontana	Sire

Sep 88. (7") *(TCB 1)* **DON'T SAY NO. / DEVIL DOES YOUR DOG BITE?** [ ] [ ]
(12"+=) *(TCBX 1)* – ('A'version) / Beats and pieces.
(cd-s+=) *(TCBCD 1)* – Beats and pieces / Percapella.

Oct 88. (lp/c)(cd) *(SF LP/MC 8)(836 416-2) <25888>* **BOOM BOOM CHI BOOM BOOM** [ ] [ ]
– Suboceana / Shock the world / Don't say no / Challenge of the love warriors / Femme fatale / Born for love / Broken promises / She belongs to me / Little Eva / Misty teardrop.

—— **KIRSTY MacCOLL** makes a guest vocal appearance

Jan 92. (cd/c) <2-/4-26951> **DARK SNEAK LOVE ACTION**   `-`   `[]`
– Love wave / Sunshine and ecstasy / You sexy thing / Who wants an ugly girl? / Say I am / Irrisistable party dip / Dark sneak love action / Innocent sex kiss / Dogs in the trash / My mama told me / As the disco ball turns / Daddy come home.

JERRY HARRISON

		Sire	Sire
Oct 81.	(7") *(SIR 4053)* **THINGS FALL APART. / WORLDS IN COLLISION**	`[]`	`[]`

Oct 81. (lp/c) <(SRK/SRC 3631)> **THE RED AND THE BLACK**
– Things fall apart / Slink / The new adventure / Magic hymie / Fast karma / No questions / Worlds in collision / The red nights / No more returns / No walking no alarm. *(cd-iss. Apr96 on 'Warners'; 7599 23631-2)*

		Fontana	Sire
Feb 88.	(7") *(JERRY 1)* **REV IT UP. / BOBBY**	`[]`	`[]`

(12"+=)(12"pic-d+=)(cd-s+=) *(JERRY 1-12)(JERYP 1-12)(JERCD 1)* – ('A'versions). *(re-iss. Jul88; same)*

Feb 88. (lp/c)(cd) *(SF LP/MC 2)(832992-2)* <25663> **JERRY HARRISON: CASUAL GODS**   `78`
– Rev it up / Songs of angels / Man with a gun / Let it come down / Cherokee chief / A perfect lie / Are you running? / Breakdown in the passing lane / A.K.A. love / We're always talkin' / Bobby. *(cd+=)* – Bobby (12"version).

May 88. (7") *(JERRY 2)* **MAN WITH A GUN. / ('A'radio edit)**   `[]`
(12"+=)(cd-s+=) *(JERRY 2-12)(JERCD 2)* – Breakdown on the passing line / Wire always talking.

—— backing incl. **BROOKS, WORRELL, BAILEY, SIEGER + WEIR**

Jun 90. (7") *(JERRY 3)* **WALK ON WATER. / MAN WITH A GUN**   `[]`
(12"+=)(cd-s+=) *(JERRY 3-12)(JERCD 3)* – Racing the fire.

Jun 90. (cd/c/lp) *(846321-2/-4/-1)* <25943> **WALK ON WATER**
– Flying under radar / Cowboy's got to go / Kick start / I don't mind / Sleep angel / Confess / I cry for Iran / Never let it slip / If the rain returns / The doctor's lie.

HEADS

HARRISON, WEYMOUTH, FRANTZ + guest vocalists & lyricists (see below)

		Radioactive-MCA	M.C.A.
Oct 96.	(c-s) *(MCS 48024)* **DON'T TAKE MY KINDNESS FOR WEAKNESS / ('A'mix)**	`60`	

(cd-s+=) *(MCSTD 48024)* – ('A'-Lunatic Calm remix).

Nov 96. (cd/c) *(MCD/MCC 11504)>* **NO TALKING, JUST HEAD**
– Damage I've done (w/ JOHNETTE NAPOLITANO) / The king is gone (w/ MICHAEL HUTCHENCE) / No talking just head (w/ DEBBIE HARRY) / Never mind (w/ RICHARD HELL) / No big bang (w/ MARIA McKEE) / Don't take my madness for weakness (w/ SHAUN RYDER) / No more lonely nights (w/ MALIN ANNETEG) / Indie hair (w/ ED KOWALCZYK) / Punk lolita (w/ DEBBIE HARRY, JOHNETTE NAPOLITANO & TINA WEYMOUTH) / Only the lonely (w/ GORDON GANO) / Papersnow (w/ ANDY PARTRIDGE) / Blue blue moon (w/ GAVIN FRIDAY).

TALK SHOW (see under ⇒ STONE TEMPLE PILOTS)

TALK TALK

Formed: London, England ... 1981 by MARK HOLLIS, who, with the help of older brother and session man ED (ex-EDDIE & THE HOT RODS), recruited WEBB, HARRIS and BREMNER. They signed to 'E.M.I.' soon after, manager Keith Aspen hiring producer Colin Thurston to work on the debut album. At the height of New Romantic posturing in the summer of '82, the band broke through with the uptempo keyboard pop of 'TODAY'. Despite reaching No.21 in the charts, the debut album, 'THE PARTY'S OVER' (1982), came across like a more pretentious version of their labelmates DURAN DURAN and unfortunately favoured lip-gloss style over content. It was to be another two years before the next album, 'IT'S MY LIFE' (1984), by which time BREMNER had bowed out and the band had wisely cast off their New Romantic trappings. Spawning three singles which barely breached the charts, the album was nevertheless an improvement on the debut. The band finally broke through with the 1986 single, 'LIFE'S WHAT YOU MAKE IT', a chunky, deliberate piece of moodiness that preceded the classic album, 'THE COLOUR OF SPRING'. Featuring an array of guest musicians that included STEVE WINWOOD and DANNY THOMPSON, the record was a combination of their earlier commercial leanings and a developing talent for abstract rock/pop. Following the album's success, EMI furnished TALK TALK with a larger budget for 1988's 'SPIRIT OF EDEN' and the band embellished their sound with an ensemble of musical exotica that included clarinet, oboe and even The Chelmsford Cathedral Choir (!). This complex sonic tapestry was laced with rich, gliding melodies, a soothing elixir that drew deserved critical praise. EMI didn't quite view things in the same way, however, and the band were dropped in 1989. After being picked up by 'Polydor', the group released 'LAUGHING STOCK' (1991) on the label's jazz imprint, 'Verve'. More heavily orchestrated with cello, viola etc., the album saw TALK TALK move ever further into avant-garde territory. Meanwhile, bassist PAUL WEBB formed 'O' RANG, having left the band in 1990. The debut album, 'HERD OF INSTINCT' (1994) didn't exactly make for easy listening; skeletal percussion, barely audible, vaguely threatening voices, screeching feedback and ethnic chants saw WEBB pushing musical boundaries that his old band hadn't yet encountered. • **Songwriters:** Initially group penned, with MARK and brother ED writing most. In 1983, MARK and 4th member TIM FRIESE-GREEN wrote all material. • **Trivia:** The song 'TALK TALK', was first heard in late 1977, when MARK's group, The REACTION, recorded a prototype of the song on the Various Artists album, 'Streets'. A single also surfaced, 'I CAN'T RESIST' / 'I AM A CASE' for 'Island'; (WIP 6437)

Album rating: THE PARTY'S OVER (*5) / IT'S MY LIFE (*6) / THE COLOUR OF SPRING (*8) / SPIRIT OF EDEN (*8) / NATURAL HISTORY – THE VERY BEST OF TALK TALK compilation (*9) / HISTORY REVISITED – THE REMIXES (*5) / LAUGHING STOCK (*8) / THE VERY BEST OF TALK TALK compilation (*8) / LONDON 1986 concert album (*6) / 'O'Rang: HERD OF INSTINCT (*7)

MARK HOLLIS (b.1955) – vocals, piano, guitar (ex-REACTION) / **SIMON BREMNER** – keyboards / **PAUL WEBB** – bass, vocals / **LEE HARRIS** – drums

		E.M.I.	EMI America
Feb 82.	(7") *(EMI 5265)* **MIRROR MAN. / STRIKE UP THE BAND**	`[]`	`-`
Apr 82.	(7"/ext-12") *(EMI/12EMI 5284)* **TALK TALK. / ('A'version)**	`52`	`-`
Jun 82.	(7"/ext-12") *(EMI/12EMI 5314)* **TODAY. / IT'S SO SERIOUS**	`14`	`-`
Jul 82.	(lp/c) *(EMC/TC-EMC 3413)* <17083> **THE PARTY'S OVER**	`21`	

– Talk talk / It's so serious / Today / The party's over / Hate / Have you heard the news? / Mirror man / Another word / Candy. *(re-iss. 1985 lp/c; ATAK/TC-ATAK 65) (cd-iss. Mar87; CDP 746366-2) (re-iss. Sep87 on 'Fame' lp/c; FA/TC-FA 3187) (cd re-iss. Apr88; CDFA 3187)*

Oct 82. (7"/7"pic-d) *(EMI/P 5352)* <8136> **TALK TALK (remix). / MIRROR MAN**   `23`   `75`
(12") *(12EMI 5352)* – ('A'side) / ('A'-BBC version).

Feb 83. (7") *(EMI 5373)* **MY FOOLISH FRIEND. / CALL IN THE NIGHTBOYS**   `57`   `-`
(12"+=) *(12EMI 5373)* – ('A'extended).

—— Now basic trio when BREMNER departed. His place was taken by 4th member **TIM FRIESE-GREEN** – keyboards, producer, co-composer. Added session people **ROBBIE McINTOSH + HENRY LOWTHER**

Jan 84. (7") *(EMI 5443)* <8195> **IT'S MY LIFE. / DOES CAROLINE KNOW?**   `46`   `-`
(12"+=) *(12EMI 5443)* – ('A'extended).

Feb 84. (lp/c) *(EMC 240002-1/-4)* <17113> **IT'S MY LIFE**   `35`   `42`
– Dum dum girl / Such a shame / Renee / It's my life / Tomorrow started / The last time / Call in the night boy / Does Caroline know? / It's you. *(cd-iss. Feb85; CDP 746063-2) (re-iss. 1989 lp/c; ATAK/TC-ATAK 116)*

Mar 84. (7") <8195> **IT'S MY LIFE. / AGAIN, A GAME AGAIN**   `-`   `31`

Mar 84. (7") *(EMI 5433)* <8215> **SUCH A SHAME. / AGAIN, A GAME . . . AGAIN**   `49`   `-`
(12"+=) *(12EMI 5433)* – ('A'extended).
(d7"+=) *(EMID 5433)* – Talk talk (demo) / Mirror man (demo).

Jun 84. (7") <8215> **SUCH A SHAME. / CALL IN THE NIGHT BOYS**   `-`   `89`

Jul 84. (7") *(EMI 5480)* **DUM DUM GIRL. / WITHOUT YOU**   `74`   `-`
(12"+=) *(12EMI 5480)* – ('A'-US mix) / Such a shame (dub).

Jan 85. (7") <8244> **WHY IS IT SO HARD. / IT'S MY LIFE**   `-`   `[]`

—— guests on next album incl. **DAVID RHODES** – guitar / **DAVID ROACH** – saxophone / **MORRIS PERT** – percussion

Jan 86. (7"/ext.12") *(EMI/12EMI 5540)* <8303> **LIFE'S WHAT YOU MAKE IT. / IT'S GETTING LATE IN THE EVENING**   `16`   `90`
('A'early mix-12"+=) *(12EMIX 5540)* – ('A'-extended dance mix).
(d12"+=) *(12EMID 5540)* – It's my life / Does Caroline know?.

Feb 86. (lp/c)(cd) *(EMC/TC-EMC 3506)(CDP746228-2)* <17179> **THE COLOUR OF SPRING**   `8`   `58`
– Happiness is easy / I don't believe in you / Life's what you make it / April 5th / Living in another world / Give it up / Chameleon day / Time it's time. *(re-iss. cd Feb90; CZ 287) (re-iss. Mar90 lp/c; ATAK/TC-ATAK 145) (re-iss. Apr93 on 'Fame' cd/c; CD/TC FA 3291) (re-iss. Feb93; LPCENT 14)*

Mar 86. (7"/7"sha-pic-d) *(EMI/+P 5551)* **LIVING IN ANOTHER WORLD. / FOR WHAT IT'S WORTH**   `48`
(12"+=) *(12EMI 5551)* – ('A'extended).
(12"+=) *(12EMIX 5551)* – ('A'-US mix).

		Parlophone	EMI America
May 86.	(7") *(R 6131)* **GIVE IT UP. / PICTURES OF BERNADETTE**	`59`	

(12"+=) *(12R 6131)* – ('A'dance mix).

Nov 86. (7") *(R 6144)* **I DON'T BELIEVE IN YOU. / DOES CAROLINE KNOW? (live)**   `[]`
(12"+=) *(12R 6144)* – Happiness is easy.

—— Basic quartet added ensemble **MARTIN DITCHAM** – percussion (also on last) / **ROBBIE McINTOSH** – dobro, 12-string guitar (also on last lp) / **MARK FELTHAM** – harmonica / **SIMON EDWARDS** – Mexican bass / **HENRY LOWTHER** – trumpet / **NIGEL KENNEDY** – violin / **DANNY THOMPSON** – double bass / **HUGH DAVIS** – shozygs / **MICHAEL JEANS** – oboe / **ANDREW STOWALL** – bassoon / **ANDREW HARRINER** – clarinet / **CHRIS HOOKER** – cor anglais / plus CHOIR OF CHELMSFORD CATHEDRAL

Sep 88. (lp/c)(cd) *(PCSD/TC-PCSD 105)(CDP 746977-2)* **SPIRIT OF EDEN**   `19`
– The rainbow / Eden / Desire / Inheritance / I believe in you / Wealth. *(re-iss. Jun93 on 'Fame' cd/c; CD/TC FA 3293)*

Sep 88. (7") *(R 6189)* **I BELIEVE IN YOU. / JOHN COPE**   `[]`
(12"+=/cd-s+=) *(12R/CDR 6189)* – Eden (edit).

Dec 88. (m-lp/c) *(ST/4XT 6542)* **IT'S MY LIFE (remixes)**   `-`

May 90. (7"/c-s) *(R/TCR 6254)* **IT'S MY LIFE (remix). / RENEE (live)**   `13`
(cd-s+=) *(CDR 6254)* – ('A'live).
(12") *(12R 6254)* – ('A'-Tropical Love Forest mix) / ('A'side) / Talk Talk recycled:- Life's what you make it – Living in another world – Such a shame – It's my life.

Jun 90. (cd)(lp/c) *(CDP 793976-2)(PCSD/TC-PCSD 109)* **NATURAL HISTORY – THE VERY BEST OF TALK TALK** (compilation)   `3`
– Today / Talk talk / My foolish friend / Such a shame / Dum dum girl / It's my life / Give it up / Living in another world / Life's what you make it / Happiness is easy / I believe in you / Desire.

Sep 90. (7"/c-s) *(R/TCR 6264)* **LIFE'S WHAT YOU MAKE IT. / ('A'live)**   `23`
(cd-s+=) *(CDR 6264)* – Tomorrow started (live).
(12") *(12R 6264)* – ('A'-BBG remix) / ('A'side) / Tomorrow started (live).
(12") *(12RX 6264)* – ('A'-Fluke mix) / ('A'-Dominic Woosey remix).

Nov 90. (7"/c-s) *(R/TCR 6276)* **SUCH A SHAME. / DUM DUM GIRL (live)**   `[]`   `[]`
(12"+=) *(12R 6276)* – ('A'-Gary Miller remix).
(cd-s++=) *(CDR 6276)* – Talk talk (live).

Feb 91. (7"/c-s) *(R/TCR 6282)* **LIVING IN ANOTHER WORLD ('91 remix). / ('A'live remix)** (12"+=/cd-s+=) – *(12R/CDR 6282)* – ('A'-Mendelsohn mix).

—— Basic quartet only retained **DITCHAM, EDWARDS + LOWTHER** and brought in **LEVINE ANDRADE, STEPHEN TEES, GEORGE ROBERTSON, GAVYN WRIGHT, JACK GLICKMAN, GARFIELD JACKSON + WILF GIBSON** – viola / **ERNEST MOTHLE** – acoustic bass / **ROGER SMITH + PAUL KEGG** – cello / **DAVE WHITE** – contra, bass, clarinet

Mar 91. (cd)(lp/c) *(CDP 793976-2)(PCS/TCPCS 7349)* **HISTORY REVISITED – THE REMIXES** | 35 |
– Living in another world '91 / Such a shame / Happiness is easy (dub) / Today / Dum dum girl (spice remix) / Life's what you make it / Talk talk / It's my life (tropical rainforest mix) / Living in another world (curious world dub mix) / Life's what you make it (the Fluke remix).

                        Verve   **Verve**

Sep 91. (cd/c/lp) *(847717-2/-4/-1)* **LAUGHING STOCK** | 26 |
– Myrrhman / Ascension day / After the flood / Taphead / New grass / Runeii.
Sep 91. (pic-cd-s) *(TALKD 1)* **AFTER THE FLOOD / MYRRHMAN**
Oct 91. (pic-cd-s) *(TALKD 2)* **NEW GRASS. / STUMP**
Nov 91. (pic-cd-s) *(TALKD 3)* **ASCENTION DAY. / 5.09**

– compilations, etc –

Nov 96. (d-cd) *E.M.I.; (CDEMC 3670)* **ASIDES AND BESIDES**
Jan 97. (cd) *E.M.I.; (CDEMC 3763)* **THE VERY BEST OF TALK TALK** | 54 |
– It's my life / Talk talk / Dum dum girl / Have you heard the news / Such a shame / For what it's worth / Life's what you make it / Eden / April 5th / Living in another world / I believe in you / Give it up / John Cope / Wealth / Time it's time.
Feb 99. (cd) *Pond Life; (PLVP 001CD)* **LONDON 1986 (live)**
– Tomorrow started / Life's what you make it / Caroline knows / Living in another world / Give it up / It's my life / Such a shame / Renee.

'O'RANG

LEE HARRIS + PAUL WEBB

                        Echo   **not iss.**

Aug 94. (cd/c/lp) *(ECH CD/MC/LP 002)* **HERD OF INSTINCT**
– Orang / Little brother / Mind on pleasure / All change / Aneon, the oass / Loaded values / Nahoojek – Fogou.
Nov 94. (12"ep/cd-ep) **SPORE**
– O'rang / Little brother / Mind our pleasure / All change / And on the oasis / Loaded values / Nahoojak fejou.
Jan 97. (12"ltd) *(ECSYDJ 029)* **P53.**
Feb 97. (cd/lp) *(ECH CD/LP 010)* **FIELDS AND WAVES**
– Barren / Jalap / P.53 / Moider / Seizure / Moratorium / Superculture / Quondam / Forest / Hoo / Boreades / Fields and waves.

MARK HOLLIS

                        Polydor   **Polydor**

Feb 98. (cd) *(537688-2)* **MARK HOLLIS** | 53 |
– The colour of Spring / Watershed / Inside looking out / The gift / Life 1895-1915 / Westward bound / Daily planet / New Jerusalem.

TALL DWARFS / Chris KNOX (dig out; Great Alt & Indie . . .)

TANGERINE DREAM

Formed: Berlin, Germany . . . Autumn 1967 by art student EDGAR FROESE, who took the name, TANGERINE DREAM, from lyrics used in The BEATLES' classic, 'Lucy In The Sky With Diamonds'. He was invited to play some classical improvisations by surrealist painter SALVADOR DALI in his Spanish villa, EDGAR subsequently going through many egotistical rock musicians before he finally met KLAUS SCHULZE in '69. Together, they soon found KONRAD SCHNITZLER and JOSEPH BEUYS, who, with other guests, worked on the sessions for the 1970 debut, 'ELECTRONIC MEDITATION'. With others going solo, EDGAR then found CHRIS FRANKE and another album, 'ALPHA CENTAURI' surfaced for UK 'Polydor'. In 1972, PETER BAUMANN joined for their third album, 'ATEM', the record heavily playlisted on John Peel's night-time Radio One show and leading to new entrepeneur, Richard Branson, signing them to his 'Virgin' label. Surprisingly, the following year, 'PHAEDRA' made it into the UK Top 40 lists, much aided by the fact 'Virgin' was now an influential part of the British/continental scene. With this album, TANGERINE DREAM made a departure from their PINK FLOYD-like experimentalism, discovering picturesque, electronic waves of sound, rhythmically haunting and repetitive. 'RUBYCON' (1975) was similarly influential, although from there on in the band started to gravitate towards soundtrack work, their atmospheric mood pieces fitting the genre with ease. Over the course of the following decade, they recorded music for such diverse screen projects as 'SORCERER' (1977), 'THIEF' (1981), 'RISKY BUSINESS' (1983) and 'FIRESTARTER' (1984), although their music increasingly verged upon 'New Age' sterility.

Album rating: ELECTRONIC MEDITATION (*4) / ALPHA CENTAURI (*4) / ZEIT (*3) / ATEM (*5) / PHAEDRA (*9) / RUBYCON (*9) / RICOCHET (*8) / STRATOSFEAR (*7) / SORCERER (*7) / ENCORE (*6) / CYCLONE (*5) / FORCE MAJEURE (*6) / TANGRAM (*6) / QUICHOTTE (aka 'PERGAMON – LIVE AT THE PALAST DER REPUBLIK') (*5) / THIEF soundtrack (*4) / EXIT (*6) / WHITE EAGLE (*5) / LOGOS – LIVE (*5) / WAVELENGTH soundtrack (*4) / HYPERBOREA (*4) / RISKY BUSINESS (*4) / FIRESTARTER soundtrack (*4) / POLAND – THE WARSAW CONCERT (*4) / FLASHPOINT soundtrack (*4) / LE PARC (*5) / HEARTBREAKERS soundtrack (*4) / DREAM SEQUENCES compilation (*6) / LEGEND soundtrack with other artists (*3) / UNDERWATER SUNLIGHT (*4) / GREEN DESERT early work

(*5) / TYGER (*5) / THREE O'CLOCK HIGH soundtrack with other artists (*3) / THE TANGERINE DREAM COLLECTION compilation (*7) / NEAR DARK soundtrack (*4) / LIVE MILES (*4) / SHY PEOPLE soundtrack (*4) / OPTICAL RACE (*5) / MIRACLE MILE (*3) / THE BEST OF TANGERINE DREAM compilation (*6) / LILY ON THE BEACH (*4) / MELROSE (*5) / DEAD SOLID PERFECT soundtrack (*3) / THE PARK IS MINE (*3) / ROCKOON (*6) / DEADLY CARE soundtrack (*3) / CANYON DREAMS (*6) / 220 VOLT LIVE (*6) / TURN OF THE TIDES (*6) / TYRANNY OF BEAUTY (*6) / BOOK OF DREAMS collection (*6) / THE DREAM MIXES remixes (*6) / THE DREAM ROOTS COLLECTION compilation (*6) / GOBLIN'S CLUB (*6) / OASIS (*4) / TOURNADO (*4) / AMBIENT MONKEYS (*4) / Edgar Froese: AQUA (*6) / EPSILON IN MALAYSIAN PALE (*6) / MACULA TRANSFER (*4) / AGES (*6) / STUNTMAN (*5) / KAMIKAZE 1989 soundtrack (*4) / PINNACLES (*5) / BEYOND THE STORM (*5)

EDGAR FROESE (b. 6 Jun'44, Tilsit, Germany) – guitar, piano, organ (ex-The ONES) / **VOLKER HOMBACH** – flute, violin / **KIRT HERKENBERG** – bass / (Mar69) **SVEN JOHANNSON** – drums; repl. LANSE HAPRHASH

—— In 1970, after HOMBACH became film cameraman for W.R.FASSBINDER, and brief wind instrumentalist STEVE JOLIFFE departed to join STEAMHAMMER. Group reformed **EDGAR FROESE** brought in newcomers **KLAUS SCHULTZE** (b. 4 Aug'47) – drums, percussion / **CONRAD SCHNITZLER** – cello, flute, violin. with guests **JIMMY JACKSON** – organ / **THOMAS VON KEYSERLING** – flute

                        Ohr   **not iss.**

Jun 70. (lp) *(OMM 556 004)* **ELECTRONIC MEDITATION** | – | – German
– Geburt (Genesis) / Reise durch ein brennendes gehirn (Journey through a burning brain) / Kalter rauch (Cold smoke) / Asche zu asche (Ashes to ashes) / Auferstehung (Resurrection). *(UK cd-iss. Jan87 on 'Jive'; CTANG 4) (cd re-iss. Feb96 on 'Essential'; ESMCD 345)*

—— **FROESE** added bass to repertoire, and again supplanted new members **CHRISTOPHER FRANKE** (b. 6 Apr'53) – drums, percussion, synthesizer repl. CONRAD / **STEVE SCHROEDER** – organs repl. KLAUS SCHULTZE who went solo / added new guests **UDO DENNEBORG** – flute, words / **ROLAND PAULICK** – synthesizer

Apr 71. (lp) *(OMM 556 012)* **ALPHA CENTAURI** | – | – German
– Sunrise in the third system / Fly and collision of Comas Sola / Alpha Centauri. *(UK-iss.Nov73 on 'Polydor Super'; 2383 314) (cd-iss. Jan87 on 'Jive'; CTANG 5) (re-iss. cd Feb96 on 'Essential'; ESMCD 346)*

—— **PETER BAUMANN** – synthesizer, organ repl. SCHROYDER (guested on below)
Feb 72. (7") *(OSS 7006)* **ULTIMA THULE (tell 1). / ULTIMA THULE (tell 2)** | – | – German

—— More guests were added on next; **FLORIAN FRICKE** – synthesizers / cellists / **CHRISTIAN VALBRACHT / JOCKEN VON GRUMBCOW / HANS JOACHIM BRUNE / JOHANNES LUCKE**

Feb 72. (d-lp) *(OMM 2-556 021)* **ZEIT** | – | – German
– 1st movement: Birth of liquid plejades / 2nd movement: Nebulous dawn / 3rd movement: Origins of supernatural probabilities / 4th movement: Zeit. *(UK-iss.Jun76 on 'Virgin'; VD 2503) (cd-iss. Jan87 on 'Jive'; CTANG 3) (cd re-iss. Feb96 on 'Essential'; ESMCD 347)*

Mar 73. (lp) *(OMM 556 031)* **ATEM** | – | – German
– Atem / Fauni-Gena / Wahn / Circulation of events. *(UK-iss.Nov73 on 'Polydor Super'; 2383 297) (cd-iss. Jan87 on 'Jive'; CTANG 2) (re-iss. cd Feb96 on 'Essential'; ESMCD 348)*

—— In Aug'73, they recorded 'GREEN DESERT' album, unreleased until 1986.

                        Virgin   **Virgin**

Mar 74. (lp/c) *(V/TCV 2010) <13108>* **PHAEDRA** | 15 |
– Phaedra / Mysterious semblance at the strand of nightmares / Movements of a visionary / Sequent C. *(re-iss. Mar84 lp/c; OVED/+C 25) (cd-iss. Jul87; CDV 2010) (cd re-iss. Feb95; TAND 5)*

—— **MICHAEL HOENIG** – synthesizer repl. BAUMANN (on tours only 1974-75)
Mar 75. (lp/c) *(V/TCV 2025) <13166>* **RUBYCON** | 12 |
– Rubycon (part 1) / Rubycon (part 2). *(re-iss. Mar84 lp/c; OVED/+C 27) (cd-iss. Jul87; CDV 2025) (cd re-iss. Feb95; TAND 6)*

Dec 75. (lp/c) *(V/TCV 2044)* **RICOCHET (live at Liverpool, Coventry & Yorkminster Cathedrals)** | 40 |
– Ricochet (part 1) / Ricochet (part 2). *(re-iss. Mar84 lp/c; OVED/+C 26) (cd-iss. Jul87; CDV 204) (cd re-iss. Feb95; TAND 7)*

—— **BAUMANN** re-united with outfit, to depose HOENIG
Nov 76. (lp/c) *(V/TCV 2068) <34427>* **STRATOSFEAR** | 39 |
– Stratosfear / The big sleep in search of Hades / 3 a.m. at the border of the marsh from Okefnokee / Invisible limits. *(cd-iss. Jul87; CDV 2068) (re-iss. Aug88 lp/c; OVED/+C 70) (cd re-iss. Feb95; TAND 8)*

Jul 77. (lp/c) *(MCF/+C 2806) <2277>* **SORCERER (Soundtrack)** | 25 |
– Main title / Search / The call / Creation / Vengeance / The journey / Grind / Rain forest / Abyss / The mountain road / Impressions of Sorcerer / Betrayal (Sorcerer's theme). *(re-iss. Feb82 lp/c; MCL/+C 1646) (cd-iss. Aug92; MCLD 19159)* (above lp & below 45, were from the MCA film 'Wages Of Fear')

Aug 77. (7") *<40740>* **BETRAYAL. / GRIND** | – |
Nov 77. (d-lp/d-c) *(VD/TCVD 2506) <35014>* **ENCORE (live)** | 55 |
– Cherokee lane / Moonlight / Coldwater canyon / Desert dream. *(cd-iss. Jul87; CDV 2506) (cd re-iss. Apr95; TAND 9)*

Jan 78. (7") *(VS 199)* **ENCORE. / HOBO MARCH** | – |
Mar 78. (7") *<9516>* **MOONLIGHT. / COLDWATER CANYON** | – |

—— **STEVE JOLIFFE** – vocals, keyboards, wind returned after several years to repl. BAUMANN who went solo. Added **KLAUS KRIEGER** – drums
Mar 78. (lp/c) *(V/TCV 2097)* **CYCLONE** | 37 |
– Bent cold sidewalk / Rising runner missed by endless sender / Madrigal meridian. *(cd-iss. Jul87; CDV 2097) (re-iss. Aug88 lp/c; OVED/+C 71) (cd re-iss. Apr95)*

Feb 79. (lp,clear-lp/c) *(V/TCV 2111)* **FORCE MAJEURE** | 26 |
– Force majeure / Cloudburst flight / Thru metamorphic rocks. *(cd-iss. Jul87; CDV 2111) (re-iss. Aug88 lp/c; OVED/+C 111) cd re-iss. Apr95; TAND 10)*

—— (now trio) **FROESE + FRANKE** recruited **JOHANNES SCHMOELLING** – keyboards
May 80. (lp/c) *(V/TCV 2147)* **TANGRAM** | 36 |
– Tangram set 1 / Tangram set 2. *(cd-iss. Oct85; CDV 2147) (re-iss. Aug88 lp/c; OVED/+C 112) (cd re-iss. Apr95; TAND 11)*

                        Virgin   **Elektra**

Apr 81. (lp/c) *(V/TCV 2198) <521>* **THIEF (Soundtrack)** | 43 |
– Beach theme / Dr. Destructo / Diamond diary / Burning bar / Scrap yard / Trap

feeling / Igneous / Confrontation. *(re-iss.Aug88 lp/c; OVED/+C 72) (cd re-iss. Jun88; CDV 2198) (cd re-iss. Aug95; TAND 12)*

Sep 81. (lp/c) *(V/TCV 2212)* <557> **EXIT** | 43 |
 – Kiev mission / Pilots of purple twilight / Chronozon / Exit / Network 23 / Remote viewing. *(re-iss. Aug88 lp/c; OVED/+C 166) (cd-iss. Aug88; CDV 2212) (re-iss. cd Aug95; TAND 13)*

Sep 81. (7") *(VS 444)* **CHRONOZON. / NETWORK 23** | - |

Apr 82. (lp/c) *(V/TCV 2226)* **WHITE EAGLE** | 57 |
 – Midnight in Tulo / Convention of the 24 / White eagle / Mojave plan. *(re-iss. Aug88 lp/c; OVED/+C 150) (cd-iss. Aug88; CDV 2226) (re-iss. cd Aug95; TAND 2)*

Dec 82. (lp/c) *(V/TCV 2257)* **LOGOS – LIVE (At The Dominion)**
 – Logos part 1 / Logos part 2 / Dominion. *(re-iss. Apr86 lp/c; OVED 167) (cd-iss. Jun88; CDV 2257) (re-iss. cd Aug95; TAND 3)*

1983. (lp/c) <STV/CTV 81207> **WAVELENGTH (Soundtrack)** | - |
 – Alien voices / Wavelength (main title) / Desert drive / Mojave (end title) / Healing / Breakout / Alien goodbyes / Spaceship / Church theme / Sunset drive / Airshaft / lley walk / Cyro lab / Running through the hills / Campfire theme / Mojave (end title reprise). *(UK cd-iss. Jan89 on 'Varese Sarabande'; VCD 47223)*

Oct 83. (lp/c/cd) *(V/TCV/CDV 2292)* **HYPERBOREA** | 45 |
 – No man's lannd / Hyperborea / Cinnamon road / Sphinx lightning. *(re-iss. Jun88 lp/c; OVED/+C 175) (re-iss. cd Aug95; TAND 4)*

Dec 83. (lp/c) *(V/TCV 2302)* **RISKY BUSINESS (Soundtrack)**
 – The dream is always the same / No future / Love on a real train / Guido the killer pimp / Lana / (tracks by other artists; PHIL COLLINS / JOURNEY / MUDDY WATERS / JEFF BECK / BOB SEGER). *(cd-iss. May87; CDV 2302) (re-iss. Apr90 lp/c; OVED/+C 2302)*

	M.C.A.	M.C.A.

Jul 84. (lp/c) *(MCF/+C 3233)* **FIRESTARTER (Soundtrack)**
 – Crystal voice / The run / Test lab / Charley the kid / Escaping point / Rainbirds move / Burning force / Between realities / Shop territory / Flash final / Out of the heat. *(re-iss. Jan89; MCA/+C 6163) (cd-iss. Apr90; DMCL 1899)*

	Jive Electro	Relativity

Sep 84. (7"/7"sha-pic-d) *(JIVE/+P 74)* **WARSAW IN THE SUN. /**
POLISH DANCE
 (12"+=) *(JIVET 74)* – ('A'-part 2) / Rare bird.

Oct 84. (lp/d-pic-lp/c) *(HIP/+X/C 22)* **POLAND – THE WARSAW**
CONCERT (live) | 90 |
 – Poland / Tangent / Barbakane / Horizon. *(cd-iss. 1988; CHIP 22) (re-iss. cd May96 on 'Essential'; ESMCD 365)*
 (below album released on 'Heavy Metal' UK / 'EMI America' US)

Feb 85. (lp/pic-lp/c) *(HM1 HP/PD/MC 29)* <ST 17141> **FLASHPOINT**
(Soundtrack) | |Dec84
 – Going west / Afternoon in the desert / Plane ride / Mystery tracks / Lost in the dunes / Highway patrol / Love phantasy / Madcap story / Dirty cross-roads / Flashpoint. *(cd-iss. Apr87; HM1 XD 29) (re-iss. cd Sep95 on 'One Way';)*

Aug 85. (lp/c) *(HIP/+C 26)* **LE PARC**
 – Bois de Boulogne (Paris) / Central Park (New York) / Gaudi Park (Guell Garden, Barcelona) / Tiergarten (Berlin) / Zen Garden (Myoonj, Temple Kyoto) / Le Parc (L.A. Streethawk) / Hyde Park (London) / The Cliffs of Sydney (Sydney) / Yellowstone Park (Rocky Mountains). *(cd-iss. Mar88; CHIP 26) (re-iss. cd May96 on 'Essential'; ESMCD 364)*

  —— guest on above album CLARE TORY – vocals

Aug 85. (7") *(JIVE 101)* **STREETHAWK. / TIERGARTEN**
 (12"+=) *(JIVET 101)* – Gaudi Park / Warsaw in the sun (part 1 & 2).

1985. Virgin; (lp) *(207 212-620)* **HEARTBREAKERS (soundtrack)** | - | - |German
 – Heartbreakers / Footbridge to Heaven / Twilight painter / Gemeni / Rain in N.Y. city / Pastime / The loser / Breathing the night away / Desire / Thorny affair / Daybreak. *(UK cd-iss. Jun95 on 'Silva Screen'; FILMCD 163)*

  —— PAUL HASLINGER – multi-instrumentalist repl. SCHMOELLING who went solo

Jul 86. (lp/c)(cd) *(HIP/+C 40)(CHIP 40)* **UNDERWATER SUNLIGHT** | 97 |
 – Song of the whale / From dawn . . . to dusk / Ride on the ray / Dolphin dance / Underwater sunlight / Scuba scuba. *(cd re-iss. May96 on 'Essential'; ESMCD 366)*

Aug 86. (12"ep) <88561-8120-1> **DOLPHIN DANCE. / DOLPHIN**
SMILE / SONG OF THE WHALE | - |

Jun 87. (lp/c)(cd) *(HIP/+C 47)(CHIP 47)* **TYGER** | 88 |
 – Tyger / London / Alchemy of the heart / Smile. *(cd+=)* – 21st century common man I & II. *(cd re-iss. May96 on 'Essential'; ESMCD 367)*

  —— guest vox – BERNADETTE SMITH

Jun 87. (7") *(JIVE 143)* **TYGER. / 21st CENTURY COMMON MAN II**
 (12"+=) *(JIVET 143)* – ('A'extended).

1987. (lp) <47357> **THREE O'CLOCK HIGH (Soundtrack shared**
with SYLVESTER LEVAY) | - |
 – It's Jerry's day today / 46-32-15 / No detention / Any school bully will do / Go to the head of the class / Sit / The fight / Jerry's decisions / The fight is on / Paper / Big bright brass knuckles / Buying paper like it's going out of style / Dangerous trend / Who's chasing who? / Bonding by candlelight / You'll never believe it / Starting the day off right / Weak at the knees / Kill him (the football dummy) / Not so quiet in the library – Get lost in a crowd / Something to remember me by / Arrival. *(UK cd-iss. Oct90 also on 'Varese Sarabande'; VCD 47307)*

Apr 88. (lp/c)(cd) *(HIP/+C 62)(CHIP 62)* **LIVE MILES (live)**
 – Live miles: (part 1) – The Albuquerque concert / Live miles: (part 2) – The West Berlin concert. *(re-iss. cd May96 on 'Essential'; ESMCD 368)*

	Silva Screen	Silva Screen

Feb 88. (lp/c/cd) *(<FILM/+C/CD 026>)* **NEAR DARK (Soundtrack)** | |Nov87
 – Cabeb's blues / Pick up at high noon / Rain in the third house / Bus station / Good times / She's my sister / Father and son / Severin dies / Flight at dawn / Mae's transformation / Mae comes back. *(re-iss. Jun90; same)*

Jul 88. (lp/c/cd) *(<FILM/+C/CD 027>)* **SHY PEOPLE (Soundtrack)** | |Nov87
 – Shy people / Joe's place / The harbor / Nightfal / Dancing on a white moon / Civilized illusion's / Swamp voices / Transparent days / Shy people (reprise).

  —— now a duo of FROESE + HASLINGER

	Arista	Private Music

Feb 89. (lp/c/cd) *(209/409/259 557)* <2042-1/-4/-2 P> **OPTICAL RACE** | |Aug88
 – Marakesh / Atlas eyes / Mothers of rain / Twin soul tribe / Optical race / Cat scan / Sun gate / Turning of the wheel / The midnight trail / Ghtrezi (long song).

Jul 89. (lp/c/cd) *(209/409/259 887)* **MIRACLE MILE**
 – Teetering scales / One for the book / After the call / On the spur of the moment / All of a dither / Final statement. *(re-iss. cd Feb96; 260.016)*

Dec 89. (lp/c/cd) <210/410/260 103> **LILY ON THE BEACH** | - |
 – Too hot for my chinchilla / Lily on the beach / Alaskan summer / Desert drive / Mount Shasta / Crystal curfew / Paradise cove / Twenty nine palms / Valley of the kings / Radio city / Blue mango cafe / Gecko / Long island sunset.

Nov 90. (cd/lp) *(261/211 105)* **MELROSE**
 – Melrose / Three bikes in the sky / Dolls in the shadow / Yucatan / Electric lion / Rolling down Cahenga / Art of vision / Desert train / Cool at heart.

	Silva Screen	Silva Screen

Mar 91. (cd) *(FILMCD 079)* **DEAD SOLID PERFECT (Soundtrack)**
 – Theme from Dead Solid Perfect / In the pond / Beverly leaves / Of cads and caddies / (Tournament montage) / A whore in one / Sand trap / In the rough / Nine iron / US Open / My name is bad hair / In the hospital room / Welcome to Bushwood / Deja vu / Birdie / Divot / Kenny and Donny montage / Phone to Beverly / Nice shots / Sinking putts / Kenny's winning shot.

Oct 91. (cd) *(FILMCD 080)* **THE PARK IS MINE**

  —— Now a duo of FROESE + JEROME FROESE his son and LINDA SPA – sax / ZLASLO PERICA – synth.

Feb 92. Essential; (cd/c/lp) *(ESM CD/MC/LP 403)* **ROCKOON**
 – Big city dwarves / Red roadster / Touchwood / Graffiti sreeet / Funky Atlanta / Spanish love / Lifted veil / Penguin reference / Body corporate / Rockoon / Girls on Broadway. *(re-iss. cd Feb96; same)*

Dec 92. (cd) *(FILMCD 121)* **DEADLY CARE (Soundtrack)**
 – Main theme / Paddles – Stolen pills / A strong drink – A bad morning / Wasted and sick / Hope for future / The hospital in bed / Annie and father / More pills / In the Head nurse's – At the father's grave / Clean and sober.

	Miramar	Miramar

Jul 93. (cd) *(MPCD 2801)* **CANYON DREAMS**
 – Shadow flyer / Canyon carver / Water's gift / Canyon voices / Sudden revelation / A matter of time / Purple nightfall / Colorado dawn.

Oct 93. (cd/c) *(MP CD/MC 2804)* **220 VOLT LIVE (live)**
 – Oriental haze / Two bunch palms / 220 volt / Homeless / Treasure of innocence / Sundance kid / Backstreet hero / The blue bridge / Hamlet / Dreamtime / Purple haze.

	CoastCoast	Miramar

Nov 94. (cd) *(CTCZ 108)* **TURN OF THE TIDES**
 – Pictures at an exhibition / Firetongues / Galley slave's horizon / Death of a nightingale / Twilight brigade / Jungle journey / Midwinter night / Turn of the tides. *(re-iss. Nov96; same)*

	Amp	Miramar

Sep 95. (cd) **TYRANNY OF BEAUTY**
 (re-iss. Oct96 on 'Tangerine Dream Int.'; TDI 002CD)

	When!

Sep 96. (cd) *(WENCD 011)* **GOBLINS CLUB**
 – Towards the evening star / At Darwin's motel / On Crane's passage / Rising haul in silence / United goblin's parade / Lamb with radar eyes / Elf June and the midnight patrol / Sad Merlin's Sunday.

Mar 97. (c-s) *(WENM 1022)* **TOWARDS THE EVENING STAR /**
('A'mix)
 (12"+=/cd-s+=) *(WEN T/X 1022)* – ('A'remixes).

	Tandream	not iss.

Jun 97. (cd) *(TDI 007CD)* **OASIS**
 – Flashblood / Zion / Reflections / Cliff dwellers / Waterborne / Cedar breaks / Summer storm / Hopi mesa heart.

Sep 97. (cd) *(TDI 008CD)* **TOURNADO (live)**
 – Flashflood / 220 volt / Firetongues / Girls on Broadway / Little blond in the park of attractions / Rising haul in silence / Lamb with radar eyes / Touchwood / Towards the evening star.

– compilations, others, etc. –

  —— on 'Virgin' unless mentioned otherwise

Jul 76. (d-lp) *(VD 2504)* **ATEM / ALPHA CENTAURI** | - | - |
Dec 80. (4xlp-box) *(VBOX 2)* **TANGERINE DREAM '70-80** | - | - |
Nov 85. (t-lp/d-c/d-cd) *(TDLP/TDC/CDTD 1)* **DREAM SEQUENCE** | - | - |
 (re-iss. d-cd Apr92; same)
Mar 86. (6xlp-box) *Jive Electro; (TANG 1)* **IN THE BEGINNING** | - | - |
 – (ELECTRONIC MEDITATION / ALPHA CENTAURI / ZEIT (d-lp) / ATEM / GREEN DESERT)
May 86. (lp) *M.C.A.; <6165>* **LEGEND (Soundtrack with other**
artists) | - | 96 |
 – Unicorn theme / Blue room / Darkness / The dance / Goblins / Fairies / The kitchen (medley).
1986. (lp) *(207684620)* **PERGAMON – LIVE AT THE PALAST DER**
REPUBLIK *(live & originally issued in East Germany 1980 as 'QUICHOTTE'; Amiga 855891)* | - | - |German
 (UK cd-iss. May96 as 'PERGAMON' on 'Essential'; ESMCD 413)
Dec 86. (cd) *Zomba; (CTANG 1)* **GREEN DESERT** (rec.1973) | - | - |
 (re-iss. May89 on 'Jive' lp/c; HOP/+C 226) (re-iss. Feb96 on 'Essential'; ESMCD 349)
Mar 87. (d-lp/c/cd) *(CCS LP/MC/CD 161)* **THE TANGERINE DREAM**
COLLECTION | | - |
Nov 89. (lp/c)(cd) *Jive; (HIP/+C 75)(CHIP 75)* **THE BEST OF**
TANGERINE DREAM | | |
Nov 90. (3xcd-box) *(TPAK 11)* **COLLECTORS' EDITION** | | |
 – (CYCLONE / FORCE MAJEURE / ENCORE)
Oct 91. (cd/c) *Music Club; (MC CD/TC 034)* **FROM DAWN . . . TILL**
DUSK 1973-88 | | |
Feb 93. (cd) *Private Music; (01005 82105-2)* **THE PRIVATE MUSIC OF**
TANGERINE DREAM | | |
Mar 93. (cd) *Silva Screen; (FILMCD 125)* **DREAM MUSIC**
 – from films; THE PARK IS MINE / DEADLY CARE / DEAD SOLID PERFECT.
Oct 94. (5xcd-box) *(CDBOX 4)* **TANGENTS** | | - |
Mar 95. (cd) *Emporio; (EMPRCD 564)* **ATMOSPHERICS** | | |
Nov 95. (cd) *Silva Screen; (FILMCD 166)* **DREAM MUSIC 2** | | |
Dec 95. (d-cd) *Essential; (EDFCD 353)* **BOOK OF DREAMS** | | |
 – (THE PINK YEARS: 1970-1973) // THE BLUE YEARS: 1983-1987)
Jul 96. (cd) *Tangerine Dream Int.; (TDI 001CD)* **THE DREAM MIXES** | | - |
Nov 96. (5xcd-box) *Essential; (ESFCD 420)* **THE DREAM ROOTS**
COLLECTION | | - |

EDGAR FROESE

—— solo (all music by himself)

			Virgin	Virgin
Jun 74.	(lp) (V 2016) <13111> **AQUA**		☐	☐

– NGC 891 / Upland / Aqua / Panorphelia. *(re-iss. Mar84; OVED 20) (cd-iss. Jun87; CDV 2016)*

Sep 75. (lp) (V 2040) **EPSILON IN MALAYSIAN PALE** ☐ ☐
– Epsilon in Malaysian pale / Maroubra Bay. *(re-iss. Mar84; OVED 22) (cd-iss. Jun87; CDV 2040)*

1976. Brain; (lp) (60.008) **MACULA TRANSFER** – ☐ – German
– Os / Af / Pa / Quantas / If. *(re-iss. Mar82; 0060.008)*

Jan 78. (d-lp) (VD 2507) **AGES** ☐ –
– Metropolis / Era of the slaves / Tropic of Capricorn / Nights of automatic women / Icarus / Childrens deeper study / Ode to Granny "A" / Pizarro and Atahwallpa / Golgatha and the circle closes. *(cd-iss. Jun97; CDOVD 480)*

Sep 79. (lp) (V 2139) **STUNTMAN** ☐ –
– Stuntman / It would be like Samoa / Detroit snackbar dreamer / Drunken Mozart in the desert / A Dali-esque sleep fuse / Scarlet score for Mescalero. *(re-iss. Mar84; OVED 21) (cd-iss. Jun87 & Mar94; CDV 2139)*

Oct 82. (lp) (V 2255) **KAMIKAZE 1989 (Soundtrack)** ☐ –
– Videophonic / Vitamen 'C' / Krismopompas / Polizei disco / Intuition / Polizei therapie center / Blauer panther / Schlangenbad / Underwarter tod / Flying kamikaze / Der konzern / Der 31. stock. *(re-iss. Aug88; OVED 125) (cd-iss. Aug88; CDV 2255)*

Aug 83. (lp) (V 2277) **PINNACLES** ☐ –
– Specific gravity of smile / The light cone / Walkabout / Pinnacles. *(re-iss. Aug88; OVED 144) (cd-iss. May88; CDV 2277)*

– FROESE compilations, others –

Aug 82. (lp) Virgin; (V 2197) **SOLO 1974-1979** ☐ –
(re-iss. Mar84; OVED 21) (cd-iss. Aug88; CDV 2197)

Jun 95. (d-cd) Ambient; (AMBT 5) **BEYOND THE STORM** ☐ –

TAPPI TiKARRASS (see under ⇒ BJORK)

TASTE (see under ⇒ GALLAGHER, Rory)

James TAYLOR

Born: 12 Mar'48, Boston, Massachusetts, USA. Despite a privileged upbringing, the troubled TAYLOR admitted himself to a mental institute in 1965, aged only 17. It was during his near-year long stay that the budding singer began writing his own material although it would be early '67 before he'd get the chance to lay some of his ideas down on vinyl. This opportunity presented itself after TAYLOR moved to New York and hooked up with old friend DANNY KORTCHMAR in The FLYING MAHCINE, the group subsequently recording two TAYLOR tracks, 'NIGHT OWL' and 'BRIGHTEN YOUR NIGHT WITH MY DAY'. A combination of poor sales and TAYLOR's worsening heroin addiction caused the band to splinter a few months later, the singer subsequently moving to Notting Hill in London the following year. Persuaded to send a demo to Peter Asher, then A&R man at 'Apple' (and future manager of LINDA RONSTADT), TAYLOR soon found himself recording for The BEATLES' fledgling label. His Asher-produced, eponymous debut was released at the tail end of the year, a promising collection of understated strumming and wistful introspection. Almost country-rock but not quite, such memorable originals as 'SOMETHING IN THE WAY SHE MOVES' (NOT the BEATLES song!) and the yearning 'CAROLINA IN MY MIND' marked TAYLOR out as a kind of male JONI MITCHELL, if not quite as adventurous. As it turned out, the pair found they had more in common than just music, TAYLOR and MITCHELL becoming romantically involved in the early 70's. As well as performing together, the couple guested on each other's releases with MITCHELL partly documenting the affair on her landmark 'BLUE' album. Despite its potential, 'JAMES TAYLOR' sank without trace amid the chaotic situation at 'Apple', both TAYLOR and ASHER moving back to the States. After another period in a mental institution, TAYLOR emerged to find himself with a 'Warner Bros' contract, pre-arranged by ASHER (now his manager). Surrounding himself with the likes of RUSS KUNKEL, RANDY MEISNER and CAROLE KING, TAYLOR duly cut a belated follow-up album. Though it took a while to warm up, 'SWEET BABY JAMES' (1970) became one of the best selling US albums of the early 70's as well as a blueprint of sorts for the Laurel Canyon elite (whose tortured musings would come to dominate the American rock scene). Following the Top 3 success of the enduring 'FIRE AND RAIN', the album went on to reside in the upper reaches of the US chart for more than a year, its unassuming confessionals striking at the strife-torn heart of the post-hipppie dream. Not blessed with the most striking of voices, TAYLOR nevertheless relied on it to power his songs, backed by the sparsest of accompaniment, an acoustic strum here, a hint of pedal steel there. What he lacked in impact he made up for in intimacy (although his vocals improved over time); it's just a pity he moved ever further into MOR schmooze-pop. 'MUD SLIDE SLIM AND THE BLUE HORIZON' (1971) consolidated TAYLOR's standing in the L.A. firmament, a transatlantic Top 5 which featured his rather weak reading of CAROLE KING's 'YOU'VE GOT A FRIEND', a US No.1 later that summer. Ironically, many of TAYLOR's subsequent hits would be cover versions although his original material was far more affecting, the lovely 'YOU CAN CLOSE YOUR EYES' for example. This period saw TAYLOR at the height of his fame and apart from the inevitable media attention over his marriage to CARLY SIMON on the 3rd of November '72, he subsequently avoided the spotlight. Both 'ONE

MAN DOG' (1972) and 'WALKING MAN' (1974) failed to spawn any major hits, TAYLOR's only Top 5 single during this time a duet with SIMON entitled 'MOCKINGBIRD'. 'GORILLA' (1975) marked a return to form of sorts, the buoyant 'MEXICO' demonstrating what TAYLOR was capable of when he decided to step up a gear. The album's hit was a laboured cover of Marvin Gaye's 'HOW SWEET IT IS TO BE LOVED BY YOU', the song going Top 5 in the summer of '75. Two years on, TAYLOR repeated the success with yet another cover, a strident run-through of the Jimmy Jones & Otis Blackwell's R&B number, 'HANDY MAN'. The album which housed it, 'J.T.' (1977), was TAYLOR's last commercial blockbuster, subsequent releases selling respectably but failing to produce any singles. For the ensuing two years, the singer turned his talents towards collaboration; Autumn '77 saw him produce and play guitar on sister KATE TAYLOR's debut US Top 50 single, 'IT'S IN HIS KISS', while early the folowing year he was credited alongside PAUL SIMON and ART GARFUNKEL on a hit cover of SAM COOKE's 'WONDERFUL WORLD'. 'FLAG' (1979) gave him another Top 10 album although the formula was wearing a mite thin, his marriage with SIMON soon going the same way. In late '78 the couple had ridden into the Top 40 together with the duet 'DEVOTED TO YOU', but in 1982, CARLY filed for divorce. TAYLOR had hit the US charts the previous year with his last Top 10 album, 'DAD LOVES HIS WORK', the singer spending the first half of the 80's on a massive world tour. Though his albums didn't command the mass audience of yore, TAYLOR retained a loyal following throughout the 80's and beyond. Fans lapped up 'THAT'S WHY I'M HERE' (1986), although he only really hit the mark with 'NEW MOON SHINE' (1991), a strong set which tackled many current issues in impressive fashion and proved that TAYLOR, along with his old mucker, JACKSON BROWNE, could still cut the mustard. A (US) Top 20 live album in 1993 marked his biggest success for years and certainly, it's on a stage in lone acoustic fashion that TAYLOR really comes into his own, the singer playing some rare, warmly received Scottish dates in early '98 at the annual Celtic Connections festival in Glasgow. • **Songwriters:** Prolific pensmith, who also covered others; LO AND BEHOLD (Bob Dylan) / MOCKINGBIRD duet (Inez & Charlie Foxx) / DEVOTED TO YOU duet (Everly Brothers) / UP ON THE ROOF (Goffin-King) / DAY TRIPPER (Beatles) / JELLY MAN KELLY (with daughter Sarah) / EVERYDAY (Buddy Holly). • **Trivia:** TAYLOR starred in the 1971 road movie, 'Two Lane Blacktop' and also acted on US TV production, 'Working' (1981).

Album rating: JAMES TAYLOR (*7) / SWEET BABY JAMES (*8) / MUD SLIDE SLIM AND THE BLUE HORIZON (*7) / ONE MAN DOG (*6) / WALKING MAN (*6) / GORILLA (*6) / IN THE POCKET (*5) / GREATEST HITS compilation (*8) / JT (*7) / FLAG (*6) / DAD LOVES HIS WORK (*5) / THAT'S WHY I'M HERE (*6) / BEST OF JAMES TAYLOR – CLASSIC SONGS compilation (*7) / NEVER DIE YOUNG (*5) / NEW MOON SHINE (*6) / (LIVE) (*6) / HOURGLASS (*6)

JAMES TAYLOR – vocals, acoustic guitar (with session people)

		Apple	Apple
Dec 68.	(lp) (SAPCOR 3) <3352> **JAMES TAYLOR**	☐	62 Sep 70

– Don't talk now / Something's wrong / Knockin' round the zoo / Sunshine sunshine / Taking it in / Something in the way she moves / Carolina in my mind / Brighten your night with my day / Night owl / Rainy day man / Circle 'round the Sun / The blues is just a bad dream. *(re-iss. Jun71; same) (re-iss. Oct91)*

Apr 69. (7") <1805> **CAROLINA ON MY MIND. / SOMETHING'S WRONG** – ☐
<re-iss. Nov70; same> – <hit No.67>

—— now with **DANNY KOOTCH** (b.KORTCHMAR) – guitar / **CAROLE KING** – piano / **RUSS KUNKEL** – drums / **RANDY MEISNER, BOBBY WEST** & **JOHN LONDON** – bass / **CHRIS DARROW** – fiddle / **RED RHODES** – steel guitar / **JACK BIELAN** – brass arrangement

		Warners	Warners
Jul 70.	(7") <7387> **SWEET BABY JAMES. / SUITE FOR ZOG**	–	
Sep 70.	(7") <7423> **FIRE AND RAIN. / ANYWHERE LIKE HEAVEN**	–	3
Nov 70.	(7") (WB 6104) **FIRE AND RAIN. / SUNNY SKIES**	42	–
Nov 70.	(lp) (K 46043) <1843> **SWEET BABY JAMES**	7	3 Mar 70

– Sweet baby James / Lo and behold / Sunny skies / Steamroller / Country road / Oh, Susannah / Fire and rain / Blossom / Anywhere like Heaven / Oh baby, don't you loose your lip on me / Suite for 20 G. *(re-iss. Dec71, hit UK No.34) (re-iss. Jul88 cd/c; K2/K4 46043)*

Feb 71. (7") <7460> **COUNTRY ROAD. / SUNNY SKIES** – 37

—— **LEE SKLAR** – bass repl. 3 bassmen. Guest **JONI MITCHELL** – b.vox (2 – 45's)

May 71. (lp/c) (K/K4 46085) <2561> **MUD SLIDE SLIM AND THE BLUE HORIZON** 4 2
– Love has brought me around / You've got a friend / Places in my (WB past / Riding on a railroad / Soldiers / Mud slide Slim / Hey mister, that's me upon the jukebox / You can close your eyes / Machine gun Kelly / Long ago and far away / Let me ride / Highway song / Isn't it nice to be home again. *(re-iss. Mar72, hit UK No.49) (cd-iss. 1989; K2 56004)*

Aug 71. (7") (K/K4 16085) <7498> **YOU'VE GOT A FRIEND. / YOU CAN CLOSE YOUR EYES** 4 1 Jun71
Sep 71. (7") <7521> **LONG AGO AND FAR AWAY. / LET ME RIDE** – 31
Nov 72. (lp/c) (K/K4 46185) <2660> **ONE MAN DOG** 27 4
– One man parade / Nobody but you / Chili dog / Fool for you / Instrumental I / New tune / Back on the street again / Don't let me be lonely tonight / Woh, don't you know / One morning in May / Instrumental II / Someone / Hymn / Fanfare / Little David / Mescalito / Dance / Jig. *(quad-lp US Feb76) (cd-iss. Feb92)*

Nov 72. (7") (K 16231) <7655> **DON'T LET ME BE LONELY TONIGHT. / WOH, DON'T YOU KNOW** – 14
Feb 73. (7") <7682> **ONE MAN PARADE / NOBODY BUT YOU** – 67
May 73. (7") <7695> **HYMN. / FANFARE** – –

—— In Jan'74, did duet with wife CARLY SIMON on UK No.34 / US No.5 hit MOCKINGBIRD.

Jul 74. (lp/c) (K/K4 56042) <2794> **WALKING MAN** ☐ 13
– Walking man / Rock'n'roll is music now / Let it fall down / Me and my guitar /

Daddy's baby / Ain't no song / Hello old friend / Migration / The promised land / Fading away.

Aug 74. (7") <8028> **WALKING MAN. / DADDY'S BABY** | - |

Aug 74. (7") (K 16444) **AIN'T NO SONG. / HELLO OLD FRIEND** | - |

May 75. (7") (K 16632) <2866> **GORILLA** | 6 |
– Mexico / Music / How sweet it is (to be loved by you) / Wandering / Gorilla / You make it easy / I was a fool to care / Lighthouse / Angry blues / Love song / Sarah Maria. (cd-iss. Jul88; K 256137) (quad-lp Feb76)

Jul 75. (7") (K 16582) <8109> **HOW SWEET IT IS (TO BE LOVED BY YOU). / SARAH MARIA** | 5 | Jun75

Oct 75. (7") (K 16632) <8137> **MEXICO. / GORILLA** | 49 |

Apr 76. (7") (K 16708) **WANDERING. / ANGRY BLUES** | - |

Jun 76. (lp/c) (K/K4 56197) <2912> **IN THE POCKET** | 16 |
– Shower the people / A junkie's lament / Money machine / Slow burning love / Everybody has the blues / Daddy's all gone / Woman's gotta have it / Captain Jim's drunken dream / Don't be sad 'cause your sun is down / Nothing like a hundred miles / Family man / Golden moments.

Jun 76. (7") (K 16776) <8222> **SHOWER THE PEOPLE. / I CAN DREAM OF YOU** | 22 |

Aug 76. (7") (K 16808) **EVERYBODY HAS THE BLUES. / I CAN DREAM OF YOU** | - |

Oct 76. (7") (K 16819) **EVERYBODY HAS THE BLUES. / MONEY MACHINE** | - |

Nov 76. (7") <8278> **WOMAN'S GOTTA HAVE IT. / YOU MAKE IT EASY** | - |

Dec 76. (lp/c) (K/K4 56309) <2979> **GREATEST HITS** (compilation) | 23 |
– Something in the way she moves / Carolina in my mind / Fire and rain / Sweet baby James / Country roads / You've got a friend / Don't let me be lonely tonight / Walking man / How sweet it is (to be loved by you) / Mexico / Shower the people / Steamroller. (re-iss. Mar82) (re-iss. +cd.Jan87)

—— Retained **KORTCHMAR, KUNKEL + SKLAR** and recruited **DAVID SANBORN** – sax / **CLARENCE McDONALD** – percussion

　　　　　　　　　　　　　　C.B.S.　Columbia

Jun 77. (7") (CBS 5363) <10557> **HANDY MAN. / BARTENDER'S BLUES** | 4 |

Jul 77. (lp/c) (CBS/40 86029) <34811> **J.T.** | 4 |
– Your smiling face / There we are / Honey don't leave L.A. / Another grey morning / Bartender's blues / Secret of life / Handy man / I was only telling a lie / Looking for love on Broadway / Terra Nova / Traffic jam / If I keep my heart out of sight. (re-iss. +cd.Feb85) (re-iss. cd+c Oct93 on 'Sony Collectors')

Oct 77. (7") (CBS 5737) <10602> **YOUR SMILING FACE. / IF I KEEP MY HEART OUT OF SIGHT** | 20 | Sep 77

—— Autumn'77, saw him produce, play guitar, etc. for sister KATE TAYLOR's debut US Top 50 hit single IT'S IN HIS KISS. Early in 1978, he was credited on another cover hit 45; 'WHAT A WONDERFUL WORLD' with PAUL SIMON & ART GARFUNKEL.

Feb 78. (7") <10689> **HONEY DON'T LEAVE L.A. / ANOTHER GREY MORNING** | 61 |

—— In Sep78, another CARLY SIMON / J.T. duet 'DEVOTED TO YOU' hit US No.36.

Jun 79. (7") (CBS 7389) <11005> **UP ON THE ROOF. / CHANSON FRANCAISE** | 28 | May 79

Aug 79. (lp/c) (CBS/40 86091) <36058> **FLAG** | 10 | May 79
– Company man / Johnnie comes back / Day tripper / I will not lie for you / Brother Trucker / Is that the way you look / B.S.U.R. / Rainy day man / Millworker / Up on the roof / Chanson francaise / Slep come free me. (re-iss. Feb86) (cd-iss. Sep93 on 'Sony Collectors')

Aug 79. (7") (CBS 7773) **B.S.U.R. / SLEEP COME FREE ME** | |

Mar 81. (7"; JAMES TAYLOR & J.D. SOUTHER) (CBS A1048) <60514> **HER TOWN TOO. / BELIEVE IT OR NOT** | 11 | Feb 81

Apr 81. (lp/c) (CBS/40 86131) <37009> **DAD LOVES HIS WORK** | 10 | Mar 81
– Hard times / Her town too / Hour that the morning comes / I will follow / Believe it or not / Stand and fight / Only for me / Summer's here / Sugar trade / London town / That lonesome road. (cd-iss. May87) (re-iss. Jan94 on 'Sony Europe')

May 81. (7") <02093> **HARD TIMES. / SUMMER'S HERE** | 72 |

—— Late '85, he duets on RICKY SCAGGS track 'New Star Shining', for current lp

Jan 86. (lp/c/cd) (CBS/40/CD 25547) <40052> **THAT'S WHY I'M HERE** | 34 | Nov 85
– That's why I'm here / Song for you far away / Only a dream in Rio / Turn away / Going around one more time / Everyday / Limousine driver / Only one / Mona / The man who shot Liberty Valance / That's why I'm here (reprise).

Mar 86. (7") (CBS A6683) <05681> **EVERYDAY. / LIMOUSINE DRIVER** | 61 | Nov85

Mar 86. (7") <05785> **MONA. / ONLY ONE** | |

May 86. (7") <05884> **THAT'S WHY I'M HERE. / GOING AROUND ONE MORE TIME** | |

Sep 86. (7") <06278> **ONLY A DREAM IN RIO. / TURN AWAY** | |

Feb 88. (lp/c/cd) (46043-1-4-2) <40851> **NEVER DIE YOUNG** | 25 |
– Never die young / T-bone / Baby boom baby / Runaway boy / Valentine's day / Sun on the Moon / Sweet potato pie / Home by another day / Letter in the mail / First of May.

Feb 88. (7") (651204) <07616> **NEVER DIE YOUNG. / VALENTINE'S DAY** | 80 |
(12"+=) (651 204-1/-2) – Everyday. (re-iss. Jun88)

May 88. (7") <07948> **LETTER IN THE MAIL. / BABY BOOM BABY** | |

Sep 88. (7") <08493> **FIRST OF MAY. / SWEET POTATO PIE** | |

Sep 91. (c-s) <74214> **(I'VE GOT TO) STOP THINKIN' 'BOUT THAT. / SLAP LEATHER** | |

Oct 91. (cd/c/lp) (468977-2-4-1) <46038> **NEW MOON SHINE** | 37 |
– Copperline / Down in the hole / (I've got to) Stop thinkin' 'bout that / Shed a little light / The frozen man / Slap leather / Like every one she knows / One more round to cha cha cha / Native son / Oh brother / The water is wide. (re-iss. cd Jul94 on 'Sony Europe')

—— with **CLIFFORD CARTER** – keyboards / **DON GROLNICK** – piano / **JIMMY JOHNSON** – bass / **MICHAEL LANDALL** – guitar / **VALERIE CARTER, DAVID LASLEY, KATE MARKOWITZ & ANDREW McCULLEY** – vocals / **CARLOS VEGA** – drums

　　　　　　　　　　　Columbia　Columbia

Sep 93. (d-cd/d-c) (474216-2) <47056> **(LIVE)** | 20 | Aug93
– Sweet baby James / Traffic jam / Handy man / Your smiling face / Secret of life / Shed a little light / Everybody has the blues / Steamroller blues / Mexico /

Millworker / Country road / Fire and rain / Shower the people / How sweet it is / New hymn / Walking man / Riding on a railroad / Something in the way she moves / Sun on the Moon / Up on the roof / Don't let me be lonely tonight / She thinks I still care / Copperline / Slap leather / Only one / You make it easy / Carolina on my mind / I will follow / That lonesome road / You've got a friend. ('BEST LIVE' of above issued Apr94; 476657-2)

Jun 97. (cd/c) (487748-2/-4) **HOURGLASS** | 46 | 9 |
– Line 'em up / Enough to be your way / Little more time with you / Gaia / Ananas / Jump up behind me / Another day / Up er mei / Up from your life / Yellow and rose / Boatman / Walking my baby back home / Hangnail.

– compilations, etc. –

Feb 71. (lp) DJM; / Euphoria; **JAMES TAYLOR & THE ORIGINAL FLYING MACHINE** | |
– (early material 1967 when a member of The FLYING MACHINE) (re-iss. Nov76 as 'RAINY DAY MAN' on 'DJM'/'Trip', tracks differed slightly)

1974. (7"ep) Warners; **YOU'VE GOT A FRIEND / SUNNY SKIES. / FIRE AND RAIN / SWEET BABY JAMES** | - |

Oct 75. (d-lp) Warners; (K 66029) **TWO ORIGINALS OF . . .** | - |
– (contains the 2 albums below)

Oct 82. (d-c) Warners; **SWEET BABY JAMES / MUD SLIDE SLIM & THE BLUE HORIZON**
(d-cd-iss. Apr84)

Mar 86. (7") Old Gold; (OG 9576) **YOU'VE GOT A FRIEND. / FIRE AND RAIN** | - |

Jan 87. (7") CBS; (YZ 105) **UP ON THE ROOF. / FIRE AND RAIN** | - |

Mar 87. (lp/c/cd) CBS-WEA TV; (JTV 1/+C)(241 0892) **THE BEST OF JAMES TAYLOR – CLASSIC SONGS** | 53 | - |
– Fire and rain / Mexico / You've got a friend / How sweet it is (to be loved by you) / Carolina on my mind / Something in the way she moves / Shower the people / Sweet baby James / That's why I'm here / Everyday / Up on the roof / Your smiling face / Her town too / Handyman / Don't let me be lonely tonight / Only a dream in Rio.

John TAYLOR (see under ⇒ DURAN DURAN)

Roger TAYLOR (see under ⇒ QUEEN)

TEARDROP EXPLODES (see under ⇒ COPE, Julian)

TEARS FOR FEARS

Formed: Bath, Avon, England . . . 1981 by ROLAND ORZABAL and CURT SMITH, childhood friends who had initially played together in ska-pop outfit, GRADUATE. Inspired by psychotherapist Arthur Janov's controversial "primal scream" therapy, ORZABAL and SMITH named the group accordingly, subsequently signing to 'Mercury' on the strength of some demos. After two early singles, 'SUFFER THE CHILDREN' and 'PALE SHELTER (YOU DON'T GIVE ME LOVE)', failed to chart, the duo eventually hit the UK Top 3 with the claustrophobic synth-pop of 'MAD WORLD' (produced by CHRIS 'Merrick' HUGHES; ex-ADAM & THE ANTS, as was the debut album). They scored another Top 5 single early the following year with 'CHANGE', the subsequent album, 'THE HURTING' (1983), reaching No.1. Po-faced in true 80's style, with ORZABAL's lyrics centring on mental functioning, therapy, healing etc., the group were often accused of angst-ridden pretension despite their pin-up status. By the release of the million selling 'SONGS FROM THE BIG CHAIR' (1985), however, their focus had widened somewhat, a preceding single, 'SHOUT', surprisingly taking them to the top of the US charts (UK Top 5). The uncharacteristically breezy guitar pop of 'EVERYBODY WANTS TO RULE THE WORLD' was another massive transatlantic hit, further boosting sales of the album. Masterfully crafted, the record displayed a more considered approach to both songwriting and arranging, while ORZABAL and SMITH had more or less ditched the bedsit whine of old. It was to be almost four years before TEARS FOR FEARS released a follow-up, the much anticipated 'THE SEEDS OF LOVE' finally hitting the shelves in the Autumn of '89. A preceding single, 'SOWING THE SEEDS OF LOVE', was a clever take on The BEATLES' 'I AM THE WALRUS', pre-empting OASIS' more cumbersome efforts by a good few years. The whole album, in fact, displayed an even greater level of pop sophistication than its predecessor, boasting contributions from the likes of OLETA ADAMS and JON HASSELL. While the record initially sold well, however, it failed to generate much chart staying power, exacerbating the growing rift between SMITH and ORZABAL. The pair finally split in the early 90's, engendering a covert slanging match similar to the current JOHN SQUIRE/IAN BROWN jousting. ORZABAL carried on under the TEARS FOR FEARS moniker, although subsequent releases, 'ELEMENTAL' (1993) and 'RAOUL AND THE KINGS OF SPAIN' (1995) failed to scale the heights of the group's mid-80's heyday, the latter not even breaking the Top 40. • **Songwriters:** All written by ORZABAL, except CREEP (Radiohead) / ASHES TO ASHES (David Bowie).

Album rating: THE HURTING (*7) / SONGS FROM THE BIG CHAIR (*7) / THE SEEDS OF LOVE (*6) / TEARS ROLL DOWN – GREATEST HITS 1982-1992 compilation (*8) / ELEMENTAL (*4) / RAOUL AND THE KINGS OF SPAIN (*4) / SATURNINE, MARSHALL & LUNATIC collection (*4)

GRADUATE

ROLAND ORZABAL (b. ROLAND ORZABAL DE LA QUINTANA, 22 Aug'61, Portsmouth, England) – vocals, guitar / **CURT SMITH** (b.24 Jun'61) – vocals, bass / **JOHN BAKER** – vocals, guitar / **STEVE BUCK** – keyboards, flute / **ANDY MARSDEN** – drums

		Precision	not iss.
Mar 80.	(7") *(PAR 100)* **ELVIS SHOULD PLAY SKA. / JULIE JULIE**		–
May 80.	(7") *(PAR 104)* **EVER MET A DAY. / SHUT UP**		–
May 80.	(10"lp) *(PART 001)* **ACTING MY AGE**		–

– Acting my age / Sick and tired / Ever met a day / Dancing nights / Shut up / Elvis should play ska / Watching your world / Love that is bad / Julie Julie / Bad dreams. *(re-iss. Jul86 on 'P.R.T.')*

| Oct 80. | (7") *(PAR 111)* **AMBITION. / BAD DREAMS** | | – |
| Mar 81. | (7") *(PAR 117)* **SHUT UP. / EVER MET A DAY** | | – |

TEARS FOR FEARS

ROLAND & CURT with **DAVID LORD** – synthesizers(Duo also on synthesizers)

		Mercury	Mercury
Nov 81.	(7") *(IDEA 1)* **SUFFER THE CHILDREN. / WIND**		

(remixed-12"+=) *(IDEA 12)* – ('A'instrumental). *(re-iss. Aug85, 7"/12"; same; hit UK No.52)*

—— Trimmed to a basic duo of **ORZABAL & SMITH**

| Mar 82. | (7") *(IDEA 2)* **PALE SHELTER (YOU DON'T GIVE ME LOVE). / THE PRISONER** | | |

(12"+=) *(IDEA 2-12)* – ('A'extended). *(re-iss. Aug85, 7"/12"; same); hit No.73)*

| Sep 82. | (7") *(IDEA 3)* **MAD WORLD. / IDEAS AS OPIATES** | 3 | |

(12"+=) *(IDEA 3-12)* – Saxophones as opiates.
(d7"+=) *(IDEA 33)* – ('A'-world remix) / Suffer the children.

| Jan 83. | (7") *(IDEA 4)* <812677> **CHANGE. / THE CONFLICT** | 4 | 73 Jun83 |

(12"+=) *(IDEA 4-12)* – ('A'extended).

—— augmented by **IAN STANLEY** – keyboards / **MANNY ELIAS** – drums

| Mar 83. | (lp/c) *(MERS/+C 17)* <811039> **THE HURTING** | 1 | 73 |

– The hurting / Mad world / Pale shelter / Ideas as opiates / Memories fade / Suffer the children / Watch me bleed / Change / The prisoner / Start of the breakdown. *(cd-iss. Sep89; 811039-2)*

| Apr 83. | (7"/7"red/7"green/7"white/7"blue/7"pic-d) *(IDEA 5/+R/G/W/B/P)* **PALE SHELTER. / WE ARE BROKEN** | 5 | |

(12"+=) *(IDEA 5-12)* – ('A'extended).

| Nov 83. | (7") *(IDEA 6)* **(THE) WAY YOU ARE. / THE MARAUDERS** | 24 | |

(ext.12"+=) *(IDEA 6-12)* – Start of the breakdown (live).
(d7"++=) *(IDEAS 6)* – Change (live).

| Aug 84. | (7",7"green,12"/7"clear-pic-d)(ext.12") *(IDEA/+P 7)(IDEA 7-12)* <884638> **MOTHER'S TALK. / EMPIRE BUILDING** | 14 | 27 Mar86 |
| Nov 84. | (7"/10") *(IDEA/+C 8)* <880294> **SHOUT. / THE BIG CHAIR** | 4 | 1 May85 |

(12"+=) *(IDEA 8-12)* – ('A'extended).

—— added mainly on tour **WILLIAM GREGORY** – saxophone / **NICKY HOLLAND** – keyboards

| Mar 85. | (lp/c)(cd) *(MERH/+C 58)* <(824300-2)> **SONGS FROM THE BIG CHAIR** | 2 | 1 |

– Shout / The working hour / Everybody wants to rule the world / Mother's talk / I believe / Broken / Head over heels / Broken (live) / Listen. *(c+=)* – (6 extra mixes).

| Mar 85. | (7"/10") *(IDEA 9/+10)* <880659> **EVERYBODY WANTS TO RULE THE WORLD. / PHAROAHS** | 2 | 1 |

(12"+=) *(IDEA 9-12)* – ('A'extended or urban mix).
(d7"+=) *(IDEA 9-9)* – ('A'-urban mix) / (duo interviewed).

| Jun 85. | (7"/7"sha-pic-d)(10") *(IDEA/+P 10)(IDEA 10-10)* <880899> **HEAD OVER HEELS (remix). / WHEN IN LOVE WITH A BLIND MAN** | 12 | 3 Sep85 |

(12"+=) *(IDEA 10-12)* – ('A'preacher mix).

| Oct 85. | (7") *(IDEA 11)* **I BELIEVE (A soulful re-recording). / SEA SONG** | 23 | |

(10"+=) *(IDEA 11-10)* – I believe (US mix).
(12"++=) *(IDEA 11-12)* – Shout (US mix).
(d7"+=) *(IDEA 11-11)* – Shout (dub) / I believe (original).

| May 86. | (7"/12") *(RACE 1/+12)* **EVERYBODY WANTS TO RUN THE WORLD. / EVERYBODY . . . (Running version)** | 5 | |

—— **ORZABAL + SMITH** retained **IAN** and **NICKY** and brought in sessioners **OLETA ADAMS** – some dual vocals, piano / **SIMON CLARK** – organ / **PINO PALLADINO** – bass / **ROBBIE McINTOSH, NEIL TAYLOR + RANDY JACOBS** – guitar / **PHIL COLLINS, CHRIS HUGHES + MANU KATCHE** – drums

		Fontana	Fontana
Aug 89.	(7"/7"g-f/c-s) *(IDEA/IDEAG/IDMC 12)* <874710> **SOWING THE SEEDS OF LOVE. / TEARS ROLL DOWN**	5	2

(ext.12"+=/12"pic-d+=/3"cd-s+=) *(IDEAT/IDPT/IDCD 12)* – Shout (US mix).

| Sep 89. | (lp/c/cd) *(838730-1/-4/-2)* <838730> **THE SEEDS OF LOVE** | 1 | 8 |

– Woman in chains / Bad man's song / Sowing the seeds of love / Advice for the young at heart / Standing on the corner of the third world / Swords and knives / Year of the knife / Famous last words.

—— (next featured **OLETA ADAMS** – co-vox)

| Nov 89. | (7"/c-s; as TEARS FOR FEARS featuring OLETA ADAMS) *(IDEA/IDMC 13)* <876248> **WOMAN IN CHAINS. / ALWAYS IN THE PAST** | 26 | 36 |

(12"+=/12"pic-d+=/cd-s+=/3"cd-s+=) *(IDEA/IDPT/IDCD/IDSTN 13)* – ('A'instrumental) / My life in the suicide ranks.

| Feb 90. | (7"/c-s) *(IDEA/IDMC 14)* <876894> **ADVICE FOR THE YOUNG AT HEART. / JOHNNY PANIC AND THE BIBLE OF DREAMS** | 36 | 89 |

(12"+=/12"pic-d+=/cd-s+=) *(IDPT/IDPIC/IDCD 14)* – Music for tables.
(3"cd-s++=) *(IDCDS 14)* – Johnny Panic (instrumental).

| Jul 90. | (7") *(IDEA 15)* **FAMOUS LAST WORDS. / MOTHER'S TALK (US remix)** | | |

(c-s+=/12"+=/12"pic-d+=/cd-s+=) *(IDEMC/IDEAT/IDPIC/IDECD 15)* – Listen.

| Feb 92. | (7"/c-s) *(IDEA/IDMC 17)* **LAID SO LOW. / THE BODY WAH** | 17 | |

(12"pic-d+=/cd-s+=) *(IDEAT/IDCD 17)* – Lord of the Kharma.

| Mar 92. | (cd/c/lp) *<510 939-2/-4/-1>* **TEARS ROLL DOWN – GREATEST HITS 1982-1992** (compilation) | 2 | 53 |

– Sowing the seeds of love / Everybody wants to rule the world / Woman in chains / Shout / Mad world / Pale shelter / I beieve / Laid so low (tears roll down) / Mothers talk / Change / Advice for the young at heart.

| Apr 92. | (7"/c-s; as TEARS FOR FEARS featuring OLETA ADAMS) *(IDEA/IDMC 16)* **WOMAN IN CHAINS. / BADMAN'S SONG** | 57 | |

(cd-s+=) *(IDCD 16)* – Ghost papa.

—— **ROLAND ORZABAL** now sole survivor, when CURT launched solo career with his album, 'SOUL ON BOARD'.

		Mercury	Mercury
May 93.	(7"/c-s) *(IDEA/IDMC 18)* <862330> **BREAK IT DOWN AGAIN. / BLOODLETTING GO**	20	25

(cd-s+=) *(IDECD 18)* – ('A'mix).

| Jun 93. | (cd/c/lp) *(<514875-2/-4/-1>)* **ELEMENTAL** | 5 | 45 |

– Elemental / Cold / Break it down again / Mr. Pessimist / Dog's a best friend's dog / Fish out of water / Gas giants / Power / Brian Wilson said / Goodnight song.

| Jul 93. | (7"/c-s) *(IDEA/IDMC 19)* **COLD. / NEW STAR** | 72 | |

(cd-s+=) *(IDECD 19)* – Deja vu / The sins of silence.

		Epic	Sony
Sep 95.	(c-s) *(662 476-4)* **RAOUL AND THE KINGS OF SPAIN / QUEEN OF COMPROMISE**	31	

(cd-s+=) *(662 476-2)* – All of the angels.
(cd-s) *(662 476-5)* – ('A'side) / Creep / The madness of Roland.

| Oct 95. | (cd/c) *(480 982-2/-4)* <67318> **RAOUL AND THE KINGS OF SPAIN** | 41 | 79 |

– Raoul and the Kings of Spain / Falling down / Secrets / God's mistake / Sketches of pain / Los Reyes Catolicos / Sorry / Humdrum and humble / I choose you / Don't drink the water / Me and my big ideas / Los Reyes Catolicos (reprise).

| Jan 96. | (c-s/cd-s) *(662 797-4/-2)* **SECRETS / RAOUL AND THE KINGS OF SPAIN (acoustic) / BREAK IT DOWN AGAIN (acoustic)** | | |

(cd-s) *(662 797-5)* – ('A'side) / Until I drown / War of attrition.

| Jun 96. | (c-s/cd-s) *(663 418-4/-2)* **GOD'S MISTAKE / UNTIL I DROWN** | 61 | – |

(cd-s) *(663 418-5)* – ('A'side) / Raoul and the kings of Spain (acoustic) / Break it down again (acoustic).

– compilations, etc. –

| Aug 95. | (d-cd) *Fontana; (528599-2)* **THE HURTING / SONGS FROM THE BIG CHAIR** | | – |
| Jun 96. | (cd/c) *Fontana; (528114-2/-4)* **SATURNINE, MARSHALL & LUNATIC** (rare material) | | |

TEENAGE FANCLUB

Formed: Glasgow, Scotland . . . 1989 although earlier they had posed as The BOY HAIRDRESSERS. After a one-off single, 'GOLDEN SHOWERS' (1988), bassist GERRY LOVE was recruited and BRENDAN O'HARE replaced FRANCIS McDONALD (who went off to join that other Glasgow institution, The PASTELS) on the drums. As TEENAGE FANCLUB, they cut the inspired chaos of the 'EVERYTHING FLOWS' (1990) single and followed it up with the debut album, 'A CATHOLIC EDUCATION' later the same year. The term "slacker rock" was surely coined with this bunch of cheeky Glaswegian wide boys in mind and if it was lazy to compare their honey-in-the-dirt melodic dischord with DINOSAUR JR., that was nothing compared to the laid back, laissez faire philosophy that fuelled (if that's not too strong a word) TEENAGE FANCLUB's ramshackle racket, both on stage and in the studio. By the release of the DON FLEMING-produced 'BANDWAGONESQUE' (1991), ('THE KING' was a sub-standard effort released to fulfill contractual obligations), the band were sounding more professional, crafting an album of languorous harmonies and chiming guitar that was a thinly veiled homage to BIG STAR as well as taking in such obvious reference points as The BYRDS, The BEACH BOYS, BUFFALO SPRINGFIELD etc. Ironically, rather than propelling TEENAGE FANCLUB into the big league, the album seemed instead to merely rekindle interest in BIG STAR's back catalogue and after a honeymoon period of being indie press darlings, the backlash was sharp and swift. The fact that the self-produced 'THIRTEEN' (1993) lacked their trademark inspired sloppiness didn't help matters any. Not that the band were overly concerned, they crafted modern retro more lovingly than most and had a loyal following to lap it up. The FANNIE's further developed their niche with 'GRAND PRIX' (1995) and if it was that reliably trad, West Coast via Glasgow roots sound you were after then TEENAGE FANCLUB were your band. While they wear their influences more proudly than any other group, (O.K., so I forgot about OASIS . . .) they do it with such verve and style that it'd be churlish to write them off as mere plagiarists and they remain one of Scotland's best loved exports. Their latest effort, 'SONGS FROM NORTHERN BRITAIN' (1997) was their most considered release to date, sharpening up their sound and arrangements to an unprecedented degree. But if that's what it takes to come up with something as engagingly swoonsome as 'I DON'T CARE' or 'IS THAT ENOUGH', no one's going to make much of a fuss. • **Songwriters:** BLAKE or BLAKE-McGINLEY or group compositions except; DON'T CRY NO TEARS (Neil Young) / THE BALLAD OF JOHN AND YOKO (Beatles) / LIKE A VIRGIN (Madonna) / LIFE'S A GAS (T.Rex) / FREE AGAIN + JESUS CHRIST (Alex Chilton) / CHORDS OF FAME (Phil Ochs) / BAD SEEDS (Beat Happening) / HAVE YOU EVER SEEN THE RAIN? (Creedence Clearwater Revival) / BETWEEN US (Neil Innes) / FEMME FATALE (Velvet Underground). • **Trivia:** ALEX CHILTON (ex-BOX TOPS) guested on 1992 sessions and contributed some songs.

Album rating: A CATHOLIC EDUCATION (*6) / THE KING instrumental (*5) / BANDWAGONESQUE (*8) / THIRTEEN (*7) / DEEP FRIED FANCLUB collection (*4) / GRAND PRIX (*8) / SONGS FROM NORTHERN BRITAIN (*8)

NORMAN BLAKE (b.20 Oct'65, Bellshill, Scotland) – vocals, guitar (ex-BMX BANDITS) / **RAYMOND McGINLEY** (b. 3 Jan'64, Glasgow) – bass, vocals / **FRANCIS McDONALD** (b.21 Nov'70, Bellshill, Scotland) – drums / **JOE McALINDEN** – violin / **JIM LAMBIE** – vibraphone

	53rd & 3rd	not iss.
Jan 88. (12"; as BOY HAIRDRESSERS) (AGARR 12T) **GOLDEN SHOWERS. / TIDAL WAVE / THE ASSUMPTION AS AN ELEVATOR**		-

—— **NORMAN + RAYMOND** – guitars, vocals plus **GERARD LOVE** (b.31 Aug'67, Motherwell, Scotland) – bass, vocals / **BRENDAN O'HARE** (b.16 Jan'70, Bellshill, Scotland) – bass repl. McDONALD who joined The PASTELS

	Paperhouse	Matador
Jun 90. (7"m) (PAPER 003) **EVERYTHING FLOWS. / PRIMARY EDUCATION / SPEEEDER** (cd-ep+=) (PAPER 003CD) – Don't Cry No Tears. (rel.Feb91)		-
Jul 90. (cd/c/lp) (PAP CD/MC/LP 004) <OLE 012> **A CATHOLIC EDUCATION** – Heavy metal / Everything flows / A catholic education / Too involved / Don't need a drum / Critical mass / Heavy metal II / A catholic education 2 / Eternal light / Every picture I paint / Everybody's fool. (re-iss. cd Mar95; same)		Aug90
Oct 90. (one-sided-7") (PAPER 005) **THE BALLAD OF JOHN AND YOKO**		
Nov 90. (7") <OLE 007> **EVERYBODY'S FOOL. /**	-	
Nov 90. (7") (PAPER 007) <OLE 023> **GOD KNOWS IT'S TRUE. / SO FAR GONE** (12"+=/cd-s+=) (PAPER 007 T/CD) – Weedbreak / Ghetto blaster.		Jan91

	Creation	Geffen
Aug 91. (cd/lp) (CRE CD/LP 096) **THE KING** (instrumental) – Heavy metal 6 / Mudhoney / Interstellar overdrive / Robot love / Like a virgin / The king / Opal inquest / The ballad of Bow Evil (slow and fast) / Heavy metal 9. (above originally only meant for US ears, deleted after 24 hours)	53	-
Aug 91. (7") (CRE 105) **STAR SIGN. / HEAVY METAL 6** (12"+=)(cd-s+=) (CRE 105T)(CRESCD 105) – Like a virgin / ('A'demo version). (7"ltd) (CRE 105L) – ('A'side) / Like a virgin.	44	-
Oct 91. (7"/c-s) (CRE/+CS 111) <4370> **THE CONCEPT. / LONG HAIR** (12"+=)(cd-s+=) (CRE 111T)(CRESCD 111) – What you do to me (demo) / Robot love.	51	Jan92
Nov 91. (cd)(c/lp) (CRECD 106)(C+/CRE 106) <24461> **BANDWAGONESQUE** – The concept / Satan / December / What you do to me / I don't know / Star sign / Metal baby / Pet rock / Sidewinder / Alcoholiday / Guiding star / Is this music?.	22	
Jan 92. (7"/c-s) (CRE/+CS 115) <21708> **WHAT YOU DO TO ME. / B-SIDE** (12"+=)(cd-s+=) (CRE 115T)(CRESCD 115) – Life's a gas / Filler.	31	
Jun 93. (7"/c-s) (CRE/+CS 130) **RADIO. / DON'S GONE COLUMBIA** (12"+=)(cd-s+=) (CRE 130T)(CRESCD 130) – Weird horses / Chords of fame.	31	
Sep 93. (7"/c-s) (CRE/+CS 142) **NORMAN 3. / OLDER GUYS** (12"+=)(cd-s+=) (CRE 142T)(CRESCD 142) – Golden glades / Genius envy.	50	-
Oct 93. (cd)(c/lp) (CRECD 144)(C+/CRE 144) <24533> **THIRTEEN** – Hang on / The cabbage / Radio / Norman 3 / Song to the cynic / 120 minutes / Escher / Commercial alternative / Fear of flying / Tears are cool / Ret live dead / Get funky / Gene Clark.	14	Nov93

—— In Mar'94, they teamed up with DE LA SOUL on single 'FALLIN'. This was from the rock-rap album 'Judgement Day' on 'Epic' records (hit UK 59).

1994. (cd-ep) <21887> **AUSTRALIAN TOUR SAMPLER**	-	

—— **PAUL QUINN** – drums (ex-SOUP DRAGONS) repl. O'HARE who later joined MOGWAI

Mar 95. (7"/c-s) (CRE/+CS 175) **MELLOW DOUBT. / SOME PEOPLE TRY TO FUCK WITH YOU** (cd-s+=) (CRESCD 175) – Getting real / About you. (cd-s) (CRESCD 175X) – ('A'side) / Have you ever seen the rain? / Between us / You're my kind.	34	-
May 95. (7"/c-s) (CRE/+CS 201) **SPARKY'S DREAM. / BURNED** (cd-s+=) (CRESCD 201) – For you / Headstand. (cd-s) (CRESCD 201X) – ('A'-alternative version) / Try and stop me / That's all I need to know / Who loves the sun.	40	-
May 95. (cd)(c/lp) (CRECD 173)(C+/CRE 173) <24802> **GRAND PRIX** – About you / Sparky's dream / Mellow doubt / Don't look back / Verisinilitude / Neil Jung / Tears / Discolite / Say no / Going places / I'll make it clear / I gotta know / Hardcore – ballad. (lp w/ free 7") – DISCOLITE (DEMO). / I GOTTA KNOW (demo)	7	Jul95
Aug 95. (7"/c-s) (CRE/+CS 210) **NEIL JUNG. / THE SHADOWS** (cd-s+=) (CRESCD 210) – My life / Every step is a way through love. (cd-s) (CRESCD 210X) – ('A'side) / Traffic jam / Hi-fi / I heard you looking.	62	-
Dec 95. (7"ep/c-ep/cd-ep) (CRE/+CS/SCD 216) **TEENAGE FANCLUB HAVE LOST IT EP** (acoustic) – Don't look back / Everything flows / Starsign / 120 mins.	53	-

	Creation	Sony
Jun 97. (cd-s) (CRESCD 228) **AIN'T THAT ENOUGH / KICKABOUT / BROKEN** (cd-s) (CRESCD 228X) – ('A'side) / Femme fatale / Jesus Christ.	17	-
Jun 97. (cd/c/lp) (CRECD/CCRE/CRELP 196) <68202> **SONGS FROM NORTHERN BRITAIN** – Start again / Ain't that enough / Can't feel my soul / I don't want control of you / Planets / It's a bad world / Take the long way round / Winter / I don't care / Mount Everest / Your love is the place where I come from / Speed of light.	3	
Aug 97. (7") (CRE 238) **I DON'T WANT CONTROL OF YOU. / THE COUNT** (cd-s+=) (CRESCD 238) – Middle of the road. (cd-s) (CRESCD 238X) –	43	-
Nov 97. (7") (CRE 280) **START AGAIN. / AIN'T THAT ENOUGH (TOTP acoustic)** (cd-s+=) (CRESCD 280) – Take the long way round (radio). (cd-s) (CRESCD 280X) – ('A'side) / How many more years / Nothing to be done.	54	-

—— added **FINLAY McDONALD** – keyboards (was p/t on tour)

| Jun 98. (7") (CRE 298) **LONG SHOT. /** | | - |

– compilations, others, etc. –

May 92. (7") K; <IPU 26> **FREE AGAIN. / BAD SEEDS**	-	
Nov 92. (12"ep/cd-ep) Strange Fruit; (SFPS/+CD 081) **THE JOHN PEEL SESSION** – God knows it's true / Alcoholiday / So far gone / Long hair. (re-iss. Dec93 & Jul95; same)	-	

—— (in 1995, they backed FRANK BLACK on his PEEL SESSION)

Mar 95. (cd/c) Fire; (FLIPCD 002) **DEEP FRIED FANCLUB** – Everything flows / Primary education / Speeeder / Critical mass (orig.) / The ballad of John and Yoko / God knows it's true / Weedbreak / So far gone / Ghetto blaster / Don't cry no tears / Free again / Bad seed.		-
Apr 97. (cd) Nectar; (NTMCD 543) **FANDEMONIUM**		
Sep 97. (7"ep) Radiation; (RARE 033) **TEENAGE FANCLUB EP**		

TELEVISION

Formed: New York City, New York, USA based ... late '73 by TOM VERLAINE, RICHARD HELL and BILLY FICCA who had all been members of The NEON BOYS. In 1975, William Terry Ork gave them a deal on his own self-named indie label, for whom they issued a one-off flop single, 'LITTLE JOHNNY JEWEL'. By this point, HELL (who went on to form the equally seminal RICHARD HELL & THE VOID-OIDS) had been replaced by ex-MC5 man, FRED 'SONIC' SMITH, TELEVISION subsequently signing with 'Elektra' and unleashing their classic debut album, 'MARQUEE MOON'. Although virtually ignored in America (more astute British punk/new wave fans placed it in the UK Top 30) upon its 1977 release, the album has since been acknowledged as a landmark release. The hypnotic near-10 minute title track (also a UK Top 30 hit) breathtakingly showcased the driving/free-from cool guitar interplay between LLOYD and virtuoso VERLAINE (the track first debuted at their early CBGB's shows and perfected/modified over the next couple of years), while the album as a whole testified to VERLAINE's barely disguised passion for The ROLLING STONES, PINK FLOYD and the darker moments of The VELVET UNDERGROUND. While VERLAINE's tortured vocals were reminiscent of LOU REED/PATTI SMITH, his molten-spark histrionics resolutely distinguished the band from the more wilfully amateurish new wave pack and TELEVISION remain the most musically adept band of the era. Unsurprisingly, however, they found it difficult following up such a milestone and although 'ADVENTURE' (1978) contained sporadic moments of genius, TELEVISION were beginning to lose clarity. Ironically, as the New York scene was at its height, LLOYD effectively pulled the plug on the group after walking out mid-tour later that year. VERLAINE tried unsuccessfully to translate his distinctive sound into a more mainstream rock setting with his solo career, retaining his characteristic vocals and of course, his trademark guitar alchemy. TELEVISION eventually reformed in the 90's with the classic line-up of VERLAINE, LLOYD, SMITH and FICCA, recording the acclaimed 'TELEVISION' (1992) for 'Capitol' and suggesting that what VERLAINE's solo career was lacking was the anchor and foil of LLOYD's rhythm playing. • **Songwriters:** VERLAINE lyrics / group compositions, except early live material; FIRE ENGINE (13th Floor Elevators) / KNOCKIN' ON HEAVEN'S DOOR (Bob Dylan) / SATISFACTION (Rolling Stones). • **Trivia:** VERLAINE played guitar on PATTI SMITH's 1974 single 'Hey Joe'.

Album rating: MARQUEE MOON (*10) / ADVENTURE (*6) / THE BLOW UP exploitation (*4) / TELEVISION (*5) / Tom Verlaine: TOM VERLAINE (*7) / DREAMTIME (*6) / WORDS FROM THE FRONT (*6) / COVER (*7) / FLASH LIGHT (*7) / THE WONDER (*7) / WARM AND COOL (*5) / THE MILLER'S TALE: A TOM VERLAINE ANTHOLOGY compilation (*8) / Richard Lloyd: ALCHEMY (*6) / FIELD OF FIRE (*5) / REAL TIME (*5)

TOM VERLAINE (b. THOMAS MILLER, 13 Dec'49, Mt.Morris, New Jersey) – vocals, lead guitar / **RICHARD LLOYD** – guitar, vocals / **RICHARD HELL** (b. RICHARD MYERS, 2 Oct'49, Lexington, Kentucky) – bass, vocals / **BILLY FICCA** – drums

	not iss.	Ork
Oct 75. (7") <81975> **LITTLE JOHNNY JEWEL. / (part 2)**	-	-

—— **FRED SMITH** (b.10 Apr'48) – bass, vocals (ex-BLONDIE) repl. RICHARD HELL who went solo

	Elektra	Elektra
Feb 77. (lp/c) (K/K4 52046) <7E 1098> **MARQUEE MOON** – See no evil / Venus / Friction / Marquee moon / Elevation / Guiding light / Prove it / Torn curtain. (cd-iss. 1989; 960616-2)	28	
Mar 77. (12",2-part-7") (K 12252) **MARQUEE MOON (stereo). / MARQUEE MOON (mono)**	30	-
Jul 77. (7"/12",12"green) (K 12262/+T) **PROVE IT. / VENUS**	25	-
Apr 78. (lp,red-lp/c) (K/K4 52072) <6E 133> **ADVENTURE** – Glory / Days / Foxhole / Careful / Carried away / The fire / Ain't that nothin' / The dream's a dream. (cd-iss. Nov93 on 'WEA'; 7559 60523-2)	7	
Apr 78. (7"/12"red) (K 12287/+T) **FOXHOLE. / CAREFUL**	36	-
Jul 78. (7") (K 12306) **GLORY. / CARRIED AWAY**	-	
Jul 78. (7") <45516> **GLORY. / AIN'T THAT NOTHIN'**	-	

—— Broke ranks in Aug'78. FICCA joined The WAITRESSES, FRED joined The PATTI SMITH GROUP and RICHARD LLOYD went solo.

– compilations, others, etc. –

Jan 83. (c) R.O.I.R.; <A-114> **THE BLOW UP** (live) (UK cd-iss. Feb90 on 'Danceteria'; DANCD 030) (cd re-iss. Nov94 on 'R.O.I.R.'; RE 114CD)	-	-
1979. (12"m) Ork-WEA; (NYC 1T) **LITTLE JOHNNY JEWEL (parts 1 & 2). / ('A'live version)**		

TOM VERLAINE

—— went solo augmented mainly by **FRED SMITH** – bass / **JAY DEE DAUGHERTY** – drums / **BRUCE BRODY** – keyboards / **ALLAN SCHWARTZBERG** – drums, percussion

	Elektra	Elektra

Sep 79. (lp/c) *(K/K4 52156)* <2156> **TOM VERLAINE**
– The grip of love / Souvenir from a dream / Kingdom come / Mr. Bingo / Yonki time / Flash lightning / Red leaves / Last night / Breakin' in my heart.

	Warners	Warners

Sep 81. (lp/c) *(K/K4 56919)* **DREAMTIME**
– There's a reason / Penetration / Always / The blue robe / Without a word / Mr. Blur / Fragile / A future in noise / Down on the farm / Mary Marie.

Sep 81. (7"/12") *(K 17855/+T)* **ALWAYS. / THE BLUE ROBE** ☐ 99 ☐

—— **JIMMY RIPP** – guitar repl. BRODY

	Virgin	Warners

May 82. (lp/c) *(V/TCV 2227)* <BSK 3685> **WORDS FROM THE FRONT**
– Present arrived / Postcard from Waterloo / True story / Clear it away / Words from the front / Coming apart / Days on the mountain. *(cd-iss. Aug88; OVED 87)* *(re-iss. cd Jun89; CDV 2227)*

May 82. (7"/12") *(VS 501/+12)* **POSTCARD FROM WATERLOO. / DAYS ON THE MOUNTAIN**

Jun 84. (7") *(VS 696)* **LET'S GO TO THE MANSION. / ('A'version)**
(12"+=) *(VS 696/+12)* – Lindi Lu.

Aug 84. (7") *(VS 704)* **FIVE MILES OF YOU. / YOUR FINEST HOUR**
(12"+=) *(VS 704/+12)* – Dissolve reveal.

Sep 84. (lp/c) *(V/TCV 2314)* <25144> **COVER**
– Five miles of you / Let's go the mansion / Travelling / O foolish heart / Dissolve – Reveal / Miss Emily / Rotation / Swim. *(re-iss. Apr86 lp/c; OVED/+C 168)* *(cd-iss. Jun89; CDV 2314)*

—— **ANDY NEWMARK** – drums repl. JAY DEE

	Fontana	Mercury-IRS

Feb 87. (7") *(FTANA 1)* **A TOWN CALLED WALKER. / SMOOTHER THAN JONES**
(12"+=) *(FTANA 1-12)* – ('A'version) / Caveman flashlight.

Feb 87. (lp/c)(cd) *(SF LP/MC 1)(830861-2)* <42050> **FLASH LIGHT** ☐ 99 ☐
– Cry mercy, judge / Say a prayer / A town called Walker / Song / The scientist writes a letter / Bomb / 4 a.m. / The funniest thing / Annie's tellin' me / One time at sundown.

Mar 87. (7") *(FTANA 2)* **CRY MERCY JUDGE. / CALL ME THE CIRCLING**
(12"+=) *(FTANA 2-12)* – At this moment (live) / Lover of the night (live) / Strange things happening.

Jun 87. (7") *(VLANE 3)* **THE FUNNIEST THING. / ONE TIME AT SUNDOWN**
(12"+=) *(VLANE 3-12)* – Marquee Moon ('87 version).

Aug 87. (7") *(VLANE 4)* **THE SCIENTIST WRITES A LETTER. / ('A'-Paris version)**

Oct 89. (7") *(VLANE 5)* **SHIMMER. / BOMB**
(12"+=)(cd-s+=) *(VLANE 5-12)(VLACD 5)* – The scientist writes a letter.

Mar 90. (7") *(VLANE 6)* **KALEIDOSCOPIN'. / SIXTEEN TULIPS**
(12"+=)(cd-s+=) *(VLANE 6-12)(VLACD 6)* – Vanity fair.

Apr 90. (cd/c/lp) *(842420-2/-4/-1)* **THE WONDER**
– Kaleidoscopin' / August / Ancient Egypt / Shimmer / Stalingrad / Pillow / Storm / 5 hours from Calais / Cooleridge / Prayer.

	Rough Trade	Rykodisc

Apr 92. (cd/lp) *(R 288-2/-1)* <10216> **WARM AND COOL**
– Those harbour lights / Sleepwalkin' / The deep dark clouds / Saucer crash / Depot (1951) / Boulevard / Harley Quinn / Sor Juanna / Depot (1957) / Spiritual / Little dance / Ore.

– compilation –

Apr 96. (cd) *Virgin; (CDVDM 9034)* **A MILLER'S TALE (The Tom Verlaine Story)**

RICHARD LLOYD

—— solo augmented by **JIM MAESTRO** – guitar (ex-BONGOS) / **MATTHEW MacKENZIE** – guitar, piano / **MICHAEL YOUNG** – guitar, synthesizer / **FRED SMITH** – bass / **VINNY DeNUNZIO** – drums

	Elektra	Elektra

Jan 80. (lp) *(K 52196)* **ALCHEMY**
– Misty eyes / In the night / Alchemy / Womans ways / Number nine / Should've known better / Blue and grey / Summer rain / Pretend / Dying words.

Apr 80. (7") **BLUE AND GREY. / PRETEND** ☐- ☐

—— Enlisted new line-up.

	Mistlur	Mistlur

Jan 86. (lp) *(MLR 046)* **FIELD OF FIRE**

	Celluloid	GrandSlamm

Oct 87. (lp/c/cd) *(CELL 6135/+C/CD)* **REAL TIME (live)**
– Fire engine / Misty eyes / Alchemy / Spider talk / Lost child / No.9 / The only feeling / Soldier blue / Field of fire / Pleading / Watch yourself / Louisianna Anna / Black to white. *(cd+=)* – Watch yourself / Losin' Anne / Black to white.

—— LLOYD went onto join JOHN DOE (ex-X)

TELEVISION

—— re-formed for one-off with **VERLAINE, LLOYD, FICCA + SMITH**

	Capitol	Capitol

Sep 92. (cd/c/lp) <(CD/TC+/EST 2181)> **TELEVISION**
– 1880 or so / Shane, she wrote this / In world / Call Mr. Lee / Rhyme / No glamour for Willi / Beauty trip / The rocket / This fire / Mars.

TEMPLE OF THE DOG (see under ⇒ SOUNDGARDEN)

TEMPTATIONS

Formed: Birmingham, Alabama, USA ... 1960, initially as The ELGINS, by EDDIE KENDRICKS and PAUL WILLIAMS (from The PRIMES), plus MELVIN FRANKLIN and OTIS WILLIAMS (from The DISTANTS). They moved to Detroit in 1961 after two flop 45's for 'Miracle'. Securing a deal with the Berry 'Gordy' label (aka Tamla Motown), they finally scored their first US hit in 1964 with 'THE WAY YOU DO THE THINGS YOU DO'. By early 1965, 'MY GIRL' had given them their first chart topper. Penned by SMOKEY ROBINSON (who dominated most of the band's songwriting during this period), the song was the first in an incredible run of chart hits that included 'IT'S GROWING', 'SINCE I LOST MY BABY' and 'MY BABY', all released in 1965. Though the acts were 'manufactured' to a certain degree by 'Motown', they possessed an impressive three-pronged vocal attack in DAVID RUFFIN's gravel-flecked rasp, EDDIE KENDRICKS' high tenor and PAUL WILLIAMS' heavy baritone. But it was RUFFIN's vocals which were pushed to the fore as producer NORMAN WHITFIELD began to lead the group's sound in a rougher direction, 'AIN'T TOO PROUD TO BEG' (1966), an early example of what was to come. As the band enjoyed a further string of hits including '(I KNOW) I'M LOSING YOU' (1966), 'YOU'RE MY EVERYTHING' (1967) and 'I WISH IT WOULD RAIN' (1968), RUFFIN became increasingly jealous of the way DIANA ROSS was being nurtured for solo stardom by 'Motown', things coming to a head when RUFFIN failed to show for a gig. The group duly sent him packing, recruiting DENNIS EDWARDS and with the 'CLOUD NINE' (1969) single, hitched a ride on the magic roundabout of "psychedelic soul" pioneered by SLY STONE's thrilling honky hybrids. With WHITFIELD and his partner BARRETT STRONG penning most of the material, the band released a clutch of hard-hitting, socially aware classics like 'PSYCHEDELIC SHACK' (1970), 'BALL OF CONFUSION (THAT'S WHAT THE WORLD IS TODAY)' (1970), the funk getting dirtier and nastier with the hard-bitten tale of a broken home, 'PAPA WAS A ROLLING STONE' (1972). KENDRICKS departed in 1971 after his swansong for the band, 'JUST MY IMAGINATION (RUNNING AWAY WITH ME)' and PAUL WILLIAMS left later the same year, the band drafting in replacements DAMON HARRIS and RICHARD STREET. While the singles dried up, in the pop charts at least, the band still shifted albums up until the late 70's. As their creative muse began to falter, the band extricated itself from 'Motown' and despite a well-received self-produced album, 'THE TEMPTATIONS DO THE TEMPTATIONS' (1976), their two albums for 'Atlantic', 'HEAR TO TEMPT YOU' (1978) and 'BARE BACK' (1978) were marred by insipid disco stylings. EDWARDS had been absent for these albums (replaced by LOUIS PRICE), although he returned towards the end of the decade and the band hooked up with 'Motown' again for a comeback single, 'POWER' (1980) which scraped into the charts. RUFFIN and KENDRICKS returned to the fold for a short-lived reunion in 1982 and following their departure, OTIS WILLIAMS and MELVIN FRANKLIN carried the TEMPTATIONS flame through the 80's and beyond, completing studio and live work with a changing cast of musicians. Although they were inducted into the Rock'n'Roll Hall Of Fame in 1989, the band were merely retreading their 60's heyday, cabaret style. With KENDRICKS dying of cancer in 1992 and MELVIN FRANKLIN dying three years later, WILLIAMS is the sole remaining member from the original line-up. • **Covered:** THE WEIGHT (Band) / I'LL TRY SOMETHING NEW (Miracles) / I'M GONNA MAKE ME LOVE ME (Madeleine Bell) / etc. • **Trivia:** In 1987, actor and fan, BRUCE WILLIS, invited The TEMPTATIONS to sing back-up on his hit version of The DRIFTERS' 'Under The Boardwalk'.

Album rating: MEET THE TEMPTATIONS (*7) / THE TEMPTATIONS SING SMOKEY (*7) / TEMPTIN' TEMPTATIONS (*7) / GETTIN' READY (*7) / THE TEMPTATIONS GREATEST HITS compilation (*8) / TEMPTATIONS LIVE! (*5) / WITH A LOT OF SOUL (*6) / THE TEMPTATIONS IN A MELLOW MOOD (*5) / WISH IT WOULD RAIN (*7) / DIANA ROSS & THE SUPREMES JOIN THE TEMPTATIONS with Diana Ross & The Supremes (*6) / TCB special with Diana Ross & The Supremes (*6) / LIVE AT THE COPA (*4) / CLOUD NINE (*8) / THE TEMPTATIONS SHOW special (*6) / PUZZLE PEOPLE (*6) / TOGETHER with Diana Ross & The Supremes (*5) / ON BROADWAY special with Diana Ross & The Supremes (*5) / PSYCHEDELIC SHACK (*8) / LIVE AT LONDON'S TALK OF THE TOWN (*5) / TEMPTATIONS GREATEST HITS II compilation (*6) / SKY'S THE LIMIT (*6) / SOLID ROCK (*6) / ALL DIRECTIONS (*6) / MASTERPIECE (*6) / ANTHOLOGY compilation (*8) / 1990 (*6) / A SONG FOR YOU (*5) / HOUSE PARTY (*4) / WINGS OF LOVE (*4) / THE TEMPTATIONS DO THE TEMPTATIONS (*4) / HEAR TO TEMPT YOU (*4) / BARE BACK (*3) / POWER (*5) / ALL THE MILLION SELLERS compilation (*8) / THE TEMPTATIONS (*4) / REUNION (*6) / SURFACE THRILLS (*4) / BACK TO BASICS (*5) / TRULY FOR YOU (*5) / TOUCH ME (*4) / 25th ANNIVERSARY compilation (*7) / TO BE CONTINUED (*5) / TOGETHER AGAIN (*5) / SPECIAL (*4) / MILESTONE (*4) / MOTOWN'S GREATEST HITS compilation (*8) / FOR LOVERS ONLY (*4) / PHOENIX RISING (*5)

MELVIN FRANKLIN (b. DAVID ENGLISH, 12 Oct'42, Montgomery, Alabama) – vocals / **OTIS WILLIAMS** (b. OTIS MILES, 30 Oct'49, Texarkana, Texas) – vocals / **ELDRIDGE BRYANT** – vocals

	not iss.	Thelma

1960. (7"; as DISTANTS) <2282> **ANSWER ME. / SAVE ME FROM THIS MISERY** ☐- ☐

	not iss.	Northern

1960. (7"; as DISTANTS) <3732> **COME ON. / ALWAYS** ☐- ☐

not iss. Warwick

1960. (7"; as DISTANTS) <546> **COME ON. / ALWAYS** – –

1960. (7"; as DISTANTS) <577> **ALRIGHT. / OPEN UP YOUR HEART** – –

—— added **EDDIE KENDRICKS** (b.17 Dec'39, Union Springs, Alabama) – lead vocals (ex-PRIMES) / **PAUL WILLIAMS** (b. 2 Jul'39) – vocals (ex-PRIMES)

not iss. Miracle

Aug 61. (7") <05> **OH, MOTHER OF MINE. / ROMANCE WITHOUT FINANCE** – –

Nov 61. (7") <12> **CHECK YOURSELF. / YOUR WONDERFUL LIFE** – –

Stateside Gordy

Apr 62. (7") <7001> **DREAM COME TRUE. / ISN'T SHE PRETTY** – –

Sep 62. (7"; as The PIRATES) <Mel-O-Die; 105> **MIND OVER MATTER (I'M GONNA MAKE YOY MINE). / I'LL LOVE YOU TILL I DIE** – –

Jan 63. (7") <7010> **PARADISE. / SLOW DOWN HEART** – –

Mar 63. (7") <7015> **I WANT A LOVE I CAN SEE. / THE FURTHER YOU LOOK THE LESS YOU SEE** – –

Jul 63. (7") <7020> **MAY I HAVE THIS DANCE. / FAREWELL MY LOVE** – –

—— **DAVID RUFFIN** (b.18 Jan'41, Meridian, Missouri) – vocals (lead in 1965) had already deposed BRYANT

Apr 64. (7") (SS 278) <7028> **THE WAY YOU DO THE THINGS YOU DO. / JUST LET ME KNOW** [ ] **11** Jan64

—— Early 1964, they backed and were credited on LIZ LANDS 'Gordy' single 'MIDNIGHT JOHNNY'. / KEEP ME'. <7030>

Jul 64. (7") (SS 319) <7032> **I'LL BE IN TROUBLE. / THE GIRL'S ALRIGHT WITH ME** [ ] **33** May64

Oct 64. (7") (SS 348) <7035> **GIRL (WHY YOU WANNA MAKE ME BLUE). / BABY BABY I NEED YOU** [ ] **26** Aug64

Jan 65. (7") (SS 378) <7038> **MY GIRL. / TALKIN' 'BOUT NOBODY BUT MY BABY** **43** **1** Dec64

Tamla Motown Gordy

Mar 65. (7") (TMG 504) <7040> **IT'S GROWING. / WHAT LOVE HAS JOINED TOGETHER** **45** **18**

May 65. (lp) **MEET THE TEMPTATIONS** **95** Apr64
– The way you do the things you do / I want a love I can see / Dream come true / Paradise / May I have this dance / Isn't she pretty / Just let me know / Your wonderful love / The further you look the less you see / Check yourself / Slow down heart / Farewell my love.

Aug 65. (7") (TMG 526) <7043> **SINCE I LOST MY BABY. / YOU'VE GOT TO EARN IT** **17** Jul65

Oct 65. (lp) (TML 11016) <912> **TEMPTATIONS SING SMOKEY** **35** Mar65
– The way you do the things you do / Baby baby I need you / You'd lose a precious love / My girl / It's growing / Who's loving you / What love has joined together / What's so good 'bout goodbye. (re-iss. Feb80 & Oct81 lp/c; STMR/CSTMR 9005)

Nov 65. (7") (TMG 541) <7047> **MY BABY. / DON'T LOOK BABY** **13** **83** Oct65

Mar 66. (lp; stereo/mono) (S+/TML 11023) <914> **TEMPTIN' TEMPTATIONS** **11** Nov65
– Since I lost my babe / Girl's alright with me / Just another lonely night / My baby / You've got to earn it / Everybody needs love / Girl / Don't look back / I gotta know now / Born to love you / I'll be in trouble / You're the one I need.

Apr 66. (7") (TMG 557) <7049> **GET READY. / FADING AWAY** **29** Feb66

Jun 66. (7") (TMG 565) <7054> **AIN'T TOO PROUD TO BEG. / YOU'LL LOSE A PRECIOUS LOVE** **21** **13** May66

Sep 66. (lp; stereo/mono) (S+/TML 11035) <918> **GETTIN' READY** **40** **12** Jul66
– Say you / Little Miss Sweetness / Ain't too proud to beg / Get ready / Lonely, lonely man am I / Too busy thinking about my baby / I've been good to you / It's a lonely world without your love / Fading away / Who you gonna run to / You're not an ordinary girl / Not now I'll tell you later. (re-iss. Jul82 on 'Motown')

Sep 66. (7") (TMG 578) <7055> **BEAUTY IS ONLY SKIN DEEP. / YOU'RE NOT AN ORDINARY MAN** **18** **3** Aug66

Dec 66. (7") (TMG 587) <7057> **(I KNOW) I'M LOSING YOU. / LITTLE MISS SWEETNESS** **19** **8** Nov66

May 67. (7") (TMG 610) <7061> **ALL I NEED. / SORRY IS A SORRY WORD** **8** Apr67

Jul 67. (lp; stereo/mono) (S+/TML 11053) <921> **TEMPTATIONS LIVE! (live)** **20** **10** Mar67
– Medley: Girl (why you wanna make me blue) – Girl's alright with me – I'll be in trouble – I want a love I can see / What love has joined together / My girl / Yesterday / What now my love / Beauty is only skin deep / Group introduction / I wish you love / Ain't too proud to beg / Ol' man river / Get ready / Fading away / My baby / You'll lose a precious love / Baby, baby I need you / Don't look back.

Sep 67. (7") (TMG 620) <7063> **YOU'RE MY EVERYTHING. / I'VE BEEN GOOD TO YOU** **26** **6** Jul67

Oct 67. (lp; stereo/mono) (S+/TML 11057) <922> **WITH A LOT O' SOUL** **19** **7** Aug67
– You're my everything / All I need / I'm losing you / Ain't no Sun since you've gone / No more water in the well / It's you that I need / Save my love for a rainy day / Just one last look / Sorry is a sorry word / Now that you've won me / Two sides to love / Don't send me away.

Dec 67. (7") (TMG 633) <7065> **(LONELINESS MADE ME REALISE) IT'S YOU THAT I NEED. / I WANT A LOVE I CAN SEE** **14** Sep67

Feb 68. (7") (TMG 641) <7068> **I WISH IT WOULD RAIN. / I TRULY, TRULY BELIEVE** **45** **4** Dec67

Mar 68. (lp; stereo/mono) (S+/TML 11068) <924> **IN A MELLOW MOOD** **13** Dec67
– Hello young lovers / A taste of honey / For once in my life / Somewhere / Ol' man river / I'm ready for love / Try to remember / Who can I turn to (when nobody needs needs me) / What now my love / That's life / With these hands / The impossible dream.

—— **DENNIS EDWARDS** (b. 3 Feb'43) – vocals repl. RUFFIN who went solo

May 68. (7") (TMG 658) <7072> **I COULD NEVER LOVE ANOTHER (AFTER LOVING YOU). / GONNA GIVE HER ALL THE LOVE I GOT** **47** **13** May68

Aug 68. (lp; stereo/mono) (S+/TML 11079) <927> **THE TEMPTATIONS WISH IT WOULD RAIN** **13** Apr68
– I could never love another (after loving you) / Cindy / I wish it would rain / Please return your love to me / Fan the flame / He who picks a rose / Why did you leave me darling / I truly, truly believe / This is my beloved / Gonna give her all the love I've got / I've passed this way before / No man can love her like I do.

Jul 68. (7") <7074> **PLEASE RETURN YOUR LOVE TO ME. / HOW CAN I FORGET** **26**

Oct 68. (7") (TMG 671) **WHY DID YOU LEAVE ME DARLING. / HOW CAN I FORGET** –

Dec 68. (7") <7082> **RUDOLPH, THE RED-NOSED REINDEER. / SILENT NIGHT** –

—— In Jan69 UK / Nov68 US, they teamed up with DIANA ROSS & THE SUPREMES (see ⇒) on Top 3 single I'M GONNA MAKE YOU LOVE ME. Around the same time the album DIANA ROSS AND THE SUPREMES JOIN THE TEMPTATIONS hit UK No.1 & US No.2. Throughout 1969, this combination also had Top 50 hits with I'LL TRY SOMETHING NEW / I SECOND THAT EMOTION (UK No.18) / THE WEIGHT / WHY (MUST WE FALL IN LOVE) (UK No.31). Their albums TCB (Soundtrack) hit UK No.11 + US No.1 / ON BROADWAY (TV Show) hit US No.38 / TOGETHER hit both UK + US No.38 early 1970.

Feb 69. (7") (TMG 688) **GET READY. / MY GIRL** **10** –

May 69. (7") (TMG 699) **AIN'T TOO PROUD TO BEG. / FADING AWAY** –

May 69. (lp; stereo/mono) (S+/TML 11104) <938> **LIVE AT THE COPA (live)** **15** Dec68
– (Introduction) / Get ready / You're my everything / I truly, truly believe / I wish it would rain / For once in my life / I could never love another / For once in my life / I could never love another / Hello young lovers / With these hands / Swanee / The impossible dream / Please return your love to me / (I know) I'm losing you.

May 69. (7") <7086> **DON'T LET THE JONESES GET YOU DOWN. / SINCE I'VE LOST YOU** **20**

—— line-up update:- MELVIN FRANKLIN, OTIS WILLIAMS, EDDIE KENDRICKS, PAUL WILLIAMS + DENNIS EDWARDS

Aug 69. (7") (TMG 707) <7081> **CLOUD NINE. / WHY DID SHE HAVE TO LEAVE ME (WHY DID SHE HAVE TO GO)** **15** **6** Oct68

Sep 69. (lp; stereo/mono) (S+/TML 11109) <939> **CLOUD NINE** **32** **4** Mar69
– Cloud nine / I heard it through it the grapevine / Why did she have to leave me (why did she have to go) / Runaway child, running wild / Love is a hurtin' thing / Hey girl / I need your lovin' / Don't let him take your love from me / Gonna keep on tryin' till I win your love / I gotta find away (to get you back). (re-iss. Oct81 lp/c; STML/CSTML 5020) (cd-iss. Aug93; 530153-2)

Nov 69. (7") (TMG 716) <7084> **RUNAWAY CHILD, RUNNING WILD. / I NEED YOUR LOVIN'** **6** Feb69

Jan 70. (7") (TMG 722) <7093> **I CAN'T GET NEXT TO YOU. / RUNNING AWAY (AIN'T GONNA HELP ME)** **13** **1** Aug69

Feb 70. (lp; stereo/mono) (S+/TML 11133) <949> **PUZZLE PEOPLE** **20** **5** Oct69
– I can't get next to you / Hey Jude / Don't let the Joneses get you down / Message from a black man / It's your thing / Little green apples / You don't love me no more / Running away (ain't gonna help you) / Since I've lost you / Slave / That's the way love is. (re-iss. Mar82 lp/c; STML/CSTMS 5050)

Apr 70. (lp; stereo/mono) (S+/TML 11141) <953> **LIVE AT THE (LONDON'S) TALK OF THE TOWN (live)** **21** Aug70
– I'm gonna make you love me / The impossible dream / Run away child running wild / Don't let the Joneses get you down / Love theme from Romeo & Juliet / I can't get next to you / This guy's in love with you / I've got to be me / I'm losing you / Cloud nine / Everything is going to be alright. (re-iss. Jan79 on 'Music For Pleasure' lp/c; MFP/TCMFP 50419)

Jun 70. (7") (TMG 741) <7096> **PSYCHEDELIC SHACK. / THAT'S THE WAY LOVE IS** **33** **7** Jan70

Jun 70. (lp) (STML 11147) <947> **PSYCHEDELIC SHACK** **56** **9** Mar70
– Psychedelic shack / Hum along and dance / War / It's summer / You make your own Heaven and Hell right here on Earth / You need love like I do (don't you) / Take a stroll thru your mind / Friendship train. (re-iss. Mar82 lp/c; STMS/CSTMS 5051)

Sep 70. (7") (TMG 7049) <7099> **BALL OF CONFUSION (THAT'S WHAT THE WORLD IS TODAY). / IT'S SUMMER** **7** **3** May70

Oct 70. (7") <7102> **UNGENA ZA ULIMWENGU (UNITE THE WORLD). / HUM ALONG AND DANCE** **33**

Dec 70. (7") <951> **CHRISTMAS CARD** (Festive songs) – –
(UK-iss.1988 on 'Pickwick' lp/c; SHM/HSC 3202)

May 71. (7") (TMG 773) <7105> **JUST MY IMAGINATION (RUNNING AWAY WITH ME). / YOU MAKE YOUR OWN HEAVEN AND HELL RIGHT HERE ON EARTH** **8** **1** Jan71

—— EDWARDS, FRANKLIN & WILLIAMS recruited new members **DAMON HARRIS** (b. 3 Jul'50, Baltimore, Maryland) – vocals repl. EDDIE KENDRICKS who went solo.

Jul 71. (7") <7109> **IT'S SUMMER. / I'M THE EXCEPTION TO THE RULE** **51**

Aug 71. (lp) (STML 11184) <957> **SKY'S THE LIMIT** **16** Apr71
– Gonna keep on tryin' till I win your love / Just my imagination / I'm the exception to the rule / Smiling faces sometimes / Man / Throw a farewell kiss / Ungenza za Ulimwenga / Love can be anything. (re-iss. May91 cd/c; WD/WK 72743))

Sep 71. (7") (TMG 783) **IT'S SUMMER. / UNGENA ZA ULIMWENGU (UNITE THE WORLD)** –

—— RICHARD STREET (b. 5 Oct'42, Detroit) – vocals (ex-DISTANTS) repl. PAUL. He later committed suicide 17 Aug'73.

Jan 72. (7") (TMG 800) <7111> **SUPERSTAR (REMEMBER HOW YOU GOT WHERE YOU ARE). / GONNA KEEP ON TRYIN' TILL I WIN YOUR LOVE** **32** **18** Nov71

Apr 72. (7") (TMG 808) <7115> **TAKE A LOOK AROUND. / SMOOTH SAILING FROM NOW ON** **13** **30** Feb72

Apr 72. (lp) (STML 11202) <961> **SOLID ROCK** **34** **30** Jan72
– Take a look around / Ain't no sunshine / Stop the war now / What it is / Smooth sailing / Superstar (remember how you got where you are) / It's summer / The end of our road.

Jun 72. (7") <7119> **MOTHER NATURE. / FUNKY MUSIC SHO NUFF TURNS ME ON** **92**

Oct 72. (7") (TMG 832) **MOTHER NATURE. / SMILING FACES SOMETIMES** –

Jan 73. (7") (TMG 839) <7121> **PAPA WAS A ROLLIN' STONE. / ('A'instrumental)** **14** **1** Oct72

Dec 72. (lp) *(STML 11218)* <962> **ALL DIRECTIONS** | 19 | 2 | Aug72
– Funky music sho nuff turns me on / Run Charlie run / I ain't got nothing / Papa was a rollin' stone / Love woke me up this morning / The first time ever I saw your face / Mother nature / It's your thing. (re-iss. Mar82 lp/c; STMS/CSTMS 5052) (cd-iss. Sep93; 530155-2)

Apr 73. (7") *<TMG 854>* <7126> **MASTERPIECE.** / ('A'instrumental) | | 7 | Feb73
Jun 73. (lp) *(STML 11229)* <965> **MASTERPIECE** | 28 | 7 | Mar73
– Masterpiece / Hey girl (I like your style) / Ha / The plastic man / Law of the land / Hurry tomorrow. (re-iss. Oct81 lp/c; STMS/CSTMS 5021) (cd-iss. Jan93; 530100-2)

Jun 73. (7") *<7129>* **THE PLASTIC MAN.** / **HURRY TOMORROW** | - | 40 |
Aug 73. (7") *<7131>* **HEY GIRL (I LIKE YOUR STYLE).** / **MA** | - | 35 |
Aug 73. (7") *(TMG 866)* **LAW OF THE LAND.** / **FUNKY MUSIC SHO NUFF TURN ME ON** | 41 | - |
Nov 73. (7") *<7133>* **LET YOUR HAIR DOWN.** / **AIN'T NO JUSTICE** | - | 27 |
Dec 73. (lp) *(STMA 8016)* <966> **1990** | | 19 |
– Let your hair down / I need you / Heavenly / You've got my soul on fire / Ain't no justice / 1990 / Zoom.

Mar 74. (7") *(TMG 887)* **HEY GIRL (I LIKE YOUR STYLE).** / **I NEED YOU** | | - |
Apr 74. (7") *<7135>* **HEAVENLY.** / **ZOOM** | | 43 |
Jun 74. (7") *<7136>* **YOU'VE GOT MY SOUL ON FIRE.** / **I NEED YOU** | | 74 |

──── **GLEN LEONARD** – vocals repl. HARRIS

Jan 75. (7") *(TMG 931)* *<7138>* **HAPPY PEOPLE.** / ('A'instrumental) | | 40 |
Feb 75. (lp) *(STMA 8021)* <969> **A SONG FOR YOU** | | 13 |
– Happy people / Glasshouse / Shakey ground / The prophet / Happy people (Instrumental) / A song for you / Memories / I'm a bachelor.

Apr 75. (7") *<7142>* **SHAKEY GROUND.** / **I'M A BACHELOR** | | 26 |
May 75. (7") *(TMG 948)* **MEMORIES.** / **AIN'T NO JUSTICE** | | - |
Aug 75. (7") *<7144>* **GLASSHOUSE.** / **THE PROPHET** | | 37 |

──── **LOUIS PRICE** – vocals repl. EDWARDS who went solo

Jan 76. (7") *<7146>* **KEEP HOLDING ON.** / **WHAT YOU NEED MOST (I DO BEST OF ALL)** | | 54 |
Feb 76. (lp) *(STML 12006)* <973> **HOUSE PARTY** | | 40 | Nov75
– Keep holding on / It's just a matter of time / You can't stop a man in love / World of you, love and music / What you need most (I do best of all) / Ways of a grown up man / Johnny Porter / Darling stand by me / If I don't love you this way.

Jun 76. (7") *<7150>* **UP THE CREEK (WITHOUT A PADDLE).** / **DARLING STAND BY ME** | | 94 |
Jun 76. (lp) *(STMA 8025)* <971> **WINGS OF LOVE** | | 29 | Mar76
– Sweet gypsy Jane / Sweetness in the dark / Up the creek / China doll / Mary Ann / Dream world / Paradise.

Oct 76. (7") *(TMG 1057)* *<7152>* **WHO ARE YOU.** / **LET ME COUNT THE WAYS (I LOVE YOU)** | | |
Oct 76. (lp) *(STML 12040)* <975> **THE TEMPTATIONS DO THE TEMPTATIONS** | | 53 | Sep76
– Why can't you and me get together / Who are you / I'm on fire / Put your trust in me, baby / There's no stopping / Let me count the ways / Is there anybody else / I'l take you in.

Jan 77. (7") *(TMG 1063)* **SHAKEY GROUND.** / **I'M A BACHELOR** | | - |
Atlantic Atlantic

Nov 77. (7") *<3436>* **IN A LIFETIME.** / **I COULD NEVER STOP LOVING YOU** | | - |
Feb 78. (lp) *(K 50413)* *<19143>* **HEAR TO TEMPT YOU** | | | Dec77
– Think for yourself / In a lifetime / Can we come and share in love / She's all I've got / Snake in the grass / It's time for love / Let's live in peace / Road between the lines / I could never stop loving you.

Feb 78. (7") *<3461>* **LET'S LIVE IN PEACE.** / **THINK FOR YOURSELF** | - | |
Aug 78. (7") *<3517>* **BARE BACK.** / **I SEE MY CHILD** | - | |
Aug 78. (lp) *(K 50504)* *<19185>* **BARE BACK** | | |
– Bare back / Mystic woman (love me over) / I just don't know how I let you go / That's when you need love / Ever ready love / Wake up to me / You're so easy to love / I see the child / Touch me again.

Sep 78. (7") *(K 11186)* **BARE BACK.** / **EVER READY LOVE** | | - |
Sep 78. (7") *<3538>* **EVER READY LOVE.** / **TOUCH ME AGAIN** | - | |
Jan 79. (7") *<3567>* **JUST DON'T KNOW HOW TO LET YOU GO.** / **MYSTIC WOMAN** | - | |
Motown Gordy

May 80. (7"/12") *(TMG/+T 1186)* <7183> **POWER.** / ('A'instrumental) | | 43 |
Jun 80. (lp/c) *(STML/CSTML 12136)* <994> **POWER** | | 45 | May80
– Power / Struck by lightning twice / How can I resist your love / Isn't the night fantastic / Shadow of your love / Go for it / Can't you see sweet thing / I'm coming her.

Aug 80. (7") *(TMG 1197)* *<7188>* **STRUCK BY LIGHTNING TWICE.** / **I'M COMING HOME** | | |
(re-iss. Oct82)

Jan 81. (7") *(TMG 1216)* **TAKE ME AWAY.** / **THERE'S MORE WHERE THAT CAME FROM** | | - |

──── **DENNIS EDWARDS** returned on lead vocals

Oct 81. (7") *(TMG 1243)* *<7208>* **AIMING AT YOUR HEART.** / **LIFE OF A COWBOY** | | 67 |
Jan 82. (lp/c) *(STML/CSTML 12159)* <1006> **THE TEMPTATIONS** | | | Aug81
– Aiming at your heart / Evil woman (gonna take your love) / The best of both worlds / Ready, willing and able / Oh what a night / Open their eyes / The life of a cowboy / What else / Just ain't havin' fun / Your lovin' is magic.

Feb 82. (7") *<7213>* **OH, WHAT A NIGHT.** / **ISN'T THE NIGHT FANTASTIC** | - | |

──── **OTIS WILLIAMS, MELVIN FRANKLIN, RICHARD STREET & DENNIS EDWARDS** re-united with **DAVID RUFFIN & EDDIE KENDRICKS** for one-off album

May 82. (lp) *<6008>* **REUNION** | | 37 | Apr82
– Standing on the top / You better beware / Lock it in the pocket / I've never been to me / Backstage / More on the inside / Money's hard to get.

May 82. (7"; TEMPTATIONS featuring RICK JAMES) *(TMG 1263)* *<1616>* **STANDING ON THE TOP.** / (part 2) | 53 | 66 |
Jul 82. (7") *<1631>* **MORE ON THE INSIDE.** / **MONEY'S HARD TO GET** | - | |

Nov 82. (7") *<1654>* **SILENT NIGHT.** / **EVERYTHING FOR CHRISTMAS** | - | |
<re-iss. Nov83; 1713>

──── The quartet added **RON TYSON** (their composer in '78) – vocals

Mar 83. (7"/12") *(TMG/+T 1297)* <1666> **LOVE ON MY MIND TONIGHT.** / **BRING YOUR BODY HERE** | | 88 |
Mar 83. (lp/c) *(STML/CSTML 12182)* <6032> **SURFACE THRILLS** | | |
– Surface thrills / Love on my mind tonight / One man woman / Show me your love / The seeker / What a way to put it / Made in America / Bring your body here (exercise chant).

May 83. (7") *<1683>* **SURFACE THRILLS.** / **MADE IN AMERICA** | - | |
Oct 83. (7") *<1707>* **MISS BUSY BODY (GET YOUR BODY BUSY).** / (part 2) | - | |
Dec 83. (lp/c) *(STML/CSTML 12196)* <6085> **BACK TO BASICS** | - | |
– Miss busy body (get your body busy) / Sail away / Outlaw / Stop the world right here (I wanna get off) / The battle song (I'm the one) / Hollywood / Isn't the night fantastic / Make me believe in love again.

Apr 84. (7") *<1720>* **SAIL AWAY.** / **ISN'T THE NIGHT FANTASTIC** | - | 54 |

──── **ALI OLLIE WODSIN** – lead vocals repl. EDWARDS

Nov 84. (7"/12") *(TMG/+T 1365)* <1765> **TREAT HER LIKE A LADY.** / **ISN'T THE NIGHT FANTASTIC** | 12 | 48 |
Dec 84. (lp/c) *(ZL/ZK 72342)* <6119> **TRULY FOR YOU** | 75 | 55 | Nov84
– Running / Treat like a lady / How can you say it's over / My life is true (truly for you) / Memories / Just to keep you in my life / Set you love right / I'll keep my light on in my window. (re-iss. Oct88 lp/c/cd; WL/WK/WD 76244)

Feb 85. (7") *<1781>* **MY LOVE IS TRUE (TRULY FOR YOU).** / **SET YOUR LOVE RIGHT** | - | |
Mar 85. (7"/12") *(TMG 1373)* **MY LOVE IS TRUE (TRULY FOR YOU).** / **I'LL KEEP A LIGHT ON IN MY WINDOW** | | - |
(12"+=) *(TMGT 1373)* – Treat her like a lady (remix).
Jun 85. (7") *<1789>* **HOW CAN YOU SAY IT'S OVER.** / **I'LL KEEP MY LIGHT IN THE WINDOW** | - | |

──── In Sep'85, RUFFIN & KENDRICKS were credited on HALL & OATES live album 'LIVE AT THE APOLLO WITH . . . '

Nov 85. (7"/12") *(ZB/ZT 40453)* <1818> **DO YOU REALLY LOVE YOUR BABY.** / **I'LL KEEP A LIGHT ON IN MY WINDOW** | | |
Nov 85. (lp/c) *(ZL/ZK 72413)* <6164> **TOUCH ME** | | |
– Magic / Give her some attention / Deeper than love / I'm fascinated / Touch me / Don't break your promise to me / She got tired of loving me / Do you really love your baby / Oh lover.

Feb 86. (7") *<1834>* **TOUCH ME.** / **SET YOUR LOVE RIGHT** | - | |
Mar 86. (7"/12") *(ZB/ZT 40622)* **I'M FASCINATED.** / **HOW CAN YOU SAY IT'S OVER** | | |
Jun 86. (7") *<1837>* **WISHFUL THINKING.** / **A FINE MESS** | - | |
Aug 86. (7") *<ZB 40850>* **LADY SOUL.** / **A FINE MESS** | | - |
(12"+=) *(ZT 40850)* – Papa was a rolling stone.
Sep 86. (lp/c) *(ZL/ZK 72515)* <6207> **TO BE CONTINUED** | | 74 | Jul86
– Lady soul / Message to the world / To be continued / Put us together again / Someone / Girls (they like it) / More love, your love / A fine mess / You're the one / Love me right.

Oct 86. (7") *<1856>* **LADY SOUL.** / **PUT US TOGETHER AGAIN** | - | 47 |
Jan 87. (7") *<1871>* **TO BE CONTINUED.** / **YOU'RE THE ONE** | - | |
Apr 87. (7") *<1881>* **SOMEONE.** / **LOVE ME RIGHT** | - | |

──── **DENNIS EDWARDS** returned again to repl. OTIS

Aug 87. (7") *<ZB 41431>* **PAPA WAS A ROLLIN' STONE (remix).** / **DON'T SAY NOTHING'S CHANGED** | 31 | - |
(12"+=) *(ZT 41431)* – Papa was a rollin' stone (remix 2).
Oct 87. (lp/c/cd) *(ZL/ZK/ZD 72616)* <6246> **TOGETHER AGAIN** | | |
– I got your number / Look what you started / I wonder who she's seeing now / 10 x 10 / Do you wanna go with me / Little things / Everytime I close my eyes / Lucky / Put your foot down.

Oct 87. (7"/12") *(ZB/ZT 41547)* <1908> **I WONDER WHO SHE'S SEEING NOW.** / **GIRLS (THEY LIKE IT)** | | |
Jan 88. (7"/c-s) *(ZB/ZV 41734)* <1920> **LOOK WHAT YOU STARTED.** / **MORE LOVE, YOUR LOVE** | 63 | |
(12"+=) *(ZT 41734)* – ('A'extended).
Apr 88. (7") *<1933>* **DO YOU WANNA GO WITH ME.** / **PUT YOUR FOOT DOWN** | - | |

──── Late 1987, RUFFIN & KENDRICKS released eponymous duo album on 'RCA'.

──── **RON TYSON** – vocals repl. EDWARDS

Oct 89. (7") *(ZB 43233)* *<1974>* **ALL I WANT FROM YOU.** / ('A'instrumental) | | 71 |
(12"+=/cd-s+=) *(ZT/ZD 43234)* – Papa was a rollin' stone / Treat her like a lady.
Oct 89. (lp/c/cd) *(ZL/ZK/ZD 72667)* <6286> **SPECIAL** | | |
– Friends / Special / All I want from you / She's better than money / One step at a time / Fill me up / Go ahead / Loveline / Soul to soul. (cd+=) – O.A.A. lover.

Jan 90. (7") *<2004>* **SPECIAL.** / **O.A.A. LOVER** | - | |
Mar 90. (7") *<2023>* **SOUL TO SOUL.** / ('A'instrumental) | - | |
Jun 90. (7") *<903>* **ONE STEP AT A TIME.** / ('A'instrumental) | - | |
Jan 92. (cd/c/lp) *(ZD/ZK/ZL 72768)* **MILESTONE** | | |
– Eenie, meenie, minie moe / Any old lovin' (just won't do) / Hoops of fire / We should be makin' love / The Jones / Get ready / Corner of my heart / Whenever you're ready / Do it easy / Wait a minute. (cd+=) – Celebrate. (re-iss. cd Apr95; 530005-2)

Feb 92. (7"/c-s) *(TMG/+C 1403)* **THE JONES'.** / ('A'-Surgery mix) | 69 | |
(12"+=/cd-s+=) *(TMG T/CD 1403)* – ('A'instrumental).

──── Tragically, EDDIE KENDRICKS died of cancer in Oct '92.

──── **THEO PEOPLES** – vocals; repl. STREET

──── Later, another original MELVIN FRANKLIN also died on 23rd February 1995.

──── **OTIS WILLIAMS, PEOPLES + ALI WOODSIN** with **RON TYSON** recruited **RAY DAVIS** (b.29 Mar'40, Sumter, South Carolina, USA)

Sep 95. (cd/c) *<530568-2/-4>* **FOR LOVERS ONLY** | | |
– Some enchanted evening / I've grown accustomed to her face / At last / Night and day / Time after time / Melvin's interlude / Life is but a dream / What a difference a day makes / I'm glad there is you / South shell interlude / That's why (I love you so) / For your love – You send me.

—— **HARRY GILBERRY Jr. + BARRINGTON SCOTT** – vocals; repl. PEOPLES + WOODSON

Oct 98.	(cd/c) <(530937-2/-4)> **PHOENIX RISING**	□	**44** Aug98

– Here after (interlude) / Stay / False faces / How he could hurt you / I'm calling you (interlude) / This is my promise / My love / Tempt me / If I give you my heart / Take me in your arms / That's what friends are for / Just like I told you / Stay.

– compilations, others, etc. –

Note; on 'Tamla Motown' UK/ 'Gordy' Us unless otherwise mentioned.

Apr 65.	(7"ep) (TME 2004) **THE TEMPTATIONS**	□	–

– My girl / Girl (why you wanna make me blue) / I'll be in trouble / The girl's alright with me.

Feb 66.	(7"ep) (TME 2010) **IT'S THE TEMPTATIONS**	□	–

– My baby / Since I lost my baby / It's growing / The way you do the things you do.

Feb 67.	(lp; stereo/mono) (S+/TML 11042) <919> **THE TEMPTATIONS' GREATEST HITS**	**26**	**5** Dec66

– The way you do the things you do / My girl / Ain't too proud to beg / Don't look back / Get ready / Beauty is only skin deep / Since I lost my baby / The girl's alright with me / My baby / Its growing / I'll be in trouble / Girl (why you wanna make me blue). (re-iss. Sep88 lp/c/cd; WL/WK/WD 72646)

Aug 69.	(lp) <933> **THE TEMPTATIONS SHOW** (TV Soundtrack)	–	**24**
Dec 70.	(lp) (STML 11170) <954> **THE TEMPTATIONS' GREATEST HITS VOL.2**	**35**	**15** Sep70
May 74.	(d-lp/d-c) (TMSP/CTMSP 6003) <974> **ANTHOLOGY 64-73**		**65** Sep73

(re-iss. Sep88 lp/c/cd; WL/WK/WD 72647)

(re-iss. Oct82; same)

Sep 76.	(7") **GET READY. / JUST MY IMAGINATION**		–
1977.	(lp) (STML 12061) **GREATEST HITS VOL.III**		–
Sep 80.	(7") (TMG 967) **BALL OF CONFUSION. / TAKE A LOOK AROUND**		–
Oct 80.	(d-lp/d-c) (STML/CSTML 12140) **20 GOLDEN GREATS**		–

(cd-iss. 1986; ZL 72160)

Oct 81.	(d-lp/d-c) (TMSP/CTMSP 6003) **ALL THE MILLION SELLERS**		–

(re-iss. Apr84 lp/c; WL/WK 72096) (cd-iss. Feb86; WD 72096)

Nov 82.	(lp/c) (STMS/CSTMS 5085) **GIVE LOVE AT CHRISTMAS**		–
Feb 83.	(7") (TMG 982) **CLOUD NINE. / PSYCHEDELIC SHACK**		–
Mar 83.	(7") (TMG 1043) **JUST MY IMAGINATION. / GET READY**		–
May 83.	(c-ep) (CTME 2024) **TEMPTATIONS EP**		–

– Take a look around / Ball of confusion / Get ready / Beauty is only skin deep.

Oct 83.	(7"/12") (TMG/+T 1320) **MEDLEY OF HITS (with 'The Four Tops'). / PAPA WAS A ROLLIN' STONE**		–
Apr 85.	(7"/12") (TMG/+T 990) **LAW OF THE LAND. / BEAUTY IS ONLY SKIN DEEP**		–
Apr 85.	(7"/12") (TMG/+T 997) **BALL OF CONFUSION. / AIN'T TOO PROUD TO BEG**		–
May 86.	(d-lp/d-c) (WL/WK 72435) <5389> **25th ANNIVERSARY**		–
Jun 86.	(7") (ZB 40743) **MY GIRL. / (B-side by Marvin Gaye)**		–

(12"+=) (ZT 40744) – The way you do the things you do / My baby.

Nov 86.	(lp/c) Telstar; (STAR/STAC 2281) **BEST OF THE TEMPTATIONS**		–
Nov 86.	(cd) (ZD 72460) **CLOUD NINE / PUZZLE PEOPLE**		–
Nov 86.	(cd) (ZD 72486) **PSYCHEDELIC SHACK / ALL DIRECTIONS**		–
Dec 86.	(cd) (ZD 72499) **SONG FOR YOU / MASTERPIECE**		–
Jan 87.	(cd) (ZD 72501) **LIVE AT THE COPA / WITH A LOT O' SOUL**		–
Jan 87.	(cd) (ZD 72525) **ANTHOLOGY 1 & 2**		–
Apr 89.	(cd) (WD 72365) **COMPACT COMMAND PERFORMANCES**		–

—— Below from the film 'My Girl' starring McAuley Caulkin.

Feb 92.	(7"/c-s/cd-s) Epic; (657676-7/-4/-2) <74108> **MY GIRL. / JAMES NEWTON HOWARD** (theme from 'My Girl')	**2**	
Apr 92.	(7") **GET READY. / ('A'version)**		

(12"+=/cd-s+=) – ('A'instrumental).

Apr 92.	(cd/c) (530015-2/-4) **MOTOWN'S GREATEST HITS**	**8**	

– My girl / The Jones / Get ready (new version) / Ain't too proud to beg / Beauty is only skin deep / I wish it would rain / (I know) I'm losing you / Cloud nine / Paa was a rollin' stone / Law of the land / Just my imagination (running away with me) / Take a look around / Ball of confusion (that's what the world is today) / I can't get to you / Psychedelic shack / Treat her like a lady / Get ready / You're my everything / Superstar (remember how you got where you are) / Standing on the top (part 1).

Dec 92.	(cd/c) Kwest; (KWEST 5409/4409) **ORIGINAL LEAD SINGERS**		–
Apr 94.	(cd) Paradiso; (PA 7142) **GREATEST HITS**		–
Oct 94.	(4xcd-box) (530338-2) **EMPERORS OF SOUL**		–
Apr 95.	(cd) Top Masters; (31272) **THE BEST OF . . .**		–
Aug 98.	(cd) (530853-2) **THE ULTIMATE COLLECTION**		–

10cc

Formed: Manchester, England ... early 1970 as HOTLEGS by the experienced ERIC STEWART, LOL CREME and KEVIN GODLEY. STEWART had been a member of WAYNE FONTANA & THE MINDBENDERS between April 1964 and November 1968, (the latter 6 months with pensmith GRAHAM GOULDMAN. GOULDMAN, while a solo artist, had written hits for The YARDBIRDS ('For Your Love', 'Heartful Of Soul' and 'Evil Hearted You'), The HOLLIES ('Bus Stop' and 'Look Through Any Window') and HERMAN'S HERMITS ('No Milk Today'). The aforementioned HOTLEGS scored a 1970 No.2 hit with 'NEANDERTHAL MAN' before folding the following year. In 1972, now trading as 10cc, the trio added GOULDMAN, signing to Jonathan King's newly formed 'UK' imprint. The revamped quartet subsequently became a massive selling outfit, making the Top 3 with the pastiche-like 'DONNA' and the follow-up, 'RUBBER BULLETS', topped the charts. The group amassed an impressive series of hits during the 70's including 'THE DEAN AND I', 'WALL STREET SHUFFLE' and 'LIFE IS A MINESTRONE', although they reached their pinnacle in 1975 (after signing to 'Mercury') with 'I'M NOT IN LOVE', a classy, sophisticated pop ballad lifted from their top selling album, 'THE ORIGINAL

'SOUNDTRACK'. Further chart success came with 'ART FOR ARTS SAKE' and 'I'M MANDY, FLY ME', although GODLEY & CREME left after the release of the accompanying 'HOW DARE YOU' (1976) set. In typically 70's fashion, the pair then indulged themselves in the luxury of a triple album, 'CONSEQUENCES' (1977), promoting their new "gizmo" guitar device in the process. GODLEY & CREME subsequently went on to become top video directors, producing, amongst others, HERBIE HANCOCK, FRANKIE GOES TO HOLLYWOOD and their own 'CRY' single (a groundbreaking effort featuring a series of human faces morphing into each other). Meanwhile, GOULDMAN and STEWART added TONY O'MALLEY, RICK FENN and STUART TOSH, scoring further hits with 'THE THINGS WE DO FOR LOVE', 'GOOD MORNING JUDGE' and the woeful cod-reggae of 'DREADLOCK HOLIDAY' (their third UK No.1); needless to say, most of the spark had vanished. In the early 80'zzz, GODLEY & CREME notched up further pop hits with 'UNDER YOUR THUMB' and 'WEDDING BELLS', STEWART also producing SAD CAFE while GOULDMAN collaborated with ANDREW GOLD in WAX. The original 10CC line-up reformed in 1992 for the album, 'MEANWHILE', although all the songs were written by STEWART and GOULDMAN and by the following year's 'MIRROR MIRROR', GODLEY & CREME had left once more.

Album rating: Hotlegs: THINKS: SCHOOL STINKS (*4) / 10cc: 10cc (*6) / SHEET MUSIC (*7) / THE ORIGINAL SOUNDTRACK (*7) / 100cc – THE GREATEST HITS OF 10cc compilation (*6) / HOW DARE YOU! (*5) / DECEPTIVE BENDS (*5) / LIVE AND LET LIVE (*4) / BLOODY TOURISTS (*5) / GREATEST HITS 1972-1978 compilation (*8) / LOOK HEAR! (*4) / TEN OUT OF 10 (*4) / WINDOW IN THE JUNGLE (*3) / MEANWHILE (*3) / MIRROR, MIRROR (*3) / THE VERY BEST OF 10cc compilation (*7) / Eric Stewart: GIRLS (*4) / Graham Gouldman: ANIMALYMPICS (*4) / Godley & Creme: CONSEQUENCIES (*4) / L (*4) / FREEZE FRAME (*4) / ISMISM (*5) / BIRDS OF PREY (*4) / THE HISTORY MIX VOLUME 1 (*5) / THE CHANGING FACES OF 10cc AND GODLEY & CREME compilation (*8) / GOODBYE BLUE SKY (*4)

HOTLEGS

ERIC STEWART (b.20 Jan'45) – vocals, guitar, bass (ex-MINDBENDERS) / **LOL CREME** (b. LAWRENCE CREME, 19 Sep'47) – vocals, guitar, keyboards, bass / **KEVIN GODLEY** (b. 7 Oct'45) – drums, vocals (ex-MOCKINGBIRDS, ex-Solo)

		Fontana	Capitol
Jun 70.	(7") (6007 019) <2886> **NEANDERTHAL MAN. / YOU DIDN'T LIKE IT**	**2**	**22**
Mar 71.	(7") <3043> **HOW MANY TIMES. / RUN BABY RUN**	–	

		Philips	Capitol
Mar 71.	(lp) (6308 047) <378> **THINKS: SCHOOL STINKS**		

– Neanderthal man / How many times / Desperate Dan / Take me back / Um wah, un woh / Suite F.A. / Fly away / Run baby run / All God's children.

Sep 71.	(7") (6006 140) **LADY SADIE. / THE LOSER**		–

—— Split late 1971. A further exploitation lp 'YOU DIDN'T LIKE IT BECAUSE YOU DIDN'T THINK OF IT' was issued 1976 on 'Philips' (9282 001); GOULDMAN guested bass on track 'Today'.

—— The trio became . . .

10cc

—— adding **GRAHAM GOULDMAN** – bass, vocals (ex-Solo artist, ex-MINDBENDERS)

		UK-Decca	UK
Sep 72.	(7") (UK 6) <49005> **DONNA. / HOT SUN ROCK**	**2**	
Dec 72.	(7") (UK 22) **JOHNNY, DON'T DO IT. / 4% OF SOMETHING**		–
Apr 73.	(7") (UK 36) <49015> **RUBBER BULLETS. / WATERFALL**	**1**	**73** Sep73
Aug 73.	(lp/c) (UKA L/C 1005) <53105> **10cc**	**36**	

– Rubber bullets / Donna / Johnny, don't do it / Sand in my face / Speed kills / The dean and I / Ships don't disappear in the night (do they?) / The hospital song / Fresh air for my momma / Headline hustler. (re-iss. Apr82 on 'Philips'; 6359014) (re-iss. Dec83 on 'Mercury' lp/c; PRICE/PRIMC 7)

Aug 73.	(7") (UK 48) **THE DEAN AND I. / BEE IN MY BONNET**	**10**	
Jan 74.	(7") (UK 57) **THE WORST BAND IN THE WORLD. / 18 CARAT MAN OF MEANS**	**10**	
Apr 74.	(7") <49019> **HEADLINE HUSTLER. / SPEED KILLS**		–
Jun 74.	(7") (UK 69) <49023> **WALL STREET SHUFFLE. / GISMO MY WAY**	**10**	
Jun 74.	(lp/c) (UKA L/C 1007) <53107> **SHEET MUSIC**	**9**	**81**

– Wall street shuffle / The worst band in the world / Hotel / Old wild men / Clockwork creep / Silly love / Somewhere in Hollywood / Baron Samedi / The sacro-iliac / Oh! Effendi. (re-iss. Apr82 on 'Philips'; 6310508) (re-iss. Dec83 on 'Mercury' lp/c; PRICE/PRIMC 8)

		Mercury	Mercury
Sep 74.	(7") (UK 77) **SILLY LOVE. / THE SACRO-ILIAC**	**24**	–
Mar 75.	(lp/c) (9102 500) <SRMI 1029> **THE ORIGINAL SOUNDTRACK**	**4**	**15**

– Une nuit a Paris: One night in Paris – The same night in Paris – Later the same night in Paris / I'm not in love / Blackmail / The second sitting for the last supper / Brand new day / Flying junk / Life is a minestrone / The film of my love. (re-iss. Dec83 lp/c; PRICE/PRIMC 48) (cd-iss. 1988; 830 775-2) (cd re-iss. Aug98 on 'Mobile Fidelity'; USCD 729)

Mar 75.	(7") (6008 010) **LIFE IS A MINESTRONE. / CHANNEL SWIMMER**	**7**	–
May 75.	(7") (6008 014) **I'M NOT IN LOVE. / GOOD NEWS**	**1**	–
May 75.	(7") <73678> **I'M NOT IN LOVE. / CHANNEL SWIMMER**	–	**2**

(re-iss. Oct84)

Nov 75.	(7") (6080 017) <73725> **ART FOR ART'S SAKE. / GET IT WHILE YOU CAN**	**5**	**83**
Jan 76.	(lp/c) (9102 501) <SRMI 1061> **HOW DARE YOU!**	**5**	

– How dare you / Lazy ways / I wanna rule the world / I'm Mandy fly me / Iceberg / Art for art's sake / Rock'n'roll lullaby / Head room / Don't hang up. (re-iss. Dec83 lp/c; PRICE/PRIMC 60)

Mar 76. (7") *(6008 019)* <73779> **I'M MANDY FLY ME. / HOW DARE YOU** — `6` `60`

—— **STEWART + GOULDMAN** carried on with session people including live drummer **PAUL BURGESS**. They replaced GODLEY & CREME who formed own duo.

Jul 76. (7") <73805> **LAZY WAYS. / LIFE IS A MINESTRONE** — `-` `☐`

Nov 76. (7") *(6008 022)* <73875> **THE THINGS WE DO FOR LOVE. / HOT TO TROT** — `6` `5`

Apr 77. (7") *(6008 025)* **GOOD MORNING JUDGE. / DON'T SQUEEZE ME LIKE TOOTHPASTE** — `5` `-`

May 77. (lp/c) *(9102 502)* <SRMI 3702> **DECEPTIVE BENDS** — `3` `31`
– Good morning judge / The things we do for love / Marriage bureau rendezvous / People in love / Modern man blues / Honeymoon with B troop / I bought a flat guitar tutor / You've got a cold / Feel the benefit: Reminisce and speculation – A Latin break. *(re-iss. May83; PRICE 5)*

May 77. (7") <73917> **PEOPLE IN LOVE. / DON'T SQUEEZE ME LIKE TOOTHPASTE** — `-` `40`

Jun 77. (7") *(6008 028)* **PEOPLE IN LOVE. / I'M SO LAID BACK I'M LAID OUT** — `☐` `☐`

Jul 77. (7") <73943> **GOOD MORNING JUDGE. / I'M SO LAID BACK I'M LAID OUT** — `-` `69`

—— added **RICK FENN** – guitar / **TONY O'MALLEY** – keyboards (ex-ARRIVAL, ex-KOKOMO) / **STUART TOSH** – 2nd drummer (ex-PILOT)

Dec 77. (d-lp/d-c) *(6641698)* <SRM 28600> **LIVE AND LET LIVE** (live) — `14` `☐`
– The second sitting for the last supper / You've got a cold / Honeymoon with B troop / Art for art's sake / Wall Street shuffle / Ships don't disappear in the night (do they?) / I'm Mandy fly me / Marriage bureau rendezvous / Good morning judge / Feel the benefit / The things we do for love / Waterfall / I'm not in love / Modern man blues.

Dec 77. (7") <73980> **WALL STREET SHUFFLE (live). / YOU'VE GOT A COLD** — `-` `☐`

—— **DUNCAN MACKAY** – keyboards (ex-COCKNEY REBEL) repl. BURGESS

	Mercury	Polydor
Jul 78. (7") *(6008 035)* <14511> **DREADLOCK HOLIDAY. / NOTHING CAN MOVE ME**	1	44
Sep 78. (lp/c) *(9102 503)* <SRMI 6160> **BLOODY TOURISTS**	3	69

– Dreadlock holiday / For you and I / Take these chains / Shock in the night (don't want love) / Last night / The anonymous alcoholic / Reds in my bed / Life line / Tokyo / Old Mister Time / From Rochdale to Ocho Rios / Everything you've wanted to know about. *(re-iss. May83)*

Oct 78. (7") *(6008 036)* **REDS IN MY BED. / TAKE THESE CHAINS** — `☐` `-`

Jan 79. (7") <14528> **FOR YOU AND I. / TAKE THESE CHAINS** — `-` `85`

Sep 79. (lp)(c) *(9102 504)(7231 304)* <6244> **GREATEST HITS 1972-1978** (compilation) — `5` `☐`
– Rubber bullets / Donna / Silly love / The dean and I / Life is a minestrone / Wall Street shuffle / Art for art's sake / I'm Mandy fly me / Good morning judge / The things we do for love / Dreadlock holiday / I'm not in love.

	Mercury	Warners
Feb 80. (7") *(LOOK 1)* **ONE TWO FIVE. / ONLY CHILD**	☐	☐
Mar 80. (lp)(c) *(9102 505)(7231 305)* <3442> **LOOK HEAR!**	35	☐

– One two five / Welcome to the world / How'm I ever going to say goodbye / Don't send we back / I took you home / It doesn't matter at all / Dressed to kill / Lovers anonymous / I hate to eat alone / Strange lover / L.A. inflatable.

—— At same time ERIC STEWART and GRAHAM GOULDMAN had own solo albums.

May 80. (7") *(LOOK 2)* **IT DOESN'T MATTER AT ALL. / FROM ROCHDALE TO OCHO RIOS** — `☐` `☐`

May 80. (7") **IT DOESN'T MATTER AT ALL. / STRANGE LOVER** — `-` `☐`

May 81. (7") *(TENT 10)* **NOUVEAU RICHE. / I HATE TO EAT ALONE** — `☐` `☐`

Nov 81. (7") *(MER 86)* **DON'T TURN ME AWAY. / TOMORROW'S WORLD TODAY** — `☐` `☐`

Nov 81. (lp)(c) *(6350 048)(7150 048)* **TEN OUT OF 10** — `☐` `☐`
– I don't ask / Overdraft in overdrive / Don't turn me away / Memories / No tell hotel / Les nouveaux riches / Action man in Motown suit / Listen with your eyes / Lying here with you / Survivor. *(cd-iss. 1983)*

Mar 82. (7") *(MER 95)* **THE POWER OF LOVE. / YOU'RE COMING HOME AGAIN** — `☐` `-`

Jun 82. (7") **THE POWER OF LOVE. / ACTION MAN IN MOTOWN SUIT** — `-` `☐`

Jul 82. (7") *(MER 113)* **RUN AWAY. / ACTION MAN IN MOTOWN SUIT** — `50` `☐`

Oct 82. (7") *(MER 121)* **WE'VE HEARD IT ALL BEFORE. / OVERNIGHT IN OVERDRIVE** — `☐` `☐`

Apr 83. (7") *(MER 139)* **24 HOURS. / DREADLOCK HOLIDAY** — `☐` `☐`
(12"+=) *(MERT 139)* – I'm not in love.

Sep 83. (7") *(MER 143)* **FEEL THE LOVE. / SHE GIVES THE PAIN** — `☐` `☐`

Oct 83. (lp/c) *(MERL/+C 28)* **WINDOW IN THE JUNGLE** — `70` `☐`
– 24 hours / Feel the love / Oomachasa ooma / Yes I can / Americana panorama / City lights / Food for thought / Working girls / Taxi! taxi!.

—— split late '83 but reunited 8 years later; originals re-formed in 1991 with STEWART & GOULDMAN

	Polydor	Polydor
Apr 92. (7"/c-s/cd-s) **WOMAN IN LOVE. / MAN WITH A MISSION**	☐	☐
May 92. (cd/c/lp) *(513279-2/-4/-1)* **MEANWHILE**	☐	☐

– Woman in love / Wonderland / Fill her up / Something special / Welcome to Paradise / The stars didn't show / Green aged monster / Charity begins at home / Shine a light in the dark / Don't break the promises.

Jun 92. (7") **WELCOME TO PARADISE. / DON'T BREAK THE PROMISES** — `☐` `-`
(cd-s+=) – Lost in love.

	Humbug	not iss.
Feb 94. (cd) *(CMCD 010)* **ALIVE – GREATEST HITS PERFORMED LIVE** (live)	☐	-

—— GOULDMAN + STEWART acoustic only

	Avex	not iss.
Feb 95. (7"/c-s) *(AVEX S/MC 2)* **I'M NOT IN LOVE. (acoustic) / BLUEBIRD**	29	-

(cd-s+=) *(AVEXCD 2)* – ('A'–The reward of art).

May 95. (c-s/cd-s/12") *(AVEX MC/CD/X 8)* **READY TO GO HOME. / ('A'album mix) / AGE OF CONSENT** — `☐` `-`

Sep 95. (cd/c/d-lp) *(AVEX CD/MC/LP 6)* **MIRROR, MIRROR**
– Yvonne's the one / Code of silence / Blue bird / Age of consent / Take this woman / The monkey and the onion / Everything is not enough / Ready to go home / Grow old with me / Margo wants the mustard / Peace in our time / Why did I break your heart / Now you're gone / I'm not in love (acoustic '95).

– compilations, etc. –

Note; Below 3 on 'UK Decca'.

May 75. (lp/c) *(UKAL/+C 1007)* <53110> **100cc – THE GREATEST HITS OF 10cc** — `9` `☐`

May 75. (7") **WATERFALL. / 4% OF NOTHING** — `☐` `-`

Jul 87. (7"/12") *(UKP/+T 002)* **THE WORST BAND IN THE WORLD. / HOT SUN ROCK** — `☐` `-`

Apr 79. (lp) *Flyover; (RJ 7437)* **THE SONGS WE DO FOR LOVE** — `☐` `☐`

Sep 79. (7") *Mercury; (6008 043)* **I'M NOT IN LOVE. / FOR YOU AND I** — `☐` `☐`

1981. (c) *Mercury; (7215 039)* **THE MUSIC OF 10cc (1975-77)** — `☐` `☐`

Oct 82. (lp) *Contour; (CN 2056)* **10cc IN CONCERT** (live) — `☐` `☐`
(cd-iss. Apr91 on 'Pickwick'; PWKS 4050P)
Note; below 4 on 'Old Gold'.

Jun 88. (7") *(OG 9475)* **I'M NOT IN LOVE. / DREADLOCK HOLIDAY** — `☐` `☐`

Jun 88. (7") *(OG 9786)* **RUBBER BULLETS. / DONNA** — `☐` `☐`

Jun 88. (7") *(OG 9788)* **WALL STREET SHUFFLE. / THE DEAN AND I** — `☐` `☐`

May 92. (cd-s) *(OG 6165)* **I'M NOT IN LOVE / DREADLOCK HOLIDAY / I'M MANDY FLY ME** — `☐` `☐`

Jul 89. (d-lp/cd) *Castle; (CCS LP/MC 214)* **THE COLLECTION** — `☐` `☐`
– (albums 10cc + SHEET MUSIC)

Apr 93. (cd/c) *Dojo; (EARLD 12)* **THE EARLY YEARS** — `☐` `☐`

May 93. (cd/c) *Music Club;* **THE BEST OF THE EARLY YEARS** — `☐` `☐`

May 93. (cd/c) *Spectrum; (550004-2/-4)* **FOOD FOR THOUGHT** — `☐` `☐`

Jul 94. (cd/c) *BR Music; (BR CD/MC 126)* **GREATEST HITS** — `☐` `☐`

Aug 95. (cd-s) *Old Gold; (OG 6307)* **RUBBER BULLETS / THE DEAN AND I** — `☐` `☐`

Sep 95. (cd-s) *Old Gold; (1262363272)* **DONNA / WALL STREET SHUFFLE** — `☐` `☐`

Mar 97. (cd/c) *Mercury; (534612-2/-4)* **THE VERY BEST OF 10CC** — `37` `☐`

Aug 98. (cd) *King Biscuit; (KBFHCD 015)* **KING BISCUIT PRESENTS . . .** — `☐` `☐`

KEVIN GODLEY & LOL CREME

with guests **PETER COOK + SARAH VAUGHAN** also introduced new Gizmo guitar orchestrator.

	Mercury	Mercury
Oct 77. (t-lp/d-c) *(CON S/C 017)* <1700> **CONSEQUENCES**	☐	☐

– Seascape / Wind / Fireworks / Stampede / Burial scene / Sleeping Earth / Honolulu Lulu / The flood / Five o'clock in the morning / When things go wrong / Lost weekend / Rosie / Office chase / Cool, cool, cool / Cool, cool, cool (reprise) / Sailor / Mobilisation / Please, please, please / Blint's tune (movement 1-17). *(re-iss. 1-lp Feb79 as 'MUSIC FROM CONSEQUENCES' tracks *)*

Dec 77. (7") *(SAMP 17)* **FIVE O'CLOCK IN THE MORNING. / THE FLOOD** — `☐` `☐`

GODLEY & CREME

—— with guest **ANDY MACKAY** – saxophone

	Mercury	Polydor
Aug 78. (lp) *(9109611)* <6177> **L**	☐	☐

– This sporting life / Sandwiches of you / Art school canteen / Group life / Punchbag / Foreign accents / Hit factory – Business is business.

	Polydor	Mirage
Jan 79. (7") *(6008104)* **SANDWICHES OF YOU. / FOREIGN ACCENTS**	☐	☐

Oct 79. (7") *(POSP 80)* **AN ENGLISHMAN IN NEW YORK. / SILENT RUNNING** — `☐` `☐`

Nov 79. (lp/c) *(POLD/+C 5027)* <6257> **FREEZE FRAME** — `☐` `☐`
– An Englishman in New York / Random brainwave / I pity inanimate objects / Freeze frame / Clues / Brazilia (wish you were here) / Mugshots / Get well soon. *(re-iss. Aug83 lp/c; SPE LP/C 30) (cd-iss. 1987 & May91; 831 555-2)*

Mar 80. (7") *(POSP 145)* **WIDE BOY. / I PITY INANIMATE OBJECTS** — `☐` `-`

Sep 80. (7") *(POSP 171)* **SUBMARINE. / MARCIANO** — `☐` `☐`

Aug 81. (7") *(POSP 322)* **UNDER YOUR THUMB. / POWER BEHIND THE THRONE** — `3` `☐`

Sep 81. (lp/c) *(POLD/+C 5043)* **ISMISM** — `29` `☐`
– Snack attack / Under your thumb / Joey's camel / The problem / Ready for Ralph / Wedding bells / Lonnie / Sale of the century / The party. *(re-iss. Oct84)*

Nov 81. (7") *(POSP 369)* **WEDDING BELLS. / BABIES** — `7` `☐`

Feb 82. (7") **WEDDING BELLS. / LONNIE** — `-` `☐`
(re-iss. Nov85 on 'Mirage')

Feb 82. (7"/12") *(POSP/+X 412)* **SNACK ATTACK. / STRANGE APPARATUS** — `☐` `☐`

Sep 82. (7") *(POSP 490)* **SAVE A MOUNTAIN FOR ME. / WELCOME TO BREAKFAST TELEVISION** — `☐` `☐`

Mar 83. (7") *(POSP 550)* **SAMSON. / SAMSON (dance mix)** — `☐` `☐`

Apr 83. (lp/c) *(POLD/+C 5070)* **BIRDS OF PREY** — `☐` `☐`
– My body the car / Worm and the rattlesnake / Cat's eyes / Samson / Save a mountain for me / Madame Guillotine / Woodwork / Twisted nerve / Out in the cold.

May 84. (7"/12") *(POSP/+X 677)* **GOLDEN BOY. / MY BODY THE CAR** — `☐` `-`

Mar 85. (7"/12") *(POSP/+X 732)* <881786> **CRY. / LOVE BOMBS** — `15` `16`
(re-iss. Aug86, hit UK 66)

Jun 85. (lp/c) *(POLH/+C 22)* <825981> **THE HISTORY MIX VOLUME 1** — `☐` `☐`
– Wet rubber soup (recycled from):- Rubber bullets – Minestrone – I'm not in love /

Cry: Expanding business – The dare you man – Hum drum boys in Paris – Mountain tension / Light me up / An Englishman in New York / Save a mountain for me / Golden boy. *(cd-iss. May91)*

Sep 85. (7"/12") *(POSP/+X 760)* **GOLDEN BOY (remix). / LIGHT ME UP** ☐ –

Dec 87. (7") *(POSP 901)* **A LITTLE BIT OF HEAVEN. / BITS OF BLUE SKY (excerpts)** ☐ –
(12"+=/cd-s+=) *(POSPX/POCD 901)* – ('A'extended).
(c-s+=) *(POSPC 901)* – Rhino rhino. *(re-iss. Jul88)*

Feb 88. (lp/c)(cd) *(POLH/+C 40)(8353482)* **GOODBYE BLUE SKY** ☐ –
– H.E.A.V.E.N. / A little piece of Heaven / Don't set fire (to the one I love) / Golden rings / Crime & punishment / The big bang / 10,000 angels / Sweet memory / Airforce one / The last page of history / Desperate times.

Mar 88. (7") *(POSP 913)* **10,000 ANGELS. / HIDDEN HEARTBREAK** ☐ –
(12"+=) *(POSPX 913)* – Can't sleep.
(cd-s++=) *(POCD 913)* – Cry.

– compilations, others, etc. –

Aug 82. (d-c) *Polydor;* **FREEZE FRAME / ISMISM** ☐ –
Aug 87. (7"/12") *Polydor; (POSP/+X 875)* **SNACK ATTACK. / WET RUBBER SOAP** ☐ –
Sep 87. (lp/c)(cd) *Polydor; (TGC LP/MC 1)(8163552)* **CHANGING FACES OF 10 cc & GODLEY AND CREME** ☐4☐
– Dreadlock holiday / The Wall Street shuffle / Under your thumb (GODLEY & CREME) / Life is a minestrone / An Englishman in New York (GODLEY & CREME) / Art for art's sake / Donna / Snack attack (GODLEY & CREME) / Cry (GODLEY & CREME) / The things we do for love / Wedding bells (GODLEY & CREME) / I'm Mandy, fly me / Good morning judge / Rubber bullets / Save a mountain for me (GODLEY & CREME) / I'm not in love. *(re-iss. Mar94 on 'Polygram TV' cd/c;)*
May 93. (cd/c) *Spectrum; (550007-2/-4)* **IMAGES** ☐ –
Apr 95. (cd) *Disky;* **ROCK AND POP LEGENDS** ☐ –

TENPOLE TUDOR (dig out; Great Alt & Indie . . .)

10,000 MANIACS

Formed: Jamestown, New York, USA . . . 1981 by NATALIE MERCHANT and J.C. LOMBARDO, who had been part of the band, STILL LIFE. Initially a new wave covers outfit, the group (which was completed by ROBERT BUCK, STEVEN GUSTAFSON, DENNIS DREW and JERRY AUGUSTYNAK) debuted on the obscure 'Christian Burial' label in 1982 with the mini-album, 'HUMAN CONFLICT NUMBER FIVE'. After a further full-length set, 'THE SECRETS OF THE I-CHING' (1984), which scaled the UK indie chart and won praise from Radio 1 guru John Peel, the group secured an international deal with 'Elektra'. Produced by veteran folk man, Joe Boyd, 'THE WISHING CHAIR' (1985) saw the band develop their eclectic, rootsy sound, although it wasn't until the release of 'IN MY TRIBE' (1987) that 10,000 MANIACS began to reap some commercial rewards to match their growing critical acclaim. By this point LOMBARDO had departed after the previous years heavy touring alongside R.E.M., the group further changing their strategy by enlisting the services of another seasoned producer, Pete Asher. The result was a sparer sound and sharpened songwriting which emphasised MERCHANT's hypnotically plangent vocals, the group scoring minor US hits with 'LIKE THE WEATHER' and 'WHAT'S THE MATTER HERE'. A cover of Cat Stevens' 'PEACE TRAIN' failed to chart, the band later withdrawing the track from subsequent pressings following hardline Islamic comments made by the former singer/songwriter. Perhaps as a result, the follow-up set, 'BLIND MAN'S ZOO' (1989), took a more political stance, though the enigmatic MERCHANT stopped short of preaching, the album becoming a transatlantic Top 20 hit. Following the accompanying tour, the band took a brief sabbatical, eventually returning in September '92 with another successful set, 'OUR TIME IN EDEN'. The minor hit, 'CANDY EVERYBODY WANTS', was backed with a suitably lugubrious reading of Morrissey's 'EVERYDAY IS LIKE SUNDAY' while CD formats included a MERCHANT/MICHAEL STIPE duet on a version of R.E.M.'s country-tinged classic,~~ 'DON'T GO BACK TO ROCKVILLE'. By the release of the languorous 'UNPLUGGED' (1993) set, however, MERCHANT was disillusioned with the group's attitude and left soon after for a solo career. While 10,000 MANIACS replaced MERCHANT with ex-member, JOHN LOMBARDO and new frontwoman MARY RAMSEY, the group's former focal point almost made the US Top 20 in summer '95 with her debut solo set, 'TIGERLILY'. • **Songwriters:** lyrics – NATALIE / music – JC LOMBARDO until his departure. MERCHANT was then the main writer with DREW or BUCK. Covered: I HOPE THAT I DON'T FALL IN LOVE WITH YOU (Tom Waits) / STARMAN – MOONAGE DAYDREAM (David Bowie) / THESE DAYS (Jackson Browne) / BECAUSE THE NIGHT (Patti Smith Group) / MORE THAN THIS (Bryan Ferry).

Album rating: HUMAN CONFLICT NUMBER FIVE mini (*4) / SECRETS OF THE I-CHING (*5) / THE WISHING CHAIR (*6) / IN MY TRIBE (*8) / BLIND MAN'S ZOO (*7) / HOPE CHEST: THE FREDONIA RECORDINGS 1982-1983 collection (*5) / OUR TIME IN EDEN (*7) / MTV UNPLUGGED (*5) / LOVE AMONG THE RUINS (*5) / THE EARTH PRESSED FLAT (*4) / John And Mary: VICTORY GARDENS (*6) / THE WEEDKILLER'S DAUGHTER (*5)

NATALIE MERCHANT (b.26 Oct'63) – vocals / **ROBERT BUCK** (b. 1 Aug'58) – guitar, synthesizers / **J.C. LOMBARDO** (b. JOHN, 30 Sep'52) – rhythm guitar, bass / **STEVEN GUSTAFSON** (b.10 Apr'57, Madrid, Spain) – bass, guitar / **DENNIS DREW** (b. 8 Aug'57, Buffalo, N.Y.) – organ / **JERRY AUGUSTYNAK** (b. 2 Sep'58, Lackawanna, N.Y.) – drums

		not iss.	Christian Burial
1982.	(m-lp) (> **HUMAN CONFLICT NUMBER FIVE**	–	

– Orange / Planed obsolescence / Anthem for doomed youth / Groove dub / Tension. *(UK-iss.Jun84 on 'Press'; P 2010)*

Jan 84. (lp) **SECRETS OF THE I-CHING** – ☐
– Grey victory / Pour de Chirico / Death of Manolette / Tension / Daktari / Pit viper / Katrina's fair / The Latin one / My mother the war. *(UK-iss.Aug84 on 'Press'; P 3001)*

		Reflex	Reflex
Mar 84.	(12"m) *(RE 1)* **MY MOTHER THE WAR (remix). / PLANNED OBSOLESCENCE / NATIONAL EDUCATION WEEK**	☐	☐

		Elektra	Elektra
Jun 85.	(7") *(EKR 11)* **CAN'T IGNORE THE TRAIN. / DAKTARI**	☐	☐

(12"+=) *(EKR 11T)* – Grey victory / The colonial wing.

Nov 85. (lp/c) *(EKT 14/+C)* **THE WISHING CHAIR** ☐ ☐
– Can't ignore the train / Just as the tide was a-flowing / Scorpio rising / Lilydale / Maddox table / Everyone a puzzle lover / Arbor day / Back o' the Moon / Tension takes a tangle / Among the Americans / Grey victory / Cotton alley / My mother the war. *(cd-iss. 1989; 960 428-2)*

Nov 85. (7"w/drawn) *(EKR 19)* **JUST AS THE TIDE WAS A-FLOWING. / AMONG THE AMERICANS** – ☐
Jan 86. (7") *(EKR 28)* **SCORPIO RISING. / ARBOR DAY** ☐ ☐

—— trimmed to a quintet when LOMBARDO departed to form JOHN AND MARY

Aug 87. (7") *(EKR 61)* **PEACE TRAIN. / THE PAINTED DESERT** ☐ ☐
Aug 87. (lp/c)(cd) *(EKT 41/+C)(960 738-2) <60738>* **IN MY TRIBE** ☐ ☐37☐
– What's the matter here? / Hey Jack Kerouac / Like the weather / Cherry tree / Painted desert / Don't talk / Peace train / Gun shy / Sister Rose / A campfire song / City of angels / Verdi cries. *(initial copies cont. Elektra sampler with X / The CALL; SAM 390)*

Nov 87. (7") *(EKR 64)* **DON'T TALK. / CITY OF ANGELS** ☐ ☐
(12"+=) *(EKR 64T)* – Goodbye (Tribal outtake).

Mar 88. (7") *(EKR 71)* **WHAT'S THE MATTER HERE?. / VERDI CRIES** ☐ –
(12"+=/cd-s+=) *(EKR 71T)* – Like the weather (live) / Gun shy (live).

Jul 88. (7") *(EKR 77) <69418>* **LIKE THE WEATHER. / A CAMPFIRE SONG** ☐68☐ May88
(12"+=/12"w-poster) *(EKR 77T/+W)* – Poison in the well (live) / Verdi cries (live).

Jul 88. (7") *<69388>* **WHAT'S THE MATTER HERE? / CHERRY TREE** – ☐80☐

May 89. (lp/c)(cd) *(EKT 57/+C)(960 815-2) <60815>* **BLIND MAN'S ZOO** ☐18☐ ☐13☐
– Eat for two / Please forgive us / The big parade / Trouble me / You happy puppet / Headstrong / Poison in the well / Dust bowl / The lion's share / Hateful hate / Jubilee.

Jun 89. (7"/c-s) *(EKR 93) <69298>* **TROUBLE ME. / THE LION'S SHARE** ☐ ☐44☐
(12"+=/3"cd-s+=) *(EKR 93 T/CD/CDX)* – Party of God.

Sep 89. (7") *<69253>* **YOU HAPPY PUPPET. / GUNSHY** ☐ –
Nov 89. (7"ep) *(EKR 100)* **EAT FOR TWO / WILDWOOD FLOWER. / DON'T CALL US / FROM THE TIME YOU SAY GOODBYE** – ☐
(12"/12"w/poster/3"cd-s) *(EKR 100 T/TW/CD)* – (1st & 2nd track) / Gun shy (acoustic) / Hello in there.
(10") *(EKR 100TE)* – (1st & 4th track) / What's the matter here? (acoustic) / Eat for two (acoustic).

Sep 92. (7"/c-s) *(EKR 156/+C) <64700>* **THESE ARE DAYS. / CIRCLE DREAM** ☐58☐ ☐66☐
(cd-s+=) *(EKR 156CD)* – I hope that I don't fall in love with you.
(cd-s) *(EKR 156CDX)* – ('A'side) / Medley:- Starman – Moonage daydream / These days.

Sep 92. (cd/c/lp) *<(7559 61385-2/-4/-1)>* **OUR TIME IN EDEN** ☐33☐ ☐28☐
– Noah's dove / These are days / Eden / Few and far between / Stockton gala days / Gold rush brides / Jezebel / How you've grown / Candy everybody wants / Circle dream / If you intend / I'm not the man. *(cd+=)* – Tolerance.

Feb 93. (c-s,cd-s) *<64665>* **CANDY EVERYBODY WANTS / I HOPE THAT I DON'T FALL IN LOVE WITH YOU** – ☐67☐

Mar 93. (7"/c-s) *(EKR 160/+C)* **CANDY EVERYBODY WANTS. / EVERYDAY IS LIKE SUNDAY** ☐47☐ –
(cd-s+=) *(EKR 160CD1)* – Don't go back to Rockville (with MICHAEL STIPE co-vocals) / Sally Ann.
(cd-s+=) *(EKR 160CD2)* – Don't go back to Rockville (with MICHAEL STIPE) / ('A' MTV version).
(cd-s) *(EKR 160CD3)* – ('A'side) / Eat for two (live) / My sister Rose (live) / Hey Jack Kerouac (live).

Aug 93. (cd-ep) *<66296>* **FEW AND FAR BETWEEN / CANDY EVERYBODY WANTS / TO SIR WITH LOVE / LET THE MYSTERY BE** – ☐95☐

Oct 93. (7"/c-s) *(EKR 175/+C)* **BECAUSE THE NIGHT. / STOCKTON GALA DAYS** ☐65☐ –
(cd-s+=) *(EKR 175CD)* – Let the mystery be / Sally Ann.

Oct 93. (c-s,cd-s) *<64595>* **BECAUSE THE NIGHT / EAT FOR TWO** – ☐11☐
Oct 93. (cd/c) *<(7559 61569-2/-4)>* **MTV UNPLUGGED (live)** ☐40☐ ☐13☐
– These are days / Eat for two / Candy everybody wants (MTV version) / I'm not the man / Don't talk / Hey Jack Kerouac / What's the matter here / Gold rush brides / Like the weather / Trouble me / Jezebel / Because the night / Stockton gala days / Noah's dove.

—— 10,000 MANIACS split when NATALIE went solo. The rest re-formed in 1995 and added ex-original JOHN LOMBARDO and his (JOHN AND MARY) partner MARY RAMSEY on vocals and violin.

		Geffen	Geffen
Sep 97.	(c-s) *(GFSC 22284) <19411>* **MORE THAN THIS / BEYOND THE BLUE**	☐	☐25☐ Jul97

(12"+=/cd-s+=) *(GFST/+D 22284)* – ('A'–Tee's radio edit).

Oct 97. (cd) *<(GED 25009)>* **LOVE AMONG THE RUINS** ☐ ☐ Jul97
– Rainy day / Love among the ruins / Even with my eyes closed / Girl on a train / Green children / Room for everything / More than this / Big star / You won't find me there / All that never happens / Shining light / Across the fields.

		not iss.	Bar/None
Jul 99.	(cd/c) *<106>* **THE EARTH PRESSED FLAT**	–	☐

– The Earth pressed flat / Ellen / Once a vity / Glow / One & on (mercy song) / Somebody's Heaven / Cabaret / Beyond the blue / Smallest step / In the quiet morning / Time turns / Hidden in my heart / Who knows where the times goes? *(cd+=)* – (bonus song).

– compilations, others, etc. –

Oct 90. (lp/c)(cd) *Elektra; (EKT 79/+C)<(7599 60962-2)>* **HOPE CHEST** ☐ ☐
– (HUMAN CONFLICT NUMBER FIVE / THE SECRETS OF I-CHING)

JOHN AND MARY

JOHN LOMBARDO – vocals, bass, guitars / **MARY RAMSEY** – vocals, keyboards, violin, viola / with **ROBERT BUCK, JEROME AUGUSTYNIAK** – drums / etc.

		Rykodisc	Rykodisc

Jul 91. (cd) *<(RCD 10203)>* **VICTORY GARDENS**
– Red wooden beads / Azalea festival / Piles of dead leaves / We have nothing / Rags of flowers / I became alone / Open window / July 6th / Pram / Canadien errant.

—— guests:- **ALEX CHILTON, MARY MARGARET O'HARA, ANDREW CASE, BOB WISEMAN, SCOTT MILLER, DAVID KANE, JOANNE RAMSEY + BUCK**

Mar 93. (cd) *<(RCD 10259)>* **THE WEEDKILLER'S DAUGHTER** ☐ ☐
– Two worlds parted / Angels of stone / Your return / Clare's scarf / Cemetery ridge / Nightfall / I wanted you / One step backward / Fly me to the north / Clouds of reason / Maid of mist / Poor murdered woman.

TEN YEARS AFTER

Formed: Nottingham, England ... summer '65 (originally as covers act The JAYBIRDS in 1961) by ALVIN LEE (vocals and guitar) and LEO LYONS (bass). The following year, they relocated to London, recruiting RIC LEE (drums) and CHICK CHURCHILL (keyboards) and adopting the name, TEN YEARS AFTER. A key forerunner of the forthcoming British blues revival (i.e. FLEETWOOD MAC, CHICKEN, SAVOY BROWN, etc.), LEE, known for his nimble fingered, lightning strike guitar playing, secured a deal (through manager, Chris Wright) with Decca offshoot label, 'Deram'. An eponymous debut set was released in '67, although the prevailing trend for for everything flower-power ensured the record met with limited interest. Building up a strong grassroots following through electric stage shows, TEN YEARS AFTER took a calculated risk by releasing a live set recorded at Klook's Kleek, 'UNDEAD' (1968), the album rewarding TYA with a Top 30 breakthrough. Early in '69, they released a third set, 'STONEDHENGE', a surprise Top 10 success (the record also saw them crack the American market) that included their best piece to date, 'HEAR ME CALLING'. To coincide with a forthcoming Woodstock appearance, the band delivered their second set of the year, 'SSSSH', not exactly a hush hush affair but a blistering melange of blues, boogie and country that became the first of three consecutive UK Top 5 albums (US Top 20, well nearly!). LEE's celebrated performance of the epic 11 minute track 'GOIN' HOME' at the aforesaid Woodstock Festival went down in rock history, thrusting the band into the premier league of blues rock acts (the song featured on the subsequent film and soundtrack). The band blazed their way through the early 70's on albums, 'CRICKLEWOOD GREEN' and 'WATT', the former spawning a UK Top 10 hit, 'LOVE LIKE A MAN' in 1970. A subsequent change of both label ('Chrysalis') and music style (following the prevailing trend for electronic progressive rock) for late '71's 'A SPACE IN TIME', saw the band losing substantial ground (critically and commercially). However, due to a Top 40 hit, 'I'D LOVE TO CHANGE THE WORLD', the album still maintained Top 20 status in the US. The ensuing few years saw TEN YEARS AFTER treading water, albums such as 'ROCK & ROLL MUSIC TO THE WORLD' (1972), 'TEN YEARS AFTER (RECORDED LIVE)' (1973) and 'POSITIVE VIBRATIONS' (1974) poor reflections of his/their former achievements. It was clear by the last of these that LEE was eager to experiment outside the band framework, a 1973 collaborative project with US gospel singer, MYLON LeFEVRE, resulting in 'ON THE ROAD TO FREEDOM'. The guitarist then formed a new outfit, ALVIN LEE & CO., releasing a handful of unconvincing albums in the mid 70's. From that point on, LEE alternated between various solo incarnations until 1989 (after a trial at a 4-day German festival the previous year), he reformed a revamped TEN YEARS AFTER for a one-off album, appropriately titled, 'ABOUT TIME'. LEE continues to spread the blues gospel to an ever faithful band of ageing worldwide disciples. • **Songwriters:** Apart from basic covers act The JAYBIRDS, ALVIN LEE penned and co-wrote with STEVE GOULD in the 80's. Covered; HELP ME (Sonny Boy Williamson) / SPOONFUL (Willie Dixon) / AT THE WOODCHOPPER'S BALL (Woody Herman) / SWEET LITTLE SIXTEEN (Chuck Berry) / GOOD MORNING LITTLE SCHOOLGIRL (Don & Bob) / GOING BACK TO BIRMINGHAM (Little Richard) / etc.

Album rating: TEN YEARS AFTER (*6) / UNDEAD (*7) / STONEDHENGE (*6) / SSSSH (*7) / CRICKLEWOOD GREEN (*7) / WATT (*6) / A SPACE IN TIME (*5) / ALVIN LEE & COMPANY compilation (*6) / ROCK'N'ROLL MUSIC TO THE WORLD (*4) / RECORDED LIVE (*4) / ON THE ROAD TO FREEDOM (*4; by Alvin Lee & Mylon LeFevre) / POSITIVE VIBRATIONS (*4) / IN FLIGHT (*4; by Alvin Lee & Co.) / GOIN' HOME! THEIR GREATEST HITS compilation (*7) / PUMP IRON! (*5; by Alvin Lee & Co.) / LET IT ROCK (*4; by Alvin Lee) / ROCKET FUEL (*4; by Alvin Lee – Ten Years Later) / RIDE ON (*4; Alvin Lee – Ten Years Later) / FREE FALL (*4; by Alvin Lee Band) / RX5 (*3; by Alvin Lee Band) / DETROIT DIESEL (*4; by Alvin Lee) / ZOOM (*5) / ABOUT TIME (*5) / THE ESSENTIAL TEN YEARS AFTER compilation (*7) / NINETEEN NINETY FOUR (*4; by Alvin Lee) / I HEAR YOU ROCKIN' (*3; by Alvin Lee) / LIVE IN VIENNA (*3; by Alvin Lee) / PURE BLUES (*4; by Alvin Lee & Ten Years After)

JAYBIRDS

ALVIN LEE – vocals, guitar / **LEO LYONS** – bass / **DAVE QUICKMIRE** – drums

			Embassy	not iss.
Jan 64.	(7") *(WB 621)*	**NOT FADE AWAY. / OVER YOU**	☐	-
Feb 64.	(7") *(WB 624)*	**TELL ME WHEN. / YOU CAN'T DO THAT**	☐	-
Mar 64.	(7") *(WB 625)*	**CAN'T BUY ME LOVE. / Del Martin: I LOVE YOU BECAUSE**	☐	-
Apr 64.	(7") *(WB 626)*	**GOOD GOLLY MISS MOLLY. / WORLD WITHOUT LOVE**	☐	-
May 64.	(7") *(WB 628)*	**MOCKIN' BIRD HILL. / HUBBLE BUBBLE (TOIL AND TROUBLE)**	☐	-
May 64.	(7") *(WB 632)*	**BABY LET ME TAKE YOU HOME. / Bud Ashton & His Group: RISE AND FALL OF FINGEL BLUNT**	☐	-
Jun 64.	(7") *(WB 635)*	**JULIET. / HERE I GO AGAIN**	☐	-
Jul 64.	(7") *(WB 645)*	**SOMEDAY WE'RE GONNA LOVE AGAIN. / Ray Pilgrim & The Beatmen: KISSIN' COUSINS**	☐	-
Aug 64.	(7") *(WB 651)*	**SHE'S NOT THERE. / Paul Rich: I WOULDN'T TRADE YOU FOR THE WORLD**	☐	-
Oct 64.	(7") *(WB 663)*	**ALL DAY & ALL OF THE NIGHT. / GOOGLE EYE**	☐	-
Dec 64.	(7") *(WB 672)*	**WHAT HAVE THEY DONE TO THE RAIN. / Bud Ashton & His Group: GENIE WITH THE LIGHT BROWN LAMP**	☐	-
Jan 65.	(7") *(WB 673)*	**GO NOW. / Terry Brandon: FERRY 'CROSS THE MERSEY**	☐	-

TEN YEARS AFTER

—— (Aug'65) **ALVIN** (b. GRAHAM BARNES, 19 Dec'44) – vocals, guitar + **LEO** (b.30 Nov'43, Bedfordshire) – bass; recruited **RIC LEE** (b.20 Oct'45, Cannock, England) – drums (ex-MANSFIELDS), repl. JAYBIRDS drummer DAVE QUIGMIRE

—— added **CHICK CHURCHILL** (b. 2 Jan'49, Mold, Wales) – keyboards

			Deram	Deram
Oct 67.	(lp; mono/stereo) *(DML/SML 1015) <18009>*	**TEN YEARS AFTER**	☐	☐

– I want to know / I can't keep from crying sometimes / Adventures of a young organ / Spoonful / Losing the dogs / Feel it for me / Love until I die / Don't want you woman / Help me. *(cd-iss. May88; 820 532-2)*

Feb 68.	(7") *(DM 176) <85027>*	**PORTABLE PEOPLE. / THE SOUNDS**		
Aug 68.	(lp; mono/stereo) *(DML/SML 1023) <18016>*	**UNDEAD (live at Klook's Kleek)**		26

– I may be wrong, but I won't be wrong always / Woodchopper's ball / Spider in my web / Summertime – Shantung cabbage / I'm going home. *(cd-iss. Jun88; 820 533-2)*

Nov 68.	(7") *(DM 221) <85035>*	**HEAR ME CALLING. / I'M GOING HOME**		
Feb 69.	(lp; mono/stereo) *(DML/SML 1029) <18021>*	**STONEDHENGE**	6	61

– Going to try / I can't live without Lydia / Woman trouble / Skoobly-oobly-doobob / Hear me calling / A sad song / Three blind mice / No title / Faro / Speed kills. *(cd-iss. Apr89; 820 534-2) (cd-iss. Jul97 on 'Beat Goes On'; BGOCD 356)*

Aug 69.	(lp) *(SML 1052) <18029>*	**SSSSH**	4	20

– Bad scene / Two time woman / Stoned woman / Good morning little schoolgirl / If you should love me / I don't know that you don't know my name / The stomp / I woke up this morning. *(re-iss. Jul75 on 'Chrysalis' lp/c; CHR/ZCHR 1083) (cd-iss. Mar94 on 'Chrysalis'; CD25CR 05) (cd re-iss. Feb97 on 'Beat Goes On'; BGOCD 338)*

Apr 70.	(lp) *(SML 1065) <18038>*	**CRICKLEWOOD GREEN**	4	14

– Sugar the road / Working on the road / 50,000 miles beneath my brain / Year 3,000 blues / Me and my baby / Love like a man / Circles / As the sun still burns away. *(re-iss. Jul75 on 'Chrysalis' lp/c; CHR/ZCHR 1084) (re-iss. Dec92 on 'Fame' cd/c; CD/TC FA 3287) (re-iss. Jul94 cd/c; CD/TC CHR 1084)*

May 70.	(7") *(DM 299) <7529>*	**LOVE LIKE A MAN. / LOVE LIKE A MAN (live at 33 rpm)**	10	98

(re-iss. while still into UK chart run; DM 310)

Jan 71.	(lp) *(SML 1078) <18050>*	**WATT**	5	21

– I'm coming on / My baby left me / Think about the times / I say yeah / The band with no name / Gonna run / She lies in the morning / Sweet little sixteen. *(re-iss. Jul75 on 'Chrysalis' lp/c; CHR/ZCHR 1085) (cd-iss. Apr97 on 'Beat Goes On'; BGOCD 345)*

			Chrysalis	Columbia
Nov 71.	(lp/c) *(CHR/ZCHR 1001) <30801>*	**A SPACE IN TIME**	36	17 Aug71

– One of these days / Here they come / I'd love to change the world / Over the hill / Baby won't you let me rock'n'roll you / Once there was a time / Let the sky fall / Hard monkeys / I've been there too / Uncle Jam. *(cd-iss. Jun97 on 'Beat Goes On'; BGOCD 351)*

Sep 71.	(7") *<45457>*	**I'D LOVE TO CHANGE THE WORLD. / LET THE SKY FALL**	-	40
Jan 72.	(7") *<45530>*	**BABY WON'T YOU LET ME ROCK'N'ROLL YOU. / ONCE THERE WAS A TIME**	-	61
Oct 72.	(lp/c) *(CHR/ZCHR 1009) <31779>*	**ROCK & ROLL MUSIC TO THE WORLD**	27	43

– You give me loving / Convention prevention / Turned off T.V. blues / Standing at the station / You can't win them all / Religion / Choo choo mama / Tomorrow I'll be out of town / Rock & roll music to the world. *(cd-iss. May97 on 'Beat Goes On'; BGOCD 348)*

Nov 72.	(7") *<45736>*	**CHOO CHOO MAMA. / YOU CAN'T WIN THEM ALL**	-	89
Feb 73.	(7") *<45787>*	**TOMORROW, I'LL BE OUT OF TOWN. / CONVENTION PREVENTION**	-	☐
Jul 73.	(7") *<45915>*	**I'M GOING HOME. / YOU GIVE ME LOVING**	-	☐
Jul 73.	(d-lp/d-c) *(CTY/ZCTY 1049) <32288>*	**TEN YEARS AFTER (RECORDED LIVE)**	36	39 Jun73

– One of these days / You give me loving / Good morning little schoolgirl / Hobbit / Help me / Classical thing / Scat thing / I can't keep from cryin' sometimes (part 1) / Extension on one chord / I can't keep from cryin' sometimes (part 2) / Silly thing / Slow blues in 'C' / I'm going home / Choo choo mama. *(cd-iss. Apr97 on 'Beat Goes On'; BGOCD 341)*

Apr 74.	(lp) *(CHR 1060) <32851>*	**POSITIVE VIBRATIONS**	☐	81

– Nowhere to run / Positive vibrations / Stone me / Without you / Going back to Birmingham / It's getting harder / You're driving me crazy / Look into my life / Look me straight into the eyes / I wanted to boogie.

Apr 74. (7") <46061> **I WANTED TO BOOGIE. / IT'S GETTING HARDER** | - | |

—— Disbanded after CHICK CHURCHILL made a solo album 'YOU AND ME' in Feb'74 (CHR 1051).

ALVIN LEE & MYLON LeFEVRE

with the US solo gospel singer plus TRAFFIC members on session plus GEORGE HARRISON and RON WOOD
Nov 73. (7") <45987> **SO SAD. / RIFFIN** | - | |
Nov 73. (lp) (CHR 1054) <32729> **ON THE ROAD TO FREEDOM** | | |
– On the road to freedom / The world is changing / So sad (no love of his own) / Fallen angel / Funny / We will shine / Carry me load / Lay me back / Let 'em say what they will / I can't take it / Riffin / Rockin' til the sun goes down.
Jan 74. (7") (CHS 2020) **THE WORLD IS CHANGING. / RIFFIN** | | |

ALVIN LEE & CO.

with **NEIL HUBBARD** – guitar / **ALAN SPENNER** – bass / **TIM HINKLEY** – keyboards / **IAN WALLACE** – drums / **MEL COLLINS** – saxophone
Nov 74. (d-lp) (CTY 1069) <33187> **ALVIN LEE & CO: IN FLIGHT (live gig)** | | 65 |
– (intro) / Let's get back / Ride my train / There's a feeling / Running around / Mystery train / Slow down / Keep a knocking / How many times / I've got my eyes for you baby / I'm writing you a letter / Got to keep moving / Going through the door / Don't be cruel / Money honey / I'm writing you a letter / You need love love love / Freedom for the stallion / Every blues you've ever heard / All life's trials.

touring band HINKLEY / **ANDY PYLE** – bass / **BRYSON GRAHAM** – drums / studio **RONNIE LEAHY** – keyboards / **STEVE THOMPSON** – bass / **IAN WALLACE** – drums
Oct 75. (lp) (CHR 1094) <33796> **PUMP IRON!** | | Sep75 |
– One more chance / Try to be righteous / You told me / Have mercy / Julian Rice / Time and space / Burnt fungus / The darkest night / It's alright now / Truckin' down the other way / Let the sea burn down.

—— An album 'SAGUITAR' was shelved in 1976.
Dec 78. (lp/c; ALVIN LEE) (CHR/ZCHR 1190) **LET IT ROCK** | | - |
– Chemicals, chemistry, mystery & more / Love the way you rock me / Ain't nobody / Images shifting / Little boy / Downhill lady racer / World is spinning faster / Through with your lovin' / Time to mediate / Let it rock.

ALVIN LEE – TEN YEARS LATER

with **TOM COMPTON** – drums / **MICK HAWKSWORTH** – bass (ex-ANDROMEDA)

			Polydor	R.S.O.
Apr 78. (lp) (2344 103) <3033> **ROCKET FUEL** | | |
– Rocket fuel / Gonna turn you on / Friday the 13th / Somebody's calling me / Ain't nothin' shakin' / Alvin's blue thing / Baby don't you cry / The Devil's screaming.
Sep 79. (lp) (2310 678) <3049> **RIDE ON (live studio)** | | May79 |
– Ain't nothin' shakin' / Scat encounter / Hey Joe / Going home / Too much / It's a gaz / Ride on cowboy / Sitin' here / Can't sleep at nite.
Sep 79. (7") (2001 930) **RIDE ON COWBOY. / SITTIN' HERE** | | - |
Sep 79. (7") **RIDE ON COWBOY. / CAN'T SLEEP AT NITE** | - | |

ALVIN LEE BAND

—— retained **COMPTON** and added **STEVE GOULD** – guitar (ex-RARE BIRD) / **MICKEY FEAT** – bass (ex-STREETWALKERS)

			Avatar	Atlantic
Oct 80. (lp) (AALP 5002) **FREE FALL** | | |
– I don't wanna stop / Take the money / One lonely hour / Heartache / Stealin' / Ridin' truckin' / No more lonely nights / City lights / Sooner or later / Dustbin city.
Nov 80. (7") (AAA 106) **I DON'T WANNA STOP. / HEARTACHE** | | |
Mar 81. (7") **RIDIN' TRUCKIN'. /** | | - |
Jul 81. (7") (AAA 109) **TAKE THE MONEY. / NO MORE LONELY NIGHTS** | | |
Oct 81. (7") **CAN'T STOP. /** | | |
Nov 81. (lp) (AALP 5006) <19306> **RX5** | | |
– Hang on / Lady luck / Can't stop / Wrong side of the law / Nutbush city limits / Rock-n roll guitar picker / Double loser / Fool no more / Dangerous world / High times.
Dec 81. (7") (AAA 117) **ROCK'N'ROLL GUITAR PICKER. / DANGEROUS WORLD** | | |
Mar 82. (7") (AAA 122) **NUTBUSH CITY LIMITS. / HIGH TIMES** | | |

—— **MICK TAYLOR** – guitar (ex-ROLLING STONES) / **FUZZY SAMUELS** – bass (ex-CROSBY, STILLS & NASH) repl. GOULD & FEAT. Split early 1982.

ALVIN LEE

recorded another solo with **LYONS + GEORGE HARRISON**

			Viceroy	21 records
Aug 86. (cd) (VIN 8032-2) <210019> **DETROIT DIESEL** | | Feb87 |
– Detroit diesel / Shot in the dark / Too late to run for cover / Talk don't bother me / Ordinary man / Heart of stone / She's so cute / Back in my arms again / Don't want to fight / Let's go. (cd-iss. Apr97 on 'Viceroy'; same)
Sep 86. (7") **DETROIT DIESEL. / LET'S GO** | | |
Jan 87. (7") **HEART OF STONE. / SHE'S SO CUTE** | | |

—— Signed to 'No Speak' records, but had no releases. In Apr'89, ALVIN guested on Various Artists live cd,c,-d-lp 'NIGHT OF THE GUITAR' for 'I.R.S.' label.

TEN YEARS AFTER

originals re-formed with **ALVIN LEE + STEVE GOULD** plus?

			Chrysalis	Chrysalis
Nov 89. (lp/c/cd) (CHR/ZCHR/CCD 1722) <21722> **ABOUT TIME** | | |

– Highway of love / Let's shake it up / I get all shook up / Victim of circumstance / Going to Chicago / Wild is the river / Saturday night / Bad blood / Working in a parking lot / Outside my window / Waiting for the judgement day.
Nov 89. (7") (CHS 3447) **HIGHWAY OF LOVE. / ROCK & ROLL MUSIC TO THE WORLD** | | |

ALVIN LEE

			Sequel	Domino
Oct 92. (cd/c) (NED CD/MC 225) **ZOOM** | | |
– A little bit of love / Jenny Jenny / Remember me / Anything for you / The price of this love / Real life blues / It don't come easy / Lost in love / Wake up moma / Moving the blues / Use that power. (re-iss. Oct95 on 'Thunderbolt' cd)(c; CDTB 171)(CTC 0201)

			H.T.D.	not iss.
Oct 93. (cd/c) (HTD CD/MC 14) **NINETEEN NINETY FOUR** | | |
– Keep on rockin' / Long legs / I hear you knockin' / I want you (she's so heavy) / I don't give a damn / Give me your love / Play it like it used to be / Take it easy / My baby's come back to me / Boogie all day / Bluest blues / Ain't nobody's business if I do. (cd re-iss. Mar95 on 'Thunderbolt'; CDTB 150)

			Viceroy	Viceroy
Mar 94. (cd) (VIC 8012-2) **I HEAR YOU ROCKIN'** | | |
(re-iss. Apr97; same)

			Coast To Coast	not iss.
Mar 95. (cd) (CTC 0201) **LIVE IN VIENNA (live)** | | - |
– Keep on rockin' / Long legs / I hear you knockin' / Hear me calling / Love like a man / Johnny B.Goode / I don't give a damn / Good morning little schoolgirl / Skooboly oobly dooboob / Help me baby / Classical thing / Going home / Rip it up. (re-iss. Apr97 on 'Viceroy'; VIC 80302)

ALVIN LEE & TEN YEARS AFTER

			Chrysalis	Chrysalis
Jul 95. (cd/c) (CD/TC CHR 6102) **PURE BLUES** | | |
– Don't want you woman / Bluest blues / I woke up this morning / Real life blues / Stomp / Slow blues in 'C' / Wake up moma / Talk don't bother me / Every blues you've ever heard / I get all shook up / Lost in love / Help me / Outside my window.

—— Aug'95, ALVIN was credited on GUITAR CRUSHER cd 'MESSAGE TO MAN' on 'In-Akustik'; INAK 9034

– compilations, others, etc. –

Mar 72. (lp/c; by ALVIN LEE) Deram; (SML/KSCM 1096) **ALVIN LEE & COMPANY** | | 55 |
– The sounds / Rock your mama / Hold me tight / Standing at the crossroads / Portable people / Boogie on. (cd-iss. Jan89; 820 566-2)
Aug 75. (lp/c) Chrysalis; (CHR/ZCHR 1077) / Deram; <18072> **GOIN' HOME – THEIR GREATEST HITS** | | Jul75 |
Sep 76. (lp/c) Chrysalis; (CHR/ZCHR 1107) **ANTHOLOGY** | | |
Feb 77. (lp/c) Chrysalis; (CHR/ZCHR 1134) **THE CLASSIC PERFORMANCES OF . . .** | | |
(cd-iss. 1987; CCD 1134)
Feb 79. (c) Teldec; (CP4 22436) **GREATEST HITS VOL.1** | | - |
Feb 79. (c) Teldec; (CP4 23252) GREATEST HITS VOL.2 | | - |
May 80. (lp/c) Hallmark; (SHM/HSC 3038) **TEN YEARS AFTER** | | - |
Mar 81. (lp) Decca; (TAB 12) **HEAR ME CALLING** | | - |
Oct 83. (7") Old Gold; (OG 9342) **LOVE LIKE A MAN. / (B-side by THEM)** | | - |
Nov 85. (d-lp/c) Castle; (CCS LP/MC 115) **THE COLLECTION** | | - |
– Hear me calling / No title / Spoonful / I can't keep from crying sometimes / Standing at the crossroads / Portable people / Rock your mama / Love like a man / I want to know / Speed kills / Boogie on / I may be wrong but I won't be wrong always / At the woodchopper's ball / Spider in your web / Summertime / Shantung cabbage / I'm going home. (re-iss. Jul91 cd/c; CCS CD/MC 293) (cd re-iss. Aug95 on 'Griffin';)
Feb 87. (lp) See For Miles; (SEE 80) **ORIGINAL RECORDINGS: VOL.1** | | - |
Jun 87. (lp) See For Miles; (SEE 90) **ORIGINAL RECORDINGS: VOL.2** | | - |
(cd-iss. Nov93; SEECD 387)
May 88. (d-lp/c/cd) Chrysalis; (CHR/ZCHR/MPCD 1639) **PORTFOLIO** | | - |
Dec 90. (cd/c/lp) Raw Fruit; (FRS CD/MC/LP 003) **LIVE AT READING 1983 (live)** | | - |
Oct 92. (cd/c) Chrysalis; (CD/TC CHR 1857) **THE ESSENTIAL TEN YEARS AFTER** | | - |
Jul 93. (cd) Code 90; (NINETY 3) **LIVE (live)** | | - |
Sep 93. (cd) Traditional Line; (TL 001327) **LOVE LIKE A MAN** | | - |
Mar 95. (cd; by ALVIN LEE) Magnum; (MMGV 064) **RETROSPECTIVE** | | - |
Nov 95. (3xcd-box) Chrysalis; (CDOMB 011) **CRICKLEWOOD GREEN / WATT / A SPACE IN TIME** | | - |

TERMINATOR X (see under ⇒ PUBLIC ENEMY)

TERRAPLANE (see under ⇒ THUNDER)

TERRORVISION

Formed: Bradford, England . . . August 1990 as The SPOILT BRATZ, by TONY WRIGHT, MARK YATES, LEIGH MARKLEW and SHUTTY, who, after locating manager Al Rhodes, changed their moniker to TERRORVISION (taking the name from an obscure 60's B-movie). Signed to 'E.M.I.' on the strength of a demo, they persuaded the company to furnish them with their very own imprint, 'Total Vegas', subsequently debuting with the 'THRIVE EP' early in '92. Melding disparate metal influences into a sticky sweet pop assault,

TERRORVISION were akin to THERAPY? and CHEAP TRICK fighting it out in a bouncy castle (fans included?!). A series of singles and a debut album, 'FORMALDEHYDE' (1992/93), failed to launch them into superstardom just yet, although one track, 'NEW POLICY ONE' gave them their first taste of the Top 50. Their first single of '94, 'MY HOUSE' (originally a flop in '92), fared a lot better (Top 30) and the accompanying GIL NORTON-produced album, 'HOW TO MAKE FRIENDS AND INFLUENCE PEOPLE' became a regular fixture in the charts over the coming year. In addition, TERRORVISION proved themselves to be a remarkably consistent singles outfit, five Top 30 smashes, 'OBLIVION', 'MIDDLEMAN', 'PRETEND BEST FRIEND', 'ALICE WHAT'S THE MATTER' and 'SOME PEOPLE SAY' all lifted from the album. Festival stalwarts, the "wacky" quartet took every opportunity to frequent the summer circuit, frontman WRIGHT a manic ball of energy and a dependably entertaining live bet. In 1996, the Kerrang! darlings were back, wreaking chart havoc with a Top 5 single, 'PERSEVERANCE' (perhaps a reference to the horror of festival bogs!) and a Top 10 album, 'REGULAR URBAN SURVIVORS'. Two Top 20 tracks, 'CELEBRITY HIT LIST' and 'BAD ACTRESS', ensured TERRORVISION remained in the public eye, WRIGHT becoming a bit of a lad while guesting in a TV quiz show hosted by Mark Lamaar, 'Never Mind The Bollocks'. 'SHAVING PEACHES' was next up for the tongue-n-cheeky Northerners, the 1998 album was a tad disappointing although it did contain the original version of No.2 hit, 'TEQUILA' – the band had now invented a pub-dance singalong number! (were SPLODGENESSABOUNDS the last group to do so?). • **Covered:** PSYCHO KILLER (Talking Heads) / THE MODEL (Kraftwerk) / THE PASSENGER (Iggy Pop) / SURRENDER (Cheap Trick) / WISHING WELL (Free) / I'LL BE YOUR SISTER (Chris Bell) / YOU'VE REALLY GOT A HOLD OF ME (Smokey Robinson) / MOONAGE DAYDREAM (David Bowie).

Album rating: FORMALDEHYDE (*7) / HOW TO MAKE FRIENDS AND INFLUENCE PEOPLE (*8) / REGULAR URBAN SURVIVORS (*6) / SHAVING PEACHES (*5)

TONY WRIGHT (b. 6 May'68) – vocals / **MARK YATES** (b. 4 Apr'68) – guitars / **LEIGH MARKLEW** (b.10 Aug'68) – bass / **SHUTTY** (b.20 Mar'67) – drums

	Total Vegas	E.M.I.
Feb 92. (12"ep/cd-ep) (12/CD VEGAS 1) **THRIVE EP**		-
– Urban space crime / Jason / Blackbird / Pain reliever.		
Oct 92. (7") (VEGAS 2) **MY HOUSE. / COMING UP**		-
(12"+=/cd-s+=) (12/CD VEGAS 2) – Tea dance.		
Dec 92. (cd/c/green-lp) (ATVR CD/MC/LP 1) **FORMALDEHYDE**		-
– Problem solved / Ships that sink / New policy one / Jason / Killing time / Urban space crime / Hole for a soul / Don't shoot my dog / Desolation town / My house / Human being / Pain reliever / Tea dance. (re-iss. May93 cd/s-cd/c/lp; VEGAS CD/CDS/MC/LP 1) (w/out last 2 tracks, hit UK No.75)		
Jan 93. (12"ep/cd-ep) (12/CD ATVR 1) **PROBLEM SOLVED / CORPSE FLY. / WE ARE THE ROADCREW / SAILING HOME**		-
Jun 93. (12"ep/12"ep w-poster) (12/12P VEGAS 3) **AMERICAN T.V. / DON'T SHOOT MY DOG AGAIN / KILLING TIME**	63	-
(cd-ep) (CDVEGAS 3) – ('A'side) / Psycho killer / Hole for a soul.		
Oct 93. (7"green) (VEGAS 4) **NEW POLICY ONE. / PAIN RELIEVER (live)**	42	
(12"/12"w poster) (12 VEGAS/+SP 4) – ('A'side) / Ships that sink (live) / Problem solved (live).		
(cd-s) (CDVEGAS 4) – ('A'side) / Psycho killer (live) / Tea dance (live) / My house (live).		
(cd-s) (CDVEGASS 4) – ('A'side) / American TV (live) / New policy one (live) / Still the rhythm (live).		
Jan 94. (7"green) (VEGAS 5) **MY HOUSE. / TEA DANCE**	29	
(12") (12VEGAS 5) – ('A'side) / ('A'machete mix) / Psycho killer (extended mix).		
(cd-s) (CDVEGAS 5) – ('A'-Attic mix) / Down under / ('A'Machete mix).		
(cd-s) (CDVEGASS 5) – ('A'side) / Discotheque wreck / ('A'-Machete mix).		
Mar 94. (7") (VEGAS 6) **OBLIVION (mix). / WHAT DO YOU DO THAT FOR?**	21	
(cd-s+=) (CDVEGAS 6) – Problem solved (by DIE CHEERLEADER) / Oblivion (demo).		
(cd-s) (CDVEGASS 6) – ('A'side) / The model (with DIE CHEERLEADER) / Remember Zelda (written by DIE CHEERLEADER).		
(12") (12VEGAS 6) – (above 3) / Problem solved (by DIE CHEERLEADER).		
Apr 94. (cd/c/lp/s-lp) (VEGAS CD/MC/LP/LPX 2) **HOW TO MAKE FRIENDS AND INFLUENCE PEOPLE**	18	
– Alice what's the matter / Oblivion / Stop this bus / Discotheque wreck / Middleman / Still the rhythm / Ten shades of grey / Stab in the back / Pretend best friend / Time o the signs / What the doctor ordered / Some people say / What makes you tick.		
Jun 94. (c-s) (TCVEGAS 7) **MIDDLEMAN / OBLIVION**	25	
(12"copper/cd-s) (12/CD VEGAS 7) – ('A'side) / Surrender / The passenger.		
(cd-s) (CDVEGASS 7) – ('A'side) / I'll be your sister / Wishing well.		
Aug 94. (c-s) (TCVEGAS 8) **PRETEND BEST FRIEND / MIDDLEMAN (live)**	25	
(12") (12VEGAS 8) – ('A'side) / Alice what's the matter (live) / Stop the bus (live) / Discotheque wreck (live).		
(cd-s) (CDVEGAS 8) – ('A'side) / Time o' the signs (live) / Oblivion (live) / ('A'-Danny Does Vegas mix).		
(cd-s) (CDVEGASS 8) – ('A'side) / What makes you tick (live) / Still the rhythm (live) / ('A'-Alice pretends mix).		
Oct 94. (c-s) (TCVEGAS 9) **ALICE, WHAT'S THE MATTER (oh yeah mix) / SUFFOCATION**	24	
(12") (12VEGAS 9) – ('A'-Junkie J mix) / ('B'side) / ('A'-Psycho bitch mix) / ('A'-All Carmen on the Western Front).		
(cd-s) (CDVEGAS 9) – ('A'side) / Psycho killer (acoustic) / ('A'-Kill your Terrorvision mix) / What shall we do with the drunken sailor?		
(cd-s) (CDVEGASS 9) – ('A'side) / ('A'-Junkie J mix) / Discotheque wreck (acoustic) / ('A'demo).		

	Total Vegas	E.M.I.
Mar 95. (7"/c-s) (VEGAS/TCVEGAS 10) **SOME PEOPLE SAY. / MR. BUSKERMAN / OBLIVION**	22	
(cd-s) (CDVEGAS 10) – ('A'side) / This drinking will kill me / ('A'-Oblivious mix) / Oblivion.		
(cd-s) (CDVEGASS 10) – ('A'side) / Blood on my wheels / ('A'extended) / Oblivion.		
Feb 96. (7"blue) (VEGAS 11) **PERSEVERANCE. / WAKE UP**	5	
(cd-s+=) (CDVEGAS 11) – What goes around comes around.		
(cd-s) (CDVEGASS 11) – ('A'side) / Sick and tired / Hard to feel.		
Mar 96. (cd/c/lp) (VEGAS CD/TC/LP 3) **REGULAR URBAN SURVIVORS**	8	
– Enteralterego / Superchronic / Perseverance / Easy / Hide the dead girl / Conspiracy / Didn't bleed red / Dog chewed the handle / Junior / Bad actress / If I was you / Celebrity hit list / Mugwump.		
Apr 96. (c-s) (TCVEGAS 12) **CELEBRITY HIT LIST / YOU REALLY GOT A HOLD ON ME**	20	
(cd-s+=) (CDVEGAS 12) – Tom Petty loves Veruca Salt.		
(cd-s) (CDVEGASS 12) – ('A'side) / Don't come here / Crossed line on the grapevine.		
Jul 96. (12"ep) (12VEGAS 13) **BAD ACTRESS / TOO STONED TO DANCE (un-do-able handbag mix). / CONSPIRACY (hexadecimal dub) / CONSPIRACY (hexadecimal mix)**	10	
(cd-s) (CDVEGAS 13) – ('A'side) / Fobbed off / Too stoned to dance / Bad actress (alternative strings).		
(cd-s) (CDVEGASS 13) – ('A'side) / Oblivion / Middleman / Funny feels fine.		
Jan 97. (10"clear-ep) (10VEGAS 14) **EASY / EASY (live). / CELEBRITY HIT LIST (live) / SOME PEOPLE SAY (live)**	12	
(cd-ep) (CDVEGAS 14) – ('A'side) / Middleman (live) / My house (live) / Bad actress (live).		
(cd-ep) (CDVEGASS 14) – ('A'side) / Discotheque wreck (live) / Pretend best friend (live) / Enteralterego (live).		
Sep 98. (7") (VEGAS 15) **JOSEPHINE. / REASONS TO DECEIVE**	23	
(cd-s+=) (CDVEGAS 15) – Go Jerry.		
(cd-s) (CDVEGASS 15) – ('A'side) / Falling down / 28 hours.		
Oct 98. (cd/c) (496132-2/-4) **SHAVING PEACHES**	34	
– III wishes / Josephine / Hypnotised / Can't get you out of my mind / In your shoes / Swings and roundabouts / Day after day / Left to the right / Cantankerous / Tequila / Vegas / Babyface / Spanner in the works / When I die / On a mission. (cd re-iss. Feb99; 499608-2)		
Jan 99. (12"/cd-s) (12/CD VEGAS 16) **TEQUILA (the Mint Royale chaser) / TEQUILA (album version) / TEQUILA (Mint Royale slammer)**	2	
(cd-s) (CDVEGASS 16) – ('A'-Mint Royale shot) / (album version) / Risk worth taking.		
May 99. (c-s) (TCVEGAS 17) **III WISHES / MOONAGE DAYDREAM / TEQUILA (Mint Royale shot mix)**	42	
(cd-s) (CDVEGAS 17) – (first & third tracks) / If that's what it takes.		
(cd-s) (CDVEGASS 17) – ('A'side) / ('A'-Scuba Z remix) / 100 things.		

TESLA (dig out; Great Metal . . .)

TESTAMENT (dig out; Great Metal . . .)

TEXAS

Formed: Glasgow, Scotland . . .1988 by SHARLEEN SPITERI, JOHHNY McELHONE, ALLY McERLAINE and STUART KERR. Initially lumped in with the new wave of young Scottish rock bands tipped for big things (GUN, SLIDE etc.), TEXAS debuted in early '89 with the rootsy pop of 'I DON'T WANT A LOVER', its infectious slide guitar refrain infiltrating the Top 10 but subsequently becoming a millstone round the band's neck as they struggled to shake off the 'one-hit-wonder' tag. The debut album, 'SOUTHSIDE' (1989) was a Top 5 hit nevertheless, a highly listenable set of inoffensive, blues/country-tinged pop/rock which became one of the top selling albums of that year. This was without the help of any further hit singles, both 'THRILL HAS GONE' and 'EVERYDAY NOW' (very reminiscent of BOB DYLAN's 'I Shall Be Released') stalling outside the Top 40. In fact, the group's next major hit single came more than three years later with a cover of Al Green's 'TIRED OF BEING ALONE'. There was certainly no disputing the sensuous beauty and power of SPITERI's voice, or indeed her striking looks and while TEXAS had their critics, they also boasted an extensive grassroots following, especially in their native Scotland where gigs often took on the fervour of religious gatherings. Predictably then, the follow-up set, 'MOTHER'S HEAVEN' (1991), was well received by devotees but failed to convince many waverers. Likewise 'RICK'S ROAD' (1993), an underated set which leant more on the country-rock side of things. With its BYRDS-esque jangle and gorgeous vocal, 'SO CALLED FRIEND' remains one of TEXAS's most affecting moments, though thousands would no doubt disagree. Many of those thousands, in fact, who probably own a copy of 'WHITE ON BLONDE', TEXAS's million selling 1997 album which must surely rank as one of the most incredible commercial turnarounds in the history of rock. Abandoning the roots trappings for a super slick soul-pop sound, TEXAS transformed themselves from yet another flagging Scottish rock band into an international phenomenon. Buoyed by the success of radio-friendly, highly infectious singles like 'SAY WHAT YOU WANT', 'HALO' and 'BLACK EYED BOY', the album was 1997's ultimate coffee table companion. Not only that, SPITERI was seemingly born again as a style mag sex symbol, her ravishing visage staring out from front cover after front cover. Bizarrely enough, among TEXAS's biggest fans were New York's hardest rap crew, The WU TANG CLAN, surely resulting in a rather unlikely pairing (of all-time, quite possibly) on a Top 5 version of 'SAY WHAT YOU WANT (ALL DAY AND EVERY DAY)'. Having already topped the charts with their last album, TEXAS repeated the formula with their follow-up, 'THE HUSH' (1999), a deliberately more sensual set of songs that included three massive hits, 'IN OUR LIFETIME, 'SUMMER SON' and 'WHEN WE ARE TOGETHER'. • Songwriters: SPITERI lyrics / McELHONE music, except SWEET CHILD O' MINE (Guns N' Roses).

Album rating: SOUTHSIDE (*6) / MOTHER'S HEAVEN (*5) / RICK'S ROAD (*5) / WHITE ON BLONDE (*7) / THE HUSH (*7)

SHARLEEN SPITERI (b. 7 Nov'67) – vocals, guitar / ALLY McERLAINE (b. ALISTAIR, 31 Oct'68) – guitar / JOHNNY McELHONE (b.21 Apr'63) – bass, vocals (ex-ALTERED IMAGES, ex-HIPSWAY) / STUART KERR (b.16 Mar'63) – drums (ex-LOVE AND MONEY)

		Mercury	Mercury
Jan 89.	(7") (TEX 1) <872350> I DON'T WANT A LOVER. / BELIEVE ME	8	77

(ext;12"+=/cd-s+=) (TEX 1-12/CD1) – All in vain.

Mar 89.	(lp/c/cd) (<838 171-1/-4/-2>) SOUTHSIDE	3	88

– I don't want a lover / Tell me why / Everyday now / Southside / Prayer for you / Faith / The thrill has gone / Fight the feeling / Fool for love / One choice / Future is promises.

Apr 89.	(7") (TEX 2) THRILL HAS GONE. / NOWHERE LEFT TO HIDE	60	

(12"+=/12"s+=)(cd-s+=) (TEX/+P 2-12)(TEXCD 2) – Dimples.

Jul 89.	(7"/c-s) (TEX/+MC 3) EVERYDAY NOW. / WAITING FOR THE FALL	44	

(12"+=) (TEX 3-12) – Faith.
(cd-s+=) (TEXCD 3) – Future is promises (acoustic) / Food for love (live at Radio Clyde).
(12") (TEXR 3-12) – ('A'live) / Living for the city (live) / It hurts me too (live).

Nov 89.	(7"/c-s) (TEX/+MC 4) PRAYER FOR YOU. / RETURN	73	

(12"+=/cd-s+=) (TEX 4-12/CD4) – I don't want a lover (live) / ('A'-acoustic).
(12"/cd-s) (TEX R/CDR 4-12) – ('A'-Southside & Northside remixes).

Aug 91.	(7"/c-s) (TEX/+MC 5) WHY BELIEVE IN YOU. / HOW IT FEELS	66	

(12"+=/cd-s+=) (TEX 5-12/CD5) – Hold me Lord.
(cd-s) (TEXCB 5) – ('A'side) / Is what I do wrong / Hold me LOrd / Living for the city (live).

Sep 91.	(cd/c/lp) (<848 578-2/-4/-1>) MOTHER'S HEAVEN	32	

– Mother's heaven / Why believe in you / Dream hotel / This will all be mine / Beliefs / Alone with you / In my heart / Waiting / Wrapped in clothes of blue / Return / Walk the dust.

Oct 91.	(7"/c-s) (TEX/+MC 6) IN MY HEART. / IS WHAT I DO WRONG	74	

(12"+=) (TEX 6-12) – Alone with you.
(12"+=/cd-s+=) (TEX 6-12/CD6) – You gave me love / ('A'remix).

Feb 92.	(7"/c-s) (TEX/+MC 7) ALONE WITH YOU. / DOWN IN THE BATTLEFIELD	32	

(cd-s) (TEXCD 7) – ('A'side) / Why believe in you / Everyday now / I don't want a lover.
(cd-s) (TEXCDX 7) – ('A'live) / Can't get next to you (live) / What goes on (live) / Sweet child o' mine (live).

Apr 92.	(7"/c-s) (TEX/+MC 8) TIRED OF BEING ALONE. / WRAPPED IN CLOTHES OF BLUE	19	

(cd-s) (TEXCD 8) – ('A'side) / Thrill has gone / In my heart (12"mix) / Prayer for you (Northside remix).
(cd-s) (TEXCB 8) – ('A'acoustic) / Walk the dust (acoustic) / Why believe in you (acoustic) / Return (acoustic).

—— RICHARD HYND (b.17 May'68, Aberdeen, Scotland) – drums (ex-SLIDE) repl. KERR

—— added EDDIE CAMPBELL (b. 6 Jun'65) – keyboards

		Vertigo	Mercury
Aug 93.	(7"/c-s) (TEX AS/MC 9) SO CALLED FRIEND. / YOU'RE THE ONE I WANT IT FOR	30	

(cd-s+=) (TEXCD 9) – Tonight I stay with you / I've been missing you.
(box;cd-s+=) (TEXCDP 9) – Mother's heaven (French mix) / Tired of being alone.

Oct 93.	(7"/c-s) (TEX AS/MC 10) YOU OWE IT ALL TO ME. / DON'T HELP ME THROUGH	39	

(cd-s+=) (TEXCD 10) – Make me want to scream / Strange that I want you.
(cd-s) (TEXCL 10) – ('A'side) / I don't want a lover (acoustic) / So called friend (acoustic) / Revolution (acoustic).

Nov 93.	(cd/c/lp) (<518 252-2/-4/-1>) RICK'S ROAD	18	

– So called friend / Fade away / Beautiful angel / You owe it all to me / Beautiful angel / So in love with you / You've got to live a little / I want to go to Heaven / Hear me now / Fearing these days / I've been missing you / Winter's end.

Feb 94.	(7"/c-s) (TEX AS/MC 11) SO IN LOVE WITH YOU. / ('A'instrumental)	28	

(cd-s) (TEXCD 11) – ('A'side) / So called friend / One love / You owe it all to me.
(cd-s) (TEXCX 11) – ('A'side) / Why believe in you (live) / Prayer for you (live) / Everyday now (live).

		Mercury	Mercury
Jan 97.	(c-s) (MERMC 480) SAY WHAT YOU WANT / COLD DAY DREAM	3	

(cd-s+=) (MERCD 480) – Tear it up / ('A'-Boilerhouse remix).
(cd-s) (MERDD 480) – ('A'side) / Good advice / ('A'-Rae & Christian mixes).

Feb 97.	(cd/c) (<534 315-2/-4>) WHITE ON BLONDE	1	

– Halo / Say what you want / Drawing crazy patterns / Put your arms around me / Insane / Black eyed boy / Polo mint city / White on blonde / Postcard / Ticket to lie / Good advice.

Apr 97.	(c-s) (MERMC 482) HALO / ASKING FOR FAVOURS	10	

(cd-s+=) (MERCD 482) – Coming down / ('A'-orchestral version).
(cd-s) (MERDD 482) – ('A'side) / ('A'-Rae & Christian mixes) / ('A'-808 mixes).

Aug 97.	(c-s) (MERMC 490) BLACK EYED BOY / FAITHLESS	5	

(cd-s+=) (MERCD 490) – ('A'side) / Sorry / Black eyed disco (disco boy dub mix) / Say what you want (session).
(cd-s) (MERDD 490) – ('A'side) / ('A'-disco/dance mixes).

Nov 97.	(c-s) (MERMC 497) PUT YOUR ARMS AROUND ME / NEVER NEVER	10	

(cd-s+=) (MERCD 497) – You're all I need to get by (session).
(cd-s) (MERDD 497) – ('A'mixes; Two Lone Swordsmen & Ballistic Brothers).

Mar 98.	(c-s; TEXAS featuring WU-TANG) (MERMC 499) SAY WHAT YOU WANT (ALL DAY EVERY DAY) / INSANE	4	

(cd-s+=) (MERCD 499) – Polo mint city (extended) / ('A'-Trailermen mix).
(cd-s) (MERDD 499) – ('A'extended) / ('B'-The econd scroll) / ('A'&'B'-RZA instrumentals & dub versions).
(12") (MERX 499) – ('A'-Trailermen mix) / ('A'-RZA instrumental).

Apr 99.	(c-s) (MERMC 517) IN OUR LIFETIME / LOVE DREAM #2	4	

(cd-s+=) (MERDD 517) – ('A'-enhanced).
(cd-s+=) (MERCD 517) – ('A'side) / ('A'-Jules disco trip mix) / ('A'-Return To Tha dub mix).

May 99.	(cd/c) (<538 972-2/-4>) THE HUSH	1	

– In our lifetime / Tell me the answer / Summer son / Sunday afternoon / Move in / When we are together / Day after day / Zero zero / Saint / Girl / The hush / The day before I went away. (cd hidden+=) – Let us be thankful.

Aug 99.	(c-s) (MERMC 520) SUMMER SON / ('A'-Giorgio Moroder mix)	5	

(cd-s+=) (MERCD 520) – Don't you want me (live).
(cd-s+=) (MERDD 520) – ('A'-Tee's freeze mix).

Nov 99.	(c-s) (MERMC 525) WHEN WE ARE TOGETHER / SAY WHAT YOU WANT (ALL DAY AND EVERY DAY) (live)	12	

(cd-s+=) (MERCD 525) – In our lifetime (live) / ('A'-video).
(cd-s) (MERDD 525) – ('A'mixes) / Summer son (Euro bootleg).

– **compilations, etc. –**

Sep 95.	(d-cd) Vertigo; (528604-2) SOUTHSIDE / RICK'S ROAD		-

---

THAT PETROL EMOTION (dig out; Great Alt & Indie . . .)

THEAUDIENCE

Formed: London, England . . . 1996 by BILLY REEVES (a former press officer for 'Fire' records), who asked delicious posh-piece, SOPHIE ELLIS BEXTOR (daughter of Janet Ellis, a former presenter of children's TV show, 'Blue Peter'!), to join his band. Concocting a style that fused NATALIE MERCHANT-esque vocals with SMITHS-esque backing, the youthful THEAUDIENCE carved their way into the ears of an even greater audience. Their second attempt at the pop charts, 'IF YOU CAN'T DO IT WHEN YOU'RE YOUNG; WHEN CAN YOU DO IT?', dented the Top 50 in early 1998, while their wittily-titled, 'A PESSIMIST IS NEVER DISAPPOINTED', fared even better. A third success, 'I KNOW ENOUGH (I DON'T GET ENOUGH)', preceded their "SOPHIE-sticated" eponymous debut set containing all the aforementioned tunes; REEVES quit the band to write songs for ex-Eastenders babe, MARTINE McCUTCHEON, while forming his own side-project, STARCHILDREN 2021. • Covered: I CAN SEE CLEARLY (Grooveyard) / THERE ARE WORSE THINGS I COULD DO (from 'Grease') / HUNTING HIGH AND LOW (A-Ha).

Album rating: THEAUDIENCE (*5)

SOPHIE ELLIS BEXTOR (b.10 Apr'79) – vocals / BILLY REEVES – guitar / DEE MOLLE – guitar / KERIN SMITH – bass / PATRICK 'PATCH' HANNAN – drums / NYGE BUTLER – keyboards

		elleffe – Mercury	Mercury
Oct 97.	(7") (AUD 1) I GOT THE WHEREWITHALL. / JE SUIS CONTENT		-

(cd-s+=) (AUDCD 1) – ('A'side) / Out of space / Helen and Polly.

Feb 98.	(7"blue) (AUD 2) IF YOU CAN'T DO IT WHEN YOU'RE YOUNG; WHEN CAN YOU DO IT? /	48	-

(cd-s+=) (AUDCD 2) –

May 98.	(7") (AUD 3) A PESSIMIST IS NEVER DISAPPOINTED. / PENIS SIZE AND CARS	27	-

(cd-s+=) (AUDCD 3) – Ne jamais decu / I miss Leo.
(cd-s) (AUDDD 3) – ('A'side) / Ten minutes which improved my life / Never gonna give it to you / I'm always ready.

Jul 98.	(7") (AUD 4) I KNOW ENOUGH (I DON'T GET ENOUGH). /	25	

(cd-s+=) (AUDCD 4) – Don't fetch the water.
(cd-s) (AUDD 4) – ('A'side) / Boutique in my backyard / The last seven minutes with you.

Aug 98.	(cd/c/lp) (558 771-2/-4/-1) THEAUDIENCE	22	

– A pessimist is never disappointed / Now that you are 18 / Mr. Doasyouwouldbedoneby / I know enough (I don't get enough) / Keep in touch / I got the wherewithal / Harry don't fetch the water / If you can't do it when you're young; when can you do it? / Running out of space / You get what you deserve / The more there is to do / Bells for David Keenan / Shoebox song / How's that? (d-cd+=; 558 845-2) – Mr. Doasyouwouldbedoneby (original version) / I know enough (I don't get enough) (original version) / A pessimist is never disappointed (Blah St acoustic version) / Keep in touch (piano version) / I can see clearly (piano version).

—— (late '98) REEVES left the band and concentrated on own project, STARCHILDREN 2021, who released 'FUNKY BUS' on his 'Wedding Reception' label

---

THEM

Formed: Belfast, N.Ireland . . . 1963 by VAN MORRISON, BILLY HARRISON, ALAN HENDERSON, ERIC WRIXEN and RONNIE MELLINGS. After their debut single flopped, producers TOMMY SCOTT and BERT BERNS, recruited session men JIMMY PAGE (future LED ZEPPELIN)

and PETER BARDENS (future CAMEL) to feature on their hot-wired cover of BIG JOE WILLIAMS' 'BABY PLEASE DON'T GO', the single rocketing into the Top 10 in early '65. The B-side, 'GLORIA' was even more primal, a riotous piece of garage that inspired generations of spotty youths to pick up guitars and has subsequently been covered by everyone from The SHADOWS OF KNIGHT to The DOORS and PATTI SMITH. Although the band found it difficult to equal this incredible double shot, their next single, 'HERE COMES THE NIGHT' climbed to No.2 in the UK charts. The eponymous debut album followed later that summer and although it failed to chart, it was a precocious collection of early VAN-penned originals and incendiary covers. Their fame was short-lived though, as successive singles failed to chart and the second album, 'THEM AGAIN' (1966) lacked the consistency of its predecessor. There were occasional flashes of VAN's maverick genius and it was clear he was the lynchpin holding the thing together. When he left to go solo in 1966, the band inevitably split, only to reform a number of times (minus VAN) around differing line-ups, trading on past glories but predictably producing no new material of any great note. • Songwriters: MORRISON penned (until his departure), except HERE COMES THE NIGHT + (IT WON'T HURT) HALF AS MUCH + few early songs (Bert Berns). DON'T START CRYING NOW (Slim Harpo) / BABY PLEASE DON'T GO (Big Joe Williams) / DON'T LOOK BACK (John Lee Hooker) / I PUT A SPELL ON YOU (Screaming Jay Hawkins) / IT'S ALL OVER NOW, BABY BLUE (Bob Dylan), etc.

Album rating: THEM (*7) / THEM AGAIN (*6) / NOW AND THEM (*5) / TIME OUT, TIME IN FOR THEM (*4) / THEM on 'Happy Tiger' (*4) / IN REALITY (*4) / THEM FEATURING VAN MORRISON compilation (*7) / SHUT YOUR MOUTH (*4)

VAN MORRISON (b.GEORGE IVAN, 31 Aug'45) – vocals, harmonica / **BILLY HARRISON** – guitar / **ERIC WRIXEN** – piano, keyboards / **RONNIE MELLINGS** – drums / **ALAN HENDERSON** (b.26 Nov'44) – bass

	Decca	Parrot
Aug 64. (7") (F 11973) <9702> **DON'T START CRYING NOW. / ONE TWO BROWN EYES**	☐	☐

—— **JACKIE McAULEY** – organ + **PATRICK McAULEY** – organ repl. ERIC and RONNIE WRIXEN who joined The WHEELS, while MELLINGS became a milkman.

Dec 64. (7") (F 12018) <9727> **BABY PLEASE DON'T GO. / GLORIA** <US re-dist.Apr66, flipped over; hit 71> (re-iss.Jul73 on 'Deram'; DM 394) (re-iss.May82; F 13923) (re-iss.Oct83 on 'Old Gold'; OG 9341)	10	93	Mar65
Mar 65. (7") (F 12094) <9747> **HERE COMES THE NIGHT. / ALL FOR MYSELF** (re-iss.Sep73 on 'Deram'; DM 400)	2	24	May65
Jun 65. (lp; mono/stereo) (LK 4700) <PS/PAS 6/7 1005> **THEM** – Here comes the night [US only] / Mystic eyes / If you and I could be as two / Little girl / Just a little bit / I gave my love a diamond (UK-only) / Go on home baby / Gloria / You just can't win / Don't look back / I like it like that / Bright lights big city / My little baby [UK-only] / Route 66. (cd-iss. Feb89 on 'London'; 820 563-2)	☐	54	Jul65

above lp featured sessioners **PETER BARDENS** – keyboards + **JIMMY PAGE** – guitar

—— **PETER BARDENS** – keyboards + **JOHN WILSON** (b. 6 Nov'47) – drums now repl. The McAULEY's who formed The BELFAST GYPSIES

Jun 65. (7") (F 12175) **ONE MORE TIME. / HOW LONG BABY?**	☐	☐
Aug 65. (7") (F 12215) <9784> **(IT WON'T HURT) HALF AS MUCH. / I'M GONNA DRESS IN BLACK**	☐	☐
Nov 65. (7") (F 12281) <9796> **MYSTIC EYES. / IF YOU AND I COULD BE AS TWO**	☐	33	Oct65

—— **MORRISON, HENDERSON + WILSON** were joined by **RAY ELLIOTT** (b.13 Sep'43) – piano, sax repl. BARDENS to solo & later CAMEL / **JIM ARMSTRONG** (b.24 Jun'44) – guitar repl. HARRISON

Jan 66. (lp; mono/stereo) (LK 4751) <PS/PAS 6/7 1008> **THEM AGAIN** – Could you would you / Something you got / Call my name / Turn on your love light / I put a spell on you / I can only give you everything / My lonely sad eyes / I got a woman / Out of sight / It's all over now, baby blue / Bad or good / How long baby / Hello Josephine / Don't you know / Hey girl / Bring 'em on in. (cd-iss. Feb89 on 'London'; 820 564-2)	☐	☐
Mar 66. (7") (F 12355) <9819> **CALL MY NAME. / BRING 'EM ON IN**	☐	☐

—— (Jan 66) **TERRY NOONE** – drums repl. WILSON later to TASTE (RORY GALLAGHER) Apr 66, **DAVE HARVEY** – drums repl. NOONE.

May 66. (7") (F 12403) <3003> **RICHARD CORY. / DON'T YOU KNOW**	☐	☐

—— Disbanded mid 1966 when VAN MORRISON went solo. In 1967, they re-formed. **KEN McDOWELL** – vocals repl. him

	Major Minor	not iss.
1967. (7") (MM 509) **GLORIA. / FRIDAY'S CHILD**	☐	–
1967. (7") (MM 513) **THE STORY OF THEM. / (part 2)**	☐	–

	not iss.	Tower-Capitol
Jan 68. (lp) <ST 5104> **NOW AND THEM** – I'm your witch doctor / What's the matter baby / Truth machine / Square room / You're just what I was looking for baby / Dirty old man / At the age of sixteen / Nobody loves you when you're down and out / Walking the Queen's garden / I happen to love you / Come to me. (UK-iss.Dec88 on 'Zap!'; ZAP 6)	–	☐
Feb 68. (7") <384> **WALKING IN THE QUEEN'S GARDEN. / HAPPEN TO LOVE YOU**	–	☐
Apr 68. (7") <407> **SQUARE ROOM. / BUT IT'S ALRIGHT**	–	☐

—— trimmed to a quartet when ELLIOTT departed

Nov 68. (lp) <ST 5116> **TIME OUT! TIME IN FOR THEM** – Time out for time in / She put a hex on you / Bent over you / Waltz of the flees / Black widow spider / We've all agreed to help / Market place / Just one conception / Young woman / The moth. (UK-iss.Dec88 on 'Zap!'; ZAP 7)	–	☐
Nov 68. (7") <461> **WALTZ OF THE FLIES. / WE ALL AGREED TO HELP**	–	☐
Mar 69. (7") <493> **DARK ARE THE SHADOWS. / CORINA**	–	☐

—— added on session **JERRY COLE** – guitar, vocals / **JOHN STARK** – drums (tour) In 1969, ARMSTRONG, ELLIOT, McDOWELL went off to Chicago to form The TRUTH alongside bassman CURTIS BACHMAN and rummer RENO SMITH. An album 'TRUTH OF TRUTHS' surfaced in 1971 for US 'Oak'. In March '95, an exploitation cd 'OF THEM AND OTHER TALES' was released for 'Epilogue' (EPI 003)

	not iss.	Happy Tiger
1970. (lp) <HT 1004> **THEM** – I keep singing / Lonely weekends / Take a little time / You got me good / Jo Ann / Memphis lady / In the midnight hour / Nobody cares / I am waiting / Just a little.	–	☐
1970. (7") <525> **I AM WAITING. / LONELY WEEKENDS**	–	☐
1970. (7") <534> **MEMPHIS LADY. / NOBODY CARES**	–	☐
1971. (lp; as THEM featuring ALAN HENDERSON) <HT 1012> **THEM IN REALITY** – Gloria / Baby please don't go / Laugh / Let my song through / California man / Lessons of the sea / Rayn / Back to the country / Can you believe.	–	☐

—— **THEM** re-formed originals **HENDERSON, HARRISON & WRIXEN + MEL AUSTIN** – vocals / **BILLY BELL** – drums

	Decca	not iss.
1979. (lp) **SHUT YOUR MOUTH** – Hamburg connection / I'm a lover not a worker / Shut your mouth / Needed on the farm / Streetwalking lady / Firewater / Child of the sixties / Slowdown / Losing you / Weekend entertainer / Holy roller / Cincinnati diceman.	☐	–

—— split 1979 after **JIM ARMSTRONG** – guitar + **BRIAN SCOTT** – keyboards, flute repl. WRIXEN + HARRISON. The latter became BILLY WHO

– compilations, others, etc. –

on 'Decca' UK / 'Parrot' US, unless otherwise mentioned

Feb 65. (7"ep) (DFE 8612) **THEM** – Don't start crying now / Philosophy / One two brown eyes / Baby please don't go.	☐	–
Jan 69. (7") (F 12875) **GLORIA. / HERE COMES THE NIGHT** <US re-iss. 1977 on 'London'; 59028>	☐	–
Feb 70. (lp; stereo/mono) (S+/PA 86) **THE WORLD OF THEM**	☐	–
Aug 72. (7"; as VAN MORRISON & THEM) <365> **GLORIA. / IF YOU AND I COULD BE AS TWO**	–	☐
Oct 73. (d-lp; as THEM FEATURING VAN MORRISON) (DPA 3001-2) <BP 71053-4> **THEM FEATURING VAN MORRISON** – Don't start crying now / Baby please don't go / Here comes the night / One more time / It won't hurt half as much / Mystic eyes / Call my name / Richard Cory / One two brown eyes / All for myself / If you and I could be as two / Don't you know / Friday's child / The story of Them (part 1) / Philosophy / How long baby / I'm gonna dress in black / Bring 'em on in / Little girl / I gave my love a diamond / Gloria / You just can't win / Go on home baby / Don't look back / I like it like that / Bright lights big city / My little baby / Route 66.(re-iss.Jul82; lp/c TAB/KTBC 45) (cd-iss. 1987 on 'London'; 810 165-2)	☐	Jul72
1974. (lp) London; <APS 639> **BACKTRACKIN'**	–	–
May 76. (lp/c) (ROOTS/KRTC 3) **ROCK ROOTS**	–	–
1977. (lp) London; <LC 50001> **THE STORY OF THEM FEATURING VAN MORRISON**	–	–
Oct 83. (7") Old Gold; (OG 9342) **HERE COMES THE NIGHT. / (B-side by Ten Years After)**	–	–
Aug 86. (d-lp/d-c; as THEM featuring VAN MORRISON) Castle; (CCS LP/MC 131) **THE COLLECTION** (cd-iss. Aug92;)	–	–
Sep 87. (lp/c) See For Miles; (SEE/+K 31) **THE SINGLES**	–	–
Jan 91. (7"/c-s) London; (LON/+C 292) **BABY PLEASE GO. / GLORIA** (12"+=/cd-s+=) (LON X/CD 292) – Mystic eyes.	65	☐
Apr 97. (cd) Spalax; (14967) **REUNION CONCERT** (live)	☐	–

THERAPY?

Formed: Belfast, N. Ireland . . . summer '89 by ANDY CAIRNS, MICHAEL McKEEGAN and FYFE EWING. After failing to attract major label interest, they took the DIY route and issued a double A-side debut single, 'MEAT ABSTRACT' / 'PUNISHMENT KISS' (1990) on their own bitterly named 'Multifuckingnational' label. With the help of Radio One guru, John Peel and Silverfish's LESLIE RANKINE, the band secured a deal with London indie label, 'Wiiija'. The following year, they released two mini-sets in quick succession, 'BABYTEETH' and 'PLEASURE DEATH', the latter nearly breaking them into the Top 50 (both topping the independent charts). This initial early 90's period was characterised by a vaguely industrial hardcore/proto-grunge sound lying somewhere between American noiseniks, BIG BLACK and HUSKER DU. Their mushrooming street kudos tempted 'A&M' into offering them a deal and in 1992 THERAPY? made their major label debut with the Top 30 single, 'TEETHGRINDER', following it up with their first album proper, 'NURSE'. A Top 40 injection, its blunt combination of metal/punk and ambitious arrangements something of a love it or hate it affair. The following year, they released a trio of Top 20 singles, starting off with the 'SHORTSHARPSHOCK EP' which opened with the classic 'SCREAMAGER' track. In the first few months of '94, THERAPY? once again crashed into the charts with 'NOWHERE', an adrenaline rush of a single, that preceded their Mercury-nominated Top 5 album, 'TROUBLEGUM'. However, by the release of 1995's 'INFERNAL LOVE', the band affected something of a musical departure from their stock-in-trade indie-metal extremity with aching ballads (including a heart rending cover of Husker Du's 'DIANE') and string flourishes courtesy of MARTIN McCARRICK. The cellist (who also appeared on their 1994 set) was made full-time member in early 1996, while EWING was replaced by GRAHAM HOPKINS. A long time in the making, 'SEMI-DETACHED' was delivered to a muted response from the critics in '98 and was the last for a major label. Although it opened in fine style with Top 30 hit, 'CHURCH OF NOISE', the rest of the tracks were below par. THERAPY? tried hard to re-establish themselves with 1999's 'SUICIDE PACT – YOU FIRST' set, the group's fanbase becoming rhetorical with each listen. • **Songwriters:** Mostly CAIRNS or group penned, except TEENAGE KICKS (Undertones) / INVISIBLE SUN (Police) / WITH OR WITHOUT YOU (U2) / BREAKING THE LAW (Judas Priest) / C.C. RIDER (hit; Elvis Presley) / ISOLATION (Joy Division) / TATTY SEASIDE TOWN (Membranes) / NICE 'N' SLEAZY (Stranglers) / REUTERS (Wire) / VICAR IN A TUTU (Smiths). • **Trivia:** In 1994, they featured w/ OZZY OSBOURNE on 'IRON MAN' for a BLACK SABBATH tribute album.

Album rating: BABYTEETH mini (*5) / PLEASURE DEATH mini (*6) / NURSE (*7) / TROUBLEGUM (*8) / INFERNAL LOVE (*5) / SEMI-DETACHED (*5) / SUICIDE PACT – YOU FIRST (*5)

ANDY CAIRNS (b.22 Sep'65, Antrim, N.Ireland) – vocals, guitar / **MICHAEL McKEEGAN** (b.25 Mar'71, Antrim) – bass / **FYFE EWING** – drums

	Multifuck-ingnational	not iss.
Aug 90. (7") *(MFN 1)* **MEAT ABSTRACT. / PUNISHMENT KISS**	☐	–

	Wiiija	not iss.
Jul 91. (m-lp) *(WIJ 9)* **BABYTEETH**	☐	–

– Meat abstract / Skyward / Punishment kiss / Animal bones / Loser cop / Innocent X / Dancin' with Manson. *(re-iss. Mar93 + Jun95 on 'Southern' cd/c/red-m-lp; 18507-2/-4/-1)*

Jan 92. (m-lp) *(WIJ 11)* **PLEASURE DEATH**	52	–

– Skinning pit / Fantasy bag / Shitkicker / Prison breaker / D.L.C. / Potato junkie. *(re-iss. Sep92 on 'A&M';) (re-iss. Mar93 + Jun95 on 'Southern' cd/c/m-lp; 18508-2/-4/-1)*

	A&M	A&M
Oct 92. (7"purple) *(AM 0097)* **TEETHGRINDER. / SUMMER OF HATE**	30	–

(12") *(AMY 0097)* – ('A'side) / Human mechanism / Sky high McKay(e).
(cd-s+=) *(AMCD 0097)* – (all four songs above).
(12") – *(AMX 0097)* – ('A'-Tee hee dub mix) / ('A'-Unsane mix).

Nov 92. (cd/c/lp) *(540044-2/-4/-1)* **NURSE**	38	–

– Nausea / Teethgrinder / Disgracelands / Accelerator / Neck freak / Perversonality / Gone / Zipless / Deep skin / Hypermania.

Mar 93. (7"pink-ep/c-ep/12"ep/cd-ep) *(AM/+MC/Y/CD 208)* **SHORTSHARPSHOCK EP**	9	–

– Screamager / Auto surgery / Totally random man / Accelerator.

— In May93, they appeared on the B-side of PEACE TOGETHER single 'BE STILL', covered The Police's 'INVISIBLE SUN' on 'Island' records.

Jun 93. (7"grey-ep/c-ep/12"ep/cd-ep) *(580304-7/-4/-1/-2)* **FACE THE STRANGE EP**	18	–

– Turn / Speedball / Bloody blue / Neck freak (re-recording).

Aug 93. (7"clearorblue-ep/c-ep/cd-ep) *(580360-7/-4/-2)* **OPAL MANTRA / INNOCENT X (live). / POTATO JUNKIE (live) / NAUSEA (live)**	13	–

Sep 93. (cd) *<POCM 1033>* **HATS OFF TO THE INSANE** (compilation)	–	–

– Screamager / Auto surgery / Totally random man / Turn / Speedball / Opal mantra.

Jan 94. (7"ep/c-ep/cd-ep) *(580504-7/-4/-2)* **NOWHERE / PANTOPON ROSE. / BREAKING THE LAW / C.C. RIDER**	18	–

(cd-s) *(580 504-2)* – ('A'side) / ('A'-Sabres Of Paradise mix) / ('A'-Therapeutic Distortion mix).

Feb 94. (cd/c/lp,green-lp) *(540196-2/-4/-1)* **TROUBLEGUM**	5	–

– Knives / Screamager / Hellbelly / Stop it you're killing me / Nowhere / Die laughing / Unbeliever / Trigger inside / Lunacy booth / Isolation / Turn / Femtex / Unrequited / Brainsaw.
above album guests **PAGE HAMILTON** – lead guitar (of HELMET) / **MARTIN McCARRICK** (b.29 Jul'62, Luton, England) – guitar, cello (of THIS MORTAL COIL) / **LESLEY RANKINE + EILEEN ROSE** – vocals

Feb 94. (7"yellow-ep/c-ep/cd-ep) *(580534-7/-4/-2)* **TRIGGER INSIDE / NICE'N'SLEAZY. / REUTERS / TATTY SEASIDE TOWN**	22	–

(12"ep) *(580534-1)* – ('A'side) / ('A'-Terry Bertram mix 1 & 2) / Nowhere (Sabres of Paradise mix 1 & 2).

May 94. (7"red-ep/c-ep/cd-ep) *(580588-7/-4/-2)* **DIE LAUGHING / STOP IT YOU'RE KILLING ME (live). / TRIGGER INSIDE (live) / EVIL ELVIS (the lost demo)**	29	–

(12") *(580588-1)* – ('A'-David Holmes mix 1 & 2).

— In May '95, they hit No.53 UK with remix of 'INNOCENT X', with ORBITAL on the B-side, 'Belfast' / 'Wasted (vocal mix)'.

May 95. (7"orange) *(581504-7)* **STORIES (cello version)**	14	–

(c-s+=/cd-s+=) *(581105-4/-2)* – Isolation (Consolidated synth mix).

Jun 95. (cd/c/red-lp) *(540379-2/-4/-1)* **INFERNAL LOVE**	9	–

– Epilepsy / Stories / A moment of clarity / Jude the obscene / Bowels of love / Misery / Bad mother / Me vs you / Loose / Diane / 30 seconds.

Jul 95. (c-s/cd-s) *(581163-4/-2)* **LOOSE / OUR LOVE MUST DIE / NICE GUYS / LOOSE (Photek remix)**	25	–

(cd-s) *(581165-2)* – ('A'side) / Die laughing (live) / Nowhere (live) / Unbeliever (live).
(7"green/one-sided-12") *(581162-7/-1)* – ('A'side) / ('A'-Photek remix).

Nov 95. (7"red-ep/c-ep/cd-ep) *(581293-7/-4/-2)* **DIANE / JUDE THE OBSCENE (acoustic) / LOOSE (acoustic) / 30 SECONDS (acoustic)**	26	–

(cd-ep) *(581291-2)* – ('A'side) / Misery (acoustic) / Die laughing (acoustic) / Screamager (acoustic).

— Jan 96, **GRAHAM HOPKINS** (b.20 Dec'75, Dublin, Ireland) – drums (ex-MY LITTLE FUNHOUSE) repl. FYFE. Also added full-time **MARTIN McCARRICK**

Mar 98. (7"red) *(582538-7)* **CHURCH OF NOISE. / 60 WATT BULB / ('A'-Messenger mix)**	29	–

(cd-s) *(582539-2)* – (first & third tracks) / Suing God / ('A'-CD-Rom video).

Mar 98. (cd/c) *(540891-2/-4)* **SEMI-DETACHED**	21	–

– Church of noise / Tightrope walker / Black eye, purple sky / Lonely, cryin', only / Born too soon / Stay happy / Safe / Straight life / Heaven's gate / Don't expect roses / Tramline / The boy's asleep. *(also iss.6x7"box; 582548-7)*

May 98. (7"blue) *(582684-7)* **LONELY, CRYIN', ONLY. / SKYWARD**	32	–

(cd-s) *(582685-2)* – ('A'side) / High noon / Diane (new version) / Teethgrinder (new version).
(cd-s) *(044121-2)* – ('A'side) / Kids stuff / Disgracelands / ('A'-CD-Rom video).

	Ark 21	not iss.
Oct 99. (cd) *(153972-2)* **SUICIDE PACT – YOU FIRST**	61	–

– He's not that kind of girl / Wall of mouths / Jam jar jail / Hate kill destroy / Big cave in / Six mile water / Little tongues first / Ten year plan / God kicks / Other people's misery / Sister / While I pursue my way unharmed.

– compilations, etc. –

Mar 92. (cd) *1/4 Stick; <QUARTERSTICK 8>* **CAUCASIAN PSYCHOSIS**	–	☐

– (BABYTEETH + PLEASURE DEATH)

THESE ANIMAL MEN   (dig out; Great Alt & Indie . . .)

THE THE

Formed: Swadlincote, Derbyshire, England . . . 1979 as a studio project by MATT JOHNSON who was part of post-punk outfit The GADGETS, at the same time. JOHNSON signed to indie label, '4 a.d.' in 1980, unleashing the poignant single, 'CONTROVERSIAL SUBJECT'. JOHNSON released a further debut album for the label in summer '81, 'BURNING BLUE SOUL', although in effect it was a THE THE recording in all but name, JOHNSON being the sole permanent member of the group. Signing briefly to 'Some Bizzare', THE THE released another three singles, 'COLD SPELL AHEAD', 'PERFECT' and the brilliant 'UNCERTAIN SMILE', before securing a deal with 'Epic'. The long awaited and much anticipated 'SOUL MINING' was eventually released in late '83, JOHNSON's critical favour and cult standing seeing the album reach the UK Top 30. An entrancing, ambitious pop record with a brooding undertow, the keening 'THIS IS THE DAY' stands among the best of JOHNSON's work, the album's claustrophobic lyrics marking out JOHNSON as a bedsit commentator par excellence. For live work, JOHNSON recruited the likes of ex-ORANGE JUICE man, ZEKE MANYIKA, JIM THIRLWELL and JOOLS HOLLAND, the latter actually having guested on the album. Three years in the making, 'INFECTED' (1986) was JOHNSON's tour de force, a scathing attack on the industrial, economic and moral wasteland that was Thatcher's Britain. Nowhere was this better articulated than in the malignant power of the album's centrepiece, 'HEARTLAND', JOHNSON berating 80's material gain and America's all-pervasive influence through gritted teeth. The pumping electro-soul of the title track, meanwhile, dealt with sexual obsession and the AIDS crisis, the attendant devil-masturbating video causing a storm of controversy. Other highlights included the tortured 'OUT OF THE BLUE (INTO THE FIRE)' and the breathy duet with NENEH CHERRY, 'SLOW TRAIN TO DAWN', JOHNSON's mastery of mood and atmosphere, together with a crack troupe of guest musicians making this one of the most realised albums of the decade. Accompanied by a full-length video/film (which was aired on Channel 4), the record also gave JOHNSON some belated Top 20 success. Spurred on, the restless maverick subsequently recruited a permanent band to turn THE THE into a group proposition, namely DAVID PALMER, JAMES ELLER and ex-SMITHS guitarist JOHNNY MARR. Though the resulting album, 'MIND BOMB' (1989) was THE THE's most successful to date (Top 5), its caustic barrage of political ranting lacked the twisted pop subtlety of its predecessor and left some critics unimpressed (a guest spot from SINEAD O'CONNOR on 'KINGDOM OF RAIN' made up for the pop tones of 'THE BEAT(EN) GENERATION'). Retaining the same core of musicians while adding keyboard player, D.C. COLLARD, THE THE eventually resurfaced with a full length album in the form of 'DUSK' (1993). Previewed by the harmonica howl of 'DOGS OF LUST', the album saw JOHNSON once again wrestling with his inner demons in his disturbingly insinuating way. A mid-life dark-night-of-the-soul, JOHNSON has rarely bared his soul or expressed his despair as affectingly as on the very SMITHS-esque 'SLOW EMOTION REPLAY', MARR literally wringing the pathos from his chiming guitar. This cathartic collection of urban blues nevertheless ended on something of a more hopeful note with 'LONELY PLANET', JOHNSON coming to some kind of peace with himself and the world. The record deservedly reached No.2, becoming the most successful THE THE release to date and making up the critical and commercial ground lost with 'MIND BOMB'. Of course, the ever restless JOHNSON turned his hand to something completely different, so to speak, for his next full-length release; 'HANKY PANKY' (1995) was a tribute album to his hero, country star HANK WILLIAMS, although only the track 'I SAW THE LIGHT' was of much note. Given short thrift by critics (the same ones probably), the record saw JOHNSON going out on a limb, no doubt alienating many of his long-time fans, although he was distant from them after relocating to Sherman Oaks in California. Then again, anyone familiar with the work of this elusive genius knows to expect the unexpected.

Album rating: Matt Johnson: BURNING BLUE SOUL (*7) / The The: SOUL MINING (*7) / INFECTED (*8) / MIND BOMB (*8) / DUSK (*7) / HANKY PANKY (*4)

GADGETS

MATT JOHNSON – guitars / **COLIN TUCKER** – synthesizers / **JOHN HYDE** – synthesizers (both ex-PLAIN CHARACTERS)

	Final Solution	not iss.
Dec 79. (lp) *(FSLP 001)* **GADGETREE**	☐	–

– Kyleaking / Making cars / Narpath / UFO import No.1 / Slippery / Singing in the rain / Only one me / Shouting 'Nispers' / There over there / Termite mound / Sleep / Devil's dyke / Six mile bottom / UFO import No.2 / Autumn 80 / Duplicate / Bog track / Thin line. (re-iss. Jun89 on 'Plastic Head' lp/cd; PLAS LP/CD 013)

—— They continued as a studio set-up with MATT's help.

Dec 80. (lp) (FSLP 002) **LOVE, CURIOSITY, FRECKLES & DOUBT**
– Bodorgan / Gadget speak / Checking to make sure / Aeron / Leave it to Charlie / Prayers / Happy endido / Quatt / Pictures of you / Aaft / Railway line through blubber houses / She's queen of toyland / Sex / It wasn't that way at all / The death and resurrection of Jennifer Gloom / Bill posters will be prosecuted. (re-iss. Jun89 on 'Plastic Head' lp/cd; PLAS LP/CD 014)

—— next featured **PETER ASHWORTH** dubbed in instead of MATT

		Glass	not iss.
Jan 83. (lp/c) (GLA LP/C 006) **THE BLUE ALBUM**			-

– We had no way of knowing / Space in my heart / Bodies without heads / The boyfriend / Uneasy listening / Juice of love / Discuss the sofa / Long empty train / Bite the sawdust / Broken fall. (re-iss. Jun89 on 'Plastic Head' lp/cd; PLAS LP/CD 016)

Jun 83. (7"/12"; unissued) (GLASS/+12 026) **WE HAD NO WAY OF KNOWING. / ACID BATH**		-	-

THE THE

MATT JOHNSON (b.15 Aug'61, Essex, England . . . raised London) – vocals, guitar, etc. (also of The GADGETS) / **KEITH LAWS** – synthesizers, drum machine / **PETER 'Triash' ASHWORTH** – drums / **TOM JOHNSTON** – bass

		4 a.d.	not iss.
Jul 80. (7") (AD 10) **CONTROVERSIAL SUBJECT. / BLACK AND WHITE**			-

—— next with guests **GILBERT & LEWIS** (of WIRE) on 2nd last track

Aug 81. (lp; as MATT JOHNSON) (CAD 113) **BURNING BLUE SOUL**			-

– Red cinders in the sand / Song without an ending / Time again for the golden sunset / Icing up / Like a Sun risin' thru my garden / Out of control / Bugle boy / Delirious / The river flows east in Spring / Another boy drowning. (re-iss. Sep83; same) (re-iss. credited to THE THE, Jun93 cd)(c; HAD 113CD)(HADC 113); hit UK No.65 <us cd-iss. 1993 on 'Warners'; 45266>

		Some Bizzare	not iss.
Sep 81. (7") (BZ 4) **COLD SPELL AHEAD. / HOT ICE**			-

(re-iss. Aug92, 12"pic-d/cd-s;)

—— **MATT JOHNSON** was now virtually **THE THE**, although he was augmented by others on tour.

		Epic	Epic
Oct 82. (7") (EPCA 2787) **UNCERTAIN SMILE. / THREE ORANGE KISSES FROM KAZAN**		68	-
(12"+=,12"yellow+=) (EPC13 2787) – Waiting for the upturn.			
Dec 82. (7") **UNCERTAIN SMILE. / WAITING FOR THE UPTURN**		-	
Feb 83. (7") (EPCA 3119) **PERFECT. / THE NATURE OF VIRTUE**			-
(12"+=) (EPCA13 3119) – The nature of virtue II.			
Sep 83. (7") (A 3710) **THIS IS THE DAY. / MENTAL HEALING PROCESS**		71	

(w/ free-7") (same) – Leap into the wind / Absolute liberation.
(12") (TA 3710) – ('A'side) / I've been waiting for tomorrow (all of my life).

—— added live **ZEKE MANYIKA** – drums (of ORANGE JUICE) / **JIM THIRLWELL** / **JOOLS HOLLAND** – piano (ex-SQUEEZE) / **THOMAS LEER** – synthesizers, keyboards

Oct 83. (lp/c) (EPC/40 25525) <EK 39266> **SOUL MINING**		27	

– I've been waiting for tomorrow (all of my life) / This is the day / The sinking feeling / Uncertain smile / The twilight hour / Soul mining / Giant. (free-12"ep.w.a.) **PERFECT. / SOUP OF MIXED EMOTIONS / FRUIT OF THE HEART** (c+=) – Perfect / Three orange kisses from Kazan / Nature of virtue / Fruit of the heart / Soup of mixed emotions / Waiting for the upturn. (cd-iss. Jun87+=; CD 25525) – Perfect. (re-iss. Mar90 cd/c/lp; 466337-2/-4/-1)

Nov 83. (7") (A 3588) **UNCERTAIN SMILE. / DUMB AS DEATH'S HEAD**			-

(12") (TA 3588) – ('A'side) / Soul mining.

—— guests for next album **ROLI MOSSIMAN / NENEH CHERRY / DAVID PALMER / STEVE HOGARTH / ANNA DOMINO / JAMIE TALBOT / WAYNE LIVESEY / ZEKE MANYIKA** / etc.

May 86. (12"m) (TRUTH 1) **SWEET BIRD OF TRUTH. / HARBOUR LIGHTS / SLEEPING JUICE**			-
Jul 86. (7") (TRUTH 2) **HEARTLAND. / BORN IN THE NEW S.A.**		29	-

(12"+=) (TRUTH T2) – Flesh and bones.
(d12"++=) (TRUTH D2) – Perfect / Fruit of the heart.
(12"+=) (TRUTH Q2) – Sweet bird of truth.
(c-s+=) (TRUTH C2) – Harbour lights.

Oct 86. (7") (TRUTH 3) **INFECTED. / DISTURBED**		48	

(12"+=/12"uncensored+=) (TRUTH T/Q 3) – ('A'-energy mix).
(d12"++=) (TRUTH D3) – Soul mining (remix) / Sinking feeling.
(c-s+=) (TRUTH C3) – ('A'-Skull crusher mix) / Soul mining / Sinking feeling.

Nov 86. (lp/c/cd) (EPC/40/CD 26770) <40471> **INFECTED**		14	89

– Infected / Out of the blue (into the fire) / Heartland / Angels of deception / Sweet bird of truth / Slow train to dawn / Twilight of a champion / The mercy beat. (cd+=) – ('A'-INFECTED singles remixed) (TA 3588)

Jan 87. (7") (TENSE 1) **SLOW TRAIN TO DAWN. / HARBOUR LIGHTS**		64	

(12"+=/12"w-stencil+=) (TENSE T/D 3) – The nature of virtue.

May 87. (7") (TENSE 2) **SWEET BIRD OF TRUTH. / SLEEPING JUICE**		55	

(12"+=) (TENSE T2) – Harbour lights.
(c-s+=)(cd-s++=) (TENSE C2/CDTHE 2) – Soul mining (12"mix).

—— THE THE were again a group when **MATT** with past session man **DAVID PALMER** – drums (ex-ABC) / recruited **JOHNNY MARR** – guitar (ex-SMITHS) / **JAMES ELLER** – bass (ex-JULIAN COPE)

Feb 89. (7") (EMU 8) **THE BEAT(EN) GENERATION. / ANGEL**		18	

(12"box+=/cd-s+=/3"cd-s+=) (EMUB/EMUCD/CBEMU 8) – Soul mining (mix).
(12"+=/pic-cd+=) (EMUT/CPEMU 8) – ('A'-Palmer mix) / ('A'-campfire mix).

May 89. (lp/c/cd) (463319-1/-4/-2) <45241> **MIND BOMB**		4	

– Good morning beautiful / Armageddon days are here (again) / The violence of truth / Kingdom of rain / The beat(en) generation / August & September / Gravitate to me / Beyond love.

Jul 89. (7"/c-s) (EMU/+C 9) **GRAVITATE TO ME. / THE VIOLENCE OF TRUTH**		63	

(12"+=/cd-s+=) (EMUT/CDEMU 9) – I've been waiting for tomorrow (all of my life).
(etched-12") (EMUE 9) – ('A'dub) / I've been waiting for tomorrow.

Sep 89. (7"/c-s) (EMU/+C 10) **ARMAGEDDON DAYS ARE HERE (AGAIN). / ('A'orchestral)**		70	

(12"+=) (EMUT 10) – The nature of virtue / Perfect.
(cd-s+=) (CDEMU 10) – Perfect / Mental healing process.
(10"ep) (EMUQT 10) **THE THE V. THE WORLD EP** – ('A'side) / The nature of virtue / Perfect / Mental healing process.
(etched-12") (EMUE 10) – ('A'edit) / Perfect.

Feb 91. (12"/c-s) (655 798-6/-4) **JEALOUS OF YOUTH. / ANOTHER BOY DROWNING** (live)		54	

(cd-s+=) **SHADES OF YOUTH EP** (655 796-8) – Solitude / Dolphins.

—— added **D.C. COLLARD** – instruments

Jan 93. (7"marble) (658 457-7) **DOGS OF LUST. / THE VIOLENCE OF TRUTH**		25	

(12"pic-d+=/cd-s+=) (658 457-6/-2) – Infected (live).
(cd-s) (658 457-5) – ('A'side) / Jealous of youth (live) / Beyond love (live) / Armageddon days are here (again) (D.N.A. remix).

Jan 93. (cd/c/lp) (472468-2/-4/-1) <53164> **DUSK**		2	

– True happiness this way lies / Love is stronger than death / Dogs of lust / This is the night / Slow emotion replay / Helpline operator / Sodium light baby / Lung shadows / Bluer than midnight / Lonely planet.

Apr 93. (12"red-ep/cd-ep) (659 077-6/-9) **SLOW MOTION REPLAY. / DOGS OF LUST (3 mixes by Jim Thirlwell)**		35	

(cd-ep) (659077-0) – ('A'side) / Scenes from Active Twilight (parts I-V).

Jun 93. (12"ep/cd-ep) (659 371-6/-2) **LOVE IS STRONGER THAN DEATH. / THE SINKING FEELING (live) / THE MERCY BEAT (live) / ARMAGEDDON DAYS ARE HERE (AGAIN) (live)**		39	

(cd-ep) (659 371-5) – ('A'side) / Infected / Soul mining / Armageddon days are . . .

Jan 94. (c-ep/12"/cd-ep) (659811-4/-6/-2) **DIS-INFECTED EP**		17	

– This was the day / Dis-infected / Helpline operator (sick boy mix) / Dogs of lust (germicide mix).

Jan 95. (c-ep/10"ep/cd-ep) (661091-0/-6/-9) <61119> **I SAW THE LIGHT / I'M FREE AT LAST. / SOMEDAY YOU'LL CALL MY NAME / THERE'S NO ROOM IN MY HEART FOR THE BLUES**		31	Aug95

Feb 95. (cd/c/10"lp) (478139-2/-4/-0) <66908> **HANKY PANKY**		28	

– Honky tonkin' / Six more miles / My heart would know / If you'll be a baby to me / I'm a long gone daddy / Weary blues from waitin' / I saw the light / Your cheatin' heart / I can't get you off of my mind / There's a tear in my beer / I can't escape from you.

– compilations, others, etc. –

Dec 88. (d-cd) Epic; (CDTT 241) **SOUL MINING / INFECTED**			-

THEY MIGHT BE GIANTS   (dig out; Great Alt & Indie . . .)

THIN LIZZY

Formed: Dublin, Ireland . . . 1969 by PHIL LYNOTT and BRIAN DOWNEY together with ERIC BELL and ERIC WRIXON (the latter leaving after the first 45). After a debut single for 'Parlophone' Ireland, the group relocated to London in late 1970 at the suggestion of managers, Ted Carroll and Brian Tuite, having already signed to 'Decca'. 'THIN LIZZY' (1971) and 'SHADES OF A BLUE ORPHANAGE' (1972) passed without much notice, although the group scored a surprise one-off UK Top 10 with 'WHISKEY IN THE JAR'. A traditional Irish folk song, THIN LIZZY's highly original adaptation married plangent lead guitar and folk-rock arrangements to memorable effect. The accompanying album, 'VAGABONDS OF THE WESTERN WORLD' (1973), failed to capitalise on the song's success, although it gave an indication of where the band were headed with the hard-edged likes of 'THE ROCKER'. BELL departed later that year, his replacement being ex-SKID ROW axeman GARY MOORE, the first of many sojourns the guitarist would enjoy with 'LIZZY' over the course of his turbulent career. He was gone by the Spring tour of the following year (subsequently joining COLOSSEUM II), the trademark twin guitar attack introduced on that tour courtesy of JOHN CANN and ANDY GEE. They were soon replaced more permanently by SCOTT GORHAM and BRIAN ROBERTSON, THIN LIZZY signing a new deal with 'Vertigo' and releasing the 'NIGHTLIFE' set in late '74. Neither that album nor 1975's 'FIGHTING' succeeded in realising the group's potential, although the latter gave them their first Top 60 entry on the album chart. Partly due to the group's blistering live shows and partly down to the massive success of 'THE BOYS ARE BACK IN TOWN', 'JAILBREAK' (1976) was a transatlantic Top 20 smash. One of the band's most consistent sets of their career, it veered from the power chord rumble and triumphant male bonding of 'THE BOYS . . .' to the epic Celtic clarion call of 'EMERALD'. The brooding, thuggish rifferama of the title track was another highlight, LYNOTT's rich, liquor-throated drawl sounding by turns threatening and conspiratorial. 'JOHNNY THE FOX' (1976) followed into the UK Top 20 later that year, a record which lacked the continuity of its predecessor but nevertheless spawned another emotive, visceral hard rock single in 'DON'T BELIEVE A WORD'. This is what marked THIN LIZZY out from the heavy-rock pack; LYNOTT's outlaw-with-a-broken-heart voice and the propulsive economy of the arrangements were light-years away from the warbling and posturing of 70's proto-metal. Accordingly, 'LIZZY were one of the few rock bands who gained any respect from punks and indeed, LYNOTT subsequently formed an extra-curricular project with The DAMNED's RAT SCABIES as well as working with ex-SEX PISTOLS, PAUL COOK and STEVE JONES (as The GREEDIES on the Christmas 1980 single, 'A MERRY JINGLE'). A 1977 US tour saw MOORE fill in for ROBERTSON who'd injured his hand in a fight, although the Scots guitarist was back in place for a headlining spot at the 'Reading Festival' later that year. 'BAD REPUTATION' was released the following month, preceded by the R&B-flavoured 'DANCING IN THE MOONLIGHT' single and furnishing the group with their highest chart placing to date (UK Top 5). But it was through blistering live work that THIN LIZZY had made their name and they finally got around to releasing a concert set in 1978. 'LIVE AND DANGEROUS' remains deservedly revered as a career landmark, as vital, razor sharp and unrestrained as any live set in the history of rock. Later that summer, THIN LIZZY again took to the road with MOORE (ROBERTSON departed to form WILD HORSES) undertaking his third stint in the band alongside MARK NAUSEEF who was deputising for an absent DOWNEY. Previewed by the keening exhilaration of 'WAITING FOR AN ALIBI', the 'BLACK ROSE (A ROCK LEGEND)' (1979) set was the last great THIN LIZZY album. Placing all-out rockers alongside more traditionally influenced material, the set produced another two major UK hits in the defiant 'DO ANYTHING YOU WANT TO DO' and the poignant 'SARAH', a beautifully realised tribute to LYNOTT's baby daughter. MOORE, meanwhile, had been enjoying solo chart success with 'PARISIENNE WALKWAYS', the THIN LIZZY frontman guesting on vocals. By late '79, MOORE was out, however, and LYNOTT secured the unlikely services of another Scot, MIDGE URE, to fulfill touring commitments. When the latter subsequently departed to front ULTRAVOX, LYNOTT replaced him with ex-PINK FLOYD man, SNOWY WHITE. 1980 saw LYNOTT marrying Caroline Crowther (daughter of LESLIE) and releasing his first solo set, 'SOLO IN SOHO'. Although it hit the UK Top 30, the record sold poorly, a shame as it contained some of his most endearingly experimental work. The classic 'YELLOW PEARL' (co-written with URE) nevertheless scored a Top 20 placing and was later used as the theme tune for 'Top Of The Pops'. Later that year saw the release of 'CHINATOWN', the title track giving THIN LIZZY yet another hit. A further patchy album, 'RENEGADE' followed in late '81, THIN LIZZY's popularity clearly on the wane as it struggled to break the Top 40. With the addition of ex-TYGERS OF PAN TANG guitarist JOHN SYKES and keyboardist DARREN WHARTON, the group released something of a belated comeback album in 'THUNDER AND LIGHTNING' (1983). It was to be THIN LIZZY's swansong, however; by the release of live set, 'LIFE' (1983), the group had already split, LYNOTT and DOWNEY forming the short-lived GRAND SLAM. LYNOTT eventually carried on with his solo career (he'd previously released a second set, 'THE PHIL LYNOTT ALBUM' in 1982) in 1985, after settling his differences with MOORE. The pair recorded the driving 'OUT IN THE FIELDS', a UK Top 5 hit and a lesson in consummate heavy-rock for the hundreds of 80's bands wielding a guitar and a poodle haircut. A follow-up single, '19', proved to be LYNOTT's parting shot, the Irishman dying from a drugs overdose on the 4th of January '86. As family, rock stars and wellwishers crowded into a small chapel in Southern Ireland for LYNOTT's low-key funeral, the rock world mourned the loss of one of its most talented, charismatic and much-loved figureheads. • **Songwriters:** PHIL LYNOTT and Co. and also covers of ROSALIE (Bob Seger) / I'M STILL IN LOVE WITH YOU (Frankie Miller).

Album rating: THIN LIZZY (*4) / SHADES OF A BLUE ORPHANAGE (*4) / VAGABONDS OF THE WESTERN WORLD (*5) / NIGHTLIFE (*5) / FIGHTING (*6) / JAILBREAK (*8) / JOHNNY THE FOX (*8) / BAD REPUTATION (*6) / LIVE AND DANGEROUS (*9) / BLACK ROSE – A ROCK LEGEND (*6) / CHINATOWN (*5) / ADVENTURES OF THIN LIZZY compilation (*8) / RENEGADE (*5) / THUNDER AND LIGHTNING (*7) / LIFE (*7) / DEDICATION – THE VERY BEST OF THIN LIZZY compilation (*8) / Phil Lynott: SOLO IN SOHO (*4) / THE PHIL LYNOTT ALBUM (*6) / THE BEST OF PHIL LYNOTT & THIN LIZZY – SOLDIER OF FORTUNE compilation (*7)

PHIL LYNOTT (b.20 Aug'51, from Brazilian + Irish parents. Raised from 3 by granny in Crumlin, Dublin) – vocals, bass (ex-ORPHANAGE, ex-SKID ROW brief) / **ERIC BELL** (b. 3 Sep'47, Belfast, N.Ireland) – guitar, vocals (ex-DREAMS) / **BRIAN DOWNEY** (b.27 Jan'51) – drums (ex-ORPHANAGE) / **ERIC WRIXON** – keyboards

	Parlophone	not iss.
1970. (7"; as THIN LIZZIE) <DIP 513> **THE FARMER. / I NEED YOU**	–	– Ireland

—— now a trio (+ without WRIXON)

	Decca	London
Apr 71. (lp) (SKL 5082) <594> **THIN LIZZY**		

– The friendly ranger at Clontarf Castle / Honesty is no excuse / Diddy Levine / Ray-gun / Look what the wind blew in / Eire / Return of the farmer's son / Clifton Grange Hotel / Saga of the ageing orphan / Remembering. (cd-iss. Jan89 on 'Deram'+=; 820 528-2) – Dublin / Remembering (part 2) / Old moon madness / Things ain't working out down at the farm.

Aug 71. (7"ep) (F 13208) **NEW DAY**		–

– Things ain't working out down on the farm / Remembering pt.II / Old moon madness / Dublin.

Mar 72. (lp) (TXS 108) **SHADES OF A BLUE ORPHANAGE**		–

– The rise and dear demise of the funky nomadic tribes / Buffalo gal / I don't want to forget how to jive / Sarah / Brought down / Baby face / Chatting today / Call the police / Shades of a blue orphanage. (cd-iss. Nov88 on 'Deram'; 820 527-2)

Nov 72. (7") (F 13355) <20076> **WHISKEY IN THE JAR. / BLACK BOYS IN THE CORNER**	6	
May 73. (7") (F 13402) <20078> **RANDOLPH'S TANGO. / BROKEN DREAMS**		

Sep 73. (lp) (SKL 5170) <636> **VAGABONDS OF THE WESTERN WORLD**		

– Mama nature said / The hero and the madman / Slow blues / The rocker / Vagabonds (of the western world) / Little girl in bloom / Gonna creep up on you / A song for while I'm away. (cd-iss. May91 on 'Deram'+=; 820969-2) – Whiskey in the jar / Black boys on the corner / Randolph's tango / Broken dreams.

Nov 73. (7") (F 13467) **THE ROCKER. / HERE I GO AGAIN**		

—— **GARY MOORE** (b. 4 Apr'52, Belfast) – guitar, vocals (ex-SKID ROW) repl. BELL (later MAINSQUEEZE)

Apr 74. (7") (F 13507) <20082> **LITTLE DARLIN'. / BUFFALO GIRL**		

—— (on tour May'74) **JOHN CANN** – guitar (ex-ATOMIC ROOSTER, ex-BULLITT) / + **ANDY GEE** – guitar (ex-ELLIS) both repl. GARY MOORE who joined COLOSSEUM II. These temp. guitarists were deposed by **SCOTT GORHAM** (b.17 Mar'51, Santa Monica, Calif.) + **BRIAN ROBERTSON** (b.12 Sep'56, Glasgow, Scotland)

	Vertigo	Vertigo
Oct 74. (7") (6059 111) **PHILOMENA. / SHA LA LA**		–
Nov 74. (lp) (6360 116) <SRMI 1107> **NIGHTLIFE**		

– She knows / Night life / It's only money / Still in love with you / Frankie Carroll / Showdown / Banshee / Philomena / Sha-la-la / Dear heart. (re-iss. Aug83 lp/c; PRICE/PRIMC 31) (cd-iss. Jun89; 838029-2)

Jan 75. (7") <202> **SHOWDOWN. / NIGHT LIFE**		–
Jun 75. (7") (6059 124) **ROSALIE. / HALF CASTE**		–
Aug 75. (lp/c) (6360 121)(7138 070) <SRMI 1108> **FIGHTING**	60	

– Rosalie / For those who love to live / Suicide / Wild one / Fighting my way back / King's vengeance / Spirit slips away / Silver dollar / Freedom song / Ballad of a hard man. (re-iss. Aug83 lp/c; PRICE/PRIMC 32) (cd-iss. Jun89; 842433-2) (cd re-iss. Mar96 on 'Mercury'; 532296-2)

Oct 75. (7") (6059 129) **WILD ONE. / FOR THOSE WHO LOVE TO DIE**		–
Nov 75. (7") <205> **WILD ONE. / FREEDOM SONG**		–

	Vertigo	Mercury
Mar 76. (lp/c) (9102 008)(7138 075) <SRMI 1081> **JAILBREAK**	10	18

– Jailbreak / Angel from the coast / Running back / Romeo and the lonely girl / Warriors / The boys are back in town / Fight or fall / Cowboy song / Emerald. (re-iss. Oct83 lp/c; PRICE/PRIMC 50) (cd-iss. Jun89; 822785-2) (cd re-iss. Mar96 on 'Mercury'; 532294-2)

Apr 76. (7") (6059 139) **THE BOYS ARE BACK IN TOWN. / EMERALD**	8	–
Apr 76. (7") <73786> **THE BOYS ARE BACK IN TOWN. / JAILBREAK**	–	12
Jul 76. (7") (6059 150) **JAILBREAK. / RUNNING BACK**	31	–
Sep 76. (7") <73841> **THE COWBOY SONG. / ANGEL FROM THE COAST**	–	77
Oct 76. (lp/c) (9102 012)(7138 082) <SRMI 1119> **JOHNNY THE FOX**	11	52

– Johnny / Rocky / Borderline / Don't believe a word / Fools gold / Johnny the fox meets Jimmy the weed / Old flame / Massacre / Sweet Marie / Boogie woogie dance. (re-iss. May83 lp/c; PRICE/PRIMC 11) (cd-iss. May90; 822687-2) (cd re-iss. Mar96 on 'Mercury'; 532295-2)

Nov 76. (7") <73867> **ROCKY. / HALF-CASTE**	–	–
Jan 77. (7") (LIZZY 1) **DON'T BELIEVE A WORD. / OLD FLAME**	12	–
Jan 77. (7") <73882> **JOHNNY THE FOX MEETS JIMMY THE WEED. / OLD FLAME**	–	

—— BRIAN ROBERTSON became injured, GARY MOORE deputised (on 6 mths. tour only)

Aug 77. (7") (6059 177) <73945> **DANCING IN THE MOONLIGHT. / BAD REPUTATION**	14	–
Sep 77. (lp)(c) (9102 016)(7231 011) <SRMI 1186> **BAD REPUTATION**	4	39

– Soldier of fortune / Bad reputation / Opium trail / Southbound / Dancing in the moonlight (it's caught me in its spotlight) / Killer without a cause / Downtown sundown / That woman's gonna break your heart / Dear Lord. (re-iss. May83 lp/c; PRICE/PRIMC 12) (cd-iss. Apr90; 842434-2) (cd re-iss. Mar96 on 'Mercury'; 532298-2)

Apr 78. (7") (LIZZY 2) **ROSALIE; COWBOY'S SONG (live medley). / ME AND THE BOYS**	20	–

	Vertigo	Warners
Jun 78. (d-lp) (9199 645) <3213> **LIVE AND DANGEROUS (live)**	2	84

– Jailbreak / Emerald / South bound / Rosalie – Cowgirls' song / Dancing in the moonlight (it's caught me in its spotlight) / Massacre / Still in love with you / Johnny the fox meets Jimmy the weed / Cowboy song / The boys are back in town / Don't believe a word / Warriors / Are you ready / Suicide / Sha la la / Baby drives me crazy / The rocker. (re-iss. Nov84; d-lp/d-c; PRID/+C 6) (cd-iss. Jun89; 838030-2) (cd re-iss. Mar96 on 'Mercury'; 532297-2)

Jul 78. (7") <8648> **COWBOY SONG. / JOHNNY THE FOX (MEETS JIMMY THE WEED)**	–	

—— In Autumn'78 tour, DOWNEY was deputised by MARK NAUSEEF. **GARY MOORE** – guitar, vocals returned to repl. ROBERTSON who formed WILD HORSES

Feb 79. (7") (LIZZY 3) **WAITING FOR AN ALIBI. / WITH LOVE**	9	–
Apr 79. (lp/c) (9102/7231 032) <3338> **BLACK ROSE (A ROCK LEGEND)**	2	81

– Do anything you want to / Toughest street in town / S & M / Waiting for an alibi / Sarah / Got to give it up / Get out of here / With love / A roisin dubh (Black rose) A rock legend part 1. Shenandoah – part 2. Will you go lassy go – part 3. Danny boy – part 4. The mason's apron. (re-iss. Sep86 lp/c; PRICE/PRIMC 90) (cd-iss. Jun89; 830392-2) (cd re-iss. Mar96 on 'Mercury'; 532299-2)

—— Apr'79, LYNOTT's vox feat. on GARY MOORE's Top 10 hit 'Parisienne Walkways'.

Jun 79. (7") (LIZZY 4) **DO ANYTHING YOU WANT TO. / JUST THE TWO OF US**	14	–
Jun 79. (7") <49019> **DO ANYTHING YOU WANT TO. / S & M**	–	–
Sep 79. (7") (LIZZY 5) **SARAH. / GOT TO GIVE IT UP**	24	–
Sep 79. (7") <49078> **WITH LOVE. / GO TO GIVE IT UP**	–	

—— (for 2 months-late'79) **MIDGE URE** (b. JAMES URE, 10 Oct'53, Glasgow) – guitar (ex-SLIK, ex-RICH KIDS) repl. GARY MOORE who went solo. URE joined ULTRAVOX when repl. by **SNOWY WHITE**

May 80. (7") (LIZZY 6) **CHINATOWN. / SUGAR BLUES**	21	–

Sep 80. (7") *(LIZZY 7)* **KILLER ON THE LOOSE. / DON'T PLAY AROUND** `10` `–`
(d7"+=) *(LIZZY 7/+701)* – Got to give it up (live) / Chinatown (live).
Oct 80. (lp/c) *(6359/7150 030) <3496>* **CHINATOWN** `7` ☐
– We will be strong / Chinatown / Sweetheart / Sugar blues / Killer on the loose / Having a good time / Genocide (the killing of buffalo) / Didn't I / Hey you. *(re-is.Sep86, cd-iss. Jun89)*
Oct 80. (7") *<49643>* **KILLER ON THE LOOSE. / SUGAR BLUES** `–` `–`
Nov 80. (7"; as The GREEDIES) *(GREED 1)* **A MERRY JINGLE. / A MERRY JANGLE** `28` `–`
above also featured STEVE JONES + PAUL COOK (ex-SEX PISTOLS)
Feb 81. (7") *<49679>* **WE WILL BE STRONG. / SWEETHEART** `–` `–`
Apr 81. (7"ep/12"ep) *(LIZZY 8/+12)* **LIVE KILLERS** (live) `19` `–`
– Are you ready / Opium trail / Dear Miss lonely heart / Bad reputation.
Jul 81. (7") *(LIZZY 9)* **TROUBLE BOYS. / MEMORY PAIN** `53` `–`
Nov 81. (lp/c) *(6359/7150 083) <3622>* **RENEGADE** `38`
– Angel of death / Renegade / The pressure will blow / Leave this town / Hollywood (down on your luck) / No one told him / Fats / Mexican blood / It's getting dangerous. *(cd-iss. Jun90; 842435-2)*
Feb 82. (7"/7"pic-d) *(LIZZY/+PD 10) <50056>* **HOLLYWOOD (DOWN ON YOUR LUCK). / THE PRESSURE WILL BLOW** `53`
(10"one-sided) *(LIZZY 10)* – ('A'side only)

—— **LYNOTT + DOWNEY** recruited new members **JOHN SYKES** – guitar (ex-TYGERS OF PAN TANG) repl. GORHAM **DARREN WHARTON** – keyboards repl. SNOWY WHITE went solo + re-joined PINK FLOYD

Feb 83. (d7"/12") *(LIZZY 11 11-12/22)* **COLD SWEAT. / BAD HABITS / DON'T BELIEVE A WORD** (live). / **ANGEL OF DEATH** (live) `27` `–`
Mar 83. (lp/c) *(VERL/+C 3) <23831>* **THUNDER AND LIGHTNING** `4` ☐
– Thunder and lightning / This is the one / The sun goes down / The holy war / Cold sweat / Someday she is going to hit back / Baby please don't go / Bad habits / Heart attack. *(initial copies with free live 12")* – EMERALD / KILLER ON THE LOOSE. / THE BOYS ARE BACK IN TOWN / HOLLYWOOD *(cd-iss. Jun89; 810490-2)*
Apr 83. (7"/12") *(LIZZY 12/+12)* **THUNDER AND LIGHTNING. / STILL IN LOVE WITH YOU** (live) `39` `–`
Jul 83. (7") *(LIZZY 13)* **THE SUN GOES DOWN** (remix). / **BABY PLEASE DON'T GO** `52` `–`
(12"+=) *(LIZZY 13/+12)* – ('A'remix).
Nov 83. (d-lp/d-c) *(VERD/+C 6) <23986>* **LIFE** (live) `29` ☐
– Thunder & lightning / Waiting for an alibi / Jailbreak / Baby please don't go / The holy war / Renegade / Hollywood / Got to give it up / Angel of death / Are you ready / Boys are back in town / Cold sweat / Don't believe a word / Killer on the loose / The sun goes down / Emerald / Roisin dubh (Black rose) A rock legend part 1. Shenandoah – part 2. Will you go lassy go – part 3. Danny boy – part 4. The mason's apron / Still in love with you / The rocker. *(4th side featured past members) (cd-iss. Aug90; 812882-2)*

—— Had already concluded proceedings. LYNOTT and DOWNEY formed short-lived GRAND SLAM. Tragically, PHIL LYNOTT died of heart failure on the 4th January '86.

– compilations, others –

Aug 76. (lp/c) *(SKL/KSKC 5249)* **REMEMBERING – PART ONE** ☐ `–`
Jan 78. (7"m) Decca; *(F 13748)* **WHISKEY IN THE JAR. / SITAMOIA / VAGABOND OF THE WESTERN WORLD** ☐ `–`
Aug 79. (7"m) Decca; *(THIN 1)* **THINGS AIN'T WORKING OUT DOWN ON THE FARM. / THE ROCKER / LITTLE DARLIN'** ☐ `–`
Sep 79. (lp) Decca; *(SKL 5298)* **THE CONTINUING SAGA OF THE AGEING ORPHANS** ☐ `–`
Apr 81. (lp/c) Vertigo; *(LIZ TV/MC 001)* **ADVENTURES OF THIN LIZZY** `6` `–`
– Whiskey in the jar / Wild one / Jailbreak / The boys are back in town / Don't believe a word / Dancing in the moonlight / Waiting for an alibi / Do anything you want to / Sarah / Chinatown / Killer on the loose.
Dec 81. (lp/c) Decca; *(KTBC/TAB 28)* **ROCKERS** ☐ `–`
(re-iss. Oct93 on 'Deram' cd/c; 820 526-2/-4)
Mar 83. (cd) Vertigo; *(800 060-2)* **LIZZY KILLERS** ☐ `–`
Oct 83. (7") Old Gold; *(OG 9330)* **WHISKEY IN THE JAR. / THE ROCKER** ☐ `–`
Nov 83. (lp/c) Contour; *(CN/+4 2066)* **THE BOYS ARE BACK IN TOWN** ☐ `–`
Jan 85. (7") Old Gold; *(OG 9484)* **DANCING IN THE MOONLIGHT. / DON'T BELIEVE A WORD** ☐ `–`
Nov 85. (d-lp/c) Castle; *(CCS LP/MC 117)* **THE COLLECTION** ☐ `–`
(cd-iss. Jul87; CCSCD 117)
Nov 85. (lp/c) Karussel Gold; *(822694-1/-4)* **WHISKEY IN THE JAR** ☐ `–`
Apr 86. (lp/c) Contour; *(CN/+4 2080)* **WHISKEY IN THE JAR** ☐ `–`
Aug 86. (12"ep) Archive 4; **WHISKEY IN THE JAR / THE ROCKER. / SARAH / BLACK BOYS ON THE CORNER** ☐ `–`
Nov 87. (lp/c/cd) Telstar; *(STAR/STAC/TCD 2300)* **THE BEST OF PHIL LYNOTT & THIN LIZZY – SOLDIER OF FORTUNE** `55` `–`
– Whiskey in the jar / Waiting for an alibi / Sarah / Parisieene walkways / Do anything you want to / Yellow pearl / Chinatown / King's call / The boys are back in town / Rosalie (cowboy's song) / Dancing in the moonlight / Don't believe a word / Jailbreak. *(cd+=)* – Out in the fields / Killer on the loose / Still in love with you.
Feb 88. (7") Old Gold; *(OG 9764)* **THE BOYS ARE BACK IN TOWN. / ('B'by Bachman-Turner Overdrive)** ☐ `–`
Jun 89. (lp) Grand Slam; *<SLAM 4>* **LIZZY LIVES** (1976-84) `–` `–`
Jan 91. (7"/c-s) Vertigo; *(LIZZY/LIZMC 14)* **DEDICATION. / COLD SWEAT** `35` `–`
(12"+=/cd-s+=) *(LIZZY1/LIZCD 14)* – Emerald (live) / Still in love with you.
(12"pic-d+=) *(LIZP1 14)* – Bad reputation / China town.
Feb 91. (cd/c/lp) Vertigo; *(848 192-2/-4/-1)* **DEDICATION – THE VERY BEST OF THIN LIZZY** `8` `–`
– Whiskey in the jar / The boys are back in town / Jailbreak / Don't believe a word / Dancing in the moonlight / Rosalie – Cowgirl song (live) / Waiting for an alibi / Do anything you want to / Parisieene walkways (with GARY MOORE) / The rocker / Killer on the loose / Sarah / Out in the fields (with GARY MOORE) / Dedication. *(cd+=/c+=)* – Still in love with you (live) / Bad reputation / Emerald / Chinatown.

Mar 91. (7"/c-s) Vertigo; *(LIZZY/LIZMC 15)* **THE BOYS ARE BACK IN TOWN. / SARAH** `63` `–`
(12"/cd-s) *(LIZZY1/LIZCD 15)* – ('A'side) / Johnny the fox / Black boys on the corner / Me and the boys.
Oct 92. (cd) Windsong; *(WINCD 024)* **BBC RADIO 1 LIVE IN CONCERT** ☐ `–`
Nov 94. (cd/c) Strange Fruit; *(SFR CD/MC 130)* **THE PEEL SESSIONS** ☐ `–`
Jan 96. (cd/c) Polygram; *(528113-2/-4)* **WILD ONE – THE VERY BEST OF THIN LIZZY** `18` `–`
Mar 96. (cd) Spectrum; *(552085-2/-4)* **WHISKEY IN THE JAR** ☐ `–`

PHIL LYNOTT

(solo) but with THIN LIZZY members.

		Vertigo	Warners
Mar 80. (7"/12") *(SOLO 1/+12)* **DEAR MISS LONELY HEARTS. / SOLO IN SOHO** `32` `–`
Apr 80. (lp)(pic-lp) *(9102 038)(PHIL 1) <3405>* **SOLO IN SOHO** `28`
– Dear Miss lonely hearts / King's call / A child's lullaby / Tattoo / Solo in Soho / Girls / Yellow pearl / Ode to a black man / Jamaican rum / Talk in '79. *(re-iss. Sep85 lp'c; PRICE/PRIMC 88) (cd-iss. Jul90; 842564-2)*
Jun 80. (7") *(SOLO 2) <49272>* **KING'S CALL. / ODE TO A BLACK MAN** `35` `–`
Mar 81. (7"yellow) *(SOLO 3)* **YELLOW PEARL. / GIRLS** `56` `–`
(re-iss. Dec81 – 12"; SOLO 3-12)
(above was later the TV theme for 'Top Of The Pops')
Aug 82. (7") *(SOLO 4)* **TOGETHER. / SOMEBODY ELSE'S DREAM** ☐ `–`
(12"+=) *(SOLO 4-12)* – ('A'dance version).
Sep 82. (7") *(SOLO 5)* **OLD TOWN. / BEAT OF THE DRUM** ☐ `–`
Oct 82. (lp/c) *(6359/7150 117)* **THE PHIL LYNOTT ALBUM** ☐ `–`
– Fatalistic attitude / The man's a fool / Old town / Cathleen / Growing up / Together / Little bit of water / Ode to liberty (the protest song) / Gino / Don't talk about me baby. *(cd-iss. Jul90; 842564-2)*

—— May'85, GARY MOORE & PHIL hit UK Top 5 with 'OUT IN THE FIELDS'.

		Polydor	not iss.
Nov 85. (7") *(POSP 777)* **19. / 19 (dub)** ☐ `–`
(12"+=) *(POSPX 777)* – A day in the life of a blues singer.
(d7"+=; 1 pic-d) *(POSPD 777)* – THIN LIZZY; Whiskey in the jar – The rocker.

– (PHIL LYNOTT) posthumous –

Jan 87. (7") Vertigo; *(LYN 1)* **KING'S CALL. / YELLOW PEARL** `68` `–`
(12"+=) *(LYN 1-12)* – Dear Miss lonely hearts (live).

THIN WHITE ROPE   (dig out; Great Alt & Indie . . .)

THIRD EYE BLIND

Formed: San Francisco, California, USA . . . mid-90's by frontman, STEPHAN JENKINS. After supporting OASIS in their home city, 3EB signed a lucrative deal with 'Elektra' for whom they delivered their first US Top 5 hit, 'SEMI-CHARMED LIFE'. That Spring of '97 also saw the band gain massive sales for their eponymous debut set which also climbed into the Top 30. Musically, they were nothing startling or adventurous (lying inbetween STEVE MILLER and the SPIN DOCTORS), although classy acoustic alt-rock/pop tunes did help the band achieve some kind of steady fanbase. So far (late '99), only America has had the chance to hear the sophomore set, 'BLUE', apparently not as good as the debut.

Album rating: THIRD EYE BLIND (*6) / BLUE (*5)

STEPHAN JENKINS – vocals, guitar / **KEVIN CADOGAN** – guitar / **REN KLYCE** – keyboards / **ARION SALAZAR** – bass, keyboards

		Elektra	Elektra
Jun 97. (c-s) *(E 4181C) <64137>* **SEMI-CHARMED LIFE. / TATTOO OF THE SUN** ☐ `4` Mar97
(cd-s+=) *(E 4181CD)* – London.
Jun 97. (cd/c) *<(7559 62012-2/-4)>* **THIRD EYE BLIND** ☐ `25` Apr97
– Losing a whole year / Narcolepsy / Semi-charmed life / Jumper / Graduate / How's it going to be / Thanks a lot / Burning man / Good for you / London / I want you / Background / Motorcycle drive-by / God of wine.
Sep 97. (7"/c-s) *(E 3907/+C)* **SEMI-CHARMED LIFE. / TATTOO OF THE SUN** `33` `–`
(cd-s+=) *(E 3907CD)* – London.
(re-iss. May98; same)
Nov 97. (7") *(E 3883)* **GRADUATE. / HORROR SHOW** ☐ `–`
(c-s+=/cd-s+=) *(E 3883 C/CD)* – ('A'remix).
Mar 98. (c-s/cd-s) *(E 3863 C/CD) <64130>* **HOW'S IT GOING TO BE / SEMI-CHARMED LIFE / HORROR SHOW** `51` `9` Nov97
Jul 98. (7") *(E 3832)* **LOSING A WHOLE YEAR. / HORROR SHOW** ☐ `–`
(cd-s+=) *(E 3832CD)* – Graduate (remix).
Nov 98. (-) *<radio play>* **JUMPER / GRADUATE (remix)** `–` `5`
Nov 99. (cd/c) *<62415>* **BLUE** `–` `40`
– Anything / Wounded / 10 days late / Never let you go / Deep inside of you / 1000 Julys / Ode to maybe / Red summer sun / Camouflage / Farther / Slow motion / Darkness / Darwin.

13th FLOOR ELEVATORS

Formed: Austin, Texas, USA . . . 1965 by ROKY ERICKSON and TOMMY HALL, together with STACY SUTHERLAND, BENNY THURMAN and JOHN IKE WALTON. ERICKSON had originally written and recorded 'YOU'RE GONNA MISS ME' with his first band, The SPADES, the single being released on the small 'Zero' label. A local hit, the record gained national

notoriety in early '66 after being picked up by the 'International Artists' label. Around this time, self-styled psychedelic explorer, TOMMY HALL, had introduced ERICKSON to the aforementioned musicians (all three were ex-LINGSMEN) and The 13th FLOOR ELEVATORS were launched into orbit. The frenzied garage thrash of 'YOU'RE GONNA MISS ME' stood out from the pack by dint of ERICKSON's apocalyptic vocal threats and HALL's bizarre amplified jug playing. In addition to his idiosyncratic musical accompaniment, HALL penned most of the lyrics, setting out his agenda according to the chemically-enhanced evolution-of-man ethos espoused by the likes of acid guru, TIM LEARY. Debuting with 'THE PSYCHEDELIC SOUNDS OF THE 13TH FLOOR ELEVATORS' in 1966, the band had unleashed nothing less than a musical manifesto for mind expansion. But if the idea was to promote the use of halucinogenics, then the sirens on the DMT-tribute, 'FIRE ENGINE', surely encouraged any sane person never to go near the stuff, sounding more like the tortured wailing of lost, limbo-locked souls. Likewise 'MONKEY ISLAND', with ERICKSON howling like a man possessed. Elsewhere on the album, tracks like 'ROLLERCOASTER' and 'REVERBATION (DOUBT)' made for thrilling, if uneasy listening, and it was obvious that a trip to the 13th floor with ROCKY and Co. was somewhat different from the rosy hue that the psychedelic experience had taken on in popular mythology. The follow-up, 'EASTER EVERYWHERE' (1967), was a slightly more contemplative affair, opening with the hypnotic brilliance of 'SLIP INSIDE THIS HOUSE' (the subject of an equally essential 90's interpretation by PRIMAL SCREAM) through the trippy 'SHE LIVES (IN A TIME OF HER OWN)' and on to the frantic 'LEVITATION'. Inevitably, the Texan police were none too amused with the band's flagrant advocacy of drugs and after escalating harassment, ERICKSON found himself in court shortly after the album's release. Charged with possession of a small amount of hashish, he was faced with a choice of jail or mental hospital and rather unadvisedly chose the latter. This effectively signalled the end for the band, although a disappointing live album was released the following year and a final studio album appeared in 1969. 'BULL OF THE WOODS' was made up largely of SUTHERLAND-penned tunes although it contained the sublime 'MAY THE CIRCLE REMAIN UNBROKEN', ERICKSON's vocal all the more haunting in light of his tragic incarceration. Subjected to years of mind-numbing drugs and electro shock therapy, ROCKY was finally released in 1972 after a judge declared him sane. Ironically no doubt somewhat less sane after this experience, ERICKSON started making music again, forming a band, BLEIB ALIEN, and immersing himself in B-movie horror nonsense. After a stint in the studio with fellow Texan, DOUG SAHM, of SIR DOUGLAS QUINTET fame, ERICKSON released the inspired psychosis of the 'RED TEMPLE PRAYER (TWO HEADED DOG)' single in 1975. An album, 'ROCKY ERICKSON AND THE ALIENS' surfaced in 1980 and included such wholesome fare as 'DON'T SHAKE ME LUCIFER', 'CREATURE WITH THE ATOM BRAIN' and 'STAND FOR THE FIRE DEMON'. Yet this was no po-faced heavy-metal posturing, ERICKSON actually believed what he was singing about, lending the record a certain level of intensity, despite the cliched hard rock backing. A series of singles and compilations appeared sporadically throughout the 80's, and after ERICKSON was hospitalised again for a short period, 'Warner Bros.' executive and longtime ELEVATORS fan, BILL BENTLEY, masterminded a tribute album, 'Where The Pyramid Meets The Eye', featuring the likes of The JESUS AND MARY CHAIN and JULIAN COPE. Although a collection of early material, 'ALL THAT MAY DO MY RHYME', appeared in 1975 on The BUTTHOLE SURFERS' 'Trance Syndicate' label, ERICKSON appears to have had no interest in writing new material. Music biz legend paints the man as an acid casualty, and while he definitely appears to live in a world of his own making, his wayward genius continues to win the respect and admiration of fans the world over.
• Songwriters: ERICKSON penned except; I'M GONNA LOVE YOU TOO (Buddy Holly) / HEROIN (Velvet Underground) / BLOWIN' IN THE WIND (Bob Dylan) / etc.
Album rating: THE PSYCHEDELIC SOUNDS OF (*7) / EASTER EVERYWHERE (*6) / LIVE exploitation (*4) / BULL OF THE WOODS exploitation (*5) / THE BEST OF THE 13th FLOOR ELEVATORS compilation (*7) / HIS EYE IS ON THE PYRAMID compilation (*8) / Roky Erickson: ROCKY ERICKSON & THE ALIENS (*6) / THE EVIL ONE (*5) / CLEAR NIGHT FOR LOVE mini (*4) / GREMLINS HAVE PICTURES (*4) / DON'T SLANDER ME (*5) / CASTING THE RUNES collection (*4) / THE HOLIDAY INN TAPES fan-club (*4) / OPENERS exploitation (*4) / LIVE AT THE RITZ (*4) / YOU'RE GONNA MISS ME: THE BEST OF ROKY ERICKSON compilation (*7) / MAD DOG compilation (*4) / ALL THAT MAY DO MY RHYME (*6) / NEVER SAY GOODBYE (*7)

The SPADES

— (had already recorded a single 'I NEED A GIRL', before ROKY joined)

— **ROKY ERICKSON** (b. ROGER KYNARD ERICKSON, 15 Jul'47, Dallas, Texas) – vocals, harmonica / **JOHN KERNEY** – guitar, vocals

		not iss.	Zero
1965.	(7") <10002> **YOU'RE GONNA MISS ME. / WE SELL SOUL**	–	☐

13th FLOOR ELEVATORS

— were formed by **ROKY** and **STACEY SUTHERLAND** – lead guitar (ex-LINGSMEN) / **BENNY THURMAN** – bass, electric violin (ex-LINGSMEN) / **JOHN IKE WALTON** – drums (ex-LINGMEN) / **TOMMY HALL** – blow jug, lyrics

		not iss.	Contact
Jan 66.	(7") <5269> **YOU'RE GONNA MISS ME. / TRIED TO HIDE** <re-iss. Apr66 on 'Hanna Barbara'; HBR 492> <re-iss. Jun66 on 'International Artists'; 107>; hit No.55> (UK-iss.Nov78 on 'Radar' 7"green; ADA 13)	–	

— **RONNIE LEATHERMAN** – bass repl. BENNY who formed PLUM NELLY

		not iss.	Int.Artists
Aug 66.	(lp) <IALP 1> **THE PSYCHEDELIC SOUNDS OF** – You're gonna miss me / Roller coaster / Splash 1 / Don't fall down / Reverberation (doubt) / Fire engine / Thru the rhythm / You don't know / Kingdom of Heaven / Monkey island / Tried to hide. <re-iss. 1977; same> (UK-iss.Nov78 on 'Radar'; RAD 13) (re-iss. Feb88 on 'Decal'; LIK 19) (cd-iss. 1990's on 'Decal-Charly'; CDGR 110) (cd re-iss. Jan99 on 'Spalax'; 14819) (lp re-iss. Nov99; same as US)	–	
Oct 66.	(7") <111> **REVERBERATION (DOUBT). / FIRE ENGINE**	–	

— **DAN GALINDO** – bass + **DANNY THOMAS** – drums repl. RONNIE + JOHN IKE

Feb 67.	(7") <113> **I'VE GOT LEVITATION. / BEFORE YOU ACCUSE ME**	–	
Apr 67.	(lp) <IALP 5> **EASTER EVERYWHERE** – Slip inside the house / Slide machine / She lives in a time of her own / Nobody to love / It's all over now, baby blue / Earthquake / Dust / I've got levitation / I had to tell you / Postures (leave your body behind). <re-iss. 1977; same> (UK-iss.May79 on 'Radar'; RAD 15) (re-iss. Apr88 on 'Decal'; LIK 28) (cd-iss. Jan99 on 'Spalax'; 14888) (lp re-iss. May99; same as US)	–	
Oct 67.	(7") <121> **SHE LIVES (IN A TIME OF HER OWN). / BABY BLUE**		
Dec 67.	(7") <122> **SLIP INSIDE THIS HOUSE. / SPLASH 1**		

— Disbanded early '68, due to ROKY being imprisoned for possession of a miniscule of hash. He once escaped but was then kept there for another 3 years, and suffered thorazine plus electric shock treatment. **DUKE DAVIS** – bass had briefly repl. GALINDO. DANNY THOMAS and DUKE were to become The GOLDEN DAWN. The original 13th FLOOR ELEVATORS reformed in 1972. In 1984, they gigged again with line-up (ERICKSON, WALTON, LEATHERMAN and GREG 'Catfish' FORREST-guitar). In Autumn 1978, STACEY was shot dead by his wife.

– others, compilations, etc. –

on 'International Artists' unless otherwise mentioned

1968.	(lp) <IALP 8> **LIVE** (studio out-takes, b-sides, demos; with false applause) – Before you accuse me / She lives in a time of her own / Tried to hide / You gotta take that girl / I'm gonna love you too / Everybody needs somebody to love / I've got levitation / You can't hurt me anymore / Roller coaster / You're gonna miss me. (UK-iss.May88 on 'Decal'; LIK 30)	–	
1968.	(7") <126> **MAY THE CIRCLE BE UNBROKEN. / I'M GONNA LOVE YOU TOO**	–	
1969.	(lp) <IALP 9> **BULL OF THE WOODS** (rec. early'68) – Livin' on / Barnyard blues / Till then / Never another / Rose and the thorn / Down by the river / Scarlet and gold / Street song / Doctor Boom / With you / May the circle remain unbroken. (UK-iss.Jul88 on 'Decal'; LIK 40) (cd-iss. Jan99 on 'Spalax'; 14886) (lp re-iss. Aug99; same as US)	–	
1969.	(7") <130> **LIVIN' ON. / SCARLET AND GOLD**	–	
Oct 78.	(7"ep) Austin; <RE 1> **YOU REALLY GOT ME. / WORD / ROLL OVER BEETHOVEN**	–	
1985.	(lp) Texas Archives; <TAR LP-4> **FIRE IN MY BONES**	–	
1987.	(lp) Texas Archives; <TAR LP-7> **ELEVATOR TRACKS (some live 1966)**	–	
1988.	(lp) Big Beat; (WIK 82) **I'VE SEEN YOUR FACE BEFORE** (live bootleg '66) (cd-iss. Jun89; CDWIK 82)		
1988.	(lp) 13th Hour; <(13-LP-1)> **DEMOS EVERYWHERE** (US-title 'THE ORIGINAL SOUND OF . . .')		
Nov 88.	(cd) Charly; (CDCHARLY 150) **EASTER EVERYWHERE / BULL OF THE WOODS**		–
Jun 89.	(cd) Charly; (CDCHARLY 159) **THE PSYCHEDELIC SOUNDS OF / LIVE**		–
Aug 91.	(4xcd-box) Decal; (LIKBOX 2) **THE COLLECTION** – (all 1960's albums) <In 1979, these appeared on a 12-lp box of 'International Artists'>		
Jul 93.	(cd) Thunderbolt; (CDTB 124) **OUT OF ORDER (LIVE AT THE AVALON BALLROOM)**		–
Jun 94.	(cd) Thunderbolt; (CDTB 147) **LEVITATION – IN CONCERT (live)**		–
Apr 95.	(cd) Thunderbolt; (CDTB 153) **THE REUNION CONCERT**		–
Dec 95.	(cd) Nectar; (NTMCD 516) **THE BEST OF THE 13th FLOOR ELEVATORS** – You're gonna miss me / Levitation / I had to tell you / She lives (in a time of her own) / Never another / I'm gonna love you too (live) / Thry the rhythm / The kingdom of Heaven / Slip inside this house / Mpnkey island / Splash 1 / Fire engine / Dr. Doom / Roller coaster / Earthquake / Reverberation (doubt) / May the circle remain unbroken / You're gonna miss me (live). (re-iss. Jul99 on 'Eva'; 642370)		
Sep 96.	(cd) Thunderbolt; (CDTB 508) **THE INTERPRETER** (re-iss. Jun99; CDTB 198)		–
Nov 97.	(cd) Music Club; (MCCD 324) **ALL TIME HIGHS**		
Nov 97.	(cd) Eagle; (EAGCD 069) **THE MASTERS**		
Oct 99.	(cd) Thunderbolt; (CDTB 199) **THE INTERPRETER VOL.2**		
Nov 99.	(d-cd) Recall; (SMDCD 190) **HIS EYE IS ON THE PYRAMID**		

ROKY ERICKSON

		not iss.	Mars
1975.	(7"; with BLIEB ALIEN) <1000> **RED TEMPLE PRAYER (TWO HEADED DOG). / STARRY EYES**	–	☐

		Virgin	Rhino
Sep 77.	(7") (VS 180) <003> **BERMUDA. / INTERPRETER**		

		Sponge	not iss.
Dec 77.	(7"ep) (101) **TWO HEADED DOG / I HAVE ALWAYS BEEN HERE BEFORE. / MINE, MINE, MIND / CLICK YOUR FINGERS APPLAUDING THE PLAY**	–	– France

ROKY ERICKSON AND THE ALIENS

—— with **DUANE ASLAKSEN** – guitar / **STEVE BURGESS** – bass / **ANDRE LEWIS** – keyboards / **FUZZY FURIOSO** – drums / **BILL MILLER** – autoharp

	C.B.S.	Columbia
Aug 80. (7") *(CBS 8888)* **CREATURE WITH THE ATOM BRAIN. / THE WIND AND MORE**	☐	–
Aug 80. (lp) *(CBS 84463)* **ROKY ERICKSON & THE ALIENS**	☐	–

– Two headed dog / I think of demons / Don't shake me Lucifer / I walked with a zombie / Night of the vampire / Cold night for alligators / White faces / Creatures with the atom brain / Mine, mine, mind / Stand for the fire demon. *(re-iss. Jan87 as 'I THINK OF DEMONS' on 'Edsel'+=; ED 222) – (2 tracks). (cd-iss. Jun97; EDCD 528)*

| Oct 80. (7") *(CBS 9055)* **MINE MINE MIND. / BLOODY HAMMER** (long version) | ☐ | – |

ROKY ERICKSON

	not iss.	415 Records
1981. (lp; as ROKY ERICKSON AND THE ALIENS) *<0005>* **THE EVIL ONE**	–	☐

– Two-headed dog (red temple prayer) / I think of demons / Creature with the atom brain / Wind and more / Don't shake me Lucifer / Bloody hammer / Stand for the the fire demon / Click your fingers applauding the play / If you have ghosts / I walked with a zombie / Night of the vampire / It's a cold night for alligators / Mine mine mind / Sputnik / White faces. *<cd-iss. 1987 was a compilation on 'Enigma-Pink Dust'; 72212-2>*

	not iss.	Dynamite
1984. (7") *<DY 002>* **DON'T SLANDER ME. / STARRY EYES**	–	☐

	New Rose	not iss.
1985. (m-lp) *(ROSE 69)* **CLEAR NIGHT FOR LOVE**	☐	– France

– You don't love me yet / Clear night for love / The haunt / Starry eyes / Don't slander me.

	One Big Guitar	Live Wire
Apr 86. (12") *(OBG 004T)* *<LW 5>* **THE BEAST. / HEROIN** (live)	☐	☐ Nov85

	Demon	Enigma
Jan 87. (lp) *(FIEND 66)* *<72109-1>* **GREMLINS HAVE PICTURES** (live 1975-1982 with his bands)	☐	☐ Nov86

– Night of the vampire / Interpreter / Song to Abe Lincoln / John Lawman / Anthem / Warning / Sweet honey pie / Cold night for alligators / I am / Heroin / I have always been there before / Before the beginning / Click your fingers applauding the play / If you have ghosts / Damn thing / Sputnik. *(cd-iss. Oct90 with extra tracks; FIENDCD 66)*

| Jun 87. (lp) *(FIEND 86)* **DON'T SLANDER ME** | ☐ | – |

– (contains some of 'THE EVIL ONE' lp)

	Fan Club	not iss.
Sep 87. (lp) *(FC 030)* **THE HOLIDAY INN TAPES**	☐	–

—— next with **WILL SEXTON + CHRIS HOLYHAUS** – guitar / **FREDDIE KRC** – drums

| 1988. (lp) *(FC 046)* **LIVE AT THE RITZ** (live Feb'87) | ☐ | – |

– You're gonna miss me / Don't slander me / Don't shake me Lucifer / Night of the vampire / Two headed dog / Splash 1 / Take a good look at yourself / Clear night for love / Bloody hammer.

—— next with **ET** (aka EVILHOOK WILDLIFE) **BRIAN S.CURLEY / KERRY GRAFTON / TIM GAGAN + DAVE CAMERON**

	Fundam.	not iss.
Feb 88. (12") *(PRAY 007)* **CLEAR NIGHT FOR LOVE. / YOU DON'T LOVE ME YET**	☐	–

	not iss.	Rok
Dec 88. (7"ep) *<88>* **ACOUSTIC EP**	–	☐

	Sympathy..	Sympathy..
1992. (7") **HASN'T ANYONE TOLD YOU. / THE INTERPRETER**	☐	☐

	Trance Syndicate	Trance Syndicate
Nov 94. (7"ltd.) *(TR 28)* **WE ARE NEVER TALKING. / PLEASE JUDGE** (acoustic version)	☐	☐
Feb 95. (lp/cd) *<(TR 33/+CD)>* **ALL THAT MAY DO MY RHYME**	☐	☐

– I'm gonna free her / Starry eyes / You don't love me yet / Please judge / Don't slander me / We are never talking / For you (I'd do anything) / For you / Clear night for love / Haunt / Starry eyes.

– compilations, others, etc. –

| Aug 87. (lp/pic-lp) *5 Hours Back; (TOCK 007/+P)* **CASTING THE RUNES** | ☐ | – |

(cd-iss. Jan99 on 'R.E.'; RE 1)

(above live Nov79 with The EXPLOSIVES; aka **CAM KING** – lead guitar / **WILLIE COLLIE** – bass / **FREDDIE KRC** – drums)

Mar 88. (lp) *5 Hours Back; (TOCK 010)* **OPENERS**	☐	–
Jun 88. (red-lp) *5 Hours Back; (TICK 001)* **TWO TWISTED TALES** (interview)	☐	–
1988. (cd) *Fan Club; (ROKY 1)* **CLICK YOUR FINGERS APPLAUDING THE PLAY**	☐	–
Sep 91. (cd/c) *Restless; <72532-2/-4>* **YOU'RE GONNA MISS ME: THE BEST OF ROKY ERICKSON**	–	☐

– Don't shake me Lucifer / Bermuda / Nothing in return / Click your fingers applauding the play / I am / I have always been here before / White faces / Night of the vampire / Don't slander me / Starry eyes / If you have ghosts / Can't be brought down / Creature with the atom brain / I walked with a zombie / Two-headed dog (red temple prayer) / You're gonna miss me / Wake up to rock'n'roll / Gonna die more / I'm a demon / Leave my kitten alone.

May 92. (cd/c) *Swordfish; (SFMD CD/LP 001)* **MAD DOG** (1976-83)	☐	–
Oct 92. (cd/lp) *New Rose; (422404)* **LIVE DALLAS 1979** (live with The NERVEBREAKERS)	☐	–
Feb 93. (cd) *Swordfish; (SFMCD 2)* **LOVE TO SEE YOU BLEED**	☐	–

– Bloody hammer / Every time I look at you / Miss Elude / Haunt / Laughing things / You don't love me yet / Creature with the atom brain / I think of demons / Two headed dog / Red temple prayer / Bumblebee zombie / Click your fingers applauding / The

play / Mine mine mind / Things that go bump in the night / Here today . . . gone tomorrow / Realise your my sweet brown angel eyes / I love to see you bleed / Please don't kill my baby.

| Feb 99. (cd) *Emperor Jones; <(EJ 26)>* **NEVER SAY GOODBYE** (rare material) | ☐ | ☐ |

– Unforced peace / I love the living you / I pledge allegiance / Pushing and pulling / Save me / Think of as one / Birds'd crash / Be and bring me home / I've never known this 'til now / "2 gone and number / I lovbe the blind man / Something extra / You're an unidentified flying object.

| Apr 99. (cd) *Triple X; <(TX 70024CD)>* **DEMON ANGEL** | ☐ | ☐ |

• **38 SPECIAL** (dig out; 4th edition or Great Metal . . .)

31st FEBRUARY (see under ⇒ **ALLMAN BROTHERS BAND**)

THIS MORTAL COIL

Formed: Wandsworth, London, England . . . 1983 by IVO WATTS-RUSSELL, aided by producer JOHN FRYER. The brainchild of '4 a.d.' mainman, IVO, THIS MORTAL COIL was basically a loose collective of mainly 4ad artists gathered together with the intention of creating atmospheric and inspiring gothic-esque sounds, most effectively through their startling cover versions (see further below). With the COCTEAU TWINS (ELIZABETH FRASER and ROBIN GUTHRIE) initially taking a lead role, THIS MORTAL COIL made their mark with a haunting cover of Tim Buckley's 'SONG TO THE SIREN', wherein LIZ FRASER's lyrical mystical mantra was actually coherent to the unfamiliar ear. Originally intended as a B-side to a version of MODERN ENGLISH's '16 DAYS' (with the latter act's ROBBIE GREY on vocals), the track secured a minor chart place and has since become a cult classic (even providing inspiration for The CHEMICAL BROTHERS, or The DUST BROTHERS as they were known at the time!). Encouraged by the response, IVO took the opportunity to provide a wider platform for the emerging talent on his label, roping in selected personnel from DEAD CAN DANCE, COLOURBOX, WOLFGANG PRESS and X-MAL DEUTSCHLAND alongside vocalists HOWARD DEVOTO (ex-MAGAZINE) and GORDON SHARPE (of CINDYTALK – a non '4ad' act) to record a full-length THIS MORTAL COIL album, 'IT'LL END IN TEARS'. Preceded by the 'KANGAROO' single (from the pen of Alex Chilton), the 1984 set cracked the UK Top 40, its combination of low-key covers (featuring another Chilton number, 'HOLOCAUST') and moody instrumentals receiving lavish praise from the critics. IVO continued to expand his record company with new US acts (i.e. The PIXIES, THROWING MUSES, etc), lending a different flavour to the 1986 follow-up, 'FILIGREE & SHADOW'. Featuring new singer/writer DOMINIC APPLETON (from another non '4ad' act, BREATHLESS), this double-set contained a number of more well-known but just as inventive interpretations including Van Morrison's 'COME HERE MY LOVE', Tim Buckley's 'I MUST HAVE BEEN BLIND' and Talking Heads' 'DRUGS'. It was five years before TMC's third and final album, the UK Top 30 double-set, 'BLOOD' (1991), starring a stripped down cast of musicians including stalwart, APPLETON, alongside KIM DEAL, TANYA DONELLY, CAROLINE CRAWLEY (from SHELLEYAN ORPHAN) and HEIDI BERRY. More accessible than its two predecessors, the record was nevertheless a graceful swansong, featuring as it did engaging renditions of CHRIS BELL classics, 'YOU AND YOUR SISTER' and 'I AM THE COSMOS'. The proverbial 7-year itch came to an end when IVO resurfaced with a new outfit, The HOPE BLISTER. Similar in some respects to TMC, it gathered together friends such as LOUISE RUTKOWSKI, AUDREY RILEY and LAURENCE O'KEEFE on "comeback" dreamy-pop album, 'SMILE'S OK' (1998). • **Songwriters:** IVO and some 4 a.d. musicians, except; GATHERING DUST (Modern English) / ANOTHER DAY (Roy Harper) / NOT ME (Colin Newman) / THE JEWELLER (Tom Rapp) / HELP ME LIFT YOU UP (Mary Margaret O'Hara) / NATURE'S WAY (Spirit) / STRENGTH OF STRINGS + WITH TOMORROW (Gene Clark) / MY FATHER (. . . Collins) / I WANT TO LIVE (. . . Ogan) / FIRE BROTHERS (. . . Duncan) / MR. SOMEWHERE (. . . Walsh) / SEVERAL TIMES (. . . Nooten) / CAROLYN'S SONG (. . . Roback) / LATE NIGHT + TARANTULA (Syd Barrett) / TILL I GAIN CONTROL AGAIN (. . . Crowell) / I COME AND STAND AT EVERY DOOR (Byrds). The HOPE BLISTER covered DAGGER (Neil Halstead) / ONLY HUMAN (Heidi Berry) / SWEET UNKNOWN (Cranes) / LET THE HAPPINESS IN (David Sylvian) / IS JESUS YOUR PAL (Slow Blow) / THE SPIDER AND I (Eno) / HANKY PANKY NO HOW (John Cale).

Album rating: IT'LL END IN TEARS (*8) / FILIGREE & SHADOW (*7) / BLOOD (*7) / Hope Blister: SMILE'S OK (*6) / UNDERARMS (*3)

IVO WATTS-RUSSELL (b.1955) – tapes, loops, etc. / **JOHN FRYER** – instruments, producer with **COCTEAU TWINS:- ELIZABETH FRAZER** – vox / **ROBIN GUTHRIE** – guitar

	4 a.d.	4ad-Reprise
Sep 83. (7") *(AD 310)* **SONG TO THE SIREN. / 16 DAYS** (reprise)	66	–

(12"+=) *(BAD 310)* – Gathering dust.
(above 'B'sides featured **ROBBIE GREY** – vocals (of MODERN ENGLISH) (below 'A'side featured **MARTIN McCARRICK** – cello, strings (of WILLING SINNERS; **MARC ALMOND**) / **GORDON SHARPE** – vocals (of CINDYTALK) / **SIMON RAYMONDE** – guitar, tapes (of COCTEAU TWINS)

| Aug 84. (7") *(AD 410)* **KANGAROO. / IT'LL END IN TEARS** | ☐ | – |

below album featured above musicians, plus **GINI BALL** – violin (of WILLING

SINNERS) / DEAD CAN DANCE: **LIZA GERRARD** – accordion, vocals / **BRENDAN PERRY** – bass drone, drum / **PETER ULRICH** – percussion / COLOURBOX: **STEVEN YOUNG** – piano / **MARTYN YOUNG** – sitar, guitar, bass / X-MAL DEUTSCHLAND: **MANUELA RICKERS** – guitar / WOLFGANG PRESS: **MARK COX** – organ / **HOWARD DEVOTO** – vocals (ex-MAGAZINE)

Oct 84. (lp/c) (CAD/+C 411) <96269> **IT'LL END IN TEARS**　　| 38 |　| - |
– Kangaroo / Song to the siren / Holocaust / FYT / Fond affections / The last ray / Waves become wings / Another day / Barramundi / Dreams made flesh / Not me / A single wish. (cd-iss. 1986; CAD 411CD) <US cd-iss. 1993 on 'Warners'; 45454>

—— Retained guests **SIMON RAYMONDE / PETER ULRICH / MARK COX / STEVEN YOUNG** plus new BREATHLESS: **DOMINIC APPLETON** – vocals / **RICHENEL** – vocals / DIF JUZ: **DAVID CURTIS** – guitar / **ALAN CURTIS** – guitar / **RICHARD THOMAS** – saxophone / MODERN ENGLISH: **ANDREW GRAY** – guitar / / **JEAN** – vocals / **ALISON LIMERICK** – vocals / **CAROLINE SEAMAN** – vocals / **KEITH MITCHELL** – guitar / **DIERDRE RUTOWSKI** – backing vocals / **LOUISE RUTOWSKI** – backing vocals / **KEITH MITCHELL** – guitar / **NIGEL K.HINE** – guitar / **CHRIS PYE** – guitar / **JOHN TURNER** – organ, keyboards / **TONY WAEREA** – didgeridoo / **ANNE TURNER + LES McKUEN** – choir

Sep 86. (d-lp/c)(cd) (DAD/+C 609)(DAD 609CD) **FILIGREE & SHADOW**　　| 53 |　| - |
– Velvet belly / The jeweller / Ivy and neet / Meniscus / Tears / Tarantula / My father / Come here my love / At first, and then / Strength of strings / Morning glory / Inch-blue / I want to live / Mama K I / Filigree & shadow / Firebrothers / Thais I / I must have been blind / A heart of glass / Alone / Mama K II / The horizon bleeds and sucks its thumb / Drugs / Red rain / Thais II. <US cd-iss. 1993 on 'Warners'; 45453>

Sep 86. (ltd-10") (BAD 608) **COME HERE MY LOVE. / DRUGS**　　| | | - |

—— They used past musicians, plus **CAROLINE CRAWLEY, KIM DEAL + TANYA DONELLY, DOMINIC APPLETON, HEIDI BERRY + The RUTOWSKI's**, etc.

Apr 91. (d-lp/c/cd) (DAD/+C/CD 609) **BLOOD**　　| 28 |　| - |
– The lacemaker / Mr. Somewhere / Ardialu / With tomorrow / Loose joints / You and your sister / Nature's way / I come and steal at every door / Bitter / Baby Ray baby / Several times / The lacemaker II / Late night / Ruddy and wretched / Help me lift you up / Carolyn's song / DD and E / Til I gain control again / Dreams are like water / I am the cosmos / (Nothing but) Blood. <US cd-iss. 1993 on 'Warners'; 45452>
above was their final release

– compilations, etc. –

Dec 89. (cd) Alex; <1426> **THIS MORTAL COIL**　　| - | | |
Mar 93. (cd) Warners; <45135> **1983-1991**　　| - | | |

HOPE BLISTER

IVO – producer / with **LOUISE RUTOWSKI** – vocals / **AUDREY RILEY** – strings / **LAURENCE O'KEEFE** – bass (ex-LEVITATION) / **SUE DENCH** – viola / **LEO PAYNE + CHRIS TOMBLING** – violin / **RITCHIE THOMAS** – drums, percussion, sax

　　　　　　　　　　　　　　　　　　　4 a.d.　　Mammoth
Jul 98. (cd) (CAD 8008) <980197> **SMILE'S OK**　　| | | | |
– Dagger / Only human / Outer skin / Sweet unknown / Let the happiness in / In Jesus your pal / The spider and I / Hanky panky no how.
Apr 99. (cd) **UNDERARMS** (remixes)　　| | | - |

David THOMAS (see under ⇒ PERE UBU)

Richard THOMPSON

Born: 3 Apr'49, London, England. A founder member of FAIRPORT CONVENTION from 1967 until his departure early in 1971, THOMPSON was an important catalyst in the translation of English folk music into a rock format. He contributed many of FAIRPORT CONVENTION's finest songs including 'MEET ON THE LEDGE' and 'SLOTH'. After session work for ex-FAIRPORT friends, SANDY DENNY and IAIN MATTHEWS, the bearded guitarist finally issued his 1972 debut album, 'HENRY THE HUMAN FLY', for 'Island' records. Just prior to this, he had worked with other recent ex-FAIRPORT members ASHLEY HUTCHINGS and DAVE MATTACKS who, as The BUNCH, released the budget covers lp 'ROCK ON'. The following year, he teamed up both artistically and romantically with LINDA PETERS, the couple becoming RICHARD & LINDA THOMPSON after their marriage in 1974. Their first of seven albums together, 'I WANT TO SEE THE BRIGHT LIGHTS AGAIN', was acclaimed by many, and by rights, should have provided them with a hit single in the evocative title track. During the recording of their next album, 'HOKEY POKEY' (1975), they converted to Sufism, even initiating their own Sufi community. Over the course of the next seven years, the royal couple of British folk created a string of finely crafted, harmony-laden albums, the pick of which was arguably 1982's 'SHOOT OUT THE LIGHTS'. The album featured the enduring 'WALL OF DEATH', appropriately enough the final track on their final album together, their marriage already having foundered. Picking up the pieces, RICHARD went solo again the following year, recording 'HAND OF KINDNESS' for 'Hannibal' Records, a set which included the excellent 'TWO LEFT FEET'. After finally achieving a more widespread recognition, he moved to 'Capitol' in the second half of the 80's and made significant inroads with the 1988 set, 'AMNESIA'. THOMPSON gained a belated UK Top 40 solo success with his 1991 album, 'RUMOUR AND SIGH', a wonderfully eclectic set running the gamut of THOMPSON's influences. 1994 saw the release of 'MIRROR BLUE', another critically acclaimed set including highlights such as 'MINGUS EYES' and 'THE WAY THAT IT SHOWS'. His 1996 release, 'YOU? ME? US?', introduced his son, TEDDY, to the proceedings and offered up further classic tracks in the shape of 'COLD KISSES' and 'WOODS OF

DARNEY'. His home city of London was the lyrical core of THOMPSON's next work, 'MOCK TUDOR' (1999). His witty tales of the capital's downside, 'WALKING THE LONG MILES HOME' and 'SIGHTS AND SOUNDS OF LONDON TOWN', could have been written years ago (but weren't!) but somehow RICHARD gives them a modern-day sheen that his contemporaries can only dream of. In his time, THOMPSON (now a practising Muslim) has influenced many guitarists including Americans, FRANK BLACK (of The PIXIES) and BOB MOULD (of HUSKER DU) and has come to be regarded as one of England's finest songwriting guitarists. • **Trivia:** A RICHARD THOMPSON tribute album in 1994, which will feature many top stars, playing their best RT tracks.

Album rating: HENRY THE HUMAN FLY (*7) / Richard & Linda Thompson: I WANT TO SEE THE BRIGHT LIGHTS TONIGHT (*8) / HOKEY POKEY (*7) / POUR DOWN LIKE SILVER (*7) / FIRST LIGHT (*6) / SUNNYVISTA (*5) / SHOOT OUT THE LIGHTS (*9) / Richard Thompson: (guitar, vocal) collection (*4) / STRICT TEMPO! (*4) / HAND OF KINDNESS (*7) / SMALL TOWN ROMANCE (*7) / ACROSS A CROWDED ROOM (*6) / DARING ADVENTURES (*7) / THE MARKSMAN soundtrack for TV with Peter Filleul (*4) / AMNESIA (*6) / RUMOUR AND SIGH (*7) / WATCHING THE DARK (THE HISTORY OF RICHARD THOMPSON 1969-1982) boxed-set (*8) / MIRROR BLUE (*6) / YOU? ME? US? (*6) / INDUSTRY with Danny Thompson (*5) / MOCK TUDOR (*7)

RICHARD THOMPSON – vocals, guitar (ex-FAIRPORT CONVENTION) with **LINDA PETERS / PAT DONALDSON** – bass / **TIM DONALD** – drums / plus **SANDY DENNY / ASHLEY HUTCHINGS / JOHN KIRKPATRICK / JOHN DEFERERI / BARRY DRANSFIELD / DAVID SNELL / CLAY TOYANI / ANDY ROBERTS / SUE DRAHEIM / JEFF COLE**

　　　　　　　　　　　　　　　　　　　Island　　Reprise
Jun 72. (lp/c) (ILPS/ZCI 9197) <2112> **HENRY THE HUMAN FLY**　　| | | |
– Roll over Vaughn Williams / Nobody's wedding / The poor ditching boy / Shaky Nancy / The angels took my racehorse away / Wheely down / The new St. George / Painted ladies / Cold feet / Mary and Joseph / The old changing ways / Twisted. (re-iss. Jan87 on 'Hannibal'; HNBL 4405) (re-iss. May87 c/cd; HNBC/HNCD 4405)

RICHARD & LINDA THOMPSON

husband & wife duo. LINDA (nee. PETERS) (ex-ALBION COUNTRY BAND) with SOUR GRAPES: **SIMON NICOL** – dulcimer / **STEVE BORRELL** – bass / **WILLIAM MURRAY** – drums (ex-KEVIN AYERS)/ plus most of main musicians on above album

　　　　　　　　　　　　　　　　　　　Island　　Island
Jan 74. (7") (WIP 6186) **I WANT TO SEE THE BRIGHT LIGHTS TONIGHT. / WHEN I GET TO THE BORDER**　　| | | |
Apr 74. (lp/c) (<ILPS/ZCI 9266>) **I WANT TO SEE THE BRIGHT LIGHTS TONIGHT**　　| | | |
– When I get to the border / The Calvery Cross / Withered and died / I want to see the bright lights tonight / Down where the drunkards roll / We sing hallelujah / Has he got a friend for me? / The little beggar girl / The end of the rainbow / The Great Valero. (cd-iss. May88; CID 9266) (re-iss. Oct89 on 'Carthage'; CGLP 4407) (cd re-iss. Mar93 on Island)

—— **IAN WHITEMAN** – keyboards, flute / **ALY BAIN** – fiddle repl. guests

Feb 75. (7") (WIP 6220) **HOKEY POKEY. / I'LL REGRET IT ALL IN THE MORNING**　　| | | |
Mar 75. (lp/c) (<ILPS/ZCI 9305>) **HOKEY POKEY**　　| | | |
– Hokey pokey (the ice-cream song) / I'll regret it all in the morning / Smiffy's glass eye / Egypt room / Never again / Georgie on a spree / Old man inside a young man / The Sun never shines on the poor / A heart needs a home / Mole in a hole. (re-iss. Jun86 on 'Hannibal'; HNBL 4408) (re-iss. May89 c/cd; HNBC/HNBD 4408)

Nov 75. (lp/c) (<ILPS/ZCI 9348>) **POUR DOWN LIKE SILVER**　　| | | |
– Streets of Paradise / For shame of doing wrong / The poor boy is taken away / Night comes in / Jet plane in a rocking chair / Beat the retreat / Hard luck stories / Dimming of the day / Dargai. (re-iss. Jun86 on 'Hannibal'; HNBL 4404) (re-iss. May89 c/cd; HNBC/HNBD 4404)

—— Their main band was:- **WILLIE WEEKS** – bass / **ANDY NEWMARK** – drums / **NEIL LARSON** – keyboards / **SIMON NICOL** – guitar, dulcimer / **JOHN KIRKPATRICK** – accordion

　　　　　　　　　　　　　　　　　　　Chrysalis　Chrysalis
Nov 78. (lp/c) (<CHR/ZCHS 1177>) **FIRST LIGHT**　　| | | |
– Restless highway / Sweet surrender / Don't let a thief steal into your heart / The choice wife / Died for love / Strange affair / Layla / Pavanne / House of cards / First light. (cd-iss. Jun86; CCD 1177) (re-iss. May89 on 'Carthage' lp/c; CGLP/CGC 4412)
Jan 79. (7") (CHS 2278) **DON'T LET A THIEF STEAL INTO YOUR HEART. / FIRST LIGHT**　　| | | |

—— **TIM DONALD, PAT DONALSON + RABBIT BUNDRICK** repl. NEWMARK, WEEKS + LARSON / guests:- **DAVE MATTACKS** – drums / **DAVE PEGG** – bass

Sep 79. (lp/c) (<CHR/ZCHS 1247>) **SUNNYVISTA**　　| | | |
– Civilization / Borrowed time / Saturday rolling around / You're going to need somebody / Why do you turn your back / Sunnyvista / Lonely hearts / Sisters / Justice in the streets / Traces of my love. (re-iss. May89 on 'Carthage' lp/c/cd; CGLP/CGC/CGCD 4403)
　　　　　　　　　　　　　　　　　　　Elixir　　not iss.
Sep 79. (7") (CHS 2369) **CIVILIZATION. / GEORGIE ON A SPREE**　　| | | - |
Sep 81. (lp) (LP 1) **STRICT TEMPO (RICHARD THOMPSON solo / instrumental)**　　| | | - |
– Scott Skinner medley / Banish misfortune / Dundee hornpipe / Do it for my sake / New fangled flogging reel / Vailance polka militair / Belfast polka / Rockin' in rhythm / The random jig / The grinder / Andalus / Marrakesh / The knife edge. (re-iss. Jul89 on 'Carthage' lp/c/cd; CGLP/CGC/CGCD 4409)

—— next w / **NICOL / MATTACKS / PEGG / + bassman PETE ZORN**
　　　　　　　　　　　　　　　　　　　Hannibal　Hannibal
Apr 82. (7") (HNS 703) **DON'T RENEGE ON YOUR LOVE. / LIVING IN LUXURY**　　| | | - |
Nov 82. (lp) (<HNBL 1303>) **SHOOT OUT THE LIGHTS**　　| | | |
– Man in need / Walking on a wire / Don't renege on your love / Just the motion / Shoot out the lights / Back street slide / Did she jump or was she pushed / Wall of death. (re-iss. Jun86 lp/c/cd+=; HNBL/HNBC/HNBD 1303) – Living in luxury. (cd-iss. Dec94 on 'Hannibal')

RICHARD THOMPSON

—— returned to solo work after separating with LINDA. He retained last band and label, while LINDA went on in 1985 to release an album ONE CLEAR MOMENT' for Warners'.

Jun 83. (lp) (<*HNBL 1313*>) **HAND OF KINDNESS**
   – A poisoned heart and a twisted memory / Tear stained letter / How I wanted to / Both ends burning / The wrong heartbeat / Hand of kindness / Devonside / Two left feet. *(re-iss. Jun86 lp/c/cd+=; HNBL/HNBC/HNBD 1313)* – Where the wind don't whine.

Jul 83. (7") (*HNS 704*) **THE WRONG HEARTBEAT. / DEVONSIDE**   [ ] [-]

Dec 84. (lp) (<*HNBL 1316*>) **SMALL TOWN ROMANCE (live)**
   – Time to ring some changes / Beat the retreat / A heart needs a home / Woman or a man / For shame of doin' wrong / Genesis Hall / Honky tonk blues / Small town romance / I want to see the bright lights tonight / Down where the drunkards roll / Love is bad for business / Never again / The Great Valero / Don't let a thief steal into your heart. i*(re-iss. Jun86 lp/c/cd; HNBL/HNBC/HNBD 1316)*

	Polydor	Polydor
Mar 85. (lp/c) (*POLD/+C 5175*) <*825421*> **ACROSS A CROWDED ROOM**   [80]
   – When the spell is broken / You don't say / I ain't going to drag my feet no more / Love in a faithless country / Fire in the engine room / Walking through a wasted land / Little blue number / She twists the knife again / Ghosts in the wind. *(cd-iss. Jun86; 825421-2) (cd re-iss. Jun92 on 'Beat Goes On' cd/c/lp; BGO CD/MC/LP 139)*

Jun 85. (7") (*POSP 750*) **YOU DON'T SAY. / WHEN THE SPELL IS BROKEN**   [ ] [ ]

—— now with **MITCHELL FROOM** – organ / **JERRY SCHEFF** – bass / **MICKEY CURRY + JIM KELTNER** – drums / **JOHN KIRKPATRICK** – accordion / **ALEX ACUNA** – percussion

Oct 86. (lp)(cd) (*POLD 5202*)(<*829728-2*>) **DARING ADVENTURES**   [92]
   – A bone through her nose / Valerie / Missie how you let me down / Dead man's handle / Long dead love / Lover''s lane / Nearly in love / Jennie / Baby talk / Cash down / Never never / How wll I ever be simple again / Al Bowly's in Heaven. *(re-iss. Jun92 on 'Beat Goes On' cd/c/lp; BGO CD/MC/LP 138)*

	B.B.C.	not iss.
Oct 87. (lp/c; by RICHARD THOMPSON & PETER FILLEUL) (*REB/ZCF 660*) **THE MARKSMAN (TV soundtrack)**   [ ] [-]
   – My time / Gordon / Rude health / Night school / Cornish pastiche / Crossing the water / The marksman / Kyrie / On yer eyes / Cutters on the run / Don't ever change / Up there.

	Capitol	Capitol
Oct 88. (cd/c/lp) (*CD/TC/+EST 2075*) <*48845*> **AMNESIA**   [89]
   – Turning of the tide / Gypsy love songs / Reckless kind / Jerusalem on the jukebox / I still dream / Don't tempt me / Yankee, go home / Can't win / Waiting for dreamers / Pharoah. *(re-iss. Mar91 lp/c; ATAK/TC-ATAK 169) (cd re-iss. Aug91; CZ 399)*

Nov 88. (7") (*CL 516*) **TURNING OF THE TIDE. / PHAROAH**   [ ] [ ]

Sep 89. (7") (*CL 550*) **RECKLESS KIND (live). / TURNING OF THE TIDE (live)**
   (12"+=) (*12CL 550*) – Pharoah (live) / Can't win (live).
   (cd-s+=) (*CDCL 550*) – Jerusalem on the jukebox (live).

May 91. (cd/c/lp) (*CD/TC+/EST 2142*) **RUMOUR AND SIGH**   [32]
   – Read about love / I feel so good / I misunderstood / Behind grey walls / You dream too much / Why must I plead / Vincent / Backlash love affair / Mystery wind / Jimmy Shands / Keep your distance / Mother knows best / God loves a drunk / Psycho Street.

Jun 91. (7") **I FEEL SO GOOD. / HARRY'S THEME (from film 'Sweet Talker')**   [ ] [ ]
   (cd-s+=) – Backlash love affair.

Mar 92. (7") **I MISUNDERSTOOD. / 1952**   [ ] [ ]
   (cd-s+=) – Vincent / Black lightning.

—— with **PETE THOMAS** – drums, percussion / **JERRY SCHEFF** – bass, double bass / **MITCHELL FROOM** – keyboards, producer / **ALISTAIR ANDERSON** – concertina, pipes / **TOM McCONVILLE** – fiddle / **MARTIN DUNN** – flute / **PHIL PICKETT** – shawms / **JOHN KIRKPATRICK** – accordion, concertina / **DANNY THOMPSON** – double bass (1) / **CHRISTINE COLLISTER + MICHAEL PARKER** – backing vocals

Jan 94. (cd/c) (*CD/TC EST 2207*) <*81492*> **MIRROR BLUE**   [23]
   – For the sake of Mary / I can't wake up to save my life / MGB-GT / The way that it shows / Easy there, steady now / King of Bohemia / Shane and Dixie / Mingus eyes / I ride in your slipstream / Beeswing / Fast food / Mascara tears / Taking my business elsewhere.

—— (a tribute album was released in 1995)

Apr 96. (d-cd/d-c) (*CD/TC EST 2282*) <*33704*> **YOU? ME? US?** (part compilation / acoustic)   [32] [97]
   – Razor dance / She steers by lightning / Dark hand over my heart / Hide it away / Put it there pal / Business on you / No's not a word / Am I wasting my love on you? / Bank vault in Heaven / The ghost of you walks / Baby don't know what to do with herself / She cut off her long silken hair / Hide it away / Burns supper / Train don't leave / Cold kisses / Sam Jones / Razor dance / Woods of Darney.

	Parlophone	Capitol
May 97. (cd; RICHARD & DANNY THOMPSON) (*CDPCS 7383*) **INDUSTRY**   [69]
   – Chorale / Sweetheart on the barricade / Children of the dark / Big chimney / Kitty "quick get up I can hear clogs going up in the street" / Drifting through the days / Lotteryland / Pitfalls / Saboteur / Mew rhythms / Last shift.

Aug 99. (cd) (*4 98860-2*) **MOCK TUDOR**   [28]
   – METROLAND:- Cooksferry queen / Sibella / Bathsheba smiles / Two-faced love / Hard on me / HEROES IN THE SUBURBS:- Crawl back (under my stone) / Uninhabited man / Dry me tears and move on / Walking the long miles home / STREET CRIES AND STAGE WHISPERS:- Sights and sounds of London town / That's all, amen, close the door / Hope you like the new me. *(d-lp-iss.Nov99 on 'Bongload'; BL 44)*

– compilations, etc. –

(below album recorded between 1967-1976)

May 76. (d-lp) (*Island; (ICD 8)* **(guitar, vocal)** <US title 'LIVE MORE OR LESS'>   [ ] [-]
   – A heart needs a home / Flee as a bird / Night comes in / Pitfall / Excursion / Calvery Cross / Time will show the wiser / Throw-away street puzzle / Mr. Lacy / The ballad of Easy Rider / Poor Will and the jolly hangman / Sweet little rock'n'roller / Dark

end of the street / I'll be me. *(incl.Live Oxford Street concert & early demos) (re-iss. Jun86 on 'Hannibal'; HNBL 4801) cd-iss. May89; HNBD 4413)*

Apr 93. (3xcd-box) *Hannibal; (HNCD 5303)* **WATCHING THE DARK (THE HISTORY OF RICHARD THOMPSON 1969-1982)**   [ ] [-]
   – A man in need / Can't win / Waltzing's for dreamers / Crash the party / I still dream / Bird in God's garden / Lost and found / Now be thankful / A sailor's kife / Genesis Hall / The knife-edge / Walking on a wire / Small town romance / Shepherd's march – Maggie Cameron / Wall of death / For shame of doing wrong / Back street slide / Strange affair / The wrong heartbeat / Borrowed time / From Galway to Graceland / Tear-stained letter / Keep your distance / Bogie's bonnie / Poor wee Jockey Clarke / Jet plane in a rocking chair / Dimming of the day / Old man inside a young man / Never again / Hokey pokey (the ice cream song) / A heart needs a home / Beat the retreat / Al Bowlly's in Heaven / Walking through a wasted land / When the spell is broken / Devonside / Little blue number / I ain't going to drag my feet no more / Withered and died / Nobody's wedding / The poor ditching boy / The Great Valerio / The Calvary Cross / Twisted / Jennie / Hand of kindness / Two left feet / Shoot out the lights.

May 93. (cd) *Windsong; (WINCD 034)* **BBC LIVE IN CONCERT**   [ ] [-]

Tracy THORN (see under ⇒ EVERYTHING BUT THE GIRL)

THOUSAND YARD STARE   (dig out; Great Alt & Indie . . .)

---

3 (see under ⇒ EMERSON, LAKE & PALMER)

---

3 COLOURS RED

Formed: London, England . . . 1995 by vocalist/bassist PETE VUCKOVIC and Geordie guitarist CHRIS McCORMACK, who recruited drummer KEITH BAXTER and guitarist BEN HARDING (ex-SENSELESS THINGS). Named after the Kieslowski film of the same name, the band issued their debut 45, 'THIS IS MY HOLLYWOOD' early '97, which immediately led to them signing with 'Creation'. Their first release for the label, the 3-chord pop punk/rock thrash 'NUCLEAR HOLIDAY' homed in on the UK Top 20, narrowly missing its target. 'SIXTY MILE SMILE' however, achieved this feat as did their debut album, 'PURE'. The band subsequently gained a groundswell of support, gigging heavily with the likes of KISS, ANTHRAX and SKUNK ANANSIE, becoming crown princes of the metal press in the process. Early in 1999, 3 COLOURS RED were previewing their Dave Eringa-produced Top 20 sophomore set, 'REVOLT', with a near Top 10 hit, 'BEAUTIFUL DAY'. 'THIS IS THE TIME' followed it into the charts soon afterwards, however, this would be their last release as the quartet disbanded after the Reading/Leeds festivals.

Album rating: PURE (*7) / REVOLT (*7)

PETE VUCKOVIC (b.16 Feb'71, Tiveton, Devon, England) – vocals, bass (ex-DIAMOND HEAD) / **CHRIS McCORMACK** (b.21 Jun'73, South Shields, England) – guitar, vocals (ex-HONEYCRACK) / **BEN HARDING** (b.31 Jan'65, Stoke-On-Trent, England) – guitar, vocals (ex-SENSELESS THINGS) / **KEITH BAXTER** (b.19 Feb'71, Morcambe, England) – drums

	Fierce Panda	not iss.
Mar 96. (7"/cd-s) (*NING 17/+CD*) **THIS IS MY HOLLYWOOD. / HATE SLICK**   [ ] [-]

	Creation	Sony
Jan 97. (7"/c-s) (*CRE/+CS 250*) **NUCLEAR HOLIDAY. / HUMAN FACTORY**   [22] [-]
   (cd-s+=) (*CRESCD 250*) – My own gauge.

Mar 97. (7") (*CRE 254*) **SIXTY MILE SMILE. / ANISEED (live)**   [20] [-]
   (cd-s) (*CRESCD 254*) – ('A'side) / Zip the morals / Till I'm ready.
   (cd-s) (*CRESCD 254X*) – ('A'side) / This is my Hollywood (live) / Nerve gas (live).

Apr 97. (7") (*CRE 265*) **PURE. / HATESLICK (live)**   [28] [-]
   (cd-s) (*CRESCD 265*) – ('A'side) / Throughbreeze / Fake apology.
   (cd-s) (*CRESCD 265X*) – ('A'side) / Mental blocks (live) / Nuclear holiday (live).

May 97. (cd/lp)(c) (*CRE CD/LP 208*)(*C-CRE 208*) <*67958*> **PURE**   [16]
   – This is my Hollywood / Nerve gas / Nuclear holiday / Copper girl / Sixty mile smile / Sunny in England / Alright ma / Mental blocks / Fit boy & faint girl / Halfway up the downs / Hateslick / Love's cradle / Aniseed. *(cd re-iss. Sep99; same)*

Jun 97. (7") (*CRE 270*) **COPPER GIRL. / SUNNY IN ENGLAND (live)**   [30] [-]
   (cd-s) (*CRESCD 270*) – ('A'side) / Inside / This opera.
   (cd-s) (*CRESCD 270X*) – ('A'side) / Sixty mile smile (live) / Alright ma (live).

Oct 97. (7") (*CRE 277*) **THIS IS MY HOLLYWOOD. / INSIDE (live)**   [48] [-]
   (cd-s) (*CRESCD 277*) – ('A'side) / On no ones side / Sunny in England (demo).
   (cd-s) (*CRESCD 277X*) – ('A'side) / ('A'-Ice-T sober mix) / Yellow hair carriage / Pure (live).

Oct 98. (7"ep/cd-ep) (*CRE/+SCD 304*) **PARALYSE EP**   [ ] [-]
   – Paralyse / Throwing the world away / Say something / Room with a view.

Jan 99. (7"/c-s) (*CRE/+CS 308*) **BEAUTIFUL DAY. / BEAUTIFUL DAY (acoustic)**   [11] [-]
   (cd-s) (*CRESCD 308*) – ('A'side) / God shape hole / A fine time for it.
   (cd-s) (*CRESCD 308X*) – ('A'side) / I want you / Paralyse (Junkie XL mix).

Feb 99. (cd/c/lp) (*CRECD/CCRE/CRELP 227*) **REVOLT**   [17]
   – Paralyse / Pirouette / Beautiful day / Cancel the exhibition / Intermission / Song on the radio / Paranoid people / Back to the city / This is my time / Be myself / Calling to the outside / Age of madness.

May 99. (c-s) (*CRECS 313*) **THIS IS MY TIME / PARANOID PEOPLE (demo)**   [36] [ ]
   (cd-s) (*CRESCD 313*) – ('A'side) / Everything / www.sad.
   (cd-s) (*CRESCD 313X*) – ('A'side) / All the fun of the unfair / If.

311

Formed: Omaha, Nebraska, USA . . . 1990 by NICK HEXUM, TIMOTHY J. MAHONEY, P-NUT, CHAD SEXTON and S.A. MARTINEZ. Taking their moniker from the American emergency number, the band signed to the newly resurrected 'Capricorn' label, issuing their debut disc, 'MUSIC' in 1993. Fed mainly on a rap/funk-metal diet of RAGE AGAINST THE MACHINE and RED HOT CHILI PEPPERS, the album, along with their 1994 follow-up, 'GRASSROOTS' built up some local support which translated into a chart call-out two years later with the eponymous US Top 20, '311' set. In 1997, it was all systems go, as 311 were mobilized into the Top 5 with 'TRANSISTOR', although Britain still remained oblivious to their street-chase thrills.

Album rating: MUSIC (*5) / GRASSROOTS (*5) / 311 (*6) / TRANSISTOR (*6) / LIVE (*5) / SOUNDSYSTEM (*5)

NICK HEXUM – vocals, guitar / **TIMOTHY J. MAHONEY** – guitar / **P-NUT** – bass / **CHAD SEXTON** – drums / **S.A. MARTINEZ** – vocals, turntables

			Capricorn	Capricorn
Nov 93.	(cd/c) <42008> **MUSIC**			

– Welcome / Freak out / Visit / Paradise / Unity / Hydrophonic / My stoney baby / Nix hex / Plain / Feels so good / Do you right / Fat chance.

| Jun 95. | (cd/c) (477894-2/-4) <42026> **GRASSROOTS** | | | Jul94 |

– Lucky / Homebrew / Nutsympton / 8:16 a.m. / Omaha stylee / Apples science / Taiyed / Silver / Grassroots / Salsa / Lose / Six / Offbeat / 1-2-3.

| Oct 96. | (cd/c) (532 530-2/-4) <42041> **311** | | 12 | Jul95 |

– Down / Random / Jack O'Lantern's weather / All mixed up / Hive / Guns / Misdirected hostility / Purpose / Loco / Brodels / Don't stay home / D.L.M.D. / Sweet / T & P combo.

| Nov 96. | (c-s,cd-s) **ENLARGED TO SHOW DETAIL /** | | - | 95 |
| Aug 97. | (cd) (536181-2) **TRANSISTOR** | | - | 4 |

– Transistor / Prisoner / Galaxy / Beautiful disaster / Inner light spectrum / Electricity / What was I thinking / Jupiter / Use of time / Continuous life / No control / Running / Color / Light years / Creature feature / Tune in / Rub a dub / Starshines / Strangers / Borders / Stealing happy hour.

| Nov 98. | (cd) <(538263-2)> **LIVE (live)** | | | 77 |

– Down / Homebrew / Beautiful disaster / Misdirected hostility / Freak out / Nix hex / Applied science / Omaha stylee / Tribute / Galaxy / Light years / Hydrophonic / Who's got the herb / Feels so good.

| Oct 99. | (cd) <(546645-2)> **SOUNDSYSTEM** | | | 9 |

– Freeze time / Come original / Large in the margin / Flowing / Can't fade me / Life's not a race / Strong all along / Sever / Eons / Evolution / Leaving Babylon / Mindspin / Livin' and rockin'.

THREE FISH (see under ⇒ PEARL JAM)

THROBBING GRISTLE

(dig out; 4th edition or Great Alt & Indie . . .)

THROWING MUSES

Formed: Boston, Massachusetts, USA . . . 1983 by KRISTIN HERSH and her half-sister, TANYA DONELLY, who duly recruited a rhythm section of ELAINE ADAMEDES and DAVID NARCIZO. After an independently released US-only EP, the group were signed up (alongside fellow Bostonians, The PIXIES) to British indie label, '4 a.d.', the first American band to be bestowed such an honour. Produced by Gil Norton, the band's eponymous debut album (featuring new bassist LESLIE LANGSTON) centred around the emotional anguish of chief writer HERSH; her tortured, BUFFY SAINTE-MARIE-like wailing and oblique lyrics conjured up an air of ill-defined unease on the likes of 'RABBIT'S DYING' and 'SOUL SOLDIER' while the twisting, folk-noir minimalism of the music lent proceedings an uncomfortable unpredictability. Raved over in Britain (John Peel was a particularly vocal fan) but largely ignored at home, the 'MUSES consolidated their cult appeal with a further couple of EP's the following year before 1988's slightly disappointing follow-up proper, 'HOUSE TORNADO'. The record signalled a move towards the more accessible territory staked out in 'HUNKPAPA' (1989), US college radio's increasing influence seeing their native fanbase mushrooming. Feeling creatively stifled by HERSH's lion's share of the songwriting, DONELLY subsequently formed her own outfit, The BREEDERS, while simultaneously working on her final 'MUSES album, 'THE REAL RAMONA' (1991). A breakthrough set which contained some of the group's most immediate compositions ('COUNTING BACKWARDS' was perhaps the nearest HERSH has come to writing a pop song), DONELLY's contributions were a blueprint for the more straightforward alternative pop she would perfect in BELLY. Taking then 'MUSES bassist, ABONG with her, DONELLY finally left the band in 1992, leaving a core of HERSH and NARCIZO. Welcoming LANGSTON back into the fold, HERSH proved THROWING MUSES was still a going concern with the soft grunge-friendly distortion of 'RED HEAVEN' (1992), the band's highest (UK) charting album to date. Nevertheless, the 'MUSES muse took time out in 1994 to complete a solo debut, 'HIPS AND MAKERS'. Produced by LENNY KAYE and featuring a guest appearance from MICHAEL STIPE, the album found HERSH probing her troubled psyche through a skewed, childlike lens, distorting the sparse acoustic backing and making for compelling listening. Hailed by critics, the record made the UK Top 10 and saw the singer gaining belated recognition from an often reluctant music press. 1995 saw the release of the sixth THROWING MUSES album, 'UNIVERSITY', another fine set which maintained the hi-octane approach of its predecessor. The following

year's 'LIMBO' was exactly that, the group becoming a little directionless and stale, although its highlights were the minor hit, 'SHARK'. During the last two years of the decade, KRISTIN delivered a couple of fine long-players, 'STRANGE ANGELS' (1998) and 'SKY MOTEL' (1999), the latter her best work to date; it also was a truly "solo" affair. • **Songwriters:** KRISTIN lyrics / group compositions except; AMAZING GRACE (trad. hit Judy Collins) / CRY BABY CRY (Beatles) / RIDE INTO THE SUN (Velvet Underground) / MANIC DEPRESSION (Jimi Hendrix) / WHEN THE LEVEE BREAKS (Led Zeppelin). HERSH solo:- PANIC PURE (Vic Chesnutt) / JESUS CHRIST (Alex Chilton) / CAN THE CIRCLE BE UNBROKEN (. . . Carter) / AMAZING GRACE (trad) / PENNYROYAL TEA (Nirvana) / EVERYBODY'S GOT SOMETHING TO HIDE EXCEPT ME AND MY MONKEY (Beatles).

Album rating: THROWING MUSES (*8) / THE FAT SKIER mini (*6) / HOUSE TORNADO (*6) / HUNKPAPA (*5) / THE REAL RAMONA (*8) / RED HEAVEN (*7) / THE CURSE (*5) / UNIVERSITY (*7) / LIMBO (*6) / Kristin Hersh: HIPS AND MAKERS (*6) / STRANGE ANGELS (*6) / SKY MOTEL (*8)

KRISTIN HERSH (b. 7 Aug'66, Atlanta, Georgia) – vocals, lead guitar, piano / **ELAINE ADAMEDES** – bass / **TANYA DONELLY** (b.14 Jul'66) – rhythm guitar, vocals / **DAVID NARCIZO** (b. 6 May'66) – drums, percussion, vocals

		not iss.	Throwing Muses
Feb 86.	(7"ep) **STAND UP / PARTY. / SANTA CLAUS / DIRT ON THE DANCE FLOOR**	-	

——— **LESLIE LANGSTON** (b. 1 Apr'64) – bass, vocals repl. ELAINE

		4 a.d.	4ad-Sire
Sep 86.	(lp/c)(cd) (CAD/+C 607)(CAD 607CD) **THROWING MUSES**		-

– Call me / Green / Hate my way / Vicky's box / Rabbit's dying / America (she can't say no) / Fear / Stand up / Soul soldier / Delicious cutters.

| Mar 87. | (12"ep/c-ep) (BAD 701/+C) **CHAINS CHANGED** | | |

– Cry baby cry / Finished / Reel / Snail head.

| Aug 87. | (m-lp/c) (CAD/+C 706) <25640> **THE FAT SKIER** | | |

– Soul soldier / Garoux des larmes / Pool in eyes / A feeling / You cage / Soap and water / And a she-wolf after the war.

| Mar 88. | (lp/c)(cd) (CAD/+C 802)(CAD 802CD) <25710> **HOUSE TORNADO** | | |

– Colder / Mexican woman / The river / Juno / Marriage tree / Run letter / Saving grace / Drive / Downtown / Giant / Walking in the dark. (cd+=) – THE FAT SKIER

| Jan 89. | (lp/c)(cd) (CAD/+C 901)(CAD 901CD) <25855> **HUNKPAPA** | 59 | |

– Devil's roof / Bea / Dizzy / No parachutes (say goodbye) / Dragonhead / Fall down / I'm alive / Angel / Mania / The burrow. (c+=) – Take. (cd++=) – Santa Claus.

| Feb 89. | (7") (AD 903) **DIZZY. / SANTA CLAUS** | | - |

(12"+=/10"+=)(cd-s+=) (BAD/+D 903)(BAD 903CD) – Mania (live) / Downtown (live).

——— TANYA with DAVID (only in '89) formed off-shoot The BREEDERS. She stayed with the MUSES until next album's completion. **FRED ABONG** – bass repl. her

| Jan 91. | (7") (AD 7001) <21833> **COUNTING BACKWARDS. / AMAZING GRACE** | 70 | |

(12"+=/cd-s+=) (BAD/+CD 1001) – Some sun / Cotton mouth.

| Feb 91. | (cd)(lp/c) (CAD 1002CD)(CAD/+C 1002) <26489> **THE REAL RAMONA** | 26 | |

– Counting backwards / Him dancing / Red shoes / Graffiti / Golden thing / Ellen West / Dylan / Hook in her head / Not too soon / Honey chain / Say goodbye / Two step.

| Nov 91. | (7") (AD 1015) <40135> **NOT TOO SOON. / CRY BABY CRY** | | |

(12"+=/cd-s+=) (BAD 1015/+CD) – Dizzy (remix) / Him dancing (remix).

——— (Sep'91) DONELLY and ABONG had now quit to form BELLY in 1992.

——— **KRISTIN + NARCIZO** recruited newcomer **BERNARD GEORGES** (b.29 Mar'65, Gonaive, Haiti) – bass

| Jul 92. | (12"ep/cd-ep) (BAD 2012/+CD) **FIREPILE / MANIC DEPRESSION. / SNAILHEAD / CITY OF THE DEAD** | 46 | - |

(12"ep)(cd-ep) (BADR 2012)(BAD 2012CDR) – ('A'remix) / Jack / Ride into the Sun / Handsome woman.

| Aug 92. | (cd)(lp/c) (CAD 2013CD)(CAD/+C 2013) <26897> **RED HEAVEN** | 13 | |

– Furious / Firepile / Die / Dirty water / Stroll / Pearl / Summer Street / Vic / Backroad / The visit / Dovey / Rosetta stone / Carnival wig. (free-lp w.a.) **LIVE (live)** – Juno / Marriage tree / Pearl / Stand up – Dovey – Mexican woman / Run letter / Soap and water / Rabbit dying / Cry baby cry / Counting backwards – Handsome woman / Take / Soul soldier / Bea / Delicate cutters.

| Nov 92. | (cd) (TAD 2019CD) **THE CURSE (live)** | 74 | - |

– Manic depression / Counting backwards / Fish / Hate my way / Furious / Devil's roof / Snailhead / Firepile / Finished / Take / Say goodbye / Mania / Two step / Delicate cutters / Cottonmouth / Pearl / Vic / Bea.

| Dec 94. | (7") (AD 4018) **BRIGHT YELLOW GUN. / LIKE A DOG** | 51 | - |

(12"+=/cd-s+=) (BAD 4018/+CD) – Red eyes / Crayon sun.

| Jan 95. | (cd)(lp/c) (CAD 5002CD)(CAD/+C 5002) <45796> **UNIVERSITY** | 10 | |

– Bright yellow gun / Start / Hazing / Shimmer / Calm down, come down / Crabtown / No way in Hell / Surf cowboy / That's all you wanted / Teller / University / Snake face / Fever few.

| Jul 96. | (7") (AD 6016) **SHARK. / TAR MOOCHERS** | 53 | - |

(7") (ADD 6016) – ('A'side) / Limbobo.
(cd-s++=) (BAD 6016CD) – Serene swing.

		4 a.d.	Rykodisc
Aug 96.	(cd)(lp/c) (CAD 6014CD)(CAD/+C 6014) <10354> **LIMBO**	36	

– Buzz / Ruthie's knocking / Freeloader / The field / Limbo / Tar kisser / Tango / Serene / Mr. Bones / Night driving / Cowbirds / Shark.

| Sep 96. | (7"etched) (TAD 6017) <51052> **RUTHIE'S KNOCKING** | | |
| Jan 97. | (cd-s) <51055> **FREELOADER /** | - | |

——— disbanded later in '97

– compilations, etc. –

Jul 98. (d-cd) *Rykodisc; <8017>* **IN A DOGHOUSE**   [-] [ ]
 – (THROWING MUSES album tracks) / (CHAINS CHAINED ep tracks) / Call me / Sinkhole / Green / Hate my way / Vicky's box / America (she can't say no) / Fear / Raise the roses / And a she wolf after the war / Fish / Catch / Lizzie Sage / Clear and great / Doghouse / People.

KRISTIN HERSH

first below featured **MICHAEL STIPE** (R.E.M.) / **JANE SCARPANTONI** – cello

		4 a.d.	Sire

Jan 94. (12"ep/cd-ep) *(BAD 4001/+CD)* **YOUR GHOST / THE KEY. / UNCLE JUNE AND AUNT KIYOTI / WHEN THE LEVEE BREAKS**   [45] [-]
Feb 94. (cd)(lp/c) *(CAD 4002CD)(CAD/+C 4002) <45413>* **HIPS AND MAKERS**   [7] [ ]
 – Your ghost / Beestung / Teeth / Sundrops / sparky / Houdini blues / A loon / Velvet days / Close your eyes / Me and my charms / Tuesday night / The letter / Lurch / The cuckoo / Hips and makers. *(cd re-iss. Jul98; same)*
Apr 94. (7"/c-s) *(AD 4006) <45667>* **A LOON. / VELVET DAYS**   [60] [ ] Jun94
 (12"ep+=/cd-ep+=) *(BAD 4006/+CD)* **STRINGS EP** – Sundrops / Me and my charms.

		4 a.d.	Rykodisc

Dec 95. (cd-ep) *(TAD 5017CD) <1049>* **THE HOLY SINGLE**   [ ] [ ]
 – Jesus Christ / Amazing grace / Sinkhole / Can the circle be unbroken.
Feb 98. (cd) *(CAD 8003CD) <10429>* **STRANGE ANGELS**   [64] [ ]
 – Home / Like you / Aching for you / Cold water coming / Some catch flies / Stained / Shake / Hope / Pale / Baseball field / Heaven / Gazebo tree / Gut pageant / Rock candy brains / Cartoons.
Mar 98. (cd-ep) *(TAD 8005CD)* **LIKE YOU / SHAKE (live to tape) / YOUR GHOST (live to tape)**   [ ] [-]
Jun 99. (7") *(AD 9007)* **ECHO. / PENNYROYAL TEA**   [ ] [ ]
 (cd-s+=) *(BAD 9007CD)* – Everybody's got something to hide except for me and my monkey.
Jun 99. (cd) *(CAD 9008CD)* **SKY MOTEL**   [ ] [ ]
 – Echo / White trash moon / Fog / Costa Rica / A cleaner light / San Francisco / Cathedral heat / Husk / Caffeine / Spring / Clay feet / Faith.

THROWN UPS (see under ⇒ MUDHONEY)

THUNDER

Formed: South London, England . . . mid '89 by main songwriter LUKE MORLEY, LUKE BOWES and GARY JAMES, who had all been part of Reading festival specialists, TERRAPLANE. This derivative Brit-rock outfit, who formed around 1982, released two melodic, workmanlike albums, 'BLACK AND WHITE' (1986) and 'MOVING TARGET' (1987), before they disintegrated in early '88, a planned career in America coming to an abrupt end. From the ashes of TERRAPLANE's crash came THUNDER, the core of the former act recruiting BEN MATTHEWS and MARK LUCKHURST (aka SNAKE) and signing to 'E.M.I.' through agent Malcolm McKenzie. Hailed as rock's great white hopes, THUNDER rolled around the country relentlessly, building up a grassroots fanbase which subsequently saw their debut ANDY 'Duran Duran' TAYLOR-produced set, 'BACK STREET SYMPHONY' (1990) go gold. Rootsy heavy rock in the mould of BAD COMPANY, AEROSMITH and LED ZEPPELIN, the album spawned a series of hit singles, 'DIRTY LOVE', 'BACKSTREET SYMPHONY', Spencer Davis Group's 'GIMME SOME LOVIN'' and a re-issue of 'SHE'S SO FINE'. They subsequently played the Cathouse in New York and were given a deal with EMI's US counterpart 'Capitol', although they tasted only minor success with the 'DIRTY LOVE' single. Sticking to their hard-rock guns, THUNDER went from strength to strength, two further albums, 'LAUGHING ON JUDGEMENT DAY' (1992) and 'BEHIND CLOSED DOORS' (1995), both storming the UK Top 5, although the latter was recorded without SNAKE, who had been superseded by MIKAEL HOGLUND. Although the group maintained healthy singles/albums sales, they surprised many by downshifting to the former compilation label, 'Raw Power' (now home to BRUCE DICKINSON and HELLOWEEN amongst others). The resulting album, 'THE THRILL OF IT ALL' (early '97), still managed to crack the Top 20, having already spawned a hit single, 'DON'T WAIT UP'. • **Covers:** GET IT ON (T.Rex) / WITH A LITTLE HELP FROM MY FRIENDS (Beatles) / GIMME SHELTER (Rolling Stones) / 5.15 (Who) / ALL THE WAY FROM MEMPHIS (Mott The Hoople) / IN A BROKEN DREAM (hit; Python Lee Jackson) / STAY WITH ME (Rod Stewart & The Faces) / PLAY THAT FUNKY MUSIC (Wild Cherry) / MY BROTHER JAKE (Free) / ONCE IN A LIFETIME (Talking Heads) / DANCE TO THE MUSIC (Sly & The Family Stone). • **Trivia:** SNAKE once appeared on Top Of The Pops as bass player on OWEN PAUL's hit, 'You're My Favourite Waste Of Time'.

Album rating: Terraplane: BLACK AND WHITE (*5) / MOVING TARGET (*4) / Thunder: BACK STREET SYMPHONY (*6) / LAUGHING ON JUDGEMENT DAY (*7) / BEHIND CLOSED DOORS (*5) / THEIR FINEST HOUR (AND A BIT) compilation (*6) / THE THRILL OF IT ALL (*5) / LIVE (*4) / GIVING THE GAME AWAY (*4)

TERRAPLANE

DANNY BOWES – vocals / **LUKE MORLEY** – guitar / **RUDY RIVIERE** – guitar / **NICK LINDEN** – bass, piano / **GARY JAMES** – drums

		City	not iss.

Mar 83. (7") *(NIK 8)* **I SURVIVE. / GIMME THE MONEY**   [ ] [-]

		Epic	Epic

Dec 84. (7") *(A 4936)* **I CAN'T LIVE WITHOUT YOUR LOVE. / BEGINNING OF THE END**   [ ] [-]
 (12"+=) *(TX 4936)* – Let the wheels go round.
Mar 85. (7"/12") *(A/TX 6110)* **I SURVIVE. / ALL NIGHT AND DAY (live)**   [ ] [-]
Jul 85. (7") *(A 6352)* **WHEN YOU'RE HOT. / TOUGH KIND OF LOVE**   [ ] [-]
 (12"+=) *(TX 6352)* – If you could see yourself.
Oct 85. (7") *(A 6584)* **TALKING TO MYSELF. / GET YOUR FACE OUT OF MY DREAMS**   [ ] [-]
 (12"+=) *(TX 6584)* – Gimme the money.
—— RUDY only appeared on 1 track from next album.
Jan 86. (lp/c) *(EPC/40 26439)* **BLACK AND WHITE**   [74] [ ]
 – Don't walk away / When you're hot / I can't live without your love / Talking to myself / You can't hurt me anymore / I survive / Right betweeen the eyes / Black and white / I'm the one / Get your face out of my dream / Couldn't handle the tears. *(c+=)* – Tough kind of love / Beginning of the end / All night and day.
Jan 87. (7"/7"sha-pic-d) *(TERRA/+P 1)* **IF THAT'S WHAT IT TAKES. / LIVING AFTER DARK**   [ ] [ ]
 (12"+=) *(TERRAT 1)* – ('A'-19th Nervous Breakdown mix) / Drugs.
Jun 87. (7") *(TERRA 2)* **GOOD THING GOING. / A NIGHT OF MADNESS**   [ ] [ ]
 (12"+=) *(TERRAT 2)* – The good life.
 (c-s+=) *(MCTERRAC 2)* ('A'version).
Aug 87. (7") *(TERRA 3)* **MOVING TARGET. / WHEN I SLEEP ALONE**   [ ] [ ]
 (d7"+=/12"+=) *(TERRA G/T 3)* – I survive (live) / I can't live without your love.
Sep 87. (lp/c/cd) *(EPC 460157-1/-4/-2)* **MOVING TARGET**   [ ] [ ]
 – If that's what it takes / Good thing going / Promised land / Moving target / Hostage to fortune / Heartburn / Hearts on fire / I will come out fighting / Nothing on but the radio. *(cd+=)* – Moving target (extended) / When I sleep alone / I can't live without your love (live) / I survive (live).
Feb 88. (7") *(TERRA 4)* **IF THAT'S WHAT IT TAKES. / LIVING AFTER DARK**   [ ] [ ]
 (12"+=/cd-s+=) *(TERRA T/Q 4)* – ('A'-19th Nervous Breakdown mix) / Drugs.
—— Disbanded early 1988 after a stint in the US

THUNDER

BOWES + MORLEY brought back **GARY 'Harry' JAMES** – drums, with also **BEN MATTHEWS** – guitar, keyboards / **MARK 'Snake' LUCKHURST** – bass

		E.M.I.	Capitol

Oct 89. (7"/7"s) *(EM/+S 111)* **SHE'S SO FINE. / GIRL'S GOING OUT OF HER HEAD**   [ ] [-]
 (12"+=)(cd-s+=) *(2EMP 111)(CDEM 1)* – Another shot of love (live).
Jan 90. (7"/7"pic-d/c-s) *(EM/EMPD/TCEM 126)* **DIRTY LOVE. / FIRED UP**   [32] [-]
 (12"+=/12"pic-d+=) *(12EM/+P 126)* – She's so fine (live).
 (cd-s+=) *(CDEM 126)* – Brown sugar (live).
Feb 90. (cd/c/lp) *(CD/TC+/EMC 3570) <24384>* **BACK STREET SYMPHONY**   [21] [ ] Apr91
 – She's so fine / Dirty love / Don't wait for me / Higher ground / Until my dying day / Back street symphony / Love walked in / An Englishman on holiday / Girl's going out of her head / Gimme some lovin'. *(cd+=/c+=)* – Distant thunder. *(pic-lp Nov90; PDEMC 3570)* *(re-iss. Sep94 cd/c; same)*
Apr 90. (c-s/7") *(TC+/EM 137)* **BACK STREET SYMPHONY. / NO WAY OUT OF THE WILDERNESS**   [25] [ ]
 (12"+=/12"pic-d+=) *(12EM/+PD 137)* – An Englishman on holiday (live).
 (cd-s++=) *(CDEM 137)* – Girl's going out of her head (live).
Jul 90. (c-s/7") *(TC+/EM 148)* **GIMME SOME LOVIN'. / I WANNA BE HER SLAVE**   [36] [ ]
 (c-s+=/12"+=/cd-s+=) *(TC/12/CD EM 148)* – Dirty love (live).
 (10"red+=) *(10EM 148)* – Until the night is through.
Sep 90. (c-s/7") *(TC+/EM 158)* **SHE'S SO FINE. / I CAN STILL HEAR THE MUSIC**   [34] [-]
 (12"+=/12"pic-d+=) *(12EM/+P 158)* – Don't wait for me (live . . .).
 (ext.10"blue+=) *(10EM 158)* – Back street symphony (live . . .).
 (cd-s) *(CDEM 158)* – ('A'side) / Back street symphony (live at Donington) / Don't wait for me (live at Donington).
Oct 90. (c-s,cd-s) *<44547>* **SHE'S SO FINE. / GIMME SOME LOVIN'**   [-] [-]
Feb 91. (c-s/7") *(TC+/EM 175)* **LOVE WALKED IN. / FLAWED TO PERFECTION (demo)**   [21] [-]
 (12"+=/12"pic-d+=/cd-s+=) *(12EM/12EMPD/CDEM 175)* – Until my dying day (live).
 (10"white+=) *(10EM 175)* – World problems: a solution.
Apr 91. (cd-s) *<19026>* **DIRTY LOVE. / GIRL'S GOING OUT OF HER HEAD**   [-] [55]
Aug 92. (c-s/7") *(TC+/EM 242)* **LOWLIFE IN HIGH PLACES. / BABY I'LL BE GONE**   [22] [ ]
 (cd-s) *(CDEM 242)* – ('A'side) / Back street symphony / She's so fine / Love walked in.
 (cd-s) *(CDEMS 242)* – ('A'side) / With a little help from my friends / She's my inspiration / Low life in high places (demo).
Aug 92. (cd/c/d-lp) *(CD/TC+/EMD 1035)* **LAUGHING ON JUDGEMENT DAY**   [2] [ ]
 – Does it feel like love? / Everybody wants her / Low life in high places / Laughing on judgement day / Empty city / Today the world stopped turning / Long way from home / Fire to ice / Feeding the flame / A better man / The moment of truth / Flawed to perfection / Like a satellite / Baby I'll be gone. *(re-iss. Mar94 cd/c; same)*
Oct 92. (c-s/7") *(TC+/EM 249)* **EVERYBODY WANTS HER. / DANGEROUS RHYTHM**   [36] [ ]
 (12"pic-d+=) *(12EMPD 249)* – Higher ground (acoustic).
 (cd-s) *(CDEM 249)* – ('A'side) / Dirty love (acoustic) / Higher ground (acoustic) / Dirty love.
Feb 93. (c-s/7") *(TC+/BETTER 1)* **A BETTER MAN. / LOW LIFE IN HIGH PLACES (live)**   [18] [ ]
 (12"/cd-s) *(12/CD BETTER 1)* – ('A'side) / New York, New York (Harry's theme) / Lazy Sunday (live) / Higher ground (live).

Jun 93. (12"ep/cd-ep) *(12/CD EM 272)* **LIKE A SATELLITE** `28` ☐
– Like a satellite / The damage is done / Like a satellite (live) / Gimme shelter.
Jan 95. (7"pic-d/c-s) *(EMPD/TCEM 365)* **STAND UP. / (interview)** `23` ☐
(cd-s+=) *(CDEM 365)* – The fire is gone (demo) / Life in a day (demo).
(cd-s) *(CDEMS 365)* – ('A'side) / One pretty woman / It happened in this town.

—— now without SNAKE, who was repl. by **MIKAEL HOGLUND**

Jan 95. (cd/c/lp) *(CD/TC+/EMD 1076)* **BEHIND CLOSED DOORS** `5` ☐
– Moth to the flame / Fly on the wall / I'll be waiting / River of pain / Future train /
'Til the river runs dry / Stand up / Preaching from a chair / Castles in the sand / Too
scared to live / Ball and chain / It happened in this train.
Feb 95. (c-s) *(TCEM 367)* **RIVERS OF PAIN / DOES IT FEEL LIKE
LOVE** `31` ☐
(cd-s+=) *(CDEM 367)* – Everybody wants her (live) / All the way from Memphis
(live).
(cd-s) *(CDEMS 367)* – ('A'side) / 5.15 (live) / You don't know what love is (demo).
(12"pic-d) *(12EMPD 367)* – ('A'side) / Move on / All the way from Memphis (live).
Apr 95. (c-ep) *(TCEM 372)* **CASTLES IN THE SAND / A BETTER
MAN / SHE'S SO FINE / DIRTY LOVE** `30` ☐
(cd-s) *(CDEM 372)* – ('A'side) / Stand up (live acoustic) / Move over (live).
(cd-s) *(CDEMS 372)* – ('A'side) / I hear you knocking (live acoustic) / River of pain
(live acoustic).
Sep 95. (c-s) *(TCEM 384)* **IN A BROKEN DREAM / 'TIL THE RIVER
RUNS DRY** `26` ☐
(cd-s) *(CDEM 384)* – ('A'side) / Love walked in / Dirty love (demo).
(cd-s) *(CDEMS 384)* – ('A'side) / Stay with me / An Englishman on holiday.
Sep 95. (cd/c/d-lp) *(CD/TC+/EMD 1086)* **THEIR FINEST HOUR (AND
A BIT)** (compilation) `22` ☐
– Dirty love / River of pain / Love walked in / Everybody wants her / In a broken
dream / Higher ground '95 / Back street symphony / A better man / Gimme shelter /
Like a satellite / Low life in high places / Stand up / Once in a lifetime / Gimme
some lovin' / Castles in the sand / She's so fine.

                                    Raw Power   not iss.

Jan 97. (c-s/cd-s) *(RAW M/X 1019)* **DON'T WAIT UP / WELCOME
TO THE PARTY / HIRSUITE BOOGIE** `27` `–`
(flexi-cd-s) *(RAWX 1020)* – ('A'version); repl. 3rd track.
(12") *(RAWX 1020)* – ('A'extended) / Every word's a lie.
Feb 97. (cd/c/d-lp) *(RAW CD/MC/LP 115)* **THE THRILL OF IT ALL** `14` `–`
– Pilot of my dreams / Living for today / Love worth dying for / Don't wait up /
Something about you / Welcome to the party / The thrill of it all / Hotter than the
sun / This forgotten town / Cosmetic punk / You can't live your life.
Mar 97. (c-s/cd-s) *(RAW M/X 1043)* **LOVE WORTH DYING FOR /
SOMEBODY TO LOVE / LETHAL COMBINATION** `60` `–`
(cd-s+=) *(RAWX 1030)* – ('A'side) / Bed of roses / Bring it on home.

—— **CHRIS CHILDS** – bass, vocals; repl. HOGLAND

                                    Eagle   unknown

Jan 98. (c-s) *(EAGCS 016)* **THE ONLY ONE / YOU CAN'T LIVE
YOUR LIFE IN A DAY (the Nomis sessions)** `31` ☐
(cd-s) *(EAGXA 016)* – ('A'side) / Too bad / This forgotten town (acoustic) /
Something about you (the Nomis session).
(cd-s) *(EAGXB 016)* – ('A'live) / Pilot of my dreams (live) / Stand up (live) /
Everybody wants her (live).
Feb 98. (d-cd) *(EDGCD 016)* **LIVE (live)** `35` ☐
– Welcome to the party / Higher ground / Don't wait up / Low life in high places /
Gimme some lovin' / Empty city / Until my dying day / A better man / Does it
feel like love? / Dance to the music / She's so fine // Backstreet symphony / An
Englishman on holiday / I'll be waiting / Laughing on judgement day / Like a
satellite / Moth to the flame / Living for today / The only one / Love walked in /
River of pain / Dirty love.
Jun 98. (c-s) *(EAGCS 030)* **PLAY THAT FUNKY MUSIC / ONCE IN
A LIFETIME** `39` ☐
(cd-s+=) *(EAGXS 030)* – Like a satellite.
(cd-s) *(EAGXA 030)* – ('A'side) / My brother Jake / I'm one.
Mar 99. (c-s) *(EAGCS 037)* **JUST ANOTHER SUICIDE (YOU WANNA
KNOW) / MONTANA MOUNTAIN WOMAN** `49` `–`
(cd-s+=) *(EAGXS 037)* – Duelling harmonicas.
(cd-s) *(EAGXA 037)* – ('A'side) / With a little help from my friends (live) / She's
so fine (live).
Mar 99. (cd/c) *(EAG CD/MC 046)* **GIVING THE GAME AWAY** `48` `–`
– Just another suicide (you wanna know) / All I ever wanted / Giving the game away /
You'll still need a friend / Rolling the dice / Numb / Play that funky music / 'Til it
shines / Time to get tough / It's another day / It could be tonight.

– compilations, etc. –

Jun 99. (cd) *E.M.I.; (521046-2)* **THE RARE, THE RAW AND THE BEST** ☐ `–`

THUNDERCLAP NEWMAN (dig out; Great Psychedelic . . .)

Johnny THUNDERS

Born: JOHN ANTHONY GENZALE, 15 Jul'52, Leesburg, Florida, USA.
Having been an integral part of The NEW YORK DOLLS in the first half
of the 70's, vocalist/guitarist THUNDERS formed new wave/punk act, The
HEARTBREAKERS, alongside ex-'DOLLS drummer, JERRY NOLAN, and
ex-TELEVISION bassist, RICHARD HELL. After an initial gig as a trio, they
picked up extra guitarist, WALTER LURE, although this incarnation was short-
lived as RICHARD promptly departed to form his own RICHARD HELL
& THE VOID-OIDS. Filling the void with BILLY RATH, they were invited
to London by ex-'DOLLS manager, MALCOLM McLAREN, who offered
them a support slot with his punk proteges, The SEX PISTOLS (on their
'Anarchy' tour of late '76). The HEARTBREAKERS subsequently signed to
UK label, 'Track', issuing their debut 45, 'CHINESE ROCKS' (a tribute to
oriental narcotics co-written with DEE DEE RAMONE), in early '77; both
the lead track and the B-side, 'BORN TO LOSE', drawled out with inimitably

wasted NY cool. In September of that "Jubilee" year, the group released their
much-anticipated debut album, 'L.A.M.F.' (New York street slang for 'Like A
Mother F*****'), and although it suffered from terrible production provided
by SPEEDY KEEN (ex-THUNDERCLAP NEWMAN), the set still managed
a Top 60 placing in Britain. So bad was the record's sound that NOLAN left
in protest, further calamity befalling the band as they found themselves on
the wrong side of the immigration authorities having abandoned their label.
Deported back to NY, the band inevitably splintered despite having recruited
a replacement drummer, TY STYX. THUNDERS subsequently returned to
London where he recorded a solo album, 'SO ALONE' (1978), aided and
abetted by the cream of the UK new wave scene including PETER PERRETT
(The Only Ones), CHRISSIE HYNDE (Pretenders), PAUL COOK and STEVE
JONES (Sex Pistols) and even PHIL LYNOTT (Thin Lizzy)! In the interim,
THUNDERS teamed up with SID VICIOUS in the ill-fated, unfortunately
named, The LIVING DEAD (SID was to die shortly afterwards). Just prior to
the turn of the decade, the HEARTBREAKERS regrouped in New York with
THUNDERS masterminding the affair and prefixing the band name with his
own; the resulting stage set, 'LIVE AT MAX'S KANSAS CITY' stands as
testament to what might have been. In the 80's, THUNDERS released a series
of sporadic albums/singles mostly for UK indie label, 'Jungle', although he
never managed to shake off the cult-legend tag. Sadly, THUNDERS died in
New Orleans on the 23rd of April 1991, the circumstances remaining shrouded
in mystery until a subsequent autopsy revealed what most people suspected –
that he'd overdosed on heroin. • Covered CAN'T KEEP MY EYES OFF YOU
(Andy Williams) / DO YOU LOVE ME (Brian Poole & The Tremeloes) /
DOWNTOWN (Petula Clark) / LIKE A ROLLING STONE (Bob Dylan) /
CRAWFISH (Elvis Presley) / QUE SERA SERA (hit; Doris Day). 'COPY
CATS' was a complete covers album.

Album rating: L.A.M.F. – REVISITED (*7) / LIVE AT MAX'S KANSAS CITY (*7) /
D.T.K. (*6)

HEARTBREAKERS

JOHNNY THUNDERS – vocals, guitar / **JERRY NOLAN** (b. 7 May'46) – drums / **WALTER
LURE** (b.22 Apr'49) – guitar, vocals / **BILLY RATH** – bass, vocals repl. RICHARD HELL
who formed his own group

		Track	not iss.
May 77. (7"/12") *(2094 135/+T)* **CHINESE ROCKS. / BORN TO LOSE**		`55`	`–`
Sep 77. (lp) *(2409 218)* **L.A.M.F.**			`–`

– Born to lose / Baby talk / All by myself / I wanna be loved / It's not enough / Get off
the phone / Chinese rocks / Pirate love / One track mind / I love you / Goin' steady /
Let go. *(re-iss. May85 as 'L.A.M.F. – REVISITED' on 'Jungle' lp,pink-lp/pic-lp;
FREUD 4/+P) <(re-iss. Sep96 as 'THE LOST '77 MIXES' cd/c/lp; FREUD CD/C/LP
044)>*
Nov 77. (7") *(2094 137)* **ONE TRACK MIND. / CAN'T KEEP MY
EYES OFF YOU (live) / DO YOU LOVE ME (live)** ☐ `–`
Mar 78. (7"w-drawn) *(2094 142)* **IT'S NOT ENOUGH. / LET GO** ☐ `–`

—— split early '78 after being deported back to New York, NOLAN joined SNATCH,
while RATH and LURE disappeared

JOHNNY THUNDERS

—— returned to London and went solo using session people

		Real-W.E.A.	not iss.
May 78. (7") *(ARE 1)* **DEAD OR ALIVE. / DOWNTOWN**		☐	`–`
Sep 78. (7"/12"pink,12"blue) *(ARE 3/+T)* **YOU CAN'T PUT YOUR
ARMS AROUND A MEMORY. / HURTIN'**		☐	`–`
Oct 78. (lp) *(RAL 1)* **SO ALONE**		☐	`–`

– Pipeline / You can't put your arms around a memory / Great big kiss / Ask me
no questions / Leave me alone / Daddy rolling stone / London boys / Untouchable /
Subway train / Downtown. *<(re-iss. Jul92 & Feb95 on 'Warners' lp/cd; 7599
26982-2)>*

JOHNNY THUNDERS & THE HEARTBREAKERS

—— re-formed '79, with **WALTER, BILLY / + STYX** – drums

		Beggars Banquet	Max's Kansas
Jul 79. (7") *(BEG 21)* **GET OFF THE PHONE (live). / I WANNA
BE LOVED (live)**		☐	`–`
Sep 79. (lp) *(BEGA 9)* ‹*DTK 213*› **LIVE AT MAX'S KANSAS CITY
(live)**		☐	☐

– (intro) / Milk me / Chinese rocks / Get off the phone / London / Take a chance /
One track mind / All by myself / Let go / I love you / Can't keep my eyes on you /
I wanna be loved / Do you love me?. *(cd-iss. Jul91; BBL 9CD) <(cd-iss. Dec95 on
'ROIR USA'; RUSCD 8219)>*

—— Split again '79. In 1980, THUNDERS joined WAYNE KRAMER'S GANG WAR.

JOHNNY THUNDERS

solo again with **WALTER LURE** – guitar / **BILLY ROGERS** – drums

		New Rose	not iss.
Dec 82. (7") *(NEW 14)* **IN COLD BLOOD / ('A'live)**		`–`	`–` France
Jan 83. (d-lp) *(NR 18)* **IN COLD BLOOD (some live)**		`–`	`–` France

– In cold blood / Just another girl / Green onions / Diary of a lover / Look at my
eyes / Live: (intro) / Just another girl / Too much junkie business / Sad vacation /
Louie Louie / Gloria / Treat me like a nigger / Do you love me / Green onions / 10
commandments. *(re-iss. Apr94 lp/cd; 422367) (re-iss. cd Jun95 on 'Dojo'; DOJOCD
221) <(cd re-iss. Aug97 on 'Essential'; ESMCD 589)>*
Jan 84. (7"m) *(NEW 27)* **HURT ME. / IT'S NOT ENOUGH / LIKE
A ROLLING STONE** ☐ `–`

Jan 84. (lp) *(ROSE 26)* **HURT ME** ☐ –
– So alone / It ain't me babe / Eve of destruction / You can't put your arms round a memory / You're so strange / I'm a boy in a girl / Lonely planet boy / Sad vacation / Hurt me / Diary of a lover / Ask me no questions. *(cd-iss. May94; 422366)* *(re-iss. cd Jul95 on 'Dojo'; DOJOCD 217) <cd re-iss. Aug97 on 'Essential'; ESMCD 588)>*

Oct 85. (7"/7"pic-d; by JOHNNY THUNDERS with PATTI PALLADIN) *(JUNG 23/+P)* **CRAWFISH. / TIE ME UP (LOVE KNOT)** ☐ –
(ext.12"+=) *(JUNG 23T)* – ('A'-Bayou mix).

—— (w/ PATTI PALLADIN – vocals (ex-SNATCH, FLYING LIZARDS))

Dec 85. (lp) *(FREUD 9)* **QUE SERA, SERA** ☐ –
– Que sera, sera / Short lives / M.I.A. / I only wrote this song for you / Little bit of whore / Cool operator / Blame it on mom / Tie me up / Alone in a crowd / Billy boy / Endless party. *(pic-lp iss.Jun87; FREUDP 09) <cd-iss. Dec94; FREUDCD 49)>*

Jun 87. (7") *(JUNG 33)* **QUE SERA SERA. / SHORT LIVES** ☐ –
(12"+=) *(JUNG 33T)* – I only wrote this song.

JOHNNY THUNDERS & PATTI PALLADIN

May 88. (7") *(JUNG 38)* **SHE WANTS TO MAMBO. / UPTOWN** ☐ –
(12"+=) *(JUNG 38T)* – Love is strange.

Jun 88. (lp/c/cd) *(FREUD/+C/CD 20)* **YEAH, YEAH, I'M A COPY CAT** ☐ –
– Can't seem to make you mine / Baby it's you / She wants to mambo / Treat her right / Uptown to Harlem / Crawfish / Alligator wine / Two time loser / Love is strange / (I was) Born to cry / He cried (she cried) / Let me entertain you (part 1 & 2). *(re-iss. cd Nov96; same)*

Jan 89. (7") *(JUNG 43)* **(I WAS) BORN TO CRY. / TREAT HER RIGHT** ☐ –
(12"+=) *(JUNG 43T)* – Can't seem to make her mine.

—— THUNDERS died on the 23rd April '91, aged 38. He left three children from his first marriage plus another 3 year-old daughter, Jamie, conceived while he'd lived in Sweden with his girlfriend, Suzanne. JERRY NOLAN died on the 14th January '92 of a stroke (aged 45) after a bout of pneumonia and meningitis. Original drummer, BILLY MURCIA, also died in the 90's.

– compilations, etc. –

on 'Jungle' unless otherwise mentioned

Nov 82. (lp,pink-lp/white-lp/pic-lp) *(FREUD/+P 1)* **D.T.K. – LIVE AT THE SPEAKEASY** (live) ☐ –
<(cd-iss. Aug94 on 'Receiver'; R 191)>

May 83. (7"ep) *(JUNG 1)* **VINTAGE '77** ☐ –
– Let go / Chinese rocks / Born to lose.

1983. (c) *R.O.I.R.; <A 118>* **TOO MUCH JUNKIE BUSINESS** – ☐
(cd-iss. Feb95 on 'ROIR Europe'; same) <US 'Combat'; 5029>

Mar 84. (7"/7"pic-d) *(JUNG 14/+P)* **GET OFF THE PHONE. / ALL BY MYSELF** ☐ –
(12"+=) *(JUNG 14X)* – Pirate love.

Jun 84. (lp) *A.B.C.; (ABCLP 2)* **LIVE AT THE LYCEUM BALLROOM 1984** (live) ☐ –
<(re-iss. Jun91 on 'Receiver' lp/c/cd; RR LP/LC/CD 134)>

Feb 85. (7") *Twins; (T 1702)* **BORN TO LOSE. / IT'S NOT ENOUGH** ☐ –

May 85. (7"ep/12"ep) *(JUNG 18/+X)* **CHINESE ROCKS / BORN TO LOSE / ONE TRACK MIND / I WANNA BE LOVED** ☐ –

Feb 87. (c) *R.O.I.R.; (A 146) / Combat; <5028>* **STATIONS OF THE CROSS** – ☐
(re-iss. cd Jul94 on 'Receiver'; RRCD 188) (re-iss. cd Feb95 on 'ROIR Europe'; same)

May 88. (box-lp) *(JTBOX 1)* **THE JOHNNY THUNDERS ALBUM COLLECTION** ☐ –

Feb 90. (lp/cd) *(FREUD/+CD 30)* **BOOTLEGGIN' THE BOOTLEGGERS** ☐ –

Jan 92. (cd) *Fan Club;* **LIVE AT MOTHERS** (live) ☐ –

Feb 92. (cd) *Bomp; (BCD 4039)* **WHAT GOES AROUND** (live) ☐ –

Oct 92. (cd) *Fan Club; (422365)* **HAVE FAITH** (live solo) ☐ –
<(re-iss. Aug96 on 'Mutiny'; MUT 8005CD)>

Dec 93. (cd) *Anagram; (CDGRAM 70)* **CHINESE ROCKS – THE ULTIMATE LIVE COLLECTION** (live) ☐ –

Sep 94. (cd) *Skydog; (62251)* **VIVE LE REVOLUTION – LIVE PARIS, 1977** (live JOHNNY THUNDERS & THE HEARTBREAKERS) ☐ –

Nov 94. (cd) *Essential; (ESDCD 226)* **ADD WATER AND STIR – LIVE IN JAPAN 1991** (live) ☐ –

Apr 96. (cd) *Dojo; (DOJOCD 231)* **THE STUDIO BOOTLEGS** ☐ –

Sep 99. (7"pink) *(JUNG 62)* **CHINESE ROCKS. /** ☐ –

Sep 99. (7") *(JUNG 63)* **ONE TRACK MIND. /** ☐ –

TIGER LILY (see under ⇒ ULTRAVOX)

Tanita TIKARAM

Born: 12 Aug'69, Munster, Germany, to an Indian-Fijian father and a Bornean/Malayan mother, TIKARAM subsequently moved to Basingstoke in England as a teenager. A budding singer/songwriter, she was soon making a name for herself on London's small venue circuit and through agent, Paul Charles, signed to 'W.E.A.'. Featuring veterans, PETER VAN HOOKE and ROD ARGENT working in both a production and writing capacity, TIKARAM's promising debut set, 'ANCIENT HEART', was released in summer '88. Previewed by the uncharacteristically upbeat fireside waltz of Top 10 single, 'GOOD TRADITION', the album revealed the smoulderingly exotic TIKARAM to be a moody, sensual and intense pop-folkie in a kind of latter day LEONARD COHEN/JONI MITCHELL style. Brooding follow-up single, 'TWIST IN MY SOBRIETY', arguably remains her finest moment, its

relatively lowly Top 30 chart placing hardly reflecting the quality of a song that's since been the subject of countless cover versions. Though her voice was sufficently husky to lend her songs an air of rootsiness, subsequent albums, 'THE SWEET KEEPER' (1990) and 'EVERYBODY'S ANGEL' (1991) veered ever closer to coffee-table safety, the latter set failing to match the sales of her previous efforts. Despite a fairly rigorous touring schedule, 1992's 'ELEVEN KINDS OF LONELINESS' saw both her critical stock and popular appeal drop away further and TIKARAM has been subsequently marginalised to cult status. 'LOVERS IN THE CITY' (1995) continued her trend toward orchestral arrangements, scraping a Top 75 placing but hardly reclaiming her lost commercial standing. • **Songwriters:** she collaborated with ARGENT and VAN HOOKE and covered LOVING YOU (Elvis Presley) / THE DAY BEFORE YOU CAME (Abba). • **Trivia:** In the late 80's, TANITA guested on an album by BRENDAN CROKER and The FIVE O'CLOCK SHADOW.

Album rating: ANCIENT HEART (*7) / THE SWEET KEEPER (*6) / EVERYBODY'S ANGEL (*5) / ELEVEN KINDS OF LONELINESS (*5) / LOVERS IN THE CITY (*6) / THE BEST OF TANITA TIKARAM compilation (*7) / THE CAPPUCCINO SONGS (*5)

TANITA TIKARAM – vocals, acoustic guitar; with producers **PETER VAN COOKE** – drums / **ROD ARGENT** – keyboards plus **RORY McFARLANE** – bass / **MITCH DALTON** – guitar / **MARTIN DITCHAM** – percussion / guests were **PAUL BRADY** + **MARK CRESWELL** – guitar / **HELEN O'HARA** – violin / **BRENDAN CROKER** – accordion, etc.

	W.E.A.	Reprise
Aug 88. (7"/7"s/7"g-f) *(YZ 196/+L/G)* **GOOD TRADITION. / VALENTINE HEART**	10	☐
(12"+=) *(YZ 196T)* – Poor cow (demo).		
(cd-s+=) *(YZ 196CD)* – Cathedral song.		
Sep 88. (lp/c/cd) *(WX 210/+C)(K 243877-2) <25839>* **ANCIENT HEART**	3	59

– Good tradition / Cathedral song / Sighing innocents / I love you / World outside your window / For all these years / Twist in my sobriety / Poor cow / He likes the sun / Valentine heart / Preyed upon. *(re-iss. cd Feb95;)*

Oct 88. (7") *(YZ 321)* **TWIST IN MY SOBRIETY. / FRIENDS**	22	☐
(ext.12"+=) *(YZ 321T)* – For all these years.		
(10"++=/cd-s++=) *(YZ 321 TE/CD)* – The kill in your heart.		
Jan 89. (7") *(YZ 331)* **CATHEDRAL SONG. / SIGHING INNOCENTS**	48	☐
(12"+=) *(YZ 331T)* – Fireflies in the kitchen (live) / Let's make everybody smile today (live).		
(7"box+=/cd-s+=) *(YZ 331 B/CD)* – Let's make everybody smile today (live) / Over you all (live).		
Mar 89. (7") *(YZ 363)* **WORLD OUTSIDE YOUR WINDOW (remix). / FOR ALL THESE YEARS (instrumental)**	58	☐
(ext.12"+=) *(YZ 363T)* – Good tradition (live).		
(cd-s+=) *(YZ 363CD)* – ('A'-extended).		
(box-cd-s+=) *(YZ 363CDX)* – He likes the sun (live).		

—— **JOHN GIBLIN** – bass repl. DITCHAM and DALTON / guests **CLEM CLEMPSON** – guitar / **MARK ISHAM** – trumpet repl. CROKER + BRADY

Jan 90. (7"/7"g-f) *(YZ 443/+G)* **WE ALMOST GOT IT TOGETHER. / LOVE STORY**	52	☐
(12"+=/cd-s+=) *(YZ 443 T/CD)* – Over you all.		
Feb 90. (cd)(lp/c) *(9031 70800-2)(WX 330/+C) <26091>* **THE SWEET KEEPER**	3	☐

– Once & not speak / Thursday's child / It all came back today / We almost got it together / Consider the rain / Sunset's arrived / Little sister leaving town / I owe it all to you / Love story / Harm in your hands.

Mar 90. (7"/c-s) *(YZ 459/+MC)* **LITTLE SISTER LEAVING TOWN. / I LOVE THE HEAVEN**	☐	☐
(12"+=/cd-s+=) *(YZ 459 T/CD)* – Hot pork sandwiches / Twist in my sobriety.		
(cd-s+=) *(YZ 459CDP)* –		
Jun 90. (7"/c-s) *(YZ 481/+C)* **THURSDAY'S CHILD. / ONCE & NOT SPEAK**	☐	☐
(12"+=/cd-s+=) *(YZ 481 T/CD)* – Cathedral song (live).		

—— She retained VAN HOOKE, ARGENT, CRESWELL + ISHAM, bringing in DAVID HAYES – bass / NICK FRANCE – drums / KATIE KISSOON + CAROL KENYON – b.vocals

	East West	Reprise
Jan 91. (7"/c-s) *(YZ 558/+C)* **ONLY THE ONES WE LOVE. / ME IN MIND**	69	☐
(12"+=) *(YZ 558T)* – Mud in any water.		
(cd-s+=) *(YZ 558CD)* – Cathedral song.		
Feb 91. (cd)(lp/c) *(9031 73341-2)(WX 401/+C) <26486>* **EVERYBODY'S ANGEL**	19	☐

– Only the ones we love / Deliver me / This story in me / To wish this / Mud in any water / Sunface / Never known / This stranger / Swear by me / Hot pork sandwiches / Me in mind / Sometime with me / I love the Heaven's solo / I'm going home.

Mar 91. (7"/c-s) *(YZ 569/+C)* **I LOVE THE HEAVEN'S SOLO. / ONLY IN NAME**	☐	☐
(12"+=/cd-s+=) *(YZ 569 T/CD)* – To wish this / I'm going home.		
Feb 92. (7"/c-s) *(YZ 644/+C)* **YOU MAKE THE WHOLE WORLD CRY. / ROCK ME 'TIL I STOP / ME, YOU & LUCIFER**	☐	☐
(cd-s) *(YZ 644CD)* – (1st 2 tracks) / This stranger (alt.version).		
(cd-s) *(YZ 644CDX)* – (1st & 3rd tracks) / This stranger (alt.version).		
Mar 92. (cd/c/lp) *(9031 76427-2/-4/-1)* **ELEVEN KINDS OF LONELINESS**	☐	☐

– You make the whole world cry / Elephant / trouble / I grant you / Heal you / To drink the rainbow / Out on the town / Hot stones / Men & women / Any reason / Love don't need no tyranny / The way that I want you.

—— now with guitarist **MICHAEL LANDAU** / + orchestra **THOMAS NEWMAN**

Jan 95. (c-s/cd-s) *(YZ 879 C/CD)* **I MIGHT BE CRYING / FIVE FEET AWAY**	64	☐
(cd-s+=) *(YZ 879CDX)* – Not waving but drowning.		
Feb 95. (cd/c) *(4509 98804-2/-4)* **LOVERS IN THE CITY**	75	☐

– Lovers in the city / Yodelling song / Wonderful shadow / Women who cheat on the world / Leaving the party / I might be crying / Bloodlines / Feeding the witches / Happy taxi / My love tonight.

Mar 95. (c-s) *(YZ 922C)* **WONDERFUL SHADOW / GOOD TRADITION**
(cd-s) *(YZ 922CD1)* – ('A'side) / Have you lost your way?
(cd-s) *(YZ 922CD2)* – ('A'side) / Out on the town.

Jul 95. (cd-s) *(YZ 968CD)* **THE YODELLING SONG / TO DRINK THE RAINBOW / BLOODLINES**

Jun 96. (cd/c) *(<0630 15106-2/-4>)* **THE BEST OF TANITA TIKARAM** (compilation)
– Twist in my sobriety / Cathedral song / World outside your window / Good tradition / Love don't need no tyranny / Little sister leaving town / Only the ones we love / You make the whole world cry / Trouble / Wonderful shadow / Men and women / I might be crying / Happy taxi / My love tonight / Lovers in the city / And I think of you – e penso a te / Twist in my sobriety (Tikaramp radio).

Sep 96. (c-s) *(EW 064C)* **TWIST IN MY SOBRIETY** / ('A'mix)
(cd-s/12") *(EW 064 T/CD)* – ('A'mixes; Tikaramp radio / Phil Kelsey vocal / Extende bumps fluidity mix / Tikaramp vocal / SFX Sobriety).

	Mother	Polygram
May 98. (cd-s) *(MUMCD 102)* **STOP LISTENING / THE CAPPUCCINO SONG / FEELING IS GONE / STOP LISTENING** (director's cut)	67	-
(cd-s) *(MUMXD 102)* – ('A'side) / Twist in my sobriety (new version) / Good tradition (new version).		
Aug 98. (cd-s) *(MUMCD 105)* **I DON'T WANNA LOSE AT LOVE / I DON'T WANNA LOSE AT LOVE** (love loss ADF remix) / **IN YOUR TIME**	73	-
(cd-s+=) *(MUMXD 105)* – ('A'side) / ('A'-XT Talvin Singh mix) / Only one boy in the crowd.		
Sep 98. (cd/c) *(MUM CD/C 9801)* *<559303>* **THE CAPPUCCINO SONGS**	69	

– Stop listening / Light up my world / Amore si / Back in your arms / The cappuccino song / I don't wanna lose at love / The day before you came / If I ever / I like this / I knew you. *(cd bonus track+=)* – I don't wanna lose at love.

'TIL TUESDAY (see under ⇒ MANN, Aimee)

TINDERSTICKS

Formed: Nottingham, England … 1988 as ASPHALT RIBBONS, by STUART STAPLES, DAVE BOULTER and DICKON HINCHCLIFFE, the line-up completed by NEIL FRASER, MARK COLWILL and AL McCAULEY. Abandoning their previous TRIFFIDS/GO-BETWEENS-esque indie attempts, the group adopted a darkly brooding hybrid of faded-glamour easy listening and semi-acoustic strumming, incorporating swooning strings, mournful violin, frantic flamenco and hints of country. Surely the heartbroken, doomed romantic to top all doomed romantics, STAPLES' low-key mumblings were somehow utterly compelling, his often barely audible melange of NICK CAVE, LEE HAZLEWOOD and TOM WAITS capable of expressing every nuance in the music regardless of what he was actually saying. The TINDERSTICKS came to critical notice with only their second single, 'MARBLES', a lo-fi STAPLES monologue cosetted by an aching melody. Released on their own 'Tippy Toe' label, the track was unanimously awarded Single Of The Week by both NME and Melody Maker, creating a buzz which would eventually see the group sign to the newly formed 'This Way Up' label. Previewed by the string-drenched melancholy of the 'CITY SICKNESS' single, the eponymous 'TINDERSTICKS' (1993) was released in late '93. A dense, bleakly beautiful, seedily glamourous near 80-minute epic, the record was so strikingly different from anything else it sounded timeless (save for maybe GALLON DRUNK or NICK CAVE). From the edgy resignation of 'WHISKEY & WATER' to the lovelorn lament of 'RAINDROPS', this was one of the most luxuriantly dark albums of the 90's, reeking of failed relationships and nicotine-stained despair. With gushing praise from the music press, both for the album and their hypnotic live shows, The TINDERSTICKS even managed to scrape a Top 60 chart placing. Released simultaneously with the album was a cover of John Barry's 'WE HAVE ALL THE TIME IN THE WORLD' alongside GALLON DRUNK on a 'Clawfist' 7", the latter group's TERRY EDWARDS having guested on the album and subsequently adding string arrangements on their next long player. Preceded by a cover of the late Townes Van Zandt's 'KATHLEEN', 'TINDERSTICKS' (same title, different album) was finally released in Spring '95, its grainy noir narratives and downtrodden country enhanced with exquisite orchestration. There were no great stylistic leaps, just a further exploration and refinement of the blurred shadows and twilit corners that graced the debut. An undisputed highlight was the goose-bump country duet with The WALKABOUTS' CARLA TORGERSON, 'TRAVELLING LIGHT', released as a single that summer. The TINDERSTICKS were also in the process of refining their live sound, or rather expanding it, with the help of a full orchestra; the gorgeous results can be heard on concert set, 'THE BLOOMSBURY THEATRE 12.3.95'. Unable to sustain such a money draining enterprise for too long, the TINDERSTICKS-plus-orchestra phase reached its zenith during a hugely successful week long residency at London's ICA theatre in late '96. The same year also saw the group's first foray into soundtrack work, scoring the music for French art film, 'Nenette et Boni'. Largely instrumental, the piano and bass-led main theme was fleshed out with the moving 'TINY TEARS' (or 'PETITES GOUTTES D'EAU' in French) from the second album; hardly essential but a pleasant listen all the same. Following the group's own fears that the fragile balance of The TINDERSTICKS' muse was becoming unworkable, the difficult third album, 'CURTAINS' was finally completed in a fevered rush of creativity and released in Summer '97. Less sprawling and more cohesive than previous efforts, it was also bolder and more accessible, STAPLES actually singing comprehensibly on the bulk of the tracks. Predictably, there were also more strings than ever, HINCHCLIFFE's orchestral flourishes crescendoing majestically on 'DON'T LOOK DOWN' and achieving a pathos only previously glimpsed before on 'LET'S PRETEND', JESUS ALEMANY's mariachi-style trumpet a bittersweet counterpart. There was even another country duet, 'BURIED BONES', a brilliantly executed NANCY/LEE-style sparring match featuring the velvet tones of BONGWATER's ANNE MAGNUSON. Lyrically, the themes remained reliably unchanged, tales of everyday lust and disillusionment dripping from STAPLES' lips like the honey from his claws as described in the gripping, unsettling 'BEARSUIT'. And, with 'BALLAD OF TINDERSTICKS', STAPLES indicated that they don't take this music business lark TOO seriously. After a stop-gap 'best of' album, 'DONKEYS' was released in '98, TINDERSTICKS were back to their mournful best courtesy of 1999's 'SIMPLE PLEASURE'. Opening with the minor hit, 'CAN WE START AGAIN?' and then a cover of Odyssey's dancefloor hit(!), 'IF YOU'RE LOOKING FOR A WAY OUT', it was clear to see the familiar 'STICKS territory had been given a modern day injection. If there was any justice, TINDERSTICKS would be bigger than OASIS; as it is they remain a treasured secret for anyone who's ever glimpsed the universe through the bottom of a wine glass. • **Other covers:** KOOKS (David Bowie) / I'VE BEEN LOVING YOU TOO LONG (Otis Redding & Jerry Butler) / HERE (Pavement). • **Trivia:** JON LANGFORD of The THREE JOHNS, produced early ASPHALT RIBBONS material.

Album rating: Asphalt Ribbons: OLD HORSE & OTHER SONGS (*4) / Tindersticks: TINDERSTICKS (*8) / THE SECOND TINDERSTICKS ALBUM (*7) / THE BLOOMSBURY THEATRE 12.3.95 (*6) / NANETTE ET BONI soundtrack (*6) / CURTAINS (*8) / DONKEYS 92-97 compilation (*7) / SIMPLE PLEASURE (*8)

ASPHALT RIBBONS

STUART STAPLES – vocals / **DICKON HINCHCLIFFE** – violin / **DAVE BOULTER** – keyboards / **BLACKHOUSE** – guitar / **FRASER** – bass / **WATT** – drums

	In-Tape	not iss.
Oct 89. (7"ep) *(IT 063)* **THE ORCHARD**		-
– Over again / Red sauce / Greyhound / I used to live T.		
May 90. (7"m) *(IT 068)* **GOOD LOVE. / LONG LOST UNCLE / THE DAY I TURNED BAD**		-

—— (Alongside new stablemates MY LIFE WITH PATRICK, their new label below issued a free flexi sampler with 'Zip Code' fanzine; cat no. LILY 001)

	Tiger Lily	not iss.
Apr 91. (12"ep) *(LILY 002)* **PASSION, COOLNESS, INDIFFERENCE, BOREDOM, MOCKERY, CONTEMPT, DISGUST**		-

	E.T.T.	not iss.
Aug 91. (m-lp) *(E 101)* **OLD HORSE & OTHER SONGS**		-
(cd-iss. Apr92; E 101-2)		

TINDERSTICKS

—— were formed by **STUART, DICKON and DAVE**, plus Londoners **NEIL FRASER** – guitar / **MARK COLWILL** – bass / **AL McCAULEY** – drums

	Tippy Toe	No.6
Nov 92. (7") *(TIPPY TOE 1)* **PATCHWORK. / MILKY TEETH**		-
Mar 93. (10"ep) *(TIPPY TOE – che 2)* **MARBLES / JOE STUMBLE. / FOR THOSE … / BENN**		-

—— Below featured dual vox of **NIKI SIN** of HUGGY BEAR.

	Rough Trade Sing. Club	not iss.
Mar 93. (7") *(45REV 16)* **A MARRIAGE MADE IN HEAVEN. / (instrumental)**		-

	Domino	No.6
Jul 93. (7"ep) *(RUG 6)* **UNWIRED E.P.**		-
– Feeling relatively good / Rottweilers and mace / She / Kooks.		

	This Way Up	Bar None
Sep 93. (7") *<KAR 028>* **MARBLES. / FOR THOSE NOT BEAUTIFUL**	-	
Sep 93. (7"/cd-s) *(WAY 1811/1833)* **CITY SICKNESS. / UNTITLED / THE BULLRING**		
Oct 93. (cd/c/lp) *(518306-2/-4/-1)* *<46>* **TINDERSTICKS**	56	

– Nectar tyed / Sweet, sweet man (pt.1) / Whiskey & water / Blood / City sickness / Patchwork / Marbles / The Walt blues / Milky teeth (pt.2) / Sweet, sweet man (pt.2) / Jism / Piano song / Tie dye / Raindrops / Sweet, sweet man (pt.3) / Her / Tea stain / Drunk tank / Paco de Renaldo's dream / The not knowing. *(lp+=)* – Fruitless. *(re-iss. Jun97; same)*

—— In Oct'93, alongside GALLON DRUNK, they issued 'Clawfist' 7" WE HAVE ALL THE TIME IN THE WORLD (XPIG 21). 'Tippy Toe' also gave away 7" 'LIVE IN BERLIN' at gigs.

Jan 94. (7"ep/10"ep/cd-ep) *(WAY 2811/2888/2833)* **KATHLEEN EP**	61	-
– Kathleen / Summat Moon / A sweet sweet man / E-type Joe.		

—— In Aug'94, they appeared on Various Artists EP on 'Blue Eyed Dog'; track 'LOVE BITES', and others by STRANGELOVE / GOD MACHINE + BREED.

	This Way Up	London
Mar 95. (7") *(WAY 38-11)* **NO MORE AFFAIRS. / (instrumental)**	58	-
(cd-s+=) *(WAY 38-33)* – Fruitless.		
Apr 95. (cd/c/d-lp) *(526303-2/-4/-1)* *<6303>* **THE SECOND TINDERSTICKS ALBUM**	13	Oct95

– El diablo en el ojo / My sister / Tiny tears / Snowy in F minor / Seaweed / Vertrauen 2 / Talk to me / No more affairs / Singing / Travelling light / Cherry blossoms / She's gone / Mistakes / Vertraven 3 / Sleepy song. *(ltd.lp w/ free one-sided-7")* – PLUS DE LIAISONS

Jun 95. (7") *<SP 297>* **THE SMOOTH SOUNDS OF TINDERSTICKS**	-	
– Here / Harry's dilemma.		

—— *<above issued for 'Sub Pop'>*

Jul 95. (7"/cd-s) (WAY 45-11) **TRAVELLING LIGHT. / WAITING 'ROUND YOU / I'VE BEEN LOVING YOU TOO LONG**   `51` `-`

Oct 95. (cd/d-10"lp) (528597-2/-1) **THE BLOOMSBURY THEATRE 12.3.95 (live)**   `32` `-`
– El diablo en el ojo / A night in / Talk to me / She's gone / My sister * / No more affairs / City sickness / Vertrauen II / Sleepy song / Jism / Drunk tank / Mistakes / Tiny tears / Raindrops / For those . . . (d-lp+ = *)

	This Way Up	Bar None

Oct 96. (cd/lp) (524300-2/-1) <99> **NENENTE ET BONI (Original Soundtrack)**
– Ma souer / La passerelle / Les gateaux / Camions / Nenette est la / Petites chiennes / Nosterfrau / Petites gouttes d'eau / Les Cannes a peche / La mort de Felix / Nenette s'en va / Les bebes / Les fleurs / Rumba.

	This Way Up	Polygram

May 97. (12"ep/cd-ep) (WAY 61-22/-33) **BATHTIME. / MANALOW / SHADOWS / PACO'S THEME**   `38` `-`
(cd-ep) (WAY 61-66) – ('A'side) / Kathleen / Here / Tyed.

Jun 97. (cd/c/lp) (<524344-2/-4/-1>) **CURTAINS**   `37`
– Another night in / Rented rooms / Don't look down / Dick's slow song / Fast one / Ballad of Tindersticks / Dancing / Let's pretend / Desperate man / Buried bones / Bearsuit / (Tonight) Are you trying to fall in love again / I was your man / Bathtime / Walking.

Oct 97. (7") (WAY 65-22) **RENTED ROOMS. / ('A'-Swing version)**   `56`
(cd-s+=) (WAY 65-33) – Make believe.
(cd-s) (WAY 65-66) – ('A'side) / Cherry blossoms (live) / She's gone (live) / Rhumba (live).

	Island	Polygram

Sep 98. (cd/lp) (CID/ILPS 8074) <524588> **DONKEYS 92-97 (A COLLECTION OF SINGLES ° RARITIES ° UNRELEASED RECORDINGS)** (compilation)
– Patchwork / Marbles / Her / City sickness / Travelling light / I've been loving you too long / Plus de liaisons / Here / Tiny tears / Bathtime / A marriage made in Heaven / For those . . .

Aug 99. (7") (IS 756) **CAN WE START AGAIN? / ONE WAY STREET**   `54`
(cd-s+=) (CID 756) – A little time.
(cd-s) (CIDX 756) – ('A'demo) / Puppy fat / Desperate man (alternate version).

Aug 99. (cd) (CID 8085) **SIMPLE PLEASURE**   `36`
– Can we start again? / Looking for a way out / Pretty words / From the inside / If she's torn / Before you close your eyes / You take this heart of mine / I know that lovin' / CFGF. (lp-iss.Sep99 on 'Simply Vinyl'; SVLP 112)

TIN MACHINE (see under ⇒ BOWIE, David)

TOAD THE WET SPROCKET (dig out; 4th edition)

TOILING MIDGETS (see under ⇒ AMERICAN MUSIC CLUB)

TOMORROW (dig out; 4th edition or Great Psychedelic . . .)

TOM TOM CLUB (see under ⇒ TALKING HEADS)

TONES ON TAIL (see under ⇒ BAUHAUS)

TOOL

Formed: Hollywood, California, USA . . . 1990 by ADAM JONES, MAYNARD JAMES KEENAN, PAUL D'AMOUR and DANNY CAREY. Signing to 'Zoo' records, TOOL showcased their claustrophobic, nihilistic nu-metal on the 1992 mini-set, 'OPIATE'. Creating a buzz with high-profile supports to the likes of HENRY ROLLINS, TOOL subsequently hammered out a full album's worth of HELMET-like savage intensity with 'UNDERTOW' (1993), a record with such bluntly titled tracks as 'PRISON SEX' (also a single), 'INTOLERANCE' and 'BOTTOM' (the latter featuring the aforementioned ROLLINS). The album went on to sell over a million copies in the States, having only reached the Top 50. Three years later, after extensive touring, they resurfaced in dramatic fashion with 'AENIMA', the record bolting straight to No.2, surprising many who had yet to acquire a taste for TOOL.

Album rating: OPIATE mini (*5) / UNDERTOW (*6) / AENIMA (*7)

MAYNARD JAMES KEENAN – vocals / **ADAM JONES** – guitar / **PAUL D'AMOUR** – bass / **DANNY CAREY** – drums

	Zoo-RCA	Zoo
Jul 92. (m-cd/m-c/m-lp) <(72445 11027-2/-4/-1)> **OPIATE**		

– Sweat / Hush / Part of me / Cold and ugly (live) / Jerk-off (live) / Opiate.

Apr 93. (cd/c) <(72445 11052-2/-4)> **UNDERTOW**   `50`
– Intolerance / Prison sex / Sober / Bottom / Crawl away / Swamp song / Undertow / 4 degrees / Flood / Disgustipated.

Mar 94. (12"grey/cd-s) (74321 19432-1/-2) **PRISON SEX. / UNDERTOW (live) / OPIATE (live)**

Jul 94. (12"/cd-s) (74321 22043-1/21849-2) **SOBER. / INTOLERANCE**

— **JUSTIN CHANCELLOR** – bass repl. D'AMOUR

Oct 96. (cd/c/lp) (61422 31144-2/-4/-1) <72445 11087-2/-4/-1> **AENIMA**   `2`
– Stinkfist / Eulogy / H. / Useful idiot / Forty six & 2 / Message to Harry Manback / Hooker with a penis / Intermission / Jimmy / Die eier von Satan / Pushit / Cesaro summability / Aenima / (-)Ions / Third eye.

TORTOISE

Formed: Chicago, Illinois, USA . . . 1990 by DOUG McCOMBS and JOHN HERNDON, who started jamming together with JOHN McENTIRE, BUNDY K BROWN and DAN BITNEY. This cult outfit initially crawled out of their collective shell with a series of early 90's EP's before finally unleashing their eponymous debut in '94. Remixed by STEVE ALBINI on the following year's blistering EP, 'RHYTHMS, RESOLUTIONS & CLUSTERS', the record proved TORTOISE to be the foremost purveyors of cut'n'mix avant-jazz. In 1996, their second album, 'MILLIONS NOW LIVING WILL NEVER DIE' (featuring the STEREOLAB trio of TIM, LAETITIA and MARY) was even better, opening with the psychedelic/Krautrock marathon of 'DJED'. This 20-minute track was subsequently given the 'Mo Wax' treatment, the extent of the band's appeal illustrated by their impressive run of collaborations over the course of the next year. The hard-working McENTIRE, who was also a part-time member of RED CRAYOLA and The SEA AND CAKE, returned to the studio at the end of the year, beavering away on what was yet another classic TORTOISE set, 'TNT' (1998). A segued journey from cool avant-jazz rock that unsuspectingly flowed into complex rhythmical landscapes, the record proved a hard listen for alt-rock buffs. JOHN McENTIRE (who also sidelined with the SEA AND CAKE), subsequently found his niche in soundtrack work, although 'REACH THE ROCK' (1999) was too pretentious and complex for some.

Album rating: TORTOISE (*7) / RHYTHMS, RESOLUTIONS & CLUSTERS remixes (*6) / MILLIONS NOW LIVING WILL NEVER DIE (*8) / TNT (*7) / John McEntire: REACH THE ROCK soundtrack (*5)

JOHN McENTIRE – synthesizers, drums, vibraphone (ex-BASTRO, ex-SHRIMP BOAT) / **BUNDY K BROWN** – guitar, bass (ex-GASTR DE SOL) / **DOUG McCOMBS** – bass (ex-ELEVENTH DREAM DAY) / **JOHNNY HERNDON** – drums, synthesizers, vibraphone (ex-POSTER CHILDREN) / **DAN BITNEY** – synthesizers, percussion, multi / 6th member **CASEY** – soundman

	not iss.	Torsion
1993. (7") <003> **MOSQUITO. / ONIONS WRAPPED IN RUBBER / GOOSENECK**	`-`	

	not iss.	Soul Static
1994. (7") <SOUL 7> **WHY WE FIGHT. / WHITEWATER** (UK-iss.Jan95; same)	`-`	

	City Slang	Thrill Jockey
1994. (12") <THRILL 006> **LONESOME SOUND. / RESERVOIR / SHEETS**	`-`	

Jan 95. (cd/lp) (EFA 04950-2/-1) <THRILL 013> **TORTOISE**
– Magnet pulls through / Night air / Ry Cooder / Onions wrapped in rubber / Tin cans and twine / Spiderwebbed / His second story island / On noble / Flyrod / Cornpole brunch. (cd-iss. remixed May97; TKCB 71016) (lp re-iss. Jun97 on 'Thrill Jockey'; THRILL 013)

Apr 95. (12") (Dodgey Beast; DS 3309) **GAMERA. / CLIFF DWELLER SOCIETY**
(12") (DS 3309S) – ('A'mixes).

Jun 95. (m-cd/m-lp) (EFA 04957-2/-1) <THRILL 019> **RHYTHMS, RESOLUTIONS & CLUSTERS: REMIXED AND RARE**
– Alcohall / Your new rod / Cobwebbed / Match incident / Not quite east of the Ryan / Initial gesture protraction.

— **DAVE PAJO** – guitar (ex-SLINT) repl. BROWN who formed DIRECTIONS IN MUSIC. He and McCOMBS were also part of alt-supergroup, PULLMAN.

Jan 96. (cd/lp) (EFA 04972-2/-1) <THRILL 025> **MILLIONS NOW LIVING WILL NEVER DIE**
– Djed / Glass museum / A survey / The taut and the tame / Dear grandma and grandpa / Along the banks of rivers. (cd-iss. Japanese version May97; TKCB 70931)

Apr 96. (12"; by TORTOISE Vs U.N.K.L.E./JOHN McENTIRE) (SHELL 001) <TJ 12.1> **DJED (bruise blood mix). / TJED**

Jul 96. (12"; by TORTOISE Vs BUNDY BROWN) <TJ 12.2> **ROME**   `-`

Jul 96. (12"; by TORTOISE Vs OVAL) (SHELL 002) <TJ 12.3> **MUSIC FOR WORK GROUPS EP**
– The bubble economy (mix by Marcus Popp) / Learning curve (mix by Marcus Popp).

Sep 96. (12"; by TORTOISE VS SPRING HEEL JACK) (SHELL 003) <TJ 12.4> **GALAPAGOS 1 (Spring Heel Jack remix). / REFERENCE RESISTANCE GATE (John O'Rourke remix)** (re-iss. Jun97 on 'Thrill Jockey'; TJ 124)

Oct 96. (12"; by TORTOISE Vs LUKE VIBERT/BUNDY K BROWN) (SHELL 004) <TJ 12.5> **THE TAUT AND THE TAME. / FIND THE ONE (WAIT, ABSTRACTION NO . . .)**

— In 1996, they also shared a single with STEREOLAB, 'VAUS' / 'SPEEDY CAR', released on 'Duophonic'; D-UHF-D12)

— **JEFF PARKER** – guitar; repl. PAJO who formed AERIAL M

Mar 98. (cd/d-lp) (EFA 08705-2/-1) <THRILL 050> **TNT**
– Swung from the gutters / Ten-day interval / I set my face to the hillside / The equator / A simple way to go faster than light that does not work / The suspension bridge at Iguazu Falls / Four-day interval / In Sarah, Mencken, Christ, and Beethoven there were women and men / Almost always is nearly enough / Jetty / Everglade.

Jul 98. (ltd-12"; TORTOISE VS. DERRICK CARTER) (087096) **IN SARAH, MENCKEN, CHRIST, AND BEETHOVEN THERE WERE WOMEN AND MEN**   `-`
– (D's winter crazy mix) / (D's winter outtake).
(above issued on 'Rephlex')

– compilations, others, etc. –

May 97. (cd) Thrill Jockey; <(TKCB 70932)> **A DIGEST COMPENDIUM OF TORTOISE'S WORLD**   `1996`
– Tin cans & twine / Alcohall / Night air / Gooseneck / Onions wrapped in rubber / Spiderwebbed / Cobwebbed / Your new rod / Ry Cooder (the beer incident) / Not

quite east of the Ryan / Reservoir / Cornpone brunch / Whitewater / Initial gesture protraction.

Apr 98. (cd) *Thrill Jockey;* <*(TKCB 71016)*> **TORTOISE REMIXED** (all the 4 collaboration/Vs singles) | | | |1996

JOHN McENTIRE

—— his debut solo album (although shared with others)

	Hefty	Hefty
Feb 99. (7"pic-d) <*(HEF 13)*> **split w/ SEA AND CAKE**		
Mar 99. (cd) <*(HEFT 14CD)*> **REACH THE ROCK** (Original Soundtrack)		

– In a thimble (TORTOISE) / Criminal record / Overview / Stolen car / Drift (BUNDY K. BROWN) / Quinn goes to town / Window lights (SEA AND CAKE) / Reverse migraine (POLVO) / Lise arrives / The kiss / Main title / Dreams of being king (DIANOGAH). (lp-iss.Nov99; HEFT 014LP)

Peter TOSH

Born: WINSTON HUBERT MacINTOSH, 9 Oct'44, Westmoreland, Jamaica. A founding member of The WAILERS alongside BOB MARLEY in 1962, TOSH was as equally pivotal as his more famous peer in spreading the reggae gospel if not more so. During his time with The WAILERS, he maintained a prolific recording schedule for the famous 'Studio One' label, eventually founding his own imprint, 'Intel-Diplo H.I.M.' in 1971. This became the main outlet for TOSH's music following his break with MARLEY & Co; throughout his lengthy spell with the band, TOSH had provided them with consistently quality material, his last contribution being 'GET UP STAND UP' on the 'Burnin' (1973) album. His career only really got off the ground again, however, when 'Virgin' signed him in 1976, his debut album proper, 'LEGALIZE IT' (1976) nearly hitting the UK Top 50. TOSH made no bones about what exactly he proposed to legalize, his hardline Rasta stance, booming baritone voice and bass-quaking reggae/dub sound winning die hard fans across the whole musical spectrum. Recorded with backing band, WORD, SOUND & POWER, 'EQUAL RIGHTS' (1977) was an even more fiercely political set featuring such scathing missives as 'DOWNPRESSOR MAN', 'STEPPING RAZOR' and a tuffed-up revamp of 'GET UP STAND UP'. One of the man's more famous admirers was MICK JAGGER of The ROLLING STONES, who signed TOSH to his own label and even provided (clearly audible) backing vocals on his first Top 50 hit single, 'DON'T LOOK BACK'. The track was featured on the 'BUSH DOCTOR' (1978) set, one of a trio of albums for The 'STONES label alongside 'MYSTIC MAN' (1979) and 'WANTED DREAD & ALIVE' (1981). After signing to 'E.M.I.' in the early 80's, he scored a further minor hit single with a cover of Chuck Berry's 'JOHNNY B. GOODE' and although his mainstream successes were few and far between, the man remained one of the scene's most visible figures. Tragically, 1987 protest set, 'NO NUCLEAR WAR', was to become the man's swansong; TOSH was shot dead on 11th September the same year during a robbery at his Kingston home. Speculation that the killing was politically motivated has continued to flourish, however, TOSH having clashed with both the Government and police in the past. He was only 42, his death coming as a sore loss to a movement that had lost figurehead, BOB MARLEY only six years earlier. • **Songwriters:** Writes himself, except several including; DON'T LOOK BACK (Temptations).

Album rating: LEGALIZE IT (*7) / EQUAL RIGHTS (*7) / BUSH DOCTOR (*7) / MYSTIC MAN (*6) / WANTED, DREAD & ALIVE (*6) / MAMA AFRICA (*5) / CAPTURED LIVE (*5) / NO NUCLEAR WAR (*6) / THE TOUGHEST compilation (*7) / THE GOLD COLLECTION compilation (*7)

PETER TOSH – vocals, keyboards, guitar (ex-WAILERS) / with some ex-WAILERS, SLY & ROBBIE, etc.

	Virgin	Virgin
Mar 76. (7") (*VS 140*) **LEGALIZE IT. / BRAND NEW SECOND HAND**		-
Aug 76. (lp/c) (*V/TCV 2061*) <*34253*> **LEGALIZE IT**	54	

– Legalize it / Burial / Watcha gonna do / No sympathy / Why must I care / Igziabeher (let him be praised) / Ketchy shuby / Till your well runs dry / Brand new second hand. (re-iss.Aug88; OVED 108) (cd-iss. Oct88; CDV 2061)

Apr 77. (7") (*VS 179*) **AFRICAN. / STEPPING RAZOR** | | - |
Apr 77. (lp/c) (*V/TCV 2081*) <*34670*> **EQUAL RIGHTS** (with WORDS, SOUND & POWER) | | |

– Get up, stand up / Downpressor man / I am that I am / Stepping razor / Equal rights / African / Jah guide / Apartheid. (re-iss.Aug88; OVED 109) (cd-iss. Oct88; CDV 2081)

	E.M.I.	Columbia
Sep 78. (7") (*EMI 2859*) <*19308*> **(YOU GOTTA WALK) DON'T LOOK BACK. / SOON COME**	43	81

above featured duet with MICK JAGGER

	Rolling Stones	Rolling Stones
Nov 78. (lp/c) (*CUN 39109*) <*39109*> **BUSH DOCTOR**		

– (You gotta walk) Don't look back / Pick myself up / I'm the toughest / Soon come / Moses the prophet / Bush doctor / Stand firm / Dem ha fe get a beatin' / Creation. (re-iss.Nov85 on 'Fame' lp/c; FA 41 3139-1-4) (cd-iss. Oct88 on 'E.M.I.'; CDP 791085-2) (cd re-iss. Nov90 on 'Trojan'; CDTRP 100)

Mar 79. (7") (*RSR 103*) **I'M THE TOUGHEST. / TOUGHEST (version)** | | |
(12"+=) (*12RSR 103*) – Word, sound and power.

Aug 79. (7") (*RSR 104*) **BUK-IN-HAMM PALACE. / THE DAY THE DOLLAR DIE** | | |
Aug 79. (lp/c) (*CUN 39111*) <*39111*> **MYSTIC MAN** | | |

– Mystic man / Recruiting soldiers / Can't you see / Fight on / Jah say no / Buk-in-hamm Palace / The day the dollar die / Crystal ball / Rumours of war.

	Rolling Stones	EMI America
Sep 80. (7") (*RSR 107*) **NOTHING BUT LOVE. (w/ GWEN GUTHRIE) / COLD BLOOD**		
Jun 81. (7"/12") (*RSR/12RSR 107*) **NOTHING BUT LOVE. / COLD BLOOD**		
Jun 81. (lp/c) (*CUN/TC-CUN 39113*) <*17055*> **WANTED DREAD & ALIVE**		91

– Coming in hot / Nothing but love / Reggaemylitis / Rock with me / Oh bumbo klaat / Wanted dread and alive / Rastafari is / Guide me from my friends / Fools die.

	Radic-EMI	EMI America
Mar 83. (7") (*RIC 115*) <*8159*> **JOHNNY B. GOODE. / PEACE TREATY**	48	84
Apr 83. (lp/c) (*RDC/TCRDC 2005*) <*17095*> **MAMA AFRICA**		59

– Mama Africa / Glasshouse / Not gonna give it up / Stop that train / Johnny B. Goode / Where you gonna run / Peace treaty / Feel no way / Maga dog.

May 83. (7") (*RIC 116*) **WHERE YOU GONNA RUN. / STOP THAT TRAIN** | | |

	E.M.I.	EMIAmerica
Sep 83. (7"/10") (*RIC/10RIC 117*) **MAMA AFRICA. / NOT GONNA GIVE IT UP**		-
Jul 84. (lp) (*PTOSH 1*) <*17126*> **CAPTURED LIVE (live)**		

– Coming in hot / Bush doctor / African / Get up, stand up / Johnny B. Goode / Equal rights – Downpresser man / Rastafari is.

	Parlophone	Capitol
Jul 87. (7") (*R 6156*) **IN MY SONG. / COME TOGETHER**		
(12"+=) (*12R 6156*) – Nah goa jail.		
Sep 87. (cd/c/lp) (*CD/C+/PCS 7309*) **NO NUCLEAR WAR**		

– No nuclear war / Nah goa jail / Fight apartheid / Vampire / In my song / Lesson in my life / Testify / Come together.

—— TOSH was shot dead on the 11th September, 1987

– compilations, others, etc. –

Oct 79. (7") *Virgin;* (*VS 304*) **STEPPING RAZOR. / LEGALIZE IT** | | - |
Mar 88. (cd/c/lp) *Parlophone;* (*CD/MC+/PCS 7318*) **THE TOUGHEST** | | |

– Coming in hot / (You gotta walk) Don't look back / Pick myself up / Crystal ball / Mystic man / Reggaemythilis / Bush doctor / Equal rights / Downpressor man / In my song. (cd re-iss. Mar96 on 'Heartbeat'; CDHB 150)

Mar 96. (cd/c) *EMI Gold;* (*CD/TC GOLD 1007*) **THE GOLD COLLECTION** | | - |

– Johnny B. Goode / Bush doctor / (You gotta walk) Don't look back / No nuclear war / Come together / Na Goa jail / Coming in hot / Pick myself up / In my song / Reggaemylitis / Equal rights / Crystal ball / Vampire / Lesson in my life / Testify / Maga dog.

TOTO

Formed: Los Angeles, California, USA … 1977 by noted ex-session men, brothers JEFF and STEVE PORCARO, BOBBY KIMBALL, STEVE LUKATHER, DAVID PAICH and DAVID HUNGATE, taking their name partly from the dog in the 'Wizard Of Oz' and partly from KIMBALL's real name (TOTEAUX). The band signed a worldwide deal on 'CBS-Epic' in 1978, their debut single, 'HOLD THE LINE', breaking through into the US and UK Top 20 in early 1979 and selling over a million copies in the process. Their eponymous debut album also became a massive seller, their blend/bland of airbrushed melody and supersession soft-rock going down a storm in America's heartlands. Enjoyed further moderate success until 1982, when they released the monster selling, 'TOTO IV', a record which became their most successful album to date and turned over three million copies in America alone. Highlights included 'ROSANNA' (a song written about actress, Rosanna Arquette) which lodged at the US No.2 spot for 5 weeks, and AOR classic, 'AFRICA', which became another million seller and furnished them with their first US No.1 the following year. TOTO's fortunes declined as the decade wore on, key group members bailing out along the way. Undoubtedly the biggest blow came with the mysterious (heart-attack) death of JEFF PORCARO in 1992, the band nevertheless opting to carry on in various incarnations. • **Songwriters:** PAICH was main songwriter, with others contributing, with group taking more of a hand in the 90's. Covered; WITH A LITTLE HELP FROM MY FRIENDS (Beatles).

Album rating: TOTO (*6) / HYDRA (*5) / TURN BACK (*4) / TOTO IV (*7) / ISOLATION (*5) / DUNE soundtrack (*2) / FAHRENHEIT (*4) / THE SEVENTH ONE (*5) / PAST TO PRESENT: 1977 TO 1990 compilation (*7) / KINGDOM OF DESIRE (*3) / ABSOLUTELY LIVE (*2) / TAMBU (*4)

BOBBY KIMBALL (b. ROBERT TOTEAUX, 29 Mar'47, Vinton, Louisiana) – vocals / **STEVE LUKATHER** (b.21 Oct'57) – lead guitar, vocals / **STEVE PORCARO** (b. 2 Sep'57) – keyboards, vocals / **JEFF PORCARO** (b. 1 Apr'54) – drums, percussion (ex-RURAL LIFE) / **DAVID PAICH** (b.25 Jun'54) – keyboards, vocals (ex-RURAL LIFE) / **DAVID HUNGATE** – bass

	C.B.S.	Columbia
Jan 79. (7") (*CBS 6784*) <*10830*> **HOLD THE LINE. / TAKIN' IT BACK**	14	5 Sep78
Mar 79. (lp/c) (*CBS/40 83148*) <*35317*> **TOTO**	37	9 Oct78

– Child's anthem / I'll supply the love / Georgy porgy / Manuela run / You are the flower / Girl goodbye / Takin' it back / Rockmaker / Hold the line / Angela. (re-iss. Jun84 lp/c; CBS/40 32165) (cd-iss. Oct86; CD83148) (cd re-iss. May94 on 'Sony'; 982730-2)

Mar 79. (7") (*CBS 7157*) <*10898*> **I'LL SUPPLY THE LOVE. / YOU ARE THE FLOWER** | | 45 Feb79 |
Apr 79. (7",7"pic-d) <*10944*> **GEORGY PORGY. / CHILD'S ANTHEM** | - | 48 |

Jun 79. (7") *(CBS 7378)* **GEORGY PORGY. / (part 2)** ☐ –

Dec 79. (7",7"pic-d) *<11040>* **ST. GEORGE AND THE DRAGON. /**
WHITE SISTER – ☐

Jan 80. (7") *(CBS 8085)* **ST. GEORGE AND THE DRAGON. / A**
SECRET LOVE ☐ –

Feb 80. (7") *(CBS 8132)* **99. / HYDRA** ☐ 26 Dec79

Feb 80. (lp/c) *(CBS/40 83900) <36229>* **HYDRA** ☐ 37 Nov79
– Hydra / St. George and the dragon / 99 / Lorraine / All us boys / Mama / White sister / A secret love. *(re-iss. Feb85 lp/c; CBS/40 32222)*

Mar 80. (7") *<11238>* **ALL US BOYS. / HYDRA** – ☐

Feb 81. (7") *(CBS 9492) <11437>* **GOODBYE ELENORE. / TURN**
BACK – ☐

Apr 81. (7") *<01056>* **TURN BACK. / IT'S THE LAST NIGHT** – 41 Jan81

Apr 81. (lp/c) *(CBS/40 84609) <36813>* **TURN BACK** ☐
– Gift with a golden gun / English eyes / Live for today / A million miles away / Goodbye Elenore / I think I could stand you forever / Turn back / If it's the last night. *(cd-iss. May87; CD 84609)*

Apr 82. (lp/c) *(CBS/40 85529) <37728>* **TOTO IV** (peaked UK Feb'83) 4 4
– Rosanna / Make believe / I won't hold you back / Good for you / It's a feeling / Afraid of love / Lovers in the night / We made it / Waiting for your love / Africa. *(cd-iss. Mar83; CD 85529) (re-iss. Nov86 lp/c; 450088-1/-4) (cd re-iss. Mar91; 450088-2) (cd re-iss. Dec95 on 'Columbia'; CK 64423)*

Apr 82. (7"/7"pic-d) *(A/WA 2079) <02811>* **ROSANNA. / IT'S A**
FEELING ☐ 2
(re-iss. Mar83; same) – hit UK No.12

Oct 82. (7") *(A 2868) <03143>* **MAKE BELIEVE. / WE MADE IT** ☐ 30 Aug82

Oct 82. (7") *<03335>* **AFRICA. / GOOD FOR YOU** – 1

Jan 83. (7"/7"sha-pic-d) *(A/WA 2510)* **AFRICA. / WE MADE IT** 3 –

Jun 83. (7"/7"pic-d) *(A/WA 3392) <03597>* **I WON'T HOLD YOU**
BACK. / AFRAID OF LOVE 37 10 Mar83
(12"+=) (TA 3392) – 99 / Hold the line / Goodbye Elenore.

Jul 83. (7") *(A 3627) <03981>* **WAITING FOR YOUR LOVE. /**
LOVERS IN THE NIGHT ☐ 73

—— (late'82) **MIKE PORCARO** (b.29 May'55) – bass had already repl. HUNGATE

—— (In '84) **DENNIS 'Fergie' FREDRICKSON** (b.15 May'51) – vocals repl. KIMBALL who later became part of the awful FAR CORPORATION

Nov 84. (7"/12") *(A/TX 4461) <04672>* **STRANGER IN TOWN. /**
CHANGE OF HEART ☐ 30

Nov 84. (lp/c) *(CBS/40 86305) <38962>* **ISOLATION** 67 42
– Carmen / Lion / Stranger in town / Angel don't cry / How does it feel / Endless / Isolation / Mr. Friendly / Change of heart / Holyanna. *(cd-iss. 1988; CD 86305)*

—— Dec '84, saw their instrumental 'DUNE' (Film Soundtrack) released on 'Polydor' *<823770>*. It was accompanied by The VIENNA SYMPHONY ORCHESTRA and it flopped. Around this time they laid down backing instruments for USA IN AFRICA single.

Jan 85. (7") *<04752>* **HOLYANNA. / MR. FRIENDLY** – 71

Feb 85. (7") *(A 6043)* **HOW DOES IT FEEL. / MR. FRIENDLY** – –

Apr 85. (7") *(A 6174)* **ENDLESS. / ISOLATION** – –

—— **JOSEPH WILLIAMS** – vocals (ex-Solo artist) repl. FREDRICKSON

Oct 86. (7") *(650043-7) <06280>* **I'LL BE OVER YOU. / IN A WORD** ☐ 11 Aug86
(12"+=) (650043-6) – Africa / 99.

Oct 86. (lp/c/cd) *(CBS/40/CD 57091) <40273>* **FAHRENHEIT** 99 40 Sep86
– Till the end / We can make it tonight / Without your love / Can't stand it any longer / I'll be over you / Fahrenheit / Somewhere tonight / Could this be love / Lea / Don't stop me now.

Dec 86. (7") *<06570>* **WITHOUT YOUR LOVE. / CAN'T STAND IT**
ANY LONGER – 38

—— trimmed to quintet, when STEVE PORCARO went solo

Mar 87. (7") *<07030>* **TILL THE END. / DON'T STOP ME NOW** – ☐

Feb 88. (7") *<07715>* **PAMELA. / THE SEVENTH ONE** – ☐

Feb 88. (7"/7"pic-d) *(651411-7/-0)* **STOP LOVING YOU. / THE**
SEVENTH ONE ☐ –
(12"+=) (651411-6) – ('A'version).
(cd-s+=) (651411-2) – I'll be over you.

Mar 88. (lp/c/cd) *(460645-1/-4/-2) <40873>* **THE SEVENTH ONE** 73 64
– Pamela / You got me / Anna / Stop loving you / Mushanga / Stay away / Straight for the heart / Only the children / A thousand years / These chains / Home of the brave.

Apr 88. (7") *<07945>* **STRAIGHT FROM THE HEART. / THE**
SEVENTH ONE – ☐

May 88. (7") *(651607-7)* **PAMELA. / STAY AWAKE** – –
(12"+=) (651607-6) – America.
(cd-s+=) (651607-2) – Africa / Rosanna.

—— **KIMBALL** returned Sep'88 but was repl. by temp. **TOMMY NELSON** ; he in turn was deposed by **JEAN-MICHEL BYRON** (b.South Africa) – vocals

Sep 90. (7"/c-s/12") **CAN YOU HEAR WHAT I'M SAYING. /**
AFRICA ☐ ☐
(cd-s+=) – Georgy porgy / Waiting for your love.

Oct 90. (cd/c/lp) *(465988-2/-4/-1) <45368>* **PAST TO PRESENT: 1977**
TO 1990 (compilation) ☐ Sep90
– Love has the power / Africa / Hold the line / Out of love / Georgy Porgy / I'll be over you / Can you hear what I'm saying / Rosanna / I won't hold you back / Stop loving you / 99 / Pamela / Animal.

—— **KIMBALL** returned to repl. BYRON who formed self-named group. In Aug'92, JEFF died mysteriously of either poisoning or a heart attack.

Sep 92. (cd/c/lp) *(471633-2/-4/-1)* **KINGDOM OF DESIRE** ☐Columbia ☐Columbia
– Gypsy train / Don't chain my heart / Never enough / How many times / 2 hearts / Wings of time / She knows the Devil / The other side / Only you / Jake to the bone.

Nov 93. (d-cd/d-c) *(474514-2/-4)* **ABSOLUTELY LIVE (live)** ☐
– Hydra / Rosanna / Kingdom of desire / Georgy Porgy / 99 / I won't hold you back / Don't stop me now / Africa / Don't chain my heart / I'll be over you / Home of the brave / Hold the line / With a little help from my friends.

Oct 95. (cd/c) *(481202-2/-4) <64957>* **TAMBU** ☐ Jun96
– Gift of faith / I will remember / Slipped away / If you belong to me / Baby, he's your man / The other end of time / The turning point / Time is the enemy / Drag him to the roof / Just can't get to you / Dave's gone skiing / The road goes on.

(cd+=) – Hold the line / Africa / Rosanna / I won't hold you back / I'll be over you.

Nov 95. (c-s) *(662655-4)* **I WILL REMEMBER / DAVE'S GONE SKIING** 64 ☐
(cd-s) (662655-2) – ('A'side) / Rosanna / Africa / Georgy porgy.

– compilations, etc. –

Sep 84. (lp/c) *Hallmark; (SHM/HSC 3152))* **HOLD THE LINE** ☐ –

Sep 85. (7") *Old Gold; (OG 9555)* **HOLD THE LINE. / ROSANNA** ☐ –

Mar 90. (7") *Old Gold; (OG 9867)* **AFRICA. / I WON'T HOLD YOU**
BACK ☐ –

Dec 90. (3xcd-box) *C.B.S.; (467386-2)* **TOTO / TURN BACK / HYDRA** ☐ ☐

Nov 91. (3xcd-box) *C.B.S.; (468331-2)* **FAHRENHEIT / TOTO IV /**
SEVENTH ONE ☐ ☐

TOURISTS (see under ⇒ EURYTHMICS)

Allen TOUSSAINT

Born: 14 Jan'38, New Orleans, USA. Learning piano as a teenager, TOUSSAINT began his professional life in the mid-50's as a PROFESSOR LONGHAIR-influenced keyboardist for ace Crescent City producer/arranger Dave Bartholomew. If the FATS DOMINO mentor had defined the sound of New Orleans in the 50's, then TOUSSAINT updated and remoulded it for the new decade with a rolling, rollicking piano and horn-led sound. In 1958 he released – by TOUSAN – 'THE WILD SOUND OF NEW ORLEANS' on 'R.C.A. Victor', helping to establish his reputation and furnishing AL HIRT with a mid-60's million-selling single ('JAVA'). TOUSSAINT really began making his mark on the scene after becoming A&R man for the 'Minit' label at the dawn of the 60's; in his capacity as writer, producer, arranger and musician, he masterminded a string of hits including CHRIS KENNER's 'I Like It Like That', JESSIE HILL's 'Ooh Poo Pah Do', IRMA THOMAS' 'Ruler Of My Heart' and BARBARA GEORGE's 'I Know' amongst many others. Even a spell in the army couldn't deter TOUSSAINT from recording and he cut sides for the 'Instant' label as The STOKES. The mid-60's found him working with LEE DORSEY, whose TOUSSAINT-penned singles for the 'Amy' imprint ('Ride Your Pony', 'Get Out Of My Life Woman', the US Top 10 ~'Working In A Coal Mine' and 'Holy Cow') made him one of the era's best-loved soul artists. The late 60's, meanwhile, found TOUSSAINT working with New Orleans funkmeisters par excellence, The METERS. Hired as the in-house rhythm section for 'Sansu Enterprises' (the operation TOUSSAINT had set up with fellow New Orleans producer, Marshall Sehorn), this bunch backed the likes of DORSEY and EARL KING before becoming stars in their own right. With TOUSSAINT at the helm they alchemised some of the funkiest grooves ever committed to vinyl i.e. 'Sophisticated Cissy', 'Cissy Strut', 'Look Ka Py Py', 'Chicken Strut', etc. Although the group subsequently signed to 'Reprise', TOUSSAINT remained as their producer and helped bring out their talents as backing musicians on early 70's albums by the likes of DR. JOHN, ROBERT PALMER and WINGS. As well as helping invent the sound of southern funk, TOUSSAINT had initiated his 70's solo recording career with an eponymous 1971 album for the 'Tiffany' label. He subsequently joined The METERS at 'Reprise', for whom he cut 'LOVE, LIFE AND FAITH' (1972) before moving to 'Warners' for 1975's classic 'SOUTHERN NIGHTS' set. The gorgeous country-soul of the title track (GLEN CAMPBELL would later popularise the track while simultaneously butchering it) still stands among TOUSSAINT's finest compositions yet unfortunately the record wasn't afforded the same commercial attention as his hits for other artists. Artists like LaBELLE, for whom TOUSSAINT co-wrote and produced the massive 1975 No.1 funk/R&B classic, 'Lady Marmalade'. A further 70's solo set, 'MOTION' (1978) again fell largely on deaf ears and TOUSSAINT increasingly withdrew from the music scene. He's since surfaced occasionally, appearing in a 1987 Broadway musical, 'Staggerlee', and also touring in the mid-90's alongside fellow Southern Soul legends such as DAN PENN. While even most music buffs would be pushed to put a face to his name, ALLEN TOUSSAINT's influence over the course of popular music remains as formidable as the stylistic range and quality of the artists who've performed his compositions.

Album rating: THE WILD SOUND OF NEW ORLEANS (*7) / TOUSSAINT (*6) / LIFE, LOVE AND FAITH (*4) / SOUTHERN NIGHTS (*8) / MOTION (*6) / THE ALLEN TOUSSAINT COLLECTION compilation (*8) / THE COMPLETE "TOUSAN" SESSIONS early work (*6) / CONNECTED (*7)

ALLEN TOUSSAINT – piano (+ later vocals) – with a plethora of various personnel throughout the years

	not iss.	R.C.A.

1958. (lp; as TOUSAN) *<1767>* **THE WILD SOUND OF NEW**
ORLEANS – ☐
– Whirlaway / Up the creek / Tim tam / Me and you / Bono / Java / Happy times / Wham Tousan / Nowhere to go / Nashua / Po' boy walk / Pelican parade. *(Uk-iss.Apr88 on 'Edsel'; ED 275) (cd-iss. Apr91; EDCD 275)*

	London	Minit

Feb 61. (7"; as AL TOUSAN) *(HLU 9291)* **NAOMI. / INDINNA** ☐ ☐

—— now with DR. JOHN as guest + others

	Soul City	Soul City

1969. (7") *<(SC 119)>* **WE THE PEOPLE. / TEQUILA** ☐ ☐

	Wand	Scepter

1970. (7") *<12317>* **FROM A WHISPER TO A SCREAM. / SECRET**
TOUCH OF LOVE – –

1971. (7") *<12334>* **WORKING IN A COAL MINE. / WHAT IS**
SUCCESS – ☐

Feb 72. (lp) *(WNS 14)* <014> **TOUSSAINT** ☐ ☐ 1971
– From a whisper to a scream / Chokin' kind / Sweet touch of love / What is success / Working in a coal mine / Everything I do gonna be funky / Either / Louie / Cast your fate to the wind / Number nine / Pickles. *(re-iss. Sep77 on 'D.J.M.'; DJF 22070)* *(re-iss. Mar85 as 'FROM A WHISPER TO A SCREAM' on 'Kent'; KENT 036)* *(cd-iss. Mar91; CDKENM 036)*

	Reprise	Reprise
Sep 72. (7") *(K 14200)* <1109> **SOUL SISTER. / SHE ONCE BELONGED TO ME**	☐	☐

Nov 72. (lp) *(K 44202)* <MS 2062> **LIFE, LOVE AND FAITH** ☐ ☐
– Victims of the darkness / Am I expecting too much / My baby is the real thing / Goin' down / She once belonged to me / Out of the city (into country life) / Soul sister / Fingers and toes / I've got to convince myself / On your way down / Gone too far / Electricity. *(cd-iss. Feb94 on 'Charly'; CPCD 8032)* <(cd re-iss. Jan96; 7599 26608-2)>

Jan 73. (7") *<1132>* **OUT OF THE CITY. / AM I EXPECTING TOO MUCH**	–	☐
May 75. (7") *<1334>* **COUNTRY JOHN. / WHEN THE PARTY'S OVER**	☐	☐
May 75. (7") *(K 14395)* **SOUTHERN NIGHTS. / OUT OF THE CITY**	☐	☐

May 75. (lp) *(K 54021)* <MS 2186> **SOUTHERN NIGHTS** ☐ ☐
– Last train / World wide world wide / Back in my baby's arms / Country John / Basic lady / Southern nights / You will not lose / What do you want the girl to do / When the party's over / Cruel way to go down. *(re-iss. Mar85 on 'Edsel'; ED 155)* <(cd-iss. Apr96; 7599 26596-2)>

	Warners	Warners
Apr 78. (12") *(IPR 2031)* <8561> **NIGHT PEOPLE. / THE OPTIMISM BLUES**	☐	☐

Jun 78. (lp) *(K 56473)* <3142> **MOTION** ☐ ☐ Aug78
– Night people / Just a kiss away / With you in my mind / Lover of love / To be with you / Motion / Viva la money / Declaration of love / Happiness / The optimism blues. <(cd-iss. Jan96 on 'Reprise'; 7599 26897-2)>

	Magnet	not iss.
Nov 78. (7") *<8609>* **HAPPINESS. / LOVER OF LOVE**	–	☐
May 80. (7") *(MAG 170)* **WORKING IN A COAL MINE. / DOWN IN THE SEWER**	☐	–

—— TOUSSAINT retired from solo work after above, although he did duet with CHET ATKINS on his 1994 version of 'SOUTHERN NIGHTS'.

	not iss.	Nyno
May 96. (cd) *<9601>* **CONNECTED**	–	☐

– Pure uncut love / Do the do / Computer lady / Get out of my life woman / We're all connected / Sweet dreams / Funky bars / Ahya / If I leave / Aign Nyee / In your love / Oh my / All of it / Wrong number / Rolling with the punches.

– compilations, etc. –

Jul 84. (lp) *Bandy; (70014)* **WITH THE STOKES**		–
Apr 92. (cd) *Bear Family; <(BCD 15641)>* **THE COMPLETE "TOUSAN" SESSIONS: THE 50's MASTERS**		☐ Mar92
Oct 92. (cd/c; as the ALLEN TOUSSAINT ORCHESTRA) *Muskateer; (MU 5036/4036)* **20 GOLDEN LOVE THEMES**		–
Jun 94. (cd) *Charly; (CPCD 8045)* **MR. NEW ORLEANS**		–
Jan 95. (cd) *Reprise; <(7599 26549-2)>* **THE ALLEN TOUSSAINT COLLECTION**		☐ Apr91

– On your way down / Soul sister / Last train / You will not lose / Night people / Lover of love / Happiness / Viva la money / From a whisper to a scream / Am I expecting too much / With you in mind / Motion / Southern nights / Country John / What is success / What do you want the girl to do.

Apr 95. (cd/c; as the ALLEN TOUSSAINT ORCHESTRA) *Muskateer; (MU 5038/4038)* **THE SOUND OF MOVIES**		–

Pete TOWNSHEND (see under ⇒ WHO)

TOYAH

Born: TOYAH ANN WILLCOX, 18 May'58, King's Heath, Birmingham. Following a stint in drama school and a bit part in a BBC play, TOYAH's big break came when the late Derek Jarman offered a her a prestigious role in his influential punk flick, 'Jubilee' (she later starred in his version of 'The Tempest'). Through this, the budding singer met ADAM ANT with whom she played in a short-lived outfit named The MAN EATERS. Soon after, TOYAH formed her own group with the help of JOEL BOGEN, PETE BUSH, MARK HENRY and STEVE BRAY. Securing a deal with burgeoning indie label, 'Safari', they released their debut single, 'VICTIMS OF THE RIDDLE', in the summer of '79. Unsurprisingly for such a cringe-inducingly titled track, it failed to break the chart, with an accompanying album, ahem . . . 'SHEEP FARMING IN BARNET' (1979) meeting a similar fate. Wisely perhaps, TOYAH continued to juggle an acting career simultaneously, scoring roles in TV and film including a part in 'The Corn Is Green' and PETE TOWNSHEND's seminal mod-revisionist movie, 'Quadrophenia'. Though a follow-up album, 'THE BLUE MEANING', and a live effort, 'TOYAH! TOYAH! TOYAH!' (1981) gave the singer her first Top 40 action, it was only with the release of the 'FOUR FROM TOYAH' EP (1981) that the kids really took to her new wave/goth histrionics. The lead track, 'IT'S A MYSTERY', was infect-t-tious enough to take her into the Top 5, though it was largely her aggressively hyped image (dauntingly flame-haired, quintessentially 80's ice-queen) which turned her into an unlikely pop star. Next up was 'I WANT TO BE FREE', a rebel song up there with Cliff Richard's 'SUMMER HOLIDAY' in terms of anti-establishment ire but naively charming and annoyingly hummable nonetheless. TOYAH's third and final Top 10 single was 'THUNDER IN THE MOUNTAINS', a song as majestically bombastic as the title suggests. The latter two tracks both featured on the 'ANTHEM' (1981) set, TOYAH's most successful album by far, narrowly missing the No.1 spot. The singer continued

her mythical/futuristic lyrical musings with 'THE CHANGELING' (1982) the following year, the set spawning two further Top 30 hits, 'BRAVE NEW WORLD' and 'BE LOUD BE PROUD (BE HEARD)'. Though she suffered constant music press jibes about her slight lisp, TOYAH retained a loyal following who put later albums like 'LOVE IS THE LAW' (1983) and 'MINX' (1985) into the Top 30 despite not having any major singles hits. Taking a sabbatical in the mid-80's during which she married ex-KING CRIMSON guitar maestro ROBERT FRIPP, TOYAH eventually returned in the summer of '87 with 'DESIRE', an album that followed a set, 'THE LADY OR THE TIGER', co-credited to both her and her new spouse. Though she never sees any chart action these days, TOYAH continues to collaborate with FRIPP, most recently on the 1994 set, 'DREAMCHILD'. The singer has also been sidelined into TV presenting of late, living it up on far-flung exotic beaches for BBC 1's 'Holiday' programme, while also presenting videos on Sky channel show, 'VH1'. • **Songwriters:** She and band wrote music, except ECHO BEACH (Martha + The Muffins) / SCHOOL'S OUT (Alice Cooper). • **Trivia:** Her other acting attributions were in 1983's 'TRAFFORD TANZI' and in 1987, she acted in the West End play, 'CABARET'. Amongst other roles, she subsequently appeared in the TV detective series, 'Shoestring'.

Album rating: SHEEP FARMING IN BARNET (*6) / THE BLUE MEANING (*7) / TOYAH! TOYAH! TOYAH! (*5) / ANTHEM (*5) / THE CHANGELING (*5) / WARRIOR ROCK – TOYAH ON TOUR (*4) / LOVE IS THE LAW (*3) / TOYAH compilation (*6) / MINX (*4) / THE LADY OR THE TIGER with Fripp (*4) / DESIRE (*3) / PROSTITUTE (*2) / OPHELIA'S SHADOW (*3) / DREAMCHILD (*3) / THE VERY BEST OF TOYAH compilation (*6)

TOYAH – vocals / with band **JOEL BOGEN** – guitar / **PETE BUSH** – keyboards / **MARK HENRY** – bass / **STEVE BRAY** – drums

	Safari	not iss.
Jun 79. (7") *(SAFE 15)* **VICTIMS OF THE RIDDLE. / VICTIMS OF THE RIDDLE (VIVESECTION)**	☐	–
Jul 79. (7"ep) *(SAP 1)* **SHEEP FARMING IN BARNET**	☐	–

– Neon womb / Indecision / Waiting / Our movie / Vivisection / Danced.

Dec 79. (lp/c) *(IC 064/264)* **SHEEP FARMING IN BARNET** ☐ –
– Neon womb / Indecision / Waiting / Computer / Victims of the riddle / Elusive stranger / Our movie / Danced / Last goodbye / Victims of the riddle (vivisection) / Race through space. *(re-iss. Aug90 on 'Great Expectations' cd/c/lp; PIP MC/CD/LP 014)*

Jan 80. (7") *(SAFE 22)* **BIRD IN FLIGHT. / TRIBAL LOOK**	☐	–

—— **CHARLIE FRANCIS** – bass; repl. MARK HENRY

May 80. (7"/ext.12"white) *(SAFE/+LS 28)* **IEYA. / SPACE WALKING (HELIUM SONG)** ☐ –
(re-iss. Jul82 + 7"pic-d; SAFEX 28) – hit UK No.48.

May 80. (lp/c) *(IEYA/CIEYA 666)* **THE BLUE MEANING** |40| –
– Ieya / Space walking (helium song) / Ghosts / Mummys / Blue meanings / She / Tiger tiger / Vision / Insects / Love me. *(re-iss. Jul90 on 'Great Expectations' cd/c/lp; PIP CD/MC/LP 015)*

Nov 80. (7"m) *(SAFE 32)* **DANCED (live). / GHOSTS (live) / NEON WOMB (live)**	☐	–

Jan 81. (lp/c) *(LIVE/CLIVE 2)* **TOYAH! TOYAH! TOYAH! (live)** |22| –
– Victims of the riddle / Indecision / Love me / Vision / Tribal look / Bird in flight / Danced / Insects / Race through space / Ieya. *(re-iss. Aug90 on 'Great Expectations' cd/c/lp; PIP CD/MC/LP 016)*

—— TOYAH retained only **BOGEN**, and recruited **ADRIAN LEE** – keys / **PHIL SPALDING** – bass (ex-ORIGINAL MIRRORS) / **NIGEL GLOCKER** – drums (ex-ASSOCIATES)

Feb 81. (7"ep) *(TOY 1)* **FOUR FROM TOYAH**	|4|	–

– It's a mystery / War boys / Angels and demons / Revelations.

May 81. (7"m) *(SAFE 34)* **I WANT TO BE FREE. / WALKIE TALKIE / ALIEN**	|8|	☐

May 81. (pic-lp/c) *(VOOR/+C 1)* **ANTHEM** |2| ☐
– I want to be free / Obsolete pop star / Elocution lesson (the door is a whore) / Jungles of Jupiter / I am / It's a mystery / Masai boy / Marionette / Demolition man / We are. *(cd-iss. Nov85 +=; VOORD 1)* – Thunder in the mountains / War boys / Angels and demons / Revelations.

—— **SIMON PHILIPS** – drums, percussion; repl GLOCKER who left to join SAXON. **ANDY CLARKE + SIMON DARLOW** – keyboards; repl LEE.

Sep 81. (7"pic-d) *(SAFE 38)* **THUNDER IN THE MOUNTAINS. / STREET ADDICT** (w/ free 7"flexi) *(SAFELS 38)* – STAND PROUD	|4|	–
Nov 81. (7"ep) *(TOY 2)* **FOUR MORE FROM TOYAH**	|14|	–

– Good morning universe / Urban tribesman / In the fairground / The furious futures.

May 82. (7"pic-d) *(SAFE 45)* **BRAVE NEW WORLD. / WARRIOR ROCK**	|21|	☐

Jun 82. (lp/c) *(VOOR/+C 9)* **THE CHANGELING** |6| ☐
– Creepy room / Street creature / Castaways / The druids / Angel and me / The pact / Life in the trees / Dawn chorus / Run wild run free / Brave new world.

—— **KEITH HALE** – keyboards, vocals; repl. CLARKE

Sep 82. (7"pic-d) *(SAFE 52)* **BE LOUD BE PROUD (BE HEARD). / LAUGHING WITH THE FOOLS**	|30|	–
Nov 82. (d-lp/d-c) *(TNT/CTNT 1)* **WARRIOR ROCK – TOYAH ON TOUR (live)**	|20|	☐

– Good morning universe / Warrior rock / Danced / Jungles of Jupiter / Castaways / Angel and me / Brave new world / The pact / Thunder in the mountains / We are / I want to be free / Dawn chorus / War boy / Ieya / Be loud be proud (be heard).

—— **ANDY DUNCAN** – drums repl. PHILIPS

	Safari	Safari
Sep 83. (7") *(SAFE 56)* **REBEL RUN. / MOUNTAINS HIGH**	|24|	☐
Oct 83. (lp/c) *(VOOR/+C 10)* **LOVE IS THE LAW**	|28|	☐

– Broken diamonds / I explode / Rebel of love / Rebel run / Martian cowboy / Dream scape / Time is ours / Love is the law / Remember / The vow.

Nov 83. (7") *(SAFE 58)* **THE VOW. / I EXPLODE** (12"+=) *(SAFELS 58)* – Haunted.	|50|	–

—— now w/ **DARLOW / LEE / PETER VAN HOOKE** – drums / **AL HODGE + PHIL PALMER** – guitar / **IAN WHERRY + ANDY BROWN** – bass

	Portrait	Portrait
Apr 85. (7"/12") *(A/TX 6160)* **DON'T FALL IN LOVE (I SAID). / SNOW COVERS THE KISS**	22	
Jun 85. (7"pic-d) *(A 6359)* **SOUL PASSING THROUGH SOUL. / ALL IN A RAGE**	57	
(12"+=) *(TA 6359)* – ('A'extended).		
Jul 85. (lp/c/cd) *(PRT/40/CD 26415)* **MINX**	24	

– Soldier of fortune, terrorist of love / Don't fall in love (I said) / Soul passing through soul / Sympathy / I'll serve you well / All in a rage / Space between the sounds / School's out / World in action / America for beginners. *(c+=/cd+=)* – Over twenty-one / Vigilante.

| Sep 85. (7"/12") *(A/TA 6545)* **WORLD IN ACTION. / SOLDIERS OF FORTUNE** | | - |

—— in Sep'85, she guested on TONY BANKS (of Genesis) EP track, 'You Call This Victory'.

below was credited with her new hubby, ROBERT FRIPP (ex-KING CRIMSON)

	E.G.	not iss.
Jan 87. (lp/c; TOYAH & FRIPP) *(EGED/+C 44)* **THE LADY OR THE TIGER**		-

– The lady or the tiger / Discourager of hesitancy.

| Apr 87. (7"/12") *(EGO/+X 31)* **ECHO BEACH. / PLENTY** | 54 | - |
| Jun 87. (lp/c/cd) *(EG LP/MC/CD 71)* **DESIRE** | | - |

– Echo beach / Moonlight dancing / Revive the world / The view / Moon migration / Love's unkind / Dear diary / Deadly as a woman / Goodbye baby / When a woman cries / Desire.

| Jun 87. (7") *(EGO 35)* **MOONLIGHT DANCING. / SUN UP** | | - |
| (12"+=) *(EGOX 35)* – R.E.-N.T.R.Y. – Into dance. | | |

—— now w / backing from **STEVE SIDEH** – drums, percussion, keyboards

| Nov 88. (lp/c/cd; as TOYAH WILLCOX) *(EGED/EGEDC/EEGCD 59)* **PROSTITUTE** | | |

– Hello / Prostitute / Wife / The show / Dream house / Homecraft / Obsession / Let the power bleed / Restless / Falling to Earth / Jazz singers in the trees / Vale of Evesham / Ghosts in the universe.

—— FRIPP appeared on above (their tour was billed as FRIPP & FRIPP)

—— new band:- **GUNN, GEBALLE + BEAVIS** and guest **ROBERT FRIPP**

| Feb 91. (cd/c/lp) *(EGCD/EGMC/EGLP 78)* **OPHELIA'S SHADOW** | | - |

– Ophelia's shadow / The shaman says / Brilliant day / Prospect / Turning tide / Take what you will / Ghost light / The woman who had an affair with herself / Homeward / Lords of the never known.

—— now with **MIKE BENNETT** – guitar, producer, main writer / **PAUL MORAN** – keyboards, producer / **JAY STAPLEY** – guitar / **BOB SKEAT** – bass / **SASHA ADAMS** – tape operator

	Cryptic	not iss.
Nov 93. (12"/cd-s) *(12/CD TOY 1)* **OUT OF THE BLUE (Trancentral mix). / OUT OF THE BLUE (deep ocean mix)**		-
(12+=) *(12XTOY 1)* – Out of The Blue (Transcentral radio mix).		
Apr 94. (c-s/12"/cd-s) *(12/MC/CD TOY 2)* **NOW AND THEN. / ('A'mixes)**		-
May 94. (cd/c) *(TOY CD/MC 1001)* **DREAMCHILD**		-

– Now and then / Let me go / Unkind / Out of the blue / Dreamchild / World of tension / Lost and found / Over you / I don't know / Disappear / Tone poem.

—— TOYAH now concentrates on her television work

– compilations, etc. –

Feb 84. (lp/c) *K-Tel; (NE/C1 1268)* **TOYAH TOYAH**	43	-
Nov 85. (lp/c) *Safari; (VOOR/+C 77)* **MAYHEM**		-
Mar 94. (cd) *Connoisseur; (CSAPCD 115)* **THE BEST OF TOYAH**		-
Nov 96. (cd) *Tring; (ANT 012)* **THE ACOUSTIC ALBUM**		-
Nov 96. (cd) *Tring; (QED 065)* **LOOKING BACK**		-
Apr 97. (cd) *Receiver; (<RRCD 235>)* **PHOENIX**		May97
Feb 98. (cd) *Reactive; (REMCD 501)* **THE VERY BEST OF TOYAH**		-

– It's a mystery / Good morning universe / I want to be free / Be proud be loud be heard / Bird in flight / Rebel run / Brave new world / Thunder in the mountains / Ieya / Street creature / Elusive stranger / Martian cowboy / Love me / Broken diamonds / Castaways / She / Jungles of Jupiter / Ieya.

| Jun 98. (cd) *Connoisseur; (CSAPCD 125)* **LIVE AND MORE (live)** | | - |

—— In Jun'82, a single as "The ANTEATERS", 'NINE TO FIVE', was lifted from the 1977 film, 'Jubilee', in which she appeared with ADAM ANT.

TRAFFIC

Formed: Based Midlands, England . . . April '67, by STEVE WINWOOD, DAVE MASON, JIM CAPALDI and CHRIS WOOD. Initially, TRAFFIC purveyed musically accomplished, thinking-man's psychedelia, debuting with the yearning 'PAPER SUN' (1967) single after signing to 'Island'. Utilising MASON's lilting, sitar-like guitar playing, the record perfectly anticipated the mood of the times and duly hit the Top 5. Dippy but delightful, the follow-up, 'HOLE IN MY SHOE' (1967) (later covered with great affection by NIGEL PLANER aka 'NEIL' of 'Young Ones' comedy fame) hit No.2 and after their third Top 10 hit in a row, 'HERE WE GO ROUND THE MULBERRY BUSH' (from the film of the same name), the band released their debut album, 'MR FANTASY' (1967). The record was a well crafted melting pot of ideas and genres put through the psychedelic blender and given a soulful reading by WINWOOD's wholesome vocal chords. The conspicuous absence of any of the previous hit singles, however, signalled that, as was the case with groups in those serious muso days, TRAFFIC wished to be considered an 'Albums' band. Around this time, MASON split, only to return six months later whence the band fashioned their second album, 'TRAFFIC' (1968), a marked progression that highlighted the band's instrumental dexterity and flowering songwriting talent. Once again, MASON came up with one of the record's most memorable tunes, 'FEELIN' ALRIGHT', later covered by JOE COCKER amongst others.

The ever dependable MASON upped sticks and left once more during the recording of TRAFFIC's third album, 'LAST EXIT' (1969). Aptly titled, this careless rag-bag of below par live and studio tracks did indeed mark the end of MASON's time with the band (save for a brief spell of live work in the early 70's), in fact the end of the band itself, for the time being at least. After a spell in short-lived 'supergroup', BLIND FAITH, WINWOOD went into the studio to commence the recording of a mooted solo album with a working title of 'MAD SHADOWS'. When WOOD and CAPALDI were drafted in for work on the sessions, the project became a fully fledged TRAFFIC concern. The resulting album, re-titled 'JOHN BARLEYCORN MUST DIE' (1970), was a triumphant return to form, mixing up folk, R&B and jazz into a prog-rock classic. In the year or so before their next album, the band recruited bassist RICK GRECH (ex-FAMILY/BLIND FAITH), African percussionist REEBOP KWAKU-BAAH, drummer JIM GORDON (ex-DEREK AND THE DOMINOES) and their old mucker DAVE MASON. 'WELCOME TO THE CANTEEN' (1971) was fairly heavy going but no less self-indulgent than your average early 70's live effort, while the next studio outing, 'THE LOW SPARK OF HIGH HEELED BOYS' (1971), saw the band add to their not inconsiderable studio accomplishments despite the cringe-inducing title. DAVID HOOD and ROGER HAWKINS (both of whom had played on CAPALDI's solo project, 'OH HOW WE DANCED') replaced GRECH and GORDON for 1973's 'SHOOT OUT AT THE FANTASY FACTORY'. The 'Muscle Shoals' veterans had tightened up the rhythm section considerably, cutting it on stage and in the studio, as evidenced by the best live album of TRAFFIC's career, 'ON THE ROAD' (1973). By 1974's 'WHEN THE EAGLE FLIES', TRAFFIC were beginning to sound congested, finally stalling the following year. CAPALDI and WINWOOD both went on to successful solo careers, resurrecting TRAFFIC briefly in 1994. WINWOOD's output in particular was undeniable coffee table rock at its shiniest, though surprisingly, he was given top billing at the 1997 Glastonbury festival. In the event he didn't show, apparently due to illness, his place taken by KULA SHAKER.
• **Songwriters:** Individually or group compositions, except GIMME SOME LOVIN' (Spencer Davis Group). CAPALDI covered LOVE HURTS (Everly Brothers).

Album rating: MR. FANTASY (*8) / TRAFFIC (*9) / LAST EXIT (*5) / THE BEST OF TRAFFIC compilation (*8) / JOHN BARLEYCORN MUST DIE (*7) / WELCOME TO THE CANTEEN (*5) / THE LOW SPARK OF THE HIGH HEELED BOYS (*7) / SHOOT OUT AT THE FANTASY FACTORY (*6) / ON THE ROAD (*5) / WHEN THE EAGLE FLIES (*5) / HEAVY TRAFFIC compilation (*7) / MORE HEAVY TRAFFIC compilation (*5) / SMILING PHASES compilation (*9) / FAR FROM HOME (*5)

STEVE WINWOOD (b.12 May'48, Birmingham, England) – vocals, keyboards (ex-SPENCER DAVIS GROUP) / **DAVE MASON** (b.10 May'47, Worcester, England) – guitar, vocals (ex-HELLIONS) / **JIM CAPALDI** (b.24 Aug'44, Evesham, England) – drums, vocals (ex-HELLIONS) / **CHRIS WOOD** (b.24 Jun'44, Birmingham, England) – flute, sax (ex-SOUNDS OF BLUE)

		Island	U.A.
May 67. (7") *(WIP 6002)* *<50195>* **PAPER SUN. / GIVING TO YOU**		5	94 Aug67
Aug 67. (7") *(WIP 6017)* *<50218>* **HOLE IN MY SHOE. / SMILING PHASES**		2	
Nov 67. (7") *(WIP 6025)* *<50232>* **HERE WE GO ROUND THE MULBERRY BUSH. / COLOURED RAIN**		8	
Dec 67. (lp; mono/stereo) *(ILP/+S 9061)* *<6651>* **MR. FANTASY**		8	88 Apr68

– Heaven is in your mind / Berkshire poppies / House for everyone / No name, no face, no number / Dear Mr. Fantasy / Dealer / Utterly simple / Coloured rain / Hope I never find me there / Giving to you. *<US version +=)* – Paper sun / Hole in my shoe. *(re-iss. 1970; same)* *(re-iss. Feb87 lp/c; ILPM/ICM 9061)* *(cd-iss. Nov87; CID 9061)* *(cd re-iss. Sep89; IMCD 43)* *(US version-iss.Aug92; 3DCID 1003)*

Feb 68. (7") *(WIP 6030)* **NO NAME, NO FACE, NO NUMBER. / ROAMIN' IN THE GLOAMIN' WITH 40,000 HEADMEN**		40	-
Feb 68. (7") *<50261>* **NO NAME, NO FACE, NO NUMBER. / HEAVEN IS IN YOUR MIND**		-	-
Sep 68. (7") *(WIP 6041)* *<50460>* **FEELIN' ALRIGHT. / WITHERING TREE**		-	-
Oct 68. (lp; mono/stereo) *(ILPS 9081/+T)* *<6676>* **TRAFFIC**		9	17

– You can all join in / Pearly queen / Don't be sad / Who knows what tomorrow may bring / Feelin' alright / Vagabond virgin / Forty thousand headmen / Cryin' to be heard / No time to live / Means to an end. *(re-iss. Feb87 lp/c; ILPM/ICM 9081)* *(cd-iss. Nov87; CID 9081)* *(cd re-iss. Sep89; IMCD 45)*

| Dec 68. (7") *(WIP 6050)* **MEDICATED GOO. / SHANGHAI NOODLE FACTORY** | | - | - |
| Jan 69. (7") *<50500>* **MEDICATED GOO. / PEARLY QUEEN** | | - | - |

—— Below album was recorded before their split late 1968.

| May 69. (lp; mono/stereo) *(ILP/+S 9097)* *<6702>* **LAST EXIT (some live)** | | | 19 |

– Just for you / Shanghai noodle factory / Something's got a hold of my toe / Withering tree / Medicated goo / Feelin' good / Blind man. *(cd-iss. May88; CID 9097)* *(cd re-iss. Sep89; IMCD 41)*

| Oct 69. (lp; mono/stereo) *(ILP/+S 9112)* *<5500>* **THE BEST OF TRAFFIC** (compilation) | | | 48 |

– Paper Sun / Heaven is in your mind / No face, no name, no number / Coloured rain / Smiling phases / Hole in my shoe / Medicated goo / Forty thousand headmen / Feelin' alright / Shanghai noodle factory / Dear Mr. Fantasy. *(cd-iss. Mar93; IMCD 169)*

—— In 1969, WINWOOD formed BLIND FAITH with ERIC CLAPTON and GINGER BAKER. WOOD also joined the latter's group AIRFORCE. WOOD, MASON and CAPALDI then formed WOODEN FROG. DAVE MASON went solo as TRAFFIC re-formed as a trio.

| Jul 70. (lp) *(ILPS 9116)* *<5504>* **JOHN BARLEYCORN MUST DIE** | | 5 | 11 |

– Glad / Freedom rider / Empty pages / Stranger to himself / John Barleycorn / Every mother's son. *(re-iss. Sep86 lp/c/cd; ILPM/ICM/CID 9116)* *(cd-iss. Sep89; IMCD 40)*

| Aug 70. (7") *<50692>* **EMPTY PAGES. / STRANGER TO HIMSELF** | | - | 74 |

—— added **RIC GRECH** (b. 1 Nov'46) – bass (ex-FAMILY, ex-BLIND FAITH, ex-GINGER BAKER'S AIRFORCE) / **REEBOP KWAKU-BAAH** (b. Konongo, Ghana) – percussion (ex-GINGER BAKER'S AIRFORCE) / **JIM GORDON** – drums (ex-DEREK & THE DOMINOES) / **DAVE MASON** guested on some live.

Sep 71. (lp) *(ILPS 9166) <5550>* **WELCOME TO THE CANTEEN** (live)   `26`
– Medicated goo / Sad and deep as you / Forty thousand headmen / Shouldn't have took more than you gave / Dear Mr. Fantasy / Gimme some lovin'. *(cd-iss. May88; CID 9166)* (cd re-iss. Sep89; IMCD 39)

Oct 71. (7") *<50841>* **GIMME SOME LOVIN'. / (part 2)**   `-` `68`
               Island Island

Dec 71. (lp/c) *(ILPS.ZCI 9180) <9306>* **THE LOW SPARK OF THE HIGH HEELED BOYS**   `7`
– Hidden treasure / The low spark of the high heeled boys / Rock & roll stew / Many a mile to freedom / Light up or leave me alone / Rainmaker. *(re-iss. Sep86 lp/c; ILPM/ICM 9180)* (cd-iss. Nov87; CID 9180) (cd re-iss. Sep89; IMCD 42)

Jan 72. (7") *<1201>* **ROCK & ROLL STEW. / (part 2)**   `-` `93`

——— **DAVID HOOD** – bass + **ROGER HAWKINS** – drums (both of JIM CAPALDI band) repl. JIM GORDON and GRECH. (The latter formed KGB)

Feb 73. (lp/c) *(ILPS/ZCI 9224) <9323>* **SHOOT OUT AT THE FANTASY FACTORY**   `6`
– Shoot out at the fantasy factory / Roll right stone / Evening blue / (ragic magic) / Uninspired (sometimes I feel so). *(cd-iss. May88; CID 9224)* (cd re-iss. Sep89; IMCD 44)

——— added **BARRY BECKETT** – keyboards

Oct 73. (d-lp)(d-c) *(ILSD 2)(ZCID 102)* **ON THE ROAD** (live) `40` `29`
– Glad / Freedom rider / Tragic magic / (Sometimes I feel so) Uninspired / Shoot out at the fantasy factory / Light up or leave me alone / The low spark of the high heeled boys. *(cd-iss. Jun88; CIDD 2)* (cd re-iss. Aug91 & Apr94; IMCD 183)

Dec 73. (7") *<50883>* **GLAD. / (part 2)**   `-`

——— **WINWOOD, CAPALDI & WOOD** enlisted **ROSKO GEE** – bass (ex-GONZALES)
               Island Asylum

Sep 74. (lp/c) *(ILPS/ZCI 9273) <7E 1020>* **WHEN THE EAGLE FLIES** `31` `9`
– Walking in the wind / Something new / Dream Gerrard / Memories of a rock'n'roller / When the eagle flies / Graveyard people / Love. *(cd-iss. Jun88; CID 9273)* (re-iss. Aug91 cd; IMCD 142)(ICM 9273)

Oct 74. (7") *(WIP 6207)* **WALKING IN THE WIND. / WALKING IN THE WIND** (instrumental)

——— Disbanded early 1975. STEVE WINWOOD went solo, also collaborating with STOMU YAMASHTA. WOOD and GEE took up session work. On 12 Jul'83, CHRIS WOOD died of liver failure. JIM CAPALDI continued his solo career

– compilations, etc. –

——— on 'Island' unless stated otherwise

May 74. (7") **HOLE IN MY SHOE. / HERE WE GO ROUND THE MULBERRY BUSH**   `-`
May 75. (lp) *United Artists; <4211>* **HEAVY TRAFFIC**   `-`
Sep 75. (lp) *United Artists; <LA 526>* **MORE HEAVY TRAFFIC**   `-`
Mar 78. (7"ep,7"pic-d-ep) *(IEP 7)* **EXTENDED PLAY**
– I'm a man / Hole in my shoe / Gimme some lovin' / No name, no face, no number.
Jun 92. (d-cd) *(IMCCD 158)* **SMILING PHASES**   `-`
– Paper sun / Hole in my shoe / Smiling phases / Heaven is in your mind / Coloured rain / No face, no name, no number / Here we go round the mulbury bush / Dear Mr. Fantasy / You can all join in / Feelin' alright / Pearly queen / Forty thousand headmen / Vagabond virgin / Shanghai noodle factory / Withering tree / Medicated goo / Glad / Freedom rider / Empty pages / John Barleycorn / The low spark of the high heeled boys / Light up or leave me alone / Rock & roll stew / Shoot out at the fantasy factory / Walking in the wind / When the eagle flies.

TRAFFIC

——— **WINWOOD + CAPALDI** re-formed for the studio
              Virgin Virgin

May 94. (cd/c) *(CD/TC V 2727)* **FAR FROM HOME** `29`
– Riding high / Here comes a man / Far from home / Nowhere is their freedom / Holy ground / Some kinda woman / Every night, every day / This train won't stop / State of grace / Mosambique.

May 94. (7"/c-s) *(VS/+C 1494)* **HERE COMES A MAN. / GLAD** (live)
(cd-s+=) *(VSCDG 1494)* – ('A'mix).

Sep 94. (c-s) *(VSC 1506)* **SOME KINDA WOMAN. / FORTY THOUSAND HEADMEN** (live)
(cd-s+=) *(VSCDX 1506)* – Low spark of high heeled boys (live)/ ('A'mix).

TRANSVISION VAMP

Formed: Brighton, England ... 1984 by frontwoman – in every sense of the word – WENDY JAMES along with songwriter/guitarist NICK CHRISTIAN SAYER, the line-up completed by the wonderfully named TEX AXILE and DAVE PARSONS. All fizzing energy and pop/punk posturing, TRANSVISION VAMP burst onto the stale UK music scene of summer '88 with 'I WANT YOUR LOVE'. Pouting and preening for all she was worth on 'Top Of The Pops', platinum blonde JAMES became an instant sex godess for a generation weaned on the offensively inoffensive RICK ASTLEY and the pre-leather hot pants KYLIE MINOGUE. The track's Top 5 success no doubt saw 'M.C.A.' breathe a sigh of relief, the group having already flopped with two previous efforts, 'REVOLUTION BABY' and 'TELL THAT GIRL TO SHUT UP'. Just prior to the release of the debut album, 'POP ART' (1988), the company dusted down the former and re-issued it in remixed form, hitting No.30. The album itself went Top 5, a heady bubblegum-punk combination of IGGY POP, MARC BOLAN and BLONDIE, the ubiquitous JAMES seemingly never out of the TV spotlight (while many painted her as a bimbo, the media-conscious starlet more often than not acquitted herself well). T.V's biggest hit was the breathy 'BABY, I DON'T CARE', in early '89, its Top 5

success a taster for 'VELVETEEN' (1989), a No.1 album later that summer. The set spawned a further two hits in 'LANDSLIDE OF LOVE' and 'BORN TO BE SOLD', although as the decade drew to a close the band's profile began to fade. So much so that 'M.C.A.' famously scrapped the UK release of T.V.'s third set, 'THE LITTLE MAGNETS VERSUS THE BUBBLE OF BABBLE' (1991). In the event, the Americans weren't too keen on it either and the record sank without trace. It was clearly over for T.V., although JAMES made a comeback solo set in 1993, 'NOW AIN'T THE TIME FOR YOUR TEARS'. Penned by ELVIS COSTELLO and his wife (and ex-POGUE), CAIT O'RIORDAN, the album failed to break the Top 40. Perhaps the WENDY JAMES appeal, or lack of it, is summed up in the rather desperately titled 'LONDON'S BRILLIANT', a No.62 chart smash. • **Songwriters:** CHRISTIAN-SAYER compositions, except TELL THAT GIRL TO SHUT UP (Holly & The Italians) / CRAWL OUT YOUR WINDOW (Bob Dylan). (See 1993 solo work for WENDY JAMES). • **Trivia:** WENDY posed nude for photographer David Bailey in the magazine 'The Tatler'.

Album rating: POP ART (*6) / VELVETEEN (*7) / THE LITTLE MAGNETS VERSUS THE BUBBLE OF BABBLE (*4) / Wendy James: NOW AIN'T THE TIME FOR YOUR TEARS (*5)

WENDY JAMES (b.21 Jan'66, London) – vocals / **NICK CHRISTIAN SAYER** (b. 1 Aug'64) – guitar (ex-FAN CLUB, ex-PLASTICS UK) / **TEX AXILE** (b.30 Jul'63) – drums (ex-SNIVELLING SHITS, ex-EDDIE &..HOT RODS) / **DAVE PARSONS** (b. 2 Jul'62) – bass
             M.C.A. Uni

Aug 87. (7") *(TVV 1)* **REVOLUTION BABY. / VID KID VAMP**   `-`
(remix-12"+=) *(TVVT 1)* – No it U lover.

Apr 88. (7"/7"w-poster) *(TVV/+PR 2)* **TELL THAT GIRL TO SHUT UP. / GOD SAVE THE ROYALTIES** `45` `87` Sep88
(ext.12"+=) *(TVVT 2)* – ('A'-knuckle duster mix).
(pic-cd-s+=) *(DVVT 2)* – ('A'extended).

Jun 88. (7") *(TVV 3)* **I WANT YOUR LOVE / SWEET THING / EVOLUTION EVIE** `5`
(12"/12"w-poster/3"cd-s) *(TVVT/TVVTR/DTVV 3)* – ('A'-Don't want your money mix) / Sweet thing / Evolution Evie (electric version).

——— added **POL BURTON** – drums (TEX now on keyboards)

Sep 88. (7"/7"w-poster)('A'-Electra-glide mix; 12"/12"pic-d) *(TVV/+PR 4)(TVVT/+P 4)* **REVOLUTION BABY (remix). / HONEY HONEY / LONG LONELY WEEKEND** `30`
(3"cd-s+=) *(DTTV 4)* – Vid kid vamp.

Oct 88. (lp/pic-lp/c)(cd) *(MCF/+P/C 3421)(DMCF 3421) <UNI 5 C/D>* **POP ART** `4`
– Trash city / I want your love / Sister Moon / Psychosonic Cindy / Revolution baby / Tell that girl to shut up / Wild star / Hanging out with Halo Jones / Andy Warhol's dead / Sex kick. *(re-iss. Aug93 cd/c; MCLD/MCLC 19224)*

Nov 88. (7"/7"pic-d) *(TVV/+P 5)* **SISTER MOON. / OH YEAH / WALK ON BY** `41`
('A'-groove on; 12"+=/12"g-f+=)(cd-s+=) *(TVVT/+G 5)(DTVV 5)* – Sex kick (Ciao Portabello).

——— Reverted to a quartet, when POL departed.

Mar 89. (7"/7"g-f) *(TVV/+G 6)* **BABY, I DON'T CARE. / TIME FOR A CHANGE / STRINGS OF MY HEART** `3`
('A'-Abigail's Party mix; 12"+=/12"w-poster+=) *(TVVT/+G 6)* – Sex kick (demo).
(cd-s++=) *(DTVV 6)* – Saturn 5 (demo).

Jun 89. (c-s/7"/ext.12") *(C+/TVV/+T 7)* **THE ONLY ONE. / THE MYSTERY SONG / LOVE ME** `15`
(cd-s+=) *(DTVV 7)* – ('A'extended).

Jul 89. (lp/pic-lp/c)(cd) *(MCG/+P/C 6050)(DMCG 6050) <UNI C/D 605>* **VELVETEEN** `1`
– Baby, I don't care / The only one / Landslide of love / Falling for a goldmine / Down on you / Song to the stars / Kiss their sons / Born to be sold / Pay the ghosts / Bad valentine / Velveteen. *(re-iss. Aug93 cd/c; MCLD/MCLC 19215)*

Jul 89. (7"/7"pic-d-c-s) *(TVV/+P/C 8)* **LANDSLIDE OF LOVE. / HARDTIME / HE'S THE ONLY ONE FOR ME** `14`
(12"+=/12"g-f+=)(cd-s+=) *(TVVT/+G 8)(DTVV 8)* – ('A'extended) / West II blues.

Oct 89. (7"/c-s) *(TVV/+C 9)* **BORN TO BE SOLD. / DOWN ON YOU / LAST TIME** `22`
(12"+=/12"box+=)(cd-s+=) *(TVVT/+B 9)(DTVV 9)* – Kiss me.

Apr 91. (7"/c-s) *(TVV/+C 10)* **(I JUST WANNA) B WITH U. / SWAMP THING / STRAIGHT THRU YOUR HEART** `30`
(cd-s+=) *(DTVV 10)* – ('A'-night ripper mix).
(12"++=) *(TVVT 10)* – Punky says.

Jun 91. (7"/c-s) *(TVV/+C 11)* **IF LOOKS COULD KILL. / MY FRIEND THE TOM CAT / PUPPY DOG TAILS** `41`
(12"+=) *(TVVT 11)* – I want your love (live).
(cd-s+=) *(DTVV 11)* – Tell that girl to shut up (live).

Aug 91. (cd/c) *(MCA D/C 10331)* **THE LITTLE MAGNETS VERSUS THE BUBBLE OF BABBLE**   `-`
– (I just wanna) B with U / Ain't no rules / If looks could kill / Every little thing / Twangy wipeout / Don't believe the type / Pressure times / Crawl out your window / You put a spell on me / Back on my knees again.

WENDY JAMES

(solo) with **PETE THOMAS** – drums, percussion / **CASS LEWIS** – bass / **NEIL TAYLOR** – guitars / **ANDY BOWN** – organ / **JON ASTLEY** – piano

——— penned by **ELVIS COSTELLO** with help from wife **CAIT O'RIORDAN**
             M.C.A. Geffen

Feb 93. (7"/c-s) *(MCS/+C 1732)* **THE NAMELESS ONE. / I JUST DON'T WANT IT ANYMORE** `34`
(cd-s+=) *(MCSTD 1732)* – May I have your autograph.
(cd-s) *(MCSXD 1732)* – ('A'side) / Only a fool / I need you now.

Mar 93. (cd/c/lp) *(MCD/MCC/MCA 10800) <24507>* **NOW AIN'T THE TIME FOR YOUR TEARS** `43` May93
– This is a test / London's brilliant / Basement kiss / Puppet girl / Earthbound / Do

you know what I'm saying? / we despise you / Fill in the blanks / The nameless one / I want to stand forever.

Apr 93. (7"/c-s) (MCS/+C 1763) **LONDON'S BRILLIANT. / MY BALLAD TO 46th STREET** — 62 — □
(12"+=) (MCST 1763) – I will never be your lover.
(cd-s) (MCSTD 1763) – ('A'side) / All beginnings / Never a stranger.

Jun 93. (c-s) (MCSC) **DO YOU KNOW WHAT I'M SAYING / SUGAR TAKES HER COFFEE BLACK** — □ — -
(cd-s) (MCSTD) – ('A'side) / I started the lie / The reigning beauty queen.

—— WENDY seems to have retired from music biz

TRAVELING WILBURYS

Formed: Los Angeles, California, USA . . . 1988 by ageing superstars BOB DYLAN, TOM PETTY, GEORGE HARRISON, JEFF LYNNE and ROY ORBISON. The various members originally came together to record a B-side for HARRISON's 'WHEN WE WAS FAB' single, the session going suffiently well that they subsequently decided to take things further. The resulting debut album, ' . . . VOLUME 1' (1988) unsurprisingly became a huge seller, the hit single, 'HANDLE WITH CARE', one of the easy-rocking highlights alongside 'TWEETER AND THE MONKEY MAN'. Each member of the band took on a pseudonym, mainly to get round contract difficulties; DYLAN was LUCKY WILBURY, PETTY became CHARLIE T. WILBURY JR, HARRISON changed to NELSON WILBURY, LYNNE took the moniker OTIS WILBURY and ORBISON was LEFTY WILBURY. ROGER McGUINN subsequently declined the offer to take over from the deceased ROY ORBISON before the release of their second (yes, second!) album, 'TRAVELING WILBURYS VOLUME 3' (1990). Their blend of good-time adult-rock took up where the previous set left off and although no hit singles were forthcoming, fans could content themselves with such enjoyable fare as 'COOL DRY PLACE' and 'NEW BLUE MOON'. This time around the names had changed to BOO (DYLAN), SPIKE (HARRISON), CLAYTON (LYNNE) and MUDDY WILBURY (PETTY), although by now the concept was wearing as thin as their crowns.

Album rating: TRAVELING WILBURYS VOLUME I (*6) / VOLUME 3 (*5)

BOB DYLAN (b.ROBERT ALLAN ZIMMERMAN, 24 May'41, Duluth, Minnesota, USA) – vocals, guitar (also solo artist) / **GEORGE HARRISON** (b.25 Feb'43, Liverpool, England) – vocals, guitar (ex-BEATLES, also solo artist) / **ROY ORBISON** (b.23 Apr'36, Vernon, Texas, USA) – vocals, guitar (solo artist) / **TOM PETTY** (b.20 Oct'53, Gainsville, Florida, USA) – vocals, guitar (solo . . .) / **JEFF LYNNE** (b.30 Dec'47, Birmingham, England) – vocals, guitar (solo artist, ex-ELECTRIC LIGHT ORCHESTRA)

	Warners	Warners

Oct 88. (7") (W 7637) <27732> **HANDLE WITH CARE. / MARGARITA** — 21 — 45
(12"+=/cd-s+=) (W 7732 T/CD) – ('A'extended).

Oct 88. (lp/c/cd) (WX 224/+C)(925769-2) <25796> **TRAVELING WILBURYS VOLUME 1** — 16 — 3
– Handle with care / Dirty world / Rattled / Last night / Not alone anymore / Conratulations / Heading for the light / Margarita / Tweeter and the monkey man / End of the line.

Feb 89. (7"/12"/cd-s) (W 7637/+T/CD) <27637> **END OF THE LINE. / CONGRATULATIONS** — 52 — 63

—— now augmented by **JIM KELTNER** – drums, percussion / **JIM HORN** – saxophone / **RAY COOPER** – percussion (and a quartet, after the death of ROY O)

Jun 90. (7") (W 9773) **NOBODY'S CHILD. / ('B'by 'Dave Stewart & The Spiritual Cowboy')** — 44 — □
(12"+=/cd-s+=) (W 9773 T/CD) – (track by 'Ringo Starr').
Above single was from The ARMENIAN DISASTER album by Various Artists.

Nov 90. (7"/c-s) **SHE'S MY BABY. / NEW BLUE MOON** — □ — □
(12"+=/cd-s+=) – Runaway.

Nov 90. (lp/c)(cd) (WX 384/+C)<(7599 26324-2)> **TRAVELING WILBURYS VOLUME 3** — 14 — 11
– She's my baby / Inside out / If you belonged to me / The Devil's been busy / 7 deadly sins / Poor house / Where were you last night? / Cool dry place / New blue moon / You took my breath away / Wilbury twist.

Mar 91. (7"/c-s) **WILBURY TWIST. / NEW BLUE MOON (instrumental)** — □ — □
(12"+=/cd-s+=) – Cool dry place.

—— all members subsequently returned to their normal solo work

Pat TRAVERS (dig out; 4th edition)

TRAVIS

Formed: Glasgow, Scotland . . . 1991 as GLASS ONION by ANDY DUNLOP and NEIL PRIMROSE, who had both been members of RUNNING RED. Songwriting singer FRAN HEALY was invited to join the fresh-faced guitar-pop quintet (with the MARTYN brothers), replacing the original female vocalist soon after. In 1993, FRAN's mother advanced the lads some cash to cut a demo and this led to a publishing contract with 'Sony'. Winning a trip to the New Music Seminar in New York via first place in a talent contest might've given them an early break had they attended, although they did manage to squeeze out an eponymous EP the same year. With the band going nowhere fast, changes had to be made and, by March '96, the MARTYN brothers had made way for FRAN's Glasgow School Of Art chum, DOUGIE PAYNE (ANDY had also been a student); TRAVIS were now in circulation. Following a self-financed debut single, 'ALL I WANT TO DO IS ROCK', the quartet were taken under the wing of (ex-Go! Discs man) Andy

McDonald's 'Independiente' (still through 'Sony') early in '97. Subsequently relocating to London, TRAVIS released their controversial follow-up single, 'U16 GIRLS', apparently a paeon to the charms of underage females. A re-vamp of their hard-to-find debut single followed it into the Top 40 and suddenly TRAVIS were one of the hippest new names on the block. Though HEALY was a charismatic frontman, the Top 10 debut album, 'GOOD FEELING', illustrated at the time the one-dimensional nature of much of their material. Nevertheless, the record did spawn two further Top 40 hits, 'TIED TO THE 90's' and 'HAPPY', indicating that there was at least some potential for the future. After a relatively quiet '98 – although 'MORE THAN US' became their biggest hit to date at No.16 – TRAVIS were back the following March. Taking a softer, laid-back approach (70's BREAD come to mind!), the quartet achieved a deserved second Top 20 spot with the beautiful ballad 'WRITING TO REACH YOU'. Further successes came in the shape of 'DRIFTWOOD', 'WHY DOES IT ALWAYS RAIN ON ME?' and 'TURN', all songwriting masterpieces from the critically acclaimed No.1 follow-up set, 'THE MAN WHO' (1999). TRAVIS were fast becoming the United Kingdom's No.1 band and by the start of the year 2000 they were given that accolade by winning the now prestigious Brit award. OASIS (who had been tops until recently!) invited nice guy HEALY and Co to support them on a US tour, the American audiences eventually being won over by their sheer honest enthusiasm and talent. • **Covered:** BE MY BABY (Ronettes) / BABY ONE MORE TIME (Britney Spears).

Album rating: GOOD FEELING (*7) / THE MAN WHO (*9)

GLASS ONION

FRAN HEALY (b. Stafford, England) – vocals, guitar; repl. female / **ANDY DUNLOP** – guitar / **NEIL PRIMROSE** – drums / . . . **MARTYN** – bass / . . . **MARTYN** – keyboards

	own label	not iss.

Nov 93. (cd-ep) (GLASSCD 001) **GLASS ONION** — □ — □
– Dream on / The day before / Free soul / Whenever she comes around.

TRAVIS

—— **DOUGIE PAYNE** – bass; repl. the MARTYN brothers

	Red Telephone	not iss.

Oct 96. (10"ep) (PHONE 001) **ALL I WANT TO DO IS ROCK. / THE LINE IS FINE / FUNNY THING** — □ — -

	Independiente	Epic

Mar 97. (7"pic-d/c-s) (ISOM 1 S/CS) **U16 GIRLS. / HAZY SHADES OF GOLD / GOOD TIME GIRLS** — 40 — -
(c-s+=/cd-s+=) (ISOM 1MS) – Good feeling.

Jun 97. (7") (SOM 3S) **ALL I WANT TO DO IS ROCK. / BLUE ON A BLACK WEEKEND** — 39 — Apr98
(cd-s+=) (ISOM 3MS) – Combing my hair.
(cd-s) (ISOM 3SMS) – ('A'side) / "20" / 1922.

Aug 97. (7"/cd-s) (ISOM 5S/+MS) <6084> **TIED TO THE 90's. / ME BESIDE YOU** — 30 — Apr98
(cd-s) (ISOM 5MS) – ('A'side) / City in the rain / Whenever she comes around / Standing on my own.

Sep 97. (cd/c/lp) (ISOM 1 CD/MC/LP) <68239> **GOOD FEELING** — 9 — Oct97
– All I want to do is rock / U16 girls / Line is fine / Good day to die / Good feeling / Midsummer nights dreamin' / Tied to the 90's / I love you anyways / Happy / More than us / Falling down / Funny thing. (re-iss. Nov99; same)

Oct 97. (c-s) (ISOM 6CS) <6081> **HAPPY / UNBELIEVERS** — 38 — Apr98
(cd-s+=) (ISOM 6MS) – Everyday faces.
(cd-s) (ISOM 6SMS) – ('A'side) / When I'm feeling blue (days of the week) / Mother.

Mar 98. (7"ep/c-ep/cd-ep) (ISOM 11 S/CS/MS) **MORE THAN US E.P.** — 16 — -
– More than us (with Anne Dudley) / Give me some truth / All I want to do is rock (with Noel Gallagher) / Funny thing (mixed by Tim Simenon).
(cd-s) (ISOM 11SMS) – (lead track) / Beautiful bird (demo version) / Reason (with Susie Hug) / More than us (acoustic version).

Mar 99. (7"/c-s) (ISOM 22 S/CS) **WRITING TO REACH YOU. / ONLY MOLLY KNOWS** — 14 — -
(cd-s+=) (ISOM 22MS) – Green behind the ears.
(cd-s) (ISOM 22SM) – ('A'side) / Yeah yeah yeah yeah / High as a kite.

May 99. (c-s) (ISOM 27CS) **DRIFTWOOD / WRITING TO REACH YOU (Deadly Avenger remix)** — 13 — -
(cd-s+=) (ISOM 27SMS) – Wtiting to reach you (Deadly Avenger instrumental remix).
(cd-s) (ISOM 27MS) – ('A'side) / Be my baby / Where is the love.

May 99. (cd/c/lp) (ISOM 9 CD/MC/LP) **THE MAN WHO** — 1 — -
– Writing to reach you / The fear / As you are / Driftwood / The last laugh of the laughter / Turn / Why does it always rain on me? / Luv / She's so strange / Slide show. (lp w/free 12"; ISOM 27T) – WRITING TO REACH YOU (Deadly Avenger mixes). (special ltd-cd+=; ISOM 9CDX) – Blue flashing light / Writing to reach you / Driftwood.

Aug 99. (c-s) (ISOM 33CS) **WHY DOES IT ALWAYS RAIN ON ME? / VILLAGE MAN** — 10 — -
(cd-s+=) (ISOM 33MS) – Driftwood (live).
(cd-s) (ISOM 33SMS) – ('A'side) / The urge for going / Slide show (live).

Nov 99. (c-s) (ISOM 39CS) **TURN / DAYS OF OUR LIVES** — 8 — -
(cd-s+=) (ISOM 39MS) – River.
(cd-s) (ISOM 39SMS) – ('A'side) / We are monkeys / Baby one more time.

TREACHEROUS JAYWALKERS (see under ⇒ SPAIN)

T. REX (see under ⇒ BOLAN, Marc)

a TRIBE CALLED QUEST

Formed: Queens, New York, USA ... 1988 by ALI, PHIFE, JAROBI and Q-TIP. They had met at high school, while Q-TIP had already sung alongside DE LA SOUL and The JUNGLE BROTHERS. Two 1989/90 singles floated by, before debut album 'PEOPLE'S INSTINCTIVE TRAVELS' cracked the US charts. It gained further success in Britain, due to hit singles 'BONITA APPLEBUM' and 'CAN I KICK IT?', which sampled LOU REED's 'Walk On The Wild Side'. Afro-centric hip-hop pioneers of acid-jazz (R&B psychedelia) influenced by JUNGLE BROTHERS, their next album 'LOW END THEORY', was their breakthrough into the US Top 50 and featured jazz veteran, RON CARTER, on upright bass. Q-TIP and others were requested by many (DEEE-LITE – 'Groove Is In The Heart', JUNGLE BROTHERS and DE LA SOUL) as guest artists, while they surfaced once again in 1993 with 'MIDNIGHT MARAUDERS'. This went to the top of the R&B charts, while gaining a US Top 10 spot, a feat easily surpassed when 1996's 'BEATS, RHYMES AND LIFE' topped the chart. • **Songwriters:** Group penned (DAVIS / TAYLOR / JONES / MUHAMMAD). Samples; SIR DUKE (Stevie Wonder) / INNER CITY BLUES (Marvin Gaye) / Others:- Grace Jones + Carly Simon on 'BONITA APPLEBUM'.

Album rating: PEOPLE'S INSTINCTIVE TRAVELS AND THE PATHS OF RHYTHM (*6) / LOW END THEORY (*7) / REVISED QUEST FOR THE SEASONED TRAVELLER remixes (*4) / MIDNIGHT MARAUDERS (*7) / BEATS, RHYMES AND LIFE (*8) / THE LOVE MOVEMENT (*6) / THE ANTHOLOGY compilation (*7)

Q-TIP (b. JONATHAN DAVIS, 20 Nov'70) – vocals / **ALI** (b. ALI SHAHEED MUHAMMAD, 11 Aug'70) – DJ / **PHIFE** (b. MALIK TAYLOR, 10 Apr'70) – vocals / **JAROBI** – vocals

		Jive	Jive
Aug 89.	(7") *(JIVE 215)* <1241> **DESCRIPTION OF A FOOL (talkie). / ('A'instrumental)**		
	(12"+=) *(JIVET 215)* – ('A'-silent version).		
Mar 90.	(12") *(JIVET 242)* **PUBIC ENEMY. /**		-
May 90.	(cd)(lp/c) *(CHIP 96)(HIP/+C 96)* <1331> **PEOPLE'S INSTINCTIVE TRAVELS AND THE PATHS OF RHYTHM**	54	91 Apr90
	– Push it along / Luck of Lucien / After hours / Footprints / I left my wallet in El Segundo / Bonita Applebum / Can I kick it? / Youthful expression / Rhythm (devoted to the art of moving butts) / Mr. Muhammad / Ham 'n' eggs / Go ahead in the rain / Description of a fool. (cd re-iss. Mar97 & Aug99; same)		
Aug 90.	(7")<c-s> *(JIVE 256)* <1368> **BONITA APPLEBUM. / ('A'mix)**	47	
	(12"+=/cd-s+=) *(JIVE T/CD 256)* <1384> – Between the sheets.		
Jan 91.	(7"/c-s) *(JIVE/+C 265)* <1430> **CAN I KICK IT?. / ('A'-Boilerhouse mix)**	15	
	(12"+=/cd-s+=) *(JIVE T/CD 265)* <1400> – ('A'-Phase 5 mix) / ('A'-If the tapes come remix).		
Mar 91.	(7"/c-s)<c-s> *(JIVE/+C 270)* <1300> **I LEFT MY WALLET IN EL SEGUNDO. / ('A'-talkie)**		
	(12"+=/cd-s+=) *(JIVE T/CD 270)* – ('A'-Vampire mix) / ('A'-Silent mix).		
	———— now without JAROBI		
Sep 91.	(7") *(JIVE 284)* <42011> **CHECK THE RHIME. / ('A'instrumental)**		
	(12"+=/cd-s+=) *(JIVE T/CD 284)* – ('A'mixes).		
Sep 91.	(lp/c/cd) *(HIP/+C/CD 117)* <1418> **LOW END THEORY**	58	45
	– Excursions / Buggin' out / Rap promoter / Butter / Verses from the abstract / Show business / Vibes and stuff / The infamous date rape / Check the rhime / Everything is fair / Jazz (we've got) / Skypager / Scenario. (cd re-iss. Mar97; same)		
Dec 91.	(12"ep/cd-ep) *(JIVE T/CD)* **JAZZ (WE'VE GOT) (4 versions) / BUGGIN' OUT**		
May 92.	(12"ep/cd-ep) *(JIVE T/CD 302)* <42065> **SCENARIO (MC mix). / (8 mixes)**		57
Sep 92.	(7") *(JIVE 317)* **LUCK OF LUCIEN. / BUTTER**		
	(12"+=/cd-s+=) *(JIVE T/CD 317)* – ('A'mixes).		
Oct 92.	(cd)(lp/c) *(CHIP 130)(HIP/+C 130)* **REVISED QUEST FOR THE SEASONED TRAVELLER** (remixes)		-
	– Bonita Applebum / I left my wallet in El Segundo / Description of a fool / Pubic enemy / Check the rhime / Luck of Lucien / Can I kick it / Scenario / If the papers came / Jazz (we've got) / Butter. (cd re-iss. Mar97; same)		
Nov 92.	(7") *(JIVE 324)* **CAN I KICK IT?. / HOT SEX**		
	(12"+=/cd-s+=) *(JIVE T/CD 324)* – ('A'-Boilerhouse extended) / ('A'side again).		
Oct 93.	(cd)(d-lp/c) *(CHIP 143)(HIP/+C 143)* <42197> **MIDNIGHT MARAUDERS**	70	8
	– Midnight marauders tour guide / Steve Biko (stir it up) / Award tour / 8 million stories / Sucka nigga / Midnight / We can get down / Electric relaxation (relax yourself girl) / (interlude) / Clap your hands / Oh my God / (interlude) / Keep it rollin' / The chase pt.II / Lyrics to go / God lives through / Hot sex. (cd re-iss. Mar97; same)		
Nov 93.	(c-s) *(JIVEC 344)* <42187> **AWARD TOUR. / THE CHASE (pt.II)**		47
	(cd-s+=) *(JIVECD 344)* – ('A'instrumental).		
	(12"++=) *(JIVET 344)* – ('A'radio mix).		
Feb 94.	(12"ep/cd-ep) *(JIVE T/CD 351)* <42179> **ELECTRIC RELAXATION (RELAX YOURSELF GIRL) / ('A'version) / MIDNIGHT / ('B'version)**		65
May 94.	(12"/c-s) *(JIVE T/C 355)* **OH MY GOD. / ('A'-UK flavour radio mix)**	68	
	(cd-s) *(JIVECD 355)* – ('A'side) / Bonita Applebum / Can I kick it? / Left my wallet in El Segundo.		
Nov 94.	(7"ep/12"ep/cd-ep) *(JIVE/+T/CD 374)* **A TRIBE CALLED QUEST EP**		-
	– We can get down / Clap your hands / Verses from the abstract / Footprints.		
Jul 96.	(12"/cd-s) *(JIVE T/CD 399)* **1NCE AGAIN. / ('A'radio) / ('A'instrumental) / I left my wallet in El Segundo**	34	
	(cd-s) *(JIVERCD 399)* – ('A'side) / Bonita applebum / Can I kick it? / Scenario (remix).		

Aug 96.	(cd)(lp/c) *(CHIP 170)(HIP/+C 170)* <41587> **BEATS, RHYMES AND LIFE**	28	1
	– Phony rappers / Get a hold / Motivators / Jam / Crew / The pressure / 1nce again (featuring TAMMY LUCAS) / Mind power / The hop / Keeping it moving / Baby Phife's return / Separate – together / What really goes on / Word play / Stressed out (featuring FAITH EVANS).		
Nov 96.	(c-s; by A TRIBE CALLED QUEST featuring FAITH EVANS & RAPHAEL SAADIQ) *(JIVEC 404)* **STRESSED OUT / ('A'mix)**	33	
	(12"/cd-s) *(JIVE T/CD 404)* – ('A'mixes).		
	———— Mar'97, credited on FUGESS Top 3 hit 'Rumble In The Jungle'.		
Aug 97.	(12"ep/cd-ep) *(JIVE TCD 427)* **THE JAM EP**	61	
	– Jam / Get a hold / Mardi gras at midnight / Same ol' thing.		
Aug 98.	(c-s) *(051898-4)* 42534> **FIND A WAY / STEPPIN' IT UP (with BUSTA RHYMES & REDMAN)**	41	71
	(12"+=/cd-s+=) *(051898-0/-2)* – ('A'instrumental).		
Sep 98.	(cd/c/lp) *(052103-2/-4/-1)* <41638> **THE LOVE MOVEMENT**	38	3
	– Start it up / Find a way / Da booty / Steppin' it up / Like it like that / Common ground (get it goin' on) / Moms / His name is Mutty Ranks / Give me / Pad & pen / Busta's lament / Hot 4 U / Against the world / Love / Rock rock y'all / Scenario / Money maker / Hot sex / Oh my God / Jazz (we've got) / One two s**t.		
Oct 99.	(d-cd/t-lp) *(052384-2/-1)* <41679> **THE ANTHOLOGY** (compilation)		81
	– Check the rhime / Bonita applebum / Award tour / Can I kick it? / Scenario / Buggin' out / If the papes come / Electric relaxation / Jazz (we've got) / I left my wallet in El Segundo / Hot sex / Oh my God / Stressed out / Luck of Lucien / Description of a fool / Keep it moving / Find a way / Sucka nigga / Vibrant thing / Bonita applebum / I left my wallet in El Segundo / Public enemy / Can I kick it? / Scenario / Bonita applebum / Oh my God.		

TRICKY

Born: ADRIAN THAWES, 27 Jan'68, Knowle West, Bristol, England. After a troubled youth growing up on one of Bristol's poorer housing estates, THAWES began spending less time lawbreaking and more time busying himself with the city's club culture, helping run sound systems and hanging out with The WILD BUNCH, a loose collective of musicians and DJ's that included MASSIVE ATTACK and famed producer NELLEE HOOPER. In between trips to court in OXFORD, where he was defending an assault charge, TRICKY KID (as he was nicknamed by his Bristolian cohorts) occasionally collaborated with MASSIVE ATTACK on their seminal 'BLUE LINES' album, contributing stoned raps on several tracks. He also contributed to MASSIVE's follow-up, 'PROTECTION', although his first solo effort was a 'Betty Boo'-sampling track entitled 'LOYALTY IS VALUABLE', engineered by future PORTISHEAD mainman GEOFF BARROWS and featured on the 1991 Sickle Cell charity album, 'HARD SELL', alongside the likes of MASSIVE ATTACK, SMITH & MIGHTY etc. Yet the track that brought him to the attention of a discerning public was the sublime claustrophobia of 'AFTERMATH'. Eventually released in early '94, the track had previously been recorded a couple of years earlier with TRICKY's musical partner, MARTINA, predating the trip-hop scene that TRICKY would later be lumped in with. Next came the jarring loops and nervous paranoia of 'PONDEROSA', another taster for the pioneering debut album, 'MAXINQUAYE' (1994), released later that summmer. A dense, brooding collection of slow motion beat-poetry from the darkside, the record was immediately hailed as a classic. Taking bastardised hip-hop beats as his raw material then suffocating them with layers of samples, disjointed rhythms, freak instrumental lines and obscure noises, TRICKY created music that was wired yet lethargic, with lyrics equally contradictory and ambiguous to match. Collaborating with TERRY HALL, NENEH CHERRY and ALISON MOYET amongst others, TRICKY released his 'NEARLY GOD' project in 1996. The album revisited the dark intensity of 'MAXINQUAYE' without quite the same effect, possibly a case of too many cooks (or too many spliffs) spoiling the broth. 'PRE-MILLENNIUM TENSION', released later the same year, was on a par with 'MAXINQUAYE' and if it didn't exactly break new ground, the album illustrated that TRICKY's wellspring of paranoid psychosis is far from running dry. Tracks like 'BAD THINGS', 'MAKES ME WANNA DIE' and 'MY EVIL IS STRONG' speak for themselves, and though it's a well worn cliche, it would appear that this man really does suffer for his art. Then again, maybe he shouldn't smoke so much. 1999 was a busy year for TRICKY, everything from making "real" gangster LP, 'PRODUCT OF THE ENVIRONMENT' (with Mad Frankie Fraser for one!) to delivering his final album for 'Island', 'JUXTAPOSE'. The latter – which was recorded with DJ MUGGS (of CYPRESS HILL) and GREASE – achieved the usual plaudits, its return to his experimental trip-hop roots gaining him a near UK Top 30 place. • **Songwriters:** Self-penned & samples except; BLACK STEEL + THE MOMENT I FEARED (Public Enemy) / PONDEROSA (co-with HOWIE B) / HELL IS ROUND THE CORNER (same source that PORTISHEAD found 'Glory Box'?) / SINGING THE BLUES (Mary McReary) / POP MUZIK (M) / he also sampled a song by Billie Holiday on 'Carriage For Two'.

Album rating: MAXINQUAYE (*9) / NEARLY GOD (*7; as Nearly God) / PRE-MILLENNIUM TENSION (*7) / ANGELS WITH DIRTY FACES (*7) / JUXTAPOSE (*7)

TRICKY – vocals (ex-MASSIVE ATTACK) / with **MARTINE TOPLEY-BIRD** – vocals / and others

		4th & Broad	4th & Broad
Jan 94.	(7") *(BRW 288)* <590> **AFTERMATH. / ('A'-I could be looking for people mix)**	69	
	(12"+=) *(12BRW 288)* – ('A'mix).		
	(cd-s++=) *(BRCD 288)* – ('A'mix).		

Apr 94. (7") *(BRW 299)* <595> **PONDEROSA.** / ('A'-Dobie's roll pt.1 mix)   [ ]   [ ] Jul94
(12"+=/cd-s+=) *(12BRW/BRCD 299)* – (3 'A'mixes; Ultragelic / Original / Dobie's roll pt.2).

Jan 95. (7"/c-s) *(BR W/CA 304)* **OVERCOME.** / ABBA ON FAT TRACKS   [34]   [-]
(12"+=/cd-s+=) *(12BRW/BRCD 304)* – ('A'-Zippy & Bungle mix).

—— guests on below ALISON GOLDFRAPP + RAGGA – vocals / PETE BRIQUETTE – bass / MARK SAUNDERS – keyboards / FTV – guitar, drums / TONY WRAFTER – flute / JAMES STEVENSON – guitar

Feb 95. (cd/c/lp) *(BR CD/CA/LP 610)* <524089> **MAXINQUAYE**   [3]   [ ] Apr95
– Overcome / Ponderosa / Black steel / Hell is round the corner / Pumpkin / Aftermath / Abbaon fat tracks / Brand new you're retro / Suffocated love / You don't / Strugglin' / Feed me.

Mar 95. (c-s) *(BRCA 320)* **BLACK STEEL.** / ('A'-Been caught stealing mix)   [28]   [-]
(12"+=/cd-s+=) *(12BRW/BRCD 320)* – ('A'live) / ('A'-In the draw mix).
(cd-s++=) *(BRCDX 320)* – ('A'edit).

Jul 95. (7"pic-d-ep/12"red-ep/cd-ep; as TRICKY VS. THE GRAVEDIGGAZ) *(BRW/12BRW/BRCD 326)* <383> **THE HELL E.P.**   [12]   [ ]
– Hell is round the corner (original) / ('A'-Hell and water mix) / Psychosis / Tonite is a special nite (chaos mass confusion mix).

Nov 95. (c-s) *(BRCA 330)* **PUMPKIN / MOODY BROODY BUDHIST CAMP / NEW KINGDOM**   [26]   [ ]
(cd-s+=) *(BRCD 330)* – Brand new you're retro (Alex Reece mix).
(12"colrd) *(12BRW 330)* – ('A'side) / (above track) / Slick 66.

NEARLY GOD

TRICKY with **TERRY HALL / MARTINE / BJORK / NENEH CHERRY / ALISON MOYET + CATH COFFEY**

	Durban Poison	Island

Apr 96. (7") *(DP 003)* **POEMS / CHILDREN'S STORY**   [28]   [ ]
(12"+=/cd-s+=) *(DP X/CD 003)* – ('A'extended).

Apr 96. (cd/c/lp) *(DP CD/MC/LP 1001)* <531064> **NEARLY GOD**   [11]   [ ]
– Tattoo / Poems / Together now / Keep your mouth shut / I be the prophet / Make a chane / Black cofee / Bubbles / I sing for you / Yoga.
above was to have been under his DURBAN POISON project.

—— Aug 96, TRICKY PRESENTS GRASS ROOTS 12"ep for 'Ultra'.

TRICKY

—— with a plethora of musicians incl. **PATRICE CHEVALIER** – guitar / **JOHN TONKS** – drums / **PAT McMANUS** – piano, violin

	4th & Broad	Island

Oct 96. (7"pic-d) *(BRW 340)* **CHRISTIANSANDS.** / FLYNN   [36]   [ ]
(12"+=/cd-s+=) *(12BRW/BRCD 340)* – Ghetto youth.

Nov 96. (cd/c/lp) *(BR CD/CA/LP 623)* <524302> **PRE-MILLENNIUM TENSION**   [30]   [ ]
– Vent / Christiansands / Tricky kid / Bad dreams / Makes me wanna die / Ghetto youth / Sex drive / Bad things / Lyrics of fury / My evil is strong / Piano. (d-cd-iss. ; BRCDX 623)

—— late '96, featured on the hit single by GARBAGE; 'Milk'.

Dec 96. (cd-ep) *(BRCDX 341)* **TRICKY KID.** / MAKES ME WANNA DIE (Tricky's extremix) / GRASS ROOTS   [28]   [ ]
(12"ep+=) *(12BRW 341)* – Smoking Beagles (Sub Sub vs Tricky).
(cd-ep) *(BRCD 341)* – ('A'side) / Devils helper / Smoking Beagles (Sub Sub vs Tricky) / Suffocated love (live on 'Later with Jools').

Apr 97. (cd-s) *(BRCDX 348)* **MAKES ME WANNA DIE / MAKES ME WANNA DIE (The Weekend mix – remixed by The Stereo MC's) / PIANO (the Green sticky mix remixed by A Guy Called Gerald)**   [29]   [ ]
(12"clear+=) *(BRX 348)* – Here comes the aliens (AFRIKA IZLAM & TRICKY).
(cd-s) *(BRCD 348)* – ('A'side) / ('A'acoustic) / Here come the aliens (AFRIKA IZLAM & TRICKY).

	Island	Island

May 98. (7"; TRICKY featuring POLLY JEAN HARVEY) *(IS 701)* **BROKEN HOMES.** / MONEY GREEDY   [25]   [ ]
(cd-s+=) *(CID 701)* – Anti histamine / Taxi.
(cd-s+=) *(CIDX 701)* – 360 degrees.

May 98. (cd/c/d-lp) *(CID/ICT/ILPS 8071)* <524520> **ANGELS WITH DIRTY FACES**   [23]   [84] Jun98
– Money greedy / Mellow / Singing the blues / Broken homes / 6 minutes / Analyze me / The moment I feared / Talk to me (angels with dirty faces) / Carriage for two / Demise / Tear out my eyes / Record companies / Peyote sings / Taxi.

Dec 98. (cd-s) <572515> **6 MINUTES (mixes)**   [-]   [ ]

Aug 99. (12"/cd-s) *(12IS/CID 753)* **FOR REAL (mixes; Hip Hop / Genaside II / Rollo)**   [45]   [ ]
(cd-s) *(CIDX 753)* – ('A'side) / Bombing bastards / Pop muzik.

Aug 99. (cd/lp; by TRICKY with DJ MUGGS & GREASE) *(CID/ILPS 8087)* **JUXTAPOSE**   [22]   [ ]
– For real / Bom bom diggy / Contradictive / She said / I like the girls / Hot like a sauna / Call me / Wash my soul / Hot like a sauce (metal mix) / Scrappy love.

TRIFFIDS

Formed: Perth, Australia . . . 1980 by New Zealand-born DAVID McCOMB, his brother ROBERT, MARTYN CASEY, ALSY McDONALD and PHIL KAKULAS (soon replaced by JILL BIRT). Following a string of domestic singles releases on obscure labels, The TRIFFIDS were signed to appropriately named Aussie independent imprint, 'Hot', making their vinyl debut in 1983 with the eerie, sun-parched sounds of the 'TREELESS PLAIN' album. Screeching violins circled over McCOMB's gloomy intonations like vultures,

the atmospheric likes of 'RED PONY' echoed years later in the work of The TINDERSTICKS amongst others. Follow-up set, 'RAINING PLEASURE', surfaced the following year but it was 1986's acclaimed 'BORN SANDY DEVOTIONAL' which saw The TRIFFIDS make their mark on European territory. With the subtle nuances of pedal steel/slide guitar player, 'EVIL' GRAHAM LEE, lending the sound a new depth, the full extent of the band's transatlantic influences were apparent on the awesome 'WIDE OPEN ROAD', while the melancholy sparseness of BIRT's vocal lent proceedings a ghostly hue. Getting er . . ., back to nature, they recorded the hastily released follow-up, 'IN THE PINES' in a sheep-shearing shed in the Australian outback (!), thankfully minus any live bleating. With the subsequent addition of extra guitarist ADAM PETERS and a major label deal courtesy of 'Island', at last The TRIFFIDS looked to be set for major alternative success. The resulting 'CALENTURE' (1987) album didn't disappoint, McCOMB's stark portraits thrown into sharp relief by Gil Norton's superior production. Yet despite a UK Top 75 hit with 'A TRICK OF THE LIGHT', success proved as elusive as ever, the band roping in MORRISSEY producer, Stephen Street, for 1989's 'BLACK SWAN'. The album scraped the lower regions of the chart but failed to score with such potential hit singles as 'GOODBYE LITTLE BOY' and 'BURY ME DEEP IN LOVE'. With recognition seemingly as far off as ever, The TRIFFIDS split at the turn of the decade, the posthumously released live album, 'STOCKHOLM' (1990) serving as a fair epitaph. While DAVID McCOMB went on to work with The BLACKEYED SUSANS and record a solo album, 'LOVE OF WILL' (1994), for 'Mushroom', the brooding spirit of The TRIFFIDS has infused the work of such gothic country luminaries as The WALKABOUTS, WILLARD GRANT CONSPIRACY and The HANDSOME FAMILY. DAVID would subsequently give up the music world to concentrate on family life, although this was cut short on the 1st of February, 1999, when he died following a car crash. • **Songwriters:** DAVID McCOMB penned except covers; / INTO THE GROOVE (Madonna) / BRIGHT LIGHTS BIG CITY / GOOD MORNING, GOOD MORNING (Beatles).

Album rating: TREELESS PLAIN (*7) / RAINING PLEASURE mini (*8) / BORN SANDY DEVOTIONAL (*7) / IN THE PINES (*6) / CALENTURE (*8) / THE BLACK SWAN (*7) / STOCKHOLM (*5) / AUSTRALIAN MELODRAMA compilation (*8) / David McComb: LOVE OF WILL (*6)

DAVID McCOMB (b. 1962) – vocals, guitar, piano, etc. / **ROBERT McCOMB** – violin, guitar, keyboards, vocals / **JILL BIRT** – keyboards, some vocals repl. PHIL KAKULAS / **MARTIN CASEY** – bass, vocals / **ALSY McDONALD** – drums, percussion, vocals

	Shake Some Action	not iss.

Jul 81. (7") *(SG-MX 57828)* **STAND UP.** / FARMERS NEVER VISIT NIGHT CLUBS   [-]   [-] Austra

	not iss.	Resonant

Dec 81. (7"ep) **REVERIE**   [-]   [-] Austra
– Reverie / Place in the sun / Joan of Arc / This boy.

	not iss.	No Records

1982. (7") **SPANISH BLUE.** / TWISTED BRAIN   [-]   [-] Austra
1982. (7"ep) **BAD TIMING**   [-]   [-] Austra
– Bad timing / Left to rot / Being driven / Snake pit.

	Hot UK	not iss.

Nov 83. (lp) *(HOT 1003)* **TREELESS PLAIN**   [-]   [-]
– Red pony / Branded / My baby thinks she's a train / Roseval / I am a lonesome hobo / Place in the sun / Play thing / Old ghostrider / Hanging shed / Hell of a summer / Madeline / Nothing can take your place. (cd-iss. Nov91)

Dec 83. (7") **BEAUTIFUL WASTE.** / PROPERTY IS CONDEMNED   [-]   [-] Austra

Dec 84. (m-lp) *(MINIHOT 1)* **RAINING PLEASURE**   [-]   [-]
– Jesus calling / Embedded / St. James Infirmary / Everybody has to eat / Ballad of Jack Frost / Raining pleasure. (re-iss. Jun94; same)

Apr 85. (12"m) *(HOT12 007)* **FIELD OF GLASS.** / BRIGHT LIGHTS BIG CITY / MONKEY ON MY BACK   [ ]   [-]

—— added **'Evil' GRAHAM LEE** – steel guitar (of The APARTMENTS)

Aug 85. (7") *(HOT7 26)* **YOU DON'T MISS YOUR WATER (TILL YOUR WELL RUNS DRY).** / CONVENT WALLS   [ ]   [-]
(12"+=) *(HOT12 26)* – Beautiful water / ('A'instrumental). (re-iss. 7"ep Oct94; HEP7 26)

May 86. (7") *(HOT7 30)* **WIDE OPEN ROAD.** / TIME OF WEAKNESS   [ ]   [-]
(12"+=) *(HOT12 30)* – Dear Miss Lonely Hearts / Native bride.

Jun 86. (lp) *(HOTLP 1023)* **BORN SANDY DEVOTIONAL**   [ ]   [-]
– The seabirds / stuary bed / Chicken killer / Tarrilup Bridge / Lonely stretch / Wide open road / Life of crime / Personal things / Stolen property / Tender is the night (the long fidelity). (cd-iss. Mar95 on 'Mushroom'; D 19457)

Nov 86. (lp) *(HOTLP 1028)* **IN THE PINES**   [ ]   [-]
– Suntrapper / In the pines / Kathy knows / 25 to 5 / Do you want me near you? / Once a day / Just might fade away / Better off this way / Only one life / Keep your eyes on the hole / One soul less on your fiery list / Born Sandy Devotional / Love and affection. (re-iss. Jun94; same) (cd-iss. Mar95 on 'Mushroom'; D 19480)

—— added **ADAM PETERS** – guitar (ex-FLOWERPOT MEN)

	Island	not iss.

Oct 87. (7") *(IS 337)* **BURY ME DEEP IN LOVE** / BABY CAN I WALK YOU HOME   [ ]   [-]
(12"+=) *(12IS 337)* – Region unknown.
(cd-s++=) *(CID 337)* – Vagabond holes.

Nov 87. (lp/c/cd) *(ILPS/ICT/CID 9885)* **CALENTURE**   [ ]   [-]
– Bury me deep in love / Kelly's blues / A trick of the light / Hometown farewell kiss / Unmade love / Open for you / Holy water / Blinded by the hour / Vagabond holes / Jerducuttup man / Calenture / Save what you can. (cd re-iss. Dec89; IMCD 46) (cd-iss. Mar95 on 'Mushroom'; D 19458)

Jan 88. (7") *(IS 350)* **A TRICK OF THE LIGHT.** / LOVE DECEIVER   [73]   [-]
(10"+=) *(10IS 350)* – Bad news always reminds me of you.
(12"+=/cd-s+=) *(12IS/CID 350)* – Everything you touch turns to time.

Aug 88. (7") *(IS 367)* **HOLY WATER.** / GOOD MORNING, GOOD MORNING   [ ]   [-]
(12"+=/cd-s+=) *(12IS/CID 367)* – Raining pleasure / Red pony.

—— added guests **PHIL KAKULAS** (who returned) + **RITA MENENDEZ**

Mar 89. (7"; by DAVE McCOMB * ADAM PETERS) *(IS 410)* **I DON'T NEED YOU. / WILLIE THE TORCH** ☐ –
     (12"+=) *(12IS 410)* – Liberty and a thousand fares.

Apr 89. (lp/c/cd) *(ILPS/ICT/CID 9928)* **THE BLACK SWAN** 63 –
     – Too hot to move, too hot to think / American sailors / Falling over you / Goodbye little boy / Bottle of love / The spinning top song / Butterflies into worms / The clown prince / Good fortune Rose / New Year's greetings / Blackeyed Susan Brown / Fairytale love. *(re-iss. cd Mar95 on 'Mushroom')*

Apr 89. (7") *(IS 413)* **FALLING OVER YOU. / GO HOME EDDIE** ☐ –
     (12"+=/cd-s+=) *(12IS/CID 413)* – Shell of a man / You minus me.

May 89. (7") *(IS 420)* **GOODBYE LITTLE BOY. / GO HOME EDDIE** ☐ –
     (12"+=) *(12IS 420)* – Shell of a man.
     (10"++=/cd-s++=) *(10IS/CID 420)* – You minus me.

Aug 89. (7") *(IS 424)* **BURY ME DEEP IN LOVE. / RENT** ☐ –
     (12"+=/cd-s+=) *(12IS/CID 424)* – Into the groove.

	M.N.W.	not iss.

Jul 90. (lp/c/cd) *(MNW X/MCX/MCDX 9)* **STOCKHOLM** (live on Swedish radio late 1989) ☐ –
     – Property is condemned / Hell of a summer / Personal things / Raining pleasure / Lonely stretch / Sure the girl I love / Wide open road / Keep your eyes on the hole / In the pines / Billy / I am a lonesome hobo / How could I help but love you. *(cd-iss. Mar95 on 'Mushroom'; D 30231)*

—— disbanded late in 1989

– compilations, etc. –

Oct 87. (12"ep) *Strange Fruit; (SFPS 036) / Dutch East India; <8340>* **THE PEEL SESSIONS** (5/5/85) ☐ –
     – Life of crime / Chicken killer / Lonely stretch.

Dec 94. (cd) *Mushroom; (D 31182)* **AUSTRALIAN MELODRAMA (THE BEST OF THE TRIFFIDS)** ☐ –
     – Red pony / Hell of a summer / Beautiful waste / Raining pleasure / Bright lights, big city / The seabirds / Wide open road / Lonely stretch / Tender is the night / Bury me deep in love / trick of the light / Hometown farewell kiss / Unmade love / Jerdacuttup man / Save what you can / Falling over you / Goodbye little boy / New Year's greetings / In the pines.

DAVID McCOMB

	Foundation	not iss.

Sep 91. (12") **THE MESSAGE. / SONG OF NO RETURN / ('A'club version)** ☐ –
     (cd-s+=) – I've heard things turn out this way.

	Mushroom	not iss.

Mar 94. (c-ep/cd-ep) *(C/D 11589)* **SETTING YOU FREE / HOME FOR FALLEN ANGELS / YOU'VE GOT A FUNNY WAY OF SHOWING YOU LOVED ME / MY FRIEND SLEEP** ☐ –

Mar 94. (cd/c) *(D/C 31071)* **LOVE OF WILL** ☐ –
     – Clear out my mind / Setting you free / Day of the ascension / Deep in a dream / Nothing good / The Lord burns every clue / Lifelike / Lover sister number one / Heard you had a bed / Inside of me / Leaning / I want to conquer you / Pack up your troubles.

—— DAVE died on the 1st February 1999

TRIP SHAKESPEARE (see under ⇒ SEMISONIC)

TRIUMPH (dig out; Great Metal . . .)

TROGGS

Formed: Andover, Hampshire, England . . . 1964 briefly as The TROGLODYTES, by REG BALL (PRESLEY), CHRIS BRITTON, PETE STAPLES and RONNIE BOND. In 1965, they were signed by KINKS manager, Larry Page, who leased them to 'C.B.S.' in early '66 for the debut single, 'LOST GIRL'. Their second 45, 'WILD THING', with TV exposure on 'Thank Your Lucky Stars', gave them a No.2 hit, which also went on to become a US No.1. This primal three-chord assault carried on where 'LOUIE LOUIE' left off, the band taking on American garage-rock in a bizarre inversion of the British invasion. It has since become one of the most covered songs ever, a blueprint for almost any band with a guitar and an amp that went up to 11. They then went No.1 with the harmony-laden, 'WITH A GIRL LIKE YOU', which again featured PRESLEY's grizzled drawl of a vocal. Their next single, 'I CAN'T CONTROL MYSELF', gave them their third consecutive Top 3 hit, closely followed by another CHIP TAYLOR-penned song (like 'WILD THING'), 'ANY WAY THAT YOU WANT ME'. They continued in their bid for chart domination with a further string of Top 50 hits, the band's sound rapidly evolving with the onset of psychedelia. One of the aforementioned 45's, 'LOVE IS ALL AROUND', became an even bigger smash in 1994, when Scots popsters WET WET WET took it to the top for several weeks. This subsequently furnished PRESLEY with enough money to indulge his crop circle obsession. Previously in 1990, The TROGGS' profile was raised somewhat, through a collaboration with R.E.M. on an album, 'AU' (this also featured 'LOVE IS ALL AROUND'). • **Songwriters:** PRESLEY was the main writer, except HI HI HAZEL (Geno Washington) / GOOD VIBRATIONS (Beach Boys) / I CAN'T GET NO SATISFACTION (Rolling Stones) / THE KITTY CAT SONG (Hal Roach-Allen Toussaint) / RIDE YOUR PONY (Aaron Neville) / EVIL (. . . Singleton) / LOUIE LOUIE (Richard Berry) / JAGUAR AND THUNDERBIRD + MEMPHIS + NO PARTICULAR PLACE TO GO (Chuck Berry) / GOT LOVE IF YOU WANT IT (Slim Harpo) / WALKING THE DOG (Rufus Thomas) / etc. • **Trivia:** Their 1990's reformation included collaborations with R.E.M. on single 'Nowhere Road'.

Album rating: FROM NOWHERE . . . THE TROGGS (*7) / TROGGLODYNAMITE (*7) / BEST OF THE TROGGS compilation (*7) / CELLOPHANE (*7) / LOVE IS ALL AROUND (*6) / MIXED BAG (*5) / BEST OF THE TROGGS, VOL.II compilation (*6) / TROGGLOMANIA (*5) / CONTRASTS (*4) / TROGGS (*3) / THE TROGGS TAPES (*2) / LIVE AT MAX'S KANSAS CITY (*2) / BLACK BOTTOM (*3) / AU (*4) / ATHENS ANDOVER (*5) / ARCHEOLOGY (1967-1977) boxed-set compilation (*8)

REG BALL (b.12 Jun'43; became REG PRESLEY after hit) – vocals, ocarina / **CHRIS BRITTON** (b.21 Jun'45, Watford, England) – guitar repl. TONY MANSFIELD / **PETE STAPLES** (b. 3 May'44) – bass (ex-TEN FOOT FIVE) repl. DAVID WRIGHT / **RONNIE BOND** (b. 4 May'43) – drums

	C.B.S.	not iss.
Feb 66. (7") *(202038)* **LOST GIRL. / THE YELLA IN ME**	–	

	Fontana	Fontana
Apr 66. (7") *(TF 689) <1548>* **WILD THING. / FROM HOME**	2	1 Jun66

     <above & below 'A' was also double 'A'side on 'Atco'; 6415>

Jul 66. (7") *(TF 717) <1552>* **WITH A GIRL LIKE YOU. / I WANT YOU** 1 | 29

Jul 66. (lp; stereo/mono) *(S+/TL 5355)* **FROM NOWHERE . . . THE TROGGS** 6 | –
     – Wild thing / The kitty cat song / Ride your pony / Hi hi Hazel / I just sing / Evil / The yella in me / With a girl like you / Our love will still be there / Louie Louie / Jingle jangle / When I'm with you / From home / Jaguar and Thunderbird / I can't control myself / Night of the long grass. *(cd-iss. 1989; 832957-2)*

	–	Atco
Aug 66. (lp) *(67556)<Atco; SD 33193>* **WILD THING**	–	52

     – Wild thing / From home / Just sing / Hi hi Hazel / Lost girl / Evil / With a girl like you / I want you / Your love / Our love will be there.

	Page One	Atco
Sep 66. (7") *(POF 001) <6444>* **I CAN'T CONTROL MYSELF. / GONNA MAKE YOU MINE**	2	43

     <also on US 'Fontana'; 1557>

	Page One	Fontana
Dec 66. (7") *(POF 010) <1585>* **ANY WAY THAT YOU WANT ME. / 6-5-4-3-2-1**	8	Apr67

Feb 67. (7") *(POF 015) <1576>* **GIVE IT TO ME. / YOU'RE LYIN'** 12 | ☐

Feb 67. (lp) *(POL 001)* **TROGGLODYNAMITE** 10 | ☐
     – I can only give you everything / Last summer / Meet Jacqueline / Oh no / It's too late / No.10 Downing Street / Mona / I want you to come into my life / Let me tell you babe / Little Queenie / Cousin Jane / You can't hurt me / Baby come closer / It's over.

May 67. (7") *(POF 022) <1593>* **NIGHT OF THE LONG GRASS. / GIRL IN BLACK** 17 | Jun67

Jul 67. (lp) *(FOR 001)* **BEST OF THE TROGGS** (compilation) 24 | ☐
     – Night of the long grass / Gonna make you / Anyway that you want me / 6-5-4-3-2-1 / I want you / With a girl like you / I can't control myself / Girl in black / Give it to me / You're lying / From home / Wild thing. *(re-iss. Feb85 on 'Rhino' + 1988 on 'Bigtime')*

Jul 67. (7") *(POF 030)* **HI HI HAZEL. / AS I RIDE BY** 42 | –

Oct 67. (7") *(POF 040) <1607>* **LOVE IS ALL AROUND. / WHEN WILL THE RAIN COME** 5 | 7 Feb68

Dec 67. (lp; mono/stereo) *(POL/S 003)* **CELLOPHANE** ☐ | –
     – Little red donkey / Too much of a good thing / Butterflies and bees / All of my time / Seventeen / Somewhere my girl is waiting / It's showing / Her emotion / When will the rain come / My lady / Come the day / Love is all around.

Feb 68. (7") *(POF 056)* **LITTLE GIRL. / MAYBE THE MADMEN** 37 | ☐

May 68. (7") *(POF 064)* **SURPRISE SURPRISE. / MARBLES AND SOME GUM?** ☐ | ☐

May 68. (lp) *<67576>* **LOVE IS ALL AROUND** – | ☐
     – Love is all around / Night of the long grass / Gonna make you / Anyway that you want me / 6-5-4-3-2-1 / When will the rain come / Little girl / I can't control myself / Girl in black / Give it to me / Cousin Jane.

Aug 68. (7") *(POF 082) <1622>* **YOU CAN CRY IF YOU WANT TO. / THERE'S SOMETHING ABOUT YOU** ☐ | ☐

Sep 68. (7") *(POF 092) <1630>* **SURPRISE SURPRISE. / COUSIN JANE** ☐ | ☐

Oct 68. (7") *(POF 092) <1634>* **HIP HIP HOORAY. / SAY DARLIN'!** ☐ | ☐

Dec 68. (lp) *(POLS 012)* **MIXED BAG** ☐ | ☐

	Page One	Page One
Jan 69. (7") *(POF 114)* **EVIL WOMAN. / SWEET MADELAINE**	☐	☐

Jan 69. (lp) *(FOR 007)* **BEST OF THE TROGGS VOL.II** (compilation) ☐ | ☐
     – I can only give you everything / Meet Jacqueline / Jingle jangle / I want you to come into my life / Cousin Jane / Louie Louie / Love is all around / From home / Jaguar and the thunderbird / Hi hi Hazel / Mona.

Feb 69. (7") *<21026>* **EVIL WOMAN. / HEADS OR TAILS** ☐ | ☐

—— Split Mar'69.

Mar 69. (7"; by RONNIE BOND) *(POF 123)* **ANYTHING FOR YOU. / CAROLYN** ☐ | –

Apr 69. (7"; by REG PRESLEY) *(POF 131)* **LUCINDA LEE. / WICHITA LINEMAN** ☐ | ☐

—— CHRIS BRITTON also issued solo album 'AS I AM' in 1969.

—— The TROGGS re-formed. **TONY MURRAY** – bass (ex-PLASTIC PENNY) repl. PETE

Feb 70. (7") *(POF 164) <21030>* **EASY LOVIN'. / GIVE ME SOMETHING** ☐ | ☐

1970. (lp) *(POS 602)* **TROGGLOMANIA** (live) ☐ | ☐
     – Give it to me / Jingle jangle / No.10 Downing Street / Wild thing / Oh no / Last Summer / Anyway that you want me / Hi hi Hazel / With a girl like you / Mona / Baby come closer / Cousin Jane / I can't control myself / I want you to come into my life / I just sing.

May 70. (7") *(POF 171) <21032>* **LOVER. / COME NOW** ☐ | ☐

Jul 70. (7") *(POF 182) <21035>* **THE RAVER. / YOU** ☐ | ☐

—— **RICHARD MOORE** – guitar repl. BRITTON

	D.J.M.	Silverline
1970. (lp) *(DJML 009)* **CONTRASTS** (1966-70)	☐	☐

     – I can't control myself / The raver / Surprise, surprise (I need you) / Evil woman / Lover / Wild thing / Love is all around / Little girl / You can cry if you want to / I've waited for someone / Easy loving / Any way that you want me *(re-iss. Nov76; same)*

Jun 71. (7") *(DJS 248)* **LAZY WEEKEND. / LET'S PULL TOGETHER** ☐ | ☐

	Jam	not iss.
Nov 72. (7"m) *(JAM 25)* **WILD THING (new version).** / **WITH A GIRL LIKE YOU** / **LOVE IS ALL AROUND**	☐	–

	Pye	Pye
1972. (7") *(7N 45147)* **EVERYTHING'S FUNNY.** / **FEELS LIKE A WOMAN**	☐	–

	Pye	Bell
1973. (7") *(7N 45244) <45405>* **LISTEN TO THE MAN.** / **QUEEN OF SORROW**	☐	☐
Oct 73. (7") *(7N 45295) <45426>* **STRANGE MOVIES.** / **I'M ON FIRE**	☐	☐

	Penny Farthing	Pye
Dec 74. (7") *(PEN 861)* **GOOD VIBRATIONS.** / **PUSH IT UP TO ME**	☐	☐
May 75. (7") *(PEN 884)* **WILD THING (reggae version).** / **JENNY COME DOWN**	☐	–
Jul 75. (7") *(PEN 889)* **SUMMERTIME.** / **JENNY COME DOWN**	☐	
1975. (lp) *(PEN 543)* **TROGGS**	☐	

– I got lovin' if you want it / Good vibrations / No particular place to go / Summertime / Satisfaction / Full blooded band / Memphis Tennessee / Peggy Sue / Jenny come down / Wild thing.

Nov 75. (7") *(PEN 901)* **(I CAN'T GET NO) SATISFACTION.** / **MEMPHIS, TENNESSEE**	☐	
Jun 76. (lp) *(PELS 551)* **THE TROGGS TAPES**	☐	

– Get you tonight / We rode through the night / A different me / Downsouth to Georgia / Gonna make you / Supergirl / I'll buy you an island / Rolling stone / After the rain / Rock and roll lady / Walkin' the dog.

Jun 76. (7") *(PEN 919)* **I'LL BUY YOU AN ISLAND.** / **SUPERGIRL**	☐	–
1977. (7") *(PEN 929)* **FEELING FOR LOVE.** / **SUMMERTIME**	☐	–

	Raw	not iss.
1978. (7") *(RAW 25)* **JUST A LITTLE TOO MUCH.** / **THE TRUE TROGG TAPES**	☐	–

—— added **COLIN 'Dill' FLETCHER** – rhythm guitar

	Max's Kansas City	Basement
Mar 81. (lp) *(MKC 100)* **LIVE AT MAX'S KANSAS CITY (live)**	☐	1980

– Got love if you want it / Satisfaction / Love is all around / Feels like a woman / Strange movies / Summertime / Walking the dog / Memphis / No particular place to go / Wild thing / Gonna make you. *(cd-iss. Oct94 on 'President' += ; MKCD 1001)* – I do I do / Call me.

	New Rose	not iss.
Mar 82. (lp) *(MKC 100)* **BLACK BOTTOM** *(cd-iss. Mar85; ROSE 4CD)*	☐	–
Mar 82. (7") *(NEW 6)* **I LOVE YOU BABY.** /	☐	–

	Stage Coach	not iss.
May 82. (7") *(MAIL 38)* **BLACK BOTTOM** / **WITH YOU**	☐	–

	10-Virgin	not iss.
1984. (7") *(TEN 21)* **EVERY LITTLE THING.** / **BLACKJACK AND POKER**	☐	–

(7"pic-d+=/12"+=) (TEN T/Y 21) – With a girl like you.

—— In 1986, REG featured on SUZI QUATRO's version of 'WILD THING'.

—— **PRESLEY + BOND** recruited **PETER LUCAS** – bass / **DAVE MAGGS** – drums

	Big Wave	not iss.
Nov 89. (7"/12") *(BWR/+T 27)* **WILD THING '89.** / **FROM HOME**	☐	–

	New Rose	not iss.
May 90. (lp/cd) *(ROSE/+CD 186)* **AU**	☐	

– Always something there to remind me / Walking the dog / Wild thing / Love is all around / With a girl like you / I can't control myself / Strange movies / Maximum overdrive / The Disco Kid versus Sid Chicane / What you doing here. *(re-iss. cd Dec95 on 'Javelin'; HADCD 195)*

—— now without BOND

	Essential	Rhino
Feb 92. (7"/c-s/12"/cd-s) *(ESS CD/MC/LP 180)* **DON'T YOU KNOW.** / **NOWHERE ROAD**	☐	☐
Mar 92. (cd/c/lp) *(ESS CD/MC/LP 180)* **ANTHENS ANDOVER**	☐	☐

– Crazy Annie / Together / Tuned into love / Deja vu / Nowhere road / Dust bowl / I'm in control / Don't you know / What's your game / Suspicious / Hot stuff. *(cd re-iss. Aug96; same)*

	Lifetime	not iss.
Nov 92. (7"/c-s; by TROGS featuring OLIVER REED & HURRICANE HIGGINS) *(LIF/+C 37)* **WILD THING.** / **('A'mix)**	☐	–

(12"+=/cd-s+=) (LIF T/CD 37) – ('A'original). *(re-is.Oct94; same)*

	Weekend	not iss.
Oct 93. (7"/c-s/cd-s; TROGGS featuring WOLF) **WILD THING.** / **(other by EDWIN STARR & SHADOW)**	69	–

– compilations, etc. –

1966. (7"ep) *Page One; (POE 001)* **TROGGS TOPS**	☐	–
1967. (7"ep) *Page One; (POE 002)* **TROGGS TOPS VOLUME 2**	☐	–
1969. (7") *Page One; (POF 23126)* **WILD THING.** / **I CAN'T CONTROL MYSELF**	☐	–
Nov 75. (lp) *D.J.M.; (DJML 26047)* **WITH A GIRL LIKE YOU**	☐	–
1976. (d-lp) *Sire; <SASH 3714-2>* **VINTAGE YEARS**	–	–
Jul 76. (lp) *D.J.M.; (44314)* **THE (ORIGINAL) TROGGS TAPES**	☐	–
Nov 81. (c) *D.J.M.; (TWO 410)* **VOLUME 1 / VOLUME 2**	☐	–
Jul 82. (7") *Old Gold; (OG 9001)* **WILD THING.** / **WITH A GIRL LIKE YOU** *(re-iss. Nov85 & Jun88; same)*	☐	–
Jul 82. (7") *Old Gold; (OG 9024)* **I CAN'T CONTROL MYSELF.** / **GIVE IT TO ME**	☐	–
Jul 82. (7") *Old Gold; (OG 9038)* **LOVE IS ALL AROUND.** / **ANY WAY THAT YOU WANT ME**	☐	–
Jan 84. (7"/12") *D.J.M.; (DJS/DJR 6)* **WILD THING.** / **I CAN'T CONTROL MYSELF** / **LOVE IS ALL AROUND**	☐	–
Aug 84. (lp) *Action Replay; (ARLP 103)* **ROCK IT BABY**	☐	–

Nov 84. (lp/c) *Astan; (2/4 0046)* **GOLDEN HITS . . . TROGGS**	–	–
Feb 85. (lp/c) *Rhino; <RN LP/C 118>* **THE BEST OF THE TROGGS** *(UK-iss.1988 on 'Big Time' lp/c/cd; 221/211/261 526)*	–	–
Apr 85. (c) *Autograph; (ASK 779)* **HOT DAYS**		–
Aug 87. (lp) *Konnexion; (KOMA 788021)* **WILD THINGS** *(re-iss. Jul89 on 'See For Miles' lp/cd; SEE/+CD 256)*	☐	–
Aug 87. (lp/c) *Masters; (MA/+MC 928487)* **GREATEST HITS**	☐	–
Oct 88. (lp/c) *BR Music; (BR LP/MC 03)* **GREATEST HITS**	☐	–
Dec 88. (cd) *Spectrum; (SPEC 85031)* **14 GREATEST HITS**	☐	–
Oct 89. (lp/c/cd; shared with DAVE DEE, DOZY, BEAKY, MICK & TICH) *Platinum; (PLA T/C/CD 3908)* **DOUBLE HITS COLLECTION**	☐	–
Oct 90. (cd) *O.B.J.; (OR 0112)* **WILD THING** *(re-iss. Jun96 on 'Music De Luxe'; MSCD 030)*	☐	–
May 91. (cd/c) *Fontana; (848 164-2/-4)* **HIT SINGLE ANTHOLOGY**	☐	–

—— In 1991, WILD THING was re-issued on 'Fontana'.

May 92. (cd-ep) *Old Gold; (OG 6164)* **WILD THING** / **WITH A GIRL LIKE YOU** / **I CAN'T CONTROL MYSELF**	☐	–
Feb 93. (3xcd-box) *Fontana; (514 423-2)* **ARCHEOLOGY (1967-1977)**	☐	–
Nov 93. (cd) *Fat Boy;* **THE VERY BEST OF THE TROGGS**	☐	–
Mar 94. (cd) *Charly; (CDCD 1147)* **WILD THING**	☐	–
Jul 94. (cd/c) *Polygram TV; (522 739-2/-4)* **GREATEST HITS**	27	–
Aug 94. (cd) *Wisepack; (LECD 074)* **LEGENDS IN MUSIC**	☐	–
Feb 95. (cd) *B.A.M.; (KLMCD 030)* **PEARLS OF THE PAST**	☐	–
Apr 95. (cd/c) *Muskateer; (MU 5/4 022)* **GREATEST HITS – WILD THING**	☐	–
Jul 95. (cd) *Summit;* **THE BEST OF THE TROGGS**	☐	–
Aug 95. (cd/c) *Spectrum; (551045-2/-4)* **LOVE IS ALL AROUND** *(cd re-iss. Apr97 on 'Music'; CD 6065)*	☐	–
Sep 95. (cd/c) *Hallmark;* **THEIR GREATEST HITS**	☐	–
Jun 96. (cd/c) *Music Club; (MC CD/TC 242)* **ATHENS GEORGIA AND BEYOND**	☐	–
Nov 96. (cd) *See For Miles; (SEECD 453)* **THE E.P. COLLECTION**	☐	–
Feb 97. (cd) *Beat Goes On; (BGOCD 340)* **FROM NOWHERE / TROGGLODYNAMITE**	☐	–
Apr 97. (cd/c) *Prism; (PLA TCD/C 203)* **WILD THING**	☐	–
Apr 97. (cd) *Beat Goes On; (BGOCD 343)* **CELLOPHANE / MIXED BAG**	☐	–
Apr 97. (cd) *Prestige; (CDSGP 0337)* **ALL THE HITS PLUS MORE**	☐	–

Robin TROWER

Born: 9 Mar'45, London, England. After an initial period with 60's outfit The PARAMOUNTS, who subsequently metamorphosed into PROCOL HARUM. He had been an integral part of this rock act since the 'HOMBURG' hit single, staying for five albums, 'PROCOL HARUM' (1967), 'SHINE ON BRIGHTLY' (1968), 'A SALTY DOG' (1969), 'HOME' (1970) and 'BROKEN BARRICADES' (1971), before the now HENDRIX-inspired TROWER set up his own band, JUDE. This deeply blues-rooted short-lived supergroup featured FRANKIE MILLER on husky vox, CLIVE BUNKER (ex-JETHRO TULL) on drums and JAMES DEWAR (ex-STONE THE CROWS) on bass. The latter stayed with TROWER when the guitarist launched his solo career after re-signing to 'Chrysalis' (incidentally, also the home of PROCOL HARUM) in 1972. A debut album, 'TWICE REMOVED FROM YESTERDAY', appeared the following year and featuring REG ISADORE on drums plus DEWAR on bass and soulful vocals!, TROWER (face-contortionist extraordinaire) nearly having his first solo breakthrough into the US Top 100. 1974's 'BRIDGE OF SIGHS' made up for it tenfold, this and his 1975 set, 'FOR EARTH BELOW' (1975) both cracking the US Top 10. ISADORE had been replaced on the latter by former SLY & THE FAMILY STONE man, BILL LORDAN and a live set in 1976 repeated the same feat. TROWER and his band continued to gain further album chart experience, sets such as 'LONG MISTY DAYS' (1976), 'IN CITY DREAMS' (1977), 'CARAVAN TO MIDNIGHT' (1978) and 'VICTIMS OF THE FURY' (1980), all making the US Top 40 (also selling moderately well in Britain). In 1981, TROWER and LORDAN teamed up with JACK BRUCE (ex-CREAM), delivering yet another success story, 'B.L.T.', while the following year's 'TRUCE' was strictly a BRUCE / TROWER effort. The rest of 80's plodded on a bit for the man with the souped-up Fender Stratocaster, a change of labels to 'GNP Crescendo' in '86, gave him his last US Top 100 appearance with his umpteenth set, 'PASSION'. Another shift two years later, this time to 'Atlantic' was not so fruitful, albums 'TAKE WHAT YOU NEED' and 'IN THE LINE OF FIRE' (1990) for the TROWER or blues connoisseur only. More recently, TROWER, who had rejoined PROCOL HARUM for a reunion set, 'THE PRODIGAL STRANGER' in 1991/92, made two albums for UK 'Demon' records, '20th CENTURY BLUES' (1994) and 'SOMEDAY BLUES' (1997).
• **Songwriters:** Mostly TROWER-DEWAR compositions, except; MAN OF THE WORLD (Fleetwood Mac) / ROCK ME BABY (B.B. King) / I CAN'T WAIT MUCH LONGER (Frankie Miller) / FURTHER ON UP THE ROAD (BB King) / SAILING (Sutherland Brothers) / RECONSIDER BABY (Lowell Folsom) / etc.

Album rating: TWICE REMOVED FROM YESTERDAY (*6) / BRIDGE OF SIGHS (*7) / FOR EARTH BELOW (*6) / ROBIN TROWER LIVE! (*7) / LONG MISTY DAYS (*5) / IN CITY DREAMS (*4) / CARAVAN TO MIDNIGHT (*4) / VICTIMS OF THE FURY (*5) / B.L.T. (*5; as B.L.T.) / TRUCE with Jack Bruce (*4) / BACK IT UP (*5) / BEYOND THE MIST (*5) / PASSION (*5) / PORTFOLIO compilation (*7) / TAKE WHAT YOU NEED (*5) / IN THE LINE OF FIRE (*4) / 20th CENTURY BLUES (*5) / SOMEDAY BLUES (*4)

ROBIN TROWER – guitar (ex-JUDE, ex-PROCOL HARUM) / **JAMES DEWAR** (b.12 Oct'46, Glasgow, Scotland) – vocals, bass (ex-JUDE, ex-STONE THE CROWS) / **REG ISADORE** (b. West Indies) – drums (ex-QUIVER)

			Chrysalis	Chrysalis

Mar 73. (lp/c) (<CHR/ZCHR 1039>) **TWICE REMOVED FROM YESTERDAY**
– I can't wait much longer / Daydream / Hannah / Man of the world / I can't stand it / Rock me baby / Twice removed from yesterday / Sinner's song / Ballerina.

Mar 73. (7") (CHS 2009) **MAN OF THE WORLD. / TAKE A FAST TRAIN**

Mar 74. (7") <> **TOO ROLLING STONED. / MAN OF THE WORLD** – –

Apr 74. (lp/c) (<CHR/ZCHR 1057>) **BRIDGE OF SIGHS** 7
– Day of the eagle / Bridge of sighs / In this place / The fool and me / Too rolling stoned / About to begin / Lady love / Little bit of sympathy. (re-iss. Jan82; same) (cd-iss. Mar94; CD25CR 15)

May 74. (7") (CHS 2046) **TOO ROLLING STONED. / LADY LOVE** –

— **BILL LORDAN** – drums (ex-SLY & THE FAMILY STONE) repl. REG to HUMMINGBIRD

Feb 75. (lp/c) (<CHR/ZCHR 1073>) **FOR EARTH BELOW** 26 5
– Shame the devil / It's only money / Confessin' midnight / Fine day / Alethea / A tale untold / Gonna be more suspicious / For Earth below.

Mar 76. (lp/c) (<CHR/ZCHR 1089>) **ROBIN TROWER LIVE!** (live) 15 10
– Too rolling stoned / Daydream / Rock me baby / Lady love / I can't wait much longer / Alethea / Little bit of sympathy.

Oct 76. (lp/c) (<CHR/ZCHR 1107>) **LONG MISTY DAYS** 31 24
– Some rain falls / Long misty days / Hold me / Caledonia / Pride / Sailing / S.M.O. / I can't live without you / Messin' the blues.

Nov 76. (7") (CHS 2124) **CALEDONIA. / MESSIN' THE BLUES** 82

— added **RUSTEE ALLEN** – bass (ex-SLY & THE FAMILY STONE)

Sep 77. (lp/c) (<CHR/ZCHR 1148>) **IN CITY DREAMS** 58 25
– Somebody calling / Sweet wine of love / Bluebird / Falling star / Further up the road / Smile / Little girl / Love's gonna bring you round / In city dreams.

— added **PAULHINO DACOSTA** – percussion

Aug 78. (lp/c) (<CHR/ZCHR 1189>) **CARAVAN TO MIDNIGHT** 37
– My love (burning love) / Caravan to midnight / I'm out to get you / Lost in love / Fool / It's for you / Birthday boy / King of the dance / Sail on.

Sep 78. (7",7"red) (CHS 2247) **IT'S FOR YOU. / MY LOVE (BURNING LOVE) / IN CITY DREAMS**

Jan 79. (7") (CHS 2256) **IT'S FOR YOU. / MY LOVE (BURNING LOVE)**

— reverted to the trio of the mid-70's; (**TROWER, DEWAR + LORDAN**)

Jan 80. (7") (CHS 2402) **VICTIMS OF THE FURY. / ONE IN A MILLION**

Jan 80. (lp/c) (<CHR/ZCHR 1215>) **VICTIMS OF THE FURY** 61 34
– Jack and Jill / Roads to freedom / Victims of the fury / The ring / Only time / Into the flame / The shout / Madhouse / Ready for the taking / Fly low.

Apr 80. (7") (CHS 2423) **JACK AND JILL. / THE SHOUT**

— **JACK BRUCE** (b.14 May'43, Glasgow, Scotland) – vocals, bass (ex-CREAM, ex-JOHN MAYALL'S BLUESBREAKERS, ex-Solo artist) repl. DEWAR

Feb 81. (lp/c; as B.L.T.) (<CHR 1324>) **B.L.T.** 37
– Into money / What it is / Won't let you down / No island lost / It's too late / Life on earth / Once the bird have flown / Carmen / Feel the heat / End game.

Feb 81. (7"; as B.L.T.) (CHS 2497) **WHAT IT IS. / INTO MONEY**

— trimmed to a duo plus drummer **REG ISADORE**

Jan 82. (lp/c; by JACK BRUCE & ROBIN TROWER)
(<CHR/ZCHR 1352>) **TRUCE**
– Gonna shut you down / Gone too far / Thin ice / The last train to the stars / Take good care of yourself / Fall in love / Fat gut / Shadows touching / Little boy lost.

ROBIN TROWER

— went solo again, augmented by **DEWAR / DAVE BRONZE** – bass / **BOBBY CLOUTER + ALAN CLARKE** – drums

Sep 83. (lp/c) (<CHR/ZCHR 1420>) **BACK IT UP**
– Back it up / River / Black to red / Benny dancer / Time is short / Islands / None but the brave / Captain midnight / Settling the score.

		Music For Nations	Passport

Jun 85. (lp/c) (MFN/TMFN 51) **BEYOND THE MIST**
– The last time / Keeping a secret / The voice (live) / Beyond the mist (live) / Time is short (live) / Back it up (live) / Bridge of sighs (live).

— still retained **BRONZE**, and also with **DAVEY PATTISON** – vox (ex-GAMMA) / **PETE THOMPSON** – drums

		P.R.T.	GNP Cres..

Feb 87. (lp/c/cd) (PRTN/ZCN/PRTCD 6563) <GNPD 2187> **PASSION** 100 Dec86
– Caroline / Secret doors / If forever / Won't even think about you / Passion / No time / Night / Bad time / One more world. (cd-iss. GNPD 2187)

— retained **PATTISON**

		Atlantic	Atlantic

Jun 88. (lp/c/cd) (781 838-1/-4/-2) <81838> **TAKE WHAT YOU NEED** May88
– Tear it up / Take what you need (from me) / Love attack / I want you home / Shattered / Over you / Careless / Second time / Love won't wait forever.

— now with **PATTISON** – vox / **JOHN REGAN** – bass / **AL FRITSCH + PEPPY CASTRO** – backing vocals / **BOBBY MAYO + MATT NOBLE** – keyboards / **TONY BEARD** – drums

Mar 90. (cd/c/lp) <782 000-2/-4/-1> **IN THE LINE OF FIRE** –
– Sea of love / Under the gun / Turn the volume up / Natural fact / If you really want to find love / Every body's watching you / Isn't it time / (I would) Still be here for you / All that I want / (Let's) Turn this fight into a brawl / Climb above the rooftops.

— ROBIN then re-joined the reformed PROCOL HARUM in 1991

— now w/ **LIVINGSTONE BROWNE** – bass / **CLIVE MAYUYU** – drums

		Demon	V-12

Nov 94. (cd/c) (FIEND CD/C 753) **20th CENTURY BLUES**
– 20th century blues / Prisoner of love / Precious gift / Waiting up a storm / Extermination blues / Step into the dark / Rise up like the Sun / Secret place / Chase the bone / Promise you the stars / Don't lose faith in tomorrow / Reconsider baby.

Jun 97. (cd) (FIENDCD 931) **SOMEDAY BLUES**
– Next in line / Feel so bad / Someday blues / Crossroads / I want you to love me / Inside out / Shining through / Looking for a true love / Extermination blues / Sweet little angel.

– compilations, etc. –

Jul 87. (d-lp/c)(cd) Chrysalis; (CNW/ZCNW 3)(MPCD 1600) **PORTFOLIO**
– Bridge of sighs / Too rolling stoned / For Earth below / Caravan to midnight / Day of the eagle / Shame the Devil / Fine day / Daydream (live) / Lady Love (live) / Alethea (live) / Caledonia (live) / Messin' the blues / Gonna shut you down / Thin ice / Benny dancer. (re-iss. cd Mar93; same)

Aug 91. (cd/c/d-lp) Castle; (CCS CD/MC/LP 291) **THE ROBIN TROWER COLLECTION** (live) –

Apr 92. (cd) Windsong; (WINCD 013) **BBC RADIO 1 LIVE IN CONCERT** – –

May 94. (cd) Connoisseur; (VSOPCD 197) **ANTHOLOGY** –

Feb 97. (cd) Beat Goes On; (BGOCD 339) **TWICE REMOVED FROM YESTERDAY / BRIDGE OF SIGHS** –

Mar 97. (cd) Beat Goes On; (BGOCD 347) **FOR EARTH BELOW / ROBIN TROWER LIVE!** –

Apr 97. (cd) Beat Goes On; (BGOCD 349) **LONG MISTY DAYS / IN CITY DREAMS** –

May 97. (cd) Beat Goes On; (BGOCD 352) **CARAVAN TO MIDNIGHT / VICTIMS OF THE FURY** –

TUBES

Formed: Phoenix, Arizona, USA ... 1972 by BILL SPOONER, VINCE WELNICK and ex-drama student FEE WAYBILL, who moved the outfit to the Bay Area, San Francisco, the line-up completed by RICK ANDERSON, MICHAEL COTTEN, ROGER STEEN, PRAIRIE PRINCE and REG STYLES. Coming on like a perverted, pseudo-punk precursor to MEAT LOAF's theatrical overload, the group became infamous for their garish shows which placed scantily clad ladies against such unsavoury stage characters as Dr. Strangekiss and Quay Lude. Signed to 'A&M', their debut single was the legendary 'WHITE PUNKS ON DOPE', a UK Top 30 hit some three years later when Britain was in the grip of three-chord fever. The accompanying AL KOOPER-produced, eponymous debut album narrowly missed the US Top 100, while follow-up, 'YOUNG AND RICH' (produced by KEN SCOTT), broke them into the US Top 50 in 1976. But the music often took second place to the theatrics and in 1979, obviously bored with the limitations of the genre, swapped anthemic punk/new wave for easier going pop/rock on that years' TODD RUNDGREN-produced 'REMOTE CONTROL' album. A proposed 1980 set, 'SUFFER FOR SOUND', was shelved by 'A&M' prior to the band being dropped. Inking a new deal with 'Capitol', the group moved even further towards the mainstream with 'THE COMPLETION BACKWARD PRINCIPLE' (1981), an album which spawed a one-off Top 10 hit in 'SHE'S A BEAUTY'. After a final couple of albums, 'OUTSIDE INSIDE' (1983) and 'LOVE BOMB' (1986), The TUBES realised the joke had run its course and packed it in. Having already released a solo set, 'READ MY LIPS' (1984), WAYBILL went on to write material for RICHARD MARX (!), while SPOONER and WELNICK subsequently went on to work with Bay Area veterans, The GRATEFUL DEAD. • **Songwriters:** WAYBILL penned except I SAW HER STANDING THERE (Beatles) / etc. • **Trivia:** In 1980, they undertook a cameo performance in the film, 'Xanadu', soundtrack courtesy of ELECTRIC LIGHT ORCHESTRA and OLIVIA NEWTON-JOHN.

Album rating: THE TUBES (*5) / YOUNG AND RICH (*6) / NOW (5) / WHAT DO YOU WANT FROM LIVE (*5) / REMOTE CONTROL / THE COMPLETION BACKWARD PRINCIPLE (*6) / T.R.A.S.H. (TUBES RARITIES AND SMASH HITS) compilation (*7) / OUTSIDE INSIDE (*5) / LOVE BOMB (*4) / THE BEST OF THE TUBES compilation / GENIUS OF AMERICA (*3) / Fee Waybill: READ MY LIPS (*3)

FEE WAYBILL (b. JOHN WALDO, 17 Sep'50, Omaha, Nebraska) – vocals / **BILL 'Sputnik' SPOONER** (b.16 Apr'49) – guitar / **VINCE WELNICK** (b.21 Feb'51) – keyboards / **RICK ANDERSON** (b. 1 Aug'47, St. Paul, Minnesota) – bass / **MICHAEL COTTEN** (b.25 Jan'50, Kansas City, Missouri) – synthesizer / **ROGER STEEN** (b.13 Nov'49, Pipestone, Minnesota) – guitar / **PRAIRIE PRINCE** (b. 7 May'50, Charlotte, New Connecticut) – drums / **REG STYLES** (b. 3 Mar'50) – vocals, guitar

		A&M	A&M

Jul 75. (7") <1733> **WHITE PUNKS ON DOPE. / (part 2)** –

Jul 75. (lp/c) (AMLH/CAM 64534) <4534> **THE TUBES**
– Up from the deep / Haloes / Space baby / Malaguena Salerosa / Mondo bondage / What do you want from life / Boy crazy / White punks on dope. (re-iss. May83 on 'Fame') (d-cd-iss. Dec85 on 'Mobile Fidelity', incl.next album)

Nov 75. (7") <> **WHAT DO YOU WANT FROM LIFE. / SPACE BABY** –

Jan 76. (7") (AMS 7209) **WHAT DO YOU WANT FROM LIFE. / WHITE PUNKS ON DOPE**

May 76. (lp/c) (AMLH/CAM 64580) <4580> **YOUNG AND RICH** 46
– Tubes world tour / Brighter day / Pimp / Stand up and shout / Don't touch me there / Slipped my disco / Proud to be an American / Poland whole / Madam I'm Adam / Young and rich.

Jun 76. (7") (AMS 7239) <1826> **DON'T TOUCH ME THERE. / PROUD TO BE AMERICAN** 61

Jan 77. (7") **YOUNG AND RICH. / LOVE WILL KEEP US TOGETHER** –

— added **MINGO LEWIS** – percussion

May 77. (lp/c) (AMLH/CAM 64632) <4632> **THE TUBES NOW**
– Smoke (la vie en fumer) / Hit parade / Strung out on strings / Golden boy / My head is my house (unless it rains) / God-bird-change / I'm just a mess / Cathy's clone / This town / Pound of flesh / You're no fun.

Aug 77. (7") <1956> **I'M JUST A MESS. / THIS TOWN** | - | |

Nov 77. (7m)(12"m) (AMS7323) **WHITE PUNKS ON DOPE. / DON'T TOUCH ME THERE / WHAT DO YOU WANT FROM LIFE** | 28 | - |

Feb 78. (d-lp/d-c) (AMLM/CLM 68460) <6003> **WHAT DO YOU WANT FROM LIVE (live)** | 38 | 82 |
– (overture) / Got yourself a deal / Show me a reason / What do you want from life / God-bird-change / Special ballet / Don't touch me there / Mondo bondage / Smoke (la vie en fumer) / Crime medley: (themes from 'Dragnet' – 'Peter Gunn' – 'Perry Mason' – 'The Untouchables') / I was a punk before you were a punk / I saw her standing there / (drum solo) / Boy crazy / You're no fun / Stand up and shout / White punks on dope. *(cd-iss. Apr97; 396003-2)*

Apr 78. (7") (AMS 7349) **SHOW ME A REASON (live). / MONDO BONDAGE (live)** | | - |

Jul 78. (7") <2037> **SHOW ME A REASON (live). / I SAW HER STANDING THERE (live)** | - | - |

Feb 79. (7")(7"cold-7 diff.) (AMS 7423,) <2120> **PRIME TIME. / NO WAY OUT** | | 34 |

May 79. (lp/c) (AMLH/CAM 64751) <4751> **REMOTE CONTROL** | 40 | 46 | Mar 79
– Turn me on / TV is king / Prime time / I want it all / No way out / Getoverture / No mercy / Only the strong survive / Be mine tonight / Love's a mystery (I don't understand) / Telecide.

May 79. (7") <2149> **LOVE'S A MYSTERY (I DON'T UNDERSTAND). / TELECIDE** | | |

Jul 79. (7")(7"yellow) (AMS 7462,) **TV IS KING. / TELECIDE** | - | - |

—— trimmed slightly when LEWIS + STYLES left.

	Capitol	Capitol

May 81. (7") <5016> **TALK TO YA LATER. / POWER TOOLS** | - | |

May 81. (7") (CL 201) **TALK TO YA LATER. / WHAT'S WRONG WITH ME** | | - |

May 81. (lp/c) (EST/TCEST 26285) <12151> **THE COMPLETION BACKWARD PRINCIPLE** | | 36 |
– Talk to ya later / Let's make some noise / Matter of pride / Mr. Hate / Attack of the fifty foot woman / Think about me / Sushi girl / Don't want to wait anymore / Power tools / Amnesia. *(re-iss. +cd.Mar91 on 'B.G.O.')*

Jul 81. (7") (CL 208) <5007> **DON'T WANT TO WAIT ANYMORE. / THINK ABOUT ME** | 60 | 35 | Jun81

Oct 81. (7") (CL 219) **SUSHI GIRL. / MR. HATE** | | |

Apr 83. (7") (CL 288) <5217> **SHE'S A BEAUTY. / WHEN YOU'RE READY TO COME** | | 10 |
(12"+=) (12CL 288) – Fantastic delusion.

May 83. (lp/c) (EST/TCEST 12260) <12260> **OUTSIDE INSIDE** | 77 | 18 | Apr83
– She's a beauty / No not again / Out of the business / The monkey time / Glass house / Wild women of Wongo / Tip of my tongue / Fantastic delusion / Drums / Theme park / Outside lookin' inside. *(cd-iss. Jul92 on 'B.G.O.')*
above feat. guests **MAURICE WHITE** (of EARTH, WIND & FIRE) + **MARTHA DAVIS** – vocals (of MOTELS)

Jul 83. (7") <5258> **TIP OF MY TONGUE. / KEYBOARD KIDS** | - | 52 |

Sep 83. (7") <5254> **THE MONKEY TIME. / SPORTS FAN** | - | 68 |

—— In 1984, WAYBILL released solo album READ MY LIPS (see further on)

Mar 85. (7") <5443> **PIECE BY PIECE. / NIGHT PEOPLE** | - | 87 |

Mar 86. (lp/c) <12381> **LOVE BOMB** | | 87 | May85
– Piece by piece / Stella / Come as you are / One good reason / Bora Bora 2000 – Love bomb / Night people / Say hey / Eyes / Muscle girls / Theme from a wooly place – Wolly bully – Theme from a summer place / For a song / Say hey (part 2) / Feel it / Night people (reprise). *(cd-iss. Aug93 on 'B.G.O.')*

—— group disbanded after above album. WAYBILL continued to write and guest on albums by RICHARD MARX (1988). WELNICK joined GRATEFUL DEAD. The TUBES re-formed in 1993; WAYBILL, STEEN, PRINCE, ANDERSON / + **GARY CAMBRA** – vocals, keyboards / **JENNIFER McFEE** + **AMY FRENCH** – vocals

	not iss.	Popular Critique

Oct 96. (cd) <12007> **GENIUS OF AMERICA** | - | - |
– Genius of America / Arms of the enemy / Say what you want / How can you live with yourself / Big brothers still watching / After all you said / Fishhouse / The fastest gun alive / I never saw it comin' / Who names the hurricanes / It's too late / Around the world.

– compilations, etc. –

Nov 81. (lp/c) A&M; (AMLH/CAM 64870) <4870> **T.R.A.S.H. (TUBES RARITIES AND SMASH HITS)** | | |
– Drivin' all night / What do you want from life / Turn me on / Slipped my disco / Mondo bondage / Love will keep us together / I'm just a mess / Only the strong survive / Don't touch me there / White punks on dope / Prime time.

Sep 85. (7") Old Gold; (OG 9545) **PRIME TIME. / ('B'by 'Styx')** | | - |

Jan 87. (7") Old Gold; **(above tracks)** | | - |
(12"+=) (OG 4013) – White punks on dope / (other by 'Styx').

Nov 86. (lp) Plastic Head; (PLASLP 006) **PRIME TIME** | | - |

Apr 93. (cd) Capitol; (C 298359) **THE BEST OF THE TUBES** | | - |

TUBEWAY ARMY (see under ⇒ NUMAN, Gary)

TUMOUR CIRCUS (see under ⇒ DEAD KENNEDYS)

(Ike &) Tina TURNER

Initiated: 1956-58, when billed as "IKE TURNER, CARLSON OLIVER & LITTLE ANN" they recorded a 1958 single, 'BOXTOP' for 'Tune Town' records. LITTLE ANN was renamed TINA TURNER the following year, although the couple weren't married until 1962(!), having conceived a child in '59. TINA was born ANNIE MAE BULLOCK, 26th November '38, Brownsville, Tennessee, USA, although she was raised in Nutbush and became a local choir singer. IKE TURNER was born on 5th November '31, Clarksville, Mississippi, USA where he became a regular DJ aged only sixteen. In 1950,

with solid session work behind him, the crack blues guitarist formed his own 5-piece outfit, IKE & THE KINGS OF RHYTHM (WILLIE WIZARD, EUGENE FOX, JACKIE BENSTON and one other). They made a couple of singles for 'Chess'; 'HEARTBROKEN AND WORRIED' / 'I'M LONESOME BABY' plus 'ROCKET 88' / 'COME BACK WHERE YOU BELONG' before signing to Sam Phillips management, the 'Sun' head honcho taking on the role of both producer and A&R man. Five years later, IKE flitted from Memphis to St. Louis where he was to strike up a working and loving partnership with TINA (after she persuaded him to let her have a go at fronting his band) and in 1960, now billed as IKE & TINA TURNER, they hit the US Top 30 with 'A FOOL IN LOVE'. As well as presenting a much feted stage show (which served to highlight both IKE's musical and choreographic skills alongside TINA's raunchy vocals and stunning appearance), the duo proceeded to notch up a string of R&B hits, even hitting the pop charts the following year with their Top 20 smash hit, 'IT'S GONNA WORK OUT FINE'. After one further major hit, things dried up until the mid-60's, when they were introduced to the legendary PHIL SPECTOR. He produced their magnus-opus, 'RIVER DEEP MOUNTAIN HIGH', a "wall of sound" soul classic, which, although a relative flop in the States, peaked at No.3 in the UK. With varying degrees of fortune, they moved from one label to another, finally scoring a massive Top 5 US hit on 'Liberty' in early '71 with an earthy cover of JOHN FOGERTY's classic 'PROUD MARY'. The enthusiastic patronage of The ROLLING STONES did much to raise their profile (the pair performed at the ill-fated Altamont gig in 1969) and they finally broke out again in 1973 when TINA's autobiographical composition, 'NUTBUSH CITY LIMITS', was a massive seller on both sides of the Atlantic. In 1974, she landed the part of 'The Acid Queen' in The WHO's rock opera, 'TOMMY', her new-found independence giving her time to reflect on her well-documented ill-treatment by IKE. In 1976, after converting to Buddhism, she finally divorced him, in effect ending not only their marriage but their lucrative musical partnership. After a time on welfare (US equivalent of the dole), she began to make tentative moves to carving out a solo career, already having released an impressive album of covers, 'ACID QUEEN', the previous year. Yet although she remained a star attraction on the live club circuit scene, she still found it hard to sell records. Until that is, 'Capitol' contracted her late in '82 following some show-stopping support slots for The 'STONES. Following the surprise international success of her Al Green cover, 'LET'S STAY TOGETHER' in late '83, the multi-million 'PRIVATE DANCER' album was rush-recorded and released in summer '84. The record included her recent Grammy winner and US No.1, 'WHAT'S LOVE GOT TO WITH IT' alongside the Top 10 title track and the Top 5 'BETTER BE GOOD TO ME, going platinum in both America and Britain. It also showcased a more sophisticated, smoother approach although TURNER's range was as impressive as ever and incredibly, she was looking better than many female stars half her age. In '85, she starred in the film 'Mad Max: Beyond The Thunderdome', receiving an award by NAACP for best actress; TURNER was also reputed to have turned down the offer of a major part in the film, 'The Color Purple'. She was now arguably the most famous female Rock & Pop singer on Earth, a claim to which the 180,000 audience attending the Rio De Janeiro January '86 concert would testify. In contrast with her continuing triumphs – TURNER went on to release further million selling 80's albums, 'BREAK EVERY RULE' (1986) and 'FOREIGN AFFAIR' (1989) – IKE was unceremoniously sentenced to a year in prison in 1988 after admitting his dealings with cocaine. The troubled history of IKE and TINA's former partnership was documented in the 1993 biopic, 'WHAT'S LOVE GOT TO DO WITH IT' (based on TINA's book), the accompanying soundtrack topping the UK charts. • **Songwriters:** IKE wrote most of the early material, but with (selective) covers intespersed I'VE BEEN LOVING YOU TOO LONG (Otis Redding) / PLEASE PLEASE PLEASE (James Brown) / COME TOGETHER (Beatles) / I WANT TO TAKE YOU HIGHER (Sly & The Family Stone) / HONKY TONK WOMAN + LET'S SPEND THE NIGHT TOGETHER + UNDER MY THUMB (Rolling Stones) / OOH POO PAH DOO (Jesse Hill) / SAVE THE LAST DANCE FOR ME (Drifters) / etc. TINA's solo covers; ACID QUEEN + I CAN SEE FOR MILES (Who) / SOMETIME WHEN WE TOUCH (Dan Hill) / THE BITCH IS BACK (Elton John) / VIVA LA MONEY (Allen Toussaint) / EARTHQUAKE AND HURRICANE (Willie Dixon) / FIRE DOWN BELOW (Bob Seger) / WHOLE LOTTA LOVE (Led Zeppelin) / FUNNY HOW TIME SLIPS AWAY (... Nelson) / BACKSTABBERS (O'Jays) / HELP! + COME TOGETHER (Beatles) / TAKE ME TO THE RIVER (Al Green) / I CAN'T STAND THE RAIN (Ann Peebles) / TONIGHT I'LL BE STAYING HERE WITH YOU (Bob Dylan) / PRIVATE DANCER (Mark Knopfler) / WHAT'S LOVE GOT TO DO WITH IT? (Terry Britten, her co-producer & Graham Lyle; ex-Gallagher & Lyle) / ADDICTED TO LOVE (Robert Palmer) / IN THE MIDNIGHT HOUR (Wilson Pickett) / STEAMY WINDOWS (Tony Joe White) / IT TAKE TWO (Marvin Gaye & Tammi Terrell) / WHY MUST WE WAIT UNTIL TONIGHT (Bryan Adams – Mutt Lange) / GOLDEN EYE (U2) / etc. • **Trivia:** In the 60's, The IKETTES also had US hits with I'M BLUE (THE GONG-GONG SONG) (No.19, Feb62) / PEACHES'N'CREAM (No.36, Apr65). In 1981, TINA appeared on BEF's (HEAVEN 17) various vocalists album 'MUSIC OF QUALITY ... ' re-actifying The Temptations number BALL OF CONFUSION.

Album rating: PROUD MARY: BEST OF IKE & TINA TURNER (best CD compilation; *7) /Tina Turner: TINA TURNS THE COUNTRY ON (*4) / ACID QUEEN (*5) / ROUGH (*4) / LOVE EXPLOSION (*4) / PRIVATE DANCER (*7) / BREAK EVERY RULE (*6) / TINA LIVE IN EUROPE (*4) / FOREIGN AFFAIR (*6) / SIMPLY THE BEST compilation (*8) / WHAT'S LOVE GOT TO DO WITH IT soundtrack (*6) / WILDEST DREAMS (*6) / TWENTY FOUR SEVEN (*5)

IKE & TINA TURNER

IKE TURNER – guitar, vocals / **TINA TURNER** – vocals plus sessioners & singing group The IKETTES (aka **P.P.ARNOLD, MERRY CLAYTON & BONNIE BRAMLETT** and loads more at various times).

			London	Sue	
Nov 60.	(7") *(HLU 9226)* <730> **A FOOL IN LOVE. / THE WAY YOU LOVE ME**			27	Aug 60
Dec 60.	(7") <735> **I IDOLISE YOU. / LETTER FROM TINA**		-	82	
1961.	(7") **I'M JEALOUS. / YOU'RE MY BABY**			-	
1961.	(lp) <2001> **THE SOUL OF IKE & TINA TURNER**			-	

– I'm jealous / I idolize you / If / Letter from Tina / You can't love two / I had a motion / A fool in love / Sleepless / Chances are / You're my baby / The way you love me. (UK-iss.Apr84 on 'Kent')

			London	Sue	
Oct 61.	(7") *(HL 94510)* <749> **IT'S GONNA WORK OUT FINE. / WON'T YOU FORGIVE ME**		-	14	Jul 61
Nov 61.	(7") <753> **POOR FOOL. / YOU CAN'T BLAME ME**		-	38	
1962.	(lp) <2005> **DON'T PLAY ME CHEAP**				

– Wake up / I made a promise up above / Desire / Those ways / Mamma tell him / Pretend / Don't play me cheap / The real me / Forever mine / No amending / Love letters / My everything to me.

				Sue	
Mar 62.	(7") <757> **TRA LA LA LA LA. / PUPPY LOVE**			-	
Jun 62.	(7") <765> **YOU SHOULD'VE TREATED ME RIGHT. / SLEEPLESS**			89	
1962.	(lp) <2007> **IT'S GONNA WORK OUT FINE**				

– Gonna find me a substitute / Mojo queen / Kinda strange / Why should I / Tinarro / I'm gonna cut you loose / Foolish / It's gonna work out fine / I'm fallin' in love / This man's crazy / Good good lovin' / The rooster / Steel guitar rag / Trackdown twist / Going home.

			Sue	Kent
Nov 62.	(7") **I IDOLIZE YOU. / TINA'S DILEMMA**		-	
1963.	(7") **MIND IN A WHIRL. / THE ARGUMENT**		-	
1963.	(7") **PLEASE DON'T HURT ME. / WORRIED AND HURTIN' INSIDE**		-	
1963.	(7") **DON'T PLAY ME CHEAP. / WAKE UP**		-	
Feb 64.	(7"ep) *(IEP 706)* **THE SOUL OF IKE & TINA TURNER**			-
Aug 64.	(7") *(SR 322)* **THE ARGUMENT. / POOR FOOL**			-
Nov 64.	(7") *(SR 350)* <402> **I CAN'T BE BELIEVE WHAT YOU SAY (FOR SEEING WHAT YOU DO). / MY BABY NOW**			95	Sep 64
Nov 64.	(lp) <> **IKE & TINA TURNER REVUE!!! (live)**			

– Please, please, please / Feel so good / The love of my man / Think / Drown in my own tears / I love the way you love / Your precious love / All in my mind / I can't believe what you say. (UK-iss.Jul66 on 'Ember') (re-iss. Dec72 on 'New World') (cd-iss. Jul93 on 'Kent')

				Sue	
May 65.	(7") *(SR 376)* **PLEASE PLEASE PLEASE. / AM I A FOOL IN LOVE**			-	

—— They had already signed to . . .

			Warners	Warners	
Jan 65.	(7") *(WB 153)* **FINGER POPPIN'. / OOH POO PAH DOO**				
Jan 65.	(7"ep) *(WEP 619)* **THE IKE & TINA TURNER SHOW (live)**				
Apr 65.	(lp) *(W 1579)* <1579> **LIVE! THE IKE & TINA TURNER SHOW (live)**				Feb 65

– Finger poppin' / Down in the valley / Good times / You are my sunshine / Good time tonight / Twist and shout / Something's got a hold on me / I know (you don't want me no more) / (Tight pants) High heel sneakers / My man he's a loving man / I can't stop loving you / Tell the truth. *(re-iss. Jul66) (re-iss. May70 on 'Valient') (cd-iss. Apr85 on 'Edsel')*

Jan 66.	(7"ep) *(WEP 620)* **SOMEBODY NEEDS YOU**	

—— Warners continued to issue material after 1966 success and new dealings . . .

			Warners	Warners
Jul 66.	(7") *(WB 5753)* **TELL HER I'M NOT HOME. / FINGER POPPIN'**		48	
Nov 66.	(7") *(WB 5766)* **SOMEBODY (SOMEWHERE) NEEDS YOU. / JUST TO BE WITH YOU**			
Feb 67.	(lp) *(WB 5904)* <1568> **THE IKE & TINA TURNER SHOW VOL.II (live)**			

– Shake a tail feather / You must believe in me / Ooh poo pah doo / Early in the morning / All I can do is cry / Somebody somewhere needs you / Keep on pushing / It's all over / You're no good / Fool for you.

—— Signed to different labels at same time . . .

			H.M.V.	Tangerine
Aug 66.	(7") *(POP 1544)* **ANYTHING THAT YOU WASN'T BORN WITH. / BEAUTY IS JUST SKIN DEEP**			
Mar 67.	(7") *(POP 1583)* **I'M HOOKED. / DUST MY BROOM**			

			Stateside	Modern
Oct 66.	(7") *(SS 551)* **GOODBYE, SO LONG. / HURT IS ALL YOU GAVE ME**			

			London	Philles
May 66.	(7") *(HLU 10046)* <131> **RIVER DEEP, MOUNTAIN HIGH. / I'LL KEEP YOU HAPPY** *(re-iss. Dec 69 on 'A & M' US)*		3	88
Sep 66.	(lp) *(HAU 8396)* **RIVER DEEP MOUNTAIN HIGH**		27	-

– River deep, mountain high / I idolize you / A love like yours (don't come knockin' every day) / A fool in love / Make 'em wait / Hold on baby / I'll never need more than this / Save the last dance for me / Oh! baby (things ain't what they used to be) / Every day I have to cry / Such a fool for you / It's gonna work out fine. *(US-iss.Sep 69 on 'A&M', UK-re-iss. Mar70 on 'Mayfair-A&M', Jan 75 on 'Hamlet-A&M', Dec79 on 'M.F.P.', re-iss. +c.May 84 on 'Spot', cd-iss. 1988 on 'Mobile Fidelity') (re-iss. cd+c Sep 93 on 'Yesterday's Gold')*

			London	
Oct 66.	(7") *(HLU 10083)* **A LOVE LIKE YOURS (DON'T COME KNOCKIN' EVERY DAY). / HOLD ON BABY**		16	
Sep 67.	(7") *(HLU 10155)* **I'LL NEVER NEED MORE THAN THIS. / SAVE THE LAST DANCE FOR ME**			
Apr 68.	(7") *(HLU 10189)* **SO FINE. / SO BLUE OVER YOU**			
Aug 68.	(7") *(HLU 10217)* **WE NEED AN UNDERSTANDING. / IT SHO' AIN'T ME**			
Jan 69.	(7") *(SHU 8370)* <6000> **SO FINE**			

– Bet'cha can't kiss me (just one time) / T'ain't nobody's business / It sho' ain't me / Too hot to hold / A fool in love / Poor little fool / I better get ta steppin' / Shake a tail feather / So fine / We need an understanding / You're so fine / Poor Sam. *(cd-iss. Sep87 on 'Entertainer')*

—— Were again on the books of 2 labels.

			Minit	Minit
Apr 69.	(7") *(MLF 11016)* <32060> **I'M GONNA DO ALL I CAN (TO DO RIGHT BY MY MAN). / YOU'VE GOT TOO MANY TIES THAT BIND**			98
Jun 69.	(7") **I WISH IT WOULD RAIN. / WITH A LITTLE HELP FROM MY FRIENDS**		-	
Sep 69.	(7") **I WANNA JUMP. / TREATING US FUNKY**		-	
Oct 69.	(lp) *(40014)* <24018> **IN PERSON (live)**			Jul 69

– Everyday people / Gimme some lovin' / Sweet soul music / Son of a preacher man / I heard it through the grapevine / Respect / Medley: There was a time – African boo's / Funky street / A fool in love / Medley: The summit – All I could do was cry – Please, please, please – Baby I love you / Goodbye, so long.

			Harvest	Blue Thumb
Feb 70.	(7") *(LBF 15303)* **COME TOGETHER. / HONKY TONK WOMAN**		-	57
May 69.	(7") <101> **I'VE BEEN LOVING YOU TOO LONG. / GRUMBLING**		-	68
Jul 69.	(7") <102> **THE HUNTER. / CRAZY 'BOUT YOU BABY**		-	93
Nov 69.	(7") <104> **BOLD SOUL SISTER. / I KNOW**		-	59
May 70.	(7") *(HAR 5018)* **THE HUNTER. / BOLD SOUL SISTER**		-	
Sep 70.	(lp) *(LBS 83350)* <7637> **COME TOGETHER**			May 70

– It ain't right / Too much woman (for a henpecked man) / Unlucky creature / Young and dumb / Honky tonk woman / Come together / Why can't we be happy / Contact high / Keep on walkin' / I want to take you higher / Evil man / Doin' it.

				Blue Thumb
Sep 70.	(lp) *(SHSP 4001)* <11> **THE HUNTER**			Nov 69

– The hunter / You don't love me (yes I know) / You got me running / Bold soul sister / I smell trouble / Things I used to do / Early in the morning / You're still my baby / I know.

			Liberty	Blue Thumb
Jun 69.	(lp) *(LBS 83241)* <5> **OUTTA SEASON**			Apr 69

– I've been loving you too long / Mean old world / 3 o'clock im the morning blues / Five long years / Dust my broom / Grumbling / I am a motherless child / Crazy 'bout your baby / Reconsider baby / Honest I do / Please love me / My babe / Rock me baby. *(re-iss. Sep73 on 'Sunset')*

			Liberty	Liberty
Jul 69.	(7") *(LBF 15223)* **CRAZY ABOUT YOU BABY. / I'VE BEEN LOVIN' YOU TOO LONG**			Apr 69
Jun 70.	(7") *(LBF 15367)* <56177> **I WANT TO TAKE YOU HIGHER. / CONTACT HIGH**			34	May 70
Sep 70.	(7") **WORKIN' TOGETHER. / THE WAY YOU LOVE ME**		-	
Jan 71.	(7") *(LBF 15432)* <56216> **PROUD MARY. / FUNKIER THAN MOSQUITA'S TWEETER**			4
Feb 71.	(lp) *(LBS 83455)* <7650> **WORKIN' TOGETHER**			25	Dec 70

– Workin' together / Get you when I want you / Get back / The way you love me / You can have it / Game of love / Funkier than a mosquito's tweeter / Ooh poo pah doo / Proud Mary / Goodbye so long / Let it be. *(cd-iss. Dec95 on 'EMI Europe')*

			U.A.	U.A.
Jun 71.	(7") *(UP 35245)* <50782> **OOH POO PAH DOO. / I WANNA JUMP**			60
Sep 71.	(d-lp) *(UAD 600056)* <9953> **LIVE AT THE CARNEGIE – WHAT YOU HEAR IS WHAT YOU GET (live)**			25	Jul 71

– Piece of my heart / Everyday people / Doin' The Tina Turner / Sweet soul music / Ooh poo pah doo / Honky tonk women / A love like yours (don't come knockin' every day) / Proud Mary / I smell trouble / Ike's tune / I want to take you higher / I've been loving you too long / Respect / What you see is what you get.

Nov 71.	(7") *(UP 35310)* **I'M YOURS. / DOIN' IT**	
Jan 72.	(7") *(UP 35219)* **CRAZY ABOUT YOU BABY. / I'VE BEEN LOVIN' YOU TOO LONG**	
Mar 72.	(lp/c) *(UAG 29256)* <5530> **'NUFF SAID**		Dec 71

– I love what you do to me / Baby (what you want me to do) / Sweet flustrations / What you don't see (is better yet) / Nuff said (part 1) / Tell the truth / Pick me up (take me where your home is) / Moving into hip style – A trip child / I love baby / Can't you hear me callin' / Nuff said (part 2).

				U.A.
Feb 72.	(7") <50881> **UP IN HEAH. / DOO WAH DIDDY**		-	83
Jun 72.	(7") *(UP 35373)* **FEEL GOOD. / OUTRAGEOUS**			
Oct 72.	(lp) *(UAS 29377)* <5598> **FEEL GOOD**			Jul 72

– Chopper / Kay got laid, Joe got paid / Feel good / I like it / If you can hully gully (I can hully gully too) / Black coffee / She came in through the bathroom window / If I knew then (what I know now) / You better think of something.

Oct 72.	(7") *(UP 9)* **LET ME TOUCH YOUR MIND. / CHOPPER**	
Feb 73.	(lp) *(UAS 29423)* <5660> **LET ME TOUCH YOUR MIND**	

– Let me touch your mind / Annie had a baby / Don't believe her / I had a notion / Popcorn / Early one morning / Help him / Up on the roof / Born free / Heaven help us all

Jul 73.	(7") *(UP 35550)* **WORK ON ME. / BORN FREE**	
Oct 73.	(7") *(UP 35582)* <298> **NUTBUSH CITY LIMITS. / HELP HIM**		4	22	Sep 73
Nov 73.	(lp/c) *(UA S/C 29557)* <180> **NUTBUSH CITY LIMITS**	

– Nutbush city limits / Make me over / Drift away / That's my purpose / Fancy Annie / River deep mountain high / Get it out of your mind / Daily bread / You are my sunshine / Club Manhattan.

Dec 73.	(7") *(UP 35632)* **FANCY ANNIE. / RIVER DEEP MOUNTAIN HIGH**	
Apr 74.	(7") *(UP 35650)* **SWEET RHODE ISLAND RED. / GET IT OUT OF YOUR MIND**	
Sep 74.	(7") *(UP 35726)* <528> **SEXY IDA. / (part 2)**		65
Oct 74.	(lp/c) *(UA S/C 30040)* <707> **SWEET RHODE ISLAND RED**	

– Let me be there / Living for the city / I know / Mississippi rolling stone / Sugar hill / Sweet Rhode Island red / Ready for you baby / Smooth out the wrinkles / Doozie / Higher ground.

Jul 75.	(7") *(UP 35766)* <598> **BABY-GET IT ON. / ('A'disco version)**		88	Jun 75
Oct 75.	(7") *(UP 36028)* **DELILAH'S POWER. / THAT'S MY PURPOSE**	
Mar 77.	(lp/c) *(UA S/C 30040)* <707> **DELILAH'S POWER**	

– Delilah's power / Never been to Spain / Unhappy birthday / (You've got to) Put something into it / Nothing comes to you when you're asleep but a dream / Stormy weather (keeps rainin' all the time) / Sugar sugar / Too much for one woman / Trying to find my mind / Pick me up (take me where your home is) / Too many women / I want to take you higher.

Above album was already recorded mid 70's, before their divorce/split.

TINA TURNER

—— went solo in 1974 with session people

U.A.   U.A.

Aug 74. (lp/c) <200> **TINA TURNS THE COUNTRY ON**
– Bayou song / Help me make it through the night / Tonight I'll be staying here with you / If you love me (let me know) / He belongs to me / Don't talk now / Long long time / I'm moving on / There'll always be music / The love that lights our way.

Oct 75. (lp/c) (UN S/C 29875) <495> **ACID QUEEN**   Sep 75
– Under my thumb / Let's spend the night together / Acid queen / I can see for miles / Whole lotta love / Baby git it on / Bootsey Whitelaw / Pick me tonight / Rockin' and rollin'. (re-iss. cd+c Jul94)

Jan 76. (7") (UP 36043) **ACID QUEEN. / ROCKIN' AND ROLLIN'**

Sep 78. (lp/c) (UA G/C 30211) **ROUGH**
– Fruits of the night / The bitch is back / The woman I'm supposed to be / Viva la money / Funny how time slips away / Earthquake & hurricane / Root toot undisputable rock'n'roller / Fire down below / Sometimes when we touch / A woman in a man's world / Night time is the right time.

Feb 79. (7") (UP 36485) **ROOT TOOT UNDISPUTABLE ROCK'N'ROLLER. / FIRE DOWN BELOW**

Mar 79. (lp/c) (UA G/C 30267) **LOVE EXPLOSION**
– Love explosion / Fool for your love / Sunset on sunset / Music keeps me dancin' / I see home / Backstabbers / Just a little lovin' (early in the morning) / You get what I'm gonna get / On the radio.

Apr 79. (7") (UP 36513) **SOMETIMES WHEN WE TOUCH. / EARTHQUAKE AND HURRICANE**

Nov 79. (7") (BP 322) **BACKSTABBERS. / SUNSET ON SUNSET**

—— In May'82, she sang on BALL OF CONFUSION single by 'BEF' (aka HEAVEN 17).

Capitol   Capitol

Nov 83. (7")(12")(12"pic-d) (CL/12CL/12CLP 316) <5322> **LET'S STAY TOGETHER. / I WROTE A LETTER**   6   26 Jan 84

Feb 84. (7"/12"/7"pic-d) (CL/12CL/CLP 325) **HELP!. / ROCK'N'ROLL WIDOW**   40

May 84. (7") <5354> **WHAT'S LOVE GOT TO DO WITH IT. / ROCK'N'ROLL WIDOW**   -   1

Jun 84. (7"/'A'ext-12"/12"pic-d) (CL/12CL/12CLP 334) **WHAT'S LOVE GOT TO DO WITH IT. / DON'T RUSH THE GOOD THINGS**   3   -

Jun 84. (lp/c)(cd) (TINA/TCTINA 1)(CDP 7460412) <12330> **PRIVATE DANCER**   2   3
– I might have been queen / What's love got to do with it / Show some respect / Private dancer / I can't stand the rain / Let's stay together / Better be good to me / Steel claw / Help! / 1984. (pic-lp Apr85)

Sep 84. (7")(12")(7"sha-pic-d) (CL/12CL/CLP 338) <5387> **BETTER BE GOOD TO ME. / WHEN I WAS YOUNG**   45   5

Nov 84. (7"/12") (CL/12CL 343) <5433> **PRIVATE DANCER. / NUTBUSH CITY LIMITS**   26   7

Feb 85. (7"/12") (CL/12CL 352) **I CAN'T STAND THE RAIN. / LET'S PRETEND WE'RE MARRIED**   57

Apr 85. (7") <5461> **SHOW SOME RESPECT. / LET'S PRETEND WE'RE MARRIED**   -   37

Jun 85. (7"/12"/7"sha-pic-d) (CL/12CL/CLP 364) <5491> (CL 364) **WE DON'T NEED ANOTHER HERO (THUNDERDOME). / ('A'instrumental**   3   2

—— Above + below 45s, from her film 'Mad Max: Beyond The Thunderdome'.

Sep 85. (7"/12") (CL/12CL 376) <5518> **ONE OF THE LIVING. / (part 2)**   55   15

—— In Oct85, teamed up with BRYAN ADAMS on UK No.29 + US 19 hit IT'S ONLY LOVE

Aug 86. (7") (CL 419) <5615> **TYPICAL MALE. / DON'T TURN AROUND**   33   2
('A'extended-12"+=) (12CL 419) – ('A'dub version).
(12"++=)(12"pic-d++=) (12CLP 419,) – ('A'dance mix).

Sep 86. (lp/c)(cd) (EST/TCEST 2018)(CDP 7463232) <12530> **BREAK EVERY RULE**   2   4
– Typical male / What you get is what you see / Two people / Till the right man comes along / Afterglow / Girls / Back where you started / Break every rule / Overnight sensation / Paradise is here / I'll be thunder.

Oct 86. (7"/12") (CL/12CL 430) <5644> **TWO PEOPLE. / HAVIN' A PARTY**   43   30
(d12"+=) (12CLD 430) – Let's stay together (live) / Private dancer (live).

Feb 87. (7"/12") (CL/12CL 439) <5668> **WHAT YOU GET IS WHAT YOU SEE. / TINA TURNER MONTAGE MIX – I Can't Stand The Rain – Two People – We Don't Need Another Hero – What's Love Got To Do With It – Typical Male – Let's Stay Together**   30   13
(d7"+=) (7CLD 439) – ('A'live) / Take me to the river.

Apr 87. (7") <44003> **BREAK EVERY RULE. / TAKE ME TO THE RIVER**   -   74

May 87. (7"/7"sha-pic-d) (CL/+P 452) **BREAK EVERY RULE. / GIRLS**   43   -

Sep 87. (7"/12"/7"pic-d) (CL/12CL/CLP 459) **PARADISE IS HERE. / IN THE MIDNIGHT HOUR**

Mar 88. (7") (CL 484) **ADDICTED TO LOVE (live). / OVERNIGHT SENSATION (live)**   71
(12"+=/cd-s+=) (12CL/CDCL 484) – Legs (live).

Mar 88. (d-c/d-cd/d-lp) (TC/CD+/ESTD 1) <90126> **TINA LIVE IN EUROPE (live)**   8   86
– What you get is what you see / Break every rule / I can't stand the rain / Two people / Girls * / Typical male / Back where you started * / Better be good to me / Addicted to love / Private dancer / We don't need another hero (Thunderdome) / What's love got to do with it / Land of 1,000 dances / In the midnight hour / 634-5789 (with ROBERT CRAY) / A change is gonna come / River deep, mountain high * / Tearing us apart (with ERIC CLAPTON) / Proud Mary / Help! / Tonight + Let's dance (with DAVID BOWIE) / Overnight sensation * / It's only love (with BRYAN ADAMS) / Nutbush city limits / Paradise is here. (c+cd+= *)

Jun 88. (7"/12") (CL/12CL 495) **A CHANGE IS GONNA COME (live). / NUTBUSH CITY LIMITS (live)**

Aug 89. (7"/c-s) (CL/TCCL 543) <44442> **THE BEST. / UNDERCOVER AGENT FOR THE BLUES**   5   15
(12"+=)(cd-s+=) (12CL/CDCL 543) – Bold and reckless.

Sep 89. (c/cd/lp) (TC/CD+/ESTU 2103) <91873> **FOREIGN AFFAIR**   1   31
– Steamy windows / The best / You know who (is doing you what) / Undercover agent for the blues / Look me in the heart / Be tender with my baby / You can't stop me loving you / Ask me how I feel / Falling like rain / I don't wanna lose you / Not enough romance / Foreign affair. (re-iss. Sep94)

Oct 89. (7"/c-s) (CL/TCCL 553) **I DON'T WANNA LOSE YOU. / NOT ENOUGH ROMANCE**   8
(12"+=/12"pic-d+=) (12CL/+P 553) – Stronger than the wind.
(cd-s+=) (CDCL 553) – We don't need another hero.

Jan 90. (7") (CL 560) <44473> **STEAMY WINDOWS. / THE BEST (muscle mix)**   13   39 Nov89
('B'extended-cd-s+=) (CDCL 560) – ('A'house mix).
(12")(c-s) (12CL/TCCL 560) – ('A'side) / ('A'vocal mix) / ('A'house mix).

Jul 90. (c-s,cd-s) <>> **LOOK ME IN THE HEART / STRONGER THAN THE WIND**   -

Aug 90. (7"/c-s) (CL/TCCL 584) **LOOK ME IN THE HEART. / STEEL CLAW (live)**   31   -
(12"+=/cd-s+=) (12CL/CDCL 584) – ('A'instrumental).
('A'remixed-cd-s) (CDCLX 584) – ('A'instrumental) / Tina Turner montage mix.

Oct 90. (7"/c-s/7"pic-d) (CL/TCCL/CLP 593) **BE TENDER WITH MY HEART. / ('A'live)**   28
(12"+=/cd-s+=) (12CL/CDCL 593) – You know who is doing you know what.

—— In Nov90, she teamed up with ROD STEWART on hit single IT TAKES TWO.

Sep 91. (7"/c-s) (CL/TCCL 630) **NUTBUSH CITY LIMITS (THE 90's VERSION). / THE BEST**   23
(12"+=/cd-s+=) (12/CD CL 630) – Addicted to love (live) / Nutbush city limits ('91).

Oct 91. (cd/c/d-lp) (CD/TC+/ESTV 1) <97152> **SIMPLY THE BEST – (compilation)**   1

Nov 91. (7"/c-s) (CL/TCCL 637) **WAY OF THE WORLD. / I DON'T WANNA LOSE YOU**   13
(12"+=)(cd-s+=) (12CL/CDCL 637) – Foreign affair.

Feb 92. (7") (CL 644) **LOVE THING. / I'M A LADY**   29
(c-s+=/cd-s+=) (TC/CD CL 644) – It's only love / Private dancer (live).

May 92. (7"/c-s) (CL/TCCL 659) **I WANT YOU NEAR ME. / LET'S STAY TOGETHER**   22
(cd-s+=) (CDCL 659) – Tonight + Let's dance (live with DAVID BOWIE).
(cd-s) (CDCLX 659) – ('A'side) / Land of a 1,000 dances / In the midnight hour / 634-5789 (live with ROBERT CRAY).

Parlophone   Virgin

May 93. (7"/c-s) (R/TCR 6346) **I DON'T WANNA FIGHT. / THE BEST**   7   -
(cd-s+=) (CDR 6346) – I don't wanna lose you / What's love got to do with it.
(cd-s) (CDRS 6346) – ('A'side) / Tina's wish / ('A'urban mix).

May 93. (c-s,cd-s) <12652> **I DON'T WANNA FIGHT / TINA'S WISH**   -   9

Jun 93. (cd/c/lp) (CD/TC+/PCSD 128) <88189> **WHAT'S LOVE GOT TO DO WITH IT (soundtrack)**   1   17
– I don't wanna fight / Rock me baby / Disco inferno / Why must we wait until tonight / Stay awhile / Nutbush city limits / You know I love you / Proud Mary / A fool in love / It's gonna work out fine / Shake a tail feather / I might have been Queen / What's love got to do with it (live) / Tina's wish.
– (a selection of new recordings of old & new songs from her biopic film)

Aug 93. (7"/c-s) (R/TCR 6357) **DISCO INFERNO. / I DON'T WANNA FIGHT**   12
(12"+=/cd-s+=) (12R/CDR 6357) – ('A'mixes).

Oct 93. (7"/c-s) (R/TCR 6366) <12683> **WHY MUST WE WAIT UNTIL TONIGHT? / SHAKE A TAIL FEATHER**   16   97
(cd-s+=) (CDR 6366) – The best.
(cd-s+++) (CDRS 6366) – ('A'remix).

Nov 95. (7"/c-s) (R/TCR 0071001) **GOLDENEYE. / ('A'-Morales club mix)**   10
(cd-s+=) (CDR 0071001) – ('A'urban mix) / ('A'-A/C mix) / ('A'-urban A/C mix).

Mar 96. (c-s) (TCR 6429) **WHATEVER YOU WANT / GOLDENEYE**   23
(cd-s+=) (CDR 6429) – ('A'extended Olympic mix).
(cd-s+=) (CDRS 6429) – Unfinished sympathy.

Apr 96. (cd/c) (CD/TC+/EST 2279) <41920> **WILDEST DREAMS**   4   61 Sep96
– Missing you / In your wildest dreams / Whatever you want / Do what you do / Thief of hearts / On silent wings / Something beautiful remains / Confidential / The difference between us / All kinds of people / Unfinished symphony / Goldeneye / Dancing in my dreams.

May 96. (c-s/cd-s) (TCR/CDR 6434) **ON SILENT WINGS / PRIVATE DANCER / THE BEST / I DON'T WANNA LOSE YOU**   13
(cd-s) (CDRS 6434) – ('A'side) / Whatever you want / Do something.

Jul 96. (c-s) (TCR 6441) **MISSING YOU / WHATEVER YOU WANT**   12
(cd-s+=) (CDR 6441) – The difference between us.
(cd-s) (CDRS 6441) – ('A'side) / We don't need another hero (live) / What's love got to do with it (live).

Sep 96. (c-s,cd-s) <38553> **MISSING YOU / DO SOMETHING**   -   84

Oct 96. (c-s) (TCR 6448) **SOMETHING BEAUTIFUL REMAINS / ADDICTED TO LOVE (live)**   27
(cd-s) (CDR 6448) – ('A'side) / Steamy windows / Better be good to me.
(cd-s) (CDRS 6448) – ('A'mixes).

Dec 96. (c-s; by TINA TURNER featuring BARRY WHITE) (TCR 6451) **IN YOUR WILDEST DREAMS / WHAT'S LOVE GOT TO DO WITH IT?**   32
(cd-s+=) (CDR 6451) – Goldeneye (live) / Missing you (live).
(cd-s) (CDRS 6451) – ('A'side) / ('A'mixes).

Oct 99. (c-s; as TINA) (TCR 6529) **WHEN THE HEARTACHE IS OVER / ('A'-Metro mix)**   10
(cd-s+=) (CDR 6529) – ('A'-7th district club mix).
(cd-s) (CDRS 6529) – ('A'mix) / I can't stand the rain (live) / On silent wings (live).

Nov 99. (cd/c) *(523180-2/-4)* **TWENTY FOUR SEVEN** | 9 | |
– Whatever you need / All the woman / When the heartache is over / Absolutely nothing's changed / Talk to my heart / Don't leave me this way / Go ahead / Without you / Falling / Will be there / Twenty four seven.

– (IKE & TINA) compilations, etc. –

Nov 65. (lp) *London; (HAC 8248) / Warners; <1810>* **GREATEST HITS**
– (re-iss. Jun68 on 'Hallmark')
1965. (7") *Sue;* **TWO IS A COUPLE. / TIN TOP HOUSE** | - | |
1965. (7") *Sue;* **THE NEW BREED. / (part 2)** | - | |
1965. (7") *Sue;* **CAN'T CHANCE A BREAKUP. / STAGGER LEE & BILLY** | - | |
1966. (7") *Sue;* **DEAR JOHN. / I MADE A PROMISE UP ABOVE** | - | |
Jan 69. (7") *London; (HLU 10242)* **RIVER DEEP MOUNTAIN HIGH. / SAVE THE LAST DANCE FOR ME** | 33 | - |
Dec 69. (lp) *Warners;* **IKE & TINA'S GREATEST HITS**
– (re-iss. Feb73)
Feb 71. (7") *A&M;* **RIVER DEEP MOUNTAIN HIGH. / OH BABY** | | |
Mar 71. (lp/c) *Sunset; (SLS 50205) <5265>* **THE FANTASTIC IKE AND TINA** | | - |
Jun 71. (lp) *Capitol; (VMP 1013) <571>* **HER MAN HIS WOMAN** | | - |
– (re-iss. c Oct84 on 'Audio Fidelity')
Aug 71. (lp) *Liberty; (LBS 834689)* **LIVE IN PARIS** (live) | | - |
Feb 73. (7"m) *A&M;* **RIVER DEEP MOUNTAIN HIGH. / A LOVE LIKE YOURS / SAVE THE LAST DANCE FOR ME** | | - |
Jun 73. (lp) *Mojo; (2916020)* **PEACHES** | | - |
Oct 73. (lp) *U.A.; (UAD 60043)* **THE WORLD OF IKE AND TINA TURNER** | | - |
Mar 75. (lp) *Warners;* **STAR COLLECTION** | | - |
Apr 75. (lp/c) *ABC; (ABCL 5123) <4014>* **16 GREAT PERFORMANCES** | | - |
Oct 75. (lp) *DJM; ()* **SOULED FROM THE VAULTS** | | - |
– (re-iss. Nov76) (re-iss. Apr82 on 'Audio Fidelity')
May 76. (lp/c) *U.A.; (UA S/C 29948)* **THE VERY BEST OF IKE & TINA TURNER** | | - |
Oct 76. (lp) *Musidisc; (CV 1323)* **BLACK BEAUTY** | | - |
Jan 77. (lp) *Musidisc; (CV 1342)* **BLACK ANGEL** | | - |
1978. (lp) *U.A.; <917>* **SOUL SELLERS** | - | |
Oct 79. (lp/c) *Liberty; (LBR/TCR 1002)* **AIRWAVES** | | - |
Nov 81. (lp) *Audio Fidelity; (AFEMP 1021)* **JUKE BOX GIANTS** | | - |
Feb 82. (c) *Orchid; (ORC 001)* **TOO HOT TO HOLD** (TINA solo?) | | - |
– (re-iss. +lp Jun87 on 'Thunderb.') (cd-iss. on Feb93 on 'Charly')
Jul 82. (7") *Old Gold; (OG 9147)* **RIVER DEEP MOUNTAIN HIGH. / A LOVE LIKE YOURS** | | - |
Sep 82. (lp) *Bulldog; (BDL 1045)* **ROCK ME BABY** | | - |
– (re-iss. +c/cd.Nov84 on 'Topline')
Jun 83. (lp/c) *Happy Bird; (B 80054/MB 980054)* **SO FINE** (not the 1969 lp) | | - |
(cd-iss. Mar88 on 'Line')
Oct 83. (7"ep) *Sue;* **THE SUE SESSIONS** | | - |
– It's gonna work out fine / I idolize you / A fool in love / (1).
Mar 84. (lp/c) *Liberty; (L/TC BR 260021-1/-4)* **NICE'N'ROUGH** | | - |
Jun 84. (lp) *Musidisc; (ALB 148)* **THE GREAT ALBUM** | | - |
Sep 84. (lp/c) *Liberty; (EG 260251-1/-4)* **TOUGH ENOUGH** | | - |
May 85. (lp/c) *Liberty; <51156>* **GET BACK** | | - |
Feb 86. (lp/c) *Crown; (GEM/+C 004)* **THE DYNAMIC DUO** | | - |
Apr 86. (7"/12") *Spartan; (SP/12SP 136)* **LIVING FOR THE CITY. / PUSH** | | - |
Feb 87. (lp/c)(cd) *Kent; (KEN T/C 065)(CDKEN 065)* **THE IKE & TINA SESSIONS** | | - |
1987. (d-lp/c/cd) *Castle; (CCS LP/MC/CD 170)* **IKE & TINA TURNER COLLECTION** | | - |
Jul 87. (cd) *C5; (12001)* **A FOOL IN LOVE** | | - |
Jul 87. (cd) *Intertape; (500055)* **IKE AND TINA TURNER** | | - |
– (re-iss. May91 on 'EMI'+ Apr93 on 'Laserlight')
Feb 88. (cd) *Edsel; (ED 243)* **FINGER POPPIN' – THE WARNER BROS YEARS** | | - |
Apr 88. (lp) *Ace; (CHD 244)* **TALENT SCOUT BLUES** | | - |
Aug 88. (lp/cd) *Starburst; (SMT/CDSM 014)* **CUSSIN' CRYIN' AND CARRYIN' ON** | | - |
Oct 88. (lp/c)(cd) *Start; (STMD L/C 18)(SMCD 18)* **WHAT YOU SEE IS WHAT YOU GET** | | - |
Dec 88. (c) *Capitol; (4XLL 9191)* **PROUD MARY AND OTHER HITS** | | - |
– A fool in love / I idolize you / I'm jealous / It's gonna work out fine / Poor fool / Tra la la la la / You shoulda treated me right / Come together / Honky tonk woman / I want to take you higher / Workin' together / Proud Mary / Funkier than a mosquito's tweeter / Ooh poo pah doo / I'm yours (use me any way you wanna) / Up in heah / River deep, mountain high / Nutbush city limits / Sweet Rhode Island red / Sexy Ida (parts 1 & 2) / Baby – Get it on / Acid queen. *(re-iss. Oct91 as 'PROUD MARY – THE BEST OF IKE & TINA TURNER' on 'EMI')*
Feb 91. (cd/c/m-lp) *Connoisseur; (NSP CD/MC/LP 501)* **GOES COUNTRY** (rec.'79) | | - |
(re-iss. cd Mar95 on 'Top Masters')
Oct 92. (cd) *Repertoire; ()* **PHILADELPHIA FREEDOM**(re-Jul93) | | - |
Apr 93. (cd/c) *Tring; (GRF/MCGRF 218)* **M.R.S.** | | - |
Sep 93. (d-cd) *Laserlight; (24052)* **GOLDEN EMPIRE** | | - |
Oct 93. (cd) *Prestige; (CD/CAS SGP 058)* **IT'S ALL OVER** | | - |
Oct 93. (cd) *ZYX; ()* **LIVE AT CIRCUS KRONE** (live) | | - |
Jul 94. (cd/c) *Success; ()* **YOU GOT WHAT YOU WANTED (w/ IKE)** | | - |
Jul 94. (cd/c) *Success; ()* **ROCK ME BABY** | | - |
Jul 94. (cd/c) *Success; ()* **LIVING FOR THE CITY (w / IKE)** | | - |
Aug 94. (cd)(cd-vid) *EMI; ()* **TINA LIVE – PRIVATE DANCER TOUR** (live) | | - |
Aug 94. (cd/c) *Javelin; (HADCD 166)* **COUNTRY CLASSICS** | | - |
Nov 94. (3xcd-box) *Capitol; (CDEST 2240)* **THE COLLECTED RECORDINGS** | | - |

Feb 95. (cd) *B.A.M.; (KLMCD 019)* **PEARLS OF THE PAST** | | - |
Apr 95. (cd/c) *Muskateer; (MU 5/4 068)* **SHAKE** | | - |
Jul 95. (4xcd-box) *Low Price; ()* **THE BEST OF IKE & TINA TURNER** | | - |

——— Note that a number of IKE TURNER albums were issued after their split. The best being IKE TURNER & THE KINGS OF RHYTHM released Dec88 on 'Ace'.

TURTLES (dig out; Great Psychedelic . . .)

Shania TWAIN

Born: EILLEEN REGINA EDWARDS, 28 Aug'65, Timmins, Ontario, Canada, daughter of Clarence and Sharon Edwards. SHANIA (pronounced shu-nye-uh) has emerged through the now traditional rough route of country music (you gotta "walk the talk") into one of the hottest properties in both country and mainstream music of today. Her father deserted the family in '67 leaving her mother and elder sister to fend for themselves in the harsh reality of living in the gold mining town of Timmins. It was to be her new stepfather, Jerry Twain, an Ojibway Indian who would recognise the talent and potential of the young EILLEEN. Faced with hunger her parents saw her vocal abilities as a way of earning money for their survival; and so, an often unwilling EILLEEN would be taken to sing after hours at local hotels. Her first song was written in '75, with her influences stemming from soul, pop, country and rock – although her main inspirations were cited as KAREN CARPENTER and GLADYS KNIGHT; by '84 she was fronting her own band doing covers of CSN&Y and FOREIGNER. Life was still hard, when not performing she would help her stepfather on his forest plantation rising at 4am; EILLEEN also worked in department stores and McDonalds where she has since been made an Honorary Life Employee. In '85 she recorded a duet 'HEAVY ON THE SUNSHINE' with a local musician, TIM DENIS, on his self-titled album. She subsequently sung backing vocals on LETITIA HAVERLAND's 'Too Hot To Handle' and it was at this time she wrote 'GOD BLESS THE CHILD' which was later to be released as a US single. Sadly and tragically neither of her parents would witness what was to take place in later years after they were killed in a head-on collision in November '87. Once again EILLEEN would be the hope for the family as she worked to ensure that her younger siblings made it through college. In '89 she undertook professional training and was discovered by 'Limelight' records boss Harry Hynde. He introduced her to Paul Sabu – songwriter/producer/guitar hero and together they wrote and recorded a demo album. A year later, EILLEEN became SHANIA (an Ojibway Indian name for "I'm On The Way") and soon saw another demo resulting in a lucrative contract with 'Mercury' records. Her self-titled album followed in '93 and received good reviews from the country music press which would help it achieve gold in the US. A single 'WHAT MADE YOU SAY THAT?' reached the Top 60 in the US country charts, but it was the video that accompanied it which was to change her life. MUTT LANGE, the well-respected rock producer who had a talent for reformatting rock bands (most notably DEF LEPPARD) was highly impressed with what he saw – he also admired much that country music had to offer and had a great respect for TAMMY WYNETTE, and he was developing an interest in the new country music genre. Contacting SHANIA, they were to keep in touch by phone, writing songs over the line. The first song that was put together was to be a future single, 'HOME AIN'T WHERE THE HEART IS', followed in August '93 by the catchy 'DANCE WITH THE ONE THAT BROUGHT YOU', a Top 60 entry. In December '93, MUTT and SHANIA were married before a third US single, 'YOU GOTTA WHOLE LOTTA LOVE ON ME', was released to promote her city to city tour. By this time, SHANIA's sound was changing to become more raunchy and rocky. Her second album 'THE WOMAN IN ME' (1995) was billed as the most expensive country album ever, while reaching the Top 5 in the US charts and going on to sell millions. A single, 'WHOSE BED HAVE YOUR BOOTS BEEN UNDER?' bubbled outside the Top 10 and was followed by her first No.1 single 'ANY MAN OF MINE'. The title track went Top 20, while her fourth single from the set, '(IF YOU'RE NOT IN IT FOR LOVE) I'M OUTTA HERE!', shot to No.1 by the end of '95; yet another 'NO ONE NEEDS TO KNOW' gave her a third US chart-topper early '96. The following year, saw the release of what was to become the phenomenally successful 'COME ON OVER' which debuted at No.2 late '97. The first of eight(!) singles followed in January '98 'DON'T BE STUPID' – a catchy lightweight number – was followed by several others all of varying styles. From romantic ballad 'YOU'RE STILL THE ONE' to tongue in cheek role reversal parody 'HONEY I'M HOME' to 'FROM THIS MOMENT ON', all were massive hits. Disco solid 'THAT DON'T IMPRESS ME MUCH, the rockin 'MAN! I FEEL LIKE A WOMAN' (complete with ROBERT PALMER-type video) and 'YOU'VE GOT A WAY' – which would be the soundtrack for the film 'Notting Hill' – and 'WE'RE GONNA ROCK THIS COUNTRY' were also big smashes on both sides of the Atlantic. SHANIA is now a star!

Album rating: SHANIA TWAIN (*4) / THE WOMAN IN ME (*6) / COME ON OVER (*8)

SHANIA TWAIN – vocals / with a plethora of session people

		Mercury	Mercury
Apr 93. (cd/c) *514422-2/-4>* **SHANIA TWAIN**		-	

– What made you say that? / You lay a whole lot of love on me / Dance with the one that brought you / Still under the weather / God ain't gonna getcha for that / Got a hold on me / There goes the neighborhood / Forget me / When he leaves you / Crime of the century. *(UK cd-iss. Jul99; same as US)*

May 93. (c-s) <864992> **WHAT MADE YOU SAY THAT? / CRIME OF THE CENTURY** | - | [ ]

Aug 93. (c-s) <862346> **DANCE WITH THE ONE THAT BROUGHT YOU / STILL UNDER THE WEATHER** | - | [ ]

Nov 93. (c-s) <856806> **YOU LAY A WHOLE LOT OF LOVE ON ME / GOD AIN'T GONNA GETCHA FOR THAT** | - | [ ]

May 95. (c-s) <856448> **ANY MAN OF MINE / WHOSE BED HAVE YOUR BOOTS BEEN UNDER?** | - | 31 / 87

(cd-s+=) <856448> – ('A'dance mix).

Jul 95. (cd/c) (534899-2/-4) <522886-2/-4> **THE WOMAN IN ME** | | 5 | Mar95
– Home ain't where his heart is (anymore) / Any man of mine / Whose bed have your boots been under? / (If you're not in it for love) I'm outta here! / The woman in me (needs the man in you) / Is there life after love? / If it don't take two / You win my love / Raining on our love / Leaving is the only way out / No one needs to know / God bless the child. *(cd re-iss. Jul99; same as US)*

Jul 95. (c-s) (MERMC 433) **ANY MAN OF MINE / STILL UNDER THE WEATHER** | | -
(cd-s+=) (MERCD 433) – Raining on our love / God ain't gonna getcha for that.

Oct 95. (c-s)(cd-s) <852 206><578 786> **THE WOMAN IN ME (NEEDS THE MAN IN YOU) / (IF YOU'RE NOT IN IT FOR LOVE) I'M OUTTA HERE** | - | 90 / 74

May 96. (c-s/cd-s) <574 521-4/-2> **YOU WIN MY LOVE / HOME AIN'T WHERE THE HEART IS (ANYMORE)** | - | [ ]

Aug 96. (7"/c-s/cd-s) <852 138-7/-4/-2> **NO ONE NEEDS TO KNOW / LEAVING IS THE ONLY WAY OUT** | - | [ ]

Dec 96. (c-s) <578 748-4> **GOD BLESS THE CHILD IF IT DON'T TAKE TWO** | - | 75
(cd-s+=) <578 749-2> – (If you're not in it for love) I'm outta here! (remix) / Whose bed have your boots been under? (dance mix) / The woman in me (needs the man in you) (steel guitarless mix).

Sep 97. (7"/c-s/cd-s) <568 062-7/-4/-2> **LOVE GETS ME EVERY TIME / ('A'dance mix)** | - | 25

Nov 97. (7"/c-s/cd-s) <568 242-7/-4/-2> **DON'T BE STUPID (YOU KNOW I LOVE YOU) / IF IT DON'T TAKE TWO** | - | 40

Feb 98. (c-s) (568 493-4) <568 452-4/-2> **YOU'RE STILL THE ONE / (IF YOU'RE NOT IN IT FOR LOVE) I'M OUTTA HERE! (Mutt Lange remix)** | 10 | 2
(cd-s+=) (568 493-2) – You win my love (Mutt Lange remix) / ('A'-version).

Mar 98. (cd/c) (558 000-2/-4) <536 003-2/-4> **COME ON OVER** | 15 | 2 | Nov97
– You're still the one / When / From this moment on / Black eyes, blue tears / I won't leave you lonely / I'm holdin' on to love (to save my life) / Come on over / You've got a way / Whatever you do! don't! / Man! I feel like a woman! / Love gets me every time / Don't be stupid (you know I love you) / That don't impress me much / Honey, I'm home / If you want to touch her, ask! / Rock this country! *(re-iss. w/some remixes.May99 cd/c; 170 081-2/-4)* – hit No.1

Jun 98. (c-s) (568 840-4) **WHEN / DON'T BE STUPID (YOU KNOW I LOVE YOU)** | 18 | -
(cd-s+=) (568 841-2) – That don't impress me much.
(cd-s+=) (566 119-2) – You're still the one (Soul Solution mixes).

Nov 98. (c-s) (566 560-4) <566 450-4/-7/-2> **FROM THIS MOMENT ON / YOU'RE STILL THE ONE** | 9 | 4
(cd-s+=) (566 561-2) – You're still the one (Soul Solution dance mix).
(cd-s+=) (566 563-2) – Don't be stupid (you know I love you).

May 99. (c-s) (870 802-4) <172 118-4/-2> **THAT DON'T IMPRESS ME MUCH (dance mix) / FROM THIS MOMENT ON** | 3 | 7 | Mar99
(cd-s+=) (870 803-2) – From this moment on (dance mix) / You're still the one.
(cd-s) (870 759-2) – ('A'side) / Medley:- Home ain't where his heart is (anymore) – The woman in me (needs the man in you) – You've got a way – That don't impress me much.

Jul 99. (-) <radio cut> **YOU'VE GOT A WAY** | - | 49

Sep 99. (c-s) (172 126-4) <radio cut> **MAN! I FEEL LIKE A WOMAN! / DON'T BE STUPID (YOU KNOW I LOVE YOU)** | 3 | 23 | Apr99
(cd-s+=) (562 324-2) – Any man of mine / ('A'-country version).
(cd-s) (562 325-2) – ('A'side) / Love gets me every time (live & direct TV mix) / Any man of mine ('A'-video).

Oct 99. (-) <radio cut> **COME ON OVER** | - | 58

TWISTED SISTER (dig out; 4th edition or Great Metal . . .)

TWO MEN, A DRUM MACHINE & . . .
(see under ⇒ **FINE YOUNG CANNIBALS**)

2PAC

Born: TUPAC AMARU SHAKUR, 16 Jun'71, Brooklyn, New York, USA. The son of a Black Panther member, after a successful start to his career as a member of West Coast rap act, DIGITAL UNDERGROUND, 2PAC signed to 'Interscope' in 1991, making his solo debut with '2PACALYPSE NOW' (1992). A veritable journey into the heart of black inner city darkness, the record combined the bleak violence of gangsta with strong pro-Afro-American sentiments, as did the follow-up, 'STRICTLY 4 MY N.I.G.G.A.Z.' (1993), 2PAC almost breaking the US Top 10 with the 'I GET AROUND' single. He also had a penchant for getting on the wrong side of the law, running up an incredible string of charges including shooting two off-duty police officers, forceful sodomy (not with the police officers!) and attacking the co-director of the film, 'Menace II Society', Allen Hughes (2PAC had already made appearances in 'Juice', 'Under The Rim' and an acclaimed role in 'Poetic Justice'). While the shooting charge was dropped, 2PAC was subsequently sentenced to spend some time in prison for the sexual assault, ironically beginning his sentence while his third album, the aptly titled 'ME AGAINST THE WORLD' (1995) went to the top of the Billboard charts. The following

year, the rapper was back at No.1 in defiant form with the landmark double set, 'ALL EYEZ ON ME', answering his many critics with 'ONLY GOD CAN JUDGE ME'. The album also spawned a No.1 single in the epochal 'CALIFORNIA LOVE', an utterly compelling 70's style pimp-rolling groove singing the praises of 2PAC's beloved home state, cut in collaboration with ex-ZAPP frontman, ROGER TROUTMAN. But if 2PAC was pro-Cali, he was viciously anti-New York, or at least its rap contingency, as witnessed on the track 'HIT 'EM UP' (included on the CD single of 'HOW DO YOU WANT IT'), a ferocious litany of hate primarily directed against his one-time friend, BIGGIE SMALLS (tried to shoot him?) but also stretching to MOBB DEEP and 'Bad Boy' records, the label at the centre of the East v West feud along with DR DRE's 'Death Row'. It had to end in tears of course, and it came as little surprise when 2PAC was shot and killed in a drive-by incident (13 September, 1996). Although no-one was subsequently charged with the murder, the rapper's list of enemies was almost as big as his police charge sheet and it was probably inevitable that a man who lived so closely by the gun wouldn't live to see 30. Violence and politics aside, there's no getting around the fact that 2PAC was an immensely talented artist, having scored his third US No.1 album in a row with 'THE DON KILLUMANATI: THE 7 DAY THEORY' (1996) under the alias MAKAVELI. His status as an American cultural icon was underlined recently when a US college introduced a 2PAC course, exploring the man's life and work. Crazy? Well, certainly no crazier than the esteem afforded the Kray Twins in Britain, and besides, did they pen anything as groovy as 'CALIFORNIA LOVE' (?!).

Album rating: 2PACALYPSE NOW (*6) / STRICTLY 4 MY N.I.G.G.A.Z. (*7) / VOLUME 1 by Thug Life (*6) / ME AGAINST THE WORLD (*7) / ALL EYEZ ON ME (*7) / DON KILLUMMINATI: THE 7 DAY THEORY (*4; as Makaveli) / R U STILL DOWN (REMEMBER ME) (*5) / IN HIS OWN WORDS (*5) / GREATEST HITS compilation (*8)

TUPAC SHAKUR – vocals (with various guests, etc)

　　　　　　　　　　　　　　　　　　Interscope Interscope

Feb 92. (cd/c) <(IND/INC 91767)> **2PACALYPSE NOW** | | 64
– Young black male / Trapped / Soulja's story / I don't give a fuck / Violent / Words of wisdom / Something wicked / Crooked ass nigga / If my home calls / Brenda's got a baby / Lunatic / Rebel of the underground / Part time mutha. *(cd re-iss. Feb97; same) (cd re-iss. Mar98 on 'Jive'; CHIP 199)*

Feb 93. (cd/c) <(IND/INC 92209)> **STRICTLY 4 MY N.I.G.G.A.Z.** | | 24
– Holler if ya hear me / 2Pac's theme / Point the finga / Something 2 die 4 / Last wordz / Souljah's revenge / Peep game / Strugglin' / Guess who's back / Representin' / Keep ya head up / Strictly 4 my N.I.G.G.A.Z. / Streetz R deathrow / I get around / Papa'z song / Five deadly venomz. *(cd re-iss. Feb97; same) (cd re-iss. Mar98 on 'Jive'; CHIP 197)*

Jun 93. (c-s,cd-s) <98372> **I GET AROUND / NOTHING BUT LOVE** | - | 11
<with free c-s+=; 96036> – KEEP YA HEAD UP <hit No.12>

Apr 94. (c-s,cd-s) <98303> **PAPA'Z SONG / ('A'instrumental)** | | 87

——— 2PAC briefly set up THUG LIFE with SKYE, MOPREME, MACADOSHIS + THE RATED R

Nov 94. (cd/c; as THUG LIFE) <(6544 92360-2/-4)> **THUG LIFE VOLUME 1** | | 42
– Bury me a G / Don't get it twisted / Shit don't stop (THUG LIFE & YNV) / Pour out a little liquor / Stay true / How long will they mourn me? (THUG LIFE & NATE DOGG) / Under pressure / Street fame / Cradle to the grave / Str8 ballin'. *(cd re-iss. Feb97; IND 92360) (cd re-iss. Mar98 on 'Jive'; CHIP 198)*

Mar 95. (cd/c/lp) <(6544 92399-2/-4/-1)> **ME AGAINST THE WORLD** | | 1
– Intro / If I die 2nite / Me against the world / So many tears / Temptations / Young niggaz / Heavy in the game / Lord knows / Dear mama / It ain't easy / Can U get away / Old school / Fuck the world / Death around the corner / Outlaw. *(cd re-iss. Feb97; IND 92399) (cd re-iss. Mar98 on 'Jive'; CHIP 200)*

Jun 95. (c-s,cd-s) <95748> **SO MANY TEARS / (track by Dramacydal)** | - | 44

Aug 95. (c-s) (A 8156C) **DEAR MAMA / OLD SCHOOL** | | 9 | Mar95
(12"+=/cd-s+=) (A 8156 T/CD) – ('A'mixes).
(above on 'Atlantic' UK)

Sep 95. (12",cd-s) <98120> **TEMPTATIONS. / ME AGAINST THE WORLD** | - | 68

　　　　　　　　　　　　　　　　　　Death Row Death Row

Mar 96. (d-cd/d-c) (524249-2/-4) <524204> **ALL EYEZ ON ME** | 33 | 1 | Feb96
– Book 1:- Ambitionz az a ridah / All bout u / Skandalouz / Got my mind made up / How do u want it / 2 of Amerikaz most wanted / No more pain / Heartz of men / Life goes on / Only God can judge me / Tradin war stories / California love / I ain't mad at cha / What'z ya phone # // Book 2:- Can't c me / Shorty wanna be a thug / Holla at me / Wonda why they call U bitch / When we ride / Thug passion / Picture me rollin' / Check out time / Ratha be ya nigga / All eyez on me / Run tha streetz / Ain't hard 2 find / Heaven ain't hard 2 find.

Apr 96. (c-s; 2PAC featuring DR.DRE) (DRWMC 3) **CALIFORNIA LOVE / ('A'mix)** | 6 | -
(12"+=/cd-s+=) (12DRW/DRWCD 3) – ('A'mixes).

Jul 96. (c-s; 2PAC featuring KC and JOJO / 2PAC featuring DR.DRE and ROGER TRAUTMAN) (DRWMC 4) <854652> **HOW DO U WANT IT / CALIFORNIA LOVE** | 17 | 1 / 6
(12"+=/cd-s+=) (12DRW/DRWCD 4) – 2 of Amerikaz most wanted / Hit 'em up.

——— 2PAC was shot dead on the 13th September, 1996 (below were posthumous releases)

Nov 96. (c-s) (DRWMC 5) **I AIN'T MAD AT CHA / SKANDALOUZ** | 13 | -
(12"+=) (12DRW 5) – Got my mind made up.
(cd-s++=) (DRWCD 5) – Heartz of men.

　　　　　　　　　　Jive　　Amaru Death Row – Interscope

Nov 97. (d-cd/d-c) (CHIP/HIPC 195) <41630> **R U STILL DOWN (REMEMBER ME)** | 44 | 2
– Open fire / R U still down (remember me) / I wonder if Heaven got a ghetto / Fuck all y'all / Fake ass bitches / Hellrazor / Nothing to lose / I'm gettin' money / Lie to kick it / Crooked nigga too / Don't make enemies with me / Is it cool to fuck / Ready

4 whatever / When I get free (Souljah's revenge) / Hold on be strong / I'm losin' it / Thug style / What you won't do for love / Po' nigga blues / Thugs 4 life / Nothin' but love / 16 on death row / Let them tangs go / When I get free II / Only fear of death.

Dec 97. (c-s) *(JIVEC 446)* <42500> **I WONDER IF HEAVEN GOT A GHETTO** / ('A'mix)		21	67
(12"+=/cd-s+=) *(JIVE T/CD 446)* – ('A'mixes).			
Jun 98. (c-s) *(051851-4)* <42516> **DO FOR LOVE** / ('A'mix)		12	21 Mar98
(12"+=/cd-s+=) *(051851-6/-2)* – ('A'mixes).			
(above credited in the States to 2PAC featuring ERIC WILLIAMS)			
Jun 99. (c-s) *(052334-4/-2)* **DEAR MAMA** / (mixes)		27	-
(cd-s) *(052370-2)* – ('A'mixes).			

– compilations, etc. –

Sep 97. (cd) *Aim; (AIM 4001CD)* **1 IN 2 1 (2PAC – A TUPAC SHAKUR STORY)**			
Jun 98. (cd; as 2PAC & NOTORIOUS B.I.G.) *Cashmoneybruthas; (CMBCD 1)* **WHO SHOT YA**			
Jul 98. (c-s; 2PAC & NOTORIOUS B.I.G.) *Black Jam; (BJAM 9005)* **RUNNIN'** (rec.1995) / ('A'mixes)		15	
(12"+=/cd-s+=) *(BJAM 1205/6605)* – ('A'mixes).			
Jul 98. (cd/c) *Eagle; (EAG CD/MC 050)* **IN HIS OWN WORDS**		65	
Nov 98. (12"/c-s/cd-s) *Eagle; (EAG CS/12/XS 058)* **HAPPY HOME (mixes)**		17	
Nov 98. (d-cd/d-c/q-lp) *Jive; (052266-2/-4/-1)* / *Amaru – Death Row – Interscope; <490307>* **GREATEST HITS** (compilation)		17	3
– Trapped 2pacalypse / Brenda got a baby / Keep your head up / I get around / How long will they mourn me / Me against the world / So many tears / Temptations / Dear mama / How do you want it / All about you all / 2 of Americaz most wanted / I ain't mad at cha / Life goes on / Picture me rollin' / California love / Hit 'em up / To live and die in L.A. / Toss it up / Hail Mary / Changes / God bless the dead / Troublesome '96 / Unconditional love.			
Feb 99. (c-s) *(052283-4)* <radio cut> **CHANGES** / ('A'mix)		3	32 Nov98
(12"+=/cd-s+=) *(052283-0/-2)* – ('A'mixes).			
Sep 99. (cd; as 2PAC & The NOTORIOUS B.I.G.) *ZYX; (20531-2)* **THE HERE AFTER**			
Dec 99. (cd/d-lp; as 2PAC & THE OUTLAWZ) *Interscope; <(490417-2/-1)>* **STILL I RISE**			
– Letter to the president / Still I rise / Secrets of war / Baby don't cry (keep your head up) / As the world turns / Black Jesus / Homeboyz / Hell 4 a hustler / High speed / The good die young / Killuminati / Teardrops and closed caskets / Tattoo tears / U can be touched / Y'all don't know us. *<(clean version; 490413-2)>*			
(above will hit the charts early in 2000)			

MAKAVELI

	Interscope	Interscope
Nov 96. (cd/c) *<(IND/INC 90039)>* **THE DON KILLUMINATI: THE 7 DAY THEORY**	53	1
– (intro) – Bomb first (my second reply) / Hail Mary / Toss it up / To live & die in L.A. / Blasphemy / Life of an outlaw / Just like daddy / Krazy / White man'z world / Me and my girlfriend / Hold ya head / Against all odds. *(re-iss. Feb97 on 'Interscope' cd/c; same)*		
—— In Jan'97, 2PAC plus NOTORIOUS B.I.G., RADIO, DRAMACYDAL & STRETCH, released collaboration single, 'RUNNIN', which hit US No.84		
Apr 97. (c-s) *(INC 95529)* **TO LIVE & DIE IN L.A.** / ('A'mix)	10	
(12"+=/cd-s+=) *(INT/IND 95529)* – ('A'mixes).		
—— In Apr'97, 2PAC & SNOOP DOGGY DOGG had a combined UK No.16 hit 'WANTED DEAD OR ALIVE'. 2PAC then guested on the SCARFACE single 'Smile' which hit No.12 US.		
Aug 97. (c-s) *(INC 95521)* **TOSS IT UP** / ('A'mix)	15	
(12"+=) *(INT 95521)* – ('A'mixes).		
(cd-s+=) *(IND 95521)* – ('A'mixes).		
Feb 98. (c-s) *(INC 95575)* **HAIL MARY** / ('A'mix)	43	
(12"+=) *(INT 95575)* – ('A'mix).		
(cd-s+=) *(IND 95575)* – ('A'mixes).		

TYGERS OF PAN TANG (dig out; Great Metal . . .)

TYPE O NEGATIVE

Formed: Brooklyn, New York, USA . . .1988 by PETER STEELE (ex-CARNIVORE). One of the more compelling original bands skulking around the fringes of the metal scene, TYPE O NEGATIVE caused controversy from the off with the shocking artwork for the unambiguously titled debut album, 'SLOW, DEEP, HARD' (1991). Issued by 'Roadracer', the record's sleeve resembled a phallic symbol (talking of symbols, sex ones that is, the musclebound STEELE appeared naked in the August '95 edition of Playgirl!). A follow-up, meanwhile, 'THE ORIGIN OF THE FECES' (1992), featured a cover which left even less to the imagination, while music contained within its grooves lent the band's goth/industrial NIN-esque metal hybrid a demonic ambience. With something of a cult building around the band, 'BLOODY KISSES' (1993), became their most successful to date, while 1996's 'OCTOBER RUST' made it into the UK Top 30. In the more experimental climate of the mid 90's metal scene, TYPE O NEGATIVE have emerged from the margins to become a significant player. Autumn '97 saw the release of an EP devoted to different mixes of TYPE O's Neil Young cover, 'CINNAMON GIRL'. Select the wittily titled 'DEPRESSED MODE' mix for maximum black humour value. • **Covered:** BLACK SABBATH (Black Sabbath).

Album rating: SLOW, DEEP, HARD (*6) / THE ORIGIN OF THE FECES (*5) / BLOODY KISSES (*7) / OCTOBER RUST (*6) / WORLD COMING DOWN (*5)

PETE STEELE – vocals, bass / with unknown line-up

	Roadracer	Roadracer
May 91. (cd/lp) *<(RO 9313-2/-1)>* **SLOW, DEEP, HARD**		
– Unsuccessfully coping with the natural beauty of infidelity / Der untermensch / Xero tolerance / Prelude to agony / Glass walls of limbo (dance mix) / The misinterpretation of silence and its disastrous consequences / Gravitational constant: G = 6.67 x 10-8 cm 3 gm-1 sec-2.		

	Roadrunner	Roadrunner
Feb 92. (cd/lp) *<(RR 9006-2/-4)>* **THE ORIGIN OF THE FECES** (live)		
– I know you're fucking someone someone else / Are you afraid / Gravity / Pain / Kill you tonight / Hey Pete / Kill you tonight (reprise) / Paranoid. *(re-iss. Nov94 cd/c; same) (cd re-iss. Nov97; RR 8762-2)*		

—— line-up STEELE + JOSH SILVER – keyboards / KENNY HICKEY – guitar / JOHNNY KELLY – drums

Aug 93. (cd/c/lp) *<(RR 9100-2/-4/-1)>* **BLOODY KISSES**		
– Machine screw * / Christian woman / Black No.1 (Little Miss Scare-all) / Fay Wray come out to play * / Kill all the white people * / Summer breeze / Set me on fire / Dark side of the womb * / We hate everything * / Bloody kisses (a death in the family) / 3.0.1.F. * / Too late: Frozen / Blood & fire / Can't lose you. *(cd+=/c+= *) (lp+=)* – Suspended in dusk.		
Feb 94. (cd-s) *(RR 2378-3)* **CHRISTIAN WOMAN** / ('A'mixes) / **SUSPENDED IN DUSK**		
Aug 96. (cd-ep) **MY GIRLFRIEND'S GIRLFRIEND** / **BLACK SABBATH (from 'The Satanic Perspective')** / **BLOOD & FIRE** (remix)		
Sep 96. (cd/c/d-lp) *<(RR 8874-2/-4/-1)>* **OCTOBER RUST**	26	42
– Bad ground / Love you to death / Be my druidess / Green man / Red water (Christmas mourning) / My girlfriend's girlfriend / Die with me / Burnt flowers fallen / In praise of Bacchus / Cinnamon girl / The glorious liberation of the people's technocratic republic of Vinnland by the combined forces of the United Territories of Europa / Wolf moon (including zoanthrobe paranoia) / Haunted / ?.		
Nov 96. (cd-ep) **LOVE YOU TO DEATH (radio)** / **SUMMER BREEZE (rejected radio)** / **LOVE YOU TO DEATH (album)**	-	- mail-o
Sep 97. (cd-ep) *(RR 2270-3)* **CINNAMON GIRL (Depressed Mode mix)** / **CINNAMON GIRL (US radio mix)** / **CINNAMON GIRL (extended mix)**		
Sep 99. (cd) *<(RR 8660-2)>* **WORLD COMING DOWN**	49	39
– Skip it / White slavery / inus / Everyone I love is dead / Save the sane / Liver / World coming down / Creepy green light / Everything dies / Lung / Pyretta blaze / Hallows eve / Day tripper (medley).		
Nov 99. (cd-s) *(RR 2130-3)* **EVERYTHING DIES** / **12 BLACK RAINBOWS** / **EVERYTHING DIES (album version)**		

TYRANNOSAURUS REX (see under ⇒ BOLAN, Marc)

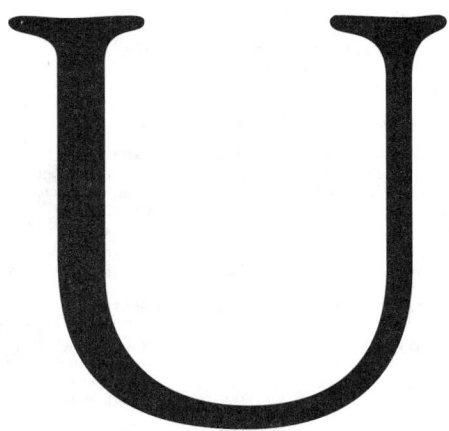

U

UB40

Formed: Mosley, Birmingham, England . . . early 1979 by ALI and ROBIN, sons of Scots folk singer, IAN CAMPBELL. The self-taught brothers built around them a multi-racial ensemble, who, due to their own jobless status and the country's unemployment figures, decided to name themselves after the dole card form, UB40. BRIAN TRAVERS, EARL FALCONER and JIM BROWN had been in their band while at Art College in 1977 and around two years later (including a lengthy stint playing in local pubs and clubs), they signed to David and Susan Virr's new label, 'Graduate'. Their protest reggae style was introduced to a wider audience as the group embarked on a prestigious tour with The PRETENDERS and 1980 saw UB40 hitting the UK Top 5 with the classic double A-side, 'FOOD FOR THOUGHT' / 'KING'. A Top 40 follow-up, 'THE EARTH DIES SCREAMING', was preceded by a Bob Lamb-produced debut album, appropriately enough titled 'SIGNING OFF' (as one does after procuring employment). In 1981, they formed their own label, 'DEP International' and recording studio, 'The Abbatoir', where they laid down the material for a second album, 'PRESENT ARMS'. The cosmopolitan reggae conglomerate continued to have massive hits throughout the 80's, including two chart topping covers, 'RED RED WINE' (from the pen of NEIL DIAMOND) and the CHRISSIE HYNDE collaboration, 'I GOT YOU BABE' (previously a 60's No.1 for SONNY & CHER). The former was taken from their album of cover versions, 'LABOUR OF LOVE' (1983) and marked their first real inroads into the lucrative US market. UB40 consolidated their position as Britain's foremost mainstream reggae act with an impressive run of hit singles and albums, continuing to translate traditional Jamaican stylings into more chart friendly pop. A temporary change in personnel was required in July 1988 when bassist FALCONER was jailed for six months on a drink driving charge. Upon his return UB40 went on to achieve further success in the 90's, their version of the ELVIS PRESLEY hit 'CAN'T HELP FALLING IN LOVE' topping the charts and a definite highlight of their equally successful long player, 'PROMISES AND LIES' (1993). ALI went solo in 1995, releasing the 'BIG LOVE' album before returning to the band for UB40's umpteenth outing, 'GUNS IN THE GHETTO' (1997). 'LABOUR OF LOVE III' was released in 1999 (same as before). • **Songwriters:** ALI penned most material except singles I THINK IT'S GOING TO RAIN TODAY (Randy Newman) / MANY RIVERS TO CROSS (Jimmy Cliff) / CHERRY OH BABY (Eric Donaldson) / PLEASE DON'T MAKE ME CRY (Junior Tucker) / SMALL AXE + SOUL REBEL (Bob Marley) / KEEP ON MOVING (Mayfield-Marley) / JOHNNY TOO BAD (Wilson, Bedford, Bailey & Crooks) / VERSION GIRL (R.Thompson aka- Dandy Livingstone) / BREAKFAST IN BED (Dusty Springfield) / HOMELY GIRL (Chi-Lites) / KINGSTON TOWN (Andy Patrick) / HERE I AM (Al Green) / THE WAY YOU DO THE THINGS YOU DO (Smokey Robinson) / HOLLY HOLY (Neil Diamond). LABOUR OF LOVE and LABOUR OF LOVE II & III were cover albums featuring some already mentioned. ALI CAMPBELL covered HAPPINESS (Stevie Wonder-Syreeta) / SOMETHIN' STUPID (hit; Frank & Nancy Sinatra) / THAT LOOK IN YOUR EYE (Starks-Grey) / YOU CAN CRY ON MY SHOULDER (Berry Gordy) / LET YOUR YEAH BE YEAH (Jimmy Cliff) / DRIVE IT HOME (Ernest Ranglin).

Album rating: SIGNING OFF (*8) / PRESENT ARMS (*7) / PRESENT ARMS IN DUB (*7) / THE SINGLES ALBUM compilation (*7) / UB44 (*6) / LABOUR OF LOVE (*8) / GEFFREY MORGAN (*7) / BAGGARIDDIM (*6) / RAT IN THE KITCHEN (*7) / CCCP: LIVE IN MOSCOW (*4) / THE BEST OF UB40 VOLUME 1 compilation (*7) / UB40 (*7) / LABOUR OF LOVE II (*6) / PROMISES AND LIES (*6) / THE BEST OF UB40 VOL.2 compilation (*7) / GUNS IN THE GHETTO (*6) / LABOUR OF LOVE III (*5) / Ali Campbell: BIG LOVE (*5)

ALI CAMPBELL (b.ALISTAIR, 15 Feb'59) – vocals, guitar / **ROBIN CAMPBELL** (b.25 Dec'54) – guitar, vocals / **ASTRO** (b. TERENCE WILSON, 24 Jun'57) – toaster/**vocals** repl. YOMI BABAYEMI / **MICHAEL VIRTUE** (b.19 Jan'57) – keyboards repl. JIMMY LYNN / **EARL FALCONER** (b.23 Jan'59) – bass / **BRIAN TRAVERS** (b. 7 Feb'59) – saxophone / **JIM BROWN** (b.20 Nov'57) – drums / **NORMAN HASSAN** (b.26 Jan'58) – percussion

		Graduate	Sound
Jan 80.	(7") *(GRAD 6)* **FOOD FOR THOUGHT. / KING**	4	
Jun 80.	(7"/12") *(GRAD/12GRAD 8)* **MY WAY OF THINKING. / I THINK IT'S GOING TO RAIN TODAY**	6	
Aug 80.	(lp/c) *(GRAD LP/C 2)* **SIGNING OFF**	2	
	– Tyler / King / 12 bar / Burden of shame / Adella / I think it's going to rain today / 25% / Food for thought / Little by little / Signing off. *(free-12"ep w.a.)* **MADAM MEDUSA. / STRANGE FRUIT / REEFER MADNESS** *(cd-iss. 1986 on 'Target')*		
Oct 80.	(7"/12") *(GRAD/12GRAD 10)* **THE EARTH DIES SCREAMING. / DREAM A LIE**	10	
	(all above 45's re-iss. 1984)		

		DEP Inter.	A & M
May 81.	(7"/12") *(DEP 1/112)* **DON'T LET IT PASS YOU BY. / DON'T SLOW DOWN**	16	-
May 81.	(lp/c) *(LP/CA DEP 1)* **PRESENT ARMS**	2	-
	– Present arms / Sardonicus / Don't let it pass you by / Wild cat / One in ten / Don't slow down / Silent witness / Lambs bread. *(free 12" w.a.)* **DON'T WALK ON THE GRASS. / DOCTOR X** *(lp re-iss. Jan83)* *(cd-iss. Apr88 on 'Virgin')*		
Jul 81.	(7") *(DEP 2)* **ONE IN TEN. / PRESENT ARMS IN DUB**	7	-
Oct 81.	(lp/c) *(LP/CA DEP 2)* **PRESENT ARMS IN DUB**	38	-
	– Present arms / Smoke it / B-line / Kings Row / Return of Doctor X / Walk out / One in ten / Neon haze. *(re-iss. Jan83)*		
Feb 82.	(7"/12") *(DEP 3/+12)* **I WON'T CLOSE MY EYES. / POLITICIAN**	32	-
May 82.	(7") *(DEP 4)* **LOVE IS ALL IS ALRIGHT. / HOT-CROSS DUB**	29	-
	(12"+=) *(DEP 412)* – ('A'live version).		
Aug 82.	(7") *(DEP 5)* **SO HERE I AM. / SILENT WITNESS**	25	-
	(12"+=) *(DEP 512)* – Doctor X (live).		
Sep 82.	(lp/c) *(LP/CA DEP 3)* **UB44**	4	-
	– So here I am / I won't close my eyes / Forget the cost / Love is all is alright / The piper calls the tune / The key / Don't do the crime / Politician / The prisoner. *(re-iss. Jan83)* *(re-iss. +cd.remixed Apr86)*		

––––– DEP International were now distributed by 'Virgin'.

Jan 83.	(7") *(DEP 6)* **I'VE GOT MINE. / DUBMOBILE**	45	-
	(12"+=) *(DEP 612)* – Forget the cost.		
Feb 83.	(lp/c) *(LPCA DEP 4)* **UB40 LIVE (live in Ireland)**	44	-
	– Food for thought / Sardonicus / Don't slow down / Politician / Tyler / Present arms / The piper calls the tune / Love is all is alright / Burden of shame / One in ten. *(re-iss. Aug84)* *(cd-iss. 1988)*		
Aug 83.	(7"/12") *(DEP 7/+12)* *<2600>* **RED RED WINE. / SUFFERING**	1	34 Nov 83
	(US re-iss. Aug88, hit No.1) *(at same time, below album hits US No.14)*		
Sep 83.	(lp/c) *(LP/CA DEP 5)* **LABOUR OF LOVE**	1	39 Nov 83
	– Cherry oh baby / Keep on moving / Please don't make me cry / Sweet sensation / Johnny too bad / Red red wine / Guilty / She caught the train / Version girl / Many rivers to cross. *(cd-iss. Jul86)*		
Oct 83.	(7"/12") *(DEP 8/+12)* **PLEASE DON'T MAKE ME CRY. / SUFFERING (featuring NYA & NATTY)**	10	-
Dec 83.	(7") *(DEP 9)* **MANY RIVERS TO CROSS. / FOOD FOR THOUGHT (live)**	16	
	(12"+=) *(DEP 9-12)* – Johnny Too Bad (version).		
Feb 84.	(7") *(DEP 10/+12)(10"pic-d)* **CHERRY OH BABY. / FOOD FOR THOUGHT**	-	
Mar 84.	(7"/12")(10"pic-d) *(DEP 10/+12)(DEPY 10)* **CHERRY OH BABY. / FRILLA**	12	
Apr 84.	(7") *(DEP 11/+12)* **PLEASE DON'T MAKE ME CRY. / FOOD FOR THOUGHT**	-	
Sep 84.	(7"/12") *(DEP 11/+12)* **IF IT HAPPENS AGAIN. / NKOMO A GO-GO**	9	
Oct 84.	(lp/c)(cd) *(LP/CA DEP 6)(DEPCD 6)* *<5033>* **GEFFERY MORGAN**	3	60
	– Riddle me / As always you were wrong again / If it happens again / D.U.B. / The pillow / Nkomo a go-go / Seasons / You're not an army / I'm not fooled so easily / Your eyes were open.		
Nov 84.	(7"/12") *(DEP 15/+12)* **RIDDLE ME. / D.U.B. (dub)**	59	

––––– In Feb85, they appeared on charity single STARVATION with various BEAT members, etc. Released on 'Zarjazz' label, it hit UK No.33.

Mar 85.	(7"/12") *(DEP 16/+12)* **I'M NOT FOOLED. / THE PILLOW**		
Jul 85.	(7"; UB40 & CHRISSIE HYNDE) *(DEP 20)* **I GOT YOU BABE. / THEME FROM LABOUR OF LOVE**	1	-
	(12"+=) *(DEP 2012)* – Up and coming MC.		
Jul 85.	(7"; UB40 & CHRISSIE HYNDE) *<2758>* **I GOT YOU BABE. / NKOMO A GO-GO**	-	28
Aug 85.	(m-lp/c)(cd) *<5090>* **LITTLE BAGGARIDM**	-	40
	– Don't break my heart / I got you babe / Hip hop lyrical robot / One in ten.		
Sep 85.	(lp/c)(cd) *(LP/CA DEP 10)(DEPCD 10)* **BAGGARIDDIM**	14	
	– The king step mk.1 / The buzz feeling / Lyric officer mk.2 / Demonstrate / Two in a one mk.1 / Hold your position mk.3 / Hip hop lyrical robot / Style mk.4 / Fight fe come in mk.2 / V's version. *(12"w.a.)* **DON'T BREAK MY HEART. / I GOT YOU BABE / MI SPLIFF** *(re-iss. Apr90)*		
Oct 85.	(7"/12") *(DEP 22/+12)* **DON'T BREAK MY HEART. / MEK YA ROK**	3	
Jun 86.	(7"/12") *(DEP 23/+12)* **SING OUR OWN SONG. / ('A' instrumental)**	5	
Jul 86.	(lp/c)(cd) *(LP/CA DEP 11)(DEPCD 11)* *<5137>* **RAT IN THE KITCHEN**	8	53
	– All I want to do / You could meet somebody / Tell it like this / The elevator / Watchdogs / Rat in me kitchen / Looking down at my reflection / Don't blame me / Sing our own song.		
Sep 86.	(7"/12") *(DEP 24/+12)* **ALL I WANT TO DO. / ('A'version)**	41	
Jan 87.	(7"/12") *(DEP 25/+12)* **RAT IN MI KITCHEN. / ('A' long version)**	12	
Apr 87.	(7") *(DEP 26)* **WATCHDOGS. / DON'T BLAME ME**	39	
	(12"+=) *(DEP 26-12)* – ('A'live version).		
Aug 87.	(lp/c)(cd) *<5168>* **CCCP: LIVE IN MOSCOW (live)**	-	
	– All I want to do / Cherry oh baby / Keep on moving / Watchdogs / Don't blame me / Tell it like it is / Please don't make me cry / Johnny too bad / I got you babe / Don't break my heart / If it happens again / Rat in me kitchen / Sing our own song.		
Sep 87.	(7") *(DEP 27)* **MAYBE TOMORROW. / DREAD DREAD TIME**	14	
	(12"+=)(c-s+=) *(DEP 27-12)(DEPC 27)* – Anything mi chat.		

May 88. (7"; UB40 & CHRISSIE HYNDE) *(DEP 29)* **BREAKFAST IN BED.** / ('A'instrumental)   `6`

(12"+=)(cd-s+=) *(DEP 29-12)(DEPX 29)* – ('A'other versions).

May 88. (lp/c)(cd) *(LP/CA DEP 13)(DEPCD 13)* <5213> **UB40**   `12` `44`
– Dance with the Devil / Come out to play / Breakfast in bed / You're always pulling me down / I would do for you / 'Cause it isn't true / Where did I go wrong / Contaminated minds / Matter of time / Music so nice / Dance with the Devil (reprise). (pic-cd.Dec88)

Aug 88. (7") *(DEP 30)* **WHERE DID I GO WRONG.** / ('A'instrumental)   `26` `-`

(12"+=) *(DEP 3012)* – Contaminated dub.
(cd-s++=) *(DEPX 30)* – Hit it (instrumental).

Nov 88. (7") <> **WHERE DID I GO WRONG. / DANCE WITH THE DEVIL**   `-`

—— **LARRY BUSHELL** – bass temp.repl. EARL for 4 mths. Jul88.

Nov 88. (7"/c-s) *(DEP/+C 31)* **COME OUT TO PLAY.** / CONTAMINATED MINDS

(12"+=) *(DEP 31-12)* – Sing our own song (live).
(10"++=) *(DEP 31-10)* – ('A'instrumental).
(cd-s+=) *(DEPX 31)* – Dance with the Devil / Rat in mi kitchen.

Jun 89. (7"/c-s) *(DEP/+C 32)* **I WOULD DO FOR YOU. / HIT IT**   `45`

(12"+=)(3"cd-s+=) *(DEP 32-12)(DEPX 32)* – ('B'version).

	Virgin	Virgin

Nov 89. (7"/c-s) *(DEP/+C 33)* **HOMELY GIRL. / GATOR**   `6`

(12"+=)(3"cd-s+=) *(DEP 33-12)(DEPX 33)* – ('A'extended).

Dec 89. (lp/c)(cd) *(LP/CA DEP 14)(DEPCD 14)* <91324> **LABOUR OF LOVE II**   `4` `30`
– Here I am (come and take me) / Tears from my eyes / Groovin' / The way you do the things you do / Wear you to the ball / Singer man / Kingston Town / Baby / Wedding day / Sweet Cherrie / Stick by me / Just another girl / Homely girl / Impossible love.

Jan 90. (7"/c-s) *(DEP/+C 34)* **HERE I AM (COME AND TAKE ME).** / CRISIS   `46` `-`

(12"+=)(cd-s+=) *(DEP 34-12)(DEPX 34)* – ('B'dub version).

Mar 90. (7"/c-s) *(DEP/+C 35)* **KINGSTON TOWN. / LICKWOOD**   `4`

(12"+=)(cd-s+=) *(DEP 35-12)(DEPXT 35)* – ('A'extended mix).

Jul 90. (7"/c-s) *(DEP/+C 36)* **WEAR YOU TO THE BALL. / SPLUGIN**   `35`

(12"+=)(cd-s++=) *(DEP 36-12)(DEPXT 36)* – ('A'extended)./ / ('A'dub version).

Sep 90. (c-s,cd-s) <98978> **THE WAY YOU DO THE THINGS YOU DO**   `-` `6`

—— (Oct90, teamed up with ROBERT PALMER on UK No.6 I'LL BE YOUR BABY TONIGHT)

Nov 90. (7"/c-s) *(DEP/+C 37)* **IMPOSSIBLE LOVE. / FIRST SHOT**   `47`

(12"+=)(cd-s+=) *(DEP 37-12)(DEPXT 37)* – Council house.

Jan 91. (7"/c-s) *(DEP/+C 38)* **THE WAY YOU DO THE THINGS YOU DO. / MISSPENT YOUTH**   `49` `-`

(cd-s+=) *(DEPXT 38)* – ('A'remix).

Mar 91. (c-s,cd-s) <99141> **HERE I AM (COME AND TAKE ME) / GATOR**   `-` `7`

Nov 91. (7"/c-s) *(DEP/+C 39)* **BABY. / SHE CAUGHT THE TRAIN**   `-`

(12"+=)(cd-s+=) *(DEP 39-12)(DEPXT 39)* – Here I am (come and take me) (mix) / Dubmobile (live).

Nov 91. (c-s,cd-s) <98654> **GROOVIN' / COUNCIL HOUSE**   `-` `90`

—— In Nov'92, teamed up with 808 STATE on a UK Top 20 version of 'ONE IN TEN'.

May 93. (7"/c-s) *(DEP/+C 40)* <12653> **(I CAN'T HELP) FALLING IN LOVE WITH YOU. / JUNGLE LOVE**   `1` `1`

(12"+=)/ /(cd-s++=) *(DEP 40-12)/ /(DEPDG 40)* – ('A'extended)./ / Red red wine.

Jul 93. (cd/c)(lp) *(LP/CA DEP 15)(DEPCD 15)* <88229> **PROMISES AND LIES**   `1` `6`
– C'est la vie / Desert sand / Promises and lies / Bring me your cup / Higher ground / Reggae music / Can't help falling in love / Now and then / Things ain't what they used to be / It's a long long way / Sorry.

Aug 93. (7"/c-s) *(DEP/+C 41)* <12681> **HIGHER GROUND. / CHRONIC**   `8` `45` Oct93

(12"+=)(cd-s+=) *(DEP 4112)(DEPD 41)* – Punjab dub (mix).

Nov 93. (7"/c-s) *(DEP/+C 42)* **BRING ME YOUR CUP. / BAD EKKO**   `24`

(cd-s+=) *(DEPD 42)* – ('A'mixes).

Mar 94. (7"/c-s) *(DEP/+C 43)* **C'EST LA VIE. / PROMISES AND LIES (live)**   `37`

(12"+=)(cd-s+=) *(DEP 43-12)(DEPD 43)* – Tyler.

Aug 94. (7"/c-s) *(DEP/+C 44)* **REGGAE MUSIC. / MATTER OF TIME**   `28`

(cd-s+=) *(DEPDG 44)* – Things ain't like they used to be.

—— In Oct94, they featured on UK No.1 'Baby Come Back' by PATO BANTON.

Oct 95. (c-s) *(DEPC 45)* **UNTIL MY DYING DAY / ('A'instrumental)**   `15`

(cd-s+=) *(DEPD 45)* – Sorry (live) / Bring me your cup (live).
(cd-s+=) *(DEPDX 45)* – ('A'-C.J.'s closet mix).

Oct 95. (cd/c) *(DUBTV/UBTVC 2)* **THE BEST OF UB 40 VOL.2** (compilation)   `12` `-`
– Breakfast in bed / Where did I go wrong / I would do for you / Homely girl / Here I am (come and take me) / Kingston town / Wear you to the ball / Can't help falling in love / Higher ground / Bring me your cup / C'est la vie / Reggae music / Superstition / Until my dying day.

Jul 97. (cd/c) *(DEPCD/CADEP/LPDEP 16)* **GUNS IN THE GHETTO**   `7`
– Always there / Hurry come on up / I love it when you smile / I've been missing you / Guns in the ghetto / Tell me is it true / Oracabessa moonshine / Friendly fire / I really can't say / Lisa.

Aug 97. (c-s) *(DEPC 48)* **TELL ME IS IT TRUE / IT'S TRUE**   `14`

(cd-s+=) *(DEPD 48)* –

Nov 97. (c-s) *(DEPC 49)* **ALWAYS THERE / MAGIC CARPET**   `53`

(cd-s+=) *(DEPD 49)* – Hills and valley.

Sep 98. (c-s/cd-s) *(DEP C/D 50)* **COME BACK DARLING / IN THE PARK**   `10`

Oct 98. (cd/c) *(DEPCD/CADEP 18)* **LABOUR OF LOVE III**   `8`
– Holly holy / It's my delight / Come back darling / Never let you go / Soul rebel / My best girl / Good ambition / The train is coming / Blood and fire / Mr. Fix it / Stay a little bit longer / Someone like you / The time has come / Crying over you / Legalise it.

Dec 98. (c-s) *(DEPC 51)* **HOLLY HOLY / NOW YOU SEE IT**   `31`

(cd-s+=) *(DEPD 51)* – Legalise it (mixes).
(cd-s+=) *(DEPX 51)* – King of the hill.

Apr 99. (c-s) *(DEPC 52)* **THE TRAIN IS COMING / LEGALISE IT**   `30`

(cd-s+=) *(DEPD 52)* – ('A'&'B'mixes).
(cd-s) *(DEPDX 52)* –

– compilations, others, etc. –

Aug 82. (lp/c) *Graduate; (GRAD LP/C 3)* **THE SINGLES ALBUM**   `17` `-`
– Food for thought / King / My way of thinking / I think it's going to rain today / Dream a lie / Tyler / Adella / Little by little / The earth dies screaming.

Feb 83. (12"m) *Graduate; (12GRAD 15)* **TYLER. / ADELLA / LITTLE BY LITTLE** (re-iss. 1984)   `-`

Mar 85. (d-lp/c) *Graduate; (VGD/+C 3511)* **THE UB40 FILE** (cd-iss. Jul86)   `-`

Oct 87. (lp/c/cd) *Virgin TV; (UBTV/UBTVC/DUBTV 1)* **THE BEST OF UB40 VOLUME 1**   `3` `-`
– Red red wine / I got you babe / One in ten / food for thought / Rat in mi kitchen / Don't break my heart / Cherry oh baby / Many rivers to cross / Please don't make me cry / If it hapens again / My way of thinking / King. (cd+=extra tracks) (re-iss. +cd.Jan89) (re-iss. cd+c Aug93, hit UK No.51)

Nov 91. (d-cd) *Virgin; (DEPDDX 1)* **LABOUR OF LOVE I & II** (re-iss. Nov94, hit UK No.6)   `-`

Oct 94. (3xcd-box) *Virgin;* **THE COMPACT COLLECTION**   `-` `-`

1999. (cd/c) **UB40 present THE DANCEHALL ALBUM**   `-` `-`
– Magic carpet (with PINCHERS) / Force ripe (with MERCILESS) / Smile for me (with GENERAL DEGREE) / Waw waw waw (with Lt. STITCHIE) / More opportunity (with ANTHONY B) / Maybe tomorrow / My way of thinking / Love that I need (with BEENIE MAN) / Ladda bay (with MAD COBRA) / More love (with RED DRAGON) / Nuff love (with LADY SAW) / Who (SPRAGGA BENZ) / Hills and valley (with NINJA MAN) / No stray (with ROUNDHEAD).

ALI CAMPBELL

May 95. (7"/c-s) *(KUFF/+C 1)* **THAT LOOK IN YOUR EYE. / DRIVE IT HOME**   `5`

(cd-s+=) *(KUFFDG 1)* – ('A'mix).

Jun 95. (cd/c/d-lp) *(CD/TC/+V 2783)* **BIG LOVE**   `6`
– Big love (intro) / Happiness / That look in your eye / Let your yeah be yeah / You can cry on my shoulder / Somethin' stupid / Big love / You could meet somebody / Talking blackbird / Pay the rent / Drive it home / Stop the guns.

Aug 95. (7"/c-s) *(KUFF/+C 2)* **LET YOUR YEAH BE YEAH. / YOU COULD MEET SOMEBODY**   `25`

(10"+=/cd-s+=) *(KUFFA/D 2)* – ('A'version).

Nov 95. (c-s) *(KUFFC 5)* **SOMETHIN' STUPID ("ALI & KIBIBI CAMPBELL"). / PAY THE RENT**   `30`

(cd-s+=) *(KUFFD 5)* – ('A'version).

U.F.O.

Formed: North London, England . . . 1969 initially as HOCUS POCUS, by PHIL MOGG, PETE WAY, MICK BOLTON and ANDY PARKER. Gaining a deal with 'Beacon' records in the early 70's, UFO had a surprising degree of success in Japan and Germany, where their blend of boogified space-rock (embellished with extended jams) sold like hotcakes. Their version of Eddie Cochran's 'C'MON EVERYBODY' (1972) was a massive hit in the far east, although Britain had previously shunned their pretentiously unremarkable first two albums, the thoughtfully titled 'UFO 1' and 'UFO 2 – FLYING' (both 1971). When BOLTON departed in 1972, his place was filled by a succession of guitarists, MICHAEL SCHENKER (ex-SCORPIONS) finally getting the permanent job the following year when BERNIE MARSDEN (who had replaced LARRY WALLIS; ex-PINK FAIRIES) departed for a bit of WILD TURKEY. Signing to 'Chrysalis' in 1974, UFO changed their style dramatically, hard-rock becoming their paymaster with classic songs such as 'DOCTOR, DOCTOR' and 'ROCK BOTTOM' featuring "heavily" on their label debut that year, 'PHENOMENON'. Between mid '74 and early '75, they added a fifth member, PAUL CHAPMAN (ex-SKID ROW), although the group soon reverted to a quartet when the guitarist joined LONE STAR. 'FORCE IT' was pushed out in the same year, the album immediately securing a Top 75 placing in the States where SCHENKER's fingering on his 'Flying V' style guitar was as much talked about as the record. For their follow-up set, the mildly disappointing 'NO HEAVY PETTIN' (1976), they added keyboard player, DANNY PEYRONEL, although he was subsequently replaced by PAUL RAYMOND on the 1977 disc, 'LIGHTS OUT'. A definite improvement, UFO landed in America properly this time, hitting their Top 30 with a blistering attack on tracks such as 'TOO HOT TO HANDLE' and a cover of Love's 'ALONE AGAIN OR'. 1978's 'OBSESSION' (featuring the classic hard-rock anthem, 'ONLY YOU CAN ROCK ME'), was again plucked from the stars, although after a live set, 'STRANGERS IN THE NIGHT' (1979), SCHENKER decided to return to The SCORPIONS. PAUL CHAPMAN returned for one GEORGE MARTIN-produced album, 'NO PLACE TO RUN' (1980), although it was clear the only thing taking off in UFO was the group members. PAUL RAYMOND joined SCHENKER in his new group and was replaced by NEIL CARTER prior to the recording of their 1981 set, 'THE WILD, THE WILLING AND THE INNOCENT', an aggressive piece of class that made its mark in Britain. All seemed well after 'MECHANIX' peaked at No.8 in the British charts in '82; however, PETE WAY was another to jump ship, the bassist eventually reappearing in his WAYSTED outfit. Former punk PAUL GRAY (from The DAMNED and EDDIE & THE HOT RODS), filled in on the 1983 set, 'MAKING CONTACT', although this was hardly the standard their fans had come to expect. They split soon after, MOGG and cohorts reforming many times over the next decade but never quite getting off the ground. • **Songwriters:** Mostly WAY / MOGG or CHAPMAN / MOGG, with both variations sometimes adding SCHENKER or CARTER. • **Trivia:** PHIL MOGG's nephew, NIGEL MOGG, became relatively famous in the band, The QUIREBOYS.

Album rating: U.F.O. 1 (*2) / U.F.O. 2 – FLYING (*3) / LIVE IN JAPAN (*5) / PHENOMENON (*6) / FORCE IT (*6) / NO HEAVY PETTIN' (*5) / LIGHTS OUT (*7) / OBSESSION (*8) / STRANGERS IN THE NIGHT (*8) / NO PLACE TO RUN (*6) / THE WILD, THE WILLING + THE INNOCENT (*8) / MECHANIX (*6) / MAKING CONTACT (*5) / HEADSTONE – THE BEST OF U.F.O. compilation (*7) / MISDEMEANOUR (*4) / AIN'T MISBEHAVIN' (*4) / HIGH STAKES AND DANGEROUS MEN (*5) / LIGHTS OUT IN TOKYO (*5) / WALK ON WATER (*3)

PHIL MOGG (b.1951) – vocals / **PETE WAY** – bass / **MICK BOLTON** – guitar / **ANDY PARKER** – drums

		Beacon	Rare Earth
1970.	(7") *(BEA 161)* **SHAKE IT ABOUT. / EVIL**		–
Jan 71.	(lp) *(BES 12) <524>* **UFO**		

– Unidentified flying object / Boogie / C'mon everybody / Shake it about / Melinda / Timothy / Follow you home / Treacle people / Who do you love / Evito. (cd-iss. Apr91 on 'Line'; GACD 900691)

Jan 71.	(7") *(BEA 165)* **COME AWAY MELINDA. / UNIDENTIFIED FLYING OBJECT**		–
Jun 71.	(7") *(BEA 172)* **BOOGIE FOR GEORGE. / TREACLE PEOPLE**		–
Oct 71.	(7") *(BEA 181)* **PRINCE KAJUKU. / THE COMING OF PRINCE KAJUKU**		–
Oct 71.	(lp) *(BEAS 19)* **U.F.O. 2 FLYING**		–

– Silver bird / Star storm / Prince Kajuku / Coming of Prince Kajuku / Flying. (re-iss. Feb72; same) (cd-iss. Apr91 on 'Line'; GACD 900694)

		Nova	not iss.
1972.	(lp) *(621454)* **UFO: LIVE (live in Japan)**	–	– German

– C'mon everybody / Who do you love / Loving cup / Prince Kajuku – The coming of Prince Kajuku / Boogie for George / Follow you home. (UK-iss.1982 on 'AKA'; AKP 2)

—— In 1972, they issued a few 45's in Japan, incl. 'C'MON EVERYBODY'.

—— (Jun'73) **MICHAEL SCHENKER** (b.10 Jan'55, Savstedt, Germany) – guitar repl. BERNIE MARSDEN to WILD TURKEY. BERNIE had repl. LARRY WALLIS (Nov'72) who had repl. BOLTON (Feb'72). WALLIS went on to PINK FAIRIES.

		Chrysalis	Chrysalis
Mar 74.	(7") *(CHS 2040)* **DOCTOR DOCTOR. / LIPSTICK TRACES**		
May 74.	(lp/c) *(<CHR/ZCHR 1059>)* **PHENOMENON**		

– Too young to know / Crystal light / Doctor doctor / Space child / Rock bottom / Oh my / Time on my hands / Built for comfort / Lipstick traces / Queen of the deep. (cd-iss. Oct91 on 'Episode'; LUSCD 10)

| Jul 75. | (lp/c) *(<CHR/ZCHR 1074>)* **FORCE IT** | | 71 |

– Let it roll / Shoot shoot / High flyer / Love lost love / Out in the street / Mother Mary / Too much of nothing / Dance your life away / This kid's – Between the walls.

—— (Sep'75) added **DANNY PEYRONEL** – keyboards (ex-HEAVY METAL KIDS)

| May 76. | (lp/c) *(<CHR/ZCHR 1103>)* **NO HEAVY PETTING** | | |

– Natural thing / I'm a loser / Can you roll her / Belladonna / Reasons love / Highway lady / On with the action / A fool in love / Martian landscape.

—— (Jul'76) **PAUL RAYMOND** – keyboards, guitar (ex-SAVOY BROWN) repl. DANNY

| Apr 77. | (7") *(CHS 2146)* **ALONE AGAIN OR. / ELECTRIC PHASE** | | |
| May 77. | (lp/c) *(<CHR/ZCHR 1127>)* **LIGHTS OUT** | 54 | 23 |

– Too hot to handle / Just another suicide / Try me / Lights out / Gettin' ready / Alone again or / Electric phase / Love to love. (cd-iss. 1987; ACCD 1127) (cd-re-iss. Jul91 on 'Episode'; LUSCD 9)

| Jun 77. | (7") *(CHS 2146)* **TOO HOT TO HANDLE. / ELECTRIC PHASE** | – | |
| Jun 78. | (lp/c) *(<CDL/ZCDL 1182>)* **OBSESSION** | 26 | 41 |

– Only you can rock me / Pack it up (and go) / Arbory Hill / Ain't no baby / Lookin' out for No.1 / Hot 'n' ready / Cherry / You don't fool me / Lookin' out for No.1 (reprise) / One more for the rodeo / Born to lose. (cd-iss. Sep91 on 'Episode'; LUSCD 11)

| Jul 78. | (7"red) *(CHS 2241)* **ONLY YOU CAN ROCK ME. / CHERRY / ROCK BOTTOM** | 50 | |
| Dec 78. | (d-lp/d-c) *(CJT/ZCJT 1) <1209>* **STRANGERS IN THE NIGHT (live)** | 8 | 42 |

– Natural thing / Out in the street / Only you can rock me / Doctor doctor / Mother Mary / This kid's / Love to love / Lights out / Rock bottom / Too hot to handle / I'm a loser / Let it roll / Shoot shoot. (cd-iss. Sep91; CCD 1209) (cd re-iss. Mar94; CD25CR 22)

| Jan 79. | (7"clear) *(CHS 2287)* **DOCTOR DOCTOR (live). / ON WITH THE ACTION (live) / TRY ME** | 35 | |
| Mar 79. | (7"clear) *(CHS 2318)* **SHOOT SHOOT (live). / ONLY YOU CAN ROCK ME (live) / I'M A LOSER (live)** | 48 | |

—— (Nov'78) **PAUL CHAPMAN** – guitar returned to repl. SCHENKER who joined The SCORPIONS and later formed his own self-named group.

| Jan 80. | (7"red) *(CHS 2399)* **YOUNG BLOOD. / LIGHTS OUT** | 36 | |
| Jan 80. | (lp/c) *(<CDL/ZCDL 1239>)* **NO PLACE TO RUN** | 11 | 51 |

– Alpha Centauri / Lettin' go / Mystery train / This fire burns tonight / Gone in the night / Young blood / No place to run / Take it or leave it / Money money / Anyday.

—— (Aug'80) **WAY, MOGG, CHAPMAN + PARKER** recruited **NEIL CARTER** – keyboards, guitar (ex-WILD HORSES) repl. PAUL RAYMOND who joined MICHAEL SCHENKER GROUP

| Oct 80. | (7"clear) *(CHS 2454)* **COULDN'T GET IT RIGHT. / HOT 'N' READY (live)** | | |
| Jan 81. | (lp/c) *(<CHR/ZCHR 1307>)* **THE WILD, THE WILLING AND THE INNOCENT** | 19 | 77 |

– Chains chains / Long gone / The wild, the willing and the innocent / It's killing me / Makin' moves / Lonely heart / Couldn't get it right / Profession of violence.

| Jan 81. | (7"clear) *(CHS 2454)* **LONELY HEART. / LONG GONE** | 41 | |
| Jan 82. | (7"clear) *(CHS 2576)* **LET IT RAIN. / HEEL OF A STRANGER / YOU'LL GET LOVE** | 62 | |

| Feb 82. | (lp/c) *(<CHR/ZCHR 1360>)* **MECHANIX** | 8 | 82 |

– The writer / Something else / Back into my life / You'll get love / Doing it all for you / We belong to the night / Let it rain / Terri / Feel it / Dreaming.

| Apr 82. | (7"/7"pic-d) *(CHS/+P 2607)* **BACK INTO MY LIFE. / THE WRITER** | | |

—— (Jun'82) on tour **BILLY SHEEHAN** – bass (ex-TALAS) repl. PETE WAY who formed FASTWAY and briefly joined OZZY OSBOURNE (later WAYSTED)

| Jan 83. | (lp/c) *(<CHR/ZCHR 1402>)* **MAKING CONTACT** | 32 | |

– Blinded by a lie / Diesel in the dust / A fool for love / You and me / When it's time to rock / The way the wild wind blows / Call my name / All over you / No getaway / Push, it's love.

| Mar 83. | (7"/7"pic-d) *(CHS/+P 2672)* **WHEN IT'S TIME TO ROCK. / EVERYBODY KNOWS** | 70 | |

(12"+=) *(CHS12 2672)* – Push it's love.

—— Disbanded when MOGG suffered a nervous breakdown on stage. He resurrected the band in 1984 with **PAUL RAYMOND / PAUL GRAY** – bass (ex-DAMNED) / **JIM SIMPSON** – drums (ex-MAGNUM) / **ATOMIK TOMMY M.** – guitar (b. Japan)

| Oct 85. | (7"/7"sha-pic-d) *(UFO/+P 1)* **THIS TIME. / THE CHASE** | | – |

(12"+=) *(UFOX 1)* – ('A'extended).

| Nov 85. | (lp/c) *(<CHR/ZCHR 1518>)* **MISDEMEANOR** | 74 | |

– This time / One heart / Night run / The only ones / Meanstreets / Name of love / Blue / Dream the dream / Heaven's gate / Wreckless.

| Feb 86. | (7"red) *(UFO 2)* **NIGHT RUN. / HEAVEN'S GATE** | | |

(12"+=) *(UFOX 2)* – ('A'extended).

—— (late '86) **DAVID 'Jake' JACOBSON** – guitar (ex-ERIC MARTIN) repl. RAYMOND

		FM Revolver	not iss.
Mar 88.	(lp/c/cd) *(WKFM LP/MC/XD 107)* **AIN'T MISBEHAVIN'**		–

– Between a rock and a hard place / Another Saturday night / At war with the world / Hunger in the night / Easy money / Rock boyz, rock. (cd+=) – Lonely cities (of the heart). (pic-lp Jan89; WKFMHP 107)

—— Disbanded Spring 1988. PHIL went into production mainly for his nephew NIGEL MOGG's new band QUIREBOYS

MOGG + WAY re-united UFO adding **LAURENCE ARCHER** – guitar (ex-GRAND SLAM) / **CLIVE EDWARDS** – drums (ex-WILD HORSES) / **JEM DAVIS** – keyboards

		Essential	Victory
Nov 91.	(12"ep/cd-ep) **ONE OF THOSE NIGHTS. / AIN'T LIFE SWEET / LONG GONE**		–
Feb 92.	(cd/c/lp) *(ESM CD/MC 178)* **HIGH STAKES AND DANGEROUS MEN**		–

– Borderline / Primed for time / She's the one / Ain't life sweet / Don't want to lose you / Burnin' fire / Running up the highway / Back door man / One of those nights / Revolution / Love deadly love / Let the good times roll.

| Feb 93. | (cd/c) *(ESS CD/MC 191) <VICP 5204>* **LIGHTS OUT IN TOKYO LIVE (live)** | | Nov92 |

– Running up the highway / Borderline / Too hot to handle / She's the one / Cherry / Back door man / One of those nights / Love to love / Only you can rock me / Lights out / Doctor, doctor / Rock bottom / Shoot, shoot / C'mon everybody. (cd re-iss. Apr95; ESSCD 386)

—— The UFO who released '3RD PERSPECTIVE' in 1997 was not the same group

		Eagle	Zero
1997.	(cd) *(EAGCD 009)* **WALK ON WATER**		1995

– A self made man / Venus / Pushed to the limit / Stopped by a bullet (of love) / Darker days / Running on empty / Knock, knock / Dreaming of summer / Doctor, doctor / Lights out / Fortune town / I will be there / Public enemy #1.

– compilations, others, etc. –

1973.	(d-lp) *Decca; (SD 30311/2)* **U.F.O. 1 / FLYING**		–
Dec 82.	(d-c) *Chrysalis; (ZCDP 107)* **MECHANIX / LIGHTS OUT**		
Aug 83.	(d-lp/d-c) *Chrysalis; (CTY/ZCTY 1437)* **HEADSTONE – THE BEST OF U.F.O.**	39	–

– Doctor doctor / Rock bottom / Fool for your loving / Shoot shoot / Too hot to handle / Only you can rock me / Love drive (SCORPIONS) / She said she said (LONE STAR) / Lights out / Armed and ready (MICHAEL SCHENKER GROUP) / Young blood / Criminal tendencies / Lonely heart / We belong to the night / Let it rain / Couldn't get it right / Electric phase / Doing it all for you.

| Nov 85. | (d-lp/d-c) *Castle; (CCS LP/MC 101)* **THE COLLECTION** | | – |
| Apr 87. | (d-lp/c/cd) *Raw Power; (RAW LP/TC/CD 029)* **ANTHOLOGY** | | – |

– Rock bottom / Built for comfort / Highway lady / Can you roll her / Fool for love / Shoot shoot / Too hot to handle / Gettin' ready / Only you can rock me / Looking for number one / Hot 'n' ready / Mystery train / No place to run / Profession and violence / Chains chains / Something else / Doing it for all of you / When it's time to rock / Diesel in the dust. (cd re-iss. Jan94; CCSCD 316)

Sep 89.	(cd) *Line; (GACD 900704)* **SPACE METAL**		–
Apr 92.	(cd) *Windsong; (WINCD 016)* **BBC LIVE IN CONCERT (live)**		–
Oct 92.	(cd) *Chrysalis; (CD/TC CHR 1888)* **ESSENTIAL U.F.O.**		–
Nov 92.	(cd) *Dojo; (EARLD 9)* **EARLY YEARS**		–
Mar 94.	(cd/c) *Music Club; (MC CD/TC 153)* **TOO HOT TO HANDLE: THE BEST OF U.F.O.**		–
May 94.	(cd) *Beat Goes On; (BGOCD 229)* **OBSESSION / NO PLACE TO RUN**		–
1994.	(cd) *Essential; (ESDCD 218)* **TNT**		–
Aug 94.	(cd) *Beat Goes On; (BGOCD 228)* **NO HEAVY PETTING / LIGHTS OUT**		–
Sep 94.	(cd) *Beat Goes On; (BGOCD 230)* **THE WILD, THE WILLING AND THE INNOCENT / MECHANIX**		–
Oct 94.	(cd) *Beat Goes On; (BGOCD 227)* **PHENOMENOM / FORCE IT**		–
May 95.	(cd) *Spectrum; (550743-2)* **DOCTOR, DOCTOR**		–
Nov 95.	(cd) *M&M; (M&MCD 1)* **HEAVEN'S GATE LIVE (live)**		–
Jul 96.	(cd) *EMI Gold; (CDGOLD 1050)* **THE BEST OF U.F.O.**		–
Jul 96.	(cd) *Beat Goes On; (BGOCD 319)* **MAKING CONTACT / MISDEMEANOUR**		–
May 97.	(d-cd) *Snapper; (SMDCD 122)* **THE X-FACTOR – OUT THERE . . . AND BACK**		–

UGLY KID JOE (dig out; Great Metal . . .)

UK SUBS (dig out; Great Alt & Indie . . .)

ULTIMATE SPINACH (dig out; Great Psychedelic . . .)

ULTRAMARINE (dig out; Great Alt & Indie . . .)

ULTRASOUND

Formed: Newcastle, England . . . early 90's by the bulky (ex-POSSESSION) singer, TINY and guitarist RICHARD GREEN, whom he had met at a music course at Wakefield College. The pair decided to form wacky CARDIACS-induced outfit, SLEEPY PEOPLE, adding drummer ANDY PEACE in the process. Relocating to London (Acton, actually), they added VANESSA BEST on bass and MATT JONES on keyboards, although times were tough playing gigs for next to nothing and trying to explain that to the dole office the next day. TINY, with a look between EDDIE IZZARD on a very bad night and a chubby MORRISSEY, began to attract the right people to ULTRASOUND gigs. Among the A&R pack was 'Virgin' supremo himself, Richard Branson, who was enticed to go and see them perform by staff at his offshoot imprint, 'V2'. Fortunately, they played at NME's Unsigned Bands Gig early the following year, releasing a debut 45, 'SAME BAND', for 'Fierce Panda' soon after. This in turn, led to 'Nude' records subsequently giving them a deal, their second single, 'BEST WISHES', breaking the hard working quintet into the UK Top 75. In the summer of '98, they cracked the Top 30 with the excellent 'STAY YOUNG', although 'I'LL SHOW YOU MINE IF YOU SHOW ME YOURS', failed to register. Released the following March, 'FLOOTLIT WORLD' (a non-album cut) continued ULTRASOUND's chart campaign and previewed the double-CD debut album, 'EVERYTHING PICTURE'. A tad ambitious, overblown and retro 70's (especially in format!), the 100-minute plus set was just too much for the average punter although it did break into the Top 30. ULTRASOUND split soon after. • **Covered:** Neil Young's 'HEY, HEY, MY, MY (INTO THE BLACK)', Pere Ubu's 'FINAL SOLUTION' and the Beatles' 'GETTING BETTER'.

Album rating: EVERYTHING PICTURE (*6)

TINY (b. ANDREW VICTOR WOOD, 1962, Birkenhead, Liverpool) – vocals / **RICHARD GREEN** – guitar / **MATT JONES** – keyboards / **VANESSA BEST** – bass / **ANDY PEACE** – drums

		Fierce Panda	not iss.
Jul 97.	(ltd-7"/cd-s) *(NING 35/+CD)* **SAME BAND. / OVER THERE / FLOODLIT WORLD**		–
		Nude	not iss.
Feb 98.	(ltd;10"/cd-s) *(NUD 33 T/CD)* **BEST WISHES / KURT RUSSELL / BLACK HOLE**	68	–
Jun 98.	(7") *(NUD 35S)* **STAY YOUNG. / UNDERWATER LOVE STORY**	30	–
	(cd-s+=) *(NUD 35CD1)* – Can't say no.		
	(cd-s+=) *(NUD 35CD2)* – ('A'side) / Football meat / Hey, hey, my, my (into the black).		
Oct 98.	(12"/cd-s) *(NUD 39 T/CD)* **I'LL SHOW YOU MINE IF YOU SHOW ME YOURS. / LOVESICK / ONE PLUS ONE / FINAL SOLUTION**		–
Mar 99.	(7") *(NUD 41S)* **FLOODLIT WORLD. / DEATH OF A DRAG RACER**	39	–
	(cd-s+=) *(NUD 41CD1)* – We will find love / Getting better.		
	(cd-s+=) *(NUD 41CD2)* – I'll show you mine (CD-Rom).		
Apr 99.	(d-cd/c/d-lp) *(NUDE 12 CDX/MC/LP)* **EVERYTHING PICTURE**	23	–
	– Cross my heart / Same band / Stay young / Suckle / Fame thing / Happy times (are coming) // Aire & Calder / Sentimental song / Floodlit world / My impossible dream / Everything picture.		

ULTRAVOX

Formed: London, England . . . mid '76 out of TIGER LILY (whose one and only single was a bizarre cover of Fats Waller's 'AIN'T MISBEHAVIN', subsequently withdrawn from release) comprising frontman JOHN FOXX, CHRIS CROSS, STEVE SHEARS, BILLY CURRIE and WARREN CANN. With the addition of violin (courtesy of CURRIE) and added synth power, the group became ULTRAVOX, initially with a ! at the end!. The fact that the band were picked up by 'Island' records and their eponymous 1977 debut album produced by BRIAN ENO says a lot about where ULTRAVOX! were coming from; artsy avant-pop combining elements of a punked-up ROXY MUSIC, the group were something of a cult live act. This didn't translate into sales, however, and despite an improved second effort, 'HA! HA! HA!' (1977), the group languished in relative obscurity. With ROBIN SIMON replacing SHEARS, they decamped to Germany to begin work on a third set under the auspices of electronic maestro, CONNY PLANK. The underwhelming result, 'SYSTEMS OF ROMANCE' (1978), failed to change the group's fortunes and by the Spring of '79, FOXX had abandoned ship for a solo career while SIMON went on to join MAGAZINE. The ubiquitous MIDGE URE was brought in as lead man, the singer having already cut his music business teeth in such diverse outfits as SLIK, The RICH KIDS and THIN LIZZY. He was also an integral part of moody synth-poppers, VISAGE, co-writing some of their material alongside mainman, STEVE STRANGE. Ironically, all this upheaval

seemed to work wonders for all concerned, FOXX going his experimental electronic way and scoring a Top 40 hit almost immediately with the brilliant 'UNDERPASS' (early '80), while the newly revamped ULTRAVOX (now without a ! and signed to 'Chrysalis') broke the Top 30 that summer with 'SLEEPWALK'. 'VIENNA' (1980; again produced by CONNY PLANK) was released later that year, its Top 5 placing indicating that the new-look outfit had effectively cornered the burgeoning new romantic/electropop market. This was confirmed early in '81 when the album's title track narrowly missed the UK No.1 spot, its chilly, grandiose Euro feel and indelible melody managing to combine pretentiousness with mass public appeal. This was a talent which was to serve the group well over the ensuing five years, ULTRAVOX scoring an impressive run of seven Top 10 albums and a string of Top 30 hits. 'RAGE IN EDEN' (1981) was another Top 5 success, spawning three Top 20 singles including the po-faced 'ALL STOOD STILL'. The album also marked the end of the group's tenure with PLANK, GEORGE MARTIN overseeing production duties on 'QUARTET' (1982). The result was a markedly warmer sound and more commercial appeal, evident on the preceding single, 'REAP THE WILD WIND'. By the release of 'LAMENT' (1984), ULTRAVOX were a fully fledged pop band, the evocative heartbreak of 'DANCING WITH TEARS IN MY EYES' giving the group their biggest hit since 'VIENNA'. A bonus new track on the best selling compilation, 'THE COLLECTION' (1984), 'LOVE'S GREAT ADVENTURE', was another pop odyssey, its rolling synth crescendos a taster for the latest chapter in URE's solo career. Strangely enough, ULTRAVOX's last hit single was the sombre 'ALL FALL DOWN', its subject matter the war-torn Northern Ireland, an almost militaristic rhythm and uillean pipes utilised for greater effect. The track was lifted from the 'U-VOX' (1986) set, an album featuring the drumming talents of BIG COUNTRY's MARK BRZEZICKI. Realising they'd reached a creative impasse, ULTRAVOX disbanded the following year, URE taking up the solo career that had begun so successfully in 1982 with a Top 10 cover of Tom Rush's 'NO REGRETS' (made famous by the WALKER BROTHERS) and continued with the soaring pop of 'IF I WAS', a No.1 single in summer '85 (URE had also helped to mastermind the Band Aid single, 'Do They Know It's Christmas'). He struggled, however, to resurrect his flagging solo career, the 1988 set, 'ANSWERS TO NOTHING' barely scraping into the Top 40 while a Spring '89 single, 'SISTERS AND BROTHERS' was withdrawn by 'Chrysalis'. Subsequently securing a new contract with 'Arista', URE returned in 1991 with the Top 20 hit, 'COLD COLD HEART' and a Top 40 album, 'PURE'. While ULTRAVOX made a low-key comeback in 1993 with a new singer, TONY FENELLE, and a new album, 'REVELATION', URE has been conspicuous by his absence from the charts for most of the 90's. • **Songwriters:** FOXX and group until URE replaced FOXX. Covered only KING'S LEAD HAT (Brian Eno). MIDGE URE's solo career included THE MAN WHO SOLD THE WORLD (David Bowie) / STRANGE BREW (Cream).

Album rating: ULTRAVOX! (*5) / HA! HA! HA! (*5) / SYSTEMS OF ROMANCE (*5) / THREE INTO ONE compilation (*7) / VIENNA (*7) / RAGE IN EDEN (*6) / QUARTET (*5) / MONUMENT – THE SOUNDTRACK (*4) / LAMENT (*5) / THE COLLECTION compilation (*7) / U-VOX (*4) / REVELATION (*3) / INGENUITY (*2) / Midge Ure: THE GIFT (*6) / ANSWERS TO NOTHING (*5) / PURE (*4) / IF I WAS: THE VERY BEST OF MIDGE URE & ULTRAVOX compilation (*7) / BREATHE (*5)

TIGER LILY

DENNIS LEIGH (JOHN FOXX) – vocals / **STEVE SHEARS** – guitar / **BILLY CURRIE** (b. 1 Apr'52, Huddersfield, Yorkshire, England) – keyboards / **WARREN CANN** (b.20 May'52, Victoria, Canada) – drums / **CHRIS ST. JOHN** (b. CHRISTOPHER ALLEN, 14 Jul'52) – bass

		Gull	not iss.
Mar 75.	(7") *(GULS 54)* **AIN'T MISBEHAVIN'. / MONKEY JIVE**		–
——	(w/drawn before release) (iss.Oct77) (re-iss. Oct80 on 'Dead Good')		

ULTRAVOX!

LEIGH became **JOHN FOXX** and ST.JOHN now **CHRIS CROSS**. (CURRIE now added violin, synthesizers.)

		Island	Antilles
Feb 77.	(7") *(WIP 6375)* **DANGEROUS RHYTHM. / MY SEX**		–
Mar 77.	(lp/c) *(ILPS/ICT 9449)* **ULTRAVOX!**		–
	– Saturday night in the city of the dead / Life at Rainbow End (for all the tax exiles on Main Street) / Slip away / I want to be a machine / Wide boys / Dangerous rhythm / The lonely hunter / The wild the beautiful and the damned / My sex.		
May 77.	(7") *(WIP 6392)* **YOUNG SAVAGE. / SLIPAWAY**		–
Oct 77.	(7") *(WIP 6404)* **ROCKWROK. / HIROSHIMA MON AMOUR**		–
	(all 3 ULTRAVOX! singles were re-iss. Jul81)		
Oct 77.	(lp/c) *(ILPS/ICT 9505)* **HA! HA! HA!**		–
	– Rockwrok / The frozen ones / Fear in the western world / Distant smile / The man who dies every day / Artificial life / While I'm still alive / Hiroshima mon amour. *(free-7"w.a.)*– **QUIRKS. / MODERN LOVE** (live)		
Feb 78.	(7"ep) *(IEP 8)* **RETRO E.P.** (live)		–
	– The wild the beautiful and the damned / Young savage / My sex / The man who dies every day.		
——	**ROBIN SIMON** – guitar (ex-NEO) repl. SHEARS to COWBOYS INTERNATIONAL		
Aug 78.	(7"/12"violet) *(WIP/12WIP 6454)* **SLOW MOTION. / DISLOCATION**		–
Sep 78.	(lp/c) *(ILPS/ICT 9555)* <7069> **SYSTEMS OF ROMANCE**		
	– Slow motion / I can't stay long / Someone else's clothes / Blue light / Some of them / Quiet men / Dislocation / Maximum acceleration / When you walk through me / Just for a moment.		

Oct 78. (7"/12"white) *(WIP/12WIP 6459)* **QUIET MEN. / CROSS FADE** ☐ ☐

—— (Apr79) **MIDGE URE** (b.JAMES, 10 Oct'53, Cambuslang, Scotland) – vocals, guitar (ex-SLIK, ex-RICH KIDS, ex-THIN LIZZY, ex-VISAGE) repl. JOHN FOXX who went solo. ROBIN also departed to MAGAZINE. Now as ULTRAVOX, after dropping the exclamation mark!

	Chrysalis	Chrysalis
Jun 80. (7",7"clear) *(CHS 2441)* **SLEEPWALK. / WAITING**	29	☐
Sep 80. (7",7"clear/12") *(CHS 2457/122457)* **PASSING STRANGERS. / SOUND ON SOUND**	57	☐
Oct 80. (lp/c) *(CHR/ZCHR 1296)* <1296> **VIENNA**	3	☐

– Astradyne / New Europeans / Private lives / Passing strangers / Sleepwalk / Mr. X / Western promise / Vienna / All stood still. (cd-iss. 1985) (re-iss. cd Mar94 + Jul94)

Jan 81. (7",7"clear) *(CHS 2481)* **VIENNA. / PASSIONATE REPLY** 2 ☐
(12"+=) *(CHS 122481)* - Herr X.

Apr 81. (7",7"clear) *(CHS 2457)* **PASSING STRANGERS. / FACE TO FACE** ☐ –
(12"+=) *(CHA 122457)* – King's lead hat.

May 81. (7",7"clear) *(CHS 2522)* **ALL STOOD STILL. / ALLES KLAR** 8 ☐
(12"+=) *(CHS 122522)* – Keep talking.

Aug 81. (7",7"clear/ext-12") *(CHS 2549/122549)* **THE THIN WALL. / I NEVER WANTED TO BEGIN** 14 ☐

Sep 81. (lp/c) *(CHR/ZCHR 1338)* <1338> **RAGE IN EDEN** 4 ☐
– The voice / We stand alone / Rage in Eden / I remember (death in the afternoon) / The thin wall / Stranger within / Accent on youth / The ascent / Your name has slipped my mind again. (cd-iss. Jun87)

Nov 81. (7",7"clear) *(CHS 2559)* **THE VOICE. / PATHS AND ANGELS** 16 ☐
(12"+=,12"clear+=) *(CHS 122559)* – All stood still (live) / Private lives (live).

Sep 82. (7",7"clear/c-s/12") *(CHS 2639/122639)* <42682> **REAP THE WILD WIND. / HOSANNA (IN EXCELIS DEO)** 12 | 71 Mar 83

Oct 82. (lp/c/pic-lp) *(CDL/ZCDL/PCDL 1394)* <1394> **QUARTET** 6 | 61 Mar83
– Reap the wild wind / Serenade / Mine for life / Hymn / Visions of blue / When the scream subsides / We came to dance / Cut and run / The song (we go).

Nov 82. (7",7"clear) *(CHS 2557)* **HYMN. / MONUMENT** 11 ☐
(12"+=,12"clear+=) *(CHS 122557)* – The thin wall.

Mar 83. (7",7"clear,7"pic-d) *(CHS 2676)* **VISIONS IN BLUE. / BREAK YOUR BACK** 15 ☐
(12"+=,12"clear+=) *(CHS 122676)* – Reap the wild wind.

May 83. (7",7"pic-d,7"clear/12",12"clear) *(VOX/+X 1)* **WE CAME TO DANCE. / OVERLOOK** 18 ☐

Oct 83. (lp/c) *(CUX/ZCUX 1452)* **MONUMENT – THE SOUNDTRACK (live)** 9 ☐
– Monument / Reap the wild wind / The voice / Vienna / Mine for life / Hymn.

Feb 84. (7",7"clear/12") *(VOX/+X 2)* **ONE SMALL DAY. / EASTERLY** 27 ☐

Apr 84. (lp/c/pic-lp/cd) *(CDL/ZCDL/PCDL/CCD 1459)* <41459> **LAMENT** 8 ☐
– White China / One small day * / Dancing with tears in my eyes / Lament * / Man of two worlds / Heart of the country / When the time comes / A friend I called Desire. (c+cd+=)– (tracks * remixed).

May 84. (7",7"clear/12") *(UV/+X 1)* **DANCING WITH TEARS IN MY EYES. / BUILDING** 3 ☐

Jul 84. (7",7"clear) *(UV 2)* **LAMENT. / HEART OF THE COUNTRY** 22 ☐
(12"+=) *(UVX 2)* – ('A'instrumental.)

Oct 84. (7",7"clear,7"pic-d/12") *(UV/+X 3)* **LOVE'S GREAT ADVENTURE. / WHITE CHINA** 12 ☐

Nov 84. (lp/c/cd) *(UTV/ZUTV 1)(CCD 1490)* **THE COLLECTION (compilation)** 2 ☐
– Dancing with tears in my eyes / Hymn / The thin wall / The voice / Vienna / Passing strangers / Sleepwalk / Reap the wild wind / All stood still / Visions in blue / We came to dance / One small day / Love's great adventure / Lament. (w/ free 12")

—— guest **MARK BRZEZICKI** (b.21 Jun'57) – drums (of BIG COUNTRY) repl. CANN to HELDEN

Sep 86. (7",7"clear,7"pic-d) *(UV 4)* **SAME OLD STORY. / 3** 31 ☐
(12",12"clear) *(UVX 4)* – ('A'side) / All in one day.

Oct 86. (lp/c/cd) *(CDL/ZCDL/CCD 1545)* **U-VOX** 9 ☐
– Same old story / Sweet surrender / Dream on / The prize / All fall down / Time to kill / Moon madness / Follow your heart / All in one day.

Nov 86. (7",7"clear) *(UV 5)* **ALL FALL DOWN. / DREAM ON** 30 ☐
(12"+=) *(UVX 5)* – ('A'version.)

May 87. (7",7"clear) *(UV 6)* **ALL IN ONE DAY. / THE PRIZE (live)** ☐ ☐
(12"+=) *(UVX 6)* – Stateless.

—— Disbanded 1987, although U-VOX was formed by BILLY CURRIE, ROBIN SIMON and MARCUS O'HIGGINS – vocals. They toured 1989 playing ULTRAVOX songs.

—— **TONY FENELLE** – vocals repl. MIDGE URE who was by now continuing solo.

	D.S.B.	not iss.
May 93. (cd/c/lp) *(DSB 3098-2/-4/-1)* **REVELATION**	☐	☐

– I am alive / Revelation / Systems of love / Perfecting the art of common ground / The great outdoors / The closer I get to you / No turning back / True believer / Unified / The new frontier.

Jun 93. (7"/c-s/7"clear) *(DSB 3097-7/-3/-1)* **I AM ALIVE. / SYSTEMS OF LOVE** ☐ ☐
(cd-s+=) *(DSB 30975)* – ('A'extended.)

—— line-up: **CURRIE / BLUE / BURNS**

	Resurgence	not iss.
Nov 95. (cd) *(RES 109CD)* **INGENUITY**	☐	☐

– Ingenuity / There goes a beautiful world / Give it all back / Future picture forever / The silent cries / Distance / Ideals / Who'll save you / A way out, a way through / Majestic.

– compilations, others, etc. –

Jun 80. (lp/c) *Island/ US= Antilles; (ILPS/ICM 9614)* <7079> **THREE INTO ONE** ☐ ☐
– Young savage / Rockwrok / Dangerous rhythm / The man who dies every day / The wild the beautiful and the damned / Slow motion / Just for a moment / My sex / Quiet men / Hiroshima mon amour. (re-iss. Nov86, cd-iss. 1990)

Mar 81. (12"ep,12"clear-ep) *Island; (DWIP 6691)* **SLOW MOTION / DISLOCATION. / QUIET MEN / HIROSHIMA MON AMOUR** 33 –

Apr 88. (12"ep) *Strange Fruit; (SFPS 047)* **THE PEEL SESSIONS (21.7.77)** ☐ ☐
– My sex / Artificial life / Young savage.

Sep 93. (cd/c) *Spectrum; (550112-2/-4)* **SLOW MOTION** ☐ ☐

Aug 94. (cd) *Chrysalis; (CDCHR 6053)* **RARE VOLUME 2** ☐ ☐

Jun 95. (cd) *Receiver; (RRCD 199)* **FUTURE PICTURE** ☐ ☐

Aug 95. (cd-s) *Old Gold;* **VIENNA / REAP THE WILD WIND** ☐ ☐

Oct 95. (cd) *MFP; (CDMFP 6175)* **DANCING WITH TEARS IN MY EYES** ☐ ☐

Nov 95. (3xcd-box) *Island; (5241522)* **ULTRAVOX! / HA! HA! HA! / SYSTEMS OF ROMANCE** ☐ ☐

MIDGE URE

—— had already started own solo career. Debut w / ex-COCKNEY REBEL **STEVE HARLEY** – dual vocals

	Chrysalis	Chrysalis
Mar 82. (7") **I CAN'T EVEN TOUCH YOU. / I CAN'T BE ANYONE**	☐	–
Jun 82. (7"/12") *(CHS 2618/122618)* **NO REGRETS. / MOOD MUSIC**	9	☐
Jul 83. (7"/12") *(FEST/+X 1)* **AFTER A FASHION ("MIDGE URE & MICK KARN"). / TEXTURES**	39	☐

Above 45 on 'Musicfest' w / ex-JAPAN bassist

—— Dec'84 saw MIDGE co-write and create BAND AID with BOB GELDOF (BOOMTOWN RATS). They hit UK No.1 with famine relief single DO THEY KNOW IT'S CHRISTMAS.

Aug 85. (7",7"clear) *(URE 1)* **IF I WAS. / PIANO** 1 ☐
(12"+=,12"clear+=) *(UREX 1)* – The man who sold the world.

Oct 85. (lp/c/cd) *(CDL/ZCDL/CCD 1508)* **THE GIFT** 2 ☐
– If I was / When the winds blow / Living in the past / That certain smile / The gift / Antilles / Wastelands / Edo / The chieftain / The gift (reprise). (re-iss. cd+c Apr93)

Nov 85. (7",7"clear/7"pic-d) *(URE/+P 2)* **THAT CERTAIN SMILE. / THE GIFT** 28 ☐
(12"+=,d12"+=,12"clear+=) *(UREX 2)* – ('A'instrumental) / Fade to grey.

Jan 86. (7",7"clear) *(URE 3)* **WASTELANDS. / THE CHIEFTAIN** 46 ☐
(12"+=)(12"clear+=) *(UREX 3)* – Dancer.

May 86. (7",7"clear) *(URE 4)* **CALL OF THE WILD. / WHEN THE WIND BLOWS** 27 ☐
(12"+=,12"clear+=) *(UREX 4)* – After a fashion (w/ MICK KARN).

Aug 88. (7",7"clear) *(URE 5)* **ANSWERS TO NOTHING. / HONORARE** 49 ☐
(12"+=,12"clear+=) *(UREX 5)* – Oboe.
(cd-s+=) *(URECD 5)* – (excerpts from lp below).

Sep 88. (lp/c/cd) *(CDL/ZCHR/CCD 1649)* <41649> **ANSWERS TO NOTHING** 30 | 88
– Answers to nothing / Take me home / Sister and brother / Dear God / The leaving (so long) / Just for you / Hell to Heaven / Lied / Homeland / Remembrance day. <US cd re-iss. Aug98 on 'EMI'; 96824>

Nov 88. (7",7"clear) *(URE 6)* <43319> **DEAR GOD. / MUSIC 1** 55 | 95
(12"+=) *(UREX 6)* – All fall down (live) / Strange brew (live).
(cd-s+=) *(URECD 6)* – Remembrance day.

—— In Apr'89, SISTERS AND BROTHERS single was withdrawn.

—— **URE** now with **MARK BRZEZICKI** – drums / **STEVE BRZEZICKI + JEREMY MEEHAN** – bass / **ROBBIE KILGORE** – keys / **SIMON PHILLIPS** – drums / **STEVE WILLIAMS** – perc./ etc

	Arista	R.C.A.
Aug 91. (7") *(114 555)* **COLD COLD HEART. / FLOWERS**	17	☐

(12"+=/cd-s+=) – Supernatural *(written by GREEN; SCRITTI POLITTI)*

Sep 91. (cd/lp) *(261/211 922)* <61010> **PURE** 36 ☐
– I see hope in the morning light / Cold, cold heart / Pure love / Sweet 'n' sensitive thing / Let it go? / Rising / Light in your eyes / Little one / Hands around my heart / Waiting days / Tumbling down.

Oct 91. (7"/c-s) **I SEE HOPE IN THE MORNING LIGHT. / THE MAN I USED TO BE** ☐ ☐
(12"+=/cd-s+=) – Madame de Sade.

May 96. (c-s) *(74321 37117-4)* **BREATHE / COLD COLD HEART (live)** 70 ☐
(cd-s+=) *(74321 37117-2)* – No regrets / Trail of tears (live).

Jun 96. (cd/c) *(74321 34629-2/-4)* **BREATHE** ☐ –
– Breathe / Fields of fire / Fallen angel / Free / Guns and arrows / Lay my body down / Sinner man / Live forever / Trail of tears / May your good Lord / Maker.

Oct 96. (c-s) *(74321 42316-4)* **GUNS & ARROWS /** ☐ ☐
(cd-s) *(74321 42316-2)* –

– (MIDGE URE & ULTRAVOX) compilations, etc. –

Jan 93. (7"/c-s) *Chrysalis; (TCCHS 3936)* **VIENNA. / WASTELANDS** 13 ☐
(cd-s+=) *(CDCHS 3936)* – Answers to nothing / The voice.
(cd-s) *(CDCHSS 3936)* – ('A'side) / Call of the wild / One small day / Hymn.

Feb 93. (cd/c/lp) *Chrysalis; (CD/TC/+CHR 1987)* **IF I WAS: THE VERY BEST OF MIDGE URE AND ULTRAVOX** 10 ☐
– If I was / No regrets / Love's great adventure / Dear God / Cold cold heart / Vienna / Call of the wild / Dancing with tears in my eyes / All fall down / Yellow pearl / Fade to grey / Reap the wild wind / Answers to nothing / Do they know it's Christmas? (BAND AID). (cd+=) After a fashion (with MICK KARN) / That certain smile.

Dec 82. (d-c) *Chrysalis; (ZCDP 109)* **VIENNA / RAGE IN EDEN** ☐ ☐

Feb 87. (7") *Old Gold; (OG 9675)* **VIENNA. / THE VOICE** ☐ ☐

Apr 87. (7") *Old Gold; (OG 9698)* **DANCING WITH TEARS IN MY EYES. / REAP THE WILD WIND** (12"-iss.Jan88) ☐ –

UNBELIEVABLE TRUTH (dig out; Great Alt & Indie . . .)

UNCLE TUPELO

Formed: Belleville, Illinois, USA ... 1987 by schoolmates JEFF TWEEDY and JAY FARRAR (who had played in punk outfit, The PRIMITIVES – US), MIKE HEIDORN completing the line-up. A band that have achieved almost legendary status among alternative country afficionados, UNCLE TUPELO christened a whole movement with the release of their seminal debut album, 'NO DEPRESSION' (1990). Issued on the small 'Rockville' label, the record translated the raw expression and sonic assault of punk into a contemporary country context; the spirit of what TWEEDY and FARRAR were trying to do was best illustrated on the title track, an impressive excavation of an ancient CARTER FAMILY song yearning for the sanctuary of Heaven, performed with as much conviction as any bonafide gospel act. Follow-up set, 'STILL FEEL GONE' (1991) continued in the same vein, developing and updating country in a fashion a damn sight closer to GRAM PARSONS' cosmic vision than the polished dross coming out of Nashville. Yet it was the stark testimony of the PETER BUCK-produced 'MARCH 16-20' (1992) that really cut to the heart of American roots tradition, a breathtaking album of grainy originals and hard-bitten folk covers. While the quality of the songwriting arguably outstripped almost anything released under the banner of country/alt-country in the past twenty years, it was the bruised beauty of the vocals (especially FARRAR) that really brought on the goose-bumps and belied UNCLE TUPELO's relative youthfulness. The likes of 'GRINDSTONE', 'BLACK EYE' and the traditional 'MOONSHINER' resonated with what sounded like the careworn resignation of a lifetime's toil and trouble, the whole album religious in its rawness. Released to rave reviews, it didn't take long for word to spread and with major labels eager for a piece of the action, FARRAR and TWEEDY opted to sign for 'Reprise' (home to spiritual forefathers PARSONS and NEIL YOUNG amongst others). With FARRAR and TWEEDY maintaining a hard-drinking, volatile relationship at the best of times, 'ANODYNE' (1993) proved to be the final product of their mercurial partnership. A return to more upbeat material, the album featured a rousing cover of Doug Sahm's 'GIVE BACK THE KEY TO MY HEART' (featuring the cult Texan roots man on guitar) alongside more reflective fare like the gorgeously plaintive 'SLATE', one of the most perfectly formed compositions in the FARRAR/TWEEDY canon with fiddle arrangements to break the hardest heart. While many mourned the band's passing, fans could look forward to the prospect of two solo projects, FARRAR's SON VOLT and TWEEDY's WILCO. The latter outfit (comprising TWEEDY, JAY BENNETT, JOHN STIRRATT and UNCLE TUPELO veterans MAX JOHNSTON and KEN COOMER) were first off the starting block with 1994's 'A.M.'. An enjoyable enough set of uptempo country-rock, it was nevertheless eclipsed by the 1996 follow-up, 'BEING THERE', a sprawling double set drawing comparisons with The STONES 'Exile On Main Street' and hailed as one of the albums of the year. Reaching far beyond TWEEDY's patented musical boundaries to encompass everything from bar-room belters to Spector-esque rock/pop, the record proved conclusively that FARRAR's other half was blessed with his own distinct musical vision. Fans yearning for the down-at-heel spirit of UNCLE TUPELO's moodier moments were comforted by the fact that FARRAR himself was still treading the dirt-road backstreets of country's dark underbelly with SON VOLT, releasing 'TRACE' in 1994 and 'STRAIGHTWAYS' in 1997; 'WIDE SWING TREMELO' (1998) was their most recent set. While some critics railed against what they perceived as the unrelenting miserabilism of FARRAR's approach (especially with regards to the SON VOLT live experience), there was no disputing the quality or honesty of the writing. While both camps continue to come up with the goods, the prospect of an UNCLE TUPELO reunion is still tantalisingly within reach. However, WILCO returned in the summer of '98, an unlikely collaboration with English bard BILLY BRAGG on a memorable WOODY GUTHRIE tribute album, 'MERMAID AVENUE', kept the duo ticking over fine style. The following March, the leaders of the alt-country/folk scene released their long-awaited third set, 'SUMMERTEETH' (1999), a UK Top 40 record (Top 100 in the US) that boasted some breezy pop tales opening with minor UK hit, 'CAN'T STAND IT'. • **Songwriters:** All compositions FARRAR/TWEEDY except arrangements of traditional tunes, plus covers: NO DEPRESSION (A.P.Carter) / JOHN HARDY (Leadbelly) / ATOMIC POWER (Louvin Brothers/B.Bain) / BLUE EYES (Gram Parsons) / EFFIGY (Creedence Clearwater Revival). • **Other info:** TWEEDY was also an integral part of y'allternative supergroup, GOLDEN SMOG, alongside members of the JAYHAWKS, SOUL ASYLUM, RUN WESTY RUN and BIG STAR.

Album rating: NO DEPRESSION (*7) / STILL FEEL GONE (*7) / MARCH 16-20 (*9) / ANODYNE (*8) / Wilco: A.M. (*6) / BEING THERE (*8) / SUMMERTEETH (*8) / Son Volt: TRACE (*6) / STRAIGHTAWAYS (*7) / WIDE SWING TREMELO (*7)

JEFF TWEEDY (b.25 Aug'67) – vocals, guitar, bass / **JAY FARRAR** (b.26 Dec'66) – vocals, guitar / **MICHAEL HEIDORN** – drums

			Rockville	Rockville
1990.	(lp) <ROCK 6050-1> **NO DEPRESSION**		-	

– Graveyard shift / That year / Before I break / No depression / Factory belt / Whiskey bottle / Outdone / Train / Life worth livin' / Flatness / So called friend / Screen door / John Hardy. *(UK cd-iss. Sep97; ROCK 6050-2)*

1990.	(7") <ROCK 6055-7> **I GOT DRUNK. / SIN CITY**		-	
1991.	(7") <ROCK 6069-7> **GUN. / I WANNA DESTROY YOU**		-	
1991.	(lp) <ROCK 6070-1> **STILL FEEL GONE**		-	

– Gun / Looking for a way out / Fall down easy / Nothing / Still be around / Watch me fail / Punch drunk / Postcard / D. Boon / True to life / Cold shoulder / Discarded / If that's alright. *(UK-iss.cd Nov92 on 'Yellow Moon'; BUFF 001CD)*

Nov 92.	(7") <ROCK 6089-7> **SAUGET WIND. /**			

Mar 93.	(cd/c/lp) <(6110-2/-4/-1)> **MARCH 16-20, 1992**			Aug92

– Grindstone / Coalminers / Wait up / Criminals / Shaky ground / Satan, your kingdom must come down / Black eye / Moonshiner / I wish my baby was born / Atomic power / Lilli Schull / Warfare / Fatal wound / Sandusky / Wipe the clock.

KEN COOMER – drums + **JOHN STIRRATT** – bass repl. HEIDORN

			Warners	Sire
Oct 93.	(cd/c) *(9362 45330-2/-4)* <45424> **ANODYNE**			

– Slate / Acuff-Rose / The long cut / Give back the key to my heart / Chickamauga / New Madrid / Anodyne / We've been had / Fifteen keys / High water / No sense in lovin' / Steal the crumbs.

—— arguments arose, FARRAR subsequently forming SON VOLT with MICHAEL HEIDORN.

– compilations, etc. –

May 95.	(c) *Dutch East; <6110>* **STILL FEEL GONE / MARCH 16-20, 1992**		-	

WILCO

JEFF TWEEDY with remaining UNCLE TUPELO members **STIRRATT + COOMER**

			Warners	Reprise
Apr 95.	(cd) <(9362 45857-2)> **A.M.**			

– I must be high / Casino queen / Box full of letters / Shouldn't be ashamed / Pick up the change / I thought IU held you / That's not the issue / It's just that simple / Should've been in love / Passenger side / Dash 7 / Blue eyed soul / Too far apart.

Jul 95.	(c-s) *(W 0306MC)* **BOX FULL OF LETTERS / I AM NOT WILLING**			

(cd-s+=) *(W 0306)* – Who were you thinking of (live).

—— added **JAY BENNETT** – guitar

Feb 97.	(d-cd) <(9362 46236-2)> **BEING THERE**		73	Nov96

– Misunderstood / Forget the flowers / I got you (at the end of the century) / Red eyed and blue / (Was I) In your dreams / Dreamer in my dreams / Lonely one / Why would you wanna live / Kingpin / Someone else's song / Outta mind (outta sight) / Someday soon / Sunken treasure / Say you miss me / Hotel Arizona / What's the world got in store / Far far away / Monday.

Apr 97.	(cd-ep) *(W 0397CD)* **OUTTA SIGHT (OUTTA MIND) / OUTTA MIND (OUTTA SIGHT) / THIRTEEN / A LASTING FONDER**		-	

—— In the middle of '98, WILCO collaborated with BILLY BRAGG on a tribute album ('MERMAID AVENUE') to WOODY GUTHRIE

Mar 99.	(cd/c/lp) <(9362 47282-2/-4/-1)> **SUMMERTEETH**		38	78

– Can't stand it / She's a jar / A shot in the arm / We're just friends / I'm always in love / Nothing'severgonnastandinmyway (again) / Pieholden suite / How to fight loneliness / Via Chicago / ELT / My darling / When you wake up feeling old / Summer teeth / In a future age.

Apr 99.	(cd-s) *(W 475CD1)* **CAN'T STAND IT / STUDENT LOAN ZERO / TRIED AND TRUE**		67	

(cd-s) *(W 475CD2)* – ('A'side) / Sunken treasure (solo acoustic) / I'm always in love (solo acoustic).

Jun 99.	(cd-s/cd-s) *(W 496 C/CD2)* **A SHOT IN THE ARM / VIA CHICAGO (demo) / SHE'S A JAR**			

(cd-s) *(W 496CD1)* – ('A'side) / ELT (demo) / True love will find you in the end.

SON VOLT

JIM FARRAR – vocals, guitar, organ, harmonica, songwriter / **DAVE BOQUIST** – guitars, fiddle, banjo, lap steel / **JIM BOQUIST** – bass, backing vocals / **MIKE HEIDORN** – drums

			Warners	Warners
Oct 95.	(cd/c) *(9362-46010-2/-4)>* **TRACE**			Sep95

– Windfall / Live free / Tear stained eye / Route / Ten second news / Drown / Loose string / Out of the picture / Catching on / Too early / Mystifies me.

—— with guests **ERIC HEYWOOD** – pedal steel, mandolin / **PAULI RYAN** – tambourine

Aug 97.	(cd) <(9362-46518-2/-4)> **STRAIGHTWAYS**		44	May97

– Caryatid easy / Back into the world / Picking up the signal / Left a slide / Cresote / Cemetery savior / Last minute shakedown / Been set free / No more parades / Way down Watson.

Oct 98.	(cd/c) <(9362 47059-2/-4)> **WIDE SWING TREMELO**			93

– Straightface / Driving the view / Jodel / Medicine hat / Strands / Flow / Dead man's clothes / Right on through / Chanty / Carry you down / Question / Streets that time walks / Hanging blue side / Blind hope.

UNDERTONES

Formed: Londonderry, N.Ireland ... late '75 by the O'NEILL brothers, DAMIAN and JOHN, alongside FEARGAL SHARKEY, MIKE BRADLEY and BILLY DOHERTY. Taking up the offer of a one-off singles deal with Belfast label, 'Good Vibrations', they released a debut EP in September '78 with the seminal 'TEENAGE KICKS' as the lead track. Immediately championed by DJ John Peel, this compelling slice of adolescent angst reached the collective ear of 'Sire' records leading to a prestigious deal. Their major label debut, 'GET OVER YOU', scraped into the Top 60 although they eventually cracked the chart later that Spring with 'JIMMY JIMMY', a boisterous post-punk stomper reminiscent of a wittier, more laid-back SHAM 69. This was closely followed by an eponymous debut album, establishing The UNDERTONES as one of the most promising and intelligent new-wave punk/pop bands in the UK. Like a more hyperactive KINKS, the band chronicled the nitty gritty, highs and lows of everyday life in such unforgettable pop nuggets as 'HERE COMES THE SUMMER', 'TRUE CONFESSIONS' and 'FAMILY ENTERTAINMENT'. Arguably, 'YOU'VE GOT MY NUMBER (WHY DON'T YOU USE IT)', remains The UNDERTONES' finest moment, a jarring, insistent riff marking it out from the group's standard pop rush. While the song barely made the UK Top 40, The UNDERTONES were back in the Top 10 the following year with the sneering

'MY PERFECT COUSIN', a humorous tale of a goody-two shoes relative which obviously struck a chord with more than a few disaffected youngsters. The accompanying album, 'HYPNOTISED' (1980), consolidated the group's standing, critically and commercially, a more assured set which also spawned another classic single in 'WEDNESDAY WEEK'. Inevitably, however, along with many of their contemporaries, The UNDERTONES increasingly moved away from the roughshod charm of old to a more refined sound. This was evident in the group's third album, 'THE POSITIVE TOUCH' (1981), only one track making the Top 20 ('IT'S GOING TO HAPPEN') despite such enduring material as the lovely 'JULIE OCEAN'. By 1983's 'THE SIN OF PRIDE', FEARGAL's quavering vocals and the group's boy-next-door image had been shelved for a blend of "alternative soul". Predictably, this didn't sit well with the group's more traditional fans who were unsurprisingly becoming increasingly critical of The UNDERTONES newfound sophistication. The imminent split eventually came in mid '83 with SHARKEY initially hooking up with VINCE CLARKE in The ASSEMBLY before launching a solo career. Following a minor hit on MADNESS' 'Zarjazz' label, SHARKEY signed to 'Virgin' and scored a massive No.1 hit with Maria McKee's 'A Good Heart'. A fully fledged, if brief, pop star, SHARKEY's eponymous solo debut hit the Top 10 around the same time in late '85, while he scored a follow-up Top 5 hit with 'YOU LITTLE THIEF'. Successive albums failed to chart, however, and SHARKEY moved into A&R work for 'Virgin'. The O'NEILL brothers, meanwhile, formed the critically acclaimed THAT PETROL EMOTION. • Songwriters: O'NEILL brothers except UNDER THE BOARDWALK (Drifters). In the mid-80's, FEARGAL, solo, collaborated with DAVE STEWART of The EURYTHMICS. In 1991, he teamed up with writers SHERRILL and DiPIERO. Covered; TAKE ME TO THE RIVER (Al Green). • More Info: While spending time in Londonderry in February '86, FEARGAL's mother and sister were abducted by terrorists, although they were thankfully released after a number of hours.

Album rating: THE UNDERTONES (*9) / HYPNOTISED (*7) / POSITIVE TOUCH (*6) / THE SIN OF PRIDE (*5) / ALL WRAPPED UP compilation (*7) / CHER O'BOWLES – THE PICK OF THE UNDERTONES compilation (*8) / Feargal Sharkey: FEARGAL SHARKEY (*6) / WISH (*4) / SONGS FROM THE MARDI GRAS (*5)

FEARGAL SHARKEY (b.13 Aug'58) – vocals / **DAMIAN O'NEILL** (b.15 Jan'61, Belfast, N.Ireland) – guitar, bass / **JOHN O'NEILL** (b.26 Aug'57) – guitar / **MIKE BRADLEY** (b.13 Aug'59) – bass / **BILLY DOHERTY** (b.10 Jul'58, Larne, N.Ireland) – drums

	Good Vibrations	not iss.
Sep 78. (7"ep) (GOT 4) **TEENAGE KICKS / TRUE CONFESSIONS. / SMARTER THAN U / EMMERGENCY CASES**	☐	-

(re-iss. Oct78 on 'Sire', hit No.31) (re-iss. Jul83 on 'Ardeck', hit 60) (re-iss. 7"ep+cd-ep Apr94 on 'Dojo')

	Sire	Sire
Jan 79. (7"m) (SIR 4010) **GET OVER YOU. / REALLY REALLY / SHE CAN ONLY SAY NO**	57	☐
Apr 79. (7",7"lime green) (SIR 4015) **JIMMY JIMMY. / MARS BARS**	16	☐
May 79. (lp/c) (SRK/+C 6071) <6081> **THE UNDERTONES**	13	Jan 80

– Family entertainment / Girls don't like it / Male model / I gotta getta / Teenage kicks / Wrong way / Jump boys / Here comes the summer / Get over you / Billy's third / Jimmy Jimmy / True confessions / She's a runaround / I know a girl / Listening in. (re-iss. Jul83 on 'Ardeck') (re-iss. +cd.Oct87 on 'Fame') (re-iss. cd+c May94 on 'Dojo', with 7 extra tracks) – Smarter than u / Emergency cases / Top twenty / Really really / Mars Bars / She can only say no / One way ticket.

Jul 79. (7"m) (SIR 4022) **HERE COMES THE SUMMER. / ONE WAY LOVE / TOP TWENTY**	34	☐
Sep 79. (7") (SIR 4024) **YOU'VE GOT MY NUMBER (WHY DON'T YOU USE IT). / LET'S TALK ABOUT GIRLS**	32	☐
Mar 80. (7"m) (SIR 4038) **MY PERFECT COUSIN. / HARD LUCK / I DON'T WANNA SEE YOU AGAIN**	9	

(d7"+=) (SIR 4038) – Here comes the summer.

Apr 80. (lp/c) (SRK/+C 6088) <6088> **HYPNOTISED**	6	

– More songs about chocolate and girls / There goes Norman / Hypnotised / See that girl / Whizz kids / Under the boardwalk / The way girls talk / Hard luck / My perfect cousin / Boys will be boys / Tearproof / Wednesday week / Nine times out of ten / Girls that don't talk / What's with Terry?. (re-iss. Mar86 on 'Fame') (re-iss. cd+c May94 on 'Dojo', with 5 extra tracks) – You've got my number (why don't you use it?) / Hard luck (again) / Let's talk about girls / I told you so / I don't want to see you again.

Jun 80. (7") (SIR 4042) **WEDNESDAY WEEK. / I TOLD YOU SO**	11	

	Ardeck-EMI	Rykodisc
Apr 81. (7") (ARDS 8) **IT'S GOING TO HAPPEN. / FAIRLY IN THE MONEY NOW**	18	☐
May 81. (lp/c) (ARD/TCARD 103) <12159> **THE POSITIVE TOUCH**	17	

– Fascination / Life's too easy / You're welcome / The positive touch / Julie Ocean / Crisis of mine / His good looking friend / When Saturday comes / It's going to happen / Sigh and explode / I don't know / Hannah Doot / Boy wonder / Forever Paradise. (re-iss. May90 on 'Dojo'+=;) – Kiss in the dark / Beautiful friend / Life's too easy / Fairly in the money now.

Jul 81. (7") (ARDS 9) **JULIE OCEAN. / KISS IN THE DARK**	41	☐
Feb 82. (7") (ARDS 10) **BEAUTIFUL FRIEND. / LIFE'S TOO EASY**	☐	-
Jan 83. (7") (ARDS 11) **THE LOVE PARADE. / LIKE THAT**	☐	-

(12"+=) (12ARDS 11) – You're welcome / Family entertainment / Crises of mine.

Mar 83. (7") (ARDS 12) **GOT TO HAVE YOU BACK. / TURNING BLUE**	☐	-

(12"+=) (12ARDS 12) – Bye bye baby blue.

Mar 83. (lp/c) (ARD/TCARD 104) **THE SIN OF PRIDE**	43	-

– Got to have you back / Valentine's treatment / Luxury / Love before romance / Untouchable / Bye bye baby blue / Conscious / Chain of love / Soul seven / The love parade / Save me / The sin of pride. (re-iss. cd+c May94 on 'Dojo', with 6 extra tracks) – Turning blue / Like that / Window shopping for new clothes / Bitter sweet / You stand so close (but you're never there) / I can only dream.

Apr 83. (7") (ARDS 13) **CHAIN OF LOVE. / WINDOW SHOPPING FOR NEW CLOTHES**	☐	-

—— Split mid'83 with FEARGAL SHARKEY joining The ASSEMBLY; (see YAZOO) before going solo. The O'NEILL brothers formed THAT PETROL EMOTION.

– compilations, others, etc. –

Nov 83. (d-lp)(c) Ardeck-EMI; (ARD 1654283)(1654289) **ALL WRAPPED UP**	67	-

– Teenage kicks / Get over you / Jimmy Jimmy / Here comes the summer / You've got my number (why don't you use it) / My perfect cousin / Wednesday week / It's going to happen / Julie Ocean / Beautiful friend / The love parade / Got to have you back / Chain of love.

—— (Note all singles were re-iss. on 'Ardeck-EMI')

May 86. (lp/c) Ardeck-EMI; (EMS/TCEMS 1172) **CHER O'BOWLIES – THE PICK OF THE UNDERTONES**	96	-

– Teenage kicks / True confessions / Get over you / Family entertainment / Jimmy Jimmy / Here comes the Summer / You got my number (why don't you use it) / My perfect cousin / See that girl / Tearproof / Wednesday week / It's going to happen / Julie Ocean / You're welcome / Forever Paradise / Beautiful friend / Save me / The love parade / Valentine's treatment / Love before romance. (re-iss. +cd.Oct89 on 'Fame')

Jun 86. (7") Ardeck-EMI; (ARDS 14) **SAVE ME. / TEARPROOF**	☐	-

(12"+=) (12ARDS 14) – I know a girl.

Dec 86. (12"ep) Strange Fruit; (SFPS 016) **THE PEEL SESSIONS** (21.1.79)	☐	-

– Listening in / Family entertainment / Here comes the summer / Billy's third. (cd-ep iss.Mar88)

Dec 89. (lp/c/cd) Strange Fruit; (SFR LP/MC/CD 103) **DOUBLE PEEL SESSIONS**	☐	-

(re-iss. cd Mar94 as 'THE PEEL SESSIONS ALBUM')

Sep 93. (cd/c) Castle / Rykodisc; (CTV CD/MC 121) **THE BEST OF THE UNDERTONES – TEENAGE KICKS**	45	
Jul 95. (cd-ep) Dojo; (TONESCD 1) **HERE COMES THE SUMMER / GET OVER YOU / JIMMY JIMMY / YOU'VE GOT MY NUMBER (WHY DON'T YOU USE IT)**	☐	-

FEARGAL SHARKEY

—— moved to California, but returned to London in 1989.

	Zarjazz	not iss.
Sep 84. (7"/12") (JAZZ 1/112) **LISTEN TO YOUR FATHER. / CAN I SAY I LOVE YOU**	23	-

	Virgin	A&M
Jun 85. (7"/12") (VS 770/+12) **LOVING YOU. / IS THIS AN EXPLANATION**	26	☐
Sep 85. (7") (VS 808/+12) <2804> **A GOOD HEART. / ANGER IS HOLY**	1	74 Feb86

(12"+=) (VST 808) – Ghost train.
(cd-s++) (VSCD 808) – ('A'original).

Nov 85. (cd/c/lp) (CD/TC/+V 2360) <5108> **FEARGAL SHARKEY**	7	75 Feb86

– A good heart / You little thief / Ghost train / Ashes and diamonds / Made to measure / Someone to somebody / Don't leave it to nature / Love and hate / Bitter man / It's all over now. (re-iss. Jun88 lp/c; OVED/+C 218)

Dec 85. (7"/12") (VS 840/+12) **YOU LITTLE THIEF. / THE LIVING ACTOR**	5	☐
Mar 86. (7"/12") (VS 828/+12) **SOMEONE TO SOMEBODY. / COLD WATER**	64	☐

	Virgin	Virgin
Jan 88. (7") (VS 992) **MORE LOVE. / A BREATH OF SCANDAL**	44	☐

(12"+=)/ /(cd-s+=) (VS 99212)/ /(CDEP 18) – ('A'piano version)./ / Good heart (original).

Mar 88. (cd/c/lp) (CD/TC/+V 500) **WISH**	☐	☐

– Cold, cold streets / More love / Full confession / Please don't believe in me / Out of my system / Strangest girl in Paradise / Let me be / Blue days / If this is love / Safe to touch.

Mar 88. (7") (VS 1051) **OUT OF MY SYSTEM. / A TOUCH OF BLUE**	☐	☐

(12"+=) (VST 1051) – ('A'version)./ ('A'dub version).
(cd-s++=) (VSCD 1051) – Blue days.

Sep 88. (7") <> **IF THIS IS LOVE. / A TOUCH OF BLUE**	-	-
Feb 91. (7"/c-s) (VS/+C 1294) **I'VE GOT NEWS FOR YOU. / I CAN'T BEGIN TO STOP**	12	-

(12") (VST 1294) – ('A'side) / Loving you / A good heart / You little thief (remixes).
(cd-s+=) (VSCD 1294) – Medley:- Don't leave it to nature – Take me to the river.

Apr 91. (cd/c/lp) (CD/TC/+V 2642) **SONGS FROM THE MARDI GRAS**	27	-

– After the Mardi Gras / One night in Hollywood / Miss you fever / Women and I / I've got news for you / To miss someone / Sister Rosa / I'll take it back / Cry like a rainy day / She moved through the fair.

May 91. (7"/c-s) **WOMEN AND I. / I'LL TAKE IT BACK** (live)	☐	-

(12"+=)/ /(cd-s+=) – ('A'piano version)./ / Never never (ASSEMBLY).
(cd-s+=) – (2-'A'versions pt.1 & 2) / ('A'demo).

Aug 91. (7"/c-s) **TO MISS SOMEONE. / I'LL TAKE IT BACK**	☐	-

(cd-s+=) – Never never (ASSEMBLY) / Miss you fever (instrumental)
(cd-s+=) – Never never (ASSEMBLY) / Women and I (piano version).

—— In May93, FEARGAL appeared on PEACE TOGETHER single 'BE STILL' alongside SINEAD O'CONNOR, PETER GABRIEL & NANCI GRIFFITH.

– compilations, others, etc. –

1988. (3"cd-ep) Virgin; (CDT 36) **YOU LITTLE THIEF / MORE LOVE / LISTEN TO YOUR FATHER**	☐	-

UNDERWORLD

Formed: Romford, London, England . . . 1987 by RICK SMITH, KARL HYDE, ALFIE THOMAS and BRYN BURROWS, who had all been in Cardiff outfit FREUR (which was actually a symbol translated into a word!; no, PRINCE wasn't the first!). Even before this, RICK and KARL had played in synth-pop band, The SCREEN GEMS. In 1987, they took on the more conventional moniker, UNDERWORLD and hit America in the late 80's after signing for Seymour Stein's 'Sire' records. After a No.1 smash, 'RADAR', in Australia, they toured the States supporting EURYTHMICS, but it was clear this was not the direction for them. After recruiting DJ DARREN EMERSON, the band signed with the 'Boys Own' label, releasing the seminal techno crescendo of 'REZ' in February '93. They followed this up with the critically acclaimed, early '94 album, 'DUBNOBASSWITHMYHEADMAN', a nouveau-psychedelic classic climaxing with the delirious trance-athon of 'COWGIRL'. However, their big break came with the track 'BORN SLIPPY', a song featured on the 'Trainspotting' soundtrack. When re-released as a single in 1996, the track stormed to No.2, boosting sales of their recently released follow-up album, 'SECOND TOUGHEST IN THE INFANTS'. The band remain one of Britain's best loved techno acts, and with the Stateside success of The PRODIGY, there was still a chance that the band might break into America. Indeed, 1999's long-awaited 'BEAUCOUP FISH' took them into the US Top 100 having already made Top 3 in Britain. Highlights from the set were undoubtedly hit singles, 'PUSH UPSTAIRS', 'JUMBO' and 'SHUDDER – KING OF SNAKE', while 'MOANER' (theme from 1997's 'Batman & Robin' movie) was its 10-star pièce de resistance. • **Songwriters:** SMITH / HYDE / THOMAS then SMITH / HYDE / EMERSON. • **Trivia:** Produced by RUPERT HINES in 1988. HYDE worked on a 1991 'Paisley P.' album with TERRI NUNN (ex-Berlin). GEOFF DUGMORE (ex-ART OF NOISE) was a guest on 1989 album. Also appeared on WILLIAM ORBIT's 'Watch From A Vine Leaf' & ORBITAL's 'Lush 3' and remixed BJORK's 'Human Behaviour'.

Album rating: Freur: DOOT DOOT (*4) / GET US OUT OF HERE (*4) / Underworld: UNDERNEATH THE RADAR (*5) / CHANGE THE WEATHER (*4) / DUBNOBASSWITHMYHEADMAN (*8) / SECOND TOUGHEST IN THE INFANTS (*8) / BEAUCOUP FISH (*8)

FREUR

RICK SMITH (b.25 May'59, Ammanford, Wales) – keyboards, vocals / **KARL HYDE** (b.10 May'57, Worcester, England) – vocals, guitar / **ALFIE THOMAS** – guitar, vocals / **JOHN WARWICKER LE BRETON** – synthesizers / **BRYN B. BURROWS** – drums

	C.B.S.	Epic
Mar 83. (7"pic-d/ext.12") (WA/A13 3141) **DOOT DOOT. / HOLD ME MOTHER**	59	
Jun 83. (7"/7"pic-d) (A/WA 3456) **MATTERS OF THE HEART. / YOU'RE A HOOVER**		
(12"+=) (TA 3456) – ('A'extended).		
Sep 83. (7"/12") **RUNAWAY. / YOU'RE A HOOVER**	-	
Nov 83. (lp/c) (CBS/40 25522) <81566> **DOOT DOOT**		
– Doot doot / Runaway / Riders in the night / Theme from the film of the same name / Tender surrender / Matters of the heart / My room / Steam machine / Whispering / All too much.		
Jan 84. (7"/ext.12") (A/TA 4073) **DOOT DOOT. / HOLD ME MOTHER**		
Apr 84. (7") (A 4333) **RIDERS IN THE NIGHT. / INNOCENCE**		
(12"+=) (TA 4333) – This is the way I like to live my life.		

 — added **JAKE BOWIE** – bass

Oct 84. (7") (A 4726) **DEVIL AND DARKNESS. / JAZZ 'N' KING**		
(12"+=) (TX 4726) – ('A'extended).		
Feb 85. (7") (A 4983) **LOOK IN THE BACK FOR ANSWERS. / HEY HO AWAY WE GO**		
(12"+=) (TX 4983) – Uncle Jeff.		
Feb 85. (lp/c/cd) **GET US OUT OF HERE**		
– Look in the back for answers / Emeralds and pearls / Kiss me / A.O.K.O. / The Devil and darkness / The piano song / Happiness / Endless groove / This is the way I'd like to live my life / Bella Donna.		

UNDERWORLD

 — **BAZ ALLEN** – bass; repl. JOHN

	Sire	Sire
Mar 88. (lp/c/cd) (<925627-1/-4/-2>) **UNDERNEATH THE RADAR**		
– Glory! glory! / Call me No.1 / Rubber ball (space kitchen) / Show some emotion / Underneath the radar / Miracle party / I need a doctor / Bright white flame / Pray / The God song.		
Jul 88. (7") (W 7968) <27968> **UNDERNEATH THE RADAR. / BIG RED X**		74 Apr88
(12"+=) (W 7968T) – ('A'dub version).		
Aug 88. (7") **SHOW SOME EMOTION. / SHOCK THE DOCTOR**	-	

 — **PASCAL CONSOLI** – percussion, drums repl. BURROWS who joined WORLDWIDE ELECTRIC

Aug 89. (7"/c-s) (W 2854/+C) <22852> **STAND UP. / OUTSKIRTS**		67
(12") (W 2854T) – Stand up (and dance) / Stand up (ya house) / Outskirts.		
(cd-s) (W 2854CD) – (all mixes & B-side)		
Sep 89. (lp/c)(cd) (WX 289/+C)(K 925945-2) <25945> **CHANGE THE WEATHER**		
– Change the weather / Stand up / Fever / Original song / Mercy / Mr. Universe / Texas / Thrash / Sole survivor / Beach.		
Nov 89. (7") **CHANGE THE WEATHER. / TEXAS**	-	

 — ALLEN + CONSOLI became D-INFLUENCE

 — **SMITH + HYDE** brought in **DARREN EMERSON** (b.30 Apr'71, Hornchurch, Essex, England) – keyboards

	Boys Own	not iss.
1992. (12"ep/cd-ep) **DIRTY. / DIRTY GUITAR**		-
1992. (12"ep/cd-ep) **REZ. / WHY WHY WHY**		-
Jan 93. (12"ep/cd-ep) (BOI X/CD 13) **MMM . . . SKYSCRAPER I LOVE YOU. / ('A'-Telegraph mix 6.11.92) / ('A'-Jamscraper mix)**		
Sep 93. (12"/12"pink)(cd-s) (Collect 002/+P) **REZ. / COWGIRL** (re-iss. Aug95 on 'Junior Boys Own'; JBO 1001)		

	Junior Boys Own	Wax Trax!
1993. (12"; as LEMON INTERRUPT) (JBO 12-002) **ECLIPSE. / BIGMOUTH**		
1993. (12"; as LEMON INTERRUPT) (JBO 7-12) **DIRTY / MINNEAPOLIS. / MINNEAPOLIS (AIRWAVES)**		
Dec 93. (12"/cd-s) (JBO 17/+CD) **SPIKEE. / DOGMAN GO WOOF**	60	
Feb 94. (cd/c/d-lp) (JBO CD/CS/LP 1) <7217> **DUBNOBASSWITHMYHEADMAN**	12	
– Dark and long / Mmm . . . skyscraper I love you / Surf boy / Spoon man / Tongue / Dirty epic / Cowgirl / River of bass / M.E. (cd re-iss. May97; same)		
Jun 94. (cd-ep) (JBO 19CDS) **DARK & LONG (mixes)**	57	
– Hall's mix / Dark train / Most 'ospitable / 215 miles.		
(12") (JB 019) – ('A'-spoon deep mix) / ('A'-thing in a back mix).		
(12") (JB 019X) – ('A'-dark train mix) / ('A'-Burt's mix).		
(re-iss. Sep99 12"/cd-s; JBO 501027-3/-6)		
Dec 94. (cd-s) <8722> **DIRTY EPIC /**	-	
May 95. (12") (JBO 29) **BORN SLIPPY (telenatic). / COWGIRL (Vinjer mix)**	52	
(12") (JBO 29R) – ('A'side) / ('A'-Nuxx mix).		
(cd-s) (JBO 29CDS) – (above 2) / ('A'side again).		
Mar 96. (cd/c/d-lp) (JBO CD/MC/LP 4) <7240> **SECOND TOUGHEST IN THE INFANTS**	9	
– Juanita – Kiteless -- To dream of love / Banstyle – Sappys curry / Confusion the waitress / Rowla / Pearls girl / Air towel / Blueski / Stagger. (cd re-iss. May97; same)		
May 96. (12"ep) (JBO 38) **PEARLS GIRL. / MOSAIC / DEEP ARCH**	24	-
(cd-ep) (JBO 38CDS1) – ('A'-Carp Dreams . . . Koi) / Oich oich / Cherry pie.		
(cd-ep) (JBO 38CDS2) – ('A'mixes).		

	Junior Boys Own	TVT
Jun 96. (12") <8737> **ROWLA. / JUANITA**	-	
Jul 96. (12"/cd-s) (JBO 44/+CDS1) <8731> **BORN SLIPPY. / ('A'mixes)**	2	
(cd-s) (JBO 38CDS2) – ('A'side) / ('A'-Deep pan mix) / ('A'-Darren Price mix) / ('A'-Darren Price remix).		
(re-iss. Apr99 on 'Junior Boys Own-V2' 12"/cd-s/cd-s; JBO 50056 2-6/0-3/1-3)		
Oct 96. (12"/cd-s) (JBO 45/+CDS1) <8748> **PEARLS GIRL. / ('A'mixes; Puppies / Oich oich / Cherry Pie)**	22	Feb97
(cd-s) (JBO 45CDS2) – ('A'mixes; Mosaic / Deep arch).		
Jan 97. (12") **COWGIRL (mixes)**	-	
1997. (cd-ep) (9362 43905-2) **MOANER (short) / (album) / (relentless legs) / (long)** (above from the Warners movie, 'Batman & Robin')		

	Junior Boys Own– V2	V2
Mar 99. (cd/c/d-lp) (JBO 100543-2/-4/-1) <27042> **BEAUCOUP FISH**	3	93
– Cups / Push upstairs / Jumbo / Shudder – King of snake / Winjer / Skym / Bruce Lee / Kittens / Push downstairs / Something like a mama / Moaner.		
Mar 99. (12"/cd-s) (JBO 500544-6/-3) **PUSH UPSTAIRS (mixes; The Large Unit / Darren Price) / PLEASE HELP ME**	12	
(cd-s) (JBO 500617-3) – ('A'mixes).		
May 99. (12"/cd-s) (JBO 500719-6/-3) **JUMBO (mixes; edit / Rob Rives & Francois K Main Dish / Jedis Electro dub)**	21	
(cd-s) (JBO 500720-3) – ('A'mixes).		
Aug 99. (cd-s) (JBO 500879-3) **KING OF SNAKE (mixes; Straight (Mate) / Fatboy Slim / Slam)**	17	
(12"/cd-s) (JBO 500879-6/-8) – ('A'mixes) / Shudder – King of snake.		
Nov 99. (12"/cd-s) (JBO 501003-6/-3) **BRUCE LEE (Micronauts remixes) / CUPS (Salt City Orchestra mix)**		

– compilations, etc. –

Oct 97. (cd) April; <002> **DARK & LONG**	-	
Mar 99. (cd-s) TVT; (8722-2) **DIRTY EPIC / COWGIRL / REZ**		

UNKLE (see under ⇒ DJ SHADOW)

Midge URE (see under ⇒ ULTRAVOX)

URIAH HEEP

Formed: London, England . . . early 1970 by guitarist MICK BOX and vocalist DAVID BYRON, who had both cut their proverbial teeth in mid 60's outfit, The STALKERS (BYRON had also featured in a cover version hits compilation singing alongside REG DWIGHT, er . . . ELTON JOHN!). In 1968, the pair became SPICE, having found musicians PAUL NEWTON (ex-GODS), ROY SHARLAND and ALEX NAPIER. A solitary 45 was issued on 'United Artists', 'WHAT ABOUT THE MUSIC' failing to sell in any substantial quantities, although it has since become very rare. Taking their new moniker, URIAH HEEP, from a character in Dickens' 'David Copperfield' novel, the band enlisted some seasoned musicians, KEN HENSLEY (ex-GODS, ex-TOE FAT) and NIGEL OLLSON (ex-SPENCER DAVIS GROUP, ex-PLASTIC PENNY) to replace ROY SHARLAND and ALEX NAPIER. Now signed to 'Vertigo' and on a hefty diet of hard rock that critics lambasted for allegedly plagiarising LED ZEPPELIN, URIAH HEEP delivered their debut album, 'VERY 'EAVY, VERY 'UMBLE', in 1970. Although this did little to change music press opinions, the record contained at least two gems,

'GYPSY' and a cover of Tim Rose's 'COME AWAY MELINDA'. Drummer KEITH BAKER filled in for the ELTON JOHN bound OLLSON, prior to their follow-up set, 'SALISBURY' (1971), which, like its predecessor sold better in Germany and other parts of Europe. People were beginning to take BYRON's at times, high-pitched warblings seriously, the classic track 'BIRD OF PREY' (which was criminally left off the US version), being a perfect example. Later that year, 'LOOK AT YOURSELF' (on the new 'Bronze' imprint and featuring new drummer, IAN CLARKE) was released to some decent reviews, the celebrated 10 minute plus epic, 'JULY MORNING' (with an outstanding guest synth/keys spot from MANFRED MANN), helping it to touch the UK Top 40, while breaking the US Top 100. A steadier formation was found while recording their fourth album, 'DEMONS AND WIZARDS' (1972), GARY THAIN (ex-KEEF HARTLEY) took over from short-stop, MARK CLARKE (who had replaced NEWTON in November '71), while HENSLEY's old mate, LEE KERSLAKE superseded CLARKE. The results were outstanding, the disc going Top 30 and gold on both sides of the Atlantic, with tracks such as 'THE WIZARD' and 'EASY LIVIN' (also a US Top 40 hit), URIAH HEEP standards. 'THE MAGICIAN'S BIRTHDAY' (1972) did much of the same, lifted from the record, 'SWEET LORRAINE' and 'BLIND EYE' both became minor US favourites. 1973 saw another two gold albums being released, a live one and their first for 'Warner Bros' in the States, 'SWEET FREEDOM', while HENSLEY even found time to release a solo set, 'PROUD WORDS ON A DUSTY SHELF'. Their live disc contained a live rock'n'roll medley, featuring their interpretations of ROLL OVER BEETHOVEN, BLUE SUEDE SHOES, MEAN WOMAN BLUES, HOUND DOG, AT THE HOP and WHOLE LOTTA SHAKIN' GOIN' ON, some of their more discerning fans awaiting 1974's more sombre studio set, 'WONDERWORLD'. A bad period indeed for URIAH HEEP, THAIN was near-fatally electrocuted on stage in Dallas, Texas, subsequently resulting in major conflicts with the manager, Gerry Bron. His personal problems and drug-taking (while recovering from his injuries) led to URIAH HEEP being kept in a state of limbo for some months and after lengthy group discussions, THAIN was finally asked to leave in February '75 (tragically, on the 19th of March, 1976, he died of a drug overdose). Another bloke with considerable talents, JOHN WETTON (ex-KING CRIMSON, ex-FAMILY, ex-ROXY MUSIC etc.), was quickly drafted in to record 'RETURN TO FANTASY' (1975) and although the record hit the UK Top 10, it barely scratched out a Top 100 US placing. HENSLEY delivered a second solo set that year, 'EAGER TO PLEASE'. Appropriately titled, it failed to get off the starting blocks, a thing that could be said of 'HEEP's next album, 'HIGH AND MIGHTY' (1976), which only checked in at No.55 in the British charts. Disillusioned by their lack of success and the sacking of BYRON (he had formed ROUGH DIAMOND), WETTON too decided to jump ship. Their places were filled by vocalist, JOHN LAWTON and bassist more famous to BOWIE fans, TREVOR BOLDER; the 'HEEP that the band had become soldiered on while punk rock in '77 became yet another stumbling block. Subsequent albums (with various comings and goings) 'FIREFLY' (1977), 'INNOCENT VICTIM' (1977), 'FALLEN ANGEL' (1978) and 'CONQUEST' (1980) all failed both commercially and critically. After a break from music in the early 80's, URIAH HEEP returned with a new line-up, BOX enlisting the services of LEE KERSLAKE, PETE GOALBY (vocals), JOHN SINCLAIR (keyboards) and BOB DAISLEY (bass) to complete a comeback album of sorts, 'ABOMINOG', a record that returned them to the charts on both sides of the Atlantic in 1982. Another, 'HEAD FIRST' (1983), showed the rock world they had not given up just yet, in fact, URIAH HEEP are still going strong a decade and a half later, although their output has led to derision from all circles except that of a loyal fanbase in Kerrang!. They even became the first ever heavy-rock act to play in the U.S.S.R. A few years later, the band plucked up some degree of courage in covering a heavy rock version of Argent's 'HOLD YOUR HEAD UP', which became a track on the 1989 set, 'THE RAGING SILENCE'. URIAH HEEP will be best remembered for their "very 'eavy, very 'ard" 70's sound and style, much mimicked by a plethora of 80's rock acts too numerous and risky to mention (apart from SPINAL TAP, maybe). • **Songwriters:** Majority by HENSLEY or BOX/THAIN. In 1976 all members took share of work.

Album rating: VERY 'EAVY... VERY 'UMBLE (*5) / SALISBURY (*5) / LOOK AT YOURSELF (*6) / DEMONS AND WIZARDS (*7) / MAGICIAN'S BIRTHDAY (*6) / URIAH HEEP LIVE! (*5) / SWEET FREEDOM (*5) / WONDERWORLD (*5) / RETURN TO FANTASY (*5) / THE BEST OF URIAH HEEP compilation (*7) / HIGH AND MIGHTY (*5) / FIREFLY (*4) / INNOCENT VICTIM (*3) / FALLEN ANGEL (*3) / CONQUEST (*3) / ABOMINOG (*4) / HEAD FIRST (*4) / EQUATOR (*4) / LIVE IN MOSCOW (*3) / RAGING SILENCE (*4) / STILL HEAVY, STILL PROUD (*4) / DIFFERENT WORLD (*4) / SEA OF LIGHT (*4) / THE BEST OF URIAH HEEP, VOL.1 compilation (*6)

DAVID BYRON (b.29 Jan'47, Epping, Essex, England) – vocals / **MICK BOX** (b. 8 Jun'47, London, England) – guitar, vocals / **ROY SHARLAND** – organ / **PAUL NEWTON** – bass, vocals / **ALEX NAPIER** – drums

	U.A.	not iss.
Dec 68. (7"; as SPICE) *(UP 2246)* **WHAT ABOUT THE MUSIC. / IN LOVE**	☐	☐

— now without SHARLAND who joined ARTHUR BROWN, etc. / added **KEN HENSLEY** (b.24 Aug'45) – keyboards, guitar, vox (ex-GODS, ex-TOE FAT) / **NIGEL OLSSON** – drums (ex-SPENCER DAVIS GROUP, ex-PLASTIC PENNY) repl. NAPIER (on all lp except 2 tracks).

	Vertigo	Mercury
Jun 70. (lp) *(6360 006) <61294>* **VERY 'EAVY... VERY 'UMBLE** <US-title 'URIAH HEEP'>	☐	☐

– Gypsy / Walking in your shadow / Come away Melinda / Lucy blues / Dreammare /

Real turned on / I'll keep on trying / Wake up (set your sights). *(re-iss. 1971 on 'Bronze'; ILPS 9142) (re-iss. Apr77 on 'Bronze'; BRNA 142) (re-iss. Apr86 on 'Castle' lp/c; CLA LP/MC 105) (cd-iss. Dec90;) (re-iss. cd Jan96 on 'Essential'; ESMCD 316)*

Jul 70. (7") *<73103>* **GYPSY. / REAL TURNED ON**	–	☐
Nov 70. (7") *<73145>* **COME AWAY MELINDA. / WAKE UP (SET YOUR SIGHTS)**	–	☐

— **KEITH BAKER** – drums (ex-BAKERLOO) repl. OLSSON who joined ELTON JOHN

Jan 71. (7") *<73174>* **HIGH PRIESTESS. /**		–
Jan 71. (lp) *(6360 028) <61319>* **SALISBURY**		–

– Bird of prey * / The park / Time to live / Lady in black / High Priestess / Salisbury. <US copies repl. *, with =) – Simon the bullet freak. *(re-iss. 1971 on 'Bronze'; ILPS 9152) (re-iss. Jul77 on 'Bronze'; BRNA 152) (re-iss. Apr86 on 'Castle' lp/c; CLA LP/MC 106) (cd-iss. Apr89; CLACD 106) (re-iss. cd Jan96 on 'Essential'; ESMCD 317)*

Mar 71. (7") *(6059 037)* **LADY IN BLACK. / SIMON THE BULLET FREAK**	☐	–

— **IAN CLARKE** – drums (ex-CRESSIDA) repl. BAKER

— guest was **MANFRED MANN** – moog synthesizer / keyboards

	Bronze	Mercury
Nov 71. (lp) *(ILPS 9169) <614>* **LOOK AT YOURSELF**	**39**	**93** Sep71

– Look at yourself / I wanna be free / July morning / Tears in my eyes / Shadows of grief / What should be done / Love machine. *(re-iss. Apr77; BRNA 169) (re-iss. Apr86 on 'Castle' lp/c; CLA LP/MC 107) (cd-iss. Apr89; CLACD 107) (re-iss. cd Jan96 on 'Essential'; ESMCD 318)*

Dec 71. (7") *(WIP 6111)* **LOOK AT YOURSELF. / SIMON THE BULLET FREAK**		
Dec 71. (7") *<73243>* **LOVE MACHINE. / LOOK AT YOURSELF**		–
Feb 72. (7") *<73254>* **I WANNA BE FREE. / WHAT SHOULD BE DONE**		–

— (Nov71) **LEE KERSLAKE** – drums, vocals (ex-GODS, ex-TOE FAT) repl. IAN (Feb'72) / **GARY THAIN** (b. New Zealand) – bass, vocals (ex-KEEF HARTLEY) repl. MARK CLARKE (ex-COLOSSEUM to TEMPEST) who had repl. NEWTON (Nov'71)

May 72. (lp) *(ILPS 9193) <630>* **DEMONS AND WIZARDS**	**20**	**23**

– The wizard / Traveller in time / Easy livin' / Poet's justice / Circle of hands / Rainbow demon / All my life / (a) Paradise – (b) The spell. *(re-iss. Apr77; BRNA 193) (re-iss. Apr86 on 'Castle' lp/c; CLA LP/MC 108) (cd-iss. Apr89; CLACD 108) (re-iss. cd Jan96 on 'Essential'; ESMCD 319) (lp re-iss. Jan97 on 'Original'; ORRLP 003)*

May 72. (7") *<73271>* **THE WIZARD. / WHY**	–	
Jun 72. (7") *(WIP 6126)* **THE WIZARD. / GYPSY**	–	
Jul 72. (7") *<73307>* **EASY LIVIN' / ALL MY LIFE**		**39**
Aug 72. (7") *(WIP 6140)* **EASY LIVIN'. / WHY**	–	
Nov 72. (lp) *(ILPS 9213) <652>* **THE MAGICIAN'S BIRTHDAY**	**28**	**31**

– Sunrise / Spider woman / Blind eye / Echoes in the dark / Rain / Sweet Lorraine / Tales / The magician's birthday. *(re-iss. Jul77; BRNA 213) (re-iss. Apr86 on 'Castle' lp/c; CLA LP/MC 109) (cd-iss. Apr89; CLACD 109) (re-iss. cd Jan96 on 'Essential'; ESMCD 339)*

Jan 73. (7") *<73349>* **BLIND EYE. / SWEET LORRAINE**	–	**97 91**
May 73. (d-lp) *(ISLD 1) <7503>* **URIAH HEEP LIVE (live)**	**23**	**37**

– Sunrise / Sweet Lorraine / Traveller in time / Easy livin' / July morning / Tears in my eyes / Gypsy / Circle of hands / Look at yourself / The magician's birthday / Love machine / Rock'n'roll medley:- Roll over Beethoven – Blue suede shoes – Mean woman blues – Hound dog – At the hop – Whole lotta shakin' goin' on. *(re-iss. Apr77; BRSP 1) (cd-iss. Jun96 on 'Essential'; ESMCD 320)*

May 73. (7") *<73406>* **JULY MORNING (live). / TEARS IN MY EYES (live)**		

	Bronze	Warners
Sep 73. (lp) *(ILPS 9245) <2724>* **SWEET FREEDOM**	**18**	**33**

– Dreamer / Stealin' / One day / Sweet freedom / If I had the time / Seven stars / Circus / Pilgrim. *(re-iss. Apr77; BRNA 245) (cd-iss. Jan96 on 'Essential'; ESMCD 338)*

May 74. (7") *(BRO 7) <7738>* **STEALIN'. / SUNSHINE**		**91** Oct73
Jun 74. (lp) *(ILPS 9280) <2800>* **WONDERWORLD**	**23**	**38**

– Wonderworld / Suicidal man / The shadows and the winds / So tired / The easy road / Something or nothing / I won't mind / We got we / Dreams. *(re-iss. Apr77; BRNA 280) (cd-iss. May96 on 'Essential'; ESMCD 380)*

Aug 74. (7") *(BRO 10) <8013>* **SOMETHING OR NOTHING. / WHAT CAN I DO**		

— **JOHN WETTON** (b.12 Jul'49, Derby, England) – bass, vocals (ex-KING CRIMSON, ex-ROXY MUSIC, ex-FAMILY) repl. THAIN (He died of a drug overdose 19 May'76) Line-up now **BYRON, BOX, HENSLEY, KERSLAKE & WETTON**

Jun 75. (lp) *(ILPS 9335) <2869>* **RETURN TO FANTASY**	**7**	**85**

– Return to fantasy / Shady lady / Devil's daughter / Beautiful dream / Prima Donna / Your turn to remember / Showdown / Why did you go / A year or a day. *(re-iss. Jul77; BRNA 385) (cd-iss. May96 on 'Essential'; ESMCD 381)*

Jun 75. (7") *<8132>* **PRIMA DONNA. / STEALIN'**		–
Jun 75. (7") *(BRO 17)* **PRIMA DONNA. / SHOUT IT OUT**	–	
May 76. (lp) *(ILPS 9384) <2949>* **HIGH AND MIGHTY**	**55**	

– One way or another / Weep in silence / Misty eyes / Midnight / Can't keep a good band down / Woman of the world / Footprints in the snow / Can't stop singing / Make a little love / Confession. *(re-iss. Apr77; BRNA 384) (re-iss. Mar91 on 'Castle' cd/lp; CLA CD/LP 191) (re-mast.Jul97 on 'Essential'; ESMCD 468)*

Jun 76. (7") *(BRO 27)* **ONE WAY OR ANOTHER. / MISTY EYES**		

— **JOHN LAWTON** – vocals (ex-LUCIFER'S FRIEND) repl. BYRON to ROUGH DIAMOND / **TREVOR BOLDER** – bass (ex-David Bowie's SPIDERS FROM MARS, ex-WISHBONE ASH) repl. WETTON who joined BRYAN FERRY BAND, and later UK and ASIA

Feb 77. (lp) *(ILPS 9483) <3013>* **FIREFLY**		

– Been away too long / Sympathy / Who needs me / Wise man / The hanging tree / Rollin' / Do you know / Firefly. *(re-iss. Apr77; BRNA 483) (re-iss. Mar91 on 'Castle' cd/lp; CLA CD/LP 190) (re-mast.Jul97 on 'Essential'; ESMCD 559)*

Apr 77. (7") *(BRO 37)* **WISE MAN. / CRIME OF PASSION**		–
Oct 77. (7") *(BRO 47) <8581>* **FREE ME. / MASQUERADE**	☐	☐

Nov 77. (lp) *(BRON 504)* <3145> **INNOCENT VICTIM**
– Keep on ridin' / Flyin' high / Roller / Free 'n' easy / Illusion / Free me / Cheat 'n' lie / The dance / Choices. *(re-iss. Dec90 on 'Castle' cd/lp; CLA CD/LP 210)*

	Bronze	Chrysalis

Sep 78. (lp) *(BRNA 512)* <1204> **FALLEN ANGEL**
– Woman of the night / Falling in love / One more night (last farewell) / Put your lovin' on me / Come back to me / Whad'ya say / Save it / Love or nothing / I'm alive / Fallen angel. *(re-iss. Feb90 on 'Castle' cd/c/lp; CLA CD/MC/LP 176) (re-mast.Jul97 on 'Essential'; ESMCD 561)*

Oct 78. (7") *(BRO 62)* **COME BACK TO ME. / CHEATER**

—— **JOHN SLOMAN** – vocals (ex-LONE STAR) repl. LAWTON / **CHRIS SLADE** (b.30 Oct'46) – drums (ex-MANFRED MANN'S EARTH BAND) repl. LEE to OZZY OSBOURNE

Jan 80. (7") *(BRO 88)* **CARRY ON. / BEING HURT** | | - |
Feb 80. (lp/c) *(BRON/+C 524)* **CONQUEST**
– No return / Imagination / Fools / Carry on / Won't have to wait too long / Out on the street / It ain't easy. *(re-iss. Dec90 on 'Castle' cd/lp; CLA CD/LP 208) (re-mast.Aug97 on 'Essential'; ESMCD 570)*

Jun 80. (7") *(BRO 96)* **LOVE STEALER. / NO RETURN**

—— **GREGG DETCHETT** – keyboards (ex-PULSAR) repl. HENSLEY to solo & BLACKFOOT

Jan 81. (7") *(BRO 112)* **THINK IT OVER. / MY JOANNA NEEDS TUNING** | | - |

—— split 1981 when SLOMAN developed a throat infection (he later formed BADLANDS). CHRIS SLADE joined GARY NUMAN then DAVID GILMOUR and later joined The FIRM. DETCHETT later joined MIKE + The MECHANICS. BOLDER re-joined WISHBONE ASH. Early 1982, URIAH HEEP re-formed with **BOX** bringing back **LEE KERSLAKE** plus new **PETE GOALBY** – vocals (ex-TRAPEZE) / **JOHN SINCLAIR** – keyboards (ex-HEAVY METAL KIDS) / **BOB DAISLEY** – bass (ex-OZZY OSBOURNE, ex-RAINBOW, ex-WIDOWMAKER, etc)

	Bronze	Mercury

Feb 82. (7"ep) *(BRO 143)* **THE ABOMINATOR JUNIOR EP**
– On the rebound / Tin soldier / Song of a bitch.
Mar 82. (lp/c) *(BRON/+C 538)* <4057> **ABOMINOG** | 34 | 56 |
– Too scared to run / Chasing shadows / On the rebound / Hot night in a cold town / Running all night (with the lion) / That's the way that it is / Prisoner / Hot persuasion / Sell your soul / Think it over. *(re-iss. Apr86 on 'Castle' lp/c; CLA LP/MC 110) (cd-iss. Apr89; CLACD 110) (re-mast.Aug97 on 'Essential'; ESMCD 571)*

May 82. (7") *(BRO 148)* **THAT'S THE WAY THAT IT IS. / HOT PERSUASION** | | - |
May 82. (7") <76177> **THAT'S THE WAY THAT IT IS. / SON OF A BITCH** | - | |
May 83. (lp/c) *(BRON/+C 545)* <812313> **HEAD FIRST** | 46 | |
– The other side of midnight / Stay on top / Lonely nights / Sweet talk / Love is blind / Roll-overture / Red lights / Rollin' the rock / Straight through the heart / Weekend warriors. *(re-iss. Dec90 on 'Castle' cd/lp; CLA CD/LP 209) (re-mast.Jul97 on 'Essential'; ESMCD 572)*

Jun 83. (7"/7"pic-d) *(BRO/+P 166)* **LONELY NIGHTS. / WEEKEND WARRIORS** | | - |
Aug 83. (7") *(BRO 168)* **STAY ON TOP. / PLAYING FOR TIME** | | - |
(d7"+=) *(BROG 168)* – Gypsy / Easy livin' / Sweet Lorraine / Stealin'.

—— **TREVOR BOLDER** – bass returned to repl. DAISLEY

	Portrait	CBS Assoc.

Mar 85. (7"/7"sha-pic-d) *(TA/WA 6103)* **ROCKERAMA. / BACK STAGE GIRL**
Mar 85. (lp) *(PRT 26414)* **EQUATOR** | 79 | |
– Rockarama / Bad blood / Lost one love / Angel / Holding on / Party time / Poor little rich girl / Skools burnin' / Heartache city / Night of the wolf.

May 85. (7"/7"pic-d) *(A/WA 6309)* **POOR LITTLE RICH GIRL. / BAD BLOOD** | | - |

—— **BERNIE SHAW** – vocals (ex-GRAND PRIX, ex-PRAYING MANTIS) repl. GOALBY / **PHIL LANZON** – keyboards (ex-GRAND PRIX, etc) repl. SINCLAIR (above 2 now alongside **BOX, BOLDER, KERSLAKE**)

	Legacy	Legacy-Sony

Jul 88. (lp/c/cd) *(LLP/LLK/LLCD 118)* <848811> **LIVE IN MOSCOW (live)**
– Bird of prey / Stealin' / Too scared to run / Corrina / Mister Majestic / The wizard / July morning / Easy livin' / That's the way that it is / Pacific highway. *(cd+=)* – Gypsy. *(cd re-iss. 1992 on 'Castle'; CLACD 276)*

Sep 88. (7") *(LGY 65)* **EASY LIVIN' (live). / CORRINA (live)** | | - |
(12"red+=) *(LGYT 65)* – Gypsy (live).
Apr 89. (7") *(LGY 67)* **HOLD YOUR HEAD UP. / MIRACLE CHILD** | | - |
(12"+=) *(LGYT 67)* – ('A'extended).
Apr 89. (lp/pic-lp/c/cd) *(LLP/LLPPD/LLK/LLCD 120)* <848812> **RAGING SILENCE**
– Hold your head up / Blood red roses / Voice on my TV / Rich kid / Cry freedom / Bad bad man / More fool you / When the war is over / Lifeline / Rough justice. *(cd re-iss. Feb93 on 'Castle'; CLACD 277)*

Jul 89. (7") *(LGY 101)* **BLOOD RED ROSES. / ROUGH JUSTICE** | | - |
(12"+=) *(LGYT 101)* – Look at yourself.
1990. (cd) *(LLCD 133)* **STILL 'EAVY, STILL PROUD (live)** | - | - | Swedish
– Gypsy / Lady in black / July morning / Easy livin' / The easy road / Free me / The other side of midnight / Mr Majestic / Rich kid / Blood red roses.
Feb 91. (cd) *(LLCD 137)* **DIFFERENT WORLD** | | - |
– Blood on stone / Which way will the wind blow / All God's children / All for one / Different world / Step by step / Seven days / First touch / One on one / Cross that line / Stand back. *(UK-iss.on 'Castle'; CLACD 279)*

	H.T.D.	not iss.

Apr 95. (cd/c/lp) *(HTD CD/MC/LP 33)* **SEA OF LIGHT**
– Against the odds / Sweet sugar / Time of revelation / Mistress of all time / Universal wheels / Fear of falling / Spirit of freedom / Logical progression / Love in silence / Words in the distance / Fires of hell / Dream on.

Oct 95. (cd-s) *(CDHTD 102)* **DREAM ON /** | | - |

	S.P.V.	Spitfire

Jul 96. (cd) *(0857699-2)* <5034> **SPELLBINDER (live)** | | Jun99 |
– Devil's daughter / Stealin' / Bad bad man / Rainbow demon / Words in a distance / The wizard / Circle of hands / Gypsy / Look at yourself / Lady in love / Easy livin'.

– compilations, etc. –

Nov 75. (lp) *Bronze; (ILPS 9375) / Mercury; <1070>* **THE BEST OF URIAH HEEP**
– Gypsy / Bird of prey / July morning / Look at yourself / Easy livin' / The wizard / Sweet Lorraine / Lady in black / Return to fantasy. *(re-iss. Apr77; BRNA 375) (cd-iss. Apr90 on 'Sequel';)*

1983. (12"ep) *Bronze; (HEEP 1)* **EASY LIVIN' / SWEET LORRAINE. / GYPSY / STEALIN'** | | |
Apr 86. (d-lp/c/cd) *Raw Power; (RAW LP/TC/CD 012)* **ANTHOLOGY** | | |
1986. (cd) *Legacy; (LLHCD 3003)* **ANTHOLOGY** | | |
Mar 87. (lp/c/cd) *Raw Power; (RAW LP/MC/CD 030)* **LIVE IN EUROPE 1979 (live)** | | |
May 88. (d-lp/c/cd) *That's Original; (TFO LP/MC/CD 7)* **LOOK AT YOURSELF / VERY 'EAVY, VERY 'UMBLE** | | |
1988. (d-lp/c) *Castle; (CCS LP/MC 177)* **THE URIAH HEEP COLLECTION** | | |
Dec 88. (cd-ep) *Special Edition; (CD 3-16)* **LADY IN BLACK / JULY MORNING / EASY LIVIN'** | | |
Dec 88. (lp/c/cd) *Castle; (HEEP LP/TC/CD 1)* **LIVE AT SHEPPERTON '74 (live)** | | |
(re-iss. Dec90 cd/lp; CLA CD/LP 192) (re-mast.Jul97 on 'Essential'; ESMCD 590)
Aug 89. (d-lp/c/cd) *Castle; (CCS LP/MC/CD 226)* **THE COLLECTION** | | |
Jun 90. (3xcd/5xlp) *Essential; (ESB CD/LP 022)* **TWO DECADES IN ROCK** | | |
Jul 90. (cd/c) *Raw Power; (RAW CD/MC 041)* **URIAH HEEP LIVE (live)** | | - |
Oct 91. (cd/c) *Elite; (ELITE 020 CD/MC)* **ECHOES IN THE DARK** | | - |
– Echoes in the dark / The wizard / Come away Melinda / Devil's daughter / Hot persuasion / Showdown / I'm alive / Look at yourself / Spider woman / Woman of the night / I want to be free / Gypsy / Sunrise / Bird of prey / Love machine / Lady in black *(re-iss. Sep93; same)*
Nov 91. (cd) *Sequel; (NEXCD 184)* **EXCAVATIONS FROM THE BRONZE AGE** | | - |
Feb 92. (3xcd-box) *Castle; (CLABX 903)* **3 ORIGINALS** | | - |
– (FIREFLY / HEAD FIRST / DEMONS AND WIZARDS)
Jan 95. (cd) *Spectrum; (550 730-2)* **LADY IN BLACK** | | - |
May 95. (cd) *Spectrum; (550 731-2)* **FREE ME** | | - |
Oct 95. (d-cd) *H.T.D.; (CDHTD 561)* | | - |
Mar 96. (4xcd-box) *Essential; (ESFCD 298)* **A TIME OF REVELATION – 25 YEARS ON** | | - |
May 96. (cd) *Red Steel; (RMCCD 0193)* **THE LANSDOWNE TAPES** | | - |
Oct 96. (cd) *Essential; (ESSCD 418)* **THE BEST OF URIAH HEEP, VOL.1** | | - |
Jun 97. (cd) *King Biscuit; (88027-2)* **URIAH HEEP IN CONCERT (live)** | | - |

URUSEI YATSURA (dig out; Great Alt & Indie . . .)

Us3 (dig out; 4th edition)

UTOPIA (see under ⇒ AMON DUUL II)

UTOPIA (see under ⇒ RUNDGREN, Todd)

U2

Formed: Dublin, Ireland . . . 1977 by BONO (b. PAUL HEWSON), THE EDGE (b. DAVID EVANS), ADAM CLAYTON and LARRY MULLEN. Indisputably one of the biggest and the most talked about 'musical phenomenon's of the last two decades, U2 nevertheless graduated from humble beginnings as a covers band. Finally adopting the U2 moniker in 1978, they subsequently attracted the attention of Paul McGuinness, one of the most respected managers in the business. It wasn't long before they found themselves signed to 'C.B.S.' Ireland via A&R man, Jackie Hayden, releasing a debut single, 'U2-3' in late '79. The track scaled the Irish charts, as did a follow-up, 'ANOTHER DAY', the group subsequently snapped up by 'Island' records for a worldwide deal. Initially, U2 made little impact, singles '11 O'CLOCK TICK TOCK' and 'A DAY WITHOUT ME' failing to chart. By the release of the Steve Lillywhite-produced debut album, 'BOY' (1980), however, U2 were already assuming the mantle of cult status. Strikingly original, the group carved out their own plot of fertile territory within the suffocatingly oversubscribed rock format, cultivating a watertight, propulsive minimalism to partner their politically direct lyrics. Carried equally by BONO's crusading vocal theatrics, THE EDGE's serrated guitar cascades and the rhythmic drive of CLAYTON and MULLEN, the likes of 'I WILL FOLLOW' was a blueprint for the U2 formula. And it was a formula which seemed to command devotion; those who followed the band did so with the same zeal as U2 set out their humanitarian agenda, the group eschewing party politics for a more expansive but no less focused commentary on the world's ills with an overriding religious/spiritual bent. Live, the group were also being hailed as one of the most innovative and exciting acts to emerge from the post-punk morass. Though 'OCTOBER' (1981) almost broke into the Top 10, the album failed to spawn any major hits, the clarion call of 'GLORIA' surprisingly stiffing outside the Top 50. So it was then, that U2 seemed to come out of nowhere in early '83 with a Top 10 single, the highly emotive 'NEW

YEAR'S DAY' (inspired by the Lech Walenska's Polish Solidarity Union) and a No.1 album, 'WAR'. U2's first masterstroke, the album was consistently compelling, through the rousing rhythmic militarism of 'SUNDAY BLOODY SUNDAY' (interpreted by many as a republican rebel song, BONO famously declared otherwise when introducing the track live) and the celebratory 'TWO HEARTS BEAT AS ONE' to the more meditative acoustics of 'DROWNING MAN'. The record's anthemic Irish qualities also appealed to the Americans, 'WAR' almost making the US Top 10; from the electric atmosphere of the live 'UNDER A BLOOD RED SKY' (1983), it certainly seemed U2's sound could galvanise a transatlantic audience, probably (and eventually) a world audience. Previewed by perhaps U2's most anthemic, politically pointed song, 'PRIDE (IN THE NAME OF LOVE)' (a tribute to assassinated black civil rights hero, Martin Luther King), 'THE UNFORGETTABLE FIRE' (1984) consolidated the band's commerical and creative maturity. For the most part, however, the record took a completely different approach, BRIAN ENO presiding over a collection of more exploratory, occasionally near-ambient excursions, the highlight arguably being the epic atmospherics of the stunning title track. Equally evocative was 'BAD', an almost hymn-like incantation with which U2 entranced the world at Live Aid in summer '85. One of the key events in the band's career, their celebrated performance undoubtedly won them a massive new audience almost overnight, much in the same way as QUEEN rejuvenated their career through the concert. Understandably, then, the anticipation for U2's forthcoming album, 'THE JOSHUA TREE' (1987), was fevered. Fortunately it was also justified, U2 delivering what was undeniably the most accomplished set of their career and probably one of the greatest rock albums ever released. Like many such masterworks, U2 scaled this pinnacle of creativity by means of a subtle balance, between panoramic euphoria and hushed reflection, between the personal and the political and between insinuation and crystal clarity. The record's undertow of spiritual soul-searching evident on the likes of 'I STILL HAVEN'T FOUND WHAT I'M LOOKING FOR' (a US No.1) obviously struck a chord in a decade more concerned with ruthless material gain, while the air of soft-focus melancholy permeating 'WITH OR WITHOUT YOU' and 'RUNNING TO STAND STILL' further enhanced the album's almost tangible warmth. Even the more full-on tracks such as 'WHERE THE STREETS HAVE NO NAME' and 'IN GOD'S COUNTRY' seemed to emanate from a deep-seated yearning through the shards of THE EDGE's guitar scree. 'THE JOSHUA TREE' was a transatlantic No.1 (a worldwide No.1), facilitating U2's move to the top of the world premier league. As well as being a formidable commercial proposition, U2 were hailed by some commentators as the most 'important' rock group on the planet, both lyrically and musically. Of course, such inflated claims were matched by equally vociferous critics of the group's perceived pomposity and preaching self-importance. Such criticism was nothing new, although it reached its height in the aftermath of 'THE JOSHUA TREE' and its attendant tour, when BONO was being hailed as some kind of messiah. The sight of the singer charging around the stage with a floodlight and a white flag, together with his increasingly politicised between song (or even half-way through) speeches became too much for some, although in a music scene bereft of direction or purpose, BONO probably made up for the prevailing insipidity. Attempting to follow up this musical landmark, U2 released a kind of stop-gap half-live/half-studio affair, 'RATTLE AND HUM' (1988). A soundtrack to the rockumentary of the same name which marked the culmination of the group's obsession with America, the album was accused of being half-baked in parts. Possibly, but the gut-level punch of 'GOD PART II' and the bleakly beautiful 'VAN DIEMEN'S LAND' were unquestionably full-baked, if oddities nonetheless. Following the poignant love song, 'ALL I WANT IS YOU' (a UK Top 5) in summer '89, U2 went to ground, hard at work on a new strategy. Sporting wraparound shades and skin-tight black leather, BONO finally emerged in late '91 with 'THE FLY', a grinding guitar groove with urgent, hoarsely whispered lyrics. The track entered the UK chart at No.1, paving the way for the massively successful 'ACHTUNG BABY' (1991). Stylistically diverse, the album marked the beginnings of U2's flirtation with dance culture, a sign that the band were wary of falling into the rock dinosaur mould. BONO had also obviously been listening to his critics, changing his persona from earnest poet to lounge lizard sophisticate. Though the likes of 'WHO'S GONNA RIDE YOUR WILD HORSES' and the deeply affecting 'ONE' (probably the most intimate song the group have ever penned) signalled a move into more personal lyrical territory, the album's attendant 'Zoo TV' tour was themed around political events in Europe, albeit with a more post-modern, multi-media stoked irony. Inspired by the tour, 'ZOOROPA' (1993) was U2's most contemporary release to date, a fractured, dance-orientated affair which rather unfairly received a bit of a pasting from more short-sighted critics. Following on from the celebrated dance mixes of 'EVEN BETTER THAN THE REAL THING' (from 'ACHTUNG BABY'), the 12" remix of 'LEMON' was hot property when originally released in limited lemon-coloured vinyl. As well as catering for dance trainspotters, U2 even recorded a duet with JOHNNY CASH, the darkly brilliant 'THE WANDERER', in effect kickstarting the aging country star's career. In the ensuing two years, BONO popped up with GAVIN FRIDAY on the theme to the acclaimed 'IN THE NAME OF THE FATHER', while U2 scored a UK No.2 hit with 'HOLD ME, THRILL ME, KISS ME, KILL ME' from the huge box office smash, 'Batman Forever'. This fascination with soundtrack music continued via the PASSENGERS project, a collaboration between U2, BRIAN ENO, italian opera singer PAVAROTTI and Glaswegian beatz guru HOWIE B. Entitled 'ORIGINAL SOUNDTRACKS VOL.1' (1995), a few of the album's tracks (highlight being the hit single, 'MISS SARAJEVO') were actually written as themes to avant-garde films while the remainder were written for

imaginary celluloid pieces. As low-key as U2 have ever dared go, the album passed by without much fuss, its ambient noodlings not really indicating a new direction as such but proving that the group were firmly committed to constant experimentation. For their next album proper, U2 retained HOWIE B as co-producer, crafting an album that once again used dance music as a touchstone. Preview single, 'DISCOTHEQUE', sounded like a watered-down 'FLY' although the accompanying VILLAGE PEOPLE-pastiche video showed, shock horror!, U2 having a right old laugh! Despite this newfound sense of humour, the 'POP' (1996) album met with mixed reviews, some hailing it as a bold new dawn, others accusing the band of treading water. The record certainly had its moments, the searing desolation of 'STARING AT THE SUN' and the apocalyptic 'LAST NIGHT ON EARTH' (the video featuring an appearance from counter-culture guru, William Burroughs, just weeks before his death, U2 having previously persuaded the voraciously anti-rock Charles Bukowski to attend a gig, no mean feat!) for example, but there was a feeling of incompleteness about the whole affair. Likewise, the accompanying 'Pop Mart' tour which got off to a shaky start in Las Vegas, its consumerist theme carried by another media extravaganza, albeit downscaled from the Zoo TV era. While U2 undoubtedly lead the way in terms of stadium rock, constantly innovative in new ways to keep the medium fresh, they arguably need to rediscover themselves musically and give up recycling second hand ideas. Whether they have either the willingness or ability to do this is another matter, although being past masters of coming out fighting in the face of adversity, it's highly likely. • **Songwriters:** All written by BONO / THE EDGE, except HELTER SKELTER (Beatles) / ALL ALONG THE WATCHTOWER (Bob Dylan) (hit; Jimi Hendrix) / STAR SPANGLED BANNER (US National anthem) / DANCING BAREFOOT (Patti Smith) / NIGHT AND DAY (Cole Porter) / PAINT IT BLACK (Rolling Stones) / FORTUNATE SON (Creedence Clearwater Revival) / HALLELUJAH (Leonard Cohen) by BONO. • **Trivia:** BONO contributed vox to BAND AID single late '84. That year, the band also started own record label, mainly for other Irish groups and was a starter for HOTHOUSE FLOWERS, CACTUS WORLD NEWS etc. In 1988, BONO and THE EDGE co-wrote for ROY ORBISON on his last living studio album, 'Mystery Girl'. They wrote the theme for the James Bond film 'GOLDEN EYE', which became a hit for TINA TURNER in 1995.

Album rating: BOY (*8) / OCTOBER (*6) / WAR (*9) / UNDER A BLOOD RED SKY (*6) / THE UNFORGETTABLE FIRE (*9) / WIDE AWAKE IN AMERICA (*6) / THE JOSHUA TREE (*10) / RATTLE & HUM (*8) / ACHTUNG BABY (*8) / ZOOROPA (*9) / ORIGINAL SOUNDTRACKS 1 (*7; as the Passengers) / POP (*6) / THE BEST OF 1980-1990 compilation (*9)

BONO VOX (b. PAUL HEWSON, 10 May'60) – vocals / **THE EDGE** (b. DAVID EVANS, 8 Aug'61, Barking, Essex) – guitar, keyboards / **ADAM CLAYTON** (b.13 Mar'60, Chinnor, Oxfordshire, England) – bass / **LARRY MULLEN** (b. LAURENCE MULLEN, 31 Oct'61) – drums

		C.B.S.	not iss.	
Oct 79.	(7"ep/12"ep) (CBS/+12 7951) **U2: THREE**	-		Irish
	– Out of control / Stories for boys / Boy-girl. (re-iss. 1980 7"orange,yellow,white; same) (re-iss. c-ep 1985; CBS 40-7951)			
Feb 80.	(7",7"yellow,7"orange,7"white) (CBS 8306) **ANOTHER**			
	DAY. / TWILIGHT (demo)	-	-	Irish
		Island	Island	
May 80.	(7") (WIP 6601) **11 O'CLOCK TICK TOCK. / TOUCH**	-	-	
Aug 80.	(7") (WIP 6630) **A DAY WITHOUT ME. / THINGS TO MAKE**			
	AND DO	-	-	
Oct 80.	(7") (WIP 6656) **I WILL FOLLOW. / BOY-GIRL** (live)	-	-	
Nov 80.	(lp/c) (ILPS/ICT <9646>) **BOY**	52	63	Feb81
	– I will follow / Twilight / An cat dubh / Into the heart / Out of control / Stories for boys / The ocean / A day without me / Another time, another place / The Electric Co. / Shadows and tall trees. (cd-iss. May86; CID 110) (re-iss. May95 cd)(c)(lp; IMCD 211)(ILPM 9646)			
Apr 81.	(7") (WIP 6679) **I WILL FOLLOW. / OUT OF CONTROL**	-	-	
Jul 81.	(7") (WIP 6679) **FIRE. / J. SWALLO**	35		
	(d7"+=) (U-WIP 6679) – 11 o'clock tick tock (live) / The ocean (live) / Cry (live) / The Electric Co. (live).			
Sep 81.	(7") (WIP 6733) **GLORIA. / I WILL FOLLOW** (live)	55		
Oct 81.	(lp/c) (ILPS/ICT <9680>) **OCTOBER**	11		
	– Gloria / I fall down / I threw a brick through a window / Rejoice / Fire / Tomorrow / October / With a shout / Stranger in a strange land / Scarlet / Is that all?. (cd-iss. May86; CID 111) (re-dist.Jun92; same) (cd re-iss. Mar96; IMCD 223)			
Mar 82.	(7") (WIP 6770) **A CELEBRATION. / TRASH, TRAMPOLENE**			
	AND THE PARTY GIRL	47		
Jan 83.	(7") (WIP 6848) <99915> **NEW YEAR'S DAY. / TREASURE**			
	(WHATEVER HAPPENED TO PETE THE CHOP)	10	53	
	(d7"+=/12"+=) (U-WIP/12WIP 6848) – Fire (live) / I threw a brick through the window (live) / A day without me (live).			
Feb 83.	(lp/c) (ILPS/ICT 9733) <90067> **WAR**	1	12	
	– Sunday bloody Sunday / Seconds / Like a song / New Year's day / Two hearts beat as one / The refugee / Drowning man / Red light / '40' / Surrender. (cd-iss. Dec85; CID 112) (re-iss. Aug91 cd/c; IMCD/ICT 141; hit no.51 Jun92, hit UK No.38 Aug93)			
Mar 83.	(7") (IS 109) <99861> **TWO HEARTS BEAT AS ONE. /**			
	ENDLESS DEEP	18		
	(d7"+=) (ISD 109) – Two hearts beat as one (U.S. remix) / New Year's day (U.S. remix).			
	(12") (12IS 109) – ('A'-club mix) / New Year's day (U.S. remix) / ('A'-U.S. remix).			
Nov 83.	(lp/c) (IMA/IMC 3) <90127> **UNDER A BLOOD RED SKY**			
	(live)	2	28	
	– Gloria / 11 o'clock tick tock / I will follow / Party girl / Sunday bloody Sunday / The Electric Co. / New Year's day / '40'. (cd-iss. May86; CID 113) (re-dist.Jun92; same)			
Dec 83.	(7") <99789> **I WILL FOLLOW (live). / TWO HEARTS BEAT**			
	AS ONE (live)	-	81	

Sep 84. (7"/7"pic-d) (IS/+P 202) <99704> **PRIDE (IN THE NAME OF LOVE). / BOOMERANG 2** `3` `33`
(d7"+=/c-s+=/12"white+=) (ISD/CIS/12IS 202) – 4th of July / Boomerang 1.
(12"blue+=) (12ISX 202) – Boomerang 1 / 11 o'clock tick tock (extended) / Touch.

Oct 84. (lp/c)(cd) (U2/+C 5)(CID 102) <90231> **THE UNFORGETTABLE FIRE** `1` `12`
– A sort of homecoming / Pride (in the name of love) / Wire / The unforgettable fire / Promenade / 4th of July / Bad / Indian summer sky / Elvis Presley and America / MLK. (re-dist.Jun92 hit No.38 UK; same)

May 85. (7"/7"sha-pic-d) (IS/+P 220) **THE UNFORGETTABLE FIRE. / A SORT OF HOMECOMING** (live) `6`
(12"+=) (12IS 220) – The three sunrises / Bass trap / Love comes tumbling.
(d7"+=) (ISD 220) – The three sunrises / Love comes tumbling / 60 seconds in kingdom come.

May 85. (m-lp/c) (ISSP/+C 22) <90279> **WIDE AWAKE IN AMERICA** `11` `37`
– Bad (live) / A sort of homecoming (live) / The three sunrises / Love comes tumbling. (cd-iss. Oct87; CIDU 22) (cd re-iss. Nov89; IMCD 75)

——— Later in the year, BONO guested for CLANNAD on hit 'IN A LIFETIME'. In Sep'86, THE EDGE issued soundtrack album CAPTIVE (see further below).

Mar 87. (7"/c-s/12"/cd-s) (IS/CIS/12IS/CID 319) <99469> **WITH OR WITHOUT YOU. / LUMINOUS TIMES (HOLD ON TO LOVE) / WALK TO THE WATER** `4` `1`

Mar 87. (lp/c)(cd) (U2/+C 6)(CIDU 26) <90581> **THE JOSHUA TREE** `1` `1`
– Where the streets have no name / I still haven't found what I'm looking for / With or without you / Bullet the blue sky / Running to stand still / Red Hill mining town / In God's country / Trip through your wires / One tree hill / Exit / Mothers of the disappeared. (also on 4x7"box) (re-charted UK Jan92, peaked Jun92 at No.19) (re-iss. Aug93 cd/c/lp, hit UK No.27; same)

May 87. (7"/c-s/12") (IS/CIS/12IS 328) <99430> **I STILL HAVEN'T FOUND WHAT I'M LOOKING FOR. / SPANISH EYES / DEEP IN THE HEART** `6` `1`

Sep 87. (7") (IS 340) <99408> **WHERE THE STREETS HAVE NO NAME. / SILVER AND GOLD / SWEETEST THING** `4` `13`
(c-s+=/12"+=/cd-s+=) (CIS/12IS/CID 340) – Race against time.

Jan 88. (7"-US-imp) (<7-99385>) **IN GOD'S COUNTRY. / BULLET THE BLUE SKY / RUNNING TO STAND STILL** `48` `44` Nov87

Sep 88. (IS 400) <99250> **DESIRE. / HALLELUJAH (HERE SHE COMES)** `1` `3`
(12"+=/12"g-f+=/pic-cd-s+=) (12IS/12ISG/CIDP 400) – ('A'-Hollywood remix).

Oct 88. (d-lp/c)(cd) (U2/+C 7)(CIDU 27) <91003> **RATTLE AND HUM** (some live) `1` `1`
– Helter skelter / Hawkmoon 269 / Van Diemen's land / Desire / Angel of Harlem / I still haven't found what I'm looking for / When love comes to town / God part II / Bullet the blue sky / Silver and gold / Love rescue me / Heartland / Star spangled banner / All I want is you / Freedom for my people / All along the watchtower / Pride (in the name of love). (re-charted UK No.37 on Jun92) (re-iss. Aug93, hit UK No.34)

Oct 88. (7") (IS 402) <99254> **ANGEL OF HARLEM. / A ROOM AT THE HEARTBREAK HOTEL** `9` `14`
(12"+=/pic-cd-s+=/US-3"cd-s+=) (12IS/CIDP/CIDX 402) – Love rescue me (live with KEITH RICHARDS & ZIGGY MARLEY).

Apr 89. (7"/c-s; U2 & B.B. KING) (IS 411) <99225> **WHEN LOVE COMES TO TOWN. / DANCING BAREFOOT** `6` `68`
(12"+=/pic-cd-s+=/US-3"cd-s+=) (12IS/CIDP/CIDX 411) – ('A'-live from the kingdom mix) / God part II (the hard metal dance mix).

Jun 89. (7"/7"box/c-s) (IS/ISB/CIS 422) <99199> **ALL I WANT IS YOU. / UNCHAINED MELODY** `4` `83`
(ext;12"+=/12"box+=) (12IS/+B 422) – Everlasting love.
(pic-cd-s++=) (CIDP 422) – ('A'extended).

Oct 91. (c-s/7") (C+/IS 500) <868885> **THE FLY. / ALEX DESCENDS INTO HELL FOR A BOTTLE OF MILK / KOROVA 1** `1` `61`
(12"+=/cd-s+=) (12IS/CID 500) – The Lounge Fly mix.

Nov 91. (cd)(lp/c) (CIDU 28)(U2/+C 8) <10347> **ACHTUNG BABY** `2` `1`
– Zoo station / Even better than the real thing / One / Until the end of the world / Who's gonna ride your wild horses / So cruel / The fly / Mysterious ways / Tryin' to throw your arms around the world / Ultra violet (light my way) / Acrobat / Love is blindness. (re-iss. Aug93, hit UK No.17; same)

Dec 91. (c-s/7") (C+/IS 509) <866188> **MYSTERIOUS WAYS. / ('A'-solar plexus magic hour remix)** `13` `9` Nov91
(12"+=) (12IS 509) – ('A'-Apollo 440 remix) / ('A'-Tabla Motown remix).
(pic-cd-s+++=) (CID 509) – ('A'-Solar Plexus extended club mix).
(12") (12ISX 509) – ('A'-Perfecto mix) / ('A'-Ultimatum mix) / ('A'-Apollo 400 Magic Hour remix) / ('A'-Solar Plexus extended club mix).

Feb 92. (c-s/7") (C+/IS 515) <866533> **ONE. / LADY WITH THE SPINNING HEAD (UVI)** `7` `10`
(12"+=) (12IS 515) – Satellite of love.
(cd-s++=) (CID 515) – Night and day (steel string remix).

Jun 92. (c-s/7") (C+/IS 525) <866977> **EVEN BETTER THAN THE REAL THING. / SALOME** `12` `32`
(12"+=/cd-s+=) (12IS/CID 525) – Where did it all go wrong (demo) / Lady with the spinning head (UVI) (extended dance mix).

Jul 92. (12") (REAL U2) **EVEN BETTER THAN THE REAL THING (the perfecto mix) / ('A'-trance mix) / ('A'-sexy dub mix)** `8` `–`
(cd-s) (CREAL 2) – (first 2) / ('A'-Apollo 440 Stealth Sonic remix) / ('A'-V16 Exit Wound remix) / ('A'-Apollo 440 vs. U2 instrumental remix).

Nov 92. (c-s/7") (C+/IS 550) <864521> **WHO'S GONNA RIDE YOUR WILD HORSES. / PAINT IT BLACK** `14` `35`
(cd-s+=) (CID 550) – Fortunate son / ('A'version).
(pic-cd-s++=) (CIDX 550) – Salome (Zooromancer remix) / Can't help falling in love (Triple Peaks remix).

Jun 93. (12"ltd) **LEMON. / SALOME (Boys Own Mix)** `–` `–`
Jul 93. (cd)(lp/c) (CIDU 29)(U2/+C 9) <518047> **ZOOROPA** `1` `1`
– Zooropa / Babyface / Numb / Lemon / Stay (faraway, so close!) / Daddy's gonna pay for your crashed car / Some days are better than others / The first time / Dirty day / The wanderer.

Aug 93. (video-ep) (088 162-3) **NUMB / NUMB (video remix) / LOVE IS BLINDNESS** `-` `-`

Nov 93. (c-s/7") (C+/IS 578) <858076> **STAY (FARAWAY, SO CLOSE!). / FRANK SINATRA WITH BONO: I'VE GOT YOU UNDER MY SKIN** `4` `61`
(cd-s+=) (CID 578) – Lemon (Bad Yard club) / Lemon (Perfecto mix).
(pic-cd-s) (CIDX 578) – ('A'side) / Slow dancing / Bullet the blue sky (live) / Love is blindness (live).

——— In Mar 94, BONO teamed up with GAVIN FRIDAY (Virgin Prunes) on single 'IN THE NAME OF THE FATHER' from the film of the same name. It made No.46 in UK and was taken from soundtrack album. (below from the 'Batman Forever' movie released on 'Atlantic' UK)

Jun 95. (7"red/c-s) (A 7131/+C) <87131> **HOLD ME, THRILL ME, KISS ME, KILL ME / (themes from 'Batman Forever' by Elliot Goldenthal)** `2` `16`
(cd-s) (A 7131CD) – ('Tell Me Now' track by MAZZY STAR).

PASSENGERS

——— aka U2, ENO + guests incl. vocalists PAVAROTTI + HOLI

	Island	Island

Nov 95. (cd/c/lp) (CID/ICT/ILPS 8043) <524166> **ORIGINAL SOUNDTRACKS 1** `12` `76`
– United colours / Slug / Your blue room / Always forever now / A different kind of blue / Beach sequence / Miss Sarajevo / Ito Okashi / One minute warning / Corpse (these chains are way too long) / Elvis ate America / Plot 180 / Theme from the swan / Theme from let's go native.

Nov 95. (c-s/7") (C+/IS 625) **MISS SARAJEVO. / ONE (live)** `6`
(cd-s+=) (CID 625) – Bottoms (Watashitachi No Ookina Yume) (Zoo Station remix) / Viva Davidoff.

U2

Feb 97. (c-s) (CIS 649) **DISCOTHEQUE / HOLY JOE (Garage mix)** `1` `10`
(cd-s+=) (CID 649) – Holy Joe (Guilty mix).
(cd-s) (CIDX 649) – ('A'-DM Deep Club mix) / ('A'-Howie B, hairy mix) / ('A'-Hexidecimal mix) / ('A'-DM Tec radio mix).
(3x12"box) (12IST 649) – 1:- (David Morales mixes; 4) // 2:- (12"version & David Holmes mix) // 3:- (Howie B & Steve Osborne's Hexidecimal mix).

Mar 97. (cd/c/d-lp) (CIDU/UC/U 210) **POP** `1` `1`
– Discotheque / Do you feel loved / Mofo / If God will send his angels / Staring at the sun / Last night on Earth / Gone / Miami / The Playboy mansion / If you wear that velvet dress / Please / Wake up dead man.

Apr 97. (c-s) (CIS 658) **STARING AT THE SUN / NORTH AND SOUTH (OF THE RIVER)** `3` `26`
(cd-s+=) (CID 658) – Your blue room.
('A'-Monster Truck mix; cd-s+=) (CIDX 658) – ('A'-Sad bastards mix) / ('A'-Lab rat mix).

Jul 97. (c-s) (CIS 664) **LAST NIGHT ON EARTH / POP MUZIK (Pop Mart mix)** `10` `57`
(cd-s+=) (CID 664) – Happiness is a warm gun (the gun mix).
('First Night In Hell mix; cd-s+=) (CIDX 664) – Numb (the Soul Assassins mix) / Happiness is a warm gun (the Danny Saber mix).
(12") (12IS 664)

Sep 97. (c-s) (CIS 673) **PLEASE / DIRTY DAY (JUNK DAY)** `7`
(cd-s+=) (CID 673) – Dirty day (bitter kiss) / I'm not your baby (Sky splintered mix).
(cd-ep) POPHEART EP (CIDX 673) – ('A'live) / Where the streets have no name (live) / With or without you (live) / Staring at the sun (live).

Dec 97. (c-s) (CIS 684) **IF GOD WILL SEND HIS ANGELS / MOFO (Romin remix)** `12`
(cd-s) (CID 684) – ('A'side) / Slow dancing (with WILLIE NELSON) / Two shots of happy, one shot of sad / Sunday bloody Sunday (live with THE EDGE on vox).
(cd-s) (CIDX 684) – ('A'-The Grand Jury mix) / Mofo (Phunk Phorce mix) / Mofo (Mother's mix).
(12") (12IS 684) – Mofo (Funk Force mix) / (Black hole dub) / (Mothers mix) / (House flava mix) / Roamin).

Oct 98. (c-s) (CIS 727 <radio cut>) **SWEETEST THING / STORIES FOR BOYS (live 1981)** `3` `63`
(cd-s+=) (CIDX 727) – Out of control (live 1981).
(cd-s) (CID 727) – Twilight (live 1983) / An cat dubh (live 1983).

Nov 98. (cd/c/d-lp) (CIDU/UC/U 211) <524612> **THE BEST OF 1980-1990** (compilation) `1` `2`
– Pride (in the name of love) / New years day / With or without you / I still haven't found what I'm looking for / Sunday bloody Sunday / Bad / Where the streets have no name / I will follow / The unforgettable fire / Sweetest thing (new recording) / Desire / When love comes to town / Angel of Harlem / All I want is you. (also on d-cd; CIDDU 211)<524613> – (hit UK No.8 & US No.45).

The EDGE

with guest SINEAD O'CONNOR – vocals

	Virgin	Virgin

Sep 86. (cd/c/lp) (CD/TC+/V 2401) **CAPTIVE (Soundtrack)**
– Rowena's theme / Heroine (theme from 'Captive') / One foot in Heaven / The strange party / Hiro's theme 1 & 2 / Drift / The dream theme / Djinn / Island.

Sep 86. (7"/12") (VS/+T 897) **HEROINE. / HEROINE (mix II)** `–`

——— In 1983, The EDGE had collaborated with JAH WOBBLE & HOLGER CZUKAY on m-lp 'SNAKE CHARMER'.

ADAM CLAYTON & LARRY MULLEN

	Mother	Mother

May 96. (c-s) (MUMSC 75) <576670> **THEME FROM "MISSION: IMPOSSIBLE" / "MISSION: IMPOSSIBLE" THEME (MISSION ACCOMPLISHED)** `7` `7`
(12"+=/cd-s+=) – ('A'-Junior's hard mix) / ('A'-cut the red not the blue mix) / ('A'-Dave Clarke remix).

Nov 93. (12"pic-ep/cd-ep) *(659614-6/-2)* **IN MY DREAMS WITH YOU. / EROTIC NIGHTMARES / I WOULD LOVE TO** ☐ ☐
Apr 95. (cd/c) *(478586-2/-4)* *<1245>* **ALIEN LOVE SECRETS** 39 ☐
– Mad horsie / Juice / Die to live / The boy from Seattle / Ya yo gakk / Kill the guy with the ball – The God eaters / Tender surrender.
Sep 96. (cd/c) *(485062-2/-4)* **FIRE GARDEN** 41 ☐
– There's a fire in my house / Crying machine / Dyin' day / Whookam / Blowfish / Mysterious murder of Christian Tierra's lover / Hand on heart / Bangkok / Fire garden suite / Deepness / Little alligator / All about Eve / Aching burger / Brother / Damn you / When I was a little boy / Genocide / Warm regards.
May 97. (cd/c; shared with JOE SATRIANI & ERIC JOHNSON) *(487539-2/-4)* **G3 LIVE IN CONCERT** (live 2nd November, 1996 at the Northrop Auditorium, Minneapolis) ☐ ☐
– (tracks by JOE SATRIANI) / (tracks by ERIC JOHNSON) / Answers / For the love of God / The attitude song / The jam songs (featuring all 3 G's):- Going down. *(video+=)* – My guitar wants to kill your mama / Red house.
Sep 99. (cd/c) *<69817>* **THE ULTRA ZONE** - ☐
– Blood & tears / The ultra zone / Oooo / Frank / Jiboom / Voodoo acid / Windows to the soul / Silent within / I'll be around / Lucky charms / Fever dream / Here I am / Asian sky.

VALENTINOS (see under ⇒ WOMACK, Bobby)

VAN DER GRAAF GENERATOR

Formed: Manchester, England ... 1967 by PETER HAMMILL, CHRIS 'JUDGE' SMITH and NICK PEAME, who met at Manchester University. A one-off 45, 'THE PEOPLE YOU WERE GOING TO', surfaced in 1968, before they disbanded. Re-grouping soon after with a slightly modified line-up, HAMMILL and SMITH enlisted the more experienced KEITH ELLIS, GUY EVANS and NICK BANTON. However, it wasn't long before SMITH left HAMMILL as the focal point and sole remaining founder member. This line-up recorded what was initially intended to be a HAMMILL solo album, 'AEROSOL GREY MACHINE', which surprisingly only saw a full release in the States. It was a remarkable debut, showcasing cuts such as 'NECROMANCER', 'RUNNING BACK' and 'AFTERWARDS', in which HAMMILL exercised his wide-ranging vocal talent to startling effect. A change of line-up ensued, with NIC POTTER (like EVANS, he had played in The MISUNDERSTOOD) replacing the JUICY LUCY bound ELLIS. Signing to 'Charisma', they released their conceptual follow-up, 'THE LEAST WE CAN DO IS WAVE TO EACH OTHER', which dented the UK Top 50 in early 1970. The album saw the band developing a hybrid of pseudo-gothic lyrics and progressive rock styles, the stand-out tracks being 'REFUGEES' and 'AFTER THE FLOOD'. POTTER departed during their next project, 'H TO HE', a record which featured the services of the (then) in-demand guitarist ROBERT FRIPP (KING CRIMSON). He also contributed session work to their subsequent effort, 'PAWN HEARTS' (1971), which included the 20-minute piece, 'A PLAGUE OF LIGHTHOUSE KEEPERS'. The composition traversed a varying degree of moods and tempos, hitting a breathtaking finale. After a GEORGE MARTIN (yes, that one!) penned 45, 'THEME ONE', failed to sell, they disbanded for the second time in the summmer of '72. With the help of some VAN DER GRAAF members, HAMMILL had previously recorded a solo album, 'FOOL'S MATE', returning to the studio once again for a follow-up, 'CHAMELEON IN THE SHADOW OF THE NIGHT', released in 1972. For a few years, HAMMILL continued in an increasingly experimental and inventive vein, much in evidence on his 1975 album, 'NADIR'S BIG CHANCE'. VAN DER GRAAF reformed around this time, releasing three albums during the next two years, one of which was the highly regarded 'WORLD RECORD' (1976). After the plug was finally pulled on the 'GENERATOR', HAMMILL went to work on a series of solo albums, bringing in his group K. His work was quite prolific in the 80's and was virtually VAN DER GRAAF in all but name. He has been an inspiration to many alternative acts, JOHN LYDON citing HAMMILL's vocal technique as a guiding influence. • **Trivia:** Named after a generator built by Dr. Robert Jemison Van Der Graaf.

Album rating: AEROSOL GREY MACHINE (*8) / THE LEAST WE CAN DO IS WAVE TO EACH OTHER (*7) / H TO HE, WHO AM THE ONLY ONE (*6) / PAWN HEARTS (*6) / Peter Hammill: FOOL'S MATE (*6) / CHAMELEON IN THE SHADOW OF THE NIGHT (*6) / THE SILENT CORNER AND THE EMPTY STAGE (*6) / IN CAMERA (*5) / NADIR'S BIG CHANCE (*7) / Van Der Graaf Generator: GODBLUFF (*6) / STILL LIFE (*6) / WORLD RECORD (*7) / Van Der Graaf: THE QUIET ZONE – THE PLEASURE DOME (*6) / VITAL (*5) / REPEAT PERFORMANCE posthumous collection (*7) / Peter Hammill: OVER (*6) / THE FUTURE NOW (*6) / pH7 (*6) / A BLACK BOX (*6) / SITTING TARGETS (*7) / ENTER K (*6) / LOOPS AND REELS (*5) / PATIENCE (*6) / THE LOVE SONGS collection (*6) / THE MARGIN – LIVE (*6) / SKIN (*6) / AND CLOSE AS THIS (*6) / SPUR OF THE MOMENT with Guy Evans (*5) / IN A FOREIGN TOWN (*6) / OUT OF WATER (*6) / THE FALL OF THE HOUSE OF USHER (*3) / FIRESHIPS (*4) / THE NOISE (*4) / THE CALM (AFTER THE STORM) compilation (*6) / THE STORM (BEFORE THE CALM) compilation (*6) / THERE GOES THE DAYLIGHT (*6) / ROARING FORTIES (*6) / ROOM TEMPERATURE LIVE (*6) / X MY HEART (*6) / EVERYONE YOU HOLD (*6) / TIDES (*5)

PETER HAMMILL (b. 5 Nov'48, London, England) – vocals, guitar, piano /**NICK PEAME** – organ / **CHRIS JUDGE SMITH** – drums, vocals, oricanos

	Polydor	Mercury
Jan 69. (7") *(56758)* **PEOPLE YOU WERE GOING TO. / FIREBRAND**	☐	-

—— **HUGH BANTON** – keyboards, repl. PEAME

—— added **KEITH ELLIS** – bass (ex-KOOBAS) / **GUY EVANS** – drums (ex-MISUNDERSTOOD)

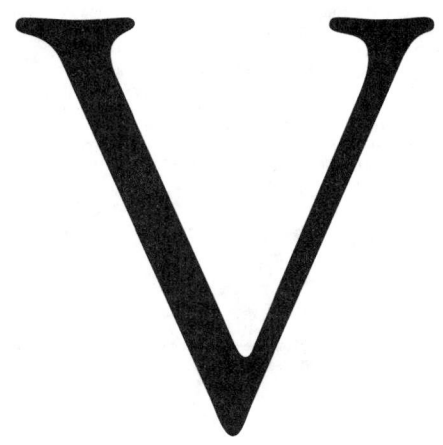

Steve VAI

Born: STEVEN CIRO VAI, 6 Jun'60, Carve Place, Long Island, New Jersey, USA. Taught as a young teenager by the great JOE SATRIANI (his neighbour), he went on to join FRANK ZAPPA's ever-changing band of musicians, playing on albums from 'Tinseltown Rebellion' (1981) to 'Frank Zappa Meets The Mothers Of Prevention' (1986). During a ZAPPA interim (and there's not many of these!), VAI found time to issue a solo album, 'FLEX-ABLE', which, after its initial copies were sold out on the small 'Akashic', it went like hotcakes on the larger stable, 'Relativity'. Now much in demand, the superb axeman became part of ALCATRAZZ, briefly replacing YNGWIE MALMSTEEN for one album in '85. During a spell of activity that would even put ZAPPA to shame, the young man played the guitar-grinding Devil in Walter Hill's movie 'Crossroads', while also finding time to lay down all the six string work for PUBLIC IMAGE LTD.'s 'Album' set. The egocentric DAVID LEE ROTH was the next person to seek out his services, VAI staying and co-writing on two albums, 'Eat 'Em And Smile' (1986) and 'Skyscraper' (1987) before moving on to WHITESNAKE and playing on their 'Slip Of The Tongue' (1989) set. The following year, while still a member of the aforementioned outfit, VAI released his long-awaited follow-up, 'PASSION AND WARFARE', a remarkable and innovative disc which brought delightfully fresh experimentation to the world of guitarslinging hard-rock. Its reviews and his consummate CV ensured it a Top 20 placing on both sides of the Atlantic, marking out VAI, alongside his teacher SATRIANI, as one the greatest young guitarists in the world. In 1993, he turned his head to more commercially viable roots, his band VAI taking on an old ZAPPA vocalist, TERRY BOZZIO for the album, 'SEX & RELIGION'. Over the course of the next few years, VAI released a few more sets, 'ALIEN LOVE SECRETS' (1995) and 'FIRE GARDEN' (1996), both moderate sellers in Britain. More recently, VAI has turned up on a collaboration live set, '3G' alongside ERIC JOHNSON and who else but JOE SATRIANI.

Album rating: FLEX-ABLE mini (*6) / PASSION AND WARFARE (*7) / SEX & RELIGION (*5) / ALIEN LOVE SECRETS (*5) / FIRE GARDEN (*6) / G3: LIVE IN CONCERT with Joe Satriani & Eric Johnson (*7) / THE ULTRA ZONE (*5)

STEVE VAI – guitar, keyboards, bass, etc.

	Music For Nations	Akashic
1984. (lp) *(MFN 31)* **FLEX-ABLE**	☐	☐

– Little green men / Viva women / Lovers are crazy / The boy / Salamanders in the sun / Girl song / Attitude song / Call it sleep / Junkie / Bill is private parts / Next stop Earth / There's something dead in here. *(re-iss. Sep86 on 'Food For Thought' lp/c; GRUB/TGRUB 3) (cd-iss. 1989; CDGRUB 3) (cd re-iss. Jun97 on 'Relativity-Epic'; 487871-2)*

—— now with **DAVE ROSENTHAL** – keyboards / **STU HAMM** – bass / **CHRIS FRAZIER** – drums

	Food For Thought	Relativity
May 90. (cd/c/lp) *(CD/C+/GRUB 17)* *<1037>* **PASSION AND WARFARE**	8	18

– Liberty / Erotic nightmares / The animal / Answers / The riddle / Ballerina 12-24 / For the love of God / The audience is listening / I would love to / Blue powder / Greasy kid's stuff / Alien water kiss / Sisters / Love secrets. *(pic-lp Nov90; GRUB 17P) (re-iss. Oct93 on 'Epic' cd/c; 467109-2/-4)*

—— His new band were **TIM STEVENS** – bass / **TERRY BOZZIO** – drums / with **DEVIN TOWNSEND** – vocals / **WILL RILEY** – keyboards / **SCOTT THUNES** – bass / **ABE LABORIEL JR.** – drums

	Relativity-Epic	Relativity-Epic
Jul 93. (cd/c/lp; as VAI) *(473947-2/-4/-1)* *<1132>* **SEX & RELIGION**	17	48

– An earth dweller's return / Here & now / In my dreams with you / Still my bleeding heart / Sex and religion / Dirty black hole / Touching tongues / State of grace / Survive / Pig / The road to Mt.Calvary / Deep down into the pain / Rescue me or bury me.

Aug 93. (12"pic-ep/cd-ep) *(659491-6/-2)* **DEEP DOWN INTO THE PAIN. / JUST CARTILAGE / DEEP DOWN IN THE PAIN (edit)** ☐ ☐

—— Now a quartet when CHRIS formed HEEBALOB. He later wrote for HAMMILL.

		not iss.	Mercury
Jan 69.	(lp) *<SR 61238>* **AEROSOL GREY MACHINE**	-	

– Afterwards / Orthenthian St. (part 1 & 2) / Running back / Into a game / Aerosol grey machine / Black smoke yen / Aguarian / Necromancer / Octopus. *(UK-iss.Feb75 on 'Fontana'; 6430 083) (cd-iss. Mar97 on 'Repertoire'+=; RR 4647)* – People you were going to / Firebrand. *(cd re-iss. May97 on 'Fie!'+=; FIE 9116)* – Ferret / Featherbird / Giant squid.

Apr 69. (7") *<72979>* **AFTERWARDS. / NECROMANCER**   -

—— **NIC POTTER** – bass (ex-MISUNDERSTOOD) repl. ELLIS who joined JUICY LUCY / added **DAVE JACKSON** – saxophone (ex-HEEBALOB)

		Charisma	Dunhill
Feb 70.	(lp)(c) *(CAS 1007)* **THE LEAST WE CAN DO IS WAVE TO EACH OTHER**	47	

– Darkness / Refugees / White hammer / Whatever would Robert have said / Out of my book / After the flood. *(re-iss. Aug82 lp/c; CHC/+MC 5) (cd-iss. Apr87; CASCD 1007)*

Apr 70. (7") *(CB 122)* **REFUGEES. / THE BOAT OF MILLIONS OF YEARS**

—— A quartet again, when POTTER left only completing half of next album. Guest on next 2 albums **ROBERT FRIPP** – guitar (of KING CRIMSON)

		Charisma	Mercury
Dec 70.	(lp) *(CAS 1027)* *<50097>* **H TO HE, WHO AM THE ONLY ONE**		

– Killer / House with no door / The emperor in his war-room: The emperor – The room / Lost: Dance in sand and sea – Dance in frost / The pioneers over C. *(re-iss. Jun81 & Sep83 on 'Polydor'; 6321 126) (cd-iss. Nov88; CASCD 1027)*

		Charisma	Mercury
Oct 71.	(lp) *(CAS 1051)* **PAWN HEARTS**		-

– Lemmings / Man-erg / A plague of lighthouse keepers: 1) Eyewitness – 2) Pictures – Lighthouse – 3) Eyewitness – 4) S.H.M. – 5) Presence of the night – 6) Kosmos tours – 7) (Custards) Last stand – 8) The clot chickens – 9) Lands End – 10) We go now. *(re-iss. Oct86; CHC 54) (cd-iss. Apr88; CASCD 1051)*

Feb 72. (7") *(CB 175)* **THEME ONE. / W**

PETER HAMMILL

had by this went solo when VAN DER GRAAF split. He continued to use VDGG members.

		Charisma	Charisma
Jul 71.	(lp) *(<CAS 1037>)* **FOOL'S MATE**		

– Imperial zeppelin / Candle / Happy / Solitude / Vision / Re-awakening / Sunshine / Child / Summer song (in the autumn) / Viking / The birds / I once wrote some poems. *(re-iss. Sep83 lp/c; CHC/+MC 2) (cd-iss. Oct88; CASCD 1037)*

May 73. (lp) *(<CAS 1067>)* **CHAMELEON IN THE SHADOW OF THE NIGHT**
– German overalls / Slender threads / Rock and role / In the end / What's it worth / Easy to slip away / Dropping the torch / In the black room / The tower. *(cd-iss. Apr89; CASCD 1067)*

Feb 74. (lp) *(<CAS 1083>)* **THE SILENT CORNER AND THE EMPTY STAGE**
– Modern / Wilhemina / The lie (Bernini's Saint Teresa) / Forsaken gardens / Red shift / Rubicon / A louse is not a home. *(re-iss. Oct86; CHC 61) (cd-iss. Nov88; CASCD 1083)*

Sep 74. (lp) *(<CAS 1089>)* **IN CAMERA**
– Ferret and featherbed / (No more) The sub-mariner / Tapeworm / Again / Faintheart and the sermon / The comet, the course. the tail / Gog Magog (in bromine chambers). *(re-iss. Nov80 on 'Polydor'; 9198 770) (re-iss. Aug88 lp/c; CHC/+MC 33) (cd-iss. Nov88; CASCD 1089)*

Feb 75. (lp) *(<CAS 1099>)* **NADIR'S BIG CHANCE**
– Nadir's big chance / The institute of mental health's burning / Open your eyes / Nobody's business / Been alone so long / Pompeii / Shingle song / Airport / People you were going to / Birthday special / Two or three spectres. *(re-iss. Mar83 lp/c; CHC/+MC 19) (cd-iss. Nov88; CASCD 1099)*

Apr 75. (7") *(CB 245)* **BIRTHDAY SPECIAL. / SHINGLE SONG**

—— **HAMMILL, BANTON, JACKSON + EVANS** reformed

VAN DER GRAAF GENERATOR

		Charisma	Mercury
Oct 75.	(lp) *(CAS 1109)* *<1069>* **GODBLUFF**		

– The undercover man / Scorched Earth / Arrow / The sleepwalkers. *(re-iss. Mar83 lp/c; CHC/+MC 13) (cd-iss. Apr88; CASCD 1109)*

Apr 76. (lp)(c) *(CAS 1116)(7208 605)* *<1096>* **STILL LIFE**
– Pilgrims / Still life / La rossa / My room (waiting for Wonderland) / Childlike faith in childhood's end. *(re-iss. Oct86; CHC 55) (cd-iss. Apr87; CASCD 1116)*

Oct 76. (lp)(c) *(CAS 1120)(7208 610)* *<1116>* **WORLD RECORD**
– When she comes / A place to survive / Masks / Meurglys III (the songwriters guild) / Wondering. *(re-iss. Aug88; CHC 62) (cd-iss. 1988; CASCD 1120)*

Oct 76. (7") *(CB 297)* **WONDERING. / MEURGLYS III**

VAN DER GRAAF

GRAHAM SMITH – violin (ex-STRING DRIVEN THING) repl. JACKSON / **NIC POTTER** – bass returned after US session work to repl. BANTON

Sep 77. (lp) *(CAS 1131)* **THE QUIET ZONE – THE PLEASURE DOME**
– Lizard play / The habit of the broken heart / The siren song / Last frame / The wave / Yellow fever (running) / The sphinx in the face / Chemical world / The sphinx returns. *(re-iss. 1987 lp/c; CHC/+MC 32) (cd-iss. 1987; CASCD 1131)*

—— added **DAVE JACKSON** who returned w / **CHARLES DICKIE** – cello, piano

		Charisma	P.V.C.
Jul 78.	(d-lp) *(CVLD 101)* **VITAL (live)**		

– Ship of fools / Still life / Mirror images / Medley: Parts of A plague of lighthouse keepers and Sleepwalkers / Pioneers over C / Door / Urban / Nadir's big chance. *(cd-iss. Apr89; CVCLD 101) (re-iss. cd Mar94 on 'Virgin';)*

– compilations, etc. –

Aug 72.	(lp) *Charisma; (CS 2)* **68-71**		-
Aug 80.	(lp/c) *Charisma; (BG/+C 3)* **REPEAT PERFORMANCE**		-

– Afterwards / Refugees / The boat of millions of years / W / White hammer / Necromancer / The Emperor in his war room / The empereor / The room / Manerg. *(c+=)* – The clot thickens (extended).

Mar 83.	(d-c) *Charisma; (CASMC 106)* **PAWN HEARTS / STILL LIFE**		
May 85.	(lp) *Demi-Monde; (DM 003)* **TIME VAULTS** (rare)		

(cd-iss. Apr97 on 'Spalax'; 14847)

Feb 87.	(cd) *Virgin; (COMCD 2)* **FIRST GENERATION**		
Feb 87.	(cd) *Virgin; (COMCD 3)* **SECOND GENERATION**		
May 88.	(lp/cd) Thunderbolt; (THBL/CDTB 042) **NOW AND THEN**		
Sep 93.	(cd) *Virgin; (CDVM 9026)* **I PROPHESY DISASTER**		
Jun 94.	(cd) *Band Of Joy; (BOJCD 008)* **MAIDA VALE**		

PETER HAMMILL

went solo after the VDGG split

		Charisma	Charisma
Sep 76.	(lp) *(<CAS 1125>)* **OVER**		

– Crying wolf / Autumn / Time heals / Alice (letting go) / This side of the looking-glass / Betrayed (on Tuesdays she used to) / Yoga / Lost and found. *(cd-iss. Feb91; CASCD 1125)*

		Charisma	P.V.C.
Sep 78.	(lp) *(CAS 1137)* *<2202>* **THE FUTURE NOW**		

– The future now / Still in the dark / Mediaevil / A motor-bike in Africa / The cut / Palinurus / Pushing thirty / The second hand / Trappings / The mousetrap (caught in) / Energy vampires / If I could. *(re-iss. Oct86; CHC 59) (cd-iss. Nov88; CASCD 1137)*

Nov 79. (lp) *(CAS 1146)* *<2205>* **pH7**
– My favourite / Careering / Porton Down / Mirror images / Handicap and equality / Not for Keith / The old school tie / Time for a change / Imperial walls / Mr. X gets tense / Faculty X. *(cd-iss. Apr89; CASCD 1146)*

Nov 79. (7"; as RICKY NADIR) *(CB 339)* **THE POLAROID. / THE OLD SCHOOL TIE**

		Mercury	not iss.
1980.	(lp) *(6302 067)* **A BLACK BOX**	-	Europe

– Golden promise / Losing faith in words / The Jargon king / Fog walking / The spirit / In slow time / The wipe / Flight: Flying blind – White cave fandango – Control – Cockpit – Silk worm wings / Nothing is nothing – A black box. *(UK-iss.Jun83; same) (re-iss. Aug88 on 'Virgin' lp/cd; OVED/CDOVD 140)*

		Virgin	not iss.
May 81.	(7") *(VS 424)* **MY EXPERIENCE. / GLUE**		-
Jun 81.	(lp) *(V 2205)* **SITTING TARGETS**		-

– Breakthrough / My experience / Ophelia / Empress's clothes / Glue / Hesitation / Sitting targets / Stranger still / Sign / What I did for love / Central hotel. *(re-iss. Aug88; OVED 139) (cd-iss. Oct88; CDV 2205)*

—— **HAMMILL** with **GUY EVANS** / **NIC POTTER** plus **JOHN ELLIS** – guitar (ex-VIBRATORS), formed **K**

		Naive	not iss.
Sep 82.	(7") *(NAV 3)* **PARADOX DRIVE. / NOW MORE THAN EVER**		-
Oct 82.	(lp/c) *(NAV L/C 1)* **ENTER K**		-

– Paradox Drive / The unconscious life / Accidents / The great experiments / Don't tell me / She wraps it up / Happy hour / Seven wonders. *(cd-iss. May92 on 'Fie!'; FIE 9101)*

Sep 83. (lp) *(NAVL 3)* **PATIENCE**
– Labour of love / Film noir / Just good friends / Jeunesse D'Oree / Traintime / Now more than ever / Comfortable / Patient. *(cd-iss. May92 on 'Fie!'; FIE 9102) (above 2 re-iss. Jan86 on 'Spartan' d-lp/d-c; SPD P/C 1)*

		Foundry	not iss.
Sep 83.	(7") *(NAV 8)* **FILM NOIR. / SEVEN WONDERS**		-
Feb 85.	(d-lp) *(FONDL 1)* **THE MARGIN (live)**		-

– Future now / Porton Down / Stranger still / Sign / The Jargon king / The second hand / Empress's clothes / The sphinx in the face / Labour of love / Sitting targets / Patience / Flight. *(cd-iss. Feb91 on 'Virgin'; CDOVD 345)*

Mar 86. (lp/c) *(FOND L/C 3)* **SKIN**
– Skin / After the show / Painting by numbers / Shell / All said and done / A perfect date / Four pails / New lover. *(cd-iss. Nov87 on 'Line'; DACD 900145) (cd re-iss. Feb91 on 'Virgin'; CDOVD 344)*

Mar 86. (7") *(FOUND 3)* **PAINTING BY NUMBERS. / YOU HIT ME WHERE I LIVE**
(ext.12"+=) – (FOUND 3-12) – Shell.

		Virgin	not iss.
Nov 86.	(lp/c) *(V/TCV 2409)* **AND CLOSE AS THIS**		-

– Too many of my yesterdays / Faith / Empire of delight / Silver / Beside the one you love / Other old cliches / Confident / Sleep now. *(cd-iss. Nov88; CDV 2409) (cd re-iss. 1989 on 'Line'; DACD 900254)*

		Red Hot	not iss.
Jun 88.	(c/cd; PETER HAMMILL & GUY EVANS) *(ZCRH/CDR 102)* **SPUR OF THE MOMENT**		-

– Sweating it out / Little did he know / Without a glitch / Anatol's proposal / You think next / Multiman / Deprogramming Archie / Always so polite / An imagined brother / Bounced / Roger and out. *(re-iss. May93; same)*

		Enigma	Enigma
Nov 88.	(lp/c/cd) *(ENVLP/TCENV/CDENV 512)* **IN A FOREIGN TOWN**		

– Hemlock / Invisible ink / Sci-finance (re-visited) / This book / Time to burn / Auto / Vote brand X / Sun City night life / The play's the thing / Under cover names. *(c+=/cd+=)* – Smile / Time to burn (instrumental). *(cd re-iss. Jun95 on 'Fie!'; FIE 9108)*

Feb 90. (cd/c/lp) *(CDENV/TVENVENVLP 1003)* **OUT OF WATER**
– Evidently goldfish / Not the man / No Moon in the water / Our oyster / Something about Ysabel's dance / Green fingers / On the surface / A way out. *(cd re-iss. Jun95 on 'Fie!'; FIE 9109)*

		Some Bizzare	not iss.
Nov 91.	(cd/c/lp) *(SBZ CD/MC/LP 007)* **THE FALL OF THE HOUSE OF USHER**		-

– An unenviable role / That must be the house / Architecture / The sleeper / One thing at a time / I shun the light / Leave this house / Dreaming / A chronic catalepsy / The herbalist / The evil that is done / Five years ago / It's over now / An influence / No rot / She is dead / Beating of the heart / The haunted palace / I dared not speak / She comes towards the door / The fall.

	Fie!	not iss.
Mar 92. (cd/c) *(FIE/+C 9103)* **FIRESHIPS**	☐	–

– I will find you / Curtains / His best girl / Oasis / Incomplete surrender / Fireship / Given time / Reprise / Gaia.

Mar 93. (cd/c) *(FIE/+C 9104)* **THE NOISE**	☐	–

– A kick to kill the kiss / Like a shot / The entertainer / Noise / Celebrity kissing / Where the mouth is / Great European department store / Planet Coventry / Primo on the carpet.

Nov 93. (cd; as PETER HAMMILL & THE NOISE) *(FIE 9106)* **THERE GOES THE DAYLIGHT (live)**	☐	–

– Sci-finance (revisited) / The habit of a broken heart / Sign / I will find you / Lost and found / Planet Coventry / Empress's clothes / Cat's eye – Yellow fever / Primo on the parapet / Central hotel.

Sep 94. (cd) *FIE 9107* **ROARING FORTIES**	☐	–

– Sharply unclear / The gift of fire / You can't want what you always get / A headlong stretch / Your tall ship.

Jun 95. (d-cd) *(FIE 9110)* **ROOM TEMPERATURE (live)**	☐	–

– Wave / Just good friends / Vision / Time to burn / Four pails / The comet, the course, the tail / Ophelia / Happy hour / If I could / Something about Ysabel's dance / Patient / Cat's eye, yellow fever (running) / Running / Skin / Hemlock / Our oyster / Unconscious life / After the snow / Way out / Future now / Traintime / Modern.

Mar 96. (cd) *(FIE 9111)* **X MY HEART**	☐	–

– Better time / Amnesiac / Ram origami / Forest of pronouns / Earthbound / Narcissus (bar & grill) / Material possession / Come clean.

	Sine	not iss.
Sep 96. (cd) *(SINE 006)* **TIDES**	☐	–

– compilations, etc. –

1978. (lp) *G.I.R.; <9211 1016>* **VISION**		
1983. (c) *Sofa;* **LOOPS AND REELS**		–

(cd-iss. Nov93 on 'Fie!'; FIE 9105)

Aug 84. (lp) *Charisma; (CAS 1166)* **THE LOVE SONGS** (remixes)		–

– Just good friends / My favourite / Been alone so long / Ophelia / Again / If I could / Vision / Don't tell me / The birds / (THis side of) The looking glass. *(re-iss. Jun88 lp/c; CHC/+MC 69) (cd-iss. Nov88; CASCD 1166)*

May 85. (7") *Charisma; (CB 414)* **JUST GOOD FRIENDS. /**		–
('A'instrumental)		
Jul 93. (cd) *Virgin; (CDVM 9017)* **THE CALM (AFTER THE STORM)**		–
Jul 93. (cd) *Virgin; (CDVM 9018)* **THE STORM (BEFORE THE CALM)**		–
Jan 95. (cd) *Golden Hind; (GH 70112)* **OFFENSICHTLLICH GOLDFISCH**		–

– Offensichtilich goldfisch / Dich zu finden / Die kalte killt den kub / Favorit / Kaufhaus Europa / Der larm / Oase / Die prominenz kubt sich / Die tunte verlischt / Auto (wieder im wagen) / Gaia / Schlaft nun.

Nov 95. (cd) *Strange Fruit; (SFRCD 136)* **THE PEEL SESSIONS**		–
Jan 96. (cd) *Virgin; (CDOVD 460)* **AFTER THE SHOW**		–
Sep 96. (cd) *Fie!; (FIE 9112)* **PAST GO: COLLECTED**		–

– A kick to kill the kiss / I will find you / Accidents / His best girl / Sharply unclear / Patient / Planet Coventry / A ritual mask / The noise / The gift of fire / Traintime / Gaia / Your tall ship.

VANGELIS

Born: EVANGELOS PAPATHANASSIOU, 29 Mar'43, Volos, Greece. A child prodigy, the young VANGELIS was performing his own compositions in front of a large audience from the age of six. Groomed by his artistic parents, he subsequently studied classical music alongside other areas of the Arts at The Academy Of Fine Arts in Athens. Having already cultivated a love of jazz, like many other budding musicians of the day, he was inspired by the revoltionary pop takeover of The BEATLES. In 1963, he duly instigated a 6-piece beat combo, The FORMINX, who scored a major hit in Greece with the single, 'YENKA BEAT'. They continued for four years, becoming one of their country's leading popular music acts and initiated a dance craze with their biggest hit, 'JERONIMO YANKA' in 1965. Following the band's demise, VANGELIS PAPATHANASSIOU took on board a more keyboard-orientated style, the result being a solo single, 'THE CLOCK', in 1968. Working with him at this time were drummer LUCAS SIDERAS and vocalist/bassist DEMIS ROUSSOS, this trio soon evolving into APHRODITE'S CHILD. A classical adaptation of PACHELBEL's 'Canon' (similar in style to PROCOL HARUM's 'A Whiter Shade Of Pale'), 'RAIN AND TEARS' was released by 'Mercury' in 1968, the single denting the UK Top 30 after being a Europe-wide hit. An album soon followed, 'END OF THE WORLD', being an unlikely hybrid of progressive rock and Latin-styled folk. Further singles appeared, although VANGELIS was eager to branch into more complex solo work. He scored the soundtrack for a soft-porn movie, 'Sex Power', released under the name, 'L'APOCALYPSE DES ANIMAUX' (1971). The following year, APHRODITE'S CHILD surfaced from their Paris studio, delivering the double set, '666', which explored the Bible's Book Of Revelations against a prog-rock backdrop. It was a critical success, although DEMIS ROUSSOS took off for a fruitful solo career (e.g. the chart-topper, 'Forever And Ever'). VANGELIS signed to 'R.C.A.' in 1974, enjoying a revived chart success with his UK debut for the label, 'HEAVEN AND HELL' (1975), which featured vocals by JON ANDERSON (of YES fame) on the track 'SO LONG AGO, SO CLEAR'. 'ALBEDO 0.39' (1976) was an overly ambitious, jazzy concept album while 'BEAUBOURG' (1978) saw VANGELIS in similarly abstruse territory, the album featuring only one track, divided into two parts. In 1979, he again hooked up with JON ANDERSON to form the duo JON AND VANGELIS, recording three successful albums, 'SHORT STORIES' (1980), 'SEE YOU LATER' (1980) and 'THE FRIENDS OF MR. CAIRO' (1981), before splitting in 1983. Meanwhile, VANGELIS recorded his masterstroke with the 1981 soundtrack, 'CHARIOTS OF FIRE'. The regal, whooshing

electronica of the title track was an international smash, leading to more soundtrack work for a host of movies throughout the 80's and 90's, including 'MASK' (1985), 'ANTARTICA' (1988) and '1492: THE CONQUEST OF PARADISE' (1992). He also recorded a further one-off album with JON ANDERSON in 1991, 'PAGE OF LIFE'. • **Trivia:** In 1975, he was asked but refused to take the place of RICK WAKEMAN in YES, instead of PATRICK MORAZ. In 1985, he also wrote the ballet score for new version of 'Frankenstein'.

Album rating: Aphrodite's Child: END OF THE WORLD – RAIN AND TEARS (*4) / IT'S FIVE O'CLOCK (*4) / 666 (er . . . *6) / Vangelis: THE DRAGON (*4) / L'APOCALYPSE DES ANIMAUX (*4) / EARTH (*5) / HEAVEN & HELL (*7) / ALBEDO 0.39 (*6) / SPIRAL (*5) / HYPOTHESIS early work (*4) / BEAUBOURG (*4) / CHINA (*5) / SHORT STORIES by Jon & Vangelis (*6) / SEE YOU LATER (*4) / CHARIOTS OF FIRE soundtrack (*7) / THE FRIENDS OF MR. CAIRO by Jon & Vangelis (*5) / OPERA SAUVAGE – COSMOS (*4) / TO THE UNKNOWN MAN collection (*6) / PRIVATE COLLECTION by Jon & Vangelis (*5) / THE BEST OF JON & VANGELIS compilation (*6) / SOIL FESTIVITIES (*4) / MASK soundtrack (*3) / INVISIBLE CONNECTIONS (*4) / RHAPSODIES (*4) / DIRECT (*4) / THEMES compilation (*5) / THE CITY (*4) / PAGE OF LIFE by Jon & Vangelis (*4) / 1492: THE CONQUEST OF PARADISE soundtrack (*6) / BLADE RUNNER soundtrack (*6) / PORTRAIT (SO LONG AGO, SO CLEAR) compilation (*6) / VOICES (*4) / OCEANIC (*4) / EL GRECO (*4)

FORMINX

VANGELIS – keyboards / **TASSOS PAPASTHAMATIS** – vocals / **VASILLIS BAKOPOULOS** – rhythm guitar / **SOTORIS ARNIS** – bass / **KOSTAS SKODOS** – drums / **NIKOS MASTORASKIS** – co-songs

	Vocalion	not iss.
Apr 65. (7") *(V 9235)* **JENKA BEAT. / GERONIMO JENKA**	☐	–

──── also released a number of Greek 45's, an album finally surfacing in 1975.

APHRODITE'S CHILD

VANGELIS PAPATHANASSIOU (b. EVANGELOS, 15 Jun'47, Velos) – keyboards, wind, percussion / **DEMIS ROUSSOS** (b.15 Jun'47, Alexandria, Egypt) – vocals, bass / **LUCAS SIDERAS** (b. 5 Dec'44, Athens) – drums, vocals

	Mercury	Mercury
Oct 68. (7") *(MF 1039)* **RAIN AND TEARS. / DON'T TRY TO CATCH A RIVER**	30	☐
Feb 69. (7") *(MF 1075)* **END OF THE WORLD. / YOU ALWAYS STAND IN THE WAY**	☐	☐
Feb 69. (lp) *(SMCL 20140)* **END OF THE WORLD / RAIN AND TEARS**	☐	☐

– End of the world / Don't try to catch a river / Mister Thomas / Rain and tears / The grass is not green / Valley of sadness / You always stand in my way / The shepherd and the Moon / Day of the fool.

	Polydor	Polydor
Jun 69. (7") *(BM 56769) <15005>* **I WANT TO LIVE. / MAGIC MIRROR**	☐	☐
Nov 69. (7") *(BM 56785)* **LET ME LOVE, LET ME LIVE. / MARIE JOLIE**	☐	–
Mar 70. (7") *(BM 56791)* **IT'S FIVE O'CLOCK. / FUNKY MARY**	☐	–
Jan 70. (lp) *(238 4005)* **IT'S FIVE O'CLOCK**	☐	–

– It's five o'clock / Wake up / Take your time / Annabella / Let me love, let me live / Funky Mary / Good time so fine / Marie Jolie / Such a funny night. *(re-iss. Jul78 on 'Impact'; 6886 650)*

1970. (7") *(6033 003)* **SPRING, SUMMER, WINTER AND FALL. / AIR**	–	– France

──── Disbanded for a time, until reappeared adding **SILVER KOULOURIS** – guitar, percussion. Guests **HARRIS HALKITIS** – bass, saxophone, percussion, vocals / **MICHEL RIPOCHE** – trombone, saxophone/ **JOHN FORST** – narration / **YANNIS TSAROUCHIS** – Greek text / **IRENE PAPAS** – vox on (1).

	Vertigo	Vertigo
Jun 72. (d-lp) *(6673 001) <500>* **666**	☐	☐

– The system / Babylon / Loud, loud, loud / The four horsemen / The lamb / The seventh seal / Aegian Sea / Seven bowls / The wakening beast / Lament / The marching beast / The battle of the locusts / Do it / Tribulation / The beasts / Ofis / Seven trumpets / Altamont / The wedding of the lamb / The capture of the beast / oo / Hic and nunc / All the seats were occupied / Break. *(re-iss. Feb77; 6641 581)* *(re-iss. May83 on 'Impact' d-lp/c; 6673/7528 001) (cd-iss. Aug98 on 'Mercury'; 838430-2)*

Aug 72. (7") *<107>* **BREAK. / BABYLON**	–	☐

(UK-iss.Jun75; 6032 900)

──── Disbanded again in 72/73. VANGELIS went solo, as did DEMIS ROUSSOS.

– compilations, others –

Jun 75. (lp) *Vertigo; (6333 002)* **THE BEST OF APHRODITE'S CHILD FEATURING DEMIS ROUSSOS**	☐	–
Jun 75. (lp) *Philips; (6483 025)* **RAIN AND TEARS**	☐	–

(re-iss. Aug81 as 'GREATEST HITS 1968-1970' on 'Fontana' lp/c; 6420 006)(7240 955)

VANGELIS

VANGELIS – keyboards, synthesizers (ex-APHRODITE'S CHILD, ex-FORMYNX)

	Charly	not iss.
1971. (lp) *(CRL 5013)* **THE DRAGON**	☐	–

– The dragon / Stuffed aubergine / Stuffed tomato. *(re-iss. 1980)*

	Polydor	not iss.
1973. (lp) *(2489 113)* **L'APOCALYPSE DES ANIMAUX (Soundtrack)**	☐	–

– Apocalypse des animaux – Generique / La petite fille de la mer / Le singe bleu / La mort du loup / L'ours musicien / Creation du monde / La mer recommence. *(re-iss. Oct76 + Apr84 lp/c; SPE LP/MC 72) (cd-iss. 1988; 831 503-2)*

—— He now moved to London and signed to ...

		Vertigo	Vertigo

1974. (lp) (6499 693) <1019> **EARTH**
– Come on / We were all uprooted / Sunny Earth / He-o / Ritual / Let it happen / The city / My face in the rain / Watch out / A song.

		R.C.A.	R.C.A.

Nov 75. (lp/c) (RS 1025) <5110> **HEAVEN & HELL** [31]
– Heaven and Hell pt.1 – Bacchanale symphony to the powers of B – 2nd movement – 3rd movement – So long ago so clear * / Heaven and Hell pt.2 – Intestinal heart – Needles and bones – 12 o'clock – Aries – Away. *(re-iss. Sep81; 3012) (re-iss. 1984 lp/c; PL/PK 70009) (re-iss. Oct86 lp/c; NL/NK 71148) (cd-iss. Sep89; ND 71148)*
above featured The ENGLISH CHAMBER CHOIR and VANA VEROUTIS – lead vocals (track* was first to use vocals of **JON ANDERSON** (of YES)

Aug 76. (7") <10733> **SO LONG AGO, SO CLEAR. / HEAVEN AND HELL THEME** [-]
Sep 76. (lp/c) (RS/RC 1080) <5136> **ALBEDO 0.39** [18]
– Pulstar / Freefall / More tranquililitatis / Main sequence / Sword of Orion / Alpha / Nucleogenesis (pt.1 & 2) / Albedo 0• 39. *(re-iss. Sep81 lp/c; RCA LP/K 3017) (re-iss. Sep89 lp/c/cd; NL/NK/ND 74208)*

Oct 76. (7") (RCA 2762) <10882> **PULSTAR. / ALPHA**
Dec 77. (lp/c) (PL2 5116) <2627> **SPIRAL**
– Spiral / Ballad / Dervish D / To the unknown man / 3 plus 3. *(re-iss. Sep81 + Nov84 lp/c; NL/NK 70568) (cd-iss. Oct89; ND 70568)*

Jan 78. (7") (PB 5064) **TO THE UNKNOWN MAN. / (part 2)** [-]
Jul 78. (lp/c) (PL2/PK2 5155) <3020> **BEAUBOURG**
– Beaubourg (part 1) / Beaubourg (part 2). *(re-iss. Sep86 on 'Fame' lp/c; FA/TC-FA 3168) (re-iss. Feb90 cd/c; ND/NK 74516)*

		Polydor	Polydor

Apr 79. (lp/c) (POLD/+C 5018) <6199> **CHINA**
– Chung Kuo / The long march / The dragon / The plum blossom / The Tao of love / The little fete / Yin and Yang / Himalaya / Summit. *(re-iss. Aug83 lp/c/cd; SPE LP/MC 19/(813653-2)*

May 79. (7") (POSP 57) **THE LONG MARCH. / (part 2)**

JON & VANGELIS

JON = JON ANDERSON – vocals (also of YES)

		Polydor	Polydor

Dec 79. (7") (POSP 96) <2098> **I HEAR YOU NOW. / THUNDER** [8] [58] Aug80
Jan 80. (lp/c) (POLD/+C 5030) <PD1 6272> **SHORT STORIES** [4]
– Curious electic / Each and everyday / Bird song / I hear you now / The road / Far away in Bagdhad / Love is / One more time / Thunder / A play within a play. *(cd-iss. Jun87 lp/c; SPE LP/MC 105)*

Feb 80. (7") <2130> **ONE MORE TIME. / THE ROAD** [-]

VANGELIS

solo (same label until stated)
Jun 80. (7") (2001 973) **MY LOVE. / DOMESTIC LOGIC 1** [-]
Nov 80. (lp)(c) (2302 101)(3100 567) **SEE YOU LATER**
– I can't take it anymore / Multitrack suggestion / Memories of green / Not a bit – all of it / Suffocation / See you later.
Mar 81. (lp/c) (POLS/+C 1026) <PD1 6335> **CHARIOTS OF FIRE (Original Motion Picture Soundtrack)** [5] [1] Oct81
– Titles / Five circles / Abraham's theme / Eric's theme / 100 metres / Jerusalem / Chariots of Fire. *(re-iss. Apr84; POLD 5160; hit UK No.39) (cd-iss. 1983; 8000202-2)*

Apr 81. (7") (POSP 246) <2189> **CHARIOTS OF FIRE – TITLES. / ERIC'S THEME** [12] [1] Dec81
(re-prom.UK Feb82 hit UK No.41 & re-iss. Aug84; same)

JON & VANGELIS

May 81. (7") (POSP 258) <2181> **THE FRIENDS OF MR. CAIRO. / BESIDE**
Jul 81. (lp/c) (POLD/+C 5039) <PD1 6326> **THE FRIENDS OF MR. CAIRO** [6] [64]
– The friends of Mr. Cairo / Back to school boogie / Outside of this (inside of that) / State of independence / Beside / The Mayflower. *(cd-iss. May83; 800021-2) (re-iss. Oct89 lp/c; POLD/+C 5053)*

Jul 81. (7") (POSP 323) **STATE OF INDEPENDENCE. / BESIDE**
Nov 81. (7") (JV 1) **I'LL FIND MY WAY HOME. / BACK TO SCHOOL BOOGIE** [6] [-]
Apr 82. (7") <2205> **I'LL FIND MY WAY HOME. / I HEAR YOU NOW** [-] [51]

—— In 1982, he wrote unissued vinyl score for film 'Blade Runner'.
May 83. (7") (JV 3) **AND WHEN THE NIGHT COMES. / SONG IS** [-]
May 83. (lp/c)(cd) (POLH/+C 4)(813174-2) <813174> **PRIVATE COLLECTION** [22]
– He is sailing / And when the night comes / Deborah / The king is coming / Horizon.
Jul 83. (7") (JV 4) **HE IS SAILING. / POLANAISE** [61]
(12"+=) (JVX 4) – Song is.

—— Above was last collaboration between the duo, until 1991.
Aug 84. (7"/12") (JV/+X 5) **STATE OF INDEPENDENCE. / THE FRIENDS OF MR. CAIRO** [67]
Aug 84. (lp/c/cd) (POLH/+C 6)(821929-2) **THE BEST OF JON & VANGELIS (compilation)** [42]
– Italian song / I'll find my way home / State of independence / One more time / Play within a play / The friends of Mr. Cairo / Outside of this (inside of that) / He is sailing / I hear you now.

VANGELIS

continued solo. BOUNTY Soundtrack was also unissued. He continued to write unissued soundtracks throughout the 80's as well as below.
Oct 84. (lp/c)(cd) (POLH/+C 11)(823396-2) **SOIL FESTIVITIES** [55]
– Movements 1-5. *(re-iss. Jun87 lp/c; SPE LP/MC 106)*

Mar 85. (lp/c)(cd) (POLH/+C 19)(825245-2) **MASK (Soundtrack)** [69]
– Movements 1-6.

		Deutsche	not iss.

Mar 85. (lp/c/cd) (415196-1/-4/-2) **INVISIBLE CONNECTIONS** [-] [-]
– Invisible connections / Atom blaster / Thermo vision.

1986. (lp/c/cd) **RHAPSODIES**
– Ti ipermacho stratigo / O! gliki mou ear / Ton nimfona sou vlepo / Rapsodia / Tin oreotita tis partenias sou / Christos anesti / Asma asmaton.

		Arista	Arista

Sep 88. (lp/c/cd) (209/409/259 149) **DIRECT**
– The motion of stars / The will of the wind / Metallic rain / Elsewhere / Glorianna (hymn a la femme) / Rotations logic / The oracle of Apollo / Ave / First approach / Dial out / Intergallactic radio station / Message.

Sep 88. (c-s) (111 767) **WILL OF THE WIND / INTERGALACTIC RADIO STATION**
(12"+=/cd-s+=) (611/661 767) – Metallic rain.

JON & VANGELIS

Aug 91. (7") **WISDOM CHAIN. / PAGE OF LIFE**
(cd-s+=) – ('A'full version) / Sing with your eyes.
Sep 91. (cd/c/lp) (261/411/211 373) **PAGE OF LIFE**
– Wisdom chain / Page of life / Money / Garden of senses / Is it love / Anyone can light a candle / Journey to Ixtlan / Shine for me / Genevieve.

VANGELIS

		East West	Atlantic

Nov 90. (cd)(lp/c) (903173026-2)(WX 398/+C) **THE CITY**
– Dawn / Morning papers / Nerve centre / Side streets / Good to see you / Twilight / Red lights / Procession. *(re-iss. cd Nov93 & Feb95; same)*

Oct 92. (cd)(c) (4509 91014-2)(WX 497C) **1492: THE CONQUEST OF PARADISE (Soundtrack)** [33]
– Opening theme / 1492: The conquest of Paradise / Monastery of la Rabida / City of Isabel / Light and shadow / Deliverance / West across the ocean sea / Eternity / Hispanola / Moxica and the horse / 28th parallel / Pinta, Nina, Santa Maria (into eternity) *(re-iss. cd Jun94).*

Oct 92. (7"/c-s) (YZ 704C) **CONQUEST OF PARADISE. / MOXICA AND THE HORSE** [60]
(cd-s+=) (YZ 704CD) – Line open / Landscape. *(re-iss. May95; same)*

Mar 93. (c-s/cd-s) (YZ 736 C/CD) **28th PARALLEL / WEST ACROSS THE OCEAN SEA**

Oct 95. (c-s) (EW 007C) **VOICES / VOICES II (ECHOES)**
(cd-s+=) (EW 007CD) – Voices III.
Feb 96. (cd)(c) (0630 12786-2/-4) <82853> **VOICES** [58]
– Voices / Echoes / Come to me / P.S. / Ask the mountains / Prelude / Losing sleep (still, my heart) / Messages / Dream in an open place.
above featured PAUL YOUNG on vocals

Mar 96. (c-s; as VANGELIS & STINA NORDENSTAM) (EW 031C) **ASK THE MOUNTAINS / SLOW PIECE**
(cd-s+=) (EW 031CD) – ('A'-Album version).

Oct 96. (cd/c) (0630 16761-2/-4) **OCEANIC**
– Bon voyage / Sirens' whispering / Dreams of surf / Spanish harbour / Islands of the Orient / Fields of coral / Aquatic dance / Memories of blue / Song of the seas.
below featured MONSERRAT CABELLE (soprano); – about 16th century master painter

Dec 98. (cd) **EL GRECO**
– Movements:- I / II / III / IV / V / VI / VII / VIII / IX / X (epilogue).

– compilations, others, etc. –

—— on 'R.C.A.' unless mentioned otherwise
1978. (lp/c) (PL2 5174) **THE BEST OF VANGELIS**
(re-iss. Sep81 lp/c; RCA LP/K 3028) (cd-iss. May93; 74321 13885-2)
May 78. (cd) *Affinity; (AFF 11)* **HYPOTHESIS** (rec.1971) [-]
Jul 81. (7") *B.B.C.; (BBC 1)* **HEAVEN AND HELL, THIRD MOVEMENT (THEME FROM THE BBC-TV SERIES – THE COSMOS). / ALPHA** [48] [-]
Aug 81. (lp) *Polydor; (AFL1 4003)* **OPERA SAUVAGE – COSMOS**
(re-iss. Nov84 lp/c; SPE LP/MC 81) (cd-iss. 1987; 829663-2) <US-iss.Dec86; 829663> hit UK No.42>
Aug 82. (d-c; JON & VANGELIS) *Polydor; (3574 139)* **SHORT STORIES / THE FRIENDS OF MR. CAIRO** [-]
Nov 82. (d-lp/d-c) (RCA LP/K 1002-3) <4397> **TO THE UNKNOWN MAN VOLS.1 & 2**
1982. (7") <13402> **TO THE UNKNOWN MAN. / (part 2)** [-]
Nov 82. (t-lp) *Polydor; (BOX 1)* **CHARIOTS OF FIRE / CHINA / OPERA SAUVAGE**
1983. (lp) (PL 30036) **THE SAVAGE BEAST**
Jun 84. (c) (NK 70345) **MAGIC MOMENTS**
Jul 84. (lp) (NL 70078) **GREATEST HITS**
1984. (7") *B.B.C.; (RESL 144)* **FRAME OF THE DAY: BBC SNOOKER THEMES (TO THE UNKNOWN MAN) (part 1). / (part 2)**
Jun 88. (7"; JON & VANGELIS) *Old Gold; (OG 9785)* **I HEAR YOU NOW. / I'LL FIND MY WAY HOME**
Nov 88. (lp/c/cd) *Polydor; (815 732-1/-4/-2)* **ANTARCTICA (Original Soundtrack)** [-]
Jul 89. (lp/c)(cd) *Polydor; (LP/MC VGTV 1)(839518-2)* **THEMES** [-]
– (excerpts from films, including some from previously unissued)
Oct 89. (cd-box/c-box) (VGPK 1) **SPIRAL / ALBEDO 0• 39 / HEAVEN AND HELL** [-]
Apr 93. (cd) *C.A.M.;* **ENTENDS-TU LES CHEINS** [-]
Jun 94. (cd/c) *East West; (4509 96574-2/-4)* **BLADE RUNNER (Soundtrack)** [20]
Aug 94. (cd/c) (74321 22415-2/-4) **THE COLLECTION** [-]
Sep 94. (cd/c; JON & VANGELIS) *Spectrum; (550196-2/-4)* **CHRONICLES** [-]
Apr 95. (cd) (74321 25954-2) **ALBEDO 0.39 / HEAVEN AND HELL** [-]

Apr 96. (cd/c) *Polydor; (531154-2/-4)* **PORTRAIT (SO LONG AGO, SO CLEAR)**　　`14`　`☐`
– To the unknown man / Italian song / Pulsar / La petite fille de la mer / Alpha / I hear you now / I'll find my way home / State of indepenence / Himalaya / Conquest of Paradise / Hymn / Antartica / Sauvage et beau / Chariots of fire / So long ago, so clear.
Jun 96. (cd) *Camden; (74321 39337-2)* **GIFT . . . THE BEST OF VANGELIS**　　`☐`　`-`
Aug 96. (cd/c) *Autograph; (MAC CD/MC 246)* **CHARIOTS OF FIRE (THE MUSIC OF VANGELIS)**　　`☐`　`-`

VAN HALEN

Formed: Pasadena, California, USA . . . 1975 by brothers ALEX and EDDIE VAN HALEN. Recruiting blonde-maned high priest of metal cool, DAVE LEE ROTH, and bass player MICHAEL ANTHONY, the quartet initially traded under the MAMMOTH moniker. As VAN HALEN, the group built up a solid reputation as a covers outfit on L.A.'s Sunset Strip, gradually introducing original material into their set. Eventually signed to 'Warners' after being spotted by in-house producer, Ted Templeman, the group released their eponymous debut album in 1977. Coming at a time when hard rock was in seemingly terminal stagnation with punk snapping at its heels, 'VAN HALEN' redefined the boundaries of the genre; from the back cover shot of a shirtless ROTH (chest-wig de rigeur!) sporting leather flares to the opening three chord mash-up of The KINKS' 'YOU REALLY GOT ME', VAN HALEN dripped effortless cool, the golden elixir of sun-bleached California coursing through their collective veins. Then there was 'AIN'T TALKIN' 'BOUT LOVE', EDDIE casually reeling off the razor-edged, caterwauling riff (recently resurrected by dance bods, APOLLO FOUR FORTY) while ROTH drawled his most lascivious, sneering drawl. And basically, this was what set VAN HALEN apart from the spandex pack; ROTH actually sang rather than screeching like an asphyxiated budgie, while in EDDIE VAN HALEN, the group boasted one of the most inventive and single-mindedly talented guitarists in the history of metal. O.K., 'ERUPTION' may be responsible for countless fret-wank crimes but it's still impossible not to be impressed by the man's vision, his innovations (flying-fingered hammer-ons, leaving a still smoking cigarette nudged in at the top of the fretboard etc.) becoming base material for any aspiring 80's guitar hero. Essentially, VAN HALEN were glamourous as opposed to glam, and for a few heady years they made heavy metal desirable. Though the debut album barely nudged into the US Top 20, it would go on to sell in excess of five million copies and remains one of THE classic hard-rock releases. A follow-up, 'VAN HALEN II' (1979) didn't pack quite the same punch, although it made the US Top 10 and spawned the group's first hit single, the dreamy 'DANCE THE NIGHT AWAY'. 'WOMEN AND CHILDREN FIRST' (1980) and 'FAIR WARNING' (1981) consolidated the band's standing, both commercially and critically although it wasn't until 'DIVER DOWN' (1982) that VAN HALEN began to cast their net wider. A cover of Roy Orbison's 'PRETTY WOMAN' gave them another US Top 20 hit, the album going US Top 5 as a result. The following year, EDDIE famously flashed his fretboard skills on MICHAEL JACKSON's 'Beat It', gaining valuable crossover exposure although by this point, VAN HALEN were already one of the biggest hard rock acts in the world. This was proved with the massive success of the '1984' (released in 1984, funnily enough!) opus and attendant synth-heavy No.1 single, 'JUMP'. For many people, especially in Britain, this was the first time they'd witnessed "Diamond" DAVE in action, the loose-limbed singer, as ever, performing death-defying feats of stage acrobatics in the accompanying video. While the album saw VAN HALEN successfully tackling obligatory 80's experimentation (which did for many of their peers), the likes of 'HOT FOR TEACHER' carried on the grand tradition of tongue-in-cheek lewdness and six-string trickery. Incredibly, at the peak of their success, ROTH buggered off for a solo career, taking his not inconsiderable wit, charisma and sly humour with him. Though VAN HALEN chose to rumble on, it was a rather different beast which reared its head in early '86 with the single, 'WHY CAN'T THIS BE LOVE'. With ex-MONTROSE man, SAMMY HAGAR on vocals, VAN HALEN had created their most consistently accessible and musically ambitious set to date in '5150' (1986), although the absence of ROTH's cheeky innuendo was glaringly obvious. If not gone completely, the group chemistry had been irrevocably altered, in effect, making VAN HALEN just another hard rock band, albeit highly professional and massively successful. '5150' gave the revamped group their first US No.1 album, the record not doing too badly in the UK either. 'OU812' (1988) was another multi-million selling No.1, VAN HALEN now virtually a US institution guaranteed multi-platinum sales with every successive release. 'FOR UNLAWFUL CARNAL KNOWLEDGE' (1991), or 'F.U.C.K.' in its abbreviated form (very clever, lads) saw the group adopt a heavier approach although this didn't prevent it from selling in bucketloads, VAN HALEN holding their own in the age of grunge when many of their contemporaries suddenly seemed embarassingly outdated. A long overdue live album, 'RIGHT HERE, RIGHT NOW', finally appeared in 1993, while a rare European tour no doubt helped boost UK sales of 'BALANCE' (1995), yet another US No.1 album and their first Top 10 placing in Britain. DAVE LEE ROTH returned during the same year, however after a compilation set in which he appeared on a few new songs, the man departed once more, this time to be replaced by ex-EXTREME frontman, GARY CHERRONE.
• **Covered:** FAIR WARNING (Aerosmith) / A POLITICAL BLUES (Little Feat) / WON'T GET FOOLED AGAIN (Who). • **Trivia:** In April '81, EDDIE married actress Valerie Bertinelli.

Album rating: VAN HALEN (*8) / VAN HALEN II (*7) / WOMEN AND CHILDREN FIRST (*7) / FAIR WARNING (*6) / DIVER DOWN (*6) / 1984 (*7) / 5150 (*5) / OU812 (*6) / FOR UNLAWFUL CARNAL KNOWLEDGE (*6) / LIVE: RIGHT HERE, RIGHT NOW (*6) / BALANCE (*5) / THE BEST OF: VOLUME ONE compilation (*8) / VAN HALEN III (*5)

EDDIE VAN HALEN (b.26 Jan'57, Nijmegen, Netherlands) – guitar / **DAVID LEE ROTH** (b.10 Oct'55, Bloomington, Indiana) – vocals / **MICHAEL ANTHONY** (b.20 Jun'55, Chicago, Illinois) – bass / **ALEX VAN HALEN** (b. 8 May'55, Nijmegen) – drums

		Warners	Warners
Feb 78. (7") *(K 17107) <8515>* **YOU REALLY GOT ME. / ATOMIC PUNK**		`☐`	`36` Jan78
Apr 78. (lp/c) *(K/K4 56470) <3075>* **VAN HALEN**	`34`	`19` Feb78

– Runnin' with the Devil / Eruption / You really got me / Ain't talkin' 'bout love / I'm the one / Jamie's cryin' / Atomic punk / Feel your love tonight / Little dreamer / Ice cream man / On fire. *(cd-iss. Jul86; K2 56470) (cd re-iss. Feb95; K2 56470)*

Apr 78. (7") *(K 17162) <8556>* **RUNNIN' WITH THE DEVIL. / ERUPTION**	`☐`	`84`
Jul 78. (7") *<8631>* **JAMIE'S CRYIN'. / I'M THE SAME**	`-`	
Sep 78. (7") *<8707>* **AIN'T TALKIN' 'BOUT LOVE. / FEEL YOUR LOVE TONIGHT**	`-`	
Apr 79. (lp/c) *(K/K4 56616) <3312>* **VAN HALEN II**	`23`	`6`

– You're no good / Dance the night away / Somebody get me a doctor / Bottoms up! / Outta love again / Light up the sky / Spanish fly / D.O.A. / Women in love / Beautiful girls. *(cd-iss. Mar87; K2 56616)*

May 79. (7"/7"pic-d) *(K 17371/+P) <8823>* **DANCE THE NIGHT AWAY. / OUTTA LOVE AGAIN**	`15`	Apr79
Sep 79. (7") *<49035>* **BEAUTIFUL GIRLS. / D. O. A.**	`-`	`84`
Apr 80. (lp/c) *(K/K4 56793) <3415>* **WOMEN AND CHILDREN FIRST**	`15`	`6`

– And the cradle will rock . . . / Everybody wants some / Fools / Romeo delight / Tora! Tora! / Loss of control / Take your whiskey home / Could this be magic? / In a simple rhyme. *(cd-iss. Jun89; K 923415-2)*

Apr 80. (7") *<49501>* **AND THE CRADLE WILL ROCK. / COULD THIS BE MAGIC**	`-`	`55`
Aug 80. (7") *(K 17645)* **AND THE CRADLE WILL ROCK. / EVERYBODY WANTS SOME!!**	`☐`	`☐`
May 81. (7") *<49751>* **SO THIS IS LOVE. / HEAR ABOUT IT LATER**	`-`	`☐`
May 81. (lp/c) *(K/K4 56899) <3540>* **FAIR WARNING**	`49`	`6`

– Mean street / Dirty movies / Sinner's swing / Hear about it later / Unchained / Push comes to shove / So this is love? / Sunday afternoon in the dark / One foot out of the door. *(cd-iss. Jun89; K 923540-2)*

Feb 82. (7") *(K 17909) <50003>* **(OH) PRETTY WOMAN. / HAPPY TRAILS**	`☐`	`12` Jan82
May 82. (7") *<29986>* **DANCING IN THE STREET. / THE BULL BUG**	`-`	`38`
May 82. (lp/c) *(K/K4 57003) <3677>* **DIVER DOWN**	`36`	`3`

– Where have all the good times gone / Hang 'em high / Cathedral / Secrets / Intruder / (Oh) Pretty woman / Dancing in the street / Little guitars (intro) / Little guitars / Big bad Bill (is sweet William now) / The bull bug / Happy trails. *(cd-iss. Jan84; K2 57003)*

May 82. (7") *(K 17957)* **DANCING IN THE STREET. / BIG BAD BILL (IS SWEET WILLIAM NOW)**	`☐`	`-`
Aug 82. (7") *<29929>* **BIG BAD BILL (IS SWEET WILLIAM NOW). / SECRETS**	`-`	`-`
Jan 84. (lp/c/cd) *(923985-1/-4/-2) <23985>* **1984 (MCMLXXXIV)**	`15`	`2`

– 1984 / Jump / Panama / Top Jimmy / Drop dead legs / Hot for teacher / I'll wait / Girl gone bad / House of pain. *(re-iss. cd/c Feb95; same)*

Jan 84. (7") *<29384>* **JUMP. / HOUSE OF PAIN**	`-`	`1`
Jan 84. (7") *(W 9384)* **JUMP. / RUNNIN' WITH THE DEVIL**	`7`	`☐`

(12"+=) *(W 9384T)* – House of pain.

Apr 84. (7") *<29307>* **I'LL WAIT. / GIRL GONE BAD**	`-`	`13`
Apr 84. (7") *(W 9273) <29250>* **PANAMA. / GIRL GONE BAD**	`61`	`13` Jun84

(12"+=) *(W 9273T)* – Dance the night away.

Jun 84. (7") *(W 9213)* **I'LL WAIT. / DROP DEAD LEGS**	`☐`	`-`

(12"+=) *(W 9213T)* – And the cradle will rock / (Oh) Pretty woman.

Jun 85. (7") *(W 9199) <29199>* **HOT FOR TEACHER. / LITTLE PREACHER**	`☐`	`56` Oct84

(12"+=) *(W 9199T)* – Hear about it later.

──── (Jun'85) Trimmed to a trio, when DAVID LEE ROTH went solo full-time. Early '86 added **SAMMY HAGAR** (b.13 Oct'47, Monterey, Calif.) – vocals (ex-MONTROSE, ex-Solo Artist)

Mar 86. (7"/7"sha-pic-d/12") *(W 8740/+P/T) <28740>* **WHY CAN'T THIS BE LOVE. / GET UP**	`8`	`3`
Apr 86. (lp/c)(cd) *(W 5150/+C)(925394-2) <25394>* **5150**	`16`	`1`

– Good enough / Why can't this be love / Get up / Dreams / Summer nights / Best of both worlds / Love walks in / "5150" / Inside. *(re-iss. cd/c Feb95; same)*

Jun 86. (7"/7"sha-pic-d/12") *(W 8642/+P/T) <28702>* **DREAMS. / INSIDE**	`62`	`22` May86
Aug 86. (7") *<28626>* **LOVE WALKS IN. / SUMMER NIGHTS**	`-`	`22`
Oct 86. (7") *<28505>* **BEST OF BOTH WORLDS. / ('A'live)**	`-`	`☐`
May 88. (7"/12") *(W 7891/+T) <27891>* **BLACK AND BLUE. / APOLITICAL BLUES**	`☐`	`34`
Jun 88. (lp/c)(cd) *(WX 177/+C)(K 925732-2) <25732>* **OU812**	`16`	`1`

– Mine all mine / When it's love / A.F.U. (naturally wired) / Cabo wabo / Source of infection / Feels so good / Finish what ya started / Black and blue / Sucker in a 3-piece. *(cd+=)* – Apolitical blues.

Jul 88. (7") *<27827>* **WHEN IT'S LOVE. / CABO WABO**	`-`	`5`
Jul 88. (7") *(W 7816)* **WHEN IT'S LOVE. / APOLITICAL BLUES**	`28`	`-`

(12"+=/12"pic-d+=/cd-s+=) *(W 7816 T/TP/CD)* – Why can't this be love.

Sep 88. (7") *<27746>* **FINISH WHAT YA STARTED. / SUCKER IN A 3-PIECE**	`-`	`☐`
Feb 89. (7") *(W 7565) <27565>* **FEELS SO GOOD. / SUCKER IN A 3 PIECE**	`☐`	`☐`

(12"+=/cd-s+=) *(W 7565 T/CD)* – Best of both worlds (live).

Jun 91. (7"/c-s) *(W 0045/+C)* **POUNDCAKE. / PLEASURE DOME**	`☐`	`☐`

(12"+=/cd-s+=) *(W 0045 T/CD)* – (interview).

Jul 91. (cd)(lp/c) *(7599 26594-2)(WX 420/+C) <26594>* **FOR UNLAWFUL CARNAL KNOWLEDGE**
– Poundcake / Judgement day / Spanked / Runaround / P[...] Man on a mission / The dream is over / Right now / 316 [...]

Sep 91. (7") <19151> **TOP OF THE WORLD. / POUNDCAKE** | – | 27 |

Oct 91. (7"/c-s) (W 0066/+C) **TOP OF THE WORLD. / IN 'N' OUT** | 63 | – |
(cd-s+=) (W 0066CD) – Why can't this be love (extended) / When it's love / Dreams.

Feb 92. (c-s,cd-s) <19059> **RIGHT NOW / MAN ON A MISSION** | – | 55 |

Feb 93. (d-cd/d-c) <(9362 45198-2/-4)> **LIVE: RIGHT HERE, RIGHT NOW** (live) | 24 | 5 |
– Poundcake / Judgement day / When it's love / Spanked / Ain't talkin' 'bout love / In'n'out / Dreams / Man on a mission / Ultra bass / Pressure dome – Drum solo / Panama / Love walks in / Runaround / Right now / One way to rock / Why can't this be love / Give to love / Finished what ya started / Best of both worlds / 316 / You really got me – Cabo wabo / Won't get fooled again / Jump / Top of the world.

Mar 93. (7"/c-s/cd-s) (W 0155/+C/CD) **JUMP (live). / LOVE WALKS IN** (live) | 26 | – |
(cd-s+=) (W 0155CDX) – Eagles fly (live) / Mine, all mine (live).

Jan 95. (7"purple/c-s) (W 0280 X/C) **DON'T TELL ME (WHAT LOVE CAN DO). / BALUCHITHERIUM** | 27 | – |
(cd-s+=) (W 0280CD) – Why can't this be love (live)/ Poundcake (live)/ Panama (live).
(cd-s) (W 0280CDX) – ('A'side)/ Judgement day (live)/ Dreams (live)/ Top of the world (live).

Jan 95. (cd/c/lp) <(9362 45760-2/-4/-1)> **BALANCE** | 8 | 1 |
– The seventh seal / Can't stop lovin' you / Don't tell me (what love can do) / Amsterdam / Big fat money / Strung out / Not enough / Aftershock / Doin' time / Baluchitherium / Take me back (deja vu) / Feelin'.

Mar 95. (7"/c-s) (W 0288/+C) <17909> **CAN'T STOP LOVIN' YOU. / CROSSING OVER** | 33 | 30 |
(cd-s+=) (W 0288CD) – Man on a mission / Right now.
(cd-s) (W 0288CDX) – ('A'side) / Best of both worlds (live) / One way to rock (live) / When it's love (live).

Jun 95. (c-s) (W 0302C) **AMSTERDAM / RUNAROUND (live)** | – | – |
(cd-s) (W 0302CDX) – ('A'side) / Finish what ya started (live).

Aug 95. (c-s,cd-s) <17810> **NOT ENOUGH / AMSTERDAM** | – | 97 |

———— **DAVID LEE ROTH** returned on 2 tracks below ('Me Wise Magic' & 'Can't Get This Stuff No More') to repl. **HAGAR**.

Oct 96. (cd/c) <(9362 46474-2/-4)> **THE BEST OF: VOLUME ONE** (compilation) | 45 | 1 |

———— ROTH's ego led to the old reunion failing. **GARY CHERONE** (ex-EXTREME) became frontman and co-writer.

Mar 98. (cd/c) <(9362 46662-2/-4)> **VAN HALEN III** | 43 | 4 |
– Neworld / Without you / One I want / From afar / Dirty water dog / Once / Fire in the hole / Josephina / Year to the day / Primary / Ballot or the bullet / How many say I.

– others, etc. –

Jun 80. (7") Atlantic; (HM 10) **RUNNIN' WITH THE DEVIL. / D.O.A.** | 52 | – |

VANILLA FUDGE

Formed: New York City, New York, USA . . . 1965 as The PIGEONS. They became VANILLA FUDGE in late '66, and after their debut at The Village Theater (Fillmore East), they were signed up by 'Atlantic'. Their po-faced, psychedelic-symphonic rock often degenerated into dirty, leaden dirges and VANILLA SLUDGE would've been a more accurate name for this proto-metallic band. Nevertheless, in 1967 they were unique, if nothing else than for their unqualified heaviness and they enjoyed chart success with their first release, a characteristically over the top and drawn out rendition of The SUPREMES' 'YOU KEEP ME HANGIN' ON'. The self-titled debut album followed later that summer and contained similarly overblown and amusing covers, The BEATLES' 'ELEANOR RIGBY' and 'TICKET TO RIDE' among them. Follow-up albums were inconsistent, the band's original material falling woefully short of matching the strength of the covers they'd made their name with and, after the band split in mid '69 , TIM BOGERT and CARMINE APPICE formed the short lived CACTUS with RUSTY DAY and JIM McCARTY. Purveying straight-down-the-line hard rock, the band cut three albums, 'CACTUS' (1970), 'ONE WAY . . .OR ANOTHER' (1971) and 'RESTRICTIONS' (1972) before BOGERT and APPICE joined JEFF BECK in the supergroup BECK, BOGERT & APPICE. • **Songwriters:** STEIN or group compositions, with mainly other covers :- BANG BANG (Cher) / SEASON OF THE WITCH (Donovan) / I CAN'T MAKE IT ALONE (Goffin-King) / THE WINDMILLS OF YOUR MIND (Legrand-Bergyan). CACTUS also covered several standards. • **Trivia:** In the summer of '69, they played the Seattle Pop Festival at Woodenville, Washington.

Album rating: VANILLA FUDGE (*7) / THE BEAT GOES ON (*5) / RENAISSANCE (*5) / NEAR THE BEGINNING (*5) / ROCK & ROLL (*4) / Cactus: CACTUS (*5) / ONE WAY . . . OR ANOTHER (*4) / RESTRICTIONS (*3) / 'OT 'N' SWEAPY (*3) / Vanilla Fudge: MYSTERY (*3) / THE BEST OF (PSYCHEDELIC SUNDAE) compilation (*7)

MARK STEIN (b.11 Mar'47, Bayonne, New Jersey) – vocals, organ / **VINCE MARTELL** (b.11 Nov'45, Bronx, NY) – guitar, vocals / **TIM BOGERT** (b.27 Aug'44) – bass, vocals / **CARMINE APPICE** (b.15 Dec'46, Staten Island, NY) – drums, vocals

	Atlantic	Atco
Jun 67. (7") <6590> **YOU KEEP ME HANGIN' ON. / COME BY DAY, COME BY NIGHT**	–	67
<US re-prom.Jul68, hit No.6>		
67. (7") (584 123) <6590> **YOU KEEP ME HANGIN' ON. / TAKE ME FOR A LITTLE WHILE**	18	–
7. (lp; mono/stereo) (587/588 086) <33224> **VANILLA FUDGE**	31	6

– Ticket to ride / People get ready / She's not there / Bang bang / Illusions of my childhood – part one / You keep me hanging on / Illusions of my childhood – part two / Take me for a little while / Illusions of my childhood – part three / Eleanor Rigby. (cd-iss. May93; 7567 90390-2)

| ⁷") (584 139) **ILLUSIONS OF MY CHILDHOOD. / ELEANOR ⁻BY** | – | – |

Feb 68. (lp; mono/stereo) (587/588 100) <33237> **THE BEAT GOES ON** | – | 17 |
– Sketch / Variation on a theme from Mozart's Divertimento No.13 in F / Old black Joe / Don't fence me in / 12th Street rag / In the mood / Hound dog / I want to hold your hand – I feel fine – Day tripper – She loves you / The beat goes on / Beethoven's fur Elise and theme from Moonlight Sonata / The beat goes on / Voices in time: – Neville Chamberlain – Winston Churchill – F.D. Roosevelt – Harry S. Truman – John F.Kennedy / Merchant / The game is over / The beat goes on. (cd-iss. Jun92 & Jul93 on 'Repertoire'+=; RR 4261)

Apr 68. (7") (584 179) <6554> **WHERE IS MY MIND?. / THE LOOK OF LOVE** | 73 Jan68 |

Jun 68. (lp; mono/stereo) (587/588 110) <33244> **RENAISSANCE** | 20 |
– The sky cried – When I was a boy / Thoughts / Paradise / That's what makes a man / The spell that comes after / Faceless people / Season of the witch. (cd-iss. Jul93 on 'Repertoire'+=; REP 4126) – You keep me hangin' on (7" version) / Come by day, come by night / People.

Sep 68. (7") <6616> **TAKE ME FOR A LITTLE WHILE. / THOUGHTS** | – | 38 |
Nov 68. (7") <6632> **SEASON OF THE WITCH. / (part 2)** | – | 65 |
| | Atco | Atco |

Feb 69. (lp) (228 020) <33278> **NEAR THE BEGINNING** (half studio / half live) | | 16 |
– Shotgun / Some velvet morning / Where is happiness / Break song. (cd-iss. Jul93 on 'Repertoire' +=) – Look of love.

Mar 69. (7") (584 257) <6655> **SHOTGUN. / GOOD GOOD LOVIN'** | | 68 |
Jun 69. (7") <6679> **SOME VELVET MORNING. / PEOPLE** | – | – |
Jul 69. (7") (584 276) **SOME VELVET MORNING. / THOUGHTS** | – | – |
Oct 69. (lp) (228 029) <33303> **ROCK & ROLL** | | 34 |
– Need love / Lord in the country / I can't make it alone / Street walking woman / Church bells of St. Martin's / The windmills of your mind / If you gotta make a fool of somebody. (cd-iss. Jul93 on 'Repertoire'+=; REP 4168) – Good good lovin' / Shotgun / Where is my mind / Need love (7" version).

Nov 69. (7") <6703> **I CAN'T MAKE IT ALONE. / NEED LOVE** | – | – |
Jan 70. (7") <6728> **LORD IN THE COUNTRY. / THE WINDMILLS OF YOUR MIND** | – | – |

———— Had already folded mid '69. STEIN formed BOOMERANG and MARTELL retired.

CACTUS

were formed Feb'70 by **BOGERT & APPICE** with **RUSTY DAY** – vocals, mouth harp (ex-AMBOY DUKES / TED NUGENT) / **JIM McCARTY** – guitar (not of YARDBIRDS)

	Atlantic	Atco
Jul 70. (lp) (2400 020) <SD 33340> **CACTUS**		54

– Parchman farm / My lady from south of Detroit / Bro. Bill / You can't judge a book by the cover / Let me swim / No need to worry / Oleo / Feel so good. (cd-iss. Jan96; 7567 80290-2)

Oct 70. (7") <6792> **YOU CAN'T JUDGE A BOOK BY THE COVER. / BRO BILL** | – | – |
Mar 71. (7") <6811> **LONG TALL SALLY. / ROCK'N'ROLL CHILDREN** | – | – |
Jul 71. (lp) (2400 114) <SD 33356> **ONE WAY . . . OR ANOTHER** | | 88 Mar71 |
– Long tall Sally / Rock out whatever you feel like / Rock'n'roll children / Big mam boogie / Feel so bad / Hometown bust / One way . . .or another.
Sep 71. (7") <6842> **TOKEN CHOKIN'. / ALASKA** | – | – |

———— (May71) added **DUANE HITCHINGS** – piano

Jan 72. (7") <6872> **EVIL. / SWEET SIXTEEN** | – | – |
Apr 72. (lp) (K 40307) <SD 33377> **RESTRICTIONS** | | Nov71 |
– Restrictions / Token chokin' / Guiltness glider / Evil / Alaska / Sweet sixteen / Bag drag / Mean man in Cleveland. (cd-iss. Jul93 on 'Repertoire')

———— **PETE FRENCH** – vocals (ex-ATOMIC ROOSTER) McCARTY and DAY

Oct 72. (lp) (K 50013) <SD 7011> **'OT & SWEATY** (live/studio) | – | – |
– Swim / Bad mother boogie / Our lil' rock and roll thing / Bad stuff / Bring me down / Bedroom Mazurka / Telling you / Underneath / The arches.
Oct 72. (7") <6901> **BAD MOTHER BOOGIE. / BRINGING ME DOWN** | – | – |

———— Disbanded and DUANE retained some of name NEW CACTUS BAND issuing an album, 'SON OF CACTUS' and single 'BILLIE GYPSY WOMAN' in 1973. TIM and CARMINE teamed up with JEFF BECK ⇒ in supergroup BECK, BOGERT & APPICE. CARMINE joined MIKE BLOOMFIELD's band KGB in the mid-70's. He later joined ROD STEWART and in the 80's with RICK DERRINGER formed DNA.

VANILLA FUDGE

re-formed originals 1982 and again in 1984.

	Atco	Atco
Jul 84. (lp/c) (90149-1/-4) **MYSTERY**		

– Golden age dreams / Jealousy / Mystery / Under suspicion / It gets stronger / Walk on by / My world is empty / Don't stop now / Hot blood / The stranger.

Jul 84. (7") <99729> **MYSTERY. / THE STRANGER** | – | – |

———— Folded again, although they briefly got together for Atlantic 40 year bash mid-'88.

– compilations, others, etc. –

1970. (lp; as PIGEONS) Wand; <687> **WHILE THE WORLD WAS EATING**	–	–
1974. (lp) Midi; (MID 0033) **STAR COLLECTION**	–	–
1982. (lp/c) Atco; <90006-2> **GREATEST HITS**	–	–
1991. (cd) Rhino; <R2 70798> **VANILLA FUDGE LIVE** (live)	–	–
Mar 93. (cd) Atlantic; (8122 71154-2) **THE BEST OF VANILLA FUDGE (PSYCHEDELIC SUNDAE)**	–	–

– You keep me hangin' on / Where is my mind? / The look of love / Ticket to ride / Come by day, come by night / Take me for a little while / That's what makes a man / Season of the witch / Shotgun / Thoughts / Faceless people / Good good lovin' / Some velvet morning / I can't make it alone / Lord in the country / Need love / Street walking woman / All in your mind.

Aug 95. (cd) Atlantic; (7567 90006-2) **THE BEST OF VANILLA FUDGE**	–	–
Jul 94. (cd/c) Success; **YOU KEEP ME HANGIN' ON**	–	–
Jul 96. (cd; CACTUS) Atlantic; (8122 72411-2) **CACTOLOGY**	–	–

Townes VAN ZANDT

Born: JOHN TOWNES VAN ZANDT, 7 Mar'44, Fort Worth, Texas, USA. Born into a Texas oil dynasty, VAN ZANDT's upbringing was characterised by constant relocation as his family moved around from state to state. As a teenager he also spent an unhappy couple of years in military school where he was allegedly diagnosed as a manic depressive, later dropping out of college courses in both Colorado and Houston in order to devote himself to writing and performing. Inspired initially by HANK WILLIAMS and later ELVIS PRESLEY, VAN ZANDT had begun learning the guitar before he'd even reached his teens. By the time he'd started making a name for himself on the mid 60's Houston folk circuit, BOB DYLAN was a glaring influence as – judging by the wry 'TALKIN' KARATE BLUES' – was DYLAN's own mentor, WOODY GUTHRIE. The latter track appeared on TOWNES' debut album, 'FOR THE SAKE OF THE SONG' (1968), a promising set produced by semi-legendary Nashville veteran, Jack Clement. Set up with the help of songwriter, MICKIE NEWBURY (whom VAN ZANDT had befriended on the Houston scene along with up and coming singer/songwriters GUY CLARK and JERRY JEFF WALKER), the sessions resulted in such enduring classics as 'TECUMSEH VALLEY' and the Spanish-tinged title track. While not blessed with the strongest of voices, VAN ZANDT's vocals resonated with the painful honesty of the archetypal tortured artist. The chilling 'WAITIN' AROUND TO DIE' could possibly be construed as morbidly prophetic with regards to VAN ZANDT's premature demise and yet while his lyrics told of a constant struggle with depression, the songs were rarely depressing in themselves. Equally, the enigmatic Texan was no archetype, rather a lone-wolf troubadour who set striking lyrical images to subtle, introspective country-folk melodies, gaining a substantial cult following over the course of his all too short life. The small 'Poppy' label was once again home for VAN ZANDT's sophomore effort, 'OUR MOTHER THE MOUNTAIN' (1969), generally considered by critics and fans alike to be his finest hour and featuring the dark, orchestrated beauty of 'KATHLEEN' (recently covered by the mighty TINDERSTICKS) as well as 'ST. JOHN THE GAMBLER'. An incredibly prolific period for the singer, he released his eponymous third album later that year, a record that revisited the finest tracks of the debut alongside a clutch of new material including the heart-rending 'NONE BUT THE RAIN'. Another of TOWNES' early mentor's was LIGHTNIN' HOPKINS, whose influence hovers over 1971's 'DELTA MOMMA BLUES' while 'HIGH LOW AND IN BETWEEN' (1972) found the surprisingly versatile Texan getting a gospel groove going on 'TWO HANDS'. His final early period album, 'THE LATE, GREAT TOWNES VAN ZANDT' (1973) featured the first incarnation of his classic outlaw ballad, 'PANCHO AND LEFTY', subsequently the subject of a sublime cover by EMMYLOU HARRIS (on her 1977 album, 'LUXURY LINER') while WILLIE NELSON and MERLE HAGGARD also got to grips with it atop the country chart. By this point, the 'outlaw' movement had permanently altered the course of country music (well, at least for a while) and VAN ZANDT had definitely played his part. Yet in reality he was more hermit than outlaw, holeing up in the hills for weeks at a time as his albums lingered in obscurity amid label distribution problems and bankruptcy. He continued to perform though and in 1977 released a typically low-key concert set, 'LIVE AT THE OLD QUARTER, HOUSTON, TEXAS'. His next set of bonafide new material came with the following year's 'FLYIN' SHOES', its haunting title track (with rare piano accompaniment) arguably the man's finest composition. After another period in the wilderness, TOWNES was back with an album on 'Sugar Hill', 'AT MY WINDOW' (1987), followed by an all too rare UK tour. 1989 saw the release of 'LIVE AND OBSCURE', its title a typical example of VAN ZANDT's self-deprecating sense of humour and ambivalent attitude to the machinations of the music industry. Tragically, although he continued to occasionally perform and record into the 90's, VAN ZANDT died suddenly on New Year's day, 1997; he was only 52. Following his death, there've been a slew of posthumous releases including 'Arista's 'FAR CRY FROM DEAD' (1999) featuring previously unreleased material.

Album rating: FOR THE SAKE OF THE SONG (*6) / OUR MOTHER THE MOUNTAIN (*8) / TOWNES VAN ZANDT (*7) / DELTA MOMMA BLUES (*6) / HIGH, LOW AND INBETWEEN (*8) / THE LATE, GREAT TOWNES VAN ZANDT (*8) / LIVE AT THE OLD QUARTER (*9) / FLYING SHOES (*6) / AT MY WINDOW (*8) / LIVE AND OBSCURE (*6) / RAIN ON A CONGA DRUM (*7) / THE NASHVILLE SESSIONS (*6) / REAR VIEW MIRROR (*6) / ROADSONGS (*6) / NO DEEPER BLUE (*6) / THE BEST OF. . . compilation (*7) / THE HIGHWAY KIND (*6) / LAST RIGHTS: THE LIFE & TIMES OF . . . compilation (*7) / A FAR CRY FROM DEAD compilation (*7)

TOWNES VAN ZANDT – vocals, acoustic guitar

			not iss.	Poppy

1968. (lp) <PYS 40.001> **FOR THE SAKE OF THE SONG**
– For the sake of the song / Tecumseh valley / Many a fine lady / Quick silver daydreams of Maria / Waitin' around to die / I'll be there in the morning / Sad Cinderella / The velvet voices / Talkin' karate blues / All your young servants / Sixteen summers, fifteen falls. *(UK cd-iss. Aug93 on 'Tomato'; 598 109129) <cd-iss. 1994 on 'Rhino'; R2 71541> (cd-iss. Jun98 on 'Charly'; CDGR 241)*

1969. (lp) <PYS 40.004> **OUR MOTHER THE MOUNTAIN**
– Be here to love me / Kathleen / She came and she touched me / Like a summer Thursday / Our mother the mountain / Second lovers song / St. John the gambler / Tecumseh valley / Snake mountain blues / My proud mountains / Why she's acting this way. <re-iss. Mar79 on 'Tomato'; TOM 7015> (UK-iss.Jan88 on 'Decal' lp/c; LIK/TCLIK 17) (cd-iss. Jan88 on 'Charly'; CDCHARLY 104) <cd-iss. 1994 on 'Rhino'; R2 71241> (cd-iss. Mar98 on 'Charly'; CDGR 211)

1970. (lp) <PYS 40.007> **TOWNES VAN ZANDT**
– For the sake of the song / Columbine / Waiting around to die / Don't take it too bad / Colorado girl / Lungs / I'll be here in the morning / Fare thee well, Miss

Carousel / (Quick silver daydreams of) Maria / None but the rain. *<re-iss. Mar79 on 'Tomato'; TOM 7014> (UK-iss.Jun88 on 'Decal' lp/c; LIK/TCLIK 32) (cd-iss. Jun88 on 'Charly'; CDCHARLY 119) <cd-iss. 1994 on 'Rhino'; R2 71240> (cd re-iss. Mar98 on 'Charly'; CDGR 212)*

1971. (lp) <PYS 40.012> **DELTA MOMMA BLUES**
– FFV / Delta momma blues / Only him or me / Turnstyled, junkpiled / Tower song / Come tomorrow / Brand new companion / Where I lead me / Rake / Nothin'. <(UK + re-iss. Mar79 on 'Tomato'; TOM 7013)> (re-iss. Apr88 on 'Decal'; LIK/TCLIK 25) (cd-iss. Apr88 on 'Charly'; CDCHARLY 110) <cd-iss. 1994 on 'Rhino'; R2 71244> (cd re-iss. Nov97 on 'Musidisc'; 17404-2) (cd re-iss. Jun98 on 'Charly'; CDGR 213)

1971. (lp) <PYS 5700> **HIGH, LOW AND INBETWEEN**
– Two hands / You are not needed now / Greensboro woman / Highway kind / Standin' / No deal / To live is to fly / When he offers his hand / Mr. Gold and Mr. Mudd / Blue ridge mountains / High, low and inbetween. <(UK + re-iss. Mar79 on 'Tomato'; TOM 7012)> (UK re-iss. Nov88 on 'Decal' lp/c; LIK/TCLIK 50) (cd-iss. Nov88 on 'Charly'; CDCHARLY 151) <cd-iss. 1994 on 'Rhino'; R2 71243> (cd re-iss. Aug98 on 'Charly'; CDGR 214)

		U.A.	Poppy

1973. (lp) <UAS 29442> <LA 004> **THE LATE, GREAT TOWNES VAN ZANDT** | 1972
– No lonesome tune / Sad Cinderella / German mustard / Don't let the sunshine fool you / Honky tonkin' / Snow don't fall / Fraulein / Poncho and Lefty / If I needed you / Silver ships of Andilar / Heavenly houseboat blues. <(UK + re-iss. Mar79 on 'Tomato'; TOM 7011)> (UK-iss.Aug88 on 'Edsel'; ED 293) (re-iss. Oct88 on 'Decal' lp/c; LIK/TCLIK 49) (cd-iss. Oct88 on 'Charly'; CDCHARLY 145) <cd-iss. 1994 on 'Rhino'; R2 71242> (cd re-iss. Nov97 on 'Charly'; CDGR 215)

		not iss.	Tomato

1977. (d-lp) <TOM 7001> **LIVE AT THE OLD QUARTER (live at Houston, Texas)**
– Announcement / Pancho and Lefty / Mr. Mudd and Mr. Gold / Don't you take it too bad / Two girls / Fraulein / If I needed you / Brand new companion / White freightliner blues / To live is to fly / She came and touched me / Talking thunderbird blues / Rex's blues / Nine pound hammer / For the sake of the song / No place to fall / Loretta / Kathleen / Tower song / Waiting 'round to die / Tecumseh valley / Lungs / Only him or me. (UK-iss.Oct89 on 'Decal' d-lp/d-c; LIKD/TCLIKD 57) (d-cd-iss. Oct89 on 'Charly'; CDCHARLY 183) <cd-iss. 1994 on 'Rhino'; R2 71245> (d-cd-iss. Aug98 on 'Charly'; CDGR 216)

1978. (lp) <TOM 7017> **FLYING SHOES**
– Loretta / No place to fall / Flyin' shoes / Who do you love / When she don't need me / Dollar bill blues / Rex's blues / Pueblo waltz / Brother flower / Snake song. (UK-iss.Jul89 on 'Decal' lp/c; LIK/TCLIK 59) (cd-iss. Jul89 on 'Charly'; CDCHARLY 193) <cd-iss. 1994 on 'Rhino'; R2 71291> (cd re-iss. Nov98 on 'Charly'; CDGR 217)

		Heartland	Sugar Hill

Nov 87. (lp/cd) (HLD/+CD 003) <SH 1020/+CD> **AT MY WINDOW**
– Snowin' on Baton / Blue wind blew / At my window / For the sake of the song / Ain't leavin' your love / Buckskin stallion blues / Little sundance / Still lookin' for you / Gone gone blues / The catfish song. (cd-iss. May92 on 'Edsel'; EDCD 351)

Nov 89. (lp/cd) (HLD/+CD 004) <SH 1026/+CD> **LIVE AND OBSCURE (live in Nashville 1985)**
– Dollar bill blues / Many a fine lady / Nothin' / Pueblo waltz / Talking Thunderbird blues / Rex's blues / White freight liner blues / Loretta / Snake mountain blues / Waitin' round to die / Tecumseh valley / Panch and Lefty / You are not needed now. (cd re-iss. Mar92 as 'PANCHO AND LEFTY (LIVE AND OBSCURE)' on 'Edsel'; EDCD 244)

		Exile – Silenz	not iss.

Oct 91. (lp – c/cd) (EXLP 02 – 269575-4/-2) **RAIN ON A CONGA DRUM (live in Berlin)**
– Mr. Mudd and Mr. Gold / If I needed you / Buckskin stallion blues / Short haired woman blues / Ain't leavin' your love / Pancho and Lefty / Dollar bill blues / Fraulein / Shrimp song / Blaze's blues / No place to fall / To live is to fly / Lungs / Tecumseh valley / Dead flowers / White freightliner blues / Catfish blues.

		Sugar Hill	Sugar Hill

Apr 94. (cd/c) <(SH 1042 CD/C)> **ROADSONGS (live covers)**
– Ira Hayes / Dead flowers / Automobile blues / Coo coo / Fraulein hello / Central Indian cowboy / Racing in the streets / My starter won't start this morning / Texas river song / Wabash cannonball / Short haired woman blues / Man gave names to all the animals / Little Willie the gambler / Cocaine / You win again / High, low and inbetween / When he offers his hand. (cd re-iss. Feb97 on 'Normal'; NORMAL 195)

Aug 95. (cd) <(SHCD 1046)> **NO DEEPER BLUE** | 1994
– Song for / Blaze's blues / Hole / Marie / Goin' down to Memphis / Hey Willy boy / Niles river blues / Nilly, Boney and ma / Katie Belle Vue / If I was Washington / Lover's lullaby / Cowboy Junkies lament / BW railroad blues / Gone too long. (re-iss. Jun96 on 'Intercord'; IRS 993151)

—— TOWNES died on the 1st of January, 1997 leaving behind posthumous . . .

Apr 97. (cd) <(SHCD 1056)> **THE HIGHWAY KIND**
– Lost highway / My proud mountains / The highway kind / Dublin blues / Blaze's blues / Wreck on the highway / Hole / (I heard that) Lonesome whistle / Rake / Banks of the Ohio / Ira Hayes / Darcey Farrow / Song for / Still lookin' for you / Joke / No deal / At my window.

		Exile	Exile

May 99. (7") (EX7 013) **RIDING THE RANGE. / DIRTY OLD TOWN**

– compilations, etc. –

Dec 90. (c) Charly; (TCAD 21) **TOWNES / LIVE IN THE LATIN QUARTER**

Aug 93. (cd) Tomato; <(598 107929)> **THE NASHVILLE SESSIONS**
– At my window / Rex's blues / No place to fall / Buckskin stallion / White freight liner / The snake song / Loretta / Two girls / The spider song / When she don't need me / Pueblo waltz / Upon my soul.

1993. (cd/c) Sundown; <SD 2100-2/-4> **REAR VIEW MIRROR (live renditions)**
(UK-iss.Jun96 on 'Intercord'; IRS 993150) (re-iss. Feb97 on 'Sugar Hill'; SHCD 1054) (re-iss. Nov97 on 'Normal'; NORMAL 203)

Jun 96. (cd) Charly; <(CPCD 8176)> **THE BEST OF TOWNES VAN ZANDT** | 1999
– Kathleen / St. John the gambler / Waiting 'round to die / Don't take it too bad / Colorado girl / I'll be here in the morning / Delta momma blues / Tower song / Brand new companion / Two hands / Standin' / No deal / To live is to fly / No lonesome

tune / Honky tonkin' / Pancho and Lefty / If I needed you / Heavenly houseboat blues / Loretta / No place to fall / Flying shoes.

Oct 96.	(cd) *Return To Sender;* <(RTS 24)> **ABNORMAL** (re-iss. Aug98 on 'Normal'; NORMAL 216CD)		
Oct 96.	(cd) *Capitol;* <53930> **HIGH, LOW AND INBETWEEN / THE LATE, GREAT TOWNES VAN ZANDT**	-	
Jul 97.	(cd) *Normal;* (NORMAL 211CD) **DOCUMENTARY**	-	-
Nov 97.	(cd) *Eagle;* (EABCD 043) **THE MASTERS**	-	-
Feb 98.	(d-cd) *Charly;* (CDGR 207-2) **ANTHOLOGY 1968-1979**	-	-
Mar 98.	(cd) *Gregor;* (GREGORCD 41290) **LAST RIGHTS: THE LIFE & TIMES OF TOWNES VAN ZANDT**		-
Jul 99.	(cd) *Arista;* <(07822 18888-20)> **A FAR CRY FROM DEAD**		Jun99

– Dollar bill blues / To live is to fly / Rex's blues / Sanitarium blues / Ain't leavin' your love / Greensboro woman / Snake mountain blues / Pancho and Lefty / For the sake of the song / Waitin' round to die / Many a fine lady / Tower song / Squash.

VASELINES (dig out; Great Alt & Indie . . .)

Stevie Ray VAUGHAN

Born: 3 Oct'54, Dallas, Texas, USA. No white bluesman, not even ERIC CLAPTON, enjoyed the amount of peer adulation afforded STEVIE RAY, the closest probably being ALAN 'BLIND OWL' WILSON of CANNED HEAT. He idolised ALBERT KING, HOWLIN' WOLF and MUDDY WATERS and his early career mirrored that of JOHNNY WINTER in that he arrived with a sensational impact, consumed an equally sensational amount of alcohol followed by collapse and eventual rehabilitation. VAUGHAN moved to Austin in 1972, playing in local bands including the NIGHTCRAWLERS and PAUL RAY & THE COBRAS (with whom he recorded 'TEXAS CLOVER' in 1974). BUDDY GUY, JOHN LEE HOOKER, MUDDY WATERS and ALBERT KING were among VAUGHAN's admirers after seeing him play at Antone's in Austin where his blend of HENDRIX, ALBERT KING, HUBERT SUMLIN and LONNIE MACK was the best show in town. His band, DOUBLE TROUBLE, (which, after many personnel changes numbered JOHNNY RENO on sax, JACKIE NEWHOUSE on bass, FREDDIE PHAROAH on drums and LOU ANN BARTON on vocals) started out, in 1976, as the TRIPLE THREAT REVUE, co-starring BARTON and local bluesman W.C. CLARK. However, the band wasn't big enough for both VAUGHAN and BARTON, the latter leaving for a solo deal with 'Elektra'/'Asylum' records and taking RENO with her (PHAROAH also left, his replacement being CHRIS 'WHIPPER' SMITH). DOUBLE TROUBLE's final line-up was finally completed with the addition of TOMMY SHANNON in place of NEWHOUSE. STEVIE RAY was then introduced to JERRY WEXLER and secured a spot at the 1982 Montreux Jazz Festival through his contacts (a feat unheard of for an unsigned band although VAUGHAN certainly didn't disgrace himself), while JACKSON BROWNE offered them some free time in his L.A. studio after hearing that they were still without a deal. JOHN HAMMOND, hearing tapes of the Montreux show and the rough mixes from BROWNE's studio, signed him for 'Epic' and BOWIE procured his services for the 'LET'S DANCE' sessions. VAUGHAN left BOWIE before the Serious Moonlight tour, either through loyalty to his own band or through BOWIE's insistence on an exclusive contract, going on to tour in his own right and promote his first album, 1983's 'TEXAS FLOOD'. An earthy, no-nonsense blues album containing the classic 'PRIDE AND JOY', the record sold half a million copies, reaching Top 40 in the States and winning a Grammy for Best Traditional Blues recording. After DOUBLE TROUBLE played at the Reading Festival in 1983, they went into the studio to record the follow-up, 'COULDN'T STAND THE WEATHER', another US Top 40 money spinner. VAUGHAN became a sought after guest and played on albums by JAMES BROWN, JOHNNY COPELAND and LONNIE MACK, while the awards continued to pile up. Although the band became a tighter unit on 'COULDN'T STAND..' and its 1985 follow-up, 'SOUL TO SOUL' and VAUGHAN was stretching his talent further, the pressures of the music biz, together with his father's death, pushed him into a spiral of cocaine and booze intake that ended in him collapsing during a European tour. STEVIE subsequently retreated into a rehabilitation clinic to re-assess his life; the 1986 album 'LIVE ALIVE', which included a 9-minute version of Jimi Hendrix's 'VOODOO CHILE', was later considered by the band to be their worst, mainly because they were out of their heads on cocaine and alcohol when it was recorded and mixed, although many fans thought that it was better than the studio albums which preceded it. His marriage and management relationship suffered but after a slow recovery he reappeared in 1989 with his life and talent still intact and his first studio album in four years, 'IN STEP' (his finest work yet and a US Top 40 success with tracks such as 'THE HOUSE IS ROCKIN', 'CROSSFIRE', 'TIGHTROPE' and 'WALL OF DENIAL' forming the record's backbone). The following year, he recorded the NILE RODGERS-produced 'FAMILY STYLE' with brother JIMMIE, (ex-FABULOUS THUNDERBIRDS), under the banner of The VAUGHAN BROTHERS. His recording career was to last little more than seven years, for only minutes after blowing ERIC CLAPTON, BUDDY GUY, ROBERT CRAY and JIMMIE off the stage at a show in Alpine Valley, Wisconsin on the 27th of August 1990, his helicopter crashed into a man-made hill on leaving the gig, killing all on board. His death instigated an outpouring of grief and the great artists who inspired him, from JOHN LEE HOOKER and BUDDY GUY (who dedicated their next albums to him), to JEFF BECK and ERIC CLAPTON, queued up to pay tribute to the guy who played the beat-up Stratocaster and who inspired a new generation of blues fans and artists. JACKSON BROWNE, STEVIE WONDER and BONNIE RAITT sang 'AMAZING GRACE' during the memorial service at Oak Cliff, Dallas four days after his death and his hometown of Austin erected a nine foot bronze statue of him in 1992. 'COULDN'T STAND THE WEATHER' became his first million seller and 'THE SKY IS CRYING', an album of out-takes from his first four studio albums (including everything from Lonnie Mack's 'WHAM' – the first record that VAUGHAN ever bought – to Jimi Hendrix's 'LITTLE WING') reached US No.10. Other albums also did well after his death, notably 'FAMILY STYLE' which made the US Top 10. In 1997, the Fender guitar company paid VAUGHAN the ultimate honour by issuing a signature Stratocaster.
• **Songwriters:** Wrote half the material except TEXAS FLOOD (Davis-Scott) / CHANGE IT + LOOKING OUT THE WINDOW (D.Bramhall) / LOOK AT LITTLE SISTER (Hank Ballard) / YOU'LL BE MINE (Willie Dixon) / COME ON (E.King) / TAXMAN (George Harrison) / etc.

Album rating: TEXAS FLOOD (*6) / COULDN'T STAND THE WEATHER (*6) / SOUL TO SOUL (*7) / LIVE ALIVE (*5) / IN STEP (*6) / FAMILY STYLE (*6; as the Vaughan Brothers) / posthumous:- THE SKY IS CRYING (*7) / IN THE BEGINNING (*5) / GREATEST HITS compilation (*8) / LIVE AT CARNEGIE HALL (*5) / THE REAL DEAL: GREATEST HITS VOLUME 2 compilation (*6)

STEVIE RAY VAUGHAN & DOUBLE TROUBLE

STEVIE RAY VAUGHAN – vocals, guitar / **TOMMY SHANNON** – bass (ex-JOHNNY WINTER) / **CHRIS 'Whipper' LAYTON** – drums (ex-GREAZY BROTHERS)

		Epic	Epic
Jul 83.	(7") <04031> **PRIDE AND JOY. / RUDE MOOD**	-	-
Aug 83.	(lp/c) (EPC/40 25534) <38734> **TEXAS FLOOD**		38 Jul83

– Love struck baby / Pride and joy / Texas flood / Tell me / Testify / Rude mood / Mary had a little lamb / Dirty pool / I'm cryin' / Lenny. *(cd-iss. Jul89; CD 25534) (re-iss. Apr91 cd/c; 460951-2/-4) (cd re-iss. Mar99 on 'Legacy'; 494129-2)*

| Aug 83. | (7") (EPC 3689) **LOVE STRUCK BABY. / RUDE MOOD** | | - |

—— added brother **JIMMIE VAUGHAN** – guitar, bass

| Jun 84. | (lp/c) (EPC/40 25940) <39304> **COULDN'T STAND THE WEATHER** | | 31 |

– Scuttle buttin' / Couldn't stand the weather / The things (that) I used to do / Voodoo chile (slight return) / Cold shot / Tin Pan alley / Honey bee / Stang's swang. *(cd-iss. Jul89; CD 25940) (re-iss. Apr91 cd/c; 465571-2/-4) (cd re-iss. Feb95; EK 64425) (cd re-iss. Mar99 on 'Legacy'; 494130-2)*

—— **JOE SUBLETT** – saxophone; repl. JIMMIE

—— added **REESE WYNANS** – keyboards

| Sep 85. | (lp/c) (EPC/40 26441) <40036> **SOUL TO SOUL** | | 34 |

– Say what! / Lookin' out the window / Look at little sister / Ain't gone 'n' give up on love / Gone home / Change it / You'll be mine / Empty arms / Come on (part III) / Life without you. *(cd-iss. Apr86; CD 26441) (re-iss. Apr91 cd/c; 466330-2/-4) (cd re-iss. Mar99 on 'Legacy'; 494131-2)*

Sep 85.	(7") <05731> **CHANGE IT. / LOOK AT LITTLE SISTER**	-	
Mar 86.	(7") <06601> **SUPERSTITION (live). / PRIDE AND JOY (live)**	-	
Jan 87.	(7") <06696> **WILLIE THE WIMP. / SUPERSTITION**	-	
Jan 87.	(d-lp/d-c/d-cd) (450238-1/-4/-2) <40511> **LIVE ALIVE (live)**		52 Dec86

– Say what! / Ain't gone 'n' give up on love / Pride and joy / Mary had a little lamb / Superstition / I'm leaving you (commit a crime) / Cold shot / Willie the wimp / Look at little sister / Texas flood / Voodoo chile (slight return) / Love struck baby / Change it / Life without you. *(re-iss. Apr93 cd/c; 466839-2/-4)*

Jun 87.	(7") <07340> **LOVE STRUCK BABY. / PIPELINE (W/ DICK DALE)**	-	
Jun 89.	(7") <69025> **TRAVIS WALK. / CROSSFIRE**	-	
Jul 89.	(lp/c/cd) (463395-1/-4/-2) <45024> **IN STEP**	63	33 Jun89

– The house is rockin' / Crossfire / Tightrope / Let me love you baby / Leave my girl alone / Travis walk / Wall of denial / Scratch-n-sniff / Love me darlin' / Riviera paradise. *(cd re-iss. Mar99 on 'Legacy'; 494132-2)*

| Aug 89. | (7") <73212> **THIS HOUSE IS ROCKIN'. / TIGHTROPE** | - | |

—— Late in the 80's, STEVIE jammed with The ERIC CLAPTON Band. On 27 Aug'90, after a concert in Alpine Valley, Wisconsin, STEVIE and other travellers were killed in a helicopter crash. He and brother JIMMIE had just cut album below.

VAUGHAN BROTHERS

		Epic	Epic
Oct 90.	(cd/c/lp) (467014-2/-4/-1) <46225> **FAMILY STYLE**	63	7

– Hard to be / White boots / D-FW / Good Texan / Hillbillies from Outer Space / Long way from home / Tick tock / Telephone song / Baboom / Mama said / Brothers.

| Oct 90. | (c-s) <73576> **TICK TOCK. / BROTHERS** | | 65 |
| Jan 91. | (c-s) <73673> **GOOD TEXAN. / MAMA SAID / BABOOM** | - | |

– (STEVIE RAY VAUGHAN) compilations, etc. –

on 'Legacy-Epic' unless mentioned otherwise

| Nov 91. | (cd/c/lp) (468649-2/-4/-1) <47390> **THE SKY IS CRYING** | | 10 |

– Boot hill / The sky is crying / Empty arms / Little wing / Wham / May I have a talk with you / Chitlins con carne / So excited / Life by the drop.

| Nov 92. | (7") <74142> **THE SKY IS CRYING. / CHITLINS CON CARNE** | - | |
| Oct 92. | (cd/c/lp) (472624-2/-4/-1) <53168> **IN THE BEGINNING (live 1st April, 1980)** | | 58 |

– In the open / Slide thing / They call me guitar Hurricane / All your love (I miss loving) / Tin pan alley / Love struck baby / Tell me / Shake for me / Live another day.

| Jan 93. | (7") **EMPTY ARMS. / WHAM** | - | |
| Nov 95. | (cd/c) (481023-2/-4) <66217> **GREATEST HITS** | | 39 |

– Taxman / Texas flood / The house is rockin' / Pride and joy / Tightrope / Little wing / Crossfire / Change it / Cold shot / Couldn't stand the weather / Life without you.

| Aug 97. | (cd/c) (488206-2/-4) <68163> **LIVE AT CARNEGIE HALL (live)** | | 40 |

– (intro) / Scuttle buttin' / Testifyin' / Love struck baby / Honey bee / Cold shot / Letter to my girl / Dirty pool / Pride and joy / Things that I used to do / C.O.D. / Iced over / Lenny / Rude mood.

Mar 99. (cd/c) *(494133-2/-4)* <65873> **THE REAL DEAL: GREATEST HITS VOLUME 2** ☐ 53
– Lovestruck baby / Ain't gonna give up on love / Scuttle buttin' / Wall of denial / Lenny / Superstition / Empty arms / Riviera paradise / Look at little sister / Willie the wimp / Pipeline / Shake for me / Leave my girl alone / Telephone song / Voodoo chile (slight return) / Life by the drop.

Alan VEGA (see under ⇒ SUICIDE)

Suzanne VEGA

Born: 12 Aug'59, Upper West Side, New York, USA. Studying dance at the High School of Performing Arts, VEGA spent her spare time gaining valuable musical experience in the folk clubs of New York's Greenwich Village. Hooking up with managers Ron Fierstein and Steve Addabbo, VEGA eventually secured a contract with 'A&M', Addabbo and LENNY KAYE (ex-PATTI SMITH GROUP and 'Nuggets' curator) overseeing production duties on her eponymous 1985 debut album. Critically acclaimed, this starkly compelling folk set saw VEGA hailed as the new JONI MITCHELL with some observers drawing comparisons with LAURA NYRO and even DORY PREVIN. Highly intelligent and acutely observed, VEGA's musings were reminiscent of LEONARD COHEN although she possessed a distinctive lyrical voice with a delicately understated vocal to match. Buoyed by the UK success (on its second release) of 'MARLENE ON THE WALL', the album almost made the British Top 10 although it struggled to penetrate the US Top 100. A couple of months later, she scored another UK Top 40 with the moodily intense 'LEFT OF CENTER', written for the soundtrack of 80's movie, 'Pretty In Pink' and featuring JOE JACKSON on piano. VEGA finally broke through in her home country with 'LUKA', a poignant character portrayal of an abused child which made No.3 in the American charts. The accompanying album, 'SOLITUDE STANDING' (1987) consolidated VEGA's standing as one of the most promising young talents in the new singer/songwriter movement alongside the likes of TRACY CHAPMAN etc. One track, the acappella 'TOM'S DINER', only a minor UK hit upon its original release in 1987, was later reworked by dance act, D.N.A., its success prompting a remixed version credited to SUZANNE VEGA & D.N.A. This in turn was even more successful, going Top 5 in Britain and America and leading to an album of the same name featuring interpretations of various VEGA tracks by such esteemed artists as R.E.M. A third album proper, 'DAYS OF OPEN HAND' (1990), met with mixed reactions however, its more ambitious jazz arrangements and enigmatic lyrics standing in contrast to the economical simplicity of her earlier work. No hit singles were forthcoming although the success of the aforementioned 'TOM'S DINER' track made sure VEGA's career stayed on the commercial straight and narrow. No doubt inspired by the rhythmic innovation applied to the track, her fourth set, '99.9F' (1992) saw VEGA experimenting with all manner of sound effects. The result was arguably her most consistent set since the debut, the likes of 'BLOOD MAKES NOISE' and 'FAT MAN & DANCING GIRL' fastening spiky rhythmic structures to VEGA's trademark sound, while the more traditional 'WHEN HEROES GO DOWN' showed VEGA could still pen affecting folk-pop. In 1997, SUZANNE was back with her most accessible work to date, 'NINE OBJECTS OF DESIRE', one of its tracks, 'NO CHEAP THRILL', even appearing on Britain's lottery show! • **Covered:** CHINA DOLL (Grateful Dead) / STORY OF ISAAC (Leonard Cohen). • **Trivia:** In 1987, she contributed two song lyrics for a PHILIP GLASS album, 'Songs From Liquid Days'.

Album rating: SUZANNE VEGA (*8) / SOLITUDE STANDING (*7) / DAYS OF OPEN HAND (*5) / 99.9 F (*6) / NINE OBJECTS OF DESIRE (*6) / THE BEST OF SUZANNE VEGA – TRIED AND TRUE compilation (*8)

SUZANNE VEGA – vocals, guitar with **JIM GORDON** – guitar / **FRANK CHRISTIAN** – guitar / **PAUL DUGAN + FRANK GRAVIS** – bass / **SUE EVANS** – drums / **C.P. ROTH** – synth
She replaced above with touring + studio band from mid'85-late 80's. **MARC SHULMAN** – guitar / **MIKE VISCEGLIA** – bass / **ANTON SANKO** – keyboards / **STEPHEN FERRARA** – percussion / **SUE EVANS** – drums

		A&M	A&M
Jul 85.	(lp/c) <(AMA/AMC 5072)> **SUZANNE VEGA**	11	91 Jun85

– Cracking / Freeze tag / Marlene on the wall / Small blue thing / Straight lines / Undertow / Some journey / The queen and the soldier / Knight moves / Neighborhood girls. (cd-iss. Feb86 & Mar93; CDA 5072)

Aug 85. (7") *(AM 275)* <2759> **MARLENE ON THE WALL. / NEIGHBORHOOD GIRLS** ☐ ☐
Jan 86. (7") *(AM 294)* **SMALL BLUE THING. / THE QUEEN AND THE SOLDIER** 65 -
(d7"+=) *(DAM 294)* – Some journey / Black widow station.
Feb 86. (7") <2834> **SMALL BLUE THING. / LEFT OF CENTER** - -
Mar 86. (7") *(AM 309)* **MARLENE ON THE WALL. / SMALL BLUE THING** 21 -
(10"+=) *(AMY 309)* – Neighborhood girls / Straight lines (live).
May 86. (7") *(AM 320)* **LEFT OF CENTER. / UNDERTOW** 32 -
(10"+=) *(AMX 320)* – ('A'live) / Freeze tag (live).
(cd-s+=) *(CDQ 320)* – Cracking.
(above 'A'side featured JOE JACKSON – piano. SUE EVANS had now left.
Oct 86. (7") *(AM 349)* **GYPSY. / CRACKING (live)** - -
(12"+=) *(AMY 349)* – Knight movies (live).
May 87. (lp/c/cd) *(SUZ LP/MC/CD 2)* <5136> **SOLITUDE STANDING** 2 11
– Tom's diner / Luka / Ironbound / Fancy poultry / In the eye / Night vision / Solitude standing / Calypso / Language / Gypsy / Wooden horse.
May 87. (7") <2937> **LUKA. / NIGHT VISION** - 3
May 87. (7") *(VEGA 1)* **LUKA. / STRAIGHT LINES (live)** 23 -
(12"+=) *(VEGA 12)* – Neighbourhood girls.

Jul 87. (7") *(VEGA 2)* **TOM'S DINER. / LEFT OF CENTER** 58 -
(10"+=/=/c-s+=) *(VEGA 210/212)* – Luka (live).
(cd-s+=) *(VEGCD 2)* – ('A'live).
Sep 87. (7") <2960> **SOLITUDE STANDING. / TOM'S DINER** - 94
Nov 87. (7") <2888> **GYPSY. / LEFT OF CENTER** - -
Nov 87. (7"/c-s) *(VEGA/+C 3)* **SOLITUDE STANDING. / LUKA** - -
(12"+=) *(VEGA 3-12)* – Ironbound – Fancy poultry.
(10"/cd-s) *(VEG A3-10/CD 3)* – ('A'side) / Marlene on the wall (live) / Some journey (live).

—— **FRANK VILARDI** – drums repl. FERRARA
—— added **MICHAEL BLAIR** – percussion

Apr 90. (cd/c/lp) *(CDA/AMC/AMA 5293)* <15293> **DAYS OF OPEN HAND** 7 50
– Tired of sleeping / Men in a war / Rusted pipe / Institution green / Book of dreams / Those whole girls (run in grace) / Room off the street / Big space / Predictions / Fifty-fifty chance / Pilgrimage. (re-iss. cd May95; 395293-2)
Apr 90. (7"/c-s) *(AM/+MC 559)* **BOOK OF DREAMS. / BIG SPACE** 66 ☐
(cd-s+=) *(AMCD 559)* – Marlene on the wall (live) / Ironbound (live).
(10"++=) *(AMX 559)* – Fancy poultry.
Jun 90. (7") *(AM 565)* **TIRED OF SLEEPING. / THOSE WHOLE GIRLS (RUN IN GRACE)** ☐ ☐
(10"+=/cd-s+=) *(AM X/CD 565)* – Left of center / Room off the street.
Jul 90. (7"/c-s; D.N.A. featuring SUZANNE VEGA) *(AM/+MC 592)* <1592> **TOM'S DINER.** / ('A'version) 2 5 Sep90
(12"+=/cd-s+=) *(AM X/CD 592)* – (2 other mixes by the Bristol duo).
Sep 90. (7"/c-s) *(AM/+MC 584)* **MEN IN A WAR. / UNDERTOW (live)** ☐ ☐
(12"+=/cd-s+=) *(AM X/CD 584)* – ('A'live).
Aug 92. (7"/c-s) *(AM/+C 0029)* **IN LIVERPOOL. / SOME JOURNEY** 52 ☐
(cd-s+=) *(AMCD 0029)* – The Queen and the soldier / Luka.
Sep 92. (cd/c/lp) *(540012-2/-4/-1)* <0005> **99.9 F** 20 86
– Rock in this pocket (song of David) / Blood makes noise / In Liverpool / 99.9 F / Blood sings / Fat man & dancing girl / (If you were) In my movie / As a child / Bad wisdom / When heroes go down / As girls go / Songs of sand / Private goes public.
Oct 92. (7"/c-s) *(AM/+C 0085)* **99.9 F. / MEN WILL BE MEN** 46 ☐
(cd-s+=) *(AMCD 0085)* – Rock in this pocket (acoustic) / In Liverpool (acoustic).
(cd-s) *(AMCDX 0085)* – ('A'side) / Tired of sleeping / Straight lines / Tom's diner (all live).
Dec 92. (7"/c-s) *(AM/+C 0112)* **BLOOD MAKES NOISE. / TOM'S DINER** 60 ☐
(cd-s) *(AMCD 0112)* – ('A'side) / Neighbourhood girls / Predictions / China doll.
(12") *(AMY 0112)* – ('A'side) / ('A'-Mitchell Froom remix) / ('A'house mix) / ('A'master mix).
Feb 93. (7"/c-s) *(AM/+C 0158)* **WHEN HEROES GO DOWN. / KNIGHT MOVES (live)** 58 ☐
(cd-s+=) *(AMCD 0158)* – Men in a war (live) / Gypsy (live).
(cd-s) *(AMCDX 0158)* – ('A'side) / Marlene on the wall / Luka / Left of center.
Feb 97. (c-ep/cd-ep) *(581869-4/-2)* **NO CHEAP THRILL / LUKA / MARLENE ON THE WALL / TOM'S DINER** 40 ☐
Feb 97. (cd/c) *(540583-2/-4)* **NINE OBJECTS OF DESIRE** 43 92 Sep96
– Birth-day (love made real) / Headshots / Caramel / Stockings / Casual match / Thin man / No cheap thrill / World before Colombus / Lolita / Honeymoon suite / Tombstone / My favorite plum.
Jun 97. (c-s) *(582249-4)* **BIRTH-DAY (LOVE MADE REAL) / WOMEN ON A TIER** ☐ ☐
(cd-s) *(582267-2)* – ('A'side) / Caramel / Small blue thing / Blood makes noise.
(cd-s) *(582269-2)* – ('A'side) / Casual match / World before Columbus.

– compilations, others, etc. –

Oct 88. (cd-ep) *A&M; (AMCD 912)* **COMPACT HITS** ☐ -
– Luka / Left of center / Neighbourhood girls / The queen and the soldier.
Sep 91. (cd/c/lp; Various Artists) *(395363-2/-4/-1)* **TOM'S ALBUM** ☐ ☐
– (contained re-workings by other artists of the track TOM'S DINER).
Oct 98. (cd/c) *A&M; <(540945-2/-4)>* **THE BEST OF SUZANNE VEGA – TRIED AND TRUE** 46 ☐
– Luka / Tom's diner (DNA featuring SUZANNE VEGA) / Marlene on the wall / Caramel / 99.9f / Small blue thing / Blood makes noise / Left of the center / In Liverpool / Gypsy / Book of dreams / No cheap thrill / World before Columbus / When heroes go down / The queen and the soldier / Book & a cover / Rosemary.

VEGAS (see under ⇒ HALL, Terry)

VELVET UNDERGROUND

Formed: New York City, New York, USA ... early 1965, by LOU REED and JOHN CALE, who nearly hit as The PRIMITIVES with the single, 'The Ostrich'. They met modern pop artist, ANDY WARHOL, who invited German chanteuse NICO to join the set-up alongside STERLING MORRISON and MO TUCKER. Early in 1966, they signed to 'MGM-Verve', and soon began work on what was to be their debut album, 'THE VELVET UNDERGROUND AND NICO'. The album was a revelation, strikingly different from the love and peace psychedelia of the day, The VELVETS' vision was decidedly darker and more disturbing. Combining sublime melodies and nihilistic noise, it featured eleven superb ahead-of-their-time classics, notably the brutally frank and frenetic 'HEROIN', the S&M 'VENUS IN FURS' and the garage raunch of 'WAITING FOR THE MAN'. It also contained three NICO sung beauties, 'FEMME FATALE', 'ALL TOMORROW'S PARTIES' and 'I'LL BE YOUR MIRROR'. The record only managed a brief stay in the US Top 200, as did the 1967 follow-up, 'WHITE LIGHT, WHITE HEAT', which included the 17-minute white noise freak-out of 'SISTER RAY'. With CALE now out of the picture, the focus fell on REED's songwriting for the self-titled third

album. An altogether mellower set of more traditionally structured songs, the highlight was undoubtedly REED's beautiful lullaby, 'PALE BLUE EYES'. The band's last studio album, 'LOADED', was the closest The VELVET UNDERGROUND ever came to mainstream rock and an indicator of the direction REED would take in his solo career. 'SWEET JANE' and 'ROCK 'N' ROLL' marked his creative peak, a final glorious burst of guitar noise before the group disbanded and the myth started to crystallise. And that was that. Except it wasn't, not come 1992 anyway, when many a precious, pasty faced obsessive went even whiter with horror as The VELVET UNDERGROUND reformed. Many fans, however, eagerly shelled out their hard earned cash for a reunion tour and album as CALE and REED became buddies once more. The live shows were apparently rather joyous and the accompanying vinyl document, 'LIVE MCMXCII' (1993), was an enjoyable romp through all the favourites. After the death of STERLING MORRISON in 1995, however, the prospect of further VELVETS activity looks doubtful. Yet despite the reunion, despite LOU REED's dodgy hairdo, despite everything, The VELVET UNDERGROUND of the 60's remain perenially cool and insidiously influential. Basically, alternative music begins and ends with VU and they have been cited as the inspiration for punk rock. A decade after that, a generation of indie groups (i.e. JESUS & MARY CHAIN, early PRIMAL SCREAM, MY BLOODY VALENTINE, etc.) paid barely disguised homage to their heroes.
• Songwriters: REED compositions, except some by group. Many rock acts have covered their material, but so far not surprisingly, none have managed to score a major chart hit yet. • Miscellaneous: In 1990, REED and CALE re-united on a tribute album to the deceased ANDY WARHOL. NICO had earlier died on the 18th of July '88 after suffering a brain haemorrhage due to a fall from her bike while on holiday in Ibiza. • Trivia: The debut lp sleeve, featured a gimmick peeling banana skin sticker. They reformed for a gig in Paris, 15 June 1990. UK's Channel 4, featured a night-long session of all their previous work.

Album rating: THE VELVET UNDERGROUND AND NICO (*10) / WHITE LIGHT – WHITE HEAT (*9) / THE VELVET UNDERGROUND (*8) / LOADED (*8) / ANDY WARHOL'S VELVET UNDERGROUND FEATURING NICO compilation (*7) / LIVE AT MAX'S KANSAS CITY exploitation (*2) / SQUEEZE (*3) / THE VELVET UNDERGROUND AND LOU REED compilation (*6) / 1969 – THE VELVET UNDERGROUND LIVE exploitation (*7) / GREATEST HITS compilation (*6) / V.U. unreleased set (*7) / ANOTHER VIEW exploitation (*4) / THE BEST OF THE VELVET UNDERGROUND (THE WORDS AND MUSIC OF LOU REED) compilation (*7) / LIVE MCMXCIII reunion (*5)

LOU REED (b. LOUIS FIRBANK, 2 Mar'44, Long Island, N.Y.) – vocals, guitar (ex-JADES, ex-PRIMITIVES) / **JOHN CALE** (b. 9 Dec'42, Garnant, Wales) – bass, viola, vocals, etc. / **STERLING MORRISON** – guitar / **MAUREEN TUCKER** – drums / plus **NICO** (b. CHRISTA PAFFGEN, 16 Oct'38, Cologne, Germany) – vocals (also – Solo artist)

		Verve	Verve
Oct 66.	(7") <10427> **ALL TOMORROW'S PARTIES. / I'LL BE YOUR MIRROR**	-	
Dec 66.	(7") <10466> **SUNDAY MORNING / FEMME FATALE**	-	
Oct 67.	(lp; stereo/mono) (S+/VLP 9184) <5008> **THE VELVET UNDERGROUND AND NICO**		Dec66

– Sunday morning / I'm waiting for the man / Femme fatale / Venus in furs / Run run run / All tomorrow's parties / Heroin / There she goes again / I'll be your mirror / Black angel's death song / European son to Delmore Schwartz. (re-iss. Oct71 on 'M.G.M.'; 2315 056) (re-iss. Aug83 on 'Polydor' lp/c; SPE LP/MC 20) (cd-iss. 1986 on 'Polydor'; 823 290-2) (cd re-iss. May96 on 'Polydor'; 531 250-2)

　　Trimmed to a quartet when NICO preferred the solo life

Jan 68.	(7") <10543> **WHITE LIGHT – WHITE HEAT. / HERE SHE COMES NOW**	-	
Mar 68.	(7") <10560> **I HEARD HER CALL MY NAME. / HERE SHE COMES NOW**	-	
Jun 68.	(lp; stereo/mono) (S+/VLP 9201) <5046> **WHITE LIGHT / WHITE HEAT**		Dec67

– White light – white heat / The gift / Lady Godiva's operation / Here she comes now / I heard her call my name / Sister Ray. (re-iss. Oct71 on 'MGM Select'; 2353 024) (re-iss. Apr84 on 'Polydor' lp/c; SPE LP/MC 73) (cd-iss. 1986 on 'Polydor'; 825 119-2) (cd re-iss. May96 on 'Polydor'; 531 251-2)

　　DOUG YULE – bass, vocals, keyboards, guitar repl. CALE who went solo

		M.G.M.	M.G.M.
Apr 69.	(lp) (CS 8108) <4617> **THE VELVET UNDERGROUND**		Mar 69

– Candy says . . . / What goes on / Some kinda love / Pale blue eyes / Jesus / Beginning to see the light / I'm set free / That's the story of my life / The murder mystery / Afterhours. (re-iss. Nov71 on 'MGM Select'; 2353 022) (re-iss. Mar76;) (re-iss. Sep83 on 'Polydor'; SPE LP/MC 39) <US re-iss. Apr85; 815454> (cd-iss. May96 on 'Polydor'; 531 252-2)

| May 69. | (7") <14057> **JESUS. / WHAT GOES ON** | - | - |

　　BILLY YULE – drums repl. TUCKER who had a baby. **MO TUCKER** returned in 1970 and BILLY only appeared on MAX's live album (see compilations)

		Atlantic	Cotillion
Jan 71.	(7") <44107> **WHO LOVES THE SUN? / OH! SWEET NUTHIN'**	-	
Apr 71.	(lp) (2400 111) <9034> **LOADED**		Aug70

– Who loves the sun? / Sweet Jane / Rock and roll / Cool it down / New age / Head held high / Lonesome cowboy Bill / I found a reason / Train around the bend / Oh! sweet nuthin'. (re-iss. 1972 lp/c; K/K4 40113) (cd-iss. Jun88 on 'Warners') (cd-iss. Feb93 on 'Warners') (d-cd-iss. May97 as 'LOADED (THE FULLY LOADED EDITION)' on 'Rhino'+=; 812272563-2) – (diff. mixes & demos, etc.)

| Apr 71. | (7") (2091 008) **WHO LOVES THE SUN. / SWEET JANE** | | - |

　　(Aug70) now with no originals The **YULE's** brought in newcomers **WALTER POWERS** – bass repl. LOU REED who went solo in 1971. (1971) **WILLIE ALEXANDER** – guitar repl. MORRISON who took a doctorate in English. MO TUCKER finally departed to raise her new family and eventually had five children in total, before going solo in 1980.

		Polydor	not iss.
Feb 73.	(lp) (2383 180) **SQUEEZE**		-

– Little Jack / Mean old man / She'll make you cry / Wordless / Dopey Joe / Crash / Friends / Jack and Jane / Send no letter / Louise.

　　Folded soon after above, DOUG sessioned for ELLIOTT MURPHY and later joined AMERICAN FLYER.

　　they re-formed early in 1993; **REED, CALE, MORRISON + TUCKER**

		Sire	Sire
Oct 93.	(d-cd/d-c) <(9362 45464-2/-4)> **LIVE MCMXCIII (live 1993)**	70	

– We're gonna have a good time together / Venus in furs / Guess I'm falling in love / After hours / All tomorrow's parties / Some kinda love / I'll be your mirror / Beginning to see the light / The gift / I heard her call my name / Femme fatale / Hey Mr. Rain / Sweet Jane / Velvet nursery rhyme / White light – white heat / I'm sticking with you / Black angel's death song / Rock'n'roll / I can't stand it / I'm waiting for the man / Heroin / Pale blue eyes / Coyote.

| Feb 94. | (7"/c-s) (W 0224/+C) **VENUS IN FURS (live). / I'M WAITING FOR THE MAN (live)** | 71 | |
| | (cd-s+=) (W 0224CD) – Heroin (live) / Sweet Jane (live). | | |

　　On the 30th August 1995, STERLING MORRISON died of lymphoma.

　　Group inducted into the Rock'n'roll Hall Of Fame, and performed 'LAST NIGHT I SAID GOODBYE TO A FRIEND', REED's tribute to recently deceased STERLING.

– compilations, others, etc. –

| Dec 71. | (d-lp) M.G.M.; (2683 006) **ANDY WARHOL'S VELVET UNDERGROUND FEATURING NICO** | | - |

– I'm waiting for the man / Candy says / Run, run, run / White light – white heat / All tomorrow's parties / Sunday morning / I heard her call my name / Femme fatale / Heroin / Here she comes now / There she goes again / Sister Ray / Venus in furs / European son / Pale blue eyes / Black angel's death song / Beginning to see the light.

| Aug 72. | (lp) Atlantic; (K 30022) / Cotillion; <9500> **LIVE AT MAX'S KANSAS CITY (live 22 Aug'70)** | | May72 |

– I'm waiting for the man / Sweet Jane / Lonesome Cowboy Bill / Beginning to see the light / I'll be your mirror / Pale blue eyes / Sunday morning / New age / Femme fatale / After hours. (cd-iss. Jun93 on 'Warners'; 7567 90370-2)

Jun 73.	(7"m; as LOU REED & VELVET UNDERGROUND) M.G.M.; (2006 283) **CANDY SAYS. / I'M WAITING FOR THE MAN / RUN RUN RUN**		
Aug 73.	(7") Atlantic; (K 10339) **SWEET JANE (live). / ROCK AND ROLL (live)**		
Oct 73.	(lp) Verve; (2315 258) / Pride; <0022> **THE VELVET UNDERGROUND AND LOU REED**		
1974.	(lp) M.G.M.; <4950> **ARCHETYPES**	-	
1976.	(ltd-7"m) A.E.B.; **FOGGY NOTION – INSIDE YOUR HEART. / I'M STICKING WITH YOU / FERRYBOAT BILL**		
Feb 79.	(d-lp) Mercury; (6643 900) <SRM2 7504> **1969 – THE VELVET UNDERGROUND LIVE (live)**		Apr74

– I'm waiting for the man / Lisa says / What goes on / Sweet Jane / We're gonna have a real good time together / Femme fatale / New age / Rock and roll / Beginning to see the light / Ocean / Pale blue eyes / Heroin / Some kinda love / Over you / Sweet Bonnie Brown – It's just too much / I'll be your mirror / White light – white heat. (re-iss. 1987; 834 823-1) (re-iss. 1988 as 'VOL.1' & 'VOL.2' cd/c; 834823-2/-4 & 834824-2/-4)

Nov 80.	(d-lp)(d-c) Polydor; (2664 438)(3578 485) **GREATEST HITS**		-
Oct 82.	(12"ep) Polydor; (POSPX 603) **HEROIN / VENUS IN FURS. / I'M WAITING FOR THE MAN / RUN RUN RUN**		
Feb 85.	(lp/c) Polydor; (POLD/+C 5167) <823721> **V.U. (rare rec.68-69)**	47	85

– I can't stand it / Stephanie says / She's my best friend / Lisa says / Ocean / Foggy notion / Temptation inside your heart / One of these days / Andy's chest / I'm sticking with you. (cd-iss. Jun87; 825 092-2)

| May 86. | (5xlp-box)(5xcd-box) Polydor; (VUBOX 1)(815 454-2) **BOXED SET** | | |

– (first 3 albums, plus V.U. & ANOTHER VIEW)

| Aug 86. | (lp/c/cd) Polydor; (829 405-1/-4/-2) **ANOTHER VIEW** | | |

– We're gonna have a good time together / I'm gonna move right in / Hey Mr. Rain (version 1) / Ride into the Sun / Coney Island steeplechase / Guess I'm falling in love / Hey Mr. Rain (version 2) / Ferryboat Bill / Rock and roll (original).

Feb 88.	(12") Old Gold; (OG 4049) **I'M WAITING FOR THE MAN. / HEROIN**		
Mar 88.	(12") Old Gold; (OG 4051) **VENUS IN FURS. / ALL TOMORROW'S PARTIES**		
Sep 88.	(lp) Plastic Inevitable; <FIRST 1> **THE VELVET UNDERGROUND ETC.**	-	

– The ostrich / Cycle Annie / Sneaky Pete / Noise.

| Sep 88. | (lp) Plastic Inevitable; <SECOND 1> **THE VELVET UNDERGROUND AND SO ON** | - | |

– It's alright (the way you live) / I'm not too sorry / Stephanie says.

| Oct 89. | (lp/c/cd) Verve; <(841 164-1/-4/-2)> **THE BEST OF THE VELVET UNDERGROUND (THE WORDS AND MUSIC OF LOU REED)** | | |

– I'm waiting for the man / Femme fatale / Run run run / Heroin / All tomorrow's parties / I'll be your mirror / White light – white heat / Stephanie says / What goes on / Beginning to see the light / Pale blue eyes / I can't stand it / Lisa says / Sweet Jane / Rock and roll.

| Oct 95. | (cd/c) Global; (RAD CD/MC 21) **THE BEST OF LOU REED & VELVET UNDERGROUND** | 56 | |
| Oct 95. | (4xcd-box) Polydor; (527887-2) **PEEL SLOWLY AND SEE** | | - |

　　(see also LOU REED discography for other tracks on comps & B's)

　　Also tribute albums 'HEAVEN AND HELL' 1, 2 & 3 were issued Oct'90-Feb'92, all on 'Imaginary' records, as was another '15 MINUTES'.

VENOM (dig out; Great Metal . . .)

Tom VERLAINE (see under ⇒ TELEVISION)

VERUCA SALT (dig out;
4th edition or Great Alt & Indie . . .)

VERVE

Formed: Wigan, England . . . 1990 by local college lads RICHARD ASHCROFT (the main writer), NICK McCABE, SIMON JONES and PETER SALISBURY. They were soon supporting the likes of RIDE and SPIRITUALIZED, signing to 'Hut' in 1991. The following year, they released three singles, the spiralling psychedelia of 'ALL IN THE MIND', 'SHE'S A SUPERSTAR' & 'GRAVITY GRAVE'. In early summer of '93, they had a minor hit with 'BLUE', a taster for the debut album, 'A STORM IN HEAVEN', which made the UK Top 30. The album delivered on the promise of the early singles; an amorphous melange of trippy rock and liquid space-jazz ambience. Ambitious and cocksure, they toured the States, subsequently coming unstuck with US label 'Verve', who forced them to slightly change their name to THE VERVE. In 1995, they unleashed a second album, 'A NORTHERN SOUL', a much darker, more intense affair featuring more conventional song structures. Although the album went Top 20, they announced they were splitting several months later, the 'HISTORY' single apparently their swan song. Just when the band were poised to enter the big league, it looked as if they'd missed the boat, McCABE and ASHCROFT's quarreling, together with well documented drug problems, seemingly to blame for the band's demise. By February '97, however, they got it together sufficiently to re-form, and their first single of the year was to many their best song yet, the grandiose, string-laden 'BITTER SWEET SYMPHONY' (written by MICK JAGGER and KEITH RICHARDS for The ANDREW LOOG OLDHAM ORCHESTRA). The song crashed into the UK chart at No.2 thanks to a glorious video featuring a tense, jaywalking ASHCROFT barging into everyone in sight! A follow-up, 'THE DRUGS DON'T WORK', went straight in at No.1, as did parent album, 'URBAN HYMNS' (1997). It seemed THE VERVE could do no wrong, although tensions between ASHCROFT and the others were coming to a head; McCABE would subsequently announce his retirement from stage work in July '98 (veteran pedal steel man BJ COLE was enlisted). The Americans had already taken the band into their hearts by this time, the aforementioned third set hitting the Top 30 and going platinum in the process. However by May 1999, THE VERVE were history, "astral man" ASHCROFT opting for a solo career with his SPIRITUALIZED wife KATE RADLEY in tow.

Album rating: A STORM IN HEAVEN (*7) / A NORTHERN SOUL (*8) / URBAN HYMNS (*9)

RICHARD ASHCROFT (b.11 Sep'71) – vocals, guitar / **NICK McCABE** (b.14 Jul'71) – lead guitar / **SIMON JONES** (b.29 Jul'72) – bass / **PETER SALISBURY** (b.24 Sep'71) – drums

	Hut	Vernon Yard
Mar 92. (7") (HUT 12) **ALL IN THE MIND. / ONE WAY TO GO**		-
(12"+=/cd-s+=) (HUT T/CD 12) – A man called Sun.		
Jun 92. (7"/ext-12"/ext-cd-s) (HUT/+H/CD 16) **SHE'S A SUPERSTAR. / FEEL**	66	-
Oct 92. (10"ep) (HUTEN 21) **GRAVITY GRAVE EP**		-
– Gravity grave / Endless life / She's a superstar (live). (12"+=/cd-s++) (HUT T/CD 21) – ('A'extended) / Endless life / A man called Sun (live).		
Jan 93. (m-cd) (<HUTUS 1>) **THE VERVE E.P.** (compilation)	-	-
– Gravity grave / A man called Sun / She's a superstar / Endless life / Feel. (UK-iss.Sep97 on 'Vernon Yard'; YARDCD 001)		
May 93. (12"ep) (HUTT 29) **BLUE. / TWILIGHT / WHERE THE GEESE GO**	69	-
(10"ep+=/cd-ep+=) (HUT EN/CD 29) – No come down.		
Jun 93. (cd/c/lp) (CDHUT/HUTMC/HUTLP 10) <87950> **A STORM IN HEAVEN**	27	
– Star sail / Slide away / Already there / Beautiful mind / The sun, the sea / Virtual world / Make it 'til Monday / Blue / Butterfly / See you in the next one (have a good time).		
Sep 93. (7"pink) (HUT 35) **SLIDE AWAY. / 6 O'CLOCK**		-
(12"/cd-s) (HUT T/CD 35) – ('A'side) / Make it 'til Monday (acoustic) / Virtual world (acoustic).		
May 94. (cd) (CDHUT 18) **NO COMEDOWN** (rare / b-sides)		-
– No come down / Blue (USA mix) / Make it 'til Monday (acoustic) / Butterfly (acoustic) / Where the grease go / 6 o'clock / One way to go / Gravity grave (live) / Twilight. (re-iss. Sep97 on 'Vernon Yard'; YARDCD 007)		

THE VERVE

Apr 95. (7"burgundy) (HUT 54) **THIS IS MUSIC. / LET THE DAMAGE BEGIN**	35	-
(12"+=/cd-s+=) (HUT T/CD 54) – You and me.		
Jun 95. (7"green/c-s) (HUT/+C 55) **ON YOUR OWN. / I SEE THE DOOR**	28	-
(cd-s+=) (HUTCD 55) – Little gem / Dance on your bones.		
Jul 95. (cd/c/d-lp) (CDHUT/HUTMC/HUTLP 27) <40437> **A NORTHERN SOUL**	13	
– A new decade / This is music / On your own / So it goes / A northern soul / Brainstorm interlude / Drive you home / History / No knock on my door / Life's an ocean / Stormy clouds / Stormy clouds (reprise).		
Sep 95. (c-s) (HUTC 59) **HISTORY / BACK ON MY FEET AGAIN**	24	-
(cd-s+=) (HUTCD 59) – On your own (acoustic) / Monkey magic (Brainstorm mix). (cd-s) (HUTDX 59) – ('A'extended) / Grey skies / Life's not a rehearsal.		

—— originals re-formed adding **SIMON TONG** – guitar, keyboards

	Hut	Virgin
Jun 97. (7") (HUTLH 82) <38634> **BITTER SWEET SYMPHONY. / SO SISTER**	2	12 Mar98
('A'extended; cd-s+=) (HUTDX 82) – Echo bass. (c-s/cd-s) (HUT C/DG 82) – ('A'side) / Lord I guess I'll never know / Country song / ('A'radio version).		
Sep 97. (c-s/cd-s) (HUT C/DG 88) **THE DRUGS DON'T WORK / THREE STEPS / THE DRUGS DON'T WORK (original demo)**	1	
(cd-s) (HUTDX 88) – ('A'extended) / Bitter sweet symphony (James Lavelle remix) / The crab / Stamped.		
Sep 97. (cd/c/lp) (<44913-2/-4/-1>) **URBAN HYMNS**	1	23
– Bitter sweet symphony / Sonnet / The rolling people / The drugs don't work / Catching the butterfly / Neon wilderness / Space and time / Weeping willow / Lucky man / One day / This time / Velvet morning / Come on.		
Nov 97. (c-s/cd-s) (HUT C/DG 92) **LUCKY MAN / NEVER WANNA SEE YOU CRY / HISTORY**	7	
(cd-s) (HUT DX 92) – ('A'side) / MSG / The longest day / Lucky man (happiness more or less).		

—— THE VERVE announced their demise in '99, ASHCROFT going solo in 2000

– compilations, etc. –

Mar 98. (ltd-12"ep) **BITTER SWEET SYMPHONY (original) / LORD I GUESS I'LL NEVER KNOW. / BITTER SWEET SYMPHONY (James Lavelle mix) / COUNTRY SONG**		-
Mar 98. (ltd-12"ep) **THE DRUGS DON'T WORK / THREE STEPS. / THE DRUGS DON'T WORK (demo) / THE CRAB**		-
Mar 98. (ltd-12"ep) **LUCKY MAN / NEVER WANNA SEE YOU CRY. / MSG / THE LONGEST DAY**		-
Mar 98. (ltd-12"ep) **SONNET / STAMPED. / SO SISTER / ECHO BASS**		-
(the import cd-single version of the above single <895075-2> actually hit UK No.74 in May'98)		

VERVE PIPE

Formed: East Lansing, Michigan, USA . . . 1992 out of JOHNNY WITH AN EYE by brothers BRIAN and BRAD VANDER ARK, the pair recruiting former WATER 4 THE POOL members, DONNY BROWN and BRIAN STOUT. Debuting later that year with the mini-set, 'I'VE SUFFERED A HEAD INJURY', The VERVE PIPE began to lay the foundations of a healthy fanbase through a punishing tour schedule. Beefing up their oddball but intelligent alterna-rock sound with the addition of A.J. DUNNING and DOUG CORELLA (to replace STOUT), the hard working quintet delivered a second independent set, 'POP SMEAR' (1993). With acclaim flowing in across the board, 'R.C.A.' were quick to spot their commercial potential, putting them into the studio for 1996's 'VILLAINS' album. Criminally, the band were ignored across the water although obviously the towering profile of Brit-rockers, THE VERVE, didn't help matters. Then again, the guys probably weren't that bothered as the aforementioned record climbed into the US Top 30, spurred on by a massive Stateside Top 5 smash, 'THE FRESHMEN'.

Album rating: I'VE SUFFERED A HEAD INJURY mini (*5) / POP SMEAR (*6) / VILLAINS (*5) / VERVE PIPE (*4)

BRIAN VANDER ARK – vocals, guitar / **BRIAN STOUT** – guitar, vocals / **BRAD VANDER ARK** – bass, vocals / **DONNY BROWN** – drums

	not iss.	Transom
Nov 92. (m-cd) <VP 001> **I'VE SUFFERED A HEAD INJURY**	-	
– Ark of the envious / Even the score / Acting as your slave / Oceanside / I've suffered a head injury / Clean break / Martyr material. <re-iss. 1997 on 'R.C.A.'; 67543>		

—— **A.J. DUNNING** – guitar / + **DOUG CORELLA** – keyboards; repl. STOUT

	not iss.	LMNO Pop~!
1993. (cd) **POP SMEAR**	-	-
– Pretty for you / Spoonful of sugar / Victoria / Honest / River / Sleepy town / Bullies on vacation / What you wanted / Wanna be / Out like a lamb / Senator speak / Is it worth it? <re-iss. 1997 on 'R.C.A.'; 67544>		

	R.C.A.	R.C.A.
Nov 96. (7"/cd-s) (74321 43069-7/-2) **PHOTOGRAPH. / DRIVE YOU MILD / BLUE BERET**		
Nov 96. (cd) <(07863 66809-2)> **VILLAINS**		24 Mar96
– Barely (if at all) / Drive you mild / Villains / Reverend girl / Cup of tea / Myself / The freshmen / Photograph / Ominous man / Real / Penny is poison / Castle / Veneer.		
Jan 97. (cd-s) <64733> **THE FRESHMEN /**	-	5
Jun 98. (cd-s) (45351) **THE FRESHMEN / ('A'–Pop mix)**	-	-
(cd-s) (2 – 'A' mixes) / Ominous man / Spoonful of sugar (live).		
Jul 99. (cd/c) <67664> **VERVE PIPE**	-	
– Supergig / She loves everybody / Hero / Television / In between / Kiss me idle / Headlines / The F word / Generations / Half a mind / She has faces / La la.		

VIBRATORS (dig out; Great Alt & Indie . . .)

VICTOR (see under ⇒ RUSH)

Gene VINCENT

Born: EUGENE VINCENT CRADDOCK, 11 Feb'35, Norfolk, Virgin[ia], USA. In 1955, he left the US Navy after suffering leg injuries in a se[rious] motor-cycle crash. Incidentally, this never fully healed, and after a [...] plaster, he had a leg-brace fitted and took up singing during his recu[...] often sitting in with WCMS Radio house band, The VIRGINIA[NS]

1956, he briefly married 15 year-old Ruth Ann Hand, also gaining a contract for 'Capitol' in April. He formed The BLUE CAPS (name taken from President Eisenhower's favourite blue golf cap) for tour work, his live commitments becoming more extensive after the US Top 10 success of his debut single (B-side), 'BE-BOP-A-LULA' (which ELVIS PRESLEY's mother reportedly thought was her own son singing). VINCENT subsequently became a cult star in the 50's, his black leather-clad image and sporadic chart appearances (his last US chart single was 'DANCE TO THE BOP' in January 1958) fueling the myth. Later that year, the media attention focused on his recent drinking bouts which made him irritable to everyone bar his great friend, EDDIE COCHRAN; late in 1959, he toured the UK with EDDIE, resurrecting his chart status in the process with 'PISTOL PACKIN MAMA' (with GEORGIE FAME on piano) and 'SHE SHE LITTLE SHEILA'. Tragedy struck however, on the 17th of April 1960, when EDDIE was killed in a London cab, with GENE and EDDIE's fiancee sustaining injuries. Shaken but vowing to continue, he had a short series of UK hits that year although success soon eluded him and his last UK chart single was 1961's 'I'M GOING HOME'. The following year, he appeared on a bill at The Cavern Club with an up and coming beat combo, The BEATLES, although his 'Capitol' contract expired in '63 and was not renewed. He married for a fourth time in 1965, signing to US label 'Challenge', although his move into country rock'n'roll in 1966 was treated with apathy. In the early 70's, his career took off again when UK BBC Radio DJ John Peel contracted him to his newly formed 'Dandelion' imprint, releasing 'I'M BACK AND I'M PROUD' in the same year. VINCENT then signed to 'Kama Sutra' in the US and released his final albums, 'GENE VINCENT' and 'THE DAY THE WORLD TURNED BLUE', and although critically well received, the records failed to sell. After more hard-living and domestic problems, GENE VINCENT died on the 12th of October 1971 (of a burst stomach ulcer) in Newall hospital California. Many had copied his image including The BEATLES and ALVIN STARDUST and there were many tributes, none more poignant than IAN DURY's 'SWEET GENE VINCENT'.
• **Songwriters:** His first hit, was written by fellow hospital patient in the same ward. He then wrote own material, except covers OVER THE RAINBOW (Judy Garland) / SUMMERTIME (Gershwin) / FRANKIE & JOHNNY (?) / ANOTHER SATURDAY NIGHT (Sam Cooke) / SLIPPIN' AND SLIDIN' + LONG TALL SALLY + GOOD GOLLY MISS MOLLY (Little Richard) / SUSIE Q (Dale Hawkins) / YOU ARE MY SUNSHINE (hit; Ray Charles) / WHITE LIGHTNING (Big Bopper) / etc. • **Trivia:** He and his BLUE CAPS made appearances in the film 'The Girl Can't Help It' & 'Hot Rod Gang'.

Best CD compilation: THE SCREAMING END: THE BEST OF . . . (*8)

GENE VINCENT & HIS BLUE CAPS

GENE VINCENT – vocals, guitar / **CLIFF GALLUP** – lead guitar / **WILLIE WILLIAMS** – acoustic rhythm guitar / **JACK NEAL** – upright bass / **DICKIE HARRELL** – drums

		Capitol	Capitol	
Jun 56.	(7",78) (CL 14599) <3450> **BE BOP A LULA. / WOMAN LOVE**	16	7	May 56
	(above B-side, was originally the A, until BE BOP . . . was radio playlisted)			
Aug 56.	(7",78) (CL 14628) <3530> **RACE WITH THE DEVIL. / GONNA BACK UP MY BABY**	28	96	Jul 56
Oct 56.	(7",78) (CL 14637) <3558> **BLUE JEAN BOP. / WHO SLAPPED JOHN?**	16	49	Sep 56
Nov 56.	(lp) <(T 764)> **BLUE JEAN BOP**		16	Sep 56

– Blue jean bop / Jezebel / Who slapped John / Ain't she sweet / I flipped / Waltz of the wind / Jump back, honey, jump back / That old gang of mine / Jumps, giggles and shouts / Up a lazy river / Bop street / Peg o' my heart (re-iss. 1983 on 'E.M.I.')

_____ **PAUL PEAK** – rhythm guitar, vocals repl. WILLIAMS. (NEAL now on bass)

Mar 57.	(7",78) (CL 14693) <3617> **CRAZY LEGS. / IMPORTANT WORDS**			Nov 56
Jan 57.	(7",78) (CL 14681) **JUMPS, GIGGLES AND SHOUTS. / WEDDING BELLS**		-	
Apr 57.	(lp) <(T 811)> **GENE VINCENT AND HIS BLUE CAPS**			

– Red blue jeans and a pony tail / Hold me, hug me, rock me / Unchained melody / You told a fib / Cat man / You better believe / Cruisin' / Double talkin' baby / Blues stay away from me / Pink Thunderbird / I sure miss you / Pretty, pretty baby. (re-iss. 1983 on 'E.M.I.')

_____ On tour **RUSSELL WILAFORD** then **TEDDY CRUTCHFIELD** had repl. GALLUP

May 57.	(7",78) (CL 14722) <3678> **BI-BICKEY-BI-BO-BO-GO. / FIVE DAYS, FIVE DAYS**			

_____ **JOHNNY MEEKS** – lead guitar repl. GALLUP **BOBBY LEE JONES** – bass repl. BILLY MACK who had repl. NEAL (PEEK was now relegated to clapper boy alongside TOMMY FACIENDA)

Sep 57.	(7",78) (CL 14763) <3763> **LOTTA LOVIN'. / WEAR MY RING**		13	Jul 57
Nov 57.	(7",78) (CL 14808) <3839> **DANCE TO THE BOP. / I GOT IT**		23	
Dec 57.	(lp) <(T 970)> **GENE VINCENT ROCKS AND THE BLUE CAPS ROLL**			

– Brand new beat / By the light of the silvery Moon / You'll never walk alone / Frankie and Johnny / In my dreams / Flea brain / Rollin' Dany / You belong to me / Your cheatin' heart / Time will bring you everything / Should I ever love again / It's no lie.

_____ briefly on tour **DUDE KAHN** – drums had repl. HARRELL until quick return. / added **MAX LIPSCOMB** – rhythm guitar, piano

58.	(7",78) (CL 14830) <3874> **I GOT A BABY. / WALKING HOME FROM SCHOOL WITH YOU**			

_____ **... SIMMONS** – piano + **GRADY OWEN** – drums repl. MAX, PAUL & ...MY

Apr 58.	(7") (CL 14868) <3959> **BABY BLUE. / TRUE TO YOU**		
1958.	(lp) <(T 1059)> **A GENE VINCENT RECORD DATE**		

– Five feet of lovin' / The wayward mind / Somebody help me / Keep it a secret / Hey good lookin' / Git it / Teenage partner / Peace of mind / Look what you gone and done to me / Summertime / I can't help it / I love you

_____ on tour **JUVEZ GOMEZ** – drums repl. HARRELL

_____ **BLUE CAPS:- HOWARD REED** – lead guitar / **BILL MACK** – bass / **MAX LIPSCOMB** – rhythm guitar / **CLIFF SIMMONS** – piano / **GRADY OWEN** – bass / **DUDE KAHN** – drums

Aug 58.	(7") (CL 14908) <4010> **ROCKY ROAD BLUES. / YES I LOVE YOU BABY**		

_____ (Sep58) **JOHNNY MEEKS** – lead guitar returned to repl. REED / **CLYDE PENNINGTON** – drums repl. KAHN and D.J.FONTANA. (sax – **JACKIE KELSO**)

Oct 58.	(7") (CL 14935) <4051> **GIT IT. / LITTLE LOVER**		
Oct 58.	(lp)<(T 1207)> **SOUNDS LIKE GENE VINCENT**		

–] My baby don't 'low / I can't believe you wanna leave / I might have known / In love again / You are the one for me / Ready Teddy / I got to you yet / Vincent's blues / Now is the hour / My heart / Maybelline.

Jan 59.	(7") (CL 14974) <4105> **SAY MAMA. / BE BOP BOOGIE BOY**		
Mar 59.	(7") (CL 15000) <4153> **WHO'S PUSHIN' YOUR SWING. / OVER THE RAINBOW**		
Jun 59.	(7") (CL 15035) <4213> **SUMMERTIME. / FRANKIE AND JOHNNY**		-

_____ The BLUE CAPS had already disbanded late 1958,

GENE VINCENT

now solo augmented by **JACKIE MERRITT** – guitar / **SANDY NELSON** – drums / **JACKIE KELSO** – sax

Aug 59.	(7") (CL 15053) <4237> **RIGHT NOW. / THE NIGHT IS LONELY**		
Dec 59.	(7") (CL 15099) <4313> **WILD CAT. / RIGHT HERE ON EARTH**	21	
Feb 60.	(7") (CL 15115) <7P 159> **MY HEART. / I'VE GOT TO GET TO YOU YET**	16	
May 60.	(7") (CL 15136) **PISTOL PACKIN' MAMA. / WEEPING WILLOW**	15	-
May 60.	(lp) <(T 1342)> **CRAZY TIMES**	12	Sep 59

– Crazy times / She she little Sheila / Darlene / Everybody's got a date but me / Why don't you people learn how to drive / Green back dollar / Big fat Saturday night / Mitchiko from Tokyo / Hot dollar / Accentuate the postive / Blue eyes crying in the rain / Pretty Pearly. (re-iss. +c.1970's on 'M.F.P.', re-iss. Oct87 on 'Tower')

Oct 60.	(7") <4442> **ANNA ANNABELLE. / PISTOL PACKIN' MAMA**	-	
Nov 60.	(7") (CL 15169) **ANNA ANNABELLE. / ACCENT-TCHUATE THE POSITIVE**		
Jan 61.	(7") (CL 15179) **JEZEBEL. / MAYBE**		-
Feb 61.	(7") (CL 15185) <4525> **IF YOU WANT LOVIN'. / MISTER LONELINESS**		
May 61.	(7") (CL 15202) **SHE SHE LITTLE SHEILA. / HOT DOLLAR**	22	Jul 60
Aug 61.	(7") (CL 15215) **I'M GOING HOME. / LOVE OF A MAN**	36	
Nov 61.	(7") (CL 15231) **BRAND NEW BEAT. / UNCHAINED MELODY**		
Mar 62.	(7") (CL 15243) **LUCKY STAR. / BABY DON'T BELIEVE HIM**		
Aug 62.	(7") (CL 15264) **KING OF FOOLS. / BE BOP A LULA 2 (with The CHARLES BLACKWELL ORCHESTRA)**		
Feb 63.	(7") (CL 15290) **HELD FOR QUESTIONING. / YOU'RE STILL IN MY HEART**		
Jul 63.	(7") (CL 15307) **CRAZY BEAT. / HIGH BLOOD PRESSURE**		
Aug 63.	(lp) <(T 20453)> **THE CRAZY BEAT OF GENE VINCENT**		

– Crazy beat / Important words / It's been nice / Lonesome boy / Good lovin' / I'm gonna catch me a rat / Rip it up / High blood pressure / That's the trouble with love / Weeping willow / Tear drops / Gone, gone, gone.
(re-iss. 1983 as 'CRAZY BEAT' on 'E.M.I.')

_____ now w / **TIM BATES** – guitar, vocals / **JOHN REECE** – bass, vocals / **JEM FIELD** – tenor sax, vocals / **ERIC BAKER** – keyboards / **VICTOR CLARK** – drums, percussion

		Columbia	Columbia
Nov 63.	(7") (DB 7174) **WHERE HAVE YOU BEEN ALL MY LIFE. / TEMPTATION BABY**		
Apr 64.	(7") (DB 7218) **HUMPITY DUMPITY. / LOVE 'EM LEAVE 'EM KINDA GUY**		
Jul 64.	(7") (DB 7293) **LA DEN LA DEN DA DA. / BEGINNING OF THE END**		
Sep 64.	(7") (DB 7343) **PRIVATE DETECTIVE. / YOU ARE MY SUNSHINE**		
Oct 64.	(lp) (33SX 1646) **SHAKIN' UP A STORM**		

– Hey-hey-hey-hey / Lavender blue / Private detective / Shimmy shammy shingle / Someday (you'll want me to want you) / Another Saturday night / Slippin' and slidin' / Long tall Sally / Send me some lovin' / Love love love / Good golly, miss Molly / Baby blue / Susie Q / You are my sunshine. (re-iss. +c.Jun83 as 'PLAYIN' UP A STORM' on 'E.M.I.')

		London	Challenge
Sep 66.	(7") (HLH 10079) **BIRD DOGGIN'. / AIN'T THAT MUCH TO DO**		
Dec 66.	(7") (HLH 10099) **LONELY STREET. / I'VE GOT MY EYES ON YOU**		
Sep 67.	(lp) (HAH 8333) **GENE VINCENT**		

– I've got my eyes on you / Ain't that too much / Bird doggin' / Love is a bird / Lonely street / Hurtin' for you baby / Poor man's prison / Born to be a rolling stone / Hi lili hi lo / I'm a lonesome fugitive. (re-iss. +c.Aug82 as 'BIRD-DOGGIN' on 'Bulldog')

1967.	(7") **BORN TO BE A ROLLING STONE. / HURTIN' FOR YOU BABY**	-	-
	(re-iss. later on 'Playground')		

		not iss.	Forever
1968.	(7") **STORY TO THE ROCKERS. / PICKIN' POPPIES**	-	

—— w / **MARS BONFIRE** – guitar / **GRANT JOHNSON** – keyboards / **RED RHODES** – steel guitar / **SKIP BATTIN** – bass / **JIM GORDON** – drums

	Dandelion	Elektra
1969. (7") *(S 4596)* **BE BOP A LULA '69. / RUBY BABY**	□	–
Jan 70. (7") *(S 4974)* **WHITE LIGHTNING. / SCARLET RIBBONS**	□	–
Jan 70. (lp) *(63754) <102>* **I'M BACK AND I'M PROUD**	□	–

– Rockin' Robin / In the pines / Be bop a lula / Rainbow at midnight / Black letter / White lightning / Sexy ways / Ruby baby / Lotta lovin' / Circle never broken / I heard that lonesome whistle / Scarlet ribbons. *(cd-iss. 1987 on 'Nightlife Communications') (cd-iss. Dec94 on 'See For Miles')*

—— now w/several musicians incl. **CHRIS DARROW**

	Kama Sutra	Kama Sutra
1970. (lp) *(2361009) <2019>* **IF ONLY YOU COULD SEE ME TODAY**	□	□

– Sunshine / I need woman's love / Slow times comin' / Danse Colinda / Geese / 500 miles / Listen to the music / If only you could see me today / A million shades of blue.

| Jan 70. (7") **SUNSHINE. / GEESE** | – | □ |
above was recorded with UK band KANSAS HOOK early in Oct'71.

| Nov 70. (7") *(2013 018)* **THE DAY THE WORLD TURNED BLUE. / HIGH OF LIFE** | | □ |
| Jan 71. (lp) *<(KSBS2027)>* **THE DAY THE WORLD TURNED BLUE** | | □ |

– How I love them old songs / High on life / North Carloina line / You can make it if you try / Our souls / Looking back / The day the world turned blue / Boppin' the blues / There is something on your mind / Oh lonesome me / The woman in black.

| Jan 71. (7") **THE DAY THE WORLD TURNED BLUE. / HOW I LOVE THEM OLD SONGS** | – | □ |

—— Sadly on the 12th Oct'71, GENE VINCENT died of a bleeding ulcer. He was just 36.

– compilations, others, etc. –

All below on 'Capitol' unless otherwise stated.

1958. (7"ep) *(EAP 1-985)* **HOT ROD GANG**
– Hot rod gang / Dance in the street / Baby blue / Lovely Loretta / Dance to the bop.

Nov 58. (7"ep) *(EAP 1-1059)* **A GENE VINCENT RECORD DATE No.1**
– Five feet of lovin' / The wayward wind / Somebody help me / Keep it a secret

Nov 58. (7"ep) *(EAP 2-1059)* **A GENE VINCENT RECORD DATE No.2**

Nov 58. (7"ep) *(EAP 3-1059)* **A GENE VINCENT RECORD DATE No.3**
– Look what you gone and done to me / Summertime / Peace of mind / I love you.

1960. (7"ep) **(CRAZY TIMES No.1)**
– If you want my lovin' / Hey good lookin' / Ain't she sweet / Hold me, hug me, rock me.

1960. (7"ep) **(CRAZY TIMES No.2)**
– Race with the Devil / Crazy legs / Yes I love you baby / Rocky road blues.

1960. (7"ep) **(CRAZY TIMES No.3)**
– True to you / She she Sheila / Little lover / Weeping willow.

1963. (7"ep) *(EAP 1-20453)* **THE CRAZY BEAT OF GENE VINCENT No.1**
– Crazy beat / Important words / It's been nice / Lonesome boy / Good lovin' / I'm gonna catch me a rat / Rip it up / High blood pressure / That's the trouble with love / Weeping willow / Teardrops / Gone, gone, gone.

1963. (7"ep) *(EAP 2-20453)* **THE CRAZY BEAT OF GENE VINCENT No.2**
– Good lovin' / Gonna catch me a rat / Rip it up / High blood pressure.

1963. (7"ep) *(EAP 3-20453)* **THE CRAZY BEAT OF GENE VINCENT No.3**
– That's the trouble with love / Weeping willow / Teardrops / Gone gone gone.

Oct 67. (lp) *(T 20957)* **THE BEST OF GENE VINCENT**		
May 68. (7") *(CL 15546)* **BE BOP A LULA. / SAY MAMA**		–
1969. (lp) *(ST 21144)* **THE BEST OF GENE VINCENT VOL.2**		
Feb 77. (7"m) *(CL 15906)* **SAY MAMA. / LOTTA LOVIN' / RACE WITH THE DEVIL**		
Feb 77. (lp/c) *(CAPTS/C 1001)* **GENE VINCENT GREATEST** *(re-iss. May82 on 'Fame')*		
Jul 77. (lp/c) *(ST/+C 11287)* **THE BOP JUST WON'T STOP 1956** *(re-iss. Jul82 on 'Magnum Force')*		
May 79. (lp/c) *(CAPS/+C 1028)* **GENE VINCENT GREATEST VOL.2**		
Apr 80. (lp/c) *(EST/TCEST 26223)* **THE GENE VINCENT SINGLES ALBUM**		
– (some cont.free 7"ep)
Jun 81. (7"m) *(CL 203)* **SHE SHE LITTLE SHEILA. / SAY MAMA / DANCE TO THE BOP**		–
1981. (lp) *(CGB 1007)* **THEIR FINEST YEARS 1956-58 (shared w / EDDIE COCHRAN)** *(re-iss. 1983)*		–
1983. (lp) *(2C 06886309)* **GENE SINGS VINCENT '56**		–
1983. (lp) *(2C 06886310)* **GENE SINGS VINCENT '57-'59**		–
1985. (lp) **ROCK'N'ROLL MASTERS**		–
Oct 85. (lp/c) *(EG 260760-/-4)* **THE BEST OF GENE VINCENT AND HIS BLUE CAPS**		
– Race with the Devil / Be-bop-a-lula / Woman love / I sure miss you / Crazy legs / Gonna back up baby / Who slapped John / Important words / Rollin' Dany / In my dreams / Baby blues '57 / Git it / Somebody help me / Summertime / Beautiful brown eyes / Say mama. *(cd-iss. Jul88)*
| Sep 86. (lp/cd) **THE SONGS OF THE JAMES DEAN ERA** | | |
| Aug 90. (6xcd-box) *(CDS 7945932)* **THE GENE VINCENT BOX SET** | | |
– (BE BOP A LULA / DANCE TO THE BOP / GIT IT / SAY MAMA / WILD CAT / KING OF . . .)
Jun 64. (lp) *Starline; ()* **THE KING OF FOOLS**		–
1972. (lp) *Starline; (SRS 5117)* **THE PIONEERS OF ROCK VOL.1**		–
1974. (lp) *Starline; (SRS 5177)* **THE PIONEERS OF ROCK VOL.4**		
1973. (4xlp-box) *Pathe Marconi France; ()* **THE STORY OF GENE VINCENT VOL.1 (1956-57), VOL.2 (1958), VOL.3 (1959) & VOL.4 (1960-62)**	–	–
Oct 73. (7") *Spark; (SRL 1091)* **STORY OF THE ROCKERS. / PICKIN' POPPIES**		–
Sep 74. (7"ep) *BBC; (BEEB 001)* **ROLL OVER BEETHOVEN. / SAY MAMA / BE BOP A LULA (all live from Johnny Walker's Radio 1 show 1971)**	–	–

Feb 80. (lp/c) *MFP; (MFP/TCMFP 50463)* **ROCK ON WITH GENE VINCENT**	□	–
Apr 86. (lp/c) *MFP; (MFP 415749-1/-4)* **GENE VINCENT: ROCK'N'ROLL GREATS**	□	
Jan 81. (7"ep) *Magnum Force; (MFEP 003)* **RAINY DAY SUNSHINE / GREEN GRASS. / MISTER LOVE / ROLL OVER BEETHOVEN**		–
Nov 82. (m-lp) *Magnum Force; (MFLP 016)* **DRESSED IN BLACK**	□	–
Nov 83. (lp) *Magnum Force; (MFLP 1023)* **FROM L.A. TO FRISCO**	□	–
Jun 84. (lp) *Magnum Force; (MFM 020)* **FOR THE COLLECTOR'S ONLY** (live + interviews)	□	
1988. (lp) *Magnum Force; (MFM 027)* **LONESOME FUGITIVE**	□	–
1983. (lp) *EMI; (IC 06485997)* **20 ROCK'N'ROLL HITS**	□	
1983. (lp) *EMI; (2C 15681001-2)* **GENE VINCENT MEMORIAL ALBUM**	□	
1983. (lp) *EMI; (2C 15485071-4)* **ROCK'N'ROLL LEGENDS**	□	
Sep 90. (6xcd-box) *EMI; (CDGV 1)* **THE GENE VINCENT BOXED SET**	□	
1984. (lp/c) *Premier; (CBR/KCBR 1006)* **AIN'T THAT TOO MUCH**	□	
Jan 85. (c) *Topline; (KTOP 122)* **BORN TO BE A ROLLING STONE** *(re-iss. lp+cd.Apr87)*	□	
Apr 86. (lp/c) *Castle; (SH LP/TC 122)* **BABY BLUE**	□	
Jul 87. (12"ep) *Nighttracks; (SFNT 001)* **THE LAST SESSION**	□	
Oct 87. (lp) *Demand; (DEMAND 0045)* **SINGS SONGS FROM THE HOT ROD GANG**	□	
Nov 87. (9xlp-box; w/ 12"ep) *Charly; (BOX 108)* **THE CAPITOL YEARS**	□	
Nov 87. (pic-lp) *Exclusive; (AR 30076)* **THE ABC OF ROCK**	□	
Jul 88. (lp/c/cd) *See For Miles; (SEE/+K/+CD 233)* **INTO THE SEVENTIES**	□	–
May 89. (lp/c/cd) *See For Miles; (SEE/+K/+CD 253)* **THE EP COLLECTION**	□	–
1985. (lp) *Rockstar; (RSRLP 1007)* **CRUISIN' WITH GENE VINCENT**	□	
Nov 89. (mail order-lp) *Rockstar; (RSRLP 1020)* **IMPORTANT WORDS**	□	
1989. (cd) *Object; ()* **BE BOP A LULA**	□	
1990. (cd/c/lp) *Capitol;* **GENE VINCENT: COLLECTORS SERIES**	□	
1992. (cd) *Entertainers; (ENTCD 260)* **HIS 30 ORIGINAL HITS**	□	
Nov 92. (cd) *Magnum Force; (CDMF 087)* **REBEL HEART VOL.1**	□	
Apr 95. (cd) *Magnum Force; (CDMF 093)* **REBEL HEART VOL.2**	□	
Apr 96. (cd) *Magnum Force; (CDMF 096)* **REBEL HEART VOL.3**	□	
Mar 97. (cd) *Magnum Force; (CDMF 097)* **REBEL HEART VOL.4**	□	
Feb 97. (cd) *Razor & Tie; <(RE 2123)>* **THE SCREAMING END: THE BEST OF GENE VINCENT**	□	Jan97
Jun 94. (cd) *Rockhouse;* **GENE'S ON THE JUKEBOX**	□	
Aug 94. (cd) *Dynamite; (LECD 038)* **GENE VINCENT**	□	
Aug 97. (cd) *EMI; (DORIG 124)* **SHAKIN' UP A STORM**	□	

VIOLENT FEMMES (dig out; 4th edition or Great Alt & Indie . . .)

VIRGIN PRUNES / Gavin FRIDAY (dig out; Great Alt & Indie . . .)

VIVA SATURN (see under ⇒ RAIN PARADE)

VIXEN (dig out; Great Metal . . .)

VOICE OF THE BEEHIVE (dig out; Great Alt & Indie . . .)

V-TWIN (see under ⇒ BELLE & SEBASTIAN)

WAH! (dig out; Great Alt & Indie . . .)

WAILERS (see under ⇒ MARLEY, Bob)

Loudon WAINWRIGHT III

Born: 5 Sep '46, Chapel Hill, North Carolina, USA. The son of a journalist, WAINWRIGHT served his musical apprenticeship on the US college and folk-club circuit following in the footsteps of BOB DYLAN and JOAN BAEZ. The budding singer/songwriter (hailed as the new DYLAN and later as the Woody Allen of folk, the Charlie Chaplin of rock and the male MELANIE!) hitched to San Francisco in 1967 and signed to 'Atlantic' two years later, soon becoming publicly recognised. After moving to 'Columbia' in 1973, he scored a US Top 20 hit with the novelty song, 'DEAD SKUNK' (which allegedly took 15 minutes to write), lifted from the helpfully titled 'ALBUM III'. His subsequent efforts, 'ATTEMPTED MOUSTACHE' and 'UNREQUITED', failed to consolidate his position, although the former contained some excellent material including 'SWIMMING SONG'. After an unsuccessful move to 'Arista', WAINWRIGHT relocated to London and spent five years on 'Demon/Rounder', sometimes augmented by RICHARD THOMPSON on albums such as 'FAME AND WEALTH', 'I'M ALRIGHT' and 'MORE LOVE SONGS'. Although still critically lauded, these albums were met with diminishing commercial returns; while WAINWRIGHT was admittedly not the greatest of singers, his inimitable comic satire usually compensated. Continuing to release fine material into the 90's, WAINWRIGHT's last effort to date was the 1995 set, 'GROWN MAN', featuring the hilarious 'IWIWAL (I WISH I WAS A LESBIAN)' which almost equalled his hit 'DEAD SKUNK' (this one took him eight! minutes to write) for deadpan humour. • **Trivia:** In the mid-70's, he appeared on a couple of TV episodes of comedy Korean War series, 'M.A.S.H.'. WAINWRIGHT resurrected an intended acting career in the 80's by appearing in stage productions, 'Pump Boys & Dinettes' and 'Owners'. In '88, he featured in the film, 'Jacknife'.

Album rating: LOUDON WAINWRIGHT III (*6) / ALBUM II (*6) / ALBUM III (*6) / ATTEMPTED MOUSTACHE (*5) / UNREQUITED (*5) / T-SHIRT (*4) / FINAL EXAM (*4) / A LIVE ONE (*7) / FAME AND WEALTH (*6) / I'M ALRIGHT (*6) / MORE LOVE SONGS (*6) / THERAPY (*6) / HISTORY (*6) / CAREER MOVES (*6) / GROWN MAN (*6) / LITTLE SHIP (*5)

LOUDON WAINWRIGHT III – vocals, acoustic guitar

		Atlantic	Atlantic
May 71.	(lp) (2400 103) <8260> **LOUDON WAINWRIGHT III**		Nov70

– School days / Hospital lady / Ode to a Pittsburgh / Glad to see you've got religion / Uptown / Black Uncle Remus / Four is a magic number / I don't care / Central Square song / Movies are a mother to me / Bruno's place. (re-iss. 1972; K 40107)

Sep 71. (lp) (2400 142) <8291> **ALBUM II**

– Me and my friend the cat / Motel blues / Nice Jewish girls / Be careful / Plane too / Cook that diner, Dora / There's a baby in the house / I know I'm unhappy / Suicide song / Glenville reel / Saw your name in the paper / Samson and the warden / Plane, too / Cook that diner, Dora / Old friend / Old paint / Winter song. (re-iss. 1974; K 40272) (re-iss. May89 on 'Edsel'; ED 310)

—— added **RICHARD CROOKS** – drums / to session people from last album.

		C.B.S.	Columbia
Jan 73.	(lp) (CBS 65238) <31462> **ALBUM III**		

– Dead skunk / Red guitar / East Indian princess / Muse blues / Hometeam crowd / B side / Needless to say / Smokey Joe's cafe / New paint / Trilogy (circa 1967) / Drinking song / Say that you love me. (re-iss. Dec85 on 'Edsel' lp/c; ED/CED 168) (cd-iss. Feb91; EDCD 168)

Jan 73.	(7") (CBS 1120) <45726> **DEAD SKUNK. / NEEDLESS TO SAY**		16 Jan73
	(7") <45849> **SAY THAT YOU LOVE ME. / NEW PAINT**	-	
	(lp) (CBS 65837) <32710> **ATTEMPTED MOUSTACHE**		

– The swimming song / A.M. world / Bell bottom pants / Liza / I am the way / [...]work chartreuse / Down drinking at the bar / The man who couldn't cry / Come

a long way / Nocturnal stumblebutt / Dialated to meet you / Lullaby. (re-iss. May88 on 'Edsel'; ED 269)

May 74.	(7") (CBS 2172) <45949> **DOWN DRINKING AT THE BAR. / I AM THE WAY**		
Jul 74.	(7") <46064> **THE SWIMMING SONG. / BELL BOTTOM PANTS**	-	
Mar 75.	(lp) (CBS 80696) <33369> **UNREQUITED**		

– Sweet nothings / The lowly tourist / Kings and queens / Kick in the head / Whatever happened to us / Crime of passion / Absence makes the heart grow fonder / On the rocks / Guru / Mr. Guilty / Untitled (aka The Hardy boys at the Y) / Unrequited to the Nth degree / Old friends / Rufus is a tit man. (re-iss. May88 on 'Edsel'; ED 273) (cd-iss. Mar91; EDCD 273)

—— Now with band: **ELLIOTT RANDALL** – guitar / **RICHARD DAVIS** – bass / **R.CROOKS / ERIC WEISSBERG** – banjo / **STEPHEN TUBIN + GLEN MITCHELL** – keyboards / etc.

		Arista	Arista
Apr 76.	(7") (ARIST 53) <0174> **BICENTENNIAL (SUMMER'S ALMOST OVER). / TALKING THE BIG APPLE '75**		
Jun 76.	(lp) (ARTY 127) <4063> **T-SHIRT**		

– Bicentennial / Summer's almost over / Hollywood hopeful / Reciprocity / At both ends / Wine with dinner / Hey Packy / California prison blues / Talking big apple / Prince Hal's dirge / Just like President Thieu.

Apr 78.	(lp) (SPART 1042) <4173> **FINAL EXAM**		

– Final exam / Mr.Guilty / Pen pal blues / Golfin' blues / The heckler / Natural disaster / Fear with flying / Heaven and mud / Two-song set / Pretty little Martha / Watch me rock I'm over thirty.

May 78.	(7") <0340> **FINAL EXAM. /**	-	

—— Next featured singing trio The ROCHES.

		Radar	Rounder
Sep 79.	(lp) (RAD 24) <ROUNDER 3050> **A LIVE ONE** (live)		

– Motel blues / Hollywood hopeful / Whatever happened to us? / Natural disaster / Suicide song / School days / Kings and queens / Down drinking at the bar / B-side / Nocturnal stumblebutt / Red guitar / Clockwork chartreuse / Lullaby. (re-iss. Jun87 on 'Edsel' lp/c; ED/CED 223) <US re-iss. Aug88; same> <US cd-iss. Aug88; CD 3050> (cd-iss. Jul92 on 'Demon';)

		Demon	Rounder
Apr 83.	(lp) (FIEND 5) <ROUNDER 3076> **FAME AND WEALTH**		

– Reader and advisor / The Grammy song / Dump the dog / Thick and thin / Revenge / Five years old / Ingenue / Idttywim / Westchester County / Saturday morning fever / April Fools Day morn / Fame and wealth. <US re-iss. Aug88; same> <cd-iss. Aug88; CD 3076>

Apr 83.	(7") (D 1016) **FIVE YEARS OLD. / RAMBUNCTIOUS**		

—— Now collaborated with **RICHARD THOMPSON** – producer, guitar

Jul 85.	(7") (D 1039) **CARDBOARD BOXES. / COLOURS**		
Sep 85.	(lp) (FIEND 54) <ROUNDER 3096> **I'M ALRIGHT**		

– One man guy / Lost love / I'm alright / Not John / Cardboard boxes / Screaming issue / How old are you? / Animal song / Out of this world / Daddy take a nap / Ready or not (so ripe) / Career moves. <US re-iss. Aug88; same> <cd-iss. Aug88; CD 3096>

Aug 86.	(7") (D 1044) **UNHAPPY ANNIVERSARY. / THE ACID SONG**		
Sep 86.	(lp/c/cd) (FIEND/+CASS/CD 79) <ROUNDER 3106/+C/CD> **MORE LOVE SONGS**		

– Hard day on the Planet / Synchronicity / Your mother and I / I eat out / No / The home stretch / Unhappy anniversary / Man's world / Vampire blues / Overseas calls / Expatriot / The back nine. (cd+=) – The acid song.

Sep 87.	(7") (D 1051) **YOUR MOTHER AND I. / AT THE END OF A LONG LONELY DAY**		

		Silvertone	Silvertone
May 89.	(lp/c/cd) (ORE LP/C/CD 500) **THERAPY**		

– Therapy / Bill of goods / T.S.D.H.A.V. (This Song Don't Have A Video) / Harry's wall / Aphrodisiac / Fly paper / Nice guys / Thanksgiving / Your father's car / Me and all the other mothers / You don't want to know / Mind read (it belonged to you) / This year.

Sep 89.	(7") (ORE 15) **T.S.D.H.A.V. (THIS SONG DON'T HAVE A VIDEO). / NICE GUYS**		

—— with **CHAIM TANNENBAUM** – banjo, harmonica / **DAVID MANSFIELD** – fiddle, mandolin

		Virgin	Charisma
Sep 92.	(cd/c/lp) (CD/TC+/V 2703) **HISTORY**		

– People in love / Men / The picture / When I'm at your house / The doctor / Hitting you / I'd rather be lonely / Between / Talking new Bob Dylan / So many songs / 4 x 10 / A father and a son / Sometimes I forget / Handful of dust.

Jul 93.	(cd/c) (CD/TC 2718) **CAREER MOVES** (live)		

– Road ode / I'm alright / Five years old / Your mother and I / Westchester County / He said, she said / Christmas rap / Suddenly it's Christmas / Thanksgiving / A fine Celtic name / T.S.M.N.W.A. / some balding guys / The swimming song / Absence makes the heart grow fonder / Happy birthday Elvis / Unhappy anniversary / I'd rather be lonely / Just say no / April fool's Day morn / The man who couldn't cry / The acid song / Tip that waitress / Career moves.

Oct 95.	(cd/c) (CD/TC 2789) **GROWN MAN**		

– The birthday present / That hospital / Housework / Cobwebs / A year / Father / Father – daughter dialogue / 1994 / Iwiwal / Just a John / I suppose / Dreaming / The end has begun / Human cannonball / Treasure untold.

Oct 97.	(cd) (CDV 2844) **LITTLE SHIP**		

– Breakfast in bed / Four mirrors / Mr. Ambivalent / O.G.M. / Our own war / So damn happy / Primrose hill / Underwear / World /What are families for / Bein' a dad / Birthday present / I can't stand myself / Little ship / Song.

– compilations, etc. –

Jan 92.	(cd) Demon; (FIENDCD 711) **FAME & WEALTH / I'M ALRIGHT**		-
Jul 94.	(cd/c) Music Club; (MC CD/TC 166) **ONE MAN GUY (THE BEST OF LOUDON WAINWRIGHT III (1983-1986)**		-

Tom WAITS

Born: 7 Dec'49, Pomona, California, USA. Signed to 'Asylum' in 1973, after being spotted at the Troubadour club. His debut album 'CLOSING TIME' produced by Jerry Yester (ex-LOVIN' SPOONFUL), didn't sell greatly, but it did contain 'OL '55' which was soon covered by The EAGLES on their album 'On The Border'. 'THE HEART OF SATURDAY NIGHT' (1974) was more proficient, his downtrodden JACK KEROUAC meets CHARLES BUKOWSKI persona beginning to develop. With his distinctive Billy Goat Gruff vocals he sounded frighteningly like he'd been drinking industrial strength paint stripper since childhood. A born raconteur, his sharply observed tales of American lowlife were set against a musical backdrop of smokey blues and jazz stylings. The live album 'NIGHTHAWKS AT THE DINER' (1975) was WAITS in his element, reeling off wry vignettes with casual ease. 'SMALL CHANGE' (1976) was a confident step forward, his booze-sodden recollections more focused and his songwriting more complex on tracks like 'TOM TRAUBERT'S BLUES'. He even attempted to cultivate his parched vocals on 'FOREIGN AFFAIR' (1977), duetting with BETTE MIDLER for 'I NEVER TALK TO STRANGERS'. With 'BLUE VALENTINE' (1978) and 'HEARTATTACK AND VINE' (1980), WAITS opted for a combination of supple R&B tracks and heartbroken love ballads, the latter set spawning the haunting 'JERSEY GIRL' which was later covered by BRUCE SPRINGSTEEN. This was the end of an era for the maverick singer/songwriter as he signed to ISLAND and employed a more experimental strategy. The gloriously titled 'SWORDFISHTROMBONES' (1983) introduced the new WAITS sound, a surrealistic cut up of mutant jazz, skewed rhythms, jarring guitar and wildly inspired lyrics. 'RAIN DOGS' (1985) advanced this formula, again employing an array of session musicians to realise his eccentric musical vision. Adapted from a song on 'SWORDFISHTROMBONES', 'FRANK'S WILD YEARS' (1987) was the soundtrack to a musical stage show that included the brilliant horn-driven weirdness of 'HANG ON ST. CHRISTOPHER'. 'BIG TIME' (1988) was similar in tone, taking material from all his 'Island' recordings to date. With a string of acting credits already behind him as well as 1983's 'ONE FROM THE HEART' soundtrack, he scored JIM JARMUSCH'S 'NIGHT ON EARTH' in 1992. His next album proper was 'BONE MACHINE', released later the same year. The title was apt, a stark collection of minimalistic clankings and dark, muted musings. 'BLACK RIDER' (1993) held the musical fruits of a collaboration between director ROBERT WILSON and uber-Beat poet WILLIAM BURROUGHS. It was six long years before WAITS returned to the fold, the 'Epitaph' label (more identified with today's hardcore/punk scene) astonishingly taking up the reins for his marvellous comeback set, 'MULE VARIATIONS' (1999); if his gruff vox could be singled out as one type of music, it would indeed be "hard core". Now over fifty years of age (and looking every part of it!), WAITS had his first UK Top 10 success with 'MULE . . .', and even more importantly, his debut into the American Top 30. WAITS is an artist with defiantly singular vision and is a rare commodity in a marketplace where so often the blind lead the blind in a musical wild goose chase for the next trend. • **Songwriters:** Pens own songs except; WHAT KEEPS MAN ALIVE (Kurt Weill) / HEIGH-HO (from 'Snow White') / IT'S ALL RIGHT WITH ME (Cole Porter). From 1987, his material was co-written with wife and Irish playwright Kathleen Brennan, whom he married on the 31st December '81. • **Filmography:** PARADISE ALLEY (bit-part 1978) / WOLFEN (cameo 1979) / STONE BOY (cameo 1980) / ONE FROM THE HEART (1981 cameo + soundtrack) / THE OUTSIDERS (1983) / RUMBLEFISH (1983) / THE COTTON CLUB (1984 cameo) / DOWN BY LAW (1986) / IRONWEED (1988) / COLD FEET (1989) / SHORT CUTS (1993) / THE FISHER KING (1990). • **Trivia:** In the late 70's, he parted company with girlfriend/singer RICKIE LEE JONES. In 1991, he sued a radio ad company for using a soundalike in a chips commercial and won nearly $2.5 million.

Album rating: CLOSING TIME (*7) / THE HEART OF SATURDAY NIGHT (*6) / NIGHTHAWKS AT THE DINER (*6) / SMALL CHANGE (*8) / FOREIGN AFFAIRS (*6) / BLUE VALENTINE (*6) / HEARTATTACK AND VINE (*7) / BOUNCED CHECKS compilation (*6) / ONE FROM THE HEART soundtrack with Crystal Gayle (*6) / SWORDFISHTROMBONES (*9) / THE ASYLUM YEARS compilation (*8) / RAIN DOGS (*9) / FRANKS WILD YEARS soundtrack (*7) / BIG TIME (*7) / NIGHT ON EARTH soundtrack (*5) / BONE MACHINE (*8) / THE BLACK RIDER (*5) / BEAUTIFUL MALADIES – THE ISLAND YEARS compilation (*8) / MULE VARIATIONS (*7)

TOM WAITS – vocals, piano, accordion

		Asylum	Elektra
May 73.	(lp) (SYL 9007) <SD 5061> **CLOSING TIME**	☐	☐

– Ol' 55 / I hope that I don't fall in love with you / Virginia Ave/ Old shoes (and picture postcards) / Midnight lullaby / Martha / Rosie / Lonely / Ice cream man / Little trip to Heaven (on the wings of your love) / Grapefruit moon / Closing time. (cd-iss. Jun76; K 53030) (re-iss. Feb93 on 'WEA'; 960836-2)

| May 73. | (7") **OL '55. / MIDNIGHT LULLABY** | - | ☐ |
| Jan 74. | (lp) (K 53035) <7E 1015> **THE HEART OF SATURDAY NIGHT** | ☐ | ☐ |

– New coat of paint / San Diego serenade / Semi suite / Shiver me timbers / Diamonds on my windshield / (Looking for) The heart of Saturday night / Fumblin' with the blues / Please call me baby / Depot, depot / Drunk on the Moon / The ghosts of Saturday night (after hours at Napoleon's pizza house). (re-iss. Jun76; same) (cd-iss. 1989 on 'WEA'; 960 597-2)

Mar 74.	(7") <45213> **DIAMONDS ON MY WINDSHIELD. / SAN DIEGO SERENADE**	-	☐
Jun 75.	(7") <45233> **NEW COAT OF PAINT. / BLUE SKIES**	-	☐
Oct 75.	(7") <45262> **(LOOKING FOR) THE HEART OF SATURDAY NIGHT. / DIAMONDS ON MY WINDSHIELD**	-	☐

—— with **MIKE MELVOIN** – piano / **JIM HUGHART** – bass / **BILL GOODWIN** – drums

| Dec 75. | (d-lp) (SYSP 903) <7E 2008> **NIGHTHAWKS AT THE DINER (live)** | ☐ | ☐ Oct75 |

– (opening intro) / Emotional weather report / (intro) / On a foggy night / (intro) / Eggs and sausage / (intro) / Better off without a wife / Nighthawk postcards (from Easy street) / (intro) / Warm beer and cold women / (intro) / Puttnam County / Spare parts 1 (a nocturnal emission) / Nobody / (intro) / Big Joe and Phantom 309 / Spare parts 2 and closing. (re-iss. Jun76; K 63002) (cd-iss. 1989 on 'WEA'; 960 620-2)

—— retained **HUGHART** + new **SHELLY MANNE** – drums / **LEW TABACKIN** – tenor sax

| Nov 76. | (7") <45371> **STEP RIGHT UP. / THE PIANO HAS BEEN DRINKING (NOT ME)** | - | ☐ |
| May 77. | (lp) (K 52050) <7E 1078> **SMALL CHANGE** | **89** Nov 76 | |

– Tom Traubert's blues / Step right up / Jitterbug boy / I wish I was in New Orleans / The piano has been drinking (not me) / Invitation to the blues / Pasties and a g-string / Bad liver and a broken heart / The one that got away / Small change / I can't wait to get off work. (cd-iss. 1989 on 'WEA'; 960 612-2)

—— **FRANK VICARI** – tenor sax / **JACK SHELDON** – trumpet repl. TABACKIN

| Oct 77. | (lp) (K 53068) <7E 1117> **FOREIGN AFFAIRS** | ☐ | ☐ |

– Cinny's waltz / Muriel / I never talk to strangers / Jack and Neal – California here I come / A sight for sore eyes / Potter's field / Burma shave / Barber shop / Foreign affair. (cd-iss. Mar95 on 'WEA'; 7559 60618-2)

—— **RICK LAWSON** – drums repl. MANNE / added **ROLAND BAUTISTA** + **RAY CRAWFORD** – guitar / **BYRON MILLER** – bass / **DA WILLIE CONGA** – piano / **HAROLD BATTISTE** – piano

| Apr 79. | (7") <45539> **SOMEWHERE. / RED SHOES BY THE DRUGSTORE** | - | ☐ |
| Aug 79. | (lp) (K 53088) <6E 162> **BLUE VALENTINE** | ☐ | ☐ |

– Somewhere / Red shoes by the drugstore / Christmas card from a hooker in Minneapolis / Romeo is bleeding / Wrong side of the road / Whistlin' past the graveyard / Kentucky avenue / A sweet little bullet from a pretty blue gun / Blue valentines. (cd-iss. Feb93; 7559 60533-2)

—— retained **HUGHART** + **BAUTISTA** + new **LARRY TAYLOR** – upright bass / **RONNIE BARRON** – organ / **GREG COHEN** – bass / **PLAS JOHNSON** – sax / **BIG JOHN THOMASSIE** – drums

| Oct 80. | (lp/c) (K/K4 52252) <6E 295> **HEARTATTACK AND VINE** | ☐ | **96** |

– Saving all my love for you / On the nickel / In shades / Downtown / Jersey girl / Til the money runs out / Mr. Segal / Ruby's arms. (cd-iss. 1989 on 'WEA') (re-iss. cd May93; 7559 60547-2)

| Dec 80. | (7") <47077> **JERSEY GIRL. / HEARTATTACK AND VINE** | - | ☐ |
| Nov 81. | (lp/c) (K/K4 52316) **BOUNCED CHECKS** (compilation, some live) | ☐ | - |

– Heartattack and vine / Jersey girl / Eggs and sausage / I never talk to strangers / The piano has been drinking (not me) / Whistlin' past the graveyard / Mr. Henry / Diamonds on my windshield / Burma shave / Tom Traubert's blues.

—— now with many session people from above incl. **VICTOR FELDMAN** – percussion

		C.B.S.	Columbia
Feb 83.	(lp; TOM WAITS & CTYSTAL GAYLE) (70215) <37703> **ONE FROM THE HEART** (Film Soundtrack)	☐	☐

– (opening montage): Tom's piano intro – Once upon a town – The wages of love / Is there any way out of this dream / Picking up after you / Old boyfriends / Broken bicycles / I beg your pardon / Little boy blue / (instrumental montage): The tango – Circus girl / You can't unring a bell / This one's from the heart / Take me home / Presents / (others by CRYSTAL GAYLE only). (cd-iss. Jan91)

—— **FRED TACKETT** – guitar + **STEPHEN TAYLOR HODGES** – drums repl. BAUTISTA + LAWSON / added **FRANCIS THUMM** – pump organ / **RANDY ALDCROFT** – horns

		Island	Island
Sep 83.	(lp/c) (ILPS/ICM 9762) <90095> **SWORDFISHTROMBONES**	**62**	☐

– Underground / Shore leave / Dave the butcher / Johnsburg, Illinois / 16 shells from a thirty-ought-six / Town with no cheer / In the neighbourhood / Just another sucker on the vine / Frank's wild years / Swordfishtrombones / Down, down, down / Soldier's things / Gin soaked boy / Trouble's braids / Rainbirds. (re-iss. Sep86 lp/c; same) (cd-iss. Nov87; CID 9762) (re-iss. cd Jun89; IMCD 48) (re-iss. lp Jan94 + May94; ILPM 9762)

| Oct 83. | (7") (IS 141) **IN THE NEIGHBOURHOOD. / FRANK'S WILD YEARS** | ☐ | ☐ |

—— **MARC RIBOT** – guitar + **MICHAEL BLAIR** – drums, percussion repl. TACKETT, THUMM + HODGES / **WILLIAM SCHIMMEL** – accordion / **RAPLH CARNEY** – sax, clarinet + **BOB FUNK** – trombone repl. FELDMAN + ALDCROFT

| Oct 85. | (lp/c)(cd) (ILPS/ICT 9803)(CID 131) <90299> **RAIN DOGS** | **29** | ☐ |

– Singapore / Clap hands / Cemetery polka / Jockey full of bourbon / Tango till they're sore / Big black Mariah / Diamonds and gold / Hang down your head / Time / Rain dogs / Midtown / Ninth and headpin / Gun Street girl / Union square / Blind love / Walking Spanish / Downtown train / Bride of Rain dog / Anywhere I lay my head. (re-iss. cd.Aug89 & Apr91; IMCD 49)

| Nov 85. | (7"/12") (IS/12IS 253) **DOWNTOWN TRAIN. / TANGO 'TILL THEY'RE SORE** | ☐ | ☐ |
| Feb 86. | (7") (IS 260) **IN THE NEIGHBOURHOOD. / SINGAPORE** | ☐ | ☐ |

(d7"+=) (ISD 260) – Tango till they're sore (live) / Rain dogs (live).
(12") (12IS 260) – ('A'side) / Jockey full of bourbon / Tango till they're sore (live) / 16 shells from a thirty-ought-six (live).

—— Past live group **FRED TACKETT** – guitar / **RICHIE HAYWARD** – drums / **LARRY TAYLOR** – upright bass. Retained only **TAYLOR, CARNEY, SCHIMMEL** / new: **MORRIS TEPPER** – guitar / **FRANCIS THUMM** – pump organ (on some) / guest **DAVID HIDALGO** – accordion

| Aug 87. | (lp/c/cd) (ITW/+C/CD 3) <90572> **FRANKS WILD YEARS** (soundtrack) | **20** | ☐ |

– Hang on St. Christopher / Straight to the top (rhumba) / Blow wind blow / Temptation / Innocent when you dream (barroom) / I'll be gone / I'll take New York / Telephone call from Istanbul / Cold cold ground / Train song / Yesterday is here / Please wake me up / Frank's theme / More than rain / Way down in the hole / Straight to the top (Vegas). (re-iss. cd.Jun89 & Apr91; IMCD 50)

—— 1988 live band **WILLIE SCHWARZ** – keyboards, accordion repl. SCHIMMEL TEPPER

| Sep 88. | (lp/c/cd) (ITW/+C/CD 4) <90987> **BIG TIME** (live) | **84** | ☐ |

– 16 shells from a thirty-ought-six / Red shoes / Cold cold ground / Wav the hole / Falling down / Strange weather / Big black Mariah / Rain (song / Telephone call from Istanbul / Gun street girl / Time. (cd+=) – I

Straight to the top / Yesterday is here / Johnsburg, Illinois / Ruby's arms / Clap hands. *(cd-iss. Mar97; IMCD 249)*

Sep 88. (7") *(IS 370)* **16 SHELLS FROM A THIRTY-OUGHT-SIX (live). / BIG BLACK MARIAH (live)**
(12"+=) *(12IS 370)* – Ruby's arms (live).

May 92. (cd/c) *(510929-2/-4)* **NIGHT ON EARTH (soundtrack)**
– Back in the good old world / Los Angeles mood (chromium descentions) / Los Angeles theme (another private dick) / New York theme (hey, you can have that heart attack outside, buddy) / New York mood (a new haircut and a busted lip) / Baby, I'm not a baby anymore (Beatrice theme) / Good old world (waltz) / Carnival (Brunello del Montalcino) / On the old side of the world (vocal) / Good old world (gypsy instrumental) / Paris mood (un de fromage) / Dragging a dead priest / Helsinki mood / Carnival Bob's confession / Good old world (waltz vocal) / On the other side of the world (instrumental).

Aug 92. (7") **GOIN' OUT WEST. / A LITTLE RAIN**
(10"+=/cd-s+=) – The ocean doesn't want me / Back in the good old world (gypsy).

Sep 92. (cd/c/lp) *(CID/ICT/ILPS 9993)* <*512580*> **BONE MACHINE** `26`
– Earth died screaming / Dirt in the ground / Such a scream / All stripped down / Who are you / The ocean doesn't want me / Jesus gonna behave / A little rain / In the Colosseum / Goin' out west / Murder in the red barn / Black wings / Whistle down the wind / I don't wanna grow up / Let me get up on it / That feel.

Nov 93. (cd/c/lp) *(CID/ICT/ILPS 8021)* <*518559*> **THE BLACK RIDER** `47`
– Lucky day overture / The black rider / November / Just the right bullets / Black box theme / 'T ain't no sin / Flash pan hunter intro / That's the way / The briar and the rose / Russian dance / Gospel train-orchestra / I'll shoot the Moon / Flash pan hunter / Crossroads / Gospel train / Interlude / Oily night / Lucky day / The last rose of summer / Carnival.

——— 3 of above tracks were co-written with author WILLIAM S. BURROUGHS

Apr 99. (cd/c/lp) <*(8 6547-2/-4/-1)*> **MULE VARIATIONS** `Epitaph 9` `Epitaph 30`
– Big in Japan / Lowside of the road / Hold on / Get behind the mule / House where nobody lives / Cold water / Pony / What's he building? / Black market baby / Eyeball kid / Picture in a frame / Chocolate Jesus / Georgia Lee / Filipino box spring hog / Take it with me / Come on up to the house.

Jun 99. (cd-s) *(1020-2)* **HOLD ON / BIG IN JAPAN / FLEDDERJON**

– compilations, etc. –

Apr 84. (d-lp/c) *Asylum; (960 321-1/-4)* **THE ASYLUM YEARS**
– Diamonds on my windshield / (Looking for) The heart of Saturday night / Martha / The ghosts of Saturday night / Grapefruit Moon / Small change / Burma slave / I never talk to strangers / Tom Traubert's blues / Blue valentine / Potter's field / Kentucky avenue / Somewhere / Ruby's arms. *(cd-iss. Oct86; 960 494-2)* – (omitted 9 tracks but added 3 others).

Jul 91. (cd/c/lp) *Edsel; (ED/C+/ED 332)* **THE EARLY YEARS (rare & demos)** `-`
– Goin' down slow / Poncho's lament / I'm your late night evening prostitute / Had me a girl / Ice cream man / Rockin' chair / Virginia Ave. / Midnight lullaboy / When you ain't got nobody / Little trip to Heaven / Frank's song / Looks like I'm up shit creek again / So long I'll see you. *(re-iss. Feb97 & Mar98 on 'Manifesto'; PT 340601)*

Nov 92. (d-cd) *Island; (ITSCD 5)* **SWORDFISHTROMBONES / RAIN DOGS**

Feb 93. (cd/c) *Edsel; (ED CD/MC 371)* **THE EARLY YEARS VOL.2** `-`
– Hope I don't fall in love with you / Ol' 55 / Mockin bird / In between love / Blue skies / Nobody / I want you / Shiver me timbers / Grapefruit moon / Diamonds on my windshield / Please call me, baby / So it goes / Old shoes. *(re-iss. Feb97 & Mar98 on 'Manifesto'; PT 340602)*

Mar 93. (7"/c-s) *Asylum;* **HEARTATTACK AND VINE. / BLUE VALENTINES**
(cd-s+=) – On a foggy night (live) / Intro to a foggy night (live).

Jun 98. (d-cd) *Island; (524 519-2)* **BEAUTIFUL MALADIES – THE ISLAND YEARS** `63`
– Hang on St. Christopher / Temptation / Clap hands / The black rider / Underground / Jockey full of bourbon / Earth died screaming / Innocent when you dream (78) / Straight to the top / Frank's wild years / Singapore / Shore leave / Johnsburg, Illinois / Way down in the hole / Strange weather (live) / Cold, cold ground (live) / November / Downtrain train / 16 shells from a thirty-ought six / Jesus gonna be here / Good old world (waltz) / I don't wanna grow up / Time.

Rick WAKEMAN

Born: 18 May'49, Perivale, Middlesex, England. Aged 16, he attended The Royal College of Music, although interest in playing live and doing sessions led to him dropping out. His in-demand pop session work (i.e. WHITE PLAINS, EDISON LIGHTHOUSE, etc.), saw him working on albums by CAT STEVENS, DAVID BOWIE, T.REX, etc. In 1970, he joined The STRAWBS, but the following year he couldn't turn down YES, as they matched his classical ambitions. He was an on-off YES member during the 70's, subsequently starting his own solo career on 'A&M' records. Prior to this, he had augmented The JOHN SCHROEDER ORCHESTRA on the 1971 'Polydor' lp, 'PIANO VIBRATIONS'; (2460 135). Taking themes of history, fiction and legend, he released three well-received (at the time) Top 10 albums between 1973-1975. His second album, 'JOURNEY TO THE CENTRE OF THE EARTH' (an adaptation of the Jules Verne classic), was premiered live at The Royal Festival Hall in January '74, topping the UK charts upon its release that year. With orchestra and choir in tow, he performed it at an open-air Crystal Palace Garden Party, subsequently touring the show around major US venues. His virtuoso, exhibitionist keyboard-playing and flash-rock image (long blonde hair and ankle-length silver capes) was perfectly suited to the live arena, a comparison that could be made with the other famous keys-basher of the era, KEITH EMERSON. Nevertheless, this gruelling tour took its toll, when RICK suffered a minor heart attack nearing the end of pocket-draining extravaganza. On his recovery, he released the third of epics, 'KING ARTHUR' in 1975, regarded by many as overblown ck, although it did have its redeeming moments (i.e. 'MERLIN THE N' and 'SIR LANCELOT & THE BLACK KNIGHT'). Following

a move into soundtrack work, notably on Ken Russell's 'LISZTOMANIA' (starring ROGER DALTREY) and 'WHITE ROCK' (a docu-film focussing on the 1976 Winter Olympics), he found time to squeeze in his fourth studio set, 'NO EARTHLY CONNECTION', a record that still managed a Top 10 placing. WAKEMAN returned in 1977 with his ' . . . CRIMINAL RECORD', which was a failure both critically and commercially, leading to public attention drifting somewhat, thus his steady decline. He continued to release a plethora of albums, most taking a neo-classical rock/pop or new-age stance. He will probably be remembered in the 21st century, not for his theatrical rock indulgence, but for the romantic classical style he helped revive. • **Songwriters:** All his own work, interspersed with little snatches of past classical works. • **Trivia:** Most distinguished session work included; LIFE ON MARS (David Bowie) / CHANGES (Black Sabbath) / MORNING HAS BROKEN (Cat Stevens) / LOU REED's debut album. WAKEMAN was married in the 70's to Ros and settled down in a Buckingham mansion alongside his collection of Rolls Royce's. The couple had three children before their divorce. In the 80's, RICK married ex-model, NINA CARTER, (also of twin-sister outfit, BLONDE ON BLONDE). He fathered another two kids (so far), later finding Christianity. BILL ODDIE (of the GOODIES TV programme) contributed vocals on WAKEMAN's 'JOURNEY' and 'CRIMINAL RECORD'.

Album rating: THE SIX WIVES OF HENRY VIII (*8) / JOURNEY TO THE CENTRE OF THE EARTH (*7) / THE MYTHS & LEGENDS OF KING ARTHUR … (*6) / LISZTOMANIA soundtrack (*5) / NO EARTHLY CONNECTION (*5) / WHITE ROCK soundtrack (*5) / RICK WAKEMAN'S CRIMINAL RECORD (*4) / RHAPSODIES (*4) / 1984 (*4) / THE BURNING soundtrack (*3) / ROCK'N'ROLL PROPHET (*3) / G'OLE soundtrack (*3) / THE COST OF LIVING (*4) / SILENT NIGHTS (*4) / LIVE AT HAMMERSMITH (*4) / COUNTRY AIRS (*5) / THE GOSPELS (*3) / CRIMES OF PASSION soundtrack (*4) / THE FAMILY ALBUM (*4) / A SUITE OF GODS with Ramon Remedios (*4) / ZODIAQUE with Tony Fernandez (*4) / TIME MACHINE (*4) / SEA AIRS (*4) / NIGHT AIRS (*4) / ASPIRANT SUNSET (*4) / ASPIRANT SUNRISE (*4) / BLACK KNIGHTS IN THE COURT OF FERNINAND IV with Mario Fasciano (*4) / PHANTOM POWER soundtrack (*4) / SOFTSWORD: KING JOHN AND THE MAGNA CHARTER (*4) / A WORLD OF WISDOM with Norman Wisdom (*3) / 2000 A.D. INTO THE FUTURE (*4) / AMBIENT SUNSHADOWS (*4) / WAKEMAN WITH WAKEMAN with Adam Wakeman (*4) / HERITAGE SUITE (*4) / AFRICAN BACH (*4) / NO EXPENSE SPARED with Adam (*4) / ROMANCE OF THE VICTORIAN AGE with Adam (*4) / THE SEVEN WONDERS OF THE WORLD (*3) / CIRQUE SURREAL – STATE CIRCUS OF IMAGINATION (*6) / VISIONS (*4) / VOYAGE: THE VERY BEST RICK WAKEMAN compilation (*7)

RICK WAKEMAN – keyboards (a member of YES; Aug71-Jun74, Nov76-Mar80, 1990+)

——— now used various YES people on sessions plus numerous choirs & ensembles.

Feb 73. (lp/c) *(AMLH/CAM 64361)* **THE SIX WIVES OF HENRY VIII** `A&M 7` `A&M 30`
– Catherine of Aragon / Anne of Cleves / Catherine Howard / Jane Seymour / Anne Boleyn / Catherine Parr. *(quad-lp; QU-84361)* *(cd-iss. 1988; CDA 3229)* *(re-iss. cd Aug89; 393 229-2)* *(re-iss. cd Jan92; CDMID 136)*

Mar 73. (7") *(AMS 7061)* **CATHERINE. / ANNE** `-`
(below A-side was an excerpt of 'CATHERINE PARR')

——— Introduced **ASHLEY HOLT** – vocals / **ROGER NEWELL** – bass / **BARNEY JAMES** – drums / plus The ENGLISH ROCK ENSEMBLE with The LONDON SYMPHONY ORCHESTRA. Narration by actor DAVID HEMMINGS.

May 74. (lp/c) *(AMLH/CAM 63621)* **JOURNEY TO THE CENTRE OF THE EARTH** `1` `3`
– The journey / Recollections / The battle / The forest. <*US quad-lp 1974; SPQU 3621*> *(re-iss. Feb85 on 'Hallmark' lp/c; SHM/HSC 3164)* *(cd-iss. Jan88; CDA 3156)* <*US cd-iss. 1988 on 'Mobile Fidelity'; MFCD 848*> *(re-iss. cd Jan92; CDMID 161)* *(re-iss. May93 on 'Spectrum' cd/c; 550 061-2/-4)*

Oct 74. (7") **THE JOURNEY. / THE RETURN** `-`

Dec 74. (7") **THE BATTLE. / AND NOW A WORD FROM OUR SPONSOR** `-`

Apr 75. (lp/c) *(AMLH/CAM 64515)* **THE MYTHS AND LEGENDS OF KING ARTHUR AND THE KNIGHTS OF THE ROUND TABLE** `2` `21`
– Arthur / Lady of the lake / Guinevere / Sir Lancelot & the Black Knight / Merlin the magician / Sir Galahad / The last battle. <*US quad-lp 1975; SPQU 54515*> *(cd-iss. 1988; CDA 3230)* *(re-iss. cd; CDMID 135)*

Jun 75. (7") **MERLIN THE MAGICIAN. / SIR GALAHAD**
(below 1975 releases with ROGER DALTREY on vocals)

Nov 75. (lp) *(AMLH 64546)* **LISZTOMANIA (Soundtrack)**
– Rienzi / Chopsticks fantasia / Love's dream / Dante period / Orpheus song / Hell / Hibernation / Excelsior song / Master race / Rape, pillage and clap funerailles / Free song / Peace at last.

Nov 75. (7") *(AMS 7206)* **ORPHEUS SONG. / LOVE'S DREAM**

——— For North & South American tour he trimmed his ENGLISH ROCK ENSEMBLE down to **ASHLEY HOLT** – vocals / **JOHN DUNSTERVILE** – guitar / **ROGER NEWELL** – bass / **TONY FERNANDEZ** – drums / **REG BROOKS + MARTYN SHIELDS** – brass section

Apr 76. (lp/c) *(AMLK/CLK 64583)* **NO EARTHLY CONNECTION** `9` `67`
– Music reincarnate: (part 1) The warning – (part 2) The maker – (part 3) The spaceman – (part 4) The realization – (part 5) The reaper / The prisoner / The lost cycle.

Jan 77. (lp/c) *(AMLH/CAM 64614)* **WHITE ROCK (Film Soundtrack)** `14`
– White rock / Searching for gold / The loser / The shoot / Lax'x / After the ball / Montezuma's revenge / Ice run. *(cd-iss. 1988; CDA 4614)*
(above from 1976 Winter Olympics docu-film, narrated by James Coburn)

Jun 77. (7") <*1937*> **AFTER THE BALL. / WHITE ROCK** `-`

Nov 77. (lp/c) *(AMLH/CAM 64660)* **RICK WAKEMAN'S CRIMINAL RECORD** `25`
– Statute of justice / Crime of passion / Chamber of horrors / Birdman of Alcatraz / The breathalizer / Judas Iscariot. *(re-iss. Mar82 lp/c; AMID/CMID 125)*

Apr 79. (7") *(AMS 7435)* **BIRDMAN OF ALCATRAZ (theme from My Son My Son).** / **FALCONS DE NEIGE** □ -

Apr 79. (7") *<2010>* **BIRDMAN OF ALCATRAZ. / AND NOW A WORD FROM OUR SPONSOR** □ -

May 79. (d-lp/c) *(AMLX/CXM 68508)* **RHAPSODIES** □ **25**
– Pedra da Gavea / Front line / Bombay duck / Animal showdown / Big Ben / Rhapsody in blue / Wooly Willy tango / The pulse / Swan lager / March of the gladiators / Flacons de Neige / The flasher / The palais / Stand by / Sea horses / Half holiday / Summertime.

May 79. (7"/7"pic-d) *(AMS/+P 7436)* **ANIMAL SHOWDOWN. / SEA HORSES** □ -

Nov 79. (7") *(AMS 7497)* **SWAN LAGER. / WOOLLY WILLY TANGO** □ -

Feb 80. (7") *(AMS 7510)* **I'M SO STRAIGHT I'M A WEIRDO. / DO YOU BELIEVE IN FAIRIES?** □ -

WEA   not iss.

Oct 80. (7") *(K 18354)* **THE SPIDER. / DANIELLE** □ -
featured **FERNANDEZ / STEVE BARNACLE** – bass / **GARY BARNACLE** – sax / **TIM STONE** – guitar / etc.

Charisma Charisma?

Jun 81. (lp)(c) *(CDS 4022)(7144 136)* **1984** □ **24**
– 1984 overture – part 1 & 2 / War games / Julia / The hymn / The room – part 1 & 2 / Robot man / Sorry / No name / 1984 / Forgotten memories / The proles / 1984. *(re-iss. Jun88; CHC 41)*
(below vocals by; CORI JOSIAS)

Jul 81. (7"; by The RICK WAKEMAN BAND) *(CB 384)* **JULIA. / SORRY** □ -

Nov 81. (7"; by The RICK WAKEMAN BAND) *(CB 392)* **ROBOT MAN. / 1984 OVERTURE (part 1)** □ -

Jan 82. (lp) *(CLASS 12)* **THE BURNING** (soundtrack) □ -
– Themes from 'The Burning' / The chase continues / Variations on the fire / Sheer terror and more / The burning (end title theme) / Campfire story / The fire / Doin' it / Devil's creek breakdown / The chase / Sheer terror.

Moon   not iss.

Nov 82. (7") *(LUNA 6)* **I'M SO STRAIGHT I'M A WEIRDO. / MAYBE '80 (edit)** □ -

Dec 82. (lp/c) *(LUNLP/ZCLUN 1)* **ROCK'N'ROLL PROPHET** (rec.1979) □ -
– I'm so straight I'm a weirdo / The dragon / Dark / Maybe '80 / Early warning / Spy of '55 / Do you believe in fairies? / Rock'n'roll prophet. *(cd-iss. Apr93 on 'President'; RWCD 12)(+=)* – Return of the prophet / Alpha sleep / March of the child soldiers / Stalemate.

—— solo with music from 1982 football World Cup in Spain

Charisma   not iss.

Apr 83. (7") *(CB 411)* **LATIN REEL (theme from G'OLE). / NO POSSIBLA** □ -

Apr 83. (lp/c) *(CAS/+MC 1162)* **G'OLE** (film soundtrack) □ -
– International flag / The dove / Wayward spirit / Red island / Latin reel (theme from G'ole) / Spanish holiday / No possibla / Shadows / Black pearls / Frustration / Spanish montage / G'ole.

Jun 83. (lp) *(CAS 1163)* **THE COST OF LIVING** □ -
– Twij / Pandomonia / Gone but not forgotten / One for the road / Bedtime stories / Happening man / Shakespeare's run / Monkey nuts / Elegy (written in a country church yard). *(re-iss. Aug88; CHC 63) (cd-iss. Jun97 on 'Griffin'; GCDWR 1892)*

—— Oct '84, WAKEMAN collaborated on album BEYOND THE PLANETS by KEVIN PEEK (Sky); hit UK No.64

—— His Spring 1985 tour band: **TONY FERNANDEZ** – drums / **CHAS CRONK** – bass / **RICK FENN** – lead guitar / **GORDON NEVILLE** – vocals / **LYNN SHEPHERD** – b.vocals

President   not iss.

Dec 84. (7") *(WAKE 1)* **GLORY BOYS. / GHOST OF A ROCK AND ROLL STAR** □ -
(12"+=) (12WAKE 1) – Elgin mansions.

Mar 85. (lp/c) *(RW/+K 1)* **SILENT NIGHTS** □ -
– Tell 'em all you know / The opening line / The opera / Man's best friend / Glory boys / Silent nights / Ghost of a rock and roll star / The dancer / That's who I am. *(cd-iss. Jan87; RWCD 1)* – Elgin mansions.

Jun 85. (7"/12") *(WAKE/12WAKE 2)* **THE THEME FROM 'LYTTON'S DIARY'. / DATABASE** □ -

Dec 85. (lp) *(RW 2)* **LIVE AT HAMMERSMITH** (live) □ -
– Arthur / Three wives of Henry VIII / The journey / Merlin the magician. *(cd-iss. Jan87; RWCD 2) (re-iss. Nov93)*

Coda   not iss.

Apr 86. (lp/c)(cd) *(NAGE/+C 10)(NAGE 10CD)* **COUNTRY AIRS** □ -
– Dandelion dreams / Stepping stones / Ducks and drakes / Morning haze / Waterfalls / Quite valleys / Nature trail / Heather carpets / Wild moors / Lakeland walks. *(re-iss. Oct92 on 'Art Of Language' cd/c; NAGE 102CD) (re-iss. re-recorded cd Dec92 on 'President'; RWCD 10)* – The spring / Green to gold / Harvest festival / The glade.

Apr 86. (7") *(CODS 19)* **WATERFALLS. / HEATHER CARPETS** □ -

Stylus   not iss.

Nov 86. (d-lp/d-c/d-cd) *(SMR/SMC/SMD 729)* **THE GOSPELS** □ **94**
– The baptism / The welcoming / The sermon on the mount / The Lord's Prayer / The way / The road to Jerusalem / Trial and error / Galilee / The gift / The magnificat / Welcome a star / Power (the acts of the apostles) / The word / The hour / The children of mine / The last verse. *(re-iss. d-cd Mar94 on 'Fragile'; BM 2-3)*

President   not iss.

Mar 87. (lp/c/cd) *(RW/+K/CD 3)* **CRIMES OF PASSION** (Soundtrack) □ -
– It's a lovely life (featuring MAGGIE BELL) / Eastern shadows / Joanna / The stretch / Policeman's ball / Stax / Taken in hand / Paradise lost / The box / Web of love. *(cd+=)* – Dangerous woman (featuring MAGGIE BELL). *(re-iss. cd Feb93)*

Aug 87. (lp/c/cd) *(RW/+K/CD 4)* **THE FAMILY ALBUM** □ -
– Adam (Rick's second son) / Black Beauty (black rabbit) / Jemma (Rick and Nina's daughter) / Benjamin (Rick's third son) / Oscar (Rick & Nina's son) / Oliver (Rick's eldest son) / Nina (Rick's wife) / Chloe (German shepherd) / Rookie (cat) / Tilly (Golden Retriever) / Mum / Dad. *(c+=)* – Wiggles (black & white rabbit). *(cd++=)* – The day after the fair / Mackintosh.

Feb 88. (lp/c/cd; RICK WAKEMAN & RAMON REMEDIOS) *(RW/+K/CD 5)* **A SUITE OF GODS** □ -
– Dawn of time / The oracle / Pandora's box / Chariot of the sun / The flood / The voyage of Ulysses / Hercules.

Apr 88. (lp/c/cd; RICK WAKEMAN & TONY FERNANDEZ) *(RW/+K/CD 6)* **ZODIAQUE** □ -
– Sagittarius / Capricorn / Gemini / Cancer / Pisces / Aquarius / Aries / Libra / Leo / Virgo / Taurus / Scorpio.

—— retained **FERNANDEZ** + recruited **DAVEY PATON** – bass / **JOHN KNIGHTSBRIDGE** – guitar (2) / guest vocals **TRACEY ACKERMAN** + **ASHLEY HOLT** below vocals by ROY WOOD (A-side) / JOHN PARR (B-side)

Jul 88. (7") *(WAKE 3)* **CUSTER'S LAST STAND. / OCEAN CITY** □ -

Jul 88. (lp/c/cd) *(RW/+K/CD 7)* **TIME MACHINE** □ -
– Custer's last stand / Ocean city / Angel of time * / Slaveman * / Ice / Open up your eyes * / Elizabethan rock / Make me a woman * / Rock age *. *(cd has extended versions of *)*

Nov 89. (lp/c/cd) *(RW/+K/CD 8)* **SEA AIRS** □ -
– Harbour lights / The pirate / Storm clouds / Last at sea / The mermaid / Waves / The fisherman / Flying fish / The Marie Celeste / Time and tide / The lone sailor / The sailor's lament.

Nov 90. (lp/c/cd) *(RW/+K/CD 9)* **NIGHT AIRS** □ -
– The sad dream / Twilight / The sleeping child / Mr. Badger / Jack Frost / The lone star / Rain shadows / Fox by night / Night owls / An evening romance.

—— (in the US; he released cd 'IN THE BEGINNING' for 'Asaph'; <AR-1049>, which received a UK date Dec91). In 1991, the 'Badger' label issued cassette 'THE SUN TRILOGY'; AMB 4MC)

Ambient   not iss.

Nov 90. (cd) *(AMB1-MCD)* **ASPIRANT SUNSET** □ -
– Floating clouds / Still waters / The dream / The sleeping village / Sea of tranquility / Peace / Sunset / Dying embers / Dusk / Evening moods. *(re-iss. 1992 on 'Rio Digital'; RIOCD 1008) (re-iss. Jun93 on 'President'; RWCD 18)*

Nov 90. (cd) *(AMB2-MCD)* **ASPIRANT SUNRISE** □ -
– Thoughts of love / Gentle breezes / Whispering cornfields / Peaceful beginnings / Dewy morn / Musical dreams / Distant thoughts / The dove / When time stood still / Secret moments / Peaceful. *(re-iss. 1992 on 'Rio Digital'; RIOCD 1009) (re-iss. Jun93 on 'President'; RWCD 17)*

Jan 91. (lp/cd; by RICK WAKEMAN & MARIO FASCIANO) *(A-IOM-2/+CD)* **BLACK KNIGHTS IN THE COURT OF FERNINAND IV** □ -
(re-iss. cd Nov92 on 'Rio Digital'; RIOCD 1002) (re-iss. cd Jun94 on 'West Coast'; WCPCD 1009)

Feb 91. (lp/cd) *(A-IOM-2/+CD)* **PHANTOM POWER** □ -
– The visit / Heaven / The rat / The stiff / Evil love / The voice of love / Heat of the moment / Fear of love / The love trilogy:- One night – The dream sequence – One night of love / The hangman / The sand-dance / You can't buy my love / Phantom power / The chase. *(re-iss. cd Nov92 on 'Rio Digital'; RIOCD 1003)*

May 91. (lp/cd) *(A-IOM-3/+CD)* **SOFTSWORD: KING JOHN AND THE MAGNA CHARTER** □ -
– Magna charter / After prayers / Battle sonata / The siege / Rochester college / The story of love (King John) / March of time / Don't fly away / Isabella / Softsword / Hymn of hope. *(re-iss. cd Nov92 on 'Rio Digital'; RIOCD 1001) (re-iss. cd Feb91 on 'President'; RWCD 24)*

Sep 91. (lp/cd) *(A-IOM-5/+CD)* **A WORLD OF WISDOM** □ -
(re-iss. cd Feb94 on 'D-Sharp'; DSHCD 7013)
(above credited to veteran English comedian/singer NORMAN WISDOM)

Oct 91. (7"; by RICK WAKEMAN featuring CHRISSIE HAMMOND) *(A-IOMS 1)* **DON'T FLY AWAY. / AFTER PRAYERS** □ -

Nov 91. (cd) **2000 A.D. INTO THE FUTURE** □ -
– Into the future / Toward peace / 2000 A.D. / A.D rock / The time tunnel / Robot dance / A new beginning / Forward past / The seventh dimension. *(re-iss. Dec92 on 'Rio Digital'; RIOCD 1007) (re-iss. Sep93 on 'President'; RWCD 21)*

Rio Digital   not iss.

1992. (cd) *(RIOCD 1010)* **AMBIENT SUNSHADOWS** □ -
– The nightwind / Churchyard / Tall shadows / Shadowlove / Melancholy mood / Mount Fuji by night / Hidden reflections / The evening harp / The moonraker pond / The last lamplight / Japanese sunshadows. *(re-iss. Jul93 as 'ASPIRANT SUNSHADOWS' on 'President'; RWCD 19)*

Nov 92. (cd; RICK WAKEMAN & ADAM WAKEMAN) *(RIOCD 1011)* **WAKEMAN WITH WAKEMAN** □ -
– Lure of the wild / The beach comber / Meglomania / Raga and rhyme / Sync or swim / Jigajig / Caesarea / After the atom / The suicide shuiffle / Past and present / Paint it black. *(re-iss. Feb93 on 'President'; RWCD 11)*
(above was with son ADAM)

Myrrh   not iss.

May 93. (cd) *(MYRCD 1296)* **PRAYERS** □ -

President   not iss.

May 93. (cd) *(RWCD 16)* **HERITAGE SUITE** □ -
– The chasms / Thorwald's cross / St.Michael's isle / Spanish head / The Ayres / Mona's isle / The Dhoon / The bee orchid / Chapel Hill / The Curraghs / The painted lady / The Peregrine falcon.

Aug 93. (cd) *(RWCD 17)* **AFRICAN BACH** (rec.& rel.South Africa 1991) □ -
– African Bach / Message of mine / My homeland / Liberty / Anthem / Brainstorm / Face in the crowd / Just a game / Africa east / Don't touch the merchandise.

Nov 93. (cd; by WAKEMAN WITH WAKEMAN) *(RWCD 22)* **NO EXPENSE SPARED** □ -

May 94. (cd-ep; by RICK WAKEMAN & HIS BAND) *(WAKEY 4)* **LIGHT UP THE SKY / SIMPLY FREE / STARFLIGHT / THE BEAR** □ -

Nov 94. (cd; by WAKEMAN WITH WAKEMAN) *(RWCD 25)* **ROMANCE OF THE VICTORIAN AGE** □ -
– Burlington arcade / If only / The last teardrop / Still dreaming / Memories of the Victorian age / Lost in words / A tale of love / Mysteries unfold / Forever in my heart / Days of wonder / The swans / Another mellow day / Dance of the elves.

Jun 95. (cd) *(RWCD 27)* **THE SEVEN WONDERS OF THE WORLD** (with narration) □ -
– The Pharoahs Of Alexandria / The Colossus Of Rhodes / The Pyramids Of Egypt / The Gardens Of Babylon / The Temples Of Artemis / The Statue Of Zeus / The Mausoleum At Halicarnassus.

Jul 95. (cd) *(DSHLCD 7018)* **CIRQUE SURREAL – STATE CIRCUS OF IMAGINATION** □ -
– Gnash / Balance of power / Wings of fortune / Static / Party / Wired for Juliet / Tubular balls / Carlos / Love that I know / The jig.
(above released on 'D-Sharp' label)

Oct 95. (cd) *(RWCD 28)* **VISIONS**   [ ]   [-]
– Fantasy / Peace of mind / Innermost thoughts / Vision of light / Higher planes /
Astral traveller / Dream on / Thought waves / Drifting patterns / Future patterns /
Levitation / Moondreams.

Nov 96. (cd; by RICK & ADAM WAKEMAN) *(RWCD 30)*   [ ]   [-]
VIGNETTES
– Waiting alone / Wish I was you / Sun comes crying / A breath of Heaven / Moment
in time / Artist's dream / Change of face / Madman blues / A painting of our love /
Riverside / Need you / Simply acoustic / Just another tear.

		Hope	not iss.
Mar 97.	(cd) *(HRHCD 004)* **LIGHT AT THE END OF THE TUNNEL**	[ ]	[-]
Mar 97.	(cd) *(HRHCD 005)* **CAN YOU HEAR ME?**	[ ]	[-]

		EMI Classics	unknown
Mar 99.	(cd/lp) *(CDC/EX 556763-2/-1)* **RETURN TO THE CENTRE OF THE EARTH**	[34]	[ ]

– Vision / Return overture / Mother Earth / Shadow of June / Gallery / Avenue of
prismed light / Earthquake / Buried alive (with OZZY OSBOURNE) / Enigma /
Is anybody there (with BONNIE TYLER) / Ravine / Dance of a thousand lights /
Shepherd / Mr Slow / Bridge of time / Never is a long time (with TREVOR
RABIN) / Tales of the Lidenbrook sea / River of hope / Hunter and hunted / Fight
for life / Kill / Timeless history / Still waters run deep (with JUSTIN HAYWARD) /
Time within time / Ebbing tide / Electric storm / Ride of your life (with KATRINA
LESKANICH) / Globes of fire / Cascades of fear / Floodflames / Volcano / Tongues
of fire / Blue mountains / End of the return.

– compilations, others, etc. –

1978.	(lp) *A&M; (AMLX 68447)* **THE ROYAL PHILHARMONIC ORCHESTRA PERFORMING BEST KNOWN WORKS OF RICK WAKEMAN**	[ ]	[-]
May 81.	(d-c) *A&M; (CAMCR 8)* **THE SIX WIVES OF HENRY VIII / THE MYTHS AND LEGENDS OF KING ARTHUR . . .**	[ ]	[-]
Feb 89.	(4xcd-box) *A&M; (RWCD 20)* **20th ANNIVERSARY**	[ ]	[-]

– (THE SIX WIVES OF HENRY VIII / JOURNEY TO THE CENTRE OF
THE EARTH / THE MYTHS AND LEGENDS OF KING ARTHUR AND THE
KNIGHTS OF THE ROUND TABLE / WHITE ROCK)

Mar 83.	(d-c) *Charisma; (CASMC 111)* **1984 / THE BURNING**	[ ]	[-]
May 91.	(cd) *Ambient; (A-IOM-4CD)* **THE PRIVATE COLLECTION**	[ ]	[-]

*(re-iss. Nov92 on 'Rio Digital'; RIOCD 1004) (re-iss. Feb94 on 'President';
RWCD 23)*

Oct 91.	(d-cd) *Ambient; (AMB5-MCD)* **THE CLASSICAL CONNECTION**	[ ]	[-]

*(re-iss. Dec92 on 'Rio Digital'; RIOCD 1005) (re-iss. 1-cd May93 on 'President';
RWCD 13)*

Oct 91.	(cd) *Ambient; (A-IOM-6MCD)* **THE CLASSICAL CONNECTION II**	[ ]	[-]

*(re-iss. Dec92 on 'Rio Digital'; RIOCD 1006) (re-iss. May93 on 'President';
RWCD 14)*

Sep 93.	(cd) *Icon; (ICONCD 005)* **THE VERY BEST OF RICK WAKEMAN – CHRONICLES**	[ ]	[-]

– (see below cd for tracks, although not YES songs)

Dec 93.	(d-cd) *Fragile; (CDFRL 001)* **RICK WAKEMAN'S GREATEST HITS** (some with YES)	[ ]	[-]

– Roundabout / Wondrous stories / Don't kill the whale / Going for the one / Siberian
khatru / Madrigal / Starship trooper / / Overture / The journey / The Hansbach /
Lost in time / The recollection / Stream of voices / The battle / Liddenbrook / The
forest / Mount Etna / Journey's end / Sea horses / Catherine of Aragon / Gone but
not forgotten / Merlin the magician.

Apr 94.	(cd/c) *Prestige; (CDSGP 115)* **THE CLASSIC TRACKS**	[ ]	[-]
Jun 94.	(d-cd; WAKEMAN WITH WAKEMAN) *Cyclops; (CYCLD 006)* **THE OFFICIAL LIVE BOOTLEG**	[ ]	[-]

(re-iss. Mar95 on 'Griffin'; GCDRW 156)

Dec 94.	(cd; as RICK WAKEMAN & THE ENGLISH ROCK ENSEMBLE) *Windsong; (WHISCD 007)* **LIVE ON THE TEST (live)**	[ ]	[-]
Jun 95.	(cd) *Disky; (RPCD 13)* **ROCK AND POP LEGENDS**	[ ]	[-]
Sep 95.	(d-cd) *Hope; (HR 001)* **THE NEW GOSPELS**	[ ]	[-]
Oct 95.	(cd) *Essential; (ESSCD 322)* **THE PIANO ALBUM – LIVE (live)**	[ ]	[-]
Nov 96.	(cd) *A&M; <5852>* **VOYAGE: THE VERY BEST OF RICK WAKEMAN**	[-]	[ ]

– Catherine of Aragon / Catherine Howard / Jane Seymour / Anne Boleyn / Arthur /
Merlin the magician / The last battle / White rock / Searching for gold / After the
ball / Ice run / March of the gladiators / Summertime / Temperament of mind /
Journey – Recollection / The battle – The forest / Crime of passion / Judas Iscariot /
Hibernation / Free song / Maker.

May 97.	(cd) *RP Media; (CDRPM 0018)* **TRIBUTE**	[ ]	[-]
May 99.	(3xcd-box) *Music Fusion; (MFCD 001)* **NATURAL WORLD TRILOGY**	[ ]	[-]
May 99.	(3xcd-box) *Music Fusion; (MFCD 002)* **ART IN MUSIC TRILOGY**	[ ]	[-]

– (THE SCULPTOR / THE WRITER / SKETCHES)

May 99.	(2xcd-box) *Music Fusion; (MFCD 003)* **OFFICIAL LIVE BOOTLEG (live)**	[ ]	[-]
Jun 99.	(cd) *Music Fusion; (MFCD 004)* **WHITE ROCK VOL.2**	[ ]	[-]
Jun 99.	(d-cd) *Eagle; (EDMCD 086)* **THE MASTERS**	[ ]	[-]

WALKABOUTS (dig out; Great Alt & Indie . . .)

Scott WALKER / The WALKER BROTHERS

Formed: Los Angeles, California, USA . . . .1964 as The WALKER
~~BROT~~HERS by GARY LEEDS, SCOTT ENGEL and JOHN MAUS. LEEDS
~~(drumm~~er for P.J. PROBY (previously a co-founder of The STANDELLS)
~~ENGE~~L and MAUS were playing bass and lead guitar respectively for

---

The DALTON BROTHERS. After signing to 'Smash' Records, they were
advised to try their luck in Britain and they subsequently relocated to London.
Their debut single, 'PRETTY GIRLS EVERYWHERE' (with MAUS on lead
vocal) flopped although their second, 'LOVE HER'(1965), scraped into the
UK Top 20. After SCOTT took over on vocals they soon made No.1 twice
in the UK with the 1965-66 cult easy-listening classics, 'MAKE IT EASY
ON YOURSELF' (US Top 20) and 'THE SUN AIN'T GONNA SHINE
ANYMORE' (also US Top 20 and written by FRANKIE VALLI). Their debut
album, 'TAKE IT EASY WITH THE WALKER BROTHERS' (1966) hit the
UK Top 5, followed by further smashes, 'PORTRAIT' (1966) and 'IMAGES'
(1967). Later that year, SCOTT WALKER left JOHN MAUS and GARY
LEEDS (after some arguments with JOHN) and went solo, hitting the heights
until the 70's (his melancholy ballads later influencing the likes of JULIAN
COPE). SCOTT scored late 60's solo hits with the controversial 'JACKIE',
'JOANNA' and 'LIGHTS OF CINCINATTI' as well as the albums, 'SCOTT'
(1967), 'SCOTT 2' (1968; a UK No.1) and 'SCOTT 3' (1969). He also
contributed backing vocals to The Beatles' 'ALL YOU NEED IS LOVE' world
broadcast in 1967, by this point even hosting his own TV show on BBC1. With
the release of cult classic, 'SCOTT 4' (1969), however, he faded from popular
stardom and languished in MOR hell for much of the early 70's. The man
briefly re-emerged mid-decade as part of a reformed WALKER BROTHERS,
enjoying a UK Top 10 with a cover of Tom Rush's 'NO REGRETS'. SCOTT
eschewed the lure of the beckoning nostalgia circuit, however, leading the band
in a radically different direction for 1978's 'NITE FLIGHTS' (the brothers'
final album together). WALKER eventually resurfaced in solo mode with the
tortured 'CLIMATE OF HUNTER' in 1984, hardly a record to kickstart his
career. 'Virgin' were suitably unimpressed with the commercial returns and he
subsequently signed to 'Fontana' in 1985. Although he recorded with BRIAN
ENO, the project was never completed; similarly, SCOTT's collaborative
work with former JAPAN warbler, DAVID SYLVIAN produced no concrete
results. It would be a further eleven years before he came out with new work
in the form of 95's 'TILT'. As out-there as WALKER has yet ventured, fans
and critics alike agreed that while he mightn't be the most prolific artist,
his darkly compelling experiments are worth waiting for. • **Songwriters:**
WALKER BROTHERS covered (45's only); LOVE HER (Mann-Weill) /
MAKE IT EASY ON YOURSELF (Jerry Butler) / MY SHIP IS COMING IN
(Jimmy Radcliffe) / THE SUN AIN'T GONNA SHINE ANYMORE (Frankie
Valli) / LOVE MINUS ZERO (Bob Dylan) / ANOTHER TEAR FALLS (Gene
McDaniels) / STAY WITH ME BABY (Lorraine Ellison) / WALKING IN THE
RAIN (Ronettes) / NO REGRETS (Tom Rush) / etc. SCOTT WALKER covers;
JACKIE and others from 'SCOTT 2' lp (Jacques Brel). JOANNA (Tony Hatch
& Jackie Trent). On his 'STRETCH' country roots album, several songs were
written by BILLY JOE SHAVER. • **Trivia:** In 1987, SCOTT appeared in TV
ads for Britvic juice.

Best CD compilation(s): Walker Brothers: AFTER THE LIGHTS GO OUT: THE
BEST OF 1965-1967 (*7) / NO REGRETS: THE BEST OF . . . (*6; shared with Scott
Walker)

Album rating: Scott Walker: SCOTT (*7) / SCOTT 2 (*8) / SCOTT (*7) / . . .SINGS
SONGS FROM HIS TV SERIES special (*4) / SCOTT 4 (*8) / 'TIL THE BAND COMES
IN (*6) / THE MOVIEGOER (*4) / ANY DAY NOW (*4) / STRETCH (*4) / WE HAD
IT ALL (*4) / FIRE ESCAPE IN THE SKY: THE GODLIKE GENIUS OF SCOTT
WALKER compilation (*7) / SCOTT WALKER SINGS JACQUES BREL collection
(*6) / CLIMATE OF HUNTER (*7) / BOY CHILD; THE BEST OF SCOTT WALKER
1967-1970 compilation (*8) / TILT (*5)

SCOTT ENGEL

(aka SCOTT WALKER) – vocals

		Vogue	Orbit
Aug 58.	(7") **CHARLIE BOP. / ALL I DO IS DREAM OF YOU**	[-]	[ ]
Oct 58.	(7") *(V 9125)* **BLUEBELL / PAPER DOLL**	[ ]	[ ]
Jun 59.	(7") *(V 9145)* **LIVIN' END. / GOOD FOR NOTHIN'**	[ ]	[ ]
1959.	(7") **SUNDAY. / GOLDEN RULE OF LOVE**	[-]	[ ]
1959.	(7") **I DON'T WANNA KNOW. / COMIN' HOME**	[-]	[ ]

—— Continued to do session work until 1962 when he joined The ROUTERS alongside
JOHN STEWART. They released 2 singles late 62-early 63, 'LET'S GO WITH
THE ROUTERS' & 'MAKE IT SNAPPY'. After a spell with the SANDY
NELSON band, he and JOHN joined The MOONGOONERS. They issued singles
MOONGOON STOMP and MOONGOON TWIST in 1963. The following year,
they became The DALTONS duo releasing one 45, 'I ONLY CAME TO DANCE
WITH YOU'. SCOTT was now part of the famous trio.

WALKER BROTHERS

SCOTT ENGEL (WALKER)(b. 9 Jan'44, Hamilton, Ohio) – vocals, bass, keyboards / **JOHN
MAUS** (WALKER)(b.12 Nov'43, New York City, N.Y.) – vocals, guitar / **GARY LEEDS**
(WALKER) (b. 3 Sep'44, Glendale, Calif.) – drums, vocals

		Philips	Smash
Feb 65.	(7") *<1952>* **PRETTY GIRLS EVERYWHERE. / DOIN' THE JERK**	[-]	[ ]
Apr 65.	(7") *(BF 1409) <1976>* **LOVE HER. / THE SEVENTH DAWN**	[20]	[ ]
Aug 65.	(7") *(BF 1428) <2000>* **MAKE IT EASY ON YOURSELF. / BUT I DO**	[1]	[Jul65]
Sep 65.	(7") *<2009>* **MAKE IT EASY ON YOURSELF. / DOIN' THE JERK**	[-]	[16]
Nov 65.	(7") *(BF 1454) <2016>* **MY SHIP IS COMING IN. / YOU'RE ALL AROUND ME**	[3]	[63]
Dec 65.	(lp) *(SBL 7691)* **TAKE IT EASY WITH THE WALKER BROTHERS**	[4]	[-]

– Make it easy for yourself / There goes my baby / First love never dies / Dancing in
the street / Lonely winds / The girl I lost in the rain / Land of 1000 dances / You're

all around me / Love minus zero / I don't want to hear it anymore / Here comes the night / Tell the truth.

Feb 66. (7") *(BF 1473) <2032>* **THE SUN AIN'T GONNA SHINE ANYMORE. / AFTER THE LIGHTS GO OUT**	1	13
Jul 66. (7") *(BF 1497) <2048>* **(BABY) YOU DON'T HAVE TO TELL ME. / MY LOVE IS GROWING**	13	
Aug 66. (lp) *(SBL 7732)* **PORTRAIT**	3	

– In my room / Saturday's child / Just for a thrill / Hurting each other / Old folks / Summertime / People get ready / I can see it now / Where's the girl / Living above your head / Take it like a man / No sad songs for me.

Sep 66. (7") *(BF 1514) <2063>* **ANOTHER TEAR FALLS. / SADDEST NIGHT IN THE WORLD**	12	
Nov 66. (7") *(BF 1537)* **DEADLIER THAN THE MALE (theme from the film). / ARC ANGEL**	34	–
Jan 67. (7") *(BF 1548)* **STAY WITH ME BABY. / TURN OUT THE MOON**	26	–
Mar 67. (lp) *(SBL 7770)* **IMAGES**	6	

– Everything under the sun / Once upon a summertime / Experience / Blueberry Hill / Orpheus / Stand by me / I wanna know / I willwait for you / It makes no difference now / I can't let it happen to you / Genevieve / Just say goodbye.

May 67. (7") *(BF 1576)* **WALKING IN THE RAIN. / BABY MAKE IT THE LAST TIME**	26	–

—— Disbanded May '67

SCOTT WALKER

re-issued old recordings.

	Liberty	Liberty
1966. (7"ep; as SCOTT ENGEL) *(LEP 2261)* **SCOTT ENGEL**		–

– I broke my own heart / What do you say / Are these really mine / Crazy in love with you.

	Capitol	Capitol
May 66. (7"; with JOHN STEWART) *(CL 15440)* **I ONLY CAME TO DANCE WITH YOU. / GREENS**		not iss.
	Philips	
Dec 66. (7"ep; 1-side by JOHN MAUS) *(BE 12597)* **SOLO SCOTT – SOLO JOHN**		–

– (SCOTT WALKER:- The gentle rain / Mrs. Murphy.

SCOTT WALKER

solo after the WALKER's split.

	Philips	Smash
Aug 67. (lp; stereo/mono) *(S+/BL 7816)* **SCOTT**	3	

– Mathilde / Montague Terrace (in blue) / Angelica / Lady came from Baltimore / When Joanna loved me / My death / Through a long and sleepless night / The big hurt / Such a small love / You're gonna hear from me / Always coming back to me / Amsterdam. *(re-iss. Mar92 on 'Fontana' cd/c; 510 879-2/-4)*

Nov 67. (7") *(BF 1628) <2156>* **JACKIE. / THE PLAGUE**	22	
Mar 68. (lp; stereo/mono) *(S+/BL 7840)* **SCOTT 2**	1	

– Jackie / Best of both worlds / The amorous Humphrey Plugg / Black sheep boy / Next / The girls from the street / Plastic palace people / Wait until dark / The girls and the dogs / Windows of the world / The bridge / Come next Spring. *(re-iss. Aug92 cd/c; 510880-2/-4)*

Apr 68. (7") *(BF 1662) <2168>* **JOANNA. / ALWAYS COMING BACK TO YOU**	7	
Mar 69. (lp) *(SBL 7882)* **SCOTT 3**	3	

– It's raining today / Copenhagen / Rosemary / Big Louise / We came through / Butterfly / Two ragged soldiers / 30th century man / Winter night / Two weeks since you've gone / Sons of / Funeral tango / If you go away. *(re-iss. Aug92 cd/c; 510881-2/-4)*

Jun 69. (7") *(BF 1793) <2228>* **LIGHTS OF CINCINNATI. / TWO WEEKS SINCE YOU'VE GONE**	13	
Jun 69. (lp) *(SBL 7900)* **... SINGS SONGS FROM HIS TV SERIES**	7	

– I have dreamed / The impossible dream / Will you still be mine / When the world was young / Who (will take my place) / If she walked into my life / The song is you / The look of love / Country girl / Someone to light up my life / Only the young / Lost in the stars.

Nov 69. (lp; as NOEL SCOTT ENGEL) *(SBL 7913)* **SCOTT 4**		

– The seventh seal / On your own again / World's strongest man / Angels of ashes / Boy child / The old man's back again / Hero of the war / Duchess / Get behind me / Rhymes of goodbye. *(re-iss. Aug92 cd/c; 510882-2/-4)*

Dec 70. (lp) *(6308 035)* **'TIL THE BAND COMES IN**		

– Prologue / Little things (that keep us together) / Jean the machine / Joe / Thanks for Chicago, Mr. James / Long about now / Time operator / Cowbells shakin' / 'Til the band comes in / The war is over / Stormy / The hills of yesterday / What are you doing the rest of your life / Rueben James / It's over. *(cd-iss. Aug96 on 'Beat Goes On'; BGOCD 320)*

Oct 71. (7") *(6006 168)* **I STILL SEE YOU. / MY WAY HOME**		–
Oct 72. (lp) *(6308 127)* **THE MOVIEGOER**		

– This way Mary / Speak softly love / Glory road / That night / The summer of '42 / Easy come easy go / The ballad of Sacco and Vanzetti (here's to you) / Face in the crowd / Joe Hill / All his children / Come Saturday morning / The look of love. *(re-iss. on 'Contour'; 6870 633)*

May 73. (7") *(6006 311)* **THE ME I NEVER KNEW. / THIS WAY MARY**		
May 73. (lp) *(6308 148)* **ANY DAY NOW**		

– Any day now / All my love's laughter / Do I love you / Ain't no sunshine / Maria Bethania / Cowboy / When you get right down to it / The me I never knew / If ships were made to sail / We could be flying.

	C.B.S.	Columbia
Oct 73. (7") *(1795)* **A WOMAN LEFT LONELY. / WHERE LOVE HAS DIED**		
Nov 73. (7") *(65725)* **STRETCH**		

– Sunshine / Just one smile / A woman left lonely / No easy way down / That's how I got to Memphis / Use me / Frisco depot / Someone who cared / Where does brown begin / Where love has died / I'll be home.

Jul 74. (7") *(2521)* **DELTA DAWN. / WE HAD IT ALL**		–
Aug 74. (lp) *(80254)* **WE HAD IT ALL**		

– Low down freedom / We had it all / Black rose / Ride me down easy / You're

young and you'll forget / The house song / Old five and dimers like me / Whatever happened to Saturday night / Sundown / Delta dawn.

—— SCOTT shelved solo career when the WALKERS re-formed in 1975.

WALKER BROTHERS

—— (SCOTT, JOHN & GARY) / on session were **BIG JIM SULLIVAN** – guitar / **ALAN SKIDMORE / BRIAN BENNETT + CHRIS MERCER**

	G.T.O.	G.T.O.
Oct 75. (lp) *(GTLP 007)* **NO REGRETS**	49	

– No regrets / Hold an old friend's hand / I've got to have you / Boulder to Birmingham / Lover's lullaby / Walkers' in the Sun / Half break your heart / Everything that touches you / Lovers / Burn our bridges. *(re-iss. Jul77; same) (re-iss. May94 on 'Sony' cd/c; 983276-2/-4) (cd re-iss. Sep94 on 'Rewind'; 477354-2)*

Nov 75. (7") *(GT 42)* **NO REGRETS. / REMEMBER ME**	7	
Jul 76. (lp) *(GTLP 014)* **LINES**		

– Lines / Taking it all in stride / Inside of you / Have you seen my baby / We're all alone / Many rivers to cross / Hard to be friends / First day / Brand new Tennessee waltz / Dreaming as one. *(cd-iss. Mar96 on 'Columbia'; 483674-2)*

Sep 76. (7") *(GT 67)* **LINES. / FIRST DAY**		–
Jun 77. (7") *(GT 78)* **WE'RE ALL ALONE / HAVE YOU SEEN MY BABY**		Nov76
Jul 78. (7") *(GT 230)* **THE ELECTRICIAN. / DEN HAAGUE**		–
Jul 78. (lp) *(GTLP 033)* **NITE FLIGHTS**		–

– Shutout / Fat mama kick / Nite flights / The electrician / Death of romance / Den Haague / Rhythms of vision / Child of flames / Disciples of death / Fury and the fire. *(cd-iss. Jul96 on 'Epic'; 484438-2)*

—— Split again in 1978 for the last time.

– (WALKER BROTHERS) compilations, etc. –

Jun 66. (7"ep) Philips; *(BE 12596)* **I NEED YOU**		–
May 67. (7"ep) Philips; *(BE 12603)* **THE WALKER BROTHERS**		–
Sep 67. (d-lp) Philips; *(DBL 002)* **THE WALKER BROTHERS STORY**	9	–
1968. (lp) Wing; *(WL 1188)* **THE FABULOUS WALKER BROTHERS**		–
1968. (lp) Philips; *(6870 564)* **THE IMMORTAL WALKER BROTHERS** *(re-iss. 1970 on 'Contour';)*		
1972. (lp) Philips; *(6336 214)* **MAKE IT EASY ON YOURSELF** *(re-iss. Jun76 on 'Contour'; CN 2017)*		
Oct 75. (lp) Philips; *(6640 009)* **GREATEST HITS**		
1976. (lp) Philips; *(6640 013)* **SPOTLIGHT ON THE WALKER BROTHERS**		
Apr 76. (7"m) Philips; *(6160 050)* **THE SUN AIN'T GONNA SHINE ANYMORE. / MAKE IT EASY ON YOURSELF / STAY WITH ME BABY**		
Oct 80. (7") Philips; *(CUT 104)* **MAKE IT EASY ON YOURSELF. / THE SUN AIN'T GONNA SHINE ANYMORE**		
Jun 81. (7"ep) G.T.O.; *(GT 295)* **SHUTOUT / THE ELECTRICIAN. / NITE FLIGHTS / FAT MAMA KICK**		
Jan 85. (7") Old Gold; *(OG 9474)* **THE SUN AIN'T GONNA SHINE ANYMORE. / MY SHIP IS COMING IN**		
Sep 85. (7") Old Gold; *(OG 9557)* **NO REGRETS. / WE'RE ALL ALONE**		
Mar 88. (7") Old Gold; *(OG 9779)* **MAKE IT EASY ON YOURSELF. / FIRST LOVE NEVER DIES**		
May 87. (7") Bam Caruso; *(OPRA 090)* **THE SUN AIN'T GONNA SHINE ANYMORE. / IN MY ROOM**		
Jul 87. (cd) Mercury; *(830212-2)* **THE WALKER BROTHERS GALA**		
Jul 90. (cd/c/lp) Fontana; *(842831-2/-4/-1)* **AFTER THE LIGHTS GO OUT – THE BEST OF 1965-1967**		
Dec 91. (7"/c-s) Fontana; **THE SUN AIN'T GONNA SHINE ANYMORE. / Scott Walker: JACKIE** *(12"+=/cd-s+=)* – First love never dies / SCOTT WALKER: Joanna.		
Dec 91. (cd/c/lp) Fontana; *(510831-2/-4/-1)* **NO REGRETS – THE BEST OF SCOTT WALKER AND THE WALKER BROTHERS 1965-1976**	4	

– (* denotes SCOTT WALKER track) – No regrets / Make it easy on yourself / The Sun ain't gonna shine anymore / My ship is comin' in / * Joanna / * Lights of Cincinatti / Another tear falls / * Boy child / * Montague Terrace in blue / * Jackie / Stay with me baby / * If you go away / First love never dies / Love her / Walking in the rain / (Baby) You don't have to tell me / Deadlier than the male / We're all alone.

Sep 93. (cd/c) Pickwick; *(PWK S/MC 4165)* **A VERY SPECIAL COLLECTION**		–
Mar 96. (cd/c) Spectrum; *(550200-2/-4)* **THE COLLECTION**		–

SCOTT WALKER

went solo again in '84.

	Virgin	Virgin
Mar 84. (7") *(VS 666)* **TRACK 3. / BLANKET ROLL BLUES**	60	
Mar 84. (lp/c) *(T/TCV 2303)* **CLIMATE OF HUNTER**		

– Rawhide / Dealer / Track 3 / Sleepwalker's woman / Track 5 / Track 6 / Track 7 / Blanket roll blues. *(re-iss. Aug88 lp/c; OVED/+C 149) (cd-iss. Nov89; CDV 2303)*

—— Retired from music for a decade.

	Fontana	Mercury
May 95. (cd/lp) *(526 859-2/-1)* **TILT**	27	

– Farmer in the city / The cockfighter / Bouncer see bouncer . . . / Manhattan / Face on breast / Bolivia '95 / Patriot (a single) / Tilt / Rosary.

– (SCOTT WALKER) compilations, etc. –

on 'Philips' unless otherwise stated

Dec 67. (c-ep) *(MCP 1006)* **GREAT SCOTT!**		–

– Jackie / When Joanna loved me / The plague / Mathilde.

Dec 67. (lp) Ember; *(EMB 3393)* **LOOKING BACK WITH SCOTT WALKER**		

Jan 70. (lp) *(SBL 7910)* **THE BEST OF SCOTT WALKER** ☐ -
(re-iss. Nov71 as 'THIS IS SCOTT WALKER'; 6382 007) (re-iss. Jun82; 6381 073)
(re-iss. Oct83; PRICE 43)
Oct 72. (lp) *(6382 052)* **THIS IS SCOTT WALKER – VOL.2** ☐ -
Jan 76. (lp) Contour; *(6870 679)* **THE BEST OF SCOTT WALKER** ☐ -
Mar 76. (d-lp) *(6625 017)* **SPOTLIGHT ON SCOTT WALKER** ☐ -
Nov 81. (lp) *(6359 090)* **SINGS JAQUES BREL** ☐ -
(cd-iss. Sep92 on 'Fontana' cd/c; 838212-2/-4)
Sep 81. (lp) Zoo; *(ZOO 2)* **FIRE ESCAPE IN THE SKY – THE GODLIKE**
GENIUS OF SCOTT WALKER ☐ -
Aug 82. (7") Old Gold; *(OG 9244)* **JOANNA. / LIGHTS OF**
CINCINNATI ☐ -
Jun 90. (cd/c/lp) Fontana; *(842832-2/-4/-1)* **BOY CHILD – THE BEST**
OF 1967-70 ☐ -

WALLFLOWERS (dig out; 4th edition)

WALL OF VOODOO (dig out; Great Alt & Indie . . .)

Joe WALSH

Born: 20th Nov'47, Wichita, Kansas, USA, the classically-trained son of a piano playing mother. In 1969, having spent the previous four years imitating the fret work of guitar idols, JEFF BECK and JIMMY PAGE, while studying at Kent State University (in Cleveland, Ohio), WALSH joined The JAMES GANG. He quit the 'GANG for a solo career late in '71, after contributing his much lauded star quality to three studio albums, 'YER ALBUM', 'RIDES AGAIN' and 'THIRDS'. Keeping his hard-rock roots firmly intact and adding harmonies, WALSH named his new backing band, BARNSTORM (KENNY PASSARELLI on bass and JOE VITALE on drums), also the title of his debut US Top 100 album released in '72. A follow-up, the strangely-titled 'THE SMOKER YOU DRINK, THE PLAYER YOU GET' (with the addition of ROCKE GRACE on keyboards and JOE LALA on percussion), thundered up the American charts into the Top 10. The single from it, 'ROCKY MOUNTAIN WAY' (Top 30), complete with his new 'talkbox', became a classic in its own right, the guitar work and countrified wail of WALSH making him a focal point par excellence. His third set, 'SO WHAT' (1974), featured guest spots from The EAGLES, J.D. SOUTHER and DAN FOGELBERG (JW produced and performed on his 'Souvenirs'), while BARNSTORM took a back seat on around half the tracks. The record just failed to match its predecessor, WALSH subsequently forming a new stage band comprising drummer RICKY FATAAR (ex-BEACH BOYS), bassist BRYAN GAROFALO and keyboard players DAVID MASON and PAUL HARRIS, a concert set, 'YOU CAN'T ARGUE WITH A SICK MIND', belatedly reaching the Top 20 in the Spring of '76. By this time, WALSH had shocked the rock world, taking the place of BERNIE LEADON in The EAGLES, his contributions to their classic 'Hotel California' (1976), certainly giving the once proud kings of country-rock a harder edge. He remained with the group for the rest of the 70's, reactivating his solo career in 1978 with the celebrated hit single 'LIFE'S BEEN GOOD' taken from another platinum album, 'BUT SERIOUSLY FOLKS . . .'. From 1980 to 1988, he became a semi-serious candidate at the US presidential elections, his recording work understandably a little sporadic and unremarkable during this time (although he did find time to perform a cameo appearance in the 'Blues Brothers' film). Mellowed-down soft-rock albums such as 'THERE GOES THE NEIGHBORHOOD' (1981), 'YOU BOUGHT IT – YOU NAME IT' (1983), 'THE CONFESSOR' (1985) and 'GOT ANY GUM' (1987) all sold moderately well in the States, the first more successful due to the appearance of another major hit, 'LIFE OF ILLUSION'. In 1991, WALSH released his umpteenth set, 'ORDINARY AVERAGE GUY', probably never a truer self-analysis of one of the great guitarists of the 70's. A few years later, the man was back on the "Vote For Me" campaign trail, subsequently rejoining The EAGLES on a reunion set; the album did little to win back the critics, although their concerts sold out everywhere. • Covered: WILL YOU STILL LOVE ME TOMORROW? (Goffin-King) / WE GOTTA GET YOU A WOMAN (Todd Rundgren) / IN-A-GADDA-DA-VIDA (Iron Butterfly) / SHAKE YOUR BOOTY (KC & The Sunshine Band) / etc.

Album rating: BARNSTORM (*6) / THE SMOKER YOU DRINK, THE PLAYER YOU GET (*7) / SO WHAT (*5) / YOU CAN'T ARGUE WITH A SICK MIND (*6) / BUT SERIOUSLY FOLKS . . . (*5) / SO FAR SO GOOD – THE BEST OF JOE WALSH compilation (*8) / THERE GOES THE NEIGHBOURHOOD (*5) / YOU BOUGHT IT – YOU NAME IT (*4) / THE CONFESSOR (*4) / GOT ANY GUM? (*4) / ORDINARY AVERAGE GUY (*5) / SONGS FOR A DYING PLANET (*3) / A FUTURE TO THIS LIFE (*3) / LOOK WHAT I DID~: THE JOE WALSH ANTHOLOGY compilation (*8)

JOE WALSH – vocals, guitar (ex-JAMES GANG) with his band BARNSTORM: **KENNY PASSARELLI** – bass / **JOE VITALE** – drums

		Probe	Dunhill
Oct 72. (7") *<4327>* **MOTHER SAYS. / I'LL TELL THE WORLD ABOUT YOU**			-
Jan 73. (lp) *(6268) <50130>* **BARNSTORM**			79 Oct72

– Here we go / Midnight visitor / One and one / Giant bohemoth / Mother says / Birdcall morning / Home / I'll tell the world about you / Turn to stone / Comin' down. (re-iss. Oct74 on 'A.B.C.'; ABCL 5022)

—— added **ROCKE GRACE** – keyboards / **JOE LALA** – percussion

Aug 73. (7") *(PRO 600) <4361>* **ROCKY MOUNTAIN WAY. / (DAYDREAM) PRAYER**			23
(UK-iss.Jul75 on 'A.B.C.'; 4061)			
(lp) *<50140>* **THE SMOKER YOU DRINK, THE PLAYER YOU GET**			6 Jun73

– Rocky mountain way / Bookends / Wolf / Midnight moodies / Happy ways /

Meadows / Dreams / Days gone by / (Daydream) Prayer. (re-iss. quad.Oct74 on 'A.B.C.'; ABCL 5033) (cd-iss. Apr92 on 'M.C.A.'; MCLD 19020)

| Jan 74. (7") *(PRO 611) <4373>* **MEADOWS. / BOOKENDS** | | 89 Dec73 |
| (re-iss. Mar76 on 'A.B.C.'; 4105) | | |

—— In 1974, he sessioned for EAGLES, B.B. KING, etc., and produced DAN FOGELBERG

—— Solo; used past BARNSTORM members on a couple of tracks, plus new studio & live line-up **DAVID MASON + PAUL HARRIS** – keyboards / **BRYAN GAROFOLO** – bass / **RICKY FATAAR** – drums (ex-BEACH BOYS) / **TOM STEPHENSON** – keyboards

	Anchor	Dunhill
Dec 74. (lp) *(ABCL 5055) <50171>* **SO WHAT**		11

– Welcome to the club / Falling down / Pavane / Time out / All night laundromat blues / Turn to stone / Help me thru the night / County fair / Song for Emma.

| Feb 75. (7") *(ABC 4035) <15026>* **TURN TO STONE. / ALL NIGHT LAUNDROMAT BLUES** | | 93 |

—— although he was still a solo artist, WALSH joined EAGLES late '75.

	A.B.C.	A.B.C.
Apr 76. (lp) *(ABLC 5156) <932>* **YOU CAN'T ARGUE WITH A SICK MIND (live)**	28	20

– Walk away / Meadows / Rocky mountain way / Tell me / Help me through the night / Turn to stone. (re-iss. Jan83 on 'Fame' lp/c; FA/TCFA 3051) <US cd-iss. Jun88; 31120>

| Apr 76. (7") *<12115>* **TIME OUT (live). / HELP ME THRU THE NIGHT (live)** | - | |
| Jun 76. (7") *(ABC 4121)* **WALK AWAY (live). / HELP ME THRU THE NIGHT (live)** | | - |

—— WALSH used mainly session people + VITALE

	Asylum	Asylum
Jun 78. (7") *(K 13129) <45493>* **LIFE'S BEEN GOOD. / THEME FROM BOAT WEIRDOS**	14	12
Jun 78. (lp/c) *(K/K4 53081) <141>* **BUT SERIOUSLY, FOLKS . . .**	16	8

– Over and over / Second hand store / Indian summer / At the station / Tomorrow / Inner tube / Theme from Boat Weirdos / Life's been good. (cd-iss. Feb93 on 'WEA'; 7559 60527-2)

| Nov 78. (7") *(K 13141) <45536>* **OVER AND OVER. / AT THE STATION** | ☐ | ☐ |

below from the film 'Urban Cowboy'. B-side by GILLEY'S URBAN COWBOY BAND. On 'Full Moon' in America.

| Jun 80. (7") *(K 79146) <46639>* **ALL NIGHT LONG. / ORANGE BLOSSOM SPECIAL / HOEDOWN** | | 19 May80 |

—— now an ex-EAGLES man after that group's split

May 81. (7") *<47144>* **A LIFE OF ILLUSION. / ROCKETS**	-	34
May 81. (7") *(K 12533)* **A LIFE OF ILLUSION. / DOWN ON THE FARM**		-
May 81. (lp/c) *(K/K4 52285) <523>* **THERE GOES THE NEIGHBORHOOD**		20

– Things / Made your mind up / Down on the farm / Rivers (of the hidden funk) / A life of illusion / Bones / Rockets / You never know.

| Jul 81. (7") *<47197>* **MADE YOUR MIND UP. / THINGS** | - | - |
| Jan 82. (7") *<69951>* **WAFFLE STOMP. / THINGS** | - | |

	Full Moon	Warners
Jun 83. (7") *<29611>* **SPACE AGE WHIZ KIDS. / THEME FROM ISLAND WEIRDOS**	-	52
Jul 83. (lp/c) *(923884-1/-4) <23884>* **YOU BOUGHT IT – YOU NAME IT**		48

– I can play that rock & roll / Told you so / Here we are now / The worry song / I.L.B.T.'s / Space age whiz kids / Love letters / Class of '65 / Shadows / Theme from Island weirdos. (cd-iss. Jul84; 923884-2) (cd re-iss. Jul96 on 'WEA'; 7559 23884-2)

Aug 83. (7") *<29519>* **I CAN PLAY THAT ROCK & ROLL. / HERE WE ARE NOW**	-	
Sep 83. (7") *(W 9841)* **LOVE LETTERS. / TOLD YOU SO**	-	
Nov 83. (7") *<29454>* **LOVE LETTERS. / I.L.B.T.'s**	-	
Jun 85. (7") *<28910>* **I BROKE MY LEG. / GOOD MAN DOWN**	-	
Jun 85. (lp/c) *(925281-1/-4) <25281>* **THE CONFESSOR**		65 May85

– Problems / I broke my leg / Bubbles / Slow dancing / 15 years / Confessor / Rosewood bitters / Good man down / Dear John. (cd-iss. Jul88; 925606-2)

—— now with **CHAD CROMWELL** – drums / **DAVID COCHRAN + RICK THE . . . PLAYER** – bass / **MARK RIVERA** – saxophone / **JOHN DAVID SOUTHER + JIMI JAMISON** – backing vocals

| Aug 87. (lp/c/cd) *(925606-1/-4/-2) <25606>* **GOT ANY GUM?** | | Jul87 |

– The radio song / Fun / In my car / Malibu / Half of the time / Got any gum? / Up to me / No peace in the jungle / Memory lane / Time. (cd re-iss. Jan96 on 'WEA'; 7599 25606-2)

| Aug 87. (7") *<28304>* **THE RADIO SONG. / HOW YA DOIN'** | - | |
| Nov 87. (7") *<28225>* **IN MY CAR. / HOW YA DOIN'** | - | |

	Epic	Pyramid-Epic
Jul 91. (cd/c/lp) *(468128-2/-4/-1) <47384>* **ORDINARY AVERAGE GUY**		May91

– Two sides to every story / Ordinary average guy / The gamma goochee / All of a sudden / Alphabetical order / Look at us now / I'm actin' different / Up all night / You might need somebody / Where I grew up (prelude to schooldays).

| Jul 91. (7") *<73843>* **ORDINARY AVERAGE GUY. / ALPHABETICAL ORDER** | - | - |
| May 92. (cd/c) *<ZK 78916>* **SONGS FOR A DYING PLANET** | - | - |

– Shut up / Fairbanks, Alaska / Coyote love / I know / Certain situations / Vote for me / Theme from baroque weirdos / Friend song / It's all right / Will you still you love me tomorrow? / Decades / Song for a dying planet.

| Apr 95. (cd-ep; JOE WALSH & LITA FORD) **A FUTURE TO HIS LIFE /** | - | - |
| Apr 95. (cd) *<71888>* **A FUTURE TO THIS LIFE** (ROBOCOP: THE SERIES SOUNDTRACK) | - | - |

– A future to this life / Guilty of the crime / Fire and brimstone / Chutes and ladders / Flannel / Jacket / We gotta get you a woman / I only have eyes for you / Stuff ya gotta watch / In-a-gadda-da-vida / Shake your booty / Robocop adventure.

– compilations, others, etc. –

Jun 77. (7") *A.B.C.; (12426>* **ROCKY MOUNTAIN WAY. / TURN TO STONE** | - | | - |

Jun 77. (12"ep) *A.B.C.; (ABE 12-002)* **PLUS FOUR EP** | 39 | | - |
– Rocky mountain way / Turn to stone / Meadows / Walk away.

Oct 78. (lp/c) *A.B.C.; (ABCL/+C 5240) <1083>* **SO FAR SO GOOD – THE BEST OF JOE WALSH** | 71 |
– Rocky mountain way / Welcome to the club / Bookends / Walk away / Mother says / Turn to stone / Here we go / Pavane / Time out / Meadows. *(re-iss. 1983 on 'M.C.A.' lp/c; MCL/+C 1751) (cd-iss. 1987; MCAD 1601) (cd re-iss. Jun97 on 'Half Moon'; HMNCD 007)*

Aug 82. (7") *M.C.A.; (MCA 787)* **ROCKY MOUNTAIN WAY. / TURN TO STONE** | | | - |
(12"pic-d+=) *(MCATP 787)* – Funk 49.

Apr 86. (7") *Old Gold; (OG 9599)* **ROCKY MOUNTAIN WAY. / (b-side by Poco)** | | | - |

Oct 87. (d-cd) *M.C.A.; (DMCL 1874)* **THE SMOKER YOU DRINK . . . / YOU CAN'T ARGUE WITH A SICK MIND** | | | - |
(re-iss. Apr92; MCLD 19020) (re-iss. Jul96; MCD 33728)

Sep 89. (lp/c) *Raw Power; (RAW LP/TC 036)* **WELCOME TO THE CLUB** | | | - |

May 94. (cd/c; JOE WALSH & THE JAMES GANG) *Pickwick; (PWK S/MC 4207)* **ALL THE BEST** | | | - |

Jul 95. (d-cd) *M.C.A.; (MCD 11233)* **LOOK WHAT I DID: THE JOE WALSH ANTHOLOGY** | | - |
– Tuning, part 1 / Take a look around / Funk #48 / Bomber / Tend my garden / Funk #49 / Ashes, the rain and I / Walk away / It's all the same / Midnight man / Here we go / Midnight visitor / Mother says / Turn to stone / Comin' down / Meadows / Rocky mountain way / Welcome to the club / All night laundry mat blues / Country fair / Help me thru the night / Life's been good / Over and over / A life of illusion / Theme from the Island Weirdos / I can play that rock and roll / I.L.B.T.'s / Space age whiz kids / Rosewood bitters / Shut up / Decades / Song for a dying planet / Ordinary average guy (live with GLENN FREY).

WANNADIES

Formed: Skellefteå, Sweden . . . 1989 by PAR WILKSTEN, CHRISTINA BERGMARK, STEFAN SCHONFELT, FREDERIK SCHONFELT and GUNNAR KARLSSON. Moving to Stockholm, the group secured a deal with independent label, 'Snap', releasing an eponymous debut set the same year. Four years in the making, 'AQUANAUTIC' found the group working with ROXETTE songwriter, PER GESSLE; as might be expected, the results were less than rocking, although 'R.C.A.'-offshoot, 'Indolent', had enough faith in their indie-pop potential to sign them up in 1995. While it missed the chart first time round, the giddy, starry-eyed rush of 'YOU & ME SONG' introduced The WANNADIES as jangling indie fops in the finest tradition of the genre. On the right side of twee, just, the single was a taster for debut album, 'BE A GIRL', released the same month; with the same stilted-English charm as forebears, ABBA, the Swedish popsters traced a time-honoured lineage through the likes of The BYRDS, The DREAM ACADEMY, The GO-BETWEENS etc., right up to modern day practitioners like TEENAGE FANCLUB and served with an extra helping of BLUR-style attitude. After a further couple of minor hits with 'MIGHT BE STARS' and 'HOW DOES IT FEEL', the group finally made the Top 20 in Spring '96 with a re-released 'YOU & ME SONG'. The following year, they continued their steady rise to major league status with the single, 'HIT', a hit! no less from the follow-up set, BAGSY ME. • **Songwriters:** Group, except; LEE REMICK (Go-Betweens) / NEW LIFE (Depeche Mode) / BLISTER IN THE SUN (Violent Femmes) / I'M A MAN (Spencer Davis Group) / CHILDREN OF THE REVOLUTION (T.Rex) / I GOT A RIGHT (Iggy Pop).

Album rating: WANNADIES (*6) / AQUANAUTIC (*6) / BE A GIRL (*8) / BAGSY ME (*7) / THE WANNADIES compilation (*7)

PAR WILKSTEN – vocals / **CHRISTINA BERGMARK** – keyboards, vocals / **STEFAN SCHONFELT** – guitar / **FREDRIK SCHONFELDT** – bass / **GUNNAR KARLSSON** – drums / **MALMQUIST**

	Snap		not iss.

1989. (lp) *(SNAP 002)* **WANNADIES** | | | - |
– Together / Heaven / My home town / Things that you love / How beautiful is the Moon / Innocent me / So many lies / Smile / Anything / Black waters / The beast cures the lover / Children of the revolution / Lee Remick. *(re-iss. cd Jan94; RESNAP 002)*

Jan 93. (cd) *(SNAP 005)* **AQUANAUTIC** | | | - |
– Everything's true / Cherry man / Things that I would love to have undone / ove is dead / So hapy now / Lucky you / 1.07 / December days / Something to tell / Suddenly I missed her / God knows / Never killed anyone / I love you love me.

Apr 93. (cd-s) **SO HAPPY NOW / IN THE ALTOGETHER / BIRDS** | | | |

Jul 93. (cd-ep) **CHERRY MAN** | | | |
– Cherry man / Love is dead / Lee Remick / I'm a man / Blister in the sun.

Jun 94. (cd-s) **LOVE IN JUNE / I GOT A RIGHT** | | | |

—— now without MALMQUIST

	Indolent		R.C.A.

Aug 95. (7"colrd/c-s) *(DIE 002/+MC)* **YOU & ME SONG. / BLISTER IN THE SUN** | | | - |
(cd-s+=) *(DIE 002CD)* – Lift me up (don't let me down).

Aug 95. (cd/c/lp) *(DIE CD/MC/LP 002)* **BE A GIRL** | | | - |
– You and me song / Might be stars / Love in June / How does it feel? / Sweet nymphet / New world record / Dying for more / Soon you're dead / Do it all the time / Dreamy Wednesdays / Kid. *(re-dist.Apr96)*

Oct 95. (c-s) *(DIE 003MC)* **MIGHT BE STARS / CHERRY MAN** | 51 | | - |
(cd-s+=) *(DIE 003CD1)* – Lee Remick / Love is dead.
(cd-s) *(DIE 003CD2)* – ('A'side) / New life / So happy now / Things that I would love to have undone.

Feb 96. (c-s/cd-s) *(DIE 004 MC/CD1)* **HOW DOES IT FEEL? / DYING FOR MORE (live) / LOVE IN JUNE (live) / MIGHT BE STARS (live)** | 53 | | - |
(cd-s) *(DIE 004CD2)* – ('A'side) / Let go oh oh / I'm a man / Never killed anyone.

Apr 96. (7"colrd/c-s) *(DIE 005/MC)* **YOU & ME SONG. / BLISTER IN THE SUN** | 18 | | - |
(cd-s) *(DIE 005CD)* – ('A'side) / Everybody loves me / I like you a lalalala lot / You & me song (lounge version).

Aug 96. (7"/c-s) *(DIE 006/+MC)* **SOMEONE SOMEWHERE. / DISAPPOINTED** | 38 | | - |
(cd-s) *(DIE 006CD)* – ('A'side) / Why / Goodbye.

Oct 96. (7"/c-s) *(DIE 007/+MC)* **FRIENDS. / WE WERE SITTING IN A CAR ON OUR WAY FROM MOLD TO BATH AS A !** | | | - |
(cd-s) *(DIE 007CD)* – ('A'side) / Trick me / Can't get enough of that.

Apr 97. (7"colrd) *(DIE 009)* **HIT. / CRUCIFY ME** | 20 | | - |
(cd-s+=) *(DIE 009CD1)* – Pathetico.
(cd-s) *(DIE 009CD2)* – ('A'side) / As if you care / (Yeah yeah yeah) In your face.

May 97. (cd/c)(lp-box) *(DIE CD/MC 008)(DIELP 008S)* **BAGSY ME** | 37 | | - |
– Because / Friends / Someone somewhere / Oh yes (it's a mess) / Shorty / Damn it I said / Silent people / What you want / Hit / Bumble bee boy / Combat honey / That's all. *(lp+=)* – What's the fuss.

Jun 97. (7") *(DIE 010)* **SHORTY. / ARE YOU EXCLUSIVE** | 41 | | - |
(cd-s+=) *(DIE 010CD1)* – Short people.
(cd-s) *(DIE 010CD2)* – ('A'side) / Taking the easy way out / That's all.

Sep 97. (7"/c-s) *(DIE 011/+MC)* **YOU AND ME SONG. / JUST CAN'T GET ENOUGH** | | | - |
(cd-s) *(DIE 011CD)* – ('A'side) / Love in June / How does it feel / Love is dead.

Oct 97. (cd,c) *<67433>* **THE WANNADIES** (compilation) | - | | - |
– Might be stars / Because / Friends / You and me song / Someone somewhere / Damn it I said / How does it feel / Oh yes (it's a mess) / Shorty / Silent people / What you want / Hit / That's all.

WAR

Formed: 1969 . . . out of Compton/South Bay, L.A. outfit The CREATORS. An eclectic R&B combo with a strong Latino influence, The CREATORS released a few singles in the mid-60's but failed to make much of an impact outside of their native California. They did, however, pre-figure their soul/blues/rock partnership with white R&B merchant ERIC BURDON by hooking up with LOVE sax player TJAY CONTRELLI for a series of L.A. club dates (actual recordings of this bizarre partnership are rumoured to exist although they've never been commercially released). In 1968, The CREATORS metamorphosed into The NIGHTSHIFT, the group subsequently backing up American football figurehead, Deacon Jones, who was attempting to re-invent himself as a club crooner. WAR were saved from such a fate by producer/songwriter Jerry Goldstein, who introduced the band to ex-ANIMALS singer ERIC BURDON, fresh from England and looking to get hip to the West Coast scene. Renaming themselves WAR, the group (who at this stage comprised LONNIE JORDAN, HOWARD SCOTT, CHARLES MILLER, HAROLD BROWN, LEE OSKAR, B.B. DICKERSON and PAPA DEE ALLEN) recorded two albums with BURDON, 'ERIC BURDON DECLARES WAR' (1970) and 'BLACK MAN'S BURDON' (1971; 1970 US). Though the strangely infectious rhythms of Top 3 hit, 'SPILL THE WINE', boded well, the debut sounded stodgy and directionless despite its US Top 20 success. The group nevertheless toured America and Europe to critical acclaim and mass adulation, while the follow-up album showed more promise. The union was to be short-lived however, and following the death of close friend JIMI HENDRIX in September 1970, BURDON bailed out of the tour. WAR battled on alone, fulfilling their live commitments and beginning work on their own album. Although the group were still officially working as BURDON's backing band, Goldstein (now their manager) secured them a separate deal with 'United Artists'. 'WAR' was released in Spring '71, a promising collection of soul, funk, gospel and jazz, underpinned with the group's trademark latino rhythms. The album opened with 'SUN OH SON', mellow flute, harmonica and close harmonies kicking into a stone-heavy bass/organ groove; dynamic tactics which would see WAR develop into one of the fiercest progressive soul combos of the 70's. One of WAR's secret weapons was the Danish-born OSKAR, his harmonica playing at its bittersweet best on the beautiful 'BACK HOME', a sun-kissed, hymn-like ballad which stands among the cream of WAR's mellower work. Their more experimental tendencies emerged on 'WAR DRUMS' and 'FIDEL'S FANTASY', the latter a bizarre spoken monologue berating Cuban leader Fidel Castro, its mocking message driven on a hypnotic groundswell of insistent piano and latin percussion. There were apparently fears for ALLEN's (writer and narrator) safety after the record's release; WAR were certainly big enough to attract unwanted attention, especially after the considerable success of 'ALL DAY MUSIC' (1971). For many fans the consummate WAR set, it was certainly their most consistent, boasting the seminal spookiness of 'SLIPPIN' INTO DARKNESS', a shadowy blues/funk epic which had the atmosphere of an old-time confessional, alongside the defiant funk clarion call of 'GET DOWN' and the groovy 'NAPPY HEAD'. 'THAT'S WHAT LOVE WILL DO', meanwhile, was an old CREATORS tune, updated in moody, melancholy style. Again produced by Goldstein, some of the flab had been trimmed off since the debut, resulting in a leaner more radio-friendly sound. Upon its release as a single, 'SLIPPIN' . . .' eventually hit the Top 20, becoming WAR's first gold release as well as boosting sales of the album and cementing the gro position as one of the foremost funk/soul attractions in America. It ca little surprise then, when WAR scaled the US charts with their third s WORLD IS A GHETTO' (1973), the record spawning two Top in the compelling mock-Western fantasy of 'CISCO KID' and the title track. 'DELIVER THE WORD' (1973) and 'WHY CAN'T WE BE FRIENDS' (1975) both went Top 10, continuing WAR's singles chart succes with a gold disc for the the latter's title track (a heartfelt plea for an end to racial segregation which was even beamed into space for US and Russian astronauts' listening pleasure!). The brilliant 'LOW RIDER' meanwhile, became one of only two WAR singles to break the UK Top 20. Things started to go awry in the latter half of the decade, beginning with a move to 'Blue Note'. Though 'PLATINUM JAZZ' (1977) was the label's only platinum release, musically it fell way short of expectations with its noodling, instrumental hotch-potch of old and previously unreleased tracks. 'GALAXY' (1978) wasn't much of an improvement, the group found all at sea attempting to come to grips with the all-pervasive disco revolution. The 80's were a barren time for WAR as sax maestro MILLER was murdered during a robbery and the group tried in vain for a successful comeback on 'R.C.A.' with 'OUTLAW' (1982). Further strife came as ALLEN died from a brain aneurysm on stage, the group having split from Goldstein and given up recording. WAR were eventually coaxed back into the studio in 1995 for 'PEACE SIGN', their profile having been revived via an extensive re-issue programme for 'ARG' records (through BMG in the UK) and the continuing patronage of various hip hop artists. At their leanest, WAR were among the most adventurous, exciting black musicians of their day; it's just a pity their passion for social justice and racial integration is so often substituted for "bitches" and "uzis" among their musical descendants.

Album rating: Eric Burdon & War: ERIC BURDON DECLARES WAR (*6) / THE BLACK MAN'S BURDON (*5) / War: WAR (*6) / ALL DAY MUSIC (*7) / THE WORLD IS A GHETTO (*8) / DELIVER THE WORD (*6) / WAR LIVE! (*4) / WHY CAN'T WE BE FRIENDS? (*8) / GREATEST HITS compilation (*7) / PLATINUM JAZZ collection (*5) / GALAXY (*6) / YOUNGBLOOD soundtrack (*4) / THE MUSIC BAND (*4) / THE MUSIC BAND 2 (*4) / OUTLAW (*5) / LIFE (IS SO STRANGE) (*4) / THE BEST OF WAR ... AND MORE remixes (*5) / WAR ANTHOLOGY 1970-1994 compilation (*8) / PEACE SIGN (*4)

LONNIE JORDAN (b.LEROY JORDAN, 21 Nov'48, San Diego, Calif.) – keyboards / **HOWARD SCOTT** (b.15 Mar'46, San Pedro, Calif.) – guitar, vocals / **CHARLES MILLER** (b. 2 Jun'39, Olathe, Kansas) – saxophone, clarinet / **HAROLD BROWN** (b.17 Mar'46) – drums, percussion / **LEE OSKAR** (b.24 Mar'46, Copenhagen, Denmark) – harmonica / **B.B.DICKERSON** (b. MORRIS, 3 Aug'49, Torrance, Calif.) – bass, vocals repl. PETER ROSEN who died drug overdose mid '69. / **PAPA DEE ALLEN** (b. THOMAS SYLVESTER ALLEN, 18 Jul'31, Wilmington, Delaware) – keyboards

— Recorded 2 albums in 1970 + 71 with (ex-ANIMALS ⇒) vocalist ERIC BURDON. 'ERIC BURDON DECLARES WAR' & 'THE BLACK MAN'S BURDON' both hit UK/US charts.

		U.A.	U.A.
Apr 71.	(7") (LBF 15443) <50746> **SUN OH SON. / LONELY FEELIN'**		
May 71.	(lp) (LBG 83478) <5508> **WAR**		Apr 71

– Sun oh son / Lonely feelin' / Back home / War drums / Vibeka / Fidel's fantasy. *(re-iss.Jun76 on 'Island'; ILPS 9164) (re-iss.Oct79 on 'M.C.A.'; MCG 4003)*

| Aug 71. | (7") (UP 35281) <50815> **ALL DAY MUSIC. / GET DOWN** | | 35 |
| Oct 71. | (lp) (UAS 29269) <5546> **ALL DAY MUSIC** | | 16 |

– All day music / Get down / That's what love will do / There must be a reason / Nappy need / Slipping into darkness / Baby brother. *(re-iss.Jun76 on 'Island'; ILPS 9177) (re-iss.Oct79 on 'MCA'; MCF 3020) (cd-iss.Oct95 on 'Avenue'; 74321 30520-2)*

| Apr 72. | (7") (UP 35327) <50867> **SLIPPIN' INTO DARKNESS. / NAPPY HEAD** | | 16 Jan 72 |

(re-iss.Nov76;)

| Dec 72. | (7") (UP 35469) <50975> **THE WORLD IS A GHETTO. / FOUR CORNERED ROOM** | | 7 Nov 72 |
| Jan 73. | (lp/c) (UAS/+C 29400) <5652> **THE WORLD IS A GHETTO** | | 1 Nov 72 |

– The Cisco kid / Where was you at / City, country city / Four cornered room / The world is a ghetto / Beetles in a bog. *(re-iss.Oct79 on 'MCA'; MCF 3021) (cd-iss.Oct95 on 'Avenue'; 74321 130521-2)*

Mar 73.	(7") (UP 35521) <163> **THE CISCO KID. / BEETLES IN THE BOG**		2
Aug 73.	(7") (UP 35576) <281> **GYPSY MAN. / DELIVER THE WORD**		8 Jul 73
Aug 73.	(lp/c) (UAS/+C 29521) <128> **DELIVER THE WORD**		6

– Three dog night eyes / Gypsy man / Me and baby brother / Deliver the word / Southern part of Texas / Blisters. *(re-iss.Oct79 on 'MCA'; MCF 3022) (cd-iss.Oct95 on 'Avenue'; 74321 30522-2)*

| Dec 73. | (7") (UP 35623) <350> **ME AND BABY BROTHER. / IN YOUR EYES** | | 15 Nov 73 |

(UK re-iss.Jun76; WIP 6303) – hit No.21

| Apr 74. | (d-lp/c) (UAD/+C 60067/8) <193> **WAR LIVE! (live)** | | 13 Mar 74 |

– (introductions by E.Rodney Jones) / Sun oh son / The Cisco kid / Slippin' into darkness / All day music / Ballero / Lonely feelin' / Intro – Get down / Get down. *(re-iss.Jun76 on 'Island'; ILSD 8) (re-iss.Oct79 on 'MCA'; MCF 3040)*

| Apr 74. | (7") <432> **BALLERO (live). / SLIPPIN' INTO DARKNESS (live)** | - | 33 |
| Jul 75. | (7") (UP 35836) <629> **WHY CAN'T WE BE FRIENDS?. / IN MAZATLAN** | | 6 May 75 |

(re-iss.Mar76 on 'Island'; WIP 6289)

| Jul 75. | (lp/c) (UAG/+C 29843) <441> **WHY CAN'T WE BE FRIENDS?** | | 8 Jun 76 |

– Don't let no one get you down / Lotus blossom / Heartbeat / Leroy's Latin lament: Lonies dream – The dream – The way we feel – La fiesta / Lament / Smile happy / So / Low rider / In Mazatlan / Why can't we be friends. *(re-iss.Jun76 on 'Island'; ILPS 9378) (re-iss.Oct79 on 'MCA'; MCF 3023) (cd-iss.Oct95 on 'Avenue'; 74321 30523-2)*

		Island	U.A.
Jan 76.	(7") (WIP 6267) <706> **LOW RIDER. / SO**	12	7 Sep75
˙ug 76.	(7") (WIP 6315) <834> **SUMMER. / ALL DAY MUSIC**		7 Jul 76
76.	(lp/c) (ILPS/ICT 9413) <648> **GREATEST HITS** (compilation)		6

– All day music / Slippin' into darkness / The world is a ghetto / The Cisco kid / ˙ypsy man / Me and baby brother / Southern part of Texas / Why can't we be ˙nds? / Low rider / Summer.*(re-iss.Jul76 on 'Island'; ILPS 9413) (re-iss.Oct79 ˙CA'; MCF 3030)*

		Island	Blue Note
Jul 77.	(d-lp) <690> **PLATINUM JAZZ**	-	23

– (compilation) War is coming / Slowly we walk together / Platinum jazz / I got you / L.A. sunshine / River Niger / H2 overture / City, country, city / Smile happy / Deliver the word / Nappy head / Four cornered room.*(re-iss.Sep77 as 'PLATINUM FUNK' on 'Island'; ILPS 9507) (re-iss.Oct79 on 'MCA'; MCSP 305) (cd-iss.Oct95 on 'Avenue'; 74321 30524-2)*

| Jul 77. | (7") <1009> **L.A.SUNSHINE. / SLOWLY WE WALK TOGETHER** | - | 45 |

		M.C.A.	M.C.A.
Dec 77.	(7") (MCA 339) <40820> **GALAXY. / ('A'instrumental)**	14	39
Jan 78.	(lp/c) (MCF/+C 2822) <3030> **GALAXY**	15	Nov 77

– Galaxy / Baby Face (she said do do do do) / Sweet fighting lady / Hey senorita / The seven tin soldiers.

| Mar 78. | (7"/12") (MCA/+T 359) <40883> **HEY SENORITA. / SWEET FIGHTING LADY** | 40 | |
| Jul 78. | (lp/c) (MCF/+C 2804) <904> **YOUNGBLOOD (Soundtrack)** | | 69 |

– Youngblood / Sing a happy song / Keep on movin' / The Kingsmen sign / Walking to war / This funky music makes you feel good / Junk yard / Superdude / Youngblood & Sybil / Flying machine / Searching for Youngblood & Rommel / Youngblood (rerise). *(re-iss.Dec79 on 'MCA'; MCF 2804)*

| Aug 78. | (7") (MCA 383) **BABY FACE (SHE SAID DO DO DO DO). / ('A'version)** | | - |
| Oct 78. | (7"/12") (MCA/+T 399) <1213> **YOUNGBLOOD. / ('A'version)** | | |

— added **ALICE TWEED SMYTH** – vocals + **LUTHER RABB** – bass

| Apr 79. | (7"/12") (MCA/+T 418) **GOOD GOOD FEELIN'. / SWEET FIGHTIN' LADY** | | |
| Apr 79. | (lp/c) (MCG/+C 4001) <3085> **THE MUSIC BAND** | | 41 |

– The music band / Corns & callouses / I'm the one who understands / Good good feelin' / Millionaire / All around the world. *(re-iss.Oct79 on 'MCA'; MCF 3050)*

| Aug 79. | (7"/12") (MCA/+T 514) <41061> **I'M THE ONE WHO UNDERSTANDS. / CORNS & CALLOUSES** | | |

— added **PAT RIZZO** – horns / **RON HAMMOND** – percussion to repl. DICKERSON.

| Jan 80. | (7"/12") (MCA/+T 557) **THE WORLD IS A GHETTO. / I'LL TAKE CARE OF YOU** | | - |
| Jan 80. | (lp/c) (MCF/+C 3050) <3193> **THE MUSIC BAND 2** | | Dec 79 |

– Don't take it away / I'll take care of you / The world is a ghetto / I'll be around / Night people / The music band. Don't take it away / I'll take care of you / The world is a ghetto / I'll be around / Night people / The music band 2.

| May 80. | (7") (MCA 593) <41209> **I'LL BE AROUND. / THE MUSIC BAND 2** | | |
| Nov 80. | (lp) <5156> **THE MUSIC BAND – LIVE (live)** | | |

– Spill the wine / All day music / Slippin' into darkness / Low rider / Cisco kid / All night long / Gypsy man / Why can't we be friends.

		R.C.A.	Lax
Mar 82.	(7"/12") (RCA/+T 201) <13061> **YOU GOT THE POWER. / CINCO DE MAYO**	58	66
Mar 82.	(lp/c) (RCA LP/K 3050) <4208> **OUTLAW**		48

– You got the power / Outlaw / The jungle (medley):- Beware it's a jungle out there – The street of walls – The street of lights – The street of now / Just because / Baby it's cold outside / I'm about somebody / Cinco de Mayo.

| May 82. | (7") <13238> **OUTLAW. / I'M ABOUT SOMEBODY** | - | 94 |
| Jul 82. | (7") (RCA 240) **JUST BECAUSE. / I'M ABOUT SOMEBODY** | - | - |

— SMYTH + MILLER now departed

| Jun 83. | (lp/c) (RCA LP/K 3113) <4598> **LIFE (IS SO STRANGE)** | | |

– Life (is so strange) / Happiness / W.W.III (medley) / The dawning of night / Waiting at the church / When the nightmare comes / Shaking it down / Summer dreams / U-2 (medley):- U-2 (part 1) – Automatic eyes – U-2 (part 2) – U-2 (part 3)

— **RICKY GREEN** – bass repl. RABB

		Bluebird	not iss.
Mar 85.	(7"/12") (BR/T 16) **GROOVIN'. / ('A'instrumental)**	43	-

(re-iss.Aug86)

		Lax	Lax
May 87.	(7") (XLAX 1) **LOW RIDER (remix). / SLIPPIN' INTO DARKNESS**		

(12"+=) (XLAX 100) – ('A'original mix). (cd-s+=) (CDLAX 100) – Galaxy / Me and baby brother.

— **JORDAN** moved to bass when GREEN departed

		not iss.	Virgin
Aug 91.	(c-s) <98751> **LOWRIDER (IN THE BOULEVARD). /**	-	54

— now without OSKAR

		Avenue	Avenue
1992.	(cd) <R2 71040> **RAP DECLARES WAR**	-	

— added **BROWN / TETSUYA NAKAMURA / RAE VALENTINE / KERRY CAMPBELL / SAL RODRIGUEZ + CHARLES GREEN**

| Jun 95. | (cd) <76024> **PEACE SIGN** | | 1994 |

– Peace sign / East L.A. / Wild Rodriguez / I'm the one (who understands) / Da roof / The smuggler (the light in the window) / U B O K / Let me tell you / Smile for me / What if / Angel / Homeless hero.

– compilations, etc. –

1983.	(lp) MCA; **THE MUSE BAND – JAZZ**	-	-
Jun 87.	(lp) Thunderbolt; (THBL 1041) **ON FIRE**		
May 87.	(cd) Chord; (CDLAX 100) / Priority; <9467> **THE BEST OF WAR & MORE – THE REMIXES**		

(re-iss.Apr92 on 'Avenue-Rhino'; 70072)

| Oct 94. | (d-cd) Rhino; <71774> **WAR ANTHOLOGY: 1970-1994** | - | - |

– Tobacco road / Spill the wine / They can't take away our music / Sun oh son / Lonely feelin' / All day music / Get down / Slippin' into darkness / Cisco kid / The world is a ghetto / City, country, city / Where was you at / Gypsy man / Me and my baby brother / Deliver the word / Ballero / Why can't we be friends? / Low rider / Don't let no one get you down / Summer / L.A. sunshine / River Niger / Galaxy / Youngblood (livin' in the streets) / This funky music makes you feel good / Music band / Outlaw / You got the power / Cinco de Mayo / Life (is so strange) / Don't let no one get you down / Peace sign.

Clifford T. WARD

Born: CLIFFORD THOMAS WARD, 10 Feb'44, Kidderminster, Worcestershire, England. While studying in Stourport, he formed his first group, CLIFF WARD & THE CRUISERS, although it was as leader of soul/R&B covers outfit MARTIN RAYNOR & THE SECRETS that he'd gain his initial foothold in the music business; the nom de plume was instigated by their label, 'Columbia-EMI', to prevent any mix up with their top star, CLIFF RICHARD. After a one-off Holland-Dozier-Holland-penned 45, 'CANDY TO ME', the group signed to 'C.B.S.' as The SECRETS. With WARD as the chief writer, they released a string of singles over the period late '66 to late '68 in an increasingly bubblegum/psychedelic mould; the final two were billed as SIMON'S SECRETS. It would be another three years before CLIFFORD (who was also employed as a schoolteacher!) re-emerged, re-inventing himself as a bedsit troubadour via a deal with 'Dandelion' records (the label co-owned by noneother than Radio One DJ JOHN PEEL). The appropriately-titled 'SINGER-SONGWRITER' (1972) album showcased his new style, leading off with the upbeat but melancholy love song 'COATHANGER'. The demise of 'Dandelion' led WARD on to 'Charisma' (home of GENESIS, VAN DER GRAAF, etc) where he shocked his fans and critics by having a Top 10 hit, 'GAYE'. This helped propel the well-received 'HOME THOUGHTS' (1973) album into the Top 40, and transformed the shy-haired long-haired singer into an unlikely teen-mag sex symbol. He stuck with this rather unfashionable and anti-glam approach on his follow-up hit single, 'SCULLERY', continuing the home-sweet-home theme on the accompanying album, 'MANTLE PIECES' (1974). Although his chart career ended here and he became more of a cult artist, WARD still managed to deliver the odd (very odd!) album; JUSTIN HAYWARD and Sir CLIFF were among those to cover his songs. However, the singer-songwriter suffered a serious setback in 1986 when he was diagnosed with multiple sclerosis. In 1992, the first in a series of out-takes CD's were issued in an attempt to keep him financially afloat.

Album rating: SINGER-SONGWRITER (*5) / HOME THOUGHTS (*7) / MANTLEPIECES (*5) / ESCALATOR (*6) / NO MORE ROCK'N'ROLL (*4) / WAVES (*4) / NEW ENGLAND DAYS (*4) / BOTH OF US (*5) / GAYE AND OTHER STORIES compilation (*6) / SOMETIME NEXT YEAR (*3) / LAUGH IT OFF demos (*4)

SECRETS

CLIFF WARD (i.e. MARTIN RAYNOR) – vocals / **FRED NASH** – guitar / **MALCOLM RUSSELL** – bass / **KEN WRIGHT** – drums

	Columbia	not iss.
May 65. (7"; as MARTIN RAYNOR & THE SECRETS) *(DB 7563)* **CANDY TO ME. / YOU'RE A WONDERFUL ONE**		-

	C.B.S.	not iss.
Dec 66. (7") *(CBS 202466)* **I SUPPOSE. / SUCH A PITY**		-
Feb 67. (7") *(CBS 202585)* **INFATUATION. / SHE'S DANGEROUS**		-
May 67. (7") *(CBS 2818)* **I INTEND TO PLEASE. / I THINK I NEED THE CASH**		-

—— **WARD** was now joined by stable line-up of **IAN SIMMONDS** – lead guitar / **DAVIE CONWAY** – rhythm guitar / **DAVE HOLDER** – bass / **ROB ELCOCK** – drums

Apr 68. (7"; as SIMON'S SECRETS) *(CBS 3406)* **NAUGHTY BOY. / SYMPATHY**		-
Dec 68. (7"; as SIMON'S SECRETS) *(CBS 3856)* **I KNOW WHAT HER NAME IS. / KEEPING MY HEAD ABOVE WATER**		-

—— In Sep'71, WARD appeared on a JESS RODEN BAND b-side; the track in question being by GAMMOND-WARD, 'A MATTER OF PERSPECTIVE'.

CLIFFORD T. WARD

—— - vocals, keyboards / with various personnel throughout

	Dandelion	not iss.
Aug 72. (7") *(2001 327)* **CARRIE. / SIDETRACK**		-
Sep 72. (7") *(2310 216)* **SINGER-SONGWRITER**		-
– Coathanger / Sam / Leader / Dream / Anticipation / Rayne / Session singer / Carrie / God help me / Cause is good / Sympathy / Circus girl / You knock when you should come in. *(cd-iss. May95 on 'See For Miles' +=; SEECD 418)* – Sidetrack.		
Oct 72. (7") *(2001 382)* **COATHANGER. / RAYNE**		-

	Charisma	Charisma
Jun 73. (7") *(CB 209)* **GAYE. / HOME THOUGHTS FROM ABROAD**	8	
Jul 73. (lp/c) *(CAS/ZC-CAS 1066)* <6061> **HOME THOUGHTS**	40	
– Gaye / Wherewithal / The dubious circus company / Where would that leave me / The traveller / Home thoughts from abroad / Where's it going to end / Time the magician / Give me one for chance / Cold wind blowing / The open university / Crisis. *(re-iss. Oct86 lp/c; CHC/+MC 56)*		
Sep 73. (7") *(CB 212)* **WHEREWITHAL. / THINKING OF SOMETHING TO DO**		-
Jan 74. (7") *(CB 221)* **SCULLERY. / TO AN AIR HOSTESS**	37	-
Feb 74. (lp/c) *(CAS/ZC-CAS 1077)* **MANTLE PIECES**	42	-
– Scullery / Not waving – drowning / Are you really interested / A sad cliche / To an air hostess / All modern conveniences / Wayward / Screen test / For Debbie and her friends / Tea cosy. *(re-iss. 1985 lp/c; CHC/+MC 37)*		
Aug 74. (7") *(CB 233)* **JAYNE (FROM ANDROMEDA SPIRAL). / MAYBE I'M RIGHT**		-
Mar 75. (7") *(CB 248)* **JIGSAW GIRL. / CELLOPHANE**		-
Apr 75. (lp/c) *(CAS/ZC-CAS 1098)* **ESCALATOR**		-
– The way of love / Jigsaw girl / Escalator / Trespass / We could be talking / Day to myself / Miner / Mr. Bilbo Baggins / Cellophane / Sad affair. *(re-iss. Oct86; CHC 57)*		

	Philips	not iss.
Nov 75. (7") *(6006 490)* **NO MORE ROCK'N'ROLL. / GANDALF**		-
Dec 75. (lp) *(9109 500)* **NO MORE ROCK'N'ROLL**		-

– Gentle / Secretary / Birmingham / Up in the world / Summer solstice / Jayne (from Andromeda spiral) / Tomorrow night / No more rock'n'roll / Gandalf / For Emily / When I found you / Easy baby.

Sep 76. (7") *(6006 542)* **OCEAN OF LOVE. / TOMORROW NIGHT**		-
Nov 76. (lp) *(9109 216)* **WAVES**		-
– Avenue dreams / Everything goes out the window / Heaven / Moonlight / Next to you / Not waving, drowning (revisited) / Ocean of love / Song for Susan / Waves / Witches and ghosts.		

	Mercury	not iss.
Mar 77. (7") *(6007 132)* **UP IN THE WORLD. / NOT WAVING, DROWNING (REVISITED)**		-
Sep 77. (7") *(6007 149)* **I GOT LOST TONIGHT. / DETRIMENT**		-
Oct 77. (lp/c) *(9109/7109 320)* **NEW ENGLAND DAYS**		-
– Detriment / I got lost tonight / If I had known / New England days / Nothing new / Reckless / Sal / Somebody stole my woman / Someone I know / Water wheel / You're no angel.		

	LUV 1	not iss.
Jan 78. (7") *(LUV 1)* **SOMEONE I KNOW. / IF I HAD KNOWN**		-

	WEA	not iss.
Jul 80. (7") *(K 18294)* **CONVERTIBLE. / TAKING THE LONG WAY ROUND**		-
Jan 81. (7") *(K 18426)* **THE BEST IS YET TO COME. / LOST AGAIN**		-
Apr 81. (7") *(K 18486)* **CONTRARY. / CLIMATE OF HER FAVOUR**		-

	Philips	not iss.
Dec 83. (7") *(814 776-7)* **THE BEST IS YET TO COME. / HOME**	-	- Irish
Mar 84. (lp/c) *(814 777-1/-4)* **BOTH OF US**	-	-
– Still not free / Messenger / Watchin' the TV news / Leaving / Both of us / Where do angels really come from / Contrary / Before the world was round / Waiting for the garda / Change of heart / Twenty minutes / The best is yet to come.		
Apr 84. (7") *(822 567-7)* **STILL NOT FREE. / WATCHIN' THE TV NEWS**	-	- Irish
Dec 84. (7") *(880 550-7)* **MESSENGER. / WHERE DO ANGELS REALLY COME FROM**	-	- Irish

	Tembo	not iss.
Mar 86. (7") *(TML 114)* **CRICKET. / COMPUTER**		-
Oct 86. (lp/c) *(TMB/+C 111)* **SOMETIME NEXT YEAR**		-
– Prams / Who cares / Another radio station / Quiz show / They must think I'm a fool / Sometime next year / Losin' after all (nothin' new) / Stars / Turbo / Like an old song / Today in parliament / Lost in the flow of your love.		
Nov 86. (7") *(TML 123)* **SOMETIME NEXT YEAR. / TURBO**		-

WARD retired from the studio; multiple sclerosis was the cause.

– compilations, etc. –

Apr 76. (7") *Charisma; (CB 280)* **HOME THOUGHTS FROM ABROAD. / WHERE WOULD THAT LEAD ME**		
Jul 78. (7") *Old Gold; (OG 9008)* **GAYE. / SCULLERY** *(re-iss. Jul82; same)*		
May 82. (7") *Charisma; (CB 409)* **THE TRAVELLER. / CLEAR WHITE LIGHT**		
Mar 83. (c) *Charisma; (CASMC 107)* **HOME THOUGHTS / MANTLE PIECES**		
Mar 87. (cd) *Charisma; (COMCD 4)* **GAYE & OTHER STORIES**		
– Gaye / Wherewithal / Cellophane / The dubious circus company / Not waving – drowning / Time the magician / Home thoughts from abroad / The way of love / The open university / Jigsaw girl / A day to myself / Nightingale / We could be talking / Where's it going to end? / Crisis / Scullery / Where would that leave me / To an air hostess / A sad affair. *(re-iss. Jul92 +=; CDVM 9009)* – (extra track).		
Nov 87. (7") *Old Gold; (OG 9733)* **GAYE. / (other track by Gary Shearston)**		
Mar 92. (cd) *Ameless; (AME 001)* **LAUGH IT OFF** (outtakes)		
Sep 94. (cd/c) *Graduate; (GRAD CD/MC 4)* **JULIA & OTHER NEW STORIES** (outtakes plus)		
Aug 98. (cd) *RP Media; (CDRPM 0041)* **HIDDEN TREASURES**		
May 99. (cd) *RP Media; (CDRPM 0052)* **BITTERSWEET**		

WARRANT (dig out; Great Metal . . .)

W.A.S.P.

Formed: Los Angeles, California, USA . . . 1983 as W.A.S.P. (We Are Sexual Perverts/White Anglo Saxon Protestants?, just two of the many possibilities touted by fans and commentators alike over the years, the debate now enshrined in metal myth) by 6' 4" New Yorker (ex-NEW YORK DOLLS reincarnation), BLACKIE LAWLESS, together with CHRIS HOLMES, RANDY PIPER and TONY RICHARDS. Coming on like a cartoon ALICE COOPER with about as much subtlety as a sledgehammer, W.A.S.P. held fast by every heavy metal cliche in the book (as well as inventing a few of their own), confirming every parent's worst nightmare about "that awful music". In spite of this, or more likely because of it, they were one of the most entertaining and amusing metal bands of the 80's. Who else would've had the balls to sign to a respected major like 'Capitol' then expect them to release 'ANIMAL (FUCK LIKE A BEAST)'? In the event, 'Music For Nations' did the honours and 'Capitol' consoled themselves with a marginally less offensive debut album, 'W.A.S.P.' (1984). LAWLESS and Co. didn't trade on outrage alone, no, surprisingly they actually had songs, hooks and melodies to back them up, tracks like 'I WANNA BE SOMEBODY' exploiting the same teen rebel formula perfected by KISS / TWISTED SISTER in equally anthemic style. Lyrics aside, W.A.S.P. caused even greater consternation among the pseudo-liberals at the PMRC with their gleefully unreconstructed stage show. A tongue-in-cheek gorefest with plenty of fake blood, topless women being 'tortured', BLACKIE flaunting his famous cod-piece etc., the W.A.S.P. live experience became the stuff of legend, although by the time the group had graduated from seedy L.A. clubs to theatres and stadiums, things had been considerably toned down. With STEPHEN

RILEY replacing RICHARDS, the group released a follow-up set in September '85, 'THE LAST COMMAND'. A transatlantic Top 50 chart hit, the album was a slight improvement on the debut, featuring such enduring stage favourites as the howling 'WILD CHILD' and 'BLIND IN TEXAS'. Amid continuing battles with their would-be censors and a new bassist, JOHNNY ROD, W.A.S.P. released a third set, 'INSIDE THE ELECTRIC CIRCUS', in late '86, showing their unlikely musical influences with covers of Uriah Heep's 'EASY LIVIN'' and Ashford & Simpson's 'I DON'T NEED NO DOCTOR'(made famous by Humble Pie). 'LIVE . . . IN THE RAW' (1987) marked a kind of last stand of the old W.A.S.P., the closing of the first turbulent period of their career before they turned all 'professional' on us. With the help of keyboard veteran (KEN HENSLEY), W.A.S.P. substituted the blood and guts for a surprisingly mature set of state-of-society ruminations. Still, LAWLESS bellowing along to 'REBEL IN THE F.D.G.' (Fucking Decadent Generation, apparently), sounds just a tad ridiculous if not hypocritical. The set provided the group with their biggest UK success to date (boosted by a furious Top 20 cover of The Who's 'REAL ME') although the change of approach didn't go down too well in the States. HOLMES subsequently departed in less than amicable circumstances, while LAWLESS revamped the band in 1990 as BLACKIE LAWLESS AND WASP, recruiting a line-up of ROD, HENSLEY, FRANKIE BANALI and BOB GULLICK for 1992's 'CRIMSON IDOL'. A concept album of all things, the record nevertheless gave LAWLESS a brief tenure in the UK Top 30. After touring the record and releasing the 'FIRST BLOOD, LAST CUTS' (1993) compilation, BLACKIE officially went solo, releasing 'STILL NOT BLACK ENOUGH' (1995) on the 'Raw Power' label. While he still commands a diehard fanbase, LAWLESS' golden days of controversy and outrage seem to be over. W.A.S.P.'s shlock-rock pales into almost non-existent insignificance next to the genuinely stomach churning output of modern death-metal acts, but can these young whippersnappers boast a fire-breathing cod-piece!?, can they heck as like! • **Songwriters:** Most written by LAWLESS and PIPER, except PAINT IT BLACK (Rolling Stones) / LOCOMOTIVE BREATH (Jethro Tull) / LONG WAY TO THE TOP + WHOLE LOTTA ROSIE (Ac-Dc) / SOMEBODY TO LOVE (Jefferson Airplane). • **Trivia:** Late in 1989, the lucky HOLMES married metal-songstress LITA FORD.

Album rating: W.A.S.P. (*5) / THE LAST COMMAND (*6) / INSIDE THE ELECTRIC CIRCUS (*6) / LIVE . . . IN THE RAW (*4) / THE HEADLESS CHILDREN (*5) / THE CRIMSON IDOL (*6) / FIRST BLOOD, LAST CUTS compilation (*6) / STILL NOT BLACK ENOUGH (*4) / KILL, F**, DIE (*3) / DOUBLE LIVE ASSASSINS (*3) / HELLDORADO (*3)

BLACKIE LAWLESS (b. STEVE DUREN, 4 Sep'54, Florida) – vocals, bass (ex-SISTER, ex-NEW YORK DOLLS) / **CHRIS HOLMES** (b.23 Jun'61) – lead guitar (ex-SISTER) / **RANDY PIPER** – rhythm guitar / **TONY RICHARDS** – drums

	Music For Nations	not iss.
Apr 84. (12",12"white/7"sha-pic-d/7") *(12/P+KUT 109)* **ANIMAL (F**K LIKE A BEAST). / SHOW NO MERCY**		–
(re-iss. 12"pic-d.May85; PIG 109) (re-iss. 12"/12"w-poster, Feb88; 12KUT/+P 109)		
LIVE ANIMAL. / DB BLUES / ANIMAL; *hit UK 61*		

	Capitol	Capitol
Aug 84. (lp/c) *(EJ 240195-1/-4)* <12343> **W.A.S.P.**	51	74
– I wanna be somebody / L.O.V.E. machine / The flame / B.A.D. / School daze / Hellion / Sleeping (in the fire) / On your knees / Tormentor / The torture never stops. *(re-iss. Jun88 on 'Fame' lp/c; FA/TCFA 3201) (cd-iss. May89; CDFA 3201) (re-iss. Jul94 cd/c; CDP 746661-2/-4)*		
Sep 84. (7")(12"/12"pic-d) *(CL 336)(12CL/+P 336)* **I WANNA BE SOMEBODY. / TORMENTOR (RAGEWARS)**		–
Jan 85. (7"/12") *(CL/12CL 344)* **SCHOOLDAZE. / PAINT IT BLACK**		–

——— **STEPHEN RILEY** – drums (ex-KEEL) repl. RICHARDS

Sep 85. (lp/c) *(EJ 240429-1/-4)* <12435> **THE LAST COMMAND**	48	49
– Wild child / Ballcrusher / Fistful of diamonds / Jack action / Widowmaker / Blind in Texas / Cries in the night / The last command / Running wild in the streets / Sex drive. *(re-iss. May89 on 'Fame' cd/c/lp; CD/TC+/FA 3218) (re-iss. Jul94 cd/c; CD/TC EST 2025)*		
Oct 85. (7"/7"pic-d) *(CL/+P 374)* **BLIND IN TEXAS. / SAVAGE**		–
(12"+=/12"pic-d+=) (12CL/+P 374) – I wanna be somebody (live).		
Jun 86. (7") *(CL 388)* **WILD THING. / MISSISSIPPI QUEEN**	71	–
(d7"+=) (CLD 388) – On your knees / Hellion.		
(12"+=) (12CL 388) – ('A'-wild mix).		

——— **JOHNNY ROD** (b. 8 Dec'57, Missouri) – bass (ex-KING KOBRA) repl. PIPER

——— **BLACKIE** now also rhythm guitar

Sep 86. (7"/7"pic-d) *(CL/+P 432)* **9.5 N.A.S.T.Y. / EASY LIVING**	70	–
(12"+=) (12CL 432) – Flesh and fire.		
Oct 86. (lp/c; as WASP) *(EST/TCEST 2025)* <12531> **INSIDE THE ELECTRIC CIRCUS**	53	60
– The big welcome / Inside the electric circus / I don't need no doctor / 95 nasty / Restless gypsy / Shoot it from the hip / I'm alive / Easy living / Sweet cheetah / Mantronic / King of Sodom and Gomorrah / The rock rolls on. *(cd-iss. Apr87; CDP 746346-2) (re-iss. May89 lp/c)(cd; ATAK/TCATAK 133)(CZ 212) (re-iss. Jul90 on 'Fame' cd/c/lp; CD/TC+/FA 3238) (re-iss. Jul94 cd/c; same)*		
Aug 87. (7") *(CL 458)* <44063> **SCREAM UNTIL YOU LIKE IT. / SHOOT IT FROM THE HIP (live)**		32
(12"+=/12"pic-d+=) (12CL/+P 458) – Sleeping (in the fire).		
Sep 87. (cd/c/lp) *(CD/TC+/EST 2040)* <48053> **LIVE . . . IN THE RAW (live)**	23	77
– Inside the electric circus / I don't need no doctor / L.O.V.E. machine / Wild child / 9.5 N.A.S.T.Y. / Sleeping (in the fire) / The manimal / I wanna be somebody / Harder faster / Blind in Texas. *(cd+=)* – Scream until you like it (theme from 'Ghoulies II'). *(re-iss. Jul94 cd/c; same).*		
Oct 87. (7"/7"s/7"w-poster/7"sha-pic-d) *(CL/+B/S/P 469)* **I DON'T NEED NO DOCTOR. / WIDOW MAKER (live)**	31	–
(12"+=/12"w-poster+=) (12CL/+P 469) – Sex drive (live).		

——— now basic trio of **BLACKIE, CHRIS & JOHNNY** when STEPHEN joined L.A. GUNS.

———　**FRANKIE BANALI** – drums (of QUIET RIOT) filled in temp. / added guest **KEN HENSLEY** – keyboards (ex-URIAH HEEP, ex-BLACKFOOT)

Feb 89. (7"/7"pic-d/7"purple) *(CL/+P/M 521)* **MEAN MAN. / LOCOMOTIVE BREATH**	21	–
(12"+=/12"g-f+=/cd-s+=) (12CL/12CLP/CDCL 521) – For whom the bells toll.		
Apr 89. (cd/c/lp) *(CD/TC+/EST 2087)* <48942> **THE HEADLESS CHILDREN**	8	48
– The heretic (the lost child) / The real me / The headless children / Thunderhead / Mean man / The neutron bomber / Mephisto waltz / Forever free / Maneater / Rebel in the F.D.G. *(pic-lp Oct89; ESTPD 2087) (re-iss. Jul94 cd/c; same).*		
May 89. (7"/7"blue/7"pic-d) *(CL/+G/P 534)* **THE REAL ME. / THE LAKE OF FOOLS**	23	–
(12"+=/12"w-poster+=/cd-s+=) (12CL/12CLS/CDCL 534) – War cry.		
Aug 89. (7"/7"s/7"sha-pic-d)(etched-12")(c-s) *(CL/+S/P 546)(12CLS 546)(TCCL 546)* **FOREVER FREE. / L.O.V.E. MACHINE (live '89)**		–
(12"+=/cd-s+=) (12/CD CL 546) – Blind in Texas (live'89).		

——— JOHNNY ROD left in 1989 as band split. Reformed in August 1990 as BLACKIE LAWLESS & WASP, but they soon returned to original name. **BLACKIE, JOHNNY, KEN, FRANKIE** + new member **BOB KULICK** – guitar

	Parlophone	Capitol
Mar 92. (7"/7"pic-d) *(RS/+P 6308)* **CHAINSAW CHARLIE (MURDERS IN THE NEW MORGUE). / PHANTOM IN THE MIRROR**	17	–
(12"+=/cd-s+=) (12/CD RS 6308) – The story of Jonathan (prologue to the crimson idol – part I).		

——— the April tour added **DAN McDADE** – guitar / **STET HOWLAND** – drums

May 92. (7"crimson/7"pic-d) *(RS/RPD 6314)* **THE IDOL. / THE STORY OF JONATHAN (PROLOGUE TO THE CRIMSON IDOL – PART II)**	41	–
(12"+=/pic-cd+=) (12/CD RS 6314) – The eulogy.		
Jun 92. (cd/c/red-lp) *(CD/TC+/PCS 118)* **THE CRIMSON IDOL**	21	–
– The Titanic overture / The invisible boy / Arena of pleasure / Chainsaw Charlie (murders in the New Morgue) / The gypsy meets the boy / Doctor Rockter / I am one / The idol / Hold on to my heart / The great misconceptions of me.		
Oct 92. (7"/7"pic-d) *(R/RPD 6324)* **I AM ONE. / WILD CHILD**	56	–
(10"+=) (10RG 6324) – Charlie chainsaw / I wanna be somebody.		
(cds-) *(CDRS 6324)* – ('A'side) / The invisible boy / The real me / The great misconception of me.		

	Capitol	Capitol
Oct 93. (7") *(CL 698)* **SUNSET & BABYLON. / ANIMAL (F**K LIKE A BEAST)**	38	–
(cd-s+=) (CDCL 698) – Sleeping in the fire / I wanna be somebody.		
(12"+=) (12CL 698) – School daze / On your knees.		
(12"pic-d) (12CLP 698) – ('A'side) / Hellion / Show no mercy.		
Oct 93. (cd/c/lp) *(CD/TC+/ESTG 2217)* **FIRST BLOOD . . ... LAST CUTS** (compilation)	69	–
– Animal (f**k like a beast) / L.O.V.E. machine (remix) / I wanna be somebody (remix) / On your knees / Blind in Texas (remix) / Wild child (remix) / I don't need no doctor (remix) / Sunset and Babylon / The real me / The headless children / Mean man / Forever free / Chainsaw Charlie / The idol / Hold on to my heart / Rock and roll to death.		

	Raw Power	not iss.
Jun 95. (7"sha-pic-d) *(RAWT 1007)* **BLACK FOREVER. / GOODBYE AMERICA**		–
(cd-s+=) (RAWX 1005) – Skin walker / One tribe.		
(cd-s) (RAWX 1006) – ('A'side) / Long way to the top / Whole lotta Rosie.		
Jun 95. (cd/c/lp) *(RAW CD/MC/LP 103)* **STILL NOT BLACK ENOUGH**	52	–
– Still not black enough / Somebody to love / Black forever / Scared to death / Goodbye America / Keep holding on / Rock and roll to death / Breathe / I can't / No way out of here.		

——— line-up: **LAWLESS + HOWLAND** plus **MICHAEL DUDA** – bass + the returning **CHRIS HOLMES**

Mar 97. (cd-s) *(RAWX 1041)* **KILL, F**K, DIE /**		–
Apr 97. (cd) *(RAWCD 114)* **KILL, F**K, DIE**		–
– Kill, f**k, die / Take the addiction / My tortured eyes / Killahead / Kill your pretty face / Foetus / Little death / U / Wicked death / Horror.		

	Snapper	CMC Int.
Feb 98. (cd) <86237> **DOUBLE LIVE ASSASSINS**		–
– Medley / Wild child / Animal / L.O.V.E. / Killahead / I wanna be somebody / U / The real me / Kill your pretty face / Horrow / Blind in Texas / The headless children / Idol / Crimson idol medley: Little death – Mean man – Rock'n'roll to death.		
May 99. (cd) *(SMACD 818)* <86269> **HELLDORADO**		
– Drive by / Helldorado / Don't cry (just suck) / Damnation alley / Dirty balls / High on the flames / Cocaine cowboys / Don't die tonight / Saturday night cockfight / Hot rods to Hell.		

WATERBOYS

Formed: London, England . . . 1982 by Scots-born MIKE SCOTT, Englishman ANTHONY THISTLETHWAITE and Welshman KARL WALLINGER. SCOTT had previously fronted Edinburgh new wave outfit, ANOTHER PRETTY FACE, along with old Ayr school pals, JOHN CALDWELL and JIM GEDDES. Taking their name from a track on LOU REED's sleaze-noir masterpiece, 'Berlin', The WATERBOYS soon secured a deal with the Irish-run label, 'Ensign', following the release of a self-financed debut single in Spring '83, 'A GIRL CALLED JOHNNY'. A tribute to punk priestess, PATTI SMITH (an obvious early influence), the track received a fair amount of airplay and almost broke into the lower regions of the charts. An eponymous debut album followed later that summer, an esoteric set of avant folk/rock which drew comparisons with TIM BUCKLEY's more ambitious meanderings and introduced SCOTT as a promising singing/songwriting seer. Embellished by additional instrumentation such as horns and violin, 'A PAGAN PLACE' (1984) was a confident follow-up, SCOTT venturing ever further out on his spiritual journey with the likes of 'THE BIG MUSIC' and 'CHURCH NOT MADE WITH HANDS'. A burgeoning live reputation and gushing critical praise saw The WATERBOYS' third set, 'THIS IS THE SEA' (1985) break into the UK Top 40, its centrepiece epic, 'THE WHOLE OF THE MOON', becoming the group's first Top 30 single. Despite this overdue success, WALLINGER subsequently departed to form his own outfit, WORLD PARTY. Relocating to Galway, Ireland for an extended sabbatical at the behest of fiddler, STEVE WICKHAM (who'd played on 'THIS..'), SCOTT and THISTLETHWAITE increasingly infused their music with traditional Irish folk influences. It was an earthier WATERBOYS, then, who eventually emerged in late '88 with the acclaimed 'FISHERMAN'S BLUES', SCOTT seemingly having at last found his true musical calling. From the strident Celtic clarion call of the title track to the soulful cover of Van Morrison's 'SWEET THING', it sounded as if The WATERBOYS had been playing this music for centuries. The record almost made the UK Top 10, an album which established The WATERBOYS as a major league act and which remains their biggest seller. 'ROOM TO ROAM' (1990) continued in the same vein, making the UK Top 5 although it lacked the depth of its predecessor. Bang on cue, 'Ensign' re-released 'THE WHOLE OF THE MOON' to massive success (Top 3), the track being played to death by radio all over again. By this point, however, the original WATERBOYS line-up had splintered following a final UK tour (wherein the group drew criticism for their return to an all-out rock sound), THISTLETHWAITE forming The BLUE STARS while SCOTT eventually moved to New York and gathered together a new group of musicians. Now signed to 'Geffen', he recorded 'DREAM HARDER' (1993), the sixth WATERBOYS album but a SCOTT solo set in all but name. Exploring many familiar themes, the album spawned two Top 30 singles in 'THE RETURN OF PAN' and 'GLASTONBURY SONG', even boasting a brief contribution from Scots comedy legend, BILLY CONNOLLY. All has since been silent on The WATERBOYS front, although SCOTT released a fine solo album in 1995, 'BRING 'EM ALL IN', this highly original musical visionary remaining one of Scotland's most talented exports. • Covered: LOST HIGHWAY (Hank Williams) / DEATH IS NOT THE END (Bob Dylan) / WAYWARD WIND (Lebawsky-Newman) / BECAUSE THE NIGHT (Patti Smith – Bruce Springsteen) / PURPLE RAIN (Prince) / and a several traditional renditions.

Album rating: THE WATERBOYS (*6) / A PAGAN PLACE (*6) / THIS IS THE SEA (*7) / FISHERMAN'S BLUES (*6) / ROOM TO ROAM (*6) / THE BEST OF THE WATERBOYS compilation (*9) / DREAM HARDER (*5) / THE SECRET LIFE OF THE WATERBOYS early stuff (*4) / Mike Scott: BRING 'EM ALL IN (*6) / STILL BURNING (*5)

ANOTHER PRETTY FACE

MIKE SCOTT (b.14 Dec'58, Edinburgh, Scotland) – vocals, guitar, piano / **JOHN CALDWELL** – guitar / **JIM GEDDES** – bass / **CRIGG** (b.IAN WALTER GREIG) – drums

		New Pleasures	not iss.
May 79.	(7") *(Z1)* **ALL THE BOYS LOVE CARRIE. / THAT'S NOT ENOUGH**	☐	-
		Virgin	not iss.
Feb 80.	(7") *(VS 320)* **WHATEVER HAPPENED TO THE WEST?. / GODBBYE 1970's**	☐	-

—— trimmed to basic duo of **SCOTT + CALDWELL** plus **MAIRI ROSS** – bass / added **ADRIAN JOHNSON** – drums

		Chicken Jazz	not iss.
Dec 80.	(7") *(JAZZ 1)* **ONLY HEROES LIVE FOREVER. / HEAVEN GETS CLOSER EVERY DAY**	☐	-
Mar 81.	(c-ep) *(JAZZ 2)* **I'M SORRY THAT I BEAT YOU, I'M SORRY THAT I SCREAMED, FOR A MOMENT THERE I REALLY LOST CONTROL(live)**	☐	-

– This could be Hell / My darkest hour / Lightning that strikes twice / Graduation day / Carrie. *(on most copies, studio tracks +=)* – Another kind of circus / Only heroes live forever / Out of control.

Apr 81.	(7") *(JAZZ 3)* **SOUL TO SOUL. / A WOMAN'S PLACE / GOD ON THE SCREEN**	☐ -

FUNHOUSE

—— were formed by **SCOTT + CALDWELL**

		Ensign	not iss.
Feb 82.	(7"/ext.12") *(ENY/+T 222)* **OUT OF CONTROL. / THIS COULD BE HELL**	☐	-

The WATERBOYS

MIKE SCOTT plus **ANTHONY THISTLETHWAITE** (b. 8 Aug'55, Leicester, England) – saxophone (ex-ROBYN HITCHCOCK / of SOFT BOYS) / **KARL WALLINGER** (b.19 Oct'57, Prestatyn, Wales) – keyboards, bass

		Chicken Jazz	not iss.
May 83.	(7") *(CJ 1)* **A GIRL CALLED JOHNNY. / THE LATE TRAIN TO HEAVEN**	☐	-

(12") *(CJT 1)* – ('A'side) / Ready for the monkey house / Somebody might wave back / Out of control (APF; John Peel session).

		Ensign	Chrysalis
Jul 83.	(lp/c) *(ENC L/C 1)* **THE WATERBOYS**	☐	-

– December / A girl called Johnny / The three day man / Gala / I will not follow / It should have been you / The girl in the swing / Savage Earth heart. *(re-iss. Aug86 on 'Chrysalis-Ensign' lp/c; CHEN/ZCHEN 1) (cd-iss. Feb87; CCD 1541) <US cd-iss. 1987; 21541>*

Sep 83.	(7") *(ENY 506)* **DECEMBER. / WHERE ARE YOU NOW WHEN I NEED YOU**	☐	-

(12") *(12ENY 506)* – ('A'side) / Red army blues / The three day man (Peter Powell session).

——	added **KEVIN WILKINSON** – drums / **RODDY LORIMER** (b. Glasgow, Scotland) – trumpet / **TIM BLANTHORN** – violin		
Apr 84.	(7") *(ENY 508)* **THE BIG MUSIC. / THE EARTH ONLY ENDURES**	☐	-

(12"+=) *(12ENY 508)* – Bury my heart.

May 84.	(lp/c) *(ENC L/C 3)* **A PAGAN PLACE**	100	-

– Church not made with hands / All the things she gave me / The thrill is gone / Rags / Somebody might wave back / The big music / Red army blues / A pagan place. *(re-iss. Aug86 on 'Chrysalis-Ensign' lp/c; CHEN/ZCHEN 2) (cd-iss. Feb87; CCD 1542) (re-iss. Jul94 cd/c;) <US cd-iss. 1987; 21542>*

—— (Oct84) **MIKE + KARL** recruited new people for tour/lp **TERRY MANN** – bass / **CHARLIE WHITTEN** – drums / **STEVE WICKHAM** (b. Dublin, Ireland) – violin / **LORIMER / DELAHAYE** – organ

Sep 85.	(lp/c) *(ENC L/C 5)* **THIS IS THE SEA**	37	-

– Don't bang the drum / The whole of the Moon / Spirit / The pan within / Medicine bow / Old England / Be my enemy / Trumpets / This is the sea. *(re-iss. Aug86 on 'Chrysalis-Ensign' lp/c; CHEN/ZCHEN 3) (cd-iss. Feb87; CCD CCD 1543) (re-iss. cd Mar94;) <US cd-iss. 1987; 21543>*

Oct 85.	(7") *(ENY 502)* **THE WHOLE OF THE MOON. / MEDICINE BOW**	26	-

(ext.12"+=) *(12ENY 520)* – Spirit (extended) / The girl in the swing (live).

—— **MIKE SCOTT** now only original survivor (retained THISTLETWAITE + HUTCHISON), when KARL formed WORLD PARTY.

—— additional band **STEVE WICKHAM** – violin (ex-IN TUA NUA) / **J.D. DOHERTY** – drums / **COLIN BLAKEY** (b. Falkirk, Scotland) – flute (ex-WE FREE KINGS) / ('88) added **SHARON SHANNON** (b. Ireland) – accordion / **NOEL BRIDGEMAN** (b. Dublin, Ireland) – drums repl. DOHERTY

Nov 88.	(lp/c)(cd) *(CHEN/ZCHEN 5)(CCD 1589) <41589>* **FISHERMAN'S BLUES**	13	76

– Fisherman's blues / We will not be lovers / Strange boat / World party / Sweet thing / And a bang on the ear / Has anybody here seen Hank? / When we will be married? / When ye go away / The stolen child. *(cd+=)* – The lost highway.

Dec 88.	(7"/12"/cd-s) *(ENY/+X/CD 621)* **FISHERMAN'S BLUES. / THE LOST HIGHWAY**	32	-
Jun 89.	(7"/c-s/12"/cd-s) *(ENY/+MC/X/CD 624)* **AND A BANG ON THE EAR. / THE RAGGLE TAGGLE GYPSY**	51	-

—— **MIKE SCOTT / THISTLETWAITE / HUTCHISON / + KEV BLEVINS** – drums repl. last additional band members

Sep 90.	(cd)(c/lp) *(CCD 1768)(Z+/CHEN 16) <21768>* **ROOM TO ROAM**	5	

– In search of a rose / Songs from the edge of the world / A man is in love / Bigger picture / Natural bridge blues / Something that is gone / The star and the sea / Life on Sundays / Island man / The raggle taggle gypsy / How long will I love you? / Upon the wind and waves / Spring rooms to Spiddal / Further up, further on / Trip to Broadford / Room to roam. *(cd+=)* – The kings of Kerry. *(re-iss. Sep94 cd/c;)*

Mar 91.	(7"/c-s) *(ENY/+MC 642) <Alex; 1516>* **THE WHOLE OF THE MOON. / A GOLDEN AGE**	3	Jul91

(12"+=/cd-s+=) *(ENY X/CD 642)* – Higher in time / High far soon / Soon as I get home.

Apr 91.	(cd/c/lp) *(CCD 1845)(Z+/CHEN 19) <21845>* **THE BEST OF THE WATERBOYS ('81-'90)** (compilation)	2	

– A girl called Johnny / The big music / All the things she gave me / The whole of the Moon / Spirit / Don't bang the drum / Fisherman's blues / Killing my heart / Strange boat / And a bang on the ear / Old England / A man is in love.

May 91.	(7"/c-s) *(ENY/+MC 645) <Alex; 1581>* **FISHERMAN'S BLUES. / LOST HIGHWAY**	75	Jun91

(12"+=/cd-s+=) *(ENY X/CD 645)* – Medicine bow (live).

—— Disbanded soon after last studio album above. In mid'91, MIKE SCOTT re-formed group and signed for US-based label 'Geffen'. THISTLETHWAITE formed The BLUE STARS.

—— **MIKE SCOTT** with **CHRIS BRUCE** – guitars / **SCOTT THUNES** – bass / **CARLA AZAR** – drums / **BASHIRI JOHNSON** – percussion / **LJUBISA 'Lubi' RISTIC** – sitar / **GEORGE STATHOS** – Greek clarinet / **JAMES CAMPAGNOLA** – saxophone / **JERE PETERS** – rattles / **PAL SHAZAR + JULES SHEAR** – backing vox / **BILLY CONNOLLY** – guest 10 second voiceover

		Geffen	Geffen
May 93.	(7"/c-s) *(GFS/+C 42)* **THE RETURN OF PAN. / KARMA**	24	

(12"+=/cd-s+=) *(GFS T/CD 42)* – Mister Powers / ('A'demo).

May 93.	(cd/c/lp) *(<GED/GEC/GEF 24476>)* **DREAM HARDER**	5	

– The new life / Glastonbury song / Preparing to fly / The return of Pan / Corn circles / Suffer / Winter winter / Love and death / Spiritual city / Wonders of Lewis / The return of Jimi Hendrix / Good news. *(cd re-iss. Jul96; GFLD 19318)*

Jul 93.	(7"/c-s) *(GFS/+C 49)* **GLASTONBURY SONG. / CHALICE HILL**	29	-

(12"+=/cd-s+=) *(GFS T/CD 49)* – Burlington Bertie – Accrington Stanley / Corn circle symphony (extended).

– compilations, etc. –

Oct 94.	(cd/c) Ensign; *(CD/TC CHEN 35)* **THE SECRET LIFE OF THE WATERBOYS** (81-85 material)	☐	☐
Aug 98.	(d-cd) Griffin; *<40>* **LIVE ADVENTURES OF THE WATERBOYS** (live)	☐	☐

– Death is not the end / Earth only endures / Medicine bow / Fisherman's blues / This is the sea / Meet me at the station / We will not be lovers / Wayward wind / A girl called Johnny / Purple rain / Be my enemy / Old England / The thrill is gone – And the healing has begun / Pain within (including Because the night) / Whole of the moon / Spirit / Savage earth heart / Saints and angels.

MIKE SCOTT

—— mostly all solo

		Chrysalis	Chrysalis
Sep 95.	(c-s/7") *(TC+/CHS 5025) <58503>* **BRING 'EM ALL IN. / CITY FULL OF GHOSTS (DUBLIN)**	56	Nov95

(cd-s+=) *(CDCHS 5025)* – Mother Cluny / Beatles reunion blues.

Sep 95.	(cd/c/lp) *(<CD/TC+/CHR 6108>)* **BRING 'EM ALL IN**	23	

– Bring 'em all in / Iona song / Edinburgh Castle / What do you want me to do? / I know she's in the building / City full of ghosts (Dublin) / Wonderful disguise / Sensitive children / Learning to love him / She is so beautiful / Wonderful disguise (reprise) / Long way to the light / Building the city of light.

Nov 95. (7") *(CHS 5026)* **BUILDING THE CITY OF LIGHT. / WHERE DO YOU WANT THE BOOMBOX, BUDDY**   `60` `-`
(cd-s+=) *(CDCHSS 5026)* – Goin' back to Glasters (live) / The whole of the Moon (live).
(cd-s) *(CDCHSS 5026)* – ('A'side) / Two great waves / My beautiful guide / Building the city of light (Universal Hall demo).

——— now with **CHRIS BRUCE** – lead guitar / **PINO PALLADINO** – bass / **JIM KELTNER** – drums / **JAMRES HALLAWELL** – organ / etc

Sep 97. (c-s) *(TCCHS 5064)* **LOVE ANYWAY / KING OF STARS**   `50` `-`
(cd-s) *(CDCHS 5064)* – ('A'side) / King electric (including Moonage Daydream) / Blues is my business.
(cd-s) *(CDCHS 5064)* – ('A'side) / Big lover / Careful with the mellotron, Eugene / Since I found my school.

Oct 97. (cd/c) *(<CD/TC CHR 6122>)* **STILL BURNING**   `34` `☐`
– Questions / My dark side / Open / Love anyway / Rare, precious and gone / Dark man of my dreams / Personal / Strawberry man / Sunrising / Everlasting arms.

Feb 98. (cd-ep) *(CDCHS 5073)* **RARE, PRECIOUS AND GONE / KISS THE WIND / WHEN WILL WE BE MARRIED (live) / LOVE ANYWAY (demo)**   `74` `-`
(cd-ep) *(CDCHS 5073)* – ('A'side) / All things she gave me (live) / She is so beautiful (live) / Nectar (7 days).

Muddy WATERS

Born: McKINLEY MORGANFIELD, 4th April 1915, Rolling Fork, Mississippi, USA. While perhaps not as widely celebrated as his peers, JOHN LEE HOOKER and BB KING, it was WATERS who was the main catalyst in converting blues to urban electric and then to rock'n'roll. Brought up by his mother in Clarksdale (birthplace of HOOKER), he began singing and playing harmonica at the age of 7, acquired his nickname due to his fondness for playing in a nearby muddy creek. By his late teens, WATERS had switched to guitar and was supplementing his wages as a cotton picker (although he had ambitions beyond that – in his late teens he was running his own whiskey still!) and by playing at local juke joints and parties. Initially, his style was a combination of CHARLEY PATTON, SON HOUSE (his mentor and tutor) and his hero, ROBERT JOHNSON (although he never met him, he once saw him play, the experience apparently changing his life) although he had evolved his own approach to the blues by the time he'd moved to Chicago in 1943. Another turning point came in 1941 when ALAN LOMAX visited the plantation where MUDDY worked; LOMAX had already recorded SON HOUSE and wanted to record ROBERT JOHNSON for the Library Of Congress, unaware that JOHNSON was already dead. When he found out, he asked about ELMORE JAMES and finally ended up recording the young MUDDY WATERS, both solo and in a band with the SON SIMS FOUR (the recorded songs were 'I BE'S TROUBLED' and 'COUNTRY BLUES'). WATERS was suitably impressed with the sound of the recordings to decide on a career as a professional musician. In Chicago he worked in a paper mill by day and played in clubs at night (encouraged by BIG BILL BROONZY and SUNNYLAND SLIM), quickly discovering that his acoustic guitar wasn't loud enough for these venues and subsequently going electric. WATERS gradually assembled the finest blues band of the era, featuring, at various times, MARVIN 'LITTLE WALTER' JACOBS (harmonica/vocals), OTIS SPANN (piano) and WILLIE DIXON (bass), among others; his bands attracted the greatest talents, WATERS giving them a platform to develop their reputations (even allowing them to record their own music during their studio time and training them to be leaders in their own right. When LITTLE WALTER, JIMMY ROGERS, OTIS SPANN and JAMES COTTON set off on their own he wished them the best and simply replaced them. He recorded briefly for 'Columbia' in 1946 ('HARD DAY BLUES' displayed signs of what was to come) before signing to 'Aristocrat' (later 'Chess' in 1950) although he didn't start recording under his own name until 1948. Such was the strength of WATERS' reputation that his first single, 'I CAN'T BE SATISFIED' sold out its first pressing within 24 hours while the follow up, 'I FEEL LIKE GOING HOME' saw him making his R&B chart debut. WATERS' first 'Chess' single was 'ROLLIN' STONE' in 1950, the bluesman achieving his second major R&B success with 'LOUISIANA BLUES' (WATERS had a further thirteen R&B hits up to 1956) the following year. His band toured the UK in 1958 and although critics weren't so supportive, viewers of the shows were taken aback by the power of the performances which effected an incalculable impact upon a future generation of British performers including ALEXIS KORNER and CYRIL DAVIES, who were inspired to form BLUES INCORPORATED. Songs like 'HOOCHIE COOCHIE MAN', 'ROLLIN' AND TUMBLIN', 'BABY PLEASE DON'T GO', 'I GOT MY MOJO WORKING', 'I JUST WANT TO MAKE LOVE TO YOU' and 'MANNISH BOY', many written by WILLIE DIXON, became standards among early UK R&B bands while The ROLLING STONES, The MOJOS, The HOOCHIE COOCHIE MEN and The MANNISH BOYS even took their name from WATERS songs. He also had a direct influence on JUNIOR WELLS, BUDDY GUY, JIMI HENDRIX and ERIC CLAPTON. Yet it took a long time for him to reap the financial benefits (he was often out-sold by JIMMY REED, JIMMY ROGERS and LITTLE WALTER) and at the end of the 50's Chess decided to market WATERS as an album based performer, releasing two albums in 1960 including 'MUDDY WATERS AT NEWPORT' (arguably his finest live album). When the 'STONES arrived to record at the Chess studios in 1964 (the year that saw the release of

the all-acoustic 'MUDDY WATERS, FOLK SINGER') they famously found WATERS up a ladder, painting the studio(!); some of the musicians he had inspired subsequently recorded collaborative albums with him. They were of inconsistent quality, but they did, at least, get WATERS noticed outwith blues circles. 'FATHERS & SONS' was a joint effort with MIKE BLOOMFIELD, PAUL BUTTERFIELD, DONALD 'DUCK' DUNN, BUDDY MILES and OTIS SPANN, marking his only entry to the US Top 100. 'THE LONDON MUDDY WATERS SESSIONS' featuring RORY GALLAGHER, GEORGIE FAME, MITCH MITCHELL, RICK GRECH and STEVE WINWOOD also helped him break out of the blues ghetto. In an attempt to keep WATERS in the public eye, 'Chess' rather ill-advisedly persuaded him to record such projects as the psychedelic 'ELECTRIC MUD' (which included a version of The STONES' 'LET'S SPEND THE NIGHT TOGETHER') album in the late 60's. Nevertheless, he won Grammy's in 1972 for 'THEY CALL ME MUDDY WATERS' and 'LONDON SESSIONS' although tragedy struck the following year when he was seriously injured in a car crash; the accident left three people dead and put him into semi-retirement for two years. The guitarist returned with the Grammy Award winning 'MUDDY WATERS WOODSTOCK ALBUM' and performed 'MANNISH BOY' at The BAND's farewell concert. WATERS left 'Chess' (after the CHESS brothers sold out to a New York corporation) in 1977 and signed to STEVE PAUL's 'Blue Sky' (PAUL was the manager of JOHNNY WINTER) imprint. WINTER, who had long idolised WATERS, jumped at the chance to work with his hero and set about recreating the veteran bluesman's 50's recording sound aided by the likes of JAMES COTTON, WALTER HORTON, LUTHER JOHNSON, JIMMY ROGERS, PINETOP PERKINS and WILLIE 'BIG EYES' SMITH. Four albums, 'HARD AGAIN', 'I'M READY', 'MUDDY MISSISSIPPI WATERS' (all Grammy winners) and 'I'M A KING BEE' were released between 1977 and 1980. 'HARD AGAIN' was recorded amid a great atmosphere, lots of excitement at the end of each track as the band went through classics like 'I WANT TO BE LOVED', 'I CAN'T BE SATISFIED' (with WINTER on slide guitar), 'DEEP DOWN IN FLORIDA' and 'MANNISH BOY'. Incidentally, it was this recording of 'MANNISH BOY' that was used for a Levi jeans TV advert in 1988 and was subsequently released as a single, becoming WATERS' only UK chart entry at number 51. By 1980, he had moved from the south side to a comfortable home in the suburbs with his 25 year old wife and numerous grandchildren. WATERS died peacefully in his sleep on the 30th of April 1983 (only after his death it was discovered that he had contracted cancer), receiving a posthumous induction to the Rock And Roll Hall Of Fame in 1987 and a Lifetime Achievement Award at the Grammy's in 1992.

Best CD compilation: MUDDY WATERS – THE CHESS BOX box-set (*9)

MUDDY WATERS – vocals, guitar; with **SUNNYLAND SLIM** – piano

			not iss.	Aristocrat
1948.	(78) *<1302>* **GYPSY WOMAN. / LITTLE ANNA MAE**		`-`	`☐`
1948.	(78) *<1305>* **I CAN'T BE SATISFIED. / FEEL LIKE GOIN' HOME**		`☐`	`☐`
1948.	(78) *<1306>* **TRAIN FARE HOME. / SITTIN' HERE AND DRINKIN'**		`-`	`☐`
1949.	(78) *<1307>* **YOU'RE GONNA MISS ME. / MEAN RED SPIDER**		`-`	`☐`
1949.	(78) *<1310>* **STREAMLINE WOMAN. / MUDDY JUMPS ONE**		`-`	`☐`
1949.	(78) *<1311>* **LITTLE GENEVA. / CANARY BIRD**		`-`	`☐`
1949.	(78) *<406>* **SCREAMIN' AND CRYIN'. / WHERE'S MY WOMAN BEEN**		`-`	`☐`
1951.	(78) *<412>* **ROLLIN' AND TUMBLIN'. / (pt. 2)**		`-`	`☐`

——— with band **JIMMY RODGERS** – guitar / **WILLIE DIXON** – bass / **LITTLE WALTER** – harmonica / **LEONARD CHESS** – drums / **ERNEST CRAWFORD** – bass

			not iss.	Chess
1950.	(78) *<1434>* **YOU'RE GONNA NEED MY HELP I SAID. / SAD LETTER BLUES** (UK-iss.May52 on 'Vogue Coral'; V 2101)		`-`	`☐`
1951.	(78) *<1441>* **LOUISIANA BLUES. / EVAN'S SHUFFLE**		`-`	`☐`
1951.	(78) *<1452>* **LONG DISTANCE CALL. / TOO YOUNG TO KNOW** (UK-iss.Nov54 on 'Vogue Coral'; V 2273)		`-`	`☐`
1951.	(7") *<1468>* **HONEY BEE. / APPEALING BLUES** (UK-iss.May56 on 'Vogue Coral'; V 2372)		`-`	`☐`
1951.	(78) *<1480>* **MY FAULT. / STILL A FOOL**		`-`	`☐`

——— ELGIN EVANS – drums repl. CHESS

1952.	(78) *<1490>* **SHE MOVES ME. / EARLY MORNING BLUES**		`-`	`☐`
1952.	(78) *<1509>* **ALL NIGHT LONG. / COUNTRY BOY**		`-`	`☐`
1952.	(78) *<1514>* **PLEASE HAVE MERCY. / I CAN'T BE SATISFIED (LOOKING FOR MY BABY)**		`-`	`☐`
1952.	(78) *<1526>* **STANDING AROUND CRYING. / GONE TO MAIN STREET**		`-`	`☐`
1953.	(78) *<1537>* **SHE'S ALL RIGHT. / SAD, SAD DAY**		`-`	`☐`
1953.	(78) *<1542>* **TURN THE LAMP DOWN LOW. / WHO'S GONNA BE YOUR SWEET MAN**		`-`	`☐`
1953.	(78) *<1550>* **BLOW WIND BLOW. / MAD LOVE (I JUST WANT YOU TO LOVE ME)**		`-`	`☐`

——— OTIS SPANN – piano (to mid-60's) repl. SLIM

1954.	(78) *<1560>* **HOOCHIE COOCHIE MAN. / SHE'S SO PRETTY**		`-`	`☐`
1954.	(78) *<1571>* **I JUST WANT TO MAKE LOVE TO YOU. / OH YEAH**		`-`	`☐`
1954.	(78) *<1579>* **I'M READY. / I DON'T KNOW WHY**		`-`	`☐`
1954.	(78) *<1585>* **I'M A NATURAL BORN LOVER. / LOVING MAN**		`-`	`☐`

Mar 55. (7"ep) *Vogue; (EPV 1046)* **MUDDY WATERS WITH LITTLE WALTER**
 – I can't be satisfied / Louisiana blues / Evans shuffle / I feel like going home.
1955. (78) *<1596>* **I WANT TO BE LOVED. / MY EYES (KEEP ME IN TROUBLE)**
1955. (78) *<1602>* **MANNISH BOY. / YOUNG FASHIONED WAYS**
1955. (78) *<1612>* **SUGAR SWEET. / TROUBLE NO MORE**
1956. (78) *<1620>* **40 DAYS AND 40 NIGHTS. / ALL ABOARD**
1956. (78) *<1630>* **DON'T GO NO FURTHER. / DIAMONDS AT YOUR FEET**
1956. (78) *<1644>* **JUST TO BE WITH YOU. / I GOT TO FIND MY BABY**

Oct 56. (7"ep) *(RU-E 1060)* **MISSISSIPPI BLUES**
 – All aboard / 40 days and 40 nights / Mannish boy / Young fashioned ways.
1957. (7") *<1652>* **GOT MY MOJO WORKING. / ROCK ME**
1957. (7") *<1667>* **GOOD NEWS. / COME HOME BABY**
1957. (7") *<1680>* **EVIL. / I LIVE THE LIFE I LOVE**
1958. (7") *<1692>* **I WON'T GO. / SHE'S GOT IT**
1958. (7") *<1704>* **SHE'S 19 YEARS OLD. / CLOSE TO YOU**
1958. (7") *<1718>* **WALKING THRU THE PARK. / MEAN MISTREATER**
1958. (7") *<1724>* **CLOUDS IN MY HEART. / OOH WEE**
1959. (7") *<1733>* **TAKE THE BITTER WITH THE SWEET. / SHE'S INTO SOMETHING**
1959. (7") *<1739>* **TELL ME BABY. / LOOK WHAT YOU'VE DONE**
1959. (7") *<1748>* **WHEN I GET TO THINKING. / I FEEL SO GOOD**
1960. (7") *<1752>* **I'M YOUR DOCTOR. / READ WAY BACK**
1960. (7") *<1758>* **LOVE AFFAIR. / RECIPE FOR LOVE**

—— **WALTER HORTON** – repl. LITTLE WALTER until **JAMES COTTON** repl. HORTON / **PAT HARE** came in on drums and ROGERS departed. He toured in the UK.
Mar 59. (lp) *(LJZ-M 15152)* **THE BEST OF MUDDY WATERS** (compilation)
 – I just want to make love to you / Long distance call / Louisiana blues / Honey bee / Rollin' stone / I'm ready / Hoochie coochie / She moves me / I want you to love me / Standing around crying / Still a fool / I can't be satisfied. *(re-iss. Oct87 lp/c; GCH/+K7 8044) (cd-iss. Jun88; CDCHESS 1012)*

—— toured now with **FRANCIS CLAY** – drums / **ANDREW STEPHENSON** – bass / **PAT HARE** – guitar / **SPANN + COTTON**
Jun 60. (7") *<1765>* **TIGER IN YOUR TANK. / MEANEST WOMAN**
Aug 60. (7") *<1774>* **GOT MY MOJO WORKING (pt.1). / WOMAN WANTED**
1961. (7") *<1796>* **LONESOME ROOM BLUES. / MESSIN' WITH THE MAN**
Sep 61. (lp) *(NJL 34) <1449>* **MUDDY WATERS AT NEWPORT (live 1960)**
 – Tiger in your tank / I've got my mojo working / I got my brand on you / Baby, please don't go / Soon forgotten / I feel so glad / Goodbye Newport blues. *(re-iss. Nov65 on 'Chess'; CRL 4513) (re-iss. Jan67 on 'Marble Arch'; MAL 661) (re-iss. 1973 on 'Checker')*
1962. (7") *<1819>* **TOUGH TIMES. / GOING HOME**
1962. (7") *<1827>* **YOU SHOOK ME. / MUDDY WATERS TWIST**
1962. (7") *<1839>* **YOU NEED LOVE. / LITTLE BROWN BIRD**
1963. (7") *<1862>* **FIVE LONG YEARS. / TWENTY FOUR HOURS**
1964. (7") *<1895>* **THE SAME THING. / YOU CAN'T LOSE WHAT YOU NEVER HAD**
May 64. (lp) *(NPL 28038) <1483>* **MUDDY WATERS – FOLK SINGER**
 – My home is my delta / Long distance / My captain / Good morning little schoolgirl / You're gonna need my help / Cold weather blues / Peg leg woman / Country boy / Feel like going home. *(re-iss. Aug87 on 'Chess'; GCH/+K7 8040)*
Sep 64. (lp) *(NPL 28040)* **MUDDY WATERS**
 – I got my brand on you / Baby, please don't go / Tiger in your tank / I've got my mojo working (part 1) / Goodbye Newport blues / The same thing / Sittin' and thinkin' / 19 years old / I'm your hoochie coochie man / Soon forgotten / I feel so good / I've got my mojo working (part 2) / Long distance call / Wee wee baby / Clouds in my heart. *(cd-iss. Mar90 on 'Roots'; RTS 33018)*
Feb 65. (7") *(CRS 8001) <1914>* **MY JOHN THE CONQUER ROOT. / SHORT DRESS WOMAN**
1965. (7") *<1921>* **PUT ME IN YOUR LAY-A-WAY. / STILL A FOOL**
Aug 65. (7"ep) *(CRE 6006)* **I'M READY**
 – She moves me / I can't be satisfied / I want you to love me.
Aug 65. (7") *(CRS 8019) <1937>* **I GOT A RICH MAN'S WOMAN. / MY DOG CAN'T BARK**
Jan 66. (lp) *(CRL 4515) <1501>* **THE REAL FOLK BLUES**
 – Mannish boy / Screamin' and cryin' / Just to be with you / Walking in the park / Same thing / Walking blues / Canary bird / Gypsy women / Rollin' and tumblin' / Forty days and forty nights / You can't lose what you never had / Little Geneva.
May 66. (7"ep) *(CRE 6022)* **THE REAL FOLK BLUES VOL.4**
 – I just want to make love to you / Louisiana blues / Still a fool / Standing around crying.
1966. (7") *<1973>* **CORINA, CORINA. / HOOTCHI KOOTCHIE MAN**
Jan 67. (lp) *(CRL 4525) <1507>* **MUDDY, BRASS AND THE BLUES**
 – Corrine, Corrina / Piney brown blues / Black night / Trouble in mind / Goin' back to Memphis / Betty and Dupree / Sweet little angel / Take me advice / Trouble / Hard loser.
Aug 67. (lp; MUDDY WATERS, BO DIDDLEY & LITTLE WALTER) *(CRL 4529)* **SUPERBLUES**
1967. (7") *<2018>* **BIRDNEST ON THE GROUND. / WHEN THE EAGLE FLIES**

May 68. (lp; MUDDY WATERS, BO DIDDLEY & HOWLIN' WOLF) *(CRL 4537) <LPS 3010>* **THE SUPER BLUES BAND**
Jan 69. (lp) *(CRL 4542) <314>* **ELECTRIC MUD**
 – I just want to make love to you / Hoochie coochie man / Let's spend the night together / She's all right / I'm a man / Herbert Harper's free press / Tom cat / Same thing.
Jan 69. (7") *(CRS 8083)* **LET'S SPEND THE NIGHT TOGETHER. / I'M A MAN**
Aug 69. (lp) *(CRL 4553) <320>* **AFTER THE RAIN**
 – I a the blues / Ramblin' mind / Rollin and tumblin' / Bottom of the sea / Honey bee / Blues and trouble / Hurtin' soul / Screamin' and cryin'
Oct 69. (d-lp) *(CRL 4556) <127>* **FATHERS AND SONS (live with PAUL BUTTERFIELD & MIKE BLOOMFIELD)**
 – All aboard / Mean disposition / Blow wind blow / Can't lose what you ain't never had / Walking through the park / 40 days and 40 nights / Standin' round crying / I'm ready / Twenty four hours / Sugar sweet / Long distance call / Baby, please don't go / Honey bee / The same thing / Got my mojo working (pt.1 & 2). (above also featured **BUDDY MILES + PHIL UPCHURCH**)
1970. (7") *<2085>* **GOING HOME. / I FEEL SO GOOD**
1972. (7") *<2107>* **MAKING FRIENDS. / TWO STEPS FORWARD**
Jul 72. (lp) *(6310 121) <60013>* **THE LONDON MUDDY WATERS SESSIONS**
 – Blind man blues / Key to the highway / Walkin' blues / I'm gonna move to the outskirts of town / Who's gonna be your sweet man when I'm gone / Young fashioned ways / Sad sad day / I don't know why. *(re-iss. Apr82 on 'Charly'; CXMP 2005) (re-iss. May92 on 'Chess-MCA'; CHLD/CHLC 19105)*

—— On 11 Oct'73, he was involved in a car accident which 3 people were killed. After releasing one more album, he went into semi-retirement for 2 years. Released 'LONDON REVISITED' Jan74 with HOWLIN' WOLF.
Nov 73. (7") *<2143>* **CAN'T GET NO GRINDIN'. / GARBAGE MAN**
Jan 74. (lp) *(6310 129) <50023>* **CAN'T GET NO GRINDIN'**
 – Can't get no grindin' / Mothers bad luck / Funky butt / Sad letter / Someday I'm gonna kitch you / Love weapon / Garbage man / After hours / Whiskey ain't no good / Muddy Waters' shuffle. *(re-iss. Sep90 lp/cd; CH/+D 9319)*
Mar 74. (lp) *<60031>* **"UNK" IN FUNK**
Apr 77. (lp) *(SKY 81853) <34449>* **HARD AGAIN**
 – Mannish boy / Bus driver / I want to be loved / Jealous-hearted man / I can't be satisfied / The blues had a baby, and they named it rock'n'roll / Deep down in Florida / Crosseyed cat / Little girl. *(re-iss. Sep83; 32357) (cd-iss. Mar91) (re-iss. Feb94 on 'Columbia' cd/c; CD/40 32357)*
Feb 78. (lp) *(SKY 82235) <34928>* **I'M READY**
 – I'm ready / 33 years / Who do you trust / Cooper Brown / I'm your hoochie coochie man / Mame / Rock me / Screamin' and cryin' / Good morning little schoolgirl. *(cd-iss. Nov91 on 'B.G.O.')*
Jan 79. (lp) *(SKY 83422) <35712>* **MUDDY MISSISSIPPI WATERS LIVE (live)**
 – Mannish boy / She's 19 years old / Nine below zero / Streamline woman / Howling wolf / Baby please don't go / Deep down in Florida. *(cd-iss. Mar91 on 'Beat Goes On';)*
May 81. (lp) *(SKY 84918) <37064>* **KING BEE**
 – I'm a king bee / Too young to know / Mean old Frisco blues / Forever lonely / I feel like goin' home / Champagne and reefer / Sad sad day / My eyes keep me in trouble / Deep down in Florida / No escape from the blues.

—— On the 30th Apr'83, MUDDY died of a heart attack in his Chicago home.

– compilations, etc. –

Nov 64. (lp) *Pye; (NPL 28048)* **MUDDY SINGS BIG BILL (BROONZY)** *(re-iss. Nov67 on 'Marble Arch'; MAL 723)*
Jan 67. (lp) *Chess; <1511>* **MORE REAL FOLK BLUES**
Aug 68. (lp) *Bounty; (BY 6031)* **DOWN ON STOVALL'S FARM** (1942 rec.) *(re-iss. May86 on 'Testament'; T 2210)*
Jun 69. (lp) *Polydor; (236 574)* **BLUES MAN**
Oct 69. (lp) *Chess; <1539>* **SAIL ON** (nearly same as BEST OF)
Dec 69. (lp) *Sunnyland; (KS 100) <100>* **VINTAGE MUD**
May 70. (lp) *Syndicate/ US= Chess; (SC 001) <001>* **BACK IN THE GOOD OLD DAYS**
 – *(re-iss. 1979)*
May 70. (lp) *Syndicate/ US= Chess; (SC 002) <002>* **GOOD NEWS**
 – Trouble no more / Don't go no further / Diamonds at your feet / Evil / All aboard / I love the life I live / Mean mistreater / Recipe for love / Good news / Come home baby / I won't go / She's got it / Close to you. *(re-iss. 1979)*
Jun 70. (lp) *Syndicate/ US= Chess; (SC 005) <005>* **WE THREE KINGS ("with HOWLIN' WOLF & LITTLE WALTER")** *(re-iss. Sep82)*
Feb 71. (lp) *Chess; <1553>* **THEY CALL ME MUDDY WATERS**
Oct 71. (lp) *Chess; <50012>* **LIVE (AT MISTER KELLY'S)**
Apr 75. (lp) *Chess; <60035>* **THE MUDDY WATERS WOODSTOCK ALBUM**
Nov 77. (d-lp) *Syndicate; (SC 001/2)* **BACK IN THE EARLY DAYS VOL.1&2**
 – (albums 'BACK IN THE GOOD OLD DAYS' & 'GOOD NEWS') *(re-iss. Sep82) (re-iss. Jul83 on 'Red Lightning')*
1979. (lp) *Muse/ US= Jazz Horizons; (MR 5021)* **CHICKEN SHACK**
1979. (lp) *Muse/ US= Jazz Horizons; (MR 5008) <5008>* **MUD IN YOUR EAR** *(cd-iss. Feb91; 600630)*
Sep 79. (lp) *Chess; (6671 001) <60006>* **McKINLEY MORGANFIELD**
Apr 81. (lp) *Chess; (CXMD 4000)* **CHESS MASTERS** *(re-iss. +cd.Mar88 on 'Stylus')*
Apr 82. (lp) *Chess; (CXMD 4006)* **CHESS MASTERS VOL.2**
Apr 83. (lp) *Chess; (CXMD 4015)* **CHESS MASTERS VOL.3**
Jul 83. (lp/c) *Blue Sky; (SKY/40 25565)* **HOOCHIE COOCHIE MAN**
 – Mannish boy / I'm ready / Champagne and reefer / Baby please don't go / I want

to be loved / Sad sad day / I'm a king bee / Blues had a baby and they named it rock'n'roll / She's 19 years old / I can't be satisfied / Screamin' and cryin' / I'm your hoochie coochie man. (re-iss. +cd.Aug88 + Apr93 on 'Epic')

Mar 85. (lp) *Chess; (CXMP 2057)* **RARE AND UNISSUED**
Aug 86. (lp) *Chess;* **RARE AND UNISSUED VOL.2**
Oct 87. *Chess; (GCH/+K7 8040)* **FOLK SINGERS**
Aug 92. (9xcd-box) *Chess; (CDREDBOX 3)* **THE COMPLETE MUDDY WATERS: 1947-1967**
1989. (6xlp/3xcd) *Chess; (CH/+D 680002)* **THE CHESS BOX**
1982. (lp) *Krazy Kat; (KK 7405)* **MUDDY WATERS IN CONCERT 1958 (live)**
Jul 83. (lp) *Blue Moon; (BMLP 1006)* **ROLLIN' STONE** (cd-iss. 1988 on 'Charly'; CDRED 1)
Sep 84. (lp) *Blue Moon; (BMLP 1014)* **MISSISSIPPI ROLLIN' STONE**
Jun 93. (cd) *Blue Moon; (CDBM 101)* **GOODBYE NEWPORT BLUES**
Nov 84. (lp) *Astan; (20027)* **SWEET HOME CHICAGO**
Nov 84. (lp) *Astan; (20028)* **ORIGINAL HOOCHIE COOCHIE**
Nov 85. (lp) *Deja Vu; (DVLP 2034)* **20 BLUES GREATS (THE COLLLECTION)**
Aug 87. (cd) *Deja Vu; (DVCD 2034)* **THE MUDDY WATERS COLLECTION**
Apr 93. (cd/c) *Deja Vu; (D2 CD/MC 15)* **THE GOLD COLLECTION**
Apr 86. (lp) *Showcase; (SHLP 141)* **I CAN'T BE SATISFIED**
Aug 87. (lp) *Onsala; (CFPC 401)* **LIVE 1965-68**
Apr 88. (7") *Epic; (MUD 1)* **MANNISH BOY. / I'M YOUR HOOCHIE COOCHIE MAN** [51]
(12") (MUDT 1) – ('A'side) / The blues had a baby and they named it rock'n'roll / Little girl.
Jun 88. (lp/cd) *Bold Reprieve; (FC/FCD 116)* **LIVE IN ANTIBES 1974 (live)**
Jul 88. (12"m) *Bold Reprieve;* **MANNISH BOY (live) / GARBAGE MAN (live). / I'M YOUR HOOCHIE COOCHIE MAN**
Jan 90. (cd/c/lp) *Mainline; (265233-2/-4/-1)* **20 BLUES CLASSICS**
Dec 90. (cd) *Jazz Velvet; (JH 02)* **LIVE IN SWITZERLAND (live 1976 with The CHICAGO BLUES BAND)**
1989. (lp) *Charly; (LPM 7002)* **CAN'T GET NO GRINDIN'**
Jun 89. (cd) *Chess; (CD 9291)* **TROUBLE NO MORE / SINGLES (1955-1959)**
Jul 89. (cd/c/lp) *Instant; (CD/TC/+ INS 5003)* **CHICAGO BLUES**
Dec 90. (c) *Charly; (TCAD 27)* **MUDDY AT NEWPORT / WHOSE MUDDY . . .**
Dec 90. (c) *Charly; (GCHK 78115)* **UNK IN FUNK / SINGS BIG BILL (BROOZY)**
1992. (cd/c) *Charly; (CD/TC BM 10)* **ROCK ME**
Feb 93. (cd/c) *Charly; (CD/TC BM 39)* **FUNKY BUTT**
Feb 93. (cd) *Charly; (CDCD 1039)* **GOT MY MOJO WORKING**
Jul 93. (cd) *Charly; (CDCD 1100)* **HOOCHIE COOCHIE MAN**
Jan 92. (cd) *Quality; (QSCD 6004)* **THE ESSENTIAL RECORDINGS**
Feb 92. (cd) *Fan Club;* **GOIN' HOME: LIVE IN PARIS 1970 (live)**
Aug 92. (cd) *Columbia; (4768922)* **BLUES SKY**
Apr 93. (cd) *Columbia;* **16 GREATEST HITS**
May 93. (cd) *Document;* **FIRST RECORDINGS 1941-46**
Sep 93. (cd) *Landscape; (LS 2921)* **LIVE IN SWITZERLAND 1976 – VOLUME II (live)**
Sep 93. (cd) *See For Miles; (SEECD 379)* **THE EP COLLECTION (1-side by HOWLIN' WOLF)**
Oct 93. (cd) *L.R.C.; (CDC 9015)* **MUDDY WATERS**
May 94. (cd) *Charly; (CDTT 3)* **TWO ON ONE (w/JOHN LEE HOOKER)**
Aug 94. (cd) *Charly;* **LIVE AT NEWPORT (live w/OTIS SPANN)**
Nov 94. (cd) *Charly;* **CHICAGO 1979 (live)**
Apr 95. (cd) *Charly; (CDRB 15)* **ELECTRIC MUD & MORE**
Apr 95. (4xcd-box+book) *Charly; (CDDIG 9)* **THE KING OF CHICAGO BLUES**
Jul 95. (lp) *Discovery; (HDR 1001)* **THE FOLK SINGER**
Jul 95. (d-cd) *Charly; (VBCD 302)* **THE VERY BEST OF MUDDY WATERS**
Jul 95. (cd) *Charly; (CDCD 1257)* **IN CONCERT**
Jul 95. (cd) *Best; (BSTCD 9104)* **MUDDY WATERS**

Roger WATERS

Born: 6 Sep'44, Great Bookham, Cambridge, England. A founding member of PINK FLOYD in 1965, WATERS became the outfit's mainman in 1968 following SYD BARRETT's break with reality. PINK FLOYD's frontman and main contributor until his departure in 1983, he put together the soundtrack to the film 'THE BODY' in 1970 together with synth/keys man, RON GEESIN. With PINK FLOYD absent from the recording front in the mid-80's, fans locked onto WATERS for worthwhile material. His debut album, 'PROS & CONS OF HITCH HIKING' (1984) didn't exactly set the world alight but managed a UK Top 20 placing. Not straying too far from latter day PF territory, WATERS carried on in even more lugubrious fashion with 1987's 'RADIO KAOS' set. Come the turn of the decade, with The BERLIN WALL being dismantled, ROGER thought it neccessary to revive the 1979 PINK FLOYD album, 'THE WALL'. With an array of famous guests, he played there to a live audience of 200,000, plus TV millions all contributing to The Disaster Relief Fund. • **Songwriters:** WATERS wrote all material. • **Trivia:** In 1987, WATERS took the existing members of PINK FLOYD to court, for their use of group name.

Album rating: THE BODY soundtrack with Ron Geesin (*4) / THE PROS AND CONS OF HITCH HIKING (*7) / RADIO K.A.O.S. (*5) / THE WALL: LIVE IN BERLIN (*4) / AMUSED TO DEATH (*5)

ROGER WATERS – vocals, bass, etc. (ex-PINK FLOYD) with **ERIC CLAPTON** – guitar / **ANDY NEWMARK** – drums / **RAY COOPER** – percussion / **MADELINE BELL** – vocals

	Harvest	Columbia

Apr 84. (7") *(HAR 5228)* **5:01 a.m. (THE PROS AND CONS OF HITCH HIKING). / 4:30 a.m. (APPARENTLY THEY WERE TRAVELLING ABROAD)**
(12"+=) *(12HAR 5228)* – 4:33 a.m. (Running shoes).
May 84. (lp/c/cd) *(SHVL 240105-1/-4/-2)* <39290> **THE PROS AND CONS OF HITCH HIKING** [13] [31]
– 4:30 a.m. (Apparently they were travelling abroad) / 4:33 a.m. (Running shoes) / 4:37 a.m. (Arabs with knives and West German skies) / 4:39 a.m. (For the first time today) / 4:41 a.m. (Sexual revolution) / 4:47 a.m. (The remains of our love) / 4:50 a.m. (Go fishing) / 4:56 a.m. (For the first time today pt.2) / 4:58 a.m. (Dunroamin' duncarin' dunlivin') / 5:06 a.m. (Every strangers eyes) / 5:11 a.m. (The moment of clarity).
Jun 84. (7") *(HAR 5230)* **5:06 a.m. (EVERY STRANGERS EYES). / 4:39 a.m. (FOR THE FIRST TIME TODAY)**

—— In Oct'86, WATERS and his BLEEDING HEART BAND featured on 1 side of 'WHEN THE WIND BLOWS' album / animated cartoon film on 'Virgin'.

—— His new band: **ANDY FAIRWEATHER-LOW** – guitar / **JAY STAPLEY** – electric guitar / **MEL COLLINS** – sax / **IAN RITCHIE** – keyboards, drum prog. / **GRAHAM BROAD** – drums

	E.M.I.	Columbia

May 87. (7") *(EM 6)* **RADIO WAVES (edit). / GOING TO LIVE IN L.A.** [74]
(12"+=/cd-s+=) *(12/CD EM 6)* – ('A'demo version).
Jun 87. (cd/c/lp) *(CD/TC+/KAOS 1)* <40795> **RADIO KAOS** [25] [50]
– Radio waves / Who needs information / Me or him / The powers that be / Sunset Strip / Home / Four minutes / The tide is turning.
Nov 87. (7") *(EM 37)* **THE TIDE IS TURNING (After Live Aid). / GET BACK ON THE RADIO (demo)** [54]
(12"+=/cd-s+=) *(12/CD EM 37)* – Money (live).

	Mercury	Mercury

Sep 90. (d-cd/d-c/d-lp; ROGER WATERS AND THE BLEEDING HEART BAND) *(<846611-2/-4/-1>)* **THE WALL: LIVE IN BERLIN (live)** [27] [56]
– In the flesh? (SCORPIONS) / The thin ice (UTE LEMPER) / Another brick in the wall – part 1 / The happiest days of our lives (JOE CHEMAY) / Another brick in the wall – part 2 (CYNDI LAUPER) / Mother (SINEAD O'CONNOR) / Goodbye blue sky (JONI MITCHELL) / Empty spaces + Young lust (BRYAN ADAMS) / One of my turns / Don't leave me now / Another brick in the wall – part 3 / Goodbye cruel world / Hey you (PAUL CARRACK) / Is there anybody out there? (MICHAEL KAMEN /The RUNDFUNK ORCHESTRA +*) / Nobody home / Vera (*) / Bring the boys back home / Comfortably numb (VAN MORRISON) / In the flesh? (*) / Run like Hell / Waiting for the worms (*) / Stop to / The trial (TIM CURRY & THOMAS DOLBY) / The tide is turning (The COMPANY). (re-iss. d-cd Sep95)
Sep 90. (7"/12") **ANOTHER BRICK IN THE WALL (part 2). / RUN LIKE HELL (live)**
(cd-s+=) – ('A'extended).

	Columbia	Columbia

Aug 92. (7"/c-s) *(658 139-7/-4)* **WHAT GOD WANTS, PART 1. / ('A'video edit)** [35]
(cd-s+=) *(658 139-2)* – What god wants, part III.
Sep 92. (cd/c/lp) *(468761-2/-4/-1)* <47127> **AMUSED TO DEATH** [8] [21]
– The ballad of Bill Hubbard / What God wants, part 1 / Perfect sense, part I & II / The bravery of being out of range / Late home tonight, part I & II / Too much rope / What God wants, part II & III / Watching TV / Three wishes / It's a miracle / Amused to death.
Dec 92. (7"/c-s) *(658 819-7/-4)* **THE BRAVERY OF BEING OUT OF RANGE. / WHAT GOD WANTS (part 1)**
(cd-s+=) *(658 819-2)* – Perfect sense. (part 1).
—— it looks as though ROGER has decided to give up

Ben WATT (see under ⇒ EVERYTHING BUT THE GIRL)

WEATHER PROPHETS (dig out; Great Alt & Indie . . .)

Jimmy WEBB

Born: 15 Aug'46, Elk City, Oklahoma. Son of a baptist preacher/minister, WEBB had learned piano as a kid and, inspired by the California surf boom, had already begun writing songs by the time he signed up for a course at San Bernardino college in 1963. Jacking it in shortly after to ply his trade as a songwriter, he soon found himself working for 'Jobete' music, the publishing wing of 'Tamla Motown'. A subsequent move to L.A. eventually led to a job with a similar company set up by JOHNNY RIVERS, the singer unsuccessfully covering WEBB's haunting 'BY THE TIME I GET TO PHOENIX'. A classic example of this farmer turned songwriter's orchestral L.A. sound, the track was later given a definitive reading by easy rocking country celeb GLEN CAMPBELL. WEBB's first real success had actually come around the same time when black soul-pop outfit, FIFTH DIMENSION took 'UP, UP AND AWAY' into the US Top 10. TWA subsequently used the track on a commercial and WEBB's career went stratospheric almost overnight. A keen student of the PHIL SPECTOR/BRIAN WILSON school of production technique, WEBB's highly distinctive, expansive arrangements were indelibly marked with the desolation and panoramic melancholy of his native Oklahoma. You could hear it in 'WITCHITA LINEMAN', another WEBB weepie transformed by the golden tonsils of GLEN CAMPBELL, the singer completing his hat trick in 1969 when he carried 'GALVESTON' into the Top 5. The previous year RICHARD HARRIS had narrowly missed the top of the US charts with WEBB's 'MACARTHUR PARK', the most deliciously overwrought composition of his songwriting career and a song subsequently covered by artists as diverse as DIANA ROSS and WAYLON JENNINGS. As for WEBB's own recording career (not including a one-one 45 with bubblegum trio, The STRAWBERRY CHILDREN), 'Epic' kickstarted it without telling him in 1968 with 'JIM WEBB SINGS JIM WEBB', a collection of early demos. With the rise of the singer songwriter brigade in the early 70's, WEBB quite understandably attempted to cut himself a piece of the action as the role of the traditional songwriter diminished. Signed to L.A. powerhouse, 'Reprise', he finally released a debut album proper, 'WORDS AND MUSIC', in 1970. Markedly more lo-fi than the grandiose pieces that had made him famous, the album made little impact. A further two albums of excellent singer songwriter fare, 'AND SO ON' (1971) and 'LETTERS' (1972), were similarly overlooked and ultimately WEBB failed to make the transition from backroom to centre stage undertaken so successfully by his former East coast contemporary, CAROLE KING. He nevertheless enjoyed at least some sporadic chart grace as ART GARFUNKEL hit in 1973 with 'ALL I KNOW', no doubt helping to ease the pressure of being dropped by 'Reprise'. Briefly taken under the wing of 'Asylum' for 'LAND'S END' (1974), WEBB's recording fortunes failed to improve and even his production forays fell by the wayside as an attempted FIFTH DIMENSION reunion project stiffed in the mid-70's. Although he continued to write for film and television, WEBB's profile was almost non existent for the bulk of the 80's following 1982's 'ANGEL HEART' album. It was more than a decade before he released another album of songs, 1993's well received 'SUSPENDING DISBELIEF'. The man behind some of America's most evocative and enduring songs, WEBB's place in music biz history is assured even if he's never actually been a household name. He still tours occasionally and even played some rare UK dates in 1998, performing timeless songs to an ageing audience.

Album rating: JIM WEBB SINGS JIM WEBB (*3) / WORDS AND MUSIC (*5) / AND SO ON (*5) / LETTERS (*4) / LAND'S END (*4) / EL MIRAGE (*7) / ANGEL HEART (*4) / ARCHIVE compilation (*8) / SUSPENDED DISBELIEF (*5) / TEN EASY PIECES (*7)

JIMMY WEBB – vocals, acoustic guitar / (with various others)

	Liberty	Soul City
1967. (7"; by The STRAWBERRY CHILDREN) (LBF 15012) <758> **LOVE YEARS COMING. / ONE STANDS HERE**		

	C.B.S.	Epic
Jul 68. (lp; as JIM WEBB) (63335) <26401> **JIM WEBB SINGS JIM WEBB** (unauthorised demos) – I keep it hid / You're so young / I'll be back / Life is hard / I need you / Our time is running out / I can do it on my own / Then / I'm in need / Run, run, run.		
Aug 68. (7"; as JIM WEBB) (3672) <10329> **I KEEP IT HID. / I NEED YOU**		

	Reprise	Reprise
Jan 71. (7"; as JIMMY L. WEBB) <(RS 20-978)> **P.F. SLOAN. / PSALM ONE-FIVE-O**		
Jan 71. (lp; as JIMMY L. WEBB) <(RSLP 6421)> **WORDS AND MUSIC** – Words and music / Sleepin' in the daytime / P.F. Sloan / Love song / Careless weed / Psalm one-five-o / Music for an unmade movie part 1:- Songseller – part 2:- Dorothy Chandler blues – part 3:- Jerusalem / Three songs:- Let it be me – Never my love – I wanna be free / Once before I die. (re-iss. 1971; K 44101)		Feb70
Aug 71. (lp) (K 44134) <RSLP 6448> **AND SO ON** – Met her on a plane / All night show / All my love's laughter / Highpockets / Marionette / Laspitch / One lady / If ships were made to sail / Pocketful of keys / See you then.		
Sep 72. (lp) (K 44173) <RSLP 2055> **LETTERS** – Galveston / Campo de Encino / Love hurts / Hurt me well / Once in the morning / Catharsis / Song seller / When can brown begin / Piano. <US cd-iss. 1999 on 'WEA Int.'; 10305>		
Sep 72. (7") <1116> **CAMPO DE ENCINO. / LOVE HURTS**	–	
Jul 73. (7") (K 14279) **CAMPO DE ENCINO. / ONCE IN THE MORNING**		–

	Asylum	Asylum
Nov 73. (7") <11027> **CRYING IN MY SLEEP. / OCEAN IN HIS EYES**	–	
May 74. (7") <11042> **FEET IN THE SUNSHINE. / LADY FITS HER BLUE JEANS**	–	
May 74. (7") (AYM 529) **FEET IN THE SUNSHINE. / OCEAN IN HIS EYES**		–
Jul 74. (lp) (SYL 9014) <5070> **LAND'S END** – Ocean in his eyes / Feet in the sunshine / Cloudman / Lady fits her blue jeans / Just this one time / Crying in my sleep / It's a sin / Alyce blue gown / Land's end – Asleep on the wind.		Apr74

	Atlantic	Atlantic
Apr 77. (7") (K 10931) **THE HIGHWAYMAN. / CHRISTIAN NO**	–	–
May 77. (lp) (K 50370) <18218> **EL MIRAGE** – The highwayman / If you see me getting smaller I'm leaving / Mixed-up guy / Christian no / Moment in a shadow / Sugarbird / Where the universes are / P.F. Sloan / Dance to the radio. <US cd-iss. 1999 on 'WEA Int.'; 2768>		
Jun 77. (7") <3407> **IF YOU SEE ME GETTING SMALLER I'M LEAVING. / CHRISTIAN NUMBER**		–
Jul 77. (7") (K 10978) **WHERE THE UNIVERSES ARE. / THE MOON IS A HARSH MISTRESS**		–
Aug 77. (7") <3426> **THE HIGHWAYMAN. / THE MOON IS A HARSH MISTRESS**	–	–

—— in 1979, JIMMY featured on the 1979 film, 'Voices'.

	not iss.	Columbia
Aug 82. (lp) <FC 37695> **ANGEL HEART** – Angel heart / God's gift / One of the few / Scissors cut / Work for a dollar / His world / Our movie / Nasty love / In cars / Old wing mouth. <cd-iss. 1992 on 'Sony'; 66654>	–	

	WEA	WEA
Oct 93. (cd/c) <(7559 61506-2/-4)> **SUSPENDED DISBELIEF** – Too young to die / I don't know how to love you anymore / Elvis and me / It won't bring her back / Sandy cove / Friends to burn / What does a woman see in a man / Postcards from Paris / Just like always / Adios / I will arise.		Sep93

	Guardian-EMI	Guardian-EMI
Oct 97. (cd) <(8 52826-2)> **TEN EASY PIECES** (re-takes) – Galveston / The highwayman / Wichita lineman / The moon is a harsh mistress / By the time I get to Phoenix / If these walls could speak / Didn't we? / The worst thing that could happen / All I know / MacArthur Park.		Oct96

—— A Various Artists tribute, 'AND SOMEONE LEFT THE CAKE OUT IN THE RAIN', was issued by 'Debutante' early '98

– compilations, etc. –

Jul 93. (cd) WEA; (9548 32063-2) **ARCHIVE** (1970-1977) – P.F. Sloan / Love song / Three songs / Met her on a plane / All my love's laughter / One lady / If ships were made to sail / Galveston / Once in the morning / When brown can begin / Piano / The highwayman / Christian no / Where the universes are / The moon is a harsh mistress / Feet in the sunshine / Lady fits her blue jeans / Just this one time / Crying in my sleep / Land's end – Asleep on the wind.		–

WEBB BROTHERS

Formed: California, USA ... 1998 by the sons of singer/composer JIMMY WEBB, CHRISTIAN and JUSTIN. The "partnership" between the two gifted musicians apparently started when CHRISTIAN began writing brilliant pop songs at the age of 11! Time passed quickly, and a demo of 11 tracks that the pair had recorded (titled ~'EXCERPTS FROM THE BIOSPHERE') reached A&R hands in January '98. Some twelve months later the majestic, space ridden, 'EXCERPTS ...' was released through the 'Easy! Tiger' imprint, although available only on a limited 1000 copies basis. This was subsequently followed up by the similarly titled debut album, 'BEYOND THE BIOSPHERE' (on 'East West'), which seemed to be heavily inspired by HARRY NILSSON's conceptual album, 'The Point', it's strange cocktail of pop harmonies and lo-fi acoustics (a fusion of CROSBY, STILLS & NASH and NIRVANA quite possibly!) thrown in for good measure.

Album rating: BEYOND THE BIOSPHERE (*8)

CHRISTIAN WEBB – vocals, keyboards / **JUSTIN WEBB** – vocals, guitar / with BEITR FUHRMAN – bass / MICHAEL DUGGAN – cello / NEAL OSTROVSKY – drums, guitar / KENNY ANDERSON – trumpet / BILL McFARLAND – trombone

	Easy! Tiger	not iss.
Jan 99. (ltd-7") (MUSE 005) **EXCERPTS FROM BEYOND THE BIOSPHERE. /**		–

	eastwest	eastwest
Jul 99. (cd/lp) <(3984 28323-2/-1)> **BEYOND THE BIOSPHERE** – Beyond the biosphere / She drifts into my room / Sour grapes / Cold fingers / What have we become / The filth of it all / Biosphere (reprise) / You took it wrong / Drink and drown / Got no worries / I'm over and I know it.		
Nov 99. (7") (WEA 243) **COLD FINGERS. / HEALTY AND HANDSOME** (cd-s+=) (WEA 243CD) – I'm over and I know it (+ CD-Rom video).		–

WEDDING PRESENT

Formed: Leeds, England ... 1984 by ex-teachers DAVID GEDGE and PETE SOLOWKA (father Ukrainian) along with KEITH GREGORY and SHAUN CHARMAN. They gained a deal with local indie label, 'Reception', in 1985 and, with appearances on John Peel's radio 1 show, quickly grew into a cult act. Debut album, 'GEORGE BEST' (1987) was one of the key 80's indie releases, GEDGE's tunefully challenged monotone combining with the fast and furious punk-jangle racket to somehow create something more than the sum of its parts. Towards the end of the decade, they were finally signed to a major record company, 'R.C.A.', their first release on the label, 'UKRAINSKI ...', surprising many with its marriage of Ukranian folk styles and indie-rock. GEDGE reverted to his trademark lovelorn lyrical fashion for follow-up proper, 'BIZARRO', a record that disappointed many longtime fans. Nevertheless, The WEDDING PRESENT were nothing if not prolific, even achieving the accolade of a Guinness Book Of Records entry in 1992 when every one of their monthly single (7"only) releases hit the UK Top 30 (The 12 hits also contained an unusual cover version on the B-side, see below). Despite the departure of all founding members save GEDGE (SALOWKA left in the early 90's to form The UKRANIANS), 1994's 'WATUSI' again found the band in favour with the critics if not commanding the fanbase they once had. In 1998, GEDGE re-invented himself as a SERGE GAINSBOURG or BURT BACHARACH-type crooner in the project/duo, CINERAMA, alongside SALLY MURRELL, his sort of JANE BIRKIN, you could say. An album, 'VA VA VOOM', was a marked change of direction from the WEDDOES bust-a-gut blasts, into EDWYN COLLINS glutty vocals. • **Songwriters:** GEDGE compositions, except GETTING NOWHERE FAST (Girls At Our Best) / WHAT BECOME OF THE BROKEN HEARTED (Jimmy Ruffin) / I FOUND THAT ESSENCE RARE (Gang Of Four) / IT'S NOT UNUSUAL (Tom Jones) / FELICITY (Orange Juice) / MAKE ME SMILE (COME UP AND SEE ME) (Steve Harley & Cockney Rebel) / BOX ELDER (Pavement) / SHE'S MY BEST FRIEND (Velvet Underground) / MOTHERS (Jean Michel Satre) / CUMBERLAND GAP (Leadbelly) / CATTLE AND CANE (Go-Betweens) / DON'T CRY NO TEARS (Neil Young) / THINK THAT IT MIGHT (Altered Images) /

FALLING (Julee Cruise) / PLEASANT VALLEY SUNDAY (Monkees) / LET'S MAKE SOME PLANS (Close Lobsters) / ROCKET (Mud) / THEME FROM SHAFT (Isaac Hayes) / CHANT OF THE EVER CIRCLING SKELETAL FAMILY (Bowie) / GO WILD IN THE COUNTRY (Bow Wow Wow) / U.F.O. (Barry Gray) / STEP INTO CHRISTMAS (Elton John) / JUMPER CLOWN (Marc Riley). • **Trivia:** STEVE ALBINI (ex-BIG BLACK) produced their early 90s material.

Album rating: GEORGE BEST (*9) / TOMMY collection (*8) / UKRAINSKI VISTUPU V JOHNA PEELA (*5) / BIZARRO (*7) / SEAMONSTERS (*7) / THE HIT PARADE 1 compilation (*7) / THE HIT PARADE 2 compilation (*6) / WATUSI (*5) / MINI (*4) / SATURNALIA (*5) / Cinerama: VA VA VOOM (*6)

DAVID GEDGE (b.23 Apr'60) – vocals, guitar / **PETE SOLOWKA** (b.Manchester) – guitar / **KEITH GREGORY** (b. 2 Jan'63, County Durham) – bass / **SHAUN CHARMAN** (b.Brighton) – drums

	Reception	not iss.
May 85. (7") *(REC 001)* **GO OUT AND GET 'EM BOY. / (THE MOMENT BEFORE) EVERYTHING'S SPOILED AGAIN** (re-iss. Sep85 on 'City Slang'; CSL 001)		-
Feb 86. (7") *(REC 002)* **ONCE MORE. / AT THE EDGE OF THE SEA**		-
Apr 86. (12"ep) *(REC 002-12)* **DON'T TRY AND STOP ME MOTHER** – Go out and get 'em boy / (The moment before) Everything's spoiled again / Once more / At the edge of the sea.		-
Jul 86. (7") *(REC 003)* **THIS BOY CAN'T WAIT. / YOU SHOULD ALWAYS KEEP IN TOUCH WITH YOUR FRIENDS** (ext.12"+=) *(REC 003-12)* – Living and learning.		-
Feb 87. (7",7"white/12") *REC 005/+12* **MY FAVOURITE DRESS. / EVERY MOTHER'S SON / NEVER SAID** (2,000 copies of above single were also given free with debut lp)		-
Sep 87. (7") *(REC 006)* **ANYONE CAN MAKE A MISTAKE. / ALL ABOUT EVE** (c-s+=/12"+=) *(REC 006 C/12)* – Getting nowhere fast.		-
Oct 87. (lp/c/cd) *(LEEDS 001/+C/CD)* **GEORGE BEST** – Everyone thinks he looks daft / What did your last servant die of? / Don't be so hard / A million miles / All this and more / Getting nowhere fast * / My favourite dress / Shatner / Something and nothing / It's what you want that matters / Give my love to Kevin / Anyone can make a mistake / You can't moan can you / All about Eve *. (c+=/cd+= * tracks) <US cd-iss. 1997 on 'Cooking Vinyl'+=; COOKCD 134> – (9 extra).	47	-

—— **SIMON SMITH** (b. 3 May'65, Lincolnshire) – drums repl. SHAUN to POPGUNS

	Reception	not iss.
Feb 88. (7") *(REC 009)* **NOBODY'S TWISTING YOUR ARM. / I'M NOT ALWAYS SO STUPID** (12"+=/cd-s+=) *(REC 009 12/CD)* – Nothing comes easy / Don't laugh.	46	-
Jul 88. (lp/c/cd) *(LEEDS 002/+C/CD)* **TOMMY** (compilation 4 singles + Peel sessions) – Go out and get 'em boy / (The moment before) Everything's spoiled again / Once more / At the edge of the sea / Living and learning / This boy can't wait / You should always keep in touch with your friends / Felicity / What becomes of the broken hearted? / Never said / Every mother's son / My favourite dress. <US cd-iss. 1997 on 'Cooking Vinyl'; COOKCD 135>	42	-
Sep 88. (7") *(REC 011)* **WHY ARE YOU BEING SO REASONABLE NOW?. / NOT FROM WHERE I'M STANDING** (12"+=) *(REC 011-12)* – Give my love to Kevin (acoustic) / Getting better. (c-s+++/cd-s++) *(REC 011 C/CD)* – Pourquoi es tu devenue si raisonable?. (s7") *(REC 011F)* – Pourquoi es tu devenue si raisonable?. / Give my love to Kevin (acoustic)	42	-

—— added guest **LEN LIGGINS** – vocals, violin (ex-SINISTER CLEANERS, Solo artist) others played assortment of instruments in Ukrainian style.

	R.C.A.	R.C.A.
Apr 89. (lp/c/cd) *(PL/PK/PD 74104)* **UKRAINSKI VISTUPI V JOHNA PEELA** (Ukrainian style John Peel sessions) – Davny chasy / Yikhav kozak za dunai / Tiutiunyk / Zadmav didochok svitit misyats / Katrusyai Vasya vasyl'ok / Hude dn ipro hude Verkhovyno. (was to have been issued as 10"m-lp, Nov88 on 'Reception'; REC 010)	22	-

—— (Reverted to usual 4-piece & style).

	R.C.A.	R.C.A.
Sep 89. (7"/c-s) *(PB/PK 43117)* **KENNEDY. / UNFAITHFUL** (c-s+=/12"+=/cd-s+=) *(PT/PK/PD 43118)* – One day all this will all be yours / It's not unusual.	33	-
Oct 89. (lp/c/cd) *(PL/PK/PD 74302)* <2173> **BIZARRO** – Brassneck / Crushed / No / Thanks / Kennedy / What have I said now / Granadaland / Bewitched / Take me / Be honest. (cd+=) – Brassneck (extended) / Box elder / Don't talk, just kiss / Gone.	22	
Feb 90. (7"/c-s) *(PB/PK 43403)* **BRASSNECK. / DON'T TALK, JUST KISS** (c-s+=/12"+=/cd-s+=) *(PK/PT/PD 43404)* – Gone / Box elder.	24	-
Sep 90. (7"ep/c-ep)(12"ep/cd-ep) *(PB/PD 44021)(PT/PD 44022)* **THE 3 SONGS EP** – Corduroy / Make me smile (come up and see me) / Crawl. (10"+=) *(PJ 44022)* – Take me (live).	25	-

	R.C.A.	First Warning
Apr 91. (7") *(PB 44495)* **DALLIANCE. / NIAGARA** (c-s+=)(12"+=/cd-s+=) *(PK 44495)(PT/PD 44496)* – She's my best friend. (10"++=) *(PJ 44495)* – What have I said now? (live).	29	-
May 91. (cd/c/lp) *(PD/PK/PL 75012)* <75708> **SEAMONSTERS** – Dalliance / Dare / Suck / Blonde / Rotterdam / Lovenest / Corduroy / Carolyn / Heather / Octopussy.	13	
Jul 91. (12"ep/cd-ep) *(PT/PD 44750)* **LOVENEST (edit) / MOTHERS. / DAN DARE / FLESHWORLD**	58	-

—— **PAUL DORRINGTON** – guitar (ex-AC TEMPLE) repl. SOLOWKA to UKRAINIANS

	Reception	not iss.
Jan 92. (7") *(PB 45185)* **BLUE EYES. / CATTLE AND CANE**	26	-
Feb 92. (7") *(PB 45183)* **GO-GO DANCER. / DON'T CRY NO TEARS**	20	-
Mar 92. (7") *(PB 45181)* **THREE. / THINK THAT IT MIGHT**	14	-
Apr 92. (7") *(PB 45311)* **SILVER SHORTS. / FALLING**	14	-
May 92. (7") *(PB 45313)* **COME PLAY WITH ME. / PLEASANT VALLEY SUNDAY**	10	

Jun 92. (7") *(PB 45313)* **CALIFORNIA. / LET'S MAKE SOME PLANS**	16	-
Jun 92. (cd/c/lp) *(PD/PK/PL 75343)* <75711> **THE HIT PARADE 1** – (last 6 singles 'A'&'B')	22	-
Jul 92. (7") *(PB 10115)* **FLYING SAUCER. / ROCKET**	22	-
Aug 92. (7") *(PB 10117)* **BOING!. / THEME FROM SHAFT**	19	-
Sep 92. (7") *(PB 10116)* **LOVESLAVE. / CHANT OF THE EVER CIRCLING SKELETAL FAMILY**	17	-
Oct 92. (7") *(PB 11691)* **STICKY. / GO WILD IN THE COUNTRY**	17	-
Nov 92. (7") *(PB 11692)* **THE QUEEN OF OUTER SPACE. / U.F.O.**	23	-
Dec 92. (7"red) *(PB 11693)* **NO CHRISTMAS. / STEP INTO CHRISTMAS**	25	

—— The above 12 singles, were limited to 15,000 copies, and hit peak chart position on its first week of issue.

Jan 93. (cd/c/lp) *(PD/PK/PL 74321)* <75711> **THE HIT PARADE 2** – (all last 6 'A'&'B' singles above) (free lp w/lp+=) BBC SESSIONS – (all 12 of the years' A-sides).	19	

—— **DARREN BELLE** – bass; repl. GREGORY who later formed CHA CHA COHEN

	Island	Polygram
Sep 94. (c-ep/12"ep/cd-ep) *(CIS/12IS/CID 585)* **YEAH YEAH YEAH YEAH YEAH / THE BIKINI / FLAME ON / HIM OR ME (WHAT'S IT GONNA BE)** (cd-ep) *(CIDX 585)* – ('A'side) / Gazebo / So long baby / Spangle.	51	-
Sep 94. (cd/c/lp) *(CID/ICT/ILPS 8014)* <524044> **WATUSI** – So long, baby / Click click / Yeah yeah yeah yeah yeah / Let him have it / Gazebo / Shake it / Spangle / It's a gas / Swimming pools, movie stars / Big rat / Catwoman / Hot pants.	47	-
Nov 94. (c-s/7") *(C+/IS 591)* **IT'S A GAS. / BUBBLES** (12"purple+=/cd-s+=) *(12IS/CID 591)* – ('A'acoustic) / Jumper clown.		-

—— SMITH was another to leave and turn up in CHA CHA COHEN

	Cooking Vinyl	Cooking Vinyl
Jan 96. (10"m-lp/m-cd) *(<COOK/+CD 094>)* **MINI** – Drive / Love machine / Go, man, go / Mercury / Convertible / Sports car. (cd+=) – Sucker / Waiting on the guns / Jet girl.		
Aug 96. (7") *(FRY 048)* **2, 3, GO. / UP** (cd-s+=) *(FRYCD 048)* – Jet girl / Real thing.	67	-
Sep 96. (2x10"lp/c/cd) *(<COOK/+C/CD 099>)* **SATURNALIA** – Snake eyes / Big boots / Spaceman / Skin diving / Real thing / Dreamworld / Kansas / Hula doll / Up / Venus / 50's / Montreal / 2, 3, go.	36	
Jan 97. (7") *(FRY 063)* <5053> **MONTREAL. / PROJECT CENZO** (7") *(FRY 053X)* – ('A'side) / Where everybody knows your name. (cd-s) *(FRYCD 053)* – ('A'side) / Sports car / My favourite dress (live) / Brassneck (live).	40	

—— they officially split after above

– compilations, etc. –

Oct 86. (12"ep) *Strange Fruit; (SFPS 009)* **THE PEEL SESSIONS** (26.2.86) – What becomes of the broken hearted / This boy can't wait / Felicity / You should always keep in touch with your friends. (c-ep iss.Jun87; SFPSC 009) (cd-ep iss.Aug88; SFPSC 009)		-
Nov 88. (12"ep/cd-ep) *Nightracks; (SFNT/+CD 016)* **THE EVENING SHOW SESSIONS** (20.4.86) – Everyone thinks he looks daft / I found that essence rare / Shatner / My favourite dress.		-
Oct 93. (lp/cd) *Strange Fruit; (SFR LP/CD 122)* **JOHN PEEL SESSIONS 1987-1990** – Give my regards to Kevin / Getting nowhere fast / A million miles / Something and nothing / Take me I'm yours / Unfaithful / Why are you being so reasonable now? / Happy birthday / Dalliance / Heather Blonde / Niagara.		

CINERAMA

DAVID LEWIS GEDGE – vocals, guitar / **SALLY MURRELL** – vocals, programming / with **DARE MASON** – guitar, theremin / **MARTY WILLSON-PIPER** – guitar (of The CHURCH) / **ANTHONY COOTE** – bass (of ANIMALS CAN SWIM) / **DAVEY RAY MOORE** – keyboards (of PUSHA) / **RICHARD MARKANGELO + CHE ALBRIGHTON** – drums, percussion / **JULIA PALMER + ABIGAIL TRUNDLE** – cello / **RACHEL DAVIES** – violin / **DUNCAN BRIDGEMAN** – flute / **THIBAULT DE MONTFORT** – oboe / **DEREK CRABTREE** – trumpet / **EMMA POLLOCK** – vocals (of DELGADOS)

	Cooking Vinyl	SpinArt
Jul 98. (7") *(FRY 072)* **KERRY KERRY. / 7X** (7") *(FRY 072X)* – ('A'side) / Mr Kiss Kiss Bang Bang. (cd-s) *(FRYCD 072)* – ('A'side) / Love / Au pair.	71	-
Aug 98. (lp/cd) *(COOK/+CD 150)* <68> **VA VA VOOM** – Maniac / Comedienne / Hate / Kerry Kerry / Barefoot in the park / You turn me on / Ears / Me next / Hard, fast and beautiful / Dance, girl, dance / Honey rider.		Oct98
Oct 98. (7") *(FRY 077)* **DANCE, GIRL, DANCE. / EARS (acoustic version)** (cd-s) *(FRYCD 077)* – ('A'side) / Crusoe / Model spy. (cd-s) *(FRYCD 077X)* – Pacific / King's Cross.		-
Aug 99. (ltd-7") *(ER 210)* **PACIFIC. / KING'S CROSS** (above issued on 'Elefant')		-

---

WEEN   (dig out; Great Alt & Indie . . .)

WEEZER

Formed: Los Angeles, California, USA . . .1993 by RIVERS CUOMO, MATT SHARP and PATRICK WILSON. Signing to 'Geffen' and recruiting final member, BRIAN BELL, the group released their eponymous RIC OCASEK-produced debut album in September '94. Helped by the transatlantic success of singles such as 'UNDONE – THE SWEATER SONG' and the pogo-pop of 'BUDDY HOLLY', the album became one of the year's biggest sellers. Often described as The PIXIES meeting The BEACH BOYS, their blaring college 'nerd'-rock saw WEEZER riding the crest of an American 'new wave' triggered by the likes of GREEN DAY and OFFSPRING. Meanwhile, MATT SHARP was also busy with a side project, The RENTALS (comprising CHERIELYNN WESTRICH, ROD CERVERA, PETRA HADEN, PAT WILSON and JIM RICHARDS), releasing an album of New Wave-esque songs in 'RETURN OF THE RENTALS' (1995/96). A second WEEZER album, 'PINKERTON' (1996), was much of the same, although it brought the band a bit of grief when the American security firm of the same name brought legal action; the band have been inactive since. • Songwriters: CUOMO, a few w/ WILSON.

Album rating: WEEZER (*7) / PINKERTON (*7) / Rentals: RETURN OF THE RENTALS (*5) / SEVEN MORE MINUTES (*6)

RIVERS CUOMO – vocals / **BRIAN BELL** – guitar, vocals / **MATT SHARP** – bass, vocals / **PATRICK WILSON** – drums

		Geffen	D.G.C.
Jan 95.	(7"blue) (GFS 85) <19378> **UNDONE – THE SWEATER SONG. / HOLIDAY**	35	57 Sep94
	(c-s+=/cd-s+=) – Mykel & Carli / Susanne.		
Feb 95.	(cd/c/lp) <(GED/GEC/GEF 24629)> **WEEZER**	23	16 Aug94
	– My name is Jonas / No one else / The world has turned and left me here / Buddy Holly / Undone – the sweater song / In the garage / Holiday / Only in dreams.		
Apr 95.	(7"/c-s) (GFS/+C 88) **BUDDY HOLLY. / JAMIE**	12	-
	(cd-s+=) (GFSTD 88) – My name is Jonas / Surf wax America.		
Jul 95.	(10"ep/c-ep/cd-ep) (GFS V/C/TD 95) **SAY IT AIN'T SO (remix). / NO ONE ELSE (live acoustic) / JAMIE (live acoustic)**	37	
Sep 96.	(7"/c-s) (GFS/+C 22167) **EL SCORCHO. / YOU GAVE YOUR LOVE TO ME SOFTLY**	50	-
	(cd-s+=) (GFSTD 22167) – Devotion.		
Oct 96.	(cd/c) <(GED/GEC 25007)> **PINKERTON**	43	19
	– Tired of sex / Getchoo / No other one / Why bother / Across the sea / Good life / El Scorcho / Pink triangle / Falling for you / Butterfly.		

RENTALS

MATT SHARP – vocals, bass, Moog synthesizer / plus **CHERIELYNN WESTRICH** – vocals / **ROD CERVERA** – guitar / **PETRA HADEN** – violin, vocals / **JIM RICHARDS** – keyboards / **PAT WILSON** – drums

		Warners	Maverick
Jan 96.	(cd/c) <(9362 46093-2/-4)> **RETURN OF THE RENTALS**		Nov95
	– Love I'm searching for / Waiting / Friends of P. / Move on / Please let that be you / My summer girl / Brilliant boy / Naive / These days / Sweetness and tenderness.		
Mar 96.	(c-s) (W 0340C) **FRIENDS OF P. / SO SOON**		
	(cd-s+=) (W 0340CD) – Love I'm searching for.		

		Sire	Sire
Apr 99.	(cd/c) <(9362 46680-2/-4)> **SEVEN MORE MINUTES**		
	– Getting by / Hello hello / She says it's alright / Cruise / Barcelona / Say goodbye forever / Overlee / Big daddy C / Keep sleeping / The man with two brains / Must be wrong / Insomnia / She says it's alright (reprise) / My head is in the sun / Jumping around.		

Scott WEILAND (see under → STONE TEMPLE PILOTS)

Paul WELLER

Born: 25 May'58, Woking, Surrey, England. (see The JAM for further details). Formed STYLE COUNCIL in early '83 with former MERTON PARKAS keys player, MICK TALBOT, and talented young sticksman, STEVE WHITE. Though it was merely a matter of months since WELLER had folded The JAM, the STYLE COUNCIL followed a radical new direction, taking the agit-soul of CURTIS MAYFIELD as their inspiration and fashioning a very 80's hybrid of cocktail jazz, breezy pop and white funk. Scoring immediately with the Top 5 'SPEAK LIKE A CHILD', the group went Top 3 later that year with the 'LONG HOT SUMMER' EP, its sultry lead track arguably the best the group ever penned and the creative pinnacle of what they were trying to achieve. Previewing The STYLE COUNCIL's debut album, 'CAFE BLEU' (1984), the mellow atmospherics of 'MY EVER CHANGING MOODS' gave the group another huge hit in early '84. The album itself was a lush fusion of summery jazz and easy soul, the keening strum of 'YOU'RE THE BEST THING' making the Top 5. WELLER became increasingly political as the decade wore on, the rousing soul/funk of 'SHOUT TO THE TOP' and 'WALLS COME TUMBLING DOWN' an indication of the direction The JAM may have have taken had they still been in existence. With the miners strike in full effect, politics were very much still an issue in rock/pop and WELLER and Co. released a benefit single, 'SOUL DEEP', at Christmas '84 under the COUNCIL COLLECTIVE banner. With production handled by HEAVEN 17's MARTYN WARE, the project included the likes of JIMMY RUFFIN, JUNIOR (GISCOMBE), VAUGHN TOULOUSE, DIZZY HEIGHTS and DEE C. LEE. The latter became not only WELLER's other half but a full-time backing singer for The STYLE COUNCIL, her sweet soul tones helping make 'OUR FAVOURITE SHOP' (1985) a mid-80's classic. The overall sound was more satisfying and the writing was sharper; 'COME TO MILTON KEYNES' was WELLER's most cutting slice of social commmentary since The JAM heyday. Come 1986, The STYLE COUNCIL became heavily involved in the 'Red Wedge' movement alongside the likes of The COMMUNARDS and BILLY BRAGG, attempting to educate music fans into voting for the right party in the upcoming elections i.e. Labour. Such an openly party political stance was probably doomed to failure from the start, the attendant tour floundering and the Tories of course, predictably romping home. It was the last time WELLER

would lay his beliefs on the line and the failure of the project seemed to lie at the heart of the lugubrious meanderings of the double set, 'THE COST OF LOVING' (1987). The following year's 'CONFESSIONS OF A POP GROUP' (1988) was similarly lacking in focus, its string arrangements and classical pretensions seeing The STYLE COUNCIL sinking in a mire of self-indulgence. The record failed to spawn any major hits and didn't even make the Top 10; when 'Polydor' refused to release a proposed fifth set, WELLER finally adjourned the 'COUNCIL and retired to re-evaluate his career. Now without a band or a recording deal, WELLER eventually regained his thirst for music via the low-key PAUL WELLER MOVEMENT, a band comprising STEVE WHITE, JACKO PEAKE, PAUL FRANCIS, MAX BEESLEY, DAMON BROWN, CHRIS LAWRENCE and DJ PAULO HEWITT along with backing singers DEE C. LEE, DR. ROBERT and CAMELLE HINDS. The subsequent '90/'91 shows saw the singer once again armed with a guitar and suggested that he'd been reacquainting himself with his record collection, more specifically late 60's R&B and psychedelia. The 'MOVEMENT released a sole single, 'INTO TOMORROW' on the DIY 'Freedom High' label. It squeezed into the Top 40 nonetheless and WELLER eventually whittled down the bulk of the group for a more basic sound, signing with 'Go! Discs' and debuting with 'UH HUH OH YEH' in late summer '92. Hailed as the best thing he'd done in years, the single went into the Top 20 and the PAUL WELLER revival was up and running. The music press had given the singer a wide berth since the heyday of The STYLE COUNCIL and, as the plaudits began to roll in for his eponymous debut album, were eventually forced to admit that, yes, WELLER was undergoing something of a creative rebirth. Matching the visceral, emotional punch of the music, the lyrics were of a decidedly more personal nature, eschewing politics for matters of the soul and the heart. With the ebullient 'SUNFLOWER' single and the attendant 'WILD WOOD' (1993) album, WELLER's star was most definitely in the ascendant. Characterised by a crisp, uncluttered Brendan Lynch production, the record saw WELLER distil his influences into vintage singer/songwriter maturity. With his voice now sufficiently rough around the edges to complement such material, the likes of the resonating, meditative folkiness of the title track assumed a greater depth. The album reached No.2, featuring in many end of year polls (Mercury Prize), the chino wearing ghost of The STYLE COUNCIL now finally laid to rest. While the UK music press were still largely fixated on US grunge, WELLER was nothing if not instrumental in the upcoming Brit-pop debacle. Cited by the likes of OASIS as a guiding influence, the Modfather, as WELLER came to be known, was everything that the hordes of mop-topped chancers aspired to. It was a role that WELLER fitted into naturally, OCEAN COLOUR SCENE's STEVE CRADDOCK was already a regular musical collaborator, while NOEL GALLAGHER would guest on WELLER's forthcoming No.1 album, 'STANLEY ROAD'. Released in Spring '95 as Brit-pop was reaching its zenith, the album was earthier than anything WELLER had recorded in his career to date. Again produced by LYNCH, the record was previewed by the blistering single, 'THE CHANGINGMAN', its lyrics signalling an even more personal bent to WELLER's writing as the looking-good-for-30-something star even began appearing in the British style press. Elsewhere on the album, WELLER covered Dr. John's 'I WALK ON GILDED SPLINTERS' although it was the spirit of ERIC CLAPTON or NEIL YOUNG that most often came to mind. WELLER was at his most affecting on the ballads, the deeply felt 'YOU DO SOMETHING TO ME', the beautiful gospel-soul of album closer 'WINGS OF SPEED' and the brilliantly evocative hammond/wurlitzer musings of 'BROKEN STONES'. Of course, a backlash was inevitable, and certain sections of the music press derided WELLER's new material as tired 'Dad-rock', an incestuous Brit-pop conspiracy which continually looked to the past instead of breaking new ground. While this may have been true to a certain degree, and WELLER was partly responsible for the vexing success of the terminally workmanlike OCEAN COLOUR SCENE, the man was simply integrating retro influences into his muse as he'd done all the way through his career; it's the fact that these influences changed which seems to annoy some writers. Keeping his profile high with various festival appearances (as well as a predictable guest spot at OASIS' Knebworth show), WELLER (now signed to 'Island' following the demise of 'Go! Discs') eventually returned to the fray in summer '97 with the storming 'BRUSHED' single. Arguably standing among the best of WELLER's work to date, the track was propelled by a stone solid/funky as hell rhythmic thrust (courtesy of WHITE), combining mod, psychedelia and rock in a fashion that he's only previously hinted at. 'Raw' is probably the best word to describe it and the best word to describe the accompanying album, 'HEAVY SOUL' (1997), WELLER's voice as impressive as ever on a set which nevertheless too often relies on 'authentic' sound over songwriting. 1998 saw the release of two Top 30 singles, 'BRAND NEW DAY' and the 'WILD WOOD' remixes EP, mainly to complement the delivery of his best of the package, 'MODERN CLASSICS – THE GREATEST HITS'. • **Songwriters:** WELLER penned except for TALBOT's STYLE COUNCIL instrumentals. They also covered MOVE ON UP (Curtis Mayfield) / PROMISED LAND (Joe Smooth) / OHIO (Neil Young). WELLER solo:- FEELIN' ALRIGHT (Traffic) / SEXY SADIE (Beatles) / I'M ONLY DREAMING (Small Faces) / I SHALL BE RELEASED (Bob Dylan).

Album rating: Style Council: CAFE BLEU (*5) / OUR FAVOURITE SHOP (*6) / HOME AND ABROAD – LIVE (*4) / THE COST OF LOVING (*5) / CONFESSIONS OF A POP GROUP (*3) / THE SINGULAR ADVENTURES OF THE STYLE COUNCIL compilation (*7) / HERE'S SOME THAT GOT AWAY collection (*4) / Paul Weller: PAUL WELLER (*6) / WILD WOOD (*9) / LIVE WOOD (*6) / STANLEY ROAD (*8) / HEAVY SOUL (*7) / MODERN CLASSICS – THE GREATEST HITS compilation (*8)

STYLE COUNCIL

PAUL WELLER (b.25 May'58, Woking, Surrey, England) – vocals, guitar (ex-JAM) / **MICK TALBOT** (b.11 Sep'58) – keyboards (ex-MERTON PARKAS) / **STEVE WHITE** – drums / plus various guests.

			Polydor	Polydor
Mar 83.	(7") (TSC 1) **SPEAK LIKE A CHILD. / PARTY CHAMBERS**		4	☐
May 83.	(7") (TSC 2) **MONEY GO ROUND.** / (part 2)		11	☐
	(12") (TSCX 2) – ('A'side) / Headstart for happiness / Mick's up.			
Aug 83.	(7"ep/12"ep) (TSC/+X 3) **LONG HOT SUMMER / PARTY CHAMBERS. / PARIS MATCH / LE DEPART**		3	☐
Nov 83.	(7") (TSC 4) **SOLID BOND IN YOUR HEART. / IT JUST CAME TO PIECES IN MY HAND** / ('A'instrumental)		11	☐
Oct 83.	(m-lp) <815277> **INTRODUCING THE STYLE COUNCIL** – (above songs)		–	☐

			Polydor	Geffen
Feb 84.	(7") (TSC 5) <29359> **MY EVER CHANGING MOODS. / MICK'S COMPANY**		5	29
	(12"+=) (TSCX 5) – Spring, Summer, Autumn.			
Mar 84.	(lp/c/cd) (TSC LP/MC 1)(817535-2) <4029> **CAFE BLEU** <US-title 'MY EVER CHANGING MOODS'>		2	56

– Mick's blessings / My ship came in / Blue cafe / The Paris match / My ever changing moods / Dropping bombs on the Whitehouse / A gospel / Strength of your nature / You're the best thing / Here's the one that got away / Headstart for happiness / Council meetin'. (cd+=) – The whole point of no return. (re-iss. cd Sep95; same)

			Polydor	Geffen
May 84.	(7") (TSC 6) <29248> **YOU'RE THE BEST THING. / BIG BOSS GROOVE**		5	76
	(12") (TSCX 6) – ('A'dub version).			
Oct 84.	(7") (TSC 7) **SHOUT TO THE TOP. / GHOSTS OF DACHAU**		7	☐
	(12"+=) (TSCX 7) – Piccadilly trail / ('A'instrumental.			
Dec 84.	(7"; as COUNCIL COLLECTIVE) (MINE 1) **SOUL DEEP.** / (part 2)		24	–
	(12"+=) (MINEX 1) – ('A'version) / (striking miners interview).			

(above single gave proceeds to miners' strike & the deceased miner David Wilkie's widow) The COLLECTIVE featured guests JIMMY RUFFIN, JUNIOR GISCOMBE, VAUGHN TOULOUSE, DEE C.LEE and DIZZY HEIGHTS. Production handled by MARTYN WARE (Heaven 17).

May 85.	(7~"ep/12"ep) (TSC/+X 8) **WALLS COME TUMBLING DOWN. / THE WHOLE POINT II / BLOODSPORTS**		6	–
Jun 85.	(lp/c/cd) (TSC LP/MC 2)(825700-2) <24061> **OUR FAVOURITE SHOP** <US title 'INTERNATIONALISTS'>		1	☐

– Homebreakers / All gone away / Come to Milton Keynes / Internationalists / A stone's throw away / The stand up comic's instructions / Boy who cried wolf / A man of great promise / Down in the Seine / The lodgers / Luck / With everything to lose / Our favourite shop / Walls come tumbling down. (cd+=) – Shout to the top. (c+=) – (interview). (cd re-iss. Aug90; same)

Jun 85.	(7") (TSC 9) **COME TO MILTON KEYNES. / WHEN YOU CALL ME**		23	–
	(12"+=) (TSCG 9) – Our favourite shop / ('A'club) / The lodgers (club mix).			
Aug 85.	(7") <28941> **OUR FAVOURITE SHOP. / BOY WHO CRIED WOLF**		–	☐
Sep 85.	(7") (TSC 10) **THE LODGERS (remix). / YOU'RE THE BEST THING (live)**		13	☐
	(d7"+=) (TSCDP 10) – Big boss groove (live) / Long hot summer (live).			
	(12"+=) (TSC?? 10) – Big boss groove (live) / Move on up (live).			
	(12"+=) (TSCX 10) – Medley: Money go round – Soul deep – Strength of your nature.			
Mar 86.	(7"ep/12"ep) (CINEX 1/+12) **HAVE YOU EVER HAD IT BLUE. / MR. COOL'S DREAM**		14	☐
May 86.	(lp/c)(cd) (TCS LP/MC 3)(829143-2) **HOME AND ABROAD – LIVE (live)**		8	–

– The big boss groove * / My ever changing moods / The lodgers / Headstart for happiness / (When you) Call me / The whole point of no return / Our favourite shop * / With everything to lose / Homebreakers / Shout to the top / Walls come tumbling down / Internationalists. (cd+= *) (cd re-iss. Aug90; same)

Jun 86.	(7") <28674> **INTERNATIONALISTS. / (WHEN YOU) CALL ME**		–	☐

			Polydor	Polydor
Jan 87.	(7"/12") (TSC/+X 12) **IT DIDN'T MATTER. / ALL YEAR ROUND**		9	☐
Feb 87.	(2x12"lp/c)(cd) (TSC LP/MC 4)(<831433-2>) **THE COST OF LOVING**		2	☐

– It didn't matter / Right to go / Waiting / Walking the night / The cost of loving / Heaven's above / Fairy tales / Angel / A woman's song. (re-iss. Oct90)

Mar 87.	(7") (TSC 13) **WAITING. / FRANCOISE**		52	☐
	(12"+=) (TCSX 13) – Theme from 'Jerusalem'.			
Oct 87.	(7") (TSC 14) **WANTED (FOR WAITER) / THE COST OF LOVING**		20	☐
	(12"+=/c-s+=) (TSC X/CS 14) – There's soup in my flies.			
	(cd-s++=) – The cost.			
May 88.	(7") (TSC 15) **LIFE AT A TOP PEOPLE'S HEALTH FARM. / SWEET LOVING WAYS**		28	☐
	(12"+=/cd-s+=) (TSC X/CD 15) – Spark (live) / ('A'version).			
Jun 88.	(lp/c)(cd) (TSC LP/MC 5)(<835785-2>) **CONFESSIONS OF A POP GROUP**		15	☐

– It's a very deep sea / The story of someone's shoe / Changing of the guard / The little boy in a castle – A dove flew down from the elephant / The gardener of Eden (a three piece suite):- In the beginning – The gardener of Eden – Mourning the passing of time / Life at a top people's health farm / Why I went missing / How she threw it all away / I was a doledads toyboy / Confessions of a pop group (parts 1, 2 & 3) / Confessions of a pop group. (cd re-iss. Oct90)

Jul 88.	(7"ep/12"ep) (TSC 16) **HOW SHE THREW IT ALL AWAY / IN LOVE FOR THE FIRST TIME / LONG HOT SUMER / I DO LIKE TO BE B-SIDE THE A-SIDE**		41	☐
Feb 89.	(7") (TSC 17) **PROMISED LAND / CAN YOU STILL LOVE ME**		27	☐
	(12") (TSCXS 17) – ('A'-Joe Smooth's alternate club) / ('B'club) / ('B'-dub).			
	(cd-s) (TSCCD 17) – ('A'-Juan Atkins mix) / ('A'-Pianopella mix) / ('B'-dub).			

	(cd-s) (TSCD 17) – ('A'side) / ('A'extended) / ('B'vocal) / ('B'dub).			
	(7"box) (TSCB 17) – ('A'-Juan Atkins mix) / ('B'side).			
Mar 89.	(lp/c)(cd) (TSC TV/TC 1)(837896-2) **THE SINGULAR ADVENTURES OF THE STYLE COUNCIL** (compilation)		3	–

– You're the best thing / Have you ever had it blue (extended) / Money go round (parts 1 & 2) / My ever changing moods (extended) / Long hot summer (extended) / The lodgers / Walls come tumbling down / Shout to the top / Wanted / It didn't matter / Speak like a child / A solid bond in your heart / Life at a top people's health farm / Promised land. (c+=/cd+=) – How she threw it all away / Waiting.

May 89.	(7") (LHS 1) **LONG HOT SUMMER ('89 mix). / EVERYBODY'S ON THE RUN**		48	☐
	(12"+=/cd-s+=) (LHS X/CD 1) – ('A'&'B' different mixes).			

—— Disbanded Mar'90. WELLER went solo, see below.

– compilations, etc. –

on 'Polydor' unless mentioned otherwise

Nov 87.	(cd-ep) (TSCCD 101) **CAFE BLEU**		☐	–

– Headstart for happiness / Here's one that got away / Blue cafe / Strength of your nature.

Nov 87.	(cd-ep) (TSCCD 102) **BIRDS AND BEES**		☐	–

– Piccadilly trail / It just came to pieces in my hands / Spin drifting / Spring, Summer, Autumn.

Nov 87.	(cd-ep) (TSCCD 103) **MICK TALBOT IS AGENT '88**		☐	–

– Mick's up / Party chambers / Mick's blessing / Mick's company.

Jan 90.	(7") Old Gold; (OG 9924) **LONG HOT SUMMER. / SPEAK LIKE A CHILD**		☐	–
Jan 90.	(7") Old Gold; (OG 9929) **YOU'RE THE BEST THING. / MY EVER CHANGING MOODS**		☐	–
Jul 93.	(cd/c) (519 372-2/-4) **HERE'S SOME THAT GOT AWAY**		39	–
Feb 96.	(cd/c) (529 483-2/-4) **THE STYLE COUNCIL COLLECTION**		60	–

PAUL WELLER

with **STEVE WHITE** – drums, percussion / **JACKO PEAKE** – sax, flute, b.vox / **DEE C.LEE, DR.ROBERT + CAMELLE HINDS** – b.vox

			Freedom High	London
May 91.	(7"/c-s; as PAUL WELLER MOVEMENT) (FHP/+C 1) **INTO TOMORROW. / HERE'S A NEW THING**		36	1992
	(12"+=/cd-s+=) (FHP T/CD 1) – That spiritual feeling / ('A'demo).			

			Go! Discs	London
Aug 92.	(7"/c-s) (GOD/+MC 86) **UH HUH OH YEH. / FLY ON THE WALL**		18	–
	(12"+=/cd-s+=) (GOD X/CD 86) – Arrival time / Always there to fool you.			
Sep 92.	(cd/c/lp) (<828 343-2/-4/-1>) **PAUL WELLER**		8	Oct92

– Uh huh oh yeh / I didn't mean to hurt you / Bull-rush / Round and round / Remember how we started / Above the clouds / Clues / Into tomorrow / Amongst butterflies / The strange museum / Bitterness rising / Kosmos. (re-iss. Apr94; same)

Oct 92.	(7"/c-s) (GOD/+MC 91) **ABOVE THE CLOUDS. / EVERYTHING HAS A PRICE TO PAY**		47	–
	(12"+=/cd-s+=) (GOD X/CD 91) – All year round (live) / Feelin' alright.			

—— now with **STEVE WHITE** – drums, percussion / **MARCO NELSON** – bass

			Go! Discs	Go! Discs
Jul 93.	(7"/c-s) (GOD/+MC 102) **SUNFLOWER. / BULL-RUSH – MAGIC BUS (live)**		16	–
	(12"+=/cd-s+=) (GOD X/CD 102) – Kosmo's sxdub 2000 / That spiritual feeling (new mix).			
Aug 93.	(7"/c-s/10"/cd-s) (<GOD/+MC/T/CD 104>) **WILD WOOD. / ENDS OF THE EARTH**		14	
Sep 93.	(cd/c/lp) (<828 435-2/-4/-1>) **WILD WOOD**		2	Oct93

– Sunflower / Can you heal us (holy man) / Wild wood – instrumental (pt.1) / All the pictures on the wall / Has my fire really gone out? / Country / 5th season / The weaver – instrumental (pt.2) / Foot of the mountain / Shadow of the Sun – Holy man (reprise) / Moon on your pyjamas. (re-iss. Apr94 +=; same) – Hung up.

Nov 93.	(7"ep/c-ep/10"ep/cd-ep) (GOD/+MC/T/CD 107) **THE WEAVER EP**		18	☐
	– The weaver / This is no time / Another new day / Ohio (live).			
Mar 94.	(7"ep/c-ep/cd-ep) (GOD/+MC/X/CD 111) **HOME OF THE CLASSIC EP**		11	–
	– Hung up / Foot of the mountain (live from Albert Hall) / The loved / Kosmos (Lynch Mob bonus beats).			
Sep 94.	(cd/c/lp) (828 561-2/-4/-1) <00601> **LIVE WOOD (live)**		13	☐

– Bull rush – Magic bus / This is no time / All the pictures on the wall / Remember how we started / Dominoes / Above the clouds / Wild wood / Shadow of the Sun / (Can you hear us) Holy man – War / 5th season / Into tomorrow / Fool of the mountains / Sunflower / Has the fire really gone out?.

Oct 94.	(7"ep/c-ep/12"ep/cd-ep) (GOD/+MC/X/CD 121) **OUT OF THE SINKING. / SUNFLOWER (Lynch Mob dub) / SEXY SADIE**		20	–

—— with **STEVE WHITE** – drums / **DR.ROBERT** – bass, vocals (ex-BLOW MONKEYS) / **STEVE CRADDOCK** – guitar / **MARK NELSON** – bass / **HELEN TURNER** – strings, organ / **BRENDAN LYNCH** – organ, co-producer / + guests **MICK TALBOT / CARLEEN ANDERSON / STEVE WINWOOD / NOEL GALLAGHER / YOLANDA CHARLES / CONSTANTINE WEIR**

Apr 95.	(12"ep/c-ep/cd-ep) (GOD X/MC/CD 127) **THE CHANGINGMAN / I'D RATHER GO BLIND / IT'S A NEW DAY, BABY / I DIDNT MEAN TO HURT YOU (live)**		7	☐
May 95.	(cd/c/lp)(6x7"pack) (<828 619-2/-4/-1>)(850070-7) **STANLEY ROAD**		1	☐

– The changingman / Porcelain gods / I walk on gilded splinters / You do something to me / Woodcutter's son / Time passes / Stanley Road / Broken stones / Out of the sinking / Pink on white walls / Whirlpool's end / Wings of speed.

Jul 95.	(7"ep/c-ep/cd-ep) (GOD/+MC/CD 130) **YOU DO SOMETHING TO ME / A YEAR LATE. / MY WHOLE WORLD IS FALLING DOWN / WOODCUTTER'S SON**		9	–
Sep 95.	(7"/c-s) (GOD/+MC 132) **BROKEN STONES. / STEAM**		20	☐
	(cd-s+=) (GODCD 132) – Whirlpool's end / Porcelain gods.			

—— WELLER was also part of one-off supergroup The SMOKIN' MOJO FILTERS alongside PAUL McCARTNEY and NOEL GALLAGHER. They had a Top 20 hit late '95 with 'COME TOGETHER'.

Feb 96. (7"ep/cd-ep) *(GOD/+CD 143)* **OUT OF THE SINKING EP**   16   -
– Out of the sinking / I shall be released / Porcelain gods / Broken stones.

Aug 96. (7"/c-s/cd-s) *(GOD/+MC+CD 149)* **PEACOCK SUIT. / EYE OF THE STORM**   5   -
                     Island   Polygram

Jun 97. (cd/c/lp) *(CID/ICT/ILPS 8058)* <524277> **HEAVY SOUL**   2   Aug97
– Heavy soul / Peacock suit / Up in Suzie's room / Brushed / Driving nowhere / I should have been there to inspire you / Heavy soul (part 2) / Friday Street / Science / Golden sands / As you lean into the light / Mermaids.

Aug 97. (7"ep/c-ep/cd-ep) *(IS/CIS/CID 666)* **BRUSHED EP**   14   -
– Brushed / Ain't no love in the heart of the city / Shoot the dove / Into the light.

Oct 97. (c-s/7") *(C+/IS 676)* **FRIDAY STREET. /**   21   -
(cd-s) *(CID 676)* – ('A'side) / Sunflower (live) / Brushed (live) / Mermaids (live).

Nov 97. (c-s/cd-s/7") *(CIS/CID/IS 683)* **MERMAIDS. / EVERYTHING HAS A PRICE TO PAY ('97 version) / SO YOU WANT TO BE A DANCER**   30   -

Nov 98. (c-s/7") *(C+/IS 711)* **BRAND NEW START. / RIGHT UNDERNEATH IT**   16   ☐
(cd-s+=) *(CID 711)* – The riverbank (new version).

Nov 98. (cd/c/d-lp) *(CID/ICT/ILPSD 8080)* <524558> **MODERN CLASSICS – THE GREATEST HITS** (compilation)   7   ☐
– Out of the sinking / Peacock suit / Sunflower / The weaver / Wild wood / Above the clouds / Uh huh oh yeh / Brushed / The changingman / Friday Street / You do something to me / Brand new start / Hung up / Mermaids / Broken stones / Into tomorrow. (lp-box; IBX 8080) (d-cd; CIDD 8080)

Dec 98. (7"ep/12"ep/cd-ep) *(IS/12IS/CID 734)* **WILD WOOD EP**   22   ☐
– Wild wood (mixes; original / Portishead / Science (Psychonauts).

Leslie WEST (see under ⇒ MOUNTAIN)

Paul WESTERBERG (see under ⇒ REPLACEMENTS)

WET WET WET

Formed: Glasgow, Scotland ... 1982 by MARTI PELLOW, GRAEME CLARK, NEIL MITCHELL and TOM CUNNINGHAM. Late in '84, the group met Elliot Davis, who became their manager and co-owner of the 'The Precious Organisation' label. They subsequently spent the next couple of years perfecting their blue-eyed soul-pop sound after brokering a major distribution deal with 'Phonogram' in 1985. The group finally made their vinyl debut with the infectious 'WISHING I WAS LUCKY' in Spring '87, PELLOW's grinning good looks immediately marking him out as one of Scotland's major sex symbols. Unfortunately, PELLOW had little to grin about as the group were forced to cough up an out of court settlement to both VAN MORRISON and SQUEEZE from whom the singer had filched some lines. Nevertheless, the single gave WET WET WET their first Top 10 hit, a cocksure cover of John Martyn's 'SWEET LITTLE MYSTERY' giving them a Top 5 hit later that summer. This success ensured a No.1 placing for their debut album, 'POPPED IN SOULED OUT' (1987), an enjoyable collection of Caledonian white-boy soul that reached its zenith on the epic 'TEMPTATION'. A mite slick for some tastes, the band nevertheless became something of a mainstream phenomenon, packing out major venues full of canoodling couples who'd just put a down payment on their joint mortgage. Obviously bruised but not battered from their earlier brush with copyright law, WET WET WET subsequently made something of a career from cover versions, taking their pop-friendly reading of The Beatles' 'WITH A LITTLE HELP FROM MY FRIENDS' to No.1 in Spring '88 (a 'Childline' charity single, it was probably the only time the group would appear on the same record as BILLY BRAGG!). Later that year the band released 'THE MEMPHIS SESSIONS', reworkings of the more soulful elements of the debut together with a couple of new tracks and a STEVIE WONDER cover, 'HEAVEN HELP US ALL'. Previewed by the sickly 'SWEET SURRENDER' single, 'HOLDING BACK THE RIVER' (1989) was the group's next album proper, narrowly missing the No.1 spot and cementing the WET WET WET's standing as coffee table soul providers par excellence. Although the hits started to dry up, PELLOW and Co. bounced back in customarily annoying fashion with the asinine 'GOODNIGHT GIRL', their second No.1 single. The accompanying album, 'HIGH ON THE HAPPY SIDE' (1992) also topped the chart, a record which trawled new depths of blandness. It was probably only a matter of time before WET WET WET achieved BRYAN ADAMS-style chart meltdown, the group topping the UK singles list for a near record breaking fifteen weeks in the summer of '94 with the nauseous 'LOVE IS ALL AROUND', theme tune from the hugely successful 'Four Weddings And A Funeral' flick. The track might've lingered further had the group not done the nation a favour and deleted it from sale. Though their career wasn't exactly flagging, the single's success boosted WET WET WET's profile to the extent that the previous year's greatest hits set, 'END OF PART ONE', soared back to the top of the charts. Fans 'unlucky' enough to have missed out on 'LOVE IS ALL AROUND' could find it on the group's subsequent album, 'PICTURE THIS' (1995), which gave them yet another No.1 album. Strangely enough, the album's other big hit, 'JULIA SAYS', was actually the most affecting track the group had penned for years. A veritable Scottish institution, WET WET WET remain the country's biggest success story since the heyday of The BAY CITY ROLLERS, though there's really no comparison ... • **Songwriters:** PELLOW – lyrics / group compositions, except HEAVEN HELP US ALL (Stevie Wonder) / I FEEL FINE (Beatles) / MAGGIE MAY (Rod Stewart) / STONED ME (Van

Morrison) / LOVE IS ALL AROUND (Troggs) / IT'S NOW OR NEVER + IN THE GHETTO (both hits; Elvis Presley) / SHARE YOUR LOVE (Malone-Braggs) / YOU'VE GOT A FRIEND (Carole King) / ATLANTIC AVENUE (Average White Band) / IF YOU ONLY KNEW (. . .Allison) / WOULDN'T HAVE MADE ANY DIFERENCE (Todd Rundgren) / TOWN CRIER (Elvis Costello) / ANGELINE (John Martyn) / BEG YOUR PARDON DEAR (Craig-Smith) / HOURGLASS + PULLING MUSSELS FROM A SHELL (Squeeze). • **Trivia:** Took their name from a line in a SCRITTI POLITTI song 'Gettin', Havin', Holdin'.

Album rating: POPPED IN SOULED OUT (*6) / THE MEMPHIS SESSIONS (*4) / HOLDING BACK THE RIVER (*6) / HIGH ON THE HAPPY SIDE (*5) / LIVE AT THE ROYAL ALBERT HALL (*4) / END OF PART ONE (THEIR GREATEST HITS) compilation (*7) / PICTURE THIS (*4) / 10 (*4)

MARTI PELLOW (b. MARK McLOUGHLIN, 23 Mar'66, Clydebank, Scotland) – vocals / **GRAEME CLARK** (b.15 Apr'66) – bass, guitar / **NEIL MITCHELL** (b. 8 Jun'67, Helensburgh, Scotland) – keyboards / **TOM CUNNINGHAM** (b.22 Jun'65) – drums

                                         Precious   Uni

Mar 87. (7") *(JEWEL 3)* <50000> **WISHING I WAS LUCKY. / WORDS OF WISDOM**   6   58 May88
(12"+=) *(JEWEL 3-12)* – Still can't remember your name.
(d12"++=) *(JWLD 3)* – ('A'-metal mix).

Jul 87. (7"/7"sha-pic-d) *(JEWEL 4/+P)* **SWEET LITTLE MYSTERY. / DON'T LET ME BE LONELY TONIGHT**   5   ☐
(12"+=) *(JEWEL 4-12)* – World in another world.
(7"ep++=) *(JEWEL 4EP)* – ('A'different mix).

Sep 87. (lp/c)(cd) *(JWWW L/M 1)(832 726-2)* <5000> **POPPED IN SOULED OUT**   1   ☐
– Wishing I was lucky / East of the river / I remember / Angel eyes (home and away) / Sweet little mystery / I don't believe (Sonny's letter) / Temptation / I can give you everything / The moment you left me. (cd+=) – Don't let me be lonely tonight / World in another world / Wishing I was lucky (live).

Nov 87. (7"/ext.12") *(JEWEL 6/+12)* **ANGEL EYES (HOME AND AWAY). / WE CAN LOVE**   5   ☐
((c-s+=/cd-s+=) *(JWL MC/C 6)* – ('A'extended.

Mar 88. (7"/s7") *(JEWEL 7/+77)* **TEMPTATION. / BOTTLED EMOTIONS (KEEN FOR LOVING)**   12   ☐
(12"+=) *(JEWEL 7-12)* – I remember.
(cd-s++=) *(JEWELCD 7)* – Heaven help us all.

May 88. (7") *(CHILD 1)* **WITH A LITTLE HELP FROM MY FRIENDS. / ('B'by Billy Bragg)**   1   ☐
(above 45 on the 'Childline' label, gave all monies to that charity).

Nov 88. (10"lp/c)(cd) *(JWWW L/M 2)(836726-2)* **THE MEMPHIS SESSIONS**   3   ☐
– I don't believe (Sonny's letter) / Sweet little mystery (Memphis version) / East of the river (Memphis version) / This time / Temptation (Memphis version) / I remember / For you are / Heaven help us all.

Sep 89. (7"/c-s) *(JWL/+MC 9)* **SWEET SURRENDER. / THIS TIME (live)**   6   ☐
(12"+=)(cd-s+=) *(JEWEL 9-12)(JWKCD 9)* – H.T.H.D.T.G.T. / ('A'extended version).

Oct 89. (lp/c/cd) *(842011-1/-4/-2)* **HOLDING BACK THE RIVER**   2   ☐
– Sweet surrender / Can't stand the night / Blue for you / Broke away / You've had it / I wish / Key to your heart / Maggie May / Hold back the river.

Dec 89. (7"/7"g-f/7"pic-d/c-s) *(JEWEL/JWLG/JWPD/JWLWC 10)* **BROKE AWAY. / YOU'VE HAD IT**   19   ☐
(12"+=) *(JEWEL 10-12)* – And now for something completely different.
(cd-s+=/pic-cd-s+=) *(JWLCD/JWCD 10)* – Sweet surrender (club mix).

Mar 90. (7"/c-s) *(JEWEL/JWLMC 11)* **HOLD BACK THE RIVER. / KEY TO YOUR HEART**   31   ☐
(12"+=)(cd-s+=) *(JEWEL 11-22)(JWCD 11)* – With a little help from my friends (live).
(12"+=) *(JEWEL 11-12)* – Party city / I can give you everything.

Aug 90. (7"/c-s) *(JEWEL/JWLMC 13)* **STAY WITH ME HEARTACHE. / I FEEL FINE**   30   ☐
(12"+=)(cd-s+=) *(JEWEL 13-12)(JWLCD 13)* – Hold back the river (acoustic) / ('A'-TC YOUNG & T-mix).
(10"+=) *(JEWEL 13-10)* – Stay with me heartache (stay where you are) / Stoned me.

Sep 91. (7"/c-s) *(JEWEL/JWLMC 15)* **MAKE IT TONIGHT. / ORDINARY LOVE**   37   ☐
(12"+=)(cd-s+=) *(JEWEL 15-12)(JWLCD 15)* – Big sister midnight.

Oct 91. (7"/etched-7") *(JEWEL 16)* **PUT THE LIGHT ON. / JUST LIKE ANY OTHER DAY**   56   ☐
(12"pic-d+=)(cd-s+=) *(JEWEL 16-12)(JWLCD 16)* – You've got a friend.

Dec 91. (7") *(JEWEL 17)* **GOODNIGHT GIRL. / AMBROSE WYKES**   1   ☐
(cd-s+=) *(JWLCD 17)* – With a little help from my friends / Sweet surrender / Goodnight (no strings attached).
(cd-s+=) *(JWCD 17)* – Wishing I was lucky / Temptation (Memphis version) / Angel eyes (home and away).

Jan 92. (cd/c/lp) *(510427-2/-4/-1)* **HIGH ON THE HAPPY SIDE**   1   ☐
– More than love / Lip service / Put the light on / High on the happy side / Maybe tomorrow / Goodnight girl / Celebration / Make it tonight / How long / Brand new sunrise / 2 days after midnite. (free-7"w.a.) – CLOAK AND DAGGER as 'MAGGIE PIE & THE IMPOSTERS')

Mar 92. (7"/c-s) *(JEWEL/JWLMC 18)* **MORE THAN LOVE. / GOODNIGHT GIRL (mix)**   19   ☐
(cd-s+=) *(JWLCD 18)* – Broke away / Sweet little mystery (Memphis session).

Jun 92. (7"ep/c-ep/cd-ep) *(JEWEL/JWLMC/JWLCD 19)* **LIP SERVICE EP**   15   ☐
– Lip service (Youth mix) / High on the happy side / Lip service (live) / More than love (live).

Apr 93. (7"/c-s) *(JEWEL/JWLMC 20)* **BLUE FOR YOU (live). / THIS TIME (live)**   38   ☐
(cd-s+=) *(JWLCD 20)* – I can give you everything.

May 93. (cd/c/lp) *(514774-2/-4/-1)* **LIVE AT THE ROYAL ALBERT HALL (live)**   10   ☐

– Angel eyes / This time / Brand new sunrise / Hold back the river / Blue for you / Goodnight girl / How long / East of the river / I can give you everything.

Oct 93. (7"c-s) *(JEWEL/JWLMC 21)* **SHED A TEAR. / EVERYDAY**   `22`
(cd-s+=) *(JWLCD 21)* – Deadline.

Nov 93. (cd/c/lp) *(518477-2/-4/-1)* **END OF PART ONE (THEIR GREATEST HITS)** (compilation)   `4`
– Wishing I was lucky / Sweet little mystery / Angel eyes / Temptation / With a little help from my friends / Sweet surrender / Broke away / Hold back the river / Stay with me heartache / This time / Make it tonight / Put the light on / Goodnight girl / More than love / Lip service / Blue for you (live) / Shed a tear / Cold, cold heart. *(initial copies contained free cd/c/lp)*

Jan 94. (7"/c-s) *(JEWEL/JWLMC 22)* **COLD COLD HEART. / ROLL 'UM EASY**   `20`
(cd-s+=) *(JWLCD 22)* – (2-'A'mixes).
(cd-s) *(JWLDD 22)* – ('A'side) / Another love in me / Wishing I was lucky (2 Arthur Baker mixes).

May 94. (7"/c-s) *(JEWEL/JWLMC 23)* <857580> **LOVE IS ALL AROUND. / I CAN GIVE YOU EVERYTHING** (Arthur Baker soul remix)   `1`   `41` Aug94
(cd-s) *(JWLCD 23)* – ('A'mix).

—— Above track hit No.1 for a near record breaking 15 weeks. Just prior to this occurance, it was withdrawn by the group. In Aug94, 'END OF PART ONE' compilation regained its No.1 placing.

Mar 95. (7"/c-s) *(JEWEL/JWLMC 24)* **JULIA SAYS. / IT'S NOW OR NEVER**   `3`
(cd-s+=) *(JWLCD 24)* – Dixie / ('A'version).
(cd-s+=) *(JWLDD 24)* – I don't want to know / ('A'-synth string version).

Apr 95. (cd/c/lp) *(526851-2/-4/-1)* **PICTURE THIS**   `1`
– Julia says / After the love goes / Somewhere somehow / Gypsy girl / Don't want to forgive me now / She might never know / Someone like you / Love is my shepherd / She's on my mind / Morning / Home tonight / Love is all around.

Jun 95. (c-s) *(JWLMC 25)* **DON'T WANT TO FORGIVE ME NOW / IN THE GHETTO**   `7`
(cd-s+=) *(JWLCD 25)* – Gypsy girl (acoustic).
(cd-s) *(JWLDD 25)* – ('A'side) / Love is all around / Angel eyes.

Sep 95. (c-s) *(JWLMC 26)* **SOMEWHERE SOMEHOW / MORNING (the Youth 1995 remix) / ('A'-synth string version)**   `7`
(cd-s) *(JWLCD 26)* – ('A'side) / All you need is love (live) / She might never know (live) / Somewhere somehow (live).

Nov 95. (c-s) *(JWLMC 27)* **SHE'S ALL ON MY MIND / IF YOU ONLY KNEW / WOULDN'T HAVE MADE ANY DIFFERENCE (last 2 by MAGGIE PIE & THE IMPOSTERS)**   `17`
(cd-s) *(JWLCD 27)* – ('A'side) / Share your love / You've got a friend / Beg your pardon dear.
(cd-s) *(JWLDD 27)* – ('A'side) / Atlantic avenue / Town crier / Angeline.

Mar 96. (c-s) *(JWLMC 28)* **MORNING ('96 mix) / JULIA SAYS**   `16`
(cd-s+=) *(JWLCD 28)* – Hourglass (live) / Pulling mussels from a shell (live).
(cd-s) *(JWLDD 28)* – ('A'side) / Love is my shepherd (live) / She's all on my mind (live) / Morning (live).

Mar 97. (c-s/cd-s) *(JWL MC/CD 29)* **IF I NEVER SEE YOU AGAIN / QU'EST QUE C'EST**   `3`
(cd-s+=) *(JWLDD 29)* – Straight from the heart.

Apr 97. (cd/c/lp) *(534585-2/-4/-1)* **10**   `2`
– If I never see you again / Back on my feet / Fool for your love / Only sounds / If only I could be with you / I want you / Maybe I'm in love / Beyond the sea / Lonely girl / Strange / Theme from Ten / It hurts.

Jun 97. (c-s/cd-s) *(JWLMC 30)* **STRANGE / THEME FROM GRAND PRIX**   `13`
(cd-s+=) *(JWLDD 30)* – Lip service / Don't want to forgive me now.

Aug 97. (c-s) *(JWLMC 31)* **YESTERDAY / MAYBE I'M IN LOVE**   `4`
(cd-s+=) *(JWLDD 31)* – Goodnight girl '94.
(cd-s) *(JWLDD 31)* – ('A'side) / Beyond the sea / Love is all around.

– compilations, others, etc. –

Feb 92. (7") *Old Gold;* **WISHING I WAS LUCKY. / SWEET LITTLE MYSTERY**   `-`

WE'VE GOT A FUZZBOX . . . (dig out; Great Alt & Indie . . .)

WHALE (dig out; Great Alt & Indie . . .)

WHAM! (see under ⇒ MICHAEL, George)

WHIPPING BOY (dig out; Great Alt & Indie . . .)

WHISTLER (see under ⇒ EMF)

Alan WHITE (see under ⇒ YES)

WHITE LION (dig out; Great Metal . . .)

WHITESNAKE

Formed: London, England . . . late 70's by ex-DEEP PURPLE vocalist, DAVID COVERDALE (b.22 Sep'49, Slatburn-On-Sea, Yorkshire, England). After leaving 'PURPLE, COVERDALE recorded two fine sets of bluesy hard-rock, 'DAVID COVERDALE'S WHITESNAKE' (1977) and 'NORTHWINDS' (1978), taking the name for his new outfit from the former and retaining a core of musicians which included such seasoned veterans as MICKY MOODY, BERNIE MARSDEN and NEIL MURRAY. Signing to 'EMI International', he/they debuted with the 'SNAKEBITE' EP in summer

'78, the record's highlight being a smoky cover of Bobby Bland's 'AIN'T NO LOVE IN THE HEART OF THE CITY'. The group subsequently hit the UK Top 50 with their debut album, 'TROUBLE' (1978), the record adding the keyboard skills of ex-DP man, JON LORD. While they followed it up with the overlooked 'LOVE HUNTER' in 1979, they only really broke through with 'READY AN' WILLING' (1980), the success of its attendant single pushing the album into the UK Top 10. The band were certainly ready, willing and able to fill the gap in the market left by the now defunct DEEP PURPLE, their musical prowess securing them an enviable live reputation if not quite measuring up in the songwriting department. Consequently then, the band's only official concert set, 'LIVE . . . IN THE HEART OF THE CITY' (1980), ranks as one of the most consistent recordings of their career. Although their most successful album to date (narrowly missing No.1), 'COME AN' GET IT' (1981) was something of a disappointment, the group moving away from their bluesy roots towards a neutered hard-rock sound. Critics also rounded on COVERDALE's notoriously sexist, cliche ridden lyrics, complaints which were water off a duck's back to the blonde-maned, mouth-full-of-plums cock-rocker. Despite personnel shuffles which saw new faces such as MEL GALLEY, COLIN 'Bomber' HODGKINSON and COZY POWELL, 'SAINTS 'N' SINNERS' (1982) failed to remedy matters although it went Top 10 nevertheless. With the addition of ex-TYGERS OF PAN TANG guitarist, JOHN SYKES, COVERDALE had finally found a sympathetic writing partner as evidenced on the much improved 'SLIDE IT IN' (1984). Blatant innuendo was still high on the agenda, but then again, that's what COVERDALE excelled at, his panting and moaning all over the shop on the epic climax-blues stomp, 'SLOW AN' EASY', actually as effective as it was hilarious. Never the most stable of bands, the tour that followed saw WHITESNAKE eventually reduced to SYKES and COVERDALE, even LORD bogging off to join the reformed DEEP PURPLE. Recruiting TONY FRANKLIN and CARMINE APPICE, the group eventually returned with the eponymous 'WHITESNAKE 1987' (1987, funnily enough), sleeker, (some might say sexier), and considerably more commercial than ever before. Previewed by the Top 10 LED ZEPPELIN-esque, 'STILL OF THE NIGHT', the album stormed both the British and US charts. The latter track was the hardest fare on offer, however, the bulk of the album made up of limp MTV ballads like 'IS THIS LOVE' and re-vamps of old songs, the infectious reworking of 'HERE I GO AGAIN' (the original can be found on 'SAINTS AN' SINNERS') giving the group their first and only No.1. While the album no doubt alienated many of their previously loyal older fans, it sold millions, finally giving COVERDALE the success he'd long been after. It didn't do much for the group's stability, however, as SYKES split for BLUE MURDER and COVERDALE once again recruited a whole new line-up numbering ADRIAN VANDENBURG, RUDY SARZO, TOMMY ALDRIDGE and VIVIAN CAMPBELL. Guitar wizard STEVE VAI subsequently replaced CAMPBELL and this line-up gave a rather lacklustre headlining performance at the 1989 Monsters Of Rock Festival, the highly anticipated 'SLIP OF THE TONGUE' (1989) equally uninspiring. Unsurprisingly, the record failed to match the giddy commercial heights of its predecessor and COVERDALE put the band on ice while he subsequently hooked up with JIMMY PAGE for the successful 'COVERDALE ° PAGE' album in 1993. Last sighted on a tour of Europe in support of a 1994 greatest hits collection, DAVID COVERDALE & WHITESNAKE delivered a UK Top 40 comeback album, 'RESTLESS HEART' in 1997. With the metal/hard-rock scene changing almost beyond recognition, it looks unlikely that WHITESNAKE can repeat the glory days of the late 80's . . . the nostalgia circuit beckons. • **Trivia:** On the 17th of February '89, COVERDALE married actress Tawny Kittaen, who had previously featured on their video of 'IS THIS LOVE'.

Album rating: NORTHWINDS (*7; by David Coverdale) / TROUBLE (*5) / LOVEHUNTER (*6) / READY AN' WILLING (*6) / LIVE . . . IN THE HEART OF THE CITY (*6) / COME AND GET IT (*6) / SAINTS 'N' SINNERS (*4) / SLIDE IN IT (*5) / 1987 (*5) / SLIP OF THE TONGUE (*5) / WHITESNAKE'S GREATEST HITS compilation (*8) / COVERDALE – PAGE (*5) / RESTLESS HEART (*5)

DAVID COVERDALE

(solo) – vocals (ex-DEEP PURPLE) with **MICK MOODY** – guitar (ex-JUICY LUCY, ex-SNAFU) / **TIM HINKLEY** – keyboards / **SIMON PHILLIPS** – drums / **DELISLE HARPER** – bass / plus **RON ASPERY** – sax / **ROGER GLOVER** – producer, bass, keyboards

                                                      Purple   not iss.

May 77. (lp) *(TPS 3509)* **DAVID COVERDALE'S WHITESNAKE**   `-`
– Lady / Blindman / Goldie's place / Whitesnake / Time on my side / Peace lovin' man / Sunny days / Hole in the sky / Celebration.

May 77. (7") *(PUR 133)* **HOLE IN THE SKY. / BLINDMAN**   `-`

—— **COVERDALE** retained only **MOODY** and recruited **BERNIE MARSDEN** – guitar (ex-PAICE, ASHTON & LORD, ex-UFO, ex-WILD TURKEY) / **NEIL MURRAY** – bass (ex-COLOSSEUM, ex-NATIONAL HEALTH) / **BRIAN JOHNSON** – keyboards + **DAVID DOWELL** – drums (both ex-STREETWALKERS)

Feb 78. (7") *(PUR 136)* **BREAKDOWN. / ONLY MY SOUL**   `-`

Mar 78. (lp) *(TPS 3513)* **NORTHWINDS**   `-`
– Keep on giving me love / Northwinds / Give me kindness / Time & again / Queen of hearts / Only my soul / Say you love me / Breakdown. *(re-iss. Apr84 on 'Fame' lp/c; FA41 3097-1/-4)*

Jun 78. (7") **BREAKDOWN. / BLOODY MARY**   `-`

DAVID COVERDALE'S WHITESNAKE

PETE SOLLEY – keyboards repl. JOHNSTON

	EMI Int.	Sunburst

Jun 78. (lp) <5C 062-61290> **SNAKEBITE**
– Come on / Bloody Mary / Ain't no love in the heart of the city / Steal away / Keep on giving me love / Queen of hearts / Only my soul / Breakdown.
Jun 78. (7"ep,7"white-ep) (INEP 751) <915> **SNAKEBITE EP** | 61 | |
– Bloody Mary / Steal away / Come on / Ain't no love in the heart of the city.

— **JON LORD** (b. 9 Jun'41, Leicester, England) – keyboards (ex-PAICE, ASHTON & LORD, ex-DEEP PURPLE) repl. SOLLEY
Oct 78. (7") (INT 568) **LIE DOWN. / DON'T MESS WITH ME** | | – |
Oct 78. (lp) (INS 3022) <937> **TROUBLE** | 50 | |
– Take me with you / Love to keep you warm / Lie down (a modern love song) / Day tripper / Night hawl (vampire blues) / The time is right for love / Trouble / Belgian Tom's hat trick / Free flight / Don't mess with me. (re-iss. Sep80 on 'United Artists'; UAG 30305) (re-iss. May82 on 'Fame' lp/c; FA/TCFA 3002) (re-iss. May90 cd/c/lp; CD/TC+/FA 3234) (re-iss. Jun87 on 'E.M.I.' lp/c; EMS/TCEMS 1257) (cd-iss. Apr88 on 'E.M.I.'; CZ 9)
Mar 79. (7") (INT 578) **THE TIME IS RIGHT FOR LOVE. / COME ON** (live) | | – |
Apr 79. (7") **THE TIME IS RIGHT FOR LOVE. / BELGUIN TOM'S HAT TRICK** | | – |

	U.A.	U.A.

Oct 79. (lp/c) (UAG 30264) <981> **LOVE HUNTER** | 29 | |
– Long way from home / Walking in the shadow of the blues / Help me thro' the day / Medicine man / You 'n' me / Mean business / Love hunter / Outlaw / Rock'n'roll women / We wish you well. (re-iss. Apr84 on 'Fame' lp/c; FA/TCFA 3095) (cd-iss. Apr88; CDFA 3095) (cd re-iss. Jul94 on 'E.M.I.'; CDEMS 1529)
Oct 79. (7"m) (BP 324) **LONG WAY FROM HOME. / TROUBLE** (live) / **AIN'T NO LOVE IN THE HEART OF THE CITY** (live) | 55 | |
Nov 79. (7") **LONG WAY FROM HOME. / WE WISH YOU WELL** | – | |

WHITESNAKE

— with **IAN PAICE** (b.29 Jun'48, Nottingham, England) – drums (ex-PAICE, ASHTON & LORD, ex-DEEP PURPLE) repl. DOWELL

	U.A.	Mirage-Atlantic

Apr 80. (7"m) (BP 352) **FOOL FOR YOUR LOVING. / MEAN BUSINESS / DON'T MESS WITH ME** | 13 | |
Jun 80. (lp/c) (UAG 30302) <19276> **READY AN' WILLING** | 6 | 90 |
– Fool for your loving / Sweet talker / Ready an' willing / Carry your load / Blindman / Ain't gonna cry no more / Love man / Black and blue / She's a woman. (re-iss. Sep85 on 'Fame' lp/c; FA/TCFA 3134) (cd-iss. Apr88; CDFA 3134) (cd re-iss. Jul94 on 'E.M.I.'; CDEMS 1526)
Jul 80. (7"m) (BP 363) **READY AN' WILLING. / NIGHT HAWK (VAMPIRE BLUES) / WE WISH YOU WELL** | 43 | – |
Jul 80. (7") <3672> **FOOL FOR YOUR LOVING. / BLACK AND BLUE** | – | 53 |
Oct 80. (7") <3766> **SWEET TALKER. / AIN'T GONNA CRY NO MORE** | – | |
Nov 80. (d-lp/d-c) (SNAKE/TC2SNAKE 1) <19292> **LIVE . . . IN THE HEART OF THE CITY** (live) | 5 | |
– Come on * / Sweet talker / Walking in the shadow of the blues / Love hunter / Fool for your loving / Ain't gonna cry no more / Ready an' willing / Take me with you * / Might just take your life / Lie down * / Ain't no love in the heart of the city / Trouble * / Mistreated. <cd-iss. Jul88 on 'Underdog'; CDS 790860-2> – <omits *> (re-iss. Nov91 on 'Fame' cd/c; CD/TC FA 3265) (re-iss. Jul94 on 'E.M.I.' cd/c; CD/TC EMS 1525)
Nov 80. (7"/12") (BP/12BP 381) <3794> **AIN'T NO LOVE IN THE HEART OF THE CITY** (live). / **TAKE ME WITH YOU** (live) | 51 | |

	Liberty	Atlantic

Apr 81. (7") (BP 395) **DON'T BREAK MY HEART AGAIN. / CHILD OF BABYLON** | 17 | |
Apr 81. (lp/c) (LBG/TCLBG 30327) <16043> **COME AN' GET IT** | 2 | |
– Come an' get it / Hot stuff / Don't break my heart again / Lonely days, lonely nights / Wine, women an' song / Would I lie to you / Girl / Hit an' run / Till the day I die. (re-iss. May89 on 'Fame' cd/c/lp; CD/TC+/FA 3219) (re-iss. Jul94 on 'E.M.I.' cd/c; CD/TC EMS 1528)
May 81. (7") (BP 399) **WOULD I LIE TO YOU. / GIRL** | 37 | |
Jun 81. (7") <3844> **DON'T BREAK MY HEART AGAIN. / LONELY DAYS, LONELY NIGHTS** | – | |

— **COVERDALE** retained **MOODY + LORD** and brought in **MEL GALLEY** – guitar (ex-TRAPEZE) repl. MARSDEN who formed ALASKA / **COLIN 'Bomber' HODGKINSON** (b.14 Oct'45) – bass (ex-BACK DOOR) repl. MURRAY to GARY MOORE / **COZY POWELL** (b.29 Dec'47, Cirencester, England) – drums (ex-JEFF BECK, ex-RAINBOW, Solo Artist, ex-BEDLAM) repl. PAICE who joined GARY MOORE

	Liberty	Geffen

Oct 82. (7"pic-d) (BP 416) **HERE I GO AGAIN. / BLOODY LUXURY** | 34 | – |
Nov 82. (lp/c/pic-lp) (LBG/TCLBG/LBGP 30354) <2-24173> **SAINTS AN' SINNERS** | 9 | |
– Young blood / Rough an' ready / Blood luxury / Victim of love / Crying in the rain / Here I go again / Love an' afection / Rock'n'roll angels / Dancing girls / Saints an' sinners. (re-iss. 1985 lp/c; ATAK/TCATAK 10) (re-iss. May87 on 'Fame' lp/c; FA/TCFA 3177) (cd-iss. Apr88; CDFA 3177) (cd re-iss. Jul94 on 'E.M.I.'; CDEMS 1521)
Aug 83. (7"/7"sha-pic-d) (BP/+P 420) **GUILTY OF LOVE. / GAMBLER** | 31 | – |

— now a quintet, when MICK MOODY departed
Jan 84. (7"/12") (BP/12BP 422) **GIVE ME MORE TIME. / NEED YOUR LOVE SO BAD** | 29 | – |

— **NEIL MURRAY** – bass returned to repl. HODGKINSON / added **JOHN SYKES** (b.29 Jul'59) – guitar (ex-TYGERS OF PAN TANG)
Feb 84. (lp/c) (WHITE/TCWHITE 1) <4018> **SLIDE IT IN** | 9 | 40 | Aug84
– Gambler / Slide it in / Standing in the shadow / Give me time / Love ain't no stranger / Slow an' easy / Spit it out / All or nothing / Hungry for love / Guilty of love. (cd-iss. Apr88 on 'E.M.I.'; cd/c; CZ 88) (pic-lp 1984 w/extra US mixes; LBGP 240-000-0)
Apr 84. (7"/7"pic-d) (BP/+P 423) **STANDING IN THE SHADOWS. / ALL OR NOTHING** (US mix) | 62 | – |
(12"+=) – ('A'-US remix).

Aug 84. (7") <29171> **LOVE AIN'T NO STRANGER. / GUILTY OF LOVE** | – | – |
Feb 85. (7"/12") (BP/12BP 424) **LOVE AIN'T NO STRANGER. / SLOW AN' EASY** | 44 | – |
(12"white+=) (BP12 424) – Slide it in.

— split for a while in 1984 when JON LORD re-joined DEEP PURPLE. **WHITESNAKE** were re-formed by **COVERDALE + SYKES** and new musicians **TONY FRANKLIN** – bass (ex-The FIRM) repl. MURRAY and GALLEY / **CARMINE APPICE** – drums (ex-BECK, BOGERT & APPICE) repl. POWELL to E.L.P.

	EMI Int.	Geffen

Mar 87. (7"/7"white) (EMI/+W 5606) **STILL OF THE NIGHT. / HERE I GO AGAIN** (1987) | 16 | – |
(12"+=/12"pic-d+=) (12EMI/+P 5606) – You're gonna break my heart again.
Apr 87. (cd/c/lp) (CD/TC+/EMC 3528) <24099> **WHITESNAKE 1987** | 8 | 2 |
– Still of the night / Bad boys / Give me all your love / Looking for love / Crying in the rain / Is this love / Straight for the heart / Don't turn away / Children of the night. (also on pic-lp; EMCP 3528) (cd+=) – Here I go again '87 / You're gonna break my heart again. (re-iss. Jul94 cd/c; CD/TC EMS 1531)
May 87. (7"/7"sha-pic-d) (EM/+P 3) **IS THIS LOVE. / STANDING IN THE SHADOWS** | 9 | – |
(12"+=/12"white+=) (12EMI/+P 3) – Need your love so bad.
(cd-ep++=/7"ep++=) (EMX/CDEM 3) – Still of the night.
Jun 87. (7") <28331> **STILL OF THE NIGHT. / DON'T TURN AWAY** | – | 79 |
Jul 87. (7") <28339> **HERE I GO AGAIN. / CHILDREN OF THE NIGHT** | – | 1 |
Oct 87. (7") <28233> **IS THIS LOVE. / BAD BOYS** | – | 2 |
Oct 87. (c-s/12"/7") (TC/12+/EM 35) **HERE I GO AGAIN '87 (US mix). / GUILTY OF LOVE** | 9 | |
(7"etched/10"white/cd-s) (EMP/10EM/CDEM 35) – ('A'side) / ('A'-US remix).
Jan 88. (7"/7"white) (EM/+W 23) **GIVE ME ALL YOUR LOVE. / FOOL FOR YOUR LOVING** | 18 | |
(12"+=/12"white) (12EMP/+W 23) – Don't break my heart again.
(3"cd-s+=) (CDEM 23) – Here I go again (USA remix).
Jan 88. (7") <28103> **GIVE ME ALL YOUR LOVE. / STRAIGHT FROM THE HEART** | – | 48 |

— **COVERDALE** completely re-modelled line-up when SYKES formed BLUE MURDER. He was replaced by **ADRIAN VANDENBURG** (b. Netherlands) – guitar (ex-VANDENBERG) / **RUDY SARZO** (b. 9 Nov'52, Havana, Cuba) – bass (ex-OZZY OSBOURNE, ex-QUIET RIOT) repl. FRANKLIN / **TOMMY ALDRIDGE** – drums (ex-OZZY OSBOURNE, ex-BLACK OAK ARKANSAS) repl. APPICE (Dec88) / **STEVE VAI** (b. 6 Jun'60, Carle Place, N.Y.) – guitar (solo Artist, ex-FRANK ZAPPA, DAVID LEE ROTH) repl. VIVIAN CAMPBELL
Nov 89. (cd/c/lp) (CD/TC+/EMD 1013) <24249> **SLIP OF THE TONGUE** | 10 | 10 |
– Slip of the tongue / Cheap an' nasty / Fool for your loving / Now you're gone / Kitten's got claws / Wings of the storm / The deeper the love / Judgement day / Slow poke music / Sailing ships. (re-iss. Jul94 cd/c; CD/TC EMS 1527)
Nov 89. (7"/7"s)<US-c-s> (EM/+P 123) <22715> **FOOL FOR YOUR LOVING ('89). / SLOW POKE MUSIC** | 43 | 37 |
(c-s+=) (TCEM 123) – ('A'version).
(12"+=/12"white+=) (12EM+/P 1243) – Walking in the shadow of the blues.
Jan 90. (7") <19951> **THE DEEPER THE LOVE. / SLIP OF THE TONGUE** | – | 28 |
Feb 90. (c-s/7"/7"pic-d) (TC+/EM/+PD 128) **THE DEEPER THE LOVE. / JUDGEMENT DAY** | 35 | – |
(12"white+=) (12EMS 128) – Sweet lady luck.
(12"++=/cd-s++=) (12/CD EM 128) – Fool for your lovin' (Vai voltage mix).
Aug 90. (c-s/7"/7"sha-pic-d) (TC+/EM/+PD 150) <19976> **NOW YOU'RE GONE (remix). / WINGS OF THE STORM** | 31 | 96 | May90
(12"+=/12"pic-d+=/cd-s+=) (12EM/12EMPS/CDEM 150) – Kittens got claws / Cheap an' nasty.

DAVID COVERDALE

	Epic	Epic

Sep 90. (7"/c-s) (656 292-7/-4) **THE LAST NOTE OF FREEDOM. / (track by HANS ZIMMER)** | | |
(12"+=) (656 292-6) – (track by other artist).
(cd-s++=) (656 292-2) – ('A'version).

COVERDALE • PAGE

DAVID COVERDALE – vocals / **JIMMY PAGE** – guitar (ex-LED ZEPPELIN, ex-solo artist) / **JORGE CASAS** – bass / **DENNY CARMASSI** – drums (ex-MONTROSE) / **RICKY PHILIPS** – bass / **LESTER MENDEL** – keyboards / **JOHN HARRIS** – acoustic harmonica / **TOMMY FUNDERBUCK** – backing vocals

	E.M.I.	Geffen

Mar 93. (cd/c/lp) (CD/TC+/EMD 1041) <24487> **COVERDALE • PAGE** | 4 | 5 |
– Shake my tree / Waiting on you / Take me for a little while / Pride and joy / Over now / Feeling hot / Easy does it / Take a look at yourself / Don't leave me this way / Absolution blues / Whisper a prayer for the dying (re-iss. Jul94 cd/c; same)
Jun 93. (c-s/12"pic-d) (12EMPD/TCEM 270) **TAKE ME FOR A LITTLE WHILE. / EASY DOES IT** | 29 | |
(cd-s) (CDEM 270) – ('A'side) / ('A'acoustic) / Shake my tree (the crunch mix) / ('A'edit).
Sep 93. (7"pic-d/c-s) (EMPD/TCEM 279) **TAKE A LOOK AT YOURSELF. / WAITING ON YOU** | | |
(cd-s+=) (CDEM 279) – ('A'acoustic) / ('A'girls version).

DAVID COVERDALE & WHITESNAKE

	E.M.I.	Capitol

May 97. (c-s/cd-s) (TC/CD EM 471) **TOO MANY TEARS / THE DEEPER THE LOVE / IS THIS LOVE** | 46 | |
(cd-s) (CDEMS 471) – ('A'part 1) / Can't stop now / ('A'part 2).
Jun 97. (cd/c) (CD/TC EMD 1104) **RESTLESS HEART** | 34 | |
– Don't fade away / All in the name of love / Restless heart / Too many tears / Crying / Stay with me / Can't go on / You're so fine / Your precious love / Take me back again / Woman trouble blues.

Oct 97. (c-s) *(TCEM 495)* **DON'T FADE AWAY / OI**
(cd-s+=) *(CDEM 495)* – Anything you want / Don't fade away.

– compilations, etc. –

Apr 88. (d-lp/c/cd) *Connoisseur; (VSOP LP/MC/CD 118)* **THE CONNOISSEUR COLLECTION**
– (DAVID COVERDALE's first 2 solo albums)

Jun 88. (cd) *M.C.A.;* **GREATEST HITS** | - |

Jul 94. (cd/c/lp) *E.M.I.; (CD/TC+/EMD 1065)* **WHITESNAKE'S GREATEST HITS** | 4 |
– Still of the night / Here I go again / Is this love / Love ain't no stranger / Looking for love / Now you're gone / Slide it in / Slow an' easy / Judgement day / You're gonna break my heart again / The deeper the love / Crying in the rain / Fool for your loving / Sweet lady luck.

Jul 94. (7"/7"white/c-s) *E.M.I.; (EM/EMS/TCEM 329)* **IS THIS LOVE. / SWEET LADY LUCK** | 25 |
(cd-s+=) *(CDEM 329)* – Now you're gone.

Nov 95. (3xcd-box) *E.M.I.; (CDOMB 016)* **SLIDE IT IN / 1987 / SLIP OF THE TONGUE**

WHITE TOWN (dig out; Great Alt & Indie . . .)

WHITE ZOMBIE

Formed: New York City, New York, USA . . . 1985 by frontman ROB 'ZOMBIE' STRAKER, guitarist TOM GUAY, drummer IVAN DePLUME and female bassist SEAN YSEULT. Fresh from an unhealthy diet of BLACK SABBATH and horror B-movies, this cartoon-esque bunch of schlock-rockers set out on their demonic trail in 1987 with a debut mini-set, 'PSYCHO-HEAD BLOWOUT', for the US indie 'Silent Explosion'. A year later, their first full-length album, 'SOUL CRUSHER', was unleashed to an unsuspecting public, although the British still awaited their landing party by early '89. A third set, 'MAKE THEM DIE SLOWLY' came out around this time, produced by the seasoned BILL LASWELL and released on 'Caroline' records, its funky death-metal slowly unearthing itself and finding underground success from both metal and alternative rock audiences. J (JOHN RICCI) had replaced GUAY at this point, although his stay was short-lived when he was in turn superseded by JAY YUENGER. In the early 90's and now on the bulging, money-spinning roster of 'Geffen', WHITE ZOMBIE went to work on a new album with producer, ANDY WALLACE. The results were mindblowing in every conceivable sense, 'LA SEXORCISTO: DEVIL MUSIC VOLUME 1' (1992), being the musical carcass that The STOOGES and KISS once spewed out. Inevitably, twisted tracks such as 'WELCOME TO PLANET MOTHERFUCKER (PSYCHOHOLIC SLAG)', 'THUNDERKISS '65', etc. (lyrics, care of the warped brain of ROB), saw the band reach the American Top 30, cracking open the skull of any youth into terror-metal (even "real" cartoon pair, Beavis & Butt-head loved them, 'ZOMBIE being a highlight on the duo's various artists album). The band were rewarded with a heavy metal Grammy the following year as the band went on a mighty touring schedule across the globe, only halting to find a replacement for the departing DePLUME. In 1995, having substituted temp PHILO with (ex-TESTAMENT) drummer JOEY TEMPESTA, they rooted out a second long-player for the label, 'ASTROCREEP 2000: SONGS OF LOVE, DESTRUCTION, AND OTHER SYNTHETIC DELUSIONS OF THE ELECTRIC HEAD' (whew!). Conceptual and groundbreaking yet again, it duly scurried up the charts and into the Top 10 (also cracked the UK Top 30), demented titles such as 'EL PHANTASMO AND THE CHICKEN-RUN BLAST-O-RAMA' carrying on where the predecessor left off. During the summer of '96, they surprised many by issuing some danceable remixes of earlier tracks going under the title of 'SUPER SEXY SWINGIN' SOUNDS', a Top 20 hit in their own country. WHITE ZOMBIE split in 1997, although the solo ROB ZOMBIE (retaining TEMPESTA) released an album, 'HELLBILLY DELUXE' (1998) and after failing to come up with the score for 'The Crow 3' movie, launched his own label, 'Zombie A Go-Go'. Meanwhile, YSEULT resurrected her moonlighting project, FAMOUS MONSTERS, releasing a second CRAMPS/B-52's style 45, 'KNOCK KNOCK HALLOWEEN' (the first, 'MONSTER GIRLS – ARE GO!', was issued a few years previously) and a debut album, 'IN THE NIGHT' (1998). • **Covers:** STRAKER/ZOMBIE except CHILDREN OF THE GRAVE (Black Sabbath) / GOD OF THUNDER (Kiss). FM covered CLOCK STRIKES TEN (Cheap Trick).

Album rating: PSYCHO-HEAD BLOWOUT mini (*4) / SOUL CRUSHER (*4) / LA SEXORCISTO: DEVIL MUSIC VOLUME 1 (*7) / ASTROCREEP 2000: SONGS OF LOVE AND DESTRUCTION . . . (*6) / SUPER SEXY SWINGIN' SOUNDS dance remixes (*7) / Rob Zombie: HELLBILLY DELUXE (*6)

ROB 'ZOMBIE' STRAKER (b.1966) – vocals, guitar / **TOM GUAY** – guitar / **SEAN YSEULT** – bass / **IVAN DePLUME** – drums

	not iss.	Silent Explosion
Feb 87. (m-lp) *<SILENT 001>* **PSYCHO-HEAD BLOWOUT**	-	
Jan 88. (lp) *<SILENT 002>* **SOUL CRUSHER**		

– Gun crazy – Eighty eight / Fast jungle / Kick – Memphis – Magdalene / True crime / Rat mouth / Shack of hate / Drowning the colossus / Crow III / Die zombie die – Skin / Truck on fire – Scum kill – Diamond ass.

--- **J** (b. JOHN RICCI) – guitar; repl. TOM

	Caroline	Caroline
Feb 89. (lp/c/cd) *(CAR LP/C/CD 3)* **MAKE THEM DIE SLOWLY**		

– Demonspeed / Disaster blaster / Murderworld / Revenge / Acid flesh / Power hungry / Godslayer.

--- **JAY YUENGER** (b.1967, Chicago, Illinois) – guitar; repl. RICCI

	Geffen	Geffen
Jul 89. (12"ep) *(CLNT 1)* **GOD OF THUNDER. / LOVE RAZOR / DISASTER BLASTER 2**		
Mar 92. (lp/cd) *<(GEF/+C/D 24460)>* **LA SEXORCISTO: DEVIL MUSIC VOL.1**		26

– Welcome to Planet Motherfucker (psychoholic slag) / Knuckle duster (Radio 1-A) / Thunderkiss '65 / Black sunshine / Soul-crusher / Cosmic monsters inc. / Spiderbaby (yeah-yeah-yeah) / I am legend / Knuckle duster (Radio 2-B) / Thrust! / One big crunch / Grindhouse (a go-go) / Starface / Warp asylum.

--- **JOHN TEMPESTA** – drums (ex-TESTAMENT, ex-EXODUS) repl.PHILO (PHIL BUERSTATTE), who had briefly repl. DePLUME

May 95. (c-s) *(GFSC 92)* **MORE HUMAN THAN HUMAN / BLOOD, MILK AND SKY (KERO KERO KEROPFI AND THE SMOOTH OPERATOR)**	51	-
(10"+=/cd-s+=) *(GFST/+D 92)* – ('A'-Jeddak of the Tharks super mix).

May 95. (cd/c/lp) *(GEF/GEC/GEF 24806)>* **ASTROCREEP 2000: SONGS OF LOVE AND DESTRUCTION AND OTHER SYNTHETIC DELUSIONS OF THE ELECTRIC HEAD**	25	6
– Electric head part I (the agony) / Super charger Heaven / Real solution No.9 / Creature of the wheel / Electric head part II (the ecstasy) / Grease paint and monkey brains / I, zombie / More human than human / El Phantasmo and the chicken-run blast-o-rama / Blur the technicolor / Blood, milk and sky. (c+=/cd+=) – The sidewalk ends where the bug parade begins.

May 96. (12"ep) *(GFST 22140)* **ELECTRIC HEAD PART II (THE ECSTASY) / EL PHANTASMO AND THE CHICKEN-RUN BLAST-O-RAMA. / SUPER CHARGER HEAVEN / MORE HUMAN THAN HUMAN (The Warlord Of Mars mega mix)**	31	-
(cd-ep) *(GFSTD 22140)* – (first 2 tracks) / More human than human (Princess of Helium ultra) / Blood, milk & sky (Im-Ho-Tep 3,700 year old boogie mix).
(cd-ep) *(GFSXD 22140)* – (tracks except second) / Thunder kiss '65 (Swinging Lovers extended mix).

Oct 96. (cd/c) *<(GED/GEC 24976)>* **SUPERSEXY SWINGIN' SOUNDS** (dance remixes!)		17	Aug96
– Phantasma / Blood, milk & sky / Real solution / Electronic head pt.1 / I'm your boogie man / Electronic head pt.2 / More human than human / I, zombie / Grease paint & monkey brains / Blur the technicolour / Super charger Heaven.

--- WHITE ZOMBIE looked to have split, J YUENGER went onto produce FU MANCHU while YSEULT moonlighted in the all-girl surf-rock act, FAMOUS MONSTERS

ROB ZOMBIE

--- with **TEMPESTA + DANNY LOHNER** – guitar (ex-NINE INCH NAILS, ex-SKREW) / **BLASKO** – bass

	Geffen	Geffen
Aug 98. (cd/c) *<(GED/GEC 25212)>* **HELLBILLY DELUXE**	37	5

– Call of the zombie / Superbeast / Dragula / Living dead girl / Perversion / Demonoid phenomenon / Spookshow baby / How to make a monster / Meet the creeper / The ballad of resurrection Joe and Rosa Whore / What lurks on Channel X? / Return of the phantom stranger / Beginning of the end.

Dec 98. (7"pic-d) *(GFS 22367)* *<1213>* **DRAGULA. / DRAGULA (Hot Rod Herman mix)**	44	
(cd-s+=) *(GFSTD 22367)* – ('A'-video).
(7"pic-d) *(GFX 22367)* – ('A'side) / Halloween (she's so mean).

	Interscope	Interscope
Oct 99. (cd) *<(490349-2)>* **AMERICAN MADE MUSIC TO STRIP BY** (HELLBILLY DELUXE remixed)		38

WHITFORD / ST. HOLMES (see under ⇒ AEROSMITH)

WHO

Formed: Chiswick & Hammersmith, London, England . . . 1964 as The HIGH NUMBERS, by ROGER DALTREY, PETE TOWNSHEND, JOHN ENTWISTLE and DOUG SANDON. After making his impromptu mid-set debut at an early gig, manic sticksman, KEITH MOON, was immediately recruited in favour of the struggling SANDON. At his first show proper, MOON reportedly mystified colleagues by roping his drums to some pillars before the show. All became clear when the drummer proceeded to knock seven shades of proverbial shit out of them during a solo, the kit actually bouncing off the floor! And thus was completed the line-up that would make their mark as one of the most pivotal, not to mention aggressive bands in rock history. Manager PETE MEADON introduced the band to the burgeoning "Mod" scene and shaped their image accordingly as a musical voice for the sharply dressed, scooter-riding young rebels, a movement that TOWNSHEND in particular felt a strong affinity with, and whose frustrations he'd document in his early, indignant blasts of raw rock'n'roll. A strutting, gloriously arrogant piece of R&B, the band's debut one-off 45 for 'Fontana', 'I'M THE FACE', was released the same month as the experienced managerial team of KIT LAMBERT and CHRIS STAMP took the reins from MEADON and began a concerted campaign for chart domination. Later that year, the band were re-christened The WHO and by this time had begun to perfect their powerful stageshow, TOWNSHEND developing his ferocious "windmilling" power-chord guitar style while the band courted controversy and delighted crowds by smashing their instruments in a cathartic rage. Rejected by major labels, they eventually secured a deal with 'Decca', through producer SHEL TALMY. Released in Britain via 'Decca's' UK subsidiary, 'Brunswick', 'I CAN'T EXPLAIN' (1965) introduced a more melodic sound and gave the band their first chart hit. The single climbed into the top 10 after TV appearances on 'Ready Steady Go' (which later adopted the track as its theme tune) and Top Of The Pops, 'ANYWAY, ANYHOW, ANYWHERE' following it later that summer. For most people however, The WHO really arrived with the seminal rebel anthem, 'MY GENERATION'. A stuttering, incredibly focused piece of amphetamine aggression, it galvanised legions of disaffected youths and only The SEX PISTOLS ever equalled it for sheer snide factor. It reached No.2 and was closely followed by the similarly titled debut album which included 'THE KIDS ARE ALRIGHT', probably TOWNSHEND's most explicit alignment with his "Mod" following. But if the kids were alright, The WHO's deal with SHEL TALMY certainly wasn't, or at least that's what the band thought, and after releasing their next single, 'SUBSTITUTE' (1966), on a new label, they became embroiled in a court battle over TALMY's right to produce the group. Despite TALMY winning a royalty on all the band's recordings for another five years, The WHO came out fighting, releasing a string of hits including 'I'M A BOY' (1966), 'HAPPY JACK' (1966) and the wistful ode to masturbation, 'PICTURES OF LILY' (1967). The title track from 'A QUICK ONE' (1966) was a patchy prototype of the rock opera concept TOWNSHEND would later refine towards the end of the decade. Elsewhere on the album, tracks like ENTWISTLE's 'BORIS THE SPIDER' and TOWNSHEND's 'HAPPY JACK' possessed the same quirky Englishness that was the essence of The KINKS, and The WHO only really began to make some headway in America after their incendiary performance at the Monterey Pop Festival in the summer of '67. 'THE WHO SELL OUT' (1967), a mock concept album, contained the sublime 'I CAN SEE FOR MILES', a spiralling piece of neo-psychedelia that had a spiritual partner in the equally trippy 'ARMENIA CITY IN THE SKY'. With 'TOMMY' (1969), TOWNSHEND ushered in the dreaded concept of the 'Rock Opera'. Yet with his compelling story of a "deaf, dumb and blind kid" who finds release through pinball, he managed to carry the whole thing off. 'PINBALL WIZARD' and 'SEE ME, FEEL ME' were classic TOWNSHEND. The album was even made into a film by maverick director Ken Russell and later into a successful West End show. After this artful tour de force, the band released the legendary 'LIVE AT LEEDS' (1970) album while they worked on TOWNSHEND's latest idea, the 'LIFEHOUSE' project. An ambitious attempt at following up 'TOMMY', the venture was later aborted, although some of the material was used as the basis for the landmark 'WHO'S NEXT' album. Released in 1971, the record heralded a harder rocking sound with the anthemic 'WON'T GET FOOLED AGAIN' and 'BABA O'REILLY'. Immaculately produced, it still stands as The WHO's most confident and cohesive work and only No.1 album. TOWNSHEND finally created a follow-up to TOMMY with 'QUADROPHENIA' in 1973. A complex, lavishly embellished piece that saw him retrospectively examining the Mod sub-culture he'd so closely identified with. The project was later made into a film, inspiring a whole new wave of neo-Mod bands at the turn of the decade. 'THE WHO BY NUMBERS' (1975) was exactly that, a confused set that found the band treading water while trying to find direction in a music scene that was to become increasingly dominated by punk rock. While 'WHO ARE YOU' (1978) sounded more assured, the album's release was marred by the death of KEITH MOON, whose hard drinking and drugging ways finally proved his undoing. Speculation of a split was rife but ex-FACE, KENNY JONES, was drafted in and the band eventually came up with 'FACE DANCES' in 1981. Neither this album, nor 1982's 'IT'S HARD' were successful in rekindling The WHO spark of old and, already demoralised after a number of fans were crushed at a gig in Cincinatti, the band finally called it a day in 1983. The WHO have since occasionally reformed for one-off live appearances including 'Live Aid' and as DALTREY has mainly concentrated on his acting career, TOWNSHEND is the only ex-WHO member who's maintained a serious solo career. His most recent release was the critically acclaimed 'PSYCHODERELICT' (1993) album which was a rock opera of sorts updated for the 90's and included material from the shelved 'LIFEHOUSE' project. • **DALTREY's filmography:** LISZTOMANIA (1975) / THE LEGACY (1979) / McVICAR (1980) / BUDDY (1991 TV serial + 1992 film). • **Songwriters:** TOWNSHEND wrote most of material except, I'M THE FACE (Slim Harpo's 'Got Live If You Want It') / I'M A MAN (Bo Diddley) / IN THE CITY (Speedy Keen; aka of Thunderclap Newman) / BARBARA ANN (Beach Boys) / BABY DON'T YOU DO IT (Marvin Gaye) / THE LAST TIME + UNDER MY THUMB (Rolling Stones) / SUMMERTIME BLUES (Eddie Cochran). KEITH MOON's only album consisted wholly of cover versions. DALTREY's solo career started with songs written for him by LEO SAYER and DAVE COURTNEY. • **Trivia:** DALTREY continues to run a trout farm in Dorset. The WHO were inducted into the Guinness Book Of Records after performing the loudest concert (120 decibels) at Charlton Athletic's Football Club.

Album rating: MY GENERATION (*7) / A QUICK ONE (*6) / THE WHO SELL OUT (*7) / MAGIC BUS – THE WHO ON TOUR (*5) / TOMMY (*8) / THE WHO LIVE AT LEEDS (*8) / WHO'S NEXT (*10) / MEATY, BEATY, BIG AND BOUNCY compilation (*9) / QUADROPHENIA (*9) / ODDS AND SODS collection (*5) / THE WHO BY NUMBERS (*5) / THE STORY OF THE WHO compilation (*7) / WHO ARE YOU (*6) / THE KIDS ARE ALRIGHT docu-soundtrack (*6) / FACE DANCES (*5) / IT'S HARD (*4) / WHO'S BETTER WHO'S BEST compilation (*8) / MY GENERATION – THE VERY BEST OF THE WHO compilation (*9) / Pete Townshend: WHO CAME FIRST (*6) / ROUGH MIX with Ronnie Lane (*6) / EMPTY GLASS (*7) / ALL THE BEST COWBOYS HAVE CHINESE EYES (*4) / SCOOP rarities (*4) / WHITE CITY – A NOVEL (*4) / PETE TOWNSHEND'S DEEP END LIVE! (*3) / THE IRON MAN a musical (*4) / ANOTHER SCOOP rarities (*3) / PSYCHODERELICT (*5) / THE BEST OF PETE TOWNSHEND–COOLWALKINGSMOOTH ... compilation (*7) / Roger Daltrey: DALTREY (*5) / RIDE A ROCK HORSE (*6) / ONE OF THE BOYS (*5) / McVICAR soundtrack (*4) / THE BEST OF . . . compilation (*6) / PARTING SHOULD BE PAINLESS (*4) / UNDER A RAGING MOON (*5) / CAN'T WAIT TO SEE THE MOVIE (*3) / John Entwistle: THE OX (*4) / WHISTLE RHYMES (*4) / RIGOR MORTIS SETS IN (*5) / MAD DOG (*4) / TOO LATE THE HERO (*3) / Keith Moon: TWO SIDES OF THE MOON (*2)

ROGER DALTREY (b. 1 Mar'45) – vocals / **PETE TOWNSHEND** (b.19 May'45) – guitar, vocals / **JOHN ENTWISTLE** (b. 9 Oct'44) – bass, vocals / **KEITH MOON** (b.23 Aug'47) – drums, vocals repl. DOUGIE SANDON

		Fontana	not iss.
Jul 64.	(7"; as The HIGH NUMBERS) *(TF 480)* **I'M THE FACE. / ZOOT SUIT**	☐	–
	(re-iss. Feb65) (re-iss. Mar80 on 'Back Door', hit UK No.49) (US re-iss. Mar80 as The WHO on 'Mercury')		

		Brunswick	Decca
Jan 65.	(7") *(05926) <31725>* **I CAN'T EXPLAIN. / BALD HEADED WOMAN**	8	93 Feb65
	(US re-iss. 1973 on 'MCA')		
May 65.	(7") *(05935)* **ANYWAY ANYHOW ANYWHERE. / DADDY ROLLING STONE**	10	–
Jun 65.	(7") *<31801>* **ANYWAY ANYHOW ANYWHERE. / ANYTIME YOU WANT ME**	–	–
Oct 65.	(7") *(05944)* **MY GENERATION. / SHOUT & SHIMMY**	2	–
Nov 65.	(7") *<31877>* **MY GENERATION. / OUT IN THE STREET**	–	74
Dec 65.	(lp) *(LAT 8616) <74664>* **MY GENERATION**	5	
	– Out in the street / I don't mind / The good's gone / La-la-la-lies / Much too much / My generation / The kid's are alright / Please please please / It's not true / I'm a man / A legal matter / The ox. *(US title 'THE WHO SING MY GENERATION') (UK re-iss. Oct80 on 'Virgin' lp/c; V/TCV 2179) – (hit UK No.20) (cd-iss. 1990;)*		

		Reaction	Decca
Mar 66.	(7") *(591 001) <6409>* **SUBSTITUTE. / WALTZ FOR A PIG** ("The WHO ORCHESTRA")	5	☐
——	(some copies 'INSTANT PARTY' or 'CIRCLES' on b-side) *<above on US 'Atco'; re-iss. Aug67; 6509>*		
Aug 66.	(7") *(591 004) <32058>* **I'M A BOY. / IN THE CITY**	2	Dec66
Dec 66.	(7") *(591 010)* **HAPPY JACK. / I'VE BEEN AWAY**	3	–
Dec 66.	(lp) *(593 002) <74892>* **A QUICK ONE** <US-title 'HAPPY JACK'>	4	67 May67
	– Run run run / Boris the spider / Whiskey man / I need you / Heatwave / Cobwebs and strange / Don't look away / See my way / So sad about us / A quick one, while he's away. *(re-iss. Aug88 on 'Polydor' lp/c)(cd); (SPE LP/MC 114)(835 782-2) (cd re-iss. Jun95 & Apr97; 527758-2)*		

		Track	Decca
Mar 67.	(7") *<32114>* **HAPPY JACK. / WHISKEY MAN**	–	24
Apr 67.	(7") *(604 002) <32156>* **PICTURES OF LILY. / DOCTOR DOCTOR**	4	51 Jun67
Jul 67.	(7") *(604 006)* **THE LAST TIME. / UNDER MY THUMB**	44	–
Oct 67.	(7") *(604 011)* **I CAN SEE FOR MILES. / SOMEONE'S COMING**	10	–
Oct 67.	(7") *<32206>* **I CAN SEE FOR MILES. / MARY ANN WITH THE SHAKY HANDS**	–	9
Jan 68.	(lp; mono/stereo) *(612/613 002) <74950>* **THE WHO SELL OUT**	13	48
	– Armenia, city in the sky / Heinz baked beans / Mary Anne with the shaky hands / Odorono / Tattoo / Our love was, is / I can see for miles / I can't reach you / Medac / Silas Stingy / Sunrise / Tattoo / Rael (1 and 2). *(re-iss. Aug88 on 'Polydor' lp/c)(cd; (SPE LP/MC 115) (cd re-iss. Jun95 & Apr97 on 'Polydor'; 527 759-2)*		
Mar 68.	(7") *<32288>* **CALL ME LIGHTNING. / DR. JEKYLL & MR. HIDE**	–	40
Jun 68.	(7") *(604 023)* **DOGS. / CALL ME LIGHTNING**	25	–
Jul 68.	(7") *<32362>* **MAGIC BUS. / SOMEONE'S COMING**	–	25
Oct 68.	(7") *(604 024)* **MAGIC BUS. / DR. JEKYLL & MR. HIDE**	26	–
Oct 68.	(lp) *<75064>* **MAGIC BUS – (THE WHO ON TOUR)** (live)	–	39
	– Disguises / Run run run / Dr. Jekyll & Mr. Hyde / I can't reach you / Our love was, is / Call me Lightning / Magic bus / Someone's coming / Doctor doctor / Bucket T. / Pictures of ily.		
Nov 68.	(lp; mono/stereo) *(612/613 006)* **DIRECT HITS** (compilation)	☐	–
	– Bucket T. / I'm a boy / Pictures of Lily / Doctor doctor / I can see for miles / Substitute / Happy Jack / The last time / In the city / Call me Lightning / Mary-Anne with the shaky hand / Dogs.		
Mar 69.	(7") *(604 027) <32465>* **PINBALL WIZARD. / DOGS (part 2)**	4	19
	<US re-iss. 1973 on 'MCA'>		
May 69.	(d-lp) *(613 013-014) <7205>* **TOMMY**	2	4
	– Overture / It's a boy / 1921 / Amazing journey / Sparks / Eyesight for the blind / Miracle cure / Sally Simpson / I'm free / Welcome / Tommy's holiday camp / We're not gonna take it / Christmas / Cousin Kevin / The acid queen / Underture / Do you think it's alright / Fiddle about / Pinball wizard / There's a doctor / Go to the mirror / Tommy can you hear me / Smash the mirror / Sensation. *(re-iss. Jul84 on 'Polydor'; 2486 161/2) (d-cd-iss. Apr89; 800 077-2)*		
Jul 69.	(7") *<32519>* **I'M FREE. / WE'RE NOT GONNA TAKE IT**	–	37
Mar 70.	(7") *(604 036) <32670>* **THE SEEKER. / HERE FOR MORE**	19	44
May 70.	(lp) *(2406 001) <79175>* **LIVE AT LEEDS** (live)	3	4
	– Young man / Substitute / Summertime blues / Shakin' all over / My generation / Magic bus. *(re-iss. Nov83 on 'Polydor' lp/c; SPE LP/MC 50) (re-iss. May88 on 'Polydor'; 825 339-2) (cd re-iss. Feb95 on 'Polydor', hit No.59 & Apr97; 527 169-2)*		
Jul 70.	(7") *(2094 002)* **SUMMERTIME BLUES (live). / HEAVEN AND HELL**	38	–
Jul 70.	(7") *<32708>* **SUMMERTIME BLUES (live). / HERE FOR MORE**	–	27
Sep 70.	(7") *<32729>* **SEE ME, FEEL ME. / WE'RE NOT GONNA TAKE IT / OVERTURE FROM TOMMY**	–	12
	<US re-iss. 1973 on 'MCA'>		
Sep 70.	(7"w-drawn) *(2094 004)* **SEE ME, FEEL ME. / OVERTURE FROM TOMMY**	–	–
Jul 71.	(7") *(2094 009) <32846>* **WON'T GET FOOLED AGAIN. / I DON'T EVEN KNOW MYSELF**	9	15
Sep 71.	(lp) *(2408 102) <79182>* **WHO'S NEXT**	1	4 Aug71
	– Baba O'Riley / Bargain / Love ain't for keeping / My wife / Song is over / Getting in tune / Going mobile / Behind blue eyes / Won't get fooled again. *(re-iss. Nov83 on 'Polydor' lp/c)(cd; SPE LP/MC 49)(813 651-2) (cd re-iss. Aug96; 527760-2)*		
Oct 71.	(7") *(2094 012)* **LET'S SEE ACTION. / WHEN I WAS A BOY**	16	–
Nov 71.	(7") *<32888>* **BEHIND BLUE EYES. / MY WIFE**	–	34
Dec 71.	(lp/c) *(2406/3191 006) <79184>* **MEATY, BEATY, BIG AND BOUNCY** (compilation)	9	11 Nov71
	– I can't explain / The kids are alright / Happy Jack / I can see for miles / Pictures of		

Lily / My generation / The seeker / Anyway, anyhow, anywhere / Pinball wizard /
A legal matter / Boris the spider / Magic bus / Substitute / I'm a boy. *(re-iss. 1974)*

Jun 72. (7") *(2094 102)* <*32983*> **JOIN TOGETHER. / BABY DON'T
YOU DO IT**

9	17

—— In Oct72, PETE TOWNSHEND was another like ENTWISTLE to issue debut
solo album 'WHO CAME FIRST'. It scraped into UK Top30. He issued more
throughout 70's-80's (see . . .) In Apr'73, ROGER DALTREY hit the singles chart
with GIVING IT ALL AWAY. It was a cut from debut album DALTREY.

Jan 73. (7") *(2094 106)* <*33041*> **RELAY. / WASPMAN**

21	39 Dec72

	Track	M.C.A.

Oct 73. (7") *(2094 115)* **5:15. / WATER**

	Track	M.C.A.
	20	-

Oct 73. (7") <*40152*> **5:15. / LOVE REIGN O'ER ME**

-	-

Nov 73. (d-lp) *(2657 002)* <*10004*> **QUADROPHENIA**

2	2

– I am the sea / The real me / Quadrophenia / Cut my hair / The punk and the
godfather / I'm one / Dirty jobs / Helpless dancer / Is it in my head? / I've had
enough / 5:15 / Sea and sand / Drowned / Bell boy / Doctor Jimmy / The rock / Love,
reign o'er me. *(re-iss. Sep79 on 'Polydor' d-lp)(d-c; 2657013)(3526001) (d-cd-iss.
Jan87 on 'Polydor'; 831074-2)*

Nov 73. (7") <*40152*> **LOVE, REIGN O'ER ME. / WATER**

-	76

Jan 74. (7") <*40182*> **THE REAL ME. / I'M ONE**

-	92

—— In Apr75, KEITH MOON was the last WHO member to release solo vinyl. The
dismal 'TWO SIDES OF THE MOON' sold poorly.

	Polydor	M.C.A.

Oct 75. (lp/c) *(2490/3194 129)* <*2161*> **THE WHO BY NUMBERS**

	Polydor	M.C.A.
	7	8

– Slip kid / However much I booze / Squeeze box / Dreaming from the waist /
Imagine a man / Success story / They are all in love / Blue, red and grey / How
many friends / In a hand or a face. *(re-iss. Mar84 lp/c; SPE LP/MC 68) (cd-iss. Jul89;
831552-2)*

Jan 76. (7") *(2121 275)* <*40475*> **SQUEEZE BOX. / SUCCESS STORY**

10	16 Nov75

Aug 76. (7") <*40603*> **SLIP KID. / DREAMING FROM THE WAIST**

-	

Sep 76. (d-lp)(d-c) *(2683 069)(3519 020)* **THE STORY OF THE WHO**
(compilation)

2	-

– Magic bus / Substitute / Boris the spider / Run run run / I'm a boy / Heatwave / My
generation / Pictures of Lily / Happy Jack / The seeker / I can see for miles / Bargain /
Squeeze box / Amazing journey / The acid queen / Do you think it's alright / Fiddle
about / Pinball wizard / I'm free / Tommy's holiday camp / We're not gonna take it /
See me, feel me / Summertime blues / Baba O'Riley / Behind blue eyes / Slip kid /
Won't get fooled again.

Jul 78. (7") *(WHO 1)* <*40948*> **WHO ARE YOU?. / HAD ENOUGH**

18	14

—— On 5th Aug'78, manager PETE MEADON committed suicide.

Sep 78. (lp/c)(pic-lp) *(WHOD/+C 5004)* <*3050*> **WHO ARE
YOU**

6	2

– New song / Had enough / 905 / Sister disco / Music must change / Trick of the
light / Guitar and pen / Love is coming down / Who are you. *(re-iss. Aug84 lp/c;
SPE LP/MC 77) (cd-iss. Jul89; 831557-2)*

—— After a party on 7th Sep'78, KEITH MOON died on an overdose of heminevrin.

Dec 78. (7") <*40978*> **TRICK OF THE LIGHT. / 905**

-	

—— Early'79, KENNY JONES (b.16 Sep'48) – drums (ex-SMALL FACES, ex-FACES)
took place of KEITH. Added 5th tour member JOHN 'Rabbit' BUNDRICK –
keyboards

	Polydor	Warners

Feb 81. (7") *(WHO 4)* <*49698*> **YOU BETTER YOU BET. / THE QUIET
ONE**

	Polydor	Warners
	9	18

Mar 81. (lp/c) *(WHOD/+C 5037)* <*3516*> **FACE DANCES**

2	4

– You better you bet / Don't let go the coat / Cache cache / The quiet one / Did you
steal my money / How can you do it alone / Daily records / You / Another tricky day.
(re-iss. May88 lp/c; SPE LP/MC 112) (re-iss. cd Jun97;) (cd re-iss. May97; 537695-2)

May 81. (7") *(WHO 5)* <*49743*> **DON'T LET GO THE COAT. / YOU**

47	84

Sep 82. (lp/c) *(WHOD/+C 5066)* <*23731*> **IT'S HARD**

11	8

– Athena / It's your turn / Cooks county / It's hard / Dangerous / Eminence front /
I've known no war / One life's enough / One at a time / Why did I fall for that / A
man is a man / Cry if you want. *(cd-iss. 1983 & Jun93; 800 106-2) (cd re-iss. May97;
537696-2)*

Sep 82. (7")/7"pic-d) *(WHO/+P 6)* **ATHENA. / A MAN IS A MAN**
(12"+=/12"pic-d+=) *(WHO X/PX 6)* – Won't get fooled again.

40	-

Sep 82. (7") <*29905*> **ATHENA. / IT'S YOUR TURN**

-	28

Dec 82. (7") <*29814*> **EMINENCE FRONT. / ONE AT A TIME**

-	68

Feb 83. (7") <*29731*> **IT'S HARD. / DANGEROUS**

-	-

—— They officially split late 1983 from studio work. They occasionally returned for
one-off live work.

– other compilations, etc. –

below 4 on 'Brunswick' label.

Mar 66. (7") *(05956)* **A LEGAL MATTER. / INSTANT PARTY**

32	-

Aug 66. (7") *(05965)* **THE KIDS ARE ALRIGHT. / THE OX**

41	-

Aug 66. (7") <*31988*> **THE KIDS ARE ALRIGHT. / A LEGAL MATTER**

-	-

Nov 66. (7") *(05968)* **LA LA LA LIES. / THE GOOD'S GONE**

-	-

Nov 66. (7"ep) *Reaction; (592 001)* **READY STEADY WHO**

-	-

– Circles / Disguises / Batman / Bucket 'T' / Barbara Ann. *(re-iss. Nov83 on
'Reaction-Polydor'; WHO 7); hit 58*

Nov 70. (7"ep) *Track; (2252 001)* **EXCERPTS FROM "TOMMY"**

-	-

– See me, feel me / I'm free / Christmas / Overture from Tommy.

Oct 74. (lp/c) *Track; (2406/3191 116)* <*2126*> **ODDS AND SODS**
(rarities)

10	15

– Postcard / Now I'm a farmer / Put the money down / Little Billy / Too much of
anything / Glow girl / Pure and easy / Faith in something bigger / I'm the face /
Naked eye / Long live rock. *(re-iss. cd Jun93;)*

Nov 74. (7") *Track; <40330>* **POSTCARD. / PUT THE MONEY DOWN**

-	

Dec 74. (d-lp)(d-c) *Track; (2683 038)(3533 022)* <*4067*> **A QUICK
ONE / THE WHO SELL OUT**

below with guest singers ELTON JOHN, TINA TURNER, OLIVER REED,
ANN-MARGRET, etc

Aug 75. (d-lp)(d-c) *Polydor; (2657 007)* <*9502*> **TOMMY (Film
Soundtrack)**

30	2 Mar75

– Prologue / Captain Walker – It's a boy / Bernie's holiday camp / 1951 – What
about the boy? / Amazing journey / Christmas / Eyesight to the blind / Acid queen /

Do you think it's alright / Cousin Kevin / Do you think it's alright / Fiddle about /
Do you think it's alright / Sparks / Extra, extra, extra / Pinball wizard / Champagne /
There's a doctor / Go to the mirror / Tommy can you hear me / Smash the mirror /
I'm free / Mother and son / Sensation / Miracle cure / Sally Simpson / Welcome –
T.V. studio / Tommy's holiday camp / We're not gonna take it / Listening to you –
See me, feel me.

—— Note; below on 'Polydor' UK/ 'MCA' US, unless mentioned otherwise

Oct 76. (7"m) *(2058 803)* **SUBSTITUTE. / I'M A BOY / PICTURES
OF LILY**

7	-

Apr 79. (7"m) *(WHO 2)* <*41053*> **LONG LIVE ROCK. / I'M THE
FACE / MY WIFE**

48	54

Jun 79. (d-lp)(d-c)<US-pic-d-lp> *(2675 179)(3577 343)* <*11005*> **THE
KIDS ARE ALRIGHT**

26	8

– (some live tracks with interviews) *(re-iss. cd Jun93)*

Sep 79. (7") <*2022*> **I'M ONE. / 5:15**

	45 b-side

Sep 79. (d-lp)(d-c) *(2625 037)(3577 352)* <*6235*> **QUADROPHENIA
(Film Soundtrack)**

23	46

– (includes tracks by other artists)

Feb 81. (lp)(c) *(2486 140)(3195 235)* **MY GENERATION (compilation)**

-	-

Oct 81. (lp) <*12001*> **HOOLIGANS**

-	52

(UK-iss.Dec88;

Feb 83. (d-c) *(3577 378)* **WHO'S NEXT / THE WHO BY NUMBERS**

-	-

Feb 83. (d-c) **WHO ARE YOU / LIVE AT LEEDS**

-	-

May 83. (lp) <*5408*> **WHO'S GREATEST HITS**

-	94

Aug 83. (lp)/(c) *(SPE LP/MC 9) (2311 132)<3100 630>* **RARITIES
VOL.1 (1966-68)**

	Oct82

Aug 83. (lp/c) *(SPE LP/MC 10)* **RARITIES VOL.2 (1970-73)**

	Oct82

(re-iss. cd+c.VOL.1 & 2 Jan91)

Nov 84. (d-lp/d-c) *(WHO/+C 1)* <*8018*> **WHO'S LAST**

48	81

(cd-iss. Dec88; DWHO 1)

Nov 84. (7") *(MCA 927)* **TWIST AND SHOUT. / I CAN'T EXPLAIN**

Nov 84. (lp/c)(cd) *(WHOH/+C 17)(815 965-2)* **THE SINGLES**

Oct 85. (d-lp/d-c) *Impression; (IMDP/IMDK 1)* **THE WHO
COLLECTION**

44	-

(d-cd-iss. Oct88; IMCD 41)

Aug 85. (lp/c) *Karusel Gold; (825 746-1/-4)* **THE BEST OF THE SIXTIES**

-	-

Apr 86. (lp/c) *Arcade; (ADAH/+C 427)* **GREATEST HITS**

-	-

Feb 88. (7") *(POSP 907)* **MY GENERATION. / SUBSTITUTE**
(12"+=/c-s+=/cd-s+=) *(POSPX/POSPC/POCD 907)* – Baba O'Riley / Behind blue
eyes.

68	-

Mar 88. (lp/c)(cd) *(WTV/+C 1)(835 389-2)* **WHO'S BETTER WHO'S
BEST**

10	

– My generation / Anyway, anyhow, anywhere / The kids are alright / Substitute /
I'm a boy / Happy Jack / Pictures of Lily / I can see for miles / Who are you / Won't
get fooled again / Magic bus / Pinball wizard / I'm free / I can't explain / See me
feel me / Squeeze box / Join together / You better you bet. *(cd+=)* – Baba O'Riley.

Jun 88. (7") *(POSP 917)* **WON'T GET FOOLED AGAIN. / BONEY
MORONIE (live)**
(ext-12"+=/cd-s+=) *(POSPX/POCD 917)* – Dancing in the street (live) / Mary Ann
with the shaky hand.

Oct 88. (lp/c/cd) *(SPE LP/MC/CD 116)* <*5641*> **WHO'S MISSING**

	Dec85

Mar 90. (7") *Virgin; (VS 1259)* **JOIN TOGETHER. / I CAN SEE FOR
MILES**
(12"+=) *(VST 1259)* – Behind blue eyes.
(cd-s++=) *(VSCD 1259)* – Christmas.

Mar 90. (d-lp/d-c/d-lp) *Virgin; (CD/TC+/VDT 102) / M.C.A.; <19501>*
JOIN TOGETHER
– (contains some solo material)

59	

Jul 94. (4xcd-box) *(521751-2)* **30 YEARS OF MAXIMUM R&B**

48	

Jul 96. (7"/c-s) *(863918-7/-4)* **MY GENERATION. / PINBALL
WIZARD (live)**
(cd-s+=) *(854637-2)* – Boris the spider.

31	-

Aug 96. (cd/c) *(533150-2/-4)* **MY GENERATION – THE VERY BEST
OF THE WHO**

11	

– I can't explain / Anyway, anyhow, anywhere / My generation / Substitute / I'm a
boy / Boris the spider / Happy Jack / Pictures of Lily / I can see for miles / Magic
bus / Pinball wizard / The seeker / Baba O'Riley / Won't get fooled again / Let's see
action / 5.15 / Join together / Squeeze box / Who are you / You better you bet.

PETE TOWNSHEND

(solo). Before his 1972 official debut, TOWNSHEND issued 2 lp's on 'Universal';
HAPPY BIRTHDAY (1970) & I AM (1972).

	Track	Track

Oct 72. (lp) *(2408 201)* <*79189*> **WHO CAME FIRST**

	Track	Track
	30	69

– Pure and easy / Evolution / Forever's no time at all / Let's see action / Time is
passing / There's a heartache followin' me / Sheraton Gibson / Content / Parvardigar.
(cd-iss. Oct92 & Mar97 on 'Rykodisc'; RCD 20246)

—— next collaboration with Solo artist and ex-SMALL FACES bassman and singer.

PETE TOWNSHEND & RONNIE LANE

	Polydor	M.C.A.

Sep 77. (7") <*40818*> **MY BABY GIVES IT AWAY. / APRIL FOOL**

	Polydor	M.C.A.
	-	-

Sep 77. (lp) *(2442 147)* <*2295*> **ROUGH MIX**

44	45

– My baby gives it away / Nowhere to run / Rough mix / Annie / Keep me turning /
Catmelody / Misunderstood / April fool / Street in the city / Heart to hang on to /
Till the rivers all run dry. *(re-iss. Nov80 & Nov83)*

Nov 77. (7") *(2058 944)* **STREET IN THE CITY. / Ronnie Lane: ANNIE**

-	-

Nov 77. (7") <*40878*> **NOWHERE TO RUN . / KEEP ME TURNING**

-	-

PETE TOWNSHEND

	Island	not iss.

Dec 79. (12"ep) *(12WIP 6598)* **THE SECRET POLICEMAN'S BALL** (the
songs)
– Drowned / Pinball wizard / Won't get fooled again.

	Island	not iss.
		-

		Atco	Atco	
Mar 80.	(7") (K 11460) <7318> **ROUGH BOYS. / AND I MOVED**	39	89	Nov80
Apr 80.	(lp/c) (K/K4 50699) <32100> **EMPTY GLASS**	11	5	

– Rough boys / I am an animal / And I moved / Let my love open your door / Jools and Jim / Keep on working / Cat's in the cupboard / A little is enough / Empty glass / Gonna get ya. (cd-iss. 1984; K 250 699) (cd re-iss. Nov93 & Oct95; 7567 9038-2-2)

Jun 80.	(7") <7217> **LET MY LOVE OPEN THE DOOR. / AND I LOVED**	-	9	
Jun 80.	(7"m) (K 11486) **LET MY LOVE OPEN THE DOOR. / CLASSIFIED / GREYHOUND GIRL**	46		
Sep 80.	(7") <7312> **A LITTLE IS ENOUGH. / CAT'S IN THE CUPBOARD**	-	72	
Oct 80.	(7") (K 11609) **KEEP ON WORKING. / JOOLS AND JIM**	-	-	
May 82.	(7") (K 11734) <99989> **FACE DANCES (pt.2). / MAN WATCHING**			
Jun 82.	(lp/c) (K/K4 50889) <38149> **ALL THE BEST COWBOYS HAVE CHINESE EYES**	32	26	

– The sea refuses no river / Communication / Exquisitely bored / North country girl / Slit skirts / Uniforms / Prelude / Somebody saved me / Face dances 2 / Stardom in action / Stop hurting people. (cd-iss. 1984; K 250 699) (cd re-iss. Nov93 & Oct95; 7567 82812-2)

Aug 82.	(7",7"pic-d) (K 11751) **UNIFORMS (CORPS D'ESPRIT). / DANCE IT ALL AWAY**	48	-	

(12",12"pic-d) (K 11751T) – ('A'side) / Stop hurting people.

Aug 82.	(7") <99973> **UNIFORMS (CORPS D'ESPRIT). / SLIT SKIRTS**	-	-	
Apr 83.	(7") <99884> **BARGAIN. / DIRTY WATER**	-	-	
Oct 85.	(7"/12") (U/UT 8859) **FACE THE FACE. / HIDING OUT**	-	26	
Nov 85.	(lp/c/cd) (252392-1/-4/-2) <90473> **WHITE CITY – A NOVEL**	70	26	

– Give blood / Brilliant blues / Face the face / Hiding out / Secondhand love / Crashing by design / I am secure / White City fighting Come to mama. (re-iss. cd Nov93; same)

Jan 86.	(7") <99553> **SECOND HAND LOVE. / WHITE CITY FIGHTING**	-	-	
Apr 86.	(7") (U 8744) **GIVE BLOOD. / MAGIC BUS (live)**	-	-	

(12"+=) (UT 8744) – Won't get fooled again.

May 86.	(7") <99499> **BEHIND BLUE EYES. / BAREFOOTIN'**	-	-	
Oct 86.	(lp,c,cd) <90553> **PETE TOWNSEND'S DEEP END LIVE! (live)**	-	98	

– Barefootin' / After the fire / Behind blue eyes / Stop hurtin' people / I'm one / I put a spell on you / Save it for later / Pinball wizard / Little is enough / Eyesight to the blind.

—— Next featured singers JOHN LEE HOOKER (Iron Man) / NINA SIMONE (The Dragon) / DALTREY + JOHN ENTWISTLE who play on 2 new WHO tracks.

		Virgin	Atlantic	
Jun 89.	(lp/c/cd) (CD/TC+/V 2592) <81996> **THE IRON MAN (The Musical)**		58	

– I won't run anymore / Over the top / Man machines / Dig / A friend is a friend / I eat heavy metal / All shall be well / Was there life / Fast food / A fool says . . . / Fire / New life (reprise). (re-iss. Mar91 lp/c; OVED/+C 355)

Jul 89.	(7"/c-s) (VS/+C 1198) **A FRIEND IS A FRIEND. / MAN MACHINES**			

(12"+=/12"g-f+=/3"cd-s+=) (VS T/TG/CD 1198) – Real world.

Nov 89.	(7"/12"/12"g-f) (VS/+T/TG 1209) **I WON'T RUN ANYMORE. / A FOOL SAYS . . .**			

		Atlantic	Atlantic	
Jul 93.	(cd/c) <(7567 82494-2/-4)> **PSYCHODERELICT**			

– English boy / Meher Baba M3 / Let's get pretentious / Meher Baba M4 (signal box) / Early morning dreams / I want that thing / Introduction to outlive the dinosaur / Outlive the dinosaur / Flame (demo) / Now and then / I am afraid / Don't try to make me real / Introduction to predictable / Predictable / Flame / Meher Baba M5 (Vivaldi) / Fake it / Introduction to now and then (reprise) / Now and then (reprise) / Baba O'Riley (demo) / English boy (reprise). (cd re-iss. Jan97; same)

Jul 93.	(7"/c-s) (A 7370/+C) **ENGLISH BOY ('A'-dialogue mix). / ('A' dialogue mix)**			

(cd-s+=) (A 7370CD1) – Fake it / Psycho montage.
(cd-s+=) (A 7370CD2) – ('A' dialogue version) / Fake it / Flame / Early morning dreams.

May 96.	(cd/c) (7567-82712-2/-4) **THE BEST OF PETE TOWNSHEND – COOLWALKINGSMOOTHSTRAIGHTSMOKINGFIRESTOKING** (compilation)			

– Rough boys / Let my love open the door / Mis understood / Give blood / A friend is a friend / Sheraton Gibson / English boy / Street in the city / Pure and easy / Slit skirts / The sea refuses no river / A little is enough / Face the face / Uneasy street / Let my love open the door (E. Cola mix).

Jun 96.	(c-s) (A 5511C) **LET MY LOVE OPEN THE DOOR /**	-	-	

(cd-s+=) (A 5511CD) –

– (other PETE TOWNSHEND compilations, etc.) –

Apr 83.	(d-lp) Atco; (B 0063) <90063> **SCOOP**		35	

– (unfinished WHO demos and solo rarities)

Jul 89.	(d-lp/d-c) Polydor; (839350-1/-4) **ANOTHER SCOOP**			

ROGER DALTREY

		Track	Track	
Apr 73.	(7") (2094 110) <40053> **GIVING IT ALL AWAY. / THE WAY OF THE WORLD**	5	83	
Apr 73.	(lp) (2406 207) <328> **DALTREY**		45	

– One man band / The way of the world / You are yourself / Thinking / You and me / It's a hard life / Giving it all away / The story so far / When the music stops / Reasons. (re-iss. Aug82 lp/c; 2485/3201 219) (cd-iss. Apr95 on 'Polydor')

Jun 73.	(7") (ODS 66302) <Ode; 66040> **I'M FREE. / (OVERTURE)**	13		
Sep 73.	(7") (2094 014) <40084> **THINKING. / THERE IS LOVE**			
Nov 73.	(7") (2094 016) **IT'S A HARD LIFE. / ONE MAN BAND**			

		Polydor	M.C.A.	
Mar 75.	(7") (2001 561) **LISTENING TO YOU. / (OVERTURE)**	-	-	
May 75.	(7") **COME AND GET YOUR LOVE. / THE WORLD OVER**	-	-	

Jul 75.	(lp)(c) (2442 135)(2660 111) <2147> **RIDE A ROCK HORSE**	14	28	

– Come and get your love / Hearts right / Oceans away / Proud / The world over / Near to surrender / Feeling / Walking the dog / Milk train / I was to sing your song.

Jul 75.	(7") (2058 628) **WALKING THE DOG. / PROUD**			
Sep 75.	(7") <40453> **COME AND GET YOUR LOVE. / FEELING**	-	68	
Nov 75.	(7") <40512> **OCEANS AWAY. / FEELING**	-	-	
Oct 75.	(7") <1779> **ORPHEUS SONG. / LOVE'S DREAM**	-	-	

—— (above from the Ken Russell film LISTZOMANIA. Released at the same time, it was scored by RICK WAKEMAN for 'A&M' (AMLH 64546)and featured some with DALTREY vocals).

Apr 77.	(7") (2121 319) **WRITTEN ON THE WIND. / DEAR JOHN**	46	-	
May 77.	(7") <40761> **ONE OF THE BOYS. / DOING IT ALL AGAIN**	-	-	
May 77.	(lp) (2441 146) <2271> **ONE OF THE BOYS**	45	46	

– Parade / Single man's dilemma / Avenging Annie / The prisoner / Leon / One of the boys / Giddy / Written on the wind / Satin and lace / Doing it all again.

Jun 77.	(7") (2058 896) **ONE OF THE BOYS. / TO PUT SOMETHING BETTER INSIDE ME**			
Jul 77.	(7") <40765> **SAY IT ISN'T SO, JOE. / SATIN AND LACE**	-	-	
Sep 77.	(7") <40800> **AVENGING ANNIE. / THE PRISONER**	-	88	
Jan 78.	(7") <40862> **THE PRISONER. / LEON**	-	-	
Feb 78.	(7") (2058 986) **SAY IT AIN'T SO, JOE. / THE PRISONER**			

		Polydor	Polydor	
Jul 80.	(7") (2001 980) <2105> **FREE ME. / McVICAR**	39	53	Jun80
Jul 80.	(lp/c) (POLD/+C 5034) <6284> **McVICAR (Soundtrack)**	39	22	

– Bitter and twisted / Just a dream away / Escape (part 1) / White City lights / Free me / My time is gonna come / Waiting for a friend / Escape (part 2) / Without your love / McVicar. (cd-iss. Apr95)

Sep 80.	(7") <2121> **WITHOUT YOUR LOVE. / ESCAPE (part 2)**	-	20	
Oct 80.	(7") (POSP 181) **WITHOUT YOUR LOVE. / SAY IT AIN'T SO, JOE. / FREE ME**	55	-	
Jan 81.	(7") <2153> **WAITING FOR A FRIEND. / BITTER AND TWISTED**	-	-	

		Polydor	M.C.A.	
Mar 82.	(lp/c) (2490/3194 162) <5301> **THE BEST OF ROGER DALTREY** <US-title 'BEST BITS'>(compilation)			

– Martyrs and madmen / Say it isn't so, Joe / Oceans away / Treasury / Free me / Without your love / It's a hard life / Giving it all away / Avenging Annie / Proud / You put something better inside me. (UK cd-iss. May91)

Apr 82.	(7") <52051> **MARTYRS AND MADMEN. / AVENGING ANNIE**	-	-	

		WEA	Atlantic	
Feb 84.	(7") (U 9686) <89704> **WALKING IN MY SLEEP. / SOMEBODY TOLD ME**	56	62	

(12"+=) (U 9686T) – Gimme some lovin'.

Feb 84.	(lp) (2502 981) <80128> **PARTING SHOULD BE PAINLESS**			

– Walking in my sleep / Parting would be painless / Is there anybody out there / Would a stranger do / Going strong / Looking for you / Somebody told me / How does the cold wind cry / Don't wait on the stairs.

Jun 84.	(7") (U 9541) <89667> **PARTING SHOULD BE SO PAINLESS. / IS THERE ANYBODY OUT THERE**			

(12"+=) (U 9541T) – I won't be the one to say goodbye.

		Ten-Virgin	Atlantic	
Sep 85.	(7") (TEN 69) <89491> **AFTER THE FIRE. / IT DON'T SATISFY ME**	50	48	

(12"+=) (TEN 69-12) – Love me like you do.

Oct 85.	(lp/c/cd) (DIX/CDIX/DIXCD 17) <81269> **UNDER A RAGING MOON**	52	42	

– After the fire / Don't talk to strangers / Breaking down Paradise / The pride you hide / Move better in the night / Fallen angel / It don't satisfy me / Rebel / Under a raging moon. (cd+=) – Behind blue eyes / 5:15 / Won't get fooled again. (re-iss. 1989 lp/c; XID/CXID 22)

Dec 85.	(7") <89471> **LET ME DOWN EASY. / FALLEN ANGEL**		86	
Feb 86.	(7"/12") <89457> **UNDER A RAGING MOON. / MOVE BETTER IN THE NIGHT**	43	-	

(d7"+=) (TEND 81) – Behind blue eyes / 5:15 / Won't get fooled again.

Apr 86.	(7") <89457> **QUICKSILVER LIGHTNING. / LOVE ME LIKE YOU DO**	-	-	
May 86.	(7") (TEN 103) **THE PRIDE YOU HIDE. / BREAK OUT**	-	-	

(d7"+=/12"+=) (TEN D/T 103) – Don't talk to strangers (live) / Pictures of Lily (live).

Jun 86.	(7") <89419> **UNDER A RAGING MOON. / THE PRIDE YOU HIDE**			
Jun 87.	(7") (TEN 147) **HEARTS OF FIRE. / LOVERS STORM**			

(12"+=) (TENT 147) – Quick silver lightning.

Jul 87.	(lp/c/cd) (DIX/CDIX/DIXCD 54) **CAN'T WAIT TO SEE THE MOVIE**			

– Hearts of fire / When the thunder comes / Ready for love / Balance on wires / Miracle of love / The price of love / The heart has its reasons / Alone in the night / Lover's storm / Take me home.

Jul 87.	(7") (TEN 202) **DON'T LET THE SUN GO DOWN ON ME. / THE HEART HAS ITS REASONS**			

(12"+=) (TENT 202) – ('A'extended).

JOHN ENTWISTLE

		Track	Decca	
Nov 70.	(lp; The WHO) (2407 014) **THE OX**		-	

– (compilation of WHO songs written by ENTWISTLE)

May 71.	(lp) (2406 005) <2024> **SMASH YOUR HEAD AGAINST THE WALL**			

– My size / Pick me up (big chicken) / What kind of people are they? / Heaven and Hell / Ted end / You're mine / No.29 (external youth) / I believe in everything.

May 71.	(7") (2094 008) **I BELIEVE IN EVERYTHING. / MY SIZE**			

—— ENTWISTLE with RIGOR MORTIS:- BRYAN WILLIAMS – keyboards / ALAN ROSS – guitar / HOWIE CASEY – sax / GRAHAM DEACON – drums / TONY ASHTON – percussion

WHO (cont)

	Track	Track
Nov 72. (lp) *(2406 104)* <79190> **WHISTLE RHYMES**
– Ten little friends / Mr. Bones & Mrs. Apron strings / And I feel better / Thinking it over / Who cares / I wonder now / I was just being friendly / The window shopper / I found out / Nightmare.

	Track	M.C.A.
Nov 72. (7") *(33052)* **WHO CARES. / I WONDER NOW** | - | |
Jun 73. (lp) *(2406 106)* <321> **RIGOR MORTIS SETS IN**
– Give me that rock and roll / Mr. Bass man / Do the dangle / Hound dog / Made in Japan / My wife / Roller skate Kate / Peg leg Peggy / Lucille / Big black Cadillac.
Jun 73. (7") *(2094 107)* **MADE IN JAPAN. / HOUND DOG**
Jun 73. (7") <40066> **MADE IN JAPAN. / ROLLER SKATE KATE** | - | |

—— with **DEACON, ASHTON & CASEY** plus **JIM RYAN** – guitar / **MIKE WEDGWOD** – guitar / **EDDIE JOBSON** – keyboards (guest)

Feb 75. (7"; as JOHN ENTWISTLE'S OX) *(FR 13567)* **MAD DOG. / CELL NO.7**
Mar 75. (lp; as JOHN ENTWISTLE'S OX) *(2129)* **MAD DOG**
– I fall to pieces / Cell number seven / You can be so mean / Lady killer / Who in the hell? / Mad dog / Jungle bunny / I'm so scared / Drowning.

—— (solo, with session stars incl. **JOE WALSH** – guitar

	WEA	Atco
Sep 81. (7",7"pic-d) *(K 79249)* **TOO LATE THE HERO. / COMIN' BACK** | | |
Nov 81. (lp/c) *(K/K4 99179)* <38142> **TOO LATE THE HERO** | | 71 |
– Try me / Talk dirty / Lovebird / Sleepin man / I'm coming back / Dancing master / Fallen angel / Love is a heart attack / Too late the hero. *(cd-iss. Mar97 on 'Repertoire'; RR 4634)*
Dec 81. (7") **TALK DIRTY. /** | - | |

KEITH MOON

	Polydor	M.C.A.
Apr 75. (lp) *(2442 134)* <2136> **TWO SIDES OF THE MOON** | | |
– Crazy like a fox / Solid gold / Don't worry baby / One night stand / The kid's are alright / Move over Ms. L / Teenage idol / Back door Sally / In my life / Together.
May 75. (7") *(2058 584)* **DON'T WORRY BABY. / TOGETHER** | | - |
May 75. (7") <40316> **DON'T WORRY BABY. / TEENAGE IDOL** | - | |
Jul 75. (7") <40387> **MOVE OVER MS. L. / SOLID GOLD** | - | |
Sep 75. (7") <40433> **CRAZY LIKE A FOX. / IN MY LIFE** | - | |

WILCO (see under ⇒ UNCLE TUPELO)

WILDHEARTS

Formed: London, England … 1989 by Northern-born guitarist GINGER, guitarist CJ (CHRIS JAGDHAR), vocalist SNAKE, bassist JULIAN and drummer STIDI (ANDREW STIDOLPH): all veterans of the late 80's hard-rock/glam-metal scene. STIDI and SNAKE subsequently dropped out the following year, GINGER taking over lead vocal duties, while a guy called PAT filled in on drums prior to BAM (of DOGS D'AMOUR fame) grabbing the sticks. By the summer of '91, a new line-up introduced 19 year-old DANNY McCORMICK to the proceedings and after difficulties with their initial record label, 'Atco', they signed to 'East West' (GINGER would later slate them at most opportunities). The following year, The WILDHEARTS were finally on their hard-rockin' way with the much-touted, 'MONDO-AKIMBO-A-GO-GO', an EP that was premiered while supporting their mates, The MANIC STREET PREACHERS. Like a punk/metal fusion of The RUTS, The CULT or The MANICS, GINGER and Co. delivered a mini-set, 'DON'T BE HAPPY… JUST WORRY' (a play on words from a Bobby McFerrin hit!), featuring the gorefest, 'SPLATTERMANIA'. Slagging everyone from IZZY STRADLIN of GUNS N' ROSES (he chucked them off his tour after only one gig!) to their producer, Simon Efeny, the wild ones toasted the release of their first full-length effort, 'EARTH VS THE WILDHEARTS' (1993), a set that saw the return of STIDI. The record managed to scrape into the UK Top 50, aided by some loveable tracks such as 'GREETINGS FROM SHITSVILLE', 'TV TAN' and a near Top 30 hit, 'CAFFEINE BOMB'. Much of 1994 was spent in personnel turmoil, STIDI was substituted by RITCH BATTERSBY, while CJ was in and out of the band more times than even he could recall. McCORMACK too had his moments, the hardy bassman dislocating his knee during their first number at the Reading Festival, while six months later, he smashed the computer of a Kerrang! journalist, who had said he was about to leave the band. Meanwhile, at the start of '95, a couple of singles had torn into the UK charts, 'IF LIFE IS LIKE A LOVE BANK I WANT A OVERDRAFT' and 'I WANNA GO WHERE THE PEOPLE GO', the latter one of the many highlights on their glorious Top 10 "comeback" album, 'P.H.U.Q.'. CJ's departure had caused a few problems, none more so than when interim (ex-SENSELESS THINGS) guitarist MARK KEDS was posted missing in Japan causing the band to cancel a Phoenix Festival spot; they subsequently found JEFF STREATFIELD. Growing hostility between them and their record company (who issued the 'FISHING FOR LUCKIES' set just one too many times), led to The WILDHEARTS branching out on their own label, 'Round', issuing two hit singles, 'SICK OF DRUGS' and 'RED LIGHT – GREEN LIGHT' in '96. Late the following year, and now on 'Mushroom' records, the group released a couple of Top 30 singles, 'ANTHEM' and 'URGE', which surprisingly didn't push up the sales of third album proper, 'ENDLESS, NAMELESS'. • **Songwriters:** GINGER, except some by others. • **Trivia:** In 1993, the group featured in a Channel 4 play, 'Comics'.

Album rating: DON'T BE HAPPY… JUST WORRY (*6) / EARTH VERSUS THE WILDHEARTS (*6) / P.H.U.Q. (*8) / THE BEST OF THE WILDHEARTS compilation (*8) / ENDLESS, NAMELESS (*5)

GINGER (b.DAVID WALLS, 17 Dec'64, South Shields, England) – vocals, guitar (ex-QUIREBOYS) / **BAM** – drums (ex-DOGS D'AMOUR) / **CJ (CHRIS JAGDHAR)** – guitar, vocals (ex-TATTOOED LOVE BOYS) / **DANNY McCORMACK** (b.28 Feb'72, South Shields) – bass, vocals (ex-ENERGETIC KRUSHER)

	East West	Atlantic
Mar 92. (12"ep/12"white-ep/cd-ep) *(YZ 669 T/TX/CD)* **MONDO-AKIMBO-A-GO-GO**
– (Nothing ever changes but the) Shoes / Turning American / Crying over nothing / Liberty cap.
Nov 92. (2xm-cd/c/2x12"m-lp) *(4509 91202-2/-4/-1)* **DON'T BE HAPPY… JUST WORRY**
– (above 4 tracks; with 4 new ones:-) Splattermania / Weekend (5 days long) / etc. *(cd w/ anti-dance mixes of 'MONDO…') (re-iss. Apr 94 cd/c; 4509 96067-2/-4)*

—— **ANDREW 'STIDI' STIDOLPH** – drums; returned to repl. BAM who returned to DOGS D'AMOUR

Sep 93. (cd/c/lp) *(4509 93201-2/-4/-1)* **EARTH VERSUS THE WILDHEARTS** | 46 | |
– Greetings from Shitsville / TV tan / Everlone / Shame on me / Loveshit / The miles away girl / My baby is a headf*** / Suckerpunch / News of the world / Love u til I don't. *(cd+=/c+=)* – Drinking about life. *(re-iss. Feb94 cd/c; 4509 94859-2/-4)*
Oct 93. (7"brown) *(YZ 773)* **GREETINGS FROM SHITSVILLE. / THE BULLSHIT GOES ON** | | |
Nov 93. (7"pic-d/c-s) *(YZ 784 P/C)* **TV TAN. / SHOW A LITTLE EMOTION** | 53 | |
(12"+=/cd-s+=) (YZ 784 T/CD) – Dangerlust / Down on London.

—— **RITCH BATTERSBY** (b.RICHARD, 29 Jun'68, Birmingham, England) – drums (ex-RADIO MOSCOW) repl. STIDI

Feb 94. (7"green/c-s) *(YZ 794/+C)* **CAFFEINE BOMB / GIRLFRIENDS CLOTHES** | 31 | |
(12"+=/cd-s+=) (YZ 794 T/CD) – Shut your fuckin' mouth and use your fuckin' brain / And the bullshit goes on.

—— added on tour **WILL DOWNING** – keyboards (ex-GRIP) on tour

Jun 94. (etched10"ep/c-ep/cd-ep) *(YZ 828 TE/C/CD)* **SUCKERPUNCH / BEAUTIFUL THING YOU. / TWO-WAY IDIOT MIRROR / 29 x THE PAIN** | 38 | |

—— (Jul'94) temp **DEVON TOWNSEND** – guitar (ex-STEVE VAI) repl. CJ who formed, although only briefly, HONEYCRACK. He returned for the Reading Festival August 1994 before taking WILL to the aforementioned outfit

Dec 94. (mail order m-cd) *(4509 99039-2)* **FISHING FOR LUCKIES** | - | - |
– Sky babies / Inglorious / Do the channel bop / Shizophronic / Geordie in wonderland / If life is like a love bank I want an overdraft.
Jan 95. (10"ep/c-ep/cd-ep/s-cd-ep) *(YZ 874 TEX/C/CD/CDX)* **IF LIFE IS LIKE A LOVE BANK I WANT AN OVERDRAFT / GEORDIE IN WONDERLAND. / HATE THE WORLD DAY / FIRE UP** | 31 | |
Apr 95. (10"ep/c-ep/cd-ep/s-cd-ep) *(YZ 923 TEX/C/CD/CDX)* **I WANNA GO WHERE THE PEOPLE GO / SHANDY BANG. / CAN'T DO RIGHT FOR DOING WRONG / GIVE THE GIRL A GUN** | 16 | |
May 95. (cd/c/lp)(s-cd) *(0630 10404-2/10653-4/10654-1)(0630 10437-2)* **P.H.U.Q.** | 6 | |
– I wanna go where the people go / V-day / Rust in lust / Baby strange / Nita nitro / Jonesing for Jones / Woah shit, you got through / Cold patootie tango / Caprice / Be my drug / Naivety play / In Lilly's garden / Getting it.

—— **MARK KEDS** – guitar (ex-SENSELESS THINGS) finally repl. C.J.

Jul 95. (10"ep/c-ep/cd-ep/cd-ep) *(YZ 967 TEX/C/CD/CDX)* **JUST IN LUST / MINDSLIDE. / FRIEND FOR FIVE MINUTES / S.I.N. (IN SIN)** | 28 | |

—— **JEF STREATFIELD** (b. 8 Jun'71, Southampton, England) – guitar repl. KEDS who went AWOL in July

Nov 95. (cd/c)(lp) *(0630 14855-2/-4)(0630 14888-1)* **FISHING FOR MORE LUCKIES** | | - |

—— Disbanded at the end of '95, although they quickly reformed.

	Round-East West	Warners
Apr 96. (c-ep/cd-ep) *(WILD 1 C/CD)* **SICK OF DRUGS / UNDERKILL / BAD TIME TO BE HAVING A BAD TIME / SKY CHASER HIGH** | 14 | |
May 96. (3D-cd/c/d-lp) *(0630 14855-2/-4/-1)* **FISHING FOR LUCKIES** (re-issue from late '94) | 16 | |
– Inglorious / Sick of drugs / Red light – green light / Schitzophonic / Soul searching on Planet Earth / Do the channel bop / Mood swings & roundabouts / In like Flynn / Sky babies / Nite songs.
Jun 96. (7"ep/c-ep/cd-ep) *(WILD 2/+C/CD)* **RED LIGHT – GREEN LIGHT EP** | 30 | |
– Red light – green light / Got it on Tuesday / Do anything / The British all-American homeboy crowd.
Nov 96. (cd/c) *(0630 17212-2/-4)* **THE BEST OF THE WILDHEARTS** (compilation) | | |
– I wanna go where the people go / T.V. tan / Sick of drugs / 29 x the pain / Caffeine bomb / Geordie in wonderland / Suckerpunch / Just in lust / Greetings from Shitsville / In Lilly's garden / My baby is a headfuck / If life is like a love bank I want an overdraft / Nothing ever changes but the shoes / Red light – green light / Beautiful me, beautiful you / Splattermania.

	Mushroom	Mushroom
Aug 97. (7") *(MUSH 6S)* **ANTHEM. / HE'S A WHORE** | 21 | - |
(cd-s) (MUSH 6CD) – ('A'side) / So good to be back home / Time to let you go.
(cd-s) (MUSH 6CDX) – ('A'side) / The song formerly known as / White lies.
Oct 97. (7") *(MUSH 14S)* **URGE. / FUCAZI (DO THE FAKE)** | 26 | - |
(cd-s+=) (MUSH 14CDS) – Kill me to death.
(cd-s) (MUSH 14CDX) –
Oct 97. (cd/c) *(MUSH 13 CD/MC/LP)* **ENDLESS, NAMELESS** | 41 | - |
– Junkenstein / Nurse maximum / Anthem / Urge / Pissjoy / Soundog Babylon / Now is the colour / Heroin / Why you lie / Thunderfuck.

—— split after above, DANNY formed The YO-YO'S (with TOM, NEIL and BLADS)

in '98, releasing their debut single, 'OUT OF MY MIND', in December. GINGER is currently in the band, SUPERSHIT 666, alongside DREGEN (Backyard Babies) and NICKE ANDERSON (Hellacopters)

– compilations, etc. –

Mar 98.	(cd/d-lp) *Kuro Neko; (NKEK/+LP 3)* **ANARCHIC AIRWAVES – THE WILDHEARTS AT THE BBC**	☐	-
Sep 98.	(cd) *Kuro Neko; (KNEK 4)* **LANDMINES & PANTOMIMES – THE LAST OF THE WILDHEARTS . . .?**	☐	-

Hank WILLIAMS

Born: HIRAM WILLIAMS, 17 Sep'23, Garland, Alabama, USA. From the age of seven, WILLIAMS was raised by his domineering mother, Lillybelle after his father had finally left the recession-hit household having suffered one too many beatings at the hands of his wife (what about zero tolerance, eh~?!). HANK, together with his mother and older sister, Irene, subsequently moved to Georgiana, where he bunked school to do odd jobs and learn guitar from an older negro friend, Tee Tot. In 1937, the family moved again, this time to Montgomery, where Lily opened a boarding house. There, she took in many male guests, too many for HANK's liking and he soon took off for a singing career on local radio. Even in his teens, WILLIAMS was drinking heavily, mainly to alleviate the pain of a chronic back ailment. He subsequently formed a band, The DRIFTING COWBOYS, who toured the Honky Tonk saloon bars as the 30's turned into the 40's. When the US of A decided to join the Second World War, HANK was fortunate enough not to be called up due to his bad back and he soon met soon-to-be divorced Audrey, whom he married in 1944. It was she who pestered publisher FRED ROSE to listen to him singing in a hotel lobby. The famous partner of ROY ACUFF was duly impressed and in 1946, after the war had ended, he was asked to scout out a new country star by 'Sterling' records. ROSE, of course, sent them HANK, who shortly after cut his first discs (see below). Three singles later, he was taken by Frank Walker to the new 'M.G.M.' stable in 1947, where they released 'MOVE IT ON OVER'. Walker then had him booked into the Louisiana Hayride, a weekly country radio show that was second only to The Grand Ole Opry. Troubles at home took precedence, however, as his wife and mother argued about his late night drinking binges. It wasn't only booze that was taking him over but a cocktail of uppers and downers. Early in 1949, he entered the country charts with standard, 'LOVESICK BLUES', propelling him overnight to Opry status. Following the birth of his son, HANK Jnr., he brought the house down at the Opry and made history with six encores, the country charts littered with HANK's songs over the period 1949-1950. Around this time, he had reluctantly agreed to kickstart his wife's singing career by convincing 'Decca' (who had earlier turned him down!) to record and release two of her songs in addition to two from his own pen; at the time HANK was writing with friend Vic McAlpin although he subsequently bought out the latter's half credit for 500 dollars. The following year, the rising country star co-authored a book, 'HOW TO WRITE COUNTRY AND FOLK MUSIC TO SELL' while Tony Bennett topped the pop charts with HANK's 'COLD COLD HEART'. In 1952 his relationship with Audrey had deteriorated to such an extent that he was drinking himself into oblivion and turning up on stage completely out of it. When Audrey and Hank Jnr. moved out of the family home, his drinking took over completely. By the time he returned to the studio in June of that year, however, the songs were coming thick and fast; classics 'JAMBALAYA', 'YOUR CHEATIN' HEART' and 'YOU WIN AGAIN' were all recorded during these sessions, demonstrating the troubled WILLIAMS at his heartbreaking best. Although he was fired from The Grand Ole Opry shows in August he returned to the Hayride to promote his new C&W No.1, 'JAMBALAYA'. He also met a young divorcee, Billie Jean, whom he married in October. He tried desperately to beat his alcoholism by spending time at a detox sanitarium, all to no avail. Tragically, in the early hours of the 1st January 1953, his 17 year-old chauffeur Charles Carr found him dead in the back seat. Two days previously, while his plane was being delayed due to bad weather, he had downed a bottle of spirits while taking morphine in his Knoxville hotel room. Desperate to make an Ohio gig, he had phoned Carr to pick his Cadillac up and drive him there. Mystery then, shrouded his death, when a rushed coroner gave a verdict as heart failure, although many still think it was an attempted suicide slow to hit fatal impact. Several others had also suspected murder, although this seems unlikely. Meanwhile, his record company 'M.G.M.' announced he was killed in a car crash! It wasn't laid to rest there, as even at his well attended funeral (estimated 20,000+), he wasn't even buried in his plot as it was too small!. Instead they dug up two nearby graves and put him in there!. A few days later, legal battles ensued between the unusual alliance of his ex-wife Audrey and his mother Lily, who fought out court battles with his recent wife Billie Jean. After around 20 pain-staking years (although not for their lawyers), Billie Jean won his estate. To make matters even crazier, a biopic film 'YOUR CHEATIN' HEART' was released early in 1965, starring GEORGE HAMILTON as HANK; his son HANK WILLIAMS Jnr. sang the soundtrack of his father's material. Billie Jean duly sued 'M.G.M.', claiming it portrayed her as a slut, although this was hardly surprising as ex-wife Audrey was employed as the film's technical advisor! HANK Jnr. carried on with his own solo career over the next 30 years, recording many of his father's classics (grandson HANK WILLIAMS III has also emerged in the late 90's!). Leaving this sometimes troubled 29-year legacy aside, the late great HANK has been a towering inspiration for many, including JERRY LEE LEWIS, BOB DYLAN, JOHN FOGERTY, BRUCE SPRINGSTEEN and even THE THE (aka MATT JOHNSON) who released a whole album attributed to the great man. Countless other artists have also made vast sums of money after hitting the pop charts with his songs. Here are a list:- JAMBALAYA (ON THE BAYOU) for (Fats Domino) (Carpenters) (John Fogerty) / YOU WIN AGAIN for (Fats Domino) / YOUR CHEATING HEART + TAKE THESE CHAINS FROM MY HEART for (Ray Charles) / HEY GOOD LOOKIN' for (Bo Diddley) / etc, etc. Many rock historians and commentators hold that HANK's premature demise represented the first bonafide rock'n'roll death, a grisly portent to the countless drug/alcohol deaths during rock's 60's/70's heyday.

Best CD compilation: THE ORIGINAL SINGLES COLLECTION box-set (*9)

HANK WILLIAMS – vocals, acoustic guitar with session people

—— (all records before his death were 78 r.p.m.)

		not iss.	Sterling
Dec 46.	(78) *<201>* **CALLING YOU. / NEVER AGAIN WILL I KNOCK ON YOUR DOOR**	-	☐
Dec 46.	(78) *<204>* **WEALTH WON'T SAVE YOUR SOUL. / WHEN GOD COMES AND (F)GATHERS HIS JEWELS**	-	☐
Mar 47.	(78) *<208>* **I DON'T CARE (IF TOMORROW NEVER COMES). / MY LOVE FOR YOU (HAS TURNED TO HATE)**	-	☐
May 47.	(78) *<210>* **HONKY TONKIN'. / PAN AMERICAN**	-	☐

		M.G.M.	M.G.M.
Jul 47.	(78) *<10033>* **MOVE IT ON OVER. / LAST NIGHT I HEARD YOU CRYING IN YOUR SLEEP**	-	☐
Sep 47.	(78) *<10073>* **FLY TROUBLE. / ON THE BANKS OF THE OLD PONTCHARTRAIN**	-	☐
Feb 48.	(78) *<10124>* **ROOTIE TOOTIE. / MY SWEET LOVE AIN'T AROUND**	-	☐
Apr 48.	(78) *<10171>* **HONKY TONKIN'. / I'LL BE A BACHELOR TILL I DIE**	-	☐
Jun 48.	(78) *<10212>* **I'M A LONG GONE DADDY. / BLUES COME AROUND**	-	☐
Jul 48.	(78) *<10226>* **PAN AMERICAN. / I DON'T CARE IF TOMORROW NEVER COMES**	-	☐
Sep 48.	(78) *<10271>* **I SAW THE LIGHT. / SIX MORE MILES (TO THE GRAVEYARD)**	-	☐
Dec 48.	(78) *<10328>* **MANSION ON THE HILL. / I CAN'T GET YOU OFF MY MIND**	-	☐
Feb 49.	(78) *<10352>* **LOVESICK BLUES. / NEVER AGAIN WILL I KNOCK ON YOUR DOOR**	-	☐
Apr 49.	(78) *<10401>* **WEDDING BLUES. / I'VE JUST TOLD MAMA GOODBYE**	-	☐
May 49.	(78; by "HANK AND AUDREY") *<10434>* **DEAR BROTHER. / LOST ON THE RIVER**	-	☐
Jul 49.	(78) **MIND YOUR OWN BUSINESS. / THERE'LL BE NO TEARDROPS TONIGHT**	-	☐
Sep 49.	(78) *<10506>* **YOU'RE GONNA CHANGE (OR I'M GONNA LEAVE). / LOST HIGHWAY**	-	☐
Nov 49.	(78) *<10560>* **MY BUCKET'S GOT A HOLE IN IT. / I'M SO LONESOME I COULD CRY**	-	☐
Jan 50.	(78) *<10609>* **I JUST DON'T LIKE THIS KIND OF LIVING. / MAY YOU NEVER BE ALONE**	-	☐
Feb 50.	(78; as LUKE THE DRIFTER) *<10630>* **THE FUNERAL. / BEYOND THE SUNSET**	-	☐

Late in 1949, his wife AUDREY WILLIAMS signed to 'Decca' and released 2 singles with the aid of HANK. These were 'I LIKE THAT KIND'. / 'MY TIGHT WAD DADDY', and his songs 'HOW CAN YOU REFUSE HIM NOW'. / HELP ME UNDERSTAND'.

		not iss.	Sterling
Mar 50.	(78) *(MGM 269)* **LOVESICK BLUES. / WEDDING BELLS**	☐	-
Mar 50.	(78) *<10645>* **LONG GONE LONESOME BLUES. / MY SON CALLS ANOTHER MAN DADDY**	-	☐
May 50.	(78) *<10696>* **WHY DON'T YOU LOVE ME. / A HOUSE WITHOUT LOVE**	-	☐
Jun 50.	(78; as LUKE THE DRIFTER) *10718>* **EVERYTHING'S OKAY. / TOO MANY PARTIES**	-	☐
Aug 50.	(78) *<10760>* **THEY'L NEVER TAKE HER LOVE AWAY FROM ME. / WHY SHOULD WE TRY ANYMORE**	-	☐
Oct 50.	(78; as "LUKE THE DRIFTER") *<10806>* **NO NO JOE. / HELP ME UNDERSTAND**	-	☐
Oct 50.	(78; as "HANK AND AUDREY") *<10813>* **I HEARD MY MOTHER PRAYING FOR ME. / JESUS REMEMBERED ME**	-	☐
Oct 50.	(78) *<10832>* **MOANIN' THE BLUES. / NOBODY'S LONESOME FOR ME**	-	☐
Dec 50.	(78) *<10904>* **DEAR JOHN. / COLD, COLD HEART**	-	☐
Mar 51.	(78; as LUKE THE DRIFTER) **JUST WAITIN'. / MEN WITH BROKEN HEARTS**	-	☐
Mar 51.	(78) *(MGM 381)* **MOANIN' THE BLUES. / BLUES COME AROUND**	☐	-
Apr 51.	(78) *<10961>* **HOWLIN' AT THE MOON. / I CAN'T HELP IT (IF I'M STILL IN LOVE WITH YOU)**	-	☐
Jun 51.	(78) *<11000>* **HEY GOOD LOOKIN'. / MY HEART WOULD KNOW**	-	☐
Jun 51.	(78) *(MGM 405)* **DEAR JOHN. / FLY TROUBLE**	☐	-
Jul 51.	(78; as LUKE THE DRIFTER) *<11017>* **I'VE BEEN DOWN THAT ROAD BEFORE. / I DREAMED ABOUT MAMA LAST NIGHT**	-	☐
Sep 51.	(78) *<11054>* **LONESOME WHISTLER. / CRAZY HEART**	-	☐
Nov 51.	(78) *<11100>* **BABY WE'RE REALLY IN LOVE. / I'D STILL WANT YOU**	-	☐
Dec 51.	(78; as LUKE THE DRIFTER) *<11120>* **RAMBLIN' MAN. / PICTURE FROM LIFE'S OTHER SIDE**	-	☐
Nov 51.	(78) *(MGM 454)* **HEY, GOOD LOOKIN'. / HOWLING AT THE MOON**	☐	-
Dec 51.	(78) *(MGM 459)* **COLD, COLD HEART. / I'M A LONG GONE DADDY**	☐	-

Feb 52. (78) *(MGM 471)* **I CAN'T HELP IT (IF I'M STILL IN LOVE WITH YOU). / BABY, WE'RE REALLY IN LOVE** □ | -

Mar 52. (78) *<11202>* **HALF AS MUCH. / LET'S TURN BACK THE YEARS** - | □

Mar 52. (78) *(MGM 483)* **WHY DON'T YOU LOVE ME. / I'D STILL WANT YOU** □ | -

May 52. (78) *(MGM 505)* *<11160>* **HONKY-TONK BLUES. / I'M SORRY FOR YOU, MY FRIEND** □ | Feb 52

Jul 52. (78) *(MGM 527)* **HALF AS MUCH. / LONG GONE LONESOME BLUES** □

Jul 52. (78) *<11283>* **JAMBALAYA (ON THE BAYOU). / WINDOW SHOPPING** □

Aug 52. (78; as LUKE THE DRIFTER) *<11309>* **WHY DON'T YOU MAKE UP YOUR MIND. / BE CAREFUL OF STONES THAT YOU THROW** □

Sep 52. (78) *<11318>* **SETTIN' THE WOODS ON FIRE. / YOU WIN AGAIN** □ | -

Sep 52. (78) *(MGM 553)* **NOBODY'S LONESOME FOR ME. / MIND YOUR OWN BUSINESS** □ | -

Oct 52. (10"lp) *(D 105)* **HANK WILLIAMS SINGS** □
– A house without love / Wedding bells / The mansion on the hill / Wealth won't save your soul / I saw the light / Six more miles (to the graveyard) / Lost highway / I've just told mama goodbye.

Oct 52. (78) *(MGM 566)* **JAMBALAYA (ON THE BAYOU). / SETTIN' THE WODS ON FIRE** □ | -

Dec 52. (78) *(SP 1016)* *<11366>* **I'LL NEVER GET OUT OF THIS WORLD ALIVE. / I COULD NEVER BE ASHAMED OF YOU** □ | Oct 52

—— tragically the above 'A'side was poignantly true, when, in the early hours of New Year's Day 1953 he was found dead

– posthumous work & compilations, etc. –

Note; below released on 'MGM' until otherwise stated

Mar 53. (7")(78) *(SP 1034)(MGM 609)* **KAW-LIGA. / TAKE THESE CHAINS FROM MY HEART** □

May 53. (78) *(MGM 630)* **I SAW THE LIGHT. /** In Memory Of Hank Williams (by "Arthur 'Guitar Boogie' Smith) □

Jul 53. (7")(78) *(SP 1049)(MGM 652)* **RAMBLIN' MAN. / I WON'T BE HOME NO MORE** □

Sep 53. (7")(78) *(SP 1048)(MGM 666)* **MY BUCKET'S GOT A HOLE IN IT. / LET'S TURN BACK THE YEARS** □

Oct 53. (10"lp) *(D 119)* **HANK WILLIAMS AS 'LUKE THE DRIFTER'** □

Oct 53. (78) *(MGM 678)* **YOU WIN AGAIN. / WINDOW SHOPPING** □

Jan 54. (7")(78) *(SP 1067)(MGM 704)* **WEARY BLUES (FROM WAITIN'). / I CAN'T ESCAPE FROM YOU** □

Apr 54. (7")(78) *(SP 1085)(MGM 733)* **THERE'LL BE NO TEARDROPS TONIGHT. / CRAZY HORSE** □

Oct 54. (7")(78) *(SP 1102)(MGM 768)* **I'M SATISFIED WITH YOU. / I AIN'T GOT NOTHIN' BUT TIME** □

Dec 54. (7"ep) *(MGM-EP 512)* **HANK WILLIAMS AND HIS DRIFTING COWBOYS** □

Feb 55. (78) *(MGM 799)* **I'M GONNA SING. / CALIFORNIA ZEPHYR** □

1955. (lp) **RAMBLIN' MAN** -
– Ramblin' man / Lonesome whistler / My son calls another man daddy / I just don't like this kind of livin' / I can't escape from you / Nobody's lonesome for me / Take these chains from my heart / Why don't you love me? / I can't help it (if I'm still in love with you) / There'll be no teardrops tonight / You're gonna change (or I'm gonna leave) / My heart would know.

Mar 56. (7"ep) *(MGM-EP 551)* **AS LUKE THE DRIFTER** □ | -
– Why don't you make up your mind? / I've been down that road before / Just waitin' / Everything's okay.

Apr 56. (78) *(MGM 896)* **YOUR CHEATIN' HEART. / A TEARDROP ON A ROSE** □

Sep 56. (7",78) *(MGM 921)* **I WISH I HAD A NICKEL. / THERE'S NO ROOM IN MY HEART (FOR THE BLUES)** □

Sep 56. (10"lp) *(D 137)* **HANK WILLIAMS MEMORIAL ALBUM** □ | 1953
– You win again / Cold cold heart / I could never be ashamed of you / Settin' the woods on fire / Hey, good lookin' / Kaw-liga / Half as much.

Oct 56. (7"ep) *(MGM-EP 569)* **I SAW THE LIGHT (No.1)** □ | -
– How can you refuse him now / When God comes and gathers his jewels / Jesus remembered me / A house of gold.

Nov 56. (7",78) *(MGM 931)* **BLUE LOVE (IN MY HEART). / SINGING WATERFALL** □

Jan 57. (7") *(MGM 942)* **LAY DOWN BLUES. / MY SWEET LOVE AIN'T AROUND** □

Feb 57. (7"ep) *(MGM-EP 582)* **HONKY TONKIN'** □ | -
– Honky tonkin' / Howlin' at the Moon / I ain't got nothin' but time / Better keep it on your mind.

Mar 57. (7") *(MGM 957)* **ROOTIE TOOTIE. / LONESOME WHISTLE** □ | -

Apr 57. (10"lp) *(D 144)* **MOANIN' THE BLUES** □
– Someday you'll call my name / Weary blues / Alone and forsaken / Moanin' the blues / I'm so lonely I could cry / Honky tonk blues / Lovesick blues / The blues come around / I'm a lone gone daddy / Long gone lonesome blues.

Jun 57. (7"ep) *(MGM-EP 608)* **I SAW THE LIGHT (No.2)** □ | -
– I'm gonna sing / Message to my mother / Thank God / The angel of death.

Sep 57. (7") *(MGM 966)* **LEAVE ME ALONE WITH THE BLUES. / WITH TEARS IN MY EYES** □

Sep 57. (7"ep) *(MGM-EP 614)* **MY BUCKET'S GOT A HOLE IN IT (HONKY TONK BLUES)** □ | -
– My bucket's got a hole in it / Baby, we're really in love / Honky tonk blues / I'll never get out of this world alive.

Mar 58. (7"ep) *(MGM-EP 639)* **SONGS FOR A BROKEN HEART (No.1)** □ | -
– Nobody's lonesome for me / You win again / Why don't you love me / Take these chains from my heart.

Mar 58. (10"lp) *(D 150)* **SING ME A BLUE SONG** □ | -
– Lay down blues / May you never be alone / I won't be home no more / Why should we try anymore / Blue love / My sweet love ain't around / (Last night) I heard you crying in your sleep / Mind your own business / They'll never take her love from me / Singing waterfall.

May 58. (7"ep) *(MGM-EP 649)* **SONGS FOR A BROKEN HEART (No.2)** □ | -
– I'd still want you / I'm sorry for you my friend / I could never be ashamed of you / I can't escape from you.

Nov 58. (10"lp) *(D 154)* **THE IMMORTAL HANK WILLIAMS** □ | -
– There's no room in my heart / Waltz of the mind / With tears in my eyes / I wish I had a nickel / California Zephyr / Please don't let me love you / I'm satisfied with you / No one will ever know / Faded love and winter roses / First fall of snow.

Nov 58. (7"ep) *(MGM-EP 675)* **HANK'S LAMENT** □
– I can't help it / Dear John / Let's turn back the years / A teardrop on a rose.

Jul 59. (lp) *(C 784)* **THE UNFORGETTABLE HANK WILLIAMS** □ | -
– I just don't like this kind of living / My love for you (has turned to hate) / Dear brother / Never again (will I knock on your door) / I can't get out of my mind / Rootie tootie / I'll be a bachelor boy till I die / My son calls another man daddy / Lonesome whistle / Lost on the river / Mother is gone / Ready to go home.

Jan 60. (7"ep) *(MGM-EP 710)* **THE UNFORGETTABLE HANK WILLIAMS** □ | -

Apr 60. (lp) *(C 811)* **THE LONESOME SOUND OF HANK WILLIAMS** □ | -

Jun 60. (7"ep) *(MGM-EP 726)* **THE UNFORGETTABLE HANK WILLIAMS No.2** □ | -

Oct 60. (7"ep) *(MGM-EP 732)* **THE UNFORGETTABLE HANK WILLIAMS No.3** □ | -

Oct 60. (lp) *(C 834)* **WAIT FOR THE LIGHTS TO SHINE** □ | -

Sep 61. (7"ep) *(MGM-EP 757)* **HANK WILLIAMS' FAVOURITES** □ | -

Oct 62. (lp) *(C 893)* **ON STAGE (live)** □ | -

Feb 63. (7"ep) *(MGM-EP 770)* **THE AUTHENTIC SOUND OF THE COUNTRY HITS** □ | -

Nov 63. (lp) *(C 956)* **THE SPIRIT OF HANK WILLIAMS** □ | -

Oct 65. (lp; with HANK WILLIAMS Jnr.) *(C 1008)* **SINGING TOGETHER (dubbed)** □ | -

May 66. (7") *(MGM 1309)* **I'M SO LONESOME I COULD CRY. / YOU WIN AGAIN** □ | -

Aug 66. (7") *(MGM 1322)* **KAW-LIGA. / LET'S TURN BACK THE TEARS** □ | -

Nov 66. (lp) *(C 8019)* **MAY YOU NEVER BE ALONE** □ | -

Nov 66. (lp) *(C 8020)* **IN MEMORY OF HANK WILLIAMS** □ | -

Nov 66. (lp) *(C 8021)* **I'M BLUE INSIDE** □ | -

Nov 66. (lp) *(C 8022)* **LUKE THE DRIFTER** □ | -

Nov 66. (lp) *(C 8023)* **THE MANY MOODS OF HANK WILLIAMS** □ | -

Feb 67. (lp; mono/stereo) *(C/CS 8031)* **THE LEGEND LIVES ANEW** (over-dubbed w/ strings) □ | -

May 67. (lp; mono/stereo) *(C/CS 8038)* **MORE HANK WILLIAMS AND STRINGS** (as above w/ strings) □ | -

Jun 67. (lp) *(C 8040)* **LOVE SONGS, COMEDY AND HYMNS** □ | -

Feb 68. (lp; mono/stereo) *(C/CS 8057)* **I WON'T BE HOME NO MORE** (over-dubbed w/ strings) □ | -

Apr 68. (lp) *M.F.P.;* **HANK WILLIAMS** □ | -

May 68. (lp; mono/stereo) *(C/CS 8075)* **HANK WILLIAMS AND STRINGS VOL.3** (over-dubbed w/ strings) □ | -

Feb 70. (lp) *(CS 8114)* **THE ESSENTIAL HANK WILLIAMS** □ | -

Oct 70. (lp) *(2352 053)* **GREATEST HITS VOL.1** □ | -
(re-iss. Jun81 on 'Polydor' lp/(c; 2482 505)(3192 631) (re-iss. May88 on 'Grand Canyon' lp/c; 3/6 5001)

Apr 71. (lp) *(2353 073)* **GREATEST HITS VOL.2** □ | -
(re-iss. Jun81 on 'Polydor' lp/c; 2482 506)(3192 632) (re-iss. May88 on 'Grand Canyon' lp/c; 3/6 5002)

Mar 72. (lp) *(2315 077)* **THE LAST PICTURE SHOW (soundtrack)** □ | -

Jun 73. (d-lp) *(2683 016)* **MEMORIAL ALBUM** □ | -

Jul 74. (d-lp) *(2683 046)* **HANK WILLIAMS ON STAGE (live featuring AUDREY)** □ | -

Nov 75. (lp) *(2353 118)* **THE COLLECTOR'S HANK WILLIAMS** □ | -

Sep 76. (lp) *(2353 128)* *<MG1 5019>* **LIVE AT THE GRAND OLE OPRY (live)** □ | -
(re-iss. Oct86; same as US)

Jan 78. (d-lp/d-c) *(2683 071)(3271 302)* **40 GREATEST HITS** □ | -
– Baby, we're really in love / Cold, cold heart / Crazy heart / Dear John / Half as much / Hey, good lookin' / Honky tonk blues / Howlin' at the Moon / I can't help it / I just don't like this kind of living / I saw the light / I won't be home no more / I'll never get out of this world alive / I'm so lonesome I could cry / I'm sorry for you my friend / Jambalaya (on the bayou) / Kaw-liga / Lonesome whistle / Long gone lonesome blues / Lost highway / Lovesick blues / A mansion on the hill / Mind your own business / Moanin' the blues / Move it on over / My bucket's got a hole in it / My son calls another man daddy / Nobody's lonesome for me / Ramblin' man / Settin' the woods on fire / Take these chains from my heart / They'll never take her love from me / Weary blues / Wedding bells / Why don't you love me / Why should we try anymore / Window shopping / You win again / Your cheatin' heart / You're gonna change. (d-cd iss.Mar89 on 'Polydor'; 821 233-2)

May 78. (lp) *Polydor; (2315 397)* **THE COLLECTOR'S HANK WILLIAMS VOL.2** □ | -

Jan 79. (lp) *Westwood; (WRS 140)* **THE BEST OF HANK WILLIAMS' ORIGINAL DRIFTING COWBOYS** □ | -

May 79. (6xlp-box) *World Service; (SM 551-556)* **THE LEGENDARY HANK WILLIAMS** □ | -
—— In 1979, 'R.C.A.' made a various artists d-lp 'A TRIBUTE TO . . .'

Aug 80. (lp) *Polydor; (2315 419)* **THE COLLECTOR'S HANK WILLIAMS VOL.3** □ | -

Jul 81. (lp/c) *Polydor; (2391/3177 519)* **THE COLLECTOR'S HANK WILLIAMS VOL.4** □ | -

Aug 81. (lp) *K-Tel; (NE 1121)* **THE LEGENDARY HANK WILLIAMS** □ | -

Mar 83. (7"ep) *Arhoolie; <EP 548>* **HOME IN HEAVEN E.P.** - | □
– Home in Heaven / In my dreams / I'm going home / Mother is gone.

Jul 85. (lp) *Jambalaya; (CW 201)* **RARE RADIO BROADCASTS 1949** □ | -

Aug 85. (lp/c) *Contour; (CN/+4 2076)* **THE GREAT HITS OF HANK WILLIAMS** □ | -
(cd-iss. Jun89 on 'Pickwick'; PWK 114)

Apr 86. (lp/c) *Arcade; (ADAH/+C 446)* **VERY BEST OF HANK WILLIAMS** □ | -

May 86. (lp) *Jambalaya; (JAM 201)* **MORE RARE RADIO BROADCASTS VOL.1**   □   -

May 86. (lp) *Jambalaya; (JAM 202)* **MORE RARE RADIO BROADCASTS VOL.2**   □   -

Jul 86. (d-lp/c) *Polydor; (825554-1/-4)* **LOST HIGHWAY** (DECEMBER '48 – MARCH '49)   □   □
(cd-iss. Jan93)

Jul 86. (d-lp) *Polydor; (825557-1)* **I'M SO LONESOME I COULD CRY** (MARCH '49 – AUGUST '49)   □   □
(cd-iss. Jul90; 825577-2)

Jan 87. (lp/c/cd) *Deja Vu; (DVLP/DVMC 2081)* **THE HANK WILLIAMS COLLECTION (20 GOLDEN GREATS)**   □

Feb 87. (lp/c) *Jambalaya; (CW/JAM 202)* **HANK WILLIAMS & THE DRIFTING COWBOYS**   □

Mar 87. (lp/c) *Contour; (CN/+4 2084)* **THE VERY BEST OF HANK WILLIAMS VOL.1**   □   -
(cd-iss. Jun90 on 'Pickwick'; PWK 138)

1987. (cd) *Bescol; (CD 43)* **16 GREATEST HITS**   □   -

Sep 87. (c) *Timeless; (MC 1625)* **16 ORIGINAL HITS**   □   -

Dec 87. (d-lp) *Polydor; (831633-1)* **LONG GONE LONESOME BLUES** (AUGUST '49 – DECEMBER '50)   □   □
(cd-iss. Jan93; 831633-2)

Dec 87. (d-lp) *Polydor; (831636-1)* **HEY GOOD LOOKING** (DECEMBER '50 – JULY '51)   □   □
(cd-iss. Jan93; 831636-2)

Dec 87. (d-lp) *Polydor; (831749-1)* **LET'S TURN BACK THE YEARS** (JULY '51 – JUNE '52)   □   □
(cd-iss. Jan93; 831749-2)

Dec 87. (d-lp) *Polydor; (831752-1)* **I WON'T BE HOME NO MORE** (JUNE '52 – SEPTEMBER '52)   □   □

Jan 88. (d-lp/c) *Polydor; (825548-1/-4)* **I AIN'T GOT NOTHIN' BUT TIME**   □   □
(cd-iss. Mar90; 825548-2)

Jan 88. (d-lp) *Polydor; (823695-1)* **RARE TAKES AND RADIO CUTS**   □   □

Jan 88. (d-lp) *Polydor; (825551-1)* **LOVESICK BLUES**   □   -
(cd-iss. Mar90; 825551-2)

Jan 88. (d-lp) *Polydor; (827531-1)* **ON THE AIR**   □   -

Jun 88. (cd/c/lp) *Country Store; (CD/TC+/CST 50)* **HANK WILLIAMS**   □   -

Sep 89. (cd/c/lp) *A Touch Of Magic; (D/C+/ATOM 6)* **RADIO SHOWS**   □   -

Aug 90. (cd/c) *Graffiti; (GRCD/GRMC 14)* **THE GRAFFITI COLLECTION**   □   -

Mar 91. (d-cd/d-c) *Polydor; (847194-2/-4)* **THE ORIGINAL SINGLES COLLECTION . . . PLUS**   □   -

Jan 93. (c) *Country Music Foundation; (CMFC 006)* **JUST ME AND MY GUITAR**   □

Jan 93. (c) *Country Music Foundation; (CMFC 007)* **THE FIRST RECORDINGS**   □

Jan 93. (cd/c) *Country Music Foundation; (CMF CD/C 67)* **RARE DEMOS: FIRST TO LAST**   □   -

Jan 93. (cd; by HANK WILLIAMS Snr. & HANK WILLIAMS Jnr.) *Curb; <77552>* **THE BEST OF HANK & HANK**   -   □

Jul 93. (d-cd) *Polydor; (517862-2)* **THE HEALTH & HAPPINESS SHOWS (live)**   □   □

Oct 93. (cd/c) *Spectrum; (550099-2/-4)* **CHEATING HEARTS**   □   □

Jul 94. (cd) *Polydor; (811900-2)* **I SAW THE LIGHT**   □   □

Jul 94. (cd) *Polydor; (823293-2)* **24 GREATEST HITS VOL.1**   □   □

Jul 94. (cd) *Polydor; (823294-2)* **24 GREATEST HITS VOL.2**   □   □

Jul 94. (cd) *Polydor; (849575-2)* **THE BEST OF HANK WILLIAMS VOL.1**   □   □

Jan 96. (cd) *Polydor; (528037-2)* **ALONE AND FORSAKEN**   □   □

Nov 96. (cd) *Curb; <(CURCD 029)>* **MEN WITH BROKEN HEARTS (THREE HANKS)**   □   □

Jan 97. (cd/c) *Music; (CD6/MC7 053)* **LEGEND OF COUNTRY MUSIC**   □   □

Jan 98. (cd) *Blue Moon; (BMCD 3052)* **THE BEST RECORDINGS VOL.1**   □

Jan 98. (cd) *Blue Moon; (BMCD 3053)* **THE BEST RECORDINGS VOL.2**   □

Apr 98. (cd) *Polydor; (554381-2)* **THE BEST OF HANK WILLIAMS**   □

Sep 98. (10xcd-box) *Mercury; (536077-2)* **THE COMPLETE HANK WILLIAMS**   □

Mar 99. (cd) *Charly; (CPCD 8356)* **HONKY TONKIN'**   □   -

May 99. (cd/c) *Pulse; (PLS CD/MC 328)* **FAMOUS COUNTRY MUSIC MAKERS**   □   -

Jul 99. (d-cd; shared with WILLIE NELSON) *Music; (2CD 28002)* **COUNTRY LEGENDS (LIVE IN CONCERT)**   □

Sep 99. (3xcd-box) *Goldies; (GLD 25351)* **LOVESICK BLUES**   □   -

Oct 99. (d-cd) *Mercury; (546466-2)* **LIVE AT THE GRAND OLE OPRY (live)**   □   □

Nov 99. (4xcd-box) *Chrome Dreams; (ABCD 021)* **THE HANK WILLIAMS STORY**   □   -

Lucinda WILLIAMS

Born: 26 Jan '53, Lake Charles, Louisiana, USA. The daughter of an English lit prof/poet, WILLIAMS' childhood was spent in such diverse locations as Texas, Mexico City and the Chilean capital, Santiago. Influenced primarily by both the literature and music of the deep South, WILLIAMS began playing in her teens around the clubs of Houston (where the likes of TOWNE VAN ZANDT and GUY CLARK had founded a burgeoning folk-country scene) and Austin. By the release of her debut album, 'RAMBLIN' ON MY MIND' (1979), she was already on the way to becoming a seasoned performer and the record's trad country/blues standards – mainly borrowed from ROBERT JOHNSON, HANK WILLIAMS and MEMPHIS MINNIE – reflected her apprenticeship. In contrast, the following year's 'HAPPY WOMAN BLUES' consisted entirely of original material backed up by a full acoustic band.

After a brief flirtation with the Greenwich Village folk scene and a further period down South, she eventually settled in L.A. where she concentrated on writing, performing and building up a permanent band. Deflecting regular major label offers, WILLIAMS' insistence on full creative control finally led her to a deal with UK indie, 'Rough Trade', who issued the long awaited 'LUCINDA WILLIAMS' early in 1989. While the music married the unmistakable influence of L.A.'s rock'n'roll heart with her trademark take on rootsy Americana, many of the lyrics centred on her recent divorce (from the Long Ryders' GREG SOWDERS), and the likes of 'PASSIONATE KISSES' and 'THE NIGHT'S TOO LONG' made for compelling listening. The former track was later covered by MARY-CHAPIN CARPENTER while PATTI LOVELESS took the latter into the country charts. WILLIAMS herself sold her work by the sheer hard graft of touring rather than any singles success although her stock with critics and roots fans had never been higher. The collapse of 'Rough Trade' certainly didn't help raise her profile, however, and after a doomed dalliance with 'R.C.A.', she again signed to an indie label, 'Chameleon'. The result was 1992's 'SWEET OLD WORLD', a roots-rock masterclass which managed to be both accomplished and inventively diverse, even pulling off a NICK DRAKE cover ('WHICH WILL'). Incredibly, her label went bust yet again and WILLIAMS moved on to Rick Rubin's 'American' before settling at 'Mercury'. She'd also based herself in Nashville and 1998's acclaimed 'CAR WHEELS ON A GRAVEL ROAD' was arguably the best thing to come out of music city in a good few years. Grittier than the likes of SHERYL CROW and certainly a lot more credible than SHANIA TWAIN, the record was roundly praised by both the rock and country camps, cropping up in many end of year polls and enjoying a prolonged stay in Mojo magazine's playlist. While her profile remains lower than it really should be, WILLIAMS' unquestionable musical integrity continues to endear her to critics and roots afficionados alike.

Album rating: RAMBLIN' (*4) / HAPPY WOMAN BLUES (*6) / LUCINDA WILLIAMS (*7) / SWEET OLD WORLD (*8) / CAR WHEELS ON A GRAVEL ROAD (*7)

LUCINDA WILLIAMS – vocals, acoustic guitar / with **JOHN GRIMAUDO** – guitar

| | | not iss. | Heartbeat |

1979. (lp) *<3507>* **RAMBLIN' ON MY MIND**   □   □
– Ramblin' on my mind / Me and my chauffeur / Motherless children / Malted milk blues / Disgusted / Jug band music / Stop breaking down / Drop down daddy / Little darlin' pal of mine / Make me a pallet on the floor / Jambalaya (on the bayou) / Great speckled bird / You're gonna need that pure religion / Satisfied mind. *<(cd/c-iss.1991 & UK Dec94/Dec98 as 'RAMBLIN' on 'Smithsonian-Folkways'; SFW CD/MC 40042)>*

—— she was now backed by session people

| | | not iss. | Folkways |

1980. (lp) *<FTS 31067>* **HAPPY WOMAN BLUES**   -   □
– Lafayette / I lost it / Maria / Happy woman blues / King of hearts / Rolling along / One night stand / Howlin' at midnight / Hard road / Louisiana man / Sharp cutting wings (song to a poet). *(UK cd-iss. 1990 on 'Network'; NETCD 12) <(cd/c-iss.1990 & UK Dec94/Dec98 on 'Simthsonian-Folkways'; SFW CD/MC 40003)>*

—— although she continued to work, she awiated a decent recording deal

—— next with **GURF MORLIX** – guitar / **JOHN CIAMBOTTI** – bass / **DONALD LINDLEY** – drums / + session people

| | | Rough Trade | Rough Trade |

Jan 89. (lp/c/cd) *(ROUGH/+C/CD 130) <ROUGHUS 47/+C/CD>* **LUCINDA WILLIAMS**   □   □
– I just wanted to see you so bad / The night's too long / Abandoned / Big red sun blues / Like a rose / Changed the locks / Passionate kisses / Am I too blue / Crescent city / Side of the road / Price to pay / I asked for water (he gave me gasoline). *(cd re-iss. Jul94 +=; R 316-2)* – Nothing in rambling / Disgusted / Goin' back home / Something that happens when we talk / Sundays / Side of the road. *(cd re-iss. Jun98 on 'Kock Int.'; 38005-2)*

Apr 89. (7"/12") *(RT/+T 224)* **I JUST WANTED TO SEE YOU SO BAD. / SOMETHING ABOUT WHAT HAPPENS WHEN WE TALK**   □   -
(cd-s+=) *(RTCD 224)* Sundays / Changed the locks / Like a rose.

Aug 89. (7"/12") *(RT/+T 232)* **PASSIONATE KISSES. / SIDE OF THE ROAD**   □   -
(cd-ep+=) *(RT 232CD) <ROUGHUS 66CD>* – Nothing in rambling (live) / Goin' back home (live) / Disgusted (live). *<re-iss. 1992 on 'Chameleon'; 61387-2>*

| | | Chameleon-WEA | Chameleon-WEA |

Jan 93. (cd/c) *<(3705 61351-2/-4)>* **SWEET OLD WORLD**   □   Aug92
– Six blocks away / Something about what happens when we talk / He never got enough love / Sweet old world / Little angel, little brother / Pineola / Lines around your eyes / Prove my love / Sidewalks of the city / Memphis pearl / Hot blood / Which will.

| | | Mercury | Mercury |

Jul 98. (cd) *<(558338-2)>* **CAR WHEELS ON A GRAVEL ROAD**   □   65
– Right in time / Car wheels on a gravel road / 2 kool 2 be 4-gotten / Drunken angel / Concrete and barbed wire / Lake Charles / Can't let go / I lost it / Metal firecracker / Greenville / Still I long for your kiss / Joy / Jackson.

Robbie WILLIAMS

Born: 13 Feb '74, Stoke-On-Trent, England. As the cheeky chappy of legendary Manchester boy band TAKE THAT, WILLIAMS enjoyed massive chart success from the early innocence of the 'Take That And Party' era through to the more risque bare-arsed antics of the band's latter days. Yet even the adoration of schoolgirl legions wasn't enough to tether the boy wonder to the restrictions of the manufactured pop industry; as WILLIAMS embarked on an extended booze-athon with rock'n'roll bad boys OASIS etc., his position as a boy band popster was deemed untenable and he soon found himself looking at solo prospects. After eventually recovering from his much publicised indulgences, the singer launched his revamped career with a hugely successful cover of George Michael's 'FREEDOM', subsequently hooking up with songwriter GUY CHAMBERS to pen the likes of 'OLD BEFORE I DIE' and 'LAZY DAYS'. While the former was a sunny, vaguely humorous stab at deflating the rock'n'roll myth, the latter showed our ROBBIE could be mean'n'moody when he wanted to be. Along with fourth single, 'SOUTH OF THE BORDER', all the tracks (save 'FREEDOM') were included on his 1997 debut album, 'LIFE THRU A LENS', the general critical concensus being that WILLIAMS was having the last laugh, beating his former TAKE THAT cronies hands down (both GARY BARLOW and MARK OWEN were taking the solo road with middling success) and winning over a cross section of musical palates with his irrepressible style. He sealed his success that Christmas with the tearjerking ballad, 'ANGELS', a massive Top 5 hit which proved conclusively, if any further proof was needed, that the lad was most definitely back for good. 'LET ME ENTERTAIN YOU' (complete with QUEEN/KISS-style video) was ROBBIE's next single to reach the Top 3 (America still took a backseat for a while). In September '98, the classy JOHN BARRY ('You Only Live Twice')-styled 'MILLENNIUM', deservedly topped the UK chart for a week – ROBBIE now kitted out in James Bond tin flute. The track was also one of the highlights on his sophomore set, 'I'VE BEEN EXPECTING YOU' (1998), a record that boasted three further Top 5 hits, 'NO REGRETS', 'STRONG' and 'SHE'S THE ONE'. The last was a recent WORLD PARTY track, having failed to be issued as a single by KARL WALLINGER and Co, it was now a No.1 smash all around Europe. 1999 was not all party-time for the reformed Mr. WILLIAMS, celebrations were probably subdued a little when he lost a court battle with former TAKE THAT manager, Nigel Martin-Smith; the £90,000 claim would turn into £1 million adding of course legal fees, commission, interest and probably a counter damage claim. • **Songwriters:** Self-penned except collaborations and covers; MAKING PLANS FOR NIGEL (Xtc) / KOOKS (David Bowie) / I WOULDN'T NORMALLY DO THIS KIND OF THING (Pet Shop Boys) / EV'RY TIME WE SAY GOODBYE (Cole Porter) / ANT MUSIC (Adam & The Ants) / etc.

Album rating: LIFE THRU A LENS (*7) / I'VE BEEN EXPECTING YOU (*7)

			Chrysalis	Ccapitol
Aug 96.	(c-s) *(TCFREE 1)* **FREEDOM '96** / ('A'-The Next Big Gen mix) / ('A'-Arthur Baker's Shake and Bake mix)		2	-
	(cd-s+=) *(CDSFREE 1)* – (interview part 2).			
	(cd-s) *(CDFREE 1)* – ('A'side) / ('A'-Arthur Baker mix) / ('A'instrumental) / (interview part 1).			
Apr 97.	(c-s/cd-s) *(TCCHS/CDCHSS 5055)* **OLD BEFORE I DIE** / **KOOKS** / **MAKING PLANS FOR NIGEL**		2	-
	(cd-s) *(CDCHSS 5055)* – ('A'side) / Better days / Average B side.			
Jun 97.	(c-s/cd-s) *(TC/CD CHS 5063)* **LAZY DAYS** / **TEENAGE MILLIONAIRE** / **FALLING IN BED (AGAIN)**		8	-
	(cd-s) *(CDCHSS 5063)* – ('A'side) / She makes me high / Everytime we say goodbye..			
Sep 97.	(c-s/cd-s) *(TC/CD CHS 5068)* **SOUTH OF THE BORDER** / ('A'-Mother's milkin' it mix) / **CHEAP LOVE SONG**		14	-
	(cd-s) *(CDCHSS 5068)* – ('A'side) / Cheap love song / ('A'-187 Lockdown mix) / ('A'-Phil "The Kick Drum" Dane & Mart Smith's nosebag dub).			
Oct 97.	(cd/c) *(CD/TC CHR 6127)* **LIFE THRU A LENS**		1	-
	– Lazy days / Life thru a lens / Ego a go go / Angels / South of the border / Old before i die / One of God's better people / Let me entertain you / Killing me / Clean / Baby girl window.			
Dec 97.	(7") *(CHSLH 5072)* **ANGELS.** / **SOUTH OF THE BORDER**		4	
	(c-s/cd-s) *(TC/CD CHS 5072)* – ('A'side) / Back for good (live) / Walk this sleigh.			
	(cd-s) *(CDCHSS 5072)* – ('A'side) / Karaoke overkill / ('A'acoustic) / Get the joke.			
Mar 98.	(7") *(CHSLH 5080)* **LET ME ENTERTAIN YOU.** / **LAZY DAYS**		3	
	(c-s/cd-s) *(TCCHS/CDCHSS 5080)* – The Full Monty medley: Make me smile (come up and see me) – You can leave your hat on – Land of a 1000 dances) / I wouldn't normally do this kind of thing / I am the (res)erection.			
	(cd-s) *(CDCHS 5080)* – ('A'extended) / ('A'-Stretch'n'Vern's rock'n'roll mix) / ('A'-Amethyst's dub) / ('A'-Robbie loves his mother mix) / ('A'-The Bizarro mix).			
Sep 98.	(c-s/cd-s) *(TC/CD CHS 5099) <radio cut>* **MILLENNIUM** / **LAZY DAYS (original)** / **ANGELS (live)**		1	72 May99
	(cd-s) *(CDCHSS 5099)* – ('A'side) / Love cheat (demo) / Rome Munich Rome (demo).			
Oct 98.	(cd/c) *(497837-2/-4)* **I'VE BEEN EXPECTING YOU**		1	-
	– Strong / No regrets / Millennium / Phoenix from the flames / Win some lose some / Grace / Jesus in a camper van / Heaven from here / Karma killer / She's the one / Man machine / These dreams. (cd+=) – Stand your ground / Stalker's day.			
Nov 98.	(7") *(CHS 5100)* **NO REGRETS.** / **ANTMUSIC**		4	-
	(c-s+=/cd-s+=) *(TCCHS/CDCHSS 5100)* – Deceiving is believing.			
	(cd-s) *(CDCHS 5100)* – ('A'side) / There she goes / Sexed up.			
Mar 99.	(c-s/cd-s) *(TC/CD CHS 5107)* **STRONG** / **LET ME ENTERTAIN YOU (live at The Brit Awards)** / **HAPPY SONG**		5	-
Jul 99.	(cd) *<97726-2>* **THE EGO HAS LANDED** (compilation)		-	63
Nov 99.	(-) *<album cut>* **ANGELS**		-	55
Nov 99.	(c-s) *(TCCHS 5112)* **SHE'S THE ONE** / **IT'S ONLY US** / **MILLENNIUM (live)**		1	-
	(cd-s+=) *(CDCHS 5112)* – ('A'video).			
	(cd-s) *(CDCHSS 5112)* – ('A'side) / Coke and tears / It's only us / It's only us (video).			

Victoria WILLIAMS (dig out; Great Alt & Indie . . .)

Sonny Boy WILLIAMSON

Born: WILLIE 'RICE' MILLER on the 5th of December 1901, Glendora, Mississippi, USA. He mastered harmonica early in life and could also play guitar and drums, and if he had had more belief in himself then he would have gone on to be one of the most respected post-war bluesmen. During the 30's he used many names such as LITTLE BOY BLUE, WILLIE WILLIAMSON, WILLIE WILLIAMS and WILLIE MILLER (after his brother) but he decided in 1941, who knows why, to borrow the name of an established fellow harpist, JOHN LEE 'SONNY BOY' WILLIAMSON (who could do nothing about the interloper) and after the latter's death in 1948, MILLER actually claimed to be the original SONNY BOY WILLIAMSON. WILLIAMSON started to host the 'King Biscuit Time' radio show (sponsored by the King Biscuit flour company) on KFFA Radio, West Helena, Arkansas in 1941. He was a unique stylist with a resonating baritone and piercing harp; what's more, he was a better performer than the man whose name he had taken. WILLIAMSON made his first records (of which 'MIGHTY LONG TIME' was one of his finest) in 1951, for Lillian McMurray's 'Trumpet' label in Jackson, Mississippi along with WILLIE LOVE and ELMORE JAMES. He was already a seasoned performer by then, having played with ROBERT JOHNSON as well as teaching harmonica to his brother-in-law, HOWLIN' WOLF in exchange for guitar lessons. WILLIAMSON had also frequently crossed the paths of ELMORE JAMES, JOHNNY SHINES, SUNNYLAND SLIM and ROBERT 'JR.' LOCKWOOD, with whom he worked frequently during the 30's and who played lead guitar on many of his late 50's 'Chess' recordings. Although he had a reputation as a mean, bitter man, he was, in actual fact, generous to up and coming musicians; B.B. KING owed his start to a spot on WILLIAMSON's radio show, while he virtually adopted JAMES COTTON as a son. SONNY subsequently moved to Chicago where he started to record for 'Chess' (who bought his contract from a third party after 'Trumpet' had sold it on). By 1955, he was in the studio with MUDDY WATERS, OTIS SPANN, JIMMY ROGERS and WILLIE DIXON backing him on his first 'Chess' single, 'DON'T START ME TALKIN''. This was a minor hit and he became a cult figure in Europe during the 60's, choosing to relocate to London in 1963 and recruiting The ANIMALS and The YARDBIRDS as backing bands. He returned to the Delta in 1964 and was found dead in his bed in Helena, Arkansas by drummer PECK CURTIS on the 25th of May 1965. His album 'DOWN AND OUT BLUES' went into the UK Top 20 one month after his death. • **Please note:** Not to be confused with another bluesman of the same name. The other was born JOHN LEE WILLIAMSON, 30 Mar'14, Jackson, Tennessee, USA, who as a teenager augmented other musicians HOMESICK JAMES WILLIAMSON and SLEEPY JOHN ESTES. He moved to Chicago in the late 30's, releasing classic songs 'GOOD MORNING LITTLE SCHOOLGIRL' and 'SUGAR MAMA' for the 'RCA-Bluebird' label. This SONNY BOY was to die on the 1st of June '48 after being attacked and robbed.

Best CD compilation: VERY BEST OF SONNY BOY WIIIAMSON box (*7)

SONNY BOY WILLIAMSON (RICE MILLER) – vocals, guitar, harmonica with **CLIFF BIVENS** – bass / **FROCK** – drums

			not iss.	Trumpet
Feb 51.	(78) *<129>* **EYESIGHT TO THE BLIND.** / **CRAZY ABOUT YOU BABY**		-	-
———	added **DAVE CAMPBELL** – piano / **JOE WILLIE WILKINS** – guitar			
Jun 51.	(78) *<139>* **COOL, COOL BLUES.** / **DO IT IF YOU WANNA**		-	
Jul 51.	(78) *<140>* **STOP CRYING.** / **COME ON BACK HOME**		-	
Nov 51.	(78) *<144>* **WEST MEMPHIS BLUES.** / **I CROSS MY HEART**		-	
———	**CLARENCE LONNIE** – piano; repl. CAMPBELL (after next w/out BIVENS)			
Dec 51.	(78) *<145>* **PONTIAC BLUES.** / **SONNY BOY'S CHRISTMAS BLUES**		-	
Apr 52.	(78) *<166>* **NINE BELOW ZERO.** / **MIGHT LONG TIME**		-	
Jun 52.	(78) *<168>* **STOP NOW BABY.** / **MR. DOWNCHILD**		-	
———	**DUKE HUDDLESTON** – tenor sax / **OLIVER HARRIS** – bass / **S.P.** – drums; repl. LONNIE + FROCK			
Dec 53.	(78) *<212>* **CAT HOP.** / **TOO CLOSE TOGETHER**		-	
Mar 54.	(78) *<215>* **GETTIN' OUT OF TOWN.** / **SHE BROUGHT LIFE BACK TO THE DEAD**		-	
May 54.	(78) *<216>* **GOING IN YOUR DIRECTION.** / **RED HOT KISSES**		-	
———	now w/ **CLARENCE LONNIE** – piano / **B.B. KING** – guitar / **GLEN RICKETTS** – drums			
Oct 54.	(78) *<228>* **EMPTY BEDROOM.** / **FROM THE BOTTOM**		-	
———	now w/ **DAVE CAMPBELL + WILKINS**			
			not iss.	Ace
Dec 54.	(78) *<511>* **NO NIGHTS BY MYSELF.** / **BOPPIN' WITH SONNY**		-	
———	now w/ **OTIS SPANN** – piano / **JIMMY ROGERS + MUDDY WATERS** – guitar / **FRED BELOW** – drums			
			not iss.	Checker
Mar 55.	(7") *<824>* **DON'T START ME TO TALKIN'.** / **ALL MY LOVE IN VAIN**		-	
———	**ROBERT LOCKWOOD + Jr. LUTHER TUCKER** – guitar / **WILLIE DIXON** – bass repl. WATERS + ROGERS + SPANN			
Jul 55.	(7") *<834>* **LET ME EXPLAIN.** / **YOUR IMAGINATION**		-	
1956.	(7") *<847>* **KEEP IT TO YOURSELF.** / **THE KEY TO YOUR DOOR**		-	
1957.	(7") *<864>* **FATTENING FROGS FOR SNAKES.** / **I DON'T KNOW**		-	
———	added **OTIS SPANN** – piano			

1957.	(7") <883> **BORN BLIND. / NINETY NINE**	– □
1958.	(7") <894> **YOUR FUNERAL AND MY TRIAL. / WAKE UP BABY**	– □
1958.	(7") <910> **CROSS MY HEART. / DISSATISFIED**	– □
1959.	(7") <927> **LET YOUR CONSCIENCE BE YOUR GUIDE. / UNSEEING EYE**	– □
1959.	(7") <943> **THE GOAT. / IT'S SAD TO BE ALONE**	– □
1960.	(7") <956> **TEMPERATURE 110. / LONESOME CABIN**	– □
1960.	(7") <963> **TRUST ME BABY. / TOO CLOSE TOGETHER**	– □
1961.	(7") <975> **STOP RIGHT NOW. / THE HUNT**	– □
1961.	(7") <1003> **ONE WAY OUT. / NINE BELOW ZERO**	– □

—— now w/ LAFAYETTE LEAKE – organ / MATT MURPHY – guitar / MILTON RECTOR – bass / AL DUNCAN – drums

		Pye Int.	Checker
Apr 63.	(7") (7N 25191) <1036> **HELP ME. / BYE BYE BIRD**	□	□
Oct 63.	(7") <1065> **TRYING TO GET BACK ON MY FEET. / DECORATION DAY**		–
1963.	(lp) <1417> **ONE WAY OUT**		–

– Born blind / Work with me / Your killing me / Keep it to yourself / Don't lose your eye / Good evening everybody / Too close together / Let your conscience be your guide / I wonder why / This is my apartment / One way out / Like Wolf / Have you ever been in love / Cool disposition / I know what love is all about. *(re-iss. Aug86 lp/c; GCH/+K7 8006) (re-iss. Sep90 c/cd; CH/+D 9116) (cd re-iss. Sep92; CHLD 19174) (cd-iss. Feb93 on 'Charly'; CDCD 1070)*

—— BUDDY GUY – guitar / JACK MEYERS – bass / CLIFTON JAMES; repl. all except LEAKE

Dec 63.	(7") <1080> **I WANT YOU CLOSE TO ME. / MY YOUNGER DAYS**	–
Feb 64.	(7") <1134> **DOWN CHILD. / BRING IT ON HOME**	–
May 64.	(lp) (NPL 28036) <1437> **DOWN AND OUT BLUES**	20

– Don't start me talkin' / All I know / All my love in vain / The key / Keep it to yourself / Dissatisfied / Fattening frogs for snakes / Wake up baby / Your funeral and my trial / 99 / Cross my heart / Let me explain. *(re-iss. Jan67 on 'Marble Arch'; MAL 662) (cd-iss. Jun88 on 'Chess'; CHD 31272) (cd re-iss. Jul90 on 'Chess'; CH 9257) (cd re-iss. Oct92; CHLD 19106)*

Oct 64.	(7") (7N 25268) **LONESOME CABIN. / THE GOAT**	–
Nov 64.	(7"ep) (NEP 44037) **SONNY BOY WILLIAMSON**	–

—— SONNY died on 25 May '65.

– compilations, others, etc. –

1963.	(lp) *Vogue; (LD 63930)* **SONNY BOY & MEMPHIS SLIM IN PARIS**	–	– French

– Your funeral and my trial / Explain yourself to me / My one room cabin / Getting out of town / The skies are crying / Nine below zero / Fattening frogs for snakes. *(re-iss. Sep76)*

1964.	(lp) *Storyville; (SLP 148)* **PORTRAIT IN BLUES, VOL.4**	

(re-iss. 1966 on 'Fontana'; 670 158) (re-iss. May86; SLP 4016)

Apr 65.	(7") *Sue; (WI 365)* **NO NIGHTS BY MYSELF. / BOPPIN' WITH SONNY BOY**	–
1965.	(7"ep) *Chess; (CRE 6001)* **HELP ME**	–
1966.	(7"ep) *Chess; (CRE 6013)* **IN MEMORIAM**	–

– Sad to be alone / Too young to die / Too old to think / One way out.

1966.	(7"ep) *Chess; (CRE 6018)* **REAL FOLK BLUES, VOL.2**	–

– Checkin' up on my baby / Dissatisfied / Trust me baby / Bring it on home.

Apr 66.	(7") *Chess; (CRS 8030)* **BRING IT ON HOME. / DOWN CHILD**	–
1966.	(lp) *Storyville; (SLP 170)* **THE BLUES OF SONNY BOY WILLIAMSON (live '63)**	–

(re-iss. 1967 on 'Fontana'; 670 170) (re-iss. Jul87 lp/cd; SLP/STCD 4062)

1967.	(7") *Blue Horizon; (45-1008)* **FROM THE BOTTOM. / EMPTY BEDROOM**	–
1968.	(lp; mono/stereo) *Marmalade; (607/608 004)* **DON'T SEND ME NO FLOWERS (with BRIAN AUGER & JIMMY PAGE)**	–

(cd-iss. Jan93 on 'Decal'; CDLIK 80)

1972.	(lp) *Chess; <1536>* **BUMMER ROAD**	–

(cd-iss. 1991; CHD 9324) (cd re-iss. Oct92; CHLD 19107)

1974.	(lp) *Rarity; (RLP 1)* **THE LAST SESSIONS – 1963**	–
Dec 75.	(lp) *Charly; (CR 30011)* **THE JAM SESSION (with BRIAN AUGER)**	–
Apr 81.	(lp) *Chess; <(CXMD 4001)>* **CHESS MASTERS**	–
Apr 83.	(d-lp) *Chess; <(CXMD 4012)>* **CHESS MASTERS VOL.2**	–
Aug 86.	(lp/c) *Deja Vu; (DVLP/DVMC 2074)* **THE COLLECTION: 20 BLUES GREATS**	
Dec 86.	(lp/c) *Greenline-Chess; (CDCHESS 35)* **THE BEST OF SONNY BOY WILLIAMSON**	–

– Don't start me to talkin' / All my love in vain / Let me explain / Keep it to yourself / The key (to your door) / Fattening frogs for snakes / Cross my heart / Born blind / Ninety nine / Your funeral and my trial / Let your conscience be your guide / The goat / It's sad to be alone / Checkin' up on my baby / Lonesome cabin / Trust my baby / Too close together / Nine below zero / Help me / Bring it on home / Decoration day / One way out.

1987.	(4xlp-box) *Chess; (BOX 1)* **THE CHESS YEARS**	□ □

(4xcd-box iss.Feb91; CDREDBOX 1)

Jul 87.	(7"ep) *Blue Moon; (BMEP 001)* **TAKE IT EASY BABY / BYE BYE BIRD. / I DON'T CARE NO MORE / BABY DON'T WORRY / 23 HOURS TOO LONG**	–
Oct 88.	(d-lp) *Vogue; (427004)* **CHICAGO GOLDEN YEARS**	–
Oct 88.	(lp) *Vogue; (515018)* **MORE REAL FOLK BLUES**	–
1989.	(lp) *Document; (DLP 575)* **SOLO HARP 1963-65**	–
May 89.	(cd/c) *Deja Vu; (DVRE CD/MC 25)* **THE SONNY BOY WILLIAMSON STORY**	–
Sep 89.	(cd) *Charly; (CDRED 14)* **WORK WITH ME**	–
Oct 89.	(6xlp-box) *Chess; (CXHT 109)* **SONNY BOY WILLIAMSON**	
Feb 90.	(cd/c) *Roots; (RTS 4/3 3005)* **DON'T START ME TO TALKIN'**	–
1990.	(cd) *Blue Moon; (CDBM 088)* **BOPPIN' WITH SONNY**	
1992.	(cd) *Blues Encore; (CD 52018)* **THE HARP FROM THE DEEP SOUTH**	–
Aug 92.	(lp/c/cd) *Alligator; (AL/+CS/CD 4787)* **KEEP IT TO OURSELVES**	

Nov 92.	(cd/c) *Blue Moon; (CD/TC BM 22)* **NINE BELOW ZERO: CHARLY BLUES – MASTERWORKS VOL.1**	□	□
Jul 93.	(cd; with WILLIE LOVE) *Alligator; (ALCD 2700)* **CLOWNIN' WITH THE WORLD**		□
Mar 94.	(cd) *See For Miles; (SEECD 395)* **THE EP COLLECTION . . . PLUS**		–
May 94.	(cd; with The ANIMALS) *16; (CD 9011)* **16 GREATEST HITS**		
Jul 94.	(cd) *Alligator; (AL 2803)* **GOIN' IN YOUR DIRECTION**		
Feb 95.	(cd) *The Collection; (COL 044)* **THE COLLECTION**		
Jul 95.	(3xcd-box; with other artists) *Charly; (VBCD 304)* **THE VERY BEST OF SONNY BOY WILLIAMSON**		
Jul 95.	(cd) *Charly; (CDRB 21)* **LIVE IN ENGLAND**		
Sep 96.	(cd) *Charly; (CHLDD 19330)* **THE ESSENTIAL SONNY BOY WILLIAMSON**		
Jul 97.	(cd) *M.C.A.; (MCD 09377)* **HIS BEST**		
May 98.	(cd; with GRAHAM BOND) *Spalax; (14552)* **ROCK GENERATION**		

Brian WILSON (see under ⇒ BEACH BOYS)

Jackie WILSON

Born: JACK LEROY WILSON, 9 Jun'34, Detroit, Michigan, USA. His first taste of fame (albeit minor) came in 1950 when he won an American amateur 'Golden Gloves' boxing title; due to his young age he was registered under a false name, Sonny Wilson. His mother, however, was more interested in directing him towards the musical arena and the teenage WILSON joined The EVER READY GOSPEL SINGERS the same year. He subsequently went on to sing alongside The THRILLERS and HANK BALLARD before being spotted by L.A. R&B mainstay, JOHNNY OTIS; he was introduced to BILLY WARD, who in turn recruited WILSON for his band, The DOMINOES. He nevertheless cut a one-off solo single – as JACKIE WILSON – in 1951 on DIZZY GILLESPIE's 'Dee Gee' label, a straining pop cover of Irish traditional standard, 'DANNY BOY'. In April '53 he took over as The DOMINOES lead singer following the departure of CLYDE McPHATTER (to form The DRIFTERS). Although WILSON was a more than adequate replacement, the group managed only one Top 20 hit ('ST. THERESE OF THE ROSES') during his tenure. In late '56 JACKIE departed for a solo career, scoring a sizeable UK Top 10 late the following year with 'REET PETITE (THE FINEST GIRL YOU EVER WANT TO KNOW)'. Co-penned by Berry Gordy Jr. (future 'Motown' guru), this strutting slice of pop/R&B was to make the record books in 1986 when it became a re-issued UK chart topper 29 years after its original release. In the meantime, a follow-up, 'TO BE LOVED', made both the US and UK Top 30 although it'd be America where WILSON would make a lasting impression on the charts. One of his biggest and most enduring hits came in late '58 with the classic 'LONELY TEARDROPS' while the near-operatic dimension to his vocal style (many of his 60's songs were adapted from operas or classical works) was showcased on 1960's Top 5 'NIGHT'. Although he continued to score minor hits throughout the early 60's, his only entry into the Top 10 was 1963's 'BABY WORKOUT', a proto-soul belter that went a long way to capturing the excitement of the JACKIE WILSON live experience. A ball of sexually kinetic energy as potent as JAMES BROWN, WILSON's loose-footed athleticism and sweat-stained, gospel-rooted fervor made him a magnetic performer who attracted legions of female fans. The man almost came a cropper in 1961 when one of those fans, Juanita Jones, attempted to shoot herself in JACKIE's New York apartment; when WILSON intervened he was shot in the stomach and spent a long period in hospital. If his studio output didn't always live up to expectations, WILSON was guaranteed to pull off at least the occasional powerful performance; a link-up with veteran Windy City producer, Carl Davis, resulted in the near Top 10 'WHISPERS' (1966) and the joyous near Top 5 '(YOUR LOVE KEEPS LIFTING ME) HIGHER AND HIGHER' (1967). In 1969, JACKIE was back in the British charts (with the latter track) for the first time in almost a decade while summer 72's 'I GET THE SWEETEST FEELING' made the UK Top 10. Ironically, longtime fan VAN MORRISON scored a minor US chart hit at almost exactly the same time with his sublime WILSON tribute, 'JACKIE WLISON SAID (I'M IN HEAVEN WHEN YOU SMILE)'. Tragically, on September 29th 1975 (by which time WILSON was touring the oldies circuit), the singer suffered a heart attack onstage; he'd been midway through 'LONELY TEARDROPS', performing as part of a Dick Clark Revue at the Latin Casino in Cherry Hill, New Jersey. He never fully regained his faculties due to brain damage and spent over eight years in hospital before his death on 21st January 1984. BARRY WHITE and The SPINNERS were among the stars who performed benefit concerts to pay for his hospital bills although the $60,000 that was raised actually went towards a $300,000 unpaid tax demand. • **Songwriters:** JACKIE wrote most of material himself and collaborating with others, notably ALONZO TUCKER in 1962-65. BERRY GORDY JR. & TYRAN CARLO (alias cousin BILLY DAVIS), penned his late 1950's 'Brunswick' songs. Many of his 1960's songs were adapted from operas or classical works. Covered:- DANNY BOY (Irish trad.) / SHAKE A HAND (Faye Adams) / THINK TWICE (Brook Benton) / FOR YOUR PRECIOUS LOVE (Impressions) / CHAIN GANG (Sam Cooke) / I GET THE SWEETEST FEELING (co-with; Van McCoy) / FOR ONCE IN MY LIFE (Stevie Wonder) / YOU GOT ME WALKING (Eugene Record; Chi-Lites) / etc. • **Trivia:** In 1959, he appeared in the Alan Freed film 'Go Johnny Go'.

Best CD compilation: THE VERY BEST OF JACKIE WILSON (*8)

JACKIE WILSON – vocals (with various personnel)

	not iss.	Dee Gee
1951. (78) **DANNY BOY.** /	-	

—— In Apr '53, he replaced CLYDE McPHATTER in The DOMINOES. Early '54, they released single RAGS TO RICHES on 'King' records. They signed to 'Jubilee' in '56, and made one single before moving to 'Decca', issuing another single ST. THERESE OF THE ROSES.

—— **JACKIE WILSON** reverted to solo career

	Coral	Brunswick	
Nov 57. (7",78) (Q 72290) <55024> **REET PETITE (THE FINEST GIRL YOU EVER WANT TO KNOW).** / **BY THE LIGHT OF THE SILVERY MOON**	6	62	Oct57
Mar 58. (7",78) (Q 72306) <55052> **TO BE LOVED.** / **COME BACK TO ME**	23	22	
Sep 58. (7",78) (Q 72332) <55070> **I'M WANDERIN'.** / **AS LONG AS I LIVE**			
Oct 58. (lp) (LVA 9087) <54042> **HE'S SO FINE**			

– Etc., etc. / To be loved / Come back to me / If I can't have you / As long as I live / Reet petite / It's too bad we had to say goodbye / Why can't you be mine / I'm wanderin' / Right now / Danny boy / He's so fine.

	Coral	Brunswick	
Oct 58. (7",78) (Q 72338) <55086> **WE HAVE LOVE.** / **SINGING A SONG**		93	Sep58
Dec 58. (7",78) (Q 72347) <55105> **LONELY TEARDROPS.** / **IN THE BLUE OF EVENING**		7	Nov58
May 59. (7",78) (Q 72366) <55121> **THAT'S WHY (I LOVE YOU SO).** / **LOVE IS ALL**		13	Mar59
Jul 59. (7",78) (Q 72372) <55136> **I'LL BE SATISFIED.** / **ASK**		20	Jun59
Sep 59. (lp) (LVA 9108) <54045> **LONELY TEARDROPS**			

– Lonely teardrops / Each time (I love you more) / (That's why) I love you so / In the blue of evening / The joke (is not on me) / Someone to need me / You better know it / By the light of the silvery moon / Singing a song / Love is all We have love / Hush-a-bye.

	Coral	Brunswick	
Oct 59. (7",78) (Q 72380) <55149> **YOU BETTER KNOW IT.** / **NEVER GO AWAY**		37	Sep59
Dec 59. (7",78) (Q 72384) <55165> **TALK THAT TALK.** / **ONLY YOU, ONLY ME**		34	Nov59
Mar 60. (7") <55166> **NIGHT.** / **DOGGIN' AROUND**	-	4 / 15	
Apr 60. (7") (Q 72393) **DOGGIN' AROUND.** / **THE MAGIC OF LOVE**		-	
May 60. (lp) (LVA 9121) <754050> **SO MUCH**			

– I know I'll always be in love with you / Happiness / Only you, only me / The magic of love / Wishing well / Talk that talk / Ask / I'll be satisfied / It's all a part of love / Never go away / Thrill of love.

	Coral	Brunswick	
Sep 60. (7") (Q 72407) <55167> **(YOU WERE MADE FOR) ALL MY LOVE.** / **A WOMAN, A LOVER, A FRIEND**		12 / 15	Jul60
Sep 60. (lp) (LVA 9130) <754055> **JACKIE SINGS THE BLUES**			Jul60

– Please tell me why / Doggin' around / New girl in town / Nothin' but the blues / Passin' through / Excuse her for lovin' / She done me wrong / Sazzle dazzle / Please stick around / Come on and love me baby / Comin' to your house / It's been a long time.

	Coral	Brunswick	
Nov 60. (7") (Q 72412) <55170> **ALONE AT LAST.** / **AM I THE MAN**	50	8 / 32	Oct60
Dec 60. (lp) (LVA 9135) <754058> **MY GOLDEN FAVOURITES** (compilation)			

– Reet petite / To be loved / I'll be satisfied / Only you, only you / Talk that talk / Ask / (That's why) I love you so much / It's all a part of love / Lonely teardrops / I'm wanderin' / You better know it / We have love.

	Coral	Brunswick	
Jan 61. (7") (Q 72421) <55201> **MY EMPTY ARMS.** / **THE TEAR OF THE YEAR**		9 / 44	
Feb 61. (7") (Q 72424) **THE TEAR OF THE YEAR.** / **YOUR ONE AND ONLY LOVE**		-	
Mar 61. (7") <55208> **PLEASE TELL ME WHY.** / **YOUR ONE AND ONLY LOVE**	-	20 / 40	
May 61. (lp) (LVA 9144) <754059> **A WOMAN, A LOVER, A FRIEND**			

– A woman, a lover, a friend / Your one and only love / You cried / The river / When you add religion to love / One kiss / Night / (You were made for) All my love / Am I the man / Behind a smile is a tear / We kissed / (So many) Cute little girls.

	Coral	Brunswick	
May 61. (7") (Q 72430) **CUTE LITTLE GIRLS.** / **PLEASE TELL ME WHY**			
Jul 61. (7") (Q 72434) <55216> **I'M COMING ON BACK TO YOU.** / **LONELY LIFE**		19 / 80	Jun61
Sep 61. (lp) (LVA 9148) <754100> **YOU AIN'T HEARD NOTHIN' YET**			

– Toot, toot, tootsie goodbye / Sonny boy / California, here I come / Keep smiling at trouble (trouble's a bubble) / You made me love you (I didn't want to do it) / My Yiddishe momme / Swane / April showers / Anniversary song / Rock-a-bye with a Dixie melody / For me and my gal / In our house.

	Coral	Brunswick	
Sep 61. (7") (Q 72439) <55219> **YEARS FROM NOW.** / **YOU DON'T KNOW WHAT IT MEANS**		37 / 79	Aug61
Nov 61. (7") (Q 72444) <55220> **THE WAY I AM.** / **MY HEART BELONGS TO ONLY YOU**		58 / 65	Oct61
Feb 62. (7") (Q 72450) <55221> **THE GREATEST HURT.** / **THERE'LL BE NO NEXT TIME**		34 / 75	Jan62
Apr 62. (lp) (LVA 9151) <754101> **BY SPECIAL REQUEST**			

– Cry / My heart belongs to only you / Stormy weather / Tenderly / Lonely life / The way I am / Try a little tenderness / Mood indigo / You belong to my heart / Indian love call / One more time / I'm comin' on back to you.

	Coral	Brunswick	
May 62. (7"; by JACKIE WILSON & LINDA HOPKINS) <55224> **I FOUND LOVE.** / **THERE'S NOTHING LIKE LOVE**		93	Apr62
May 62. (7") <55225> **HEARTS.** / **SING**	-	58	
Aug 62. (7") (Q 72454) <55229> **I JUST CAN'T HELP IT.** / **THE TALE OF WOE**		70	Jun62
Sep 62. (lp) (LVA 9202) <754105> **BODY AND SOUL**			

– Body and soul / I don't know you anymore / I apologize / I got it bad (and that ain't good) / The greatest hurt / I'll always be in love with you / Crazy she calls me / The tear of the year / Blue Moon / I'll be around / There'll be no next time / We'll be together.

Sep 62. (7") <55233> **FOREVER AND A DAY.** / **BABY, THAT'S ALL**	-	82
Jan 63. (7") <55236> **WHAT GOOD AM I WITHOUT YOU?.** / **A GIRL NAMED TAMIKO**		
Feb 63. (lp) (LVA 9209) <754108> **AT THE COPA** (live)		Nov62

– Tonight / Medley: Body and soul – I apologize / Love for sale / And this is my beloved / The way I am / I love them all (part 1): What'd I say – Night – That's why (I love you so) / I love them all (part 2): Danny boy – Doggin' around – To be loved – Lonely teardrops / St. James infirmary / A perfect day.

Mar 63. (7") <55239> **BABY WORKOUT.** / **I'M GOING CRAZY (GOTTA GET YOU OFF MY MIND)**	-	5
Mar 63. (7") (Q 72460) **BABY WORKOUT.** / **WHAT GOOD AM I WITHOUT YOU**	-	
Apr 63. (lp) <754110> **BABY WORKOUT**	-	36

– Shake! shake! shake! / The kictapoo / Yeah! yeah! yeah! / You only live once / Say you will / Baby workout / Love train / Now that I want her / (I feel like I'm in) Paradise / (So many) Cute little girls / What good am I without you.

Jun 63. (7") (Q 72464) <55243> **SHAKE A HAND. ("JACKIE WILSON & LINDA HOPKINS")** / **SAY I DO**		42 May63
Aug 63. (7") (Q 72465) <55246> **SHAKE! SHAKE! SHAKE!.** / **HE'S A FOOL**		33 Jul63
Sep 63. (lp; mono/stereo) (LVA/SVL 9214) <754106> **SINGS THE WORLD'S GREATEST MELODY**		

– Forever and a day / Take my heart / Pianissmo / My eager heart / I dream of you / My tale of woe / A girl named Tamiko / All my love / A heart of love / Alone at last / A thing of beauty.

Nov 63. (7") (Q 72467) 55250> **BABY GET IT (AND DON'T QUIT IT).** / **THE NEW BREED**		61 Sep63
Dec 63. (7") <55254> **SILENT NIGHT.** / **O HOLY NIGHT**	-	
Jan 64. (7") <55260> **I'M TRAVELIN' ON.** / **HAUNTED HOUSE**	-	
Mar 64. (7") <55263> **CALL HER UP.** / **THE KICKAPOO**	-	
Jun 64. (7") (Q 72474) <55266> **BIG BOSS LINE.** / **BE MY GIRL**		94 May64
Jun 64. (lp; by JACKIE WILSON & LINDA HOPKINS) <754113> **SHAKE A HAND**	-	

– Swing low sweet cariot / Nobody knows the trouble I've seen / Yes indeed / Joshua fit the battle of Jericho / Old time religion / Shake a hand / He's got the whole world in his hands / When the saints go marching in / Do Lord / Everytime I feel the spirit / Dry bones / Down by the riverside.

Sep 64. (7") (Q 72476) <55269> **SQUEEZE HER, TEASE HER (BUT LOVE HER).** / **GIVE ME BACK MY HEART**		89 Aug64
Nov 64. (7") <55273> **SHE'S ALRIGHT.** / **WATCH OUT**	-	
Feb 65. (7") <55277> **DANNY BOY.** / **SOUL TIME**	-	94
Mar 65. (lp) <754117> **SOMETHIN' ELSE**	-	

– Big boss line / Groovin' / Deep down love / Take one step / Love (is where you find it) / Give me back my heart / Squeeze her – tease her (but love her) / Be my girl / Baby (I just can't help it) / Rebecca / My best friend's girl / Twistin' and shoutin' (doing the monkey).

May 65. (7"; by JACKIE WILSON & LINDA HOPKINS) (Q 72480) <55278> **YES INDEED.** / **WHEN THE SAINTS GO MARCHING IN**		
Aug 65. (7") (Q 72481) <55280> **NO PITY (IN THE NAKED CITY).** / **I'M SO LONELY**		59 Jun65
Sep 65. (lp) <754118> **SOUL TIME**	-	

– No pity / Danny boy / An ocean I'll cry / Teardrop avenue / She'll be there / Star dust / A kiss, a thrill and goodbye / Mama of my song / She's all right / Better play it safe / No time out.

Nov 65. (7") (Q 72482) <55283> **I BELIEVE I'LL LOVE ON.** / **LONELY TEARDROPS**		96 Oct65
Jan 66. (lp) (LVA 9231) <754119> **SPOTLIGHT ON JACKIE WILSON**		

– Over the rainbow / Pledging my love / Georgia on my mind / Georgia on my mind / You'll never walk alone / Rags to riches / You don't know me / What kind of fool am I / I wanna be around / Until the real thing comes along / I apologize / Lonely teardrops / We have love.

Jan 66. (7"; by JACKIE WILSON & LAVERN BAKER) <55287> **THINK TWICE.** / **PLEASE DON'T HURT ME**	-	93
May 66. (7") (Q 72476) <55269> **TO MAKE A BIG MAN CRY.** / **BE MY LOVE**		
Jul 66. (lp; mono/stereo) (LVA/SVL 9232) <754120> **SOUL GALORE**		

– Brand new thing / 3 days 1 hour 30 minutes / I've got to get back (country boy) / So you say you wanna dance (workout #2) / Stop lying / Let me build / Brand new thing (2) / Soul galore / What's done in the dark / I got my mind made up / Everything's gonna be fine / Your loss, my gain.

Jul 66. (7") <55289> **I'VE GOT TO GET BACK (COUNTRY BOY).** / **3 DAYS, 1 HOUR, 30 MINUTES**	-	
Aug 66. (7") <55290> **BRAND NEW THING.** / **SOUL GALORE**	-	-
Sep 66. (7") <55294> **I BELIEVE.** / **BE MY LOVE**	-	
Nov 66. (7") (Q 72487) <55300> **WHISPERS (GETTIN' LOUDER).** / **THE FAIREST OF THEM ALL**		11 Oct66
Feb 67. (7") <55309> **JUST BE SINCERE.** / **I DON'T WANT TO LOSE YOU**	-	91 / 84
Apr 67. (7") <55321> **I'VE LOST YOU.** / **THOSE HEARTACHES**		82
Jul 67. (lp) (LVA 9235) <754122> **WHISPERS**		Jan67

– I don't want to lose you / My heart is calling / Who am I / Whispers (gettin' louder) / The fairest of them all / (Too much) Sweet loving / I can do better / Just be sincere / Only your love can save me / To make a man cry / I've gotta talk to you / Tears will tell it all.

Sep 67. (7") (Q 72493) <55336> **(YOUR LOVE KEEPS LIFTING ME) HIGHER AND HIGHER.** / **I'M THE ONE TO DO IT**		6 Aug67
Dec 67. (7") (Q 72496) <55354> **SINCE YOU SHOWED ME HOW TO BE HAPPY.** / **THE WHO WHO SONG**		32 Nov67

	M.C.A.	Brunswick	
Mar 68. (7"; by JACKIE WILSON & COUNT BASIE) (MU 10140) <55365> **FOR YOUR PRECIOUS LOVE.** / **UPTIGHT**		49	Feb68

Apr 68. (lp; mono/stereo) (MUP/+S 304) <754130> **HIGHER AND HIGHER** [ ] [Dec67]
– (Your love keeps lifting me) Higher and higher / I don't need you around / I've lost you / Those heartaches / Soulville / Open the door to your heart / I'm the one to do it / You can count on me / I need your loving / Somebody up there likes you / When will our day come.

Apr 68. (7"; by JACKIE WILSON & COUNT BASIE) <55373> **CHAIN GANG. / FUNKY BROADWAY** [-] [84]

Jul 68. (7") <55381> **I GET THE SWEETEST FEELING. / NOTHING BUT HEARTACHES** [-] [34]

Sep 68. (lp; mono/stereo; as JACKIE WILSON & COUNT BASIE) (MUP/MUPS 333) <754134> **TOO MUCH** <US-title 'MANUFACTURERS OF SOUL'> [Jun68]
– Funky Broadway / For your precious love / In the midnight hour / Ode to Billie Joe / Chain gang / I was made to love her / Uptight (everything's alright) / I never loved a woman (the way I love you) / Respect / Even when you cry / My girl. (UK re-iss. Feb74)

Oct 68. (7") <55393> **FOR ONCE IN MY LIFE. / YOU BROUGHT ABOUT A CHANGE IN ME** [-] [70]

Apr 69. (7") (MUPS 361) <754138> **I GET THE SWEETEST FEELING**
– You keep me hangin' on / Once in a lifetime / Who can I turn to (when nobody needs me) / People / Don't go to strangers / I get the sweetest feeling / You brought about the change in me / Nothing but blue skies / A woman needs to be loved / Growin' tall / Since you showed me how to be happy.

Apr 69. (7") (MU 1131) **(YOUR LOVE KEEPS LIFTING ME) HIGHER AND HIGHER. / WHISPERS (GETTIN' LOUDER)** [11]

Dec 69. (7") (MU 1105) <55418> **HELPLESS. / DO IT THE RIGHT WAY**

Feb 70. (7") <55423> **WITH THESE HANDS. / (WHY DON'T YOU) DO YOUR THING** [-]

Apr 70. (7") <55435> **LET THIS BE A LETTER (TO MY BABY). / DIDN'T I** [-] [91]

Jun 70. (lp) (MUPS 405) <754154> **DO YOUR THING**
– To change my love / This guy's in love with you / Why don't you do your thing / This better Earth / Helpless / Light my fire / That lucky old Sun (just rolls around Heaven all day) / With these hands / Hold on, I'm coming / Eleanor Rigby.

Dec 70. (7") <55443> **(I CAN FEEL THOSE VIBRATIONS) THIS LOVE IS REAL. / LOVE UPRISING** [-] [56]

Apr 71. (7") <55449> **SAY YOU WILL. / THIS GUY'S IN LOVE WITH YOU** [-]

Nov 71. (7") <55461> **LOVE IS FUNNY THAT WAY. / TRY IT AGAIN** [-] [95]

Feb 72. (7") <55467> **YOU GOT ME WALKING. / THE FOUNTAIN** [-] [93]

Jul 72. (7"m) (MU 1160) **I GET THE SWEETEST FEELING. / GALORE / SOUL GALORE** [9] [-]

Brunswick Brunswick

May 73. (7") <55467> **YOU GOT ME WALKING. / THE FOUNTAIN**

Jul 73. (7") <55475> **FOREVER AND A DAY. / THE GIRL TURNED ME ON**

Aug 73. (lp) (BRLS 3001) <754172> **YOU GOT ME WALKING**
– You got me walking / What a lovely day / You left the fire burning / My way / Try it again / Forever and a day / The girl turned me on / Hard to get a thing called love / Love is funny that way / The fountain.

Oct 73. (7") <55480> **WHAT A LOVELY DAY. / YOU LEFT THE FIRE BURNING** [-]

Mar 74. (7") (BR 3) <55490> **BEAUTIFUL DAY. / WHAT'CHA GONNA DO ABOUT LOVE** [-]

Apr 74. (lp) <754189> **BEAUTIFUL DAY**
– Beautiful day / Because of you / Go away / Pretty little angel eyes / Let's love again / It's all over / I get lonely sometimes / This love is mine / Don't you know I love you / What'cha gonna do about me.

1974. (7") <55495> **BECAUSE OF YOU. / GO AWAY** [-]

1974. (7") <55499> **NO MORE GOODBYES. / SING A LITTLE SONG** [-]

Apr 75. (7") (BR 18) **I GET THE SWEETEST FEELING. / (YOUR LOVE KEEPS LIFTING ME) HIGHER AND HIGHER** [25] [-]

Jul 75. (7") <55504> **IT'S ALL OVER. / SHAKE A LEG** [-]

Nov 75. (7"; by JACKIE WILSON & The CHI-LITES) (BR 28) <55522> **DON'T BURN NO BRIDGES / ('A'instrumental)**

Jan 76. (7") <55536> **NOBODY BUT YOU. / I'VE LEARNED ABOUT LOVE** [-]

—— On the 29th September '75, JACKIE had a heart attack. He lapsed into a coma and due to brain damage stayed in the same state until his death on 21st of January '84.

– compilations, etc. –

Mar 59. (7"ep) Coral; (FEP 2016) **JACKIE WILSON** [-]

Feb 60. (7"ep) Coral; (FEP 2043) **THE DYNAMIC JACKIE WILSON** [-]
– I'll be satisfied / Talk that talk / Never go away / Only you, only me.

May 62. (7") Ember; (JBS 705) **TENDERLY. / Clyde McPhatter: HARBOUR LIGHTS** [-]

1962. (lp; shared with Clyde McPhatter) Ember; (NR 5001) **MEET BILLY WARD & THE DOMINOES**

1964. (lp) Brunswick; <754115> **MY GOLDEN FAVORITES VOL.2** [-]

May 69. (7") MCA Soul Bag; (BAG 2) **(YOUR LOVE KEEPS LIFTED ME) HIGHER AND HIGHER. / WHISPERS (GETTIN' LOUDER)** [11]

Jul 69. (7") MCA Soul Bag; (BAG 7) **SINCE YOU SHOWED ME HOW TO BE HAPPY. / CHAIN GANG** [-]

Mar 73. (lp) Brunswick; (BRLS 3004) <754185> **GREATEST HITS**

Mar 73. (7") Brunswick; (BR 23) **WHISPERS (GETTIN' LOUDER). / REET PETITE** [-]

Aug 75. (lp) (BRLS 3016) **THE VERY BEST OF JACKIE WILSON**
– Reet petite / Lonely teardrops / That's why I love you so / Night / You better know it / Talk that talk / To be loved / I'll be satisfied / Whispers (gettin' louder) / Your love keeps lifting me higher and higher / I get the sweetest feeling / Doggin' around / Am I the man / I'm comin' on back to you / A woman a lover a friend / No pity (in the naked city). (cd-iss. Jun87 on 'Ace' & Jun91 on 'Music Club')

Jul 77. (7") Brunswick; (BR 43) **IT ONLY HAPPENS WHEN I LOOK. / JUST AS SOON AS THE FEELING'S OVER** [-]

Aug 77. (lp) Brunswick; (5002) <754212> **NOBODY BUT YOU**

Sep 83. (lp/c) Skratch; (JAK/TCJAK 101) **THE CLASSIC JACKIE WILSON** [-]

Jan 85. (lp/c) Kent; (KEN T/C 027) **THE SOUL YEARS** [-]

Mar 85. (7"m) Skratch; (SKM 1) **I GET THE SWEETEST FEELING. / WHISPERS (GETTIN' LOUDER) / (YOUR LOVE KEEPS LIFTING ME) HIGHER AND HIGHER** [-]
(12"+=) (SKM12 1) – The who who song / Nothin' but blue skies. (UK re-iss. Feb87; same) – hit No.3

Mar 85. (7"m/12"m) Skratch; (SKM/+12 3) **REET PETITE. / YOU BROUGHT ABOUT A CHANGE IN ME / I'M THE ONE TO DO IT**
(UK re-iss. Nov86; same) – hit No.1

Mar 85. (lp/c) Ace; (CH/+C 125) **REET PETITE** [-]
(cd-iss. May86; CDCH 902)

Apr 85. (7"m) Kent; (TOWN 101) **I DON'T WANT TO LOSE YOU. / ADAM'S APPLE / DON'T TAKE IT OUT ON THE WORLD** [-]

May 86. (lp) Kent; (KENT 054) **THE SOUL YEARS VOL.2** [-]

May 86. (cd) Kent; (CDKEN 901) **HIGHER AND HIGHER** [-]

Jan 87. (lp) Portrait; (450455-1) **15 CLASSIC TRACKS** [-]

Jun 87. (7"/12") Skratch; (SKM 10/+12) **(YOUR LOVE KEEPS LIFTING ME) HIGHER AND HIGHER. / THE WHO WHO SONG** [15]

Nov 87. (7"/12") Skratch; (SKM 11/+12) **BABY WORKOUT. / LONELY TEARDROPS** [-]
(cd-s+=) (SKMCD 11) –

Oct 87. (lp/c) Rhino; <(RN LP/C 70230)> **THRU THE YEARS** [-]

Mar 88. (lp; shared with BILLY WARD) King; <(K 5007)> **14 ORIGINAL GREATEST HITS**

May 88. (lp/c) Streetlife; **GREATEST HITS** [-]

Oct 88. (lp/c/cd) BR Music; (BR LP/MC/CD 48) **20 GREATEST HITS** (re-iss. Apr90 on 'Mainline' cd/c/lp; 266254-2/-4/-1)

May 89. (12") Old Gold; (OG 4118) **I GET THE SWEETEST FEELING. / (YOUR LOVE KEEPS LIFTING ME) HIGHER AND HIGHER / WHISPERS (GETTING LOUDER)** [-]

Feb 91. (cd/c) Music Club; (MC CD/TC 017) **THE VERY BEST OF JACKIE WILSON** [-]

Aug 91. (cd/c/lp) Arista; (261/411/211 854) **GREATEST HITS** [-]

Apr 93. (cd) Kenwest; **ORIGINAL HITS** [-]

Apr 93. (cd) Roots; (RTS 33051) **THE JACKIE WILSON HIT STORY** [-]

Apr 93. (cd) Roots; (RTS 33052) **THE JACKIE WILSON HIT STORY VOLUME 2** [-]

Oct 93. (cd) Charly; (CDPD 8005) **HIGHER AND HIGHER** (different) [-]

Nov 93. (cd) Charly; (CPCD 8018) **THE DYNAMIC JACKIE WILSON** [-]

Nov 93. (cd) Charly; (CDCD 1142) **REET PETITE AND OTHER CLASSICS** [-]

May 94. (cd; with SAM COOKE) Charly; **TWO ON ONE** [-]

Feb 95. (cd/c) Pickwick; (PWK S/MC 4238) **A PORTRAIT OF JACKIE WILSON** [-]

Oct 95. (cd) Charly; (JWCD 1) **THE JACKIE WILSON STORY – THE NEW YORK YEARS, VOLUME 1** [-]

Oct 95. (cd) Charly; (JWCD 2) **THE JACKIE WILSON STORY – THE NEW YORK YEARS, VOLUME 2** [-]

Oct 95. (cd) Charly; (JWCD 5) **THE JACKIE WILSON STORY – THE CHICAGO YEARS, VOLUME 1** [-]

Oct 95. (cd) Charly; (JWCD 6) **THE JACKIE WILSON STORY – THE CHICAGO YEARS, VOLUME 2** [-]

Jun 96. (cd) Charly; (JWCD 3) **THE JACKIE WILSON STORY – THE NEW YORK YEARS, VOLUME 3** [-]

Jul 96. (d-cd) Double Gold; (DBG 53035) **THE JACKIE WILSON STORY** [-]

Sep 96. (cd) Charly; (JWCD 4) **THE JACKIE WILSON STORY – THE NEW YORK YEARS, VOLUME 4** [-]

Nov 96. (cd) More Music; (MOCD 3018) **THE VERY BEST OF JACKIE WILSON** [-]

Apr 97. (cd/c) Carlton; (303600100-2/-4) **THE HIT COLLECTION** [-]

Nov 97. (d-cd) Eagle; (EDMCD 007) **THE MASTERS** [-]

WINGER (dig out; Great Metal . . .)

WINGS (see under ⇒ McCARTNEY, Paul)

Edgar WINTER

Born: 28 Dec'46, Beaumont, Texas, USA. Having spent the latter half of the 60's playing in his older brother JOHNNY's bands including BLACK PLAGUE, the albino keyboard wizard (strapped to his shoulder on stage!) went solo in 1969. His debut album, 'ENTRANCE' (1970) scraped into the US Top 200 and in 1972, after forming WHITE TRASH, he made the Top 30 with double live set, 'ROADWORK' (a record oft cited as one of the seminal progressive rock releases). The following year, he surpassed brother JOHNNY's triumphs when the EDGAR WINTER GROUP topped the US charts with the classic instrumental 45, 'FRANKENSTEIN', a track lifted from his finest album, 'THEY ONLY COME OUT AT NIGHT'. Mainstream success was to be relatively short-lived, however and WINTER parted company with 'Epic' following the release of 'SHOCK TREATMENT' in 1974, signalling the end of the high profile period of his career. He subsequently re-joined JOHNNY, recording 'TOGETHER' (1976) and signing to 'Blue Sky' Records, releasing albums that showed a return to his blues and jazz roots. Arguably ahead of his time, WINTER's maverick streak effectively prevented him from becoming the star that his talent merited. Nevertheless, his band has provided a launching pad for many a future star including BOZ SCAGGS, DAN HARTMAN, RICK DERRINGER and RONNIE MONTROSE. • **Covered:** I CAN'T TURN YOU LOOSE (Otis Redding) / TOGETHER album with JOHNNY featured loads of covers.

Album rating: ENTRANCE (*6) / EDGAR WINTER'S WHITE TRASH (*6) / ROADWORKS (*7) / THEY ONLY COME OUT AT NIGHT (*7) / SHOCK TREATMENT (*6) / JASMINE NIGHTDREAMS (*4) / THE EDGAR WINTER GROUP WITH RICK DERRINGER (*5) / RECYCLED (*4) / THE EDGAR WINTER ALBUM (*3) / STANDING ON ROCK (*4) / HARLEM NOCTURNE (*4) / THE BEST OF EDGAR WINTER compilation (*6) / LIVE IN JAPAN (*4) / I'M NOT A KID ANYMORE (*3) / THE REAL DEAL (*4)

EDGAR WINTER – (solo) – keyboards, saxophone, all (ex-JOHNNY WINTER) except guests **JOHNNY WINTER + RANDAL DOLANON** – guitar / **JIMMY GILLEN** – drums / **RAY AVONGE, EARL CHAPIN + BROOKS TILLOTSON** – horns

		Epic	Epic
Jun 70.	(lp) (EPC 64083) <26503> **ENTRANCE**		

– Entrance / Where have you gone / Rise to fall / Fire and ice / Hung and up / Back in the blues / Re-entrance / Tobacco Road / Jump right out / Peace pipe / A different game / Jimmy's gospel.

| Jun 70. | (7") <10618> **TOBACCO ROAD. / NOW IS THE TIME** | - | |

EDGAR WINTER'S WHITE TRASH

EDGAR with **JERRY LaCROIX** – vox, sax / **JON ROBERT SMITH** – sax, vox / **MIKE McLELLAN** – trumpet, vox / **GEORGE SHECK** – bass / **FLOYD RADFORD** – guitar / **BOBBY RAMIREZ** – drums also **RICK DERRINGER** – guitar

| May 71. | (7") (EPC 7269) <10740> **WHERE WOULD I BE. / GOOD MORNING MUSIC** | | |
| Jun 71. | (lp) (EPC 81191) <30512> **EDGAR WINTER'S WHITE TRASH** | | Apr 71 |

– Give it everything you got / Fly away / Where would I be / Let's get it on / I've got news for you / Save the planet / Dying to live / Keep playin' that rock'n'roll / You were my light / Good morning music. (cd-iss. Oct93 on 'Sony Europe')

| Nov 71. | (7") (EPC 7550) <10788> **KEEP PLAYIN' THAT ROCK'N'ROLL. / DYING TO LIVE** | | |
| May 72. | (d-lp) (EPC 67244) <31249> **ROADWORK** (live) | 23 | 70 Mar72 |

– Save the planet / Jive jive jive / I can't turn you loose / Still alive & well / Back in the U.S.A. / Rock and roll hoochie koo / Tobacco Road / Cool fool / Do yourself a favour / Turn on your lovelight.

| Jun 72. | (7") (EPC 8136) <10855> **I CAN'T TURN YOU LOOSE. / COOL FOOL** | | 81 May72 |

—— WHITE TRASH folded when on 24th Jul'72, RAMIREZ was killed in pub brawl.

EDGAR WINTER GROUP

added synthesizer to his new line-up **DAN HARTMAN** – vocals, bass / **RONNIE MONTROSE** – guitar / **CHUCK RUFF** – drums / **+ RICK**

| Aug 72. | (7") (EPC 8315) **FREE RIDE. / CATCHIN' UP** | | |
| Jan 73. | (lp) (EPC 65074) <31584> **THEY ONLY COME OUT AT NIGHT** | | 3 Nov72 |

– Hangin' around / When it comes / Alta Mira / Free ride / Frankenstein / Autumn / Round and round / Rock'n'roll boogie woogie blues / We all had a really good time. (re-iss. quad.Sep84; EPC 32518)

Jan 73.	(7") (EPC 1064) <10922> **ROUND AND ROUND. / CATCHIN' UP**		Nov72
Jan 73.	(7") <10945> **FRANKENSTEIN. / HANGIN' AROUND**	-	
May 73.	(7") (EPC 1440) <10967> **FRANKENSTEIN. / UNDERCOVER MAN**	18	1 Mar73
Aug 73.	(7") (EPC 1712) <11024> **FREE RIDE. / WHEN IT COMES**		14
Feb 74.	(7") (EPC 2031) <1069> **HANGIN' AROUND. / WE ALL HAD A REAL GOOD TIME**		65 Dec73

—— Billed on tour as EDGAR WINTER GROUP Featuring RICK DERRINGER
RICK – guitars, vocals, etc. (ex-JOHNNY WINTER, ex-McCOYS) repl. JERRY WEEMS. In Oct'74, WEEMS had repl. RONNIE who formed own band MONTROSE

| Jul 74. | (lp/c) (EPC/40 65640) <32461> **SHOCK TREATMENT** | | 13 May74 |

– Some kinda animal / Easy street / Sundown / Miracle of love / Do like me / Rock & roll woman / Someone take my heart away / Queen of my dreams / Maybe someday you'll call my name / River's risin' / Animal.

Jul 74.	(7") (EPC 2537) <11143> **RIVER'S RISIN'. / ANIMAL**		33
Nov 74.	(7") (EPC 2802) <50034> **EASY STREET. / DO LIKE ME**		83 Oct74
Feb 75.	(7") (EPC 3146) <50060> **SOMEONE TAKE MY HEART AWAY. / MIRACLE OF LOVE**		

EDGAR WINTER

(solo) with **HARTMAN, RUFF, DERRINGER + J.WINTER**

		Blue Sky	Blue Sky
Jun 75.	(7") <2758> **JASMINE NIGHTDREAMS. / ONE DAY TOMORROW**	-	
Jun 75.	(lp/c) (SKY/40 80772) <33483> **JASMINE NIGHTDREAMS**		69

– One day tomorrow / Little brother / Hello mellow feelin' / Tell me in a whisper / Shuffle-low / Keep on burnin' / How do you like your love / I always wanted you / Outa control / All out / Sky train / Solar strut.

| Sep 75. | (7") <2761> **I ALWAYS WANTED YOU. / OUTA CONTROL** | - | |

The EDGAR WINTER GROUP WITH RICK DERRINGER

| Nov 75. | (7") <2762> **COOL DANCE. / PEOPLE MUSIC** | - | |
| Nov 75. | (lp/c) (SKY/40 69181) <33798> **THE EDGAR WINTER GROUP WITH RICK DERRINGER** | | |

– Cool dance / People music / Good shot / Nothin' good comes easy / Infinite peace in rhythm / Paradise skies / Modern love / Let's do it together again / Can't tell one from the other / J.A.P. (Just another punk) / Chainsaw.

| May 76. | (7") (SKY 4217) <2763> **DIAMOND EYES. / INFINITE PEACE IN RHYTHM** | | |

—— Next set was a collaboration, 'TOGETHER' with his brother, JOHNNY

EDGAR WINTER'S WHITE TRASH

| 1977. | (7") <2769> **PUTTIN' IT BACK. / STICKIN' IT OUT** | - | |
| 1977. | (lp/c) (SKY/40 82228) <34858> **RECYCLED** | | |

– Puttin' it back / Leftover love / Shake it off / Stickin' it out / New wave / Open up / Parallel love / The in and out of love blue / Competition.

EDGAR WINTER GROUP

in 1979 with different line-up **CRAIG SNYDER** – guitar / **JAMES WILLIAMS** – bass / **KEITH BENSON** – drums / **LARRY WASHINGTON** – percussion (same label)

| Aug 79. | (7") (SKY 7803) <2780> **IT'S YOUR LIFE TO LIVE. / FOREVER IN LOVE** | | |
| Sep 79. | (lp/c) (SKY/40 83648) <35989> **THE EDGAR WINTER ALBUM** | | |

– It's your life to live / Above and beyond / Take it the way it is / Dying to live / Please don't stop / Make it last / Do what / It took your love to bring me out / Forever in blue.

| Mar 80. | (7"/12") (SKY/+12 8246) <2786> **ABOVE AND BEYOND. / ('A'instrumental)** | | |

—— now with **AL FERRANTE** – guitar / **GREG CARTER** – drums / **SCOTT SPRAY** – bass / **RONNIE LAWSON** – keyboards, vocals / **MONIQUE WINTER** – backing vocals

| 1981. | (lp) (SKY 84503) <36494> **STANDING ON ROCK** | | |

– Step garbage / Standing on rock / Love is everywhere / Martians / Rock'n'roll revival / In love / Everyday man / Tomorrowland.

—— EDGAR retired from solo work for the rest of the 80's

		Thunderbolt	Cypress
Nov 90.	(cd) (CDTB 089) **HARLEM NOCTURNE**		

– Searching / Tingo tango / Cry me a river / Save your love for me / Quiet gas / Satin doll / Jordu / Girl from Ipanema / Harlem nocturne / Come back baby / Before the sunset / Who dunnit / Please come home for Christmas.

| Nov 91. | (cd; EDGAR WINTER & RICK DERRINGER) (CDTB 134) **LIVE IN JAPAN** (live) | | |

– Keep playing that rock and roll / Teenage love affair / Free ride / Fly away / Blood from a stone / Undercover man / Jump jump jump / Hang on Sloopy / Against the law / Play guitar / Rock and roll hoochie koo / Frankenstein.

		Thunderbolt	Intersound
Jan 94.	(cd) (CDTB 152) **I'M NOT A KID ANYMORE**		

– Way down south / I'm not a kid anymore / Against the law / Brother's keeper / I wanta rock / Crazy / Just like you / Big city woman / Innocent lust / Wild man / Frankenstein.

—— In Apr 94; his former keyboard wizard, DAN HARTMAN, died of a brain tumour.

| May 97. | (cd) (CDTB 182) **THE REAL DEAL** | | |

– Hoochie coo / The real deal / We can't win / Good ol' rock'n'roll / Nitty gritty / Eye of the storm / Sanctuary / Hot passionate love / Music is you / What do I tell my heart.

– compilations, etc. –

1975.	(7") Epic; (152337) **FRANKENSTEIN. / FREE RIDE**		-
Jul 91.	(cd/c; with JOHNNY) Elite; **BROTHERS IN ROCK'N'ROLL** (re-iss. Sep93)		
Apr 91.	(cd/c/lp) Columbia; (467507-2/-4/-1) **THE BEST OF EDGAR WINTER**		-
Aug 93.	(cd) Rhino; (8122 70709-2) **MISSION EARTH**		-
May 95.	(cd) Rhino; (8122 70895-2) **THE COLLECTION**		-

Johnny WINTER

Born: JOHN DAWSON WINTER III, 23 Feb'44, Leland, Mississippi, USA. Something of a musical child prodigy, WINTER grew up in Beaumont, Texas on a diet of blues and hard rock, gigging anywhere (often backed by bands including younger brother EDGAR on piano and sax) and churning out singles for small local labels, sounding like anyone from BOB DYLAN to BOBBY 'BLUE' BLAND (an early band, JOHNNY AND THE JAMMERS, released the single 'SCHOOLDAY BLUES' on 'Dart' in 1959). WINTER hammered out power blues at amazing velocity and played some of the most ferocious slide guitar ever laid down on vinyl, a compression of MUDDY WATERS, ROBERT JOHNSON and ELMORE JAMES sped up to breakneck speed. By the late 60's he was totally into the blues, fronting a power trio including TOMMY SHANNON (bass – later to back STEVIE RAY VAUGHAN) and drummer JOHN 'RED' TURNER. This was the combination with which he made his major label breakthrough, signing to 'Columbia' on a five year, $300,000 contract in 1969 (a bargain as WINTER became the top live act of the early 70's). 'Imperial' Records stole 'Columbia's' thunder by releasing 'THE PROGRESSIVE BLUES EXPERIMENT' (a US Top 50 hit) as a one-off album prior to WINTERS' new company getting a record out. After two albums, the eponymous debut and 'SECOND WINTER', his manager steered him towards hard rock and, dumping SHANNON and TURNER, teamed him up with the 60's teen band, The McCOYS, to form, JOHNNY WINTER AND . . . . Two albums later (including the eponymous set which was to become his biggest seller outwith the US and included such choice fare as 'ROCK N ROLL HOOCHIE KOO', 'STORMY MONDAY' and Eddie Floyd's 'FIVE LONG YEARS'), WINTER was in rehab with a severe heroin habit. His creative capacity was obviously suffering judging by the patchy-at-best quality of 'STILL ALIVE AND WELL' (1973) and 'JOHN DAWSON WINTER III' (1974), his first couple of releases for new label, 'Blue Sky'. He was subsequently reunited with brother, EDGAR for 'TOGETHER' in 1976 (a rag-bag of soul and old time rock'n'roll favourites). WINTER duly re-emerged with a renewed commitment to the blues and his biggest 70's achievements were the production of MUDDY WATERS' post 'Chess' albums beginning with 1977's 'HARD AGAIN' and his own 'NOTHIN BUT THE BLUES', recorded with the same band during the same sessions. 1978's 'WHITE HOT AND BLUE' marked the guitarist's final US chart entry (Top 200) for six years; a new band comprising WINTER, JON PARIS on bass and BOBBY TORDELLO on drums was formed for 'RAISIN CAIN' in 1980, subsequently signing to 'Alligator' Records prior to 1984's 'WHOOPIN'. 'GUITAR SLINGER', 'SERIOUS BUSINESS' and 'THIRD DEGREE' (a Grammy winner) followed over the next two years and although they were his best blues albums in years, they all failed to chart. WINTER subsequently attempted to re-enter the rock market with 'MCA's 'WINTER OF 88'; the results were poor and the man now records blues for 'Point Blank', his first release for the label being 1991's 'LET ME IN'. The same year he featured on JOHN LEE HOOKER's 'Mr. Lucky' and in 1992, sang 'HIGHWAY 61 REVISITED' at the BOB DYLAN Anniversary Tribute in Madison Square Garden. WINTER may not be the greatest white blues guitarist although he probably should have been and can still take the breath away on a good night. • Songwriters: J.WINTER or DERRINGER, with mostly covers; JUMPIN' JACK FLASH + SILVER TRAIN + LET IT BLEED + STRAY CAT BLUES + SILVER TRAIN (Rolling Stones) / HIGHWAY 101 (Van Morrison) / IT'S ALL OVER NOW (Bobby & Shirley Womack) / GREAT BALLS OF FIRE + WHOLE LOTTA SHAKIN' GOIN' ON (Jerry Lee Lewis) / LONG TALL SALLY + SLIPPIN' & SLIDIN' (Little Richard) / BONY MORONIE (Larry Williams) / JOHNNY B. GOODE + THIRTY DAYS (Chuck Berry) / ROCK & ROLL PEOPLE (John Lennon) / IT'S MY OWN FAULT (B.B. King) / HIGHWAY 61 REVISITED (Bob Dylan) / SHAME SHAME SHAME (Shirley Ellis) / RAISED ON ROCK (Elmore James) / ROCK ME BABY (Big Bill Broozy-Arthur Crudup) / GOOD MORNING LITTLE SCHOOLGIRL (Don & Bob) / BAREFOOTIN' (Robert Parker) / PLEASE COME HOME FOR CHRISTMAS (Charles Brown) / GOT MY BRAND ON YOU (Muddy Waters) / etc.

Album rating: WINTER, THE PROGRESSIVE BLUES EXPERIMENT (*4) / JOHNNY WINTER (*7) / SECOND WINTER (*8) / JOHNNY WINTER AND . . . (*7) / JOHNNY WINTER AND . . . LIVE (*6) / STILL ALIVE AND WELL (*6) / SAINTS AND SINNERS (*6) / JOHN DAWSON WINTER III (*5) / CAPTURED LIVE! (*5) / TOGETHER with Edgar Winter (*5) / NOTHIN' BUT THE BLUES (*6) / WHITE, HOT & BLUE (*4) / RAISIN' CAIN (*4) / WHOOPIN' (*4) / GUITAR SLINGER (*6) / SERIOUS BUSINESS (*5) / THIRD DEGREE (*4) / WINTER OF '88 (*5) / LET ME IN (*4) / HEY, WHERE'S YOUR BROTHER? (*5) / A ROCK'N'ROLL COLLECTION compilation (*7)

JOHNNY WINTER – vocals, guitar, mandolin / with **EDGAR WINTER** – keyboards, alto saxophone / **TOMMY SHANNON** – bass, ukelele / **JOHN 'Red' TURNER** – percussion

			Liberty	Imperial
May 69.	(lp) *(LBS 83240)* <12431> **WINTER, THE PROGRESSIVE BLUES EXPERIMENT**			49 Apr69

– Rollin' and tumblin' / Tribute to Muddy / I got love if you want it / Bad luck and trouble / Help me / Mean town blues / Broke down engine / Black cat bones / It's my own fault / Forty-four. *(re-iss. 1973 on 'Sunset'; 50264) (re-iss. Oct79 on 'Liberty'; LBR 1001) (re-iss. Nov86 on 'Razor'; MACH 7) (cd-iss. Sep93 on 'I.T.M.')*

			C.B.S.	Columbia
Jun 69.	(lp) *(CBS 63619)* <9826> **JOHNNY WINTER**			24 May69

– I'm yours and I'm hers / Be careful with a fool / Dallas / Mean mistreater / Leland Mississippi blues / Good morning little schoolgirl / When you got a good friend / I'll drown in my tears / Back door friend. *(re-iss. Jan76; same) (re-iss. Nov85 on 'Edsel' lp/c; ED/CED 163) (cd-iss. Jan97 on 'Columbia'; 471218-2)*

Jul 69. (7") *(CBS 4386)* <44900> **I'M YOURS AND I'M HERS. / I'LL DROWN IN MY TEARS**

Jan 70.	(d-lp;3-playing sides) *(CBS 66231)* <9947> **SECOND WINTER**	59	55 Nov69

– Memory pain / I'm not sure / The good love / Slippin' and slidin' / Miss Ann / Johnny B. Goode / Highway 61 revisited / I love everybody / Hustled down in Texas / I hate everybody / Fast life rider. *(re-iss. 1974; same) (re-iss. Apr89 on 'Edsel' lp/cd; ED/CD 312)*

Jan 70.	(7") *(CBS 4794)* <45058> **JOHNNY B.GOODE. / I'M NOT SURE**		92 Dec69

—— band now **RICK DERRINGER** – guitar, producer repl. EDGAR who went solo / **RANDY JO HOBBS** – bass / **RANDY ZEHRINGER** (RICK's bro) – drums (all ex-McCOYS)

Oct 70.	(lp) *(CBS 64117)* <30221> **JOHNNY WINTER AND**	29	Sep70

– Guess I'll go away / Ain't that a kindness / No time to live / Rock and roll hoochie koo / Am I here? / Look up / Prodigal son / On the limb / Let the music play / Nothing left / Funky music. *(re-iss. Sep91 on 'Beat Goes On' lp/cd; BGO LP/CD 105)*

Nov 70. (7") <45260> **ROCK AND ROLL HOOCHIE KOO. / 21st CENTURY MAN** –

—— **BOBBY CALDWELL** – drums repl. RANDY

May 71.	(lp) *(CBS 64289)* <64289> **JOHNNY WINTER AND LIVE (live)**	20	40 Mar71

– Good morning little schoolgirl / It's my own fault / Jumpin' Jack Flash / Rock'n'roll medley: Great balls of fire – Long tall Sally – Whole lotta shakin' goin' on – Mean town blues / Johnny B.Goode. *(re-iss. 1974; same) (re-iss. Jan89 on 'Beat Goes On'; BGOLP 29) (re-iss. Jun92; BGOCD 29)*

May 71.	(7") *(CBS 7227)* <45368> **JUMPIN' JACK FLASH (live). / GOOD MORNING LITTLE SCHOOLGIRL (live)**		89 Apr71

—— Due to drugs problems, JOHNNY semi-retired. DERRINGER joined EDGAR WINTER Re-united w/DERRINGER in 1973, **RICHARD HUGHES** – drums repl. CALDWELL

Apr 73.	(lp) *(CBS 65484)* <32188> **STILL ALIVE AND WELL**		22

– Rock me baby / Can't you feel it / Cheap tequila / All tore down / Rock and roll / Silver train / Ain't nothing to me / Still alive and well / Too much seconal / Let it bleed. *(also on quad.Sep74; CQ 32188) (cd-iss. Apr93 on 'Sony Europe')*

Jun 73. (7") *(CBS 1620)* <45860> **SILVER TRAIN. / ROCK AND ROLL**

Sep 73. (7") <45899> **CAN YOU FEEL IT. / ROCK AND ROLL** – –

Mar 74. (7") <46036> **BONY MORONIE. / HURTIN' SO BAD** –

Mar 74.	(lp/c) *(CBS/40 65842)* <32715> **SAINTS AND SINNERS**		42 Feb74

– Stone County / Blinded by love / Thirty days / Stray cat blues / Bad luck situation / Rollin' cross the country / Riot in cell block #9 / Hurtin' so bad / Bony Moronie / Feedback on Highway 101. *(cd-iss. Apr93 on 'Sony Europe') (cd-iss. Jul94; CK 66420)*

Apr 74. (7") *(CBS 2162)* <46006> **STONE COUNTY. / BAD LUCK SITUATION** Jan74

			Blue Sky	Blue Sky
Nov 74.	(7") *(CBS 2800)* **MIND OVER MATTER. / PICK UP ON MY MOJO**			–
Dec 74.	(lp/c) *(SKY/40 80586)* <33292> **JOHN DAWSON WINTER III**			78

– Rock & roll people / Golden days of rock & roll / Self-destructable blues / Raised on rock / Stranger / Mind over matter / Roll with me / Love song to me / Pick up on my mojo / Lay down your sorrows / Sweet Papa John. *(cd-iss. Apr93 on 'Sony Europe')*

Dec 74. (7") <2754> **RAISED ON ROCK. / PICK UP ON MY MOJO** –

Feb 75. (7") <2756> **GOLDEN DAYS OF ROCK & ROLL. / STRANGER** –

—— **FLOYD RADFORD** – guitar repl. DERRINGER.

Mar 76.	(lp/c) *(SKY/40 69230)* <33944> **CAPTURED LIVE! (live)**		93

– Bony Moronie / Roll with me / Rock & roll people / It's all over now / Highway 61 revisited / Sweet Papa John.

—— Mid'76, teamed up with brother EDGAR on below set

—— + **RICK DERRINGER** + **FLOYD RADFORD** – guitar / **CHUCK RUFF** + **RICHARD HUGHES** – drums / **RANDY JO HOBBS** – bass (DAN HARTMAN was now solo disco artist)

Jul 76.	(lp/c; JOHNNY & EDGAR WINTER) *(SKY/40 81338)* <34033> **TOGETHER (live)**		89

– Harlem shuffle / Soul man / You've lost that lovin' feeling / Rock'n'roll medley:- Slippin' & slidin' – Jailhouse rock – Tutti frutti – Sick & tired – I'm ready – Reelin' and rockin' – Blue sude shoes – Jenny take a ride – Good golly Miss Molly / Let the good times roll / Mercy, mercy / Baby whatcha want me to do. *(cd-iss. Jun93 on 'Sony Europe')*

Aug 76. (7") <2764> **SOUL MAN. / LET THE GOOD TIMES ROLL** –

—— Early 1977, JOHNNY also produced and joined MUDDY WATERS band.

—— with **CHARLES CALMESE** – bass / **WILLIE SMITH** – drums / MUDDY WATERS – guitar

Aug 77.	(lp/c) *(SKY/40 82141)* <34813> **NOTHIN' BUT THE BLUES**		Jul77

– Tired of tryin' / TV mama / Everybody's blues / Sweet love and evil woman / Drinkin' blues / Mad blues / It was rainin' / Blondie Mae / Walking thru the park. *(re-iss. Aug91 on 'Beat Goes On' lp/cd; BGO LP/CD 104)*

—— with **BOBBY TORELLO** – drums / **I.P.SWEAT** – bass / **PAT RUSH** – guitar / + **EDGAR**

Aug 78.	(lp/c) *(SKY/40 82963)* <35475> **WHITE, HOT AND BLUE**		

– Walkin' by myself / Slidin' in / Divin' duck blues / One stop at a time / Nickel blues / E-Z rider / Last night / Messin' with the kid / Honest I do. *(cd-iss. Jun93 on 'Sony Europe')*

—— now with **BOBBY TORTELLO** – drums / **JON PARIS** – bass, etc.

May 80.	(lp/c) *(SKY/40 84103)* <36343> **RAISIN' CAIN**		

– The crawl / Sitting in this jail house / Like a rolling stone / New York, New York / Talk is cheap / Rollin' and tumblin' / Don't hide your love. *(cd-iss. Apr93 on 'Sony Europe')*

			Sonet	Alligator
Mar 84.	(lp) **WHOOPIN'**			

– I got my eyes on you / Sonny's whoopin' the doop / Burnt child / Whoee whoee / Crow Jane / So tough with me / Whoo wee baby / I think I got the blues / Ya ya / Roll me baby.

Aug 84.	(lp) *(SNTF 914)* <4735> **GUITAR SLINGER**		

– It's my life baby / Don't like advantage / Iodine in my coffee / Trick bag / Mad dog / Boothill / I smell trouble / Lights out / My soul / Kiss tomorrow goodbye. *(cd-iss. Oct86; SNTCD 914) <US cd-iss. 1990's; ALCD 4735>*

Sep 85.	(lp) *(SNTF 948)* <4742> **SERIOUS BUSINESS**		

– Master mechanic / Sound the bell / Murdering the blues / It ain't your business / Good time woman / Unseen eye / My time after a while / Serious as a heart attack / Give it back / Route 90. *(re-iss. Jun88 cd/c; SNTCD/ZCSN 948) <US cd-iss. 1988; ALCD 4742>*

Oct 86.	(lp/cd) *(SNT F/CD 965)* **THIRD DEGREE**		

– Mojo boogie / Love, life and money / Evil on my mind / See see baby / Tin pan alley / I'm good / Third degree / Shake your moneymaker / Bad girl blues / Broke and lonely.

—— now with **JON PARIS** – bass / **TOM COMPTON** – drums

			M.C.A.	Voyager-MCA
Nov 88.	(lp/c/cd) *(MCF/MCFC/DMCF 3436)* <42241> **WINTER OF '88**			

– Close to me / Stranger blues / Lightning / Anything for your love / Rain / Ain't that just like a woman / Looking for trouble / Look away.

			Point Blank	Virgin
Aug 91.	(cd/lp) *(VPB CD/LP 5)* **LET ME IN**			

– Illustrated man / Barefootin' / Life is hard / Hey you / Blue mood / Sugarlee / Medicine man / You're humbuggin' me / If you got a good woman / Got to find my baby / Shame shame shame / Let me in. *(cd+=) – You lie too much.*

—— with **JEFF GANZ** – bass / **TOM COMPTON** – drums, percussion / guests **EDGAR** – sax / **BILLY BRANCH** – harmonica

Sep 92.	(cd/c/lp) *(VPB CD/TC/LP 11)* **HEY, WHERE'S YOUR BROTHER?**			

– Johnny Guitar / She likes to boogie real low / White line blues / Please come home for Christmas / You must have a twin / You keep sayin' that you're leavin' / Hard way / Sick and tired / Blues this bad / no more dogin' / Check out her mama / Got my brand on you. *(cd+=) – One step forward (two steps back).*

– compilations, etc. –

			GRT; ROADRUNNER	
1969.	(7") *GRT; ROADRUNNER.* / **GANGSTER OF LOVE**		–	
1971.	(lp) *Marble Arch; / GRT; <10010>* **THE JOHNNY WINTER STORY**			Sep69
1970.	(lp) *Buddah; (2359 011)* **FIRST WINTER**			
1971.	(lp) *Janus; <3008>* **ABOUT BLUES**			
1971.	(lp) *Janus; <3023>* **EARLY TIMES**			
Feb 81.	(d-lp) *Blue Sky; (SKY 88457)* **THE JOHNNY WINTER STORY – RAISED ON ROCK**			
Jul 84.	(lp) *President; (PRCV 116)* **EARLY WINTER** *(cd-iss. Jan87; PRCD 116)*			
Apr 86.	(lp) *Showcase; (SHLP/SHTC 132)* **LIVIN' IN THE BLUES** *(cd-iss. Oct90 on 'Thunderbolt'; CDTB 083)*			
Mar 87.	(lp/c)(cd) *Topline; (TOP/KTOP 168)(TOPCD 515)* **OUT OF SIGHT**			

Date	Details	UK	US
1988.	(d-lp/c/cd) *Castle*; (CCS LP/MC/CD 167) **THE JOHNNY WINTER COLLECTION** – Rock and roll hoochie koo / Cheap tequila / On the lamb / Slippin' and slidin' / Johnny B.Goode / Rock me baby / Let it bleed / Stray cat blues / Riot in cell block 9 / Bony Moronie / Highway 61 revisited / Raised on rock / Pick up on my mojo / Thirty days / Good morning little school girl / Jumpin' Jack Flash / It's my own fault / Medley:- Great balls of fire – Long tall Sally – Whole lotta shakin' goin' on.	☐	-
Jan 89.	(lp) *Relix*; **BIRDS CAN'T ROW BOATS**	-	-
Nov 89.	(lp/cd) *Thunderbolt*; (THBL/CDTB 073) **FIVE AFTER 4 A.M.**	-	-
Apr 90.	(cd/lp; JOHNNY WINTER & UNCLE JOHN TURNER) (THBL/CDTB 077) **BACK IN BEAUMONT**	☐	-
Jul 91.	(cd) *Thunderbolt*; (CDTB 100) **LIVE IN HOUSTON, BUSTED IN AUSTIN (live)**	☐	-
Feb 92.	(cd; JOHNNY WINTER & CALVIN JOHNSON) *Thunderbolt*; (CDTB 126) **RAW TO THE BONE**	☐	-
Aug 92.	(cd/c) *Sony*; (471661-2/-4) **SCORCHIN' BLUES**	☐	-
Nov 92.	(cd) *Fan Club*; **LIVE AT LIBERTY HALL, HOUSTON, TX. 1972 (live with JIMMY REED)**	☐	-
Feb 93.	(cd) *Charly*; (CDCD 1033) **THE TEXAS TORNADO**	☐	-
Apr 93.	(cd) *Pulsar*; **THE GOLDEN DAYS OF ROCK'N'ROLL**	☐	-
Nov 93.	(cd) *Thunderbolt*; (CDTB 149) **WHITE LIGHTNING**	☐	-
Jul 94.	(cd/c) *Success*; **LIVIN' THE BLUES**	☐	-
Jun 96.	(cd) *Sony*; (483897-2) **A ROCK AND ROLL COLLECTION**	☐	-
Jan 97.	(cd) *Thunderbolt*; (CDTB 509) **ELECTRIC BLUES MAN**	☐	-
Mar 96.	(cd) *Thunderbolt*; (CDTB 165) / *Magnum*; <41> **BROKE AND LONELY**	☐	-
Jan 97.	(cd) *Sundazed*; (SC 6070) **LIVIN' IN THE BLUES**	☐	-
Jan 97.	(cd) *Sundazed*; (SC 6071) **EASE MY PAIN**	☐	-
Feb 97.	(cd) *Castle*; (CCSCD 445) **WINTER BLUES**	☐	-
Apr 97.	(cd) *Carlton*; (303600085-2) **JOHNNY B. GOODE**	☐	-
Feb 98.	(d-cd) *Snapper*; (SMDCD 185) **TEXAS BLUES**	☐	-

Steve WINWOOD

Born: 12 May'48, Birmingham, Warwickshire, England. The young WINWOOD had his first encounter with rock'n'roll via his music loving uncle before beginning his illustrious career with his father's band. At the age of 15 (already an accomplished vocalist, guitarist and keyboard player), he joined The SPENCER DAVIS GROUP with brother MUFF, where he had three massive hits on the fledgling 'Island' records between 1963 and April 1967; the brilliant 'KEEP ON RUNNING', 'SOMEBODY HELP ME' and 'GIMME SOME LOVING'. Around this time he formed TRAFFIC and scored three more, newly psychedelicised UK Top 10 smashes, 'PAPER SUN', 'HOLE IN MY SHOE' and 'HERE WE GO ROUND THE MULBERRY BUSH'. In 1969, (still only 21) WINWOOD joined ERIC CLAPTON, GINGER BAKER and RIC GRECH in the short-lived supergroup, BLIND FAITH. Early the following year, he joined GINGER BAKER's AIRFORCE, subsequently returning to TRAFFIC in 1971. WINWOOD's first solo album was to have been 'MUD SHADOWS' in 1970 although it eventually surfaced as TRAFFIC album, 'JOHN BARLEYCORN MUST DIE', following the input of JIM CAPALDI and CHRIS WOOD. After leaving TRAFFIC, he made session appearances for TOOTS & THE MAYTALS, The SUTHERLAND BROTHERS and SANDY DENNY plus a guest spot on 'GO' by STOMU YAMASHTA. Having re-signed to 'Island' in 1976, his first solo venture (released at the onset of punk) was an undistinguished eponymous effort in 1977. His second release (taking two years to complete) 'ARC OF A DIVER' (1981) was produced, engineered and performed by WINWOOD himself with excellent results (the album and the extracted single 'WHILE YOU SEE A CHANCE' both reached US Top 10 while the album hit the UK Top 20). 'TALKING BACK TO THE NIGHT' (1982) was similar to the preceding album and had, in 'VALERIE', an outstanding highlight. 1986 saw WINWOOD joining the 80's tasteful coffee table elite with 'BACK IN THE HIGH LIFE', a record which sold three million copies in the US alone. One of the set's standouts, 'HIGHER LOVE' (with guest vocals by CHAKA KHAN), topped the US singles chart and earned him a Grammy. His contract with 'Island' expired shortly after and the label were outbid by 'Virgin', who reportedly secured WINWOOD's artistic services with an offer worth 13 million. His first release for the label, 'ROLL WITH IT', saw him teaming up with The MEMPHIS HORNS, such enduring songs as 'DANCING SHOES' and the fantastic title track ensured that WINWOOD would enjoy the fruits of his first No.1 album. The 1990 follow-up, 'REFUGEES OF THE HEART' was extremely disappointing, however, and together with CAPALDI, WINWOOD reformed TRAFFIC in 1994. • **Songwriters:** For his debut in 1977, he co-wrote with JIM CAPALDI (an ex-member of TRAFFIC). He collaborated on some further releases with lyricist VIV STANSHALL, WILL JENNINGS and JOE WALSH. • **Trivia:** He was also a renowned session man, having played on albums by JIMI HENDRIX (1968 + 1970) / JOE COCKER (1969) / McDONALD & GILES (1970) / LEON RUSSELL (1970) / HOWLIN' WOLF (1971) / ALVIN LEE (1973) / JOHN MARTYN (1973) / AMAZING BLONDEL (1973) / JADE WARRIOR (1975) / TOOTS & THE MAYTALS (1976) / SANDY DENNY (1977) / VIVIAN STANSHALL (1978) / GEORGE HARRISON (1979) / MARIANNE FAITHFULL (1979) / PIERRE MOERLEN'S GONG (1979) / etc. (see other 'Island' label artists).

Album rating: STEVE WINWOOD (*7) / ARC OF A DIVER (*8) / TALKING BACK TO THE NIGHT (*6) / BACK IN THE HIGH LIFE (*8) / CHRONICLES compilation (*7) / ROLL WITH IT (*6) / REFUGEES OF THE HEART (*6) / THE FINER THINGS boxed-set compilation/history (*8) / JUNCTION SEVEN (*4)

STEVE WINWOOD (debut solo recording was actually compiled from his past bands' work)

Date	Details	Island	U.A.
May 71.	(d-lp) (ILPS 9964) <9950> **WINWOOD** – (tracks by SPENCER DAVIS GROUP / TRAFFIC / BLIND FAITH / AIRFORCE)	☐	93

— Later that year, WINWOOD reformed TRAFFIC and went into lots of session work mainly for 'Island' artists. In 1976, he and ex-SANTANA drummer MIKE SHRIEVE collaborated with solo classical percussionist STOMU YAMASH'TA. As **"GO"**, they issued eponymous live album in Jun76. When WINWOOD was releasing solo albums, GO also issued live 12" CROSSING THE LINE. Another album GO LIVE IN PARIS (live), was given light in Spring'78. (see STOMU YAMASH'TA discography)

STEVE WINWOOD

STEVE WINWOOD – vocals, keyboards solo with **WILLIE WEEKS** – bass / **ANDY NEWMARK** – drums / **REEBOP KWAKU BANU** – congas

Date	Details	Island	Island
Jun 77.	(7") (WIP 6394) **TIME IS RUNNING OUT. / PENULTIMATE ZONE**	☐	☐
Jul 77.	(7") **TIME IS RUNNING OUT. / HOLD ON**	-	-
Jul 77.	(lp/c) (ILPS/ZCI 9494) **STEVE WINWOOD** – Hold on / Time is running out / Midland maniac / Vacant chair / Luck's in / Let me make something in your life. (cd-iss. May87; CID 9494) (re-iss. cd Mar93; IMCD 161)	12	22

— His next projects/albums featured WINWOOD on all instruments, vocals

Date	Details	Island	Island
Dec 80.	(lp/c) (ILPS/ICT 9576) **ARC OF A DIVER** – While you see a chance / Arc of a diver / Second-hand woman / Slowdown sundown / Spanish dancer / Night train / Dust. (cd-iss. May87; CID 9576)	13	3
Dec 80.	(7"/c-s) (WIP/CWIP 6655) <49656> **WHILE YOU SEE A CHANCE. / VACANT CHAIR**	45	7
Mar 81.	(7"/12") (WIP/12WIP 6680) **SPANISH DANCER (remix). / HOLD ON**	☐	☐
May 81.	(7") <49726> **ARC OF A DIVER. / DUST**	-	48
Sep 81.	(7"/12") (WIP/12WIP 6710) **NIGHT TRAIN. / ('A'instrumental)**	☐	☐
Nov 81.	(7") (WIP 6747) **THERE'S A RIVER. / TWO WAY STRETCH**	☐	
Jul 82.	(7") (WIP 6786) <29940> **STILL IN THE GAME. / DUST**		47
Aug 82.	(lp/c) (ILPS/ICT 9777) **TALKING BACK TO THE NIGHT** – Valerie / Big girls walk away / And I go / While there's a candle burning / Still in the game / It was happiness / Help me angel / Talking back to the night / There's a river. (cd-iss. May87; CID 9777)	6	28 Jul82
Sep 82.	(7"/12") (WIP/12WIP 6818) <29879> **VALERIE. / SLOWDOWN SUNDOWN**	51	70
Jun 83.	(7") (WIP 6849) **YOUR SILENCE IS YOUR SONG. / ('A'instrumental)**	☐	

— Around the mid-80's, his work took a back seat as his marriage broke down. In 1986, he brought in session musicians to augment.

Date	Details	Island	Island
Jun 86.	(7") (IS 288) <28710> **HIGHER LOVE. / AND I GO** (ext.12"+=) (12IS 288) – ('A'instrumental). (c-s+=) (CIS 288) – Valerie / While you see a chance / Talking back to the night.	13	1
Jul 86.	(lp/c/cd) (ILPS/ICT/CID 9844) <25448> **BACK IN THE HIGH LIFE** – Higher love / Take it as it comes / Freedom overspill / Back in the high life again / The finer things / Wake me up on judgement day / Split decision / My love's leavin'.	8	3
Aug 86.	(7") <28595> **FREEDOM OVERSPILL. / HELP ME ANGEL**	-	20
Aug 86.	(7") (IS 294) **FREEDOM OVERSPILL. / SPANISH DANCER** (some w/ c-s+=) (IS 294) – (last lp excerpts & interview). (12"+=) (12IS 294) – ('A'-Liberty mix). (12"w/ free 7") (ISG 294) – Low spark of high heeled boys / Gimme some lovin'. (d7"+=) (ISD 294) – Higher love / And I go.	69	-
Jan 87.	(7") (IS 303) **BACK IN THE HIGH LIFE AGAIN. / HELP ME ANGEL** (12"+=) (12IS 303) – Night train (instrumental).	53	-
Feb 87.	(7") <28498> **THE FINER THINGS. / NIGHT TRAIN**	-	8
May 87.	(7") <28472> **BACK IN THE HIGH LIFE AGAIN. / NIGHT TRAIN (instrumental)**	-	13
Sep 87.	(7") (IS 336) <28231> **VALERIE (remix). / TALKING BACK TO THE NIGHT (instrumental)** (c-s+=/12"+=/cd-s+=) (CIS/12IS/CID 336) – The finer things.	19	9
Oct 87.	(lp)(c)(cd) (SSW/+MC/CD 1) <25660> **CHRONICLES** (compilation) – Wake me up on judgement day / While you see a chance / Vacant chair / Help me angel / My love's leavin' / Valerie / Arc of a diver / Higher love / Spanish dancer / Talking back to the night.	12	26
Feb 88.	(7") <28122> **TALKING BACK TO THE NIGHT. / THERE'S A RIVER**	-	57

Date	Details	Virgin	Virgin
May 88.	(7"/ext.12") (VS/+T 1085) <99326> **ROLL WITH IT. / THE MORNING SIDE** (cd-s+=) (VSCD 1085) – ('A'extended). (c-s+=) (VSTC 1085) – ('A'dub version).	53	1
Jun 88.	(cd/c/lp) (CD/TC/V 2532) <90946> **ROLL WITH IT** – Roll with it / Holding on / The morning side / Put on your dancing shoes / Don't you know what the night can do? / Hearts on fire / One more morning / Shining song.	4	1
Aug 88.	(7") (VS 1107) <99290> **DON'T YOU KNOW WHAT THE NIGHT CAN DO? (remix). / ('A'instrumental)** (12"+=) (VST 1107) – ('A'extended). (cd-s+=) (VSCD 1107) – Roll with it.	☐	6
Oct 88.	(7") (VS 1135) <99261> **HOLDING ON. / ('A'instrumental)** (3"cd-s+=/12"+=) (VS T/CD 1135) – ('A'dance version) / Go Juan.	☐	11
Mar 89.	(7") <99234> **HEARTS ON FIRE. / (instrumental)**	-	53
Oct 90.	(7") <98892> **ONE AND ONLY MAN. / ALWAYS** (12"+=/cd-s+=) –	-	18
Nov 90.	(cd/c/lp) (CD/TC/V 2650) <91405> **REFUGEES OF THE HEART** – You'll keep on searching / Every day (oh Lord) / One and only man / I will be here / Another deal goes down / Running on / Come out and dance / In the light of day.	26	27

Apr 91. (7") **I WILL BE HERE. / IN THE LIGHT OF DAY**
(Instrumental)
(12"+=/cd-s+=) –
Mar 97. (c-s/cd-s) *(VSC/+DT 1642)* **SPY IN THE HOUSE OF LOVE /**
COME OUT AND DANCE
Jun 97. (cd/c) *(CDV/TCV 2832)* **JUNCTION SEVEN** `32`
– Spy in the house of love / Angel of mercy / Just wanna have some fun / Let your love come down / Real love / Fill me up / Gotta get back to my baby / Someone like you / Family affair / Plenty lovin' / Lord of the street.

– compilations, others –

May 65. (7"; by ANGLOS) *Fontana; (TF 589)* **INCENSE. / YOU'RE**
FOOLING ME
(re-iss. May69 on 'Island'; WIP 6061)
Aug 91. (cd/c/lp) *Island; (CID/ICT/ILPS 9975)* **KEEP ON RUNNING**
– (tracks by SPENCER DAVIS GROUP / TRAFFIC / BLIND FAITH / + 2 solo)
(re-iss. cd Mar96; IMCD 224)
Mar 95. (4xcd-box) *Island; (IBXCD 1)* **THE FINER THINGS**
– (tracks by SPENCER DAVIS GROUP / ERIC CLAPTON & POWERHOUSE /
BLIND FAITH / TRAFFIC / STOMU YAMASH'TA's GO / solo)

WIPERS (dig out; Great Alt & Indie . . .)

WIRE

Formed: London, England . . . October '76, by GRAHAM LEWIS, COLIN NEWMAN, BRUCE GILBERT and ROBERT GOTOBED. WIRE made their vinyl debut in April '77 when safety pin-pierced ears were subjected to their punk anthems, '12XU' and 'LOWDOWN' on the seminal Various Artists lp, 'Live At The Roxy'. The EMI backed label 'Harvest', desperate for some hip punk credibility, decided to give WIRE a contract and although unsuccessful with their first single attempt ('MANNEQUIN'), unleashed the Mike Thorne-produced 'PINK FLAG' at the end of '77. The record contained 21 short, sharp shocks of minimalist punk rock/new wave, possessed of a musical intelligence that dwarfed their more retro-fixated contemporaries. Early in 1978, they followed this with the classic 'I AM THE FLY', lyrically a simple piece of what can only be described as progressive punk. After another fruitless stab at the charts with 'DOT DASH', they returned with an even more engaging second set, the oblique, atmospheric 'CHAIRS MISSING'. This record surely deserved better than its Top 50 placing, featuring as it did the classy avant-punk tunes, 'PRACTICE MAKES PERFECT', 'I FEEL MYSTERIOUS TODAY' and the "minor" hit 45, 'OUTDOOR MINER'. In the Autumn of '79, WIRE's third set, '154' hit the Top 40, effectively displaying an even more experimental side to the one-time three-chord wonders. Sadly, however, it was their final outing for 'Harvest', the group moving on to the more appropriate indie label, 'Rough Trade', who released the 1981 single, 'OUR SWIMMER'. An anti-commercial, unproduced live set appeared around the same time, the band members having already taken off for solo projects. One of these, DOME (aka GILBERT & LEWIS), had been in the pipeline for some time, while NEWMAN went onto indie success with several albums. In 1986, the much-in-demand WIRE returned, completing a few EP's for top indie, 'Mute' before the following year's 'THE IDEAL COPY' album. They continued to enjoy cult success, which even spread across the Atlantic, the band signing to US label, 'Enigma'. In 1991, GOTOBED retired (to Bedfordshire, no doubt?!) and the band became WIR, releasing the disappointing 'THE FIRST LETTER' that year. For the remainder of the 90's, each took on individual projects, all fairly obscure of course. • **Songwriters:** Group compositions. • **Trivia:** COLIN NEWMAN produced The VIRGIN PRUNES in 1982 and FAD GADGET in 1984. He moved to India at this time, returning after a few years to live in Belgium, where he founded 'Crammed Discs' records.

Album rating: PINK FLAG (*8) / CHAIRS MISSING (*9) / 154 (*7) / DOCUMENT AND EYEWITNESS: ELECTRIC BALLROOM (*6) / THE IDEAL COPY (*7) / A BELL IS A CUP . . . UNTIL IT IS STRUCK (*5) / ON RETURNING (1977-1979) compilation (*8) / IT'S BEGINNING TO & BACK AGAIN 6) / MANSCAPE (*5) / THE FIRST LETTER (*4; as Wir)

COLIN NEWMAN (b.16 Sep'54, Salisbury, England) – vox, guitar, keyboards / **BRUCE GILBERT** (b.18 May'46, Watford, England) – guitar, vocals, synths. / **GRAHAM LEWIS** (b.22 Feb'53, Grantham, England) – bass, vocals, synthesizers / **ROBERT GOTOBED** (b. MARK FIELD, 1951, Leicester, England) – drums, percussion (ex-SNAKES, ex-ART ATTACKS) / **GEORGE GILL** – guitar (left before debut)

	Harvest	Harvest
Nov 77. (7"m) *(HAR 5144)* **MANNEQUIN. / 12XU / FEELING CALLED LOVE**	☐	-

Nov 77. (lp/c) *(SHSP/TC-SHSP 4076)* <11757> **PINK FLAG**
– Reuters / Field day for the Sundays / Three girl rhumba / Ex-lion tamer / Lowdown / Start to move / Brazil / It's so obvious / Surgeon's girl / Pink flag / The commercial / Straight line / 106 beats that / Mr. Suit / Strange / Fragile / Mannequin / Different to me / Champs / Feeling called love / 12XU. *(cd-iss. 1990 on 'Restless'+=; 72360)* – Options R. *(re-iss. cd Aug94 on 'E.M.I.'; CDGO 2063) <cd-iss. 1995 on 'Capitol'; 29857-2>*
Feb 78. (7") *(HAR 5151)* **I AM THE FLY. / EX-LION TAMER**
Jun 78. (7") *(HAR 5161)* **DOT DASH. / OPTIONS R**
Sep 78. (lp/c) *(<SHSP/TC-SHSP 4093>)* **CHAIRS MISSING** `48`
– Practice makes perfect / French film blurred / Another the letter / Men 2nd / Marooned / Sand in my joints / Being sucked in again / Heartbeat / Mercy / Outdoor miner / I am the fly / I feel mysterious today / From the nursery / Used to / Too late. *(cd-iss. 1990 on 'Restless'+=; 72361)* – Go ahead / A question of degree / Former airline. *(re-iss. cd Aug94 on 'E.M.I.'; CDGO 2065) <cd-iss. 1995 on 'Capitol'; 29858-2>*
Jan 79. (7",7"white) *(HAR 5172)* **OUTDOOR MINER. / PRACTICE MAKES PERFECT** `51`

	Harvest	Warners
Jun 79. (7") *(HAR 5187)* **A QUESTION OF DEGREE. / FORMER AIRLINE**	☐	☐

Sep 79. (lp/c) *(SHSP/TC-SHSP 4105)* <3398> **154** `39`
– I should have known better / Two people in a room / The 15th / The other window / Single k.o. / A touching display / On returning / A mutual friend / Blessed state / Once is enough / Map reference 41°N, 93°W / Indirect enquiries / 40 versions. *(free-7"ep w.a.)* *(Dome; PSR 444)* – Song 2 / Get down (parts 1 & 2) / Let's panic / Later / Small electric piece. *(cd-iss. 1990 on 'Restless'+= 72362)* – (7"ep above). *(re-iss. cd Aug94 on 'E.M.I.'; CDGO 2064) <cd-iss. 1995 on 'Capitol'; 39859>*
Oct 79. (7") *(HAR 5192)* **MAP REFERENCE 41°N 93°W. / GO AHEAD**

—— In 1980, WIRE also diversed into own activities; GILBERT & LEWIS became CUPOL and DOME, etc. The pair also joined THE THE. COLIN NEWMAN went solo taking ROBERT GOTOBED with him. The latter also became member of FAD GADGET. (see further on for these activities)

	Rough Trade	not iss.
May 81. (7") *(RT 079)* **OUR SWIMMER. / MIDNIGHT BAHNHOF CAFE**	☐	-

Jul 81. (lp) *(ROUGH 29)* **DOCUMENT AND EYEWITNESS: ELECTRIC BALLROOM (live)**
– 5 10 / 12XU (fragment) / Underwater experiences / Zegk hoqp / Everything's going to be nice / Instrumental (thrown bottle) / Piano tuner (keep strumming those guitars) / And then . . . / We meet under tables / Revealing trade secrets / Eels sang lino / Eastern standard / Coda. *(free 12"m-lp)* **DOCUMENT AND EYEWITNESS: NOTRE DAME HALL (live)** – Underwater experiences / Go ahead / Ally in exile / Relationship / Our swimmer / Witness to the fact / 2 people in a room / Heartbeat. *(re-iss. 1984 lp/c; same/ COPY 004) (cd-iss. Apr91 on 'Grey Area-Mute'; WIRE 80CD)*
Mar 83. (12"m) *(RTT 123)* **CRAZY ABOUT LOVE. / SECOND LENGTH (OUR SWIMMER) / CATAPULT 30**

—— WIRE were now back to full-time membership.

	Mute	Enigma
Nov 86. (12"ep) *(12MUTE 53)* <72245> **SNAKEDRILL**		

– A serious of snakes / Advantage in height / Up to the sun / Drill.
Mar 87. (7") *(MUTE 57)* **AHEAD. / FEED ME (live)**
(12"+=) *(12MUTE 57)* – Ambulance chasers (live) / Vivid riot of red (live).
Apr 87. (cd/c/lp) *(CD/C+/STUMM 42)* <273270> **THE IDEAL COPY** `87`
– Points of collapse / Ahead / Madman's honey / Feed me / Ambitious / Cheeking tongues / Still shows / Over theirs. *(cd+=)* – Ahead II / SNAKEDRILL EP tracks.
Mar 88. (7") *(MUTE 67)* **KIDNEY BONGOS. / PIETA**
(3"cd-s+=) *(CDMUTE 67)* – Drill (live).
(12"++=) *(12MUTE 67)* – Over theirs (live).
May 88. (cd/c/lp) *(CD/C+/STUMM 54)* <73314-1> **A BELL IS A CUP . . . UNTIL IT IS STRUCK**
– Silk skin paws / The finest drops / The queen of Ur and the king of Um / Free falling divisions / It's a boy / Boiling boy / Kidney bongos / Come back in two halves / Follow the locust / A public place. *(cd+=)* – The queen of Ur and the king of Um (alternate take) / Pieta / Over theirs (live) / Drill (live).
Jun 88. (7") *(MUTE 84)* **SILK SKIN PAWS. / GERMAN SHEPHERDS**
(12"+=) *(12MUTE 84)* – Ambitious (remix).
(3"cd-s+=) *(CDMUTE 84)* – Come back in two halves.
Apr 89. (7"clear; withdrawn) *(MUTE 87)* **EARDRUM BUZZ. / THE OFFER** `68`
(12"+=) *(12MUTE 87)* – It's a boy (instrumental).
(cd-s) *(CDMUTE 87)* – ('A'side) / Silk skin paws / A serious of snakes / Ahead (extended).
(live-12") *(LMUTE 87)* – BUZZ BUZZ BUZZ – Eardrum buzz / Ahead / Kidney bongos.

	Mute	Mute
May 89. (cd/c/lp) *(CD/C+/STUMM 66)* <73516-2> **IT'S BEGINNING TO AND BACK AGAIN (live)**		

– Finest drops / Eardrum buzz / German shepherds / Public place / It's a boy / Illuminated / Boiling boy / Over theirs / Eardrum buzz (12"version) / The offer / In vivo.
Jul 89. (7") *(MUTE 98)* **IN VIVO. / ILLUMINATED**
(12"+=/cd-s+=) *(12/CD MUTE 98)* – Finest drops (live).
May 90. (7"; w-drawn) *(MUTE 107)* **LIFE IN THE MANSCAPE. / GRAVITY WORSHIP**
(12"+=/cd-s+=) *(12/CD MUTE 107)* – Who has wine.
May 90. (cd/c/lp) *(CD/C+/STUMM 80)* <73559-2> **MANSCAPE**
– Patterns of behaviour / Goodbye ploy / Morning bell / Small black reptile / Torch it / Other moments / Sixth sense / What do you see? / Where's the deputation? / You hung your lights in the trees – A craftman's touch. *<US cd+=>* – Life in the manscape / Stampede / Children of groceries.
Apr 91. (cd/c/lp) *(CD/C+/STUMM 74)* **DRILL**
– (7 versions of out-takes from last album)

WIR

Slightly different name when GOTOBED left.
Sep 91. (7") **SO AND SLOW IT GOES. / NICE FROM HERE**
(12") – ('A'side) / ('A'-Orb mix) / Take it (for greedy)
(cd-s+=) – (all 4 tracks).
Oct 91. (cd/c/lp) *(CD/C+/STUMM 87)* <61238> **THE FIRST LETTER**
– Take it (for greedy) / So and slow it goes (extended) / A bargain at 3 and 20 yeah! / Rootsi-rootsy / Ticking mouth / It continues / Looking at me (stop!) / Naked, whooping and such-like / Tailor made / No cows on the ice / A big glue canal.

– compilations, others, etc. –

Mar 86. (m-lp) *Pink; (PINKY 7)* **PLAY POP**
Aug 86. (lp) *Dojo; (DOJOLP 36)* **IN THE PINK (live)**
Nov 87. (12"ep) *Strange Fruit; (SFPS 041)* **THE PEEL SESSIONS**
(18.1.78)
– I am the fly / Culture vultures / Practice makes perfect / 106 beats that.
Jul 89. (cd)(c/lp) *Harvest; (CDP 792 535-2)(TC+/SHSP 4127) / Restless; <72358-1>* **ON RETURNING (1977-1979)**

– 12XU / It's so obvious / Mr. Suit / Three girl rhumba / Ex lion tamer / Lowdown / Strange / Reuters / Feeling called love / I am the fly / Practise makes perfect / French film blurred / I feel mysterious today / Marooned / Sand in my joints / Outdoor miner / A question of degree / I should have known better / The other window / 40 versions / A touching display / On returning. (cd+=) – Straight line / 106 beats that / Field day for the Sundays / Champs / Dot dash / Another the letter / Men 2nd / Two people in a room / Blessed state.

Feb 90. (cd/c/lp) *Strange Fruit; (SFR CD/MC/LP 108)* **DOUBLE PEEL SESSIONS** | | – |
(*cd re-iss. May96; same*)

May 93. (cd/c/d-lp) *Mute; (CD/C+/STUMM 116)* **1985-1990 THE A LIST** | | – |

Sep 94. (cd; w/book) *Audioglobe; (SCONC 25)* **EXPLODING VIEWS** | | – |

May 95. (cd) *E.M.I.; (CDGO 2066)* **BEHIND THE CURTAIN** | | – |

Dec 95. (12"; WIRE with HAFLER TRIO) *Touch; (TONE 5)* **THE FIRST LETTER / THE LAST LAST NUMBER** | | – |

May 96. (cd/c/d-lp) *W.M.O.; (WMO 004CD)* **TURNS AND STROKES** | | – |
– Safe / Lorries / Panamanian craze / Remove for improvement / Spare one / Over my head / 12XU / Inventory / Ritual view / Part of our history / Second length (our swimmer) / Catapult 30.
(*d-lp-iss.Apr97; same*)

Oct 97. (cd) *W.M.O.; (WMO 014CD)* **World Domination; <67>**
COATINGS | | |
– Ambulance chasers / Series of snakes / Ambitious / Madman's honey / Kidney bongos / It's a boy / German shepherds / Boling boy / Drill / In vivo / Who has nine? / It can't be true can it? / Gravity worship. (*w/ free cd-s*) – AMBITIOUS

WISHBONE ASH

Formed: Torquay, Devon, England ... summer 1969 out of the EMPTY VESSELS, by MARTIN TURNER and STEVE UPTON. They quickly moved to London with two new members; ANDY POWELL and TED TURNER (no relation). In 1970, they signed to 'M.C.A.' and delivered their eponymous debut into the UK Top 40. They were described at the time as Britain's answer to The ALLMAN BROTHERS, albeit with a mystical lyrical element. Fusing heavy-rock with fine harmonies and self-indulgent solos, the second album, the Top 20 'PILGRIMAGE' was more of the same. Their third album, 'ARGUS' (1972) broke them through big time, a compelling hybrid of arcane medieval themes and water-tight prog-rock. This classic Top 3 album featured, 'WARRIOR', 'THE KING WILL COME' and 'THROW DOWN THE SWORD' alongside the more freely flowing, 'BLOWIN' FREE' (a record that should have given them a hit). 'WISHBONE FOUR' was completed the following year, a mellower set with a rootsier country-rock feel, especially on the track, 'BALLAD OF THE BEACON'. After a double live set in '73, they took an even more down-home approach on 'THERE'S THE RUB', although it did contain one highlight, 'F*U*B*B*' (Fucked Up Beyond Belief). Although they managed to retain some (very!) loyal fans, by the end of the decade they had lost all their credibility when most of the original members left. In 1981, they even drafted in folky/new-age vocalist, CLAIRE HAMILL, in an attempt to develop other areas of their sound. They are still treading the boards, churning out new versions of their once classic songs, two live albums of recent material being recorded in Chicago and Geneva respectively. • **Songwriters:** Group compositions / TURNER's.

Album rating: WISHBONE ASH (*5) / PILGRIMAGE (*6) / ARGUS (*8) / WISHBONE FOUR (*6) / LIVE DATES (*8) / THERE'S THE RUB (*5) / LOCKED IN (*4) / NEW ENGLAND (*4) / CLASSIC ASH compilation (*8) / FRONT PAGE NEWS (*5) / NO SMOKE WITHOUT FIRE (*5) / JUST TESTING (*4) / LIVE DATES II (*5) / NUMBER THE BRAVE (*4) / TWIN BARRELS BURNING (*4) / RAW TO THE BONE (*4) / NOUVEAU CALLS (*4) / HERE TO HEAR (*4) / STRANGE AFFAIR (*4) / THE ASH LIVE IN CHICAGO (*4) / BLOWIN' FREE – THE VERY BEST OF... compilation (*7) / LIVE IN GENEVA (*4) / ILLUMINATIONS (*3)

MARTIN TURNER (b. 1 Oct'47) – vocals, bass / **ANDY POWELL** (b. 8 Feb'50) – guitar, vocals repl. GLEN TURNER (no relation) / **TED TURNER** (b.DAVID, 2 Aug'50) – guitar, vocals (ex-KING BISCUIT) / **STEVE UPTON** (b.24 May'46, Wrexham, Wales) – drums

			M.C.A.	Decca
Dec 70.	(lp) *(MKPS 2014) <75249>* **WISHBONE ASH**		**34**	

– Blind eye / Lady Whiskey / Error of my ways / Queen of torture / Handy / Phoenix. (*re-iss. Feb74 lp/c; MCG/TCMCG 3507*) (*re-iss. 1980; MCA 2343*) (*cd-iss. Jul91; BGOCD 234*)

Jan 71. (7") *(MK 5061) <32826>* **BLIND EYE. / QUEEN OF TORTURE** | | |

| Sep 71. | (lp) *(MDKS 8004) <75295>* **PILGRIMAGE** | | **14** | |

– Vas dis / The pilgrim / Jail bait / Alone / Lullaby / Valediction / Where were you tomorrow. (*re-iss. Feb74 lp/c; MCG/TCMCG 3504*) (*re-iss. Dec83 lp/c; MCL/+C 1762*) (*cd-iss. Jul91; DMCL 1762*) (*cd re-iss. 1990's; MCLD 19084*) (+=) – Baby what you want me to do / Jail bait (live).

Oct 71. (7") *<32902>* **JAIL BAIT. / VAS DIS** | – | |
May 72. (lp) *(MDKS 8006) <75437>* **ARGUS** | | **3** |

– Time was / Sometime world / Blowin' free / The king will come / Leaf and stream / Warrior / Throw down the sword. (*re-iss. Feb74 lp/c; MCG/TCMCG 3510*) (*re-iss. Feb84 lp/c; MCL/+C 1787*) (*re-iss. 1987 on 'Castle' lp/c; CLA LP/MC 140*) (*cd-iss. 1991; DMCL 1787*) (*cd re-iss. 1990's; MCLD 19085*)

Jun 72. (7") *(MKS 5097) <33004>* **BLOWIN' FREE. / NO EASY ROAD** | | |

			M.C.A.	M.C.A.
May 73.	(lp) *(MDKS 8011) <327>* **WISHBONE FOUR**		**12**	**44**

– So many things to say / Ballad of the beacon / No easy road / Everybody needs a friend / Doctor / Sorrel / Sing out the song / Rock and roll widow. (*re-iss. Feb74 lp/c; MCG/TCMCG 3505*)

Jul 73. (7") *<40041>* **ROCK AND ROLL WIDOW. / NO EASY ROAD** | – | |
Jul 73. (7") *(MUS 1210)* **SO MANY THINGS TO SAY. / ROCK'N'ROLL WIDOW** | | |
Dec 73. (d-lp) *(ULD 1-2) <2-8006>* **LIVE DATES (live)** | | **82** Nov73 |

– The king will come / Warrior / Throw down the sword / Rock'n'roll widow / Ballad of the beacon / Baby what you want me to do / The pilgrim / Blowin' free / Jail bait / Lady Whiskey / Phoenix. (*re-iss. Jun74 d-lp/c; MCSP/+C 254*)

──── (Jun74) **LAURIE WISEFIELD** – guitar (ex-HOME) repl. TED who found religion

Nov 74. (7") *(MCA 165)* **HOMETOWN. / PERSEPHONE** | | |
Nov 74. (lp/c) *(MCF/TCMCF 2585) <464>* **THERE'S THE RUB** | **16** | **88** |
– Silver shoes / Don't come back / Persephone / Hometown / Lady Jay / F*U*B*B.
Feb 75. (7") *(MCA 176) <40362>* **SILVER SHOES. / PERSEPHONE** | | |

──── added on session **PETER WOODS** – keyboards

			M.C.A.	Atlantic
Mar 76.	(lp/c) *(MCF/TCMCF 2750)* **LOCKED IN**		**36**	

– Rest in peace / No water in the well / Moonshine / She was my best friend / It started in Heaven / Half past lovin' / Trust in you / Say goodbye.

Nov 76. (lp/c) *(MCG/TCMCG 3523) <18200>* **NEW ENGLAND** | **22** | |
– Mother of pearl / (In all of my dreams) You rescue me / Runaway / Lorelei / Outward bound / Prelude / When you know love / Lonely island / Candle-light. (*re-iss. Jul82 lp/c; MCL/+C 1699*)

Nov 76. (7") *(MCA 261) <3381>* **OUTWARD BOUND. / LORELEI** | | |

			M.C.A.	M.C.A.
Sep 77.	(7") *(MCA 326)* **FRONT PAGE NEWS. / DIAMOND JACK**			
Oct 77.	(lp/c) *(MCG/+C 3524) <2311>* **FRONT PAGE NEWS**		**31**	

– Front page news / Midnight dancer / Goodbye baby hello friend / Surface to air / 714 / Come in from the rain / Right or wrong / Heart beat / The day I found your love / Diamond Jack. (*re-iss. Feb82 lp/c; MCL/+C 1655*)

Oct 77. (7") *<40829>* **FRONT PAGE NEWS. / GOODBYE BABY, HELLO FRIEND** | – | |
Nov 77. (7") *(MCA 327)* **GOODBYE BABY, HELLO FRIEND. / COME IN FROM THE RAIN** | | |
Sep 78. (7"/12") *(MCA/12MCA 392)* **YOU SEE RED. / BAD WEATHER BLUES (live)** | | |
Oct 78. (lp/c) *(MCG/+C 3528) <3060>* **NO SMOKE WITHOUT FIRE** | **43** | |
– You see red / Baby the angels are here / Ships in the sky / Stand and deliver / Anger in harmony / Like a child / The way of the world (part 1 & 2) / A stormy weather. (*w/ free live 7"*) – COME IN FROM THE RAIN. / LORELEI (*cd-iss. May98; MCLD 19374*)

Aug 79. (7") *(MCA 518)* **COME ON. / FAST JOHNNY** | | |
Jan 80. (7") *<41214>* **HELPLESS. / INSOMNIA** | – | – |
Jan 80. (7") *(MCA 549)* **LIVING PROOF. / JAIL BAIT (live)** | – | |
Jan 80. (lp/c) *(MCF/TCMCF 3052)* **JUST TESTING** | **41** | |
– Living proof / Haunting me / Insomnia / Helpless / Pay the price / New rising star / Master of disguise / Lifeline. (*cd-iss. May98; MCLD 19375*)

Apr 80. (7"/12") *(MCA/+T 577)* **HELPLESS (live). / BLOWIN' FREE (live)** | | |
Oct 80. (d-lp/c) *(MCG/+C 4012)* **LIVE DATES II (live)** | **40** | |
– Doctor / Living proof / Runaway / Helpless / F*U*B*B / The way of the world / Lorelei / Persephone / You rescue me / Time was / Goddbye baby hello friend / No easy road. (*ltd. w/ free live lp*) (*re-iss. Jun84; MCL 1799*)

──── **JOHN WETTON** – bass, vocals (ex-URIAH HEEP, ex-FAMILY, ex-KING CRIMSON) repl. MARTIN TURNER to production. / added **CLAIRE HAMILL** – vocals (solo artist)

Mar 81. (7") *(MCA 695)* **UNDERGROUND. / MY MIND IS MADE UP** | | |
Apr 81. (lp/c) *(MCF/+C 3103)* **NUMBER THE BRAVE** | **61** | |
– Loaded / Where is the love / Underground / Kicks on the street / Open road / Get ready / Rainstorm / That's that / Rollercoaster / Number the brave.

May 81. (7") *(MCA 726/+/MCL 14)* **GET READY. / KICKS ON THE STREET** | | |
May 81. (7") *<51149>* **GET READY. / LOADED** | – | |

──── **UPTON, POWELL + WISEFIELD** recruited new member **TREVOR BOLDER** – bass (ex-SPIDERS FROM MARS / Bowie, ex-URIAH HEEP, etc. repl. WETTON to ASIA, etc.

			A.V.M.	Fantasy
Oct 82.	(7") *(WISH 1)* **ENGINE OVERHEAT. / GENEVIEVE**			
Nov 82.	(lp/c) *(ASH/+C 1) <F 9629>* **TWIN BARRELS BURNING**		**22**	1983

– Engine overheat / Can't fight love / Genevieve / Me and my guitar / Hold on / Streets of shame / No more lonely nights / Angels have mercy / Wind up. (*cd-iss. Aug93 on 'Castle'; CLACD 389*)

Dec 82. (7") *(1002)* **NO MORE LONELY NIGHTS. / STREETS OF SHAME** | | – |

──── **MERVYN 'Spam' SPENCER** – bass (ex-TRAPEZE) repl. BOLDER to URIAH HEEP

			Neat	not iss.
Jan 85.	(lp/pic-lp/c) *(NEAT/+P/C 1027)* **RAW TO THE BONE**		**–**	

– Cell of fame / People in motion / Don't cry / Love is blue / Long live the night / Rocket in my pocket / It's only love / Don't you mess / Dreams (searching for an answer) / Perfect timing. (*re-iss. Aug93 on 'Castle'; CLACD 390*)

──── **ANDY PYLE** – bass (ex-SAVOY BROWN, ex-BLODWYN PIG) repl. SPENCE

──── Originals (**ANDREW, STEVE, MARTIN & TED**) reformed WISHBONE ASH.

			I.R.S.-MCA	I.R.S.-MCA
Feb 88.	(lp/c/cd) *(MIRF/CMIRF/DMIRF 1028)* **NOUVEAU CALLS** (instrumental)			

– Tangible evidence / Closseau / Flags of convenience / From Soho to Sunset / Arabesque / In the skin / Something's happening in Room 602 / Johnny left home without it / The spirit flies free / A rose is a rose / Real guitars have wings. (*re-iss. 1990 lp/c/cd; ILP/+MC/CD 39*)

May 88. (7") *(IRM 164)* **IN THE SKIN. / TANGIBLE EVIDENCE** | | |

──── In Apr89, TED & ANDY guested on their labels' Various Artists live cd,c,d-lp, video 'NIGHT OF THE GUITAR'.

			I.R.S.	I.R.S.
Jun 89.	(7") *(EIRS 104)* **COSMIC JAZZ. / T-BONE SHUFFLE**			

(12"+=) *(EIRST 104)* – Bolan's monument.

Aug 89. (lp/c/cd) *(EIRSA/+C/CD 1006) <82006>* **HERE TO HEAR** | | |
– Cosmic jazz / Keeper of the light / Mental radio / Walk on water / Witness on wonder / Lost cause in Paradise / Why don't we / In the case / Hole in my heart (part 1 & 2).

──── **RAY WESTON** – drums repl. MARTIN

May 91. (lp/c/cd) *(EIRSA/+C/CD 1045)* **STRANGE AFFAIR**　☐　☐
– Strange affair / Wings of desire / Dream train / You / Hard times / Standing in the rain / Renegade / Say you will / Rollin' / Some conversion.

—— **POWELL + TED TURNER + RAY** bring in **ANDY PYLE** – bass / **DAN C. GILLOGLY** – keyboards

	Permanent	Griffin
Mar 92. (cd/c/lp) *(PERM CD/MC/LP 6)* **THE ASH LIVE IN CHICAGO** (live)　☐　☐ 1994
– The king will come / Strange affair / Standing in the rain / Lost cause in Paradise / Keeper of the light / Throw down the sword / In the skin / Why don't we? / Hard times / Blowing free / Living proof.

—— **POWELL** recruited an entire new line-up:- **ROGER FILGATE** – guitar / **TONY KISHMAN** – bass / **MIKE STRURGIS** – drums

	Hengest	not iss.
Mar 96. (cd) *(HNRCD 03)* **LIVE IN GENEVA** (live)　☐　☐
– The king will come / Strange affair / Thrown down the sword / In the skin / Hard times / Blowin' free / Keeper of the light / Medley: Blind eye – Lady Whiskey – Jail bait – Phoenix – The pilgrim / Runaway / Sometime world / Vas dis.

—— **MARK TEMPLETON + MIKE MINDEL** – keyboards (FILGATE now bass); repl. KISHMAN

	H.T.D.	not iss.
Oct 96. (cd) *(HTDCD 67)* **ILLUMINATIONS**　☐　☐
– Mountainside / On your own / Top of the world / No joke / Tales of the wise / Another time / A thousand years / The ring / Comfort zone / Mystery man / Wait out the storm / The crack of dawn.

	Invisible Hands	unknown
Apr 98. (cd) *(IHCD 12)* **TRANCE VISIONARY**　☐　☐
– Numerology / Wonderful stash / Heritage / Interface / Powerbright / Remnants of a paranormal maagerie / Narcissus nervosa / Trance visionary / Flutterboy / Banner headlines / Loner / Powerbright volition / Gutterfly / Wronged by righteousness.

– compilations, others, etc. –

—— on 'M.C.A.' unless stated otherwise

Apr 77. (7"ep) *(MCA 291)* **PHOENIX. / BLOWIN' FREE / JAIL BAIT**　☐　–
May 77. (lp/c) *(MCF/TCMCF 2795)* **CLASSIC ASH**　☐　–
– Blind eye / Phoenix / The pilgrim / Blowin' free / The king will come / Rock'n'roll widow / Persephone / Outward bound / Throw down the sword (live). *(re-iss.Aug81 lp/c; MCL/+C 1621) (re-iss. Jan83 on 'Fame' lp/c; FA/TCFA 3053)*
Jan 82. (lp) *(5283-27126)* **HOT ASH**　–
Apr 82. (d-c) *(MCA 2103)* **PILGRIMAGE / ARGUS**　–
May 82. (lp) *(MCF 3134)* **THE BEST OF WISHBONE ASH**　–
Oct 91. (cd) *Windsong; (WINCD 004)* **LIVE IN CONCERT** (live)　☐
1993. (d-cd) *<MCAD2 10765>* **TIME WAS** (w/ remixed 'ARGUS')　☐
Mar 94. (cd/c) *Nectar; (NTR CD/MC 014)* **BLOWIN' FREE – THE VERY BEST OF WISHBONE ASH**　☐
Sep 94. (cd/c) *(MCLD/MCLC 19249)* **THERE'S THE RUB / LOCKED IN**　☐
Nov 94. (cd) *Start; (HP 93452)* **IN CONCERT**　☐
Jan 97. (cd) *Receiver; (RRCD 216)* **LIVE – TIMELINE** (live)　☐
Apr 98. (cd) *Rhino; (CP 1002)* **MOTHER OF PEARL**　☐
Jun 98. (4xcd-box) *Repertoire; (REP 4649WX)* **DISTILLATION**　☐

WIZZARD (see under ⇒ MOVE)

Jah WOBBLE

Born: JOHN WORDLE, 1962, London, England. Having learned to play on SID VICIOUS's bass, he was subsequently invited by JOHN LYDON (the artist formerly known as JOHNNY ROTTEN) to join PUBLIC IMAGE LTD early in 1978. WOBBLE's contributions to albums 'PUBLIC IMAGE' and the excellent 'METAL BOX 1' were a little understated at the time, probably due to LYDON's full-dental attacks. One lasting impression of the bassman's memorable TV appearances was undoubtedly his gap-toothed wide grin on 'Top Of The Pops' while plucking along to their Top 20 hit 'Death Disco'. JAH's sudden departure in 1980 was due to LYDON's annoyance at his use of PIL rhythm tracks on his awful punk/dub debut, 'THE LEGEND LIVES ON'. Subsequently flying out to Germany, he cut the 'FULL CIRCLE' album with CAN members, HOLGER CZUKAY and JAKI LIEBEZEIT, while in 1983, he was the main thrust behind another collaboration, 'SNAKE CHARMER', with CZUKAY and THE EDGE (of U2). In the mid-80's, WOBBLE was forced to endure the trials of a "real" job when he worked for the London Underground (mind the gap!). Sporadic releases also paid the bills, although it wasn't until 1991's comeback set, 'RISING ABOVE BEDLAM' (which introduced vocalist, NATACHA ATLAS of Transglobal Underground) that WOBBLE became a fully-fledged musician once more. The bassman and his ever-expanding INVADERS OF THE HEART even hit the Top 40 with the beautiful 'VISIONS OF YOU' single featuring vocals by SINEAD O'CONNOR. With WOBBLE's spiritual leanings now looming large over proceedings, 1994's 'TAKE ME TO GOD' album hit the Top 20 following a rapturous appearance at Glastonbury Festival. An accompanying single, 'THE SUN DOES RISE', featured DOLORES O'RIORDAN of The CRANBERRIES, a sublime track which surely should've given him a massive hit. WOBBLE subsequently went on to work with the great BRIAN ENO on Derek Jarman's home film project, 'SPANNERS', more recently the man finding his true vocation as a knowledgable guest on Sunday morning religious TV shows. • **Trivia:** In 1992 he appeared on 12"ers by ONE DOVE and SECRET KNOWLEDGE FEATURING WONDER. Guested on albums by ORB, PRIMAL SCREAM, SINEAD O'CONNOR, JOOLZ, HOLGER CZUKAY, DODGY, SHAMEN, GINGER BAKER + IAN McNABB.

Album rating: THE LEGEND LIVES ON ... JAH WOBBLE IN BETRAYAL (*4) / JAH WOBBLE'S BEDROOM ALBUM ... INVADERS OF THE HEART mini (*5) / SNAKE CHARMER mini with The Edge & Holger Czukay (*5) / NEON MOON with Ollie Marland (*5) / PSALMS (*4) / WITHOUT JUDGEMENT (*4) / RISING ABOVE BEDLAM (*8) / TAKE ME TO GOD (*8) / HEAVEN AND EARTH (*6) / THE INSPIRATION OF WILLIAM BLAKE (*5) / THE CELTIC POETS (*5) / THE LIGHT PROGRAMME (*4) / UMBRA SUMUS (*5)

JAH WOBBLE – bass, vocals

	Virgin	Caroline
Oct 78. (7"/12") *(VOLE/12VOLE 9)* **DREADLOCK DON'T DEAL IN WEDLOCK. / PTHILIUS PUBIS**　☐　–
Feb 79. (7"/12" by; DON LETTS & JAH WOBBLE) *(VS 239/+12)* **STEEL LEG: STRATETIME & THE WIDE MAN. / ELECTRIC DREAD: HAILE UNLIKELY**　☐　–
Oct 79. (7"ep/12"ep; as DAN McARTHUR) *(VS 275/+12)* **DAN McARTHUR**　☐　–

—— added **MARTIN ATKINS** – drums / **SNOWY WHITE** – vocals

Apr 80. (7"/12") *(VS 337/+12)* **BETRAYAL. / Mr.X: BATTLE OF BRITAIN**　☐　–
May 80. (lp) *(V 2158) <CAROL 1669>* **THE LEGEND LIVES ON ... JAH WOBBLE IN BETRAYAL**　☐　☐
– Betrayal / Beat the drum for me / Blueberry Hill / Today is the first day of the ... ? / Not another / Tales from Outer Space / Dan McArthur / Pineapple. *(re-iss. 1988; OVED 205) (cd-iss. 1989 & Mar94 +=; CDV 2158)* – Blueberry hill (computer version) / I need you by my side / Message from Pluto / Seaside special / Something profound / Dreadlock don't deal in wedlock / Mr.X: Battle of Britain.
Jul 80. (12"ep) *(VS 361-12)* **V.I.E.P.**　　☐
– Blueberry Hill / etc.

	Island	not iss.
Jul 81. (12"ep; by JAH WOBBLE, JAKI LIEBEZEIT & HOLGER CZUKAY) *(WIP 6701)* **HOW MUCH ARE THEY? / WHERE'S THE MONEY? / TRENCH WARFARE / TWILIGHT WORLD**　☐　–
(re-iss. May88 on 'Licensed'; LD 8816)

	Jah Wobble	not iss.
May 82. (7") *(JAH 1)* **FADING. / NOCTURNAL**　☐　–
Oct 82. (12" by; JAH WOBBLE with ANIMAL) *(JAH 2)* **LONG LONG AWAY. / ROMANY**　☐　–

	Virgin	not iss.
Jan 83. (lp) *(none)* **FULL CIRCLE**　☐　–
– (tracks as above +=) / Full circle R.P.S. (No.7) / Mystery R.P.S. (No.8). *(cd-iss. May92; CDOVD 437)*

—— In 1982, formed BARTOK with RAT SCABIES – drums (ex-DAMNED) / SIMON WERBER + JOHN GRANT (both ex-STRAPS). Released 7" on 'On-U-Sound' in Oct82; INSANITY. / I AM THE BOMB.

—— Next with **ANIMAL** – guitar (of MOTORHEAD) / **OLLIE MARLAND** – keyboards / **ANNIE WHITEHEAD** – trombone

	Lago	not iss.
May 83. (m-lp) *(LAGO 3)* **JAH WOBBLE'S BEDROOM ALBUM – INVADERS OF THE HEART**　☐　–
– City / Fading / Long long way / Sense of history / Hill in Korea / Journey to death / Invaders of the heart / Sunshine / Concentration camp / Desert song / Heart of the jungle.
Jun 83. (12"ep) *(LAGO 4)* **INVADERS OF THE HEART EP**

—— next w / **THE EDGE** – guitar (of U2) / **HOLGER CZUKAY** – percussion, etc (ex-CAN) / **LIEBEZEIT** – (ex-CAN) / **BEN MENDELSON** – (ex-MAGAZINE) / **OLLIE MARTLAND** – keyboards / **JIM WALKER** – drums (ex-PUBLIC IMAGE LTD) / **FRANCOIS KEVORKIAN** – electric drums

	Island	Island
Oct 83. (7") *(WOB 1)* **SNAKE CHARMER. / HOLD ON TO YOUR DREAMS**　☐　–
Oct 83. (m-lp/c; by JAH WOBBLE THE EDGE HOLGER CZUKAY) *(IMA/IMC 1)* **SNAKE CHARMER**　☐　–
– Snake charmer / Hold on to your dreams / It was a camel / Sleazy / Snake charmer – reprise.

JAH WOBBLE & OLLIE MARLAND

with sessions **ANIMAL** – guitar / **B.J. COLE** – steel / **HARRY BECKETT** – timpani / **NEVILLE MURRAY** – percussion / **GENERAL SMUTLEY** – drums

	Lago	not iss.
Sep 84. (12") *(LAGO 5)* **VOODOO. / EAST**　☐　–

	Island	not iss.
Apr 85. (7"/12") *(IS/12IS 9828)* **LOVE MYSTERY. / LOVE MYSTERY (instrumental)**　☐　–
May 85. (lp/c) *(ILPS/ICT 9828)* **NEON MOON**　☐　–
– Love mystery / Love mystery (instrumental) / Running away / Neon Moon / Life on the line / Life on the line (dub) / The beat inside / Despite.

JAH WOBBLE

	Lago	not iss.
Nov 85. (12") *(LAGO 6)* **BLOW OUT. / BLOW OUT (instrumental)**　☐　–
May 86. (12" by; JAH WOBBLE with BRETT DICKENS) *(G 2001)* **BETWEEN TWO FREQUENCIES. / 6020**　☐　–
(above issued on 'General Kinetics')
Oct 86. (lp; by JAH WOBBLE & OLLIE MARLAND) *(LAGO 7)* **TRADEWINDS**　☐　–

	Wobble	not iss.
Sep 87. (lp) *(WOB 7)* **PSALMS**　☐　–
(re-iss. Aug94 on 'Southern' cd/lp; 18522-2/-1)
Sep 87. (12"ep) *(WOB 8)* **ISLAND PARADISE / ALCOHOL. / JIHAD / ('A'remix)**　☐　–

JAH WOBBLE'S INVADERS OF THE HEART

—— w / **JUSTIN ADAMS** – guitar (ex-sessions FRANK CHICKENS) / **MICK SCHOOTS** – drums / **DAVID HARROW** – keyboards, etc / **NATASHA** – vocals (a Spanish/Belgian belly dancer) of TRANSGLOBAL UNDERGROUND

	KK	not iss.

Nov 89. (lp/cd) (KKUK 001/+CD) **WITHOUT JUDGEMENT**   -   - Belgium
– Bungalow park / What the problem is / Anything can happen / A13 / The drowned and the saved / So many years / Message from our sponsor / Coypu / Burger var / What will you say / Spirit / Voodoo / Psyche / Good ghosts / Saracen / Eternal vendor / Invisible cities / Inferno / Location / Uncommercial road / Will the circle be unbroken? (imported into UK Jun93; same) <US 1994 on 'Restless'; 72750>

	Boys Own	not iss.

Oct 90. (7"/cd-s) (BOI/+CD 2) **BOMBA (Miles away mix). /**   ('A'live)
(12") (BOIX 2) – ('A'-Nonsonicus Maximus mix) / ('A'live).

—— Late 1990, he also splintered in MAX with ANDY ROURKE (ex-SMITHS) on 'ZTT'.

	Oval-East West	Atlantic

Oct 91. (cd/c/lp) (9031 75470-2/-4/-1) <82386> **RISING ABOVE BEDLAM**
– Visions of you / Relight the flame / Bomba / Ungodly kingdom / Rising above bedlam / Erzulie / Everyman's an island / Soledad / Sweet divinity / Wonderful world.

Nov 91. (7") (OVAL 102) **ERZULIE. / REMIND ME TO BE NICE TO MYSELF**
(12"+=/cd-s+=) (OVAL 102 T/CD) – ('A'extended dependent mix).

—— Below 'A' + next 'B'-side featured **SINEAD O'CONNOR** – vocals

Jan 92. (7") (OVAL 103) **VISIONS OF YOU. / ('A'-Ade phases the parameters of sound mix)**   35   -
(12"+=/cd-s+=) (OVAL 103 T/CD) – ('A'-Secret love child of Hank & Johnny mix) / ('A'-Pick'n'mix 1 & 2).

Sep 92. (7"ep/12"ep/cd-ep) (OVAL 107/+T/CD) **THE UNGODLY KINGDOM EP**
– Ungodly kingdom (Transformed mix) / Saeta / Josey Walsh / Love life.

—— next with **JUSTIN ADAMS** – guitars, vocals / **MARK FERDA** – guitars, mandolin / **NEVILLE MURRAY** – percussion / **ANNELI DRECKER** (of Norwegian band BEL CANTO) or **XIMENA TADSON** or **ABDEL ALI SLIMANI** or **GAVIN FRIDAY** (ex-VIRGIN PRUNES) or **ANDREA OLIVER** (ex-RIP, RIG & PANIC) or **NAJMA AKHTAR** – vocals / **KRIS NEEDS** – dub (of SECRET KNOWLEDGE) / **JAKI LIEBEZEIT** or **JOHN REYNOLDS** – drums / etc.

	Island	Polygram

Apr 94. (7") (IS 571) **BECOMING MORE LIKE GOD. / WINE, WOMEN AND SONG**   36   -
(c-s+=) (CIS 571) – Football.
(12"+=) (12IS 571) – ('A'-Secret Knowledge To Hell & Back mix).
(cd-s++=) (CID 571) – (all 4 tracks).

May 94. (cd/c/d-lp) (CID/ICT/ILPSD 8017) <524000> **TAKE ME TO GOD**   13
– God in the beginning / Becoming more like God / Whisky priests / I'm an Algerian / Amor / Amor dub / Take me to god / The Sun does rise / When the storm comes / I love everybody / Yoga of the nightclub / I am the music / The bonds of love / Angels / No change is sexy / Raga / Forever.

—— below featured **DOLORES O'RIORDAN** (of CRANBERRIES)

Jun 94. (c-s/7") (C+/IS 587) **THE SUN DOES RISE. / YALILI YA AINI / RAGA**   41   -
(12"+=/cd-s+=) (12IS/CID 587) – Om namah shiva (tranformation).
(cd-s) (CIDX 587) – ('A'side) / A13 / Snake charmer (reprise) / So many years.

Oct 94. (c-s/cd-s) (CIS/CIDX 602) **AMOR / ('A'mix)**
(12"+=) (12IS 602) – ('A'-Rockas jungle remix).
(cd-s++=) (CID 602) – Sahara.
(cd-s) – (4-'A'mixes).

JAH WOBBLE

Nov 95. (cd/c/d-lp) (CID/ICT/ILPSD 8044) <531650> **HEAVEN AND EARTH**
– Heaven and Earth / A love song / Dying over Europe / Divine mother / Gone to Croatan / Hit me / Om namah shiva.

—— Had also just collaborated with BRIAN ENO (who hasn't!) on Top 75 album 'SPANNER' on below label; AS/+C/CD 023)

	All Saints	Thirsty Ear

Sep 96. (lp/c/cd) (AS/+C/CD 029) <66629> **PRESENTS THE INSPIRATION OF WILLIAM BLAKE**
– Songs of innocence / Lonely London / Bananas / Tyger tyger / Holy Thursday / Breathing out the world / Swallow in the world / Kings of Asia / Swallow in the world (reprise) / Bob and Harry / Angel / Gateway / Auguires of innocence.

	30 Hertz	30 Hertz

Jun 97. (cd; as JAH WOBBLE'S INVADERS OF THE HEART) (<30HZCD 001>) **THE CELTIC POETS**   - Nov98
– Dunes / The man I knew / Market rasen / Thames / Gone in the wind / Saturn / Bagpipe music / Third Heaven / Star of the east / London rain.

Jul 97. (cd) (<30HZCD 002>) **REQUIEM**
– Requiem I / Requiem II / Requiem III / Father / Mother.

Oct 97. (cd) (<30HZCD 003>) **THE LIGHT PROGRAMME**
– Veneer / One in 7 / Night / Appearance and thing-it-itself / Nice cop: nasty cop / Magical thought / Maieusia / 15 dohs / Tranquilliser.

Nov 97. (cd-s) (30HZCD 004) **MAGICAL THOUGHT (mixes) / 15 DOHS**

Jun 98. (cd) (<30HZCD 005>) **UMBRA SUMUS**
– Il jevedro il oblanco / Mehemda jaika bubage / Paternal kindness / Moon slowbeat (part 1) / Moon slowbeat (part 2) / Just a prayer / St. Mary-le-bow / I offer you everything / Organ meditation / Compound / Chela / Umbra sumus (part 1) / Umbra sumus (part 2) / 4 basses an organ jaki and a train / Mount Zion / Limehouse cut.

Jun 98. (cd-s) (30HZCD 006) **I OFFER YOU EVERYTHING / IL JEVEDRO IL OBLANCO / TRAIN**

Jul 98. (cd-s) (30HZCD 007) **MOUNT ZION / MOUNT ZION (dance mix) / MOUNT ZION (edited live version)**

WOLFGANG PRESS (dig out; Great Alt & Indie . . .)

WOLFSBANE (dig out; Great Metal . . .)

Bobby WOMACK

Born: 4 Mar'44, Cleveland, Ohio, USA. Along with his four siblings, CECIL, CURTIS, HARRIS, FRIENDLY Jnr and BOBBY formed The WOMACK BROTHERS as a gospel quintet in 1959. It wasn't long before he met SAM COOKE who subsequently snapped him up to play guitar in his own gospel outfit, The SOUL STIRRERS. In early 1960, COOKE formed the L.A.-based 'SAR' label with manager J.W. Alexander and promptly added the brothers to his roster, renaming them The VALENTINOS after the following year's debut single, 'SOMEBODY'S WRONG'. A handful of classy R&B singles followed while two of them, 'IT'S ALL OVER NOW' and 'LOOKIN' FOR A LOVE' became major hits for The ROLLING STONES and The J.GEILS BAND respectively. After SAM COOKE's controversial death in 1964, Alexander had a dispute with COOKE's widow, Barbara (whom BOBBY married three months later) and subsequently shut down 'SAR'. Although The VALENTINOS soon followed suit, BOBBY's songwriting and performing credentials were already well established and although he began recording for new label, 'Him', most of his time was taken up by session work for the likes of ARETHA FRANKLIN, RAY CHARLES and WILSON PICKETT. As well as playing on the latter's 'Funky Broadway' single, WOMACK penned a series of tracks for PICKETT including 'I'M IN LOVE' and 'I'M A MIDNIGHT MOVER'. The two also became great buddies and it isn't difficult to hear similarities in their gritty soul-shout vocal style; WOMACK himself was nicknamed 'The PREACHER'. After a brief spell at 'Chess', he signed to Liberty's R&B subsidiary, 'Minit', where he cut a series of fair to middling solo singles, none of which were big hits. His final effort for the label was 'THE WOMACK LIVE (LIVE '68)', a Hollywood-recorded concert set that pitted masterful interpretations of soul classics like Sam Cooke's 'LAUGHING AND CLOWNING' and Percy Mayfield's 'TO LIVE THE PAST' against his characteristic penchant for seemingly incongruous cover material i.e. The Mamas And The Papas' 'CALIFORNIA DREAMIN' and Fred Neil's 'Everybody's Talkin'. The square-spectacled soul man had more success with his 'United Artists' (who took over from 'Liberty') recordings which he kicked off in late 1971 with his first (US) Top 30 hit, 'THAT'S THE WAY I FEEL ABOUT 'CHA'. WOMACK's impressive development as both a singer and songwriter was illustrated the following year with the release of two great albums, 'COMMUNICATION' and 'UNDERSTANDING', the latter featuring BOBBY's fond ode to his brother HARRY (who was subsequently stabbed to death by his own wife in 1978), 'HARRY HIPPIE'. 1972 was also the year of SLY & THE FAMILY STONE's seminal 'There's A Riot Goin' On', to which WOMACK added his famous wah-wah guitar; his well documented friendship with the wayward SLY STONE led them both off the rails in the early 70's as they became increasingly dependent on drugs and the high-rolling L.A. lifestyle. Following the lead of contemporaries MARVIN GAYE and CURTIS MAYFIELD, WOMACK cut a blaxploitation soundtrack in 1973 for the movie, 'ACROSS 110th STREET' and although the classic title track remains arguably one of the finest marriages of soul and pop ever committed to vinyl, the project failed to bring BOBBY the same fame as ISAAC HAYES' 'Shaft' which was screened around the same time. A series of back to basics Muscle Shoals-recorded efforts followed in the form of 'FACTS OF LIFE' (1973), 'LOOKIN' FOR A LOVE AGAIN' (1974), 'I DON'T KNOW WHAT THE WORLD IS COMING TO' (1975) and 'SAFETY ZONE' (1976) although only the old VALENTINOS song, 'LOOKIN' FOR A LOVE' was a major hit (US Top 10) in 1974. 1976, meanwhile saw the release of his brave country-soul set, 'B.W. GOES C & W', one of the poorest selling albums of his career. Things didn't get much better as he recorded another couple of flop albums for 'Columbia', 'HOME IS WHERE THE HEART IS' (1977) and 'PIECES' (1978), closing the decade with a patchy one-off set for 'Arista', 'ROADS OF LIFE' (1979) as he tried to come to terms with the cot death of his baby son. Salvation came in the form of CRUSADERS man, WILTON FELDER who asked WOMACK to sing on his solo album, 'Inherit The Wind'; the title track was a UK hit and its success provided the impetus for BOBBY's creative and critical rebirth with 'THE POET' (1982). One of that sterile decade's few soul records of any lasting worth, WOMACK had succeeded in updating his classic soulman stance without being swamped by new technology, singing his pain on the massive R&B hit, 'IF YOU THINK YOU'RE LONELY NOW'. Yet more strife followed however as he fought a protracted court battle with his new label, 'Beverly Glen' over non-payment of royalties. Nevertheless, a second instalment, 'THE POET II' (1984), finally emerged on 'Motown', hitting the UK Top 40 and enjoying further critical acclaim due in part to some stunning duets with PATTI LaBELLE. Following another collaboration with FELDER, WOMACK returned to his Memphis roots for 'WOMAGIC' (1986), hooking up with veteran country-soul man, Chips Moman. For the remainder of the decade, WOMACK kept a low profile, occasionally popping up on other artists' albums (notably the ROLLING STONES' 'Dirty Work'). The 90's brought another period of personal upheaval before the true soul survivor finally re-emerged with 'RESURRECTION' (1994). • **Songwriters:** All his own work, except covers:- CALIFORNIA DREAMIN' (Mamas & The

Papas) / SWEET CAROLINE (Neil Diamond) / I WISH IT WOULD RAIN (Temptations) / LIVING IN A BOX (Living In A Box) / etc. • **Trivia:** His brother CECIL became part of WOMACK & WOMACK team with wife LINDA.

Album rating: FLY ME TO THE MOON (*6) / MY PRESCRIPTION (*6) / THE WOMACK "LIVE" (*5) / COMMUNICATION (*6) / UNDERSTANDING (*6) / ACROSS 110th STREET soundtrack (*6) / FACTS OF LIFE (*6) / LOOKIN' FOR A LOVE AGAIN (*5) / BOBBY WOMACK'S GREATEST HITS compilation (*6) / I DON'T KNOW WHAT THE WORLD IS COMING TO (*5) / SAFETY ZONE (*5) / BW GOES C&W (*4) / HOME IS WHERE THE HEART IS (*4) / PIECES (*4) / ROADS OF LIFE (*4) / THE POET (*7) / THE POET II (*8) / SOMEDAY WE'LL ALL BE FREE (*4) / SO MANY RIVERS (*5) / WOMAGIC (*4) / THE SOUL MAN (*4) / MIDNIGHT MOVER: THE BOBBY WOMACK COLLECTION compilation (*8)

VALENTINOS

BOBBY, CECIL, CURTIS, HARRY + FRIENDLY Jnr

		not iss.	S.A.R.
Nov 61.	(7"; as WOMACK BROTHERS) <118> **SOMEBODY'S WRONG. / YIELD NOT TO TEMPTATION**	-	
Jul 62.	(7") <132> **LOOKIN' FOR A LOVE. / SOMEWHERE THERE'S A GIRL**	-	72
Sep 62.	(7") <137> **I'LL MAKE IT ALRIGHT. / DARLING COME BACK HOME**	-	97
Feb 63.	(7") <144> **SHE'S SO GOOD TO ME. / BABY, LOT'S OF LUCK**	-	
Jun 64.	(7") <152> **IT'S ALL OVER NOW. / TIRED OF LIVING IN THE COUNTRY**	-	94
	(UK-iss.1968 on 'Soul City'; SC 106)		
Sep 64.	(7") <155> **EVERYBODY WANTS TO FALL IN LOVE. / BITTER DREAMS**	-	

—— they split later in the year. On February '65, BOBBY married SAM COOKE's widow, BARBARA. That year, he recorded for new label 'Him', but time was mostly taken up by session work for RAY CHARLES, WILSON PICKETT and other 'Atlantic' artists. In 1966, he signed for the label, but he mainly wrote for PICKETT before briefly moving to 'Chess'.

BOBBY WOMACK

		Minit	Minit
Sep 67.	(7") <32024> **TRUST ME. / BABY, I CAN'T STAND IT**	-	
Feb 68.	(7") (MLF 11001) <32030> **BROADWAY WALK. / SOMEBODY SPECIAL**		
Apr 68.	(7") (MLF 11005) <32037> **WHAT IS THIS? / WHAT YOU GONNA DO (WHEN YOUR LOVE HAS GONE)**		
Sep 68.	(7") (MLF 11010) <32048> **FLY ME TO THE MOON. / TAKE ME**		52 Aug68
Dec 68.	(lp) <24014> **FLY ME TO THE MOON**	-	
Jan 69.	(7") (MLF 11012) <32055> **CALIFORNIA DREAMIN'. / BABY~I YOU OUGHTA THINK IT OVER**		43 Nov68
Apr 69.	(7") <32059> **I LEFT MY HEART IN SAN FRANCISCO. / LOVE, THE TIME IS NOW**	-	
Jul 69.	(7") <32071> **IT'S GONNA RAIN. / THANK YOU**	-	
Nov 69.	(7") <32081> **HOW I MISS YOU BABY. / TRIED AND CONVICTED**	-	93
Apr 70.	(7") <32093> **MORE THAN I CAN STAND. / ARKANSAS STATE PRISON**	-	90

		not iss.	Liberty
Jun 70.	(7") <56186> **I'M GONNA FORGET ABOUT YOU. / DON'T LOOK BACK**	-	
Dec 70.	(7") <56206> **SOMETHING (live). / EVERYBODY'S TALKIN' (live)**	-	
Apr 71.	(7") <7645> **THE WOMACK "LIVE" (live '68)**	-	

– Intro – Let it out / Oh how I miss you baby / California dreamin' / Something / Everybody's talking / Laughin' and clownin' / To live the past / I'm a midnight mover / More than I can stand. (UK-iss.Feb89 on 'Charly' lp/c; CRB/TCCRB 1201) (cd; CDCHARLY 155)

—— with a number of exceptions, his band over the 70's included **ROGER HAWKINS** – drums / **CLAYTON IVEY** – keyboards / **JIMMY JOHNSON** – guitar / **BARRY BECKETT** – keyboards / **TRUMAN THOMAS** – bass

		U.A.	U.A.
Feb 72.	(7") (UP 35339) <50847> **THAT'S THE WAY I FEEL ABOUT CHA. / COME L'AMORE**		27 Nov71
Jun 72.	(lp) (UAS 29306) <5539> **COMMUNICATION**		83 Nov71
	– Communication / Come l'amore / Fire and rain / (If you don't want my love) Give it back / (They long to be) Close to you / Everything is beautiful / That's the way I feel about cha / Held not to temptation.		
Jul 72.	(7") (UP 35375) <50902> **WOMAN'S GOT TO HAVE IT. / (IF YOU DON'T WANT MY LOVE) GIVE IT BACK**		60 Apr72
Sep 72.	(lp) (UAG 29365) <5577> **UNDERSTANDING**		43 Jun72
	– I can understand it / Woman's gotta have it / And I love her / Got to get you back / Simple man / Ruby Dean / A thing called love / Sweet Caroline (good times never seemed so good) / Harry hippie. (re-iss.Jan75 as 'I CAN UNDERSTAND IT'; UAG 29715)		
Aug 72.	(7") <50946> **SWEET CAROLINE (GOOD TIMES NEVER SEEMED SO GOOD). / HARRY HIPPIE**	-	51
			31
Dec 72.	(7") (UP 35456) **HARRY HIPPIE. / I CAN UNDERSTAND IT**		-
	(re-iss.Jan75 but flipped over; UP 36462)		
Apr 73.	(7") (UP 35512) <196> **ACROSS 110th STREET. / HANG ON IN THERE**		56 Mar73
May 73.	(lp) (UAS 29451) <5225> **ACROSS 110th STREET|** (Soundtrack)		50 Jan73
	– Across 110th Street / If you don't want my love give it back / Quicksand / Do it right / Hang on in there / Across 110th Street / Harlem clarinet (J.J. JOHNSON ORCHESTRA) / Harlem love theme (J.J. JOHNSON ORCHESTRA). (cd-iss. May98 on 'Charly'; CPCD 8340)		

Jul 73.	(7") (UP 35565) <255> **NOBODY WANTS YOU WHEN YOU'RE DOWN AND OUT. / I'M THROUGH TRYING TO PROVE MY LOVE TO YOU**		29 Jun73
Sep 73.	(lp) (UAS 29456) <LA 043> **FACTS OF LIFE**		37 Jun73
	– Nobody wants you when you're down and out / I'm through trying to prove my love to you / If you can't give her love give her up / That's Heaven to me / Holdin' on to my baby's love / Nobody (reprise) / Facts of life / He'll be there when the sun goes down / Can't stop a man in love / The look of love / Natural man / All along the watchtower / Interlude No.1.		
Mar 74.	(7") <375> **LOOKIN' FOR A LOVE. / LET IT ALL HANG OUT**		10 Jan74
Apr 74.	(lp) (UAS 29574) <LA 199> **LOOKIN' FOR A LOVE AGAIN**		85 Jan74
	– Lookin' for a love / I don't wanna be hurt by your love again / Doing it my way / Let it all hang out / Point of no return / You're welcome, stop on by / You're messing up a good thing / Don't let me down / Copper kettle / There's one thing that beats falling. (re-iss.Aug88 on 'Edsel'; ED 291) (re-iss. Jan89 on 'Charly' lp/c; CRB/TCRB 1193) (cd; CDCHARLY 153)		
Jun 74.	(7") <439> **YOU'RE WELCOME, STOP ON BY. / I DON'T WANNA BE HURT BY YA LOVE AGAIN**	-	59
Nov 74.	(lp) <LA 346> **BOBBY WOMACK'S GREATEST HITS** (compilation)	-	
May 75.	(lp) (UAG 29762) <LA 353> **I DON'T KNOW WHAT THE WORLD IS COMING TO**		
	– I don't know – (interlude 1 & 2) / Superstar / I want my love, put something down on it / Git it / What's your world / Check it out / Interlude No.2 / Jealous love / It's all over now / Yes Jesus loves me.		
Jun 75.	(7") (UP 35859) <621> **CHECK IT OUT. / INTERLUDE No.2**		91 Apr75
Jul 75.	(7") <674> **GIT IT. / IT'S ALL OVER NOW**	-	
Jan 76.	(7") (UP 36042) <735> **WHERE THERE'S A WILL THERE'S A WAY. / EVERYTHING'S GONNA BE ALRIGHT**		Nov75
Feb 76.	(lp) (UAG 29907) <LA 544> **SAFETY ZONE**		Jan76
	– Everything's gonna be alright / I wish it would rain / Trust me / Where there's a will there's a way / Love ain't something you can get for free / Something you got / Daylight / I feel a groove comin' on / Don't make this the last date for you and me.		
Mar 76.	(7") (UP 36098) <763> **DAYLIGHT. / TRUST ME**		
Aug 76.	(lp) (UAS 29979) <LA 638> **B.W. GOES C & W**		Apr76
	– Behind closed doors / Bouquet of roses / Tired of living in the country / Tarnished rings / Big bayou / Song of the mockingbird / I'd be ahead if I could quit while I'm behind / You / I take it on home.		

		C.B.S.	Columbia
Sep 76.	(7") <804> **TRUST ME. / I FEEL A GROOVE COMIN' ON**	-	
Jan 77.	(7"; as BOBBY WOMACK & BROTHERHOOD) (CBS 4827) <10437> **HOME IS WHERE THE HEART IS. / WE'VE ONLY JUST BEGUN**		Oct76
Feb 77.	(lp/c) (CBS/40 81693) <34384> **HOME IS WHERE THE HEART IS**		Sep76
	– Home is where the heart is / A little bit salty / Standing in the safety zone / One more chance on love / How long (has this been goin' on) / I could never be satisfied / Something for my head / A change is gonna come / We've only just begun. (re-iss. Feb86 on 'Edsel' lp/c; ED/CED 172) (cd-iss. Feb91; EDCD 172)		
Mar 77.	(7"; as BOBBY WOMACK & BROTHERHOOD) <10493> **STANDING IN THE SAFETY ZONE. / A CHANGE IS GONNA COME**	-	
Apr 78.	(7") <10672> **TRUST YOUR HEART. / WHEN LOVE BEGINS, FRIENDSHIP ENDS**	-	
Jun 78.	(7") <10732> **WIND IT UP. / STOP BEFORE WE START**	-	
Jul 78.	(lp) <39083> **PIECES**	-	
	– It's party time / Trust your heart / Stop before we start / When love begins, friendship ends / Wind it up / Is this the thanks I get / Caught up in the middle / Never let nothing get the best of you.		

		Arista	Arista
Jun 79.	(7") <0421> **I HONESTLY LOVE YOU. / HOW COULD YOU BREAK MY HEART**		
Jul 79.	(lp) (ARTY 165) <4222> **ROADS OF LIFE**		
	– Roads of life / How could you break my heart / Honey dripper boogie / Roots in me / What are you doin' / Give it up / Mr. D.J. don't stop the music / I honestly love you. (cd-iss. Aug97 on 'Razor & Tie'; RE 2140)		
Aug 79.	(7") <0446> **ROADS OF LIFE. / GIVE IT UP**	-	

—— took time out to stifle increasing drug intake, re-actifying again after his brother Harris was murdered. Oct'80, he provided the vocals for WILTON FELDER's (of The Crusaders) hit single 'INHERIT THE WIND'.

		Motown	Beverly Glen
Jun 82.	(lp) (STML 12168) <BG 10000> **THE POET**		29 Dec81
	– So many sides of you / Lay your lovin' on me / Secrets / Just my imagination / Stand up / Games / If you think you're lonely now / Where do we go from here. (cd-iss.Jul87 on 'Pacific'; BGD 10000) (re-iss. Sep94 on 'M.C.I.' cd/c; MUS CD/MC 505) (cd re-iss. Jun96 on 'Razor & Tie'; RE 2029) (cd-iss. May99 on 'Charly'; CPCD 8054)		
Jul 82.	(7"/12") (TMG/+T 1267) **SO MANY SIDES OF YOU. / JUST MY IMAGINATION**		-
Sep 82.	(7") (TMG 1278) <2000> **SECRETS. / STAND UP**		Feb82
Sep 82.	(7") <2001> **WHERE DO WE GO FROM HERE. / JUST MY IMAGINATION**	-	

—— In 1982, BOBBY took 'Beverly Glen' label owner Otis Smith to court, fighting literally over non-payment of royalties.

Mar 84.	(7"; by BOBBY WOMACK and PATTI LaBELLE) <2012> **LOVE HAS FINALLY COME AT LAST. / AMERICAN DREAM**	-	88
Apr 84.	(lp/c) (ZL/ZK 72205) <BG 10003> **THE POET II**	31	60 Mar84
	– Love has finally come at last / It takes a lot of strength to say goodbye / Through the eyes of a child / Surprise surprise / Tryin' to get over you / Tell me why / Who's foolin' who / I wish I had someone to go home to / American dream. (cd-iss.Jul87 on 'Pacific'; BGD 10003) (re-iss. Sep94 on 'M.C.I.' cd/c; MUS CD/TC 506) (cd re-iss. Jun96 on 'Razor & Tie'; RE 2030)		
Jun 84.	(7"/12") (TMG/+T 1339) **TELL ME WHY. / THROUGH THE EYES OF A CHILD**	60	
Sep 84.	(7") (TMG 1353) **SURPRISE SURPRISE. / AMERICAN DREAM**		-
	(12"+=) (TMGT 1353) – If you think you're lonely now.		

Sep 84. (7"; by BOBBY WOMACK and PATTI LaBELLE) *<2018>*
**IT TAKES A LOT OF STRENGTH TO SAY GOODBYE /
WHO'S FOOLIN' WHO**　　　　—　　☐
Jan 85. (7") *<2021>* **I WISH I HAD SOMEONE TO GO HOME
TO. / SOMEDAY WE'LL ALL BE FREE**　　　—　　☐
Mar 85. (7") *<2023>* **SEARCHING FOR MY LOVE. / I'M SO PROUD**　☐　☐

—— early in 1985, he re-united with WILTON FELDER on 7+12" '(NO MATTER HOW
HIGH I GET) I WILL STILL BE LOOKING UP TO YOU'.

	M.C.A.	M.C.A.

Sep 85. (lp/c) *(MCF/+C 3282) <5617>* **SO MANY RIVERS**
– I wish he didn't trust me so much / So baby don't leave home without it / So many
rivers / Got to be with you tonight / Whatever happened to the times / Let me kiss
it where it hurts / The only survivor / That's where it's at / Check it out / Gypsy
woman. *(cd-iss. 1986; DMCF 3282) (cd re-iss. Aug89; DMCL 1894) (cd-iss. Mar93;
MCLD 19136)*
Sep 85. (7"/12") *(MCA/+T 944)* **I WISH HE DIDN'T TRUST ME SO
MUCH. / GOT TO BE WITH YOU TONIGHT**　　**64**　☐
May 86. (7"/12") *(MCA/+T 1050)* **GYPSY WOMAN. / WHATEVER
HAPPENED TO THE TIMES**　　☐　☐
Nov 86. (lp/c) *(MCG/+C 6020)* **WOMAGIC**　　☐　Jul86
– I wanna make love to you / When the weekend comes / All the things you do / I
can't stay mad too long / Hear the music / Outside myself / I ain't got to live nobody
else / More than love / It ain't me. *(cd-iss. Nov87; DMCG 6020)*
Jan 87. (7"/12") *(MCA/+T 1108)* **I WANNA MAKE LOVE TO YOU. /
WHATEVER HAPPENED TO THE TIMES**　　☐　☐
Oct 87. (7") *(MCA 1210)* **LIVING IN A BOX. / ('A'instrumental)**　**70**　☐
(12"+=) *(MCAT 1210)* – ('A'-Another box) / ('A'-Hacienda mix).
Nov 87. (lp/c/cd) *(MCF/MCFC/DMCF 3408)* **THE LAST SOUL MAN**　☐　☐
– Living in a box / When the weekend comes / I still love you / Gina / A world where
no one cries / A woman likes to hear that / Real love please stand up / The things
we do (when we're lonely) / Falling in love again / Outside myself.

—— In Nov'89, WOMACK teamed up with SHIRLEY BROWN on the single, 'AIN'T
NOTHIN' LIKE THE LOVIN' WE GOT' on 'Chrysalis' ('Cooltempo' US)

—— In Mar'93, he was credited on the LULU single, 'I'm Back For More', which hit
the UK Top 30

	Continuum	Slide

Aug 94. (c-s/12"/cd-s) *(T/12/CD CTUM 105)* **FOREVER LOVE /
COLOUR HIM FATHER / (other mixes)**　　☐　☐
Sep 94. (cd/c) *(CD/T CTUM 8)* **RESURRECTION**　　☐　☐
– Good ole days / You made me love again / So high on your love / Don't break
your promise (too soon) / Forever love / Please change your mind / Trying not to
break down / Cousin Henry / Centerfield / Goin' home / Walking on the wildside /
Cry myself to sleep / Wish / Color him father.

—— In May'95, he collaborated with JEANIE TRACY on the single, 'IT'S A MAN'S
MAN'S WORLD' on 'Pulse'.

– compilations, etc. –

1968. (lp; by the VALENTINOS / SIMS TWINS) *Soul City; (SCM
001)* **THE VALENTINOS / THE SIMS TWINS**　☐　☐
Dec 68. (7"; by the VALENTINOS) *Stateside; (SS 2137)* **TIRED OF
BEING NOBODY. / THE DEATH OF LOVE**　☐　—
Mar 71. (7"; as the VALENTINOS) *Polydor; (2058 090)* **RAISE YOUR
HAND IN ANGER. / STAND UP AND BE COUNTED**　☐　—
Feb 74. (7") *Jet Boy; (BOY 75)* **WHAT IS THIS? / I WONDER**　☐　—
Jan 79. (7") *United Artists; (UP 36462)* **I CAN UNDERSTAND IT. /
HARRY HIPPIE**　☐　—
Jul 79. (lp) *United Artists; (UAG 30245)* **A PORTRAIT OF BOBBY
WOMACK**　☐　—
Sep 84. (lp/c) *Liberty; (EG 260250-1/-4)* **SOMEBODY SPECIAL**　☐　—
Oct 84. (lp/c; as BOBBY WOMACK & THE VALENTINOS)
Chess; (CXMB 7202) **CHESS MASTERS**　☐　—
(re-iss. Dec88 as 'BOBBY WOMACK & THE VALENTINOS' lp/c; GCH/+K7 8031)
1986. (lp/c) *Stateside; (SSL/TCSSL 6013)* **CHECK IT OUT**　☐　—
Jun 87. (7") *Arista; (RIS 17)* **HOW COULD YOU BREAK MY HEART. /
GIVE IT UP**　☐　—
(12"+=) *(RIST 17)* – Mr. DJ don't stop the music.
Jan 89. (d-lp/c)(cd) *Charly; (CDX/TCCDX 36)(CDCHARLY 152)*
UNDERSTANDING / COMMUNICATION　☐　—
(cd re-iss. Feb98; CDGR 183)
Jan 89. (cd-ep) *Charly; (CDS 10)* **LOOKIN' FOR A LOVE / HARRY
HIPPIE / THAT'S THE WAY I FEEL ABOUT CHA / IF YOU
DON'T WANT MY LOVE, GIVE IT BACK**　☐　—
Feb 89. (d-lp/c)(cd) *Charly; (CDX/TCCDX 37)(CDCHARLY 154)*
**WOMACK WINNERS – THE BEST OF BOBBY WOMACK
1968-1975**　☐　—
(cd-iss. Jul93 on 'Instant'; CDINS 5074)
Mar 89. (d-lp/c)(cd) *Charly; (CDX/TCCDX 39)(CDCHARLY 157)* **FACTS
OF LIFE / I DON'T KNOW WHAT THE WORLD IS COMING
TO**　☐　—
(cd re-iss. Mar98; CDGR 208)
Sep 89. (d-lp/c)(cd) *Charly; (CDX/TCCDX 46)(CDCHARLY 155)*
WOMACK IN MEMPHIS　☐　—
Nov 89. (d-lp/c)(cd) *Charly; (CDX/TCCDX 47)(CDCHARLY 199)*
SAFETY ZONE / B.W. GOES C&W　☐　—
Jul 89. (cd/c/lp) *Instant; (CD/TC+/INS 5000)* **THE MIDNIGHT MOVER**　☐　—
May 91. (cd/c/lp) *Essential; (ESD CD/MC/LP 141)* **SUPER SOUL
SEDUCTION**　☐　—
Jun 91. (cd/c) *Music Club; (MC CD/TC 018)* **THE VERY BEST OF
BOBBY WOMACK**　☐　—
– I can understand it / Harry hippie / I'm a midnight mover / What is this /
Somebody special / That's the way I feel about cha / Communication / California
dreaming / If you don't want my love give it back / I wish it would rain / Nobody
wants you when you're down and out / Across 110th Street / If you want my love,
put something down on it / Lookin' for a love / I don't wanna be hurt by ya love
again / Got to get you back / Woman's gotta have it / There's one thing that beats
failing / You're messing up a good thing / Love ain't something you can get for
free.

Mar 94. (d-cd) *E.M.I.; (CDEM 1514)* **MIDNIGHT MOVER – THE
BOBBY WOMACK STORY**　☐　☐
Apr 94. (cd/c) *Castle; (CCS CD/MC 404)* **THE COLLECTION**　☐　☐
Jul 94. (3xcd-box) *Charly; (CPCD 80803)* **THE POET TRILOGY**　☐　☐
Apr 95. (cd) *Charly; (CPCD 8083)* **I FEEL A GROOVE COMIN' ON**　☐　☐
(cd-iss. Apr97; CPCD 8294)
Jun 96. (cd) *Razor & Tie; (RE 2009)* **LOOKIN' FOR A LOVE (THE
BEST OF BOBBY WOMACK 1968-1975)**　☐　—
Nov 96. (d-cd) *Charly; (CPCD 8255-2)* **THE VERY BEST OF BOBBY
WOMACK**　☐　—
Apr 97. (cd) *M.C.A.; (MCLD 19355)* **THE ONLY SURVIVOR (THE
M.C.A. YEARS)**　☐　—
Sep 97. (cd) *Charly; (CDGR 165)* **FLY ME TO THE MOON / MY
PRESCRIPTION**　☐　—
Nov 97. (d-cd) *Eagle; (EDMCD 020)* **THE MASTERS**　☐　—
Nov 97. (cd) *Charly; (CDGR 179)* **LOOKIN' FOR A LOVE / B.W.
GOES C.W.**　☐　—
Jan 98. (cd) *Sequel; (NEMCD 996)* **SOUL SENSATION**　☐　—
Jun 98. (cd) *Charly; (CDGR 237)* **THE SAFETY ZONE / THE
WOMACK "LIVE"**　☐　—
Jun 98. (cd) *Charly; (CDGR 255)* **GREATEST HITS**　☐　☐
Aug 98. (cd) *Columbia; (487394-2)* **AT HOME IN MUSCLE SHOALS**　☐　—
Oct 99. (12"/cd-s) *Joeboy-Skratch; (JBV/JBCCD 019)* **ACROSS 110th
STREET. /**　☐　—

Stevie WONDER

Born: STEVELAND JUDKINS MORRIS, 13 May'50, Saginaw, Michigan,
USA. Blind since birth, he became a member of his local Baptist choir, and
in 1960 he also formed a duo with JOHN GLOVER, who recommended him
to his cousin; MIRACLES singer RONNIE WHITE. He in turn contacted,
BERRY GORDY, who immediately signed STEVIE for a long-term contract
to 'Tamla Motown' and gave him the famous title of (LITTLE) STEVIE
WONDER. After two albums and a few flop 45's, STEVIE broke through
in 1963 with US chart-topper, 'FINGERTIPS – Pt.2', an updated version of
a track from his debut album that featured STEVIE's dazzling harmonica
playing. This preceded the No.1 album, 'RECORDED LIVE – THE 12 YEAR
OLD GENIUS' (1963), a record which featured the child prodigy in concert
playing an array of instruments with breathtaking ease. After a few years of
mediocre fortunes, and now somewhat older, he emerged as simply STEVIE
WONDER, notching up a top 3 hit with the high-octane soul of 'UPTIGHT'
(1966). The album of the same name was released later the same year and
included an early indication of WONDER's developing social awareness and
eclectic diversity with a cover of Bob Dylan's 'BLOWIN' IN THE WIND'. 'I
WAS MADE TO LOVE HER' (1968) contained some passionately executed
covers, while the goose-bump gem of a title track was a Top 10 hit in its
own right. The celebratory title track from 'FOR ONCE IN MY LIFE' (1969)
was similarly successful while the sun-ripened loveliness of 'MY CHERIE
AMOUR' went Top 5 on both sides of the Atlantic. 'SIGNED, SEALED,
DELIVERED (I'M YOURS)' (1970) saw WONDER begin taking more
control of his affairs in the studio, handling the whole operation almost single-
handedly. This self-determination was consolidated in 1971 when he turned 21
and renegotiated his contract with 'Motown'. Setting up his own publishing
operation, WONDER made sure that he'd never be on the wrong end of a
bum deal again, especially one where he received only one million dollars out
of the thirty million he'd earned at 'Motown' in his youth. 'MUSIC OF MY
MIND' (1972) was the first album to fully realise WONDER's kaleidoscopic
vision, fusing jazz, rock and soul with pioneering synthesizer sounds and other
rhythms while still maintaining an overt pop sensibility. That summer he toured
with The ROLLING STONES, bringing his music to a predominantly white
rock audience who subsequently lapped up WONDER's heaviest offering
to date, the taut funk of 'SUPERSTITION' (1973). The album 'TALKING
BOOK' was released the same month and was the first of STEVIE's mercurial
70's masterpieces. From the heart-melting opening chords of 'YOU ARE THE
SUNSHINE OF MY LIFE' to the gospel-like closer, 'I BELIEVE (WHEN I
FALL IN LOVE IT WILL BE FOREVER)', WONDER had created one of
the most accomplished, searching albums in the soul pantheon. It was a hard
act to follow but follow it he did, in fine style with 'INNERVISIONS' (1973),
a similarly spiritual journey of epic proportions. 'HIGHER GROUND' kept
the funk intact while 'VISIONS' and 'JESUS CHILDREN OF AMERICA'
were meditative quests for truth. 'LIVING FOR THE CITY' was a hard-bitten
knot of genius while the closing 'HE'S MISSTRA KNOW-IT-ALL' featured
some beautifully careworn piano playing. These themes were developed
on 'FULFILLINGNESS FIRST FINALE' (1974), an album that repeated
'INNERVISIONS' Grammy Award winning success and included the defiantly
anti-Nixon 'YOU HAVEN'T DONE NOTHIN'' as well as a rare nod to
sexuality on 'BOOGIE ON REGGAE WOMAN'. WONDER completed this
quadruple whammy with his groundbreaking double album, 'SONGS IN THE
KEY OF LIFE' (1976). A breathtaking summation of all that WONDER had
been working towards up to that point, it embraced everything from jazz
and funk ('SIR DUKE' and 'I WISH' respectively, both American No.1's)
to charming MOR with 'ISN'T SHE LOVELY'. The ominously chiding
'PASTIME PARADISE' was later reinterpreted by rapper COOLIO to massive
success. In many ways, releasing another double album, especially one as
esoteric and lacking in focus as 'THE SECRET LIFE OF PLANTS' (1979)
was commercial suicide. The album was a moderate success however, and
stil outshone WONDER's contemporaries. Returning to more commercial fare
with a vengeance on 'HOTTER THAN JULY' (1980), WONDER offered

up the reggae-flavoured 'MASTERBLASTER (JAMMIN')' (1980) and the anthemic Martin Luther King tribute, 'HAPPY BIRTHDAY' (1980). A string of singles followed, among them the duet with PAUL McCARTNEY, 'EBONY AND IVORY' (1982) and the similarly radio-friendly 'I JUST CALLED TO SAY I LOVE YOU' (1984), which won an Oscar the following year. While 1985's 'IN SQUARE CIRCLE' produced the No.1 hit 'PART-TIME LOVER', it was generally inconsistent and along with 'CHARACTERS' (1987) and his soundtrack to Spike Lee's 'JUNGLE FEVER' (1991) failed to capture the pioneering spirit of his 70's work. WONDER's most recent album, 1995's 'CONVERSATION PEACE' contained flashes of brilliance but fans are still waiting (probably in vain) for another 'TALKING BOOK' or 'INNERVISIONS'. Live, WONDER is still worth selling your granny for the ticket price, his charismatic energy rarely failing to deliver the goods. As well as being a tireless promoter of worthy causes he remains one of the most respected figures in the music industry, and his influence on the course of popular music is incalculable. • **Songwriters:** STEVIE wrote all his own work except, when in the 60's he collaborated with producer HENRY COSBY. His cover versions were; MR. TAMBOURINE MAN (Bob Dylan) / WE CAN WORK IT OUT (Beatles) / SIXTEEN TONS (Ernie Ford) / CAN I GET A WITNESS (Marvin Gaye) / PLEASE, PLEASE, PLEASE (James Brown) / RESPECT (Otis Redding) / MY GIRL (Temptations) / LIGHT MY FIRE (Doors) / GOD BLESS THE CHILD (Billie Holiday) / BRIDGE OVER TROUBLED WATER (Simon & Garfunkel). The album 'TRIBUTE TO UNCLE RAY', had many covers of RAY CHARLES' songs. • **Miscellaneous:** On the 14th September '70, STEVIE married singer, SYREETA WRIGHT, who became his co-writer in the early 70's. They split-up 4 years later and STEVIE found new girlfriend, YOLANDA SIMMONS, who moved with him and their new daughter, to Manhattan. On the 6th August '73, STEVIE was nearly killed in a serious road accident. He recovered from head injuries, after spending a few days in a coma. STEVIE also wrote million sellers for Minnie Riperton (LOVIN' YOU) & Rufus (TELL ME SOMETHING GOOD).

Album rating: TRIBUTE TO UNCLE RAY (*5) / THE JAZZ SOUL OF LITTLE STEVIE (*5) / THE 12 YEAR OLD GENIUS (RECORDED LIVE) (*6) / WITH A SONG IN MY HEART (*4) / AT THE BEACH (HEY HARMONICA MAN) (*4) / UP-TIGHT EVERYTHING'S ALRIGHT (*6) / DOWN TO EARTH (*5) / I WAS MADE TO LOVE HER (*7) / GREATEST HITS compilation (*8) / FOR ONCE IN MY LIFE (*7) / MY CHERIE AMOUR (*7) / STEVIE WONDER LIVE (AT THE TALK OF THE TOWN) (*6) / SIGNED SEALED & DELIVERED (*7) / WHERE I'M COMING FROM (*7) / STEVIE WONDER'S GREATEST HITS, VOL.2 compilation (*8) / MUSIC OF MY MIND (*7) / TALKING BOOK (*9) / INNERVISIONS (*10) / FULFILLINGNESS' FIRST FINALE (*7) / SONGS IN THE KEY OF LIFE (*8) / LOOKING BACK (aka ANTHOLOGY) compilation (*8) / JOURNEY THROUGH THE SECRET LIFE OF PLANTS (*6) / HOTTER THAN JULY (*7) / ORIGINAL MUSIQUARIUM 1 compilation (*9) / WOMAN IN RED soundtrack with others (*4) / IN SQUARE CIRCLE (*5) / CHARACTERS (*4) / JUNGLE FEVER soundtrack (*5) / CONVERSATION PEACE (*4) / NATURAL WONDER (*4)

LITTLE STEVIE WONDER

– vocals, piano, harmonica

		Oriole	Tamla
Aug 62.	(7") <54061> **I CALL IT PRETTY MUSIC (BUT OLD PEOPLE CALL IT THE BLUES). / (part 2)**	-	
1962.	(lp) <232> **TRIBUTE TO UNCLE RAY**	-	

– Hallelujah I love her so / Ain't that love / Don't you know / Sunset / Frankie and Johnny / Drown in my own tears / Come back baby / Mary Ann / My baby's gone / (I'm afraid) The masquerade is over. (UK-iss.Aug63 on 'Oriole'; PS 40049) (re-iss. May82 on 'Motown') (cd-iss. Sep95)

| Oct 62. | (7") <54070> **LITTLE WATER BOY (w/ CLARENCE PAUL). / LA LA LA LA LA** | | |
| 1963. | (lp) <233> **THE JAZZ SOUL OF LITTLE STEVIE** | | |

– Fingertips / Square / Soul bongo / Manhattan at six / Some other time / Wandering / Session number 112 / Bam. (UK-iss.May64 on 'Stateside'; SL 10078) (re-iss. Mar82 on 'Motown')

Dec 62.	(7") <54074> **CONTRACT ON LOVE. / SUNSET**	-	
Aug 63.	(7") (CBA 1853) <54080> **FINGERTIPS (part 2). / FINGERTIPS (part 1)**		1 Jun63
Aug 63.	(lp) (PS 40050) <240> **THE 12 YEAR OLD GENIUS (RECORDED LIVE) (live)**		1 Jul63

– Fingertips / Soul bongo / Drown in my own tears / La la la la / (I'm afraid) The masquerade is over / Hallelujah I love her so / Don't you know. (re-iss. Oct81 on 'Motown')

		Stateside	Tamla
Nov 63.	(7") (SS 238) <54086> **WORKOUT STEVIE, WORKOUT. / MONKEY TALK**	-	33 Oct63
Jan 64.	(lp) <250> **WITH A SONG IN MY HEART**	-	

– Dream / With a song in my heart / Get happy / Put on a happy face / When you wish upon a star / Smile / Make someone happy / Without a song / On the sunny side of the street / Give your heart a chance. (UK-iss.Oct81 on 'Motown')

| Apr 64. | (7") (SS 285) <54090> **CASTLES IN THE SAND. / THANK YOU (FOR LOVING ME ALL THE WAY)** | - | 52 Feb64 |

STEVIE WONDER

Aug 64.	(7") (SS 323) <54096> **HEY HARMONICA MAN. / THIS LITTLE GIRL**	-	29 Jun64
Sep 64.	(7") <54103> **SAD BOY. / HAPPY STREET**		-
Jan 65.	(lp) (SL 10108) **AT THE BEACH (HEY HARMONICA MAN)**		

– Red sails in the sunset / Party at the beach house / Happy Street / Beachcomber / Castles in the sand / Beyond the sea / Sad boy / Beach stomp / Hey, harmonica man.

		Tamla Motown	Tamla
Jan 65.	(7") <54108> **PRETTY LITTLE ANGEL. / TEARS IN VAIN**	-	

Mar 65.	(7") (TMG 505) **KISS ME BABY. / TEARS IN VAIN**		
Sep 65.	(7") (TMG 532) <54119> **HIGH HEEL SNEAKERS. / MUSIC TALK**		59 Aug65
Jan 66.	(7") (TMG 545) <54124> **UPTIGHT (EVERYTHING'S ALRIGHT). / PURPLE RAINDROPS**	14	3 Dec65
Apr 66.	(7") (TMG 558) <54130> **NOTHING'S TOO GOOD FOR MY BABY. / WITH A CHILD'S HEART**		20 Mar66
Aug 66.	(7") (TMG 570) <54136> **BLOWIN' IN THE WIND. / AIN'T THAT ASKING FOR TROUBLE**	36	9 Jun66
Nov 66.	(lp) (TML 11036) **UP-TIGHT EVERYTHING'S ALRIGHT**		33 Jun 66

– Love a go-go / Hold me / Blowin' in the wind / Nothing's too good for my baby / Teach me tonight / Uptight (everything's alright) / Ain't that asking for trouble / I want my baby back / Pretty little angel / Music talk / Contract on love / With a child's heart. (re-iss. Oct81) (re-iss. 1973 on 'M.F.P.')

Dec 66.	(7") (TMG 588) <54139> **A PLACE IN THE SUN. / SYLVIA**	20	9 Oct66
Dec 66.	(7") <54142> **SOME DAY AT CHRISTMAS. / THE MIRACLE OF CHRISTMAS**	-	
Apr 67.	(lp) (TML 11045) <272> **DOWN TO EARTH**		92 Jan67

– A place in the Sun / Bang bang / Thank you love / Mr. Tambourine man / Hey love / Sixteen tons / Down to Earth / Sylvia / Lonesome road / The world is empty without you / Angel baby (don't you ever leave me) / Be cool, be calm (and keep yourself together). (re-iss. Oct81)

Apr 67.	(7") (TMG 602) <54147> **TRAVELLIN' MAN. / HEY LOVE**		32 / 90 Mar67
Jul 67.	(7") (TMG 613) <54151> **I WAS MADE TO LOVE HER. / HOLD ME**	5	2 Jun 67
Oct 67.	(7") (626) <54157> **I'M WONDERING. / EVERY TIME I SEE YOU I GO WILD**	22	12
Apr 68.	(lp) (TML 11059) <279> **I WAS MADE TO LOVE HER**		45 Sep67

– I was made to love her / Send me some lovin' / I'd cry / Everybody needs somebody (I need you) / Respect / My girl / Baby don't you do it / A fool for you / Can I get a witness / I pity the fool / Please, please, please / Every time I see you I go wild. (re-iss. Oct81)

| Apr 68. | (7") (TMG 653) <54165> **SHOO-BE-DOO-BE-DOO-DA-DAY. / WHY DON'T YOU LEAD ME TO LOVE** | 46 | 9 |
| Aug 68. | (lp) (TML 11075) <282> **STEVIE WONDER'S GREATEST HITS** (compilation) | 25 | 37 Apr68 |

– Shoo-be-doo-be-doo-da-day / A place in the Sun / Uptight (everything's alright) / Travellin' man / High heel sneakers / Sad boy / Kiss me, baby / Workout Stevie, workout / Fingertips (part 2) / Hey, harmonica man / Contract on love / Castles in the sand / Nothing's too good for my baby / I was made to love her / Blowin' in the wind / I'm wonderin'. (re-iss. Oct81 & 1986) (cd-iss. 'VOL.1' Sep89) (cd-iss. Nov93)

| Aug 68. | (7") (TMG 666) <54168> **YOU MET YOUR MATCH. / MY GIRL** | | 35 Jul68 |
| Dec 68. | (7") (TMG 679) <54174> **FOR ONCE IN MY LIFE. / ANGIE GIRL** | 3 | 2 Oct68 |

(re-iss. Oct81)

| Feb 69. | (lp) (TML 11098) <291> **FOR ONCE IN MY LIFE** | | 50 Oct68 |

– For once in my life / Shoo-be-ddo-be-doo-da-day / You met your match / I wanna make her love me / I'm more than happy (I don't know why (I love you) / Sunny / I'd be a fool right now / Ain't no lovin' / God bless the child / Do I love her / The house on the hill. (re-iss. Oct81, re-iss. +cd.Aug88)

| Mar 69. | (7") (TMG 690) <54180> **I DON'T KNOW WHY (I LOVE YOU). / MY CHERIE AMOUR** | 14 | 39 Feb69 |

(above flipped over Jun69 hit both UK + US No.4) (re-iss. Oct81)

| Nov 69. | (7") (TMG 717) <54188> **YESTER-ME, YESTER-YOU, YESTERDAY. / I'D BE A FOOL RIGHT NOW** | 2 | 7 Oct69 |
| Nov 69. | (lp) (TML 11128) <296> **MY CHERIE AMOUR** | 17 | 34 Oct69 |

– My Cherie amour / Hello young lovers / At last / Light my fire / The shadow of your smile / You and me / Pearl / Somebody knows, somebody cares / Yester-me, yester-you, yesterday / Angie girl / Give your love / I've got you. (re-iss. Oct81 & Apr84, cd-iss. Aug88)

| Mar 70. | (7") (TMG 731) <54191> **NEVER HAD A DREAM COME TRUE. / SOMEBODY KNOWS, SOMEBODY CARES** | 6 | 26 Feb70 |
| Mar 70. | (lp) (TML 11164) <298> **LIVE (AT THE TALK OF THE TOWN)** | | 81 Apr70 |

– Pretty world / Never had a dream come true / Shoo-be-doo-be-doo-da-day / My Cherie amour / Alfie / (drum solo) / Bridge over troubled water / I was made to love her / Yester-me, yester-you, yesterday / For once in my life / Signed, sealed, delivered (I'm yours). (re-iss. Oct81)

| Jun 70. | (7") (TMG 744) <54196> **SIGNED, SEALED, DELIVERED (I'M YOURS). / I'M MORE THAN HAPPY (I'M SATISFIED)** | 15 | 3 |
| Nov 70. | (lp) (TML 11169) <304> **SIGNED, SEALED, DELIVERED (I'M YOURS)** | | 25 Aug70 |

– Never had a dream come true / We can work it out / Signed, sealed, delivered (I'm yours) / Heaven help us all / You can't judge a book by it's cover / Sugar / Don't wonder why / Anything you want me to do / I can't let my Heaven walk away / Joy (takes over me) / I gotta have a song / Something to say. (re-iss. Oct81, re-iss. +cd.Aug88)

Nov 70.	(7") (TMG 757) <54200> **HEAVEN HELP US ALL. / I GOTTA HAVE A SONG**	29	9 Oct70
Mar 71.	(7") <54202> **WE CAN WORK IT OUT. / NEVER DREAMED YOU'D LEAVE IN SUMMER**	-	13 / 78
May 71.	(7") (TMG 772) **WE CAN WORK IT OUT. / DON'T WONDER WHY**	27	-
Jul 71.	(7") (TMG 779) **NEVER DREAMED YOU'D LEAVE IN SUMMER. / IF YOU REALLY LOVE ME**		-
Jul 71.	(lp) (TML 11183) <308> **WHERE I'M COMING FROM**		62 May71

– Look around / Do yourself a favour / Think of me as your soldier / Something out of the blue / If you really love me / I wanna talk to you / Take up a course in happiness / Never dreamed you'd leave in Summer / Sunshine in their eyes. (re-iss. Jul81) (re-iss. +cd.Apr91) (cd-iss. Sep93)

Nov 71.	(7") <54214> **WHAT CHRISTMAS MEANS TO ME. / BEDTIME FOR TOYS**	-	
Jan 72.	(7") (TMG 798) <54208> **IF YOU REALLY LOVE ME. / THINK OF ME AS YOUR SOLDIER**	20	8 Aug71
Jan 72.	(lp) (STML 11196) <313> **GREATEST HITS VOL.2** (compilation)	30	69 Nov71

– Signed, sealed, delivered (I'm yours) / We can work it out / For once in my life /

If you really love me / You met your match / My Cherie amour / Yester-me, yester-you, yesterday / Never had a dream come true / Heaven help us all / Don't know why I love you / Never dreamed you'd leave in Summer. (re-iss.Oct81 & 1986, cd-iss. Sep89 as 'VOL.2') (cd-iss. Nov93)

May 72. (7") <54216> **SUPERWOMAN (WHERE WERE YOU WHEN I NEEDED YOU). / I LOVE EVERY LITTLE THING ABOUT YOU** | [–] | [ ]

May 72. (lp/c) (STMA/TC-STMA 8002) <314> **MUSIC OF MY MIND** | [ ] | [21] Mar72
– Love having you around / Superwoman (where were you when I needed you) / I love every thing about you / Sweet little girl / Happier than the morning sun / Girl blue / Seems so long / Keep on running / Evil. (re-iss. Oct81, cd-iss. Nov87 & Jul92)

Sep 72. (7") (TMG 827) **SUPERWOMAN (WHERE WERE YOU WHEN I NEEDED YOU). / SEEMS SO LONG** | [ ] | [–]

Sep 72. (7") <54223> **KEEP ON RUNNING. / EVIL.** | [–] | [90]

Jan 73. (7") (TMG 841) <54226> **SUPERSTITION. / YOU'VE GOT IT BAD GIRL** | [11] | [1] Nov72
(re-iss. Mar83)

Jan 73. (lp/c) (STMA/TC-STMA 8007) <319> **TALKING BOOK** | [16] | [3] Nov72
– You are the sunshine of my life / Maybe your baby / You and I / Tuesday heartbreak / You've got it bad girl / Superstition / Big brother / Blame it on the sun / Lookin' for another pure love / I believe (when I fall in love it will be forever). (re-iss. Oct81, cd-iss. May86 & Jul92, re-Oct87) (pic-lp 1980's)

Mar 73. (7") <54232> **YOU ARE THE SUNSHINE OF MY LIFE. / TUESDAY HEARTBREAK** | [–] | [1]

May 73. (7") (TMG 852) **YOU ARE THE SUNSHINE OF MY LIFE. / LOOK AROUND** | [7] | [–]
(re-iss. Oct81)

Aug 73. (lp/c) (STMA/TC-STMA 8011) <326> **INNERVISIONS** | [8] | [4]
– Too high / Visions / Living for the city / Higher ground / Jesus children of America / All in love is fair / Don't you worry 'bout a thing / He's a misstra know-it-all. (re-iss. Oct81, cd-iss. Oct87 & Jul92, re-.May88)

Sep 73. (7") (TMG 869) <54235> **HIGHER GROUND. / TOO HIGH** | [29] | [4] Aug73

Dec 73. (7") (TMG 881) <54242> **LIVING FOR THE CITY (edit). / VISIONS** | [15] | [8] Nov73

Apr 74. (7") (TMG 892) **HE'S MISSTRA KNOW IT ALL. / YOU CAN'T JUDGE A BOOK BY IT'S COVER** | [10] | [–]
(re-iss. Oct81)

Apr 74. (7") <54245> **DON'T YOU WORRY 'BOUT A THING. / BLAME IT ON THE SUN** | [ ] | [16]

Jul 74. (7") (TMG 908) **DON'T YOU WORRY 'BOUT A THING. / DO YOURSELF A FAVOUR** | [ ] | [ ]

Aug 74. (lp/c) (STMA/TCSTMA 8019) **FULFILLINGNESS' FIRST FINALE** | [5] | [1]
– Smile please / Heaven is 10 zillion light years away / Too shy to say / Boogie on reggae woman / Creepin' / You haven't done nothin' / It ain't no use / They won't go when I go / Bird of beauty / Please don't go. (re-iss. Oct81, re-iss. +cd.Oct87) (re-iss. cd+c Nov93)

Aug 74. (7") <54252> **YOU HAVEN'T DONE NOTHIN? / BIG BROTHER** | [–] | [1]

Oct 74. (7") (TMG 921) **YOU HAVEN'T DONE NOTHIN'. / HAPPIER THAN THE MORNING SUN** | [30] | [–]

Nov 74. (7") <54254> **BOOGIE ON REGGAE WOMAN. / SEEMS SO LONG** | [–] | [3]

Dec 74. (7") (TMG 928) **BOOGIE ON REGGAE WOMAN. / EVIL** | [12] | [–]

Oct 76. (d-lp/d-c) (TMPS/TC-TMSP 6002) <340> **SONGS IN THE KEY OF LIFE** | [2] | [1]
– Love's in need of love today / Have a talk with God / Village ghetto land / Confusion / Sir Duke / Isn't she lovely / Joy inside my tears / Black man / I wish / Knocks me off my feet / Pastime Paradise / Summer soft / Ordinary pain / Ngiculela es una historia – I am singing / If it's magic / As / Another star. (7"ep w.a.) (re-iss. Oct81, d-cd-iss. 1988 & Jul92)

Dec 76. (7") (TMG 1054) <54274> **I WISH. / YOU AND I** | [5] | [1] Nov76

Mar 77. (7") <54281> **SIR DUKE. / HE'S MISSTRA KNOW-IT-ALL** | [–] | [1]

Mar 77. (7") (TMG 1068) **SIR DUKE. / TUESDAY HEARTBREAK** | [2] | [ ]

Aug 77. (7") (TMG 1083) <54286> **ANOTHER STAR. / CREEPIN'** | [29] | [32]

Nov 77. (7") (TMG 1091) <54291> **AS. / CONFUSION** | [ ] | [36]
(last 5 singles, except Aug77 re-iss. Oct81)

Jan 79. (t-lp) <M-804 LP3> **LOOKING BACK** (compilation) | [–] | [34]

── In Feb79, STEVIE WONDER teamed up with DIANA ROSS, MARVIN GAYE & SMOKEY ROBINSON on minor hit single POPS WE LOVE YOU.

Nov 79. (d-lp/d-c) (TMSP/+TC-TMSP 6009) <371> **STEVIE WONDER'S JOURNEY THROUGH THE SECRET LIFE OF PLANTS** | [8] | [4]
– Earth's creation / The first garden / Voyage to India / Same old story / Venus' flytrap and the bug / Ai no sono / Seasons / Power flower / Send one your love / Race babbling / Outside my window / Black orchid / Ecclesiastes / Kesse ye lolo de ye / Come back as a flower / A seed's a star – Tree (medley) / The secret life of plants / Tree / Seasons. (d-cd-iss. 1986 & Sep95)

Nov 79. (7") (TMG 1146) <54303> **SEND ONE YOUR LOVE. / ('A'instrumental)** | [52] | [4]

Jan 80. (7") (TMG 1173) **BLACK ORCHID. / BLAME IT ON THE SUN** | [63] | [–]

Mar 80. (7") (TMG 1179) <54308> **OUTSIDE MY WINDOW. / SAME OLD STORY** | [52] | [52] Feb80

Sep 80. (7")(12") (TMG 1204) <54317> **MASTERBLASTER (JAMMIN'). / MASTERBLASTER (dub)** | [2] | [5]
(last 3 singles re-iss. Oct81)

Oct 80. (lp/c) (STMA/TC-STMA 8035) <373> **HOTTER THAN JULY** | [2] | [3]
– Did I hear you say you love me / All I do / Rocket love / I ain't gonna stand for it / As if you read my mind / Masterblaster (jammin') / Do like you / Cash in your face / Lately / Happy birthday. (re-iss. Oct81, cd-iss. Oct87, re-1988)

Dec 80. (7") (TMG 1215) <54320> **I AIN'T GONNA STAND FOR IT. / KNOCKS ME OFF MY FEET** | [10] | [11]

Feb 81. (7") (TMG 1226) <54323> **LATELY. / IF IT'S MAGIC** | [3] | [64]
(re-iss. Oct81)

May 81. (7") <54328> **DID I HEAR YOU SAY YOU LOVE ME. / AS IF YOU READ MY MIND** | [–] | [ ]

Jul 81. (7"/12") (TMG/+T 1235) **HAPPY BIRTHDAY. / HAPPY BIRTHDAY (SINGALONG)** | [2] | [–]

Jan 82. (7") (TMG 1254) <1602> **THAT GIRL. / ALL I DO** | [39] | [4]

── In Mar82, hit UK/US No.1 with PAUL McCARTNEY on single EBONY AND IVORY.

May 82. (7"/12") (TMG/+T 1269/) <1612> **DO I DO. / ROCKET LOVE** | [10] | [13]

May 82. (d-lp/d-c) (TMSP/TC-TMSP 6012) <6002> **ORIGINAL MUSIQUARIUM 1** (compilation) | [8] | [ ]
– Superstition / You haven't done nothin' / Living for the city / Front line / Superwoman (where were you when I needed you) / Send one your love / You are the sunshine of my life / Ribbon in the sky / Higher ground / Sir Duke / Master blaster / Boogie on reggae woman / That girl / I wish / isn't she lovely / Do I do. (re-iss. +d-cd-'2 VOLUMES' Nov84 & Jul92)

Sep 82. (7"/12") (TMG/+T 1280) **RIBBON IN THE SKY. / THE SECRET LIFE OF PLANTS** | [45] | [–]

Sep 82. (7") <1639> **RIBBON IN THE SKY. / BLACK ORCHID** | [–] | [54]
Dec 82, he & other Motown artist CHARLENE had US Top50 hit with USED TO BE.

Jan 83. (7"/12") (TMG/+T 1289) **FRONT LINE. / ('A'instrumental)** | [ ] | [ ]

── In Aug83, STEVIE co-wrote and sang on GARY BYRD's UK Top 10 hit 12" 'The CROWN'. Early next year, he guested on ELTON JOHN's 'I GUESS THAT'S WHY THEY..'.

Aug 84. (7"/12") (TMG/+T 1349) <1745> **I JUST CALLED TO SAY I LOVE YOU. / ('A'instrumental)** | [1] | [1]

── Shared half of next lp with DIONNE WARWICK (also duet on *)

Sep 84. (lp/c) (ZL /ZK 72285) <6108> **WOMAN IN RED – SELECTIONS FROM ORIGINAL MOTION PICTURE SOUNDTRACK** | [2] | [4]
– The woman in red / It's you (with DIONNE WARWICK) / It's more than you / I just called to say I love you / Love light in flight / Weakness (with DIONNE WARWICK) / Don't drive drunk / Moments aren't moments (DIONNE WARWICK solo). (cd-iss. Oct87)

Nov 84. (7"/12") (TMG/+T 1364) <1769> **LOVE LIGHT IN FLIGHT. / IT'S MORE THAN YOU** | [44] | [17]

Dec 84. (7"/12") (TMG/+T 1372) **DON'T DRIVE DRUNK. / ('A'instrumental)** | [62] | [ ]

── In Mar85, STEVIE featured on USA FOR AFRICA charity single WE ARE THE WORLD

Aug 85. (7"/12") (ZB/ZT 40351) <1808> **PART-TIME LOVER. / ('A'instrumental)** | [3] | [1]

Sep 85. (lp/c/cd) (ZL /ZK/ZD 72005) <6134> **IN SQUARE CIRCLE** | [5] | [5]
– Part-time lover / I love you too much / Whereabouts / Stranger on the shore of love / Never in the sun / Spiritual walkers / Land of la la / Go home / Overjoyed / It's wrong (apartheid). (re-iss. cd.Nov92)

Nov 85. (7"/12") (ZB/ZT 40501) <1817> **GO HOME. / ('A'instrumental)** | [67] | [10]

Feb 86. (7"/12") (ZB/ZT 40567) <1832> **OVERJOYED. / ('A'instrumental)** | [17] | [24]

Jun 86. (7"/12") (WOND/+T 1) <1846> **LAND OF LA LA. / ('A'instrumental)** | [ ] | [86]

Jan 87. (7"/12") (WOND/+T 2) **STRANGER ON THE SHORE OF LOVE. / DID I HEAR YOU SAY YOU LOVE ME** | [55] | [–]

Oct 87. (7"/12"/c-s) (ZB/ZT/ZC 41439) <1907> **SKELETONS. / ('A'instrumental)** | [59] | [19]

Nov 87. (lp/c/cd) (ZL /ZK/ZD 72001) <6248> **CHARACTERS** | [33] | [17]
– You will know / Dark 'n' lovely / In your corner / With each part of my heart / One of a kind / Skeletons / Get it / Galaxy Paradise / Cryin' through the night. (c+=/cd+=) – Come let me make your love come down / My eyes don't cry.

Jan 88. (7"/12") (ZB/ZT 41723) <1919> **YOU WILL KNOW. / ('A'instrumental)** | [ ] | [77]
(cd-s+=) (ZD 41723) – (interview).

── In Feb88, collaborated with JULIO IGLESIAS on single MY LOVE.

May 88. (7"/12"; STEVIE WONDER & MICHAEL JACKSON) (ZB/ZT 41883) <1930> **GET IT. / GET IT (instrumental)** | [37] | [80]

Oct 88. (7") (ZB 42259) **MY EYES DON'T CRY. / ('A'instrumental)** | [ ] | [ ]
(12"/cd-s) (ZT/ZD 42260) – ('A'side) / ('A'dub) / ('A'radio edit).

May 89. (7"/c-s) (ZB/ZK 42855) **FREE. / HAPPY BIRTHDAY** | [49] | [ ]
(12"+=/cd-s+=) (ZT/ZD 42856) – It's wrong (aparteid).

Oct 90. (7"/c-s) **KEEP YOUR LOVE ALIVE. / ('A'instrumental)** | [ ] | [ ]
(12"+=)(cd-s+=) – ('A'version).

May 91. (cd/c/lp) (ZD/ZK/ZL 71750) <6291> **JUNGLE FEVER (Soundtrack)** | [56] | [24]
– Fun day / Queen in the black / These three words / Each other's throats / If she breaks your hearts / Gotta have you / Make sure you're sure / Jungle fever / I go sailing / Chemical love / Lighting up the candles.

Jun 91. (7"/c-s) <2081> **GOTTA HAVE YOU. / FEEDING OFF THE LOVE OF THE LAND** | [ ] | [92]
(12"+=/cd-s+=) – ('A'extended mix).

Sep 91. (7"/c-s) (ZB/ZK 44957) **FUN DAY. / ('A'instrumental)** | [63] | [ ]
(12"+=/cd-s+=) – ('A'remix) / ('A'club mix).

Feb 95. (7"/c-s) (TMG/+CS 1437) <0290> **FOR YOUR LOVE. / ('A'mix)** | [23] | [53]
(cd-s+=) – My Cherie amour/ Uptight (everything's alright).

Mar 95. (cd/c) (530238-2/-4) <0238> **CONVERSATION PEACE** | [8] | [16]
– Rain your love down / Edge of eternity / Taboo to love / Take the time out / I'm new / My love is with you / Treat myself / Tomorrow Robins will sing / Sensuous whisper / For your love / Cold chill / Sorry / Conversation peace.

Jul 95. (c-s) (860 356-4) **TOMORROW ROBINS WILL SING / ('A'-Wonder West side version)** | [71] | [ ]
(12") (860 373-1) – ('A'-Ronin smooth) / ('A'-Dance Hall) / ('A'-Slo jungle).
(cd-s) (860 373-2) – ('A'side) / (above 3 tracks).

Oct 95. (c-s) (860 464-4) **COLD CHILL / ('A'mix)** | [ ] | [ ]
(12"+=/cd-s+=) (860 465-1/-2) – ('A'mixes).

Oct 95. (d-cd/d-c) (530546-2/-4) <0546> **NATURAL WONDER – LIVE IN CONCERT (live)** | [ ] | [ ]
– Love's in need of love today / Master blaster (jammin') / Higher ground / Rocket love / Ribbon in the sky / Pastime paradise / If it's magic / Village ghetto land / Tomorrow robins will sing / Overjoyed / My Cherie amour / Signed, sealed, delivered (I'm yours) / Living for the city / Sir Duke / I wish / You are the sunshine of my life / Superstition / I just called to say I love you / For your love / Another star / Stevie Ray blues / Ms. and Mr. little ones / Stay gold.

– compilations, etc. –

Note; on 'Tamla Motown' until otherwise stated.

Dec 68.	(lp) *(TML 11085)* **SOMEDAY AT CHRISTMAS** (re-iss. +c.Nov82 & 1986)	☐ ☐ Dec67
Sep 76.	(7") *(TMG 1042)* **YESTER-ME, YESTER-YOU, YESTERDAY. / UPTIGHT (EVERYTHING'S ALRIGHT)**	☐ ☐
Dec 77.	(d-lp/d-c) *(M9 804)* <804> **ANTHOLOGY** (both above re-iss. Oct81)	☐ ☐
Sep 80.	(7") *(TMG 959)* **I WAS MADE TO LOVE HER. / NEVER HAD A DREAM COME TRUE**	☐
Sep 80.	(7") *(TMG 966)* **SIGNED, SEALED, DELIVERED (I'M YOURS). / FINGERTIPS (part 2)** (both above re-iss. Oct81)	☐
May 83.	(c-ep) **CASSINGLE** – For once in my life / Signed, sealed, delivered (I'm yours) / My Cherie amour / Yester-me, yester-you, yesterday.	☐ -
Dec 83.	(12") *(TMGT 1235)* **HAPPY BIRTHDAY. / (Martin Luther King speech extracts)**	☐
Apr 85.	(7"/12") *(TMG/+T 989)* **FOR ONCE IN MY LIFE. / I WAS MADE TO LOVE HER**	☐
Apr 85.	(7"/12") *(TMG/+T 1384)* **I WISH. / SIR DUKE**	☐
Apr 85.	(7"/12") *(TMG/+T 1388)* **HE'S MISSTRA KNOW IT ALL. / BOOGIE ON REGGAE WOMAN**	☐
Oct 86.	(cd) *(ZD 72489)* **FOR ONCE IN MY LIFE / UPTIGHT**	☐
Oct 86.	(cd) *(ZD 72453)* **MY CHERIE AMOUR / SIGNED, SEALED, DELIVERED, I'M YOURS**	☐
Jun 87.	(d-lp-d-c/d-cd) *(WL/WK/ZD 72585)* **THE ESSENTIAL**	☐
Jul 87.	(cd) *(ZD 72558)* **DOWN TO EARTH / I WAS MADE TO LOVE YOU**	☐
Apr 88.	(7") *(ZB 41937)* **FINGERTIPS (part 2). / BLOWIN' IN THE WIND**	☐
Apr 88.	(7") *(ZB 41939)* **NEVER HAD A DREAM COME TRUE. / SIGNED, SEALED, DELIVERED, I'M YOURS**	☐
Jun 89.	(cd-s) *(ZD 41959)* **UPTIGHT (EVERYTHING'S ALRIGHT) / etc.**	☐
Feb 79.	(lp/c) *MFP; (MFP 50420)* **LIGHT MY FIRE**	☐ -
Nov 84.	(lp/c) *Telstar; (STA R/C 2251)* **LOVE SONGS – 16 CLASSIC HITS** (re-iss. +cd.Jul86 as '20 CLASSIC HITS' on 'Motown'+4)	20 -
Nov 87.	(cd) *Priority; (VPRVCD 201)* **THEIR VERY BEST – BACK TO BACK**	☐ -
	—— (above shared with GLADYS KNIGHT & THE PIPS)	
Jul 95.	(cd) *Connoisseur; (VSOPCD 216)* **STEVIE WONDER SONGBOOK**	☐ -
Sep 95.	(cd) *Motown;* **EIVETS REDNOW**	☐ -
Nov 96.	(cd/c) *Motown; (530757-2/-4)* **SONG REVIEW – A GREATEST HITS COLLECTION**	19 ☐

WONDER STUFF

Formed: Stourbridge, Midlands, England ...early 1986 by ex-EDEN drummer turned frontman, MILES HUNT, together with MALCOLM TREECE, THE BASS THING and MARTIN GILKS. After a couple of EP's on their own 'Farout' label, the group signed to 'Polydor' in late '87, initially lumped in with contemporaries like POP WILL EAT ITSELF and CRAZYHEAD under the music press-created 'grebo' banner. It soon became clear, however, that The WONDER STUFF were a unique proposition in their own right, as evidenced on the debut album, 'THE EIGHT LEGGED GROOVE MACHINE' (1988), a diverse collection of sparkling, hard-edged indie pop. HUNT was as bitingly uncompromising in his lyrics as he was in his relations with the media, the sardonic singer ever reliable for a controversial comment. While 'A WISH AWAY' narrowly missed the Top 40, another single, the wry 'IT'S YER MONEY I'M AFTER BABY', just nosed its way into the chart, the track backed by the self-explanatory 'ASTLEY IN THE NOOSE'. 'WHO WANTS TO BE THE DISCO KING?' asked HUNT in his inimitable bad attitude style, taking the WONDER STUFF into the Top 30 for the first time in early '89. A comparatively sensitive side was glimpsed on the jaunty 'DON'T LET ME DOWN' later that year, a Top 20 hit and a taster for the follow-up album, 'HUP' (1989). With the addition of JAMES TAYLOR on organ and MARTIN BELL on banjo/mandolin (no, not THAT JAMES TAYLOR and not THAT MARTIN BELL!), the record combined their high-octane pop/rock with a loose folky feel. It also marked their first major success, reaching the Top 5 and establishing the group as a headlining act. The success brought internal tensions to a head, however, with THE BASS THING (aka ROB JONES) departing for New York where he later formed 8-piece outfit The BRIDGE AND THE TUNNEL CREW (JONES subsequently died from heart problems in 1993). With PAUL CLIFFORD coming in as a replacement, the group entered the most high profile period of their career. Following on from the Top 20 success of the groovy 'CIRCLESQUARE' single, The WONDER STUFF scored a massive hit with the insanely catchy and ultimately annoying 'SIZE OF A COW'. A third set, 'NEVER LOVED ELVIS' (1991), made the Top 3 later that summer, a more mature set which nevertheless lacked the raw charm of old. A marriage made in heaven/hell (delete according to taste), The WONDER STUFF teamed up with comedic loonies VIC REEVES & BOB MORTIMER for a cover of TOMMY ROE's 'DIZZY', giving the group their one and only No.1 single later that year. With the help of rootsy chanteuse KIRSTY MacCOLL, the 'WELCOME TO THE CHEAP SEATS' EP (1992) continued the band's folk/indie hybrid, as did the group's final album, 'CONSTRUCTION FOR THE MODERN IDIOT' (1993). Increasingly disillusioned by their failure to break the American market

and the direction of the British music scene, The WONDER STUFF finally signed off with the surprisingly ebullient 'HOT LOVE NOW! EP' (1994) and a farewell performance at the 1994 Phoenix festival. While HUNT went on to work as a presenter for MYV before forming VENT 414, the other members subsequently founded the group WEKNOWWHEREYOULIVE.
• **Songwriters:** Group music / HUNT lyrics except; GIMME SOME TRUTH (John Lennon) / THAT'S ENTERTAINMENT (Jam) / INSIDE YOU (Pop Will Eat Itself) / COZ I LUV YOU (Slade).
Album rating: THE EIGHT LEGGED GROOVE MACHINE (*6) / HUP (*6) / NEVER LOVED ELVIS (*7) / CONSTRUCTION FOR THE MODERN IDIOT (*5) / IF THE BEATLES HAD READ HUNTER . . . THE SINGLES compilation (*8)

MILES HUNT – vocals, guitar / **MALCOLM TREECE** – guitar, vocals / **THE BASS THING** (b.ROB JONES) – bass / **MARTIN GILKS** – drums, percussion (ex-MIGHTY LEMON DROPS)

		Farout not iss.
Feb 87.	(7"ep) *(GONE ONE)* **IT'S NOT TRUE . . . / A WONDERFUL DAY. / LIKE A MERRY GO ROUND / DOWN HERE**	☐ -
Sep 87.	(7") *(GONE 002)* **UNBEARABLE. / TEN TRENCHES DEEP** (12"+=) *(GOBIG 002)* – I am a monster / Frank.	☐ -
		Polydor Polygram
Apr 88.	(7") *(GONE 3)* **GIVE GIVE GIVE ME MORE MORE MORE. / A SONG WITHOUT AN END** (12"+=/cd-s+=) *(GONE X/CD 3)* – Meaner than mean / See the free world.	72 -
Jul 88.	(7") *(GONE 4)* **A WISH AWAY. / JEALOUSY** (12"+=/cd-s+=) *(GONE X/CD 4)* – Happy-sad / Goodbye fatman.	43 -
Aug 88.	(lp/c)(cd) *(GON LP/MC 1)(837135-2)* <837802> **THE EIGHT LEGGED GROOVE MACHINE** – Redbury joy town / No for the 13th time / It's yer money I'm after baby / Rue the day / Give give give me more more more / Like a merry go round / The animals and me / A wish away / Grin / Mother and I / Some sad someone / Ruby horse / Unbearable / Poison. *(cd-iss. Apr95; same)*	18
Sep 88.	(7"ep/12"ep/cd-ep) *(GONE/+X/CD 5)* **IT'S YER MONEY I'M AFTER BABY / ASTLEY IN THE NOOSE. / OOH, SHE SAID / RAVE FROM THE GRAVE**	40 -
Feb 89.	(7") *(GONE 6)* **WHO WANTS TO BE THE DISCO KING?. / UNBEARABLE (live)** (12"+=/cd-s+=) *(GONEX/GONCD 6)* – Ten trenches deep (live) / No for the 13th time (live).	28 -
	—— added guests **JAMES TAYLOR** – organ (ex-PRISONERS) / **MARTIN BELL** – banjo	
Sep 89.	(7"/c-s) *(GONE/GONCS 7)* **DON'T LET ME DOWN, GENTLY. / IT WAS ME** (12"+=/cd-s+=) *(GONEX/GONCD 7)* – ('A'extended).	19 -
Oct 89.	(lp/c/cd) *(841 187-1/-4/-2)* **HUP** – 30 years in the bathroom / Radio ass kiss / Golden green / Let's be other people / Piece of sky / Can't shape up / Good night though / Don't let me down, gently / Cartoon boyfriend / Unfaithful / Them, big oak trees / Room 410. *(re-iss. cd Apr95; same)*	5 -
Nov 89.	(7"/c-s) *(GONE/GONCS 8)* **GOLDEN GREEN. / GET TOGETHER** (12"+=/cd-s+=) *(GONEX/GONCD 8)* – Gimme some truth.	33 -
	—— (Mar'90) **PAUL CLIFFORD** – bass finally repl. THE BASS THING (left '89). He later formed 8-piece The BRIDGE AND THE TUNNEL CREW.	
May 90.	(7"/c-s) *(GONE/GONCS 10)* **CIRCLESQUARE. / OUR NEW SONG** (12"+=/cd-s+=) *(GONEX/GONCD 10)* – ('A'-Paranoia mix).	20 -
Mar 91.	(7"/c-s) *(GONE/GONCD 11)* **THE SIZE OF A COW. / RADIO ASS KISS** (12"+=/cd-s+=) *(GONEX/GONCD 11)* – Give give give me more more more (live).	5 -
May 91.	(7"/c-s) *(GONE/GONCS 12)* **CAUGHT IN MY SHADOW. / GIMME SOME TRUTH (live)** (12"+=/cd-s+=) *(GONEX/GONCD 12)* – ('A'extended).	18 -
Jun 91.	(cd/c/lp) *(847 252-2/-4/-1)* **NEVER LOVED ELVIS** – Mission drive / Play / False start / Welcome to the cheap seats / The size of a cow / Sleep alone / Reaction / Inertia / Maybe / Grotesque / Here come everyone / Caught in my shadow / Line poem. *(re-iss. cd Apr95; same)*	3 -
Aug 91.	(7"/c-s) *(GONE/GONCS 13)* **SLEEP ALONE. / EL HERMANO DE FRANK** (12"+=/cd-s+=) *(GONEX/GONCD 13)* – The takin' is easy.	43 -
	—— In Oct'91, they teamed up with comedian VIC REEVES (& BOB MORTIMER) on No.1 hit cover of Tommy Roe's 'DIZZY'. Next single with guest, KIRSTY MacCOLL	
Jan 92.	(7"ep/c-ep) *(GONE/GONCS 14)* **WELCOME TO THE CHEAP SEATS** – Welcome to the cheap seats / Me, my mum, my dad and my brother / Will the circle be unbroken / That's entertainment. (cd-ep+=) *(GONECD 14)* – ('A'naked mix) / Caught in my shadw (bare mix) / Circlesque (butt naked mix) / Can't shape up again.	8 -
	—— added **MARTIN BELL** – fiddle, accordion, mandolin, guitar, sitar, keyboards and 6th member **PETE WHITTAKER** – keyboards	
Sep 93.	(7"ep/c-ep/12"ep/cd-ep) *(GONE/GONCS/GONEX/GONCD 15)* **ON THE ROPES EP** – On the ropes / Professional disturber of the peace / Hank and John / Whites.	10 -
Oct 93.	(cd/c/lp) *(519 894-2/-4/-1)* **CONSTRUCTION FOR THE MODERN IDIOT** – Change every light bulb / I wish them all dead / Cabin fever / Hot love now / Full of life (happy now) / Storm drain / On the ropes / Your big assed mother / Swell / A great drinker / Hush / Sing the absurd.	4 -
Nov 93.	(7") *(GONE 16)* **FULL OF LIFE (HAPPY NOW). / CLOSER TO FINE** (cd-s+=) *(GONCD 16)* – Burger standing / A curious weird and ugly scene. (cd-s) *(GONCDX 16)* – ('A'-Dignity mix) / Change every light bulb (dub mix) / I wish them all dead (dub mix).	28 -
	—— Note: Ex-member ROB JONES (THE BASS THING) died mysteriously on 30 Jul'93 in his New York apartment.	

Mar 94. (7"ep/c-ep/cd-ep) *(GONE/GONEX/GONCD 17)* **HOT LOVE NOW! EP**   `19` `-`
– Hot love now! / Just helicopters / I must've had something really useful to say / Room 512, all the news that's fit to print.
(cd-ep) *(GONCDX 17)* – ('A'cardinal error mix) / Unrest song / Flour babies / The Tipperary triangle.

—— Disbanded after July Phoenix Festival. MILES went on to work for MTV.

– compilations, etc. –

Sep 94. (7"/c-s/cd-s) Polydor; *(GONE/GONCS/GONCD 18)* **UNBEARABLE. / INSIDE YOU / HIT BY A CAR**   `16` `-`
(cd-s) *(GONCDX 18)* – ('A'original) / Ten trenches deep / I am a monster / Frank.
Sep 94. (cd/c) Polydor; *(521 397-2/-4/-1)* **IF THE BEATLES HAD READ HUNTER . . . THE SINGLES**   `8` `-`
– Welcome to the cheap seats / A wish away / Caught in my shadow / Don't let me gently / Size of a cow / Hot love now! / Dizzy / Unbearable / Circlesquare / Who wants to be the disco king? / Golden green / Give give give me more more more / Sleep alone / Coz I luv you / Full of life / On the ropes / It's yer money I'm after baby / It's not true.
Jul 95. (cd) Windsong; *(WINCD 074)* **LIVE IN MANCHESTER (live)**   `74` `-`

Roy WOOD (see under ⇒ MOVE)

WOODENTOPS (dig out; Great Alt & Indie . . .)

WORLD PARTY

Formed: London, England . . . 1986 by producer/keyboard virtuoso, KARL WALLINGER. With a varied CV which included a stint in an embryonic version of Welsh pomp-rockers, The ALARM, and a period as musical director of The Rocky Horror Show in London's West End, WALLINGER made his name as 'the other half' of The WATERBOYS alongside MIKE SCOTT. Eager to realise his own creative vision, WALLINGER subsequently formed WORLD PARTY, signing to 'Ensign' UK on the strength of his WATERBOYS' pedigree. With SINEAD O'CONNOR enjoying a co-credit, the debut WORLD PARTY single, 'PRIVATE REVOLUTION' (also the title of the subsequent album) emerged in summer '86. It was closely followed by the US Top 30 hit, 'SHIP OF FOOLS', a slice of environmentally-conscious folk-pop which served as a taster for the debut album, 'PRIVATE REVOLUTION' (1987). Written, performed and produced almost wholly by WALLINGER (with a little help from O'CONNOR and ex-WATERBOYS' MARTIN SWAIN and GUY CHAMBERS), the record saw him revisiting his beloved 60's past with a style and vision entirely his own; BOB DYLAN and The BEATLES were the favoured critical comparisons, no doubt spurred on by his cover of the former's 'ALL I REALLY WANT TO DO'. Lyrically, WALLINGER was travelling along roughly the same ley lines as SCOTT, espousing environmental awareness in a neo-pagan style. It would be another three years before WALLINGER re-emerged with a follow-up, and apart from helping out O'CONNOR on her album, 'The Lion And The Cobra', he maintained a fairly low profile. Few contested that 'GOODBYE JUMBO' (1990) wasn't worth the wait, its tougher, more familiar pop-friendly melodies resulting in a Top 10 placing for the compelling 'WAY DOWN NOW'. Both lyrically and musically, WALLINGER had matured into one of the UK's most affecting songwriters, and arguably this album marked some kind of artistic peak. It was also his last one-man show, WALLINGER opting to delegate some of the musical duties on 1993's 'BANG' to new members CHRIS SHARROCK and DAVE CAITLIN-BIRCH. The album turned out to be the most commercially successful WORLD PARTY release to date, climbing to No.2 in the UK charts following the Top 20 success of melancholy strumathon 'IS IT LIKE TODAY'. It was also the most diversely ambitious WORLD PARTY release to date, proving that WALLINGER wasn't just a one-trick pony even if he did sound most at home on the acid-folk numbers. • **Songwriters:** All WALLINGER, except ALL I REALLY WANT TO DO (Bob Dylan) / HAPPINESS IS A WARM GUN (Beatles) / sampled SAY WHAT (by Troublefunk) on GIVE IT ALL AWAY.

Album rating: PRIVATE REVOLUTION (*7) / GOODBYE JUMBO (*8) / BANG! (*5) / EGYPTOLOGY (*7)

KARL WALLINGER (b.19 Oct'57, Prestatyn, Wales) – vocals, keyboards, synth. with **MARTYN SWAIN + GUY CHAMBERS** (also both ex-WATERBOYS)

	Ensign	Chrysalis
Aug 86. (7"; WORLD PARTY featuring SINEAD O'CONNOR) *(ENY 604)* **PRIVATE REVOLUTION. / HOLY WATER**	`-`	
(12"+=) *(ENYX 604)* – Trouble down here.		
Aug 86. (lp/c)(cd) *(CHEN/ZCHEN 4) <41552>* **PRIVATE REVOLUTION**	`56`	`39` Dec86

– Private revolution / Making love (to the world) / Ship of fools / All come true / Dance of the hoppy lads / It can be beautiful (sometimes) / Ballad of the little man / Hawaiian island world / All I really want to do / World party / It's all mine. *(cd-iss. Apr87; CCD 1552)*

Feb 87. (7") *(ENY 606)* **SHIP OF FOOLS. / WORLD GROOVE (DO THE MIND GUERILLA)**	`42`	`-`
(12"+=) *(ENYX 606)* – Now here man.		
(cd-s+=) *(SCD 1)* – Trouble down here / Private revolution.		
Feb 87. (7") *<43052>* **SHIP OF FOOLS (SAVE ME FROM TOMORROW). / HOLY WATER**	`-`	`27`

—— KARL toured w/ 6-piece incl. **CHRIS SHARROCK** – drums (ex-ICICLE WORKS)

	Ensign	Ensign
May 90. (c-s/7") *(T+/ENY 631)* **MESSAGE IN A BOX. / NATURE GIRL**	`39`	

(12"+=/cd-s+=) *(ENYX/CDENY 631)* – You're all invited to the party / Happiness is a warm gun.
May 90. (cd)(c/lp) *(CCD 1654)(Z+/CHEN 10) <21654>* **GOODBYE JUMBO**   `36` `73`
– Is it too late? / Way down now / When the rainbow comes / Put the message in the box / Ain't gonna come till I'm ready / And I fell back alone / Take it up / God on my side / Show me to the top / Love street / Sweet soul dream / Thank you world. *(re-iss. cd Mar94; same)*
Aug 90. (c-s/7") *(T+/ENY 634)* **WAY DOWN NOW. / WATCHING AND WAITING**   `66`
(12"+=) *(ENYX 634)* – ('A'remix) / S.E.X.
(cd-s++=) *(CDENY 634)* – Love street (live).
Apr 91. (c-s/7") *(T+/ENY 643)* **THANK YOU WORLD. / ('A' Peter Lorimer mix)**   `68`
(12"+=/cd-s=) *(ENYX/CDENY 643)* – ('A'live).

—— In 1991, CHAMBERS left forming LEMON GRASS the following year.

—— **KARL WALLINGER, CHRIS SHARROCK + DAVE CATLIN-BIRCH,** plus guests **GUY CHAMBERS, DOMINIC MILLER, KAREN RAMELISE**

Mar 93. (c-s/7") *(T+/ENY 658)* **IS IT LIKE TODAY. / BASICALLY**   `19`
(cd-s) *(CDENY 658)* – ('A'side) / Ship of fools / World without love.
(cd-s) *(CDENYS 658)* – ('A'side) / Message in a box / The little man (1985 demo).
Apr 93. (cd)(c/lp) *(CD/TC+/CHEN 33)* **BANG!**   `2`
– Kingdom come / Is it like today? / What is love all about? / And God said . . . / Give it all away / Sooner or later / Hollywood / Radiodays / Rescue me / Sunshine / All I gave / Give it all away (reprise).
Jul 93. (12"/c-s) *(ENYX/TENY 659)* **GIVE IT ALL AWAY. / MYSTERY GIRL**   `43`
(cd-s+=) *(CDENY 659)* – Closer still / Basically.
(cd-s) *(CDENYS 659)* – ('A'side) / My pretty one / World groove (do the mind guerilla).
Sep 93. (c-s/7") *(T+/ENY 660)* **ALL I GAVE. / NO MORE CRYING**   `37`
(cd-s+=) *(CDENY 660)* – Sunset.
(cd-s) *(CDENYS 660)* – ('A'side) / Time on my hands / Is it too late / Radio days (live).

	Chrysalis	Chrysalis
May 97. (cd-s) *(CDCHS 5053)* **BEAUTIFUL DREAM / IS IT LIKE TODAY / PUT THE MESSAGE IN THE BOX / SHIP OF FOOLS**	`31`	

(cd-s) *(CDCHSX 5053)* – ('A'side) / Penny Lane / Sweetheart like you / No.9 dream.
(cd-s) *(CDCHSS 5053)* – ('A'side) / Nicotine / Seaview story.
Jun 97. (cd/c) *(CD/TC CHR 6124)* **EGYPTOLOGY**   `34`
– Is it time / Beautiful dream / Call me up / Vanity fair / She's the one / Curse of the mummy's tomb / Hercules / Love is best / Rolling off a log / Strange groove / Whole of the night / Piece of mind / This world / Always.

Link WRAY

Born: LINCOLN WRAY, 2 May'30, Dunn, North Carolina, USA. The (part Shawnee Indian) guitarist's first music venture was a country band (LUCKY WRAY & THE LAZY PINE WRANGLERS) consisting of his brothers DOUG and VERNON; the trio – who subsequently renamed themselves LUCKY WRAY & THE PALOMINO RANCH HANDS – recruited SHORTY HORTON and cut a debut EP for the local 'Kay' label. After losing a lung from TB in the Korean War, WRAY increasingly concentrated on his guitar technique; by the release of 1958's 'RUMBLE' (a one-off debut for 'Cadence'), he'd developed a primitive yet pioneering style of 6-string distortion which would see the aforementioned track have a seismic influence on the development of white guitar-rock and in turn, Heavy Metal. A Top 20 US hit, LINK WRAY & HIS WRAYMEN moved on to 'Epic' for their follow-up, 'RAW-HIDE', another classic Top 30 instrumental that was again slated for apparently appealing to juvenile delinquents. After the major label failed to tone the man down for popular consumption, WRAY set up his own 'Rumble' records and released the original version of 'JACK THE RIPPER'. The Philadelphia-based 'Swan' imprint turned this platter into a minor hit in 1963, although subsequent 45's would fail to impress the majority of the American record buying public. He made several attempts to revive his flagging career, although all were in vain (probably too busy looking after his nine children from three marriages). 1971's eponymous comeback set (which included a version of Willie Dixon's 'TRAIL DRAGGER') was recorded in his home studio (a converted chicken coop), a more mellow effort that attempted to resurrect the various American Roots traditions. Having spent a short spell on Richard Branson's 'Virgin' label in the mid-70's, WRAY was back in the spotlight in '77 after scoring a minor hit ('RED HOT') with rockabilly punk man ROBERT GORDON (ex-TUFF DARTS). With groups like The CRAMPS, The GUN CLUB, etc, citing him as a major influence, WRAY was never short of a recording contract (or three . . .), 1993's 'INDIAN CHILD' recorded in Denmark where he now resides.

Best CD compilation: RUMBLE! – THE BEST OF LINK WRAY (*8)

LINK WRAY & HIS RAY MEN

between 1957-1964, his WRAYMEN were; **DOUG WRAY** – drums, sax, flute / **SHORTY HORTON** – bass (added in 1963; **VERNON WRAY** – keyboards)

	London	Cadence
May 58. (7") *(HLA 8623) <1347>* **RUMBLE. / THE SWAG**		`16` Apr58
	not iss.	Epic
Jan 59. (7") *<9300>* **RAW-HIDE. / THE DIXIE-DOODLE** *(UK-iss.1975; 15-2210)*	`-`	`23`
1959. (7") *<9321>* **COMMANCHE. / LILLIAN**	`-`	`-`
1959. (7") *<9343>* **SLINKY. / RENDEZVOUS**	`-`	`-`

1960. (7") <9361> **GOLDEN STRINGS. / TRAIL OF THE LONESOME PINE**

1960. (7") <9419> **MARY ANN. / AIN'T THAT LOVIN' YOU BABY**

1960. (lp) <LN 3661> **LINK WRAY & THE WRAY MEN**
– The Dixie-doodle / Ramble / Caroline / Raw-hide / Right turn / Golden strings / Comanche / Hambone / Mary Ann / Rumble mambo / Ain't that lovin' you baby / Slinky / Hand clapper / Lillian / Radar / Studio blues. *(UK version iss.1973 + Apr76 as 'ROCKIN' AND HANDCLAPPIN' on 'Epic'; EPC 63627) (UK-iss.Jun85 on 'Edsel'; ED 149) (cd-iss. Jan88; EDCD 149)*

		not iss.	Rumble

1961. (7") <9454> **EL TORO. / TIAJUANA**

		Stateside	Swan

1962. (7") <1000> **JACK THE RIPPER. / THE STRANGER**

Aug 63. (7") (SS 217) <4137> **JACK THE RIPPER. / THE BLACK WIDOW**   64 Jun63

1963. (lp) <SLP 510> **JACK THE RIPPER**
– Mr guitar / My Beth / Deacon Jones / Steel trap / Cross ties / Jack the ripper / Ace of spades / Hidden charms / Fat back / Run chicken run / Dinosaur / Big Ben / Mash potato party / I'll do anything for you / Rendez-vous / Slinky *(UK-iss.Jun90 on 'Hangman'; HANG 033UP)*

Sep 63. (7") <4154> **TURNPIKE U.S.A. / WEEKEND**
Nov 63. (7") <4163> **THE SWEEPER. / RUN CHICKEN RUN**
Jan 64. (7") (SS 256) **THE SWEEPER. / WEEKEND**
Feb 64. (7"ep) (SE 1015) **MR. GUITAR**
– Mr. Guitar / Dinosaur / Run chicken run / Rumble.
1964. (7") <4171> **THE SHADOW KNOWS. / MY ALBERTA**
1964. (7") <4187> **DEUCES WILD. / SUMMER DREAM**

—— **BOBBY HOWARD** – vocals; repl. VERNON

Mar 65. (7") (SS 397) <4201> **GOOD ROCKIN' TONIGHT. / I'LL DO ANYTHING FOR YOU**

LINK WRAY

1965. (7") <4211> **BRANDED. / HANG ON**
1965. (7") <4232> **GIRL FROM NORTH COUNTRY. / YOU HURT ME SO**
1966. (7") <4239> **ACE OF SPADES. / THE FUZZ**
1966. (7") <4244> **BATMAN THEME. / ALONE**
1966. (7") <4261> **HIDDEN CHARMS. / ACE OF SPADES**
1967. (7") <4273> **LET THE GOOD TIMES ROLL. / SOUL TRAIN**
1967. (7") <4284> **JACK THE RIPPER. / I'D DO ANYTHING FOR YOU**

		not iss.	Heavy

1968. (7") <101> **RUMBLE '68. / BLOW YOUR MIND**

		not iss.	Mr.G

1969. (7") <101> **RUMBLE '69. / BLOW YOUR MIND**

—— returned for the 70's, w/**DOUG + BOBBY + BILLY HODGES** – keyboards / **STEVE VERROCA** – drums

	Polydor	Polydor

Sep 71. (lp) (2489 029) <244064> **LINK WRAY**   Jul71
– La de da / Take me home Jesus / Jukebox mama / Rise and fall of Jimmy Stokes / Fallin' rain / Fire and brimstone / Ice people / God out west / Crowbar / Black river swamp / Tail dragger.
Sep 71. (7") (2066 120) <14084> **FIRE AND BRIMSTONE. / JUKEBOX MAMA**
Nov 71. (7") <14096> **FALLIN' RAIN. / JUKE BOX MAMA**

—— w/loads on session incl. guests **PETER KAUKONEN + COMMANDER CODY**
Jul 73. (lp) (2391 063) <5047> **BE WHAT YOU WANT TO**
– Be what you want to / All cried out / Lawdy Miss Clawdy / Tucson, Arizona / Riverbed / You walked by / Walk easy, walk slow / All the love in my life / You realy got a hold on me / Shine the light / Morning.
Aug 73. (7") <14188> **LAWDY MISS CLAWDY. / SHINE THE LIGHT**
Nov 73. (7") <14256> **SHE'S THAT KIND OF WOMAN. / I GOT TO RUMBLE**

—— w/1971 line-up, except **MORDICAI JONES** – piano, mandolin repl. BOBBY

	Virgin	not iss.

Sep 73. (lp) (V 2006) **BEANS & FATBACK**
– Beans and fatback / I'm so glad / Shaw Nee tribe / Hobo man / Georgia pines / Alabama circus / Water boy / From Tulsa to North Carolina / Right or wrong / In the pines / Take my hand.
Nov 73. (7") (VS 103) **I'M SO GLAD I'M SO PROUD. / SHAWNEE TRIBE**
Apr 75. (lp) (C 1511) **INTERSTATE 10**   French
(above issued on 'Caroline')

—— LINK now w/**ARCHIE LEGGAT** – bass / **FREDDIE SMITH** – drums, percussion / **GORDON SMITH** – steel guitar / **RUAN O'LOCHLAINN** – keyboards, alto sax
Mar 76. (lp) (V 2050) **STUCK IN GEAR**
– Southern lady / Tecolote / Quicksand / I know you're leaving me now / Did you see the man / Midnight lover / Cottoncandy apples / Bo Jack / Jack the ripper.
Apr 76. (7") (VS 142) **I KNOW YOU'RE LEAVING ME NOW. / QUICKSAND**

—— between 1977 & 1978, LINK WRAY teamed up with ex-TUFF DARTS singer ROBERT GORDON on two albums, 'ROBERT GORDON WITH LINK WRAY' and 'FRESH FISH SPECIAL'; the single 'THE WAY I WALK' was also a dual effort.

—— now with **ANTON FIG** – drums / **CHRIS ROBINSON** – keyboards, synthesizers / + producer **RICHARD GOTTEHEIR** – piano, etc.

	Chiswick	not iss.

Mar 78. (7"; w-drawn) (NS 32) **BATMAN THEME. / HIDDEN CHARMS**

	Charisma	Visa

May 79. (7"blue) (CB 333) **IT'S ALL OVER NOW, BABY BLUE. / JUST THAT KIND OF SWITCHBLADE**

May 79. (lp) (CAS 1143) <7009> **BULLSHOT**
– Good good lovin' / Fever / Snag / Just that kind of switchblade / It's all over now, baby blue / Rawhide / Wild party / The sky is falling / Don't. *(cd-iss. Nov89 on 'Line'; LICD 9.00142)*

—— w/**ANTON FIG** / + **JIMMY LOWELL** – bass

	Magnum Force	Visa

Oct 80. (lp) (MFLP 008) <7010> **LIVE AT THE PARADISO (live)**
– Blue suede shoes / Ace of spades / Walk away from love / I saw her standing there / Run chicken run / She's no good / Rumble / Rawhide / Subway blues / Money / Shake, rattle and roll / Be bop a lula. *(re-iss.Jul82; MFM 012) (cd-iss. Apr91; CDMF 008)*

—— w/ **KEITH LENTIN** – bass, vocals / **MARTY FEIER** – drums

	Big Beat	not iss.

Jan 86. (lp) (WIKM 42) **LIVE IN '85 (live)**
– Rumble / It's only words / Fire / Mystery train / I gotta woman / Baby let's play house / Jack the ripper / Love me / King Creole / I'm counting on you / Rawhide / Born to be wild.
Sep 87. (lp) (WIK 65) **GROWLING GUITAR** (60's tracks)
– Climbing a high wall / Genocide / The Earth is crying / Growlin' guts / Hungry / Ace of spades / Ruby baby / Hang on / Summer dreams / Sorrento / Peggy Sue / Alone / Girl from North Country / You hurt me so / The fuzz. *(cd-iss. May91+=; CDWIK 972)* – LIVE IN '85

—— with **KIM HYTTEL** – keyboards / **FLEMMING NILSSON** – percussion / **SHAKY GROUND band: JAN MOLS** – rhythm guitar, vocals / **CARSTEN EGHOLM** – bass / **ERIK LODBERG** – drums (he now writes music & lyrics with wife OLIVE

	Ball Product	Sony Denmark

Jun 93. (cd) (SHED 001CD) **INDIAN CHILD**
– Torture / Trying to find your love / Indian child / God's litle baby / I apologize / Saving all my love / Diamonds and pearls / It was Elvis / Guitar man from New Orleans / Bring on the night.

– compilations, etc. –

1971. (lp) *Union Pacific; (UP 002)* **THERE'S GOOD ROCKIN' TONITE**
(re-iss. Sep82; same)
Nov 76. (lp) *Polydor; (2391 128) <6025>* **THE LINK WRAY RUMBLE**   Oct74
Mar 79. (lp) *Ace-Chiswick; (CH 6)* **THE EARLY RECORDINGS**
Apr 79. (lp) *Charly; (CR 30171)* **ROCK'N'ROLL RUMBLE**
(re-iss. May83 as 'GOOD ROCKIN' TONITE' on 'Ace'; CH 69)
Apr 80. (7") *Revival; (REV 6001)* **RUMBLE. / (B-side by Bobby Fuller Four)**
(re-iss. Jul82; same)
1980's. (lp) *Vermillion; <1924>* **GREAT GUITAR HITS**
1980's. (lp) *Vermillion; <1925>* **SINGS & PLAYS**
1980's. (lp) *Record Factory; <1929>* **YESTERDAY & TODAY**
May 89. (lp) *Ace; (CH 266)* **RUMBLE MAN**
Nov 89. (cd) *Ace; (CDCH 924)* **THE ORIGINAL RUMBLE**
Nov 89. (lp) *Hangman; (HANG 31UP)* **SWAN DEMOS '64**
Jan 90. (lp) *Norton; (210)* **HILLBILLY WOLF: MISSING LINKS VOL.1**
Jan 90. (lp) *Norton; (211)* **BIG CITY AFTER DARK: MISSING LINKS VOL.2**
Jan 90. (lp) *Norton; (212)* **SOME KINDA NUT: MISSING LINKS VOL.3**
Mar 90. (lp) *Ace; (CH 286)* **APACHE**
Jun 90. (lp) *Ace; (CH 296)* **WILD SIDE OF THE CITY LIGHTS**
Jun 90. (cd) *Ace; (CDCHD 931)* **APACHE / WILD SIDE OF THE CITY LIGHTS**
May 93. (cd) *Columbia; (472866-2)* **WALKING WITH LINK**
Oct 94. (cd-ep) *Rollercoaster; (RCEP 116)* **MR. GUITAR EP**
– Jack The Ripper / Ace of spades / Branded / Black widow.
Mar 95. (cd-ep) *Rollercoaster;* **PULP FICTION EP**
– Rumble / Ace of spades / +
Jan 96. (7"ep) *Rollercoaster; (RCEP 119)* **LINK WRAY SINGS**
– Let the good times roll / What a price / 5-10-15-20 / Hidden charms.
Apr 96. (cd) *Polydor; (527717-2)* **GUITAR PREACHER: THE POLYGRAM YEARS**
Jan 97. (cd) *Ace-Charly; (CDCHD 638)* **SHADOWMAN**
Feb 97. (cd) *Visionary; (VICD 010)* **WALKING DOWN A STREET CALLED LOVE**
Sep 97. (cd) *Norton; (CED 242)* **MR. GUITAR**
Sep 97. (cd) *Norton; (CED 253)* **STREETS OF CHICAGO: THE MISSING LINKS VOL.4**
Oct 97. (cd) *Rollercoaster; (CDROLL 3011)* **THE SWAN SINGLES COLLECTION**
May 98. (cd) *Rollercoaster; (RCCD 3032)* **THEY'RE OFF AND RUMBLIN'**
Jul 98. (cd) *Hallmark; (30916-2)* **ROCK AND RUMBLE**

WRECKLESS ERIC   (dig out; Great Alt & Indie . . .)

Richard WRIGHT (see under ⇒ PINK FLOYD)

WU-TANG CLAN

Formed: Staten Island, New York, USA . . . 1992 by the RZA (aka THE ABBOT) and a posse of several young rappers under the pseudonyms; METHOD MAN, GENIUS/GZA, CHEF RAEKWON, OL' DIRTY BASTARD, GHOSTFACE KILLAH and U-GOD. The RZA was originally a solo artist (who at one point stood trial for murder) and the man responsible for forming GRAVEDIGGAZ, a gothic hip hop outfit who later worked with TRICKY. All chess-loving, blunt-smoking wordsmiths, the 'CLAN were highly influenced by martial art movies and took their name from the WU-TANG or SHAOLIN sword. In 1991, GENIUS released a debut album for

'Cold Chillin', 'WORDS FROM THE GENIUS', followed a year later by the 'CLAN's first single, the self-financed, 'PROTECT YA NECK'. The following year, the conglomerate signed for 'R.C.A.', although each member was allowed to retain his separate contract, if he had one. In 1993, complete with Kung-Fu style movie samples, WU-TANG CLAN's acclaimed debut 'ENTER THE WU-TANG (36 CHAMBERS)', scaled the US charts and showed the socially aware, wise-cracking gang in full flow. With their lavish use of sampled jazz/soul, loping beats and breathtaking, expletive-filled spitfire rapping, the crew opened up a whole new chapter of the ever unfolding hip hop saga and, for a while at least, breathed some spliff-heavy air into a stagnant scene. However, in March the following year, tragedy struck when U-GOD's toddler son, Dante, was seriously injured by a bullet in a crossfire battle. 1995 proved to be a busy and commercially fruitful year for most of the gang, especially OL' DIRTY BASTARD, METHOD MAN, CHEF RAEKWON and GENIUS/GZA, the latter unleashing the highly praised 'LIQUID SWORDS' set later that year. WU-TANG themselves made a belated return in 1997 with the feverishly anticipated 'WU-TANG FOREVER', an album which broke records by gatecrashing/topping both the US and UK charts simultaneously, an incredible feat for a hip hop act. Even more surprisingly, the set was a double; on reflection, the material could have been pared down to a blistering single disc although the schizophrenic combination of melodic but hard-bitten soul and frenetic rapping was rarely less engaging. Early in '98, GHOSTFACE KILLAH was jailed for three months on a 1995! attempted robbery charge, while on June 30th, OL' DIRTY BASTARD was wounded in the back and arm after being shot by an intruder (in his cousin's New York apartment); he, er, discharged himself a day later! ODB was up on a number of separate charges the following year in which he was alleged to have threatened security guards then (a few months later) his girlfriend before topping it all off with a shoot-out with the police; the latter would see him charged with attempted murder, although after a short-stay in jail (a six-figure bail was paid) this case – and later the others – was thrown out due to lack of evidence. Were they out to get 'im, who knows? The rapper (who was admitted to a drug rehabilitation centre in August '99) was back on the record front soon after, 'N***A PLEASE' (1999) the RICK JAMES-meets-IGGY POP-stylings making it the best WU-TANG platter for some time. In fact, mostly all the 'CLAN were at the solo game in the last few years, INSPECTAH DECK philosophising with his 'UNCONTROLLED SUBSTANCE' (in September also), the GENIUS/GZA swordsman with 'BENEATH THE SURFACE' (in July '99) and master CLANsman RZA (also in July) – RZA, wrote, produced, directed and starred in his own movie, 'BOBBY DIGITAL', which also featured WU-TANG members and was released late in '98. Around the same time, METHOD MAN made a re-appearance with 'TICAL 2000: JUDGEMENT DAY', while KILLAH PRIEST (via 'HEAVY MENTAL') and CAPPADONNA (via 'THE PILLAGE') were both out and about in March of 1998 – note also that GHOSTFACE KILLAH issued his solo 'IRONMAN' in October '96. Phew! and as if that wasn't enough, towards the end of the decade, CHEF RAEKWON added 'IMMOBILARITY' to WU-TANG's stock-pile release schedule, while METHOD MAN (and "outsider" REDMAN) had their 'BLACKOUT!' collaboration – all albums, monster sellers in the big U.S. of A.

Album rating: ENTER THE WU-TANG (36 CHAMBERS) (*8) / WU-TANG FOREVER (*7) / WU-TANG RECORDS PRESENTS: WU-CHRONICLES various artists compilation (*5) / Genius/GZA: WORDS FROM THE GENIUS (*6) / LIQUID SWORDS (*8) / BENEATH THE SURFACE (*7) / Ol' Dirty Bastard: RETURN TO THE 36 CHAMBERS (*7) / N***A PLEASE (*8) / Method Man: TICAL (*7) / TICAL 2000: JUDGEMENT DAY (*7) / BLACKOUT! with Redman (*6) / Chef Raekwon: ONLY BUILT 4 CUBAN LINX (*7) / IMMOBILARITY (*5) / Ghostface Killah: IRONMAN (*7) / Killah Priest: HEAVY MENTAL (*6) / Cappadonna: THE PILLAGE (*6) / RZA: RZA AS BOBBY DIGITAL IN STEREO (*6) / THE RZA HITS various artists compilation (*7) / Inspectah Deck: UNCONTROLLED SUBSTANCE (*7)

RZA (b. ROBERT DIGGS, 22 Aug'66) – producer, mixer / rappers **GENIUS** (aka GZA and MAXIMILLIAN) (b. GARY PRICE, 22 Aug'66) **METHOD MAN** (aka JOHNNY BLAZE and SHAQUAN) (b. CLIFFORD SMITH) / **OL' DIRTY BASTARD** (aka DIRT McDIRT and OSIRIS) (b. RUSSELL JONES, 15 Nov'68) / **RAEKWON** (aka CHEF and LEX DIAMONDS) (b. COREY WOODS) / **GHOSTFACE KILLAH** (aka TONY STARKS) (b. DENNIS COLES) / **U-GOD** (aka GOLDEN ARMS) (b. LAMONT HAWKINS) / **INSPECTAH DECK** (aka REBEL INS) (b. JASON HUNTER) / **CAPPADONNA** (aka CAPPUCCINO and TRACK SLASHER) (b. DARRYL HILL) / with other early members **MASTA KILLAH** (aka NOODLES and JAMAL) (b. ELGIN TURNER) / **SHYLEIM THE RUGGED PRINCE (PAUL)** / **DOLLY FINGERS** / **DREDDY KRUGER** / **KILLAH PRIEST** / **4th DISCIPLE**

	not iss.	own label
1992. (12") **PROTECT YA NECK.** /		
	Loud-RCA	Loud-RCA
Sep 93. (c-s,cd-s) <62544> **METHOD MAN / PROTECT YA NECK**	–	69
Feb 94. (c-s,12",cd-s) <62829> **C.R.E.A.M. (CASH RULES EVERYTHING AROUND ME). / DA MYSTERY OF CHESSBOXIN'**	–	60
May 94. (cd/c) (74321 20367-2/-4) <66336> **ENTER THE WU-TANG (36 CHAMBERS)**		41 Nov93

– Bring da ruckus / Shame on a nigga / Clan in da front / Wu-Tang: 7th chamber / Can it all be so simple / (intermission) / Da mystery of chessboxin / Wu-Tang Clan ain't nuthing ta f'wit / C.R.E.A.M. / Method Man / Protect ya neck / Tearz / Wu-Tang: 7th chamber – part II. (cd+=) – Method Man (skunk mix) / (conclusion).

—— were back (**RZA** The Abbott / **GZA** The Genius / **DIRTY** Osirus / **U-GOD** Golden Arms / **METHOD MAN** Hott Nikkels / **RAEKWON** Lex Diamonds / **GHOSTFACE KILLAH** Ironman / **INSPECTAH DECK** Fifth Brother / **MASTA KILLAH** High Chief / **CAPPADONNA** Jaybird, plus STREET LIFE, TEKITHA or POPPA WU and UNCLE PETE / **TRUEMASTER** (b. DAVID HARRIS) a new member now on tour

Jun 97. (d-cd/d-c) (74321 45769-2/-4) **WU-TANG FOREVER**	1	1

– Wu-revolution / Reunited / For Heaven's sake / Cash still rules – Scary hours (still don't nothing move but the money) / Visionz / As high as Wu-Tang get / Severe punishment / Older gods / Maria / A better tomorrow / It's yourz / Intro / Triumph / Impossible / Little ghetto boys / Deadly melody / The city / The projects / Bells of war / The M.G.M. / Dog sh*t / Duck seazon / Hellz wind staff / Heaterz / Black shampoo / Second coming / Sunshower / Projects international remix.

Aug 97. (12"/cd-s) (74321 49678-1/-2) **TRIUMPH. / PROJECTS INTERNATIONAL**	☐	☐
(cd-s+=) (74321 51021-2) – Diesel.		
(above featured CAPPADONNA)		

—— In Mar'98, the WU-TANG CLAN featured on TEXAS's new UK Top 5 version of 'SAY WHAT YOU WANT'.

	Wu-Tang	Wu-Tang
Aug 98. (cd/c/d-lp; as RZA presents WU-TANG KILLA BEES) <(50013)> **THE SWARM VOLUME 1**	☐	4 Jul98

– (Various cuts from some of the WU-TANG CLAN and new talents including SUNZ OF MAN and BLACK KNIGHTS OF THE NORTH STAR)

Mar 99. (cd/d-lp) (WT 004 CD/LP) <51143> **WU-TANG RECORDS PRESENTS: WU-CHRONICLES** (V/A compilation)	☐	25

– other associated releases, etc. –

OL' DIRTY BASTARD

	Elektra	Elektra
Feb 95. (c-s,cd-s) <64477> **BROOKLYN ZOO / ('A'remix)**	–	54
Mar 95. (cd/c) <(7559 61659-2/-4)> **RETURN TO THE 36 CHAMBERS** (dirty version)		7

– Intro / Shimmy shimmy ya / Baby c'mon / Brooklyn zoo / Hippa to da hoppa / Raw hide / Damage / Don't u know / The stomp / Goin' down / Drunk game (sweet sugar pie) / Snakes / Brooklyn zoo II (tiger crane) / Proteck ya neck II the zoo / Cuttin' headz / Dirty dancin' / Harlem world. (cd+=) – (2 extra).

May 95. (c-s,12"/cd-s) <66419> **SHIMMY SHIMMY YA. / ('A'version)**	–	62

—— In Jun'97, ODB featured on The ALKOHOLIKS minor US hit, 'Hip Hop Drunkies'. A month later, he was also on the BLACKstreet hit single, 'Fix'.

Sep 99. (cd/c) <(7559 62414-2/-4)> **N***A PLEASE**		10

– Recognize / I can't wait / Cold blooded / Got your money / Rollin' wit' you / Getting high / You don't want to fuck with me / Nigga please / Dirt dog / I want pussy / Good morning heartache / All in together now.

Nov 99. (c-s/12"/cd-s; as OL' DIRTY BASTARD featuring KELIS) (E 3719 C/T/CD) <radio cut> **GOT YOUR MONEY / ROLLIN' WITH YOU**	☐	33 Oct99

METHOD MAN

—— with RZA on co-writing credits

	Def Jam	Def Jam
Nov 94. (c-s,cd-s) <85-3964> **BRING THE PAIN / ('A'radio version)**	–	45
Apr 95. (12") (12DEF 6) <85-4184> **RELEASE YO' DELF / (3 'A'mixes)**	46	98 Feb95
(cd-s+=) (DEFCD 6) – (2 'A'mixes) / Bring the pain (remix).		
Jul 95. (cd-s; METHOD MAN featuring MARY J. BLIGE) (DEFDX 11) <85-1878> **I'LL BE THERE FOR YOU / YOU'RE ALL I NEED TO GET BY**	10	3 Apr95
(12"+=) (12DEF 11) – Bring the pain (remix).		
(cd-s+++=) (DEFCD 11) – Release yo' delf.		
Aug 95. (cd/c) (529 174-2/-4) <523839> **TICAL**	☐	4

– Tical / Biscuits / Bring the pain / All I need / What the blood clot / Meth Vs. Chef / Sub crazy / Release yo' delf / P.L.O. style / I get my thang in action / Mr. Sandman / Stimulation / Method Man (remix) / I'll be there for you – You're all I need to get by (featuring MARY J. BLIGE).

—— In Aug'95, METHOD MAN was credited with REDMAN on the single, 'HOW HIGH', which hit US No.13. In Oct'95, MM featured on CAPLETON's minor hit 'Wings Of The Morning'. Below from the movie, 'Batman Forever' on 'Atlantic' records.

Oct 95. (c-s,cd-s) <87100> **THE RIDDLER / ('A'-Riddler Hide-Out mix)**	–	56
Nov 98. (cd/d-lp) <(558 920-2/-1)> **TICAL 2000: JUDGEMENT DAY**	49	2

– 1999: Judgement day (intro) / Perfect world / Cradle rock (featuring LEFT EYE) / Dangerous grounds (featuring STREETLIFE) / Sweet love (skit) / Sweet love (featuring CAPPADONNA & STREETLIFE) / Shaolin what (skit) / Torture / Where's Method Man? (skit featuring ED LOVER) / Suspect chin music (featuring STREETLIFE) / Retro godfather / Dooney boy / Spazzola (featuring STREETLIFE, RAEKWON, MASTA KILLA, KILLER SIN & INSPECTAH DECK) / Check writer (skit) / 2000: You play too much (CHRIS ROCK & METHOD MAN) / Party crasher / Grid iron rap (featuring STREETLIFE) / Step by step / Play IV keeps (featuring INSPECTAH DECK, STREETLIFE & MOBB DEPP) / Donald Trump / Snuffed out (skit featuring STREETLIFE) / Elements (featuring STAR & POLITE) / Killin' fields / Big dogs (featuring REDMAN) / Break ups 2 make ups (featuring D'ANGELO) / Message from Penny / Judgement day / C.E.O.utro.

Feb 99. (c-s/cd-s; as METHOD MAN featuring D'ANGELO) <563405> **BREAK UPS 2 MAKE UPS**	–	98
Mar 99. (12"/cd-s) (566 851-1/845-2) **JUDGEMENT DAY / (mixes)**	☐	☐
May 99. (12"/cd-s; by METHOD MAN featuring D'ANGELO) (870927-1/-2) **BREAK UPS 2 MAKE UPS**	33	☐
(cd-s) (870929-2) –		
Sep 99. (cd/lp; by METHOD MAN & REDMAN) <(546609-2/-1)> **BLACKOUT!**	45	3

– Special joint / Tear it off / Masad crew / 1 2 1 2 / Da rockwilder / Run 4 cover / Dat's dat shit / Blackout! / YOU / Cereal killer / Fire ina hole / Where we at / Well all rite cha / Big dogs / How high.

—— in Nov'99, METHOD MAN featured on US singles by D'ANGELO ('Left & Right') and LIMP BIZKIT ('N 2 Gether Now')

CHEF RAEKWON

		Loud-RCA	Loud-RCA
Jul 95.	(c-s,cd-s) <64375> **GLACIERS OF ICE / CRIMINOLOGY**	–	43
Aug 95.	(cd/c) <(07863 66663-2/-4)> **ONLY BUILT 4 CUBAN LINX . . .**		4

– Striving for perfection / Knuckleheadz / Knowledge god / Criminology / Incarcerated scarfaces / Rainy dayz / Guillotine (swordz) / Can it all be so simple (remix) / Shark niggas (biters) / Ice water / Glaciers of ice / Verbal intercourse / Wisdom body / Spot rusherz / Ice cream / Wu-Gambinos / Heaven G Hell. (cd+=) – North Star (jewels).

Oct 95.	(c-s,cd-s) <64426> **INCARCERATED SCARFACES / ICE CREAM**	–	37
			71

—— RAEKWON featured on FAT JOE's minor US hit 'FIREWATER' / 'ENVY'

		Loud-Epic	Loud-Columbia
Nov 99.	(cd/c/lp) (496361/-2/-4/-1) <63844> **IMMOBILARITY**		9

– Intro / Yae yo / Casablanca / 100 rounds / Real life / Power / Skit No.1 / All I got is you pt.II / Jury / Fuck them / Skit No.2 / Live from New York / My favourite dred / Friday / The table / Sneakers / Raw / Pop shit / Heart to heart / Forecast / Outro.

GENIUS/GZA

with some of the posse

		Geffen	Geffen
Oct 95.	(c-s)(cd-s) <19390> **LIQUID SWORDS / LABELS**	–	48
Nov 95.	(cd/c/lp) <(GED/GEC/GEF 24813)> **LIQUID SWORDS**	73	9

– Killah Hills 10304 / Liquid swords / Living in the world today / Investigative reports / Duel of the Iron Mic / Labels / Cold world / Gold / I gotcha back / Swordsman / 4th chamber / Shadowboxin' / B.I.B.L.E. (Basic Instructions Before Leaving Earth) / Hell's wind staff / Unexplained.

Feb 96.	(c-s; GENIUS/GZA featuring Inspektah Deck a.k.a. Rollie Fingers) (GFSC 2214) <19391> **COLD WORLD (RZA mix) / COLD WORLD (power mix)**	40	97 Dec95

(12"+=/cd-s+=) (GFST/+D 2214) – B.I.B.L.E.
above featuring D'ANGELO

Mar 96.	(c-s,cd-s; GENIUS/GZA featuring METHOD MAN) <19396> **SHADOWBOXIN' / (instrumental) / SHADOWBOXIN' (2 versions)**	–	67

		M.C.A.	M.C.A.
Jul 99.	(cd/d-lp as GZA) <(MCD/MCA 11969)> **BENEATH THE SURFACE**	56	9

– Intro / Amplified sample / Beneath the surface / Skit 1 / Skit 2 / Crash your crew / Breaker breaker / High price small reward / Hip hop fury / Skit 3 / 1112 / Skit 4 / Victim / Publicity / Feel like an enemy / Stingplay (like dis – like dat) / Mic trippin' / Outro.

RZA

		not iss.	Big Beat
Aug 96.	(c-s,cd-s; RZA featuring METHOD MAN & CAPPADONNA) <98045> **WU-WEAR: THE GARMENT RENAISSANCE / GET DOWN FOR MINE (REAL LIVE)**	–	60

(above from the film, 'High School High')

		Gee Street	V2
Nov 98.	(cd/d-lp) (GEE 100380-2/-1) <32521> **RZA AS BOBBY DIGITAL IN STEREO**	70	16

– Intro / B.O.B.B.Y. / Unspoken word / Slow grind African / Airwaves / Love Jones / N.Y.C. everything / Mantis / Slow grind French / Holocaust (silkworm) / Terrorist / Bobby did it (Spanish fly) / Handwriting on the wall / Kiss of a black widow / Slow grindi Italian / My lovin' is digi / Domestic violence / Project talk / Lab drunk / Fuck what you think / Daily routine.

		Epic	Epic
Jun 99.	(cd/c) (492542-2/-4) <69610> **THE RZA HITS** (V/A compilation)		61

– RZA: (narration) / WU-TANG CLAN: Wu-Tang Clan ain't nothin' to fuck with / Protect ya neck / OL' DIRTY BASTARD: Shimmy / GENIUS/GZA: Liquid swords / METHOD MAN: Method man / RAEKWON THE CHEF: Incarcerated surfaces / Ice cream / RZA: (narration) / METHOD MAN: Bring the pain / GHOSTFACE KILLAH; Winter warz / OL' DIRTY BASTARD: Brooklyn zoo / METHOD MAN: All I need / WU-TANG CLAN: Cream / GHOSTFACE KILLAH: All that I got is you / RZA: (narration) / WU-TANG CLAN: Wu wear the garment renaissance.

GHOSTFACE KILLAH

		Epic	Epic
Oct 96.	(cd/c) (485389-2/-4) **IRONMAN**	38	2

– Iron maiden / Wildflower / Faster blade / 260 / Assassination day / Poisonous darts / Winter warz / Box in hand / Fish / Camay / Daytona 500 / Motherless child / Black Jesus / After the smoke is clear / All that I got is you / Soul controller / Marvel.

Jun 97.	(c-s) (664684-4) **ALL THAT I GOT IS YOU / DAYTONA 500**	11	

(12"+=/cd-s+=) (664684-6/-2) – Camay.

KILLAH PRIEST

		Geffen	Geffen
Jan 98.	(12"/cd-s) (GFST/+D 22318) **ONE STEP (mixes)**	45	
Mar 98.	(cd/c) <(GED/GEC 24971)> **HEAVY MENTAL**		24

– Intro / One step / Blessed are those / From then till now / Cross my heart / Fake MC's / It's over / It's over / Crusaids / Tai Chi / Heavy mental / If you don't know / Atoms to Adam / High explosives / Wisdom / B.I.B.L.E. / Mystic city / Information / Science project / Almost there / Professional.

CAPPADONNA

—— featuring RZA and the clan

		Epic	Epic
Mar 98.	(cd/c/lp) (488850-2/-4/-1) <67947> **THE PILLAGE**	43	3

– Slang editorial / The pillage / Run / Blood on blood war / Supa ninjaz / M.C.F. / Splish splash / Oh Donna / Milk the cow / South of the border / Check for a nigga / Dart throwing / Young hearts / Everything is everything / Pump up your fist / Black boy.

INSPECTAH DECK

		Loud-Epic	Loud-Columbia
Oct 99.	(cd/c) (496180-2/-4) <1865> **UNCONTROLLED SUBSTANCES**		19

– Intro / Movas & shakers / 9th chamber / Uncontrolled substance / Femme fatale / Grand prix / Forget me not / Longevity / Word on the street / Elevation / Lovin you / Trouble man / R.E.C. room / Friction / Hyperdermix / Show n prove / Cause.

Robert WYATT

Born: ROBERT ELLIDGE, 28 Jan'45, Bristol, England. While at school he formed The WILDE FLOWERS with the HOPPER brothers, which soon spliced into two groups, CARAVAN and SOFT MACHINE. The latter was the band WYATT joined in 1966, but after four albums ('THE SOFT MACHINE', 'VOLUME 2', 'THIRD' & 'FOURTH'), he estranged himself from the group in '71, forming his own MATCHING MOLE. The previous year, his record label 'C.B.S.', had issued his first solo album, 'THE END OF THE EAR', which was assisted by fellow SOFT MACHINE members supplying the jazz-rock feel. In the summer of '73, WYATT was paralysed from the waist down after falling from a window, convalescing for several months at Stoke Mandeville hospital. He returned the following year (now confined to a wheelchair), his single, a version of The MONKEES' 'I'M A BELIEVER' hitting the Top 30. Richard Branson had given him a break on 'Virgin' records earlier in the year, WYATT subsequently critically heralded for his NICK MASON-produced album, 'ROCK BOTTOM' (1974). The set featured such gems as 'SEA SONG' and 'LITTLE RED RIDING HOOD HITS THE ROAD' (in two parts). His second for the label, 'RUTH IS STRANGER THAN RICHARD' (1975), showed an even deeper side, WYATT covering CHARLIE HAYDEN's jazz track, 'SONG FOR CHE'. In 1977, he had another stab at the pop charts, a dire cover version of CHRIS ANDREWS' 'YESTERDAY MAN' being his final recording for some time. He signed to indie, 'Rough Trade' in 1980, releasing a number of singles prior to his comeback album, 'NOTHING CAN STOP US NOW' (1982). This featured his classy re-working of ELVIS COSTELLO and CLIVE LANGER's 'SHIPBUILDING'. In 1983, through constant airplay by Radio 1 DJ John Peel, the anti-Falklands war song gained a Top 40 placing. He continued to spread his political messages through his music, although he has never been one to preach, his songs retaining an intensely personal quality. • **Songwriters:** WYATT penned except: GRASS (Ivor Cutler) / STRANGE FRUIT (Billie Holiday) / AT LAST I AM FREE (Chic) / STALIN WASN'T STALLIN' (Golden Gate Quartet) / BIKO (Peter Gabriel). • **Trivia:** WYATT also provided session drums for SYD BARRETT (1969) / KEVIN AYERS (early 70's) / HENRY COW (1975) / NICK MASON (1981) / RAINCOATS (1981 and '83).

Album rating: THE END OF AN EAR (*6) / Matching Mole: MATCHING MOLE (*6) / MATCHING MOLE'S LITTLE RED RECORD (*6) / Robert Wyatt: ROCK BOTTOM (*7) / RUTH IS STRANGER THAN RICHARD (*7) / NOTHING CAN STOP US (*8) / ANIMALS mini (*4) / OLD ROTTENHAT (*6) / DONDESTAN (*6) / A SHORT BREAK mini (*5) / FLOTSAM JETSAM (*5) / GOING BACK A BIT: A LITTLE HISTORY OF ROBERT WYATT compilation (*8) / SHLEEP (*7)

ROBERT WYATT (solo) – vocals, drums (ex-SOFT MACHINE) w / **DAVID SINCLAIR** – oboe (of CARAVAN) / **MARK CHARIG** – cornet (of SOFT MACHINE) / **ELTON DEAN** – sax / plus **NEVILLE WHITEHEAD** – bass / **CYRIL AYERS** – percussion

		C.B.S.	Columbia
Oct 70.	(lp) (64189) <31846> **THE END OF AN EAR**		

– Las Vegas tango (part 1) / To Mark everywhere / To saintly Bridget / To Oz alien Daevyd and Gilly / To Nick everyone / To caravan and Brother Jim / To the old world (thank you for the use of your body) / To Carla, Marsha and Caroline (for making everything beautifuller) / Las Vegas tango (part 2). (re-iss. Aug80 on 'Embassy' lp/c; CBS/40 31846) (cd-iss. Apr93 on 'Sony Europe')

MATCHING MOLE

WYATT with retained guest **D.SINCLAIR** and band **DAVE McRAE** – keyboards / **BILL McCORMICK** – bass (ex-QUIET SUN) / **PHIL MILLER** – guitar (ex-DYBLE, COXHILL & THE MB's) (same label)

Apr 72.	(lp) (64850) <32148> **MATCHING MOLE**		

– O Caroline / Instant pussy / Signed curtain / Part of the dance / Instant kitten / Dedicated to Hugh, but you weren't listening / Beer as in braindeer / Immediate curtain. (re-iss. Mar82; CBS 32105) (cd-iss. Mar93 on 'Beat Goes On'; BGOCD 175)

Apr 72.	(7") (8101) **O CAROLINE. / SIGNED CURTAIN**		–
Oct 72.	(lp) (65260) **MATCHING MOLE'S LITTLE RED RECORD**		

– Gloria gloom / God song / Flora fidgit / Smoke signal / Starting in the middle of the day we can drink all our politics away / Marchides / Nan's true hole / Righteous rumba / Brandy as in Benji. (cd-iss. Jul93 on 'Beat Goes On'; BGOCD 174) (cd re-iss. Mar97 on 'Columbia Rewind'; 471488-2)

—— In the summer of '73, WYATT was paralysed from the waist down after falling from a window. After a year convalescing, but still in a wheelchair;

ROBERT WYATT

returned as solo vocalist. He was augmented by guests/friends **FRED FRITH** – percussion / **HUGH HOPPER** – bass / **GARY WINDO** – wind / **LAURIE ALLEN** – drums / **MIKE OLDFIELD** – guitar / **RICHARD SINCLAIR** – bass / **IVOR CUTLER** – vox, keyboards / **ALFREDA BENGE** – vocals

		Virgin	Virgin
Jul 74.	(lp/c) (V/TCV 2017) <13112> **ROCK BOTTOM**		

– Sea song / A last straw / Little Red Riding Hood hit the road (part 1) / Alifib / Alife / Little Red Riding Hood hit the road (part 2). (cd-iss. Feb89; CDV 2017)

Sep 74.	(7") (VS 114) **I'M A BELIEVER. / MEMORIES**	29	

⌐ FRITH, ALLEN & WINDO and contributions from **PHIL**
⌐ – guitar / **BILL McCORMICK** – bass / **BRIAN ENO** – synthesizers /
⌐ES – bass / **MONEZI FEZI** – trumpet / **GEORGE KHAN** – saxophone

⌐CV 2034) **RUTH IS STRANGER THAN RICHARD** ☐ –
⌐house: (a) Solar flames – (b) Five black notes and one white tone – (c)
⌐mouth / Soup song / Sonia / Team spirit 1 & 2 / Soup for Che. *(cd-iss. Feb89;*
CDv ⌐J34)

Apr 77. (7") *(VS 115)* **YESTERDAY MAN. / SONJA** ☐ –

—— accompanied only by **McCORMICK** – bass / **HARRY BECKETT** – flugelhorn (B-side)

	Rough Trade	not iss.
Mar 80. (7") *(RT 037)* **ARAUCO. / CAIMENERA** ☐ –

—— now used only **MOGOTSI MOTHLE** – double bass / **FRANK ROBERTS** – keyboards
Nov 80. (7") *(RT 052)* **AT LAST I AM FREE. / STRANGE FRUIT** ☐ –
Feb 81. (7") *(RT 046)* **STALIN WASN'T STALLIN'. / STALINGRAD** ☐ –
(**P. Blackman**)

—— now with **ESMAIL SHEK** – tabla / **KADIR DURUESH** – shenzi
Aug 81. (7") *(RT 81)* **GRASS. / TRADE UNION (Dishari featuring** ☐ –
Abdus Salique) ☐ –
Apr 82. (lp) *(ROUGH 35)* **NOTHING CAN STOP US**
– Born again cretin / At last i am free / Quantanera / Grass / Stalin wasn't stalling /
The red flag / Strange fruit / Arauco / Strange fruit / Trade union / Stalingrad. *(re-iss.*
Apr83 lp+=/c+=; ROUGH/+C 35) – Shipbuilding. *(cd-iss. May87; ROUGHCD 35)*

—— Above album featured musicians as 1980-82.

—— In Apr'82, WYATT was credited on BEN WATT ep 'SUMMER INTO WINTER'.

—— guests **STEVE NIEVE** – piano / **MARK BEDDERS** – double bass / **MARTIN HUGHES**
– drums / **CLIVE LANGER** – organ / **ELVIS COSTELLO** – b.vox
Aug 82. (7") *(RT 115)* **SHIPBUILDING. / MEMORIES OF YOU** ☐ –
(12"-iss.Nov82+=; RTT 115) – Round midnight. *(re-iss. Apr83; same); hit No.35)*

—— now with ? plus **HUGH HOPPER**, etc.
May 84. (m-lp) *(ROUGH 40)* **THE ANIMAL FILM (Soundtrack)** ☐ –
– (no tracks listed) *(cd-iss. Jul94)*
Aug 84. (12"ep) *(RTT 149)* **WORK IN PROGRESS** ☐ –
– Biko / Amber and the amberines / Yolanda / Te rescuerdo Amanda.
Oct 85. (7"/12"; ROBERT WYATT with The SWAPO SINGERS)
(RT/+T 168) **THE WIND OF CHANGE. / NAMIBIA** ☐ –

	Rough Trade	Gramavision
Dec 85. (lp/c) *(ROUGH/+C 69)* **OLD ROTTENHAT**
– Alliance / The United States of amnesia / East Timor / Speechless / The age of
self / Vandalusia / The British road / Mass medium / Gharbzadegi / P.I.A. *(cd-iss.*
Nov86; ROUGHCD 69)
Sep 91. (cd/c/lp; one-side with BENGE) *(R 274-2/-4/-1)*
DONDESTAN
– Costa / The sight of the wind / Worship / Catholic architecture / Shrink rap / Left
on man / Lisp service / CP jeebies / Dondestan.

	Blueprint	not iss.
Nov 92. (cd+book) *(BP 108CD)* **A SHORT BREAK** ☐ –
– A short break / Tubab / Kutcha / Ventilatir / Unmasked. *(re-iss. Apr96; same)*

	Hannibal	unknown
Sep 97. (cd) *(HNCD 1418)* **SHLEEP**
– Heaps of sheeps / Duchess / Maryan / Was a friend / Free will and testament /
September the ninth / Alien / Out of season / Sunday in Madrid / Blues in Bob minor /
Whole point of no return.

—— the next A-side featured **PAUL WELLER** – guitars, vocals

	Trade 2	not iss.
Sep 97. (7") *(TRDSC 010)* **FREE WILL AND TESTAMENT. / THE**
SIGHT OF THE WIND ☐ –

– compilations, others, etc. –

Mar 81. (d-lp) *Virgin; (VGD 3505)* **ROCK BOTTOM / RUTH IS**
STRANGER THAN RICHARD ☐ –
Apr 82. (7"ep; ROBERT WYATT & MEMBERS OF CAST) *Virgin;*
(VS 499) **FROM MAN TO WOMAN** ☐ –
Dec 84. (lp) *Rough Trade; (RTSP 25)* **1982-1984** – –
Feb 85. (12") *Recommended; (RE 1984)* **THE LAST NIGHTINGALE. /**
ON THE BEACH AT CAMBRIDGE ☐ –

—— next 'B'side by "The GRIMETHORPE COLLIERY BAND".
Sep 85. (7") *T.U.C.;* **THE AGE OF SELF. / RAISE YOUR BANNERS**
HIGH ☐ –
Sep 87. (12"ep) *Strange Fruit; (SFPS 037)* **THE PEEL SESSIONS**
(10.9.74) ☐ –
– Soup song / Sea song / Alife / I'm a believer.
Jan 93. (cd) *Rough Trade; (R 2952)* **MID EIGHTIES** ☐ ☐
Jul 94. (cd; by MATCHING MOLE) *Windsong; (WINCD 063)* **BBC**
RADIO 1 LIVE IN CONCERT (live) ☐ –
Jul 94. (d-cd) *Virgin; (CDVM 9031)* **GOING BACK A BIT: A LITTLE**
HISTORY OF . . . ☐ –
Aug 94. (cd) *Rough Trade; (R 3112)* **FLOTSAM AND JETSAM** ☐ –

Steve WYNN (see under ⇒ DREAM SYNDICATE)

X

Formed: Los Angeles, California, USA . . . 1977 by EXENE CERVENKA, BILLY ZOOM, JOHN DOE and original drummer MICK BASHER (the latter subsequently replaced by DJ BONEBRAKE). After a one-off debut in 1978, 'ADULT BOOKS' (for the US 'Dangerhouse' imprint), X marked their spot with the then newly formed indie label, 'Slash'. Pioneers of the cowpunk scene alongside WALL OF VOODOO, The GUN CLUB, etc, the quartet enlisted the help of RAY MANZAREK, the former DOORS organist producing their debut set, 'LOS ANGELES' (1980). A rock hybrid of country and raw punk, X were obviously influenced by 60's garage punks the FUGS and MC5 with a tone of 50's rockabilly, this combination of musical styles used most effectively on follow-up set, 'WILD GIFT' (also recorded with MANZAREK at the helm). The MANZAREK connection continued when X moved to 'Elektra', their third album, 'UNDER THE BIG BLACK SUN' (1982) breaking them into the US Top 100. A fourth set, 'MORE FUN IN THE NEW WORLD' (1983), fared just as well commercially, although the band were in turn accused of selling out. The previous year, EXENE and LYDIA LUNCH had a book of poetry, 'Adulterers Anonymous' (with that title, it's not surprising that EXENE and JOHN were divorced in '84) published in the States, the X frontwoman subsequently teaming up with DOE, DAVE ALVIN (Blasters), HENRY ROLLINS (Black Flag) and JONNY RAY BARTEL to form country-rock outfit, The KNITTERS. The latter project obviously had an effect on X themselves (ALVIN had now replaced ZOOM), who emerged with a more countrified sound on 1985's 'AIN'T LOVE GRAND'. The following year ALVIN was deposed by ex-LONE JUSTICE guitarist, TONY GILKYSON, a fuller heavy sound beginning to manifest itself on 1987's 'SEE HOW WE ARE'. A commercially disastrous double-live set was their last for some time, although the band returned after other solo projects with a disappointing comeback set, 'HEY ZEUS!' (1993). • **Covered:** WILD THING (Troggs) / ALL OR NOTHING (Small Faces) / IT'S IN HIS KISS (Betty Everett) / SOUL KITCHEN (Doors) / POSITIVELY 4th STREET (Bob Dylan) / U.S. MALE (hit; Elvis Presley) / HOME MOTEL (Willie Nelson).

Album rating: LOS ANGELES (*6) / WILD GIFT (*8) / UNDER THE BIG BLACK SUN (*6) / MORE FUN IN THE NEW WORLD (*5) / AIN'T LOVE GRAND (*6) / SEE HOW WE ARE (*5) / LIVE AT THE WHISKEY A GO-GO (*5) / HEY ZEUS! (*4) / UNCLOGGED (*4)

EXENE CERVENKA (b. CHRISTINE CERVENKA, 1 Feb'56, Chicago, Illinois) – vocals / **BILLY ZOOM** – guitar / **JOHN DOE** (b.JOHN NOMMENSEN, 25 Feb'53, Decatur, Illinois) – bass, vocals / **D.J. BONEBRAKE** (b. DON, 8 Dec'55, Hollywood, Calif.) – drums repl. MICK BASHER

		not iss.	Dangerhouse
Apr 78.	(7") *<D 88>* **ADULT BOOKS. / WE'RE DESPERATE**	-	

		not iss.	Slash
Jun 80.	(7") **THE WORLD'S A MESS. / IT'S IN MY KISS**	-	
Jun 80.	(lp) *<SR 106>* **LOS ANGELES**	-	

– Your phone's off the hook, but you're not / Johnny hit and run Pauline / Soul kitchen / Nausea / Sugarlight / Los Angeles / Sex and dying in high society / The unheard music / The world's a mess / It's in my kiss.

May 81.	(lp) *<SR 107>* **WILD GIFT**		

– The once over twice / We're desperate / Adult books / Universal corner / I'm coming over / It's who you know / In this house that I call home / Some other time / White girl / Beyond and back / Back 2 the base / When our love passed out on the coach / Year 1.

Jun 81.	(7") **WE'RE DESPERATE. / GET USED TO IT**	-	
Aug 81.	(7") *<SRS 106>* **WHITE GIRL. / YOUR PHONE'S OFF THE HOOK**	-	

		Elektra	Elektra
Jul 82.	(7") *<69885>* **BLUE SPARK. / DANCING WITH TEARS IN MY EYES**		
Jul 82.	(lp) *(K 52401)* *<60150>* **UNDER THE BIG BLACK SUN**		76

– The hungry wolf / Motel room in my bed / Riding with Mary / Come back to me / Under the big black sun / Because I do / Blue spark / Dancing with tears in my eyes / Real child of Hell / How I (learned my lesson) / The have nots.

Jun 83.	(7") *<69825>* **BREATHLESS. / RIDING WITH MARY**	-	

Sep 83.	(lp/c) *(K 960283-1/-4)* *<60283>* **MORE FUN IN THE NEW WORLD**		86

– The new world / We're having much more fun / True love / Poor girl / Make the music go bang / Breathless / I must not think bad thoughts / Devil doll / Painting the town blue / Hot house / Drunk in my past / I see red / True love #2.

Jan 84.	(7") *(E 9779)* **THE NEW WORLD. / I MUST NOT THINK BAD THOUGHTS**		
Jun 84.	(12") **WILD THING. / TRUE LOVE** (part 2)		
Jun 84.	(7") *<69709>* **WILD THING. / DEVIL DOLL**	-	

In 1985, JOHN DOE splintered with country-western project The KNITTERS. They included HENRY ROLLINS (of BLACK FLAG), DAVE ALVIN (of BLASTERS) + JOHNNY RAY BARTEL and made one album POOR LITTLE CRITTER ON THE ROAD. In fact, X brought in **DAVE ALVIN** – guitar to repl. BILLY

Aug 85.	(7") *(EKR 18)* **BURNING HOUSE OF LOVE. / LOVE SHACK**		
	(12"+=) *(EKRT 18)* – Wild thing.		
Sep 85.	(lp) *(EKT 12)* *<60430>* **AIN'T LOVE GRAND**		89 Aug85

– Burning house of love / Love shack / My soul cries your name / My goodness / Around my heart / What's wrong with me . . . / All or nothing / Watch the sun go down / I'll stand up for you / Little honey / Supercharged.

TONY GILKYSON (b. 6 Aug'52) – guitar (ex-LONE JUSTICE) repl. ALVIN who went solo

Jul 87.	(lp/c) *(K 960492-1/-4)* *<60492>* **SEE HOW WE ARE**		

– I'm lost / You / 4th of July / In the time it takes / Anyone can fill your shoes / See how we are / Left & right / When it rains . . . / Holiday story / Surprise surprise / Cyrano de Berger's back.

Jul 87.	(7") *<69462>* **4th OF JULY. / POSITIVELY 4th STREET**	-	
May 88.	(d-lp/c/cd) *(K 960788-1/-4/-2)* *<60788>* **LIVE AT THE WHISKEY A GO-GO ON THE FABULOUS SUNSET STRIP** (live)		

– Los Angeles / House I call home / The new world / Around my heart / Surprise surprise / Because I do / Burning house of love / My goodness / Blue spark / The once over twice / In the time it takes / Devil doll / Hungry wolf / Just another perfect day / Unheard music / Riding with Mary / The world's a mess / True love / White girl / Skin deep town / So long / Call of the wreckin' ball / Year 1 / Johnny hit a run / Pauline.

		R.C.A.	D.G.C.
Oct 89.	(7") **WILD THING. / (part 2)**		
	(ext;12"+=/cd-s+=) – Oh you angel / U.S. male.		

split after this final flop, although they re-formed in 1993

		Big Life	Mercury
Jun 93.	(cd/c) *<519261-2/-4>* **HEY ZEUS!**		

– Someone's watching / Big blue house / Clean like tomorrow / New life / Country at war / Arms for hostages / Into the light / Lettuce and vodka / Everybody / Baby you lied / Drawn in the dark.

Jul 93.	(c-s) *(BLRC 94)* **COUNTRY AT WAR / YOU WOULDN'T TELL ME**		
	(12"+=/cd-s+=) *(BLR T/D 94)* – Drawn in the dark (acoustic).		

		not iss.	Infidelity
Jun 95.	(cd) *<10812>* **UNCLOGGLED** (acoustic live)	-	

– White girl / Because I do / Lying in the road / Unheard music / I must not think bad thoughts / Burning house of love / Stage / See how we are / True love / Have nots / The world's a mess, it's in my kiss / I see red / What's wrong with me.

when they finally split, EXENE fronted the band AUNTIE CHRIST who had signed to 'Lookout!'; included in their ranks, MATT FREEMAN (of RANCID).

– compilations, etc. –

Oct 97.	(d-cd) *Elektra; <62103>* **BEYOND & BACK: THE X ANTHOLOGY**	-	

– Los Angeles / The world's a mess, it's in his kiss / Yr ignition / Year one / Hungry wolf / We're desperate / Beyond and back / Back 2 the base / Blue spark / Some other time / Sex and dying in high society / Motel room in my bed / Heater / Once over twice / Because I do / In this house I call home / Soul kitchen / Universal corner / Delta 88 / Real child of hell / I'm coming over / White girl / Nausea / Johnny hit and run Paulene / You phone's off the hook but you're / Riding with Mary / New world / Breathless / Poor girl / What's wrong with me / How I (learned my lesson) / Have nots / Someone like you / Stage / See how we are / Surprise, surprise / 4th of July / Arms for hostages / Wild thing / Burning house of love / Devil doll / True love / Call of the wreckin' ball / In the time it takes / I must not think bad thoughts.

JOHN DOE

with band; **JOHN DEE GRAHAM** – guitar / **RICHARD LLOYD** – guitar (ex-TELEVISION) /**TONY MARSICO** – bass / **JEFF DONAVAN** – drums

		D.G.C.	D.G.C.
Jun 90.	(cd/c/lp) *<(7599 24291-2/-4/-1)>* **MEET JOHN DOE**		

– Let's be mad / A matter of degrees / Dyin' to get home / It's only love / The real one / Take #52 / Worldwide brotherhood / With someone like you / By the light / Knockin' around / Touch me, baby / My offering.

next with various session people including EXENE + DJ BONEBRAKE (actress SANDRA BERNHARD also makes an appearance)

		Forward	Rhino
1995.	(cd) *<72134>* **KISSINGSOHARD**	-	

– Fallen tears / Safety / Love knows / Mo goodness / Tragedy by definition / Kissing / Hits the ground / Going down fast / TV set / Beer, gas, ride forever / Field of dirt / Williamette / Liar's market.

		not iss.	Kill Rock Stars
Jan 98.	(cd-ep; as JOHN THING DOE) *<KRS 290>* **FOR THE REST OF US**	-	

– Step outside / Let's get lost / Unhappy song / Bad, bad feeling / This loving thing.

EXENE CERVENKA

		not iss.	Freeway
Jan 86.	(lp; EXENE CERVENKA WANDA COLEMAN) *<FRWY 1057>* **TWIN SISTERS: LIVE AT McCABE'S** (live poetry)	-	

with **TONY GILKYSON / STEVE NELSON / JIM CHRISTIE / KEN STRANGE / JULIE CHRISTENSEN / ELIZA GILKYSON** etc

	not iss.	Rhino
/R4/R1 70913> **OLD WIVES' TALES**	-	

...d / Biggest memory / Here come the crucifiers / Cocktail trees / Famous
Leave Heaven alone / Good luck / White trash wife / He's got a she /
Coyote on the town.

1990. :R2/R4 70757> **RUNNING SCARED**
- ...e labor / Clinic / Red dirt / Real estate / Curtains / The boy and his sister /
Same denomination / Missing nature / It fell / The ballad of Roberta / Just another
perfect day / Will Jesus wash the bloodstains from our souls.

—— EXENE also released an album, 'RUDE HIEROGLYPHICS', with LYDIA
LUNCH

	2.13.61	Thirsty Ear
Jun 96. (cd) <(213CD 04)> **SURFACE TO AIR SERPENTS**		

- Big stain / Dream bodies / In the year of the ant / Unfortunate / Flies without
borders / Living / Closing numbers / Truce / Magdalene / Deep end / Like morning /
Three stories / Clay / I want questions / I want answers / I want / Good, then its
unanimous/ Being and everythingness / Waiting / Hello / Debate / What is there to
be at one with?

X-RAY SPEX

(dig out; 4th edition or Great Alt & Indie . . .)

XTC

Formed: Swindon, Wiltshire, England . . . 1976 after 3 years of calling
themselves The HELIUM KIDZ. Not an early version of acid house as the
name might suggest, XTC traded in a quirky blend of pop that owed more
to quintessential English psychedelia than the nihilistic three chord assault of
their punk peers. Nevertheless, they were picked up by 'Virgin' in the signing
scramble that followed The SEX PISTOLS early success in 1977. The debut
album, 'WHITE MUSIC' (1978), introduced their tentative art-pop sound,
PARTRIDGE's songwriting talent much in evidence even at this early stage.
The JOHN LECKIE (STONE ROSES, RADIOHEAD, etc.) produced 'GO
2' (1978) was a more sonically adventurous follow-up, heavily influenced by
BRIAN ENO and moulding their pop with quirky electronica. Soon after the
record's release, ANDREWS left to join ROBERT FRIPP's 'LEAGUE OF
GENTLEMEN' and was replaced by DAVE GREGORY. The new improved
unit cut the successful 'DRUMS AND WIRES' (1979) album which spawned a
top 20 hit single, the hypnotic, MOULDING-penned 'MAKING PLANS FOR
NIGEL'. The rest of the tracks were just as catchy in their distinctive, left-of-
centre way. This signalled the onset of a punishing touring/recording schedule
during which time the band released a succession of impressive singles, some
of which went top 20 and an album, 'BLACK SEA' (1980), that hinted at the
psychedelic nostalgia which would characterise their later output. 'ENGLISH
SETTLEMENT' (1982) is generally held to be band's finest hour. A double set,
the record artfully blended rustic folk, ethnic rhythms and synthesizer pop, all
shot through with the spectral hue of psychedelia. Although the stellar single,
'SENSES WORKING OVERTIME' was one of the band's biggest hits and
XTC looked to be headed for the big time, PARTRIDGE, never comfortable
with live performance, was dreading the inevitable round of touring. In the
event, after a few disastrous shows he decided he could suffer it no longer and
shortly after announced that the band would never tour again. CHAMBERS
promptly left, unhappy with such a prospect and although PARTRIDGE
was now suffering from Agoraphobia, the band struggled on. With no full-
time drummer and a string of producers, 'MUMMER' (1983) and 'THE
BIG EXPRESS' (1983) were inconsistent and lacking in direction although
'EVERYDAY STORY OF SMALLTOWN' from the latter set was a charming
piece of nostalgia-pop. It was clear the band needed some fresh inspiration
and with the help of JOHN LECKIE they cut the '25 O'CLOCK' mini-album
in 1985 under the pseudonym DUKES OF STRATOSPHERE. More overtly
psychedelic than any previous XTC material, PARTRIDGE was given free
range to indulge his obvious passions. Re-energised, the band were paired
with TODD RUNDGREN on 'SKYLARKING' (1986) and although there
were some well documented clashes between PARTRIDGE and the maverick
American, the resultant album was a triumphant return to form. Embellishing
the gentle hybrid of 'ENGLISH SETTLEMENT' with a 'PET SOUNDS'-
like sonic richness, the album spawned the sultry single 'GRASS'. Its B-side,
the semi-acoustic sweep of 'DEAR GOD' was picked up by American radio,
with the end result that 'SKYLARKING' was a considerable stateside success.
After a final DUKES OF STRATOSPHERE album, 'PSONIC PSUNSPOT',
XTC began work on the 'ORANGES AND LEMONS' set. Released in 1989,
the album was another resounding success, creatively at least, and spawned
the charming 'MAYOR OF SIMPLETON' single. While the album was a
relative success in America, it failed to make any lasting impact in the UK
and after 'NONESUCH' (1992) stiffed completely, XTC faded into obscurity.
Although sightings are rare, PARTRIDGE has surfaced occasionally, notably
on the HAROLD BUDD collaboration, 'THROUGH THE HILL', in 1994.
Without even an inkling that songwriters PARTRIDGE and MOULDING were
about to unleash a new episode of quirky pop tunes, the public were happy
to find out XTC were once again planning their comeback. Delivered early
'99 for 'Cooking Vinyl', 'APPLE VENUS VOLUME 1' saw Swindon's finest
regain the ground they had lost while securing a Top 30 entry in the process.
• **Covered:** ALL ALONG THE WATCHTOWER (Bob Dylan) / ELLA GURU
(Captain Beefheart).

Album rating: WHITE MUSIC (*8) / GO 2 (*4) / DRUMS AND WIRES (*8) / BLACK
SEA (*7) / ENGLISH SETTLEMENT (*8) / WAXWORKS (SOME SINGLES 1977-82)
compilation (*8) / BEESWAX (SOME B-SIDES 1977-82) compilation (*5) / MUMMER
(*7) / THE BIG EXPRESS (*7) / SLYLARKING (*8) / THE COMPACT XTC – THE
SINGLES 1978-1985 (*8) / ORANGES AND LEMONS (*7) / EXPLODE TOGETHER
(THE DUB EXPERIMENTS '78-'80) exploitation (*4) / RAG 'N' BONE BUFFET
collection (*5) / NONESUCH (*8) / FOSSIL FUEL: THE XTC SINGLES 1977-1992
compilation (*8) / APPLE VENUS VOLUME 1 (*7) / Andy Partridge: TAKE AWAY
(THE LURE OF SALVAGE) (*5) / Dukes Of Stratosfear: 25 O'CLOCK mini (*4) /
PSONIC PSUNSPOT (*5)

ANDY PARTRIDGE (b.11 Dec'53) – vocals, guitar / **COLIN MOULDING** (b.17 Aug'55) –
bass, vocals / **BARRY ANDREWS** (b.12 Sep'56, London) – keyboards repl. JONATHAN
PERKINS / **TERRY CHAMBERS** (b.18 Jul'55) – drums

		Virgin	Virgin-Epic
Oct 77.	(7") (VS 188) **SCIENCE FRICTION. / SHE'S SO SQUARE** (12"ep+=) (VS 188-12) **3-D** – Dance band.		
Jan 78.	(7") (VS 201) **STATUE OF LIBERTY. / HANG ON TO THE NIGHT**		-
Feb 78.	(lp/c) (V/TCV 2095) **WHITE MUSIC**	38	

– Radios in motion / Cross wires / This is pop? / Do what you do / Statue of liberty /
All along the watchtower / Into the atom age / I'll set myself on fire / I'm bugged /
New town animal in a furnished cage / Neon shuffle. (re-iss. Mar84 lp/c; OVED/+C
60) (cd-iss. Mar87 +=; CDV 2095) – Science friction / She's so square / Dance
band / Hang on to the night / Heatwave / Traffic light rock / Instant tunes.

Apr 78.	(7") (VS 209) **THIS IS POP?. / HEATWAVE**		-
Oct 78.	(7") (VS 231) **ARE YOU RECEIVING ME. / INSTANT TUNES**		-
Oct 78.	(lp/c) (V/TCV 2108) **GO 2**	21	

– Mekanic dancing (oh we go!) / Battery brides / Buzzcity talking / Crowded room /
The rhythm / Beatown / My weapon / Life is good in the greenhouse / Jumping in
Gomorrah / My weapon / Super-tuff. (free-12"ep w/ lp) **GO +** – Dance with me
Germany / Beat the bible / A dictionary of modern marriage / Clap, clap, clap /
We kill the beast. (re-iss. Mar84 lp/c; OVED/+C 61) (cd-iss. Jul87 +=; CDV 2108)
– Are you receiving me.

—— **DAVE GREGORY** – synthesizers, guitar repl. ANDREWS who joined LEAGUE
OF GENTLEMEN (w/ ROBERT FRIPP). He later went solo and formed
SHRIEKBACK

May 79.	(7",7"clear) (VS 259) **LIFE BEGINS AT THE HOP. / HOMO SAFARI**	54	-
		Virgin	Virgin Atlantic
Aug 79.	(lp/c) (V/TCV 2129) <VA 13134> **DRUMS AND WIRES**	34	

– Making plans for Nigel / Helicopter / Life begins at the hop / When you're near
me I have difficulty / Ten feet tall / Roads girdle the globe / Reel by reel / Millions /
That is the way / Outside world / Scissor man / Complicated game. (free-7"w/ lp) –
LIMELIGHT. / CHAIN OF COMMAND (re-iss. 1986 lp/c; OVED/+C 113) (cd-iss.
Jun88 +=; CDV 2129) – Limelight / Chain of command.

Sep 79.	(7"m) (VS 282) **MAKING PLANS FOR NIGEL. / BUSHMAN PRESIDENT (HSS 2) / PULSING, PULSING**	17	-
Nov 79.	(7") **TEN FEET TALL. / HELICOPTER / THE SOMNAMBULIST**	-	-
Feb 80.	(7"m) <VA 67009> **MAKING PLANS FOR NIGEL. / THIS IS POP? / MEKANIC DANCING (OH WE GO!)**	-	-
Mar 80.	(7") (VS 322) **WAIT TILL YOUR BOAT GOES DOWN. / TEN FEET TALL (U.S. version)**		
Aug 80.	(7") (VS 365) **GENERALS AND MAJORS. / DON'T LOSE YOUR TEMPER** (d7"+=) (VS 365) – Smokeless zone. / The somnambulist.	32	
Sep 80.	(lp/c) (V/TCV 2173) <VA 13147> **BLACK SEA**	16	41

– Respectable Street / General and majors / Living through another Cuba / Love at
first sight / Rocket from a bottle / No language in our lungs / Towers of London /
Paper and iron (notes and coins) / Burning with optimism's flames / Sgt. Rock
(is going to help me) / Travels in Nihilon. (re-iss. 1986 lp/c; OVED/+C 83) (cd-
iss. Mar87 +=; CDV 2172) – Smokeless zone / Don't lose your temper / The
somnambulist.

Oct 80.	(7") (VS 372) **TOWERS OF LONDON. / SET MYSELF ON FIRE (live)** (d7"+=) (VS 372) – Battery brides (live) / Scissor man.	31	
Oct 80.	(7"; as The COLONEL) (VS 380) **TOO MANY COOKS IN THE KITCHEN. / I NEED PROTECTION** (above by The COLONEL; aka MOULDING + CHAMBERS)		-
Nov 80.	(7") (RSO 71) **TAKE THIS TOWN. / (b-side by The Ruts)** (above single was from 'Times Square' film soundtrack on 'R.S.O.')		
Dec 80.	(7") (VS 384) **LOVE AT FIRST SIGHT. / ROCKET FROM A BOTTLE**	-	
Jan 81.	(7"m) (VS 384) **SGT. ROCK (IS GOING TO HELP ME). / LIVING THROUGH ANOTHER CUBA (live) / GENERALS AND MAJORS (live)**	16	
Mar 81.	(7"m) (VS 407) **RESPECTABLE STREET. / STRANGE TALES, STRANGE TAILS / OFFICER BLUE**		
		Virgin	Epic
Jan 82.	(7"m) (VS 462) **SENSES WORKING OVERTIME. / BLAME THE WEATHER / TISSUE TIGERS** (12"+=) (VS 462-12) – Egyptian solution (HSS 3).	10	-
Feb 82.	(d-lp/c)<US-lp> (V/TCV 2223) <37943> **ENGLISH SETTLEMENT**	5	48 Mar82

– Runaways / Ball and chain / Senses working overtime / Jason and the Argonauts /
No thugs in our house / Yacht dance / All of a sudden (it's too late) / Melt the guns /
** Leisure * / It's nearly Africa * / Knuckle down * / Fly on the wall * / ** Down
in the cockpit * / English roundabout / Snowman. <US single-lp version omits *>
(cd-iss. Jun88; CDV 2223); omits tracks *>

Mar 82.	(7"m) (VS 482) **BALL AND CHAIN. / PUNCH AND JUDY / HEAVEN IS PAVED WITH BROKEN GLASS** (12"+=) (VS 482-12) – Cockpit dance mixture.	58	
May 82.	(7"ep,9"ep) (VS 490) **NO THUGS IN OUR HOUSE / CHAIN OF COMMAND. / LIMELIGHT / OVER RUSTY WALLS**		-
May 82.	(7") **SENSES WORKING OVERTIME. / ENGLISH ROUNDABOUT**	-	

Nov 82. (lp/c) *(V/TCV 2251)* **WAXWORKS (SOME SINGLES 1977-82)** (compilation)   `54` `-`
(free lp w/ above) **BEESWAX (SOME B-SIDES 1977-82)** (re-iss. Dec82 lp/c; *OVED/+C 9*)

—— trimmed to basic trio of **PARTRIDGE, MOULDING + GREGORY** plus on session **PETER PHIPPES** – drums (ex-GLITTER BAND) (CHAMBERS emigrated to Australia)

	Virgin	Geffen

Apr 83. (7") *(VS 553)* **GREAT FIRE. / GOLD**   ` ` `-`
(12"+=) *(VS 553-12)* – Frost circus (HSS 5) / Procession towards learning land (HSS 6).

Jul 83. (7"/7"pic-d) *(VS/+Y 606)* **WONDERLAND. / JUMP**   ` ` ` `

Aug 83. (lp/c) *(V/TCV 2264)* <4027> **MUMMER**   `51`
– Beating of hearts / Wonderland / Love on a farmboy's wages / Great fire / Deliver us from the elements / Human alchemy / Ladybird / In loving memory of a name / Me and the wind / Funk pop a roll. *(re-iss. 1986 lp/c; OVED/+C 142)* (cd-iss. Mar87 +=; *CDV 2264)* – Frost circus (HSS 5) / Jump / Toys / Gold / Procession towards learning land (HSS 6) / Desert island.

Sep 83. (7") *(VS 613)* **LOVE ON A FARMBOY'S WAGES. / IN LOVING MEMORY OF A NAME**   `50` ` `
(d7"+=) *(VS 613)* – Desert island / Toys.
(12") *(VS 613-12)* – ('A'side) / Burning with optimism's flames (live / English roundabout (live) / Cut it out (live).

Nov 83. (7"; as THREE WISE MEN) *(VS 642)* **THANKS FOR CHRISTMAS. / COUNTDOWN TO CHRISTMAS PARTYTIME**   ` ` `-`

Sep 84. (7") *(VS 709)* **ALL YOU PRETTY GIRLS. / WASHAWAY**   `55`
(12"+=) *(VS 709-12)* – Red brick dream.

Oct 84. (lp/c) *(V/TCV 2325)* <24054> **THE BIG EXPRESS**   `38`
– Wake up / All you pretty girls / Shake you donkey up / Seagulls screaming kiss her, kiss her / This world over / The everyday story of Smalltown / I bought myself a liarbird / Reign of blows / You're the wish you are I had / I remember the sun / Train running low on soul coal. *(re-iss. 1987 +=; CDV 2325)* – Red brick dreams / Washaway / Blue overall. *(re-iss. 1988 lp/c; OVED/+C 182)*

Oct 84. (7"/12") *(VS 721/+12)* **THIS WORLD OVER. / BLUE OVERALL**   ` ` ` `

Jan 85. (7"m) *(VS 746)* **WAKE UP. / TAKE THIS TOWN / MANTIS ON PAROLE (HSS 4)**   ` ` ` `
(12"+=) *(VS 746-12)* – Making plans for Nigel / Sgt. Rock (is going to help me) / Senses working overtime.

—— **IAN GREGORY** (DAVE's brother) – drums repl. PHIPPES

DUKES OF STRATOSPHEAR

Apr 85. (7") *(VS 763)* **THE MOLE FROM THE MINISTRY. / MY LOVE EXPLODES**   ` ` `-`

Apr 85. (m-lp/c) *(WOW/+C 1)* **25 O'CLOCK**   ` ` ` `
– 25 o'clock / Bike ride to the Moon / My love explodes / What in the world . . . / Your gold dress / The mole from the ministry.

XTC

Aug 86. (7") *(VS 882)* **GRASS. / DEAR GOD**   ` ` ` `
(12"+=) *(VS 882-12)* – Extrovert.

Oct 86. (lp/c/cd) *(V/TCV/CDV 2399)* <24117> **SKYLARKING**   `90` `70`
– Summer's cauldron / Grass / The meeting place / That's really super, Supergirl / Ballet for a rainy day / 1000 umbrellas / Season cycle / Earn enough for us / Big day / Another satellite / Mermaid smiled * / The man who sailed around his soul / Dying / Sacrificial bonfire. <re-iss. 1987; 'Dear God' repl. *>

Jan 87. (7"/7"clear) *(VS/+V 912)* **THE MEETING PLACE. / THE MAN WHO SAILED AROUND HIS SOUL**   ` ` ` `
(12"+=) *(VS 912-12)* – Terrorism.

Jun 87. (7") *(VS 960)* **DEAR GOD. / BIG DAY**   ` ` ` `
(12"+=) *(VS 960-12)* – Another satellite (live).
(cd-s) *(CDEP 3)* – ('A'side) / Homo safari series (HSS 1-6):- Homo safari / Bushman president / Egyptian solution / Mantis on parole / Frost circus / Procession towards learning land.

Jul 87. (7") **DEAR GOD. / MERMAID SMILED**   `-` ` `

DUKES OF STRATOSPHEAR

Jul 87. (7"/7"colrd) *(VS/+Y 982)* **YOU'RE A GOOD MAN ALBERT BROWN (CURSE YOU RED BARREL). / VANISHING GIRL**   ` ` `-`
(12"+=) *(VS 982-12)* – The mole from the ministry / My love explodes.

Aug 87. (lp/colrd-lp/c) *(V/VP/TCV 2440)* **PSONIC PSUNSPOT**   ` ` ` `
– Vanishing girl / Have you seen Jackie? / Little lighthouse / You're a good man Albert Brown (curse you red barrel) / Collideascope / You're my drug / Shiny cage / Brainiac's daughter / The affiliated / Pale and precious.

1989. (cd) *(COMCD 11)* **CHIPS FROM THE CHOCOLATE FIREBALL**   ` ` ` `
– (25 O'CLOCK / PSONIC PSUNSPOT)

XTC

—— **PAT MASTELOTTO** – drums (of MR. MISTER) repl. IAN

Jan 89. (7") *(VS 1158)* **THE MAYOR OF SIMPLETON. / ONE OF THE MILLIONS**   `46` `72`
(12"+=) *(VST 1158)* – Ella guru.
(3"cd-s) *(VSCD 1158)* – ('A'side) / Ella guru / Living in a haunted heart / The good thing.
(12") *(VSR 1158)* – ('A'side) / Dear God / Senses working overtime / Making plans for Nigel.

Feb 89. (d-lp/c/cd) *(V/TCV/CDV 2581)* <24218> **ORANGES AND LEMONS**   `28` `44`
– Garden of earthly delights / The Mayor of Simpleton / King for a day / Here comes President Kill again / The loving / Poor skeleton steps out / One of the millions / Scarecrow people / Merely a man / Cynical days / Across this antheap / Hold me my daddy / Pink thing / Miniature sun / Chalkhills and children. *(re-iss. Oct89, 3xcd-ep-box; CDVT 2581)*

Apr 89. (7") *(VS 1177)* **KING FOR A DAY. / HAPPY FAMILIES**   ` ` `-`
(12"+=) *(VST 1177)* – ('A'extended).
(c-s+=) *(VSC 1177)* – Generals and majors / Towers of London.
(3"cd-s) *(VSCD 1177)* – ('A'extended) / ('A'side) / My paint heroes (home demo) / Skeletons (home demo).

Aug 89. (7") *(VS 1201)* **THE LOVING. / CYNICAL DAYS**   ` ` ` `
(c-s) *(VSC 1201)* – ('A'side) / The world is full of angry young men.
(12"/cd-s) *(VS T/CD 1201)* – (all 3 tracks).

Sep 89. (cd-ep) <9-21236-2> **KING FOR A DAY (Czar mix) / ('A' Versailles mix) / TOYS / DESERT ISLAND**   `-` ` `

Mar 92. (7"/c-s) *(VS/+C 1404)* **THE DISAPPOINTED. / THE SMARTEST MONKEYS**   `33` ` `
(10"+=) *(VST 1404)* – Humble Daisy.
(cd-s++=) *(VSCD 1404)* – ('B'demo).

May 92. (cd/c/d-lp) *(CD/TC+/V 2699)* <24474> **NONESUCH**   `28` `97`
– The ballad of Peter Pumpkinhead / My bird performs / Dear Madam Barnum / Humble Daisy / The smartest monkeys / The dismal / Holly up on poppy / Crocodile / Rook / Omnibus / That wave / Then she appeared / War dance / Wrapped in grey / The ugly underneath / Bungalow / Books are burning.

Jun 92. (7"/c-s) *(VS/+C 1415)* **THE BALLAD OF PETER PUMPKINHEAD. / WAR DANCE**   `71` ` `
(cd-s+=) *(VSCD1 1415)* – Down a peg (demo) / ('A'demo).
(cd-s+=) *(VSCD2 1415)* – My bird performs (demo) / Always winter never Christmas (demo).

—— **PARTRIDGE + MOULDING** re-formed six years later
—— additional musicians **DAVE GREGORY, PRAIRIE PRINCE**, etc

	Cooking Vinyl	T.V.T.

Feb 99. (lp/c/cd) *(COOK/+C/CD 172)* <3250> **APPLE VENUS VOLUME 1**   `42` ` `
– River of orchids / I'd like that / Easter theatre / Knights in shining karma / Frivolous tonight / Greenman / Your dictionary / Fruit nut / I can't own her / Harvest festival / Last balloon.

Apr 99. (cd-s) *(FRYCD 080)* **EASTER THEATRE / EASTER THEATRE (home demo) / HOW EASTER THEATRE CAME TO BE**   ` ` `-`

Jun 99. (cd-s) *(FRYCD 083)* **I'D LIKE THAT / I'D LIKE THAT (home demo) / HOW I'D LIKE THAT CAME TO B**   ` ` `-`

– compilations, others, etc. –

on 'Virgin' unless otherwise mentioned

Jan 87. (cd) *(CDV 2251)* **THE COMPACT XTC – THE SINGLES 1978-1985**   ` ` `-`
– Science friction / Statue of liberty / This is pop? / Are you receiving me / Life begins at the hop / Making plans for Nigel / Wait till your boat goes down / Generals and majors / Towers of London / Sgt. Rock (is going to help me) / Senses working overtime / Ball and chain / Great fire / Wonderland / Love on a farmboy's wages / All you pretty girls / This world over / Wake up.

Jul 88. (3"cd-ep) *(VSCDT 9)* **SENSES WORKING OVERTIME / BLAME THE WEATHER / TISSUE TIGERS**   ` ` `-`

Nov 88. (7") *Old Gold; (OG 9819)* **MAKING PLANS FOR NIGEL. / SENSES WORKING OVERTIME**   ` ` ` `

Aug 90. (cd) *(CDOVD 308)* **EXPLODE TOGETHER (THE DUB EXPERIMENTS 78-80)**   ` ` `-`
– (included the ANDY PARTRIDGE album below)

Aug 90. (cd) *(CDOVD 311)* / Geffen; <24417> **RAG & BONE BUFFET** (rare)   ` ` ` `

Nov 94. (cd) *Night Tracks; (CDNT 008)* **DRUMS AND WIRELESS: BBC RADIO SESSIONS 77-89**   ` ` ` `

Jun 96. (d-cd) *Geffen; <25137>* **UPSY DAISY ASSORTMENT (A SELECTION OF SWEETEST HITS)**   `-` ` `

Sep 96. (cd/c) *(CD/TC VD 2811)* **FOSSIL FUEL: THE XTC SINGLES 1977-92**   `33` ` `
– (nearly same tracks as 1987 collection + add more recent) *(d-cd; CDVDX 2811)*

Nov 98. (4xcd-box) *Cooking Vinyl; (COOKCD 152)* / TVT; <3240> **TRANSISTOR BLAST: BEST OF THE BBC SESSIONS**   ` ` ` `

MR. PARTRIDGE

Feb 80. (lp/c) *(V/TCV 2145)* **TAKE AWAY (THE LURE OF SALVAGE)**   ` ` ` `
– Commerciality / The day the pulled the North Pole down / Cairo / Madhattan / The forgotten language of light / Steam fist futurist / The rotary / Shore leave ornithology (another 1950) / I sit in the snow / Work away Tokyo day / New broom. *(re-iss. Aug88; OVED 130)*

—— In Jun'94, ANDY PARTRIDGE co-released with HAROLD BUDD the cd 'THROUGH THE HILL' for 'All Saints' label.

—— Also in '94, PARTRIDGE with MARTIN NEWELL, issued album 'THE GREATEST LIVING ENGLISHMAN' for 'Pipeline'.

Winnerloser / Solitude / Nature / Air voice / Crossing the line / Man of Leo / Stellar / Space requiem.

May 78. (12") *(IPR 2014)* **CROSSING THE LINE (live). / WINNERLOSER (live)** ☐ -

—— returned to Japan for several years

—— with **TAKASHI KOKUBO + SEN IZUMI** – synths / **PAUL BUCKMASTER** & orchestra

		Kuckuck	not iss.
Aug 85. (lp) *(626154)* **SEA AND SKY**		-	- German

– A photon / Appeared / And / Touched / Ah . . . / Time / To see / To know. *(UK cd-iss. Jun87; CDKUCK 072)* *(UK lp/c 1988; LP/MC KUCK 072)*

– compilations, etc. –

1973. (lp) *Help-Island; (HELP 12)* **COME TO THE EDGE** ☐ -

Y & T (dig out; Great Metal . . .)

YARDBIRDS

Formed: Richmond, Surrey, England . . . 1963, by KEITH RELF and PAUL SAMWELL-SMITH (both ex-METROPOLITAN BLUES QUARTET) together with JIM McCARTY, CHRIS DREJA and ANTHONY TOPHAM. The latter was soon replaced by ERIC CLAPTON and after a residency at Richmond's 'Crawdaddy' club backing bluesman, SONNY BOY WILLIAMSON, the YARDBIRDS were signed up by EMI's 'Columbia' label in early '64. After two well received singles that year, 'I WISH YOU WOULD' and 'GOOD MORNING LITTLE SCHOOLGIRL', the band released the acclaimed 'FIVE LIVE YARDBIRDS' the following year. Recorded at London's Marquee club, the album was a thrilling snapshot of the group's pioneering, souped-up blues and R&B sound. Although it contained no original material, the band marked interpretations of standards like 'SMOKESTACK LIGHTNING' and 'RESPECTABLE' with an indelible stamp. But this line-up promptly came to an end upon the release of the classic 'FOR YOUR LOVE' (1965) single. Considering the record a betrayal of the band's blues roots, CLAPTON upped sticks and left for JOHN MAYALL'S BLUESBREAKERS. Enter JEFF BECK, another supremely gifted guitarist, and the band embarked upon the most successful period of their career, notching up hits with the likes of 'HEART FULL OF SOUL', 'EVIL HEARTED YOU', 'STILL I'M SAD' and 'SHAPES OF THINGS'. BECK had brought a new spirit of experimentation to the band and employed such psychedelic tactics as Eastern-style guitar mantras, distortion and Gregorian Chant. With 'THE YARDBIRDS' (1966), the band further embraced psychedelia and the album stands as a career pinnacle, innovative while maintaining the essence of their R&B heritage. This was especially evident on the single, 'OVER UNDER SIDEWAYS DOWN' (1966), which was backed by another of the album's best tracks, the self explanatory 'JEFF'S BOOGIE'. SAMWELL-SMITH, who'd produced the album, departed soon after and was replaced by yet another future guitar God, JIMMY PAGE. Soon shifting from bass to co-lead alongside BECK, the new line-up cut the electrifying psychedelia of 'HAPPENINGS TEN YEARS AGO' (1966). This honeymoon period was short-lived however, as BECK parted ways with the band during a particularly laborious US tour. 'LITTLE GAMES' (1967) was an ill-advised attempt at commerciality while covers of MANFRED MANN's 'HA! HA! SAID THE CLOWN' and NILSSON's 'TEN LITTLE INDIANS' were equally puzzling. Though these releases achieved a modicum of success in America, the band split in mid '68, PAGE and DREJA going on to form The NEW YARDBIRDS which in turn evolved into LED ZEPPELIN. The inevitable reunion took place in the mid-80's and under the BOX OF FROGS moniker, a line-up of BECK, McCARTY, DREJA, SAMWELL-SMITH, RORY GALLAGHER and MAX MIDDLETON cut a self-titled album in 1984 and the 'STRANGE LAND' lp in 1986. • **Songwriters:** RELF wrote some, except covers, I WISH YOU WOULD (Billy Boy Arnold) / SMOKESTACK LIGHTNING (Howlin' Wolf) / A CERTAIN GIRL (Ernie K-Doe) / GOOD MORNING LITTLE SCHOOLGIRL (Don & Bob) / TRAIN (Johnny Burnette) / FOR YOUR LOVE + HEART FULL OF SOUL (c. Graham Gouldman, ⇒ 10cc) / I'M A MAN (Bo Diddley) / THE SUN IS SHINING (Elmore James) / plus loads of other blues greats. • **Trivia:** Made two group appearances in the 66/67 films 'SWINGING LONDON' & 'BLOW-UP'. Early in 1966, manager GIORGIO GOMELSKY was replaced by SIMON NAPIER-BELL.

Album rating: FIVE LIVE YARDBIRDS (*8) / FOR YOUR LOVE (*6) / HAVING A RAVE UP WITH THE YARDBIRDS (*5) / SONNY BOY WILLIAMSON & THE YARDBIRDS exploitation (*5) / THE YARDBIRDS (aka OVER UNDER SIDEWAYS DOWN) (*5) / GREATEST HITS compilation (*7) / LITTLE GAMES (*(*5) / THE VERY BEST OF THE YARDBIRDS (*9)

KEITH RELF (b.22 Mar'43, Richmond) – vocals, harmonica / **ERIC CLAPTON** (b.30 Mar'45, Ripley, England) – lead guitar, vocals repl. ANTHONY TOPHAM / **CHRIS DREJA** (b.11 Nov'45, Surbiton, Surrey) – rhythm guitar / **PAUL SAMWELL-SMITH** (b. 8 May'43, Richmond) – bass / **JIM McCARTY** (b.25 Jul'43, Liverpool) – drums

		Columbia	Epic
Jun 64. (7") *(DB 7283)* *<9709>* **I WISH YOU WOULD. / A CERTAIN GIRL**		☐	☐ Oct64
Oct 64. (7") *(DB 7391)* **GOOD MORNING LITTLE SCHOOLGIRL. / I AIN'T GOT YOU**		44	-
Feb 65. (lp) *(33SX 1677)* **FIVE LIVE YARDBIRDS (live)**		☐	-

– Too much monkey business / I got love if you want it / Smokestack lightning / Good morning little schoolgirl / Respectable / Five long years / Pretty girl / Louise / I'm a man / Here 'tis. *(re-iss. Aug79 on 'Charly' lp)(c; CR 30173)(CFK 1017)* *(re-iss. Aug89; LIK 55)* *(cd-iss. on 'Charly'; CDCHARLY 182)*

Stomu YAMASH'TA

Born: TSUTOMU YAMASHITA, 15 Mar'47, Kyoto, Japan. His father was the leader of the Kyoto Philharmonic Orchestra, leading to him studying percussion in his early teens at the Kyoto Academy of Music. In the mid-60's, he arrived in the States, having already performed his first concert as a soloist. Around this time, he also wrote two scores, 'YOJIMBO' & 'SANJURO', for the great film director, KUROSAWA. Having adapted his more westernised classical/jazz style, he worked with composers PETER MAXWELL DAVIES and HANS WERNE HENZE, who created the 'CONTEMPORARY' piece for him under the 'L'OISEAU-LIVRE' banner/label in 1972. YAMASH'TA's "floating music" concept was a hybrid of Eastern rock and neo-classical Western styles which led to a contract with 'Island'. In 1973, they issued 'MAN FROM THE EAST', a record well-received by the British press. In 1975, his music was used on the film, 'The Man Who Fell To Earth', which starred DAVID BOWIE. It led to collaborations with the likes of STEVE WINWOOD, MIKE SHRIEVE, KLAUS SCHULZE, GARY BOYLE (ex-Isotope) and MURRAY HEAD. He returned to more classical themes in the 80's, having set up his own "new age" company, CELESTIAL HARMONIES.

Album rating: FLOATING MUSIC (*6) / EAST WIND (*6)

STOMU YAMASH'TA – percussion, instruments

		Decca-L'Oiseau-Livre	not iss.
1972. (lp) *(DSLO 01)* **CONTEMPORARY**		☐	-

– Hans-Werner Henze: Prison song / Toru Takemitsu: Seasons / Peter Maxwell Davies: Turris campanarum sonatium.

		Barclay	Vanguard
1972. (lp) *(16063)* *<VSD 79343>* **RED BUDDHA**		-	☐ France

– Red buddha / As expanding as.

—— now augmented by various musicians, including **MORRIS PERT** – percussion / **GARY BOYLE** – guitar / **ROBIN THOMPSON** – sax / **PETER ROBINSON** – piano / **HISAKO YAMASH'TA** – violin / etc

		Island	Island
1973. (lp) *(ILPS 9228)* **THE MAN FROM THE EAST (soundtrack)**		☐	-

– Scoop / Ana Orori / What a way to live in modern times / My little partner / Mandala / Memory of Hiroshima / Mountain pass.

| 1973. (lp) *(86455)* **FLOATING MUSIC** | | - | - German |

– Poker dice / Keep in lane / Xingu / One way.

| Dec 73. (lp) *(ILPS 9242)* **EAST WIND** | | ☐ | - |

– Freedom is frightening / Rolling nuns / Pine on the horizon / Wind words.

| Jun 74. (lp) *(ILPS 9269)* **ONE BY ONE** | | ☐ | - |

– One by one / Hey man / One by one (reprise) / Black flame / Rain race / Tangerine beach / Superstar / Loxy cycle / Nuremberb ring / Seasons / Accident / At Tangerine Beach.

| Mar 75. (lp) *(ILPS 9319)* **RAINDOG** | | ☐ | - |

– Dunes / 33 & 1/3 / Rainsong / The monk's song / Shadows / Ishi.

—— **STEVE WINWOOD** – vocals, keyboards / **MICHAEL SHRIEVE** – drums / with also **KLAUS SCHULZE** – keyboards / **PAT THRALL + AL DiMEOLA + PHIL MANZANERA** – guitar / **ROSCO GEE** – bass

Jun 76. (lp/c; STOMU YAMASH'TA / STEVE WINWOOD / MICHAEL SHRIEVE) *(ILPS/ZCI <9387>)* **GO** [60]
– Solitude / Nature / Air over / Crossing the line / Stellar / Man of Leo / Space theme / Sace requiem / Space song / Carnival / Ghost machine / Surfspin / Time is here / Winnerloser.

—— **JESS RODEN** – vocals / **DONI HARVEY** – guitar, vocals / **PAUL JACKSON** – bass / **PETER ROBINSON** – keyboards, vocals; repl. WINWOOD (now solo) / no MANZANERA, GEE, THRALL

		Arista	Arista
Jul 77. (lp) *(SPARTY 1011)* *<4138>* **GO TOO**			

– Prelude / See you before / Madness / Mysteries of love / Wheels of fortune / Beauty / You and me / Ecliptic.
below recorded 1976; **JEROME RIMSON** – bass, repl. GEE + MANZANERA

		Island	Island
Apr 78. (d-lp) *(ISLD 10)* **GO LIVE (FROM PARIS) (live 1976)**		☐	-

– Space song / Carnival / Wind spin / Ghost machine / Surfspin / Time is here /